# HANDWÖRTERBUCH
# DEUTSCH ▶ENGLISCH
# ENGLISCH ▶DEUTSCH
# GERMAN ▶ENGLISH
# ENGLISH ▶GERMAN
# DICTIONARY

# PONS

# COLLINS

## DEUTSCH ▶ ENGLISCH
## ENGLISCH ▶ DEUTSCH

Handwörterbuch
Ernst Klett Verlag für Wissen und Bildung
Stuttgart • Dresden

# COLLINS

## GERMAN ▶ ENGLISH
## ENGLISH ▶ GERMAN
# DICTIONARY

HarperCollins*Publishers*

First published in this edition 1994

© Copyright 1994 HarperCollins Publishers

HarperCollins Publishers
P.O. Box, Glasgow G4 ONB, Great Britain

ISBN 0 00 470294-8

10 East 53rd Street, New York, NY 10022

ISBN 0-06-275515-3

First HarperCollins edition published 1995

---

Library of Congress Cataloging-in-Publication Data

Collins German-English, English-German dictionary / [by Peter Terrell
... et al.]. — 2nd ed.

   p.    cm.
  ISBN 0-06-275515-3
   1. German language—Dictionaries—English. 2. English language—
Dictionaries—German.   I. Terrell, Peter.
PF3640.C68 1995
433'.21—dc20                               94-15588
                                              CIP

---

  94 95 96 97 98   TBP   10 9 8 7 6 5 4 3 2 1

---

Die Deutsche Bibliothek - CIP-Einheitsaufnahme

**Handwörterbuch Deutsch-Englisch, Englisch-Deutsch** = German-
English, English-German dictionary. - 2. überarb. Aufl. / [bearb. von Eva
Vennebusch...]. - Stuttgart: Klett-Verl. für Wissen und Bildung, 1995
  Nebent.: Pons Collins Deutsch-Englisch, Englisch-Deutsch
  1. Aufl. u.d.T.: Pons-Handwörterbuch Deutsch-Englisch, Englisch-Deutsch
  ISBN 3-12-517921-1
NE: Vennebusch, Eva [Bearb.]; German-English, English-German dictionary;
  Pons Collins Deutsch-Englisch, Englisch-Deutsch

---

Lizenzausgabe für Ernst Klett Verlag für Wissen und Bildung GmbH, Stuttgart 1995
Alle Rechte vorbehalten

---

2. Auflage 1995
Ernst Klett Verlag für Wissen und Bildung GmbH, Stuttgart
ISBN 3-12-517921-1

Computer typeset by Morton Word Processing Ltd., Scarborough
Printed in Great Britain by The Bath Press

FIRST EDITION     ERSTE AUSGABE

Peter Terrell     Horst Kopleck

*Assistant Editors / Bearbeitung*

Jimmy Burnett     Philip Ladd
Andrea Ender     Reinhold Trott

*Copy Editor / Redaktionsassistentin*

Daphne Trotter

*based on / auf der Basis von*
Collins German Dictionary
*by / von*
Peter Terrell  Veronika Calderwood-Schnorr
Wendy V. A. Morris  Roland Breitsprecher

*prepared for Collins by / Projektleitung*

**LEXUS**

SECOND EDITION     ÜBERARBEITETE AUFLAGE

*Prepared by / Bearbeitet von*

Eva Vennebusch
Robin Sawers

*with / mit*

Horst Kopleck

*Editorial Staff / Verlagsangestellte*

Joyce Littlejohn
Nicola Cooke

# INHALT

# CONTENTS

## Warenzeichen

## Trademarks

# Vorwort

Diese umfassend aktualisierte und erweiterte Auflage enthält eine Vielzahl der Ergänzungen, welche in die zweite Auflage (1991) unseres Großwörterbuchs aufgenommen wurden, sowie weitere Materialien aus anderen Quellen. Mehr als 14.000 Stichwörter und Wendungen wurden hinzugefügt, um den Veränderungen des Wortschatzes Rechnung zu tragen, die sich aus gesellschaftlichen und politischen Veränderungen sowie aus Entwicklungen in Wissenschaft und Technik ergeben haben, soweit diese Eingang in die Alltagssprache gefunden haben, und um eine Vielzahl sprachlicher Aspekte noch besser als zuvor abzudecken. Hier ist vorrangig die stets wachsende Bedeutung des amerikanischen Englisch zu nennen, welcher in beiden Teilen dieses Wörterbuchs verstärkt Rechnung getragen wurde. Spezielle Aufmerksamkeit wurde Abkürzungen und Eigennamen zuteil, insbesondere geographischen Begriffen, und beide Kategorien wurden voll in die Stichwortliste integriert. Nützliche Ergänzungen wie das Buchstabieralphabet, die aktuellen postalischen Abkürzungen der US-Bundesstaaten sowie Substantive und Adjektive mit Bezug auf neuere Länder und Nationen sind alle erstmals in einem Wörterbuch dieser Größe enthalten. Spezielleres Vokabular aus vielfältigen Interessensgebieten wie Ökologie, Sport, Autos, Fotografie, Hi-Fi, Kino, Handel und Computer wurde aufgenommen, da es sich bei diesen Bereichen um wichtige Aspekte des täglichen Lebens handelt.

Schließlich wurde auch den umwälzenden Veränderungen in Deutschland Rechnung getragen, welche seit der Erstausgabe dieses Wörterbuchs stattgefunden haben. DDR-Vokabular, entsprechend gekennzeichnet, wurde weitgehend beibehalten, da diese Begriffe in zeitgenössischem Schrifttum nach wie vor auffindbar sind. Andere Institutionen, die inzwischen der Vergangenheit angehören, wurden mit *(Hist)* gekennzeichnet.

# Preface

This thoroughly updated and enlarged edition includes much additional material taken from the second (1991) edition of our renowned larger edition as well as other sources. More than 14,000 references have been added to take account of new vocabulary resulting from social and political change, as well as developments in science and technology as they affect everyday life, and to give even better coverage of many general aspects of the language. Chief among these is the ever increasing importance of American English, the representation of which has been increased significantly on both sides of the dictionary. Particular attention has been paid to abbreviations and proper names, especially geographical names, and both these categories have been included in the main word list. Such useful items as the telephone alphabet, the latest forms of abbreviations for the states of the USA used in postal addresses, and nouns and adjectives for many of the newer nations, are all included for the first time in a dictionary of this size. Much specialized vocabulary from areas of widespread interest such as ecology, sport, motoring, photography, hi-fi, cinema, commerce and computers has been added, since these areas all play an important part in our daily life.

Last but by no means least, due note has been taken of the cataclysmic changes which have taken place in Germany since the first edition appeared. Most of the GDR vocabulary has been retained, marked *(DDR)*, since readers of the literature of the time will encounter these terms. Other institutions which have disappeared are marked *(Hist)*.

# Einleitung

Dieses Wörterbuch ist insbesondere für Benutzer geeignet, die bereits Grundkenntnisse in der Fremdsprache besitzen und ein handliches Wörterbuch mittlerer Größe benötigen, welches ihnen jedoch eine umfassende Darstellung der modernen englischen und deutschen Alltagssprache bieten soll. Dieses Ziel wird erreicht, indem der Schwerpunkt auf den heutigen Sprachgebrauch — ob Umgangssprache oder förmlichere Ausdrucksweise — gelegt wird und alle Sachbereiche, die in der Welt von heute wichtig sind, wie z.B. Computertechnik, Sport und Handel, ausführlich abgedeckt werden. Aus diesem Grund ist dieses Wörterbuch gleichermaßen für die Schule, die Universität, für Büro und Geschäftswelt sowie zum allgemeinen Gebrauch daheim geeignet.

Dieses Wörterbuch soll jedoch nicht nur ein Verständnis der Fremdsprache vermitteln, sondern dem Benutzer darüber hinaus ihren sicheren Gebrauch in Wort und Schrift ermöglichen. Zu diesem Zweck wird die Verwendungsweise der angegebenen Übersetzungen auf vielfache Art aufgezeigt, z.B. durch Indikatoren zur Unterscheidung verschiedener Bedeutungen, durch Angabe typischer Subjekte und Objekte bei Verben sowie typischer Substantive, die gemeinsam mit Adjektiven verwendet werden; daneben wird eine Fülle von Beispielen gegeben, die Verwendungs- und Übersetzungsvarianten je nach Kontext aufzeigen. Überdies werden elementare, am häufigsten verwendete Wörter besonders ausführlich behandelt, da gerade sie häufig Schwierigkeiten bei der Kommunikation und Ausdrucksweise in der Fremdsprache bereiten. Der Inhalt dieses Wörterbuchs basiert auf unserem berühmten Großwörterbuch, dem Maßstab, an dem andere gemessen werden. Diese Ausgabe besitzt dieselben Vorzüge wie das Großwörterbuch, darunter eine außergewöhnlich klare Anordnung der Einträge und eine moderne Sprachauffassung.

# Introduction

This dictionary is intended especially for users who already have a grasp of the basics of the language and who require a handy dictionary of medium size, which will nonetheless provide them with a comprehensive survey of modern everyday German and English. It achieves this by placing the emphasis on current usage — from the colloquial to the more formal — and by giving extensive treatment of subjects such as computer technology, sport and commerce which are relevant to the modern world. Hence the dictionary is equally suitable for the student both at school and at college, the business person at the office, and the interested general reader at home.

However, the dictionary is designed to enable the user not only to understand the foreign language, but also to write and speak it with confidence. To this end there are numerous features which show how the translations given are used, such as the guiding system of indicating words to distinguish between alternatives, the typical subjects and objects for verbs and nouns that go with adjectives, and the rich store of examples, all of which show how usage and hence translation vary according to context. Also the basic, most frequently used words are treated in depth, as these so often cause problems when trying to communicate or express oneself in the foreign language. The content of the dictionary is based on our famous large edition which has become the market leader and the standard by which others are judged. This dictionary shares the outstanding features of the larger edition, including exceptional clarity of layout and modernity of approach.

# Benutzungshinweise

## „Ich werde einen Lammsattel haben und für Wüste eine Apfelnutte"

Zugegeben — es ist unwahrscheinlich, daß jemand in einem deutschen Restaurant auf so groteske Weise eine Bestellung aufzugeben versucht, es sei denn, es handelt sich um einen Briten oder Amerikaner mit minimalen Deutschkenntnissen und ohne Erfahrung mit Wörterbüchern. Dieses Beispiel veranschaulicht jedoch die Gefahr, Bedeutungen zu verwechseln, da man auch mit einem guten Wörterbuch nachlässig umgehen kann und im Falle eines schlechten Wörterbuchs Bedeutungsunterschiede unter Umständen gar nicht oder nur unzulänglich aufgezeigt werden. In unserem Beispiel wurde **I'll have** mit „ich werde haben" übersetzt — ohne auf den Kontext zu achten. Wenn Sie sich die Beispiele (unter **have**) in diesem Wörterbuch ansehen, werden Sie einen ähnlichen Satz finden: **I'll have the steak**, übersetzt mit „ich möchte gern das Steak"; dies ist offensichtlich der hier gewünschte Zusammenhang. Bestellt werden sollte ein Lammrücken (**saddle** ist sowohl ein Pferde- oder Bergsattel als auch — abgegrenzt durch einen entsprechenden Bedeutungshinweis — ein Rücken bei Fleischgerichten) sowie ferner zum Nachtisch (**dessert** (Nachtisch) und **desert** (Wüste) kann man beim schnellen Nachschlagen leicht verwechseln) ein Stück Apfelkuchen. Besonders peinlich ist hier die Verwechslung von zwei völlig unterschiedlichen Bedeutungen des Wortes **tart**. Die Moral ist, daß es verheerende Folgen haben kann, einfach die erste Übersetzung zu verwenden, auf die der Blick fällt.

## Wie findet man das richtige Wort?

Das obige Beispiel klingt vielleicht etwas weit hergeholt, aber ähnliche Fehler werden ständig gemacht. Nehmen wir zum Beispiel ein einfaches englisches Wort: **to cut**. Sie werden sagen: „Ich weiß, wie das auf deutsch heißt: **schneiden**". Wenn Sie jedoch im Wörterbuch nachsehen, finden Sie dort zunächst einen ganzen Absatz, der mit **1** *n* beginnt. Dies sind Übersetzungen für das Substantiv; da Sie aber nach einer Übersetzung für **to cut** suchen, sind Sie hier falsch. **2** *adj* kann auch nicht stimmen, da Adjektive lediglich beschreibend sind.

Bei **3** *vt* sind Sie am richtigen Ort; *vt* bedeutet transitives Verb, also ein Verb, das ein Objekt hat — bei **to cut** z.B. in den Ausdrücken **to cut the grass, to cut one's hair, to cut prices** und so weiter. Hier finden Sie natürlich „schneiden", jedoch daneben noch viele weitere Übersetzungen. Kein Grund zur Verzweiflung — solange Sie das zugehörige Objekt kennen, wird Ihnen das Wörterbuch die richtige Übersetzung nennen. Die Objekte sind jeweils vor der Übersetzung angegeben, z.B. **to cut the grass** = „das Gras mähen"; **to cut the cake** = „den Kuchen anschneiden" und so weiter.

Verschiedene Bedeutungen von **to cut** werden dann aufgelistet, unterteilt in Absätze, die jeweils mit einem Buchstaben in Klammern beginnen, gefolgt von einem ebenfalls eingeklammerten Wort, das die Bedeutung wiedergibt. Sucht man nach einer Übersetzung für **to cut prices**, so ist die entsprechende Bedeutung *reduce* (reduzieren), d.h. Absatz **(g)** (*reduce*) enthält die richtige Übersetzung: „senken". Ist das gewünschte Objekt jedoch nicht *prices*, sondern *salary*, so ist das korrekte Wort im Deutschen „kürzen".

Schließlich gibt es noch den Absatz **4** *vi*. *vi* bedeutet intransitives Verb, also ein Verb, das kein Objekt hat. Hier sind ebenfalls Hinweise in Klammern angegeben, doch diesmal sind dies Substantive wie z.B. (*knife, scissors*). Diese bezeichnen offensichtlich nicht die jeweilige Bedeutung des Verbs, sondern sind typische Subjekte. In Absatz **(b)** finden wir eine Kombination von Verb und Substantiven: „(*intersect: lines, roads*) sich schneiden". Dies bedeutet, daß hier eine Bedeutung wie etwa in dem Satz **the lines cut at right angles** gemeint ist — also **to cut** im Sinne von **to intersect** mit *lines* als Subjekt. Die korrekte Übersetzung ist „sich schneiden" (im ganzen Satz also: „die Linien schneiden sich im rechten Winkel").

# Wie findet man die richtige Wendung?

Wenn Sie eine Redensart oder eine feststehende Wendung übersetzen möchten, ist es oft nicht einfach, zu entscheiden, wo genau diese im Wörterbuch aufgeführt ist. Die Grundregel ist, unter dem ersten bedeutungstragenden Wort nachzusehen (d.h. nicht in Einträgen wie der, das, ein oder Präpositionen) bzw. unter dem ersten Wort der gewünschten Wendung, welches stets unverändert bleibt, auch wenn andere Teile des Satzes variiert werden können. So findet man z.B. die Redensart sich aufs Ohr legen unter Ohr, aber jemandem reinen Wein einschenken unter Wein, da man ja ebenfalls sagen kann jemandem klaren Wein einschenken.

Einige sehr häufig verwendete Verben wurden hierbei nicht als bedeutungstragend eingestuft, da sie in so vielen Wendungen vorkommen, daß sie als Wörterbucheinträge unüberschaubar wären. Hierzu zählen im Englischen be, get, have, make und put und im Deutschen bringen, haben, geben, machen und tun. Die Wendung to make hay while the sun shines ist also unter hay zu finden und to give somebody something for safe-keeping unter safe-keeping.

Wie aus diesen Beispielen ersichtlich ist, werden Wendungen im allgemeinen im Infinitiv aufgeführt. Im Englischen ist dies am to zu erkennen. Ausnahmen bilden Sprichwörter und andere Wendungen, die nur in einer Form existieren (z.B. the early bird catches the worm unter early), und natürlich Beispielsätze.

Was ist der Unterschied zwischen einer Wendung und einem Beispielsatz? Beispielsätze sind im Prinzip dazu da, zu zeigen, wie ein Stichwort verwendet wird und wie es in Verbindung mit anderen Wörtern zu übersetzen ist, *wobei diese Wörter veränderbar sind*; eine Wendung dagegen besteht aus einer mehr oder weniger festen Wortkombination. Beispielsätze sollen also auch dort helfen, wo der gesuchte Wortlaut von dem tatsächlich aufgeführten Beispiel abweicht, wie wir oben in dem Beispiel I'll have the steak sahen, übersetzt mit „ich möchte gern das Steak"; dieser Beispielsatz liefert die korrekte Übersetzung von I'll have, was auch immer bestellt werden soll. Es lohnt sich, die jeweils angegebenen Beispiele durchzugehen, um mit Bezug auf den zu übersetzenden Satz einen ähnlichen oder parallelen Wortlaut herauszusuchen. Auf den Seiten xiv-xxi sind weitere Informationen zur Benutzung des Wörterbuchs enthalten.

*ENGLISH–GERMAN* 1

---

**cut** [kʌt] *(vb: pret, ptp ~)* **1** *n* **(a)** Schnitt *m*. **to make a ~ in sth** einen Einschnitt in etw *(acc)* machen; **the ~ and thrust of politics** das Spannungsfeld der Politik; **the ~ and thrust of the debate** die Hitze der Debatte. **(b)** *(reduction) (in gen) (in prices)* Senkung *f*; *(in wages etc)* Kürzung *f*; *(in production, output)* Einschränkung *f*. **he had to take a ~ in (his) salary** er mußte eine Gehaltskürzung hinnehmen. **(c)** *(of meat)* Stück *nt*. **(d)** *(col: share)* Anteil *m*. **(e)** *(short route)* Abkürzung *f*. **(f)** *(Elec)* Unterbrechung *f (in gen)*. **power ~** Stromausfall *m*. **(g)** *(Cards)* **it's your ~** du hebst ab. **(h) he's a ~ above the rest of them** er ist den anderen um einiges überlegen.

**2** *adj usu attr flowers* Schnitt-; *bread* geschnitten; *grass* gemäht; *prices* herabgesetzt.

**3** *vt* **(a)** schneiden; *grass* mähen; *cake* anschneiden; *(~ out) fabric, suit* zuschneiden; *(~ off)* abschneiden. **to ~ one's finger** *(with knife etc)* sich *(dat)* in den Finger schneiden; **to ~ one's nails** sich *(dat)* die Nägel schneiden; **to ~ sth in half/three** etw halbieren/dritteln; **to ~ to pieces** zerstückeln; **to get one's hair ~** sich *(dat)* die Haare schneiden lassen; **to ~ sb free/loose** jdn losschneiden.

**(b)** *(shape)* steps schlagen; *channel, trench* ausheben; *figure (in wood)* schnitzen *(in aus)*; *(in stone)* hauen *(in aus)*; *diamond* schleifen; *key* anfertigen. **to ~ one's coat according to or to suit one's cloth** *(fig)* sich nach der Decke strecken.

**(c)** *(fig: break off)* electricity abstellen; *ties, links* abbrechen. **to ~ a long story short,** ... der langen Rede kurzer Sinn ist ....

**(d)** *person* schneiden. **to ~ sb dead** jdn wie Luft behandeln.

**(e)** *class* schwänzen *(col)*.

**(f)** *(intersect)* schneiden.

**(g)** *(reduce)* prices senken; *expenses, salary* kürzen; *production, output* einschränken.

**(h)** *part of text* streichen; *part of film* herausschneiden.

**(i)** *(cause pain to)* **it ~ me to the quick** es schnitt mir ins Herz.

**(j) to ~ a tooth** einen Zahn bekommen.

**(k)** *(Cards)* **to ~ the cards/the pack** abheben.

**(l) aren't you ~ting it a bit fine?** ist das nicht ein bißchen knapp?

**4** *vi* **(a)** *(knife, scissors)* schneiden. **to ~ both ways** *(fig)* auch umgekehrt zutreffen; *(have disadvantages too)* ein zweischneidiges Schwert sein. **(b)** *(intersect: lines, roads)* sich schneiden. **(c)** *(Cards)* abheben. **(d) to ~ and run** abhauen *(col)*.

# How to use the dictionary

**"I receive a lamb club and my woman pig's sidewhiskers"**

Admittedly it's unlikely that you'll hear anything as grotesque as this in a British or American restaurant, unless not only the speaker but the writer of the menu is a German with minimal English and no idea of how to use a dictionary. But it does illustrate the pitfalls of careless use of even a good dictionary — and of any use of a bad dictionary which fails to distinguish adequately between the translations given. The German in the above example has simply translated **ich bekomme** by taking the main translation given in most dictionaries ("I receive"), but if one looks at the examples under "bekommen" in our dictionary there is a similar one: **ich bekomme bitte ein Glas Wein** translated as **I'll have a glass of wine**, which is obviously the right phrase here. Then the speaker has in mind for himself leg of lamb (**Keule** means both the sort of club you hit people with and — distinguished by a (*Cook*) label — a leg if it's for eating), and for his wife (the second meaning of **Frau**, shown by the fuller form **Ehefrau**), pork chops (**Kotelette** is the word for sidewhiskers, which is easily confused with **Kotelett** meaning "chop"). The moral of this is that it can be disastrous simply to take the first translation you come across.

## Finding the right word

The above example may sound a bit far-fetched, but similar mistakes are made all the time. So let's look at a nice simple English word: **to cut**. Of course, you say, I know that in German it's **schneiden**. But if you look in the dictionary you will find first a whole section marked **1** *n*. These are the translations for the noun, and as you want to say **to cut** something you know that isn't right. **2** *adj* can't be right either, as an adjective always describes something. **3** *vt* is what you want, as *vt* stands for transitive verb, a verb which has an object: **to cut the grass, one's hair, prices** and so on. Here you find **schneiden**, but many other translations as well. Don't despair; as long as you know what you want to cut, this dictionary will give you the right word. The object in each case is given before the translations: **to cut the grass** is "das Gras mähen", **to cut the cake** is "den Kuchen anschneiden" and so on.

Different senses of **to cut** then follow in sections starting with a letter in brackets, and a word in brackets, which gives you the sense in question. **To cut prices** means to reduce prices, so we find this in section **(g)** (*reduce*). The right word is "senken", but if it's your *salary* that is being cut, you want "kürzen".

Finally there is a section **4** *vi*, standing for intransitive verb — verbs that do not take an object. Here there are also words in brackets, but this time they are nouns (*knife, scissors*), so obviously not signposts for the sense of the verb. They are in fact typical subjects. In **1 (b)** we even have a combination of a verb and a noun: "(*intersect: lines, roads*) sich schneiden". This means that in an example such as **the lines cut at right angles**, i.e. cut in the sense of intersect with lines as the subject, the translation is "sich schneiden" ("die Linien schneiden sich im rechten Winkel").

## Finding the right phrase

When you want to translate a phrase or idiom, it is often difficult to know where to find it in the dictionary. The general rule is to look under the first significant word, (i.e. not "a" or "the" or a preposition for instance), or the first word in the phrase which does not change even when other parts of it do. Thus **to throw out the baby with the bathwater** is included under **baby**, whereas **to lend somebody a hand** is treated under **hand** because it is equally possible to say **to give somebody a hand**.

Certain very common verbs have not been counted as significant words for this purpose, since they occur in so many phrases that their entries would otherwise become enormous. These include **be, get, have, make, put,** and, in German, **bringen, haben, geben, machen,** and **tun.** So **to make hay while the sun shines** is under **hay** and **to give somebody something for safe-keeping** is under **safe-keeping**.

As you will have noticed from the above examples, phrases are usually given in the infinitive with **to**. The same applies in German, but German word order puts the verb in the infinitive at the end (**etwas in Gang bringen** under **Gang**). Exceptions are proverbs and any other phrases which only exist in one form (**the early bird catches the worm** under **early**) and of course examples of usage.

What is the difference between a phrase and an example? Basically an example is there to show how the headword functions and is translated in combination with other words *where these words may vary*, while a phrase contains a more or less set combination of words. So examples may help to translate different words combinations from the one they give, as we saw above with **ich bekomme bitte ein Glas Wein** translated by "I'll have a glass of wine, please" which gives us the right translation for **ich bekomme** whatever one wants to order. The trick is to look through the examples to see if there is one parallel or similar to what one wants to translate or to say.

See pages xiv-xxi for further information on how to use the dictionary.

*ENGLISH–GERMAN* 1

**cut** [kʌt] *(vb: pret, ptp ~)* **1** *n* **(a)** Schnitt *m*. **to make a ~ in sth** einen Einschnitt in etw *(acc)* machen; **the ~ and thrust of politics** das Spannungsfeld der Politik; **the ~ and thrust of the debate** die Hitze der Debatte. **(b)** *(reduction) (in gen) (in prices)* Senkung *f*; *(in wages etc)* Kürzung *f*; *(in production, output)* Einschränkung *f*. **he had to take a ~ in (his) salary** er mußte eine Gehaltskürzung hinnehmen. **(c)** *(of meat)* Stück *nt*. **(d)** *(col: share)* Anteil *m*. **(e)** *(short route)* Abkürzung *f*. **(f)** *(Elec)* Unterbrechung *f (in gen)*. **power ~** Stromausfall *m*. **(g)** *(Cards)* **it's your ~** du hebst ab. **(h) he's a ~ above the rest of them** er ist den anderen um einiges überlegen.

**2** *adj usu attr flowers* Schnitt-; *bread* geschnitten; *grass* gemäht; *prices* herabgesetzt.

**3** *vt* **(a)** schneiden; *grass* mähen; *cake* anschneiden; *(~ out) fabric, suit* zuschneiden; *(~ off)* abschneiden. **to ~ one's finger** *(with knife etc)* sich *(dat)* in den Finger schneiden; **to ~ one's nails** sich *(dat)* die Nägel schneiden; **to ~ sth in half/three** etw halbieren/dritteln; **to ~ to pieces** zerstückeln; **to get one's hair ~** sich *(dat)* die Haare schneiden lassen; **to ~ sb free/loose** jdn losschneiden.

**(b)** *(shape) steps* schlagen; *channel, trench* ausheben; *figure (in wood)* schnitzen *(in aus)*; *(in stone)*

hauen *(in aus)*; *diamond* schleifen; *key* anfertigen. **to ~ one's coat according to** *or* **to suit one's cloth** *(fig)* sich nach der Decke strecken.

**(c)** *(fig: break off) electricity* abstellen; *ties, links* abbrechen. **to ~ a long story short,** ... der langen Rede kurzer Sinn ist ....

**(d)** *person* schneiden. **to ~ sb dead** jdn wie Luft behandeln.

**(e)** *class* schwänzen *(col)*.

**(f)** *(intersect)* schneiden.

**(g)** *(reduce) prices* senken; *expenses, salary* kürzen; *production, output* einschränken.

**(h)** *part of text* streichen; *part of film* herausschneiden.

**(i)** *(cause pain to)* **it ~ me to the quick** es schnitt mir ins Herz.

**(j)** **to ~ a tooth** einen Zahn bekommen.

**(k)** *(Cards)* **to ~ the cards/the pack** abheben.

**(l) aren't you ~ting it a bit fine?** ist das nicht ein bißchen knapp?

**4** *vi* **(a)** *(knife, scissors)* schneiden. **to ~ both ways** *(fig)* auch umgekehrt zutreffen; *(have disadvantages too)* ein zweischneidiges Schwert sein. **(b)** *(intersect: lines, roads)* sich schneiden. **(c)** *(Cards)* abheben. **(d) to ~ and run** abhauen *(col)*.

## Layout and order

**1.1 Alphabetical order** is followed throughout. Where a letter occurs in brackets in a head-word, this letter is counted for the alphabetical oreder, eg **Beamte(r)** will be found in the place of **Beamter, vierte(r, s)** in the place of **vierter**.

**1.2 Abbreviations, acronyms** and **proper nouns** will be found in their alphabetical place in the word list.

**1.3** Superior numbers are used to differentiate between words spelt the same way.

**rowing[1], rowing[2]; durchsetzen[1], durchsetzen[2].**

**1.4 Compounds** will be found in their alphabetical place in the word list. The term "compound" is taken to cover not only those written in one word or hyphenated (eg **Bettwäsche, large-scale**) but also attributive uses of English nouns (eg **defence mechanism**) and other set word combinations (eg **long jump**). Where the alphabetical order permits, compounds are run on in blocks with the first element printed in boldface type at the beginning of each block. Where possible a general translation has been given for the first element.

**Silber-** *in cpds* silver.

From this the user can derive the translation for compounds not given in the word list.

**1.5 Phrasal verbs** (marked ▶) will be found immediately after the main headword entry.

## Explanatory material

General explanatory notes or 'signposts' in the dictionary are printed *in italics* and take the following forms:

**2.1 Indicators** in brackets:

**2.1.1** synonyms and partial definitions

**gefühlvoll** *adj (empfindsam)* sensitive; *(ausdrucksvoll)* expressive; *(liebevoll)* loving.

**2.1.2** within verb entries, typical subjects of the headword

**peel 3** *vi (wallpaper)* sich lösen; *(paint)* abblättern; *(skin, person)* sich schälen *or* pellen *(col)*

## Aufbau und Anordnung der Einträge

**1.1 Die alphabetische Anordnung** der Einträge ist durchweg gewahrt. In Klammern stehende Buchstaben in einem Stichwort unterliegen ebenfalls der Alphabetisierung, so findet man z.B. **Beamte(r)** an der Stelle von **Beamter, vierte(r, s)** unter **vierter**.

**1.2 Abkürzungen, Akronyme** und **Eigennamen** sind in alphabetischer Ordnung im Wörterverzeichnis zu finden.

**1.3** Hochgestellte Ziffern werden verwendet, um zwischen Wörtern gleicher Schreibung zu unterscheiden.

**1.4 Zusammengesetzte Wörter** stehen an ihrer Stelle im Alphabet. Der Begriff „zusammengesetzte Wörter" bezeichnet nicht nur zusammengeschriebene oder durch Bindestrich verbundene Komposita (z.B. **Bettwäsche, large-scale**) sondern auch die attributive Verwendung englischer Substantive (z.B. **defence mechanism**) und andere feste Verbindungen (z.B. **long jump**). Wo die alphabetische Ordnung es gestattet, werden die Zusammensetzungen in Blöcken angeordnet, wobei der erste Bestandteil am Anfang jedes Blocks in Fettdruck erscheint. Wo immer möglich, ist für das erste Element eine allgemeine Übersetzung angegeben.

Daraus kann der Benutzer die Übersetzung hier nicht angegebener Zusammensetzungen erschließen.

**1.5 *Phrasal verbs*** (feste Verb-Partikel-Verbindungen im Englischen, durch ▶ gekennzeichnet) folgen unmittelbar auf das Hauptstichwort.

## Erklärende Zusätze

Allgemeine erklärende Zusätze im Wörterbuch sind *kursiv* gedruckt und erscheinen in folgender Form:

**2.1 Indikatoren**, in Klammern stehend:

**2.1.1** Synonyme und Teildefinitionen

**2.1.2** bei Verben: typische Substantiv-Ergänzungen

**2.1.3** within noun entries, typical noun complements of the headword

**2.1.3** bei Substantiven: typische Substantiv-Ergänzungen des Stichworts

**Schar** f -en crowd, throng *(liter)*; *(von Vögeln)* flock; *(von Insekten etc)* swarm.

**2.2 Collocators** or typical complements, not in brackets:

**2.2 Kollokatoren** oder typische Ergänzungen, ohne Klammern stehend:

**2.2.1** in transitive verb entries, typical objects of the headword

**2.2.1** bei transitiven Verben: typische Objekte des Stichworts

**dent 2** vt car eindellen, verbeulen; *(col)* pride anknacksen *(col)*.

**2.2.2** in adjective entries, typical nouns modified by the headword

**2.2.2** bei Adjektiven: typische, durch das Stichwort näher bestimmte Substantive

**neu** adj new; *Kräfte, Hoffnung auch* fresh; *Wäsche* clean; *Wein* young.

**2.2.3** in adverb entries, typical verbs or adjectives modified by the headword

**2.2.3** bei Adverbien: typische, durch das Stichwort näher bestimmte Verben oder Adjektive

**vaguely** adv vage; *remember also* dunkel; *speak also* unbestimmt; *understand* ungefähr, in etwa.

**2.3 Field labels** are used:

**2.3 Sachbereichsangaben** werden verwendet:

**2.3.1** to differentiate various meanings of the headword

**2.3.1** um die verschiedenen Bedeutungen des Stichworts zu unterscheiden

**Jungfrau** f virgin; *(Astrol)* Virgo.

**2.3.2** when the meaning in the source language is clear but may be ambiguous in the target language

**2.3.2** wenn die Bedeutung in der Ausgangssprache klar ist, jedoch in der Zielsprache mehrdeutig sein könnte

**Virgo** n *(Astrol)* Jungfrau f.

A list of the field labels used in this dictionary is given on pages xxvii-xxx.

Eine Liste dieser Sachbereichsangaben befindet sich auf den Seiten xxvii-xxx.

**2.4 Style labels** are used to mark all words and phrases which are not neutral in style level or which are no longer current in the language. This labelling is given for both source and target languages and serves primarily as an aid to the non-native speaker.

**2.4 Stilangaben** werden verwendet zur Kennzeichnung aller Wörter und Wendungen, die keiner neutralen Stilebene oder nicht mehr dem modernen Sprachgebrauch angehören. Die Angaben erfolgen sowohl in der Ausgangs- als auch in der Zielsprache und sollen in erster Linie dem Nicht-Muttersprachler helfen.

When a style label is given at the beginning of an entry or category it covers all meanings and phrases in that entry or category.

Stilangaben zu Beginn eines Eintrages oder einer Kategorie beziehen sich auf alle Bedeutungen und Wendungen innerhalb dieses Eintrages oder dieser Kategorie.

Style labels used in this dictionary are explained on pages xviii-xxx.

In diesem Wörterbuch verwendete Stilangaben werden auf den Seiten xxvii-xxx erläutert.

**2.5** *also, auch* used after explanatory material denotes that the translation(s) following it can be used in addition to the first translation given in the respective entry, category or phrase.

**2.5** *also, auch* nach erklärenden Zusätzen gibt an, daß die folgende(n) Übersetzung(en) zusätzlich zu der ersten Übersetzung, die in dem Eintrag oder der Kategorie angegeben ist, benutzt werden kann/können.

## Grammatical Information

## Grammatische Angaben

### Gender

### Geschlecht

**3.1** All German **nouns** are marked for gender in both sections of the dictionary.

**3.1** Alle deutschen **Substantive** sind in beiden Teilen des Wörterbuchs mit der Geschlechtsangabe versehen.

**3.2** Where two or more German nouns of the same gender are given consecutively as interchangeable translations, the gender is given only after the last translation.

**3.2** Wo mehrere deutsche Substantive gleichen Geschlechts als austauschbare Übersetzungen hintereinander stehen, wird das Geschlecht nur nach der letzten Übersetzung angegeben.

**computer** *n* Computer, Rechner *m*.

**3.3** Where a German translation consists of an adjective plus a noun, the adjective is given in the indefinite form which shows gender and therefore no gender is given for the noun.

**3.3** Wenn eine deutsche Übersetzung aus einem Adjektiv und einem Substantiv besteht, wird das Adjektiv in der unbestimmten Form angegeben, die das Geschlecht erkennen läßt. Für das Substantiv erfolgt daher keine Geschlechtsangabe.

**große Pause; zweites Frühstück.**

**3.4** Nouns listed in the form **Reisende(r)** *mf decl as adj* can be either masculine or feminine and take the same endings as adjectives.

**3.4** Substantive nach dem Muster **Reisende(r)** *mf decl as adj* können sowohl männlich wie weiblich sein und haben die gleichen Deklinationsendungen wie Adjektive.

*m* **der Reisende, ein Reisender, die Reisenden** *pl*
*f* **die Reisende, eine Reisende, die Reisenden** *pl*

**3.5** Nouns listed in the form **Beamte(r)** *m decl as adj* take the same endings as adjectives.

**3.5** Substantive nach dem Muster **Beamte(r)** *m decl as adj* haben die gleichen Deklinationsendungen wie Adjektive.

**der Beamte, ein Beamter, die Beamten** *pl*

**3.6** **Adjectives** listed in the form **letzte(r, s)** do not exist in an undeclined form and are only used attributively.

**3.6** **Adjektive** nach dem Muster **letzte(r, s)** haben keine unflektierte Form und werden nur attributiv verwendet.

**der letzte Mann, ein letzter Mann**
**die letzte Frau, eine letzte Frau**
**das letzte Kind, ein letztes Kind**

**3.7** Nouns listed in the form **Schüler(in** *f)* *m* are only used in the bracketed form in the feminine.

**3.7** Substantive nach dem Muster **Schüler(in** *f)* *m* werden nur im Femininum in der eingeklammerten Form benutzt.

**der/ein Schüler**
**die/eine Schülerin**

**3.8** The **feminine forms** are shown, where relevant, for all German noun headwords; unless otherwise indicated, the English translation will be the same as for the masculine form.

Where there is no distinction between the translations given for the masculine and feminine forms and yet the context calls for a distinction, the user should prefix the translation with "male/female *or* woman *or* lady ..."

**3.8** Für alle deutschen Substantive, die ein natürliches Geschlecht haben, wird die **weibliche** neben der **männlichen Form** angegeben. Wenn nicht anders angegeben, lautet die englische Form für beide gleich.

Wo die für die männliche und die für die weibliche Form angegebene Übersetzung dieselbe ist, im entsprechenden Zusammenhang aber betont werden soll, daß es sich um einen Mann bzw. eine Frau handelt, sollte der Benutzer der Übersetzung „male/female *or* woman *or* lady" voranstellen.

**Lehrer(in) = male teacher/female *or* woman *or* lady teacher**

## Nouns

**4.1** Nouns marked *no pl* are not normally used in the plural or with an indefinite article or with numerals.

**4.2** Nouns marked *no art* are not normally used with either a definite or an indefinite article except when followed by a relative clause.

**4.3** The **plural endings** are given for all German noun headwords except for those with certain regular noun endings. A complete list of these is given on page xxv, which also includes genitive endings. Rules for the formation of these are given on page xxvi.

The plural endings of German compound nouns are only given where the final element does not exist as a headword in its own right.

**4.4 Irregular plural forms** of English nouns are given on the English-German side.

**4.4.1** Most English nouns take *-s* in the plural.

## Substantive

**4.1** Substantive mit der Angabe *no pl* werden im allgemeinen nicht im Plural, mit dem unbestimmten Artikel oder mit Zahlwörtern verwendet.

**4.2** Mit *no art* bezeichnete Substantive stehen im allgemeinen weder mit dem unbestimmten noch mit dem bestimmten Artikel, außer wenn ein Relativsatz von ihnen abhängig ist.

**4.3** Bei allen deutschen Substantiv-Stichwörtern ist **der Plural** angegeben, mit Ausnahme von Substantiven, die bestimmte regelmäßige Endungen haben. Diese sind in cincr vollständigen Liste auf Seite xxv erfaßt, wo auch Genitivendungen angegeben werden. Regeln für die Bildung des Genitivs werden auf Seite xxvi gegeben.

Der Plural ist bei zusammengesetzten Substantiven nur dann angegeben, wenn das letzte Element der Zusammensetzung nicht als Einzelwort vorkommt.

**4.4 Unregelmäßige Pluralformen** englischer Substantive sind im englisch-deutschen Teil angegeben.

**4.4.1** Die meisten englischen Substantive bilden den Plural durch Anhängen von *-s*.

**bed -s, site -s, key -s, roof -s**

**4.4.2** Nouns ending in *-s, -z, -x, -sh, -ch* take *-es*

**4.4.2** Substantive, die auf *-s, -z, -x, -sh, -ch* enden, erhalten die Endung *-es*.

**gas -es, box -es, patch -es**

**4.4.3** Nouns ending in *-y* preceded by a consonant change the *-y* to *ie* and add *-s* in the plural, except in the case of proper nouns.

**4.4.3** Substantive, die auf Konsonant + *-y* enden, verwandeln im Plural das auslautende *-y* in *-ie*, auf das die Pluralendung *-s* folgt. Ausnahmen bilden Eigennamen.

**lady — ladies, berry — berries
Henry — two Henrys**

## Adjectives and adverbs

**5.1** As a general rule, adjective translations consisting of more than one word should be used after the noun, not before it.

**ordnungsgemäß** *adj* in accordance with the rules

**5.2** On the German-English side of the dictionary adverbs have only been treated as separate grammatical entries distinct from adjective entries:
**(a)** when their use is purely adverbial

**höchst, wohl, sehr**

**(b)** when the adverbial use is as common as the adjectival use

**schön**

**(c)** when the English translation of the adverbial use cannot be derived from the adjectival translations by the rules of adverb formation

**gut**

Where no separate entry is given for the adverbial use of a German adjective, the user should form the English adverb from the translations given according to the rules given on page xxiv.

**5.3** On the English-German side of the dictionary adverbs have not been entered in every case alongside the related adjective. Normally the German translation of an English adverb takes the same form as the translation of the related adjective. For example:

**he is astute** er ist scharfsinnig
**..., he remarked astutely** ..., bemerkte er scharfsinnig

## Verbs

**6.1** All German verbs which form the past participle without *ge-* are marked with an asterisk in the text.

**umarmen\*** *vt insep ptp* **umarmt**
**manövrieren\*** *vti ptp* **manövriert**

## Adjektive und Adverbien

**5.1** Grundsätzlich sollten Übersetzungen von Adjektiven, die aus mehreren Wörtern bestehen, nur nachgestellt oder adverbial gebraucht und nicht dem Substantiv vorangestellt werden.

**5.2** Im deutsch-englischen Teil des Wörterbuchs sind Adverbien als selbständige grammatische Einträge von Adjektiven nur dann unterschieden worden:
**(a)** wenn es sich um echte Adverbien handelt

**(b)** wenn der adverbiale Gebrauch genauso häufig ist wie der adjektivische

**(c)** wenn die englische Übersetzung eines adverbial verwendeten Adjektivs nicht mit Hilfe der Regeln erschlossen werden kann, nach denen im Englischen Adverbien aus Adjektiven gebildet werden

Wo für den adverbialen Gebrauch eines deutschen Adjektivs kein gesonderter Eintrag vorliegt, ist es dem Benutzer selbst überlassen, aus den angegebenen Übersetzungen die englischen Adverbien nach den auf Seite xxiv angeführten Regeln zu bilden.

**5.3** Im englisch-deutschen Teil des Wörterbuchs sind Adverbien nicht immer als gesonderte Einträge aufgenommen worden. Normalerweise ist die deutsche Übersetzung eines englischen Adverbs gleichlautend mit der des entsprechenden Adjektivs. Zum Beispiel:

## Verben

**6.1** Alle Verben im Deutschen, die das 2. Partizip ohne *ge-* bilden, sind in Text durch Sternchen gekennzeichnet.

**6.2** All German verbs beginning with a prefix which can be separable are marked *sep* or *insep* as appropriate.

**6.2** Alle deutschen Verben, die mit einer trennbaren Vorsilbe beginnen, werden durch *sep* oder *insep* (= trennbar/untrennbar) bezeichnet.

> **unterliegen** *vi insep* es unterliegt keinem Zweifel, daß ...
> **umschalten** *vti sep* wir schalten jetzt um nach Hamburg

Verbs beginning with the prefixes *be-, er-, ver-, zer-* are always inseparable.

Verben mit den Vorsilben *be-, er-, ver-, zer-* sind immer untrennbar.

**6.3** All German verbs which form their perfect, pluperfect and future perfect tenses with "sein" as the auxiliary are marked *aux sein*.

**6.3** Alle deutschen Verben, die die zusammengesetzten Zeiten mit dem Hilfsverb „sein" bilden, sind durch *aux sein* gekennzeichnet.

> **gehen** *pret* **ging**, *ptp* **gegangen** *aux sein* **er ist gegangen** he went.

Where the auxiliary is not stated, "haben" is used.

Erfolgt keine Angabe, ist „haben" zu verwenden.

**6.4** German **irregular verbs** composed of prefix and verb are marked *irreg*, and the forms can be found under the simple verb. For example, the irregular forms of "eingehen" will be found under "gehen".

**6.4** Zusammengesetzte **unregelmäßige** Verben im Deutschen sind durch *irreg* bezeichnet, ihre Stammformen sind beim Simplex angegeben. So sind beispielsweise die Stammformen von „eingehen" unter „gehen" zu finden.

**6.5** If the present or past participle of a verb occurs simply as an adjective it is treated as a separate headword in its alphabetical place.

**6.5** Wenn 1. oder 2. Partizip eines Verbs den Status eines Adjektivs haben, werden sie als eigenständige Stichwörter in alphabetischer Reihenfolge aufgeführt.

> **gereift** *adj (fig)* mature.
> **growing** *adj (lit, fig)* wachsend; *child* heranwachsend.

## Phrasal verbs

## Phrasal verbs

**7.1 Phrasal verbs** are covered in separate entries marked ► following the main headword.

**7.1** *Phrasal verbs* (feste Verb-Partikel-Verbindungen) sind in eigenen Einträgen abgehandelt. Sie sind durch ► gekennzeichnet und folgen dem Stichworteintrag für das Verb.

**7.2 Phrasal verbs** are treated in four grammatical categories:

**7.2** *Phrasal verbs* werden unter vier grammatischen Kategorien abgehandelt:

**7.2.1** *vi* (intransitive verb)

**7.2.1** *vi* (intransitives Verb)

> ► **grow apart** *vi (fig)* sich auseinanderentwickeln.

**7.2.2** *vi +prep obj*
This indicates that the verbal element is intransitive but that the particle requires an object.

**7.2.2** *vi +prep obj*
Hiermit soll gezeigt werden, daß das Verbelement intransitiv ist, daß aber die Partikel ein Objekt erfordert.

> ► **hold with** *vi +prep obj (col)* **I don't ~ ~ that** ich bin gegen so was *(col)*.

**7.2.3** *vt*
This indicates that the verbal element is transitive. In most cases the object can be placed

**7.2.3** *vt*
Dies gibt an, daß das Verbelement transitiv ist. In den meisten Fällen kann das Objekt vor

either before or after the particle; these cases are marked *sep*.

oder hinter der Partikel stehen; diese Fälle sind mit *sep* bezeichnet.

▶ **hand in** *vt sep* abgeben; *forms, resignation* einreichen.

In some cases the object must precede the particle; these cases are marked *always separate*.

In einigen Fällen muß das Objekt der Partikel vorangehen; solche Fälle sind durch *always separate* bezeichnet.

▶ **get over with** *vt always separate* hinter sich *(acc)* bringen.
let's ~ it ~ (~) bringen wir's hinter uns.

Occasionally the object must come after the particle, these cases are marked *insep*.

Gelegentlich muß das Objekt der Partikel nachgestellt werden; solche Fälle sind durch *insep* bezeichnet.

▶ **strike up** *vt insep* (a) *(band) tune* anstimmen.
(b) *friendship* schließen; *conversation* anfangen.

**7.2.4** *vt + prep obj*
This indicates that both the verbal element and the particle require an object.

**7.2.4** *vt + prep obj*
Hiermit wird gezeigt, daß *sowohl* das Verbelement als auch die Partikel ein Objekt verlangen.

▶ **take upon** *vt + prep obj* **he has taken it** ~ **himself to ...**
er hat die Verantwortung auf sich genommen, zu ...

In cases where a prepositional object is optional its translation is covered under *vi* or *vt*.

In Fällen, wo ein Präpositionalobjekt, möglich, aber nicht nötig ist, findet man die entsprechende Übersetzung unter *vi* oder *vt*.

▶ **get off** *vi (from bus, train etc)* aussteigen *(prej obj aus)*;
*(from bicycle, horse)* absteigen *(prep obj von)*.
▶ **go down** *vi* hinuntergehen *(prep obj acc)*.

For example:

Zum Beispiel:

**he got off** er stieg aus/ab
**he got off the bus** er stieg aus dem Bus aus
**he got off his bicycle** er stieg von seinem Fahrrad ab
**she went down** sie ging hinunter
**she went down the street** sie ging die Straße hinunter

## 8.1 Punctuation and Symbols

## 8.1 Satzeichen und Symbole

, between translations indicates that the translations are interchangeable; between alternative phrases to be translated indicates that the phrases have the same meaning.

, zwischen Übersetzungen zeigt an, daß die Übersetzungen gleichwertig sind; zwischen Wendungen in der Ausgangssprache zeigt an, daß die Wendungen die gleiche Bedeutung haben.

; between translations indicates a difference in meaning which is clarified by explanatory material unless:
(a) the distinction has already been made within the same entry;
(b) the distinction is self-evident.

; zwischen Übersetzungen zeigt einen Bedeutungsunterschied an, der durch erklärende Zusätze erläutert ist, außer:
(a) wenn die Unterscheidung innerhalb desselben Eintrags schon gemacht worden ist;
(b) wenn die Unterscheidung offensichtlich ist.

| | | |
|---|---|---|
| between a headword and a phrase indicates that the headword is normally only used in that phrase. | : | zwischen Stichwort und Wendung gibt an, daß das Stichwort im allgemeinen nur in der aufgeführten Wendung vorkommt. |
| is used within an entry to represent the headword whenever it occurs in an unchanged form.<br><br>In German headwords of the form **Reisende(r)** *mf decl as adj*, and **höchste(r, s)** *adj* it only replaces the element outside the bracket.<br><br>In blocks of German compounds it represents the first element exactly as given at the beginning of the block. If it is given there with a capital, any subsequent occurence in a compound or phrase where it requires a small letter is clearly shown eg **Wochen-**: ...; **w~lang** *adj, adv* ... | ~ | wird innerhalb von Einträgen verwendet, um das unveränderte Stichwort zu ersetzen.<br><br>Bei deutschen Stichwörtern des Typs **Reisende(r)** *mf decl as adj* und **höchste(r, s)** *adj* ersetzt der Strich den außerhalb der Klammer stehenden Teil des Wortes.<br><br>In deutschen Komposita-Blöcken ersetzt der Strich das erste Element der Zusammensetzung genau, wie es am Anfang des Blocks erscheint. Soll von Großschreibung auf Kleinschreibung übergegangen werden, ist dies angegeben, z.B. **Wochen-**: ...; **w~lang** *adv, adv* ... |
| separates two speakers | — | unterscheidet zwischen zwei Sprechern. |
| indicates that the translation is approximate or the cultural equivalent of the term and may not have exactly the same sense; in the case of institutions, they are those of the country indicated and obviously not the same. | ≃ | weist darauf hin, daß die Übersetzung eine Entsprechung ist oder auf Grund kultureller Unterschiede nicht genau die gleiche Bedeutung hat. Bei Institutionen werden die des jeweiligen Landes angegeben, die natürlich nicht identisch sind. |
| after a German verb indicates that the past participle is formed without *ge-*. | * | nach einem deutschen Verb gibt an, daß das 2. Partizip ohne *ge-* gebildet wird. |

# Phonetic Symbols    Zeichen der Lautschrift

Phonetic transcriptions in square brackets are given for all headwords in the English-German section, apart from compounds and from words spelt the same way and with the same pronunciation. In the German-English section, phonetics are only given where the pronunciation is not in accordance with the rules listed on page xxiii.

Die Lautschrift wird für alle Hauptstichwörter im englisch-deutschen Teil angegeben, außer dann, wenn Wörter in Schreibweise und Aussprache genau übereinstimmen. Im deutsch-englischen Teil wird die Lautschrift nur dann angegeben, wenn die Aussprache von den auf Seite xxiii gegebenen Regeln abweicht.

## Vowels/Vokale

| | | |
|---|---|---|
| matt | [a] | |
| Fahne | [a:] | |
| Vater | [ɐ] | |
| | [ɑ:] | calm, part |
| | [æ] | sat |
| Chanson | [ã] | |
| Chance | [ɑ̃] | |
| | [ɑ̃:] | double entendre |
| Etage | [e] | egg |
| Seele, Mehl | [e:] | |
| Wäsche, Bett | [ɛ] | |
| zählen | [ɛ:] | |
| Teint | [ɛ̃:] | |
| mache | [ə] | above |
| | [ɜ:] | burn, earn |
| Kiste | [ɪ] | pit, awfully |
| Vitamin | [i] | |
| Ziel | [i:] | peat |
| Oase | [o] | |
| oben | [o:] | |
| Fondue | [õ] | |
| Chanson | [õ:] | |
| Most | [ɔ] | |
| | [ɒ] | cot |
| | [ɔ:] | born, jaw |
| ökonomisch | [ø] | |
| blöd | [ø:] | |
| Götter | [œ] | |
| Parfum | [œ̃:] | |
| | [ʌ] | hut |
| zuletzt | [u] | |
| Mut | [u:] | pool |
| Mutter | [ʊ] | put |
| Typ | [y] | |
| Kübel | [y:] | |
| Sünde | [ʏ] | |

## Consonants/Konsonanten

| | | |
|---|---|---|
| Ball | [b] | ball |
| mich | [ç] | |
| | [tʃ] | child |
| fern | [f] | field |
| gern | [g] | good |
| Hand | [h] | hand |
| ja, Million | [j] | yet, million |
| | [dʒ] | just |
| Kind | [k] | kind, catch |
| links, Pult | [l] | left, little |
| matt | [m] | mat |
| Nest | [n] | nest |
| lang | [ŋ] | long |
| Paar | [p] | put |
| rennen | [r] | run |
| fast, fassen | [s] | sit |
| Chef, Stein, Schlag | [ʃ] | shall |
| Tafel | [t] | tab |
| | [θ] | thing |
| | [ð] | this |
| wer | [v] | very |
| | [w] | wet |
| Loch | [x] | loch |
| fix | [ks] | box |
| singen | [z] | pods, zip |
| Zahn | [ts] | |
| genieren | [ʒ] | measure |

### Other signs/Andere Zeichen

| | |
|---|---|
| \| | glottal stop/Knacklaut |
| [ʳ] | [r] pronounced before a vowel/vor Vokal ausgesprochenes [r] |
| ['] | main stress/Hauptton |
| [ˌ] | secondary stress/Nebenton |

## Diphthongs/Diphthonge

| | | |
|---|---|---|
| weit | [ai] | |
| | [aɪ] | buy, die, my |
| Haus | [au] | |
| | [aʊ] | house, now |
| | [eɪ] | pay, mate |
| | [ɛə] | pair, mare |
| | [əʊ] | no, boat |
| | [ɪə] | mere, shear |
| Heu, Häuser | [ɔy] | |
| | [ɔɪ] | boy, coin |
| | [ʊə] | tour, poor |

NB: Vowels and consonants which are frequently elided (not spoken) are given in *italics:*

Vokale und Konsonanten, die häufig elidiert (nicht ausgesprochen) werden, sind *kursiv* dargestellt:

**convention** [kən'venʃən]
**attempt** [ə'tempt]

# The Pronunciation of German

German pronunciation is largely regular, and a knowledge of the basic patterns is assumed.

## Stress

1. The stress and the length of the stressed vowel are shown for every German headword.
2. The stressed vowel is usually marked in the headword, either with a dot if it is a short vowel:
   **sofọrt, Mạtte**

or a dash if it is a long vowel or diphthong:
   **họchmütig, ka̲ufen**

## Glottal Stop

1. A glottal stop *(Knacklaut)* occurs at the beginning of any word starting with a vowel.
2. A glottal stop always occurs in compounds between the first and second elements when the second element begins with a vowel.
3. When a glottal stop occurs elsewhere it is marked by a hairline before the vowel:
   **Be|ạmte(r)**

## Vowel length

1. When phonetics are given for the headword a long vowel is indicated in the transcription by the length mark after it:
   **Chemie [çe'miː]**

2. Where no phonetics are given a short stressed vowel is marked with a dot in the headword:
   **Mụtter**

and a long stressed vowel is marked with a dash:
   **Va̲ter**

3. Unstressed vowels are usually short; if not, phonetics are given for that vowel:
   **Almosen [-oː-]**

## Diphthongs and double vowels

1. Where phonetics are not given, vowel combinations which represent a stressed diphthong or a stressed long vowel are marked with an unbroken dash in the headword:
   **be̲iderlei, Ha̲ar, si̲eben**

2. **ie**
Stressed **ie** pronounced [iː] is marked by an unbroken dash:
   **si̲eben**

When the plural ending **-n** is added, the pronunciation changes to [-iːən]:
   **Allegorie̲, pl Allegorien [-iːən]**

When **ie** occurs in an unstressed syllable the pronunciation of that syllable is given:
   **Hortẹnsie [-iə]**

3. **ee** is pronounced [eː]
When the plural ending **-n** is added the change in pronunciation is shown:
   **Alle̲e f -n [-eːən]**

## Consonants

Where a consonant is capable of more than one pronunciation the following rules have been assumed:

1. **v**
(i) **v** is generally pronounced [f]:
   **Vater ['faːtɐ]**

Where this is not the case phonetics are given:
   **Sklave ['sklaːvə]**

(ii) Words ending in **-iv** are pronounced [iːf] when undeclined, but when an ending is added the pronunciation changes to [iːv]:
   **aktiv [ak'tiːf]**
   **aktive (as in der aktive Sportler) [ak'tiːvə]**

2. **ng**
(i) **ng** is generally pronounced [ŋ]:
   **Finger ['fɪŋɐ]**

Where this is not the case phonetics are given:
   **Angora [aŋ'goːra]**

(ii) In compound words where the first element ends in **-n** and the second element begins with **g-** the two sounds are pronounced individually:
   **Eingang ['aingaŋ]**
   **ungeheuer ['ʊngəhɔyɐ]**

3. **tion** is always pronounced [-tsioːn] at the end of a word and [-tsion-] in the middle of a word:
   **Nation [na'tsioːn]**
   **national [natsio'naːl]**

4. **st, sp**
(i) Where **st** or **sp** occurs in the middle or at the end of a word the pronunciation is [st], [sp]:
   **Fest [fɛst], Wespe ['vɛspə]**

(ii) At the beginning of a word or at the beginning of the second element of a compound word the standard pronunciation is [ʃt], [ʃp]:
   **Stand [ʃtant], sperren ['ʃpɛrən]**
   **Abstand ['ap-ʃtant], absperren ['ap-ʃpɛrən]**

5. **ch**
(i) **ch** is pronounced [ç] after *ä-, e-, i-, ö-, ü-, y-, ai-, ei-, äu, eu-* and after consonants:
   **ich [ɪç], Milch [mɪlç]**

(ii) **ch** is pronounced [x] after *a-, o-, u-, au-*:
   **doch [dɔx], Bauch [baux]**

Phonetics are given for all words beginning with **ch**.

6. **ig** is pronounced [ɪç] at the end of a word:
   **König ['køːnɪç]**

When an ending beginning with a vowel is added, it is pronounced [ig]:
   **Könige ['køːnɪgə]**

7. **h** is pronounced [h]:
(i) at the beginning of a word

(ii) between vowels in interjections:
   **oho [o'hoː]**

(iii) in words such as **Ahorn** ['aːhɔrn] and **Uhu** ['uːhu].

It is mute in the middle and at the end of non-foreign words:
   **leihen ['laiən], weh [veː]**

Where **h** is pronounced in words of foreign origin, this is shown in the text.

8. **th** is pronounced [t].

9. **qu** is pronounced [kv].

10. **z** is pronounced [ts].

Phonetics are given where these rules do not apply and for foreign words which do not follow the German pronunciation patterns.

# Adjectives and Adverbs  Adjektive und Adverbien

## Declension of German adjectives

Adjectives ending in -abel, -ibel, -el drop the -e- when declined.

| | |
|---|---|
| miserable | ein miserabler Stil |
| | eine miserable Handschrift |
| | ein miserables Leben |
| heikel | ein heikler Fall |
| | eine heikle Frage |
| | ein heikles Problem |

Adjectives ending in -er, -en usually keep the -e- when declined, except:

1 in language of an elevated style level

| | |
|---|---|
| finster | seine finstren Züge |

2 in adjectives of foreign origin

| | |
|---|---|
| makaber | eine makabre Geschichte |
| integer | ein integrer Beamter |

Adjectives ending in -auer, -euer usually drop the -e- when declined.

| | |
|---|---|
| teuer | ein teures Geschenk |
| sauer | saure Gurken |

## German adverbs

German adverbs are in most cases identical in form to the adjective, so except where there is a particular problem of translation the adverbial usage does not receive separate treatment in this dictionary.

## Comparison of German adjectives and adverbs

Irregular comparative and superlative forms are given in the text, including those of adjectives and adverbs with the vowels a, o, u which take an umlaut:

hoch adj comp höher, superl höchste(r, s) or (adv) am höchsten

Where no forms are given in the text, the comparative and superlative are formed according to the following rules:

1 Both adjectives and adverbs add -er for the comparative before the declensional endings:

schön — schöner
eine schöne Frau — eine schönere Frau

2 Most adjectives add -ste(r, s) for the superlative:

schön — schönste(r, s)
ein schöner Tag — der schönste Tag

3 Most adverbs form the superlative according to the following pattern:

schön — am schönsten
schnell — am schnellsten

4 Adjectives and adverbs of one syllable or with the stress on the final syllable add -e before the superlative ending:

(i)  always if they end in -s, -ß, -st, -tz, -x, -z
(ii)  usually if they end in -d, -t, -sch

spitz  adj spitzeste(r, s)
       adv am spitzesten
gerecht  adj gerechteste(r, s)
       adv am gerechtesten

The same applies if they are used with a prefix or in compounds, regardless of where the stress falls:

unsanft  adj unsanfteste(r, s)
       adv am unsanftesten

## Adverbialbildung im Englischen

1 Die meisten Adjektive bilden das Adverb durch Anhängen von -ly:

strange -ly, odd -ly, beautiful -ly

2 Adjektive, die auf Konsonant +y enden, wandeln das auslautende -y in -i um und erhalten dann die Endung -ly:

happy — happily
merry — merrily

3 Adjektive, die auf -ic enden, bilden normalerweise das Adverb durch Anhängen vom -ally:

scenic -ally
linguistic -ally

## Steigerung der englischen Adjektive und Adverbien

Adjektive und Adverbien, deren Komparativ und Superlativ im allgemeinen durch Flexionsendungen gebildet werden, sind im Text durch (+er) bezeichnet, z.B.

young adj (+er)

Komparativ und Superlativ aller nicht durch (+er) bezeichneten Adjektive und Adverbien sind mit more und most zu bilden. Das gilt auch für alle auf -ly endenden Adverbien, z.B.

grateful — more grateful — most grateful
fully — more fully — most fully

Unregelmäßige Formen des Komparativs und Superlativs sind im Text angegeben, z.B.

bad adj comp worse, superl worst
well adv comp better, superl best

Die flektierten Formen des Komparativs und Superlativs werden nach folgenden Regeln gebildet:

1 Die meisten Adjektive und Adverbien fügen -er zur Bildung des Komparativs und -est zur Bildung des Superlativs an:

small — smaller — smallest

2 Bei auf Konsonant +y endenden Adjektiven und Adverbien wird das auslautende -y in -i umgewandelt, bevor die Endung -er bzw. -est angefügt wird:

happy — happier — happiest

3 Mehrsilbige Adjektive auf -ey wandeln diese Endsilbe in -ier, -iest um:

homey — homier — homiest

4 Bei Adjektiven und Adverbien, die auf stummes -e enden, entfällt dieser Auslaut:

brave — braver — bravest

5 Bei Adjektiven und Adverbien, die auf -ee enden, entfällt das zweite -e:

free — freer — freest

6 Adjektive und Adverbien, die auf einen Konsonanten nach einfachem betontem Vokal enden, verdoppeln den Konsonanten im Auslaut:

sad — sadder — saddest

Nach Doppelvokal wird der auslautende Konsonant nicht verdoppelt:

loud — louder — loudest

# Regular German Noun Endings

The genitive and plural of a large number of German nouns are formed according to regular patterns. These patterns are:

| nom | | gen | pl |
|---|---|---|---|
| -ade | f | -ade | -aden |
| -ant | m (wk) | -anten | -anten |
| -anz | f | -anz | -anzen |
| -ar | m | -ars | -are |
| -är | m | -ärs | -äre |
| -at | nt | -at(e)s | -ate |
| -atte | f | -atte | -atten |
| -chen | nt | -chens | -chen |
| -ei | f | -ei | -eien |
| -elle | f | -elle | -ellen |
| -ent | m (wk) | -enten | -enten |
| -enz | f | -enz | -enzen |
| -esse | f | -esse | -essen |
| -ette | f | -ette | -etten |
| -eur | m | -eurs | -eure |
| -eurin | f | -eurin | -eurinnen |
| -euse | f | -euse | -eusen |
| -graph | m (wk) | -graphen | -graphen |
| -heit | f | -heit | -heiten |
| -ie | f | -ie | -ien |
| -ik | f | -ik | -iken |
| -in | f | -in | -innen |
| -ine | f | -ine | -inen |
| -ion | f | -ion | -ionen |
| -ist | m (wk) | -isten | -isten |
| -ium | nt | -iums | -ien |
| -ius | m | -ius | -iusse |
| -ive | f | -ive | -iven |
| -ivum | nt | -ivums | -iva |
| -keit | f | -keit | -keiten |
| -lein | nt | -leins | -lein |
| -ling | m | -lings | -linge |
| -ment | nt | -ments | -mente |
| -mus | m | -mus | -men |
| -nis | f | -nis | -nisse |
| -nis | nt | -nisses | -nisse |
| -nom | m (wk) | -nomen | -nomen |
| -oge | m (wk) | -ogen | -ogen |
| -or | m | -ors | -oren |
| -rich | m | -richs | -riche |
| -schaft | f | -schaft | -schaften |
| -sel | nt | -sels | -sel |
| -tät | f | -tät | -täten |
| -tiv | nt, m | -tivs | -tive |
| -tum | nt | -tums | -tümer |
| -ung | f | -ung | -ungen |
| -ur | f | -ur | -uren |

# General rules for forming the genitive

**Genitive endings** are formed

> for masculine and neuter nouns by adding **-s** or **-es**

>> **der Mann:** *(gen)* **des Mann(e)s**
>> **das Rad:** *(gen)* **des Rad(e)s**

> for feminine nouns: no change

>> **die Frau:** *(gen)* **der Frau**

Masculine or neuter nouns ending in **-s**, **-ß**, **-x** and **-z** always take the full form of **-es** for the genitive

>> **das Glas:** *(gen)* **des Glases**
>> **das Maß:** *(gen)* **des Maßes**
>> **der Komplex:** *(gen)* **des Komplexes**
>> **der Geiz:** *(gen)* **des Geizes**

Masculine or neuter nouns ending in **-sch** or **-st** normally take the full form of **-es**, as do those ending in a double consonant

>> **der Wunsch:** *(gen)* **des Wunsches**
>> **der Gast:** *(gen)* **des Gastes**
>> **das Feld:** *(gen)* **des Feldes**
>> **der Kampf:** *(gen)* **des Kampfes**

Masculine or neuter nouns ending in **-en**, **-em**, **-el**, **-er** and **-ling** always take the short form of **-s**

>> **der Regen:** *(gen)* **des Regens**
>> **der Atem:** *(gen)* **des Atems**
>> **der Mantel:** *(gen)* **des Mantels**
>> **der Sänger:** *(gen)* **des Sängers**
>> **der Flüchtling:** *(gen)* **des Flüchtlings**

Masculine or neuter nouns ending in **-ß** preceded by a short vowel will change the ß to **ss**

>> **der Fluß:** *(gen)* **des Flusses**

If the genitive is not formed according to these patterns it will be shown in the entry after the gender and before the plural ending

>> **Herz** *nt* **-ens, en**
>> **Klerus** *m* **-,** *no pl*

## Plural endings

We have not shown plural endings where the regular patterns shown on page xxv apply. All other plural endings are shown in the entry after the gender and the genitive ending (where given). If only one ending is given this will be the plural, unless otherwise indicated.

## Weak nouns

**Weak** nouns (marked as *wk*) have the same **-en** ending in the accusative, genitive and dative cases in both singular and plural forms

>> **der Mensch:** *(acc)* **den Menschen**
>> *(gen)* **des Menschen**
>> *(dat)* **dem Menschen**

# Abkürzungen

# Abbreviations

| Abkürzung | *abbr* | abbreviation |
|---|---|---|
| Akkusativ | *acc* | accusative |
| Adjektiv | *adj* | adjective |
| Verwaltung | *Admin* | administration |
| Adverb | *adv* | adverb |
| Landwirtschaft | *Agr* | agriculture |
| Anatomie | *Anat* | anatomy |
| Archäologie | *Archeol* | arch(a)eology |
| Architektur | *Archit* | architecture |
| Artikel | *art* | article |
| Kunst | *Art* | art |
| Astrologie | *Astrol* | astrology |
| Astronomie | *Astron* | astronomy |
| attributiv | *attr* | attributive |
| österreichisch | *Aus* | Austrian |
| australisch | *Austral* | Australian |
| Kraftfahrzeugwesen | *Aut* | automobiles |
| Hilfsverb | *aux* | auxiliary |
| Luftfahrt | *Aviat* | aviation |
| Kindersprache | *baby-talk* | |
| biblisch | *Bibl* | biblical |
| Biologie | *Biol* | biology |
| Botanik | *Bot* | botany |
| Bundesrepublik Deutschland | *BRD* | Federal Republic of Germany |
| britisch | *Brit* | British |
| Hoch- und Tiefbau | *Build* | building |
| Kartenspiel | *Cards* | |
| Chemie | *Chem* | chemistry |
| Schach | *Chess* | |
| umgangssprachlich | *col* | colloquial |
| derb | *col!* | potentially offensive |
| anstößig | *col!!* | highly offensive |
| Handel | *Comm* | commerce |
| Komparativ | *comp* | comparative |
| Computer | *Comp* | computers |
| Konjunktion | *conj* | conjunction |
| Zusammenziehung | *contr* | contraction |
| Kochen | *Cook* | cooking |
| Kompositum | *cpd* | compound |
| Dativ | *dat* | dative |
| altmodisch | *dated* | |
| Deutsche Demokratische Republik (1949-90) | *DDR* | German Democratic Republic (1949-90) |
| dekliniert | *decl* | declined |
| bestimmt | *def* | definite |
| demonstrativ | *dem* | demonstrative |
| Dialekt | *dial* | dialect |
| Verkleinerung | *dim* | diminutive |
| Akkusativobjekt | *dir obj* | direct object |
| kirchlich | *Eccl* | ecclesiastical |
| Volkswirtschaft | *Econ* | economics |
| Elektrizität | *Elec* | electricity |
| betont | *emph* | emphatic |
| besonders | *esp* | especially |
| etwas | *etw* | something |
| Euphemismus | *euph* | euphemism |
| Femininum | *f* | feminine |
| Mode | *Fashion* | |
| übertragen | *fig* | figurative |
| Finanzen | *Fin* | finance |
| Fischerei | *Fishing* | |
| Forstwesen | *Forest* | forestry |

# Abkürzungen

# Abbreviations

| | | |
|---:|:---:|:---|
| förmlich | *form* | formal |
| Fußball | *Ftbl* | football |
| gehoben | *geh* | elevated |
| Genitiv | *gen* | genitive |
| Geographie | *Geog* | geography |
| Geologie | *Geol* | geology |
| Grammatik | *Gram* | grammar |
| Heraldik | *Her* | heraldry |
| Geschichte | *Hist* | history |
| Gartenbau | *Hort* | horticulture |
| scherzhaft | *hum* | humorous |
| Jagd | *Hunt* | hunting |
| Imperativa | *imper* | imperative |
| unpersönlich | *impers* | impersonal |
| Industrie | *Ind* | industry |
| unbestimmt | *indef* | indefinite |
| Dativobjekt | *indir obj* | indirect object |
| Infinitiv | *infin* | infinitive |
| untrennbar | *insep* | inseparable |
| Versicherungswesen | *Insur* | insurance |
| Interjektion | *interj* | interjection |
| interrogativ | *interrog* | interrogative |
| unveränderlich | *inv* | invariable |
| irisch | *Ir* | Irish |
| ironisch | *iro* | ironical |
| unregelmäßig | *irreg* | irregular |
| jemand, jemandes, | *jd, jds* | somebody, |
| jemandem, jemanden | *jdm, jdn* | somebody's |
| Rechtswesen | *Jur* | law |
| Sprachwissenschaft | *Ling* | linguistics |
| wörtlich | *lit* | literal |
| literarisch | *liter* | literary |
| Literatur | *Liter* | literature |
| Maskulinum | *m* | masculine |
| Mathematik | *Math* | mathematics |
| Maß | *Measure* | |
| Mechanik | *Mech* | mechanics |
| Medizin | *Med* | medicine |
| Meteorologie | *Met* | meteorology |
| Metallurgie | *Metal* | metallurgy |
| militärisch | *Mil* | military |
| Bergbau | *Min* | mining |
| Mineralogie | *Miner* | mineralogy |
| Straßenverkehr | *Mot* | motoring and transport |
| Musik | *Mus* | music |
| Mythologie | *Myth* | mythology |
| Substantiv | *n* | noun |
| nautisch | *Naut* | nautical |
| verneint | *neg* | negative |
| nordenglisch | *N Engl* | Northern English |
| norddeutsch | *N Ger* | North German |
| Nationalsozialismus | *NS* | Nazism |
| Neutrum | *nt* | neuter |
| Zahlwort | *num* | numeral |
| Objekt | *obj* | object |
| obsolet | *obs* | obsolete |
| veraltet | *old* | |
| Optik | *Opt* | optics |
| Vogelkunde | *Orn* | ornithology |
| Parlament | *Parl* | parliament |
| Passiv | *pass* | passive |
| pejorativ | *pej* | pejorative |

# Abkürzungen     Abbreviations

| | | |
|---|---|---|
| persönlich/Person | *pers* | personal/person |
| Pharmazie | *Pharm* | pharmacy |
| Philosophie | *Philos* | philosophy |
| Phonetik | *Phon* | phonetics |
| Fotografie | *Phot* | photography |
| Physik | *Phys* | physics |
| Physiologie | *Physiol* | physiology |
| Plural | *pl* | plural |
| poetisch | *poet* | poetic |
| Dichtung | *Poet* | poetry |
| Politik | *Pol* | politics |
| Possessiv- | *poss* | possessive |
| prädikativ | *pred* | predicative |
| Vorsilbe | *pref* | prefix |
| Präposition | *prep* | preposition |
| Präsens | *pres* | present |
| Presse | *Press* | |
| Präteritum, | *pret* | preterite, |
| Imperfekt | | imperfect |
| Pronomen | *pron* | pronoun |
| sprichwörtlich | *prov* | proverbial |
| Sprichwort | *Prov* | proverb |
| Partizip Präsens | *prp* | present participle |
| Psychologie | *Psych* | psychology |
| Partizip Perfekt | *ptp* | past participle |
| Warenzeichen | ® | trademark |
| Rundfunk | *Rad* | radio |
| Eisenbahn | *Rail* | railways |
| selten | *rare* | |
| regelmäßig | *reg* | regular |
| Relativ- | *rel* | relative |
| Religion | *Rel* | religion |
| jemand(em, -en) | *sb* | somebody |
| Schulwesen | *Sch* | school |
| Naturwissenschaften | *Sci* | science |
| schottisch | *Scot* | Scottish |
| Bildhauerei | *Sculpt* | sculpture |
| trennbar, veränderbare Folge | *sep* | separable |
| Handarbeiten | *Sew* | sewing |
| süddeutsch | *S Ger* | South German |
| Singular | *sing* | singular |
| Skisport | *Ski* | skiing |
| Slang, Jargon | *sl* | slang |
| Sozialwissenschaften | *Sociol* | social sciences |
| Raumfahrt | *Space* | space flight |
| Fachausdruck | *spec* | specialist term |
| Börse | *St Ex* | Stock Exchange |
| etwas | *sth* | something |
| Konjunktiv | *subjunc* | subjunctive |
| Nachsilbe | *suf* | suffix |
| Superlativ | *superl* | superlative |
| Landvermessung | *Surv* | surveying |
| schweizerisch | *Sw* | Swiss |
| Technik | *Tech* | technology |
| Nachrichtentechnik | *Telec* | telecommunications |
| Textilien | *Tex* | textiles |
| Theater | *Theat* | theatre, theater |
| Fernsehen | *TV* | television |
| Typographie, Buchdruck | *Typ* | typography and printing |
| Hochschule | *Univ* | university |

# Abkürzungen   Abbreviations

| | | |
|---|---|---|
| (nord)amerikanisch | *US* | (North) American |
| gewöhnlich | *usu* | usually |
| Verb | *vb* | verb |
| Tiermedizin | *Vet* | veterinary medicine |
| intransitives Verb | *vi* | intransitive verb |
| reflexives Verb | *vr* | reflexive verb |
| transitives Verb | *vt* | transitive verb |
| schwache | *wk* | weak |
| Deklination | | declension |
| Zoologie | *Zool* | zoology |
| Partizip Perfekt | * | past participle |
| ohne ge- | | without ge- |

# A

**A, a** [aː] *nt* -, - A, a. **das A und O** the be-all and end-all; *(eines Wissensgebietes)* the basics *pl*; **von A bis Z** *(fig col)* from beginning to end; **wer A sagt, muß auch B sagen** *(prov)* in for a penny, in for a pound *(prov)*; **A wie Anton** ≃ A for Andrew, A for Able *(US)*.

**A** *f* = **Autobahn** ≃ M *(Brit)*.

**à** [a] *prep (esp Comm)* at.

**AA¹** [aːˈǀaː] *nt no pl* = **Auswärtiges Amt** ≃ FO *(Brit)*.

**AA²** [aːˈǀaː] *m* -s = **Anonyme Alkoholiker** AA.

**Aal** *m* -e eel. **sich winden wie ein** ~ to wriggle like an eel.

**aalen** *vr (col)* to stretch out. **sich in der Sonne** ~ to bask in the sun.

**aalglatt** *adj (pej)* slippery (as an eel), slick.

**a.a.O.** = **am angegebenen** *or* **angeführten Ort** loc. cit.

**Aas** *nt* -e **(a)** *(Tierleiche)* carrion, rotting carcass. **(b)** *pl* **Äser** *(col: Luder)* bugger *(col!)*. **kein** ~ not a single bloody person *(col)*.

**aasen** *vi (col)* to be wasteful. **mit etw** ~ to waste sth.

**Aasgeier** *m (lit, fig)* vulture.

**ab** [ap] **1** *prep +dat (räumlich)* from; *(zeitlich auch)* as of. **Kinder** ~ **14 Jahren** children from (the age of) 14; **Soldaten** ~ **Gefreitem** soldiers from private up; ~ **Werk** *(Comm)* ex works; ~ **sofort** as of now/then. **2** *adv* off. **die nächste Straße rechts** ~ the next street off to the right; **München** ~ **12²⁰ Uhr** *(Rail)* leaving Munich 12.20; ~ **wann?** from when?, as of when?; ~ **nach Hause** off home with you; ~ **ins Bett mit euch!** off to bed with you; **Tell** ~ *(Theat)* exit Tell; **N und M** ~ *(Theat)* exeunt N and M; ~ **durch die Mitte!** *(col)* beat it! *(col)*, hop it! *(col)*; ~ **und zu** from time to time, now and then.

**ab|ändern** *vt sep* to alter *(in +acc to)*; *Gesetzentwurf* to amend *(in +acc to)*; *Strafe, Urteil* to revise *(in +acc to)*.

**Ab|änderung** *f siehe vt* alteration *(gen to)*; amendment; revision.

**Ab|änderungsantrag** *m (Parl)* proposed amendment. **einen** ~ **einbringen** to submit an amendment.

**ab|arbeiten** *sep* **1** *vt Schuld* to work off. **2** *vr* to slave (away).

**Ab|art** *f* variety *(auch Biol)*; *(Variation)* variation *(gen on)*.

**ab|artig 1** *adj* **(a)** abnormal, deviant. **(b)** *(widersinnig)* perverse. **2** *adv (col)* **das tut** ~ **weh** that hurts like hell *(col)*.

**Abb.** = **Abbildung** fig.

**Abbau** *m no pl* **(a)** *(von Personal, Produktion etc)* reduction *(gen in, of)*, cutback *(gen in)*. **(b)** *(von Kohlen etc)* mining. **(c)** *(Chem)* decomposition. **(d)** *(lit, fig: Demontage)* dismantling.

**abbaubar** *adj* **biologisch** ~ biodegradable.

**abbauen** *sep* **1** *vt* **(a)** *(demontieren)* Gerüst, System to dismantle; *Gerüst auch, Zelt* to take down; *Lager* to break, to strike. **(b)** *(verringern)* Produktion, Personal, Bürokratie to cut back, to reduce. **Arbeitsplätze** ~ to make job cuts. **(c)** *Kohle etc* to mine. **(d)** *(Chem)* to break down, to decompose. **2** *vi (col: erlahmen)* to flag, to wilt.

**abbeißen** *sep irreg* **1** *vt* to bite off. **2** *vi* to take a bite.

**abbeizen** *vt sep Farbe* to strip.

**Abbeizmittel** *nt* paint stripper *or* remover.

**abbekommen*** *vt sep irreg* to get. **etwas** ~ to get some (of it); *(beschädigt werden)* to get damaged; *(verletzt werden)* to get hurt; **das Auto/er hat dabei ganz schön was** ~ *(col)* the car/he really copped it *(col)*; **nichts** ~ not to get any (of it); *(nicht beschädigt werden)* not to get damaged; *(nicht verletzt werden)* to come off unscathed; **sein(en) Teil** ~ *(lit, fig)* to get one's fair share.

**abberufen*** *vt sep irreg Diplomaten etc* to recall. **(von Gott)** ~ **werden** *(euph)* to be called to one's maker.

**Abberufung** *f* recall.

**abbestellen*** *vt sep* to cancel; *jdn* to put off.

**Abbestellung** *f* cancellation.

**abbetteln** *vt sep* **jdm etw** ~ to scrounge sth off *or* from sb *(col)*.

**abbezahlen*** *vt sep Raten, Auto etc* to pay off.

**abbiegen** *sep irreg* **1** *vt* **(a)** to bend; *(abbrechen)* to break off. **(b)** *(col: verhindern)* Frage, Thema to head off, to avoid. **das Gespräch** ~ to change the subject. **2** *vi aux sein* to turn off *(in +acc into)*; *(Straße)* to bend. **nach rechts** ~ to turn (off to the) right.

**Abbiegespur** *f (Mot)* turning lane.

**Abbild** *nt (Kopie)* copy, reproduction; *(Spiegelbild)* reflection; *(Wiedergabe)* picture, portrayal. **er ist das genaue** ~ **seines Vaters** he's the spitting image of his father.

**abbilden** *vt sep (lit, fig)* to depict, to portray; *(wiedergeben)* to reproduce.

**Abbildung** *f* **(a)** *(Illustration)* illustration; *(Schaubild)* diagram. **(b)** *(Wiedergabe)* reproduction.

**abbinden** *vt sep irreg* **(a)** *(losbinden)* to undo, to untie. **(b)** *(Med)* Arm, Bein etc to ligature.

**Abbitte** *f* apology. **(bei jdm wegen etw)** ~ **tun** *or* **leisten** to make *or* offer one's apologies (to sb for sth).

**abblasen** *vt sep irreg (col)* Veranstaltung, Feier, Streik to call off.

**abblättern** *vi sep aux sein (Putz, Farbe)* to flake (off).

**abblenden** *sep* **1** *vt Lampe* to shade, to screen; *(Aut) Scheinwerfer* to dip *(Brit)*, to dim *(US)*. **2** *vi (Aut)* to dip *(Brit)* or dim *(US)* one's headlights.

**Abblend-:** ~**licht** *nt (Aut)* dipped *(Brit)* or dimmed *(US)* headlights *pl*; ~**schalter** *m (Aut)* dipswitch

*(Brit)*, dimmer (switch) *(US)*.

**abblitzen** *vi sep aux sein (col)* to be sent packing *(bei* by*) (col)*. **jdn ~ lassen** to send sb packing.

**abblocken** *vt sep (Sport, fig)* to block.

**abbrausen** *vt sep* to give a shower. **sich ~** to have *or* take a shower.

**abbrechen** *sep irreg* **1** *vt* **(a)** to break off. **etw von etw ~** to break sth off sth; **sich** *(dat)* **einen ~** *(col) (Umstände machen)* to make heavy weather of it *(col)*; *(sich sehr anstrengen)* to bust a gut *(col)*. **(b)** *Zelt* to take down; *Lager* to strike; *(niederreißen)* to demolish, to pull down. **(c)** *(beenden)* to break off; *Raumflug, Experiment, (Comp)* Operation to abort; *Streik* to call off; *Schwangerschaft* to terminate. **2** *vi* **(a)** *aux sein* to break off; *(Bleistift, Fingernagel)* to break. **(b)** *(aufhören)* to break off, to stop.

**abbremsen** *vti sep* to brake, to slow down; *(fig)* to curb.

**abbrennen** *sep irreg* **1** *vt Gehöft, Dorf* to burn down; *Feuerwerk, Rakete* to let off; *Kerze etc* to burn. **ein Feuerwerk ~** to have a fireworks display. **2** *vi aux sein* to burn down.

**abbringen** *vt sep irreg* **jdn davon ~, etw zu tun** to stop sb doing sth; *(abraten auch)* to persuade sb not to do sth; **jdn von etw ~** to make sb change his/her mind about sth; **jdn vom Rauchen ~** to get sb to stop smoking.

**abbröckeln** *vi sep aux sein* to crumble away; *(fig)* to fall off. **der Ruf der Firma ist am A~** the firm's reputation is gradually declining.

**Abbruch** *m no pl* **(a)** *(das Niederreißen)* demolition. **(b)** *(Beendigung)* breaking off; *(von Schwangerschaft)* termination; *(von Raumflug etc)* abortion, aborting; *(von Veranstaltung etc)* stopping. **es kam zum ~ des Kampfes** the fight had to be stopped. **(c)** *(Schaden)* harm, damage. **einer Sache** *(dat)* **~ tun** to do (some) harm *or* damage to sth.

**Abbruch-: ~arbeiten** *pl* demolition work; **a~reif** *adj* only fit for demolition; **~unternehmer** *m* demolition contractor.

**abbrühen** *vt sep* to scald; *siehe* **abgebrüht.**

**abbuchen** *vt sep (im Einzelfall)* to debit *(von* to, against*)*; *(durch Dauerauftrag)* to pay by standing order *(von* from*)*.

**Abbuchung** *f siehe vt* debit; (payment by) standing order.

**abbürsten** *vt sep Staub* to brush off *(von etw* sth*)*; *Schuhe* to brush.

**abbüßen** *vt sep Strafe* to serve.

**Abc** [aːbeːˈtseː] *nt -, - (lit, fig)* ABC. **Namen nach dem ~ ordnen** to put names in alphabetical order.

**abchecken** [ˈaptʃɛkn] *vt sep* to check.

**Abc-Schütze** *m (hum)* school-beginner.

**ABC-Waffen** *pl* atomic, biological and chemical weapons.

**Abdampf** *m* exhaust steam.

**abdampfen** *vi sep aux sein (fig col: losgehen, -fahren)* to hit the road *(col)*.

**abdanken** *vi sep* to resign; *(König etc)* to abdicate.

**Abdankung** *f (Thronverzicht)* abdication; *(Rücktritt)* resignation.

**abdecken** *vt sep* **(a)** *(freilegen) Tisch* to clear; *Bett* to turn down; *Haus* to tear the roof off. **(b)** *(zudecken) Grab, Loch* to cover (over). **(c)** *(ausgleichen, einschließen)* to cover. **(d)** *(fig) Bereich, Thema* to cover.

**Abdecker** *m* - knacker.

**Abdeckung** *f* cover.

**abdichten** *vt sep (isolieren)* to insulate; *Loch, Leck, Rohr* to seal (up); *Ritzen* to stop up. **gegen Luft/ Wasser ~** to make airtight/watertight.

**Abdichtung** *f (Isolierung)* insulation; *(Verschluß, Dichtung)* seal.

**abdienen** *vt sep (Mil: ableisten)* to serve.

**abdrängen** *vt sep* to push away *(von* from*)*. **einen Spieler vom Ball ~** to push a player off the ball.

**abdrehen** *sep* **1** *vt* **(a)** *Gas, Wasser, Hahn* to turn off; *Licht, Radio auch* to switch off. **(b)** *Film* to shoot, to film. **(c)** *Hals* to wring. **jdm den Hals ~** to wring sb's neck *(col)*; *(col: ruinieren)* to bankrupt sb. **2** *vi aux sein or haben (Richtung ändern)* to change course. **nach Osten ~** to turn east.

**abdriften** *vi sep aux sein (Naut, Aviat, fig)* to drift off.

**abdrosseln** *vt sep Motor* to throttle down; *(fig) Produktion* to cut down (on).

**Abdruck¹** *m, pl* **Abdrücke** imprint, impression; *(Stempel~)* stamp; *(Finger~, Fuß~)* print. **einen ~ machen** to take *or* make an impression.

**Abdruck²** *m -e (Kopie)* copy; *(Nachdruck)* reprint.

**abdrucken** *vt sep* to print. **wieder ~** to reprint.

**abdrücken** *sep* **1** *vt* **(a)** *Gewehr* to fire. **(b)** *Vene* to constrict. **jdm die Luft ~** *(col) (lit)* to squeeze all the breath out of sb; *(fig)* to force sb into bankruptcy, to squeeze the lifeblood out of sb. **2** *vi* to pull *or* squeeze the trigger.

**abdunkeln** *vt sep Lampe* to dim; *Zimmer auch* to darken.

**abduschen** *vt sep* = **abbrausen.**

**ab|ebben** *vi sep aux sein* to die *or* fade away.

**Abend** *m -e* evening. **am ~** in the evening; *(jeden ~)* in the evening(s); **am ~ des 4. April** on the evening *or* night of April 4th; **gegen ~** towards (the) evening; **~ für ~** every evening *or* night, night after night; **eines ~s** one evening; **den ganzen ~ (über)** the whole evening; **guten ~** good evening; **letzten ~** yesterday evening, last night; **zu ~ essen** to have supper *or* dinner; **je später der ~, desto schöner or netter die Gäste** *(prov)* the best guests always come late; **man soll den Tag nicht vor dem ~ loben** *(Prov)* don't count your chickens before they're hatched *(Prov)*.

**abend** *adv* **gestern/morgen/Mittwoch ~** yesterday/ tomorrow/Wednesday evening, last/tomorrow/Wednesday night.

**Abend-: ~andacht** *f* evening service; **~anzug** *m* dinner jacket, DJ *(col)*, tuxedo *(US)*; **~blatt** *nt* evening (news)paper; **~brot** *nt* supper; **~brot essen** to have (one's) supper; **~dämmerung** *f* dusk, twilight; **~essen** *nt* supper, evening meal; *(größer)* dinner; **mit dem ~essen auf jdn warten** to wait with supper *or* dinner for sb; **a~füllend** *adj* taking up the whole evening; *Film, Stück* full-length; **~gymnasium** *nt* night school; **~kasse** *f (Theat)* box office; **~kleid** *nt* evening dress *or* gown; **~kurs(us)** *m* evening classes *pl (für* in*)*; **~land** *nt no pl (geh)* West, western world; **a~ländisch** *(geh) adj* western, occidental *(liter)*.

**abendlich** *adj no pred* evening *attr*. **die ~e Stille** the quiet of the evening; **es war schon um drei Uhr ~ kühl** at three there was already an evening chill.

**Abend-: ~mahl** *nt (Eccl)* (Holy) Communion; **das Letzte ~mahl** the Last Supper; **~mahlzeit** *f* evening meal; **~programm** *nt (Rad, TV)* evening('s) programmes *(Brit) or* programs *(US) pl*; **~rot** *nt* sunset.

**abends** *adv* in the evening; *(jeden Abend)* in the evening(s). **spät ~** late in the evening; **~ um neun** at nine in the evening.

**Abend-: ~schule** *f* night school; **~schüler** *m* night-school student; **~stern** *m* evening star; **~stunde** *f* evening (hour); **sich bis in die ~stunden**

**hinziehen** to go on (late) into the evening; **~vorstellung** f evening performance; **~zeitung** f evening paper.

**Abenteuer** nt - adventure; (Liebes~ auch) affair. **ein militärisches ~** a military venture; **auf ~ aussein** to be looking for adventure.

**abenteuerlich** adj (a) adventurous; (erlebnishungrig auch) adventuresome. (b) (phantastisch) bizarre; Erzählung auch fantastic.

**Abenteuer-:** **~lust** f thirst for adventure; **~roman** m adventure story; **~spielplatz** m adventure playground; **~urlaub** m adventure holiday.

**Abenteurer** m - adventurer (auch pej).

**Abenteu(r)erin** f (female) adventurer.

**aber 1** conj (a) but. **~ dennoch** or **trotzdem** but still; **schönes Wetter heute, was? — ja, ~ etwas kalt** nice weather, eh? — yes, a bit cold though; **da er ~ nicht wußte ...** however, since he didn't know ...; **oder ~** or else. (b) (zur Verstärkung) **~ ja!** oh, yes!; (sicher) but of course; **~ selbstverständlich!** but of course; **~ nein!** oh, no!; (selbstverständlich nicht) of course not!; **~ Renate!** but Renate!; **~, ~!** tut, tut!; **das ist ~ schrecklich!** but that's awful!; **das mach' ich ~ nicht!** I will not do that!; **das ist ~ heiß/schön!** that's really hot/nice; **du hast ~ einen schönen Ball** you've got a nice ball, haven't you?; **bist du ~ braun!** aren't you brown!; **das geht ~ zu weit!** that's really going too far!

**2** adv (liter) **tausend und ~ tausend** thousands upon thousands.

**Aber** nt - or (col) **-s** but. **kein ~!** no buts (about it); **die Sache hat ein ~** there's just one snag.

**Aberglaube(n)** m superstition; (fig auch) myth.

**abergläubisch** adj superstitious.

**ab|erkennen*** vt sep or (rare) insep irreg **jdm etw ~** to strip sb of sth.

**Ab|erkennung** f deprivation, stripping.

**aber-:** **~malig** adj attr repeated; **~mals** adv once more.

**ab|ernten** vti sep to harvest.

**Abertausende** pl thousands upon thousands pl.

**aberwitzig** adj (liter) siehe **wahnwitzig**.

**Abessinien** [-iən] nt Abyssinia.

**Abessinier(in** f) [-iɐ, -iərɪn] m - Abyssinian.

**abessinisch** adj Abyssinian.

**Abf.** (Rail) = **Abfahrt** dep.

**abfackeln** vt Gas to burn off.

**abfahrbereit** adj ready to leave.

**abfahren** sep irreg aux sein **1** vi (a) to leave, to depart (form); (Schiff auch) to sail. **der Zug fährt um 8⁰⁰ von Bremen ab** the train leaves Bremen at 8 o'clock; **der Zug ist abgefahren** (lit) the train has left; (fig) we've/you've etc missed the boat. (b) (col: abgewiesen werden) **jdn ~ lassen** to tell sb to get lost (col). (c) (col: mögen) **auf jdn/etw ~** to go for sb/sth in a big way (col).

**2** vt (a) Stück von Mauer etc to knock off. **der Traktor hat ihm ein Bein abgefahren** the tractor severed his leg. (b) aux sein or haben Strecke (bereisen) to cover; (Polizei etc) to patrol. **wir mußten die ganze Strecke noch einmal ~, um ... zu suchen** we had to go over the whole stretch again to look for ... (c) (abnutzen) (völlig) to wear out; (teilweise) to wear; (benutzen) Fahrkarte to use. **abgefahrene Reifen/Schienen** worn tyres/rails. (d) (Film, TV) Kamera to roll; Film to start. **bitte ~!** roll 'em!

**3** vr (Reifen etc) to wear.

**Abfahrt** f (a) (von Zug, Bus etc) departure. **bis zur ~ sind es noch fünf Minuten** there's still five minutes before the train/bus goes; **Vorsicht bei der ~ des Zuges!** stand clear, the train is about to leave! (b)

(Ski) (Talfahrt) descent; (~sstrecke) (ski-) run. (c) (Autobahn~) exit. **die ~ Gießen** the exit for Gießen.

**Abfahrts-:** **~lauf** m (Ski) downhill; **~tafel** f departure board; **~zeit** f departure time.

**Abfall** m, pl **Abfälle** (a) refuse; (Haus~) rubbish (esp Brit), garbage (esp US); (Straßen~) litter. (b) no pl (Lossagung) break (von with). (c) no pl (Rückgang) drop (gen in), fall (gen in); (Verschlechterung auch) deterioration.

**Abfall-:** **~beseitigung** f refuse or garbage (US) disposal; **~eimer** m rubbish bin, trashcan (US).

**abfallen** vi sep irreg aux sein (a) (herunterfallen) to fall or drop off; (Blätter, Blüten etc) to fall. (b) (col: herausspringen) **wieviel fällt bei dem Geschäft für mich ab?** how much do I get out of the deal? (c) (fig: übrigbleiben) to be left (over). (d) (schlechter werden) to go downhill; (Sport: zurückbleiben) to drop back. (e) **alle Unsicherheit/Furcht fiel von ihm ab** all his uncertainty/fear left him. (f) (Fraktion: von Partei etc) to break away (von from). **vom Glauben ~** to leave the faith. (g) (sich senken: Gelände) to fall away; (sich vermindern: Druck, Temperatur) to fall.

**abfällig** adj Bemerkung, Kritik disparaging; Lächeln derisive; Urteil adverse. **über jdn ~ reden/sprechen** to be disparaging about sb.

**Abfall-:** **~produkt** nt waste-product; (von Forschung) by-product, spin-off; **~verwertung** f waste utilization.

**abfälschen** vti sep (Sport) to deflect.

**abfangen** vt sep irreg (a) Flugzeug, Funkspruch, Brief, Ball to intercept; Menschen auch to catch (col); Schlag to block; (col: anlocken) Kunden to lure away. (b) (bremsen) Fahrzeug to bring under control; Flugzeug auch to pull out; Aufprall to absorb; Trend to check.

**Abfangjäger** m (Mil) interceptor fighter.

**abfärben** vi sep (a) (Wäsche) to run. **paß auf, die Wand färbt ab!** be careful, the paint comes off the wall. (b) (fig) **auf jdn ~** to rub off on sb.

**abfassen** vt sep (verfassen) to write; Entwurf to draft.

**abfaulen** vi sep aux sein to rot away or off.

**abfeiern** vt sep (col) Überstunden **~** to take time off in lieu of overtime pay.

**abfeilen** vt sep to file off or (glättend) down.

**abfertigen** vt sep (a) (versandfertig machen) Pakete, Waren to prepare for dispatch, to process; Gepäck to check (in); (be- und entladen) Flugzeug auch ready for take-off. (b) (bedienen) Kunden etc to attend to; (col: Sport) Gegner to deal with. **jdn kurz ~** (col) to snub sb. (c) (kontrollieren) Waren, Reisende to clear.

**Abfertigung** f (a) siehe vt (a) making ready for dispatch, processing (form); checking; making ready for take-off. (b) (Bedienung) (von Kunden) service; (von Antragstellern) dealing with. (c) (von Waren, Reisenden) clearance. **die ~ an der Grenze** customs clearance at the border. (d) (~sstelle) (für Waren) dispatch office; (im Flughafen) check-in.

**abfeuern** vt sep to fire.

**abfinden** sep irreg **1** vt to pay off; Gläubiger auch to settle with; (entschädigen) to compensate. **er wurde von der Versicherung mit 20.000 DM abgefunden** he was paid 20,000 marks (in) compensation by the insurance company; **jdn mit leeren Versprechungen ~** to fob sb off with empty promises. **2** vr **sich mit jdm/etw ~** to come to terms with sb/sth; **er konnte sich nie damit ~, daß ...** he could never accept the fact that ...

**Abfindung** f (von Gläubigern) paying off; (Entschä-

*digung)* compensation; *(bei Entlassung)* severance pay; *(wegen Rationalisierung)* redundancy payment.

**abflachen** *sep* **1** *vt* to level (off), to flatten (out). **2** *vr (Land)* to flatten out. **3** *vi aux sein (fig: sinken)* to decline.

**abflauen** *vi sep aux sein* **(a)** *(Wind)* to die down. **nach (dem) A~ des Windes** when the wind had died down. **(b)** *(fig) (Erregung)* to die away; *(Interesse auch)* to wane; *(Börsenkurse)* to drop; *(Geschäfte, Konjunktur)* to fall off.

**abfliegen** *sep irreg* **1** *vi aux sein (Aviat)* to take off *(nach* for); *(Zugvögel)* to migrate. **sie sind gestern nach München abgeflogen** they flew off to Munich yesterday. **2** *vt Gelände* to fly over.

**abfließen** *vi sep irreg aux sein (wegfließen)* to drain or flow away; *(durch ein Leck)* to leak away. **ins Ausland ~** *(Geld)* to flow out of the country.

**Abflug** *m* take-off; *(von Zugvögeln)* migration.

**Abflug-:** **~anzeige** *f* departure board; **a~bereit** *adj* ready for take-off; **~halle** *f* departure lounge; **~schalter** *m* check-in desk; **~zeit** *f* departure time.

**Abfluß** *m* **(a)** *(Abfließen)* draining away; *(durch ein Leck)* leakage. **der ~ von Kapital ins Ausland** the flow of capital out of the country. **(b)** *(~stelle)* drain; *(von Teich etc)* outlet; *(~rohr)* drainpipe; *(von sanitären Anlagen)* wastepipe.

**Abfluß-:** **~rinne** *f* gutter; **~rohr** *nt* outlet; *(im Gebäude)* wastepipe; *(außen am Gebäude)* drainpipe; *(unterirdisch)* drain.

**Abfolge** *f (geh)* sequence, succession.

**abfordern** *vt sep* **jdm etw ~** to demand sth from sb.

**Abfrage** *f (Comp)* query.

**abfragen** *vt sep* **(a)** *(esp Sch)* **jdn etw ~** to question sb on sth; *(Lehrer)* to test sb orally on sth. **(b)** *(Comp)* Information to call up; *Datenbank* to query, to interrogate.

**abfrieren** *sep irreg* **1** *vi aux sein* **abgefroren sein** *(Körperteil)* to be frostbitten; **ihm sind die Füße abgefroren** his feet got frostbite. **2** *vt* **sich** *(dat)* **einen ~** *(col)* to freeze to death *(col)*.

**Abfuhr** *f* **-en** **(a)** *no pl (Abtransport)* removal. **(b)** *(col: Zurückweisung)* snub, rebuff. **jdm eine ~ erteilen** to snub or rebuff sb; *(Sport)* to thrash sb *(col)*; **sich** *(dat)* **eine ~ holen** to meet with a snub.

**abführen** *sep* **1** *vt* **(a)** *(wegführen)* to lead away; *(ableiten) Gase etc* to draw off. **~! away with him/her etc!** **(b)** *(abgeben) Betrag* to pay *(an +acc* to). **2** *vi* **(a)** *(wegführen)* **der Weg führt hier (von der Straße) ab** the path leaves the road here; **das würde vom Thema ~** that would take us off the subject. **(b)** *(den Darm anregen)* to have a laxative effect.

**abführend** *adj* laxative *no adv.* **~ wirken** to have a laxative effect.

**Abführmittel** *nt* laxative.

**Abfüll-:** **~anlage** *f* bottling plant; **~betrieb** *m* bottling factory.

**abfüllen** *vt sep* **(a)** *(in Flaschen)* to bottle; *Flasche* to fill. **Wein in Flaschen ~** to bottle wine. **(b)** **jdn ~** *(col)* to get sb pickled *(col)* or sloshed *(col)*.

**Abgabe** *f* **(a)** *no pl (Abliefern)* handing in; *(von Gepäck auch)* depositing; *(Übergabe: von Brief etc)* delivery. **zur ~ von etw aufgefordert werden** to be told to hand sth in. **(b)** *no pl (Verkauf)* sale. **(c)** *no pl (von Wärme etc)* giving off; *(von Schuß, Salve)* firing; *(von Erklärung etc)* giving; *(von Stimme)* casting. **(d)** *(Sport: Abspiel)* pass. **(e)** *(Steuer)* tax; *(auf Tabak etc auch)* duty; *(soziale ~)* contribution.

**abgabe(n)-:** **~frei** *adj, adv* tax-free, exempt from tax; **~pflichtig** *adj* liable to taxation.

**Abgabetermin** *m* closing date; *(für Dissertation etc)*

submission date.

**Abgang** *m no pl* **(a)** *(Absendung)* dispatch. **vor ~ der Post** before the post goes. **(b)** *(Abfahrt)* departure. **(c)** *(aus einem Amt)* departure; *(Schul~)* leaving. **seit seinem ~ vom Gymnasium** since he left the grammar school. **(d)** *(Theat, fig)* exit.

**Abgangszeugnis** *nt* leaving certificate.

**Abgas** *nt* exhaust *no pl,* exhaust fumes *pl,* waste gas *(esp Tech)*. **Luftverschmutzung durch ~e** exhaust gas pollution.

**Abgas-:** **a~arm** *adj Fahrzeug* low-emission; **a~frei** *adj Fahrzeug* exhaust-free; **~reinigung** *f (Aut)* exhaust emission control; **~sonderuntersuchung** *f (Aut)* compulsory annual test of a car's emission levels; **~wolke** *f* cloud of exhaust fumes.

**ABGB** ['a:be:ge:'be:] *nt (Aus)* = **Allgemeines Bürgerliches Gesetzbuch** *Austrian Civil code.*

**abge|arbeitet** *adj (verbraucht)* workworn; *(erschöpft)* exhausted.

**abgeben** *sep irreg* **1** *vt* **(a)** *(abliefern)* to hand in; *Gepäck* to deposit; *(übergeben)* to deliver; *(weggeben)* to give away; *(gegen Gebühr)* to sell; *(an einen anderen Inhaber)* to hand over; *(überlassen) Auftrag* to pass on *(an +acc* to); *(abtreten) Posten* to hand over *(an +acc* to). **Kinderwagen abzugeben** pram for sale; **jdm etw von seinem Kuchen ~** to give sb some of one's cake. **(b)** *(Sport) Punkte, Rang* to concede; *(abspielen)* to pass. **(c)** *Schuß, Salve* to fire; *Erklärung* to give; *Stimmen* to cast. **(d)** *Rahmen, Hintergrund, Stoff, Material etc* to provide; *(verkörpern)* to make. **den Vermittler ~** *(col)* to act as mediator. **2** *vr* **sich mit jdm/etw ~** *(sich beschäftigen)* to bother oneself with sb/sth; *(sich einlassen)* to associate with sb/sth. **3** *vi (Sport)* to pass.

**abgebrannt** *adj pred (col)* broke *(col)*.

**abgebrochen** *adj (nicht beendet) Studium* incomplete. **er ist ~er Mediziner** *(col)* he broke off his medical studies.

**abgebrüht** *adj (col: skrupellos)* hard-boiled *(col)*, hardened.

**abgedroschen** *adj (col)* hackneyed, well-worn; *Witz auch* corny *(col)*. **eine ~e Phrase** a cliché.

**abgefeimt** *adj* cunning, wily.

**abgegriffen** *adj Buch* (well-)worn; *(fig) Phrasen etc* hackneyed.

**abgehackt** *adj* clipped. **~ sprechen** to clip one's words.

**abgehangen** *adj* **(gut)** **~** *(Fleisch)* well-hung.

**abgehärmt** *adj* careworn.

**abgehärtet** *adj* tough, hardy; *(fig)* hardened. **gegen Erkältungen ~ sein** to be immune to colds.

**abgehen** *sep irreg aux sein* **1** *vi* **(a)** *(abfahren)* to leave, to depart *(form) (nach* for). **(b)** *(Theat: abtreten)* to exit. **(c)** *(ausscheiden)* to leave. **von der Schule ~** to leave school. **(d)** *(sich lösen: Knopf etc)* to come off; *(herausgehen: Farbe etc auch)* to come out. **(e)** *(abgesandt werden)* to be sent or dispatched; *(Funkspruch)* to be sent. **etw ~ lassen** dispatch sth. **(f)** *(col: fehlen)* **jdm geht Verständnis/Taktgefühl ab** sb lacks understanding/tact. **(g)** *(abgezogen werden)* **(von etw) ~** *(von Preis)* to be taken off (sth); *(von Verdienst auch)* to be deducted (from sth); **davon gehen 5% ab** 5% is taken off that. **(h)** *(abzweigen)* to branch off; *(bei Gabelung auch)* to fork off. **(i)** *(abweichen)* **von einem Plan/einer Forderung ~** to give up a plan/demand; **von seiner Meinung ~** to change one's opinion. **(j)** *(verlaufen)* to go. **es ging nicht ohne Streit ab** there was an argument. **(k)** *(col)* **das geht gut ab** that's really great.

**2** *vt (entlanggehen)* to walk along; *(Mil) Gelände* to patrol.

**abgehetzt** *adj* out of breath.

**abgekämpft** *adj* exhausted.

**abgekartet** *adj (col)* eine ~e Sache, ein ~es Spiel a put-up job *(col)*.

**abgeklärt** *adj* serene, tranquil.

**abgelagert** *adj Wein* mature; *Holz, Tabak* seasoned.

**abgelegen** *adj (entfernt) Dorf, Land* remote; *(einsam)* isolated.

**abgeleiert** *adj (pej)* banal, trite.

**abgelten** *vt sep irreg Ansprüche* to satisfy.

**abgemacht 1** *interj* OK, that's settled; *(bei Kauf)* it's a deal. **2** *adj* eine ~e Sache a fix *(col)*.

**abgemagert** *adj (sehr dünn)* thin; *(ausgemergelt)* emaciated.

**abgemergelt** *adj* emaciated.

**abgemessen** *adj Schritt, Worte* measured, deliberate.

**abgeneigt** *adj* averse *pred (dat* to*)*. **ich wäre gar nicht ~** *(col)* actually I wouldn't mind.

**abgenutzt** *adj* worn, shabby; *Besen* worn out; *Reifen* worn; *(völlig)* worn out; *(fig) Klischees* well-worn.

**Abge|ordnete(r)** *mf decl as adj* (elected) representative; *(von Parlament)* member of parliament.

**abgerissen** *adj Kleidung* tattered; *Worte, Gedanken* disjointed.

**Abgesandte(r)** *mf decl as adj* envoy.

**abgeschieden** *adj (geh: einsam)* secluded. **~ leben/wohnen** to live in seclusion.

**Abgeschiedenheit** *f* seclusion.

**abgeschlafft** *adj (col)* whacked *(col)*.

**abgeschlagen** *adj* **(a)** *(besiegt)* defeated; *(zurück)* behind. **weit ~ liegen** to be way behind; **er landete ~ auf dem 8. Platz** he finished up way down in 8th place. **(b)** *(erschöpft)* shattered *(col)*.

**abgeschlossen** *adj (einsam)* isolated; *(attr: geschlossen) Wohnung* self-contained.

**Abgeschlossenheit** *f* isolation.

**abgeschmackt** *adj* tasteless; *Witz auch* corny; *Worte* fatuous.

**abgeschnitten** *adj* isolated. **von der Außenwelt ~** cut off from the outside world.

**abgesehen 1** *ptp of* absehen. **es auf jdn ~ haben** to have it in for sb *(col)*; *(interessiert sein)* to have one's eye on sb; **du hast es nur darauf ~, mich zu ärgern** you're only trying to annoy me. **2** *adv:* **~ von jdm/etw** apart from sb/sth; **~ davon, daß ...** apart from the fact that ...

**abgespannt** *adj* weary, tired.

**Abgespanntheit** *f* weariness, tiredness.

**abgespielt** *adj Schallplatte* worn.

**abgestanden** *adj Luft, Wasser* stale; *Bier, Limonade etc* flat.

**abgestorben** *adj Glieder* numb; *Pflanze, Ast, Gewebe* dead.

**abgestumpft** *adj (gefühllos) Person* insensitive; *Gefühle, Gewissen* dulled.

**abgetakelt** *adj (pej col)* seedy.

**abgetan** *adj pred* finished with. **damit ist die Sache ~** that settles the matter.

**abgetragen** *adj* worn. **~e Kleider** old clothes.

**abgewinnen** *vt sep irreg* **(a)** *(lit)* jdm etw ~ to win sth from sb. **(b)** *(fig)* jdm ein Lächeln ~ to persuade sb to smile; **dem Meer Land ~** to reclaim land from the sea; **einer Sache keinen Reiz ~ können** to be unable to see anything attractive in sth.

**abgewogen** *adj Urteil, Worte* balanced.

**abgewöhnen** *vt sep* jdm etw ~ to cure sb of sth; *das Rauchen, Trinken* to get sb to give up sth; **sich** *(dat)* **das Trinken ~** to give up drinking; **noch einen zum A~** *(hum)* one last one; *(von Alkohol auch)* one

for the road; **das/die ist ja zum A~** *(col)* that/she is enough to put anyone off.

**abgewrackt** *adj (abgetakelt) Mensch* broken down, washed up *(esp US col)*.

**abgezehrt** *adj* emaciated.

**abgießen** *vt sep irreg* **(a)** *Flüssigkeit* to pour off; *Kartoffeln* to strain. **(b)** *(Art, Metal)* to cast.

**Abglanz** *m* reflection *(auch fig)*. **nur ein schwacher** *or* **matter ~** *(fig)* a pale reflection.

**abgleichen** *vt sep irreg (fig) Termine, Vorgehensweise* to coordinate; *Dateien, Einträge* to compare.

**abgleiten** *vi sep irreg aux sein (geh: abrutschen)* to slip; *(Gedanken)* to wander; *(Fin: Kurs)* to drop, to fall. **von etw ~** to slip off sth.

**Abgott** *m,* **Abgöttin** *f* idol. **jdn zum ~ machen** to idolize sb.

**abgöttisch** *adj* idolatrous. **jdn ~ lieben** to idolize sb.

**abgraben** *vt sep irreg Erdreich* to dig away. **jdm das Wasser ~** *(fig col)* to take away sb's livelihood.

**abgrasen** *vt sep Feld* to graze; *(fig col) Geschäfte* to scour, to comb; *Thema* to do to death *(col)*.

**abgrenzen** *sep* **1** *vt Gelände* to fence off; *(fig) Rechte, Befugnisse, Begriff* to delimit *(gegen, von* from*)*. **etw durch einen Zaun/eine Mauer/Hecke ~** to fence/wall/hedge sth off. **2** *vr* to dissociate oneself *(gegen* from*)*.

**Abgrenzung** *f* **(a)** *no pl siehe vt* fencing/walling/hedging off; *(fig)* delimitation. **(b)** *siehe vr* dissociation *(gegen* from*)*. **(c)** *(Zaun)* fencing *no pl*.

**Abgrund** *m* precipice; *(Schlucht, fig)* abyss, chasm. **sich am Rande eines ~es befinden** *(fig)* to be on the brink of disaster; **in einen ~ von Verrat blicken** *(fig)* to stare into a bottomless pit of treachery.

**abgründig** *adj Humor, Ironie* cryptic.

**abgrundtief** *adj Haß, Verachtung* profound.

**abgucken** *vti sep* to copy. **jdm etw ~** to copy sth from sb; **bei jdm (etw) ~** *(Sch)* to copy (sth) from *or* off *(col)* sb.

**Abguß** *m* **(a)** *(Art, Metal) (Vorgang)* casting; *(Form)* cast. **(b)** *(dial: Ausguß)* sink.

**abhaben** *vt sep irreg (col)* **(a)** *Brille, Hut* to have off; *(abgemacht haben)* to have got off. **(b)** *(abbekommen)* to have. **willst du ein Stück ~?** do you want a bit?

**abhacken** *vt sep* to chop off, to hack off; *siehe* **abgehackt.**

**abhaken** *vt sep (markieren)* to tick *or (esp US)* check off; *(fig)* to cross off.

**abhalten** *vt sep irreg* **(a)** *Kälte, Hitze, Fliegen* to keep off. **(b)** *(hindern)* to stop, to prevent. **jdn von etw/von der Arbeit ~** to keep sb from sth/from working; **jdn davon ~, etw zu tun** to prevent sb from doing sth; **laß dich nicht ~!** don't let me/us *etc* stop you. **(c)** *(veranstalten)* to hold.

**Abhaltung** *f no pl (Durchführung)* holding.

**abhandeln** *vt sep* **(a)** *Thema* to treat, to deal with. **(b)** *(abkaufen)* jdm etw ~ to do a deal with sb for sth. **(c)** jdm 8 Mark ~ to beat sb down 8 marks.

**abhanden** *adv:* **~ kommen** to get lost; **jdm ist etw ~ gekommen** sb has lost sth.

**Abhandlung** *f* treatise, discourse *(über +acc* (up)on*)*.

**Abhang** *m* slope, incline.

**abhängen** *sep* **1** *vt* **(a)** *Bild* to take down; *(Rail) Wagen* to uncouple; *Anhänger* to unhitch. **(b)** *(col: hinter sich lassen) jdn* to shake off *(col)*. **2** *vi* **(a)** *irreg (Fleisch etc)* to hang; *siehe* **abgehangen. (b)** *irreg* **von etw ~** to depend on sth, to be dependent on sth; **das hängt ganz davon ab** it all depends. **(c)** *(Telec col)* to hang up *(col)*.

**abhängig** *adj* dependent *(auch euph: süchtig)*; *Satz*

*auch* subordinate; *Rede* indirect. **von etw ~ sein** to be dependent on sth; *(Gram)* to be governed by sth; **voneinander ~ sein** to be dependent on each other.

**Abhängigkeit** f **(a)** *no pl (Bedingtheit)* dependency *no pl (von on)*; *(Gram: von Sätzen)* subordination *(von to)*. **(b)** *(Angewiesensein, euph: Sucht)* dependence *(von on)*. **gegenseitige ~** interdependence.

**abhärten** *sep* **1** *vt* to toughen up. **2** *vi* **das härtet ab** that toughens you up. **3** *vr* to toughen oneself up. **sich gegen etw ~** to toughen oneself against sth; *(fig)* to harden oneself to sth; *siehe* **abgehärtet.**

**Abhärtung** f *siehe vb* toughening up; hardening.

**abhauen** *sep irreg* **1** *vi aux sein (col)* to clear out, to vamoose *(US col)*; *(verschwinden auch)* to push off. **hau ab!** beat it! *(col)*. **2** *vt Kopf* to chop off; *Baum* to chop down; *Verputz, Schicht* to knock off.

**abheben** *sep irreg* **1** *vti* **(a)** *(anheben)* to lift (up), to raise; *(abnehmen)* to take off; *Telefonhörer* to pick up, to lift; *Telefon* to answer; *(beim Stricken) Masche* to slip. **(b)** *Geld* to withdraw. **wenn Sie ~ wollen** if you wish to make a withdrawal. **2** *vi* **(a)** *(Flugzeug)* to take off; *(Rakete)* to lift off. **(b)** *(Cards: vor Spielbeginn etc)* to cut. **3** *vr* **sich von jdm/etw** *or* **gegen jdn/etw ~** to stand out from/against sb/sth; **sich wohltuend gegen etw ~** to contrast pleasantly with sth.

**abheften** *vt sep* **(a)** *Rechnungen etc* to file away. **(b)** *(Sew)* to tack, to baste.

**abhelfen** *vi sep irreg +dat* to remedy; *einem Fehler auch* to rectify.

**abhetzen** *sep* **1** *vt Tiere* to exhaust, to tire out. **hetz' mich nicht so ab!** *(col)* stop hustling me like that! *(col)*. **2** *vr* to wear *or* tire oneself out; *siehe* **abgehetzt.**

**abheuern** *sep (Naut)* **1** *vi* to be paid off. **2** *vt* to pay off.

**Abhilfe** f *no pl* remedy, cure. **~ schaffen** to take remedial action.

**abholen** *vt sep* to collect *(bei from)*; *Bestelltes auch* to call for *(bei at)*; *Fundsache* to claim *(bei from)*; *jdn* to call for; *(mit dem Wagen auch)* to pick up. **jdn am Bahnhof/Flughafen ~** to meet sb at the station/airport; *(mit dem Wagen auch)* to pick sb up from the station/airport; **etw ~ lassen** to have sth collected; **„Geldbörse gefunden, abzuholen bei ...“** "purse found, claim from ...".

**Abholung** f collection.

**abholzen** *vt sep Wald* to clear, to deforest.

**Abhör-** *in cpds* bugging; **~aktion** f bugging operation; **~anlage** f bugging system.

**abhorchen** *vt sep* to sound, to listen to. **einen Patienten ~** to listen to a patient's chest.

**abhören** *vt sep* **(a)** *(auch vi: überwachen) Gespräch* to bug; *(mithören)* to listen in on; *Telefon* to tap. **abgehört werden** *(col)* to be bugged. **(b)** *(zuhören) Band etc* to listen to. **(c)** *(Med)* to sound, to listen to. **einen Patienten ~** to listen to a patient's chest. **(d)** *(Sch: abfragen)* **einem Schüler etw ~** to test a pupil orally on sth.

**Abhör-:** **~gerät** nt bugging device; **a~sicher** adj bugproof.

**abhungern** *vr sep* **er mußte sich** *(dat)* **sein Studium ~** he had to starve his way through college *etc*; **sich** *(dat)* **10 Kilo ~** to lose 10 kilos by going on a starvation diet.

**Abi** nt **-s** *(Sch col)* = Abitur.

**ab|irren** *vi sep aux sein (geh)* to lose one's way; *(fig: Gedanken)* to wander. **vom Weg(e) ~** to wander off the path.

**Abitur** nt **-e** *school-leaving exam and university entrance qualification*, ≃ A-levels *pl (Brit)*. **(das) ~ ma-**

**chen** to take one's school-leaving exam, ≃ to take one's A-levels *(Brit)*.

**Abiturient(in** f) m *person who is doing/has done the Abitur.*

**Abiturzeugnis** nt *certificate of having passed the Abitur,* ≃ A-level certificate *(Brit)*, high-school graduation certificate *(US)*.

**abjagen** *vt sep jdm etw ~* to get sth off sb.

**Abk.** = **Abkürzung** abbr.

**abkämmen** *vt sep (fig)* to comb, to scour.

**abkämpfen** *vr sep* to fight hard; *siehe* **abgekämpft.**

**abkanzeln** *vt sep (col) jdn ~* to give sb a dressing-down.

**abkapseln** *vr sep (fig)* to cut oneself off.

**abkarten** *vt sep (col)* to rig *(col)*, to fix. **die Sache war von vornherein abgekartet** the whole thing was a put-up job *(col)*; *siehe* **abgekartet.**

**abkassieren\*** *vti sep (col)* to cash up *(col)*. **bei jdm ~** to get sb to pay; **darf ich (bei Ihnen) ~?** could I ask you to pay now?

**abkauen** *vt sep Fingernägel* to bite; *Bleistift* to chew.

**abkaufen** *vt sep jdm etw ~* to buy sth from sb; *(col: glauben)* to buy sth *(col)*.

**Abkehr** f *no pl* turning away *(von from)*; *(von Glauben etc)* renunciation *(von of)*.

**abkehren** *sep* **1** *vt (geh) Blick, Gesicht* to avert, to turn away. **2** *vr (fig)* to turn away *(von from)*.

**abklappern** *vt sep (col) Läden, Straße* to scour, to comb *(nach for)*; *Kunden, Museen etc* to do the rounds of *(col)*.

**abklären** *sep* **1** *vt (klarstellen)* to clear up, to clarify. **2** *vr* **(a)** *(sich setzen)* to clarify. **(b)** *(sich beruhigen)* to calm down; *siehe* **abgeklärt.**

**Abklatsch** m **-e** *(Art)* cast, casting; *(fig pej)* poor imitation *or* copy.

**abklemmen** *vt sep Nabelschnur, Leitung* to clamp.

**abklingen** *vi sep irreg aux sein* **(a)** *(leiser werden)* to die *or* fade away. **(b)** *(nachlassen)* to wear off, to abate; *(Erregung, Fieber auch)* to subside.

**abklopfen** *vt sep* **(a)** *Staub etc* to brush off; *Putz* to knock off; *Teppich, Polstermöbel* to beat. **(b)** *(beklopfen)* to tap; *(Med)* to sound, to percuss *(spec)*.

**abknabbern** *vt sep (col)* to nibble off; *Knochen* to gnaw at.

**abknallen** *vt sep (col)* to shoot down *(col)*.

**abknappen, abknapsen** *vt sep (col)* **sich** *(dat)* **jeden Pfennig ~ müssen** to have to scrimp and save; **er hat mir 20 Mark abgeknapst** he got 20 marks off me.

**abknicken** *sep* **1** *vt (abbrechen)* to break *or* snap off; *(einknicken)* to break. **2** *vi aux sein (abzweigen)* to fork *or* branch off.

**abknöpfen** *vt sep* **(a)** *(lit)* to unbutton. **(b)** *(col: ablisten)* **jdm etw ~** to get sth off sb.

**abknutschen** *vt sep (col)* to canoodle with *(col)*. **sich ~** to canoodle *(col)*.

**abkochen** *vt sep (keimfrei machen)* to sterilize (by boiling).

**abkommandieren\*** *vt sep (Mil) (zu Einheit)* to post; *(zu bestimmtem Dienst)* to detail *(zu for)*.

**abkommen** *vi sep irreg aux sein* **(a)** **von etw ~** *(abirren)* to wander off sth; **vom Kurs ~** to deviate from one's course; **(vom Thema) ~** to get off the subject, to digress. **(b)** *(aufgeben)* **von etw ~** to drop sth; *(von Angewohnheit)* to give sth up; *(von Idee, Plan)* to abandon sth; **von einer Meinung ~** to revise one's opinion.

**Abkommen** nt **-** agreement *(auch Pol)*.

**abkömmlich** adj available. **nicht ~ sein** to be unavailable.

**Abkömmling** m *(Nachkomme)* descendant; *(fig)* adherent.

**ạbkönnen** *vt sep irreg (col)* **(a)** *(trinken)* **er kann nicht viel ab** he can't take much (drink). **(b)** *(mögen)* **das kann ich nicht ab** I can't stand it.

**ạbkoppeln** *vt sep (Rail)* to uncouple; *Anhänger* to unhitch; *Pferd* to untie; *Raumfähre* to undock.

**ạbkratzen** *sep* **1** *vt Schmutz etc* to scratch off; *(mit einem Werkzeug)* to scrape off. **2** *vi aux sein (col: sterben)* to kick the bucket *(col)*.

**ạbkriegen** *vt sep (col) siehe* **abbekommen**.

**ạbkühlen** *sep* **1** *vt* to cool; *Speise auch* to cool down. **2** *vi aux sein* to cool down. **3** *vr* to cool down; *(Beziehungen)* to become cool(er).

**Ạbkühlung** *f* cooling.

**Ạbkunft** *f no pl (liter)* descent, origin; *(Nationalität auch)* extraction.

**ạbkupfern** *vt sep (col)* to crib *(col)*, to copy.

**ạbkürzen** *sep* **1** *vt* **(a)** *(abschneiden)* **den Weg** ~ to take a short cut. **(b)** *(verkürzen)* to cut short; *Verfahren* to shorten; *Aufenthalt, Urlaub auch* to curtail. **(c)** *Namen* to abbreviate. **2** *vi (verkürzt schreiben)* to use abbreviations.

**Ạbkürzung** *f* **(a)** *(Weg)* short cut. **(b)** *(von Wort)* abbreviation.

**ạbküssen** *vt sep* to smother with kisses.

**ạbladen** *vti sep irreg Last, Wagen* to unload; *Schutt* to dump; *(esp Comm) Passagiere, Ware* to off-load; *(fig col) Ärger auch* to vent *(bei jdm on sb)*.

**Ạblage** *f -n* **(a)** *(Gestell)* place to keep/put sth. **wir brauchen eine** ~ **für die Akten** we need somewhere for our files; **etw als** ~ **benutzen** *(für Akten, Bücher etc)* to use sth for storage. **(b)** *(Aktenordnung)* filing.

**Ạblagekorb** *m* filing tray.

**ạblagern** *sep* **1** *vt (deponieren)* to leave, to store. **2** *vi aux sein or haben (ausreifen)* to mature; *(Holz auch)* to season. ~ **lassen** to allow to mature; *Holz auch* to (allow to) season. **3** *vr* to be deposited.

**Ạblagerung** *f (abgelagerter Stoff)* deposit.

**ạblandig** *adj (Naut)* Wind offshore.

**ạblassen** *sep irreg* **1** *vt* **(a)** *(herauslaufen lassen) Flüssigkeit, Luft* to let out; *Wasser, Motoröl auch* to drain; *Dampf* to let off. **(b)** *(ermäßigen)* to knock off *(col)*. **er hat mir 20 Mark abgelassen** he knocked 20 marks off for me *(col)*. **2** *vi (liter)* **(a)** *(mit etw aufhören)* to desist. **von einem Vorhaben** *etc* ~ to abandon a plan *etc*. **(b)** *(jdn in Ruhe lassen)* **von jdm** ~ to leave sb alone.

**Ạblativ** *m -e (Gram)* ablative (case).

**Ạblauf** *m* **(a)** *(Abfluß)* drain; *(Rinne)* drainage channel. **(b)** *(Verlauf)* course; *(von Verbrechen)* sequence of events *(gen in)*; *(von Handlung in Buch etc)* development. **der** ~ **der Ereignisse** the course of events; **es gab keinerlei Störungen im** ~ **des Programms** the programme went off without any disturbances. **(c)** *(von Zeitraum, Frist etc)* expiry. **nach** ~ **von 4 Stunden** after 4 hours (have/had passed *or* gone by); **nach** ~ **des Jahres/dieser Zeit** at the end of the year/this time.

**Ạblaufbrett** *nt (an Spüle)* draining board.

**ạblaufen** *sep irreg* **1** *vt* **(a)** *(abnutzen) Schuhsohlen, Schuhe* to wear out; *Absätze* to wear down. **sich** *(dat)* **die Beine** *or* **Hacken nach etw** ~ *(col)* to walk one's legs off looking for sth. **(b)** *aux sein or haben (entlanglaufen) Strecke* to go *or* walk over; *Stadt, Straßen, Geschäfte* to comb, to scour. **2** *vi aux sein* **(a)** *(abfließen: Flüssigkeit)* to drain *or* run away; *(trocken werden: Geschirr)* to dry off. **(b)** *(vonstatten gehen)* to go off. **(c)** ~ **lassen** *(abspulen, abspielen) Platte, Tonband* to play; *Film, (Comp) Programm* to run. **(d)** *(ungültig werden: Paß etc)* to expire, to run out; *(enden: Frist, Vertrag etc auch)* to run out, to be

up. **(e)** *(Zeitraum)* to pass, to go by.

**Ạbleben** *nt no pl (form)* demise *(form)*.

**ạblecken** *vt sep* to lick; *Teller* to lick (clean).

**ạblegen** *sep* **1** *vt* **(a)** *(niederlegen)* to put down; *Last, Waffen auch* to lay down; *(Zool) Eier* to lay. **(b)** *Schriftwechsel* to file (away); *(Comp) daten* to store. **(c)** *(ausziehen) Kleider* to take off, to remove. **(d)** *(nicht mehr tragen) Anzug, Kleid* to discard, to cast off. **abgelegte Kleider** cast-off clothes. **(e)** *(aufgeben) Mißtrauen, Scheu, Stolz* to lose, to shed; *Namen* to give up. **(f)** *Schwur, Eid* to swear; *Gelübde auch* to make; *Zeugnis* to give; *Bekenntnis, Beichte* to make; *Prüfung* to take, to sit; *(erfolgreich)* to pass. **2** *vi* **(a)** *(Schiff)* to cast off; *(Space)* to separate. **(b)** *(Garderobe* ~*)* to take one's things off.

**Ạbleger** *m* - *(Bot)* layer; *(fig: Zweigunternehmen)* branch, subsidiary.

**ạblehnen** *vt sep* **(a)** *auch vi (zurückweisen, nein sagen)* to decline; *Antrag, Vorschlag, Bewerber* to reject; *(Parl) Gesetzentwurf* to throw out. **eine** ~**de Antwort** a negative answer; **ein** ~**der Bescheid** a rejection; **dankend** ~ to decline with thanks. **(b)** *(mißbilligen)* to disapprove of. **jede Form von Gewalt** ~ to be against any form of violence.

**Ạblehnung** *f* **(a)** *(Zurückweisung)* refusal; *(von Antrag etc)* rejection. **(b)** *(Mißbilligung)* disapproval. **auf** ~ **stoßen** to meet with disapproval.

**ạbleiern** *vt sep (col) Gedicht etc* to reel off.

**ạbleisten** *vt sep (form) Zeit* to serve; *Wehrdienst* to do.

**ạbleiten** *sep vt* **(a)** *(herleiten)* to derive; *(logisch folgern auch)* to deduce *(aus from)*. **(b)** *(umleiten) Fluß* to divert; *(herausleiten) Rauch, Flüssigkeit* to draw off *or* out; *(ablenken) Blitz* to conduct.

**Ạbleitung** *f* **(a)** *siehe vt* derivation; deduction; diversion; drawing off *or* out; conduction. **(b)** *(Wort, Math)* derivative.

**ạblenken** *sep* **1** *vt* **(a)** *(ab-, wegleiten)* to deflect *(auch Phys)*, to turn aside. **(b)** **er ließ sich durch nichts** ~ he wouldn't let anything distract him; **das lenkt mich ab** *(zerstreut mich)* it takes my mind off things; **jdn von seinem Schmerz/seinen Sorgen** ~ to take sb's mind off his pain/worries. **(c)** *(abbringen)* to divert; *Verdacht* to avert. **2** *vi* **(a)** **(vom Thema)** ~ to change the subject. **(b)** **das lenkt ab** *(zerstreut)* it takes your mind off things; *(stört)* it's distracting. **3** *vr* to take one's mind off things.

**Ạblenkung** *f* **(a)** *(Ab-, Wegleitung)* deflection *(auch Phys)*. **(b)** *(Zerstreuung)* diversion, distraction. ~ **brauchen** to need something to take one's mind off things.

**Ạblenkungsmanöver** *nt* diversionary tactic; *(um von Thema abzulenken auch)* red herring.

**ạblesen** *vt sep irreg* **(a)** *(auch vi: vom Blatt)* to read. **er muß (alles/seine Rede)** ~ he has to read everything/his speech (from notes *etc*); **(jdm) etw von den Lippen** ~ to lip-read sth (that sb says). **(b)** *(auch vi: registrieren) Meßgeräte, Barometer, Strom* to read. **nächste Woche wird abgelesen** the meter(s) will be read next week. **(c)** *(herausfinden, erkennen, folgern)* to see. **jdm etw vom Gesicht** ~ to read sth in sb's face; **das konnte man ihr vom Gesicht** ~ it was written all over her face; **jdm jeden Wunsch von den Augen** ~ to anticipate sb's every wish.

**ạbleugnen** *vt sep Schuld, Tat* to deny.

**Ạbleugnung** *f* denial.

**ạblichten** *vt sep (form)* to photocopy; *(fotografieren)* to photograph.

**Ạblichtung** *f (form) siehe vt* photocopy; photograph.

**ạbliefern** *vt sep* to hand in *(bei to)*; *(liefern)* to deliver *(bei to)*; *(col) Kinder* to deposit *(col) (bei with)*.

**Ablieferung** *f (von Waren)* delivery.

**abliegen** *vi sep irreg (entfernt sein)* **das Haus liegt weit ab** the house is quite a distance away; *siehe* **abgelegen**.

**ablisten** *vt sep* **jdm etw** ~ to trick sb out of sth.

**ablocken** *vt sep* **jdm etw** ~ to get sth out of sb.

**ablöschen** *vt sep* **(a)** *(mit dem Löschblatt)* to blot. **(b)** *(Cook)* to add water to.

**ablösen** *sep* **1** *vt* **(a)** *(abmachen)* to take off, to remove; *Etikett etc auch* to detach. **(b)** *(Fin) Schuld, Hypothek* to pay off, to redeem. **(c)** *(ersetzen) Wache* to relieve; *Amtsinhaber* to replace. **(d)** *(fig: an Stelle treten von)* to take the place of; *(Methode, System)* to supersede. **2** *vr* **(a)** *(abgehen)* to come off; *(Lack etc auch)* to peel off. **(b)** *(auch einander ~)* to take turns; *(Fahrer, Kollegen auch, Wachen)* to relieve each other.

**Ablösesumme** *f (Sport)* transfer fee.

**Ablösung** *f* **(a)** *(von Hypothek, Schuld)* paying off, redemption. **(b)** *(Wache)* relief; *(Entlassung)* replacement. **bei dieser Arbeit braucht man alle zwei Stunden eine** ~ you need relieving every two hours in this work.

**abluchsen** *vt sep (col)* **jdm etw** ~ to get *or* wangle *(col)* sth out of sb.

**Abluft** *f no pl (Tech)* used air.

**ablutschen** *vt sep* to lick.

**ABM** [aːbeːʼ|ɛm] = **(a) Antiballistic Missile** ABM. **(b) Arbeitsbeschaffungsmaßnahme.**

**abmachen** *vt sep (col)* **(a)** *(entfernen)* to take off. **(b)** *(vereinbaren) Termin etc* to agree (on). **(c)** *(besprechen)* to settle. **etw mit sich allein** ~ to sort sth out for oneself.

**Abmachung** *f* agreement.

**abmagern** *vi sep aux sein* to get thinner, to lose weight.

**Abmagerung** *f no pl* emaciation.

**Abmagerungskur** *f* diet. **eine** ~ **machen** to be on a diet, to be dieting; *(anfangen)* to go on a diet.

**abmahnen** *vt sep (form)* to caution.

**Abmahnung** *f (form)* caution.

**abmalen** *vt sep (abzeichnen)* to paint; *(nach Vorlage)* to copy.

**Abmarsch** *m* departure; *(von Soldaten auch)* march-off. **beim** ~ when marching off; **zum** ~ **antreten** *(Mil)* to fall in ready to march off.

**abmarschbereit** *adj* ready to move off.

**abmarschieren\*** *vi sep aux sein* to move off.

**abmelden** *sep* **1** *vt* **(a)** *Telefon* to have disconnected; *(bei Verein) jdn* to cancel the membership of. **sein Auto** ~ to take one's car off the road; **ein Kind von einer Schule** ~ to take a child away from a school. **(b)** *(col)* **er/sie ist bei mir abgemeldet** I don't want anything to do with him/her. **2** *vr* to ask for permission to be absent; *(im Hotel)* to check out. **sich bei jdm** ~ to tell sb that one is leaving; **sich (beim Einwohnermeldeamt)** ~ to notify the local authorities that one is moving away.

**Abmeldung** *f (von Telefon)* disconnection; *(beim Einwohnermeldeamt)* cancellation of one's registration. **seit der** ~ **meines Autos** since I took my car off the road.

**abmergeln** *vr sep* to slave away.

**abmessen** *vt sep irreg* **(a)** to measure; *(fig) Worte* to weigh. **(b)** *(abteilen)* to measure off.

**Abmessung** *f usu pl* measurement; *(Ausmaß)* dimension.

**abmildern** *vt sep Geschmack, Worte* to tone down; *Aufprall* to cushion, to soften; *Schock* to lessen.

**abmontieren\*** *vt sep Räder, Teile* to remove *(von*

*etw from sth)*; *Maschine* to dismantle.

**ABM-Stelle** [aːbeːʼ|ɛm-] *f* temporary post *(obtained through a job creation scheme)*.

**abmühen** *vr sep* to struggle (away).

**abmustern** *sep (Naut)* **1** *vt Besatzung* to pay off. **2** *vi* to sign off, to leave the ship.

**abnabeln** *sep* **1** *vt* **ein Kind** ~ to cut a baby's umbilical cord. **2** *vr* to cut oneself loose, to make the break. **sich vom Elternhaus** ~ to leave the parental home, to leave the nest *(col)*.

**abnagen** *vt sep* to gnaw off; *Knochen* to gnaw.

**Abnäher** *m -* *(Sew)* dart.

**Abnahme** *f -n* **(a)** *(Wegnahme)* removal; *(Amputation)* amputation. **(b)** *(Verringerung)* decrease *(gen* in*)*; *(bei Anzahl, Menge auch)* drop *(gen* in*)*; *(von Kräften, Energie, Interesse, Nachfrage)* decline *(gen* in*)*. **(c)** *(von Prüfung)* holding; *(von Neubau, Fahrzeug etc)* inspection. **(d)** *(Comm)* purchase. **bei** ~ **von 50 Exemplaren** if you/we *etc* purchase *or* take 50 copies; **keine/gute** ~ **finden** not to sell/to sell well.

**abnehmbar** *adj* removable, detachable.

**abnehmen** *sep irreg* **1** *vt* **(a)** *(herunternehmen)* to take off, to remove; *Hörer* to lift, to pick up; *Obst* to pick; *(lüften) Hut* to raise; *Vorhang, Bild, Wäsche* to take down; *Maschen* to decrease; *(amputieren)* to amputate.

**(b)** *(an sich nehmen)* **jdm etw** ~ to take sth from sb; *(fig) Arbeit, Sorgen* to relieve sb of sth; **darf ich Ihnen den Mantel** ~**?** can I take your coat?; **kann ich dir etwas** ~**?** *(tragen)* can I take something for you?; *(helfen)* can I do anything for you?; **jdm die Beichte** ~ to hear confession from sb; **jdm ein Versprechen** ~ to make sb promise something.

**(c)** *(wegnehmen)* to take away *(jdm* from sb*)*; *(rauben, abgewinnen)* to take *(jdm* off sb*)*.

**(d)** *(begutachten) Gebäude, Auto* to inspect; *(abhalten) Prüfung* to hold.

**(e)** *(abkaufen)* to take *(dat* off*)*, to buy *(dat* from, off*)*.

**(f)** *(fig col: glauben)* to buy *(col)*. **dieses Märchen nimmt dir keiner ab!** nobody'll buy that!

**(g)** *Fingerabdrücke* to take.

**2** *vi* **(a)** *(sich verringern)* to decrease; *(Niveau, Kräfte)* to decline; *(Fieber)* to go down; *(Mond)* to wane; *(beim Stricken)* to decrease. **(an Gewicht)** ~ to lose weight. **(b)** *(Telec)* to answer.

**Abnehmer** *m -* *(Comm)* buyer, customer. **viele/wenige** ~ **finden** to sell well/badly.

**Abneigung** *f* dislike *(gegen* of*)*; *(Widerstreben)* aversion *(gegen* to*)*.

**abnorm, abnormal** *adj* abnormal.

**Abnormität** *f* abnormality.

**abnötigen** *vt sep (geh)* **jdm etw** ~ to force sth from sb; **jdm Respekt** ~ to gain sb's respect.

**abnutzen** *vtr sep* to wear; *(völlig)* to wear out.

**Abnutzung** *f* wear; *(Verschleiß)* wear and tear.

**Abnutzungserscheinung** *f* sign of wear.

**Abo** *nt -s (col)* = **Abonnement.**

**Abonnement** [abɔnəˈmãː] *nt -s or -e* **(a)** *(Zeitungs~)* subscription. **eine Zeitung im** ~ **beziehen** to subscribe to a newspaper. **(b)** *(Theater~)* subscription series ticket.

**Abonnent(in** *f)* *m (Zeitungs~)* subscriber; *(Theater~)* subscription holder.

**abonnieren\*** **1** *vt Zeitung* to subscribe to; *Konzertreihe etc* to have a subscription ticket to. **2** *vi* **auf eine Zeitung/Konzertreihe abonniert sein** to have a subscription for a newspaper/a ticket for a subscription concert series.

**ab|ordnen** *vt sep* to delegate.

**Ab|ordnung** *f* delegation.

**Abort¹** *m* -e *(dated)* lavatory, toilet.

**Abort²** *m* -e *(Fehlgeburt)* miscarriage; *(Abtreibung)* abortion.

**abpacken** *vt sep* to pack. **ein abgepacktes Brot** a wrapped loaf.

**abpassen** *vt sep* **(a)** *(abwarten) Gelegenheit, Zeitpunkt* to wait for. **den richtigen Zeitpunkt** ~ to bide one's time; **etw gut** ~ to time sth well. **(b)** *(auf jdn warten)* to catch; *(jdm auflauern)* to waylay.

**abpausen** *vt sep* to make a tracing of.

**abperlen** *vi sep aux sein* to run off *(von etw sth)*.

**abpfeifen** *sep irreg (Sport)* **1** *vi (Schiedsrichter)* to blow one's whistle. **2** *vt* **das Spiel/die erste Halbzeit** ~ to blow the whistle for the end of the game/for half-time.

**Abpfiff** *m (Sport)* final whistle. ~ **zur Halbzeit** half-time whistle.

**abpflücken** *vt sep* to pick.

**abplagen** *vr sep* to struggle (away).

**abplatzen** *vi sep aux sein (Lack, Ölfarbe)* to flake or crack off; *(Knopf)* to fly or burst off.

**abprallen** *vi sep aux sein von* or **an etw** *(dat)* ~ *(Ball)* to bounce or *(Kugel)* to ricochet off sth; **an jdm** ~ *(fig)* to make no impression on sb.

**Abpraller** *m* - *(Sport)* rebound.

**abpumpen** *vt sep Wasser, Öl* to pump off; *Muttermilch* to express.

**abputzen** *sep vt* to clean; *Schmutz* to clean off. **sich** *(dat)* **die Nase/den Hintern** ~ to wipe one's nose/bottom; **putz dir die Schuhe ab!** wipe your feet!

**abquälen** *sep* **1** *vr* to struggle (away). **2** *vt* **sich** *(dat)* **ein Lächeln** ~ to force a smile.

**abqualifizieren*** *vt sep* to dismiss, to write off.

**abquetschen** *vt sep* to crush. **sich** *(dat)* **den Arm** ~ to get one's arm crushed.

**abrackern** *vr sep (col)* to slave away. **sich mit etw** ~ to struggle with sth.

**abrasieren*** *vt sep* to shave off; *(col) Gebäude* to flatten.

**abraten** *vti sep irreg* **jdm (von) etw** ~ to advise sb against sth.

**Abraum** *m (Min)* overburden.

**abräumen** *vti sep* to clear up or away. **den Tisch** ~ to clear the table.

**abreagieren*** *sep* **1** *vt Spannung, Wut* to work off, to get rid of. **seinen Ärger an anderen** ~ to take it out on others. **2** *vr* to work it off. **er war ganz wütend, aber jetzt hat er sich abreagiert** he was furious, but he's simmered down now.

**abrechnen** *sep* **1** *vi* **(a)** *(Kasse machen)* to cash up. **darf ich** ~**?** would you like your bill *(Brit)* or check *(US)* now? **(b) mit jdm** ~ to settle up with sb; *(fig)* to get even with sb. **2** *vt (abziehen)* to deduct.

**Abrechnung** *f* **(a)** *(Aufstellung) statement (über +acc for)*; *(Rechnung)* bill, invoice; *(Bilanz)* balancing; *(fig: Rache)* revenge. **der Tag der** ~ *(fig)* the day of reckoning. **(b)** *(Abzug)* deduction. **nach** ~ **von** after (the deduction of); **in** ~ **stellen** *(form)* to deduct.

**Abrechnungszeitraum** *m* accounting period.

**Abrede** *f* **etw in** ~ **stellen** to deny or dispute sth.

**abregen** *vr sep (col)* to calm or cool down. **reg dich ab!** relax!, cool it! *(col)*.

**abreiben** *vt sep irreg Schmutz, Rost* to clean or rub off; *(trocknen)* to rub down.

**Abreibung** *f (col: Prügel)* hiding, thrashing.

**Abreise** *f* departure *(nach for)*. **bei meiner** ~ on my departure.

**abreisen** *vi sep aux sein* to leave *(nach for)*.

**abreißen** *sep irreg* **1** *vt* **(a)** *(abtrennen)* to tear off; *Tapete, Blätter auch* to strip (off). **er hat sich** *(dat)* **den Knopf abgerissen** he's torn his button off; **er wird dir nicht (gleich) den Kopf** ~ *(col)* he won't bite your head off *(col)*. **(b)** *(niederreißen) Gebäude* to pull down. **2** *vi aux sein (sich lösen)* to come off; *(fig: unterbrochen werden)* to break off. **das reißt nicht ab** *(fig)* there is no end to it; **den Kontakt** *etc* **nicht** ~ **lassen** to stay in touch.

**Abreißkalender** *m* tear-off calendar.

**abrichten** *vt sep* to train. **der Hund ist auf Einbrecher abgerichtet** the dog is trained to go for burglars.

**Abrichtung** *f* training.

**abriegeln** *vt sep (verschließen) Tür* to bolt; *(absperren) Straßen, Gebiet* to cordon off.

**abringen** *vt sep irreg* **jdm etw** ~ to wring or force sth out of sb; **sich** *(dat)* **ein Lächeln** ~ to force a smile; **dem Meer Land** ~ *(liter)* to wrest land from the sea *(liter)*.

**Abriß** *m* **(a)** *(Abbruch)* demolition. **(b)** *(Übersicht)* outline, summary. **(c)** *(von Eintrittskarte etc)* tear-off part.

**abrollen** *sep* **1** *vt (abwickeln)* to unwind; *Papier, Stoff* to unroll. **2** *vi aux sein* **(a)** *(abfahren: Züge, Waggons)* to roll off or away. **(b)** *(col: vonstatten gehen) (Programm)* to run; *(Veranstaltung)* to go off; *(Ereignisse)* to unfold. **mein ganzes Leben rollte noch einmal vor meinen Augen ab** my whole life passed before me again.

**abrücken** *sep* **1** *vt (wegschieben)* to move away. **2** *vi aux sein* **(a)** *(fig: sich distanzieren)* to dissociate oneself *(von from)*. **(b)** *(Mil etc)* to move out.

**Abruf** *m* **(a) sich auf** ~ **bereit halten** to be ready to be called (for); **auf** ~ **zur Verfügung stehen** to be available on call. **(b)** *(Comm)* **etw auf** ~ **bestellen/kaufen** to order/buy sth (to be delivered) on call. **(c)** *(Comp)* retrieval; **auf** ~ **bereit** readily retrievable.

**abruf-:** ~**bar** *adj* **(a)** *(Comp) daten* retrievable; **(b)** *(Fin)* ready on call; **(c)** *(fig)* accessible; ~**bereit** *adj* **(a)** *Arzt etc* on call; *(abholbereit)* ready to be called for; **(b)** *(Comm, Fin)* ready on call.

**abrufen** *vt sep irreg* **(a)** *(wegrufen)* to call away. **(b)** *(Comm)* to request delivery of; *(Fin: abheben)* to withdraw. **(c)** *Daten, Informationen* to call up, to retrieve.

**abrunden** *vt sep (lit, fig)* to round off. **eine Zahl nach unten** ~ to round a number down.

**Abrundung** *f (lit, fig)* rounding off. **zur** ~ **von etw** to round sth off.

**abrupt** *adj* abrupt.

**abrüsten** *sep vi (Mil, Pol)* to disarm.

**Abrüstung** *f no pl (Mil, Pol)* disarmament.

**Abrüstungsgespräche** *pl* disarmament talks.

**abrutschen** *vi sep aux sein (abgleiten)* to slip; *(fig) (Leistungen)* to go downhill; *(moralisch)* to let oneself go.

**ABS** [aːbeːˈɛs] *nt no pl (Aut)* = **Antiblockiersystem** ABS.

**Abs.** = **(a)** *Absatz* par., para. **(b)** *Absender.*

**absäbeln** *vt sep (col)* to hack or chop off.

**absacken** *vi sep aux sein (sinken)* to sink; *(Boden, Gebäude auch)* to subside; *(fig col: nachlassen)* to fall off; *(verkommen)* to go to pot *(col)*.

**Absage** *f* -n refusal; *(auf Einladung auch)* negative reply. **das ist eine** ~ **an die Demokratie** that's a denial of democracy; **jdm/einer Sache eine** ~ **erteilen** to reject sb/sth.

**absagen** *sep* **1** *vt (rückgängig machen) Veranstaltung, Besuch* to cancel, to call off; *(ablehnen) Einladung* to decline. **2** *vi* to decline. **jdm** ~ to tell sb that one can't come; **in letzter Minute** ~ to cry off

at the last minute.
**absägen** *vt sep* (a) *(abtrennen)* to saw off. (b) *(fig col)* to chuck *or* sling out *(col)*; *Minister, Beamten* to oust, to give the chop *(col)*; *Schüler* to make fail.
**absahnen** *sep (fig col)* **1** *vt Geld* to rake in; *(sich verschaffen)* to cream off. **2** *vi* to make a killing *(col)*.
**absatteln** *vti sep* to unsaddle.
**Absatz** *m, pl* **Absätze** (a) *(Abschnitt)* paragraph; *(Jur)* section. **einen ~ machen** to start a new paragraph. (b) *(Treppen~)* half-landing. (c) *(Schuh~)* heel. **spitze Absätze** stiletto heels; **auf dem ~ kehrtmachen** to turn on one's heel. (d) *(Verkauf)* sales *pl.* **guten ~ finden** to sell well.
**Absatz-:** **a~fähig** *adj* marketable, saleable; **~flaute** *f* slump in sales; **~gebiet** *nt* sales area; **~markt** *m* market; **~schwierigkeiten** *pl* sales problems *pl*; **~steigerung** *f* increase in sales.
**absaufen** *vi sep irreg aux sein (col) (ertrinken)* to drown; *(Motor)* to flood; *(Schiff etc)* to go down.
**absaugen** *vt sep Flüssigkeit* to suck out *or* off; *Teppich, Sofa* to hoover ® *(Brit)*, to vacuum.
**ABS-Bremse** *f* ABS brakes *pl.*
**abschaben** *vt sep* to scrape off.
**abschaffen** *sep vt* (a) to abolish, to do away with. (b) *(nicht länger halten)* to get rid of.
**Abschaffung** *f* abolition.
**abschälen** *vtr sep* to peel off.
**abschalten** *sep* **1** *vt* to switch off. **2** *vi (fig)* to unwind. **3** *vr* to switch itself off.
**abschätzen** *vt sep* to estimate; *Menschen, Fähigkeiten* to assess. **seine Lage ~** to take stock of one's position; **ein ~der Blick** an appraising look.
**abschätzig** *adj* disparaging. **sich ~ über jdn äußern** to make disparaging remarks about sb.
**Abschaum** *m no pl* scum. **der ~ der Menschheit** the scum of the earth.
**abscheiden** *vt sep irreg (ausscheiden)* to give off, to produce; *(Biol auch)* to secrete.
**Abscheu** *m or f no pl* repulsion, abhorrence *(vor +dat at)*. **vor jdm/etw ~ haben** *or* **empfinden** to loathe sb/sth.
**abscheuerregend** *adj* repulsive, loathsome.
**abscheuern** *vt sep* (a) *Schmutz* to scrub off. (b) *(abschürfen)* Haut to rub *or* scrape off. (c) *Kleidung* to wear thin. **abgescheuerte Knie** threadbare knees.
**abscheulich** *adj* abominable, loathsome; *Verbrechen auch* heinous; *Anblick auch* repulsive. **wie ~!** how awful!; **~ kalt** hideously cold.
**Abscheulichkeit** *f (Untat)* atrocity, abomination; *(no pl: Widerwärtigkeit)* loathsomeness; *(von Verbrechen auch)* heinousness; *(von Geschmack, Anblick)* repulsiveness.
**abschicken** *vt sep* to send; *Paket, Brief* to send off, to dispatch.
**Abschiebehaft** *f (Jur)* remand pending deportation.
**abschieben** *sep irreg* **1** *vt* (a) *(wegschieben)* to push away *(von* from*)*; *(fig) Verantwortung, Schuld* to shift *(auf +acc* onto*)*. (b) *(ausweisen) Ausländer* to deport. (c) *(col: loswerden)* to get rid of. **jdn in eine andere Abteilung ~** to shunt sb off to another department *(col).* **2** *vi aux sein (col)* to clear off *(col).*
**Abschiebung** *f (Ausweisung)* deportation.
**Abschied** *m* **-e** (a) *(Trennung)* farewell, parting. **von jdm/etw ~ nehmen** to say goodbye to sb/sth, to take one's leave of sb/sth; **ein ... zum ~** a farewell ...; **es war ein ~ für immer** it was goodbye for ever; **beim ~ meinte er, ...** as he was leaving he said ...; **ihr ~ von der Bühne/vom Film** her farewell from the stage/from film; *(letzte Vorstellung)* her farewell performance; **der ~ von der Vergangenheit** the

break with the past. (b) *(von Beamten)* resignation; *(von Offizieren)* discharge. **seinen ~ nehmen** to hand in one's resignation/to apply for a discharge.
**Abschieds-:** **~besuch** *m* farewell visit; **~brief** *m* farewell letter; **~feier** *f* farewell party; **~geschenk** *nt (für Kollegen etc)* leaving present; *(für Freund)* going-away present; **~gruß** *m* farewell; **~kuß** *m* farewell kiss; **~schmerz** *m* pain of parting; **~stunde** *f* hour of parting; **~szene** *f* farewell scene.
**abschießen** *vt sep irreg* (a) *(auf +acc* at*) Geschoß, Gewehr* to fire; *Pfeil* to shoot; *Rakete* to launch; *(auf ein Ziel)* to fire. (b) *(außer Gefecht setzen) Flugzeug* to shoot down. (c) *(totschießen) Wild* to shoot. (d) *(fig col: abschieben)* to get rid of.
**abschinden** *vr sep irreg (col)* to slave away *(col).*
**Abschirmdienst** *m (Mil)* counter-espionage service.
**abschirmen** *sep* **1** *vt* to shield; *(schützen auch)* to protect; *(vor Licht auch)* to screen. **2** *vr* to shield oneself *(gegen* from*)*; *(sich schützen)* to protect oneself *(gegen* from *or* against*)*; *(sich isolieren)* to cut oneself off *(gegen* from*)*.
**Abschirmung** *f no pl* (a) *(Schutz)* protection. (b) *(fig: Isolierung)* isolation.
**abschlachten** *vt sep* to slaughter.
**Abschlachtung** *f* slaughter.
**abschlaffen** *vi sep aux sein (col)* to flag.
**Abschlag** *m* (a) *(Preisnachlaß)* reduction. (b) *(Zahlung)* part payment *(auf +acc* of*)*.
**abschlagen** *vt sep irreg* (a) *(mit Hammer etc)* to knock off; *(mit Beil etc)* to chop off; *Baum* to chop down; *(herunterschlagen)* to knock down. (b) *(ablehnen)* to refuse; *Einladung, Bitte auch, Antrag* to turn down. **jdm etw ~** to refuse sb sth. (c) *(zurückschlagen) Angriff, Feind* to drive off; *Konkurrenten* to wipe out. (d) *siehe* **abgeschlagen**.
**abschlägig** *adj* negative. **jdn/etw ~ bescheiden** *(form)* to turn sb/sth down.
**Abschlag(s)zahlung** *f* part payment.
**abschleifen** *sep irreg* **1** *vt Unebenheiten* to grind down; *Holzboden* to sand (down). **2** *vr (fig) (Angewohnheit etc)* to wear off; *(Mensch)* to have the rough edges taken off. **das schleift sich (noch) ab** *(fig)* that'll wear off.
**Abschleppdienst** *m* breakdown service *(Brit)*, (vehicle) recovery service.
**abschleppen** *sep* **1** *vt* (a) *Fahrzeug, Schiff* to tow, to take in tow; *(bei widerrechtlichem Parken)* to tow away. (b) *(col) Menschen* to drag along; *(aufgabeln)* to pick up *(col).* **2** *vr* **sich mit etw ~** *(col)* to struggle with sth.
**Abschlepp-:** **~fahrzeug** *nt* breakdown *(Brit)* or recovery vehicle, wrecker *(US)*; **~seil** *nt* towrope. **~stange** *f* towbar *(for towing a vehicle)*; **~wagen** *m* = **~fahrzeug**.
**abschließbar** *adj* lockable.
**abschließen** *sep irreg* **1** *vt* (a) *(zuschließen)* to lock. (b) *(beenden) Sitzung, Vortrag etc* to conclude, to bring to a close; *Kursus* to complete. **sein Studium ~** to graduate; **mit abgeschlossenem Studium** with a degree. (c) *(vereinbaren) Geschäft* to transact; *Versicherung* to take out; *Wette* to place. **einen Vertrag ~** *(Pol)* to conclude a treaty; *(Jur, Comm)* to conclude a contract. **2** *vr (sich isolieren)* to cut oneself off. **sich von der Außenwelt ~** to shut oneself off from the outside world; *siehe* **abgeschlossen**. **3** *vi* (a) *(zuschließen)* to lock up. **sieh mal nach, ob auch abgeschlossen ist** will you see if everything's locked? (b) *(enden)* to come to a close. (c) *(Comm: Vertrag schließen)* to conclude the deal. (d) *(Schluß machen)* to finish, to end. **mit der Vergangenheit ~**

to break with the past.

**abschließend 1** *adj* concluding. **2** *adv* in conclusion, finally.

**Abschluß** *m* (**a**) *(Beendigung)* end; *(col: ~prüfung)* final examination; *(Univ)* degree. **zum ~ möchte ich ... finally** *or* to conclude I would like ...; **zum ~ kommen** to come to an end; **etw zum ~ bringen** to finish sth. (**b**) *no pl (Vereinbarung)* conclusion. **bei ~ des Vertrages** on completion of the contract. (**c**) *(Rand etc)* border.

**Abschluß-:** **~feier** *f (Sch)* school-leavers' ceremony; **~prüfung** *f (Sch)* final examination; *(Univ auch)* finals *pl*; **~rechnung** *f* final account; **~zeugnis** *nt (Sch)* leaving certificate, diploma *(US)*.

**abschmecken** *vt sep (kosten)* to taste; *(würzen)* to season.

**abschmettern** *vt sep (col) (Sport)* to smash; *(fig: zurückweisen)* to throw out.

**abschmieren** *sep* **1** *vt* (**a**) *(Tech)* Auto to grease. (**b**) *(col: abschreiben)* to crib *(col)*. **2** *vi aux sein (Aviat)* to go down.

**abschminken** *vt sep* (**a**) *Gesicht, Haut* to remove the make-up from. **sich ~** to remove one's make-up. (**b**) *(col: aufgeben)* **sich** *(dat)* **etw ~** to get sth out of one's head.

**abschmirgeln** *vt sep* to sand down.

**abschnallen** *sep* **1** *vt* to unfasten, to undo. **2** *vr* to unfasten one's seat belt. **3** *vi (col)* (**a**) *(nicht mehr folgen können)* to give up. (**b**) *(fassungslos sein)* to be staggered *(col)*. **da schnallste ab!** it's unbelievable!

**abschneiden** *sep irreg* **1** *vt (lit, fig)* to cut off; *Blumen, Fingernägel, Haar* to cut. **jdm das Wort ~** to cut sb short. **2** *vi* **bei etw gut/schlecht ~** *(col)* to come off well/badly in sth.

**Abschnitt** *m* (**a**) section; *(Math)* segment; *(Mil)* sector, zone; *(Geschichts~, Zeit~)* period. (**b**) *(Kontroll~) (von Scheck etc)* counterfoil; *(von Karte)* section; *(von Papier)* slip.

**abschnitt(s)weise** *adv* in sections.

**abschnüren** *vt sep* to cut off *(von from)*. **jdm das Blut ~** to cut off sb's circulation; **jdm die Luft ~** *(lit)* to take sb's breath away; *(fig)* to ruin sb.

**abschöpfen** *vt sep* Fett to skim off; *(fig)* Dank, Ruhm to reap. **den Rahm** *or* **das Fett ~** *(fig)* to cream off the best part; **den Gewinn ~** to siphon off the profits.

**abschotten** *vt sep* **sich gegen etw ~** *(fig)* to cut oneself off from sth; **etw ~** *(fig)* to shield *or* screen sth.

**abschrägen** *vt sep* to slope; *Holz, Brett* to bevel. **ein abgeschrägtes Dach** a sloping roof.

**abschrauben** *vt sep* to unscrew.

**abschrecken** *sep* **1** *vt* (**a**) *(fernhalten)* to deter, to put off; *(verjagen) Hund, Vogelscheuche* to scare off. **ich lasse mich dadurch nicht ~** I won't be deterred by that. (**b**) *(abkühlen) Stahl* to quench; *(Cook)* to rinse with cold water. **2** *vi (Strafe)* to act as a deterrent.

**abschreckend** *adj (warnend)* deterrent. **ein ~es Beispiel** a warning; **eine ~e Wirkung haben, ~ wirken** to act as a deterrent.

**Abschreckung** *f (das Fernhalten, Mil)* deterrence; *(~smittel)* deterrent.

**Abschreckungs-:** **~mittel** *nt* deterrent; **~waffe** *f* deterrent (weapon).

**abschreiben** *sep irreg* **1** *vt* (**a**) to copy *(bei, von from)*; *(kopieren)* to copy out. (**b**) *(Comm: absetzen, abziehen)* to deduct. (**c**) *(verloren geben)* to write off. **er ist bei mir abgeschrieben** I'm finished with him. **2** *vi* (**a**) *(Sch)* to copy, to crib *(col)*. (**b**) **jdm ~**

to write to sb to tell him/her that one cannot come.

**Abschreibung** *f (Steuer~)* tax write-off; *(Comm)* deduction; *(Wertverminderung)* depreciation.

**Abschreibungsprojekt** *nt* tax avoidance scheme.

**abschreiten** *vt sep irreg (entlanggehen) Gelände* to patrol; *(inspizieren) Front* to inspect.

**Abschrift** *f* copy.

**abschrubben** *vt sep (col) Schmutz* to scrub off; *Rücken, Fußboden* to scrub (down).

**abschuften** *vr sep (col)* to slog one's guts out *(col)*.

**abschürfen** *vt sep* to graze.

**Abschürfung** *f (Wunde)* graze.

**Abschuß** *m* (**a**) *(das Abfeuern)* firing, shooting; *(von Rakete)* launch(ing). (**b**) *(das Außer-Gefecht-Setzen)* shooting down; *(von Panzer)* knocking out. **die Luftwaffe erzielte zwölf Abschüsse** the air force shot down twelve planes. (**c**) *(von Wild)* shooting. **Fasanen sind jetzt zum ~ freigegeben** pheasant-shooting is now permitted; **zum ~ freigegeben sein** *(fig)* to be fair game.

**abschüssig** *adj* sloping. **eine sehr ~e Straße** a steep road.

**Abschuß-:** **~liste** *f (col)* hit list *(col)*. **er steht auf der ~liste** his days are numbered; **~rampe** *f* launch(ing) pad.

**abschütteln** *vt sep (lit, fig)* to shake off.

**abschütten** *vt sep Flüssigkeit etc* to pour off; *(Cook)* to drain off; *Kartoffeln etc* to drain.

**abschwächen** *sep* **1** *vt* to weaken; *Formulierung* to tone down. **2** *vr* to fall off, to diminish; *(Lärm)* to decrease; *(Preisauftrieb, Andrang)* to ease off.

**Abschwächung** *f siehe vb* weakening; toning down; decrease; easing off.

**abschwatzen** *vt sep (col)* **jdm etw ~** to talk sb into giving one sth.

**abschweifen** *vi sep aux sein (lit, fig) (von* from*)* to stray, to wander (off); *(Redner auch)* to digress.

**Abschweifung** *f* digression.

**abschwellen** *vi sep irreg aux sein (Entzündung, Fluß)* to go down; *(Lärm)* to die away.

**abschwenken** *sep* **1** *vi aux sein* to turn away; *(Kamera)* to pan. **er ist nach links abgeschwenkt** *(lit)* he turned off to the left; *(fig)* he swung (over) to the left; (**nach rechts**) **~** *(Mil)* to wheel (right). **2** *vt (Cook)* to drain (off).

**abschwindeln** *vt sep* **jdm etw ~** to swindle sb out of sth.

**abschwirren** *vi sep aux sein* to whirr off; *(fig col: weggehen)* to buzz off *(col)*.

**abschwören** *vi sep irreg (old, liter)* to renounce *(dat* sth*)*. **dem Glauben/Teufel ~** to renounce one's faith/the devil; **dem Alkohol ~** *(col)* to give up drinking.

**Abschwung** *m (Sport)* dismount; *(Econ)* downward trend, recession.

**absegnen** *vt sep (col)* to give one's blessing to.

**absehbar** *adj* foreseeable. **in ~er/auf ~e Zeit** in/for the foreseeable future; **die Folgen sind noch gar nicht ~** there's no telling what the consequences will be.

**absehen** *sep irreg* **1** *vt* (**a**) *(abgucken)* (**bei**) **jdm etw ~** to pick sth up from sb. (**b**) *(voraussehen)* to foresee. **es ist ganz klar abzusehen, daß ...** it's easy to see that ...; **das Ende läßt sich noch nicht ~** the end is not yet in sight; *siehe* **abgesehen 1. 2** *vi* **von etw ~** *(verzichten)* to refrain from sth; *(nicht berücksichtigen)* to disregard sth; **davon ~, etw zu tun** to dispense with doing sth; *siehe* **abgesehen 2.**

**abseifen** *vt sep* to soap down.

**abseilen** *sep* **1** *vt* to lower down on a rope. **2** *vr (Bergsteiger)* to abseil (down).

**absein** *vi sep irreg aux sein (col)* **(a)** *(weg sein)* to be off. **die Farbe/der Knopf ist ab** the paint/button has come off. **(b)** *(abgelegen sein)* to be far away.

**abseits** *adv (abgelegen)* out of the way, remote; *(Sport)* offside. **~ vom Wege** off the beaten track; **~ stehen** *(fig)* to be on the outside; *(Sport)* to be offside; **~ bleiben, sich ~ halten** *(fig)* to keep to oneself.

**Abseits** *nt -* *(Sport)* offside. **im ~ stehen** to be offside; **im ~ leben** *(fig)* to live in the shadows; **ins politische ~ geraten** to end up in the political wilderness.

**Abseits-** *(Sport)* **~falle** *f* offside trap; **~position**, **~stellung** *f* offside position; **~tor** *nt* offside goal.

**absenden** *vt sep* to send; *(mit der Post auch)* to post *(Brit)*, to mail *(esp US)*.

**Absender(in** *f)* *m -* sender; *(Adresse)* (sender's) address.

**absenken** *sep* **1** *vt Grundwasserstand* to lower; *Fundamente* to sink. **2** *vr* to subside.

**abservieren\*** *sep* **1** *vi* to clear the table. **2** *vt* **(a)** *Geschirr, Tisch* to clear. **(b)** *(col: entlassen, kaltstellen)* **jdn ~** to push sb out, to get rid of sb. **(c)** *(col: umbringen)* to do in *(col)*. **(d)** *(Sport col: besiegen)* to thrash *(col)*.

**absetzbar** *adj Ware* saleable; *Betrag* deductible.

**absetzen** *sep* **1** *vt* **(a)** *(abnehmen)* Hut, Brille to take off; *(hinstellen)* Gepäck, Glas to set *or* put down. **(b)** *(aussteigen lassen)* Fahrgast to drop. **(c)** *Theaterstück* to take off; *Fußballspiel, Versammlung, Termin* to cancel. **(d)** *(entlassen)* König to dismiss; König to depose. **(e)** *(Med)* Medikament to stop taking; *Behandlung* to discontinue. **(f)** *(Comm)* Waren to sell. **sich gut ~ lassen** to sell well. **(g)** *(abziehen)* Betrag to deduct. **das kann man ~ that** is tax-deductible.
**2** *vr* **(a)** *(Chem, Geol)* to be deposited; *(Feuchtigkeit, Staub etc)* to collect. **(b)** *(col: weggehen)* to get *or* clear out *(aus of) (col)*; *(Sport: Abstand vergrößern)* to pull ahead. **sich nach Brasilien ~** to make off to Brazil.
**3** *vi* **er trank das Glas aus, ohne abzusetzen** he emptied his glass in one gulp.

**Absetzung** *f* **(a)** *(Entlassung) (von Beamten)* dismissal; *(von König)* deposing, deposition. **(b)** *(Fin: Abschreibung)* deduction. **(c)** *(von Theaterstück etc)* withdrawal; *(von Fußballspiel, Termin etc)* cancellation.

**absichern** *sep* **1** *vt* to safeguard; *(garantieren)* to cover; *Bauplatz, Gefahrenstelle* to make safe; *(Comp)* daten to store; *(schützen)* to protect. **2** *vr (sich schützen)* to protect oneself; *(sich versichern)* to cover oneself.

**Absicht** *f -en* *(Vorsatz)* intention; *(Zweck)* purpose; *(Jur)* intent. **in der besten ~** with the best of intentions; **die ~ haben, etw zu tun** to intend to do sth; **eine ~ mit etw verfolgen** to have something in mind with sth; **ernste ~en haben** *(col)* to have serious intentions; **das war nicht meine ~!** I didn't intend that; **etw mit/ohne ~ tun** to do/not to do sth deliberately *or* on purpose.

**absichtlich** *adj* deliberate, intentional. **etw ~ tun** to do sth on purpose *or* deliberately.

**Absichts-:** **~erklärung** *f* declaration of intent; **a~los** *adj* unintentional.

**absingen** *vt sep irreg (vom Blatt)* to sight-read.

**absinken** *vi sep irreg aux sein (Schiff)* to sink; *(Boden auch)* to subside; *(Interesse, Leistungen)* to fall *or* drop off; *(fig: moralisch ~)* to go downhill.

**absitzen** *sep irreg* **1** *vt* **(a)** *(verbringen)* Zeit to sit out; *(verbüßen)* Strafe to serve. **(b)** *(abnutzen)* Hose etc to wear thin. **2** *vi aux sein* **(vom Pferd)** **~** to dis-

mount (from a horse).

**absolut** *adj* absolute; *(völlig auch)* complete, total. **~ nicht/nichts** absolutely not/nothing; **das ist ~ unmöglich** that's quite *or* absolutely impossible.

**Absolutheits|anspruch** *m* claim to absolute right. **einen ~ vertreten** to claim absoluteness.

**Absolution** *f (Eccl)* absolution. **jdm die ~ erteilen** to grant *or* give sb absolution.

**Absolvent(in** *f)* [apzɔl'vɛnt(ɪn)] *m (Univ)* graduate. **die ~en eines Lehrgangs** the students who have completed a course.

**absolvieren\*** [apzɔl'viːrən] *vt insep Studium, Probezeit* to complete; *Schule* to finish, to graduate from *(US)*; *Prüfung* to pass.

**absonderlich** *adj* peculiar, strange.

**absondern** *sep* **1** *vt* **(a)** *(trennen)* to separate; *(isolieren)* to isolate. **(b)** *(ausscheiden)* to secrete. **2** *vr (Mensch)* to cut oneself off. **sie sondert sich immer sehr ab** she always keeps herself very much to herself.

**Absonderung** *f* **(a)** *siehe vt* separation; isolation; secretion. **(b)** *(abgeschiedener Stoff)* secretion.

**absorbieren\*** *vt insep (lit, fig)* to absorb.

**Absorption** *f* absorption.

**abspalten** *vtr sep* to split off; *(Chem)* to separate (off).

**Abspann** *m -e (TV, film)* final credits *pl*.

**abspannen** *sep* **1** *vt Pferd, Wagen* to unhitch. **2** *vi (fig: entspannen)* to relax; *siehe* **abgespannt**.

**Abspannung** *f (Ermüdung)* weariness, tiredness.

**absparen** *vt sep* **sich ~ (dat) ein Auto vom Lohn ~** to save up for a car from one's wages; **sich (dat) etw vom Munde ~** to scrimp and save for sth.

**abspecken** *sep (col)* **1** *vt* to shed; *(fig: verkleinern)* to slim down, to trim. **2** *vi* to lose weight.

**abspeisen** *vt sep (fig: abfertigen)* **jdn mit etw ~** to fob sb off with sth.

**abspenstig** *adj* **jdm jdn/etw ~ machen** to lure sb/sth away from sb; **jdm die Freundin ~ machen** to pinch sb's girlfriend *(col)*.

**absperren** *sep* **1** *vt* **(a)** *(versperren)* to block off. **(b)** *Strom etc* to turn *or* shut off. **(c)** *(zuschließen)* to lock. **2** *vi* to lock up.

**Absperrung** *f* **(a)** *(Abriegelung)* blocking *or* closing off. **(b)** *(Sperre)* barrier.

**Abspiel** *nt (Sport)* pass.

**abspielen** *sep* **1** *vt* **(a)** *Tonband etc* to play; *(vom Blatt)* Musik to sight-read; *siehe* **abgespielt**. **(b)** *(Sport)* Ball to pass. **2** *vr (sich ereignen)* to happen.

**absplittern** *vti sep (vi: aux sein)* to chip off; *Holz auch* to splinter off.

**Absprache** *f* arrangement. **ohne vorherige ~** without prior consultation.

**absprechen** *sep irreg* **1** *vt* **(a)** **jdm ein Recht ~** *(verweigern)* to deny sb a right; **jdm seine Begabung ~** *(in Abrede stellen)* to question sb's talent; **er ist wirklich sehr klug, das kann man ihm nicht ~** there's no denying that he's very clever. **(b)** *(verabreden)* Termin to arrange. **2** *vr* **sich mit jdm ~** to make an arrangement with sb; **die beiden hatten sich vorher abgesprochen** they had agreed on what to do/say in advance.

**abspringen** *vi sep irreg aux sein* **(a)** *(herunterspringen)* to jump down *(von from)*; *(herausspringen)* to jump out *(von of)*; *(Aviat)* to jump *(von from)*; *(bei Gefahr)* to bale out. **(b)** *(sich lösen)* to come off; *(Farbe, Lack auch)* to flake *or* peel off. **(c)** *(fig col: sich zurückziehen)* to get out; *(von Partei, Kurs etc)* to back out.

**abspritzen** *vt sep* **etw/jdn ~** to spray sth/sb down; *Schmutz* to spray off *(von etw sth)*.

**Absprung** m jump (auch Aviat), leap; (Sport) take-off. **den ~ schaffen** (fig) to make the break (col); **er hat den ~ gewagt** (fig) he took the leap.
**abspulen** vt sep Kabel, Garn to unwind.
**abspülen** sep 1 vt Hände, Geschirr to rinse; Fett etc to rinse off. 2 vi to wash up.
**abstammen** vi sep no ptp to be descended (von from).
**Abstammung** f descent; (Abkunft auch) origin, extraction. **ehelicher/unehelicher ~** (Jur) of legitimate/illegitimate birth; **französischer ~** of French extraction or descent.
**Abstammungslehre** f theory of evolution.
**Abstand** m (a) (Zwischenraum) distance; (kürzer) gap, space; (Zeit~) interval; (fig: Distanz) distance. **mit ~** by far, far and away; **~ von etw gewinnen** (fig) to distance oneself from sth; **in Abständen von 10 Minuten** at 10 minute intervals; **~ halten** to keep one's distance; **mit großem ~ führen** to lead by a wide margin. (b) (form: Verzicht) **davon ~ nehmen, etw zu tun** to refrain from doing sth.
**Abstandssumme** f (form) indemnity.
**abstatten** vt sep (form) **jdm einen Besuch ~** to pay sb a visit; **jdm seinen Dank ~** to give thanks to sb.
**abstauben** vti sep (a) Möbel etc to dust. (b) (col) (wegnehmen) to nick (col); (schnorren) to cadge (von, bei, dat off, from).
**Abstauber** m - (Ftbl col) (a) (auch ~tor) easy goal. (b) (Spieler) goal-hanger (col).
**abstechen** sep irreg 1 vt (a) **ein Tier ~** to cut an animal's throat. (b) (abtrennen) Torf to cut; Rasen to trim (the edges of). 2 vi to stand out (gegen, von against).
**Abstecher** m - (Ausflug) trip; (Umweg) detour, side-trip.
**abstecken** vt sep (a) (lit, fig) Gelände, Verhandlungsposition to mark out. (b) Kleid, Naht to pin.
**abstehen** sep irreg 1 vi (entfernt stehen) to be a distance away (von from); (nicht anliegen) to stick out. **~de Ohren** ears that stick out; siehe **abgestanden**. 2 vt (col) **sich** (dat) **die Beine ~** to stand for hours.
**Absteige** f -n cheap hotel.
**absteigen** vi sep irreg aux sein (a) (heruntersteigen) to get off (von etw sth). (b) (abwärts gehen) to make one's way down; (Bergsteiger auch) to climb down. **in ~der Linie** in the line of descent; **auf dem ~den Ast sein** (col) to be going downhill, to be on the decline. (c) (einkehren) to stay; (im Hotel auch) to put up (in +dat at). (d) (Sport: Mannschaft) **aus der ersten Liga ~** to be relegated from the first division.
**Absteiger** m - (Sport) relegated team.
**abstellen** vt sep (a) (hinstellen) to put down. (b) (unterbringen) to put; (Aut: parken auch) to park. (c) (abrücken, entfernt stellen) to put away from. (d) (abkommandieren) to order off, to detail; Offizier auch to second. (e) (abdrehen) to turn off. (f) (sich abgewöhnen) to give up, to stop. (g) (unterbinden) Mangel, Unsitte etc to bring to an end. **das läßt sich nicht/läßt sich ~** nothing/something can be done about that.
**Abstell-:** **~gleis** nt siding; **jdn aufs ~gleis schieben** (fig) to put sb out to grass; **~kammer** f boxroom; **~raum** m storeroom.
**abstempeln** vt sep to stamp; Post to postmark; (fig) to brand (zu, als as).
**absterben** vi sep irreg aux sein (eingehen, Med, fig) to die; (gefühllos werden: Glieder) to go or grow numb; siehe **abgestorben**.
**Abstieg** m -e (das Absteigen) way down, descent;

(Niedergang) decline; (Sport) relegation.
**abstillen** sep 1 vt Kind to wean, to stop breastfeeding. 2 vi to stop breastfeeding.
**abstimmen** sep 1 vi to take a vote. **über etw** (acc) **~** to vote on sth; **über etw** (acc) **~ lassen** to put sth to the vote; **geheim ~** to have a secret ballot. 2 vt Instrumente to tune (auf +acc to); Radio to tune (in) (auf +acc to); Farben, Kleidung to match (auf +acc with); Termine to coordinate (auf +acc with); (anpassen) to suit (auf +acc to). **gut auf etw** (acc)/ **aufeinander abgestimmt sein** (Instrumente) to be in tune with sth/with each other; (Farben, Speisen etc) to go well with sth/to go well together; (Termine) to fit in well with sth/with each other; (einander angepaßt sein) to be well-suited to sth/to each other; **etw miteinander ~** (vereinbaren) to settle sth amongst ourselves/themselves etc. 3 vr **sich (mit jdm/miteinander) ~** to come to an agreement (with sb/amongst ourselves/themselves etc).
**Abstimmung** f (Stimmabgabe) vote; (geheime ~) ballot. **eine ~ durchführen** to take a vote.
**Abstimmungs-:** **~ergebnis** nt result of the vote; **~niederlage** f **eine ~niederlage erleiden** to be defeated in a/the vote; **~sieg** m **einen ~sieg erringen** to win a/the vote.
**abstinent** adj teetotal.
**Abstinenz** f no pl teetotalism, abstinence.
**Abstinenzler(in** f) m - teetotaller (Brit), teetotaler (US).
**abstoppen** vti sep (auch Sport) to stop; (mit Stoppuhr) to time.
**Abstoß** m (Ftbl) goal kick; (nach Fangen des Balls) clearance.
**abstoßen** sep irreg 1 vt (a) (wegstoßen) Boot to push off or out; (abschlagen) Ecken to knock off. (b) (zurückstoßen) to repel; (Comm) Ware, Aktien to sell off; (Med) Organ to reject; (fig: anwidern) to repel. **dieser Stoff stößt Wasser ab** this material is water-repellent; **sich von etw abgestoßen fühlen** to find sth repulsive. (c) (Ftbl) **den Ball ~** to take the goal kick; (nach Fangen) to clear the ball. 2 vr (esp Sport: Mensch) **sich mit den Füßen vom Boden ~** to push oneself off. 3 vi (anwidern) to be repulsive.
**abstoßend** adj Aussehen, Äußeres repulsive.
**Abstoßung** f (Phys) repulsion; (Med) rejection.
**abstottern** vt sep (col) to pay off.
**abstrahieren*** [apstra'hi:rən] vti insep to abstract (aus from).
**abstrahlen** vt sep Wärme etc to emit.
**abstrakt** [ap'strakt] adj abstract.
**Abstraktum** [-st-] nt, pl **Abstrakta** (Begriff) abstract (concept); (Ling: Substantiv) abstract noun.
**abstrampeln** vr sep (fig col) to sweat (away) (col).
**abstreichen** vt sep irreg (wegstreichen) to wipe off.
**abstreifen** vt sep (a) (abtreten) Schuhe, Füße to wipe. (b) (abziehen) Kleidung, Schmuck to take off, to slip off; (entfernen) Haut to shed; (fig) Gewohnheit, Fehler to get rid of.
**abstreiten** vt sep irreg (leugnen) to deny. **das kann man ihm nicht ~** you can't deny it.
**Abstrich** m (a) (Kürzung) cutback. **~e machen** to cut back (an +dat on); (weniger erwarten etc) to lower one's sights. (b) (Med) swab; (Gebärmutter~) smear. **einen ~ machen** to take a swab/smear.
**abstrus** [ap'stru:s] adj (geh) abstruse.
**abstufen** vt sep Gelände to terrace; Farben to shade; Gehälter, Steuern, Preise to grade.
**Abstufung** f (Nuance) shade; (Stufe) grade.
**abstumpfen** sep 1 vt Menschen to dull; siehe **abgestumpft**. 2 vi aux sein (fig: Geschmack etc) to become dulled. **diese Arbeit stumpft ab** this work dulls

the mind.

**Absturz** m *siehe* vi crash; fall. **ein Flugzeug zum ~ bringen** to bring a plane down.

**abstürzen** vi *sep aux sein (Flugzeug)* to crash; *(Bergsteiger)* to fall.

**abstützen** *sep* **1** vt to support *(auch fig)*; *Haus, Mauer auch* to shore up. **2** vr to support oneself.

**absuchen** vt *sep* to search; *Gegend auch* to comb, to scour; *Himmel* to scan; *(Scheinwerfer)* to sweep.

**absurd** adj absurd. **~es Drama** *or* **Theater** theatre of the absurd.

**Absurdität** f absurdity *(auch Philos)*.

**Abszeß** m **-sse** abscess.

**Abt** m **=e** abbot.

**Abt.** = **Abteilung** dept.

**abtakeln** vt *sep Schiff* to unrig; *siehe* **abgetakelt.**

**abtasten** vt *sep* to feel; *(Elec)* to scan; *(bei Durchsuchung)* to frisk *(auf +acc for)*.

**abtauchen** vi *sep aux sein* **(a)** *(U-Boot)* to dive. **(b)** *(col)* to go underground.

**abtauen** *sep* **1** vt to thaw out; *Kühlschrank* to defrost. **2** vi *aux sein* to thaw.

**Abtei** f abbey.

**Abteil** nt **-e** compartment.

**abteilen** vt *sep (abtrennen)* to divide off.

**Abteilung** f *(in Firma, Kaufhaus)* department; *(in Krankenhaus, Jur)* section; *(Mil)* unit, section.

**Abteilungsleiter** m head of department.

**abtelefonieren*** vi *sep* to telephone to say one cannot come.

**abtippen** vt *sep (col)* to type out.

**Äbtissin** f abbess.

**abtönen** vt *sep Farbe* to tone down.

**Abtönung** f *(Farbton)* tone, shade.

**abtöten** vt *sep (lit, fig)* to destroy, to kill (off); *Nerv* to deaden.

**abtragen** vt *sep irreg* **(a)** *(abbauen)* Gebäude, Mauer to take down; *(Fluß)* Ufer to erode. **(b)** *(abbezahlen)* Schulden to pay off. **(c)** *(abnutzen)* Kleider to wear out; *siehe* **abgetragen.**

**abträglich** adj detrimental *(dat* to, for*)*; *Kritik etc* adverse.

**Abtragung** f *(Geol)* erosion.

**abtrainieren*** vt *sep (Übergewicht)* to work off (by training).

**Abtransport** m transportation; *(aus Katastrophengebiet)* evacuation. **beim ~ der Gefangenen** when the prisoners were being taken away.

**abtransportieren*** vt *sep* to transport; *(aus Katastrophengebiet)* to evacuate.

**abtreiben** *sep irreg* **1** vt **(a)** **vom Kurs ~** to carry off course. **(b)** *Kind* to abort. **sie hat das Kind abgetrieben** *or* **~ lassen** she had an abortion. **2** vi **(a)** *aux sein* **(vom Kurs)** ~ to be carried off course. **(b)** *(Abort vornehmen)* to carry out an abortion; *(Abort vornehmen lassen)* to have an abortion.

**Abtreibung** f abortion. **eine ~ vornehmen lassen** to have an abortion.

**Abtreibungs-:** **~gegner** m anti-abortionist; **~paragraph** m abortion laws pl; **~versuch** m attempted abortion.

**abtrennen** vt *sep* **(a)** *(lostrennen)* to detach; *Knöpfe, Besatz etc* to remove; *Bein, Finger etc (durch Unfall)* to sever, to cut off. **„hier ~"** "detach here". **(b)** *(abteilen)* to separate off; *(mit Zwischenwand etc auch)* to partition off.

**abtreten** *sep irreg* **1** vt **(a)** *Teppich* to wear (out); *Schnee, Schmutz* to stamp off. **sich** *(dat)* **die Füße ~** to wipe one's feet. **(b)** *(überlassen)* *(jdm or an jdn to sb)* to hand over; *Gebiet, Land auch* to cede; *Ansprüche* to transfer. **2** vi *aux sein (Theat)* to go

off(stage); *(Mil)* to dismiss; *(col: zurücktreten) (Politiker)* to resign; *(Monarch)* to abdicate. **~!** *(Mil)* dismiss!

**Abtreter** m **- *(Fuß~)*** doormat.

**Abtretung** f *(an +acc to)* transfer; *(von Ansprüchen auch, von Gebiet)* ceding, cession.

**Abtritt** m *(Theat)* exit; *(Rücktritt) (von Minister)* resignation; *(von Monarch)* abdication.

**abtrocknen** *sep* **1** vt to dry. **2** vi to dry up, to do the drying-up.

**abtropfen** vi *sep aux sein* to drip; *(Geschirr)* to drain. **etw ~ lassen** to let sth drain.

**abtrotzen** vt *sep jdm etw ~ (geh)* to wring sth out of sb.

**abtrünnig** adj renegade; *(rebellisch)* rebel. **jdm/einer Gruppe ~ werden** to desert sb/a group.

**Abtrünnige(r)** mf *decl as adj siehe adj* renegade; rebel.

**abtun** vt *sep irreg (fig: beiseite schieben)* to dismiss. **etw mit einem Achselzucken/einem Lachen ~** to shrug/laugh sth off; **etw kurz ~** to brush sth aside; *siehe* **abgetan.**

**abtupfen** vt *sep Tränen* to dab away; *Gesicht, Wunde* to dab.

**ab|urteilen** vt *sep* to pass sentence *or* judgement on.

**abverlangen*** vt *sep siehe* **abfordern.**

**abwägen** vt *sep irreg* to weigh up; *Worte* to weigh. **er wog beide Möglichkeiten gegeneinander ab** he weighed up the two possibilities; *siehe* **abgewogen.**

**Abwahl** f voting out. **es kam zur ~ des gesamten Vorstands** the whole committee was voted out.

**abwählen** vt *sep* to vote out (of office); *(Sch) Fach* to give up.

**abwälzen** vt *sep Schuld, Verantwortung* to shift *(auf +acc onto)*; *Arbeit* to unload *(auf +acc onto)*; *Kosten* to pass on *(auf +acc to)*. **die Schuld von sich ~** to shift the blame onto somebody else.

**abwandeln** vt *sep Melodie* to adapt; *Thema auch* to modify.

**abwandern** vi *sep aux sein* to move (away) *(aus* from*)*; *(Kapital)* to be transferred *(aus* out of*)*. **viele Spieler/Abonnenten etc wandern ab** a lot of players/subscribers etc are transferring.

**Abwandlung** f adaptation, variation; *(von Thema etc auch)* modification.

**Abwärme** f waste heat.

**abwarten** *sep* **1** vt to wait for. **das Gewitter ~** to wait till the storm is over; **er kann es nicht mehr ~** he can't wait any longer; **das bleibt abzuwarten** that remains to be seen. **2** vi to wait. **warten Sie ab!** just wait a bit!; **~ und Tee trinken** *(col)* to wait and see; **eine ~de Haltung einnehmen** to play a waiting game.

**abwärts** adv down; *(nach unten auch)* downwards. **„~!"** *(im Fahrstuhl)* "going down!".

**abwärtsgehen** vi *impers sep aux sein (fig)* **mit ihm/dem Land geht es abwärts** he/the country is going downhill.

**Abwärtstrend** m downward *or* downhill trend.

**Abwasch** m *no pl* washing-up *(Brit)*, dirty dishes pl. **den ~ machen** to do the washing-up *(Brit)*, to wash the dishes; **dann kannst du das auch machen, das ist (dann) ein ~** *(col)* then you could do that as well and kill two birds with one stone *(prov)*.

**abwaschbar** adj *Tapete* washable.

**abwaschen** *sep irreg* **1** vt *Gesicht* to wash; *Geschirr* to wash; *Schmutz* to wash off; *Auto* to wash down. **den Schmutz (vom Gesicht) ~** to wash the dirt off (one's face). **2** vi to wash up *(Brit)*, to do the

washing-up *(Brit)*, to wash the dishes.
**Abwaschwasser** *nt* washing-up water *(Brit)*, dishwater; *(fig col)* dishwater *(col)*.
**Abwasser** *nt* sewage *no pl*.
**Abwasser-**: ~**aufbereitung** *f* reprocessing of sewage; ~**kanal** *m* sewer.
**abwechseln** *vir sep* to alternate. **sich** *or* **einander** ~ to alternate; *(Menschen auch)* to take turns; **sich mit jdm** ~ to take turns with sb.
**abwechselnd** *adv* alternately. **er war** ~ **fröhlich und traurig** he alternated between being happy and sad.
**Abwechslung** *f* change; *(Zerstreuung)* diversion. **eine angenehme/schöne** ~ a pleasant/nice change; **zur** ~ for a change; **für** ~ **sorgen** to provide variety *or (Unterhaltung)* entertainment; **eine kleine** ~ a bit of a change; *(bei Arbeit etc)* a little light relief; **hier haben wir wenig** ~ there's not much variety in our life here.
**abwechslungs-**: ~**halber** *adv* for a change; ~**los** *adj* monotonous; ~**reich** *adj* varied.
**Abweg** ['apveːk] *m* **jdn auf** ~**e führen** to lead sb astray *(auch moralisch)*; **auf** ~**e geraten** *or* **kommen** to go astray; *(moralisch auch)* to stray from the straight and narrow.
**abwegig** ['apveːgɪç] *adj (geh)* erroneous; *(bizarr)* eccentric; *Verdacht* groundless.
**Abwehr** *f no pl* **(a)** defence *(Brit)*, defense *(US) (gen* against); *(~truppen)* defence *(Brit)* or defense *(US)* troops; *(Spionage~)* counter-intelligence (service); *(Schutz)* protection *(gen* against*)*. **der** ~ **von etw dienen** to provide *or* give protection against sth. **(b)** *(Zurückweisung)* repulse; *(Abweisung)* rejection. **die** ~ **des Feindes** repelling the enemy; **auf** ~ **stoßen** to be repulsed.
**abwehrbereit** *adj (Mil)* ready for defence *(Brit)* or defense *(US)*.
**abwehren** *sep* **1** *vt* **(a)** *Gegner* to fend *or* ward off; *Ball* to clear; *Schlag* to parry, to ward off. **(b)** *(fernhalten)* to keep away; *Krankheitserreger* to protect against; *Gefahr, üble Folgen* to avert. **(c)** *(abweisen) Anschuldigung* to dismiss. **eine** ~**de Geste** a dismissive wave of the hand. **2** *vi (Sport)* to clear; *(Torwart auch)* to make a save. **mit dem Kopf** ~ to head clear; **zur Ecke** ~ to clear and concede a corner.
**Abwehr-**: ~**kampf** *m (Mil, Sport)* defence *(Brit)*, defense *(US)*; ~**kräfte** *pl (Physiol)* (the body's) defences; ~**reaktion** *f (Psych)* defence *(Brit)* or defense *(US)* reaction; ~**spieler** *m* defender; ~**stoff** *m (Med)* antibody.
**abweichen** *vi sep irreg aux sein (sich entfernen)* to deviate; *(sich unterscheiden)* to differ. **voneinander** ~ *(Theorien)* to diverge, to differ; **vom Kurs** ~ to deviate *or* depart from one's course; **vom Thema** ~ to digress; **vom rechten Weg** ~ *(fig)* to wander off the straight and narrow; **ich weiche erheblich von seiner Meinung ab** I hold quite a different view from him; ~**des Verhalten** *(Psych, Sociol)* deviant behaviour.
**Abweichler(in** *f)* *m* - deviant.
**abweichlerisch** *adj (Pol)* deviant.
**Abweichung** *f* siehe *vi* deviation; difference; *(von Theorien)* divergence. **zulässige** ~ *(Tech)* tolerance; *(zeitlich, zahlenmäßig)* allowance.
**abweisen** *vt sep irreg* to turn down; *(wegschicken)* to turn away; *(Jur) Klage* to dismiss. **er läßt sich nicht** ~ he won't take no for an answer.
**abweisend** *adj Ton, Blick* cold, chilly.
**abwenden** *sep reg or irreg* **1** *vt* **(a)** *(zur Seite wenden)* to turn away; *Blick* to avert; *Kopf* to turn. **(b)** *(verhindern) Unheil* to avert. **2** *vr* to turn away.

**abwerben** *vt sep irreg* to woo away *(dat* from*)*; *(Spitzenkräfte)* to head-hunt.
**Abwerbung** *f* wooing away; *(von Spitzenkräften)* head-hunting.
**abwerfen** *sep irreg* **1** *vt* to throw off; *Reiter* to throw; *Bomben, Flugblätter etc* to drop; *Ballast* to jettison; *Blätter, Nadeln* to shed; *(Cards)* to discard; *(Comm) Gewinn* to yield. **2** *vti (Sport) Ball* to throw out; *Latte* to knock off *or* down.
**abwerten** *vt sep* **(a)** *auch vi (Fin)* to devalue. **(b)** *(fig) Ideale* to debase, to cheapen.
**abwertend** *adj* pejorative.
**Abwertung** *f (Fin)* devaluation.
**abwesend** *adj* absent; *(iro: zerstreut auch)* far away; *Blick* absent-minded. **die A~en** the absentees.
**Abwesenheit** *f* absence. **in** ~ *(+gen)* in the absence of; **durch** ~ **glänzen** *(iro)* to be conspicuous by one's absence.
**abwetzen** *vt sep Hose, Ärmel* to wear thin.
**abwickeln** *sep* **1** *vt* **(a)** *(abspulen)* to unwind; *Verband auch* to remove. **(b)** *(fig: erledigen)* to deal with, to handle; *(abschließen)* to conclude. **2** *vr* to unwind; *(vonstatten gehen)* to go *or* pass off.
**Abwicklung** *f (Erledigung)* handling; *(Abschluß)* completion, conclusion. **die Polizei sorgte für eine reibungslose** ~ **der Veranstaltung** the police made sure that the event went *or* passed off smoothly.
**abwiegeln** *sep* **1** *vt* to appease. **2** *vi* to calm things down.
**abwiegen** *vt sep irreg* to weigh out.
**abwimmeln** *vt sep (col) jdn* to get rid of; *Auftrag* to get out of. **seine Sekretärin hat mich abgewimmelt** his secretary found an excuse to get rid of me; **laß dich nicht** ~ don't let yourself be fobbed off.
**abwinken** *sep* **1** *vi (col) (abwehrend)* to wave it/him etc aside; *(fig: ablehnen)* to say no. **als er merkte, wovon ich reden wollte, winkte er gleich ab** when he realised what I wanted to talk about he immediately put me off. **2** *vti* **ein Rennen** ~ to wave the chequered *(Brit)* or checkered *(US)* flag.
**abwirtschaften** *vi sep (col)* to go downhill. **abgewirtschaftet haben** to have reached rock bottom.
**abwischen** *vt sep Staub, Schmutz etc* to wipe off *or* away; *Augen, Tränen* to dry.
**abwracken** *vt sep Schiff, Auto, technische Anlage* to break (up); *siehe* **abgewrackt**.
**Abwurf** *m* throwing off; *(von Reiter)* throw; *(von Bomben etc)* dropping; *(von Ballast)* jettisoning; *(Sport: von Speer etc)* throwing. **ein** ~ **vom Tor** a goal-throw, a throw-out.
**abwürgen** *vt sep (col)* to scotch; *Motor* to stall. **etw von vornherein** ~ to nip sth in the bud.
**abzahlen** *vt sep* to pay off.
**abzählen** *vt sep* to count. **das läßt sich an den (fünf) Fingern** ~ *(fig)* any fool can see that *(col)*; **abgezähltes Geld** exact money; **das Fahrgeld abgezählt bereithalten** to have the exact fare ready.
**Abzählreim** *m* counting rhyme *(such as "eeny meeny miney mo", for choosing a person)*.
**Abzahlung** *f* **(a)** *(Rückzahlung)* repayment, paying off. **(b)** *(Ratenzahlung)* hire purchase *(Brit)*, HP *(Brit)*, installment plan *(US)*; *(Rate)* (re)payment, instalment. **etw auf** ~ **kaufen** to buy sth on HP *(Brit)* or on hire purchase *(Brit)* or on the installment plan *(US)*.
**Abzahlungsgeschäft** *nt* hire purchase *(Brit)*, HP *(Brit)*, installment plan *(US)*.
**abzapfen** *vt sep* **jdm Blut** ~ to take blood from sb; **jdm Geld** ~ to get some money out of sb.
**abzäunen** *vt sep* to fence off.

**Abzäunung** *f* fencing.
**Abzeichen** *nt* badge; *(Mil)* insignia *pl.*
**abzeichnen** *sep* **1** *vt* (a) to draw; *(nach Vorlage)* to copy. (b) *(signieren)* to initial. **2** *vr* to stand out; *(fig) (deutlich werden)* to emerge, to become apparent; *(drohend bevorstehen)* to loom (on the horizon).
**Abziehbild** *nt* transfer, decal *(US)*.
**abziehen** *sep irreg* **1** *vt* (a) to skin; *Fell, Haut* to remove, to strip off. (b) *Bett* to strip. (c) *Ring etc* to take off. (d) *Schlüssel* to take out, to remove. (e) *(zurückziehen) Kapital* to withdraw; *Truppen auch* to pull out; *(subtrahieren) Zahlen* to take away, to subtract; *Steuern* to deduct. **DM20 vom Preis** ~ to take 20 marks off the price. (f) *(Typ: vervielfältigen)* to run off; *(Phot) Bilder* to make prints of, to print. **etw zwanzigmal** ~ to run off twenty copies of sth. (g) *(schleifen)* to sharpen; *Parkett* to sand (down). **2** *vi* (a) *aux sein (sich verflüchtigen: Rauch)* to escape; *(Hoch, Tief)* to move away. (b) *aux sein (Soldaten)* to pull out *(aus of)*, to withdraw *(aus from)*; *(col: weggehen)* to go off *or* away. **zieh ab!** *(col)* clear off! *(col)*. (c) *(abdrücken)* to pull the trigger, to fire.
**abzielen** *vi sep* **auf etw** *(acc)* ~ *(Mensch)* to aim at sth; *(in Rede)* to get at sth; *(Bemerkung, Maßnahme etc)* to be aimed *or* directed at sth.
**Abzug** [ˈaptsuːk] *m* (a) *no pl (von Truppen, Kapital etc)* withdrawal. **jdm freien** ~ **gewähren** to give *or* grant sb safe conduct. (b) *(usu pl: vom Lohn etc)* deduction; *(Rabatt)* discount. (c) *(Typ)* copy; *(Korrekturfahne)* proof; *(Phot)* print. (d) *(Öffnung für Rauch, Gas)* flue. (e) *(am Gewehr)* trigger.
**abzüglich** *prep* +*gen (Comm)* minus, less.
**Abzugs-:** **a~fähig** *adj* allowable; **~haube** *f* cooker *or* extractor hood; **~rohr** *nt* flue (pipe).
**Abzweig** *m* junction.
**abzweigen** *sep* **1** *vi aux sein* to branch off. **2** *vt (col)* to set *or* put on one side.
**Abzweigung** *f* junction, turn-off; *(Gabelung)* fork.
**abzwingen** *vt sep irreg* **jdm Respekt** *etc* ~ to enforce sb's respect *etc*; **er zwang sich** *(dat)* **ein Lächeln ab** he forced a smile.
**Accessoires** [aksɛˈsoaːɐ(s)] *pl (Fashion)* accessories *pl.*
**ach** [ax] *interj* oh. ~ **nein!** oh no!; *(überrascht)* no!, really!; *(ablehnend)* no, no!; ~ **so!** I see!; ~ **was** *or* **wo!** of course not; ~ **was** *or* **wo, das ist doch nicht so schlimm!** come on now, it's not that bad; ~ **wirklich?** oh really?
**Ach** *nt:* **mit** ~ **und Krach** *(col)* by the skin of one's teeth *(col)*.
**Achat** *m* **-e** agate.
**Achillesferse** *f* Achilles heel.
**Achse** [ˈaksə] *f* **-n** (a) axis. (b) *(Tech)* axle. **auf** ~ **sein** *(col)* to be out and about.
**Achsel** [ˈaksl] *f* **-n** (a) shoulder. **die** ~**n** *or* **mit den** ~**n zucken** to shrug (one's shoulders). (b) *(~höhle)* armpit.
**Achsel-:** **~haare** *pl* underarm hair; **~höhle** *f* armpit; **~klappe** *f*, **~stück** *nt* epaulette; **~zucken** *nt* shrug; **mit einem** ~**zucken** with a shrug (of one's shoulders); **a~zuckend** *adj* **er stand a~zuckend da** he stood there shrugging his shoulders; **er nahm es a~zuckend zur Kenntnis** he acknowledged it with a shrug of his shoulders.
**Achsen-:** **~bruch** *m* broken axle; **~kreuz** *nt* coordinate system; **~mächte** *pl (Hist)* Axis powers *pl.*
**Achs-:** **~lager** *nt* axle bearing; **~last** *f* axle weight.
**acht**[1] *num* eight. **für** *or* **auf** ~ **Tage** for a week; **heute/morgen in** ~ **Tagen** a week today/tomorrow, today/tomorrow week; **heute vor** ~ **Tagen war ich ...**

a week ago today I was ...; *siehe* **vier.**
**acht**[2]**: sich in** ~ **nehmen** to take care, to look out; **etw außer** ~ **lassen** to disregard sth.
**Acht**[1] *f* **-en** eight; *(beim Eislaufen etc)* figure (of) eight; *siehe* **Vier.**
**Acht**[2] *f no pl (Hist)* outlawry, proscription.
**achtbar** *adj (geh)* worthy; *(Leute)* respectable; *(Leistung)* creditable.
**Acht|eck** *nt* octagon.
**acht|eckig** *adj* octagonal, eight-sided.
**achtel** *adj* eighth; *siehe* **viertel.**
**Achtel** *nt* - eighth.
**Achtel-:** **~finale** *nt* round before the quarterfinal; **ins** ~**finale kommen** to get a place in the last sixteen; **~note** *f (Mus)* quaver, eighth note *(US)*.
**achten** **1** *vt* to respect. **2** *vi* **auf etw** *(acc)* ~ to pay attention to sth; **auf die Kinder** ~ to keep an eye on the children; **darauf** ~, **daß ...** to see that ..., to take care that ...
**ächten** *vt (Hist)* to outlaw, to proscribe; *(fig)* to ostracize.
**achtenswert** *adj Person* worthy; *Bemühungen, Handlung auch* commendable.
**achte(r, s)** *adj* eighth; *siehe* **vierte(r, s).**
**Achte(r)** *mf decl as adj* eighth; *siehe* **Vierte(r).**
**Achter** *m* - *(Rudern)* eight.
**Achter-:** **~bahn** *f* big dipper *(Brit)*, roller coaster; **~deck** *nt (Naut)* afterdeck.
**achtern** *adv (Naut)* aft, astern. **nach** ~ **gehen** to go aft; **von** ~ from astern.
**achtfach** *adj* eightfold; *siehe* **vierfach.**
**achtgeben** *vi sep irreg* to take care, to be careful *(auf* +*acc* of); *(aufmerksam sein)* to pay attention *(auf* +*acc* to). **auf jdn/etw** ~ *(beaufsichtigen)* to keep an eye on sb/sth, to look after sb/sth.
**acht-:** **~hundert** *num* eight hundred; **~kantig** *adj* **~kantig rausfliegen** *(col)* to be flung out on one's ear *(col)*.
**achtlos** *adj* careless, thoughtless. **viele gehen** ~ **daran vorbei** many people just pass by without noticing.
**Achtlosigkeit** *f* carelessness, thoughtlessness.
**achtmal** *adv* eight times.
**achtsam** *adj (sorgfältig)* careful. **mit etw** ~ **umgehen** to be careful with sth.
**Acht-:** **~stundentag** *m* eight hour day; **a~tägig** *adj* lasting a week, week-long.
**Achtung** *f no pl* (a) ~! watch out!, look out!; *(Mil: Befehl)* attention!; ~, ~! (your) attention please!; „~ **Hochspannung!**" "danger, high voltage"; „~ **Stufe!**" "mind the step"; ~, **fertig, los!** ready, steady, go! (b) *(Wertschätzung)* respect *(vor* +*dat* for*)*. **die** ~ **vor sich selbst** one's self-respect; **bei aller** ~ **vor jdm/etw** with all due respect to sb/sth; **jdm** ~ **einflößen** to command *or* gain sb's respect; **sich** *(dat)* ~ **verschaffen** to make oneself respected; **alle** ~! good for you/him *etc!*
**Ächtung** *f no pl (fig: gesellschaftlich)* ostracism.
**Achtungserfolg** *m* reasonable success.
**achtzehn** *num* eighteen; *siehe* **vierzehn.**
**achtzig** *num* eighty. **jdn auf** ~ **bringen** *(col)* to make sb's blood boil *(col)*; **auf** ~ **sein** *(col)* to be livid, to be hopping mad *(col)*; *siehe* **vierzig.**
**ächzen** *vi* to groan *(vor* +*dat* with*)*. ~ **und stöhnen** to moan and groan.
**Acker** *m* ⁼ *(Feld)* field. **den** ~**/die** ⁓ **bestellen** to till the soil/plough the fields.
**Acker-:** **~bau** *m no pl* agriculture, farming; **~bau betreiben** to farm the land; **~bau und Viehzucht** farming; **~furche** *f* furrow; **~gaul** *m (pej)* farm horse; **~gerät** *nt* agricultural implement; **~krume**

*f* topsoil; ~**land** *nt* arable land.
**ackern** *vi (col)* to slog away *(col)*.
**a conto** *adv (Comm)* on account.
**Acryl** *nt* acrylic.
**Action** ['ækʃən] *f no pl* action.
**A.D.** [aː'deː] = **Anno Domini** AD.
**a.D.** = **außer Dienst** retd.
**a.d.** = **an der** *(in place names)*.
**ad absurdum** *adv* ~ **führen** *Argument etc* to reduce to absurdity.
**ADAC** [aːdeː|aː'tseː] = **Allgemeiner Deutscher Automobil-Club** *German motoring organization* ≈ AA *(Brit)*, RAC *(Brit)*, AAA *(US)*.
**ad acta** *adv:* **etw** ~ **legen** *(fig)* to consider sth finished; *Frage, Problem* to consider sth closed.
**Adam** *m* Adam. **seit** ~**s Zeiten** *(col)* since the year dot *(col)*; **bei** ~ **und Eva anfangen** *(col)* to start right from scratch *(col)* or from square one *(col)*.
**Adams-:** ~**apfel** *m (col)* Adam's apple; ~**kostüm** *nt (col)* **im** ~**kostüm** in one's birthday suit *(col)*.
**Adapter** *m* - adapter, adaptor.
**adaptieren*** *vt* to adapt.
**adäquat** *adj (geh) Belohnung, Übersetzung* adequate; *Stellung, Verhalten* suitable; *Kritik* valid. **einer Sache** *(dat)* ~ **sein** to be adequate to sth.
**addieren*** *vti* to add (up).
**Addis Abeba** *nt* Addis Ababa.
**Addition** *f* addition.
**Additiv** *nt* -**e** additive.
**ade** *interj (old, S Ger)* farewell *(old, liter)*.
**Adel** *m no pl (Geschlecht, Stand)* nobility; *(Brit auch)* peerage; *(hoher auch)* aristocracy. **von** ~ **sein** to be a member of the nobility; **er stammt aus altem** ~ he comes from an old aristocratic family; ~ **verpflichtet** noblesse oblige.
**adelig** *adj* = **adlig**.
**Adelige(r)** *mf decl as adj* = **Adlige(r)**.
**adeln** *vt (lit, fig)* to ennoble; *(den Titel „Sir" verleihen)* to knight; *(niedrigen Adel verleihen)* to give a title to.
**Adels-:** ~**prädikat** *nt* mark of nobility *(in a name)*; ~**stand** *m* nobility; *(Brit auch)* peerage; *(hoher auch)* aristocracy; **in den** ~**stand erheben** siehe **adeln**; ~**titel** *m* title.
**Aden** *nt* **Golf von** ~ Gulf of Aden.
**Ader** *f* -**n** vein; *(fig: Veranlagung)* bent. **eine** ~ **für etw haben** to have feeling for sth; **eine poetische/ musikalische** ~ **haben** to have a feeling for poetry/ music, to have a poetic/musical bent; **jdn zur** ~ **lassen** *(old, fig col)* to bleed sb.
**Aderlaß** *m* -**lässe** *(old Med)* blood-letting *(auch fig)*, bleeding.
**Adhäsion** *f (Phys)* adhesion.
**Adhäsionsverschluß** *m* adhesive seal.
**ad hoc** *adv (geh)* ad hoc.
**Adjektiv** *nt* adjective.
**Adjutant** *m* adjutant; *(von general)* aide(-de-camp).
**Adler** *m* - eagle.
**Adler-:** ~**auge** *nt (fig)* ~**augen haben** to have eyes like a hawk, to be eagle-eyed; ~**blick** *m (fig)* eagle eye; ~**horst** *m* eyrie; ~**nase** *f* aquiline nose.
**adlig** *adj (lit, fig)* noble. ~ **sein** to be of noble birth.
**Adlige(r)** *mf decl as adj* member of the nobility, nobleman/-woman; *(hoher auch)* aristocrat.
**Administration** *f* administration.
**administrativ** *adj* administrative.
**Admiral** *m, pl* -**e** *or* **Admiräle** (a) admiral. (b) *(Zool)* red admiral.
**Admiralität** *f* (a) *(die Admirale)* admirals *pl*. (b) *(Marineleitung)* admiralty.
**adoptieren*** *vt* to adopt.

**Adoption** *f* adoption.
**Adoptiv-:** ~**eltern** *pl* adoptive parents *pl*; ~**kind** *nt* adopted child.
**Adr.** = **Adresse** add.
**Adrenalin** *nt no pl* adrenalin.
**Adreßbuch** *nt* directory; *(privat)* address book.
**Adresse** *f* -**n** *(Anschrift, Comp)* address. **eine Warnung an jds** ~ *(acc)* **richten** *(fig)* to address a warning to sb; **dieser Vorwurf geht an Ihre** ~ this reproach is aimed *or* directed at you (personally); **an der falschen** ~ **sein** *(col)* to have gone/come to the wrong person.
**Adressen-:** ~**aufkleber** *m* address label; ~**verwaltung** *f (Comp)* address filing system.
**adressieren*** *vt* to address *(an +acc to)*.
**adrett** *adj (dated)* neat.
**Adria** *f* Adriatic (Sea).
**Adriatisches Meer** *nt (form)* Adriatic Sea.
**Advent** [at'vɛnt] *m* -**e** Advent. **erster/vierter** ~ first/ fourth Sunday in Advent.
**Advents-:** ~**kalender** *m* Advent calendar; ~**kranz** *m* Advent wreath; ~**sonntag** *m* Sunday in Advent; ~**zeit** *f* Advent.
**Adverb** [at'vɛrp] *nt* -**ien** adverb.
**adverbial** *adj* adverbial.
**Advokat** [atvo'kaːt] *m (wk)* -**en**, -**en** *(old Jur, fig)* advocate.
**Aerobic** *nt* aerobics *sing*.
**Aero-:** ~**dynamik** *f* aerodynamics; **a**~**dynamisch** *adj* aerodynamic.
**Affäre** *f* -**n** (a) *(Angelegenheit)* affair, business *no pl*; *(Liebesabenteuer)* affair. **in eine** ~ **verwickelt sein** to be mixed up in *or* involved in an affair; **sich aus der** ~ **ziehen** *(col)* to get (oneself) out of it. (b) *(Zwischenfall)* incident, episode.
**Affe** *m (wk)* -**n**, -**n** (a) monkey; *(Menschen~)* ape. **der Mensch stammt vom** ~**n ab** man is descended from the apes; **klettern wie ein** ~ to climb like a monkey. (b) *(col: Kerl)* clown *(col)*, berk *(Brit col)*.
**Affekt** *m* -**e** emotion, affect *(form)*. **im** ~ **handeln** to act in the heat of the moment.
**Affekthandlung** *f* act committed under emotional stress.
**affektiert** *adj (pej)* affected. **sich** ~ **benehmen** to be affected, to behave affectedly.
**Affektiertheit** *f* affectation, affectedness.
**Affen-:** **a**~**artig** *adj* like a monkey; *(wie ein Menschenaffe)* apelike; **mit a**~**artiger Geschwindigkeit** *(col)* like greased lightning *(col)*, in a flash *(col)*; **a**~**geil** *adj (col!)* wicked *(col!)*, right on *(col!)* *pred*, right-on *attr*; ~**haus** *nt* ape house; ~**hitze** *f (col)* sweltering heat; ~**käfig** *m* monkey's/ape's cage; ~**liebe** *f* blind adoration *(zu of)*; ~**schande** *f (col)* crying shame *(col)*; ~**tempo** *nt (col)* **in** *or* **mit einem** ~**tempo** at breakneck speed *(col)*; *(fahren auch)* like the clappers *(col)*; ~**theater** *nt (col)* carry-on *(col)*, fuss; **ein** ~**theater aufführen** to make a fuss; ~**zahn** *m (col)* siehe ~**tempo**.
**affig** *adj (col) (eitel)* stuck-up *(col)*, conceited; *(geziert)* affected; *(lächerlich)* ridiculous, ludicrous.
**Äffin** *f* female monkey/ape.
**Affront** [a'frõː] *m* -**s** *(geh)* affront, insult *(gegen to)*.
**Afghane** *m (wk)* -**n**, -**n**, **Afghanin** *f* Afghan.
**afghanisch** *adj* Afghan. ~**er Windhund** Afghan (hound).
**Afghanistan** *nt* Afghanistan.
**Afrika** *nt* Africa.
**Afrikaander(in** *f)* *m* Afrika(a)ner.
**Afrikaans** *nt* Afrikaans.
**Afrikaner(in** *f)* *m* - African.
**afrikanisch** *adj* African.

**Afro-:** ~**amerikaner** *m* Afro-American; **a~amerikanisch** *adj* Afro-American; ~**asiat** *m* Afro-Asian; **a~asiatisch** *adj* Afro-Asian; ~**-Look** *m* Afro-look.
**After** *m* - *(form)* anus.
**AG** [aːˈgeː] *f* **-s** = **Aktiengesellschaft** ≈ plc *(Brit)*, corp., inc. *(US)*.
**Ägäis** [ɛˈgɛːɪs] *f* Aegean (Sea).
**ägäisch** [ɛˈgɛːɪʃ] *adj* **Ä~es Meer** Aegean Sea.
**Agent(in** *f)* *m* agent.
**Agenten-:** ~**netz** *nt* spy network; ~**ring** *m* spy ring; ~**tätigkeit** *f* espionage; **seine ~tätigkeit** his activity as an agent.
**Agentur** *f* agency.
**Agenturbericht** *m* (news) agency report.
**Aggregat** *nt (Geol)* aggregate; *(Tech)* unit, set of machines.
**Aggregatzustand** *m* state.
**Aggression** *f* aggression *(gegen* towards*).* ~**en gegen jdn empfinden** to feel aggressive *or* aggression towards sb.
**Aggressions-:** **a~geladen** *adj* charged with aggression; ~**trieb** *m (Psych)* aggressive impulse.
**aggressiv** *adj* aggressive.
**Aggressivität** *f* aggression, aggressiveness.
**Aggressor** *m* aggressor.
**agieren*** *vi* to operate, to act; *(Theat)* to act. **als jd ~** *(Theat)* to act *or* play the part of sb.
**agil** *adj (körperlich)* agile, nimble. **(geistig)** ~ sharp, mentally agile.
**Agitation** *f (Pol)* agitation. ~ **treiben** to agitate.
**Agitator(in** *f)* [-ˈtoːrɪn] *m (Pol)* agitator.
**agitatorisch** *adj (Pol) Rede* inflammatory, agitating *attr.*
**agitieren*** *vi* to agitate.
**agnostisch** *adj* agnostic.
**Agonie** *f (lit, fig geh)* death throes *pl.* **in (der)** ~ **liegen** to be in the throes of death.
**Agrar-:** ~**land** *nt* agrarian country; ~**politik** *f* agricultural policy; ~**staat** *m* agrarian state.
**Ägypten** *nt* Egypt.
**Ägypter(in** *f)* *m* - Egyptian.
**ägyptisch** *adj* Egyptian.
**ah** [aː] ah, oh.
**äh** [ɛː] *interj (beim Sprechen)* er, um; *(Ausdruck des Ekels)* ugh.
**aha** *interj* aha; *(verstehend auch)* I see.
**Aha-Erlebnis** *nt* sudden insight.
**Ahn** *m (wk)* **-en, -en** *(geh)* ancestor, forefather *(liter).*
**ahnden** *vt (geh) Freveltat, Verbrechen* to avenge; *Übertretung, Verstoß* to punish.
**Ahndung** *f siehe* vt avenging; punishment.
**Ahne** *f* **-n** *(geh: weiblicher Vorfahr)* ancestress.
**ähneln** *vi* +*dat* to resemble. **sich** *or* **einander** *(geh)* ~ to resemble one another; **in diesem Punkt ähnelt sie sehr ihrem Vater** she's very like her father in this respect.
**ahnen** *vt (voraussehen)* to foresee, to know; *Gefahr, Tod etc* to have a presentiment *or* premonition of; *(vermuten)* to suspect; *(erraten)* to guess. **das kann ich doch nicht ~!** how am I expected to know that!; **nichts Böses ~** to be unsuspecting; **nichts Böses ~d** unsuspectingly; **ohne es zu** ~ without suspecting; **davon habe ich nichts geahnt** I didn't have the slightest inkling of it.
**Ahnen-:** ~**forschung** *f* genealogy; ~**galerie** *f* ancestral portrait gallery; ~**reihe** *f* ancestral line.
**Ahn-:** ~**frau** *f (liter)* ancestress; ~**herr** *m (liter)* ancestor.
**ähnlich** *adj* similar (+*dat* to). **ein dem Rokoko ~er**

**Stil** a style similar to rococo; ~ **wie er/sie** like him/her; **sie sind sich** ~ they are similar *or* alike; **ein ~ aussehender Gegenstand** a similar-looking object; **ich denke** ~ I think likewise; **jdm ~ sehen** to be like sb, to resemble sb; **das sieht ihm (ganz)** ~! *(col)* that's just like him!, that's him all over! *(col)*; **(etwas) Ä~es** something similar, something like it/ that.
**Ähnlichkeit** *f* similarity *(mit* to*).* **mit jdm/etw ~ haben** to resemble sb/sth, to be like sb/sth.
**Ahnung** *f* **(a)** *(Vorgefühl)* hunch, presentiment; *(düster)* foreboding, premonition. **(b)** *(Vorstellung, Wissen)* idea; *(Vermutung)* suspicion. **keine** ~! *(col)* no idea! *(col)*, I haven't a clue! *(col)*; **er hat keine blasse** *or* **nicht die geringste** ~ he hasn't the faintest idea *(col)*; **ich hatte keine ~, daß ...** I had no idea that ...; **hast du eine ~, wo er sein könnte?** have you any idea where he could be?; **du hast keine ~, wie schwierig das ist** you have no idea how difficult it is; **hast du eine ~!** *(iro col)* a (fat) lot you know (about it)! *(col)*.
**Ahnungs-:** **a~los** *adj (nichtsahnend)* unsuspecting; *(unwissend)* clueless *(col)*; ~**losigkeit** *f (Unwissenheit)* ignorance; **a~voll** *adj (geh)* full of presentiment *or (Böses ahnend)* foreboding.
**ahoi** [aˈhɔy] *interj (Naut)* **Schiff ~!** ship ahoy!
**Ahorn** *m* **-e** maple.
**Ahornblatt** *nt* maple leaf.
**Ähre** *f* **-n** ear; *(allgemeiner, Gras~)* head.
**Aids** [eɪdz] *nt* -, *no pl* Aids.
**Aids-** *in cpds* Aids; ~**-Erreger** *m* Aids virus; ~**infizierte(r)** *mf decl as adj* person infected with Aids; ~**kranke(r)** *mf* Aids victim.
**Airbus** [ˈɛːɾbʊs] *m (Aviat)* airbus.
**ais, Ais** [ˈaːɪs] *nt* - A sharp.
**Ajatollah** *m* **-s** ayatollah.
**Akad.** = **Akademie.**
**akad.** = **akademisch.**
**Akademie** *f* academy; *(Fachschule)* college.
**Akademiker(in** *f)* *m* - person with a university education; *(Student)* (university) student; *(Hochschulabsolvent)* (university) graduate; *(Universitätslehrkraft)* academic.
**akademisch** *adj (lit, fig)* academic. **das ~e Proletariat** (the) jobless graduates *pl*; ~ **gebildet sein** to have (had) a university education.
**Akazie** [-iə] *f* acacia.
**Akelei** *f* columbine.
**Akk.** = **Akkusativ.**
**Akklamation** *f (form)* **Wahl per** *or* **durch** ~ **election** by acclamation.
**akklimatisieren*** *vr (lit, fig)* to become acclimatized *(in* +*dat* to*).*
**Akkord** *m* **-e (a)** *(Mus)* chord. **(b)** *(Stücklohn)* piece rate. **im** ~ **arbeiten** to do piecework.
**Akkord-:** ~**arbeit** *f* piecework; ~**arbeiter** *m* pieceworker.
**Akkordeon** [-ɛɔn] *nt* **-s** accordion.
**Akkord-:** ~**lohn** *m* piece wages *pl*, piece rate; ~**zuschlag** *m* piece rate bonus.
**akkreditieren*** *vt (Pol)* to accredit *(bei* to, at*).*
**Akkreditierung** *f (Pol)* accrediting, accreditation *(bei* to, at*).*
**Akkreditiv** *nt* **(a)** *(Pol)* credentials *pl.* **(b)** *(Fin)* letter of credit.
**Akku** [ˈaku] *m* **-s** *(col)* = **Akkumulator.**
**Akkumulation** *f* accumulation.
**Akkumulator** *m* accumulator, storage battery.
**akkumulieren*** *vtir* to accumulate.
**akkurat** *adj* precise; *(sorgfältig auch)* meticulous.
**Akkusativ** *m* accusative.

**Akkusativ|objekt** *nt* accusative *or* direct object.
**Akne** *f* -n acne.
**Akontozahlung** *f* payment on account.
**Akquisition** [akvizitsi'oːn] *f (old)* acquisition; *(Comm)* canvassing.
**Akribie** *f no pl (geh)* meticulousness.
**akribisch** *adj (geh)* meticulous.
**Akrobat(in** *f) m (wk)* -en, -en acrobat.
**Akrobatik** *f no pl* acrobatics *pl*.
**akrobatisch** *adj* acrobatic.
**Akt** *m* -e **(a)** *(Tat)* act; *(Zeremonie)* ceremony. **(b)** *(Theat, Zirkus~)* act. **(c)** *(Art: ~bild)* nude. **(d)** *(Geschlechts~)* sexual act, coitus *no art (form)*.
**Akt|aufnahme** *n* nude (photograph).
**Akte** *f* -n file, record. **die ~ Schmidt** the Schmidt file; **das kommt in die ~n** this goes on file *or* record; **etw zu den ~n legen** to put sth on file.
**Akten-:** **~deckel** *m* folder; **~koffer** *m* attaché case; **a~kundig** *adj* on record; **~mappe** *f* **(a)** *(Umschlag)* folder, file; **(b)** *siehe* **~tasche;** **~notiz** *f* memo(randum); **~ordner** *m* file; **~schrank** *m* filing cabinet; **~tasche** *f* briefcase, portfolio; **~zeichen** *nt* reference.
**Akteur(in** *f)* [ak'tøːr, -tøːrin] *m (geh)* participant, protagonist.
**Aktfoto** *nt* nude (photograph).
**Aktie** ['aktsiə] *f* share; *(~nschein)* share certificate. **~n** shares, stock *sing*; **die ~n fallen/steigen** share prices are falling/rising; **die ~n stehen gut** shares are buoyant; **wie stehen die ~n?** *(hum col)* how are things?
**Aktien-:** **~besitz** *m* shareholdings *pl*; **~gesellschaft** *f* joint-stock company; **~index** *m* share index; **~kapital** *nt* share capital; **~kurs** *m* share price; **~markt** *m* stock market.
**Aktion** *f (Handlung)* action *(auch Mil)*; *(Kampagne)* campaign; *(Werbe~)* promotion; *(geplantes Unternehmen, Einsatz)* operation *(auch Mil)*. **in ~** in action.
**Aktionär(in** *f) m* shareholder, stockholder *(esp US)*.
**Aktionärsversammlung** *f* shareholders' meeting.
**Aktions-:** **~einheit** *f (Pol)* working unity; **a~fähig** *adj* capable of action; **~preis** *m (Werbung)* promotional price; **~radius** *m (Aviat, Naut)* range; *(fig: Wirkungsbereich)* scope.
**aktiv** *adj* active; *(Econ) Bilanz* positive; *(Mil) Soldat etc* on active service. **sich ~ an etw** *(dat)* **beteiligen** to take an active part in sth.
**Aktiv** *nt (Gram)* active.
**Aktiva** *pl* assets *pl*. **~ und Passiva** assets and liabilities.
**Aktive(r)** *mf decl as adj (Sport)* active participant.
**aktivieren\*** [akti'viːrən] *vt* to activate; *(fig) Arbeit, Kampagne* to step up; *Mitarbeiter* to get moving.
**Aktivist(in** *f) m* activist.
**Aktivität** *f* activity.
**Aktiv-:** **~posten** *m (lit, fig)* asset; **~saldo** *m* credit balance; **~seite** *f* assets side.
**Aktmodell** *nt* nude model.
**aktualisieren\*** *vt* to make topical; *Datei, Nachschlagewerk* to update.
**Aktualisierung** *f* updating.
**Aktualität** *f* relevance (to the current situation), topicality. **~en** *pl (geh: neueste Ereignisse)* current events.
**aktuell** *adj* relevant (to the current situation); *Frage auch* topical; *Buch, Film auch* of topical interest; *Problem, Theorie* current; *(Fashion: modern) Mode* latest *attr*, current. **von ~em Interesse/~er Bedeutung** of topical interest/of relevance to the present situation; **dieses Problem ist nicht mehr ~** this is no longer a problem; **eine ~e Sendung** *(Rad, TV)* a current-affairs programme.
**Aktzeichnung** *f* nude (drawing).
**akupunktieren\*** **1** *vt* to acupuncture. **2** *vi* to perform acupuncture.
**Akupunktur** *f* acupuncture.
**Akustik** *f no pl* acoustics *pl*.
**akustisch** *adj* acoustic. **ich habe dich rein ~ nicht verstanden** I simply didn't catch what you said (properly).
**akut** *adj (Med, fig)* acute; *Frage auch* pressing.
**AKW** [aːkaː'veː] *nt* -s = **Atomkraftwerk**.
**Akzent** *m* -e accent; *(Betonung)* stress; *(Zeichen)* stress mark. **den ~ auf etw** *(acc)* **legen** *(lit)* to stress sth. **~e setzen** *(fig)* to bring out *or* emphasize the main points.
**akzentfrei** *adj* without an accent.
**akzentuieren\*** *vt* to articulate, to enunciate; *(betonen)* to stress; *(fig: hervorheben)* to accentuate.
**Akzentverschiebung** *f (fig)* shift of emphasis.
**akzeptabel** *adj* acceptable.
**akzeptieren\*** *vt* to accept.
**Akzeptierung** *f* acceptance.
**AL** [aː'|ɛl] *f* -s = **Alternative Liste**.
**à la** [a la] *adv* à la.
**Alabaster** *m* - alabaster.
**Alarm** *m* -e *(Warnung)* alarm; *(Flieger~)* air-raid warning; *(Zustand)* alert. **~!** fire! *etc*; **~ schlagen** to give *or* raise the alarm.
**Alarm-:** **~anlage** *f* alarm system; **a~bereit** *adj* on the alert; **~bereitschaft** *f* alert; **in ~bereitschaft sein** *or* **stehen** to be on the alert; **in ~bereitschaft versetzen** to put on the alert, to alert; **~glocke** *f* alarm bell.
**alarmieren\*** *vt Polizei etc* to alert; *(fig: beunruhigen)* to alarm. **~d** *(fig)* alarming.
**Alarm-:** **~ruf** *m* warning cry; **~signal** *nt* alarm signal; **~stufe** *f* alert stage; **höchste ~stufe** maximum alert; **~übung** *f* practice exercise *or* drill; **~zustand** *m* alert; **im ~zustand sein** to be on the alert.
**Alaska** *nt* Alaska.
**Albaner(in** *f) m* - Albanian.
**Albanien** [-iən] *nt* Albania.
**albanisch** *adj* Albanian.
**Albatros** *m* -se albatross.
**Alben** *pl* of **Album**.
**albern** *adj* silly. **sich ~ benehmen** to act silly; **~es Zeug** (silly) nonsense.
**Albernheit** *f* **(a)** *no pl* silliness, foolishness. **(b)** *(Tat)* silly prank; *(Bemerkung)* inanity.
**Albino** *m* -s albino.
**Album** *nt, pl* **Alben** album.
**Alchemie** *(esp Aus)*, **Alchimie** *f* alchemy.
**alert** *adj (geh)* vivacious, lively.
**Aleuten** *pl* **die ~** the Aleutians, the Aleutian Islands.
**Alge** *f* -n alga.
**Algebra** *f no pl* algebra.
**Algerien** [-iən] *nt* Algeria.
**Algerier(in** *f)* [-iɐ, -iərin] *m* - Algerian.
**algerisch** *adj* Algerian.
**Algier** ['alʒiːɐ] *nt* -s Algiers.
**Algorithmus** *m* algorithm.
**alias** *adv* alias, also *or* otherwise known as.
**Alibi** *nt* -s *(Jur, fig)* alibi.
**Alibi-** *in cpds* alibi; **~frau** *f* token woman; **~funktion** *f (fig)* **~funktion haben** to be used as an alibi.
**Alimente** *pl* maintenance *sing*.
**alkalisch** *adj* alkaline.

**Alkohol** ['alkoho:l, alko'ho:l] *m* **-e** alcohol; *(Getränke auch)* drink. **seinen Kummer im ~ ertränken** to drown one's sorrows; **unter ~ stehen** to be under the influence (of alcohol).

**Alkohol-: a~arm** *adj* low in alcohol; **~ausschank** *m* sale of alcohol; **~einfluß** *m* **unter ~einfluß** under the influence of alcohol; **a~frei** *adj* nonalcoholic; *Getränk auch* soft; **~gehalt** *m* alcohol(ic) content; **~genuß** *m* consumption of alcohol; **a~haltig** *adj* alcoholic.

**Alkoholika** *pl* alcoholic drinks *pl.*
**Alkoholiker(in** *f)* *m* - alcoholic.
**alkoholisch** *adj* alcoholic.
**Alkoholismus** *m* alcoholism.
**Alkohol-: ~konsum** *m* consumption of alcohol; **~kontrolle** *f* drink-driving check; **~mißbrauch** *m* alcohol abuse; **~spiegel** *m* jds **~spiegel** the level of alcohol in sb's blood; **~steuer** *f* duty *or* tax on alcohol; **~sünder** *m (col)* drunk(en) driver; **~test** *m* breath test; **~verbot** *nt* ban on alcohol; **der Arzt hat ihm ~verbot verordnet** the doctor told him not to touch alcohol; **~vergiftung** *f* alcohol(ic) poisoning.

**all** *indef pron* **all mein/sein Geld** all my/his money.
**All** *nt no pl (Sci, Space)* space *no art*; *(außerhalb unseres Sternsystems)* outer space *no art*; *(liter, geh)* universe. **Spaziergang im ~** space walk.

**all-: ~abendlich 1** *adj* regular evening; **2** *adv* every evening; **~bekannt** *adj* universally known.

**alle 1** *pron siehe* **alle(r, s). 2** *adv (col)* all gone. **die Milch ist ~** the milk's all gone, there's no milk left; **etw/jdn ~ machen** *(col)* to finish sth/sb off.

**alledem** *pron* **bei/trotz** *etc* **~** with/in spite of *etc* all that; **von ~ stimmt kein Wort** there's not a word of truth in any of it; **zu ~** moreover.

**Allee** *f* **-n** [-e:ən] avenue.
**Allegorie** *f* allegory.
**allegorisch** *adj* allegorical.

**allein 1** *adj pred* alone; *Gegenstand, Wort auch* by itself, on its own; *(ohne Begleitung, Hilfe auch)* by oneself, on one's own; *(einsam)* lonely. **von ~** by oneself/itself; **ganz ~** *(einsam)* all alone; *(ohne Begleitung, Hilfe)* all by oneself, all on one's own. **2** *adv (nur)* alone. **das ist ~ seine Verantwortung** that is his responsibility alone; **~ schon der Gedanke** the very *or* mere thought ..., the thought alone ...; **das Porto ~ kostet ...** the postage alone costs ..., just the postage is ...

**Allein-: ~erbe** *m* sole *or* only heir; **~erziehend** *adj Mutter, Vater* single; **~erziehende(r)** *mf decl as adj* single parent; **~gang** *m (col) (Sport)* solo run; *(von Bergsteiger)* solo climb; *(fig: Tat)* solo effort; **etw im ~gang machen** *(fig)* to do sth on one's own; **~herrscher** *m* autocrat, absolute dictator.

**alleinig** *adj attr* sole, only.
**Allein-: ~recht** *nt* exclusive right; **~sein** *nt* being on one's own *no def art*, solitude; *(Einsamkeit)* loneliness; **a~stehend** *adj* living alone; *(nicht verheiratet)* single; **~stehende(r)** *mf decl as adj* single person; **~unterhalter** *m* solo entertainer; **~verdiener** *m* sole earner; **~vertretung** *f (Comm)* sole agency.

**allemal** *adv (ohne Schwierigkeit)* without any problem *or* trouble. **was er kann, kann ich noch ~** anything he can do I can do too; **ein für ~** once and for all.

**allenfalls** *adv (nötigenfalls)* if need be; *(höchstens)* at most; *(bestenfalls)* at best.

**alle(r, s) 1** *indef pron* **(a)** *attr* all; *(bestimmte Menge, Anzahl)* all the. **~ Kinder unter 10 Jahren** all children under 10; **im Geschäft war ~s Brot ausverkauft**

all the bread in the shop was sold out; **wir haben ~n Haß vergessen** we have forgotten all (our) hatred; **~ Anwesenden** all those present; **mit ~m Nachdruck** with all possible emphasis; **trotz ~r Mühe** in spite of every effort; **ohne ~n Grund** without any reason, with no reason at all; **mit ~r Deutlichkeit** quite distinctly; **in ~r Unschuld** in all innocence; **ohne ~n Zweifel** without any doubt.

**(b)** *(substantivisch)* **~s** *sing* everything; **~** *pl* all; *(alle Menschen)* all, everybody, everyone; **~s, was ...** all *or* everything that/everybody *or* everyone who ...; **das ~s** all that; **~s Schöne** everything beautiful; **~s Gute** all the best; **~s und jedes** anything and everything; **in ~m** *(in jeder Beziehung)* in everything; **~s in ~m** all in all; **trotz ~m** in spite of everything; **vor ~m** above all; **das ist ~s, das wäre ~s** that's all, that's it *(col)*; **das ist ~s andere als ...** that's anything but ...; **es hat ~s keinen Sinn mehr** nothing makes sense any more; **was habt ihr ~s gemacht?** what did you get up to?; **wer war ~s da?** who was there?; **was er (nicht) ~s weiß!** the things he knows!; **die haben mir ~ nicht gefallen** I didn't like any of them; **~ beide/drei** both of them/ all three of them; **~ diejenigen, die ... all** (those) who ...; **diese ~** all (of) these; **der Kampf ~r gegen ~** the free-for-all; **~ für einen und einer für ~** all for one and one for all; **sie kamen ~** they all came, all of them came; **sie haben ~ kein Geld mehr** none of them has any money left.

**(c)** *(mit Zeit-, Maßangaben)* usu *pl* every. **~ fünf Minuten/fünf Meter** every five minutes/five metres; **~ Jahre wieder** year after year.

**2** *adv siehe* **alle.**

**aller-: ~beste(r, s)** *adj* very best, best ... of all; **ich wünsche Dir das A~beste** (I wish you) all the best; **der/die/das A~beste** the very best/the best of all; **~dings** *adv* **(a)** *(einschränkend)* though, mind you; **das ist ~dings wahr, aber ...** that may be true, but ...; **(b)** *(bekräftigend)* certainly; **~erste(r, s)** *adj* very first; **~frühestens** *adv* at the very earliest.

**Allergie** *f (Med, fig)* allergy. **eine ~ gegen etw haben** to be allergic to sth *(auch fig hum)*; *(fig auch)* to have an aversion to sth.

**allergisch** *adj (Med, fig)* allergic *(gegen* to*)*. **auf etw** *(acc)* **~ reagieren** to be allergic to sth.

**Aller-: a~hand** *adj inv (substantivisch) (allerlei)* all kinds of things; *(ziemlich viel)* rather a lot; *(attributiv)* all kinds *or* sorts of; rather a lot of; **das ist ja a~hand!** *(zustimmend)* that's quite something!, not bad at all! *(col)*; *(empört)* that's too much! **~heiligen** *nt* All Saints' Day; **a~höchste(r, s)** *adj* **von a~höchste Stelle** from the very highest authority; **es wird a~höchste Zeit, daß ...** it's really high time that ...; **a~höchstens** *adv* at the very most; **a~lei** *adj inv (substantivisch)* all sorts *or* kinds of things; *(attributiv)* all sorts *or* kinds of; **a~letzte(r, s)** *adj* very last; *(a~neueste)* very latest; *(col: unmöglich)* most awful *attr (col)*; **der/das ist das ~letzte** *(col)* he's/it's the pits! *(col)*; **~liebste(r, s)** *adj* **es wäre mir das a~liebste** *or* **am a~liebsten, wenn ...** I would much prefer it if ...; **a~meiste(r, s)** *adj* most ... of all; **die ~meisten** the vast majority; **a~nächste(r, s)** *adj (in Folge)* very next; *(räumlich)* nearest; *Verwandte* very closest; **in a~nächster Zeit** in the very near future; **a~neu(e)ste(r, s)** *adj* very latest; **~seelen** *nt* All Souls' Day; **a~seits** *adv* on all sides, on every side; **guten Abend a~seits!** good evening everybody; **a~spätestens** *adv* at the very latest.

**Allerwelts-** *in cpds (Durchschnitts-)* common; *(nichtssagend)* commonplace; **~kerl** *m* jack of all trades.

**Aller-:** a~**wenigstens** *adv* at the very least; a~**wenigste(r, s)** *adj* least ... of all; *(pl)* fewest ... of all; *(äußerst wenig)* very little; *(pl)* very few; **die a~wenigsten Menschen wissen das** very few people know that; **das ist doch das ~wenigste, was man erwarten könnte** but that's the very least one could expect; **das am a~wenigsten!** least of all that!; ~**werteste(r)** *m decl as adj (hum)* posterior *(hum)*.

**alles** *indef pron siehe* **alle(r, s)**.

**allesamt** *adv* all (of them/us *etc*). **ihr seid ~ Betrüger!** you're all cheats!

**Alles-:** ~**fresser** *m* omnivore; ~**kleber** *m* all-purpose adhesive; ~**wisser** *m* - *(iro)* know-all *(col)*, know-it-all *(US col)*.

**allgegenwärtig** *adj* omnipresent, ubiquitous.

**allgemein 1** *adj* general; *Feiertag* public; *Wahlrecht* universal; *Wehrpflicht* compulsory. **im ~en** in general, generally; **im ~en Interesse** in the common interest; **auf ~en Wunsch** by popular request; **die ~e Meinung** the general opinion; **zur ~en Überraschung** to everyone's surprise. **2** *adv* generally; *(ausnahmslos von allen)* universally; *(nicht spezifisch)* in general terms. **es ist ~ bekannt** it's common knowledge; **es ist ~ üblich** it's the general rule; ~ **verbreitet** widespread; ~ **zugänglich** open to all .

**Allgemein-:** ~**befinden** *nt* general condition; ~**bildung** *f* general *or* all-round education; **a~gültig** *adj attr* general, universal; ~**heit** *f (no pl: Öffentlichkeit)* general public; *(alle)* everyone, everybody; ~**medizin** *f* general medicine; **Arzt für ~medizin** general practitioner, GP; **a~verständlich** *adj no pred* generally intelligible; ~**wissen** *nt* general knowledge; ~**wohl** *nt* public good *or* welfare.

**Allheilmittel** *nt* cure-all, panacea *(esp fig)*.

**Allianz** *f* **(a)** alliance. **(b)** *(NATO)* Alliance.

**Alligator** *m* alligator.

**Alliierte(r)** *mf decl as adj* ally. **die ~n** *(im 2. Weltkrieg)* the Allies.

**Alliteration** *f (Poet)* alliteration.

**All-:** **a~jährlich** *adj* annual, yearly; ~**macht** *f (esp von Gott)* omnipotence; **a~mächtig** *adj* all-powerful, omnipotent; ~**mächtige(r)** *m decl as adj (Gott)* **der ~mächtige** Almighty God, the Almighty; ~**mächtiger!** good Lord!

**allmählich 1** *adj attr* gradual. **2** *adv* gradually; *(col: endlich)* at last. **es wird ~ Zeit** *(col)* it's about time; **ich werde (ganz) ~ müde** *(col)* I'm beginning to get tired; **wir sollten ~ gehen** *(col)* we should be thinking of going.

**allmonatlich** *adj* monthly.

**Allotria** *nt no pl (col) (Unfug)* monkey business *(col)* no *indef art*; *(Lärm)* racket *(col)*, din.

**Allrad|antrieb** *m* all-wheel drive.

**allseitig** *adj (allgemein)* general; *(ausnahmslos)* universal; *(vielseitig)* all-round *attr*. ~ **begabt sein** to be an all-rounder; **zur ~en Zufriedenheit** to the satisfaction of all *or* everyone.

**allseits** *adv (überall)* everywhere, on all sides; *(in jeder Beziehung)* in every respect.

**Alltag** *m (fig)* everyday life. **der ~ der Ehe** the mundane *or* day-to-day side of married life.

**alltäglich** *adj* **(a)** *(tagtäglich)* daily. **(b)** *(üblich)* everyday *attr*, ordinary; *Gesicht, Mensch* ordinary; **es ist ganz ~** it's nothing unusual.

**alltags** *adv* on weekdays.

**Alltags-** *in cpds* everyday.

**all|umfassend** *adj* all-embracing, global.

**Allüren** *pl* odd behaviour *(Brit)* or behavior *(US)*; *(geziertes Verhalten)* affectations *pl*; *(eines Stars etc)* airs and graces *pl*.

**all-:** **A~wetter-** *in cpds* all-weather; ~**wissend** *adj* omniscient; **A~wissenheit** *f* omniscience; ~**wöchentlich** *adj* weekly; ~**zeit** *adv (geh)* always.

**allzu** *adv* all too; *(+neg)* too. ~ **viele Fehler** far too many mistakes.

**allzu-:** ~**gern** *adv mögen* only too much; *(bereitwillig)* only too willingly; **nicht ~gern** not all that much/willingly, not too much/willingly; **er ißt Muscheln nur ~gern** he's only too fond of mussels; ~**oft** *adv* all too often; ~**sehr** *adv* too much; *mögen* all too much; *sich freuen* only too; *versuchen* too hard; *sich ärgern, enttäuscht sein* too; **nicht ~sehr mögen/enttäuscht sein** not to like too much/ not to be too disappointed; ~**viel** *adv* too much; ~**viel ist ungesund** *(Prov)* you can have too much of a good thing *(prov)*.

**Allzweck-** *in cpds* all-purpose.

**Alm** *f* -en alpine pasture.

**Almosen** [-oː-] *nt* - *(geh: Spende)* alms *pl (old)*. ~ *pl (fig)* charity.

**Alpaka** *nt* -s alpaca.

**Alpdruck** *m (lit, fig)* nightmare. **wie ein ~druck auf jdm lasten** to weigh sb down, to oppress sb.

**Alpen** *pl* **die ~** the Alps *pl*.

**Alpen-:** ~**glühen** *nt* - alpenglow; ~**paß** *m* alpine pass; ~**rose** *f* Alpine rose; ~**veilchen** *nt* cyclamen; ~**vorland** *nt* foothills *pl* of the Alps.

**Alphabet** *nt* -e alphabet. **nach dem ~** alphabetically, in alphabetical order.

**alphabetisch** *adj* alphabetical. ~ **geordnet** arranged in alphabetical order.

**alphabetisieren*** *vt* to make literate.

**alphanumerisch** *adj (Comp)* alphanumeric.

**Alphastrahlen** *pl* alpha rays *pl*.

**Alphorn** *nt* alp(en)horn.

**alpin** *adj* alpine.

**Alpinist(in** *f)* *m* alpinist.

**Alptraum** *m (lit, fig)* nightmare.

**als** *conj* **(a)** *(nach comp)* than. **ich kam später ~ er** I came later than he (did) *or* him.

**(b)** *(bei Vergleichen)* **soviel/soweit ~ möglich** as much/far as possible; **nichts/niemand/nirgend anders ~** nothing/nobody/nowhere but; **eher** *or* **lieber ... ~** rather ... than; **anders sein ~** to be different from; **das machen wir anders ~ ihr** we do it differently from you; **alles andere ~** anything but.

**(c)** **es sieht aus, ~ würde es bald schneien** it looks as if *or* though it will snow soon; ~ **ob ich das nicht wüßte!** as if I didn't know!

**(d)** **sie ist zu alt, ~ daß sie das noch verstehen könnte** she is too old to understand that; **die Zeit war zu knapp, ~ daß wir ...** the time was too short for us to ...

**(e)** *(in Temporalsätzen)* when; *(gleichzeitig)* as. **damals, ~** in the days when; **gerade, ~** just as.

**(f)** *(in der Eigenschaft)* as. ~ **Beweis** as proof; ~ **Antwort/Warnung** as an answer/a warning; **sich ~ wahr/falsch erweisen** to prove to be true/false; ~ **Kind/Mädchen** *etc* as a child/girl *etc*.

**alsbaldig** *adj (form)* immediate; „**zum ~en Verbrauch bestimmt"** "for immediate use (only)".

**also 1** *conj (folglich)* so, therefore. **2** *adv* so; *(nach Unterbrechung anknüpfend)* well; *(zusammenfassend, erklärend)* that is. ~ **doch** so ... after all; **du machst es ~?** so you'll do it then?; ~ **wie ich schon sagte** well (then), as I said before. **3** *interj* well. **na ~!** there you are!, you see?; ~ **gut** *or* **schön** well all right then; ~ **so was/so eine Frechheit!** well (I never)/what a cheek!

**Alster(wasser)** *nt (N Ger)* shandy *(Brit)*, beer and lemonade.

**alt** *adj, comp* ⸚**er,** *superl* ⸚**este(r, s)** *or (adv)* **am** ⸚**esten** **(a)** old; *(sehr ~)* *Sage, Aberglaube auch, Griechen, Geschichte* ancient; *Sprachen* classical. **das ~e Rom** ancient Rome; **das A~e Testament** the Old Testament; **die A~ Welt** the Old World; **~ und jung** (everybody) old and young; **ein drei Jahre ~es Kind** a three-year-old child; **wie ~ bist du?** how old are you?; **etw ~ kaufen** to buy sth second-hand; **ich werde heute nicht ~ (werden)** *(col)* I won't last long today/tonight *etc (col)*; **~e Liebe rostet nicht** *(Prov)* true love never dies *(prov)*. **(b)** *(dieselbe, gewohnt)* same old. **sie ist ganz die ~e (Ingrid)** she's the same old Ingrid; **er ist nicht mehr der ~e** he's not the man he was; **alles beim ~en lassen** to leave everything as it was. **(c)** **~ aussehen** *(col: dumm dastehen)* to look stupid.

**Alt** *m* **-e** *(Mus)* alto; *(von Frau auch)* contralto.

**Altar** *m, pl* **Altäre** altar.

**Alt-:** **a~backen** *adj* **(a)** stale; **(b)** *(fig) Mensch, Ansichten* old-fashioned; **~bau** *m* old building; **~bauwohnung** *f* flat in an old building; **a~bekannt** *adj* well-known; **a~bewährt** *adj Methode etc* well-tried; *Tradition etc* long-standing; **~bier** *nt* top-fermented German dark beer; **~bundeskanzler** *m* former German/Austrian Chancellor; **a~deutsch** *adj* old German; *Möbel, Stil* German Renaissance.

**Alte** *siehe* **Alte(r), Alte(s).**

**Alt-:** **a~ehrwürdig** *adj* venerable; *Bräuche* time-honoured *(Brit)*, time-honored *(US)*; **a~eingesessen** *adj* old-established; **~eisen** *nt* scrap-metal.

**Alten-:** **~heim** *nt* old people's home; **~pfleger** *m* old people's nurse; **~tagesstätte** *f* old people's day home; **~teil** *nt* **sich aufs ~teil setzen** *or* **zurückziehen** *(fig)* to retire from public life; **~wohnheim** *nt =* **~heim.**

**Alte(r)** *mf decl as adj (alter Mann, col: Ehemann, Vater)* old man; *(alte Frau, col: Ehefrau, Mutter)* old woman; *(col: Vorgesetzter)* boss. **die ~n** *(Eltern)* the folk(s) *pl (col)*; *(Tiereltern)* the parents *pl*; *(ältere Generation)* the old people *pl or* folk *pl*.

**Alter** *nt* **-** age; *(letzter Lebensabschnitt)* old age. **im ~ in one's old age; in deinem ~** at your age; **er ist in deinem ~** he's your age; **im ~ von 18 Jahren** at the age of 18; **45, das ist doch kein ~** *(col)* 45, that's not old.

**älter** *adj* **(a)** *comp of* **alt** older; *Bruder, Tochter etc auch* elder. **werden Frauen ~ als Männer?** do women live longer than men?; **Holbein der Ä~e** Holbein the Elder. **(b)** *attr (nicht ganz jung)* elderly.

**altern** *vi aux sein* to age; *(Wein)* to mature.

**alternativ** *adj* alternative. **~ leben** to live an alternative lifestyle; **A~e Liste** *(Pol) electoral pact of alternative political groupings.*

**Alternativ-** *in cpds* alternative.

**Alternative** *f* alternative *(etw zu tun* of doing sth*).*

**Alternative(r)** *mf decl as adj* person with alternative views.

**alternierend** *adj* alternate; *Strom, Verse* alternating.

**alt|erprobt** *adj* well-tried.

**alters** *adv (geh):* **von** *or* **seit ~ (her)** from time immemorial.

**Alters-:** **a~bedingt** *adj* related to a particular age; related to *or* caused by old age; **~erscheinung** *f* sign of old age; **~forschung** *f* gerontology; **~fürsorge** *f* care of the elderly; **~genosse** *m* contemporary; **~grenze** *f* age limit; *(Rentenalter)* re-

tirement age; **flexible ~grenze** flexible retirement age; **~gründe** *pl* **aus ~gründen** for reasons of age; **~gruppe** *f* age-group; **~heim** *nt* old people's home; **~klasse** *f (Sport)* age-group; **~präsident** *m* president by seniority; **~prozeß** *m* ageing process; **~rente** *f* old age pension; **~ruhegeld** *nt* retirement pension; **a~schwach** *adj Mensch* old and infirm; *Auto, Möbel* decrepit; **~schwäche** *f siehe adj* infirmity; decrepitude; **~sitz** *m:* **sein ~sitz war München** he spent his retirement in Munich; **~stufe** *f* age group; *(Lebensabschnitt)* age; **~versorgung** *f* provision for (one's) old age; *(Rente)* old age pension; **betriebliche ~versorgung** occupational pension scheme; **~werk** *nt* late works *pl*; *(einzelnes Werk)* late work.

**Altertum** *nt no pl* antiquity *no art.*

**Altertümer** *pl* antiquities *pl.*

**altertümlich** *adj (aus dem Altertum)* ancient; *(veraltet)* antiquated.

**Altertums-:** **~forscher** *m* archaeologist; **~forschung** *f* archaeology; **~wert** *m:* **das hat schon ~wert** *(hum)* it has antique value *(hum)*.

**Alte(s)** *nt decl as adj* **das ~** *(das Gewohnte, Traditionelle)* the old; *(alte Dinge)* old things *pl*; **er hängt sehr am ~n** he clings to the past.

**Älteste(r)** *mf decl as adj* oldest; *(Sohn, Tochter auch)* eldest.

**älteste(r, s)** *adj superl of* **alt** oldest; *Bruder etc auch* eldest.

**Alt-:** **a~gedient** *adj* long-serving; **~glas** *nt* used glass; **~glascontainer** *m* bottle bank *(Brit)*; **~griechisch(e)** *nt* classical *or* ancient Greek; **a~hergebracht** *adj* traditional; **~herrenmannschaft** *f (Sport)* team of players over thirty; **~hochdeutsch(e)** *nt* Old High German.

**Altist(in** *f) m (Mus)* alto.

**Alt-:** **a~jüngferlich** *adj* old-maidish; **a~klug** *adj* precocious; **~lasten** *pl (Ökologie)* legacy of dangerous waste.

**ältlich** *adj* oldish.

**Alt-:** **~material** *nt* scrap; **~meister** *m* doyen; *(Sport)* ex-champion; **~metall** *nt* scrap metal; **a~modisch** *adj* old-fashioned; *(rückständig)* outmoded; **~papier** *nt* wastepaper; **~philologe** *m* classical scholar; **~philologie** *f* classical studies *pl*; **a~rosa** *adj* dark pink, old rose; **~schlüssel** *m (Mus)* alto clef; **~schnee** *m* old snow; **~stadt** *f* old town; **die Ulmer ~stadt** the old part of Ulm; **~steinzeit** *f* Palaeolithic Age, Old Stone Age; **~stimme** *f (Mus)* alto; *(von Frau auch)* contralto; **a~testamentarisch** *adj* Old Testament *attr*; **a~väterlich** *adj Bräuche* ancestral; *(altmodisch)* old-fashioned *no adv*; *Erscheinung etc* patriarchal; **~waren** *pl* second-hand goods *pl*; **~warenhändler** *m* second-hand dealer.

**Altweiber-:** **~geschwätz** *nt* old woman's talk; **~sommer** *m (Nachsommer)* Indian summer.

**Alu** *nt (col) =* **Aluminium.**

**Alufolie** *f* tinfoil, kitchen foil.

**Aluminium** *nt no pl* aluminium *(Brit)*, aluminum *(US)*.

**Aluminiumfolie** *f* tinfoil.

**Alzheimer-Krankheit** *f* Alzheimer's disease.

**am** *prep =* **an dem (a)** *(zur Bildung des Superlativs)* **er war ~ tapfersten** he was (the) bravest; **er hat ~ tapfersten gekämpft** he fought (the) most bravely; **sie war ~ schönsten** she was (the) most beautiful; **~ besten machen wir das morgen** it would be best to do it tomorrow; **~ seltsamsten war ...** the strangest thing was ... **(b)** *(als Zeitangabe)* on. **~ letzten Sonntag** last Sunday; **~ 8. Mai** on the eighth of

May, on May *(the Brit)* eighth; *(geschrieben)* on May 8th; ~ **Morgen/Abend** in the morning/evening. **(c)** *(als Ortsangabe)* on the; *(bei Gebirgen)* at the foot of the. **(d)** *(col: als Verlaufsform)* **ich war gerade** ~ **Schlafen** I was just sleeping.

**Amalgam** *nt -e* almalgam.

**Amateur** [-'tøːʀ] *m* amateur.

**Amateur-** [ama'tøːʀ]: ~**funker** *m* radio amateur *or* ham *(col)*; **a~haft** *adj* amateurish.

**Amazonas** *m* (River) Amazon.

**Amber** *m* **-(n)** ambergris.

**Ambiente** *nt no pl* ambience.

**Ambition** *f (geh)* ambition. ~**en auf etw** *(acc)* **haben** to have aspirations to sth.

**ambivalent** [-va'lɛnt] *adj* ambivalent.

**Ambivalenz** [-va'lɛnts] *f* ambivalence.

**Amboß** *m* **-sse** anvil.

**ambulant** *adj (Med) Versorgung, Behandlung* out-patient *attr.* ~**e Patienten** out-patients.

**Ambulanz** *f (Klinikstation)* out-patient department, out-patients *sing.*

**Ambulanzwagen** *m* ambulance.

**Ameise** *f* **-n** ant.

**Ameisen-:** ~**bär** *m* anteater; ~**haufen** *m* anthill; ~**säure** *f* formic acid; ~**staat** *m* ant colony.

**amen** *interj* amen.

**Amen** *nt* - amen. **sein** ~ **zu etw geben** to give one's blessing to sth; **das ist so sicher wie das** ~ **in der Kirche** *(col)* you can bet your bottom dollar on that *(col).*

**Amerika** *nt* America.

**Amerikaner(in** *f)* *m* - **(a)** American. **(b)** *(Gebäck)* flat iced cake.

**amerikanisch** *adj* American.

**amerikanisieren\*** *vt* to Americanize.

**Amerikanisierung** *f* Americanization.

**Amerikanismus** *m* **-men** Americanism.

**Amerikanistik** *f* American studies *pl.*

**Amethyst** *m* **-e** amethyst.

**Ami** *m* **-s** *(col)* Yank *(col)*; *(Soldat)* GI *(col).*

**Amme** *f* **-n** *(old)* foster-mother; *(Nährmutter)* wet nurse.

**Ammenmärchen** *nt* fairy tale *or* story.

**Ammoniak** *nt no pl* ammonia.

**Amnesie** *f (Med)* amnesia.

**Amnestie** *f* amnesty.

**amnestieren\*** *vt* to grant an amnesty to.

**Amöbe** *f* **-n** *(Biol)* amoeba.

**Amok** *m:* ~ **laufen** to run amok *or* amuck.

**Amok-:** ~**fahrer** *m* mad *or* lunatic driver; ~**läufer** *m* madman; ~**schütze** *m* crazed gunman.

**Amor** *m* - Cupid.

**Amortisation** *f (Econ)* amortization.

**amortisieren\*** *vr* to pay for itself.

**amourös** [amu'røːs] *adj (geh)* amorous.

**Ampel** *f* **-n** **(a)** *(Verkehrs~)* (traffic) lights *pl (Brit)*, (traffic) light *(US)*. **(b)** *(Hängeblumentopf)* hanging (flower) basket.

**Ampelphase** *f* traffic light sequence. **die langen ~n an dieser Kreuzung** the length of time the lights take to change at this junction.

**Ampere** [am'pɛːʀ] *nt* - amp.

**Amperemeter** [am'pɛːʀ-] *nt* ammeter.

**Amphetamin** *nt* **-e** amphetamine.

**Amphibie** [-iə] *f (Zool)* amphibian.

**Amphibienfahrzeug** *nt* amphibious vehicle.

**amphibisch** *adj* amphibious.

**Amphitheater** *nt* amphitheatre *(Brit)*, amphitheater *(US).*

**Ampulle** *f* **-n** *(Behälter)* ampoule.

**Amputation** *f* amputation.

**amputieren\*** *vt* to amputate. **jdm den Arm** ~ to amputate sb's arm.

**Amsel** *f* **-n** blackbird.

**Amsterdam** *nt* Amsterdam.

**Amt** *nt* **ᵗer** **(a)** *(Stellung)* office; *(Posten)* post. **im** ~ **sein** to be in office; **jdm aus einem** ~ **entfernen** to remove sb from office. **(b)** *(Aufgabe)* duty, task. **seines ~es walten** *(geh)* to carry out *or* discharge *(form)* one's duties. **(c)** *(Behörde) (Einwohnermelde~, Finanz~)* registration/tax office; *(Stadtverwaltung)* council offices *pl.* **zum zuständigen** ~ **gehen** to go to the relevant authority; **von ~s wegen** *(auf behördliche Anordnung hin)* officially. **(d)** *(Telefon~)* operator; *(Zentrale)* exchange. **(e)** *(Eccl: Messe)* High Mass.

**amtieren\*** *vi* **(a)** *(Amt innehaben)* to be in office. ~**d** incumbent; **der ~de Bürgermeister/Weltmeister** the (present) mayor/the reigning world champion; **als Außenminister** ~ to hold the post of foreign minister. **(b)** *(fungieren)* **als ...** ~ to act as ...

**amtlich** *adj* official; *(wichtig) Miene, Gebaren* officious; ~**es Kennzeichen** registration (number), license number *(US).*

**Amtmann** *m, pl* **-männer** *or* **-leute, Amtmännin** *f (Admin)* senior civil servant.

**Amts-:** ~**anmaßung** *f* unauthorized assumption of authority; ~**arzt** *m* medical officer; **a~ärztlich** *adj Zeugnis* from the medical officer; **a~ärztlich untersucht werden** to have an official medical examination; ~**bereich** *m* area of competence; ~**dauer** *f* term of office; ~**deutsch(e)** *nt* (German) officialese; ~**eid** *m* oath of office; **den ~eid ablegen** to be sworn in, to take the oath of office; ~**einsetzung** *f* inauguration; ~**enthebung** *f* dismissal from office; ~**geheimnis** *nt* **(a)** *(geheime Sache)* official secret; **(b)** *(Schweigepflicht)* official secrecy; ~**gericht** *nt* county *(Brit)* or district *(US)* court; ~**geschäfte** *pl* official duties *pl;* ~**handlung** *f* official duty; ~**hilfe** *f* cooperation between authorities; ~**leitung** *f (Telec)* exchange line; ~**mißbrauch** *m* abuse of one's position; ~**periode** *f* term of office; ~**person** *f* official; ~**richter** *m* ≈ county *(Brit)* or district *(US)* court judge; ~**schimmel** *m (hum)* officialdom; **der ~schimmel wiehert** officialdom rears its ugly head; ~**sitz** *m* official residence; *(von Behörde)* offices *pl;* ~**sprache** *f* official language; ~**träger** *m* office bearer *or* holder *(US);* ~**vorstand, ~vorsteher** *m* head *or* chief of a/the department *etc;* ~**weg** *m* **auf dem ~weg** through official channels; ~**zeichen** *nt (Telec)* dialling tone *(Brit)*, dial tone *(US);* ~**zeit** *f* period of office; ~**zimmer** *nt* office.

**Amulett** *nt* **-e** amulet, charm.

**amüsant** *adj* amusing.

**Amüsement** [amyzə'mãː] *nt* **-s** *(geh)* amusement, entertainment.

**amüsieren\* 1** *vt* to amuse. **amüsiert zuschauen** to look on with amusement. **2** *vr (sich vergnügen)* to have a good time, to have fun. **sich über etw** *(acc)* ~ to find sth funny; *(unfreundlich)* to make fun of sth.

**Amüsierviertel** *nt* nightclub district.

**an 1** *prep +dat* **(a)** *(räumlich: wo?)* at; *(~ etw dran)* on. **am Haus/Bahnhof** at the house/station; **am Fenster sitzen** to sit at *or* by the window; **am Tatort** at the scene of the crime; ~ **der Tür/Wand** on the door/wall; ~ **der Donau/Autobahn/am Ufer** by *or* *(direkt* ~ *gelegen)* on the Danube/motorway/bank; **zu nahe** ~ **etw stehen** to be too near to sth; **jdn** ~ **der Hand nehmen** to take sb by the hand; **unten am Fluß** down by the river; **sie wohnen Tür** ~ **Tür** they live next door to one another; **sich** *(dat)* **die Hand**

**am Tuch abwischen** to wipe one's hand on the cloth.
 (b) *(zeitlich)* on. ~ **diesem Abend** (on) that evening; ~ **dem Abend, als ich ...** the evening I ...; *siehe* **am.**
 (c) **jung** ~ **Jahren sein** to be young in years; **fünf** ~ **der Zahl** five in number; ~ **etw arbeiten/ schreiben/kauen** to be working on/writing/chewing sth; ~ **etw sterben** to die of sth; **arm/reich** ~ **Rohstoffen** short of/rich in resources; **was haben Sie** ~ **Weinen da?** what wines do you have?; ~ **der ganzen Sache ist nichts** there is nothing in it; **es** ~ **der Leber** *etc* **haben** *(col)* to have liver *etc* trouble; **das gefällt mir nicht** ~ **ihm** that's what I don't like about him; **sie hat etwas** ~ **sich, das ...** there is something about her that ...; **es ist** ~ **ihm, etwas zu tun** *(geh)* it's up to him to do something.
 **2** *prep* +*acc* (a) *(räumlich: wohin?)* to; *(gegen)* on, against. **etw** ~ **die Wand/Tafel schreiben** to write sth on the wall/blackboard; **etw** ~ **etw hängen** to hang sth on sth; **A**~ **den Vorsitzenden ...** *(bei Anschrift)* The Chairman ... (b) *(zeitlich: woran?)* ~ **die Zukunft/Vergangenheit denken** to think of the future/past; **bis** ~ **mein Lebensende** to the end of my days. (c) ~ **die Arbeit gehen** to get down to work; **ich habe eine Bitte/Frage** ~ **Sie** I have a request to make of you/question to ask you; **ein Gruß/eine Frage** ~ **jdn** greetings/a question to sb; ~ **(und für) sich** actually.
 **3** *adv* (a) *(ungefähr)* about. ~ **(die) hundert** about a hundred. (b) *(Ankunftszeit)* **Frankfurt** ~: **18.30** *(Rail)* arriving Frankfurt 18.30. (c) **von diesem Ort** ~ from here onwards; **von diesem Tag/heute** ~ from this day/today on(wards). (d) *(col: angeschaltet, angezogen)* on. **Licht** ~! lights on!; **ohne etwas** ~ with nothing on.
**Anabolikum** *nt* -**bolika** anabolic steroid.
**Anachronismus** [-kr-] *m (geh)* anachronism.
**anachronistisch** [-kr-] *adj (geh)* anachronistic.
**Anagramm** *nt (Liter)* anagram.
**analog** *adj* (a) analogous *(+dat, zu* to). (b) *(Comp, Elec)* analog.
**Analogie** *f* analogy.
**Analog-:** ~**rechner** *m* analog computer; ~**uhr** *f* analogue clock.
**Analphabet(in** *f)* *m (wk)* -**en, en** illiterate (person).
**Analphabetentum** *nt* illiteracy.
**Analyse** *f* -**n** analysis *(auch Psych)*.
**analysieren\*** *vt* to analyze.
**Analytiker(in** *f)* *m* - analyst.
**analytisch** *adj* analytical.
**Anämie** *f* anaemia *(Brit)*, anemia *(US)*.
**Ananas** *f* - *or* -**se** pineapple.
**Anarchie** *f* anarchy.
**anarchisch** *adj* anarchic.
**Anarchismus** *m* anarchism.
**Anarchist(in** *f)* *m* anarchist.
**anarchistisch** *adj* anarchistic.
**Anästhesie** *f* anaesthesia *(Brit)*, anesthesia *(US)*.
**Anästhesist(in** *f)* *m* anaesthetist *(Brit)*, anesthesiologist *(US)*.
**Anatolien** [-iən] *nt* Anatolia.
**Anatomie** *f* (a) anatomy. (b) *(Institut)* anatomical institute.
**anatomisch** *adj* anatomical.
**anbahnen** *sep* **1** *vt* to initiate. **2** *vr (sich andeuten)* to be in the offing; *(Unangenehmes)* to be looming; *(Möglichkeiten, Zukunft etc)* to be opening up. **zwischen den beiden bahnt sich etwas an** *(Liebesverhältnis)* there is the beginnings of something going on between those two.

**Anbahnung** *f* initiation *(von, gen* of).
**anbandeln** *(S Ger, Aus)*, **anbändeln** *vi sep* to start flirting *(mit* with).
**Anbau¹** *m no pl (Anpflanzung)* cultivation, growing.
**Anbau²** *m* -**ten** *(Nebengebäude)* extension; *(freistehend)* annexe.
**anbauen** *sep* **1** *vt* (a) to grow. (b) *(Build)* to add, to build on. **etw ans Haus** ~ to build sth onto the house. **2** *vi* to build an extension.
**Anbau-:** ~**fläche** *f* (area of) cultivable land; ~**gebiet** *nt* area ~**gebiet für etw** a good area for growing sth; ~**möbel** *pl* unit furniture.
**Anbeginn** *m (geh)* beginning.
**anbehalten\*** *vt sep irreg* to keep on.
**anbei** *adv (form)* enclosed. ~ **schicken wir Ihnen ...** please find enclosed ...
**anbeißen** *sep irreg* **1** *vi (Fisch)* to bite; *(fig auch)* to take the bait. **2** *vt Apfel etc* to bite into. **ein angebissener Apfel** a half-eaten apple; **sie sieht zum A~ aus** *(col)* she looks nice enough to eat.
**anbelangen\*** *vt sep* to concern. **was das/mich anbelangt ...** as far as that is/I am concerned ...
**anbellen** *vt sep* to bark at.
**anberaumen\*** *vt sep or insep (form)* to arrange, to fix.
**anbeten** *vt sep* to worship; *Menschen auch* to adore.
**Anbetracht** *m:* **in** ~ *(+gen)* in consideration *or* view of; **in** ~ **dessen, daß ...** in consideration *or* view of the fact that ...
**anbetreffen\*** *vt sep irreg siehe* **anbelangen.**
**anbetteln** *vt sep* **jdn** ~ to beg from sb; **jdn um etw** ~ to beg sth from sb.
**Anbetung** *f siehe vt* worship; adoration.
**anbiedern** *vr sep (pej)* **sich (bei jdm)** ~ to get pally (with sb) *(col)*.
**anbieten** *sep irreg* **1** *vt* to offer *(jdm etw* sb sth). **2** *vr* (a) *(Mensch)* **sich (als etw)** ~ to offer one's services (as sth); **sich** ~, **die Arbeit zu tun** to offer to do the work; **der Ort bietet sich für die Konferenz an** that is the obvious place for the conference. (b) *(in Betracht kommen: Gelegenheit)* to present itself. **das bietet sich als Lösung an** that would provide a solution.
**Anbieter** *m* - supplier.
**anbinden** *vt sep irreg (an* +*acc or dat* to) (a) to tie (up); *Pferd auch* to tether; (b) *(verbinden)* to connect; *siehe* **angebunden.**
**Anbindung** *f (Verbindung)* connection.
**Anblick** *m* sight. **beim ersten** ~ at first sight; **du bist ein** ~ **für die Götter** you really look hilarious.
**anblicken** *vt sep* to look at. **jdn lange/feindselig** ~ to gaze/glare at sb.
**anblinzeln** *vt sep* (a) *(blinzelnd ansehen)* to squint at. (b) *(zublinzeln)* to wink at.
**anbraten** *vt sep irreg* to brown.
**anbrechen** *sep irreg* **1** *vt Packung, Flasche etc* to open; *Vorrat, Ersparnisse, Geldsumme* to break into; *siehe* **angebrochen. 2** *vi aux sein (Epoche etc)* to dawn; *(Tag auch)* to break; *(Nacht)* to fall; *(Jahreszeit)* to begin; *(Winter)* to close in.
**anbrennen** *vi sep irreg aux sein* to catch fire; *(Holz, Kohle etc)* to catch light; *(Essen)* to burn; *(Stoff)* to get scorched. **mir ist das Essen angebrannt** I burnt the food; *siehe* **angebrannt.**
**anbringen** *vt sep irreg* (a) *(befestigen)* to fix, to fasten *(an* +*dat* (on)/to); *(aufstellen, aufhängen)* to put up; *Telefon, Feuermelder etc* to put in, to install. (b) *(äußern)* Bemerkung, Beschwerde to make *(bei* to); *Kenntnisse, Wissen* to display; *Argument* to use. **er konnte seine Kritik/seinen Antrag nicht mehr** ~ he couldn't get his criticism/motion in; *siehe* **an-**

**gebracht. (c)** *(col: loswerden)* Ware to get rid of.

**Anbruch** *m no pl (geh: Anfang)* beginning; *(von Zeitalter, Epoche)* dawn(ing). **bei ~ des Tages/Morgens** at daybreak, at break of day; **bei ~ der Nacht/ Dunkelheit** at nightfall.

**anbrüllen** *vt sep (Löwe etc)* to roar at; *(col: Mensch)* to shout or bellow at.

**Anchovis** [an'çoːvis, an'ʃoːvis] *f* - anchovy.

**Andacht** *f -en* **(a)** *no pl (das Beten)* (silent) prayer or worship. **(b)** *(Gottesdienst)* prayers *pl*. **(c)** *(Versenkung)* rapt interest; *(Ehrfurcht)* reverence. **in tiefe(r) ~ versunken sein** to be completely absorbed.

**andächtig** *adj* **(a)** *(im Gebet)* in prayer. **(b)** *(versunken)* rapt; *(ehrfürchtig)* reverent.

**Andalusien** [-iən] *nt* Andalusia.

**andauern** *vi sep* to continue; *(anhalten)* to last. **das dauert noch an** that is still going on; **der Regen dauert noch an** the rain hasn't stopped.

**andauernd** *adj (ständig)* continuous; *(anhaltend)* continual. **wenn du mich ~ unterbrichst** ... if you keep on interrupting me ...

**Anden** *pl* **die ~** the Andes.

**Andenken** *nt no pl* **(a)** memory. **zum ~ an jdn/etw** *(an Verstorbenen etc)* in memory or remembrance of sb/sth; *(an Freunde/Urlaub etc)* as a reminder of sb/sth. **(b)** *(Reise~)* souvenir *(an +acc* of*)*; *(Erinnerungsstück)* memento, keepsake *(an +acc* from*)*.

**ander(e)n-:** **~falls** *adv* otherwise; **~orts** *adv (geh)* elsewhere.

**andere(r, s)** *indef pron* **1** *(adjektivisch)* different; *(weiterer)* other. **ein ~r Mann/ein ~s Auto/eine ~ Frau** a different man/car/woman; *(ein weiterer etc)* another man/car/woman; **jede ~ Frau hätte** ... any other woman would have ...; **das machen wir ein ~s Mal** we'll do that another time; **er ist ein ~r Mensch geworden** he is a changed man.

**2** *(substantivisch)* **(a)** *(Ding)* **ein ~r** a different one; *(noch einer)* another one; **etwas ~s** something or *(in Fragen)* anything else; **alle ~n** all the others; **das ist etwas ganz ~s** that's something quite different; **hast du etwas ~s gedacht?** did you think otherwise?; **ich habe ~s zu tun** I've other things to do; **nichts ~s** nothing else; **nichts ~s als** ... nothing but ...; **es blieb mir nichts ~s übrig, als selbst hinzugehen** I had no alternative but to go myself; **alles ~ als zufrieden** anything but pleased, far from pleased; **unter ~m** among other things; **es kam eins zum ~n** one thing led to another; **sie hat sich eines ~n besonnen** she changed her mind; **von einem Tag zum ~n** overnight.

**(b)** *(Person)* **ein ~r/eine ~** a different person; *(noch einer)* another person; **jeder ~/kein ~r** anyone/no-one else; **niemand ~s** no-one else; **das haben mir ~ auch schon gesagt** other people or others have told me that too; **die ~n** the others; **alle ~n** all the others, everyone else; **jemand ~s** somebody or *(in Fragen)* anybody else; **sie hat einen ~n** she has someone else; **der eine oder (der) ~ von unseren Kollegen** one or other of our colleagues; **einer nach dem ~n** one after the other; **eine schöner als die ~** each one more beautiful than the next.

**and(e)rerseits** *adv* on the other hand.

**andermal** *adv:* **ein ~** some other time.

**ändern** **1** *vt* to change, to alter; *Kleidungsstück* to alter. **ich kann es nicht ~** I can't do anything about it; **das ändert nichts an der Tatsache, daß** ... that doesn't alter the fact that ... **2** *vr* **(a)** to change, to alter. **(b)** *(Mensch)* to change; *(sich bessern)* to change for the better. **wenn sich das nicht ändert** ... if things don't improve ...

**andern-** *in cpds siehe* **ander(e)n-**.

**anders** *adv* **(a)** *(sonst)* else. **jemand/niemand ~ somebody** or anybody/nobody else; **wer/wo ~?** who/where else?; **irgendwo ~** somewhere else. **(b)** *(verschieden)* differently; *(andersartig) sein, aussehen, klingen, schmecken* different *(als* to*)*. **~ als jd denken/reagieren/aussehen** to think/react differently/look different from sb; **~ als jd** *(geh: im Gegensatz zu)* unlike sb; **~ ausgedrückt** to put it another way; **das machen wir so und nicht ~** we'll do it this way and no other; **wie nicht ~ zu erwarten** as was to be expected; **sie ist ~ geworden** she has changed; **wie könnte es ~ sein?** how could it be otherwise?; **es geht nicht ~** there's no other way; **ich kann nicht ~** *(kann es nicht lassen)* I can't help it; *(muß leider)* I have no choice.

**Anders-:** **a~artig** *adj no comp* different; **~denkende(r)** *mf decl as adj* dissident, dissenter; **a~farbig** *adj* of a different colour *(Brit)* or color *(US)*; **a~gläubig** *adj* of a different faith or religion; **a~(he)rum** *adv* the other way around; **a~lautend** *adj attr (form)* contrary; **a~lautende Berichte** reports to the contrary; **a~wo** *adv* elsewhere; **a~woher** *adv* from elsewhere; **a~wohin** *adv* elsewhere.

**anderthalb** *num* one and a half. **~ Pfund Kaffee** a pound and a half of coffee.

**Änderung** *f* change, alteration *(an +dat, gen* in, to*)*; *(an Kleid, Gebäude)* alteration *(an +dat* to*)*.

**Änderungs-:** **~antrag** *m (Parl)* amendment; **~schneider** *m* tailor (who does alterations); **~vorschlag** *m* suggested change or alteration; **einen ~vorschlag machen** to suggest a change or an alteration.

**anderweitig** **1** *adj attr (andere, weitere)* other. **2** *adv (anders)* otherwise; *(an anderer Stelle)* elsewhere. **~ vergeben/besetzt werden** to be given to/filled by someone else; **etw ~ verwenden** to use sth for a different purpose.

**andeuten** *sep* **1** *vt (zu verstehen geben)* to hint, to intimate *(jdm etw sth* to sb*)*; *(kurz erwähnen) Problem* to mention briefly; *(erkennen lassen)* to indicate. **2** *vr* to be indicated; *(Gewitter)* to be in the offing.

**Andeutung** *f (Anspielung, Anzeichen)* hint; *(flüchtiger Hinweis)* brief mention; *(Spur)* sign, trace. **eine ~ machen** to hint *(über +acc* at*)*, to drop a hint *(über +acc* about*)*.

**andeutungsweise** *adv (als Anspielung, Anzeichen)* by way of a hint; *(als flüchtiger Hinweis)* in passing. **jdm ~ zu verstehen geben, daß** ... to hint to sb that ...

**andichten** *vt sep* **jdm etw ~** *(col) Fähigkeiten* to credit sb with sth.

**Andorra** *nt* Andorra.

**Andorraner(in** *f)* *m* Andorran.

**andorranisch** *adj* Andorran.

**Andrang** *m no pl (Zustrom, Gedränge)* crowd, crush.

**andrehen** *vt sep* **(a)** *(anstellen)* to turn on. **(b) jdm etw ~** *(col)* to palm sth off on sb.

**androhen** *vt sep* to threaten *(jdm etw* sb with sth*)*.

**Androhung** *f* threat. **unter ~ von Gewalt** with the threat of violence; **unter ~** *(Jur)* under penalty *(von, gen* of*)*.

**Andruck** *m (Typ)* proof.

**andünsten** *vti sep (Cook)* to braise lightly.

**an|ecken** *vi sep aux sein (col)* **bei jdm/allen ~** to rub sb/everyone up the wrong way.

**an|eignen** *vt sep sich (dat)* **etw ~** *(etw erwerben)* to acquire sth; *(etw wegnehmen)* to appropriate sth; *(sich mit etw vertraut machen)* to learn sth.

**An|eignung** *f siehe vr* acquisition; appropriation;

learning.

**an|einander** *adv* ~ **denken** to think of each other; **sich** ~ **gewöhnen** to get used to each other; ~ **vorüber-/vorbeigehen** to go past each other; ~ **befestigen** to stick together; **zu dicht** ~ too close together.

**an|einander-** *in cpds* together; **~fügen** *vt* to put together; **~geraten\*** *vi sep irreg aux sein* to come to blows *(mit* with*)*; *(streiten)* to have words *(mit* with*)*; **~grenzen** *vi sep* to border on each other; **~hängen** *vi sep irreg* **(a)** *(zusammenhängen)* to be linked (together); **(b)** *(fig: Menschen)* to be attached to each other; **~kleben** *sep* **1** *vt* to stick together; **2** *vi* to be stuck together; *(col: unzertrennlich sein)* to be glued together *(col)*; **~reihen** *vt sep* to string together.

**Anekdote** *f* **-n** anecdote.

**an|ekeln** *vt sep (anwidern)* to disgust, to nauseate.

**Anemone** *f* **-n** anemone.

**an|erkannt** *adj* recognized; *Tatsache auch* established; *Werk* standard; *Experte* acknowledged.

**an|erkennen\*** *vt sep or insep irreg Staat, König, Rekord* to recognize; *Forderung auch* to accept; *Vaterschaft* to accept, to acknowledge; *(würdigen) Leistung, Bemühung* to appreciate. **...**, **das muß man** ~ *(zugeben)* ... you can't argue with that; *(würdigen)* ... you have to grant him/her *etc* that; **als gleichwertiger Partner anerkannt sein** to be accepted as an equal partner.

**anerkennend** *adj (Blick)* appreciative.

**an|erkennenswert** *adj* commendable.

**An|erkennung** *f siehe vt* recognition; acceptance; acknowledgement; appreciation.

**an|erziehen\*** *vt insep irreg:* **jdm etw** ~ *(Kindern)* to instil sth into sb.

**an|erzogen** *adj* acquired. **das ist alles** ~ this is all the result of upbringing.

**anfachen** *vt sep (geh)* **(a)** *(Glut, Feuer)* to fan. **(b)** *(fig)* to arouse.

**anfahren** *sep irreg* **1** *vi aux sein (losfahren)* to start (up). **angefahren kommen** *(Wagen, Fahrer)* to drive up; *(Zug)* to pull up; **beim A~** when starting (up); **das A~ am Berg üben** to practise a hill start. **2** *vt* **(a)** *(liefern)* Kohlen, Kartoffeln to deliver. **(b)** *(ansteuern)* Ort to stop or call at; *Hafen auch* to put in at. **(c)** *(anstoßen)* Passanten, Baum etc to run into, to hit.

**Anfahrt** *f (~sweg, ~szeit)* journey; *(Zufahrt)* approach.

**Anfall** *m* **(a)** attack; *(Wut~, epileptisch)* fit. **einen** ~ **haben/bekommen** *(lit)* to have an attack or a fit; *(fig col)* to have or throw a fit *(col)*; **in einem** ~ **von** *(fig)* in a fit of. **(b)** *(Ertrag, Nebenprodukte)* yield *(an +dat* of*)*; *(von Zinsen auch)* accrual. **(c)** *(von Reparaturen, Kosten)* amount *(an +dat* of*)*; *(form: Anhäufung)* accumulation. **bei** ~ **von Reparaturen** if repairs are necessary.

**anfallen** *sep irreg* **1** *vt (überfallen)* to attack; *(Sittenstrolch etc)* to assault. **2** *vi aux sein (Zinsen)* to accrue; *(Nebenprodukte)* to be obtained; *(sich anhäufen)* to accumulate. **die ~den Kosten/Reparaturen** the costs/repairs incurred; **die ~de Arbeit** the work which comes up.

**anfällig** *adj (nicht widerstandsfähig)* delicate; *Motor, Maschine* temperamental. **für etw/eine Krankheit** ~ **sein** to be susceptible to sth/prone to an illness.

**Anfälligkeit** *f siehe adj* delicateness; temperamental nature; susceptibility; proneness.

**Anfang** *m, pl* **Anfänge** *(Beginn)* beginning, start; *(Ursprung)* beginnings *pl*, origin. **zu** or **am** ~ to start with; *(anfänglich)* at first; ~ **Fünfzig** in one's early

fifties; ~ **Juni/1992** *etc* at the beginning of June/1992 *etc*; **von** ~ **an** (right) from the beginning or start; **von** ~ **bis Ende** from start to finish; **den** ~ **machen** to start or begin; *(den ersten Schritt tun)* to make the first move; **einen neuen** ~ **machen** to make a new start; **aller** ~ **ist schwer** *(Prov)* the first step is always the most difficult; **das ist der** ~ **vom Ende** it's the beginning of the end.

**anfangen** *sep irreg* **1** *vt* **(a)** *(beginnen)* to start, to begin; *Streit* to start. **(b)** *(anstellen, machen)* to do. **das mußt du anders** ~ you'll have to go about it differently; **nichts mit sich/jdm anzufangen wissen** not to know what to do with oneself/sb; **damit kann ich nichts** ~ *(nützt mir nichts)* that's no good to me; *(verstehe ich nicht)* it doesn't mean a thing to me; **mit dir ist heute (aber) gar nichts anzufangen!** you're no fun at all today! **2** *vi* to begin, to start. **du hast angefangen!** *(bei Streit)* you started it!; **es fing zu regnen an** or **an zu regnen** it started raining or to rain; **das fängt ja schön an!** *(iro)* that's a good start!; **jetzt fängt das Leben erst an** life is only just beginning; **mit etw** ~ to start sth; **bei einer Firma** ~ to start working for a firm.

**Anfänger(in** *f) m* - beginner; *(Neuling)* novice; *(Aut)* learner; *(col: Nichtskönner)* rank amateur *(pej)*.

**Anfängerkurs(us)** *m* beginners' course.

**anfänglich 1** *adj attr* initial. **2** *adv* at first, initially.

**anfangs 1** *adv* at first, initially. **wie ich schon** ~ **erwähnte** as I mentioned at the beginning. **2** *prep +gen* ~ **der zwanziger Jahre/des Monats** in the early twenties/at the beginning of the month.

**Anfangs-:** **~buchstabe** *m* first letter; **kleine/große ~buchstaben** small/capital initials; **~gehalt** *nt* starting salary; **~stadium** *nt* initial stage; **meine Versuche sind schon im ~stadium steckengeblieben** my attempts never really got off the ground.

**anfassen** *sep* **1** *vt* **(a)** *(berühren)* to touch. **(b)** *(bei der Hand nehmen)* **jdn** ~ to take sb's hand or sb by the hand; **sich** ~ to take each other by the hand. **(c)** *(fig: anpacken)* Problem to tackle, to go about. **2** *vi* **(a)** *(berühren)* **nicht ~!** don't touch! **(b)** *(mithelfen)* **mit** ~ to give a hand. **(c)** **zum A~** accessible; *(Mensch auch)* approachable.

**anfauchen** *vt sep (Katze)* to spit at; *(fig col)* to snap at.

**anfechtbar** *adj* contestable.

**anfechten** *vt sep irreg (nicht anerkennen)* to contest; *Aussage auch* to challenge; *Urteil* to appeal against; *Vertrag* to dispute.

**Anfechtung** *f* **(a)** *siehe vt (a)* contesting; challenging; appeal *(gen* against*)*; disputing. **(b)** *(Versuchung)* temptation.

**anfeinden** *vt sep* to treat with hostility.

**Anfeindung** *f* hostility. **trotz aller ~en** in spite of all the hostility.

**anfertigen** *vt sep* to make; *Schriftstück* to draw up; *Hausaufgaben* to do; *Protokoll* to take down. **sich** *(dat)* **einen Anzug** *etc* ~ **lassen** to have a suit *etc* made.

**Anfertigung** *f siehe vt* making; drawing up; taking down.

**anfeuchten** *vt sep* to moisten.

**anfeuern** *vt sep (fig: ermutigen)* to spur on.

**Anfeuerung** *f (fig)* spurring on.

**Anfeuerungsruf** *m* cheer.

**anflehen** *vt sep* to beseech, to implore *(um* for*)*. **ich flehe dich an, tu das nicht!** I beg you, don't!

**anfliegen** *sep irreg* **1** *vi aux sein (auch* **angeflogen kommen)** *(Flugzeug)* to come in to land; *(Vogel, Geschoß)* to come flying up. **2** *vt (Flugzeug)* Flugha-

*fen, (Mil) Stellung* to approach; *(landen)* to land *(in/ auf* in/on*)*. **diese Fluggesellschaft fliegt Bali an** this airline flies to Bali.

**Anflug** *m* (a) *(Flugweg)* flight; *(das Heranfliegen)* approach. **wir befinden uns im ~ auf Paris** we are now approaching Paris. (b) *(Spur)* trace.

**anfordern** *vt sep* to request; *Waren* to order.

**Anforderung** *f* (a) *no pl (das Anfordern)* request *(gen, von* for*)*. **bei der ~ von Ersatzteilen** when ordering spare parts. (b) *(Anspruch)* requirement; *(Belastung)* demand. **große ~en an jdn/etw stellen** to make great demands on sb/sth.

**Anfrage** *f (auch Comp)* inquiry; *(Parl)* question.

**anfragen** *vi sep* to inquire *(bei jdm* of sb*)*, to ask *(bei jdm* sb*)*.

**anfressen** *vt sep irreg* (a) *(Maus)* to nibble at; *(Vogel)* to peck (at). (b) *(zersetzen)* to eat away.

**anfreunden** *vr sep* to make *or* become friends. **sich mit etw ~** *(fig)* to get to like sth.

**anfügen** *vt sep* to add.

**anfühlen** *sep* 1 *vt* to feel. 2 *vr* to feel. **sich glatt/ weich** *etc* ~ to feel smooth/soft *etc*.

**Anfuhr** *f* **-en** transport(ation).

**anführen** *vt sep* (a) *(vorangehen, befehligen)* to lead. (b) *(zitieren)* to quote, to cite; *Tatsachen, Beispiel auch* to give; *Grund, Beweis* to give, to offer; *(benennen) jdn* to name, to cite. (c) **jdn ~** *(col)* to have sb on *(col)*, to take sb for a ride *(col)*.

**Anführer(in** *f)* *m* leader; *(pej: Anstifter)* ringleader.

**Anführung** *f* (a) *(Befehligung auch)* leadership; *(Befehligung auch)* command. **unter ~ von ...** under the leadership of ... (b) *(Zitat)* quotation.

**Anführungs-:** ~**strich** *m*, ~**zeichen** *nt* quotation mark, inverted comma; ~**striche** *or* ~**zeichen unten/oben** quote/unquote.

**anfüllen** *vt sep* to fill (up). **mit etw angefüllt sein** to be full of sth, to be filled with sth.

**Angabe** ['anga:-] *f* **-n** (a) *usu pl (Aussage)* statement; *(Zahl, Detail)* detail. ~**n über etw** *(acc)* **machen** to give details about sth; **laut** ~**n** *(+gen)* according to; **nach Ihren eigenen** ~**n** by your own account; ~**n zur Person** *(form)* personal details *or* particulars. (b) *(Nennung)* giving. **wir bitten um ~ der Einzelheiten/Preise** please give *or* quote details/ prices; **ohne ~ von Gründen** without giving any reasons. (c) *no pl (col: Prahlerei)* showing-off; *(Reden auch)* boasting. (d) *(Sport: Aufschlag)* service, serve. **wer hat (die)** ~? whose service *or* serve is it?

**angeben** ['ange:-] *sep irreg* 1 *vt* (a) *(nennen)* to give; *(als Zeugen)* to name, to cite; *(erklären)* to explain; *(beim Zoll)* to declare; *(anzeigen) Temperatur etc* to indicate; *(aussagen)* to state; *(behaupten)* to maintain. (b) *(bestimmen) Tempo, Kurs* to set; *(Mus) Tempo, Note* to give. **den Takt ~** *(klopfen)* to beat time. 2 *vi* *(prahlen)* to show off; *(durch Reden auch)* to boast, to brag *(mit* about*)*.

**Angeber(in** *f)* ['ange:-] *m* *(Prahler)* show-off, poser *(col)*; *(durch Reden auch)* boaster.

**Angeberei** [ange:-] *f no pl (Prahlerei)* showing-off, posing *(col) (mit* about*)*; *(verbal auch)* boasting, bragging *(mit* about*)*.

**angeberisch** ['ange:-] *adj Reden* boastful; *Benehmen, Tonfall* pretentious, showy.

**angeblich** ['ange:-] 1 *adj attr* so-called, alleged. 2 *adv* supposedly, allegedly. **er ist ~ Musiker** he's supposed to be a musician.

**angeboren** ['angə-] *adj* innate, inherent; *(Med, fig col)* congenital *(bei* with*)*.

**Angebot** ['angə-] *nt* (a) offer; *(bei Auktion)* bid; *(Comm: Offerte auch)* tender *(über +acc, für* for*)*;

*(: Kostenvoranschlag auch)* quote. (b) *no pl (Comm, Fin)* supply *(an +dat, von* of*)*; *(Auswahl)* selection *(an +dat* of*)*. ~ **und Nachfrage** supply and demand; **im ~** *(col)* on special offer.

**Angebotspreis** *m* asking price.

**angebracht** ['angə-] *adj* appropriate; *(sinnvoll)* reasonable.

**angebrannt** ['angə-] *adj* burnt. **es riecht hier so ~** there's a smell of burning here.

**angebrochen** ['angə-] *adj Packung, Flasche* open(ed). **was machen wir mit dem ~en Abend?** what shall we do with the rest of the evening?; **das Parken kostet für jede ~e Stunde eine Mark** parking costs one mark for every hour or part of an hour.

**angebunden** ['angə-] *adj* **kurz ~ sein** *(col)* to be abrupt *or* curt.

**angegossen** ['angə-] *adj* **wie ~ sitzen** *or* **passen** to fit like a glove.

**angegraut** ['angə-] *adj* grey; *Haar auch* greying.

**angegriffen** ['angə-] *adj Gesundheit* weakened; *Mensch, Aussehen* frail; *(nervlich)* strained.

**angehalten** ['angə-] *adj* ~ **sein, etw zu tun** to be required *or* obliged to do sth.

**angehaucht** ['angə-] *adj* **links/rechts ~ sein** to have left-/right-wing tendencies *or* leanings.

**angeheiratet** ['angə-] *adj* related by marriage. **ein ~er Cousin** a cousin by marriage.

**angeheitert** ['angə-] *adj (col)* merry *(col)*, tipsy.

**angehen** ['ange:-] *sep irreg* 1 *vi aux sein* (a) *(col: beginnen) (Feuer)* to start burning, to catch; *(Licht)* to come on, to go on. (b) *(entgegentreten)* **gegen jdn/ etw ~** to fight sb/sth; **gegen etw ~** *Mißstände, Zustände* to take measures against sth. 2 *vt* (a) *aux haben or (S Ger) sein (anpacken) Aufgabe* to tackle. (b) *aux haben or (S Ger) sein (bitten)* to ask *(jdn um etw* sb for sth*)*. (c) *aux sein (in bezug auf Personen), aux haben (in bezug auf Sachen) (betreffen)* to concern. **was mich angeht** as far as I'm concerned; **das geht ihn gar nichts an** that's none of his business. 3 *vi impers aux sein* **das geht nicht/keinesfalls an** that's quite out of the question.

**angehend** ['ange:-] *adj Musiker, Künstler* budding; *Lehrer, Ehemann, Vater* prospective.

**angehören*** ['angə-] *vi sep +dat* to belong to; *(einer Partei, einer Familie auch)* to be a member of.

**Angehörige(r)** ['angə-] *mf decl as adj* (a) *(Mitglied)* member. (b) *(Familien~)* relative, relation. **der nächste ~** the next of kin.

**Angeklagte(r)** ['angə-] *mf decl as adj* accused, defendant.

**angeknackst** ['angə-] *adj (col) Mensch* uptight *(col)*; *Selbstbewußtsein* weakened. **er/seine Gesundheit ist ~** he is in bad shape.

**angekratzt** ['angə-] *adj (col)* seedy *(col)*.

**Angel** ['aŋəl] *f* **-n** (a) *(Tür~, Fenster~)* hinge. **die Welt aus den ~n heben** *(fig)* to turn the world upside down. (b) *(Fischfanggerät)* fishing rod, fishing pole *(US)*. **die ~ auswerfen** to cast (the line).

**Angelegenheit** ['angə-] *f* matter; *(politisch, persönlich)* affair; *(Aufgabe)* concern. **das ist nicht meine ~** that's not my concern *or* business.

**angelegt** ['angə-] *adj* calculated *(auf +acc* for*)*.

**angelernt** ['angə-] *adj Arbeiter* semi-skilled.

**Angel-:** ~**gerät** *nt* fishing tackle *no pl*; ~**haken** *m* fish-hook.

**angeln 1** *vi* (a) to fish. ~ **gehen** to go angling *or* fishing. (b) *(zu greifen versuchen, hervorziehen)* to fish. **nach etw ~** to fish (around) for sth. 2 *vt Fisch* to fish for; *(fangen)* to catch. **sich** *(dat)* **einen Mann ~** *(col)* to hook a man *(col)*.

**Angel-:** ~**punkt** *m* crucial *or* central point; *(Frage)* key *or* central issue; ~**rute** *f* fishing rod, fishing pole *(US)*.

**Angelsachse** *m decl as adj*, **Angelsächsin** *f* Anglo-Saxon.

**angelsächsisch** *adj* Anglo-Saxon.

**Angel-**: ~**schein** *m* fishing permit; ~**schnur** *f* fishing line.

**angemessen** ['angə-] *adj (passend)* appropriate *(dat* to, for*)*; *(adäquat)* adequate *(dat* for*)*; *Preis* reasonable, fair. **eine der Leistung** ~**e Bezahlung** payment commensurate with input.

**angenehm** ['angə-] *adj* pleasant, agreeable. **das wäre mir sehr** ~ I should greatly appreciate it; **es ist mir gar nicht** ~, **daß er mich besuchen will** I don't like the idea of him wanting to visit me; **wenn Ihnen das** ~**er ist** if you prefer; **(sehr)** ~**!** *(form)* delighted (to meet you); **das A**~**e mit dem Nützlichen verbinden** to combine business with pleasure.

**angenommen** ['angə-] **1** *adj* assumed; *Kind* adopted. **2** *conj* assuming.

**angepaßt** ['angə-] *adj* conformist.

**Angepaßtheit** ['angə-] *f* conformism.

**angeregt** ['angə-] *adj* lively, animated. ~ **diskutieren** to have a lively *or* an animated discussion.

**angereichert** ['angə-] *adj Uran* enriched.

**angeschlagen** ['angə-] *adj (col) Mensch, Aussehen, Nerven* shattered *(col)*; *Gesundheit* poor.

**angeschlossen** ['angə-] *adj* affiliated *(dat* to *or* with*)*, associated *(dat* with*)*.

**angeschmiert** ['angə-] *adj pred (col)* in trouble. **der/die A**~**e sein** to have been had *(col)*.

**angeschmutzt** ['angə-] *adj* soiled; *(Comm)* shop-soiled.

**angeschrieben** ['angə-] *adj (col)* **bei jdm gut/ schlecht** ~ **sein** to be in sb's good/bad books.

**angesehen** ['angə-] *adj* respected.

**Angesicht** ['angə-] *nt* **-er** *(geh)* face. **von** ~ **zu** ~ face to face; **im** ~ **+gen** *(fig)* in the face of.

**angesichts** ['angə-] *prep* **+gen** in the face of; *(im Hinblick auf)* in view of.

**angespannt** ['angə-] *adj Nerven, Lage* tense, strained; *Aufmerksamkeit* close, keen; *(Comm) Markt, Lage* tight, overstretched.

**angestammt** ['angə-] *adj (überkommen)* traditional; *(ererbt) Rechte* hereditary; *Besitz* inherited.

**angestellt** ['angə-] *adj pred* ~ **sein** to be an employee *or* on the staff *(bei* of*)*; **fest** ~ **sein** to be a permanent employee.

**Angestellte(r)** ['angə-] *mf decl as adj* (salaried) employee; *(Büro~)* office-worker, white-collar worker.

**Angestellten-** ['angə-]: ~**gewerkschaft** *f* white-collar union; ~**versicherung** *f* (salaried) employee's insurance.

**angestrengt** ['angə-] *adj Gesicht* strained; ~ **arbeiten/denken** to work/think hard; ~ **diskutieren** to have an intense discussion.

**angetan** ['angətan] *adj pred* **(a) von jdm/etw** ~ **sein** to be taken with sb/sth. **(b) dazu** ~ **sein, etw zu tun** *(geh)* to be suitable for doing sth; *(Atmosphäre, Benehmen etc)* to be apt to do sth.

**angetrunken** ['angə-] *adj* inebriated.

**angewandt** ['angə-] *adj attr Wissenschaft etc* applied.

**angewidert** ['angə-] *adj* nauseated, disgusted.

**angewiesen** ['angə-] *adj* **auf jdn/etw** ~ **sein** to have to rely on sb/sth, to be dependent on sb/sth; **auf sich selbst** ~ **sein** to be left to one's own devices; **darauf bin ich nicht** ~ I don't need it.

**angewöhnen\*** ['angə-] *vt sep* **jdm etw** ~ to get sb used to sth, to accustom sb to sth; **sich** *(dat)* **etw** ~**/es sich** *(dat)* ~, **etw zu tun** to get into the habit of sth/of doing sth.

**Angewohnheit** ['angə-] *f* habit.

**angewurzelt** ['angə-] *adj* **wie** ~ **dastehen** to be rooted to the spot.

**angiften** ['angɪ-] *vt sep (pej inf)* to snap at.

**Angina** [aŋ'giːna] *f, pl* **Anginen** *(Med)* angina. ~ **pectoris** angina (pectoris).

**angleichen** ['angl-] *sep irreg* **1** *vt* to bring into line, to align *(dat, an* +*acc* with*)*. **2** *vr (gegenseitig: Kulturen, Geschlechter, Methoden)* to grow closer together. **sich jdm/einer Sache** ~ *(einseitig)* to become like sb/sth.

**Angleichung** *f* alignment *(an* +*acc* with*)*.

**Angler(in** *f)* *m* - angler.

**angliedern** ['angl-] *vt sep (dat, an* +*acc* to*)* *(Verein, Partei)* to affiliate; *Land* to annex.

**Angliederung** *f siehe* vt affiliation; annexation.

**Anglikaner(in** *f)* [aŋgli-] *m* Anglican.

**anglikanisch** [aŋgli-] *adj* Anglican. **die A**~**e Kirche** the Anglican Church, the Church of England.

**anglisieren\*** [aŋgli-] *vt* to anglicize.

**Anglist(in** *f)* [aŋ'glɪ-] *m* English specialist, Anglicist; *(Student)* student of English; *(Professor etc)* lecturer/professor of English.

**Anglistik** [aŋ'glɪ-] *f* English (language and literature).

**Anglizismus** [aŋgli-] *m* anglicism.

**Anglo-** [aŋglo-]: ~**-Amerikaner** *m* member of the English-speaking community; ~**amerikaner** *m* Anglo-American; **a**~**phil** *adj* anglophil(e).

**Angola** [aŋ'goːla] *nt* Angola.

**Angolaner(in** *f)* [aŋgo-] *m* Angolan.

**angolanisch** [aŋgo-] *adj* Angolan.

**Angora-** [aŋ'goːra]: ~**katze** *f* Angora cat; ~**wolle** *f* Angora (wool).

**angreifbar** ['angr-] *adj* open to attack.

**angreifen** ['angr-] *sep irreg* **1** *vt* **(a)** to attack. **(b)** *(schwächen) Organismus, Nerven* to weaken; *Gesundheit, Pflanzen* to affect; *siehe* **angegriffen. 2** *vi* to attack.

**Angreifer(in** *f)* ['angr-] *m* - attacker *(auch Sport, fig)*.

**angrenzen** ['angr-] *vi sep* **an etw** *(acc)* ~ to border on sth, to adjoin sth.

**angrenzend** *adj attr* adjacent *(an* +*acc* to*)*, adjoining *(an etw (acc)* sth*)*.

**Angriff** ['angr-] *m (Mil, Sport, fig)* attack *(gegen, auf* +*acc* on*)*; *(Luft~)* (air) raid. ~ **ist die beste Verteidigung** *(prov)* attack is the best means of defence; **etw in** ~ **nehmen** to tackle sth.

**Angriffs-**: ~**fläche** *f* target; **jdm/einer Sache eine** ~**fläche bieten** *(lit, fig)* to provide sb/sth with a target; ~**krieg** *m* war of aggression; ~**lust** *f* aggressiveness, aggression; **a**~**lustig** *adj* aggressive; ~**spiel** *nt (Sport)* aggressive *or* attacking game; ~**spieler** *m (Ftbl)* forward.

**angrinsen** ['angr-] *vt sep* to grin at.

**Angst** *f* ¨**e** *(innere Unruhe, Psych)* anxiety *(um* about*)*; *(Sorge)* worry *(um* about*)*; *(Befürchtung)* fear *(um* for, *vor* +*dat* of*)*; *(Existenz~)* angst. **(vor etw** *dat)* ~ **haben** to be afraid *or* scared (of sth); ~ **um jdn/etw haben** to be anxious *or* worried about sb/sth; ~ **bekommen** *or* **kriegen** to become afraid *or* scared; **aus** ~, **etw zu tun** for fear of doing sth; **keine** ~**!** don't worry; **jdm** ~ **einflößen** *or* **einjagen** to frighten sb.

**angst** *adj pred* **ihr wurde** ~ **(und bange)** she became worried *or* anxious; **jdm** ~ **(und bange) machen** to worry sb, to make sb anxious.

**Angsthase** *m (col)* scaredy-cat *(col)*, chicken.

**ängstigen 1** *vt* to frighten; *(unruhig machen)* to worry. **2** *vr* to be afraid; *(sich sorgen)* to worry.

**sich vor etw** *(dat)* ~ to be afraid of sth; **sich wegen etw** ~ to worry about sth.

**ängstlich** *adj (verängstigt)* anxious, apprehensive; *(schüchtern)* timid, timorous. ~ **darauf bedacht sein, etw zu tun** to be at pains to do sth.

**Ängstlichkeit** *f siehe adj* anxiety, apprehension; timidity, timorousness.

**Angst-:** ~**macher** *m (col)* scaremonger; ~**schrei** *m* cry of fear; ~**schweiß** *m* cold sweat; **mir brach der** ~**schweiß aus** I broke out in a cold sweat; **a**~**voll** *adj* apprehensive, fearful; ~**zustand** *m* state of panic; ~**zustände bekommen** to get into a state of panic.

**angucken** ['angʊ-] *vt sep* to look at.

**angurten** ['angʊ-] *vtr sep* = **anschnallen**.

**Anh.** = **Anhang** app.

**anhaben** *vt sep irreg* **(a)** *(angezogen haben)* to have on, to wear. **sie hatte ein schwarzes Kleid an** she was wearing a black dress, she had on a black dress. **(b)** *(zuleide tun)* to do harm. **jdm etw** ~ **wollen** to want to harm sb; **die Kälte kann mir nichts** ~ the cold doesn't worry *or* bother me. **(c)** *(am Zeug flicken)* **Sie können/die Polizei kann mir nichts** ~**!** *(col)* you/the police can't touch me.

**anhaften** *vi sep* **(a)** *(lit)* to stick *(an +dat* to*)*. **(b)** *(fig) +dat* to stick to, to stay with.

**anhalten** *sep irreg* **1** *vi* **(a)** *(stehenbleiben)* to stop. **(b)** *(fortdauern)* to last. **(c)** *(werben)* **um die Hand eines Mädchens** ~ to ask for a girl's hand in marriage. **2** *vt* **(a)** *(stoppen)* to stop. **(b)** *(anleiten)* to urge, to encourage; **jdn zur Arbeit/Höflichkeit** ~ to get sb to work/teach sb to be polite; *siehe* **angehalten**.

**anhaltend** *adj* continuous, incessant.

**Anhalter(in** *f) m* - hitch-hiker. **per** ~ **fahren** to hitch-hike, to hitch *(col)*.

**Anhaltspunkt** *m (Vermutung)* clue *(für* about*)*; *(für Verdacht)* grounds *pl*. **ich habe keinerlei** ~**e** I have no idea.

**anhand, an Hand** *prep +gen siehe* **Hand (d)**.

**Anhang** *m, pl* **Anhänge (a)** *(Nachtrag)* appendix. **(b)** *no pl (Gefolgschaft)* following; *(Angehörige)* family.

**anhängen** *sep* **1** *vt* **(a)** *(an +acc* to*) (ankuppeln)* to attach; *(Rail auch)* to couple on; *Anhänger* to hitch up; *(Comp)* to append; *(fig: anfügen)* to add *(dat, an +acc* to*)*. **(b)** *(col)* **jdm etw** ~ *(nachsagen, anlasten)* to blame sb for sth, to blame sth on sb; *schlechten Ruf, Spitznamen* to give sb sth; *Verdacht, Schuld* to pin sth on sb *(col)*. **2** *vi irreg (fig)* **(a)** *(anhaften)* **jdm** ~ to stay with sb; *(schlechter Ruf, Gefängnisstrafe auch)* to stick with sb. **(b)** *(sich zugehörig fühlen) +dat* to adhere to, to subscribe to.

**Anhänger** *m* - **(a)** supporter; *(von Sportart auch)* fan; *(von Partei auch)* follower. **(b)** *(Wagen)* trailer. **(c)** *(Schmuckstück)* pendant. **(d)** *(Koffer*~ *etc)* tag, label.

**Anhängerin** *f* = **Anhänger (a)**.

**Anhänger-:** ~**kupplung** *f* towbar; ~**schaft** *f siehe* **Anhänger (a)** supporters *pl*; fans *pl*; followers *pl*.

**anhängig** *adj (Jur)* sub judice. **etw** ~ **machen** to start legal proceedings over sth.

**anhänglich** *adj Kind, Freund* clinging; *Haustier* devoted.

**Anhänglichkeit** *f siehe adj* tendency to cling to one; devotion.

**Anhängsel** *nt* **(a)** *(Überflüssiges, Mensch)* appendage *(an +dat* to*)*. **(b)** *(Schildchen)* tag; *(an Kette)* pendant.

**anhauchen** *vt sep* to breathe on; *siehe* **angehaucht**.

**anhauen** *vt sep (col: ansprechen)* to accost *(um* for*)*. **jdn um etw** ~ to (try to) touch sb for sth *(col)*.

**anhäufen** *sep* **1** *vt* to accumulate, to amass; *Vorräte, Geld* to hoard. **2** *vr* to pile up, to accumulate; *(Zinsen)* to accumulate, to accrue.

**Anhäufung** *f siehe vt* accumulation, amassing; hoarding.

**anheben** *vt sep irreg* **(a)** *(hochheben)* to lift (up); *Glas* to raise. **(b)** *(erhöhen)* to raise.

**Anhebung** *f* increase *(gen, von* in*)*.

**anheften** *vt sep* to fasten (on) *(an +acc or dat* to*)*.

**anheimelnd** *adj (geh)* homely; *Klänge* familiar.

**anheimfallen** *vi sep irreg aux sein +dat (liter)* to pass *or* fall to; *einem Betrug* to fall victim to.

**anheimstellen** *vt sep +dat (geh)* **jdm etw** ~ to leave sth to sb's discretion.

**anheizen** *vt sep* **(a)** *Ofen* to light. **(b)** *(fig col) Wirtschaft* to stimulate; *(verschlimmern) Krise* to aggravate.

**anheuern** *vti sep (Naut, fig)* to sign on *or* up.

**Anhieb** *m:* **auf** ~ *(col)* straight *or* right away, first go *(col)*; **das kann ich nicht auf** ~ **sagen** I can't say offhand.

**anhimmeln** *vt sep (col)* to idolize, to worship.

**Anhöhe** *f* hill.

**anhören** *sep* **1** *vt* **(a)** to hear; *CD, Konzert* to listen to. **(b)** *(zufällig mithören)* to overhear. **ich kann das nicht mehr mit** ~ I can't listen to that any longer. **(c)** *(anmerken)* **man konnte ihr/ihrer Stimme die Verzweiflung** ~ one could hear the despair in her voice. **2** *vr* **(a)** **sich** *(dat)* **etw** ~ to listen to sth; **das höre ich mir nicht mehr länger mit an** I'm not going to listen to that any longer. **(b)** *(klingen)* to sound. **das hört sich ja gut an** *(col)* that sounds good.

**Anhörung** *f* hearing.

**animalisch** *adj* animal; *(pej auch)* bestial, brutish.

**Animierdame** *f* nightclub *or* bar hostess.

**animieren*** *vt* **(a)** *(anregen)* to encourage. **jdn zum Kaufen** ~ to encourage sb to buy; to put sb up to a trick; **durch das schöne Wetter animiert** prompted by the good weather. **(b)** *(Film)* to animate.

**Animier-:** ~**lokal** *nt* hostess bar, clipjoint *(pej)*; ~**mädchen** *nt* nightclub *or* bar hostess.

**Animosität** *f (geh: Feindseligkeit)* animosity, hostility *(gegen* towards*)*.

**Anis** [a'niːs] *m* **-e** *(Gewürz)* aniseed; *(Pflanze)* anise.

**Anisett** *m* **-s** *m* anisette, aniseed liqueur.

**Ank.** *(Rail)* = **Ankunft** arr.

**ankämpfen** *vi sep* **gegen etw** ~ to fight (against) sth; *gegen Wind, Strömung* to battle against sth.

**Ankara** *nt* Ankara.

**ankarren** *vt sep (col)* to cart along.

**Ankauf** *m* purchase. **An- und Verkauf von ...** we buy and sell ...

**ankaufen** *vti sep* to purchase, to buy.

**Anker** *m* - *(Naut, Archit, fig)* anchor. **vor** ~ **gehen** to drop anchor; **vor** ~ **liegen** to lie *or* ride at anchor; **den/die** ~ **lichten** to weigh anchor.

**ankern** *vi (Anker werfen)* to anchor; *(vor Anker liegen)* to be anchored.

**Anker-:** ~**platz** *m* anchorage; ~**winde** *f* capstan.

**anketten** *vt sep* to chain up *(an +acc or dat* to*)*. **angekettet sein** *(fig)* to be tied up.

**ankläffen** *vt sep (pej)* to bark at; *(kleiner Hund)* to yap at.

**Anklage** *f* **(a)** *(Jur)* charge; *(~vertretung)* prosecution. **gegen jdn** ~ **erheben** to bring *or* prefer charges against sb; **(wegen etw) unter** ~ **stehen** to have been charged (with sth). **(b)** *(fig) (Beschuldigung)* accusation; *(Anprangerung)* indictment *(an +acc* of*)*.

**Anklagebank** f dock. **auf der** ~ **(sitzen)** *(lit, fig)* (to be) in the dock.

**anklagen** vt sep *(Jur)* to charge, to accuse. **jdn einer Sache** *(gen)* or **wegen etw** ~ to charge sb with sth; *(fig: beschuldigen)* to accuse sb of sth.

**anklagend** adj Ton accusing; *Blick* reproachful.

**Anklagepunkt** m charge.

**Ankläger** m - *(Jur)* prosecutor.

**Anklage-:** ~**schrift** f indictment; ~**vertreter** m (public) prosecutor, counsel for the prosecution.

**anklammern** sep **1** vt *(mit Büroklammer)* to clip *(an +acc or dat* (on)to*)*; *(mit Heftmaschine)* to staple *(an +acc or dat* on(to), to*)*. **2** vr **sich an jdn/etw** *(acc or dat)* ~ to cling to sb/sth.

**Anklang** m **(a)** *no pl (Beifall)* approval. ~ **(bei jdm) finden** to meet with (sb's) approval; **großen/ wenig/keinen** ~ **finden** to be very well/poorly/badly received. **(b)** *(Reminiszenz)* **Anklänge an etw** *(acc)* **enthalten** to be reminiscent of sth.

**ankleben** vt sep to stick up *(an +acc or dat* on*)*. **Plakate** ~ **verboten** stick no bills.

**Ankleidekabine** f changing cubicle.

**ankleiden** vtr sep *(geh)* to dress.

**Ankleideraum** m dressing-room; *(im Schwimmbad, Geschäft)* changing room.

**anklicken** vti sep *(Comp)* to click on.

**anklingeln** vti sep *(col)* to give a ring *(Brit col)*, to call up *(US)*.

**anklingen** vi sep aux sein *(erinnern)* to be reminiscent *(an +acc* of*)*; *(angeschnitten werden)* to be touched (up)on.

**anklopfen** vi sep to knock *(an +acc or dat* at, on*)*.

**anknabbern** vt sep *(col) (annagen)* to gnaw or nibble (at). **zum A~ (aussehen)** *(fig)* (to look) good enough to eat.

**anknacksen** vt sep *(col) Knochen* to crack; *Fuß, Gelenk etc* to crack a bone in.

**anknipsen** vt sep to switch on; *Schalter* to flick.

**anknüpfen** sep **1** vt *Beziehungen* to establish; *Gespräch* to start up. **2** vi **an etw** *(acc)* ~ to take sth up.

**Anknüpfung** f *(fig)* siehe vt establishing; starting up. **in** ~ **an etw** *(acc)* following on from sth.

**Anknüpfungspunkt** m link.

**ankommen** sep irreg aux sein **1** vi **(a)** to arrive. **bist du gut angekommen?** did you arrive safely or get there all right?; **bei etw angekommen sein** to have reached sth, to have got to sth; **das Kind soll in 6 Wochen** ~ the baby is due (to arrive) in 6 weeks. **(b)** *(Anklang, Resonanz finden) (bei* with*)* to go down well; *(Mode, Neuerungen)* to catch on. **damit kommst du bei ihm nicht an!** you won't get anywhere with him like that; **er kommt bei seinen Schülern ausgezeichnet an** he is a great success with his pupils. **(c)** *(sich durchsetzen)* **gegen etw** ~ *gegen Gewohnheit, Sucht etc* to be able to fight sth; **er ist zu stark, ich komme gegen ihn nicht an** he's too strong, I'm no match for him.

**2** vi impers **(a)** *(wichtig sein)* **es kommt auf etw** *(acc)* **an** sth matters; **es kommt darauf an, daß wir ... ** what matters is that we ...; **darauf soll es mir/ uns** *etc* **nicht** ~ that doesn't matter. **(b)** *(abhängig sein)* to depend *(auf +acc* on*)*. **es kommt darauf an** it (all) depends; **es käme auf einen Versuch an** we'd have to give it a try. **(c)** *(col)* **es darauf** ~ **lassen** to chance it; **laß es nicht drauf** ~! don't push your luck! *(col)*; **er ließ es auf einen Streit/einen Versuch** ~ he was prepared to argue about it/to give it a try.

**ankoppeln** vt sep *(Rail)* to couple up *(an +acc* to*)*; *(Space)* to link up *(an +acc* with, to*)*.

**ankotzen** vt sep *(col: anwidern)* to make sick *(col)*.

**ankratzen** vt sep *(fig)* jds Ruf etc to damage; siehe **angekratzt.**

**ankreiden** vt sep *(fig)* **jdm etw (dick** or **übel)** ~ to hold sth against sb.

**ankreuzen** vt sep to mark with a cross.

**ankündigen** sep **1** vt **(a)** *(ansagen, anmelden)* to announce; *(auf Plakat, in Zeitung etc)* to advertise. **(b)** *(auf etw hindeuten)* to be a sign of. **2** vr *(fig)* to be heralded *(durch* by*)*. **der Frühling kündigt sich an** spring is in the air.

**Ankündigung** f announcement; *(vorherige Benachrichtigung)* advance notice.

**Ankunft** f, pl **Ankünfte** arrival.

**Ankunfts-:** ~**halle** f arrival lounge; ~**zeit** f time of arrival.

**ankuppeln** vt sep = **ankoppeln.**

**ankurbeln** vt sep *Maschine* to wind up; *(fig) Wirtschaft, Konjunktur* to boost, to reflate.

**Ankurbelung** f *(fig)* reflation.

**Anl.** = **Anlage** encl.

**anlächeln** vt sep to smile at.

**anlachen** vt sep to smile at. **sich** *(dat)* **jdn** ~ *(col)* to pick sb up *(col)*.

**Anlage** f -**n (a)** *(Fabrik~)* plant. **(b)** *(Grün~, Park~)* (public) park; *(um ein Gebäude herum)* grounds *pl.* **(c)** *(Einrichtung) (Mil, Elec)* installation(s); *(Sport~ etc)* facilities *pl.* **(d)** *(col: Stereo~)* (stereo) system or equipment; *(EDV-~)* system. **(e)** *(usu pl: Veranlagung)* aptitude, gift *(zu* for*)*; *(Neigung)* predisposition, tendency *(zu* to*)*. **(f)** *(Kapital~)* investment. **(g)** *(Beilage zu einem Schreiben)* enclosure. **als** ~ or **in der** ~ **erhalten Sie ...** please find enclosed ...

**Anlage-:** ~**berater** m investment consultant; ~**kapital** nt investment capital; ~**papier** nt long-term investment bond.

**anlangen** sep **1** vi aux sein *(an einem Ort)* to arrive. **am Gipfel angelangt sein** to have reached the summit. **2** vt = **anbelangen.**

**Anlaß** m, pl **Anlässe (a)** *(Veranlassung)* (immediate) cause *(zu* for*)*. **welchen** ~ **hatte er, das zu tun?** what prompted him to do that?; **es besteht kein** ~ **...** there is no reason ...; **etw zum** ~ **nehmen, zu ...** to use sth as an opportunity to ...; **beim geringsten/bei jedem** ~ for the slightest reason/at every opportunity. **(b)** *(Gelegenheit)* occasion. **aus gegebenem** ~ in view of the occasion; **aus diesem** ~ on this occasion.

**anlassen** sep irreg **1** vt **(a)** *Motor* to start (up). **(b)** *(col) Mantel* to keep on; *Wasserhahn, Motor, Licht, Radio* to leave on. **2** vr **sich gut/schlecht** ~ to get off to a good/bad start.

**Anlasser** m - *(Aut)* starter.

**anläßlich** prep +gen on the occasion of.

**anlasten** vt sep jdm etw ~ to blame sb for sth; **jdm etw als Schwäche** ~ to regard or see sth as a weakness on sb's part.

**Anlauf** m, pl **Anläufe (a)** *(Sport)* run-up. **mit/ohne** ~ with a run-up/from standing; ~ **nehmen** to take a run-up. **(b)** *(fig: Versuch)* attempt, try. **beim ersten/zweiten** ~ at the first/second attempt.

**anlaufen** sep irreg **1** vi aux sein **(a)** *(beginnen)* to begin, to start; *(Saison auch, Film)* to open; *(Motor)* to start. **(b)** **rot/blau** ~ to turn or go red/blue. **(c)** *(Sport: Anlauf nehmen)* to take a run-up. **2** vt *(Naut) Hafen etc* to put into, to call at.

**Anlauf-:** ~**stelle** f shelter, refuge; ~**zeit** f *(fig)* time to get going or started.

**anläuten** vti sep *(dial: anrufen)* **jdn** or **bei jdm** ~ to ring sb (up) *(Brit)*, to call sb up *(US)*.

**Anlegebrücke** f landing stage, jetty.

**anlegen** sep **1** vt (a) Leiter to put up (an +acc against); Brett, Karte to lay (down) (an +acc next to, beside); Lineal to position, to set. **das Gewehr ~** to raise the gun to one's shoulder; **strengere Maßstäbe ~** to lay down or to impose stricter standards (bei in). (b) Kartei, Akte to start; Vorräte to lay in; Garten etc to lay out. (c) (investieren) Geld to invest; (ausgeben) to spend (für on). (d) **es darauf ~, daß** ... to be determined that ...; siehe **angelegt**. **2** vi (a) (Naut) to berth, to dock. (b) (Gewehr ~) to aim (auf +acc at). **3** vr **sich mit jdm ~** to pick an argument with sb.
**Anlegeplatz** m berth.
**Anleger(in** f) m - (Fin) investor.
**Anlegestelle** f mooring.
**anlehnen** sep **1** vt to lean or rest (an +acc against). **angelehnt sein** (Tür) to be ajar; (Fenster) to be slightly open. **2** vr (lit) to lean (an +acc against); **sich an etw** (acc) ~ (fig) to follow sth.
**Anlehnung** f (a) (Anschluß) dependence (an +acc on). ~ **an jdn suchen** to seek sb's support. (b) (Imitation) **in** ~ **an jdn/etw** following sb/sth.
**Anlehnungs-:** ~**bedürfnis** nt need of loving care; **a~bedürftig** adj needing loving care.
**anleiern** vt sep (col: in die Wege leiten) to get going.
**Anleihe** f -n (Fin) loan; (Wertpapier) bond. **eine ~ aufnehmen** to take out a loan; **bei jdm eine ~ machen** to borrow (money) from sb.
**anleinen** vt sep (festmachen) to tie up. **den Hund ~** to put the dog's lead on.
**anleiten** vt sep (a) (unterweisen) to teach, to instruct. (b) (erziehen) **jdn zu etw ~** to teach sb sth.
**Anleitung** f (Erklärung, Hilfe) instructions pl. **unter der ~ seines Vaters** under his father's guidance or direction.
**anlernen** vt sep (ausbilden) to train; siehe **angelernt**.
**Anlernling** m trainee.
**anlesen** vt sep irreg (aneignen) **sich** (dat) **etw ~** to learn sth by reading.
**anliefern** vt sep to deliver.
**Anlieferung** f delivery.
**Anliegen** nt - (a) (Bitte) request. (b) (wichtige Angelegenheit) matter of concern.
**anliegen** vi sep irreg (a) (anstehen, vorliegen) to be on. (b) (Kleidung) to fit closely or tightly (an etw (dat) sth); (Haar) to lie flat (an +dat against, on).
**anliegend** adj (a) Ohren flat. (eng) ~ Kleidung tight- or close-fitting. (b) (in Briefen) enclosed. (c) Grundstück adjacent.
**Anlieger** m - neighbour (Brit), neighbor (US); (Anwohner) (local) resident. ~ **frei** no thoroughfare – residents only.
**Anlieger-:** ~**staat** m **die** ~**staaten des Schwarzen Meers** the countries bordering (on) the Black Sea; ~**verkehr** m (local) residents' vehicles.
**anlocken** vt sep to attract; Tiere auch to lure.
**Anlockung** f attraction.
**anlügen** vt sep irreg to lie to, to tell lies to.
**Anm.** = **Anmerkung**.
**Anmache** f no pl (col) pick-up (col); (Belästigung) harassment.
**anmachen** vt sep (a) (col: befestigen) to put up (an +acc or dat on). (b) (zubereiten) to mix; Salat to dress. (c) (anstellen) Radio, Licht, Heizung etc to put or turn on; Feuer to light. (d) (col: ansprechen) to chat up (col); (belästigen) to harass. **mach mich nicht an** leave me alone. (e) (col: begeistern) to drive wild; (sexuell) to turn on (col). **das Publikum ~** to get the audience going.
**anmahnen** vt sep to send a reminder about.

**anmalen** sep **1** vt to paint. **2** vr (pej: schminken) to paint one's face or oneself.
**Anmarsch** m no pl (Mil) advance. **im ~ sein** to be advancing (auf +acc on); (hum) to be on the way.
**anmarschieren*** vi sep aux sein (Mil) to advance.
**anmaßen** vr sep sich (dat) **etw ~** Befugnis, Recht to claim sth (for oneself); Titel, Macht, Autorität to assume sth; **sich** (dat) **ein Urteil über etw** (acc) ~ to presume to pass judgement on sth.
**anmaßend** adj presumptuous.
**Anmaßung** f presumption, presumptuousness. **es ist eine ~ zu meinen, ...** it is presumptuous to maintain that ...
**Anmeldeformular** nt application form.
**anmelden** sep **1** vt (a) (ankündigen) Besuch to announce. (b) (bei Schule, Kurs etc) to enrol (bei at, zu for). (c) (eintragen lassen) Patent to apply for; neuen Wohnsitz, Auto to register (bei at); Fernseher to get a licence (Brit) or license (US) for. **Konkurs ~** to declare oneself bankrupt. (d) (Telec) **ein Gespräch nach Deutschland ~** to book a call to Germany. (e) (geltend machen) Recht, Ansprüche, (zu Steuerzwecken) to declare. **ich melde starke Bedenken an** I have serious doubts about that. **2** vr (a) (ankündigen: Besucher) to announce one's arrival. (b) (an Schule, zu Kurs etc) to enrol (oneself) (an +dat at, zu for). **sich (beim Einwohnermeldeamt) ~** to register with the local authorities. (c) (sich einen Termin geben lassen) to make an appointment.
**anmeldepflichtig** adj Krankheit notifiable.
**Anmeldung** f (an Schule, zu Kurs etc) enrolment (an +dat at, zu for); (beim Einwohnermeldeamt) registration. **nur nach vorheriger ~** by appointment only.
**anmerken** vt sep (sagen) to say; (als Fußnote) to note. **jdm seine Verlegenheit** etc ~ to notice sb's embarrassment etc; **sich** (dat) **etw ~ lassen** to let sth show.
**Anmerkung** f note.
**anmieten** vt sep to rent.
**anmustern** vti (Naut) to sign on.
**Anmut** f no pl grace; (Grazie auch) gracefulness; (Schönheit) beauty, loveliness.
**anmuten** sep **1** vt (geh) to appear, to seem (jdn to sb). **2** vi **eine eigenartig ~de Geschichte** a story that strikes one as odd.
**anmutig** adj (geh) (geschmeidig) Bewegung graceful; (hübsch anzusehen) lovely, charming.
**annageln** vt sep to nail on (an +acc or dat -to). **er stand wie angenagelt da** he stood there rooted to the spot.
**annagen** vt sep to gnaw (at).
**annähen** vt sep to sew on (an +acc or dat -to); Saum to sew up.
**annähern** sep **1** vt to bring closer (dat, an +acc to). **2** vr (a) (lit, fig: sich nähern) to approach (einer Sache (dat) sth). (b) (sich angleichen, näherkommen) to come closer (dat, an +acc to).
**annähernd 1** adj (ungefähr) approximate, rough. **2** adv (etwa) roughly; (fast) almost. **nicht ~ soviel** not nearly as much.
**Annäherung** f (lit, fig) approach (an +acc towards); (von Standpunkten) convergence (dat, an +acc with). **die ~ zwischen Ost und West** the rapprochement of East and West.
**Annäherungsversuch** m overtures pl.
**Annahme** f -n (a) (Vermutung, Voraussetzung) assumption. **in der ~, daß ...** on the assumption that ...; **von einer ~ ausgehen** to work on an assumption. (b) siehe **annehmen 1** (a) acceptance; taking; approval; passing; adoption. ~ **an Kindes Statt**

(child) adoption.

**Annahme-:** ~**frist** *f* ~**frist bis zum 17. Juli** closing date 17th July; **die** ~**frist einhalten** to meet the deadline; ~**schluß** *m* closing date; ~**stelle** *f (für Pakete, Telegramme)* counter; *(für Lotto etc)* (national lottery *etc)* agency; *(für Reparaturen)* reception; *(für Material)* delivery point; ~**verweigerung** *f* refusal.

**Annalen** *pl* annals *pl.* **in die** ~ **eingehen** *(fig)* to go down in the annals *or* in history.

**annehmbar** *adj* acceptable; *(nicht schlecht)* reasonable, not bad.

**annehmen** *sep irreg* **1** *vt* **(a)** to accept; *Nahrung, einen Rat, Telefonat* to take; *(billigen)* to approve; *Gesetz* to pass; *Resolution* to adopt. **(b)** *(vermuten, voraussetzen)* to assume. **von jdm etw** ~ *(erwarten)* to expect sth of sb; *(glauben)* to believe sth of sb; *siehe* **angenommen. (c)** *(sich aneignen)* to adopt; *Gewohnheit etc auch* to pick up; *Staatsangehörigkeit auch* to take on; *Gestalt, Namen* to assume, to take on. **jdn an Kindes Statt** ~ to adopt sb. **2** *vr* **sich jds/ einer Sache** ~ to look after a person/a matter.

**Annehmlichkeit** *f (Bequemlichkeit)* convenience. ~**en** *pl* comforts *pl.*

**annektieren*** *vt* to annex.

**Annektierung, Annexion** *f* annexation.

**anno** *adj* in the year. **von** ~ **dazumal** *(col)* or **Tobak** *(col)* from the year dot *(col)*; **ein Überbleibsel von** ~ **dazumal** *(col)* a hangover from the olden days.

**Anno Domini** *adv* in the year of Our Lord.

**Annonce** [a'nõːsə] *f* -**n** advertisement.

**annoncieren*** [anõ'siːrən] *vti* to advertise.

**annullieren*** *vt (Jur)* to annul.

**Annullierung** *f* annulment.

**Anode** *f* -**n** anode.

**an|öden** *vt sep (col: langweilen)* to bore stiff.

**anomal** *adj (regelwidrig)* unusual, abnormal; *(nicht normal)* strange, odd.

**Anomalie** *f* anomaly.

**anonym** *adj* anonymous. **A~e Alkoholiker** Alcoholics Anonymous.

**Anonymität** *f* anonymity.

**Anorak** *m* -**s** anorak *(Brit)*, parka.

**an|ordnen** *vt sep* **(a)** *(befehlen, festsetzen)* to order. **(b)** *(nach Plan ordnen, aufstellen)* to arrange; *(systematisch)* to order.

**An|ordnung** *f* **(a)** *(Befehl)* order. **laut (polizeilicher)** ~ by order (of the police); **auf** ~ **des Arztes** on doctor's orders; ~**en treffen** to give orders. **(b)** *(Aufstellung)* arrangement; *(systematische* ~*)* order; *(Formation)* formation.

**Anorexie** *f no pl* anorexia (nervosa).

**an|organisch** *adj (Chem)* inorganic.

**anormal** *adj (col)* = **anomal.**

**anpacken** *sep (col)* **1** *vt* **(a)** *(anfassen)* to take hold of, to grab. **(b)** *(handhaben, beginnen)* to tackle, to set about. **(c)** *(umgehen mit) jdn* to treat. **2** *vi (helfen: auch mit* ~*)* to lend a hand.

**anpassen** *sep* **1** *vt* **(a)** *Kleidung* to fit *(dat* on*)*. **(b)** *(abstimmen)* **etw einer Sache** *(dat)* ~ to suit sth to sth. **(c)** *(angleichen)* **etw einer Sache** *(dat)* ~ to bring sth into line with sth. **2** *vr* to adapt (oneself) *(dat* to*)*; *(einer Situation etc)* to adjust *(dat* to*)*; *(gesellschaftlich)* to conform. **wir mußten uns (ihren Wünschen)** ~ we had to fit in with their wishes *or* them; *siehe* **angepaßt.**

**Anpassung** *f (an +acc* to*)* adaptation; *(an Gesellschaft, Normen etc)* adjustment.

**Anpassungs-: a~fähig** *adj* adaptable; ~**fähigkeit** *f* adaptability; ~**schwierigkeiten** *pl* difficulties *pl* in adapting; ~**vermögen** *nt* adaptability.

**anpeilen** *vt sep (mit Radar, Funk etc)* to take a bearing on. **etw** ~ *(fig inf)* to have one's sights on sth.

**anpeitschen** *vt sep* to drive on, to push (hard).

**anpfeifen** *sep irreg (Sport)* **1** *vi* to blow the whistle. **2** *vt* **das Spiel** ~ to start the game (by blowing one's whistle).

**Anpfiff** *m (Sport)* (starting) whistle; *(Spielbeginn)* kick-off.

**anpflanzen** *vt sep (bepflanzen)* to plant; *(anbauen)* to grow.

**Anpflanzung** *f* **(a)** *siehe vt* planting; growing. **(b)** *(Fläche)* cultivated area.

**anpirschen** *vr sep* to creep up *(an +acc* on*)*.

**anpöbeln** *vt sep (col)* to abuse.

**Anprall** *m* impact. **beim** ~ **gegen** on impact with.

**anprallen** *vi sep aux sein* to crash *(an or gegen jdn/ etw* into sb/against sth*)*.

**anprangern** *vt sep* to denounce.

**anpreisen** *vt sep irreg* to extol *(jdm etw* sth to sb*)*. **sich (als etw)** ~ to sell oneself as sth.

**Anprobe** *f* **(a)** fitting. **(b)** *(*~ *raum)* fitting room.

**anprobieren*** *vt sep* to try on.

**anpumpen** *vt sep (col)* to borrow from. **jdn um 50 Mark** ~ to touch sb for 50 marks *(col)*.

**anquatschen** *vt sep (col)* to speak to; *Mädchen* to chat up *(col)*.

**Anrainer** *m* - neighbour *(Brit)*, neighbor *(US)*. **die** ~ **der Nordsee** the countries bordering (on) the North Sea.

**anraten** *vt sep irreg* **jdm etw** ~ to recommend sth to sb; **auf A**~ **des Arztes** on the doctor's advice *or* recommendation.

**anrechnen** *vt sep* **(a)** *(in Rechnung stellen)* to charge for *(jdm* sb*)*. **(b)** *(gutschreiben)* to count, to take into account *(jdm* for sb*)*. **das alte Auto rechnen wir (Ihnen) mit DM 500 an** we'll allow (you) 500 marks for the old car. **(c)** *(bewerten)* **jdm etw hoch** ~ to think highly of sb for sth; **jdm etw als Fehler** ~ *(Lehrer)* to count sth as a mistake; *(fig)* to consider sth as a fault on sb's part; **ich rechne es ihm als Verdienst an, daß ...** I think it is greatly to his credit that ...

**Anrecht** *nt (Anspruch)* right, entitlement *(auf +acc* to*)*. **ein** ~ **auf etw** *(acc)* **haben** to be entitled to sth, to have a right to sth.

**Anrede** *f* form of address; *(Brief*~ *auch)* salutation *(form)*.

**anreden** *vt sep* to address. **jdn mit „du"** ~ to address sb as "du"; **jdn mit seinem Titel** ~ to address sb by his title.

**anregen** *vt sep* **(a)** *(ermuntern)* to prompt *(zu* to*)*. **jdn zum Denken** ~ to make sb think. **(b)** *(geh: vorschlagen) Verbesserung* to propose, to suggest. **(c)** *(beleben)* to stimulate; *Appetit auch* to whet, to sharpen. **Kaffee regt an** coffee has a stimulating effect; *siehe* **angeregt.**

**anregend** *adj* stimulating.

**Anregung** *f* **(a)** *(Antrieb, Impuls)* stimulus. **(b)** *(Vorschlag)* idea. **auf** ~ **von** *or* +*gen* at *or* on the suggestion of. **(c)** *(Belebung)* stimulation.

**Anregungsmittel** *nt* stimulant.

**anreichen** *vt sep* to pass, to hand.

**anreichern** *vt sep (gehaltvoller machen)* to enrich.

**Anreise** *f* **(a)** *(Anfahrt)* journey there/here. **die** ~ **zu diesem abgelegenen Ort ist sehr mühsam** it is very difficult to get to this remote place. **(b)** *(Ankunft)* arrival.

**anreisen** *vi sep aux sein* **(a)** *(ein Ziel anfahren)* to make a/the journey *or* trip (there/here). **mit dem eigenen PKW** ~ to travel (there/here) in one's own car. **(b)** *(eintreffen) (auch* **angereist kommen*)** to arrive.

**anreißen** vt sep irreg (**a**) (kurz zur Sprache bringen) to touch on. (**b**) (pej col) Kunden to attract.

**Anreiz** m incentive. **ein ~ zum Lernen** a learning incentive.

**anreizen** sep **1** vt (anspornen) to encourage. **2** vi to act as an incentive (zu to); (Menge) to cheer on.

**anrempeln** vt sep (anstoßen) to bump into; (absichtlich) Menschen to jostle.

**anrennen** vi sep irreg aux sein **gegen etw ~ gegen** Wind etc to run against sth; (Mil) to storm sth; **angerannt kommen** (col) to come running.

**Anrichte** f -n (Schrank) dresser; (Büfett) sideboard.

**anrichten** vt sep (**a**) Speisen to prepare. **es ist angerichtet** (form) dinner/luncheon is served (form). (**b**) (fig) Unheil etc to cause, to bring about. **da hast du aber etwas angerichtet!** (col) (verursacht) you've started something there all right; (angestellt) you've really made a mess there.

**anrollen** vi sep aux sein (zu rollen beginnen) to start to roll; (heranrollen) to roll up; (Aviat) to taxi; (fig: beginnen) to start.

**anrosten** vi sep aux sein to get (a bit) rusty.

**anrüchig** adj (von üblem Ruf) of ill repute; Lokal etc notorious.

**anrücken** vi sep aux sein (Truppen) to advance; (Polizei etc) to move in.

**Anruf** m call; (Mil: eines Wachtpostens) challenge. **etw auf ~ tun** to do sth when called.

**Anrufbe|antworter** m (telephone) answering machine, answerphone.

**anrufen** sep irreg **1** vt (**a**) to shout to; (Telec) to call, to phone, to ring (Brit); (Mil: Posten) to challenge. **darf ich dich ~?** is it all right if I call you or I give you a ring (Brit)?; **kann man Sie ~?** are you on the phone? (**b**) (fig: appellieren an) to appeal to (um for). **2** vi (telefonieren) to phone col. **bei jdm ~** to phone sb.

**Anrufer(in** f) m caller.

**Anrufung** f (Gottes, der Heiligen etc) invocation; (Jur) appeal (gen to).

**anrühren** vt sep (**a**) (berühren, sich befassen mit) to touch; (fig) Thema to touch on. **er rührt kein Fleisch/keinen Alkohol an** he doesn't touch meat/alcohol. (**b**) (mischen) Farben to mix; Sauce to blend; (verrühren) to stir.

**ans** = **an das**.

**Ansage** f -n announcement; (Cards) bid.

**ansagen** sep **1** vt (**a**) to announce. **jdm den Kampf ~** to declare war on sb. (**b**) (Cards) to bid; (Skat) to declare. (**c**) (col) **angesagt sein** (modisch sein) to be in; (erforderlich sein) to be called for; (auf dem Programm stehen) to be the order of the day. **2** vr (Besuch ankündigen) to say that one is coming.

**Ansager(in** f) m - (Rad etc) announcer.

**ansammeln** sep **1** vt (**a**) (anhäufen) to accumulate. (**b**) (zusammenkommen lassen) to gather together; Truppen to concentrate. **2** vr (**a**) (sich versammeln) to gather, to collect. (**b**) (aufhäufen) to accumulate; (Staub, Wasser auch) to collect; (Druck, fig: Wut) to build up; (Zinsen) to build up.

**Ansammlung** f (**a**) (Anhäufung) accumulation; (Sammlung) collection; (von Druck, Wut) build-up; (Haufen) pile. (**b**) (Auflauf) gathering, crowd; (von Truppen) concentration.

**ansässig** adj (form) resident. **alle in diesem Ort A~en** all local residents.

**Ansatz** m (**a**) (von Hals, Arm, Henkel etc) base. (**b**) (Tech) (Zusatzstück) attachment; (zur Verlängerung) extension; (Naht) join. (**c**) (erstes Anzeichen, Beginn) first sign(s pl), beginning(s pl); (Ausgangspunkt)

starting-point.

**Ansatz-**: **~punkt** m starting-point; **~stück** nt (Tech) attachment; (zur Verlängerung) extension; **a~weise** adv to some extent.

**ansaugen** vt sep to suck or draw in.

**anschaffen** sep **1** vt (**sich** dat) etw ~ to get oneself sth; (kaufen) to buy sth; **sich** (dat) **Kinder ~** (col) to have children. **2** vi (col: durch Prostitution) ~ **gehen** to be on the game (col).

**Anschaffung** f acquisition. **ich habe mich zur ~ eines Autos entschlossen** I have decided to buy a car. **~en machen** to acquire things; (kaufen) to make purchases.

**Anschaffungs-**: **~kosten** pl cost sing of purchase; **~preis** m purchase price.

**anschalten** vt sep to switch on.

**anschauen** vt sep to look at; (prüfend) to examine. **sich** (dat) **etw ~** to have a look at sth.

**anschaulich** adj clear; (lebendig, bildhaft) vivid; Beschreibung graphic; Beispiel concrete. **etw ~ machen** to illustrate sth.

**Anschauung** f (Ansicht, Auffassung) view; (Meinung) opinion. **nach neuerer ~** according to the current way of thinking; **aus eigener ~** from one's own experience.

**Anschauungs-**: **~material** nt illustrative material, visual aids pl; **~unterricht** m visual instruction.

**Anschein** m appearance; (Eindruck) impression. **allem ~ nach** to all appearances, apparently; **den ~ erwecken, als ...** to give the impression that ...; **es hat den ~, als ob ...** it appears that or seems as if ...

**anscheinend** adv apparently.

**anscheißen** vt sep irreg (fig col!) jdn ~ (betrügen) to do the dirty on sb (col); (beschimpfen) to give sb a bollocking (col!).

**anschicken** vr sep **sich ~, etw zu tun** (geh: im Begriff sein) to be about to do sth.

**anschieben** vt sep irreg Fahrzeug to push.

**anschießen** sep irreg **1** vt (**a**) (verletzen) to shoot (and wound); Vogel (in Flügel) to wing; **siehe angeschossen**. (**b**) (col: kritisieren) to hit out at (col). **2** vi aux sein (col) (heranrasen) to shoot up. **angeschossen kommen** to come shooting along or (auf einen zu) up.

**anschimmeln** vi sep aux sein to (start to) go mouldy.

**Anschiß** m -sse (col) bollocking (col!).

**Anschlag** m (**a**) (Plakat) poster; (Bekanntmachung) notice. **einen ~ machen** to put up a poster/notice. (**b**) (Überfall) attack (auf +acc on); (Attentat) attempt on sb's life. **einem ~ zum Opfer fallen** to be assassinated. (**c**) (von Klavier(spieler), Schreibmaschine) touch. **200 Anschläge in der Minute** ≈ 40 words per minute. (**d**) (bei Hebel, Knopf etc) stop. **etw bis zum ~ durchdrücken** to push sth right down. (**e**) (Mil) **ein Gewehr im ~ haben** to have a rifle at the ready.

**Anschlagbrett** nt notice-board (Brit), bulletin board (US).

**anschlagen** sep irreg **1** vt (**a**) (befestigen) to fix on (an +acc -to); (mit Nägeln) to nail on (an +acc -to); (aushängen) Plakat to put up, to post (an +acc on). (**b**) Taste, accord to strike. **eine schnellere Gangart ~** (fig) to speed up; **einen anderen Ton ~** (fig) to change one's tune. (**c**) (beschädigen, verletzen) Geschirr to chip. (**d**) (aufnehmen) Maschen to cast on. **2** vi (**a**) (Welle) to beat (an +acc against). (**b**) (Laut geben) (Hund) to give a bark; (Vogel) to give a screech. (**c**) (wirken: Arznei etc) to work, to take effect.

**a̧nschlagfrei** *adj Drucker* non-impact.

**a̧nschleichen** *sep irreg* **1** *vi aux sein* to creep along *or (auf einen zu)* up. **angeschlichen kommen** *(col)* to come creeping along/up. **2** *vr* **sich an jdn/etw** ~ to creep up on sb/sth; *(sich anpirschen)* to stalk sth.

**a̧nschleppen** *vt sep* **(a)** *Auto* to tow-start. **(b)** *(col: unerwünscht mitbringen)* to bring along; *(nach Hause)* to bring home; *Freund etc auch* to turn up with *(col)*.

**a̧nschließen** *sep irreg* **1** *vt* **(a)** *(an +acc to) (Tech, Elec, Telec etc: verbinden)* to connect; *(in Steckdose)* to plug in; *(Waschmaschine etc)* to plumb in. **(b)** *(fig: hinzufügen)* to add; *siehe* **angeschlossen. 2** *vr* **sich jdm** *or* **an jdn** ~ *(folgen)* to follow sb; *(zugesellen)* to join sb; *(beipflichten)* to side with sb; **sich einer Sache** *(dat)* **or an etw** *(acc)* ~ *(folgen)* to follow sth; *(beitreten, sich beteiligen)* to join sth; *(beipflichten)* to endorse sth; *(angrenzen)* to adjoin sth; **sich an ein Datennetz** ~ to link up with a data network. **3** *vi* **an etw** *(acc)* ~ to follow sth.

**a̧nschließend 1** *adv* afterwards. **2** *adj* following. **Essen mit ~em Tanz** dinner with a dance afterwards.

**A̧nschluß** *m* **(a)** *(Verbindung)* connection; *(Beitritt)* entry *(an +acc into)*; *(an Klub)* joining *(an +acc of)*. ~ **haben nach** *(Rail)* to have a connection to; **den** ~ **verpassen** *(Rail etc)* to miss one's connection; *(fig)* to miss the boat *(col)*. **ihm gelang der** ~ **an die Spitze** *(Sport)* he managed to catch up with the leaders. **(b)** *(Telec, Elec, Comp)* connection; *(weiterer Apparat)* extension; *(Wasser~)* supply point; *(für Waschmaschine)* point connection. ~ **bekommen** to get through; **kein** ~ **unter dieser Nummer** number unobtainable. **(c) im** ~ **an** *(+acc) (nach)* subsequent to, following. **(d)** *(fig: Kontakt)* contact *(an +acc with)*; ~ **finden** to make friends *(an +acc with)*; **er sucht** ~ he wants to make friends.

**A̧nschluß-:** ~**flug** *m* connecting flight; ~**stelle** *f (Mot)* junction; ~**zug** *m (Rail)* connecting train, connection.

**a̧nschmiegen** *vr sep* **sich an jdn/etw** ~ *(Kind, Hund)* to snuggle *or* nestle up to *or* against sb/sth; *(Kleidung)* to cling to sb/sth.

**a̧nschmiegsam** *adj Wesen* affectionate; *Material* smooth.

**a̧nschmieren** *vt sep* **(a)** *(bemalen)* to smear. **(b)** *(col) (betrügen)* to con *(col)*; *(Streiche spielen)* to play tricks on; *siehe* **angeschmiert.**

**a̧nschnallen** *sep* **1** *vt Rucksack* to strap on; *Skier* to clip on. **2** *vr (Aviat, Aut)* to fasten one's seat belt. **bitte ~!** fasten your seat belts, please!

**A̧nschnallpflicht** *f* obligatory wearing of seat belts. **für Kinder besteht** ~ children must wear seat belts.

**a̧nschnauzen** *vt sep (col)* to yell at.

**a̧nschneiden** *vt sep irreg* **(a)** *Brot etc* to (start to) cut. **(b)** *(fig) Frage, Thema* to touch on. **(c)** *(Aut) Kurve, (Sport) Ball* to cut.

**A̧nschnitt** *m (Schnittfläche)* cut part; *(erstes Stück)* first slice.

**Anschovis** [an'ʃoːvɪs] *f* - anchovy.

**a̧nschrauben** *vt sep* to screw on *(an +acc -to)*.

**a̧nschreiben** *sep irreg* **1** *vt* **(a)** *(aufschreiben)* to write up *(an +acc on)*. **etw mit Kreide** ~ to chalk sth up; *siehe* **angeschrieben. (b)** *(col: in Rechnung stellen)* to chalk up. **(c)** *Behörde, Versandhaus etc* to write to. **2** *vi (col)* **sie läßt immer** ~ she always buys on tick *(col)*.

**a̧nschreien** *vt sep irreg* to shout *or* yell at.

**A̧nschrift** *f* address.

**A̧nschriftenliste** *f* mailing list.

**a̧nschuldigen** *vt sep* to accuse *(gen of)*.

**A̧nschuldigung** *f* accusation.

**a̧nschwärzen** *vt sep (fig col)* **jdn** ~ to blacken sb's name *(bei with)*.

**a̧nschweigen** *vt sep irreg* to say nothing to. **sich (gegenseitig)** ~ to say nothing (to each other).

**a̧nschweißen** *vt sep* to weld on *(an +acc -to)*.

**a̧nschwellen** *vi sep irreg aux sein* to swell (up); *(Lärm)* to rise. **dick angeschwollen** very swollen.

**a̧nschwemmen** *vt sep* to wash up *or* ashore.

**a̧nschwimmen** *sep irreg* **1** *vt* to swim towards. **2** *vi aux sein* **gegen etw** ~ to swim against sth.

**a̧nschwindeln** *vt sep (col)* **jdn** ~ to tell sb fibs *(col)*.

**a̧nsehen** *vt sep irreg* **(a)** *(betrachten)* to look at. **er sah mich ganz böse an** he gave me an angry look; **hübsch** *etc* **anzusehen** pretty *etc* to look at; **sieh mal einer an!** *(col)* well, I never! *(col)*. **(b)** *(fig)* to regard, to look upon *(als, für as)*. **ich sehe es als meine Pflicht an** I consider it to be my duty; *siehe* **angesehen. (c) (sich** *dat)* **etw** ~ to (have a) look at sth; *Fernsehsendung* to watch sth; *Film, Stück, Veranstaltung* to see sth; **sich** *(dat)* **jdn/etw gründlich** ~ *(lit, fig)* to take a close look at sb/sth. **(d) das sieht man ihm an/nicht an** he looks it/ doesn't look it; **man kann ihm die Strapazen der letzten Woche** ~ he's showing the strain of the past week; **man sieht ihm sein Alter nicht an** he doesn't look his age; **jdm etw an den Augen** *or* **an der Nasenspitze** *(hum)* ~ to tell *or* guess sth by looking at sb. **(e) etw (mit)** ~ to watch sth, to see sth happening; **ich kann das nicht länger mit** ~ I can't stand it any more.

**A̧nsehen** *nt no pl* **(a)** *(Aussehen)* appearance. **jdn vom** ~ **kennen** to know sb by sight. **(b)** *(guter Ruf)* good reputation, standing. **großes** ~ **genießen** to enjoy a good reputation; **an** ~ **verlieren** to lose credit *or* standing. **(c)** *(Jur)* **ohne** ~ **der Person** without respect of person.

**a̧nsehnlich** *adj (beträchtlich)* considerable; *Leistung* impressive.

**a̧nseilen** *vt sep* **jdn/sich** ~ to rope sb/oneself up.

**a̧nsein** *vi sep irreg aux sein (col)* to be on.

**a̧nsetzen** *sep* **1** *vt* **(a)** *(anfügen)* to attach *(an +acc to)*; *(annähen)* to sew on. **(b)** *(in Stellung bringen)* to place in position. **das Glas** ~ to raise the glass to one's lips; **an welcher Stelle muß man den Wagenheber** ~? where should the jack be put *or* placed? **(c)** *(festlegen) Kosten, Termin* to fix *(mit at, auf +acc for)*. **(d)** *(einsetzen)* **jdn auf jdn/etw** ~ to put sb on(to) sb/sth. **(e)** *(entstehen lassen) Blätter etc* to put on. **Fett** ~ to put on weight; **Rost** ~ to get rusty. **(f)** *(Cook) (vorbereiten)* to prepare; *(auf den Herd setzen)* to put on. **2** *vr (Rost)* to form; *(Kalk etc)* to be deposited. **3** *vi* **(a)** *(beginnen)* to start, to begin. **zur Landung** ~ *(Aviat)* to come in to land; **zum Sprung/Spurt** ~ to get ready to jump/to start one's spurt. **(b)** *(Cook: sich festsetzen)* to stick.

**A̧nsicht** *f* **-en (a)** view. ~ **von hinten/vorn** rear/front view; ~ **von oben/unten** view from above/below, top/bottom view *(Tech)*. **(b)** *(das Betrachten, Prüfen)* inspection. **zur** ~ *(Comm)* for *(your/our etc)* information; **jdm Waren zur** ~ **schicken** *(Comm)* to send sb goods on approval. **(c)** *(Meinung)* opinion, view. **nach** ~ *+gen* in the opinion of; **meiner** ~ **nach** in my opinion *or* view; **anderer/der gleichen** ~ **sein** to be of a different/the same opinion, to disagree/ agree; **ich bin ganz Ihrer** ~ I entirely agree with you; **die ~en sind geteilt** opinions differ, opinion is divided.

**A̧nsichts-:** ~**karte** *f* picture postcard; ~**sache** *f* **das**

ist ~sache that is a matter of opinion.

**ansiedeln** sep **1** vt to settle; Tierart to introduce. **2** vr to settle; (Industrie etc) to become established.

**Ansiedlung** f settlement.

**Ansinnen** nt (dated, geh: Vorschlag) suggestion.

**ansonsten** adv otherwise.

**anspannen** vt sep **(a)** (straffen) to tauten, to tighten; Muskeln to tense. **(b)** (anstrengen) to strain, to tax; Geduld, Mittel auch to stretch. **alle seine Kräfte** ~ to strain every nerve; siehe **angespannt. (c)** Wagen, Pferd to hitch up.

**Anspannung** f (fig) strain; (körperliche Anstrengung auch) effort.

**ansparen** vt to save.

**Anspiel** nt (Sport) start of play. **das** ~ **haben** to start play; (Ftbl) to kick off.

**anspielen** sep **1** vt (Sport) to play the ball etc to; Spieler to pass to. **2** vi **auf jdn/etw** ~ to allude to sb/sth; **worauf wollen Sie** ~**?** what are you driving at?, what are you insinuating?

**Anspielung** f allusion (auf +acc to); (böse) insinuation, innuendo (auf +acc regarding).

**anspitzen** vt sep Bleistift etc to sharpen.

**Ansporn** m no pl incentive.

**anspornen** vt sep (fig) to spur on, to encourage (zu to); Menge to cheer on.

**Ansprache** f (Rede) address, speech. **eine** ~ **halten** to make a speech.

**ansprechbar** adj **(a) er ist beschäftigt/wütend und zur Zeit nicht** ~ he's so busy/angry it's no use talking to him just now. **(b)** Patient responsive.

**ansprechen** sep irreg **1** vt **(a)** (anreden) to speak to; (belästigend) to accost. **jdn auf etw** (acc) ~ to ask or approach sb about sth; **damit sind Sie alle angesprochen** this is directed at all of you. **(b)** (gefallen) to appeal to; (Eindruck machen auf) to make an impression on. **2** vi (auf +acc to) (reagieren) (Patient, Gaspedal etc) to respond; (Meßgerät auch) to react. **diese Tabletten sprechen bei ihr nicht an** these tablets don't have any effect on her.

**ansprechend** adj (reizvoll) Äußeres, Verpackung etc attractive, appealing; Umgebung etc pleasant.

**Ansprechpartner** m (form) contact.

**anspringen** sep irreg **1** vt (anfallen) to jump; (Raubtier) to pounce on; (Hund: hochspringen) to jump up at. **2** vi aux sein (Motor) to start. **das Auto springt nicht an** the car won't start.

**Anspruch** m, pl **Ansprüche (a)** (esp Jur) claim; (Recht) right (auf +acc to). ~ **auf Schadenersatz erheben/haben** to make a claim for damages/to be entitled to damages. **(b)** (Anforderung) demand; (Standard) standard, requirement. **große** or **hohe Ansprüche stellen** to be very demanding; (hohes Niveau verlangen) to demand high standards; **den Ansprüchen gerecht werden** to meet the requirements. **(c)** (Behauptung) claim. **diese Theorie erhebt keinen** ~ **auf Unwiderlegbarkeit** this theory does not claim to be irrefutable. **(d) etw in** ~ **nehmen** Recht to claim sth; jds Hilfe to enlist sth; Möglichkeiten, Kantine etc to take advantage of sth; Zeit, Kräfte to take up sth; **darf ich Ihre Aufmerksamkeit in** ~ **nehmen?** may I have your attention?; **das nimmt mich sehr in** ~ it keeps me very busy.

**anspruchslos** adj (bescheiden) modest, unassuming; (wenig Pflege etc erfordernd) undemanding; Literatur, Musik lowbrow; Produkte downmarket.

**anspruchsvoll** adj (viel verlangend) demanding; (übertrieben ~) hard to please, fastidious; (hohe Ansprüche stellend) Stil, Buch ambitious; Geschmack, Musik highbrow; (kultiviert) sophisticated; (hochwertig) upmarket.

**anspucken** vt sep to spit at or on.

**anspülen** vt sep to wash up or ashore.

**anstacheln** vt sep to spur (on); (antreiben) to drive or goad on.

**Anstalt** f -en **(a)** institution (auch euph); (Institut) institute. **(b)** ~en pl (Maßnahmen) measures pl; (Vorbereitungen) preparations pl; ~**en/keine** ~**en machen, etw zu tun** to make a/no move to do sth.

**Anstand** m no pl (Schicklichkeit) decency, propriety; (Manieren) (good) manners pl. **keinen** ~ **haben** to have no sense of decency/no manners.

**anständig 1** adj decent; Witz auch clean; (ehrbar) respectable; (col: beträchtlich) sizeable, large. **das war nicht** ~ **von ihm** that was pretty bad of him; **eine** ~**e Tracht Prügel** (col) a good hiding. **2** adv decently. **sich** ~ **benehmen** to behave oneself; **sich** ~ **hinsetzen** to sit properly.

**Anständigkeit** f decency; (Ehrbarkeit) respectability.

**Anstands-:** ~**besuch** m formal call; (aus Pflichtgefühl) duty visit; ~**dame** f chaperon(e); ~**formen** pl manners pl; **a**~**halber** adv out of politeness; **a**~**los** adv without difficulty.

**anstarren** vt sep to stare at.

**anstatt 1** prep +gen instead of. **2** conj ~ **zu arbeiten** instead of working.

**anstauen** vr sep to accumulate; (Blut in Adern etc) to congest; (fig auch: Gefühle) to build up. **angestaute Wut** pent-up rage.

**anstechen** vt sep irreg to make a hole in, to pierce; Kartoffeln, Fleisch to prick; Reifen to puncture; Faß to tap, to broach.

**anstecken** sep **1** vt **(a)** (befestigen) to pin on; Ring to put or slip on. **(b)** (anzünden) to light; (in Brand stecken) to set fire to. **(c)** (Med, fig) to infect. **2** vr **sich (mit etw)** ~ to catch sth (bei from). **3** vi (Med, fig) to be infectious or catching; (durch Berührung, fig) to be contagious.

**ansteckend** adj (Med, fig) infectious, catching pred (col); (durch Berührung, fig) contagious.

**Anstecknadel** f pin, badge.

**Ansteckung** f (Med) infection; (durch Berührung) contagion.

**Ansteckungsgefahr** f risk of infection.

**anstehen** vi sep irreg **(a)** (in Schlange) to queue (up) (Brit), to stand in line (nach for). **(b)** (Verhandlungspunkt) to be on the agenda. ~**de Probleme** problems that have arisen.

**ansteigen** vi sep irreg aux sein to rise; (Temperatur, Preis, Zahl auch) to go up, to increase.

**anstelle** prep +gen instead of, in place of.

**anstellen** sep **1** vt **(a)** to place; (anlehnen) to lean (an +acc against). **(b)** (beschäftigen) to employ, to take on; siehe **angestellt. (c)** (anmachen, andrehen) to turn on; (in Gang setzen auch) to start. **(d)** Betrachtung, Vermutung etc to make; Vergleich auch to draw. **(e)** (machen, unternehmen) to do; (fertigbringen) to manage. **(f)** (col: Unfug treiben) to get up to. **etwas** ~ to get up to mischief; **was hast du da wieder angestellt!** what have you done now?, what have you been up to now? **2** vr **(a)** (Schlange stehen) to queue (up) (Brit), to stand in line. **(b)** (col: sich verhalten) to act, to behave. **sich dumm/ungeschickt** ~ to act stupid/clumsily, to be stupid/clumsy. **(c)** (col: sich zieren) to make a fuss, to act up (col). **stell dich nicht so an!** don't make such a fuss!

**Anstellung** f employment; (Stelle) position.

**ansteuern** vt sep to make or steer or head (auch hum) for.

**Anstich** m (von Faß) tapping, broaching.

**Anstieg** *m* -e (a) *(Aufstieg)* climb, ascent; *(Weg)* ascent. (b) *(von Temperatur, Kosten, Preisen etc)* rise, increase *(gen* in*)*.

**anstiften** *vt sep (anzetteln)* to instigate; *(verursachen)* to cause. **jdn zu etw** ~ to incite sb to (do) sth, to put sb up to sth *(col)*.

**Anstifter(in** *f) m* instigator *(+gen, zu* of*)*.

**Anstiftung** *f (von Mensch)* incitement *(zu* to*)*; *(von Tat)* instigation.

**anstimmen** *vt sep* (a) *(singen)* to begin singing; *(Chorleiter)* Grundton to give; *(Kapelle)* to strike up, to start playing. (b) *(fig)* **ein Geschrei/Proteste** *etc* ~ to start crying/protesting *etc.*

**Anstoß** *m* (a) impetus, impulse. **den (ersten)** ~ **zu etw geben** to initiate sth, to get sth going; **den** ~ **zu etw bekommen** to be prompted *or* encouraged to do sth; **es bedurfte eines neuen** ~**es** new impetus was needed. (b) *(Ftbl)* kick-off. (c) *(Ärgernis)* annoyance *(für* to*)*. ~ **erregen** to cause offence *(bei* to*)*; ~ **nehmen an** *(+Dat)* to take offence at; **ein Stein des** ~**es** *(umstrittene Sache)* a bone of contention.

**anstoßen** *sep irreg* **1** *vi* (a) *aux sein* **an etw** *acc* ~ to bump into sth. (b) **(mit den Gläsern)** ~ to clink glasses; **auf jdn/etw** ~ to drink to sb/sth. (c) *(Ftbl)* to kick off. (d) *(angrenzen)* **an etw** *(acc)* ~ to adjoin sth; *(Land auch)* to border on sth. **2** *vt* **jdn** to knock (into); *(mit dem Fuß)* to kick; *(in Bewegung setzen)* to give a push.

**anstößig** *adj* offensive; *Kleidung* indecent.

**Anstößigkeit** *f siehe adj* offensiveness; indecency.

**anstrahlen** *vt sep* to floodlight; *(im Theater)* to spotlight; *(strahlend ansehen)* to beam at.

**anstreben** *vt sep* to strive for.

**anstreichen** *vt sep irreg* (a) *(mit Farbe etc)* to paint. (b) *(markieren)* to mark. **(jdm) etw als Fehler** ~ to mark sth wrong.

**Anstreicher(in** *f) m* - (house) painter.

**anstrengen** *sep* **1** *vt* (a) to strain; *Muskel, Geist* to exert; *(strapazieren)* jdn to tire out; *esp Patienten* to fatigue. **das viele Lesen strengt meine Augen/mich an** all this reading puts a strain on my eyes/is a strain (for me); *siehe* **angestrengt.** (b) *(Jur)* **eine Klage** ~ to initiate *or* institute proceedings *(gegen* against*)*. **2** *vr* to make an effort; *(körperlich auch)* to exert oneself. **sich mehr** ~ to make more of an effort.

**anstrengend** *adj (körperlich)* strenuous; *(geistig)* demanding; *(erschöpfend)* exhausting, tiring. **das ist** ~ **für die Augen** it's a strain on the eyes.

**Anstrengung** *f* effort; *(Strapaze)* strain. **große** ~**en machen** to make every effort.

**Anstrich** *m (das Anmalen, Tünchen)* painting; *(Farbüberzug)* paint; *(fig: Anflug)* touch. **ein zweiter** ~ a second coat (of paint).

**Ansturm** *m* onslaught; *(auf Kaufhaus etc)* rush; *(auf Bank)* run; *(Menschenmenge)* crowd.

**anstürmen** *vi sep aux sein* **gegen etw** ~ *(Mil)* to attack *or* storm sth; *(Wellen, Wind)* to pound sth; *(fig: ankämpfen)* to attack sth.

**ansuchen** *vi sep (form, Aus)* **bei jdm um etw** ~ *(bitten um)* to request sth from sb; *(beantragen)* to apply to sb for sth.

**Ansuchen** *nt* - *(form, Aus)* request; *(Gesuch)* application.

**Antagonismus** *m* antagonism.

**antanzen** *vi sep aux sein (col)* to turn *or* show up *(col)*.

**Antarktika** *f no pl* Antarctica.

**Antarktis** *f no pl* Antarctic.

**antarktisch** *adj* antarctic.

**antasten** *vt sep* (a) *Ehre, Würde* to offend; *Rechte* to infringe. (b) *(berühren)* to touch.

**Anteil** *m* -e (a) share. (b) *(Beteiligung)* ~ **an etw** *(dat)* **haben** *(beitragen)* to contribute to sth; *(teilnehmen)* to take part in sth. (c) *(Teilnahme: an Leid etc)* sympathy *(an* +dat with*)*. **an etw** *(dat)* ~ **nehmen** *an Leid etc* to be deeply sympathetic over sth; *an Freude etc* to share in sth. (d) *(Interesse)* interest *(an* +dat in*)*, concern *(an* +dat about*)*. **regen** ~ **an etw** *(dat)* **nehmen** to take a lively interest in sth.

**anteilig, anteilmäßig** *adj* proportionate, proportional.

**Anteilnahme** *f no pl* (a) *(Beileid)* sympathy *(an* +dat with*)*. (b) *(Beteiligung)* participation *(an* +dat in*)*.

**antelefonieren\*** *vti sep (col)* to phone. **bei jdm** ~ to phone sb up.

**Antenne** *f* -n *(Rad, TV)* aerial, antenna *(US)*; *(Zool)* feeler, antenna. **eine/keine** ~ **für etw haben** *(fig inf)* to have a/no feeling for sth.

**Anthologie** *f* anthology.

**Anthrazit** *m* -e anthracite.

**anthrazit(farben)** *adj* charcoal-grey, charcoal.

**Anthropologe** *m,* **Anthropologin** *f* anthropologist.

**Anthropologie** *f* anthropology.

**anthropologisch** *adj* anthropological.

**Anthroposophie** *f* anthroposophy.

**Anti-** *pref* anti; ~**alkoholiker** *m* teetotaller *(Brit)*, teetotaler *(US)*; ~**amerikanismus** *m no pl* anti-Americanism; a~**autoritär** *adj* anti-authoritarian; ~**babypille** *f (col)* (contraceptive)pill; ~**biotikum** *nt, pl* ~**biotika** antibiotic; ~**blockiersystem** *nt (Aut)* anti-lock braking system; a~**demokratisch** *adj* antidemocratic; ~**faschismus** *m* antifascism; ~**faschist** *m* antifascist; a~**faschistisch** *adj* antifascist; ~**held** *m* antihero; ~**heldin** *f* antiheroine; ~**histamin** *nt* -e antihistamine.

**antik** *adj (Hist)* ancient; *(Comm, col)* antique.

**Antike** *f no pl* antiquity. **die Kunst der** ~ the art of the ancient world.

**Anti-:** ~**kommunismus** *m* anticommunism; ~**körper** *m (Med)* antibody.

**Antillen** *pl* **die** ~ the Antilles *pl.*

**Antilope** *f* -n antelope.

**Anti-:** ~**pathie** *f* antipathy *(gegen* to*)*; ~**pode** *m (wk)* -n, -n antipodean; **die Engländer sind die** ~**poden Australiens** the English live on the opposite side of the world from Australia.

**antippen** *vt sep* to tap; *Pedal, Bremse* to touch; *(fig) Thema* to touch on.

**Antiquar(in** *f) m* antiquarian *or (von moderneren Büchern)* second-hand bookseller.

**Antiquariat** *nt* antiquarian *or (modernerer Bücher)* second-hand bookshop *(Brit)* or bookstore *(US)*. **modernes** ~ remainder bookshop *(Brit)* or bookstore *(US)*.

**antiquarisch** *adj* antiquarian; *(von moderneren Büchern)* second-hand. **ein Buch** ~ **kaufen** to buy a book second-hand.

**antiquiert** *adj (pej)* antiquated.

**Antiquität** *f usu pl* antique.

**Antiquitäten-:** ~**geschäft** *nt* antique shop *(Brit)* or store *(US)*; ~**handel** *m* antique business *or* trade; ~**händler** *m* antique dealer.

**Anti-:** ~**(raketen) rakete** *f* anti(-missile)-missile; ~**semit** *m* antisemite; a~**semitisch** *adj* antisemitic; a~**semitismus** *m* antisemitism; a~**septisch** *adj* antiseptic; a~**statisch** *adj* antistatic; ~**teilchen** *nt (Phys)* anti-particle.

**Antiterror-** *in cpds* antiterrorist.

**Antithese** *f* antithesis.

**Antlitz** *nt* **-e** *(poet)* countenance *(liter)*, face.

**Antrag** *m, pl* **Anträge (a)** *(auf +acc for)* application; *(Gesuch auch)* request; *(Formular)* application form. **einen ~ auf etw** *(acc)* **stellen** to make an application for sth. **(b)** *(Jur)* petition; *(bei Gericht)* claim. **einen ~ auf etw** *(acc)* **stellen** to file a petition/claim for sth. **(c)** *(Parl)* motion.

**antragen** *vt sep irreg (geh)* **jdm etw ~** to offer sb sth.

**Antragsformular** *nt* application form.

**Antragsteller(in** *f)* *m* - applicant; *(für Beihilfe)* claimant.

**antreffen** *vt sep irreg* to find; *Situation auch* to meet. **er ist schwer anzutreffen** it's difficult to catch him in; **ich habe ihn in guter Laune angetroffen** I found him in a good mood.

**antreiben** *vt* **(a)** *(vorwärtstreiben)* *Tiere, Gefangene* to drive; *(fig)* to urge. **jdn zur Eile/Arbeit ~** to urge sb to hurry up/to work; **ich lasse mich nicht ~** I won't be pushed. **(b)** *(bewegen)* *Rad etc* to drive; *(mit Motor auch)* to power.

**Antreiber** *m (pej)* slave-driver *(pej)*.

**antreten** *sep irreg* **1** *vt Reise, Strafe* to begin; *Stellung, Amt* to take up; *Erbe, Erbschaft* to come into. **den Beweis ~, daß ...** to prove that ...; **seine Lehrzeit ~** to start one's apprenticeship. **2** *vi aux sein* **(a)** *(sich aufstellen)* to line up; *(Mil)* to fall in. **(b)** *(erscheinen)* to assemble; *(bei einer Stellung)* to start; *(zum Dienst)* to report. **(c)** *(zum Wettkampf)* to compete.

**Antrieb** *m* **(a)** impetus *no pl*; *(innerer)* drive. **aus eigenem ~** on one's own initiative, off one's own bat *(col)*. **(b)** *(Triebkraft)* drive. **Auto mit elektrischem ~** electrically driven *or* powered car.

**Antriebs-:** **~kraft** *f (Tech)* power; **~rad** *nt* drive wheel; **~welle** *f* driveshaft.

**antrinken** *vt sep irreg (col)* to start drinking. **sich** *(dat)* **einen (Rausch/Schwips) ~** to get (oneself) drunk/tipsy; **sich** *(dat)* **Mut ~** to give oneself Dutch courage; **eine angetrunkene Flasche** an opened bottle; *siehe* **angetrunken.**

**Antritt** *m no pl (Beginn)* beginning. **bei ~ der Reise** when beginning one's journey; **nach ~ der Stellung** after taking up the post.

**antun** *vt sep irreg* **(a)** *(erweisen)* **jdm (große) Ehre ~** to pay (great) tribute to sb. **(b)** *(zufügen)* **jdm etw ~** to do sth to sb. **sich** *(dat)* **ein Leid ~** to injure oneself; **jdm Schaden/Unrecht ~** to do sb an injury/injustice. **(c)** *(Sympathie erregen)* **es jdm ~** to appeal to sb; **sie hat es ihm angetan** he has fallen for her; *siehe* **angetan.**

**anturnen** ['antœrnən] *sep (col)* **1** *vt (Drogen, Musik)* to turn on *(col)*. **2** *vi* to turn you on *(col)*.

**Antwerpen** *nt* Antwerp.

**Antwort** *f* **-en (a)** answer, reply; *(Lösung, bei Examen)* answer. **sie gab mir keine ~ auf die Frage** she didn't reply to *or* answer my question; **in ~ auf etw** *(acc)* *(form)* in reply to sth; **um umgehende ~ wird gebeten** please reply by return. **(b)** *(Reaktion)* response. **als ~ auf etw** *(acc)* in response to sth.

**antworten** *vti* **(a)** to answer, to reply. **jdm ~** to answer sb, to reply to sb; **was soll ich ihm ~?** what should I tell him?; **mit Ja/Nein ~** to answer yes/no. **(b)** *(reagieren)* to respond *(auf +acc to, mit with)*.

**Antwort-:** **~schein** *m* (international) reply coupon; **~schreiben** *nt* reply, answer.

**anvertrauen*** *sep* **1** *vt* **jdm etw ~** *(übergeben)* to entrust sth to sb *or* sb with sth; *(vertraulich erzählen)* to confide sth to sb. **2** *vr* **sich jdm ~** *(sich mitteilen)* to confide in sb.

**Anverwandte(r)** *mf decl as adj (geh)* relative, rela-

tion.

**anvisieren*** ['anvi-] *vt sep (fig)* to set one's sights on.

**anwachsen** *vi sep irreg aux sein* **(a)** *(festwachsen)* to grow on; *(Pflanze etc)* to take root. **(b)** *(zunehmen)* *(auf +acc to)* to increase, to grow.

**Anwachsen** *nt* increase, growth. **im ~ sein** to be on the increase, to be growing.

**anwählen** *vt sep* to dial; *jdn* to call.

**Anwalt** *m, pl* **Anwälte, Anwältin** *f* **(a)** = **Rechtsanwalt. (b)** *(fig: Fürsprecher)* advocate.

**Anwaltsbüro** *nt* **(a)** lawyer's office. **(b)** *(Firma)* firm of lawyers *or* solicitors *(Brit)*.

**Anwalts-:** **~kammer** *f* professional association of lawyers ≃ Law Society *(Brit)*; **~kosten** *pl* legal expenses *pl*; **~praxis** *f* legal practice; *(Räume)* lawyer's office.

**Anwandlung** *f (Laune)* mood; *(Drang)* impulse. **aus einer ~ heraus** on (an) impulse; **in einer ~ von etw** in a fit of sth.

**anwärmen** *vt sep* to warm up.

**Anwärter(in** *f)* *m (Kandidat)* candidate *(auf +acc for)*; *(Sport)* contender *(auf +acc for)*; *(Thron~)* heir *(auf +acc to)*.

**anweisen** *vt sep irreg* **(a)** *(anleiten)* *Schüler* to instruct; *(befehlen auch)* to order. **(b)** *(zuweisen)* *(jdm etw sb sth)* to allocate; *Zimmer auch* to give. **jdm einen Platz ~** to show sb to a seat. **(c)** *Geld* to transfer. **(d)** *siehe* **angewiesen.**

**Anweisung** *f* **(a)** *(Fin)* payment; *(auf Konto etc)* transfer. **(b)** *(Anordnung)* instruction, order. **(c)** *(Zuweisung)* allocation. **(d)** *(Anleitung)* instructions *pl*.

**anwendbar** *adj Theorie, Regel* applicable *(auf +acc to)*. **das ist in der Praxis nicht ~** that is not practicable.

**anwenden** *vt sep auch irreg* **(a)** *(gebrauchen)* to use *(auf +acc on)*. **(b)** *Theorie, Prinzipien* to apply *(auf +acc to)*; *Erfahrung, Einfluß* to use, to bring to bear *(auf +acc on)*. **sich auf etw** *(acc)* **~ lassen** to be applicable to sth; *siehe* **angewandt.**

**Anwender(in** *f)* *m (esp Comp)* user.

**Anwender-:** *(Comp)* **~programm** *nt* user *or* application program; **~software** *f* user *or* application software.

**Anwendung** *f siehe vt* use; application. **etw zur ~ bringen** *(form)* to use/apply sth.

**Anwendungs-:** **~möglichkeit** *f* possible application; **~vorschrift** *f* instructions *pl* for use.

**anwerben** *vt sep irreg* to recruit *(für to)*.

**Anwerbung** *f* recruitment.

**anwerfen** *vt sep irreg (Tech)* to start up.

**Anwesen** *nt* - *(geh)* estate.

**anwesend** *adj (form)* present. **ich war nicht ganz ~** *(hum col)* I wasn't quite with it *(col)*.

**Anwesende(r)** *mf decl as adj* person present. **die ~n** those present.

**Anwesenheit** *f* presence. **in ~ +gen** *or* **von** in the presence of.

**Anwesenheitsliste** *f* attendance list.

**anwidern** *vt sep* **jdn ~** *(Essen, Anblick)* to make sb feel sick; **es/er widert mich an** I can't stand it/him; *siehe* **angewidert.**

**anwinkeln** *vt sep* to bend.

**Anwohner** *m* - resident. **die ~ des Rheins** the people who live along *or* on the Rhine.

**Anzahl** *f no pl* number. **eine ganze ~** quite a number.

**anzahlen** *vt sep Ware* to pay a deposit on, to make a down payment on. **100 DM ~** to pay 100 marks down *or* as a deposit.

**Anzahlung** f deposit, down payment *(für, auf +acc on)*; *(erste Rate)* first instalment *(Brit) or* installment *(US)*. **eine ~ machen** *or* **leisten** *(form)* to pay a deposit.

**anzapfen** vt sep Faß to broach; *Telefon, elektrische Leitung* to tap. **jdn (um Geld) ~** *(col)* to touch sb (for money) *(col)*; **jdn ~** *(col: Telec)* to tap sb's phone.

**Anzeichen** nt sign; *(Med auch)* symptom. **alle ~ deuten darauf hin, daß ...** all the signs are that ...

**Anzeige** f **(a)** *(bei Behörde)* report *(wegen* of*)*; *(bei Gericht)* legal proceedings pl. **~ gegen jdn/wegen etw erstatten** to report sb/sth (to the police); **jdn/etw zur ~ bringen** *(form)* *(bei Polizei)* to report sb/sth to the police; *(bei Gericht)* to take sb/bring sth to court. **(b)** *(Bekanntgabe)* *(Karte, Brief)* announcement; *(in Zeitung auch)* notice; *(Inserat, Reklame)* advertisement. **(c)** *(~tafel etc, Comp)* display.

**anzeigen** vt sep **(a)** jdn ~ *(bei der Polizei)* to report sb (to the police); *(bei Gericht)* to institute legal proceedings against sb. **(b)** *(bekanntgeben)* Heirat etc to announce. **(c)** *(angeben)* Temperatur, Zeit, Geschwindigkeit to indicate, to show. **(d)** *(Comp)* to display.

**Anzeigen-:** ~**blatt** nt advertiser, free newspaper; ~**kampagne** f advertising campaign; ~**preise** pl advertising rates pl; ~**teil** m advertisement section; ~**werbung** f newspaper and magazine advertising.

**anzeigepflichtig** adj notifiable.

**Anzeiger** m *(Tech)* indicator.

**Anzeigetafel** f indicator board; *(Sport)* scoreboard.

**anzetteln** vt sep to instigate.

**anziehen** sep irreg **1** vt **(a)** *Kleidung* to put on. **sich** *(dat)* **etw ~** to put sth on. **(b)** *(straffen)* to pull (tight); *Bremse (betätigen)* to apply, to put on; *Zügel* to pull; *Schraube* to tighten. **(c)** *(Magnet, fig)* to attract; *Geruch, Feuchtigkeit* to absorb. **sich von jdm/etw angezogen fühlen** to feel attracted to sb/sth. **2** vi **(a)** *(beschleunigen)* to accelerate. **(b)** *(Chess etc)* to make the first move. **(c)** *(Fin: Preise)* to rise. **3** vr **(a)** *(sich kleiden)* to get dressed. **(b)** *(fig: Gegensätze)* to attract each other.

**anziehend** adj *(ansprechend)* attractive.

**Anziehung** f attraction.

**Anziehungskraft** f *(Phys)* force of attraction; *(fig)* attraction, appeal. **eine große ~ auf jdn ausüben** to attract sb strongly.

**Anzug** m, pl **Anzüge** **(a)** *(Herren~)* suit. **(b)** *(das Heranrücken)* approach. **im ~ sein** to be coming; *(Gewitter, Gefahr)* to be in the offing; *(Krankheit)* to be coming on. **(c)** *(Chess etc)* opening move. **Weiß ist als erster im ~** white has first move.

**anzüglich** adj lewd, suggestive. **~ werden** to get personal.

**Anzüglichkeit** f lewdness, suggestiveness. ~**en** lewd *or* suggestive remarks.

**anzünden** vt sep Feuer to light. **das Haus ~** to set fire to the house, to set the house on fire.

**Anzünder** m lighter.

**anzweifeln** vt sep to question, to doubt.

**AOK** [a:|o:'ka:] f **-s** = **Allgemeine Ortskrankenkasse.**

**Aorta** f, pl **Aorten** aorta.

**apart** adj distinctive, unusual; *Mensch, Aussehen, Kleidungsstück auch* striking.

**Apartheid** [a'pa:ɐthait] f no pl apartheid.

**Apartment** [a'partmənt] nt **-s** flat *(Brit)*, apartment *(esp US)*.

**Apathie** f apathy; *(von Patienten)* listlessness.

**Apenninen** pl **die ~** the Apennines pl.

**apathisch** adj apathetic; *Patient* listless.

**Aperitif** m **-s** or **-e** aperitif.

**Apfel** m ≐ apple. **in den sauren ~ beißen** *(fig col)* to grasp the nettle; **etw für einen ~ und ein Ei kaufen** *(col)* to buy sth dirt cheap *(col)* or for a song *(col)*; **der ~ fällt nicht weit vom Stamm** *(Prov)* it's in the blood; like father, like son.

**Apfel-:** ~**baum** m apple tree; ~**blüte** f **(a)** apple blossom; **(b)** *(das Blühen)* blossoming of the apple trees; ~**kompott** nt stewed apples; ~**kuchen** m apple cake; ~**mus** nt apple purée or *(als Beilage)* sauce; ~**presse** f cider press; ~**saft** m apple juice; ~**schimmel** m dapple-grey (horse).

**Apfelsine** f orange.

**Apfel-:** ~**strudel** m apfelstrudel; ~**tasche** f apple turnover; ~**wein** m cider.

**APO, Apo** ['a:po] f no pl *(Hist)* = **außerparlamentarische Opposition** extraparliamentary opposition.

**Apokalypse** f **-n** apocalypse.

**apokalyptisch** adj apocalyptic.

**apolitisch** adj non-political, apolitical.

**Apostel** m - apostle.

**Apostel-:** ~**brief** m epistle; ~**geschichte** f Acts of the Apostles pl.

**Apostroph** m **-e** apostrophe.

**Apotheke** f **-n** dispensing chemist's *(Brit)*, pharmacy *(US)*.

**apothekenpflichtig** adj available only at a chemist's *(Brit)* or pharmacy *(US)*.

**Apotheker(in** f) m - pharmacist, (dispensing) chemist *(Brit)*.

**App.** = **Apparat** *(Telefon)* ext.

**Appalachen** pl **die ~** the Appalachians pl, the Appalachian Mountains pl.

**Apparat** m **-e** **(a)** apparatus no pl, appliance; *(kleineres, technisches, mechanisches Gerät auch)* device, gadget; *(Röntgen~ etc)* machine. **(b)** *(Radio)* radio; *(Fernseher)* set; *(Foto~)* camera. **(c)** *(Telefon)* (tele)phone; *(Anschluß)* extension. **am ~** on the phone; *(als Antwort)* speaking; **wer war am ~?** who did you speak to?; **bleiben Sie am ~!** hold the line. **(d)** *(Personen und Hilfsmittel)* set-up; *(Verwaltungs~, Partei~)* machinery, apparatus; *(technischer etc)* equipment, apparatus.

**Apparatur** f equipment no pl, apparatus no pl.

**Appartement** [aparto'mã:] nt **-s** **(a)** *siehe* **Apartment. (b)** *(Zimmerflucht)* suite.

**Appell** m **-e** **(a)** *(Aufruf)* appeal *(an +acc* to, *zu* for*)*. **einen ~ an jdn richten** to (make an) appeal to sb. **(b)** *(Mil)* roll call. **zum ~ antreten** to line up for roll call.

**appellieren*** vi to appeal *(an +acc* to*)*.

**Appetit** m no pl *(lit, fig)* appetite. **~ auf etw** *(acc)* **haben** to feel like sth; **guten ~!** enjoy your meal; **jdm den ~ verderben** to spoil sb's appetite.

**Appetit-:** **a~anregend** adj Speise etc appetizing; ~**happen** m canapé; **a~lich** adj *(lit, fig)* appetizing; ~**losigkeit** f lack of appetite; ~**zügler** m - appetite suppressant.

**applaudieren*** vti to applaud.

**Applaus** m no pl applause.

**apportieren*** vti to retrieve, to fetch.

**Appretur** f *(Mittel)* finish; *(Tex)* starch; *(Wasserundurchlässigkeit)* waterproofing.

**approbiert** adj Arzt registered, certified.

**Apr.** = **April** Apr.

**Après-Ski** [apre'ʃiː] nt **-s** après-ski.

**Aprikose** f **-n** apricot.

**Aprikosenmarmelade** f apricot jam.

**April** m **-e** April. **~, ~!** April fool!; **der erste ~** April

Fool's Day; **jdn in den ~ schicken** to make an April fool of sb; *siehe* **März**.

**April-:** ~**scherz** *m* April fool's trick; **das ist doch wohl ein** ~**scherz** *(fig)* it's got to be a joke; ~**wetter** *nt* April weather.

**apropos** [apro'po:] *adv* by the way, that reminds me. ~ **Afrika** talking about Africa.

**Aquädukt** *nt* **-e** aqueduct.

**Aqua-:** ~**marin** *nt* **-e** aquamarine; ~**planing** *nt no pl (Aut)* aquaplaning.

**Aquarell** *nt* **-e** watercolour *(Brit)*, watercolor *(US)*.

**Aquarell-:** ~**farbe** *f* watercolour *(Brit)*; watercolor *(US)*; ~**maler** *m* watercolourist *(Brit)*, water colorist *(US)*; ~**malerei** *f* watercolour *(Brit)* or watercolor *(US)* painting.

**Aquarium** *nt* aquarium; *(im Haus)* fish tank.

**Äquator** *m no pl* equator.

**äquatorial** *adj* equatorial.

**Aquavit** [akva'vi:t] *m* **-e** aquavit.

**Äquivalent** [ɛkviva'lɛnt] *nt* **-e** equivalent; *(Ausgleich)* compensation.

**äquivalent** *adj* equivalent.

**Äquivalenz** [ɛkviva'lɛnts] *f* equivalence.

**Ar** *nt or m* **-e** *(Measure)* are *(100 m²)*.

**Ära** *f, pl* **Ären** era. **die ~ Adenauer** the Adenauer era.

**Araber** *m* **-** *(auch Pferd)*, **Araberin** *f* Arab.

**Arabien** [-iən] *nt* Arabia.

**arabisch** *adj* Arab; *Ziffer, Sprache etc* Arabic; *(Geog: Meer, Wüste)* Arabian. **die A~e Halbinsel** the Arabian Peninsula, Arabia.

**Arabisch(e)** *nt* Arabic; *siehe* **Deutsch(e)**.

**Arbeit** *f* **(a)** work; *(~sstelle, Aufgabe)* job; *(Pol, Econ, ~skosten)* labour *(Brit)*, labor *(US)*. ~ **und Kapital** capital and labour; **Tag der ~** Labour Day; **die ~en an der Autobahn** the work on the motorway; **viel ~ machen** to be a lot of work *(jdm for sb)*; **das ist/ kostet viel ~** it's a lot of work *or* a big job; **an** *or* **bei der ~ sein** to be working; **sich an die ~ machen**, **an die ~ gehen** to get down to work, to start working; **an die ~!** to work!; **etw ist in ~** work on sth is in progress; **erst die ~, dann das Vergnügen** *(prov)* business before pleasure *(prov)*; **ganze** *or* **gründliche ~ leisten** *(lit, fig iro)* to do a good job. **(b)** *no pl (Mühe)* trouble, bother. **jdm ~ machen** to put sb to trouble; **machen Sie sich keine ~!** don't go to any trouble *or* bother; **einer (geregelten) ~ nachgehen** to have a (steady) job; **ohne ~ sein** to be out of work; **zur ~ gehen/von der ~ kommen** to go to/ come back from work; **seine ~ besteht darin, zu ...** his job is to ...
**(c)** *(Produkt)* work; *(handwerkliche)* piece of work; *(Prüfungs~)* (examination) paper; *(wissenschaftliche)* paper; *(Sch)* test. ~**en korrigieren** to mark test papers; **eine ~ schreiben/schreiben lassen** to do/set a test.

**arbeiten 1** *vi* to work *(an +dat on)*. **die Zeit arbeitet für/gegen uns** time is on our side/against us; **er arbeitet für zwei** *(col)* he does the work of two; **die Anlage arbeitet elektrisch/mit Kohle** the plant runs on electricity/coal; **bei einer Firma/Zeitung ~** to work for a firm/newspaper; **die ~de Bevölkerung** the working population. **2** *vr* **(a) sich zu Tode ~** to work oneself to death. **(b)** *(sich fortbewegen)* to work oneself *(in +acc into, durch through, zu to)*. **sich nach oben/an die Spitze ~** *(fig)* to work one's way up/to the top. **(c)** *impers* **es arbeitet sich gut/schlecht** you can/can't work well.

**Arbeiter(in** *f***)** *m* **-** worker; *(im Gegensatz zum Angestellten)* blue-collar worker; *(auf Bau, Bauernhof)* labourer *(Brit)*, laborer *(US)*; *(bei Straßenbau, im*

*Haus)* workman. ~ **und** ~**innen** male and female workers.

**Arbeiter-:** ~**bewegung** *f* labour *(Brit)* or labor *(US)* movement; ~**familie** *f* working-class family; ~**führer** *m (Pol)* leader of the working classes; ~**gewerkschaft** *f* blue-collar (trade) union, labor union *(US)*; ~**jugend** *f* young workers *pl*; ~**kind** *nt* child from a working-class family; ~**klasse** *f* working class(es *pl*); ~**lied** *nt* workers' song; ~**partei** *f* workers' party; ~**schaft** *f* workforce; ~**-und-Bauern-Staat** *m (DDR)* workers' and peasants' state; ~**unruhen** *pl* unrest among the workers; ~**viertel** *nt* working-class area; ~**wohlfahrt** *f* workers' welfare association.

**Arbeitgeber(in** *f***)** *m* employer.

**Arbeitgeber-:** ~**anteil** *m* employer's contribution; ~**verband** *m* employers' federation.

**Arbeitnehmer(in** *f***)** *m* employee.

**Arbeitnehmer-:** ~**anteil** *m* employee's contribution; ~**schaft** *f* employees *pl*.

**Arbeits|ablauf** *m* work routine; *(von Fabrik)* production *no art*.

**arbeitsam** *adj* industrious, hard-working.

**Arbeitsamkeit** *f* industriousness.

**Arbeits-:** ~**amt** *nt* employment exchange, job centre *(Brit)*; ~**anzug** *m* working suit; ~**atmosphäre** *f* work(ing) atmosphere, work climate; ~**auffassung** *f* attitude to work; ~**aufwand** *m* expenditure of energy; *(Ind)* use of labour *(Brit)* or labor *(US)*; **mit geringem/großem ~aufwand** with little/a lot of work; ~**ausfall** *m* loss of working hours; ~**bedingungen** *pl* working conditions *pl*; ~**beginn** *m* start of work; ~**belastung** *f* workload; ~**beschaffung** *f (Arbeitsplatzbeschaffung)* job creation; ~**beschaffungsmaßnahme** *f (Admin)* job creation scheme; ~**besuch** *m* working visit; ~**eifer** *m* enthusiasm for one's work; ~**erlaubnis** *f* work permit; ~**erleichterung** *f* **das bedeutet eine große ~erleichterung** that makes the work much easier; ~**essen** *nt (esp Pol)* working lunch/dinner; ~**exemplar** *nt* desk copy; **a~fähig** *adj Person* able to work; *(gesund)* fit to work; ~**friede(n)** *m* peaceful labour *(Brit)* or labor *(US)* relations *pl, no art*; ~**gang** *m (Abschnitt)* operation; ~**gebiet** *nt* field of work; ~**gemeinschaft** *f* team; *(Sch, Univ)* study-group; ~**genehmigung** *f* work permit; ~**gericht** *nt* industrial tribunal *(Brit)*, labor court *(US)*; ~**gruppe** *f* team; ~**haltung** *f* attitude to work; **a~intensiv** *adj* labour-intensive *(Brit)*, labor-intensive *(US)*; ~**kampf** *m* industrial action; ~**kleidung** *f* working clothes *pl*; ~**klima** *nt* work climate, work(ing) atmosphere; ~**kollege** *m (bei Angestellten etc)* colleague; *(bei Arbeitern)* fellow worker, workmate; ~**kosten** *pl* labor *(Brit)* or labour *(US)* costs *pl*; ~**kraft** *f* **(a)** *no pl* capacity for work; **seine ~kraft verkaufen** to sell one's labour *(Brit)* or labor *(US)*; **(b)** *(Arbeiter)* worker; ~**kräftemangel** *m* labour shortage; ~**kreis** *m* = ~**gemeinschaft**; ~**lager** *nt* labour *(Brit)* or labor *(US)* camp; ~**leistung** *f (quantitativ)* output; *(qualitativ)* performance; ~**lohn** *m* wages *pl*.

**arbeitslos** *adj* unemployed, out of work. ~ **werden** to lose one's job.

**Arbeitslosen-:** ~**geld** *nt* unemployment benefit; ~**hilfe** *f* supplementary benefit; ~**quote** *f* unemployment rate; ~**unterstützung** *f* unemployment benefit, dole money *(Brit col)*; ~**versicherung** *f* compulsory insurance against unemployment; ~**zahlen** *pl*, ~**ziffer** *f* unemployment figures *pl*.

**Arbeitslose(r)** *mf decl as adj* unemployed person/ man/woman *etc*. **die ~n** the unemployed; **die Zahl**

der ~n the number of unemployed *or* of people out of work.

**Arbeitslosigkeit** *f* unemployment.

**Arbeits-**: ~**mangel** *m* lack of work; ~**markt** *m* job market; ~**material** *nt* material for one's work; *(Sch)* teaching aids *pl*; ~**methode** *f* method of working; ~**minister** *m* Employment Secretary *(Brit)*, Labor Secretary *(US)*; ~**mittel** *nt siehe* ~**material**; ~**moral** *f* attitude to work; *(in Betrieb)* work climate; ~**niederlegung** *f* walkout; ~**papiere** *pl* cards, employment papers *(form) pl*.

**arbeitsparend** *adj* labour-saving *(Brit)*, labor-saving *(US)*.

**Arbeits**: ~ **platte** *f* worktop; ~**platz** *m* (a) *(~stätte)* place of work, workplace; *(im Büro)* workspace; *(im Großraumbüro)* work station; **am** ~**platz** at work; **(b)** *(Stelle)* job; **freie** ~**plätze** vacancies.

**Arbeitsplatz-**: ~**computer** *m* personal computer; ~**garantie** *f* job security; ~**sicherung** *f* safeguarding of jobs; ~**teilung** *f* job sharing.

**Arbeits-**: ~**probe** *f* sample of one's work; ~**prozeß** *m* work process; ~**raum** *m* workroom; *(für geistige Arbeit)* study; ~**recht** *nt* industrial law; ~**rhythmus** *m* work rhythm; **a**~**scheu** *adj* work-shy; ~**schluß** *m* end of work; **nach** ~**schluß** after work; ~**schutz** *m* maintenance of industrial health and safety standards; **a**~**sparend** *adj* = **arbeitsparend**; ~**speicher** *m (Comp)* main memory; ~**stätte** *f* place of work; ~**stelle** *f* (a) place of work; **(b)** *(Stellung)* job; ~**stil** *m* work-style, style of working; ~**suche** *f* search for work *or* a job; **auf** ~**suche sein** to be looking for a job, to be job-hunting; ~**tag** *m* workday; ~**takt** *m (Tech)* **(a)** *(von Motor)* power stroke; **(b)** *(bei Fließbandarbeit)* time for an/the operation, phase time; ~**tätigkeit** *f* work; ~**technik** *f* technique of working; ~**teilung** *f* division of labour *(Brit)* or labor *(US)*; ~**tempo** *nt* rate of work; ~**tier** *nt (fig)* glutton for work; *(Geistesarbeiter auch)* workaholic *(col)*; ~**tisch** *m* work-table; *(für geistige Arbeit)* desk; *(für handwerkliche Arbeit)* workbench; ~**überlastung** *f (von Mensch)* overworking.

**Arbeit-**: ~**suche** *f* = **Arbeitssuche**; ~**suchende(r)** *mf decl as adj* person *etc* looking for a job.

**Arbeits-**: **a**~**unfähig** *adj* unable to work; *(krank)* unfit for work; ~**unfähigkeit** *f siehe adj* inability to work; unfitness for work; ~**unfall** *m* industrial accident; **a**~**unwillig** *adj* reluctant *or* unwilling to work; ~**verhältnis** *nt* employee-employer relationship; **ein** ~**verhältnis eingehen** to enter employment; ~**verhältnisse** *pl* working conditions *pl*; ~**vermittlung** *f (Amt)* employment exchange; *(privat)* employment agency; ~**vertrag** *m* contract of employment; ~**vorgang** *m* work process; ~**weise** *f (Praxis)* way *or* method of working; *(von Maschine)* mode of operation; **die** ~**weise dieser Maschine** the way this machine works; ~**welt** *f* working world; **die industrielle** ~**welt** the world of industry; ~**willig** *adj* willing to work; ~**wut** *f* work mania; **ihn hat die** ~**wut gepackt** he's turned into a workaholic; **a**~**wütig** *adj* ~**wütig sein** to be a workaholic *(col)*; ~**zeit** *f* working hours *pl*; **während der** ~**zeit** in *or* during working hours; **5 Stunden** ~**zeit** 5 hours' labour; ~**zeitverkürzung** *f* reduction in working hours; ~**zeugnis** *nt* reference from one's employer; ~**zimmer** *nt* study.

**archaisch** *adj* archaic.

**Archäologe** *m*, **Archäologin** *f* archaeologist.

**Archäologie** *f* archaeology.

**archäologisch** *adj* archaeological.

**Arche** *f* **-n die** ~ **Noah** Noah's Ark.

**Archipel** *m* **-e** archipelago.

**Architekt(in** *f) m (wk)* **-en, -en** *(lit, fig)* architect.

**architektonisch** *adj* architectural.

**Architektur** *f* architecture *(auch Comp)*.

**Archiv** *nt* archives *pl*; *(Comp)* archive.

**Archivar(in** *f)* [-'va:ɐ, -'va:rɪn] *m* archivist.

**archivieren*** [-'vi:rən] *vt* to archive.

**ARD** ['a:ɛr'de:] *f no pl* = **Arbeitsgemeinschaft der Rundfunkanstalten Deutschlands** *German Broadcasting Association.*

**Areal** *nt* **-e** area.

**Arena** *f, pl* **Arenen** *(lit, fig)* arena; *(Zirkus~, Stierkampf~)* ring.

**arg** *comp* ⁼**er**, *superl* ⁼**ste(r, s)** *or (adv)* **am** ⁼**sten 1** *adj (esp S Ger) (schlimm)* bad; **Wetter auch, Gestank, Katastrophe, Verlust, Blamage, Verlegenheit, Schicksal** terrible; **Enttäuschung** bitter. **sein** ⁓**ster Feind** his worst enemy; **etw liegt im** ~**en** sth is in a bad way. **2** *adv* **(a)** *(schlimm)* badly. **er hat sich** ~ **vertan** *(col)* he's made a bad mistake; **es zu** ~ **treiben** to go too far. **(b)** *(col: sehr)* very.

**Argentinien** [-iən] *nt* Argentina, the Argentine.

**Argentinier(in** *f)* [-iɐ, -iərɪn] *m* - Argentinian.

**argentinisch** *adj* Argentine, Argentinian.

**Ärger** *m no pl* **(a)** annoyance; *(stärker)* anger. **wenn ihn der** ~ **packt** when he gets annoyed/angry. **(b)** *(Unannehmlichkeiten)* trouble; *(Erlebnisse auch)* bother. **jdm** ~ **machen** *or* **bereiten** to cause sb a lot of trouble *or* bother; ~ **bekommen** *or* **kriegen** *(col)* to get into trouble; **mach keinen** ~! *(col)* don't cause any trouble!; **so ein** ~! *(col)* what a nuisance!; **es gibt** ~ *(col)* there'll be trouble.

**ärgerlich** *adj* **(a)** *(verärgert)* annoyed, cross. ~ **über** *or* **auf jdn/über etw** *(acc)* **sein** to be annoyed with sb/about sth. **(b)** *(unangenehm)* annoying; *(stärker)* maddening, infuriating.

**ärgern 1** *vt* to annoy, to irritate; *(stärker)* to make angry. **jdn krank/zu Tode** ~ to drive sb mad. **2** *vr (ärgerlich sein/werden)* to be/get annoyed; *(stärker)* to be/get angry *(über jdn/etw* with sb/about sth*).* **über so etwas könnte ich mich krank/zu Tode** ~ that sort of thing drives me mad.

**Ärgernis** *nt* **(a)** *no pl (Anstoß)* offence, outrage. **wegen Erregung öffentlichen** ~**ses angeklagt werden** to be charged with offending public decency. **(b)** *(etwas Anstößiges)* outrage; *(etwas Ärgerliches)* terrible nuisance.

**Arglist** *f no pl (Hinterlist)* cunning, craftiness; *(Boshaftigkeit)* malice; *(Jur)* fraud.

**arglistig** *adj* cunning, crafty; *(böswillig)* malicious. ~**e Täuschung** fraud.

**arglos** *adj* innocent; *(ohne Täuschungsabsicht)* guileless.

**Arglosigkeit** *f siehe adj* innocence; guilelessness.

**Argument** *nt* argument.

**Argumentation** *f* argument; *(Darlegung)* argumentation *no pl*.

**argumentieren*** *vi* to argue.

**Argus|auge** *nt (geh)* eagle eye. **mit** ~**n** eagle-eyed.

**Argwohn** *m no pl* suspicion. **jds** ~ **erregen** to arouse sb's suspicions; ~ **gegen jdn hegen** to be suspicious of sb; **mit** *or* **voller** ~ suspiciously.

**argwöhnen** *vt insep (geh)* to suspect.

**argwöhnisch** *adj* suspicious.

**Arie** [-iə] *f (Mus)* aria.

**Aristokrat(in** *f) m (wk)* **-en, -en** aristocrat.

**Aristokratie** *f* aristocracy.

**aristokratisch** *adj* aristocratic.

**Aristoteles** *m* - Aristotle.

**Arithmetik** *f no pl* arithmetic.

**arithmetisch** *adj* arithmetic(al).

**Arkade** f *(Bogen)* arch(way). **~n** pl *(Bogengang)* arcade.
**Arktis** f *no pl* Arctic.
**arktisch** *adj* arctic.
**arm** *adj, comp* ⁼**er**, *superl* ⁼**ste(r, s)** *or (adv)* **am** ⁼**sten** *(lit, fig)* poor. **die A~en** the poor *pl*; **du machst mich noch mal ~** *(col)* you'll be the ruin of me; **~ an etw** *(dat)* **sein** to be somewhat lacking in sth; **der Boden ist ~ an Nährstoffen** the soil is poor in nutrients; **~ an Vitaminen** low in vitamins; **um jdn/etw ~er werden/sein** to lose/have lost sb/sth; **um 55 Mark ~er sein** to be 55 marks worse off *or* poorer; **ach, du/Sie A~er!** *(iro)* you poor thing!; **~ dran sein** *(col)* to have a hard time of it.
**Arm** m **-e** *(Anat, Tech, fig)* arm; *(Fluß~ auch)* branch; *(Ärmel)* sleeve. **~ in ~** arm in arm; **jdn im ~ or in den ~en halten** to hold sb in one's arms; **jdn in die ~e nehmen** to take sb in one's arms; **sich in den ~en liegen** to lie in each other's arms; **jdn auf den ~ nehmen** *(fig col)* to pull sb's leg *(col)*; **jdm unter die ~e greifen** *(fig)* to help sb out; **jdn mit offenen ~en empfangen** *(fig)* to welcome sb with open arms; **der ~ des Gesetzes** the long arm of the law; **einen langen/den längeren ~ haben** *(fig)* to have a lot of/more pull *(col) or* influence.
**Armada** f, *pl* **-s** *or* **Armaden** *(lit, fig)* armada.
**Armaturen** *pl (Tech) (Hahn, Leitung etc)* fittings; *(Instrument)* instruments.
**Armaturenbrett** *nt* instrument panel; *(Aut)* dashboard.
**Arm-:** **~band** *nt* bracelet; *(von Uhr)* (watch)strap; **~banduhr** f wristwatch; **~beuge** f **(a)** inside of one's elbow; **(b)** *(Sport)* arm bend; **~binde** f armband; *(Med)* sling; **~bruch** m *(Med)* broken arm; **~brust** f crossbow.
**Armee** f **-n** [-e:ən] *(Mil, fig)* army; *(Gesamtheit der Streitkräfte)* (armed) forces pl.
**Ärmel** m **-** sleeve. **sich** *(dat)* **die ~ hochkrempeln** *(lit, fig)* to roll up one's sleeves; **etw aus dem ~ schütteln** to produce sth just like that.
**Ärmelkanal** m (English) Channel.
**ärmellos** *adj* sleeveless.
**Armenhaus** *nt (old)* poorhouse.
**Armenien** [-iən] *nt* Armenia.
**Armenier(in** f) [-iɐ, -iərin] m Armenian.
**armenisch** *adj* Armenian.
**Armen-:~recht** *nt (Jur)* legal aid; **~viertel** *nt* poor district or quarter.
**Arm-:** **~gelenk** *nt* elbow joint; **a~lang** *adj* arm-length; **~lehne** f armrest; **~leuchter** m *(pej col:Dummkopf)* twit *(Brit col)*, fool; *(euph: Arschloch)* bastard *(col!)*.
**ärmlich** *adj (lit, fig)* poor; *Kleidung, Wohnung* shabby; *Verhältnisse* humble. **einen ~en Eindruck machen** to look poor/shabby; **aus ~en Verhältnissen** from a poor family.
**armselig** *adj (dürftig)* miserable; *(mitleiderregend)* pathetic, pitiful; *Summe, Ausrede* paltry.
**Armsessel** m, **Armstuhl** *(old)* m armchair.
**Armut** f *no pl (lit, fig)* poverty. **charakterliche ~** lack of character; **geistige ~** intellectual poverty.
**Armuts-:** **~falle** f poverty trap; **~grenze** f *no pl* poverty line; **~zeugnis** *nt (fig)* **jdm/sich ein ~zeugnis ausstellen** to show sb's/one's shortcomings; **das ist ein ~zeugnis für ihn** that shows him up.
**Aroma** *nt, pl* **Aromen** *or* **-s** **(a)** *(Geruch)* aroma. **(b)** *(Geschmack)* flavour *(Brit)*, flavor *(US)*. **(c)** *no pl* flavouring *(Brit)*, flavoring *(US)*.
**Aromatherapie** f aromatherapy.
**aromatisch** *adj* aromatic; *(wohlschmeckend)* sa-

voury *(Brit)*, savory *(US)*.
**Arrangement** [arãʒə'mãː] *nt* **-s** arrangement.
**arrangieren*** [arã'ʒiːrən] **1** *vti* to arrange *(jdm* for sb*)*. **2** *vr* **sich mit jdm ~** to come to an arrangement with sb; **sich mit etw ~** to come to terms with sth.
**Arrest** m **-s** *(Mil, Jur)* detention.
**Arrestzelle** f detention cell.
**arretieren*** *vt (Tech)* to lock (in place).
**Arretierung** f **(a)** locking. **(b)** *(Vorrichtung)* locking mechanism.
**arriviert** [-'viːɐt] *adj* successful; *(pej)* upstart.
**arrogant** *adj* arrogant.
**Arroganz** f *no pl* arrogance.
**Arsch** m ⁼**e** *(col!)* arse *(col!)*, ass *(US col!)*. **auf den ~ fallen** *(fig: scheitern)* to fall flat on one's face; **leck mich am ~!** *(laß mich in Ruhe)* get stuffed! *(col)*, fuck off! *(col!!)*; **jdm in den ~ kriechen** to lick sb's arse *(col!)*; **am ~ der Welt** *(col)* in the back of beyond; **im or am ~ sein** to be screwed up *(col)*.
**Arsch-:** **~backe** f *(col!)* buttock, cheek; **~kriecher** m *(col!)* arse-licker *(col!)*; **~loch** *nt (col!) (Mensch)* bastard *(col!)*; *(Dummkopf)* stupid bastard *(col!)*.
**Arsen** *nt no pl* arsenic.
**Arsenal** *nt* **-e** *(lit, fig)* arsenal.
**Art** f **-en** **(a)** kind, sort, type; *(von Pflanze, Insekt etc auch)* variety; *(Biol)* species. **diese ~ Leute/Buch** that kind or sort of person/book; **ein Heuchler schlimmster ~** the worst type or kind of hypocrite; **einzig in seiner ~ sein** to be one of a kind, to be unique; **aus der ~ schlagen** not to take after anyone in the family; *(pej)* to be the black sheep of the family. **(b)** *(Methode)* way; *(Stil)* style. **die einfachste ~, etw zu tun** the simplest way to do sth or of doing sth; **auf diese ~ und Weise** in this way; **es entspricht nicht meiner ~** it's not my nature; **das ist eigentlich nicht seine ~** it's not like him; **Schnitzel nach ~ des Hauses** schnitzel à la maison. **(c)** *(Benehmen)* behaviour *(Brit)*, behavior *(US)*. **das ist doch keine ~!** that's no way to behave!
**Art. = Artikel.**
**arten** *vi aux sein (geh)* **nach jdm ~** to take after sb; *siehe* **geartet**.
**Artenschutz** m protection of endangered species.
**Arterie** [-iə] f artery.
**arteriell** *adj* arterial.
**Arterienverkalkung** [-iən-] f *(col)* hardening of the arteries.
**Arteriosklerose** f arteriosclerosis.
**Art-:** **~genosse** m animal/plant of the same species; *(Mensch)* person of the same type; **a~gleich** *adj* of the same species; *Mensch* of the same type.
**Arthritis** f, *pl* **Arthritiden** arthritis.
**arthritisch** *adj* arthritic.
**Arthrose** f **-n** arthrosis.
**artig** *adj* Kind, Hund etc good, well-behaved *no adv*. **sei schön ~** be a good boy/dog *etc*!, be good!
**Artikel** m **-** *(auch Gram)* article; *(Comm auch)* item.
**artikulieren*** *vti* to articulate.
**Artillerie** f artillery.
**Artillerist** m artilleryman.
**Artischocke** f **-n** (globe) artichoke.
**Artist(in** f) m (circus/variety) artiste or performer.
**Artistik** f artistry; *(Zirkus-, Varietékunst)* circus/variety performing.
**artistisch** *adj* **(a)** sein **~es Können** his ability as a performer; **eine ~e Glanzleistung** a feat of circus etc artistry. **(b)** *(geschickt)* masterly *no adv*. **(c)** *(formalkünstlerisch)* artistic.
**Artus** m **-** *(Hist, Myth)* (King) Arthur.
**Arznei** f *(lit, fig)* medicine.

**Arzneimittel** *nt* medicine, drug.

**Arzt** *m* ⁼e doctor. **praktischer** ~ general practitioner, GP *abbr.*

**Ärzte-:** ~**kammer** ≈ General Medical Council *(Brit)*, State Medical Board of Registration *(US)*; ~**schaft** *f* medical profession; ~**zentrum** *nt* health centre *(Brit)* or center *(US)*.

**Arzthelferin** *f* (doctor's) receptionist; nurse.

**Ärztin** *f* woman doctor; *siehe* **Arzt.**

**ärztlich** *adj* medical. **er ließ sich** ~ **behandeln** he got medical treatment.

**Arzt-:** ~**praxis** *f* doctor's practice; *(Räume)* doctor's surgery *(Brit)* or office *(US)*; ~**rechnung** *f* doctor's bill.

**As¹** *nt* **-se** *(lit, fig)* ace.

**As²** *nt (Mus)* A flat.

**Asbest** *nt no pl* asbestos.

**aschblond** *adj* ashblonde.

**Asche** *f* ash(es *pl*); *(von Zigarette, Vulkan)* ash; *(sterbliche Überreste)* ashes *pl.* **zu** ~ **werden** to turn to dust.

**Aschen-:** ~**bahn** *f* cinder track; ~**becher** *m* ashtray; ~**brödel**, ~**puttel** *nt - (Liter, fig)* Cinderella.

**Aschermittwoch** *m* Ash Wednesday.

**asch-:** ~**fahl** *adj* ashen; ~**grau** *adj* ash-grey.

**äsen** *(Hunt) vir* to graze, to browse.

**Aserbaidschan** *nt* Azerbaijan.

**Aserbaidschane** *m (wk)* **-n, -n, Aserbaidschanin** *f* Azerbaijani.

**aserbaidschanisch** *adj* Azerbaijani.

**Asiat(in** *f) m (wk)* **-en, -en** Asian.

**asiatisch** *adj* Asian, Asiatic.

**Asien** [-iən] *nt* Asia.

**Asket** *m (wk)* **-en, -en** ascetic.

**asketisch** *adj* ascetic.

**asozial** *adj* antisocial.

**Asoziale(r)** *mf decl as adj (pej)* antisocial man/ woman *etc.* ~ *pl* antisocial elements.

**Aspekt** *m* **-e** aspect. **unter diesem** ~ **betrachtet** looking at it from this aspect; **einen neuen** ~ **bekommen** to take on a different complexion.

**Asphalt** *m* **-e** asphalt.

**Asphaltdecke** *f* asphalt surface.

**asphaltieren*** *vt* to asphalt, to tarmac.

**asphaltiert** *adj* asphalt, tarmac; surfaced.

**Asphaltstraße** *f* asphalt *or* tarred *or* surfaced road.

**Aspik** *m* **-e** aspic.

**Aspirant(in** *f) m (geh)* candidate *(auf +acc* for*)*.

**aß** *pret of* **essen.**

**Ass.** = (a) **Assessor(in).** (b) **Assistent(in)** asst.

**Assel** *f* **-n** woodlouse.

**Assemblersprache** *f (Comp)* assembly language.

**Assessor(in** *f) m graduate civil servant who has completed his/her traineeship.*

**Assistent(in** *f)* [-st-] *m* assistant.

**Assistenz** [-st-] *f* assistance.

**Assistenz|arzt** [-st-] *m* houseman *(Brit)*, intern *(US)*.

**assistieren*** [-st-] *vi* to assist *(jdm* sb*)*.

**Assoziation** *f* association.

**assoziieren*** *vt (geh)* to associate. **mit Grün assoziiere ich Ruhe** I associate green with peace.

**Ast** *m* ⁼e (a) branch. **den** ~ **absägen, auf dem man sitzt** *(fig)* to dig one's own grave. (b) *(im Holz)* knot. (c) *(col)* **sich** *(dat)* **einen** ~ **lachen** to double up (with laughter).

**AStA** ['asta] *m, pl* **Asten** *(Univ)* = **Allgemeiner Studentenausschuß** ≈ student union.

**Aster** *f* **-n** aster, Michaelmas daisy.

**Astgabel** *f* fork (in a branch).

**Ästhet(in** *f) m (wk)* **-en, -en** aesthete *(Brit)*, esthete

*(US)*.

**Ästhetik** *f* aesthetics *(Brit)*, esthetics *(US)* sing; *(eines Bildes)* aesthetics *pl*; *(Schönheitssinn)* aesthetic sense.

**ästhetisch** *adj* aesthetic *(Brit)*, esthetic *(US)*.

**Asthma** *nt no pl* asthma.

**Asthmatiker(in** *f) m* - asthmatic.

**Astloch** *nt* knothole.

**astral** *adj* astral.

**astrein** *adj (col)* (a) *(fig col: moralisch einwandfrei)* straight *(col)*, on the level *(col)*. (b) *(fig: echt)* genuine. (c) *(prima)* fantastic.

**Astro-:** ~**loge** *m*, ~**login** *f* astrologer; ~**logie** *f* astrology; **a**~**logisch** *adj* astrological; ~**naut(in** *f) m (wk)* **-en, -en** astronaut; ~**nom(in** *f) m* astronomer; ~**nomie** *f* astronomy; **a**~**nomisch** *adj (lit)* astronomical; *(fig auch)* astronomic; ~**physik** *f* astrophysics *sing*; ~**physiker(in** *f) m* astrophysicist.

**ASU** ['asu] *f no pl* = **Abgassonderuntersuchung**.

**ASW** [aː'ɛs'veː] *no art, no pl* = **außersinnliche Wahrnehmung** ESP.

**Asyl** *nt* **-e** *(politisch)* (political) asylum *no art*; *(geh: Schutz)* sanctuary *no art.* **um** ~ **bitten** to ask for (political) asylum; **jdm** ~ **gewähren** to grant sb (political) asylum.

**Asylant(in** *f) m* person seeking (political) asylum, asylum-seeker.

**Asyl-:** ~**antrag** *m* application for (political) asylum; ~**bewerber(in** *f) m* applicant for (political) asylum; ~**recht** *nt (Pol)* right of (political) asylum.

**asymmetrisch** *adj* asymmetrical.

**asynchron** [-kroːn] *adj* asynchronous *(form, Comp)*.

**at** ['aːˈteː] *(Phys)* = **Atmosphäre**.

**A.T.** = **Altes Testament** OT.

**Atelier** [-'lieː] *nt* **-s** studio.

**Atelierwohnung** *f* studio apartment.

**Atem** *m no pl* (a) *(das Atmen)* breathing. **den** ~ **anhalten** *(lit, fig)* to hold one's breath; **mit angehaltenem** ~ *(lit)* holding one's breath; *(fig)* with bated breath; **wieder zu** ~ **kommen** to get one's breath back; **den längeren** ~ **haben** *(fig)* to have more staying power; **jdn in** ~ **halten** to keep sb in suspense *or* on tenterhooks; **das verschlug mir den** ~ **it** took my breath away. (b) *(lit, fig:* ~**luft)* breath. ~ **holen** *or* **schöpfen** *(lit)* to take a breath; *(fig)* to get one's breath back.

**Atem-:** **a**~**beraubend** *adj* breathtaking; ~**beschwerden** *pl* trouble in breathing; **a**~**los** *adj (lit, fig)* breathless; ~**losigkeit** *f* breathlessness; ~**not** *f* difficulty in breathing; ~**pause** *f (fig)* breathing space; **eine** ~**pause einlegen/brauchen** to take/need a breather; ~**wege** *pl (Anat)* respiratory tracts *pl*; ~**zug** *m* breath; **in einem/im selben** ~**zug** *(fig)* in one/the same breath.

**Atheismus** *m* atheism.

**Atheist(in** *f) m* atheist.

**atheistisch** *adj* atheist(ic).

**Athen** *nt* Athens.

**Athener(in** *f) m* Athenian.

**athenisch** *adj* Athenian.

**Äther** *m no pl* (a) ether. (b) *(Rad)* air.

**ätherisch** *adj (Liter, Chem)* ethereal.

**Ätherwellen** *pl (Rad)* radio waves *pl.*

**Äthiopien** [ɛ'tioːpiən] *nt* Ethiopia.

**Äthiopier(in** *f) m* [-piɐ, -iɐrin] - Ethiopian.

**äthiopisch** *adj* Ethiopian.

**Athlet(in** *f) m (wk)* **-en, -en** athlete.

**Athletik** *f no pl* athletics *sing.*

**athletisch** *adj* athletic.

**Atlantik** *m* Atlantic.

**atlantisch** *adj* Atlantic. **der A~e Ozean** the Atlantic Ocean.

**Atlas¹** *m, pl* **Atlanten** *or* **-se** atlas.

**Atlas²** *m* - *(Geog)* Atlas Mountains *pl*.

**atmen** *vi* to breathe. **frei ~** *(fig)* to breathe freely.

**Atmosphäre** *f* **-n** *(Phys, fig)* atmosphere.

**atmosphärisch** *adj* atmospheric. **~e Störungen** atmospherics *pl*.

**Atmung** *f no pl* breathing; *(Med)* respiration.

**Atmungs|organe** *pl* respiratory organs *pl*.

**Atoll** *nt* **-e** atoll.

**Atom** *nt* **-e** atom.

**Atom-** *in cpds* atomic; *siehe auch* **Kern-**; **~angriff** *m* nuclear attack; **~antrieb** *m* nuclear propulsion; **ein U-Boot mit ~antrieb** a nuclear-powered submarine.

**atomar** *adj* atomic, nuclear; *Struktur* atomic; *Drohung* nuclear.

**Atom-:** **~bombe** *f* atomic *or* atom bomb; **a~bombensicher** *adj* atomic *or* nuclear blast-proof; **~bombenversuch** *m* atomic *or* nuclear test; **~bunker** *m* atomic *or* nuclear blast-proof bunker; **~energie** *f* nuclear energy; **a~getrieben** *adj* nuclear-powered; **~industrie** *f* nuclear industry; **~kern** *m* atomic nucleus; **~kraft** *f* nuclear power *or* energy; **~kraftwerk** *nt* atomic *or* nuclear power station; **~krieg** *m* atomic *or* nuclear war; **~macht** *f* nuclear power; **~meiler** *m* nuclear reactor; **~müll** *m* nuclear *or* radioactive waste; **~physik** *f* nuclear physics *sing*; **~physiker** *m* nuclear physicist; **~pilz** *m* mushroom cloud; **~rakete** *f* nuclear-powered rocket; *(Waffe)* nuclear missile; **~reaktor** *m* atomic *or* nuclear reactor; **~rüstung** *f* nuclear armament; **~spaltung** *f* nuclear fission; **die erste ~spaltung** the first splitting of the atom; **~sprengkopf** *m* atomic *or* nuclear warhead; **~strahlung** *f* nuclear radiation; **~streitmacht** *f* nuclear capability; **~strom** *m* *(col)* electricity generated by nuclear power; **~test** *m* nuclear test; **~teststopp** *m no pl* nuclear test ban; **~-U-Boot** *nt* nuclear submarine; **~waffe** *f* nuclear *or* atomic weapon; **a~waffenfrei** *adj* nuclear-free; **~waffensperrvertrag** *m* nuclear *or* atomic weapons non-proliferation treaty; **~zeitalter** *nt* atomic *or* nuclear age.

**Atrium** *nt* atrium.

**ätsch** *interj (col)* ha-ha.

**Attaché** [ata'ʃeː] *m* **-s** attaché.

**Attacke** *f* **-n** *(Angriff)* attack. **eine ~ gegen jdn/etw reiten** *(fig)* to attack sb/sth.

**attackieren*** *vt (angreifen)* to attack.

**Attentat** [-taːt] *nt* **-e** *(gelungen)* assassination; *(~sversuch)* assassination attempt. **ein ~ auf jdn verüben** to make an attempt on sb's life.

**Attentäter(in** *f)* *m* - *(bei gelungenem Versuch)* assassin; *(bei gescheitertem Versuch)* would-be assassin.

**Attest** *nt* **-e** certificate.

**attestieren*** *vt (form)* to certify.

**Attraktion** *f* attraction.

**attraktiv** *adj* attractive.

**Attraktivität** *f* attractiveness.

**Attrappe** *f* **-n** dummy; *(fig: Schein)* sham. **bei ihr ist alles ~** everything about her is false.

**Attribut** *nt* **-e** *(geh, Gram)* attribute.

**atypisch** *adj (geh)* atypical.

**ätzen** *vti* **(a)** to etch. **(b)** *(Säure)* to corrode.

**ätzend** *adj* **(a)** *(lit)* *Säure* corrosive. **(b)** *Geruch* pungent; *Spott* caustic. **(c)** *(col) (furchtbar)* lousy *(col)*; *(toll)* magic *(col)*.

**au, aua** *interj* ow, ouch.

**Aubergine** [obɛr'ʒiːnə] *f* aubergine, eggplant.

**auch** *adv* **(a)** *(zusätzlich, gleichfalls)* also, too, as well. **~ nicht** not ... either; **das ist ~ nicht richtig** that's not right either; **er kommt — ich ~** he's coming — so am I, me too; **ich mag das nicht — ich ~ nicht** I don't like that — nor *or* neither do I; **nicht nur ..., sondern ~** not only ... but also ...; **~ das noch!** that's all I needed!

**(b)** *(tatsächlich)* too, as well. **du siehst müde aus — das bin ich ~** you look tired — (so) I am; **so ist es ~** (so) it is.

**(c)** *(sogar)* even. **~ wenn du Vorfahrt hast** even if you (do) have right of way; **ohne ~ nur zu fragen** without even asking.

**(d)** *(emph)* **so was Ärgerliches aber ~!** it's really too annoying!; **wozu ~?** whatever for?

**(e)** *(~ immer)* **wie dem ~ sei** be that as it may; **was er ~ sagen mag** whatever he might say; **so schnell er ~ laufen mag** however fast he runs *or* may run, no matter how fast he runs.

**Audienz** *f* audience *(bei* with*)*.

**Audimax** *nt no pl (Univ col)* main lecture hall.

**audiovisuell** *adj* audiovisual.

**Auditorium** *nt* **(a)** *(Hörsaal)* lecture hall. **(b)** *(geh: Zuhörerschaft)* audience.

**Auerhahn** *m* capercaillie.

**Auer|ochse** *m* aurochs.

**Auf** *nt inv*: **das ~ und Ab** the up and down; *(fig)* the ups and downs.

**auf 1** *prep* **(a)** *+dat* on. **~ (der Insel) Skye** on the Isle of Skye; **~ See** at sea; **~ meinem Zimmer** in my room; **~ der Bank/Post/Party** at the bank/post office/party; **mein Geld ist ~ der Bank** my money is in the bank; **~ der Straße** on *or* in the street; **etw ~ der Geige spielen** to play sth on the violin; **~ einem Ohr taub/einem Auge kurzsichtig sein** to be deaf in one ear/short-sighted in one eye; **was hat es damit ~ sich?** what does it mean?; **~ der Fahrt/dem Weg** *etc* on the journey/way *etc*.

**(b)** *+acc* on, onto. **etw ~ etw stellen** to put sth on(to) sth *or* on top of sth; **sich ~ etw setzen/legen** to sit/lie (down) on sth; **er fiel ~ den Rücken** he fell on(to) his back; **etw ~ einen Zettel schreiben** to write sth on a piece of paper; **er ist ~ die Orkneyinseln gefahren** he has gone to the Orkney Islands; **geh mal ~ die Seite** go to the side; **~ sein Zimmer/die Post/eine Party** *etc* **gehen** to go to one's room/the post office/a party *etc*; **~s Gymnasium gehen** to go to the grammar school *(Brit)* or high school *(US)*; **die Uhr ~ 10 stellen** to put the clock to 10; **die Sitzung ~ morgen verschieben** to postpone the meeting until tomorrow.

**(c)** *+acc* **~ 10 km/drei Tage** for 10 km/three days; **~ eine Tasse Kaffee/eine Zigarette(nlänge)** for a cup of coffee/a smoke; **ein Manuskript ~ Fehler prüfen** to check a manuscript for errors; **~ seinen Vorschlag (hin)** at his suggestion; **~ meinen Brief hin** because of *or* on account of my letter.

**(d)** **es geht ~ Weihnachten zu** Christmas is approaching; **er kam ~ mich zu und sagte ...** he came up to me and said ...; **die Nacht (von Montag) ~ Dienstag** Monday night; **~ einen Polizisten kommen 1.000 Bürger** there is one policeman to every 1,000 citizens; **~ den Millimeter/die Sekunde genau** to within one millimetre/second; **~ ein glückliches Gelingen** *etc*! here's to a great success *etc*!; **die Dauer ~ ein Jahr reduzieren** to reduce the duration to one year.

**2** *adv* **(a)** *(offen)* open. **Mund/Fenster ~!** open your mouth/the window. **(b)** *(hinauf)* up. **~ und ab** *or* **nieder** *(geh)* up and down. **(c)** **Helm ~!** helmets on; **ich war die halbe Nacht** ~ I've been up half the night; ~ **nach Chicago!** let's go to Chicago; ~ **geht's!** let's go!; ~ **und davon** up and away, off; ~, **an die Arbeit!** come on, let's get on with it; *siehe* **aufsein.**

**3** *conj (old, liter)* ~ **daß** that *(old, liter).*

**auf|arbeiten** *vt sep* **(a)** *(erneuern)* to refurbish, to do up; *Möbel etc auch* to recondition. **(b)** *(erledigen) Korrespondenz etc* to catch up with. **(c)** *(Phys) Brennelemente* to reprocess.

**Auf|arbeitung** *f siehe vt* refurbishing; reconditioning; catching up; reprocessing.

**auf|atmen** *vi sep (lit, fig)* to breathe *or* heave a sigh of relief. **ein A~** a sigh of relief.

**aufbacken** *vt sep* to warm *or* crisp up.

**aufbahren** *vt sep Sarg* to lay on the bier; *Leiche* to lay out. **einen Toten feierlich** ~ to put a person's body to lie in state.

**Aufbau** *m* **(a)** *no pl (das Aufbauen)* construction, building; *(das Wiederaufbauen)* reconstruction. **der wirtschaftliche** ~ the building up of the economy. **(b)** *no pl (Struktur)* structure.

**aufbauen** *sep* **1** *vt* **(a)** *(errichten)* to put up; *(hinstellen) Ausstellungsstücke, Brettspiel etc* to set *or* lay out. **(b)** *(fig: gestalten) Organisation, Angriff, Spannung* to build up; *Zerstörtes* to rebuild; *Theorie* to construct. **sich** *(dat)* **eine (neue) Existenz** ~ to build a new life for oneself. **(c)** *(fig: fördern) Gesundheit* to build up; *Star etc auch* to promote; *Beziehung* to build. **(d)** *(fig: gründen)* **etw auf etw** *(dat or acc)* ~ to base sth on sth. **(e)** *(strukturieren)* to construct; *Aufsatz, Rede auch, Komposition* to structure. **2** *vi (sich gründen)* to be based *(auf +dat or acc* on*).* **3** *vr* **(a)** *(inf: sich postieren)* to take up position. **sich vor jdm** ~ to draw oneself up to one's full height in front of sb. **(b)** *(sich bilden)* to build up. **(c)** *(sich gründen)* **sich auf etw** *(dat or acc)* ~ to be based on sth.

**aufbäumen** *vr sep (Tier)* to rear. **sich gegen jdn/etw** ~ *(fig)* to rebel *or* revolt against sb/sth.

**aufbauschen** *vt sep (fig)* to blow up, to exaggerate.

**aufbegehren\*** *vi sep (geh)* to rebel *(gegen* against*).*

**aufbehalten\*** *vt sep irreg Hut, Brille etc* to keep on.

**aufbekommen\*** *vt sep irreg (col)* **(a)** *(öffnen)* to get open. **(b)** *Aufgabe* to get as homework.

**aufbereiten\*** *vt sep* to process; *Trinkwasser auch* to purify; *Daten* to edit; *Text etc* to work up.

**Aufbereitungs|anlage** *f* processing plant.

**aufbessern** *vt sep* to improve; *Gehalt etc auch* to increase.

**Aufbesserung** *f siehe vt* improvement; increase.

**aufbewahren\*** *vt sep* to keep; *(in Lager)* to store; *(behalten) alte Zeitungen etc auch* to save. **kann ich hier mein Gepäck** ~ **lassen?** can I leave my luggage here?

**Aufbewahrung** *f siehe vt* keeping; storage; saving. **einen Koffer in** ~ **geben** to deposit a suitcase (at the left-luggage *(Brit)* or checkroom *(US)*).

**aufbieten** *vt sep irreg Menschen, Mittel* to muster; *Kräfte auch* to summon (up); *Polizei* to call in.

**Aufbietung** *f* **unter** ~ **aller Kräfte** ... summoning (up) all his/her *etc* strength ...

**aufbinden** *vt sep irreg* **(a)** *Schuh etc* to undo, to untie. **(b) laß dir doch so etwas nicht** ~ *(fig)* don't fall for that.

**aufblähen** *sep* **1** *vt* to blow out; *(fig)* to inflate. **2** *vr* to blow out; *(Segel auch)* to billow out; *(Med)* to become swollen; *(fig pej)* to puff oneself up.

**aufblasbar** *adj* inflatable.

**aufblasen** *vt sep irreg* to blow up; *siehe* **aufgeblasen.**

**aufbleiben** *vi sep irreg aux sein* **(a)** to stay up. **(b)** *(geöffnet bleiben)* to stay open.

**aufblenden** *vi sep (Phot)* to increase the aperture; *(Aut)* to turn the headlights on full (beam).

**aufblicken** *vi sep* to look up. **zu jdm/etw** ~ *(lit, fig)* to look up to sb/sth.

**aufblitzen** *vi sep (Licht)* to flash.

**aufblühen** *vi sep aux sein (lit, fig)* to blossom (out); *(Blume auch)* to bloom; *(Kultur etc auch)* to (begin to) flourish.

**aufbocken** *vt sep Auto* to jack up.

**aufbrauchen** *vt sep* to use up.

**aufbrausen** *vi sep aux sein* **(a)** *(Brandung etc)* to surge; *(fig: Beifall, Jubel)* to break out. **(b)** *(fig: Mensch)* to flare up, to fly off the handle *(col).*

**aufbrausend** *adj Temperament* irascible; *Mensch auch* quick-tempered, liable to flare up.

**aufbrechen** *sep irreg* **1** *vt* to break *or* force open; *Tresor auch, Auto* to break into; *Boden, Oberfläche* to break up. **2** *vi aux sein* **(a)** *(sich öffnen)* to open; *(Straßenbelag etc)* to break up. **(b)** *(fig: Konflikte etc)* to break out. **(c)** *(sich auf den Weg machen)* to start *or* set out *or* off.

**aufbringen** *vt sep irreg* **(a)** *(beschaffen)* to find; *Geld auch* to raise; *Kraft, Mut auch* to summon up. **Verständnis für etw** ~ to be able to understand sth. **(b)** *(erzürnen)* to make angry. **jdn gegen jdn/etw** ~ to set sb against sb/sth; *siehe* **aufgebracht. (c)** *(Naut) Schiff* to seize.

**Aufbruch** *m no pl (Abreise, das Losgehen)* departure. **das Zeichen zum** ~ **geben** to give the signal to set out *or* off.

**aufbrühen** *vt sep* to brew up.

**aufbrummen** *vt sep (col)* **jdm die Kosten** ~ to land sb with the costs *(col);* **eine Haftstrafe aufgebrummt bekommen** to get a sentence.

**aufbügeln** *vt sep* **(a)** *Kleidungsstück* to iron out. **(b)** *Flicken, Bild etc* to iron on.

**aufbürden** *vt sep (geh)* **jdm etw** ~ *(fig)* to encumber sb with sth; **jdm die Schuld für etw** ~ to put the blame for sth on sb.

**aufdecken** *vt sep* **(a)** *jdn* to uncover; *Bett(decke)* to turn down; *Spielkarten* to show. **(b)** *(fig) Wahrheit etc* to uncover; *Verbrechen auch* to expose; *Schwäche* to lay bare; *Geheimnis* to solve.

**Aufdeckung** *f siehe vt (b)* uncovering; exposure; laying bare; solving.

**aufdonnern** *vr sep (pej col)* to tart oneself up *(pej col);* *siehe* **aufgedonnert.**

**aufdrängen** *sep irreg* **1** *vt* **jdm etw** ~ to impose *or* force sth on sb. **2** *vr* to impose. **sich jdm** ~ *(Mensch)* to impose oneself on sb; *(fig: Erinnerung)* to come involuntarily to sb's mind; **dieser Gedanke/ Verdacht drängte sich mir auf** I couldn't help thinking/suspecting that.

**aufdrehen** *sep* **1** *vt* **(a)** *Wasserhahn* to turn on; *Ventil* to open; *Schraubverschluß* to unscrew; *Radio etc* to turn up. **(b)** *Haar* to put in rollers. **2** *vi (col: beschleunigen)* to open up; *siehe* **aufgedreht.**

**aufdringlich** *adj Benehmen, Tapete* obtrusive; *Geruch, Parfüm* powerful; *Farbe auch* loud; *Mensch* insistent, pushy *(col).*

**Aufdringlichkeit** *f siehe adj* obtrusiveness; powerfulness; loudness; insistence, pushiness.

**Aufdruck** *m (Aufgedrucktes)* imprint.

**aufdrucken** *vt sep* **etw auf etw** *(acc)* ~ to print sth on sth.

**aufdrücken** *vt sep* **(a)** **etw auf etw** *(acc)* ~ to press *or (mit Stempel etc)* stamp sth on sth. **(b)** *(öffnen) Tür etc* to push open.

**auf|einander** *adv* **(a)** on (top of) each other *or* one another. **(b) sich** ~ **verlassen können** to be able to rely on each other *or* one another; ~ **zufahren** to drive towards each other.

**auf|einander-:** ~**folgen** *vi sep aux sein* to follow each other; ~**folgend** *adj* successive; **drei schnell** ~**folgende Tore** three goals in quick succession; ~**legen** *vt sep* to lay on top of each other; ~**passen** *vi sep* to fit on top of each other; ~**prallen** *vi sep aux sein (Autos etc)* to collide; *(Truppen, Meinungen)* to clash; ~**stellen** *vt sep* to put on top of each other; ~**stoßen** *vi sep irreg aux sein* to bump into each other, to collide; ~**treffen** *vi sep irreg aux sein (Mannschaften, Gruppen etc)* to meet; *(Meinungen)* to clash; *(Kugeln, Gegenstände etc)* to hit each other.

**Aufenthalt** *m* **-e (a)** stay; *(das Wohnen)* residence. **(b)** *(esp Rail)* stop; *(bei Anschluß)* wait. **wie lange haben wir** ~**?** how long do we stop for?

**Aufenthalts-:** ~**erlaubnis** *f,* ~**genehmigung** *f* residence permit; ~**ort** *m* whereabouts *sing or pl; (Jur)* residence; ~**raum** *m* day room; *(in Betrieb)* recreation room; *(in Flughafen)* lounge.

**auf|erlegen\*** *vt sep or insep (geh)* to impose *(jdm etw* sth on sb).

**auf|erstehen\*** *vi sep or insep irreg aux sein* to rise from the dead. **Christus ist auferstanden** Christ is risen.

**Auf|erstehung** *f* resurrection.

**auf|essen** *sep irreg* **1** *vt* to eat up. **2** *vi* to eat (everything) up.

**auffädeln** *vt sep* to thread *or* string (together).

**auffahren** *sep irreg* **1** *vi aux sein* **(a)** *(aufprallen)* **auf jdn/etw** ~ to run *or* drive into sb/sth; **auf eine Sandbank** ~ to run aground on a sandbank. **(b)** *(näher heranfahren)* to drive up. **zu dicht** ~ to drive too close behind (the car in front). **(c)** *(auf Autobahn)* to enter. **(d)** *(aufschrecken)* to start. **aus dem Schlaf** ~ to awake with a start. **(e)** *(aufbrausen)* to flare up, to fly into a rage. **2** *vt (herbeischaffen) Truppen etc* to bring up; *(col) Speisen etc* to serve up.

**Auffahrt** *f* approach road; *(Autobahn~ auch)* slip road; *(bei Haus etc)* drive.

**Auffahr|unfall** *m (von zwei Autos)* (nose-to-tail) collision; *(von mehreren Autos)* pile-up.

**auffallen** *vi sep irreg aux sein* **(a)** *(sich abheben)* to stand out; *(unangenehm* ~*)* to attract attention; *(sich hervortun)* to be remarkable *(durch* for). **er ist schon früher als Extremist aufgefallen** he has already got a reputation for being an extremist; **angenehm/unangenehm** ~ to make a good/bad impression; **nur nicht** ~**!** just keep a low profile. **(b)** *(bemerkt werden)* **jdm fällt etw auf** sb notices sth, sth strikes sb; **fällt es auf?** does it show?; **das muß dir doch aufgefallen sein!** surely you must have noticed (it).

**auffallend** *adj* conspicuous, noticeable; *Schönheit, Ähnlichkeit, Farbe, Kleider* striking. **er ist** ~ **intelligent** he is remarkably intelligent; **stimmt** ~**!** *(hum)* too true!, how right you are!

**auffällig** *adj* conspicuous; *Farbe, Kleidung* loud.

**auffangen** *vt sep irreg* **(a)** *Ball, Gesprächsfetzen* to catch; *(Telec) Nachricht* to pick up. **(b)** *(abfangen) Aufprall etc* to cushion, to absorb; *Faustschlag* to block; *(fig) Preissteigerung etc* to offset. **(c)** *(sammeln) Regenwasser etc* to collect, to catch; *(fig) Flüchtlinge etc* to assemble.

**Auffanglager** *nt* reception camp *or* centre.

**auffassen** *vt sep* to interpret, to understand. **etw als etw** *(acc)* ~ to take sth as sth; **etw falsch/richtig** ~ to take sth the wrong way/in the right way.

**Auffassung** *f* view. **nach meiner/christlicher** ~ in my view/according to Christian belief.

**Auffassungs-:** ~**gabe** *f* intelligence, grasp; ~**sache** *f (col)* question of interpretation; *(Ansichtssache)* matter of opinion.

**auffegen** *vt sep* to sweep up.

**auffindbar** *adj* **es ist nicht** ~ it can't be found.

**auffinden** *vt sep irreg* to find, to discover.

**auffischen** *vt sep* to fish up; *(col) Schiffbrüchige* to fish out.

**aufflackern** *vi sep aux sein (lit, fig)* to flare up.

**aufflammen** *vi sep aux sein (lit, fig: Feuer, Unruhen etc)* to flare up.

**auffliegen** *vi sep irreg aux sein* **(a)** *(hochfliegen)* to fly up. **(b)** *(fig col) (Konferenz etc)* to break up; *(Rauschgiftring etc)* to be busted *(col)*. **einen Schmugglerring/eine Konferenz** ~ **lassen** to bust a ring of smugglers *(col)*/to break up a meeting.

**auffordern** *vt sep* **(a)** to ask. **wir fordern Sie auf, ...** you are required to ... **(b)** *(bitten)* to ask, to invite; *(zum Wettkampf etc)* to challenge. **(c)** *(zum Tanz bitten)* to ask to dance.

**auffordernd** *adj* inviting.

**Aufforderung** *f* request; *(nachdrücklicher)* demand.

**aufforsten** *vt sep Gebiet* to reafforest; *Wald* to restock.

**Aufforstung** *f siehe vt* reafforestation; restocking.

**auffressen** *vt sep irreg (lit, fig)* to eat up. **er wird dich nicht gleich** ~ *(col)* he's not going to eat you *(col)*.

**auffrischen** *sep* **1** *vt* to freshen (up); *Anstrich auch* to brighten up; *(ergänzen) Vorräte* to replenish; *(fig) Erinnerungen* to refresh; *Kenntnisse* to brush up; *persönliche Beziehungen* to renew; *Impfung* to boost. **2** *vi aux sein or haben (Wind)* to freshen. **3** *vi impers aux sein* to get fresher.

**Auffrischung** *f siehe vt* freshening (up); brightening up; replenishment; refreshing; brushing up; renewal; boosting.

**Auffrischungs-:** ~**impfung** *f* booster; ~**kurs** *m* refresher course.

**aufführen** *sep* **1** *vt* **(a)** to put on; *Drama, Oper auch* to stage, to perform. **(b)** *(auflisten)* to list; *(nennen) Zeugen* to cite; *Beispiel* to give. **einzeln** ~ to itemize. **2** *vr* to behave.

**Aufführung** *f* performance.

**Aufführungsrecht** *nt* performing rights *pl*.

**auffüllen** *vt sep* **(a)** *(vollständig füllen)* to fill up; *(nachfüllen)* to top up. **(b)** *(ergänzen) Flüssigkeit* to dilute; *Vorräte* to replenish; *Öl* to top up.

**Aufgabe** *f* **(a)** *(Arbeit, Pflicht)* job, task. **es ist nicht** ~ **der Regierung, ...** it is not the job *or* task of the government to ...; **sich** *(dat)* **etw zur** ~ **machen** to make sth one's job *or* business. **(b)** *(Zweck, Funktion)* purpose, job. **(c)** *(esp Sch) (Problem)* question; *(Math auch)* problem; *(zur Übung)* exercise; *(usu pl: Haus~)* homework *no pl*. **(d)** *(von Koffer, Postsendung)* handing in; *(Aviat)* checking-in. **(e)** *(Verzicht auf weiteren Kampf etc) (Sport)* retirement; *(Mil etc)* surrender. **die Polizei forderte die Geiselnehmer zur** ~ **auf** the police appealed to the hostage-takers to give themselves up *or* to surrender. **(f)** *(von Gewohnheit, Geschäft)* giving up; *(von Plänen, Forderungen auch)* dropping; *(von Hoffnung, Studium)* abandoning.

**aufgabeln** *vt sep (fig col) jdn* to pick up *(col)*.

**Aufgabenbereich** *m* area of responsibility.

**Aufgang** *m* **(a)** *(von Sonne, Mond)* rising; *(von Stern auch)* ascent. **(b)** *(Treppen~)* staircase.

**aufgeben** *sep irreg* **1** *vt* **(a)** *Hausaufgaben* to give; *Problem* to pose *(jdm* for sb). **jdm viel/nichts** ~ *(Sch)* to give sb a lot of/no homework. **(b)** *Koffer,*

*Gepäck* to hand in; *(Aviat)* to check in; *Brief* to post *(esp Brit)*, to mail; *Anzeige, Bestellung* to place. **(c)** *Kampf, Hoffnung, Arbeitsstelle, Patienten etc* to give up. **gib's auf!** why don't you give up? **2** *vi (sich geschlagen geben)* to give up *or* in.

**aufgeblasen** *adj (fig)* puffed up, self-important.

**Aufgebot** *nt* **(a)** *(zur Eheschließung)* **das ~ bestellen** to give notice of one's intended marriage; *(Eccl)* to put up the banns. **(b)** *(Ansammlung) (von Menschen)* contingent; *(von Material etc)* array.

**aufgebracht** *adj* outraged, incensed.

**aufgedonnert** *adj (pej col)* tarted up *(pej col)*.

**aufgedreht** *adj (col)* in high spirits.

**aufgedunsen** *adj* swollen, bloated; *Gesicht auch* puffy.

**aufgehen** *vi sep irreg aux sein* **(a)** *(Sonne, Mond, Sterne)* to come up, to rise. **(b)** *(sich öffnen)* to open; *(Theat: Vorhang)* to go up; *(Knopf, Knoten etc)* to come undone. **(c)** *(aufkeimen)* to come up. **(d)** *(Cook)* to rise. **(e)** *(klarwerden)* **jdm geht etw auf** sb realizes sth, sth dawns on sb. **(f)** *(Math, fig)* to work out. **20 durch 6 geht nicht auf** 20 divided by 6 doesn't go. **(g) in etw** *(dat)* ~ *(fig)* to be wrapped up in sth, to be taken up with sth; **in Flammen ~** to go up in flames.

**aufgehoben** *adj*: **(bei jdm) gut/schlecht ~ sein** to be/not to be in good hands (with sb).

**aufgeilen** *vt sep (col)* to get worked up *(col)*.

**aufgekratzt** *adj (col)* in high spirits, full of beans *(col)*.

**aufgelegt** *adj* **gut/schlecht ~** in a good/bad mood.

**aufgelöst** *adj* **(a)** *(außer sich)* beside oneself *(vor +dat* with*)*, distraught; *(bestürzt)* upset. **in Tränen ~** in tears. **(b)** *(erschöpft)* exhausted.

**aufgeräumt** *adj (geh: gutgelaunt)* light-hearted.

**aufgeregt** *adj (erregt)* excited; *(nervös)* nervous; *(durcheinander)* flustered.

**Aufgeregtheit** *f no pl siehe adj* excitement; nervousness; flustered state.

**aufgeschlossen** *adj (nicht engstirnig)* open-minded *(für, gegenüber* about, as regards*)*; *(empfänglich)* receptive, open *(für, gegenüber* to*)*.

**Aufgeschlossenheit** *f no pl siehe adj* open-mindedness; receptiveness, openness.

**aufgeschmissen** *adj pred (col)* in a fix, stuck.

**aufgeschwemmt** *adj* bloated, swollen.

**aufgetakelt** *adj (pej)* dressed to the nines *(col)*.

**aufgeweckt** *adj* bright, quick, sharp.

**aufgewühlt** *adj (geh)* agitated, in a turmoil *pred*; *Gefühle auch, Meer* turbulent.

**aufgießen** *vt sep irreg* **(a) etw (auf etw** *acc)* **~** to pour sth on (sth). **(b)** *Kaffee, Tee* to make.

**aufgliedern** *sep* **1** *vt (in +acc into)* to split up, to (sub)divide; *(in Kategorien auch)* to break down. **2** *vr (in +acc into)* to (sub)divide, to break down.

**aufgreifen** *vt sep irreg* **(a)** *(festnehmen)* to pick up, to apprehend. **(b)** *Thema* to take up.

**aufgrund** *prep +gen,* **auf Grund** *siehe* **Grund**.

**Aufguß** *m* brew, infusion; *(fig pej)* rehash.

**Aufgußbeutel** *m* sachet (containing coffee/herbs *etc)* for brewing; *(Teebeutel)* tea bag.

**aufhaben** *sep irreg* **1** *vt* **(a)** *Hut, Brille* to have on. **(b)** *Tür, Augen* to have open. **(c)** *(Sch: als Hausaufgabe)* **ich habe heute viel auf** I've got a lot of homework today. **2** *vi (Laden etc)* to be open.

**aufhalsen** *vt sep (col)* **jdm/sich etw ~** to saddle *or* land sb/oneself with sth *(col)*.

**aufhalten** *sep irreg* **1** *vt* **(a)** *Fahrzeug, Entwicklung* to stop, to halt; *(verlangsamen)* to hold up, to delay; *(abhalten, stören) (bei* from*)* to hold back, to keep back. **ich will dich nicht länger ~** I don't want to

keep *or* hold you back any longer. **(b)** *(col: offenhalten)* to keep open. **die Hand ~** to hold one's hand out. **2** *vr* **(a)** *(an einem Ort bleiben)* to stay. **(b)** *(sich befassen)* **sich bei etw ~** to dwell on sth.

**aufhängen** *sep* **1** *vt* **(a)** to hang up; *(Aut)* *Rad* to suspend. **(b)** *(töten)* to hang *(an +dat* from*)*. **2** *vr (sich töten)* to hang oneself *(an +dat* from*)*.

**Aufhänger** *m* tag, loop. **ein ~ für etw** *(fig col)* a peg to hang sth on.

**Aufhängung** *f (Tech)* suspension.

**aufhäufen** *vtr sep* to pile up, to accumulate.

**aufheben** *sep irreg* **1** *vt* **(a)** *(vom Boden)* to pick up; *größeren Gegenstand auch* to lift up. **(b)** *(nicht wegwerfen)* to keep. **jdm etw ~** to keep sth for sb; *siehe* **aufgehoben**. **(c)** *(ungültig machen)* to abolish, to do away with; *Urteil* to reverse, to quash. **(d)** *(beenden) Blockade, Belagerung* to raise, to lift; *Beschränkung* to remove, to lift. **(e)** *(ausgleichen)* to offset, to make up for; *Schwerkraft* to neutralize, to cancel out. **2** *vr (sich ausgleichen)* to cancel each other out *(auch Math)*, to offset each other.

**Aufheben** *nt no pl* fuss. **viel ~(s) (von etw) machen** to make a lot of fuss (about *or* over sth).

**Aufhebung** *f* **(a)** *siehe vt (c)* abolition; reversal, quashing. **(b)** *siehe vt (d)* raising, lifting; removal.

**aufheitern** *sep* **1** *vt jdn* to cheer up; *Rede, Leben* to brighten up *(jdm* for sb*)*. **2** *vr (Himmel, Wetter)* to clear up, to brighten up.

**Aufheiterung** *f usu pl (Met)* bright period.

**aufheizen** *sep* **1** *vt* to heat (up). **die Stimmung ~** to stir up feelings. **2** *vr* to heat up; *(fig)* to hot up *(col)*, to intensify.

**aufhelfen** *vi sep irreg (lit: beim Aufstehen)* to help up *(jdm* sb*)*.

**aufhellen** *sep* **1** *vt* to brighten (up); *Haare* to lighten; *(fig: klären)* to throw *or* shed light upon. **2** *vr (Himmel, Wetter, fig: Miene)* to brighten (up).

**aufhetzen** *vt sep* to stir up, to incite. **jdn gegen jdn/etw ~** to stir up sb *or* incite sb against sb/sth; **jdn zu etw ~** to incite sb to (do) sth.

**aufhetzerisch** *adj* inflammatory.

**Aufhetzung** *f* incitement, agitation.

**aufheulen** *vi sep* to howl *(vor* with*)*; *(Sirene)* to (start to) wail; *(Motor)* to give a roar.

**aufholen** *sep* **1** *vt Zeit, Vorsprung* to make up; *Lernstoff* to catch up on. **2** *vi (Mannschaft, Schüler, Arbeiter)* to catch up.

**aufhorchen** *vi sep* to prick up one's ears, to sit up (and take notice).

**aufhören** *vi sep* to stop; *(bei Firma)* to finish; *(Musik, Lärm auch, Freundschaft)* to (come to an) end. **hör doch endlich auf!** (will you) stop it!; **mit etw ~** to stop sth; **da hört sich doch alles auf!** *(col)* that's the (absolute) limit!

**aufjagen** *vt sep* to disturb.

**aufjauchzen** *vi sep* **vor Freude ~** to give a shout of joy.

**aufkaufen** *vt sep* to buy up.

**Aufkäufer** *m* buyer.

**aufkeimen** *vi sep aux sein* to germinate, to sprout; *(fig) (Hoffnung, Liebe)* to burgeon *(liter)*, to form; *(Zweifel)* to (begin to) take root.

**aufklappbar** *adj Verdeck* folding.

**aufklappen** *vt sep* to open up; *Klappe* to let down; *Verdeck* to put down; *Messer* to unclasp; *Fenster, Buch* to open; *(hochschlagen) Kragen* to turn up.

**aufklaren** *vi sep (Met)* to clear (up).

**aufklären** *sep* **1** *vt* **(a)** *Mißverständnis, Irrtum* to clear up; *Verbrechen* to solve; *Ereignis, Vorgang* to throw light upon. **(b)** *jdn* to enlighten. **Kinder ~** *(sexuell)* to tell children the facts of life; *(in der*

*Schule)* to give children sex education; **jdn über etw** *(acc)* ~ to inform sb about sth. **2** *vr (Irrtum, Geheimnis)* to be cleared up; *(Himmel)* to clear up; *(fig: Gesicht)* to brighten (up).

**Aufklärung** *f* (a) *(Philos)* **die** ~ the Enlightenment. (b) *siehe* vt *(a)* clearing up; solution; *(von Vorgang)* elucidation. (c) *(Information)* enlightenment. (d) **(sexuelle)** ~ *(in Schulen)* sex education. **die** ~ **von Kindern** explaining the facts of life to children. (e) *(Mil)* reconnaissance.

**Aufklärungs-:** ~**arbeit** *f* educational work; ~**film** *m* sex education film; ~**flugzeug** *nt* reconnaissance aircraft; ~**kampagne** *f* information campaign; ~**schiff** *nt (Mil)* reconnaissance ship.

**aufkleben** vt sep *(auf +acc to)* to stick on; *(mit Leim, Klebstoff auch)* to glue on.

**Aufkleber** *m* sticker.

**aufknacken** vt sep *Nüsse etc, (col)* Tresor to crack; *Auto* to break into.

**aufknöpfen** vt sep *(öffnen)* to unbutton, to undo.

**aufknoten** vt sep to untie, to undo.

**aufknüpfen** vt sep (a) to hang *(an +dat* from*)*, to string up *(col) (an +dat* on*)*. (b) *(aufknoten)* to untie, to undo.

**aufkochen** vt sep to bring to the boil.

**aufkommen** vi sep irreg aux sein (a) *(lit, fig: entstehen)* to arise; *(Nebel)* to come down; *(Wind)* to spring *or* get up; *(auftreten: Mode etc auch)* to appear (on the scene). **etw** ~ **lassen** *(fig) Zweifel, Kritik* to give rise to sth; **endlich kam Stimmung auf** at last things livened up. (b) ~ **für** *(Kosten tragen)* to bear the costs of, to pay for; *(Haftung tragen)* to be liable for. **für die Kinder** ~ *(finanziell)* to pay for the children's upkeep; **für die Kosten** ~ to bear the costs; **für den Schaden** ~ to pay for the damage.

**Aufkommen** *nt* (a) *no pl (das Auftreten)* appearance; *(von Methode, Mode etc auch)* advent, emergence. (b) *(Fin) (Summe, Menge)* amount; *(von Steuern)* revenue *(aus* from*)*.

**aufkratzen** vt sep *(zerkratzen)* to scratch; *(öffnen) Wunde* to scratch open; *siehe* **aufgekratzt**.

**aufkreischen** vi sep *(Mensch)* to scream, to shriek; *(Bremsen, Maschine)* to screech.

**aufkrempeln** vi sep **(sich** *dat***) die Ärmel/Hose** ~ to roll up one's sleeves/trousers.

**aufkreuzen** vi sep aux sein *(col: erscheinen)* to turn *or* show up.

**aufkriegen** vt sep *(col) siehe* **aufbekommen**.

**aufkündigen** vt sep *Vertrag etc* to terminate.

**Aufl.** = **Auflage**.

**auflachen** vi sep to (give a) laugh.

**aufladbar** adj chargeable; *(neu* ~*)* rechargeable.

**aufladen** sep irreg **1** vt (a) **etw (auf etw** *acc***)** ~ to load sth on(to) sth. **jdm/sich etw** ~ *(fig)* to saddle sb/oneself with sth. (b) *(elektrisch)* to charge; *(neu* ~*)* to recharge. **emotional aufgeladen** *(fig)* emotionally charged. **2** vr *(Batterie etc)* to be charged; *(neu)* to be recharged.

**Auflage** *f* (a) *(Ausgabe)* edition; *(Druck)* printing, impression; *(~höhe)* number of copies printed; *(von Zeitung)* circulation. (b) *(Bedingung)* condition. **jdm etw zur** ~ **machen** to impose sth on sb as a condition; **jdm zur** ~ **machen, etw zu tun** to make it a condition for sb to do sth; **die** ~ **haben, etw zu tun** to be obliged to do sth. (c) *(Überzug)* plating *no pl*, coating.

**Auflage(n)-:** ~**höhe** *f (von Buch)* number of copies printed, printrun; *(von Zeitung)* circulation; ~**ziffer** *f* circulation (figures *pl*); *(von Buch)* number of copies printed, printrun.

**auflandig** adj *(Naut) Wind* onshore.

**auflassen** vt sep irreg *(col) (offenlassen)* to leave open; *(aufbehalten) Hut* to keep *or* leave on. **die Kinder länger** ~ to let the children stay up (longer).

**auflauern** vi sep +dat to lie in wait for.

**Auflauf** *m* (a) *(Menschen~)* crowd. (b) *(Cook)* (baked) pudding *(sweet or savoury)*.

**auflaufen** vi sep irreg aux sein (a) *(auf Grund laufen: Schiff)* to run aground *(auf +acc or dat* on*)*; *(fig)* to run into trouble.

(b) *(aufprallen)* **auf jdn/etw** ~ to run into sb/sth, to collide with sb/sth; **jdn** ~ **lassen** *(Ftbl)* to bodycheck sb; *(col)* to drop sb in it *(col)*.

**Auflaufform** *f (Cook)* ovenproof dish.

**aufleben** vi sep aux sein to revive; *(munter, lebendig werden)* to liven up, to come to life again; *(neuen Lebensmut bekommen)* to find a new lease of life. **Erinnerungen wieder** ~ **lassen** to revive memories.

**auflecken** vt sep to lick up.

**auflegen** sep **1** vt (a) to put on; *Gedeck* to lay; *Hörer* to put down, to replace. (b) *Buch (herausgeben)* to publish; *(drucken)* to print. **ein Buch neu** ~ to reprint a book; *(neu bearbeitet)* to bring out a new edition of a book. **2** vi *(Telec)* to hang up.

**auflehnen** vr sep **sich gegen jdn/etw** ~ to revolt *or* rebel against sb/sth.

**Auflehnung** *f* revolt, rebellion.

**auflesen** vt sep irreg *(lit, fig col)* to pick up. **jdn/etw von der Straße** ~ to pick sb/sth up off the street.

**aufleuchten** vi sep aux sein or haben *(lit, fig)* to light up.

**aufliegen** vi sep irreg (a) to lie *or* rest on top. (b) = **ausliegen**.

**auflisten** vt sep to list.

**Auflistung** *f (auch Comp)* listing; *(Liste auch)* list.

**auflockern** sep **1** vt (a) *Boden* to break up, to loosen (up). (b) *Unterricht, Stoff, Vortrag* to make less monotonous, to give relief to *(durch* with*)*. (c) *(entspannen)* to make relaxed; *Atmosphäre auch* to ease. **in aufgelockerter Stimmung** in a relaxed mood. **2** vr (a) *(Sport)* to limber *or* loosen up. (b) *(Bewölkung)* to break up.

**Auflockerung** *f* (a) *(von Boden)* breaking up, loosening (up). **zur** ~ **der gespannten Atmosphäre** in order to ease the tense atmosphere. (b) *(von Bewölkung)* breaking up.

**auflodern** vi sep aux sein *(Flammen, fig)* to flare up; *(lodernd brennen)* to blaze.

**auflösen** sep **1** vt (a) *(in Flüssigkeit)* to dissolve; *(in Bestandteile zerlegen)* to break down *(in +acc* into*)*; *(Math) Gleichung* to (re)solve; *siehe* **aufgelöst**. (b) *(aufklären) Widerspruch etc* to clear up, to resolve; *Rätsel* to solve. (c) *(zerstreuen) Wolken, Versammlung* to disperse, to break up. (d) *(aufheben)* to dissolve *(auch Parl)*; *Einheit, Gruppe* to disband; *Firma* to wind up; *Verlobung* to break off; *Vertrag* to cancel; *Konto* to close; *Haushalt* to break up. **2** vr (a) *(in Flüssigkeit)* to dissolve; *(Zweifel, Probleme)* to disappear. (b) *(sich zerstreuen)* to disperse; *(Wolken auch)* to break up; *(Nebel auch)* to lift. (c) *(auseinandergehen) (Verband)* to disband; *(Firma)* to cease trading; *(formell: esp Parl)* to dissolve.

**Auflösung** *f siehe* vt (a) dissolving; breaking down; (re)solving. (b) clearing up, resolving; solving; *(fertige Lösung: von Rätsel etc)* solution. (c) dispersal. (d) dissolving; disbanding; winding up; breaking off; cancellation; closing; breaking up; *(Mus, von Parlament)* dissolution. (e) *(von Bildschirm)* resolution.

**Auflösungszeichen** *nt (Mus)* natural.

**aufmachen** sep **1** vt (a) *(öffnen)* to open; *(lösen, aufknöpfen etc)* to undo. (b) *(eröffnen, gründen) Ge-*

*schäft, Unternehmen* to open (up). **(c)** *(gestalten)* *Buch, Zeitung* to make up; *(in Presse) Ereignis, Pro-* *zeß etc* to feature. **2** *vi (Tür öffnen)* to open the door; *(Geschäft (er)öffnen)* to open (up). **3** *vr* **(a)** *(sich zurechtmachen)* to get oneself up. **(b)** *(sich anschicken)* to get ready, to make preparations; *(aufbrechen)* to set out.

**Aufmacher** *m (Press)* lead (story).

**Aufmachung** *f* **(a)** *(Kleidung)* turn-out. **in großer ~ erscheinen** to turn up dressed to the nines *(col)*. **(b)** *(Gestaltung)* presentation, style; *(von Buch)* presentation, make-up; *(Press etc)* layout.

**aufmalen** *vt sep* to paint on *(auf etw (acc)* sth).

**Aufmarsch** *m (Mil)* marching; *(Parade)* marchpast; *(in Stellung, Kampflinie)* deployment.

**aufmarschieren\*** *vi sep aux sein (heranmarschieren)* to march up; *(Mil: in Stellung gehen)* to deploy; *(vorbeimarschieren)* to march past.

**aufmerksam** *adj* **(a)** *Zuhörer, Beobachter, Schüler* attentive; *Blicke auch, Augen* keen; *(scharf beobachtend)* observant. **jdn auf etw** *(acc)* **~ machen** to draw sb's attention to sth; **auf etw** *(acc)* **~ werden** to become aware of sth. **(b)** *(zuvorkommend)* attentive. **(das ist) sehr ~ von Ihnen** (that's) most kind of you.

**Aufmerksamkeit** *f* **(a)** *no pl* attention, attentiveness. **das ist meiner ~ entgangen** it escaped my attention. **(b)** *no pl (Zuvorkommenheit)* attentiveness. **(c)** *(Geschenk)* token (gift).

**aufmischen** *vt sep (col: provozieren)* to stir up.

**aufmöbeln** *vt sep (col) Gegenstand* to do up *(col)*; *jdn (beleben)* to buck up *(col)*, to pep up *(col)*.

**aufmotzen** *sep (col)* **1** *vt* to zap up *(col)*. **2** *vi* to get cheeky *(esp Brit)* or fresh *(esp US)*.

**aufmucken, aufmucksen** *vt sep (col)* to protest *(gegen* at, against*)*.

**aufmuntern** *vt sep (aufheitern)* to cheer up; *(beleben)* to liven up.

**Aufmunterung** *f siehe vt* cheering up; livening up.

**aufmüpfig** *adj (col)* rebellious.

**aufnähen** *vt sep* to sew on *(auf +acc* to*)*.

**Aufnahme** *f* **-n (a)** *(Empfang, fig: Reaktion)* reception. **bei jdm freundliche ~ finden** *(lit, fig)* to meet with a warm reception from sb; **wie war die ~ beim Publikum?** how did the audience receive it *or* react? **(b)** *(in Verein)* admission *(in +acc* to*)*. **(c)** *no pl (lit, fig: Absorption)* absorption. **(d)** *no pl (von Kapital etc)* raising. **(e)** *no pl (Beginn: von Gespräch etc)* start, commencement. **(f)** *(Foto)* photo(graph); shot *(col)*; *(Film~)* take. **(g)** *(auf Tonband etc)* recording.

**Aufnahme-:** **~antrag** *m* application for membership *or* admission; **a~bereit** *adj Kamera* ready to shoot; *(fig)* receptive, open *(für* to*)*; **~bereitschaft** *f (fig)* receptiveness; **a~fähig** *adj* **für etw a~fähig sein** to be able to take sth in; **~gebühr** *f* enrolment fee; *(in Verein)* admission fee; **~lager** *nt* reception camp; **~leiter** *m (Film)* production manager; *(Rad, TV)* producer; **~prüfung** *f* entrance examination; **~stopp** *m (für Flüchtlinge etc)* freeze on immigration; **~studio** *nt* (film/recording) studio.

**aufnehmen** *vt sep irreg* **(a)** *(vom Boden)* to pick up. **(b)** *(lit: empfangen, fig: reagieren auf)* to receive. **(c)** *(unterbringen)* to take (in); *(fassen)* to take, to hold; *Einwanderer* to absorb. **(d)** *(in Verein)* to admit *(in +acc* to*)*; *(Schule auch)* to take on. **(e)** *(absorbieren)* to absorb, to take up; *(fig: eindringen lassen) Eindrücke* to take in; *(begreifen auch)* to grasp. **(f)** *(mit einbeziehen)* to include, to incorporate; *(aufgreifen) Thema* to take up. **(g)** *(esp Ftbl) Ball* to take, to re-

ceive. **(h)** *(beginnen) Beziehung* to establish; *Tätigkeit, Studium* to take up. **den Kampf ~** to commence battle; *(fig auch)* to take up the struggle. **(i)** *Hypothek etc* to raise; *Kredit auch* to get. **(j)** *(niederschreiben) Protokoll, Diktat* to take down; *Personalien* to take (down); *Telegramm* to take. **(k)** *(fotografieren)* to take (a photograph of), to photograph; *(filmen)* to film, to shoot *(col)*. **(l)** *(auf Tonband usw.)* to record. **(m)** *(beim Stricken) Maschen* to increase, to make. **(n) es mit jdm/etw ~ können** to be a match for sb/sth.

**aufnötigen** *vt sep* **jdm etw ~** to force sth on sb.

**auf|oktroyieren\*** *vt sep* **jdm etw ~** *(geh)* to impose *or* force sth on sb.

**auf|opfern** *vr sep* to sacrifice oneself.

**auf|opfernd** *adj* self-sacrificing.

**Auf|opferung** *f* **(a)** *(Aufgabe)* sacrifice. **(b)** *(Selbst~)* self-sacrifice.

**aufpäppeln** *vt sep (col) (mit Nahrung)* to feed up *(col)*; *(durch Pflege)* to nurse back to health.

**aufpassen** *vi sep* **(a)** *(beaufsichtigen)* **auf jdn/etw ~** to keep an eye on sb/sth. **(b)** *(aufmerksam sein, achtgeben)* to pay attention. **paß auf!, aufgepaßt!** look, watch; *(sei aufmerksam)* pay attention; *(Vorsicht)* look out, watch out, mind (out).

**Aufpasser(in** *f)* *m* - *(pej: Aufseher, Spitzel)* spy *(pej)*, watchdog *(col)*; *(für VIP etc)* minder; *(Beobachter)* supervisor; *(Wächter)* guard.

**aufpeitschen** *vt sep Meer, Wellen* to whip up; *(fig) Sinne* to inflame, to fire; *Menschen* to work up; *(stärker)* to whip up into a frenzy.

**aufpeppen** *vt sep (col)* to jazz up *(col)*.

**aufpflanzen** *sep* **1** *vt (Mil) Bajonett* to fix. **2** *vr* **sich vor jdm ~** to plant oneself in front of sb.

**aufpicken** *vt sep (Vogel)* to peck up.

**aufplatzen** *vi sep aux sein* to burst open.

**aufplustern** *sep* **1** *vt Federn* to ruffle up. **2** *vr (Vogel)* to ruffle (up) its feathers; *(Mensch)* to puff oneself up.

**aufpolieren\*** *vt sep (lit, fig)* to polish up.

**aufprägen** *vt sep* **jdm/einer Sache seinen Stempel ~** *(fig)* to leave one's mark on sb/sth.

**Aufprall** *m* **-e** impact.

**aufprallen** *vi sep aux sein* **auf etw** *(acc)* **~** to strike *or* hit sth; *(Fahrzeug auch)* to collide with sth.

**Aufpreis** *m* extra *or* additional charge. **gegen ~** for an extra *or* additional charge.

**aufpulvern** *vt sep (col)* to pep *or* buck up *(col)*.

**aufpumpen** *vt sep* to pump up, to inflate; *Fahrrad* to pump up the tyres *(Brit)* or tires *(US)* of.

**aufputschen** *sep* **1** *vt* **(a)** *(aufwiegeln)* to rouse; *Gefühle, öffentliche Meinung* to stir up. **(b)** *(durch Reizmittel)* to stimulate. **~de Mittel** stimulants. **2** *vr* to pep oneself up *(col)*, to dope oneself *(Sport col)*.

**Aufputschmittel** *nt* stimulant.

**aufquellen** *vi sep irreg aux sein (anschwellen)* to swell (up). **aufgequollen** swollen; **etw ~ lassen** to soak sth (to allow it to swell up).

**aufraffen** *sep* **1** *vr* to force oneself to do sth. **sich zu einer Entscheidung ~** to force oneself to make a decision. **2** *vt Papiere, Eigentum* to gather up; *(schnell aufheben)* to snatch up.

**aufragen** *vi sep aux sein or haben (in die Höhe ~)* to rise; *(sehr hoch, groß auch)* to tower (up) *(über +dat* above, over*)*. **die hoch ~den Türme** the soaring towers.

**aufrappeln** *vr sep (col)* **(a)** *siehe* **aufraffen 1. (b)** *(wieder zu Kräften kommen)* to recover, to get over it.

**aufrauchen** *vt sep (zu Ende rauchen)* to finish (smoking).

**aufrauhen** *vt sep* to roughen; *(Tex) Stoff* to nap.

**aufräumen** *sep* **1** *vt* to tidy or clear up; *(wegräumen auch)* to clear or put away. **2** *vi* **mit etw** ~ to do away with sth; *siehe* **aufgeräumt**.

**Aufräumungs|arbeiten** *pl* clearing-up operations *pl*.

**aufrechnen** *vt sep* **etw gegen etw** ~ to offset sth against sth.

**aufrecht** *adj (lit, fig)* upright; *Körperhaltung, Gangart auch* erect.

**aufrecht|erhalten\*** *vt sep irreg* to maintain; *Kontakt, Bräuche auch* to keep up; *Behauptung auch* to stick to; *(moralisch) jdn* to keep going.

**Aufrecht|erhaltung** *f siehe vt* maintenance, maintaining; keeping up; sticking *(gen to)*; keeping going.

**aufregen** *sep* **1** *vt (ärgerlich machen)* to irritate, to annoy; *(nervös machen)* to make nervous; *(beunruhigen)* to agitate; *(bestürzen)* to upset; *(erregen)* to excite. **du regst mich auf!** you're getting on my nerves. **2** *vr* to get worked up *(col)* or excited *(über +acc about)*; *siehe* **aufgeregt**.

**aufregend** *adj* exciting.

**Aufregung** *f* excitement *no pl*; *(Beunruhigung)* agitation *no pl*. **nur keine** ~! don't get excited, don't get worked up *(col)*; **jdn in** ~ **versetzen** to get sb in a state *(col)*.

**aufreiben** *vt sep irreg* **(a)** *Haut etc* to chafe, to rub sore. **(b)** *(fig: zermürben)* to wear down. **(c)** *(Mil: völlig vernichten)* to wipe out, to annihilate.

**aufreibend** *adj (fig)* wearing, trying; *(stärker)* stressful.

**aufreihen** *sep* **1** *vt (in Linie)* to line up; *Perlen* to string. **2** *vr* to line up.

**aufreißen\*** *sep irreg* **1** *vt* **(a)** *(aufbrechen)* to tear or rip open; *Straße* to tear or rip up. **(b)** *Tür, Fenster* to fling open; *Augen, Mund* to open wide. **(c)** *(col) Mädchen* to pick up *(col)*. **2** *vi aux sein (Naht)* to split, to burst; *(Hose)* to tear, to rip; *(Wunde)* to tear open; *(Wolkendecke)* to break up.

**aufreizen** *vt sep (herausfordern)* to provoke; *(aufwiegeln)* to incite.

**aufreizend** *adj* provocative.

**aufrichten** *sep* **1** *vt* **(a)** *Gegenstand* to put upright; *jdn* to help up; *Oberkörper* to straighten (up). **(b)** *(fig: moralisch)* to put new heart into. **2** *vr (gerade stehen)* to stand up (straight); *(gerade sitzen)* to sit up (straight); *(aus gebückter Haltung)* to straighten up. **sich im Bett** ~ to sit up in bed.

**aufrichtig** *adj* sincere *(zu, gegen towards)*; *(ehrlich auch)* honest.

**Aufrichtigkeit** *f siehe adj* sincerity; honesty.

**aufrollen** *vt sep* **(a)** *(zusammenrollen)* to roll up; *Kabel* to coil or wind up. **(b)** *(entrollen)* to unroll; *Fahne* to unfurl; *Kabel* to uncoil, to unwind. **(c)** *(fig) Problem* to go into. **einen Fall/Prozeß wieder** ~ to re-open a case/trial.

**aufrücken** *vi sep aux sein (lit, fig)* to move up. **zum Geschäftsleiter** ~ to be promoted to manager.

**Aufruf** *m* **(a)** appeal *(an +acc to)*. **(b)** *(von Namen)* **nach** ~ when called. **(c)** *(Comp, Aviat)* call.

**aufrufen** *sep irreg* **1** *vt* **(a)** *Namen* to call. **Sie werden aufgerufen** your name or you will be called; **einen Schüler** ~ to ask a pupil (to answer) a question. **(b)** **jdn zu etw** ~ *(zu Mithilfe, Unterstützung etc)* to appeal to or call upon sb for sth. **(c)** *(Jur) Zeugen* to summon. **(d)** *(Comp)* to call up. **2** *vi* **zum Streik** *etc* ~ to call for a strike *etc*.

**Aufruhr** *m* **-e (a)** *(Auflehnung)* revolt, rebellion, uprising. **(b)** *(Bewegtheit, fig: Erregung)* tumult, turmoil. **in** ~ **sein** to be in a turmoil; **jdn in** ~ **verset-**

zen to throw sb into a turmoil.

**aufrühren** *vt sep (lit, fig)* to stir up.

**Aufrührer(in** *f) m* - rabble-rouser.

**aufrührerisch** *adj* **(a)** *Rede, Pamphlet* rabble-rousing, inflammatory. **(b)** *attr (in Aufruhr)* rebellious; *(meuternd)* mutinous.

**aufrunden** *vt sep Zahl* to round up *(auf +acc to)*.

**aufrüsten** *vti sep* to arm.

**Aufrüstung** *f* armament. **atomare** ~ nuclear armament.

**aufrütteln** *vt sep* to rouse *(aus from)*. **jdn/jds Gewissen** ~ to stir sb/sb's conscience.

**aufs** = **auf das**.

**aufsagen** *vt sep Gedicht etc* to recite, to say.

**aufsammeln** *vt sep (lit, fig)* to pick up.

**aufsässig** *adj* rebellious.

**Aufsässigkeit** *f* rebelliousness.

**Aufsatz** *m* **(a)** *(Abhandlung)* essay; *(Schul~ auch)* composition. **(b)** *(oberer Teil)* top or upper part.

**aufsaugen** *vt sep irreg Flüssigkeit* to soak up; *(fig)* to absorb. **etw mit dem Staubsauger** ~ to vacuum sth up.

**aufschauen** *vt sep (dial)* = **aufblicken**.

**aufscheuchen** *vt sep* to startle.

**aufscheuern** *vt sep* to rub sore, to chafe.

**aufschichten** *vt sep* to stack, to pile up; *Stapel* to build up.

**aufschieben** *vt sep irreg Fenster, Tür* to slide open; *Riegel* to push or slide back; *(fig: verschieben)* to put off, to postpone. **aufgeschoben ist nicht aufgehoben** *(prov)* putting something off does not mean it's cancelled.

**Aufschlag** *m* **(a)** *(das Aufschlagen)* impact. **(b)** *(Tennis etc)* service, serve. **sie hat** ~ it's her service or serve. **(c)** *(Preis~)* surcharge, extra charge. **(d)** *(Ärmel~)* cuff; *(Hosen~)* turn-up *(Brit)*, cuff *(US)*; *(Mantel~ etc)* lapel.

**Aufschlag-** *in cpds (Sport)* service.

**aufschlagen** *sep irreg* **1** *vi* **(a)** *aux sein (auftreffen)* **auf etw** *(dat)* ~ to hit sth; **mit dem Kopf** *etc* **auf etw** *(acc or dat)* ~ to hit one's head *etc* on sth. **(b)** *aux haben or sein (Waren, Preise)* to rise, to go up *(um by)*. **(c)** *(Tennis etc)* to serve. **2** *vt* **(a)** *(durch Schlagen öffnen)* to crack. **jdm/sich den Kopf** ~ to crack sb's/one's head open. **(b)** *(aufklappen)* to open. **schlagt Seite 111 auf** open your books at page 111. **(c)** *Augen* to open. **(d)** *(aufbauen) Bett, Liegestuhl* to put up; *Zelt auch* to pitch; *Lager* to set up, to pitch. **(e)** *(Comm) Preise* to put up.

**aufschließen** *sep irreg* **1** *vt (öffnen)* to unlock. **jdm die Tür** *etc* ~ to unlock the door *etc* for sb; *siehe* **aufgeschlossen**. **2** *vi* **(a)** *(öffnen)* **(jdm)** ~ to unlock the door (for sb). **(b)** *(heranrücken)* to close up; *(Sport)* to catch up *(zu with)*.

**aufschlitzen** *vt sep* to rip open; *(mit Messer auch)* to slit open.

**aufschluchzen** *vi sep (geh)* to give a deep sob.

**Aufschluß** *m (Aufklärung)* information *no pl*. **(jdm)** ~ **über etw** *(acc)* **geben** to give (sb) information about sth.

**aufschlüsseln** *vt sep* to break down *(nach into)*; *(klassifizieren)* to classify *(nach according to)*.

**aufschlußreich** *adj* informative, instructive.

**aufschnappen** *vt sep* to catch; *(col) Wort etc* to pick up.

**aufschneiden** *sep irreg* **1** *vt* **(a)** to cut open; *Braten* to carve. **(b)** *(in Scheiben schneiden)* to slice. **2** *vi (col: prahlen)* to brag, to boast.

**Aufschneider** *m (col)* boaster, show-off *(col)*.

**Aufschnitt** *m no pl* (assorted) sliced cold meats, cold cuts.

**aufschnüren** *vt sep (lösen)* to untie, to undo; *Schuh auch* to unlace.

**aufschrauben** *vt sep Schraube etc* to unscrew; *Flasche etc* to take the top off.

**aufschrecken** *sep* **1** *vt* to startle; *(aus Gleichgültigkeit)* to jolt *(aus* out of*)*. **2** *vi aux sein* to start (up), to be startled. **aus dem Schlaf** ~ to wake up with a start.

**Aufschrei** *m* yell; *(schrill)* scream, shriek. **ein** ~ **der Empörung** *(fig)* an outcry.

**aufschreiben** *vt sep irreg* **(a)** *(niederschreiben)* etw ~ to write *or* note sth down. **(b)** *(notieren)* **sich** *(dat)* **etw** ~ to make a note of sth.

**aufschreien** *vi sep irreg* to yell out; *(schrill)* to scream *or* shriek out.

**Aufschrift** *f* inscription; *(Etikett)* label.

**Aufschub** *m (Verzögerung)* delay; *(Vertagung)* postponement. **die Sache duldet keinen** ~ *(geh)* the matter must not be delayed; **jdm** ~ **gewähren** to grant sb an extension.

**aufschürfen** *vt sep* **sich** *(dat)* **die Haut/das Knie** ~ to graze *or* scrape oneself/one's knee.

**aufschütteln** *vt sep Kissen* to shake *or* plump up.

**aufschütten** *vt sep* **(a)** *Flüssigkeit* to pour on. **Kaffee** ~ to make coffee. **(b)** *Kohle* to put on (the fire). **(c)** *Damm, Deich* to throw up.

**aufschwatzen** *vt sep (col)* **jdm etw** ~ to talk sb into taking sth.

**aufschwingen** *vr sep irreg* to swing oneself up; *(Vogel)* to soar (up). **sich zu etw** ~ *(sich aufraffen)* to bring oneself to do sth.

**Aufschwung** *m* **(a)** *(Antrieb)* lift; *(der Wirtschaft etc)* upturn, upswing *(gen* in*)*. **(b)** *(Turnen)* swing-up.

**aufsehen** *vi sep irreg* = **aufblicken**.

**Aufsehen** *nt no pl* sensation. **großes** ~ **erregen** to cause a sensation *or* stir; **ich möchte jedes** ~ **vermeiden** I want to avoid any fuss.

**aufsehen|erregend** *adj* sensational.

**Aufseher(in** *f)* *m (allgemein)* supervisor; *(Gefängnis~)* warder *(Brit)*, guard *(US)*; *(Park~, Museums~ etc)* attendant.

**aufsein** *vi sep irreg aux sein* **(a)** *(aufgestanden sein)* to be up. **(b)** *(geöffnet sein)* to be open.

**aufsetzen** *sep* **1** *vt* **(a)** *Brille etc, Miene etc* to put on; *Fuß* to put down. **(b)** *(verfassen)* to draft. **2** *vr* to sit up. **3** *vi (Flugzeug)* to touch down, to land.

**Aufsetzer** *m* - *(Sport)* bouncing ball.

**aufseufzen** *vi sep* **(tief)** ~ to heave a (deep) sigh.

**Aufsicht** *f no pl (Überwachung)* supervision *(über +acc* of*)*; *(Obhut)* charge. **die** ~ **haben** *or* **führen** to be in charge; **unter jds** ~ *(dat)* under the supervision of sb; **bei einer Prüfung** ~ **führen** to invigilate an examination; **jdn ohne** ~ **lassen** to leave sb unsupervised.

**aufsichtführend** *adj attr Behörde* supervisory; *Beamter* supervising.

**Aufsichts-:** ~**beamte(r)** *m (in Museum, Zoo etc)* attendant; ~**rat** *m* (supervisory) board; *(Mitglied)* member of the board.

**aufsitzen** *vi sep irreg* **(a)** *(aufgerichtet sitzen)* to sit up. **(b)** *aux sein (auf Reittier)* to mount; *(auf Fahrzeug)* to get on. **(c)** *aux sein (col: hereinfallen)* **jdm/ einer Sache** ~ to be taken in by sb/sth.

**aufspalten** *vtr sep* to split; *(fig auch)* to split up.

**aufspannen** *vt sep* **(a)** *Netz, Sprungtuch* to stretch *or* spread out; *Schirm* to put up, to open. **(b)** *(aufziehen)* *Leinwand* to stretch *(auf +acc* onto*)*; *Saite* to put on *(auf etw (acc)* sth*)*.

**aufsparen** *vt sep* to save (up), to keep.

**aufsperren** *vt sep Tür, Schnabel* to open wide. **die Ohren** ~ to prick up one's ears.

**aufspielen** *sep* **1** *vi (dated)* to play; *(anfangen)* to strike up. **2** *vr (col)* **(a)** *(sich wichtig tun)* to give oneself airs. **(b)** **sich als etw** ~ to set oneself up as sth; **sich als Boß** ~ to play the boss.

**aufspießen** *vt sep* to spear; *(durchbohren)* to run through; *(mit Hörnern)* to gore; *Fleisch (mit Spieß)* to skewer.

**aufsplittern** *vti sep (vi: aux sein) (Holz)* to splinter; *(Gruppe)* to split (up).

**aufspringen** *vi sep irreg aux sein* **(a)** *(hochspringen)* to jump up. **auf etw** *(acc)* ~ to jump onto sth. **(b)** *(auftreffen)* to bounce. **(c)** *(sich öffnen) (Tür)* to burst open; *(platzen)* to burst; *(Haut, Lippen etc)* to crack, to chap.

**aufspüren** *vt sep (lit, fig)* to track down.

**aufstacheln** *vt sep* = **anstacheln**.

**aufstampfen** *vi sep* to stamp. **mit dem Fuß** ~ to stamp one's foot.

**Aufstand** *m* rebellion, revolt. **den** ~ **proben** *(fig)* to flex one's muscles.

**aufständisch** *adj* rebellious, insurgent.

**Aufständische(r)** *mf decl as adj* rebel, insurgent.

**aufstapeln** *vt sep* to stack *or* pile up.

**aufstauen** *sep* **1** *vt Wasser* to dam. **etw in sich** *(dat)* ~ *(fig)* to bottle sth up inside (oneself). **2** *vr* to collect; *(fig: Ärger)* to be bottled up.

**aufstechen** *vt sep irreg* to puncture; *(Med)* to lance.

**aufstecken** *sep* **1** *vt* **(a)** *(auf etw stecken)* to put on *(auf +acc* -to*)*. **(b)** *(mit Nadeln)* to pin up; *Haar auch* to put up. **2** *vi (col: aufgeben)* to pack it in *(col)*; *(bei Rennen etc)* to drop out.

**aufstehen** *vi sep irreg aux sein* **(a)** *(sich erheben)* to get *or* stand up; *(morgens aus dem Bett)* to get up. ~ **dürfen** *(Kranker)* to be allowed (to get) up; **da mußt du früher** *or* **eher** ~! *(fig col)* you'll have to do better than that! **(b)** *(col: offen sein)* to be open. **(c)** *(sich auflehnen)* to rise (in arms).

**aufsteigen** *vi sep irreg aux sein* **(a)** *(auf Berg, Leiter)* to climb (up); *(Flugzeug)* to climb; *(Nebel, Gefühl)* to rise; *(Gewitter, Wolken)* to gather. **einen Ballon** ~ **lassen** to release a balloon; **an die Oberfläche** ~ to rise to the surface; **in jdm** ~ *(Haß, Verdacht, Erinnerung etc)* to well up in sb. **(b)** *(auf Fahrrad etc)* to get on *(auf etw (acc)* -to*)* sth*)*. **(c)** *(fig: im Rang etc)* to rise *(zu* to*)*; *(beruflich, Sport)* to be promoted *(in +acc* to*)*.

**Aufsteiger** *m* **(a)** *(Sport)* promoted team. **(b)** *(auch* ~**in** *f)* **(sozialer)** ~ social climber. **ein** ~ **sein** to be upwardly mobile.

**aufstellen** *sep* **1** *vt* **(a)** *(aufrichten)* to put up *(auf +dat* on*)*; *Maschine* to install; *Falle* to set; *(Mil)* to deploy; *(postieren) Wachposten* to post. **(b)** *Truppe* to raise; *Spieler, Mannschaft* to select; *Kandidaten* to nominate. **(c)** *(erzielen) Rekord* to set (up). **(d)** *Forderung, Behauptung* to put forward; *System* to establish; *Programm, Rechnung, Liste* to draw up. **(e)** *Essen etc (auf Herd)* to put on. **2** *vr (sich postieren)* to stand; *(hintereinander)* to line up; *(Soldaten)* to fall into line. **sich im Karree/Kreis** *etc* ~ to form a square/circle *etc.*

**Aufstellung** *f siehe vt* **(a)** putting up; installation; setting; deployment; posting. **(b)** raising; selecting; nomination; *(Mannschaft)* line-up *(col)*, team. **(c)** setting. **(d)** putting forward; establishing; drawing up; *(Liste)* list; *(Tabelle)* table.

**aufstemmen** *vt sep* to force open.

**Aufstieg** *m* **-e** **(a)** *no pl (auf Berg)* climb, ascent; *(von Flugzeug, Rakete)* climb; *(von Ballon)* ascent. **(b)** *(fig)* rise; *(Sport, beruflich)* promotion *(in +acc* to*)*. **den** ~ **ins Management schaffen** to work one's way up into the management. **(c)** *(Weg)* way up *(auf etw (acc) sth)*, ascent *(auf +acc of)*.

**Aufstiegs:**- ~**chance,** ~**möglichkeit** *f* prospect of promotion.

**aufstöbern** *vt sep Wild* to flush; *(col: entdecken)* to run to earth.

**aufstocken** *vt sep Vorräte* to build up.

**aufstöhnen** *vi sep* to give a loud groan.

**aufstoßen** *sep irreg* **1** *vt (öffnen)* to push open; *(mit dem Fuß)* to kick open. **2** *vi* **(a)** *aux sein* **auf etw** *(acc)* ~ to hit (on *or* against) sth. **(b)** *aux haben (rülpsen)* to burp.

**Aufstoßen** *nt no pl* burping, flatulence.

**aufstrebend** *adj (fig)* aspiring; *(Stadt, Land)* up-and-coming.

**Aufstrich** *m (auf Brot)* spread.

**aufstülpen** *vt sep* to put on; *Ärmel, Kragen* to turn up.

**aufstützen** *sep* **1** *vt Kranken etc* to prop up; *Arme* to rest *(auf +acc or dat on)*. **den Kopf** ~ to rest one's head on one's hand. **2** *vr* to support oneself; *(im Bett, beim Essen)* to prop oneself up.

**aufsuchen** *vt sep Bekannten* to call on; *Arzt, Ort, Toilette* to go to.

**auftakeln** *vt sep (Naut)* to rig up. **sich** ~ *(pej col)* to tart oneself up *(col)*; *siehe* **aufgetakelt.**

**Auftakt** *m* **(a)** *(Beginn)* start. **den** ~ **zu etw bilden** to mark the beginning of sth. **(b)** *(Mus)* upbeat.

**auftanken** *vti sep* to fill up; *(Aviat)* to refuel. **Benzin** ~ to fill up with petrol *(Brit) or* gas *(US)*.

**auftauchen** *vi sep aux sein* **(a)** *(aus dem Wasser)* to surface; *(Taucher etc auch)* to come up. **(b)** *(fig) (sichtbar werden)* to appear; *(aus Nebel etc auch)* to emerge; *(Zweifel, Problem)* to arise. **(c)** *(gefunden werden, kommen)* to turn up.

**auftauen** *sep* **1** *vi aux sein* to thaw; *(fig auch)* to unbend. **2** *vt* to thaw; *Tiefkühlkost* to thaw (out).

**aufteilen** *vt sep* **(a)** *(aufgliedern)* to divide *or* split up *(in +acc into)*. **(b)** *(verteilen)* to share out *(an +acc between)*.

**Aufteilung** *f siehe vt* division; sharing out.

**auftischen** *vt sep* to serve up; *(fig col)* to come up with.

**Auftrag** *m, pl* **Aufträge (a)** *no pl (Anweisung)* orders *pl*, instructions *pl*; *(zugeteilte Arbeit)* job, task; *(Jur)* brief. **einen** ~ **ausführen** to carry out an order; **ich habe den** ~**, Ihnen mitzuteilen** ... I have been instructed to tell you ...; **in jds** ~ *(dat) (für jdn)* on sb's behalf; *(auf jds Anweisung)* on sb's instructions; **im** ~ *or* **i.A.: J. Burnett** pp J. Burnett. **(b)** *(über +acc for) (Comm)* order; *(bei Künstlern etc)* commission. **etw in** ~ **geben** to order/commission sth *(bei from)*.

**auftragen** *sep irreg* **1** *vt* **(a)** *(servieren)* to serve. **(b)** *Farbe, Salbe* to apply, to put on. **etw auf etw** *(acc)* ~ to apply sth to sth. **(c) jdm etw** ~ *(form)* to instruct sb to do sth. **(d)** *Kleider* to wear out. **2** *vi (übertreiben)* **dick** ~ *(col)* to lay it on thick *(col)*.

**Auftraggeber(in** *f)* *m* client, customer.

**Auftrags:**- ~**bestätigung** *f* confirmation of order; **a**~**gemäß** *adj, adv* as instructed; *(Comm)* as per order; ~**rückgang** *m* drop in orders.

**auftreffen** *vi sep irreg aux sein* **auf etw** *(dat or acc)* ~ to hit *or* strike sth.

**auftreiben** *vt sep irreg (col: ausfindig machen)* to find, to get hold of *(col)*.

**auftrennen** *vt sep* to undo.

**auftreten** *sep irreg* **1** *vi aux sein* **(a)** *(lit)* to tread. **(b)** *(erscheinen, Theat)* to appear. **als Zeuge** ~ to appear as a witness; **gegen jdn/etw** ~ to stand up *or* speak out against sb/sth; **geschlossen** ~ to put up a united front. **(c)** *(fig: eintreten)* to occur; *(Schwierigkeiten*

*etc)* to arise. **(d)** *(sich benehmen)* to behave. **bescheiden/arrogant** ~ to have a modest/an arrogant manner. **(e)** *(handeln)* **als Vermittler** *etc* ~ to act as intermediary *etc.* **2** *vt Tür etc* to kick open.

**Auftreten** *nt no pl* **(a)** *(Erscheinen)* appearance. **(b)** *(Benehmen)* manner. **(c)** *(Vorkommen)* occurrence.

**Auftrieb** *m no pl* **(a)** *(Phys)* buoyancy; *(Aviat)* lift. **(b)** *(fig)* impetus; *(Preis~)* upward trend *(gen in)*; *(Ermunterung)* lift. **das wird ihm** ~ **geben** that will give him a lift.

**Auftritt** *m* entrance; *(Theat: Szene)* scene.

**auftrumpfen** *vi sep (seine Leistungstärke zeigen)* to show how good one is.

**auftun** *sep irreg* **1** *vt (col: ausfindig machen)* to find. **2** *vr (sich öffnen)* to open (up).

**auftürmen** *sep* **1** *vt* to pile up. **2** *vr (Gebirge etc)* to tower up; *(Schwierigkeiten)* to pile up.

**aufwachen** *vi sep aux sein (lit, fig)* to wake up. **aus einer Narkose** ~ to come out of an anaesthetic.

**aufwachsen** *vi sep irreg aux sein* to grow up.

**aufwallen** *vi sep aux sein* to bubble up; *(Cook)* to boil up; *(Leidenschaft etc)* to surge up.

**Aufwand** *m no pl* **(a)** *(von Geld)* expenditure *(an +dat of)*. **das erfordert einen großen** ~ **an Zeit/ Energie/Geld** that requires a lot of time/energy/ money. **(b)** *(Luxus, Prunk)* extravagance. **(großen)** ~ **treiben** to be (very) extravagant.

**Aufwands\entschädigung** *f* expense allowance.

**aufwärmen** *sep* **1** *vt* to heat *or* warm up; *(col: wieder erwähnen)* to bring up. **2** *vr* to warm up.

**aufwarten** *vi sep (zu bieten haben)* **mit etw** ~ to offer sth.

**aufwärts** *adv* up, upward(s); *(bergauf)* uphill. **den Fluß** ~ upstream.

**Aufwärts-:** ~**entwicklung** *f* upward trend *(gen in)*; **a**~**gehen** *vi impers sep irreg aux sein* **mit dem Staat/der Firma geht es a**~ things are improving for the country/firm; ~**haken** *m (Boxen)* uppercut; ~**trend** *m* upward trend.

**Aufwartung** *f (geh: Besuch)* **jdm seine** ~ **machen** to pay one's respects to sb.

**aufwecken** *vt sep* to wake (up); *(fig)* to rouse; *siehe* **aufgeweckt.**

**aufweichen** *sep* **1** *vt* to soften; *Brot* to soak. **2** *vi aux sein* to become soft.

**aufweisen** *vt sep irreg* to show; *(haben)* to have. **das Buch weist einige Fehler auf** the book has some mistakes in it; **etwas aufzuweisen haben** to have something to show for oneself.

**aufwenden** *vt sep irreg* to use; *Energie* to expend; *Geld, Zeit* to spend. **viel Mühe/Zeit** ~**, etw zu tun** to take a lot of trouble/spend a lot of time doing sth.

**aufwendig** *adj* lavish; *(teuer)* costly.

**Aufwendungen** *pl* expenditure.

**aufwerfen** *vt sep irreg* **(a)** *(aufhäufen)* to pile up. **(b)** *Frage, Probleme* to raise, to bring up.

**aufwerten** *vt sep* **(a)** *(auch vi) Währung* to revalue. **(b)** *(fig)* to increase the value of.

**Aufwertung** *f (von Währung)* revaluation; *(fig)* increase in value.

**aufwickeln** *vt sep* **(a)** *(aufrollen)* to roll up; *(col) Haar* to put in curlers. **(b)** *(lösen)* to untie; *Windeln, Verband* to take off.

**aufwiegeln** *vt sep* to stir up. **jdn zum Streik/ Widerstand** ~ to incite sb to strike/resist.

**aufwiegen** *vt sep irreg (fig)* to offset. **das ist nicht mit Geld aufzuwiegen** that can't be measured in terms of money.

**Aufwiegler(in** *f)* *m* - agitator; *(Anstifter)* instigator.

**aufwieglerisch** *adj* seditious; *Rede, Artikel auch* inflammatory.

**Aufwind** *m (Aviat)* upcurrent. **neuen ~ bekommen** *(fig)* to get new impetus.

**aufwirbeln** *vti sep (vi: aux sein)* to swirl *or* whirl up. **(viel) Staub ~** *(fig)* to cause a (big) stir.

**aufwischen** *vti sep* to mop up.

**aufwühlen** *vt sep* **(a)** *(lit)* Erde, Meer to churn (up). **(b)** *(geh)* Gefühle to stir; *siehe* **aufgewühlt.**

**aufzählen** *vt sep* to list; *(aufführen auch)* to enumerate.

**Aufzählung** *f siehe vt* list; enumeration.

**aufzeichnen** *vt sep* **(a)** *Plan etc* to draw, to sketch. **(b)** *(notieren, Rad, TV)* to record.

**Aufzeichnung** *f* **(a)** *usu pl (Notiz)* note; *(Niederschrift auch)* record. **(b)** *(Tonband~, Film~)* recording.

**aufzeigen** *vt sep* to show.

**aufziehen** *sep irreg* **1** *vt* **(a)** *(hochziehen)* to pull *or* draw up; *Flagge, Segel* to hoist. **(b)** *(öffnen)* Reißverschluß to undo; *Schublade* to (pull) open; *Gardinen* to draw (back). **(c)** *(aufspannen)* Saite, Reifen to put on. **(d)** *(spannen)* Feder, Uhr etc to wind up. **(e)** *(großziehen)* to raise; *Kind auch* to bring up; *Tier auch* to rear. **(f)** *(col: veranstalten)* to set up; *Fest* to arrange. **(g)** *(verspotten)* **jdn ~** *(col)* to tease sb *(mit about)*. **2** *vi aux sein (Wolke)* to come up; *(Gewitter, Wolken auch)* to gather; *(aufmarschieren)* to march up.

**Aufzucht** *f no pl (das Großziehen)* rearing, raising.

**Aufzug** *m* **(a)** *(Fahrstuhl)* lift *(Brit)*, elevator *(US)*; *(Güter~)* hoist. **(b)** *(von Gewitter etc)* gathering. **(c)** *(Theat)* act. **(d)** *no pl (pej col: Kleidung)* get-up *(col)*.

**aufzwingen** *sep irreg* **1** *vt* **jdm etw/seinen Willen ~** to force sth on sb/impose one's will on sb. **2** *vr* **das zwingt sich einem doch förmlich auf** it's the only possible conclusion.

**Aug. = August** Aug.

**Aug|apfel** *m* eyeball. **jdn/etw wie seinen ~ hüten** to cherish sb/sth like life itself.

**Auge** *nt -n* **(a)** eye. **gute/schlechte ~n haben** to have good/bad eyesight; **mit den ~n zwinkern/blinzeln** to wink/blink; **jdn mit** *or* **aus großen ~n ansehen** to look at sb wide-eyed; **mit bloßem ~** with the naked eye; **mit verbundenen ~n** *(lit, fig)* blindfold; **etw im ~ haben** *(fig)* to have one's eye on sth; **ein sicheres ~ für etw haben** to have a good eye for sth; **ich kann doch meine ~n nicht überall haben** I can't see everything at once; **er machte große ~n** his eyes popped out of his head *(col)*; **ich konnte kaum aus den ~n sehen** I could hardly see straight; **geh mir aus den ~n!** get out of my sight!; **unter jds ~n** *(dat)* *(fig)* before sb's very eyes; **vor aller ~n** in front of everybody, for all to see; **jdn/etw mit anderen ~n (an)sehen** to see sb/sth in a different light; **seine ~n waren größer als sein Magen** *(col)* his eyes were bigger than his stomach; **aus den ~n, aus dem Sinn** *(Prov)* out of sight, out of mind *(Prov)*; **das ~ des Gesetzes** the law; **soweit das ~ reicht** as far as the eye can see; **er hatte nur ~n für sie** he only had eyes for her; **ich habe kein ~ zugetan** I didn't sleep a wink; **da blieb kein ~ trocken** *(hum)* there wasn't a dry eye in the place; **ein ~ auf jdn/etw geworfen haben** to have one's eye on sb/sth; **jdm etw aufs ~ drücken** *(col)* to force *or* impose sth on sb; **ein ~/beide ~n zudrücken** *(col)* to turn a blind eye; **etw im ~ behalten** to keep *or* bear sth in mind; **sie ließen ihn nicht aus den ~n** they didn't let him out of their sight; **jdn/etw aus den ~n verlieren** to lose sight of sb/sth; *(fig)* to lose touch with sb/sth; **das springt einem gleich ins ~** it hits you right in the face *(col)*; **jdm etw vor ~n führen** *(fig)* to make sb aware of sth; **etw ins ~ fassen** to contemplate sth; **etw noch**

**genau** *or* **lebhaft vor ~n haben** to remember sth clearly *or* vividly; **jdm die ~n öffnen** *(fig)* to open sb's eyes; **ein ~ riskieren** *(hum)* to have a peep *(col)*; **das kann leicht ins ~ gehen** *(fig col)* it might easily go wrong; **in meinen ~n** in my opinion *or* view; **mit einem lachenden und einem weinenden ~** with mixed feelings; **~ in ~** face to face; **~ um ~, Zahn um Zahn** *(Bibl)* an eye for an eye and a tooth for a tooth; **dem Tod ins ~ sehen** to look death in the face.
**(b)** *(bei Kartoffel)* eye.
**(c)** *(Punkt bei Spielen)* point.
**(d)** *(von Hurrikan)* eye.

**äugen** *vi* to look.

**Augen-:** **~arzt** *m* eye specialist, ophthalmologist; **~aufschlag** *m* look.

**Augenblick** *m* moment. **jeden ~** any time *or* moment; **einen ~, bitte** one moment please!; **~ mal!** *(col)* just a minute *or* second! *(col)*; **im ~** at the moment; **im ersten ~** for a moment.

**augenblicklich 1** *adj (sofortig)* immediate; *(gegenwärtig)* present, current. **2** *adv (sofort)* immediately; *(zur Zeit)* at the moment.

**Augen-:** **~braue** *f* eyebrow; **~entzündung** *f* inflammation of the eyes; **~farbe** *f* colour *(Brit)* *or* color *(US)* of eyes; **ihre ~farbe** the colour of her eyes; **~höhe** *f:* **in ~höhe** at eye level; **~höhle** *f* eye socket; **~klappe** *f* **(a)** eye patch; **(b)** *(für Pferde)* blinker, blinder *(US)*; **~krankheit** *f* eye disease; **~licht** *nt no pl* (eye)sight; **~lid** *nt* eyelid; **~maß** *nt* eye; *(für Entfernungen)* eye for distance(s); *(fig)* perceptiveness; **nach ~maß** by eye; **ein gutes/schlechtes ~maß haben** to have a good eye/no eye for distance(s); **~merk** *nt no pl (Aufmerksamkeit)* attention; **jds/sein ~merk auf etw** *(acc)* **lenken** to direct sb's/one's attention to sth; **~operation** *f* eye operation; **~optiker** *m* optician; **~paar** *nt* pair of eyes; **~ränder** *pl* rims of the/one's eyes; **~schein** *m no pl* **(a)** *(Anschein)* appearance; **dem ~schein nach** by all appearances; **(b)** **jdn/etw in ~schein nehmen** to have a close look at sb/sth; **a~scheinlich** *adj* obvious, evident; **~tropfen** *pl* eyedrops *pl*; **~weide** *f* feast *or* treat for the eyes; **~wimper** *f* eyelash; **~winkel** *m* corner of the/one's eye; **~wischerei** *f (fig)* eyewash; **~zeuge** *m* eyewitness *(bei to)*; **~zeugenbericht** *m* eyewitness account; **~zwinkern** *nt no pl* winking; **a~zwinkernd** *adj* winking *attr; (fig)* sly.

**August** *m -e* August; *siehe* **März.**

**Auktion** *f* auction.

**Auktionator(in** *f)* [-'toːrɪn] *m* auctioneer.

**Auktionshaus** *nt* auction house, auctioneers *pl*.

**Aula** *f, pl* **Aulen** *(Sch, Univ)* (assembly) hall.

**Au-pair-** [oʊ'pɛːɐ]: **~-Mädchen** *nt* au-pair (girl); **~-Stelle** *f* au-pair job.

**Aura** *f no pl* aura.

**aus 1** *prep +dat* **(a)** *(räumlich)* from; *(aus dem Inneren von)* out of. **~ dem Fenster/der Tür** out of the window/door; **~ unserer Mitte** from our midst.
**(b)** *(Herkunft, Quelle bezeichnend)* from. **~ dem Deutschen** from (the) German; **~ guter Familie** from a good family; **~ dem Barock** from the Baroque period.
**(c)** *(auf Ursache deutend)* out of. **~ Haß/Mitleid** out of hatred/sympathy; **~ Erfahrung** from experience; **~ Furcht vor/Liebe zu** for fear/love of; **~ dem Grunde, daß ...** for the reason that ...; **~ Spaß** for fun; **~ Versehen** by mistake; **~ sich heraus** of one's own accord.
**(d)** *(beschaffen ~)* (made) of. **ein Herz ~ Stein** a heart of stone.

(e) einen anständigen Menschen ~ jdm machen to make sb into a decent person; was ist ~ ihm/dieser Sache geworden? what has become of him/this?; ~ ihm wird einmal ein guter Arzt he'll make a good doctor one day. (f) ~ dem Gleichgewicht out of balance; ~ der Mode out of fashion.

2 adv siehe auch aussein (a) (col: vorbei, zu Ende) over. ~ und vorbei over and done with. (b) (gelöscht) out; (an Geräten) off. Licht ~! lights out! (c) (Sport) out, out of play. (d) (in Verbindung mit von) von München ~ from Munich; von sich (dat) ~ of one's own accord; von ihm ~ as far as he's concerned; ok, von mir ~ OK, if you like.

**Aus** nt (a) no pl (Sport) touch no art. (b) (Ende) end.

**aus|arbeiten** vt sep to work out; (vorbereiten) to prepare.

**Aus|arbeitung** f siehe vt working out; preparation.

**aus|arten** vi sep aux sein (Party etc) to get out of control. ~ in (+acc) or zu to degenerate into.

**aus|atmen** vti sep to breathe out, to exhale.

**ausbaden** vt sep (col) to carry the can for (col).

**Ausbau** m -ten siehe vt removal; extension (zu into); conversion (zu (in)to); improvement; building up.

**ausbauen** vt sep (a) (herausmontieren) to remove (aus from). (b) (lit, fig: erweitern) to extend (zu into); (umbauen) to convert (zu (in)to); Straße to improve; Freundschaft to build up; siehe ausgebaut.

**ausbaufähig** adj Position with good prospects; Produktion, Markt, Computer expandable; Beziehungen that can be built up.

**ausbedingen** vr sep irreg sich (dat) etw ~ to insist on sth.

**ausbeißen** vr sep irreg sich (dat) an etw (dat) die Zähne ~ (fig) to have a tough time of it with sth.

**ausbessern** vt sep to repair; Wäsche etc auch to mend.

**Ausbesserung** f siehe vt repair; mending.

**Ausbesserungs-:** ~arbeiten pl repair work sing; a~bedürftig adj in need of repair etc.

**ausbeulen** vt sep Auto to knock the dent(s) out of; Kleidung to make baggy; siehe ausgebeult.

**Ausbeute** f (Gewinn) profit, gain; (Ertrag einer Grube etc) yield (an +dat in); (fig) result(s); (Einnahmen) proceeds pl.

**ausbeuten** vt sep (lit, fig) to exploit.

**Ausbeuter(in** f) m - exploiter.

**Ausbeutung** f exploitation.

**ausbezahlen*** vt sep Geld to pay out.

**ausbilden** vt sep to train; (unterrichten auch) to instruct; (akademisch) to educate; Fähigkeiten to develop. sich in etw (dat)/als or zu etw ~ lassen (esp Arbeiter, Lehrling) to train in sth/as sth; ein ausgebildeter Übersetzer a qualified translator.

**Ausbilder(in** f) m - instructor, instructress.

**Ausbildung** f siehe vt training; instruction; education; development. er ist noch in der ~ he's still a trainee; he hasn't finished his education.

**Ausbildungs-:** ~beihilfe, ~förderung f grant; ~platz m (Stelle) training vacancy; ~stand m level of training; ~zeit f training period.

**ausbitten** vr sep irreg sich (dat) (von jdm) etw ~ (geh) to request sth (from sb) (form); ich bitte mir Ruhe aus! I will have silence!

**ausblasen** vt sep irreg to blow out; Ei to blow.

**ausbleiben** vi sep irreg aux sein (fortbleiben) to stay out; (nicht erscheinen: Gäste) to fail to appear; (nicht eintreten: Erwartung etc) to fail to materialize; (aufhören: Puls, Atmung etc) to stop. es konnte nicht ~, daß ... it was inevitable that ...

**ausblenden** vti sep (TV etc) to fade out; (plötzlich) to cut out.

**Ausblick** m (a) view (auf +acc of). (b) (fig) prospect, outlook (auf +acc for).

**ausblicken** vi sep (geh) nach jdm ~ to look for sb.

**ausbooten** vt sep (col) jdn to kick or boot out (col).

**ausbrechen** sep irreg 1 vt (herausbrechen) Steine to break off (aus from). 2 vi aux sein (a) (lit, fig: sich befreien) to break out (aus of) (auch Mil), to escape (aus from). (b) (Richtung ändern: Pferd, Wagen) to swerve; (Auto auch) to get into a skid. (c) (Krieg, Feuer, Schweiß etc) to break out; (Jubel, Zorn etc) to erupt, to explode; (Vulkan) to erupt. in Gelächter/Tränen/Jubel ~ to burst out laughing/crying/cheering.

**Ausbrecher(in** f) m - (col: Gefangener) escaped prisoner, escapee.

**ausbreiten** sep 1 vt to spread (out); Arme to stretch out; (ausstellen, fig: zeigen) to display; Licht, Wärme to spread. 2 vr (a) (sich verbreiten) to spread. (b) (col: sich breitmachen) to spread oneself out. (c) sich über etw (acc) ~ (fig) to dwell on sth.

**Ausbreitung** f spread, spreading.

**ausbrennen** sep irreg 1 vi aux sein (a) (zu Ende brennen) to burn out. (b) (völlig verbrennen) to be burnt out, to be gutted. er ist ausgebrannt (fig) he's burnt out. 2 vt (Med) to cauterize.

**ausbringen** vt sep irreg Trinkspruch to propose.

**Ausbruch** m (a) (aus from) (aus Gefängnis) breakout (auch Mil), escape (auch fig). (b) (Beginn) outbreak; (von Vulkan) eruption. zum ~ kommen to break out. (c) (fig: Gefühls~) outburst.

**ausbrüten** vt sep to hatch; (fig col) Plan etc to cook up (col).

**Ausbuchtung** f bulge; (von Strand) (small) cove.

**ausbügeln** vt sep to iron out; (col) Fehler, Verlust to make good.

**ausbuhen** vt sep (col) to boo; ausgebuht werden to be booed off the stage.

**Ausbund** m no pl: ein ~ an or von Tugend/Sparsamkeit a paragon of virtue/a model of thrift.

**ausbürgern** vt sep jdn ~ to expatriate sb.

**Ausbürgerung** f expatriation.

**Ausdauer** f no pl staying power, stamina; (Beharrlichkeit) perseverance.

**ausdauernd** adj (Mensch) with staying power, with stamina; (im Ertragen) with endurance; (beharrlich) persevering; Bemühungen etc untiring.

**ausdehnbar** adj expandable; (fig) extendable (auf +acc to).

**ausdehnen** sep 1 vt (a) (vergrößern) to expand. (b) (fig) to extend; (zeitlich auch) to prolong (auf +acc to). 2 vr (a) (größer werden) to expand; (sich erstrecken) to extend, to stretch (bis as far as). der Krieg dehnte sich über das ganze Land aus the war spread over the whole country. (b) (fig) to extend (über +acc over, bis as far as, to); (zeitlich) to go on (bis until); siehe ausgedehnt.

**Ausdehnung** f (a) siehe vt expansion; extension; prolongation. (b) (Umfang) expanse.

**ausdenken** vt sep irreg sich (dat) etw ~ (erfinden) to think sth up; (in Einzelheiten) to think sth out; Wunsch to think of sth; Überraschung to plan sth; (sich vorstellen) to imagine sth; eine ausgedachte Geschichte a made-up story; das ist nicht auszudenken (unvorstellbar) it's inconceivable.

**ausdienen** vi sep ausgedient haben (fig col) to have had its day.

**ausdiskutieren*** vt sep Thema to discuss fully.

**ausdrehen** vt sep (ausschalten) to turn or switch

off; *Licht auch* to turn out.

**Ausdruck**[1] *m, pl* **Ausdrücke** (a) *no pl* expression. **als ~ meiner Dankbarkeit** as an expression of my gratitude; **mit dem ~ des Bedauerns** *(form)* expressing regret; **etw zum ~ bringen** to express sth, to give expression to sth. (b) *(Wort)* expression; *(Fach~ auch)* term. **sich im ~ vergreifen** to use the wrong word.

**Ausdruck**[2] *m* **-e** *(Comp)* printout.

**ausdrucken** *vt sep (Comp)* to print out.

**ausdrücken** *sep* 1 *vt* (a) to press out, to squeeze out; *Pickel* to squeeze; *Zigarette* to stub out. (b) *(zum Ausdruck bringen)* to express *(jdm* to sb*)*. **anders ausgedrückt** in other words; **einfach ausgedrückt** put simply. 2 *vr (Mensch)* to express oneself. **er drückt sich gut aus** he is very articulate; **in ihrem Gesicht/Verhalten drückte sich Verzweiflung aus** her face/behaviour showed her despair.

**ausdrücklich** 1 *adj attr Wunsch* express, explicit. 2 *adv* explicitly; *(besonders)* particularly.

**Ausdrucks-:** **a~fähig** *adj* expressive; *(gewandt)* articulate; **~fähigkeit** *f siehe adj* expressiveness; articulateness; **a~los** *adj* inexpressive; *Gesicht, Blick auch* expressionless; **~losigkeit** *f siehe adj* inexpressiveness; lack of expression; **~mittel** *nt* means of expression; **a~voll** *adj* expressive; **~weise** *f* way of expressing oneself.

**ausdünnen** *vt sep Pflanzen, Haare* to thin out.

**ausdünsten** *vt sep Geruch* to give off.

**Ausdünstung** *f (Dampf)* vapour *(Brit)*, vapor *(US)*; *(Geruch)* smell.

**aus|einander** *adv (getrennt)* apart. **weit ~** far apart; *Meinungen* very different; **etw ~ schreiben** to write sth as two words; **die beiden sind (im Alter) ein Jahr ~** there is a year between the two of them; **~ sein** *(col: Paar)* to have split up.

**aus|einander-:** **~brechen** *sep irreg* 1 *vt* to break in two; 2 *vi aux sein (lit, fig)* to break up; **~fallen** *vi sep irreg aux sein (zerfallen)* to fall apart; *(fig auch)* to collapse; **~ gehen** *vi sep irreg aux sein* (a) *(lit, fig: sich trennen) (Menschen)* to part, to separate; *(Menge)* to disperse; *(Versammlung, Ehe etc)* to break up; (b) *(sich verzweigen: Weg etc)* to divide; *(zwei Wege)* to diverge; *(fig: Ansichten etc)* to differ; **~halten** *vt sep irreg* to keep apart; *(unterscheiden) Begriffe* to distinguish between; *esp Zwillinge etc* to tell apart; **~klaffen** *vi sep aux sein* to gape open; *(fig: Meinungen)* to be far apart, to diverge (wildly); **~laufen** *vi sep irreg aux sein* (a) *(zerlaufen)* to melt; *(Farbe)* to run; (b) *(col: sich trennen) (Menge)* to disperse; **~leben** *vr sep* to drift apart; **~nehmen** *vt sep irreg* to take apart; *Maschine etc auch* to dismantle; *(kritisch)* to tear apart *or* to pieces; **~setzen** *sep* 1 *vt (fig) (jdm* to sb*)* to explain; *(schriftlich auch)* to set out; 2 *vr* **sich mit etw ~setzen** *(sich befassen)* to work on; **sich kritisch mit etw ~setzen** to have a critical look at sth; **sich mit jdm ~setzen** to talk *or (sich streiten)* to argue with sb.

**Aus|einandersetzung** *f* (a) *(Diskussion)* discussion, debate *(über +acc* about, on*)*; *(Streit)* argument; *(feindlicher Zusammenstoß)* clash *(wegen* over*)*. (b) *(das Befassen)* examination *(mit* of*)*; *(kritisch)* analysis *(mit* of*)*.

**aus|erkoren** *adj (liter)* chosen, selected.

**aus|erlesen** *adj (ausgesucht)* select; *Speisen, Weine auch* choice *attr*.

**aus|ersehen*** *vt sep irreg (geh)* **dazu ~ sein, etw zu tun** to be chosen to do sth.

**Aus|erwählte(r)** *mf decl as adj (geh)* chosen one.

**ausfahrbar** *adj* extendable; *Antenne, Fahrgestell* retractable.

**ausfahren** *sep irreg* 1 *vi aux sein* (a) *(spazierenfahren)* to go for a ride *or (im Auto auch)* drive. (b) *(abfahren) (Zug)* to pull out *(aus* of*)*, to leave; **aus dem Hafen ~** *(Schiff)* to leave harbour. 2 (a) *(ausliefern) Waren* to deliver. (b) **ein Auto** *etc* **(voll) ~** to drive a car *etc* flat out. (c) *(Tech)* to extend; *(Aviat) Fahrgestell* to lower.

**Ausfahrt** *f* (a) *(auch Autobahn~)* exit. **~ Gütersloh** Gütersloh exit; **„~ freihalten"** "Keep clear". (b) *no pl (Abfahrt)* departure. **der Zug hat keine ~** the train has not been cleared for departure. (c) *(Spazierfahrt)* drive, ride.

**Ausfall** *m* (a) *(Verlust)* loss; *(das Versagen) (Tech, Med)* failure; *(von Motor)* breakdown; *(Produktionsstörung)* stoppage. (b) *no pl (von Sitzung, Unterricht etc)* cancellation. (c) *no pl (das Ausscheiden)* dropping out.

**ausfallen** *vi sep irreg aux sein* (a) *(herausfallen)* to fall out. **mir fallen die Haare aus** my hair is falling out. (b) *(nicht stattfinden)* to be cancelled. **etw ~ lassen** to cancel sth; **die Schule fällt morgen aus** there's no school tomorrow. (c) *(nicht funktionieren)* to fail; *(Motor)* to break down. (d) *(wegfallen: Verdienst)* to be lost. (e) *(ausscheiden)* to drop out. (f) **gut/schlecht** *etc* **~** to turn out well/badly *etc*; **die Bluse fällt zu eng aus** the blouse is too tight. (g) *siehe* **ausgefallen.**

**ausfallend, ausfällig** *adj* abusive.

**ausfällen** *vi sep (Chem)* to precipitate.

**Ausfallstraße** *f* arterial road.

**ausfechten** *vt sep irreg (fig)* to fight (out).

**ausfegen** *vt sep Zimmer* to sweep out.

**ausfeilen** *vt sep* to file (out); *siehe* **ausgefeilt.**

**ausfertigen** *vt sep (form) Dokument* to draw up; *Rechnung etc* to make out; *Paß* to issue.

**Ausfertigung** *f (form)* (a) *no pl siehe vt* drawing up; making out; issuing. (b) *(Abschrift)* copy. **in doppelter/dreifacher ~** in duplicate/triplicate.

**ausfetten** *vt sep* to grease.

**ausfindig** *adj:* **~ machen** to find; *(Aufenthaltsort feststellen)* to trace.

**ausfliegen** *sep irreg* 1 *vi aux sein* **ausgeflogen sein** *(fig col)* to have gone out; **der Vogel ist ausgeflogen** *(fig col)* the bird has flown. 2 *vt (Aviat) Verwundete etc* to fly out *(aus* from*)*.

**ausfließen** *vi sep irreg aux sein (herausfließen)* to flow out *(aus* of*)*; *(auslaufen: Öl etc)* to leak *(aus* out of*)*; *(Eiter etc)* to be discharged.

**ausflippen** *vi sep aux sein (col)* to freak out *(col)*; *siehe* **ausgeflippt.**

**ausflocken** *vti sep (Chem)* to precipitate.

**Ausflucht** *f, pl* **Ausflüchte** excuse. **Ausflüchte machen** to make excuses.

**Ausflug** *m* trip, outing; *(esp mit Reisebüro)* excursion; *(Betriebs~, Schul~)* outing; *(Wanderung)* walk, hike. **einen ~ machen** to go on a trip *etc*.

**Ausflügler(in** *f)* *m* - tripper.

**Ausflugs-:** **~dampfer** *m* pleasure steamer; **~lokal** *nt* tourist café; *(am Meer)* seaside café; **~verkehr** *m (an Feiertagen)* holiday traffic; *(am Wochenende)* weekend holiday traffic; **~ziel** *nt* destination (of one's outing).

**Ausfluß** *m* (a) *(das Herausfließen)* outflow. (b) *(~stelle)* outlet. (c) *(Med)* discharge.

**ausforschen** *vt sep* (a) *Sache* to find out; *(erforschen)* to investigate. (b) *jdn* to question.

**ausfragen** *vt sep* to question, to quiz *(col) (nach* about*)*; *(strenger)* to interrogate.

**ausfransen** *vi sep aux sein* to fray.

**ausfressen** *vt sep irreg (col: anstellen)* **etwas ~** to get up to something; **was hat er denn wieder ausge-fressen?** what's he done now? *(col)*.

**Ausfuhr** *f* -en *no pl (das Ausführen)* export; *(~handel)* exports *pl*.

**Ausfuhr-** *in cpds* export; *siehe auch* **Export-**.

**ausführbar** *adj* **(a)** *Plan* feasible, practicable. **schwer ~** difficult to carry out. **(b)** *(Comm)* exportable.

**ausführen** *vt sep* **(a)** *jdn* to take out; *Hund auch* to take for a walk. **(b)** *(durchführen)* to carry out; *Gesetz* to implement; *(Comp)* to execute; *(Sport) Freistoß* to take. **die ~de Gewalt** *(Pol)* the executive. **(c)** *(erklären)* to explain; *(darlegen)* to set out; *(argumentierend)* to argue. **(d)** *(Comm) Waren* to export.

**Ausfuhr-:** **~genehmigung** *f* export licence; **~güter** *pl* export goods *pl*, exports *pl*; **~hafen** *m* port of exportation.

**ausführlich 1** *adj* detailed, full. **2** *adv* in detail, in full. **sehr ~** in great detail.

**Ausführlichkeit** *f* detail, fullness. **in aller ~** in (great) detail, in full.

**Ausführung** *f* **(a)** *no pl siehe vt* **(b)** carrying out; implementation; taking. **zur ~ gelangen** to be carried out. **(b)** *(Erklärung)* explanation; *(von Thema etc)* exposition. **(c)** *(von Waren)* design; *(Tech: äußere ~)* finish; *(Qualität)* quality; *(Modell)* model.

**Ausfuhrzoll** *m* export duty.

**ausfüllen** *vt sep* to fill; *Platz* to take up; *Formular* to fill out. **jdn (ganz) ~** *(Zeit in Anspruch nehmen)* to take (all) sb's time; **ein ausgefülltes Leben** a full life.

**Ausg.** = **Ausgabe** ed.

**Ausgabe** *f* -n **(a)** *no pl (Austeilung) (von Proviant etc)* distribution, giving out; *(von Befehl, Fahrkarten etc)* issuing; *(von Essen)* serving. **(b)** *(Schalter)* counter. **(c)** *(von Buch etc)* edition; *(von Zeitschrift auch, von Aktien)* issue. **(d)** *(Ausführung)* version. **(e)** *(Geldaufwand)* expense, expenditure *no pl*. **~n** *pl (Geldverbrauch)* expenditure *sing (für on)*; *(Kosten)* expenses *pl*, costs *pl*. **(f)** *(Comp)* output; *(mit Drucker)* printout.

**Ausgabe-** *in cpds (Comp)* output; **~gerät** *nt* output device.

**Ausgang** *m* **(a)** *(Auslaß, Weg nach draußen)* exit, way out *(gen, von* from*)*; *(Aviat)* gate. **(b)** *(Erlaubnis zum Ausgehen)* permission to go out; *(Mil)* pass. **~ haben** to have the day off *or (am Abend)* the evening off; *(Mil)* to have a pass. **(c)** *no pl (Ende)* end; *(von Epoche auch)* close; *(von Roman, Film auch)* ending; *(Ergebnis)* outcome, result. **ein Unfall mit tödlichem ~** a fatal accident. **(d)** *no pl (Ausgangspunkt)* starting point; *(Anfang)* beginning.

**Ausgangs-:** **~basis** *f* basis, starting point; **~lage**, **~position** *f* initial *or* starting position; **~punkt** *m* starting point; **~sperre** *f* ban on going out; *(esp bei Belagerungszustand)* curfew; *(für Soldaten)* confinement to barracks; **~sperre haben** to be forbidden to go out; *(Mil)* to be confined to barracks; **~sprache** *f* source language; **~stellung** *f (Sport)* starting position; *(Mil)* initial position.

**ausgebaut** *adj* **gut ~** *Schul-, Verkehrssystem etc* fully developed.

**ausgeben** *vt sep irreg* **(a)** *(austeilen) Proviant etc* to distribute, to give out; *(aushändigen) Dokumente, Fahrkarten, Aktien etc* to issue; *Befehl* to issue, to give; *Essen* to serve; *(Cards)* to deal; *(ausdrucken) Text* to print out. **(b)** *Geld* to spend *(für* on*)*. **eine Runde ~** to stand a round; **ich gebe heute abend einen aus** *(col)* it's my treat this evening; **darf ich dir einen Whisky ~?** would you like a whisky? **(c)** *jdn/etw als or für jdn/etw ~* to pass sb/sth off as

sb/sth; **sich als jd/etw ~** to pose as sb/sth.

**ausgebeult** *adj Kleidung* baggy; *Hut* battered.

**ausgebombt** *adj* bombed out.

**ausgebucht** *adj Reise etc* booked up.

**ausgebufft** *adj (col: trickreich)* shrewd, fly *(col)*.

**Ausgeburt** *f (pej) (der Phantasie etc)* monstrous product; **eine ~ der Hölle** a fiendish monster.

**ausgedehnt** *adj (breit, groß, fig: weitreichend)* extensive; *(zeitlich)* lengthy; *Spaziergang* long.

**ausgedörrt** *adj* dried up; *Boden, Kehle* parched; *Pflanzen* shrivelled; *Land, Gebiet* arid.

**ausgefallen** *adj (ungewöhnlich)* unusual; *(übertrieben)* extravagant.

**ausgefeilt** *adj (fig)* polished.

**ausgeflippt** *adj (col)* freaky *(col)*, freaked-out *(col)*. **~er Typ** freak *(col)*; *(aus der Gesellschaft)* drop-out *(col)*.

**ausgefuchst** *adj (col)* clever; *(listig)* crafty *(col)*.

**ausgeglichen** *adj* balanced; *Spiel, Klima* even; *Torverhältnis* equal.

**Ausgeglichenheit** *f siehe adj* balance; evenness.

**ausgehen** *vi sep irreg aux sein* **(a)** *(weggehen)* to go out; *(spazierengehen auch)* to go (out) for a walk. **(b)** *(ausfallen: Haare, Federn, Zähne)* to fall out. **(c)** *(seinen Ausgang nehmen)* to start *(von* at*)*; *(herrühren: Idee etc)* to come *(von* from*)*. **(d)** *(abgeschickt werden: Post)* to be sent off. **die ~de Post** the outgoing mail. **(e)** *(zugrunde legen)* to start out *(von* from*)*. **gehen wir einmal davon aus, daß ...** let us assume that ... **(f)** **auf etw** *(acc)* **~** to be intent on sth. **(g)** *(enden)* to end. **gut/schlecht ~** to turn out well/badly; *(Film etc)* to have a happy/sad ending; *(Abend, Spiel)* to end well/badly; **leer ~** *(col)* to come away empty-handed. **(h)** *(zu Ende sein: Vorräte etc)* to run out. **ihm ist die Luft** *or* **der Atem ausgegangen** *(lit)* he ran out of breath; *(fig col)* he ran out of steam *(col)*. **(i)** *(aufhören zu brennen)* to go out.

**Ausgeh|erlaubnis** *f* permission to go out; *(Mil)* pass.

**ausgehungert** *adj* starved; *(abgezehrt) Mensch etc* emaciated.

**Ausgeh-:** **~uniform** *f* walking-out uniform; **~verbot** *nt siehe* **Ausgangssperre**.

**ausgeklügelt** *adj (col)* ingenious.

**ausgekocht** *adj (pej col: durchtrieben)* cunning.

**ausgelassen** *adj (heiter)* lively; *Stimmung* happy; *(wild) Kinder, Stimmung, Party* wild.

**Ausgelassenheit** *f siehe adj* liveliness; happiness; wildness.

**ausgelastet** *adj Mensch* fully occupied; *Maschine, Anlage* working to capacity.

**ausgeleiert** *adj Gummiband etc* worn.

**ausgemacht** *adj* **(a)** *(abgemacht)* agreed. **es ist eine ~e Sache, daß ...** it is agreed that ... **(b)** *attr (col: vollkommen)* complete, utter.

**ausgemergelt** *adj Gesicht* emaciated, gaunt.

**ausgenommen** *conj* except, apart from, aside from *(esp US)*. **alle, du** *or* **dich ~** everyone except (for) *or* apart from you; **Anwesende ~** present company excepted.

**ausgepowert** [-paʊɐt] *adj (col)* washed out *(col)*, done in *(col)*.

**ausgeprägt** *adj Gesicht* distinctive; *Eigenschaft* distinct; *Interesse* marked, pronounced.

**ausgerechnet** *adv* **~ du/er** *etc* you/he *etc* of all people; **~ heute/gestern** today/yesterday of all days; **~ jetzt kommt er** he would have to come just now.

**ausgereift** *adj* mature.

**ausgeruht** *adj* (well) rested.

**ausgeschlossen** *adj pred (unmöglich)* impossible;

*(nicht in Frage kommend)* out of the question. **es ist nicht ~, daß ...** it's just possible that ...; **jeder Irrtum ist ~** there is no possibility of a mistake.

**ausgeschnitten** *adj Bluse, Kleid* low-cut. **ein tief ~es Kleid** a dress with a plunging neckline.

**ausgesorgt** *adj siehe* **aussorgen.**

**ausgesprochen 1** *adj Schönheit* outstanding; *Vorliebe* definite; *Begabung* particular; *Ähnlichkeit auch* marked. **~es Pech haben** to be really unlucky. **2** *adv* really.

**ausgestorben** *adj Tierart* extinct; *(fig)* deserted. **der Park war wie ~** the park was deserted.

**Ausgestoßene(r)** *mf decl as adj* outcast.

**ausgesucht 1** *adj (erlesen) Wein* choice, select; *Gesellschaft* select; *Worte* well-chosen. **2** *adv (überaus)* extremely.

**ausgetreten** *adj Schuhe, Stufe* well-worn; *Pfad auch* well-trodden.

**ausgewachsen** *adj* fully-grown; *(col) Skandal* full-blown.

**ausgewählt** *adj* select; *Satz etc* well-chosen; *Werke* selected.

**ausgewogen** *adj* balanced; *Maß* equal. **ein ~es Kräfteverhältnis** an equal balance of powers.

**Ausgewogenheit** *f* balance.

**ausgezeichnet** *adj* excellent. **es geht mir ~** I'm feeling marvellous.

**ausgiebig 1** *adj Mahlzeit etc* substantial, large; *Mittagsschlaf* long; *Gebrauch* extensive. **2** *adv ~ frühstücken* to have a substantial breakfast; **~ schlafen** to have a good (long) sleep; **etw ~ gebrauchen** to use sth extensively.

**ausgießen** *vt sep irreg (aus einem Behälter)* to pour out; *(weggießen)* to pour away; *Behälter* to empty.

**Ausgleich** *m* **-e (a)** *(Gleichgewicht)* balance; *(von Konto)* balancing; *(von Schulden)* settling; *(von Verlust, Fehler)* compensation; *(von Unterschieden)* balancing out; *(von Konflikten etc)* reconciliation. **zum/als ~ für etw** in order to compensate for sth; **er treibt zum ~ Sport** he does sport for exercise. **(b)** *no pl (Ballspiele)* equalizer; *(Tennis)* deuce.

**ausgleichen** *sep irreg* **1** *vt Unterschiede* to even out; *Unebenheit* to level out; *Konto* to balance; *Schulden* to settle; *Fehler* to make good; *Verlust, Mangel* to offset, to compensate for; *Konflikte etc* to reconcile. **~de Gerechtigkeit** poetic justice; *siehe* **ausgeglichen. 2** *vi (Sport)* to equalize. **zum 1:1 ~** to equalize to make it 1 all. **3** *vr* to balance out; *(Einnahmen und Ausgaben)* to balance.

**Ausgleichs-:** **~sport** *m* keep-fit activity; **als ~sport** to keep fit; **~tor** *nt*, **treffer** *m* equalizer.

**ausgraben** *vt sep irreg (lit, fig) Grube* to dig up; *Grube* to dig out; *Altertümer auch* to excavate; *(hervorholen)* to dig out; *alte Geschichten* to dig up.

**Ausgrabung** *f* excavation, dig; *(Fund)* find.

**ausgrenzen** *vt sep* to exclude.

**Ausgrenzung** *f* exclusion.

**Ausguck** *m* **-e** lookout.

**Ausguß** *m (Becken)* sink; *(Abfluß)* drain.

**aushaben** *sep irreg (col)* **1** *vt (fertig sein mit) Buch etc* to have finished; *(ausgezogen haben)* to have taken off. **2** *vi (Schule etc: beendet haben)* to finish.

**aushaken** *sep* **1** *vt* to unhook. **2** *vi (col)* **es hat bei ihm ausgehakt** *(er begriff nicht)* he gave up *(col)*; *(er wurde wild)* something in him snapped *(col)*.

**aushalten** *vt sep irreg* **(a)** to bear, to stand. **es läßt sich ~** it's bearable; **das ist nicht auszuhalten** or **zum A~** it's unbearable; **ich halte es vor Hitze/zu Hause nicht mehr aus** I can't stand the heat/being at home any longer; **wie kann man es bei der Firma bloß ~?** how can anyone stand working for that

firm?; **er hält viel/nicht viel aus** he can take a lot/can't take much. **(b)** *Ton* to hold. **(c)** *(col: unterhalten)* to keep. **sich von jdm ~ lassen** to be kept by sb.

**aushandeln** *vt sep* to negotiate.

**aushändigen** *vt sep* **jdm etw/einen Preis ~** to hand sth over to sb/give sb a prize.

**Aushändigung** *f* handing over.

**Aushang** *m, pl* **Aushänge** notice, announcement; *(das Aushängen)* posting. **etw durch ~ bekanntgeben** to put up a notice about sth.

**aushängen** *sep* **1** *vt* **(a)** *(bekanntmachen) Nachricht etc* to put up. **(b)** *(herausheben) Tür* to unhinge. **2** *vi irreg* **am Schwarzen Brett ~** to be on the noticeboard *(Brit)* or bulletin board *(US)*.

**Aushängeschild** *nt* sign; *(fig: Reklame)* advertisement.

**ausharren** *vi sep (geh)* to wait. **auf seinem Posten ~** to stand by one's post.

**ausheben** *vt sep irreg* **(a)** *Tür etc* to take off its hinges. **(b)** *Erde* to dig out; *Graben* to dig. **(c)** *(fig) Diebesnest* to raid; *Bande* to make a raid on.

**aushecken** *vt sep (col) Plan* to cook up *(col)*.

**ausheilen** *sep* **1** *vt Krankheit* to cure; *Organ, Wunde* to heal. **2** *vi aux sein (Krankheit)* to be cured; *(Organ, Wunde)* to heal.

**aushelfen** *vi sep irreg* to help out *(jdm sb)*.

**Aushilfe** *f* **(a)** help, aid. **jdn zur ~ haben** to have sb to help out. **(b)** *(Mensch)* temporary worker; *(esp im Büro auch)* temp *(col)*. **als ~ arbeiten** to help out; *(im Büro auch)* to temp *(col)*.

**Aushilfs-:** **~kraft** *f* temporary worker; *(esp im Büro auch)* temp *(col)*; **~lehrer** *m* supply teacher; **~personal** *nt* temporary staff; **a~weise** *adv* on a temporary basis.

**aushöhlen** *vt sep* to hollow out; *(fig: untergraben)* to undermine.

**Aushöhlung** *f* **(a)** *(ausgehöhlte Stelle)* hollow. **(b)** *no pl (das ~)* hollowing out; undermining.

**ausholen** *vi sep (zum Schlag)* to raise one's hand/arm etc; *(zum Wurf)* to reach back. **weit ~ (zum Schlag, beim Tennis)** to take a big swing; *(fig: Redner)* to go far afield; **zum Gegenschlag ~ (lit, fig)** to prepare for a counter-attack.

**aushorchen** *vt sep jdn* to sound out.

**aushungern** *vt sep* to starve out; *siehe* **ausgehungert.**

**auskennen** *vr sep irreg (an einem Ort)* to know one's way around; *(in einem Gebiet)* to know a lot *(auf or in +dat* about*)*. **man kennt sich bei ihm nie aus** you never know where you are with him.

**auskippen** *vt sep (col)* to empty (out).

**ausklammern** *vt sep Problem* to leave on one side.

**Ausklang** *m (geh)* conclusion, end.

**ausklappbar** *adj* folding. **dieser Tisch ist ~** this table can be opened out.

**auskleiden** *sep* **1** *vt* **(a)** *(beziehen)* to line. **(b)** *(geh: entkleiden)* to undress. **2** *vr (geh)* to get undressed.

**ausklingen** *vi sep irreg aux sein (Feier etc)* to end.

**ausklinken** *sep* **1** *vt Bombe* to release. **2** *vi* to release; *(col: durchdrehen)* to flip one's lid *(col)*. **3** *vr* to release (itself).

**ausklopfen** *vt sep Teppich* to beat; *Pfeife* to knock out.

**ausknobeln** *vt sep (col) Plan* to figure out *(col)*.

**ausknöpfbar** *adj Futter* detachable.

**auskochen** *vt sep* to boil; *(Med)* to sterilize *(in boiling water)*; *(fig col: sich ausdenken)* to cook up *(col)*; *siehe* **ausgekocht.**

**auskommen** *vi sep irreg aux sein* **(a)** *(genügend haben, zurechtkommen)* to get by *(mit on)*, to manage *(mit on, with)*. **ohne jdn/etw ~** to manage *or* do without sb/sth. **(b) mit jdm (gut)** ~ to get on *or* along well with sb.

**Auskommen** *nt no pl (Einkommen)* livelihood. **sein** ~ **haben/finden** to get by; **mit ihm ist kein** ~ he's impossible to get on with.

**auskosten** *vt sep (genießen)* to make the most of; *Leben* to enjoy to the full.

**auskramen** *vt sep (col)* to dig out, to unearth; *(fig) alte Geschichten etc* to dig up.

**auskratzen** *vt sep (auch Med)* to scrape out. **jdm die Augen** ~ to scratch sb's eyes out.

**auskugeln** *vr sep* **sich** *(dat)* **den Arm/die Schulter** ~ to dislocate one's arm/shoulder.

**auskühlen** *sep* **1** *vt* to cool down. **2** *vi aux sein (abkühlen)* to cool down; *(Körper, Menschen)* to chill through. **etw** ~ **lassen** to leave sth to cool.

**auskundschaften** *vt sep* to find out; *.Versteck to* spy out; *(esp Mil)* to reconnoitre.

**Auskunft** *f, pl* **Auskünfte (a)** *(Mitteilung)* information *no pl (über +acc* about*).* **nähere** ~ further details; **eine detaillierte** ~ a detailed piece of information; **jdm eine** ~ **erteilen** *or* **geben** to give sb some information. **(b)** *(Schalter)* information office/desk; *(am Bahnhof auch)* enquiry office/desk; *(Telec)* directory enquiries *no art (Brit)*, directory assistance *no art (US)*.

**Auskunfts-:** ~**beamte(r)** *m* information officer; *(am Bahnhof)* information clerk; ~**person** *f* informer; *(Beamter)* information clerk; ~**schalter** *m* information desk.

**auskuppeln** *vi sep* to disengage the clutch.

**auskurieren\*** *vt sep (col)* to cure; *Krankheit auch* to get rid of *(col)*.

**auslachen** *vt sep* **jdn** to laugh at.

**ausladen** *vt sep irreg* **(a)** *Ware, Ladung* to unload. **(b)** *(col)* **jdn** ~ to tell sb not to come.

**ausladend** *adj Gebärden, Bewegung* sweeping.

**Auslage** *f* **(a)** *(von Waren)* display; *(Schaufenster)* window; *(Schaukasten)* showcase. **(b)** *usu pl* expense. **seine** ~**n für Essen** his outlay for food.

**auslagern** *vt sep Kunstgegenstände etc* to evacuate.

**Ausland** *nt no pl* foreign countries *pl*; *(fig: die Ausländer)* foreigners *pl*. **ins/im** ~ abroad; **aus dem** *or* **vom** ~ from abroad; **wie hat das** ~ **darauf reagiert?** what was the reaction abroad?; **Handel mit dem** ~ foreign trade.

**Ausländer(in** *f)* *m* - foreigner; *(Admin, Jur)* alien.

**Ausländerbeauftragte(r)** *mf* official looking after foreign immigrants.

**ausländerfeindlich** *adj* hostile to foreigners.

**Ausländerfeindlichkeit** *f* hostility to foreigners, xenophobia.

**ausländisch** *adj attr* foreign; *Erzeugnisse, Freunde etc auch* from abroad.

**Auslands-:** ~**aufenthalt** *m* stay abroad; ~**deutsche(r)** *mf* expatriate German; ~**geschäft** *nt* foreign business *or* trade; ~**gespräch** *nt* international call; ~**investition** *f* foreign investment; ~**korrespondent** *m* foreign correspondent; ~**reise** *f* journey *or* trip abroad; ~**schulden** *pl* foreign exchange debts; ~**schutzbrief** *m* international motoring cover; ~**vertretung** *f* agency abroad; *(von Firma)* foreign branch.

**auslassen** *sep irreg* **1** *vt* **(a)** *(weglassen, übergehen)* to leave *or* miss out; *(versäumen) Chance* to miss. **(b)** *(abreagieren)* to vent *(an +dat* on*).* **seine Gefühle** ~ to let off steam *(col)*. **(c)** *Butter, Fett* to melt. **(d)** *Kleider etc* to let out; *Saum* to let down. **(e)** *siehe* **ausgelassen. 2** *vr* to talk *(über +acc* about*).* **sich über jdn/etw** ~ *(pej)* to go on about sb/sth *(pej).*

**Auslassung** *f* **(a)** *(Weglassen)* omission. **(b)** ~**en** *pl*

*(pej: Äußerungen)* remarks *pl*.

**Auslassungszeichen** *nt* apostrophe.

**auslasten** *vt sep* **(a)** *Fahrzeug* to make full use of; *Maschine auch* to use to capacity. **(b)** *jdn* to occupy fully; *siehe* **ausgelastet.**

**Auslauf** *m, pl* **Ausläufe (a)** *no pl (für Kinder, Tiere)* room to run about. **(b)** *no pl (das Auslaufen)* discharge; *(das Lecken)* leakage.

**auslaufen** *vi sep irreg aux sein* **(a)** *(Flüssigkeit)* to run out *(aus of)*; *(Behälter)* to empty; *(undicht sein)* to leak. **(b)** *(Naut: Schiff)* to sail. **(c)** *(enden) (Modell, Serie)* to be discontinued; *(Vertrag etc)* to run out. **(d)** *(zum Stillstand kommen: Rad etc)* to come to a stop. **(e)** *(Farbe)* to run.

**Ausläufer** *m* **(a)** *(Met) (von Hoch)* ridge; *(von Tief)* trough. **(b)** *(Vorberg)* foothill *usu pl*.

**auslaugen** *vt sep (lit, fig)* to exhaust.

**ausleben** *sep* **1** *vr (Mensch)* to live it up. **2** *vt (geh)* to realize.

**auslecken** *vt sep* to lick out.

**ausleeren** *vt sep Gefäß* to empty.

**auslegen** *vt sep* **(a)** *(ausbreiten)* to lay out; *Waren etc auch* to display; *Köder* to put down. **(b)** *(bedecken)* to cover; *(auskleiden)* to line. **den Boden/das Zimmer (mit Teppichen)** ~ to carpet the floor/room. **(c)** *(deuten)* to interpret. **etw falsch** ~ to misinterpret sth. **(d)** *Geld* to lend *(jdm etw* sb sth*).* **sie hat die 5 Mark für mich ausgelegt** she paid the 5 marks for me.

**Ausleger** *m* - **(a)** *(von Kran etc)* jib, boom. **(b)** *(Deuter)* interpreter.

**Auslegung** *f (Deutung)* interpretation. **falsche** ~ misinterpretation.

**ausleiern** *vti sep (col)* to wear out; *siehe* **ausgeleiert.**

**Ausleihe** *f (Schalter)* issue desk. **eine** ~ **ist nicht möglich** it is not possible to lend out anything.

**ausleihen** *vt sep irreg (verleihen)* to lend *(jdm, an jdn* to sb*)*; *(von jdm leihen)* to borrow.

**auslernen** *vi sep (Lehrling)* to finish one's apprenticeship. **man lernt nie aus** *(prov)* you live and learn *(prov).*

**Auslese** *f* -**n (a)** *no pl (Auswahl)* selection. **natürliche** ~ natural selection; **eine** ~ **treffen** *or* **vornehmen** to make a selection. **(b)** *(Wein) high-quality wine made from selected grapes.*

**auslesen** *vti sep irreg (col) Buch* to finish reading.

**ausliefern** *vt sep* **(a)** *Waren* to deliver. **(b)** *jdn* to hand over *(an +acc* to*)*; *(an anderen Staat)* to extradite *(an +acc* to*)*; *(fig: preisgeben)* to leave *(jdm* in the hands of*).* **jdm/einer Sache ausgeliefert sein** to be at sb's mercy/the mercy of sth.

**Auslieferung** *f siehe vt* **(a)** delivery. **(b)** handing over; *(von Gefangenen)* extradition.

**Auslieferungs|abkommen** *nt* extradition treaty.

**ausliegen** *vi sep irreg (zur Ansicht)* to be displayed; *(Zeitschriften etc)* to be available (to the public); *(Liste)* to be up.

**auslöffeln** *vt sep* ~ **müssen, was man sich eingebrockt hat** *(col)* to have to take the consequences.

**ausloggen** *vi sep (Comp)* to log off.

**auslöschen** *vt sep (a) Feuer etc* to put out, to extinguish. **(b)** *(auswischen) Spuren, Erinnerung* to wipe out; *Schrift* to erase *(an +dat* from*).*

**auslosen** *vt sep* to draw lots for; *Preis, Gewinner* to draw.

**auslösen** *vt sep Mechanismus, Alarm* to trigger off; *Kameraverschluß* to release; *(fig) Wirkung* to produce; *Begeisterung etc* to arouse.

**Auslöser** *m* - **(a)** trigger; *(für Bombe)* release button; *(Phot)* shutter release. **(b)** *(Anlaß)* cause.

**Auslosung** *f* draw.

**Auslösung** *f siehe vt (a)* triggering off; release; producing; arousing.

**ausloten** *vt sep (Naut) Tiefe* to sound; *(fig geh)* to plumb.

**auslutschen** *vt sep (col) Orange, Zitrone etc* to suck; *Saft* to suck out; *(fig)* to suck dry.

**ausmachen** *vt sep* **(a)** *Feuer, Kerze, Zigarette* to put out; *elektrisches Licht auch, Radio, Gas* to turn off. **(b)** *(ermitteln, sichten)* to make out. **(c)** *(vereinbaren)* to agree. **etw mit sich selbst ~ (müssen)** to (have to) sort sth out for oneself; *siehe* **ausgemacht. (d)** *(bewirken, darstellen)* (to go) to make up. **all der Luxus, der ein angenehmes Leben ausmacht** all the luxuries which go to make up a pleasant life. **(e)** *(bedeuten)* **viel/wenig** *or* **nicht viel ~** to make a big/ not much difference; **das macht nichts aus** that doesn't matter. **(f)** *(stören)* to matter *(jdm to).* **macht es Ihnen etwas aus, wenn ...?** would you mind if ...?

**ausmalen** *sep* **1** *vt (darstellen)* to describe. **2** *vr* **sich** *(dat)* **etw ~** to imagine sth.

**ausmanövrieren*** *vt sep* to outmanoeuvre *(Brit),* to outmaneuver *(US).*

**Ausmaß** *nt (Größe: von Gegenstand, Fläche)* size; *(Umfang: von Katastrophe)* extent. **ein Verlust in diesem ~** a loss on this scale.

**ausmerzen** *vt sep Unkraut, Fehler* to eradicate.

**ausmessen** *vt sep irreg* to measure (out).

**ausmisten** *vt sep Stall* to muck out; *(fig col) Schrank etc* to tidy out; *Zimmer* to clean out.

**ausmustern** *vt sep Maschine, Fahrzeug etc* to take out of service; *(Mil: entlassen)* to invalid out.

**Ausnahme** *f* **-n** exception. **mit ~ von Horst** with the exception of Horst; **~n bestätigen die Regel** *(prov)* the exception proves the rule *(prov).*

**Ausnahme-:** **~erscheinung** *f* exception; **~fall** *m* exception, exceptional case; **~genehmigung** *f* special (case) authorization; **~situation** *f* special *or* exceptional situation; **~zustand** *m (Pol)* state of emergency; **den ~zustand verhängen** to declare a state of emergency.

**ausnahmslos** **1** *adv* without exception. **2** *adj Bewilligung, Zustimmung* unanimous.

**ausnahmsweise** *adv* **darf ich das machen? — ~** may I do that? — just this once; **er darf heute ~ früher von der Arbeit weggehen** as an exception he may leave work earlier today.

**ausnehmen** *sep irreg* **1** *vt* **(a)** *Fisch, Kaninchen* to gut; *Geflügel* to draw. **(b)** *(ausschließen) jdn* to make an exception of. **(c)** *(col) jdn* to fleece; *(beim Kartenspiel)* to clean out. **2** *vr (geh: wirken)* **sich schön** *or* **gut/schlecht ~** to look good/bad.

**ausnehmend** *adj (geh)* exceptional. **das gefällt mir ~ gut** I like that very much indeed.

**ausnüchtern** *vti sep* to sober up.

**Ausnüchterung** *f* sobering up.

**Ausnüchterungszelle** *f* drying-out cell.

**ausnutzen, ausnützen** *(esp S Ger, Aus) vt sep* to make use of; *(ausbeuten)* to exploit; *Gelegenheit* to make the most of; *jds Gutmütigkeit etc* to take advantage of.

**Ausnutzung** *f* use; *(Ausbeutung)* exploitation.

**auspacken** *sep* **1** *vti Koffer* to unpack; *Geschenk* to unwrap. **2** *vi (col: alles sagen)* to talk *(col).*

**auspeitschen** *vt sep* to whip.

**auspfeifen** *vt sep irreg* to boo.

**ausplaudern** *vt sep* to let out.

**ausposaunen*** *vt sep (col)* to tell the world about *(col).*

**auspowern** [-paʊɐn] *vi sep (ausbeuten) Massen, Bo-*

den to exploit; *siehe* **ausgepowert.**

**ausprägen** *vr sep (Begabung, Charaktereigenschaft etc)* to reveal *or* show itself; *siehe* **ausgeprägt.**

**Ausprägung** *f no pl (von Charakter)* shaping.

**auspressen** *vt sep Saft, Schwamm etc* to squeeze out; *Zitrone etc* to squeeze.

**ausprobieren*** *vt sep* to try out.

**Auspuff** *m* **-e** exhaust.

**Auspuff-:** **~gase** *pl* exhaust fumes *pl*; **~rohr** *nt* exhaust pipe; **~topf** *m* silencer *(Brit),* muffler *(US).*

**auspumpen** *vt sep* to pump out.

**ausputzen** *vi sep (Ftbl)* to clear (the ball); *(Ausputzer sein)* to play sweeper.

**Ausputzer** *m* **-** *(Ftbl)* sweeper.

**ausquartieren*** *vt sep* to move out.

**ausquetschen** *vt sep Zitrone etc* to squeeze; *(col: ausfragen)* to grill *(col)*; *(aus Neugier)* to pump *(col).*

**ausradieren*** *vt sep* to rub out, to erase; *(fig: vernichten)* to wipe out.

**ausrangieren*** *vt sep Kleider* to throw out; *Maschine, Auto* to scrap. **ein altes ausrangiertes Auto** an old scrap car.

**ausrasten** *sep* **1** *vi aux sein* **(a)** *(Tech)* to come out. **(b)** *(col: zornig werden)* to blow one's top *(col).* **2** *vi impers (col)* **es rastete bei ihm aus** something snapped in him *(col).*

**ausrauben** *vt sep* to rob.

**ausraufen** *vt sep* **ich könnte mir die Haare ~** I could kick myself.

**ausräumen** *vt sep* to clear out; *(fig) Mißverständnisse, Konflikt* to clear up; *Vorurteile, Bedenken* to dispel; *(col: ausrauben)* to clean out *(col).*

**ausrechnen** *vt sep* to work out; *(ermitteln) Gewicht, Länge auch* to calculate. **sich** *(dat)* **große Chancen ~** to reckon that one has a good chance; *siehe* **ausgerechnet.**

**Ausrede** *f* excuse.

**ausreden** *sep* **1** *vi* to finish speaking. **er hat mich nicht mal ~ lassen** he didn't even let me finish (speaking). **2** *vt* **jdm etw ~** to talk sb out of sth.

**ausreichen** *vi sep* to be sufficient *or* enough. **die Zeit reicht nicht aus** there is not sufficient time.

**ausreichend** **1** *adj* adequate; *(Sch)* satisfactory. **2** *adv* adequately.

**Ausreise** *f* **bei der ~** on leaving the country; *(Grenzübertritt)* on crossing the border; **jdm die ~ verweigern** to prohibit sb from leaving the country.

**Ausreise-:** **~antrag** *m* application for an exit visa; **~erlaubnis** *f*, **~genehmigung** *f* exit permit.

**ausreisen** *vi sep aux sein* to leave (the country).

**Ausreisevisum** *nt* exit visa.

**ausreißen** *sep irreg* **1** *vt Haare, Blatt* to tear out; *Zahn* to pull out; *Blumen* to pull up. **er hat sich** *(dat)* **kein Bein ausgerissen** *(col)* he didn't exactly overstrain himself. **2** *vi aux sein (+dat from) (col: davonlaufen)* to run away; *(Sport)* to break away.

**Ausreißer(in** *f)* *m* **-** *(col)* runaway; *(Sport)* runner/ cyclist who breaks away.

**ausreiten** *vi sep irreg aux sein* to go riding.

**ausrenken** *vt sep* to dislocate. **sich** *(dat)* **(fast) den Hals ~** *(col)* to crane one's neck.

**ausrichten** *vt sep* **(a)** *(aufstellen)* to line up. **jdn/etw auf etw** *(acc)* **~** *(abstellen)* to gear sb/sth to sth. **(b)** *(veranstalten)* to organize. **(c)** *(erreichen)* to achieve. **ich konnte bei ihr nichts ~** I couldn't get anywhere with her. **(d)** *(übermitteln)* to tell; *Nachricht* to pass on. **kann ich etwas ~?** can I take a message?; **bitte richten Sie ihm einen Gruß aus** please give him my regards.

**Ausrichtung** *f siehe vt* **(a)** lining up. **(b)** organization. **(c)** *(fig) (auf Ideologie etc)* orientation *(auf +acc* towards/); (auf Bedürfnisse etc) gearing (auf +acc to).

**Ausritt** m ride (out).

**ausrollen** vt sep Teig, Teppich to roll out.

**ausrotten** vt sep to wipe out; Volk auch, Ungeziefer to exterminate; Religion, Ideen auch to stamp out.

**Ausrottung** f siehe vt wiping out; extermination; stamping out.

**ausrücken** vi sep aux sein (a) (Mil) to move out; (Polizei, Feuerwehr) to turn out. (b) (col: ausreißen) to make off; (von zu Hause) to run away.

**Ausruf** m (Ruf) cry, shout.

**ausrufen** vt sep irreg to exclaim; Schlagzeilen to shout out; (verkünden) to call out; Haltestellen, Streik to call. jdn zum König ~ to proclaim sb king; jdn ~ (lassen) (über Lautsprecher etc) to page sb.

**Ausrufezeichen** nt exclamation mark (Brit) or point (US).

**Ausrufung** f proclamation. die ~ eines Streiks a strike call.

**ausruhen** vtir sep to rest; (Mensch auch) to have a rest; siehe **ausgeruht**.

**ausrüsten** vt sep (lit, fig) to equip. ein Fahrzeug mit etw ~ to fit a car with sth.

**Ausrüstung** f (~sgegenstände) equipment; (esp Kleidung) outfit.

**Ausrüstungsgegenstand** m piece of equipment.

**ausrutschen** vi sep aux sein to slip; (Fahrzeug) to skid. das Messer/die Hand ist mir ausgerutscht my knife/my hand slipped.

**Ausrutscher** m - (col: lit, fig) slip.

**Aussaat** f no pl (das Säen) sowing.

**aussäen** vt sep (lit, fig) to sow.

**Aussage** f -n statement; (Behauptung) opinion; (Bericht) report; (Jur) (eines Angeklagten) statement; (Zeugen~) evidence no pl. eine eidliche/schriftliche ~ a sworn/written statement; der Zeuge verweigerte die ~ the witness refused to give evidence; eine ~ machen to make a statement.

**aussagekräftig** adj meaningful.

**aussagen** sep 1 vt to say (über +acc about/); (behaupten) to state; (unter Eid) to testify. 2 vi (Jur) (Zeuge) to give evidence; (Angeklager) to make a statement; (unter Eid auch) to testify. für/gegen jdn ~ to give evidence for/against sb.

**Aussatz** m no pl (Med) leprosy.

**Aussätzige(r)** mf decl as adj (lit, fig) leper.

**aussaugen** vt sep Saft etc to suck out; Wunde to suck the poison out of; (fig: ausbeuten) to drain dry. jdn bis aufs Blut ~ to bleed sb white.

**ausschaben** vt sep to scrape out; (Med auch) to curette.

**Ausschabung** f (Med) curettage.

**ausschachten** vt sep to dig, to excavate.

**Ausschachtung** f excavation.

**Ausschaltautomatik** f auto or automatic stop.

**ausschalten** vt sep (a) (abstellen) to switch or turn off. (b) (fig) to eliminate.

**Ausschaltung** f siehe vt switching off; elimination.

**Ausschank** m, pl **Ausschänke** bar; (no pl: Getränkeausgabe) sale of drinks.

**Ausschank|erlaubnis** f licence (Brit), license (US).

**Ausschau** f no pl: ~ halten to look out (nach for).

**ausschauen** vi sep (geh) to be on the lookout (nach for).

**ausscheiden** sep irreg 1 vt (aussondern) to take out; (Physiol) to excrete. 2 vi aux sein (a) (aus einem Amt) to retire (aus from); (aus Firma) to leave (aus etw sth); (Sport) to be eliminated; (wegen Verletzung etc) to drop out. (b) (nicht in Betracht kommen: Möglichkeit etc) to be ruled out. das/er

scheidet aus that/he has to be ruled out.

**Ausscheidung** f (a) no pl (das Aussondern) removal; (Physiol) excretion. (b) (Sport) elimination; (Vorkampf) qualifying contest.

**Ausscheidungs-:** ~kampf m qualifying contest; (Leichtathletik, Schwimmen) heat; ~organ nt excretory organ; ~spiel nt qualifying match or game.

**ausschenken** vti sep to pour (out); (am Ausschank) to serve.

**ausscheren** vi sep aux sein (Fahrzeug) to pull out.

**ausschicken** vt sep to send out.

**ausschiffen** vt sep to disembark; Ladung, Waren to unload.

**Ausschiffung** f siehe vt disembarkation; unloading.

**ausschildern** vt sep to signpost.

**ausschimpfen** vt sep to tell off.

**ausschlachten** vt sep (a) to gut, to dress. (b) (fig) Fahrzeuge, Maschinen etc to cannibalize. (c) (fig col: ausnutzen) Skandal, Ereignis to exploit.

**ausschlafen** sep irreg 1 vt Rausch etc to sleep off. 2 vir to have a good sleep.

**Ausschlag** m (a) (Med) rash. (b) (von Zeiger etc) swing; (von Kompaßnadel) deflection. (c) (fig) den ~ geben to be the decisive factor; die Stimme des Vorsitzenden gibt den ~ the chairman has the casting vote.

**ausschlagen** sep irreg 1 vt (a) (herausschlagen) to knock out. (b) Feuer to beat out. (c) (auskleiden) to line. (d) (ablehnen) to turn down. jdm etw ~ to refuse sb sth. 2 vi (a) aux sein or haben (Baum, Strauch) to start to bud. (b) (Pferd) to kick. (c) aux sein or haben (Zeiger etc) to swing; (Kompaßnadel) to be deflected.

**ausschlaggebend** adj decisive; Stimme auch deciding. das ist von ~er Bedeutung that is of prime importance.

**ausschließen** vt sep irreg (a) (aussperren) to lock out. (b) (ausnehmen) to exclude; (aus Gemeinschaft) to expel; (vorübergehend) to suspend; (Sport) to disqualify; Fehler, Möglichkeit etc to rule out. das eine schließt das andere nicht aus the one does not exclude the other; die Öffentlichkeit ~ (Jur) to exclude the public; siehe **ausgeschlossen**.

**ausschließlich** adj attr exclusive.

**ausschlüpfen** vi sep aux sein to slip out; (aus Ei, Puppe) to hatch out.

**Ausschluß** m siehe **ausschließen** (b) exclusion; expulsion; suspension; disqualification. unter ~ der Öffentlichkeit stattfinden to be closed to the public.

**ausschmücken** vt sep to decorate; (fig) Erzählung to embellish.

**Ausschmückung** f siehe vt decoration; embellishment.

**ausschneiden** vt sep irreg (herauschneiden) to cut out; siehe **ausgeschnitten**.

**Ausschnitt** m (a) (Zeitungs~) cutting, clipping. (b) (Kleid~) neck. ein tiefer ~ a low neckline. (c) (fig: Teil) part; (aus Film) clip.

**ausschöpfen** vt sep (a) Wasser etc to ladle out (aus of). (b) (leeren) to empty; (fig) to exhaust.

**ausschreiben** vt sep irreg (a) to write out; (ungekürzt schreiben) to write (out) in full. (b) Rechnung etc to make out. (c) (bekanntmachen) to announce; Wahlen to call; Stelle to advertise.

**Ausschreibung** f (Bekanntmachung) (von Wahlen) calling; (von Stelle) advertising.

**Ausschreitung** f usu pl (Aufruhr) rioting no pl.

**Ausschuß** m (a) (Komitee) committee. (b) no pl (Comm) rejects pl; (fig col) trash.

**ausschütteln** vt sep to shake out.

**ausschütten** vt sep (a) (auskippen) to tip out; Ei-

*mer, Glas* to empty. **jdm sein Herz ~** *(fig)* to pour out one's heart to sb. **(b)** *(Fin) Dividende etc* to distribute.

**Ausschüttung** *f (Fin)* distribution.

**ausschwärmen** *vi sep aux sein (Bienen, Menschen)* to swarm out; *(Mil)* to fan out.

**ausschweifend** *adj Leben* dissipated; *Phantasie* wild.

**Ausschweifung** *f (Maßlosigkeit)* excess; *(in Lebensweise)* dissipation.

**ausschweigen** *vr sep irreg* to remain silent *(über +acc, zu* about*).*

**ausschwenken** *vi sep aux sein* **(a)** *(Mil)* to wheel. **(b)** *(Kran etc)* to swing out.

**ausschwitzen** *vt sep* to sweat out.

**aussehen** *vi sep irreg* to look. **gut ~** to look good; *(hübsch)* to be good-looking; *(gesund)* to look well; **gesund/elend ~** to look healthy/wretched; **es sieht nach Regen aus** it looks like rain; **wie jd/etw ~** to look like sb/sth; **wie sieht's aus?** *(col: wie steht's)* how's things? *(col)*; **es soll nach etwas ~** it's got to look good; **es sieht danach** *or* **so aus, als ob ...** it looks as if ...; **so siehst du aus!** *(col)* that's what you think!; **es sieht nicht gut mit ihm aus** things don't look good for him.

**Aussehen** *nt no pl* appearance. **dem ~ nach** by the look of it; **etw dem ~ nach beurteilen** to judge sth by appearances.

**aussein** *sep irreg aux sein.* **1** *vi (col)* **(a)** *(zu Ende sein) (Schule)* to finish; *(Krieg, Stück)* to have ended; *(nicht ansein) (Feuer, Ofen)* to be out; *(Radio, Fernseher etc)* to be off. **die Schule ist aus** school has finished *or* is out. **(b) auf etw** *(acc)* **~** to be (only) interested in sth; **auf jdn ~** to be after sb *(col).* **2** *vi impers* **es ist aus (und vorbei) zwischen uns** it's (all) over between us; **es ist aus mit ihm** he is finished, he has had it *(col).*

**außen** *adv* **(a) ~ bemalt** painted on the outside; **~ an der Windschutzscheibe** on the outside of the windscreen *(Brit)* or windshield *(US)*; **von ~ sieht es gut aus** on the outside it looks good; **das Fenster geht nach ~ auf** the window opens outwards; **nach ~ hin** *(fig)* outwardly. **(b) ~ vor sein** to be left out.

**Außen-:** **~antenne** *f* outdoor aerial *(Brit)* or antenna *(US)*; **~arbeiten** *pl* work on the exterior; **~aufnahme** *f* outdoor shot; **bei ~aufnahmen sein** to be on location; **~bahn** *f* outside lane; **~bezirk** *m* outlying district; **~bordmotor** *m* outboard motor.

**aussenden** *vtr sep irreg* to send out.

**Außen-:** **~dienst** *m* external duty; **im ~dienst sein** to work outside the office; **~dienstmitarbeiter** *m* sales representative; **~handel** *m* foreign trade; **~minister** *m* foreign minister, foreign secretary *(Brit)*, secretary of state *(US)*; **~ministerium** *nt* foreign ministry, foreign office *(Brit)*, state department *(US)*; **~politik** *f (Gebiet)* foreign politics *sing*; *(bestimmte)* foreign policy/policies; **~politiker** *m* foreign affairs politician; **a~politisch** *adj* foreign policy *attr*; *Sprecher* on foreign affairs; **~seite** *f* outside.

**Außenseiter(in** *f)* *m -* *(Sport, fig)* outsider.

**Außenseiterrolle** *f* role as an outsider. **eine ~ spielen** to play the role of an outsider.

**Außen-:** **~spiegel** *m* *(Aut)* outside mirror; **~stände** *pl (esp Comm)* outstanding debts *pl*, arrears *pl*; **~stehende(r)** *mf decl as adj* outsider; **~stelle** *f* branch; **~stürmer** *m (Ftbl)* wing; **~temperatur** *f* outside temperature; **~wand** *f* outer wall; **~welt** *f* outside world.

**außer 1** *prep +dat or (rare) gen* **(a)** *(räumlich)* out of.

**~ Sicht** out of sight; **~ sich** *(acc)* **geraten** to go wild; **~ sich** *(dat)* **sein** to be beside oneself; **~ Haus sein/essen** to be/eat out; **~ Atem** out of breath. **(b)** *(ausgenommen)* except (for); *(abgesehen von)* apart from, aside from. **alle ~ mir** everyone except (for) me. **(c)** *(zusätzlich zu)* in addition to. **2** *conj* except. **~ daß ...** except that ...; **~ wenn ...** unless ...

**außerdem** *adv* besides; *(dazu)* in addition, as well; *(überdies)* anyway.

**außerdienstlich** *adj (nicht dienstlich) Angelegenheit* private; *(außerhalb der Arbeitszeit)* social.

**außer|ehelich 1** *adj* extramarital; *Kind* illegitimate. **2** *adv* outside marriage.

**äußere(r, s)** *adj (außerhalb gelegen, Geog)* outer; *Verletzung* external; *Schein, Eindruck* outward.

**Äußere(s)** *nt decl as adj* exterior; *(fig: Aussehen auch)* outward appearance.

**außer-:** **~europäisch** *adj attr* non-European; **~fahrplanmäßig** *adj* unscheduled; **~gewöhnlich 1** *adj* unusual, out of the ordinary; **2** *adv (sehr)* extremely.

**außerhalb 1** *prep +gen* outside. **~ der Stadt** outside the town, out of town. **2** *adv (außen)* outside; *(~ der Stadt)* out of town. **~ stehen** *(fig)* to be on the outside.

**außer|irdisch** *adj* extraterrestrial.

**Außerkraftsetzung** *f* repeal.

**äußerlich** *adj* **(a)** external. **(b)** *(fig) (oberflächlich)* superficial; *(scheinbar)* outward. **„nur zur ~en Anwendung"** for external use only; **rein ~ betrachtet** on the face of it.

**Äußerlichkeit** *f (fig)* triviality; *(Oberflächlichkeit)* superficiality; *(Formalität)* formality. **~en** *(outward)* appearances.

**äußern 1** *vt (sagen)* to say; *Wunsch etc* to express; *Worte* to utter; *Kritik* to voice. **seine Meinung ~** to give one's views. **2** *vr (Mensch)* to speak; *(Krankheit, Symptom)* to show itself. **sich zu etw ~** to comment on sth.

**außer-:** **~ordentlich 1** *adj* extraordinary; *(ungewöhnlich auch)* exceptional; *(bemerkenswert auch)* remarkable; *Professor* associate; **2** *adv (sehr)* exceptionally, extremely; **~parlamentarisch** *adj* extraparliamentary; **~planmäßig** *adj* Besuch, Treffen unscheduled; **~sinnlich** *adj* **~sinnliche Wahrnehmung** extrasensory perception.

**äußerst** *adv* extremely, exceedingly.

**außerstande** *adv (unfähig)* incapable; *(nicht in der Lage)* unable. **~ sein, etw zu tun** to be incapable of doing sth.

**äußerstenfalls** *adv* at most.

**äußerste(r, s)** *adj (räumlich)* furthest; *Schicht* outermost; *Norden etc* extreme; *(zeitlich)* latest possible; *(fig)* utmost. **mein ~s Angebot** my final offer; **im ~n Falle** if the worst comes to the worst; **mit ~r Kraft** with all one's strength.

**Äußerste(s)** *nt decl as adj* **bis zum ~n gehen** to go to extremes; **er hat sein ~s gegeben** he gave his all.

**außertariflich** *adj Regelung* non-union; *Zuschlag* supplementary to agreed union rates.

**Äußerung** *f (Bemerkung)* remark, comment; *(Behauptung)* statement; *(Zeichen)* expression.

**aussetzen** *sep* **1** *vt* **(a)** *Kind, Haustier* to abandon; *Pflanzen* to plant out; *(Naut) Passagiere* to put ashore. **jdn/etw einer Sache** *(dat)* **~** to expose sb/sth to sth; **jdm/einer Sache ausgesetzt sein** *(ausgeliefert)* to be at the mercy of sb/sth. **(c)** *Belohnung, Preis* to offer. **(d)** *(unterbrechen)* to interrupt; *Debatte, Prozeß* to adjourn. **(e)** *(vertagen) Verfahren* to suspend. (f) an jdm/etw etwas auszusetzen haben to find fault with sb/sth; daran ist nichts auszusetzen there is nothing wrong with it; was haben Sie daran auszusetzen? what's your objection to it? 2 vi (aufhören) to stop; (bei Spiel) to sit out; (Herz) to stop (beating); (Motor auch) to fail. mit der Pille/Behandlung ~ to stop taking the pill/to interrupt the treatment; ohne auszusetzen without a break.

**Aussetzung** f (a) siehe vt (a) abandonment; planting out; putting ashore. (b) (Jur: von Verfahren) suspension.

**Aussicht** f (a) (Blick) view (auf +acc of). mit ~ auf den Park overlooking the park. (b) (fig) prospect (auf +acc of). die ~, daß etw geschieht the chances of sth happening; unser Plan hat große ~en auf Erfolg our plan has every chance of succeeding; etw in ~ haben to have good prospects of sth; jdm etw in ~ stellen to promise sb sth; das sind ja schöne ~en! (iro col) what a prospect!

**Aussichts-:** a~los adj hopeless; (zwecklos) pointless; (völlig hoffnungslos) desperate; ~losigkeit f siehe adj hoplessness; pointlessness; desperateness; ~punkt m vantage point; a~reich adj promising; Stellung with good prospects; ~turm m lookout tower.

**aussieben** vt sep (lit, fig) to sift out.

**aussiedeln** vt sep to resettle.

**Aussiedler(in** f) m (Auswanderer) emigrant.

**Aussiedlung** f resettlement.

**aussöhnen** sep 1 vt jdn mit jdm/etw ~ to reconcile sb with sb/to sth. 2 vr sich mit jdm/etw ~ to become reconciled with sb/to sth; wir haben uns wieder ausgesöhnt we have made it up again.

**Aussöhnung** f reconciliation (mit jdm with sb, mit etw to sth).

**aussondern** vt sep to select; Schlechtes to separate out.

**aussorgen** vi sep: ausgesorgt haben to have no more money worries, to be set up for life.

**aussortieren*** vt sep to sort out.

**ausspannen** sep 1 vt (a) Tuch, Netz to spread out; Schnur, Leine to put up. (b) Pferd to unhitch; (aus Schreibmaschine) Bogen to take out. (c) (fig col) jdm die Freundin etc ~ to pinch sb's girlfriend etc (col). 2 vi (sich erholen) to have a break.

**aussparen** vt sep (fig) to omit.

**Aussparung** f (Lücke) gap.

**aussperren** vt sep to lock out.

**Aussperrung** f (Ind) lockout.

**ausspielen** sep 1 vti (a) Karte to play. ausgespielt haben (fig) to be finished. (b) (fig) jdn/etw gegen jdn/etw ~ to play sb/sth off against sb/sth. (c) Gewinne to give as a prize/as prizes. 2 vi (Cards) to lead. wer spielt aus? whose lead is it?

**Ausspielung** f (im Lotto) draw.

**ausspionieren*** vt sep Pläne etc to spy out; Person to spy on.

**Aussprache** f (a) pronunciation; (Akzent) accent. (b) (Meinungsaustausch) discussion, talks pl.

**aussprechen** sep irreg 1 vt Wörter, Urteil etc to pronounce; Scheidung to grant; (äußern) to express (jdm to sb); Verdächtigung to voice; Warnung to give. der Regierung das Vertrauen ~ to pass a vote of confidence in the government. 2 vr (Partner) to talk things out; (sein Herz ausschütten) to say what's on one's mind. sich für/gegen etw ~ to come out in favour of/against sth. 3 vi (zu Ende sprechen) to finish (speaking); siehe ausgesprochen.

**Ausspruch** m remark; (geflügeltes Wort) saying.

**ausspucken** sep 1 vt to spit out. 2 vi to spit.

**ausspülen** vt sep to rinse (out).

**ausstaffieren*** vt sep (col) to rig out; (herausputzen) to dress up.

**Ausstand** m (a) (Streik) strike, industrial action. in den ~ treten to (go on) strike, to take industrial action. (b) seinen ~ geben to hold a leaving party.

**ausstatten** vt sep to equip; (versorgen) to provide; (möblieren) to furnish. mit Humor ausgestattet sein to be endowed with a sense of humour.

**Ausstattung** f (a) siehe vt equipping; provision. (b) (Ausrüstung) equipment; (Tech auch) fittings pl; (von Zimmer etc) furnishings pl; (Theat) décor and costumes.

**ausstechen** vt sep irreg (a) Torf, Plätzchen etc to cut out. (b) Augen to gouge out. (c) (fig) jdn (übertreffen) to outdo, to outshine.

**ausstehen** sep irreg 1 vt (ertragen) to endure; Sorge, Angst to go through, to suffer. ich kann ihn/so etwas nicht ~ I can't stand him/anything like that. 2 vi (a) (noch nicht gezahlt sein) to be due; (Antwort) to be still to come; (Entscheidung) to be still to be taken. (b) (Schulden) to be outstanding.

**aussteigen** vi sep irreg (a) aux sein to get out (aus of); (aus Bus, Zug etc auch) to get off (aus etw sth). alles ~! everybody out!; (von Schaffner) all change! (b) (col) (aus Geschäft etc) to get out (aus of); (aus Gesellschaft) to drop or opt out (aus of).

**Aussteiger(in** f) m - (col) drop-out. er ist ein ~ he has opted out.

**ausstellen** vt sep (a) (zur Schau stellen) to display; (auf Messe, in Museum etc) to exhibit. (b) (ausschreiben) to make out (jdm to sb); (behördlich ausgeben) to issue (jdm etw sb with sth). einen Scheck auf jdn ~ to make out a cheque to sb. (c) (ausschalten) Gerät to turn off.

**Aussteller(in** f) m - (a) (auf Messe) exhibitor. (b) (von Scheck) drawer.

**Ausstellung** f (a) (Kunst~, Messe) exhibition. (b) no pl (von Scheck etc) making out; (behördlich) issuing.

**Ausstellungs-:** ~datum nt date of issue; ~gelände nt exhibition site; ~halle f exhibition hall; ~stück nt (in Ausstellung) exhibit; (in Schaufenster etc) display item.

**Aussterben** nt no pl extinction. vom ~ bedroht sein to be threatened by extinction; eine vom ~ bedrohte Art an endangered species.

**aussterben** vi sep irreg aux sein to die out; (esp Spezies, Geschlecht auch) to become extinct; siehe ausgestorben.

**Aussteuer** f -n dowry.

**aussteuern** vt sep Verstärker etc to control the level of.

**Ausstieg** m -e (a) (Ausgang) exit. (b) (fig) dropping or opting out (aus of). der ~ aus der Kernenergie the abandonment of nuclear energy.

**ausstopfen** vt sep Kissen etc, Tiere to stuff.

**Ausstoß** m (a) (esp Phys, Tech: das Ausstoßen) expulsion, discharge. (b) (Produktion) output.

**ausstoßen** vt sep irreg (a) (herausstoßen) to discharge; Atem to expel; (herstellen) Teile, Stückzahl to turn out, to produce. (b) (ausschließen) (aus Verein, Armee etc) to expel (aus from); (verbannen) to banish (aus from). (c) (äußern) to utter; Schrei to give.

**ausstrahlen** sep 1 vt to radiate (auch fig); esp Licht, Wärme auch to give off; (Rad, TV) to transmit, to broadcast. 2 vi aux sein to radiate; (Schmerz) to spread (bis in +acc as far as).

**Ausstrahlung** f radiation; (Rad, TV) transmission, broadcasting; (fig: von Ort) aura; (von Mensch) charisma.

**ausstrecken** *sep* **1** *vt* to extend *(nach* towards*)*; *Fühler auch* to put out; *Hand auch, Beine etc* to stretch out. **2** *vr* to stretch (oneself) out.

**ausstreuen** *vt sep* to scatter; *(fig) Gerücht* to spread.

**ausströmen** *sep* **1** *vi aux sein* **(a)** *(herausfließen)* to stream out *(aus* of*)*; *(entweichen)* to escape *(aus* from*)*. **(b)** *(ausstrahlen) etw* **strömt von jdm/etw aus** *(fig)* sb/sth radiates sth. **2** *vt Duft, Gas* to give off; *Wärme, Ruhe etc* to radiate.

**aussuchen** *vt sep (auswählen)* to choose; *(esp iro)* to pick; *siehe* **ausgesucht**.

**Austausch** *m* exchange; *(von Gedanken etc auch)* interchange; *(Ersatz)* replacement; *(Sport)* substitution. **im ~ für** *or* **gegen** in exchange for.

**austauschbar** *adj* (ex)changeable; *(untereinander ~)* interchangeable; *(ersetzbar)* replaceable.

**austauschen** *vt sep (lit, fig)* to exchange *(gegen* for*)*; *(untereinander ~)* to interchange; *(ersetzen)* to replace *(gegen* with*)*.

**Austausch-:** **~motor** *m* replacement engine; **~schüler** *m* exchange student *or* pupil; **~student** *m* exchange student.

**austeilen** *vt sep* to distribute *(an +acc* among*)*; *(aushändigen auch)* to hand out *(an +acc* to*)*; *Spielkarten* to deal (out); *Essen* to serve; *Befehle* to give, to issue.

**Austeilung** *f* distribution; *(Aushändigung auch)* handing out; *(von Essen etc)* serving.

**Auster** *f* **-n** oyster.

**austoben** *vr sep (Mensch)* to let off steam; *(sich müde machen)* to tire oneself out. **ein Garten, wo sich die Kinder ~ können** a garden where the children can romp about.

**austragen** *sep irreg vt* **(a)** *Waren, Post etc* to deliver. **(b)** *Duell, Wettkampf etc* to hold. **einen Streit mit jdm ~** to have it out with sb. **(c) ein Kind ~** *(nicht abtreiben)* to have a child. **(d)** *(löschen) Zahlen, Daten* to take out. **jdn ~** *(aus Liste)* to cancel sb's name. **2** *vr* to sign out; *(in Hotel)* to check out.

**Austräger(in** *f***)** *m* delivery man/boy *etc*; *(von Zeitungen)* newspaper man/boy *etc*.

**Austragung** *f (Sport)* holding.

**Austragungs|ort** *m (Sport)* venue.

**Australien** [-iən] *nt* Australia.

**Australier(in** *f***)** [-iɐ, -iərɪn] *m* - Australian.

**australisch** *adj* Australian.

**austräumen** *vt sep* **sein Traum von Reichtümern ist ausgeträumt** his dreams of riches are over.

**austreiben** *sep irreg* **1** *vt (vertreiben)* to drive out; *Teufel etc auch* to exorcize, to cast out *(esp old, liter)*. **jdm etw ~** to cure sb of sth; *(esp durch Schläge)* to knock sth out of sb. **2** *vi (sprießen)* to sprout.

**austreten** *sep irreg* **1** *vi aux sein* **(a)** *(herauskommen)* to come out *(aus* of*)*; *(Gas etc)* to escape *(aus* from, through*)*. **(b)** *(col: zur Toilette gehen)* to go to the loo *or* john *(US) (col)*; *(Sch auch)* to be excused *(euph)*. **(c)** *(ausscheiden)* to leave *(aus etw* sth*)*. **2** *vt Pfad, Feuer etc* to tread out; *Schuhe* to wear out; *siehe* **ausgetreten**.

**austricksen** *vt sep (col: Sport, fig)* to outsmart.

**austrinken** *vti sep irreg* to finish. **trink (deine Milch) aus!** drink (your milk) up.

**Austritt** *m* **(a)** *no pl (von Flüssigkeit)* outflow; *(das Entweichen)* escape; *(von Blut)* issue. **(b)** *(das Ausscheiden)* leaving *no art (aus etw* sth*)*.

**austrocknen** *sep* **1** *vi aux sein* to dry out; *(Fluß etc)* to dry up; *(Kehle)* to become parched. **2** *vt* to dry out; *(trockenlegen) Sumpf auch* to drain.

**austüfteln** *vt sep (col)* to work out; *(ersinnen)* to

think up.

**aus|üben** *vt sep* **(a)** *Beruf, Kunst* to practise *(Brit)*, to practice *(US)*; *Gewerbe auch* to carry on; *Aufgabe, Funktion* to perform; *(innehaben) Amt* to hold. **(b)** *Druck, Einfluß* to exert *(auf +acc* on*)*; *Macht, Recht* to exercise; *Wirkung* to have *(auf +acc* on*)*.

**Aus|übung** *f siehe vt* **(a)** practice; performance. **in ~ seines Dienstes/seiner Pflicht** *(form)* in the execution of his duty. **(b)** exertion; exercise.

**aus|ufern** *vi sep aux sein (fig)* to get out of hand; *(Konflikt etc)* to escalate *(zu* into*)*.

**Ausverkauf** *m* (clearance) sale; *(wegen Schließung)* closing-down sale; *(fig: Verrat)* sell-out.

**ausverkaufen*** *vt sep* to sell off, to clear.

**ausverkauft** *adj* sold out. **vor ~em Haus spielen** to play to a full house.

**auswachsen** *sep irreg* **1** *vi aux sein* **das ist (ja) zum A~** *(col)* it's enough to drive you crazy *(col)*; *siehe* **ausgewachsen**. **2** *vr* **sich zu etw ~** *(fig: Streit etc)* to turn into sth.

**Auswahl** *f no pl* selection *(an +dat* of*)*; *(Angebot auch)* range; *(Wahl)* choice; *(die Besten)* pick. **viele Sachen zur ~ haben** to have many things to choose from; **eine ~ treffen** to make a choice; *(mehrere auswählen)* to make a selection.

**auswählen** *vt sep* to select, to choose *(unter +dat* from among*)*; *siehe* **ausgewählt**.

**Auswahl-:** **~mannschaft** *f* representative team; **~möglichkeit** *f* choice.

**Auswanderer** *m*, **Auswanderin** *f* emigrant.

**auswandern** *vi sep aux sein* to emigrate *(nach, in +acc* to*)*; *(Volk)* to migrate.

**Auswanderung** *f* emigration; *(Massen~)* migration.

**auswärtig** *adj attr* **(a)** *(nicht ansässig)* non-local; *Schüler, Mitglied* from out of town. **(b)** *(Pol)* foreign. **das A~e Amt** the Foreign Office *(Brit)*, the State Department *(US)*.

**auswärts** *adv* **(a)** *(außerhalb der Stadt)* out of town; *(Sport)* away. **~ essen** to eat out; **von ~ anrufen** to call long distance.

**Auswärtsspiel** *nt (Sport)* away (game).

**auswaschen** *vt sep irreg* to wash out; *(spülen)* to rinse (out).

**auswechselbar** *adj* (ex)changeable; *(untereinander)* interchangeable; *(ersetzbar)* replaceable.

**auswechseln** *vt sep* to change; *(esp gegenseitig)* to exchange; *(ersetzen)* to replace; *(Sport)* to substitute *(gegen* for*)*. **er ist wie ausgewechselt** *(fig)* he's a changed *or* different person.

**Auswechselspieler** *m* substitute.

**Ausweg** *m* way out; *(fig: Lösung auch)* solution. **der letzte ~** the last resort.

**Ausweg-:** **a~los** *adj (fig)* hopeless; **~losigkeit** *f (fig)* hopelessness.

**ausweichen** *vi sep irreg aux sein* to get out of the way *(+dat* of*)*; *(fig)* to evade the point/issue *etc*. **jdm/einer Begegnung ~** to avoid sb/a meeting; **eine ~de Antwort** an evasive answer; **auf etw** *(acc)* **~** *(fig)* to switch to sth.

**Ausweich-:** **~manöver** *nt* evasive action; **~möglichkeit** *f (lit)* possibility of getting out of the way; *(fig)* alternative; **~strecke** *f* alternative route.

**ausweinen** *vr sep* **sich bei jdm ~** to have a cry on sb's shoulder; **sich** *(dat)* **die Augen ~** to cry one's eyes out *(nach over)*.

**Ausweis** *m* **-e** *(Mitglieds~/Leser~/Studenten~ etc)* (membership/library/student *etc)* card; *(Personal~)* identity card; *(Berechtigungsnachweis)* pass. **~, bitte** your papers please.

**ausweisen** *sep irreg* **1** *vt (aus Land)* to expel, to deport. **2** *vr* to identify oneself. **können Sie sich ~?** do you have any means of identification?

**Ausweis-:** ~**karte** *f* = **Ausweis;** ~**kontrolle** *f* identity check; ~**papiere** *pl* identity papers *pl.*

**Ausweisung** *f* expulsion, deportation.

**ausweiten** *sep* **1** *vt* to widen; *(fig)* to expand *(zu into).* **2** *vr* to widen; *(esp Dehnbares)* to stretch; *(fig) (Thema, Bewegung)* to expand *(zu into); (sich verbreiten)* to spread.

**Ausweitung** *f* widening; *(Ausdehnung)* stretching; *(fig)* expansion; *(Verbreitung)* spreading.

**auswendig** *adv* by heart, from memory. **etw ~ können/lernen** to know/learn sth (off) by heart.

**auswerfen** *vt sep irreg* **(a)** Anker, Netz to cast. **(b)** *(hinausschleudern)* Lava, Asche to throw out.

**auswerten** *vt sep (bewerten)* to evaluate; *(analysieren)* to analyse.

**Auswertung** *f siehe vt* evaluation; analysis.

**auswickeln** *vt sep* Paket, Bonbon etc to unwrap.

**auswiegen** *vt sep irreg* to weigh (out); *siehe* **ausgewogen.**

**auswirken** *vr sep* to have an effect *(auf +acc on).* **sich negativ ~** to have a negative effect.

**Auswirkung** *f (Folge)* consequence; *(Wirkung)* effect; *(Rückwirkung)* repercussion.

**auswischen** *vt sep* to wipe out. **jdm eins ~** *(col)* to get one over on sb *(col); (aus Rache)* to get one's own back on sb.

**auswringen** *vt sep irreg* to wring out.

**Auswuchs** *m* **(a)** (out)growth; *(Mißbildung)* deformity. **(b)** *(fig) (Erzeugnis)* product; *(Mißstand, Übersteigerung)* excess.

**auswuchten** *vt sep* Räder to balance.

**Auswurf** *m no pl (Med)* sputum.

**auszahlen** *sep* **1** *vt* Geld etc to pay out; Arbeiter, Gläubiger to pay off. **2** *vr (sich lohnen)* to pay (off).

**auszählen** *sep* **1** *vt* Stimmen to count (up); *(Boxen)* to count out. **2** *vi (bei Kinderspielen)* to count out.

**Auszahlung** *f siehe vt* paying out; paying off.

**Auszählung** *f (von Stimmen etc)* counting (up), count.

**auszeichnen** *sep* **1** *vt* **(a)** *(mit Preisschild versehen)* to price. **(b)** *(ehren)* to honour *(Brit),* to honor *(US).* **jdn mit einem Orden ~** to decorate sb (with a medal); **jdn mit einem Preis/Titel ~** to award a prize/ title to sb. **(c)** *(hervorheben)* to distinguish (from all others); *(kennzeichnen)* to be a feature of. **2** *vr* to stand out *(durch due to).* **der Wagen zeichnet sich durch ... aus** one of the car's best features is ...; *siehe* **ausgezeichnet.**

**Auszeichnung** *f* **(a)** *no pl (das Auszeichnen) (von Waren)* pricing; *(mit Orden)* decoration. **(b)** *(Markierung: an Ware)* ticket. **(c)** *(Ehrung)* honour *(Brit),* honor *(US),* distinction; *(Orden)* decoration; *(Preis)* award, prize. **mit ~ bestehen** to pass with distinction.

**Auszeit** *f (Sport)* time-out.

**ausziehbar** *adj* extendible; Antenne telescopic. **ein ~er Tisch** a pull-out table.

**ausziehen** *sep irreg* **1** *vt* **(a)** *(herausziehen)* to pull out; *(verlängern auch)* to extend. **(b)** Kleider to take off; jdn to undress. **2** *vr (sich entkleiden)* to undress, to take off one's clothes. **3** *vi aux sein (aufbrechen, abreisen)* to set out; *(aus einer Wohnung)* to move *(aus out of).*

**Auszubildende(r)** *mf decl as adj* trainee; *(als Handwerker auch)* apprentice.

**Auszug** *m* **(a)** *(das Weggehen)* departure; *(aus der Wohnung)* move. **(b)** *(Ausschnitt)* excerpt; *(aus Buch auch)* extract; *(Konto~)* statement.

**autark** *adj* self-sufficient *(auch fig),* autarkic *(Econ).*

**Autarkie** *f* self-sufficiency *(auch fig),* autarky *(Econ).*

**authentisch** *adj* authentic.

**Auto** *nt* **-s** car, automobile *(esp US, dated).* ~ **fahren** *(selbst)* to drive (a car); *(als Mitfahrer)* to go by car; **mit dem ~ fahren** to go by car.

**Auto|atlas** *m* road atlas.

**Autobahn** *f* motorway *(Brit),* expressway *(US).*

**Autobahn-:** ~**ausfahrt** *f* motorway *(Brit)* or expressway *(US)* exit; ~**dreieck** *nt* motorway *(Brit)* or expressway *(US)* junction; ~**kreuz** *nt* motorway *(Brit)* or expressway *(US)* intersection; ~**raststätte** *f* motorway *(Brit)* or expressway *(US)* services *pl;* ~**zubringer** *m* motorway *(Brit)* or expressway *(US)* approach road.

**Auto-:** ~**batterie** *f* car battery; ~**biographie** *f* autobiography; **a~biographisch** *adj* autobiographical; ~**bombe** *f* car bomb; ~**bus** *m* bus; *(Reiseomnibus)* coach *(Brit),* bus; ~**didakt(in** *f)* **-en** self-educated person, autodidact *(form);* ~**diebstahl** *m* car theft; ~**fähre** *f* car ferry; ~**fahren** *nt* driving (a car); *(als Mitfahrer)* going by car; ~**fahrer** *m* (car) driver; ~**fahrt** *f* drive; ~**fokus** *m (Phot)* autofocus; ~**friedhof** *m (col)* car dump.

**autogen** *adj* autogenous. ~**es Training** *(Psych)* relaxation through self-hypnosis.

**Autogramm** *nt* **-e** autograph.

**Autogramm-:** ~**jäger** *m* autograph hunter; ~**stunde** *f* autograph(ing) session.

**Auto-:** ~**industrie** *f* car or automobile *(esp US)* industry; ~**karte** *f* road map; ~**kino** *nt* drive-in cinema *(Brit)* or movie theater *(US);* ~**knacker** *m (col)* car thief; ~**krat** *m (wk)* **-en, -en** autocrat; ~**marke** *f* make (of car).

**Automat** *m (wk)* **-en, -en** *(auch fig: Mensch)* machine; *(Verkaufs~)* vending machine; *(Spiel~)* slot-machine.

**Automatenkarte** *f* cash card.

**Automatic, Automatik¹** *m* **-s** *(Aut)* (car with) automatic.

**Automatik²** *f* automatic mechanism *(auch fig); (Gesamtanlage)* automatic system; *(Aut)* automatic transmission.

**Automatik-:** ~**getriebe** *nt* automatic transmission; ~**gurt** *m* inertia(-reel) seat belt; ~**schaltung** *f* automatic transmission; ~**wagen** *m* (car with) automatic.

**automatisch** *adj* automatic.

**automatisieren\*** *vt* to automate.

**Automatisierung** *f* automation.

**Automechaniker** *m* motor *(Brit)* or auto *(US)* mechanic.

**Automobil-:** ~**ausstellung** *f* motor *(Brit)* or auto *(US)* show; ~**club** *m* automobile association.

**Auto-:** **a~nom** *adj* autonomous *(auch fig);* ~**nome(r)** *mf decl as adj (Pol)* independent; ~**nomie** *f* autonomy *(auch fig);* ~**nummer** *f* (car) number.

**Autopsie** *f (Med)* autopsy.

**Autor** *m* author.

**Auto-:** ~**radio** *nt* car radio; ~**reifen** *m* car tyre *(Brit)* or tire *(US);* ~**reisezug** *m* ≃ motorail train; ~**rennbahn** *f* motor-racing circuit; ~**rennen** *nt* (motor) race.

**Autorin** *f* authoress.

**autorisieren\*** *vt* to authorize.

**autoritär** *adj* authoritarian.

**Autorität** *f* authority.

**Auto-:** ~**schalter** *m* drive-in bank counter; ~**schlange** *f* queue *(Brit)* or line of cars;

~**schlosser** *m* panel beater; ~**schlosserei** *f* body shop; ~**skooter** *m* dodgem, bumper car; ~**stellplatz** *m* (car) parking space; ~**stop(p)** *m* (esp S Ger) hitch-hiking; **per** ~**stop(p) fahren** to hitch(-hike); ~**strich** *m* (col: Gegend) kerb-crawling area (col); ~**telefon** *nt* car phone; ~**unfall** *m* car accident; ~**verkehr** *m* motor traffic; ~**verleih** *m*, ~**vermietung** *f* car hire (Brit) or rental; (Firma) car hire (Brit) or rental firm; ~**werkstatt** *f* garage, car repair shop (US); ~**zoom** [-'zu:m] *nt* (Phot) automatic zoom (lens); ~**zubehör** *nt* motor (Brit) or auto (US) accessories *pl.*

**autsch** *interj* (col) ouch, ow.

**auweh, auwei(a)** *interj* oh dear.

**avancieren*** [avã'si:rən] *vi aux sein* (dated, geh) to advance (zu to).

**Avant-** [avã]: ~**garde** *f* (geh) (Art) avant-garde; (Pol) vanguard; **a**~**gardistisch** *adj* avant-garde.

**AvD** [a:fau'de:] = **Automobilclub von Deutschland** ≃ AA (Brit), RAC (Brit), AAA (US).

**Avocado, Avocato** [avo'ka:do, -to] *f* **-s** avocado.

**Axiom** *nt* **-e** axiom.

**Axt** *f* ⁼**e** axe (Brit), ax (US). **die** ~ **im Haus erspart den Zimmermann** (Prov) self-help is the best help; **die** ~ **an etw/an die Wurzel einer Sache legen** (fig) to strike at the very roots of sth.

**Azalee** [-'le:ə] *f* **-n** (Bot) azalea.

**Azoren** *pl* (Geog) Azores *pl.*

**Azteke** *m* (wk) **-n, -n, Aztekin** *f* Aztec.

**Azubi** [a'tsu:bi] *m* **-s** (col) = **Auszubildende(r).**

**azurblau** *adj* azure.

# B

**B, b** [be:] *nt* **-, -** B, b. **B-dur/b-Moll** (the key of) B flat major/minor; **B wie Bertha** ≃ B for Benjamin, B for Baker *(US)*.

**B** *f* = **Bundesstraße** ≃ A *(Brit)*.

**Baby** ['be:bi] *nt* **-s** baby.

**Baby-:** ~**ausstattung** *f* layette; ~**nahrung** *f* baby food; **b~sitten** *vi insep* to babysit; ~**sitter(in** *f)* *m* - babysitter; ~**speck** *m (col)* puppy fat; ~**trage-tasche** *f* carrycot.

**Bạch** *m* ⁼e *(lit, fig)* stream.

**Bạchstelze** *f* **-n** wagtail.

**Bạckblech** *nt* baking tray.

**Bạckbord** *nt no pl (Naut)* port (side).

**bạckbord(s)** *adv (Naut)* on the port side.

**Bạcke** *f* **-n** **(a)** cheek. **mit vollen** ~**n kauen** to eat away with bulging cheeks. **(b)** *(col: Hinter~)* buttock, cheek.

**bạcken** *vt* to bake; *Brot, Kuchen auch* to make; *(dial: braten) Fisch, Eier etc* to fry. **frisch/knusprig ge-backenes Brot** fresh/crusty bread; **gebackener Fisch** fried fish; *(im Ofen)* baked fish.

**Bạcken-:** ~**bart** *m* sideboards *pl*, sideburns *pl*; ~**knochen** *m* cheekbone; ~**zahn** *m* molar.

**Bạ̈cker(in** *f)* *m* - baker.

**Bạ̈ckerei** *f* baker's *(Brit)*, baker *(US)*; *(Backstube)* bakery.

**Bạ̈cker-:** ~**junge** *m (Lehrling)* baker's apprentice; ~**laden** *m* baker's *(Brit)*, baker *(US)*; ~**meister** *m* master baker.

**Bạck-:** **b~fertig** *adj* oven-ready; ~**fett** *nt* cooking fat; ~**fisch** *m* **(a)** fried fish; **(b)** *(dated)* teenager; ~**form** *f* baking tin; ~**hähnchen** *nt* fried chicken in breadcrumbs; ~**mischung** *f* cake mix; ~**obst** *nt* dried fruit; ~**ofen** *m* oven *(auch fig)*; ~**pflaume** *f* prune; ~**pinsel** *m* pastry brush; ~**pulver** *nt* baking powder.

**Bạckstein** *m* brick.

**Bạck-:** ~**stube** *f* bakery; ~**waren** *pl* bread, cakes and pastries *pl*.

**Bạd** *nt* ⁼er **(a)** *(Wannen~, Phot)* bath; *(das Baden)* bathing. **ein** ~ **nehmen** to have *or* take a bath; **ein** ~ **in der Menge nehmen** *(fig)* to go on a walkabout. **(b)** *(im Meer)* bathe, swim; *(das Baden)* bathing, swimming. **(c)** *(Badezimmer)* bathroom. **Zimmer mit** ~ room with (private) bath. **(d)** *(Schwimm~)* (swimming) pool *or* baths. **die städtischen** ⁼**er** the public baths. **(e)** *(Heil~)* spa; *(See~)* (seaside) resort.

**Bade-:** ~**anstalt** *f* (public) swimming baths *pl*; ~**anzug** *m* swimsuit, bathing suit; ~**gast** *m* **(a)** *(im Kurort)* spa visitor; **(b)** *(im Schwimmbad)* bather, swimmer; ~**handtuch** *nt* bath towel; *(größer)* bath sheet; ~**hose** *f* swimming trunks *pl*; ~**kappe** *f* swimming cap; ~**mantel** *m* bathrobe, dressing gown *(Brit)*; ~**matte** *f* bathmat; ~**meister** *m (im Schwimmbad)* (pool) attendant; *(am Strand)* lifeguard; ~**mütze** *f* = ~**kappe**.

**baden** 1 *vi* **(a)** to have a bath. **(b)** *(im Meer,* *Schwimmbad etc)* to swim, to bathe. ~ **gehen** to go swimming. **(c)** *(col)* ~ **gehen** to come a cropper *(col)*; **wenn das passiert, gehe ich** ~ I'll be for it if that happens *(col)*. **2** *vt* **(a)** *Kind etc* to bath. **(b)** *Augen, Wunde etc* to bathe.

**Baden-Württemberg** *nt* Baden-Württemberg.

**Bade-:** ~**ort** *m (Kurort)* spa; *(Seebad)* (seaside) resort; ~**sachen** *pl* swimming things *pl*; ~**saison** *f* swimming season; *(in Kurort)* spa season; ~**salz** *nt* bath salts *pl*; ~**strand** *m* (bathing) beach; ~**tuch** *nt* = ~**handtuch**; ~**wanne** *f* bath (tub); ~**wasser** *nt* bath water; ~**zimmer** *nt* bathroom.

**baff** *adj pred (col)* ~ **sein** to be flabbergasted.

**Bafög** ['ba:føk] *nt no pl* = **Bundesausbildungsför-derungsgesetz** German grant system for students. **er bekommt** ~ he gets a grant.

**Bagage** [ba'ga:ʒə] *f no pl (dated col: Gesindel)* crowd *(col)*.

**Bagatẹlle** *f* trifle, bagatelle.

**Bagatẹllsache** *f (Jur)* minor case.

**Bagdad** *nt* Baghdad.

**Bạgger** *m* - excavator, digger; *(für Schlamm)* dredger.

**bạggern** *vti Graben* to excavate; *Fahrrinne* to dredge.

**Bạggersee** *m* (flooded) gravel pit.

**Bahạmas** *pl* **die** ~ the Bahamas *pl*.

**Bahn** *f* **-en** **(a)** *(lit, fig)* path; *(von Fluß)* course; *(Astron auch)* orbit. **jdm/einer Sache die** ~ **frei ma-chen** *(fig)* to clear the way for sb/sth; **die** ~ **ist frei** *(fig)* the way is clear; **sich** *(dat)* ~ **brechen** *(fig)* to make headway; *(Mensch)* to forge ahead; **in ge-wohnten** ~**en verlaufen** *(fig)* to continue as before; **von der rechten** ~ **abkommen** *(geh)* to stray from the straight and narrow; **jdn auf die rechte** ~ **brin-gen** *(fig)* to put sb on the straight and narrow; **jdn aus der** ~ **werfen** *(fig)* to shatter sb.

**(b)** *(Eisen~)* railway *(Brit)*, railroad *(US)*; *(Straßen~)* tram, streetcar *(US)*; *(Zug)* train; *(Ver-kehrsnetz, Verwaltung)* railway *(Brit) usu pl*, railroad *(US)*. **mit der** ~ by train *or* rail/tram; **frei** ~ *(Comm)* carriage free to station of destination.

**(c)** *(Sport)* track; *(für Pferderennen auch)* course; *(für einzelne Läufer, Schwimmer etc)* lane.

**(d)** *(Stoff~, Tapeten~)* length, strip.

**Bahn-:** ~**arbeiter** *m* railworker; ~**beamte(r)** *m* railway *(Brit) or* railroad *(US)* official; **b~bre-chend** *adj* pioneering; ~**brechendes leisten** to pioneer new developments; ~**bus** *m* railway *(Brit) or* railroad *(US)* bus.

**Bahndamm** *m* (railway *(Brit) or* railroad *(US)*) embankment.

**bahnen** *vt* **jdm/einer Sache den/einen Weg** ~ *(fig)* to pave the way for sb/sth; **sich** *(dat)* **einen Weg** ~ to fight one's way through.

**Bahn-:** ~**fahrt** *f* rail journey; ~**fracht** *f* rail freight.

**Bahnhof** *m* station. **am** *or* **auf dem** ~ at the station; ~ **Schöneberg** Schöneberg station; **ich verstehe nur**

~ *(hum col)* it's all Greek to me *(col)*; **er wurde mit großem ~ empfangen** he was given the red carpet treatment.

**Bahnhofs-** *in cpds* station; **~gaststätte** *f* station restaurant; **~halle** *f* (station) concourse; **~mission** *f charitable organization for helping rail travellers in difficulties, traveller's aid;* **~vorsteher** *m* stationmaster; **~wirtschaft** *f* station restaurant.

**Bahn-: b~lagernd** *adj (Comm)* to be collected from the station; **~linie** *f* railway *(Brit)* or railroad *(US)* line *or* track; **~polizei** *f* railway *(Brit)* or railroad *(US)* police; **~schranke** *f* level *(Brit)* or grade *(US)* crossing barrier; **~steig** *m* platform; **~steigkarte** *f* platform ticket; **~übergang** *m* level *(Brit)* or grade *(US)* crossing; **beschrankter/unbeschrankter ~übergang** crossing with gates/unguarded crossing; **~verbindung** *f* rail *(Brit)* or train connection; **~wärter** *m* gatekeeper.

**Bahrain, Bahrein** *nt* Bahrain.

**Bahre** *f* **-n** *(Kranken~)* stretcher; *(Toten~)* bier.

**Baiser** [bɛ'zeː] *nt* **-s** meringue.

**Baisse** ['bɛːs(ə)] *f* **-n** *(St Ex)* fall; *(plötzliche)* slump.

**Bajonett** *nt* **-e** bayonet.

**Bajuware** *m (wk)* **-n, -n, Bajuwarin** *f (old, hum)* Bavarian.

**Bake** *f* **-n** *(Verkehrszeichen)* distance warning signal; *(an Autobahn auch)* countdown marker.

**Bakterie** [-riə] *f* **-n** *usu pl* germ. **~n** germs *pl*, bacteria *pl*.

**bakteriell** *adj* bacterial, bacteria *attr*.

**Bakteriologe** *m*, **Bakteriologin** *f* bacteriologist.

**bakteriologisch** *adj* bacteriological; *Krieg* biological.

**Balance** [ba'lãːs(ə)] *f* **-n** balance, equilibrium. **die ~ halten/verlieren** to keep/lose one's balance.

**Balance|akt** [ba'lãːs(ə)-] *m (lit, fig)* balancing act.

**balancieren\*** [balã'siːrən] **1** *vi aux sein* to balance. **über etw** *(acc)* **~** to work one's way across sth, keeping one's balance. **2** *vt* to balance.

**bald 1** *adv, comp* **eher,** *superl* **am ehesten (a)** soon. **er kommt ~** he'll be coming soon; **~ darauf** soon afterwards; **so ~ wie möglich, möglichst ~** as soon as possible; **wird's ~?** get a move on; **bis ~!** see you soon. **(b)** *(fast)* almost, nearly. **sie platzt ~ vor Neugier** she's just about dying with curiosity. **2** *conj (geh)* **~ hier, ~ da** now here, now there; **~ so, ~ so** now this way, now that.

**baldig** *adj attr, no comp* quick, speedy; *Antwort, Wiedersehen* early.

**baldmöglichst** *adv* as soon as possible.

**Baldrian** *m* **-e** valerian.

**Baldriantropfen** *pl* valerian (drops *pl*).

**Balearen** *pl* **die ~** the Balearics *pl*.

**Balg¹** *m* **⸚e (a)** *(Tierhaut)* pelt, skin. **(b)** *(Blase~)* bellows *pl*.

**Balg²** *m or nt* **⸚er** *(pej col: Kind)* brat *(pej col)*.

**balgen** *vr* to scrap *(um over)*.

**Balgerei** *f* scrap, tussle.

**Balkan** *m* *(~länder)* **der ~** the Balkans *pl*; **auf dem ~** in the Balkans.

**Balkanländer** *pl* Balkan States.

**Balken** *m* **- (a)** *(Holz~, Schwebe~)* beam; *(Stütz~)* prop; *(Quer~)* joist, crossbeam. **lügen, daß sich die ~ biegen** *(col)* to tell a pack of lies. **(b)** *(Strich)* bar; *(Uniformstreifen)* stripe. **(c)** *(an Waage)* beam.

**Balkendiagramm** *nt* bar chart.

**Balkon** [bal'kɔŋ, bal'koːn] *m* **-s** *or* **-e** balcony; *(Theat)* (dress) circle.

**Balkon-: ~möbel** *pl* garden furniture *sing (for the balcony)*; **~tür** *f* French window(s).

**Ball¹** *m* **⸚e** ball. **~ spielen** to play ball; **am ~ sein** *(lit)* to have the ball; **immer am ~ sein** *(fig)* to be on the ball; **am ~ bleiben** *(lit)* to keep (possession of) the ball; *(fig)* to stay on the ball; **bei jdm am ~ bleiben** *(fig)* to keep in with sb; **jdm den ~ zuspielen** *(lit)* to pass (the ball) to sb; **jdm/sich gegenseitig die ~e zuspielen** *(fig)* to feed sb/each other lines.

**Ball²** *m* **⸚e** *(Tanzfest)* ball. **auf dem ~** at the ball.

**Ballade** *f* ballad.

**Ballast** [*auch* -'-] *m (rare)* **-e** *(Naut, Aviat)* ballast; *(fig)* burden, encumbrance. **~ abwerfen** *(lit)* to discharge ballast; *(fig)* to get rid of a burden.

**Ballaststoffe** *pl (Med)* roughage *sing*.

**Ballen** *m* **- (a)** bale; *(Kaffee~)* sack. **in ~ verpacken** to bale. **(b)** *(Anat: an Daumen, Zehen)* ball; *(an Pfote)* pad.

**ballen** *vt Faust* to clench; *siehe* **geballt**.

**Ballerei** *f (col)* shoot-out *(col)*.

**Ballerina** *f*, *pl* **Ballerinen** ballerina.

**ballern** *vi (col)* to shoot, to fire.

**Ballett** *nt* **-e** ballet. **beim ~ sein** *(col)* to be a ballet dancer.

**Balletttänzer(in** *f)* *m* ballet dancer.

**Ballführung** *f (Sport)* ball control.

**Ballistik** *f no pl* ballistics *sing*.

**ballistisch** *adj* ballistic.

**Ball-: ~junge** *m (Tennis)* ball boy; **~kleid** *nt* ball gown; **~mädchen** *nt (Tennis)* ball girl.

**Ballon** [ba'lɔŋ, ba'loːn] *m* **-s** *or* **-e** balloon.

**Ball-: ~saal** *m* ballroom; **~spiel** *nt* ball game.

**Ballung** *f* concentration; *(von Truppen auch)* massing.

**Ballungs-: ~gebiet** *nt*, **~raum** *m* conurbation; **~zentrum** *nt* centre *(Brit)* or center *(US)* (of population, industry *etc)*.

**Ballwechsel** *m (Sport)* rally.

**Balsam** *m* **-e** balsam; *(fig)* balm.

**balsamieren\*** *vt* = **einbalsamieren**.

**Balte** *m (wk)* **-n, -n, Baltin** *f* **er/sie ist ~** he/she comes from the Baltic.

**Baltikum** *nt* **das ~** the Baltic States *pl*.

**baltisch** *adj* Baltic *attr*.

**Balz** *f* **-en (a)** *(Paarungsspiel)* courtship display. **(b)** *(Paarungszeit)* mating season.

**Balz-: ~ruf** *m* mating call; **~zeit** *f* mating season.

**Bambus** *m* **-ses** *or* **-, -se** bamboo.

**Bambus-: ~rohr** *nt* bamboo cane; **~sprossen** *pl* bamboo shoots *pl*.

**Bammel** *m no pl (col)* **(einen) ~ vor jdm/etw haben** to be scared of sb/sth.

**banal** *adj* banal, trite.

**banalisieren\*** *vt* to trivialize.

**Banalität** *f* banality.

**Banane** *f* **-n** banana.

**Bananen-: ~dampfer** *m* banana boat; **~republik** *f (Pol pej)* banana republic; **~schale** *f* banana skin; **~stecker** *m* jack plug.

**Banause** *m (wk)* **-n, -n** *(pej)* peasant *(col)*; *(Kultur~ auch)* philistine.

**band** *pret of* **binden**.

**Band¹** *nt* **⸚er (a)** *(Seiden~ etc)* ribbon; *(Isolier~, Maß~, Ziel~)* tape; *(Haar~, Hut~)* band; *(Schürzen~)* string. **(b)** *(Ton~)* tape. **etw auf ~ aufnehmen** to tape *or* record sth. **(c)** *(Fließ~)* conveyor belt; *(als Einrichtung)* production line; *(Montage~)* assembly line. **am ~ arbeiten** to work on the production line; **am laufenden ~** *(fig)* non-stop, continuously. **(d)** *(Rad)* **auf dem 44m-~** on the 44 meter band. **(e)** *(Anat) usu pl* ligament.

**Band²** *nt* **-e** *(liter)* **das ~ der Freundschaft/Liebe** *etc* the bonds *or* ties of friendship/love *etc*.

**Band³** m ⁼e (Buch~) volume. **darüber könnte man ~e schreiben/erzählen** you could write a book about it; **das spricht ~e** that speaks volumes.
**Band⁴** [bɛnt] f -s (Mus) band.
**Bandage** [-'daːʒə] f -n bandage. **mit harten ~n** (fig col) with no holds barred.
**bandagieren*** [-'ʒiːrən] vt to bandage (up).
**Band-:** ~**aufnahme** f tape-recording; ~**breite** f (Rad) bandwidth, frequency range; (fig) range.
**Bande¹** f -n gang; (col: Gruppe) bunch (col).
**Bande²** f -n (Sport) (von Eisbahn) barrier; (Billiard) cushion.
**Banden-:** ~**chef** m (col) gang-leader; ~**diebstahl** m (Jur) gang robbery; ~**führer** m = ~**chef**.
**Banderole** f -n tax or revenue seal.
**Bänder-:** (Med) ~**riß** m torn ligament; ~**zerrung** f pulled ligament.
**bändigen** vt to control; (zähmen) to tame.
**Bändigung** m no pl siehe vt controlling; taming.
**Bandit** m (wk) -en, -en bandit; (fig pej) brigand.
**Band-:** ~**laufwerk** nt (Comp) tape streamer; ~**maß** nt tape measure; ~**nudeln** pl tagliatelle pl, ribbon noodles pl; ~**säge** f band saw; ~**scheibe** f (Anat) disc; ~**scheibenschaden** m slipped disc; ~**wurm** m tapeworm.
**bang(e)** adj (a) (ängstlich) scared, frightened. **jdm ~ machen** to scare or frighten sb; **mir ist ~e vor ihm** I'm scared or frightened of him. **(b)** (geh: beklommen) uneasy (um about). **es wurde ihr ~ ums Herz** her heart sank.
**Bange** f no pl (esp NGer) **nur keine ~!** (col) don't worry.
**Bange-:** ~**machen** nt scaremongering; ~**macher** m scaremonger.
**bangen** vi (geh) **um jds Leben etc ~** to fear for sb's life etc.
**Bangkok** nt Bangkok.
**Bangladesch** nt Bangladesh.
**Banjo** ['bɛndʒo, 'bandʒo] nt -s banjo.
**Bank¹** f ⁼e (a) bench; (Kirchen~) pew; (Anklage~) dock. **auf** or **in der ersten/letzten ~** on the front/back bench etc; **(alle) durch die ~** (col) every single one; **etw auf die lange ~ schieben** (col) to put sth off. **(b)** (Arbeitstisch) (work) bench.
**Bank²** f -en (a) (Comm) bank. **Geld auf der ~ liegen haben** to have money in the bank; **bei der ~** at the bank. **(b)** (bei Glücksspielen) bank. **(die) ~ halten** (col) to be banker; **die ~ sprengen** to break the bank.
**Bank-:** ~**angestellte(r)** mf bank employee; ~**anweisung** f banker's order; ~**automat** m cash dispenser; ~**direktor** m director of a/the bank; ~**einbruch** m bank raid.
**Bänkelsänger** m ballad-singer, minstrel.
**Bankett¹** nt -e (an Straßen) verge (Brit), shoulder.
**Bankett²** nt -e (Festessen) banquet.
**Bank-:** ~**fach** nt (a) (Beruf) banking **(b)** (Schließfach) safe-deposit box; ~**gebühr** f bank charge; ~**geheimnis** nt confidentiality in banking; ~**geschäft** nt no pl (~wesen) banking world; ~**guthaben** nt bank balance; ~**halter** m (bei Glücksspielen) banker.
**Bankier** [-'kieː] m -s banker.
**Bank-:** ~**kauffrau** f, ~**kaufmann** m (qualified) bank clerk; ~**konto** nt bank account; ~**leitzahl** f (bank) sort code; ~**note** f banknote, bill (US); ~**raub** m bank robbery; ~**räuber** m bank robber.
**bankrott** adj (lit, fig) bankrupt. **~ gehen** to go bankrupt; **jdn ~ machen** to bankrupt sb.
**Bankrott** m -e (lit, fig) bankruptcy. **~ machen** to go bankrupt; **den ~ anmelden** or **erklären** to declare

oneself bankrupt.
**Bankrott|erklärung** f declaration of bankruptcy; (fig) sellout (col).
**Bank-:** ~**überfall** m bank raid; ~**überweisung** f bank transfer; ~**verbindung** f banking arrangements pl; ~**wesen** nt banking.
**Bann** m -e (a) no pl (geh) spell. **im ~ eines Menschen/einer Sache stehen** or **sein** to be under sb's spell/the spell of sth; **sie zog** or **zwang ihn in ihren ~** she cast her spell over him. **(b)** (Hist: Kirchen~) excommunication.
**bannen** vt (a) (geh: bezaubern) to bewitch, to entrance. **(wie) gebannt** fascinated; (stärker) spellbound. **(b)** Geister to exorcize; Gefahr to ward off.
**Banner** nt - (geh) banner.
**Bannmeile** f inviolable precincts pl (of city, Parliament etc).
**Bantamgewicht** nt bantamweight.
**Bantu** m -(s) Bantu.
**Baptist(in** f) m Baptist.
**bar** adj no comp (a). cash. **~es Geld** cash; **(in) ~ bezahlen** to pay (in) cash; **~ auf die Hand** cash on the nail; **etw für ~e Münze nehmen** (fig) to take sth at face value. **(b)** attr Unsinn absolute. **(c)** pred +gen (liter) **~ aller Hoffnung** devoid of hope, completely without hope. **(d)** (liter: bloß) bare. **~en Hauptes** bareheaded.
**Bar** f -s bar.
**Bär** m (wk) -en, -en bear. **stark wie ein ~** (col) (as) strong as an ox; **der Große/Kleine ~** (Astron) the Great/Little Bear, Ursa Major/Minor; **jdm einen ~en aufbinden** (col) to have sb on (col).
**Baracke** f -n hut, shack; (pej: kleines Haus) hovel.
**Barbar(in** f) m (wk) -en, -en (pej) barbarian.
**Barbarei** f (pej) barbarity; (no pl: Kulturlosigkeit) barbarism.
**barbarisch** adj (a) (pej) barbaric, barbarous. **(b)** (col: fürchterlich) terrible.
**bärbeißig** adj (col) grouchy (col), grumpy.
**Bardame** f barmaid.
**Barde** m (wk) -n, -n (Liter) bard; (iro) minstrel.
**Bären-:** ~**dienst** m **jdm einen ~dienst erweisen** to do sb a disservice; ~**hunger** m (col) einen ~**hunger haben** to be famished (col); ~**jagd** f bear hunt/hunting; ~**kräfte** pl the strength of an ox; **b~stark** adj strapping, strong as an ox; (fig col) terrific.
**Barett** nt -e or -s cap; (für Richter etc) biretta.
**barfuß** adj pred barefoot(ed). **~ gehen** to go/walk barefoot.
**barfüßig** adj barefooted.
**barg** pret of **bergen**.
**Bar-:** ~**geld** nt cash; **b~geldlos 1** adj cashless; **b~geldloser Zahlungsverkehr** non-cash or credit transactions pl; **2** adv without using cash; **b~häuptig** adj (geh) bareheaded; ~**hocker** m (bar) stool.
**Bärin** f (she-)bear.
**Bariton** [-tɔn] m -e [-toːnə] baritone.
**Barium** nt no pl barium.
**Barkasse** f -n launch; (Beiboot auch) longboat.
**Barkauf** m cash purchase.
**Barke** f -n (Naut) skiff; (liter) barque (liter).
**Barkeeper** ['baːɐkiːpɐ] m - barman, bartender.
**Barkredit** m cash loan.
**barmherzig** adj (liter, Rel) merciful; (mitfühlend) compassionate.
**Barmherzigkeit** f (liter, Rel) mercy, mercifulness; (Mitgefühl) compassion.
**Barmittel** pl cash (reserves pl).
**barock** adj baroque; (fig) ornate; Sprache florid.
**Barock** nt or m no pl baroque.

**Barock-** *in cpds* baroque; ~zeit *f* baroque period.
**Barometer** *nt* - *(lit, fig)* barometer. **das** ~ **steht auf Sturm** *(fig)* there's trouble brewing.
**Baron(in** *f)* *m* **-e** baron/baroness.
**Baroneß** *f* **-ssen** *(dated)*, **Baronesse** *f* baroness.
**Barras** *m no pl (col)* army.
**Barren** *m* - **(a)** *(Metall~)* bar; *(esp Gold~)* ingot. **(b)** *(Sport)* parallel bars *pl.*
**Barriere** *f* **-n** *(lit, fig)* barrier.
**Barrikade** *f* barricade. **auf die** ~**n gehen** *(lit, fig)* to go to the barricades.
**Barsch** *m* **-e** perch.
**barsch** *adj* brusque, curt; *Befehl auch* peremptory. **jdn** ~ **anfahren** to snap at sb.
**Barschaft** *f no pl* **meine ganze** ~ **bestand aus 10 Mark** all I had on me was 10 marks.
**Barscheck** *m* uncrossed cheque *(Brit)* or check *(US).*
**barst** *pret of* **bersten.**
**Bart** *m* **ᵹe (a)** beard; *(von Katze, Robbe etc)* whiskers *pl.* **(b)** *(fig col)* **(sich** *dat)* **etw in den** ~ **murmeln** to mutter sth in one's beard *(col);* **jdm um den** ~ **gehen** to butter sb up *(col);* **der Witz hat einen** ~ that's an old chestnut *(col).* **(c)** *(Schlüssel~)* bit.
**Barthaar** *nt* facial hair; *(Bart auch)* beard.
**bärtig** *adj* bearded.
**Bart-: b~los** *adj* beardless; *(glattrasiert)* clean-shaven; ~**nelke** *f* sweet william; ~**stoppeln** *pl* stubble *sing;* ~**wuchs** *m* beard; *(esp weiblicher)* facial hair *no indef art;* **er hat starken** ~**wuchs** he has a heavy growth of beard.
**Bar-:** ~**verkauf** *m* cash sale; ~**vermögen** *nt* liquid assets *pl;* ~**zahlung** *f* cash payment; **(Verkauf) nur gegen** ~**zahlung** cash (sales) only; ~**zahlungspreis** *m* cash price.
**Basar** *m* **-e** bazaar.
**Base¹** *f* **-n** *(old, dial)* cousin.
**Base²** *f* **-n** *(Chem)* base.
**Baseball** ['be:sbo:l] *m no pl* baseball.
**Basel** *nt* Basle.
**basieren\*** *vi* to be based *(auf +dat* on).
**Basilika** *f, pl* **Basiliken** basilica.
**Basilikum** *nt no pl* basil.
**Basis** *f, pl* **Basen** basis; *(Archit, Mil, Math)* base. **auf breiter** ~ on a broad basis; ~ **und Überbau** *(Pol, Sociol)* foundation and superstructure; **die** ~ *(col)* the grass roots.
**Basis|arbeit** *f (Pol)* groundwork.
**basisch** *adj (Chem)* basic.
**Basis-:** ~**demokratie** *f* grass-roots democracy; ~**gruppe** *f* action group.
**Baske** *m (wk)* **-n, -n, Baskin** *f* Basque.
**Basken-:** ~**land** *nt* Basque region; ~**mütze** *f* beret.
**Basketball** *m no pl* basketball.
**baskisch** *adj* Basque.
**Baskisch(e)** *nt decl as adj* Basque; *siehe* **Deutsch(e).**
**Baß** *m* **ᵹsse (a)** bass. **(b)** *(Instrument)* double bass.
**Baßbariton** *m* bass baritone.
**Baßgeige** *f (col)* (double) bass.
**Bassin** [ba'sɛ̃:] *nt* **-s** *(Schwimm~)* pool; *(von Brunnen)* fountain.
**Bassist(in** *f)* *m* **(a)** *(Sänger)* bass. **(b)** *(im Orchester etc)* (double) bass player.
**Baß-:** ~**schlüssel** *m* bass clef; ~**stimme** *f* bass (voice); *(Partie)* bass (part).
**Bast** *m (rare)* **-e** *(zum Binden, Flechten)* raffia.
**basta** *interj (und damit)* ~! (and) that's that.
**Bastard** *m* **-e (a)** *(pej)* bastard. **(b)** *(Tier)* cross.
**Bastel|arbeit** *f* piece of handicraft.
**Bastelei** *f (col)* handicraft; *(pej)* botched job *(col).*
**basteln 1** *vi* **(a)** *(als Hobby)* to make things with

one's hands. **sie kann gut** ~ she is good with her hands. **(b) an etw** *(dat)* ~ to work on sth; *(bauen)* to make sth; *(an etw herumbasteln)* to tinker with sth; **mit Holz** *etc* ~ to make things out of wood *etc.* **2** *vt* to make; *Geräte etc auch* to build.
**Basteln** *nt no pl* handicraft.
**Bastion** *f (lit, fig)* bastion.
**Bastler(in** *f)* *m* - *(von Modellen etc)* modeller; *(von Möbeln etc)* do-it-yourself enthusiast. **ein guter** ~ **sein** to be clever with one's hands.
**BAT** ['be:|a:'te:] = **Bundesangestelltentarif** *German salary scale for employees.*
**bat** *pret of* **bitten.**
**Bataillon** [batal'jo:n] *nt* **-e** *(Mil, fig)* battalion.
**Batik** *f or m* **-en** batik.
**Batist** *m* **-e** batiste, cambric.
**Batterie** *f (Elec, Mil)* battery; *(Reihe von Flaschen etc auch)* row.
**Batterie-: b~betrieben** *adj* battery-powered; ~**gerät** *nt* battery-powered radio *etc.*
**Batzen** *m* - *(col)* **ein** ~ **Geld** a tidy sum *(col).*
**Bau** *n* **(a)** *no pl (das Bauen)* building, construction. **im** ~ under construction; **der** ~ **des Hauses dauerte ein Jahr** it took a year to build the house. **(b)** *no pl (Auf~)* structure; *(von Satz, Apparat auch)* construction; *(Körper~)* build. **von kräftigem** ~ **sein** to be powerfully built. **(c)** *no pl (~stelle)* building site. **auf dem** ~ **arbeiten** to work on a building site. **(d)** *pl* **-ten** *(Gebäude)* building. **(e)** *pl* **-e** *(Erdhöhle)* burrow, hole; *(Biber~)* lodge; *(Fuchs~)* den; *(Dachs~)* set(t). **(f)** *no pl (Mil sl)* guardhouse. **4 Tage** ~ 4 days in the guardhouse.
**Bau-:** ~**arbeiten** *pl* building *or* construction work *sing;* *(Straßen~)* roadworks *pl (Brit),* roadwork *sing (US);* ~**arbeiter** *m* building *or* construction worker; ~**bude** *f* site hut.
**Bauch** *m, pl* **Bäuche (a)** *(von Mensch)* stomach, belly *(col);* *(Anat)* abdomen; *(Fett~)* paunch. **ihm tat der** ~ **weh** he had stomach-ache; **sich** *(dat)* **den** ~ **vollschlagen** *(col)* to stuff oneself *(col);* **sich** *(dat)* **(vor Lachen) den** ~ **halten** *(col)* to split one's sides (laughing); **einen** ~ **ansetzen** to get a paunch; **mit etw auf den** ~ **fallen** *(col)* to come a cropper with sth *(col).* **(b)** *(Hohlraum: von Schiff etc)* belly, bowels *pl.*
**Bauch-:** ~**ansatz** *m* beginning of a paunch; ~**fell** *nt* peritoneum; ~**fell|entzündung** *f* peritonitis; ~**flosse** *f* pelvic fin; ~**höhle** *f* abdomen.
**bauchig** *adj Gefäß* bulbous.
**Bauch-:** ~**laden** *m* vendor's tray; ~**landung** *f (col)* *(Aviat)* belly landing; *(bei Sprung ins Wasser)* belly-flop.
**bäuchlings** *adv* on one's front.
**Bauch-:** ~**muskel** *m* stomach muscle; ~**nabel** *m* navel, belly-button *(col);* ~**redner** *m* ventriloquist; ~**schmerzen** *pl* stomach-ache; ~**speck** *m (Cook)* belly of pork; ~**speicheldrüse** *f* pancreas; ~**tanz** *m* belly-dance/dancing; ~**tänzerin** *f* belly-dancer; ~**weh** *nt* stomach-ache.
**Baud** *nt (Telec, Comp)* baud.
**Baudenkmal** *nt* historical monument.
**bauen 1** *vt* **(a)** to build, to construct; *(anfertigen auch)* to make; *Höhle* to dig. **seine Hoffnung auf jdn/etw** ~ to pin one's hopes on sb/sth; **die Betten** ~ *(esp Mil)* to make the beds; *siehe* **gebaut.** **(b)** *(col: verursachen)* *Unfall* to cause. **da hast du Mist gebaut** *(col)* you really messed that up *(col).* **(c)** *(col: machen, ablegen)* *Prüfung etc* to pass. **seinen Doktor** ~ to get one's doctorate. **2** *vi* **(a)** to build. **wir haben neu gebaut** we built a new house; **hier wird viel gebaut** there is a lot of building going on around here.

**(b)** *(vertrauen)* **auf jdn/etw** ~ to rely *or* count on sb/ sth.

**Bauer** *m (wk)* **-n, -n (a)** *(Landwirt)* farmer; *(als Vertreter einer Klasse)* peasant; *(pej)* yokel. **die dümmsten ~n haben die dicksten Kartoffeln** *(prov col)* fortune favours fools *(prov)*. **(b)** *(Chess)* pawn; *(Cards)* jack.

**Bäuerchen** *nt (baby-talk)* burp. **(ein)** ~ **machen** to burp.

**Bäuerin** *f* farmer's wife; *(Landwirtin)* farmer; *(als Vertreterin einer Klasse)* peasant (woman).

**bäuerlich** *adj* rural; *(ländlich) Fest, Sitten* rustic, country *attr*.

**Bauern-:** ~**brot** *nt* coarse rye bread; ~**dorf** *nt* farming *or* country village; ~**fängerei** *f (col)* con *(col)*; ~**frühstück** *nt* bacon and potato omelette *(Brit) or* omelet *(US)*; ~**haus** *nt* farmhouse; ~**hof** *m* farm; ~**kriege** *pl (Hist)* Peasant War(s); ~**regel** *f* country saying; ~**schläue** *f* native cunning.

**Bauersfrau** *f* farmer's wife.

**Bau-:** **b~fällig** *adj* dilapidated; *Decke, Gewölbe* unsafe; ~**fälligkeit** *f* dilapidation; ~**firma** *f* building contractor; ~**genehmigung** *f* planning permission; ~**gerüst** *nt* scaffolding; ~**grube** *f* excavation; ~**handwerk** *nt* building trade; ~**handwerker** *m* (trained) building worker; ~**herr** *m* client *(for whom sth is being built)*; ~**holz** *nt* building timber; ~**industrie** *f* building industry; ~**ingenieur** *m* civil engineer.

**Bauj.** = **Baujahr.**

**Bau-:** ~**jahr** *nt* year of construction; *(von Auto)* date (of manufacture); **ein VW ~jahr 90** a 1990 VW; ~**kasten** *m* construction kit; *(mit Holzklötzchen)* box of bricks; ~**klotz** *m*, ~**klötzchen** *nt* (building) block; ~**klötze(r) staunen** *(col)* to gape (in astonishment); ~**kolonne** *f* gang of building workers *or* (*bei Straßenbau*) navvies; ~**kosten** *pl* building *or* construction costs *pl*; ~**land** *nt* building land; *(für Stadtplanung)* development area; ~**leiter** *m* site manager; **b~lich** *adj* structural; **in gutem b~lichem Zustand** structurally sound; ~**löwe** *m* building speculator; ~**lücke** *f* undeveloped building plot.

**Baum** *m*, *pl* **Bäume** tree. **auf dem** ~ **in** the tree; **heute könnte ich ~e ausreißen** I feel full of energy today.

**Baumarkt** *m* property market; *(Geschäft)* builder's merchant's; *(für Heimwerker)* DIY superstore.

**baumeln** *vi* to dangle *(an +dat* from).

**Baum-:** ~**grenze** *f* tree line; ~**krone** *f* treetop; **b~lang** *adj* **ein b~langer Kerl** *(col)* a beanpole *(col)*; ~**rinde** *f* tree bark; ~**schule** *f* tree nursery; ~**stamm** *m* tree-trunk; ~**sterben** *nt* loss of trees *(due to pollution)*; ~**stumpf** *m* tree stump.

**Baumwolle** *f* cotton. **ein Hemd aus** ~ a cotton shirt.

**Bau-:** ~**plan** *m* building plans *pl*; ~**platz** *m* site (for building); ~**polizei** *f* building control department; ~**ruine** *f (col)* unfinished building; ~**sachverständige(r)** *mf decl as adj* quantity surveyor; ~**satz** *m* construction kit.

**Bausch** *m*, *pl* **Bäusche** *or* **-e** *(Watte~)* ball. **in** ~ **und Bogen** lock, stock and barrel.

**bauschen 1** *vr (Segel)* to billow (out); *(Bluse etc)* to bunch (up). **2** *vt Segel, Vorhänge* to fill.

**bausparen** *vi sep* to save with a building society *(Brit) or* building and loan association *(US)*.

**Bausparer** *m* saver with a building society *(Brit) or* building and loan association *(US)*.

**Bauspar-:** ~**kasse** *f* building society *(Brit)*, building and loan association *(US)*; ~**vertrag** *m* savings contract with a building society *(Brit) or* building

and loan association *(US)*.

**Bau-:** ~**stein** *m* stone (for building); *(Spielzeug)* (building) brick *or* block; *(fig: Bestandteil)* building block; *(Tech)* module; ~**stelle** *f* building *or* construction site; *(bei Straßenbau)* roadworks *pl (Brit)*, roadwork *sing (US)*; *(bei Gleisbau)* railway *(Brit) or* railroad *(US)* construction site; ~**stil** *m* architectural style; ~**stoff** *m* building material; ~**stoffhändler** *m* builder's merchant; ~**substanz** *f* fabric, structure; ~**technisch** *adj* structural; ~**unternehmen** *nt (Firma)* building contractor; ~**unternehmer** *m* building contractor, builder; ~**weise** *f* type of construction; *(Stil)* style; ~**werk** *nt* construction; *(Gebäude auch)* edifice, building.

**Bauxit** *m* **-e** bauxite.

**Bau-:** ~**zaun** *m* hoarding, fence; ~**zeit** *f* time taken for building *or* construction; **die ~zeit betrug drei Jahre** it took three years to build.

**Bayer(in** *f)* ['baiɐ, -ərɪn] *m (wk)* **-n, -n** Bavarian.

**bay(e)risch** ['bai(ə)rɪʃ] *adj* Bavarian.

**Bayern** ['baiɐn] *nt* Bavaria.

**Bazillus** *m*, *pl* **Bazillen (a)** bacillus, microbe; *(Krankheitserreger auch)* germ. **(b)** *(fig)* cancer, growth.

**Bd.** = **Band** vol.

**BDA**[1] [beːdeːˈʔaː] *f* = **Bundesvereinigung der Arbeitgeberverbände** ≃ CBI *(Brit)*.

**BDA**[2] *m* = **Bund deutscher Architekten** ≃ RIBA *(Brit)*.

**Bde.** = **Bände** vols.

**be|absichtigen*** *vti* to intend. **eine Reise** ~ *(form)* to intend to go on a journey; **das hatte ich nicht beabsichtigt** I didn't intend that to happen.

**be|achten*** *vt* **(a)** *(befolgen)* to observe; *Gebrauchsanweisung* to follow. **(b)** *(berücksichtigen)* to take into consideration. **(c)** *(Aufmerksamkeit schenken)* jdn to notice, to pay attention to. **jdn nicht** ~ to ignore sb, to take no notice of sb.

**be|achtenswert** *adj* noteworthy, remarkable.

**be|achtlich** *adj* **(a)** *(beträchtlich)* considerable; *Erfolg* notable. **(b)** *(bedeutend) Ereignis* significant; *Leistung* considerable, excellent. **er hat im Leben/ Beruf B~es geleistet** he has achieved a considerable amount in life/his job.

**Be|achtung** *f* siehe *vt* **(a)** observance; following. **unter** ~ **der Vorschriften** in accordance with the rules. **(b)** consideration. **(c)** notice, attention *(gen* to*).* ~ **finden** to receive attention; **jdm keine** ~ **schenken** to take no notice of sb.

**Be|amten-:** ~**anwärter** *m* civil service trainee; ~**apparat** *m* bureaucracy; ~**laufbahn** *f* career in the civil service; **die ~laufbahn einschlagen** to enter the civil service; ~**tum** *nt no pl* civil service; ~**verhältnis** *nt* **im ~verhältnis stehen** to be a civil servant.

**Be|amte(r)** *m decl as adj* official; *(Staats~)* civil servant; *(Zoll~ auch, Polizei~)* officer; *(dated: Büro~, Schalter~)* clerk. **er ist ein typischer ~r** he is a typical bureaucrat.

**be|amtet** *adj (form)* appointed on a permanent basis *(by the state)*.

**Be|amtin** *f* siehe **Beamte(r).**

**be|ängstigend** *adj* alarming. **sein Zustand ist** ~ his condition is giving cause for concern.

**be|anspruchen*** *vt* **(a)** *(fordern)* to claim. **etw** ~ **können** to be entitled to sth. **(b)** *(erfordern)* to take; *Zeit, Platz auch* to take up. **(c)** *(in Anspruch nehmen)* to use; *jds Geduld* to demand; *jds Hilfe* to ask for; jdn to keep busy. **etw stark** ~ to use sth a great deal.

**Be|anspruchung** *f* **(a)** *(Forderung)* claim *(gen* to*).*

**(b)** *(Ausnutzung: von jds Geduld etc)* demand *(gen on)*. **(c)** *(Belastung)* use; *(von Beruf)* demands *pl*.

**be|anstanden\*** *vt* to object to; *Rechnung* to query; *Ware* to complain about. **er hat an allem etwas zu ~** he complains about everything.

**Be|anstandung** *f* complaint *(gen about)*.

**be|antragen\*** *vt* to apply for *(bei to)*; *(Jur) Strafe* to demand, to ask for; *(vorschlagen: in Debatte etc)* to move, to propose. **er beantragte, versetzt zu werden** he applied for a transfer.

**Be|antragung** *f siehe vt* application *(gen for)*; demand *(gen for)*; proposal.

**be|antworten\*** *vt* to answer; *Anfrage, Brief auch* to reply to; *Gruß, Beleidigung auch* to respond to.

**Be|antwortung** *f siehe vt (gen to)* answer; reply; response.

**be|arbeiten\*** *vt* **(a)** *(behandeln)* to work on; *Stein, Holz* to work, to dress. **(b)** *(sich befassen mit)* to deal with; *Fall auch* to handle; *Bestellungen etc* to process. **(c)** *(redigieren)* to edit; *(neu ~)* to revise; *(umändern) Roman etc* to adapt; *Musik* to arrange. **(d)** *(col: einreden auf)* jdn to work on. **(e)** *Land* to cultivate.

**Be|arbeiter(in** *f)* *m siehe vt* **(c)** editor; reviser; adapter; arranger.

**Be|arbeitung** *f siehe vt* **(a)** working (on); dressing. **(b)** dealing with; handling; processing. **die ~ meines Antrags hat lange gedauert** they took a long time to deal with my claim. **(c)** editing; revising; adapting; arranging; *(bearbeitete Ausgabe etc)* edition; revision; adaptation; arrangement. **neue ~** *(von Film etc)* new version; **die deutsche ~** the German version. **(d)** *(von Land)* cultivation.

**Be|arbeitungsgebühr** *f* handling charge.

**be|argwöhnen\*** *vt* to be suspicious of.

**Beat** [bi:t] *m no pl* **(a)** *(Musik)* beat *or* pop music. **(b)** *(Rhythmus)* beat.

**be|atmen\*** *vt* jdn (künstlich) **~ to** give sb artificial respiration.

**Be|atmung** *f* künstliche **~** artificial respiration.

**Be|atmungsgerät** *nt* respirator.

**Beatmusik** ['bi:t-] *f* beat *or* pop music.

**be|aufsichtigen\*** *vt* to supervise; *Kind* to mind; *Prüfung* to invigilate at.

**Be|aufsichtigung** *f siehe vt* supervision; minding; invigilation.

**be|auftragen\*** *vt* **(a)** *(heranziehen)* **jdm mit etw ~** to give sb the job of doing sth; *(geschäftlich)* to commission sb to do sth. **(b)** *(anweisen) Untergebene etc* to instruct.

**Be|auftragte(r)** *mf decl as adj* representative.

**be|äugen\*** *vt (col)* to gaze *or* look at.

**bebauen\*** *vt* **(a)** *Grundstück* to build on, to develop. **(b)** *(Agr)* to cultivate; *Land* to farm.

**Bebauung** *f no pl* **(a)** *(Vorgang)* building *(gen on)*; *(von Gelände)* development. **(b)** *(Agr)* cultivation; *(von Land)* farming.

**beben** *vi* to tremble.

**Beben** *nt* - trembling; *(Erd~)* earthquake.

**bebildern\*** *vt Buch, Vortrag* to illustrate.

**Becher** *m* - cup; *(esp Porzellan~, Ton~ auch)* mug; *(Plastik~ auch)* beaker; *(ohne Henkel)* tumbler.

**bechern** *vi (hum col)* to have a few *(col)*.

**Becken** *nt* - **(a)** *(Wasch~, Geol)* basin; *(Abwasch~)* sink; *(Toiletten~)* bowl, pan; *(Schwimm~)* pool. **(b)** *(Anat)* pelvis. **ein breites ~** broad hips. **(c)** *(Mus)* cymbal.

**Becken-** *(Anat, Med)* pelvic; **~bruch** *m* fractured pelvis; **~knochen** *m* hip-bone.

**bedacht** *adj* **(a)** *(überlegt)* cautious. **(b)** **darauf ~ sein, etw zu tun** to be concerned about doing sth.

**Bedacht** *m no pl (geh)* **mit ~** *(vorsichtig)* prudently, carefully; *(absichtlich)* deliberately; **ohne ~** without thinking.

**bedächtig** *adj Schritt, Sprache* measured *no adv*, deliberate; *(besonnen)* thoughtful.

**bedanken\*** *vr* to say thank you. **sich bei jdm (für etw) ~** to thank sb (for sth); **ich bedanke mich herzlich** thank you very much; **dafür können Sie sich bei Herrn Weitz ~** *(iro col)* you can thank Mr Weitz for that *(iro)*; **dafür wird er sich ~** *(iro)* he'll just love that *(iro)*.

**Bedarf** *m no pl* **(a)** *(Bedürfnis)* need *(an +dat for)*; *(~smenge)* requirements *pl*. **bei ~** as required; **Dinge des täglichen ~s** basic *or* everyday necessities; **alles für den häuslichen ~** all household requirements; **seinen ~ an Wein/Lebensmitteln** *etc* **einkaufen** to buy the wine/food *etc* one needs; **an etw (dat) ~ haben** to need sth, to be in need of sth. **(b)** *(Comm: Nachfrage)* demand *(an +dat for)*. **(je) nach ~** according to demand; **den ~ übersteigen** to exceed demand; **über ~** in excess of demand.

**Bedarfs-:** **~deckung** *f* satisfaction of the/sb's needs; **~fall** *m (form)* **im ~fall** if necessary; *(wenn gebraucht)* as necessary *or* required; **~güter** *pl* consumer goods *pl*; **~haltestelle** *f* request stop *(Brit)*, flag stop *(US)*.

**bedauerlich** *adj* regrettable, unfortunate.

**bedauerlicherweise** *adv* regrettably, unfortunately.

**bedauern\*** *vt* **(a)** *etw* to regret. **wir ~, Ihnen mitteilen zu müssen, ...** we regret to have to inform you ...; **er schüttelte ~d den Kopf** he shook his head regretfully; **(ich) bedau(e)re!** I'm sorry. **(b)** *(bemitleiden)* jdn to feel sorry for. **er ist zu ~** he is to be pitied.

**Bedauern** *nt no pl* regret. **(sehr) zu meinem ~** (much) to my regret.

**bedauernswert** *adj Mensch* pitiful; *Zustand* deplorable.

**bedecken\*** **1** *vt* to cover. **2** *vr* **(a)** *(sich zudecken)* to cover oneself; **sich bedeckt halten** *(fig)* to keep a low profile. **(b)** *(Himmel)* to become overcast, to cloud over.

**bedeckt** *adj* **(a)** covered. **(b)** *(bewölkt)* overcast, cloudy. **bei ~em Himmel** when the sky is overcast *or* cloudy.

**Bedeckung** *f* covering; *(Mil)* guard.

**bedenken\*** *vt irreg* **(a)** *(überlegen)* to consider, to think about. **wenn man es recht bedenkt, ...** if you think about it properly ... **(b)** *(in Betracht ziehen) Umstand, Folgen etc* to consider. **das hättest du vorher ~ sollen** you should have thought about that before; **ich gebe zu ~, daß ...** *(geh)* I would ask you to consider that ... **(c)** *(geh: beschenken)* **jdn mit einem Geschenk ~** to give sb a present; **jdn reich ~** to be generous to sb; **mit etw bedacht werden** to receive sth (as a gift).

**Bedenken** *nt* - **(a)** *usu pl (Zweifel, Einwand)* doubt, reservation, misgiving. **moralische ~** moral scruples; **~ haben** to have one's doubts *(bei about)*; **ohne ~** without hesitation; **ihm kommen ~** he is having second thoughts. **(b)** *no pl (das Überlegen)* consideration *(gen* of*)*. **nach langem ~** after much thought.

**bedenkenlos** *adj* **(a)** *(ohne Zögern)* unhesitating. **(b)** *(skrupellos)* thoughtless.

**Bedenkenlosigkeit** *f no pl* **(a)** *(Bereitwilligkeit)* readiness, promptness. **(b)** *(Skrupellosigkeit)* unscrupulousness.

**bedenkenswert** *adj* worth considering.

**bedenklich** *adj* **(a)** *(zweifelhaft)* dubious, question-

**able. (b)** *(besorgniserregend)* serious. **(c)** *(besorgt)* apprehensive, anxious. **jdn ~ stimmen** to make sb apprehensive.

**Bedenkzeit** f **um ~ bitten** to ask for time to think about it.

**bedeppert** adj *(col)* dazed, stunned; *(trottelig)* dopey *(col)*.

**bedeuten*** vt **(a)** to mean. **das hat nichts zu ~** it doesn't mean anything; *(macht nichts aus)* it doesn't matter; **das bedeutet nichts Gutes** that means trouble; **Geld bedeutet mir nichts** money means nothing to me. **(b)** *(geh: einen Hinweis geben)* to indicate. **man bedeutete mir, daß ...** I was given to understand that ...

**bedeutend 1** adj **(a)** *(wichtig)* Persönlichkeit important, eminent; *Leistung, Rolle* major. **(b)** *(groß)* Summe, Erfolg considerable. **2** adv *(beträchtlich)* considerably.

**bedeutsam** adj significant; *(vielsagend auch)* meaningful.

**Bedeutsamkeit** f siehe adj significance; meaningfulness.

**Bedeutung** f **(a)** *(Sinn, Wortsinn)* meaning. **(b)** *(Wichtigkeit)* importance, significance. **von ~ sein** to be of significance.

**Bedeutungs-:** **~lehre** f *(Ling)* semantics sing; **b~los** adj **(a)** *(unwichtig)* insignificant, unimportant; **(b)** *(nichts besagend)* meaningless; **~losigkeit** f insignificance, unimportance; **zur ~losigkeit verurteilt sein** to be condemned to insignificance; **b~voll** adj = **bedeutsam**.

**bedienbar** adj leicht/schwer ~ easy/hard to operate.

**Bedienbarkeit** f no pl usability. **leichte ~** ease of operation.

**bedienen*** **1** vt **(a)** to serve; *(Kellner auch)* to wait on. **werden Sie schon bedient?** are you being served?; **hier wird man gut bedient** the service is good here; **er läßt sich gern ~** he likes to be waited on; **damit sind Sie sehr gut bedient** that should serve you very well; **ich bin bedient!** *(col)* I've had enough. **(b)** *(handhaben)* Maschine etc to operate. **(c)** *(Cards)* **eine Farbe/Karo ~** to follow suit/to follow suit in diamonds. **2** vi **(a)** to serve. **(b)** *(Cards)* **du mußt ~** you must follow suit; **falsch ~** to fail to follow suit. **3** vr **(a)** **bitte ~ Sie sich** please help or serve yourself. **(b)** *(geh: gebrauchen)* **sich jds/einer Sache ~** to use sb/sth.

**Bediener** m - *(Comp)* operator.

**Bedienstete(r)** mf decl as adj public employee.

**Bedienung** f **(a)** no pl *(in Restaurant etc)* service; *(von Maschinen)* operation. **die ~ der Kunden** serving the customers; **mit ~** *(Tankstelle)* with forecourt service; *(Restaurant)* with waiter service. **(b)** *(~sgeld)* service (charge). **(c)** *(~spersonal)* staff; *(Kellner etc)* waiter/waitress.

**Bedienungs-:** **~anleitung** f operating instructions pl; **~zuschlag** m service charge.

**bedingen** vt **(a)** *(bewirken)* to cause; *(notwendig machen)* to necessitate; *(bestimmen: auch Psych, Physiol)* to condition. **sich gegenseitig ~** to be mutually dependent. **(b)** *(voraussetzen, verlangen)* to call for, to demand.

**bedingt** adj **(a)** *(eingeschränkt)* limited; *Lob auch* qualified. **(nur) ~ gelten** to be (only) partially valid; **~ tauglich** *(Mil)* fit for limited duties. **(b)** *(an Bedingung geknüpft)* Straferlaß conditional.

**Bedingung** f condition; *(Erfordernis)* requirement. **mit** or **unter der ~, daß ...** on condition that ...; **unter keiner ~** on no condition; **es zur ~ machen, daß ...** to make it a condition that ...; **zu günstigen ~en** *(Comm)* on favourable terms.

**bedingungslos** adj Kapitulation unconditional; *Hingabe, Gehorsam* unquestioning.

**Bedingungssatz** m conditional clause.

**bedrängen*** vt Feind to attack; *gegnerische Mannschaft, Schuldner* to put pressure on; *(belästigen)* to plague. **sich in einer bedrängten Lage befinden** to be in difficulties.

**Bedrängnis** f *(geh: seelisch)* distress, torment. **in ~ geraten** to get into difficulties.

**bedrohen*** vt to threaten; *(gefährden)* to endanger. **vom Tode/von Überschwemmung bedroht** in mortal danger/in danger of being flooded.

**bedrohlich** adj *(gefährlich)* dangerous, alarming; *(unheilverkündend)* ominous, menacing.

**Bedrohung** f threat *(gen to)*. **in ständiger ~ leben** to live under a constant threat.

**bedrucken*** vt to print on. **bedruckter Stoff** print, printed fabric.

**bedrücken*** vt to depress. **was bedrückt dich?** what's getting you down?

**bedrückend** adj depressing.

**bedrückt** adj *(niedergeschlagen)* depressed, dejected; *Schweigen* oppressive.

**Bedrückung** f siehe adj depression, dejection; oppressiveness.

**Beduine** m *(wk)* **-n, -n, Beduinin** f Bedouin.

**bedürfen** vi irreg +gen *(geh)* to need, to require. **es bedarf einiger Mühe** it needs or requires some effort; **ohne daß es eines Hinweises bedurft hätte, ...** without having to be asked ...

**Bedürfnis** nt need; *(no pl: form: Anliegen)* wish. **die ~se des täglichen Lebens** everyday needs; **ich hatte das dringende ~, das zu tun** I felt an urgent need to do it; **das ~ nach Schlaf haben** to be in need of sleep.

**Bedürfnis-:** **~anstalt** f *(dated form, hum)* public convenience *(Brit)*, comfort station *(US)*; **~befriedigung** f satisfaction of one's/sb's needs; **b~los** adj Mensch etc undemanding, modest in one's needs.

**bedürftig** adj *(hilfs~)* needy, in need. **die B~en** the needy pl.

**Bedürftigkeit** f no pl need.

**Beefsteak** ['bi:fste:k] nt steak. **deutsches ~** ≃ beefburger.

**be|ehren*** vt *(iro, geh)* to honour *(Brit)*, to honor *(US)*.

**be|eiden*** vt *(beschwören)* Aussage to swear to.

**be|eilen*** vr to hurry (up), to get a move on *(col)*.

**Be|eilung** interj *(col)* get a move on *(col)*.

**be|eindrucken*** vt to impress. **davon lasse ich mich nicht ~** I won't be impressed by that.

**be|eindruckend** adj impressive.

**be|einflußbar** adj impressionable, suggestible. **er ist nur schwer ~** he is hard to influence.

**be|einflussen*** vt jdn to influence. **er ist leicht/schwer zu ~** he is easily influenced/hard to influence.

**Be|einflussung** f *(das Beeinflussen)* influencing; *(Einfluß)* influence *(durch of)*.

**be|einträchtigen*** vt *(stören)* to spoil; *Konzentration auch* to disturb; *Rundfunkempfang* to interfere with; *(vermindern)* Sehvermögen, Reaktionen, Leistung to impair. **jdn in seiner Freiheit ~** to restrict sb's freedom.

**Be|einträchtigung** f siehe vt spoiling; disturbance; interference *(gen with)*; impairment.

**be|end(ig)en*** vt to end; *Arbeit, Studium etc* to finish, to complete. **etw vorzeitig ~** to cut sth short.

**Be|end(ig)ung** f no pl ending; *(Ende)* end; *(Fertigstellung)* completion; *(Schluß)* conclusion.

**be|engen*** vt (fig) to stifle, to inhibit. ~de Kleidung restricting clothing.

**be|engt** adj cramped; (fig) stifled. ~ wohnen to live in cramped conditions.

**Be|engtheit** f (von Räumen) cramped conditions pl.

**be|erben*** vt jdn ~ to be sb's heir.

**be|erdigen*** vt to bury.

**Be|erdigung** f burial; (~sfeier) funeral. auf der falschen ~ sein (hum) to have come to the wrong place.

**Be|erdigungs-** in cpds siehe auch **Bestattungs-** funeral; ~**feier** f funeral service.

**Beere** f -n berry; (Wein~) grape. ~n sammeln to go berry-picking.

**Beeren-:** ~**auslese** f wine made from specially selected grapes; ~**obst** nt soft fruit.

**Beet** nt -e (Blumen~) bed; (Gemüse~) patch.

**befähigen*** vt (jdn zu etw sb to do sth) to enable; (Ausbildung) to qualify, to equip.

**befähigt** adj capable, competent; (durch Ausbildung) qualified. zu etw ~ sein to be capable of doing sth.

**Befähigung** f no pl (a) die ~ zum Richteramt the qualifications to become a judge. (b) (Können, Eignung) capability, ability (zu etw to do sth).

**befahl** pret of befehlen.

**befahrbar** adj Straße passable; Seeweg, Fluß navigable. ~ sein (Straße) to be open to traffic; nicht ~ sein (Straße, Weg) to be closed (to traffic); (wegen Schnee etc auch) to be impassable.

**befahren¹*** vt irreg (a) Straße, Weg to use. der Paß kann nur im Sommer ~ werden the pass is only open to traffic in summer; diese Straße wird stark/wenig ~ this road is used a lot/isn't used much. (b) (Schiff, Seemann) Meer to sail; Fluß, Seeweg to navigate.

**befahren²** adj eine viel or stark/wenig ~e Straße a much/little used road.

**Befahren** nt no pl use (gen of).

**Befall** m no pl attack; (mit Schädlingen) infestation.

**befallen¹*** vt irreg (a) (geh: überkommen) to overcome; (Angst auch) to grip; (Fieber, Krankheit) to strike. (b) (angreifen, infizieren) to affect; (Schädlinge, Ungeziefer) to infest.

**befallen²** adj affected (von by); (von Schädlingen) infested (von with).

**befangen** adj (a) Lächeln bashful; Schweigen awkward. (b) Richter, Zeuge prejudiced, bias(s)ed; jdn als ~ ablehnen (Jur) to object to sb on grounds of interest.

**Befangenheit** f no pl siehe adj (a) bashfulness, awkwardness. (b) bias, prejudice; (Jur) interest.

**befassen*** 1 vr sich ~ mit to deal with; mit Forschungsbereich to work on; sie hat keine Zeit, sich mit ihren Kindern zu ~ she has no time for her children. 2 vt (form) mit etw befaßt sein to be dealing with sth.

**Befehl** m -e (a) (Anordnung) order, command (an +acc to, von from); (Comp) command. wir hatten den ~, ... we had orders or were ordered to ...; auf seinen ~ (hin) on his orders; auf ~ handeln to act under orders; auf höheren ~ on orders from above; zu ~, Herr Hauptmann (Mil) yes, sir; ~ ausgeführt! mission accomplished; ~ ist ~ orders are orders; dein Wunsch ist mir ~ (hum) your wish is my command. (b) (Befehlsgewalt) command. den ~ haben or führen to be in command (über +acc of).

**befehlen** pret **befahl**, ptp **befohlen** 1 vi to order; (Befehle erteilen) to give orders; (den Befehl haben) to be in command (über +acc of). er befahl, den Mann zu erschießen he ordered the man to be shot.

2 vt to order. du hast mir gar nichts zu ~ I won't take orders from you; wie Sie ~ as you wish.

**befehligen*** vt (Mil) to be in command of.

**Befehls-:** ~**empfänger** m ~**empfänger sein** to follow orders (gen from); ~**form** f (Gram) imperative; b~**gemäß** adj as ordered; ~**gewalt** f (Mil) command; ~**gewalt haben** to be in command (über +acc over); ~**haber** m - commander; ~**notstand** m (Jur) obligation to obey orders; ~**sprache** f (Comp) command language; ~**ton** m peremptory tone; ~**verweigerung** f (Mil) refusal to obey orders.

**befestigen*** vt (a) (an +dat to) (anbringen) to fasten; Boot to tie up. etw durch Nähen/Kleben etc ~ to sew/glue etc sth. (b) (fest, haltbar machen) Böschung, Deich to reinforce; Fahrbahn, Straße to make up. (c) (Mil) to fortify.

**Befestigung** f (a) (das Befestigen) fastening; (das Festmachen auch) securing; (von Boot) tying up. (b) (das Haltbarmachen) reinforcement. (c) (Mil) fortification.

**Befestigungs|anlage** f fortification.

**befeuchten*** vt to moisten; Wäsche to dampen.

**befeuern*** vt (a) (beheizen) to fuel. (b) (lit, fig: mit Geschossen) to bombard.

**befinden*** irreg 1 vr (a) (sein) to be; (liegen auch) to be situated; (esp in Maschine, Körper etc auch) to be located. unter ihnen befanden sich einige, die ... there were some amongst them who ... (b) (form: sich fühlen) to feel. 2 vt (form: erachten) to deem (form), to find. etw für nötig/gut ~ to deem or find sth (to be) necessary/good; jdn für schuldig ~ to find sb guilty. 3 vi (geh: entscheiden) to decide (über +acc about). darüber hat der Arzt zu ~ that is for the doctor to decide.

**Befinden** nt no pl (a) (form: Gesundheitszustand) (state of) health; (eines Kranken) condition. (b) (geh: Meinung) nach meinem ~ in my view.

**befindlich** adj usu attr (form) Gebäude, Park situated, located; (in Behälter) contained. der hinter dem Haus ~e Garten the garden (situated) behind the house; das im Umbau ~e Hotel the hotel which is being renovated.

**befingern*** vt (col) to finger.

**beflaggen*** vt Häuser to decorate with flags; Schiff to dress.

**beflecken*** vt (a) (lit) to stain. er hat sich mit Blut befleckt (fig) he has blood on his hands. (b) (fig geh) Ruf, Ehre to besmirch.

**befleißigen*** vr (geh) sich einer Sache (gen) ~ to cultivate sth; sich ~, etw zu tun to make a great effort to do sth.

**beflissen** adj (geh) (bemüht) zealous, keen; (pej: unterwürfig) obsequious.

**Beflissenheit** f siehe adj zeal, keenness; obsequiousness.

**beflügeln*** vt (geh) to inspire.

**befohlen** ptp of befehlen.

**befolgen*** vt to follow; Vorschrift auch to comply with.

**Befolgung** f siehe vt following (gen sth); compliance (gen with).

**befördern*** vt (a) Waren to transport, to carry; Personen to carry. etw mit der Post/per Bahn ~ to send sth by post/rail. (b) (beruflich) to promote. er wurde zum Major befördert he was promoted to major.

**Beförderung** f siehe vt (a) transportation; carriage. die ~ eines Briefes dauert 3 Tage a letter takes 3 days (to arrive). (b) promotion.

**Beförderungs-:** ~**bedingungen** pl conditions pl of

carriage; ~**kosten** pl transport costs pl; ~**mittel** nt means of transport.

**befrachten\*** vt (lit, fig geh) to load.

**befragen\*** vt (a) (über +acc, zu about) to question; Zeugen auch to examine. **auf B**~ when questioned. (b) (um Stellungnahme bitten) to consult (über +acc, nach about).

**Befragte(r)** mf decl as adj person asked; (in Umfrage auch) interviewee. **alle** ~**n** all those asked.

**Befragung** f siehe vt (a) questioning; examining. (b) consultation (gen with or of). (c) (Umfrage) survey.

**befreien\*** 1 vt (a) (frei machen) to free, to set free. **jdn aus einer schwierigen Lage** ~ to rescue sb from a tricky situation. (b) (freistellen) (von from) to excuse; (von Militärdienst, Steuern) to exempt. (c) (reinigen) (von of) (von Ungeziefer etc) to rid; (von Schnee, Eis) to free. 2 vr (a) (Volk, Land) to free oneself; (entkommen) to escape (von, aus from). (b) (erleichtern) to rid oneself (von of), to free oneself (von from).

**Befreier(in** f) m - liberator.

**befreit** adj (erleichtert) relieved.

**Befreiung** f siehe vt (a) freeing, setting free. (b) excusing; exemption. **um** ~ **von etw bitten** to ask to be excused/exempted from sth. (c) ridding; freeing. (d) (Erleichterung) relief.

**Befreiungs-:** ~**bewegung** f liberation movement; ~**front** f liberation front; ~**kampf** m struggle for liberation; ~**krieg** m war of liberation; ~**organisation** f liberation organization; ~**versuch** m escape attempt.

**befremden\*** vt to disconcert. **es befremdete mich, daß** ... I was taken aback that ...

**Befremden** nt no pl disconcertment.

**befremdet** adj disconcerted, taken aback.

**befremdlich** adj disconcerting.

**befreunden\*** vr to make or become friends; (fig: mit einem Gedanken etc) to get used to.

**befreundet** adj on friendly terms (with one another). **wir sind schon lange (miteinander)** ~ we have been friends for a long time; **gut** or **eng** ~ **sein** to be good or close friends; **alle** ~**en Familien** all the families we etc are friendly with; **ein** ~**er Staat** a friendly nation.

**befrieden\*** vt (geh) to pacify.

**befriedigen\*** 1 vt to satisfy; Gelüste auch to gratify. 2 vi to be satisfactory. 3 vr **sich (selbst)** ~ to masturbate.

**befriedigend** adj satisfactory; Verhältnisse, Leistung, Antwort auch adequate; Gefühl satisfying.

**befriedigt** adj satisfied.

**Befriedigung** f siehe vt satisfaction; gratification. **sexuelle** ~ sexual satisfaction.

**befristen\*** vt to limit, to restrict (auf +acc to).

**befristet** adj Genehmigung, Visum restricted; Arbeitsverhältnis, Anstellung temporary. ~ **sein/auf zwei Jahre** ~ **sein** (Paß etc) to be valid for a limited period/for two years.

**befruchten\*** vt (lit) Eizelle to fertilize; Blüte to pollinate; (fig: geistig anregen) to stimulate.

**Befruchtung** f siehe vt fertilization; pollination; stimulation. **künstliche** ~ artificial insemination.

**Befugnis** f (form) authority no pl. **eine** ~ **erhalten/erteilen** to receive/give authority.

**befugt** adj (form) authorized. ~ **sein(, etw zu tun)** to have the authority (to do sth).

**befühlen\*** vt to feel.

**Befund** m -e results pl, findings pl. **ohne** ~ (Med) (results) negative.

**befürchten\*** vt to fear. **es ist zu** ~**, daß** ... it is (to

be) feared that ...; **das ist nicht zu** ~ there is no fear of that.

**Befürchtung** f fear usu pl. **die schlimmsten** ~**en haben** to fear the worst.

**befürworten\*** vt to approve.

**Befürworter(in** f) m - supporter; (von Idee auch) advocate.

**Befürwortung** f approval; (von Idee) advocacy.

**begabt** adj talented; (esp geistig, musisch auch) gifted. **für etw** ~ **sein** to be talented at sth; **vielseitig** ~ **sein** to be versatile, to have many talents.

**Begabte(r)** mf decl as adj talented or gifted person.

**Begabung** f (Anlage) talent; (esp geistig, musisch auch) gift. **er hat** ~ **zum Lehrer** he has a gift for teaching; **mangelnde** ~ a lack of talent.

**begann** pret of **beginnen**.

**begatten\*** (esp Zool) 1 vt to mate with. 2 vr to mate; (geh, hum) to copulate.

**Begattung** f (esp Zool) mating; (geh, hum) copulation.

**begeben** vr irreg (a) (geh) to go. **sich nach Hause** ~ to make one's way home; **sich auf eine Reise** ~ to go on a journey; **sich zu Bett/zur Ruhe** ~ to retire; **sich in ärztliche Behandlung** ~ to take medical treatment; **sich an die Arbeit** ~ to commence work; **sich in Gefahr** ~ to expose oneself to danger. (b) (old liter: geschehen) to come to pass (old liter).

**Begebenheit** f (geh) occurrence, event.

**begegnen\*** vi aux sein +dat (a) (treffen) to meet. **sich** or **einander** (geh) ~ to meet. (b) (stoßen auf) to encounter. (c) (widerfahren) **es war mir schon einmal begegnet, daß** ... it had happened to me once already that ... (d) (geh: entgegentreten) einer Krankheit, der Not to combat; Angriff to resist; einer Gefahr, Schwierigkeiten to meet, to face. **man begegnete mir nur mit Spott** I only met with derision.

**Begegnung** f encounter; (Treffen auch) meeting; (Sport auch) match.

**Begegnungsstätte** f meeting place.

**begehen\*** vt irreg (a) (verüben) Verbrechen, Ehebruch to commit; Fehler to make. **einen Mord an jdm** ~ to murder sb; **eine Dummheit/Unvorsichtigkeit** ~ to do something stupid/careless; **an jdm ein Unrecht** ~ to wrong sb; **Verrat an jdm/etw** ~ to betray sb/sth. (b) (entlanggehen) Weg to use. (c) (geh: feiern) to celebrate.

**begehren\*** vt (geh, old) to desire.

**Begehren** nt - (a) (geh: Verlangen) desire (nach for). (b) (old: Wunsch, Forderung) wish.

**begehrenswert** adj desirable.

**begehrlich** adj (geh) covetous.

**begehrt** adj much sought-after; Partner etc auch, Ferienziel popular; Junggeselle eligible; Posten auch desirable.

**Begehung** f (form: eines Verbrechens) committing.

**begeistern\*** 1 vt to fill with enthusiasm. **er ist für nichts zu** ~ you can't get him interested in anything. 2 vr to get enthusiastic (an +dat, für about).

**begeisternd** adj inspiring; Rede auch stirring.

**begeistert** adj enthusiastic (von about).

**Begeisterung** f no pl enthusiasm (über +acc about, für for). **in** ~ **geraten** to become enthusiastic.

**Begeisterungs-:** b~**fähig** adj Publikum etc quick to show one's enthusiasm; ~**fähigkeit** f capacity for enthusiasm; ~**sturm** m storm of enthusiasm.

**Begierde** f -n (geh) desire (nach for); (Sehnsucht) longing, yearning. **vor** ~ **brennen, etw zu tun** to be longing to do sth.

**begierig** adj (voll Verlangen) hungry, greedy; (gespannt) eager, keen.

**begießen\*** vt irreg (a) (mit Wasser) to pour water

on; *Blumen, Beet* to water; *(mit Fett) Braten etc* to baste; *siehe* **begossen**. (**b**) *(fig col) freudiges Ereignis etc* to celebrate. **das muß begossen werden!** that calls for a drink!

**Beginn** *m no pl* beginning, start. **zu** ~ at the beginning.

**beginnen** *pret* **begann**, *ptp* **begonnen** *vti* to start, to begin. **mit der Arbeit** ~ to start *or* begin work; **es beginnt zu regnen** it's starting to rain; **eine ~de Erkältung** the beginnings of a cold.

**beglaubigen\*** *vt* (**a**) *Testament, Unterschrift* to witness; *Abschrift* to authenticate; *Echtheit, Übersetzung* to certify. (**b**) *Botschafter* to accredit *(bei to)*.

**Beglaubigung** *f siehe vt* (**a**) witnessing, authentication; certification. (**b**) accrediting.

**Beglaubigungsschreiben** *nt* credentials *pl*.

**begleichen\*** *vt irreg (lit, fig)* to settle. **mit Ihnen habe ich noch eine Rechnung zu** ~ *(fig)* I've a score to settle with you.

**Begleichung** *f* settlement.

**Begleitbrief** *m* covering letter.

**begleiten\*** *vt* to accompany *(auch Mus)*.

**Begleiter(in** *f)* *m -* (**a**) companion; *(zum Schutz)* escort. (**b**) *(Mus)* accompanist.

**Begleit-:** **~erscheinung** *f* concomitant *(form);* *(Med)* side-effect; **~musik** *f* accompaniment; *(in Film etc)* incidental music; **~papiere** *pl (Comm)* accompanying documents *pl;* **~person** *f* escort; **~schein** *m* dispatch note; **~schreiben** *nt* covering letter; *(für Waren auch)* advice note; **~umstände** *pl* attendant circumstances *pl.*

**Begleitung** *f* (**a**) *no pl* company. **in** ~ **seines Vaters** accompanied by his father; **ich bin in** ~ **hier** I'm with someone. (**b**) *(Begleiter)* companion; *(zum Schutz)* escort. **ohne** ~ unaccompanied. (**c**) *(Mus: Begleitmusik)* accompaniment.

**beglücken\*** *vt jdn* ~ to make sb happy; **er hat uns gestern mit seinem Besuch beglückt** *(iro)* he honoured *(Brit)* or honored *(US)* us with a visit yesterday; **ein ~des Gefühl** a wonderful feeling.

**beglückt** *adj* happy.

**beglückwünschen\*** *vt* to congratulate.

**begnadet** *adj* gifted.

**begnadigen\*** *vt* to pardon.

**Begnadigung** *f* pardon.

**begnügen\*** *vr* **sich mit etw** ~ to be content *or* satisfied with sth; **sich damit** ~, **etw zu tun** to be content *or* satisfied to do sth.

**Begonie** [-niə] *f* begonia.

**begonnen** *ptp of* **beginnen**.

**begossen** *adj* **er stand da wie ein ~er Pudel** *(col)* he looked so sheepish.

**begraben** *vt irreg* (**a**) to bury. **dort möchte ich nicht** ~ **sein** *(col)* I wouldn't like to be stuck in that hole *(col);* **damit kannst du dich** ~ **lassen** *(col)* you can stuff that *(col!).* (**b**) *(aufgeben) Hoffnung* to abandon; *(beenden) Streit etc* to end.

**Begräbnis** *nt* burial; *(~feier)* funeral.

**begradigen\*** *vt* to straighten.

**Begradigung** *f* straightening.

**begreifbar** *adj* conceivable.

**begreifen\*** *irreg* **1** *vti* to understand. **~, daß ...** *(einsehen)* to realize that ...; **es ist kaum zu** ~ it's quite incomprehensible; **schnell/langsam** ~ to be quick/slow on the uptake; *siehe* **begriffen. 2** *vr* to be understandable.

**begreiflich** *adj* understandable. **jdm etw** ~ **machen** to make sth clear to sb; **ich kann mich ihm nicht** ~ **machen** I can't make myself clear to him; **es ist mir nicht** ~, **warum ...** I cannot understand why ....

**begreiflicherweise** *adv* understandably.

**begrenzen\*** *vt* (**a**) *(Grenze sein von)* to mark the boundary of; *Straße etc* to line. (**b**) *(beschränken)* to restrict, to limit *(auf +acc* to).

**begrenzt** *adj (beschränkt)* restricted, limited.

**Begrenztheit** *f no pl (von Möglichkeiten, Talent)* limited nature; *(von Menschen)* limitations *pl*.

**Begrenzung** *f* (**a**) *(das Begrenzen) (von Gebiet, Straße etc)* demarcation; *(von Geschwindigkeit, Redezeit)* restriction. (**b**) *(Grenze)* boundary.

**Begrenzungsleuchte** *f (Aut)* sidelight.

**Begriff** *m -e* (**a**) concept; *(Terminus)* term. **etw in ~e fassen** to put sth into words; **sein Name ist mir ein/kein** ~ his name means something/doesn't mean anything to me. (**b**) *(Vorstellung, Eindruck)* idea. **sich** *(dat)* **einen** ~ **von etw machen** to imagine sth; **du machst dir keinen** ~ **(davon)** *(col)* you've no idea *(col);* **für meine ~e** in my opinion. (**c**) **im** ~ **sein, etw zu tun** to be on the point of doing sth, to be about to do sth. (**d**) **schwer von** ~ **sein** *(col)* to be slow on the uptake.

**begriffen** *adj* **ein noch in der Entwicklung ~er Plan** a plan still in the process of being developed.

**begrifflich** *adj* conceptual.

**Begriffs-:** **~bestimmung** *f* definition; **b~stutzig** *adj (col)* dense *(col);* **~vermögen** *nt* understanding.

**begründen\*** *vt* (**a**) *(Gründe anführen für)* to give reasons for; *(rechtfertigend) Forderung, Ansicht* to justify; *Verhalten* to account for; *Verdacht, Behauptung* to substantiate. **etw näher** ~ to give specific reasons for sth; *siehe* **begründet**. (**b**) *(beginnen, gründen)* to establish; *Geschäft etc auch* to found.

**Begründer** *m* founder.

**begründet** *adj* well-founded; *(berechtigt)* justified. **es besteht ~e Hoffnung, daß ...** there is reason to hope that ...; **sachlich** ~ founded on fact.

**Begründung** *f* (**a**) grounds *pl (für, gen* for). **etwas zur** *or* **als** ~ **sagen** to say something in explanation. (**b**) *(Gründung)* establishment; *(von Geschäft etc auch)* foundation.

**begrünen\*** *vt Hinterhöfe, Plätze* to plant with trees and grass, to landscape.

**Begrünung** *f* planting with trees and grass, landscaping.

**begrüßen\*** *vt* (**a**) to greet; *(als Gastgeber auch)* to welcome. (**b**) *Kritik, Entschluß etc* to welcome.

**begrüßenswert** *adj* welcome.

**Begrüßung** *f* greeting; *(der Gäste)* welcoming; *(Zeremonie)* welcome.

**Begrüßungs-** *in cpds* welcoming.

**begucken\*** *vt (col)* to (have a) look at.

**begünstigen\*** *vt* to favour *(Brit)*, to favor *(US);* *Wachstum, Handel* to encourage; *Pläne, Beziehungen* to further; *(Jur)* to aid and abet. **durch die Dunkelheit begünstigt** assisted by the darkness.

**Begünstigung** *f* (**a**) *(Jur)* aiding and abetting. (**b**) *(Bevorzugung)* preferential treatment. (**c**) *(Förderung)* favouring *(Brit)*, favoring *(US);* *(von Wachstum, Handel)* encouragement; *(von Plänen, Beziehungen)* furthering.

**begut|achten\*** *vt* to give expert advice about; *Kunstwerk* to examine; *Projekte, Leistung* to judge; *(col: ansehen)* to have a look at.

**Begut|achtung** *f* (expert) assessment.

**begütert** *adj (reich)* wealthy, affluent.

**begütigend** *adj Worte etc* soothing. ~ **auf jdn einreden** to calm sb down.

**behaart** *adj* hairy. **dicht** ~ (thickly) covered with hair.

**Behaarung** *f* hairs *pl (+gen, an +dat* on).

**behäbig** *adj Mensch* portly; *(phlegmatisch, geruh-*

*sam)* stolid; *(fig) Leben* comfortable; *Sprache, Ton* complacent.

**Behäbigkeit** *f no pl siehe adj* portliness; stolidity; comfortableness; complacency.

**behaftet** *adj:* **mit etw ~ sein** *mit Krankheit etc* to be afflicted with sth; *mit Fehlern* to be full of sth; *mit Makel* to be tainted with sth.

**Behagen** *nt no pl* contentment. **mit ~ essen** to eat with relish.

**behagen*** *vi* **etw behagt jdm** sth pleases sb; **das/er behagt mir gar nicht** I don't like it/him at all.

**behaglich** *adj* cosy; *(bequem)* comfortable. **es sich** *(dat)* **~ machen** to make oneself comfortable.

**Behaglichkeit** *f no pl siehe adj* cosiness; comfortableness.

**behalten** *vt irreg* to keep; *(nicht vergessen)* to remember. **~ Sie (doch) Platz!** please don't get up!; **den Hut auf dem Kopf ~** to keep one's hat on; **im Gedächtnis/im Kopf ~** to remember; **ich habe seine Adresse nicht ~** I've forgotten his address; **etw für sich ~** to keep sth to oneself.

**Behälter** *m* - container.

**behämmert** *adj (col)* screwy *(col)*.

**behandeln*** *vt* to treat; *Thema, Frage etc* to deal with; *(umgehen mit)* to handle. **er weiß, wie man Kinder/die Maschine ~ muß** he knows how to handle children/the machine; **der ~de Arzt** the doctor in attendance.

**Behandlung** *f* treatment. **wir sind jetzt bei der ~ dieses Themas** we are now dealing with this subject; **die schlechte ~ seiner Frau und Kinder** the maltreatment of his wife and children; **in (ärztlicher) ~ sein** to be receiving (medical) treatment; **bei wem sind Sie in ~?** who's treating you?

**Behandlungs-:** **b~bedürftig** *adj* in need of treatment; **~kosten** *pl* cost *sing* of treatment; **~methode** *f* (method of) treatment; **~raum** *m* treatment room; **~stuhl** *m* doctor's/dentist's chair; **~weise** *f* treatment.

**Behang** *m ⁼e (Vorhang)* curtain; *(Wand~)* hanging; *(Schmuck)* decorations *pl.*

**behängen*** *vt* to decorate; *Wände auch* to hang.

**beharren** *vi (hartnäckig sein)* to insist *(auf +dat* on*)*; *(nicht aufgeben)* to persist *(bei, auf +dat* in*)*.

**Beharren** *nt no pl siehe vi* insistence *(auf* on*)*; persistence *(bei, auf* in*)*.

**beharrlich** *adj (hartnäckig)* insistent; *(ausdauernd)* persistent. **~ fortfahren, etw zu tun** to persist in doing sth.

**Beharrlichkeit** *f siehe adj* insistence; persistence.

**behauen*** *vt irreg Holz* to hew; *Stein* to cut; *(mit dem Meißel)* to carve.

**behaupten*** **1** *vt* **(a)** to claim, to maintain. **von jdm ~, daß ...** to say (of sb) that ... **(b)** *Stellung, Recht* to maintain. **2** *vr* to assert oneself; *(bei Diskussion)* to hold one's own *(gegenüber, gegen* against*)*. **sich auf dem Markt ~** to establish itself/oneself on the market.

**Behauptung** *f* **(a)** claim; *(esp unerwiesene ~)* assertion. **(b)** *(Aufrechterhaltung)* assertion; *(von Stellung)* successful defence *(Brit)* or defense *(US)*.

**Behausung** *f (geh, hum: Wohnung)* dwelling.

**beheben*** *vt irreg (beseitigen)* to remove; *Mißstände* to remedy; *Schaden* to repair; *Störung* to clear.

**Behebung** *f no pl siehe vt* removal; remedying; repairing; clearing.

**beheimatet** *adj (Mensch)* resident *(in +dat* in*)*; *(Pflanzen, Tiere)* native *(in +dat* to*)*.

**beheizbar** *adj* heatable; *Heckscheibe* heated.

**beheizen*** *vt* to heat.

**Behelf** *m* substitute; *(Notlösung)* makeshift.

**behelfen*** *vr irreg* to manage.

**Behelfs-** *in cpds* temporary; **b~mäßig** *adj* makeshift; *(zeitlich begrenzt)* temporary; **b~weise** *adv* temporarily.

**behelligen*** *vt* to bother.

**behend(e)** *adj (geh) (flink)* swift, quick; *(gewandt)* nimble, agile.

**Behendigkeit** *f no pl siehe adj* swiftness, quickness; nimbleness, agility.

**beherbergen*** *vt (lit, fig)* to house; *Gäste* to accommodate; *Flüchtlinge* to give shelter to.

**beherrschen*** **1** *vt* **(a)** *(herrschen über)* to rule, to govern; *(fig: dominieren)* to dominate. **(b)** *(zügeln)* to control. **(c)** *Handwerk, Tricks* to master; *Fahrzeug, Situation* to have control of. **er beherrscht drei Sprachen/das Klavier** he has a command of three languages/he's a skilled pianist. **2** *vr* to control oneself. **ich kann mich ~!** *(iro col)* not likely! *(col)*.

**beherrscht** *adj (fig)* self-controlled.

**Beherrschtheit** *f no pl (fig)* self-control.

**Beherrschung** *f no pl* control; *(Selbst~)* self-control; *(des Markts)* domination; *(eines Fachs)* mastery. **die ~ verlieren** to lose one's temper.

**beherzigen*** *vt* to take to heart, to heed.

**beherzt** *adj (geh)* courageous, brave.

**Beherztheit** *f no pl (geh)* courage, bravery.

**behilflich** *adj* helpful. **jdm (bei etw) ~ sein** to help sb (with sth).

**behindern*** *vt* to hinder; *Sicht* to impede; *(bei Sport, im Verkehr)* to obstruct.

**behindert** *adj* handicapped; *(stärker, esp körperlich)* disabled.

**Behinderte(r)** *mf decl as adj siehe adj* handicapped/disabled person. **die ~n** the handicapped/disabled *pl.*

**Behinderung** *f* hindrance; *(im Sport, Verkehr)* obstruction; *(körperlich, Nachteil)* handicap. **mit ~en muß gerechnet werden** delays *or* hold-ups are likely to occur.

**Behörde** *f -n* authority *usu pl*; *(Amtsgebäude)* office *usu pl.*

**behördlich** *adj* official. **~ genehmigt** officially approved.

**behüten*** *vt* to look after. **jdn vor etw** *(dat)* **~** to save *or* protect sb from sth; **(Gott) behüte!** *(col)* God forbid!; **behütet** *(Jugend etc)* sheltered.

**behutsam** *adj* cautious, careful; *(zart auch)* gentle. **man muß es ihr ~ beibringen** it will have to be broken to her gently.

**Behutsamkeit** *f no pl* care(fulness), cautiousness; *(Zartheit auch)* gentleness.

**bei** *prep +dat* **(a)** *(in der Nähe von)* near; *(zum Aufenthalt)* at, with; *(Tätigkeitsbereich angebend, in Institutionen)* at; *(in Werken)* in; *(jdn betreffend)* with; *(Teilnahme bezeichnend)* at; *(unter, zwischen Menge)* among. **die Schlacht ~ Leipzig** the battle of Leipzig; **dicht ~ dem Ort, wo ...** very near the place where ...; **der Wert liegt ~ tausend Mark** the value is around a thousand marks; **~ uns** at our place; **~ seinen Eltern wohnen** to live with one's parents; **ich war ~ meiner Tante** I was at my aunt's; **~ Müller** *(auf Briefen)* c/o Müller; **sie sind ~ uns eingeladen** they're invited to our house; **er ist** *or* **arbeitet ~ der Post** he works for the post office; **~m Militär** in the army; **~m Fleischer** at the butcher's *(Brit)*, at the butcher; **~ Collins erschienen** published by Collins; **das war ~ ihm der Fall** that was the case with him; **~ einer Hochzeit sein** to be at a wedding; **jdn ~ sich haben** to have sb with one; **ich habe kein Geld ~ mir** I have no money on me.

**(b)** *(Zeitspanne: während)* during; *(Zeitpunkt)*

(up)on, at. ~m letzten Gewitter during the last storm; ~ meiner Ankunft on my arrival; ~m Erscheinen der Königin ... when the queen appeared ...; ich habe ihm ~ der Arbeit geholfen I helped him with the work; ~ der Arbeit when I'm *etc* working; ~ dem Zugunglück in the train crash; er verliert ~m Kartenspiel immer he always loses at cards.
(c) *(Zustand, Umstand bezeichnend)* in. ~ Kerzenlicht by candlelight; etw ~ einer Flasche Wein bereden to discuss sth over a bottle of wine; ~ guter Gesundheit sein to be in good health; ~ zehn Grad unter Null when it's ten degrees below zero; ~ offenem Fenster schlafen to sleep with the window open; ~ Feuer Scheibe einschlagen in case of fire break glass; ~ Nebel und Glatteis when there is fog and ice; ~ solcher Hitze/solchem Wind in such heat/such a wind; ~ seinem Talent with his talent; ~ aller Vorsicht in spite of all one's caution; ~ Gott by God.

**beibehalten\*** *vt sep irreg* to keep; *Bräuche, Regelung auch* to retain; *Leitsatz, Richtung* to keep to; *Gewohnheit* to keep up.

**Beibehaltung** *f no pl siehe vt* keeping; retention; keeping to; keeping up.

**Beiboot** *nt (Naut)* dinghy.

**beibringen** *vt sep irreg* (a) *(unterweisen in)* to teach *(jdm etw* sb sth*)*. (b) jdm etw ~ *(mitteilen)* to break sth to sb; *(zu verstehen geben)* to get sth across to sb. (c) *(zufügen) Wunde, Niederlage* to inflict *(jdm etw* sth on sb*)*. (d) *(herbeischaffen)* to produce; *Beweis, Geld etc* to furnish, to supply.

**Beichte** *f* -n confession. zur ~ gehen to go to confession.

**beichten** *vti (lit, fig)* to confess *(jdm etw* sth to sb*)*. ~ gehen to go to confession.

**Beicht-:** ~geheimnis *nt* seal of the confessional; ~stuhl *m* confessional; ~vater *m* father confessor.

**beide** *pron* (a) *(adjektivisch) (ohne Artikel)* both; *(mit Artikel)* two. alle ~n Teller both plates; seine ~n Brüder both his brothers, his two brothers; ihr ~(n)/euch ~ you two; euch ~n herzlichen Dank many thanks to both of you. (b) *(substantivisch) (ohne Artikel)* both (of them); *(mit Artikel)* two (of them). alle ~ both (of them); keiner/keines *etc* von ~n neither of them; ich habe ~ nicht gesehen I haven't seen either of them. (c) ~s both; (alles) ~s ist erlaubt both are permitted.

**beidemal** *adv* both times.

**beider-:** ~lei *adj attr inv* both; ~lei Geschlechts of both sexes; ~seitig *adj (auf beiden Seiten)* on both sides; *(gegenseitig) Vertrag etc* bilateral; *Einverständnis etc* mutual; ~seits **1** *adv* on both sides; **2** *prep +gen* on both sides of.

**beidhändig** *adj* ambidextrous.

**beidrehen** *vi sep (Naut)* to heave to.

**beidseitig** *adj (auf beiden Seiten)* on both sides; *(gegenseitig)* mutual.

**bei|einander** *adv* together.

**bei|einander-:** ~haben *vt sep irreg (col)*: du hast sie nicht alle ~ you can't be all there *(col)*; ~halten *vt sep irreg* to keep together; ~sein *vi sep irreg aux sein (col)* (gut) ~sein *(gesundheitlich)* to be in good shape *(col)*; *(geistig)* to be all there *(col)*.

**Beifahrer** *m (Aut)* (front-seat) passenger; *(beim Motorrad)* pillion passenger; *(berufsmäßiger Mitfahrer, Sport)* co-driver.

**Beifahrersitz** *m* passenger seat; *(auf Motorrad)* pillion.

**Beifall** *m no pl (Zustimmung)* approval; *(Händeklatschen)* applause; *(Zuruf)* cheering, cheers *pl.* ~

**finden** to meet with approval; ~ spenden/klatschen to applaud.

**beifällig** *adj* approving. ~e Worte words of approval.

**Beifalls-:** ~äußerung *f* expression of (one's) approval; ~ruf *m* cheer; ~sturm *m* storm of applause.

**Beifilm** *m* supporting film.

**beifügen** *vt sep (mitschicken)* to enclose *(dat* with*)*.

**Beigabe** *f* addition. unter ~ eines Löffels Senf adding a spoonful of mustard.

**beige** [be:ʃ, 'be:ʒə] *adj* beige.

**beigeben** *sep irreg* **1** *vt (zufügen)* to add *(dat* to*)*; *(mitgeben)* jdn to assign *(jdm* to sb*)*. **2** *vi*: klein ~ *(col)* to give in.

**Beigeschmack** *m* (accompanying) taste; *(fig: von Worten)* flavour *(Brit)*, flavor *(US)*.

**Beiheft** *nt* supplement.

**beiheften** *vt sep* to append, to attach.

**Beihilfe** *f* **(a)** *(finanziell)* financial assistance *no indef art*; *(Zuschuß)* allowance; *(Studien~)* grant; *(Subvention)* subsidy. **(b)** wegen ~ zum Mord *(Jur)* as an accessory to murder.

**Beiklang** *m (fig)* overtone *usu pl.*

**beikommen** *vi sep irreg aux sein* jdm ~ *(zu fassen bekommen)* to get hold of sb; *(fertig werden mit)* to get the better of sb; einer Sache *(dat)* ~ *(bewältigen)* to deal with sth.

**Beil** *nt* -e axe *(Brit)*, ax *(US)*; *(kleiner)* hatchet; *(Fleischer~)* cleaver; *(Fall~)* blade (of a/the guillotine).

**Beilage** *f* -n **(a)** *(Gedrucktes)* insert; *(Beiheft)* supplement. **(b)** *(das Beilegen)* enclosure; *(in Buch)* insertion. **(c)** *(Cook)* side-dish.

**beiläufig** *adj* casual; *Bemerkung auch* passing *attr.* etw ~ erwähnen to mention sth in passing.

**Beiläufigkeit** *f (von Bemerkung etc)* casualness; *(Nebensächlichkeit)* triviality. ~en *pl* trivia *pl.*

**beilegen** *vt sep* **(a)** *(hinzulegen)* to insert *(dat* in*)*; *(einem Brief)* to enclose *(dat* with, in*)*. **(b)** *(schlichten)* to settle. **(c)** = beimessen.

**Beilegung** *f siehe vt* **(a)** insertion; enclosure. **(b)** settlement.

**beileibe** *adv* ~ nicht! certainly not!; das darf ~ nicht passieren that mustn't happen under any circumstances; er ist ~ kein Heiliger he is by no means a saint, he is certainly no saint.

**Beileid** *nt no pl* condolences *pl.* jdm sein ~ aussprechen to offer sb one's condolences.

**Beileids-:** *in cpds* of condolence; ~bekundung *f,* ~bezeigung *f,* ~bezeugung *f* expression of sympathy; ~karte *f* sympathy *or* condolence card.

**beiliegend** *adj* enclosed. ~ senden wir Ihnen ... please find enclosed ...

**beim** = bei dem.

**beimengen** *vt sep* to add *(dat* to*)*.

**beimessen** *vt sep irreg* jdm/einer Sache Bedeutung ~ to attach importance to sb/sth.

**beimischen** *vt sep* to add *(dat* to*)*.

**Bein** *nt* -e leg. sich kaum auf den ~en halten können to be hardly able to stay on one's feet; er ist noch gut auf den ~en he's still sprightly; jdm ein ~ stellen *(lit, fig)* to trip sb up; jdm wieder auf die ~e helfen *(lit, fig)* to help sb back on his feet; auf den ~en sein *(nicht krank)* to be on one's feet; wir sollten uns auf die ~e machen *(col)* we ought to be making tracks *(col)*; jdm ~e machen *(col) (antreiben)* to make sb get a move on *(col)*; *(wegjagen)* to make sb clear off *(col)*; ~e bekommen *(col: verschwinden)* to vanish, to do a vanishing trick *(col)*; die ~e in die Hand nehmen *(col)* to take to one's heels; sich

**bekanntlich**

*(dat)* **die ~e in den Bauch stehen** *(col)* to stand about until one is fit to drop; **mit beiden ~en auf der Erde stehen** *(fig)* to have both feet firmly on the ground; **mit einem ~ im Grab/im Gefängnis stehen** *(fig)* to have one foot in the grave/to be likely to end up in jail; **auf eigenen ~en stehen** *(fig)* to be able to stand on one's own two feet; **auf einem ~ kann man nicht stehen!** *(fig col)* you can't stop at one!; **etw auf die ~e stellen** *(fig)* to get sth off the ground.

**beinah(e)** *adv* almost, nearly.

**Beiname** *m* epithet; *(Spitzname)* nickname.

**Beinbruch** *m* fracture of the leg. **das ist kein ~** *(fig col)* it could be worse *(col)*.

**be|inhalten\*** *vt* to contain.

**Beinschiene** *f (Sport)* shin pad; *(Med)* splint.

**Beipackzettel** *m* instruction leaflet.

**beipflichten** *vi sep* **jdm/einer Sache (in etw** *dat)* **~** to agree with sb/sth (on sth).

**Beiprogramm** *nt* supporting programme *(Brit)* or program *(US)*.

**Beirat** *m* advisory council *or* committee.

**be|irren\*** *vt* to disconcert. **sich in etw** *(dat)* **nicht ~ lassen** to pursue sth doggedly; **er läßt sich nicht ~** he won't be put off.

**Beirut** *nt* Beirut.

**beisammen** *adv* together.

**beisammen-** *pref* together; **~haben** *vt sep irreg (col)* Geld, Leute to have got together; **seinen Verstand ~haben** to have all one's wits about one; **er hat (sie) nicht alle ~** he's not all there; **~sein** *vi sep irreg aux sein (fig) (körperlich)* to be in good shape; *(geistig)* to be all there; **B~sein** *nt* get-together.

**Beischlaf** *m (Jur)* sexual intercourse.

**Beisein** *nt* presence. **in/ohne jds ~** in sb's presence/without sb being present.

**beiseite** *adv* aside *(auch Theat)*. **Spaß ~!** joking apart!; **jdn/etw ~ schaffen** to get rid of sb/sth; **etw ~ legen** to put sth aside, *(sparen)* to put sth by; **etw ~ sprechen** *(Theat)* to say sth in an aside.

**beisetzen** *vt sep (beerdigen)* to bury; *Urne* to install (in its resting place).

**Beisetzung** *f* funeral; *(von Urne)* installing in its resting place.

**Beisitzer(in** *f) m -* *(Jur)* assessor; *(bei Prüfung)* observer.

**Beispiel** *nt* **-e** example. **zum ~** for example *or* instance; **wie zum ~** such as; **jdm ein ~ geben** to set sb an example; **sich** *(dat)* **ein ~ an jdm/etw nehmen** to take a leaf out of sb's book/to take sth as an example; **mit gutem ~ vorangehen** to set a good example.

**beispiel-:** **~haft** *adj* exemplary; **~los** *adj* unprecedented; *(unerhört)* outrageous.

**beispielsweise** *adv* for example *or* instance.

**beispringen** *vi sep irreg aux sein* **jdm ~** to rush to sb's aid; *(mit Geldbeträgen)* to help sb out.

**beißen** *pret* **biß**, *ptp* **gebissen 1** *vti* to bite; *(brennen: Geschmack, Schmerzen)* to sting. **in den Apfel ~** to take a bite out of the apple; **der Hund hat mich ins Bein gebissen** the dog has bitten my leg *or* me in the leg; **der Rauch beißt in den Augen** the smoke makes your eyes sting; **etwas/nichts zu ~** *(col: essen)* something/nothing to eat; **an etw** *(dat)* **zu ~ haben** *(fig)* to have sth to chew over. **2** *vr (Farben)* to clash.

**beißend** *adj (lit, fig)* biting; *Bemerkung* cutting; *Geschmack, Geruch* pungent, sharp; *Schmerz* gnawing; *Ironie, Spott* bitter.

**Beißzange** *f* (pair of) pincers *or* pliers.

**Beistand** *m* **=e (a)** *no pl* help, assistance; *(moralisch)* support; *(von Priester)* presence. **jdm ~ leisten**

to give sb assistance/give sb one's support. **(b)** *(Jur)* legal adviser.

**Beistands-:** **~pakt, ~vertrag** *m* mutual assistance agreement.

**beistehen** *vi sep irreg* **jdm ~** to stand by sb.

**Beistell-** *in cpds* side; **~tisch** *m* occasional table.

**beisteuern** *vt sep* to contribute.

**beistimmen** *vi sep* = **zustimmen**.

**Beistrich** *m* comma.

**Beitrag** *m* **=e (a)** *(Anteil)* contribution; *(Aufsatz auch)* article. **einen ~ zu etw leisten** to make a contribution to sth. **(b)** *(Betrag)* contribution; *(Versicherungs~)* premium; *(Mitglieds~)* fee.

**beitragen** *vti sep irreg* to contribute *(zu to)*.

**Beitrags-:** **b~frei** *adj* non-contributory; **b~·pflichtig** *adj* contributory; **b~pflichtig sein** *(Mensch)* to have to pay contributions; **~satz** *m* membership rate; **~zahlende(r)** *mf decl as adj* fee-paying member.

**beitreiben** *vt sep irreg* to collect; *(esp Jur)* to enforce (the) payment of.

**beitreten** *vi sep irreg aux sein* +dat to join; *einem Pakt* to enter into; *einem Vertrag* to accede to.

**Beitritt** *m siehe* **beitreten** joining *(zu etw* sth*)*; entering into *(zu etw* sth*)*; accession *(zu* to*)*. **seinen ~ erklären** to become a member.

**Beitritts|erklärung** *f* confirmation of membership.

**Beiwagen** *m (beim Motorrad)* sidecar.

**Beiwerk** *nt* additions *pl*; *(modisch)* accessories *pl*.

**beiwohnen** *vi sep* +dat *(geh: dabeisein)* to be present at.

**Beize** *f* **-n** *(Beizmittel)* corrosive fluid; *(Metall~)* pickling solution; *(Holz~)* stain.

**beizeiten** *adv* in good time.

**beizen** *vt* to steep in corrosive fluid; *Metall* to pickle; *Holz* to stain.

**Beizmittel** *nt* = **Beize**.

**bejahen\*** *vti* to answer in the affirmative; *(gutheißen)* to approve of.

**bejahend** *adj* positive; *Antwort* affirmative.

**bejahrt** *adj* elderly, advanced in years.

**Bejahung** *f* affirmative answer *(gen* to*)*; *(Gutheißung)* approval.

**bejammern\*** *vt* to lament.

**bejammernswert** *adj* deplorable, lamentable; *Mensch, Schicksal* pitiable.

**bejubeln\*** *vt* to cheer; *Ereignis* to rejoice at.

**bekakeln\*** *vt (col)* to talk over.

**bekämpfen\*** *vt* to fight; *(fig auch)* to combat; *Ungeziefer* to control.

**Bekämpfung** *f* fight, battle *(von, gen* against*)*; *(von Ungeziefer)* controlling. **zur ~ der Terroristen** to fight *or* combat the terrorists.

**bekannt** *adj* **(a)** well-known *(wegen* for*)*; *Mensch auch* famous. **die ~eren Spieler** the better-known players; **sie/das ist mir ~** I know her/about that; **es ist allgemein ~, daß** ... it is common knowledge that ... **(b)** *(nicht fremd)* familiar. **jdn/sich mit etw ~ machen** to familiarize sb/oneself with sth; **jdn (mit jdm) ~ machen** to introduce sb (to sb); **wir sind miteinander ~** we already know each other.

**Bekanntenkreis** *m* circle of acquaintances.

**Bekannte(r)** *mf decl as adj* friend; *(entfernter ~)* acquaintance.

**bekanntermaßen** *adv* as is known.

**Bekanntgabe** *f* announcement.

**bekanntgeben** *vt sep irreg* to announce.

**Bekanntheit** *f* fame. **wegen seiner ~** because he is well-known.

**Bekanntheitsgrad** *m* degree of fame.

**bekanntlich** *adv* **es ist ~** ... it is well known that it is ...; ~ **gibt es** ... it is known that there are ...; **er hat ~ eine Schwäche für Frauen** he is well known to have a weakness for women.

**bekanntmachen** *vt sep* to announce; *(der Allgemeinheit mitteilen)* to publicize; *siehe* **bekannt (b)**.

**Bekanntmachung** *f* **(a)** *siehe vt* announcement; publicizing. **(b)** *(Anschlag etc)* announcement.

**Bekanntschaft** *f* acquaintance; *(mit Materie, Gebiet)* knowledge *(mit* of*)*. **jds ~ machen** to make sb's acquaintance; **mit etw ~ machen** to come into contact with sth; **meine ganze ~** *(col)* all my friends.

**bekanntwerden** *vi sep irreg aux sein* to become known; *(Geheimnis)* to leak out.

**bekehren*** *vt* to convert *(zu* to*)*.

**Bekehrung** *f* conversion.

**bekennen** *irreg* **1** *vt* to confess, to admit; *Sünde* to confess. **2** *vr* **sich (für) schuldig ~** to`admit *or* confess one's guilt; **sich als ... ~** to declare oneself to be a ...; **sich zu einem Glauben ~** to profess a faith; **sich zu jdm/etw ~** to declare one's support for sb/sth.

**Bekenner-:** **~brief** *m* letter claiming responsibility; **~geist** *m*, **~mut** *m* courage of one's convictions.

**Bekenntnis** *nt* **(a)** confession *(zu* of*)*. **sein ~ zum Sozialismus** his declared belief in socialism; **ein ~ zur Demokratie ablegen** to declare one's belief in democracy. **(b)** *(Rel: Konfession)* denomination.

**Bekenntnis-:** **~freiheit** *f* freedom of religious belief; **~schule** *f* denominational school.

**beklagen*** **1** *vt* to lament; *Tod, Verlust* to mourn. **Menschenleben sind nicht zu ~** there are no casualties. **2** *vr* to complain *(über +acc, wegen* about*)*. **sich bei jdm ~** to complain to sb; **ich kann mich nicht ~** I can't complain.

**beklagenswert** *adj Mensch* pitiful; *Zustand* lamentable, deplorable; *Unfall* terrible.

**Beklagte(r)** *mf decl as adj (Jur)* defendant.

**beklatschen*** *vt (applaudieren)* to clap.

**bekleben*** *vt* **etw mit Papier/Plakaten etc ~** to stick paper/posters *etc* on sth.

**bekleckern*** *(col)* **1** *vt* to stain. **2** *vr* **sich mit Saft etc ~** to spill juice *etc* all over oneself; **er hat sich nicht gerade mit Ruhm bekleckert** *(iro)* he didn't exactly cover himself with glory.

**bekleiden*** *vt (geh)* **(a)** *(anziehen)* to dress *(mit* in*)*. **(b)** *Amt etc* to occupy, to hold.

**Bekleidung** *f* **(a)** clothes *pl*, clothing; *(Aufmachung)* dress. **(b)** *(form: eines Amtes)* tenure.

**beklemmend** *adj* oppressive.

**Beklemmung** *f usu pl* feeling of oppressiveness; *(Gefühl der Angst)* feeling of apprehension.

**beklommen** *adj* apprehensive, anxious.

**Beklommenheit** *f* apprehensiveness.

**bekloppt** *adj (col) (Mensch)* crazy *(col)*; *(Sache)* lousy *(col)*, stupid *(col)*.

**beknackt** *adj (col)* = **bekloppt**.

**beknien*** *vt (col) jdn* to beg.

**bekommen** *irreg* **1** *vt* **(a)** to get; *Geschenk, Brief, Lob, Belohnung auch* to receive; *Zug, Krankheit auch* to catch; *gutes Essen, Schlaganfall, ein Kind, Besuch* to have; *Spritze, Tadel auch* to be given. **wir ~ anderes Wetter** the weather is changing; **wir ~ Regen/Schnee** we're going to have *or* get rain/snow; **einen Stein/Ball an den Kopf ~** to be hit on the head by a stone/ball; **kann ich das schriftlich ~?** can I have that in writing?; **ich bekomme bitte ein Glas Wein** I'll have a glass of wine, please; **was ~ Sie dafür/von mir?** how much is that/how much do I owe you?; **er bekam es einfach nicht über sich, ... he**

just could not bring himself to ...

**(b)** *Flecken/Risse* ~ to get *or* become spotty/cracked, to develop spots/cracks; *Heimweh* ~ to get *or* become homesick; *graue Haare/eine Glatze* ~ to go grey/bald; *Hunger/Durst/Angst* ~ to get *or* become hungry/thirsty/afraid.

**(c) etw zu sehen ~** to get to see sth; **es mit jdm zu tun ~** to get into trouble with sb; **wenn ich ihn zu fassen bekomme** ... if I get my hands on him ...; **etw gemacht ~** to get *or* have sth done; **seine Arbeit fertig ~** to get one's work finished.

**2** *vi aux sein (zuträglich sein)* **jdm (gut) ~** to do sb good; **das Essen ist mir gut ~** I enjoyed the meal; **jdm nicht** *or* **schlecht ~** not to do sb any good; *(Essen)* not to agree with sb; **wie bekommt ihm die Ehe?** how is he enjoying married life?; **wohl bekomm's!** your health!

**bekömmlich** *adj Mahlzeit, Speisen* (easily) digestible; *Klima* beneficial. **schwer ~ sein** to be difficult to digest.

**Bekömmlichkeit** *f siehe adj* digestibility; beneficial quality.

**beköstigen*** *vt* to cater for.

**Beköstigung** *f* catering *(gen* for*)*; *(Kost)* food.

**bekräftigen*** *vt* to confirm; *Vorschlag* to back up. **etw nochmals ~** to reaffirm sth.

**Bekräftigung** *f* confirmation. **zur ~ seiner Worte** to reinforce his words.

**bekreuzigen*** *vr* to cross oneself.

**bekriegen*** *vt* to wage war on; *(fig)* to fight.

**bekritteln*** *vt* to find fault with.

**bekümmern*** *vt* to worry.

**bekümmert** *adj* worried *(über +acc* about*)*.

**bekunden*** *vt* to show, to express. **~, daß ...** *(Jur)* to testify that ...

**Bekundung** *f* expression, manifestation; *(Jur)* testimony.

**belabern*** *vt (col) jdn* ~ to keep on at sb; *(überreden)* to talk sb into it.

**belächeln*** *vt* to smile at.

**belachen*** *vt* to laugh at.

**beladen*** *irreg* **1** *vt* to load; *(fig: mit Sorgen etc)* to burden. **2** *vr (mit Gepäck etc)* to load oneself up. **sich mit Verantwortung ~** to take on responsibilities. **3** *adj* loaded; *(fig: Mensch)* burdened.

**Belag** *m* ⁼e coating; *(Schicht)* layer; *(auf Pizza, Brot)* topping; *(auf Tortenboden, zwischen Brotscheiben)* filling; *(auf Zahn)* plaque; *(Zungen~)* fur; *(Fußboden~)* covering; *(Straßen~)* surface.

**Belagerer** *m* - besieger.

**belagern*** *vt (Mil, fig)* to besiege.

**Belagerung** *f* siege.

**Belagerungszustand** *m* state of siege.

**Belang** *m* -e **(a)** *(no pl: Wichtigkeit)* **von/ohne ~ (für jdn/etw) sein** to be of importance/of no importance (to sb/sth). **(b)** **~e** *pl* interests.

**belangen*** *vt (Jur)* to prosecute *(wegen* for*)*; *(wegen Beleidigung, Verleumdung)* to sue.

**belanglos** *adj* inconsequential, trivial. **das ist für das Ergebnis ~** that is irrelevant to the result.

**Belanglosigkeit** *f* **(a)** *no pl* inconsequentiality, triviality. **(b)** *(Bemerkung)* triviality.

**belassen*** *vt irreg* to leave. **wir wollen es dabei ~** let's leave it at that.

**belastbar** *adj* **(a)** **bis zu 500 kg ~ sein** to take a maximum load of 500 kg. **(b)** *(fig: beanspruchbar)* resilient. **die Umwelt/der Steuerzahler ist nicht unbegrenzt ~** there's a limit to what the environment/the taxpayer can stand. **(c) wie hoch ist mein Konto ~?** what is the limit on my account?; **der Etat ist nicht unbegrenzt ~** the budget is not unlimited.

**Belastbarkeit** f (a) *(von Brücke, Aufzug)* load-bearing capacity. (b) *(von Menschen, Nerven)* ability to take stress. (c) *(von Stromnetz etc)* maximum capacity; *(von Menschen, Organ)* maximum resilience.

**belasten\*** 1 vt (a) *(lit)* etw mit 50 Tonnen ~ to put a 50 ton load on sth; **die Brücke/das Fahrzeug zu sehr** ~ to put too great a load on the bridge/to overload the vehicle. (b) *(fig)* jdn mit etw ~ mit Arbeit to load sb with sth; mit Verantwortung, Sorgen to burden sb with sth; **von Sorgen belastet** weighed down with cares. (c) *(beanspruchen)* Stromnetz, Leitung to load *(mit* with*)*; Umwelt to pollute; *(Med)* Körper, Menschen to put a strain on, to strain; Steuerzahler to burden. **jdn/etw zu sehr** or **stark** ~ to overstrain sb/overload sth. (d) *(Jur)* Angeklagten to incriminate. (e) *(Fin)* Konto to debit. **steuerlich belastet** taxed; **etw (mit einer Hypothek)** ~ to mortgage sth; **jdn mit den Kosten** ~ to charge the costs to sb. 2 vr (a) **sich mit etw** ~ to take sth on; mit Sorgen to burden oneself with sth. (b) *(Jur)* to incriminate oneself.

**belastend** adj *(Jur)* incriminating.

**belästigen\*** vt to bother; *(zudringlich werden)* to harass; *(mit Fragen etc)* to pester; *(körperlich)* to molest.

**Belästigung** f annoyance; *(durch Lärm etc)* irritation; *(Zudringlichkeit)* harassment; *(mit Fragen etc)* pestering; *(körperlich)* molesting. **etw als eine** ~ **empfinden** to find sth annoying; **sexuelle** ~ sexual harassment.

**Belastung** f (a) *(Last)* weight; *(von Fahrzeug etc)* load; *(fig: Bürde)* burden. (b) *(von Nerven, Körper)* strain *(gen* on*)*; *(von Umwelt)* pollution *(gen* of*)*; *(von Stromnetz)* load *(gen* on*)*. (c) *(Jur)* incrimination. (d) *(Fin)* *(von Etat, steuerlich)* burden *(gen* on*)*; *(mit Hypothek)* mortgage *(gen* on*)*.

**Belastungs-:** ~**grenze** f *(seelisch, physisch)* limit; ~**material** nt *(Jur)* incriminating evidence; ~**probe** f endurance test; ~**zeuge** m *(Jur)* witness for the prosecution.

**belaubt** adj **~ sein** to have thick foliage.

**belauern\*** vt to eye; Wild to observe secretly.

**belaufen\*** vr irreg **sich auf etw** *(acc)* ~ to amount to sth.

**belauschen\*** vt to eavesdrop on.

**beleben\*** 1 vt (a) *(anregen)* to liven up; *(neu ~)* to revive; Konjunktur, jds Hoffnungen to stimulate. (b) *(zum Leben erwecken)* to bring to life. 2 vr *(Konjunktur)* to be stimulated; *(Augen, Gesicht)* to light up; *(Natur, Stadt)* to come to life. 3 vi **das belebt** it livens you up.

**belebend** adj invigorating.

**belebt** adj Straße etc busy.

**Belebung** f revival; *(der Konjunktur)* stimulation.

**Beleg** m -e (a) *(Beweis)* piece of evidence; *(Quellennachweis)* reference. (b) *(Quittung)* receipt.

**belegbar** adj verifiable.

**belegen\*** vt (a) *(bedecken)* to cover; Brote, Tortenboden to fill. **etw mit Fliesen/Teppich** ~ to tile/carpet sth; siehe **belegt**. (b) *(besetzen)* Wohnung, Hotelbett to occupy; *(reservieren)* to reserve; *(Univ)* Fach to take; Vorlesung to enrol for. **den fünften Platz** ~ to come fifth. (c) *(beweisen)* to verify. **mit Beispielen** ~ to illustrate.

**Belegschaft** f *(Beschäftigte)* staff; *(esp in Fabriken etc)* workforce.

**belegt** adj Zunge furred; Stimme hoarse; Zimmer occupied. ~**e Brote** open sandwiches.

**belehren\*** vt *(unterweisen)* to teach, to instruct; *(aufklären)* to inform *(über* +acc of*)*. **jdn eines anderen/Besseren** ~ to teach sb otherwise; **er ist nicht zu** ~ he won't be told; **ich bin belehrt!** I've learned my lesson.

**Belehrung** f explanation, lecture *(col)*; *(Anweisung)* instruction *(über* +acc about*)*; *(von Zeugen, Angeklagten)* caution.

**beleibt** adj stout, portly.

**beleidigen\*** vt jdn to insult; *(Verhalten, Anblick)* to offend; *(Jur)* *(mündlich)* to slander; *(schriftlich)* to libel.

**beleidigt** adj insulted; *(gekränkt)* offended. ~ **weggehen** to go off in high dudgeon; **die ~e Leberwurst spielen** *(col)* to be in a huff *(col)*; **bist du jetzt** ~? have I offended you?

**Beleidigung** f insult; *(Jur)* *(mündliche)* slander; *(schriftliche)* libel. **etw als** ~ **auffassen** to take offence at sth.

**beleihen\*** vt irreg *(Comm)* to lend money on.

**belemmert** adj *(col)* *(betreten)* sheepish; *(niedergeschlagen)* miserable; *(scheußlich)* lousy *(col)*.

**belesen** adj well-read.

**Belesenheit** f wide reading.

**beleuchten\*** vt to light up, to illuminate; Straße, Bühne etc to light; *(fig: betrachten)* to examine.

**Beleuchter(in** f) m - lighting technician.

**Beleuchtung** f (a) lighting; *(fig)* examination. (b) *(Licht)* light; *(Lichter)* lights pl.

**beleumdet, beleumundet** adj gut/schlecht ~ **sein** to have a good/bad reputation.

**Belfast** nt Belfast.

**Belgien** [-iən] nt Belgium.

**Belgier(in** f) [-iɐ, -iɐrɪn] m - Belgian.

**belgisch** adj Belgian.

**Belgrad** nt Belgrade.

**belichten\*** vt *(Phot)* to expose.

**Belichtung** f *(Phot)* exposure.

**Belichtungs-:** ~**automatik** f automatic exposure; ~**messer** m exposure meter; ~**zeit** f exposure (time).

**Belieben** nt no pl **nach** ~ just as you/they etc like.

**belieben\*** 1 vi impers *(geh)* **wie es Ihnen beliebt** as you wish. 2 vt **er beliebt zu scherzen** *(iro)* he must be joking.

**beliebig** 1 adj any. **eine/jede** ~**e Farbe** any colour at all, any colour you like; **in** ~**er Reihenfolge** in any order whatever; **die Auswahl ist** ~ the choice is free. 2 adv as you etc like. **Sie können** ~ **lange bleiben** you can stay as long as you like.

**beliebt** adj popular *(bei* with*)*.

**Beliebtheit** f popularity.

**beliefern\*** vt to supply.

**Belieferung** f supplying.

**Belize** nt Belize.

**bellen** vi to bark.

**bellend** adj Husten hacking; Stimme gruff.

**Belletristik** f fiction and poetry.

**belobigen\*** vt *(form)* to commend.

**Belobigung** f *(form)* commendation.

**belohnen\*** vt to reward.

**Belohnung** f reward; *(das Belohnen)* rewarding. **zur** or **als** ~ **(für)** as a reward (for).

**belüften\*** vt to ventilate.

**Belüftung** f ventilation.

**belügen\*** vt irreg to lie to. **sich selbst** ~ to deceive oneself.

**belustigen\*** 1 vt to amuse. 2 vr *(geh)* **sich über jdn/etw** ~ to make fun of sb/sth.

**belustigt** 1 adj amused. 2 adv in amusement.

**Belustigung** f amusement.

**bemächtigen\*** vr *(geh)* **sich eines Menschen** ~ to

seize hold of sb; *(Gefühl, Gedanke)* to come over sb.

**bemäkeln\*** *vt (col)* to find fault with.

**bemalen\*** **1** *vt* to paint. **2** *vr (pej: schminken)* to put on one's war paint *(col)*.

**Bemalung** *f* painting.

**bemängeln\*** *vt* to find fault with, to fault.

**bemannen\*** *vt U-Boot, Raumschiff* to man.

**Bemannung** *f* manning; *(Mannschaft)* crew.

**bemänteln\*** *vt* to cover up.

**bemerkbar** *adj* noticeable, perceptible. **sich ~ ma-chen** *(sich zeigen)* to make itself felt, to become noticeable; *(auf sich aufmerksam machen)* to draw attention to oneself.

**bemerken\*** *vt* **(a)** *(wahrnehmen)* to notice. **(b)** *(äußern)* to remark, to comment *(zu on)*. **nebenbei bemerkt** by the way.

**bemerkenswert** *adj* remarkable.

**Bemerkung** *f* remark, comment *(zu on)*.

**bemessen\*** *irreg* **1** *vt (zuteilen)* to allocate; *(einteilen)* to calculate. **meine Zeit ist knapp ~** my time is limited. **2** *vr (form)* to be proportionate *(nach to)*.

**bemitleiden\*** *vt* to pity, to feel sorry for. **er ist zu ~** he is to be pitied; **sich selbst ~** to feel sorry for oneself.

**bemitleidenswert** *adj* pitiable, pitiful.

**bemittelt** *adj* well-to-do, well-off.

**bemogeln\*** *vt (col)* to cheat.

**Bemühen** *nt no pl (geh)* endeavours *pl (Brit)*, endeavors *pl (US) (um for)*.

**bemühen\*** **1** *vt* to trouble, to bother; *Rechtsanwalt etc* to engage. **jdn zu sich ~** to call in sb. **2** *vr* **(a)** to try hard, to endeavour *(Brit)*, to endeavor *(US)*. **sich um eine Stelle ~** to try to get a job; **sich um jdn ~** to look after sb; *(um jds Gunst)* to court sb; **bitte ~ Sie sich nicht** please don't trouble yourself. **(b)** *(geh: gehen)* **sich zu jdm ~** to go to sb.

**bemüht** *adj* **(darum)** **~ sein, etw zu tun** to endeavour *(Brit)* or endeavor *(US)* or be at pains to do sth.

**Bemühung** *f* effort. **vielen Dank für Ihre ~en** thank you for your efforts or trouble.

**bemüßigt** *adj* **sich ~ fühlen/sehen, etw zu tun** to feel it incumbent on one to do sth; *(geh, usu iro)* to feel called upon.

**bemuttern\*** *vt* to mother.

**benachbart** *adj* neighbouring *(Brit)*, neighboring *(US)*; *Haus, Familie auch* next door.

**benachrichtigen\*** *vt* to inform *(von of)*; *(amtlich auch)* to notify *(von of)*.

**Benachrichtigung** *f* notification; *(Comm)* advice note.

**benachteiligen\*** *vt* to put at a disadvantage; *(wegen Geschlecht, Rasse, Glauben etc)* to discriminate against; *(körperliches Leiden auch)* to handicap. **benachteiligt sein** to be at a disadvantage/discriminated against/handicapped.

**Benachteiligung** *f siehe vt (das Benachteiligen)* disadvantaging; discrimination *(gen against)*; *(Zustand)* disadvantage; discrimination *no pl.*

**benebeln\*** *vt (col)* **jdn/jds Sinne ~** to make sb's head swim; **benebelt sein** to be feeling dazed or *(von Alkohol auch)* muzzy *(col)*.

**Benediktiner** *m* - *(Eccl auch ~in f)* Benedictine.

**Benefiz-:** **~konzert** *nt* benefit (concert); **~spiel** *nt* benefit (match); **~vorstellung** *f* charity performance.

**Benehmen** *nt no pl* behaviour *(Brit)*, behavior *(US)*. **kein ~ haben** to have no manners.

**benehmen\*** *vr irreg* to behave. **benimm dich!** behave yourself!; **sich gut ~** to behave oneself, to behave well; **sich schlecht ~** to behave (oneself) badly, to misbehave; *siehe* **benommen**.

**beneiden\*** *vt* to envy. **jdn um etw ~** to envy sb sth; **er ist nicht zu ~** I don't envy him.

**beneidenswert** *adj* enviable.

**Benelux-:** **~länder, ~staaten** *pl* Benelux countries *pl.*

**benennen\*** *vt irreg* to name. **jdn/etw nach jdm ~** to name sb/sth after or for *(US)* sb.

**Benennung** *f (das Benennen)* naming; *(Bezeichnung)* name, designation *(form)*.

**Bengale** *m (wk)* -n, -n, **Bengalin** *f* Bengali.

**Bengalen** *nt* Bengal.

**bengalisch** *adj* Bengali. **~er Tiger** Bengal tiger; **~e Beleuchtung** Bengal lights.

**Bengel** *m* -(s) boy, lad; *(frecher Junge)* rascal.

**Benimm** *m no pl (col)* manners *pl.*

**Benin** *nt* Benin.

**benommen** *adj* dazed.

**Benommenheit** *f* daze, dazed state.

**benoten\*** *vt* to mark.

**benötigen\*** *vt* to need, to require. **das benötigte Geld** the necessary money, the money needed.

**Benotung** *f* mark; *(das Benoten)* marking.

**benutzbar** *adj* usable; *Weg* passable.

**benutzen\*** *vt* to use.

**Benutzer(in** *f)* *m* - user; *(von Leihbücherei)* borrower.

**Benutzer-:** **b~freundlich** *adj* user-friendly; **~freundlichkeit** *f* user-friendliness; **~handbuch** *nt* user's guide; **~oberfläche** *f (Comp)* user or system interface.

**Benutzung** *f* use. **jdm etw zur ~ überlassen** to put sth at sb's disposal.

**Benzin** *nt* -e petrol *(Brit)*, gas(oline) *(US)*; *(Reinigungs~)* benzine; *(Feuerzeug~)* lighter fuel.

**Benzin-:** **~einspritzung** *f* fuel injection; **~feuerzeug** *nt* petrol *(Brit)* or gasoline *(US)* lighter; **~gutschein** *m* petrol *(Brit)* or gasoline *(US)* coupon; **~kanister** *m* petrol *(Brit)* or gasoline *(US)* can; **~motor** *m* petrol *(Brit)* or gasoline *(US)* engine; **~pumpe** *f* fuel pump; **~uhr** *f* fuel gauge; **~verbrauch** *m* petrol *(Brit)* or gasoline *(US)* consumption.

**be|obachten\*** *vt* to observe; *(bemerken auch)* to notice, to see; *(genau verfolgen, betrachten auch)* to watch. **etw an jdm ~** to notice sth in sb; **jdn ~ lassen** *(Polizei etc)* to put sb under surveillance.

**Be|obachter(in** *f)* *m* - observer.

**Be|obachtung** *f* observation; *(polizeilich)* surveillance. **die ~ habe ich oft gemacht** I've often noticed that.

**Be|obachtungs-:** **~gabe** *f* powers *pl* of observation; **er hat eine gute ~gabe** he has a very observant eye; **~posten** *m* observation post; **~station** *f* **(a)** *(Med)* observation ward; **(b)** *(Met)* weather station.

**be|ordern\*** *vt* to order. **jdn zu sich ~** to send for sb.

**bepacken\*** *vt* to load (up).

**bepflanzen\*** *vt* to plant.

**Bepflanzung** *f* **(a)** *(das Bepflanzen)* planting. **(b)** *(die Pflanzen)* plants *pl (gen in)*.

**bepinkeln\*** *(col)* **1** *vt* to pee on *(col)*. **2** *vr* to wet oneself.

**bequatschen\*** *vt (col)* **(a)** *etw* to talk over. **(b)** *(überreden)* to persuade.

**bequem** *adj* comfortable; *Weg, Methode* easy; *Ausrede* convenient; *(träge) Mensch* idle. **es sich** *(dat)* **machen** to make oneself comfortable; **machen Sie es sich ~** make yourself at home.

**bequemen\*** *vr* **sich (dazu) ~, etw zu tun** to bring oneself to do sth.

**Bequemlichkeit** *f no pl (Behaglichkeit)* comfort;

*(Trägheit)* idleness.

**berappen\*** *vti (col)* **er mußte schwer ~** he had to fork out a lot *(col)*.

**beraten\*** *irreg* **1** *vt* **(a)** jdn **~** to advise sb; **gut/ schlecht ~ sein** to be well-/ill-advised; **sich von jdm ~ lassen(, wie ...)** to ask sb's advice (on how ...), to consult sb (about how...). **(b)** *(besprechen)* to discuss. **2** *vir* to discuss. **sich mit jdm ~** to consult (with) sb *(über +acc* about*)*.

**beratend** *adj* advisory, consultative. **jdm ~ zur Seite stehen** to act in an advisory capacity to sb.

**Berater(in** *f) m* - adviser, consultant.

**Beratervertrag** *m* consultancy contract.

**beratschlagen\*** *vti insep* to discuss.

**Beratung** *f* **(a)** *(das Beraten)* advice; *(geschäftlich: bei Rechtsanwalt, Arzt etc)* consultation. **(b)** *(Besprechung)* discussion.

**Beratungs-:** ~**dienst** *m* advice *or* advisory service; ~**stelle** *f* advice centre.

**berauben\*** *vt* to rob. **jdn einer Sache** *(gen)* **~** to rob sb of sth; *seines Rechtes* to deprive sb of sth.

**berauschen\*** **1** *vt (lit, fig)* to intoxicate; *(Droge auch)* to make euphoric. **2** *vr* **sich an etw** *(dat)* **~** *(lit, fig)* to become intoxicated with sth.

**berauschend** *adj* intoxicating. **das war nicht sehr ~** *(iro)* that wasn't very exciting.

**Berber** *m* - **(a)** Berber. **(b)** *(auch ~teppich)* Berber carpet.

**berechenbar** *adj Kosten* calculable; *Verhalten* predictable.

**Berechenbarkeit** *f siehe adj* calculability; predictability.

**berechnen\*** *vt* **(a)** *(ausrechnen)* to calculate. **(b)** *(in Rechnung stellen)* to charge. **jdm zu viel ~** to overcharge sb. **(c)** *(vorsehen)* to intend, to mean.

**berechnend** *adj (pej) Mensch* calculating.

**Berechnung** *f siehe vt* **(a)** calculation. **meiner ~ nach, nach meiner ~** according to my calculations; **aus ~ handeln** to act in a calculating manner. **(b)** charge. **ohne ~** without any charge.

**berechtigen\*** *vti* to entitle. **(jdn) zu etw ~** to entitle sb to sth; **das berechtigt zu der Annahme, daß ...** this justifies the assumption that ...

**berechtigt** *adj* justifiable; *Frage, Hoffnung, Anspruch* legitimate; *Vorwurf auch* just; *Forderung, Einwand auch* justified. **~ sein, etw zu tun** to be entitled to do sth.

**berechtigterweise** *adv* legitimately, justifiably.

**Berechtigung** *f* **(a)** *(Befugnis)* entitlement; *(Recht)* right. **die ~/keine ~ haben, etw zu tun** to be entitled/not to be entitled to do sth. **(b)** *(Rechtmäßigkeit)* legitimacy, justifiability.

**bereden\*** *vt* **(a)** *(auch vr: besprechen)* to discuss, to talk over. **(b)** *(überreden)* **jdn zu etw ~** to talk sb into sth.

**beredsam** *adj (liter) (iro: redefreudig)* talkative.

**Beredsamkeit** *f (liter)* eloquence; *(iro)* talkativeness.

**beredt** *adj (geh)* eloquent.

**Beredtheit** *f (geh)* eloquence.

**Bereich** *m* -e **(a)** area. **im ~ der Innenstadt** in the town centre area. **(b)** *(Einfluß~, Aufgaben~)* sphere; *(Sach~)* area, field; *(Sektor)* sector. **im ~ des Möglichen liegen** to be within the bounds of possibility.

**bereichern\*** **1** *vt (lit, fig)* to enrich; *Sammlung etc* to enlarge. **2** *vr* to make a lot of money *(an +dat* out of*)*. **sich auf Kosten anderer ~** to feather one's nest at the expense of other people.

**Bereicherung** *f* **(a)** *(das Bereichern)* enrichment;

*(von Sammlung)* enlargement. **(b)** *(Gewinn)* boon. **eine wertvolle ~** a valuable addition.

**bereifen\*** *vt (Aut)* to put tyres *(Brit) or* tires *(US)* on.

**Bereifung** *f (Aut)* set of tyres *(Brit) or* tires *(US)*. **die ~ bei diesem Auto** the tyres on this car.

**bereinigen\*** *vt* to clear up; *(Meinungsverschiedenheiten)* to settle.

**Bereinigung** *f siehe vt* clearing up; settlement.

**bereisen\*** *vt ein Land* to travel around; *(Comm) Gebiet* to travel, to cover. **die Welt/fremde Länder ~** to travel the world/in foreign countries.

**bereit** *adj usu pred* **(a)** *(fertig)* ready; *(vorbereitet auch)* prepared. **sich ~ machen** to get ready. **(b)** *(willens)* willing, prepared. **sich ~ erklären, etw zu tun** to agree to do sth.

**bereiten** *vt* **(a)** *(zu~)* to prepare *(dat for)*. **(b)** *(verursachen)* to cause; *Überraschung, Empfang, Freude, Kopfschmerzen* to give. **einer Sache** *(dat)* **ein Ende ~** to put an end to sth.

**bereit-:** ~**halten** *sep* **1** *vt irreg Fahrkarten etc* to have ready; *(für den Notfall)* to keep ready; *Überraschung* to have in store; **2** *vr* to stand by; ~**legen** *vt sep* to lay out ready; ~**liegen** *vi sep irreg* to be ready; ~**machen** *vtr sep* to get ready.

**bereits** *adv* already. **~ vor drei Wochen** even three weeks ago; **das haben wir ~ gestern gemacht** we did that yesterday; **~ am nächsten Tage** on the very next day.

**Bereitschaft** *f* **(a)** *no pl* readiness; *(Bereitwilligkeit auch)* willingness. **in ~ sein, ~ haben** *(Polizei, Soldaten etc)* to be on stand-by; *(Arzt)* to be on call. **(b)** *(Mannschaft)* squad.

**Bereitschafts-:** ~**arzt** *m* doctor on call; *(im Krankenhaus)* duty doctor; ~**dienst** *m* emergency service; ~**dienst haben** *siehe* **Bereitschaft**; ~ **polizei** *f* riot police.

**Bereit-:** b~**stehen** *vi sep irreg* to be ready; *(Flugzeug auch, Truppen)* to stand by; **Ihr Wagen steht** b~ your car is waiting; b~**stellen** *vt sep* to provide, to supply; ~**stellung** *f* provision, supply.

**Bereitung** *f* preparation.

**Bereit-:** b~**willig** *adj* willing; ~**willigkeit** *f* willingness.

**bereuen\*** *vt* to regret; *Schuld, Sünden* to repent of. **~, etw getan zu haben** to regret having done sth; **das wirst du noch ~!** you'll regret it!

**Berg** *m* -e **(a)** mountain; *(esp kleiner auch)* hill. **~e versetzen (können)** to (be able to) move mountains; **mit etw hinterm ~ halten** *(fig)* to keep quiet about sth; **in die ~e fahren** to go to the mountains; **über den ~ sein** *(col)* to be out of the woods; **über alle ~e sein** *(col)* to be miles away *(col)*; **da stehen einem ja die Haare zu ~e** it's enough to make your hair stand on end. **(b)** *(große Menge)* heap, pile; *(von Sorgen)* mass.

**Berg-** *in cpds* mountain; *(Bergbau-)* mining; b~**ab** *adv* downhill; **es geht mit ihm** b~**ab** *(fig)* he is going downhill; ~**arbeiter** *m* miner; b~**auf** *adv* uphill; **es geht wieder** b~**auf** *(fig)* things are getting better *or* looking up; ~**bahn** *f* mountain railway; *(Seilbahn auch)* cable railway; ~**bau** *m* mining.

**bergen** *pret* **barg**, *ptp* **geborgen** *vt* **(a)** *(retten) Menschen* to save, to rescue; *Leichen* to recover; *Ladung, Fahrzeug* to salvage. **aus dem Wasser tot/ lebend geborgen werden** to be brought out of the water dead/alive. **(b)** *(geh: enthalten)* to hold. **diese Möglichkeit birgt die Gefahr in sich, daß ...** this possibility involves the danger that ... **(c)** *siehe* **geborgen**.

**Berg-:** ~**fried** *m* keep; ~**führer** *m* mountain guide; ~**gipfel** *m* mountain top *or* peak; ~**hang** *m* moun-

tain slope; **b~hoch** *adj Wellen* mountainous; **~hütte** *f* mountain hut.
**bergig** *adj* mountainous.
**Berg-:** **~kamm** *m* mountain ridge; **~kette** *f* mountain range; **~kristall** *m* rock crystal; **~kuppe** *f* (round) mountain top; **~land** *nt* mountainous region; **das walisische ~land** the Welsh mountains.
**Bergmann** *m, pl* **-leute** miner.
**bergmännisch** *adj* miner's *attr*.
**Berg-:** **~not** *f* in **~not sein/geraten** to be in/get into difficulties while climbing; **~predigt** *f (Bibl)* Sermon on the Mount; **~rettungsdienst** *m* mountain rescue service; **~rücken** *m* mountain ridge; **~rutsch** *m* landslide *(auch fig)*, landslip; **~schuh** *m* climbing boot; **~spitze** *f* mountain peak; **b~steigen** *vi sep irreg aux sein or haben* to go mountain climbing *or* mountaineering; **(das) ~steigen** mountaineering; **~steiger(in** *f)* *m* mountaineer; **~steigerei** *f (col)* mountaineering; **~und-Tal-Bahn** *f* big dipper, roller-coaster; **~und-Tal-Fahrt** *f* ride on the big dipper.
**Bergung** *f no pl siehe* **bergen** (a) saving, rescue; recovery; salvage, salvaging.
**Bergungs-:** **~mannschaft** *f,* **~trupp** *m* rescue team.
**Berg-:** **~wacht** *f* mountain rescue service; **~wand** *f* mountain face; **~wanderung** *f* walk *or* hike in the mountains; **~werk** *nt* mine; **im ~werk arbeiten** to work down the mines; **~wiese** *f* mountain pasture.
**Bericht** *m* **-e** report *(über +acc* about, on, *von on); (Erzählung auch)* account; *(Zeitungs~ auch)* story. **jdm über etw** *(acc)* **~ erstatten** to give sb a report (on sth).
**berichten*** *vti* to report; *(erzählen)* to tell. **jdm über etw** *(acc)* **~** to report to sb about sth; to tell sb about sth; **mir ist (darüber) berichtet worden, daß ...** I have received reports that ...; **er berichtete von der Reise** he gave an account of his journey; **uns wird soeben berichtet, daß ...** *(Rad, TV)* news is just coming in that ...
**Bericht-:** **~erstatter(in** *f)* *m* reporter; *(Korrespondent)* correspondent; **~erstattung** *f* reporting; **die ~erstattung über diese Vorgänge in der Presse** press coverage of these events.
**berichtigen*** *vt* to correct; *Fehler auch, (Jur)* to rectify.
**Berichtigung** *f siehe vt* correction; rectification.
**berieseln*** *vt* (a) to spray with water *etc; (durch Sprinkleranlage)* to sprinkle. (b) *(fig col)* **von etw berieselt werden** *(fig)* to be exposed to a constant stream of sth.
**Berieselung** *f* watering. **die ~ mit** *or* **durch etw** *(fig)* the constant stream of sth.
**Berieselungs|anlage** *f* sprinkler (system).
**Bering-:** **~meer** *nt* Bering Sea; **~straße** *f* Bering Straits *pl*.
**beritten** *adj* mounted, on horseback.
**Berlin** *nt* Berlin.
**Berliner¹** *adj attr* Berlin.
**Berliner²** *m* - *(Cook)* jam doughnut.
**Berliner(in** *f)* *m* - Berliner.
**berlinerisch** *adj (col) Dialekt* Berlin *attr*.
**berlinern*** *vi (col)* to speak in the Berlin dialect.
**Bermuda-Dreieck** *nt* Bermuda triangle.
**Bermudas** *pl* **auf den ~** in Bermuda.
**Bermudashorts** *pl* Bermuda shorts *pl*.
**Bern** *nt* Berne.
**Bernhardiner** *m* - Saint Bernard (dog).
**Bernstein** *m no pl* amber.
**bernsteinfarben** *adj* amber(-coloured).

**Berserker** *m* - **wie ein ~ arbeiten/kämpfen** to work/fight like mad *or* fury.
**bersten** *pret* **barst,** *ptp* **geborsten** *vi aux sein (geh)* to crack; *(auf~, zerbrechen)* to break; *(zerplatzen)* to burst. **vor Neugier/Zorn** *etc* **~** to be bursting with curiosity/anger *etc;* **zum B~voll** full to bursting.
**berüchtigt** *adj* notorious, infamous.
**berückend** *adj* charming, enchanting.
**berücksichtigen*** *vt (beachten, bedenken)* to take into account *or* consideration; *(in Betracht ziehen) Antrag, Bewerber* to consider. **das ist zu ~** that must be taken into account *or* consideration.
**Berücksichtigung** *f* consideration. **in** *or* **unter ~ der Tatsache, daß ...** in view of the fact that ...
**Beruf** *m* **-e** occupation; *(akademischer auch)* profession; *(handwerklicher)* trade; *(Stellung)* job. **was sind Sie von ~?** what is your occupation *etc?,* what do you do for a living?; **von ~ Arzt/Bäcker/Hausfrau sein** to be a doctor by profession/baker by trade/ housewife by occupation; **seinen ~ verfehlt haben** to have missed one's vocation; **im ~ stehen** to be working; **von ~s wegen** on account of one's job.
**berufen*** *irreg* **1** *vt* (a) *(ernennen, einsetzen)* to appoint. **zum Minister/auf einen Lehrstuhl ~ werden** to be appointed minister/to a chair. (b) = **beschreien. 2** *vr* **sich auf jdn/etw ~** to refer to sb/sth. **3** *adj* (a) *Kritiker* competent, capable; **aus ~em Munde** from an authoritative source. (b) *(ausersehen)* **zu etw ~ sein** to have a vocation for sth; *(esp Rel)* to be called to sth.
**beruflich** *adj (esp auf akademische Berufe bezüglich)* professional. **sein ~er Werdegang** his career; **sich ~ weiterbilden** to undertake further professional training; **~ ist sie sehr erfolgreich** she is very successful in her career; **er ist ~ viel unterwegs** he is away a lot on business.
**Berufs-** *in cpds* professional; **~ausbildung** *f* vocational training; **~aussichten** *pl* job prospects *pl*; **b~bedingt** *adj* occupational; **~berater** *m* careers adviser; **~beratung** *f* careers guidance; **~bezeichnung** *f* job title; **~boxen** *nt* professional boxing; **~erfahrung** *f* (professional) experience; **~feuerwehr** *f* fire service; **~fußball** *m* professional football; **~geheimnis** *nt* professional secret; *(Schweigepflicht)* professional secrecy, confidentiality; **~heer** *nt* professional *or* regular army; **~kleidung** *f* working clothes *pl*; **~krankheit** *f* occupational disease; **~leben** *nt* working *or* professional life; **im ~leben stehen** to be working *or* in employment; **b~mäßig** *adj* professional; **etw b~mäßig betreiben** to do sth on a professional basis; **~risiko** *nt* occupational hazard; **~schule** *f* vocational school, ≈ technical college *(Brit);* **~schüler** *m* student at vocational school *etc;* **~soldat** *m* regular *or* professional soldier; **~sport** *m* professional sport; **~sportler** *m* professional sportsman; **b~tätig** *adj* working; **b~tätig sein** to be working, to work; **~tätige(r)** *mf decl as adj* working person; **b~unfähig** *adj* unable to work; **~unfähigkeit** *f* inability to work; **~unfall** *m* occupational accident; **~verband** *m* professional/trade organization; **~verbot** *nt* exclusion from a profession; **jdm ~verbot erteilen** to ban sb from his/her profession; *einem Arzt, Anwalt* to strike sb off; **~verbrecher** *m* professional criminal; **~verkehr** *m* commuter traffic; **~wahl** *f* choice of occupation; **~wechsel** *m* change of occupation.
**Berufung** *f* (a) *(Jur)* appeal. **in die ~ gehen/~ einlegen** to appeal *(bei to).* (b) *(in ein Amt etc)* appointment *(auf or an +acc to).* (c) *(innerer Auftrag)* voca-

tion; *(Rel auch)* calling. **(d)** *(form)* **unter ~ auf etw** *(acc)* with reference to sth.

**Berufungs-:** **~frist** *f* period in which an appeal must be lodged; **~gericht** *nt* appeal court, court of appeal; **~klage** *f* appeal; **~kläger** *m* appellant.

**beruhen\*** *vi* to be based *or* founded *(auf + dat* on*)*. **das beruht auf Gegenseitigkeit** *(col)* the feeling is mutual; **etw auf sich ~ lassen** to let sth rest.

**beruhigen\*** **1** *vt* to calm (down); *Baby* to quieten; *(trösten)* to comfort; *(versichern)* to reassure; *Magen* to settle; *Nerven auch* to soothe; *Gewissen* to appease. **na, dann bin ich ja beruhigt** well I must say I'm quite relieved; **~d** soothing; *(tröstlich)* reassuring. **2** *vr* to calm down; *(Krise auch)* to ease off; *(Verkehr, Kämpfe)* to subside; *(Börse, Magen)* to settle down; *(Sturm)* to die down, to abate.

**Beruhigung** *f no pl* **(a)** *siehe vt* calming (down); quietening; comforting; reassuring; settling; soothing; appeasement. **zu Ihrer ~ kann ich sagen ...** you'll be reassured to know that ... **(b)** *siehe vr* calming down, easing off; subsiding; settling down.

**Beruhigungs-:** **~mittel** *nt* sedative, tranquillizer; **~pille** *f* sedative (pill), tranquillizer; **~spritze** *f* sedative (injection).

**berühmt** *adj* famous. **das war nicht ~** *(col)* it was nothing to write home about *(col)*.

**berühmt-berüchtigt** *adj* infamous, notorious.

**Berühmtheit** *f* **(a)** fame. **~ erlangen** to become famous; **zu trauriger ~ gelangen** to achieve notoriety. **(b)** *(Mensch)* celebrity.

**berühren\*** **1** *vt* **(a)** to touch; *(erwähnen)* Thema, Punkt to touch on. **B~ verboten** do not touch. **(b)** *(seelisch bewegen)* to move; *(auf jdn wirken)* to affect; *(betreffen)* to affect, to concern. **das berührt mich gar nicht!** that's nothing to do with me; **von etw peinlich berührt sein** to be embarrassed by sth. **2** *vr* to touch.

**Berührung** *f* touch; *(von Drähten etc, menschlich)* contact; *(Erwähnung)* mention. **mit jdm/etw in ~ kommen** to come into contact with sb/sth.

**Berührungs-:** **~angst** *f usu pl* fear of involvement; **~punkt** *m* point of contact.

**bes.** = **besonders** esp.

**besagen\*** *vt* to say; *(bedeuten)* to mean, to imply.

**besagt** *adj attr (form)* said *(form)*.

**besaiten\*** *vt* to string. **etw neu ~** to restring sth.

**besamen\*** *vt* to fertilize; *(künstlich)* to inseminate.

**Besamung** *f siehe vt* fertilization; insemination.

**besänftigen\*** *vt* to soothe; *Menge auch* to pacify.

**Besänftigung** *f siehe vt* soothing; pacifying.

**besät** *adj* covered; *(mit Blättern etc)* strewn.

**Besatz** *m* ⁼e edging, trimming.

**Besatzer** *m* - *(pej col)* occupying forces *pl*.

**Besatzung** *f* **(a)** *(Mannschaft)* crew; *(Verteidigungstruppe)* garrison. **(b)** *(~truppen)* occupying forces *pl*.

**Besatzungs-:** **~armee** *f* army of occupation; **~macht** *f* occupying power; **~truppen** *pl* occupying forces *pl*; **~zone** *f* occupied zone.

**besaufen\*** *vr irreg (col)* to get plastered *(col)*.

**Besäufnis** *nt (col)* booze-up *(col)*.

**beschädigen\*** *vt* to damage. **beschädigt** damaged.

**Beschädigung** *f* damage *(von* to*)*.

**beschaffen\*** **1** *vt* to get (hold of), to obtain *(jdm etw* sth for sb*)*. **2** *adj (form)* **so ~ sein wie ...** to be the same as ...; **das ist so ~, daß ...** that is such that ...

**Beschaffenheit** *f no pl* composition; *(körperlich)* constitution; *(Art, seelisch)* nature, qualities *pl*. **je nach ~ der Lage** according to the situation.

**Beschaffung** *f no pl* obtaining.

**Beschaffungskriminalität** *f* drug-related crime.

**beschäftigen\*** **1** *vr* **sich mit etw ~** to occupy oneself with sth; *(sich befassen, abhandeln)* to deal with sth; **sich mit Literatur ~** to study literature; **sich mit jdm ~** to devote one's attention to sb. **2** *vt* **(a)** *(innerlich)* **jdn ~** to be on sb's mind. **(b)** *(anstellen)* to employ. **(c)** *(eine Tätigkeit geben)* to keep occupied. **jdn mit etw ~** to give sb sth to do.

**beschäftigt** *adj* **(a)** busy. **mit Nähen/jdm ~ sein** to be busy sewing/with sb; **mit sich selbst ~ sein** to be preoccupied with oneself. **(b)** *(angestellt)* employed *(bei* by*)*.

**Beschäftigte(r)** *mf decl as adj* employee.

**Beschäftigung** *f* **(a)** work *no indef art*, job; *(Anstellung, Angestelltsein)* employment. **einer ~ nachgehen** *(form)* to be employed. **(b)** *(Tätigkeit)* activity, occupation. **jdm eine ~ geben** to give sb something to do. **(c)** *(geistige ~)* preoccupation; *(mit Frage)* consideration *(mit* of*)*.

**Beschäftigungs-:** **b~los** *adj* unoccupied; *(arbeitslos)* unemployed; **~programm** *nt* job creation scheme; **~therapie** *f* occupational therapy.

**beschämen\*** *vt* to put to shame. **es beschämt mich, zu sagen ...** I feel ashamed to have to say ...

**beschämend** *adj* shaming; *(schändlich)* shameful.

**beschämt** *adj* ashamed.

**Beschämung** *f* shame.

**beschatten\*** *vt* **(a)** *(überwachen)* to shadow, to tail. **(b)** *(Sport)* to mark closely. **(c)** *(geh: Schatten geben)* to shade.

**Beschatter** *m* - *(Polizist etc)* tail; *(Sport)* marker.

**Beschattung** *f siehe vt* **(a)** tailing. **(b)** marking.

**beschaulich** *adj* Leben, Abend quiet, tranquil; *Charakter, Mensch* pensive, contemplative.

**Beschaulichkeit** *f siehe adj* quietness, tranquillity; pensiveness.

**Bescheid** *m* -e **(a)** *(Auskunft)* information; *(Nachricht)* notification; *(Entscheidung auf Antrag etc)* decision. **jdm (über etw** *(acc)* **or von etw) ~ sagen/geben** to let sb know (about sth), to tell sb (about sth); **jdm ordentlich ~ sagen** *(col)* to tell sb where to go *(col)*. **(b)** *(über etw* *(acc)* **or in etw** *(dat)***) ~ wissen** to know (about sth); **er weiß schon ~** he knows all about it.

**bescheiden[1]\*** *irreg* **1** *vt* **(a)** *(form: entscheiden)* to decide upon. **etw abschlägig ~** to turn sth down. **(b)** *(geh)* **es war ihr nicht beschieden, ...** it was not to be her lot to ... **2** *vr (geh)* to be content.

**bescheiden[2]** *adj* modest. **~e Verhältnisse** modest circumstances; **darf ich mal ~ fragen, ob ...** may I venture to ask whether ...; **eine ~e Frage** one small question.

**Bescheidenheit** *f* modesty. **nur keine falsche ~** no false modesty now.

**bescheinen\*** *vt irreg* to shine on. **vom Mond/von der Sonne beschienen** moonlit/sunlit.

**bescheinigen\*** *vt* to certify; *Empfang* to confirm, to acknowledge; *(durch Quittung)* to give a receipt for. **hiermit wird bescheinigt, daß ...** this is to certify that ...; **jdm äußerste Kompetenz ~** to confirm sb's extreme competence.

**Bescheinigung** *f siehe vt (das Bescheinigen)* certification; confirmation; *(Schriftstück)* certificate; written confirmation; *(Quittung)* receipt.

**bescheißen\*** *vt irreg (col!)* jdn to cheat *(um* out of*)*.

**beschenken\*** *vt* jdn to give presents/a present to. **jdn mit etw ~** to give sb sth (as a present).

**bescheren\*** *vti* **(a)** jdn ~ to give sb a Christmas present/Christmas presents; **jdm eine Überraschung ~** to give sb a nice surprise. **(b)** *(zuteil werden las-*

*sen)* **jdm etw** ~ *Glück, Kinder* to bless sb with sth.
**Bescherung** *f* **(a)** giving out of Christmas presents.
**(b)** *(iro col)* **das ist ja eine schöne** ~! this is a nice
mess; **da haben wir die** ~! what did I tell you!
**bescheuert** *adj (col)* stupid.
**beschichten\*** *vt (Tech)* to coat, to cover.
**Beschichtung** *f (Tech)* coating.
**beschicken\*** *vt* **(a) eine Ausstellung mit jdm/etw** ~
to send sb/sth to an exhibition. **(b)** *Hochofen* to
charge.
**beschickert** *adj (col)* tipsy.
**beschießen\*** *vt irreg* to shoot *or* fire at; *(mit Geschützen, Phys)* to bombard.
**Beschießung** *f siehe vt* shooting *(gen* at*)*, firing *(gen*
on, at*)*; bombardment *(gen* of*)*.
**beschildern\*** *vt* to put a sign/signs on; *(mit Ver-
kehrsschildern)* to signpost.
**Beschilderung** *f siehe vt* putting a sign *(von* on*)*;
signposting; *(Schilder)* signs *pl*; signposts *pl*.
**beschimpfen** *vt jdn* to swear at.
**Beschimpfung** *f* **(a)** swearing *(gen* at*)*. **(b)**
*(Schimpfwort)* insult.
**beschirmen\*** *vt (geh: beschützen)* to shield.
**Beschiß** *m no pl (col!)* swindle, rip-off *(col)*.
**beschissen** *adj (col!)* bloody awful *(Brit col)*, lousy
*(col)*.
**Beschlag** *m ⁼e* **(a)** *(an Koffer, Truhe)* fitting; *(an Tür,
Möbelstück)* mounting; *(von Pferd)* shoes *pl*. **(b)** *(auf
Glas, Spiegel etc)* condensation. **(c) jdn/etw in** ~
**nehmen** to monopolize sb/sth; **mit** ~ **belegt sein** to
be occupied.
**beschlagen\*** *irreg* **1** *vt* **(a)** *Möbel, Türen* to put
(metal) fittings on; *Huftiere* to shoe; *Schuhe* to put
metal tips on. **(b)** *(anlaufen lassen: Dampf)* to steam
up. **2** *vir (vi: aux sein) (Brille, Glas, Fenster)* to steam
up, to mist up; *(Wand)* to get covered in conden-
sation. **3** *adj (erfahren)* **in etw** *(dat)* **(gut)** ~ **sein** to
be (well-)versed in sth.
**Beschlagenheit** *f no pl* sound knowledge *or* grasp
*(in +dat* of*)*.
**Beschlagnahme** *f* **-n** confiscation, seizure.
**beschlagnahmen\*** *vt insep* **(a)** to confiscate, to
seize. **(b)** *(col: in Anspruch nehmen) (Mensch)* to
monopolize, to hog *(col)*; *(Arbeit)* Zeit to take up.
**Beschlagnahmung** *f* = **Beschlagnahme.**
**beschleunigen\* 1** *vtr* to accelerate, to speed up;
*Tempo auch* to increase; *Verfall* to hasten, to accelerate. **2** *vi (Fahrzeug, Fahrer)* to accelerate.
**Beschleuniger** *m* **-** *(Phys)* accelerator.
**beschleunigt** *adj* faster.
**Beschleunigung** *f* acceleration *(auch Aut, Phys)*,
speeding up; *(von Tempo auch)* increase; *(von Verfall etc)* hastening.
**beschließen\*** *irreg* **1** *vt* **(a)** to decide on; *Gesetz* to
pass. ~, **etw zu tun** to decide to do sth. **(b)** *(beenden)* to end. **2** *vi* **über etw** *(acc)* ~ to decide on sth.
**beschlossen** *adj (entschieden)* decided, agreed. **das
ist** ~**e Sache** that's settled.
**Beschluß** *m* ⁼**sse** decision, resolution. **einen** ~ **fassen** to pass a resolution; **auf** ~ **des Gerichts** by order of the court.
**Beschluß-: b**~**fähig** *adj* **b**~**fähig sein** to have a
quorum; ~**fähigkeit** *f no pl* quorum; ~**fassung** *f*
*(passing of a)* resolution; **b**~**unfähig** *adj* **b**~**unfähig sein** not to have a quorum.
**beschmeißen\*** *vt irreg (col: lit, fig)* to bombard.
**beschmieren\* 1** *vt Kleidung* to smear; *Wand* to be-
daub; *Tafel* to scribble *or* scrawl all over. **2** *vr* to
get (all) dirty.
**beschmutzen\* 1** *vt* to (make *or* get) dirty, to soil;
*(fig) Ruf, Namen* to besmirch. **2** *vr* to make *or* get

oneself dirty.
**beschneiden\*** *vt irreg* **(a)** *(stutzen)* to trim; *Sträucher etc* to prune. **(b)** *(Med, Rel)* to circumcise. **(c)**
*(fig: beschränken)* to cut back, to curtail.
**Beschneidung** *f no pl siehe vt* **(a)** trimming; pruning. **(b)** circumcision. **(c)** *(von Unterstützung etc)*
cut-back; *(von Rechten)* curtailing.
**beschneit** *adj* snow-covered; *Berge auch* snow-
capped.
**beschnüffeln\*, beschnuppern\* 1** *vt* to sniff at;
*(fig col)* to sniff out; *jdn* to size up. **2** *vr (Hunde)* to
sniff each other; *(fig col)* to size each other up.
**beschönigen\*** *vt* to gloss over. ~**der Ausdruck**
euphemism.
**Beschönigung** *f* glossing over.
**beschränken\* 1** *vt (auf +acc to)* to limit, to restrict. **2** *vr (auf +acc to)* to be limited *or* restricted;
*(esp Jur, Rede, Aufsatz etc auch)* to confine oneself;
*(sich einschränken)* to restrict oneself.
**beschrankt** *adj Bahnübergang* with gates.
**beschränkt** *adj* **(a)** *(eingeschränkt, knapp)* limited;
*Gebrauch auch* restricted. **wir sind zeitlich/finanziell**
~ we have only a limited amount of time/money;
**Gesellschaft mit** ~**er Haftung** limited company *(Brit)*,
corporation *(US)*. **(b)** *(pej) (geistig) Mensch* dim; *Intelligenz* limited; *(engstirnig auch)* narrow-minded.
**Beschränktheit** *f siehe adj* **(a)** limited nature. **(b)**
limited intelligence; narrow-mindedness.
**Beschränkung** *f* limitation, restriction. **jdm** ~**en
auferlegen** to impose restrictions on sb.
**beschreiben\*** *vt irreg* **(a)** *(auch Kreis)* to describe.
**sein Glück/Schmerz war nicht zu** ~ his happiness/
pain was indescribable; **ich kann dir nicht** ~, **wie** ...
I can't tell you how ... **(b)** *(vollschreiben)* to write
on. **ein eng beschriebenes Blatt** a closely written
sheet.
**Beschreibung** *f* **(a)** description. **(b)** *(Gebrauchsanweisung)* instructions *pl*.
**beschreien\*** *vt irreg (col)* **ich will es nicht** ~, **aber** ...
I don't want to tempt fate, but ...
**beschreiten\*** *vt irreg (lit geh, fig)* to follow.
**beschriften\*** *vt* to write on; *(mit Aufschrift)* to label.
**Beschriftung** *f* **(a)** *(das Beschriften)* labelling. **(b)**
*(Aufschrift)* writing; *(Etikett)* label.
**beschuldigen\*** *vt* to accuse; *(esp Jur auch, liter)* to
charge. **jdn einer Sache** *(gen)* ~ to accuse sb of sth;
to charge sb with sth.
**Beschuldigte(r)** *mf decl as adj* accused.
**Beschuldigung** *f* accusation; *(esp Jur auch, liter)*
charge.
**beschummeln\*** *vt (col)* to cheat. **jdn um etw** ~ to
cheat *or* diddle *(col)* sb out of sth.
**Beschuß** *m no pl (Mil)* fire; *(Phys)* bombarding. **jdn/
etw unter** ~ **nehmen** *(Mil)* to (start to) bombard *or*
shell sb/sth; *Stellung auch* to fire on sth; *(fig)* to attack sb/sth; **unter** ~ **geraten** *(Mil, fig)* to come under
fire.
**beschützen\*** *vt* to protect *(vor +dat* from*)*. ~**de
Werkstätte** sheltered workshop; ~**d** protective.
**Beschützer(in** *f) m* **-** protector.
**Beschützer**|**instinkt** *m* protective instinct.
**beschwatzen\*** *vt (col)* **(a)** *(überreden)* to talk over.
**(b)** *(bereden)* to chat about.
**Beschwerde** *f* **-n (a)** *(Mühe)* hardship. **(b)** ~**n** *pl*
*(Leiden)* trouble; **das macht mir immer noch** ~**n** it's
still giving me trouble. **(c)** *(Klage)* complaint; *(Jur)*
appeal. ~ **einlegen** *(form)* to lodge a complaint.
**Beschwerde-: b**~**frei** *adj* fit and healthy; ~**frist** *f*
*(Jur)* period of time during which an appeal may be
lodged.
**beschweren\* 1** *vt (mit Gewicht)* to weigh(t) down;

*(fig) (Kummer)* to weigh on; *(Mensch)* to burden. **2** *vr (sich beklagen)* to complain.

**beschwerlich** *adj* arduous.

**Beschwerlichkeit** *f* difficulty; *(von Reise, Aufgabe auch)* arduousness *no pl.*

**beschwichtigen*** *vt jdn* to appease, to pacify; *Kinder, jds Zorn, Gewissen* to soothe.

**Beschwichtigung** *f siehe vt* appeasement, pacification; soothing.

**beschwindeln*** *vt (col)* **(a)** *(belügen) jdn* ~ to tell sb a lie *or* a fib *(col)*. **(b)** *(betrügen)* to swindle.

**beschwingt** *adj* lively; *(Mensch)* elated.

**Beschwingtheit** *f siehe adj* liveliness; elation.

**beschwipst** *adj (col)* tipsy.

**beschwören*** *vt irreg* **(a)** *(beeiden)* to swear to; *(Jur auch)* to swear on oath. **(b)** *(anflehen)* to implore, to beseech. **(c)** *(Geister, Erinnerung)* to conjure up; *Schlangen* to charm.

**Beschwörung** *f* **(a)** *(das Flehen)* entreaty. **(b)** *siehe vt (c)* conjuring up; charming.

**beseelen*** *vt (erfüllen)* **neuer Mut beseelte ihn** he was filled with fresh courage.

**besehen*** *vt irreg* to (take a) look at.

**beseitigen*** *vt* **(a)** *(entfernen)* to remove, to get rid of; *Atommüll, Abfall* to dispose of; *Schwierigkeiten auch* to sort out; *Fehler auch* to eliminate; *Mißstände* to get rid of, to do away with. **(b)** *(euph: umbringen)* to get rid of.

**Beseitigung** *f no pl siehe vt* **(a)** removal, getting rid of; disposal; sorting out; elimination; getting rid of, doing away with. **(b)** getting rid of.

**Besen** *m* - **(a)** broom. **ich fresse einen** ~**, wenn das stimmt** *(col)* if that's right, I'll eat my hat *(col)*; **neue** ~ **kehren gut** *(Prov)* a new broom sweeps clean *(Prov)*. **(b)** *(pej col: Frau)* old bag *(col)*.

**Besen-:** ~**kammer** *f*, ~**schrank** *m* broom cupboard; ~**stiel** *m* broom-stick; **er ist steif wie ein** ~**stiel** he's as stiff as a ramrod.

**besessen** *adj (von bösen Geistern)* possessed *(von by)*; *(von einer Idee etc)* obsessed *(von with)*. **wie** ~ like one possessed.

**Besessene(r)** *mf decl as adj* one possessed *no art.* **die** ~**n** the possessed.

**Besessenheit** *f no pl siehe adj* possession; obsession.

**besetzen*** *vt* **(a)** *(dekorieren)* to trim; *(mit Edelsteinen)* to stud. **(b)** *(belegen)* to occupy; *(reservieren)* to reserve; *(füllen) Plätze, Stühle* to fill. **ist dieser Platz besetzt?** is this place taken?; *siehe* **besetzt. (c)** *(esp Mil)* to occupy; *(Hausbesetzer)* to squat in. **(d)** *Stelle* to fill; *(Theat) Rolle* to cast. **eine Stelle neu** ~ to find a new person for a job.

**Besetzer(in** *f)* *m (Haus*~*)* squatter.

**besetzt** *adj (belegt) Leitung* engaged *(Brit)*, busy; *WC* occupied, engaged *(Brit)*; *Abteil, Tisch* full (up); *(vorgebucht)* booked; *Abteil etc* taken.

**Besetztzeichen** *nt (Telec)* engaged *(Brit)* or busy tone.

**Besetzung** *f* **(a)** *(von Stelle)* filling; *(von Rolle)* casting; *(Theat: Schauspieler)* cast; *(Sport: Mannschaft)* team. **die Nationalelf in der neuen** ~ the new line-up for the national team; **zweite** ~ *(Theat)* understudy. **(b)** *(esp Mil)* occupation.

**besichtigen*** *vt (ansehen) Stadt, Kirche* to have a look at, to visit; *Betrieb* to tour; *(zur Prüfung) Haus* to view; *Ware, Truppen* to inspect.

**Besichtigung** *f (von Sehenswürdigkeiten)* sightseeing tour; *(von Museum etc)* tour; *(zur Prüfung) (von Haus)* viewing; *(von Truppen)* inspection.

**besiedeln*** *vt (ansiedeln)* to populate, to settle *(mit with)*; *(kolonisieren)* to colonize. **dicht/dünn besie-**

**delt** densely/thinly populated.

**Besied(e)lung** *f no pl siehe vt* settlement; colonization. **dichte/dünne** ~ dense/thin population.

**besiegeln*** *vt* to seal.

**besiegen*** *vt (schlagen)* to defeat, to beat; *(überwinden)* to overcome.

**Besiegte(r)** *mf decl as adj* loser.

**besingen*** *vt irreg* **(a)** *Schallplatte* to record. **(b)** *(rühmen)* **jdn/etw** ~ to sing the praises of sb/sth.

**besinnen*** *vr irreg (überlegen)* to reflect, to think; *(erinnern)* to remember *(auf jdn/etw* sb/sth*)*; *(es sich anders überlegen)* to have second thoughts. **sich anders** ~ to change one's mind; **sich eines Besseren** ~ to think better of sth; **ohne sich zu** ~ without a moment's thought *or* hesitation.

**besinnlich** *adj* thoughtful, contemplative.

**Besinnlichkeit** *f no pl* thoughtfulness, contemplativeness.

**Besinnung** *f no pl* **(a)** consciousness. **bei/ohne** ~ **sein** to be conscious/unconscious; **die** ~ **verlieren** to lose consciousness; *(fig)* to lose one's head; **zur** ~ **kommen** to regain consciousness; *(fig)* to come to one's senses; **jdn zur** ~ **bringen** *(fig)* to bring sb to his senses. **(b)** *(das Sich-Besinnen)* contemplation *(auf +acc* of*)*.

**Besinnungs-:** **b**~**los** *adj* unconscious; *(fig)* blind; ~**losigkeit** *f no pl (lit)* unconsciousness.

**Besitz** *m no pl* **(a)** possession. **im** ~ **von etw sein** to be in possession of sth; **etw in** ~ **nehmen** to take possession of sth; **von etw** ~ **ergreifen** to seize possession of sth; **in privatem** ~ in private ownership. **(b)** *(Eigentum)* property; *(Landgut)* estate.

**Besitz-:** ~**anspruch** *m* claim of ownership; *(Jur)* title; **seine** ~**ansprüche** *(auf etw acc)* **anmelden** to lay claim to sth; **b**~**anzeigend** *adj (Gram)* possessive.

**besitzen*** *vt irreg* to possess, to own; *Führerschein, Wertpapiere auch* to hold; *Narbe, grüne Augen* to have; *Fähigkeiten* to have, to possess. **die** ~**den Klassen** the propertied classes.

**Besitzer(in** *f)* *m* - owner; *(von Wertpapieren auch, von Führerschein etc)* holder; *(Laden*~*, Hotel*~ *etc auch)* proprietor. **den** ~ **wechseln** to change hands.

**Besitz-:** ~**ergreifung** *f* seizure; **b**~**los** *adj* having no possessions; ~**nahme** *f no pl* seizure; ~**stand** *m (form)* assets *pl*; *(fig)* vested rights; ~**tum** *nt (Eigentum)* property *no pl*; *(Grundbesitz)* estate(s *pl*), property.

**Besitzung** *f (privater Landbesitz)* estate(s *pl*).

**besoffen** *adj (col) (betrunken)* plastered *(Brit col)*, smashed *(col)*.

**Besoffene(r)** *mf decl as adj (col)* drunk.

**besohlen*** *vt* to sole; *(neu* ~*)* to resole.

**besolden*** *vt* to pay.

**Besoldung** *f* pay.

**besondere(r, s)** *adj* special; *(bestimmt)* particular; *(hervorragend)* Qualität, Schönheit etc exceptional. **eine ganz** ~ **Anstrengung** a quite exceptional effort; **unser** ~**s Interesse gilt ...** we are particularly *or* (e)specially interested in ...; **ohne** ~ **Begeisterung** without any particular enthusiasm; **im** ~**n** *(im einzelnen)* in particular cases; *(vor allem)* in particular.

**Besondere(s)** *nt decl as adj* **etwas/nichts** ~**s** something/nothing special; **das** ~ **daran** what is special about it.

**Besonderheit** *f* special feature; *(besondere Eigenschaft)* peculiarity.

**besonders** *adv* particularly, (e)specially. **nicht** ~ **viel Geld** not a particularly large amount of money; **das Essen/der Film war nicht** ~ *(col)* the food/film was nothing special *or* nothing to write home about *(col)*; **wie geht's dir? − nicht ~** *(col)* how are you? − not too hot *(col)*.

**besonnen** *adj* considered, level-headed. **ihre ruhige, ~e Art** her calm and collected way.

**Besonnenheit** *f no pl* level-headedness, calm.

**besonnt** *adj* sunny.

**besorgen*** *vt* **(a)** *(kaufen, beschaffen etc)* to get; *(euph col: stehlen)* to acquire *(euph col)*. **jdm/sich etw ~** to get sth for sb/oneself. **(b)** *(erledigen)* to attend *or* see to. **(c)** *(versorgen)* to take care of, to look after. **(d)** *(col)* **es jdm ~** to sort sb out *(col)*, to fix sb *(col)*. **(e)** *(col!: sexuell)* **es jdm ~** to have it off with sb *(col)*.

**Besorgnis** *f* anxiety, worry.

**besorgnis|erregend** *adj* alarming, worrying.

**besorgt** *adj* **(a)** *(voller Sorge)* anxious, worried *(wegen* about*)*. **(b) um jdn/etw ~ sein** to be concerned about sb/sth.

**Besorgtheit** *f no pl* concern.

**Besorgung** *f* **(a)** *(das Kaufen)* purchase. **(b) die ~ des Haushaltes** looking after the house. **(c)** *(Einkauf)* **~en machen** to do some shopping.

**bespannen*** *vt* **(a)** *(mit Material)* to cover; *(mit Saiten, Fäden)* to string. **(b)** *(Wagen* to harness up.

**Bespannung** *f* **(a)** *no pl* covering; *(mit Saiten etc)* stringing; *(mit Pferden)* harnessing. **(b)** *(Material)* covering; *(Saiten, Fäden etc)* strings *pl*.

**bespielbar** *adj Rasen etc* playable.

**bespielen*** *vt* **(a)** *Tonband* to record on. **das Band ist mit klassischer Musik bespielt** the tape has a recording of classical music on it. **(b)** *(Sport)* to play on.

**bespitzeln*** *vt* to spy on.

**Bespitz(e)lung** *f* spying.

**besprechen*** *irreg* **1** *vt* **(a)** to discuss, to talk about. **wie besprochen** as arranged. **(b)** *(rezensieren)* to review. **(c)** *Tonband* to make a recording on. **2** *vr* **sich mit jdm ~** to confer with sb *(über +acc* about*)*.

**Besprechung** *f* **(a)** discussion, talk; *(Konferenz)* meeting. **er ist bei einer ~, er hat eine ~** he's in a meeting. **(b)** *(Rezension)* review, notice.

**Besprechungs-: ~-exemplar** *nt* review copy; **~zimmer** *nt* conference room.

**besprengen*** *vt* to sprinkle.

**bespringen*** *vt irreg (Tier)* to mount, to cover.

**bespritzen*** *vt* to spray; *(beschmutzen)* to spatter.

**besprühen*** *vt* to spray.

**bespucken*** *vt* to spit at.

**besser** *adj, adv, comp of* **gut** better. **~e Leute** a better class of people; **er hat ~e Tage gesehen** *(iro)* he has seen better days; **du willst wohl etwas B~es sein!** *(col)* I suppose you think you're better than other people; **~ ist ~** (it is) better to be on the safe side; **um so ~!** *(col)* so much the better!; **~ (gesagt)** or rather; **sie will immer alles ~ wissen** she always thinks she knows better; **das ist auch ~ so** it's better that way; **B~es zu tun haben** to have better things to do; **das solltest du ~ nicht tun** you had better not do that; **dann geh ich ~** then I'd better go; **das Essen war nur ein ~er Imbiß** the meal was just a glorified snack.

**bessergehen** *vi impers sep irreg aux sein* **es geht jdm besser** sb is feeling better; **jetzt geht's der Firma wieder besser** the firm is doing better again now.

**bessern** **1** *vt* to improve, to make better; *Verbrecher etc* to reform. **2** *vr (moralisch, im Benehmen)* to mend one's ways.

**besser-: ~stehen** *vr sep irreg (col)* to be better off; **~stellen** *vt sep* **jdn ~stellen** to improve sb's finan-

cial position.

**Besserung** *f no pl* improvement; *(von Verbrecher etc)* reformation; *(genesung)* recovery. **gute ~!** I hope you get better soon; **auf dem Wege der ~ sein** to be getting better, to be improving; *(Patient auch)* to be on the road to recovery.

**Besser-: ~wessi** *m (col)* snooty West German *(who treats Germans from the former GDR condescendingly)*; **~wisser** *m* - *(col)* know-all, know-it-all *(US)*; **b~wisserisch** *adj (col)* know-all *etc attr*.

**Bestand** *m* ∸e **(a)** *(Fortdauer)* continued existence, continuance. **von ~ sein/~ haben** to be permanent, to endure. **(b)** *(vorhandene Menge, Tiere)* stock *(an +dat* of*)*. **~ aufnehmen** to take stock.

**bestanden** *adj* **(a) mit Bäumen ~e Alleen/Abhänge** tree-lined avenues/tree-covered slopes. **(b) nach ~er Prüfung** after passing the/an exam; **bei nicht ~er Prüfung** if you *etc* don't pass the exam.

**beständig** *adj* **(a)** *no pred (dauernd)* constant, continual. **(b)** *(gleichbleibend)* constant; *Mitarbeiter* steady; *Wetter* settled. **(c)** *no adv (widerstandsfähig)* resistant *(gegen* to*)*; *(dauerhaft)* Freundschaft lasting.

**Beständigkeit** *f no pl siehe adj* **(a)** continual nature. **(b)** constancy; steadiness; settledness. **(c)** resistance; lastingness.

**Bestands|aufnahme** *f* stock-taking.

**Bestandteil** *m* component, part; *(fig)* integral part. **sich in seine ~e auflösen** to fall to pieces.

**bestärken*** *vt* to confirm. **jdn in seinem Vorsatz/Wunsch ~** to confirm sb in his intention/desire.

**Bestärkung** *f* confirmation.

**bestätigen*** **1** *vt* **(a)** to confirm; *(beurkunden auch)* to certify; *(Jur) Urteil* to uphold. **sich in etw *(dat)* bestätigt finden** to be confirmed in sth; **... sagte er ~d** ... he said in confirmation; **jdn (im Amt) ~** to confirm sb's appointment. **(b)** *(Comm) Empfang, Brief* to acknowledge (receipt of). **2** *vr* to be confirmed, to be proved true.

**Bestätigung** *f siehe vt* **(a)** confirmation; upholding. **(b)** acknowledgement (of receipt).

**bestatten*** *vt* to bury. **wann wird er bestattet** when is the funeral (service)?

**Bestatter** *m* - undertaker, mortician *(US)*.

**Bestattung** *f* burial; *(Feuer~)* cremation; *(Feier auch)* funeral.

**Bestattungs-: ~institut, ~unternehmen** *nt* undertaker's, mortician *(US)*; **~unternehmer** *m* undertaker, mortician *(US)*.

**bestäuben*** *vt* to dust; *(Bot)* to pollinate.

**Bestäubung** *f* dusting; *(Bot)* pollination.

**bestaunen*** *vt* to marvel at, to gaze in wonder.

**beste** *siehe* **beste(r, s)**.

**bestechen*** *irreg* **1** *vt* **(a)** to bribe. **ich lasse mich nicht ~** I'm not open to bribery. **(b)** *(beeindrucken)* to captivate. **2** *vi (Eindruck machen)* to be impressive *(durch* because of*)*.

**bestechend** *adj Schönheit, Eindruck* captivating; *Angebot* tempting.

**bestechlich** *adj* bribable, corruptible.

**Bestechlichkeit** *f no pl* corruptibility.

**Bestechung** *f* bribery; *(von Beamten etc auch)* corruption.

**Bestechungs-: ~geld** *nt usu pl*, **~summe** *f* bribe; **~versuch** *m* attempted bribery.

**Besteck** *nt* -e **(a)** *(Eß~)* knives and forks *pl*, cutlery *sing*; *(Set, für ein Gedeck)* set of cutlery. **(b)** *(Instrumentensatz)* set of instruments. **chirurgisches ~** (set of) surgical instruments.

**Besteckkasten** *m* cutlery canteen.

**bestehen*** *irreg* **1** *vt* **(a)** *Examen, Probe* to pass; **sie-**

*he* **bestanden. (b)** *Schicksalsschläge* to withstand; *Gefahr* to overcome; *Kampf* to win.
  **2** *vi* **(a)** *(existieren)* to exist. **die Universität besteht seit hundert Jahren** the university has been in existence *or* has existed for a hundred years; **es besteht die Hoffnung/der Verdacht, daß ...** there is (a) hope/a suspicion that ... **(b)** *(Bestand haben)* to continue to exist; *(Zweifel, Problem etc auch)* to persist. **(c)** *(sich zusammensetzen)* to consist *(aus of)*. **in etw** *(dat)* ~ to consist in sth; *(Aufgabe)* to involve sth; **seine einzige Chance besteht darin, zu ...** his only chance is to ...; **die Schwierigkeit/das Problem besteht darin, daß ...** the difficulty/problem lies in the fact that ..., the difficulty/problem is that ... **(d)** *(standhalten, sich bewähren)* to hold one's own *(in +dat* in). **vor etw** *(dat)* ~ to stand up against sth. **(e)** *(bei Prüfung etc)* to pass. **(f) auf etw** *(dat)* ~ to insist on sth; **ich bestehe darauf** I insist.
**Bestehen** *nt no pl* **(a)** existence. **seit** ~ **der Firma** ever since the firm came into existence. **(b)** *(Beharren)* insistence *(auf +dat* von). **(c)** *(von Prüfung etc)* passing.
**bestehenbleiben** *vi sep irreg aux sein* to last, to endure; *(Frage, Hoffnung)* to remain.
**bestehend** *adj* existing; *Gesetze auch, Preise* present, current.
**bestehlen\*** *vt irreg* to rob *(um etw of sth)*.
**besteigen\*** *vt irreg Berg, Leiter* to climb; *Fahrrad, Pferd* to mount, to get *or* climb on(to); *Bus, Flugzeug* to get on; *Auto* to get into; *Thron* to ascend.
**Besteigung** *f* climbing, ascent.
**bestellen\*** **1** *vt* **(a)** *(anfordern, in Restaurant)* to order. **sich** *(dat)* **etw** ~ to order sth; **das Material ist bestellt** the material has been ordered *or* is on order. **(b)** *(reservieren)* to book, to reserve. **(c)** *(ausrichten)* **bestell ihm (von mir), daß ...** tell him (from me) that ...; **soll ich irgend etwas** ~**?** can I take a message?; ~ **Sie ihm schöne Grüße von mir** give him my regards; **er hat hier nicht viel/nichts zu** ~ he doesn't have much/any say here. **(d)** *(kommen lassen)* *jdn* to send for, to summon. **ich bin für 10 Uhr bestellt** I have an appointment for *or* at 10 o'clock; **wie bestellt und nicht abgeholt dastehen** *(hum col)* to stand there looking stupid *or* like orphan Annie *(col)*. **(e)** *(einsetzen, ernennen)* to nominate, to appoint. **(f)** *(bearbeiten)* *Land* to till. **(g)** *(fig)* **es ist schlecht um ihn bestellt** he is in a bad way. **2** *vi (in Restaurant)* to order.
**Besteller** *m* - customer.
**Bestell-:** ~**menge** *f* order quantity; ~**nummer** *f* order number; ~**schein** *m* order form.
**Bestellung** *f* **(a)** *(Anforderung, das Angeforderte)* order; *(das Bestellen)* ordering. **(b)** *(Reservierung)* booking, reservation. **(c)** *(Ernennung)* nomination, appointment. **(d)** *(von Land)* tilling.
**besten** *adv:* **am** ~ *siehe* **beste(r, s) 2.**
**bestenfalls** *adv* at best.
**bestens** *adv (sehr gut)* very well.
**beste(r, s)** **1** *adj, superl of* **gut (a)** *attr* best. **im** ~**n Fall** at (the) best; **in** ~**n Händen** in the best of hands. **(b) das** ~ **wäre, wir ...** the best thing would be for us to...; **es steht nicht zum** ~**n** it does not look too promising *or* good; **jdn zum** ~**n halten** to pull sb's leg, to have sb on *(col)*; **etw zum** ~**n geben** *(erzählen)* to tell sth. **(c) der/die/das B**~ the best; **ich will nur dein B**~**s** I've your best interests at heart; **sein B**~**s geben** to give of one's best. **2** *adv* **am** ~**n** best; **am** ~**n gehe ich jetzt** I'd *or* I had best be going now.
**Beste(s)** *nt siehe* **beste(r, s) 1 (c).**
**besteuern\*** *vt* to tax.

**Besteuerung** *f* taxation; *(Steuersatz)* tax.
**Bestform** *f (esp Sport)* top *or* best form.
**bestialisch** *adj* bestial; *(col)* awful, beastly *(col)*.
**Bestialität** *f* bestiality.
**besticken\*** *vt* to embroider.
**Bestie** [-tiə] *f* beast; *(fig)* animal.
**bestimmen\*** **1** *vt* **(a)** to determine; *Zeitpunkt etc auch* to fix, to set; *(entscheiden auch)* to decide; *Landschaft etc* to characterize; *Pflanze, Funde* to classify. **(b)** *(vorsehen)* to intend, to mean *(für for)*. **er ist zu Höherem bestimmt** he is destined for higher things; **wir waren füreinander bestimmt** we were meant for each other. **2** *vi* to decide *(über +acc* on). **du hast hier nicht zu** ~ you don't make the decisions here; **er kann über sein Geld allein** ~ it is up to him what he does with his money.
**bestimmend** *adj* *Faktor, Einfluß* determining, decisive. **für etw** ~ **sein** to be characteristic of sth; *(entscheidend)* to have a determining influence on sth.
**bestimmt** **1** *adj* **(a)** definite; *(gewiß)* certain; *(festgesetzt)* *Preis, Tag* set, fixed. **suchen Sie etwas B**~**es?** are you looking for anything in particular? **(b)** *(entschieden)* *Auftreten, Ton* firm, decisive. **2** *adv* **(a)** *(sicher)* definitely, certainly. **ich weiß ganz** ~**, daß ...** I know for sure *or* for certain that ...; **ich komme ganz** ~ I'll definitely come. **(b)** *(wahrscheinlich)* no doubt. **das hat er** ~ **verloren** he's bound to have lost it.
**Bestimmtheit** *f* **(a)** *(Sicherheit)* certainty. **ich weiß aber mit** ~**, daß ...** but I know for sure *or* for certain that ... **(b)** *(Entschiedenheit)* firmness. **in** *or* **mit aller** ~ quite categorically.
**Bestimmung** *f* **(a)** *(Vorschrift)* regulation. **(b)** *no pl (Zweck)* purpose. **eine Anlage ihrer** ~ **übergeben** to officially open a new plant. **(c)** *(Schicksal)* destiny. **(d)** *(das Bestimmen)* determining; *(von Zeit etc)* fixing, setting; *(von Pflanze, Funden)* classification.
**Bestimmungs-:** ~**bahnhof** *m* (station of) destination; **b**~**gemäß** *adj* as agreed; ~**hafen** *m* (port of) destination; ~**land** *nt*, ~**ort** *m* destination.
**Best-:** ~**leistung** *f (esp Sport)* best performance; **seine persönliche** ~**leistung** his personal best; **b**~**möglich** *adj no pred* best possible.
**Best.-Nr.** = **Bestellnummer.**
**bestrafen\*** *vt* to punish; *(Jur)* jdn to sentence *(mit* to); *(Sport)* *Spieler, Foul* to penalize.
**Bestrafung** *f siehe vt* punishment, sentencing; penalization.
**bestrahlen\*** *vt* to shine on; *(beleuchten)* *Gebäude, Bühne* to light up, to illuminate; *(Med)* to give radiotherapy to; *(mit Höhensonne)* to give ultra-violet treatment to.
**Bestrahlung** *f* illumination; *(Med)* radiotherapy; *(mit Höhensonne)* ultra-violet treatment.
**Bestreben** *nt no pl* endeavour *(Brit)*, endeavor *(US)*.
**bestrebt** *adj* ~ **sein, etw zu tun** to endeavour *(Brit)* *or* endeavor *(US)* to do sth.
**bestreichen\*** *vt irreg* to spread; *(mit Farbe)* to paint. **etw mit Butter/Fett/Öl** ~ to butter/grease/oil sth.
**bestreiken\*** *vt* to black. **bestreikt** strikebound; **die Fabrik wird zur Zeit bestreikt** there's a strike on in the factory at the moment.
**bestreiten\*** *vt irreg* **(a)** *(abstreiten)* to dispute, to challenge; *(leugnen)* to deny. **jdm das Recht auf ...** ~ to dispute *etc* sb's right to ...; **das will ich nicht** ~ I'm not disputing *or* denying it. **(b)** *(finanzieren)* to pay for, to finance; *Kosten* to carry. **(c) er hat das ganze Gespräch allein bestritten** he did all the talking; **die Mannschaft hat fünf Spiele in zwei Wochen bestritten** the team has played five games in two

weeks.

**bestreuen*** *vt* to cover *(mit* with*)*; *(Cook)* to sprinkle.

**Bestseller** ['bɛst-] *m* - best-seller.

**Bestseller-:** ~**autor** *m* best-selling author; ~**liste** *f* best-seller list.

**bestücken*** *vt* to fit, to equip; *(Mil)* to arm; *Lager* to stock.

**Bestuhlung** *f* seating *no indef art.*

**bestürmen*** *vt* to storm; *(mit Fragen, Bitten)* to bombard; *(mit Briefen, Anrufen)* to inundate.

**bestürzen*** *vt* to fill with consternation, to dismay.

**bestürzend** *adj* alarming.

**bestürzt** *adj* filled with consternation, dismayed. **er sah mich** ~ **an** he looked at me in consternation.

**Bestürzung** *f* consternation.

**Bestzeit** *f (esp Sport)* best time.

**Besuch** *m* **-e** (a) visit *(gen* to*)*; *(von Schule, Veranstaltung)* attendance *(gen* at*)*. **bei jdm zu** ~ **sein** to be visiting sb; **(von jdm)** ~ **erhalten** to have *or* get a visit (from sb). (b) *(Besucher)* visitor; visitors *pl.* **er hat** ~ he has visitors/a visitor.

**besuchen*** *vt jdn* to visit. *Vortrag, Schule, Kino etc* to go to.

**Besucher(in** *f) m* - visitor; *(pl: Publikum)* audience. **etwa 1000** ~ **waren zu der Veranstaltung gekommen** about 1,000 people attended the event.

**Besuchs-:** ~**erlaubnis** *f (für Land)* visa; ~**erlaubnis haben** to be allowed to receive visitors; ~**zeit** *f* visiting time.

**besucht** *adj* **gut/schlecht** ~ **sein** to be well/badly attended.

**besudeln*** *vt (geh) Wände* to smear; *Kleidung, Hände* to soil; *(fig) Namen, Ehre* to sully.

**betagt** *adj (geh)* aged, advanced in years.

**betanken*** *vt Fahrzeug* to fill up; *Flugzeug* to refuel.

**betasten*** *vt* to feel.

**Betastrahlen** *pl* beta rays *pl.*

**betätigen*** **1** *vt* to operate; *Muskeln, Gehirn* to activate; *Bremse auch* to apply. **2** *vr* to busy oneself; *(körperlich)* to get some exercise. **sich als jd/etw** ~ to act as sb/sth; **sich politisch** ~ to be active in politics; **sich literarisch/künstlerisch** ~ to do some writing/painting.

**Betätigung** *f* (a) *(Tätigkeit)* activity. (b) *siehe vt* (a) operation; activation; application.

**betäuben*** *vt (unempfindlich machen)* to deaden; *(durch Narkose)* to anaesthetize *(Brit)*, to anesthetize *(US)*; *(fig: benommen machen)* to stun. **seinen Kummer mit Alkohol** ~ to drown one's sorrows (in drink); ~**der Lärm** deafening noise; **ein** ~**der Duft** an overpowering scent.

**Betäubung** *f (Narkose)* anaesthetic *(Brit)*, anesthetic *(US)*. **örtliche** ~ local anaesthetic.

**Betäubungsmittel** *nt* anaesthetic *(Brit)*, anesthetic *(US)*.

**Bete** *f* -**n** beet. **rote** ~ beetroot.

**beteiligen*** **1** *vt jdn an etw (dat)* ~ to involve sb in sth; *(finanziell)* to give sb a share in sth. **2** *vr* to take part, to participate *(an +dat* in*)*; *(finanziell)* to have a share *(an +dat* in*)*. **sich an den Unkosten** ~ to contribute to the expenses.

**beteiligt** *adj* **an etw (dat)** ~ **sein/werden** to be involved in sth, to have a part in sth; *(finanziell)* to have a share in sth.

**Beteiligte(r)** *mf decl as adj* person involved; *(an Diskussion auch)* participant; *(Teilhaber)* partner; *(Jur)* party.

**Beteiligung** *f no pl (Teilnahme) (an +dat* in*)* participation; *(finanziell)* share; *(an Unfall)* involvement.

**beten 1** *vi* to pray *(um, für* for, *zu* to*)*, to say one's

prayers; *(bei Tisch)* to say grace. **2** *vt* to say.

**beteuern*** *vt* to declare; *Unschuld auch* to protest.

**Beteuerung** *f siehe vt* declaration; protestation.

**Bethlehem** *nt* Bethlehem.

**betiteln*** *vt* to entitle; *(anreden)* to address as; *(col: beschimpfen)* to call.

**Beton** [be'tɔŋ, be'tõː] *m* -**s** concrete.

**betonen*** *vt* to stress; *(hervorheben)* to emphasize; *siehe* **betont.**

**betonieren*** *vti* to concrete. **betoniert** concrete.

**Beton-:** ~**klotz** *m* concrete block; ~**mischmaschine** *f* concrete-mixer.

**betont** *adj Höflichkeit* emphatic, deliberate; *Kühle, Sachlichkeit* pointed. **sich** ~ **einfach kleiden** to dress with pronounced simplicity.

**Betonung** *f* (a) *no pl siehe vt* stressing; emphasis. (b) *(Akzent, fig: Gewicht)* stress, emphasis.

**Betonungszeichen** *nt* stress mark.

**Betonwüste** *f (pej)* concrete jungle.

**betören*** *vt* to bewitch, to beguile.

**Betr.** = **Betreff** re, ref.

**betr.** = **betreffend** regarding, re.

**Betracht** *m no pl etw außer* ~ **lassen** to leave sth out of consideration, to disregard sth; **in** ~ **kommen** to be considered; **nicht in** ~ **kommen** to be out of the question; **jdn/etw in** ~ **ziehen** to take sb/sth into consideration.

**betrachten*** *vt* (a) *(sehen, beurteilen)* to look at. **so/objektiv betrachtet** from this/an objective point of view; **bei näherem B**~ on closer examination. (b) **als jdn/etw** ~ to regard *or* look upon *or* consider as sb/sth.

**Betrachter(in** *f) m* - observer.

**beträchtlich** *adj* considerable.

**Betrachtung** *f* (a) *(das Betrachten)* contemplation. **bei näherer** ~ on closer examination. (b) *(Überlegung)* reflection. **über etw (acc)** ~**en anstellen** to reflect on *or* contemplate sth.

**Betrachtungsweise** *f* **er hat eine andere** ~ he has a different way of looking at things.

**Betrag** *m* ⸚**e** amount, sum.

**betragen*** *irreg* **1** *vi* to be; *(Kosten, Rechnung auch)* to come to, to amount to. **der Unterschied beträgt 100 DM** the difference is *or* amounts to 100 marks. **2** *vr* to behave.

**Betragen** *nt no pl* behaviour *(Brit)*, behavior *(US)*; *(esp im Zeugnis)* conduct.

**betrauen*** *vt jdn mit etw* ~ to entrust sb with sth.

**betrauern*** *vt* to mourn.

**beträufeln*** *vt* **den Fisch mit Zitrone** ~ to sprinkle lemon juice on the fish.

**Betreff** *m* -**e** *(form)* ~: **Ihr Schreiben vom** ... re *or* reference your letter of ...

**betreffen*** *vt irreg (angehen)* to concern. **von dieser Regelung werde ich nicht betroffen** this does not concern *or* affect me; **was mich betrifft** ... as far as I'm concerned ...; „**Betrifft:**" "re:"; *siehe* **betroffen.**

**betreffend** *adj attr (erwähnt)* in question; *(zuständig, für etw relevant)* relevant. **das** ~**e Wort richtig einsetzen** to insert the appropriate word in the right place.

**betreffs** *prep +gen (form)* concerning, regarding.

**betreiben*** *vt irreg* (a) *(vorantreiben)* to push ahead. **auf jds B**~ **hin** at sb's instigation. (b) *Gewerbe, Handwerk* to carry on; *Handel auch* to do; *Politik* to pursue. (c) *(Tech)* to operate.

**betreten[1]*** *vt irreg* to enter, to go/come into; *Spielfeld, Bühne, Brücke* to step onto; *(fig) Zeitalter etc* to enter. „**B**~ **(des Rasens) verboten!**" "Keep off (the grass)".

**betreten²** *adj* embarrassed.
**Betretenheit** *f* embarrassment.
**betreuen\*** *vt* to look after.
**Betreuer(in** *f)* *m* carer; *(Kinder~)* child-minder.
wir suchen noch ~ für ... we are still looking for people to look after ...
**Betreuung** *f* looking after; *(von Patienten, Tieren etc)* care. **er wurde mit der ~ der Gruppe beauftragt** he was put in charge of the group.
**Betrieb** *m* -e (a) *(Firma)* business, concern; *(Fabrik)* factory, works *sing or pl.* (b) *(Tätigkeit)* work; *(von Maschine, Fabrik)* working, operation. **er hält den ganzen ~ auf** he's holding everything up; **außer ~** out of order; **die Maschinen sind in ~** the machines are running; **eine Maschine in/außer ~ setzen** to start a machine up/to stop a machine; **eine Maschine/Fabrik in ~ nehmen** to put a machine/factory into operation. (c) *(Betriebsamkeit)* bustle. **in den Geschäften herrscht großer ~** the shops are very busy.
**betrieblich** *adj attr* company *attr.* **eine Sache ~ regeln** to settle a matter within the company.
**Betriebs-** *in cpds (Fabrik-)* factory, works; *(Firmen-)* company.
**betriebsam** *adj* busy, bustling *no adv.*
**Betriebsamkeit** *f* bustle; *(von Mensch)* active nature.
**Betriebs-:** ~**angehörige(r)** *mf* employee; ~**anleitung** *f* operating instructions *pl;* ~**ausflug** *m* staff outing; **b~bereit** *adj* operational; **b~blind** *adj* **b~blind sein** to have become blind to organizational faults at work; **b~eigen** *adj* company *attr;* ~**ferien** *pl* (annual) company holiday, vacation close-down *(US);* ~**führung** *f* management; ~**geheimnis** *nt* trade secret; **b~intern** *adj* in-house; internal company *attr;* **etw b~intern regeln** to settle sth within the company; ~**klima** *nt* working atmosphere; ~**kosten** *pl (von Firma etc)* overheads *pl; (von Maschine)* running costs *pl;* ~**leiter** *m* (works or factory) manager; ~**leitung** *f* management; ~**prüfung** *f* (government) audit; ~**rat** *m* (a) *(Gremium)* works council. (b) *(col: Person)* works council member; ~**schluß** *m (von Firma)* end of business hours; *(von Fabrik)* end of factory hours; **nach ~schluß** after business/factory hours; **b~sicher** *adj* safe (to operate); ~**störung** *f* breakdown; ~**system** *nt (Comp)* operating system; ~**unfall** *m* industrial accident; *(hum col)* accident; ~**vereinbarung** *f* in-house agreement; ~**versammlung** *f* staff meeting; ~**wirt** *m* management expert; ~**wirtschaft** *f* business management.
**betrinken\*** *vr irreg* to get drunk; *siehe* **betrunken.**
**betroffen** *adj* (a) affected *(von* by). (b) *(bestürzt)* taken aback; *Schweigen* awkward.
**Betroffene(r)** *mf decl as adj* person affected.
**Betroffenheit** *f* consternation.
**betrüben\*** *vt* to sadden, to distress.
**betrüblich** *adj* sad, distressing; *Zustände* deplorable.
**betrübt** *adj* saddened, distressed.
**Betrug** *m no pl* deceit, deception; *(Jur)* fraud. **das ist ja (alles) ~** it's (all) a cheat *or* fraud.
**betrügen** *vt irreg* to deceive; *(geschäftlich auch)* to cheat; *Freund(in), Ehepartner auch* to be unfaithful to; *(Jur)* to defraud. **jdn um etw ~** to cheat sb out of sth; *(Jur)* to defraud sb of sth; **ich fühle mich betrogen** I feel betrayed; **sich um etw betrogen sehen** to feel deprived of sth.
**Betrüger(in** *f)* *m* - *(beim Spiel)* cheat; *(geschäftlich)* swindler; *(Jur)* defrauder.

**Betrügerei** *f* deceit; *(geschäftlich)* cheating *no pl,* swindling *no pl; (von Ehepartner)* deceiving *no pl; (Jur)* fraud.
**betrügerisch** *adj* deceitful; *(Jur)* fraudulent. **in ~er Absicht** with intent to defraud.
**betrunken** *adj* drunk *no adv,* drunken *attr.* **Fahren in ~em Zustand** drunk driving.
**Betrunkene(r)** *mf decl as adj* drunk.
**Bett** *nt* -en bed. **an jds ~** *(dat)* **sitzen** to sit at sb's bedside *or* by sb's bed; **im ~** in bed; **jdn ins *or* zu ~ bringen** to put sb to bed; **ins *or* zu ~ gehen** to go to bed; **mit jdm das ~ teilen** to share sb's bed; **er hat sich ins gemachte ~ gelegt** *(fig)* he had everything handed to him on a plate.
**Bett-:** ~**bezug** *m* quilt cover; ~**couch** *f* bed settee; ~**decke** *f* blanket; *(gesteppt)* (continental) quilt, duvet.
**Bettel-:** **b~arm** *adj* destitute; ~**brief** *m* begging letter.
**Bettelei** *f* begging.
**Bettelmönch** *m* mendicant *or* begging monk.
**betteln** *vi* to beg. **(bei jdm) um etw ~** to beg (sb) for sth.
**Bettelstab** *m:* **jdn an den ~ bringen** to reduce sb to beggary.
**betten** *vt (legen)* to make a bed for, to bed down; *Kopf* to lay. **wie man sich bettet, so liegt man** *(Prov)* as you make your bed so you must lie on it *(Prov);* **er hat sich weich gebettet** *(fig)* he's feathered his nest.
**Bett-:** ~**feder** *f* bedspring; ~**federn** *pl (Daunen)* bed feathers; ~**geflüster** *nt* pillow talk; ~**genosse** *m (dated, iro)* bedfellow; ~**gestell** *nt* bedstead; ~**hupferl** *nt* - *(SGer)* bedtime sweet; ~**kante** *f* edge of the bed; ~**kasten** *m* linen drawer; **b~lägerig** *adj* bedridden, confined to bed; ~**laken** *nt* sheet; ~**lektüre** *f* bedtime reading.
**Bettler(in** *f)* *m* - beggar.
**Bett-:** ~**nässen** *nt no pl* bed-wetting; ~**nässer** *m* - bed-wetter; ~**pfanne** *f* bedpan; ~**pfosten** *m* bedpost; ~**rand** *m* edge of the bed; ~**ruhe** *f* bed rest; ~**schwere** *f (col)* **die nötige ~schwere haben/bekommen** to be/get tired enough to sleep; ~**sofa** *nt* sofa bed.
**Bettuch** *nt* sheet.
**Bett-:** ~**vorleger** *m* bedside rug; ~**wäsche** *f* bed linen; ~**zeug** *nt* bedding.
**betucht** *adj (col)* well-to-do.
**betulich** *adj* (a) *(übertrieben besorgt)* fussing *attr; Redeweise* twee. (b) *(beschaulich)* leisurely *no adv.*
**betupfen\*** *vt* to dab; *(Med)* to swab.
**Beuge** *f* -n bend; *(Rumpf~)* forward bend; *(seitlich)* sideways bend; *(Knie~)* knee-bend.
**Beugehaft** *f (Jur)* coercive detention.
**beugen 1** *vt* (a) to bend; *(Phys) Wellen* to diffract; *Strahlen, Licht* to deflect; *(fig) Stolz, Starrsinn* to break. **das Recht ~** to pervert the course of justice; **vom Alter gebeugt** bent *or* bowed by age; **von Kummer/Gram gebeugt** bowed down with grief/sorrow; *siehe* **gebeugt.** (b) *(Gram)* to decline; *Verb* to conjugate. **2** *vr* to bend; *(fig)* to submit, to bow *(dat* to). **sich aus dem Fenster ~** to lean out of the window; **er beugte sich zu mir herüber** he leant across to me.
**Beugung** *f siehe vt* (a) bending, diffraction; deflection; breaking. (b) declension; conjugation.
**Beule** *f* -n *(von Stoß etc)* bump; *(Delle)* dent.
**be|unruhigen\* 1** *vt* to worry. **über etw** *(acc)* **beunruhigt sein** to be worried about sth. **2** *vr* to worry (oneself) *(über +acc, wegen* about*).*
**Be|unruhigung** *f* concern.

**be|urkunden\*** *vt* to certify; *Vertrag* to record; *Geschäft* to document.

**Be|urkundung** *f* (a) *siehe vt* certification; recording; documentation. (b) *(Dokument)* documentation.

**be|urlauben\*** *vt* to give leave; *(von Pflichten)* to excuse *(von* from*)*. **beurlaubt sein** to be on leave; *(suspendiert sein)* to have been relieved of one's duties; **sich ~ lassen** to take leave.

**Be|urlaubung** *f* granting of leave *(gen* to*)*; *(Beurlaubtsein)* leave.

**be|urteilen\*** *vt* to judge *(nach* by, from*)*; *Leistung, Wert* to assess. **etw richtig/falsch ~** to judge sth correctly/to misjudge sth.

**Be|urteilung** *f siehe vt* judgement; assessment.

**Be|urteilungs-:** **~gespräch** *nt* appraisal interview; **~maßstab** *m* criterion.

**Beute** *f no pl* (a) *(Kriegs~,* fig hum*)* spoils *pl*; *(Diebes~)* haul, loot; *(von Raubtieren etc)* prey; *(Jagd~)* bag. **~ machen** *(Dieb)* to make a haul. (b) *(liter: Opfer)* prey. **eine ~ sein** *(gen)* **sein/werden** to have fallen prey/to fall prey to sth; **eine leichte ~ sein** to be a sitting target.

**Beutel** *m -* (a) bag; *(Tabaks~,* Zool*)* pouch. (b) *(col: Geld~)* *(von Frau)* purse; *(von Mann)* wallet *(Brit)*, billfold *(US)*.

**Beuteltier** *nt* marsupial.

**Beute-:** **~stück** *nt* booty; **~zug** *m* raid *(auch fig)*.

**bevölkern\*** **1** *vt* (a) *(bewohnen)* to inhabit; *(beleben)* to crowd, to fill. **schwach/stark bevölkert** sparsely/densely populated. (b) *(besiedeln)* to populate. **2** *vr* to become inhabited; *(fig)* to fill up.

**Bevölkerung** *f (die Bewohner)* population.

**Bevölkerungs-:** **~dichte** *f* population density; **~explosion** *f* population explosion; **~schicht** *f* social stratum; **~zahl** *f* (total) population.

**bevollmächtigen\*** *vt* to authorize *(zu etw* to do sth*)*.

**Bevollmächtigte(r)** *mf decl as adj* authorized representative.

**Bevollmächtigung** *f* authorization *(durch* from*)*.

**bevor** *conj* before. **~ Sie (nicht) die Rechnung bezahlt haben** until you pay the bill.

**bevormunden\*** *vt* **jdn ~** to treat sb like a child; *(für jdn entscheiden)* to make sb's decisions (for him/her).

**Bevormundung** *f* **unsere ~ durch den Staat** the State's making up our minds for us.

**bevorstehen** *vi sep irreg* to be imminent; *(Winter etc)* to approach. **jdm ~** to be in store for sb; **das Schlimmste steht uns noch bevor** the worst is still to come.

**bevorstehend** *adj* forthcoming; *Gefahr, Krise* imminent; *Winter* approaching.

**bevorzugen\*** *vt* to prefer; *(begünstigen)* to favour *(Brit)*, to favor *(US)*, to give preferential treatment to.

**bevorzugt 1** *adj* preferred; *Behandlung* preferential; *(privilegiert)* privileged. **2** *adv* **jdn ~ behandeln** *etc* to give sb preferential treatment; **etw ~ abfertigen** *etc* to give sth priority.

**Bevorzugung** *f* preference *(gen* for*)*; *(vorrangige Behandlung)* preferential treatment *(bei* in*)*.

**bewachen\*** *vt* to guard; *(Sport) Spieler* to mark.

**Bewacher(in** *f)* *m -* guard; *(Sport: von Spieler)* marker.

**bewachsen** *adj* overgrown *(mit* in, with*)*.

**Bewachung** *f* guarding; *(Wachmannschaft)* guard; *(Sport)* marking.

**bewaffnen\*** **1** *vt* to arm. **2** *vr (lit, fig)* to arm oneself.

**bewaffnet** *adj* armed. **bis an die Zähne ~** armed to the teeth.

**Bewaffnung** *f* arming; *(Waffen)* weapons *pl*.

**bewahren\*** *vt* (a) *(beschützen)* to protect *(vor +dat* from*)*. **(Gott) bewahre!** *(col)* heaven *or* God forbid! (b) *(beibehalten)* to keep, to retain.

**bewähren\*** *vr* (a) to prove oneself/itself; *(Methode, Sparsamkeit, Fleiß)* to pay off; *(Auto, Gerät etc)* to prove a good investment. **sich im Leben ~** to make something of one's life; **es bewährt sich immer, das zu tun** it's always worth doing that; **ihre Freundschaft hat sich bewährt** their friendship stood the test of time; *siehe* **bewährt.**

**bewahrheiten\*** *vr* to prove (to be) well-founded; *(Prophezeiung)* to come true.

**bewährt** *adj* proven, tried and tested.

**Bewahrung** *f siehe vt* protection; retention.

**Bewährung** *f* (a) **bei ~ der Methode** if the method proves (to be) workable *or* valid. (b) *(Jur)* probation. **eine Strafe zur ~ aussetzen** to impose a suspended sentence; **ein Jahr Gefängnis mit ~** a suspended sentence of one year with probation.

**Bewährungs-:** **~frist** *f (Jur)* probation(ary) period; **~helfer** *m* probation officer; **~probe** *f* test; **etw einer ~probe** *(dat)* **unterziehen** to put sth to the test; **~zeit** *f* time spent on probation.

**bewaldet** *adj* wooded.

**bewältigen\*** *vt Schwierigkeiten* to cope with; *Arbeit, Aufgabe auch, Strecke* to manage; *Erlebnis etc* to get over; *(erledigen, beenden)* to deal with.

**Bewältigung** *f* **die ~ der Schwierigkeiten/der Arbeit/eines Erlebnisses** coping with the difficulties/managing the work/getting over an experience.

**bewandert** *adj* well-versed.

**Bewandtnis** *f* **damit hat es eine andere ~** there's another reason *or* explanation for that; **damit hat es folgende ~** the fact of the matter is this.

**bewässern\*** *vt* to irrigate; *(mit Sprühanlage)* to water.

**Bewässerung** *f siehe vt* irrigation; watering.

**Bewässerungs-** *in cpds* irrigation.

**bewegen¹\*** **1** *vt* (a) to move. **dieser Gedanke bewegt mich seit langem** this has been on my mind a long time; **~d** moving *siehe* **bewegt.** (b) *(bewirken, ändern)* to change. **2** *vr* (a) to move. (b) *(Bewegung haben: Mensch)* to get some exercise. (c) *(fig: schwanken)* to vary, to range *(zwischen* between*)*. **der Preis bewegt sich um die 50 Mark** the price is about 50 marks. (d) *(sich ändern)* to change. **es bewegt sich etwas** things are beginning to happen.

**bewegen²** *pret* **bewog,** *ptp* **bewogen** *vt* **jdn zu etw ~** to induce *or* persuade sb to do sth; **sich dazu ~ lassen, etw zu tun** to let oneself be persuaded to do sth.

**Beweggrund** *m* motive.

**beweglich** *adj* (a) *(bewegbar)* movable; *Truppe* mobile. (b) *(wendig)* agile; *Fahrzeug* manoeuvrable *(Brit)*, maneuverable *(US)*. **mit dem Fahrrad ist man in der Stadt ~er** you can get around more easily in town on a bicycle.

**Beweglichkeit** *f no pl siehe adj* (a) movability; mobility. (b) agility; manoeuvrability *(Brit)*, maneuverability *(US)*.

**bewegt** *adj* (a) *Wasser, See* choppy; *Zeiten, Leben* eventful. (b) *Stimme, Worte* emotional.

**Bewegung** *f* (a) movement; *(Hand~ auch)* gesture; *(Sci, Tech auch)* motion. **keine ~!** don't move!; **in ~ sein** *(Fahrzeug)* to be moving, to be in motion; *(Menge)* to mill around; **sich in ~ setzen** to start moving; **etw in ~ setzen** to set sth in motion. (b) *(körperliche ~)* exercise. **sich** *(dat)* ~ **verschaffen** to get some exercise. **(c)** *(Entwicklung)* progress. **etw kommt in** ~ sth gets moving. **(d)** *(Ergriffenheit)* emotion. **(e)** *(Pol, Art etc)* movement.

**Bewegungs-:** ~**freiheit** *f* freedom of movement; *(fig)* freedom of action; **b**~**los** *adj* motionless, immobile; ~**losigkeit** *f* motionlessness, immobility; **b**~**unfähig** *adj* unable to move; *(gehunfähig)* unable to get about.

**beweihräuchern*** *vt (fig)* to praise to the skies.

**beweinen*** *vt* to mourn (for), to weep for.

**Beweis** *m* **-e** proof *(für of)*; *(Zeugnis)* evidence *no pl.* **als** *or* **zum** ~ as proof *or* evidence; **ein eindeutiger** ~ clear evidence; **den** ~ **antreten** *or* **führen** to offer evidence *or* proof; **den** ~ **für etw erbringen** to produce evidence *or* proof of sth.

**Beweis-:** ~**aufnahme** *f (Jur)* taking *or* hearing of evidence; **b**~**bar** *adj* provable, demonstrable.

**beweisen*** *vt irreg* to prove. **was zu** ~ **war** QED; **was noch zu** ~ **wäre** that remains to be seen.

**Beweis-:** ~**führung** *f (Jur)* presentation of one's case; *(Math)* proof; *(Argumentation)* argumentation, reasoning; ~**grund** *m* argument; ~**kraft** *f* value as evidence; ~**lage** *f (Jur)* body of evidence; ~**last** *f (Jur)* onus, burden of proof; ~**material** *nt* (body of) evidence; ~**not** *f (Jur)* lack of evidence; ~**pflicht** *f (Jur)* onus, burden of proof; ~**stück** *nt* exhibit.

**bewenden** *vt impers:* **wir wollen es dabei** ~ **lassen** let's leave it at that.

**bewerben*** *vr irreg* to apply *(bei* to, *um* for, *als* for the post/job of*)*; *(bei Wahl)* to stand; *(Comm: um Auftrag)* to quote.

**Bewerber(in** *f)* *m* - applicant; *(Pol)* candidate; *(Sport)* contender.

**Bewerbung** *f* application; *(Pol)* candidacy.

**Bewerbungs-:** ~**bogen** *m* application form; ~**gespräch** *nt* (job) interview; ~**schreiben** *nt* (letter of) application; ~**unterlagen** *pl* application documents *pl.*

**bewerfen*** *vt irreg* **jdn/etw mit etw** ~ to throw sth at sb/sth.

**bewerkstelligen*** *vt* to manage; *Geschäft* to bring off. **es** ~, **daß jd etw tut** to manage *or* contrive to get sb to do sth.

**bewerten*** *vt jdn* to judge; *Gegenstand* to put a value on; *Leistung auch, Schularbeit* to assess. **etw mit der Note 5** ~ to give sth a mark of 5.

**Bewertung** *f siehe vt* judgement; valuation; assessment.

**bewilligen*** *vt* to allow; *Etat etc* to approve; *Geld etc auch* to grant; *Stipendium* to award.

**Bewilligung** *f siehe vt* allowing; approval; granting; awarding. **die** ~ **für einen Kredit bekommen** to be allowed *or* granted credit.

**bewirken*** *vt* **(a)** *(verursachen)* to cause, to bring about. ~, **daß etw passiert** to cause sth to happen. **(b)** *(erreichen)* to achieve.

**bewirten*** *vt* to entertain; **jdn mit Kaffee und Kuchen** ~ to serve sb coffee and cakes.

**bewirtschaften*** *vt Land* to farm, to cultivate.

**Bewirtschaftung** *f (von Land)* farming, cultivation.

**Bewirtung** *f (das Bewirten)* hospitality; *(im Hotel)* (food and) service. **die** ~ **so vieler Gäste** catering for so many guests.

**bewog** *pret of* **bewegen**².

**bewogen** *ptp of* **bewegen**².

**bewohnbar** *adj* habitable.

**Bewohnbarkeit** *f* habitability.

**bewohnen*** *vt* to live in; *Haus, Bau, Nest auch* to occupy; *(Volk)* to inhabit; *siehe* **bewohnt.**

**Bewohner(in** *f)* *m* - *(von Land, Gebiet)* inhabitant;

*(von Haus etc)* occupier.

**bewohnt** *adj* inhabited; *Haus etc auch* occupied.

**bewölken*** *vr (lit, fig)* to cloud over.

**bewölkt** *adj* cloudy.

**Bewölkung** *f* clouding over; *(Wolken)* cloud.

**Bewölkungs-:** ~**auflockerung** *f* break-up of the cloud; ~**zunahme** *f* increase in cloud.

**Bewuchs** *m no pl* vegetation.

**Bewund(e)rer(in** *f)* *m* - admirer.

**bewundern*** *vt* to admire *(wegen* for*)*.

**bewundernswert** *adj* admirable.

**Bewunderung** *f* admiration.

**bewußt 1** *adj* **(a)** conscious. **sich** *(dat)* **einer Sache** *(gen)* ~ **sein/werden** to be/become aware *or* conscious of sth, to realize sth; **es wurde ihm allmählich** ~, **daß** ... he gradually realized (that) ... **(b)** *(willentlich)* deliberate, intentional; *Lüge* deliberate. **(c)** *(bekannt, besagt)* **die** ~**e Kreuzung** the crossroads in question. **2** *adv* **(a)** consciously. ~ **leben** to live in total awareness. **(b)** *(willentlich)* deliberately, intentionally.

**Bewußt-:** **b**~**los** *adj* unconscious; **b**~**los werden** to become unconscious; ~**lose(r)** *mf decl as adj* unconscious man/woman/person *etc*; ~**losigkeit** *f* unconsciousness; **bis zur** ~**losigkeit** *(col)* ad nauseam; **b**~**machen** *vt sep* **jdm etw b**~**machen** to make sb conscious of sth, to make sb realize sth; **sich** *(dat)* **etw b**~**machen** to realize sth.

**Bewußtsein** *nt no pl* **(a)** *(Wissen)* awareness, consciousness. **etw kommt jdm zu(m)** ~ sb becomes aware *or* conscious of sth; **jdm etw zu** ~ **bringen/ins** ~ **rufen** to make sb conscious *or* aware of sth; **im** ~, **daß** ... in the knowledge that ...; **er tat es mit (vollem)** ~ he was (fully) aware of what he was doing. **(b)** *(Philos, Psych, Med)* consciousness. **das** ~ **verlieren/wiedererlangen** to lose/regain consciousness; **bei** ~ **sein** to be conscious; **bei vollem** ~ fully conscious.

**Bewußtseins-:** ~**bildung** *f (Pol)* shaping of political ideas; **b**~**erweiternd** *adj* **b**~**erweiternde Drogen** mind-expanding drugs; ~**erweiterung** *f* consciousness raising; ~**spaltung** *f* schizophrenia; ~**veränderung** *f* change in outlook.

**bez.** = **(a)** **bezahlt** pd. **(b)** **bezüglich** re.

**Bez.** = **Bezirk.**

**bezahlbar** *adj* affordable.

**bezahlen*** **1** *vt* **(a)** to pay. **(b)** *Sache, Leistung* to pay for. **etw bezahlt bekommen/für etw nichts bezahlt bekommen** to get/not to get paid for sth; **er hat seinen Fehler mit seinem Leben bezahlt** he paid for his mistake with his life. **2** *vi* to pay.

**bezahlt** *adj* paid. **sich** ~ **machen** to pay off.

**Bezahlung** *f* **(a)** *siehe vt* payment; paying for *(einer Sache* *(gen)* sth*)*. **(b)** *(Lohn, Gehalt)* pay; *(für Dienste)* payment. **ohne/gegen** *or* **für** ~ without/ for payment.

**bezähmen*** **1** *vt (fig geh) Begierden etc* to control, to curb. **2** *vr* to control *or* restrain oneself.

**bezaubern*** *vt (fig)* to charm, to captivate.

**bezaubernd** *adj* enchanting, charming.

**bezeichnen*** *vt* **(a)** *(kennzeichnen)* to mark; *Takt, Tonart* to indicate. **(b)** *(genau beschreiben)* to describe. **(c)** *(benennen)* to call, to describe. **ich weiß nicht, wie man das bezeichnet** I don't know what it's called. **(d)** *(bedeuten)* to mean, to denote.

**bezeichnend** *adj (für of)* characteristic, typical.

**bezeichnenderweise** *adv* typically (enough).

**Bezeichnung** *f* **(a)** *siehe vt (a, b)* marking; indication; description. **(b)** *(Ausdruck)* expression, term.

**bezeugen*** *vt* to attest, to testify to. ~, **daß** ... to attest the fact that ..., to testify that ...

**bezichtigen\*** *vt* to accuse *(einer Sache (gen)* of sth*)*.

**beziehbar** *adj* **(a)** *Wohnung etc* ready to move into. **(b)** *Waren etc* obtainable.

**beziehen\*** *irreg* **1** *vt* **(a)** *(überziehen) Polster* to cover. **die Betten frisch** ~ to change the beds. **(b)** *(einziehen in) Wohnung* to move into. **(c)** *Stellung, Standpunkt* to take up. **(d)** *(erhalten)* to get. **(e)** *(in Beziehung setzen)* **etw auf jdn/etw** ~ to apply sth to sb/sth; *siehe* **bezogen**. **2** *vr* **(a)** *(Himmel)* to cloud over. **(b) sich auf jdn/etw** ~ to refer to sb/sth.

**Bezieher(in** *f)* *m* - *(Abonnent)* subscriber; *(von Waren)* purchaser; *(von Einkommen)* drawer.

**Beziehung** *f* **(a)** *(Verhältnis)* relationship. **(b)** *usu pl (Kontakt)* relations *pl*. **diplomatische** ~**en** diplomatic relations. **(c)** *(Zusammenhang)* connection *(zu* with*)*, relation. **etw zu etw in** ~ **setzen** to relate sth to sth; **etw hat keine** ~ **zu etw** sth has no bearing on sth *or* no relationship to sth. **(d)** *usu pl (Verbindung)* connections *pl (zu* with*)*. **seine** ~**en spielen lassen** to pull strings. **(e)** *(Sympathie)* feeling, affinity *(zu* for*)*. **er hat überhaupt keine** ~ **zu seinen Kindern** he just doesn't relate to his children. **(f) in einer/keiner** ~ in one/no respect *or* way; **in jeder/mancher** ~ in every respect/some respects.

**Beziehungs-:** ~**kiste** *f (col)* relationship; **b**~**los** *adj* unrelated, unconnected.

**beziehungsweise** *conj* **(a)** *(oder aber)* or. **(b)** *(im anderen Fall)* and ... respectively. **zwei Briefmarken, die 50** ~ **70 Pfennig kosten** two stamps costing 50 and 70 Pfennig respectively. **(c)** *(genauer gesagt)* or rather, or that is to say.

**beziffern\*** **1** *vt (angeben)* to estimate *(auf +acc, mit* at*)*. **2** *vr* **sich** ~ **auf** *(+acc)* to amount to.

**Bezirk** *m* -e **(a)** *(Gebiet)* district. **(b)** *(Admin) (Stadt)* ≃ district; *(von Land)* ≃ region.

**Bezirks-:** ~**klasse,** ~**liga** *f (Sport)* regional league; ~**regierung** *f* regional administration; ~**stadt** *f* ≃ county town.

**bezirzen\*** *vt (col)* to bewitch.

**bezogen** *adj* **auf jdn/etw** ~ referring to sb/sth.

**Bezogene(r)** *mf decl as adj (Fin) (von Scheck)* drawee; *(von Wechsel)* acceptor.

**bezug** *siehe* **Bezug (g)**.

**Bezug** *m* ⸚e **(a)** *(für Kissen, Polster etc)* cover; *(für Kopfkissen)* pillow-case, pillow-slip. **(b)** *(Erwerb)* buying, purchase; *(von Zeitung)* taking. **beim regelmäßigen** ~ **der Zeitung** ... if you take the newspaper on a regular basis ... **(c)** *(von Einkommen, Rente etc)* drawing. **(d)** ⸚e *pl (Einkünfte)* income, earnings *pl*. **(e)** *(Zusammenhang)* = **Beziehung (c)**. **(f)** *(form: Berufung)* reference. ~ **nehmen auf** *(+acc)* to refer to; **mit** *or* **unter** ~ **auf** *(+acc)* with reference to. **(g) in b**~ **auf** *(+acc)* regarding, with regard to, concerning.

**bezüglich** *prep +gen (form)* regarding, with regard to, re *(Comm)*.

**Bezugnahme** *f* -n *(form)* reference. **unter** ~ **auf** *(+acc)* with reference to.

**Bezugs-:** **b**~**bereit, b**~**fertig** *adj Haus etc* ready to move into; ~**person** *f* **die wichtigste** ~**person des Kleinkindes** the person to whom a small child relates most closely; ~**punkt** *m (lit, fig)* point of reference; ~**quelle** *f* source of supply; ~**schein** *m* (ration) coupon.

**bezuschussen\*** *vt* to subsidize.

**Bezuschussung** *f* subsidizing; *(Betrag)* subsidy.

**bezwecken\*** *vt* to aim at. **etw mit etw** ~ *(Mensch)* to intend sth by sth; **was soll das** ~**?** what's the point of that?

**bezweifeln\*** *vt* to doubt. **das ist nicht zu** ~ there's no doubt about it.

**bezwingen\*** *vt irreg* to conquer; *Feind auch* to defeat, to overcome; *(Sport)* to beat, to defeat.

**Bezwinger(in** *f)* *m* - *(von Berg, Feind)* conqueror; *(Sport)* winner *(gen* over*)*.

**Bf** = **Bahnhof**.

**BGB** ['beːgeːˈbeː] *nt* -, *no pl* = **Bürgerliches Gesetzbuch**.

**BGH** [beːgeːˈhaː] *m* = **Bundesgerichtshof**.

**BH** [beːˈhaː] *m* -(s) = **Büstenhalter** bra.

**Bhf** = **Bahnhof**.

**Biathlon** *nt* -s *(Sport)* biathlon.

**bibbern** *vi (col) (vor Angst)* to tremble, to shake; *(vor Kälte)* to shiver.

**Bibel** *f* -n *(lit)* Bible; *(fig)* bible.

**Bibel-:** **b**~**fest** *adj* well versed in the Bible; ~**spruch** *m* quotation from the Bible; ~**wort** *nt, pl* ~**worte** biblical saying.

**Biber** *m* - **(a)** *(Tier, Pelz)* beaver. **(b)** *auch nt (Tuch)* flannelette.

**Biber-:** ~**bettuch** *nt* flannelette sheet; ~**pelz** *m* beaver (fur).

**Bibliographie** *f* bibliography.

**Bibliothek** *f* -en *(auch Comp)* library.

**Bibliothekar(in** *f)* *m* librarian.

**biblisch** *adj* biblical. **ein** ~**es Alter** a great age, a ripe old age.

**Bidet** [biˈdeː] *nt* -s bidet.

**bieder** *adj* **(a)** *(rechtschaffen)* honest; *Mensch, Leben auch* upright. **(b)** *(pej)* conventional.

**Bieder-:** ~**mann** *m, pl* ~**männer** *(pej geh)* petty bourgeois; **b**~**männisch** *adj (pej geh)* petty bourgeois; *Geschmack, Gesinnung auch* philistine; ~**meier** *nt no pl* Biedermeier period.

**Biege** *f* -n *(dial)* bend, curve. **die** ~ **machen** *(col)* to make oneself scarce *(col)*.

**biegen** *pret* **bog**, *ptp* **gebogen** **1** *vt* to bend; *(fig: manipulieren)* to wangle *(col)*. **auf B**~ **oder Brechen** *(col)* by hook or by crook *(col)*. **2** *vi aux sein (Mensch, Wagen)* to turn; *(Weg, Straße auch)* to curve. **3** *vr* to bend; *(Holz, Plastik)* to warp; *(Metall)* to buckle. **sich vor Lachen** ~ *(fig)* to double up with laughter.

**biegsam** *adj* flexible; *Holz auch* pliable; *Metall auch* malleable; *Glieder, Körper* supple.

**Biegsamkeit** *f siehe adj* flexibility; pliability; malleability; suppleness.

**Biegung** *f* bend, curve. **der Fluß/die Straße macht eine** ~ the river/road curves *or* bends.

**Biene** *f* -n **(a)** bee. **(b)** *(dated col: Mädchen)* bird *(Brit col)*, chick *(esp US col)*.

**Bienen-:** **b**~**fleißig** *adj* industrious; ~**honig** *m* real *or* natural honey; ~**königin** *f* queen bee; ~**korb** *m* (bee)hive; ~**schwarm** *m* swarm (of bees); ~**stich** *m (Cook)* cake coated with sugar and almonds filled with custard or cream; ~**stock** *m* (bee)hive; ~**volk** *nt* bee colony; ~**wachs** *nt* beeswax; ~**zucht** *f* beekeeping; ~**züchter** *m* beekeeper.

**Bier** *nt* -e beer. **zwei** ~**, bitte!** two beers, please; **das ist mein** ~ *(fig col)* that's my business.

**Bier-** *in cpds* beer; ~**bauch** *m (col)* beer belly *(col)*; ~**brauerei** *f* (beer-)brewing; *(Betrieb)* brewery; ~**deckel** *m* beer mat; ~**dose** *f* beer can; ~**ernst** *m (col)* deadly seriousness; ~**faß** *nt* keg; ~**filz** *m* beer mat; ~**flasche** *f* beer bottle; ~**kasten** *m* beer crate; ~**keller** *m* beer cellar; ~**krug** *m* tankard, beer mug; *(aus Steingut)* (beer) stein; ~**leiche** *f (col)* drunk; ~**ruhe** *f (col)* cool *(col)*; ~**schinken** *m* = ~**wurst**; ~**seidel** *nt* tankard; **b**~**selig** *adj Mensch* boozed up *(col)*; ~**wurst** *f* ham sausage; ~**zelt** *nt* beer tent.

**Bimmel**

**Biest** *nt* **-er** *(pej col)* **(a)** *(Tier)* creature; *(Insekt auch)* bug. **(b)** *(Mensch)* (little) wretch; *(Frau)* bitch *(col!)*.
**biestig** *adj (col)* beastly *(col)*; *(schlechter Laune)* ratty *(col)*.
**bieten** *pret* **bot**, *ptp* **geboten 1** *vt* **(a)** to offer *(jdm etw* sb sth, sth to sb*)*; *(bei Auktion)* to bid *(auf +acc* for*)*; *Gelegenheit auch* to give. **jdm die Hand ~** to offer sb one's hand; **wer bietet mehr?** *(bei Auktion)* any more bids?; **diese Stadt hat nichts zu ~** this town has nothing to offer. **(b)** *(haben, aufweisen)* to have; *Problem, Schwierigkeit* to present. **das Hochhaus bietet fünfzig Familien Wohnung** the tower block provides accommodation for fifty families. **(c)** *(zeigen, darbieten)* Anblick, Bild to present; *Film* to show; *Leistung* to give. **die Mannschaft bot ein hervorragendes Spiel** the team played an excellent game. **(d)** *(zumuten)* **sich** *(dat)* **etw ~ lassen** to put up with sth; **so etwas könnte man mir nicht ~** I wouldn't stand for that sort of thing; *siehe* **geboten. 2** *vi (Cards)* to bid. **3** *vr (Gelegenheit, Anblick etc)* to present itself *(jdm* to sb*)*.
**Bieter(in** *f)* *m* - bidder.
**Bigamie** *f* bigamy.
**Bigamist(in** *f)* *m* bigamist.
**bigott** *adj* overly pious; *(scheinheilig)* hypocritical.
**Bikini** *m* **-s** bikini.
**Bilanz** *f* **(a)** balance; *(Abrechnung)* balance sheet. **eine ~ aufstellen** to draw up a balance sheet. **(b)** *(fig: Ergebnis)* end result. **(die) ~ ziehen** to take stock *(aus of)*.
**Bilanzprüfer** *m* auditor.
**bilateral** *adj* bilateral.
**Bild** *nt* **-er (a)** *(lit, fig)* picture; *(Film)* frame. **ein ~ machen** to take a photo *or* picture; **ein ~ des Elends** a picture of misery. **(b)** *(Abbild)* image; *(Spiegel~ auch)* reflection. **sie ist das ~ ihrer Mutter** she is the image of her mother. **(c)** *(Anblick, Ansicht)* sight. **das äußere ~ der Stadt** the outward impression created by the town. **(d)** *(Theat: Szene)* scene. **(e)** *(Metapher)* metaphor, image. **im ~ bleiben** to use the same metaphor. **(f)** *(Erscheinungs~)* character. **sie gehören zum ~ dieser Stadt** they are part of the scene in this town. **(g)** *(fig: Vorstellung)* image, picture. **im ~e sein** to be in the picture *(über +acc* about*)*; **jdn ins ~ setzen** to put sb in the picture; **sich** *(dat)* **von jdm/etw ein ~ machen** to get an idea of sb/sth; **das ~ des Deutschen** the image of the German.
**Bild-:** **~archiv** *nt* picture library; **~atlas** *m* pictorial atlas; **~auflösung** *f (TV, Comp)* resolution; **~ausfall** *m (TV)* loss of vision; **~band** *m* illustrated book; **~beschreibung** *f (Sch)* description of a picture.
**bilden 1** *vt* **(a)** to form; *(fig) Charakter auch* to shape, to mould; *Vermögen* to acquire; *(ausmachen)* Höhepunkt, Ausnahme, Gefahr etc to constitute. **sich** *(dat)* **eine Meinung ~** to form an opinion. **(b)** *(erziehen)* to educate. **2** *vr* **(a)** *(entstehen)* to form, to develop. **(b)** *(lernen)* to educate oneself; *(durch Lesen etc)* to improve one's mind; *(durch Reisen etc)* to broaden one's mind. **3** *vi siehe vr* **(b)** to be educational; to improve the mind; to broaden the mind.
**bildend** *adj* **die ~e Kunst** (plastic) art; **~er Künstler** artist.
**Bilderbogen** *m* illustrated broadsheet. **ein musikalischer ~** a musical medley.
**Bilderbuch** *nt* picture book. **eine Landschaft wie im ~** a picturesque landscape.
**Bilderbuch-** *in cpds (fig)* perfect; **~landung** *f* textbook landing.

**Bilder-:** **~geschichte** *f* picture story; *(in Comic, Zeitung)* strip cartoon; **~rahmen** *m* picture-frame; **~rätsel** *nt* picture-puzzle; **b~reich** *adj Buch etc* full of pictures; *(fig) Sprache* rich in imagery.
**Bild-:** **~fläche** *f* **(a)** *(Leinwand)* projection surface; **(b)** *(fig col)* **auf der ~fläche erscheinen** to appear on the scene; **von der ~fläche verschwinden** to disappear (from the scene); **~geschichte** *f* strip cartoon; **b~haft** *adj* pictorial; *Beschreibung, Sprache* vivid; **~hauer** *m* sculptor; **~hauerin** *f* sculptress; **b~hübsch** *adj Mädchen* (as) pretty as a picture; *Kleid, Garten* really lovely.
**bildlich** *adj* pictorial; *Ausdruck etc* figurative. **sich** *(dat)* **etw ~ vorstellen** to picture sth in one's mind's eye.
**Bildnis** *nt (liter)* portrait.
**Bild-:** **~platte** *f* video disc; **~plattenspieler** *m* video disc player; **~punkt** *m (Comp)* pixel; **~qualität** *f (TV, Film)* picture quality; **(Phot)** print quality; **~reporter** *m* photojournalist; **~röhre** *f (TV)* picture tube; **~schärfe** *f* definition *no indef art.*
**Bildschirm** *m (TV, Comp)* screen.
**Bildschirm-:** **~arbeiter** *m* VDU operator; **~gerät** *nt* visual display unit, VDU, monitor; **~speicher** *m* screen memory; **~text** *m* viewdata ®.
**Bild-:** **b~schön** *adj* beautiful; **~text** *m* caption.
**Bildung** *f* **(a)** *(Erziehung)* education; *(Kultur)* culture. **~ haben** to be cultured. **(b)** *no pl (das Formen)* formation, forming; *(fig: von Charakter etc auch)* shaping; *(von Vermögen)* acquisition. **zur ~ des Passivs** to form the passive.
**Bildungs-:** **~chancen** *pl* educational opportunities *pl*; **~einrichtung** *f* educational institution; *(Kulturstätte)* cultural institution; **~gang** *m* school (and university/college) career; **~grad** *m* level of education; **~gut** *nt* **das gehört zum deutschen ~gut** that is part of the German cultural heritage; **~lücke** *f* gap in one's education; **~politik** *f* education policy; **~reise** *f* educational trip; **~roman** *m (Liter)* Bildungsroman, *novel concerned with the intellectual or spiritual development of the main character*; **~stand** *m*, **~stufe** *f* level of education; **~urlaub** *m* educational holiday; *(in Firma)* study leave; **~weg** *m* **jds ~weg** the course of sb's education; **auf dem zweiten ~weg** through night school/the Open University *etc*; **~wesen** *nt* education system.
**Bild-:** **~unterschrift** *f* caption; **~werfer** *m* projector; **~wörterbuch** *nt* pictorial *or* picture dictionary; **~zuschrift** *f* reply enclosing photograph.
**Bilge** *f* **-n** *(Naut)* bilge.
**Billard** ['bɪljart] *nt (Spiel)* billiards *sing*.
**Billard-:** **~kugel** *f* billiard ball; **~stock** *m* billiard cue; **~tisch** *m* billiard table.
**Billett** [bɪl'jɛt] *nt* **-e** *or* **-s** *(dated)* ticket.
**Billiarde** *f* **-n** thousand billion *(Brit)*, thousand trillion *(US)*.
**billig** *adj* **(a)** cheap. **~ abzugeben** going cheap; **~ davonkommen** *(col)* to get off lightly. **(b)** *(pej: primitiv)* cheap; *Ausrede* feeble.
**billigen** *vt* to approve. **etw stillschweigend ~** to condone sth; **~, daß jd etw tut** to approve of sb's doing sth.
**Billig-:** **~flagge** *f (Naut, Comm)* flag of convenience; **~flug** *m* cheap flight; **~land** *nt* country with low production costs; **~preis** *m* low price.
**Billigung** *f* approval. **jds ~ finden** to meet with sb's approval.
**Billion** *f* billion *(Brit)*, trillion *(US)*.
**bimbam** *interj* ding-dong.
**Bimmel** *f* **-n** *(col)* bell.

**bimmeln** *vi (col)* to ring.
**Bimsstein** *m* pumice stone.
**bin** *1. pers sing pres of* **sein**.
**binär** *adj* binary.
**Binärcode** [-koːd] *m* binary code.
**Binde** *f* **-n** (a) *(Med)* bandage. (b) *(Arm~)* armband; *(Augen~)* blindfold. (c) *(Monats~)* (sanitary) towel or napkin *(US)*. (d) *(dated: Krawatte)* tie. **sich** *(dat)* **einen hinter die ~ gießen** *or* **kippen** *(col)* to put a few drinks away.
**Binde-:** **~gewebe** *nt (Anat)* connective tissue; **~glied** *nt* connecting link; **~hautentzündung** *f* conjunctivitis; **~mittel** *nt* binder.
**binden** *pret* **band**, *ptp* **gebunden 1** *vt* (a) *(zusammen~)* to tie; *(fest~)* to bind; *(fig geh)* to bind, to unite. (b) *(Buch etc)* to bind; *Strauß, Kranz* to make up; *Knoten, Schal* to tie; *Krawatte* to knot. **sich** *(dat)* **die Schuhe ~** to tie (up) one's shoelaces. (c) *(fesseln, befestigen)* *(an +acc* to) to tie (up); *Menschen auch* to bind; *(fig)* *(an einen Ort)* to tie; *(Versprechen, Vertrag, Eid etc)* to bind. **jdm die Hände auf den Rücken ~** to tie sb's hands behind his back; **mir sind die Hände gebunden** *(fig)* my hands are tied; **nichts bindet mich an Glasgow** I have no special ties in Glasgow. (d) *(festhalten)* *Staub, Erdreich* to bind; *(Chem)* *(aufnehmen)* to absorb; *(sich verbinden mit)* to combine with; *(Cook)* *Soße* to bind. **2** *vr* *(sich verpflichten)* to commit oneself *(an +acc* to).
**bindend** *adj* binding *(für* on); *Zusage* definite.
**Binder** *m* - *(Krawatte)* tie, necktie *(US)*.
**Binde-:** **~strich** *m* hyphen; **~wort** *nt* conjunction.
**Bindfaden** *m* string. **es regnet** **~** *(col)* it's sheeting down *(col)*.
**Bindung** *f* (a) tie *(an +acc* with*)*; *(Beziehung zu einem Partner)* relationship *(an +acc* with*)*; *(Verpflichtung: an Beruf etc, durch Vertrag)* commitment *(an +acc* to*)*. (b) *(Ski~)* binding.
**binnen** *prep +dat or (geh) gen (form)* within. **~ kurzem** shortly.
**Binnen-:** **~gewässer** *nt* inland water; **~hafen** *m* river port; **~handel** *m* domestic trade; **~land** *nt* *(Landesinneres)* interior; **b~ländisch** *adj* inland; **~markt** *m* home market; **Europäischer ~markt** single European market; **~meer** *nt* inland sea; **~schiffahrt** *f* inland navigation; **~see** *m* lake; **~staat** *m* landlocked country *or* state.
**Binse** *f* **-n** *usu pl* rush. **in die ~n gehen** *(fig col)* *(mißlingen)* to be a washout *(col)*; *(verlorengehen)* to go west *(col)*; *(kaputtgehen)* to give out *(col)*.
**Binsen-:** **~wahrheit**, **~weisheit** *f* truism.
**Bio-** *in cpds* bio-; **~aktiv** *adj Waschmittel* biological; **~chemie** *f* biochemistry; **b~dynamisch** *adj* biodynamic; **~gas** *nt* methane gas.
**Biograph(in** *f)* *m* biographer.
**Biographie** *f* biography.
**biographisch** *adj* biographical.
**Bioladen** *m (col)* health food shop *(Brit) or* store *(US)*.
**Biologe** *m,* **Biologin** *f* biologist.
**Biologie** *f* biology.
**biologisch** *adj* biological. **~-dynamisch** *Anbau etc* organic; **~e Vielfalt** biodiversity.
**Bio-:** **~masse** *f no pl (Chem)* organic substances *pl*; **~physik** *f* biophysics *sing*; **~technik** *f* biotechnology; **~top** *nt* **-e** biotope; **~Waschmittel** *nt* biological washing powder.
**Birke** *f* **-n** birch.
**Birma** *nt* Burma.
**Birmane** *m* **-n,** **Birmanin** *f* Burmese.
**birmanisch** *adj* Burmese.
**Birnbaum** *m (Baum)* pear tree; *(Holz)* pear-wood.

**Birne** *f* **-n** (a) pear. (b) *(Glühlampe)* (light) bulb. (c) *(col: Kopf)* nut *(col)*.
**birnenförmig** *adj* pear-shaped.
**bis 1** *prep +acc* (a) *(zeitlich)* until, till; *(bis spätestens, nicht später als)* by. **~ Ende Mai bin ich noch in London** I'll be in London up to *or* until the end of May; **~ Ende Mai bin ich damit fertig** I'll have finished it by the end of May; **~ dahin ist er längst weg** he will have gone long before then; **~ wann gilt der Fahrplan/ist das fertig?** up to when is the timetable valid/when will that be finished by?; **~ wann?** till/by when?; **~ wann bleibt ihr hier?** how long are you staying here?; **~ dann!** see you then!; **von ... ~ (einschließlich) ...** from ... to *or* till *or* through *(US)* ...
  (b) *(räumlich)* to; *(in Buch, Film etc auch)* up to. **ich fahre nur ~ München** I'm only going to *or* as far as Munich; **~ dorthin sind es nur 8 km** it's only 5 miles (to get) there; **~ hierher und nicht weiter** *(lit, fig)* this far and no further; **~ mindestens Carlisle** at least as far as Carlisle.
  (c) *(bei Zahlen)* up to; *(bis zu einer unteren Grenze von)* (down) to. **Kinder ~ sechs Jahre** children up to the age of six.
**2** *adv* (a) *(zeitlich)* until, till; *(bis spätestens)* by. **~ zu diesem Zeitpunkt** up to this time; **das sollte ~ zum nächsten Sommer fertig sein** that should be finished by next summer; **~ auf weiteres** until further notice.
  (b) *(räumlich)* to; *durch, über, unter* right. **~ an unser Grundstück** (right *or* up) to our plot; **es sind noch 16 km ~ nach Schlüchtern** it's another 10 miles to Schlüchtern; **~ ins letzte/kleinste** (right) down to the last/smallest detail.
  (c) *(bei Zahlen)* **~ zu** up to; *(bis zu einer unteren Grenze von)* (down) to; **Gefängnis ~ zu 8 Jahren** a maximum of 8 years' imprisonment.
  (d) **~ auf** *(+acc)* *(außer)* except (for); *(einschließlich)* (right) down to.
**3** *conj* (a) *(beiordnend)* to. **zehn ~ zwanzig Stück** ten to twenty; **bewölkt ~ bedeckt** cloudy or overcast. (b) *(unterordnend)* until, till; *(nicht später als)* by the time. **ich warte noch, ~ es dunkel wird** I'll wait until *or* till it gets dark; **~ es dunkel wird, möchte ich zu Hause sein** I want to get home before it gets dark.
**Bisam** *m* **-e** *or* **-s** *(Pelz)* musquash.
**Bisamratte** *f* muskrat (beaver).
**Bischof** *m* **≠e** bishop.
**bischöflich** *adj* episcopal.
**bisexuell** *adj* bisexual.
**bisher** *adv* until *or* till now; *(und immer noch)* up to now. **~ nicht** not until *or* till now, not before; *(und immer noch nicht)* not as yet; **das wußte ich ~ nicht** I didn't know that before; **~ habe ich es ihm nicht gesagt** I haven't told him as yet; **ein ~ unbekannter Stern** a hitherto unknown star.
**bisherig** *adj attr (vorherig)* previous; *(momentan)* present, up to now. **in meiner ~en Karriere** in my career up to now.
**Biskaya** [bɪsˈkaːja] *f* **Golf von ~** Bay of Biscay.
**Biskuit** [bɪsˈkviːt] *nt or m* **-s** *or* **-e** sponge.
**Biskuit-:** **~gebäck** *nt* sponge cake/cakes; **~rolle** *f* Swiss roll; **~teig** *m* sponge mixture.
**bislang** *adv* = **bisher**.
**Bison** *m* **-s** bison.
**biß** *pret of* **beißen**.
**Biß** *m* **-sse** bite; *(fig)* vigour, spirit.
**bißchen 1** *adj inv* **ein ~ Geld/Liebe/Wärme** a bit of *or* a little money/love/warmth; **das ~ Geld, das wir haben** what little money we have; **ich habe kein ~**

**Hunger** I'm not a bit hungry. **2** *adv* **ein** ~ a bit, a little; **ein** ~ **(zu) wenig** rather (too) little; **ein** ~ **mehr/viel/teuer** *etc* a bit more/much/expensive *etc.*

**Bissen** *m* - mouthful; *(Imbiß)* bite (to eat). **er will keinen** ~ **anrühren** he won't eat a thing; **sich** *(dat)* **jeden** ~ **vom** *or* **am Munde absparen** to watch every penny one spends.

**bissig** *adj* **(a)** vicious; *Bemerkung* caustic. ~ **sein** to bite; „**Vorsicht,** ~**er Hund**" "Beware of the dog". **(b)** *(übellaunig)* snappy.

**Bißwunde** *f* bite.

**bist** *2. pers sing pres of* **sein.**

**Bistum** ['bɪstuːm] *nt* diocese, bishopric.

**bisweilen** *adv (geh)* from time to time.

**Bit** *nt* **-s** *(Comp)* bit.

**Bittbrief** *m* petition.

**Bitte** *f* **-n** request; *(inständig)* plea. **ich habe eine große** ~ **an dich** I have a big favour to ask you; **er kann ihr keine** ~ **abschlagen** he can't refuse her anything.

**bitte** *interj* **(a)** *(bittend, auffordernd)* please. ~ **schön** please; ~ **nicht!** no, please!, please don't; **ja** ~! yes please. **(b)** *(bei höflicher Frage etc)* ~ **schön?** *(in Geschäft)* can I help you?; *(in Gaststätte)* what would you like?; ~**(, Sie wünschen)?** what can I do for you?; **ja** ~? yes?; ~**(, nehmen Sie doch Platz)!** *(form)* please *or* do sit down; **Entschuldigung! —** ~! I'm sorry! — that's all right; **aber** ~! sure *(col)*; **na** ~! there you are! **(c)** *(sarkastisch: nun gut)* all right. ~, **wie du willst** (all right) just as you like. **(d)** *(Dank erwidernd)* ~ **(sehr** *or* **schön)** you're welcome, not at all; **aber** ~! there's no need to thank me. **(e)** *(nachfragend)* **(wie)** ~? (I beg your) pardon? *(auch iro)*, pardon me *(US)*, sorry?

**bitten** *pret* **bat,** *ptp* **gebeten 1** *vt* **(a)** to ask; *(inständig)* to beg. **jdn um etw** ~ to ask/beg sb for sth; **jdn (darum)** ~, **etw zu tun** to ask *etc* sb to do sth; **darf ich Sie um Ihren Namen** ~? might I ask your name?; **er läßt sich nicht (lange)** ~ you don't have to ask him twice; **aber ich bitte dich!** not at all; **wenn ich** ~ **darf** *(form)* if you please, if you wouldn't mind; **ich bitte darum** *(form)* if you wouldn't mind; **ich muß doch (sehr)** ~! well I must say! **(b)** *(einladen)* to ask, to invite. **jdn auf ein Glas Wein** ~ to invite sb to have a glass of wine. **(c)** *(bestellen)* **jdn zu sich** ~ to ask sb to come and see one. **2** *vi* **(a)** to ask; *(inständig)* to plead, to beg. **um etw** ~ to ask (for) *or* request sth; to plead *or* beg for sth; **bei jdm um etw** ~ to ask sb for sth. **(b)** *(einladen)* **ich lasse** ~ would you ask him/her to come in now?; **darf ich (um den nächsten Tanz)** ~? may I have the pleasure (of the next dance)?

**Bitten** *nt no pl* pleading. **auf** ~ **von** at the request of.

**bittend** *adj* pleading.

**bitter** *adj* bitter; *Schokolade* plain; *(fig) Wahrheit, Lehre, Verlust* hard, painful; *Zeit, Schicksal* hard; *Ernst* deadly; *Hohn, Spott* cruel; *Not, Notwendigkeit* dire; *Leid, Unrecht* grievous. **bis zum** ~**en Ende** to the bitter end; **jdn** ~ **machen** to embitter sb, to make sb bitter; **etw** ~ **nötig haben** to be in dire need of sth; **solche Fehler rächen sich** ~ one pays dearly for mistakes like that.

**Bitter-:** **b**~**böse** *adj* furious; **b**~**ernst** *adj* deadly serious; **damit ist es mir b**~**ernst** I am deadly serious *or* in deadly earnest; **b**~**kalt** *adj attr* bitterly cold; ~**keit** *f (lit, fig)* bitterness; **b**~**lich** *adv* bitterly; **b**~**süß** *adj (lit, fig)* bitter-sweet.

**Bitt-:** ~**gesuch** *nt,* ~**schrift** *f* petition; ~**steller(in** *f)* *m* - petitioner.

**Biwak** *nt* **-s** *or* **-e** bivouac.

**bizarr** *adj* bizarre.

**Bizeps** *m* **-e** biceps.

**Bj.** = **Baujahr.**

**Blabla** *nt no pl (col)* waffle *(col)*.

**Blag** *nt* **-en, Blage** *f* **-n** *(pej col)* brat.

**blähen 1** *vt* to swell; *Anorak, Gardine* to fill; *Nüstern* to flare. **2** *vr* to swell; *(Segel auch, Anorak, Gardine)* to billow; *(Nüstern)* to flare. **3** *vi (Speisen)* to cause flatulence *or* wind.

**blähend** *adj (Med)* flatulent.

**Blähung** *f usu pl (Med)* wind *no pl,* flatulence *no pl.*

**blamabel** *adj* shameful.

**Blamage** [bla'maːʒə] *f* **-n** disgrace.

**blamieren*** **1** *vt* to disgrace. **2** *vr* to make a fool of oneself.

**blanchieren*** [blãˈʃiːrən] *vt (Cook)* to blanch.

**blank** *adj* **(a)** shiny, shining. **etw** ~ **polieren** to polish sth till it shines. **(b)** *(nackt)* bare; *Schwert* naked; *(col: ohne Geld)* broke; *(Cards: einzeln)* single. **eine Karte** ~ **haben** to have only one card of a suit. **(c)** *(rein)* pure, sheer; *Hohn* utter.

**Blanko-** *in cpds* blank; ~**scheck** *m* blank cheque *(Brit)* *or* check *(US)*; ~**vollmacht** *f* carte blanche.

**Bläschen** ['blɛːsçən] *nt (Med)* small blister.

**Blase** *f* **-n (a)** *(Seifen*~, *Luft*~*)* bubble. **(b)** *(Med)* blister. **sich** *(dat)* ~**n laufen** *etc* to get blisters from walking *etc.* **(c)** *(Anat)* bladder. **(d)** *(pej col: Clique)* gang *(col)*, mob *(col)*.

**Blasebalg** *m* (pair of) bellows.

**blasen** *pret* **blies,** *ptp* **geblasen 1** *vi* to blow. **zum Rückzug** ~ *(lit, fig)* to sound the retreat; **zum Aufbruch** ~ *(fig)* to say it's time to go; **es bläst** *(col)* it's blowy *(col)* *or* windy. **2** *vt* **(a)** to blow. **(b)** *Posaune etc* to play. **(c)** *(col)* **dir/ihm werd ich was** ~! I'll give you/him a piece of my mind.

**Blasen-:** ~**entzündung** *f,* ~**katarrh** *m* cystitis; ~**leiden** *nt* bladder trouble *no art.*

**Bläser(in** *f)* *m* - *(Mus)* wind player. **die** ~ the wind (section).

**blasiert** *adj (pej geh)* blasé.

**Blasiertheit** *f (pej geh)* blasé character; *(von Mensch)* blasé attitude.

**Blas-:** ~**instrument** *nt* wind instrument; ~**kapelle** *f* brass band; ~**musik** *f* brass band music.

**Blasphemie** *f* blasphemy.

**blasphemisch** *adj* blasphemous.

**blaß** *adj* **(a)** *Haut, Farbe, Licht* pale. ~ **werden** to grow *or* go pale, to pale; *(vor Schreck auch)* to blanch; ~ **vor Neid werden** *(fig)* to go green with envy. **(b)** *(fig) Ahnung, Vorstellung* faint, vague; *Ausdruck* weak, insipid.

**blaß-** *in cpds* pale.

**Blässe** *f* paleness, pallor.

**Blatt** *nt* ⸚**er (a)** *(Bot)* leaf. **kein** ~ **vor den Mund nehmen** not to mince one's words. **(b)** *(Papier etc)* sheet. **ein** ~ **Papier** a sheet of paper; **(noch) ein unbeschriebenes** ~ **sein** *(unerfahren)* to be inexperienced; *(ohne Image)* to be an unknown quantity; **vom** ~ **singen/spielen** to sight-read. **(c)** *(Seite)* page. **das steht auf einem anderen** ~ *(fig)* that's another story. **(d)** *(Zeitung)* paper. **(e)** *(von Säge, Ruder)* blade. **(f)** *(Cards)* hand; *(Einzelkarte)* card. **das** ~ **hat sich gewendet** *(fig)* the tables have been turned.

**blätt(e)rig** *adj Teig* flaky; *Farbe etc* flaking.

**blättern 1** *vi* **(a)** **in einem Buch** ~ to leaf through a book. **(b)** *(Comp)* to scroll. **2** *vt Geldscheine, Spielkarten* to put down one by one.

**Blätterteig** *m* puff pastry.

**Blatt-:** ~**feder** *f (Tech)* leaf spring; ~**gemüse** *nt* greens *pl;* **ein** ~**gemüse** a leaf vegetable; ~**gold** *nt* gold leaf; ~**grün** *nt* chlorophyll; ~**laus** *f* greenfly, aphid; **b~los** *adj* leafless; **~pflanze** *f* foliage plant; **~salat** *m* green salad; **~schuß** *m (Hunt)* shot through the shoulder to the heart; **~silber** *nt* silver leaf; **~werk** *nt no pl* foliage.

**blau** *adj* **(a)** blue. **Forelle** *etc* ~ *(Cook)* trout *etc* au bleu; **ein ~es Auge** *(col)* a black eye; **mit einem ~en Auge davonkommen** *(fig)* to get off lightly; **~es Blut** blue blood; **ein ~er Brief** *(Sch) letter informing parents that their child is likely to have to repeat a year;* **ein ~er Fleck** a bruise; **er wird sein ~es Wunder erleben** *(col)* he won't know what's hit him *(col)*. **(b)** *usu pred (col: betrunken)* drunk, tight *(col)*.

**Blau** *nt* - *or (col)* **-s** blue.

**Blau-: b~äugig** *adj* blue-eyed; *(fig)* naïve; **~äugigkeit** *f (fig)* naïvety; **~beere** *f* bilberry, blueberry *(esp US)*; **b~blütig** *adj* blue-blooded.

**Blaue** *nt no pl* **(a) das ~ vom Himmel (herunter) lügen** *(col)* to tell a pack of lies; **jdm das ~ vom Himmel (herunter) versprechen** *(col)* to promise sb the moon. **(b)** *(ohne Ziel)* **ins ~ hinein** *(col)* at random; **eine Fahrt ins ~** a mystery tour.

**Bläue** *f no pl* blueness; *(des Himmels auch)* blue.

**Blaue(r)** *m decl as adj (col)* hundred mark note.

**blau-: ~grau** *adj* blue-grey; **~grün** *adj* blue-green; **B~helm** *m (col)* UN soldier.

**bläulich** *adj* bluish, bluey.

**Blau-: ~licht** *nt (von Polizei etc)* flashing blue light; *(Lampe)* blue light; **mit ~licht** *Krankenwagen etc* with its blue light flashing; **b~machen** *sep (col)* **1** *vi* to skip work, to skive *(Brit col)*; **2** *vt* **den Freitag/zwei Tage b~machen** to skip work on Friday/for two days; **~mann** *m, pl* **~männer** *(col)* boilersuit; **~meise** *f* bluetit; **~pause** *f* blueprint; **~säure** *f* prussic acid; **~strumpf** *m* bluestocking; **~tanne** *f* colorado spruce; **~wal** *m* blue whale.

**Blech** *nt* **-e (a)** *no pl* (sheet) metal. **(b)** *(Blechstück)* metal plate. **(c)** *(Backblech)* (baking) tray. **(d)** *no pl (col: Blechinstrumente)* brass. **(e)** *no pl (col: Unsinn)* rubbish *no art (col)*. **red' kein ~** don't talk crap *(col!)*.

**Blech-: ~bläser** *m* brass player; **die ~bläser** the brass (section); **~blasinstrument** *nt* brass instrument; **~büchse** *f*, **~dose** *f* tin *(Brit)*, can.

**blechen** *vti (col)* to cough up *(col)*.

**blechern** *adj* **(a)** *attr* metal. **(b)** *Geräusch* tinny.

**Blech-: ~instrument** *nt* brass instrument; **~kanister** *m* metal can; **~kiste** *f (pej col)* (old) crate *(col)*; **~lawine** *f (pej col)* endless queue *(Brit)* or line of cars; **~napf** *m* metal bowl; **~schaden** *m* damage to the bodywork; **~schere** *f* (pair of) metal shears; **~trommel** *f* tin drum.

**blecken** *vt* **die Zähne ~** to bare one's teeth.

**Blei** *nt* **-e (a)** *no pl (Metall)* lead. **jdm wie ~ in den Gliedern** *or* **Knochen liegen** *(Schreck)* to paralyze sb; *(Depression)* to weigh sb down. **(b)** *(Lot)* plumb, (plumb-)bob.

**Bleibe** *f* **-n** place to stay. **eine/keine ~ haben** to have somewhere/nowhere to stay.

**bleiben** *pret* **blieb**, *ptp* **geblieben** *vi aux sein* **(a)** to stay, to remain. **unbeachtet ~** to go unnoticed; **unbeantwortet ~** to be left *or* to remain unanswered; **in Übung/Form ~** to keep in practice/form; **wach ~** to stay *or* keep awake; **wenn das Wetter so bleibt** if the weather stays *or* keeps like this; **sitzen/stehen ~** to remain seated/standing; **bitte, ~ Sie doch sitzen** please don't get up; **von etw ~** to stay *or* keep away from sth; **wo bleibst du so lange?** *(col)* what's keeping you?; **wo sind denn all die alten Häuser geblieben?** what happened to all the old houses? **(b)** *(fig)* **bei etw ~** to keep *or* stick *(col)* to sth; **das bleibt unter uns** that's (just) between our-

selves; **wir möchten unter uns ~** we want to keep ourselves to ourselves. **(c)** *(übrigbleiben)* to be left, to remain. **es blieb keine andere Wahl** there was no other choice; **es bleibt abzuwarten** it remains to be seen; **es bleibt zu hoffen, daß ...** I/we can only hope that ... **(d)** *(col: versorgt werden)* **und wo bleibe ich?** and what about me?; **sieh zu, wo du bleibst!** that's your problem!

**bleibend** *adj Wert, Erinnerung etc* lasting; *Schaden, Zähne* permanent.

**bleibenlassen** *vt sep irreg (col)* **(a)** *(unterlassen)* **etw ~** to give sth a miss *(col)*; **das wirst du ganz schön ~** you'll do nothing of the sort! **(b)** *(aufgeben)* to give up.

**bleich** *adj* pale. **~ wie der Tod** deathly pale.

**bleichen** *vt* to bleach.

**Bleich-: ~gesicht** *nt* **(a)** *(col: blasser Mensch)* pasty-face *(col)*; **(b)** *(Weißer)* paleface; **b~gesichtig** *adj (col)* pasty-faced *(col)*; **~mittel** *nt* bleach.

**bleiern** *adj* **(a)** *attr (aus Blei)* lead. **wie eine ~e Ente schwimmen** *(hum)* to swim like a brick. **(b)** *(fig)* leaden; *Verantwortung* onerous. **es lag ihr ~ in den Gliedern** her limbs were like lead.

**Blei-: b~frei** *adj Benzin etc* lead-free, unleaded; **b~frei fahren** to drive on unleaded petrol; **~gehalt** *m* lead content; **~gießen** *nt New Year's Eve custom of telling fortunes by the shapes made by molten lead dropped into cold water;* **b~haltig** *adj Benzin etc* leaded; **b~haltig sein** to contain lead; **~kristall** *nt* lead crystal; **~satz** *m (Typ)* hot-metal setting; **b~schwer** *adj* = **bleiern (b)**; **~soldat** *m* ≈ tin soldier.

**Bleistift** *m* pencil; *(zum Malen)* crayon.

**Bleistift-: ~absatz** *m* stiletto heel; **~mine** *f* pencil lead; **~spitzer** *m* pencil sharpener.

**Bleivergiftung** *f* lead poisoning.

**Blende** *f* **-n (a)** *(Lichtschutz)* shade, screen; *(an Fenster)* blind. **(b)** *(Phot)* *(Öffnung)* aperture; *(Einstellungsposition)* f-stop; *(Vorrichtung)* diaphragm. **die ~ schließen** to stop down; **bei** *or* **mit ~ 2,8** at (an aperture of) f2.8. **(c)** *(Film, TV)* fade. **(d)** *(Sew)* trim.

**blenden 1** *vt* **(a)** *(lit, fig: bezaubern)* to dazzle; *(fig: täuschen)* to blind, to hoodwink. **(b)** *(blind machen)* to blind. **2** *vi* to dazzle.

**blendend** *adj* splendid; *Pianist, Schüler etc* brilliant; *Stimmung* sparkling. **~ aussehen** to be extremely good-looking; **sich ~ amüsieren** to have a splendid *or* wonderful time; **es geht mir ~** I feel wonderful.

**blendfrei** *adj* dazzle-free; *Glas, Bildschirm* non-reflective.

**Blesse** *f* **-n** *(Fleck)* blaze.

**bleu** [blØ:] *adj inv (Fashion)* light blue.

**Blick** *m* **-e (a)** look; *(flüchtiger ~)* glance. **auf den ersten ~** at first glance; **Liebe auf den ersten ~** love at first sight; **auf den zweiten ~** when one looks again; **mit einem ~** at a glance; **jds ~ (dat) ausweichen** to avoid sb's eye; **jds ~ erwidern** to return sb's gaze; **jdn mit seinen ~en verschlingen** to devour sb with one's eyes; **sie zog alle ~e auf sich** everybody's eyes were drawn to her; **einen ~ auf etw (acc) werfen** to throw a glance at sth; **jdm keinen ~ schenken** not to spare sb a glance; **wenn ~e töten könnten!** if looks could kill!; **mein ~ fiel auf sein leeres Glas** I noticed his empty glass; **den ~ heben** to look up; **den ~ senken** to look down. **(b)** *(Augenausdruck)* look in one's eyes. **den bösen ~ haben** to have the evil eye. **(c)** *(Ausblick)* view. **ein Zimmer mit ~ auf den Park**

a room overlooking the park.
   (d) *(Verständnis)* **seinen ~ für etw schärfen** to increase one's awareness of sth; **einen (guten) ~ für etw haben** to have an eye for sth; **er hat keinen ~ dafür** he doesn't see *or* notice that sort of thing.
**blickdicht** *adj Strümpfe* opaque.
**blicken** *vi (auf +acc* at*)* to look; *(flüchtig ~)* to glance. **sich ~ lassen** to put in an appearance; **laß dich hier ja nicht mehr ~**! don't show your face here again!; **laß dich doch mal wieder ~**! why don't you drop in some time?; **das läßt tief ~** that's very revealing.
**Blick-:** **~fang** *m* eye-catcher; **als ~fang** to catch the eye; **~feld** *nt* field of vision; **ins ~feld (der Öffentlichkeit) treten** to become the focus of (public) attention; **~kontakt** *m* visual contact; **~punkt** *m (fig)* **(a)** limelight; **im ~punkt der Öffentlichkeit stehen** to be in the public eye; **(b)** *(Standpunkt)* point of view; **~richtung** *f* line of vision; *(fig)* outlook; **~winkel** *m (fig)* viewpoint.
**blieb** *pret of* **bleiben**.
**blies** *pret of* **blasen**.
**blind** *adj* **(a)** *(lit, fig)* blind *(für* to*)*; *Zufall* pure; *Alarm* false. **jdm ~ gehorchen** to obey sb blindly; **ein ~es Huhn findet auch mal ein Korn** *(Prov)* anyone can be lucky now and again; **~er Fleck** *(Physiol)* blind spot; **~e Gewalt** brute force; **~er Eifer schadet nur** *(Prov)* it's not a good thing to be over-enthusiastic; **etw ~ herausgreifen** to pick sth at random. **(b)** *(getrübt)* dull; *Spiegel etc* clouded. **(c)** *(Archit)* false; *Fenster* blind, false. **(d) ein ~er Passagier** a stowaway.
**Blinddarm** *m (Anat)* appendix.
**Blinddarm-:** **~entzündung** *f* appendicitis; **~operation** *f* appendectomy; **~reizung** *f* grumbling appendix.
**Blindekuh** *f no art* **~ spielen** to play blind man's buff.
**Blinden-:** **~hund** *m* guide-dog; **~schrift** *f* braille; **~stock** *m* white stick.
**Blinde(r)** *mf decl as adj* blind person/man/woman *etc.* **die ~n** the blind; **das sieht doch ein ~r** *(col)* any fool can see that.
**Blind-:** **~flug** *m* blind flight; **~gänger** *m (Mil, fig)* dud; **~heit** *f (lit, fig)* blindness; **mit ~heit geschlagen** *(fig)* blind; **b~lings** *adv* blindly; **~schleiche** *f* slow-worm; **b~schreiben** *vti sep irreg* to touch-type; **b~wütig** *adj* in a blind rage.
**blinken 1** *vi* **(a)** *(funkeln)* to gleam. **(b)** *(Leuchtturm)* to flash; *(Aut)* to indicate. **2** *vt Signal* to flash. **rechts/links ~** to indicate right/left.
**Blinker** *m* - *(Aut)* indicator, turn signal *(US)*.
**Blinklicht** *nt* flashing light.
**blinzeln** *vi* to blink; *(zwinkern)* to wink; *(geblendet)* to squint.
**Blitz** *m* -e **(a)** *(das Blitzen)* lightning *no pl, no indef art*; *(~strahl)* flash of lightning; *(Lichtstrahl)* flash (of light). **vom ~ getroffen/erschlagen werden** to be struck by lightning; **wie vom ~ getroffen** *(fig)* thunderstruck; **einschlagen wie ein ~** *(fig)* to come as a bombshell; **wie ein ~ aus heiterem Himmel** *(fig)* like a bolt from the blue; **wie der ~** *(col)* like lightning. **(b)** *(Phot col)* flash, *(Blitzlichtgerät auch)* flashgun.
**Blitz-:** **~ableiter** *m* lightning conductor; **~aktion** *f* lightning operation; **~angriff** *m (Mil)* lightning attack; **b~artig** = **b~schnell; b~(e)blank** *adj (col)* spick and span.
**blitzen 1** *vi impers* **es blitzt** there's lightning; **es blitzt und donnert** there's thunder and lightning; **es fing an zu ~** lightning began. **2** *vi* **(a)** *(strahlen)* to

flash, to sparkle. **vor Sauberkeit ~** to be sparkling clean. **(b)** *(Phot col)* to use a flash.
**Blitz-:** **~gerät** *nt (Phot)* flash (unit); **~karriere** *f* **eine ~karriere machen** to have a meteoric rise; **~krieg** *m* blitzkrieg; **~licht** *nt (Phot)* flash (light); **b~sauber** *adj* spick and span; **~schlag** *m* flash of lightning; **vom ~schlag getroffen** struck by lightning; **b~schnell 1** *adj* lightning *attr*; **2** *adv* like lightning; *(plötzlich)* verschwinden in a flash; **~sieg** *m* lightning victory; **~strahl** *m* flash of lightning; **~umfrage** *f* quick poll; **~würfel** *m (Phot)* flashcube.
**Block** *m* ⁼e **(a)** block *(von, aus* of*)*. **etw im ~ kaufen** to buy sth in bulk. **(b)** *pl auch* **-s** *(Häuser~)* block. **(c)** *pl* **-s** *(Rail)* block. **(d)** *(Pol) (Staaten~)* bloc; *(Fraktion)* faction. **(e)** *(Comp)* block.
**Blockade** *f (Absperrung)* blockade.
**Block-:** **~bildung** *f (Pol)* formation of blocs/factions; **~buchstabe** *m* block letter *or* capital.
**blocken** *vti (Rail, Sport, Comp)* to block.
**Block-:** **~flöte** *f* recorder; **b~frei** *adj* non-aligned; **~freiheit** *f* non-alignment; **~haus** *nt,* **~hütte** *f* log cabin.
**blockieren\* 1** *vt* **(a)** to block. **(b)** *(mit Blockade)* to blockade. **2** *vi* to jam.
**Blockierung** *f siehe vt* blocking; blockade.
**Block-:** **~politik** *f* joint policy; **~satz** *m (Typ)* justified print; **~schokolade** *f no pl* cooking chocolate; **~schrift** *f* block capitals *pl or* letters *pl*; **~stunde** *f (Sch)* double period.
**blöd(e)** *adj (col)* silly, stupid; *(ärgerlich)* Sache, Situation stupid; Gefühl funny. **das B~e daran ist, daß ...** the silly thing about it is that ...
**blödeln** *vi (col)* to fool around; *(Witze machen)* to make jokes.
**Blödhammel** *m (pej col)* idiot *(col)*.
**Blödheit** *f* **(a)** *(Dummheit)* stupidity. **(b)** *(blödes Verhalten)* stupid thing; *(alberne Bemerkung)* silly *or* stupid remark. **(c)** *(Med)* imbecility.
**Blödian** *m* -e *(col)*, **Blödmann** *m, pl* -männer *(col)* idiot.
**Blödsinn** *m no pl* nonsense. **das ist doch ~** that's nonsense; **~ machen** to fool about.
**blödsinnig** *adj* stupid, idiotic.
**blöken** *vi (Schaf)* to bleat.
**blond** *adj (blondhaarig)* fair(-haired); *(bei Frauen auch)* blonde; *(bei Männern auch)* blond. **~es Gift** *(hum col)* blonde bombshell *(col)*.
**blond-:** **~gefärbt** *adj* dyed blonde/blond; **~gelockt** *adj* with fair curly hair; *Haar* fair curly *attr*; **~haarig** *adj* fair-haired, blonde/blond.
**blondieren\*** *vt* to bleach.
**Blondine** *f* blonde.
**bloß 1** *adj* **(a)** *(unbedeckt)* bare. **etw auf der ~en Haut tragen** to wear sth next to the skin; **mit ~en Füßen** barefoot(ed); **mit der ~en Hand** with one's bare hand; **mit ~em Auge** with the naked eye. **(b)** *attr (alleinig)* mere; *Neid, Dummheit* sheer; *Gedanke, Anblick* very. **er kam mit dem ~en Schrecken davon** he got off with no more than a fright. **2** *adv* only. **wie kann so etwas ~ geschehen?** how on earth can something like that happen?; **tu das ~ nicht wieder!** don't you dare do that again; **geh mir ~ aus dem Weg** just get out of my way.
**Blöße** *f* **-n** *(geh)* bareness; *(Nacktheit)* nakedness. **sich** *(dat)* **eine ~ geben** *(fig)* to reveal a weak spot.
**Bloß-:** **b~legen** *vt sep* to uncover; *(ausgraben auch, Med)* to expose; *(fig)* Geheimnis to reveal; *Hintergründe* to bring to light; **b~liegen** *vi sep irreg aux sein* to be uncovered; *(Ausgegrabenes auch, Med)* to be exposed; **b~stellen** *sep* **1** *vt jdn* to show up;

*Lügner, Betrüger* to unmask, to expose; **2** *vr* to show oneself up; **sich als Lügner b~stellen** to show oneself to be a liar; **~stellung** *f siehe vt* showing up; unmasking, exposing; **b~strampeln** *vr sep* to kick one's covers off.

**Blouson** [blu'zõ:] *m or nt* **-s** blouson, bomber jacket.

**blubbern** *vi (col)* (a) to bubble. (b) *(Blödsinn reden)* to waffle *(col)*.

**Blücher** *m:* **er geht ran wie ~** *(col)* he doesn't hang about *(col)*.

**Bluff** *m* **-s** bluff.

**bluffen** *vti* to bluff.

**blühen** *vi* (a) *(Blume)* to flower, to bloom; *(Bäume)* to be in blossom, to blossom. (b) *(col: bevorstehen)* to be in store *(jdm* for sb*)*. **... dann blüht dir aber was ...** then you'll be in for it *(col)*.

**blühend** *adj Baum* blossoming; *Aussehen* radiant; *Pflanze* blooming; *Garten* full of flowers; *(fig) Geschäft etc* flourishing, thriving; *Unsinn* absolute; *Phantasie* vivid, lively. **wie das ~e Leben aussehen** to look the very picture of health.

**Blume** *f* **-n** (a) flower; *(Topfblume)* pot plant. **jdm etw durch die ~ sagen** to say sth in a roundabout way to sb. (b) *(von Wein)* bouquet; *(von Bier)* head.

**Blumen-** *in cpds* flower; **~bank** *f* stand for plants; **~beet** *nt* flowerbed; **~erde** *f* potting compost; **~geschäft** *nt* florist's (shop); **~kasten** *m* window box; **~kohl** *m no pl* cauliflower; **~kübel** *m* flower tub; **~meer** *nt* sea of flowers; **~muster** *nt* floral pattern; **b~reich** *adj* full of flowers; *(fig) Sprache etc* flowery; **~strauß** *m* bouquet, bunch of flowers; **~topf** *m* flowerpot; *(größer)* plant pot; **damit ist kein ~topf zu gewinnen** *(col)* that's nothing to write home about *(col)*; **~vase** *f* (flower) vase; **~zucht** *f* flower growing; **~zwiebel** *f* bulb.

**blümerant** *adj Gefühl* queer. **mir ist/wird ~** I am feeling/feel queer.

**blumig** *adj (lit, fig)* flowery.

**Bluse** *f* **-n** blouse.

**Blut** *nt no pl (lit, fig)* blood. **er lag in seinem ~** he lay in a pool of blood; **es ist viel ~ geflossen** there was a lot of bloodshed; **er kann kein ~ sehen** he can't stand the sight of blood; **~ geleckt haben** *(fig)* to have tasted blood; **böses ~ machen** *or* **schaffen** to cause bad blood; **jdm steigt das ~ in den Kopf** the blood rushes to sb's head; **ihnen stockte** *or* **gefror** *or* **gerann das ~ in den Adern** their blood froze; **heißes** *or* **feuriges ~ haben** to be hot-blooded; **kaltes ~ bewahren** to remain unmoved; **(nur) ruhig ~** keep your shirt on *(col)*; **jdn/sich bis aufs ~ bekämpfen** to fight sb/fight ferociously; **frisches ~** *(fig)* new blood; **~ und Wasser schwitzen** *(col)* to sweat blood; **das liegt mir/ihm im ~** it's in my/his blood.

**Blut-:** **~ader** *f* vein; **~alkohol(gehalt)** *m* blood alcohol level; **~apfelsine** *f* blood orange; **b~arm** *adj (Med, fig)* anaemic *(Brit)*, anemic *(US)*; **~armut** *f (Med)* anaemia *(Brit)*, anemia *(US)*; **~austausch** *m (Med)* exchange transfusion; **~bad** *nt* bloodbath; **~bahn** *f* bloodstream; **~bank** *f* blood bank; **b~befleckt** *adj* bloodstained; **b~beschmiert** *adj* smeared with blood; **~bild** *nt* blood count; **~buche** *f* copper beech; **~druck** *m* blood pressure.

**Blüte** *f* **-n** (a) flower, bloom; *(von Baum)* blossom. **eine ~ seiner Phantasie** a figment of his imagination. (b) *(das Blühen, Blütezeit)* flowering; *(von Baum)* blossom; **in (voller) ~ stehen** to be in (full) flower/blossom; *(Kultur, Geschäft)* to be flourishing; **sich zur vollen ~ entfalten** to come into full flower; *(Mädchen, Kultur)* to blossom; **seine ~ erleben** *(Kultur etc)* to reach its peak; **in der ~ seiner Jahre** in

the prime of his life. **(c)** *(col: gefälschte Note)* dud *(col)*.

**Blut|egel** *m* leech.

**bluten** *vi* to bleed *(an +dat, aus* from*)*. **mir blutet das Herz** my heart bleeds.

**Blüten-:** **~blatt** *nt* petal; **~honig** *m* honey *(made from flowers)*; **~kelch** *m* calyx; **~staub** *m* pollen; **b~weiß** *adj* sparkling white.

**Blut|entnahme** *f* taking a blood sample.

**Bluter** *m* **-** *(Med)* haemophiliac *(Brit)*, hemophiliac *(US)*.

**Blut|erguß** *m* haematoma *(spec)*; *(blauer Fleck)* bruise.

**Bluterkrankheit** *f* haemophilia *(Brit)*, hemophilia *(US)*.

**Blütezeit** *f* (a) flowering (period); *(von Baum)* blossom(-time). **während der ~ der Kirschbäume** while the cherries were in blossom. (b) *(fig)* heyday; *(von Mensch)* prime.

**Blut-:** **~farbstoff** *m* haemoglobin *(Brit)*, hemoglobin *(US)*; **~fleck** *m* bloodstain; **~gefäß** *nt* blood vessel; **~gerinnsel** *nt* blood clot; **~gruppe** *f* blood group; **~hochdruck** *m* high blood pressure; **~hund** *m (lit, fig)* bloodhound.

**blutig** *adj* (a) *(lit, fig)* bloody. **er hat ihn ~ geschlagen** he hit him and made him bleed. (b) *(col) Anfänger* absolute; *Ernst* deadly.

**Blut-:** **b~jung** *adj* very young; **~konserve** *f* unit of (stored) blood; **~körperchen** *nt* blood corpuscle; **~krebs** *m* leukaemia; **~kreislauf** *m* blood circulation; **~lache** *f* pool of blood; **b~leer** *adj* bloodless; **~leere** *f no pl* lack of blood; **b~los** *adj* bloodless; *(fig)* anaemic *(Brit)*, anemic *(US)*; **~orange** *f* blood orange; **~probe** *f* blood test; **~rache** *f* blood feud; **~rausch** *m* frenzy; **b~rot** *adj (liter)* blood-red; **b~rünstig** *adj* bloodthirsty; **~sauger** *m (lit, fig)* bloodsucker; *(Vampir)* vampire.

**Blutsbruder** *m* blood brother.

**Blut-:** **~schande** *f* incest; **~senkung** *f (Med)* sedimentation of the blood; **eine ~senkung machen** to test the sedimentation rate of the blood; **~spenden** *nt* giving blood *no art*; **~spender** *m* blood donor; **~spur** *f* trail of blood; **b~stillend** *adj* styptic.

**Blutstropfen** ['blu:ts-] *m* drop of blood.

**Blutsturz** *m* haemorrhage *(Brit)*, hemorrhage *(US)*.

**Bluts-:** **b~verwandt** *adj* related by blood; **~verwandte(r)** *mf decl as adj* blood relation; **~verwandtschaft** *f* blood relationship.

**Blut-:** **~tat** *f* bloody deed; **~transfusion** *f* blood transfusion; **b~überströmt** *adj* streaming with blood; **~übertragung** *f* blood transfusion.

**Blutung** *f* bleeding *no pl*; *(monatliche)* period.

**Blut-:** **b~unterlaufen** *adj* suffused with blood; *Augen* bloodshot; **~untersuchung** *f* blood test; **~vergießen** *nt no pl* bloodshed *no indef art*; **~vergiftung** *f* blood-poisoning *no indef art*; **~verlust** *m* loss of blood; **~wurst** *f* blood pudding *(US)*, black pudding *(Brit)*; **~zuckerspiegel** *m* blood sugar level; **~zufuhr** *f* blood supply.

**BLZ** [be:|ɛl'tsɛt] *f* **-s** = **Bankleitzahl.**

**BND** [be:|ɛn'de:] *m* = **Bundesnachrichtendienst.**

**Bö** *f* **-en** gust (of wind); *(stärker, mit Regen)* squall.

**Boa** *f* **-s** *(Schlange, Schal)* boa.

**Bob** *m* **-s** bob(sleigh).

**Bob-:** **~bahn** *f* bob(sleigh) run; **~fahrer** *m* bobber.

**Boccia** ['bɔtʃa] *nt or f no pl* bowls *sing.*

**Bock** *m* **=e** (a) *(Reh~, Kaninchen~)* buck; *(Schafs~)* ram; *(Ziegen~)* he-goat, billy-goat. **alter ~** *(col)* old goat *(col)*; **sturer/geiler ~** *(col)* stubborn old devil *(col)*/randy *(Brit)* or horny old goat *(col)*; **den ~ zum**

**Gärtner machen** *(fig)* to choose the worst possible person for the job; **einen ~ schießen** *(fig col)* to boob *(Brit col)*, to goof *(US col)*. **(b)** *(Gestell)* stand; *(Stützgerät)* support; *(für Auto)* ramp; *(aus Holzbalken, mit Beinen)* trestle; *(Säge~)* sawhorse. **(c)** *(Sport)* buck. **(d)** *(col: Lust)* **null ~!** can't be bothered *(col)*; **~e** or **(einen) ~ haben, etw zu tun** to fancy doing sth.

**Bockbier** *nt* bock (beer) *(type of strong beer)*.

**bocken** *vi* **(a)** *(Zugtier etc)* to refuse to move; *(nicht springen wollen: Pferd)* to refuse. **vor einer Hürde ~** to refuse to jump. **(b)** *(col: Auto, Mensch)* to play up.

**bockig** *adj (col)* stubborn, awkward.

**Bockmist** *m (col: dummes Gerede)* bullshit *(col!)*; **~ machen** to make a balls-up *(col!)*.

**Bocks-:** **~beutel** *m* *wide, rounded bottle used for Franconian wine*; **~horn** *nt*: **sich von jdm ins ~horn jagen lassen** to let sb upset one.

**Bock-:** **~springen** *nt* leapfrog; *(Sport)* vaulting; **~sprung** *m* leapfrog; *(Sport)* vault; **~wurst** *f* bockwurst *(large frankfurter)*.

**Boden** *m* ~ **(a)** ground; *(Erdreich auch)* soil; *(Fuß~)* floor; *(no pl: Terrain)* soil. **auf spanischem ~** on Spanish soil; **zu ~ fallen** to fall to the ground; **festen ~ unter den Füßen haben** to be on firm ground, to be on terra firma; **den ~ unter den Füßen verlieren** *(lit)* to lose one's footing; *(fig: in Diskussion)* to get out of one's depth; **ihm wurde der ~ (unter den Füßen) zu heiß** *(fig)* things were getting too hot for him; **ich hätte (vor Scham) in den ~ versinken können** *(fig)* I was so ashamed that I wished the ground would swallow me up; **am ~ zerstört sein** *(col)* to be shattered *(col)*; **(an) ~ gewinnen/verlieren** *(fig)* to gain/lose ground; **~ gutmachen** *(fig)* to make up ground; **etw aus dem ~ stampfen** *(fig)* to conjure sth up out of nothing; **Häuser aus dem ~ stampfen** to build overnight; **auf fruchtbaren ~ fallen** *(fig)* to fall on fertile ground; **jdm/einer Sache den ~ bereiten** *(fig)* to prepare the ground for sb/sth.

**(b)** *(unterste Fläche)* bottom; *(Torten~)* base. **(c)** *(Dach~, Heu~)* loft.

**(d)** *(fig: Grundlage)* **auf dem ~ der Tatsachen stehen** to base oneself on fact; **auf dem ~ der Tatsachen bleiben** to stick to the facts; **sich auf unsicherem ~ bewegen** to be on shaky ground; **einer Sache *(dat)* den ~ entziehen** to knock the bottom out of sth.

**Boden-:** **~belag** *m* floor covering; **~ertrag** *m (Agr)* crop yield; **~fläche** *f (Agr)* area of land; *(von Zimmer)* floor space or area; **~frost** *m* ground frost; **~haftung** *f (Aut)* adhesion *(of tyres (Brit) or tires (US))* no indef art; **~heizung** *f* underfloor heating; **~kammer** *f* attic; **~kontrolle** *f (Space)* ground control; **b~los** *adj* bottomless; *(col: unerhört)* indescribable, incredible; **~nebel** *m* ground mist; **~personal** *nt (Aviat)* ground personnel *pl*; **~reform** *f* land reform; **~satz** *m* sediment; *(von Kaffee auch)* grounds *pl*; **~schätze** *pl* mineral resources *pl*; **~schicht** *f* layer of soil; *(Geol)* stratum; **~schwelle** *f* speed bump; **~see** *m*: **der ~see** Lake Constance; **~spekulation** *f* land speculation; **b~ständig** *adj* native *(in +dat* to*)*; *(fig)* rooted in the soil; **~station** *f (Space)* ground station; **~turnen** *nt* floor exercises *pl*.

**Böe** *f* -**n** = **Bö**.

**bog** *pret of* **biegen**.

**Bogen** *m* - or ~ **(a)** curve, bend; *(Math)* arc; *(Mus)* tie; *(bei verschiedenen Noten)* slur; *(Ski)* turn. **einen ~ fahren** *(Ski)* to do a turn; **den ~ heraushaben** *(col)* to have got the hang of it *(col)*; **einen ~ machen** *(Fluß etc)* to curve; **einen großen ~ um jdn/etw machen** *(meiden)* to give sb/sth a wide berth; **jdn in hohem ~ hinauswerfen** *(col)* to fling sb out. **(b)** *(Archit)* arch. **(c)** *(Waffe, Mus: Geigen~ etc)* bow. **den ~ überspannen** *(fig)* to go too far. **(d)** *(Papier~)* sheet (of paper).

**Bogen-:** **~fenster** *nt* arched window; **b~förmig** *adj* arched; **~gang** *m (Archit)* arcade; **~schießen** *nt* archery; **~schütze** *m* archer, bowman.

**Bohle** *f* -**n** (thick) board.

**Böhme** *m* -**n**, **Böhmin** *f* Bohemian *(inhabitant of Bohemia)*.

**Böhmen** *nt* Bohemia.

**böhmisch** *adj* Bohemian. **das sind für mich ~e Dörfer** *(col)* that's all Greek to me *(col)*.

**Bohne** *f* -**n** bean. **dicke/grüne/weiße ~n** broad/green or French or runner/haricot beans; **blaue ~** *(col)* bullet; **nicht die ~** *(col)* not one little bit; **du hast wohl ~n in den Ohren** *(col)* are you deaf or something?

**Bohnen-:** **~eintopf** *m* bean stew; **~kaffee** *m* real coffee; **gemahlener ~kaffee** ground coffee; **~kraut** *nt* savory; **~stange** *f (fig col)* beanpole *(col)*; **~stroh** *nt*: **dumm wie ~stroh** *(col)* (as) thick as two (short) planks *(col)*; **~suppe** *f* bean soup.

**bohnern** *vti* to polish.

**Bohnerwachs** *nt* floor polish or wax.

**bohren 1** *vt* to bore; *(mit Bohrer auch)* to drill; *(hineindrücken)* Pfahl, Schwert etc to sink *(in +acc* into*)*. **2** *vi* **(a)** to bore *(in +dat* into*)*; to drill *(nach* for*)*. **in einem Zahn ~** to drill a tooth; **in der Nase ~** to pick one's nose. **(b)** *(fig) (drängen)* to keep on; *(peinigen: Schmerz, Zweifel etc)* to gnaw. **3** *vr* **sich in/durch etw *(acc)* ~** to bore its way into/through sth.

**bohrend** *adj (fig)* Blick piercing; Schmerz, Zweifel gnawing; Frage probing.

**Bohrer** *m* - *(elektrisch)* drill; *(Hand~)* gimlet.

**Bohr-:** **~insel** *f* drilling rig; *(für Öl auch)* oilrig; **~loch** *nt* borehole; *(in Holz, Metall etc)* drill-hole; **~maschine** *f* drill; **~turm** *m* derrick.

**Bohrung** *f* **(a)** *siehe vt* boring; drilling; sinking. **(b)** *(Loch)* bore(-hole); *(in Metall etc)* drill-hole.

**böig** *adj siehe* **Bö** gusty; squally.

**Boiler** ['bɔylɐ] *m* - hot-water heater.

**Boje** *f* -**n** buoy.

**Bolivianer(in** *f)* [boliviˈaːnɐ, -ərɪn] *m* Bolivian.

**bolivianisch** [boliviˈaːnɪʃ] *adj* Bolivian.

**Bolivien** [boˈliːviən] *nt* Bolivia.

**Böller** *m* - (small) cannon *(for ceremonial use)*.

**Böllerschuß** *m* gun salute.

**Bollwerk** *nt (lit, fig)* bulwark.

**Bolschewismus** *m* Bolshevism.

**Bolzen** *m* - **(a)** *(Tech)* pin; *(esp mit Gewinde)* bolt. **(b)** *(Geschoß)* bolt.

**bolzen** *(col)* **1** *vi* to kick about. **2** *vt* Ball to slam.

**Bombardement** [bɔmbardəˈmãː] *nt* -**s** bombardment; *(mit Bomben)* bombing. **ein ~ von** *(fig)* a deluge of.

**bombardieren*** *vt (lit)* to bomb; *(fig)* to bombard.

**Bombardierung** *f* bombing; *(fig)* bombardment.

**bombastisch** *adj* bombastic.

**Bombe** *f* -**n** bomb; *(Sport col: Schuß)* cracker *(col)*. **wie eine ~ einschlagen** to come as a (real) bombshell; **eine ~ platzen lassen** *(fig)* to drop a bombshell.

**Bomben-** *in cpds (Mil)* bomb; *(col: hervorragend)* fantastic *(col)*, great *(col)*; **~alarm** *m* bomb scare; **~angriff, ~anschlag** *m* bomb attack; **~erfolg** *m (col)* smash hit *(col)*; **~flugzeug** *nt* bomber; **~geschäft** *nt (col)* **ein ~geschäft** to be a gold mine; **ein ~geschäft machen** to do a roaring trade *(col) (mit* in*);* ~**hitze** *f (col)* sweltering heat *no indef art;* ~**leger(in** *f) m* bomber; ~**krater** *m* bomb crater; ~**räumexperte** *m* bomb disposal expert; **b**~**sicher** *adj* **(a)** *(Mil)* bombproof; **(b)** *(col)* dead certain *(col);* ~**splitter** *m* bomb fragment; ~**stimmung** *f* tremendous atmosphere; ~**teppich** *m* **einen** ~**teppich legen** to blanket-bomb an/the area; ~**trichter** *m* bomb crater.

**Bomber** *m* - bomber.

**Bommel** *f* -**n** bobble.

**Bon** [bɔŋ] *m* -**s** voucher; *(Kassenzettel)* receipt.

**Bonbon** [bɔŋ'bɔŋ] *nt or m* -**s** sweet *(Brit)*, candy *(US)*.

**Bonbonniere** [bɔŋbɔ'nieːrə] *f* -**n** box of chocolates.

**Bongo** [bɔŋgo] *nt or f* -**s** bongo (drum).

**Bonität** *f no pl (Fin)* financial standing, creditworthiness.

**Bonn** *nt* Bonn.

**Bonner** *adj attr* Bonn.

**Bonsai** *nt* bonsai.

**Bonus** *m* - *or* -**se** bonus; *(Univ, Sport: Punktvorteil)* bonus points *pl*.

**Bonze** *m* -**n** big shot *(col)*.

**Boot** *nt* -**e** boat. ~ **fahren** to go out in a boat; **wir sitzen alle in einem** ~ *(fig)* we're all in the same boat.

**Boots-:** ~**bau** *m* boat-building; ~**bauer** *m* boatbuilder; ~**fahrt** *f* boat trip; ~**flüchtlinge** *pl* boat people; ~**haus** *nt* boathouse; ~**mann** *m, pl* ~**leute** *(Naut)* bo'sun, boatswain; *(Dienstgrad)* petty officer; ~**steg** *m* landing-stage; ~**verleih** *m* boat hire.

**Bord**[1] *m no pl* **an** ~ **(eines Schiffes)** aboard *or* on board (a ship); **alle Mann an** ~**!** all aboard!; **an** ~ **gehen** to go aboard; **Mann über** ~**!** man overboard!; **über** ~ **gehen** to go overboard; *(fig)* to go by the board; **über** ~ **werfen** *(lit, fig)* to throw overboard, to jettison; **von** ~ **gehen** to leave the ship/ the plane; *(esp Passagiere am Ziel)* to disembark.

**Bord**[2] *nt* -**e** *(Wandbrett)* shelf.

**Bord-:** ~**buch** *nt* log(book); ~**computer** *m* on-board computer.

**Bordell** *nt* -**e** brothel.

**Bord-:** ~**funk** *m (Naut)* (ship's) radio; *(Aviat)* (aircraft) radio equipment; ~**funker** *m (Naut, Aviat)* radio operator; ~**karte** *f* boarding pass *or* card; ~**personal** *nt* cabin crew; ~**stein(kante** *f) m* kerb *(Brit)*, curb *(US)*.

**Bordüre** *f* -**n** edging, border.

**borgen** *vti* **(a)** *(erhalten)* to borrow *(von* from*).* **(b)** *(geben)* to lend, to loan *(jdm etw* sb sth, sth to sb*)*.

**Borke** *f* -**n** bark.

**borniert** *adj* bigoted, narrow-minded.

**Borneo** *nt* Borneo.

**Börse** *f* -**n** **(a)** *(Geld*~*)* purse; *(für Männer)* wallet *(Brit)*, billfold *(US)*. **(b)** *(Fin)* stock market, stock exchange.

**Börsen-:** ~**bericht** *m* stock market report; ~**geschäft** *nt (Wertpapierhandel)* stockbroking; *(Transaktion)* stock market transaction; ~**krach** *m* stock market crash; ~**kurs** *m* stock market price; ~**makler** *m* stockbroker; **b**~**notiert** *adj* Firma listed; ~**notierung** *f* quotation (on the stock exchange); ~**spekulation** *f* speculation on the stock market; ~**tendenz** *f* stock market trend.

**Borste** *f* -**n** bristle.

**Borstenvieh** *nt (hum col)* pigs *pl*, swine *pl*.

**borstig** *adj (lit, fig)* bristly.

**Borte** *f* -**n** braid trimming.

**bös** *adj* = **böse**.

**bös|artig** *adj* malicious, nasty; *Tier* vicious; *(Med)* malignant.

**Bös|artigkeit** *f siehe adj* maliciousness, nastiness;

viciousness; malignancy.

**Böschung** *f* embankment; *(von Straße auch)* bank.

**böse** *adj* **(a)** bad; *(stärker)* evil, wicked; *(col: unartig auch)* naughty; *Überraschung, Geschichte, Wunde* nasty. **ein** ~**r Geist** an evil spirit; **das war keine** ~ **Absicht** there was no harm intended; **das war nicht** ~ **gemeint** I/he *etc* didn't mean it nastily; ~ **Folgen** dire consequences; ~ **Zeiten** bad times; **das/es sieht** ~ **aus** things look/it looks bad. **(b)** *(verärgert)* angry *(+dat, auf +acc, mit* with*).* **im** ~**n auseinandergehen** to part on bad terms.

**Böse(s)** *nt decl as adj* evil; *(Schaden, Leid)* harm. **jdm** ~**s antun** to do sb harm; **ich will dir doch nichts** ~**s** I don't mean you any harm; **ich dachte an** *or* **ahnte gar nichts** ~**s, als** ... I was quite unsuspecting when ...

**Bösewicht** *m* -**e** *or* -**er** *(old, hum)* villain.

**Bos-:** **b**~**haft** *adj* malicious; ~**haftigkeit** *f* maliciousness; ~**heit** *f* malice; *(Bemerkung, Handlung)* malicious remark/thing to do.

**Bosnien** *nt* Bosnia.

**Bosnier(in** *f) m* Bosnian.

**bosnisch** *adj* Bosnian.

**Boß** *m* -**sse** *(col)* boss *(col)*.

**böswillig** *adj* malicious; *(Jur auch)* wilful. **in** ~**er Absicht** with malicious intent.

**Böswilligkeit** *f* malice, maliciousness.

**bot** *pret of* **bieten**.

**Botanik** *f* botany.

**Botaniker(in** *f) m* - botanist.

**botanisch** *adj* botanic.

**Bote** *m (wk)* -**n**, -**n** **(a)** messenger; *(Kurier)* courier; *(Post*~*)* postman *(Brit)*, mailman *(US)*. **(b)** *(fig: Anzeichen)* herald.

**Botengang** *m* errand. **einen** ~**gang machen** to run an errand.

**Botin** *f siehe* **Bote** **(a)** messenger; courier; postwoman *(Brit)*, mailwoman *(US)*.

**Botschaft** *f* **(a)** *(Mitteilung)* message; *(esp amtlich)* communication. **eine freudige** ~ good news; **die Frohe** ~ the Gospel. **(b)** *(Pol: Vertretung)* embassy.

**Botschafter(in** *f) m* - ambassador.

**Botswana** *nt* Botswana.

**Bottich** *m* -**e** tub.

**Bottnischer Meerbusen** *m* Gulf of Bothnia.

**Bouillon** [bʊl'jɔn, bʊl'jõː] *f* -**s** stock; *(auf Speisekarte)* bouillon, consommé.

**Bouillonwürfel** *m* stock cube.

**Boulevard-** [bʊlə'vaːɐ-]: ~**blatt** *nt (col)* tabloid; ~**presse** *f (col)* popular press; ~**stück** *nt* light play/comedy; ~**theater** *nt* light theatre *(Brit)* or theater *(US)*; ~**zeitung** *f* tabloid.

**Bouquet** [bu'keː] *nt* -**s** = **Bukett**.

**Bourgeoisie** [bʊrʒoa'ziː] *f (geh)* bourgeoisie.

**Boutique** [bu'tiːk] *f* -**n** boutique.

**Bowle** ['boːlə] *f* -**n** *(Getränk)* punch.

**Bowling** ['boːlɪŋ] *nt* -**s** (tenpin) bowling. ~ **spielen gehen** to go bowling.

**Bowlingbahn** *f* bowling alley.

**Box** *f* -**en** **(a)** *(Behälter)* box. **(b)** *(für Pferde)* box; *(in Großgarage)* parking space; *(für Rennwagen)* pit. **(c)** *(Lautsprecher*~*)* speaker.

**Boxen** *nt no pl (Sport)* boxing.

**boxen 1** *vi* to box; *(zur Übung)* to spar; *(mit Fäusten zuschlagen)* to hit out, to punch. **gegen jdn** ~ to fight sb. **2** *vt jdn* to punch, to hit. **3** *vr* **(a)** *(col: sich schlagen)* to have a punch-up *(col)* or a fight. **(b)** *(sich einen Weg bahnen)* to fight one's way.

**Boxer** *m* - *(Sportler, Hund)* boxer.

**Boxer-:** ~**motor** *m (Tech)* opposed cylinder engine; ~**nase** *f* boxer's nose, broken nose.

**Box-:** ~**handschuh** *m* boxing glove; ~**kalf** *nt no pl* box calf; ~**kampf** *m* fight, (boxing) match; ~**ring** *m* boxing ring; ~**sport** *m* boxing.
**Boykott** [bɔy'kɔt] *m* -e *or* -s boycott.
**boykottieren\*** [bɔykɔ'tiːrən] *vt* to boycott.
**brabbeln** *vi (col)* to mumble, to mutter; *(Baby)* to babble.
**brach** *pret of* **brechen.**
**brachial** *adj* mit ~**er Gewalt** with brute force.
**Brach-:** ~**land** *nt* fallow (land); **b~liegen** *vi sep irreg (lit, fig)* to lie fallow; ~**vogel** *m* curlew.
**brachte** *pret of* **bringen.**
**brackig** *adj* brackish.
**Brackwasser** *nt* brackish water.
**Branche** ['brãːʃə] *f* -n *(Gewerbe)* trade; *(Wirtschaftszweig)* industry. **in welcher ~ sind Sie tätig?** what line (of business) are you in?
**Branchen-:** ~**führer** *m* market leader; ~**kenntnis** *f* knowledge of the trade/industry; **b~üblich** *adj* usual in the trade/industry; ~**verzeichnis** *nt* trade *or (Telec)* classified directory.
**Brand** *m* ⁼e **(a)** *(Feuer)* fire; *(lodernd auch)* blaze. **in ~ geraten** to catch fire; **in ~ stehen** to be on fire; **etw in ~ stecken** to set fire to sth. **(b)** *(von Porzellan etc)* firing. **(c)** *(fig col: großer Durst)* raging thirst. **(d)** *(Pflanzenkrankheit)* blight.
**Brand-:** **b~aktuell** *adj (col) Thema, Frage* red-hot *(col); Buch* hot from the presses; ~**anschlag** *m* arson attack; ~**bekämpfung** *f* firefighting; ~**blase** *f* (burn) blister; ~**bombe** *f* incendiary bomb *or* device; **b~eilig** *adj (col)* extremely urgent; ~**eisen** *nt* branding iron.
**Brandenburg** *nt* Brandenburg. ~**er Tor** Brandenburg Gate.
**Brand-:** ~**fleck** *m* burn; ~**gefahr** *f* danger of fire; ~**geruch** *m* smell of burning; ~**herd** *m* source of the fire; *(fig)* source; ~**katastrophe** *f* fire disaster; ~**mal** *nt* -e brand; *(fig auch)* stigma; **b~marken** *vt insep (fig)* jdn als etw **b~marken** *(fig)* to brand sb (as) sth; ~**meister** *m* fire chief; **b~neu** *adj (col)* brand-new; ~**opfer** *nt* **(a)** *(Rel)* burnt offering; **(b)** *(Mensch)* fire victim; ~**rede** *f* harangue; ~**salbe** *f* ointment for burns; ~**satz** *m* incendiary device; ~**schaden** *m* fire damage; ~**schutz** *m* fire protection; ~**schutzbestimmungen** *pl* fire regulations; ~**stelle** *f* fire, blaze; *(verbrannte Stelle)* burnt patch; ~**stifter** *m* arsonist; ~**stiftung** *f* arson; ~**teig** *m* choux pastry.
**Brandung** *f* surf, breakers *pl.*
**Brand-:** ~**ursache** *f* cause of a/the fire; ~**wunde** *f* burn; ~**zeichen** *nt* brand.
**brannte** *pret of* **brennen.**
**Branntwein** *m* spirits *pl.* **Whisky ist ein ~** whisky is a (type of) spirit.
**Branntwein-:** ~**brenner** *m* distiller; ~**brennerei** *f* distillery; ~**steuer** *f* tax on spirits.
**Brasil** *f* -(s) Brazil cigar.
**Brasilianer(in** *f)* *m* - Brazilian.
**brasilianisch** *adj* Brazilian.
**Brasilien** [-iən] *nt* Brazil.
**Brat|apfel** *m* baked apple.
**braten** *pret* **briet,** *ptp* **gebraten 1** *vti* to roast; *(ohne Fett)* to bake; *(in der Pfanne)* to fry. **2** *vi (col: in der Sonne)* to roast.
**Braten** *m* - roast. **kalter ~** cold meat; **ein fetter ~** *(fig)* a prize catch; **den ~ riechen** *(col)* to smell a rat *(col).*
**Braten-:** ~**fleisch** *nt* meat for roasting/frying; ~**saft** *m* meat juices *pl;* ~**soße** *f* gravy; ~**wender** *m* - ≈ fishslice.
**Brat-:** **b~fertig** *adj* oven-ready; ~**fett** *nt* fat for

frying/roasting; ~**fisch** *m* fried fish; ~**hähnchen,** ~**hendl, -(n)** *(Aus, SGer) nt* roast chicken; ~**hering** *m* fried herring; ~**huhn** *nt* roast chicken; *(zum Braten)* roasting chicken; ~**kartoffeln** *pl* fried potatoes; ~**ofen** *m* oven; ~**pfanne** *f* frying pan, skillet *(US);* ~**röhre** *f* oven; ~**rost** *m* grill.
**Bratsche** *f* -n viola.
**Brat-:** ~**spieß** *m* spit; ~**wurst** *f* (fried) sausage.
**Brauch** *m, pl* **Bräuche** custom, tradition. **das ist bei uns so ~** *(col)* that's traditional with us.
**brauchbar** *adj* **(a)** *(benutzbar)* usable; *Plan* workable; *(nützlich)* useful. **(b)** *(ordentlich) Mensch, Idee* reasonable.
**Brauchbarkeit** *f* usefulness; *(von Plan)* workability.
**brauchen 1** *vt* **(a)** *(nötig haben)* to need *(für, zu* for). **es braucht alles seine Zeit** everything takes time; **wie lange braucht man, um ...?** how long does it take to ...? **(b)** *(benutzen)* to use. **wir können das/ ihn nicht ~** *(col)* we've no use for that/him. **(c)** *(col: verbrauchen)* to use (up). **2** *aux* to need. **du brauchst es ihm nicht (zu) sagen** you needn't tell *or* don't need to tell him that; **du hättest das nicht (zu) tun ~** you needn't have done that, you didn't need to do that; **du brauchst nur an(zu)rufen** you only have *or* need to call; **es braucht nicht gleich zu sein** it doesn't need to be done immediately; **es hätte nicht sein ~** there was no need for that; *(hätte nicht geschehen müssen)* that needn't have happened.
**Brauchtum** *nt* customs *pl,* traditions *pl.*
**Braue** *f* -n (eye)brow.
**brauen** *vti Bier* to brew; *(col) Tee* to brew up; *Kaffee* to make.
**Brauer** *m* - brewer.
**Brauerei** *f* brewery.
**braun** *adj* brown; *(col: ~haarig)* brown-haired; *(pej)* Nazi. **~ werden** *(Mensch)* to get a (sun)tan, to go *or* get brown.
**Braun** *nt* - brown.
**Braun-:** **b~äugig** *adj* brown-eyed; ~**bär** *m* brown bear.
**Bräune** *f no pl* brown(ness); *(Sonnen~)* (sun)tan.
**bräunen 1** *vt (Cook)* to brown; *(Sonne etc)* to tan. **2** *vi (Cook)* to go *or* turn brown; *(Mensch)* to tan, to go brown; *(Sonne)* to tan. **sich in der Sonne ~ lassen** to get a (sun)tan.
**Braun-:** **b~gebrannt** *adj attr* (sun)tanned, brown; **b~haarig** *adj* brown-haired; *Frau auch* brunette; ~**kohle** *f* brown coal.
**bräunlich** *adj* brownish, browny.
**Braunschweig** *nt* Brunswick.
**Bräunung** *f* browning; *(von Haut)* bronzing. **eine tiefe ~ der Haut** a deep (sun)tan.
**Brause** *f* -n **(a)** shower. **sich unter die ~ stellen** to have a shower. **(b)** *(~aufsatz)* shower attachment; *(an Schlauch, Gießkanne)* rose, sprinkler. **(c)** *(Getränk)* pop; *(Limonade)* (fizzy) lemonade; *(~pulver)* lemonade powder.
**brausen** *vi* **(a)** *(tosen)* to roar; *(sprudeln: Wasser, Brandung)* to foam. ~**der Beifall** thunderous applause. **(b)** *aux sein (rasen, rennen)* to race. **(c)** *auch vr (duschen)* to (have a) shower. **2** *vt Körperteil, Kinder* to wash.
**Brause-:** ~**pulver** *nt* sherbet; ~**tablette** *f* effervescent tablet.
**Braut** *f, pl* **Bräute** bride; *(dated: Verlobte)* fiancée.
**Brautführer** *m person who gives away the bride.*
**Bräutigam** *m* -e (bride)groom; *(dated: Verlobter)* fiancé.
**Braut-:** ~**jungfer** *f* bridesmaid; ~**kleid** *nt* wedding dress; ~**leute** *pl,* ~**paar** *nt* bridal couple; *(dated: Verlobte)* engaged couple; ~**schau** *f:* **auf ~schau**

**sein** to be looking for a wife; **~schleier** *m* wedding *or* bridal veil.

**brav** *adj* **(a)** *Kind* good, well-behaved. **sei schön ~!** be a good boy/girl. **(b)** *(rechtschaffen)* worthy *(auch iro)*; *(bieder) Frisur, Kleid* plain. **~ seine Pflicht tun** to do one's duty virtuously. **(c)** *(dated: tapfer)* brave.

**bravo** ['braːvo] *interj* well done; *(für Künstler)* bravo.

**Bravoruf** *m* cheer.

**Bravour** [bra'vuːɐ] *f no pl (geh)* bravura.

**bravourös** [bravu'røːs] *adj (meisterhaft)* brilliant.

**BRD** [beːɛr'deː] *f* = **Bundesrepublik Deutschland** FRG. **die alte ~** former West Germany.

**Brech-: b~bar** *adj* breakable; **~bohne** *f* French bean; **~eisen** *nt* crowbar; *(von Dieb)* jemmy, jimmy *(US)*.

**brechen** *pret* **brach**, *ptp* **gebrochen 1** *vt* **(a)** to break; *(geh: pflücken) Blumen* to pluck. **sich/jdm den Arm ~** to break one's/sb's arm; **das wird ihm den Hals ~** *(fig)* that will be his downfall. **(b)** *(erbrechen)* to bring up. **2** *vi* **(a)** *aux sein* to break. **mir bricht das Herz** it breaks my heart; **mit jdm/etw ~** to break with sb/sth; **~d voll sein** to be full to bursting. **(b)** *(sich erbrechen)* to be sick, to throw up. **3** *vr (Wellen)* to break; *(Lichtstrahl)* to be refracted; *(Schall)* to rebound *(an +dat* off*)*.

**Brecher** *m* - *(Welle)* breaker; *(Tech)* crusher.

**Brech-: ~mittel** *nt* emetic; **er/das ist das reinste ~mittel** he/it makes me feel ill; **~reiz** *m* nausea; **~stange** *f* crowbar.

**Brechung** *f (der Wellen)* breaking; *(des Lichts)* refraction; *(des Schalls)* rebounding.

**Brei** *m* **-e** mush, paste; *(für Kinder, Kranke)* mash; *(Hafer~)* porridge; *(Grieß~)* semolina; *(Reis~)* rice pudding; *(Papier~)* pulp. **jdn zu ~ schlagen** *(col)* to beat sb to a pulp *(col)*; **um den heißen ~ herumreden** *(col)* to beat about the bush *(col)*.

**breiig** *adj* mushy.

**breit 1** *adj* broad; *(esp bei Maßangabe)* wide; *Bekanntenkreis, Publikum, Interessen auch* wide; *Schrift* broadly spaced. **etw ~er machen** to broaden *or* widen sth; **die ~e Masse** the masses *pl*. **2** *adv* **~ gebaut** sturdily built; **sich ~ hinsetzen** to sit down and spread oneself.

**breitbeinig** *adj* with one's legs apart.

**Breite** *f* **-n** **(a)** breadth; *(von Dialekt, Aussprache)* broadness; *(esp bei Maßangaben)* width. **der ~ nach** widthways; **etw in aller ~ erklären** to explain sth in great detail; **in die ~ gehen** *(col: dick werden)* to put it on a bit *(col)*. **(b)** *(Geog)* latitude; *(Gebiet)* part of the world. **es liegt 20° nördlicher ~** it lies 20° north.

**breiten** *vtr* to spread.

**Breiten-: ~grad** *m* (degree of) latitude; **~kreis** *m* parallel; **~sport** *m* popular sport; **~wirkung** *f* widespread impact.

**Breit-: b~gefächert** *adj* **ein b~gefächertes Angebot** a wide range; **b~machen** *vr sep (col)* **mach dich doch nicht so b~!** don't take up so much room; **b~schlagen** *vt sep irreg (col)* **sich b~schlagen lassen** to let oneself be talked round; **b~schult(e)rig** *adj* broad-shouldered; **~seite** *f (Naut)* broadside; **eine ~seite abgeben** to fire a broadside; **b~treten** *vt sep irreg (col)* to go on about; *Thema, Witz* to flog to death *(col)*; **~wand** *f* wide screen; **~wandfilm** *m* film for the wide screen.

**Bremen** *nt* Bremen.

**Bremer** *adj attr*, **bremisch** *adj* Bremen *attr*.

**Brems-: ~backe** *f* brake shoe; **~belag** *m* brake lining.

**Bremse[1]** *f* **-n** brake. **auf die ~(n) treten/steigen** *(col)*

to put on *or* apply/slam on the brake(s).

**Bremse[2]** *f* **-n** *(Insekt)* horsefly.

**bremsen 1** *vi* to brake. **der Wind bremst** the wind slows you *etc* down; **mit etw ~** *(col)* to cut down (on) sth. **2** *vt* **(a)** *Fahrzeug* to brake. **(b)** *(fig)* to restrict, to limit; *Entwicklung* to slow down. **er ist nicht zu ~** *(col)* there's no stopping him. **3** *vr (col)* **ich kann mich ~** not likely!

**Brems-: ~flüssigkeit** *f* brake fluid; **~klotz** *m* brake pad; **~kraft** *f* braking power; **~kraftverstärker** *m* brake servo; **~leistung** *f* braking efficiency; **~licht** *nt* brake light; **~pedal** *nt* brake pedal; **~schuh** *m* brake shoe; **~spur** *f* skid mark *usu pl*.

**Bremsung** *f* braking.

**Bremsweg** *m* braking distance.

**Brenn-: b~bar** *adj* combustible, inflammable. **leicht b~bar** highly inflammable; **~element** *nt* fuel element.

**brennen** *pret* **brannte**, *ptp* **gebrannt 1** *vi* to burn; *(Haus, Wald auch)* to be on fire; *(Glühbirne etc)* to be on; *(Zigarette)* to be alight; *(Stich)* to sting; *(Füße)* to hurt, to be sore. **das Streichholz brennt nicht** the match won't light; **auf der Haut ~** to burn the skin; **das Licht ~ lassen** to leave the light on; **es brennt!** fire!, fire!; *(fig)* it's urgent; **wo brennt's denn?** *(col)* what's the panic?; **darauf ~, etw zu tun** to be dying to do sth. **2** *vt* to burn; *Branntwein* to distil; *Porzellan, Ziegel* to fire, to bake; *Tier* to brand; *siehe* **gebrannt**.

**brennend** *adj (lit, fig)* burning; *Zigarette* lighted; *Durst* raging; *Haß* consuming. **das interessiert mich ~** *(col)* I would be extremely interested.

**Brenner** *m* - **(a)** *(Tech)* burner. **(b)** *(Branntwein~)* distiller.

**Brennerei** *f* distillery.

**Brennessel** *f* stinging nettle.

**Brenn-: ~holz** *nt* firewood; **~kammer** *f* combustion chamber *(of jet engine)*; **~material** *nt* fuel (for heating); **~ofen** *m* kiln; **~punkt** *m (Math, Opt)* focus; **im ~punkt des Interesses stehen** to be the focus of attention; **~raum** *m* combustion chamber *(of petrol or diesel engine)*; **~schere** *f* curling tongs *pl*; **~spiritus** *m* methylated spirits *sing or pl*; **~stab** *m* fuel rod; **~stoff** *m* fuel.

**brenzlig** *adj (col) Situation etc* precarious. **die Lage wurde ihm zu ~** things got too hot for him.

**Bresche** *f* **-n** breach, gap. **in die ~ springen** *(fig)* to step into the breach; **für jdn/etw eine ~ schlagen** *(fig)* to stand up for sb/sth.

**Bretagne** [bre'tanjə] *f* **die ~** Brittany.

**Bretone** *m (wk)* **-n**, **Bretonin** *f* Breton.

**bretonisch** *adj* Breton.

**Brett** *nt* **-er** **(a)** board; *(länger und dicker)* plank; *(Regal)* shelf. **hier ist die Welt mit ~ern vernagelt** this is a parochial little place; **er hat ein ~ vor dem Kopf** *(col)* he's really thick. **(b)** **~er** *pl (fig) (Bühne)* boards *pl*; *(Boden des Boxrings)* floor, canvas; *(Skier)* planks *pl (col)*; **die ~er, die die Welt bedeuten** the stage.

**Bretter-: ~bude** *f* booth; *(pej)* shack; **~zaun** *m* wooden fence; *(an Baustellen auch)* hoarding.

**Brettspiel** *nt* board game.

**Brezel** *f* **-n** pretzel.

**Brief** *m* **-e** **(a)** letter; *(Bibl)* epistle. **etw als ~ schicken** to send sth (by) letter post; **jdm ~ und Siegel auf etw *(acc)* geben** to give sb one's word. **(b)** *(St Ex:* **~kurs***)* selling rate.

**Brief-** *in cpds* letter; **~beschwerer** *m* - paperweight; **~block** *m* writing pad; **~bogen** *m* (sheet of) writing paper; **~bombe** *f* letter bomb.

**Briefchen** *nt* ein ~ Streichhölzer a book of matches; ein ~ Nadeln a packet of needles/pins.

**Brief-**: ~**drucksache** *f* circular; ~**fach** *nt* pigeonhole; ~**freund(in** *f)* *m* penfriend, penpal; ~**freundschaft** *f* eine ~**freundschaft mit jdm haben** to be penfriends with sb; ~**geheimnis** *nt* privacy of the post; ~**karte** *f* correspondence card.

**Briefkasten** *m* letter box, mail box *(US)*.

**Briefkasten-**: ~**adresse,** ~**firma** *f* accommodation address; ~**tante** *f (col)* agony aunt.

**Brief-**: ~**kopf** *m* letterhead; ~**kurs** *m (St Ex)* selling rate; ~**lich** *adj* by letter; **mit jdm** ~**lich verkehren** to correspond with sb.

**Briefmarke** *f* stamp.

**Briefmarken-** *in cpds* stamp; ~**automat** *m* stamp machine; ~**kunde** *f* philately; ~**sammler** *m* stamp collector, philatelist; ~**sammlung** *f* stamp collection.

**Brief-**: ~**öffner** *m* letter opener, paper knife; ~**papier** *nt* letter paper, notepaper; ~**porto** *nt (Gebühr)* letter rate; ~**qualität** *f (Comp)* letter quality; ~**sendung** *f* item sent by letter post; ~**tasche** *f* wallet *(Brit)*, billfold *(US)*; ~**taube** *f* carrier pigeon; ~**träger(in** *f)* *m* postman/-woman, mailman/-woman *(US)*; ~**umschlag** *m* envelope; ~**verkehr** *m* correspondence; ~**waage** *f* letter scales *pl*; ~**wahl** *f* per ~**wahl wählen** to use one's postal vote; ~**wähler** *m* postal voter; ~**wechsel** *m* correspondence.

**Bries** *nt* **-e** *(Cook)* sweetbread.

**briet** *pret of* **braten.**

**Brigade** *f* **(a)** *(Mil)* brigade. **(b)** *(DDR)* (work) team *or* group.

**Brikett** *nt* **-s** briquette.

**Brikettzange** *f* fire tongs *pl.*

**brillant** [brɪl'jant] *adj* brilliant.

**Brillant** [brɪl'jant] *m* diamond.

**Brillantschmuck** *m* diamonds *pl.*

**Brille** *f* **-n (a)** glasses *pl,* spectacles *pl*; *(Schutz~)* goggles *pl.* **eine** ~ a pair of glasses *or* spectacles; goggles; **eine** ~ **tragen** to wear glasses. **(b)** *(Klosett~)* (toilet) seat.

**Brillen-**: ~**etui** *nt* glasses *or* spectacle case; ~**gestell** *nt* (spectacle) frame; ~**glas** *nt* lens; ~**schlange** *f (hum)* four-eyes *(hum)*, woman who wears glasses; ~**träger(in** *f)* *m* **er ist** ~**träger** he wears glasses.

**Brimborium** *nt (col)* fuss.

**bringen** *pret* **brachte,** *ptp* **gebracht** *vt* **(a)** *(her~)* to bring; *(holen auch)* to get *(jdm* for sb*)*; *(mitnehmen, weg~)* to take. **der Besuch hat mir Blumen gebracht** my visitor(s) brought me flowers; **wir haben der Gastgeberin Blumen gebracht** we took our hostess flowers; **jdn zum Bahnhof/nach Hause** ~ to take sb to the station/home; **das Essen auf den Tisch** ~ to serve the food; **er bringt es nicht übers Herz** *or* **über sich** he can't bring himself to do it; **etw an sich** *(acc)* ~ to acquire sth; **etw mit sich** ~ to involve sth; **etw hinter sich** *(acc)* ~ to get sth over and done with.

**(b)** *(ein~) Gewinn* to bring in; *(Boden etc)* to produce; *Ärger* to cause; *Freude, Vorteile* to give. **das bringt nichts** *(fig col)* it's pointless.

**(c)** *(lenken, bewirken)* to bring. **das bringt dich vors Gericht/ins Gefängnis** you'll end up in court/prison if you do that; **das Gespräch auf etw** *(acc)* ~ to bring the conversation around to sth; **jdn in Gefahr** ~ to put sb in danger; **jdn zum Lachen/Weinen** ~ to make sb laugh/cry; **jdn zur Verzweiflung** ~ to drive sb to despair; **jdn zur Vernunft** ~ to bring sb to his senses; **jdn auf eine Idee** ~ to give sb an idea; **jdn dazu** ~, **etw zu tun** to get sb to do sth; **jdn um etw** ~ to make sb lose sth, to do sb out of sth; **jdn ums Leben** ~ to kill sb.

**(d)** *(leisten, erreichen)* **es auf 80 Jahre** ~ to reach the age of 80; **das Auto bringt 200 km/h** *(col)* the car can do 125 mph; **es zu etwas/nichts** ~ to get somewhere/nowhere; **es weit** ~ to do very well, to get far; **er hat es bis zum Direktor gebracht** he made it to director.

**(e)** *(senden) Bericht etc* to broadcast; *(im Fernsehen auch)* to show. **was bringt das Fernsehen/Radio heute abend?** what's on television/the radio tonight?

**(f)** *(veröffentlichen)* to print, to publish. **alle Zeitungen brachten es auf der ersten Seite** all the papers had it on the front page.

**(g)** *(aufführen) Stück* to do.

**(h)** *(col: schaffen, können)* **das bringt er nicht** he's not up to it; **er/das bringt's** he's got what it takes/it does the business *(col)*; **das bringt's doch nicht!** that's no damn use! *(col).*

**brisant** *adj (fig)* highly controversial.

**Brisanz** *f (fig)* highly controversial nature.

**Brise** *f* **-n** breeze.

**Brite** *m (wk)* **-n, -n, Britin** *f* Briton, Britisher *(US)*. **er ist** ~ he is British; **die** ~**n** the British.

**britisch** *adj* British. **die B**~**en Inseln** the British Isles.

**bröckelig** *adj* crumbly; *Mauer* crumbling.

**bröckeln** *vti* to crumble.

**Brocken** *m* - lump, chunk; *(fig: Bruchstück)* scrap; *(col: Person)* lump *(col).* **ein paar** ~ **Spanisch** a smattering of Spanish; **ein harter** ~ a tough nut to crack.

**brocken** *vt Brot* to break.

**brodeln** *vi (Wasser, Suppe)* to bubble. **es brodelt** *(fig)* there is seething unrest.

**Brokat** *m* **-e** brocade.

**Brokkoli** *pl* broccoli *sing.*

**Brom** *nt no pl* bromine.

**Brombeere** *f* blackberry, bramble.

**Bronchie** [-iə] *f usu pl* bronchial tube.

**Bronchitis** *f, pl* **Bronchitiden** bronchitis.

**Bronze** ['brõːsə] *f* **-n** bronze.

**Bronze-**: ~**medaille** *f* bronze medal; ~**zeit** *f no pl* Bronze Age.

**Brosche** *f* **-n** brooch.

**broschiert** *adj Ausgabe* paperback.

**Broschüre** *f* **-n** brochure; *(Heft)* booklet.

**Brösel** *m* **-n** crumb.

**bröselig** *adj* crumbly.

**bröseln** *vi* to crumble.

**Brot** *nt* **-e** bread; *(Laib)* loaf (of bread); *(Scheibe)* slice (of bread); *(Sandwich)* sandwich; *(fig: Unterhalt)* daily bread *(hum)*, living. **ein** ~ **mit Käse** a slice of bread and cheese; **das ist ein hartes** ~ *(fig)* that's a hard way to earn one's living.

**Brot-**: ~**aufstrich** *m* spread *(for bread)*; ~**belag** *m* topping *(for bread).*

**Brötchen** *nt* roll. **kleine** ~ **backen** *(col)* to set one's sights lower.

**Brötchengeber** *m (hum)* employer, provider *(hum).*

**Brot-**: ~**erwerb** *m* (way of earning one's) living; ~**kasten** *m* bread bin; ~**korb** *m* bread basket; **jdm den** ~**korb höher hängen** *(fig)* to keep sb short; ~**krume** *f,* ~**krümel** *m* breadcrumb; ~**kruste** *f* crust; **b**~**los** *adj* unemployed, out of work; ~**maschine** *f* bread slicer; ~**messer** *nt* bread knife; ~**rinde** *f* crust; ~**schnitte** *f* slice of bread; ~**zeit** *f (S Ger: Pause)* break (for a snack); *(Essen)* snack *(of sandwiches, beer etc)*; ~**zeit machen** to have a snack.

**BRT** = **Bruttoregistertonne**.

**Bruch** *m* ⁼e (a) *(~stelle)* break; *(in Porzellan etc auch)* crack; *(das Brechen)* breaking. **zu ~ gehen** to get broken; **~ machen** *(col)* to smash *(mit etw sth)*. (b) *(fig) (mit Vergangenheit, Partei, im Stil etc)* break; *(von Gesetz)* breaking, infringement; *(von Vertrag)* breach. **in die ~e gehen** *(Ehe, Freundschaft)* to break up; **es kam zum ~ zwischen ihnen** they broke up. (c) *(zerbrochene Ware)* broken biscuits/chocolate *etc*; *(Porzellan)* breakage. (d) *(Knochen~)* fracture, break; *(Eingeweide~)* hernia, rupture. **sich** *(dat)* **einen ~ heben** to rupture oneself. (e) *(Math)* fraction. (f) *(col: Einbruch)* break-in.

**Bruch-:** **~band** *nt* truss; **~bude** *f (pej)* hovel; **b~fest** *adj* unbreakable.

**brüchig** *adj* brittle, fragile; *Gestein, Ehe, Moral* crumbling; *Leder, (fig) Stimme* cracked. **~ werden** *(Gestein, Macht etc)* to (begin to) crumble; *(Ehe, Verhältnisse auch)* to (begin to) break up; *(Leder)* to crack *or* split.

**Bruch-:** **~landung** *f* crashlanding; **~rechnung** *f* fractions *sing or pl*; *(Aufgabe)* sum with fractions; **~stelle** *f* break; *(von Knochen auch)* fracture; **~strich** *m (Math)* line (of a fraction); **~stück** *nt* fragment; *(von Lied, Rede etc auch)* snatch; **b~stückhaft** *adj* fragmentary; **~teil** *m* fraction; **im ~teil einer Sekunde** in a fraction of a second; **~zahl** *f (Math)* fraction.

**Brücke** *f* -n (a) *(lit, fig, Naut, Zahn~)* bridge. **alle ~n hinter sich** *(dat)* **abbrechen** *(fig)* to burn one's bridges behind one; **jdm goldene ~n bauen** to make things easy for sb; **~n schlagen** *(fig)* to forge links. (b) *(Turnen)* crab; *(Teppich)* rug.

**Brücken-:** **~kopf** *m (Mil, fig)* bridgehead; **~schlag** *m (fig)* **das war der erste ~schlag** that forged the first link.

**Bruder** *m* ⁼ (a) brother. **unter ~n** *(col)* between friends. (b) *(Mönch)* friar, brother. (c) *(col: Mann)* guy *(col)*. **ein warmer ~** *(dated)* a pansy *(col)*; **euch ~ kenn' ich** *(pej)* I know *you* lot.

**Bruder-:** **~krieg** *m* war between brothers; **~kuß** *m (fig)* fraternal kiss.

**brüderlich** *adj* fraternal, brotherly *no adv.* **~ teilen** to share and share alike.

**Brüderlichkeit** *f no pl* brotherliness.

**Bruder-:** **~mord** *m* fratricide; **~mörder** *m* fratricide; **~schaft** *f (Eccl)* brotherhood; **mit jdm ~schaft trinken** to agree to use the familiar du *(over a drink)*.

**Brügge** *nt* Bruges.

**Brühe** *f* -n *(Suppe)* (clear) soup; *(als Suppengrundlage)* stock; *(pej) (schmutzige Flüssigkeit)* sludge; *(Getränk)* dishwater *(col)*, muck *(col)*.

**brühen** *vt* (a) to blanch. (b) *Tee* to brew; *Kaffee* to make *(in the jug or pot)*.

**Brüh-:** **b~heiß** *adj* scalding (hot); **b~warm** *adj (col)* hot from the press *(col)*; **er hat das sofort b~warm weitererzählt** he promptly spread it around; **~würfel** *m* stock cube; **~wurst** *f* sausage *(to be heated in water)*.

**brüllen** *vti* to shout, to roar; *(pej: laut weinen)* to yell, to bawl; *(Stier)* to bellow; *(Elefant)* to trumpet. **das ist zum B~** *(col)* it's a scream *(col)*.

**Brummbär** *m (col)* crosspatch *(col)*.

**brummeln** *vti (col)* to mumble, to mutter.

**brummen** *vti* (a) *(Insekt)* to buzz; *(Bär)* to growl; *(Motor, singen)* to drone; *(Kreisel etc)* to hum. **mir brummt der Kopf** my head is throbbing. (b) *(murren)* to grumble. (c) *(col: in Haft sein)* to be locked up *(col)*.

**Brummer** *m* - *(col)* (a) fly; wasp; bee. (b) *(Lastwagen)* large truck, juggernaut *(Brit)*.

**Brummi** *m* -s *(col: Lastwagen)* lorry *(Brit)*, truck.

**brummig** *adj* grumpy.

**Brumm-:** **~kreisel** *m (col)* humming-top; **~schädel** *m (col)* thick head *(col)*.

**brünett** *adj* dark(-haired). **sie ist ~** she is a brunette.

**Brünette** *f* brunette.

**Brunft** *f* ⁼e *(Hunt)* = **Brunst**.

**Brunnen** *m* - (a) well; *(fig liter)* fountain. (b) *(Spring~)* fountain. (c) *(Heilquelle)* spring.

**Brunnen-:** **~kresse** *f* watercress; **~schacht** *m* well shaft; **~vergifter(in** *f*) *m* - *(fig pej)* (political) trouble-maker; **~wasser** *nt* well water.

**Brunst** *f* ⁼e *(von männlichen Tieren)* rut; *(von weiblichen Tieren)* heat; *(~zeit)* rutting season.

**Brunst-:** **~schrei** *m* mating call; **~zeit** *f* rutting season.

**brüsk** *adj* brusque, curt.

**brüskieren*** *vt* to snub.

**Brüskierung** *f* snub.

**Brüssel** *nt* Brussels.

**Brüsseler** *adj attr* Brussels.

**Brust** *f* ⁼e (a) chest; *(fig: Inneres, Cook)* breast. **einen zur ~ nehmen** *(col)* to have a quick drink *or* quickie *(col)*; **sich in die ~ werfen** *(fig)* to puff oneself up; **mit geschwellter ~** *(fig)* as proud as a peacock; **schwach auf der ~ sein** *(col)* to have a weak chest; *(hum: an Geldmangel leiden)* to be a bit short *(col)*. (b) *(weibliche ~)* breast. **einem Kind die ~ geben** to breastfeed a baby. (c) *(~schwimmen)* breast-stroke.

**Brust-:** **~bein** *nt* breastbone, sternum; **~beutel** *m* money bag *(worn around the neck)*; **~bild** *nt* half-length portrait.

**brüsten** *vr* to boast, to brag *(mit etw)*.

**Brust-:** **~fellentzündung** *f* pleurisy; **~höhe** *f:* **in ~höhe** chest high; **~kasten** *(col)*, **~korb** *m* rib cage, thorax; **~krebs** *m* breast cancer, cancer of the breast; **~schwimmen** *nt* breast-stroke; **b~schwimmen** *vi* *only* to swim *or* do the breast-stroke; **~stimme** *f* chest-voice; **~stück** *nt (Cook)* breast; **~tasche** *f* breast pocket; *(Innentasche)* inside (breast) pocket; **~ton** *m* **im ~ton der Überzeugung** in a tone of utter conviction; **~umfang** *m* chest measurement; *(von Frau)* bust measurement.

**Brüstung** *f* parapet; *(Balkon~ etc auch)* balustrade; *(Fenster~)* breast.

**Brust-:** **~warze** *f* nipple; **~weite** *f* = **~umfang**.

**Brut** *f* -en (a) *no pl (das Brüten)* incubating. (b) *(die Jungen)* brood; *(pej)* lot, mob *(col)*.

**brutal** *adj* brutal; *(gewalttätig auch)* violent. **das tut ~ weh** *(col)* that hurts like hell *(col)*.

**Brutalität** *f* (a) *no pl siehe adj* brutality; violence. (b) *(Gewalttat)* act of violence or brutality.

**brüten 1** *vi* to incubate; *(fig)* to ponder *(über +dat over)*. **~de Hitze** oppressive *or* stifling heat. **2** *vt (künstlich)* to incubate; *(Tech)* to breed.

**brütendheiß** *adj attr* sweltering.

**Brüter** *m* - *(Tech)* breeder (reactor). **schneller ~** fast-breeder (reactor).

**Brut-:** **~kasten** *m (Med)* incubator; **~reaktor** *m* breeder (reactor); **~stätte** *f (lit, fig)* breeding ground *(gen for)*.

**brutto** *adv* gross.

**Brutto-** *in cpds* gross; **~einkommen** *nt* gross income; **~registertonne** *f* register ton; **~sozialprodukt** *nt* gross national product, GNP.

**Brutzeit** *f* incubation (period).

**brutzeln** *(col)* **1** *vi* to sizzle (away). **2** *vt* to fry (up).

**Btx** [beːteːˈʔɪks] *m* -, *no pl* = **Bildschirmtext**.

**Bub** *m (wk)* **-en, -en** *(SGer, Aus, Sw)* boy, lad.

**Bube** *m (wk)* **-n, -n** *(Cards)* jack, knave.

**Bubikopf** *m* bobbed hair *no pl*, bob.

**Buch** *nt* ∹er **(a)** book; *(Band)* volume; *(Dreh~)* script. **er redet wie ein ~** *(col)* he never stops talking; **ein Gentleman, wie er im ~e steht** a perfect example of a gentleman; **ein Tor, wie es im ~e steht** a textbook goal; **ein ~ mit sieben Siegeln** *(fig)* a closed book. **(b)** *usu pl (Comm: Geschäfts~)* books *pl*, accounts *pl*. **über etw** *(acc)* **~ führen** to keep a record of sth. **zu ~(e) schlagen** to make a (significant) difference.

**Buch-:** **~besprechung** *f* book review; **~binder(in** *f)* *m* bookbinder; **~druck** *m no pl* letterpress (printing); **~drucker** *m* printer; **~druckerei** *f (Betrieb)* printery.

**Buche** *f* **-n** beech (tree).

**Buch|ecker** *f* **-n** beechnut.

**buchen** *vt* **(a)** *(Comm)* to enter; *(Kasse, fig: registrieren)* to register. **etw als Erfolg ~** to put sth down as a success. **(b)** *(vorbestellen)* to book.

**Buchen-:** **~holz** *nt* beech(wood); **~wald** *m* beech wood.

**Bücher-:** **~bord, ~brett** *nt* bookshelf.

**Bücherei** *f* (lending) library.

**Bücher-:** **~freund** *m* book-lover; **~gestell** *nt* bookcase; **~gutschein** *m* book token; **~narr** *m* book-freak *(col)*; **~regal** *nt* bookshelf; **~schrank** *m* bookcase; **~verzeichnis** *nt* bibliography; **~wand** *f* wall of bookshelves; **~wurm** *m (lit, fig hum)* bookworm.

**Buchfink** *m* chaffinch.

**Buch-:** **~führung** *f* book-keeping, accounting; **~halter(in** *f)* *m* book-keeper; **~haltung** *f* **(a)** = **~führung**; **(b)** *(Abteilung)* accounts department; **~gemeinschaft** *f* book club; **~handel** *m* book trade; **im ~handel erhältlich** available in bookshops *(Brit)* or bookstores *(US)*; **~händler** *m* bookseller; **~handlung** *f* bookshop *(Brit)*, bookstore *(US)*; **~laden** *m* bookshop *(Brit)*, bookstore *(US)*; **~macher** *m* bookmaker, bookie *(col)*; **~messe** *f* book fair; **~prüfer** *m* auditor; **~prüfung** *f* audit; **~rücken** *m* spine.

**Buchs** [ˈbʊks] *m* **-e**, **Buchsbaum** *m* box (tree).

**Buchsbaumhecke** *f* box hedge.

**Buchse** [ˈbʊksə] *f* **-n** *(Elec)* socket; *(Tech) (von Zylinder)* liner; *(von Lager)* bush.

**Büchse** [ˈbʏksə] *f* **-n** **(a)** tin; *(Konserven~)* can, tin *(Brit)*; *(Sammel~)* collecting box. **(b)** *(Gewehr)* rifle, (shot)gun.

**Büchsen-:** **~fleisch** *nt* canned *or* tinned *(Brit)* meat; **~milch** *f* tinned *(Brit)* or evaporated milk; **~öffner** *m* can *or* tin *(Brit)* opener.

**Buchstabe** *m* **-n** letter; *(esp Druck~)* character. **kleiner ~** small letter; **großer ~** capital (letter); **Betrag in ~n** amount in words; **dem ~n nach** *(fig)* literally; **auf den ~n genau** *(fig)* to the letter; **nach dem ~n des Gesetzes** according to the letter of the law.

**buchstabieren*** *vt* to spell.

**buchstäblich** *adv* literally.

**Buchstütze** *f* bookend.

**Bucht** *f* **-en** bay.

**Buchung** *f (Comm)* entry; *(Reservierung)* booking.

**Buchweizen** *m* buckwheat.

**Buchwert** *m (Comm)* book value.

**Buckel** *m* - **(a)** hump(back), hunchback; *(col: Rücken)* back. **einen ~ machen** *(Katze)* to arch its back; **er kann mir den ~ (he)runterrutschen** *(col)* he can (go and) take a running jump *(col)*; **80 Jahre**

---

**auf dem ~ haben** *(col)* to be 80 (years old). **(b)** *(col: Auswölbung)* bulge, hump.

**buck(e)lig** *adj* hunchbacked; *(col)* Straße bumpy.

**buckeln** *vi (pej)* to bow and scrape.

**bücken** *vr* **sich nach etw ~** to bend down *or* to stoop to pick sth up; *siehe* **gebückt**.

**Bückling** *m* **(a)** *(Cook)* smoked herring. **(b)** *(hum col: Verbeugung)* bow.

**Budapest** *nt* Budapest.

**buddeln** *vti (col)* to dig.

**Buddhismus** *m* Buddhism.

**Buddhist(in** *f)* *m* Buddhist.

**buddhistisch** *adj* Buddhist(ic).

**Bude** *f* **-n** **(a)** hut; *(Markt~, Verkaufs~)* stall, booth; *(Zeitungs~)* kiosk. **(b)** *(pej col: Laden, Lokal etc)* dump *(col)*. **(c)** *(col) (Zimmer)* room; *(von Untermieter auch)* digs *pl (col)*; *(Wohnung)* pad *(col)*. **Leben in die ~ bringen** to liven the place up; **jdm die ~ einrennen** to pester sb; **jdm auf die ~ rücken** to come around.

**Budget** [byˈdʒeː] *nt* **-s** budget.

**Buenos Aires** *nt* Buenos Aires.

**Büfett** *nt* **-e** *or* **-s** **(a)** *(Geschirrschrank)* sideboard. **(b)** *(Schanktisch)* bar; *(Verkaufstisch)* counter. **(c) kaltes ~** cold buffet.

**Büffel** *m* - buffalo.

**Büffelei** *f (col)* swotting *(col)*, cramming *(col)*.

**büffeln** *(col)* **1** *vi* to swot *(col)*, to cram *(col)*. **2** *vt* Lernstoff to swot up *(col)*.

**Buffet, Büffet** [byˈfeː] *nt* **-s** = **Büfett**.

**Bug** *m* ∹e *or* **-e** *(Schiffs~)* bow; *(Flugzeug~)* nose.

**Bügel** *m* - **(a)** *(Kleider~)* (coat-)hanger. **(b)** *(Steig~)* stirrup. **(c)** *(Brillen~)* side *or* ear-piece.

**Bügel-:** **~brett** *nt* ironing board; **~eisen** *nt* iron; **~falte** *f* crease in one's trousers; **b~fertig** *adj* ready for ironing; **b~frei** *adj* non-iron.

**bügeln** **1** *vt* to iron; Hose to press. **2** *vi* to iron.

**bugsieren*** *vt* **(a)** *(Naut)* to tow. **(b)** *(col)* Möbelstück *etc* to edge. **jdn aus dem Zimmer ~** to manoeuvre *(Brit)* or maneuver *(US)* sb out of the room.

**buh** *interj* boo.

**buhen** *vi (col)* to boo.

**buhlen** *vi (pej: werben)* **um jds Gunst ~** to woo *or* court sb's favour.

**Buhmann** *m, pl* **-männer** *(col)* bogeyman *(col)*.

**Bühne** *f* **-n** **(a)** *(lit, fig)* stage; *(von Aula etc auch)* platform. **über die ~ gehen** *(col)* to go (off); **etw über die ~ bringen** *(col)* to bring sth off; *(unangenehmes)* to get sth over (with); **hinter der ~** *(lit, fig)* behind the scenes; **von der ~ abtreten** to make one's exit. **(b)** *(Theater)* theatre *(Brit)*, theater *(US)*; *(als Beruf)* stage. **zur ~ gehen** to go on the stage.

**Bühnen-:** **~anweisung** *f* stage direction; **~arbeiter** *m* stagehand; **~ausstattung** *f* props *pl*; **~autor** *m* playwright, dramatist; **~bearbeitung** *f* stage adaptation; **~bild** *nt* (stage) set; **~bildner** *m* set-designer; **~erfolg** *m* success; *(Stück auch)* (stage) hit; **~personal** *nt* theatre *(Brit)* or theater *(US)* staff; **b~reif** *adj* ready for the stage; **~stück** *nt* (stage) play; **~techniker** *m* stage technician.

**Buhruf** *m* boo, catcall.

**Bukarest** *nt* Bucharest.

**Bukett** *nt* **-s** *or* **-e** *(geh: Blumen~, von Wein)* bouquet.

**Bulette** *f (dial)* meat ball.

**Bulgare** *m (wk)* **-n, -n**, **Bulgarin** *f* Bulgarian.

**Bulgarien** [-ɪən] *nt* Bulgaria.

**bulgarisch** *adj* Bulgarian.

**Bulimie** *f no pl (Med)* bulimia.

**Bull|auge** *nt (Naut)* porthole.

**Bulldogge** *f* bulldog.

**Bulldozer** ['bʊldoːzɐ] *m* - bulldozer.
**Bulle** *m (wk)* **-n, -n (a)** bull. **(b)** *(col: starker Mann)* great ox of a man. **(c)** *(pej: Polizist)* cop *(col)*. **die** ~**n** the fuzz *(pej)*, the cops *(col)*.
**Bullenhitze** *f (col)* sweltering heat.
**bullern** *vi (col) (Wasser)* to bubble; *(Ofen)* to roar.
**bullig** *adj (col)* **(a)** brawny, beefy *(col)*. **(b)** *Hitze* sweltering, boiling *(col)*.
**bum** *interj* bang; *(tiefer)* boom.
**Bumerang** *m* **-s** *or* **-e** *(lit, fig)* boomerang.
**Bummel** *m* - stroll; *(Lokal* ~*)* pub-crawl. **einen** ~ **durch die Stadt machen** to go for a stroll around (the) town.
**Bummelant(in** *f) m (wk) (col)* **(a)** *(Trödler)* slowcoach *(Brit col)*, slowpoke *(US col)*. **(b)** *(Faulenzer)* loafer *(col)*, idler.
**Bummelei** *f (col) (Trödelei)* dawdling; *(Faulenzerei)* loafing about *(col)*, idling.
**bummeln** *vi* **(a)** *aux sein (spazierengehen)* to stroll; *(ausgehen)* to go out on the town. **(b)** *(trödeln)* to dawdle. **(c)** *(faulenzen)* to laze around.
**Bummel-:** ~**streik** *m* go-slow *(Brit)*, slowdown *(US)*; ~**zug** *m (col)* slow *or* stopping train.
**Bummler(in** *f) m* - **(a)** *(Spaziergänger)* stroller. **(b)** = **Bummelant(in).**
**Bums** *m* **-e** *(col: Schlag)* bang, thump.
**bumsen 1** *vi impers (col: dröhnen)* **es bumste, als ...** there was a thump *or* thud when ...; **es hat gebumst** *(von Fahrzeugen)* there's been a crash. **2** *vi* **(a)** *(schlagen)* to thump. **(b)** *aux sein (prallen, stoßen)* to bump, to bang. **(c)** *(col: koitieren)* to have it off *(col)*, to have a screw *(col!!)*. **3** *vt (col)* **jdn** ~ to lay sb *(col)*, to screw sb *(col!!)*; **gebumst werden** to get laid *(col)*.
**Bumslokal** *nt (pej col)* (low) dive.
**Bund**[1] *m* ⁼**e** **(a)** *(Bündnis)* alliance; *(Organisation)* association. **den** ~ **fürs Leben schließen** to take the marriage vows. **(b)** *(Pol: Bundesstaat)* Federal Government. **(c)** *(BRD col: Bundeswehr)* **der** ~ the army. **(d)** *(an Kleidern)* waistband.
**Bund**[2] *nt* **-e** *(von Stroh, Reisig etc)* bundle; *(von Radieschen, Spargel etc)* bunch.
**Bündchen** *nt (Hals~)* neckband; *(am Ärmel)* sleeveband.
**Bündel** *nt* - bundle, sheaf; *(Stroh~)* sheaf; *(von Radieschen etc)* bunch; *(fig: von Problemen etc)* cluster. **sein** ~ **schnüren** to pack one's bags.
**bündeln** *vt Zeitungen* to bundle up; *Stroh* to sheave; *Karotten etc* to tie into bunches/a bunch.
**bündelweise** *adv* by the bundle, in bundles.
**Bundes-** *in cpds* federal; ~**amt** *nt* Federal Office; ~**bahn** *f* Federal Railway(s *pl*); ~**bank** *f* Federal bank; ~**behörde** *f* Federal authority; ~**bürger** *m* German citizen; *(before 1990)* West German citizen; ~**deutsche(r)** *mf* German; *(before 1990)* West German; ~**gebiet** *nt* federal territory; ~**genosse** *m* ally, confederate; ~**gerichtshof** *m* Federal Supreme Court; ~**grenzschutz** *m* Federal Border Guard; ~**hauptstadt** *f* Federal capital; ~**kabinett** *nt* Federal cabinet; ~**kanzler** *m* German/Austrian Chancellor; ~**land** *nt* state; ~**liga** *f (Sport)* national league; ~**minister** *m* Federal Minister; ~**mittel** *pl* Federal funds *pl*; ~**nachrichtendienst** *m* Federal Intelligence Service; ~**post** *f:* **die (Deutsche)** ~**post** the (German) Federal Post (Office); ~**präsident** *m* (Federal) President; *(Sw)* President of the Federal Council; ~**rat** *m* Bundesrat *(upper house of the German Parliament)*; *(Sw)* Council of Ministers; ~**regierung** *f* Federal Government; ~**republik** *f* Federal Republic; ~**republik Deutschland** Federal Republic of Germany; ~**staat**

*m* federal state; ~**straße** *f* trunk road *(Brit)*, main highway *(US)*.
**Bundestag** *m* Bundestag *(lower house of the German Parliament)*.
**Bundestags-:** ~**abgeordnete(r)** *mf* member of the German Parliament *or Bundestag*; ~**fraktion** *f* group *or* faction in the *Bundestag*; ~**präsident** *m* President of the German Parliament *or Bundestag*; ~**wahl** *f* (federal) parliamentary elections *pl*.
**Bundes-:** ~**trainer** *m (Sport)* national coach; ~**verfassungsgericht** *nt* Federal Constitutional Court; ~**wehr** *f* (German *or (before 1990)* West German) army, armed forces *pl*; **b~weit** *adj* nationwide.
**Bund-:** ~**faltenhose** *f* pleated trousers *pl*; ~**hose** *f* knee breeches *pl*.
**bündig** *adj* **(a)** *(schlüssig)* conclusive; *(kurz, bestimmt)* concise, succinct. **(b)** *(in gleicher Ebene)* flush *pred*, level.
**Bündnis** *nt* alliance.
**Bundweite** *f* waist measurement.
**Bungalow** ['bʊŋgalo] *m* **-s** bungalow, ranch house *(US)*.
**Bunker** *m* - **(a)** bunker; *(Luftschutz~)* air-raid shelter. **(b)** *(Sammelbehälter)* bin; *(Kohlen~)* bunker; **(c)** *(Mil sl: Gefängnis)* guardhouse.
**Bunsenbrenner** *m* Bunsen burner.
**bunt** *adj* **(a)** *(farbig)* coloured *(Brit)*, colored *(US)*; *(mehrfarbig)* colourful *(Brit)*, colorful *(US)*; *(vielfarbig)* multi-coloured *(Brit)*, multi-colored *(US)*; *(gefleckt)* mottled, spotted. ~ **gestreift** *pred* brightly striped; ~**e Farben** bright colours; ~**es Glas** stained glass; **etw** ~ **anstreichen** to paint sth a bright colour/in bright colours; ~ **fotografieren** *(col)* to take colour photos. **(b)** *(fig: abwechslungsreich)* varied. **eine** ~**e Menge** a motley crowd; **ein** ~**es Bild** a colourful picture. **(c)** **jetzt wird's mir aber zu** ~! *(col)* that's going too far!
**Bunt-:** **b~bemalt** *adj attr* brightly painted; ~**film** *m (col)* colour *(Brit) or* color *(US)* film; ~**glasfenster** *nt* stained-glass window; **b~gemischt** *adj attr* Programm varied; **b~gestreift** *adj attr* brightly striped; ~**papier** *nt* coloured *(Brit) or* colored *(US)* paper; ~**specht** *m* spotted woodpecker; ~**stift** *m* coloured *(Brit) or* colored *(US)* pencil; ~**wäsche** *f* coloureds *pl (Brit)*, coloreds *pl (US)*.
**Bürde** *f* **-n** *(lit, fig)* burden.
**Burg** *f* **-en** castle.
**Bürge** *m (wk)* **-n, -n** guarantor; *(fig)* guarantee *(für of)*. **für jdn** ~ **sein** to be sb's guarantor.
**bürgen** *vi* **für etw** ~ to guarantee sth; **für jdn** ~ *(Fin)* to stand surety for sb; *(fig)* to vouch for sb.
**Bürger** *m* -, **Bürgerin** *f* citizen; *(Sociol, pej)* bourgeois.
**Bürger-:** ~**block** *m* conservative alliance; ~**initiative** *f* citizens' initiative *or* action group; ~**krieg** *m* civil war.
**bürgerlich** *adj* **(a)** civil; *Pflicht* civic. **B~es Gesetzbuch** Civil Code. **(b)** *(dem Bürgerstand angehörend)* middle-class *(auch pej)*, bourgeois *(esp pej)*; *(Hist)* bourgeois. ~**es Essen/Küche** good plain food/ cooking; ~**es Trauerspiel** *(Liter)* domestic tragedy.
**Bürgerliche(r)** *mf decl as adj* commoner.
**Bürger-:** ~**meister(in** *f) m* mayor; **b~nah** *adj* populist; ~**nähe** *f* populism; ~**pflicht** *f* civic duty; ~**recht** *nt usu pl* civil rights *pl*; ~**rechtler** *m* - civil rights campaigner; ~**rechtsbewegung** *f* civil rights movement; ~**schaft** *f* citizens *pl*; *(Vertretung)* City Parliament; ~**schreck** *m* bogey of the middle classes; ~**steig** *m* pavement *(Brit)*, sidewalk *(US)*; ~**tum** *nt no pl (Hist)* bourgeoisie *(Hist)*;

~**wehr** f vigilantes pl, vigilance committee (US).

**Burgfriede(n)** m (fig) truce.

**Bürgin** f siehe **Bürge**.

**Bürgschaft** f (Jur) (gegenüber Gläubigern) security, surety; (Haftungssumme) penalty. ~ **für jdn leisten** to stand surety for sb.

**Burgund** nt Burgundy.

**Burgunder** m - (auch: ~**wein**) burgundy.

**Büro** nt -s office.

**Büro-** in cpds office; ~**angestellte(r)** mf office worker; ~**bedarf** m office supplies pl; ~**gebäude** nt office building or block; ~**gehilfe** m (office) junior; ~**kauffrau** f, ~**kaufmann** m office administrator; ~**klammer** f paper clip; ~**kraft** f (office) clerk.

**Bürokrat** m (wk) -en, -en bureaucrat.

**Bürokratie** f bureaucracy.

**bürokratisch** adj bureaucratic.

**Bürokratismus** m no pl bureaucracy.

**Büro-:** ~**leiter** m office manager; ~**schluß** m office closing time; **nach** ~**schluß** after office hours; ~**stunden** pl office hours pl; ~**tätigkeit** f office work; ~**technik** f office technology.

**Bursche** m (wk) -n, -n (a) (col: Kerl) fellow, guy (col). **ein übler** ~ a bad lot. (b) (Lauf~) boy.

**Burschen-:** ~**schaft** f student fraternity; ~**schaft(l)er** m - member of a student fraternity.

**burschikos** adj (a) (jungenhaft) (tom)boyish. (b) (unbekümmert) casual.

**Bürste** f -n brush.

**bürsten** vt to brush.

**Bürsten(haar)schnitt** m crew cut.

**Bus** m -ses, -se bus; (Reise~ auch) coach (Brit).

**Busbahnhof** m bus/coach (Brit) station.

**Busch** m ⁻e bush. **etwas ist im** ~ (col) there's something up; **mit etw hinter dem** ~ **halten** (col) to keep sth quiet; **bei jdm auf den** ~ **klopfen** (col) to sound sb out; **sich in die** ⁻**e schlagen** (col) to slip away.

**Büschel** nt - (von Gras, Haaren) tuft; (von Heu, Stroh) bundle.

**buschig** adj bushy.

**Busch-:** ~**messer** nt machete; ~**werk** nt bushes pl; ~**windröschen** nt (wood) anemone.

**Busen** m - (von Frau) bust, bosom.

**Busen-:** b~**frei** adj topless; ~**freund** m (iro) bosom friend.

**Bus-:** ~**fahrer(in** f) m bus/coach (Brit) driver; ~**fahrpreis** m bus fare; ~**fahrschein** m bus ticket; ~**fahrt** f bus/coach (Brit) ride; ~**haltestelle** f bus stop; ~**linie** f bus route. **welche** ~**linie fährt zum Bahnhof?** which bus goes to the station?

**Bussard** m -e buzzard.

**Buße** f -n (a) (Rel) repentance, penitence; (Auflage) penance; (tätige ~) atonement. ~ **tun** to do penance. (b) (Jur: Geldstrafe) fine.

**büßen 1** vt to pay for. **das sollst du mir** ~ I'll make you pay for that. **2** vi **für etw** ~ (auch Rel) to atone for sth; **für Leichtsinn** etc to pay for sth.

**Büßer(in** f) m - penitent.

**Bußgeld** nt fine.

**Bußgeldbescheid** m notice of payment due (for traffic offence etc).

**Busspur** f bus lane, busway (US).

**Buß-:** ~**tag**, ~- **und Bettag** m day of prayer and repentance.

**Büste** f -n bust; (Schneider~) tailor's dummy.

**Büstenhalter** m bra.

**Busverbindung** f bus service.

**Butan** nt -e, **Butangas** nt butane (gas).

**Bütten(papier)** nt no pl handmade paper (with deckle edge).

**Büttenrede** f carnival speech.

**Butter** f no pl butter. **alles (ist) in** ~ (col) everything is fine or hunky-dory (col); **jdm die** ~ **auf dem Brot nicht gönnen** (fig col) to begrudge sb the very air he breathes; **wir lassen uns nicht die** ~ **vom Brot nehmen** (col) we're going to stick up for our rights.

**Butter-** in cpds butter; ~**berg** m (col) butter mountain; ~**blume** f buttercup; ~**brot** nt piece of bread and butter; (Sandwich) sandwich; **für ein** ~**brot** (col) for next to nothing; **das mußt du mir nicht ständig aufs** ~**brot schmieren** there's no need to keep rubbing it in; ~**brotpapier** nt greaseproof paper (Brit), oil paper (US); ~**creme** f butter cream; ~**cremetorte** f cream cake; ~**dose** f butter dish.

**Butter-:** ~**keks** m ≃ Rich Tea ® biscuit; ~**milch** f buttermilk.

**buttern** vt (a) Brot to butter. (b) (col: investieren) to put (in +acc into).

**butterweich** adj beautifully soft; (Sport) Aufschlag gentle.

**Button** ['batn] m -s badge.

**Butzenscheibe** f bull's-eye (window pane).

**Buxtehude** nt aus/nach ~ (col) from/to the back of beyond (col).

**BVG** [beːfauˈgeː] nt = **Bundesverfassungsgericht**.

**b.w.** = **bitte wenden** pto.

**Byte** [bait] nt -s (Comp) byte.

**Byzantiner(in** f) m Byzantine.

**byzantinisch** adj (a) Byzantine. (b) (üppig) extravagant.

**Byzanz** nt Byzantium.

**bzgl.** = **bezüglich**.

**bzw.** = **beziehungsweise**.

# C

(siehe auch **K, Z**; für **CH** siehe auch **SCH**)

**C, c** [tseː] nt -, - C, c. **C-Schlüssel** m alto or C clef; **C wie Cäsar** ≃ C for Charlie.
**C** = **Celsius.**
**ca.** = **circa** approx.
**Cabriolet** [-'leː] nt -s (Aut) convertible.
**Café** [ka'feː] nt -s café.
**Cafeteria** f -s cafeteria.
**cal** = **(Gramm)kalorie** cal.
**Calais** [ka'leː] nt **die Straße von** ~ the Straits of Dover.
**Callgirl** ['koːlgøːɐl] nt -s callgirl.
**Calvados** [kalva'doːs] m -, - calvados.
**Calypso** m -s calypso.
**Camcorder** m - camcorder.
**Camembert** ['kaməmbeːɐ] m -s Camembert.
**Camp** [kɛmp] nt -s camp.
**campen** ['kɛmpn] vi to camp.
**Camper(in** f) ['kɛmpɐ, -ərɪn] m - camper.
**Camping** ['kɛmpɪŋ] nt no pl camping no art. **zum** ~ **fahren** to go camping.
**Camping-** in cpds camping; **~artikel** m piece of camping equipment; pl camping equipment sing; **~bus** m camper; **~platz** m camp site.
**Campus** m -, no pl (Univ) campus.
**Cannabis** m -, no pl cannabis.
**Cape** [keːp] nt -s cape.
**Caravan** ['ka(ː)ravan] m -s (a) (Kombiwagen) estate car (Brit), station wagon. (b) (Wohnwagen) caravan (Brit), trailer (US).
**Casanova** [kaza'noːva] m -s (fig) Casanova.
**Cashewnuß** ['kɛʃuː] f cashew (nut).
**catchen** ['kɛtʃn] vi to do all-in wrestling or catch-wrestling.
**Catcher(in** f) ['kɛtʃɐ, -ərɪn] m - all-in wrestler, catch wrestler.
**Cayennepfeffer** [ka'jɛn-] m cayenne (pepper).
**CB** ['tseː'beː] = **Citizen-Band** CB.
**CB-Funk** m no pl citizens' band, CB radio.
**cbm** = **Kubikmeter** cubic metre.
**ccm** = **Kubikzentimeter** cc.
**CD** [tseː'deː] f -s = **Compact Disc** CD.
**CD-** in cpds CD; **~-ROM** [-rɔm] abbr CD-ROM; **~-Spieler** m CD player.
**CDU** ['tseːdeː'|uː] f = **Christlich-Demokratische Union.**
**Cedille** [se'diːj(ə)] f -n cedilla.
**Cellist(in** f) [tʃɛ'lɪst(ɪn)] m (wk) cellist.
**Cello** ['tʃɛlo] nt -s or **Celli** cello.
**Cellophan** ® [tsɛlo'faːn] nt no pl Cellophane ®.
**Celsius** ['tsɛlzius] no art, inv centigrade.
**Celsiusskala** f centigrade scale.
**Cembalo** ['tʃɛmbalo] nt -s cembalo, harpsichord.
**ces, Ces** [tsɛs] nt, gen - (Mus) C flat.
**Ceylon** ['tsailɔn] nt (old) Ceylon.
**Chamäleon** [ka'mɛːleɔn] nt -s (lit, fig) chameleon.
**Champagner** [ʃam'panjɐ] m - champagne.

**Champignon** ['ʃampɪnjɔŋ] m -s mushroom.
**Chance** ['ʃãːsə] f -n chance; (bei Wetten) odds pl. **keine** ~ **haben** not to have or stand a chance; **im Beruf ~n haben** to have good career prospects.
**Chancengleichheit** ['ʃãːsən-] f equal opportunities pl.
**changieren*** [ʃã'ʒiːrən] vi (schillern) to be iridescent. **~de Seide** shot silk.
**Chanson** [ʃã'sõː] nt -s (satirical) song.
**Chaos** ['kaːɔs] nt -, no pl chaos.
**Chaot(in** f) [ka'oːt(ɪn)] m (wk) -en, -en (a) (Pol pej) anarchist (pej). (b) (col) (schusseliger Mensch) scatterbrain (pej); (verrückter Mensch) nutter (col). **du bist vielleicht ein** ~ you're so disorganized/crazy.
**chaotisch** [ka'oːtɪʃ] adj chaotic. **~e Zustände** a state of (utter) chaos.
**Charakter** [ka'raktɐ] m -e [-'teːrə] character. **ein Mann von** ~ a man of character; **der vertrauliche** ~ **dieses Gespräches** the confidential nature of this conversation.
**Charakter-:** **~darsteller** m actor of complex parts; **~eigenschaft** f character trait; **c~fest** adj of strong character; **~festigkeit** f strength of character.
**charakterisieren*** [ka-] vt to characterize.
**Charakterisierung** [ka-] f characterization.
**Charakteristik** [ka-] f description; (typische Eigenschaften) characteristics pl.
**Charakteristikum** [ka-] nt, pl **Charakteristika** (geh) characteristic.
**charakteristisch** [ka-] adj characteristic (für of).
**Charakter-:** **c~lich 1** adj (of) character, personal; **c~liche Stärke/Mängel** strength of character/character defects; **2** adv in character; **jdn c~lich stark prägen** to have a strong influence on sb's character; **c~los** adj (a) (niederträchtig) unprincipled; **c~los handeln** to act in an unprincipled way; (b) (ohne Prägung) characterless; Spiel, Vortrag insipid; **~losigkeit** f (Niederträchtigkeit) lack of principle; (Handlung) unprincipled behaviour (Brit) or behavior (US) no pl; **~merkmal** nt characteristic; **~rolle** f complex part; **~schwäche** f weakness of character; **~stärke** f strength of character; **c~voll** adj (ausgeprägt) full of character; **~zug** m characteristic.
**Charge** ['ʃarʒə] f -n (a) (Mil, fig) rank. (b) (Theat) bit part.
**Charisma** ['çaːrɪsma] nt, pl **Charismen** or **Charismata** charisma.
**charismatisch** [ça-] adj charismatic.
**charmant** [ʃar'mant] adj charming.
**Charme** [ʃarm] m no pl charm.
**Charta** ['karta] f -s charter.
**Charter-** ['tʃartɐ]: **~flug** m charter flight; **~(flug)gesellschaft** f charter (flight) company; **~maschine** f charter plane.

**chartern** ['tʃartɐn] vt Schiff, Flugzeug to charter.
**Chassis** [ʃa'siː] nt -, - [-iːs] chassis.
**Chauffeur** [ʃɔ'føːɐ] m chauffeur.
**chauffieren*** [ʃɔ-] vti to chauffeur.
**Chaussee** [ʃo'seː] f -n [-eːən] (dated) high road.
**Chauvi** ['ʃoːvi] m -s (col) male chauvinist pig (pej col).
**Chauvinismus** [ʃovi-] m chauvinism; (männlicher ~) male chauvinism.
**Chauvinist(in** f) [ʃovi-] m chauvinist; (männlicher ~) male chauvinist.
**chauvinistisch** [ʃovi-] adj chauvinist(ic). **er ist sehr ~** he is a real chauvinist.
**checken** ['tʃɛkn] **1** vt (a) (überprüfen) to check. **(b)** (col: verstehen) to get (col). **2** vti (Eishockey) to block; (anrempeln) to barge.
**Check-** ['tʃɛk-]: **~liste** f checklist; **~point** [-pɔynt] m -s checkpoint.
**Chef(in** f) [ʃɛf] m -s boss; (von Bande, Delegation etc) leader; (von Organisation, col: Schuldirektor) head; (der Polizei) chief; (Mil: von Kompanie) commander. **er ist der ~ vom ganzen** he's the boss here.
**Chef-**: **~arzt** m senior consultant; **~etage** f executive floor; **~koch** m chef, head cook; **~redakteur** m editor-in-chief; (einer Zeitung) editor; **~redaktion** f **(a)** (Aufgabe) (chief) editorship; **(b)** (Büro) main editorial office; **~sekretärin** f personal assistant/secretary; **~visite** f (Med) consultant's round.
**Chemie** [çe'miː] f no pl (lit, fig) chemistry; (col: Chemikalien) chemicals pl.
**Chemie-**: **~arbeiter** m chemical worker; **~baukasten** m chemistry set; **~faser** f synthetic fibre (Brit) or fiber (US).
**Chemikalie** [çemi'kaːliə] f -n usu pl chemical.
**Chemiker(in** f) ['çeː-] m - chemist.
**chemisch** ['çeː-] adj chemical.
**Chemo-** ['çeːmo-]: **~technik** f chemical engineering; **~techniker** m chemical engineer; **~therapie** f chemotherapy.
**chic** [ʃɪk] adj = schick.
**Chicorée** ['ʃikoreː] f or m no pl chicory.
**Chiffon** ['ʃɪfõ(ː)] m -s chiffon.
**Chiffre** ['ʃɪfrə] f -n **(a)** cipher. **(b)** (in Zeitung) box number.
**chiffrieren*** [ʃif-] vti to encipher, to code. **chiffriert** coded.
**Chile** ['tʃiːle] nt Chile.
**Chilene** [tʃi'leːnə] m (wk) -n, -n, **Chilenin** f Chilean.
**chilenisch** [tʃi-] adj Chilean.
**Chili** ['tʃiːli] m no pl chil(l)i.
**China** ['çiːna] nt China.
**China-**: **~kohl** m Chinese leaves pl; **~restaurant** nt Chinese restaurant.
**Chinese** [çi-] m (wk) -n, -n Chinaman; (heutig auch) Chinese.
**Chinesin** [çi-] f Chinese woman; (heutig auch) Chinese.
**chinesisch** [çi-] adj Chinese. **die C~e Mauer** the Great Wall of China.
**Chinesisch(e)** [çi-] nt decl as adj Chinese.
**Chinin** [çi'niːn] nt no pl quinine.
**Chip** [tʃɪp] m -s **(a)** (Spiel~, Comp) chip. **(b)** usu pl (Kartoffel~) (potato) crisp (Brit), potato chip (US).
**Chipkarte** f smart card.
**Chirurg(in** f) [çi'rʊrg(ɪn)] m (wk) -en, -en surgeon.
**Chirurgie** [çɪrʊr'giː] f surgery.
**chirurgisch** [çi-] adj surgical. **ein ~er Eingriff** surgery no indef art.
**Chlor** [kloːɐ] nt no pl chlorine.

**chloren** [klo-] vt to chlorinate.
**Chloro-** [kloro-]: **~form** nt no pl chloroform; **~phyll** nt no pl chlorophyll.
**Choke** [tʃoːk] m -s choke.
**Cholera** ['koːlera] f no pl cholera.
**Choleriker(in** f) [ko-] m - hot-tempered person.
**cholerisch** [ko-] adj choleric.
**Cholesterin** [ko-] nt no pl cholesterol.
**Cholesterinspiegel** [ko-] m cholesterol level.
**Chor** [koːɐ] m ⸚e **(a)** choir; (Theat) chorus. **im ~ sprechen/rufen** to speak/shout in chorus. **(b)** (Archit: Altarraum) chancel, choir.
**Choral** [ko'raːl] m, pl **Choräle** (Kirchenlied) chorale.
**Choreo-** [koreo-]: **~graph(in** f) m choreographer; **~graphie** f choreography.
**Chor-** ['koːɐ]: **~gesang** m (Lied) choral music; (das Singen) choral singing; **~gestühl** nt choir stalls pl.
**Chorist(in** f) [ko-] m = **Chorsänger(in)**.
**Chor-** ['koːɐ]: **~knabe** m choirboy; **~leiter** m choirmaster; **~sänger(in** f) m member of a choir; (im Kirchenchor) chorister.
**Chose** ['ʃoːzə] f -n (col: Angelegenheit) thing.
**Chr.** = Christus.
**Christ** [krɪst] m (wk) -en, -en Christian.
**Christbaum** m Christmas tree.
**Christbaum-**: **~kugel** f Christmas tree ball; **~schmuck** m Christmas tree decorations pl.
**Christ-** ['krɪst-]: **~demokrat** m Christian Democrat; **c~demokratisch** adj Christian Democratic.
**Christen-** ['krɪstn-]: **~heit** f Christendom; **~pflicht** f (one's) Christian duty; **~tum** nt no pl Christianity.
**Christi** gen of **Christus**.
**Christianisierung** [krɪ-] f conversion to Christianity.
**Christin** ['krɪstɪn] f Christian.
**Christkind** ['krɪst-] nt no pl infant Jesus, Christ Child; (das Geschenke bringt) ≈ Father Christmas.
**christlich** ['krɪ-] **1** adj Christian. **C~er Verein Junger Männer** Young Men's Christian Association. **2** adv as a Christian.
**Christ-**: **~messe** f Midnight Mass; **~mette** f (katholisch) Midnight Mass; (evangelisch) Midnight Service.
**Christus** ['krɪstʊs] m, gen **Christi** Christ; (~figur auch) figure of Christ. **vor Christi Geburt, vor ~** before Christ, BC; **nach Christi Geburt, nach ~ AD**, Anno Domini; **Christi Himmelfahrt** Ascension Day.
**Chrom** [kroːm] nt no pl chrome.
**chromatisch** [kro-] adj (Mus, Opt) chromatic.
**Chromosom** [kro-] nt -en chromosome.
**Chronik** ['kroː-] f chronicle.
**chronisch** ['kroː-] adj (Med, fig) chronic.
**Chronist(in** f) [kro-] m chronicler.
**Chronologie** [kronolo'giː] f chronology.
**chronologisch** [kro-] adj chronological.
**Chrysantheme** [kryzan'teːmə] f -n chrysanthemum.
**Chuzpe** ['xʊtspə] f no pl (col) chutzpa(h) (col).
**Cineast(in** f) [sine'ast(ɪn)] m (wk) -en, -en cineaste; (Filmemacher) film maker.
**circa** ['tsɪrka] adv = zirka.
**Circulus vitiosus** ['tsɪrkulus vi'tsioːzʊs] m, pl **Circuli vitiosi** (geh: Teufelskreis) vicious circle.
**cis, Cis** [tsɪs] nt, gen - (Mus) C sharp.
**City** ['sɪti] f -s city centre.
**cl** = Zentiliter cl.
**Clan** [klaːn] m -s (lit, fig) clan.
**clean** [kliːn] adj pred (Drogen sl) off drugs.

**Clearing** ['kliːrɪŋ] *nt* **-s** *(Econ)* clearing.
**Clematis** *f* - *(Bot)* clematis.
**clever** ['klɛvɐ] *adj* clever; *(gerissen)* crafty.
**Clinch** [klɪntʃ] *m no pl (Boxen, fig)* clinch. **jdn in den ~ nehmen** *(lit)* to go into a clinch with sb; *(fig)* to get stuck into sb *(col)*; **mit jdm im ~ liegen** to be at loggerheads with sb.
**Clip** *m* **-s** clip; *(Ohr~)* (clip-on) earring.
**Clique** ['klɪkə] *f* **-n** group; *(pej)* clique.
**Cliquen-**: **~bildung** *f* forming of cliques; **~wirtschaft** *f (pej inf)* cliquey set-up *(inf)*.
**Clochard** [klɔ'ʃaːr] *m* **-s** tramp.
**Clou** [kluː] *m* **-s** *(von Geschichte)* (whole) point; *(von Show)* highlight, high spot. **das ist doch gerade der ~** but that's just it, but that's the whole point.
**Clown** [klaun] *m* **-s** *(lit, fig)* clown. **den ~ spielen** to clown around, to play the fool; **sich/jdn zum ~ machen** to make a clown of oneself/sb.
**Clownerie** [klaunə'riː] *f* clowning (around) *no pl.*
**Club** *m* **-s** = **Klub.**
**cm** = **Zentimeter** cm.
**Co.** = **Kompanie** Co.
**Coach** [koːtʃ] *m* **-s** *(Sport)* coach.
**Cockpit** *nt* **-s** cockpit.
**Cocktail** ['kɔkteːl] *m* **-s** cocktail.
**Cocktail-**: **~kleid** *nt* cocktail dress; **~party** *f* cocktail party.
**Code** [koːt] *m* **-s** = **Kode.**
**Cognac** ® ['kɔnjak] *m* **-s** cognac.
**Coiffeur** [koa'føːɐ] *m,* **Coiffeuse** [koa'føːzə] *f (geh)* hair stylist.
**Cola** *f* **-s** *(col)* Coke ® *(col).*
**Collage** [kɔ'laːʒə] *f* **-n** *(Art, fig)* collage.
**Collie** *m* **-s** collie.
**Combo** *f* **-s** combo.
**Comeback** [kam'bɛk] *nt* **-(s), -s** comeback.
**Comic** *m* comic strip.
**Comic-**: **~figur** *f* cartoon character; **~heft** *nt* comic.
**Compact Disc** *f* - **-s** compact disc.
**Computer** [kɔm'pjuːtɐ] *m* - computer.
**Computer-** *in cpds* computer-; **~generation** *f* computer generation; **c~gerecht** *adj* (ready) for the computer; **c~gesteuert** *adj* computer-controlled; **~grafik** *f* computer graphics *pl.*
**computerisieren\*** [kɔmpjutəri'ziːrən] *vti* to computerize.
**Computer-**: **~kriminalität** *f* computer crime; **~satz** *m* computer typesetting; **~spiel** *nt* computer game; **~technik** *f* computer technology.
**Conférencier** [kõferã'sieː] *m* **-s** compère, MC.
**Container** [kɔn'teːnɐ] *m* - container; *(für Schutt etc)* skip.
**Container-** *in cpds* container; **~bahnhof** *m* container depot; **~schiff** *nt* container ship; **~terminal** *m or nt* container terminal; **~verkehr** *m* container traffic.
**Contergankind** *nt (col)* thalidomide baby.
**cool** [kuːl] *adj (col: gefaßt)* cool.
**Copyright** ['kɔpirait] *nt* **-s** copyright.
**Cord** *m* **-e** *or* **-s** *(Tex)* cord, corduroy.
**Cord-** *in cpds* cord, corduroy; **~hose** *f,* **~jeans** *pl* cords *pl.*
**Cordon bleu** [kɔrdõ'blø] *nt* - -, **-s -s** *(Cook)* veal cordon bleu.
**Cornichon** [kɔrni'ʃõː] *nt* **-s** gherkin.
**Corpus delicti** *nt, pl* **Corpora** - corpus delicti; *(hum)* culprit *(col).*
**cos.** = **Kosinus** cos.
**Costa Rica** *nt* Costa Rica.
**Couch** [kautʃ] *f* **-(e)s** *or (col)* **-en** couch.
**Couch-**: **~garnitur** *f* three-piece suite; **~tisch** *m* coffee table.
**Couleur** [ku'løːɐ] *f* **-s** *(geh)* kind, sort.
**Coup** [kuː] *m* **-s** coup. **einen ~ (gegen jdn/etw) landen** to bring off a coup (against sb/sth).
**Coupé** [ku'peː] *nt* **-s** coupé.
**Coupon** [ku'põː] *m* **-s** coupon, voucher.
**Courage** [ku'raːʒə] *f no pl (geh)* courage.
**couragiert** [kura'ʒiːɐt] *adj (geh)* courageous.
**Courtage** [kʊr'taːʒə] *f* **-n** *(Fin)* commission.
**Cousin** [ku'zɛː] *m* **-s, Cousine** [ku'ziːnə] *f* cousin.
**Cover** ['kavɐ] *nt* **-s** cover.
**Crack¹** [krɛk] *m* **-s** *(Sportler)* ace.
**Crack²** [krɛk] *nt no pl (Droge)* crack.
**Cracker** ['krɛkɐ] *m* **-(s)** (a) cracker. (b) *(Feuerwerkskörper)* banger *(Brit)*, fire-cracker *(US).*
**Creme** [kreːm] *f* **-s** *(Haut~, Cook, fig)* cream. **die ~ der Gesellschaft** the cream of society.
**cremefarben** *adj* cream.
**cremig** *adj* creamy.
**Crew** [kruː] *f* **-s** crew.
**Cromargan** ® [kro-] *nt no pl* stainless steel.
**Croupier** [kru'pieː] *m* **-s** croupier.
**Crux** *f no pl (Schwierigkeit)* trouble, problem.
**CSU** [tseː|ɛs'|uː] *f* = **Christlich-Soziale Union.**
**cum laude** *adv (Univ)* cum laude *(form)*, with distinction.
**Cup** [kap] *m* **-s** *(Sport)* cup.
**Curling** ['køːɐlɪŋ] *nt no pl* curling.
**Curriculum** *nt, pl* **Curricula** *(geh)* curriculum.
**Curry** ['kari] *m or nt no pl* curry.
**Currywurst** *f* curried sausage.
**Cursor** *[auch:* 'køːɐsɐ] *m* **-s** *(Comp)* cursor.
**Cut** [kœt] *m* **-s** *(dated)* cutaway.
**Cutter(in** *f)* ['katɐ, -ərɪn] *m* - *(Film, Rad, TV)* editor.
**CVJM** [tseːfaujɔt'|ɛm] *m* = **Christlicher Verein Junger Männer** YMCA.

# D

**D, d** [deː] *nt* -, - D, d. **D wie Dora** ≃ D for David, D for Dog *(US)*.

**da 1** *adv* **(a)** *(örtlich) (dort)* there; *(hier)* here. **~ drau-ßen** out there; **hier und ~, ~ und dort** here and there; **he, Sie ~!** hey, you there!; **~ bin ich/sind wir** here I am/we are; **~ bist du ja!** there you are!; **~ kommt er ja** here he comes; **~, wo ... where ...;** **ach, ~ war der Brief!** so that's where the letter was; **~ hast du dein Geld!** (here you are,) there's your money; **~ siehst du, was du angerichtet hast** now see what you've done.

**(b)** *(zeitlich: dann, damals)* then. **ich ging gerade aus dem Haus, ~ schlug es zwei** I was just going out of the house when the clock struck two; **kommen Sie mal gleich mit** *(col)* you just come along with me.

**(c)** *(daraufhin)* **sagen** to that; *lachen* at that. **sie weinte, ~ ließ er sich erweichen** when she started to cry he softened.

**(d)** *(folglich)* so. **es war niemand im Zimmer, ~ habe ich ...** there was nobody in the room, so I ...

**(e)** *(col)* there. **~ haben wir aber Glück gehabt!** we were lucky there!; **was gibt's denn ~ zu lachen/fragen?** what's so funny about that?/what is there to ask?; **~ kann man nichts machen** nothing can be done about it; **~ kann man nur lachen/sich nur wundern** you can't help laughing/being amazed.

**2** *conj* **(a)** *(weil)* as, since, seeing that. **(b)** *(liter: als)* when.

**d.Ä.** = **der Ältere.**

**DAAD** [deːʔaːʔaːˈdeː] *m* = **Deutscher Akademischer Austauschdienst** German Academic Exchange Service.

**dabehalten\*** *vt sep irreg* to keep (here/there); *Schüler* to keep behind.

**dabei** *adv* **(a)** *(örtlich)* with it; *(bei Gruppe von Menschen, Dingen)* there.

**(b)** *(zeitlich) (gleichzeitig)* at the same time; *(während-dessen, dadurch)* in the course of this. **warum arbeiten Sie im Stehen? Sie können doch auch ~ sit-zen** why are you working standing up? you can sit down while you're doing it; **... orkanartige Winde; ~ kam es zu schweren Schäden ...** gale-force winds, which have resulted in serious damage.

**(c)** *(außerdem)* **sie ist schön und ~ auch noch klug** she's pretty, and clever as well.

**(d)** *(wenn, während man etw tut)* in the process; *ertappen, erwischen* at it. **hast du ~ etwas gelernt?** did you learn anything from it?; **~ darf man nicht vergessen, daß ...** it shouldn't be forgotten that ...; **die ~ entstehenden Kosten** the expenses arising from this/that; **wir haben ihn ~ ertappt, wie er über den Zaun stieg** we caught him in the act of climbing over the fence.

**(e)** *(in dieser Angelegenheit)* **das Schwierigste ~** the most difficult part of it; **mir ist nicht ganz wohl ~** I don't really feel happy about it; **er hat ~ einen Fehler gemacht** he's made a mistake; **es kommt** doch nichts ~ **heraus** nothing will come of it.

**(f)** *(einräumend: obwohl)* (and) yet. **er hat mich geschlagen, ~ hatte ich gar nichts gemacht** he hit me and I hadn't even done anything.

**(g)** **es bleibt ~, daß ihr morgen alle mitkommt** we'll stick to that, you're all coming tomorrow; **ich bleibe ~** I'm not changing my mind; **lassen wir es ~** let's leave it at that!; **was ist schon ~?** so what? *(col)*, what of it? *(col)*; **was ist schon ~, wenn man das tut?** what harm is there in doing that?; **ich finde gar nichts ~** I don't see any harm in it; **was hast du dir denn ~ gedacht?** what were you thinking of?

**dabeibleiben** *vi sep irreg aux sein* to stay *or* stick *(col)* with it; *(bei Firma)* to stay on; *siehe* **dabei (g).**

**dabeihaben** *vt sep irreg (col)* to have with one.

**dabeisein** *vi sep irreg aux sein* **(a)** to be there *(bei* at*)*; *(mitmachen)* to be involved *(bei* in*)*. **ich bin da-bei!** count me in!; **er will überall ~** he wants to be in on everything. **(b)** *(im Begriff sein)* **~, etw zu tun** to be just doing sth; **ich bin (gerade) dabei** I'm just doing it.

**dabeisitzen** *vi sep irreg* to sit there. **bei einer Besprechung ~** to sit in on a discussion.

**dabeistehen** *vi sep irreg* to stand there.

**dableiben** *vi sep irreg aux sein* to stay (on); **(jetzt wird) dageblieben!** (you just) stay right there!

**Dach** *nt* ⸗er **(a)** roof. **mit jdm unter einem ~ wohnen** to live under the same roof as sb; **unterm ~ woh-nen** *(col)* to live in an attic; *(im obersten Stock)* to live right on the top floor; **unter ~ und Fach sein** *(abgeschlossen)* to be in the bag *(col)*; *(Vertrag, Ge-schäft auch)* to be signed and sealed; *(in Sicherheit)* to be safe; *(Ernte)* to be safely in. **(b)** *(fig col)* **jdm eins aufs ~ geben** *(schlagen)* to bash sb over the head *(col)*; *(ausschimpfen)* to give sb a (good) talk-ing to; **jdm aufs ~ steigen** *(col)* to get onto sb *(col)*.

**Dach-** *in cpds* roof; **~boden** *m* attic, loft; **~decker** *m* - roofer; *(mit Ziegeln)* tiler; **~deckerarbeiten** *pl* roofing; *(mit Ziegeln)* tiling; **~fenster** *nt* skylight; *(ausgestellt)* dormer window; **~first** *m* ridge of the roof; **~garten** *m* roof garden; **~gepäckträger** *m* *(Aut)* roof rack; **~geschoß** *nt* attic storey; *(ober-ster Stock)* top floor *or* storey; **~giebel** *m* gable; **~kammer** *f* attic room; **~luke** *f* skylight; **~organisation** *f* umbrella *or (Comm)* parent or-ganization; **~pappe** *f* roofing felt; **~rinne** *f* gutter.

**Dachs** *m* -e **(a)** badger. **(b)** **ein junger ~** *(col)* a young whippersnapper.

**Dachsbau** *m* badger's sett.

**Dach-:** **~schaden** *m* **(a)** *(lit)* damage to the roof; **(b)** *(col)* **einen ~schaden haben** to have a screw loose *(col)*; **~schindel** *f* (roof) shingle; **~stube** *f* attic (room); **~stuhl** *m* roof truss.

**dachte** *pret of* **denken.**

**Dach-:** **~terrasse** *f* roof terrace; **~verband** *m* um-brella organization; **~wohnung** *f* attic flat *(Brit) or* apartment; **~ziegel** *m* roof tile; **~zimmer** *nt* attic (room).

**Dackel** *m* - dachshund.

**dadurch** *adv (emph* **dadurch)** **(a)** *(örtlich)* through there; *(wenn Bezugsobjekt vorher erwähnt)* through it. **(b)** *(kausal)* thereby *(form)*; *(aus diesem Grund auch)* because of this/that; *(auf diese Weise)* in this/ that way. **was willst du ~ gewinnen?** what do you hope to gain by that?; **meinst du, ~ wird alles wieder gut?** do you think that will make everything all right again?; **~, daß er das tat, hat er ...** by doing that he ...

**dafür** *adv (emph* **dafür)** **(a)** *(für das, diese Tat etc)* for that/it. **~ war er nicht zu haben** it wasn't his scene *(col)*; *(erlaubte es nicht)* he wouldn't have it; **~ ist er immer zu haben** he never says no to that; **ich bin nicht ~ verantwortlich, was mein Bruder macht** I'm not responsible for what my brother does; **~ bin ich ja hier** that's what I'm here for; **er ist ~ bestraft worden, daß er frech zum Lehrer war** he was punished for being cheeky to the teacher. **(b)** *(Zustimmung)* for that/it, in favour (of that/it). **ich bin (ganz) ~, daß wir das machen** I'm (all) for doing that. **(c)** *(als Ersatz)* instead, in its place; *(bei Tausch)* in exchange; *(als Gegenleistung)* in return. **(d)** *(zum Ausgleich)* **in Mathematik ist er schlecht, ~ kann er gut Fußball spielen** he's very bad at maths but he makes up for it at football. **(e)** *(im Hinblick darauf)* **~, daß er erst drei Jahre ist, ist er sehr klug** seeing *or* considering that he's only three he's very clever.

**dafür-:** **~halten** *vi sep irreg (geh)* to be of the opinion; **nach meinem D~halten** in my opinion; **~können** *vt sep irreg* **er kann nichts ~** he can't help it; **er kann nichts ~, daß er dumm ist** he can't help being stupid.

**DAG** [de:|a:'ge:] *f* = **Deutsche Angestellten-Gewerkschaft** *German union for white-collar workers.*

**dagegen** **1** *adv (emph* **dagegen)** **(a)** *(örtlich)* against it. **(b)** *(als Einwand, Ablehnung)* against that/it. **~ sein** to be against it; **etwas/nichts ~ haben** to object/not to object; **was hat er, ~ daß wir früher anfangen?** what has he got against us starting earlier?; **haben Sie was ~, wenn ich rauche?** do you mind if I smoke?; **sollen wir ins Kino gehen? — ich hätte nichts ~ (einzuwenden)** shall we go to the cinema? — that's okay by me *(col)*. **(c)** *(als Gegenmaßnahme)* unternehmen about it; *(Medikamente einnehmen etc)* for it. **~ läßt sich nichts machen** nothing can be done about it. **(d)** *(verglichen damit)* in comparison. **(e)** *(als Ersatz)* eintauschen for that/ it/them. **2** *conj (im Gegensatz dazu)* on the other hand, however.

**dagegen-:** **~halten** *vt sep irreg* **(a)** *(vergleichen)* to compare it/them with; **(b)** *(fig: einwenden)* to object; **~setzen** *vt sep (fig)* **er setzte ~, daß ...** he put forward the objection that ...; **~sprechen** *vi sep irreg* to be against it; **was spricht ~, daß wir es so machen?** what is there against us doing it that way?; **es spricht nichts ~, es so zu machen** there's no reason not to do it that way.

**dagewesen** *adj siehe* **dasein.**

**dahaben** *vt sep irreg* to have here/there; *(in Geschäft etc)* to have in stock.

**daheim** *adv* at home; *(nach prep)* home. **bei uns ~** back home; **~ sein** *(lit, fig)* to be at home; *(nach Reise)* to be home; **wo bist du ~?** where's your home?

**Daheim** *nt no pl* home.

**daher** **1** *adv (auch* **daher)** **(a)** *(von dort)* from there.

**(b)** *(durch diesen Umstand)* that is why. **~ weiß ich das** that's how *or* why I know that; **~ die große Eile** hence all the hurry; **~ kommt es, daß ...** that is (the reason) why ...; **das kommt ~, daß ...** that is because ... **2** *conj (deshalb)* that is why.

**daher-:** **~gelaufen** *adj* **jeder ~gelaufene Kerl** any Tom, Dick or Harry; **~kommen** *vi sep irreg aux sein* to come along; **~reden** *sep* **1** *vi* to talk away; **red doch nicht so (dumm) ~!** don't talk such rubbish!; **2** *vt* to say without thinking; **was er alles ~redet** the things he comes out with! *(col)*; **das war nur so ~geredet** I/he *etc* just said that.

**dahin** **1** *adv (emph* **dahin)** **(a)** *(räumlich)* there; *(hierhin)* here. **kommst du auch ~?** are you coming too?; **bis ~** as far as there, up to that point; **ist es noch weit bis ~?** is it far still? **(b)** *(fig: so weit)* **~ kommen** to reach such a state; **du wirst es ~ bringen, daß ...** you'll bring things to such a state that ... **(c)** *(in dem Sinne)* **er äußerte sich ~ gehend, daß ...** he said something to the effect that ...; **eine ~ gehende Aussage** a statement to that effect; **er hat den Bericht ~ (gehend) interpretiert, daß ...** he interpreted the report as saying ...; **wir haben uns ~ geeinigt, daß ...** we have agreed that ...; **seine Meinung geht ~, daß ...** he tends to the opinion that ... **2** *adj pred* **~ sein** to have gone; **das Auto ist ~** *(hum col)* the car has had it *(col)*.

**dahin-:** **~dämmern** *vi sep aux sein* to lie/sit there in a semi-conscious state; **~eilen** *vi sep aux sein (liter)* to hurry along; *(Zeit)* to pass swiftly.

**dahingegen** *adv* on the other hand.

**dahingehen** *vi sep irreg aux sein (geh: Zeit etc)* to pass.

**dahingehend** *adv siehe* **dahin 1 (c).**

**dahin-:** **~gestellt** *adj* **~gestellt sein lassen, ob ...** to leave it open whether ...; **es bleibt** *or* **sei ~gestellt, ob ...** it is an open question whether ...; **~leben** *vi sep* to exist, to vegetate *(pej)*; **~sagen** *vt sep* to say without (really) thinking; **~schleppen** *vr sep (lit: sich fortbewegen)* to drag oneself along; *(fig: Verhandlungen, Zeit)* to drag on; **~schwinden** *vi sep irreg aux sein (geh) (Geld, Kraft)* to dwindle (away); *(vergehen: Zeit)* to go past; **~stehen** *vi sep irreg* to be debatable.

**dahinten** *adv (emph* **dahinten)** over there.

**dahinter** *adv (emph* **dahinter)** behind (it/that/him *etc)*. **(da ist) nichts ~** *(fig)* there's nothing behind it.

**dahinter-:** **~klemmen, ~knien** *vr sep (col)* to put one's back into it; **~kommen** *vi sep irreg aux sein (col)* to find out; **~stecken** *vi sep (col)* to be behind it/that; **~stehen** *vi sep irreg (unterstützen)* to back it/that, to be behind it/that.

**dahinvegetieren** *vi sep* to vegetate.

**Dahlie** [-iə] *f* -**n** dahlia.

**DAK** [de:|a:'ka:] *f* = **Deutsche Angestellten-Krankenkasse** German Employees' Health Insurance.

**Dakapo** *nt* -**s** encore.

**da-:** **~lassen** *vt sep irreg* to leave (here/there); **~liegen** *vi sep irreg* to lie there.

**dalli** *adv (col)* **~, ~!** on the double! *(col)*; **mach ein bißchen ~!** get a move on! *(col)*.

**Dalmatiner** *m* - *(Hund)* dalmatian.

**damalig** *adj attr* at that time; *Sitten auch* in those days. **der ~e Kanzler** the then Chancellor.

**damals** *adv* at that time, then. **seit ~** since then; **von ~** of that time; **~, als ...** at the time when ...

**Damaskus** *nt* Damascus.

**Damast** *m* -**e** damask.

**Dame** *f* -**n** **(a)** lady. **meine ~n und Herren!** ladies and gentlemen!; **Hundert-Meter-Staffel der ~n**

women's 100 metre relay. **(b)** *(Spiel)* draughts *sing* *(Brit)*, checkers *sing (US)*; *(Doppelstein)* king; *(Cards, chess)* queen.

**Damebrett** *nt* draught(s)board, checkerboard *(US)*.

**Dämel** *m* - *(col)* jerk *(col!)*.

**Damen-** *in cpds* ladies'; **~bart** *m* facial hair; **~begleitung** *f*: in **~begleitung** in the company of a lady; **~bekanntschaft** *f* female acquaintance *(col)*; **eine ~bekanntschaft machen** to make the acquaintance of a lady; **~besuch** *m* female visitor/ visitors; **~binde** *f* sanitary towel *or* napkin *(US)*; **~fahrrad** *nt* ladies' bicycle; **~gesellschaft** *f* hen party *(col)*; *(gesellige Runde)* ladies' gathering; **d~haft** *adj* ladylike *no adv*; **sich d~haft benehmen** to behave in a ladylike way; **~oberbekleidung** *f* ladies' wear; **~rad** *nt* ladies' bicycle; **~salon** *m* ladies' hairdressing salon; **~sattel** *m* im **~sattel reiten** to ride side-saddle; **~toilette** *f (WC)* ladies' toilet *or* restroom *(US)*; **~wahl** *f* ladies' excuse-me.

**Damhirsch** *m* fallow deer.

**damit 1** *adv (emph auch* **damit)** **(a)** with it/that/ them. **was soll ich ~?** what am I meant to do with that?; **ist ihre Frage ~ beantwortet?** does that answer your question?; **meint er mich ~?** does he mean me?; **was ist ~?** what about it?; **wie wäre es ~?** how about it?; **wie sieht es ~ aus?** what's happening about it?; **muß er denn immer wieder ~ ankommen?** must he keep on about it?; **~ ist nichts** *(col)* it's no go *(col)*; **hör auf ~!** *(col)* lay off! *(col)*; **~ hat es noch Zeit** there's no hurry for that; **was willst du ~ sagen?** what's that supposed to mean?; **~ will ich nicht sagen, daß ...** I don't mean to say that ...; **~ fing der Streit an** that's how the argument started; **der Streit fing ~ an, daß er behauptete ...** the argument started when he said ... **(b)** *(bei Befehlen)* with it. **weg ~!** away with it; **her ~!** give it here! *(col)*. **(c)** *(begründend)* because of that. **~ ist es klar, daß er es war** from that it's clear that it was him. **2** *conj* so that. **~ er nicht fällt** so that he does not fall.

**dämlich** *adj (col)* stupid.

**Dämlichkeit** *f* stupidity.

**Damm** *m* ⁼e **(a)** *(Deich)* dyke; *(Stau~)* dam; *(Hafen~)* wall; *(Ufer~, Straßen~)* embankment; *(fig)* barrier. **(b)** *(fig col)* **wieder auf dem ~ sein** to be back to normal; **nicht recht auf dem ~ sein** to be a bit under the weather *(col)*.

**Dammbruch** *m* breach in a/the dyke *etc*.

**dämmen** *vt* **(a)** *(geh) (lit)* to dam; *(fig)* to check. **(b)** *(Tech)* Wärme to keep in; *Schall* to absorb.

**dämm(e)rig** *adj* Licht dim, faint; *Stunden* twilight *attr.* **es wird ~** *(abends)* dusk is falling; *(morgens)* dawn is breaking.

**Dämmerlicht** *nt* twilight; *(abends auch)* dusk; *(Halbdunkel)* half-light.

**dämmern 1** *vi* **(a)** *(Tag, Morgen)* to dawn; *(Abend)* to fall. **als der Tag** *or* **Morgen/Abend dämmerte ...** as dawn was breaking/dusk was falling; **es dämmerte ihm, daß ...** *(col)* it dawned on him that ... **(b)** *(im Halbschlaf sein)* to doze. **vor sich hin ~** *(Kranker)* to be semi-conscious. **2** *vi impers* **es dämmert** *(morgens)* dawn is breaking; *(abends)* dusk is falling; **jetzt dämmert's (bei) mir!** *(col)* now it's dawning (on me)!

**Dämmer-:** **~schein** *m (liter)* glow; **~schoppen** *m* early evening drink; **~stunde** *f* twilight, dusk.

**Dämmerung** *f* twilight; *(Abend~ auch)* dusk; *(Morgen~ auch)* dawn; *(Halbdunkel)* half-light. **in der ~** at dusk/dawn.

**Dämmerzustand** *m (Halbschlaf)* dozy state; *(Bewußtseinstrübung)* semi-conscious state.

**Dämmung** *f* insulation.

**Dämon** *m, pl* **Dämonen** demon.

**dämonisch** *adj* demonic.

**Dampf** *m* ⁼e **(a)** steam. **~ ablassen** *(lit, fig)* to let off steam. **(b)** *(col: Wucht, Schwung)* force. **jdm ~ machen** *(col)* to make sb get a move on *(col)*; **~ dahinter machen** to get a move on *(col)*; **mit ~** *(col)* at full tilt.

**Dampf-** *in cpds* steam; **~antrieb** *m* steam drive; **~bügeleisen** *nt* steam iron.

**dampfen** *vi* **(a)** to steam. **ein ~des Bad** a steaming hot bath. **(b)** *aux sein (Zug, Schiff)* to steam.

**dämpfen** *vt* **(a)** *(abschwächen)* Ton to muffle; *Geräusch, Schall auch* to deaden; *Farbe* to mute; *Licht, Stimme* to lower; *Wut* to calm; *Freude, Stimmung* to dampen; *Aufprall* to deaden; *siehe* **gedämpft. (b)** *(Cook)* to steam.

**Dampfer** *m* - steamer, steamship. **auf dem falschen ~ sein** *(fig col)* to have got the wrong idea.

**Dämpfer** *m* - *(Mus) (bei Klavier)* damper; *(bei Geige, Trompete)* mute. **dadurch hat er einen ~ bekommen** that dampened his spirits.

**Dampf-:** **~kessel** *m* *(Tech)* steam-boiler; **~kochtopf** *m* pressure cooker; **~lokomotive,** **~lok** *(col)* *f* steam engine *or* locomotive; **~maschine** *f* steam(-driven) engine; **~schiff** *nt* steamship, steamer; **~walze** *f* steamroller.

**Damwild** *nt* fallow deer.

**danach** *adv (emph auch* **danach)** **(a)** *(zeitlich)* after that/it; *(nachher auch)* afterwards. **zehn Minuten ~ war sie schon wieder da** ten minutes later she was back. **(b)** *(in der Reihenfolge) (örtlich)* behind (that/it/ him *etc*); *(zeitlich)* after that/it/him *etc*. **(c)** *(dementsprechend)* accordingly; *(laut diesem)* according to that. **~ sein** *(Wetter, Stimmung etc)* to be right; **er hat den Aufsatz in zehn Minuten geschrieben — ~ ist er auch** *(col)* he wrote the essay in ten minutes — it looks like it too; **sie sieht nicht ~ aus** she doesn't look (like) it; *(als ob sie so etwas getan hätte)* she doesn't look the type; **~ zu urteilen** judging by that; **mir war nicht ~** *(col) or* **~ zumute** I didn't feel like it. **(d)** *(in bestimmte Richtung)* towards it. **er griff schnell ~** he grabbed at it. **(e)** **sie sehnte sich ~, ihren Sohn wiederzusehen** she longed to see her son again; **~ kann man nicht gehen** you can't go by that; **wenn es ~ ginge, was mir Spaß macht, dann ...** if it were a matter of what I enjoy, then ...

**Dandy** ['dɛndi] *m* **-s** dandy.

**Däne** *m (wk)* **-n, -n** Dane, Danish man/boy.

**daneben** *adv (emph auch* **daneben)** **(a)** *(räumlich)* next to him/her/that/it *etc*; **links/rechts ~** to the left/right of sb/sth; **wir wohnen im Haus ~** we live in the house next door. **(b)** *(verglichen damit)* in comparison. **(c)** *(außerdem)* as well (as that); *(gleichzeitig)* at the same time.

**daneben-:** **~benehmen*** *vr sep irreg (col)* to make an exhibition of oneself; **~gehen** *vi sep irreg aux sein* **(a)** *(verfehlen: Schuß etc)* to miss; **(b)** *(col: scheitern)* to go wrong; **~geraten*** *vi sep irreg aux sein* to go wrong; *(Übersetzung)* not to hit the mark; **~greifen** *vi sep irreg* to miss; *(fig col: mit Schätzung etc)* to be wide of the mark; **im Ton ~greifen** to strike the wrong note; **~hauen** *vi sep irreg* **(a)** *(beim Schlagen)* to miss; **(b)** *(col: sich irren)* to be wide of the mark; **~liegen** *vi sep irreg* *(col: sich irren)* to be way out *(col)*; **~raten** *vi sep ir-*

*reg (col)* to guess wrong; ~**schießen** *vi sep irreg* to miss; *(absichtlich)* to shoot to miss; ~**sein** *vi sep irreg aux sein (col) (verwirrt sein)* to be completely confused; *(sich nicht wohl fühlen)* to be feeling out of sorts; ~**treffen** *vi sep irreg* to miss; ~**zielen** *vi sep* to aim to miss.

**Dänemark** *nt* Denmark.

**Dänin** *f* Dane, Danish woman/girl.

**dänisch** *adj* Danish.

**Dänisch(e)** *nt decl as adj* Danish.

**Dank** *m no pl* thanks *pl.* **herzlichen** *or* **vielen** ~ many thanks, thank you very much, thanks a lot *(col)*; **vielen herzlichen/tausend** ~**!** many/very many thanks!, thanks a million! *(col)*; **jdm für etw** ~ **sagen** *(liter)* to express one's *or* give *(esp Eccl)* thanks to sb for sth; **jdm zu** ~ **verpflichtet sein** *(form)* to owe sb a debt of gratitude; **mit bestem** ~ **zurück!** many thanks for the loan; *(iro: Retourkutsche)* thank you - the same to you!; **das ist der** ~ **dafür** that's all the thanks you get; **zum** ~ **(dafür)** as a way of saying thank you.

**dank** *prep +gen or dat* thanks to.

**dankbar** *adj* **(a)** *(dankerfüllt)* grateful; *(erleichtert, froh)* thankful; *Publikum, Zuhörer* appreciative. **jdm** ~ **sein** to be grateful to sb *(für for)*; **sich** ~ **erweisen** to show one's gratitude *(gegenüber to).* **(b)** *(lohnend) Aufgabe, Rolle* rewarding; *(haltbar)* hard-wearing.

**Dankbarkeit** *f* gratitude *(gegen, gegenüber to).*

**Dankbrief** *m* thank-you letter.

**danke** *interj* thank you, thanks *(col)*, ta *(Brit col)*; *(ablehnend)* no thank you. ~ **ja, ja,** ~ yes please; ~ **nein, nein,** ~ no thank you; ~ **schön** *or* **sehr** thank you *or* thanks *(col)* very much; ~ **vielmals** many thanks.

**danken 1** *vi* **(a)** to express one's thanks. **jdm** ~ to thank sb *(für for)*; **danke!** yes please!; *(ablehnend)* no thank you, no thanks *(col)*; **man dankt** *(col)* thanks *(col)*; **jdm** ~ **lassen** to send sb one's thanks; **nichts zu** ~ don't mention it; **na, ich danke** *(iro)* no thank you; ~**d erhalten** *(Comm)* received with thanks; ~**d ablehnen** to decline with thanks. **(b)** *(ablehnen)* to decline. **2** *vt* **(a)** *(geh: verdanken)* **ihm danke ich es, daß ...** I owe it to him that ... **(b)** **jdm etw** ~ to thank sb for sth; **man hat es mir schlecht gedankt, daß ich das getan habe** I got small thanks for doing it.

**dankenswert** *adj Bemühung* commendable; *Hilfe* kind; *(lohnenswert) Aufgabe, Arbeit* rewarding.

**Dankeschön** *nt no pl* thank-you.

**Dankesworte** *pl* words *pl* of thanks; *(von Redner)* vote *sing* of thanks.

**Dank-:** ~**gottesdienst** *m* service of thanksgiving; ~**sagung** *f (Brief)* note of thanks; ~**schreiben** *nt* letter of thanks.

**dann** *adv* **(a)** then. ~ **und** ~ about then; ~ **und wann** now and then; **gerade** ~, **wenn ...** just when ...; **was** ~**?** what happens then?; **bis** ~**!** see you then! **(b)** *(unter diesen Umständen)* then. **wenn ...,** ~ **if ...,** (then); **nein, selbst** ~ **nicht** no, not even then; **selbst** ~/**selbst** ~ **nicht, wenn ...** even/not even if ...; **erst** ~, **wenn ...** only when ...; **ja,** ~**!** (oh) well then!; **wenn er seine Gedichte selbst nicht versteht, wer** ~**?** if he can't understand his own poems, who can?; ~ **eben nicht** well, in that case (there's no more to be said); ~ **erst recht nicht!** in that case no way *(col)*; ~ **will ich lieber gehen** well, I'd better be getting along (then); **also** ~ **bis morgen** see you tomorrow then. **(c)** *(außerdem)* ~ **... noch** on top of that.

**dannen** *adv:* **von** ~ *(liter: weg)* away.

**daran** *adv (auch* **dran***)* **(a)** *(räumlich) hängen* on it/that; *schieben, lehnen, stellen* against it/that; *legen* next to it/that; *kleben, machen* to it/that. **nahe** *or* **dicht** ~ right up against it; **nahe** ~ **sein, etw zu tun** to be on the point of doing sth; **zu nahe** ~ too close (to it); ~ **vorbei** past it; ~ **kommen** to touch it/that. **(b)** *(zeitlich: danach anschließend)* **im Anschluß** ~ following that/this. **(c)** *(col)* = **dran (b, c). (d)** *arbeiten* on it/that; *sterben, erinnern, Bedarf, Mangel* of it/that; *sich beteiligen, arm, reich* in it/that; *sich klammern* to it/that. **wird sich etwas** ~ **ändern?** will that change at all?; **wir können nichts** ~ **machen** we can't do anything about it; ~ **sieht man, wie ...** there you (can) see how ...; **das Beste/Schönste** *etc* ~ the best/nicest *etc* thing about it; **es ist nichts** ~ *(ist nicht fundiert)* there's nothing in it; *(ist nichts Besonderes)* it's nothing special.

**daran-:** ~**gehen** *vi sep irreg aux sein* to set about it; ~**gehen, etw zu tun** to set about doing sth; ~**machen** *vr sep (col)* to set about it; **sich** ~**machen, etw zu tun** to set about doing sth; ~**setzen** *sep* **1** *vt* **seine ganzen Kräfte** ~**setzen, etw zu tun** to spare no effort to do sth; **2** *vr (sich* ~**machen)** to get down to it.

**darauf** *adv (emph* **darauf***)* **(a)** *(räumlich)* on it/that/ them *etc*; *(in Richtung)* towards it/that/them *etc*; *schießen, zielen, losfahren* at it/that/them *etc*; *(fig) basieren, aufbauen* on it/that; *zurückführen, beziehen* to it/that. **er schlug mit dem Hammer** ~ he hit it with the hammer; **seine Behauptungen stützen sich** ~, **daß ...** his claims are based on the supposition that ...

**(b)** *(Reihenfolge)* after that. **die Tage, die** ~ **folgten** the days which followed; ~ **folgte ...** that was followed by ..., after that came ...; **am Tag** ~ the next day; **kurz** ~ shortly afterwards.

**(c)** *(als Reaktion) sagen, reagieren* to that. ~ **antworten** to answer that; **eine Antwort** ~ an answer to that.

**(d)** *bestehen, verlassen, wetten, Zeit/Mühe verschwenden, Einfluß* on that/it; *hoffen, warten, sich vorbereiten, gefaßt sein* for that/it; *trinken* to that/it; *stolz sein* of that/it. **ich bin stolz** ~, **daß sie gewonnen hat** I'm proud that she won; **ich bestehe** ~, **daß du kommst** I insist that you come; **wir freuen uns schon** ~, **daß du bald kommst** we're looking forward to your *or* you coming; **wir kamen auch** ~ **zu sprechen** we talked about that too; **wie kommst du** ~**?** what makes you think that?; ~ **willst du also hinaus!** so that's what you're getting at!

**darauffolgend** *adj attr* after him/it/that *etc*; *Tag etc* following; *Wagen etc* behind *pred.*

**daraufhin** *adv (emph* **daraufhin***)* **(danach)** after that, thereupon; *(aus diesem Anlaß, deshalb)* as a result (of that/this); *(im Hinblick darauf)* with regard to that/this. **wir müssen es** ~ **prüfen, ob ...** we must test it to see whether ...

**daraus** *adv (emph auch* **daraus***)* out of that/it/them; *(aus dieser Angelegenheit)* from that/it/them. **was ist** ~ **geworden?** what became of it?; ~ **ergibt sich, daß ...** it follows from this that ...

**darben** *vi (geh: hungern)* to starve.

**darbieten** *sep irreg (geh)* **1** *vt* **(a)** *(vorführen) Tänze etc* to perform; *(vortragen) Lehrstoff* to present. **(b)** *(anbieten)* to offer; *Speisen* to serve. **2** *vr* to present itself.

**Darbietung** *f* performance; *(das Dargebotene)* act.

**darbringen** *vt sep irreg (geh) Opfer* to offer.

**darein** *adv (emph auch* **darein***) (räumlich: hinein)* in there; *(wenn Bezugsobjekt vorher erwähnt)* in it/ them.

**dar<u>ei</u>n-** pref siehe auch **drein-**; **~finden** vr sep irreg (geh) to come to terms with it.

**dar<u>i</u>n** adv (emph auch **d<u>a</u>rin**) **(a)** (räumlich) in there; (wenn Bezugsobjekt vorher erwähnt) in it/them. **(b)** (in dieser Beziehung) in that respect. **~ ist er ganz groß** (col) he's very good at that; **die beiden unterscheiden sich ~, daß** ... the two of them differ in that ...; **der Unterschied liegt ~, daß** ... the difference is that ...

**d<u>a</u>rlegen** vt sep to explain (jdm to sb); Theorie, Ansichten auch to expound (jdm to sb).

**D<u>a</u>rlegung** f explanation.

**D<u>a</u>rleh(e)n** nt - loan. **als ~** as a loan.

**D<u>a</u>rm** m ⁼e intestine(s pl), bowel(s pl); (für Wurst) (sausage) skin; (für Saiten, Schläger etc) gut.

**D<u>a</u>rm-** in cpds intestinal; **~ausgang** m anus; **~grippe** f gastric influenza; **~krebs** m cancer of the intestine; **~saite** f gut string; **~tätigkeit** f peristalsis no art; **die ~tätigkeit fördern** to stimulate the movement of the bowels; **~trägheit** f under-activity of the intestines.

**D<u>a</u>rre** f -n drying kiln or oven; (Hopfen~) oast.

**d<u>a</u>rreichen** vt sep (liter: anbieten) to offer (jdm etw sb sth, sth to sb).

**d<u>a</u>rstellbar** adj (in Literaturwerk etc) portrayable; (durch Diagramm etc) representable; (beschreibbar) describable. **schwer/leicht ~** hard/easy to portray/show/describe.

**d<u>a</u>rstellen** sep **1** vt **(a)** to show; (ein Bild entwerfen von) to portray, to depict; (Theat) to play; (beschreiben) to describe. **etw kurz ~** to give a short description of sth; **die ~den Künste** (Theater) the performing arts; (Malerei, Plastik) the visual arts; **er stellt nichts dar** (fig) he's nothing special. **(b)** (bedeuten) to constitute, to represent. **2** vr (Eindruck vermitteln) to appear (jdm to sb); (sich erweisen) to show oneself.

**D<u>a</u>rsteller** m - (Theat) actor. **der ~ des Hamlet** the actor playing Hamlet.

**D<u>a</u>rstellerin** f (Theat) actress.

**d<u>a</u>rstellerisch** adj dramatic. **eine ~e Höchstleistung** a magnificent piece of acting.

**D<u>a</u>rstellung** f portrayal; (in Buch, Bild auch) depiction; (durch Diagramm etc) representation; (Beschreibung) description; (Bericht) account. **graphische ~** diagram, graph (Math); **eine falsche ~ der Fakten** a misrepresentation of the facts; **er gab eine großartige ~ des Hamlet** his performance as Hamlet was superb.

**dar<u>ü</u>ber** adv (emph auch **d<u>a</u>rüber**) **(a)** (räumlich) over that/it/them; (höher als etw) above (there/it/them); (direkt auf etw) on top (of it/them). **~ hinweg sein** (fig) to have got over it; **~ hinaus** over and above that, in addition; **~ hinaus belog sie mich** on top of that she lied to me. **(b)** (deswegen, in dieser Beziehung) about that/it. **sich ~ beschweren/beklagen, daß** ... to complain/moan that ... **(c)** (davon) about that/it. **sie führt eine Liste ~** she keeps a list of it. **(d)** (mehr, höher) above or over that. **21 Jahre und ~** 21 years and above or over; **~ hinaus** over and above that.

**dar<u>ü</u>ber-:** **~fahren** vi sep irreg aux sein (fig) to run over it; **wenn du mit der Hand ~fährst,** ... if you run your hand over it ...; **~liegen** vi sep irreg (fig) to be higher; **~stehen** vi sep irreg (fig) to be above such things.

**dar<u>u</u>m** adv (emph auch **d<u>a</u>rum**) siehe auch **drum (a)** (räumlich) around (that/it/him/her/them. **~ herum** around about (it/him/her/them). **(b)** (um diese Angelegenheit) **es geht ~, daß** ... the thing is that ...; **~ geht es mir/geht es mir nicht** that's my point/

that's not the point for me; **es geht mir ~, Ihnen das klarzumachen** I'm trying to make it clear to you; **ich gäbe viel ~, die Wahrheit zu erfahren** I would give a lot to learn the truth. **(c)** (deshalb) that's why, because of that. **eben ~** that is exactly why; **warum willst du nicht mitkommen? — ~!** (col) why don't you want to come? — I just don't.

**dar<u>u</u>nter** adv (emph auch **d<u>a</u>runter) (a)** (räumlich) under that/it/them. **~ hervorkommen** to appear from underneath; **ein Stockwerk ~** one floor below (it). **(b)** (weniger) under that. **Leute im Alter von 35 Jahren und ~** people aged 35 and under; **~ macht sie's nicht** (col) she won't do it for less. **(c)** (dabei) among them. **~ waren viele Ausländer** there were a lot of foreigners among them. **(d) was verstehen Sie ~?** what do you understand by that/it?; **~ kann ich mir nichts vorstellen** that doesn't mean anything to me.

**dar<u>u</u>nter-:** **~bleiben** vi sep irreg aux sein (fig) to be lower; **~fallen** vi sep irreg aux sein (fig) (dazugerechnet werden) to be included; (davon betroffen werden) to come under it/them; **~liegen** vi sep irreg (fig) to be lower; **~mischen** sep **1** vt Mehl to mix in; **2** vr (Mensch) to mingle with them; **~setzen** vt sep Unterschrift to put to it.

**d<u>a</u>s** art etc siehe **der²**.

**D<u>a</u>sein** nt no pl existence; (Anwesendsein) presence.

**d<u>a</u>sein** vi sep irreg aux sein to be there. **noch ~** to be still there; (übrig sein auch) to be left; **wieder ~** to be back; **ich bin gleich wieder da** I'll be right back; **ist Post für mich da?** is there any mail for me?; **war der Briefträger schon da?** has the postman been yet?; **sie ist nur für ihren Mann da** she lives for her husband; **ein Arzt, der immer für seine Patienten da ist** a doctor who always has time for his patients; **voll ~** (col) to be all there (col); **es ist alles schon mal dagewesen** it's all been done before; **ein nie dagewesener Erfolg** an unprecedented success.

**D<u>a</u>seins-:** **~berechtigung** f right to exist; **~kampf** m struggle for survival.

**d<u>a</u>sitzen** vi sep irreg to sit there. **ohne einen Pfennig ~** (col) to be left without a penny.

**d<u>a</u>sjenige** dem pron siehe **derjenige**.

**d<u>a</u>ß** conj that. **ich bin überzeugt, ~ du das Richtige getan hast** I'm sure (that) you have done the right thing; **ich bin dagegen, ~ ihr alle kommt** I'm against you all coming; **das liegt daran, ~** ... that is because ...; **~ du es mir nicht verlierst!** see that you don't lose it!

**d<u>a</u>sselbe** dem pron siehe **derselbe**.

**d<u>a</u>stehen** vi sep irreg aux haben or sein **(a)** to stand there. **steh nicht so dumm da!** don't just stand there looking stupid. **(b)** (fig) **gut/schlecht ~** to be in a good/bad position; **allein ~** to be on one's own; **einzig ~** to be unique or unparalleled; **jetzt stehe ich als Lügner da** now I'm left looking like a liar; **wie stehe ich jetzt da!** (Selbstlob) just look at me now!; (Vorwurf) I look a proper fool!

**Dat. = Dativ**.

**Dat<u>ei</u>** f (Comp) file.

**Dat<u>ei</u>-:** **~name** m file name; **~verwaltung** f file management.

**D<u>a</u>ten (a)** pl of **Datum. (b)** (Comp etc) data usu sing.

**D<u>a</u>ten-** (Comp) in cpds data; **~abruf** m data retrieval; **~bank** f database; (größer) data bank; **~erfassung** f data capture; **~satz** m record; **~schutz** m data protection no art; **~sichtgerät** nt visual display unit; **~technik** f computer science; **~träger** m data carrier; **~typist(in** f) *m* keyboarder; ~**übertragung** *f* data transmission; ~**verarbeitung** *f* data processing; ~**verarbeitungsanlage** *f* data processing equipment.

**datieren\*** *vti* to date. **dieser Brief datiert vom 1. Januar** this letter is dated January 1st.

**Dativ** *m (Gram)* dative (case).

**Dativ\objekt** *nt (Gram)* indirect object.

**dato** *adv*: **bis** ~ *(Comm, col)* to date.

**Dattel** *f* **-n** date.

**Dattelpalme** *f* date palm.

**Datum** *nt, pl* **Daten** (**a**) date. **was für ein** ~ **haben wir heute?** what is the date today?; **das heutige** ~ today's date; **ein Brief ohne** ~ an undated letter; **ein Nachschlagewerk neueren** ~**s** a recent reference work. (**b**) *usu pl (Statistik, Comp etc)* piece of data.

**Datums-:** ~**grenze** *f (Geog)* (international) date line; ~**stempel** *m* date stamp.

**Dauer** *f no pl (das Andauern)* duration; *(Zeitspanne)* period, term; *(Länge: einer Sendung etc)* length. **während der** ~ **des Vertrages/Krieges** for the duration of the contract/war; **für die** ~ **eines Monats** for a period of one month; **seine Begeisterung war nicht von** ~ his enthusiasm was short-lived; **von langer/ kurzer** ~ **sein** to last a long time/not to last long; **auf die** ~ in the long run; **das kann auf die** ~ **nicht so weitergehen** it can't go on like that indefinitely; **auf** ~ permanently.

**Dauer-** *in cpds* permanent; ~**arbeitslose(r)** *mf* long-term unemployed person; **die** ~**arbeitslosen** the long-term unemployed; ~**auftrag** *m (Fin)* standing order; ~**belastung** *f* continual pressure *no indef art*; *(von Maschine)* constant load; ~**beschäftigung** *f (Stellung)* permanent position; ~**brenner** *m* (**a**) *(Ofen)* slow burning stove; (**b**) *(col: Dauererfolg)* long runner; **ein** ~**brenner sein** to run and run; ~**erfolg** *m* long-running success; ~**gast** *m* permanent guest; *(häufiger Gast)* regular visitor, permanent fixture *(hum)*.

**dauerhaft** *adj Zustand, Farbe* permanent; *Frieden, Beziehung* lasting; *Stoff* durable.

**Dauerhaftigkeit** *f* permanence; *(von Material)* durability.

**Dauer-:** ~**karte** *f* season ticket; ~**lauf** *m (Sport)* jog; *(das Laufen)* jogging; **im** ~**lauf** at a jog *or* trot; **einen** ~**lauf machen** to go jogging; ~**lutscher** *m* lollipop *(Brit)*, popsicle ® *(US)*; ~**mieter** *m* long-term tenant.

**dauern** *vi* (**a**) *(an~)* to last, to go on. **die Verhandlungen** ~ **schon drei Wochen** the negotiations have already been going on for three weeks. (**b**) *(Zeit benötigen)* to take a while; *(lange)* to take a long time. **das dauert noch** *(col)* it'll be some time yet; **es dauerte lange, bis er sich befreit hatte** it took him a long time to get free; **das dauert mir zu lange** I can't wait that long; **es dauert jetzt nicht mehr lange** it won't take much longer.

**dauernd 1** *adj Regelung* lasting; *Wohnsitz* permanent; *(fortwährend) Unterbrechung* constant, perpetual. **2** *adv* **etw** ~ **tun** to keep (on) doing sth.

**Dauer-:** ~**obst** *nt* fruit suitable for storing; ~**parker** *m* - long-stay parker; ~**redner** *m (pej)* interminable speaker; ~**regen** *m* continuous rain; ~**schlaf** *m* prolonged sleep; ~**speicher** *m (Comp)* permanent memory; ~**stellung** *f* permanent position; ~**ton** *m* continuous tone; ~**welle** *f* permanent wave, perm *(col)*; ~**wirkung** *f* (long-)lasting effect; ~**wurst** *f* German salami; ~**zustand** *m* permanent state of affairs.

**Däumchen** *nt dim of* **Daumen**.

**Daumen** *m* - thumb. **jdm die** ~ **drücken** to keep

one's fingers crossed for sb; ~ **drehen** to twiddle one's thumbs; **den** ~ **auf etw** *(acc)* **halten** *(col)* to hold on to sth.

**Daumen-:** ~**abdruck** *m* thumbprint; ~**nagel** *m* thumbnail; ~**register** *nt* thumb index; ~**schraube** *f* **jdm die** ~**schrauben anlegen** *(fig, col)* to put the (thumb)screws on sb.

**Daune** *f* **-n** down feather. ~**n** down *sing*.

**Daunen-:** ~**bett** *nt*, ~**decke** *f* (down-filled) duvet; ~**jacke** *f* quilted jacket; **d**~**weich** *adj* soft as down.

**davon** *adv (emph* **davon***)* (**a**) *(räumlich)* from there; *(wenn Bezugsobjekt vorher erwähnt)* from it/them; *(mit Entfernungsangabe)* away (from there/it/them). **weg** ~! *(col)* get away from there/it/them. (**b**) *(fig)* **ich bin weit** ~ **entfernt, Ihnen Vorwürfe machen zu wollen** the last thing I want to do is reproach you; **wenn wir** ~ **absehen, daß ...** if we overlook the fact that ...; **und** ~ **kommt die rote Farbe** and that's where the red comes from; **das kommt** ~! that's what you get!; ~ **hat man nur Ärger** you get nothing but trouble with it; ~ **wird man müde** it makes you tired; **was habe ich** ~? what do I get out of it? (**c**) *(mit Passiv)* ~ **betroffen werden** to be affected by it/them. (**d**) *(Anteil)* of that/it/them. **nehmen Sie doch noch etwas** ~! do have some more!; **das Doppelte** ~ twice that. (**e**) *(darüber) hören, wissen, sprechen* about that/ it/them; *verstehen, halten* of that/it/them. **genug** ~! enough of this!

**davon-:** ~**bleiben** *vi sep irreg aux sein (col)* to keep away; *(nicht anfassen)* to keep one's hands off; ~**fahren** *vi sep irreg aux sein* to drive away; *(auf Fahrrad etc)* to ride away; *(Zug)* to pull away; ~**fliegen** *vi sep irreg aux sein* to fly away; ~**gehen** *vi sep irreg aux sein (geh)* to walk away; ~**jagen** *vt sep* to chase off *or* away; ~**kommen** *vi sep irreg aux sein (entkommen)* to get away, to escape; *(nicht bestraft werden)* to get away with it; **mit dem Schrecken/dem Leben/einer Geldstrafe** ~**kommen** to escape with no more than a shock/with one's life/to get off with a fine; ~**lassen** *vt sep irreg* **die Finger** ~**lassen** *(col)* to keep one's hands *or* fingers off (it/ them); ~**laufen** *vi sep irreg aux sein* to run away *(jdm/vor jdm* from sb); *(verlassen)* to walk out *(jdm* on sb); **es ist zum D**~**laufen!** *(col)* it's all too much!; **die Preise sind den Löhnen** ~**gelaufen** prices have outstripped wages; ~**machen** *vr sep* to make off; ~**schleichen** *vir sep irreg (vi: aux sein)* to creep away *or* off; ~**stehlen** *vr sep irreg (geh)* to steal away; ~**tragen** *vt sep irreg* (**a**) *(wegtragen)* to carry away; *Preis* to carry off; *Sieg, Ruhm* to win; (**b**) *Schaden, Verletzung* to suffer; ~**ziehen** *vi sep irreg aux sein (liter)* to leave; *(Sport col)* to pull away *(jdm* from sb).

**davor** *adv (emph* **davor***)* (**a**) *(räumlich)* in front (of that/it/them); *(wenn Bezugsobjekt vorher erwähnt)* in front of it/them. (**b**) *(zeitlich)* before that; *(bevor man etw tut)* beforehand. (**c**) *bewahren, schützen* from that/it; *warnen* about that/it; *Angst haben* of that/it; *sich ekeln* by that/it. **ich habe Angst** ~, **daß der Hund beißen könnte** I'm afraid that the dog might bite.

**davor-:** ~**stehen** *vi sep irreg aux haben or sein* to stand in front of it/them; ~**stellen** *sep* **1** *vt* to put in front of it/them; **2** *vr* to stand in front of it/them.

**DAX** [daks] *m* = **Deutscher Aktienindex** German share index.

**dazu** *adv (emph* **dazu***)* (**a**) *(dabei, damit)* with it. **er**

**decodieren**

**ist dumm und** ~ **auch noch faul** he's stupid and lazy with it or into the bargain (col); ... **und** ~ **nicht unintelligent** ... and not unintelligent either; **noch** ~ as well, too; ~ **serviert man am besten Reis** it's best to serve rice with it.

(b) (dahin) to that/it. **das führt** ~, **daß weitere Forderungen gestellt werden** that will lead to further demands being made; **wie konnte es nur** ~ **kommen?** how could that happen?; **wie komme ich** ~? (empört) why on earth should I?; ... **aber ich bin nicht** ~ **gekommen** ... but I didn't get around to it.

(c) (dafür, zu diesem Zweck) for that/it. **ich bin zu alt** ~, **noch tanzen zu gehen** I'm too old to go dancing; **ich habe ihm** ~ **geraten** I advised him to (do that); ~ **bereit sein, etw zu tun** to be prepared to do sth; ~ **ist er da** that's what he's there for; **das Recht** ~ the right to do it.

(d) (darüber, zum Thema) about that/it. **was meinst du** ~? what do you think about that?

(e) **im Gegensatz/Vergleich** ~ in contrast to/ comparison with that.

**dazu-:** ~**geben** vt sep irreg to add; ~**gehören*** vi sep to belong (to it/us etc); (als Ergänzung) to go with it/them; (eingeschlossen sein) to be included (in it/them); **das gehört** ~ (versteht von selbst) it's all part of it; **es gehört schon einiges** ~, **das zu tun** it takes a lot to do that; ~**gehörig** adj attr which goes/go with it/them; Schlüssel etc belonging to it/them; Werkzeuge, Material necessary; ~**kommen** vi sep irreg aux sein (a) (ankommen) to arrive (on the scene); (b) (hinzugefügt werden) to be added; **kommt noch etwas** ~? will there be anything else?; **es kommt noch** ~, **daß er faul ist** added to that he's lazy; ~**lernen** vt sep **viel/nichts** ~**lernen** to learn a lot more/nothing new; **schon wieder was** ~**gelernt!** you learn something (new) every day!

**dazumal** adv (old) in those days. siehe auch **anno**.

**dazu-:** ~**rechnen** vt sep Betrag to add on; ~**schreiben** vt sep irreg to add; ~**setzen** vr sep to join him/us etc; ~**tun** vt sep irreg (col) to add; **er hat es ohne dein D~tun geschafft** he managed it without your doing/saying etc anything.

**dazwischen** adv in between; (in der betreffenden Menge, Gruppe) amongst them, in with them. **der Unterschied** ~ the difference between them.

**dazwischen-:** ~**fahren** vi sep irreg aux sein (a) (eingreifen) to intervene; (b) (unterbrechen) to interrupt; ~**funken** vi sep (col: eingreifen) to put one's oar in (col); ~**kommen** vi sep irreg aux sein (störend erscheinen) to get in the way; ... **wenn nichts** ~**kommt!** ... if all goes well; **mir ist leider etwas** ~**gekommen, ich kann nicht dabeisein** something has come or cropped up, I'm afraid I can't be there; ~**liegend** adj attr **die** ~**liegenden Monate** the intervening months; ~**reden** vi sep to interrupt (jdm sb); ~**rufen** vti sep irreg to yell out; ~**stehen** vi sep irreg aux haben or sein (a) (lit) to be amongst or (zwischen zweien) between them; (b) (zwischen den Parteien) to be neutral; (c) (geh: hindernd) to be in the way; (störend) to come between them.

**DB** [deː'beː] f = **Deutsche Bundesbahn**.

**dB** = **Dezibel** dB.

**DDR** [deːdeːʔ|ɛr] f (Hist) = **Deutsche Demokratische Republik** GDR, East Germany no art.

**DDR-Bürger** m (Hist) East German.

**DDT** ® [deːdeː'teː] nt - DDT.

**Deal** [diːl] m -s (Geschäft etc, col: Drogen) deal.

**dealen** ['diːlən] (col) **1** vt Drogen to push. **2** vi **mit Kokain** ~ to deal in or to push cocaine; **er dealt** he

is a dealer.

**Dealer(in** f) ['diːlɐ, -ərɪn] m - (col) drug peddler or pusher.

**Debakel** nt - debacle. **ein** ~ **erleiden** (Stück etc) to be a debacle.

**Debatte** f -n debate. **etw zur** ~ **stellen** to put sth up for discussion or (Parl) debate; **das steht hier nicht zur** ~ that's not the issue.

**debattieren*** vti to debate (über etw sth).

**Debet** nt -s (Fin) debits pl.

**Debüt** [de'byː] nt -s debut. **sein** ~ **als etw geben** to make one's debut as sth.

**Debütant(in** f) m (wk) person making his/her debut.

**debütieren*** vi (Theat, fig) to make one's debut.

**Dechant** m (Eccl) dean.

**dechiffrieren*** [deʃɪ'friːrən] vt to decode, to decipher.

**Deck** nt -s deck; (in Parkhaus) level. **an** ~ **gehen** to go on deck; **alle Mann an** ~! all hands on deck!

**Deck-:** ~**adresse** f accommodation or cover (US) address; ~**anstrich** m top coat; ~**bett** nt feather quilt; ~**blatt** nt (von Zigarre) wrapper; (Schutzblatt) cover.

**Decke** f -n (a) (lit, fig) blanket; (Tisch~) cloth; (Stepp~) quilt. **sich nach der** ~ **strecken** (fig) to cut one's coat according to one's cloth; **mit jdm unter einer** ~ **stecken** (fig) to be hand in glove with sb. (b) (Zimmer~) ceiling; **an die** ~ **gehen** (col) to hit the roof (col); **vor Freude an die** ~ **springen** (col) to jump for joy; **mir fällt die** ~ **auf den Kopf** (fig col) I feel really claustrophobic. (c) (Schicht) layer; (Straßen~) surface.

**Deckel** m - lid; (von Schachtel auch, von Flasche) top; (Buch~) cover. **du kriegst gleich eins auf den** ~ (col) you're going to catch it (col).

**decken 1** vt (a) (zu~, Fin, begatten) to cover; (Ftbl auch) to mark; Komplizen to cover up for. **ein Dach mit Ziegeln** ~ to tile a roof; **mein Bedarf ist gedeckt** I have all I need; (fig col) I've had enough. (b) Tisch, Tafel to set, to lay (Brit). **sich an einen gedeckten Tisch setzen** (fig) to be handed everything on a plate; **ein Tuch über etw** (acc) ~ to cover sth with a cloth. **2** vt to cover; (Boxen) to guard; (Ftbl auch) to mark. **3** vr (a) (Interessen, Begriffe) to coincide; (Aussagen) to correspond, to agree. (b) (Boxer etc) to cover oneself.

**Deck-:** ~**farbe** f opaque water colour; ~**hengst** m stud(horse), stallion; ~**mantel** m (fig) mask; **unter dem** ~**mantel von** ... under the guise of ...; ~**name** m assumed name; (Mil) code name; ~**offizier** m (Naut) ≃ warrant officer; ~**platte** f (Build) slab; ~**schicht** f surface layer; (von Straße) surface; (Geol) top layer.

**Deckung** f (a) (Schutz) cover; (Ftbl, Chess) defence; (Boxen etc) guard. **in** ~ **gehen** to take cover. (b) (Verheimlichung) **die** ~ **von etw** covering up for sth. (c) (Comm, Fin) (von Scheck, Wechsel) cover; (das Decken) covering; (das Begleichen) meeting. **zur** ~ **seiner Schulden** to meet his debts. (d) **eine** ~ **der Nachfrage ist unmöglich** demand cannot possibly be met. (e) (Übereinstimmung) **lassen sich diese Standpunkte zur** ~ **bringen?** can these points of view be reconciled?

**Deckungs-:** ~**fehler** m (Ftbl) defensive error; ~**feuer** nt (Mil) covering fire; **d~gleich** adj (Math) congruent; **d~gleich sein** (fig) to coincide; (Aussagen) to agree; ~**zusage** f (von Versicherung) cover note.

**Deckweiß** nt opaque white.

**Decoder** [de'koːdɐ, dɪ'koʊdə] m - decoder.

**decodieren*** vt to decode.

**dediziert** *adj (esp Comp)* dedicated.
**Deduktion** *f* deduction.
**deduzieren*** *vt* to deduce *(aus* from*)*.
**de facto** *adv* de facto.
**Defätismus** *m no pl* defeatism.
**defätistisch** *adj* defeatist *no adv*.
**defekt** *adj Gerät etc* faulty, defective.
**Defekt** *m* **-e** fault, defect; *(Med)* deficiency.
**defensiv** *adj* defensive. **sich ~ verhalten** to be on the defensive.
**Defensive** [-'ziːvə] *f no pl* defensive. **in der ~** on the defensive; **jdn in die ~ drängen** to force sb onto the defensive.
**defilieren*** *vi aux haben or sein (Mil)* to march past; *(fig)* to parade past.
**definierbar** *adj* definable.
**definieren*** *vt* to define. **etw neu ~** to redefine sth.
**Definition** *f* definition.
**definitiv** *adj* definite.
**Defizit** *nt* **-e** deficit; *(Mangel)* deficiency *(an +dat* of*)*.
**defizitär** *adj* in deficit. **eine ~e Haushaltspolitik führen** to follow an economic policy which can only lead to deficit.
**Deflation** *f (Econ)* deflation.
**deflationär** *adj* deflationary *no adv*.
**deflorieren*** *vt* to deflower.
**Deformation** *f* deformation, distortion; *(Mißbildung)* deformity; *(Entstellung)* disfigurement.
**deformieren*** *vt (lit, fig: mißbilden)* to deform; *(entstellen)* to disfigure. **eine deformierte Nase** a misshapen nose.
**Defroster** *m* - *(Aut)* demister, defroster *(US)*; *(Sprühmittel)* de-icer.
**deftig** *adj* **(a)** *Witz, Humor* ribald. **(b)** *Lüge* whopping *(col)*, huge; *Mahlzeit* solid; *Wurst etc* substantial, good solid *attr*; *Ohrfeige* cracking *(col)*.
**Degen** *m* - *(Sportfechten)* épée.
**degenerieren*** *vi aux sein* to degenerate *(zu* into*)*.
**degeneriert** *adj* degenerate.
**degradieren*** *vt (Mil)* to demote *(zu* to*)*; *(fig: herabwürdigen)* to degrade. **jdn/etw zu etw ~** *(fig)* to lower sb/sth to the level of sth.
**Degradierung** *f (Mil)* demotion *(zu* to*)*; *(fig)* degradation.
**dehnbar** *adj (lit, fig)* elastic.
**Dehnbarkeit** *f no pl* elasticity.
**dehnen 1** *vt* to stretch; *(Med auch)* to dilate; *Laut, Silbe* to lengthen. **2** *vr (auch Ozean etc)* to stretch.
**Dehnung** *f siehe vt* stretching; dilation; lengthening.
**Deich** *m* **-e** dyke, dike *(esp US)*.
**Deichsel** [-ks-] *f* **-n** shaft; *(Doppel~)* shafts *pl*.
**deichseln** [-ks-] *vt (col)* to wangle *(col)*. **das werden wir schon ~** we'll wangle it somehow.
**dein** *poss pron (adjektivisch) (in Briefen:* **D~)** your. **herzliche Grüße, D~e** Elke with best wishes, yours *or (herzlicher)* love Elke.
**deiner** *pers pron gen of* **du** *(geh)* of you. **wir werden ~ gedenken** we will remember you.
**deine(r, s)** *poss pron (substantivisch)* yours. **der/die/das ~** *(geh)* yours; **die D~n** *(geh)* your family; **das D~** *(geh: Besitz)* what is yours.
**deinerseits** *adv (auf deiner Seite)* for your part; *(von deiner Seite)* on your part.
**deinesgleichen** *pron inv* people like you.
**deinet-:** **~wegen** *adv (wegen dir)* because of you, on account of you; *(dir zuliebe)* for your sake; *(um dich)* about you; *(für dich)* on your behalf; **~willen** *adv* **um ~willen** for your sake.
**deinige** *poss pron (old, geh)* **der/die/das ~** yours; **tu du das ~** you do your share.

**deins** *poss pron* yours.
**de jure** *adv* de jure.
**Dekade** *f (10 Tage)* ten days; *(10 Jahre)* decade.
**dekadent** *adj* decadent.
**Dekadenz** *f no pl* decadence.
**Dekan** *m* **-e** *(Univ, Eccl)* dean.
**Dekanat** *nt (Univ)* office of dean; *(Eccl)* deanery.
**Deklamation** *f* declamation. **~en** *(pej)* (empty) rhetoric *sing*.
**deklamieren*** *vti* to declaim.
**Deklaration** *f* declaration.
**deklarieren*** *vt* to declare.
**deklassieren*** *vt* **(a)** *(Sociol, herabsetzen)* to downgrade. **(b)** *(Sport: übertreffen)* to outclass.
**Deklination** *f (Gram)* declension.
**deklinieren*** *vt (Gram)* to decline.
**Dekolleté** [dekɔl'teː] *nt* **-s** low-cut *or* décolleté neckline.
**dekolletiert** [dekɔl'tiːɐt] *adj Kleid* low-cut, décolleté.
**Dekor** *m or nt* **-s** *or* **-e** decoration; *(von Raum auch, Theat, Film etc)* décor *no pl*.
**Dekorateur(in** *f)* [dekora'tøːɐ, -øːrɪn] *m* interior designer; *(Schaufenster~)* window-dresser.
**Dekoration** *f* **(a)** *no pl (das Ausschmücken)* decorating, decoration. **(b)** *(Einrichtung)* décor *no pl*; *(Fenster~)* window-dressing; *(Theat: Bühnenbild)* set. **zur ~ dienen** to be decorative. **(c)** *(Ordensverleihung)* decoration.
**Dekorations-:** **~maler** *m* (interior) decorator; *(Theat)* scene-painter; **~stoff** *m (Tex)* furnishing fabric; **~stück** *nt* piece of the décor; **das ist nur ein ~stück** that's just for decoration.
**dekorativ** *adj* decorative.
**dekorieren*** *vt* to decorate; *Schaufenster* to dress.
**Dekostoff** *m (Tex)* furnishing fabric.
**Dekret** *nt* **-e** decree.
**dekretieren*** *vt* to decree.
**Delegation** *f* delegation.
**delegieren*** *vt* to delegate *(an +acc* to*)*.
**Delegierte(r)** *mf decl as adj* delegate.
**delikat** *adj* **(a)** *(wohlschmeckend)* exquisite, delicious. **(b)** *(behutsam)* delicate. **(c)** *(heikel)* Problem delicate, sensitive; *(gewagt)* risqué.
**Delikateß-** *in cpds* top-quality, fine.
**Delikatesse** *f (Leckerbissen, fig)* delicacy.
**Delikatessengeschäft** *nt* delicatessen *sing*, deli *(esp US col)*.
**Delikt** *nt* **-e** *(Jur)* offence; *(schwerer)* crime.
**Delinquent** [delɪŋ'kvɛnt] *m (geh)* offender.
**Delirium** *nt* delirium. **im ~ sein** to be delirious; *(col: betrunken)* to be paralytic *(col)*.
**Delle** *f* **-n** *(col: eingedrückte Stelle)* dent.
**Delphin¹** *m* **-e** *(Zool)* dolphin.
**Delphin²** *nt no pl*, **Delphinschwimmen** *nt* butterfly.
**Delta** *nt, pl* **-s** *or* **Delten** *(Geog)* delta.
**dem 1** *dat of def art* **der, das (a)** to the; *(mit Präposition)* the. **(b) wenn ~ so ist** if that is the way it is; **wie ~ auch sei** be that as it may. **2** *dat of dem pron* **der, das (a)** *attr* to that; *(mit Präposition)* that. **(b)** *(substantivisch)* to that one; that one; *(Menschen)* to him; him. **3** *dat of rel pron* **der, das** to whom, that *or* who(m) ... to; *(mit Präposition)* who(m); *(von Sachen)* to which, which *or* that ... to; *(mit Präposition)* which.
**Demagoge** *m* demagogue.
**demagogisch** *adj Rede etc* demagogic.
**Demarkationslinie** *f (Pol, Mil)* demarcation line.
**demaskieren*** **1** *vt* to unmask, to expose. **2** *vr* to take off one's mask.
**Dementi** *nt* **-s** denial.

**dementieren\* 1** *vt* to deny. **2** *vi* to deny it.
**dem|entsprechend 1** *adv* correspondingly; *(dem-nach)* accordingly. **2** *adj* appropriate.
**dem-:** ~**gegenüber** *adv (wohingegen)* on the other hand; *(im Vergleich dazu)* in contrast; ~**gemäß** *adv, adj* = ~**entsprechend**.
**demilitarisieren\*** *vt* to demilitarize.
**Demission** *f (Pol: Rücktritt)* resignation.
**dem-:** ~**nach** *adv* therefore; *(~entsprechend)* accordingly; ~**nächst** *adv* soon.
**Demo** *f* -s *(col)* demo *(col)*.
**Demographie** *f* demography.
**demographisch** *adj* demographic.
**Demokrat(in** *f) m (wk)* **-en, -en** democrat.
**Demokratie** *f* democracy.
**Demokratieverständnis** *nt* understanding of (the meaning of) democracy.
**demokratisch** *adj* democratic.
**demokratisieren\*** *vt* to democratize, to make democratic.
**Demokratisierung** *f* democratization.
**demolieren\*** *vt* to wreck, to smash up; *(Rowdy auch)* to vandalize.
**Demonstrant(in** *f) m (wk)* demonstrator.
**Demonstration** *f* demonstration.
**Demonstrations-:** ~**material** *nt* teaching material; ~**objekt** *nt* teaching aid; ~**recht** *nt* right to demonstrate; *(Gesetz)* law on demonstrations; ~**zug** *m* demonstration.
**demonstrativ** *adj* demonstrative *(auch Gram)*; *Beifall* acclamatory; *Protest, Fehlen* pointed. **der Botschafter verließ ~ den Saal** the ambassador pointedly left the room.
**demonstrieren\*** *vti* to demonstrate.
**Demontage** [-'ta:ʒə] *f* -n *(lit, fig)* dismantling.
**demontieren\*** *vt (lit, fig)* to dismantle; *Räder* to take off.
**demoralisieren\*** *vt* to demoralize.
**Demoskop(in** *f) m (wk)* -en -en (opinion) pollster.
**Demoskopie** *f no pl* (public) opinion research.
**demoskopisch** *adj* ~**es Institut** (public) opinion research institute; **alle** ~**en Voraussagen waren falsch** all the predictions in the opinion polls were wrong; **eine** ~**e Untersuchung** a (public) opinion poll.
**demselben** *dat of* **derselbe, dasselbe**.
**Demut** *f no pl* humility. **in** ~ with humility.
**demütig** *adj Bitte, Blick* humble.
**demütigen 1** *vt Besiegten, Volk* to humiliate; *stolzen Menschen etc* to humble. **2** *vr* to humble oneself *(vor +dat before)*.
**Demütigung** *f* humiliation.
**demzufolge** *adv* therefore.
**den 1 (a)** *acc of def art* **der** the. **(b)** *dat pl of def art* **der, die, das** the; to the. **2** *acc of dem pron* **der (a)** *attr* that. **(b)** *(substantivisch)* that one; *(Menschen)* him. **3** *acc of rel pron* **der** who(m), that; *(von Sachen)* which, that.
**denen 1** *dat pl of dem pron* **der, die, das** to them; *(mit Präposition)* them. **2** *dat pl of rel pron* **der, die, das** to whom, that *or* who(m) ... to; *(mit Präposition)* whom; *(von Sachen)* to which, that *or* which ... to; which.
**Denk-:** ~**ansatz** *m* starting point; ~**anstoß** *m* **jdm** ~**anstöße geben** to give sb food for thought; ~**art** *f* way of thinking; **d~bar 1** *adj* conceivable; **es ist durchaus d~bar, daß er kommt** it's quite likely that he'll come; **2** *adv* extremely; **der d~bar schlechteste Eindruck** the worst possible impression.
**Denken** *nt no pl* thinking.
**denken** *pret* **dachte,** *ptp* **gedacht 1** *vi* to think *(über +acc* about, of*)*. **bei sich** ~ to think to one-

self; **wo** ~ **Sie hin!** what an idea!; **ich denke schon** I think so; **der Mensch denkt, Gott lenkt** *(Prov)* man proposes, God disposes *(Prov)*; **das gibt mir/einem zu** ~ it makes you think; **wie** ~ **Sie darüber?** what do you think about it?; **kleinlich** ~ to be petty-minded; **alle, die damals liberal gedacht haben,...** all those who were thinking along liberal lines ...; **an jdn/etw** ~ to think of sb/sth; **daran ist gar nicht zu** ~ that's (quite) out of the question; **ich denke nicht daran!** no way! *(col)*, not on your life!; **ich denke nicht daran, das zu tun** there's no way I'm going to do that *(col)*; **solange ich** ~ **kann** (for) as long as I can remember; **denk daran!** don't forget!; **an das Geld habe ich gar nicht mehr gedacht** I had forgotten all about the money; **die viele Arbeit, ich darf gar nicht daran** ~ all that work, it doesn't bear thinking about.
**2** *vt* to think. **was denkst du jetzt?** what are you thinking?; **ich denke gar nichts** I'm not thinking about anything; **(nur) Schlechtes/Gutes von jdm** ~ to think ill/well of sb; **wer hätte das (von ihr) gedacht!** who'd have thought it (of her)!; **was sollen bloß die Leute** ~! what will people think!; **ich denke schon** I think so; **ich denke nicht** I don't think so, I think not; **für jdn/etw gedacht sein** to be intended *or* meant for sb/sth; **so war das nicht gedacht** it wasn't meant that way.
**3** *vr* **(a)** *(vorstellen)* **das kann ich mir** ~ I can imagine; **ich habe mir das so gedacht:** ... this is what I had in mind: ...; **das habe ich mir gedacht** I thought so; **dachte ich mir's doch!** I knew it! **(b)** *(beabsichtigen)* **sich** *(dat)* **etw bei etw** ~ to mean sth by sth; **ich habe mir nichts Böses dabei gedacht** I meant no harm (in it).
**Denker(in** *f) m* - thinker. **das Volk der Dichter und** ~ the nation of poets and philosophers.
**Denkerstirn** *f (hum)* lofty brow.
**Denk-:** **d~fähig** *adj* capable of thinking; **als d~fähiger Mensch** as an intelligent person; ~**fähigkeit** *f* ability to think, intelligence; **d~faul** *adj* (mentally) lazy; ~**fehler** *m* flaw in the/one's reasoning; ~**horizont** *m* mental horizon.
**Denkmal** [-ma:l] *nt* =**er** *or (geh)* -e *(lit, fig)* monument *(für to)*; *(Standbild)* statue. **er hat sich** *(dat)* **ein** ~ **gesetzt** he has earned himself a place in history.
**Denkmalschutz** *m* protection of historical monuments. **etw unter** ~ **stellen** to place sth under a preservation order; **unter** ~ **stehen** to be listed *or* under a preservation order.
**Denk-:** ~**pause** *f* **eine** ~**pause einlegen** to have a break to think things over; ~**prozeß** *m* thought-process; ~**schema** *nt* thought pattern; ~**schrift** *f* memorandum; ~**sport** *m* mental exercise; ~**sportaufgabe** *f* brainteaser.
**denkste** *interj (col)* that's what you think.
**Denk-:** ~**vermögen** *nt* intellectual capacity; ~**weise** *f* way of thinking; **d~würdig** *adj* memorable, notable; ~**würdigkeit** *f* memorability, notability; ~**zettel** *m (col)* warning; **jdm einen** ~**zettel verpassen** to give sb a warning.
**denn 1** *conj* **(a)** *(kausal)* because, for *(esp liter)*. **(b)** *(geh: vergleichend)* than. **schöner** ~ **je** more beautiful than ever. **(c)** *(konzessiv)* **es sei** ~, **(daß)** unless. **2** *adv (verstärkend)* **wann/wie/wo** ~? when/how/where?; **warum** ~ **nicht?** why not?; **was soll das** ~? what's all this then?
**dennoch** *adv* nevertheless, nonetheless. **und** ~, ... and yet ...
**denselben 1** *acc of* **derselbe**. **2** *dat of* **dieselben**.
**dental** *adj (Med, Ling)* dental.
**Denunziant(in** *f) m (wk) (pej)* informer.

**Denunziation** *f (pej)* informing *no pl (von* on, against*)*; *(Anzeige)* denunciation *(von* of*)*.

**denunzieren\*** *vt (pej)* to inform on *or* against, to denounce *(bei* to*)*.

**Deo** *nt -s*, **Deodorant** *nt -s or -e* deodorant.

**Deospray** *nt or m* deodorant spray.

**Dependance** [depã'dã:s] *f -n (Hotel~)* annexe.

**Depesche** *f -n (dated)* dispatch.

**deplaziert** *adj* out of place.

**Deponie** *f* dump, disposal site.

**deponieren\*** *vt (geh)* to deposit.

**Deportation** *f* deportation.

**deportieren\*** *vt* to deport.

**Depot** [de'po:] *nt -s* depot; *(Aufbewahrungsort auch)* depository; *(in Bank)* strong room; *(Schließfach)* safe-deposit box.

**Depp** *m -e(n) (dial pej)* twit *(col)*.

**Depression** *f* depression. **~en haben** to suffer from depression.

**depressiv** *adj* depressive; *(Econ)* depressed.

**deprimieren\*** *vt* to depress.

**deprimierend** *adj* depressing.

**deprimiert** *adj* depressed.

**der¹ 1 (a)** *gen of def art* **die** *sing, pl* of the. **(b)** *dat of def art* **die** *sing* to the; *(mit Präposition)* the. **2** *dat of dem pron* **die** *sing* **(a)** *(adjektivisch)* to that; *(mit Präposition)* that. **(b)** *(substantivisch)* to her; her. **3** *dat of rel pron* **die** *sing* to whom, that *or* who(m) ... to; *(mit Präposition)* who(m); *(von Sachen)* to which, which ... to; which.

**der², die, das,** *pl* **die 1** *def art* the. **die Engländer** the English *pl*; **der Hans** *(col)*/**der Faust** Hans/Faust; **der Rhein** the Rhine; **der Michigansee** Lake Michigan; **die „Bismarck"** the "Bismarck"; **der Lehrer/ die Frau** *(im allgemeinen)* teachers *pl*/women *pl*; **der Tod/die Liebe/das Leben** death/love/life; **das Rauchen** smoking; **das Viktorianische England** Victorian England; **in dem England, das ich kannte** in the England (that *or* which) I knew; **er hat sich den Fuß verletzt** he has hurt his foot; **10 Mark die Stunde** 10 marks an *or* per hour; **der und der Wissenschaftler** such and such a scientist.

**2** *dem pron* **(a)** *(attr) (jener, dieser)* that; *pl* those. **(b)** *(substantivisch)* he/she/it; *pl* those. **der/die war es** it was him/her; **der/die mit der großen Nase** the one with *or* him/her *(col)* with the big nose; **der und schwimmen?** swimming?, (what) him?; **der und der/die und die** so-and-so; **das und das** such and such. **3** *rel pron (Mensch)* who, that; *(Gegenstand, Tier)* which, that.

**der|art** *adv* **(a)** *(Art und Weise)* in such a way. **sein Benehmen war ~, daß ...** his behaviour was so bad that ... **(b)** *(Ausmaß) (vor adj)* so; *(vor vb)* so much, to such an extent. **ein ~ unzuverlässiger Mensch** such an unreliable person, so unreliable a person.

**der|artig 1** *adj* **bei ~en Versuchen** in such tests, in tests of that kind; **(etwas) D~es** something like that *or* of the kind. **2** *adv* = **derart**.

**derb** *adj* **(a)** *(kräftig)* strong; *Kost* coarse. **(b)** *(grob)* coarse; *Sprache, Humor auch* earthy, crude *(pej)*.

**Derbheit** *f siehe adj* **(a)** strength; coarseness. **(b)** coarseness; earthiness, crudeness.

**Derby** ['dɛrbi] *nt -s* derby.

**Deregulierung** *f* deregulation.

**der|einst** *adv (liter)* **(a)** *(in der Zukunft)* one day. **(b)** *(früher)* at one time, once.

**deren 1** *gen pl of dem pron* **der, die, das** their. **2 (a)** *gen sing of rel pron* **die** whose. **(b)** *gen pl of rel pron* **der, die, das** whose, of whom; *(von Sachen)* of which.

**derent-:** **~wegen** *adv (weswegen)* because of whom, on whose account; *(von Sachen)* because of which, on account of which; **~willen** *adv* **um ~willen** *(rel)* for whose sake; *(von Sachen)* for the sake of which.

**dergestalt** *adv (geh)* in such a way.

**dergleichen** *dem pron inv* **(a)** *(adjektivisch)* ~ **Dinge** things of that kind. **(b)** *(substantivisch)* that sort of thing. **er tat nichts ~** he did nothing of the kind; **und ~ (mehr)** and suchlike.

**Derivat** [-'va:t] *nt (Chem, Ling)* derivative.

**derjenige, diejenige, dasjenige,** *pl* **diejenigen** *dem pron* **(a)** *(substantivisch)* the one; *pl* those. **du warst also derjenige, welcher!** *(col)* so you're the one! **(b)** *(adjektivisch)* the one; *pl* those.

**derlei** *dem pron inv* = **dergleichen**.

**dermaßen** *adv (mit adj)* so; *(mit vb)* so much. **ein ~ dummer Kerl** such a stupid fellow.

**Dermato-:** **~loge** *m*, **~login** *f* dermatologist; **~logie** *f* dermatology.

**derselbe, dieselbe, dasselbe,** *pl* **dieselben** *dem pron* the same; **es sind immer dieselben** it's always the same ones *or* the same people; **ein und derselbe Mensch** one and the same person.

**derweil(en)** *adv* in the meantime, meanwhile.

**derzeit** *adv (jetzt)* at present, at the moment.

**derzeitig** *adj attr (jetzig)* present, current.

**des¹** *gen of def art* **der²**, **das** of the.

**des²**, **Des** *nt no pl (Mus)* D flat.

**Desaster** [de'zastə] *nt* - disaster.

**Deserteur(in** *f*) [-'tø:ɐ, -'tø:ərɪn] *m (Mil, fig)* deserter.

**desertieren\*** *vi aux sein or haben (Mil, fig)* to desert.

**Desertion** *f (Mil, fig)* desertion.

**desgleichen** *adv (ebenso)* likewise, also.

**deshalb** *adv, conj* therefore; *(aus diesem Grunde)* because of that. **ich bin ~ hergekommen, weil ich dich sprechen wollte** the reason I came here was that I wanted to speak to you; **~ muß er nicht dumm sein** that does not necessarily mean he is stupid; **~ frage ich ja** that's exactly why I'm asking.

**Design** [di'zaɪn] *nt -s* design.

**Designer(in** *f*) [di'zaɪnɐ, -ərɪn] *m* - designer.

**designiert** [dezɪ'gniːɐt] *adj attr* **der ~e Vorsitzende/ Nachkomme** the chairman designate/prospective successor.

**des|illusionieren\*** *vt* to disillusion.

**Des|infektion** *f* disinfection.

**Des|infektionsmittel** *nt* disinfectant.

**des|infizieren\*** *vt* to disinfect.

**Des|infizierung** *f* disinfection.

**Des|information** *f (Pol)* disinformation *no pl*.

**Des|interesse** *nt* lack of interest *(an +dat* in*)*.

**des|interessiert** *adj* uninterested.

**deskriptiv** *adj* descriptive.

**desodorierend** *adj* deodorant.

**desolat** *adj (geh)* desolate; *Zustand, wirtschaftliche Lage* desperate.

**Des|organisation** *f* disorganization; *(Auflösung auch)* disruption. **auf der Tagung herrschte eine völlige ~** there was complete chaos at the conference.

**des|organisieren\*** *vt* to disorganize.

**des|orientieren\*** *vt* to disorient(ate).

**Despot** [dɛs'po:t] *m (wk) -en, -en* despot.

**despotisch** [dɛs'po:tɪʃ] *adj* despotic.

**Despotismus** [dɛspo-] *m no pl* despotism.

**desselben** *gen of* **derselbe, dasselbe**.

**dessen 1** *gen of dem pron* **der²**, **das** his; *(von Sachen, Tieren)* its. **2** *gen of rel pron* **der²**, **das** whose; *(von Sachen)* of which, which ... of.

**dessent-** = **derent-**.
**dessen|unge|achtet** *adv (geh)* nevertheless.
**Dessert** [dɛ'seːɐ] *nt* **-s** dessert.
**Dessin** [dɛ'sẽ':] *nt* **-s** *(Tex)* pattern, design.
**destabilisieren\*** *vt* to destabilize.
**Destillation** [dɛstɪla'tsioːn] *f* (a) *(Chem)* distillation.
(b) *(Branntweinbrennerei)* distillery.
**destillieren\*** [dɛstɪ'liːrən] *vt* to distil.
**desto** *conj* ~ **mehr/besser** all the more/better; ~ **wahrscheinlicher ist es, daß wir ...** that makes it all the more probable that we ...; *siehe* **je**.
**destruktiv** [dɛstrʊk'tiːf] *adj* destructive.
**deswegen** *adv* = **deshalb**.
**Detail** [de'tai] *nt* **-s** detail; *(Filmeinstellung)* close-up. **ins** ~ **gehen** to go into detail(s); **im** ~ in detail; **bis ins kleinste** ~ (right) down to the smallest detail; **in allen** ~**s** in the greatest detail.
**Detail-:** ~**frage** *f* question of detail; ~**kenntnis** *f usu pl* detailed knowledge *no pl*.
**detaillieren\*** [deta'jiːrən] *vt* to specify.
**detailliert** [deta'jiːɐt] *adj* detailed.
**Detektei** *f* (private) detective agency.
**Detektiv(in** *f***)** *m* private detective.
**Detektiv-:** ~**büro** *nt* detective agency; ~**roman** *m* detective novel.
**Detektor** *m (Tech)* detector.
**determinieren\*** *vt* to determine.
**Detonation** *f* explosion, blast. **etw zur** ~ **bringen** to detonate sth.
**detonieren\*** *vi aux sein* to explode, to go off.
**Deut** *m* **(um) keinen** ~ not one iota *or* jot; **seine Ratschläge sind keinen** ~ **wert** his advice is not worth tuppence; **du bist keinen** ~ **besser** you're not one jot *or* whit better.
**deutbar** *adj* interpretable. **nicht/schwer** ~ impossible/difficult to interpret.
**deuteln** *vi (geh)* to quibble, to cavil. **daran gibt es nichts zu** ~**!** there are no ifs and buts about it!
**deuten 1** *vt (auslegen)* to interpret; *Zukunft* to read. **etw falsch** ~ to misinterpret sth. **2** *vi* (a) **(mit dem Finger) auf etw** *(acc)* ~ to point (one's finger) at sth. (b) *(fig: hinweisen)* to indicate. **alles deutet darauf, daß ...** all the indications are that ...
**deutlich** *adj* clear. ~ **sichtbar** clearly visible; **ich fühle** ~**, daß ...** I have the distinct feeling ...; **jdm etw** ~ **vor Augen führen** *or* **zu verstehen geben** to make sth perfectly clear *or* plain to sb; **muß ich** ~**er werden?** have I not made myself clear *or* plain enough?
**Deutlichkeit** *f* clarity. **etw mit aller** ~ **sagen** to make sth perfectly clear *or* plain.
**deutsch** *adj* German. ~**e Schrift** Gothic script; ~**er Schäferhund** Alsatian *(Brit)*, German shepherd; ~**e Gründlichkeit** *etc* German *or* Teutonic efficiency *etc*; **D**~**e Mark** deutschmark, German mark; **sich (auf)** ~ **unterhalten** to speak (in) German; **auf** ~ **heißt das ...** in German it means ...; **mit jdm** ~ **reden** *(fig col: deutlich)* to speak bluntly with sb; **auf gut** ~ **(gesagt)** *(fig col)* ≈ in plain English.
**Deutsch** *nt no pl* German. **gut(es)** ~ **sprechen** to speak good German.
**Deutsch-:** ~**amerikaner** *m* German American; **d**~**-amerikanisch** *adj* German-American; **d**~**-d**~ *adj (Hist)* intra-German.
**Deutsch(e)** *nt* **-en**, *no pl (Sprache)* German. **aus dem** ~**en/ins** ~**e übersetzt** translated from (the)/into German.
**Deutsche Demokratische Republik** *f (Hist)* German Democratic Republic, East Germany *no art*.
**deutsch-|englisch** *adj* (a) *(Pol)* Anglo-German. (b) *(Ling)* German-English.

**Deutsche(r)** *mf decl as adj* **er ist** ~**r** he is (a) German; **die** ~**n** the Germans.
**Deutsch-:** **d**~**feindlich** *adj* anti-German, Germanophobic; **d**~**französisch** *adj* (a) *(Pol)* Franco-German; **der D**~**Französische Krieg** the Franco-Prussian war; (b) *(Ling)* German-French; **d**~**freundlich** *adj* pro-German, Germanophile.
**Deutschland** *nt* Germany.
**Deutschland-:** ~**frage** *f (Pol)* German question; ~**lied** *nt* German national anthem; ~**politik** *f* home *or* domestic policy; *(von fremdem Staat)* policy towards Germany.
**Deutsch-:** ~**lehrer** *m* German teacher; ~**schweiz** *f* **die** ~**schweiz** German-speaking Switzerland; ~**schweizer** *m* German Swiss; **d**~**schweizerisch** *adj* German-Swiss; **d**~**sprachig** *adj Bevölkerung, Gebiete* German-speaking; *Zeitung, Ausgabe* German-language; *Literatur* German; **d**~**sprachlich** *adj* German(-language); **d**~**sprechend** *adj* German-speaking; **d**~**stämmig** *adj* of German origin; ~**stunde** *f* German lesson; ~**tum** *nt no pl* Germanness; ~**tümelei** *f (pej)* hyper-Germanness.
**Deutung** *f* interpretation. **eine falsche** ~ a misinterpretation.
**Devise** [de'viːzə] *f* **-n** (a) *(Wahlspruch)* motto. (b) *(Fin)* ~**n** *pl* foreign exchange *or* currency.
**Devisen-** *in cpds* foreign exchange; ~**ausgleich** *m* foreign exchange offset; ~**bestimmungen** *pl* foreign exchange control regulations *pl*; ~**börse** *f* foreign exchange market; ~**geschäft** *nt* foreign exchange dealing; ~**handel** *m* foreign currency *or* exchange dealings *pl*; ~**kontrolle** *f* exchange control; ~**kurs** *m* exchange rate, rate of exchange; ~**markt** *m* foreign exchange market, currency market.
**devot** [de'voːt] *adj (pej geh: unterwürfig)* obsequious.
**Dez.** = **Dezember** Dec.
**Dezember** *m* **-** December; *siehe* **März**.
**dezent** *adj* discreet.
**dezentral** *adj* decentralized.
**dezentralisieren\*** *vt* to decentralize.
**Dezentralisierung** *f* decentralization.
**Dezernat** *nt (Admin)* department.
**Dezernent(in** *f***)** *m (Admin)* head of department.
**Dezibel** ['deːtsibɛl, -'bɛl] *nt* **-** decibel.
**dezidiert** *adj (geh)* firm, determined.
**Deziliter** *m or nt* decilitre *(Brit)*, deciliter *(US)*.
**dezimal** *adj* decimal.
**Dezimale** *f* **-n** decimal.
**Dezimal-:** ~**rechnung** *f* decimals *pl*; ~**stelle** *f* **auf zwei** ~**stellen genau** correct to two decimal places; ~**system** *nt* decimal system; ~**zahl** *f* decimal number.
**dezimieren\*** *(fig)* **1** *vt* to decimate. **2** *vr* to be decimated.
**Dezimierung** *f (fig)* decimation.
**DFB** [deː|ɛf'beː] *m* = **Deutscher Fußball-Bund** German Football Association.
**DGB** [deːgeː'beː] *m* = **Deutscher Gewerkschaftsbund** Federation of German Trade Unions.
**dgl** = **dergleichen, desgleichen** the like.
**d.Gr.** = **der/die Große**.
**d.h.** = **das heißt** i.e.
**Di.** = **Dienstag** Tue(s).
**Dia** *nt* **-s** *(Phot)* slide, transparency.
**Diabetes** [dia'beːtɛs] *m no pl* diabetes.
**Diabetiker(in** *f***)** *m* **-** diabetic.
**diabetisch** *adj* diabetic.
**diabolisch** *adj (geh)* diabolical.
**Diadem** *nt* **-e** diadem.
**Diagnose** *f* **-n** diagnosis. **eine** ~ **stellen** to make a

diagnosis.

**Diagnosezentrum** *nt* diagnostic centre.

**diagnostizieren*** *vti (Med, fig)* to diagnose.

**diagonal** *adj* diagonal. **ein Buch ~ lesen** *(col)* to flick through a book.

**Diagonale** *f* -n diagonal.

**Diagramm** *nt* -e diagram.

**Diakon** *m* -e(n) *(Eccl)* deacon.

**Diakonie** *f (Eccl)* social welfare work.

**Diakonisse** *f* -n *(Eccl)* deaconess.

**Dialekt** *m* -e dialect.

**Dialekt|ausdruck** *m* dialect expression *or* word.

**dialektfrei** *adj* free from dialect.

**Dialektik** *f (Philos)* dialectics *sing or pl.*

**dialektisch** *adj (Philos)* dialectical.

**Dialog** *m* -e dialogue.

**Dialog-:** **~betrieb** *m (Comp)* conversation mode; **~regie** *f (Film)* script supervision.

**Dialyse** *f* -n *(Med)* dialysis.

**Diamant** *m (wk)* -en, -en diamond.

**diamanten** *adj attr* diamond.

**Diamant-:** **~nadel** *f* **(a)** diamond brooch; **(b)** *(an Tonarm)* diamond (stylus); **~schleifer** *m* diamond polisher; **~schmuck** *m* diamonds *pl.*

**diametral** *adj* **~ entgegengesetzt** *(fig)* diametrically opposed.

**Diaphragma** [dia'fragma] *nt, pl* **Diaphragmen** diaphragm.

**Dia-** *(Phot)*: **~positiv** *nt* slide, transparency; **~projektor** *m* slide projector.

**diät** *adv* **kochen, essen** according to a diet; *leben* on a special diet.

**Diät** *f* -en *(Med)* diet. **~ halten** to keep to a strict diet; **nach einer ~ leben** to be on a diet *or (wegen Krankheit)* special diet; **jdn auf ~ setzen** *(col)* to put sb on a diet.

**Diät|assistent(in** *f)* *m* dietician.

**Diäten** *pl (Parl)* parliamentary allowance.

**Diät-:** **~kost** *f* dietary foods; **~kost bekommen** to be on a special diet; **~kur** *f* dietary *or* dietetic treatment.

**Diavortrag** *m* slide show.

**dich 1** *pers pron acc of* **du** you. **2** *refl pron* yourself. **wie fühlst du ~?** how do you feel?

**dicht 1** *adj* **(a)** *Gefieder, Haar, Hecke* thick; *Laub, Nebel auch, Wald, Gewühl* dense; *Verkehr auch* heavy; *Gewebe* close; *(fig: konzentriert) Programm* full. **in ~er Folge** in quick succession. **(b)** *(undurchlässig)* watertight; airtight; *Vorhänge* thick, heavy. **~ machen** to seal; **~ schließen** to shut tightly; **nicht ~ sein** to leak; **er ist nicht ganz ~** *(col)* he's crackers *(col)*. **(c)** *(col: zu)* shut, closed. **2** *adv* **(a)** *(nahe)* closely. **(~ an) ~ stehen** to stand close together; **~ gefolgt von** closely followed by. **(b)** *(sehr stark) bevölkert* densely; **~ behaart sein** to be very hairy. **(c)** *(mit Präpositionen)* **~ an/bei** close to; **~ dahinter/davor** right behind/in front; **~ hintereinander** right behind one another; **~ beieinander** close together.

**dicht-:** **~auf** *adv* closely; **~auf folgen** to follow close behind; **~behaart** *adj attr* (very) hairy; **~besiedelt, ~bevölkert** *adj attr* densely populated.

**Dichte** *f* -n **(a)** *no pl siehe adj (a)* thickness; denseness; heaviness; closeness; fullness. **(b)** *(Phys)* density. **(c)** *(Comp)* **Diskette mit einfacher/doppelter ~** single-density/double-density diskette.

**dichten¹ 1** *vt* to write. **2** *vi* to write poems.

**dichten²** *vt (undurchlässig machen)* to seal, to make watertight/airtight.

**Dichter** *m* - poet; *(Schriftsteller)* writer, author.

**Dichterin** *f* poet(ess); *(Schriftstellerin)* writer, auth-

or(ess).

**dichterisch** *adj* poetic; *(schriftstellerisch)* literary. **~e Freiheit** poetic licence *(Brit) or* license *(US)*.

**Dichter-:** **~kreis** *m* circle of poets; **~lesung** *f* reading *(by a poet/writer from his/her own works)*; **~wort** *nt* -e (literary) quotation.

**dicht-:** **~gedrängt** *adj attr* closely packed; **~halten** *vi sep irreg (col)* to keep one's mouth shut *(col)*.

**Dichtkunst** *f* art of poetry; *(Schriftstellerei)* creative writing.

**dichtmachen** *vti sep (col) Laden* to shut up, to close; *Fabrik, Betrieb* to close down. **(den Laden) ~** to shut up shop.

**Dichtung¹** *f* **(a)** *no pl* literature; *(in Versform)* poetry. **~ und Wahrheit** *(fig)* fact and fantasy. **(b)** *(Dichtwerk)* poem, poetic work; literary work.

**Dichtung²** *f (Tech)* seal; *(in Wasserhahn etc)* washer; *(Mech)* gasket.

**Dichtungsmasse** *f* sealant.

**dick** *adj* **(a)** thick; *Mensch, Körperteil, Buch, Brieftasche* fat; *Baum, Stamm* big, thick; *(col) Gehalt, Rechnung, Gewinn* big, fat; *(col) Tränen, Geschäft, Fehler, Auto* big; *Zigarre* big fat. **ein ~er Brocken** *(col)* a tough nut (to crack); **~ machen** *(Speisen)* to be fattening; **er hat es ~(e)** *(col) (satt)* he's had enough of it; *(viel)* he's got enough and to spare; **das ist ein ~es Lob** that's high praise; **das ist ein ~er Hund** *(col)* that's a bit much *(col)*; **das ~e Ende kommt noch** *(prov)* the worst is yet to come; **eine ~e Suppe** *(col: Nebel)* a real pea-souper *(col)*; **durch ~ und dünn** through thick and thin. **(b)** *(geschwollen)* swollen; *Beule* big. **(c)** *(col) Freundschaft, Freund* close. **mit jdm ~ befreundet sein** to be thick with sb *(col)*.

**Dick-:** **d~bauchig** *adj Vase* bulbous; **d~bäuchig** *adj Mensch* potbellied; **~darm** *m (Anat)* colon.

**Dicke** *f* -n **(a)**. thickness. **(b)** *(von Menschen, Körperteilen)* fatness.

**Dicke(r)** *mf decl as adj (col)* fatty *(col)*, fatso *(col)*.

**dick-:** **~fellig** *adj (col)* thick-skinned; **~flüssig** *adj* thick, viscous; **~häutig** *adj* thick-skinned.

**Dickicht** *nt* -e thicket; *(fig)* jungle.

**Dick-:** **~kopf** *m* **(a)** *(Starrsinn)* obstinacy, stubbornness; **einen ~kopf haben** to be obstinate *or* stubborn; **(b)** *(Mensch)* obstinate so-and-so *(col)*; **d~köpfig** *adj (fig)* stubborn; **d~leibig** *adj Buch* massive; *Mensch* corpulent; **d~lich** *adj* plump; **~milch** *f (Cook)* sour milk; **~schädel** *m (col)* = **~kopf**; **~wanst** *m (pej col)* fatso *(col)*.

**Didaktik** *f* teaching methods *pl.*

**didaktisch** *adj* didactic.

**die** *art etc siehe* **der².**

**Dieb(in** *f)* *m* -e thief. **haltet den ~!** stop thief!

**Diebes-:** **~bande** *f* gang of thieves; **~gut** *nt* stolen goods *pl*; **d~sicher** *adj* thief-proof.

**diebisch** *adj* **(a)** *(lit) Gesindel etc* thieving *attr.* **(b)** *(col) Freude, Vergnügen* impish.

**Diebstahl** ['di:pʃta:l] *m* ⸗e theft. **einfacher/schwerer ~** petty/grand larceny; **bewaffneter ~** armed robbery; **geistiger ~** plagiarism.

**Diebstahl-:** **d~sicher** *adj* theft-proof; **~sicherung** *f (Aut)* anti-theft system/device; **~versicherung** *f* insurance against theft.

**diejenige** *dem pron siehe* **derjenige.**

**Diele** *f* -n **(a)** floorboard. **(b)** *(Vorraum)* hall.

**Dielenbrett** *nt* floorboard.

**dienen** *vi* **(a)** to serve *(jdm* sb, *einer Sache (dat)* sth*)*; *dem Fortschritt, der Erforschung* to aid; *dem Verständnis* to promote; *(nützlich sein)* to be of use *or* service *(jdm* to sb*)*. **es dient einer guten Sache** it is in a good cause; **womit kann ich Ihnen ~?** what can

**diktieren**

I do for you?; (im Geschäft auch) can I help you?; **damit ist mir wenig gedient** that's no use or good to me; **als/zu etw** ~ to serve as/for sth. **(b)** (Militärdienst leisten) to do (one's) military service.
**Diener** m - **(a)** servant. **(b)** (col: Verbeugung) bow.
**Dienerin** f maid.
**dienern** vi (fig pej) to bow and scrape (vor +dat to).
**Dienerschaft** f servants pl, domestic staff.
**dienlich** adj useful, helpful. **jdm/einer Sache** ~ **sein** to help sb/sth, to be of help to sb/sth.
**Dienst** m -e **(a)** service; (Arbeitsstelle) position. **in jds** ~**(en)** (dat) **stehen** to be in sb's service; **Oberst außer** ~ retired colonel; ~ **mit der Waffe** (Mil) armed service; **im** ~**(e) der Menschheit** in the service of humanity; **jdm einen schlechten** ~ **erweisen** to do sb a disservice; **jdm gute** ~**e leisten** or **tun** to serve sb well; ~ **am Kunden** customer service; **etw in** ~ **stellen** to put sth into service; **jdm zu** ~**en stehen** to be at sb's disposal. **(b)** (Berufsausübung, Amtspflicht) duty; (Arbeit, Arbeitszeit) work. ~ **haben** (Arzt etc) to be on duty; (Apotheke) to be open; **im** ~ **sein** (Angestellter etc) to be working; **nach** ~ after work; ~ **tun** to serve (bei in, als as); ~ **nach Vorschrift** work-to-rule.
**Dienst|abteil** nt (Rail) ≃ guard's compartment, conductor's car (US).
**Dienstag** m Tuesday. ~ **abend/morgen** (on) Tuesday evening/morning; ~ **abends/vormittags** on Tuesday evenings/mornings; **am** ~ on Tuesday; **hast du** ~ **Zeit?** have you time on Tuesday?; **alle** ~**e** every Tuesday; **eines** ~**s** one Tuesday; **die Nacht von** ~ **auf Mittwoch** the night of Tuesday to Wednesday; **den (ganzen)** ~ **über** all (day) Tuesday, the whole of Tuesday; ~ **in acht Tagen** or **in einer Woche** a week on Tuesday, Tuesday week; ~ **vor einer Woche** or **acht Tagen** a week (ago) last Tuesday.
**dienstags** adv on Tuesdays, on a Tuesday. ~ **abends** on Tuesday evenings.
**Dienst-:** ~**alter** nt length of service; ~**älteste(r)** mf (most) senior member of staff; ~**antritt** m assumption of one's duties; (jeden Tag) commencement of work; ~**anweisung** f instructions pl, regulations pl; **d**~**bar** adj **d**~**bare Geister** willing hands; **sich** (dat) **etw d**~**bar machen** to utilize sth; **d**~**beflissen** adj zealous; **d**~**bereit** adj **(a)** Apotheke open pred; Arzt on duty; **(b)** (hilfsbereit) obliging; ~**bezüge** pl salary sing; ~**bote** m servant; ~**boteneingang** m tradesmen's or service entrance; ~**eid** m oath of service; ~**eifer** m zeal; **d**~**eifrig** adj zealous, assiduous; **d**~**frei** adj free; **d**~**frei haben/bekommen** to have/be given time off; ~**gebrauch** m (Mil, Admin) **nur für den** ~**gebrauch** for official use only; ~**geheimnis** nt official secret; ~**gespräch** nt business call; (von Beamten) official call; ~**grad** m (Mil: Rangstufe) rank; **d**~**habend** adj attr Arzt, Offizier duty attr, on duty; ~**herr** m employer; ~**jahr** nt usu pl (Mil, Admin) year of service; ~**leistung** f service; ~**leistungsabend** m late opening evening; ~**leistungsbetrieb** m service industry business; ~**leistungsbranche** f service industry; ~**leistungsgewerbe** nt service industries (sector); **d**~**lich 1** adj Angelegenheiten business attr; Schreiben, Befehl official; **d**~**lich werden** (col) to become businesslike; **2** adv on business; **wir haben hier d**~**lich zu tun** we have business here; ~**mädchen** nt maid; ~**ordnung** f (Admin) official regulations pl; (Mil) service regulations pl; **d**~**pflichtig** adj (esp Mil) liable for compulsory service; ~**pistole** f service gun; ~**plan** m duty rota; ~**programm** nt

(Comp) utility (program); ~**rang** m grade; (Mil) rank; ~**reise** f business trip; **auf** ~**reise** on a business trip; ~**schluß** m end of work; **nach** ~**schluß** (von Arbeiter etc) after work; ~**stelle** f (Admin) department; ~**stunden** pl working hours pl; **d**~**tauglich** adj (Mil) fit for service; **d**~**tuend** adj Arzt duty attr, on duty; **d**~**unfähig** adj unfit for work; (Mil) unfit for duty; **d**~**untauglich** adj (Mil) unfit for service; ~**vergehen** nt breach of duty; ~**wagen** m company car; (von Beamten) official car; ~**weg** m **auf dem** ~**weg** through official channels; ~**wohnung** f police/army etc house; ~**zeit** f **(a)** period of service; **(b)** (Arbeitszeit) working hours pl; (Mil) hours pl of duty; ~**zeugnis** nt testimonial.
**dies** dem pron inv this; pl these. ~ **sind** these are; siehe **dieser.**
**diesbezüglich** adj (form) regarding this.
**diese** dem pron siehe **dieser.**
**Diesel** m - diesel.
**dieselbe** dem pron siehe **derselbe.**
**Diesel-:** ~**kraftstoff** m diesel fuel; ~**lok(omotive)** f diesel locomotive; ~**motor** m diesel engine; ~**öl** nt diesel oil.
**dieser, diese, dies(es),** pl **diese** dem pron this; (~ dort, da) that; pl these; (~ dort, da) those. **diese(r, s) hier** this (one); **diese(r, s) da** that (one); **dieser ...,** **jener ...** the latter ..., the former ...; **dies und das, dieses und jenes** this and that; **diese Nacht** tonight; **dies alles** all this/that.
**diesig** adj Wetter, Luft misty, hazy.
**dies-:** ~**jährig** adj attr **die** ~**jährige Ernte** this year's harvest; ~**mal** adv this time; ~**malig** adj attr **der** ~**malige Preis** the price this time; ~**seitig** adj Ufer etc near(side) attr, (on) this side; ~**seits** prep +gen on this side of; **D**~**seits** nt no pl **das D**~**seits** this life.
**Dietrich** m -e picklock.
**diffamieren*** vt to defame.
**diffamierend** adj defamatory.
**Diffamierung** f defamation (of character); (Bemerkung etc) defamatory statement.
**Diffamierungskampagne** f smear campaign.
**Differential** [-'tsiaːl] nt -e (Aut: auch ~**getriebe** nt) differential (gear).
**Differential-** in cpds (Tech, Math) differential; ~**rechnung** f (Math) differential calculus.
**Differenz** f difference; (Abweichung) discrepancy.
**Differenzbetrag** m difference, balance.
**differenzieren*** vti to make distinctions/a distinction (zwischen +dat between, bei in); (abändern) to make changes/a change in, to modify; (den Unterschied verstehen) to differentiate (zwischen +dat between, bei in). **genau** ~ to make a precise distinction.
**differenziert** adj subtly differentiated; (verfeinert) sophisticated; Charakter, Mensch complex.
**differieren*** vi to differ.
**diffus** adj Gedanken etc confused.
**digital** adj digital.
**Digital-** in cpds digital; ~**anzeige** f digital display; ~**aufnahme** f digital recording.
**digitalisieren** vt to digitize.
**Digitalrechner** m (Comp) digital computer.
**Diktat** nt **(a)** dictation. **etw nach** ~ **schreiben** to write sth from dictation. **(b)** (fig: Gebot) dictate; (Pol auch) diktat.
**Diktator** m dictator.
**diktatorisch** adj dictatorial.
**Diktatur** f dictatorship.
**diktieren*** vt Brief, (fig) Bedingungen to dictate.

**Diktiergerät** *nt* dictating machine.
**Diktion** *f* style.
**Dilemma** *nt* **-s** dilemma.
**Dilettant(in** *f)* *m (wk)* amateur, dilettante *(pej)*.
**dilettantisch** *adj* amateurish.
**Dill** *m* **-e** *(Bot, Cook)* dill.
**Dimension** *f* dimension.
**Dimmer** *m* - dimmer (switch).
**DIN** ® [dɪn, diːn] *f no pl* = **Deutsche Industrie-Norm** German Industrial Standard. ~ **A4** A4.
**Diner** [di'neː] *nt* **-s** *(form) (Mittagessen)* luncheon; *(Abendessen)* dinner.
**Ding** *nt* **-e** *or (col)* **-er** thing. **das ist ein** ~ **der Unmöglichkeit** that is totally impossible; **guter** ~**e sein** *(geh)* to be in good spirits; **jedes** ~ **hat zwei Seiten** *(Prov)* there are two sides to everything; **gut** ~ **will Weile haben** *(Prov)* it takes time to do a thing well; **vergangene/berufliche** ~**e** past events/professional matters; **so wie die** ~**e liegen, nach Lage der** ~**e** as things are; **über den** ~**en stehen** to be above things; **vor allen** ~**en** above all (things), first and foremost; **es müßte nicht mit rechten** ~**en zugehen, wenn** ... it would be more than a little strange if ...; **das** ~**(s) da** *(col)* that thing (over) there; **das ist ein** ~**!** now there's a thing! *(col)*; **da hast du dir aber ein** ~ **geleistet** that was quite something you got up to *(col)*; **was macht ihr bloß für** ~**er?** the things you do! *(col)*.
**dingfest** *adj* **jdn** ~ **machen** to arrest sb.
**Dingi** ['dɪŋgi] *nt* **-s** dinghy.
**dinglich** *adj* material.
**Dings, Dingsbums, Dingsda** *nt no pl (col)* thingummyjig *(col)*.
**dinieren*** *vi (geh)* to dine *(form)*.
**Dinosaurier** *m* dinosaur.
**Diode** *f* **-n** diode.
**Dioptrie** *f* **-n** *(Opt)* dioptre *(Brit)*, diopter *(US)*.
**Diözese** *f* **-n** diocese.
**Diphtherie** [dɪfteˈriː] *f* diphtheria.
**Dipl.** = **Diplom** Dip.
**Dipl. Ing.** = **Diplomingenieur** academically qualified engineer.
**Diplom** *nt* **-e** diploma. **ein** ~ **machen** to take *or* do one's diploma.
**Diplom-** *in cpds (vor Berufsbezeichnung)* qualified; ~**arbeit** *f* dissertation.
**Diplomat(in** *f)* *m (wk)* **-en, -en** diplomat.
**Diplomatie** *f (lit, fig)* diplomacy.
**diplomatisch** *adj (Pol, fig)* diplomatic.
**diplomiert** *adj* qualified.
**dir** *pers pron dat of* **du** to you; *(nach Präpositionen)* you.
**direkt 1** *adj* direct; *Erledigung* immediate; *(genau) Hinweis* plain; *Auskunft* clear. **eine** ~**e Verbindung** *(Zug)* a through train; *(Flug)* a direct flight. **2** *adv* **(a)** *(unmittelbar)* directly; *(geradewegs auch)* straight; *übertragen* live; *telefonieren* direct. ~ **von/nach** straight *or* direct from/to; ~ **an/unter** directly *or* right by/under; **(b)** *(unverblümt)* bluntly. **jdm etw** ~ **ins Gesicht sagen** to tell sb sth (straight) to his face; ~ **fragen** to ask outright *or* straight out. **(c)** *(col: geradezu)* really.
**Direktheit** *f no pl* directness.
**Direktion** *f* management; *(Direktionsbüro)* manager's office.
**Direktive** *f (geh)* directive.
**Direktmandat** *nt (Pol)* direct mandate.
**Direktor** *m*, **Direktorin** *f* director; *(von Gefängnis)* governor, warden *(US)*; *(von Hochschule)* principal; *(von Schule)* head (teacher), principal *(esp US)*.
**Direktorat** *nt* **(a)** *(Amt)* directorship; *(von Schule)*

headship, principalship *(esp US)*. **(b)** *(Diensträume: von Schule)* head (teacher)'s *or* principal's *(esp US)* study *or* room.
**Direktorium** *nt* board of directors, directorate.
**Direkt-:** ~**übertragung** *f (Rad, TV)* live transmission; ~**verbindung** *f (Rail)* through train; *(Aviat)* direct flight; ~**zugriff** *m (Comp)* direct access; ~**zugriffsspeicher** *m (Comp)* random access memory, RAM.
**Dirigent(in** *f)* *m (wk) (Mus)* conductor.
**dirigieren*** *vt* **(a)** *(auch vi) (Mus)* to conduct; *(fig)* to lead. **(b)** *Verkehr etc* to direct.
**Dirndl** *nt* - *(auch* ~**kleid)** dirndl.
**Dirne** *f* **-n** *(Prostituierte)* prostitute.
**dis, Dis** *nt* **-, -** *(Mus)* D sharp.
**Disco** *f* **-s** disco.
**Discount-** [dɪsˈkaunt] *in cpds* discount; ~**händler** *m* discount dealer; ~**laden** *m* discount shop *or* store.
**Disharmonie** *f (lit, fig)* discord.
**disharmonisch** *adj (lit, fig)* discordant.
**Diskant** *m* **-e** *(Stimmlage)* treble; *(Gegenstimme)* descant.
**Diskette** *f* (floppy) disk, diskette.
**Diskettenlaufwerk** *nt* disk drive.
**Diskjockey** ['dɪskdʒɔke] *m* **-s** disc jockey, DJ.
**Diskont** *m* **-e** *(Fin)* discount.
**Diskontsatz** *m (Fin)* discount rate.
**Diskothek** *f* **-en** discotheque.
**diskreditieren*** *vt (geh)* to discredit.
**Diskrepanz** *f* discrepancy.
**diskret** *adj* discreet; *Gespräch* confidential.
**Diskretion** *f* discretion; *(vertrauliche Behandlung)* confidentiality. **strengste** ~ **wahren** to preserve the strictest confidence.
**diskriminieren*** *vt* to discriminate against.
**diskriminierend** *adj* discriminatory.
**Diskriminierung** *f* discrimination.
**Diskus** *m, pl* **-se** *or* **Disken** discus.
**Diskussion** *f* discussion. **zur** ~ **stehen** to be under discussion; **etw zur** ~ **stellen** to put sth up for discussion.
**Diskussions-:** ~**beitrag** *m* contribution to the discussion; ~**teilnehmer** *m* participant (in a discussion).
**Diskus-:** ~**werfen** *nt no pl* throwing the discus; ~**werfer(in** *f)* *m* discus-thrower.
**diskutabel** *adj* worth discussing.
**diskutieren*** *vti* to discuss. **über etw** *(acc)* ~ to discuss sth; **darüber läßt sich** ~ that sounds like something we could talk about.
**dispensieren*** [dɪspɛnˈziːrən] *vt* **jdn** to excuse *(von from)*.
**Dispersionsfarbe** *f* emulsion paint.
**disponibel** *adj* available.
**disponieren*** [dɪspoˈniːrən] *vi (geh)* **(a)** *(verfügen)* **ich kann nicht über sie** ~ I can't tell her what to do; **über etw** *(acc)* **(frei)** ~ to do as one wishes with sth. **(b)** *(planen)* to make arrangements.
**disponiert** [dɪspoˈniːɐt] *adj (geh)* **gut/schlecht** ~ **sein** to be in good/bad form.
**Disposition** [dɪspoziˈtsioːn] *f (geh)* **(a)** *(Verfügung)* **jdm zur** *or* **zu jds** ~ **stehen** to be at sb's disposal; **jdm etw zur** ~ **stellen** to place sth at sb's disposal. **(b)** *(Anordnung)* arrangement. **seine** ~**en treffen** to make (one's) arrangements.
**Dispositionskredit** *m (Fin)* overdraft facility.
**Disput** [dɪsˈpuːt] *m* **-e** *(geh)* dispute.
**disqualifizieren*** *vt* to disqualify.
**Disqualifizierung** *f* disqualification.
**Dissertation** *f (Doktorarbeit)* thesis.
**Dissident(in** *f)* *m (wk)* dissident.

**dissonant** adj dissonant.
**Dissonanz** f (Mus) dissonance; (fig) (note of) discord.
**Distanz** f distance (auch Sport); (fig) (Abstand, Entfernung) detachment; (Zurückhaltung) reserve. ~ halten or wahren (lit, fig) to keep one's distance; **auf** ~ **gehen** (fig) to become distant.
**distanzieren\*** **1** vr sich von jdm/etw ~ to dissociate oneself from sb/sth. **2** vt (Sport) to outdistance.
**distanziert** adj Verhalten distant.
**Distel** f -n thistle.
**distinguiert** [dɪstɪŋ'giːɐt] adj (geh) distinguished.
**Distrikt** m -e district.
**Disziplin** f -en discipline (auch Sport).
**disziplinarisch** adj disciplinary. **jdn** ~ **bestrafen** to take disciplinary action against sb.
**Disziplinar-**: **~strafe** f punishment; **eine ~strafe bekommen** to be disciplined; **~verfahren** nt disciplinary proceedings pl.
**disziplinieren\*** vt to discipline.
**Disziplin-**: **d~los** **1** adj undisciplined; **2** adv in an undisciplined manner; **~losigkeit** f lack no pl of discipline.
**dito** adv (Comm, hum) ditto.
**Diva** ['diːva] f -s star; (Film) screen goddess.
**divergieren\*** [diver'giːrən] vi to diverge.
**divers** [di'vɛrs] adj attr various. **„D~es"** "miscellaneous".
**Diversifikation** f diversification.
**diversifizieren\*** vt to diversify.
**Dividende** [divi'dɛndə] f -n (Fin) dividend.
**dividieren\*** [divi'diːrən] vti to divide (durch by).
**Division** [divi'zioːn] f (Math, Mil) division.
**Diwan** m -e divan.
**d.J.** = (a) **der Jüngere.** (b) **dieses Jahres** of this year.
**DJH** [deːjɔt'haː] nt = **Deutsches Jugendherbergswerk** German Youth Hostel Association.
**DKP** [deːkaː'peː] f = **Deutsche Kommunistische Partei.**
**dl** = **Deziliter** dl.
**DM** ['deː|ɛm] no art - = **Deutsche Mark.**
**d.M.** = **dieses Monats.**
**dm** = **Dezimeter** dm.
**D-Mark** ['deːmark] f - deutschmark, German mark.
**DNS** [deː|ɛn|'ɛs] f = **Desoxyribonukleinsäure** DNA.
**Do.** = **Donnerstag** Thurs.
**Dobermann** m, pl **-männer** Doberman (pinscher).
**doch 1** conj (aber, allein) but; (jedoch, trotzdem) but still, yet. **und** ~ **hat er es getan** but he still did it, but still he did it.
**2** adv (a) (betont: dennoch) after all; (trotzdem, sowieso) anyway. **jetzt ist er** ~ **nicht gekommen** now he hasn't come after all; **du weißt es ja** ~ **besser** you know better than I do anyway; **und** ~, ... and yet ...
(b) (betont: tatsächlich) really. **also** ~! so it is/so he did! etc; **er hat es gestohlen — also** ~! he stole it — so it was him!; **es ist** ~ **so, wie ich vermutet hatte** so it (really) is as I thought; **das ist er** ~! (why,) that is him!
(c) (als bejahende Antwort) yes I do/it does etc. **hat es dir nicht gefallen? — (~,) ~!** didn't you like it? — (oh) yes I did!
(d) (auffordernd) nicht übersetzt, aber emphatisches „do" wird oft gebraucht. **komm** ~ do come; **seid** ~ **endlich still!** do keep quiet!, keep quiet, can't you?; **laß ihn ~!** just leave him!; **nicht ~!** don't (do that)!
(e) **sie ist** ~ **noch so jung** but she's still so young;

**das ist** ~ **wohl nicht wahr?** that's not true, is it?; **du hast** ~ **nicht etwa ...?** you haven't ..., have you?, surely you haven't ...(, have you)?; **es war** ~ **ganz interessant** it was really or actually quite interesting; **Sie wissen** ~, **wie das so ist** (well,) you know how it is, don't you?; **wenn** ~ if only.
**Docht** m -e wick.
**Dock** nt -s dock.
**docken\*** vti to dock.
**Docker** m - docker.
**Dogge** f -n mastiff. **deutsche** ~ great Dane.
**Dogma** nt, pl **Dogmen** dogma.
**dogmatisch** adj (Rel, fig) dogmatic.
**Dohle** f -n (Orn) jackdaw.
**Doktor** m (auch col: Arzt) doctor. **den** ~ **machen** (col) to do a doctorate or PhD.
**Doktorand(in** f) m (wk) **-en, -en** PhD student.
**Doktor-**: **~arbeit** f doctoral or PhD thesis; **~grad** m doctorate, PhD; **~hut** m (fig) doctorate.
**Doktorin** f doctor.
**Doktor-**: **~prüfung** f examination for a/one's doctorate; **~titel** m doctorate; **~vater** m supervisor; **~würde** f doctorate.
**Doktrin** f -en doctrine.
**doktrinär** adj doctrinal; (pej: stur) doctrinaire.
**Dokument** nt document; (fig: Zeugnis) record.
**Dokumentar-** in cpds documentary; **~film** m documentary (film).
**dokumentarisch 1** adj documentary. **2** adv **etw** ~ **belegen/festhalten** to provide documentary evidence for or of sth/to document sth.
**Dokumentarspiel** nt docudrama.
**Dokumentation** f documentation.
**dokumentieren\*** vt to document; (fig: zu erkennen geben) to reveal, to show.
**Dolch** m -e dagger; (col: Messer) knife.
**Dolchstoß** (esp fig) m stab (auch fig). **ein** ~ **(von hinten)** (fig) a stab in the back.
**Dollar** m -s dollar.
**Dollbord** nt (Naut) gunwale.
**Dolle** f - (Naut) rowlock, oarlock (US).
**dolmetschen** vti to interpret.
**Dolmetscher(in** f) m - interpreter.
**Dolmetscherschule** f school of interpreting.
**Dolomiten** pl (Geog) **die** ~ the Dolomites pl.
**Dom** m -e cathedral.
**Domäne** f -n (fig) domain, province.
**domestizieren\*** vt to domesticate.
**dominant** adj dominant (auch Biol), dominating.
**Dominante** f -n (a) (Mus) dominant. (b) (wichtigster Faktor) dominant or dominating feature.
**Dominanz** f (Biol, Psych) dominance.
**dominieren\*** **1** vi (vorherrschen) to predominate; (Mensch) to dominate. **2** vt to dominate.
**dominierend** adj dominating, dominant.
**Dominikaner(in** f) m - (Eccl, Geog) Dominican.
**dominikanisch** adj (Eccl, Geog) Dominican. **die D~e Republik** the Dominican Republic.
**Domino** nt -s (Spiel) dominoes sing.
**Domino-**: **~spiel** nt dominoes sing; **~stein** m (a) domino; (b) square chocolate containing layers of marzipan, gingerbread and jelly.
**Domizil** nt -e (geh, hum) domicile (form).
**Dompfaff** m (Orn) bullfinch.
**Dompteur** [dɔmp'tøːɐ] m, **Dompteuse** [-'tøːzə] f trainer; (von Raubtieren) tamer.
**Donau** f **die** ~ the Danube.
**Donner** m (lit, fig) thunder no indef art, no pl; **(~schlag)** clap of thunder. **wie vom** ~ **gerührt** (fig col) thunderstruck.
**donnern 1** vi impers to thunder. **es donnerte in der**

**Ferne** there was (the sound of) thunder in the distance. **2** *vi aux haben or (bei Bewegung) sein* to thunder. **gegen etw ~** *(schlagen)* to hammer on sth; *(schimpfen)* to inveigh *or* vituperate against sth. **3** *vt (col: schleudern, schlagen)* to slam, to crash.

**donnernd** *adj (fig) Beifall* thunderous.

**Donnerschlag** *m* clap of thunder, thunderclap. **die Nachricht traf mich wie ein ~** the news left me thunderstruck.

**Donnerstag** *m* Thursday; *siehe* **Dienstag.**

**donnerstags** *adv* on Thursdays.

**Donner-:** **~stimme** *f* thunderous voice; **~wetter** *nt (fig col: Schelte)* row; **~wetter!** *(col) (anerkennend)* my word!; *(zornig)* blast (it)! *(col).*

**doof** *adj (col)* stupid, daft *(col)*; *Mensch auch* thick *(col).*

**Doofi** *m* **-s** *(col)* thickie, dumbo *(col).*

**dopen** *(Sport)* **1** *vt* to dope. **2** *vir* to take drugs.

**Doping** *nt* **-s** *(Sport)* doping.

**Dopingkontrolle** *f (Sport)* dope check.

**Doppel** *nt* **-** **(a)** *(Duplikat)* duplicate (copy) *(gen, zu of).* **(b)** *(Tennis etc)* doubles *sing.*

**Doppel-** *in cpds* double; **~agent** *m* double agent; **~band** *m (von doppeltem Umfang)* double-sized volume; *(zwei Bände)* two volumes *pl*; **~belastung** *f* double burden *(gen on)*; **steuerliche ~belastung** double taxation; **~beschluß** *m (Pol)* two-track *or* twin-track decision; **~bett** *nt* double bed; *(zwei Betten)* twin beds *pl*; **d~bödig** *adj Koffer etc* double-bottomed, false-bottomed; *(d~deutig)* ambiguous; **~decker** *m* **-** **(a)** *(Aviat)* biplane; **(b)** *(Bus)* double-decker (bus); **d~deutig** *adj* ambiguous; **~deutigkeit** *f* ambiguity; **~fenster** *nt* double window; *(~verglasung)* double glazing; **~gänger(in** *f)* *m* **-** double, doppelgänger *(esp Liter)*; **ein ~gänger von Boris Becker** a Boris Becker lookalike; **~haus** *nt* semi-detached house, semi *(Brit col)*, duplex (house) *(US)*; **er bewohnt eine Hälfte eines ~hauses** he lives in a semi(-detached house); **~haushälfte** *f* semi-detached house; **~kinn** *nt* double chin; **~korn** *m type of schnaps*; **d~läufig** *adj* double-barrelled; **~moral** *f* double standards *pl*; **~name** *m (Nachname)* double-barrelled name; **~paß** *m (Ftbl)* one-two; **~punkt** *m* colon; **~rolle** *f (Theat, fig)* dual role; **~seite** *f* double-page spread; **d~seitig** *adj* double-sided; *Lungenentzündung* double; **d~seitige Anzeige** double page spread; **~sinn** *m* double meaning; **d~sinnig** *adj* ambiguous; **~spiel** *nt* **(a)** *(Tennis)* doubles *sing*; **(b)** *(fig)* double game; **~stecker** *m* two-way adaptor; **d~stöckig** *adj Haus* two-storey; **~strategie** *f* dual strategy; **~stunde** *f (Sch)* double period.

**doppelt 1** *adj* double; *(verstärkt) Enthusiasmus* redoubled; *(mit zwei identischen Teilen)* twin *attr*; *(zweimal soviel)* twice; *(Comm) Buchführung* double-entry; *Staatsbürgerschaft* dual. **die ~e Freude/Menge** double *or* twice the pleasure/amount; **~er Boden** false *or* double bottom; **~e Moral** double standards *pl*; **in ~er Hinsicht** in two respects; **ein ~es Spiel treiben** to play a double game. **2** *adv* **sehen, zählen** double; *(zweimal)* twice; *(direkt vor Adjektiv)* doubly. **~ so schön/soviel** *etc* twice as nice/much *etc*; **sie ist ~ so alt wie ich** she is twice as old as I am; **die Karte habe ich ~** I have two of these cards; **~ gemoppelt** *(col)* saying the same thing twice over; **sich ~ in acht nehmen** to be doubly careful; **~ genäht hält besser** *(prov)* better safe than sorry *(prov).*

**Doppelte(r)** *m decl as adj (col)* double.

**Doppelte(s)** *nt decl as adj* double. **das ~ bezahlen** to pay twice as much; **etw um das ~ erhöhen** to dou-

ble sth.

**Doppel-:** **~verdiener** *m* **sie sind ~verdiener** they have two incomes; **~verglasung** *f* double glazing; **~zentner** *m* 100 kilos; **~zimmer** *nt* double room; **d~züngig** *adj* two-faced; **d~züngig reden** to say one thing and mean another; **~züngigkeit** *f no pl* two-facedness.

**Dorado** *nt* **-s** *(fig)* eldorado.

**Dorf** *nt* **=er** village; *(fig)* backwater. **das Leben auf dem ~e** village life.

**Dorf-** *in cpds* village; **~bewohner** *m* villager; **~jugend** *f* young people *pl* of the village; **~krug** *m* village inn *or* pub *(Brit).*

**dörflich** *adj* village *attr*; *(ländlich)* rustic, rural.

**Dorn** *m* **-en** **(a)** *(Bot, fig)* thorn. **das ist mir ein ~ im Auge** *(fig)* it's a thorn in my flesh; *(Anblick)* I find it an eyesore. **(b)** *pl* **-e** *(Sporn)* spike; *(von Schnalle)* tongue; *(Tech: Werkzeug)* awl.

**Dornbusch** *m* briar, thornbush.

**Dornen-:** **~hecke** *f* thorn(y) hedge; **~krone** *f (Bibl)* crown of thorns; **d~reich** *adj* thorny.

**dornig** *adj* thorny.

**Dorn-:** **~röschen** *nt* Sleeping Beauty; **~röschenschlaf** *m (fig)* slumber; **aus seinem ~röschenschlaf erwachen** to awake from one's slumbers.

**dörren 1** *vt* to dry. **2** *vi aux sein* to dry; *(austrocknen)* to dry up.

**Dörr-:** **~fleisch** *nt* dried meat; **~obst** *nt* dried fruit; **~pflaume** *f* prune.

**Dorsch** *m* **-e** *type of cod.*

**dort** *adv* there; *siehe* **da 1 (a).**

**dort-:** **~her** *adv* **von ~her** from there; **~hin** *adv* there; **bis ~hin** as far as there; **~hinauf** *adv* up there; **~hinaus** *adv* out there; **frech bis ~hinaus** *(col)* insolent in the extreme; **das ärgert mich bis ~hinaus** *(col)* that really gets me *(col)*; **~hinein** *adv* in there; **~hinunter** *adv* down there.

**dortig** *adj* **die ~en Behörden** the authorities there.

**Dose** *f* **-n** **(a)** *(Blech~)* tin; *(Konserven~)* can, tin *(Brit)*; *(Bier~)* can; *(esp aus Holz)* box; *(mit Deckel)* jar; *(Pillen~, für Schmuck)* box; *(Zucker~)* bowl. **in ~n** *(Konserven)* canned, tinned *(Brit).* **(b)** *(Elec)* socket.

**dösen** *vi (col)* to doze.

**Dosen-** *in cpds* canned, tinned *(Brit)*; **~bier** *nt* canned beer; **~milch** *f* evaporated milk; **~öffner** *m* can-opener, tin-opener *(Brit).*

**dosieren*** *vt (lit, fig)* to measure out.

**Dosierung** *f (Dosis)* dosage, dose.

**dösig** *adj (col)* dozy *(col).*

**Dosis** *f, pl* **Dosen** *(lit, fig)* dose.

**Dossier** [dɔ'siːɛ] *nt* **-s** dossier.

**dotieren*** *vt Posten* to remunerate; *Preis* to endow.

**Dotierung** *f* endowment; *(von Posten)* remuneration.

**Dotter** *m or nt* **-** yolk.

**doubeln** ['duːbln] **1** *vt jdn* to stand in for; *Szene* to shoot with a stand-in. **ein Stuntman hat die Szene für ihn gedoubelt** a stuntman doubled for him in the scene. **2** *vi* to stand in; *(als Double arbeiten)* to work as a stand-in.

**Double** ['duːbl] *nt* **-s** *(Film etc)* stand-in.

**down** [daun] *adj pred (col)* **~ sein** to be down.

**Dozent(in** *f)* *m (wk)* lecturer *(für* in*)*, (assistant) professor *(US) (für* of*).*

**Dozentur** *f* lectureship *(für* in*)*, (assistant) professorship *(US) (für* of*).*

**dozieren*** *vi (Univ)* to lecture *(über +acc* on, *an +dat* at*)*; *(pej auch)* to pontificate *(über +acc* about*).*

**dpa** ['deːpeː|'aː] *f* = **Deutsche Presse-Agentur.**

**Dr.** ['dɔktɔr] = **Doktor. Dr.rer.nat./rer.pol./phil.** PhD;

**Dr.** theol./jur. DD/LLD; **Dr.** med. M.D.

**Drạche** m (wk) -n, -n (Myth) dragon.

**Drạchen** m - (a) (Papier~) kite; (Sport: Fluggerät) hang-glider. **einen ~ steigen lassen** to fly a kite. (b) (pej col: zänkisches Weib) dragon (col).

**Drạchen-:** ~**fliegen** nt (Sport) hang-gliding; ~**flieger** m (Sport) hang-glider.

**Dragée** [dra'ʒeː] nt -s (a) (Bonbon) sugar-coated chocolate sweet. (b) (Pharm) dragee, sugar-coated pill.

**Dragọner** m - (Hist) dragoon; (pej: Frau) battleaxe, dragon.

**Drạht** m ⁼e wire. **auf ~ sein** (col) to be on the ball (col); **du bist wohl heute nicht ganz auf ~** (col) you're not quite with it today (col).

**Drạht-** in cpds wire; ~**bürste** f wire brush; ~**esel** m (hum) trusty bicycle; ~**gitter** nt wire netting; ~**haardackel** m wire-haired dachshund; **d~haarig** adj wire-haired.

**drạhtig** adj Haar, Mensch wiry.

**Drạht-:** **d~los** adj Telegrafie wireless; Telefon, Nachrichtenübermittlung cordless; ~**schere** f wire cutters pl.

**Drạhtseil** nt wire rope, cable. **Nerven wie ~e** (col) nerves of steel.

**Drạhtseil-:** ~**akt** m (lit, fig) balancing act; ~**bahn** f cable railway; ~**künstler** m (Seiltänzer) tightrope walker.

**Drạht-:** ~**verhau** m or nt wire entanglement; ~**zaun** m wire fence; ~**zieher(in** f) m (fig) wire-puller.

**drakọnisch** adj draconian.

**drạll** adj Mädchen, Arme strapping, sturdy.

**Drạll** m -e (a) (von Kugel, Ball) spin; (Abweichung von Bahn) swerve; (col: von Auto) pull. **einen ~ nach links haben** (Auto) to pull to the left. (b) (fig: Hang) tendency.

**Drạma** nt, pl **Drạmen** (lit, fig) drama.

**Dramạtik** f (lit, fig) drama.

**Dramạtiker(in** f) m - dramatist.

**dramạtisch** adj (lit, fig) dramatic.

**dramatisịeren*** vt (lit, fig) to dramatize.

**Dramatụrg(in** f) m (wk) -en, -en artistic director; (TV) drama producer.

**dramatụrgisch** adj dramatic; Abteilung drama attr.

**drạn** adv (col) (a) (an der Reihe) **jetzt bist du ~** it's your turn now; **(wenn er erwischt wird,) dann ist er ~** (if he gets caught) he'll be for it (col). (b) **schlecht ~ sein** to be in a bad way; **gut ~ sein** to be well-off; **früh/spät ~ sein** to be early/late. (c) **an ihm ist nichts ~** he doesn't have much going for him; **was ist an ihm ~, daß ...?** what is there about him that ...?; **da ist alles ~!** that's got everything; **da wird schon etwas (Wahres) ~ sein** there must be something in that; **ich weiß nicht, wie ich (bei ihm) ~ bin** I don't know where I stand (with him).

**drạnbleiben** vi sep irreg aux sein (col) to stay close; (am Apparat) to hang on. **am Gegner ~** to stick to one's opponent.

**Drạng** m ⁼e (Antrieb) urge (auch Physiol); (Sehnsucht) yearning (nach for). **~ nach Wissen** thirst for knowledge.

**drạng** pret of **dringen.**

**drạngeben** vt sep irreg (col: opfern) to give up. **sein Leben für etw ~** to give one's life for sth.

**drạngehen** vi sep irreg aux sein (col) (a) (berühren etc) to touch (an etw (acc) sth). (b) (in Angriff nehmen) ~, **etw zu tun** to get down to doing sth.

**Drängelei** f (col) pushing, jostling.

**drängeln** (col) **1** vi to push, to jostle. **2** vr sich nach vorne ~ to push one's way to the front.

**drängen 1** vi (a) (in Menge) to push. (b) (fordern) to press (auf +acc for). **auf Antwort ~** to press for an answer; **er drängte zur Eile** he urged us/them etc to hurry. (c) **die Zeit drängt** time presses. **2** vt (a) (drücken, schieben) to push. (b) (auffordern) to press. **3** vr (Menge) to throng; (fig: Termine etc) to mount up. **sich nach vorn ~** to push or force one's way to the front; siehe **gedrängt.**

**Drängen** nt no pl urging; (Bitten) requests pl; (Bestehen) insistence.

**drängend** adj pressing, urgent.

**drangsalịeren*** vt to pester, to plague.

**drạnhalten** vr sep irreg (col: sich beeilen) to get a move on (col).

**drạnhängen** sep (col) **1** vt viel Zeit etc ~, **etw zu tun** to put a lot of time etc into doing sth. **2** vr (verfolgen) to stay close behind.

**drạnkommen** vi sep irreg aux sein (col: an die Reihe kommen) to have one's turn; (Sch: beim Melden) to be called; (Frage, Aufgabe etc) to come up. **jetzt kommst du dran** now it's your turn.

**drạnkriegen** vt sep (col) jdn ~ to get sb (col); (zu einer Arbeit) to get sb to do sth/it.

**drạnmachen** sep (col) **1** vr = **daranmachen. 2** vt etw (an etw acc) ~ to put sth on (sth).

**drạnnehmen** vt sep irreg (col) Schüler to ask.

**drạnsetzen** vtr sep (col) = **daransetzen.**

**drapịeren*** vt to drape.

**drạstisch** adj drastic; (deutlich) graphic.

**drauf** adv (col) siehe auch **darauf. ~ und dran sein, etw zu tun** to be on the point of doing sth; **etw ~ haben** (col) (können) to be able to do sth just like that (col); Kenntnisse to be well up on sth (col); Witze, Sprüche to have sth off pat (col); **160 Sachen ~ haben** (col) to be doing 100.

**Drauf-:** ~**gänger** m go-getter; **d~gängerisch** adj go-getting; (negativ) reckless; **d~geben** vt irreg sep (a) jdm eins d~geben (col) to give sb a smack; (b) (dazugeben) noch etwas d~geben to add some extra (col); **d~gehen** vi sep irreg aux sein (col); (verbraucht werden) to be used up; (kaputtgehen) to be smashed up; (sterben) to bite the dust (col); **dabei gehen mindestens zwei Tage d~** that'll take at least two days; **d~haben** vt sep (col) Sprüche, Antwort to come out with; **zeigen, was man d~hat** to show what one is made of; **d~halten** vi sep irreg (als Ziel) to aim for it; **d~kommen** vi sep irreg aux sein (col) (sich erinnern) to remember; (begreifen) to catch on, to get it (col); jdm d~kommen to get on to sb (col); **d~kriegen** vt sep (col) etw (auf etw acc) d~kriegen to get or fit sth on(to sth); **eins d~kriegen** to catch it (col); **d~legen** vti sep (col) 20 Mark d~legen to lay out an extra 20 marks.

**drauflos** adv immer feste ~! (just) keep at it!

**drauflos-:** ~**arbeiten** vi sep (col) to work away, to beaver away (col); ~**gehen** vi sep irreg aux sein (col: auf ein Ziel) to make straight for it; ~**reden** vi sep (col) to talk away; (anfangen) to start talking.

**drauf-:** ~**machen** vt sep (col) einen ~**machen** to make a night of it (col); ~**sein** vi sep irreg aux sein (col) schlecht/gut ~sein to be in a bad/good mood; **D~sicht** f view from above; ~**stehen** vi sep irreg (col) auf etw (dat) ~stehen to stand on sth; (Aufschrift) to be on sth; ~**zahlen** sep (col) (a) vti = ~**legen**; (b) vi (fig: Einbußen erleiden) to pay the price.

**draus** adv = **daraus.**

**draußen** adv outside; (im Freien auch) outdoors; (da ~, weit weg von hier) out there; **~ auf dem Lande/im Garten** out in the country/garden; **hier ~** out here; **nach ~** outside; **weit ~** far out.

**drechseln** *vt* to turn *(on a wood lathe).*
**Drechsler(in** *f) m -* (wood) turner.
**Dreck** *m no pl* **(a)** dirt; *(Schlamm)* mud; *(Kot)* muck; *(fig) (Schund)* rubbish; *(Schmutz, Obszönes)* dirt, filth. ~ **machen** to make a mess; **mit ~ und Speck** *(ungewaschen)* unwashed; **im ~ sitzen** *(col)* to be in a mess *or* jam *(col);* **aus dem gröbsten ~ heraus sein** *(col)* to be past the worst; **jdn wie den letzten ~ behandeln** *(col)* to treat sb like dirt; **der letzte ~ sein** *(pej col: Mensch)* to be the lowest of the low; ~ **am Stecken haben** *(fig)* to have a skeleton in the cupboard; **etw in den ~ ziehen** *(fig)* to drag sth through the mud. **(b)** *(col) (Kram)* business, stuff *(col);* *(Kleinigkeit)* little thing. **sich einen ~ um jdn/etw kümmern** not to give a damn about sb/sth *(col);* **mach deinen ~ alleine!** do it yourself; **das geht ihn einen ~ an** that's none of his business.
**Dreck|arbeit** *f (col)* **(a)** *(lit, fig)* dirty work. **(b)** *(pej: niedere Arbeit)* donkey work.
**dreckig** *adj (lit, fig)* dirty; *(stärker)* filthy. ~ **lachen** to give a dirty laugh; **es geht mir ~** *(col)* I'm having a dreadful time.
**Dreck-:** ~**loch** *nt (pej)* hole *(col);* ~**pfoten** *pl (col) (lit, fig)* dirty paws *pl;* ~**sack** *m (pej col)* dirty thing *(col);* ~**sau** *f (col!)* filthy swine *(col!);* ~**schleuder** *f (pej) (Mensch)* foul-mouthed person; *(Kraftwerk, Auto)* pollution-belcher; ~**schwein** *nt (col!)* dirty pig *(col!).*
**Dreckskerl** *m (col!)* dirty swine *(col!).*
**Dreckspatz** *m (col: Kind)* mucky pup *(col).*
**Dreck(s)zeug** *nt (col)* damn stuff *(col).* **das ist doch ein ~** damn this stuff *(col).*
**Dreh** *m -s or -e* *(List)* dodge; *(Kunstgriff)* trick. **den ~ heraushaben** to have got the hang of it; **so um den ~** *(col)* or thereabouts.
**Dreh-:** ~**arbeiten** *pl (Film)* shooting *sing;* ~**bank** *f* lathe; **d~bar** *adj* rotating, revolving *attr;* **d~bar sein** to rotate *or* revolve; ~**beginn** *m (Film)* start of shooting; ~**bleistift** *m* propelling *(Brit) or* mechanical *(US)* pencil; ~**brücke** *f* swing bridge; ~**buch** *nt (Film)* screenplay, (film) script; ~**buchautor** *m* scriptwriter, screenplay writer; ~**bühne** *f* revolving stage.
**drehen** **1** *vt* to turn *(auch Tech: auf Drehbank); (um eine Achse auch)* to rotate, to revolve; *Kreisel* to spin; *Zigaretten* to roll; *Film* to shoot; *(fig: verdrehen)* to twist; *(col: schaffen)* to fix *(col).* **das Gas hoch/auf klein ~** to turn the gas up high/down low; **Fleisch durch den Wolf ~** to put meat through the mincer; **ein Ding ~** *(col)* to play a prank; *(Verbrecher)* to pull a job *(col);* **wie man es auch dreht und wendet** no matter how you look at it.
  **2** *vi* to turn; *(Wind)* to shift, to change; *(Film)* to shoot, to film; *(Zigaretten ~)* to roll one's own. **am Radio ~** to keep turning the tuning knob on the radio.
  **3** *vr* **(a)** *(lit)* to turn *(um about); (um Achse auch)* to rotate, to revolve; *(Kreisel)* to spin; *(Wind)* to shift, to change. **sich um sich (selbst) ~** to revolve on its own axis; **mir dreht sich alles im Kopf** my head is spinning; **sich ~ und winden** *(fig)* to twist and turn. **(b)** *(fig)* **sich um etw ~** *(betreffen)* to concern sth, to be about sth; *(um zentrale Frage)* to centre *(Brit)* or center *(US)* on sth; **alles dreht sich um sie** she's the focus of attention; **es dreht sich darum, daß ...** the point is that ...
**Dreher(in** *f) m -* lathe operator.
**Dreh-:** ~**gelenk** *nt* swivel; ~**knopf** *m* knob; ~**kran** *m* revolving crane; ~**kreuz** *nt* turnstile; ~**moment** *nt* torque; ~**orgel** *f* barrel-organ; ~**orgelspieler** *m* organ-grinder; ~**ort** *m (Film)* lo-

cation; ~**punkt** *m* pivot; ~**restaurant** *nt* revolving restaurant; ~**scheibe** *f* **(a)** *(Rail)* turntable; **(b)** *(Töpferscheibe)* potter's wheel; ~**stuhl** *m* swivel-chair; ~**tür** *f* revolving door.
**Drehung** *f* turn; *(um eigene Achse auch)* rotation, revolution. **eine ~ um 180°** a 180° turn; **80 ~en pro Minute** 80 revolutions per minute.
**Drehwurm** *m (col):* **einen ~ kriegen/haben** to get/be giddy.
**Drehzahl** *f* number of revolutions *or (col)* revs. **bei hohen ~en** at high revolution *or* high revs *(col).*
**Drehzahlmesser** *m* rev counter *(col).*
**drei** *num* three. **aller guten Dinge sind ~!** *(prov)* all good things/all disasters come in threes!; *(nach zwei mißglückten Versuchen)* third time lucky!; **sie sieht aus, als ob sie nicht bis ~ zählen könnte** *(col)* she looks as thick as two planks *(col);* siehe **vier.**
**Drei** *f -en* three; *(Sch)* ≃ C; siehe **Vier.**
**Drei-D-** [drai'deː] *in cpds* 3-D.
**dreidimensional** *adj* three-dimensional.
**Drei|eck** *nt -e* triangle.
**drei|eckig** *adj* triangular.
**Drei|ecks-:** ~**tuch** *nt* triangular shawl; *(Med)* triangular bandage; ~**verhältnis** *nt* eternal triangle.
**Drei|einigkeit** *f* Trinity.
**Dreier-, dreier-** *in cpds* siehe **Vierer-, vierer-.**
**dreifach** **1** *adj* triple. **die ~e Menge** three times *or* triple *or* treble the amount; **ein ~es Hoch!** three cheers! **2** *adv* three times. ~ **abgesichert** trebly secure; siehe **vierfach.**
**Dreifache(s)** *nt decl as adj* **das ~** triple *or* treble the amount, three times as much; **etw um das ~ vermehren** to multiply sth by three.
**Dreifachstecker** *m* three-way adapter.
**Drei-:** ~**fuß** *m* tripod; *(Schemel)* three-legged stool; ~**gangrad** *nt* three-speed bike; ~**gangschaltung** *f* three-speed gear; **d~hundert** *num* three hundred; ~**käsehoch** *m -s (col)* tiny tot *(col);* ~**klang** *m* triad; ~**königstag** *m* feast of Epiphany; **d~mal** *adv* three times; siehe **viermal;** ~**meilenzone** *f* three-mile zone.
**drein-:** ~**blicken** *vi sep* traurig *etc* ~**blicken** to look sad *etc;* ~**reden** *vi sep (col) (dazwischenreden)* to interrupt; *(sich einmischen)* to interfere *(bei* in, with*);* **ich lasse mir da von niemandem ~reden** I won't have anyone interfering (with this); ~**schauen** *vi sep* = ~**blicken.**
**Drei-:** **d~polig** *adj Kabel* three-core; *Steckdose, Stecker* three-pin; ~**punktgurt** *m (Aut)* lap and diagonal seatbelt; ~**rad** *nt* tricycle; ~**satz** *m (Math)* rule of three; ~**springer** *m* triple-jumper; ~**sprung** *m* triple jump, hop, step and jump.
**dreißig** *num* thirty; siehe auch **vierzig.**
**dreißig-** *in cpds* siehe auch **vierzig-;** ~**jährig** *adj* **der ~jährige Krieg** the Thirty Years' War.
**dreist** *adj* bold, audacious.
**Dreistigkeit** *f* **(a)** *no pl* boldness, audacity. **(b)** *(Handlung)* bold or audacious act.
**dreiteilig** *adj Kostüm etc* three-piece *attr.*
**dreiviertel** ['drai'fɪrtl] siehe auch **viertel 1** *adj* three-quarter. **eine ~ Stunde** three quarters of an hour. **2** *adv* threequarters.
**Dreiviertel-:** **d~lang** *adj* three-quarter length; ~**literflasche** *f* three-quarter litre *(Brit)* or liter *(US)* bottle; ~**mehrheit** *f* three-quarters majority; ~**stunde** *f* three quarters of an hour *no indef art;* ~**takt** *m* **im ~takt** in three-four time.
**Dreiweg-** *in cpds (Tech, Elec)* three-way; ~**stecker** *m* three-way adapter.
**drei-:** ~**wöchentlich 1** *adj attr* three-weekly; **2** *adv* every three weeks; ~**wöchig** *adj attr* three-week;

**~zehn** adj num thirteen. **jetzt schlägt's aber ~zehn** (col) that's a bit much; siehe **vierzehn**.

**Dresche** f no pl (col) ~ **kriegen** to get a thrashing.

**dreschen** pret **drosch**, ptp **gedroschen 1** vt **(a)** Korn to thresh. **Skat** ~ (col) to play skat. **(b)** (col: prügeln) to thrash. **2** vr (col: sich prügeln) to have a fight.

**Dresch-:** ~**flegel** m flail; ~**maschine** f threshing machine.

**Dresden** nt Dresden.

**Dreß** m **-sse** (Sport) (sports) kit; (einer Fußballmannschaft) strip (Brit).

**Dresseur** [-'søːɐ] m trainer.

**dressieren*** vt **(a)** to train. **zu etw dressiert sein** to be trained etc to do sth. **(b)** Geflügel to dress.

**Dressman** ['drɛsmən] m, pl **Dressmen** male model.

**Dressur** f training; (für ~reiten) dressage.

**dribbeln** vi to dribble. **mit dem Ball** ~ to dribble the ball.

**Dribbling** nt **-s** dribbling. **ein** ~ a piece of dribbling.

**Drift** f **-en** (Naut) drift.

**driften** vi aux sein (Naut, fig) to drift.

**Drill** m no pl (Mil, fig) drill; (Sch auch) drills pl.

**drillen** vti to drill. **auf etw** (acc) **gedrillt sein** (fig col) to be practised at doing sth.

**Drillich** m **-e** (Tex) drill.

**Drilling** m **(a)** triplet. **(b)** (Jagdgewehr) triple-barrelled shotgun.

**drin** adv (col) siehe auch **darin, drinnen (a)** in it. **er/es ist da** ~ he/it is in there; **in der Flasche ist noch etwas** ~ there's still something in the bottle. **(b)** (col) **bei ihm ist alles** ~ anything's possible with him; **bis jetzt ist noch alles** ~ everything is still quite open; **das ist doch nicht** ~ (geht nicht) that's not on (col).

**dringen** pret **drang**, ptp **gedrungen** vi **(a)** aux sein (durch etw) ~ to penetrate (sth); **an die Öffentlichkeit** ~ to leak or get out. **(b)** (geh) aux sein **in jdn** ~ to press or urge sb; **mit Bitten/Fragen in jdn** ~ to ply or press sb with requests/questions. **(c) auf etw** (acc) ~ to insist on sth.

**dringend** adj (eilig, wichtig) urgent, pressing; (nachdrücklich, zwingend) strong; Gründe compelling. **ein** ~**er Fall** (Med) an emergency; ~ **verdächtig** strongly suspected; ~ **empfehlen** to recommend strongly.

**dringlich** adj urgent, pressing.

**Dringlichkeit** f urgency.

**Dringlichkeits-:** ~**antrag** m (Parl) emergency motion; ~**stufe** f priority; ~**stufe 1** top priority.

**drinnen** adv inside; (im Haus auch) indoors. **hier/dort** ~ in here/there; **ich gehe nach** ~ (col) I'm going in(side).

**drinstecken** vi sep (col) **da steckt eine Menge Geld/Arbeit** etc **drin** a lot of money/work etc has gone into it; **er steckt bis über die Ohren drin** he's up to his ears in it; **da steckt man nicht drin** you never can tell (what will happen).

**dritt** adv **wir kommen zu** ~ three of us are coming together.

**dritt-:** in cpds third; ~**älteste(r, s)** adj third oldest.

**Drittel** nt **-** third; siehe **Viertel¹**.

**drittens** adv thirdly.

**Dritte(r)** mf decl as adj third person, third man/woman etc; (Unbeteiligter) third party. **in dieser Angelegenheit ist er der lachende** ~ he comes out of this best; **im Beisein** ~**r** in the presence of a third party; siehe **Vierte(r)**.

**dritte(r, s)** adj third. **von** ~**r Seite** from a third party; **die D**~ **Welt** the Third World; siehe **vierte(r, s)**.

**Dritte-Welt-** in cpds third world; ~**-Laden** m charity shop raising money for third world countries.

**dritt-:** ~**größte(r, s)** adj third-biggest; **d**~**klassig** adj third-rate (pej), third-class; **d**~**letzte(r, s)** adj third from last; **d**~**rangig** adj third-rate.

**DRK** ['deːʔɛr'kaː] nt = **Deutsches Rotes Kreuz**.

**droben** adv (old, dial) up there.

**Droge** f **-n** drug.

**Drogen-:** **d**~**abhängig** adj addicted to drugs; ~**abhängige(r)** mf decl as adj drug addict; ~**abhängigkeit** f drug addiction no art; ~**händler** m drug peddler or pusher; ~**konsum** m drug-taking; **d**~**süchtig** adj addicted to drugs; ~**süchtige(r)** mf decl as adj drug addict; ~**szene** f drug scene.

**Drogerie** f chemist's (Brit), drugstore (US).

**Drogist(in** f) m chemist (Brit), druggist (US).

**Drohbrief** m threatening letter.

**drohen** vi to threaten (jdm sb). **er droht mit Selbstmord** he threatens to commit suicide; **jdm droht etw** sb is being threatened by sth; **jdm droht Gefahr** sb is in danger; **es droht ein Streik** there is the threat of a strike; **das Schiff drohte zu sinken** the ship was in danger of sinking.

**drohend** adj threatening, menacing; (bevorstehend) Gefahr, Krieg imminent, impending.

**Drohgebärde** f threatening gesture.

**Drohne** f **-n** drone.

**dröhnen** vi to roar; (Donner) to rumble; (Musik, Stimme) to boom; (Raum etc) to resound, to echo. **mir dröhnt der Kopf** my head is ringing.

**Drohung** f threat.

**drollig** adj comical, droll; Kätzchen etc cute.

**Dromedar** [auch: 'droː-] nt **-e** dromedary.

**Drops** m or nt **-** fruit drop.

**drosch** pret of **dreschen**.

**Droschke** f **-n** (Pferde~) (hackney) cab, hackney-carriage; (dated: Taxi) (taxi-)cab.

**Droschkenkutscher** m cab driver.

**Drossel** f **-n** (Orn) thrush.

**drosseln** vt Motor etc to throttle; Heizung to turn down; Strom, Tempo, Produktion to cut down.

**Drosselung** f siehe vt throttling, turning down; cutting down.

**drüben** adv over there; (auf der anderen Seite, Hist col: auf DDR/BRD bezogen) on the other side. **hier/dort** or **da** ~ over here/there; **nach/von** ~ over/from over there.

**drüber** adv (col) = **darüber**.

**Druck¹** m ⁼e (Phys, fig) pressure. **unter** ~ **stehen** (lit, fig) to be under pressure; **jdn unter** ~ **setzen** (fig) to put pressure on sb, to pressurize sb; **durch einen** ~ **auf den Knopf** by pressing the button.

**Druck²** m **-e (a)** (das Drucken) printing; (Art des Drucks, Schriftart) print; (Druckwerk) copy. **das Buch ist im** ~ the book is being printed; **in** ~ **gehen** to go to press. **(b)** (Kunst~) print.

**Druck-:** ~**ausgleich** m pressure balance; ~**buchstabe** m printed character or letter; **in** ~**buchstaben schreiben** to print.

**Druckeberger** m **-** (pej col) shirker.

**Druckebergerei** f no pl (pej col) shirking.

**druck|empfindlich** adj sensitive (to pressure).

**drucken** vti (Typ, Tex) to print; siehe **gedruckt**.

**drücken 1** vt **(a)** Hand, Hebel to press; Knopf auch to push. **jdm etw in die Hand** ~ to press or slip sth into sb's hand; **jdn** ~ to squeeze sb; (umarmen) to hug sb; **jdn zur Seite** ~ to push sb aside. **(b)** (Schuhe, Korsett etc) to pinch, to nip. **mich drückt der Magen** my stomach feels heavy. **(c)** (verringern) Leistung, Niveau to lower; Steuern to bring down. **(d)** (Gewichtheben) to press. **(e)** (col) Heroin to shoot. **2** vi **(a)** to press; (Wetter, Hitze) to be oppressive;

*(Brille, Schuhe etc)* to pinch. **auf die Stimmung** ~ to dampen one's mood. **(b)** *(drängeln, stoßen)* to push. **(c)** *(col: Heroin injizieren)* to shoot. **3** *vr* **(a)** *(sich quetschen)* to squeeze. **sich aus dem Zimmer** ~ to slip out of the room. **(b)** *(col)* **sich vor etw** *(dat)* ~ to shirk sth; *(vor Militärdienst)* to dodge sth; **sich (um etw)** ~ to get out of (doing) sth.

**drückend** *adj* Last, Steuern heavy; *Sorgen* serious; *Armut* grinding; *Wetter, Hitze* oppressive, close. **es ist** ~ **heiß** it's oppressively hot.

**Drucker** *m* - printer.

**Drücker** *m* - *(Knopf)* (push) button; *(Türklinke)* handle; *(col: von Pistole etc)* trigger. **am** ~ **sein** *or* **sitzen** *(fig col)* to be the key person; **auf den letzten** ~ *(fig col)* at the last minute.

**Druckerei** *f* printing works *pl*, printery.

**Druckerin** *f* printer.

**Drucker-:** ~**presse** *f* printing press; ~**schwärze** *f* printer's ink.

**Druck-:** **d~fähig** *adj* printable; ~**fahne** *f* galley (proof); ~**fehler** *m* misprint; **d~fertig** *adj* ready to print; **d~fest** *adj* Werkstoff pressure-resistant; ~**knopf** *m (Sew)* press-stud *(Brit)*, snap fastener *(US)*; *(Tech)* push button; ~**kopf** *m (Comp)* print head; ~**legung** *f* printing; ~**luft** *f* compressed air; ~**luftbremse** *f* air-brake; ~**messer** *m* - pressure gauge; ~**mittel** *nt (fig)* form of pressure; ~**platte** *f* printing plate; ~**pumpe** *f* pressure pump; **d~reif** *adj* ready for printing, passed for press; *(fig)* polished; ~**sache** *f* printed matter; ~**schrift** *f* **(a)** *(Schriftart)* printed (hand)writing; **in** ~**schrift schreiben** to print; **(b)** *(gedrucktes Werk)* pamphlet.

**drucksen** *vi (col)* to hum and haw *(col)*.

**Druck-:** ~**stelle** *f (auf Obst, Haut)* bruise; ~**taste** *f* push button; ~**verband** *m (Med)* pressure bandage; ~**vorlage** *f* setting copy; *(kamerafertig)* camera-ready copy; ~**welle** *f* shock wave.

**drum** *adv (col)* siehe auch **darum** around. ~ **(he)rumreden** to beat about the bush; **da wirst du nicht** ~ **(he)rumkommen** there's no getting out of it; **sei's** ~! *(geh)* never mind; **das D~ und Dran** the paraphernalia; *(Begleiterscheinungen)* the fuss and bother; **mit allem D~ und Dran** with all the bits and pieces *(col)*; *(Mahlzeit)* with all the trimmings.

**Drumherum** *nt no pl* trappings *pl*.

**drunten** *adv (old, dial)* down there.

**drunter** *adv* siehe auch **darunter** under(neath). ~ **und drüber** upside down, topsy-turvy.

**Drüse** *f* **-n** gland.

**Drüsenfieber** *nt* glandular fever.

**DSB** [de:ɛs'be:] *m* = **Deutscher Sportbund** German Sports Association.

**Dschungel** *m* - *(lit, fig)* jungle.

**Dschungel-:** ~**fieber** *nt* yellow fever; ~**krieg** *m* jungle war/warfare.

**Dschunke** *f (Naut)* **-n** junk.

**DSD** [de:ɛs'de:] *nt* = **Duales System Deutschland** *German waste collection and recycling service.*

**DSG** [de:ɛs'ge:] *f* = **Deutsche Schlafwagen- und Speisewagen-Gesellschaft.**

**dt.** = **deutsch.**

**Dtzd.** = **Dutzend.**

**du** *pers pron (familiar form of address)* you. **D~** *(in Briefen)* you; **jdn mit** ~ **anreden** to say "du" to sb; **mit jdm auf** ~ **und** ~ **stehen** to be pally with sb; **mit jdm per** ~ **sein** to be on familiar terms with sb; ~ **bist es** it's you; ~, **ich muß jetzt aber gehen** listen, I have to go now; ~, ~! *(hum: drohend)* naughty, naughty.

**Du** *nt* **-(s)** **jdm das** ~ **anbieten** to suggest that sb uses "du" *or* the familiar form of address.

**Dualsystem** *nt (Math)* binary system.

**Dübel** *m* - plug; *(Holz~)* dowel.

**dübeln** *vti* to plug.

**dubios** *adj (geh)* dubious.

**Dublette** *f* **(a)** duplicate. **(b)** *(Boxen)* one-two.

**Dublin** ['dablɪn] *nt* Dublin.

**ducken 1** *vr* to duck; *(fig pej)* to cringe, to cower. **sich in eine Ecke** ~ to duck *or* dodge into a corner; *siehe* **geduckt. 2** *vi (fig pej)* to cower.

**Duckmäuser** *m* - *(pej)* wimp *(col)*.

**Duckmäusertum** *nt (pej)* spinelessness.

**dudeln** *vti (pej col)* to tootle. **das Radio dudelt schon den ganzen Tag** the (damn) radio's been playing all day.

**Dudelsack** *m* bagpipes *pl.*

**Dudelsack-:** ~**pfeifer**, ~**spieler** *m* (bag)piper.

**Duell** *nt* **-e** *(lit, fig)* duel *(um over)*.

**Duellant** [duɛ'lant] *m (wk)* dueller, duellist.

**duellieren\*** [duɛ'liːrən] *vr* to (fight a) duel.

**Duett** *nt* **-e** **(a)** *(Mus, fig)* duet. **(etw) im** ~ **singen** to sing (sth as) a duet. **(b)** *(fig col: Paar)* duo *(col)*.

**Duft** *m* **⁼e** (pleasant) smell, scent; *(von Blumen, Parfüm auch)* fragrance; *(von Essen)* smell, aroma.

**dufte** *adj, adv (dated col)* great *(col)*.

**duften** *vi* to smell *(nach of)*. **das duftet** that smells nice; **nicht** ~ *(Blume)* to have no scent.

**duftend** *adj attr* nice-smelling; *Parfüm, Blumen etc* fragrant.

**duftig** *adj* Kleid, Stoff light, gossamery.

**Duft-:** ~**marke** *f* scent mark; ~**note** *f (von Parfüm)* scent; ~**stoff** *m* scent; *(für Parfüm, Waschmittel etc)* fragrance; ~**wasser** *nt, pl* ~**wässer** toilet water; ~**wolke** *f (iro)* cloud of perfume.

**dulden** *vt* **(a)** *(zulassen)* to tolerate. **etw stillschweigend** ~ to connive at sth; **er ist hier nur geduldet** he's only here on sufferance. **(b)** *(geh: erdulden)* to suffer.

**duldsam** *adj* tolerant *(gegenüber of, jdm gegenüber towards sb)*.

**Duldsamkeit** *f* tolerance.

**Duldung** *f* toleration. **mit stillschweigender** ~ **der Behörden** with the (tacit) connivance of the authorities.

**dumm** *adj comp* **⁼er,** *superl* **⁼ste(r, s)** *or (adv)* **am ⁼sten** **(a)** stupid, dumb *(esp US)*; *Mensch auch* thick *(col)*; *(unklug, unvernünftig auch)* silly, foolish. **der** ~**e August** *(col)* the clown; ~**e Gans** silly goose; ~**es Zeug (reden)** (to talk) nonsense *or* rubbish; **ein** ~**es Gesicht machen,** ~ **gucken** to look stupid; **jdn wie einen** ~**en Jungen behandeln** *(col)* to treat sb like a child; **du willst mich wohl für** ~ **verkaufen** you must think I'm stupid; **ich lasse mich nicht für** ~ **verkaufen** I'm not stupid *(col)*; **sich** ~ **stellen** to act stupid; ~ **fragen** to ask a silly question/silly questions; ~ **dastehen** to look stupid; **der D~ sein** to be left to carry the can *(col)*; **sich** ~ **und dämlich reden** *(col)* to talk till one is blue in the face *(col)*; **sich** ~ **und dämlich verdienen** to earn the earth *(col)*; **jetzt wird's mir zu** ~ I've had enough. **(b)** *(ärgerlich)* annoying; *Gefühl* nasty; *Sache, Geschichte auch* silly. **es ist zu** ~, **daß er nicht kommen kann** it's too bad that he can't come; **jdm** ~ **kommen** to get funny with sb *(col)*; **so etwas D~es** how stupid; *(wie ärgerlich)* what a nuisance.

**dummdreist** *adj* insolent.

**Dummejungenstreich** *m* silly *or* childish prank.

**dummerweise** *adv* unfortunately.

**Dummheit** *f* **(a)** *no pl* stupidity; *(Unvernunft)* foolishness. **(b)** *(dumme Handlung)* stupid thing.

**Dummkopf** *m (col)* idiot, fool.

**dümmlich** *adj* silly, stupid.

**dumpf** adj (a) Geräusch, Ton muffled. ~ **aufschlagen** to land with a thud. (b) Geruch, Geschmack etc musty; (fig) Atmosphäre stifling. (c) Gefühl, Ahnung vague; Schmerz dull.

**Dumpfheit** f no pl siehe adj muffled nature; mustiness; stifling nature; dullness.

**Dumpingpreis** ['dampıŋ-] m give-away price.

**Düne** f -n (sand-)dune.

**Dung** m no pl dung, manure.

**Düngemittel** nt fertilizer.

**düngen 1** vt to fertilize. **2** vi im Garten ~ to put fertilizer on the garden.

**Dünger** m - fertilizer.

**Düngung** f (das Düngen) fertilizing.

**dunkel** adj (a) dark. im D~n in the dark; im Zimmer ~ **machen** (col) to darken the room; sich ~ **kleiden** to dress in dark colours. (b) (tief) Stimme, Ton deep. (c) (unbestimmt, unklar) vague. in dunkler Vorzeit in the dim and distant past; im ~n tappen (fig) to be in the dark. (d) (pej: zwielichtig) shady (col), dubious.

**Dunkel** nt no pl (lit, fig) darkness. im ~ der Nacht at dead of night.

**Dünkel** m no pl (pej geh) conceit, arrogance.

**dunkel-** in cpds dark; ~**blond** adj light brown; ~**haarig** adj dark-haired.

**dünkelhaft** adj (pej geh) arrogant, conceited.

**Dunkel-**: d~**häutig** adj dark-skinned; ~**heit** f (lit, fig) darkness; bei Einbruch der ~**heit** at nightfall; ~**kammer** f (Phot) darkroom; ~**mann** m, pl ~**männer** (pej) shady character.

**dunkeln** vi impers es dunkelt (geh) darkness is falling, it is growing dark.

**Dunkel-**: d~**rot** adj dark red, maroon; ~**ziffer** f estimated number of unreported/undetected cases.

**dünken** pret **dünkte** or (obs) **deuchte**, ptp **gedünkt** or (obs) **gedeucht** vti impers (old, geh) das dünkt mir gut zu sein it seems good to me.

**dünn** adj thin; Kaffee, Tee watery, weak; (fein) Schleier, Strümpfe fine; Besiedlung auch sparse. ~ **gesät** (fig) few and far between; sich ~ **machen** (hum) to squeeze up; siehe **dünnmachen**.

**Dünn-**: d~**besiedelt** adj attr sparsely populated; ~**darm** m small intestine; d~**flüssig** adj thin; Teig, Honig runny; d~**gesät** adj attr sparse; d~**häutig** adj (lit, fig) thin-skinned; d~**machen** vr sep (col) to make oneself scarce; ~**pfiff** (col), ~**schiß** (col) m the runs (col).

**Dunst** m ∹e mist, haze; (Dampf) steam; (Smog) smog; (Zigaretten~) fug; (Geruch) smell. **jdm blauen ~ vormachen** (col) to tell sb stories (col); **keinen (blassen) ~ von etw haben** to have not a clue or not the faintest idea about sth.

**Dunstabzugshaube** f extractor hood.

**dünsten** vt (Cook) to steam; Obst to stew.

**Dunstglocke** f haze; pall of smog.

**dunstig** adj hazy, misty; (verräuchert) smoky.

**Dunst-**: ~**kreis** m atmosphere; (von Mensch) sphere of influence; ~**schleier** m veil of mist; ~**wolke** f cloud of smog.

**Dünung** f (Naut) swell.

**Duo** nt -s duo.

**düpiert** adj duped.

**Duplikat** nt duplicate (copy).

**Dur** nt no pl (Mus) major. in G-~ in G major.

**durch 1** prep +acc (a) through. ~ **den Fluß waten** to wade across the river; ~ **die ganze Welt reisen** to travel all over the world. (b) (mittels) through, by (means of); (in Passivkonstruktion: von) by. **Tod ~ den Strang** death by hanging; **Tod ~ Herzschlag** death from a heart attack; ~ **die Post** by post; **etw**

~ **die Zeitung bekanntgeben** to announce sth in the press. (c) (aufgrund, infolge von) due to, owing to. **2** adv (a) (hin~) through. **die ganze Nacht** ~ all through the night, throughout the night; **es ist 4 Uhr** ~ it's past 4 o'clock; ~ **und** ~ **kennen** through and through; verlogen, überzeugt completely, utterly; ~ **und** ~ **naß** wet through; **das geht mir** ~ **und** ~ that goes right through me. (b) (Cook col) **(gut)** ~ well-done. **das Fleisch ist noch nicht** ~ the meat isn't done yet.

**durch|ackern** sep (col) **1** vt to plough through. **2** vr **sich durch etw** ~ to plough (one's way) through sth.

**durch|arbeiten** sep **1** vti to work through. **2** vr **sich durch etw** ~ to work (one's way) through sth.

**durch|atmen** vi sep to breathe deeply.

**durch|aus** adv (emph auch **durch|aus/**) (a) (unbedingt) **wenn du das** ~ **willst** if you insist, if you absolutely must; **das ist** ~ **nötig** that is absolutely necessary; **er will** ~ **recht haben** he (absolutely) insists that he is right. (b) (bekräftigend) quite; verständlich, richtig, möglich auch perfectly; gefallen really. **das läßt sich** ~ **machen** that sounds perfectly feasible; **ich bin** ~ **Ihrer Meinung** I quite or absolutely agree with you; **es ist** ~ **anzunehmen, daß sie kommt** it's highly likely that she'll be coming. (c) (in verneinten Sätzen) ~ **nicht** (als Verstärkung) by no means; (als Antwort) not at all; (stärker) absolutely not; **etw** ~ **nicht tun wollen** to refuse absolutely to do sth; **das ist** ~ **kein Witz** that's no joke at all; **er ist** ~ **kein schlechter Mensch** he is by no means a bad person.

**durchbacken** vt sep Kuchen to bake through.

**durchbeißen** sep irreg **1** vt to bite through. **2** vr (col) to struggle through (durch etw sth).

**durchblättern** vt sep Buch to leaf through.

**Durchblick** m vista (auf +acc of); (Ausblick) view (auf +acc of). **den** ~ **haben** (fig col) to know what's what (col).

**durchblicken** vi sep (a) (lit) to look through (durch etw sth). (b) (fig) **etw** ~ **lassen** to hint at sth. (c) (col: verstehen) to understand. **blickst du da durch?** do you get it? (col).

**durchbluten** vt insep to supply with blood.

**Durchblutung** f circulation (of blood) (gen to).

**durchbohren¹\*** vt insep to drill through; (mit Schwert) to run through; (Kugel) to go through. **jdn mit Blicken** ~ (fig) to look piercingly at sb.

**durchbohren²** sep **1** vt **etw durch etw** ~ Loch, Tunnel to drill sth through sth. **2** vr to bore (one's way) through (durch etw sth).

**durchbohrend** adj piercing.

**durchboxen** vr sep (fig col) to fight (one's way) through (durch etw sth).

**durchbraten** vti sep irreg to cook through. **durchgebraten** well done.

**durchbrechen¹** sep irreg **1** vt to break (in two). **2** vi aux sein (a) (in zwei Teile) to break (in two). (b) (Knospen) to appear; (Sonne auch) to break through (durch etw sth). (c) (Med: Blinddarm etc) to burst, to perforate.

**durchbrechen²\*** vt insep irreg to break; Mauer, Blockade etc to break through.

**durchbrennen** vi sep irreg aux sein (Sicherung etc) to blow; (col: davonlaufen) to run away. **jdm** ~ (col) to run away from sb.

**durchbringen** vt sep irreg (a) (durch etw sth) to get through; (durch Krankheit) to pull through; (für Unterhalt sorgen) to provide for. (b) Geld to get through.

**Durchbruch** m (a) (Mil, fig) breakthrough. **jdm/etw**

**zum** ~ **verhelfen** to help sb/sth on the road to success. **(b)** *(von Sonne)* breaking through *(durch etw sth)*; *(von Charakter)* revelation. **zum** ~ **kommen** *(fig: Charakter etc)* to show itself.

**durchdenken\*** *vt irreg insep* to think out *or* through. **gut durchdacht** well thought out.

**durchdrehen** *sep* **1** *vt Fleisch etc* to mince. **2** *vi* **(a)** *(Aut: Räder)* to spin. **(b)** *(col)* to go mad; *(nervlich)* to crack up *(col)*. **ganz durchgedreht sein** *(col)* to be wound up *(col) or (verwirrt)* confused.

**durchdringen¹** *vi sep irreg aux sein* **(a)** to penetrate *(durch etw sth)*; *(Sonne)* to come through *(durch etw sth)*. **bis zu jdm** ~ *(fig)* to get as far as sb. **(b)** *(sich verständlich machen)* **zu jdm** ~ to get through to sb.

**durchdringen²\*** *vt insep irreg Materie, Dunkelheit etc* to penetrate; *siehe* **durchdrungen**.

**durchdringend** *adj* piercing; *Kälte, Wind auch* biting; *Geruch* pungent.

**durchdrücken** *vt sep* **(a)** *(durch Presse)* to press through; *Creme, Teig* to pipe. **(b)** *(fig) Gesetz, Reformen etc* to push through; *seinen Willen* to get. **(c)** *Knie, Kreuz etc* to straighten.

**durchdrungen** *adj pred* imbued *(von* with*)*. **ganz von einer Idee** ~ **sein** to be taken with an idea.

**durchdürfen** *vi sep irreg (col)* to be allowed through. **darf ich mal durch?** can I get through?; **Sie dürfen hier nicht durch** you can't come through here.

**durch\einander 1** *adv* muddled up, in a muddle. **Gemüse** ~ vegetable stew; **alles** ~ **essen/trinken** to eat/drink indiscriminately. **2** *adj pred* ~ **sein** *(col) (Mensch)* to be confused *or (aufgeregt)* in a state *(col)*; *(Zimmer etc)* to be in a mess *or* muddle.

**Durch\einander** *nt no pl (Unordnung)* mess, muddle; *(Wirrwarr)* confusion.

**durch\einander-:** ~**bringen** *vt sep irreg* to muddle *or* mix up; *(verwirren) jdn* to confuse; ~**geraten\***, ~**kommen** *vi sep irreg aux sein* to get mixed *or* muddled up; ~**laufen** *vi sep irreg aux sein* to run about *or* around all over the place; ~**reden** *vi sep* to all talk at once; ~**werfen** *vt sep irreg* to muddle up.

**durchfahren¹** *vi sep irreg aux sein* **(a)** to go through *(durch etw sth)*. **(b)** *(nicht anhalten/umsteigen)* to go straight through. **er ist bei Rot durchgefahren** he jumped the lights; **die Nacht** ~ to travel through the night.

**durchfahren²\*** *vt insep irreg* to travel through; *(fig: Schreck etc)* to shoot through. **ein Gedanke durchfuhr ihn blitzartig** a (sudden) thought flashed through his mind.

**Durchfahrt** *f* way through. **auf der** ~ **sein** to be passing through; ~ **bitte freihalten!** please keep access free; ~ **verboten!** no through road.

**Durchfahrts-:** ~**straße** *f* through road; ~**verbot** *nt* **seit wann besteht hier** ~**verbot?** since when has this been a no through road?

**Durchfall** *m* **(a)** *(Med)* diarrhoea *no art (Brit)*, diarrhea *no art (US)*. **(b)** *(Mißerfolg)* failure.

**durchfallen** *vi sep irreg aux sein* **(a)** to fall through *(durch etw sth)*. **(b)** *(col: nicht bestehen)* to fail; *(Theaterstück auch)* to flop; *(Wahlkandidat)* to be defeated. **jdn** ~ **lassen** to fail sb; **beim Publikum** ~ to be a flop with the public.

**Durchfallquote** *f* failure rate.

**durchfeiern** *vi sep* to celebrate all night.

**durchfinden** *vir sep irreg (lit, fig)* to find one's way through *(durch etw sth)*. **ich finde (mich) hier nicht mehr durch** *(fig)* I am simply lost.

**durchfliegen¹** *vi sep irreg aux sein* **(a)** to fly through

*(durch etw sth)*; *(ohne Landung)* to fly non-stop *or* direct. **(b)** *(col: in Prüfung)* to fail *(durch etw, in etw (dat)* sth*)*.

**durchfliegen²\*** *vt insep irreg Luft, Wolken* to fly through; *Land* to fly over; *Strecke* to cover; *(flüchtig lesen)* to skim through.

**durchfließen\*** *vt insep irreg (lit, fig)* to flow through.

**Durchflug** *m* flight through. **Passagiere auf dem** ~ transit passengers.

**durchfluten\*** *vt insep (geh: Fluß)* to flow through; *(fig: Licht, Sonne)* to flood.

**durchforschen\*** *vt insep Gegend* to search; *Land, Fachgebiet* to explore; *Akten* to search through.

**durchforsten\*** *vt insep (fig) Akten* to go through.

**durchfragen** *vr sep* to ask one's way.

**durchfressen** *vr sep irreg (durch etw sth) (Säure etc, Tier)* to eat (its way) through. **sich (bei jdm)** ~ *(pej col)* to live on sb's hospitality.

**durchfroren** *adj* frozen stiff.

**Durchfuhr** *f* transit.

**durchführbar** *adj* practicable, feasible.

**Durchführbarkeit** *f* feasibility, practicability.

**durchführen** *sep* **1** *vt* **(a)** *(durchleiten) (durch etw sth) jdn* to take through; *Leitung* to run through. **(b)** *(verwirklichen)* to carry out; *Gesetz* to implement; *(unternehmen) Expedition* to undertake; *Messung* to take; *Kursus* to run; *Wahl, Prüfung* to hold. **2** *vi* **zwischen/unter etw** *(dat)* ~ *(Straße etc)* to go between/under sth.

**Durchführung** *f siehe vt* **(a)** taking through; running through. **(b)** carrying out; implementation; undertaking; taking; running; holding.

**durchfüttern** *vt sep (col)* to feed. **sich von jdm** ~ **lassen** to feed off sb.

**Durchgabe** *f* announcement; *(telefonisch)* message (over the telephone).

**Durchgang** *m* **(a)** passage. **(b)** *(das Durchgehen)* ~ **verboten!** no right of way; **beim** ~ **durch das Tal** going through the valley. **(c)** *(von Wahl, Sport)* round; *(beim Rennen)* heat.

**durchgängig** *adj* universal, general.

**Durchgangs-:** ~**handel** *m* transit trade; ~**lager** *nt* transit camp; ~**stadium** *nt* transition stage; ~**straße** *f* through road; ~**verkehr** *m* through traffic; *(Transitverkehr)* transit traffic.

**durchgeben** *vt sep irreg (Rad, TV) Hinweis, Wetter* to give; *Nachricht, Lottozahlen* to announce. **jdm etw telefonisch** ~ to telephone etw to sb; **es wurde im Radio durchgegeben** it was announced on the radio.

**durchgefroren** *adj Mensch* frozen stiff.

**durchgehen** *sep irreg aux sein* **1** *vi* **(a)** to go through *(durch etw sth)*. **(b)** *(toleriert werden)* **jdm etw** ~ **lassen** to let sb get away with sth; **das lasse ich nochmal** ~ I'll let it pass. **(c)** *(gehalten werden für)* **für etw** ~ to pass for sth, to be taken for sth. **(d)** *(ohne Unterbrechung)* to go straight through; *(Flug, Zug)* to be direct. **(e)** *(Pferd)* to bolt. **seine Frau ist ihm durchgegangen** his wife has run off and left him; **mit etw** ~ to run *or* make off with sth. **(f)** *(außer Kontrolle geraten)* **mit jdm** ~ *(Temperament)* to get the better of sb. **2** *vt (durchsprechen etc)* to go *or* run through.

**durchgehend 1** *adj Öffnungszeiten* round-the-clock *attr*, continuous; *Straße* straight; *Verkehrsverbindung* direct; *Zug, Fahrkarte* through *attr*. **2** *adv* throughout, right through. ~ **geöffnet** open right through; open 24 hours.

**durchgeschwitzt** *adj* soaked in sweat.

**durchgreifen** *vi sep irreg* to reach through *(durch etw sth)*; *(fig)* to take (strong) action.

**durchgucken** vi sep (Mensch) to look through (durch etw sth).

**durchhaben** vt sep irreg (col) **etw ~** to have got sth through (durch etw sth); (durchgelesen etc haben) to have got through sth.

**durchhalten** sep irreg **1** vt Zeit, Kampf etc to survive; Streik to see through; Belastung to stand; (Sport) Tempo to keep up. **das Rennen ~** to stay the course. **2** vi to hold out.

**Durchhalte-:** **~parole** f rallying call (to hold out at all costs); **~vermögen** nt staying power.

**durchhängen** vi sep irreg (lit, fig) to sag.

**durchhauen** vt sep to chop in two; (spalten) to split. **jdn ~** (col) to give sb a walloping (col).

**durchhecheln** vt sep (col) to gossip about.

**durchhelfen** vi sep irreg **jdm (durch etw) ~** to help sb through (sth).

**durchhungern** vr sep to scrape by.

**durchkämmen** vt sep (a) Haare to comb out. (b) (auch **durchkämmen*** insep) (absuchen) to comb (through).

**durchkämpfen** sep **1** vt to push through. **2** vr to battle one's way through (durch etw sth).

**durchkauen** vt sep Essen to chew (thoroughly); (col: besprechen) to go over or through.

**durchklingen** vi sep irreg aux haben or sein (durch etw sth) to sound through; (fig) to come through. **etw ~ lassen** to hint at sth.

**durchkommen** vi sep irreg aux sein (durch etw sth) to come through; (durchgelangen, telefonisch, in Prüfung) to get through; (Patient) to pull through; (finanziell) to get by; (im Radio) to be announced. **mit etw ~** (mit Forderungen) to succeed with sth; (mit Betrug) to get away with sth; **er kam mit seiner Stimme nicht durch** he couldn't make his voice heard; **damit kommt er bei mir nicht durch** he won't get away with that with me.

**durchkönnen** vi sep irreg (col) to be able to get through (durch etw sth).

**durchkreuzen*** vt insep (a) Wüste, Ozean to cross. (b) (fig) Pläne etc to thwart.

**durchladen** vi sep irreg Gewehr to reload.

**Durchlaß** m, pl **Durchlässe** (Durchgang) passage, way through; (für Wasser) duct.

**durchlassen** vt sep irreg (durch etw sth) to let through; (eindringen lassen) to let in.

**durchlässig** adj Material permeable; Zelt, Schuh leaky; Grenze open. **eine ~e Stelle** (lit, fig) a leak.

**Durchlässigkeit** f permeability.

**Durchlaucht** f -en (Euer) **~** Your Highness.

**Durchlauf** m (a) (das Durchlaufen) flow. (b) (Comp) run. (c) (Sport) heat.

**durchlaufen[1]** sep irreg **1** vt Schuhe to go through, to wear out. **2** vi aux sein (durch etw sth) to go through; (Flüssigkeit auch) to run through; (Kaffee) to filter.

**durchlaufen[2]*** vt insep irreg Gebiet to run through; Strecke to cover, to run; (Astron) Bahn to describe; Schule, Phase to go through.

**Durchlauf-:** **~erhitzer** m - continuous-flow water heater; **~zeit** f (Comp) length of a/the run.

**durchleben*** vt insep to experience; Jugend to have.

**durchlesen** vt sep irreg to read through. **sich (dat) etw ~** to read sth through.

**durchleuchten*** vt insep to X-ray; (fig) Sache to investigate. **sich ~ lassen** to have an X-ray.

**Durchleuchtung** f (Med) X-ray examination; (fig: von Angelegenheit etc) investigation.

**durchliegen** vt sep irreg Matratze to wear down (in the middle).

**durchlöchern*** vt insep to make holes in; (fig) to undermine completely. **(mit Schüssen) ~** to riddle with bullets.

**durchlüften** vti sep to air thoroughly.

**durchmachen** sep **1** vt (erdulden, durchlaufen) to go through; Krankheit to have; Lehre to serve; (fig) Entwicklung to undergo. **er hat viel durchgemacht** he has been or gone through a lot; **eine ganze Nacht ~** (col: durchfeiern) to make a night of it. **2** vi (col) (durcharbeiten) to work right through; (durchfeiern) to keep going all night/day etc.

**Durchmarsch** m der **~ durch die Stadt** the march through the town.

**durchmarschieren*** vi sep aux sein to march through (durch etw sth).

**Durchmesser** m - diameter. **120 cm im ~** 120 cm in diameter.

**durchmischen** vt sep to mix thoroughly.

**durchmogeln** vr sep (col) to wangle (col) or fiddle (col) one's way through.

**durchmüssen** vi sep irreg (col) (durch etw sth) to have to get through; (durch Unangenehmes) to have to go through with. **da mußt du eben durch** (fig) you'll just have to see it through.

**durchnässen*** vt insep to soak, to drench. **völlig durchnäßt** wet through, drenched.

**durchnehmen** vt sep irreg (Sch) to do.

**durchnumerieren*** vt sep to number consecutively.

**durch|organisieren*** vt sep to organize down to the last detail.

**durchpauken** vt sep (col) (a) Lernstoff to swot up (col). (b) Gesetz, Schüler to push through.

**durchpausen** vt sep to trace.

**durchpeitschen** vt sep to flog; (fig) to rush through.

**durchpressen** vt sep to press through.

**durchprobieren** vt sep to try one after the other.

**durchprügeln** vt sep to thrash, to beat.

**durchqueren*** vt insep to cross.

**durchrasen** vi sep aux sein, **durchrasen*** vt insep to race or tear through.

**durchrechnen** vt sep to calculate.

**durchregnen** vi sep impers **es regnet durchs Dach durch** the rain is coming through the roof; **es hat die Nacht durchgeregnet** it rained all through the night.

**Durchreiche** f -n (serving) hatch (Brit), passthrough (US).

**durchreichen** vt sep to pass through (durch etw sth).

**Durchreise** f journey through. **auf der ~ sein** to be passing through.

**durchreisen** vi sep aux sein, **durchreisen*** vt insep to travel through.

**Durchreisende(r)** mf decl as adj traveller (passing through), transient (US).

**Durchreisevisum** nt transit visa.

**durchreißen** vti sep irreg (vi: aux sein) to tear in two.

**durchringen** vr sep irreg **sich dazu ~, etw zu tun** to bring or force oneself to do sth.

**durchrosten** vi sep aux sein to rust through.

**durchrufen** vi sep irreg (col) to ring (bei jdm sb).

**durchrühren** vt sep to mix thoroughly.

**durchrutschen** vi sep aux sein (lit) to slip through (durch etw sth).

**durchs** = **durch das**.

**Durchsage** f announcement. **eine ~ der Polizei** a police announcement.

**durchsagen** vt sep = **durchgeben**.

**durchsägen** *vt sep* to saw through.

**Durchsatz** *m (Ind, Comp)* throughput.

**durchsausen** *vi sep aux sein (col)* **(a)** to rush through. **(b)** *(col: nicht bestehen)* to fail, to flunk *(col) (durch etw, in etw (dat))* (in) sth/.

**durchschaubar** *adj (fig) Plan, Ereignisse* clear; *Lüge* transparent. **eine leicht ~e Lüge** a lie that is easy to see through; **schwer ~er Charakter** inscrutable character.

**durchschauen**[1]* *vt insep Absichten, Lüge, jdn* to see through; *(begreifen)* to understand. **du bist durchschaut!** you've been found out.

**durchschauen²** *vti sep* = **durchsehen**.

**durchscheinen** *vi sep irreg (durch etw* sth/ *(lit, fig)* to shine through; *(Farbe)* to show through.

**durchscheinend** *adj* transparent.

**durchscheuern** *vt sep* to wear through. **sich** *(dat)* **die Haut ~** to graze one's skin.

**durchschieben** *vt sep irreg* to push *or* shove *(col)* through *(durch etw* sth/.

**durchschießen**[1] *vi sep irreg* **durch etw ~** to shoot through sth.

**durchschießen²*** *vt insep irreg (lit, fig)* to shoot through. **ein Gedanke durchschoß mich** a thought flashed through my mind.

**durchschimmern** *vi sep (durch etw* sth/ to shimmer through; *(Farbe, fig)* to show through.

**durchschlafen** *vi sep irreg* to sleep through.

**Durchschlag** *m* **(a)** *(Kopie)* carbon (copy). **(b)** *(Küchengerät)* sieve, strainer.

**durchschlagen**[1] *sep irreg* **1** *vt etw ~ (entzweischlagen)* to chop through sth; *(Cook)* to sieve sth. **2** *vi* **(a)** *aux sein (durchkommen) (durch etw* sth/ to come through; *(fig: Charakter, Eigenschaft)* to show through. **bei ihm schlägt der Vater durch** you can see his father in him. **(b)** *aux sein (Wirkung haben)* to catch on. **auf etw** *(acc)* **~** to make one's/its mark on sth; **auf jdn ~** to rub off on sb. **(c)** *aux sein (Sicherung)* to blow, to go. **3** *vr* to fight through; *(im Leben)* to struggle through *or* along.

**durchschlagen²*** *vt insep irreg* to blast a hole in.

**durchschlagend** *adj Sieg* sweeping; *Erfolg* tremendous; *Beweis* decisive, conclusive. **eine ~e Wirkung haben** to be totally effective.

**Durchschlagpapier** *nt* copy paper, flimsy; *(Kohlepapier)* carbon paper.

**Durchschlagskraft** *f (von Geschoß)* penetration; *(fig: von Argument)* decisiveness.

**durchschlängeln** *vr sep (durch etw* sth/ *(Fluß)* to wind (its way) through, to meander through; *(Mensch)* to thread one's way through; *(fig)* to manoeuvre *(Brit)* or maneuver *(US)* one's way through.

**durchschleusen** *vt sep* **(a)** **ein Schiff ~** to pass a ship through a lock. **(b)** *(fig: durch schmale Stelle)* to guide through *(durch etw* sth/.

**Durchschlupf** *m, pl* **Durchschlüpfe** way through.

**durchschlüpfen** *vi sep aux sein* to slip through *(durch etw* sth/.

**durchschmecken** *vt sep* to taste. **man kann den Essig ~** the taste of vinegar comes through.

**durchschneiden**[1] *vt sep irreg* to cut in two.

**durchschneiden²*** *vt insep irreg* to cut through; *(Schiff) Wellen* to plough through. **jdm die Kehle ~** to cut *or* slit sb's throat.

**Durchschnitt** *m* average; *(in Statistik)* mean. **der ~** *(normale Menschen)* the average person; *(die Mehrheit)* the majority; **im ~** on average; **im ~ 100 km/h fahren** to average 62 mph; **über/unter dem ~** above/below average; **guter ~ sein** to be a good average.

**durchschnittlich** **1** *adj* average; *Wert auch* mean

**attr. 2** *adv (im Durchschnitt) verdienen, essen etc* on average. **~ begabt/groß** of average ability/height; **die Mannschaft hat sehr ~ gespielt** the team played a very average game.

**Durchschnitts-** *in cpds* average; **~alter** *nt* average age; **~geschwindigkeit** *f* average speed; **~gesicht** *nt* ordinary *or* nondescript *(pej)* face; **~mensch** *m* average person; **~wert** *m* average *or* mean *(Math)* value.

**durchschreiben** *vt sep irreg* to make a (carbon) copy of.

**durchschreiten*** *vt insep irreg (geh)* to stride through.

**Durchschrift** *f* (carbon) copy.

**Durchschuß** *m* **(a)** *(Loch)* bullet hole. **ein ~ durch den Darm** a gunshot wound right through the intestine. **(b)** *(Typ)* leading.

**durchschütteln** *vt sep Mischung* to shake thoroughly; *(in Auto, Bus etc) jdn* to shake about.

**durchschwimmen**[1] *vi sep irreg aux sein* to swim through.

**durchschwimmen²** *vt insep irreg Fluß* to swim across; *Ärmelkanal* to swim.

**durchschwitzen** *vt sep* to soak with sweat.

**durchsegeln**[1] *vi sep aux sein* **(a)** *(Schiff)* to sail through *(durch etw* sth/. **(b)** *(col: nicht bestehen)* to fail, to flunk *(col) (durch etw, bei etw* sth/.

**durchsegeln²*** *vt insep Meer* to sail across.

**durchsehen** *sep irreg* **1** *vi* **(a)** *(hindurchschauen)* to look through *(durch etw* sth/. **ein Stoff, durch den man ~ kann** see-through material. **(b)** *(col: verstehen)* = **durchblicken (c)**. **2** *vt (überprüfen) etw ~** to have a look through sth *(auf +acc* for/.

**durchsein** *vi sep irreg aux sein (col)* to be through *(durch etw* sth/; *(vorbeigekommen sein)* to have gone; *(Cook: Steak, Gemüse)* to be done.

**durchsetzen**[1] *sep* **1** *vt Maßnahmen* to put through; *Forderung* to push through; *Vorschlag, Plan* to carry through; *Ziel* to achieve. **etw bei jdm ~** to get sb to agree to sth; **seinen Willen (bei jdm) ~** to get one's (own) way (with sb). **2** *vr* **(a)** *(Mensch)* to assert oneself *(bei jdm* with sb/; *(Partei etc)* to be successful. **sich gegen etw ~** to win through against sth; **sich mit etw ~** to be successful with sth; **sich im Leben ~** to make a success of one's life. **(b)** *(Idee, Neuheit)* to be accepted, to catch on.

**durchsetzen²*** *vt insep* **mit etw durchsetzt** interspersed with sth; **mit subversiven Elementen durchsetzt** infiltrated by subversive elements.

**Durchsetzung** *f siehe* **durchsetzen**[1] **1** putting through; pushing through; carrying through; achievement.

**Durchsetzungsvermögen** *nt* self-assertion.

**durchseuchen*** *vt insep (Gebiet)* to infect completely.

**Durchsicht** *f* examination, inspection. **jdm etw zur ~ geben** to give sb sth to check through; **bei ~ der Bücher** on checking the books.

**durchsichtig** *adj (lit, fig)* transparent.

**Durchsichtigkeit** *f no pl (lit, fig)* transparency.

**durchsickern** *vi sep aux sein (lit, fig)* to trickle through; *(fig: trotz Geheimhaltung)* to leak out. **Informationen ~ lassen** to leak information.

**durchsieben**[1] *vt sep* to sieve, to sift; *(fig) Bewerber etc* to sift through.

**durchsieben²*** *vt insep (col)* **von Kugeln durchsiebt** riddled with bullets.

**durchsitzen** *vt sep irreg Sessel etc* to wear out (the seat of).

**durchspielen** *vt sep* to go *or* run through.

**durchsprechen** *vt sep irreg Problem, Möglichkeiten**

to talk over *or* through.

**durchspülen** *vt sep* to rinse (out) thoroughly.

**durchstarten** *vi sep (Aviat)* to abort a landing manoeuvre *(Brit) or* maneuver *(US) (and start climbing again)*; *(Aut)* to accelerate off again; *(beim Anfahren)* to rev up.

**durchstechen**[1] *sep irreg* **1** *vt Nadel, Spieß* to stick through *(durch etw sth)*. **2** *vi* to pierce.

**durchstechen**[2*] *vt insep irreg* to pierce; *(mit Degen etc)* to run through; *(mit Nadel)* to prick.

**durchstecken** *vt sep* to put *or* stick *(col)* through *(durch etw sth)*.

**durchstehen** *vt sep irreg Zeit, Prüfung, Situation* to get through; *Krankheit* to get over; *Tempo, Qualen* to stand; *Abenteuer* to have.

**Durchstehvermögen** *nt* staying power.

**durchsteigen** *vi sep irreg aux sein* **(a)** to climb through *(durch etw sth)*. **(b)** *(col: verstehen)* = **durchblicken (c)**.

**durchstellen** *vt sep (Telec)* to put through. **ich stelle durch** I'll put you through.

**durchstöbern*** *insep*, **durchstöbern** *sep vt* to hunt *or* rummage through *(nach for)*; *(durchwühlen)* to ransack *(nach looking for)*.

**Durchstoß** *m* breakthrough.

**durchstoßen**[1*] *vt insep irreg* to break through.

**durchstoßen**[2] *vti sep irreg (vi: aux sein)* to break through *(auch Mil)*. **etw (durch etw)** ~ to push sth through (sth).

**durchstreichen** *vt sep irreg* to cross out.

**durchstreifen*** *vt insep (geh)* to roam through.

**durchströmen*** *vt insep (lit, fig)* to flow through.

**durchstylen** [-stailən] *vt sep* to give a consistent style to. **durchgestylt** with a consistent style.

**durchsuchen*** *vt insep (nach for)* to search (through); *jdn* to search, to frisk.

**Durchsuchung** *f* search *(auf +dat for)*.

**Durchsuchungsbefehl** *m* search warrant.

**durchtrainieren*** *vt sep Sportler, Körper* to get fit. **(gut) durchtrainiert** in superb condition.

**durchtränken*** *vt insep* to soak, to saturate.

**durchtrennen** *sep*, **durchtrennen*** *insep vt (schneiden)* to cut (through); *Nerv, Sehne* to sever.

**durchtreten** *sep irreg* **1** *vt* **(a)** *Pedal* to step on; *Starter* to kick. **(b)** *(abnutzen) Schuh, Sohle* to go *or* wear through. **2** *vi aux sein (durchsickern)* to come through *(durch etw sth)*. **bitte weiter** ~ *(form: weitergehen)* pass along please.

**durchtrieben** *adj* cunning, sly.

**Durchtriebenheit** *f no pl* cunning, slyness.

**durchwachen*** *vt insep* **die Nacht** ~ to stay awake all through the night.

**durchwachsen** *adj* **(a)** *(lit) Speck* streaky; *Fleisch, Schinken* with fat running through it. **(b)** *pred (hum col: mittelmäßig)* so-so *(col)*.

**Durchwahl** *f (Telec)* direct dialling; *(Anschluß)* direct dialling number.

**durchwählen** *vi sep (Telec)* to dial direct. **nach London** ~ to dial London direct.

**Durchwahlnummer** *f* dialling code *(Brit)*, dial code *(US)*; *(Anschluß)* direct dialling number.

**durchwandern*** *vt insep Gegend* to walk through; *(hum) Zimmer, Straßen etc* to wander through.

**durchwaschen** *vt sep irreg* to wash through.

**durchweben*** *vt insep irreg* to interweave *(mit, von with)*.

**durchweg** *adv* without exception. ~ **gut** good in every way.

**durchweichen** *sep* **1** *vi aux sein* to get wet through; *(weich werden: Karton, Boden)* to go soggy. **2** *vt* to soak; *Boden, Karton* to make soggy.

**durchwetzen** *vtr sep* to wear through.

**durchwinden** *vr sep irreg* = **durchschlängeln**.

**durchwühlen** *sep*, **durchwühlen*** *insep vt* to rummage through *(nach for)*; *Zimmer auch* to ransack *(nach looking for)*.

**durchwursteln** *vr sep (col)* to muddle through.

**durchzählen** *vt sep* to count.

**durchzechen**[1] *vi sep* to carry on drinking.

**durchzechen**[2*] *vt insep* **die Nacht** ~ to spend the night drinking; **eine durchzechte Nacht** a night of drinking.

**durchziehen**[1] *sep irreg* **1** *vt* **(a)** to pull through *(durch etw sth)*. **(b)** *(col: erledigen)* **etw** ~ to get sth through. **2** *vi aux sein* **(a)** *(durchkommen)* to pass through *(durch etw sth)*. **(b)** *(Cook)* to soak. **3** *vr* to run through *(durch etw sth)*.

**durchziehen**[2*] *vt insep irreg (durchwandern)* to pass through, to go/come through; *(Straße, Fluß, fig: Thema)* to run through; *(Geruch)* to fill, to pervade.

**durchzucken*** *vt insep (Blitz)* to flash across; *(fig: Gedanke)* to flash through.

**Durchzug** *m* **(a)** *no pl (Luftzug)* draught *(Brit)*, draft *(US)*. **(b)** *(durch ein Gebiet)* passage; *(von Truppen)* march through.

**durchzwängen** *sep (durch etw sth)* **1** *vt* to force *or* squeeze through. **2** *vr* to force one's way through, to squeeze (one's way) through.

**dürfen** *pret* **durfte**, *ptp* **gedurft** *or (modal aux)* **dürfen** *vi* **(a)** *(Erlaubnis haben)* **etw tun** ~ to be allowed to do sth, to be permitted to do sth; **darf ich?** — **ja, Sie** ~ may I? — yes, you may; **darf ich ins Kino?** may I go to the cinema?

**(b)** *(verneint)* **man darf etw nicht (tun)** *(sollte, muß nicht)* one must not *or* mustn't do sth; *(hat keine Erlaubnis)* one isn't allowed to do sth, one may not do sth; **er durfte das nicht** he wasn't allowed to; **hier darf man nicht rauchen** smoking is prohibited here; **du darfst ihm das nicht übelnehmen** you must not hold it against him; **das darf doch nicht wahr sein!** that can't be true!; **da darf er sich nicht wundern** that shouldn't surprise him.

**(c)** *(in Höflichkeitsformeln)* **Ruhe, wenn ich bitten darf!** quiet, (if you) please!; **darf ich Sie bitten, das zu tun?** may *or* could I ask you to do that?; **was darf es sein?** can I help you?; **dürfte ich bitte Ihren Paß sehen** may *or* might I see your passport, please.

**(d)** *(Veranlassung haben, können)* **wir freuen uns, Ihnen mitteilen zu** ~ we are pleased to be able to tell you; **man darf doch wohl fragen** one can *or* may ask, surely?; **das** ~ **Sie mir glauben** you can *or* may take my word for it.

**(e)** **das dürfte ...** *(als Annahme)* that must ...; *(sollte)* that should ...; *(ought to ...)*; *(könnte)* that could ...; **das dürfte wohl das Beste sein** that is probably the best thing.

**dürftig** *adj* **(a)** *(ärmlich)* wretched, miserable; *Bekleidung* poor. **(b)** *(pej: unzureichend)* miserable, pathetic *(col)*; *Kenntnisse* scanty; *Ausrede auch* feeble; *Ersatz* poor *attr*.

**dürr** *adj* **(a)** dry; *Boden* arid, barren; *Ast, Strauch* withered. **(b)** *(pej: mager)* scrawny, scraggy.

**Dürre** *f* **-n** **(a)** *(Zeit der* ~*)* drought. **(b)** *no pl (Trockensein)* dryness; *(von Boden)* aridity.

**Dürre-:** ~**jahr** *nt* year of drought; ~**katastrophe** *f* drought disaster; ~**periode** *f* drought.

**Durst** *m no pl (lit, fig)* thirst *(nach for)*. ~ **haben** to be thirsty; ~ **bekommen** to get thirsty; **den** ~ **löschen** to quench one's thirst; **einen über den** ~ **getrunken haben** *(col)* to have had one too many.

**dursten** *vi (geh)* to be thirsty, to thirst *(liter)*.

**dürsten 1** *vt impers (liter)* **mich dürstet** I thirst *(liter)*; **es dürstet ihn nach Rache** he is thirsting for revenge. **2** *vi (fig)* to thirst *(nach for)*.
**durstig** *adj* thirsty. **diese Arbeit macht ~** this is thirsty work *(col)*, this work makes you thirsty.
**Durst-: d~löschend, d~stillend** *adj* thirst-quenching; **~strecke** *f* hard times *pl*.
**Durtonleiter** *f* major scale.
**Duschbad** *nt* shower(-bath); *(Gel)* shower gel.
**Dusche** *f* **-n** shower. **unter der ~ sein** to be in the shower; **unter die ~ gehen, eine ~ nehmen** to have *or* take a shower; **das war eine kalte ~** *(fig)* that really brought him/her *etc* down to earth with a bump.
**duschen** *vir* to have *or* take a shower, to shower. **(sich) kalt ~** to have *or* take a cold shower.
**Dusch-: ~gel** *nt* shower gel; **~gelegenheit** *f* shower facilities *pl*; **~kabine** *f* shower (cubicle); **~raum** *m* shower room, showers *pl*; **~vorhang** *m* shower curtain.
**Düse** *f* **-n** nozzle; *(Mech auch)* jet.
**Dusel** *m no pl (col)* **(a)** *(Glück)* luck. **da hat er (einen) ~ gehabt** he was lucky. **(b)** *(Trancezustand)* daze, dream; *(durch Alkohol)* fuddle.
**duselig** *adj (schlaftrunken)* drowsy; *(benommen)* dizzy; *(esp durch Alkohol)* befuddled.
**düsen** *vi aux sein (col)* to dash.
**Düsen-: ~antrieb** *m* jet propulsion; **~bomber** *m* jet bomber; **~flugzeug** *nt* jet aircraft, jet; **d~getrieben** *adj* jet-propelled; **~jäger** *m (Mil)* jet fighter; **~triebwerk** *nt* jet power-unit.
**Dussel** *m* - *(col)* twit *(Brit col)*, twerp *(col)*.
**dusselig, dußlig** *adj (col)* stupid.

**Dusseligkeit, Dußligkeit** *f (col)* stupidity.
**düster** *adj* gloomy; *Bild, Gedanken* sombre *(Brit)*, somber *(US)*, dismal; *(unheimlich) Gestalten* sinister.
**Düsterkeit** *f* gloominess; *(Dunkelheit)* gloom, dark(ness).
**Dutt** *m* **-s** *or* **-e** *(dial)* bun.
**Dutzend** *nt* **-e** dozen. **ein halbes ~** half-a-dozen, a half-dozen; **zwei/drei ~** two/three dozen; **~e** *pl (col)* dozens *pl*.
**Dutzend-: d~mal** *adv (col)* **(ein) d~mal** dozens of times; **~ware** *f (pej)* (cheap) mass-produced item; **d~weise** *adv* in dozens, by the dozen.
**duzen** *vt* **jdn/sich ~** to use the familiar form (of address) to sb/each other; **wir ~ uns** we call one another "du".
**Duzfreund** *m* close friend *(whom one addresses as "du")*.
**DV** [deː'fau] *f* = **Datenverarbeitung** DP.
**Dynamik** *f no pl* **(a)** *(Phys)* dynamics. **(b)** *(fig)* dynamism.
**dynamisch** *adj (Phys, fig)* dynamic; *Renten* ≈ index-linked.
**Dynamit** *nt no pl (lit, fig)* dynamite.
**Dynamo** *m* **-s** dynamo.
**Dynastie** *f* dynasty.
**dz** = **Doppelzentner**.
**dz.** = **derzeit**.
**D-Zug** ['deːtsuːk] *m* fast train; *(hält nur in großen Städten)* through train. **ein alter Mann ist doch kein ~** *(col)* I am going as fast as I can.
**D-Zug-Tempo** *nt (col)* fantastic speed *(col)*. **im ~** like greased lightning *(col)*.

# E

**E, e** [eː] *nt* -, - E, e. **E wie Emil** ≈ E for Edward, E for Easy *(US)*.

**E** = (a) **Europastraße. (b) Eilzug.**

**Ebbe** *f* -n (a) ebb tide; *(Niedrigwasser)* low tide. ~ **und Flut** ebb and flow; **bei** ~ **baden** to swim when the tide is going out; *(bei Niedrigwasser)* to swim at low tide; **es ist** ~ the tide is going out; *(es ist Niedrigwasser)* it's low tide, the tide is out. (b) *(fig)* **in meinem Geldbeutel ist** ~ my finances are at a pretty low ebb at the moment.

**eben 1** *adj (glatt)* smooth; *(gleichmäßig)* even; *(gleich hoch)* level; *(flach)* flat. **zu** ~**er Erde** at ground level. **2** *adv* (a) just. **mein Bleistift war doch** ~ **noch da** my pencil was there (just) a minute ago; **ich gehe** ~ **zur Bank** I'll just go to the bank; **das reicht so** *or* **nur** ~ **aus** it's only just enough. (b) **das ist** ~ **so** that's just the way it is; **dann bleibst du** ~ **zu Hause** then you'll just have to stay at home. (c) *(gerade or genau das)* exactly, precisely. **das ist es ja** ~! that's just *or* precisely it!; **nicht** ~ **billig** not exactly cheap.

**Ebenbild** *nt* image. **das genaue** ~ **seines Vaters** the spitting image of his father.

**ebenbürtig** *adj (gleichwertig)* equal; *Gegner* evenly matched. **jdm an Kraft** ~ **sein** to be sb's equal in strength.

**eben-:** ~**da** *adv (gerade dort)* ~**da will auch ich hin** that is exactly where I am going too; ~**darum** *adv* for that very reason; ~**der,** ~**die,** ~**das** *pron* he; she; it; ~**deshalb,** ~**deswegen** *adv* that is exactly why; ~**diese(r, s)** *adj* this very.

**Ebene** *f* -n plain; *(Hoch~)* plateau; *(Math, Phys)* plane; *(fig)* level. **auf höchster/der gleichen** ~ *(fig)* at the highest/the same level.

**eben-:** ~**erdig** *adj* at ground level; ~**falls** *adv* as well, likewise; **er hat** ~**falls nichts davon gewußt** he knew nothing about it either.

**Ebenholz** *nt* ebony.

**Ebenmaß** *nt (von Gestalt etc)* perfect proportions *pl*; *(von Versen)* even flow.

**ebenmäßig** *adj Gestalt etc* perfectly proportioned; *Verse* evenly flowing.

**ebenso** *adv (genauso)* just as; *(auch, ebenfalls)* as well. **das kann doch** ~ **eine Frau machen** a woman can do that just as well; **er hat ein** ~ **großes Zimmer wie wir** he has just as big a room as we have.

**ebenso-:** ~**gern** *adv* **ich mag sie** ~**gern** I like her just as much; **ich komme** ~**gern morgen** I'd just as soon come tomorrow; ~**gut** *adv* (just) as well; ~**lang(e)** *adv* just as long; ~**oft** *adv* just as often; ~**sehr** *adv* just as much; ~**viel** *adv* just as much; ~**wenig** *adv* just as little.

**Eber** *m* - boar.

**Eberesche** *f* rowan, mountain ash.

**ebnen** *vt* to level (off), to make level. **jdm den Weg** ~ *(fig)* to smooth the way for sb.

**EC** [eːʔtseː] *m* -, -s *(Rail)* = **Eurocity-Zug** European Intercity train.

**Echo** *nt* -s echo; *(fig)* response *(auf +acc to)*. **ein lebhaftes** ~ **finden** *(fig)* to meet with a lively response *(bei from)*.

**Echolot** *nt (Naut)* echo-sounder, sonar; *(Aviat)* sonic altimeter.

**Echse** [ˈɛksə] *f* -n *(Zool)* lizard.

**echt 1** *adj, adv* (a) real, genuine; *Haar, Perlen, Gold* real; *Unterschrift, Geldschein, Gemälde* genuine. (b) *(typisch)* typical. **ein** ~**er Bayer** a real *or* typical Bavarian; ~ **englisch** typically English. **2** *adv (col)* really. **ich hab'** ~ **keine Zeit** I really don't have any time.

**Echtheit** *f* genuineness; *(von Unterschrift, Dokument auch)* authenticity.

**Echtzeit** *f (Comp)* real time.

**Eck** *nt* -e (a) *(esp Aus, S Ger)* = **Ecke.** (b) **über** ~ diagonally across *or* opposite.

**Eck-** *in cpds* corner; ~**ball** *m (Sport)* corner; ~**bank** *f* corner seat.

**Ecke** *f* -n (a) corner *(auch Sport)*; *(Kante)* edge; *(von Kragen)* point. **Kantstraße** ~ **Goethestraße** at the corner of Kantstraße and Goethestraße; **gleich um die** ~ just around the corner; **jdn in die** ~ **drängen** *(fig)* to push sb into the background; **an allen** ~**n und Enden sparen** to pinch and scrape *(col)*; **jdn um die** ~ **bringen** *(col)* to bump sb off *(col)*; **mit jdm um ein paar** ~**n herum verwandt sein** *(col)* to be distantly related to sb, to be sb's second cousin twice removed *(hum col)*. (b) *(Käse~, Kuchen~)* wedge. (c) *(col: Gegend)* corner, area. **aus welcher** ~ **kommst du?** what part of the world are you from? (d) *(col: Strecke)* way. **eine** ~ *(fig: viel)* quite a bit; **eine ganze** ~ **entfernt** quite a (long) way away; **eine (ganze)** ~ **älter/billiger/größer** quite a bit older/cheaper/bigger.

**Eck-:** ~**fahne** *f (Sport)* corner flag; ~**haus** *nt* corner house.

**eckig** *adj* angular; *Klammer* square; *(spitz)* sharp.

**Eck-:** ~**kneipe** *f (col)* pub on the corner *(Brit)*; ~**lohn** *m* basic rate of pay; ~**pfeiler** *m (fig)* cornerstone; ~**pfosten** *m* corner post; ~**schrank** *m* corner cupboard; ~**stoß** *m (Ftbl)* corner kick; ~**wert** *m (Econ)* benchmark figure; *(fig)* basis; ~**zahn** *m* canine tooth; ~**zins** *m (Fin)* minimum lending rate.

**Economyklasse** [iˈkɔnəmɪ-] *f* economy class.

**Ecu** [eːˈkuː] *m* -(s), -(s) ecu.

**Ecuador** [ekuaˈdoːɐ] *nt* Ecuador.

**ecuadorianisch** *adj* Ecuadorian.

**edel** *adj* noble; *(hochwertig)* precious; *(col: vornehm)* swish *(col)*; *Wein, Speisen* fine.

**Edel-:** ~**fäule** *f (bei Weintrauben)* noble rot; ~**frau** *f (Hist)* noblewoman; ~**gas** *nt* rare gas; ~**holz** *nt* precious wood; ~**mann** *m, pl* ~**leute** *(Hist)* noble(man); ~**metall** *nt* precious metal; ~**mut** *m (liter)* magnanimity; **e~mütig** *adj (liter)* magnanimous; ~**pilzkäse** *m* blue (vein) cheese; ~**rost** *m* patina; ~**stahl** *m* high-grade steel; ~**stein** *m* pre-

cious stone; *(geschliffener auch)* jewel, gem;
~**tanne** *f* noble fir; ~**weiß** *nt* **-e** edelweiss.
**Eden** *nt no pl* **der Garten** ~ *(Bibl)* the Garden of
Eden.
**Edinburg(h)** *nt* Edinburgh.
**editieren\*** *vt* to edit.
**Edition** *f (das Herausgeben)* editing; *(die Ausgabe)*
edition.
**Editor(in** *f)* [-'tɔːrɪn] *m* editor.
**EDV** [eːdeː'faʊ] *f* = **elektronische Datenverarbei-
tung** EDP.
**EDV-Anlage** *f* EDP *or* computer system.
**EEG** [eːeː'geː] *nt* **-(s), -(s)** = **Elektroenzephalo-
gramm** EEG.
**Efeu** *m no pl* ivy.
**Eff|eff** *nt no pl (col)* **etw aus dem** ~ **können** to be
able to do sth standing on one's head *(col)*; **etw aus
dem** ~ **kennen** to know sth inside out.
**Effekt** *m* **-e** effect.
**Effekten** *pl (Fin)* stocks and bonds *pl.*
**Effekten-:** ~**börse** *f* stock exchange; ~**handel** *m*
stockbroking; ~**händler** *m* jobber.
**Effekthascherei** *f (col)* showmanship. **das ist reine**
~ it's just done for effect.
**effektiv 1** *adj* **(a)** effective. **(b)** *(tatsächlich)* actual.
**2** *adv* actually. ~ **kein** absolutely no.
**Effektivität** *f* effectiveness.
**Effektivlohn** *m* actual wage.
**effektvoll** *adj* effective.
**Effet** [ε'feː] *m* **-s** spin. **den Ball mit** ~ **schießen** to put
spin on a ball.
**effizient** *adj* efficient.
**EG** [eː'geː] *f* = **Europäische Gemeinschaft** EC.
**egal** *adj, adv* **(a)** *pred* **das ist** ~ that doesn't matter,
that doesn't make any difference; **das ist mir ganz**
~ it's all the same to me; ~ **wo/wie** it doesn't matter where/how, no matter where/how. **(b)** *(col:
gleichartig)* the same, identical.
**egalitär** *adj (geh)* egalitarian.
**Egge** *f* **-n** *(Agr)* harrow.
**EG-:** ~**-Kommission** *f* EC Commission; ~**-
Ministerrat** *m* (EC) Council of Ministers.
**Ego** *nt* **-s** *(Psych)* ego.
**Egoismus** *m* ego(t)ism.
**Egoist(in** *f)* *m (wk)* ego(t)ist.
**egoistisch** *adj* ego(t)istical.
**Ego-:** ~**trip** *m (col)* ego-trip *(col)*; ~**zentriker(in** *f)*
*m* - egocentric; **e~zentrisch** *adj* egocentric.
**EG-Staat** *m* EC country.
**eh 1** *interj* hey. **2** *adv* **(a)** **seit** ~ **und je** for ages,
since the year dot *(col)*; **wie** ~ **und je** just as before. **(b)** *(col: sowieso)* anyway. **ich komme** ~ **nicht
dazu** I won't get around to it anyway.
**ehe** *conj (bevor)* before. ~ **(daß) ich mich auf andere
verlasse, mache ich lieber alles selbst** rather than
rely on others, I would prefer to do everything myself.
**Ehe** *f* **-n** marriage. **er versprach ihr die** ~ he promised to marry her; **die** ~ **eingehen** *(form)* to enter
into matrimony *(form)*; **eine unglückliche** ~ **führen**
to have an unhappy marriage; **die** ~ **brechen** *(form)*
to commit adultery; **sie hat drei Kinder aus erster** ~
she has three children from her first marriage.
**Ehe-:** **e~ähnlich** *adj (form)* **in einer e~ähnlichen
Gemeinschaft leben** to cohabit *(form)*; ~**anbah-
nungsinstitut** *nt* marriage bureau; ~**beratung** *f*
marriage guidance; ~**bett** *nt* double bed; *(fig)*
marital bed; ~**brecher** *m* - adulterer; ~**brecherin**
*f* adulteress; **e~brecherisch** *adj* adulterous; ~
**bruch** *m* adultery.
**ehedem** *adv (old)* formerly.

**Ehe-:** ~**frau** *f* wife; ~**gatte** *m,* ~**gattin** *f (form)*
spouse *(form)*; ~**gemeinschaft** *f (form)* wedlock
*(form)*, matrimony; ~**glück** *nt* married bliss;
~**krach** *m* marital row; ~**leben** *nt* married life;
~**leute** *pl (form)* married couple; *(in Briefadresse)*
Mr and Mrs.
**ehelich** *adj* marital; *Pflichten, Rechte auch* conjugal;
*Kind* legitimate.
**ehelichen** *vt (dated, hum)* to wed *(old)*.
**ehelos** *adj* unmarried, single.
**Ehelosigkeit** *f no pl* unmarried state; *(Rel)* celibacy.
**ehemalig** *adj attr* former. ~**er Häftling** ex-convict;
**mein E~er/meine E~e** *(hum col)* my ex *(col)*.
**ehemals** *adv (form)* formerly, previously.
**Ehe-:** ~**mann** *m, pl* ~**männer** married man; *(Partner)* husband; ~**paar** *nt* (married) couple;
~**partner(in** *f)* *m* husband; wife; **beide** ~**partner**
both partners (in the marriage).
**eher** *adv* **(a)** *(früher)* earlier, sooner. **je** ~**, je** *or* **desto
lieber** the sooner the better; **nicht** ~ **als** not before.
**(b)** *(lieber)* rather, sooner; *(wahrscheinlicher)* more
likely; *(leichter)* more easily. **um so** ~**, als** the more
so because; **das ist** ~ **möglich** that is more likely *or*
probable. **(c)** *(vielmehr)* more. **er ist** ~ **faul als
dumm** he's more lazy than stupid, he's lazy rather
than stupid.
**Ehe-:** ~**ring** *m* wedding ring; ~**scheidung** *f* divorce; ~**schließung** *f* marriage ceremony, wedding.
**Ehestand** *m no pl* matrimony, marriage. **in den** ~
**treten** *(form)* to enter into matrimony.
**ehestens** *adv* ~ **morgen** tomorrow at the earliest.
**eheste(r, s) 1** *adj* **bei** ~**r Gelegenheit** at the earliest
opportunity. **2** *adv* **am** ~**n** *(am liebsten)* best of all;
*(am wahrscheinlichsten)* most likely; *(am leichtesten)* the easiest; **am** ~**n würde ich mir ein Auto
kaufen** what I'd like best (of all) would be to buy
myself a car; **das geht wohl am** ~**n** that's probably
the best way.
**Ehe-:** ~**streit** *m* marital argument; ~**vermittlung** *f
(Büro)* marriage bureau; ~**versprechen** *nt (Jur)*
promise to marry.
**ehrbar** *adj (achtenswert)* respectable; *(ehrenhaft)*
honourable *(Brit)*, honorable *(US)*; *Beruf auch* reputable.
**Ehre** *f* **-n** honour *(Brit)*, honor *(US)*; *(Ruhm)* glory.
**etw in** ~**n halten** to treasure *or* cherish sth; **jdm** ~**/
wenig** ~ **machen** to do sb credit/not do sb any
credit; **auf** ~ **und Gewissen** on my/his *etc* honour;
**etw um der** ~ **willen tun** to do sth for the honour of
it; **seine Kenntnisse in allen** ~**n, aber ...** I don't
doubt his expertise, but ...; **sich** *(dat)* **etw zur** ~ **anrechnen** to count sth an honour; **das rechne ich ihm
zur** ~ **an** I consider that as being to his credit; **mit
wem habe ich die** ~**?** *(iro, form)* with whom do I
have the honour of speaking? *(form)*; **um der Wahrheit die** ~ **zu geben ...** *(geh)* to be perfectly honest
...; **wir geben uns die** ~**, Sie zu ... einzuladen** *(form)*
we request the honour of your company at ...
*(form)*; **zu** ~**n** *(+gen)* in honour of; ~**, wem** ~ **gebührt** *(prov)* give credit where credit is due *(prov)*.
**ehren** *vt* to honour *(Brit)*, to honor *(US)*. **etw ehrt jdn**
sth does sb credit *or* honour; **Ihr Vertrauen ehrt
mich** I am honoured by your trust; **jdm ein** ~**des
Andenken bewahren** to treasure sb's memory; *siehe* **geehrt.**
**Ehren-:** ~**amt** *nt* honorary office *or* post;
**e~amtlich 1** *adj* honorary; **2** *adv* in an honorary
capacity.
**Ehrenbürger** *m* freeman.

**Ehrenbürgerrecht** *nt* die Stadt verlieh ihr das ~ she was given the freedom of the city.

**Ehren-:** ~**doktor** *m* honorary doctor; ~**doktorwürde** *f:* ihm wurde die ~**doktorwürde** verliehen he was made an honorary doctor *or* given an honorary doctorate; ~**garde** *f* guard of honour *(Brit)* or honor *(US)*; ~**gast** *m* guest of honour *(Brit)* or honor *(US)*; ~**gericht** *nt* tribunal; **e~haft** *adj* honourable *(Brit)*, honorable *(US)*; ~**haftigkeit** *f* honourableness *(Brit)*, honorableness *(US)*; **e~halber** *adv* er wurde e~halber zum Vorsitzenden auf Lebenszeit ernannt he was made honorary president for life; ~**legion** *f* legion of honour *(Brit)* or honor *(US)*; ~**mal** *nt* memorial; ~**mann** *m, pl* ~**männer** man of honour *(Brit)* or honor *(US)*; ~**mitglied** *nt* honorary member; ~**mitgliedschaft** *f* honorary membership; ~**platz** *m (lit)* place of honour *(Brit)* or honor *(US)*; *(fig)* special place; ~**preis** *m (Auszeichnung)* prize; *(bei Wettbewerb)* special prize; ~**rechte** *pl (Jur)* civil rights *pl;* ~**rettung** *f* zu seiner ~**rettung** sei gesagt, daß ... in his favour *(Brit)* or favor *(US)* it must be said that ...; **e~rührig** *adj* defamatory; ~**runde** *f (Sport)* lap of honour *(Brit)* or honor *(US)*; ~**sache** *f* matter of honour *(Brit)* or honor *(US)*; ~**sache!** *(col)* you can count on me; ~**tag** *m (Geburtstag)* birthday; *(großer Tag)* big day; ~**titel** *m* honorary title; ~**tor** *nt (Sport)* consolation goal; ~**tribüne** *f* VIP rostrum; ~**urkunde** *f* certificate; **e~voll** *adj* honourable *(Brit)*, honorable *(US)*; ~**vorsitzende(r)** *mf* honorary chairman/chairwoman; ~**wache** *f* guard of honour *(Brit)* or honor *(US)*; **e~wert** *adj* Mensch honourable *(Brit)*, honorable *(US)*; die E~werte Gesellschaft *(hum)* the Mafia; ~**wort** *nt* word of honour *(Brit)* or honor *(US)*; ~**wort!** *(col)* cross my heart! *(col)*; Urlaub auf ~**wort** parole; **e~wörtlich** *adj* Versprechen solemn, faithful.

**Ehr-:** **e~erbietig** *adj* respectful, deferential; ~**erbietung** *f* respect, deference.

**Ehrfurcht** *f no pl* deep respect *(vor +dat for)*; *(Scheu)* reverence *(vor +dat for)*.

**ehrfurchtgebietend** *adj* Stimme authoritative.

**ehrfürchtig** *adj* reverent.

**Ehrgefühl** *nt* sense of honour *(Brit)* or honor *(US)*.

**Ehrgeiz** *m no pl* ambition.

**ehrgeizig** *adj* ambitious.

**ehrlich 1** *adj, adv* honest; Name good; Wunsch sincere. eine ~e Haut *(col)* an honest soul; er hat ~e Absichten *(col)* his intentions are honourable *(Brit)* or honorable *(US)*; ~ verdientes Geld hard-earned money; ~ gesagt ... quite frankly or honestly ...; ~ währt am längsten *(Prov)* honesty is the best policy *(Prov)*. **2** *adv (wirklich)* honestly. ~**!** honestly!, really!

**Ehrlichkeit** *f no pl* honesty; *(von Gefühlen etc)* sincerity.

**Ehr-:** **e~los** *adj* dishonourable *(Brit)*, dishonorable *(US)*; ~**losigkeit** *f* dishonourableness *(Brit)*, dishonorableness *(US)*; *(Schlechtigkeit)* infamy.

**Ehrung** *f* honour *(Brit)*, honor *(US)*; *(Sieger~ etc)* honouring *(Brit)*, honoring *(US)*.

**ehrwürdig** *adj* venerable. ~e Mutter/~er Vater *(Eccl)* Reverend Mother/Father.

**ei** *interj (zärtlich)* there (there); *(old) (spöttisch)* well; *(bekräftigend)* oh.

**Ei** *nt* -er **(a)** egg; *(Physiol auch)* ovum. das ~ des Kolumbus finden to come up with just the thing; das ~ will klüger sein als die Henne you're trying to teach your grandmother to suck eggs *(prov)*; jdn wie ein rohes ~ behandeln *(fig)* to handle sb with kid gloves; wie auf ~ern gehen *(col)* to step

gingerly; wie aus dem ~ gepellt aussehen *(col)* to look spruce; sie gleichen sich wie ein ~ dem anderen they are as alike as two peas (in a pod); das sind ungelegte ~er! *(col)* we'll cross that bridge when we come to it. **(b)** ~er *pl (col: Geld)* marks. **(c)** ~er *pl (col!: Hoden)* balls *pl (col!)*.

**Eibe** *f* -n *(Bot)* yew.

**Eich|amt** *nt* ≈ Weights and Measures Office *(Brit)*.

**Eiche** *f* -n oak.

**Eichel** *f* -n **(a)** *(Bot)* acorn. **(b)** *(Anat)* glans.

**Eichelhäher** *m* jay.

**eichen** *vt* to calibrate; *(prüfen auch)* to check against official specifications. darauf bin ich geeicht! *(col)* that's right up my street *(col)*.

**Eichenholz** *nt* oak. ein Tisch aus ~ an oak table.

**Eichhörnchen** *nt* squirrel.

**Eich-:** ~**maß** *nt* standard measure; *(Gewicht)* standard weight; ~**strich** *m* line measure.

**Eichung** *f* calibration; *(Prüfung auch)* official verification.

**Eid** *m* -e oath. einen ~ leisten *or* schwören to take *or* swear an oath *(auf etw (acc)* on sth*)*; ich nehme es auf meinen ~, daß ... I would be prepared to swear that ...; unter ~ under oath; eine Erklärung an ~es Statt abgeben *(Jur)* to make a statutory declaration.

**Eidechse** ['aidɛksə] *f* -n *(Zool)* lizard.

**Eidesformel** *f* wording of the oath. die ~ nachsprechen to repeat the oath.

**eidesstattlich** *adj* solemn. eine ~e Erklärung abgeben to make a statutory declaration.

**Eid-:** ~**genosse** *m,* ~**genossin** *f (Schweizer)* Swiss citizen; ~**genossenschaft** *f* Schweizerische ~genossenschaft Swiss Confederation; **e~genössisch** *adj (schweizerisch)* Swiss.

**Eidotter** *m or nt* egg yolk.

**Eier-:** ~**becher** *m* eggcup; ~**farbe** *f* egg paint; ~**handgranate** *f (Mil)* (pineapple) hand grenade; ~**kopf** *m (col)* egghead *(col)*; ~**kuchen** *m* pancake; *(Omelette)* omelette made with a mixture containing flour; ~**laufen** *nt* egg and spoon race; ~**likör** *m* ≈ advocaat; ~**löffel** *m* eggspoon.

**eiern** *vi (col)* to wobble.

**Eier-:** ~**schale** *f* eggshell; **e~schalenfarben** *adj* cream, off-white; ~**speise** *f* egg dish; ~**stock** *m (Anat)* ovary; ~**tanz** *m* einen ~**tanz** aufführen *(fig col)* to go through all kinds of contortions; ~**uhr** *f* egg timer.

**Eifer** *m no pl (Begeisterung)* enthusiasm; *(Eifrigkeit)* eagerness, keenness. in ~ geraten to get agitated; mit großem ~ bei der Sache sein to put one's heart into it; im ~ des Gefechts *(fig col)* in the heat of the moment.

**Eiferer** *m* - *(liter)* fanatic; *(Rel auch)* zealot.

**eifern** *vi (liter)* **(a)** gegen jdn/etw ~ to inveigh against sb/sth. **(b)** *(streben)* nach etw ~ to strive for sth.

**Eifersucht** *f* jealousy *(auf +acc of)*.

**eifersüchtig** *adj* jealous *(auf +acc of)*.

**Eifersuchtsszene** *f* ihr Mann hat ihr eine ~ gemacht her husband's jealousy caused a scene.

**eiförmig** *adj* egg-shaped, oval.

**eifrig** *adj* eager; Leser, Sammler keen, avid; *(begeistert)* enthusiastic; *(emsig)* zealous. sie diskutierten ~ they carried on an animated discussion.

**Eigelb** *nt* egg yolk.

**eigen** *adj* **(a)** own; *(selbständig)* separate. seine ~e Wohnung haben to have a flat of one's own, to have one's own flat; etw sein ~ nennen können *(geh)* to be the proud owner of sth; sich *(dat)* etw zu ~ machen to adopt sth; ich möchte kurz in ~er Sache

**sprechen** I would like to say something on my own account. **(b)** *(typisch)* typical. **das ist ihm** ~ that is typical of him; **der ihm** ~**e Zynismus** his characteristic cynicism. **(c)** *(seltsam)* strange, peculiar. **(d)** *(ordentlich)* particular; *(übergenau)* fussy. **in Gelddingen ist er sehr** ~ he is very particular about money matters.

**Eigen|art** f *(Besonderheit)* peculiarity; *(Eigenschaft)* characteristic; *(Eigentümlichkeit von Personen)* idiosyncrasy.

**eigen|artig** *adj* peculiar; *(sonderbar auch)* strange.

**Eigen-:** ~**bau** m *no pl* **er fährt ein Fahrrad Marke** ~**bau** *(hum col)* he rides a home-made bike; ~**bedarf** m *(von Mensch)* personal use; *(von Staat)* domestic requirements *pl*; **der Hausbesitzer machte** ~**bedarf geltend** the landlord claimed that he needed the house/flat for himself; ~**brötler(in** f) m - *(col)* loner, lone wolf; *(komischer Kauz)* oddball *(col)*; **e**~**brötlerisch** *adj (col)* solitary; *(komisch)* eccentric; ~**dynamik** f momentum; **eine** ~**dynamik entwickeln** to gather momentum; ~**gewicht** nt *(Comm)* net weight; *(Sci)* dead weight; **e**~**händig** *adj Unterschrift etc* in one's own hand, handwritten; *Übergabe* personal; **eine Arbeit e**~**händig machen** to do a job oneself; ~**heim** nt one's own home; ~**heit** f = ~**art**; ~**initiative** f initiative of one's own; ~**kapital** nt personal captial; *(von Firma)* company capital; ~**leben** nt *no pl* one's own life; *(selbständige Existenz)* independent existence; **ein** ~**leben entwickeln** to develop a life of its own; ~**leistung** f *(bei Hausbau)* (borrower's) own funding; ~**lob** nt self-praise; ~**lob stinkt!** *(prov)* don't blow your own trumpet! *(prov)*; **e**~**mächtig 1** *adj (selbstherrlich)* high-handed; *(e~verantwortlich)* taken/done *etc* on one's own authority; *(unbefugt)* unauthorized; **2** *adv* high-handedly; *(entirely)* on one's own authority; without any authorization; ~**mächtigkeit** f *(Selbstherrlichkeit)* high-handedness *no pl*; *(unbefugtes Handeln)* unauthorized behaviour *(Brit)* or behavior *(US) no pl*; ~**name** m proper name; ~**nutz** m *no pl* self-interest; **e**~**nützig** *adj* selfish.

**eigens** *adv* specially.

**Eigenschaft** f *(Attribut)* quality; *(Chem, Phys etc)* property; *(Merkmal)* characteristic, feature; *(Funktion)* capacity.

**Eigenschaftswort** nt adjective.

**Eigen-:** ~**sinn** m *no pl* stubbornness, obstinacy; **e**~**sinnig** *adj* stubborn, obstinate; **e**~**ständig** *adj* independent; ~**ständigkeit** f independence.

**eigentlich 1** *adj* real, actual. **2** *adv* actually; *(überhaupt)* anyway. **was willst du** ~ **hier?** what do you want here anyway?; **wissen Sie** ~, **wer ich bin?** do you know who I am?; ~ **müßtest du das wissen** you should really know that.

**Eigentor** nt *(Sport, fig)* own goal.

**Eigentum** nt *no pl* property.

**Eigentümer(in** f) m - owner.

**eigentümlich** *adj* **(a)** curious, odd. **(b)** *(geh: typisch)* **jdm/einer Sache** ~ **sein** to be characteristic of sb/sth.

**eigentümlicherweise** *adv* oddly enough.

**Eigentümlichkeit** f **(a)** *(Kennzeichen)* characteristic. **(b)** *(Eigenheit)* peculiarity.

**Eigentums-:** ~**anspruch** m claim of ownership; **einen** ~**anspruch auf etw** *(acc)* **geltend machen** to claim ownership of sth; ~**delikt** nt *(Jur: Diebstahl)* theft; ~**recht** nt right of ownership; ~**urkunde** f title deed; ~**wohnung** f owner-occupied flat *(Brit)* or apartment; **er kaufte sich** *(dat)* **eine** ~**wohnung** he bought a flat (of his own).

**Eigen-:** **e**~**verantwortlich 1** *adj* autonomous; **2**

*adv* on one's own authority; **e**~**willig** *adj* with a mind of one's own; *(e~sinnig)* self-willed; *(unkonventionell)* unconventional.

**eignen** *vr* to be suitable *(für, zu* for, *als* as*)*. **er eignet sich nicht zum Lehrer** he's not suited to teaching; *siehe* **geeignet.**

**Eigner(in** f) m - *(form)* owner.

**Eignung** f suitability; *(Befähigung)* aptitude.

**Eignungs-:** ~**prüfung** f, ~**test** m aptitude test.

**Eiland** nt -e *(liter)* isle *(liter)*.

**Eil-:** ~**bote** m messenger; **per** *or* **durch** ~**boten** express; ~**brief** m express letter.

**Eile** f *no pl* hurry. **in** ~ **sein** to be in a hurry; **das hat keine** ~ there is no hurry, it's not urgent; **in der/meiner** ~ in the hurry/my haste; **in aller** ~ hurriedly, hastily; **nur keine** ~! don't rush!

**Eileiter** m *(Anat)* Fallopian tube.

**eilen** *vi* **(a)** *aux sein* to hurry. **er eilte dem Ertrinkenden zu Hilfe** he rushed to help the drowning man; **eile mit Weile** *(Prov)* more haste less speed *(Prov)*. **(b)** **eilt!** *(auf Briefen etc)* urgent; **es eilt** it's urgent.

**eilends** *adv* hurriedly; hastily.

**Eilgut** nt express freight. **etw als** ~ **senden** to send sth express freight.

**eilig** *adj* **(a)** *(schnell)* quick, hurried. **es** ~ **haben** to be in a hurry *or* rush; **nur nicht so** ~! don't be in such a hurry *or* rush! **(b)** *(dringend)* urgent.

**Eil-:** ~**paket** nt express parcel; ~**sendung** f express delivery item; ~**tempo** nt: **etw im** ~**tempo machen** to do sth in a rush; ~**zug** m semi-fast stopping train; ~**zustellung** f express *or* *(Brit)* special delivery.

**Eimer** m - bucket; *(Müll-)* (rubbish) bin. **ein** ~ **(voll) Wasser** a bucket(ful) of water; **es gießt wie aus** ~**n** *(col)* it's bucketing down *(col)*; **im** ~ **sein** *(col)* to be up the spout *(col)* or be ruined.

**ein**[1] *adv (an Geräten)* **E**~/**Aus** on/off; **er geht bei uns** ~ **und aus** he is always round at our place; **ich weiß nicht mehr** ~ **noch aus** I'm at my wits' end.

**ein**[2], **eine**, **ein 1** *num* one. ~ **für allemal** once and for all; **er ist ihr** ~ **und alles** he means everything to her; *siehe* **eins. 2** *indef art* a; *(vor Vokalen)* an. ~ **Europäer** a European; ~ **Hotel** a *or* an hotel; **der Sohn** ~**es Lehrers** the son of a teacher, a teacher's son; **was für** ~ **Wetter!** this is some weather!

**Ein|akter** m - *(Theat)* one-act play.

**einander** *pron* one another, each other.

**ein|arbeiten** *sep* **1** *vr* to get used to the work. **2** *vt* **jdn** to train.

**Ein|arbeitungszeit** f training period.

**ein|armig** *adj* one-armed.

**ein|äschern** *vt sep Leichnam* to cremate; *Stadt etc* to reduce to ashes.

**Ein|äscherung** f *(von Leichnam)* cremation.

**ein|atmen** *vti sep* to breathe in.

**ein|äugig** *adj* one-eyed.

**Einbahnstraße** f one-way street.

**einbalsamieren*** *vt sep* to embalm.

**Einbalsamierung** f embalming.

**Einband** m book cover.

**einbändig** *adj* one-volume *attr.*

**Einbau** m -ten installation.

**einbauen** *vt sep* to install, to put in. **eingebaut** built-in.

**Einbauküche** f (fully-)fitted kitchen.

**Einbaum** m dug-out (canoe).

**Einbau-:** ~**möbel** *pl* built-in *or* fitted furniture; *(Schränke)* fitted cupboards *pl*; ~**schrank** m built-in *or* fitted cupboard.

**einbegriffen** *adj* included.

**einbehalten*** *vt sep irreg* to keep back.

**einbeinig** *adj* one-legged.

**einberechnen\*** *vt sep* to allow for (in one's calculations). ~, **daß** ... to allow for the fact that ...

**einberufen\*** *vt sep irreg Parlament* to summon; *Versammlung* to convene, to call; *(Mil)* to call up, to draft *(US)*.

**Einberufung** *f* (a) *(einer Versammlung)* calling; *(des Parlaments)* summoning. (b) *(Mil)* conscription; *(~sbescheid)* call-up.

**Einberufungs-:** ~**bescheid**, ~**befehl** *m (Mil)* call-up *or* draft *(US)* papers *pl.*

**einbetten** *vt sep (also Comp)* to embed *(in +acc in)*; *Rohr, Kabel* to lay *(in +acc in)*; *siehe* **eingebettet.**

**Einbettzimmer** *nt* single room.

**einbeziehen\*** *vt sep irreg* to include *(in +acc in)*.

**Einbeziehung** *f* inclusion. **unter** ~ **von etw** including sth.

**einbiegen** *vi sep irreg aux sein* to turn (off) *(in +acc into)*. **links** ~ to turn (off to the) left.

**einbilden** *vr sep* (a)  **sich** *(dat)* **etw** ~ to imagine sth; **er bildet sich** *(dat)* **ein, daß** ... he's got hold of the idea that ...; **das bildest du dir nur ein** that's just your imagination; **was bildest du dir eigentlich ein?** what's got into you? (b) *(stolz sein)* **sich** *(dat)* **viel auf etw** *(acc)* ~ to be conceited about sth; **darauf können Sie sich etwas** ~**!** that's something to be proud of!; **darauf brauchst du dir nichts einzubilden** that's nothing special; *siehe* **eingebildet.**

**Einbildung** *f* (a) *(Vorstellung)* imagination; *(irrige Vorstellung)* illusion. **das sind** ~**en** that's pure imagination. (b) *(Dünkel)* conceit.

**Einbildungskraft** *f* (powers *pl* of) imagination.

**einbinden** *vt sep irreg Buch* to bind; *(fig: einbeziehen)* to integrate.

**Einbindung** *f (fig)* integration.

**einblenden** *sep (Film, TV, Rad)* **1** *vt* to insert, to slot in; *(nachträglich) Musik etc* to dub on. **2** *vr* **sich in etw** *(acc)* ~ to link up with sth.

**Einblendung** *f siehe vt* insert; *(das Einblenden)* insertion, dubbing (on).

**einbleuen** *vt sep (col)* **jdm etw** ~ *(einschärfen)* to drum sth into sb.

**Einblick** *m (fig: Kenntnis)* insight. ~ **in etw** *(acc)* **gewinnen** to gain an insight into sth; ~ **in die Akten nehmen** to examine the files; **jdm** ~ **in etw** *(acc)* **gewähren** to allow sb to look at sth.

**einbrechen** *vi sep irreg aux sein* (a) *(einstürzen)* to fall *or* cave in. **er ist (auf dem Eis) eingebrochen** he fell through the ice. (b) *aux sein or haben (Einbruch verüben)* to break in. **bei mir ist eingebrochen worden** I've been burgled *or* burglarized *(US)*; **in neue Absatzmärkte** *etc* ~ to break into new markets *etc.* (c) *(Dämmerung etc)* to fall; *Winter* to set in. **bei** ~**der Nacht** at nightfall.

**Einbrecher(in** *f)* *m* - burglar.

**einbringen** *sep irreg* **1** *vt Geld, Ernte, Schiff* to bring in; *Ruhm, Nachteil* to bring; *Zinsen* to earn; *(Parl)* to introduce. **das bringt nichts ein** there's no money in it; *(fig)* it's not worth it; **etw in die Ehe** ~ to bring sth into the marriage. **2** *vr* **sich (in eine Diskussion)** ~ to involve oneself (in a discussion).

**einbrocken** *vt sep (col)* **jdm/sich etwas** ~ to land sb/oneself in it *(col)*; **da hast du dir etwas Schönes eingebrockt!** you've really let yourself in for it there.

**Einbruch** *m* (a) *(~diebstahl)* burglary, break-in *(in +acc in)*. **der** ~ **in die Bank** the break-in at the bank. (b) *(von Wasser)* penetration. (c) *(Einsturz)* collapse. ~ **der Kurse/der Konjunktur** *(Fin)* stock exchange/economic crash. (d) *(des Winters)* onset. **bei/vor** ~ **der Nacht/Dämmerung** at/before night-

fall/dusk.

**Einbruch(s)-:** ~**diebstahl** *m (Jur)* burglary, breaking and entering *(form)*; **e~sicher** *adj* burglarproof.

**einbuchten** *vt sep (col)* to put away *(col)*, to lock up.

**Einbuchtung** *f* indentation; *(Bucht)* inlet, bay.

**einbürgern** *sep* **1** *vt Person* to naturalize; *Fremdwort, Gewohnheit* to introduce. **2** *vr (Person)* to become *or* be naturalized; *(Brauch, Tier)* to become established; **das hat sich so eingebürgert** *(Brauch)* it's just the way we/they *etc* have come to do things.

**Einbürgerung** *f siehe vt* naturalization; introduction.

**Einbuße** *f* loss *(an +dat in)*.

**einbüßen** *sep vt* to lose; *(durch eigene Schuld)* to forfeit.

**einchecken** ['-tʃɛkn] *vti sep* to check in *(an +dat at)*.

**eincremen** *vt sep* to put cream on.

**eindämmen** *vt sep Fluß* to dam; *(fig)* to check, to contain.

**Eindämmung** *f* (a) *(Damm)* dam. (b) *siehe vt* damming; checking, containing.

**eindecken** *sep* **1** *vr* **sich (mit etw)** ~ to stock up (with sth). **2** *vt (col: überhäufen)* **mit Arbeit eingedeckt sein** to be inundated with work.

**eindeutig** *adj* clear; *(nicht zweideutig)* unambiguous; *Witz* explicit. **jdm etw** ~ **sagen** to tell sb sth quite plainly.

**eindeutschen** *vt sep Fremdwort* to Germanize.

**Eindeutschung** *f* Germanization.

**eindicken** *vti sep (vi: aux sein)* to thicken.

**eindimensional** *adj* one-dimensional.

**eindösen** *vi sep aux sein (col)* to doze off.

**eindrängen** *vr sep* to crowd in *(in +acc -to)*; *(fig)* to intrude *(in +acc upon)*.

**eindrehen** *vt sep* (a) to screw in *(in +acc -to)*. (b) *Haar* to put in rollers.

**eindringen** *vi sep irreg aux sein* (a) *(einbrechen)* **in etw** *(acc)* ~ to force one's way into sth; **in unsere Linien/das Land** ~ *(Mil)* to penetrate our lines/to enter the country. (b) **in etw** *(acc)* ~ *(Messer, Wasser)* to penetrate sth; *(Fremdwort etc)* to find its way into sth. (c) *(bestürmen)* **auf jdn** ~ to go for sb, to attack sb *(mit with)*; *(mit Fragen, Bitten etc)* to besiege sb.

**eindringlich** *adj (nachdrücklich)* insistent; *(dringend auch)* urgent; *Schilderung* vivid. **ich habe ihn** ~ **gebeten** ... I urged him ...

**Eindringlichkeit** *f siehe adj* insistence; urgency; vividness.

**Eindringling** *m* intruder.

**Eindruck** *m* ~**-̈e** impression. **den** ~ **erwecken, als ob** *or* **daß** ... to give the impression that ...; **großen** ~ **auf jdn machen** to make a big impression on sb; **er will** ~ **(bei ihr) machen** *or* **schinden** *(col)* he's out to impress (her).

**eindrücken** *vt sep* to push in; *Fenster* to break; *Tür, Mauer* to push down; *(Sturm, Explosion)* to blow in/down; *(einbeulen)* to dent; *Brustkorb* to crush; *Nase* to flatten.

**eindrucksvoll** *adj* impressive.

**eine** *siehe* **ein²,** **eine(r, s).**

**ein|ebnen** *vt sep (lit)* to level (off); *(fig)* to level out.

**Ein|ehe** *f* monogamy.

**ein|eiig** *adj Zwillinge* identical.

**ein|einhalb** *num* one and a half; *siehe* **anderthalb.**

**Ein|eltern(teil)familie** *f* single-parent family.

**einen** *vtr (geh)* to unite.

**ein|engen** *vt sep (lit)* to constrict; *(fig)* to restrict. **jdn in seiner Freiheit** ~ to restrict sb's freedom.

**Ein|engung** *f (lit)* constriction; *(fig)* restriction.
**eine(r, s)** *indef pron adj* **(a)** one; *(jemand)* somebody, someone. **der/die/das** ~ the one; **das ~ Gute war ...** the one good thing was ...; **er denkt immer nur an das ~** he only thinks of one thing; **sein ~r Sohn** *(col)* one of his sons; **die ~n sagen so, die anderen ...** some (people) say one thing and others ...; **~r für alle, alle für ~n** *(prov)* all for one and one for all *(prov)*; **du bist mir vielleicht ~(r)!** *(col)* you're a fine one *(col)*; **sieh mal ~r an!** *(iro)* well what do you know! *(col)*; **in ~m fort, in ~r Tour** *(col)* nonstop. **(b)** *(man)* one *(esp form)*, you. **wie kann ~r nur so dumm sein!** how could anybody be so stupid! **(c)** **~s** *(auch* **eins)** one thing; **~s sag' ich dir** I'll tell you one thing; **noch ~s, bevor ich's vergesse** (there's) one other thing before I forget; **es kam ~s zum anderen** it was (just) one thing after another. **(d)** *(col)* **sich** *(dat)* **~n genehmigen** to have a quick one *(col)*; **jdm ~ kleben** to thump sb one *(col)*.
**Einer** *m* - **(a)** *(Math)* unit. **(b)** *(Ruderboot)* single scull.
**einerlei** *adj pred inv (gleichgültig)* **das ist mir ganz ~** it's all the same to me; **~, was/wer ...** no matter what/who ...
**Einerlei** *nt no pl* monotony.
**einerseits** *adv* ~ **... andererseits ...** on the one hand ... on the other hand ...
**einfach 1** *adj* **(a)** simple; *Mensch* ordinary; *Essen* plain. **(b)** *(nicht doppelt) Knoten* simple; *Fahrkarte, Fahrt* single *(Brit)*, one-way; *Buchführung* single-entry. **2** *adv* simply. ~ **gemein** downright mean; **das ist doch ~ dumm** that's (just) plain stupid.
**Einfachheit** *f siehe adj* simplicity; ordinariness; plainness. **der ~ halber** for the sake of simplicity.
**einfädeln** *sep* **1** *vt* **(a)** *Nadel, Faden* to thread *(in +acc* through*)*. **(b)** *(col) Plan etc* to engineer. **2** *vr* **sich in eine Verkehrskolonne ~** to filter into a stream of traffic.
**einfahren** *sep irreg* **1** *vi aux sein (Zug, Schiff)* to come in *(in +acc -to)*. **2** *vt* **(a)** *(kaputtfahren) Mauer, Zaun* to knock down. **(b)** *Ernte* to bring in. **(c)** *Fahrgestell etc* to retract. **(d)** *Wagen* to run in *(Brit)*, to break in *(US)*; *siehe* **eingefahren.**
**Einfahrt** *f* **(a)** *no pl (das Einfahren)* entry *(in +acc* to*)*; *(Min)* descent. **Vorsicht bei (der) ~ des Zuges!** stand well back, the train is arriving. **(b)** *(Eingang)* entrance; *(von Autobahn)* sliproad.
**Einfall** *m* **(a)** idea; *(Grille, Laune)* notion. **es war nur so ein ~** it was just an idea. **(b)** *(Mil)* invasion *(in +acc* of*)*.
**einfallen** *vi sep irreg aux sein* **(a)** to collapse; *siehe* **eingefallen. (b)** *(eindringen)* **in ein Land ~** to invade a country. **(c)** *(Licht)* to fall; *(in ein Zimmer etc)* to come in *(in +acc -to)*. **(d)** *(mitsingen, mitreden)* to join in; *(dazwischenreden)* to break in *(in +acc* on*)*. **(e)** *(Gedanke)* **jdm ~** to occur to sb; **hast du dir etwas ~ lassen?** have you had any ideas?, have you thought of anything?; **da mußt du dir schon etwas Besseres ~ lassen!** you'll really have to think of something better; **was fällt Ihnen ein!** what are you thinking of!; **dabei fällt mir mein Onkel ein, der ...** that reminds me of my uncle, who ...; **es fällt mir jetzt nicht ein** I can't think of it *or* it won't come to me at the moment; **es wird Ihnen schon wieder ~** it will come back to you.
**Einfalls-:** **e~los** *adj* unimaginative; **~losigkeit** *f* lack of imagination; **e~reich** *adj* resourceful; *(phantasievoll)* imaginative; **~reichtum** *m* resourcefulness; *(Phantasie)* imaginativeness.
**Einfalt** *f no pl* naivety.
**einfältig** *adj* naive.

**Einfaltspinsel** *m (col)* simpleton.
**Einfamilienhaus** *nt* single-occupier family house; *(freistehend)* detached house.
**einfangen** *vt sep irreg (lit, fig)* to catch, to capture.
**einfärben** *vt sep Stoff, Haar* to dye.
**einfarbig** *adj* one colour *(Brit)* or color *(US)*, plain; *Stoff* self-coloured *(Brit)*, self-colored *(US)*.
**einfassen** *vt sep Beet, Kleid* to edge; *Edelstein* to set. **ein Grundstück (mit einem Zaun) ~** to put a fence around a plot of land.
**Einfassung** *f (von Beet)* border; *(von Edelstein)* setting.
**einfetten** *vt sep* to grease; *Leder, Schuhe* to dubbin; *Haut, Gesicht* to rub cream into.
**einfinden** *vr sep irreg* to come; *(eintreffen)* to arrive.
**einflechten** *vt sep irreg* to twine; *(fig: ins Gespräch etc)* to work in *(in +acc -to)*.
**einfliegen** *vt sep irreg Proviant, Truppen* to fly in *(in +acc -to)*.
**einfließen** *vi sep irreg aux sein* to flow in. **er ließ nebenbei ~, daß ...** he let it drop that ...
**einflößen** *vt sep* **jdm etw ~** to pour sth down sb's throat; *Medizin auch* to give sb sth; *Ehrfurcht, Mut etc* to instil sth into sb.
**Einflugschneise** *f (Aviat)* approach path.
**Einfluß** *m* **(a)** influence. **unter dem ~ von jdm/etw stehen** to be under the influence of sb/sth; **~ auf jdn haben/ausüben** to have/exert an influence on sb; **~ nehmen** to bring an influence to bear. **(b)** *(von Luft)* influx.
**Einfluß-:** **~bereich** *m* sphere of influence; **~möglichkeit** *f* influence; **~nahme** *f* exertion of influence *(gen* by*)*; **e~reich** *adj* influential.
**einflüstern** *vt sep* **jdm etw ~** to whisper sth to sb; *(fig)* to insinuate sth to sb.
**einfordern** *vt sep Schulden* to demand payment of.
**einförmig** *adj* uniform; *(eintönig)* monotonous.
**Einförmigkeit** *f siehe adj* uniformity; monotony.
**einfrieren** *sep irreg* **1** *vi aux sein* to freeze; *(Wasserleitung)* to freeze up. **2** *vt Nahrungsmittel, Löhne etc* to freeze; *(Pol)* Beziehungen to suspend.
**einfügen** *sep* **1** *vt Steine etc* to fit *(in +acc* into*)*; *(Comp)* to insert *(in +acc* in*)*; *(nachtragen)* to add *(in +acc* to*)*. **2** *vr* to fit in *(in +acc -to)*; *(sich anpassen)* to adapt *(in +acc* to*)*.
**Einfügung** *f* insertion, addition.
**einfühlen** *vr sep* **sich in jdn ~** to empathize with sb; **sich in etw** *(acc)* **~** in *Situation, jds Probleme* to understand sth, to sympathize with sth; *in Gedicht, Rolle* to feel one's way into sth.
**einfühlsam** *adj* sensitive; *Mensch auch* understanding.
**Einfühlungsvermögen** *nt* empathy. **mit großem ~** with a great deal of sensitivity.
**Einfuhr** *f* -en import; *(das Einführen auch)* importing.
**Einfuhr-** *in cpds* import; **~artikel** *m* import.
**einführen** *vt sep* **(a)** to introduce *(in +acc* into*)*; *Mode, Sitte* to start; *(hineinstecken auch)* to insert. **jdn in sein Amt ~** to install sb (in office). **(b)** *(Comm) Waren* to import.
**Einfuhr-:** **~genehmigung** *f* import permit; **~hafen** *m* port of entry; **~kontingent** *nt* import quota; **~land** *nt* importing country; **~sperre** *f*, **~stopp** *m* ban on imports.
**Einführung** *f* introduction *(in +acc* to*)*; *(Amts~)* installation.
**Einführungs-** *in cpds* introductory.
**Einfuhr-:** **~verbot** *nt* ban on imports; **~zoll** *m* import duty.

**einfüllen** *vt sep* to pour in.
**Einfüllstutzen** *m (Aut)* filler pipe.
**Eingabe** *f* (a) *(form: Gesuch)* petition *(an +acc to)*. (b) *(Comp)* input.
**Eingabe-** *in cpds (Comp)* input; **~gerät** *nt* input device.
**Eingang** *m* (a) entrance *(in +acc to)*; *(Zutritt, Aufnahme)* entry. „**kein ~!**" "no entrance"; **in etw** *(acc)* ~ **finden** to find one's way into sth. (b) *(Comm: Waren~, Post~)* delivery; *(Erhalt)* receipt. **wir bestätigen den ~ Ihres Schreibens vom ...** we acknowledge receipt of your letter of the ...; **den ~** *or* **die ~e bearbeiten** to deal with the incoming mail.
**eingängig** *adj Melodie, Spruch* catchy.
**eingangs 1** *adv* at the beginning. **2** *prep +gen (form)* at the beginning of.
**Eingangs-:** **~bestätigung** *f (Comm)* acknowledgement of receipt; **~datum** *nt* date of receipt; **~halle** *f* entrance hall; **~stempel** *m (Comm)* receipt stamp; **~tür** *f* entrance, door.
**eingeben** *vt sep irreg* (a) *(verabreichen)* to give. (b) *(einspeichern) Daten* to input. **dem Computer etw ~** to feed *or* enter sth into the computer.
**eingebettet** *adj* **in** *or* **zwischen Hügeln ~** nestling among the hills.
**eingebildet** *adj* (a) *(hochmütig)* conceited. (b) *(imaginär)* imaginary. **ein ~er Kranker** a hypochondriac.
**eingeboren** *adj (einheimisch)* native; *(angeboren)* innate, inborn *(dat in)*.
**Eingeborene(r)** *mf decl as adj* native *(auch hum)*.
**Eingebung** *f* inspiration.
**eingedenk** *(old, liter) prep +gen* bearing in mind. **~ dessen, daß ...** bearing in mind that ...
**eingefahren** *adj Verhaltensweise* well-worn. **die Diskussion bewegte sich in ~en Gleisen** the discussion covered the same old well-worn topics.
**eingefallen** *adj Wangen* hollow; *Gesicht* gaunt.
**eingefleischt** *adj attr (überzeugt)* confirmed; *(unverbesserlich)* dyed-in-the-wool. **~er Junggeselle** *(hum)* confirmed bachelor.
**eingehen** *sep irreg aux sein* **1** *vi* (a) *(Aufnahme finden: Wort, Sitte)* to be adopted *(in +acc in)*. **in die Geschichte ~** to go down in history. (b) *(ankommen: Briefe, Waren etc)* to arrive. **eingegangene Post/Spenden** mail/donations received. (c) *(sterben: Tiere, Pflanze)* to die *(an +dat of)*; *(col: Firma etc)* to fold. **bei dieser Hitze/Kälte geht man ja ein!** *(col)* this heat/cold is just too much *(col)*. (d) *(behandeln)* **auf etw** *(acc)* ~ **auf Frage etc** to go into sth; **niemand ging auf meine Frage ein** nobody took any notice of my question; **auf jdn/etw ~** to give (one's) time and attention to sb/sth. (e) *(zustimmen)* **auf einen Vorschlag/Plan ~** to go along with a suggestion/plan. **2** *vt (abmachen, abschließen)* to enter into; *Risiko* to take; *Wette* to make.
**eingehend** *adj* detailed, in-depth.
**eingekeilt** *adj* hemmed in; *(fig)* trapped.
**Eingemachte(s)** *nt decl as adj* bottled fruit/vegetables; *(Marmelade)* preserves *pl*; *(col: Erspartes)* one's own resources *pl*. **ans ~ gehen** *(fig col)* to get down to the nitty-gritty *(col)*.
**eingemeinden*** *vt sep Ort, Gebiet* to incorporate *(in +acc, nach into)*.
**eingenommen** *adj* **für jdn/etw ~ sein** to be taken with sb/sth; **gegen jdn/etw ~ sein** to be biased against sb/sth; **er ist sehr von sich selbst ~** he really fancies himself.
**eingeschnappt** *adj (col)* cross. **~ sein** to be in a huff *(col)*.
**eingeschossig** [ˈaɪŋəʃɔsɪç] *adj Haus* single-storey

*(Brit)*, single-story *(US)*.
**eingeschränkt** *adj (eingeengt)* restricted, limited; *(sparsam)* careful.
**eingeschrieben** *adj Mitglied, Brief* registered.
**eingeschworen** *adj* confirmed; *Gemeinschaft* close. **auf etw** *(acc)* ~ **sein** to swear by sth; **auf eine Politik ~ sein** to be committed to a policy.
**eingesessen** *adj Familie* old-established.
**eingespannt** *adj* busy.
**eingespielt** *adj Mannschaft, Team* (well-)adjusted to playing/working together. **aufeinander ~ sein** to be used to one another.
**Eingeständnis** *nt* admission, confession.
**eingestehen*** *vt sep irreg* to admit, to confess.
**eingestellt** *adj* **fortschrittlich ~ sein** to be progressively minded; **links/rechts ~ sein** to have leanings to the left/right; **wer so ~ ist wie er** anyone who thinks as he does; **gegen jdn ~ sein** to be set against sb; **ich bin im Moment nicht auf Besuch ~** I'm not prepared for visitors.
**eingetragen** *adj Verein, Warenzeichen* registered.
**Eingeweide** *nt - usu pl* entrails *pl*, innards *pl*.
**Eingeweihte(r)** *mf decl as adj* initiate. **ein paar ~** a chosen few.
**eingewöhnen*** *vr sep* to settle down *or* in *(in +dat in)*.
**Eingewöhnung** *f* settling down.
**eingießen** *vt sep irreg (hineinschütten)* to pour in *(in +acc -to)*; *(einschenken)* to pour.
**eingipsen** *vt sep Arm, Bein* to put in plaster.
**eingleisig** *adj* single-track. **er denkt sehr ~** *(fig)* he has a one-track mind.
**eingliedern** *sep* **1** *vt* to integrate *(in +acc into)*. **2** *vr* to integrate oneself *(in +acc into)*.
**Eingliederung** *f* integration.
**eingraben** *irreg* **1** *vt* to bury *(in +acc in)*; *Pflanze etc* to dig in *(in +acc -to)*. **2** *vr* to dig oneself in *(auch Mil)*. **dieses Erlebnis hat sich seinem Gedächtnis eingegraben** this experience has engraved itself on his memory.
**eingravieren*** *vt sep* to engrave *(in +acc in)*.
**eingreifen** *vi sep irreg (einschreiten, Mil)* to intervene. **in jds Rechte** *(acc)* ~ to intrude (up)on sb's rights.
**Eingreifen** *nt no pl* intervention.
**eingrenzen** *vt sep* to enclose; *(fig) Problem* to delimit.
**Eingriff** *m* (a) *(Med)* operation. (b) *(Übergriff)* intervention. **ein ~ in jds Rechte** an intrusion (up)on sb's rights.
**einhaken** *sep* **1** *vt* to hook in *(in +acc -to)*. **2** *vi (col: Punkt aufgreifen)* to intervene; *(in Unterhaltung auch)* to break in. **3** *vr* **sie hakte sich bei ihm ein** she put *or* slipped her arm through his; **eingehakt gehen** to walk arm in arm.
**Einhalt** *m no pl* **jdm/einer Sache ~ gebieten** to stop sb/sth.
**einhalten** *vt sep irreg (beachten)* to keep; *Spielregeln* to follow; *Diät, Vertrag* to keep to; *Verpflichtungen* to carry out. **die Zeit ~** to keep to time *or* schedule.
**Einhaltung** *f siehe vt* keeping; following; keeping to; carrying out.
**einhämmern** *vt sep Nagel etc* to hammer in *(in +acc -to)*. **jdm etw ~** *(fig)* to hammer sth into sb.
**einhandeln** *vt sep* (a) *(gegen, für* for) to trade. (b) *(bekommen)* **sich** *(dat)* **etw ~** *(col)* to get sth.
**einhändig** *adj* one-handed.
**einhändigen** *vt sep (form)* to hand in, to submit *(form)*.
**einhängen** *sep* **1** *vt Tür* to hang; *Fenster* to put in;

*(Telec)* Hörer to put down. **2** *vi (Telec)* to hang up.

**einheften** *vt sep* **(a)** *(Sew)* to tack in. **(b)** *Akten etc* to file.

**einheimisch** *adj* native, indigenous; *Produkt, Mannschaft* local.

**Einheimische(r)** *mf decl as adj* local.

**einheimsen** *vt sep (col)* to collect; *Erfolg, Ruhm auch* to walk off with; *Geld auch* to rake in *(col)*.

**Einheirat** *f* marriage *(in +acc into)*.

**einheiraten** *vi sep* **in einen Betrieb** ~ to marry into a business.

**Einheit** *f* **(a)** unity; *(das Ganze)* whole. **eine geschlossene** ~ **bilden** to form an integrated whole. **(b)** *(Mil, Sci)* unit.

**einheitlich** *adj (gleich)* the same, uniform; *(genormt)* standard(ized); *(in sich geschlossen)* unified. ~ **gekleidet** dressed alike *or* the same way; **wir müssen** ~ **vorgehen** we must present a united front.

**Einheitlichkeit** *f siehe adj* uniformity; standardization; unity.

**Einheits-:** ~**format** *nt* standard format; ~**front** *f (Pol)* united front; *(Volksfront)* popular front; ~**gewerkschaft** *f* unified trade *(Brit)* or labor *(US)* union; ~**kleidung** *f* uniform; ~**liste** *f (Pol)* single list of candidates; ~**preis** *m* standard price; ~**staat** *m (Pol)* united state; ~**tarif** *m* flat rate.

**einheizen** *sep* **1** *vi* to put the heating on. **jdm (tüchtig)** ~ *(col) (die Meinung sagen)* to haul sb over the coals; *(zu schaffen machen)* to make things hot for sb. **2** *vt Zimmer* to heat (up).

**einhellig** *adj* unanimous.

**einhergehen** *vi sep irreg aux sein* to walk. **mit etw** ~ *(fig)* to be accompanied by sth.

**einholen** *vt sep* **(a)** *Boot, Netz* to pull in; *Fahne, Segel* to lower. **(b)** *Rat, Erlaubnis* to get. **(c)** *(erreichen) Laufenden* to catch up with; *Vorsprung, Zeit* to make up. **der Alltag/die Vergangenheit hat mich eingeholt** the daily routine/the past has caught up with me. **(d)** *auch vi* = **einkaufen**.

**Einholung** *f* **(a)** *(von Fahne)* lowering. **(b)** *(von Rat etc)* obtaining.

**Einhorn** *nt* unicorn.

**einhüllen** *vt sep* to wrap (up) *(in +acc in)*. **in Wolken eingehüllt** shrouded in clouds.

**einhundert** *num siehe* **hundert**.

**einig** *adj* **(a)** *(geeint)* united. **(b)** *(einer Meinung)* agreed, in agreement *(über +acc on, about, in +dat on)*. **sich** *(dat)* **über etw** *(acc)* ~ **werden** to agree on sth; **wir sind uns** ~**, daß** ... we are agreed that ...; **wir werden schon miteinander** ~ **werden** we will manage to come to an agreement.

**einige** *indef pron siehe* **einige(r, s)**.

**einigemal** *adv* a few times.

**einigen** **1** *vt Volk etc* to unite; *Streitende* to reconcile. **2** *vr* to reach (an) agreement *(über +acc about)*. **sich auf einen Kompromiß** ~ to agree to a compromise.

**einige(r, s)** *indef pron* **(a)** *sing (etwas)* some; *(ziemlich viel)* (quite) some. **in** ~**r Entfernung** some distance away; **das wird** ~**s kosten** that will cost something; **dazu ist noch** ~**s zu sagen** there are still one or two things to say about that; **mit** ~**m guten Willen** *(mit Anstrengung)* with a bit of effort. **(b)** *pl* some; *(mehrere)* several; *(ein paar auch)* a few. **mit Ausnahme** ~**r weniger** with a few exceptions; ~ **hundert Menschen** a few hundred people; **in** ~**n Tagen** in a few days; **vor** ~**n Tagen** the other day, a few days ago.

**einigermaßen** *adv* rather, somewhat; *(vor adj)* fairly; *(ungefähr)* to some extent. ~ **Bescheid wissen** to have a fair idea; **wie geht's dir?** — ~ **how**

are you? — all right, not too bad.

**einiges** *indef pron siehe* **einige(r, s)**.

**einiggehen** *vi sep irreg aux sein* to agree, to be agreed *(in +dat on)*.

**Einigkeit** *f no pl* unity; *(Übereinstimmung)* agreement.

**Einigung** *f* **(a)** *(Pol)* unification. **(b)** *(Übereinstimmung)* agreement. **über etw** *(acc)* ~ **erzielen** to come to *or* reach agreement on sth.

**Einigungsvertrag** *m (Pol)* unification treaty.

**ein|impfen** *vt sep* **jdm etw** ~ to inoculate sb with sth; *(fig)* to din sth into sb.

**einjagen** *vt sep* **jdm Furcht/einen Schrecken** ~ to give sb a fright.

**einjährig** *adj Kind, Tier* one-year-old; *Pflanze* annual. **nach** ~**er Pause** after a break of one year.

**einkalkulieren*** *vt sep* to reckon on; *Kosten* to take into account.

**einkassieren*** *vt sep* **(a)** *Geld, Schulden* to collect. **(b)** *(col: wegnehmen)* to take; *Dieb* to nab *(col)*.

**Einkauf** *m* **(a)** *(das Einkaufen)* buying, purchase. **Einkäufe machen** to go shopping; **ich muß noch ein paar Einkäufe machen** I still have a few things to buy. **(b)** *(usu pl: Gekauftes)* purchase. **(c)** *no pl (Comm: Abteilung)* purchasing (department).

**einkaufen** *sep* **1** *vt* to buy. **2** *vi* to shop; *(Comm)* to buy. ~ **gehen** to go shopping; **bei Müller/im Supermarkt** ~ to shop at Müllers/the supermarket.

**Einkäufer** *m (Comm)* buyer.

**Einkaufs-** *in cpds* shopping; ~**bummel** *m* **einen** ~**bummel machen** to go on a shopping spree; ~**korb** *m* shopping basket; *(im Geschäft)* basket; ~**leiter** *m (Comm)* chief buyer; ~**netz** *nt* string bag; ~**passage** *f* shopping arcade; ~**preis** *m* trade price; ~**tasche** *f* shopping bag; ~**wagen** *m* shopping trolley *(Brit)* or cart *(US)*; ~**zentrum** *nt* shopping centre *(Brit)* or mall *(esp US)*; ~**zettel** *m* shopping list.

**Einkehr** *f no pl (geh: Besinnung)* self-examination, reflection.

**einkehren** *vi sep aux sein* **(a)** *(in Gasthof)* to (make a) stop *(in +dat at)*. **(b)** *(geh: Ruhe, Frühling)* to come.

**einkellern** *vt sep* to store in a cellar.

**einkerben** *vt sep* to cut a notch/notches in.

**Einkerbung** *f* notch.

**einkerkern** *vt sep* to incarcerate.

**einkesseln** *vt sep* to encircle.

**einklagen** *vt sep Schulden* to sue for (the recovery of).

**einklammern** *vt sep* to put in brackets.

**Einklang** *m* **(a)** *(Mus)* unison. **(b)** *(geh: Übereinstimmung)* harmony. **in** ~ **bringen** to harmonize; **im** ~ **mit etw stehen** to be in accord with sth.

**einkleben** *vt sep* to stick in *(in +acc -to)*.

**einkleiden** *vt sep* to fit out. **jdn/sich völlig neu** ~ to buy sb/oneself a completely new wardrobe.

**einklemmen** *vt sep* **(a)** *(quetschen)* to jam. **er hat sich die Hand in der Tür eingeklemmt** he caught his hand in the door. **(b)** *(festdrücken)* to clamp.

**einknicken** *sep* **1** *vt Papier* to crease; *Streichholz, Äste* to snap. **2** *vi aux sein (Strohhalm)* to get bent; *(Äste)* to snap; *(Knie)* to give way, to buckle.

**einkochen** *vt sep Gemüse* to preserve; *Obst auch, Marmelade* to bottle.

**einkommen** *vi sep irreg aux sein* to come in.

**Einkommen** *nt* - income.

**Einkommens-:** ~**ausfall** *m* loss of income; ~**klasse** *f* income bracket; **e~schwach** *adj* low-income *attr*; **e~stark** *adj* high-income *attr*.

**Einkommen(s)steuer** *f* income tax.

**Einkommen(s)steuer-:** ~**erklärung** f income tax return; **e~pflichtig** adj liable to income tax.

**Einkommensverhältnisse** pl (level of) income.

**einkreisen** vt sep Feind, Wild to surround; (fig) Problem to consider from all sides.

**Einkreisung** f (von Feind etc) surrounding; (Pol) isolation.

**einkriegen** sep (col) **1** vt to catch up. **2** vr **sie konnte sich gar nicht mehr darüber** ~, **daß** ... she couldn't get over the fact that ...; **krieg dich mal wieder ein!** control yourself!

**Einkünfte** pl income sing; (einer Firma auch) receipts.

**einkuppeln** vi sep (Aut) to let the clutch in.

**einladen** vt sep irreg **(a)** to invite. **jdn zu einer Party** ~ to ask sb to a party; **jdn auf ein Bier** ~ to invite sb for a beer; **laß mal, ich lade dich ein** come on, this is on me; **wir sind heute abend eingeladen** we've been invited out this evening. **(b)** Waren to load (in +acc into).

**einladend** adj inviting; Speisen appetizing.

**Einladung** f invitation.

**Einlage** f **(a)** (in Brief etc) enclosure. **(b)** (Schuh~) insole; (zum Stützen) (arch) support. **(c)** (Sew) padding; (Versteifung) interfacing. **(d)** (Zahn~) temporary filling. **(e)** (Cook) noodles, egg etc added to a clear soup. **(f)** (Zwischenspiel) interlude. **(g)** (Fin: Kapital~) investment; (Spar~ auch) deposit.

**einlagern** vt sep to store.

**Einlagerung** f storage.

**Einlaß** m **-sses**, **⁼sse** **(a)** no pl (Zutritt) admission. **jdm** ~ **gewähren** to admit sb. **(b)** (Tech) inlet.

**einlassen** sep irreg **1** vt to let in (in +acc -to); Person auch to admit; Wasser to run (in +acc into). **2** vr **(a) sich auf etw** (acc) ~ to get involved in sth; (sich zu etw verpflichten) to let oneself in for sth; **sich auf einen Kompromiß** ~ to agree to a compromise; **ich lasse mich auf keine Diskussion ein** I'm not having any discussion about it. **(b) sich mit jdm** ~ (pej: Umgang pflegen mit) to get mixed up or involved with sb; **sie läßt sich mit jedem ein** she'll go with anyone.

**Einlauf** m **(a)** no pl (Sport) (am Ziel) finish; (ins Stadion etc) entry. **beim** ~ **in die Zielgerade** ... coming into the final straight ... **(b)** (Med) enema. **jdm einen** ~ **machen** to give sb an enema.

**einlaufen** sep irreg **1** vi aux sein **(a)** to come in (in +acc -to); (ankommen auch) to arrive (in +acc in); (Wasser) to run in (in +acc -to). **(b)** (eingehen: Stoff) to shrink. **2** vt Schuhe to wear in. **3** vr (Motor, Maschine) to be run in, to be broken in (US).

**einläuten** vt sep neues Jahr to ring in; (Sport) Runde to sound the bell for.

**einleben** vr sep to settle down (in or an +dat in).

**Einlege|arbeit** f inlay no pl. **Tisch mit** ~ inlaid table.

**einlegen** vt sep **(a)** (hineintun) to insert (in +acc in), to put in (in +acc -to); Film auch to load (in +acc into); (in Brief) to enclose (in +acc in). **(b)** Sonderschicht, Spurt to put on; Pause to have; (Aut) Gang to engage. **(c)** (in Holz etc) to inlay. **(d)** (fig) Protest to register. **ein gutes Wort für jdn** ~ to put in a good word for sb (bei with); **sein Veto** ~ to use one's veto. **(e)** (Cook) Heringe etc to pickle. **(f)** Haare to set, to put in rollers.

**Einlegesohle** f insole.

**einleiten** vt sep **(a)** (in Gang setzen) to initiate; Maßnahmen auch, Schritte to introduce, to take; neues Zeitalter to mark the start of, to inaugurate; (Jur) Verfahren to institute; (Med) Geburt to induce. **(b)** (beginnen) to start; (eröffnen) to open. **(c)** Abwässer etc to discharge (in +acc into).

**einleitend** adj introductory. **er sagte** ~, **daß** ... he said by way of introduction that ...

**Einleitung** f **(a)** siehe vt **(a)** initiation; introduction; inauguration; institution; induction. **(b)** (Vorwort) introduction; (Mus) prelude. **(c)** (von Abwässern) discharge (in +acc into).

**einlenken** vi sep (fig) to yield, to give way.

**einlesen** sep irreg **1** vr **sich in ein Gebiet** ~ to get into a subject. **2** vt Daten to read in (in +acc -to).

**einleuchten** vi sep to be clear (jdm to sb). **ja, das leuchtet mir ein!** yes, I see that.

**einleuchtend** adj reasonable, plausible.

**einliefern** vt sep Waren to deliver. **jdn ins Krankenhaus** ~ to admit sb to hospital; **jdn ins Gefängnis** ~ to put sb in prison.

**Einlieferung** f (von Waren) delivery; (ins Krankenhaus) admission (in +acc to); (ins Gefängnis) committal (in +acc to).

**Einlieferungsschein** m certificate of posting.

**einlochen** vt sep (col: einsperren) to lock up.

**einloggen** vi sep (Comp) to log on.

**einlösen** vt sep Pfand to redeem; Scheck, Wechsel to cash (in); (fig) Wort, Versprechen to keep.

**Einlösung** f siehe vt redemption; cashing (in); keeping.

**einlullen** vt sep (fig col) **jdn mit schönen Worten** ~ to soft-talk sb.

**einmachen** vt sep to preserve; (in Gläser auch) to bottle.

**Einmach-:** ~**glas** nt bottling jar; ~**zucker** m preserving sugar.

**einmal** adv **(a)** (ein einziges Mal) once; (erstens) first of all, firstly. ~ **sagt er dies,** ~ **das** sometimes he says one thing, sometimes another; **auf** ~ (plötzlich) all at once; (zugleich) at once; ~ **mehr** once again; ~ **und nie wieder** once and never again; **noch** ~ again; **wenn sie da ist, ist es noch** ~ **so schön** it's twice as nice when she's there; ~ **ist keinmal** (Prov) once doesn't count. **(b)** (früher, vorher) once; (später, in Zukunft) one day. **waren Sie schon** ~ **in Rom?** have you ever been to Rome?; **es war** ~ ... once upon a time there was ...; **das war** ~! that was then. **(c)** (verstärkend) **nicht** ~ not even; **wieder** ~ again; **sag** ~, **ist das wahr?** tell me, is it true?; **nehmen wir** ~ **an** just let's suppose; **gib mir** ~ **das Buch** give me the book.

**Einmal|eins** nt no pl (multiplication) tables pl; (fig) ABC, basics pl. **das** ~ **lernen** to learn one's tables; **das kleine/große** ~ (multiplication) tables up to ten/over ten.

**Einmalhandtuch** nt disposable towel.

**einmalig** adj unique; Anschaffung, Zahlung one-off; (col: hervorragend) fantastic, amazing.

**Einmaligkeit** f uniqueness.

**Einmannbetrieb** m **(a)** one-man business or band (col). **(b) etw auf** ~ **umstellen** to convert sth for one-man operation.

**Einmarkstück** nt one-mark piece.

**Einmarsch** m entry (in +acc into); (in ein Land) invasion (in +acc of).

**einmarschieren*** vi sep aux sein to march in (in +acc -to).

**einmauern** vt sep (ummauern) to wall in (in +acc in).

**einmieten** vr sep **sich bei jdm** ~ to take lodgings with sb.

**einmischen** vr sep to interfere (in +acc in).

**Einmischung** f interference (in +acc in).

**einmonatig** adj attr one-month.

**einmontieren*** vt sep to fit in (in +acc -to).

**einmotorig** *adj Flugzeug* single-engined.

**einmotten** *vt sep Kleider etc* to put in mothballs; *(fig auch)* to mothball.

**einmumme(l)n** *vt sep (col)* to muffle up.

**einmünden** *vi sep aux sein* **in etw** *(acc)* ~ *(Fluß)* to flow into sth; *(Straße)* to run *or* lead into sth.

**Einmündung** *f (von Fluß)* confluence; *(von Straße)* junction.

**einmütig** *adj* unanimous.

**Einmütigkeit** *f* unanimity.

**einnähen** *vt sep* to sew in *(in +acc -to)*; *(enger machen)* to take in.

**Einnahme** *f -n* **(a)** *(Mil)* seizure, capture. **(b)** ~**n** *pl* income *sing*; *(Geschäfts~)* takings *pl*; *(aus Einzelverkauf)* proceeds *pl*; *(eines Staates)* revenue *sing*; ~**n** **und Ausgaben** income and expenditure.

**Einnahmequelle** *f* source of income; *(eines Staates)* source of revenue.

**einnehmen** *vt sep irreg* **(a)** to take; *(lit, fig)* Platz *etc* to take (up), to occupy; *Stelle (innehaben)* to have, to occupy; *Haltung, Standpunkt etc* to take up; *Steuern* to collect. **die eingenommenen Gelder** the takings. **(b)** **er nahm uns alle für sich ein** he won us all over; **jdn gegen sich** ~ to set sb against oneself.

**einnehmend** *adj* likeable, charming. **er hat ein** ~**es Wesen** he's a likeable character; *(hum col)* he has taking ways *(hum col)*.

**einnicken** *vi sep aux sein (col)* to nod off.

**einnisten** *vr sep (lit)* to nest; *(Parasiten, Ei)* to lodge; *(fig)* to park oneself *(bei* on*)*.

**Ein|öde** *f* barren waste.

**ein|ölen** *sep* **1** *vt* to oil. **2** *vr* to rub oneself with oil.

**ein|ordnen** *sep* **1** *vt* **(a)** *Bücher etc* to (put in) order; *Akten* to file. **(b)** *(klassifizieren)* to classify. **2** *vr* **(a)** *(in Gemeinschaft etc)* to fit in *(in +acc -to)*. **(b)** *(Aut)* to get in(to) lane. **„bitte** ~**"** "get in lane".

**einpacken** *sep* **1** *vt* **(a)** *(einwickeln)* to wrap up *(in +acc* in*) (auch fig)*. **(b)** *(hineintun)* to pack *(in +acc* in*)*. **2** *vi* to pack. **dann können wir** ~ *(col)* in that case we may as well give up *(col)*.

**einparken** *vti sep* to park. **(in eine Parklücke)** ~ to get into a parking space.

**Einpartei-** *in cpds* one-party.

**einpassen** *vt sep* to fit in *(in +acc -to)*.

**einpauken** *vt sep (col)* **jdm etw** ~ to drum sth into sb.

**einpendeln** *vr sep (fig)* to settle down; *(Preise etc)* to level off.

**einpennen** *vi sep aux sein (col)* to drop off *(col)*.

**Einpfennigstück** *nt* one-pfennig piece.

**einpferchen** *vt sep Vieh* to pen in *(in +acc -to)*; *(fig)* to coop up *(in +acc* in*)*.

**einpflanzen** *vt sep* to plant *(in +dat* in*)*; *(Med)* to implant *(jdm* in(to) sb*)*.

**einplanen** *vt sep* to plan (on), to include in one's plans; *Verzögerungen, Verluste* to allow for.

**einpökeln** *vt sep Fisch, Fleisch* to salt.

**einprägen** *sep* **1** *vt Muster, Spuren* to imprint, to impress; *Inschrift* to stamp. **sich** *(dat)* **etw** ~ to remember sth; *(auswendig lernen)* to memorize sth, to commit sth to memory. **2** *vr* **sich jdm** ~ to make an impression on sb.

**einprägsam** *adj* easily remembered; *Slogan, Melodie auch* catchy.

**einprogrammieren*** *vt sep Daten* to input.

**einprügeln** *sep (col)* **1** *vt* **jdm etw** ~ to din sth into sb *(col)*. **2** *vi* **auf jdn** ~ to lay into sb *(col)*.

**einquartieren*** *sep* **1** *vt* to quarter; *(Mil auch)* to billet. **Gäste bei Freunden** ~ to put visitors up with friends. **2** *vr* to be quartered *(bei* with*)*; *(Mil auch)* to be billeted *(bei* on*)*; *(Gäste)* to stop *(bei* with*)*

*(col)*.

**einquetschen** *vt sep* = **einklemmen (a)**.

**einrahmen** *vt sep (lit, fig)* to frame.

**einrammen** *vt sep Pfahl etc* to ram in.

**einrasten** *vti sep (vi: aux sein)* to engage.

**einräuchern** *vt sep* to envelop in smoke; *(col) Zimmer* to fill with smoke.

**einräumen** *vt sep* **(a)** *Wäsche, Bücher etc* to put away; *Schrank, Regal etc* to fill. **(b)** *(zugestehen)* to concede, to admit; *Freiheiten etc* to allow; *Frist, Kredit* to grant, to allow. **jdm das Recht** ~, **etw zu tun** to give *or* grant sb the right to do sth.

**einrechnen** *vt sep* to include. **ihn (mit) eingerechnet** including him.

**einreden** *sep* **1** *vt* **jdm/sich etw** ~ to talk sb/oneself into believing sth, to persuade sb/oneself of sth; **das redest du dir nur ein!** you're only imagining it. **2** *vi* **auf jdn** ~ to keep on and on at sb.

**einregnen** *vr* **es hat sich eingeregnet** the rain has set in.

**einreiben** *vt sep irreg* **er rieb sich** *(dat)* **das Gesicht mit Creme ein** he rubbed cream into his face.

**einreichen** *vt sep Antrag, Unterlagen* to submit *(bei* to*)*; *(Jur) Klage* to file; *(bitten um) Versetzung, Pensionierung* to apply for, to request.

**einreihen** *sep* **1** *vt (einordnen, einfügen)* to put in *(in +acc -to)*; *(klassifizieren)* to classify. **2** *vr* **sich in etw** *(acc)* ~ to join sth.

**Einreiher** *m* - single-breasted suit/jacket/coat.

**einreihig** *adj Anzug etc* single-breasted.

**Einreise** *f* entry *(in +acc* into, to*)*. **bei der** ~ **in die USA** when entering the USA, on entry to the USA.

**Einreise-:** ~**bestimmungen** *pl* entry regulations; ~**erlaubnis**, ~**genehmigung** *f* entry permit.

**einreisen** *vi sep aux sein* to enter the country. **er reiste in die Schweiz ein** he entered Switzerland.

**Einreise-:** ~**verbot** *nt* refusal of entry; ~**verbot haben** to have been refused entry; ~**visum** *nt* entry visa.

**einreißen** *sep irreg* **1** *vt* **(a)** *Papier, Nagel* to tear. **(b)** *Zaun etc* to tear *or* pull down. **2** *vi aux sein (Papier)* to tear; *(fig col: Unsitte etc)* to catch on *(col)*, to get to be a habit *(col)*.

**einreiten** *sep irreg* **1** *vt Pferd* to break in. **2** *vi aux sein* to ride in *(in +acc -to)*.

**einrenken** *sep* **1** *vt Gelenk, Knie* to put back in place; *(fig col)* to sort out. **2** *vr (fig col)* to sort itself out.

**einrennen** *vt sep irreg (col) Tür* to break down.

**einrichten** *sep* **1** *vt* **(a)** *(möblieren) Wohnung* to furnish; *(ausstatten) Hobbyraum* to fit out; *Praxis, Labor* to equip, to fit out. **eine Wohnung modern** ~ to furnish a flat in a modern style. **(b)** *(gründen, eröffnen)* to set up; *Konto* to open. **(c)** *(fig: arrangieren)* to arrange, to fix. **ich werde es** ~, **daß wir um zwei Uhr da sind** I'll arrange for us to be there at two. **2** *vr* **(a)** *(sich möblieren)* to furnish one's house *etc*. **(b)** *(sich der Lage anpassen)* to get along *or* by, to manage; *(sparsam sein)* to cut down. **(c)** **sich auf etw** *(acc)* ~ to prepare oneself for sth; **auf Tourismus eingerichtet sein** to be geared to tourism.

**Einrichtung** *f* **(a)** *(das Einrichten) (von Wohnung)* furnishing; *(von Hobbyraum)* fitting-out; *(von Labor, Praxis)* equipping. **(b)** *(Wohnungs~)* furnishings *pl*; *(Geschäfts~ etc)* fittings *pl*; *(Labor~ etc)* equipment *no pl*. **(c)** *(Gründung, Eröffnung)* setting-up; *(von Konto)* opening. **(d)** *(behördlich, wohltätig)* institution; *(öffentliche* ~*)* facility. **(e)** *(Gewohnheit)* **zur** ~ **ständigen** ~ **werden** to become an institution.

**Einrichtungsgegenstand** *m* item of furniture.

**einritzen** *vt sep* to carve in *(in +acc -to)*.

**einrollen** vt sep (einwickeln) to roll up (in +acc in). **sich** (dat) **die Haare** ~ to put one's hair in rollers.

**einrosten** vi sep aux sein to rust up; (fig: Glieder) to stiffen up; (Kenntnisse etc) to get rusty.

**einrücken** sep **1** vi aux sein (Mil: in ein Land) to move in (in +acc -to). **2** vt Zeile to indent; Anzeige (in Zeitung) to insert.

**einrühren** vt sep to stir or mix in (in +acc -to).

**eins** num one. **es ist** ~ it's one (o'clock); ~ **zu** ~ (Sport) one all; ~ **mit jdm sein** (übereinstimmen) to be in agreement with sb; **das ist doch alles** ~ (col) it's all one or all the same; **sehen und handeln waren** ~ the moment he/she etc saw it he/she etc acted; ~ **a** (col) first-rate (col); siehe **eine(r, s) (c), vier.**

**Eins** f -en one; (Sch) ≃ A.

**einsacken**[1] vt sep (col: erbeuten) to grab (col); Geld, Gewinne to rake in (col).

**einsacken**[2] vi sep aux sein (einsinken) to sink; (Boden etc auch) to subside.

**einsalzen** vt sep irreg Fisch, Fleisch to salt.

**einsam** adj (a) lonely; (einzeln) solitary. ~ **leben** to live a lonely/solitary life. (b) (abgelegen) Haus, Insel secluded; (Dorf) isolated; (menschenleer) empty. (c) (col) ~**e Klasse/Spitze** absolutely fantastic (col), awesome (col).

**Einsamkeit** f siehe adj (a) loneliness; solitariness. **er liebt die** ~ he likes solitude. (b) seclusion; isolation; emptiness.

**einsammeln** vt sep to collect (in).

**Einsatz** m (a) (~teil) insert; (Schubladen~, Koffer~) tray; (Topf~) compartment. (b) (Spiel~) stake; (Kapital~) investment. **den** ~ **erhöhen** to raise the stakes. (c) (Mus) entry. **der Dirigent gab dem Orchester den** ~ the conductor brought in the orchestra. (d) (Verwendung) use; (esp Mil) deployment; (von Arbeitskräften) employment. **im** ~ in use; **die Ersatzspieler kamen nicht zum** ~ the reserves weren't used; **unter** ~ **aller Kräfte** by making a supreme effort. (e) (Aktion) operation; (Mil also) action; (esp von Fliegern) mission. **im** ~ in action; **zum** ~ **kommen** to go into action; **bei seinem ersten** ~ the first time he saw action; **sich zum** ~ **melden** to report for duty. (f) (Hingabe) commitment. **etw unter** ~ **seines Lebens tun** to risk one's life to do sth.

**Einsatz-:** ~**befehl** m order to go into action; **e**~**bereit** adj ready for use; (Mil) ready for action; Rakete etc operational; **e**~**fähig** adj fit for use; (Mil) fit for action; Sportler fit; ~**kommando** (Mil) nt task force; ~**leiter** m head of operations; ~**plan** m plan of action; ~**wagen** m (bei Straßenbahn, Bus) extra tram/bus.

**einschalten** sep **1** vt (a) (in Betrieb setzen) to switch on; Sender to tune in to. (b) (einfügen) to interpolate. (c) jdn ~ to bring sb in. **2** vr (a) (Heizung etc) to switch itself on. (b) (eingreifen) to intervene.

**Einschaltquote** f (TV) viewing figures pl, ratings pl.

**einschärfen** vt sep jdm etw ~ to impress sth (up)on sb.

**einschätzen** vt sep to assess (auch Fin), to evaluate. **falsch** ~ to misjudge; **wie ich die Lage einschätze** as I see the situation; **jdn hoch/niedrig** ~ to have a high/low opinion of sb; **etw zu hoch/niedrig** ~ to overestimate/underestimate sth.

**Einschätzung** f assessment, evaluation. **falsche** ~ misjudgement; **nach meiner** ~ in my estimation.

**einschenken** vt sep to pour (out). **darf ich Ihnen noch Wein** ~? can I give you some more wine?

**einscheren** vi sep aux sein to get back (into lane).

**einschicken** vt sep to send in (an +acc to).

**einschieben** vt sep irreg to put in (in +acc -to). **eine Pause** ~ to have a break.

**einschießen** sep irreg **1** vt Scheibe (mit Ball etc) to smash (in). **2** vi (a) (Sport) to score. **er schoß zum 1:0 ein** he scored to make it 1-0. (b) **auf jdn** ~ to shoot at sb.

**einschiffen** sep **1** vt to ship. **2** vr to embark.

**Einschiffung** f (von Personen) boarding, embarkation; (von Gütern) loading.

**einschl.** = **einschließlich** incl.

**einschlafen** vi sep irreg aux sein to fall asleep, to go to sleep; (Bein, Arm) to go to sleep; (euph: sterben) to pass away; (fig: Freundschaft) to peter out. **ich kann nicht** ~ I can't get to sleep; **vor dem E**~ **zu nehmen** (Medizin) to be taken before retiring.

**einschläfern** vt sep (schläfrig machen) to make sleepy; Gewissen to soothe; (narkotisieren) to give a soporific; (töten) Tier to put to sleep.

**einschläfernd** adj soporific; (langweilig) monotonous. ~ **wirken** to have a soporific effect.

**Einschlag** m (a) (von Geschoß) impact. **beim** ~ **des Blitzes** when the lightning strikes; **der** ~ **der Granate war deutlich zu sehen** the place where the grenade had landed was clearly visible. (b) (Aut: des Lenkrads) lock. **bei vollem** ~ at full lock. (c) (Zusatz, Beimischung) element. **ein südländischer** ~ a hint of the Mediterranean.

**einschlagen** sep irreg **1** vt (a) Nagel to hammer or knock in; Pfahl to drive in. (b) (zertrümmern) to smash in; Zähne to knock out. (c) (einwickeln) Ware to wrap up. (d) (Aut) Räder to turn. (e) (wählen) Weg to take; Kurs to follow; Laufbahn etc to enter on. **das Schiff änderte den eingeschlagenen Kurs** the ship changed (from its previous) course. **2** vi (a) (in etw acc) ~ (Blitz) to strike (sth); (Geschoß etc auch) to hit (sth); **es muß irgendwo eingeschlagen haben** something must have been struck by lightning; **gut** ~ (col) to go down well, to be a big hit (col). (b) **auf jdn/etw** ~ to hit out at sb/sth. (c) (zur Bekräftigung) to shake on it.

**einschlägig** adj appropriate; Literatur, Paragraph auch relevant. **er ist** ~ **vorbestraft** (Jur) he has a previous conviction for a similar offence.

**einschleichen** vr sep irreg (lit, fig) to creep in (in +acc -to). **sich in jds Vertrauen** ~ (fig) to worm one's way into sb's confidence.

**einschleifen** vt sep irreg to cut in (in +acc -to). **das hat sich (bei ihm) eingeschliffen** it's become a habit (with him).

**einschleppen** vt sep (fig) Krankheit etc to bring in.

**einschleusen** vt sep to smuggle in (in +acc -to).

**einschließen** vt sep irreg (a) to lock up (in +acc in). **er schloß sich in seinem Zimmer ein** he locked himself (up) in his room. (b) (umgeben) to surround. (c) (fig: beinhalten) to include.

**einschließlich 1** prep +gen including, inclusive of. **2** adv **bis S. 205** ~ up to and including p.205; **vom 1. bis** ~ **31. Oktober** from 1st to 31st October inclusive.

**einschlummern** vi sep aux sein (geh) to fall asleep.

**Einschluß** m **mit** or **unter** ~ **von** (form) including.

**einschmeicheln** vr sep **sich bei jdm** ~ to ingratiate oneself with sb; ~**de Stimme** silky voice.

**einschmelzen** vt sep irreg to melt down.

**einschmieren** vt sep (mit Fett) to grease; (mit Öl) to oil; Gesicht (mit Creme) to put cream on.

**einschmuggeln** vt sep to smuggle in (in +acc -to). **er hat sich in den Saal eingeschmuggelt** he sneaked into the hall.

**einschnappen** vi sep aux sein (a) (Schloß, Tür) to click shut. (b) (col: beleidigt sein) to take offence

*(Brit) or* offense *(US)*, to get into a huff *(col)*; *siehe* **eingeschnappt.**

**einschneiden** *vt sep irreg* to cut. **tief eingeschnittene Felsen** steep cliffs.

**einschneidend** *adj (fig)* drastic, radical.

**einschneien** *vi sep aux sein* to get snowed in. **eingeschneit sein** to be snowed in *or* snowbound.

**Einschnitt** *m* cut; *(Med)* incision; *(im Tal, Gebirge)* cleft; *(im Leben)* decisive point.

**einschnüren** *vt sep* **(a)** *(einengen)* to cut into. **dieser Kragen schnürt mir den Hals ein** this collar is strangling me. **(b)** *Paket* to tie up.

**einschränken** *sep* **1** *vt* to cut back; *Bewegungsfreiheit, Recht* to limit, to restrict; *Wünsche* to moderate; *Behauptung* to qualify. **~d möchte ich sagen, daß ...** I'd like to qualify that by saying ...; **das Rauchen ~** to cut down on smoking. **2** *vr (sparen)* to economize. **sich im Trinken ~** to cut down on one's drinking; *siehe* **eingeschränkt.**

**Einschränkung** *f siehe vt* cutting back; limitation; restriction; moderation; qualification; *(Vorbehalt)* reservation.

**einschrauben** *vt sep* to screw in *(in +acc -to)*.

**Einschreib(e)brief** *m* registered letter.

**einschreiben** *sep irreg* **1** *vt (eintragen)* to enter; *siehe* **eingeschrieben. 2** *vr (für Abendkurse etc)* to enrol; *(Univ)* to register.

**Einschreiben** *nt* registered letter/parcel. **einen Brief als ~ schicken** to send a letter by registered mail.

**Einschreibung** *f* enrolment; *(Univ)* registration.

**einschreiten** *vi sep irreg aux sein* to take action *(gegen* against*)*; *(dazwischentreten)* to intervene, to step in.

**Einschreiten** *nt no pl* intervention.

**einschrumpfen** *vi sep aux sein* to shrivel (up).

**Einschub** *m* insertion.

**einschüchtern** *vt sep* to intimidate.

**Einschüchterung** *f* intimidation.

**einschulen** *vti sep* to send to school. **eingeschult werden** *(Kind)* to start school.

**Einschulung** *f* first day at school. **die ~ findet im Alter von 6 Jahren statt** children start school at the age of 6.

**Einschuß** *m* **(a)** *(~stelle)* bullet hole; *(Med)* point of entry. **(b)** *(Ftbl)* (shot into) goal.

**einschütten** *vt sep* to tip in *(in +acc -to)*; *Flüssigkeiten* to pour in *(in +acc -to)*. **er hat sich** *(dat)* **noch etwas Kaffee eingeschüttet** he poured himself (out) some more coffee.

**einschweißen** *vt sep (Tech)* to weld in *(in +acc -to)*; *(in Plastikfolie)* to shrink-wrap.

**Einschweißfolie** *f* shrink-wrapping.

**einschwenken** *vi sep aux sein* to turn *or* swing in *(in +acc -to)*. **auf etw** *(acc)* **~** *(fig)* to go along with sth.

**einsehen** *vt sep irreg* to see; *(prüfen auch)* to inspect; *Fehler, Schuld auch* to recognize. **das sehe ich nicht ein** I don't see why.

**Einsehen** *nt:* **ein ~ haben** to have some understanding *(mit, für* for*)*; *(Vernunft, Einsicht)* to see reason; **hab doch ein ~!** be reasonable!

**einseifen** *vt sep* to soap; *(col: betrügen)* to con *(col)*.

**einseitig** *adj* one-sided; *Ernährung* unbalanced; *(Jur, Pol)* Erklärung, Kündigung unilateral; *(Comp)* Diskette single-sided. **~e Lähmung** paralysis of one side of the body.

**Einseitigkeit** *f* one-sidedness; *(von Ernährung)* imbalance.

**einsenden** *vt sep irreg* to send in, to submit *(an +acc* to*)*.

**Einsender(in** *f)* *m* sender; *(bei Preisausschreiben)*

competitor.

**Einsendeschluß** *m* closing date (for entries).

**Einsendung** *f* **(a)** *(bei Wettbewerb etc)* entry. **(b)** *no pl (das Einsenden)* sending in, submission.

**einsetzen** *sep* **1** *vt* **(a)** *(einfügen)* to put in *(in +acc -to)*; *Maschinenteil auch* to insert *(in +acc* into*)*, to fit in *(in +acc -to)*; *(schreiben auch)* to enter *(in +acc* in*)*. **jdm einen Goldzahn ~** to give sb a gold tooth. **(b)** *(ernennen)* to appoint; *Nachfolger* to name. **jdn in ein Amt ~** to appoint sb to an office. **(c)** *(verwenden)* to use; *Truppen, Polizei* to deploy; *Busse, Sonderzüge* to put on. **(d)** *(beim Glücksspiel)* to stake; *Leben* to risk. **2** *vi (beginnen)* to start, to begin; *(Mus)* to come in. **3** *vr* **sich (voll) ~** to show (complete) commitment *(in +dat* to*)*; **sich für jdn/etw ~** to support sb/sth; **ich werde mich dafür ~, daß ...** I will do what I can to see that ...

**Einsetzung** *f* appointment *(in +acc* to*)*.

**Einsicht** *f* **(a)** *(in Akten, Bücher)* inspection *(in +acc* of*)*. **~ in etw** *(acc)* **haben/verlangen** to look/ask to look at sth. **(b)** *(Vernunft)* sense, reason; *(Erkenntnis)* insight. **zur ~ kommen** to come to one's senses; **zu der ~ kommen, daß ...** to recognize that ...; **haben Sie doch ~!** have a heart!; *(seien Sie vernünftig)* be reasonable!; **jdn zur ~ bringen** to bring sb to his/her senses.

**einsichtig** *adj* **(a)** *(vernünftig)* reasonable; *(verständnisvoll)* understanding. **(b)** *(verständlich, begreiflich)* understandable. **jdm etw ~ machen** to make sb understand *or* see sth.

**Einsichtnahme** *f* **-n** *(form)* inspection. **er bat um ~ in die Akten** he asked to inspect *or* see the files; **„zur ~"** "for attention".

**einsickern** *vi sep aux sein* to seep in *(in +acc -to)*; *(fig)* to filter in *(in +acc -to)*.

**Einsiedler(in** *f)* *m* hermit; *(fig auch)* recluse.

**einsilbig** *adj* monosyllabic; *(Mensch)* uncommunicative.

**Einsilbigkeit** *f (von Mensch)* uncommunicativeness.

**einsinken** *vi sep irreg aux sein (im Morast, Schnee)* to sink in *(in +acc or dat -to)*; *(Boden etc)* to subside, to cave in. **eingesunkene Wangen** sunken *or* hollow cheeks.

**Einsitzer** *m* - single-seater.

**einspannen** *vt sep* **(a)** *(in Schraubstock)* to clamp in *(in +acc -to)*. **(b)** *(in Schreibmaschine)* to insert *(in +acc* in, into*)*. **(c)** *Pferde* to harness. **(d)** *(fig: arbeiten lassen)* to rope in *(für etw* to do sth*)*. **jdn für seine Zwecke ~** to use sb for one's own ends; *siehe* **eingespannt.**

**einsparen** *vt sep* to save, to economize on; *Kosten* to cut down on; *Posten* to eliminate.

**Einsparung** *f* **(a)** economy. **(b)** *siehe vt* saving; cutting down *(von* on*)*; elimination.

**einspeichern** *vt sep Daten* to feed in, to enter *(in +acc -to)*.

**einspeisen** *vt sep* to feed in *(in +acc -to)*.

**einsperren** *vt sep* to lock up *(in +acc or dat* in*)*.

**einspielen** *sep* **1** *vr (Mus, Sport)* to warm up; *(Regelung, Arbeit)* to work out. **aber das spielt sich alles noch ein** but things should sort themselves out all right; **sich aufeinander ~** to become attuned to one another; *siehe* **eingespielt. 2** *vt (Film etc)* to bring in, to gross; *Kosten* to recover.

**einsprachig** *adj* monolingual.

**einspringen** *vi sep irreg aux sein (col: aushelfen)* to stand in; *(mit Geld etc)* to help out.

**Einspritz-** *in cpds (Aut, Med)* injection; **~düse** *f* injector.

**einspritzen** *vt sep (Aut, Med)* to inject. **er spritzte ihr Insulin ein** he gave her an insulin injection.

**Einspritz-** *(Aut)*: **~motor** *m* injection engine; **~pumpe** *f* injection pump.

**Einspruch** *m* objection *(auch Jur)*. **~ einlegen** *(Admin)* to file an objection; **gegen etw ~ erheben** to raise an objection to sth.

**Einspruchs-:** **~frist** *f (Jur)* period for filing an objection; **~recht** *nt* right to object.

**einspurig** *adj (Rail)* single-track; *(Aut)* single-lane. **die Straße ist nur ~ befahrbar** the road is reduced to one lane.

**einst** *adv (geh)* **(a)** *(früher)* once. **(b)** *(in ferner Zukunft)* one day.

**einstampfen** *vt sep Bücher* to pulp (down).

**Einstand** *m* **(a)** **er hat gestern seinen ~ gegeben** yesterday he celebrated starting his new job. **(b)** *(Tennis)* deuce.

**einstanzen** *vt sep* to stamp in *(in +acc -to)*.

**einstechen** *vt sep irreg* to pierce; *Nadel* to put *or* stick in *(in +acc -to)*; *(Cook)* to prick.

**einstecken** *vt sep* **(a)** *(in etw stecken)* to put *or* stick in *(in +acc -to)*; *Gerät* to plug in. **(b)** *(in die Tasche etc)* **(sich** *dat)* **etw ~** to take sth; **hast du deinen Paß eingesteckt?** have you got your passport with you? **(c)** *(in den Briefkasten)* to post, to mail *(esp US)*. **(d)** *(col) Kritik etc* to take; *(verdienen)* Geld, Profit to pocket *(col)*. **der Boxer mußte viel ~** the boxer had to take a lot of punishment; **er steckt sie alle ein** he puts them all in the shade.

**einstehen** *vi sep irreg aux sein* **(a)** *(sich verbürgen)* **für jdn/etw ~** to vouch for sb/sth; **ich stehe dafür ein, daß** ... I will vouch that ... **(b)** *(Ersatz leisten)* **für etw ~** to make good sth.

**einsteigen** *vi sep irreg aux sein* **(a)** *(in ein Fahrzeug etc)* to get in *(in +acc -to)*; *(in Zug auch, in Bus)* to get on *(in +acc -to)*. **~!** *(Rail etc)* all aboard! **(b)** *(in ein Haus etc)* to climb *or* get in *(in +acc -to)*. **(c)** *(col)* **in die Politik/ins Verlagsgeschäft ~** to go into politics/publishing.

**Einsteiger(in** *f)* *m (col)* beginner.

**einstellbar** *adj* adjustable.

**einstellen** *sep* **1** *vt* **(a)** *(hineinstellen)* to put in. **Bücher ins Regal ~** to put books away on the shelves. **(b)** *(anstellen) Arbeitskräfte* to take on. **(c)** *(beenden)* to stop; *(endgültig auch)* to discontinue; *Expedition, Suche* to call off; *(Mil) Feuer* to cease. **(d)** *(regulieren)* to adjust *(auf +acc to)*; *Fotoapparat (auf Entfernung)* to focus *(auf +acc on)*; *Wecker* to set *(auf +acc for)*; *Sender* to tune in to. **(e)** *(Sport) Rekord* to equal. **2** *vr* **(a)** **sich auf jdn/etw ~** *(sich richten nach)* to adapt oneself to sb/sth; *(sich vorbereiten auf)* to prepare oneself for sb/sth; *siehe* **eingestellt. (b)** *(erscheinen)* to appear; *(Fieber, Regen)* to set in; *(Wort, Gedanke)* to come to mind; *(Jahreszeiten)* to come, to arrive.

**einstellig** *adj Zahl* single-digit.

**Einstellplatz** *m (auf Hof)* carport; *(in Großgarage)* (covered) parking space.

**Einstellung** *f* **(a)** *(Anstellung)* employment. **(b)** *(Beendigung) siehe vt (c)* stopping; discontinuation; calling-off; cessation. **der Sturm zwang uns zur ~ der Suche** the storm forced us to call off the search. **(c)** *(Film: Szene)* take. **(d)** *(Gesinnung, Haltung)* attitude; *(politisch, religiös etc)* views *pl*.

**Einstellungs-:** **~gespräch** *nt* (job) interview; **~stopp** *m* halt in recruitment; **~termin** *m* starting date.

**Einstich** *m* puncture, prick.

**Einstieg** *m* **-e (a)** *no pl (das Einsteigen)* getting in; *(in Bus)* getting on; *(von Dieb: in Haus etc)* entry; *(fig: zu einem Thema etc)* lead-in *(zu to)*. **kein ~** no entrance. **(b)** *(von Bus, Bahn)* door.

**Einstiegsdroge** *f* starter drug.

**einstig** *adj attr* former.

**einstimmen** *sep* **1** *vi (in ein Lied etc)* to join in. **2** *vt (Mus) Instrument* to tune. **jdn/sich auf etw** *(acc)* **~** *(fig)* to get sb/oneself in the mood for sth.

**einstimmig 1** *adv singen, rufen* in unison. **2** *adj (einmütig)* unanimous.

**Einstimmigkeit** *f* unanimity.

**Einstimmung** *f* **für die richtige ~ der Zuhörer sorgen** to get the audience in the right mood.

**einstöckig** *adj Haus* two-storey *(Brit)*, two-story *(US)*.

**einstöpseln** *vt sep (Elec)* to plug in *(in +acc -to)*.

**einstoßen** *vt sep irreg Tür* to break down; *Scheibe* to push in.

**einstreichen** *vt sep irreg (col) Geld, Gewinn* to pocket *(col)*.

**einstreuen** *vt sep* to sprinkle in *(in +acc -to)*; *(fig) Bemerkung etc* to slip in *(in +acc -to)*.

**einströmen** *vi sep aux sein* to flood in *(in +acc -to)*; *(Licht, fig auch)* to stream in *(in +acc -to)*. **~de Kaltluft** a stream of cold air.

**einstudieren\*** *vt sep Rolle* to study; *Theaterstück* to rehearse.

**Einstudierung** *f (Theat)* production.

**einstufen** *vt sep* to classify. **in eine Kategorie** *etc* **~** to put into a category *etc*.

**Einstufung** *f* classification. **nach seiner ~ in eine höhere Gehaltsklasse** after he was put on a higher salary grade.

**einstündig** *adj attr* one-hour.

**einstürmen** *vi sep aux sein* **auf jdn ~** *(Mil)* to assault sb; *(fig)* to assail sb.

**Einsturz** *m* collapse.

**einstürzen** *vi sep aux sein* to collapse. **auf jdn ~** *(fig)* to overwhelm sb.

**Einsturzgefahr** *f* danger of collapse.

**einstweilen** *adv* in the meantime; *(vorläufig)* temporarily.

**einstweilig** *adj attr* temporary. **~e Verfügung** *(Jur)* temporary *or* interim injunction.

**eintägig** *adj attr* one-day.

**Eintagsfliege** *f (Zool)* mayfly; *(fig)* nine-day wonder.

**eintauchen** *sep* **1** *vt* to dip *(in +acc in, into)*; *(völlig)* to immerse *(in +acc in)*. **2** *vi aux sein (Schwimmer)* to dive in; *(U-Boot)* to dive.

**Eintausch** *m* exchange, swap *(col)*. **im ~ gegen** *or* **für etw** in exchange for sth.

**eintauschen** *vt sep* to exchange, to swap *(col) (gegen, für* for); *(umtauschen) Devisen* to change.

**eintausend** *num siehe* **tausend.**

**einteilen** *vt sep* **(a)** to divide (up) *(in +acc into)*. **(b)** *(sinnvoll aufteilen) Zeit, Arbeit* to plan (out), to organize; *Geld* to budget. **(c)** *(dienstlich verpflichten)* to detail *(zu for)*. **er ist als Aufseher eingeteilt** he has been assigned the job of supervisor.

**einteilig** *adj Badeanzug* one-piece *attr*.

**Einteilung** *f siehe vt* **(a)** division. **(b)** planning, organization; budgeting. **(c)** assignment.

**eintippen** *vt sep* to key *or* type in *(in +acc -to)*.

**eintönig** *adj* monotonous.

**Eintönigkeit** *f* monotony.

**Eintopf(gericht** *nt)* *m* stew.

**Eintracht** *f no pl* harmony, concord.

**einträchtig** *adj* peaceable.

**Eintrag** *m ⸚e (schriftlich)* entry *(in +acc in)*.

**eintragen** *sep irreg* **1** *vt* **(a)** *(in Liste etc)* to enter; *(amtlich)* to register; *siehe* **eingetragen. (b)** **jdm Gewinn ~** to bring sb profit; **das trägt nur Schaden ein** that will only do harm. **2** *vr* to sign; *(im Hotel)* to check in. **er trug sich in die Warteliste ein** he put his name down on the waiting list.

**einträglich** *adj* profitable.

**Eintragung** *f* entry *(in +acc in)*.

**eintreffen** *vi sep irreg aux sein* **(a)** *(ankommen)* to arrive. **(b)** *(fig: wahr werden)* to come true.

**eintreiben** *vt sep irreg* **(a)** *Vieh* to drive in *(in +acc -to)*. **(b)** *Geldbeträge* to collect.

**Eintreibung** *f (von Geldbeträgen)* collection.

**eintreten** *sep irreg* **1** *vi* **(a)** *aux sein* **in etw** *(acc)* ~ to enter sth; *(in Zimmer etc auch)* to go/come into sth; *(in Verein etc)* to join sth. **(b) auf jdn** ~ to kick sb. **(c)** *aux sein (sich ereignen) (Tod)* to occur; *(Zeitpunkt)* to come; *(beginnen) (Dunkelheit, Nacht)* to fall; *(Tauwetter)* to set in. **(d)** *aux sein* **für jdn/etw** ~ to stand up for sb/sth. **2** *vt (zertrümmern)* to kick in.

**eintrichtern** *vt sep (col)* **jdm etw** ~ to drum sth into sb.

**Eintritt** *m* **(a)** *(das Eintreten)* entry *(in +acc* (in)to*)*; *(ins Zimmer etc auch)* entrance; *(in Verein etc)* joining *(in +acc* of*)*. **beim** ~ **ins Zimmer** on entering the room; **der** ~ **ins Geschäftsleben** getting into the business world. **(b)** *(~sgeld)* admission *(in +acc* to*)*. ~ **frei** admission free; „~ **verboten**" "no admittance". **(c) bei** ~ **eines solchen Falles** in such an event; **der** ~ **des Todes** the moment when death occurs.

**Eintritts-:** ~**geld** *nt* entrance money, admission charge; ~**karte** *f* (entrance) ticket; ~**preis** *m* admission charge.

**eintrocknen** *vi sep aux sein* to dry up.

**eintrudeln** *vi sep aux sein (col)* to drift in *(col)*.

**eintunken** *vt sep Brot* to dunk *(in +acc in)*.

**ein|üben** *vt sep* to practise *(Brit)*, to practice *(US)*; *Theaterstück etc* to rehearse.

**einverleiben**\* *vi sep and insep* **(a)** *Gebiet, Land* to annex *(dat to)*. **(b)** *(hum col)* **sich** *(dat)* **etw** ~ *(essen, trinken)* to put sth away *(col)*.

**Einvernehmen** *nt no pl (Eintracht)* harmony; *(Übereinstimmung)* agreement. **in gutem** ~ **leben** to live together in harmony; **im** ~ **mit jdm** in agreement with sb.

**einvernehmlich** *adj (form) Regelung* joint.

**einverstanden** *adj* ~**!** okay!, agreed!; ~ **sein** to agree; **ich bin mit deinem Verhalten gar nicht** ~ **I** don't approve of your behaviour; **sich mit etw** ~ **erklären** to give one's agreement to sth.

**Einverständnis** *nt* agreement; *(Zustimmung)* consent. **wir haben uns in gegenseitigem** ~ **scheiden lassen** we were divorced by mutual consent; **im** ~ **mit jdm handeln** to act with sb's consent.

**Einwaage** *f no pl (Comm: Reingewicht) weight of contents of can or jar excluding juice etc.*

**einwachsen**[1] *vt sep Boden, Skier* to wax.

**einwachsen**[2] *vi sep (Finger-, Zehennagel)* to become ingrown.

**Einwand** *m* ⁼e objection. **einen** ~ **erheben** to raise an objection.

**Einwanderer** *m* immigrant.

**einwandern** *vi sep aux sein* to immigrate *(nach, in +acc to)*.

**Einwanderung** *f* immigration *(nach, in +acc to)*.

**Einwanderungs-** *in cpds* immigration.

**einwandfrei** *adj* **(a)** *(ohne Fehler)* perfect; *Sprache, Arbeit auch* faultless; *Benehmen* impeccable. **er spricht ein** ~**es Spanisch** he speaks perfect Spanish. **(b)** *(unzweifelhaft) Beweis auch* definite. **etw** ~ **beweisen** to prove sth beyond doubt.

**einwärts** *adv* inwards.

**einwechseln** *vt sep Geld* to change *(in +acc, gegen* into*)*; *(Sport) Spieler* to substitute.

**einwecken** *vt sep* to preserve; *Obst auch* to bottle.

**Einweckglas** *nt* preserving jar.

**Einweg-** ['ainveːk]: ~**flasche** *f* non-returnable bottle; ~**spritze** *f* disposable syringe; ~**verpackung** *f* disposable wrapping.

**einweichen** *vt sep* to soak.

**einweihen** *vt sep* **(a)** *(feierlich eröffnen)* to open (officially); *(fig)* to christen. **(b) jdn in etw** *(acc)* ~ to initiate sb into sth; **er ist eingeweiht** he knows all about it; *siehe* **Eingeweihte(r)**.

**Einweihung(sfeier)** *f* (official) opening.

**einweisen** *vt sep irreg* **(a)** *(in Krankenhaus)* to admit *(in +acc to)*. **(b)** *(in Arbeit unterweisen)* **jdn** ~ to introduce sb to his job *or* work. **(c)** *(Aut)* to guide in *(in +acc -to)*.

**Einweisung** *f siehe vt* **(a)** admission *(in +acc to)*. **(b) die** ~ **der neuen Mitarbeiter übernehmen** to assume responsibility for introducing new employees to their jobs *or* work. **(c)** guiding in.

**einwenden** *vt sep irreg* **etwas/nichts gegen etw einzuwenden haben** to have an objection/no objection to sth, to object/not to object to sth; **er hat immer etwas einzuwenden** he always has some objection to make.

**Einwendung** *f* objection *(auch Jur)*.

**einwerfen** *sep irreg* **1** *vt* **(a)** *Fensterscheibe etc* to break, to smash. **(b)** *Brief* to post, to mail *(esp US)*; *Münze* to insert. **(c)** *(fig) Bemerkung* to throw in. **2** *vi (Sport)* to throw in, to take the throw-in.

**einwickeln** *vt sep* **(a)** to wrap (up). **(b)** *(col: überreden)* to take in; *(durch Schmeicheleien)* to butter up *(col)*.

**einwilligen** *vi sep (in +acc to)* to consent, to agree.

**Einwilligung** *f (in +acc to)* consent, agreement.

**einwinken** *vt sep* to guide or direct in.

**einwirken** *vi sep* **auf jdn/etw** ~ to have an effect on sb/sth; *(beeinflussen)* to influence sb/sth; **etw** ~ **lassen** *(Med)* to let sth work in.

**Einwirkung** *f* influence; *(einer Sache auch)* effect. **unter (der)** ~ **von Drogen** *etc* under the influence of drugs *etc*; **unter (der)** ~ **eines Schocks stehen** to be suffering from shock.

**einwöchig** *adj* one-week *attr*.

**Einwohner(in** *f)* *m -* inhabitant.

**Einwohner-:** ~**meldeamt** *nt residents' registration office*; **sich beim** ~**meldeamt (an)melden** ≃ to register with the police; ~**schaft** *f no pl* population, inhabitants *pl*; ~**zahl** *f* population.

**Einwurf** *m* **(a)** *(von Münze)* insertion; *(von Brief)* posting, mailing *(esp US)*. **(b)** *(Sport)* throw-in. **(c)** *(Schlitz)* slot; *(von Briefkasten)* slit. **(d)** *(fig)* interjection; *(Einwand)* objection.

**Einzahl** *f* singular.

**einzahlen** *vt sep* to pay in. **Geld auf ein Konto** ~ to pay money into an account.

**Einzahlung** *f* payment; *(auf Sparkonto auch)* deposit.

**Einzahlungs-** *in cpds* paying-in; ~**frist** *f* payment deadline.

**einzäunen** *vt sep* to fence in.

**Einzäunung** *f* fence, fencing; *(das Umzäunen)* fencing-in.

**einzeichnen** *vt sep* to draw in. **ist der Ort eingezeichnet?** is the place marked?

**Einzel** *nt -* *(Tennis)* singles *sing*.

**Einzel-:** ~**aktion** *f* independent action; ~**anfertigung** *f* custom-made item, one-off; ~**aufstellung** *f (Comm)* itemized list; ~**ausgabe** *f* separate edition; ~**band** *m* individual *or* single volume; ~**behandlung** *f* individual treatment; ~**bett** *nt* single bed; ~**blatteinzug** *m* cut-sheet feed;

~**erscheinung** f isolated occurrence; ~**fahrschein** m single (Brit) or one-way ticket; ~**fall** m individual case; (Sonderfall) isolated or one-off case; ~**gänger(in** f) m - loner; ~**haft** f solitary (confinement).

**Einzelhandel** m retail trade. **im ~ erhältlich** available retail.

**Einzelhandels-** in cpds retail.

**Einzel-:** ~**händler** m retailer; ~**heit** f detail, particular; **etw in allen ~heiten schildern** to describe sth right down to the last detail; ~**kind** nt only child.

**Einzeller** m - (Biol) single-celled organism.

**einzeln** adj (a) individual; (getrennt) separate; (von Paar) Schuh etc odd. **bitte ~ eintreten** please come in one (person) at a time; **die ~en Städte, die wir besucht haben** the individual cities which we visited; ~ **aufführen** to list separately or individually; ~ **angeben** to specify. (b) (alleinstehend) Baum, Haus single, solitary. (c) (mit pl n: einige, vereinzelte) some. ~**e Besucher kamen schon früher** one or two visitors came earlier. (d) (substantivisch) **der/die ~e** the individual; **ein ~er** an individual, a single person; (ein einziger Mensch) one single person; ~**e** some (people), a few (people); **jeder ~e** (each and) every one of you/them etc; ~**es** some; ~**es hat mir gefallen** I liked some of it; **das ~e** the particular; **jedes ~e** each one; **etw im ~en besprechen** to discuss sth in detail; **bis ins ~e** right down to the last detail.

**Einzel-:** ~**person** f single person; ~**preis** m (individual) price, unit price (Comm); ~**radaufhängung** f (Aut) independent suspension; ~**reisende(r)** mf single traveller; ~**stück** nt ein schönes ~**stück** a beautiful piece; ~**stücke verkaufen wir nicht** we don't sell them singly; ~**teil** nt individual or separate part; (Ersatzteil) spare part; **etw in seine ~teile zerlegen** to take sth to pieces; ~**unterricht** m one-to-one tuition; ~**wesen** nt individual; ~**zelle** f single cell (auch Biol); ~**zimmer** nt single room.

**einzementieren*** vt sep Stein to cement.

**einziehen** sep irreg **1** vt (a) (einfügen) Faden to thread; (in einen Bezug etc) to put in; (Build: einbauen) Wand etc to put in; (Kopiergerät etc) Papier to take in. (b) (zurückziehen) Krallen, Fahrgestell to retract, to draw in; Bauch, Netz to pull in; Flagge, Segel to lower, to take down. **den Kopf ~** to duck (one's head); **der Hund zog den Schwanz ein** the dog put his tail between his legs. (c) (Mil) (zu into) Personen to call up, to draft (esp US); Fahrzeuge etc to requisition. (d) (einfordern) Steuern to collect; Banknoten to withdraw (from circulation); Führerschein to take away; Vermögen to confiscate; (fig) Erkundigungen to make (über +acc about). **2** vi aux sein (a) (in Haus) to move in. (b) (auch Mil: einmarschieren) to march in (in +acc -to). (c) (einkehren) to come in (in +dat to). **wenn der Friede im Lande einzieht** when peace comes to our country. (d) (eindringen) to soak in (in +acc -to).

**Einziehung** f (a) (Mil) (von Personen) call-up, drafting (esp US); (von Fahrzeugen) requisitioning. (b) (Einforderung) (von Vermögen) confiscation; (von Banknoten, Führerschein etc) withdrawal; (von Steuern etc) collection.

**einzig 1** adj (a) attr only, sole. **ich sehe nur eine ~e Möglichkeit** I can see only one (single) possibility; **kein ~es Mal** not once, not one single time. (b) (emph) absolute. **dieses Fußballspiel war eine ~e Schlammschlacht** this football match was just one big mudbath. (c) pred (~artig) unique. (d) (substan-

tivisch) **der/die ~e** the only one; **das ~e** the only thing; **kein ~er** nobody, not a single person. **2** adv (allein) only, solely. **die ~ mögliche Lösung** the only possible solution; ~ **und allein** solely; **das ~ Wahre** the only thing; (das beste) the real McCoy.

**einzig|artig** adj unique.

**Einzig|artigkeit** f uniqueness.

**Einzimmer-** in cpds one-room.

**Einzug** m (a) (in Haus etc) move (in +acc into). (b) (Einmarsch) entry (in +acc into). (c) (fig: von Stimmung, Winter etc) advent. **der Frühling etc hält seinen ~** spring etc is coming. (d) (von Steuern) collection; (von Banknoten) withdrawal.

**Einzugs-:** ~**auftrag** m (Fin) direct debit; ~**bereich** m catchment area; ~**feier** f house-warming (party); ~**verfahren** nt (Fin) direct debit.

**einzwängen** vt sep (lit) to squeeze or jam in; (fig) jdn to constrict.

**Eis** nt - (a) no pl ice. **zu ~ gefrieren** to freeze, to turn to ice; **das ~ brechen** (fig) to break the ice; **etw auf ~ legen** (fig col) to put sth on ice or into cold storage. (b) (Speise~) ice(-cream). ~ **am Stiel** ice-lolly (Brit), popsicle ® (US).

**Eis-:** ~**bahn** f ice rink; ~**bär** m polar bear; ~**becher** m sundae; **e~bedeckt** adj ice-covered; ~**bein** nt (Cook) knuckle of pork; ~**berg** m iceberg; **die Spitze des ~bergs** (fig) the tip of the iceberg; ~**beutel** m ice pack; **e~blau** adj ice-blue; ~**block** m block of ice; ~**blume** f usu pl frost pattern; ~**brecher** m icebreaker; ~**café** nt = ~**diele**.

**Eischnee** m (Cook) beaten white of egg.

**Eis-:** ~**creme** f ice(-cream); ~**decke** f sheet of ice; ~**diele** f ice-cream parlour (Brit) or parlor (US).

**Eisen** nt - iron. **mehrere ~ im Feuer haben** (fig) to have more than one iron in the fire; **zum alten ~ gehören** (fig) to be on the scrap heap; **man muß das ~ schmieden, solange es heiß ist** (Prov) strike while the iron is hot (Prov).

**Eisenbahn** f railway (Brit), railroad (US); (~wesen) railways (Brit) pl, railroad (US); (col: Zug) train; (Spielzeug~) train set. **es ist (aller)höchste ~** (col) it's getting late.

**Eisenbahn-:** ~**abteil** nt compartment; ~**brücke** f railway (Brit) or railroad (US) bridge.

**Eisenbahner(in** f) m - railwayman (Brit), railway employee (Brit), railroader (US).

**Eisenbahn-:** ~**fähre** f train ferry; ~**fahrkarte** f rail or train ticket; ~**fahrt** f train or rail ride; ~**netz** nt rail network; ~**schaffner** m (railway) guard (Brit), (railroad) conductor (US); ~**strecke** f railway line (Brit), railroad (US); ~**überführung** f footbridge; ~**wagen** m railway (Brit) or railroad (US) carriage; ~**waggon** m (Güter~) goods wagon.

**Eisen-:** ~**erz** nt iron ore; **e~haltig** adj Gestein iron-bearing; **das Wasser ist e~haltig** the water contains iron; ~**hütte** f ironworks pl or sing, iron foundry; ~**mangel** m iron deficiency; ~**oxyd** nt ferric oxide; ~**präparat** nt (Med) iron tonic/tablets pl; ~**stange** f iron bar; **e~verarbeitend** adj attr iron processing; ~**waren** pl ironmongery sing (Brit), hardware sing (US); ~**warenhandlung** f ironmonger's (Brit), hardware store (US); ~**zeit** f Iron Age.

**eisern** adj (a) attr (aus Eisen) iron. **der E~e Vorhang** the Iron Curtain; ~**e Lunge** (Med) iron lung. (b) Disziplin, Wille iron attr; Energie unflagging; Ruhe unshakeable. ~**e Gesundheit** iron constitution; **er schwieg ~** he remained resolutely silent; **er ist ~ bei seinem Entschluß geblieben** he stuck firmly to his decision; **mit ~er Faust** with an iron hand; **in**

**etw** *(dat)* ~ **sein** to be adamant about sth; **mit** ~**em Besen kehren** to make a clean sweep; ~ **sparen** to save resolutely. **(c)** *attr Reserve* emergency; *Ration auch* iron.

**Eiseskälte** *f* icy cold.

**Eis-:** ~**fach** *nt* freezer compartment, ice-box; ~**fläche** *f* (surface of the) ice; **e**~**frei** *adj* free of ice *pred*; **e**~**gekühlt** *adj* chilled; ~**glätte** *f* black ice; ~**hockey** *nt* ice hockey, hockey *(US)*.

**eisig** *adj (lit, fig)* icy.

**Eis-:** ~**kaffee** *m* iced coffee; **e**~**kalt** *adj* **(a)** icy-cold; **(b)** *(fig) (abweisend)* icy, cold; *(kalt und berechnend)* cold-blooded, cold and calculating; *(dreist)* cool; ~**kappe** *f* ice cap; ~**kunstlauf** *m* figure skating; ~**kunstläufer** *m* figure skater; ~**lauf** *m* ice-skating; **e**~**laufen** *vi sep irreg aux sein* to ice-skate; ~**läufer** *m* ice-skater; ~**meer** *nt* polar sea; **Nördliches/Südliches** ~**meer** Arctic/Antarctic Ocean; ~**pickel** *m* ice axe *(Brit)* or ax *(US)*, ice pick.

**Eisprung** *m (Physiol)* ovulation *no art.*

**Eis-:** ~**regen** *m* sleet; ~**revue** *f* ice revue, ice show; ~**schießen** *nt* curling; ~**schmelze** *f* thaw; ~**schnellauf** *m* speed skating; ~**schnelläufer** *m* speed skater; ~**schokolade** *f* iced chocolate; ~**scholle** *f* ice floe; ~**schrank** *m* refrigerator; ~**stadion** *nt* ice rink; ~**stockschießen** *nt* curling; ~**tanz** *m* ice-dancing; ~**torte** *f* ice-cream cake; ~**verkäufer** *m* ice-cream seller *or* man *(col)*; ~**vogel** *m (Orn)* kingfisher; ~**würfel** *m* ice cube; ~**zapfen** *m* icicle; ~**zeit** *f* Ice Age.

**eitel** *adj* vain; *(eingebildet auch)* conceited.

**Eitelkeit** *f* vanity.

**Eiter** *m no pl* pus.

**eit(e)rig** *adj Ausfluß* purulent; *Wunde* festering.

**eitern** *vi* to discharge pus, to suppurate.

**Eiweiß** *nt* (egg-)white, white of egg; *(Chem)* protein.

**Eiweiß-:** **e**~**arm** *adj* low in protein; ~**arme Kost** a low-protein diet; ~**gehalt** *m* protein content; **e**~**haltig** *adj Fleisch ist sehr* **e**~**haltig** meat is high in protein *or* contains a lot of protein; ~**mangel** *m* protein deficiency; ~**präparat** *nt* protein preparation; **e**~**reich** *adj* high in protein; **e**~**reiche Kost** a high-protein diet.

**Eizelle** *f (Biol)* egg cell.

**Ejakulation** *f* ejaculation.

**EKD** [eːkaːˈdeː] *f* - = **Evangelische Kirche in Deutschland.**

**Ekel[1]** *m no pl* disgust, revulsion; *(Übelkeit)* nausea. **vor jdm/etw einen** ~ **haben** to loathe sb/sth; **dabei empfinde ich** ~ it gives me a feeling of disgust *etc*; **er hat das Essen vor** ~ **ausgespuckt** he spat out the food in disgust.

**Ekel[2]** *nt - (col)* obnoxious person, horror *(col)*.

**ekel|erregend** *adj* nauseating, revolting.

**ekelhaft, ek(e)lig** *adj* disgusting, revolting; *(col) Problem, Chef* nasty *(col)*, horrible.

**ekeln 1** *vt* to disgust, to revolt. **2** *vt impers* **es ekelt mich vor diesem Anblick** the sight of it fills me with disgust *or* revulsion. **3** *vr* to feel disgusted. **sich vor etw** *(dat)* ~ to find sth disgusting.

**EKG** [eːkaːˈgeː] *nt* **-s** = **Elektrokardiogramm** ECG.

**Eklat** [eˈklaː(ː)] *m* **-s** *(geh: Aufsehen)* sensation.

**eklatant** *adj Fall* sensational; *Beispiel* striking; *Verletzung* flagrant.

**eklig** *adj* = **ek(e)lig.**

**Eklipse** *f* **-n** eclipse.

**Ekstase** *f* **-n** ecstasy. **in** ~ **geraten** to go into ecstasies; **jdn in** ~ **versetzen** to send sb into ecstasies.

**ekstatisch** *adj* ecstatic.

**Ekzem** *nt* **-e** *(Med)* eczema.

**Elan** *m no pl* élan, zest.

**elastisch** *adj* elastic; *Gang, Metall, Holz* springy; *(fig) Muskel, Mensch* strong and supple; *(flexibel)* flexible, elastic.

**Elastizität** *f siehe* **elastisch** elasticity; springiness; flexibility. **die** ~ **seines Körpers** the supple strength of his body.

**Elch** *m* **-e** elk.

**Elefant** *m* elephant. **wie ein** ~ **im Porzellanladen** *(col)* like a bull in a china shop *(prov)*.

**Elefanten-:** ~**bulle** *m* bull elephant; ~**kuh** *f* cow elephant.

**elegant** *adj* elegant.

**Eleganz** *f* elegance.

**Elegie** *f* elegy.

**elegisch** *adj* elegiac.

**elektrifizieren*** *vt* to electrify.

**Elektrifizierung** *f* electrification.

**Elektrik** *f (Anlagen)* electrics *pl.*

**Elektriker(in** *f)* *m* - electrician.

**elektrisch** *adj* electric; *Entladung, Widerstand* electrical. ~**e Geräte** electrical appliances; ~**er Schlag/Strom** electric shock/current; **der** ~**e Stuhl** the electric chair; **wir kochen/heizen** ~ we cook/heat by electricity.

**Elektrische** *f* **-n** *(dated)* tram, streetcar *(US)*.

**elektrisieren*** **1** *vt (lit, fig)* to electrify. **ich habe mich elektrisiert** I got an electric shock; **wie elektrisiert** (as if) electrified. **2** *vi* to give an electric shock.

**Elektrizität** *f* electricity.

**Elektrizitätswerk** *nt* power station; *(Gesellschaft)* electric power company, electricity board *(Brit)*.

**Elektro-** [eˈlɛktro] *in cpds* electro- *(auch Sci)*, electric; ~**antrieb** *m* electric power; ~**artikel** *m* electrical appliance; ~**auto** *nt* electric car.

**Elektrode** *f* **-n** electrode.

**Elektro-:** ~**fahrzeug** *nt* electric vehicle; ~**gerät** *nt* electrical appliance; ~**geschäft** *nt* electrical shop *(Brit)* or store *(US)*; ~**herd** *m* electric cooker; ~**ingenieur** *m* electrical engineer; ~**installateur** *m* electrician; ~**kardiogramm** *nt (Med)* electrocardiogram; ~**lok** *f* electric locomotive; ~**magnet** *m* electromagnet; ~**mechaniker** *m* electrician; **e**~**mechanisch** *adj* electromechanical; ~**motor** *m* electric motor.

**Elektron** [elɛkˈtroːnən] *nt* **-en** electron.

**Elektronen-:** ~**blitz(gerät** *nt)* *m (Phot)* electronic flash; ~**(ge)hirn** *nt* electronic brain; ~**mikroskop** *nt* electron microscope; ~**rechner** *m* (electronic) computer; ~**röhre** *f* valve, electron tube *(US)*.

**Elektronik** *f* electronics *sing; (Teile)* electronics *pl.*

**elektronisch** *adj* electronic. ~**er Geldverkehr** electronic banking; ~**e Post** electronic mail, E-mail; ~**er Briefkasten** electronic mailbox.

**Elektro-:** ~**rasierer** *m* electric shaver *or* razor; ~**schock** *m (Med)* electric shock, electroshock; ~**technik** *f* electrical engineering; ~**techniker** *m* electrician; *(Ingenieur)* electrical engineer; **e**~**technisch** *adj* electrical.

**Element** *nt* element; *(Elec)* cell. **kriminelle** ~**e** *(pej)* criminal elements; **in seinem** ~ **sein** to be in one's element.

**elementar** *adj (grundlegend)* elementary; *Gewalt, Trieb* elemental.

**Elementar-:** ~**begriff** *m* elementary *or* basic concept; ~**kenntnisse** *pl* elementary knowledge; ~**teilchen** *nt (Phys)* elementary particle.

**elend** *adj* **(a)** wretched, miserable; *(krank)* wretched, awful. **mir ist ganz** ~ I feel really awful.

**(b)** *(col: furchtbar)* Hunger, Wetter awful. **ich habe ~ gefroren** I was miserably cold.

**Elend** *nt no pl (Unglück, Not)* misery, distress; *(Verwahrlosung)* squalor; *(Armut)* poverty. **(wie) ein Häufchen ~** *(col)* (looking) a picture of misery; **da kann man das heulende ~ kriegen** *(col)* it's enough to make you scream *(col)*.

**elendig(lich)** *adv (geh)* wretchedly. **~ zugrunde gehen** to come to a wretched end.

**Elends-:** **~quartier** *nt* slum dwelling; **~viertel** *nt* slum area.

**elf** *num* eleven; *siehe* **vier.**

**Elf** *f* **-en** *(Sport)* team, eleven.

**Elfe** *f* **-n** elf.

**Elfenbein** *nt* ivory.

**elfenbeine(r)n** *adj* ivory.

**Elfenbein-:** **~küste** *f* Ivory Coast; **~turm** *m (fig)* ivory tower.

**elfmal** *adv* eleven times; *siehe* **viermal.**

**Elfmeter** *m (Ftbl)* penalty (kick) *(für* to, for*)*. **einen ~ schießen** to take a penalty.

**Elfmeter-:** **~punkt** *m (Ftbl)* penalty spot; **~schießen** *nt (Ftbl)* penalty shoot-out; **durch ~schießen entschieden** decided on penalties; **~schütze** *m (Ftbl)* penalty-taker.

**Elftel** *nt* **-** eleventh.

**elfte(r, s)** *adj* eleventh; *siehe* **vierte(r, s).**

**eliminieren*** *vt* to eliminate.

**Eliminierung** *f* elimination.

**elitär** *adj* **1** elitist. **2** *adv* in an elitist fashion.

**Elite** *f* **-n** elite.

**Elite-:** **~denken** *nt* elitism; **~truppe** *f (Mil)* crack *or* elite troops *pl.*

**Elixier** *nt* **-e** elixir *(liter)*, tonic.

**Elle** *f* **-n** *(Anat)* ulna *(spec)*. **alles mit der gleichen ~ messen** *(fig)* to measure everything by the same yardstick.

**Ell(en)bogen** *m* **-** elbow. **die ~ gebrauchen** *(fig)* to be pushy *(col)* or ruthless.

**Ell(en)bogen-:** **~freiheit** *f (fig)* elbow room; **~gesellschaft** *f* dog-eat-dog society.

**ellenlang** *adj (fig col)* incredibly long *(col)*; **Kerl** incredibly tall *(col)*.

**Ellipse** *f* **-n** *(Math)* ellipse.

**elliptisch** *adj (Math)* elliptic(al).

**Elsaß** *nt, gen* **-** *or* **-sses das ~** Alsace.

**Elsässer(in** *f)* *m* **-** Alsatian, inhabitant of Alsace.

**Elsässer, elsässisch** *adj* Alsatian.

**Elster** *f* **-n** magpie. **eine diebische ~ sein** *(fig)* to be a thief.

**elterlich** *adj* parental.

**Eltern** *pl* parents *pl.* **nicht von schlechten ~ sein** *(col)* to be quite something *(col)*.

**Eltern-:** **~abend** *m (Sch)* parents' evening; **~beirat** *m (Sch)* parents' association; **~haus** *nt (lit, fig)* (parental) home; **e~los** *adj* orphaned; **~sprechtag** *m* open day (for parents); **~teil** *m* parent; **~urlaub** *m* *unpaid leave given to a new mother or father.*

**Email** [e'mai] *nt* **-s, Emaille** [e'maljə] *f* **-n** enamel.

**emaillieren*** [ema'ji:rən] *vt* to enamel.

**Emanze** *f* **-n** *(usu pej)* women's libber *(col)*.

**Emanzipation** *f* emancipation.

**emanzipatorisch** *adj* emancipatory.

**emanzipieren*** *vr* to emancipate oneself.

**emanzipiert** *adj* emancipated, **Frau** *auch* liberated.

**Embargo** *nt* **-s** embargo.

**Emblem** *nt* **-e** emblem; *(Firmen~)* logo.

**Embolie** *f (Med)* embolism.

**Embryo** *m* **-s** *or* **-nen** [-y'o:nən] embryo.

**embryonal** *adj attr (Biol, fig)* embryonic.

**Emigrant(in** *f)* *m* emigrant; *(politisch)* émigré.

**Emigration** *f* emigration. **in der ~ leben** to live in self-imposed exile.

**emigrieren*** *vi aux sein* to emigrate.

**eminent** *adj (geh)* **Person** eminent. **von ~er Bedeutung** of the utmost significance.

**Eminenz** *f (Eccl)* **(Seine) ~** (His) Eminence.

**Emir** *m* **-e** emir.

**Emirat** *nt* emirate.

**Emission** *f* **(a)** *(Fin)* issue. **(b)** *(Phys)* emission.

**emittieren** *vt* **(a)** *(Fin)* to issue. **(b)** *(Phys)* to emit.

**Emotion** *f* emotion.

**emotional** *adj* emotional; **Ausdrucksweise** emotive.

**emotions-:** **~geladen** *adj* emotionally-charged; **~los** *adj* free of emotion, unemotional.

**empfahl** *pret of* **empfehlen.**

**empfand** *pret of* **empfinden.**

**Empfang** *m* **=e** reception *(auch Rad, TV)*; *(von Brief, Ware etc)* receipt. **etw in ~ nehmen** to receive sth; *(Comm)* to take delivery of sth; **(zahlbar) nach/bei ~** *(+gen)* (payable) on receipt (of).

**empfangen** *pret* **empfing,** *ptp* **~ 1** *vt* to receive *(auch Rad, TV)*; *(begrüßen)* to greet, to receive *(form)*; *(herzlich)* to welcome; *(abholen)* **Besuch** to meet. **2** *vti (schwanger werden)* to conceive.

**Empfänger(in** *f)* *m* **-** recipient, receiver *(auch Rad, TV)*; *(Adressat)* addressee; *(Waren~)* consignee. **~ unbekannt** *(auf Briefen)* not known at this address.

**empfänglich** *adj (aufnahmebereit)* receptive *(für to)*; *(anfällig)* susceptible *(für to)*.

**Empfänglichkeit** *f siehe adj* receptivity; susceptibility.

**Empfängnis** *f* conception.

**Empfängnis-:** **e~verhütend** *adj* contraceptive; **e~verhütende Mittel** *pl* contraceptives *pl*; **~verhütung** *f* contraception.

**Empfangs-:** **~bereich** *m (Rad, TV)* reception area; **~bestätigung** *f* (acknowledgment of) receipt; **~chef** *m (von Hotel)* head porter; **~dame** *f* receptionist; **~gerät** *nt* (radio/TV) set, receiver; **~störung** *f (Rad, TV)* interference *no pl*; **~zimmer** *nt* reception room.

**empfehlen** *pret* **empfahl,** *ptp* **empfohlen 1** *vt* **(jdm) etw/jdn ~** to recommend sth/sb (to sb); **jdm ~, etw zu tun** to recommend *or* advise sb to do sth; **ich würde dir Vorsicht/Geduld ~** I would recommend caution/patience. **2** *vr* **(a)** to recommend itself/oneself. **sich als Experte etc ~** to offer one's services as an expert *etc*; **es empfiehlt sich, das zu tun** it is advisable to do that. **(b)** *(dated, hum: sich verabschieden)* to take one's leave. **ich empfehle mich!** I'll take my leave.

**empfehlenswert** *adj* to be recommended.

**Empfehlung** *f* recommendation; *(Referenz)* reference; *(form: Gruß)* regards *pl.* **auf ~ von** on the recommendation of; **mit freundlichen ~en** *(am Briefende)* with best regards.

**Empfehlungsschreiben** *nt* letter of recommendation, testimonial.

**empfinden** *pret* **empfand,** *ptp* **empfunden** *vt* to feel. **etw als Beleidigung ~** to find sth insulting; **jdn als Störenfried ~** to see sb as a troublemaker.

**Empfinden** *nt no pl* feeling. **meinem ~ nach** to my mind.

**empfindlich** *adj* **(a)** sensitive *(auch Phot, Tech)*; **Gesundheit, Stoff** delicate; *(leicht reizbar)* touchy *(col)*. **~ reagieren** to be sensitive *(auf +acc* to*)*; **~e Stelle** *(lit)* sensitive spot; *(fig auch)* sore point. **(b)** **Verlust, Kälte, Strafe** severe. **deine Kritik hat ihn ~ getroffen** your criticism cut him to the quick.

**Empfindlichkeit** *f siehe adj* **(a)** sensitivity *(auch*

*Phot, Tech)*; delicateness; touchiness *(col)*.
**empfindsam** *adj Mensch* sensitive.
**Empfindsamkeit** *f* sensitivity.
**Empfindung** *f* feeling; *(Sinnes~ auch)* sensation.
**empfindungslos** *adj lit, fig* insensitive *(für, gegen* to*)*; *Glieder* numb, without sensation.
**empfing** *pret of* **empfangen.**
**empfohlen** *ptp of* **empfehlen.**
**empfunden** *ptp of* **empfinden.**
**empirisch** *adj* empirical.
**empor** *adv (liter)* upwards, up.
**empor-:** ~**arbeiten** *vr sep (geh)* to work one's way up; ~**blicken** *vi sep (liter: lit, fig)* to look up *(zu* to*)*.
**Empore** *f* -n *(Archit)* gallery.
**empören*** **1** *vt* to outrage; *siehe* **empört. 2** *vr* to be indignant *or* outraged *(über +acc* at*)*.
**empörend** *adj* outrageous.
**Empor-:** **e~heben** *vt sep irreg (geh)* to raise; **e~kommen** *vi sep irreg aux sein (geh)* to rise (up); *(fig) (aufkommen)* to come to the fore; *(vorankommen)* to go up in the world; ~**kömmling** *m (pej)* upstart; **e~ragen** *vi sep aux haben or sein (geh: lit, fig)* to tower *(über +acc* above*)*; **e~steigen** *vti sep irreg aux sein (geh)* to climb (up); *(fig: Karriere machen)* to climb, to rise.
**empört** *adj* indignant, outraged *(über +acc* at*)*.
**Empörung** *f no pl (Entrüstung)* indignation *(über +acc* at*)*. **über etw in ~ geraten** to get indignant about sth.
**emsig** *adj* busy, industrious; *Treiben* bustling.
**Emsigkeit** *f siehe adj* industriousness; bustle.
**Emu** *m* -s emu.
**Emulation** *f (esp Comp)* emulation.
**Emulsion** *f* emulsion.
**E-Musik** *f* serious music.
**End-** *in cpds* final; ~**abnehmer** *m* buyer; ~**abrechnung** *f* final account; ~**bahnhof** *m* terminus; ~**benutzer** *m* end-user; ~**betrag** *m* final amount.
**Ende** *nt* -n end; *(Ergebnis)* outcome, result; *(Ausgang eines Films, Romans etc)* ending. **~ Mai/der Woche** at the end of May/the week; **er ist ~ vierzig** he is in his late forties; **er wohnt am ~ der Welt** *(col)* he lives at the back of beyond; **bis ans ~ der Welt** to the ends of the earth; **letzten ~es** in the end, at the end of the day; **einer Sache** *(dat)* **ein ~ machen** to put an end to sth; **damit muß es jetzt ein ~ haben** there has to be an end to this now, this must stop now; **ein ~ nehmen** to come to an end; **ein böses ~ nehmen** to come to a bad end; **... und kein ~ ...** with no end in sight, ... without end; **es ist noch ein gutes** *or* **ganzes ~** *(col)* there's still quite a way to go (yet); **am ~** at the end; *(schließlich)* in the end; *(col: möglicherweise)* perhaps; **am ~ sein** *(fig)* to be at the end of one's tether; **ich bin mit meiner Weisheit am ~** I'm at my wits' end; **meine Geduld ist am ~** my patience is at an end; **zu ~** finished, over; **etw zu ~ führen** to finish (off) sth; **ein Buch zu ~ lesen** to finish (reading) a book; **zu ~ gehen** to come to an end; *(Vorräte)* to run out; **~ gut, alles gut** *(Prov)* all's well that ends well *(Prov)*.
**End|effekt** *m:* **im ~** *(col)* in the final analysis, at the end of the day.
**enden** *vi* to end, to finish; *(Zug)* to terminate; *(sterben)* to meet one's end. **auf etw** *(acc)* **~** *(Wort)* to end with sth; **der Streit endete vor Gericht** the quarrel ended up in court; **wie wird das noch mit ihm ~?** what will become of him?; **das wird böse ~!** no good will come of it!
**End|ergebnis** *nt* final result.

**endgültig** *adj* final; *Antwort* definite; *Fassung* definitive.
**Endivie** [-viə] *f* endive.
**End-:** ~**lager** *nt (für Atommüll etc)* permanent (waste) disposal site; ~**lagerung** *f (von Atommüll etc)* permanent (waste) disposal; ~**lauf** *m* final.
**endlich** **1** *adv* finally, at last; *(am Ende)* eventually, in the end. **hör ~ damit auf!** will you stop that!; **komm doch ~!** come on! **2** *adj (Math, Philos)* finite.
**endlos** *adj* endless. **ich mußte ~ lange warten** I had to wait for an eternity *or* interminably.
**Endlosformular** *nt* continuous stationery.
**Endlosigkeit** *f* endlessness.
**Endlospapier** *nt no pl* continuous paper.
**End-:** ~**phase** *f* final stage(s *pl*); ~**produkt** *nt* end *or* final product; ~**punkt** *m (lit, fig)* end.
**Endrunde** *f (Sport)* finals *pl*; *(fig)* final round.
**Endrunden-:** ~**spiel** *nt* final (match); ~**teilnehmer** *m* finalist.
**End-:** ~**spiel** *nt (Sport)* final; *(Chess)* end game; ~**spurt** *m (Sport, fig)* final spurt; **er hat einen starken ~spurt** *(Sport)* he's got a good finish; ~**stadium** *nt* final *or (Med)* terminal stage; ~**station** *f (Rail etc)* terminus; *(fig)* end of the line; ~**stufe** *f* final stage; ~**summe** *f* (sum) total.
**Endung** *f (Gram)* ending.
**End-:** ~**verbraucher** *m* consumer, end-user; ~**ziel** *nt* ultimate goal; ~**zweck** *m* ultimate purpose.
**Energie** *f (Sci, fig)* energy. **mit ganzer ~** with all one's energy.
**Energie-:** ~**bedarf** *m* energy requirement; ~**bündel** *nt (col)* fireball; ~**gewinnung** *f* generation of energy; ~**haushalt** *m (Physiol)* energy balance; ~**knappheit** *f* energy shortage; ~**krise** *f* energy crisis; **e~los** *adj* lacking in energy; ~**politik** *f* energy policy/politics *sing or pl*; ~**quelle** *f* energy source; **e~sparend** *adj* energy-saving; ~**sparmaßnahmen** *pl* energy-saving measures; ~**träger** *m* source of energy; ~**verbrauch** *m* energy consumption; ~**versorgung** *f* supply of energy; ~**wirtschaft** *f* energy industry; ~**zufuhr** *f* energy supply.
**energisch** *adj (entschlossen, streng)* forceful, firm; *Protest* energetic, strong. **~ durchgreifen** to take vigorous *or* firm action; **etw ~ verteidigen** to defend sth vigorously; **etw ~ dementieren** to deny sth strenuously.
**eng** *adj* **(a)** *(lit, fig)* narrow; *Raum* cramped; *Kleidung* tight, close-fitting. **ein Kleid ~er machen** to take a dress in; **im ~eren Sinne** in the narrow sense; **in die ~ere Wahl kommen** to be short-listed; **das darfst du nicht so ~ sehen** *(fig col)* don't take it so seriously. **(b)** *(nah, vertraut)* close. **~ nebeneinander** close together; **eine Feier im ~sten Kreise** a small party for close friends; **mit jdm ~ befreundet sein** to be a close friend of sb.
**Engadin** *nt* Engadine.
**Engagement** [ãgaʒə'mã:] *nt* -s **(a)** *no pl* commitment *(für* to*)*. **(b)** *(Theat)* engagement.
**engagieren*** [ãga'ʒiːrən] **1** *vt* to engage. **2** *vr* to be/become committed *(für* to*)*; *(in einer Bekanntschaft)* to become involved. **er hat sich sehr dafür engagiert, daß ...** he completely committed himself to ...; **ein engagierter Film** a (socially/politically) committed film.
**engagiert** [ãga'ʒiːrt] *adj* committed.
**Enge** *f* -n **(a)** *no pl (lit, fig)* narrowness; *(von Wohnung)* cramped conditions, lack of space *(+gen* in*)*; *(Gedrängtheit)* crush; *(von Kleid)* tightness. **(b)** *(Engpaß)* pass, defile. **jdn in die ~ treiben** *(fig)* to drive sb into a corner.

**Engel** *m - (lit, fig)* angel. **ein guter ~** *(fig)* a guardian angel; **wir sind alle keine ~** *(prov)* none of us is perfect.

**Engelmacher(in** *f) m (euph col)* backstreet abortionist.

**Engels-:** **~geduld** *f* sie hat eine **~geduld** she has the patience of a saint; **~haar** *nt* angel's hair, *type of Christmas tree decoration;* **~zungen** *pl:* **(wie) mit ~zungen reden** to use all one's powers of persuasion.

**Eng-:** **e~herzig** *adj* petty, hidebound; **~herzigkeit** *f* pettiness.

**England** *nt* England.

**Engländer** *m -* (a) Englishman; *(Junge)* English boy. **die ~** *pl* the English, the Britishers *(US);* **er ist ~** he's English. (b) *(Tech)* adjustable spanner, monkey wrench.

**Engländerin** *f* Englishwoman; *(Mädchen)* English girl.

**englisch 1** *adj* English; *siehe* **deutsch. 2** *adv (Cook)* rare.

**Englisch(e)** *nt* English; *siehe* **Deutsch(e).**

**englisch-:** **~-deutsch** *etc adj* Anglo-German *etc;* *Wörterbuch* English-German *etc;* **~sprachig** *adj Gebiet* English-speaking.

**Eng-:** **e~maschig** *adj* close-meshed; **~paß** *m* (narrow) pass, defile; *(Mot, fig)* bottleneck.

**en gros** [ã'gro] *adv* wholesale.

**engstirnig** *adj* narrow-minded.

**Enkel** *m -* (~kind) grandchild; (~sohn) grandson; *(Nachfahr)* descendant; *(fig)* heir.

**Enkelin** *f* granddaughter.

**Enkel-:** **~kind** *nt* grandchild; **~sohn** *m* grandson; **~tochter** *f* granddaughter.

**Enklave** [ɛn'klɑːvə] *f -n* enclave.

**en masse** [ã'mas] *adv* en masse.

**enorm** *adj* enormous; *(col: herrlich, kolossal)* tremendous *(col).* **er verdient ~ viel (Geld)** *(col)* he earns an enormous amount (of money).

**en passant** [ãpɑ'sã] *adv* en passant, in passing.

**Ensemble** [ã'sãbl] *nt -s* ensemble; *(Besetzung)* cast.

**ent|arten*** *vi aux sein* to degenerate *(zu into).*

**ent|artet** *adj* degenerate.

**Ent|artung** *f* degeneration.

**entbehren*** **1** *vt (vermissen)* to miss; *(auch vi: verzichten)* to do without; *(zur Verfügung stellen)* to spare. **wir können ihn heute nicht ~** we cannot spare him today. **2** *vi* **einer Sache** *(gen)* **~** *(geh)* to lack sth.

**entbehrlich** *adj* dispensable.

**Entbehrung** *f* privation, deprivation. **~en auf sich** *(acc)* **nehmen** to make sacrifices.

**entbehrungs-:** **~reich, ~voll** *adj Zeit, Leben* (full) of privation.

**entbinden*** *irreg* **1** *vt* (a) *Frau* to deliver. (b) *(von Amt etc)* to release *(von from).* **2** *vi (Frau)* to give birth.

**Entbindung** *f* delivery, birth; *(von Amt etc)* release.

**Entbindungsstation** *f* maternity ward.

**entblößen*** *vt (form)* to expose *(auch Mil); Kopf* to bare; *(fig) sein Innenleben* to lay bare.

**entblößt** *adj* bare.

**entbrennen*** *vi irreg aux sein (liter) (Kampf, Streit)* to flare up; *(Liebe)* to be aroused.

**entbürokratisieren*** *vt* to free of *or* from bureaucracy.

**entdecken*** *vt* to discover; *Fehler auch* to detect; *(erspähen)* to spot.

**Entdecker(in** *f) m -* discoverer.

**Entdeckung** *f* discovery; *(von Fehler auch)* detection.

**Ente** *f -n* (a) duck. (b) *(col) (Falschmeldung)* hoax, false report; *(Aut)* Citroën 2CV, deux-chevaux.

**ent|ehren*** *vt* to dishonour *(Brit),* to dishonor *(US).*

**ent|eignen*** *vt* to dispossess; *Besitz* to expropriate.

**Ent|eignung** *f siehe vt* dispossession; expropriation.

**ent|eisen*** *vt* to de-ice; *Kühlschrank* to defrost.

**Enten-:** **~braten** *m* roast duck; **~ei** *nt* duck's egg; **~teich** *m* duckpond.

**ent|erben*** *vt* to disinherit.

**Enterhaken** *m* grappling iron *or* hook.

**Enterich** *m* drake.

**entern** *(Naut) vti Schiff* to board.

**Enter-Taste** *f (Comp)* enter key.

**entfachen*** *vt (geh) Feuer* to kindle; *Krieg, Streit* to provoke.

**entfahren*** *vi irreg aux sein* **jdm ~** to escape sb's lips.

**entfallen*** *vi irreg aux sein +dat* (a) **der Name ist mir ~** the name has slipped my mind. (b) *(nicht in Betracht kommen)* not to apply; *(wegfallen)* to be dropped. (c) **auf jdn/etw ~** *(Geld, Kosten)* to be allotted to sb/sth; **auf jeden ~ 100 Mark** each person will receive/pay 100 marks.

**entfalten*** **1** *vt* (a) *(lit)* to unfold. (b) *(fig) (entwickeln)* to develop; *(darlegen) Plan* to unfold; *(zeigen) Pracht* to display. **2** *vr (Knospe, Blüte)* to open, to unfold; *(fig)* to develop; *(Schönheit)* to blossom (out). **hier kann ich mich nicht ~** I can't make full use of my abilities here.

**Entfaltung** *f* unfolding *(auch von Plan); (Entwicklung)* development; *(von Schönheit)* blossoming; *(von Prunk, Tatkraft)* display. **zur ~ kommen** to develop; *(Schönheit)* to blossom.

**entfärben*** *vt* to take the colour *(Brit)* or color *(US)* out of.

**Entfärber** *m,* **Entfärbungsmittel** *nt* colour *or* dye remover.

**entfernen*** **1** *vt* to remove *(von, aus from).* **das entfernt uns (weit) vom Thema** that takes us a long way from our subject. **2** *vr* **sich (von** *or* **aus etw) ~** *(weggehen)* to go away (from sth), to leave (sth); **sich unerlaubt von der Truppe ~** *(Mil)* to go absent without leave; **sich zu weit ~** to go too far away; **sich von jdm ~** *(fig)* to become estranged from sb.

**entfernt 1** *adj Ort, Verwandter* distant; *Ähnlichkeit* remote. **16 km ~ von** 10 miles (away) from; **16 km ~** 10 miles away. **2** *adv* remotely, slightly. **~ verwandt** distantly related; **das hat nur ~ mit dieser Angelegenheit zu tun** that is only vaguely related with this matter; **nicht im ~esten!** not in the slightest.

**Entfernung** *f* (a) distance. **aus kurzer/großer ~ (schießen)** (to fire) from close/long range; **aus einiger ~** from a distance; **in einiger ~** at a distance. (b) *(das Entfernen)* removal. **unerlaubte ~ von der Truppe** absence without leave.

**Enfernungsmesser** *m - (Phot)* rangefinder.

**entfesseln*** *vt (fig)* to unleash.

**entfesselt** *adj* unleashed; *Trieb* unbridled; *Naturgewalten* raging. **vor Begeisterung ~** wild with enthusiasm.

**Entfesselungskünstler** *m* escape artist.

**entfetten*** *vt* to degrease; *Milch* to skim.

**Entfettungskur** *f* weight-reducing course.

**entflammbar** *adj* inflammable.

**entflammen*** **1** *vt (fig)* to (a)rouse. **2** *vi aux sein* to burst into flames; *(fig) (Streit)* to flare up; *(Leidenschaft)* to be (a)roused *or* inflamed. **in Liebe ~** to fall passionately in love.

**entflechten*** *vt irreg Konzern, Kartell etc* to break

up.

**Entflechtung** f *(von Konzern, Kartell)* breaking up.

**entfliegen*** vi *irreg aux sein* to fly away, to escape *(dat or aus* from*)*.

**entfliehen*** vi *irreg aux sein (geh)* to escape, to flee *(dat or aus* from*)*.

**entfremden*** **1** vt to alienate *(auch Sociol, Philos)*, to estrange. **jdn einer Person/Sache** *(dat)* ~ to alienate *or* estrange sb from sb/sth. **2** vr to become alienated *or* estranged *(dat* from*)*.

**Entfremdung** f alienation, estrangement.

**entfrosten*** vt to defrost.

**Entfroster** m - defroster.

**entführen*** vt jdn to abduct, to kidnap; *Beute etc* to carry off; *Flugzeug* to hijack; *(hum col: wegnehmen)* to make off with.

**Entführer(in** f*)* m abductor, kidnapper; *(Flugzeug~ etc)* hijacker.

**Entführung** f siehe vt abduction, kidnapping; hijack(ing).

**entgegen** **1** adv *(liter)* **der Sonne/der Zukunft** *etc* ~! on towards the sun/future *etc*! **2** prep +dat ~ **meiner Bitte** contrary to my request.

**entgegenbringen** vt sep irreg **jdm etw** ~ *(fig) Achtung, Verständnis etc* to show sth for sb.

**entgegengehen** vi sep irreg aux sein +dat to go towards, to approach; *(um jdn zu treffen)* to go to meet; *(fig) einer Gefahr, dem Tode, der Zukunft* to face. **dem Ende** ~ *(Leben, Krieg)* to approach its end; **Schwierigkeiten** ~ to be heading for difficulties.

**entgegengesetzt** adj *Richtung etc* opposite. **einander** ~**e Interessen/Meinungen** opposing *or* conflicting interests/views; **genau** ~ **denken/handeln** to think/do exactly the opposite.

**entgegenhalten** vt sep irreg +dat **(a)** *(lit)* **jdm etw** ~ to hold sth out towards sb. **(b)** *(fig) einer Sache* ~**, daß** ... to object to sth that ...; **dem hielt sie entgegen, daß** ... she made the objection that ...

**entgegenkommen** vi sep irreg aux sein +dat to come towards, to approach; *(fig)* to accommodate. **das kommt unseren Plänen sehr entgegen** that fits in very well with our plans; **können Sie uns preislich etwas** ~? can you accommodate us a little on price?

**Entgegenkommen** nt *(Gefälligkeit)* obligingness; *(Zugeständnis)* concession.

**entgegenkommend** adj *Verkehr* oncoming; *(fig)* obliging, accommodating.

**entgegenlaufen** vi sep irreg aux sein + dat to run towards; *(fig)* to run contrary or counter to.

**Entgegennahme** f no pl *(form) (Empfang)* receipt; *(Annahme)* acceptance.

**entgegennehmen** vt sep irreg *(empfangen)* to receive; *(annehmen)* to accept.

**entgegensehen** vi sep irreg *(fig)* **einer Sache** *(dat)* ~ to await sth; *(freudig)* to look forward to sth; **einer Sache** ~ **müssen** to have to expect sth.

**entgegensetzen** vt sep +dat **etw einer Sache** ~ to set sth against sth; **wir können diesen Forderungen nichts** ~ we have nothing to counter these claims with; **dem habe ich entgegenzusetzen, daß** ... against that I'd like to say that ...; **jdm/einer Sache Widerstand** ~ to put up resistance to sb/sth; *siehe* **entgegengesetzt.**

**entgegenstehen** vi sep irreg +dat *(fig)* to stand in the way of, to be an obstacle to. **dem steht nichts entgegen** there's no objection to that.

**entgegenstellen** sep +dat **1** vt = **entgegensetzen. 2** vr **sich jdm/einer Sache** ~ to oppose sb/sth.

**entgegentreten** vi sep irreg aux sein +dat einer Politik to oppose; *Behauptungen* to counter; *einer Gefahr, Unsitten* to take steps against.

**entgegenwirken** vi sep +dat to counteract.

**entgegnen*** vti to reply; *(kurz, barsch)* to retort *(auf +acc* to*)*.

**Entgegnung** f reply; *(kurz, barsch)* retort.

**entgehen*** vi irreg aux sein +dat **(a)** *(entkommen)* to escape; *Verfolgern, dem Feind* to escape from. **(b)** *(fig: nicht bemerkt werden)* **dieser Fehler ist mir entgangen** I missed this mistake; **ihr entgeht nichts** she doesn't miss a thing; **sich** *(dat)* **etw** ~ **lassen** to miss sth.

**entgeistert** adj dumbfounded.

**Entgelt** nt no pl *(form)* remuneration *(form)*. **gegen** ~ for a fee.

**entgelten** vt irreg *(geh)* **jdm etw** ~ to repay sb for sth.

**entgiften** vt to decontaminate; *(Med)* to detoxify.

**Entgiftung** f decontamination; *(Med)* detoxification.

**entgleisen*** vi aux sein **(a)** *(Rail)* to be derailed. **(b)** *(fig: Mensch)* to misbehave.

**Entgleisung** f derailment; *(fig)* faux pas, clanger *(col)*.

**entgleiten** vi irreg aux sein +dat to slip. **jdm** ~ to slip from sb's grasp; *(fig)* to slip away from sb.

**entgräten*** vt *Fisch* to fillet, to bone.

**enthaaren*** vt to remove unwanted hair from.

**Enthaarungs-:** ~**creme** f depilatory cream; ~**mittel** nt depilatory.

**enthalten*** irreg **1** vt to contain. **(mit)** ~ **sein in** *(+dat)* to be included in. **2** vr **(a)** *(geh)* **sich einer Sache** *(gen)* ~ to abstain from sth; **sich einer Bemerkung nicht** ~ **können** to be unable to refrain from making a remark. **(b)** **sich (der Stimme)** ~ to abstain.

**enthaltsam** adj abstemious; *(geschlechtlich)* chaste.

**Enthaltsamkeit** f siehe adj abstemiousness; chastity.

**Enthaltung** f abstinence; *(Stimm~)* abstention.

**enthärten*** vt *Wasser* to soften; *Metall* to anneal.

**enthaupten*** vt to decapitate; *(als Hinrichtung auch)* to behead.

**Enthauptung** f siehe vt decapitation; beheading.

**enthäuten*** vt to skin.

**entheben*** vt irreg **jdn einer Sache** *(gen)* ~ to relieve sb of sth.

**enthemmen*** vti **jdn** ~ to make sb lose his inhibitions; **Alkohol wirkt** ~**d** alcohol has a disinhibiting effect.

**enthemmt** adj uninhibited.

**Enthemmung** f loss of inhibitions.

**enthüllen*** vt to reveal; *Skandal, Lüge auch* to expose; *Denkmal* to unveil.

**Enthüllung** f siehe vt revealing; exposure; unveiling. **noch eine sensationelle** ~ another sensational revelation or disclosure.

**Enthüllungsjournalismus** m investigative journalism.

**Enthusiasmus** m enthusiasm.

**Enthusiast(in** f*)* m enthusiast.

**enthusiastisch** adj enthusiastic.

**entjungfern*** vt to deflower.

**entkalken*** vt to decalcify.

**entkernen*** vt *Orangen etc* to remove the pips from; *Kernobst* to core; *Steinobst* to stone.

**entkleiden*** vtr *(geh)* to undress.

**entkoffe|iniert** adj decaffeinated.

**entkommen*** vi irreg aux sein to escape, to get away *(+dat, aus* from*)*.

**Entkommen** nt escape.

**entkorken*** vt *Flasche* to uncork.

**entscheidend**

**entkräften\*** vt (schwächen) to weaken; (erschöpfen) to exhaust; (fig: widerlegen) Behauptung to invalidate.

**Entkräftung** f (Erschöpfung) exhaustion; (Widerlegung) invalidation.

**entkrampfen\*** vt (fig) to relax, to ease.

**Entkrampfung** f (fig) relaxation, easing.

**entladen\*** irreg **1** vt to unload; Batterie etc to discharge. **2** vr (Gewitter) to break; (elektrische Spannung, Batterie, Waffe) to discharge; (Sprengladung) to explode; (fig) (Emotion) to vent itself; (Spannung) to release itself.

**Entladung** f (a) (das Entladen) unloading. (b) siehe vr breaking; discharge; explosion; venting; release.

**entlang 1** prep along. ~ **dem Fluß, den Fluß** ~ along the river. **2** adv along. **hier** ~ this way.

**entlang-** pref along; ~**gehen** vti sep irreg aux sein to walk along, to go along.

**entlarven\*** vt (fig) to expose.

**Entlarvung** f exposure.

**entlassen\*** vt irreg (aus from) (kündigen) to dismiss; (nach Stellenabbau) to make redundant; Patienten, Soldaten to discharge; (aus dem Gefängnis, aus Verpflichtungen) to release. **aus der Schule** ~ **werden** to leave school.

**Entlassung** f siehe vt dismissal; making redundant; discharge; release. **es gab 20** ~**en** there were 20 redundancies.

**Entlassungs-:** ~**feier** f school-leaving or (US) graduation ceremony; ~**gesuch** nt (letter of) resignation; **ein** ~**gesuch stellen** to tender one's resignation; ~**zeugnis** nt (Sch) school leaving certificate.

**entlasten\*** vt to relieve the strain or load (Tech) on; (Mil, Rail) to relieve; Gewissen, Verkehr to ease; (Arbeit abnehmen) to take some of the load off; (Jur) Angeklagten to exonerate; (Comm) Vorstand to approve the activities of; (von Verpflichtungen) jdn to release.

**Entlastung** f relief (auch Mil, Rail etc); (von Achse etc, Herz) relief of the strain or load (Tech) (+gen on); (Jur) exoneration; (Comm: des Vorstands) approval; (von Verpflichtungen etc) release. **zu seiner** ~ **führte der Angeklagte an, daß** ... in his defence (Brit) or defense (US) the defendant stated that ...

**Entlastungs-:** ~**material** nt (Jur) evidence for the defence (Brit) or defense (US); ~**zeuge** m (Jur) defence (Brit) or defense (US) witness; ~**zug** m relief (Brit) or extra train.

**entlaufen\*** vi irreg aux sein to run away (dat, von from). **ein** ~**es Kind** a runaway child; **ein** ~**er Sträfling** an escaped convict; **ein** ~**er Hund** a lost dog.

**entledigen\*** (form) vr sich einer Person/Sache (gen) ~ to rid oneself of sb/sth; **sich seiner Kleidung** ~ to remove one's clothes.

**entleeren\*** vt to empty; Darm to evacuate.

**entlegen** adj remote.

**entlehnen\*** vt (fig) to borrow (dat, von from).

**entleihen\*** vt irreg to borrow (von, aus from).

**Entleiher** m - borrower.

**Entlein** nt duckling.

**entloben\*** vr to break off one's engagement.

**entlocken\*** vt jdm/einer Sache etw ~ to elicit sth from sb/sth.

**entlohnen\*** vt to pay; (fig) to reward.

**Entlohnung** f pay(ment); (fig) reward.

**entlüften\*** vt to ventilate, to air; Bremsen to bleed.

**Entlüfter** m - ventilator.

**Entlüftung** f siehe vt ventilation, airing; bleeding.

**entmachten\*** vt to deprive of power; (stürzen) to topple.

**entmannen\*** vt to castrate.

**Entmannung** f castration.

**entmenscht** adj bestial, inhuman.

**entmilitarisieren** vt to demilitarize.

**entmündigen\*** vt (Jur) to (legally) incapacitate, to declare incapable of managing one's own affairs; (wegen Geisteskrankheit auch) to certify.

**Entmündigung** f siehe vt (Jur) (legal) incapacitation; certification.

**entmutigen\*** vt to discourage, to dishearten. **sich nicht** ~ **lassen** not to be discouraged.

**Entmutigung** f discouragement.

**Entnahme** f -n (form) removal; (von Blut) extraction; (von Geld) withdrawal.

**entnehmen\*** vt irreg (aus, dat) to take (from); (aus Kasse) Geld to withdraw (from); (fig: folgern) to infer (from). **wie ich Ihren Worten entnehme, ...** I gather from what you say that ...

**entnerven\*** vt to unnerve. ~**d** nerve-racking.

**entpuppen\*** vr sich als Betrüger etc ~ to turn out to be a cheat etc.

**entrahmen\*** vt Milch to skim.

**enträtseln\*** vt to solve; Sinn, Schrift to decipher.

**entrechten\*** vt jdn ~ to deprive sb of his/her rights.

**entreißen\*** vt irreg jdm etw ~ (lit, fig) to snatch sth (away) from sb.

**entrichten\*** vt (form) to pay.

**Entrichtung** f (form) payment.

**entrinnen\*** vi irreg aux sein (geh) +dat to escape from; dem Tod to escape. **es gibt kein E**~ there is no escape.

**entrosten\*** vt to derust.

**entrückt** adj (geh verzückt) enraptured. **der Wirklichkeit** ~ **sein** to live in a world of one's own.

**entrümpeln\*** vt to clear out.

**Entrümp(e)lung** f clear-out.

**entrüsten\*** **1** vt (empören) to fill with indignation, to outrage. **2** vr sich ~ über (+acc) (sich empören) to be outraged at.

**entrüstet** adj indignant, outraged.

**Entrüstung** f indignation (über +acc at).

**Entsafter** m - juice extractor.

**entsagen\*** vi +dat (geh) der Welt ~ to renounce the world.

**Entsagung** f (geh) renunciation (of wordly things).

**entsagungsvoll** adj (geh) Leben (full) of privation; Blick resigned.

**entsalzen\*** vt irreg to desalinate.

**Entsatz** m no pl (Mil) relief.

**entschädigen\*** vt (für for) (lit, fig) to compensate, to recompense; (Kosten erstatten) to reimburse. **das Theaterstück entschädigte uns für das lange Warten** the play made up for the long wait.

**Entschädigung** f siehe vt compensation, recompense; reimbursement.

**Entschädigungssumme** f compensation.

**entschärfen\*** vt (lit, fig) to defuse.

**Entscheid** m -e (Sw, form) = Entscheidung.

**entscheiden\*** irreg **1** vti to decide. ~ **Sie, wie es gemacht werden soll!** you decide how it is to be done; **den Kampf (um etw) für sich** ~ to secure victory in the struggle (for sth); **über etw** (acc) ~ to decide (on) sth; **es ist noch nichts entschieden** nothing has been decided (as) yet; **darüber habe ich nicht zu** ~ that is not for me to decide. **2** vr (Mensch) to decide, to make up one's mind; (Angelegenheit) to be decided. **sich für jdn/etw** ~ to decide in favour of sb/sth.

**entscheidend** adj decisive; Augenblick, Fehler auch

crucial. **die ~e Stimme** *(bei Wahlen etc)* the deciding *or* casting vote; **der alles ~e Augenblick** the critical decisive moment; **das E~e** the decisive *or* deciding factor.

**Entscheidung** *f* decision. **eine ~ treffen** to make a decision; **etw steht vor der** *or* **kommt zur ~** sth is about to be decided; **wie ist die ~ ausgefallen?** which way did the decision go?

**Entscheidungs-:** **~befugnis** *f* decision-making powers *pl*; **~findung** *f* decision-making; **~freiheit** *f* freedom of decision-making; **e~freudig** *adj* able to make decisions, decisive; **~hilfe** *f* aid to decision-making; **~kampf** *m* show-down *(auch fig)*; *(Sport)* decider; **~schlacht** *f* decisive battle; *(fig)* show-down *(col)*; **~spiel** *nt* decider, play-off; **~träger** *m* decision-maker; **~unfähigkeit** *f* inability to make decisions.

**entschieden** *adj* **(a)** *(entschlossen)* determined, resolute; *Befürworter* staunch. **etw ~ ablehnen** to reject sth firmly. **(b)** *no pred (eindeutig)* decided, distinct. **das geht ~ zu weit** that's definitely going too far.

**Entschiedenheit** *f (Entschlossenheit)* determination, resolution. **etw mit aller ~ dementieren** to deny sth categorically.

**entschlacken*** *vt (Med) Körper* to purify.

**entschlafen*** *vi irreg aux sein (geh)* to fall asleep; *(euph: sterben)* to pass away.

**entschleiern*** *vt (lit, fig)* to unveil.

**entschließen*** *vr irreg* to decide *(für, zu on)*. **ich entschloß mich zum Kauf dieses Hauses** I decided to buy this house; **sich zu nichts ~ können** to be unable to make up one's mind; **ich bin fest entschlossen** I am absolutely determined; **zu allem entschlossen sein** to be ready for anything; **kurz entschlossen** on the spur of the moment.

**Entschließung** *f* resolution.

**Entschließungsantrag** *m (Pol)* resolution proposal.

**entschlossen** *adj* determined, resolute. **~ handeln** to act resolutely *or* with determination.

**Entschlossenheit** *f* determination, resolution.

**entschlüpfen*** *vi aux sein (dat from)* to escape, to slip away; *(fig: Wort etc)* to slip out.

**Entschluß** *m* decision; *(Vorsatz)* resolution, resolve. **aus eigenem ~ handeln** to act on one's own initiative; **es ist mein fester ~ ...** it is my firm intention ...

**entschlüsseln*** *vt* to decipher; *Funkspruch auch* to decode.

**Entschlüsselung** *f siehe vt* deciphering; decoding.

**Entschluß-:** **e~freudig** *adj* decisive; **~kraft** *f* decisiveness; **e~los** *adj* indecisive.

**entschuldbar** *adj* excusable, pardonable.

**entschuldigen*** **1** *vt* to excuse. **etw mit etw ~** to excuse sth as due to sth; **das ist durch nichts zu ~!, das läßt sich nicht ~!** that is inexcusable!; **jdn bei jdm ~** to make sb's excuses *or* apologies to sb; **einen Schüler ~ (lassen)** to ask for a pupil to be excused; **ich bitte mich zu ~** I beg to be excused. **2** *vi* **~ Sie (bitte)!** excuse me; *(Verzeihung auch)* sorry; *(bei Frage etc)* sorry, pardon me *(esp US)*. **3** *vr* **sich (bei jdm) ~** to excuse oneself; *(um Verzeihung bitten)* to apologize (to sb) *(wegen etw (gen)* for sth*)*; **sich ~ lassen** to send one's apologies.

**entschuldigend** *adj* apologetic.

**Entschuldigung** *f (Grund)* excuse; *(Bitte um ~)* apology; *(Sch: Brief)* note. **~!** excuse me; *(Verzeihung auch)* sorry; **(jdn) (wegen einer Sache) um ~ bitten** to apologize (to sb) (for sth); **ich bitte vielmals um ~ (, daß ich mich verspätet habe)!** I do

apologize (for being late).

**entschwefeln*** *vt* to desulphurize.

**Entschwef(e)lung** *f* desulphurization.

**entschwinden*** *vi irreg aux sein (geh: lit, fig)* to vanish.

**entsenden*** *vt irreg or reg (geh)* to dispatch.

**entsetzen*** **1** *vt* **(a)** to horrify, to appal. **(b)** *(Mil)* to relieve. **2** *vr* **sich über jdn/etw ~** to be horrified *or* appalled at sb/sth; *siehe* **entsetzt.**

**Entsetzen** *nt no pl* horror; *(Erschrecken)* terror. **mit ~ sehen, daß ...** to be horrified/terrified to see that ...

**entsetzlich** *adj* dreadful, appalling.

**entsetzt** *adj* horrified, appalled *(über +acc* at, by*)*. **ein ~er Schrei** a cry of horror.

**entseuchen*** *vt* to decontaminate.

**Entseuchung** *f* decontamination.

**entsichern*** *vt* to release the safety catch of.

**entsinnen*** *vr irreg (einer Sache (gen), an etw (acc)* sth*)* to remember, to recall. **wenn ich mich recht entsinne** if my memory serves me correctly.

**entsorgen*** *vt Atomkraftwerk* to remove the waste from. **eine Stadt ~** to dispose of a town's refuse and sewage.

**Entsorgung** *f* waste disposal. **die ~ von Chemikalien** the disposal of chemicals.

**Entsorgungspark** *m* (nuclear) waste dump.

**entspannen*** **1** *vt Muskeln, Nerven etc* to relax; *(fig) Lage auch* to ease. **2** *vr* to relax *(auch fig)*; *(ausruhen)* to rest; *(nach der Arbeit etc)* to unwind; *(Lage etc)* to ease.

**entspannt** *adj* relaxed.

**Entspannung** *f* relaxation *(auch fig)*; *(Pol)* détente, easing of tension *(+gen* in*)*.

**Entspannungs-:** **~politik** *f* policy of détente; **~übungen** *pl (Med etc)* relaxation exercises.

**entspiegeln*** *vt Brillengläser* to put an anti-reflective coating on.

**entspr.** = **entsprechend.**

**entsprechen*** *vi irreg +dat* to correspond to; *Vorschriften* to be in accordance with; *(genügen) Anforderungen* to meet; *Erwartungen* to come up to; *einer Beschreibung* to answer, to fit; *einer Bitte, einem Wunsch etc* to meet, to comply with. **sich ~** to correspond, to tally.

**entsprechend** **1** *adj* corresponding; *(zuständig)* relevant; *(angemessen)* appropriate. **2** *adv* accordingly; *(ähnlich, gleich)* correspondingly. **er wurde ~ bestraft** he was suitably *or* appropriately punished. **3** *prep +dat* in accordance with, according to; *(ähnlich, gleich)* corresponding to. **ein der Leistung ~es Gehalt** a salary commensurate with performance.

**Entsprechung** *f* equivalent; *(Analogie)* parallel; *(Übereinstimmung)* correspondence.

**entspringen*** *vi irreg aux sein* **(a)** *(Fluß)* to have its source. **(b)** *(+dat: sich herleiten von)* to spring from.

**entstaatlichen*** *vt* to denationalize.

**entstammen*** *vi aux sein +dat* to stem *or* come from.

**entstehen*** *vi irreg aux sein (ins Dasein treten)* to come into being; *(seinen Ursprung haben)* to originate; *(sich entwickeln)* to arise *(aus, durch from)*; *(hervorkommen)* to emerge *(aus, durch from)*; *(verursacht werden)* to result *(aus, durch from)*; *(Kunstwerk: geschrieben/gebaut etc werden)* to be written/built *etc*. **wir wollen nicht den Eindruck ~ lassen, ...** we don't want to give rise to the impression that ...; **für ~den** *or* **entstandenen Schaden** for damages incurred.

**Entstehung** *f (das Werden)* genesis, coming into

being; *(das Hervorkommen)* emergence; *(Ursprung)* origin; *(Bildung)* formation.
**Entstehungs-**: ~**geschichte** f genesis; ~**ort** m place of origin; ~**zeit** f date of origin.
**entsteinen*** vt to stone.
**entstellen*** vt *(lit, fig)* to distort; *(verunstalten) Gesicht* to disfigure. **etw entstellt wiedergeben** to distort *or* misrepresent sth.
**Entstellung** f *siehe* vt distortion; disfigurement.
**Entstickung** f denitrification.
**entstören*** vt *Radio, Telefon* to free from interference; *Auto, Elektrogerät* to suppress.
**enttarnen*** vt *Spion* to blow the cover of *(col)*.
**Enttarnung** f exposure.
**enttäuschen*** **1** vt to disappoint; *Vertrauen* to betray. **enttäuscht sein über** *(+acc)*/**von** to be disappointed at/by. **2** vi **unsere Mannschaft hat sehr enttäuscht** our team was very disappointing.
**Enttäuschung** f disappointment. **jdm eine** ~ **bereiten** to disappoint sb.
**entthronen*** vt *(lit, fig)* to dethrone.
**entvölkern*** vt to depopulate.
**entwachsen*** vi irreg aux sein +dat (a) to outgrow, to grow out of. (b) *(geh: herauswachsen aus)* to spring from.
**entwaffnen*** vt *(lit, fig)* to disarm.
**entwaffnend** adj *(fig)* disarming.
**Entwaffnung** f disarming; *(eines Landes)* disarmament.
**Entwaldung** f deforestation.
**entwarnen*** vi to sound the all-clear.
**Entwarnung** f all-clear.
**entwässern*** vt to drain.
**Entwässerung** f drainage.
**entweder** [auch: 'ɛntveːdə] conj ~ ... **oder** ... either ... or ...; ~ **oder!** yes or no.
**entweichen*** vi irreg aux sein to escape *(+dat, aus* from*)*.
**entweihen*** vt to desecrate.
**entwenden*** vt *(form)* **jdm etw** ~ to steal *or* purloin *(hum, form)* sth from sb.
**entwerfen*** vt irreg *Zeichnung* to sketch; *Muster, Modell* to design; *Gesetz, Schreiben etc* to draft, to draw up; *Plan* to devise, to draw up; *(fig) Bild* to draw; *(in Umrissen darstellen)* to outline.
**entwerten*** vt (a) *(im Wert mindern)* to devalue. (b) *(ungültig machen)* to make invalid; *Briefmarke, Fahrschein* to cancel.
**Entwerter** m - (ticket-)cancelling machine.
**Entwertung** f *siehe* vt devaluation; invalidation; cancellation.
**entwickeln*** **1** vt to develop *(auch Phot)*; *Gas etc* to produce, to generate; *Mut, Energie* to show, to display. **etw zu etw** ~ to develop sth into sth. **2** vr to develop *(zu* into*)*; *(Gase etc)* to be produced *or* generated. **das Projekt entwickelt sich gut** the project is coming along *or* progressing nicely.
**Entwickler** m - *(Phot)* developer.
**Entwicklung** f development; *(von Gasen etc)* production, generation; *(von Mut, Energie)* show, display; *(Phot)* developing. **in der** ~ at the development stage; *(Jugendliche etc)* still developing.
**Entwicklungs-**: ~**dienst** m voluntary service overseas *(Brit)*, VSO *(Brit)*, Peace Corps *(US)*; **e~fähig** adj capable of development; **diese Stelle ist e~fähig** this position has prospects; ~**gebiet** nt development area; ~**geschichte** f evolution; ~**helfer** m VSO worker *(Brit)*, Peace Corps worker *(US)*; ~**hilfe** f development *or* foreign aid; ~**jahre** pl adolescent *or* formative *(auch fig)* years, adolescence; ~**land** nt developing *or* third-world country;

~**stadium** nt, ~**stufe** f stage of development; ~**zeit** f period of development; *(Phot)* developing time.
**entwirren*** vt *(lit, fig)* to disentangle, to unravel.
**entwischen*** vi aux sein *(col)* to escape, to get away *(dat, aus* from*)*.
**entwöhnen*** vt **jdn** ~ to break sb of the habit *(+dat, von* of*)*, to cure sb *(+dat, von* of*)*; *Säugling, Jungtier* to wean.
**Entwöhnung** f *siehe* vt cure, curing; weaning.
**entwürdigen*** **1** vt to degrade. **2** vr to degrade oneself.
**entwürdigend** adj degrading.
**Entwürdigung** f degradation.
**Entwurf** m ⸚e (a) *(Skizze, Abriß)* outline, sketch; *(Design)* design; *(Archit, fig)* blueprint. (b) *(Vertrags~, von Plan)* draft; *(Gesetz~)* bill.
**entwurzeln*** vt *(lit, fig)* to uproot.
**entzerren*** vt to correct.
**entziehen*** irreg **1** vt *(+dat* from*)* to withdraw, to take away; *Gunst etc* to withdraw; *Flüssigkeit, (Chem)* to extract. **jdm Alkohol/Nikotin** ~ to deprive sb of alcohol/nicotine; **jdm die Erlaubnis** etc ~ to take sb's permit etc away; **dem Redner das Wort** ~ to ask the speaker to stop. **2** vr **sich jdm/einer Sache** ~ to evade *or* elude sb/sth; **sich seiner Verantwortung** ~ to shirk one's responsibilities; **das entzieht sich meiner Kenntnis** that is beyond my knowledge; **sich jds Blicken** ~ to be hidden from sight.
**Entziehung** f withdrawal; *(Behandlung)* treatment for drug addiction/alcoholism.
**Entziehungskur** f cure for drug addiction/alcoholism.
**entzifferbar** adj *siehe* vt decipherable; decodable.
**entziffern*** vt to decipher; *Funkspruch auch* to decode.
**entzücken*** vt to delight. **von jdm/über etw** *(acc)* **entzückt sein** to be delighted by sb/at sth.
**Entzücken** nt no pl delight, joy. **in** ~ **geraten** to go into raptures.
**entzückend** adj delightful, charming.
**Entzug** m no pl *(einer Lizenz etc, Med)* withdrawal.
**Entzugs|erscheinung** f withdrawal symptom.
**entzündbar** adj *(lit, fig)* inflammable. **leicht** ~ highly inflammable; *(fig)* easily roused.
**entzünden*** **1** vt *Feuer* to light; *(fig) Streit etc* to spark off; *Haß* to inflame. **2** vr (a) to catch fire; *(fig) (Streit)* to be sparked off; *(Haß)* to be inflamed. (b) *(Med)* to become inflamed. **entzündet** inflamed.
**entzündlich** adj *Gase, Brennstoff* inflammable; *(Med)* inflammatory.
**Entzündung** f (a) *(Med)* inflammation. (b) ignition *(esp Sci, Tech)*. **Funken führten zur** ~ **des Heus** sparks led to the hay catching fire.
**Entzündungs-** *(Med)*: **e~hemmend** adj anti-inflammatory; ~**herd** m focus of inflammation.
**entzwei** adj pred in two, in half; *(kaputt)* broken; *(zerrissen)* torn.
**entzweien*** vt to turn against each other.
**entzweigehen** vi sep irreg aux sein to break (in two *or* half).
**Enzian** ['ɛntsiaːn] m -e gentian; *(Branntwein) spirit distilled from the roots of gentian.*
**Enzyklika** f, pl **Enzykliken** *(Eccl)* encyclical.
**Enzyklopädie** f encyclop(a)edia.
**enzyklopädisch** adj encyclop(a)edic.
**Enzym** nt -e enzyme.
**Epen** pl of **Epos.**
**Epidemie** f *(Med, fig)* epidemic.
**epidemisch** adj *(Med, fig)* epidemic.
**Epik** f epic poetry.

**Epilepsie** f epilepsy.
**Epileptiker(in** f) m - epileptic.
**epileptisch** adj epileptic.
**Epilog** m -e epilogue.
**episch** adj (lit, fig) epic.
**Episode** f -n episode.
**Epitaph** nt -e (liter) epitaph.
**Epizentrum** nt epicentre.
**Epoche** f -n epoch.
**epochemachend** adj epoch-making.
**Epos** nt, pl **Epen** epic (poem).
**Equipe** [e'kɪp] f -n team.
**er** pers he; (von Dingen) it; (von Hund etc) it, he.
  **wenn ich ~ wäre** if I were him or he (form); **~ ist
  es** it's him, it is he (form); **sie ist größer als ~** she is
  taller than he is or than him.
**er|achten*** vt (geh) **jdn/etw für** or **als etw ~** to con-
  sider sb/sth (to be) sth.
**Er|achten** nt no pl: **meines ~s** in my opinion.
**er|arbeiten*** vt **(a)** Vermögen etc to work for; Wis-
  sen etc to acquire. **(b)** Entwurf etc to work out.
**Erb-:** **~anlage** f usu pl hereditary factor(s pl);
  **~anspruch** m claim to an/the inheritance.
**erbarmen*** 1 vt **jdn ~** to arouse sb's pity; **es kann
  einen ~** it's pitiable; **er sieht zum E~ aus** he's a
  pitiful sight. 2 vr (+gen) to take pity (on) (auch
  hum col). **Herr, erbarme dich (unser)!** Lord, have
  mercy (upon us)!
**Erbarmen** nt no pl (Mitleid) pity, compassion (mit
  on); (Gnade) mercy (mit on). **aus ~** out of pity;
  **ohne ~** pitiless(ly), merciless(ly); **er kennt kein ~**
  he knows no mercy.
**erbarmenswert** adj pitiable, wretched, pitiful.
**erbärmlich** adj (erbarmenswert, pej: dürftig) pitiful,
  wretched; (gemein, schlecht) miserable.
**Erbärmlichkeit** f (Elend) wretchedness, misery;
  (fig: Dürftigkeit, Gemeinheit etc) wretchedness, mis-
  erableness.
**Erbarmungs-:** **e~los** adj (lit, fig) pitiless, merciless; **~losigkeit** f (lit, fig) pitilessness, mercilessness; **e~voll** adj compassionate, full of pity.
**erbauen*** vt **(a)** (lit, fig: errichten) to build. **(b)** (fig:
  seelisch) to edify, to uplift. **er ist von meinem Plan
  nicht besonders erbaut** (col) he isn't particularly enthusiastic about my plan.
**Erbauer(in** f) m - builder; (fig auch) architect.
**erbaulich** adj edifying (auch iro), uplifting.
**Erbauung** f siehe vt building; edification.
**Erb-:** **e~berechtigt** adj entitled to inherit;
  **e~biologisch** adj (Jur) **e~biologisches Gutachten**
  blood test (to establish paternity).
**Erbe**[1] m (wk) **-n, -n** (lit, fig) heir (einer Person (gen)
  of or to sb, einer Sache (gen) to sth). **jdn zum** or **als
  ~n einsetzen** to make sb one's/sb's heir.
**Erbe**[2] nt no pl inheritance; (fig) heritage; (esp Unerwünschtes) legacy.
**erbeben*** vi aux sein (geh) to shudder.
**erben** 1 vt (lit, fig) to inherit (von from); (col: geschenkt bekommen) to get, to be given. **bei ihm ist
  nichts zu ~** (col) you won't get anything out of him.
  2 vi to inherit.
**erbetteln*** vt to get by begging.
**erbeuten*** vt (Tier) Opfer to carry off; (Dieb) to get
  away with; (im Krieg) to capture.
**Erb-:** **~faktor** m (Biol) hereditary factor, gene;
  **~feind** m traditional or arch enemy; **~folge** f
  (line of) succession; **~gut** nt (Biol) genotype, genetic make-up.
**erbieten*** vr irreg (geh) **sich ~, etw zu tun** to offer to
  do sth.
**Erbin** f heiress.

**erbitten*** vt irreg to ask for, to request.
**erbittern*** vt to enrage, to incense.
**erbittert** adj Widerstand, Kampf, Gegner etc fierce.
**Erbitterung** f rage.
**Erbkrankheit** f hereditary disease.
**erblassen*** vi aux sein to (go) pale, to blanch. **vor
  Neid ~** to go green with envy.
**Erblasser(in** f) m - (Jur) person who leaves an inheritance.
**erbleichen*** vi aux sein (geh) to (go) pale, to
  blanch.
**erblich** adj hereditary. **er ist ~ (vor)belastet** it runs
  in his family.
**erblicken*** vt (geh) to see; (erspähen) to spot.
**erblinden*** vi aux sein to go blind.
**Erblindung** f loss of sight.
**erblühen*** vi aux sein (geh) to bloom, to blossom.
**Erbmasse** f estate; (Biol) genetic make-up.
**erbosen*** (geh) **1** vt to infuriate. **2** vr **sich ~ über**
  (+acc) to become infuriated at.
**erbost** adj furious.
**Erbpacht** f hereditary lease(hold).
**erbrechen*** vtir irreg **(sich) ~** (Med) to vomit, to be
  sick (Brit) (nicht vt); **etw bis zum E~ tun** (fig) to do
  sth ad nauseam.
**Erbrecht** nt law of inheritance.
**erbringen*** vt irreg to produce, to furnish.
**Erbschaft** f inheritance. **eine ~ machen** to come into
  an inheritance.
**Erbschaftssteuer** f estate or death duties pl.
**Erbschleicher(in** f) m legacy-hunter.
**Erbse** f -n pea.
**Erbsensuppe** f pea soup.
**Erb-:** **~stück** nt heirloom; **~sünde** f (Rel) original
  sin; **~teil** nt (Jur: auch m) (share of an/the) inheritance.
**Erd|achse** f earth's axis.
**erdacht** adj Geschichte made-up.
**Erd-:** **~anziehungskraft** f gravitational pull (of the
  earth); **~apfel** m (Aus, S Ger) potato; **~arbeiten**
  pl excavation(s pl), earthworks pl; **~atmosphäre**
  f earth's atmosphere; **~ball** m (liter) globe, world.
**Erdbeben** nt earthquake.
**erdbebensicher** adj earthquake-proof.
**Erdbeere** f strawberry.
**Erdboden** m ground, earth. **etw dem ~ gleichmachen** to level sth, to raze sth to the ground; **als hätte ihn der ~ verschluckt** as if the earth had swallowed him up.
**Erde** f -n **(a)** (Welt) earth, world. **auf der ganzen ~**
  all over the world. **(b)** (Boden) ground. **unter der ~**
  underground, below ground; **du wirst mich noch
  unter die ~ bringen** (col) you'll be the death of me
  (col); **über der ~** above ground. **(c)** (Erdreich, Bo-
  denart) soil, earth (auch Chem). **(d)** (Elec: Erdung)
  earth (Brit), ground (US).
**erden** vt (Elec) to earth (Brit), to ground (US).
**erdenklich** adj attr conceivable, imaginable. **sich
  (dat) alle ~e Mühe geben** to take the greatest possible pains; **alles E~e tun** to do everything conceivable or imaginable.
**Erd-:** **~gas** nt natural gas; **~geschoß** nt ground
  floor (Brit), first floor (US); **im ~geschoß** on the
  ground/first floor; **~hörnchen** nt ground squirrel;
  **~innere(s)** nt interior or bowels pl of the earth;
  **~kruste** f earth's crust; **~kugel** f earth, globe;
  **~kunde** f geography; **~nuß** f peanut, groundnut;
  **~oberfläche** f earth's surface; **~öl** nt (mineral)
  oil, petroleum.
**erdolchen*** vt to stab (to death). **jdn mit Blicken ~**
  to look daggers at sb.

**Erdöl-:** e~**exportierend** *adj attr* oil-exporting; ~**leitung** *f* oil pipeline; ~**verarbeitung** *f* processing of crude oil.

**Erdreich** *nt* soil, earth.

**erdreisten*** *vr* sich ~, etw zu tun to have the audacity to do sth; **wie können Sie sich ~!** how dare you!

**erdrosseln*** *vt* to strangle, to throttle.

**erdrücken*** *vt* to crush (to death); *(fig: überwältigen)* to overwhelm. ~**de Übermacht/~des Beweismaterial** overwhelming superiority/evidence; **die Schuld erdrückte ihn** the sense of guilt weighed heavily upon him.

**Erd-:** ~**rutsch** *m* landslide, landslip; ~**schicht** *f* layer (of the earth), stratum; ~**stoß** *m* (seismic) shock; ~**teil** *m* continent.

**erdulden*** *vt* to endure, to suffer.

**Erd-:** ~**umdrehung** *f* rotation *or* revolution of the earth; ~**umlaufbahn** *f* earth orbit.

**Erdung** *f (Elec)* earth(ing) *(Brit)*, ground(ing) *(US)*.

**er|eifern*** *vr* to get worked up *(über +acc over)*.

**er|eignen*** *vr* to occur, to happen.

**Er|eignis** *nt* event; *(Vorfall auch)* incident.

**er|eignis-:** ~**los** *adj* uneventful; ~**reich** *adj* eventful.

**Erektion** *f (Physiol)* erection.

**Eremit** *m (wk)* -**en**, -**en** hermit.

**er|erben*** *vt* to inherit.

**erfahren[1]*** **1** *vt irreg* **(a)** *Nachricht etc* to learn, to find out; *(hören)* to hear *(von* about, of*)*. **etw ~ to find out about sth; darf man Ihre Absichten ~?** might one inquire as to your intentions? **(b)** *(erleben)* to experience; *(empfangen) Verständnis* to receive. **2** *vi irreg* to hear *(von* about, of*)*.

**erfahren[2]** *adj* experienced.

**Erfahrenheit** *f* experience.

**Erfahrung** *f* experience. **aus (eigener)** ~ from (one's own) experience; **nach meiner** ~ in my experience; ~**en sammeln** to gain experience; **die** ~ **hat gezeigt, daß** ... experience has shown that ...; **etw in** ~ **bringen** to learn *or* find out sth; **eine** ~ **machen** to have an experience; **ich habe die** ~ **gemacht, daß** ... I have found that ...; **mit dieser neuen Mitarbeiterin haben wir nur gute** ~**en gemacht** we have found this new employee (to be) completely satisfactory; **ich habe mit der Ehe nur schlechte** ~**en gemacht** I've had a very bad experience of marriage.

**Erfahrungs-:** ~**austausch** *m (Pol)* exchange of experiences; e~**gemäß** *adv* e~**gemäß** ... as experience shows ...

**erfaßbar** *adj* ascertainable.

**erfassen*** *vt* **(a)** *(mitreißen: Auto, Strömung)* to catch. **(b)** *(Furcht, Verlangen etc)* to seize. **Angst erfaßte sie** she was seized by fear. **(c)** *(begreifen)* to grasp. **(d)** *(registrieren)* to record, to register; *Daten* to capture. **alle Fälle werden statistisch erfaßt** statistics of all cases are being recorded.

**Erfassung** *f* registration, recording; *(von Daten)* capture.

**erfinden*** *vt irreg* to invent. **das hat sie glatt erfunden** she made it all up; **frei erfunden** completely fictitious.

**Erfinder(in** *f) m* - inventor.

**erfinderisch** *adj* inventive; *(findig auch)* ingenious.

**Erfindung** *f* invention; *(Erdichtung, Lüge auch)* fabrication.

**Erfindungs-:** ~**gabe** *f*, ~**reichtum** *m* inventiveness.

**Erfolg** *m* -**e** success; *(Ergebnis, Folge)* result, outcome. **mit/ohne** ~ successfully/without success *or* unsuccessfully; ~/**keinen** ~ **haben** to be successful/unsuccessful; **sie warnte mich mit dem** ~, **daß** ...

the result of her warning me was that ...; **viel** ~! good luck.

**erfolgen*** *vi aux sein (form) (vollzogen werden)* to be effected *(form) or* carried out; *(stattfinden)* to take place. **nach erfolgter Zahlung** when payment has been made; **es erfolgte keine Antwort** no answer was forthcoming.

**Erfolg-:** e~**los** *adj* unsuccessful, without success; ~**losigkeit** *f* lack of success, unsuccessfulness; e~**reich** *adj* successful.

**Erfolgs-:** ~**aussicht** *f* prospect of success; ~**druck** *m* pressure to succeed; ~**erlebnis** *nt* feeling of success, sense of achievement; ~**leiter** *f (fig)* ladder to success; ~**mensch** *m* success, successful person; ~**rezept** *nt* recipe for success; ~**serie** *f* string of successes.

**erfolgversprechend** *adj* promising.

**erforderlich** *adj* necessary, requisite. **unbedingt** ~ (absolutely) essential *or* imperative.

**erfordern*** *vt* to require, to call for.

**Erfordernis** *nt* requirement.

**erforschen*** *vt Land* to explore; *Probleme auch* to investigate; *Meinung, Wahrheit* to find out. **sein Gewissen** ~ to examine one's conscience.

**Erforscher** *m (eines Landes)* explorer; *(in Wissenschaft)* investigator.

**Erforschung** *f siehe vt* exploration; investigation *(+gen* into*)*; finding out.

**erfragen*** *vt Weg* to ask; *Einzelheiten etc* to obtain.

**erfreuen*** **1** *vt* to please, to delight; *Herz* to gladden. **sehr erfreut!** *(form)* pleased to meet you!; **ja, sagte er erfreut** yes, he said delightedly. **2** *vr* **sich einer Sache** *(gen)* ~ *(geh)* to enjoy sth; **sich an etw** *(dat)* ~ to enjoy sth, to take pleasure in sth.

**erfreulich** *adj* pleasant; *Neuerung, Besserung etc* welcome; *(befriedigend)* gratifying. **es ist wenig** ~, **daß wir** ... it's not very satisfactory that we ...; **es wäre** ~, **wenn die Regierung** ... it would be good if the government ...; **sehr** ~! very nice!; **wir haben** ~ **viel geleistet** it's very encouraging how much we've done.

**erfreulicherweise** *adv* happily.

**erfrieren*** **1** *vi irreg aux sein* to freeze to death; *(Pflanzen)* to be killed by frost. **erfrorene Glieder** frostbitten limbs. **2** *vt* **sich** *(dat)* **die Füße** ~ to suffer frostbite in one's feet.

**Erfrierung** *f usu pl* frostbite *no pl*.

**erfrischen*** **1** *vti* to refresh. **2** *vr* to refresh oneself; *(sich waschen)* to freshen up.

**erfrischend** *adj (lit, fig)* refreshing.

**Erfrischung** *f* refreshment.

**Erfrischungs-:** ~**getränk** *nt* refreshing drink; ~**raum** *m* refreshment room; ~**tuch** *nt* towelette.

**erfüllen*** **1** *vt* **(a)** *Raum etc* to fill. **Haß/Liebe etc erfüllte ihn** he was filled with hate/love *etc*; **es erfüllt mich mit Genugtuung, daß** ... it gives me great satisfaction to see that ...; **ein erfülltes Leben** a full life. **(b)** *(ausführen, einhalten)* to fulfil *(Brit)*, to fulfill *(US)*; *Bedingungen auch* to meet, to comply with; *Wunsch, Pflicht auch* to carry out; *Erwartungen auch* to come up to; *(Jur) Soll* to achieve; *Plan* to carry through; *Zweck* to serve. **ihr Wunsch wurde erfüllt** her/their wish came true. **2** *vr (Wunsch, Voraussagung)* to be fulfilled, to come true.

**Erfüllung** *f* fulfilment *(Brit)*, fulfillment *(US)*; *(einer Aufgabe auch)* performance; *(eines Solls)* achievement; *(eines Plans)* execution. **in** ~ **gehen** to be fulfilled.

**ergänzen*** *vt* to supplement; *(vervollständigen)* to complete; *Fehlendes* to supply; *Vorräte* to replenish; *Bericht auch* to add (sth) to; *Worte* to add; *Ge-*

*setz* to amend. **sich** ~ to complement one another; **~d hinzufügen** to add *(zu to)*.

**Ergänzung** f **(a)** *(das Ergänzen)* supplementing; *(Vervollständigung)* completion; *(von Fehlendem)* supply(ing); *(eines Berichts)* addition *(+gen to)*; *(von Gesetz)* amendment; *(von Lager, Vorräten)* replenishment. **(b)** *(Zusatz; zu Buch etc)* supplement; *(Hinzugefügtes, Person)* addition; *(zu einem Gesetz)* amendment.

**ergattern\*** *vt (col)* to get hold of.

**ergeben\*** *irreg* **1** *vt* to yield, to produce; *(zum Ergebnis haben)* to result in; *Summe* to amount to. **2** *vr* **(a)** *(kapitulieren) (dat to)* to surrender, to capitulate. **sich in etw** *(acc)* ~ to submit to sth. **(b)** *(folgen)* to result, to arise *(aus from)*. **daraus können sich Nachteile** ~ this could turn out to be disadvantageous. **(c)** *(sich herausstellen)* to come to light. **es ergab sich, daß unsere Befürchtungen ...** it turned out that our fears ... **3** *adj (hingegeben, treu)* devoted; *(demütig)* humble; *(unterwürfig)* submissive. **jdm treu ~ sein** to be loyally devoted to sb.

**Ergebenheit** f *(Hingabe, Treue)* devotion; *(Demut)* humility; *(Unterwürfigkeit)* submissiveness.

**Ergebnis** nt result; *(Sport auch)* score; *(Auswirkung auch)* consequence, outcome. **die Verhandlungen führten zu keinem** ~ the negotiations were inconclusive; **zu einem ~ kommen** to come to or reach a conclusion.

**ergebnislos** *adj* unsuccessful, fruitless. **~ bleiben/verlaufen** to come to nothing.

**ergehen\*** *irreg* **1** *vi aux sein* **(a)** *(form)* to go out *(an +acc to)*; *(Gesetz)* to be enacted. **~ lassen** to issue, to send; to enact. **(b)** **sie ließ seine Vorwürfe über sich** *(acc)* ~ she let his reproaches simply wash over her; **sie ließ seine Zärtlichkeiten über sich** *(acc)* ~ she submitted to his intimacies. **2** *vi impers aux sein* **es ist ihm schlecht/gut ergangen** he fared badly/well; **es wird ihm schlecht ~** he will suffer. **3** *vr (fig)* **sich in etw** *(dat)* ~ to indulge in sth; **sich (in langen Reden) über ein Thema ~** to hold forth at length on a subject.

**Ergehen** nt no pl *(geh)* (state of) health.

**ergiebig** *adj (lit, fig)* productive; *Geschäft* profitable, lucrative; *(fruchtbar)* fertile; *(sparsam im Verbrauch)* economical.

**ergießen\*** *vr irreg (geh)* to pour forth *(liter)* or out *(auch fig)*.

**ergo** *conj* therefore, ergo *(liter, hum)*.

**Ergonomie** f ergonomics *sing*.

**ergonomisch** *adj* ergonomic.

**ergötzen\*** *(geh)* **1** *vt* to delight. **2** *vr* **sich an etw** *(dat)* ~ to take delight in sth.

**ergrauen\*** *vi aux sein* to go grey *(Brit)* or gray *(US)*.

**ergreifen\*** *vt irreg (lit, fig)* to seize; *(fassen auch)* to grasp, to grip; *Beruf* to take up; *Maßnahmen* to take; *(innerlich bewegen)* to move. **von Furcht etc ergriffen werden** to be seized with fear etc; **er ergriff das Wort** he began to speak; *(Parl, bei Versammlung etc)* he took the floor.

**ergreifend** *adj (fig)* moving.

**ergriffen** *adj (fig)* moved.

**Ergriffenheit** f emotion.

**ergründen\*** *vt Sinn etc* to fathom; *Ursache, Motiv* to discover.

**Erguß** m ⁼sse effusion; *(Samen~)* ejaculation; *(fig)* outpouring.

**erh. = erhalten** recd.

**erhaben** *adj* **(a)** *Gedanken, Stil* lofty, elevated; *Schönheit, Anblick* sublime; *Augenblick* solemn. **(b)** *(überlegen)* superior. **~ lächeln** to smile in a superior way; **über etw** *(acc)* ~ **(sein)** (to be) above sth;

**über jeden Verdacht ~ sein** to be above suspicion.

**Erhalt** m no pl receipt; *(das Erhalten)* preservation. **bei/nach** ~ on receipt.

**erhalten\*** *irreg* **1** *vt* **(a)** to get, to receive; *Resultat, Genehmigung* to obtain, to get. **das Wort** ~ to receive permission to speak. **(b)** *(bewahren)* to preserve; *Gesundheit etc auch* to maintain. **jdn am Leben** ~ to keep sb alive; **ich hoffe, daß du uns noch lange ~ bleibst** I hope you'll be with us for a long time yet; **er hat sich** *(dat)* **seinen Optimismus ~** he retained his optimism; **gut ~** in good condition; *Antiquitäten, hum: Mensch* well preserved. **2** *vr (Brauch etc)* to last.

**erhältlich** *adj* obtainable, available. **schwer ~** difficult to obtain, hard to come by.

**Erhaltung** f *(Bewahrung)* preservation.

**erhängen\*** *vt* to hang. **Tod durch E~** death by hanging; **sich ~** to hang oneself.

**erhärten\*** **1** *vt* to harden; *(fig) Behauptung etc* to corroborate. **2** *vr (fig: Verdacht)* to harden.

**erhaschen\*** *vt* to catch *(auch fig)*.

**erheben\*** *irreg* **1** *vt* **(a)** to raise. **jdn in den Adelsstand ~** to raise or elevate sb to the peerage. **(b)** *Gebühren* to charge, to levy; *Steuern (auferlegen)* to impose. **2** *vr* **(a)** *(aufstehen)* to get up, to rise. **(b)** *(sich auflehnen)* to rise (up), to revolt. **(c)** *(aufragen)* to rise *(über +dat above)*.

**erhebend** *adj* elevating, uplifting; *(beeindruckend)* impressive.

**erheblich** *adj (beträchtlich)* considerable; *Verletzung* serious; *(relevant)* pertinent.

**Erhebung** f **(a)** *(Boden~)* elevation. **(b)** *(Aufstand)* uprising, revolt. **(c)** *(von Gebühren)* levying. **(d)** *(amtliche Ermittlung)* investigation, inquiry; *(Umfrage)* survey.

**erheitern\*** **1** *vt* to cheer (up); *(belustigen)* to amuse. **2** *vr* to be amused *(über +acc by)*.

**Erheiterung** f amusement.

**erhellen\*** **1** *vt* to illuminate; *(fig: klären auch)* to elucidate. **2** *vr (lit, fig)* to brighten; *(plötzlich)* to light up.

**Erhellung** f *(fig)* elucidation.

**erhitzen\*** **1** *vt* to heat *(auf +acc to)*. **die Gemüter ~** to whip up feeling. **2** *vr* to get hot, to heat up; *(fig: sich erregen)* to become heated *(an +dat over)*. **die Gemüter erhitzten sich** feelings were running high.

**Erhitzung** f heating up; *(fig: Erregung)* excitement.

**erhoffen\*** *vt* to hope for. **was erhoffst du dir davon?** what do you hope to gain from it?

**erhöhen\*** **1** *vt* to raise; *Preise auch, Produktion, Wirkung, Spannung* to increase. **jdn im Rang ~** to promote sb; **erhöhte Temperatur haben** to have a temperature. **2** *vr* to rise, to increase.

**Erhöhung** f **(a)** raising; *(von Produktion, Wirkung)* increase; *(von Spannung)* heightening. **(b)** *(Lohn~)* rise *(Brit)*, raise *(US)*; *(Preis~)* increase. **(c)** *(Hügel)* hill, elevation.

**Erhöhungszeichen** nt *(Mus)* sharp (sign).

**erholen\*** *vr (von from)* to recover; *(sich entspannen auch)* to relax, to have a rest; *(fig: Preise, Aktien auch)* to rally, to pick up. **du siehst sehr erholt aus** you look very rested.

**erholsam** *adj* restful, refreshing.

**Erholung** f *siehe vr* recovery *(auch fig)*; relaxation, rest. **zur ~ in die Schweiz fahren** to go to Switzerland for a relaxing holiday *(esp Brit)* or vacation *(US)* and a rest; **er braucht dringend ~** he badly needs a rest.

**Erholungs-: e~bedürftig** *adj* in need of a rest, run-down; **~gebiet** nt holiday *(Brit)* or vacation *(US)* area; **~heim** nt rest home; *(Ferienheim)* holi-

day *(Brit)* or vacation *(US)* home; **~kur** *f* rest cure; **~ort** *m* spa, health resort; **~pause** *f* break; **~reise** *f* holiday *(Brit)* or vacation *(US)* trip.
**erhören\*** *vt* Gebet *etc* to hear; *Bitte* to yield to.
**Erika** *f*, *pl* **Eriken** *(Bot)* heather.
**er|innern\*** **1** *vt* **jdn an etw** *(acc)* ~ to remind sb of sth; **jdn daran ~, daß ...** to remind sb that ... **2** *vr* **sich an jdn/etw ~** to remember *or* recall sb/sth; **soweit ich mich ~ kann** as far as I remember; **wenn ich mich recht erinnere** if I remember rightly. **3** *vi* **~ an** *(+acc)* to be reminiscent of.
**Er|innerung** *f (an +acc of)* memory, recollection; *(euph: Mahnung)* reminder; *(Andenken)* memento. **~en** *pl (Lebens~)* reminiscences *pl*; *(Liter)* memoirs *pl*; **zur ~ an** *(+acc)* in memory of; *(an Ereignis)* in commemoration of; *(als Andenken)* as a memento of; **jdn/etw in guter ~ behalten** to have pleasant memories of sb/sth.
**Er|innerungs-:** **~lücke** *f* gap in one's memory; **~schreiben** *nt (Comm)* reminder; **~stück** *nt* keepsake; **~wert** *m* sentimental value.
**Eritrea** *nt* Eritrea.
**Eritreer(in** *f)* *m* - Eritrean.
**erkalten\*** *vi aux sein (lit, fig)* to cool (down).
**erkälten\*** *vr* to catch (a) cold. **sich** *(dat)* **die Blase ~** to catch a chill in one's bladder.
**erkältet** *adj* **~ sein** to have a cold; **wir sind alle ~** we all have colds.
**Erkältung** *f* cold; *(leicht)* chill. **eine ~ bekommen** to catch a cold/chill.
**Erkältungskrankheiten** *pl* colds and coughs *pl*.
**erkämpfen\*** *vt* to win, to secure. **sich** *(dat)* **etw ~** to win sth; **er hat sich** *(dat)* **seine Position hart erkämpft** he fought hard for his position.
**erkaufen\*** *vt (fig)* to buy. **etw teuer ~** to pay dearly for sth; **den Erfolg mit seiner Gesundheit ~** to achieve success at the price of one's health.
**erkennbar** *adj (wieder~)* recognizable; *(sichtbar)* visible; *(ersichtlich)* discernible.
**erkennen\*** *irreg* **1** *vt (wieder~, einsehen)* to recognize *(an +dat* by*)*; *(wahrnehmen)* to see, to make out; *Unterschied* to see. **er hat erkannt, daß das nicht stimmte** he realized that it wasn't right; **jdm zu ~ geben, daß ...** to give sb to understand that ...; **sich zu ~ geben** to reveal oneself *(als* to be*)*; **~ lassen** to show, to reveal; **du bist erkannt!** I see what you're after, I know your game. **2** *vi* **~ auf** *(+acc) (Jur) Freispruch* to grant; *Strafe* to impose; *(Sport) Freistoß* to give, to award.
**erkenntlich** *adj* **sich (für etw) ~ zeigen** to show one's gratitude *or* appreciation (for sth).
**Erkenntlichkeit** *f* gratitude; *(Gegenleistung)* token of one's gratitude *or* appreciation.
**Erkenntnis** *f (Wissen)* knowledge *no pl*; *(das Erkennen)* recognition, realization; *(Entdeckung)* discovery. **zu der ~ kommen, daß ...** to come to the realization that ..., to realize that ...
**Erkennungs-:** **~dienst** *m* police records department; **e~dienstlich** *adv* **jdn e~dienstlich behandeln** to fingerprint and photograph sb; **~marke** *f* identity disc; **~melodie** *f* theme tune; *(esp Rad)* signature tune; **~zeichen** *nt* identification; *(Mil: Abzeichen)* badge.
**Erker** *m* - bay; *(kleiner Vorbau)* oriel.
**Erker-:** **~fenster** *nt* bay window; **~zimmer** *nt* room with a bay window.
**erklärbar** *adj* explicable, explainable. **leicht ~** easily explained; **schwer ~** hard to explain.
**erklären\*** **1** *vt* **(a)** *(erläutern)* to explain *(jdm etw* sth to sb*)*. **ich kann mir nicht ~, warum ...** I can't understand why ... **(b)** *(bekanntgeben)* to declare *(als*

to be*)*; *Rücktritt* to announce; *(Politiker, Pressesprecher etc)* to say. **einem Staat den Krieg ~** to declare war on a country; **eine Ausstellung** *etc* **für eröffnet ~** to declare an exhibition *etc* open; **jdn für schuldig** *etc* **~** to pronounce sb guilty *etc*. **2** *vr* **(a)** *(Sache)* to be explained. **das erklärt sich daraus, daß ...** it can be explained by the fact that ...; **das erklärt sich (von) selbst** that's self-explanatory. **(b)** *(Mensch)* to declare oneself. **er erklärte sich für gesund** he said that he was in good health.
**erklärend** *adj* explanatory. **einige ~e Worte** a few words of explanation.
**erklärlich** *adj* **(a)** = **erklärbar. (b)** *(verständlich)* understandable.
**erklärt** *adj attr Ziel* professed; *Gegner auch* avowed; *Favorit, Liebling* acknowledged.
**Erklärung** *f* **(a)** explanation. **(b)** *(Bekanntgabe)* declaration; *(eines Politikers etc)* statement.
**erklecklich** *adj* considerable.
**erklimmen\*** *vt irreg (geh)* to scale; *(fig) Spitze, höchste Stufe* to climb to.
**erklingen\*** *vi irreg (geh) aux sein* to ring out. **ein Lied ~ lassen** to burst (forth) into song.
**erkranken\*** *vi aux sein* to be taken ill *(an +dat* with*)*; *(Organ, Pflanze, Tier)* to become diseased *(an +dat* with*)*. **erkrankt sein** to be ill/diseased.
**Erkrankung** *f* illness; *(von Organ, Pflanze, Tier)* disease.
**erkunden\*** *vt (esp Mil) Gelände etc* to reconnoitre; *(feststellen)* to find out.
**erkundigen\*** *vr* **sich nach etw/jdm ~** to ask about sth/after sb; **ich werde mich ~** I'll find out.
**Erkundigung** *f* inquiry; *(Nachforschung auch)* investigation. **~en einholen** to make inquiries.
**Erkundung** *f (Mil)* reconnaissance.
**erlahmen\*** *vi aux sein (lit, fig)* to flag.
**erlangen\*** *vt* to attain, to achieve.
**Erlaß** *m* **-sse** **(a)** decree, enactment. **(b)** *(Straf~ etc)* remission.
**erlassen\*** *vt irreg* **(a)** *Verfügung* to pass; *Gesetz* to enact. **(b)** *Strafe etc* to remit; *Gebühren* to waive. **jdm etw ~** *Schulden etc* to release sb from sth; *Gebühren* to waive sth for sb; **jdm die Strafarbeit ~** to let sb off a punishment.
**erlauben\*** **1** *vt* to allow, to permit. **jdm etw ~** to allow *or* permit sb (to do) sth; **es ist mir nicht erlaubt, das zu tun** I am not allowed *or* permitted to do that; **~ Sie?** may I?; **~ Sie, daß ich das Fenster öffne?** do you mind if I open the window?; **~ Sie, daß ich mich vorstelle** allow me *or* permit me to introduce myself; **~ Sie mal!** do you mind!; **soweit es meine Zeit erlaubt** *(form)* time permitting. **2** *vr* **sich** *(dat)* **etw ~** *(gestatten, sich gönnen)* to allow *or* permit oneself sth; *(wagen) Bemerkung* to venture sth; *(sich leisten)* to afford sth; **sich** *(dat)* **~, etw zu tun** *(so frei sein)* to take the liberty of doing sth; *(sich leisten)* to afford to do sth; **was ~ Sie sich (eigentlich)!** how dare you!
**Erlaubnis** *f* permission; *(Schriftstück)* permit. **(jdn) um ~ bitten** to ask (sb) (for) permission.
**erläutern\*** *vt* to explain, to elucidate; *Text* to comment on. **~d** explanatory; **~d fügte er hinzu** he added in explanation.
**Erläuterung** *f siehe vt* explanation, elucidation; commentary. **zur ~** in explanation.
**Erle** *f* **-n** alder.
**erleben\*** *vt* to experience; *(noch lebend erreichen)* to live to see; *(durchmachen) schwere Zeiten* to go through; *Abenteuer, Enttäuschung, Erfolg* to have; *Jahrhundertwende* to see. **im Urlaub habe ich viel erlebt** I had an eventful time on holiday *(Brit)* or va-

cation *(US)*; **was haben Sie im Ausland erlebt?** what sort of experiences did you have abroad?; **er hat schon viel Schlimmes erlebt** he's had a lot of bad times *or* experiences; **ich habe es oft erlebt** I've often seen it happen; **so wütend habe ich ihn noch nie erlebt** I've never seen *or* known him so furious; **das werde ich nicht mehr** ~ I shan't live to see that; **er möchte mal etwas** ~ he wants to have a good time; **das muß man erlebt haben** you've got to have experienced it for yourself; **na, der kann was** ~! *(col)* he'll be for it! *(col)*.

**Erlebnis** *nt* experience; *(Abenteuer)* adventure.
**erlebnisreich** *adj* eventful.
**erledigen\*** **1** *vt* (a) to deal with; *Akte etc* to process; *(ausführen) Auftrag* to carry out; *Sache* to settle. **Einkäufe** ~ to do some shopping; **ich habe noch einiges in der Stadt zu** ~ I've still got a few things to do in town; **das ist erledigt** that's taken care of, that's been done. (b) *(col) (ermüden)* to wear out; *(ruinieren)* to finish, to ruin; *(töten)* to do in *(col)*; *(k.o. schlagen)* to finish off. **2** *vr* **das hat sich erledigt** that's all settled; **sich von selbst** ~ to take care of itself.
**erledigt** *adj (col) (erschöpft)* shattered *(col)*, done in *pred (col)*; *(ruiniert)* finished, ruined.
**Erledigung** *f (Ausführung)* execution, carrying out; *(Durchführung, Beendung)* completion; *(einer Sache)* settlement. **die** ~ **meiner Korrespondenz** dealing with my correspondence; **einige** ~**en in der Stadt** a few things to do in town; **in** ~ **Ihrer Anfrage** *(form)* further to your inquiry *(form)*.
**erlegen\*** *vt Wild* to shoot, to bag *(Hunt)*.
**erleichtern\*** *vt (einfacher machen)* to make easier; *(fig) Last, Los* to lighten; *(lindern) Not, Schmerz etc* to relieve. **sein Herz/Gewissen** ~ to unburden one's heart/conscience; **jdn um etw** ~ *(hum)* to relieve sb of sth; **erleichtert aufatmen** to breathe a sigh of relief.
**Erleichterung** *f (von Last etc)* lightening; *(Linderung)* relief. **das trägt zur** ~ **meiner Aufgabe bei** it makes my task easier.
**erleiden\*** *vt irreg* to suffer.
**erlernbar** *adj* learnable. **leicht** ~ easy to learn.
**erlernen\*** *vt* to learn.
**erlesen** *adj* exquisite. **ein** ~**er Kreis** a select circle.
**erleuchten\*** *vt* to light (up), to illuminate.
**Erleuchtung** *f (Eingebung)* inspiration.
**erliegen\*** *vi irreg aux sein +dat (lit, fig)* to succumb to; *einem Irrtum* to be the victim of. **zum E~ kommen** to come to a standstill.
**erlogen** *adj* made-up.
**Erlös** *m* -e proceeds *pl (+gen* from*)*.
**erlöschen\*** *vi irreg aux sein (Feuer)* to go out; *(Gefühle, Interesse)* to die; *(Anspruch etc)* to expire, to lapse; *(Firma)* to be dissolved. **ein erloschener Vulkan** an extinct volcano.
**erlösen\*** *vt (retten)* to save, to rescue *(aus, von* from*)*; *(Rel)* to redeem, to save; *(von Sünden, Qualen)* to deliver *(esp Bibl)*, to release.
**erlösend** *adj* relieving, liberating. **sie sprach das** ~**e Wort** she spoke the magic word.
**Erlöser(in** *f) m - (Rel)* Redeemer; *(Befreier)* saviour.
**Erlösung** *f* release, deliverance; *(Erleichterung)* relief; *(Rel)* redemption.
**ermächtigen\*** *vt* to authorize, to empower *(zu etw* to do sth*)*.
**Ermächtigung** *f* authorization.
**ermahnen\*** *vt* to exhort, to urge; *(warnend)* to warn; *(Jur)* to caution. **jdn zur Aufmerksamkeit** ~ to admonish sb to be attentive; **jdn im Guten** ~ to give sb a friendly warning.

**Ermahnung** *f* exhortation, urging; *(warnend)* warning; *(Jur)* caution.
**Ermang(e)lung** *f*: **in** ~ **+gen** because of the lack of.
**ermannen\*** *vr* to pluck up courage.
**ermäßigen** **1** *vt* to reduce. **2** *vr* to be reduced.
**Ermäßigung** *f* reduction; *(Steuer~)* relief.
**ermattet** *adj (geh)* exhausted, weary.
**ermessen\*** *vt irreg (einschätzen) Größe, Wert* to estimate; *(begreifen können)* to appreciate.
**Ermessen** *nt no pl (Urteil)* judgement; *(Gutdünken)* discretion. **nach meinem** ~ in my judgement; **nach menschlichem** ~ as far as anyone can judge; **nach eigenem** ~ **handeln** to act on one's own discretion; **in jds** ~ *(dat)* **liegen** to be at sb's discretion.
**Ermessens-:** ~**entscheidung** *f (Jur)* discretionary decision; ~**frage** *f* matter of discretion; ~**spielraum** *m* discretionary powers *pl*.
**ermitteln\*** **1** *vt* to determine *(auch Chem, Math)*, to ascertain; *Person* to trace; *Tatsache* to establish. **2** *vi* to investigate. **gegen jdn** ~ to investigate sb; **in einem Fall** ~ to investigate a case.
**Ermittlung** *f* (a) *no pl siehe vt* determination, ascertaining; tracing; establishing. (b) *(esp Jur: Erkundigung)* investigation, inquiry. ~**en anstellen** to make inquiries *(über +acc* about*)*.
**Ermittlungs-:** ~**ausschuß** *m* committee of inquiry; ~**beamte(r)** *m* investigating officer; ~**richter** *m (Jur)* examining magistrate; ~**stand** *m* stage of the investigation; ~**verfahren** *nt (Jur)* preliminary proceedings *pl*.
**ermöglichen\*** *vt* to facilitate, to make possible. **jdm das Studium** ~ to make it possible for sb to study.
**ermorden\*** *vt* to murder; *(Pol)* to assassinate.
**Ermordung** *f* murder; *(Pol)* assassination.
**ermüden\*** **1** *vt* to tire. **2** *vi aux sein* to tire, to become tired; *(Tech)* to fatigue.
**ermüdend** *adj* tiring.
**Ermüdung** *f* fatigue *(auch Tech)*, tiredness.
**Ermüdungs|erscheinung** *f* sign of fatigue.
**ermuntern\*** *vt (ermutigen)* to encourage *(jdn zu etw* sb to do sth*)*; *(aufmuntern)* to cheer up.
**Ermunterung** *f siehe vt* encouragement, cheering-up.
**ermutigen\*** *vt (ermuntern)* to encourage; *(Mut geben)* to give courage.
**Ermutigung** *f* encouragement.
**ernähren\*** **1** *vt* to feed; *(unterhalten)* to support, to keep. **schlecht/gut ernährt** undernourished/well-fed. **2** *vr* to eat. **sich von etw** ~ to live on sth; **sich von Übersetzungen** ~ to earn one's living by doing translations.
**Ernährer(in** *f) m* - breadwinner, provider.
**Ernährung** *f* feeding; *(Nahrung)* food, nourishment, nutrition *(esp Med)*. **die** ~ **einer großen Familie** feeding a big family; **falsche/richtige/pflanzliche** ~ the wrong/a proper/a vegetarian diet.
**Ernährungs-:** ~**gewohnheiten** *pl* eating habits *pl*; ~**weise** *f* diet; ~**wissenschaft** *f* dietetics *sing*.
**ernennen\*** *vt irreg* to appoint *(jdn zu etw* sb sth*)*.
**Ernennung** *f* appointment *(zu as)*.
**erneuerbar** *adj* renewable; ~**e Energien** renewables *pl*.
**erneuern\*** *vt* to renew; *(renovieren)* to renovate; *(restaurieren)* to restore; *(auswechseln) Maschinenteile* to replace; *(wiederbeleben)* to revive.
**Erneuerung** *f siehe vt* renewal; renovation; restoration; replacement; revival.
**erneut** **1** *adj attr* renewed. **2** *adv* (once) again.
**erniedrigen\*** **1** *vt (demütigen)* to humiliate; *(herab-*

*setzen)* to degrade. **2** *vr* to humble oneself; *(pej)* to lower oneself.

**Erniedrigung** *f siehe vt* humiliation; degradation.

**Erniedrigungszeichen** *nt (Mus)* flat (sign).

**Ernst** *m no pl* seriousness. **im ~** seriously; **allen ~es** in all seriousness, quite seriously; **ist das Ihr ~?** are you (really) serious?; **das kann doch nicht dein ~ sein!** you can't be serious!; **es ist mir ~ damit** I'm serious about it, I'm in earnest; **mit einer Drohung ~ machen** to carry out a threat; **der ~ des Lebens** the serious side of life; **mit ~ bei der Sache sein** to do sth seriously.

**ernst** *adj* serious. **es (mit jdm/etw) ~ meinen** to be serious (about sb/sth); **jdn/etw ~ nehmen** to take sb/sth seriously; **es steht ~ um ihn** things don't look too good for him.

**Ernst-:** **~fall** *m* emergency; **im ~fall** in case of emergency; **e~gemeint** *adj attr* serious; **e~haft** *adj* serious; *(eindringlich, eifrig)* earnest; **~haftigkeit** *f siehe adj* seriousness; earnestness; **e~lich** *adj* serious.

**Ernte** *f* **-n (a)** harvest *(an +dat* of*)*; *(von Äpfeln, fig)* crop. **die ~ seines Fleißes** the fruits of his labour. **(b)** *(das Ernten) (von Getreide)* harvest(ing); *(von Kartoffeln)* digging; *(von Äpfeln etc)* picking.

**Ernte-:** **~arbeiter** *m* harvester; *(von Kartoffeln, Obst)* picker; **~ausfall** *m* crop failure; **~(dank)fest** *nt* harvest festival.

**ernten** *vt Getreide* to harvest, to reap; *Kartoffeln* to get in; *Äpfel, Erbsen* to pick; *(fig) Früchte, Unfrieden* to reap; *(Un)dank, Spott* to get.

**ernüchtern*** *vt* to sober up; *(fig)* to bring down to earth. **~d** sobering; **ich war sehr ernüchtert** my illusions were shattered.

**Ernüchterung** *f* sobering-up; *(fig)* disillusionment.

**Er|oberer** *m* **-**, **Er|oberin** *f* conqueror.

**er|obern*** *vt* to conquer; *Festung, Stadt* to capture; *(fig) Sympathie, neue Märkte etc* to win; *(col: ergattern)* to get hold of. **im Sturm ~** *(Mil, fig)* to take by storm.

**Er|oberung** *f (lit, fig)* conquest; *(einer Festung, Stadt)* capture.

**er|öffnen*** **1** *vt* to open; *Konkursverfahren* to institute. **jdm etw ~** *(hum, geh)* to disclose *or* reveal sth to sb. **2** *vr (Aussichten etc)* to open up. **3** *vi (Währungskurs)* to open *(mit* at*)*.

**Er|öffnung** *f siehe vt* opening; institution; disclosure, revelation.

**Er|öffnungs-:** **~ansprache** *f* inaugural *or* opening address; **~feier** *f* opening ceremony; **~kurs** *m* opening price.

**erogen** *adj* erogenous.

**er|örtern*** *vt* to discuss (in detail).

**Er|örterung** *f* discussion.

**Erosion** *f (Geol, Med)* erosion.

**Erotik** *f* eroticism.

**erotisch** *adj* erotic.

**Erpel** *m* drake.

**erpicht** *adj* **auf etw** *(acc)* **~ sein** to be keen on sth.

**erpressen*** *vt* to blackmail; *Geld etc* to extort.

**Erpresser(in** *f)* *m* **-** blackmailer; *(bei Entführung)* kidnapper.

**erpresserisch** *adj Methode* blackmailing *attr.*

**Erpressung** *f* blackmail; *(von Geld etc)* extortion.

**erproben*** *vt (lit, fig)* to test. **erprobt** tried and tested.

**erquicken*** *vt (old, liter)* to refresh.

**erraten*** *vt irreg* to guess.

**errechnen*** *vt* to calculate, to work out.

**erregbar** *adj* excitable; *(sexuell)* easily aroused; *(empfindlich)* sensitive.

**Erregbarkeit** *f siehe adj* excitability; ability to be aroused; sensitivity.

**erregen*** **1** *vt* **(a)** *(aufregen) jdn, Nerven etc* to excite; *(erzürnen)* to infuriate. **er war vor Wut ganz erregt** he was in a rage; **erregte Diskussionen** heated discussions; **freudig erregt** excited. **(b)** *(erzeugen)* to arouse; *Aufsehen, Heiterkeit* to cause, to create; *Aufmerksamkeit* to attract. **2** *vr* to get worked up *or* excited *(über +acc* about, over*)*; *(sich ärgern)* to get annoyed *(über +acc* at*)*.

**Erreger** *m* **-** *(Med)* cause.

**Erregung** *f* excitement; *(sexuell auch)* arousal; *(Beunruhigung)* agitation; *(Wut)* rage. **in ~ geraten** to get excited/aroused/agitated/into a rage.

**erreichbar** *adj* reachable; *(nicht weit)* within reach; *Ziel* attainable. **leicht ~** easily reached/within easy reach/easily attainable; **schwer ~ sein** *(Ort)* not to be very accessible; *(Mensch)* to be difficult to get hold of; **der Direktor ist nie ~** the director is never available.

**erreichen*** *vt* to reach; *Zug* to catch; *Zweck* to achieve; *(einholen)* to catch up with. **ein hohes Alter ~** to live to a great age; **vom Bahnhof leicht zu ~** within easy reach of the station; **wann kann ich Sie morgen ~?** when can I get in touch with you tomorrow?; **wir haben nichts erreicht** we achieved nothing.

**erretten*** *vt (liter, esp Rel)* to save, to deliver *(liter)*.

**errichten*** *vt* to erect, to put up; *(fig: gründen)* to set up.

**Errichtung** *f no pl* erection, construction; *(fig: Gründung)* setting-up.

**erringen*** *vt irreg* to gain.

**erröten*** *vi aux sein* to blush.

**Errungenschaft** *f* achievement; *(col: Anschaffung)* acquisition.

**Ersatz** *m no pl* substitute *(auch Sport)*; *(für Altes, Mitarbeiter)* replacement; *(Mil: ~truppen)* replacements *pl*; *(das Ersetzen)* replacement, substitution; *(von Kosten)* reimbursement. **als ~ für** as a substitute/replacement; **als ~ für jdn einspringen** to stand in for sb; **für etw ~ leisten** *(Jur)* to pay compensation for sth.

**Ersatz-:** **~befriedigung** *f* vicarious satisfaction; **~dienst** *m (Mil)* community service *(for conscientious objectors)*; **~kasse** *f* private health insurance; **e~los** *adj* **e~los gestrichen** cancelled (with no alternative); **~mann** *m, pl* **~männer** *or* **~leute** replacement; *(Sport)* substitute; **~spieler** *m (Sport)* substitute; **~teil** *nt* spare (part); **e~weise** *adv* as an alternative.

**ersaufen*** *vi irreg aux sein (col)* to drown; *(Aut)* to flood.

**ersäufen*** *vt* to drown.

**erschaffen** *vt irreg* to create.

**Erschaffung** *f* creation.

**erschaudern*** *vi aux sein (geh)* to shudder *(bei* at*)*.

**erschauern*** *vi aux sein (geh) (vor Kälte)* to shiver; *(vor Ehrfurcht)* to tremble.

**erscheinen*** *vi irreg aux sein* to appear; *(Buch auch)* to come out. **es erscheint (mir) wünschenswert** it seems *or* appears desirable (to me).

**Erscheinen** *nt no pl* appearance; *(von Buch auch)* publication. **um rechtzeitiges ~ wird gebeten** you are kindly requested to attend punctually.

**Erscheinung** *f* **(a)** *no pl (das Erscheinen)* appearance. **in ~ treten** *(Merkmale)* to appear; *(Gefühle)* to show themselves. **(b)** *(das Erscheinende)* phenomenon; *(Krankheits~, Alters~)* symptom; *(Zeichen)* sign. **(c)** *(Gestalt)* figure. **(d)** *(Geister~)* apparition; *(Traumbild)* vision.

**Erscheinungs-:** ~**bild** *nt* appearance; ~**form** *f* manifestation; ~**jahr** *nt (von Buch)* year of publication.

**erschießen\*** *irreg* **1** *vt* to shoot (dead). **2** *vr* to shoot oneself; *siehe* **erschossen**.

**Erschießung** *f* shooting; *(als Todesstrafe)* execution.

**Erschießungskommando** *nt* firing squad.

**erschlaffen\*** *vi aux sein (ermüden)* to tire; *(schlaff werden)* to go limp; *(Interesse)* to flag.

**Erschlaffung** *f siehe vi* tiredness; limpness; flagging.

**erschlagen\*** **1** *vt irreg* to kill. **2** *adj* ~ **sein** *(col) (todmüde)* to be worn out *or* dead beat *(col)*; *(erstaunt)* to be flabbergasted *(col)*.

**erschleichen\*** *vt irreg* (sich *dat*) **etw** ~ to obtain sth by devious means; **sich** *(dat)* **jds Vertrauen** ~ to worm oneself into sb's confidence.

**erschließen\*** *irreg* **1** *vt Gebiet, Absatzmarkt* to develop, to open up; *Bodenschätze* to tap. **2** *vr* **sich jdm** ~ *(verständlich werden)* to become clear to sb.

**Erschließungskosten** *pl* development costs *pl*.

**erschlossen** *adj Gebiet* developed.

**erschöpfen\*** **1** *vt* to exhaust. **2** *vr* **(a)** *(körperlich)* to exhaust oneself. **(b)** *(fig)* **sich in etw** *(dat)* ~ to amount to nothing more than sth.

**erschöpfend** *adj* **(a)** *(ermüdend)* exhausting. **(b)** *(ausführlich)* exhaustive.

**Erschöpfung** *f* exhaustion. **bis zur** ~ **arbeiten** to work to the point of exhaustion.

**erschossen** *adj (col)* **(völlig)** ~ **sein** to be whacked *(col)*, to be dead (beat) *(col)*.

**erschrecken\*** **1** *vt* to frighten, to scare; *(bestürzen)* to startle. **2** *pret auch* **erschrak**, *ptp auch* **erschrocken** *vir (vi: aux sein)* to be frightened *(vor +dat by)*; *(bestürzt sein)* to be startled. **sie erschrak beim Gedanken, daß ...** the thought that ... gave her a start *or* a scare; **sie erschrak bei dem Knall** the bang made her jump; *siehe* **erschrocken**.

**erschreckend** *adj* alarming, frightening. ~ **wenig Leute** alarmingly few people.

**erschrocken** *adj* frightened, scared; *(bestürzt)* startled.

**erschüttern\*** *vt* to shake; *Glaubwürdigkeit* to cast doubt on; *Gesundheit* to upset. **über etw** *(acc)* **erschüttert sein** to be shaken *or* shattered by sth; **ihn kann nichts** ~ he is unflappable.

**erschütternd** *adj* shattering.

**Erschütterung** *f (des Bodens etc)* tremor, vibration; *(seelische Ergriffenheit)* emotion, shock. **ihr Tod löste allgemeine** ~ **aus** her death shocked everyone.

**erschweren\*** *vt* to make more difficult. ~**de Umstände** *(Jur)* aggravating circumstances; **es kommt noch** ~**d hinzu, daß ...** to compound matters ...

**Erschwerung** *f* obstruction *(gen to)*. **das bedeutet eine** ~ **meiner Arbeit** that will make my job more difficult.

**erschwindeln\*** *vt* to obtain by fraud.

**erschwinglich** *adj Preise* affordable.

**ersehen\*** *vt irreg* **etw aus etw** ~ to see sth from sth.

**ersehnt** *adj* longed-for.

**ersetzen\*** *vt* to replace; *Unkosten* to reimburse. **jdm einen Schaden** ~ to compensate sb for damages.

**Ersetzung** *f no pl* replacing; *(von Unkosten)* reimbursement.

**ersichtlich** *adj* obvious, clear.

**ersinnen\*** *vt irreg* to devise, to think up.

**ersparen\*** *vt Vermögen, Zeit, Kummer* to save. **jdm/ sich etw** ~ to spare *or* save sb/oneself sth; **ich kann**

**mir jeglichen Kommentar** ~ I don't think I need to comment; **ihr blieb auch nichts erspart** she was spared nothing; **das Ersparte** the savings *pl*.

**Ersparnis** *f* **(a)** *no pl (an Zeit etc)* saving *(an +dat of)*. **(b)** *usu pl* savings *pl*.

**erst** *adv* **(a)** first. **mach** ~ **(ein)mal die Arbeit fertig** finish your work first; **wenn du das** ~ **einmal hinter dir hast** once you've got that behind you. **(b)** *(nicht früher als, nicht mehr als, bloß)* only; *(nicht früher als auch)* not until. **gerade** ~ just; ~ **gestern** only yesterday; ~ **jetzt verstehe ich** I have only just understood; ~ **morgen** not until tomorrow; **wir fahren** ~ **später** we're not going until later; ~ **als** only when, not until. **(c)** **da ging's** ~ **richtig los** then it really got going; **da fange ich** ~ **gar nicht an** I simply won't bother to begin; **jetzt** ~ **recht/recht nicht!** that makes me all the more determined (to do it/ not to do it); **wäre er doch** ~ **zurück!** if only he were back!; **diese Gerüchte darf man gar nicht** ~ **aufkommen lassen** these rumours mustn't even be allowed to start.

**erstarren\*** *vi aux sein (Finger)* to grow stiff; *(Flüssigkeit)* to solidify; *(Gips, Zement etc)* to set; *(fig: Blut)* to freeze, to run cold; *(Lächeln)* to freeze; *(vor Entsetzen)* to be paralysed *(Brit)* or paralyzed *(US) (vor +dat with)*.

**erstatten\*** *vt* **(a)** *Unkosten* to refund. **(b)** *(form)* **(Straf)anzeige gegen jdn** ~ to report sb; **Bericht** ~ **to** (give a) report *(über +acc on)*.

**Erstattung** *f no pl (von Unkosten)* reimbursement.

**Erst-:** ~**aufführung** *f (Theat, Mus)* first performance; ~**auflage** *f* first printing.

**erstaunen\*** *vti* to astonish, to amaze; *siehe* **erstaunt**.

**Erstaunen** *nt no pl* astonishment, amazement. **jdn in** ~ **(ver)setzen** to astonish *or* amaze sb.

**erstaunlich** *adj* astonishing, amazing.

**erstaunt** *adj* astonished, amazed *(über +acc about)*. **er sah mich** ~ **an** he looked at me in astonishment *or* amazement.

**Erst-:** ~**ausgabe** *f* first edition; **e~beste(r, s)** *adj attr siehe* **erste(r, s) (b)**.

**erstechen\*** *vt irreg* to stab to death.

**erstehen\*** *irreg* **1** *vt (col)* to buy. **2** *vi aux sein (form)* to arise; *(Bibl: auf~)* to rise.

**Erste-Hilfe-Leistung** *f* administering first aid.

**ersteigen\*** *vt irreg* to climb.

**ersteigern\*** *vt* to buy at an auction.

**Ersteigung** *f* ascent.

**Erst|einsatz** *m (von Atomwaffen)* first strike.

**erstellen\*** *vt* **(a)** *(bauen)* to construct. **(b)** *Liste etc* to draw up.

**erstemal** *adv* **das** ~ the first time.

**erstens** *adv* first(ly), in the first place.

**erste(r, s)** *adj* **(a)** first; *Seite der Zeitung* front. ~ **Etage** first floor *(Brit)*, second floor *(US)*; **der** ~ **Rang** *(Theat)* the dress-circle, the (first) balcony *(US)*; ~ **Qualität** top quality; **E~ Hilfe** first aid; **der/die E~ in der Klasse sein** to be top of the class; **als** ~**s** first of all; **fürs** ~ for the time being; **in** ~**r Linie** first and foremost; **zum** ~**n, zum zweiten, zum dritten** *(bei Auktionen)* going, going, gone!; *siehe* **vierte(r, s)**. **(b)** **er hat den** ~**n besten Kühlschrank gekauft** he bought the first fridge he saw.

**Erste-Klasse-Abteil** *nt* first class compartment.

**erstere(r, s)** *adj* the former.

**erst-:** ~**geboren** *adj attr* first-born; ~**genannt** *adj attr* first-mentioned.

**ersticken\*** **1** *vt jdn* to suffocate, to smother; *Feuer* to smother; *(fig) Aufruhr* to suppress. **mit erstickter Stimme** in a choked voice. **2** *vi aux sein* to suffo-

cate; *(Feuer)* to go out. **an etw** *(dat)* ~ to be suffocated by sth; **an einer Gräte** ~ to choke (to death) on a bone; **vor Lachen** ~ to choke with laughter; **in der Arbeit** ~ *(col)* to be snowed under with work.
**Erstickung** *f* suffocation, asphyxiation.
**Erstickungs-:** ~**gefahr** *f* danger of suffocation; ~**tod** *m* death by suffocation, asphyxia.
**Erst-:** **e**~**klassig** *adj* first-class, first-rate; ~**kommunion** *f* first communion.
**Erstling** *m* first (child); *(Werk)* first work.
**Erstlingswerk** *nt* first work.
**erst-:** ~**malig 1** *adj* first; **2** *adv* for the first time; ~**mals** *adv* for the first time.
**erstrahlen**\* *vi aux sein (liter)* to shine.
**erstrangig** ['e:ɛstraŋɪç] *adj* first-rate.
**erstreben**\* *vt* to strive for.
**erstrebenswert** *adj* worthwhile; *Beruf* desirable.
**erstrecken**\* *vr* to extend *(auf, über +acc* over*)*; *(räumlich auch)* to stretch *(auf, über +acc* over*)*; *(zeitlich auch)* to last *(auf, über +acc* for*)*.
**Erst-:** ~**schlag** *m (mit Atomwaffen)* first strike; ~**schlagwaffe** *f* first-strike weapon; ~**stimme** *f* first vote; ~**stempel** *m* date stamp on a first-day cover; ~**tagsbrief** *m* first-day cover; ~**täter** *m* first offender.
**erstunken** *adj:* **das ist** ~ **und erlogen** *(col)* that's a pack of lies.
**erstürmen**\* *vt (Mil)* to (take by) storm; *Gipfel* to conquer.
**Erstwähler** *m* first-time voter.
**ersuchen**\* *vt (form)* to request *(jdn um etw* sth of sb*)*.
**Ersuchen** *nt - (form)* request.
**ertappen**\* *vt* to catch. **ich habe ihn dabei ertappt** I caught him at it.
**erteilen**\* *vt* to give; *Lizenz* to issue; *Auftrag auch* to place *(jdm* with sb*)*. **jdm einen Verweis** ~ to reproach sb.
**Erteilung** *f siehe vt* giving; issue; placing.
**ertönen**\* *vi aux sein (geh)* to sound, to ring out. ~ **lassen** to sound.
**Ertrag** *m* ⸚**e** *(von Acker)* yield; *(Einnahmen)* return.
**ertragen**\* *vt irreg* to bear; *(esp in Frage auch)* to stand. **wie erträgst du nur seine Launen?** how can you put up with his moods?
**erträglich** *adj* bearable, endurable; *(leidlich)* tolerable.
**ertragreich** *adj Geschäft* profitable, lucrative.
**ertränken**\* **1** *vt* to drown. **2** *vr* to drown oneself.
**erträumen**\* *vt* to dream of, to imagine.
**ertrinken**\* *vi irreg aux sein* to drown, to be drowned.
**Ertrinken** *nt no pl* drowning.
**Ertüchtigung** *f (geh)* getting in trim. **körperliche** ~ physical training.
**er|übrigen**\* **1** *vt Zeit, Geld* to spare. **2** *vr* to be unnecessary *or* superfluous.
**eruieren**\* *vt (form)* to investigate, to find out.
**erwachen**\* *vi aux sein* to awake, to wake (up); *(aus Ohnmacht etc)* to come around *(aus* from*)*; *(fig: Verdacht)* to be aroused. **ein böses E**~ *(fig)* a rude awakening.
**erwachsen**\* **1** *vi irreg aux sein (geh)* to arise, to develop; *(Vorteil, Kosten etc)* to result. **daraus erwuchsen ihm Unannehmlichkeiten** that caused him some trouble. **2** *adj* grown-up, adult. ~ **sein** *(Mensch)* to be grown-up *or* an adult.
**Erwachsenenbildung** *f* adult education.
**Erwachsene(r)** *mf decl as adj* adult, grown-up.
**erwägen**\* *vt irreg* to consider.
**Erwägung** *f* consideration. **etw in** ~ **ziehen** to take

sth into consideration.
**erwähnen**\* *vt* to mention, to refer to.
**erwähnenswert** *adj* worth mentioning.
**Erwähnung** *f* mention *(gen* of*)*, reference *(gen* to*)*.
**erwärmen**\* **1** *vt* to warm. **2** *vr* to warm up. **sich für jdn/etw** ~ *(fig)* to take to sb/sth; **ich kann mich für Goethe nicht** ~ Goethe leaves me cold.
**erwarten**\* *vt* to expect. **etw von jdm** ~ to expect sth from *or* of sb; **ein Kind** ~ to be expecting (a baby); **das war zu** ~ that was to be expected; **etw sehnsüchtig** ~ to long for sth; **sie kann den Sommer kaum noch** ~ she's really looking forward to the summer; **was mich da wohl erwartet?** I wonder what awaits me there; **über E**~ beyond expectation.
**Erwartung** *f* expectation; *(Spannung, Ungeduld)* anticipation. **in** ~ **Ihrer baldigen Antwort** *(form)* in anticipation of your early reply.
**erwartungs-:** ~**gemäß** *adv* as expected; ~**voll** *adj* expectant.
**erwecken**\* *vt* **(a)** *(liter: aus Schlaf etc)* to rouse. **etw zu neuem Leben** ~ to resurrect sth. **(b)** *(fig) Begeisterung etc* to arouse; *Hoffnungen, Zweifel* to raise; *Erinnerungen* to bring back.
**erwehren**\* *vr (+gen) (geh)* to ward off. **er konnte sich kaum der Tränen** ~ he could hardly hold back his tears.
**erweichen**\* *vt* to soften; *(fig: überreden auch)* to move. **sich nicht** ~ **lassen** to be unmoved.
**erweisen**\* *irreg* **1** *vt* **(a)** *(nachweisen)* to prove. **eine erwiesene Tatsache** a proven fact. **(b)** *(zuteil werden lassen)* to show. **jdm einen Dienst** ~ to do sb a service. **2** *vr* **sich als etw** ~ to prove to be sth, to turn out to be sth; **sich jdm gegenüber dankbar** ~ to show one's gratitude to sb.
**erweiterbar** *adj (auch Comp)* expandable.
**erweitern**\* *vtr* to widen, to enlarge; *Geschäft* to expand; *Kleid* to let out; *(Med)* to dilate; *(fig) Kenntnisse* to broaden; *Macht* to extend.
**Erweiterung** *f siehe vtr* widening, enlargement; expansion; letting out; dilation; broadening; extension.
**Erwerb** *m no pl* acquisition; *(Kauf)* purchase. **beim** ~ **eines Autos** when buying a car.
**erwerben**\* *vt irreg* to acquire; *Ehre, Vertrauen, (Sport) Titel* to win, to gain; *(käuflich)* to purchase. **sich** *(dat)* **etw** ~ to acquire *etc* sth; **er hat sich** *(dat)* **große Verdienste um die Firma erworben** he has done the firm great services.
**Erwerbs-:** **e**~**fähig** *adj (form)* capable of gainful employment; ~**fähigkeit** *f (form)* fitness for work; ~**leben** *nt* working life; **e**~**los** *adj* = **arbeitslos**; ~**quelle** *f* source of income; **e**~**tätig** *adj (gainfully)* employed; ~**tätigkeit** *f* gainful employment; **e**~**unfähig** *adj* unable to work; ~**unfähigkeit** *f* inability to work.
**Erwerbung** *f* acquisition.
**erwidern**\* *vt* **(a)** to reply *(auf +acc* to*)*. **(b)** *Besuch, Grüße, Blick, (Mil) Feuer* to return; *Gefühle* to reciprocate.
**Erwiderung** *f (Antwort)* reply, answer. **in** ~ **Ihres Schreibens vom ...** *(form)* in reply to your letter of the ...
**erwiesen** *adj* proven.
**erwiesenermaßen** *adv* as has been proved *or* shown.
**erwirtschaften**\* *vt Gewinn etc* to make by good management. **Gewinne** ~ to make profits.
**erwischen**\* *vt (col)* to catch. **jdn beim Stehlen** ~ to catch sb stealing; **du darfst dich nicht** ~ **lassen** you mustn't get caught; **ihn hat's erwischt!** *(verliebt)*

he's got it bad *(col)*; *(krank)* he's got it; *(gestorben)* he's had it *(col)*.

**erwünscht** *adj Wirkung etc* desired; *Eigenschaft, Kenntnisse* desirable; *(willkommen)* welcome.

**erwürgen\*** *vt* to strangle, to throttle.

**Erz** *nt* **-e** ore.

**erzählen\*** *vti* **(a)** to tell. **er hat den Vorfall erzählt** he told (us *etc*) about the incident; **jdm etw ~** to tell sb sth; **man erzählt sich, daß ...** people say that ...; **wem ~ Sie das!** *(col)* you're telling me!; **das kannst du einen anderen ~** *(col)* pull the other one *(col)*; **mir kannst du nichts ~** *(col)* don't give *or* tell me that! *(col)*; **dem werd' ich was ~!** *(col)* I'll have something to say to him; **er kann gut ~** he's a good story-teller. **(b)** *(Liter)* to narrate. **~de Dichtung** narrative fiction.

**Erzähler(in** *f)* *m* - narrator *(auch Liter)*; *(Geschichten~)* story-teller; *(Schriftsteller)* narrative writer.

**erzählerisch** *adj* narrative.

**Erzählung** *f (Liter)* story, tale; *(das Erzählen)* narration; *(Bericht)* account.

**Erz-:** **~bergbau** *m* ore mining; **~bischof** *m* archbishop; **~bistum** *nt* archbishopric; **~engel** *m* archangel.

**erzeugen\*** *vt* to produce; *Strom auch* to generate; *(fig: bewirken)* to give rise to, to create.

**Erzeuger** *m* - *(Comm)* producer; *(Vater)* father.

**Erzeuger-:** **~land** *nt* country of origin; **~preis** *m* manufacturer's price.

**Erzeugnis** *nt* product; *(Agr)* produce *no indef art, no pl.*

**Erzeugung** *f no pl* production; *(von Strom auch)* generation; *(geistige, künstlerische)* creation.

**Erz-:** **~feind** *m* arch-enemy; **~grube** *f* ore mine; **~hütte** *f* smelting works *sing or pl.*

**erziehbar** *adj Kind* educable; *Tier* trainable. **ein Heim für schwer ~e Kinder** a home for difficult children.

**erziehen\*** *vt irreg Kind* to bring up; *Tier, Körper* to train; *(ausbilden)* to educate. **ein Kind zur Sauberkeit ~** to bring a child up to be clean; **gut/schlecht erzogen** well/badly brought-up.

**Erzieher(in** *f)* *m* - educator, teacher; *(in Kindergarten)* nursery school teacher.

**erzieherisch** *adj* educational.

**Erziehung** *f no pl* upbringing; *(Ausbildung)* education; *(das Erziehen)* bringing up; *(von Tieren, Körper)* training.

**Erziehungs-:** **~anstalt** *f* approved school, reformatory *(US)*; **~beratung** *f* educational guidance *or* counselling; **e~berechtigt** *adj* having parental authority; **~berechtigte(r)** *mf* parent or (legal) guardian; **~geld** *nt* subsidy for new parents; **~heim** *nt* = **anstalt**; **~methode** *f* educational method; **~urlaub** *m* paid leave for a new parent; **~wesen** *nt* educational system.

**erzielen\*** *vt Erfolg, Ergebnis* to achieve; *Kompromiß, Geschwindigkeit* to reach; *Gewinn* to make, to realize; *(Gegenstand) Preis* to fetch; *(Sport) Tor, Punkte* to score; *Rekord* to set.

**erzittern\*** *vi aux sein (liter)* to tremble.

**erzkonservativ** *adj* ultraconservative.

**erzürnen\*** *vt (geh)* to anger, to incense.

**erzwingen\*** *vt irreg* to force. **etw von jdm ~** to force sth out of sb.

**es** *pers pron* it; *(auf männliches Wesen bezogen) (nom)* he; *(acc)* him; *(auf weibliches Wesen bezogen) (nom)* she; *(acc)* her. **wer ist da?** — **ich bin ~** who's there? — it's me; **sie ist klug, er ist ~ auch** she is clever, so is he; **wer ist die Dame?** — **~ ist meine Frau** who's the lady? — it's *or* she's my wife; **alle**

dachten, daß das ungerecht war, aber niemand sagte ~ everyone thought it was unjust, but nobody said so; **ich hoffe ~** I hope so; **~ sitzt sich bequem hier** it's comfortable sitting here; **~ wurde getanzt** there was dancing; **~ kamen viele Leute** a lot of people came; **~ lebe der König!** long live the king!

**Es** *nt - (Mus: Dur)* E flat.

**Escape-Taste** [ɛs'keːp-] *f (Comp)* escape key.

**Esche** *f* **-n** ash-tree.

**Esel** *m* - donkey; *(col: Dummkopf)* (silly) ass. **ich ~!** silly me!; **störrisch wie ein ~** as stubborn as a mule.

**Eselin** *f* she-ass.

**Esels-:** **~brücke** *f (Gedächtnishilfe)* mnemonic, aide-mémoire; **~ohr** *nt (fig)* dog-ear; **ein Buch mit ~ohren** a dog-eared book.

**Eskalation** *f* escalation.

**eskalieren\*** *vti (vi: aux sein)* to escalate.

**Eskapade** *f (fig)* escapade.

**Eskimo** *m* **-s** Eskimo.

**Eskorte** *f* **-n** *(Mil)* escort.

**eskortieren\*** *vt* to escort.

**esoterisch** *adj* esoteric.

**Espe** *f* **-n** aspen.

**Espenlaub** *nt* aspen leaves *pl.* **zittern wie ~** to shake like a leaf.

**Esperanto** *nt no pl* Esperanto.

**Espresso** *m* **-s** espresso.

**Esprit** [ɛs'priː] *m no pl* wit.

**Eß-:** **e~bar** *adj* edible, eatable; *Pilz* edible; **habt ihr irgend etwas ~bares im Haus?** have you got anything to eat in the house?; **nicht e~bar** inedible, uneatable; **~besteck** *nt* set of cutlery; **~ecke** *f* dining area.

**essen** *pret* **aß**, *ptp* **gegessen** *vti* to eat. **gut/schlecht ~** *(Appetit haben)* to have a good/poor appetite; **in dem Restaurant kann man gut ~** the food's good in that restaurant; **warm/kalt ~** to have a hot/cold meal; **etw zum Frühstück ~** to have *or* eat sth for breakfast; **~ Sie gern Äpfel?** do you like apples?; **beim E~ sein** to be in the middle of a meal; **~ gehen** *(auswärts)* to eat out; **nach dem Kino gingen wir noch ~** after the cinema we went for a meal; **das Thema ist schon lange gegessen** *(fig col)* the subject is dead and buried.

**Essen** *nt - (Mahlzeit)* meal; *(Nahrung)* food; *(Küche)* cooking. **bleib doch zum ~** stay for lunch/supper, stay for a meal; **das ~ kochen** *or* **machen** *(col)* to get the meal; **jdn zum ~ einladen** to invite sb for a meal.

**Essen(s)-:** **~ausgabe** *f* serving of meals; *(Stelle)* serving counter; **~marke** *f* meal voucher; **~zeit** *f* mealtime; **bei uns ist um 12 ~zeit** we have lunch at 12.

**essentiell** [ɛsɛn'tsiɛl] *adj (geh)* essential.

**Essenz** *f* essence.

**Esser** *m* - **ein guter/schlechter ~** a good/poor eater.

**Eßgeschirr** *nt* dinner service.

**Essig** *m* **-e** vinegar. **damit ist es ~** *(col)* it's all off.

**Essig-:** **~essenz** *f* vinegar concentrate; **~gurke** *f* (pickled) gherkin; **~säure** *f* acetic acid.

**Eßkastanie** *f* sweet chestnut.

**Eßl.** = **Eßlöffel**.

**Eß-:** **~löffel** *m* soup/dessert spoon; *(in Rezept)* tablespoon; **~lokal** *nt* eating place; **~stäbchen** *pl* chopsticks *pl*; **~tisch** *m* dining table; **~waren** *pl* food; **~zimmer** *nt* dining room.

**Este** *m* **-n**, **Estin** *f* Estonian.

**Estland** *nt* Estonia.

**estnisch** *adj* Estonian.

**Estragon** *m no pl* tarragon.

**Estrich** *m* **-e** concrete floor.
**etablieren\* 1** *vt (dated)* to establish. **2** *vr* to establish oneself; *(Comm)* to set up.
**etabliert** *adj* established. **die ~e Oberschicht** the upper echelons of the establishment.
**Etablissement** [etablɪsə'mãː] *nt* **-s** establishment.
**Etage** [e'taːʒə] *f* **-n** floor. **in** *or* **auf der 2.** ~ on the 2nd *(Brit)* or 3rd *(US)* floor.
**Etagen-:** **~bett** *nt* bunk bed; **~heizung** *f heating system which covers one floor of a building;* **~wohnung** *f flat occupying the whole of one floor of a building.*
**Etappe** *f* **-n** **(a)** stage; *(einer Strecke auch)* leg. **(b)** *(Mil)* communications zone.
**Etappen-:** **~sieg** *m (Sport)* stage-win; *(fig)* partial victory; **e~weise** *adv* step by step, stage by stage.
**Etat** [e'taː] *m* **-s** budget.
**Etat-:** **~jahr** *nt* financial year; **~posten** *m* item in the budget.
**etc.** = **et cetera** [ɛt'tseːtera] etc.
**etepetete** [eːtəpe'teːtə] *adj pred (col)* fussy, pernickety *(col).*
**Ethik** *f* ethics *pl (als Fach sing).*
**ethisch** *adj* ethical.
**ethnisch** *adj* ethnic. **~e Säuberung** ethnic cleansing.
**Ethos** ['eːtɔs] *nt no pl* ethos; *(Berufs~)* professional ethics *pl.*
**Etikett** *nt* **-e** *(lit, fig)* label.
**Etikette** *f* etiquette.
**etikettieren\*** *vt (lit, fig)* to label.
**etliche(r, s)** *indef pron* **(a)** *sing attr* quite a lot of. **(b)** etliche *pl (substantivisch)* quite a few, several people/things; *(attr)* several, quite a few. **(c)** ~s *sing (substantivisch)* quite a lot.
**Etüde** *f* **-n** *(Mus)* étude.
**Etui** [ɛt'viː, e'tyiː] *nt* **-s** case.
**etwa** *adv* **(a)** *(ungefähr, annähernd)* about, approximately. **so ~, ~ so** more or less like this. **(b)** *(zum Beispiel)* for instance. **(c)** *(entrüstet, erstaunt)* **hast du ~ schon wieder kein Geld dabei?** don't tell me you've come out without any money again!; **willst du ~ schon gehen?** (surely) you don't want to go already! **(d)** *(zur Bestätigung)* **Sie kommen doch, oder ~ nicht?** you are coming, aren't you?; **sind Sie ~ nicht einverstanden?** do you mean to say that you don't agree?; **ist das ~ wahr?** (surely) it's not true! **(e)** *(in Gegenüberstellung, einschränkend)* **nicht ~, daß ...** (it's) not that ...; **ich wollte dich nicht ~ beleidigen** I certainly didn't intend to insult you.
**etwaig** ['ɛtvaːɪç] *adj attr* possible. **~e Unkosten** any costs which might arise.
**etwas** *indef pron* **(a)** *(substantivisch)* something; *(fragend, bedingend auch, verneinend)* anything; *(unbestimmter Teil einer Menge)* some; any. **kannst du mir ~ (davon) leihen?** can you lend me some (of it)?; **ohne ~ zu erwähnen** without saying anything; **~ sein** *(col)* to be somebody *(col)*; **aus ihm wird nie ~** *(col)* he'll never get anywhere; **er kann ~** he's good; **sein Wort gilt ~ beim Chef** what he says counts for something with the boss; **das ist sicher, wie nur ~** *(col)* that's as sure as (sure) can be *(col)*; **~ Kaltes** something cold. **(b)** *(adjektivisch)* some; *(fragend, bedingend auch)* any. **~ Salz?** some salt? **(c)** *(adverbial)* **~ besser** somewhat better, a little better.
**Etwas** *nt no pl* **das gewisse ~** that certain something.
**Etymologie** *f* etymology.
**etymologisch** *adj* etymological.
**EU** *f* = **Europäische Union** EU.
**euch** *pers pron dat, acc of* **ihr** *(in Briefen:* **E~)** you;

*(dat auch)* to/for you; *(refl)* yourselves. **ein Freund von ~** a friend of yours; **wascht ~!** wash yourselves; **setzt ~!** sit down!
**Eucharistie** *f (Eccl)* Eucharist.
**euer 1** *poss pron (in Briefen:* **E~)** your. **E~** *(Briefschluß)* yours. **2** *pers pron gen of* **ihr.** ~ **aller heimlicher Wunsch** the secret wish of all of you.
**Eukalyptus** *m, pl* **Eukalypten** eucalyptus.
**Eule** *f* **-n** owl. **~n nach Athen tragen** *(prov)* to carry coals to Newcastle *(prov).*
**Euphemismus** *m* euphemism.
**Euphorie** *f* euphoria.
**euphorisch** *adj* euphoric.
**Eurasien** [-iən] *nt* Eurasia.
**Eurasier(in** *f)* *m* [-iɐ̯-iərɪn] *m* - Eurasian.
**eurasisch** *adj* Eurasian.
**eure(r, s)** *poss pron* yours. **der/die/das ~** *(geh)* yours.
**eurerseits** *adv (von eurer Seite)* on your part.
**euresgleichen** *pron inv* people like you.
**euretwegen** *adv (wegen euch)* because of you, on your account; *(euch zuliebe auch)* for your sake.
**Euro-** *in cpds* Euro-; **~cheque** *m* Eurocheque; **~krat(in** *f)* *m* Eurocrat.
**Europa** *nt* Europe.
**Europacup** [-kap] *m* = **Europapokal.**
**Europäer(in** *f)* *m* - European.
**Europaflagge** *f* European flag.
**europäisch** *adj* European. **das E~e Parlament** the European Parliament; **E~e Union** European Union; **E~es Währungssystem** European Monetary System; **E~e (Wirtschafts)gemeinschaft** European (Economic) Community, Common Market.
**Europa-:** **~meister** *m* European champion; *(Team, Land)* European champions *pl*; **~meisterschaft** *f* European championship; **~parlament** *nt* European Parliament; **~pokal** *m (Sport)* European cup; **~rat** *m* Council of Europe; **~straße** *f* Euroroute; **~wahlen** *pl* European elections; **e~weit** *adj* Europe-wide.
**Euro-:** **~scheck** *m* Eurocheque; **~scheckkarte** *f* Eurocheque card; **~vision** *f* Eurovision.
**Euter** *nt* - udder.
**Euthanasie** *f* euthanasia.
**ev.** = **evangelisch.**
**e.V.** = **eingetragener Verein.**
**evakuieren\*** [evaku'iːrən] *vt* to evacuate.
**Evakuierung** [evaku'iːrʊŋ] *f* evacuation.
**evangelisch** [evaŋ'geːlɪʃ] *adj* Protestant.
**Evangelist** [evaŋge'lɪst] *m* evangelist.
**Evangelium** [evaŋ'geːliʊm] *nt* Gospel; *(fig)* gospel.
**Eva(s)kostüm** *nt (dated hum)* **im ~** in her birthday suit *(hum).*
**Eventualfall** [evɛntu'aːl-] *m,* **Eventualität** [evɛntuali'tɛːt] *f* eventuality.
**eventuell** [evɛntu'ɛl] **1** *adj attr* possible. **2** *adv* possibly, perhaps. **~ rufe ich Sie später an** I may possibly call you later.
**Evolution** [evolu'tsioːn] *f* evolution.
**evolutionär** *adj* evolutionary.
**Evolutionstheorie** *f* theory of evolution.
**evtl.** = **eventuell.**
**EWG** [eːveː'geː] *f* = **Europäische Wirtschaftsgemeinschaft** EEC.
**ewig 1** *adj* eternal; **Eis, Schnee** perpetual; *(col)* **Nörgelei** *etc auch* never-ending. **2** *adv* for ever, eternally. **auf ~** for ever; **das dauert ja ~, bis ...** it'll take ages until ...; **~ dankbar** eternally grateful; **ich habe Sie ~ lange nicht gesehen** *(col)* I haven't seen you for ages.
**Ewigkeit** *f* eternity. **in die ~ eingehen** to go to eter-

nal rest; **bis in alle** ~ for ever; **eine** ~ *(col)* ages *(col)*.

**EWS** [eːveːˈɛs] *nt* = **Europäisches Währungssystem** EMS.

**EWU** [eːveːˈuː] *f* = **Europäische Währungsunion** EMU.

**ex** *adv (col)* **etw** ~ **trinken** to drink sth down in one.

**Ex-** *in cpds* ex.

**exakt** *adj* exact. ~ **arbeiten** to work accurately.

**exaltiert** *adj* exaggerated, effusive.

**Examen** *nt, pl - or* **Examina** exam, examination; *(Univ)* finals *pl.* ~ **machen** to do *or* take one's exams *or* finals.

**Examens-:** ~**angst** *f* exam nerves *pl*; ~**arbeit** *f* dissertation; ~**kandidat** *m* candidate (for an examination).

**examinieren*** *vt (geh)* to examine.

**exekutieren*** *vt (form)* to execute.

**Exekution** *f* execution.

**Exekutionskommando** *nt* firing squad.

**Exekutive** [-ˈtiːvə] *f* executive.

**Exempel** *nt* **die Probe aufs** ~ **machen** to put it to the test.

**Exemplar** *nt* **-e** specimen; *(Buch~)* copy.

**exemplarisch** *adj* exemplary. **jdn** ~ **bestrafen** to punish sb as an example (to others).

**exerzieren*** *vti* to drill; *(fig)* to practise *(Brit)*, to practice *(US)*.

**Exerzierplatz** *m (Mil)* parade ground.

**Exhibitionismus** [ɛkshibɪtsioˈnɪsmʊs] *m* exhibitionism.

**Exhibitionist(in** *f)* [ɛkshibɪtsioˈnɪst(ɪn)] *m* exhibitionist.

**exhumieren*** *vt* to exhume.

**Exhumierung** *f* exhumation.

**Exil** *nt* **-e** exile. **im (amerikanischen)** ~ **leben** to live in exile (in America); **ins** ~ **gehen** to go into exile.

**Exilregierung** *f* government in exile.

**existent** *adj (geh)* existing, existent.

**Existentialismus** [ɛksɪstɛntsiaˈlɪsmʊs] *m* existentialism.

**existentialistisch** [-tsiaˈlɪstɪʃ] *adj* existential(ist).

**existentiell** [ɛksɪstɛnˈtsiɛl] *adj (geh)* existential. **von** ~**er Bedeutung** of vital significance.

**Existenz** *f* existence; *(Lebensgrundlage)* livelihood; *(pej col: Person)* character, customer *(col)*. **eine gescheiterte** ~ *(col)* a failure; **sich eine** ~ **aufbauen** to make a life for oneself.

**Existenz-:** ~**berechtigung** *f* right to exist; **e~fähig** *adj* able to exist; *Firma* viable; ~**grundlage** *f* basis of one's livelihood; ~**kampf** *m* struggle for survival; ~**minimum** *nt* subsistence level; *(Lohn)* minimal living wage; **das Gehalt liegt noch unter dem** ~**minimum** that is not even a living wage.

**existieren*** [ɛksɪsˈtiːrən] *vi* to exist.

**exkl.** = **exklusiv(e)** excl.

**exklusiv** *adj* exclusive.

**Exklusivbericht** *m (Press)* exclusive (report).

**exklusive** [-ˈziːvə] *prep* +*gen* exclusive of, excluding.

**Exklusivität** [-ziviˈtɛːt] *f* exclusiveness.

**Exkommunikation** *f (Eccl)* excommunication.

**exkommunizieren*** *vt* to excommunicate.

**Exkrement** *nt usu pl (geh)* excrement *no pl*, excreta *pl.*

**Exkurs** *m* **-e** digression.

**Exkursion** *f* (study) trip.

**Exmatrikulation** *f (Univ)* being taken off the university register. **bei seiner** ~ when he left university.

**exmatrikulieren*** *vt (Univ)* to take off the university register. **sich** ~ **lassen** to withdraw from the university register.

**exorzieren*** *vt* to exorcize.

**Exorzismus** *m* exorcism.

**Exot(e)** *m (wk)* **-en, -en, Exotin** *f (Tier, Pflanze)* exotic *or* tropical animal/plant; *(Mensch)* exotic foreigner.

**exotisch** *adj* exotic.

**Expander** *m* - *(Sport)* chest-expander.

**expandieren*** *vi* to expand.

**Expansion** *f (Phys, Pol)* expansion.

**expansiv** *adj* expansionist; *Wirtschaftszweig* expanding.

**Expedition** *f (Forschungs~, Mil)* expedition.

**Experiment** *nt* experiment.

**experimentell** *adj* experimental.

**experimentieren*** *vi* to experiment.

**Experte** *m (wk)* **-n, -n, Expertin** *f* expert *(für* in).

**Experten-:** ~**kommission** *f* panel of experts; *(für ein bestimmtes Sachgebiet)* think-tank; ~**system** *nt (Comp)* expert system.

**explizit** *adj* explicit.

**explodieren*** *vi aux sein (lit, fig)* to explode.

**Explosion** *f* explosion. **etw zur** ~ **bringen** to detonate *or* explode sth.

**Explosions-:** **e~artig** *Geräusch* like an explosion; *Wirkung* explosive; ~**gefahr** *f* danger of explosion.

**explosiv** *adj (lit, fig)* explosive.

**Exponent** *m (Math, fig)* exponent.

**exponieren*** *vt (herausheben)* to expose. **an exponierter Stelle stehen** to be in an exposed position.

**Export** *m* **-e** export *(an +dat* of*)*; *(~waren)* exports *pl.*

**Export-** *in cpds* export; ~**abteilung** *f* export department; ~**artikel** *m* export.

**Exporteur** [ɛkspɔrˈtøːɐ] *m* exporter.

**Export-:** ~**geschäft** *nt*, ~**handel** *m* export trade.

**exportieren*** *vti (also Comp)* to export.

**Exportkaufmann** *m* exporter.

**Exposé** [ɛkspoˈzeː] *nt* **-s** *(für Film etc)* outline.

**Expreß-:** ~**brief** *m* express letter; ~**gut** *nt* express goods *pl.*

**Expressionismus** *m* expressionism.

**Expressionist(in** *f)* *m* expressionist.

**expressionistisch** *adj* expressionist *no adv.*

**exquisit** *adj* exquisite.

**extensiv** *adj* extensive.

**extern** *adj (Sch, Comp)* external.

**extra** *adv (besonders)* extra, (e)specially; *(eigens, ausschließlich)* (e)specially, just; *(gesondert)* separately; *(zusätzlich)* extra, in addition; *(col: absichtlich)* on purpose. **jetzt tu ich's** ~! *(col)* just for that I will do it!

**Extra-:** ~**ausgabe** *f* special edition; ~**ausstattung** *f* extras *pl*; ~**blatt** *nt* special edition; ~**tour** *f (fig col)* **sich** *(dat)* ~**touren leisten** to do one's own thing *(col)*.

**extravagant** [-vaˈgant] *adj* extravagant; *Kleidung auch* flamboyant.

**Extravaganz** [-vaˈgants] *f siehe adj* extravagance; flamboyance.

**Extrawurst** *f (col: Sonderwunsch)* special favour *(Brit) or* favor *(US)*. **er will immer eine** ~ **(gebraten haben)** he always wants something different.

**extrem** *adj* extreme; *Belastung* excessive. ~ **schlecht/gut** extremely badly/well; **die Lage hat sich** ~ **verschlechtert** the situation has deteriorated enormously; **ich habe mich** ~ **beeilt** I hurried as much as I could.

**Extrem** *nt* **-e** extreme. **von einem ~ ins andere fallen** to go from one extreme to the other.
**Extremfall** *m* extreme (case).
**Extremist(in** *f*) *m* extremist.
**extremistisch** *adj* extremist.
**Extremität** *f usu pl* extremity *usu pl*.

**extrovertiert** [-vɛr'tiːɐt] *adj* extrovert.
**Exzellenz** *f* Excellency.
**exzentrisch** *adj (Math, fig)* eccentric.
**Exzentrizität** *f* eccentricity.
**Exzeß** *m* **-sse** excess. **bis zum ~** to excess.
**E-Zug** ['eːtsuːk] *m* = **Eilzug**.

# F

**F, f** [ɛf] *nt* -, - F, f. **nach Schema F** *(col)* in the same old way; according to a set routine; **F wie Friedrich** ≃ F for Frederick, F for Fox *(US)*.

**F** = **Fahrenheit** F.

**f** *(Mus)* = **forte** f.

**f.** = **und folgende (Seite)** f.

**Fa.** = **Firma.**

**Fabel** *f* **-n** (a) fable. (b) *(col)* fantastic story.

**Fabel-:** **f~haft** *adj* splendid, magnificent; **~tier,** **~wesen** *nt* mythical creature.

**Fabrik** *f* **-en** factory.

**Fabrik|anlage** *f* plant; *(~gelände)* factory site.

**Fabrikant(in** *f)* *m* (a) industrialist. (b) *(Hersteller)* manufacturer.

**Fabrikarbeiter** *m* factory worker.

**Fabrikat** *nt* (a) *(Marke)* make; *(von Nahrungs- und Genußmitteln)* brand. (b) *(Produkt)* product; *(Ausführung)* model.

**Fabrikation** *f* manufacture, production.

**Fabrikationsfehler** *m* manufacturing fault.

**Fabrik-** *in cpds* factory; **~besitzer** *m* factory owner; **~direktor** *m* managing director (of a factory); **~gelände** *nt* factory site.

**fabrizieren\*** *vt* (a) *(dated: industriell)* to produce. (b) *(col)* Möbelstück *etc* to put together; *geistiges Produkt* to produce; *Geschichte* to concoct, to fabricate.

**fabulieren\*** *vi (geh) (erzählen)* to spin a yarn.

**Facette** [fa'sɛtə] *f* facet.

**Fach** *nt* ⁼**er** (a) compartment; *(in Handtasche etc auch)* pocket; *(in Schrank, Regal etc)* shelf; *(für Briefe etc)* pigeonhole. (b) *(Wissens-, Sachgebiet)* subject; *(Gebiet)* field; *(Handwerk)* trade. **ein Mann vom ~** an expert; **sein ~ verstehen** to know one's stuff *(col) or* one's subject/trade.

**Fach-:** **~arbeiter** *m* skilled worker; **~arzt** *m* specialist *(für in)*; **~ausbildung** *f* specialist training; **~ausdruck** *m* technical *or* specialist term; **~bereich** *m* (a) (special) field; (b) *(Univ)* school, faculty; **f~bezogen** *adj* specialized; **~buch** *nt* reference book; **wasserbautechnische ~bücher** specialist books on hydraulic engineering.

**fächeln** *(geh) vt* to fan.

**Fächer** *m* - fan; *(fig)* range, array.

**fächer-:** **~artig,** **~förmig 1** *adj* fan-shaped; **2** *adv* like a fan.

**Fach-:** **~frau** *f* expert; **~gebiet** *nt* (special) field; **f~gemäß, f~gerecht** *adj* expert; *Ausbildung* specialist *attr*; **~geschäft** *nt* specialist shop *(Brit) or* store *(US)*; **~geschäft für Lederwaren** leather shop; **~handel** *m* specialist shops *pl (Brit) or* stores *pl (US)*; **~händler** *m* specialist supplier; **~hochschule** *f* university college *(specializing in a particular subjects)*; **~idiot** *m (col)* narrow-minded specialist; **~jargon** *m* technical jargon; **~kenntnisse** *pl* specialized knowledge; **~kraft** *f* qualified employee; **~kreise** *pl*: **in ~kreisen** among experts; **f~kundig** *adj* informed *no adv*; *(erfahren)* with a knowledge of the subject; *(fachmännisch)* proficient; **jdn f~kundig beraten** to give sb informed advice; **~lehrer** *m* specialist subject teacher.

**fachlich** *adj* technical; *Ausbildung* specialist *attr*; *(beruflich)* professional. **~ hochqualifiziert** highly qualified in one's field.

**Fach-:** **~literatur** *f* specialist literature; **~mann** *m,* *pl* **~leute** expert; **f~männisch** *adj* expert; **f~männisch ausgeführt** professionally *or* expertly done; **~personal** *nt* qualified staff; **~richtung** *f* subject area; **~schule** *f* technical college; **~simpelei** *f (col)* shoptalk; **f~simpeln** *vi insep (col)* to talk shop; **f~spezifisch** *adj* technical, subject-specific; **~sprache** *f* technical terminology; **f~sprachlich 1** *adj* technical; **2** *adv* in technical terminology; **f~übergreifend** *adj* interdisciplinary; **~verband** *m* trade association; **~welt** *f* experts *pl*; **~werk** *nt no pl* half-timbering; **~werkhaus** *nt* half-timbered house; **~wissen** *nt* (specialized) knowledge of the/one's subject; **~wort** *nt* specialist term; **~wörterbuch** *nt* specialist dictionary; *(technisches auch)* technical dictionary; **~zeitschrift** *f* specialist journal; *(für Berufe)* trade journal.

**Fackel** *f* **-n** *(lit, fig)* torch.

**fackeln** *vi (col)* **da wird nicht lange gefackelt** there won't be any shilly-shallying.

**Fackel-:** **~schein** *m* torchlight; **~zug** *m* torchlight procession.

**fad(e)** *adj* (a) *Geschmack* insipid; *Essen auch* tasteless. (b) *(fig: langweilig)* dull.

**Faden¹** *m* ⁼ *(lit, fig)* thread; *(Bohnen~, an Marionetten)* string; *(Med)* stitch. **der rote ~** *(fig)* the central theme; **den ~ verlieren** *(fig)* to lose the thread; **alle ~ laufen hier zusammen** this is the nerve centre *(Brit) or* center *(US)* of the whole business; **er hält alle ~ in der Hand** he holds the reins; **sein Leben hing an einem ~** his life was hanging by a thread.

**Faden²** *m* - *(Naut)* fathom.

**Faden-:** **~kreuz** *nt* crosshair; **~nudeln** *pl* vermicelli *pl*; **f~scheinig** *adj (fig)* flimsy; *Argument auch, Moral* threadbare *no adv*.

**Fagott** *nt* **-e** bassoon.

**Fagottist(in** *f)* *m* bassoonist.

**fähig** *adj* capable, competent, able. **sie ist ein ~er Kopf** she has an able mind; **(dazu) ~ sein, etw zu tun** to be capable of doing sth; **zu allem ~ sein** to be capable of anything.

**Fähigkeit** *f* ability; *(praktisches Können)* skill. **die ~ haben, etw zu tun** to be capable of doing sth; **bei deinen ~en ...** with your talents ...

**fahl** *adj* pale.

**Fähnchen** *nt* (a) *(Wimpel)* pennant. (b) *(pej col)* flimsy dress.

**fahnden** *vi* to search *(nach for)*.

**Fahndung** *f* search.

**Fahndungs-:** **~aktion** *f* search; **~buch** *nt,* **~liste** *f* wanted (persons) list.

**Fahne** f -n (a) flag; *(von Verein etc auch)* banner; *(Mil auch)* colours *pl (Brit)*, colors *pl (US)*. **die ~ hochhalten** *(fig)* to keep the flag flying; **etw auf seine ~ schreiben** *(fig)* to take up the cause of sth; **mit fliegenden ~n zu jdm/etw überlaufen** to go over to sb/sth. (b) *(col)* **eine ~ haben** to reek of alcohol. (c) *(Typ)* galley (proof).

**Fahnen-:** ~**eid** m oath of allegiance; ~**flucht** f *(Mil, fig)* desertion; **f~flüchtig** *adj* **f~flüchtig sein** *(Mil, fig)* to be a deserter; ~**flüchtige(r)** mf *(Mil, fig)* deserter; ~**mast** m, ~**stange** f flagpole; ~**träger** m standard-bearer.

**Fähnrich** m *(Mil)* officer cadet; *(Hist)* ensign. **~ zur See** midshipman.

**Fahr-:** ~**ausweis** m *(form)* ticket; ~**bahn** f carriageway *(Brit)*, highway *(US)*; *(Fahrspur)* lane; ~**bahnmarkierung** f road marking; **f~bar** *adj* on castors; *Kran* mobile; **f~barer Untersatz** *(hum)* wheels *pl (hum)*; **f~bereit** *adj* in running order.

**Fähre** f -n ferry.

**fahren** *pret* **fuhr**, *ptp* **gefahren** 1 *vi aux sein* (a) *(Fahrzeug, Fahrgast)* to go; *(reisen)* to travel; *(Fahrer)* to drive; *(Schiff)* to sail; *(Kran, Rolltreppe etc)* to move. **mit dem Zug/Motorrad/Taxi ~** to go by train/motorbike/taxi; **mit dem Aufzug ~** to take the lift, to ride the elevator *(US)*; **wollen wir ~ oder zu Fuß gehen?** shall we go by car/bus *etc* or walk?; **links/rechts ~** to drive on the left/right; **wie lange fährt man von hier nach Basel?** how long does it take to get to Basle from here?; **gegen einen Baum ~** to drive *or* go into a tree.
(b) *(losfahren)* to go, to leave.
(c) *(verkehren)* **es ~ täglich zwei Fähren** there are two ferries a day; **die U-Bahn fährt alle fünf Minuten** the underground goes *or* runs every five minutes.
(d) **blitzartig fuhr es ihm durch den Kopf, daß** ... the thought suddenly flashed through his mind that ...; **was ist (denn) in dich gefahren?** what's got *(Brit) or* gotten *(US)* into you?; **in seine Kleider ~** to fling on one's clothes; **der Blitz fuhr in die Eiche** the lightning struck the oak; **sich *(dat)* mit der Hand über die Stirn ~** to pass one's hand over one's brow; **einen ~ lassen** *(col)* to fart *(col)*.
(e) *(zurechtkommen)* **(mit jdm/etw) gut/schlecht ~** to get on all right/not very well (with sb/sth); **(bei etw) gut/schlecht ~** to do well/badly (with sth).
2 *vt* (a) *(lenken)* Auto, Bus *etc* to drive; *Fahrrad, Motorrad* to ride. (b) *aux sein* Straße, Strecke, Buslinie *etc* to take. **welche Strecke fährt der 59er?** which way does the 59 go?; **ich fahre lieber Autobahn als Landstraße** I prefer (driving on) motorways to ordinary roads. (c) *(benutzen)* Kraftstoff *etc* to use. (d) *(befördern)* to take; *(hierher~)* to bring; *(Lastwagen, Taxi: gewerbsmäßig)* to carry. **ich fahre dich nach Hause** I'll take *or* drive you home, I'll give you a lift home. (e) *aux sein* Geschwindigkeit to do. (f) *aux haben or sein (Sport)* Rennen to take part in; *Runde etc* to do; *Zeit, Rekord etc* to clock up. (g) *(Tech) (steuern, betreiben)* to run; *(durchführen)* Sonderschicht to put on; *Überstunden* to do, to work.
3 *vr* **der neue Wagen fährt sich gut** the new car is nice to drive.

**fahrend** *adj* itinerant; *Zug, Auto* in motion. **~es Volk** travelling people; **ein ~er Sänger** a wandering minstrel.

**fahrenlassen\*** *vt sep irreg* Hoffnung to abandon.

**Fahrer(in** f) m - (a) driver. (b) *(Sport col) (Rad~)* cyclist; *(Motorrad~)* motorcyclist.

**Fahrerflucht** f hit-and-run driving. **~ begehen** to be involved in a hit-and-run.

**Fahr|erlaubnis** f *(form)* driving licence *(Brit)*, driver's license *(US)*.

**Fahrersitz** m driver's seat.

**Fahr-:** ~**gast** m passenger; ~**geld** nt fare; ~**gelegenheit** f transport *no indef art*; ~**gemeinschaft** f car pool; ~**geschwindigkeit** f *(form)* speed; ~**gestell** nt (a) *(Aut)* chassis. (b) = ~**werk** (a).

**Fährhafen** m ferry terminal.

**fahrig** *adj* nervous; *(unkonzentriert)* distracted.

**Fahrkarte** f ticket; *(fig)* passport *(nach to)*.

**Fahrkarten-:** ~**ausgabe** f ticket office; ~**automat** m ticket machine; ~**kontrolle** f ticket inspection; ~**schalter** m ticket office.

**Fahr-:** **f~lässig** *adj* negligent *(auch Jur)*; **f~lässig handeln** to be guilty of negligence; ~**lässigkeit** f negligence *(auch Jur)*; ~**lehrer** m driving instructor.

**Fährmann** m, *pl* -**männer** *or* -**leute** ferryman.

**Fahr-:** ~**plan** m timetable, schedule *(US)*; *(fig)* schedule; **f~planmäßig** 1 *adj* scheduled; 2 *adv* on schedule; *verlaufen* according to schedule; ~**praxis** f *no pl* driving experience *no indef art*; ~**preis** m fare; ~**prüfung** f driving test.

**Fahrrad** nt bicycle, bike *(col)*.

**Fahrrad-:** ~**fahrer** m cyclist; ~**geschäft** nt cycle shop *(Brit)* or store *(US)*; ~**händler** m bicycle dealer; *(Geschäft)* cycle shop *(Brit)* or store *(US)*; ~**ständer** m (bi)cycle stand; ~**weg** m cycle path.

**Fahr-:** ~**rinne** f *(Naut)* shipping channel, fairway; ~**schein** m ticket; ~**scheinautomat** m ticket machine; ~**scheinentwerter** m ticket stamping machine *(in bus/tram etc)*; ~**schule** f driving school; ~**schüler** m learner driver *(Brit)*, student driver *(US)*; ~**spur** f lane; ~**stil** m style of driving/riding/skiing *etc*; ~**streifen** m lane; ~**stuhl** m lift *(Brit)*, elevator *(US)*; ~**stunde** f driving lesson.

**Fahrt** f -en journey; *(Aut auch)* drive; *(Ausflug)* trip; *(Naut)* voyage; *(Über~)* crossing. **nach zwei Stunden ~** after travelling for two hours; **was kostet eine ~ nach London?** how much is it to London?; **gute ~!** safe journey!; **volle ~ voraus!** *(Naut)* full speed ahead!; **jdn in ~ bringen** *(col)* to get sb going; **in ~ sein** *(col)* to have got going; *(wütend)* to be mad *(col)*.

**Fahr-:** **f~tauglich** *adj* fit to drive; ~**tauglichkeit** f fitness to drive.

**Fährte** f -n tracks *pl*; *(Witterung)* scent; *(Spuren)* trail. **auf der richtigen/falschen ~ sein** *(fig)* to be on the right/wrong track; **jdn auf eine falsche ~ locken** *(fig)* to put sb off the scent.

**Fahrtechnik** f driving technique.

**Fahrten-:** ~**buch** nt driver's log; ~**messer** nt sheath knife; ~**schreiber** m tachograph.

**Fahrtest** m road test.

**Fahrt-:** ~**kosten** *pl* travelling *(Brit)* or traveling *(US)* expenses *pl*; ~**richtung** f direction of travel; *(im Verkehr)* direction of the traffic; **entgegen der/in ~richtung** *(im Zug)* with one's back to the engine/facing the engine; *(im Bus etc)* facing backwards/the front; **die Autobahn ist in ~richtung Norden gesperrt** the northbound section of the motorway is closed; ~**richtungsanzeiger** m *(Aut)* direction indicator.

**Fahr-:** **f~tüchtig** *adj* fit to drive; *Wagen etc* roadworthy; ~**tüchtigkeit** f driving ability; roadworthiness.

**Fahrtwind** m airstream.

**Fahr-:** **f~untauglich** *adj* unfit to drive; *Wagen etc* unroadworthy; ~**verbot** nt driving ban; **jdn mit**

~**verbot belegen** to ban sb from driving; ~**verbot für Privatwagen** ban on private vehicles; ~**verhalten** *nt (von Fahrer)* behaviour *(Brit)* or behavior *(US)* behind the wheel; *(von Wagen)* road manners *pl*; ~**wasser** *nt* (a) *(Naut)* = ~**rinne**; (b) *(fig)* **in jds ~wasser geraten** to get in with sb; **in ein gefährliches ~wasser geraten** to get on to dangerous ground; ~**weise** *f* **seine ~weise** his driving; ~**werk** *nt* (a) *(Aviat)* undercarriage, landing gear; (b) *(Aut)* chassis; ~**zeit** *f* time for the journey; **bei einer ~zeit von fünf Stunden** on a five-hour journey.

**Fahrzeug** *nt* vehicle; *(Luft~)* aircraft; *(Wasser~)* vessel.

**Fahrzeug-:** ~**brief** *m* registration document; ~**führer** *m (form)* driver of a vehicle; ~**halter** *m* vehicle keeper; ~**papiere** *pl* vehicle documents *pl*; ~**park** *m* fleet (of vehicles).

**Faible** ['fɛːbl] *nt* **-s** *(geh)* liking; *(Schwäche auch)* weakness; *(Vorliebe auch)* penchant.

**fair** [fɛːɐ] **1** *adj* fair *(gegen to)*. **2** *adv* fairly. ~ **spielen** *(Sport)* to play fairly; *(fig)* to play fair.

**Fäkalien** [-iən] *pl* faeces *pl*.

**Faksimile** [fak'ziːmile] *nt* **-s** facsimile.

**faktisch 1** *adj attr* actual, real. **2** *adv* (a) in reality. (b) *(esp Aus col: praktisch)* more or less.

**Faktor** *m* factor *(auch Math)*.

**Faktum** *nt, pl* **Fakten** fact.

**fakturieren*** *vt (Comm)* to invoice.

**Fakultät** *f (Univ)* faculty.

**Falke** *m* **-n** falcon; *(fig)* hawk.

**Falkland-Inseln** *pl* Falkland Islands *pl*, Falklands *pl*.

**Falkner(in** *f)* *m* - falconer.

**Fall** *m* ≃e (a) *(Sturz)* fall; *(fig: von Menschen, Regierung auch)* downfall. **zu ~ kommen** *(lit, geh)* to fall; **über die Affäre ist er zu ~ gekommen** *(fig)* the affair was his downfall; **zu ~ bringen** *(lit geh)* to trip up; *(fig) Menschen, Regierung* to cause the downfall of; *Gesetz, Plan etc* to thwart.

(b) *(Umstand, Jur, Med, Gram)* case. **gesetzt den ~** assuming (that); **für den ~, daß ich ... in** case I ...; **für alle ~e** just in case; **auf jeden/keinen ~** at any rate/on no account; **das mache ich auf keinen ~** there's no way I'm going to do that; **im ~(e)** *+gen* in the event of; **auf alle ~e** in any case, anyway; **für solche ~e** for such occasions; **im äußersten ~(e)** if the worst comes to the worst; **im günstigsten/schlimmsten ~(e)** at best/worst; **in diesem ~** in this case or instance; **jds ~ sein** *(col)* to be sb's cup of tea *(col)*; **klarer ~!** *(col)* sure thing! *(col)*, you bet! *(col)*; **der erste/zweite/dritte/vierte ~** *(Gram)* the nominative/genitive/dative/accusative case.

**Fallbeil** *nt* guillotine.

**Falle** *f* **-n** (a) *(lit, fig)* trap. **in eine ~ geraten** or **gehen** *(lit)* to get caught in a trap; *(fig)* to fall into a trap; **jdm in die ~ gehen** to walk or fall into sb's trap; **in der ~ sitzen** to be trapped; **jdm eine ~ stellen** *(fig)* to set a trap for sb. (b) *(col: Bett)* bed. **in die ~ gehen** to hit the hay *(col)*.

**fallen** *pret* **fiel**, *ptp* **gefallen** *vi aux sein* (a) to fall. **etw ~ lassen** to drop sth; **über etw** *(acc)* ~ to fall over sth; **durch eine Prüfung** ~ to fail an exam.

(b) *(abfallen, sinken)* to drop, to fall; *(Aktien, Barometer)* to fall; *(Nachfrage, Ansehen)* to fall off. **im Preis/Wert** ~ to drop or fall in price/value.

(c) *(im Krieg)* to fall, to be killed. **mein Mann ist gefallen** my husband was killed in the war.

(d) *(erobert werden: Festung, Stadt etc)* to fall.

(e) *(sich ereignen: Datum etc)* to fall *(auf +acc* on); *(gehören)* to come *(unter +acc* under, *in +acc* within, under). **in eine Zeit ~** to belong to an era.

(f) *(zufallen: Erbschaft etc)* to go *(an +acc* to*)*. **das Elsaß fiel an Frankreich** Alsace fell or *(nach Verhandlungen)* went to France.

(g) *(gemacht werden) (Entscheidung)* to be made; *(Urteil)* to be passed; *(Schuß)* to be fired; *(Sport: Tor)* to be scored; *(Wort)* to be uttered or spoken; *(Name)* to be mentioned; *(Bemerkung)* to be made.

**fällen** *vt* (a) *Baum* to fell. (b) *(fig) Entscheidung* to make; *Urteil* to pass.

**fallenlassen*** *vt sep irreg* to drop.

**Fallensteller** *m* - *(Hunt)* trapper.

**fällig** *adj* due *pred*; *Rechnung, Betrag auch* payable; *Wechsel* mature(d). **längst ~** long overdue; **die ~en Zinsen** the interest due; **~ werden** to become or fall due; *(Wechsel)* to mature.

**Fälligkeit** *f (Fin)* settlement date; *(von Wechseln)* maturity.

**Fall|obst** *nt* windfalls *pl*.

**Fallout** [fɔ'laut] *m* **-s** fallout.

**Fallrückzieher** *m (Ftbl)* overhead kick, bicycle kick.

**falls** *conj (wenn)* if; *(für den Fall, daß)* in case.

**Fallschirm** *m* parachute. **mit dem ~ abspringen** to parachute; **etw mit dem ~ abwerfen** to drop sth by parachute.

**Fallschirm-:** ~**absprung** *m* parachute jump; ~**abwurf** *m* parachute drop; ~**jäger** *m (Mil)* paratrooper; ~**springen** *nt* parachuting; ~**springer** *m* parachutist; ~**truppe** *f (Mil)* paratroops, paras *pl*.

**Fall-:** ~**strick** *m (fig)* trap, snare; ~**studie** *f* case study; ~**tür** *f* trapdoor.

**Fällung** *f no pl* (a) *(von Bäumen)* felling. (b) *(Jur: eines Urteils)* passing; *(einer Entscheidung)* reaching.

**fallweise** *adv* from case to case.

**falsch** *adj* (a) wrong. **richtig/wahr oder ~** right or wrong/true or false; **alles ~ machen** to do everything wrong; **wie man's macht, ist es ~** *(col)* whatever one does, it always seems to be wrong; ~**er Alarm** *(lit, fig)* false alarm; **etw ~ verstehen** to misunderstand sth, to get sth wrong; **etw ~ schreiben/aussprechen** to spell/pronounce sth wrongly, to misspell/mispronounce sth; **die Uhr geht ~** the clock is wrong; **~ spielen** *(Mus)* to play the wrong note/notes; *(unrein)* to play off key or out of tune; *(Cards)* to cheat; **~ singen** to sing out of tune or off key; **Sie sind hier ~** you're in the wrong place; **da sind Sie bei mir an den F~en geraten** you've picked the wrong person (in me); ~ **liegen** *(col)* to be wrong *(bei, in +dat* about, *mit* in*)*; **am ~en Ort** or **Platz sein** to have come to the wrong place; ~ **verbunden sein** to have the wrong number.

(b) *(unecht) Zähne etc* false; *Geld* forged; *Paß* fake.

(c) *(unaufrichtig) Gefühl, Freund etc* false. **ein ~es Spiel (mit jdm) treiben** to play (sb) false.

**Falsch|aussage** *f (Jur)* **(uneidliche) ~** false statement or evidence.

**fälschen** *vt* to forge, to fake; *Tatsachen* to falsify; *siehe* **gefälscht.**

**Fälscher(in** *f)* *m* - forger.

**Falsch-:** ~**fahrer** *m* ghost-driver *(esp US col)*, *person driving in the wrong direction*; ~**geld** *nt* counterfeit or forged money; ~**heit** *f no pl* falsity, falseness; *(dial: von Menschen)* nastiness.

**fälschlich 1** *adj* false. **2** *adv* wrongly, falsely; *(versehentlich)* by mistake.

**fälschlicherweise** *adv* wrongly, falsely.

**Falsch-:** ~**meldung** *f (Press)* false report; ~**münzer(in** *f)* *m* - forger, counterfeiter; ~**münzerei** *f* forgery, counterfeiting; ~**parker(in** *f)* *m* - parking offender; **f~spielen** *vi sep (Cards)* to cheat; ~**spieler** *m (Cards)* cheat; *(professional)* cardsharp(er).

**Fälschung** *f* forgery.

**fälschungssicher** *adj* forgery-proof.

**Falsett** *nt* **-e** falsetto.

**Falt-**: ~**blatt** *nt* leaflet; *(in Zeitschrift etc)* insert; ~**boot** *nt* collapsible boat.

**Falte** *f* **-n** fold; *(Knitter~)* crease; *(in Haut)* wrinkle. **die Stirn in** ~**n legen** to knit one's brow.

**falten** *vtr* to fold. **die Stirn** ~ to knit one's brow.

**Falten-**: **f**~**los** *adj Haut* unlined; **f**~**reich** *adj Haut* wrinkled; ~**rock** *m* pleated skirt.

**Falter** *m* - *(Tag~)* butterfly; *(Nacht~)* moth.

**faltig** *adj (zerknittert)* creased; *(in Falten gelegt)* hanging in folds; *Gesicht, Haut* wrinkled.

**Falz** *m* **-e** *(Kniff, Faltlinie)* fold.

**falzen** *vt Papierbogen* to fold.

**Fam.** = **Familie**.

**familiär** *adj* **(a)** family *attr.* **(b)** *(zwanglos)* informal; *(pej: plump-vertraulich)* familiar. **mit jdm** ~ **verkehren** to be on familiar terms with sb.

**Familie** [fa'mi:liə] *f* family. ~ **Müller** the Müller family; ~ **Otto Francke** *(als Anschrift)* Mr. & Mrs. Otto Francke and family; ~ **haben** *(col)* to have a family; **aus guter** ~ **sein** to come from a good family; **es liegt in der** ~ it runs in the family; **zur** ~ **gehören** to be one of the family; **es bleibt in der** ~ it'll stay in the family; **das kommt in den besten** ~**n vor** *(hum)* that can happen in the best of families.

**Familien-** [-iən-] *in cpds* family; ~**ähnlichkeit** *f* family resemblance; ~**angehörige(r)** *mf* dependant; ~**angelegenheit** *f* family affair *or* matter; ~**anschluß** *m*: **Unterkunft mit** ~**anschluß** *accommodation where one is treated as one of the family*; ~**anzeigen** *pl* personal announcements *pl*; ~**besitz** *m* family property; **in** ~**besitz sein** to be owned by the family; ~**betrieb** *m* family business; ~**feier** *f* family party; ~**kreis** *m* family circle; ~**leben** *nt* family life; ~**mitglied** *nt* member of the family; ~**name** *m* surname, family name *(US)*; ~**oberhaupt** *nt* head of the family; ~**packung** *f* family(-size) pack; ~**planung** *f* family planning; ~**stand** *m* marital status; ~**vater** *m* father of a family; ~**verhältnisse** *pl* family circumstances; ~**vorstand** *m (form)* head of the family.

**famos** *adj (dated col)* capital *(dated col)*, splendid.

**Fan** [fɛn] *m* **-s** fan.

**Fanal** *nt* **-e** *(liter)* signal *(gen* for*)*.

**Fanatiker(in** *f)* *m* - fanatic.

**fanatisch** *adj* fanatical.

**Fanatismus** *m* fanaticism.

**Fanclub** ['fɛn-] *m* fan club.

**fand** *pret of* **finden**.

**Fanfare** *f* **-n** *(Mus)* fanfare.

**Fang** *m* ⁼**e** **(a)** *no pl (das Fangen)* hunting; *(Fischen)* fishing. **(b)** *no pl (Beute) (lit, fig)* catch; *(fig: von Gegenständen)* haul. **(c)** *usu pl (Hunt: Kralle)* talon. **in den** ˜**en** +*gen (fig)* in the clutches of.

**fangen** *pret* **fing**, *ptp* **gefangen** **1** *vti* to catch; *Verbrecher, Soldat etc auch* to capture; *siehe* **gefangen. 2** *vr* **(a)** *(in einer Falle etc)* to get caught. **(b)** *(das Gleichgewicht wiederfinden)* to steady oneself; *(beim Reden etc)* to compose oneself; *(seelisch)* to get on an even keel again.

**Fänger** *m* - *(Tier~)* hunter; *(Sport)* catcher.

**Fang-**: ~**flotte** *f* fishing fleet; ~**frage** *f* catch *or* trick question; ~**gründe** *pl* fishing grounds *pl*; ~**quote** *f* (fishing) quota; ~**schiff** *nt* fishing boat; *(mit Netzen)* trawler.

**Fantasie** *f (Mus)* fantasia.

**fantastisch** *adj* fantastic.

**Farb-** *in cpds* colour *(Brit)*, color *(US)*; ~**aufnahme** *f* colour *(Brit) or* color *(US)* photo(graph); ~**bad** *nt* dye-bath; ~**band** *nt (von Schreibmaschine)* (typewriter) ribbon; ~**bild** *nt* = ~**aufnahme**.

**Farbe** *f* **-n** **(a)** colour *(Brit)*, color *(US)*. ~ **bekommen** to get a bit of colour; ~ **verlieren** to go pale. **(b)** *(Maler~)* paint; *(für Farbbad)* dye; *(Druck~)* ink. **(c)** *(Cards)* suit. ~ **bekennen** *(fig)* to nail one's colours to the mast.

**farb|echt** *adj* colourfast *(Brit)*, colorfast *(US)*.

**Färbemittel** *nt* dye.

**farb|empfindlich** *adj (Phot)* colour-sensitive *(Brit)*, color-sensitive *(US)*.

**färben 1** *vt* to colour *(Brit)*, to color *(US)*; *Stoff, Haar* to dye; *siehe* **gefärbt. 2** *vi (ab~)* to run. **3** *vr* to change colour. **sich grün/blau** ~ to turn green/blue.

**Farben-** *in cpds* colour *(Brit)*, color *(US)*; **f**~**blind** *adj* colour-blind *(Brit)*, color-blind *(US)*; **f**~**freudig**, **f**~**froh** *adj* colourful *(Brit)*, colorful *(US)*; **f**~**prächtig** *adj* gloriously colourful *(Brit) or* colorful *(US)*; ~**reichtum** *m* wealth of colours *(Brit) or* colors *(US)*; ~**sinn** *m* sense of colour *(Brit) or* color *(US) (auch Biol)*.

**Farb-**: ~**fernsehen** *nt*, ~**fernseher** *m* colour *(Brit) or* color *(US)* television; ~**film** *m* colour *(Brit) or* color *(US)* film; ~**foto** *nt* = ~**aufnahme**; ~**fotografie** *f* colour *(Brit) or* color *(US)* photography; ~**gebung** *f* colouring *(Brit)*, coloring *(US)*.

**farbig** *adj* coloured *(Brit)*, colored *(US)*; *(fig) Schilderung* vivid, colourful *(Brit)*, colorful *(US)*. ~ **kennzeichnen** to colour-code *(Brit)*, color code *(US)*.

**Farbige(r)** *mf decl as adj* coloured *(Brit) or* colored *(US)* man/woman/person *etc.* **die** ~**n** coloured people *pl*.

**Farb-**: ~**kasten** *m* paintbox; ~**kopierer** *m* colour *(Brit) or* color *(US)* copier; **f**~**lich** *adj* colour *(Brit)*, color *(US)*; **zwei Sachen f**~**lich aufeinander abstimmen** to match two things up for colour; **f**~**los** *adj (lit, fig)* colourless *(Brit)*, colorless *(US)*; ~**losigkeit** *f (lit, fig)* colourlessness *(Brit)*, colorlessness *(US)*; ~**stift** *m* coloured *(Brit) or* colored *(US)* pen; *(Bunt-stift)* crayon; ~**stoff** *m (Lebensmittel~)* (artificial) colouring *(Brit) or* coloring *(US)*; *(Haut~)* pigment; *(für Textilien)* dye; ~**ton** *m* shade; *(Tönung)* tint.

**Färbung** *f* colouring *(Brit)*, coloring *(US)*; *(Tönung)* tinge; *(fig)* slant, bias.

**Farce** ['farsə] *f* **-n** *(Theat, fig)* farce.

**Farm** *f* **-en** farm.

**Farmer** *m* - farmer.

**Farn** *m* **-e**, **Farnkraut** *nt* fern.

**Färöer** *pl* Faeroes *pl*, Faeroe Islands *pl*.

**Fasan** *m* **-e** *or* **-en** pheasant.

**Fasching** *m* **-e** *or* **-s** Shrovetide carnival.

**Faschismus** *m* fascism.

**Faschist(in** *f)* *m* fascist.

**faschistisch** *adj* fascist.

**faseln** *(pej)* **1** *vi* to drivel *(col)*. **2** *vt* **Blödsinn** ~ to talk drivel.

**Faser** *f* **-n** fibre *(Brit)*, fiber *(US)*.

**fas(e)rig** *adj* fibrous; *Fleisch, Spargel* stringy *(pej)*; *(zerfasert)* frayed.

**fasern** *vi* to fray.

**Faser-**: ~**optik** *f* fibre *(Brit) or* fiber *(US)* optics *sing*; ~**pflanze** *f* fibre *(Brit) or* fiber *(US)* plant; ~**platte** *f* fibreboard *(Brit)*, fiberboard *(US)*; ~**schreiber** *m* felt-tip (pen).

**Faß** *nt*, *pl* **Fässer** barrel; *(kleines Bier~)* keg; *(zum Gären, Einlegen)* vat; *(zum Buttern)* churn; *(für Öl, Benzin etc)* drum. **vom** ~ on tap; *Bier* on draught

*(Brit)* or draft *(US)*; **Bier vom** ~ draught beer; **ein** ~ **ohne Boden** *(fig)* a bottomless pit; **das schlägt dem** ~ **den Boden aus** *(col)* that's the last straw!

**Fassade** f *(lit, fig)* façade.

**Faß-:** f~**bar** adj comprehensible; **das ist doch nicht f~bar!** that's incomprehensible!; ~**bier** nt draught *(Brit)* or draft *(US)* beer.

**Fäßchen** nt dim of **Faß.**

**fassen 1** vt **(a)** *(ergreifen)* to take hold of; *(hastig, kräftig)* to grab, to seize; *(festnehmen)* Einbrecher etc to apprehend, to seize. **jdn am Arm** ~ to take/grab sb by the arm; **faß!** seize! **(b)** *(fig)* Entschluß to make, to take; *Mut* to take. **den Gedanken** ~, **etw zu tun** to form the idea of doing sth. **(c)** *(begreifen)* to grasp. **es ist nicht zu** ~ it's unbelievable. **(d)** *(enthalten)* to hold. **(e)** *(fig: ausdrücken)* to express. **in Verse/Worte** ~ to put into verse/words; **etw weit/eng** ~ to interpret sth broadly/narrowly. **2** vi *(greifen)* **an/in etw** *(acc)* ~ to feel sth; *(berühren)* to touch sth; **faß mal unter den Tisch** feel under the table. **3** vr *(sich beherrschen)* to compose onself. **sich in Geduld** ~ to exercise patience; **sich kurz** ~ to be brief; *siehe* **gefaßt.**

**Fasson** [fa'sõː] f -s style; *(Art und Weise)* way. **aus der** ~ **geraten** *(lit)* to lose its shape; **jeder soll nach seiner** ~ **selig werden** *(prov)* everyone has to find his own salvation.

**Fassonschnitt** [fa'sõː-] m *(für Herren)* short back and sides.

**Fassung** f **(a)** *(von Juwelen)* setting; *(von Brille, Bild)* frame; *(Elec)* holder. **(b)** *(Bearbeitung)* version. **ein Film in deutscher** ~ a film with German dubbing. **(c)** no pl *(Ruhe, Besonnenheit)* composure. **etw mit** ~ **tragen** to take sth calmly; **völlig außer** ~ **geraten** to lose all self-control; **jdn aus der** ~ **bringen** to disconcert or throw *(col)* sb.

**Fassungs-:** f~**los** adj aghast, stunned; ~**losigkeit** f complete bewilderment; ~**vermögen** nt capacity; **das übersteigt mein** ~**vermögen** that is beyond me.

**fast** adv almost, nearly. ~ **nie** hardly ever.

**fasten** vi to fast.

**Fastenzeit** f *(Eccl)* Lent.

**Fastnacht** f no pl Shrovetide carnival.

**Fastnachtszeit** f carnival period.

**Faszination** f fascination.

**faszinieren*** vti to fascinate *(an +dat about)*. ~**d** fascinating.

**fatal** adj *(geh)* *(verhängnisvoll)* fatal, fateful; *(peinlich)* embarrassing, awkward.

**Fatalismus** m fatalism.

**Fatalist(in** f**)** m fatalist.

**fatalistisch** adj fatalistic.

**Fata Morgana** f - -s *(lit, fig)* Fata Morgana *(liter)*, mirage.

**Fatzke** m -s *(col)* stuck-up twit *(col)*.

**fauchen** vti to hiss.

**faul** adj **(a)** *(verfault)* bad; *Eier, Obst auch, Holz* rotten; *Geschmack, Geruch auch, Wasser* foul; *Laub* rotting. **(b)** *(träge)* lazy, idle. **(c)** *(verdächtig)* fishy *(col)*, suspicious; *Ausrede* feeble; *Kompromiß* uneasy; *(dumm) Witz* bad. **hier ist etwas** ~ *(col)* there's something fishy here *(col)*.

**faulen** vi aux sein or haben to rot; *(Zahn)* to decay; *(Lebensmittel)* to go bad.

**faulenzen** vi to laze or loaf *(esp pej col)* about.

**Faulenzer** m - layabout.

**Faulenzerei** f lazing or loafing *(esp pej col)* about.

**Faulheit** f laziness, idleness.

**faulig** adj going bad; *Geruch, Geschmack* foul.

**Fäulnis** f no pl rot; *(von Zahn)* decay. **in** ~ **übergehen** to go rotten.

**Faul-:** ~**pelz** m *(col)* lazybones sing *(col)*; ~**tier** nt sloth; *(col: Mensch)* lazybones sing *(col)*.

**Fauna** f, pl **Faunen** fauna.

**Faust** f, pl **Fäuste** fist. **jdm mit der** ~ **ins Gesicht schlagen** to punch sb in the face; **mit der** ~ **auf den Tisch schlagen** *(lit)* to thump the table (with one's fist); *(fig)* to take a hard line; **die** ~ **in der Tasche ballen** *(fig)* to choke back one's anger; **das paßt wie die** ~ **aufs Auge** *(paßt nicht)* it's all wrong; *(Farbe)* it clashes horribly; *(paßt gut)* it's just the job *(col)*; **auf eigene** ~ *(fig)* on one's own initiative, off one's own bat *(col)*; **reisen, fahren** under one's own steam.

**Faustball** m form of volleyball.

**Fäustchen** nt: **sich** *(dat)* **ins** ~ **lachen** to laugh up one's sleeve.

**faustdick** adj *(col)* **eine** ~**e Lüge** a whopper *(col)*, a whopping (great) lie *(col)*; **er hat es** ~ **hinter den Ohren** he's a crafty one *(col)*.

**fausten** vt Ball to punch.

**Faust-:** f~**groß** adj as big as a fist; ~**handschuh** m mitt(en).

**Faustkampf** m fist-fight.

**Fäustling** m mitt(en).

**Faust-:** ~**pfand** nt security; ~**recht** nt no pl law of the jungle; ~**regel** f rule of thumb; ~**schlag** m punch.

**Fauxpas** [foˈpa] m -, - gaffe, faux pas.

**Favorit(in** f**)** [favoˈriːt(ɪn)] m *(wk)* -en, -en favourite *(Brit)*, favorite *(US)*.

**Fax** nt -, -e fax.

**Faxen** pl ~ **machen** to fool around.

**faxen** vt to fax, to send by fax.

**Fazit** nt -s or -e **das** ~ **der Untersuchungen war** ... on balance the result of the investigations was ...; **wenn wir aus diesen vier Jahren das** ~ **ziehen** if we take stock of these four years.

**FCKW** [ɛftseːkaːˈveː] m = **Fluorchlorkohlenwasserstoff** CFC.

**FDP** [ɛfdeːˈpeː] f = **Freie Demokratische Partei.**

**Feature** [ˈfiːtʃə] nt -s *(Rad, TV, Press)* feature.

**Febr.** = **Februar** Feb.

**Februar** m -e February; *siehe* **März.**

**fechten** pret **focht**, ptp **gefochten** vi *(Sport)* to fence; *(geh: kämpfen)* to fight. **das F~** fencing.

**Fechter(in** f**)** m - fencer.

**Fecht-:** ~**hieb** m (fencing) cut; ~**sport** m fencing.

**Feder** f -n **(a)** *(Vogel~)* feather. ~**n lassen müssen** *(col)* not to escape unscathed; **in den** ~**n liegen** *(col)* to be/stay in one's bed or pit *(Brit col)*. **(b)** *(Schreib~)* quill; *(an ~halter)* nib. **ich greife zur** ~ ... I take up my pen ... **(c)** *(Tech)* spring.

**Feder-:** ~**ball** m *(Ball)* shuttlecock; *(Spiel)* badminton; ~**besen** m feather duster; ~**bett** nt continental quilt *(Brit)*, comforter *(US)*; ~**fuchser** m ~ *(pej)* petty-minded pedant *(pej)*; f~**führend** adj Behörde in overall charge *(für of)*; ~**führung** f unter der ~**führung** +gen under the overall control of; **die** ~**führung haben** to be in overall charge; ~**gewicht** nt *(Sport)* featherweight; ~**halter** m (dip) pen; *(Fül!~)* (fountain) pen; ~**kernmatratze** f interior sprung mattress, innerspring mattress *(US)*; ~**kiel** m quill; ~**kissen** nt feather cushion; *(in Bett)* feather pillow; ~**krieg** m *(fig)* war of words; f~**leicht** adj light as a feather; ~**lesen** nt: **nicht viel** ~**lesens mit jdm/etw machen** to make short work of sb/sth; **ohne langes** ~**lesen** without any further ado; ~**mäppchen** nt pencil case.

**federn** vi **(a)** *(als Eigenschaft)* to be springy. **(b)** *(zurück~ etc)* to spring back; *siehe* **gefedert.**

**federnd** adj *(Tech)* sprung. **einen** ~**en Gang haben** to have a springy step.

**Federstrich** m **mit einem** ~ with a single stroke of the pen.

**Federung** f springs pl; (Aut) suspension.

**Feder-**: ~**vieh** nt (col) poultry; ~**waage** f spring balance; ~**weiße(r)** m decl as adj (dial) new wine; ~**zeichnung** f pen-and-ink drawing.

**Fee** f -n ['feːən] fairy.

**Fegefeuer** nt das ~ purgatory.

**fegen 1** vt to sweep; (auf~) to sweep up. **2** vi (a) to sweep (up). (b) aux sein (col: jagen) to sweep.

**Fehde** f -n (Hist) feud. **mit jdm eine** ~ **ausfechten** to feud or carry on a feud with sb.

**fehl** adj: ~ **am Platz(e)** out of place.

**Fehl-**: ~**anzeige** f (col) dead loss (col); ~**anzeige!** wrong!; **f~bar** adj fallible; ~**besetzung** f miscasting; ~**betrag** m deficit; ~**deutung** f misinterpretation; ~**diagnose** f wrong diagnosis; ~**einschätzung** f false estimation; (der Lage) misjudgement.

**fehlen 1** vi (a) (mangeln) to be lacking; (nicht vorhanden sein) to be missing; (in der Schule etc) to be away or absent (in +dat from). **jdm fehlt etw** sb lacks sth, sb doesn't have sth; (wird schmerzlich vermißt) sb misses sth; **mir fehlt Geld** I'm missing some money; **mir ~ 20 Pfennig am Fahrgeld** I'm 20 pfennigs short for my fare; **mir ~ die Worte** words fail me; **du fehlst mir sehr** I miss you a lot; **der/das hat mir gerade noch gefehlt!** (col) he/that was all I needed (iro). (b) **was fehlt dir?** what's the matter (with you)?; **mir fehlt nichts** there's nothing the matter (with me); **weit gefehlt!** (fig) you're way out! (col); (ganz im Gegenteil) far from it!

**2** vi impers **es fehlt an etw** (dat) there is a lack of sth; (völlig) there is no sth, sth is missing; **es ~ drei Messer** there are three knives missing; **es fehlt jdm an etw** (dat) sb lacks sth; **wo fehlt es?** what's the trouble?, what's up? (col); **es fehlte nicht viel, und ich hätte ihn verprügelt** I almost hit him.

**Fehl|entscheidung** f wrong decision.

**Fehler** m - (a) (Irrtum) mistake, error; (Sport) fault. **ihr ist ein** ~ **unterlaufen** she made a mistake. (b) (Mangel) fault, defect. **einen** ~ **aufweisen** to prove faulty; **einen** ~ **an sich** (dat) **haben** to have a fault; **in den** ~ **verfallen, etw zu tun** to make the mistake of doing sth.

**Fehler-**: **f~frei** adj perfect; Arbeit, Aussprache etc auch faultless, flawless; Messung, Rechnung correct; **f~freier Lauf/Sprung** (Sport) clear round/jump; ~**grenze** f margin of error; **f~haft** adj (Tech) faulty, defective; Ware substandard, imperfect; Messung, Rechnung incorrect; Arbeit, Aussprache poor; **f~los** adj = **f~frei**; ~**meldung** f (Comp) error message; ~**quote** f error rate.

**Fehl-**: ~**farbe** f (Cards) missing suit; (Nicht- Trumpf) plain or side suit; ~**geburt** f miscarriage; **f~gehen** vi sep irreg aux sein (geh: sich irren) to be wrong or mistaken; ~**griff** m mistake; ~**information** f incorrect information no pl; ~**investition** f bad investment; ~**konstruktion** f bad design; **der Stuhl ist eine ~konstruktion** this chair is badly designed; ~**leistung** f slip, mistake; ~**paß** m (Ftbl) bad pass; ~**planung** f bad planning; **eine ~planung** a piece of bad planning; ~**schlag** m (fig) failure; **f~schlagen** vi sep irreg aux sein to go wrong; (Hoffnung) to come to nothing; ~**schluß** m false conclusion; ~**start** m false start; (Space) faulty launch; ~**tritt** m (geh) false step; (fig) (Vergehen) slip, lapse; (Affäre) indiscretion; ~**urteil** nt miscarriage of justice; ~**verhalten** nt inappropriate behaviour (Brit) or be-

havior (US); (Psych) abnormal behaviour (Brit) or behavior (US); ~**versuch** m unsuccessful attempt; ~**zündung** f misfire; (im Auspuff) backfire.

**Feier** f -n celebration; (Party) party; (Zeremonie) ceremony. **zur** ~ **von etw** to celebrate sth.

**Feier|abend** m (Arbeitsschluß) end of work; (Geschäftsschluß) closing time. ~ **machen** to finish work, to knock off (col); (Geschäfte) to close; **ich mache jetzt** ~ I think I'll call it a day (col); **nach** ~ after work; **jetzt ist aber** ~! (fig col) enough is enough; **schönen** ~! have a nice evening!

**feierlich** adj (ernsthaft, würdig) solemn; (festlich) festive; (förmlich) ceremonial. **das ist ja nicht mehr** ~ (col) that's beyond a joke (col).

**Feierlichkeit** f (a) siehe adj solemnity; festiveness; ceremony. (b) usu pl celebrations pl.

**feiern 1** vt (a) to celebrate; Party, Orgie to hold. **das muß gefeiert werden!** that calls for a celebration. (b) (umjubeln) to fête. **2** vi to celebrate.

**Feier-**: ~**schicht** f cancelled shift; ~**stunde** f ceremony; ~**tag** m holiday.

**feig(e) 1** adj cowardly. **2** adv in a cowardly way. **er zog sich** ~ **zurück** he retreated like a coward.

**Feige** f -n fig.

**Feigen-**: ~**baum** m fig tree; ~**blatt** nt fig leaf; **ein ~blatt für etw** (fig) a front to hide sth; **als demokratisches ~blatt** (fig) to give a veneer of democracy.

**Feigheit** f cowardice.

**Feigling** m coward.

**feilbieten** vt sep irreg (old) to offer for sale.

**Feile** f -n file.

**feilen** vti to file. **an etw** (dat) ~ (fig) to perfect sth.

**feilschen** vi (pej) to haggle (um over).

**fein** adj (a) fine; Humor, Ironie delicate. (b) (erlesen) excellent, choice; Geruch, Geschmack delicate; (prima) great (col), fine. **ein ~er Kerl** a great guy (col); **das ist etwas F~es** that's really something (col); ~ **(he)raussein** to be sitting pretty. (c) Gehör etc sensitive, keen. (d) (vornehm) refined, fine (esp iro), posh (col). **(jdm) nicht** ~ **genug sein** not to be good enough (for sb); **sich** ~ **machen** to get all dressed up; **dazu ist sie sich** (dat) **zu** ~ that's beneath her.

**Fein-** in cpds fine; **f~abstimmen** vt to fine-tune; ~**abstimmung** f fine tuning; ~**arbeit** f precision work.

**Feind(in** f) m -e enemy. **jdn zum** ~ **haben** to have sb as an enemy; **sich** (dat) **jdn zum** ~ **machen** to make an enemy of sb.

**Feind-** in cpds enemy; ~**berührung** f contact with the enemy; ~**bild** nt image of an/the enemy.

**feindlich** adj (Mil) enemy; (feindselig) hostile. **jdm/einer Sache** ~ **gegenüberstehen** to be hostile to sb/sth.

**Feindschaft** f hostility. **sich** (dat) **jds** ~ **zuziehen** to make an enemy of sb.

**feindselig** adj hostile.

**Feindseligkeit** f hostility.

**Fein-**: **f~fühlig** adj sensitive; ~**gefühl** nt no pl sensitivity; ~**gold** nt refined gold.

**Feinheit** f siehe adj (a) fineness; delicacy. (b) excellence; delicateness. (c) keenness. (d) ~**en** pl niceties pl; (Nuancen) subtleties pl.

**Fein-**: ~**kost** f „~**kost**" "Delicatessen"; ~**kostgeschäft** nt delicatessen; ~**mechaniker** m precision engineer; ~**schmecker** m - gourmet; (fig) connoisseur; ~**schnitt** m (Tabak) fine cut; ~**silber** nt refined silver; **f~sinnig** adj sensitive; ~**strumpfhose** f sheer tights (esp Brit) or pantyhose (US); ~**wäsche** f delicates pl; ~**waschmittel** nt mild(-action) detergent.

**feist** adj fat; Mensch auch obese.

**feixen** *vi (col)* to smirk.

**Feld** *nt* **-er** field; *(Sport: Spiel~ auch)* pitch; *(auf Spielbrett)* square; *(offenes Gelände)* open country. **auf freiem** ~ in the open country; **gegen jdn/etw zu ~e ziehen** *(fig)* to crusade against sb/sth; **Argumente ins** ~ **führen** to bring arguments to bear; **das** ~ **räumen** *(fig)* to bow out; **jdm das** ~ **überlassen** to give way to sb; *(freiwillig)* to hand over to sb.

**Feld-** *in cpds* field; **~arbeit** *f (Agr)* work in the fields; *(Sci, Sociol)* fieldwork; **~arbeiter** *m* fieldworker; **~besteck** *nt* eating irons *pl*; **~bett** *nt* campbed; **~blume** *f* wild flower; **~flasche** *f* canteen *(Mil)*, water bottle; **~herr** *m (old)* commander; **~jäger** *m (Mil)* military policeman; **die ~jäger** the military police; **~küche** *f (Mil)* field kitchen; **~lazarett** *nt (Mil)* field hospital; **~marschall** *m (old)* field marshal; **~maus** *f* field mouse; **~salat** *m* lamb's lettuce; **~spieler** *m (Sport)* player; **~stecher** *m* - (pair of) binoculars *or* field glasses; **~verweis** *m* sending-off.

**Feld-Wald-und-Wiesen-** *in cpds (col)* common-or-garden.

**Feld-:** **~versuch** *m* field test; **~webel** *m* sergeant; **~weg** *m* track across the fields; **~zug** *m (Mil, fig)* campaign.

**Felge** *f* **-n** *(Tech)* (wheel) rim.

**Fell** *nt* **-e** fur; *(von Schaf)* fleece; *(von toten Tieren)* skin, fell. **einem Tier das** ~ **abziehen** to skin an animal; **ihm sind die ~e weggeschwommen** *(fig)* all his hopes were dashed; **ein dickes** ~ **haben** to be thick-skinned, to have a thick skin; **jdm das** ~ **über die Ohren ziehen** to pull the wool over sb's eyes.

**Fels** *m (wk)* **-en, -en** = **Felsen.**

**Fels-:** **~block, ~brocken** *m* boulder.

**Felsen** *m* - rock; *(Klippe)* cliff.

**felsenfest** *adj* firm. ~ **überzeugt sein** to be firmly convinced; **sich** ~ **auf jdn verlassen** to put one's complete trust in sb.

**felsig** *adj* rocky.

**Fels-:** **~massiv** *nt* rock massif; **~spalte** *f* crevice; **~vorsprung** *m* ledge; **~wand** *f* rock face.

**feminin** *adj* feminine; *(pej)* effeminate.

**Femininum** *nt, pl* **Feminina** *(Gram)* feminine noun.

**Feminismus** *m* feminism.

**Feminist(in** *f)* *m (wk)* **-en,-en** feminist.

**feministisch** *adj* feminist.

**Fenchel** *m no pl* fennel.

**Fenster** *nt* - window *(auch Comp)*. **weg vom** ~ *(col)* out of the game *(col)*, finished; **Geld zum** ~ **hinauswerfen** *(col)* to chuck money down the drain.

**Fenster-** *in cpds* window; **~bank** *f,* **~brett** *nt* windowsill, window ledge; **~flügel** *m side of a casement window*; **~glas** *nt* window glass; *(in Brille)* plain glass; **~heber** *m (Aut) (esp elektronisch)* window mechanism; **~kreuz** *nt* mullion and transom; **~laden** *m* shutter; **~leder** *nt* chamois, shammy (leather); **f~los** *adj* windowless; **~platz** *m* window seat; **~putzer** *m* window cleaner; **~rahmen** *m* window frame; **~scheibe** *f* window pane; **~sims** *m* window ledge, windowsill; **~umschlag** *m* window envelope.

**Ferien** ['feːriən] *pl* holidays *pl (Brit)*, vacation *sing (US, Univ)*; *(Parlaments~, Jur)* recess *sing.* **die großen** ~ the summer holidays *(Brit)*, the long vacation *(US, Univ)*; ~ **haben** to be on holiday *or* vacation; ~ **machen** to take a holiday; **in die** ~ **fahren** to go on holiday.

**Ferien-** *in cpds* holiday *(Brit)*, vacation *(US)*; **~gast** *m* holidaymaker *(Brit)*, vacationist *(US)*; *(Besuch)* person staying on holiday *(Brit)* or vacation *(US)*; **~haus** *nt* holiday *(Brit)* or vacation *(US)* home;

**~kolonie** *f* children's holiday *(Brit)* or vacation *(US)* camp; **~kurs** *m* holiday *(Brit)* or vacation *(US)* course; **~ort** *m* holiday *(Brit)* or vacation *(US)* resort; **~reise** *f* holiday *(Brit)* or vacation *(US)* trip; **~wohnung** *f* holiday flat *(Brit)*, vacation apartment *(US)*; **~zeit** *f* holiday *(Brit)* or vacation *(US)* period.

**Ferkel** *nt* - piglet; *(fig)* pig.

**Ferment** *nt* **-e** enzyme.

**fern** *adj* **(a)** *(räumlich)* distant, faraway. ~ **von hier** a long way (away) from here; **von** ~**(e) betrachtet** seen from a distance; **der F~e Osten** the Far East; **von** ~**(e) kennen** *(fig)* to know (only) slightly. **(b)** *(zeitlich)* far-off. **in nicht zu** ~**er Zeit** in the not-too-distant future; **der Tag ist nicht mehr** ~**, wo ...** the day is not far off when ...

**Fern-:** **f~ab** *adv* far away; **~amt** *nt* (telephone) exchange; **~bedienung** *f* remote control; **f~bleiben** *vi sep irreg aux sein* to stay away *(dat, von* from*)*; **~bleiben** *nt no pl* absence.

**Ferne** *f* **-n (a)** *(räumlich)* distance. **aus der** ~ from a distance. **(b)** *(zeitlich)* **in weiter** ~ **liegen** to be in the distant future.

**ferner** *adj, adv* further. **für die** ~**e Zukunft** for the long term; **unter** ~ **liefen rangieren** *(col)* to be an also-ran.

**Fern-:** **~fahrer** *m* long-distance lorry *(Brit)* or truck driver; **f~gelenkt** *adj* = **f~gesteuert; ~gespräch** *nt* long-distance call; **f~gesteuert** *adj* remote-controlled; *Rakete* guided; *(fig)* manipulated *(von* by*)*; **~glas** *nt* (pair of) binoculars; **f~halten** *vt sep irreg* to keep away; **~heizung** *f* district heating; **~kopie** *f (Telec)* fax; **f~kopieren** *vti* to fax; **~kopierer** *m* fax (machine); **~kurs(us)** *m* correspondence course; **~laster** *m* long-distance lorry *(Brit)* or truck; **~lastverkehr** *m* long-distance goods traffic; **~leitung** *f (Telec)* trunk *(Brit)* or long-distance line(s); *(Röhren)* pipeline; **~lenkung** *f* remote control; **~licht** *nt (Aut)* full *or* high beam; **mit ~licht fahren** to drive on full beam; **f~liegen** *vi sep irreg (fig)* **(jdm) f~liegen** to be far from sb's thoughts *or* mind; **es liegt mir f~, das zu tun** far be it from me to do that; **nichts liegt mir f~er** nothing could be further from my mind.

**Fernmelde-** *in cpds* telecommunications; *(Mil)* signals; **~gebühren** *pl* telephone charges *pl.*

**Fernmelder** *m (Mil col)* signaller *(Brit)*, signaler *(US)*.

**Fernmelde-:** **~satellit** *m* communications satellite; **~technik** *f* telecommunications *sing*; **~wesen** *nt* telecommunications *sing.*

**Fern-:** **~mündlich 1** *adj* telephone *attr*; **2** *adv* by telephone; **~ost** *no art* **aus/in** ~**ost** from/in the Far East; **~östlich** *adj* Far Eastern *attr*; **~rohr** *nt* telescope; **~ruf** *m (form)* telephone number; **~schreiben** *nt* telex; **~schreiber** *m* teleprinter; *(Comm)* telex; **f~schriftlich** *adj* by telex.

**Fernseh-** *in cpds* television, TV; **~ansager** *m* television announcer; **~anstalt** *f* television company; **~apparat** *m* television *or* TV (set).

**fernsehen** *vi sep irreg* to watch television *or* TV.

**Fernsehen** *nt no pl* television, TV. **vom** ~ **übertragen werden** to be televised; **im** ~ on television *or* TV.

**Fernseher** *m* - *(col) (Gerät)* television, TV, telly *(Brit col)*; *(Zuschauer)* (television) viewer.

**Fernseh-:** **~gebühr** *f* television licence *(Brit)* or license *(US)* fee; **~gerät** *nt* television *or* TV set; **~programm** *nt* **(a)** *(Kanal)* television channel *or* station *(US)*; **(b)** *(Sendung)* television programme *(Brit)* or program *(US)*; *(Sendefolge)* television programmes *pl (Brit)* or programs *pl (US)*; **(c)** *(~zeitschrift)* (television) programme *(Brit)* or program *(US)* guide; ~**satellit** *m* TV satellite; ~**schirm** *m* television *or* TV screen; ~**sendung** *f* television programme *(Brit)* or program *(US)*; ~**spiel** *nt* television play; ~**teilnehmer** *m (form)* television viewer; ~**turm** *m* television tower; ~**zeitschrift** *f* TV guide; ~**zuschauer** *m* (television) viewer.

**Fernsicht** *f* **(eine) gute** ~ **haben** to be able to see a long way.

**Fernsprech-** *in cpds (form) siehe auch* **Telefon-** telephone; ~**apparat** *m* telephone; ~**auskunft** *f* directory enquiries; ~**buch** *nt* telephone directory.

**Fernsprecher** *m* - *(form)* (public) telephone.

**Fernsprech-:** ~**gebühren** *pl* telephone charges *pl*; ~**teilnehmer** *m* telephone subscriber; ~**zelle** *f* (tele)phone box *or* booth *(US)*, callbox.

**Fern-:** **f~stehen** *vi sep irreg:* **jdm/etw f~stehen** to have no connection with sb/sth; **ich stehe ihm ziemlich f~** I'm not on very close terms with him; **f~steuern** *vt sep* to operate by remote control; *siehe* **f~gesteuert;** ~**steuerung** *f* remote control; ~**straße** *f* major road, highway *(US)*; ~**studium** *nt* multi-media course, ≈ Open University course *(Brit)*; ~**universität** *f* ≈ Open University *(Brit)*; ~**unterricht** *m* = ~**studium;** ~**verkehr** *m* long-distance traffic; ~**wärme** *f* district heating; ~**weh** *nt* wanderlust; ~**ziel** *nt* long-term goal; ~**zug** *m* long-distance train.

**Ferse** *f* -n heel. **jdm (dicht) auf den** ~**n bleiben** to stay hard on sb's heels.

**Fersengeld** *nt:* ~ **geben** to take to one's heels.

**fertig** *adj* **(a)** *(zu Ende, vollendet)* finished; *(ausgebildet)* qualified; *(reif) Mensch, Charakter* mature. **etw** ~ **kaufen** to buy sth ready-made; *Essen* to buy sth ready-cooked; ~ **ausgebildet** fully qualified; **mit etw** ~ **sein** to have finished sth; ~ **essen/lesen** to finish eating/reading; **mit jdm** ~ **sein** *(fig)* to be finished with sb; **mit jdm/etw** ~ **werden** to cope with sb/sth; **ich werde damit nicht** ~ I can't cope with it. **(b)** *(bereit)* ready. ~ **zur Abfahrt** ready to leave. **(c)** *(col)* shattered *(col)*; *(ruiniert)* finished. **mit den Nerven** ~ **sein** to be at the end of one's tether.

**Fertig-** *in cpds* finished; *(Build)* prefabricated; ~**bau** *m* **-ten** prefabricated building; **f~bekommen*** *vt sep irreg* to get finished; **f~bringen** *vt sep irreg* **(a)** *(vollenden)* to get done; **(b)** *(imstande sein)* to manage; *(iro)* to be capable of; **ich brachte es nicht f~, ihr die Wahrheit zu sagen** I couldn't bring myself to tell her the truth; **er bringt das f~** *(iro)* I wouldn't put it past him.

**fertigen** *vt (form)* to manufacture.

**Fertig-:** ~**gericht** *nt* ready-to-serve meal; ~**haus** *nt* prefabricated house.

**Fertigkeit** *f* skill.

**Fertig-:** **f~machen** *vt sep* **(a)** *(vollenden)* to finish; **(b)** *(bereit machen)* to get ready; **sich f~machen** to get ready; **(c)** *(col)* **jdn f~machen** *(erledigen)* to do for sb; *(ermüden)* to take it out of sb; *(deprimieren)* to get sb down; *(abkanzeln)* to lay into sb *(col)*; **f~stellen** *vt sep* to complete; ~**stellung** *f* completion.

**Fertigung** *f* production.

**Fertigungs-** *in cpds* production; ~**straße** *f* production line.

**Fertigware** *f* finished product.

**Fes, fes** *nt* - *(Mus)* F flat.

**fesch** *adj (col) (modisch)* smart; *(hübsch)* attractive.

**Fessel** *f* -n **(a)** *(lit, fig)* bond, fetter; *(Kette)* chain.

**jdm** ~**n anlegen** to fetter sb. **(b)** *(Anat) (von Huftieren)* pastern; *(von Menschen)* ankle.

**fesseln** *vt* **(a)** to tie (up), to bind; *(mit Handschellen)* to handcuff; *(mit Ketten)* to chain (up). **ans Bett gefesselt** *(fig)* confined to bed; **jdn an sich** ~ *(fig)* to bind sb to oneself. **(b)** *(faszinieren)* to grip.

**fesselnd** *adj* gripping.

**fest** *adj* **(a)** *(hart)* solid. ~**e Nahrung** solid food, solids *pl*. **(b)** *(stabil)* solid; *Gewebe, Schuhe* strong, sturdy; *(Comm, Fin)* stable. **(c)** *(sicher, entschlossen)* firm. ~ **versprechen** to promise faithfully; **eine ~e Meinung von etw haben** to have definite views on sth; **etw ist** ~ sth is definite; ~ **entschlossen sein** to be absolutely determined. **(d)** *(kräftig)* firm; *Schlag* hard. ~ **zuschlagen** to hit hard. **(e)** *(nicht locker)* tight; *Griff* firm; *(fig) Schlaf* sound. ~ **packen** to grip firmly; **die Tür** ~ **schließen** to shut the door tight; ~ **schlafen** to sleep soundly. **(f)** *(ständig)* regular; *Freund(in)* steady; *Bindung, Stellung, Mitarbeiter* permanent; *Kosten, Einkommen* fixed. ~ **befreundet sein** to be good friends; *(Freund und Freundin)* to be going steady.

**Fest** *nt* -e **(a)** *(Feier)* celebration; *(Party)* party. **man soll die ~e feiern, wie sie fallen** *(prov)* make hay while the sun shines *(Prov)*. **(b)** *(Weihnachts~)* Christmas.

**Fest-:** ~**akt** *m* ceremony; **f~angestellt** *adj* employed on a permanent basis; **f~beißen** *vr sep irreg (Hund etc)* to get a firm grip *(an +dat on)*; *(fig: nicht weiterkommen)* to get bogged down *(an +dat in)*; ~**beleuchtung** *f* festive lights *pl*; *(col: im Haus)* blazing lights *pl*; **f~binden** *vt sep irreg* to tie up *(an +dat to)*; ~**essen** *nt* banquet; **f~fahren** *vr sep irreg (lit, fig)* to get bogged down; **f~fressen** *vr sep irreg* to seize (up); ~**geld** *nt (Fin)* time deposit; ~**halle** *f* assembly hall.

**festhalten** *sep irreg* **1** *vt* **(a)** to keep hold of, to hold on to. **(b)** *(inhaftieren)* to hold, to detain. **(c)** *(speichern)* to record; *Atmosphäre etc* to capture. **etw schriftlich** ~ to record sth. **2** *vi* **an etw** *(dat)* ~ to hold *or* stick *(col)* to sth. **3** *vr* to hold on *(an +dat to)*. **halt dich fest!** *(lit)* hold tight!; **halt dich fest, und hör dir das an!** *(col)* brace yourself and listen to this!

**festigen** **1** *vt* to strengthen. **2** *vr* to become stronger.

**Festiger** *m* - *(Haar~)* setting lotion.

**Festigkeit** *f no pl* strength; *(fig)* steadfastness.

**Festigung** *f* strengthening.

**Festival** ['fɛstivəl, 'fɛstival] *nt* -s festival.

**Festivität** [fɛstivi'tɛːt] *f (old, hum col)* celebration, festivity.

**Fest-:** **f~klammern** *vr sep* to cling *(an +dat to)*; **f~kleben** *vti sep (vi: aux sein)* to stick (firmly) *(an +dat* (on)to)*; ~**kleid** *nt* formal dress; **f~klemmen** *sep* **1** *vt* to wedge fast; *(mit Klammer)* to clip; **2** *vir (vi: aux sein)* to jam; ~**komma** *nt (Comp)* fixed point; **f~krallen** *vr sep (Tier)* to dig one's claws in *(an +dat* -to)*; *(Mensch)* to dig one's nails in *(an +dat* -to)*; *(fig)* to cling *(an +dat* to)*.

**Festland** *nt* mainland; *(nicht Meer)* dry land.

**festlegen** *sep* **1** *vt* **(a)** *(festsetzen) Termin etc* to fix *(auf +acc, bei* for)*; *Regelung, Arbeitszeiten* to lay down. **etw schriftlich** ~ to put sth down in writing. **(b)** **jdn auf etw** *(acc)* ~ *(festnageln)* to tie sb (down) to sth; *(verpflichten)* to commit sb to sth. **(c)** *Geld* to tie up. **2** *vr* **sich darauf** ~**, etw zu tun** to commit oneself to doing sth.

**Festlegung** *f siehe vt (a, b)* **(a)** fixing; laying-down. **(b)** tying-down; commitment.

**festlich** *adj* festive; *(feierlich)* solemn; *(prächtig)*

magnificent. **etw ~ begehen** to celebrate sth.
**Festlichkeit** f celebration; *(Stimmung)* festiveness.
**Fest-: f~liegen** *vi sep irreg* **(a)** *(f~gesetzt sein)* to have been fixed *or* definitely decided; **(b)** *(Fin: Geld)* to be tied up; **(c)** *(nicht weiterkönnen)* to be stuck; *(Naut)* to be aground; **f~machen** *sep* **1** *vt* **(a)** *(befestigen)* to fix on *(an +dat -to)*, to fasten *(an +dat* (on)/to); *(Naut)* to moor; **(b)** *(vereinbaren)* to arrange; **ein Geschäft f~machen** to clinch a deal; **2** *vi (Naut)* to moor; **~mahl** *nt (geh)* banquet, feast; **f~nageln** *vt sep (lit)* to nail (down/up/on); *(fig col) jdn* to nail down *(auf +acc* to*)*; **~nahme** f **-n** arrest; **f~nehmen** *vt sep irreg* to arrest; **vorläufig f~nehmen** to take into custody; **Sie sind ~genommen** you are under arrest; **~platte** f *(Comp)* hard disk; **~preis** m *(Comm)* fixed price; **~rede** f speech (for a big occasion); **die ~rede halten** to give the main speech; **~saal** m (large) function room; *(Tanzsaal)* ballroom; **f~schrauben** *vt sep* to screw (on) tight; **f~schreiben** *vt sep irreg (fig)* to establish; *(Jur)* to enact; **~schrift** f commemorative publication; *(Univ)* festschrift.
**festsetzen** *sep* **1** *vt* **(a)** to fix *(bei, auf +acc* at*)*; *Ort, Termin auch* to arrange *(auf +acc, bei* for*)*. **(b)** *(inhaftieren)* to detain. **2** *vr (Staub, Schmutz)* to collect; *(fig: Gedanke)* to take root.
**Festsetzung** f **(a)** *siehe vt (a)* fixing; arrangement. **(b)** *(Inhaftierung)* detention.
**festsitzen** *vi sep irreg* to be stuck; *(Schmutz)* to cling.
**Festspeicher** m *(Comp)* permanent memory.
**Festspiele** *pl* festival *sing.*
**fest-: ~stecken** *sep* **1** *vt* to pin *(an +dat* (on)/to, *in +dat* in*)*; *Haare* to pin up; **2** *vi (steckenbleiben)* to be stuck; **~stehen** *vi sep irreg (sicher sein)* to be certain; *(beschlossen sein)* to have been settled *or* fixed; **~stehend** *adj* **(a)** *(Mech)* fixed; **(b)** *attr (bestimmt)* definite; *Redewendung* set; **~stellbar** *adj (herauszufinden)* ascertainable.
**feststellen** *vt sep* **(a)** *(Mech)* to lock (fast). **(b)** *(ermitteln)* to ascertain, to find out; *Personalien, Ursache auch* to establish; *Schaden* to assess; *Krankheit* to diagnose. **der Arzt konnte nur noch seinen Tod ~** the doctor found him to be dead. **(c)** *(erkennen)* to tell *(an +dat* from*)*; *Fehler* to find, to detect; *(bemerken)* to discover; *(einsehen)* to realize. **ich mußte entsetzt/überrascht ~, daß ...** I was horrified/surprised to find that ... **(d)** *(aussprechen)* to stress, to emphasize.
**Feststellung** f **(a)** *siehe vt (b)* ascertainment; establishment; assessment; diagnosis. **(b)** *(Erkenntnis)* conclusion. **(c)** *(Wahrnehmung)* observation. **die ~ machen, daß ...** to realize that ...; **ist das eine Frage oder eine ~?** is that a question or a statement (of fact)? **(d)** *(Bemerkung)* remark, observation. **die ~ machen, daß ...** to remark *or* observe that ...
**Festtag** m **(a)** *(Ehrentag)* special day. **(b)** *(Feiertag)* holiday, feast(day) *(Eccl)*.
**fest-: ~treten** *sep irreg* **1** *vt* to tread down; *(in Teppich etc)* to tread in *(in +acc* -to*)*; **2** *vr* to get trodden down/in; **~umrissen** *adj attr* clear-cut.
**Festung** f fortress; *(Burgfeste)* castle.
**Fest-: f~verwurzelt** *adj attr* deep-rooted; **f~verzinslich** *adj* fixed-interest *attr*; **~vortrag** m lecture (for a big occasion); **~wertspeicher** m *(Comp)* read-only memory; **~wiese** f *(für Volksfest)* fairground; **~woche** f festival week; **die ~wochen** the festival *sing*; **~zelt** *nt* carnival marquee; **~zins** m fixed interest.
**Fete, Fête** ['feːtə, 'fɛːtə] f **-n** party.
**Fetisch** m **-e** fetisch.

**Fetischist** m *(wk)* fetishist.
**fett** *adj* **(a)** *(~haltig) Speisen* fatty. **~ essen** to eat fatty food; **ein ~er Brocken** *(fig)* a lucrative deal. **(b)** *(dick)* fat; *(Typ)* bold. **~ gedruckt sein** to be (in) bold. **(c)** *(üppig) Boden, Weide* rich; *Beute, Gewinn* fat; *Geschäft* lucrative. **~e Jahre** fat years.
**Fett** *nt* **-e** fat; *(zum Schmieren)* grease. **~ ansetzen** to put on weight; *(Tiere)* to fatten up; **sein ~ bekommen** *(col)* to get one's comeuppance *(col)*.
**Fett-: f~arm** *adj* low-fat; **f~arm essen** to eat low-fat foods; **~auge** *nt* globule of fat; **~creme** f enriched skin cream; **~druck** m *(Typ)* bold type.
**fetten** *vt* to grease.
**Fett-: ~fleck(en)** m grease spot, greasy mark; **f~frei** *adj* fat-free; *Milch* low-fat; *Kost* non-fatty; *Creme* non-greasy; **f~gedruckt** *adj attr (Typ)* bold; **~gehalt** m fat content; **f~haltig** *adj* fatty.
**fettig** *adj* greasy; *Haut auch* oily.
**Fettigkeit** f *siehe adj* greasiness; oiliness.
**Fett-: ~kloß** m *(pej)* fatty *(col)*; **f~leibig** *adj (geh)* obese, corpulent; **~leibigkeit** f *(geh)* obesity, corpulence; **f~los** *adj* fat-free; **~näpfchen** *nt (col)*: **ins ~näpfchen treten** to put one's foot in it *(bei jdm* with sb*)*; **~polster** *nt (hum col)* flab *no pl*; **~polster haben** to be well-padded; **~presse** f grease gun; **f~reich** *adj* high-fat; **f~reich essen** to eat foods with a high fat content; **~sack** m *(pej)* fatso *(col)*; **~schicht** f layer of fat; **~stift** m lip salve; **~sucht** f *no pl (Med)* obesity; **f~süchtig** *adj (Med)* obese; **~wanst** m *(pej)* potbelly; *(Mensch)* fatso *(col)*.
**Fetzen** m **-** shred; *(Papier~, Gesprächs~)* scrap; *(Kleidung)* rag. **das Kleid ist in ~ gegangen** the dress has fallen to pieces; **etw in ~/in tausend ~ (zer)reißen** to tear sth to shreds/into a thousand pieces; **..., daß die ~ fliegen** *(col)* ... like mad *(col)*.
**fetzen** *vi aux sein (col: rasen)* to tear.
**fetzig** *adj* wild, crazy; *(Musik auch)* hot.
**feucht** *adj* damp; *Lippen* moist; *(feuchtheiß) Klima* humid; *Hände* sweaty; *Tinte, Farbe* wet. **sie hatte ~e Augen** her eyes were moist; **ein ~er Abend** *(hum)* a boozy night; **eine ~e Aussprache haben** *(hum col)* to splutter when one speaks; **das geht dich einen ~en Kehricht** *or* **Dreck an** *(col!)* it's none of your damn business *(col)*.
**Feucht-: f~fröhlich** *adj (hum)* boozy; **~gebiet** *nt* marshland; **f~heiß** *adj* muggy.
**Feuchtigkeit** f *no pl* **(a)** *siehe adj* dampness; moistness; humidity; sweatiness; wetness. **(b)** *(Flüssigkeit)* moisture; *(Luft~)* humidity.
**Feuchtigkeits-: ~creme** f moisturizer; **~gehalt, ~grad** m moisture content.
**feuchtwarm** *adj* muggy, humid.
**feudal** *adj (Pol, Hist)* feudal; *(col)* plush *(col)*.
**Feudal-** *in cpds* feudal; **~herrschaft** f feudalism; **~system** *nt* feudal system.
**Feudalismus** m feudalism.
**Feuer** *nt* **-** **(a)** *(Flamme, Kamin~)* fire. **am ~** by the fire; **~ machen** to light a/the fire; **~ hinter etw** *(acc)* **machen** *(fig)* to chase sth up; **jdm ~ unter dem Hintern machen** *(col)* to put a bomb under sb *(col)*; **du spielst mit dem ~** *(fig)* you're playing with fire; **sie sind wie ~ und Wasser** they're as different as chalk and cheese; **~ legen** to start a fire; **~ fangen** to catch fire; **für jdn durchs ~ gehen** to go through fire and water for sb; **haben Sie ~?** do you have a light?; **jdm ~ geben** to give sb a light. **(b)** *(Naut, Funk~)* beacon; *(von Leuchtturm)* light. **(c)** **das/sie hat bei ihm ~ gefangen** he was really taken with it/her; **~ und Flamme sein** *(col)* to be dead keen *(col)* *(für* on*)*. **(d)** *(Schießen)* fire. **~! fire!; ~ frei!** open fire!; **das ~ eröffnen** to open fire; **das ~ einstellen**

to cease fire; **etw unter** ~ *(acc)* **nehmen** to open fire on sth.

**Feuer-** *in cpds* fire; ~**alarm** *m* fire alarm; ~**anzünder** *m* firelighter; ~**ball** *m* fireball; ~**befehl** *m (Mil)* order to fire; ~**bekämpfung** *f* fire-fighting; **f**~**beständig** *adj* fire-resistant; ~**bestattung** *f* cremation; ~**eifer** *m* zeal; ~**einstellung** *f* cessation of fire; *(Waffenstillstand)* ceasefire; **f**~**fest** *adj* fireproof; *Geschirr* heat-resistant; ~**gefahr** *f* fire hazard *or* risk; **bei** ~**gefahr** in the event of fire; **f**~**gefährlich** *adj* inflammable; ~**haken** *m* poker; ~**leiter** *f (am Haus)* fire escape; ~**löscher** *m* - fire extinguisher; ~**meer** *nt (liter)* sea of flames; ~**melder** *m* - fire alarm.

**feuern 1** *vi* (a) *(heizen)* **mit Öl/Holz** ~ to have oil heating/use wood for one's heating. (b) *(Mil)* to fire. **2** *vt* (a) *Ofen* to light. (b) *(col) (werfen)* to fling; *(Ftbl) Ball* to slam; *(ins Tor)* to slam in. (c) *(col: entlassen)* to fire *(col)*.

**Feuer-:** ~**pause** *f* break in the firing; *(vereinbart)* ceasefire; **f**~**polizeilich** *adj Bestimmungen* laid down by the fire authorities; ~**probe** *f* **die** ~**probe bestehen** *(fig)* to pass the (acid) test; **f**~**rot** *adj* fiery red.

**Feuersbrunst** *f (geh)* conflagration.

**Feuer-:** ~**schein** *m* glow of the fire; ~**schiff** *nt* lightship; ~**schlucker** *m* - fire-eater; ~**schutz** *m* (a) *(Vorbeugung)* fire prevention; (b) *(Mil: Deckung)* covering fire; **f**~**speiend** *adj attr Drache* fire-breathing; *Berg* belching flames; ~**spritze** *f* fire hose; ~**stein** *m* flint; ~**stelle** *f* campfire site; *(Herd)* fireplace; ~**taufe** *f* **die** ~**taufe bestehen/erhalten** to go through/have a baptism of fire; ~**treppe** *f* fire escape; ~**tür** *f* fire door.

**Feuerung** *f* heating; *(Brennstoff)* fuel.

**Feuer-:** ~**versicherung** *f* fire insurance; ~**wache** *f* fire station; ~**waffe** *f* firearm; ~**wechsel** *m* exchange of fire.

**Feuerwehr** *f* fire brigade *(Brit)* or department *(US)*. **fahren wie die** ~ *(col)* to drive like the clappers *(Brit col)*, to drive flat out.

**Feuerwehr-:** ~**auto** *nt* fire engine; ~**frau** *f* firewoman; ~**mann** *m* fireman.

**Feuer-:** ~**werk** *nt* fireworks *pl*; *(fig)* cavalcade; ~**werkskörper** *m* firework; ~**zangenbowle** *f red wine punch containing rum which has been flamed off*; ~**zeug** *nt* (cigarette) lighter.

**Feuilleton** [fœjə'tõ, 'fœjətõ] *nt* -**s** *(Press)* feature section; *(Artikel)* feature (article).

**feurig** *adj* fiery.

**Fez** *m no pl (dated col: Spaß)* larking about *(col)*.

**ff.** = **folgende Seiten** ff.

**Fiaker** *m* - *(Aus) (Kutsche)* (hackney) cab; *(Kutscher)* cab driver, cabby *(col)*.

**Fiasko** *nt* -**s** *(col)* fiasco.

**Fibel** *f* -**n** *(Sch)* primer.

**Fiber** *f* -**n** fibre *(Brit)*, fiber *(US)*.

**Fiche** [fiːʃ] *m or nt* -**s** (micro)fiche.

**Fichte** *f* -**n** *(Bot)* spruce.

**Fichten-** *in cpds* spruce; ~**zapfen** *m* spruce cone.

**ficken** *vti (col!!!)* to fuck *(col!!!)*.

**fidel** *adj (dated col)* jolly, merry.

**Fidel** *f* -**n** fiddle.

**Fidschi|inseln** *pl* Fiji (Islands).

**Fieber** *nt* - temperature; *(Krankheit)* fever. ~ **haben** to have a temperature; **to be feverish; 40°** ~ **haben** to have a temperature of 40; **(jdm) das** ~ **messen** to take sb's temperature; **im** ~ **seiner Leidenschaft** in a fever of passion.

**Fieber-** *in cpds* feverish; **f**~**haft** *adj (lit, fig)* feverish.

**fieb(e)rig** *adj* feverish.

**Fieberkurve** *f* temperature curve.

**fiebern** *vi* to have a temperature; *(schwer)* to be feverish. **vor Ungeduld** *(dat)* ~ *(fig)* to be in a fever of impatience.

**Fieber-:** **f**~**senkend** *adj* fever-reducing; ~**thermometer** *nt* thermometer.

**Fiedel** *f* -**n** *(old, pej: Geige)* fiddle.

**fiedeln** *vti (hum, pej)* to fiddle.

**fiel** *pret of* **fallen**.

**fiepen** *vi* to whimper; *(Vogel)* to cheep.

**fies** *adj (col)* nasty, horrible.

**Fifa, FIFA** *f* FIFA.

**Figur** *f* figure; *(Roman~, Film~ etc)* character; *(von Männern)* physique. **auf seine** ~ **achten** to watch one's figure; **eine gute/schlechte/traurige** ~ **abgeben** to cut a good/poor/sorry figure.

**figurbetont** *adj* figure-hugging.

**Fiktion** *f* fiction.

**fiktiv** *adj* fictitious.

**Filet** [fi'leː] *nt* -**s** *(Cook)* fillet; *(Rinder~)* fillet steak; *(zum Braten)* piece of sirloin *or* tenderloin *(US)*.

**filetieren*** *vt* to fillet.

**Filet-** [fi'leː-]: ~**steak** *nt* fillet steak; ~**stück** *nt* piece of sirloin *or* tenderloin *(US)*.

**Filiale** *f* -**n** branch.

**Filialleiter** *m* branch manager.

**Filipino** *m* -**s** Filipino.

**Filius** *m* -**se** *(hum)* son, offspring *(hum)*.

**Film** *m* -**e** (a) film; *(Spiel~ auch)* movie *(esp US)*. **in einen** ~ **gehen** to go and see a film *(Brit)* or movie *(US)*; **da ist bei mir der** ~ **gerissen** *(col)* I had a mental blackout *(col)*. (b) *(~branche)* films *pl*, the movies *pl (esp US)*. **zum** ~ **gehen** to go into films.

**Film-** *in cpds* film, movie *(esp US)*; ~**atelier** *nt* film studio; ~**bewertungsstelle** *f* ≈ board of film classification; ~**biographie** *f* biopic; ~**diva** *f (dated)* screen goddess.

**Filmemacher(in** *f)* *m* film-maker.

**filmen** *vti* to film.

**Film-:** ~**festspiele** *pl* film festival; ~**geschäft** *nt* film *or* movie *(esp US)* industry; ~**geschichte** *f* history of the cinema; ~**geschichte machen** to make cinema history; ~**gesellschaft** *f* film company; ~**größe** *f* great star of the screen; ~**held** *m* screen *or* movie *(esp US)* hero.

**filmisch** *adj* cinematic.

**Film-:** ~**kamera** *f* film *or* movie *(esp US)* camera; *(Schmalfilmkamera)* cine-camera *(Brit)*; ~**kritik** *f* film criticism; *(Artikel)* film review; *(Kritiker)* film critics *pl*; ~**kulisse** *f* film set; ~**material** *nt* film, footage; ~**musik** *f* film music; **die originale** ~**musik** the original soundtrack; ~**preis** *m* film *or* movie *(esp US)* award; ~**produzent** *m* film *or* movie *(esp US)* producer; ~**regie** *f* direction of a/the film; ~**regisseur** *m* film *or* movie *(esp US)* director; ~**riß** *m (lit)* tear in a film; *(col)* mental blackout *(col)*; ~**rolle** *f (Spule)* spool of film; *(für Fotoapparat)* roll of film; *(Part)* film part; ~**schaffende(r)** *mf decl as adj* film-maker; ~**schauspieler(in** *f)* *m* film *or* movie *(esp US)* actor/actress; ~**star** *m* filmstar, movie star *(esp US)*; ~**sternchen** *nt* starlet; ~**theater** *nt (form)* cinema *(Brit)*, movie theater *(US)*; ~**trick** *m* film stunt; ~**verleih** *m* film distributors *pl*; ~**vorführer** *m* projectionist; ~**vorführung, ~vorstellung** *f* film show.

**Filou** [fi'luː] *m* -**s** *(dated col)* devil *(col)*.

**Filter** *m or (esp Tech) nt* - filter. **eine Zigarette mit/ohne** ~ a filter-tipped/plain cigarette.

**Filterkaffee** *m* filter *or* drip *(US)* coffee.

**filtern** *vti* to filter.

**Filter-:** ~**papier** *nt* filter paper; ~**tüte** *f* filter bag.
**Filterung** *f* filtering.
**Filterzigarette** *f* filter-tipped cigarette.
**filtrieren\*** *vt* to filter.
**Filz** *m* **-e** *(Tex)* felt.
**filzen** *vt (col) (durchsuchen) jdn* to frisk, to search; *Gepäck etc* to search; *(berauben)* to do over *(col)*.
**Filzhut** *m* felt hat.
**Filzokratie** *f (hum)* web of patronage and nepotism.
**Filz-:** ~**pantoffel** *m* (carpet) slipper; ~**schreiber,** ~**stift** *m* felt-tip (pen).
**Fimmel** *m* - *(col)* obsession *(mit* about*)*. **du hast wohl einen** ~! you're crazy *(col)*.
**Finale** *nt* **-s** *or* - *(Mus)* finale; *(Sport)* final.
**Finalist** *m* finalist.
**Finanz-** *in cpds* financial; ~**amt** *nt* tax office; ~**beamte(r)** *mf* tax official; ~**behörde** *f* tax authority.
**Finanzen** *pl* finances *pl. das übersteigt meine* ~ that's beyond my means.
**finanziell** *adj* financial.
**finanzieren\*** *vt* to finance, to fund. **frei** ~ to finance privately; **ich kann meinen Urlaub nicht** ~ I can't afford a holiday.
**Finanzierung** *f* financing. **zur** ~ **von etw** to finance sth.
**Finanzierungs-:** ~**gesellschaft** *f* finance company; ~**plan** *m* financing plan *or* scheme.
**Finanz-:** ~**jahr** *nt* financial year; **f**~**kräftig** *adj* financially strong; ~**minister** *m* minister of finance; ~**politik** *f* financial policy; **f**~**schwach** *adj* financially weak; ~**spritze** *f* capital injection; **f**~**stark** *adj* financially strong; ~**wesen** *nt* financial system.
**Findelkind** *nt (old)* foundling *(old)*.
**finden** *pret* **fand,** *ptp* **gefunden 1** *vt* **(a)** to find; *Anklang, Zustimmung auch, Beifall* to meet with; *Berücksichtigung, Beachtung* to receive. **ich finde es nicht** I can't find it; **es war nicht/nirgends zu** ~ it was not/nowhere to be found; **es ließ sich niemand** ~ **we/they** *etc* couldn't find anybody; **etwas an jdm** ~ to see something in sb; **nichts dabei** ~ to think nothing of it. **(b)** *(ansehen, betrachten)* to think. **es kalt/warm/ganz erträglich** ~ to find it cold/warm/quite tolerable; **etw gut/zu teuer/eine Frechheit** ~ to think (that) sth is good/too expensive/a cheek; **jdn blöd/nett** ~ to think (that) sb is stupid/nice; **wie findest du das?** what do you think?; ~ **Sie?** do you think so?; **ich finde, wir sollten ...** I think we should ...; **ich fände es besser, wenn ...** I think it would be better if ...

**2** *vi (lit, fig: den Weg* ~*)* to find one's way. **er findet nicht nach Hause** he can't find his way home; **ich finde schon allein hinaus** I can see myself out; **zu sich selbst** ~ to sort oneself out.

**3** *vr* **(a)** *(zum Vorschein kommen)* to be found; *(wiederauftauchen auch)* to turn up; *(sich befinden auch)* to be. **(b)** *(in Ordnung kommen: Angelegenheit etc)* to sort itself out; *(Mensch: zu sich* ~*)* to sort oneself out. **(c)** *(sich fügen)* **sich in etw** *(acc)* ~ to reconcile oneself to sth. **(d)** *(sich treffen) (lit, fig)* to find each other.
**Finder(in** *f)* *m* - finder.
**Finderlohn** *m* reward for the finder.
**findig** *adj* resourceful.
**Findigkeit** *f* resourcefulness.
**Finesse** *f* **(a)** *(Feinheit)* refinement; *(Kunstfertigkeit)* finesse *no pl.* **mit allen** ~**n** with all the refinements. **(b)** *(Trick)* trick.
**fing** *pret of* **fangen.**
**Finger** *m* - finger. **jdm mit dem** ~ **drohen** to wag

one's finger at sb; **jdm auf die** ~ **hauen** *(lit)*/**klopfen** *(fig)* to give sb a rap on the knuckles; **mit** ~**n auf jdn zeigen** *(fig)* to look askance at sb; **sich** *(dat)* **nicht die** ~ **schmutzig machen** *(lit, fig)* not to get one's hands dirty; **das kann sich jeder an den (fünf)** ~**n abzählen** *(col)* it sticks out a mile *(col)*; **das läßt er nicht mehr aus den** ~**n** he won't let it out of his hands; **jdm/etw in die** ~ **bekommen** to get one's hands on sb/sth; **er hat überall seine** ~ **drin** *(col)* he has a finger in every pie *(col)*; **wenn man ihm den kleinen** ~ **gibt, nimmt er (gleich) die ganze Hand** *(prov)* give him an inch and he'll take a mile *(col)*; **lange** ~ **machen** *(hum col)* to be light-fingered; **jdm in die** ~ **geraten** to fall into sb's hands *or* clutches; **die** ~ **von etw lassen** *(col)* to keep away from sth; **jdm (scharf) auf die** ~ **sehen** to keep an eye on sb; **sich** *(dat)* **etw aus den** ~**n saugen** to conjure sth up; **sich** *(dat)* **die** ~ **nach etw lecken** *(col)* to be dying for sth; **keinen** ~ **krumm machen** *(col)* not to lift a finger *(col)*; **mir juckt es in den** ~**n( etw zu tun)** *(col)* I'm itching to (do sth); **jdn um den kleinen** ~ **wickeln** to twist sb around one's little finger; **etw im kleinen** ~ **haben** to have a natural feel for sth.
**Finger-:** ~**abdruck** *m* fingerprint; **f**~**breit** *adj* the width of a finger; ~**farbe** *f* finger paint; **f**~**fertig** *adj* nimble-fingered, dexterous; ~**fertigkeit** *f* dexterity; ~**hakeln** *nt* finger-wrestling; ~**handschuh** *m* glove; ~**hut** *m* **(a)** *(Sew)* thimble; **(b)** *(Bot)* foxglove; ~**knöchel** *m* knucklebone; ~**kuppe** *f* fingertip; ~**ling** *m* fingerstall.
**fingern** *vi* **an etw** *(dat)* ~ to fiddle with sth; **nach etw** ~ to fumble (around) for sth.
**Finger-:** ~**nagel** *m* fingernail; ~**spitze** *f* fingertip; **das muß man in den** ~**spitzen haben** you have to have a feel for it; ~**spitzengefühl** *nt no pl* sensitivity; ~**zeig** *m* **-e** hint.
**fingieren\*** [fɪŋˈgiːrən] *vt (vortäuschen)* to fake; *(erdichten)* to fabricate. **fingiert** *(vorgetäuscht)* bogus; *(erfunden)* fictitious.
**Finish** [ˈfɪnɪʃ] *nt* **-s (a)** *(Endverarbeitung)* finish. **(b)** *(Sport: Endspurt)* final spurt.
**Fink** *m (wk)* **-en, -en** finch.
**Finne** *m (wk)* **-n, -n, Finnin** *f* Finn.
**finnisch** *adj* Finnish; *siehe* **deutsch.**
**Finnisch(e)** *nt* **-n** Finnish; *siehe* **Deutsch(e).**
**Finnland** *nt* Finland.
**finster** *adj* **(a)** *(lit, fig)* dark; *Zimmer, Wald, Nacht* dark (and gloomy). **im F**~**n** in the dark; **es sieht** ~ **aus** *(fig)* things look bleak. **(b)** *(dubios)* shady. **(c)** *(mürrisch, düster)* grim; *Wolken* dark, black. ~ **entschlossen sein** to be grimly determined; **jdn** ~ **ansehen** to give sb a black look. **(d)** *(unheimlich) Gestalt, Blick, Gedanken* sinister.
**Finsternis** *f* **(a)** darkness. **(b)** *(Astron)* eclipse.
**Finte** *f* **-n (a)** *(Sport)* feint. **(b)** *(List)* ruse.
**Firlefanz** *m no pl (col)* **(a)** *(Kram)* frippery. **(b)** *(Albernheit)* ~ **machen** to clown around.
**firm** *adj pred* **in etw** *(dat)* ~ **sein** to have a sound knowledge of sth.
**Firma** *f, pl* **Firmen** company, firm. **die** ~ **Wahlster** Messrs Wahlster, Wahlster(s); **die** ~ **Lexomat** Lexomat; **die** ~ **dankt** *(hum)* much obliged (to you).
**Firmament** *nt no pl (poet)* firmament *(liter)*.
**firmen** *vt (Rel)* to confirm.
**Firmen-:** ~**gründung** *f* formation of a company; ~**image** *nt* corporate image *or* identity; ~**inhaber** *m* owner of a/the company; ~**name** *m* company name; ~**register** *nt* register of companies; ~**schild** *nt* company sign; ~**übernahme** *f* takeover; ~**verzeichnis** *nt* trade directory; ~**wagen** *m* company car; ~**zeichen** *nt* trademark.

**firmieren*** *vi*: **als ... ~** *(Comm, fig)* to trade under the name of ...

**Firmung** *f (Rel)* confirmation. **jdm die ~ erteilen** to confirm sb.

**Firnis** *m* **-se** varnish.

**First** *m* **-e** *(Dach~)* (roof) ridge.

**Fis** *nt* - *(Mus)* F sharp. **in ~/f~** in F sharp major/minor.

**Fisch** *m* **-e** **(a)** fish. **~e/drei ~e fangen** to catch fish/three fish(es); **das sind kleine ~e** *(fig col)* that's child's play *(col)*; **ein großer ~** *(fig col)* a big fish; **ein kleiner ~** one of the small fry; **sich wohl fühlen wie ein ~ im Wasser** to be in one's element; **stumm wie ein ~ sein** to be as silent as a post; **weder ~ noch Fleisch** neither fish nor fowl. **(b) ~e** *pl (Astrol)* Pisces.

**Fisch-** *in cpds* fish; **~auge** *nt (Phot)* fish-eye lens; **~becken** *nt* fishpond; **~bestand** *m* fish population; **~dampfer** *m* trawler.

**fischen** *vti (lit, fig)* to fish. **mit (dem) Netz ~** to trawl; **Heringe ~** to fish for herring.

**Fischer** *m* - fisherman.

**Fischer-**: **~boot** *nt* fishing boat; **~dorf** *nt* fishing village.

**Fischerei** *f* **(a)** fishing. **(b)** *(~gewerbe)* fishing industry, fisheries *pl*.

**Fischerei-** *in cpds* fishing; **~grenze** *f* fishing limit.

**Fischernetz** *nt* fishing net.

**Fischfang** *m no pl* **vom ~ leben** to live by fishing; **zum ~ auslaufen** to set off for the fishing grounds.

**Fischfanggebiet** *nt* fishing grounds *pl*.

**Fisch-**: **~filet** *nt* fish fillet; **~frikadelle** *f* fishcake; **~geruch** *m* smell of fish, fishy smell; **~geschäft** *nt* fishmonger's (shop); **~gräte** *f* fish bone; **~grätenmuster** *nt* herringbone (pattern); **~gründe** *pl* fishing grounds *pl*, fisheries *pl*; **~händler** *m* fishmonger; *(Großhändler)* fish merchant; **~konserve** *f* canned fish; **~kutter** *m* fishing cutter; **~laden** *m* fishmonger; **~markt** *m* fish market; **~mehl** *nt* fish meal; **~otter** *m* otter; **~schuppe** *f* (fish) scale; **~schwarm** *m* shoal of fish; **~stäbchen** *nt* fish finger *(Brit)*, fish stick *(US)*; **~sterben** *nt* death of fish; **~zucht** *f* fish-farming; *(Betrieb)* fish farm; **~zug** *m (fig: Beutezug)* raid, foray.

**Fisimatenten** *pl (col) (Ausflüchte)* excuses *pl*; *(Umstände)* fuss; *(Albernheiten)* nonsense.

**Fiskus** *m no pl (fig: Staatskasse)* Treasury.

**Fistelstimme** *f* falsetto.

**fit** *adj pred* fit. **sich ~ halten** to keep fit.

**Fitness, Fitneß** *f no pl* physical fitness.

**Fitnesscenter** *nt* health *or* fitness centre.

**Fittich** *m* **-e** *(liter)* wing. **jdn unter seine ~e nehmen** *(hum)* to take sb under one's wing.

**Fitzelchen** *nt (col)* little bit.

**fix** *adj* **(a)** *(col: flink)* quick. **mach ~!** look lively! **(b)** *(col)* **~ und fertig sein** to be all finished; *(bereit)* to be all ready; *(erschöpft, emotional)* to be shattered *(col)*; **jdn ~ und fertig machen** *(nervös machen)* to drive sb mad; *(erschöpfen, emotional)* to shatter sb *(col)*. **(c) ~e Idee** obsession.

**fixen** *vi* to mainline.

**Fixer(in** *f)* *m* - *(col)* fixer *(col)*.

**Fixierbad** *nt (Phot)* fixer.

**fixieren*** *vt* **(a)** *(anstarren)* **jdn/etw ~** to stare at sb/sth. **(b)** *(festlegen)* to specify; *(schriftlich niederlegen)* to record. **er ist zu stark auf seine Mutter fixiert** *(Psych)* he has a mother fixation. **(c)** *(Phot)* to fix.

**Fixierung** *f (Festlegung) siehe vt* **(b)** specification; recording; *(Psych)* fixation.

**Fix-**: **~kosten** *pl* fixed costs *pl*; **~stern** *m* fixed star.

**Fixum** *nt, pl* **Fixa** basic salary.

**Fjord** *m* **-e** fiord.

**FKK** [εfka:'ka:] *no art* = **Freikörperkultur**.

**FKK-**: **~-Anhänger** *m* **~-Anhänger sein** to be a nudist; **~-Strand** *m* nudist beach.

**flach** *adj* **(a)** flat; *(Gebäude)* low; *(Abhang)* gentle; *(Gewässer)* shallow. **~ liegen** to lie flat; **die ~e Hand** the flat of one's hand; **eine ~e Brust** a hollow chest; *(Busen)* a flat chest; **auf dem ~en Land** in the middle of the country. **(b)** *(fig)* flat; *(Geschmack)* insipid; *(oberflächlich)* shallow. **~ atmen** to take shallow breaths.

**Flachdach** *nt* flat roof.

**Fläche** *f* **-n** *(auch Math)* area; *(Ober~)* surface; *(Gelände, Land~, Wasser~)* expanse.

**Flächen-**: **~bombardierung** *f* carpet bombing; **~brand** *m* extensive fire; **sich zu einem ~brand ausweiten** *(fig)* to spread to epidemic proportions; **~inhalt** *m* area; **~maß** *nt* square measure.

**Flach-**: **f~fallen** *vi sep irreg aux sein (col)* not to come off; *(Regelung)* to end; **~land** *nt* lowland; **f~legen** *sep (col)* **1** *vt* to lay out; **2** *vr* to lie down; **f~liegen** *vi sep irreg (col)* to be laid up; **~mann** *m, pl* **~männer** *(col)* hipflask.

**Flachs** [flaks] *m no pl* **(a)** *(Bot, Tex)* flax. **(b)** *(col: Neckerei, Witzelei)* kidding *(col)*. **jetzt mal ganz ohne ~** joking *or* kidding *(col)* apart.

**flachsblond** ['flaks-] *adj* flaxen-haired; *(Haar)* flaxen.

**flachsen** ['flaksn] *vi (col)* to kid around *(col)*.

**Flachzange** *f* flat-nosed pliers *pl*.

**flackern** *vi (lit, fig)* to flicker.

**Fladen** *m* - **(a)** *(Cook)* round flat dough-cake. **(b)** *(col: Kuh~)* cowpat.

**Fladenbrot** *nt* unleavened bread.

**Flagge** *f* **-n** flag. **die ~ streichen** *(fig)* to capitulate; **~ zeigen** to nail one's colours *(Brit) or* colors *(US)* to the mast.

**flaggen** *vi* **geflaggt haben** to fly flags/a flag.

**Flaggenmast** *m* flagpole.

**Flagg-**: **~offizier** *m* flag officer; **~schiff** *nt (lit, fig)* flagship.

**flagrant** *adj* flagrant; *siehe* **in flagranti**.

**Flair** [flɛ:ɐ] *nt no pl (geh)* atmosphere; *(Nimbus)* aura.

**Flak** *f* - *or* **-s** = **Flug(zeug)abwehrkanone** anti-aircraft gun; *(Einheit)* anti-aircraft unit.

**Flakon** [fla'kõ:] *nt or m* **-s** bottle, flacon.

**flambieren*** *vt (Cook)* to flambé.

**Flame** *m (wk)* **-n, -n, Flämin** *f* Fleming.

**Flamingo** [fla'mɪŋgo] *m* **-s** flamingo.

**flämisch** *adj* Flemish.

**Flämisch(e)** *nt* Flemish; *siehe* **Deutsch(e)**.

**Flamme** *f* **-n** *(lit, fig)* flame. **in ~n stehen/aufgehen** to be in flames/go up in flames.

**flammend** *adj* fiery. **mit ~em Gesicht** blazing.

**flammendrot** *adj (geh)* flame red, blazing red.

**Flammen-**: **~meer** *nt* sea of flames; **~werfer** *m* flame-thrower.

**Flandern** *nt* Flanders *sing*.

**Flanell** *m* **-e** flannel.

**flanieren*** *vi* to stroll, to saunter.

**Flanke** *f* **-n** *(Anat, Mil)* flank; *(Sport) (Turnen)* flankvault; *(Ftbl)* cross; *(Spielfeldseite)* wing.

**flanken** *vi (Ftbl)* to centre *(Brit)*, to center *(US)*.

**Flanken-**: **~angriff** *m (Mil)* flank attack; **~ball** *m (Ftbl)* cross; **~deckung** *f (Mil)* flank defence *(Brit) or* defense *(US)*.

**flankieren*** *vt (Mil, fig)* to flank. **~de Maßnahmen** supporting measures.

**Flansch** *m* **-e** flange.

**flapsig** *adj (col) Benehmen* cheeky; *Bemerkung* off-hand.

**Flasche** *f* **-n (a)** bottle. **mit der ~ aufziehen** to bottle-feed; **eine ~ Wein/Bier** a bottle of wine/beer; **zur ~ greifen** *(fig)* to hit the bottle. **(b)** *(col: Versager)* dead loss *(col)*.

**Flaschen-:** **~bier** *nt* bottled beer; **f~grün** *adj* bottle-green; **~hals** *m* neck of a bottle; *(fig)* bottle-neck; **~kind** *nt* bottle-fed baby; **~milch** *f* bottled milk; **~öffner** *m* bottle-opener; **~pfand** *nt* deposit on a/the bottle; **~post** *f* message in a/the bottle; **per ~post** in a bottle; **~wein** *m* wine by the bottle; **~zug** *m* block and tackle.

**Flatter-:** **f~haft** *adj* fickle; **~haftigkeit** *f* fickleness.

**flatt(e)rig** *adj* fluttery; *Puls* fluttering.

**flattern** *vi bei Richtungsangabe aux sein (lit, fig)* to flutter; *(mit den Flügeln schlagen)* to flap its wings; *(Fahne, Segel)* to flap; *(Haar)* to fly; *(col: Mensch)* to be in a flap *(col)*. **ein Brief flatterte mir auf den Schreibtisch** a letter arrived on my desk.

**Flattersatz** *m (Typ)* unjustified print.

**flau** *adj* **(a)** *Brise, Wind* slack. **(b)** *Stimmung* flat. **(c)** *(übel)* queasy; *(vor Hunger)* faint. **mir ist ~ (im Magen)** I feel queasy. **(d)** *(Comm)* slack. **in meiner Kasse sieht es ~ aus** *(col)* my finances aren't too healthy *(col)*.

**Flaum** *m no pl* fluff, down.

**Flaum-:** **~bart** *m* downy beard; **~feder** *f* down feather.

**flaumig** *adj* downy.

**Flausch** *m* **-e** fleece.

**flauschig** *adj* fleecy; *(weich)* soft.

**Flausen** *pl (col)* **(a)** *(Unsinn)* nonsense; *(Illusionen)* fancy ideas *pl (col)*. **~ im Kopf haben** to have fancy ideas. **(b)** *(Ausflüchte)* excuses *pl.*

**Flaute** *f* **-n (a)** *(Naut)* calm. **das Schiff geriet in eine ~** the ship was becalmed. **(b)** *(fig)* slack period.

**fläzen** *vr (col)* to sprawl *(in +acc* in).

**Flechte** *f* **-n** *(Bot, Med)* lichen.

**flechten** *pret* **flocht**, *ptp* **geflochten** *vt Haar* to plait; *Kranz, Korb* to weave.

**Flechtwerk** *nt* = **Geflecht.**

**Fleck** *m* **-e** *or* **-en (a)** *(Schmutz~)* mark. **dieses Zeug macht ~en** this stuff stains *(in/auf etw (acc)* sth); **einen ~ auf der Weste haben** *(fig)* to have blotted one's copybook. **(b)** *(Farb~)* patch. **(c)** *(Stelle)* spot, place. **auf demselben ~** in the same place; **sich nicht vom ~ rühren** not to budge; **nicht vom ~ kommen** not to get any further; **vom ~ weg** on the spot.

**Fleckchen** *nt* **ein schönes ~ (Erde)** a lovely little spot.

**flecken** *vi (dial)* to stain.

**Flecken** *m* - **(a)** *(old: Markt~)* small town. **(b)** = **Fleck (a, b).**

**Flecken|entferner** *m* stain remover.

**fleckenlos** *adj (lit, fig)* spotless.

**Fleckenwasser** *nt* stain remover.

**Fleckfieber** *nt* typhus fever.

**fleckig** *adj* marked; *Obst* blemished; *Tierfell* speckled; *Gesichtshaut* blotchy.

**Fledermaus** *f* bat.

**Flegel** *m* - *(Lümmel)* lout, yob *(col)*; *(Kind)* brat *(col)*.

**Flegel|alter** *nt* awkward adolescent phase.

**Flegelei** *f* uncouthness *no pl.*

**Flegel-:** **f~haft** *adj* uncouth; **~haftigkeit** *f* uncouthness; **~jahre** *pl* = **~alter.**

**flegeln** *vr* to loll, to sprawl.

**flehen** *vi (geh)* to plead *(um +acc* for, *zu* with*).*

**flehentlich** *adj* imploring, pleading. **jdn ~ bitten** to plead with sb.

**Fleisch** *nt no pl* **(a)** flesh. **vom ~ fallen** *(col)* to lose

(a lot of) weight; **sich** *(dat or acc)* **ins eigene ~ schneiden** to cut off one's nose to spite one's face *(prov)*; **sein eigen ~ und Blut** *(liter)* his own flesh and blood; **jdm in ~ und Blut übergehen** to become second nature to sb. **(b)** *(Nahrungsmittel)* meat; *(Frucht~)* flesh.

**Fleisch-** *in cpds (Cook)* meat; *(Anat)* flesh; **~beschau** *f* **(a)** meat inspection; **(b)** *(hum col)* cattle market *(col)*; **~beschauer(in** *f)* *m* meat inspector; **~brocken** *m* lump of meat; **~brühe** *f* meat stock; *(Gericht)* bouillon.

**Fleischer** *m* - butcher.

**Fleischerei** *f* butcher's (shop).

**Fleischer-:** **~haken** *m* meat hook; **~handwerk** *nt* butcher's trade; **~hund** *m (lit, fig)* brute of a dog; **ein Gemüt wie ein ~hund haben** *(col)* to be a callous brute; **~laden** *m* butcher's (shop); **~messer** *nt* butcher's knife.

**Fleisch-:** **f~farben, f~farbig** *adj* flesh-coloured *(Brit)*, flesh-colored *(US)*; **f~fressend** *adj* carnivorous; **~fresser** *m (Zool)* carnivore; **~gericht** *nt* meat dish.

**fleischig** *adj* fleshy.

**Fleisch-:** **~käse** *m* meat loaf; **~klopfer** *m* steak hammer; **~kloß** *m,* **~klößchen** *nt* (a) meatball; **(b)** *(pej col)* mountain of flesh; **f~lich** *adj attr Kost* meat; *(old liter: Begierden)* carnal; **f~los** *adj* **(a)** *(ohne Fleisch)* meatless; *Kost, Ernährung* vegetarian; **f~los essen/kochen** to eat no meat/to cook without meat; **(b)** *(mager)* thin, lean; **~saft** *m* meat juices *pl*; **~salat** *m* diced meat salad with mayonnaise; **~tomate** *f* beef tomato; **f~verarbeitend** *adj attr* meat-processing; **~vergiftung** *f* food poisoning *(from meat)*; **~waren** *pl* meat products *pl*; **~wolf** *m* mincer, meat grinder *(esp US)*; **~wunde** *f* flesh wound; **~wurst** *f* pork sausage.

**Fleiß** *m no pl* industriousness. **~ aufwenden** to apply oneself; **mit ~ kann es jeder zu etwas bringen** anybody can succeed if he works hard; **mit ~ bei der Sache sein** to work hard; **ohne ~ kein Preis** *(Prov)* success never comes easily.

**fleißig** *adj* hard-working *no adv,* industrious; *Sammler* keen. **~ studieren/arbeiten** to study/work hard; **~ wie die Bienen sein** to work like beavers; **ein ~er Arbeiter** a hard worker.

**flektieren*** *vt* to inflect.

**flennen** *vi (pej col)* to blubb(er).

**fletschen** *vti*: **die Zähne** *or* **mit den Zähnen ~** to bare one's teeth.

**Fleurop** ® ['flɔyrɔp] *f* ≈ Interflora ®.

**flexibel** *adj (lit, fig)* flexible.

**Flexibilität** *f* flexibility.

**flicken** *vt* to mend; *(mit Flicken)* to patch.

**Flicken** *m* - patch. **eine Jacke mit ~** a patched jacket.

**Flicken-:** **~decke** *f* patchwork quilt; **~teppich** *m* rag rug.

**Flick-:** **~schuster** *m (old)* cobbler; *(fig pej)* bungler *(col)*; **~schusterei** *f* **das ist ~schusterei** *(fig pej)* that's a patch-up job; **~werk** *nt* **die Reform war reinstes ~werk** the reform had been carried out piecemeal; **~zeug** *nt (Nähzeug)* sewing kit; *(für Reifen)* (puncture) repair outfit.

**Flieder** *m* - lilac.

**flieder-:** **~farben, ~farbig** *adj* lilac.

**Fliege** *f* **-n (a)** fly. **sie fielen um wie die ~n** they were dropping like flies; **sie starben wie die ~n** they fell like flies; **er tut keiner ~ etwas zuleide** *(fig)* he wouldn't hurt a fly; **zwei ~n mit einer Klappe schlagen** *(prov)* to kill two birds with one stone *(prov)*;

ihn stört die ~ an der Wand every little thing irritates him; die or 'ne ~ machen (col) to beat it (col). (b) (Schlips) bow tie.

fliegen pret flog, ptp geflogen 1 vi aux sein to fly. nach Köln fliegt man zwei Stunden it's a two-hour flight to Cologne; ich kann doch nicht ~! I haven't got wings (col); auf jdn/etw ~ (col) to be mad about sb/sth (col); von der Leiter ~ (col) to fall off the ladder; durchs Examen ~ (col) to fail one's exam; aus der Firma ~ (col) to get the sack (col); ~der Puls racing pulse; geflogen kommen to come flying; in den Papierkorb ~ to go into the wastepaper basket; ein Schuh flog ihm an den Kopf he had a shoe flung at him; aus der Kurve ~ to skid off the bend. 2 vt to fly.

fliegend adj attr Fische, Untertasse, Start flying. in ~er Eile in a tremendous hurry; ~e Hitze hot flushes pl.

Fliegen-: ~draht m wire mesh; ~fänger m (Klebestreifen) fly-paper; ~fenster nt wire-mesh window; ~gewicht nt (Sport, fig) flyweight; ~gewichtler m - (Sport) flyweight; ~gitter nt fly screen; ~klatsche f fly-swat(ter); ~pilz m fly agaric.

Flieger m - airman; (col: Flugzeug) plane.

Flieger-: (Mil): ~alarm m air-raid warning; ~angriff m air raid; ~horst m (Mil) military airfield; - jaoke f bomber jacket.

fliehen pret floh, ptp geflohen vi aux sein to flee; (entkommen) to escape (aus from). vor jdm/der Polizei ~ to flee from sb/the police; aus dem Lande ~ to flee the country.

fliehend adj Kinn receding; Stirn sloping.

Fliehkraft f centrifugal force.

Fliese f -n tile. etw mit ~n auslegen to tile sth.

fliesen vt to tile.

Fliesenleger m tiler.

Fließ-: ~band nt conveyor belt; am ~band arbeiten to work on the assembly or production line; ~bandarbeit f work on the assembly line; ~bandfertigung f assembly-line production.

fließen pret floß, ptp geflossen vi aux sein to flow; (Fluß auch, Tränen) to run. es ist genug Blut geflossen enough blood has been shed.

fließend adj flowing; Leitungswasser running; Verkehr moving; Übergang fluid. sie spricht ~ Französisch she speaks fluent French.

Fließ-: ~heck nt (Aut) fastback; ~komma nt (Comp) floating point.

Flimmer-: ~kasten m, ~kiste f (col) box (col).

flimmern vi to shimmer; (TV) to flicker. es flimmert mir vor den Augen everything is swimming in front of my eyes.

flink adj (geschickt) nimble; Zunge quick. ein bißchen ~! (col) get a move on!; mit etw ~ bei der Hand sein to be quick (off the mark) with sth.

Flinkheit f siehe adj nimbleness; quickness.

Flinte f -n (Schrot~) shotgun. die ~ ins Korn werfen (fig) to throw in the sponge.

Flipper m -, Flipperautomat m pinball machine.

flippern vi to play pinball.

flippig adj (col) Typ, Klamotten hip (col).

Flirt [flœrt] m -s (Flirten) flirtation.

flirten ['flœrtn] vi to flirt.

Flittchen nt - (pej col) slut.

Flitter m - (a) (~schmuck) sequins pl. (b) no pl (pej: Tand) trumpery.

flittern vi to glitter, to sparkle.

Flitterwochen pl honeymoon sing. in den ~ sein to be on honeymoon.

Flitz(e)bogen m bow and arrow. ich bin gespannt wie ein ~ (col) the suspense is killing me.

flitzen vi aux sein (col) to whizz (col), to dash.

Flitzer m - (col) (Fahrzeug) sporty little job (col); (Schnelläufer) streak of lightning (col).

floaten ['flo:tn] vti (Fin) to float. ~ (lassen) to float.

Flocke f -n (a) flake; (Schaum~) blob (of foam). (b) ~n pl (col: Geld) dough (col).

flockig adj fluffy.

flog pret of fliegen.

floh pret of fliehen.

Floh m ⸚e (a) (Zool) flea. es ist leichter, einen Sack ⸚e zu hüten, als ... ... is absolutely impossible; jdm einen ~ ins Ohr setzen (col) to put an idea into sb's head. (b) (col: Geld) ⸚e pl dough (col).

Floh-: ~biß m flea bite; ~halsband nt flea collar; ~kino nt (col) fleapit (Brit col); ~markt m jumble sale; (ständige Einrichtung) flea market.

Flop m flop (col).

Flor m -e (a) (dünnes Gewebe) gauze; (Trauer~) crêpe. (b) (Teppich~) pile.

Flora f pl Floren flora.

Florentiner(in f) m - Florentine.

florentinisch adj Florentine.

Florenz nt Florence.

Florett nt -e (Waffe) foil.

florieren* vi to flourish, to bloom.

Florist(in f) m (wk) -en, -en florist.

Floskel f -n set phrase. eine abgedroschene ~ a hackneyed phrase.

floskelhaft adj cliché-ridden, stereotyped.

floß pret of fließen.

Floß nt ⸚e raft.

Flosse f -n (Fisch~, Aviat) fin; (Wal~, Robben~, Taucher~) flipper; (col: Hand) paw (col).

flößen vti to raft.

Flöte f -n (a) pipe; (Quer~) flute; (Block~) recorder; (Pikkolo~) piccolo. (b) (Kelchglas) flute glass. (c) (Cards) flush.

flöten vti (Vogel, hum) to warble.

Flöten-: f~gehen vi sep aux sein (col) to go west (col) or for a burton (Brit col); ~spieler m piper; flautist; ~ton m sound of flutes/a flute; jdm die ~töne beibringen (col) to teach sb what's what (col).

Flötist(in f) m (wk) -en, -en flautist; piccolo player.

flott adj (a) (zügig) Fahrt quick; Tempo brisk; Bedienung speedy (col); Tänzer good; (flüssig) Stil, Artikel racy (col); (schwungvoll) Musik lively; Auto sporty. aber ein bißchen ~! and look lively! (b) (schick) smart. (c) (lebenslustig) fun-loving, fast-living. ein ~es Leben führen to be a fast liver. (d) pred wieder ~ werden (Schiff) to be refloated; (fig col) (Auto etc) to get back on the road; (Unternehmen) to get back on its feet.

Flotte f -n (Naut) fleet.

Flotten-: ~basis f, ~stützpunkt m naval base; ~verband m naval unit.

flottmachen vt sep Schiff to float off; (fig col) Auto etc to get back on the road.

Flöz nt -e (Min) seam.

Fluch m ⸚e curse. ein ~ lastet auf diesem Haus there is a curse on this house.

fluchen vi to curse (auf or über jdn/etw (acc) sb/sth).

Flucht f -en (a) (Fliehen) flight; (geglückt auch) escape. die ~ ergreifen to take flight; ihm glückte die ~ he succeeded in escaping; auf der ~ sein to be fleeing; (Dieb) to be on the run; jdn/etw in die ~ schlagen to put sb/sth to flight; die ~ nach vorn antreten to take the bull by the horns. (b) (Häuser~) row. (c) (Zimmer~) suite.

fluchtartig adj hasty. in ~er Eile in great haste.

flüchten vi (a) aux sein (davonlaufen) to flee; (erfolgreich auch) to escape. vor der Wirklichkeit ~ to escape reality; **sich in Alkohol** ~ to take refuge in alcohol; **sich in Ausreden** ~ to resort to excuses. **(b)** *auch vr (vi: aux sein) (Schutz suchen)* to take refuge.

**Flucht-:** ~**fahrzeug** *nt* escape vehicle; *(von Dieb)* getaway vehicle; ~**gefahr** *f* risk of escape; ~**hilfe** *f* ~**hilfe leisten** to aid an escape.

**flüchtig** *adj* **(a)** *(geflüchtet)* ~ **sein** to be at large. **(b)** *(kurz)* fleeting. **(c)** *(oberflächlich)* cursory. **etw** ~ **lesen** to skim through sth; **jdn** ~ **kennen** to have met sb briefly. **(d)** *(Chem)* volatile. **(e)** *(Comp)* ~**er Speicher** volatile memory.

**Flüchtigkeit** *f* **(a)** *(Kürze)* briefness. **(b)** *(Oberflächlichkeit)* cursoriness. **(c)** *(Chem)* volatility.

**Flüchtigkeitsfehler** *m* careless mistake.

**Flüchtling** *m* refugee.

**Flüchtlings-** *in cpds* refugee; ~**hilfe** *f* aid to refugees; ~**lager** *nt* refugee camp.

**Flucht-:** ~**linie** *f* alignment; ~**punkt** *m* vanishing point; ~**verdacht** *m* **bei** ~**verdacht** if an attempt to abscond is thought likely; ~**versuch** *m* escape attempt *or* bid; ~**weg** *m* escape route.

**Flug** *m* ⸗e flight; *(Ski~)* jump. **im** ~**(e)** in the air; **einen** ~ **antreten** to take off *(nach for)*; **wie im** ~**(e)** *(fig)* in a flash; **das Wochenende verging wie im** ~**(e)** the weekend flew past.

**Flug-:** ~**abwehr** *f* air defence; ~**bahn** *f* flight path; *(von Rakete auch)* trajectory; *(Kreisbahn)* orbit; ~**ball** *m* *(Tennis etc)* volley; ~**begleiter(in** *f)* *m* flight attendant; **f**~**bereit** *adj* ready for take-off; ~**blatt** *nt* leaflet, flier; ~**dauer** *f* flying time.

**Flügel** *m* - **(a)** wing; *(von Hubschrauber)* blade; *(Windmühlen~)* sail, vane; *(Altar~)* sidepiece; *(Fenster~)* casement; *(Mil)* flank. **einem Vogel/jdm die** ~ **stutzen** to clip a bird's/sb's wings. **(b)** *(Konzert~)* grand piano.

**Flügel-:** ~**fenster** *nt* casement window; ~**schraube** *f* wing bolt; ~**spannweite** *f* wingspan; ~**stürmer** *m* *(Sport)* wing forward; ~**tür** *f* double door.

**Flug-:** **f**~**fähig** *adj* able to fly; *Flugzeug (in Ordnung)* airworthy; ~**gast** *m* (airline) passenger.

**flügge** *adj* fully-fledged; *(fig) Jugendlicher* independent. ~ **werden** *(lit)* to be able to fly; *(fig)* to leave the nest.

**Flug-:** ~**gelände** *nt* airfield; ~**geschwindigkeit** *f* flying speed; ~**gesellschaft** *f* airline; ~**hafen** *m* airport; ~**höhe** *f* flying height, altitude; **unsere** ~**höhe beträgt 10.000 Meter** we are flying at an altitude of 10,000 metres; ~**kapitän** *m* captain; ~**karte** *f (Ticket)* plane ticket; ~**körper** *m* projectile; ~**lärm** *m* aircraft noise; ~**leitung** *f* air-traffic *or* flight control; ~**linie** *f* **(a)** *(Strecke)* air route; **(b)** *(~gesellschaft)* airline; ~**lotse** *m* air-traffic *or* flight controller; ~**minute** *f:* **30** ~**minuten von hier** 30 minutes by air from here; ~**netz** *nt* network of air routes; ~**objekt** *nt:* **ein unbekanntes** ~**objekt** an unidentified flying object, a UFO; ~**personal** *nt* flight personnel *pl*; ~**plan** *m* flight schedule; ~**platz** *m* airfield; *(größer)* airport; ~**preis** *m* air fare; ~**reise** *f* flight; **eine** ~**reise machen** to travel by air; ~**reisende(r)** *mf* (airline) passenger; ~**route** *f* air-route.

**flugs** [fluks] *adv (dated)* without delay, speedily.

**Flug-:** ~**sand** *m* drifting sand; ~**schein** *m* **(a)** pilot's licence *(Brit)* or license *(US)*; **(b)** *(~karte)* plane ticket; ~**schreiber** *m* flight recorder; ~**schrift** *f* pamphlet; ~**sicherung** *f* air traffic control; ~**steig** *m* gate; ~**strecke** *f* **(a)** flying distance; **(b)** *(Route)* route; ~**stunde** *f* **(a)** flying hour; **zehn** ~**stunden entfernt** ten hours away by air; **(b)** *(Unterricht)* flying lesson; **f**~**technisch** *adj* aeronautical; *Erfahrung, Fehler* flying *attr*; **f**~**tüchtig** *adj* air-

worthy; ~**tüchtigkeit** *f* airworthiness; ~**verbindung** *f* air connection; ~**verkehr** *m* air traffic; ~**wesen** *nt no pl* aviation *no art*; ~**zeit** *f* flying time.

**Flugzeug** *nt* -e aircraft, (aero)plane *(Brit)*, airplane *(US)*.

**Flugzeug-** *in cpds* aircraft; ~**absturz** *m* air crash; ~**besatzung** *f* aircrew; ~**entführer** *m* hijacker; ~**entführung** *f* hijacking; ~**führer** *m* (aircraft) pilot; ~**halle** *f* (aircraft) hangar; ~**katastrophe** *f* air disaster; ~**träger** *m* aircraft carrier; ~**unglück** *nt* air crash.

**fluktuieren*** *vi* to fluctuate.

**Flunder** *f* -n flounder.

**Flunkerei** *f (col)* **(a)** *(no pl: Flunkern)* story-telling. **(b)** *(kleine Lüge)* story.

**flunkern** *(col)* **1** *vi* to tell stories. **2** *vt* to make up.

**Flunsch** *m* -e *(col)* pout. **einen** ~ **ziehen** to pout.

**Fluor** *nt no pl (Chem)* fluorine; *(~verbindung)* fluoride.

**Flur¹** *m* -e corridor; *(in Privathaus)* hall; *(oben in Privathaus)* landing.

**Flur²** *f* -en *(geh)* open fields *pl.* **durch Wald/Feld und** ~ through woods/fields and meadows; **allein auf weiter** ~ **stehen** *(fig)* to be out on a limb.

**Fluß** *m* ⸗sse **(a)** river. **unten am** ~ down by the river(side). **(b)** *(von Verkehr, Rede, Strom)* flow. **etw in** ~ *(acc)* **bringen** to get sth moving; **im** ~ **sein** *(sich verändern)* to be in a state of flux; *(im Gange sein)* to be in progress.

**Fluß-** *in cpds* river; **f**~**ab(wärts)** *adv* downstream, downriver; **f**~**aufwärts** *adv* upstream, upriver; ~**bett** *nt* riverbed; ~**diagramm** *nt* flow chart.

**flüssig** *adj* **(a)** liquid; *Honig, Lack* runny; *Glas, Metall auch* molten. **(b)** *Stil, Spiel* flowing, fluid. ~ **lesen** to read fluently; **den Verkehr** ~ **halten** to keep the traffic flowing. **(c)** *Geld* available. ~**es Vermögen** liquid assets *pl*; *Wertpapiere* ~ **machen** to realize securities; **ich bin im Moment nicht** ~ *(col)* I'm out of funds at the moment.

**Flüssigkeit** *f* **(a)** liquid; *(esp Anat)* fluid. **(b)** *no pl (von Metall)* liquidity; *(von Geldern)* availability; *(von Stil)* fluidity.

**Flüssigkristallanzeige** *f* liquid-crystal display, LCD.

**flüssigmachen** *vt sep* to realize.

**Fluß-:** ~**lauf** *m* course of a/the river; ~**mündung** *f* estuary; ~**pferd** *nt* hippopotamus; ~**ufer** *nt* river bank.

**Flüstergalerie** *f* whispering gallery.

**flüstern** *vti* to whisper. **das kann ich dir** ~ *(col)* take it from me *(col)*; **dem werde ich was** ~ *(col)* I'll tell him a thing or two *(col)*.

**Flüster-:** ~**propaganda** *f* whispering campaign; ~**stimme** *f* whisper; ~**ton** *m* whisper; **sich im** ~**ton unterhalten** to talk in whispers.

**Flut** *f* -en **(a)** incoming *or* flood tide; *(Zustand)* high tide. **die** ~ **kommt** the tide's coming in; **die** ~ **geht zurück** the tide has started to go out. **(b)** *usu pl (Wassermasse)* waters *pl.* **(c)** *(fig: Menge)* flood. **eine** ~ **von Tränen** floods of tears.

**fluten** *vi aux sein (geh: lit, fig)* to flood.

**Flutlicht** *nt* floodlight.

**flutschen** *vi (col)* **(a)** *aux sein (rutschen)* to slide. **(b)** *(funktionieren)* to go well.

**Flutwelle** *f* tidal wave.

**Föderalismus** *m* federalism.

**Föderation** *f* federation.

**föderativ** *adj* federal.

**Fohlen** *nt* - foal; *(männlich auch)* colt; *(weiblich auch)* filly.

**Föhn** *m* **-e** *warm dry Alpine wind*, foehn.
**Föhre** *f* **-n** Scots pine (tree).
**Fokus** *m* **-, -se** focus.
**Folge** *f* **-n** (a) sequence; *(Cards auch)* run; *(Fortsetzung)* instalment *(Brit)*, installment *(US)*; *(TV, Rad)* episode. **in rascher** ~ in quick succession; **in der** *or* **für die** ~ *(form)* in future. (b) *(Ergebnis)* consequence. **dies hatte seine Entlassung zur** ~ this resulted in his dismissal; **die ~n werden nicht ausbleiben** there will be repercussions. (c) *(form)* **einem Befehl/einer Einladung** ~ **leisten** to obey an order/to accept an invitation.
**Folge|erscheinung** *f* result, consequence.
**folgen** *vi* (a) *aux sein* to follow *(jdm/einer Sache* sb/sth*)*. **auf jdn (im Rang)** ~ to come after sb; ~ **Sie mir (bitte)**! come with me please; **wie folgt** as follows; **daraus folgt, daß** ... it follows from this that ...; **können Sie mir** ~? do you follow (me)? (b) *(gehorchen)* to obey.
**folgend** *adj* following. ~**es** the following; **im** ~**en** in the following; *(schriftlich auch)* below.
**folgendermaßen** *adv* like this, as follows.
**folgen-:** ~**los** *adj* without consequences; **das konnte nicht** ~**los bleiben** that was bound to have serious consequences; ~**schwer** *adj* serious; **die Maßnahme erwies sich als** ~**schwer** the measure had serious consequences.
**Folge-:** **f**~**richtig** *adj* (logically) consistent; ~**richtigkeit** *f* logical consistency.
**folgern** *vti* to conclude. **daraus läßt sich** ~, **daß** ... we can conclude from this that ...
**Folgerung** *f* conclusion.
**Folgezeit** *f* following period.
**folglich** *adv, conj* consequently, therefore.
**folgsam** *adj* obedient.
**Folgsamkeit** *f* obedience.
**Folie** ['foːliə] *f* *(Plastik~)* film; *(Metall~)* foil.
**Folklore** *f no pl* folklore; *(Volksmusik)* folk music.
**folkloristisch** *adj* folkloric; *Kleidung* ethnic.
**Folter** *f* **-n** *(lit, fig)* torture. **jdn auf die** ~ **spannen** *(fig)* to keep sb on tenterhooks.
**Folterbank** *f* rack.
**Folterer** *m* **-** torturer.
**Folterkammer** *f* torture chamber.
**foltern** **1** *vt* to torture; *(quälen auch)* to torment. **2** *vi* to use torture.
**Folterung** *f* torture.
**Fön** ® *m* **-e** hair dryer.
**Fond** [fõː] *m* **-s** (a) *(geh: Wagen~)* back. (b) *(Hintergrund)* background. (c) *(Cook: Fleischsaft)* meat juices *pl*.
**Fonds** [fõː] *m* **-** (a) *(lit, fig)* fund. (b) *(Fin: Schuldverschreibung)* government bond.
**Fondue** [fõ'dyː] *nt* **-s** fondue.
**fönen** *vt* to blow-dry.
**Fontäne** *f* **-n** jet (of water); *(Springbrunnen)* fountain.
**foppen** *vt* *(col)* **jdn** ~ *(necken)* to pull sb's leg *(col)*.
**forcieren*** [fɔr'siːrən] *vt* to push; *Tempo* to force; *Konsum, Produktion* to push *or* force up.
**forciert** [fɔr'siːɐt] *adj* forced.
**Förder-:** ~**anlage** *f* conveyor; ~**band** *nt* conveyor belt.
**Förderer** *m* **-,** **Förderin** *f* sponsor; *(Gönner)* patron.
**Förder-:** ~**klasse** *f* *(Sch)* remedial class; ~**korb** *m* *(Min)* cage; ~**leistung** *f* *(Min)* output.
**förderlich** *adj* beneficial *(dat* to*)*. **guten Beziehungen** ~ **sein** to be conducive to good relations.
**fordern** **1** *vt* (a) *(verlangen)* to demand; *Preis* to ask; *(in Aufrufen)* to call for; *(Anspruch erheben auf)* to claim. **viel von jdm** ~ to ask *or* demand a lot of sb.

(b) *(fig: kosten)* *Opfer* to claim. (c) *(fig: herausfordern)* to challenge. (d) *(Sport)* to make demands on. **2** *vi* to make demands.
**fördern** *vt* (a) *(unterstützen)* to support; *(propagieren)* to promote; *(finanziell)* bestimmtes Projekt* to sponsor; *jds Talent, Neigung* to encourage, to foster; *Verdauung* to aid; *Appetit* to stimulate; *Untersuchung, Wahrheitsfindung, Wachstum* to further; *Verbrauch* to boost. **jdn beruflich** ~ to help sb in his career. (b) *Bodenschätze* to extract.
**Förder-:** ~**plattform** *f* production platform; ~**schacht** *m* winding shaft; ~**stufe** *f* *(Sch)* mixed ability class(es) *(intended to foster the particular talents of each pupil)*; ~**turm** *m* *(Min)* winding tower; *(auf Bohrstelle)* derrick.
**Forderung** *f* (a) *(Verlangen)* demand *(nach* for*)*; *(Lohn~ etc)* claim; *(in Aufrufen etc)* call. **eine** ~ **nach etw erheben** to call for sth; **jds** ~ **erfüllen** to meet sb's demands/claim. (b) *(Comm: Anspruch)* claim *(an +acc* on*)*. (c) *(Herausforderung)* challenge.
**Förderung** *f* (a) *siehe* **fördern** (a) support; promotion; sponsorship; encouragement, fostering; aid; stimulation; furtherance; boosting. (b) *(Gewinnung)* extraction.
**Forelle** *f* trout.
**forensisch** *adj Medizin* forensic.
**Form** *f* **-en** (a) form; *(Gestalt, Umriß)* shape. **in** ~ **von Dragees** in the form of pills; **seine** ~ **verlieren/aus der** ~ **geraten** to lose its shape; **einer Sache** *(dat)* ~ **(und Gestalt) geben** *(lit, fig)* to give sth shape; **feste** ~ **annehmen** *(fig)* to take shape; **gewalttätige** ~**en annehmen** *(fig)* to become violent. (b) *(Umgangs~en)* ~**en** *pl* manners *pl*; **die** ~ **wahren** to observe the proprieties; **der** ~ **wegen** for the sake of form; **in aller** ~ formally. (c) *(Kondition)* form. **in** ~ **bleiben/kommen** to keep/get (oneself) in shape; **groß in** ~ in great form; **außer** ~ off form. (d) *(Gieß~)* mould; *(Kuchen~)* baking tin *(Brit)* or pan *(US)*; *(Hut~, Schuh~)* block.
**formal** *adj* formal; *Besitzer, Grund* technical.
**Form|aldehyd** *m no pl* formaldehyde.
**formalisieren*** *vt* to formalize.
**Formalität** *f* formality. **alle** ~**en erledigen** to go through all the formalities.
**Format** *nt* **-e** (a) format. (b) *(Persönlichkeit)* stature. (c) *(fig: Niveau)* class *(col)*, quality.
**formatieren** *vti* *(Comp)* to format.
**Formation** *f* formation; *(Gruppe)* group.
**Form-:** **f**~**bar** *adj* *(lit, fig)* malleable; **f**~**beständig** *adj* **f**~**beständig sein** to hold its shape; ~**blatt** *nt* form.
**Formel** *f* **-n** formula; *(von Eid etc)* wording; *(Floskel)* set phrase. ~ **Eins** *(Sport)* Formula One; **etw auf eine** ~ **bringen** to reduce sth to a formula.
**formelhaft** *adj Sprache, Stil* stereotyped. ~ **reden** to talk in set phrases.
**formell** *adj* formal.
**formen** *vt* to form, to shape; *Eisen* to mould; *Wörter* to articulate.
**formenreich** *adj* with a great variety of forms.
**Form-:** ~**fehler** *m* irregularity; *(gesellschaftlich)* breach of etiquette; ~**gebung** *f* *(geh)* design.
**formieren*** **1** *vt Truppen* to draw up; *Kolonne, Zug* to form (into); *(bilden)* to form. **2** *vr* to form up.
**Formierung** *f* formation; *(von Truppen)* drawing-up.
**förmlich** *adj* (a) *(formell)* formal. (b) *(regelrecht)* positive. **ich hätte** ~ **weinen können** I really could have cried; **er strahlte** ~ **vor Freude** he was positively beaming with joy.

**Förmlichkeit** *f* formality. **bitte keine** ~**en!** please don't stand on ceremony.

**formlos** *adj* **(a)** shapeless. **(b)** *(zwanglos)* informal, casual. **(c)** *(Admin) Antrag* unaccompanied by a form/any forms.

**Form-:** ~**sache** *f* formality; **f**~**schön** *adj* beautifully shaped, elegantly proportioned; ~**schönheit** *f* elegant proportions *pl*; ~**tief** *nt* loss of form; **sich in einem** ~**tief befinden** to be badly off form.

**Formular** *nt* **-e** form.

**formulieren*** *vt* to word, to phrase. **... wenn ich es mal so** ~ **darf** ... if I might put it like that.

**Formulierung** *f* wording. **eine bestimmte** ~ a particular phrase.

**Formung** f **(a)** *no pl (das Formen)* forming, shaping; *(von Eisen)* moulding; *(von Wörtern)* articulation. **(b)** *(Form)* shape.

**formvollendet** *adj* perfect; *Vase etc* perfectly formed.

**forsch** *adj* dynamic.

**forschen** *vi* to search *(nach* for); *(Forschung betreiben)* to research *(über +acc* on or into*)*.

**forschend** *adj* inquiring; *(musternd)* searching.

**Forscher(in** *f***)** *m* - **(a)** researcher; *(in Naturwissenschaften)* research scientist. **(b)** *(Forschungsreisender)* explorer.

**Forschung** *f* research *no pl.* **verschiedene** ~**en** various studies; ~ **und Lehre** research and teaching; ~ **und Entwicklung** research and development, R & D.

**Forschungs-** *in cpds* research; ~**auftrag** *m* research assignment; ~**reise** *f* expedition; ~**reisende(r)** *mf decl as adj* explorer.

**Forst** *m* **-e(n)** forest.

**Forst|amt** *nt* forestry office.

**Förster(in** *f***)** *m* - forest warden or ranger *(US).*

**Forstwirtschaft** *f* forestry.

**Fort** [foːɐ] *nt* **-s** fort.

**fort** *adv* **(a)** *(weg)* away; *(verschwunden)* gone. ~ **mit ihm/damit!** away with him/it!; **er ist** ~ he has left or gone; **weit** ~ far away. **(b)** *(weiter)* on. **und so** ~ and so on; **in einem** ~ incessantly.

**fort-** *pref in cpd vbs (weg)* away; *siehe* **weg-**.

**Fort-:** **f**~**begeben*** *vr sep irreg (geh)* to depart; ~**bestand** *m no pl* continued existence; *(von Gattung etc)* survival; **f**~**bestehen*** *vi sep irreg* to continue to exist; **f**~**bewegen*** *vtr sep* to move; ~**bewegung** *f no pl* locomotion; **f**~**bilden** *vt sep* **jdn/sich f**~**bilden** to continue sb's/one's education; ~**bildung** *f no pl* further education; **berufliche** ~**bildung** further vocational training; ~**bildungskurs(us)** *m* in-service training course; **f**~**bleiben** *vi sep irreg aux sein* to stay away; ~**bleiben** *nt no pl* absence; **f**~**bringen** *vt sep irreg* to take away; *(zur Reparatur, Reinigung etc)* to take in; *Brief, Paket etc* to post; ~**dauer** *f* continuance, continuation; **f**~**dauern** *vi sep* to continue; **f**~**dauernd** *adj* continuing; *(in der Vergangenheit)* continued; **2** *adv* constantly, continuously; **f**~**entwickeln*** *vtr sep* to continue to develop; ~**entwicklung** *f no pl* further development; **f**~**fahren** *sep* **1** *vi* **(a)** *aux sein (wegfahren)* to go away; *(Fahrer)* to drive off; *(abfahren)* to leave, to go; *(einen Ausflug machen)* to go out; **(b)** *aux haben or sein (weitermachen)* to continue; **f**~**fahren, etw zu tun** to con tinue doing sth or to do sth; **2** *vt Wagen* to drive away; ~**fall** *m no pl; (von Beihilfe etc)* discontinuance; **f**~**fallen** *vi sep irreg aux sein (ausgelassen werden)* to be omitted; *(Bedenken etc)* to vanish; *(Zuschuß etc)* to be discontinued; **f**~**führen** *vt sep* **(a)** *(fortsetzen)* to continue, to carry on; **(b)**

*(wegführen)* to take away; ~**führung** *f* continuation; ~**gang** *m no pl* **(a)** *(Weggang)* departure *(aus* from*)*; **(b)** *(Verlauf)* progress; **f**~**gehen** *vi sep aux sein* to go away, to leave; **f**~**geschritten** *adj* advanced; **er kam zu f**~**geschrittener Stunde** he came at a late hour; ~**geschrittenenkurs(us)** *m* advanced course; **f**~**gesetzt** *adj* constant; *Betrug etc* repeated; **f**~**jagen** *sep* **1** *vt* to chase out *(aus, von* of*)*; *(hinauswerfen)* to throw out *(aus, von* of*)*; **2** *vi aux sein* to race off; ~**kommen** *nt (lit, fig)* progress; **f**~**kommen** *vi aux sein* **(a)** to get away; **mach, daß du f**~**kommst!** be off! **(b)** *(vorankommen)* to get on (well); **f**~**lassen** *vt sep* **(a)** *(weggehen lassen)* **jdn f**~**lassen** to let sb go; **(b)** *(auslassen)* to leave out, to omit; **f**~**laufen** *vi sep irreg aux sein* to run away; **f**~**laufend** *adj Handlung* ongoing *no adv; Zahlungen* regular; *(andauernd)* continual; **f**~**laufend numeriert** consecutively numbered; **f**~**machen** *vr sep (col)* to clear out *(col);* **f**~**nehmen** *vt sep irreg* to take away *(jdm* from sb*)*; **f**~**pflanzen** *vr sep (Mensch)* to reproduce; *(Schall, Licht)* to travel; ~**pflanzung** *f no pl* reproduction; **f**~**räumen** *vt sep* to clear away; **f**~**reißen** *vt sep irreg* to tear away; *(Menge, Flut, Strom)* to sweep or carry away; *(fig)* to carry away; **jdn/etw mit sich f**~**reißen** *(lit)* to carry or sweep sb/sth along.

**Forts.** = **Fortsetzung.**

**fort-:** ~**schaffen** *vt sep* to remove; ~**scheren** *vr sep (col)* to clear off *(aus* out of*) (col);* ~**schicken** *vt sep* to send away; **f**~**schreiten** *vi sep irreg aux sein* to progress, to advance; *(Zeit)* to march on; *siehe* ~**geschritten;** ~**schreitend** *adj* progressive; *Alter, Wissenschaft* advancing.

**Fortschritt** *m* advance, progress *no pl.* **gute** ~**e machen** to make good progress; **dem** ~ **dienen** to further progress.

**fortschrittlich** *adj* progressive *(auch Pol)*; *Mensch, Ideen auch* forward-looking.

**fortschrittsgläubig** *adj:* ~ **sein** to believe in progress.

**Fort-:** **f**~**setzen** *sep* **1** *vt* to continue; *(nach Unterbrechung auch)* to resume; **2** *vr (zeitlich)* to continue; *(räumlich)* to extend; ~**setzung** *f* **(a)** continuation; *(nach Unterbrechung auch)* resumption; **(b)** *(Rad, TV)* episode; *(eines Romans)* instalment *(Brit)*, installment *(US);* „~**setzung folgt"** ''to be continued''; ~**setzungsroman** *m* serialized novel; **f**~**stehlen** *vr sep irreg (geh)* to steal away; **f**~**währen** *vi sep (geh)* to continue, to persist; **f**~**während** *adj no pred* constant, continual; **f**~**wirken** *vi sep* to continue to have an effect; **f**~**ziehen** *sep irreg* **1** *vt* to pull away, to drag away; **2** *vi aux sein* **(a)** to move on; **(b)** *(von einem Ort)* to move away *(aus* from*)*.

**Forum** *nt, pl* **Foren** forum.

**Forumsdiskussion** *f* forum (discussion).

**Fossil** *nt* **-ien** [-iən] fossil.

**Foto** *nt* **-s** photo(graph), snap(shot) *(col)*. **ein** ~ **machen** to take a photo(graph).

**Foto-** *in cpds* photo; ~**album** *nt* photograph album; ~**amateur** *m* amateur photographer; ~**apparat** *m* camera; ~**atelier** *nt* (photographic) studio; ~**ecke** *f* (photo or mounting) corner; ~**gelegenheit** *f* photo opportunity.

**fotogen** *adj* photogenic.

**Fotograf** *m* photographer.

**Fotografie** f **(a)** photography. **(b)** *(Bild)* photo(graph).

**fotografieren*** **1** *vt* to photograph, to take a photo(graph) of. **sich** ~ **lassen** to have one's

photo(graph) taken. **2** *vi* to take photo(graph)s.
**Fotografin** *f* photographer.
**fotografisch** *adj* photographic.
**Foto-:** ~**journalist** *m* photojournalist; ~**kopie** *f* photocopy; ~**kopierer** *(col)* *m,* ~**kopiergerät** *nt* photocopier; **f**~**kopieren*** *vt insep* to photocopy; ~**labor** *nt* darkroom; ~**modell** *nt* photographic model; ~**reporter** *m* press photographer; ~**safari** *f* photographic safari; ~**termin** *m* photo call.
**Fötus** *m* **-, Föten** foetus, fetus *(esp US)*.
**Foul** [faul] *nt* **-s** *(Sport)* foul.
**Foul|elfmeter** ['faul-] *m (Ftbl)* penalty (kick).
**foulen** ['faulən] *vti (Sport)* to foul.
**Foulspiel** ['faul-] *nt (Sport)* foul play.
**Fox** *m* **-e** **(a)** *(auch* ~**terrier)** fox-terrier. **(b)** *(auch* ~**trott)** foxtrot.
**Foyer** [foa'je:] *nt* **-s** foyer; *(in Hotel auch)* lobby.
**FPÖ** = **Freiheitliche Partei Österreichs** Austrian Freedom Party.
**Fr.** = **(a) Frau** Mrs, Ms; *(unverheiratet)* Miss, Ms. **(b) Freitag** Fri. **(c) Franken** fr.
**Fracht** *f* **-en** freight *no pl*; *(von Flugzeug, Schiff auch)* cargo; *(~preis auch)* freightage *no pl*.
**Frachtbrief** *m* consignment note, waybill.
**Frachter** *m* - freighter.
**Fracht-:** **f**~**frei** *adj* carriage paid *or* free; ~**gut** *nt* freight *no pl*; ~**kosten** *pl* freight charges *pl*; ~**raum** *m* hold; *(Ladefähigkeit)* cargo space; ~**schiff** *nt* cargo ship, freighter.
**Frack** *m* **-̈e** tails *pl*, tail coat. **im** ~ in tails.
**Frack-:** ~**hemd** *nt* dress shirt; ~**sausen** *nt:* ~**sausen haben** *(col)* to be in a funk *(col)*; ~**weste** *f* waistcoat *(Brit)* or vest *(US)* *worn with tails*; ~**zwang** *m* requirement to wear tails; „~**zwang**" "tails".
**Frage** *f* **-n** question. **eine** ~ **zu etw** a question on sth; **jdm eine** ~ **stellen** to ask sb a question; **auf eine dumme** ~ **bekommt man eine dumme Antwort** *(prov)* ask a silly question (get a silly answer) *(prov)*; **das ist (doch sehr) die** ~ that's (just) the question; **das ist die große** ~ that's the sixty-four thousand dollar question *(col)*; **das ist gar keine** ~, **das steht außer** ~ there's no question about it; **ohne** ~ without question *or* doubt; **in** ~ **kommen** to be possible; **sollte er für diese Stelle in** ~ **kommen,** ... if he should be considered for this post ...; **für jdn/etw nicht in** ~ **kommen** to be out of the question for sb/sth; **in** ~ **kommend** possible; *Bewerber* worth considering; **etw in** ~ **stellen** to question sth; **eine** ~ **der Zeit** a question *or* matter of time.
**Fragebogen** *m* questionnaire; *(Formular)* form.
**fragen 1** *vti* to ask. **nach** *or* **wegen** *(col)* **jdm** ~ to ask for sb; *(nach jds Befinden)* to ask after sb; **ich fragte sie nach den Kindern** I asked her how the children were doing; **nach Arbeit/Post** ~ to ask whether there is/was any work/mail; **nach den Ursachen** ~ to inquire as to the causes; **nicht nach den Folgen** ~ not to care about the consequences; **wegen etw** ~ to ask about sth; **das frage ich dich!** I could ask you the same; **da fragst du noch?** you still have to ask?; **frag nicht so dumm!** don't ask silly questions; **da fragst du mich zuviel** *(col)* I really couldn't say; **man wird ja wohl noch** ~ **dürfen** *(col)* I only asked *(col)*; **wenn ich (mal)** ~ **darf?** if I might ask?; **ohne lange zu** ~ without asking a lot of questions.
**2** *vr* to wonder. **das/da frage ich mich** I wonder; **das frage ich mich auch** that's just what I was wondering; **es/man fragt sich, ob** ... it's questionable/one wonders whether ...; **da muß man sich** ~, **ob** ... you can't help wondering if ...

**fragend** *adj* questioning, inquiring.
**Frager(in** *f)* *m* - questioner.
**Fragerei** *f* questions *pl*.
**Frage-:** ~**steller(in** *f)* *m* - questioner; *(Interviewer)* interviewer; ~**stellung** *f* **(a)** formulation of a/the question; **(b)** *(Frage)* question; ~**stunde** *f* *(Parl)* question time; ~**zeichen** *nt* question mark *(auch fig)*; **dastehen/dasitzen wie ein** ~**zeichen** *(col)* to slouch.
**fraglich** *adj* **(a)** doubtful, questionable. **(b)** *attr (betreffend)* in question.
**fraglos** *adv* undoubtedly, unquestionably.
**Fragment** *nt* fragment.
**fragmentarisch** *adj* fragmentary.
**fragwürdig** *adj* dubious.
**Fragwürdigkeit** *f* dubiousness.
**Fraktion** *f* **(a)** *(Pol)* ≈ parliamentary *or* congressional *(US)* party; *(Sondergruppe)* group, faction. **(b)** *(Chem)* fraction.
**Fraktions-** *in cpds (Pol)* party; **f**~**los** *adj* independent; ~**mitglied** *nt* member of a parliamentary *etc* party; ~**sitzung** *f* party meeting; ~**vorsitzende(r)** *mf* party whip; ~**zwang** *m* requirement to follow the party whip.
**Fraktur** *f* **(a)** *(Typ)* Gothic print. ~ **reden** *(col)* to be blunt. **(b)** *(Med)* fracture.
**Franc** [frãː] *m* **-, -s** franc.
**frank** *adv:* ~ **und frei** frankly, openly.
**Franken**[1] *nt* Franconia.
**Franken**[2] *m* **- (Schweizer)** ~ (Swiss) franc.
**frankieren*** *vt* to stamp; *(mit Maschine)* to frank.
**Frankiermaschine** *f* franking machine.
**Frankierung** *f* franking.
**fränkisch** *adj* Franconian.
**franko** *adj inv (Comm)* carriage paid; *(von Postsendungen)* post-free, post-paid.
**Frankreich** *nt* France.
**Franse** *f* **-n** (loose) thread; *(von Haar)* strand of hair. ~**n** *(als Besatz)* fringe; *(Pony)* fringe *(Brit)*, bangs *pl (US)*.
**fransen** *vi* to fray (out).
**Franz** *m* **-'** *or* **-ens** Francis.
**Franzbranntwein** *m* alcoholic liniment.
**Franzose** *m* **-n** Frenchman; *(Junge)* French boy.
**Französin** *f* Frenchwoman; *(Mädchen)* French girl.
**französisch** *adj* French. **die** ~**e Schweiz** French-speaking Switzerland; ~**es Bett** double bed; **sich (auf)** ~ **empfehlen** *(col)* to leave without saying good-bye/paying; *siehe* **deutsch.**
**Französisch(e)** *nt decl as adj* French; *siehe* **Deutsch(e).**
**frappant** *adj* striking.
**frappieren*** *vt (verblüffen)* to astound.
**frappierend** *adj* striking.
**Fräse** *f* **-n** *(Werkzeug)* milling cutter; *(für Holz)* moulding cutter; *(Boden~)* rotary hoe.
**fräsen** *vt* to mill; *Holz* to mould.
**fraß** *pret of* **fressen.**
**Fraß** *m* **-e** **(a)** **etw einem Tier zum** ~ **vorwerfen** to feed sth to an animal; **jdn den Kritikern zum** ~ **vorwerfen** to leave sb to the mercy of the critics. **(b)** *(pej col: Essen)* muck *(col)* *no indef art.* **(c)** *(Abfressen)* **vom** ~ **befallen** eaten away.
**fraternisieren*** *vi* to fraternize.
**Fratze** *f* **-n** *(Grimasse)* grimace; *(col: Gesicht)* mug *(col)*; *(fig: Zerrbild)* caricature. **jdm eine** ~ **schneiden** to pull *or* make a face at sb.
**Frau** *f* **-en** **(a)** woman; *(Ehe~)* wife. **jdn zur** ~ **haben** to be married to sb. **(b)** *(Anrede, mit Namen)* Mrs, Ms; *(für eine unverheiratete ~)* Miss, Ms. ~ **Doktor** doctor; ~ **Vorsitzende** Madam Chairman.

**Fräuchen** nt dim of **Frau** (col) (a) (Ehefrau) little woman. (b) (Herrin von Hund) mistress.

**Frauen-** in cpds women's; (einer bestimmten Frau) woman's; (Sport auch) ladies'; ~**arbeit** f female labour (Brit) or labor (US); ~**arzt** m gynaecologist (Brit), gynecologist (US); ~**beruf** m career for women; **f~bewegt** adj feminist; ~**bewegung** f feminist movement; **f~feindlich** adj anti-women pred; Mensch, Verhalten auch misogynous; ~**haus** nt women's refuge; ~**heilkunde** f gynaecology (Brit), gynecology (US); ~**held** m lady-killer; ~**klinik** f gynaecological (Brit) or gynecological (US) clinic; ~**kloster** nt convent; ~**rechtlerin** f feminist; **f~rechtlerisch** adj feminist; **sich f~rechtlerisch betätigen** to be involved in women's rights or (in der heutigen Zeit auch) women's lib; ~**wahlrecht** nt vote for women; ~**zeitschrift** f women's magazine; ~**zentrum** nt women's advice centre; ~**zimmer** nt (old) woman; (hum, pej) female (col), broad (US col).

**Fräulein** nt - or -s (a) young lady. **ein altes** or **älteres** ~ an elderly spinster. (b) (Anrede) Miss. (c) (Verkäuferin) assistant (Brit), sales clerk (US); (Kellnerin) waitress. „~!" "Miss!"; **das** ~ **vom Amt** (dated) the switchboard girl.

**fräulich** adj feminine; (reif) womanly no adv.

**frech** adj cheeky (esp Brit), fresh (esp US); Lüge bare-faced no adv. ~ **wie Oskar sein** (col) to be a little monkey (col).

**Frechdachs** m (col) cheeky monkey (col).

**Frechheit** f (a) no pl impudence, cheek (esp Brit). **die** ~ **besitzen, zu** ... to have the impudence to ... (b) (Äußerung, Handlung) piece of cheek (esp Brit) or impudence. **sich** (dat) **einige** ~**en erlauben** to be a bit cheeky (esp Brit) or fresh (esp US).

**Freesie** ['fre:ziə] f freesia.

**Fregatte** f frigate.

**Fregattenkapitän** m commander.

**frei** adj (a) free; Blick clear. ~**e Hand haben** to have a free hand; **aus der** ~**en Hand zeichnen** to draw freehand; **jdm zur** ~**en Verfügung stehen** to be completely at sb's disposal; **aus** ~**en Stücken** or ~**em Willen** of one's own free will; ~ **nach** ... based on ...; ~ **nach Goethe** (Zitat) to adapt a phrase of Goethe's; **ich bin so** ~ (form) may I?; **von Kiel nach Hamburg hatten wir** ~**e Fahrt** we had a clear run from Kiel to Hamburg; **für etw** ~**e Fahrt geben** (fig) to give sth the go-ahead; **der** ~**e Fall** (Phys) free fall; **der Film ist** ~ **ab 16 (Jahren)** the film may be seen by people over (the age of) 16; **sich von etw** ~ **machen** to free oneself from sth.

(b) Schriftsteller etc freelance; (nicht staatlich) private. ~**er Beruf** independent profession; **als** ~**er Mitarbeiter arbeiten** to work freelance; ~**er Markt** open market; ~**e Marktwirtschaft** free market economy; **die** ~**e Wirtschaft** private enterprise.

(c) (ohne Hilfsmittel) Rede extemporary. ~ **schwimmen** to swim unaided or on one's own; ~ **in der Luft schweben** to hang in mid-air; **ein Vortrag in** ~**er Rede** a talk given without notes; ~ **sprechen** to extemporize.

(d) (verfügbar) Mittel, Geld available; Zeit, Mensch free. **morgen/Mittwoch ist** ~ tomorrow/Wednesday is a holiday; **einen Tag** ~ **nehmen/haben** to take/have a day off; **ist hier** or **ist dieser Platz noch** ~? is this seat free?; „**Zimmer** ~" "vacancies"; **eine Stelle wird** ~ a position is becoming vacant; **einen Platz** ~ **machen** (aufstehen) to vacate a seat; **einen Platz für jdn** ~ **lassen** to leave a seat for sb.

(e) (offen) open. **unter** ~**em Himmel** in the open (air); **im** ~**en Raum** (Astron) in (outer) space; **eine**

**Frage im** ~**en Raum stehenlassen** to leave a question hanging; **auf** ~**er Strecke** (Rail) between stations; (Aut) on the road.

(f) (unbekleidet) bare. **sich** ~ **machen** (beim Arzt) to take one's clothes off, to strip; ~ **lassen** to leave bare.

**Frei-:** ~**bad** nt open-air swimming pool, lido; **f~bekommen*** vt sep irreg (a) **jdn f~bekommen** to get sb freed or released; (b) **einen Tag f~bekommen** to get a day off; ~**berufler(in** f) m - self-employed person; **f~beruflich** adj self-employed; ~**betrag** m tax allowance; ~**bier** nt free beer; ~**brief** m (fig) licence (Brit), license (US).

**Freier** m - (a) (dated, hum) suitor. (b) (col: von Dirne) (prostitute's) client, john (US col).

**Freie(s)** nt decl as adj **im** ~**n** in the open (air); **ins** ~ **gehen** to go outside.

**Frei-:** ~**exemplar** nt free copy; ~**fahrschein** m free ticket; ~**flug** m free flight; ~**frau** f baroness (by marriage); ~**gabe** f siehe ~**geben** release; lifting of controls (gen on); opening; passing; **f~geben** sep irreg **1** vt to release (an +acc to); Preise to lift controls on; Straße, Strecke to open; Film to pass; **etw zum Verkauf f~geben** to allow sth to be sold on the open market; **jdm den Weg f~geben** to let sb past; **2** vi **jdm f~geben** to give sb a holiday; **f~gebig** adj generous; ~**gebigkeit** f generosity; ~**gehege** nt open-air enclosure; ~**gepäck** nt baggage allowance; **f~haben** vi sep irreg to have a holiday; **eine Stunde f~haben** (Sch) to have a free period; ~**hafen** m free port; **f~halten** sep irreg **1** vt (a) (nicht besetzen) to keep free or clear; (b) (reservieren) to keep, to save; (c) (bezahlen) to pay for; **sich von jdm f~halten lassen** to let sb pay for one; **2** vr **sich von etw f~halten** to avoid sth; von Verpflichtungen to keep oneself free of sth; ~**handel** m free trade; ~**handelszone** f free trade area; **f~händig** adj Zeichnung freehand; **f~händig radfahren** to ride with no hands; **f~hängend** adj attr suspended.

**Freiheit** f freedom; (Pol auch) liberty; **in** ~ (dat) **sein** to be free; **jdn in** ~ **setzen** to set sb free; **jdm die** ~ **schenken** to give sb his/her etc freedom; **dichterische** ~ poetic licence (Brit) or license (US); **alle** ~**en haben** to have all the freedom possible; **die** ~ **haben, etw zu tun** to be free or at liberty to do sth; **sich** (dat) **die** ~ **nehmen, etw zu tun** to take the liberty of doing sth.

**freiheitlich** adj liberal; Verfassung based on the principle of liberty; Demokratie free. ~**demokratisch** free democratic.

**Freiheits-:** ~**beraubung** f (Jur) wrongful deprivation of personal liberty; ~**bewegung** f freedom movement; ~**drang** m no pl urge or desire for freedom; ~**entzug** m imprisonment; ~**kampf** m fight for freedom; ~**kämpfer** m freedom-fighter; ~**rechte** pl civil rights and liberties pl; ~**statue** f Statue of Liberty; ~**strafe** f prison sentence.

**Frei-:** **f~heraus** adv candidly, frankly; ~**herr** m baron; ~**karte** f free or complimentary ticket; **f~kaufen** vt sep **jdn/sich f~kaufen** to buy sb's/one's freedom; **f~kommen** vi sep irreg aus sein (entkommen) to get out (aus of); (befreit werden) to be released or freed (aus, von from); ~**körperkultur** f no pl nudism; ~**landgemüse** nt outdoor vegetables; **f~lassen** vt sep irreg to set free, to free; (aus Haft auch) to release; Hund to let off the lead; ~**lassung** f release; (von Sklaven) setting free; ~**lauf** m (Tech) neutral; (bei Fahrrad) freewheel; **f~laufen** vr sep irreg (Sport) to get free; **f~laufend** adj Huhn free-range; **Eier von f~laufenden Hühnern**

free-range eggs; **f~lebend** *adj* living free; **f~legen** *vt sep* to expose; *Ruinen, Trümmer* to uncover; **~legung** *f siehe* *vt* exposure; uncovering.

**freilich** *adv* (a) *(allerdings)* admittedly. (b) *(esp S Ger: natürlich)* of course.

**Freilicht-** *in cpds* open-air; **~bühne** *f* open-air theatre *(Brit)* or theater *(US)*.

**Frei-:** **f~machen** *sep* 1 *vt* to stamp; *(mit Frankiermaschine)* to frank; 2 *vi* to take time off; **ich habe eine Woche f~gemacht** I took a week off; 3 *vr* to take time off; **~maurer** *m* Mason, Freemason.

**Freimut** *m no pl* frankness, honesty.

**freimütig** *adj* frank, honest.

**Freimütigkeit** *f* frankness, honesty.

**Frei-:** **~raum** *m (fig)* freedom *no art (zu* for*)*; **die Universität ist kein gesellschaftlicher ~raum** university isn't a social vacuum; **f~schaffend** *adj attr* freelance; **~schaffende(r)** *mf decl as adj* freelance; **~schärler** *m -* guerrilla; **f~setzen** *vt sep* to release; *(euph) Arbeitskräfte* to make redundant; *(vorübergehend)* to lay off; **~setzung** *f* release; *(euph)* dismissal; *(vorübergehend)* laying off; **f~sprechen** *vt sep irreg* to acquit; **jdn von einem Verdacht f~sprechen** to clear sb of suspicion; **~spruch** *m* acquittal; **es ergeht ~spruch** the verdict is "not guilty"; **f~stehen** *vi sep irreg* (a) **es steht jdm f~, etw zu tun** sb is free to do sth; **das steht Ihnen völlig f~** that is completely up to you; (b) *(leerstehen)* to stand empty; **~stehend** *adj Haus* detached; **f~stellen** *vt sep* (a) *(anheimstellen)* **jdm etw f~stellen** to leave sth (up) to sb; (b) *(befreien)* to exempt.

**Freistil-** *in cpds* freestyle.

**Frei-:** **~stoß** *m (Ftbl)* free kick; **~stunde** *f* free hour; *(Sch)* free period.

**Freitag** *m* Friday; *siehe* **Dienstag**.

**freitags** *adv* on Fridays.

**Frei-:** **~tod** *m* suicide; **f~tragend** *adj* self-supporting; *Brücke* cantilever; **~übung** *f* exercise; **~umschlag** *m* reply-paid envelope.

**freiweg** ['frai'vɛk] *adv* openly; *(freiheraus)* straight out, frankly.

**Frei-:** **~wild** *nt (fig)* fair game; **f~willig** *adj* voluntary; *Versicherung, Unterricht* optional; **sich f~willig melden** to volunteer *(zu, für* for*)*; **~willige(r)** *mf decl as adj* volunteer; **~zeichen** *nt (Telec)* ringing tone.

**Freizeit** *f* (a) free *or* leisure time. (b) *(Zusammenkunft)* weekend/holiday course.

**Freizeit-:** **~beschäftigung** *f* leisure activity; **~droge** *f* recreational drug; **~gestaltung** *f* organization of one's leisure time; **~kleidung** *f* casual clothes *pl*; *(Warengattung)* leisurewear *no pl*.

**Frei-:** **f~zügig** *adj* (a) *(reichlich) Gebrauch* liberal; (b) *(moralisch)* permissive; **~zügigkeit** *f siehe adj* (a) liberalness; (b) permissiveness; (c) *(Ortsungebundenheit)* freedom of movement.

**fremd** *adj* (a) *(unbekannt)* strange; *(ausländisch)* foreign; *Planeten* other; *Welt* different. **jdm ~ sein** to be foreign *or* alien to sb; **es ist mir ~, wie ...** I don't understand how ...; **ich bin hier ~** I'm a stranger here; **sich** *(dat)* **~ werden** to become strangers; **sich ~ fühlen** to feel like a stranger. (b) *(andern gehörig)* someone else's; *Bank, Firma* different; *(Comm, Pol)* outside *attr*. **unter ~em Namen** under an assumed name; **in ~e Hände übergehen** to come under outside control.

**Fremd-:** **f~artig** *adj* strange; *(exotisch)* exotic; **~artigkeit** *f siehe adj* strangeness; exoticism; **~bestäubung** *f* cross-fertilization.

**Fremde** *f no pl (liter)* **die ~** foreign parts *pl*; **in die ~**

gehen to go to foreign parts.

**Fremden-:** **f~feindlich** *adj* xenophobic; **~führer** *m* (tourist) guide; *(Buch)* guide(book); **~legion** *f* Foreign Legion; **~verkehr** *m* tourism *no def art*; **~zimmer** *nt* guest room; **„~zimmer"** "rooms to let" *(Brit)*, "rooms for rent" *(US)*.

**Fremde(r)** *mf decl as adj* stranger; *(Ausländer)* foreigner; *(Admin, Pol)* alien; *(Tourist)* visitor.

**Fremd-:** **f~gehen** *vi sep irreg aux sein (col)* to be unfaithful; **~kapital** *nt* outside capital; **~körper** *m* foreign body; *(fig)* alien element; **f~ländisch** *adj* foreign *no adv*; *(exotisch)* exotic.

**Fremdling** *m (liter)* stranger.

**Fremdsprache** *f* foreign language.

**Fremdsprachen-:** **~korrespondentin,** **~sekretärin** *f* bilingual secretary; **~unterricht** *m* language teaching.

**Fremd-:** **f~sprachig** *adj* in a foreign language; **f~sprachlich** *adj* **f~sprachlicher Unterricht** (foreign) language teaching; **~wort** *nt* foreign word; **Rücksichtnahme ist für ihn ein ~wort** *(fig)* he's never heard of the word consideration.

**frenetisch** *adj* frenetic, frenzied.

**Frequenz** *f* frequency; *(Stärke)* numbers *pl*.

**Fresko** *nt, pl* **Fresken** fresco.

**Fressalien** [-iən] *pl (col)* grub *sing (col)*.

**Fresse** *f* -n *(col!) (Mund)* gob *(col!)*; *(Gesicht)* mug *(col)*. **die ~ halten** to shut one's face *(col!)*.

**fressen** *pret* **fraß,** *ptp* **gefressen** 1 *vi* (a) to feed, to eat; *(col!: Menschen)* to eat; *(gierig)* to guzzle. **jdm aus der Hand ~** *(fig col)* to eat out of sb's hand. (b) *(zerstören)* to eat away *(an etw (dat)* sth*)*.

2 *vt (Tier, col!: Mensch)* to eat; *(sich ernähren von)* to feed on; *(col!: gierig essen)* to guzzle, to scoff; *(col: verbrauchen) Benzin, Ersparnisse* to eat up. **Kilometer ~** to burn up the miles; **ein Loch in den Geldbeutel ~** to make a big hole in one's pocket; **ich habe dich zum F~ gern** *(col)* you're good enough to eat *(col)*; **jdn/etw gefressen haben** *(col)* to have had one's fill of sb/sth; **jetzt hat er es endlich gefressen** *(col)* he's got it at last *(col)*; **einen Narren an jdm/etw gefressen haben** to dote on sb/sth.

3 *vr* (a) *(sich bohren)* to eat one's way *(in +acc* into*)*. (b) **sich voll/satt ~** to gorge oneself.

**Fressen** *nt -* (a) *no pl* food; *(col!)* grub *(col)*. (b) *(col!: Gelage)* blow-out *(col)*.

**Fresser** *m -* *(Tier)* eater; *(col!: gieriger Mensch)* pig *(col)*, greedyguts *(col)*.

**Fresserei** *f no pl (col) (übermäßiges Essen)* guzzling; *(Gefräßigkeit)* gluttony.

**Freß-:** **~gier** *f* voraciousness; *(pej: von Menschen)* gluttony; **~napf** *m* feeding bowl; **~paket** *nt (col)* food parcel; **~sack** *m (col!)* greedyguts *(col)*; **~sucht** *f (col)* gluttony; *(krankhaft)* craving for food.

**Frettchen** *nt* ferret.

**Freude** *f* -n pleasure; *(innig)* joy *(über +acc* at*)*. **~ an etw (dat) haben** to get *or* derive pleasure from sth; **~ am Leben haben** to enjoy life; **es ist mir eine ~, zu ...** it's a real pleasure for me to ...; **es macht ihnen keine/wenig ~** they don't enjoy it (at all)/much; **jdm eine ~ machen** *or* **bereiten** to make sb happy; **zu meiner großen ~** to my great delight; **aus Spaß an der ~** *(col)* for the fun *or* hell *(col)* of it; **mit ~n** with pleasure; **da kommt ~ auf** this is where the fun starts.

**Freuden-:** **~fest** *nt* celebration; **~feuer** *nt* bonfire; **~haus** *nt (dated, hum)* house of ill repute; **~mädchen** *nt (dated, hum)* lady of easy virtue *(euph)*, prostitute; **~tanz** *m* **einen ~tanz aufführen** to dance with joy; **~taumel** *m* ecstasy; **~tränen**

*pl* tears of joy.

**freudestrahlend** *adj no pred* beaming with delight.

**freudig** *adj* joyful; *(begeistert)* enthusiastic. **jdn ~ stimmen** to raise sb's spirits; **etw ~ erwarten** to look forward to sth with great pleasure; **~ überrascht sein** to have a delightful surprise.

**Freud-:** **f~los** *adj* joyless, cheerless; **~losigkeit** *f no pl* joylessness, cheerlessness.

**Freudsch** *adj attr* Freudian. **~e Fehlleistung, ~er Versprecher** Freudian slip.

**freuen 1** *vr* **(a)** to be glad *or* pleased *(über +acc* about*)*. **sich über ein Geschenk ~** to be pleased with a present; **er freut sich sehr an seinen Kindern** his children give him a lot of pleasure; **sich mit jdm ~** to share sb's happiness; **sich seines Lebens ~** to enjoy life. **(b) sich auf jdn/etw ~** to look forward to seeing sb/to sth; **sich zu früh ~** to get one's hopes up too soon. **2** *vt impers* to please. **es freut mich/ihn, daß ...** I'm/he's pleased *or* glad that ...; **es freut mich sehr, Ihre Bekanntschaft zu machen** *(form)* (I'm) pleased to meet you.

**Freund** *m* -**e** friend; *(Liebhaber)* boyfriend. **ein ~ der Kunst** an art-lover; **ein ~ der alten Musik** an early music enthusiast; **er ist kein ~ vieler Worte** he's a man of few words; **ich bin kein ~ von so etwas** I'm not one for that sort of thing.

**Freundchen** *nt (col)* my friend *(iro)*. **~! ~!** just watch it!

**Freundeskreis** *m* circle of friends.

**Freundin** *f* (woman/girl) friend; *(Liebhaberin)* girlfriend.

**freundlich** *adj* **(a)** friendly *no adv; Wetter etc* pleasant; *Zimmer, Farben* cheerful; *(Fin, Comm: günstig)* favourable *(Brit)*, favorable *(US)*. **jdn ~ behandeln** to be friendly towards sb; **bitte recht ~!** smile please! **(b)** *(liebenswürdig)* kind *(zu* to*)*. **würden Sie bitte so ~ sein und das tun?** would you be so kind as to do that?

**freundlicherweise** *adv* kindly.

**Freundlichkeit** *f* **(a)** *no pl siehe adj* friendliness; pleasantness; cheerfulness; favourableness. *(Brit)*, favorableness *(US)*. **würden Sie (wohl) die ~ haben, das zu tun?** would you be kind enough to do that? **(b)** *(Handlung, Gefälligkeit)* kindness. **jdm ein paar ~en sagen** to say a few kind words to sb.

**Freundschaft** *f* friendship. **in aller ~** in all friendliness; **da hört die ~ auf** *(col)* friendship doesn't go that far.

**freundschaftlich** *adj* friendly *no adv.* **jdm ~ gesinnt sein** to feel friendly towards sb; **jdm ~ auf die Schulter klopfen** to give sb a friendly slap on the back.

**Freundschafts-:** **~besuch** *m (Pol)* goodwill visit; **~dienst** *m*: **jdm einen ~dienst erweisen** to do sb a favour; **~preis** *m* (special) price for a friend; **~spiel** *nt (Sport)* friendly match, friendly; **~vertrag** *m (Pol)* treaty of friendship.

**Frevel** *m* - *(geh)* sin *(gegen* against*)*; *(fig)* crime *(an +dat* against*)*.

**frevelhaft** *adj (geh)* sinful; *Leichtsinn* wanton.

**Frevler(in** *f)* *m* - *(liter)* sinner.

**Friede** *m* -**ns**, **-n** *(old)* peace. **~ auf Erden** peace on earth; **~, Freude, Eierkuchen** *(col)* everything in the garden is lovely *(col)*.

**Frieden** *m* - peace. **im ~** in peacetime; **im ~ leben** to live in peace; **~ schließen** to make one's peace; *(Pol)* to make peace; **~ stiften** to make peace; **jdn in ~ lassen** to leave sb in peace; **um des lieben ~s willen** *(col)* for the sake of peace and quiet; **ich traue dem ~ nicht** *(col)* something (fishy) is going on *(col)*.

**Friedens-** *in cpds* peace; **~bemühung** *f usu pl* effort to achieve peace; **f~bewegt** *adj* pacifist; **~bewegung** *f* peace movement; **~kämpfer** *m* peace campaigner; **~nobelpreis** *m* Nobel peace prize; **~pfeife** *f* pipe of peace, peace pipe; **~politik** *f* policy of peace; **~richter** *m* justice of the peace, JP; **~schluß** *m* peace agreement; **~sicherung** *f* peacekeeping; **Maßnahmen zur ~sicherung** peacekeeping measures; **~stifter** *m* peacemaker; **~taube** *f* dove of peace; **~truppen** *pl* peacekeeping force; **~verhandlungen** *pl* peace talks *pl*; **~vertrag** *m* peace treaty.

**friedfertig** *adj* peaceable.

**Friedfertigkeit** *f* peaceableness.

**Friedhof** *m* cemetery; *(Kirchhof)* graveyard.

**friedlich** *adj* peaceful; *(friedfertig) Mensch* peaceable; *Charakter, Art* placid. **etw auf ~em Wege lösen** to solve sth by peaceful means; **damit er endlich ~ ist** *(col)* to keep him happy; **nun sei doch endlich ~!** *(col)* give it a rest! *(col)*.

**friedliebend** *adj* peace-loving.

**Friedrich** *m* Frederick. **seinen ~ Wilhelm unter etw** *(acc)* **setzen** *(col)* to put one's signature *or* name to sth.

**frieren** *pret* **fror**, *ptp* **gefroren 1** *vi* **(a)** *auch vt impers (sich kalt fühlen)* to be/get cold. **ich friere, es friert mich** I'm cold; **ich friere an den Zehen** my toes are cold. **(b)** *aux sein (gefrieren)* to freeze. **2** *vi impers* to freeze. **heute nacht hat es gefroren** it was below freezing last night.

**Fries** *m* -**e** *(Archit, Tex)* frieze.

**Friese** *m* (wk) **-n**, **-n**, **Friesin** *f* Fri(e)sian.

**frigid(e)** *adj* frigid.

**Frigidität** *f* frigidity.

**Frikadelle** *f (Cook)* rissole.

**Frikassee** *nt* -**s** *(Cook)* fricassee.

**frisch** *adj* **(a)** fresh; *(feucht) Farbe, Fleck* wet. **~e Eier** new-laid eggs; **~ gestrichen** newly painted; *(auf Schild)* wet paint; **~ gewaschen** clean; **das Bett ~ beziehen** to change the bed; **sich ~ machen** to freshen up; **mit ~en Kräften** with renewed strength; **das ist mir noch ~ in Erinnerung** that is still fresh in my memory; **jdn auf ~er Tat ertappen** to catch sb red-handed *or* in the act. **(b)** *(munter) Wesen, Art* bright, cheery; *(gesund) Aussehen* fresh. **~ und munter sein** *(col)* to be bright and cheery; **~ gewagt ist halb gewonnen** *(Prov)* a good start is half the battle. **(c)** *(kühl)* cool, chilly; *Luft, Wind auch* fresh.

**Frische** *f no pl* **(a)** freshness. **in alter ~** *(col)* as always. **(b)** *(Kühle)* coolness, chilliness; *(von Luft, Wind auch)* freshness.

**Frisch-:** **f~gebacken** *adj (col) Ehepaar* newly wed; **~haltebeutel** *m* airtight bag; **~haltefolie** *f* cling film; **~käse** *m* cream cheese; **~luft** *f* fresh air; **~milch** *f* fresh milk; **~wasser** *nt* fresh water; **f~weg** *adv (munter)* straight out *(col)*.

**Friseur(in** *f)* [fri'zøːɐ, -'zøːrɪn] *m* hairdresser.

**Friseursalon** *m* hairdresser's *(Brit)*, hairdressing salon.

**Friseuse** [fri'zøːzə] *f* hairdresser.

**Frisiercreme** *f* haircream.

**frisieren\* 1** *vt* **(a)** **jdn ~, jdm das Haar ~** to do sb's hair; **sie ist stets gut frisiert** her hair is always beautifully done. **(b)** *(col) Abrechnung* to fiddle; *Bericht* to doctor *(col)*. **die Bilanzen ~** to cook the books *(col) Auto* to tune, to soup up *(col)*. **2** *vr* to do one's hair.

**Frisier-:** **~spiegel** *m* dressing (table) mirror; **~tisch** *m* dressing table.

**Frisör** *m* -**e**, **Frisöse** *f* -**n** hairdresser.

**Frist** f -en (Zeitraum) period; (Zeitpunkt) deadline (zu for); (bei Rechnung) last date for payment. **eine ~ einhalten/verstreichen lassen** to meet a deadline/to let a deadline pass; (bei Rechnung) to pay/not to pay within the period stipulated; **innerhalb kürzester ~** without delay; **jdm eine ~ von vier Tagen geben** to give sb four days grace.

**fristen** vt **ein kümmerliches Dasein ~** to eke out a miserable existence; (Partei, Institution) to exist on the fringes.

**Fristen-:** ~**lösung,** ~**regelung** f law allowing the termination of a pregnancy within the first three months.

**Frist-:** f~**gerecht** adj within the period stipulated; f~**los** adj without notice; **jdn f~los entlassen** to dismiss sb without notice; ~**verlängerung** f extension.

**Frisur** f hairstyle.

**Friteuse** [fri'tø:zə] f chip pan (Brit), deep fat fryer.

**fritieren*** vt to (deep-)fry.

**Fritten** pl (col) chips pl (Brit), fries pl (esp US col).

**Frittenbude** f (col) chip shop (Brit), chippie (Brit col).

**frivol** [fri'vo:l] adj frivolous; (anzüglich) Witz, Bemerkung risqué.

**Frivolität** [frivoli'tɛ:t] f no pl frivolity; (von Witz etc) suggestiveness.

**Frl.** = **Fräulein** Miss, Ms.

**froh** adj happy; (dankbar auch) glad; (erfreut auch) glad, pleased. **über etw (acc) ~ sein** to be pleased with sth; **um etw ~ sein** to be grateful for sth; **seines Lebens nicht (mehr) ~ werden** not to enjoy life any more.

**frohgestimmt** adj (geh) happy, joyful (liter).

**fröhlich** 1 adj cheerful, merry. 2 adv (unbekümmert) blithely, gaily.

**Fröhlichkeit** f no pl happiness; (gesellige Stimmung) merriment, gaiety.

**Froh-:** f~**locken*** vi (geh) to rejoice (über +acc over, at); ~**natur** f (geh: Mensch) happy or cheerful soul; ~**sinn** m no pl cheerfulness; f~**sinnig** adj cheerful.

**fromm** adj (a) (gläubig) religious; Christ, Leben devout, pious; (scheinheilig) sanctimonious. ~**e Sprüche** pious words. (b) (old: gehorsam) docile. ~ **wie ein Lamm sein** to be as gentle as a lamb.

**Frömmelei** f (pej) false piety, sanctimoniousness.

**Frömmigkeit** f siehe **fromm (a)** religiousness; devoutness, piousness; sanctimoniousness.

**frömmlerisch** adj (pej) sanctimonious.

**frönen** vi +dat (geh) to indulge in.

**Fronleichnam** no art no pl Corpus Christi.

**Front** f -en front. **die hintere/rückwärtige ~** the back/the rear; **auf breiter ~** along a wide front; **an der ~** at the front; **klare ~en schaffen** (fig) to clarify the position; **~ gegen jdn/etw machen** to make a stand against sb/sth; **in ~ liegen/gehen** (Sport) to be in/take the lead.

**frontal** 1 adj no pred frontal; Zusammenstoß head-on. 2 adv frontally; zustammenstoßen head-on.

**Frontal-:** ~**angriff** m frontal attack; ~**zusammenstoß** m head-on collison.

**Front-:** ~**antrieb** m (Aut) front-wheel drive; ~**motor** m front (mounted) engine.

**fror** pret of **frieren**.

**Frosch** m -̈e frog. **einen ~ im Hals haben** (col) to have a frog in one's throat; **sei kein ~!** (col) be a sport!

**Frosch-:** ~**hüpfen** nt leapfrog; ~**könig** m Frog Prince; ~**mann** m frogman; ~**maul** nt (fig col) pout; ~**perspektive** f **etw aus der ~perspektive sehen** to get a worm's eye view of sth; ~**schenkel** m frog's leg.

**Frost** m -̈e (a) frost. **bei eisigem ~** in heavy frost; ~**(ab)bekommen** (Hände, Ohren) to get frostbitten. (b) (Med: Schüttel~) fit of shivering.

**Frost-:** f~**beständig** adj frost-resistant; ~**beule** f chilblain.

**frösteln** 1 vi to shiver. 2 vt impers **es fröstelte mich** I shivered.

**Froster** m - freezer.

**frostig** adj (lit, fig) frosty.

**Frost-:** f~**klar** adj clear and frosty; ~**schaden** m frost damage; ~**schutz** m protection against frost; ~**schutzmittel** nt (Aut) antifreeze.

**Frottee** [frɔ'te:] nt or m -s terry towelling.

**Frottee-:** ~**(hand)tuch** nt (terry) towel; ~**kleid** nt towelling dress.

**frottieren*** vt Haut to rub; jdn, sich to rub down.

**Frottier(hand)tuch** nt (terry) towel.

**Frotzelei** f (col) teasing.

**frotzeln** vti (col) to tease. **über jdn ~** to make fun of sb.

**Frucht** f -̈e (Bot, fig) fruit; (Embryo) foetus; (no pl: Getreide) crops pl. ~**e** (Obst) fruit sing; ~**e tragen** (lit, fig) to bear fruit.

**fruchtbar** adj (lit, fig) fruitful; Boden fertile. **etw für jdn ~ machen** to use sth to benefit sb.

**Fruchtbarkeit** f siehe adj fruitfulness; fertility.

**Fruchtbarmachung** f (von Wüste) reclamation.

**Frucht-:** ~**becher** m fruit sundae; ~**bonbon** m or nt fruit drop; f~**bringend** adj (geh) fruitful.

**Früchtchen** nt (col) (Tunichtgut) good-for-nothing; (Kind) rascal (col). **du bist mir ein sauberes** or **nettes ~** (iro) you're a right one (col).

**fruchten** vi to bear fruit. **nichts ~** to be fruitless.

**Fruchtfleisch** nt flesh (of a fruit).

**fruchtig** adj fruity.

**Frucht-:** ~**joghurt** m or nt fruit yog(h)urt; f~**los** adj (fig) fruitless; ~**losigkeit** f fruitlessness; ~**saft** m fruit juice.

**früh** 1 adj early. **am ~en Morgen** in the early morning; **ein Werk des ~en Picasso** an early work by Picasso. 2 adv (a) early; (in jungen Jahren) at an early age; (in Entwicklung) early on. **es ist noch ~ am Tag** it is still early in the day; **von ~ bis spät** from morning till night. (b) morgen ~ tomorrow morning; **heute ~** this morning.

**Früh-** in cpds early; f~**auf adv von f~auf** from an early age; ~**aufsteher** m - early riser, early bird (col); ~**dienst** m early shift; ~**dienst haben** to be on early shift.

**Frühe** f no pl (Morgen) **in der ~** early in the morning; **in aller ~** at the crack of dawn.

**früher** comp of **früh 1** adj (a) earlier. **in ~en Jahren/Zeiten** in the past; **in ~em Alter** when he/she etc was younger. (b) (ehemalig) former, previous. **der Kontakt zu seinen ~en Freunden ist abgebrochen** he lost contact with his old friends. 2 adv (a) earlier. **~ geht's nicht** that's the soonest possible; **das hättest du ~ sagen müssen** you should have said that before or sooner; **~ oder später** sooner or later. (b) (in vergangenen Zeiten) **Herr X, ~ Direktor eines ...** Herr X, formerly director of a ...; **ich habe ihn ~ mal gekannt** I used to know him; **~ habe ich so etwas nie gemacht** I never used to do that kind of thing; **~ stand hier eine Kirche** there used to be a church here; **Erzählungen von/ Erinnerungen an ~** stories/memories of times gone by; **ich kannte/kenne ihn von ~** I knew him before/ I've known him some time.

**Früh|erkennung** f (Med) early diagnosis.

**frühestens** adv at the earliest. **wann kann das ~**

**fertig sein?** when's the earliest it can be ready?
**frühestmöglich** *adj attr* earliest possible.
**Frühgeburt** *f* premature birth; *(Kind)* premature baby.
**Frühjahr** *nt* spring.
**Frühjahrs-**: **~müdigkeit** *f* springtime lethargy; **~putz** *m* spring-cleaning; **in etw** *(dat)* **~putz machen** to spring-clean sth.
**Frühling** *m* spring. **es wird ~, der ~ kommt** spring is coming; **im ~** in spring; **einem neuen ~ entgegengehen** *(fig)* to start to flourish again; **seinen zweiten ~ erleben** to go through one's second adolescence.
**Frühlings-** *in cpds* spring; **~anfang** *m* first day of spring; **f~haft** *adj* springlike.
**Früh-**: **~messe** *f* early mass; **f~morgens** *adv* early in the morning; **~nebel** *m* early morning mist; **f~reif** *adj* precocious; *(körperlich)* mature at an early age; **~rentner** *m* person who has retired early; **~schicht** *f* early shift; **~schoppen** *m* morning/lunchtime drink; **~sport** *m* early morning exercise.
**Frühstück** *nt* -e breakfast; *(~spause)* morning *or* coffee break. **zweites ~** ≈ elevenses *(Brit col)*, mid-morning snack.
**frühstücken** *insep* **1** *vi* to have breakfast. **2** *vt* **etw ~** to have sth for breakfast.
**Frühstücks-**: **~buffet** *nt* breakfast buffet; **~fernsehen** *nt* breakfast television; **~fleisch** *nt* luncheon meat; **~pause** *f* morning *or* coffee break.
**Früh-**: **~warnsystem** *nt* early warning system; **~werk** *nt* early work; **~zeit** *f* early days *pl*; **f~zeitig 1** *adj* early; *(vorzeitig auch)* premature; **2** *adv* early; *(vorzeitig)* prematurely; *(ziemlich am Anfang)* early on.
**Frust** *m no pl (col)* frustration.
**Frustration** *f* frustration.
**frustrieren\*** *vt* to frustrate; *(col: enttäuschen)* to upset.
**FU** [ɛfˈuː] *f* = **Freie Universität (Berlin)**.
**Fuchs** [fʊks] *m* ⁼e **(a)** *(Tier, Fell, fig)* fox. **er ist ein schlauer ~** *(col)* he's a cunning old devil *(col) or* fox *(col)*; **wo sich die ~e** *or* **wo sich Hase und ~ gute Nacht sagen** *(hum)* in the back of beyond. **(b)** *(Pferd)* chestnut; *(mit hellerem Schwanz und Mähne)* sorrel; *(col: Mensch)* redhead.
**fuchsen** [ˈfʊksn] *vt (col)* to annoy.
**Fuchsie** [ˈfʊksɪə] *f (Bot)* fuchsia.
**fuchsig** [ˈfʊksɪç] *adj (col: wütend)* mad *(col)*.
**Füchsin** [ˈfʏksɪn] *f* vixen.
**Fuchs-**: **~jagd** *f* fox-hunt/-hunting; **f~rot** *adj Fell* red; *Pferd* chestnut; *Haar* ginger; **~schwanz** *m* **(a)** fox's tail; **(b)** *(Säge)* handsaw; **f~teufelswild** *adj (col)* hopping mad *(col)*.
**Fuchtel** *f* -n *(fig col)* **unter jds ~** under sb's control *or* thumb.
**fuchteln** *vi (col)* **(mit den Händen) ~** to wave one's hands about *(col)*.
**fuchtig** *adj (col)* (hopping) mad *(col)*.
**Fug** *m*: **mit ~ und Recht** *(geh)* with complete justification.
**Fuge** *f* -n **(a)** joint; *(Ritze)* gap, crack. **in allen ~n krachen** to creak at the joints; **aus den ~n gehen** to come apart at the seams. **(b)** *(Mus)* fugue.
**fügen 1** *vt* **(a)** *(setzen)* to put, to place; *(geh) Worte, Satz* to formulate. **(b)** *(geh: bewirken)* to ordain. **2** *vr* to obey. **sich jdm/einer Sache** *(geh)* **~** to bow to sb/sth; *einem Befehl etc* to comply with sth; **es fügte sich, daß ...** *(geh)* it so happened that ...
**fügsam** *adj Mensch* obedient.
**Fügsamkeit** *f* obedience.

**Fügung** *f* **eine glückliche ~** a stroke of good fortune; **göttliche ~** divine providence; **eine ~ des Schicksals** an act of fate.
**fühlbar** *adj (spürbar)* perceptible.
**fühlen** *vtir* to feel. **sich krank/verantwortlich ~** to feel ill/responsible; **wie ~ Sie sich?** how do you feel?; **da hat er sich aber gefühlt** *(col)* he felt really great *(col)*.
**Fühler** *m* - *(Zool)* feeler; *(von Schnecke)* horn. **seine ~ ausstrecken** *(col)* to put out feelers.
**Fühlerlehre** *f* feeler gauge.
**Fühlung** *f* contact. **mit jdm in ~ bleiben/stehen** to stay/be in contact *or* touch with sb.
**fuhr** *pret of* **fahren**.
**Fuhre** *f* -n *(Ladung)* load.
**führen 1** *vt* **(a)** *(hin~, herum~)* to take. **eine alte Dame über die Straße ~** to help an old lady over the road; **~ Sie mich zum Geschäftsführer!** take me to the manager!; **eine Klasse zum Abitur ~** to see a class through to A-levels; **der Hinweis führte die Polizei auf die Spur des Diebes** that tip put the police on the trail of the thief; **was führt Sie zu mir?** *(form)* what brings you to me?; **ein Land ins Chaos ~** to reduce a country to chaos.
**(b)** *(an~)* to lead; *Firma etc* to run; *Armee etc* to command.
**(c)** *(handhaben) Pinsel, Kamera etc* to wield. **das Glas an die Lippen ~** to raise one's glass to one's lips.
**(d)** *(haben, mit~)* to carry; *Autokennzeichen, Namen* to have, to bear. **Geld/seine Papiere bei sich ~** *(form)* to carry money/one's papers on one's person; **der Fluß führt Hochwasser** the river is running high.
**(e)** *(Laden: im Angebot haben)* to stock.
**2** *vi* **(a)** *(in Führung liegen)* to lead. **die Mannschaft führt mit 10 Punkten Vorsprung** the team has a lead of 10 points. **(b)** *(verlaufen) (Straße)* to go; *(Kabel, Pipeline etc)* to run; *(Spur)* to lead. **die Brücke führt über die Elbe** the bridge crosses the Elbe. **(c)** *(als Ergebnis haben)* **zu etw ~** to lead to sth; **das führt zu nichts** that will come to nothing; **es führte zu dem Ergebnis, daß er entlassen wurde** it resulted in *or* led to his being dismissed; **wohin soll das alles nur ~?** where is it all leading *(us)*?
**3** *vr (form: sich benehmen)* to conduct oneself.
**führend** *adj* leading *attr*; *Rolle, Persönlichkeit auch* prominent. **diese Firma ist im Stahlbau ~** that is one of the leading firms in steel construction; **die Amerikaner sind im Schach ~** the Americans lead the world in chess.
**Führer(in** *f)* *m* - **(a)** *(Leiter)* leader; *(Oberhaupt)* head. **(b)** *(Fremden~, Berg~)* guide. **(c)** *(form: Lenker)* driver; *(von Flugzeug)* pilot; *(von Kran, Fahrstuhl)* operator. **(d)** *(Buch)* guide.
**Führer-**: **~haus** *nt* cab; **f~los** *adj* leaderless *no adv*; *Wagen* driverless *no adv*; **~schein** *m (für Auto)* driving licence *(Brit)*, driver's license *(US)*; **den ~schein machen** *(Aut)* to learn to drive; *(die Prüfung ablegen)* to take one's (driving) test; **ihm wurde der ~schein entzogen** he lost his licence; **~scheinentzug** *m* loss of one's licence, disqualification from driving.
**Fuhr-**: **~mann** *m, pl* **~leute** carter; **~park** *m* fleet (of vehicles).
**Führung** *f* **(a)** *no pl* direction; *(von Partei, Expedition etc)* leadership; *(Mil)* command; *(eines Unternehmens etc)* management. **(b)** *no pl (die Führer)* leaders *pl*, leadership *sing*; *(Mil)* commanders *pl*; *(eines Unternehmens etc)* directors *pl*. **(c)** *(Besichtigung)* guided tour *(durch* of*)*. **(d)** *no pl (Vorsprung)*

lead. **in** ~ **gehen/liegen** to go into/be in the lead. **(e)** *no pl (Betragen)* conduct. **(f)** *(form: Lenken)* **zur** ~ **eines Kraftfahrzeugs berechtigt sein** to be licensed to drive a motor vehicle. **(g)** *no pl (Betreuung)* running. **die** ~ **der Akten/Bücher** keeping the files/ books.

**Führungs-:** ~**anspruch** *m* claim to leadership; **seinen** ~**anspruch anmelden** to make a bid for the leadership; ~**kraft** *f* executive; ~**qualität** *f usu pl* leadership qualities *pl*; ~**schicht** *f* ruling classes *pl*; ~**spitze** *f* highest echelon of the leadership; *(eines Unternehmens)* top management; ~**stab** *m (Mil)* command *no pl*; *(Comm)* top management; ~**stil** *m* style of leadership; *(Comm auch)* management style.

**Fuhr-:** ~**unternehmen** *nt* haulage business; ~**unternehmer** *m* haulier, haulage contractor; ~**werk** *nt* wag(g)on; *(mit Pferden)* horse and cart; **f~werken** *vi insep (col)* **in der Küche f~werken** to bustle around in the kitchen.

**Fülle** *f no pl* **(a)** *(Körpermasse)* corpulence, portliness. **(b)** *(Stärke)* fullness. **(c)** *(Menge)* wealth.

**füllen 1** *vt* to fill; *(Cook)* to stuff. **etw in Flaschen** ~ to bottle sth; **etw in Säcke** ~ to put sth into sacks. **2** *vr (Theater, Badewanne)* to fill up.

**Füllen** *nt* - foal.

**Füller** *m* -, **Füllfederhalter** *m* fountain pen.

**Füll-:** ~**gewicht** *nt (Comm)* weight at time of packing; *(auf Dosen)* net weight; ~**horn** *nt (liter)* cornucopia.

**füllig** *adj Mensch* corpulent, portly; *Figur* ample.

**Füllung** *f* filling; *(Fleisch~, Polster~)* stuffing; *(Tür~)* panel; *(von Pralinen)* centre *(Brit)*, center *(US)*.

**Füllwort** *nt (Ling)* filler (word).

**Fummel** *m* - *(col)* rag.

**Fummelei** *f (col)* fidgeting, fiddling; *(col: Petting)* petting, groping *(col)*.

**fummeln** *vi (col)* to fiddle; *(hantieren)* to fumble; *(bei Petting)* to pet, to grope *(col)*.

**Fund** *m* -**e** find; *(das Entdecken)* discovery, finding.

**Fundament** *nt (lit, fig)* foundation *(usu pl)*. **das** ~ **zu etw legen** to lay the foundations for sth.

**fundamental** *adj* fundamental.

**Fundamentalist(in** *f)* *m* fundamentalist.

**Fund-:** ~**büro** *nt* lost property office *(Brit)*, lost and found *(US)*; ~**grube** *f (fig)* treasure trove.

**fundieren*** *vt (fig)* to back up.

**fundiert** *adj* sound. **schlecht** ~ unsound.

**fündig** *adj (Min)* rich. ~ **werden** to make a strike; *(fig)* to strike it lucky.

**Fund-:** ~**ort** *m* der ~**ort von etw** (the place) where sth is/was found; ~**sachen** *pl* lost property *sing*; ~**stätte,** ~**stelle** *f* = ~**ort.**

**fünf** *num* five. **seine** ~ **Sinne beisammen haben** to have all one's wits about one; ~**(e) gerade sein lassen** *(col)* to turn a blind eye; *siehe* **vier.**

**Fünf-** *in cpds* five; ~**eck** *nt* pentagon; **f~eckig** *adj* pentagonal, five-cornered.

**Fünfer** *m* - *(col)* five-pfennig piece; five-marks.

**Fünf-:** **f~fach** *adj* fivefold; **f~hundert** *num* five hundred; ~**jahr(es)plan** *m* five-year plan; **f~jährig** *adj Frist, Plan* five-year; *Kind* five-year-old; ~**kampf** *m (Sport)* pentathlon; ~**ling** *m* quintuplet; **f~mal** *adv* five times; ~**prozentklausel** *f* five-percent rule, *clause debarring parties with less than 5% of the vote from Parliament*; ~**tagewoche** *f* five-day week; **f~tägig** *adj* five-day *attr*; **f~tausend** *num* five thousand.

**Fünftel** *nt* - fifth.

**fünfte(r, s)** *adj* fifth; *siehe* **vierte(r, s).**

**fünfzehn** *num* fifteen.

**fünfzig** *num* fifty.

**Fünfziger** *m* - *(col) (Mensch)* fifty-year-old; *(Geld)* fifty.

**fungieren*** [fʊŋˈgiːrən] *vi* to function *(als* as a*)*.

**Funk** *m no pl* radio, wireless. **über** ~ by radio.

**Funk-:** ~**amateur** *m* radio ham; ~**ausstellung** *f* radio and television exhibition.

**Funke** *m* -**ns,** -**n (a)** *(lit, fig)* spark. ~**n sprühen** to spark; **arbeiten, daß die** ~**n fliegen** *(col)* to work like mad *(col)*; **zwischen den beiden sprang der** ~ **über** *(col)* something clicked between the two of them *(col)*. **(b)** *(ein bißchen)* scrap; *(von Hoffnung auch)* glimmer; *(von Anstand auch)* spark.

**funkeln** *vi* to sparkle; *(Sterne)* to twinkle; *(Augen) (vor Freude)* to gleam; *(vor Zorn)* to flash; *(Edelmetall)* to gleam.

**funkelnagelneu** *adj (col)* brand-new.

**Funken** *m* - = **Funke.**

**funken 1** *vti* to radio. **SOS** ~ to send out *or* radio an SOS. **2** *vi impers* **endlich hat es bei ihm gefunkt** *(col)* the light finally dawned (on him).

**Funker** *m* - radio *or* wireless operator.

**Funk-** *in cpds* radio; ~**gerät** *nt* **(a)** *no pl* radio equipment; **(b)** *(Sprechfunkgerät)* radio set, walkie-talkie; ~**haus** *nt* broadcasting studios *pl*; ~**kolleg** *nt* educational radio broadcasts *pl*; ~**kontakt** *m* radio contact; ~**meßgerät** *nt* radar (equipment) *no pl*; ~**sprechgerät** *nt (tragbar)* walkie-talkie; ~**sprechverkehr** *m* radiotelephony; ~**spruch** *m* radio signal; *(Mitteilung)* radio message; ~**stille** *f* radio silence; *(fig)* silence; ~**streife** *f* police radio patrol; ~**taxi** *nt* radio taxi; ~**telefon** *nt* cellphone.

**Funktion** *f (Zweck, Math)* function; *(no pl: Tätigkeit)* functioning; *(Amt)* office; *(Stellung)* position. **in** ~ **treten/sein** to come into/be in operation; **etw außer** ~ **setzen** to stop sth functioning.

**Funktionär(in** *f)* *m* functionary, official.

**funktionell** *adj* functional.

**funktionieren*** *vi* to work; *(Maschine etc auch)* to function, to operate.

**Funktions-:** **f~fähig** *adj* operational; *Maschine* working *pred*; ~**störung** *f (Med)* malfunction; ~**taste** *f (Comp)* function key; **f~tüchtig** *adj* in working order.

**Funk-:** ~**turm** *m* radio tower; ~**verbindung** *f* radio contact.

**Funzel** *f* -**n** *(col)* dim light, gloom.

**Für** *nt*: **das** ~ **und Wider** the pros and cons *pl*.

**für** *prep* +*acc* for. ~ **was ist denn dieses Werkzeug?** *(col)* what is this tool for?; ~ **zwei arbeiten** *(fig)* to do the work of two people; ~**s erste** for the moment; ~**s nächstemal** next time; **sich** ~ **etw entscheiden** to decide in favour *(Brit)* or in favor *(US)* of sth; **was Sie da sagen, hat etwas** ~ **sich** there's something in what you're saying; **er hat was** ~ **sich** he's not a bad person; **Tag** ~ **Tag** day after day; **Schritt** ~ **Schritt** step by step.

**Fürbitte** *f (Eccl, fig)* intercession.

**Furche** *f* -**n** furrow; *(Wagenspur)* rut.

**furchen** *vt* to furrow. **eine gefurchte Stirn** a furrowed brow.

**Furcht** *f no pl* fear. **aus** ~ **vor jdm/etw** for fear of sb/sth; ~ **vor jdm/etw haben** to be afraid of sb/sth; **jdn in** ~ **versetzen, jdm** ~ **einflößen** to frighten *or* scare sb.

**furchtbar** *adj* terrible, awful. **ich habe einen** ~**en Hunger** I'm ever so hungry *(col)*.

**furcht|einflößend** *adj* terrifying, fearful.

**fürchten 1** *vt* jdn/etw ~ to be afraid of sb/sth, to fear sb/sth; **es war schlimmer, als ich gefürchtet hat-**

**te** it was worse than I had feared. **2** *vr* to be afraid *(vor +dat of)*. **3** *vi* **für** *or* **um etw** ~ to fear for sth; **zum F**~ **aussehen** to look a fright *(col)*; **da kannst du das F**~ **lernen** it will scare you stiff.

**fürchterlich** *adj* terrible, awful.

**Furcht-:** **f**~**erregend** *adj* terrifying, fearful. **f**~**los** *adj* fearless; ~**losigkeit** *f* fearlessness; **f**~**sam** *adj* timorous; ~**samkeit** *f* timorousness.

**für|einander** *adv* for each other, for one another.

**Furie** ['fuːriə] *f (Myth)* fury; *(fig)* hellcat.

**Furnier** *nt* **-e** veneer.

**furnieren\*** *vt* to veneer.

**Furore** *f or nt no pl* sensation. ~ **machen** *(col)* to cause a sensation.

**Fürsorge** *f no pl* **(a)** *(Betreuung)* care; *(Sozial~)* welfare. **(b)** *(col: Sozialamt)* welfare *(col)*. **der** ~ **zur Last fallen** to be a burden on the state. **(c)** *(col: Sozialunterstützung)* social security *(Brit)*, welfare *(US)*. **von der** ~ **leben** to live on social security *(Brit)* or the welfare *(US)*.

**fürsorgend** *adj* caring. **jdn** ~ **betreuen** to care for sb.

**Fürsorger(in** *f)* *m* - (church) welfare worker.

**fürsorglich** *adj* caring. **jdn sehr** ~ **behandeln** to lavish care on sb.

**Fürsorglichkeit** *f* care.

**Fürsprache** *f* recommendation. **für jdn** ~ **einlegen** to put in a word of recommendation for sb *(bei* with).

**Fürsprecher(in** *f)* *m* advocate.

**Fürst** *m (wk)* **-en, -en** prince; *(Herrscher)* ruler. **wie ein** ~ **leben** to live like a lord.

**Fürsten-:** ~**haus** *nt* royal house; ~**tum** *nt* principality.

**Fürstin** *f* princess; *(Herrscherin)* ruler.

**fürstlich** *adj (lit, fig)* princely *no adv.* **jdn** ~ **bewirten** to entertain sb right royally; ~ **leben** to live like a lord.

**Furt** *f* **-en** ford.

**Furunkel** *nt or m* - boil.

**Fürwort** *nt* ~**er** *(Gram)* pronoun.

**Furz** *m* ~**e** *(col!)* fart *(col)*.

**furzen** *vi (col!)* to fart *(col)*.

**Fusel** *m* - *(pej)* rotgut *(col)*, hooch *(US col)*.

**Fusion** *f* amalgamation; *(von Unternehmen)* merger; *(von Atomkernen, Zellen)* fusion.

**fusionieren\*** *vti* to amalgamate; *(Unternehmen)* to merge.

**Fuß** *m* ~**e** **(a)** foot. **zu** ~ on foot; **er ist gut/schlecht zu** ~ he has no difficulty/has difficulty walking; **sich jdm zu** ~**en werfen** to prostrate oneself before sb; **jdm zu** ~**en fallen/liegen** to fall/lie at sb's feet; **das Publikum lag ihm zu** ~**en** he had the audience at his feet; **den** ~ **in die Tür stellen** to get one's foot in the door; **kalte** ~**e bekommen** *(lit, fig)* to get cold feet; **bei** ~**!** heel!; **jdm etw vor die** ~**e werfen** *(lit)* to throw sth at sb; *(fig)* to tell sb to keep sth; **jdn/etw mit** ~**en treten** *(fig)* to walk all over sb/sth; **(festen)** ~ **fassen** *(lit, fig)* to gain a foothold; *(sich niederlassen)* to settle down; **auf eigenen** ~**en stehen** *(fig)* to be able to stand on one's own two feet; **auf großem** ~ **leben** to live the high life; **mit jdm auf gutem** ~ **stehen** to be on good terms with sb.

**(b)** *(von Gegenstand)* base; *(Tisch-, Stuhlbein)* leg; *(von Schrank, Gebirge)* foot. **auf schwachen/tönernen** ~**en stehen** to be built on sand.

**(c)** *pl - (Längenmaß)* foot.

**Fuß-:** ~**abdruck** *m* footprint; ~**angel** *f (lit)* mantrap; *(fig)* catch, trap; ~**bad** *nt* foot bath.

**Fußball** *m* football; *(Sportart auch)* soccer.

**Fußballer(in** *f)* *m* - *(col)* footballer.

**Fußball-:** ~**mannschaft** *f* football team; ~**platz** *m* football *or* soccer pitch; ~**schuh** *m* football boot; ~**spiel** *nt* football *or* soccer match; *(Sportart)* football; ~**spieler** *m* football *or* soccer player; ~**toto** *m or nt* football pools *pl*; ~**verein** *m* football club.

**Fuß-:** ~**bank** *f* footstool; ~**boden** *m* floor; ~**bodenbelag** *m* floor covering, flooring; ~**bodenheizung** *f* underfloor heating; ~**bremse** *f* footbrake; ~**eisen** *nt* mantrap.

**Fussel** *f* **-n** fluff *no pl.* **eine** ~ a bit of fluff.

**fusselig** *adj* fluffy. **sich** *(dat)* **den Mund** ~ **reden** *(col)* to talk till one is blue in the face.

**fusseln** *vi (Stoff, Kleid etc)* to make fluff.

**fußen** *vi* to rest, to be based *(auf +dat* on).

**Fuß-:** ~**ende** *nt (von Bett)* foot; ~**fehler** *m (Tennis)* foot fault.

**Fußgänger(in** *f)* *m* - pedestrian.

**Fußgänger-:** ~**brücke** *f* footbridge; ~**insel** *f* traffic island; ~**übergang, ~überweg** *m* pedestrian crossing *(Brit)*, crosswalk *(US)*; *(auch ~überführung)* pedestrian bridge; ~**unterführung** *f* underpass, pedestrian subway *(Brit)*; ~**zone** *f* pedestrian precinct.

**Fuß-:** ~**gelenk** *nt* ankle; ~**leiste** *f* skirting board *(Brit)*, baseboard *(US)*.

**fußlig** *adj* = **fusselig**.

**Fuß-:** ~**marsch** *m* walk; *(Mil)* march; ~**matte** *f* doormat; ~**nagel** *m* toenail; ~**note** *f* footnote; ~**pflege** *f* chiropody, podiatry *(US)*; ~**pfleger** *m* chiropodist, podiatrist *(US)*; ~**pilz** *m (Med)* athlete's foot *no art*; ~**sohle** *f* sole of the foot; ~**spitze** *f* toes *pl*; **sich auf die** ~**spitzen stellen** to stand on tiptoe; ~**spur** *f* footprint; ~**stapfen** *m* footprint; **in jds** ~**stapfen treten** *(fig)* to follow in sb's footsteps; ~**stütze** *f* footrest; ~**tritt** *m (Stoß)* kick; **jdm einen** ~**tritt geben** to kick sb, to give sb a kick; **einen** ~**tritt bekommen** *(fig)* to be kicked out; ~**volk** *nt* **(a)** *(Mil old)* footmen *pl*; **(b)** *(fig)* **das** ~**volk** the rank and file; ~**wanderung** *f* hike; ~**weg** *m* **(a)** footpath; **(b) es sind nur 15 Minuten** ~**weg** it's only 15 minutes' walk; ~**zeile** *f (Comp)* footer.

**futsch** *adj pred (col: weg)* gone, vanished.

**Futter** *nt* - **(a)** *no pl* food, feed; *(für Kühe, Pferde etc auch)* fodder. **gut im** ~ **sein** to be well-fed. **(b)** *(Kleider~, Briefumschlag~)* lining.

**Futteral** *nt* **-e** case.

**Futter-:** ~**häuschen** *nt* bird box; ~**krippe** *f* manger; **an der** ~**krippe sitzen** *(col)* to be well-placed.

**futtern** *(hum col)* **1** *vi* to stuff oneself *(col)*. **2** *vt* to scoff.

**füttern** *vt* **(a)** to feed. „**F**~ **verboten**" "do not feed the animals". **(b)** *Kleidungsstück* to line.

**Futter-:** ~**napf** *m* bowl; ~**neid** *m (fig)* material envy, jealousy; ~**pflanze** *f* forage plant; ~**stoff** *m* lining (material); ~**trog** *m* feeding trough.

**Fütterung** *f* feeding.

**Futur** *nt* **-e** *(Gram)* **(erstes)** ~ future (tense); **zweites** ~ future perfect.

**futuristisch** *adj* futuristic.

# G

**G, g** [geː] *nt* -, - G, g. **G wie Gustav** ≃ G for Geroge.
**g** = **Gramm** g.
**gab** *pret of* **geben**.
**Gabardine** ['gabardiːn] *m or f no pl* gabardine.
**Gabe** *f* -n **(a)** *(dated: Geschenk)* gift, present *(gen of, from)*. **(b)** *(Begabung)* gift. **die ~ haben, etw zu tun** to have a gift for doing sth.
**Gabel** *f* -n fork; *(Heu~, Mist~)* pitchfork; *(Telec)* rest, cradle.
**Gabel-: g~förmig** *adj* forked *no adv*; **~frühstück** *nt* mid-morning light lunch.
**gabeln** *vtr* to fork.
**Gabelstapler** *m* - fork-lift truck.
**Gabelung** *f* fork.
**Gabentisch** *m* table for Christmas or birthday presents.
**Gabun** *nt* Gabon.
**gackern** *vi (lit, fig)* to cackle.
**gaffen** *vi* to gape, to stare *(nach at)*.
**Gaffer(in** *f*) *m* - **die neugierigen ~ bei einem Unfall** the nosy people standing gaping at an accident.
**Gag** [gɛk] *m* -s *(Film~)* gag; *(Werbe~)* gimmick.
**Gage** ['gaːʒə] *f* -n *(esp Theat)* fee.
**gähnen** *vi (lit, fig)* to yawn. **~de Leere** total emptiness; **ein ~der Abgrund** a yawning abyss; **ein G~** a yawn; **das G~ unterdrücken** to stop oneself (from) yawning.
**GAL** [geː|aː|'ɛl] *f* = **Grün-Alternative Liste** *electoral pact of Greens and alternative parties*.
**Gala** *f no pl* formal dress. **sich in ~ werfen** to get all dressed up.
**Gala-** *in cpds* formal; *(Mil)* full ceremonial; *(Theat)* gala; **~abend** *m* gala evening; **~anzug** *m* formal dress; *(Mil)* full dress; **~ empfang** *m* grand reception.
**galaktisch** *adj* galactic.
**galant** *adj (dated)* gallant.
**Galanterie** *f (dated)* gallantry.
**Galapagosinseln** *pl* Galapagos Islands *pl*.
**Gala-: ~uniform** *f (Mil)* (full) dress uniform; **~vorstellung** *f (Theat)* gala performance.
**Galeere** *f* -n galley.
**Galerie** *f* gallery. **auf der ~** in the gallery.
**Galgen** *m* - gallows *pl*; *(Film)* boom. **jdn an den ~ bringen** to bring sb to the gallows.
**Galgen-: ~frist** *f (col)* reprieve; **jdm eine ~frist geben** to give sb a reprieve, to reprieve sb; **~humor** *m* gallows humour *(Brit)* or humor *(US)*; **~strick, ~vogel** *m (col)* gallows bird *(col)*.
**Galionsfigur** *f* figurehead.
**gälisch** *adj* Gaelic.
**Galle** *f* -n gall; *(Organ)* gallbladder; *(Flüssigkeit auch)* bile. **seine ~ verspritzen** *(fig)* to pour out one's venom; **jdm kommt die ~ hoch** sb's blood begins to boil; **die ~ läuft ihm über** *(col)* he's livid.
**galle(n)bitter** *adj* bitter; *Bemerkung* caustic.
**Gallen-** *in cpds* gall; **~blase** *f* gall-bladder; **~kolik** *f* bilious attack; **~stein** *m* gallstone.

**gallig** *adj* bitter; *(fig)* caustic.
**gallisch** *adj* Gallic.
**Gallizismus** *m (Ling)* Gallicism.
**Galopp** *m* -s *or* -e gallop. **im ~** *(lit)* at a gallop; *(fig)* at top speed; **langsamer ~** canter.
**galoppieren*** *vi aux haben or sein* to gallop.
**galt** *pret of* **gelten**.
**galvanisieren*** [galvani'ziːrən] *vt* to galvanize.
**Gamasche** *f* -n gaiter.
**Gambia** *nt* (the) Gambia.
**Gambier(in** *f*) *m* Gambian.
**gambisch** *adj* Gambian.
**Gammastrahl** *m* gamma ray.
**Gammel** *m no pl (col)* junk *(col)*, rubbish.
**gamm(e)lig** *adj (col) Lebensmittel* old, ancient; *Kleidung* tatty *(col)*.
**gammeln** *vi (col)* to laze *or* loaf *(col)* about.
**Gammler(in** *f*) *m* - long-haired layabout.
**gang** *adj:* **~ und gäbe sein** to be the usual thing.
**Gang¹** *m* ~e **(a)** *(no pl: ~art)* walk, way of walking, gait; *(eines Pferdes)* gait. **einen leichten/schnellen ~ haben** to be light on one's feet/to be a fast walker; **seinen ~ verlangsamen/beschleunigen** to slow down/to speed up.
  **(b)** *(Besorgung)* errand; *(Spazier~)* walk. **einen ~ machen** to go on an errand/to go for a walk; **einen ~ zum Anwalt machen** to pay a visit to one's lawyer; **einen schweren ~ tun** to do something difficult; **das war für ihn immer ein schwerer ~** it was always hard for him; **den ~ nach Canossa antreten** *(fig)* to eat humble pie.
  **(c)** *(Ablauf)* course; *(eines Dramas)* development. **der Motor hat einen leisen ~** the engine runs quietly; **seinen gewohnten ~ gehen** *(fig)* to run its usual course; **etw in ~ bringen** *or* **setzen** to get sth going; **etw in ~ halten** *(lit, fig)* to keep sth going; **in ~ kommen** to get going; **in ~ sein** to be going; *(fig)* to be off the ground; **in vollem ~** in full swing; **es ist etwas im ~(e)** *(col)* something's up *(col)*.
  **(d)** *(Arbeits~)* operation; *(eines Essens)* course. **ein Essen mit vier ~en** a four-course meal.
  **(e)** *(Verbindungs~)* passage(way); *(Rail, in Gebäuden)* corridor; *(Hausflur) (offen)* passage(way); *(hinter Eingangstür)* hallway; *(im oberen Stock)* landing; *(Theat, Aviat, in Kirche)* aisle; *(Aviat, in Stadion)* gangway; *(in einem Bergwerk)* tunnel, gallery; *(Anat)* duct; *(Min: Erz~)* vein; *(Tech: eines Gewindes)* thread.
  **(f)** *(Mech)* gear. **den ersten ~ einlegen** to engage first (gear); **auf** *or* **in den dritten ~ schalten** to change *or* shift *(US)* into third (gear).
**Gang²** [gɛŋ] *f* -s gang.
**Gangart** *f* walk, way of walking, gait; *(von Pferd)* gait. **eine schnellere ~ vorlegen** to walk faster; **eine harte ~ einlegen** *(fig)* to take a tough line.
**gangbar** *adj (lit) Weg, Brücke* passable; *(fig)* practicable. **nicht ~** impassable/impracticable.
**Gängelband** *nt:* **jdn am ~ führen** *(fig) (Lehrer etc)* to

spoon-feed sb; *(Mutter)* to keep sb tied to one's apron strings.

**gängeln** *vt (fig)* jdn ~ to treat sb like a child; *(Mutter)* to keep sb tied to one's apron strings.

**gängig** *adj* (a) *(üblich)* common; *(aktuell)* current; *(vertretbar)* possible. (b) *(gut gehend)* Waren popular. **die ~ste Ausführung** the best-selling model.

**Gangschaltung** *f* gears *pl*.

**Gangster** ['gɛnstə] *m* - gangster.

**Gangster-:** ~**boß** *m* gang boss; ~**braut** *f* (gangster's) moll *(col)*; ~**methoden** *pl* strong-arm tactics *pl*.

**Gangway** ['gæŋweɪ] *f* **-s** *(Naut)* gangway; *(Aviat)* steps *pl*.

**Ganove** [ga'noːvə] *m* **-n** *(col)* crook.

**Ganoven-:** ~**ehre** *f* honour *(Brit)* or honor *(US)* among(st) thieves; ~**sprache** *f* underworld slang.

**Gans** *f* ⁼e goose.

**Gänschen** ['gɛnsçən] *nt* gosling; *(fig col)* little goose *(col)*.

**Gänse-** *in cpds* goose; ~**blümchen** *nt* daisy; ~**braten** *m* roast goose; ~**füßchen** *pl (col)* inverted commas *pl*; ~**haut** *f (fig)* goose-pimples *pl*, goose-flesh; ~**marsch** *m:* **im ~marsch** in single *or* Indian file.

**Gänserich** *m* **-e** gander.

**ganz 1** *adj* (a) whole, entire; *(vollständig)* complete; *Wahrheit* whole. **eine ~e Zahl** a whole number; **eine ~e Note** *(Mus)* a semi-breve *(Brit)*, a whole note *(US)*; ~ **England/London** the whole of England/London, all England/London; **die ~e Zeit** all the time, the whole time; **sein ~es Geld/Vermögen** all his money/fortune, his entire *or* whole fortune; **seine ~e Kraft** all his strength; **ein ~er Mann** a real *or* proper man; **etw im~en kaufen** to buy sth as a whole; **im (großen und) ~en (genommen)** on the whole, all in all. (b) *(col: unbeschädigt)* intact. **etw wieder ~ machen** to mend sth; **wieder ~ sein** to be mended. (c) *(col: nicht mehr als)* ~**e 200 Mark im Monat** all of 200 marks a month.

**2** *adv (völlig, ziemlich)* quite; *(ausnahmslos)* completely; *(sehr)* really; *(genau)* exactly, just. ~ **hinten/vorn** right at the back/front; **nicht ~** not quite; ~ **gewiß!** absolutely; **ein ~ gutes Buch** *(ziemlich)* quite a good book; *(sehr gut)* a very *or* really good book; **ein ~ billiger Trick** a really cheap trick; **er hat ~ recht** he's quite *or* absolutely right; ~ **allein** all alone; **du bist ja ~ naß** you're all wet; ~ **Aufmerksamkeit** *etc* **sein** to be all attention *etc*; **etwas ~ Verrücktes** something really mad; **eine Zeitschrift ~ lesen** to read a magazine right through *or* from cover to cover; ~ **und gar** completely, utterly; ~ **und gar nicht** not at all, not in the least; **noch nicht ~ zwei Uhr** not quite two o'clock yet; **ein ~ klein wenig** just a tiny bit; **das mag ich ~ besonders gerne** I'm particularly fond of that; **sie ist ~ die Mutter** she's just *or* exactly like her mother; **man sollte es ~ oder gar nicht machen** one should do it properly or not at all.

**Gänze** *f no pl (form)* entirety.

**Ganze(s)** *nt decl as adj* **das ~** the whole; *(alle Sachen zusammen)* the (whole) lot; *(ganzer Satz, ganze Ausrüstung)* the complete set. **etw als ~s sehen** to see sth as a whole; **das ~ kostet ... altogether** it costs ...; **das ~ gefällt mir gar nicht** I don't like it at all; **aufs ~ gehen** *(col)* to go all out; **es geht ums ~** everything's at stake.

**Ganzheit** *f (Einheit)* unity; *(Vollständigkeit)* entirety. **in seiner ~** in its entirety.

**ganzheitlich** *adj* integral.

**Ganzheitsmethode** *f* look-and-say method.

**ganzjährig** *adj* all-year *attr.* ~ **geöffnet** open all year (round).

**gänzlich** *adv* completely, totally.

**ganzseitig** *adj Anzeige etc* full-page.

**ganztägig** *adj* all-day *attr.*

**ganztags** *adv arbeiten* full-time.

**Ganztags-:** ~**beschäftigung** *f* full-time occupation; ~**schule** *f* all-day schooling *no pl or* schools *pl*; *(Gebäude)* all-day school; ~**stelle** *f* full-time job.

**Ganzton** *m (Mus)* (whole) tone.

**gar 1** *adv* (a) *(überhaupt)* at all; *(ganz)* quite. ~ **keines** not a single one, none whatsoever *or* at all; ~ **kein Grund** no reason whatsoever *or* at all; ~ **nichts** nothing at all; ~ **nicht schlecht** not bad at all, not at all bad. (b) **er wäre ~ zu gern noch länger geblieben** he would really have liked to stay longer; **ein ~ feiner Mensch** *(old)* a really splendid person. (c) *(sogar)* even. **wie alt ist er? — 70, wenn nicht ~ 80** how old is he? — 70, if not 80. **2** *adj Speise* done *pred*, cooked. **etw ~ kochen** to cook sth (until it is done).

**Garage** [ga'raːʒə] *f* **-n** garage; *(Hoch~, Tief~)* car park *(Brit)*, parking garage *(US)*.

**Garantie** *f (lit, fig)* guarantee. **die Uhr hat ein Jahr ~** the watch is guaranteed for a year *or* has a year's guarantee; **das fällt noch unter die ~** that's covered by the guarantee.

**Garantie-:** ~**frist** *f* guarantee period; ~**lohn** *m* guaranteed minimum wage.

**garantieren\* 1** *vt* to guarantee *(jdm etw* sb sth*)*. **er konnte mir nicht ~, daß ...** he couldn't guarantee that ... **2** *vi* to give a guarantee. **für etw ~** to guarantee sth.

**garantiert** *adv wasserdicht etc* guaranteed. **er kommt garantiert nicht** *(col)*, he's bound not to come.

**Garantieschein** *m* guarantee.

**Garaus** *m: (col)* **jdm den ~ machen** to do sb in *(col)*, to bump sb off *(col)*.

**Garbe** *f* **-n** *(Korn~)* sheaf; *(Mil: Schuß~)* burst of fire. **zu ~n binden** to bind into sheaves.

**Garde** *f* **-n** guard. **bei der ~** in the Guards; **die alte ~** *(fig)* the old guard.

**Gardemaß** *nt:* ~ **haben** *(hum)* to be as tall as a tree.

**Garderobe** *f* **-n** (a) *(Kleiderbestand)* wardrobe. (b) *(Kleiderablage)* hall-stand; *(im Theater, Kino etc)* cloakroom *(Brit)*, checkroom *(US)*. (c) *(Theat: Umkleideraum)* dressing-room.

**Garderoben-:** ~**frau** *f* cloakroom *(Brit)* or checkroom *(US)* attendant; ~**haken** *m* coat hook; ~**marke** *f* cloakroom *(Brit)* or checkroom *(US)* number; ~**schein** *m* cloakroom *(Brit)* or checkroom *(US)* ticket; ~**ständer** *m* hat-stand, hat tree *(US)*.

**Gardine** *f* curtain, drape *(US)*; *(Tüll~)* net curtain.

**Gardinen-:** ~**leiste** *f* curtain rail; ~**predigt** *f (col)* jdm eine ~**predigt halten** to give sb a talking-to; ~**stange** *f* curtain rail; *(zum Ziehen)* curtain rod.

**garen** *(Cook)* *vti* to cook.

**gären 1** *vi aux haben or sein* to ferment; *(fig: Gefühle etc)* to seethe. **die Wut gärte in ihm** he was seething with anger. **2** *vt* to ferment.

**Garn** *nt* **-e** thread; *(Baumwoll~ auch)* cotton; *(Häkel~, fig: Seemanns~)* yarn. **ein ~ spinnen** *(fig)* to spin a yarn; **jdm ins ~ gehen** *(fig)* to fall into sb's snare.

**Garnele** *f* **-n** *(Zool)* prawn, shrimp.

**garnieren\*** *vt Kuchen, Kleid* to decorate; *Gericht, (fig) Reden etc* to garnish.

**Garnierung** *f siehe vt* decoration; garnishing.

**Garnison** f *(Mil)* garrison.
**Garnison(s)-** *in cpds* garrison.
**Garnitur** f *(Satz)* set; *(Unterwäsche)* set of underwear. **die erste** ~ *(fig)* the pick of the bunch; **erste/ zweite** ~ **sein** to be first-rate/second-rate.
**Garnrolle** f spool; *(von Baumwolle, Nähgarn)* cotton reel.
**garstig** adj nasty, horrible.
**Garten** m ⁼ garden; *(Obst~)* orchard. **botanischer/ zoologischer** ~ botanic/zoological gardens *pl*; **im** ~ **arbeiten** to do some gardening; **das ist nicht in seinem** ~ **gewachsen** *(fig col: Ideen)* he didn't think of that himself.
**Garten-** *in cpds* garden; **~arbeit** f gardening *no pl*; **~bau** m horticulture; **~fest** nt garden party; **~gerät** nt gardening tool; **~haus** nt summer house; **~laube** f *(~häuschen)* summer house; **~lokal** nt beer garden; *(Café)* garden café; **~möbel** pl garden furniture; **~schere** f secateurs pl *(Brit)*, pruning shears *pl*; **~schlauch** m garden hose; **~zwerg** m garden gnome; *(pej col: Mensch)* little squirt *(col)*.
**Gärtner(in** f*)* m gardener.
**Gärtnerei** f *(Baumschule, für Setzlinge)* nursery; *(für Obst, Gemüse, Schnittblumen)* market garden *(Brit)*, truck farm *(US)*.
**gärtnerisch** adj attr gardening. **wenn man sich** ~ **betätigt** if you do some gardening.
**gärtnern** vi to do gardening.
**Gärung** f fermentation; *(fig)* ferment, turmoil.
**Gas** nt **-e** gas; *(Aut: ~pedal)* accelerator, gas pedal *(esp US)*. ~ **geben** *(Aut)* to accelerate, to step on the gas *(col)*; ~ **wegnehmen** *(Aut)* to decelerate.
**Gas-** *in cpds* gas; **g~beheizt** adj gas-heated; **~feuerzeug** nt gas lighter; **~flasche** f bottle of gas, gas cylinder; **g~förmig** adj gaseous; **~geruch** m smell of gas; **~hahn** m gas tap; **~heizung** f gas central heating; **~herd** m gas cooker; **~kammer** f gas chamber; **~kocher** m camping stove; **~kraftwerk** nt gas-fired power station; **~laterne** f gas (street) lamp; **~leitung** f *(Rohr)* gas pipe; **~licht** nt gaslight; *(Beleuchtung)* gas lighting; **~maske** f gasmask; **~ofen** m *(Heizofen)* gas fire or heater; **~pedal** nt *(Aut)* accelerator (pedal), gas pedal *(esp US)*.
**Gasse** f **-n** lane; *(Durchgang)* alley(way); *(S Ger, Aus: Straße)* street.
**Gassen-:** **~hauer** m *(old, col)* popular melody; **~junge** m *(pej)* street urchin or arab.
**Gassi** adv *(col)* **mit einem Hund** ~ **gehen** to take a dog for walkies *(col)*.
**Gast** m ⁼**e** guest; *(Besucher auch, Tourist)* visitor; *(in einer ~stätte)* customer; *(Theat)* guest (star); **vor geladenen** ⁓**en** before an invited audience; **wir haben heute abend** ⁓**e** we're having people around this evening; **bei jdm zu** ~ **sein** to be sb's guest(s); **in einem anderen Ort zu** ~ **sein** to visit another place.
**Gast|arbeiter** m immigrant or foreign worker.
**Gäste-:** **~bett** nt spare or guest bed; **~buch** nt visitors' book; **~handtuch** nt guest towel; **~haus** nt guest house; **~zimmer** nt guest or spare room.
**Gast-:** **g~freundlich** adj hospitable; **~freundlichkeit,** **~freundschaft** f hospitality; **~geber** m host; **~geberin** f hostess; **~haus** nt, **~hof** m inn; **~hörer(in** f*)* m *(Univ)* observer, auditor *(US)*.
**gastieren*** vi to make a guest appearance.
**Gast-:** **~land** nt host country; **g~lich** adj hospitable; **~lichkeit** f hospitality; **~professor** m visiting professor.

**Gastritis** f, pl **Gastritiden** gastritis.
**Gastrolle** f *(Theat)* **eine** ~ **spielen** *(lit)* to make a guest appearance; *(fig)* to put in a fleeting appearance.
**Gastronom(in** f*)* m *(Gastwirt)* restaurateur.
**Gastronomie** f *(Kochkunst)* gastronomy; *(form: Gaststättengewerbe)* catering trade.
**gastronomisch** adj gastronomic.
**Gast-:** **~spiel** nt *(Theat)* guest performance; **ein ~spiel geben** *(lit)* to give a guest performance; *(fig col)* to put in a brief appearance; **~spielreise** f *(Theat)* tour; **~stätte** f *(Speise~)* restaurant; *(Trinklokal)* pub *(Brit)*, bar; **~stube** f lounge; **~wirt(in** f*)* m *(Besitzer)* restaurant owner; *(Pächter)* restaurant manager/manageress; *(von Trinklokal)* landlord/landlady; **~wirtschaft** f = **~stätte**.
**Gas-:** **~uhr** f gas meter; **~verbrauch** m gas consumption; **~vergiftung** f gas poisoning; **~versorgung** f *(System)* gas supply *(gen to)*; **~werk** nt gasworks sing or pl; *(Verwaltung)* gas board; **~zähler** m gas meter; **~zentralheizung** f gas central heating.
**GATT** [gat] nt GATT.
**Gatte** m **-n** *(form)* husband, spouse *(form)*.
**Gatter** nt **-** *(Tür)* gate; *(Zaun)* fence; *(Rost)* grating, grid.
**Gattin** f *(form)* wife, spouse *(form)*.
**Gattung** f *(Biol)* genus; *(Liter, Mus, Art)* genre, form; *(fig: Sorte)* type, kind.
**Gattungsbegriff** m generic concept.
**GAU** [gau] m = **größter anzunehmender Unfall** maximum credible accident, MCA.
**Gaube** f **-, -n** dormer window.
**Gaudi** nt or *(SGer, Aus)* f no pl *(col)* fun.
**Gaukler** m **-** *(liter)* travelling *(Brit)* or traveling *(US)* entertainer.
**Gaul** m, pl **Gäule** *(pej)* nag, hack.
**Gaumen** m **-** palate *(auch fig)*, roof of the/one's mouth. **die Zunge klebte ihm vor Durst am** ~ his tongue was hanging out (with thirst).
**Gauner** m **-** rogue, rascal; *(Betrüger)* crook; *(hum col: Schelm auch)* scamp.
**Gaunerbande** f bunch of rogues/crooks.
**Gaunerei** f swindling no pl, cheating no pl.
**gaunerhaft** adj rascally no adv.
**gaunern** vi *(col)* *(betrügen)* to swindle, to cheat; *(stehlen)* to thieve. **er hat sich durchs Leben gegaunert** he cheated his way through life.
**Gaunersprache** f underworld jargon.
**Gaze** ['gaːzə] f **-n** gauze.
**Gazelle** f gazelle.
**Ge|ächtete(r)** mf decl as adj outlaw.
**ge|artet** adj **gutmütig/freundlich** ~ **sein** to be good-natured/have a friendly nature; **sie ist ganz anders** ~ she has a completely different nature.
**Ge|äst** nt no pl branches pl.
**geb.** = (a) **geboren** b. (b) **geborene** née.
**Gebäck** nt **-e** *(Kekse)* biscuits pl *(Brit)*, cookies pl *(US)*; *(Teilchen)* pastries pl.
**gebacken** ptp of **backen**.
**Gebälk** nt **-e** timberwork no pl, timbers pl.
**geballt** adj *(fig: konzentriert)* concentrated.
**gebannt** adj spellbound. **wie** ~ as if spellbound.
**gebar** pret of **gebären**.
**Gebärde** f **-n** gesture; *(lebhafte auch)* gesticulation.
**gebärden*** vr to behave, to conduct oneself *(form)*.
**Gebärdenspiel** nt no pl gestures pl, gesticulation(s).
**Gebaren** nt no pl behaviour *(Brit)*, behavior *(US)*; *(Geschäfts~)* conduct.
**gebären** pret **gebar,** ptp **geboren** **1** vt to give birth

to; *(fig liter: erzeugen)* to breed. **geboren werden** to be born; **wo sind Sie geboren?** where were you born?; **aus der Not geborene Ideen** ideas springing from necessity; *siehe* **geboren. 2** *vi* to give birth.

**Gebärmutter** *f (Anat)* womb, uterus.

**gebauchpinselt** *adj (hum col)* **sich ~ fühlen** to be tickled pink *(col)*, to feel flattered.

**Gebäude** *nt* - building; *(fig: Gefüge)* structure.

**Gebäude-: ~komplex** *m* (building) complex; **~reinigung** *f (das Reinigen)* commercial cleaning; *(Firma)* cleaning contractors *pl*.

**gebaut** *adj* built. **gut/stark ~ sein** to be well-built/sturdily built.

**gebefreudig** *adj* generous, open-handed.

**Gebeine** *pl (geh)* bones *pl*, mortal remains *pl (liter)*.

**Gebell** *nt no pl* barking.

**geben** *pret* **gab**, *ptp* **gegeben 1** *vt* **(a)** *(auch vi)* to give. **wer hat dir das gegeben?** who gave you that?; **gib's mir!** give it to me!, give me it!; **sich** *(dat)* **(von jdm) etw ~ lassen** to ask sb for sth; **was darf ich Ihnen ~?** what can I get you?; **~ Sie mir bitte zwei Flaschen Bier** I'd like two bottles of beer, please; **ich gebe dir das Auto für 100 Mark** I'll let you have the car for 100 marks; **ein gutes Beispiel ~** to set a good example; **jdn/etw verloren ~** to give sb/sth up as lost; **~ Sie mir bitte Herrn Braun** *(Telec)* can I speak to Mr Braun please?; **Gott gebe, daß ...** God grant that ...; **es war ihm nicht gegeben, seine Eltern lebend wiederzusehen** he was not to see his parents alive again; **in die Post ~** to post; **ein Auto in Reparatur ~** to have a car repaired; **ein Kind in Pflege ~** to put *or* place a child in care; **2 + 2 gibt 4** 2+2 makes 4; **das gibt keinen Sinn** that doesn't make sense; **Rotwein gibt Flecken** red wine leaves stains; **was wird heute im Theater gegeben?** what's on at the theatre today?; **er gibt Englisch** he teaches English.

**(b) viel/nicht viel auf etw** *(acc)* **~** to set great store/not much store by sth; **ich gebe nicht viel auf seinen Rat** I don't think much of his advice; **etw von sich ~** *Laut, Worte, Flüche* to utter sth.

**2** *vi (auch vt) (Cards)* to deal; *(Tennis: Aufschlag haben)* to serve. **wer gibt?** whose deal/serve is it?

**3** *vt impers* **es gibt** *(+acc)* there is/there are; **was gibt's?** what's the matter?, what's up?; **was gibt's zum Mittagessen?** what's for lunch?; **freitags gibt es bei uns immer Fisch** we always have fish on Fridays; **heute gibt's noch Regen** it's going to rain today; **dafür gibt es 10% Rabatt** you get 10% discount for it; **das gibt's doch nicht!** I don't believe it!; **da gibt's nichts** *(col)* there are no two ways about it *(col)*; **gleich gibt's was!** *(col)* there'll be trouble in a minute!

**4** *vr* **(a)** *(nachlassen)* to ease off, to let up; *(sich erledigen)* to sort itself out; *(aufhören)* to stop. **sich geschlagen ~** to admit defeat; **sich gefangen ~** to give oneself up; **das wird sich schon ~** it'll all work out. **(b)** *(sich benehmen)* to behave.

**Geber** *m* - giver; *(Cards)* dealer.

**Gebet** *nt* **-e** prayer. **sein ~ verrichten** to say one's prayers; **jdn ins ~ nehmen** *(fig)* to take sb to task.

**Gebetbuch** *nt* prayer book, missal *(US)*.

**gebeten** *ptp of* **bitten.**

**gebeugt** *adj Haltung* stooped; *Kopf* bowed; *Schultern* sloping. **~ sitzen/stehen** to sit/stand hunched up.

**Gebiet** *nt* **-e** area, region; *(Fläche)* area; *(Staats~)* territory; *(fig: Fach)* field; *(Teil~)* branch. **auf diesem ~** in this field.

**gebieten*** *irreg* **1** *vti (verlangen)* to demand; *(befehlen)* to command. **jdm etw ~** to command sb to do

sth. **2** *vi (liter: herrschen)* to have command *(über +acc* over*)*. **über ein Land/Volk ~** to have dominion over a country/nation.

**Gebieter** *m* - *(old)* master.

**Gebieterin** *f (old)* mistress.

**gebieterisch** *adj (geh)* imperious; *(herrisch)* domineering; *Ton* peremptory.

**Gebiets-: ~anspruch** *m* territorial claim; **~hoheit** *f* territorial sovereignty.

**Gebilde** *nt* - thing, construction.

**gebildet** *adj* educated; *(gelehrt)* learned, erudite; *(kultiviert)* cultured.

**Gebirge** *nt* - mountains *pl*, mountain range. **im/ins ~** in/into the mountains.

**gebirgig** *adj* mountainous.

**Gebirgs-** *in cpds* mountain; **~ausläufer** *pl* foothills *pl*; **~bahn** *f* mountain railway *crossing a mountain range*; **~kette** *f* mountain chain; **~rücken** *m* mountain ridge; **~straße** *f* mountain road; **~zug** *m* mountain range.

**Gebiß** *nt* **-sse** *(die Zähne)* (set of) teeth; *(künstliches ~)* dentures *pl*.

**gebissen** *ptp of* **beißen.**

**Gebläse** *nt* - fan, blower.

**geblasen** *ptp of* **blasen.**

**geblichen** *ptp of* **bleichen.**

**geblieben** *ptp of* **bleiben.**

**geblümt** *adj* flowered.

**Geblüt** *nt no pl (geh: Abstammung)* descent, lineage. **von edlem ~** of noble blood.

**gebogen 1** *ptp of* **biegen. 2** *adj Nase* Roman.

**geboren 1** *ptp of* **gebären. 2** *adj* born. **blind ~ sein** to have been born blind; **er ist blind ~** he was born blind; **~er Engländer sein** to be English by birth; **er ist der ~e Erfinder** he's a born inventor; **Hanna Schmidt, ~e** *or* **geb. Müller** Hanna Schmidt, née Müller.

**geborgen 1** *ptp of* **bergen. 2** *adj* **sich ~ fühlen/ ~ sein** to feel/be secure *or* safe.

**Geborgenheit** *f* security.

**geborsten** *ptp of* **bersten.**

**Gebot** *nt* **-e (a)** *(Gesetz)* law; *(Regel, Vorschrift)* rule; *(Bibl)* commandment; *(moralisch)* precept; *(geh: Erfordernis)* requirement. **das ~ der Stunde** the needs of the moment; **das ~ der Vernunft** the dictates of reason. **(b)** *(Verfügung)* command. **jdm zu ~e stehen** to be at sb's command *or (Geld etc)* disposal. **(c)** *(Comm: bei Auktionen)* bid.

**geboten 1** *ptp of* **bieten, gebieten. 2** *adj (geh) (ratsam)* advisable; *(notwendig)* necessary; *(dringend ~)* imperative. **bei aller ~en Achtung** with all due respect.

**Gebr.** = **Gebrüder** Bros.

**gebracht** *ptp of* **bringen.**

**gebrannt 1** *ptp of* **brennen. 2** *adj* **ein ~es Kind scheut das Feuer** *(Prov)* once bitten twice shy *(Prov)*.

**gebraten** *ptp of* **braten.**

**Gebräu** *nt* **-(e)s, -e** brew; *(pej)* strange concoction.

**Gebrauch** *m, pl* **Gebräuche** *(Benutzung)* use; *(eines Wortes auch)* usage; *(Anwendung)* application; *(Brauch)* custom. **falscher ~** misuse; misapplication; **von etw ~ machen** to make use of sth; **in ~** *(dat)* **haben** to use sth; **allgemein in ~** *(dat)* in general use; **zum äußerlichen/innerlichen ~** to be taken externally/internally; **vor ~ (gut) schütteln** shake (well) before use.

**gebrauchen*** *vt (benutzen)* to use; *(anwenden)* to apply. **sich zu etw ~ lassen** to be useful for sth; *(ausnutzen)* to be used as sth; **nicht mehr zu ~ sein** to be no longer any use; **er/das ist zu nichts zu ~** he's/that's (of) no use to anybody; **das kann ich gut**

~ I can really use that; **ich könnte ein neues Kleid** ~ I could do with a new dress.

**gebräuchlich** adj (verbreitet) common; (gewöhnlich) usual, customary. **nicht mehr** ~ (Ausdruck etc) no longer used.

**Gebrauchs-:** ~**anweisung** f (für Arznei) directions pl; (für Geräte etc) instructions pl; ~**artikel** pl (esp Comm) basic consumer goods pl; **g~fähig** adj in working order, usable; **etw g~fähig machen** to put sth into working order; **g~fertig** adj ready for use; Nahrungsmittel instant; ~**gegenstand** m utilitarian object; (Gerät) utensil.

**gebraucht** adj second-hand, used. **etw** ~ **kaufen** to buy sth second-hand.

**Gebrauchtwagen** m used or second-hand car.

**gebräunt** adj (braungebrannt) (sun-)tanned.

**Gebrechen** nt - (geh) affliction.

**gebrechlich** adj frail.

**Gebrechlichkeit** f frailty.

**gebrochen 1** ptp of **brechen**. **2** adj broken. ~**en Herzens** broken-hearted; ~ **Deutsch sprechen** to speak broken German.

**Gebrüder** pl (old) brothers pl; ~ **Müller** (Comm) Müller Brothers.

**Gebrüll** nt no pl (von Rind) bellowing; (von Mensch) yelling.

**gebückt** adj **eine** ~**e Haltung** a stoop; ~ **gehen** to stoop.

**Gebühr** f -en **(a)** charge; (Post~) postage no pl; (Honorar) fee; (Studien~) fees pl; (Vermittlungs~) commission; (Rad, TV) licence (Brit), license (US). ~**en erheben** to make a charge, to charge postage/a fee etc; **zu ermäßigter** ~ at a reduced rate; ~ **(be)zahlt Empfänger** postage to be paid by addressee. **(b)** (Angemessenheit) **nach** ~ suitably, properly; **über** ~ excessively.

**gebühren*** (geh) **1** vi to be due (dat to). **ihm gebührt Anerkennung** he deserves or is due recognition. **2** vr to be proper or fitting. **wie es sich gebührt** as is proper.

**gebührend** adj (verdient) due; (angemessen) suitable; (geziemend) proper.

**Gebühren-:** ~**einheit** f (Telec) (tariff) unit; ~**erhöhung** f increase in charges/fees; **g~frei** adj free of charge; Brief, Paket post-free; **g~frei anrufen** to call freefone; **g~pflichtig** adj chargeable; **g~pflichtige Verwarnung** (Jur) fine; **jdn g~pflichtig verwarnen** to fine sb; **g~pflichtige Autobahn** toll motorway (Brit), turnpike (US).

**gebunden 1** ptp of **binden**. **2** adj tied (an +acc to sth); Kapital tied up; Preise controlled; (Ling, Phys) bound; (Buch) cased, hardback; Wärme latent; (Mus) legato. **anderweitig** ~ **sein** to be otherwise engaged.

**Geburt** f -en (lit, fig) birth. **von** ~ by birth; **von** ~ **an** from birth; **das war eine schwere** ~! (fig col) that took some doing (col).

**Geburten-:** ~**kontrolle**, ~**regelung** f birth control; ~**rückgang** m drop in the birth rate; **g~schwach** adj Jahrgang with a low birth rate; **g~stark** adj Jahrgang with a high birth rate; ~**zahlen** pl, ~**ziffer** f birth rate.

**gebürtig** adj ~**er Londoner sein** to have been born in London, to be a native Londoner.

**Geburts-:** ~**anzeige** f birth announcement; ~**datum** nt date of birth; ~**fehler** m congenital defect; ~**helfer(in** f) m (Arzt) obstetrician; (Hebamme) midwife; ~**hilfe** f (als Fach) obstetrics sing; (von Hebamme auch) midwifery; ~**jahr** nt year of birth; ~**land** nt native country; ~**ort** m birth place.

**Geburtstag** m birthday. **herzlichen Glückwunsch zum** ~! happy birthday!, many happy returns (of the day)!; **jdm zum** ~ **gratulieren** to wish sb (a) happy birthday or many happy returns (of the day); **heute habe ich** ~ it's my birthday today; ~ **feiern** to celebrate one's/sb's birthday; **jdm etw zum** ~ **schenken** to give sb sth for his/her birthday.

**Geburtstags-** in cpds birthday.

**Geburts-:** ~**urkunde** f birth certificate; ~**wehen** pl labour (Brit) or labor (US) pains pl.

**Gebüsch** nt -e bushes pl; (Unterholz) undergrowth.

**gedacht 1** ptp of **denken, gedenken**. **2** adj Linie, Fall imaginary.

**Gedächtnis** nt memory; (Andenken auch) remembrance. **etw aus dem** ~ **hersagen** to recite sth from memory; **wenn mich mein** ~ **nicht trügt** if my memory serves me right; **zum** ~ **an die Toten** in memory or remembrance of the dead.

**Gedächtnis-:** ~**feier** f commemoration; ~**hilfe** f memory aid, mnemonic; ~**lücke** f gap in one's memory; ~**schwund** m amnesia, loss of memory; ~**stütze** f = ~**hilfe**; ~**verlust** m loss of memory.

**gedämpft** adj Geräusch muffled; Farben, Instrument, Stimmung muted; Optimismus cautious; Licht, Freude subdued. **mit** ~**er Stimme** in a low voice.

**Gedanke** m -n thought (über +acc on, about); (Idee, Plan, Einfall) idea; (Konzept) concept; (Betrachtung) reflection (über +acc on). **der bloße** ~ **an ...** the mere thought of ...; **da kam mir ein** ~ then I had an idea; **in** ~ **vertieft/verloren sein** to be deep/lost in thought; **jdn auf andere** ~**n bringen** to take sb's mind off things; **sich** (dat) **über etw** (acc) ~**n machen** to think about sth; (sich sorgen) to worry about sth; **etw ganz in** ~**n** (dat) **tun** to do sth without thinking; **jds** ~**n lesen** to read sb's mind or thoughts; **auf einen** ~**n kommen** to have or get an idea; **auf dumme** ~**n kommen** (col) to get up to mischief; **jdn auf den** ~**n bringen, etw zu tun** to give sb the idea of doing sth.

**Gedanken-:** ~**austausch** m exchange of ideas; ~**freiheit** f freedom of thought; ~**gang** m train of thought; ~**lesen** nt mind-reading; **g~los** adj (unüberlegt) unthinking; (zerstreut) absent-minded; (rücksichtslos) thoughtless; **etw g~los tun** to do sth without thinking; ~**losigkeit** f siehe adj lack of thought; absentmindedness; thoughtlessness; ~**sprung** m mental leap; ~**strich** m dash; ~**übertragung** f telepathy (auch fig), thought transference; **g~verloren** adj lost in thought; **g~voll** adj (nachdenklich) thoughtful, pensive.

**gedanklich** adj intellectual; (vorgestellt) imaginary.

**Gedärme** pl intestines pl.

**Gedeck** nt -e (Tisch~) cover; (Menü) set meal, table d'hôte; (in Lokal) cover charge; set drink served with cover charge. **ein** ~ **auflegen** to set a place.

**gedeckt** adj Farben muted; Gang covered.

**Gedeih** m: **auf** ~ **und Verderb** for better or (for) worse.

**gedeihen** pret **gedieh**, ptp **gediehen** vi aux sein to thrive, to flourish; (geh: sich entwickeln) to develop; (fig: vorankommen) to make progress. **die Sache ist so weit gediehen, daß...** the matter has reached the point or stage where ...

**Gedeihen** nt no pl (Gelingen) success.

**Gedenken** nt no pl memory. **zum** ~ **an jdn/etw** in memory or remembrance of sb/sth.

**gedenken*** vi irreg +gen **(a)** (geh: denken an) to remember, to think of; (feierlich) to commemorate. **(b)** ~, **etw zu tun** to propose to do sth.

**Gedenk-:** ~**feier** f commemoration; ~**minute** f minute's silence; ~**stätte** f memorial; ~**stein** m memorial stone; ~**stunde** f hour of commemoration; ~**tafel** f plaque; ~**tag** m commemoration day.

**Gedicht** nt -e poem. **die ~e Enzensbergers** Enzensberger's poetry or poems; **dieses Kleid ist ein** ~ *(fig col)* this dress is a dream *(col)*.

**gediegen** adj **(a)** Metall pure. **(b)** *(von Qualität)* high-quality; *(geschmackvoll)* tasteful; *(rechtschaffen)* upright; Verarbeitung solid; Kenntnisse sound.

**Gediegenheit** f siehe adj purity; high quality; tastefulness; uprightness; solidity; soundness.

**gedieh** pret of **gedeihen**.

**gediehen** ptp of **gedeihen**.

**gedr.** = **gedruckt**.

**Gedränge** nt no pl *(Menschenmenge)* crowd, crush; *(Drängeln)* jostling. **ins ~ kommen** or **geraten** *(fig)* to get into a fix.

**gedrängt** adj packed; *(fig)* Stil terse. **~ voll** packed full, jam-packed *(col)*.

**gedroschen** ptp of **dreschen**.

**gedruckt** adj **lügen wie ~** *(col)* to lie through one's teeth.

**gedrückt** adj depressed, dejected. **~er Stimmung sein** to be in low spirits, to feel depressed.

**gedrungen** **1** ptp of **dringen**. **2** adj Gestalt sturdy, stocky.

**geduckt** adj Haltung, Mensch crouching; Kopf lowered.

**Gedudel** nt no pl *(col)* *(von Klarinette etc)* tootling; *(von Radio)* noise.

**Geduld** f no pl patience. **mit jdm/etw ~ haben** to be patient or have patience with sb/sth; **mir reißt die ~, ich verliere die ~** my patience is wearing thin, I'm losing my patience.

**gedulden\*** vr to be patient.

**geduldig** adj patient. **~ wie ein Lamm** meek as a lamb.

**Gedulds-:** ~**faden** m **jetzt reißt mir aber der** ~**faden!** *(col)* I'm just about losing patience; ~**probe** f trial of (one's) patience; ~**spiel** nt puzzle.

**gedungen** adj *(pej geh)* Mörder hired.

**gedurft** ptp of **dürfen**.

**ge|ehrt** adj honoured *(Brit)*, honored *(US)*. **Sehr ~e Damen und Herren!** Ladies and Gentlemen!; *(in Briefen)* Dear Sirs; Dear Sir or Madam; **Sehr ~er Herr Kurz!** Dear Mr Kurz.

**ge|eignet** adj *(passend)* suitable; *(richtig)* right. **sie ist für diesen Posten nicht ~** she's not the right person for this job; **im ~en Augenblick** at the right moment; **er wäre zum Lehrer gut/schlecht ~** he would/wouldn't make a good teacher.

**Gefahr** f **-en** **(a)** danger *(für to, for)*; *(Bedrohung)* threat *(für to, for)*. **die ~en des Verkehrs/dieses Berufs** the dangers or perils or hazards of the traffic/this job; **in ~ sein/schweben** to be in danger or jeopardy; **außer ~** *(nicht gefährdet)* not in danger; *(nicht mehr gefährdet)* out of danger; *(Patient)* off the danger list; **sich einer ~ aussetzen** to put oneself in danger; **es besteht die ~, daß ...** there's a risk or the danger that ... **(b)** *(Wagnis, Risiko)* risk *(für to, for)*. **auf eigene ~** at one's own risk or *(stärker)* peril; **~ laufen, etw zu tun** to run the risk of doing sth.

**gefährden\*** vt to endanger; Chancen etc auch to jeopardize; *(bedrohen)* to threaten.

**gefährdet** adj Tierart etc endangered; Ehe, Jugendliche etc at risk.

**Gefährdung** f no pl **(a)** siehe vt endangering; jeopardizing. **(b)** *(Gefahr)* danger *(gen to)*.

**gefahren** ptp of **fahren**.

**Gefahren-:** ~**herd** m danger area; ~**quelle** f source of danger; ~**stelle** f danger spot; ~**zone** f danger zone or area; ~**zulage** f danger money, hazard pay *(US)*.

**gefährlich** adj dangerous; *(gewagt auch)* risky.

**Gefährlichkeit** f siehe adj dangerousness; riskiness.

**Gefahr-:** **g~los** adj safe; ~**losigkeit** f safety.

**Gefährt** nt -(e)s, e *(dated)* wagon, carriage; *(hum)* jalopy *(col)*.

**Gefährte** m *(wk)* **-n, -n, Gefährtin** f *(geh: lit, fig)* companion.

**Gefälle** nt - *(Neigung)* *(von Fluß)* drop, fall; *(von Land, Straße)* slope; *(Neigungsgrad)* gradient; *(fig: Unterschied)* difference. **das Gelände hat ein starkes ~** the land slopes down steeply; **„starkes ~!"** steep hill.

**gefallen**[1]\* vi irreg to please *(jdm sb)*. **es gefällt mir (gut)** I like it (very much or a lot); **es gefällt ihm, wie sie spricht** he likes the way she talks; **das gefällt mir gar nicht** I don't like it at all; **das könnte dir so ~!** *(col)* no way! *(col)*; **sich** *(dat)* **etw ~ lassen** *(dulden)* to put up with sth.

**gefallen**[2] **1** ptp of **fallen**, **gefallen**[1]. **2** adj *(Mil)* killed in action.

**Gefallen**[1] nt no pl *(geh)* pleasure. **an etw** *(dat)* ~ **finden** to derive pleasure from sth; **an jdm ~ finden** to take to sb.

**Gefallen**[2] m - favour *(Brit)*, favor *(US)*. **jdn um einen ~ bitten** to ask a favour of sb; **tun Sie mir den ~ und schweigen Sie** would you do me a favour and be quiet; **ihm zu ~** to please him.

**Gefallene(r)** mf decl as adj soldier killed in action.

**gefällig** adj **(a)** *(hilfsbereit)* helpful, obliging. **(b)** *(ansprechend)* pleasing; *(freundlich)* pleasant. **(c) sonst noch etwas ~?** *(iro)* will there be anything else?

**Gefälligkeit** f **(a)** *(Gefallen)* favour *(Brit)*, favor *(US)*. **jdm eine ~ erweisen** to do sb a favour. **(b)** no pl *(gefälliges Wesen)* pleasantness. **etw aus ~ tun** to do sth out of the kindness of one's heart.

**gefälligst** adv *(col)* kindly. **sei ~ still!** will you kindly keep your mouth shut! *(col)*.

**gefangen** **1** ptp of **fangen**. **2** adj *(~genommen)* captured; *(fig)* captivated. **sich ~ geben** to give oneself up, to surrender.

**Gefangenen-:** ~**austausch** m exchange of prisoners; ~**lager** nt prison camp; ~**wärter** m prison officer, *(prison)* warder.

**Gefangene(r)** mf decl as adj prisoner. **500 ~ machen** *(Mil)* to take 500 prisoners.

**Gefangen-:** **g~halten** vt sep irreg to hold prisoner; Tiere to keep in captivity; *(fig)* to captivate; ~**nahme** f **-n** capture; *(Verhaftung)* arrest; **g~nehmen** vt sep irreg Mensch to take captive or prisoner; *(verhaften)* to arrest; *(fig)* to captivate; ~**schaft** f captivity; **in ~schaft geraten** to be taken prisoner.

**Gefängnis** nt prison, jail; *(~strafe)* imprisonment. **im ~ sitzen** *(col)* to be in prison; **ins ~ kommen** to be sent to prison; **zwei Jahre ~ bekommen** to get two years' imprisonment.

**Gefängnis-** in cpds prison; ~**aufseher** m warder *(Brit)*, guard *(US)*, prison officer; ~**direktor** m prison governor, prison warden *(esp US)*; ~**insasse** m inmate; ~**strafe** f prison sentence; **er wurde zu einer ~strafe verurteilt** he was sent to prison, he was given a prison sentence; ~**wärter** m siehe ~**aufseher**; ~**zelle** f prison cell.

**gefärbt** adj coloured *(Brit)*, colored *(US)*; Haar, Stoff dyed; Lebensmittel artificially coloured *(Brit)* or colored *(US)*; *(fig)* Bericht biased.

**Gefasel** *nt no pl (pej)* drivel *(col)*.

**Gefäß** *nt* -e vessel *(auch Anat, Bot)*; *(Behälter)* receptacle.

**gefaßt** *adj (ruhig)* composed, calm. **auf etw** *(acc)* ~ **sein** to be prepared *or* ready for sth; **er kann sich auf etwas** ~ **machen** *(col)* he'll be in for it.

**Gefecht** *nt* -e *(lit, fig)* battle; *(Mil)* engagement; *(Scharmützel)* skirmish. **ein hartes** ~ fierce fighting; **jdn/etw außer** ~ **setzen** *(lit, fig)* to put sb/sth out of action; **Argumente ins** ~ **führen** to advance arguments; **im Eifer des** ~**s** *(fig)* in the heat of the moment.

**gefechtsbereit** *adj* ready for action; *(einsatzfähig)* (fully) operational.

**gefedert** *adj (Matratze)* sprung.

**gefeiert** *adj* celebrated.

**gefeit** *adj* **gegen etw** ~ **sein** to be immune to sth.

**gefestigt** *adj Tradition* established; *Charakter* steadfast.

**Gefieder** *nt* - plumage, feathers *pl*.

**gefiedert** *adj* feathered.

**Gefilde** *nt* - *(old, liter)* realm. **heimatliche** ~ *(hum)* home pastures.

**Geflecht** *nt* -e *(lit, fig)* network; *(Gewebe)* weave; *(Rohr~)* wickerwork.

**gefleckt** *adj* spotted; *Blume, Vogel* speckled; *Haut* blotchy.

**Geflimmer** *nt no pl* shimmering; *(Film, TV)* flicker(ing); *(heiße Luft)* heat-haze.

**geflissentlich** *adj (geh)* deliberate.

**geflochten** *ptp of* **flechten.**

**geflogen** *ptp of* **fliegen.**

**geflohen** *ptp of* **fliehen.**

**geflossen** *ptp of* **fließen.**

**Geflügel** *nt no pl (Zool, Cook)* poultry *no pl*.

**Geflügel-** *in cpds* poultry; ~**händler** *m* poulterer, poultry dealer; ~**schere** *f* poultry shears *pl*.

**geflügelt** *adj* winged. ~**e Worte** familiar quotations.

**Geflügelzucht** *f* poultry farming.

**Geflüster** *nt no pl* whispering.

**gefochten** *ptp of* **fechten.**

**Gefolge** *nt* - retinue; *(Trauer~)* cortège. **im** ~ in the wake *(+gen of)*; **etw im** ~ **haben** *(fig)* to bring sth in its wake.

**Gefolgschaft** *f (die Anhänger)* following; *(Hist: Gefolge)* retinue.

**gefragt** *adj* in demand *pred*.

**gefräßig** *adj* gluttonous; *(fig geh)* voracious.

**Gefräßigkeit** *f* gluttony.

**Gefreite(r)** *mf decl as adj (Mil)* lance corporal *(Brit)*, private first class *(US)*.

**gefressen** *ptp of* **fressen. jdn** ~ **haben** *(col)* to be sick of sb *(col)*.

**gefrieren*** *vi irreg aux sein (lit, fig)* to freeze.

**Gefrier-:** ~**fach** *nt* freezer compartment; **g**~**getrocknet** *adj* freeze-dried; ~**punkt** *m* freezing point; ~**schrank** *m* (upright) freezer; ~**truhe** *f* freezer, deep freeze.

**gefroren** *ptp of* **frieren, gefrieren.**

**Gefüge** *nt* - *(lit, fig)* structure.

**gefügig** *adj* submissive; *(gehorsam)* obedient. **jdn** ~ **machen** to make sb bend to one's will.

**Gefühl** *nt* -e feeling; *(~sregung auch)* emotion. **etw im** ~ **haben** to have a feel for sth; **etw nach** ~ **tun** to do sth by instinct; **ich habe ein** ~**, als ob** ... I feel as though ...; **ein** ~ **für Zahlen/Musik** a feeling for figures/music; **ein** ~ **für Gerechtigkeit/Anstand** a sense of justice/decency.

**gefühllos** *adj* insensitive, unfeeling; *Bein* numb.

**Gefühllosigkeit** *f siehe adj* insensitivity; numbness.

**Gefühls-:** **g**~**arm** *adj* unemotional; ~**ausbruch** *m* emotional outburst; **g**~**betont** *adj* emotional; *Rede, Äußerung auch* emotive; ~**duselei** *f (pej)* mawkishness; **g**~**kalt** *adj* cold; ~**kälte** *f* coldness; ~**leben** *nt* emotional life; **g**~**mäßig** *adj* instinctive; ~**mensch** *m* emotional person; ~**regung** *f* stir of emotion; *(seelische Empfindung)* feeling.

**gefühlvoll** *adj (empfindsam)* sensitive; *(ausdrucksvoll)* expressive; *(liebevoll)* loving.

**gefüllt** *adj (Cook)* stuffed; *Pralinen* with soft centres *(Brit)* or centers *(US)*; *Brieftasche* full.

**gefunden** 1 *ptp of* **finden.** 2 **adj das war ein** ~**es Fressen für ihn** that was handing it to him on a plate.

**gefürchtet** *adj* dreaded *usu attr.*

**Gegacker** *nt no pl (lit, fig)* cackle, cackling.

**gegangen** *ptp of* **gehen.**

**gegeben** 1 *ptp of* **geben.** 2 *adj* given; *(Philos: real)* factual. **unter den** ~**en Umständen** given the circumstances; **bei den** ~**en Tatsachen** given these facts; **etw als** ~ **voraussetzen** to assume sth; **zu** ~**er Zeit** in due course.

**gegebenenfalls** *adv* should the situation arise.

**Gegebenheit** *f usu pl* (actual) fact; *(Zustand)* condition.

**gegen** *prep +acc* **(a)** *(wider)* against. **X** ~ **Y** *(Sport, Jur)* X versus Y; ~ **seinen Befehl** contrary to *or* against his orders; **haben Sie ein Mittel** ~ **Schnupfen?** do you have anything for colds?; **nichts** ~ **jdn/ etw haben** to have nothing against sb/sth. **(b)** *(in Richtung auf)* towards *(esp Brit)*, toward; *(nach)* to; *(an)* against. ~ **einen Baum fahren** to drive into a tree; **etw** ~ **das Licht halten** to hold sth to *or* against the light; ~ **Osten fahren** to travel to(wards) the east; **es wird** ~ **Abend kühler** it grows cooler towards evening. **(c)** *(ungefähr)* round about, around. **ich komme** ~ **Abend vorbei** I'll come around early this evening. **(d)** *(gegenüber)* towards *(esp Brit)*, toward, to. **gerecht** ~ **alle** fair to all. **(e)** *(im Austausch für)* for. ~ **bar** for cash; ~ **Quittung** against a receipt; ~ **Bezahlung** in exchange for payment. **(f)** *(verglichen mit)* compared with.

**Gegen-:** ~**angriff** *m (Mil, fig)* counterattack; ~**argument** *nt* counterargument; ~**beispiel** *nt* counterexample; ~**besuch** *m* return visit; **jdm einen** ~**besuch machen** to return sb's visit; ~**bewegung** *f (Tech, fig)* countermovement; ~**beweis** *m* **den** ~**beweis zu etw erbringen** to produce evidence against sth.

**Gegend** *f* -en area; *(geographisches Gebiet, Körper~)* region. **die** ~ **von London** the London area; **hier in der** ~ around here; **die ganze** ~ **spricht davon** the whole neighbourhood *(Brit)* or neighborhood *(US)* is talking about it.

**Gegendarstellung** *f (Press)* reply.

**gegen|einander** *adv* against each other; *(im Austausch)* for each other; *(zueinander)* to(wards) each other.

**gegen|einander-:** ~**halten** *vt sep irreg (lit)* to hold together; *(fig)* to compare; ~**stehen** *vi sep irreg (fig)* to be on opposite sides; *(Aussagen)* to conflict; ~**stoßen** *vi sep irreg aux sein* to bump into each other; *(kollidieren)* to collide.

**Gegen-:** ~**entwurf** *m* alternative plan; ~**erklärung** *f* counterstatement; *(Dementi)* denial, disclaimer; ~**fahrbahn** *f* opposite carriageway or *(Spur)* lane; ~**frage** *f* counterquestion; **jdm eine** ~**frage stellen** to ask sb a question in reply (to his); ~**gerade** *f (Sport)* back straight; ~**gewicht** *nt* counterbalance *(auch fig)*, counterweight; ~**gift** *nt* antidote *(gegen to)*; ~**kandidat** *m* rival candidate;

~**kurs** *m (lit, fig)* opposite course; **einen** ~**kurs steuern** to take an opposing course of action; **g~läufig** *adj (fig) Tendenz* contrary, opposite; ~**leistung** *f* service in return; **als** ~**leistung für etw** in return for sth; **g~lenken** *vi sep (Aut)* to steer in the opposite direction; ~**licht** *nt* etw bei *or* im ~ **aufnehmen** *(Phot)* to take a backlit photograph of sth; ~**lichtaufnahme** *f* backlit photograph; ~**liebe** *f* requited love; *(fig: Zustimmung)* approval; **der Vorschlag stieß auf wenig** ~**liebe** the suggestion was hardly welcomed with open arms; ~**maßnahme** *f* countermeasure; ~**maßnahmen zur Bekämpfung der Inflation** measures to counter inflation; ~**meinung** *f* opposite opinion; ~**mittel** *nt (Med)* antidote *(gegen to)*; ~**partei** *f* other side; *(Sport)* opposing side; *(Jur)* opposing party; ~**probe** *f* crosscheck; ~**reaktion** *f* counter-reaction; ~**rede** *f (Antwort)* reply; *(Widerrede)* contradiction; ~**richtung** *f* opposite direction.

**Gegensatz** *m* ⸚e opposite; *(Kontrast)* contrast; *(Unvereinbarkeit)* conflict; *(Unterschied)* difference. **im** ~ **zu** unlike, in contrast to; **einen krassen** ~ **zu etw bilden** to contrast sharply with sth; ~**e ausgleichen** to even out differences.

**gegensätzlich** *adj (konträr)* contrasting; *(widersprüchlich)* opposing; *(unterschiedlich)* different; *(unvereinbar)* conflicting. **eine** ~**e Meinung** a conflicting view.

**Gegen-:** ~**schlag** *m (Mil)* reprisal; *(fig)* retaliation *no pl;* **zum** ~**schlag ausholen** to prepare to retaliate; ~**seite** *f (lit, fig)* other side; **g~seitig** *adj* mutual; **sie beschuldigten sich g~seitig** they (each) accused one another *or* each other; **sich g~seitig ausschließen** to be mutually exclusive; **in g~seitigem Einverständnis** by mutual agreement; ~**seitigkeit** *f* mutuality; **ein Vertrag auf** ~**seitigkeit** a reciprocal treaty; ~**sinn** *m* **im** ~**sinn** in the opposite direction; ~**spieler** *m* opponent; *(bei Mannschaftsspielen auch)* opposite number; ~**sprechanlage** *f* (two-way) intercom.

**Gegenstand** *m* ⸚e *(Ding)* object, thing; *(Thema)* subject; *(der Neugier etc, Philos)* object. ~ **des Gespötts** laughing stock.

**gegenständlich** *adj* concrete; *(Philos)* objective; *(Art)* representational.

**gegenstandslos** *adj (grundlos)* groundless; *(hinfällig)* irrelevant.

**Gegen-:** ~**stimme** *f (Parl)* vote against; ~**stoß** *m (Mil, Sport)* counterattack; ~**stück** *nt* opposite; *(passendes* ~*stück)* counterpart.

**Gegenteil** *nt* opposite *(von of)*; *(Umkehrung)* reverse *(von of)*. **im** ~**!** on the contrary!; **ganz im** ~ quite the reverse; **das** ~ **bewirken** to have the opposite effect; *(Mensch)* to achieve the exact opposite; **ins** ~ **umschlagen** to swing to the other extreme.

**gegenteilig** *adj Ansicht, Wirkung* opposite, contrary. **eine** ~**e Meinung** a different opinion; **ich habe nichts G~es gehört** I've heard nothing to the contrary.

**Gegentor** *nt (esp Ftbl)* **ein** ~ **hinnehmen müssen** to concede a goal; **ein** ~ **erzielen** to score.

**gegen|über 1** *prep* +*dat* **(a)** *(örtlich)* opposite. **er wohnt mir** ~ he lives opposite me; **er saß mir schräg** ~ he sat diagonally across from me. **(b)** *(zu)* to; *(in bezug auf)* with regard to, towards *(esp Brit)*, toward; *(angesichts, vor)* in the face of; *(im Vergleich zu)* in comparison with. **mir** ~ **hat er das nicht geäußert** he didn't say that to me; **er ist allem Neuen** ~ **wenig aufgeschlossen** he's not very open-minded about anything new. **2** *adv* opposite. **der Park** ~ the park opposite; **die Leute von** ~ *(col)* the people opposite.

**Gegen|über** *nt* - *(bei Kampf)* opponent; *(bei Diskussion)* opposite number. **mein** ~ **im Zug** the person opposite me in the train.

**gegen|über-:** ~**liegen** *sep irreg* **1** *vi* +*dat* to be opposite, to face; **2** *vr* **sich** *(dat)* ~**liegen** to face each other; ~**liegend** *adj attr* opposite; ~**sehen** *vr sep irreg* +*dat* **sich einer Aufgabe** ~**sehen** to be faced *or* confronted with a task; ~**sitzen** *vi sep irreg* to sit opposite *or* facing; ~**stehen** *vi sep irreg* +*dat* to be opposite, to face; **jdm feindlich/freundlich** ~**stehen** to have a hostile/friendly attitude towards sb; **einer Gefahr** ~**stehen** to be faced with a danger; ~**stellen** *vt sep (konfrontieren mit)* to confront *(dat* with*)*; *(fig: vergleichen)* to compare *(dat* with*)*; **G~stellung** *f* confrontation; *(fig: Vergleich)* comparison; ~**treten** *vi sep irreg aux sein* **jdm** ~**treten** to face sb.

**Gegen-:** ~**verkehr** *m* oncoming traffic; ~**vorschlag** *m* counter-proposal.

**Gegenwart** *f no pl* **(a)** present; *(Gram)* present (tense). **die Musik der** ~ contemporary music; **die Probleme der** ~ the problems of today. **(b)** *(Anwesenheit)* presence. **in** ~ **von** in the presence of.

**gegenwärtig 1** *adj* **(a)** *attr (jetzig)* present; *(heutig auch)* current, present-day. **(b)** *(geh: anwesend)* present *pred.* **2** *adv (augenblicklich)* at present; *(heutzutage auch)* currently.

**Gegenwarts-:** **g~bezogen** *adj Roman etc* relevant to present times; ~**bezug** *m* relevance (to present times); **g~nah(e)** *adj* relevant (to the present).

**Gegen-:** ~**wehr** *f* resistance; ~**wert** *m* equivalent; **Ware im** ~**wert von DM800** goods worth *or* to the value of 800 marks; ~**wind** *m* headwind; **g~zeichnen** *vt sep* to countersign; ~**zeuge** *m* witness for the other side; ~**zug** *m* **im** ~**zug zu etw** as a countermove to sth.

**gegessen** *ptp of* **essen.**

**geglichen** *ptp of* **gleichen.**

**gegliedert** *adj* jointed; *(fig)* structured.

**geglitten** *ptp of* **gleiten.**

**geglommen** *ptp of* **glimmen.**

**geglückt** *adj* successful; *Überraschung* real.

**Gegner(in** *f)* *m* - opponent *(auch Sport)*, adversary; *(Rivale)* rival; *(Feind)* enemy.

**gegnerisch** *adj attr* opposing; *(Mil: feindlich)* enemy *attr,* hostile; *Übermacht* of the enemy.

**Gegnerschaft** *f* opposition.

**gegolten** *ptp of* **gelten.**

**gegoren** *ptp of* **gären.**

**gegossen** *ptp of* **gießen.**

**gegr.** = **gegründet** established, est.

**gegraben** *ptp of* **graben.**

**gegriffen** *ptp of* **greifen.**

**Gehabe** *nt no pl (col)* affected behaviour *(Brit)* or behavior *(US)*.

**gehabt** *ptp of* **haben.**

**Gehackte(s)** *nt decl as adj* mince *(Brit)*, minced *or* ground *(US)* meat.

**Gehalt¹** *m* -e content. **der** ~ **an Eiweiß** the protein content.

**Gehalt²** *nt* ⸚er salary.

**gehalten 1** *ptp of* **halten. 2** *adj:* ~ **sein, etw zu tun** *(form)* to be required to do sth.

**gehaltlos** *adj Nahrung* unnutritious; *(fig)* empty.

**Gehalts-:** ~**abrechnung** *f* salary statement; ~**anspruch** *m* salary claim; ~**empfänger** *m* salary earner; ~**empfänger sein** to receive a salary, to be salaried; ~**erhöhung** *f* salary increase; *(regelmäßig)* increment; ~**gruppe,** ~**klasse** *f* salary bracket; ~**konto** *nt* current *(Brit)* or checking *(US)* account; ~**kürzung** f cut in salary; ~**streifen** m payslip; ~**wunsch** m salary requirement; ~**zulage** f (~erhöhung) salary increase; (regelmäßig) increment; (Extrazulage) bonus.

**gehaltvoll** adj Speise nutritious, nourishing; Mahlzeit substantial; (fig) rich in content.

**gehandikapt** [gə'hɛndikɛpt] adj handicapped.

**Gehänge** nt - garland; (Ohr~) drop, pendant.

**gehangen** ptp of **hängen**.

**geharnischt** adj (fig) Brief, Abfuhr etc strong; Antwort etc sharp.

**gehässig** adj spiteful.

**Gehässigkeit** f spite, spitefulness.

**gehäuft** 1 adj Löffel heaped. 2 adv in large numbers.

**Gehäuse** nt - (a) case, casing; (Lautsprecher~) enclosure. (b) (Schnecken~) shell. (c) (Obst~) core.

**gehbehindert** adj disabled.

**Gehege** nt - reserve; (im Zoo) enclosure, compound; (Wild~) preserve. **jdm ins ~ kommen** (fig col) to get under sb's feet (col); (ein Recht streitig machen) to poach on sb's preserves.

**geheiligt** adj Brauch, Recht sacred.

**geheim** adj secret. **seine ~sten Gefühle/Wünsche** his innermost or most private feelings/wishes; **streng ~ top secret; ~ abstimmen** to vote by secret ballot; **im ~en** secretly.

**Geheim-:** ~**bund** m secret society; ~**dienst** m secret service; ~**fach** nt secret compartment; **g~halten** vt sep irreg **etw** (vor jdm) **g~halten** to keep sth a secret (from sb); ~**haltung** f secrecy. **zur ~ von etw verpflichtet sein** to be sworn to secrecy about sth.

**Geheimnis** nt secret; (rätselhaftes ~) mystery. **das ~ der Schönheit/des Erfolgs** the secret of beauty/success; **aus etw ein/kein ~ machen** to make a big secret about sth/no secret of sth.

**Geheimnis-:** ~**krämer** m (col) secretive type (col), mystery-monger (col); ~**krämerei** f (col), ~**tuerei** f secretiveness; **g~tuerisch** adj secretive; **g~voll** adj mysterious; **g~voll tun** to be mysterious.

**Geheim-:** ~**nummer** f secret number; (für Geldautomaten) PIN number; ~**polizei** f secret police; ~**rat** m privy councillor; ~**ratsecken** pl (col) **er hat ~ratsecken** he is going bald at the temples; ~**rezept** nt secret recipe; ~**schrift** f code, secret writing; ~**tip** m (personal) tip; ~**waffe** f secret weapon.

**Geheiß** nt no pl (geh) **auf jds ~** (acc) at sb's behest.

**geheißen** ptp of **heißen**.

**gehemmt** adj Mensch inhibited.

**gehen** pret **ging**, ptp **gegangen** aux sein 1 vi (a) to go; (zu Fuß) to walk; (abfahren, ausscheiden auch) to leave; (blicken: Fenster) to look out (auf +acc, nach onto). **über die Straße ~** to cross the street; **auf die andere Seite ~** to cross (over) to the other side; **zu jdm ~** to go to see sb; **er ging im Zimmer auf und ab** he walked or paced up and down the room; **wie lange geht man bis zum Bus?** how long a walk is it to the bus?; **wie geht man dorthin?** how do you get there?; **das Kind lernt ~** the baby is learning to walk; **wo er geht und steht** wherever he goes or is; **schwimmen/schlafen ~** to go swimming/to bed; **mit jdm ~** (befreundet sein) to go out with sb, to be with sb; **mit der Zeit/Mode ~** to move with the times/follow the fashion; **in sich** (acc) **~** to think things over; **nach einer Regel ~** to follow a or go by a rule; **das geht gegen meine Überzeugung** that goes or runs against my convictions; **er ging so weit, zu behaupten ...** (fig) he went so far as to claim ...; **das geht zu weit** (fig) that's going too far; **wie geht das**

**Lied/Gedicht?** how does the song/poem go?; **heute geht ein scharfer Wind** there's a biting wind today; **die See geht hoch** there's a high sea, the sea is running high; **die Reise geht über Dresden** the route goes via Dresden; **~ wir!** let's go; **das Schiff geht nach Harwich** the boat is going to or is bound for Harwich; **jdm aus dem Weg ~** to get or move out of sb's way.

(b) (funktionieren) to work; (Auto, Uhr) to go. **die Uhr geht falsch/richtig** the clock is wrong/right.

(c) (dauern) to go on. **wie lange geht das denn noch?** how much longer is it going to go on?

(d) (reichen) to go. **der Rock geht ihr bis zum Knie** the skirt reaches to her knees; **in die Tausende ~** to run into (the) thousands.

(e) (Teig) to rise; (vor dem Backen auch) to prove.

(f) (urteilen) **nach etw ~** to go by sth.

(g) (sich kleiden) **in etw** (dat) **~** to wear sth; **als etw ~** (sich verkleiden) to go as sth.

(h) (ertönen: Klingel) to go, to ring.

(i) **wie ~ die Geschäfte?** how's business?; **wieviele Leute ~ in deinen Wagen?** how many people can you get in your car?; **in diese Schachtel ~ 20 Stück** this packet holds 20; **das Buch ging um ...** the book was about ...; **mein Vorschlag geht dahin, daß ...** my suggestion is that ...; **diese Schublade geht schwer** this drawer is very stiff; **nichts geht über** (+acc) **...** there's nothing to beat ..., there's nothing better than ...; **in die Politik ~** to go into politics; **in die Gewerkschaft/Partei ~** to join the union/party; **unter die Künstler/Säufer ~** (usu hum) to join the ranks of the artists/alcoholics; **als Putzfrau ~** (arbeiten) to work as a cleaner; **das geht doch nicht** (ist nicht möglich) that's not on; **Dienstag geht auch nicht** (col) Tuesday is no good either; **was geht hier vor sich?** what's going on here?

2 vi impers (a) (gesundheitlich) **wie geht es Ihnen?** how are you?; (zu Patient) how are you feeling?; **(danke,) es geht** (col) all right or not too bad (, thanks) (col); **es geht ihm gut/schlecht** he's quite well/not at all well; **sonst geht's dir gut?** (iro) are you sure you're feeling quite all right? (iro).

(b) (ergehen) **wie geht's?** how are things?; (bei Arbeit etc) how's it going?; **es geht** not too bad, so-so; **mir ist es genauso gegangen** (ich habe dasselbe erlebt) it was just the same with me; (ich habe dasselbe empfunden) I felt the same way; **laß es dir gut ~** look after yourself, take care of yourself.

(c) **es geht** (läßt sich machen) it's all right or OK (col); **solange es geht** as long as possible; **geht es?** (ohne Hilfe) can you manage?; **es geht nicht** (ist nicht möglich) it can't be done, it's impossible; (kommt nicht in Frage) it's not on; **so geht das, das geht so** that/this is how it's done; **so geht es or das** (eben) (so ist das Leben) that's how it goes; **morgen geht es nicht** tomorrow's no good.

(d) (betreffen) **ich weiß nicht, worum es geht** I don't know what this is about; **es geht um seinen Vertrag** it's about or it concerns his contract; **es geht um meine Ehre** my honour is at stake; **es geht ihm nur um eins** he's only interested in one thing; **darum geht es mir nicht** that's not the point; (spielt keine Rolle) that's not important to me; **wenn es nach mir ginge ...** if it were or was up to me ..., if I had my way ...

(e) (führen) **dann geht es immer geradeaus** (Straßenrichtung) then it's just straight on.

3 vt ein Kilometer ~ he walked a kilometre; **ich gehe immer diese Straße** I always walk along or take this road.

**Gehen** nt no pl (Zu-Fuß-~, Sport) walking; (Ab-

*schied)* leaving.

**gehenlassen\*** *sep irreg* **1** *vt (col: in Ruhe lassen)* to leave alone. **2** *vr* **(a)** to lose one's self-control. **(b)** *(nachlässig sein)* to let oneself go.

**Geher(in** *f) m - (Sport)* walker.

**gehetzt** *adj* harassed.

**geheuer** *adj* **nicht** ~ *(beängstigend)* scary *(col)*; *(spukhaft)* creepy *(col)*; *(verdächtig)* fishy *(unwohl)* uneasy; **es ist mir nicht ganz** ~ I find it a bit scary *(col)*; it gives me the creeps *(col)*; it seems a bit fishy to me; I feel uneasy about it.

**Geheul(e)** *nt no pl* howling.

**Gehilfe** *m (wk)* **-n, -n, Gehilfin** *f (kaufmännischer ~)* trainee; *(Jur)* accomplice.

**Gehirn** *nt* **-e** brain; *(Geist)* mind.

**Gehirn-:** ~**chirurg** *m* brain surgeon; ~**erschütterung** *f* concussion; ~**schlag** *m* stroke; ~**tumor** *m* brain tumour *(Brit)* or tumor *(US)*; ~**wäsche** *f* brainwashing *no pl*; **jdn einer** ~**wäsche unterziehen** to brainwash sb.

**gehoben** **1** *ptp of* **heben.** **2** *adj* Ausdrucksweise elevated, lofty; *(anspruchsvoll)* sophisticated; *Stellung* senior; *Stimmung* elated. ~**er Dienst** *professional and executive levels of the civil service.*

**Gehöft** *nt* **-e** farm.

**geholfen** *ptp of* **helfen.**

**Gehölz** *nt* **-e** *(geh)* copse; *(Dickicht)* undergrowth.

**Gehör** *nt* **-e** hearing; *(Mus)* ear. **kein musikalisches** ~ **haben** to have no ear for music; **ein schlechtes** ~ **haben** to be hard of hearing; **nach dem** ~ **spielen** to play by ear; **absolutes** ~ perfect pitch; **das** ~ **verlieren** to go deaf; ~ **finden** to gain a hearing; **er fand kein** ~ he was not given a hearing; **jdm** ~/**kein** ~ **schenken** to listen/not to listen to sb; **sich** *(dat)* ~ **verschaffen** to gain attention; *(bei Behörde)* to obtain a hearing.

**gehorchen\*** *vi* to obey *(jdm sb)*; *(Wagen, Maschine etc)* to respond *(jdm/einer Sache* to sb/sth*)*. **seine Stimme gehorchte ihm nicht mehr** he lost control of his voice.

**gehören\*** **1** *vi* **(a)** **jdm** ~ to belong to sb, to be sb's. **(b)** *(den richtigen Platz haben)* to belong; *(Gegenstand auch)* to go. **das gehört nicht hierher** *(Vorschlag)* that is irrelevant here; **das gehört nicht zur Sache** that's irrelevant; **er gehört ins Bett** he should be in bed. **(c)** ~ **zu** *(zählen zu)* to be one of; *(Bestandteil sein von)* to be part of; *(Mitglied sein von)* to belong to; **es gehört zu seinen Pflichten** it's one of his duties; **zur Familie** ~ to be one of the family; **dazu gehört Mut** that takes courage; **dazu gehört (schon) einiges** *or* **etwas** that takes some doing *(col)*. **2** *vr* to be (right and) proper. **das gehört sich einfach nicht** that's just not done.

**gehörig** *adj* **(a)** *(geh)* **nicht zur Sache** ~ irrelevant. **(b)** *attr, adv (gebührend)* proper. **mit dem** ~**en Respekt** with proper respect. **(c)** *(col: beträchtlich, groß)* good *attr*, well and truly *adv*. **eine** ~**e Achtung vor jdm haben** to have a healthy respect for sb.

**gehörlos** *adj (form)* deaf.

**Gehörlose(r)** *mf decl as adj (form)* deaf person.

**gehorsam** *adj* obedient.

**Gehorsam** *m no pl* obedience. **jdm den** ~ **verweigern** to refuse to obey sb.

**Gehorsamkeit** *f* obedience.

**Gehorsamsverweigerung** *f (Mil)* insubordination.

**Gehörsinn** *m* sense of hearing.

**Gehsteig** *m* pavement *(Brit)*, sidewalk *(US)*.

**Gehweg** *m* **(a)** = **Gehsteig. (b)** footpath.

**Geier** *m - (lit, fig)* vulture. **weiß der** ~ *(col)* God knows *(col)*.

**Geifer** *m no pl* slaver; *(fig pej)* venom.

**geifern** *vi* to slaver; *(Schaum vor dem Mund haben)* to foam at the mouth. **gegen jdn/etw** ~ to revile sb/sth.

**Geige** *f* **-n** violin. **die erste/zweite** ~ **spielen** *(lit)* to play first/second violin; *(fig)* to call the tune/play second fiddle.

**geigen** **1** *vi* to play the violin. **2** *vt Lied* to play on the violin.

**Geigen-:** ~**bauer** *m* violin-maker; ~**bogen** *m* violin bow; ~**kasten** *m* violin-case.

**Geiger(in** *f) m* - violinist.

**Geigerzähler** *m* Geiger counter.

**geil** *adj* **(a)** randy, horny; *(pej: lüstern)* lecherous. **(b)** *(col: prima)* brilliant, wicked *(col)*.

**Geilheit** *f siehe adj* randiness, horniness; lecherousness.

**Geisel** *f* **-n** hostage. **jdn als** ~ **nehmen** to take sb hostage.

**Geisel-:** ~**drama** *nt* hostage crisis; ~**nahme** *f* **-n** hostage-taking; ~**nehmer(in** *f) m* hostage-taker.

**Geiß** *f* **-en** *(Ziege)* (nanny-)goat.

**Geißbock** *m* billy-goat.

**Geißel** *f* **-n** *(lit, fig)* scourge; *(dial: Peitsche)* whip.

**geißeln** *vt (anprangern)* to castigate.

**Geist** *m* **-er** **(a)** *no pl (Denken, Vernunft)* mind. ~ **und Materie** mind and matter; **etw im** ~**(e) vor sich sehen** to see sth in one's mind's eye; **sich im** ~**(e) als etw/an einem Ort sehen** to picture oneself as sth/in a place.

**(b)** *(Rel: Seele, außerirdisches Wesen)* spirit; *(Gespenst)* ghost. ~ **und Körper** mind and body; **seinen** ~ **aufgeben** to give up the ghost; **der Heilige** ~ the Holy Ghost *or* Spirit; **der** ~ **Gottes** the Spirit of God; **von allen guten** ~**ern verlassen sein** *(col)* to have taken leave of one's senses *(col)*; **jdm auf den** ~ **gehen** *(col)* to get on sb's nerves.

**(c)** *(no pl: Intellekt)* intellect, mind; *(fig: Denker, Genie)* mind. ~ **haben** to have a good mind *or* intellect; *(Witz)* to be witty; **hier scheiden sich die** ~**er** this is where opinions differ; **sie sind verwandte** ~**er** they are kindred spirits.

**(d)** *no pl (Wesen, Gesinnung)* spirit. **in jds** ~ **handeln** to act in the spirit of sb.

**Geister-:** ~**bahn** *f* ghost train; ~**fahrer** *m (col)* ghost-driver *(US col)*, *person driving in the wrong direction*; **g~haft** *adj* ghostly; ~**hand** *f:* **wie von** ~**hand** as if by magic.

**geistern** *vi aux sein* to wander like a ghost. **der Gedanke geisterte durch sein Hirn** the thought haunted him.

**Geister-:** ~**stadt** *f* ghost town; ~**stimme** *f* ghostly voice; ~**stunde** *f* witching hour.

**Geistes-:** **g~abwesend** *adj* absent-minded; ~**abwesenheit** *f* absent-mindedness; ~**arbeiter** *m* brain-worker *(col)*; ~**armut** intellectual poverty; ~**blitz** *m* brainwave *(Brit)*, brainstorm *(US)*; ~**gabe** *f* intellectual gift; ~**gegenwart** *f* presence of mind; **g~gegenwärtig** *adj* quick-witted; **g~gegenwärtig duckte er sich unter das Steuer** with great presence of mind he ducked below the steering wheel; **g~gestört** *adj* mentally disturbed *or* *(stärker)* deranged; ~**größe** *f* **(a)** *no pl (Genialität)* greatness of mind; **(b)** *(genialer Mensch)* great mind, genius; ~**haltung** *f* mental attitude; **g~krank** *adj* mentally ill; ~**kranke(r)** *mf* mentally ill person; **die** ~**kranken** the mentally ill; ~**krankheit** *f* mental illness; *(Wahnsinn)* insanity; **g~schwach** *adj* mentally deficient; ~**verfassung** *f* frame of mind; **g~verwandt** *adj* **die beiden sind g~verwandt** they are kindred spirits; ~**wissenschaft** *f* arts subject; **die** ~**wissenschaften**

the arts; **~wissenschaftler** *m* arts scholar; *(Student)* arts student; **g~wissenschaftlich** *adj Fach* arts *attr*; **~zustand** *m* mental condition; **jdn auf seinen ~zustand untersuchen** to give sb a psychiatric examination.

**geistig** *adj* **(a)** *(unkörperlich)* spiritual. **~-moralisch** spiritual and moral; **~-seelisch** mental and spiritual. **(b)** *(intellektuell)* intellectual; *(Psych)* mental. **~e Arbeit** intellectual work; **~ anspruchsvoll/anspruchslos** intellectually demanding/undemanding, highbrow/lowbrow; **~er Diebstahl** plagiarism; **~es Eigentum** intellectual property; **~ behindert/zurückgeblieben** mentally handicapped/retarded; **etw vor seinem ~en Auge sehen** to see sth in one's mind's eye. **(c)** *attr (alkoholisch)* spirituous.

**geistlich** *adj* spiritual; *(religiös)* religious. **~es Amt/~er Orden** religious office/order; **~es Recht** canon law; **der ~e Stand** the clergy.

**Geistliche** *f (wk)* **-n, -n** woman priest; *(von Freikirchen)* woman minister.

**Geistliche(r)** *m decl as adj* clergyman; *(Priester)* priest; *(von Freikirchen)* minister; *(Gefängnis~, Militär~ etc)* chaplain.

**Geistlichkeit** *f siehe* **Geistliche(r)** clergy; priesthood; ministry.

**Geist-:** **g~los** *adj* stupid; *(langweilig)* dull; *(einfallslos)* unimaginative; **~losigkeit** *f* **(a)** *no pl siehe adj* stupidity; dullness; unimaginativeness; **(b)** *(Äußerung)* stupid remark; **g~reich** *adj (witzig)* witty; *(klug)* intelligent; *(einfallsreich)* ingenious; *Beschäftigung, Gespräch* intellectually stimulating; **g~tötend** *adj* soul-destroying; **g~voll** *adj Mensch, Äußerung* wise; *Buch, Beschäftigung* intellectual.

**Geiz** *m no pl* meanness.

**geizen** *vi* to be mean; *(mit Worten, Zeit)* to be sparing.

**Geizhals** *m* miser.

**geizig** *adj* mean, stingy *(col)*.

**Geizkragen** *m (col)* skinflint *(col)*.

**gekannt** *ptp of* **kennen**.

**Gekicher** *nt no pl* giggling.

**Gekläff** *nt no pl* yapping.

**Geklapper** *nt no pl* clatter(ing).

**gekleidet** *adj* dressed. **weiß ~** dressed in white.

**Geklimper** *nt no pl (col) (Klavier~)* tinkling; *(stümperhaft)* plonking *(col)*; *(von Geld)* jingling.

**Geklirr(e)** *nt no pl* clinking; *(von Fensterscheiben)* rattling; *(von Ketten etc)* clanking; *(von Waffen)* clashing.

**geklungen** *ptp of* **klingen**.

**Geknatter** *nt no pl (von Motorrad)* rat-tat-tat.

**geknickt** *adj (col)* glum, dejected.

**gekniffen** *ptp of* **kneifen**.

**Geknister** *nt no pl* crackling; *(von Papier etc)* rustling.

**gekommen** *ptp of* **kommen**.

**gekonnt 1** *ptp of* **können**. **2** *adj* neat; *(meisterhaft)* masterly.

**Gekrakel** *nt no pl (col)* scrawl.

**gekräuselt** *adj* ruffled.

**Gekreisch(e)** *nt no pl* screeching.

**Gekritzel** *nt no pl (Gekritzeltes)* scribble.

**gekrochen** *ptp of* **kriechen**.

**gekühlt** *adj* chilled.

**gekünstelt** *adj* artificial; *Sprache, Benehmen auch* affected.

**Gel** *nt* **-e** gel.

**Gelaber(e)** *nt no pl (col)* jabbering *(col)*.

**Gelächter** *nt* **-** laughter. **in ~ ausbrechen** to burst

out laughing; **jdn dem ~ preisgeben** *(geh)* to make sb a laughing stock.

**gelackmeiert** *adj (col)* conned *(col)*.

**geladen 1** *ptp of* **laden**. **2** *adj* loaded; *(Phys)* charged; *(col: wütend)* hopping mad *(col)*.

**Gelage** *nt* **-** feast, banquet.

**gelagert** *adj* **in anders/ähnlich ~en Fällen** in different/similar cases.

**gelähmt** *adj* paralyzed.

**Gelände** *nt* **-** **(a)** *(Land)* open country; *(Mil: Terrain)* ground. **offenes ~** open country; **schwieriges ~** difficult terrain *or* country. **(b)** *(Gebiet)* area. **(c)** *(Grundstück)* grounds *pl*; *(Bau~)* site.

**Gelände-:** **~fahrt** *f* cross-country drive; **~fahrzeug** *nt* cross-country *or* all-terrain vehicle; **g~gängig** *adj Fahrzeug* suitable for cross-country work, all-terrain; **~lauf** *m* cross-country run.

**Geländer** *nt* **-** railing(s *pl*); *(Treppen~)* bannister(s *pl*).

**Geländewagen** *m* cross-country *or* all-terrain vehicle.

**gelang** *pret of* **gelingen**.

**gelangen*** *vi aux sein* **an/auf etw** *(acc)***/zu etw ~** *(lit, fig)* to reach sth; *(fig: mit Mühe)* to attain sth; *(erwerben)* to acquire sth; **zum Ziel ~** to reach one's goal; **in jds Besitz ~** to come into sb's possession; **in die richtigen/falschen Hände ~** to fall into the right/wrong hands; **zu Ruhm ~** to achieve fame; **zu einer Überzeugung ~** to become convinced; **zur Durchführung ~** *(form)* to be carried out; **an die Macht ~** to come to power.

**gelangweilt** *adj* bored *no adv*.

**gelassen 1** *ptp of* **lassen**. **2** *adj* calm. **etw ~ hinnehmen** to take sth calmly.

**Gelassenheit** *f* calmness.

**Gelatine** [ʒela'tiːnə] *f no pl* gelatine.

**gelaufen** *ptp of* **laufen**.

**geläufig** *adj* common; *(vertraut)* familiar. **das ist mir nicht ~** I'm not familiar with that.

**gelaunt** *adj pred* **gut/schlecht ~** good-/bad-tempered; *(vorübergehend)* in a good/bad mood; **wie ist er ~?** what sort of mood is he in?

**gelb** *adj* yellow; *(bei Verkehrsampel)* amber *(Brit)*; **G~e Seiten** Yellow Pages.

**Gelb** *nt* **-** *or (col)* **-s** yellow; *(von Verkehrsampel)* amber *(Brit)*.

**Gelbe(s)** *nt decl as adj (vom Ei)* yolk. **das war nicht gerade das ~ vom Ei** *(col)* that wasn't exactly brilliant.

**Gelbfieber** *nt* yellow fever.

**gelbgrün** *adj* yellowish-green.

**gelblich** *adj* yellowish; *Gesichtsfarbe* sallow.

**Gelb-:** **~sucht** *f* jaundice; **g~süchtig** *adj* jaundiced.

**Geld** *nt* **-er** **(a)** money. **bares/großes/kleines ~** cash/notes *pl (Brit)*, bills *pl (US)*/change; **~ und Gut** wealth and possessions; **~ aufnehmen** to raise money; **zu ~ machen** to sell off; **(mit etw) ~ machen** *(col)* to make money (from sth); **etw für teures ~ kaufen** to pay a lot for sth; **er hat ~ wie Heu** *(col)* he's stinking rich *(col)*; **mit ~ um sich werfen** to chuck one's money around *(col)*; **jdm das ~ aus der Tasche ziehen** to squeeze money out of sb; **am ~ hängen** *or* **kleben** to be tight with money; **hinterm ~ hersein** *(col)* to be out for money; **das ist nicht für ~ zu haben** *(col)* that can't be bought; **sie/das ist nicht mit ~ zu bezahlen** *(col)* she/that is priceless; **nicht für ~ und gute Worte** *(col)* not for love nor money; **~ oder Leben!** your money or your life!; **~ stinkt nicht** *(Prov)* there's nothing wrong with money; **~ regiert die Welt** *(Prov)* money makes the world go round *(prov)*.

**(b)** *(~summen)* ~**er** *pl* money, monies *pl*; **staatliche** ~**er** state funds *pl or* money.

**(c)** *(St Ex: ~kurs)* buying rate.

**Geld-:** ~**angelegenheit** *f* financial matter; **jds** ~**angelegenheiten** sb's financial affairs; ~**anlage** *f* (financial) investment; ~**automat** *m* cash dispenser, automatic teller *(US)* ~**automatenkarte** *f* cash card; ~**beutel** *m*, ~**börse** *f* purse; **tief in den** ~**beutel greifen** *(col)* to dig deep (into one's pocket) *(col)*; ~**dinge** *pl* financial *or* money matters *pl*; ~**einwurf** *m* slot; **beim** ~**einwurf** when inserting the money; ~**geber(in** *f)* *m* financial backer; *(esp Rad, TV)* sponsor; *(hum: Arbeitgeber)* employer; ~**geschäft** *nt* financial transaction; ~**gier** *f* avarice; **g**~**gierig** *adj* avaricious; ~**institut** *nt* financial institution; ~**kassette** *f* cash box; ~**knappheit** *f* shortage of money; ~**kurs** *m* *(St Ex)* buying rate.

**geldlich** *adj* financial.

**Geld-:** ~**mangel** *m* lack of money; ~**markt** *m* money market; ~**menge** *f* money supply; ~**mittel** *pl* funds *pl*; ~**quelle** *f* source of income; ~**schein** *m* banknote *(Brit)*, bill *(US)*; ~**schrank** *m* safe; ~**schwierigkeiten** *pl* financial difficulties *pl*; ~**sorgen** *pl* **in** ~**sorgen sein** to have financial worries; ~**spende** *f* donation, gift of money; ~**strafe** *f* fine; **jdn zu einer** ~**strafe verurteilen** to fine sb; ~**stück** *nt* coin; ~**umlauf** *m* circulation of money; ~**verkehr** *m* transactions *pl*; ~**verleiher** *m* moneylender; ~**verschwendung** *f* waste of money; ~**waschanlage** *f* money-laundering outfit; ~**wäsche** *f* money laundering; ~**wechsel** *m* exchange of money; „~**wechsel**" "bureau de change"; ~**wechsler** *m* *(Automat)* change machine; ~**wert** *m* cash value; *(Fin: Kaufkraft)* currency value.

**geleckt** *adj* **wie** ~ **aussehen** to be neat and tidy.

**Gelee** [ʒeˈleː] *m or nt* -**s** jelly.

**gelegen 1** *ptp of* **liegen. 2** *adj* **(a)** *(befindlich)* **Haus** situated. **(b)** *(passend)* **zu** ~**er Zeit** at a convenient time; **das kommt mir sehr** ~ that's most convenient. **(c)** *pred (wichtig)* **mir ist viel/nichts daran** ~ it matters a great deal/doesn't matter to me.

**Gelegenheit** *f* **(a)** *(günstiger Umstand)* opportunity. **bei** ~ some time (or other); **bei passender/der ersten (besten)** ~ when I get the opportunity/at the first opportunity. **(b)** *(Anlaß)* occasion. **bei dieser** ~ on this occasion. **(c)** *(~skauf)* bargain.

**Gelegenheits-:** ~**arbeit** *f* **(a)** casual work *no pl*; **(b)** *(eines Autors)* minor work; ~**arbeiter** *m* casual labourer *(Brit)* or laborer *(US)*; ~**kauf** *m* bargain; ~**raucher** *m* occasional smoker; ~**trinker** *m* occasional drinker.

**gelegentlich 1** *adj attr* occasional. **2** *adv (manchmal)* occasionally, now and again; *(bei Gelegenheit)* some time (or other). **lassen Sie** ~ **etwas von sich hören!** keep in touch.

**gelehrig** *adj* quick to learn. **sich bei etw** ~ **anstellen** to be quick to grasp sth.

**Gelehrsamkeit** *f (geh)* learning, erudition.

**gelehrt** *adj* learned, erudite; *(wissenschaftlich)* scholarly.

**Gelehrte(r)** *mf decl as adj* scholar.

**Geleit** *nt* -**e** *(Hist: Gefolge)* retinue; *(Begleitung, Mil)* escort; *(Leichenzug)* cortège. **freies** *or* **sicheres** ~ safe conduct; **jdm das** ~ **geben** to escort *or* accompany sb.

**geleiten*** *vt (geh)* to escort.

**Geleitschutz** *m* escort. **jdm** ~ **gewähren** *or* **geben** to give sb an escort; *(persönlich)* to escort sb.

**Gelenk** *nt* -**e** joint; *(Hand~)* wrist; *(Fuß~)* ankle; *(Ketten~)* link; *(Scharnier~)* hinge.

**gelenkig** *adj* supple.

**Gelenkigkeit** *f* suppleness.

**gelernt** *adj* trained; *Arbeiter* skilled.

**gelesen** *ptp of* **lesen.**

**geliebt** *adj* dear, beloved *(liter, Eccl)*.

**Geliebte** *f decl as adj* sweetheart; *(Mätresse)* mistress, lover.

**Geliebte(r)** *m decl as adj* sweetheart; *(Liebhaber)* lover.

**geliefert** *adj* ~ **sein** *(col)* to have had it *(col)*.

**geliehen** *ptp of* **leihen.**

**gelieren*** [ʒeˈliːrən] *vi* to gel.

**gelind(e)** *adj (geh)* gentle; *(mild)* Urteil, Schmerz, Ausdruck mild. ~ **gesagt** to put it mildly.

**gelingen** *pret* **gelang,** *ptp* **gelungen** *vi aux sein* to succeed, to be successful. **es gelang ihm, das zu tun** he succeeded in doing it; **es gelang ihm nicht, das zu tun** he failed to do it, he didn't succeed in doing it; **dein Plan wird dir nicht** ~ you won't succeed with your plan; **es will mir nicht** ~ I can't seem to manage it.

**Gelingen** *nt no pl (geh) (Glück)* success; *(erfolgreiches Ergebnis)* successful outcome. **gutes** ~ **für Ihren Plan!** good luck with your plan!; **auf gutes** ~! to success!

**gelitten** *ptp of* **leiden.**

**gell, gelle** *interj (S Ger, Sw)* = **gelt.**

**gellen** *vi* to shrill; *(von lauten Tönen erfüllt sein)* to ring. **der Lärm gellt mir in den Ohren** the noise makes my ears ring.

**gellend** *adj* shrill, piercing.

**geloben*** *vt (geh)* to vow, to swear. **das Gelobte Land** *(Bibl)* the Promised Land.

**Gelöbnis** *nt (geh)* vow.

**gelockt** *adj Haar* curly; *Mensch* curly-haired.

**gelogen** *ptp of* **lügen.**

**gelöst** *adj* relaxed.

**gelt** *interj (S Ger)* right. **schön,** ~? nice, isn't it?

**gelten** *pret* **galt,** *ptp* **gegolten 1** *vi* **(a)** *(gültig sein)* to be valid; *(Gesetz)* to be in force; *(Preise)* to be effective; *(zählen)* to count. **die Wette gilt!** it's a bet!; **das gilt nicht!** that doesn't count!; *(nicht erlaubt)* that's not allowed!; **das Gesetz gilt für alle** the law applies to everyone. **(b)** +*dat (bestimmt sein für)* to be meant for *or* aimed at. **(c)** *(zutreffen)* **für jdn/etw** ~ to hold (good) for sb/sth, to go for sb/sth; **das gleiche gilt auch für ihn** the same goes for him too. **(d)** ~ **als** to be regarded as; **es gilt als sicher, daß** ... it seems certain that ... **(e)** ~ **lassen** to accept; **das lasse ich** ~! I'll agree to that!, I accept that!; **für diesmal lasse ich es** ~ I'll let it go this time.

**2** *vti impers (geh)* **es gilt, ... zu ...** it is necessary to ...; **jetzt gilt es, zusammenzuhalten** it is now a question of sticking together.

**3** *vt (wert sein)* to be worth. **was gilt die Wette?** what do you bet?

**geltend** *adj attr Preise* current; *Gesetz* in force; *Meinung etc* prevailing. ~ **machen** *(form)* to assert; **einen Einwand** ~ **machen** to raise an objection; ~**es Recht sein** to be the law of the land.

**Geltung** *f (Gültigkeit)* validity; *(Ansehen)* prestige. ~ **haben** to be valid; *(Gesetz)* to be in force; *(Preise)* to be effective; *(Einfluß haben)* to carry weight; *(angesehen sein)* to be recognized; **an** ~ **verlieren** to lose prestige; **einer Sache** *(dat)* ~ **verschaffen** to enforce sth; **sich** *(dat)* ~ **verschaffen** to establish one's position; **etw zur** ~ **bringen** to show sth off to advantage; *(durch Kontrast)* to set sth off; **zur** ~ **kommen** to show to advantage; *(durch Kontrast)* to be set off.

**Geltungs-:** ~**bedürfnis** *nt no pl* need for admiration; **g~bedürftig** *adj* needing admiration; ~**bereich** *m* der ~bereich einer Fahrkarte/eines Gesetzes the area within which a ticket is valid/a law is operative; ~**dauer** *f no pl* period of validity; ~**drang** *m no pl* need for admiration; ~**sucht** *f no pl* craving for admiration; **g~süchtig** *adj* craving admiration.

**Gelübde** *nt -* (*Rel, geh*) vow. **ein/das** ~ **ablegen** to take a vow.

**gelungen 1** *ptp of* **gelingen. 2** *adj attr* (a) *(geglückt)* successful. **eine nicht so recht** ~e **Überraschung** a surprise that didn't quite come off. **(b)** *(col: drollig)* funny, priceless.

**Gelüst** *nt -e (geh)* desire.

**gelüsten\*** *vt impers (liter, iro)* **mich gelüstet nach ...** I have a craving for ...

**Gemach** *nt ̈-er (geh)* chamber *(old, form)*.

**gemächlich** *adj* leisurely *no adv*; *Mensch* unhurried. **ein** ~ **fließender Strom** a gently flowing river.

**gemacht** *adj* **(a) für etw** ~ **sein** to be made for sth; **das ist für ihn wie** ~ it's made for him; **ein** ~**er Mann sein** to be made. **(b)** *(gewollt, gekünstelt)* false, contrived.

**Gemahl** *m -e (geh, form)* spouse *(old, form)*, husband; *(Prinz~)* consort.

**Gemahlin** *f (geh, form)* spouse *(old, form)*, wife; *(von König auch)* consort.

**Gemälde** *nt -* painting; *(fig: Schilderung)* portrayal.

**Gemäldegalerie** *f* picture gallery.

**gemasert** *adj Holz* grained.

**gemäß 1** *prep +dat* in accordance with. **2** *adj* appropriate *(dat to)*. **eine ihren Fähigkeiten** ~e **Arbeit** a job suited to her abilities.

**gemäßigt** *adj* moderate; *Klima, Zone* temperate; *Optimismus etc* qualified.

**Gemäuer** *nt - (geh)* masonry, walls *pl*.

**Gemauschel** *nt no pl (pej col)* scheming.

**Gemecker** *nt no pl (von Ziegen)* bleating; *(col: Nörgelei)* moaning.

**gemein** *adj* **(a)** *(niederträchtig)* mean; *(roh, unverschämt auch)* nasty; *Verräter, Lüge* contemptible. **ein** ~**er Streich** a dirty or rotten trick. **(b)** *(ordinär)* vulgar; *Bemerkung, Witz auch* dirty, coarse. **(c)** *(col: unangenehm)* horrible, awful. **die Prüfung war** ~ **schwer** the exam was horribly difficult. **(d) etw** ~ **mit jdm/etw haben** to have sth in common with sb/sth; **das ist beiden** ~ it is common to both of them. **(e) das** ~e **Volk** the common people; **der** ~e **Mann** the ordinary man.

**Gemeinbesitz** *m* common property.

**Gemeinde** *f* -**n** **(a)** *(Kommune)* municipality; *(~bewohner auch)* community. **(b)** *(Pfarr~)* parish; *(beim Gottesdienst)* congregation.

**Gemeinde-:** ~**abgaben** *pl* local taxes *pl*; ~**amt** *nt* local authority; *(Gebäude)* local administrative office; ~**beamte(r)** *m* local government officer; ~**ordnung** *f* bylaws *pl*, ordinances *pl (US)*; ~**rat** *m* district council; *(Mitglied)* district councillor *(Brit)*, councilman *(US)*; ~**schwester** *f* district nurse; ~**steuer** *f* local tax, ≈ council tax *(Brit)*; ~**verwaltung** *f* local administration; ~**wahl** *f* local election; ~**zentrum** *nt* community centre.

**Gemein|eigentum** *nt* common property.

**Gemein-:** **g~gefährlich** *adj Verbrecher* dangerous; **er/das ist g~gefährlich** he/it is a public menace; ~**gefährlichkeit** *f* danger to the public; ~**gut** *nt* *(lit, fig)* common property.

**Gemeinheit** *f* **(a)** *no pl (Niedertracht)* meanness. **(b)** *(Tat)* mean *or* dirty trick; *(Worte)* mean thing. **das**

**war eine** ~ that was a mean thing to do/say.

**Gemein-:** **g~hin** *adv* generally; ~**kosten** *pl* overheads *pl (Brit)*, overhead *(US)*; ~**nutz** *m* public *or* common good; **g~nützig** *adj* of benefit to the public; *(wohltätig)* charitable; ~**nützigkeit** *f* die ~nützigkeit einer Organisation the charitable status of an organization; ~**platz** *m* platitude, commonplace.

**gemeinsam 1** *adj* common; *Freund* mutual; *Konto, Aktion, Ausflug* joint. **ihnen ist vieles** ~ they have a great deal in common; **die Firma ist** ~**es Eigentum der beiden Brüder** the two brothers are joint owners of the firm; **unser** ~**es Leben** our life together; **der G**~e **Markt** the Common Market; **mit jdm** ~e **Sache machen** *(pej)* to make common cause with sb. **2** *adv* together. **etw** ~ **haben** to have sth in common; **es gehört den beiden** ~ it belongs jointly to the two of them.

**Gemeinsamkeit** *f (gemeinsame Interessen, Eigenschaft etc)* common ground *no pl.* **die** ~**en zwischen ihnen sind sehr groß** they have a great deal in common.

**Gemeinschaft** *f* community; *(Gruppe)* group; *(Zusammensein)* company. **in** ~ **mit** jointly with; **eheliche** ~ *(Jur)* matrimony; ~ **Unabhängiger Staaten** Commonwealth of Independent States.

**gemeinschaftlich** *adj* = **gemeinsam**.

**Gemeinschafts-:** ~**antenne** *f* party aerial *(Brit)* or antenna *(US)*; ~**arbeit** *f* teamwork; ~**aufgabe** *f* joint task; ~**gefühl** *nt* sense of community; ~**küche** *f* communal kitchen; *(Kantine)* canteen; ~**kunde** *f* social studies *pl*; ~**leistung** *f* collective achievement; ~**praxis** *f* group practice; ~**raum** *m* common room; **g~schädigend** *adj Verhalten* antisocial; ~**schule** *f* interdenominational school; ~**wohnung** *f* shared house/apartment *etc*.

**Gemein-:** ~**sinn** *m* public spirit; **g~verständlich** *adj* generally comprehensible *no adv*; **sich g~verständlich ausdrücken** to make oneself generally understood; ~**wesen** *nt* community; ~**wohl** *nt* public welfare; **das dient dem** ~**wohl** it is in the public interest.

**Gemenge** *nt -* **(a)** *(Mischung)* mixture *(aus of)*; *(Durcheinander)* jumble *(aus of)*. **(b)** *(Gewühl)* bustle; *(Hand~)* scuffle.

**gemessen 1** *ptp of* **messen. 2** *adj (würdevoll)* measured.

**Gemetzel** *nt -* bloodbath.

**gemieden** *ptp of* **meiden**.

**Gemisch** *nt -e* **(a)** *(auch Aut)* mixture *(aus of)*. **(b)** *no pl (Durcheinander)* jumble *(aus of)*.

**gemischt** *adj* mixed; *(Schule auch)* coeducational; *(col: nicht sehr gut auch)* patchy. **mit** ~**en Gefühlen** with mixed feelings.

**Gemischt-:** **g~rassig** *adj* of mixed race; *(mit mehreren Rassen)* multi-racial; ~**warenhandlung** *f* *(dated)* general store.

**gemocht** *ptp of* **mögen**.

**gemolken** *ptp of* **melken**.

**Gemse** *f -n* chamois.

**Gemunkel** *nt no pl* rumours; *(Klatsch)* gossip.

**Gemurmel** *nt no pl* murmuring.

**Gemüse** *nt -* vegetables *pl.* **frisches** ~ fresh vegetables; **ein** ~ a vegetable; **junges** ~ *(hum col)* youngsters *pl.*

**Gemüse-:** ~**beet** *nt* vegetable bed *or* patch; ~**beilage** *f* vegetables *pl*; ~**eintopf** *m* vegetable stew; ~**garten** *m* vegetable *or* kitchen garden; ~**händler** *m* greengrocer; ~**handlung** *f*, ~**laden** *m* greengrocer's *(Brit)*, greengrocer; ~**markt** *m* vegetable market; ~**platte** *f (Cook)* **eine** ~**platte** as-

sorted vegetables *pl*; **~suppe** *f* vegetable soup.
**gemußt** *ptp of* **müssen**.
**gemustert** *adj* patterned.
**Gemüt** *nt* **-er** (**a**) *(Geist)* mind; *(Charakter)* nature, disposition; *(Seele)* soul; *(Gefühl)* feeling. **viel ~ haben** to be very warm-hearted; **etwas fürs ~** *(hum)* something for the soul; *(Film, Buch etc)* something sentimental; **sich** *(dat)* **etw zu ~e führen** *(beherzigen)* to take sth to heart; *(hum col) Speise, Buch etc* to indulge in sth. (**b**) *(fig: Mensch)* person; *(pl)* people. **die ~er erregen** to cause a stir; **wir müssen warten, bis sich die ~er beruhigt haben** we must wait until feelings have cooled down.
**gemütlich** *adj* (**a**) *(behaglich)* comfortable; *(freundlich)* friendly *no adv*; *(zwanglos)* informal; *(klein und intim)* cosy *(Brit)*, cozy *(US)*. **wir verbrachten einen ~en Abend** we spent a very pleasant evening; **es sich** *(dat)* **~ machen** to make oneself comfortable; **langsam wurde es ~** gradually the atmosphere became more relaxed. (**b**) *Mensch* good-natured, pleasant; *(gelassen)* easy-going *no adv*, relaxed *no adv*. **in ~em Tempo** at a leisurely speed.
**Gemütlichkeit** *f siehe adj* (**a**) comfortableness; friendliness; informality; cosiness. (**b**) good-naturedness, pleasantness; easy-going nature. **da hört doch die ~ auf!** *(col)* that's going too far; **in aller ~** *(gemächlich)* at one's leisure.
**Gemüts-:** **~art** *f* disposition, nature; **~bewegung** *f* emotion; **g~krank** *adj* emotionally disturbed; **~krankheit** *f* emotional disorder; **~lage** *f* mood; **~mensch** *m* good-natured, phlegmatic person; **~ruhe** *f* calmness; *(Kaltblütigkeit)* composure; *(Phlegma)* placidness; **in aller ~ruhe** *(col)* (as) cool as a cucumber *(col)*; *(gemächlich)* at a leisurely pace; **~zustand** *m* frame of mind.
**gemütvoll** *adj* sentimental; *(warmherzig)* warm-hearted.
**gen** *prep* +*acc (old, liter)* toward. **~ Norden** northwards.
**Gen** *nt* **-e** gene.
**Gen-** = (**a**) **Genitiv** gen. (**b**) **General** Gen.
**genannt** *ptp of* **nennen**.
**genas** *pret of* **genesen**.
**genau 1** *adj* exact, precise. **haben Sie die ~e Zeit?** have you got the right time?; **G~eres** further details *pl*; **man weiß nichts G~es über ihn** no-one knows anything definite about him. **2** *adv* **~!** *(col)* exactly!, precisely!, quite! **~ das Gegenteil** just *or* exactly the opposite; **~ in der Mitte** right in the middle; **ich kenne ihn ~** I know just what he's like; **etw ~ wissen** to know sth for certain; **er nimmt es sehr ~** he's very particular *(mit etw* about sth*)*; **einen Entschluß ~ überlegen** to think a decision over very carefully; **meine Uhr geht ~** my watch keeps accurate time; **~ auf die Minute** exactly on time; **so ~ wollte ich es gar nicht wissen!** *(iro)* you can spare me the details.
**genaugenommen** *adv* strictly speaking.
**Genauigkeit** *f* exactness, precision.
**genauso** *adv (vor Adjektiv)* just as; *(alleinstehend)* just *or* exactly the same.
**genauso-** = **ebenso-**.
**Gendarm** [ʒanˈdarm] *m* **-en, en** *(old, Aus)* gendarme.
**genehm** *adj (geh)* suitable, acceptable. **jdm ~ sein** to suit sb.
**genehmigen\*** *vt Baupläne etc* to approve; *(erlauben)* to sanction; *(Lizenz erteilen)* to license; *Aufenthalt* to authorize; *(zugestehen)* to grant. **sich** *(dat)* **einen ~** *(hum col)* to have a little drink.
**Genehmigung** *f siehe vt* approval; sanction; li-

cence *(Brit)*, license *(US)*; authorization; *(Schein)* permit. **mit freundlicher ~ von** by kind permission of.
**genehmigungspflichtig** *adj (form)* requiring official approval; *(mit Visum, Stempel)* requiring official authorization.
**geneigt** *adj (geh) Zuhörer, Publikum* willing; *Aufmerksamkeit* kind. **~ sein, etw zu tun** to be inclined to do sth.
**General** *m* **-e** *or* **~e** *(Mil)* general. **Herr ~** General.
**General-:** **~amnestie** *f* general amnesty; **~angriff** *m (Mil, fig)* general attack; **~direktor** *m* chairman *(Brit)*, president *(US)*; **~intendant** *m (Theat, Mus)* director; **~konsulat** *nt* consulate general; **~major** *m* major general, brigadier-general *(US)*; **~probe** *f (Theat, fig)* dress rehearsal; *(Mus)* final rehearsal; **~sekretär** *m* secretary general; **~stab** *m* general staff; **~streik** *m* general strike; **g~überholen\*** *vt infin and ptp only* **etw g~überholen** to give sth a complete overhaul; **~überholung** *f* complete overhaul; **~versammlung** *f* general meeting; **~vertretung** *f* sole agency; **~vollmacht** *f* general *or* full power of attorney.
**Generation** *f* generation.
**Generationskonflikt** *m* generation gap.
**Generator** *m* generator.
**generell** *adj* general.
**genesen** *pret* **genas**, *ptp* **~** *vi aux sein (geh)* to convalesce; *(fig)* to recuperate.
**Genesende(r)** *mf decl as adj* convalescent.
**Genesung** *f* convalescence, recovery *(auch fig)*. **auf dem Wege der ~** on the road to recovery.
**Genesungs-:** **~prozeß** *m* convalescence; **~urlaub** *m* convalescent leave.
**Genetik** *f* genetics *sing*.
**genetisch** *adj* genetic; **~er Fingerabdruck** genetic fingerprint.
**Genf** *nt* Geneva.
**Genfer** *adj attr* **der ~ See** Lake Geneva; **~ Konvention** *f* Geneva Convention.
**genial** *adj Entdeckung, Mensch* brilliant; *Künstler, Stil auch* inspired; *(erfinderisch)* ingenious. **ein ~er Mensch** a genius; **ein ~es Werk** a work of genius.
**Genialität** *f* genius; *(Erfindungsreichtum)* ingenuity.
**Genick** *nt* **-e** neck. **sich** *(dat)* **das ~ brechen** to break one's neck; **jdm/einer Sache das ~ brechen** *(fig)* to finish sb/sth.
**Genick-:** **~schuß** *m* shot in the neck; **~starre** *f* stiffness of the neck; **~starre haben** *(col)* to have a stiff neck.
**Genie** [ʒeˈniː] *nt* **-s** genius.
**genieren\*** [ʒeˈniːrən] *vr* to be embarrassed. **sich vor Fremden ~** to be shy with strangers; **ich geniere mich, das zu sagen** I don't like to say it; **er genierte sich (gar) nicht, das zu tun** it didn't bother him (at all) to do that.
**genießbar** *adj (eßbar)* edible; *(trinkbar)* drinkable. **er ist heute nicht ~** *(fig col)* he is unbearable today.
**genießen** *pret* **genoß**, *ptp* **genossen** *vt* (**a**) *(lit, fig)* to enjoy. **den Wein muß man ~** you must savour *(Brit)* or savor *(US)* the wine; **er ist heute nicht zu ~** *(fig col)* he is unbearable today. (**b**) *(essen)* to eat; *(trinken)* to drink. **das Essen ist kaum zu ~** the meal is scarcely edible.
**Genießer(in** *f)* *m* **-** *(des Lebens)* pleasure-lover; *(Feinschmecker)* gourmet; *(Kenner)* connoisseur.
**genießerisch** *adj* appreciative. **~ zog er an seiner Zigarre** he puffed at his cigar with relish.
**Geniestreich** [ʒeˈniː-] *m* stroke of genius.
**Genitalien** [-iən] *pl* genitals *pl*.
**Genitiv** *m* genitive.

**Genius** *m, pl* **Genien** [ˈgeːniən] genius.

**genommen** *ptp of* **nehmen**.

**genoß** *pret of* **genießen**.

**Genosse** *m (wk)* **-n, -n** comrade; *(pej: Kumpan)* mate *(Brit col)*, buddy *(US col)*.

**genossen** *ptp of* **genießen**.

**Genossen-:** ~**schaft** *f* co-operative; **g~schaftlich** *adj* co-operative; **g~schaftlich organisiert** organized as a co-operative.

**Genossenschafts-:** ~**bank** *f* co-operative bank; ~**betrieb** *m* co-operative.

**Genossin** *f siehe* **Genosse**.

**genötigt** *adj* ~ **sein, etw zu tun** to be obliged to do sth; **sich** ~ **sehen, etw zu tun** to feel obliged to do sth.

**Genre** [ˈʒɑ̃ːrə] *nt* **-s** genre.

**Gent** *nt* Ghent.

**Gen-:** ~**technik**, ~**technologie** *f* genetic engineering.

**Genua** *nt* Genoa.

**genug** *adj inv* enough. **das ist wenig** ~ that's precious little; **und damit noch nicht** ~ and that's not/that wasn't all; **sie sind jetzt** ~, **um** ... there are enough of them now to ...; **jetzt ist('s) aber** ~! that's enough!; **(von etw)** ~ **haben** to have enough (of sth); *(überdrüssig sein)* to have had enough (of sth).

**Genüge** *f no pl* **zur** ~ enough; **etw zur** ~ **kennen** to know sth well enough; *(abwertend)* to know sth only too well; **jdm** ~ **tun** *(geh)* to satisfy sb.

**genügen*** *vi* **(a)** *(ausreichen)* to be enough *or* sufficient *(dat* for). **das genügt (mir)** that's enough (for me). **(b)** *Anforderungen* to satisfy; *Erwartungen* to fulfil *(Brit)*, to fulfill *(US)*.

**genügend 1** *adj* **(a)** *inv (ausreichend)* enough, sufficient. **(b)** *(befriedigend)* satisfactory. **2** *adv (reichlich)* enough, sufficiently.

**genügsam** *adj (anspruchslos) Tier, Pflanze* undemanding; *Mensch auch* modest. **ein** ~**es Leben führen** to live modestly.

**Genügsamkeit** *f* simple needs *pl*.

**Genugtuung** *f* satisfaction *(über +acc* at). **ich hörte mit** ~, **daß** ... it gave me great satisfaction to hear that ....

**Genus** *nt, pl* **Genera** *(Gram)* gender.

**Genuß** *m* ⁼**sse (a)** *no pl (das Zusichnehmen)* consumption; *(von Drogen)* taking, use; *(von Tabak)* smoking. **nach dem** ~ **der Pilze** after eating the mushrooms. **(b)** *(Vergnügen)* pleasure. **etw mit** ~ **essen** to eat sth with relish. **(c)** *no pl (Nutznießung)* **in den** ~ **von etw kommen** *(von Vergünstigungen)* to enjoy sth; *(von Rente, Prämie etc)* to be in receipt of sth.

**genüßlich** *adj* pleasurable. **er schmatzte** ~ he smacked his lips with relish.

**Genuß-:** ~**mittel** *nt semi-luxury food or tobacco*; **g~reich** *adj* enjoyable; **g~süchtig** *adj* hedonistic.

**Geograph(in** *f)* *m* geographer.

**Geographie** *f* geography.

**geographisch** *adj no pred* geographic(al).

**Geologe** *m*, **Geologin** *f* geologist.

**Geologie** *f* geology.

**geologisch** *adj no pred* geological.

**Geometrie** *f* geometry.

**geometrisch** *adj* geometric.

**Geophysik** *f* geophysics *sing*.

**ge|ordnet** *adj Leben, Zustände* well-ordered. **in** ~**en Verhältnissen leben** to live a well-ordered life; ~**e Verhältnisse schaffen** to put things on an orderly basis.

**Georgien** [geˈɔrgiən] *nt* Georgia.

**Georgier(in** *f)* *m* Georgian.

**georgisch** *adj* Georgian.

**Georgisch(e)** *nt* Georgian; *siehe* **Deutsch(e)**.

**Gepäck** *nt no pl* luggage *no pl (esp Brit)*, baggage *no pl*; *(Mil: Marsch~)* baggage; *(von Soldat, Pfadfinder etc)* kit; *(von Bergsteiger)* pack. **mit leichtem** ~ **reisen** to travel light.

**Gepäck-:** ~**abfertigung** *f (Stelle) (am Bahnhof)* baggage office; *(am Flughafen)* baggage check-in; ~**ablage** *f* baggage *or* luggage *(Brit)* rack; ~**annahme** *f (am Bahnhof) (zur Beförderung)* (in-counter of the) baggage office; *(zur Aufbewahrung)* (in-counter of the) left-luggage office *(Brit) or* checkroom *(US)*; *(am Flughafen)* baggage check-in; ~**aufbewahrung** *f* left-luggage office *(Brit)*, baggage checkroom *(US)*; ~**aufkleber** *m* baggage sticker; ~**ausgabe** *f (am Bahnhof) (zur Beförderung)* (out-counter of the) baggage office; *(zur Aufbewahrung)* (out-counter of the) left-luggage office *(Brit) or* baggage checkroom *(US)*; *(am Flughafen)* baggage reclaim; ~**kontrolle** *f* baggage control *or* check; ~**netz** *nt* baggage *or* luggage *(Brit)* rack; ~**raum** *m* baggage compartment; *(Aviat)* baggage hold; ~**schein** *m* baggage ticket *or (US)* check; ~**schließfach** *nt* baggage locker; ~**stück** *nt* piece of baggage; ~**träger** *m* **(a)** *(Person)* porter *(Brit)*, baggage handler; **(b)** *(am Fahrrad)* carrier; ~**wagen** *m* luggage van *(Brit)*, baggage car *(US)*.

**Gepard** *m* **-e** cheetah.

**gepfeffert** *adj (col) Preise* steep; *Fragen, Prüfung* tough; *Kritik* biting.

**gepfiffen** *ptp of* **pfeifen**.

**gepflegt 1** *adj* **(a)** *(nicht vernachlässigt)* well looked after; *Mensch, Hund, Aussehen* well-groomed. **(b)** *(col: kultiviert)* civilized; *Atmosphäre* sophisticated; *Ausdrucksweise* cultured; *Sprache* cultured, refined. **(c)** *(erstklassig) Speisen, Weine* excellent. **2** *adv (kultiviert)* **sich** ~ **unterhalten** to have a civilized conversation; **sich** ~ **ausdrücken** to have a cultured way of speaking; **sehr** ~ **wohnen** to live in style.

**Gepflogenheit** *f (geh) (Gewohnheit)* habit; *(Verfahrensweise)* practice; *(Brauch)* custom, tradition.

**Geplänkel** *nt* - skirmish; *(fig)* squabble.

**Geplapper** *nt no pl* babbling; *(fig: Geschwätz auch)* chatter(ing).

**Geplärr(e)** *nt no pl* bawling; *(von Radio)* blaring.

**geplättet** *adj pred (col)* flabbergasted *(col)*.

**Geplauder** *nt no pl (geh)* chatting.

**Gepolter** *nt no pl (Krach)* din; *(an Tür etc)* banging.

**Gepräge** *nt no pl (fig: Eigentümlichkeit)* character; *(Aura)* aura. **das hat den 60er Jahren ihr** ~ **gegeben** it gave the sixties their particular identity.

**gepriesen** *ptp of* **preisen**.

**gepuffert** *adj (Comp)* buffered.

**gepunktet** *adj Linie* dotted; *Stoff, Kleid* spotted.

**gequält** *adj Lächeln* forced; *Miene, Ausdruck* pained; *Gesang, Stimme* strained.

**Gequatsche** *nt no pl (pej col)* gabbing *(col)*; *(Blödsinn)* twaddle *(col)*.

**gequollen** *ptp of* **quellen**.

**gerade, grade** *(col)* **1** *adj* straight; *Zahl* even; *(aufrecht) Haltung* upright. ~ **gewachsen sein** *(Mensch)* to be clean-limbed; *(Baum)* to be straight; **das** ~ **Gegenteil** the very opposite, just the opposite; ~ **sitzen/stehen** to sit up/stand up straight.

**2** *adv* **(a)** *(im Augenblick, soeben)* just. **wenn Sie** ~ **Zeit haben** if you have time just now; **wo Sie** ~ **da sind** while you're here; **er wollte** ~ **aufstehen** he was just about to get up; ~ **erst** only just; **da wir** ~ **von Geld sprechen**, ... talking of money ...

**(b)** *(knapp)* just. ~ **so viel, daß er davon leben**

**kann** just enough for him to live on; ~ **noch** only just; **das hat ~ noch gefehlt!** *(iro)* that's all we wanted!

(c) *(genau)* just; *(direkt)* right. ~ **zur rechten Zeit** at exactly the right time, just at the right time; ~ **deshalb** that's just *or* exactly why; **das ist es ja ~!** that's just it!

(d) *(speziell, besonders)* especially. ~, **weil** ... just because ...; ~ **du solltest dafür Verständnis haben** you especially should understand; **sie ist nicht ~ eine Schönheit** she's not exactly a beauty; **warum ~ das?** why that of all things?; **warum ~ heute/ich?** why today of all days/me of all people?

(e) *(col: erst recht)* **nun ~!** you try and stop me now! *(col)*; **jetzt ~ nicht!** I'll be damned if I will! *(col)*.

**Gerade** *f (wk)* **-n, -n (a)** *(Math)* straight line. **(b)** *(Sport) (von Renn-, Laufbahn)* straight, straightaway *(US)*; *(beim Boxen)* **linke/rechte ~** straight left/right.

**gerade-:** ~**aus** *adv* straight ahead; *gehen, fahren auch* straight on; ~**biegen** *vt sep irreg (lit, fig)* to straighten out; ~**halten** *sep irreg* **1** *vt* to hold straight; **2** *vr* to hold oneself (up) straight; ~**heraus** *(col)* **1** *adj pred* forthright, frank; **2** *adv* frankly; ~**heraus gesagt** quite frankly; ~**richten** *vt sep* to straighten up; *(horizontal)* to straighten out.

**gerädert** *adj (col)* **wie ~ sein, sich wie ~ fühlen** to be *or* feel (absolutely) whacked *(col)*.

**gerade-:** ~**so** *adv* = **ebenso;** ~**sogut** *adv* (just) as well; ~**soviel** *adv* just as much; ~**stehen** *vi sep irreg aux haben or sein* **(a)** *(aufrecht stehen)* to stand up straight; **(b) für jdn/etw** ~**stehen** *(fig)* to be answerable for sb/sth; ~**wegs** *adv* straight; ~**zu** *adv (beinahe)* virtually, almost; **das ist doch** ~**zu Selbstmord** that's nothing short of suicide; **das ist ja** ~**zu lächerlich!** that is absolutely ridiculous!

**geradlinig** *adj* straight; *Abstammung* direct; *Entwicklung etc* linear; *(fig: aufrichtig)* straight.

**gerammelt** *adv:* ~ **voll** *(col)* (jam-)packed *(col)*.

**Gerangel** *nt no pl (Balgerei)* scrapping; *(fig: zäher Kampf)* wrangling.

**Geranie** [-ɪə] *f* geranium.

**gerannt** *ptp of* **rennen.**

**Geraschel** *nt no pl* rustle, rustling.

**Gerät** *nt* **-e (a)** piece of equipment; *(Apparat)* gadget; *(elektrisches ~)* appliance; *(Radio~, Fernseh~)* set; *(Meß~)* instrument; *(Werkzeug, Garten~)* tool. **(b)** *no pl (Ausrüstung)* equipment *no pl*; *(von Handwerker)* tools *pl*.

**geraten¹ 1** *vi irreg aux sein* **(a)** *(zufällig gelangen)* to get *(in +acc* into*)*. **an jdn ~** *(jdn kennenlernen)* to come across sb; **an etw** *(acc)* ~ to get sth, to come by sth; **an den Richtigen/Falschen ~** to come to the right/wrong person; **das Schiff ist in einen Sturm ~** the boat got caught in a storm; **unter schlechten Einfluß ~** to come under a bad influence. **(b)** *(sich entwickeln, ausfallen)* to turn out. **ihm gerät einfach alles** everything he does is a success. **2** *adj (geh: ratsam)* advisable.

**geraten²** *ptp of* **raten, geraten¹.**

**Geräte-:** ~**schuppen** *m* toolshed; ~**turnen** *nt* apparatus gymnastics *no pl*.

**Geratewohl** *nt:* **aufs ~** on the off-chance; *auswählen etc* at random.

**Gerätschaften** *pl (Ausrüstung)* equipment *sing*; *(Werkzeug)* tools *pl*.

**Geratter** *nt no pl* clatter(ing); *(von Maschinengewehr)* chatter(ing).

**geraum** *adj attr* **vor** ~**er Zeit** some time ago; **seit** ~**er Zeit** for some time.

**geräumig** *adj* spacious, roomy.

**Geräumigkeit** *f no pl* spaciousness, roominess.

**Geräusch** *nt* **-e** sound; *(esp unangenehm)* noise.

**Geräusch-:** **g~arm** *adj* quiet; **g~empfindlich** *adj* sensitive to noise; ~**kulisse** *f* background noise; *(Film, Rad, TV)* sound effects *pl*; **g~los** *adj* silent; ~**losigkeit** *f no pl* silence; ~**pegel** *m* sound level; **g~voll** *adj (laut)* loud; *(lärmend)* noisy.

**gerben** *vt* to tan.

**Gerber** *m* - tanner.

**Gerberei** *f* tannery.

**gerecht** *adj* just; *(unparteiisch auch)* fair; *(rechtschaffen)* upright. ~ **gegen jdn sein** to be fair *or* just to sb; ~**er Lohn für alle Arbeiter!** fair wages for all workers!; **den Schlaf des G~en schlafen** *(usu hum)* to sleep the sleep of the just; ~**er Zorn** righteous anger; **jdm/einer Sache ~ werden** to do justice to sb/sth; **den Bedingungen ~ werden** to fulfil *(Brit) or* fulfill *(US)* the conditions.

**gerechtfertigt** *adj* justified.

**Gerechtigkeit** *f* justice; *(das Gerechtsein)* justness; *(Unparteilichkeit)* fairness; *(Rechtschaffenheit)* righteousness. **jdm ~ widerfahren lassen** to be just to sb; *(fig)* to do justice to sb.

**Gerechtigkeits-:** ~**gefühl** *nt,* ~**sinn** *m* sense of justice.

**Gerede** *nt no pl* talk; *(Klatsch)* gossip(ing). **jdn ins ~ bringen** to get sb talked about.

**geregelt** *adj Arbeit, Mahlzeiten* regular; *Leben* well-ordered; *Katalysator* computer-controlled.

**gereichen*** *vi (geh)* **jdm zur Ehre ~** to redound to sb's honour *(form)*; **zum Vorteil ~** to be an advantage to sb.

**gereift** *adj (fig)* mature.

**gereizt** *adj (verärgert)* irritated; *(reizbar)* irritable, touchy; *(nervös)* edgy. **im Zimmer herrschte ~e Stimmung** there was a strained atmosphere in the room.

**Gereiztheit** *f siehe adj* irritation; irritability; touchiness; edginess; strainedness.

**Gericht¹** *nt* **-e** *(Speise)* dish.

**Gericht²** *nt* **-e** *(Behörde)* court (of justice); *(Gebäude)* court(house), law courts *pl*; *(die Richter)* court, bench. **vor ~ erscheinen/aussagen** to appear/testify in court; **vor ~ stehen** to stand trial; **jdn/einen Fall vor ~ bringen** to take sb/sth to court; **das Jüngste ~** the Last Judgement; **über jdn zu ~ sitzen** *(fig)* to sit in judgement on sb; **mit jdm (scharf) ins ~ gehen** *(fig)* to judge sb harshly.

**gerichtlich** *adj attr* judicial; *Entscheidung etc* court; *Medizin* forensic; *Verhandlung* legal. **laut ~em Beschluß** according to the decision of a/the court; **ein ~es Nachspiel haben** to finish up in court; ~ **gegen jdn vorgehen** to take legal proceedings against sb; **eine Sache ~ klären** to settle a matter in court.

**Gerichts-:** ~**akten** *pl* court records *pl*; ~**arzt** *m* court doctor; ~**barkeit** *f* jurisdiction; ~**beschluß** *m* court decision; ~**diener** *m (old)* court usher; ~**entscheid** *m,* ~**entscheidung** *f* court decision; ~**ferien** *pl* court vacation, recess; ~**hof** *m* court (of justice), law court; ~**kosten** *pl* court costs *pl*; ~**medizin** *f* forensic medicine; ~**mediziner** *m* forensic doctor; **g~medizinisch** *adj* forensic medical *attr*; ~**reporter** *m* legal correspondent; ~**saal** *m* courtroom; ~**schreiber** *m* clerk of the court; ~**stand** *m (form)* court of jurisdiction; ~**termin** *m* date of a/the trial; *(für Zivilsachen)* date of a/the hearing; ~**verfahren** *nt* court *or* legal proceedings *pl*; **ein ~verfahren gegen jdn einleiten** to institute legal proceedings against sb; ~**verhandlung** *f* trial; *(zivil)* hearing; ~**vollzieher** *m* bailiff; ~**weg** *m* **auf**

**dem ~weg** through the courts.
**ger|ieben 1** *ptp of* **reiben. 2** *adj (fig col)* smart, sharp; *(verschlagen auch)* sly, fly *(col)*. **der ist verdammt** ~ there are no flies on him *(col)*.
**geriet** *pret of* **geraten¹.**
**gering** *adj* **(a)** *(niedrig)* low; *Menge* small; *Wert* little *attr*; *(kurz) Zeit, Entfernung* short. **Berge von ~er Höhe** low hills; **seine Leistung erhielt eine zu ~e Bewertung** his performance wasn't rated highly enough. **(b)** *(unbedeutend, unerheblich)* slight; *Chance auch* small, slim; *Bedeutung, Rolle* minor. **das ist meine ~ste Sorge** that's the least of my worries; **die Kosten sind nicht** ~ the costs are not inconsiderable; **nicht im ~sten** not in the least *or* slightest; **nichts G~eres als** ... nothing less than; **kein G~erer als Freud** ... no less a person than Freud. **(c)** *(unzulänglich) Qualität, Kenntnisse* poor; *(abschätzig) Meinung* low, poor.
**gering|achten** *vt sep* = **geringschätzen.**
**geringelt** *adj Muster* ringed; *Socken* hooped.
**Gering-: g~fügig** *adj (unwichtig)* insignificant; *Unterschied* slight; *Vergehen, Verletzung* minor; *Betrag* small; **sein Zustand hat sich g~fügig gebessert** his condition is marginally improved; **~fügigkeit** *f* **(a)** insignificance; slightness; **ein Verfahren wegen ~fügigkeit einstellen** *(Jur)* to dismiss a case because of the trifling nature of the offence; **(b)** *(Kleinigkeit)* small thing, trifle; **g~schätzen** *vt sep (verachten) Menschen, Leistung* to have a low opinion of; *(mißachten) Gefahr, Folgen* to disregard; **g~schätzig** *adj* contemptuous; **~schätzung** *f no pl (Ablehnung)* disdain; *(schlechte Meinung)* low opinion *(für, gen* of*)*; *(für menschliches Leben)* low regard *(für, gen* for*)*.
**ger|innen\*** *vi irreg aux sein* to coagulate; *(Blut auch)* to clot; *(Milch auch)* to curdle. **mir gerann das Blut in den Adern** *(fig)* my blood ran cold.
**Gerinnsel** *nt (Blut~)* clot.
**Gerinnung** *f siehe vi* coagulation; clotting; curdling.
**Gerippe** *nt -* skeleton; *(von Schirm, Gebäude)* frame; *(fig: Grundplan)* framework. **er ist nur noch ein** ~ he's nothing but skin and bones.
**gerippt** *adj* ribbed *no adv*.
**gerissen 1** *ptp of* **reißen. 2** *adj* crafty, cunning.
**Gerissenheit** *f* cunning.
**geritten** *ptp of* **reiten.**
**geritzt** *adj pred (col)* **die Sache ist** ~ everything's fixed up *or* settled.
**German|e** *n (wk)* **-n, -n, Germanin** *f* Teuton.
**germanisch** *adj* Germanic.
**germanisieren\*** *vt* to Germanize.
**Germanist(in** *f)* *m* Germanist; *(Student auch)* German student; *(Wissenschaftler auch)* German specialist.
**Germanistik** *f* German (studies *pl*). ~ **studieren** to study German (language and literature).
**gern(e)** *adv, comp* **lieber,** *superl* **am liebsten (a)** *(freudig)* with pleasure; *(bereitwillig auch)* willingly, readily. **(aber)** ~! of course!; **kommst du mit?** — **ja,** ~ **as** you coming too? — oh yes, I'd like to; **geschehen!** you're welcome!, not at all!; **von mir aus kann er ja** ~ **älter sein** I don't mind if he's older; **etw** ~ **tun** to like doing sth *or* to do sth *(esp US)*; **etw** ~ **essen/trinken** to like sth; **sie ißt am liebsten** *Spargel* asparagus is her favourite *(Brit) or* favorite *(US)* food; **er sieht** *or* **hat es nicht** ~, **wenn wir zu spät kommen** he doesn't like us coming too late; **ein** ~ **gesehener Gast** a welcome visitor; **das glaube ich** ~ I can quite *or* well believe it; **jdn/etw** ~ **haben** *or* **mögen** to like sb/sth, to be fond of sb/sth;

**jdn/etw am liebsten haben** *or* **mögen** to like sb/sth best *or* most; **ich hätte** *or* **möchte** ~ ... I would like ...; **du kannst mich mal** ~ **haben!** *(col)* (you can) go to hell! *(col)*; *siehe* **lieber.**
**(b)** *(gewöhnlich, oft)* **etw** ~ **tun** to tend to do sth; **morgens läßt er sich** ~ **viel Zeit** he likes to leave himself a lot of time in the mornings.
**Gernegroß** *m -, -e (hum)* **er war schon immer ein kleiner** ~ he always did like to act big *(col)*.
**gerochen** *ptp of* **riechen.**
**Geröll** *nt -e* detritus *no pl*; *(größer)* boulders *pl*.
**geronnen** *ptp of* **rinnen, gerinnen.**
**Gerste** *f* **-n** barley.
**Gersten-: ~korn** *nt* **(a)** barleycorn; **(b)** *(Med)* stye; **~saft** *m (hum)* John Barleycorn *(hum)*, beer.
**Gerte** *f* **-n** switch; *(Reit~ auch)* crop.
**gertenschlank** *adj* slim and willowy.
**Geruch** *m* ̈**-e (a)** smell *(nach* of*)*; *(Duft auch)* fragrance *(nach* of*)*; *(von Speise etc auch)* aroma *(nach* of*)*. **(b)** *no pl (~ssinn)* sense of smell. **(c)** *no pl (fig: Ruf)* reputation. **in den** ~ **von etw kommen** to get a reputation for sth.
**geruchlos** *adj* odourless *(Brit)*, odorless *(US)*; *(duftlos)* scentless.
**Geruch(s)-: ~organ** *nt* organ of smell, olfactory organ *(spec)*; **~sinn** *m* sense of smell.
**Gerücht** *nt* **-e** rumour *(Brit)*, rumor *(US)*. **das halte ich für ein** ~ *(col)* I have my doubts about that.
**gerüchtweise** *adv* **etw** ~ **hören** to hear sth rumoured *(Brit) or* rumored *(US)*; ~ **ist bekanntgeworden, daß** ... rumour *(Brit) or* rumor *(US)* has it that ...
**gerufen** *ptp of* **rufen.**
**geruhen\*** *vt* ~, **etw zu tun** *(dated form, iro)* to be so gracious as to do sth.
**geruhsam** *adj* peaceful; *Spaziergang etc* leisurely *no adv*. ~ **essen** to eat in peace (and quiet).
**Gerümpel** *nt no pl* junk.
**Gerundium** *nt* gerund.
**gerungen** *ptp of* **ringen.**
**Gerüst** *nt* **-e** scaffolding *no pl*; *(Gestell)* trestle; *(fig: Gerippe)* framework *(zu* of*)*.
**ges, Ges** *nt* **-** *(Mus)* G flat.
**gesalzen** *adj (fig col) Preis, Rechnung* steep, stiff.
**gesammelt** *adj Aufmerksamkeit, Kraft* collective; *Werke* collected.
**gesamt** *adj attr* whole, entire. **die ~e Familie** the whole family; **die ~en Kosten** the total costs.
**Gesamt-: ~auflage** *f (von Zeitung etc)* total circulation; *(von Buch)* total edition; **~ausgabe** *f* complete edition; **~betrag** *m* total (amount); **g~deutsch** *adj* all-German; **~eindruck** *m* general impression; **~ergebnis** *nt* overall result; **~erlös** *m* total proceeds; **~fläche** *f* total area; **~gewicht** *nt* total weight.
**Gesamtheit** *f* totality. **die** ~ **der** ... all the ...; *(die Summe)* the totality of ...; **die** ~ **(der Bevölkerung)** the population (as a whole); **in seiner** ~ in its entirety; **das Volk in seiner** ~ the nation as a whole.
**Gesamt-: ~hochschule** *f* polytechnic; **~kosten** *pl* total costs *pl*; **~lage** *f* general situation; **~masse** *f (Comm)* total assets *pl*; **~note** *f (Sch)* overall mark; **~schaden** *m* total damage; **ein ~schaden von 5.000 Mark** damage totalling *(Brit) or* totaling *(US)* 5,000 marks; **~schule** *f* comprehensive school; **~sieger** *m (Sport)* overall winner; **~summe** *f* total (amount); **~übersicht** *f* general survey *(über + acc* of*)*; **~umsatz** *m* total turnover; **~werk** *nt* complete works *pl*; **~wert** *m* total value; **im ~wert von** ... totalling *(Brit) or* totaling *(US)* ... in value; **~wertung** *f (Sport)* overall

placings *pl*; **er liegt in der ~wertung vorn** he has the overall lead; **~zahl** *f* total number; **~zusammenhang** *m* general view.

**gesandt** *ptp of* **senden**[1].

**Gesandte(r)** *mf decl as adj* envoy; *(col: Botschafter)* ambassador.

**Gesandtschaft** *f* legation; *(col: Botschaft)* embassy.

**Gesang** *m ⁼e* **(a)** *(Lied, Vogel~)* song. **geistliche ⁼e** religious hymns and chants. **(b)** *no pl (das Singen)* singing.

**Gesang-:** **~buch** *nt (Eccl)* hymnbook; **~lehrer** *m* singing teacher.

**gesanglich** *adj* vocal; *Begabung* for singing.

**Gesangverein** *m* choral society.

**Gesäß** *nt -e* seat, bottom, posterior *(hum)*.

**Gesäßtasche** *f* back pocket.

**gesättigt** *adj (Chem)* saturated.

**gesch.** = **geschieden**.

**Geschädigte(r)** *mf decl as adj* victim.

**Geschäft** *nt -e* **(a)** *(Gewerbe, Handel)* business *no pl*; *(~sabschluß)* (business) deal *or* transaction. **wie geht das ~?** how's business?; **mit jdm ins ~ kommen** to do business with sb; **im ~ sein** to be in business; **ein ~ tätigen** to carry out a transaction; **ein gutes/schlechtes ~ machen** to make a good/bad deal; **dabei hat er ein ~ gemacht** he made a profit out of it; **das war für mich ein/kein ~** that was a good/bad bit of business for me; **~e mit etw machen** to make money out of sth. **(b)** *(Aufgabe)* duty. **seinen ~en nachgehen** to go about one's business. **(c)** *(Firma)* business; *(Laden)* shop *(Brit)*, store *(US)*. **im ~** at work; *(im Laden)* in the shop. **(d)** *(babytalk: Notdurft)* **ein ~ machen** to do a job *(baby-talk)*; **sein ~ verrichten** to do one's business *(euph)*.

**Geschäfte-:** **g~halber** *adv* verreist on business; *verhindert* because of business; **~macher** *m (pej)* wheeler-dealer; **~macherei** *f (pej)* wheeling and dealing.

**geschäftig** *adj (betriebsam)* busy. **~es Treiben** hustle and bustle.

**Geschäftigkeit** *f (geschäftiges Treiben)* hustle and bustle.

**geschäftlich 1** *adj (das Geschäft betreffend)* business *attr*; *(sachlich) Ton* businesslike. **ich habe mit ihm etwas G~es zu besprechen** I have some business to discuss with him. **2** *adv verreist* on business; *verhindert* because of business. **~ unterwegs** away on business.

**Geschäfts-:** **~abschluß** *m* business deal *or* transaction; **~aufgabe**, **~auflösung** *f* closure of a/the business; **~bank** *f* commercial bank; **~bedingungen** *pl* terms of business *pl*; **~bereich** *m (Parl)* responsibilities *pl*; **Minister ohne ~bereich** minister without portfolio; **~bericht** *m* report; *(einer Gesellschaft)* company report; **~beziehungen** *pl* business connections *pl (zu with)*; **~brief** *m* business letter; **~bücher** *pl* books *pl*, accounts *pl*; **~essen** *nt* business lunch; **~frau** *f* businesswoman; **~freund** *m* business associate; **g~führend** *adj attr* executive; *(stellvertretend)* acting; *Regierung* caretaker; **~führer** *m (von Laden)* manager; *(von Firma)* managing director; *(von Verein)* secretary; *(von Partei)* whip; **~führung** *f* management; **~geheimnis** *nt* trade secret; **~haus** *nt* **(a)** *(Gebäude)* business premises *pl*; *(von Büros)* office block; **(b)** *(Firma)* house, firm; **~inhaber(in** *f)* *m* owner; **~jahr** *nt* financial year; **~kapital** *nt* working capital; **~kosten** *pl* business expenses *pl*; **das geht alles auf ~kosten** it's all on expenses; **~lage** *f* **(a)** *(Wirtschaftslage)* trading situation; **(b) in erstklassiger ~lage** in a good business location;

**~leitung** *f* management; **~mann** *m, pl* **~leute** businessman; **g~mäßig** *adj* businesslike *no adv*; **~ordnung** *f* standing orders *pl*; **eine Frage zur ~ordnung** a question on a point of order; **~partner** *m* business associate; **~räume** *pl* (business) premises *pl*; *(Büroräume)* offices *pl*; **~reise** *f* business trip; **auf ~reise sein** to be on a business trip; **g~schädigend** *adj* bad for business; **g~schädigendes Verhalten** conduct *no art* injurious to the interests of the company *(form)*; **~schluß** *m* close of business; *(von Läden)* closing-time; **nach ~schluß** after working hours/closing-time; **~sinn** *m* business sense *or* acumen; **~stelle** *f* offices *pl*; **~straße** *f* shopping street; **~stunden** *pl* office hours *pl*; *(von Läden)* opening hours *pl*; **~tätigkeit** *f* business activity; **g~tüchtig** *adj* business-minded; **~wagen** *m* company car; **~welt** *f* business world; **~zeiten** *pl* = **~stunden**; **~zimmer** *nt* office.

**geschah** *pret of* **geschehen**.

**gescheckt** *adj* spotted; *Pferd* skewbald, pinto *(US)*.

**geschehen** *pret* **geschah**, *ptp* **~** *vi aux sein* to happen *(jdm* to sb); *(ausgeführt werden)* to be done; *(Verbrechen)* to be committed. **es ist nun einmal ~** what's done is done; **es wird ihm nichts ~** nothing will happen to him; **das geschieht ihm (ganz) recht** it serves him (jolly well *col)* right; **was soll mit ihm/damit ~?** what is to be done with him/it?; **als er sie sah, war es um ihn ~** he was lost the moment he set eyes on her; **da war es um meine Seelenruhe ~** that was an end to my peace of mind.

**Geschehen** *nt -* events *pl*, happenings *pl*.

**gescheit** *adj* clever; *Mensch, Idee auch* bright; *(vernünftig)* sensible. **du bist wohl nicht recht ~?** you must be out of your mind *or* off your head; **sei ~!** be sensible.

**Geschenk** *nt -e* present, gift; *(Schenkung)* gift. **jdm ein ~ machen** to give sb a present; **das war ein ~ des Himmels** it was a godsend.

**Geschenk-** *in cpds* gift; **~artikel** *m* gift; **~gutschein** *m* gift token; **~packung** *f* gift pack *or* box; *(von Pralinen)* gift box; **~papier** *nt* gift-wrap(ping paper); **~sendung** *f* gift parcel.

**Geschichte** *f -n* **(a)** *no pl (Historie)* history. **Alte/Neuere ~** ancient/modern history; **~ machen** to make history; **das ist längst ~** that's ancient history. **(b)** *(Erzählung, Lügen~)* story; *(Märchen, Fabel etc auch)* tale; *(Kurz~)* short story. **~n erzählen** to tell stories. **(c)** *(col: Angelegenheit, Sache)* affair, business *no pl*. **das sind alte ~n** that's old hat *(col)*; **alte ~n wieder aufwärmen** to rake up the past; **eine schöne ~!** *(iro)* a fine how-do-you-do! *(col)*; **die ~ mit seinem Magen** the business with his stomach; **mach keine ~n!** don't be silly! *(col)*; *(Dummheiten)* don't get up to anything silly!

**Geschichten|erzähler** *m (lit, fig)* storyteller.

**geschichtlich** *adj (historisch)* historical; *(bedeutungsvoll)* historic. **~ belegt** *or* **nachgewiesen sein** to be a historical fact.

**Geschichts-:** **~buch** *nt* history book; **~fälschung** *f* falsification of history; **~forscher** *m* historian; **~forschung** *f* historical research; **~kenntnis** *f* historical knowledge *no pl*; **~lehrer** *m* history teacher; **~schreiber** *m* historian; **~schreibung** *f* historiography.

**Geschick**[1] *nt -e (geh) (Schicksal)* fate; *(usu pl: politische etc Entwicklung)* fortune. **ein gütiges ~** good fortune, providence.

**Geschick**[2] *nt no pl (~lichkeit)* skill.

**Geschicklichkeit** *f siehe* **geschickt** skill; cleverness; agility. **für etw ~ haben** to be clever at sth.

**Geschicklichkeitsspiel** *nt* game of skill.
**geschickt** *adj* skilful *(Brit)*, skillful *(US)*; *(taktisch auch)* clever; *(beweglich)* agile.
**Geschicktheit** *f* = Geschicklichkeit.
**geschieden** *ptp of* scheiden.
**Geschiedene(r)** *mf decl as adj* divorcee.
**geschienen** *ptp of* scheinen.
**Geschirr** *nt* **-e (a)** *no pl (Teller etc)* crockery *(Brit)*, tableware; *(Küchen~)* pots and pans *pl*, kitchenware; *(Porzellan)* china. **(das)** ~ **spülen** to wash *or* do the dishes, to wash up *(Brit)*; **feuerfestes** ~ ovenware. **(b)** *(Service)* (dinner/tea *etc*) service; *(Gläser)* set of glasses; *(feuerfestes ~)* set of ovenware. **(c)** *(von Zugtieren)* harness.
**Geschirr-:** ~**schrank** *m* china cupboard; ~**spülen** *nt* washing-up; ~**spüler** *m*, ~**spülmaschine** *f* dishwasher; ~**spülmittel** *nt* washing-up liquid *(Brit)*; dishwashing liquid *(US)*; ~**tuch** *nt* tea towel *(Brit)*, dishtowel *(US)*.
**geschissen** *ptp of* scheißen.
**geschlafen** *ptp of* schlafen.
**geschlagen** *ptp of* schlagen.
**Geschlecht** *nt* **-er (a)** sex; *(Gram)* gender. **Jugendliche beiderlei** ~**s** young people of both sexes; **das andere** ~ the opposite sex. **(b)** *no pl (geh: Geschlechtsteil)* sex *(liter)*. **(c)** *(liter) (Gattung)* race; *(Sippe)* house; *(Abstammung)* lineage. **das menschliche** ~ the human race.
**geschlechtlich** *adj* sexual. ~**e Erziehung** sex education; **mit jdm** ~ **verkehren** to have sexual intercourse with sb.
**Geschlechtlichkeit** *f* sexuality.
**Geschlechts-:** ~**akt** *m* sex act; ~**erziehung** *f* sex education; **g~krank** *adj* suffering from VD; **g~krank sein** to have VD; ~**krankheit** *f* venereal disease; ~**leben** *nt* sex life; **g~los** *adj* asexual *(auch Biol)*, sexless; ~**losigkeit** *f* asexuality *(auch Biol)*, sexlessness; ~**merkmal** *nt* sex(ual) characteristic; ~**organ** *nt* sex organ; **g~reif** *adj* sexually mature; ~**reife** *f* sexual maturity; **g~spezifisch** *adj (Sociol)* sex-specific; ~**teil** *nt* genitals *pl*; ~**trieb** *m* sex drive; ~**umwandlung** *f* sex change; ~**verkehr** *m* sexual intercourse; ~**wort** *nt (Gram)* article.
**geschlichen** *ptp of* schleichen.
**geschliffen 1** *ptp of* schleifen². **2** *adj Manieren* polished, refined; *Sätze* polished.
**geschlossen 1** *ptp of* schließen. **2** *adj* closed; *(vereint)* unified. **in sich** *(dat)* ~ self-contained; *Mensch, Charakter* well-rounded; *Handlung* well-knit; **ein** ~**es Ganzes** a unified whole; ~**e Gesellschaft** *(Fest)* private function; ~**e Ortschaft** built-up area. **3** *adv* ~ **für etw sein/stimmen** to be/vote unanimously in favour of sth; ~ **hinter jdm stehen** to stand solidly behind sb.
**Geschlossenheit** *f* unity.
**geschlungen** *ptp of* schlingen.
**Geschmack** *m* ⁼e *or (hum, col)* ⁼er *(lit, fig)* taste; *(Aroma)* flavour *(Brit)*, flavor *(US)*; *(no pl: ~ssinn)* sense of taste. **je nach** ~ to one's own taste; **Salz (je) nach** ~ **hinzufügen** add salt to taste; **an etw** *(dat)* ~ **finden** to acquire a taste for sth; **auf den** ~ **kommen** to acquire a taste for it; **er hat einen guten** ~ *(fig)* he has good taste; **das ist nicht mein** ~ *or* **nach meinem** ~ that's not to my taste; **die ⁼er sind verschieden** tastes differ; **über** ~ **läßt sich (nicht) streiten** *(Prov)* there's no accounting for taste(s) *(prov)*.
**geschmacklich** *adj (lit, fig)* as regards taste.
**geschmacklos** *adj (lit, fig)* tasteless.
**Geschmacklosigkeit** *f* **(a)** *no pl (lit, fig)* tastelessness, lack of taste; *(Taktlosigkeit auch)* bad taste. **(b)** *(Beispiel der* ~*)* example of bad taste; *(Bemerkung)* remark in bad taste.
**Geschmacks-:** ~**frage** *f* question of (good) taste; ~**richtung** *f* taste; *(von Speisen etc)* flavour *(Brit)*, flavor *(US)*; ~**sache** *f* matter of taste; **das ist** ~**sache** it's (all) a matter of taste; ~**sinn** *m* sense of taste; ~**verirrung** *f* **unter** ~**verirrung leiden** *(iro)* to have no taste.
**geschmackvoll** *adj* tasteful.
**Geschmeide** *nt* **-** *(geh)* jewellery *no pl*.
**geschmeidig** *adj* **(a)** *Haar, Leder, Haut* supple; *Fell* sleek; *(weich) Handtuch, Haar* soft; *Teig* workable. **(b)** *(fig) (anpassungfähig)* flexible; *(wendig)* adroit.
**Geschmeidigkeit** *f* *no pl siehe adj* **(a)** suppleness; sleekness; softness. **(b)** flexibility, adroitness.
**Geschmier(e)** *nt* *no pl (col)* mess; *(Geschriebenes)* scribble, scrawl.
**geschmissen** *ptp of* schmeißen.
**geschmolzen** *ptp of* schmelzen.
**Geschmorte(s)** *nt decl as adj (Cook)* braised meat.
**Geschnatter** *nt* *no pl (lit)* cackling; *(fig)* jabbering.
**Geschnetzelte(s)** *nt decl as adj (Cook)* meat cut into strips stewed to produce a thick sauce.
**geschniegelt** *adj (pej)* flashy.
**geschnitten** *ptp of* schneiden.
**geschoben** *ptp of* schieben.
**gescholten** *ptp of* schelten.
**Geschöpf** *nt* **-e** *(Geschaffenes)* creation; *(Lebewesen)* creature.
**geschoren** *ptp of* scheren¹.
**Geschoß¹** *nt* **-sse** projectile *(form)*; *(Wurf~, Rakete etc auch)* missile; *(Kugel auch)* bullet.
**Geschoß²** *nt* **-sse** *(Stockwerk)* floor, storey *(Brit)*, story *(US)*.
**Geschoßbahn** *f* trajectory.
**geschossen** *ptp of* schießen.
**geschraubt** *adj (pej) Stil, Redeweise* pretentious.
**Geschrei** *nt* *no pl* shouts *pl*, shouting; *(von Verletzten, Babys, Popfans)* screams *pl*, screaming; *(fig: Aufhebens)* fuss, to-do *(col)*. **viel** ~ **um etw machen** to make a big fuss about sth.
**geschrieben** *ptp of* schreiben.
**geschrie(e)n** *ptp of* schreien.
**geschritten** *ptp of* schreiten.
**geschunden** *ptp of* schinden.
**Geschütz** *nt* **-e** gun. **schweres** ~ heavy artillery; **schweres** ~ **auffahren** *(fig)* to bring up one's big guns.
**Geschütz-:** ~**feuer** *nt* shell fire; ~**rohr** *nt* gun barrel.
**geschützt** *adj Winkel, Ecke* sheltered; *Pflanze, Tier* protected. ~**er Sex** safe sex.
**Geschw.** = Geschwister.
**Geschwader** *nt* **-** squadron.
**Geschwafel** *nt* *no pl (pej col)* waffle *(col)*.
**Geschwätz** *nt* *no pl (pej)* prattle; *(Klatsch)* tittle-tattle *(col)*, gossip.
**geschwätzig** *adj* talkative; *(klatschsüchtig)* gossipy.
**Geschwätzigkeit** *f* *no pl siehe adj* talkativeness; gossipy nature.
**geschweift** *adj* **(a)** curved. **(b)** *Stern* with a tail.
**geschweige** *conj* ~ **(denn)** let alone.
**geschwiegen** *ptp of* schweigen.
**geschwind** *adj* quick, fast *no adv*.
**Geschwindigkeit** *f* speed; *(Phys: von Masse)* velocity. **mit einer** ~ **von ...** at a speed of ...; **mit höchster** ~ at top speed.
**Geschwindigkeits-:** ~**begrenzung**, ~**beschränkung** *f* speed limit; **gegen die** ~**begrenzung verstoßen** to exceed the speed limit; ~**kontrolle**

*f* speed check; ~**messer** *m* - tachometer; *(Aut auch)* speedometer; ~**überschreitung** *f* exceeding the speed limit *no art*, speeding *no art*.

**Geschwịster** *pl* brothers and sisters *pl.* **haben Sie noch** ~? do you have any brothers or sisters?

**geschwịsterlich 1** *adj* brotherly/sisterly. **2** *adv* in a brotherly/sisterly way.

**Geschwịster-:** ~**liebe** *f* brotherly/sisterly love; *(gegenseitig)* love between a brother and a sister; ~**paar** *nt* brother and sister *pl*.

**geschwọllen 1** *ptp of* **schwellen. 2** *adj (pej)* turgid.

**geschwọmmen** *ptp of* **schwimmen.**

**geschwọren** *ptp of* **schwören.**

**Geschwọrene(r)** *mf decl as adj* juror. **die** ~**n** the jury *sing or pl.*

**Geschwụlst** *f* ⁼e growth; *(Hirn~, Krebs~ etc auch)* tumour *(Brit)*, tumor *(US).*

**geschwụnden** *ptp of* **schwinden.**

**geschwụngen 1** *ptp of* **schwingen. 2** *adj* curved.

**Geschwụ̈r** *nt* -e ulcer; *(Furunkel)* boil; *(fig)* ulcer.

**gesẹgnet** *adj (geh)* **mit etw** ~ **sein** to be blessed with sth; ~**es Neues Jahr!** Happy New Year; **einen** ~**en Schlaf haben** to be a sound sleeper.

**gesẹhen** *ptp of* **sehen.**

**Gesẹlle** *m (wk)* **-n, -n (a)** *(Handwerks~)* journeyman. **(b)** *(dated col: Bursche)* fellow.

**gesẹllen\*** *vr* **sich zu jdm** ~ to join sb.

**Gesẹllen-:** ~**brief** *m* journeyman's certificate; ~**prüfung** *f* examination to become a journeyman.

**gesẹllig** *adj* sociable, convivial; *Tier* gregarious; *Verkehr* social. ~**es Beisammensein** social gathering.

**Gesẹlligkeit** *f* **(a)** *no pl* sociability; *(geselliges Leben)* social intercourse. **die** ~ **lieben** to be sociable. **(b)** *(Veranstaltung)* social gathering.

**Gesẹllschaft** *f* **(a)** *(Sociol, Vereinigung)* society; *(Comm)* company. **die** ~ **verändern** to change society. **(b)** *(Abend~)* reception, party; *(Gäste)* guests *pl*, party. **geschlossene** ~ private function. **(c)** *(Umgang, Begleitung)* company. **in schlechte** ~ **geraten** to get into bad company; **jdm** ~ **leisten** to keep sb company; **darf ich Ihnen** ~ **leisten?** may I join you? **(d)** *(Kreis von Menschen)* group of people; *(pej)* crowd *(col).* **wir waren eine bunte** ~ we were a mixed bunch.

**Gesẹllschafter(in** *f)* *m* - **(a)** *(Unterhalter)* companion. **ein guter** ~ **sein** to be good company. **(b)** *(Comm) (Teilhaber)* shareholder; *(Partner)* partner. **stiller** ~ sleeping *(Brit)* or silent *(US)* partner.

**gesẹllschaftlich** *adj* social. **er ist** ~ **erledigt** he's ruined socially.

**Gesẹllschafts-:** ~**anzug** *m* formal dress; **g**~**fähig** *adj Verhalten* socially acceptable; *Mensch, Aussehen auch* presentable; ~**form** *f* social system; ~**kapital** *nt (Comm)* authorized capital; ~**klasse** *f (Sociol)* social class; ~**klatsch** *m* society gossip; ~**kleidung** *f* formal dress; ~**kritik** *f* social criticism; **g**~**kritisch** *adj* critical of society; **g**~**kritisch denken** to have a critical attitude towards society; ~**ordnung** *f* social system; ~**politik** *f* social policy; ~**recht** *nt* company law; ~**reise** *f* group tour; ~**roman** *m* social novel; ~**schicht** *f* social stratum; ~**spiel** *nt* party game; ~**stück** *nt (Theat)* comedy of manners; *(Art)* genre painting; ~**system** *nt* social system; ~**tanz** *m* ballroom dance; ~**wissenschaften** *pl* social sciences.

**Gesẹnk** *nt* -e *(Tech)* die.

**gesẹssen** *ptp of* **sitzen.**

**Gesẹtz** *nt* -e *(Jur, Natur~, Prinzip)* law; *(~buch)* stat-

ute book; *(Parl)* act; *(Vorlage)* bill; *(Satzung, Regel)* rule. **das Copyright-**~ the Copyright Act; **nach dem** ~ **under the law** *(über +acc on)*; **vor dem** ~ in (the eyes of the) law; **im Sinne des** ~**es** within the meaning of the act; **steht etwas davon im** ~? is there any law about it?; **das** ~ **der Schwerkraft** the law of gravity; **das oberste** ~ **(der Wirtschaft** *etc)* the golden rule (of industry *etc)*; **ein ungeschriebenes** ~ an unwritten rule.

**Gesẹtz-:** ~**blatt** *nt* law gazette; ~**buch** *nt* statute book; **Bürgerliches** ~**buch** Civil Code; ~**entwurf** *m* (draft) bill.

**Gesẹtzes-:** ~**brecher(in** *f)* *m* - law-breaker; ~**hüter** *m (iro)* guardian of the law; ~**lücke** *f* legal loophole; ~**novelle** *f* amendment; ~**text** *m* wording of a/the law; **g**~**treu** *adj* law-abiding; ~**treue** *f* law-abiding character; ~**übertretung** *f* infringement of a/the law; ~**vorlage** *f* (draft) bill.

**Gesẹtz-:** **g**~**gebend** *adj attr* legislative, lawmaking; **die g**~**gebende Gewalt** the legislature; ~**geber** *m* legislator, lawmaker; ~**gebung** *f* legislation *no pl.*

**gesẹtzlich 1** *adj Bestimmungen, Vertreter, Zahlungsmittel* legal; *Feiertag, Reglungen* statutory; *(rechtmäßig)* lawful, legitimate. **2** *adv* legally; *(durch Gesetze auch)* by law; *(rechtmäßig)* lawfully, legitimately. ~ **geschützt** registered.

**Gesẹtzlichkeit** *f no pl (Gesetzmäßigkeit)* legality.

**Gesẹtz-:** **g**~**los** *adj* lawless; ~**losigkeit** *f* lawlessness; **g**~**mäßig** *adj (gesetzlich)* legal; *(rechtmäßig)* lawful, legitimate. **2** *adv* legally; ~**mäßigkeit** *f siehe adj* legality; lawfulness, legitimacy.

**gesẹtzt 1** *adj (reif)* sedate, sober. **ein Herr im** ~**en Alter** a man of mature years. **2** *conj* ~ **den Fall, ...** assuming (that) ...

**Gesẹtz-:** **g**~**widrig** *adj* illegal; *(unrechtmäßig)* unlawful; ~**widrigkeit** *f siehe adj* illegality; unlawfulness *no pl.*

**ges. gesch.** = **gesetzlich geschützt** reg'd.

**gesịchert** *adj Einkommen, Existenz* secure.

**Gesịcht** *nt* -er **(a)** face. **ein trauriges/böses/wütendes** ~ **machen** to look sad/cross/angry; **ein langes** ~ **machen** to pull a long face; **was machst du denn heute für ein** ~? what's up with you today?; **jdm ins** ~ **sehen** to look sb in the face; **den Tatsachen ins** ~ **sehen** to face facts; **jdm etw ins** ~ **sagen** to tell sb sth to his face; **mir schien die Sonne ins** ~ the sun was (shining) in my eyes; **es stand ihm im** ~ **geschrieben** it was written all over his face; **jdm ins** ~ **springen** *(fig col)* to go for sb; **sein wahres** ~ **zeigen** to show (oneself in) one's true colours *(Brit)* or colors *(US)*; **jdm wie aus dem** ~ **geschnitten sein** to be the spitting image of sb; **das/sein** ~ **verlieren** to lose face; **das** ~ **wahren** to save face.

**(b)** *(fig) (Aussehen)* look, appearance; *(geh: Charakter)* character. **die Sache bekommt ein anderes** ~ the matter takes on a different complexion.

**(c)** *no pl* **das Zweite** ~ second sight; **etw aus dem** ~ **verlieren** *(lit, fig)* to lose sight of sth; **jdn/etw zu** ~ **bekommen** to set eyes on sb/sth.

**Gesịchts-:** ~**ausdruck** *m* (facial) expression; *(Mienenspiel auch)* face; **einen ängstlichen** ~**ausdruck haben** to look scared; ~**creme** *f* face cream; ~**farbe** *f* complexion; ~**feld** *nt* field of vision; ~**haut** *f* facial skin; ~**kreis** *m* **(a)** *(dated: Umkreis)* field of vision; **jdn aus dem/seinem** ~**kreis verlieren** to lose sight of sb; **(b)** *(fig)* horizons *pl*, outlook; **g**~**los** *adj (fig)* faceless; ~**packung** *f* face pack; ~**pflege** *f* facial care; ~**puder** *m* face powder; ~**punkt** *m (Betrachtungsweise)* point of view; *(Ein-*

zelheit) point; **unter diesem ~punkt betrachtet** looked at from this standpoint; **~verlust** m loss of face; **~wasser** nt face lotion; **~winkel** m visual angle; (fig) angle; **aus** or **unter diesem ~winkel betrachtet** looked at from this angle; **~züge** pl features pl.

**Gesindel** nt no pl (pej) riff-raff pl.

**gesinnt** adj usu pred **jdm gut/übel ~ sein** to be well/ill disposed to(wards) sb; **jdm freundlich/feindlich ~ sein** to be friendly/hostile to sb; **sozial ~ sein** to be socially minded; **er ist anders ~ als wir** his views are different from ours.

**Gesinnung** f (Charakter) cast of mind; (Ansichten) views pl, basic convictions pl; (Einstellung) fundamental attitude; (Denkart) way of thinking; (einer Gruppe) ethos. **seine wahre ~ zeigen** to show (oneself in) one's true colours (Brit) or colors (US).

**Gesinnungs-:** **~genosse** m like-minded person; **g~los** adj (pej) unprincipled; **sich g~los verhalten** to show a total lack of principle; **~losigkeit** f lack of principle; **~schnüffelei** f (pej) **~schnüffelei betreiben** to pry into people's political convictions; **~täter** m person motivated by political/moral convictions; **g~treu** adj true to one's convictions; **~wandel** m conversion.

**gesittet** adj (a) (wohlerzogen) well-mannered, well-behaved. (b) (zivilisiert) civilized.

**Gesocks** nt no pl (pej) riff-raff pl.

**Gesöff** nt -e (pej) muck (col); (Bier) piss (col!).

**gesoffen** ptp of **saufen**.

**gesogen** ptp of **saugen**.

**gesondert** adj separate.

**gesonnen 1** ptp of **sinnen**. **2** adj **~ sein, etw zu tun** to be of a mind to do sth.

**gespalten** adj Bewußtsein split; Lippe cleft; Zunge forked.

**Gespann** nt -e (Pferde~) horse and cart; (zur Personenbeförderung) horse and carriage; (fig col: Paar) pair. **ein gutes ~ abgeben** to make a good team.

**gespannt** adj (a) Seil, Schnur taut. (b) (fig) tense; Beziehungen auch strained. **seine Nerven waren aufs äußerste ~** his nerves were at breaking point. (c) (neugierig) curious; (begierig) eager; Aufmerksamkeit rapt. **in ~er Erwartung** in eager anticipation; **~ zuhören** to listen with rapt attention; **ich bin ~, wie er darauf reagiert** I wonder how he'll react to that; **ich bin auf seine Reaktion sehr ~** I'm dying to see how he'll react to that; **ich bin ~ wie ein Flitz(e)bogen** (hum col) I'm on tenterhooks; **da bin ich aber ~!** I'm looking forward to that; (iro) that I'd like to see!

**Gespanntheit** f no pl siehe adj (a) tension. (b) tension; strain. (c) curiosity; eagerness.

**Gespenst** nt -er ghost; (fig: Gefahr) spectre (Brit), specter (US). **~er sehen** (fig col) to imagine things.

**Gespenster-:** **~geschichte** f ghost story; **g~haft** adj ghostly no adv; (fig) eerie, eery; **das Licht flackerte g~haft** the light flickered eerily; **~stunde** f witching hour.

**gespenstisch** adj = **gespensterhaft**.

**gespie(e)n** ptp of **speien**.

**Gespiele** m -n, -n (old liter, hum), **Gespielin** f (old liter, hum) playmate.

**gespielt** adj feigned. **mit ~em Interesse** with a pretence (Brit) or pretense (US) of being interested.

**Gespinst** nt -e (fig geh) web; (der Phantasie) product, fabrication.

**gesponnen** ptp of **spinnen**.

**Gespött** nt no pl mockery; (Gegenstand des Spotts) laughing stock. **sich zum ~ der Leute machen** to make oneself a laughing stock.

**Gespräch** nt -e (a) (Unterhaltung) conversation; (Diskussion) discussion; (Dialog) dialogue. **~e** (Pol) talks; **ein ~ unter vier Augen** a confidential or private talk; **im ~ sein** to be under discussion; **mit jdm ins ~ kommen** to get into conversation with sb; (fig) to establish a dialogue with sb. (b) (~sstoff) **das ~ des Tages** the topic of the hour; **das ~ der Stadt** the talk of the town; **zum ~ werden** to become a talking point. (c) (Telec: Anruf) (telephone) call.

**gesprächig** adj talkative; (mitteilsam) communicative.

**Gesprächs-:** **g~bereit** adj (esp Pol) ready to talk; **~einheit** f (Telec) unit; **~gegenstand** m topic; **~partner** m **~partner bei der Diskussion sind die Herren X, Y und Z** taking part in the discussion are Mr X, Mr Y and Mr Z; **mein ~partner bei den Verhandlungen** my opposite number at the talks; **wer war dein ~partner?** who did you talk with?; **~pause** f break in a/the conversation; **~stoff** m topics pl; (Diskussionsstoff) topics to discuss; **~thema** nt talking point, topic.

**gespreizt** adj (fig) affected, unnatural.

**gesprenkelt** adj speckled.

**Gespritzte(r)** n decl as adj (S Ger, Aus) spritzer, wine with soda water.

**gesprochen** ptp of **sprechen**.

**gesprossen** ptp of **sprießen**.

**gesprungen** ptp of **springen**.

**Gespür** nt no pl feel(ing).

**gest.** = **gestorben**, d.

**Gestalt** f -en (a) (lit, fig) form; (Umriß auch) shape. **in ~ von** (fig) in the form of; (feste) **~ annehmen** to take shape; **einer Sache** (dat) **~ geben** to shape sth; **sich in seiner wahren ~ zeigen** (fig) to show (oneself in) one's true colours (Brit) or colors (US). (b) (Wuchs) build. (c) (Persönlichkeit, Traum~) figure; (Liter auch, pej: Mensch) character.

**gestalten* 1** vt to shape, to form (zu into); Wohnung to lay out; Programm, Abend to arrange; Schaufenster to dress; Freizeit to structure. **ich gestalte mein Leben so, wie ich will** I organize my life the way I want to; **etw interessanter** etc **~ to make** sth more interesting etc; **schöpferisches G~** creative expression. **2** vr (werden) to become; (sich entwickeln) to develop (zu into).

**Gestalter(in** f) m - creator.

**gestalterisch** adj formal, creative.

**gestaltlos** adj formless, shapeless.

**Gestaltung** f siehe vt shaping, forming (zu into); lay-out; arrangement; dressing; structuring.

**Gestammel** nt no pl stammering, stuttering.

**gestanden 1** ptp of **stehen, gestehen**. **2** adj attr **ein ~er Mann** a mature and experienced man.

**geständig** adj **~ sein** to have confessed.

**Geständnis** nt confession. **jdm ein ~ machen** to make a confession to sb.

**Gestänge** nt - (von Gerüst) bars pl, struts pl; (von Zelt) frame; (von Maschine) linkage.

**Gestank** m no pl stink, stench.

**gestatten* ** vti to allow, to permit; (einwilligen in) to agree or consent to. **jdm ~, etw zu tun** to allow or permit sb to do sth; **~ Sie, daß ich ...?** may I ...?; **wenn Sie ~ ...** with your permission ...; **sich** (dat) **etw ~** to permit or allow oneself sth; **wenn ich mir eine Bemerkung ~ darf** (geh) if I might be permitted a comment.

**Geste** ['gɛstə, 'geːstə] f -n (lit, fig) gesture.

**Gesteck** nt -e flower arrangement.

**gestehen** vti irreg to confess (jdm etw sth to sb). **offen gestanden** quite frankly.

**Gestein** *nt* -e rock(s); *(Schicht)* rock stratum.
**Gesteins-:** ~**brocken** *m* rock; ~**masse** *f* mass of rock.
**Gestell** *nt* -e **(a)** stand; *(Regal)* shelf; *(Ablage)* rack; *(Bett~, Brillen~)* frame; *(Fahr~)* chassis. **(b)** *(fig col: Beine)* pins *(col)* *pl.* **langes** ~ beanpole *(col)*.
**gestellt** *adj (unecht)* posed.
**gestelzt** *adj* stilted.
**gestern** *adv* yesterday. ~ **abend** *(früh)* yesterday evening; *(spät)* last night; **die Zeitung von** ~ yesterday's paper; **Ansichten von** ~ outdated views; **er ist nicht von** ~ *(col)* he wasn't born yesterday.
**gestiefelt** *adj* **der G~e Kater** Puss-in-Boots; ~ **und gespornt** *(fig col)* ready and waiting.
**gestiegen** *ptp of* **steigen.**
**Gestik** ['gɛstɪk] *f no pl* gestures *pl.*
**gestikulieren\*** [gɛstiku'liːrən] *vi* to gesticulate.
**gestimmt** *adj* **froh/düster** ~ in a cheerful/sombre mood.
**Gestirn** *nt* -e star, heavenly body.
**gestoben** *ptp of* **stieben.**
**Gestöber** *nt* - *(Schnee~)* snowstorm.
**gestochen** **1** *ptp of* **stechen. 2** *adj Handschrift* clear, neat. ~ **scharfe Fotos** needle-sharp photographs.
**gestohlen** **1** *ptp of* **stehlen. 2** *adj* **der/das kann mir** ~ **bleiben** *(col)* he/it can get lost *(col)*.
**gestorben** *ptp of* **sterben.**
**gestört** *adj* disturbed; *Rundfunkempfang* poor, with a lot of interference. ~**er Kreislauf** circulation problems; **Kinder aus** ~**en Familien** children from problem families.
**gestoßen** *ptp of* **stoßen.**
**Gestotter** *nt no pl* stuttering, stammering.
**Gesträuch** *nt* -e shrubbery, bushes *(pl)*.
**gestreift** *adj* striped. **eine rot-grün** ~**e Bluse** a red and green striped blouse.
**gestrichen** **1** *ptp of* **streichen. 2** *adj* **(a) frisch** ~**!** wet paint. **(b)** *(genau voll)* ~ **voll** level; *(sehr voll)* full to the brim; **ein** ~**er Teelöffel (voll)** a level teaspoon(ful); **er hat die Hosen** ~ **voll** *(col)* he's shitting himself *(col!)*; **ich habe die Nase** ~ **voll** *(col)* I'm fed up to the back teeth with it *(col)*.
**gestrig** *adj attr* yesterday's. **unser** ~**es Schreiben** our letter of yesterday; **am** ~**en Tage** *(geh)* yesterday; **die ewig G~en** the stick-in-the-muds.
**gestritten** *ptp of* **streiten.**
**Gestrüpp** *nt* -e undergrowth, brushwood; *(fig)* jungle.
**gestunken** *ptp of* **stinken.**
**Gestüt** *nt* -e stud; *(Anlage auch)* stud farm.
**Gesuch** *nt* -e petition *(auf +acc, um* for*)*; *(Antrag)* application *(auf +acc, um* for*)*. **ein** ~ **einreichen** to lodge a petition/an application.
**gesucht** *adj (begehrt)* sought after. **sehr** ~ *(very)* much sought after.
**gesund** *adj, comp* ⁼**er** *superl* ⁼**este(r, s)** *or adv* **am** ⁼**esten** healthy; *(leistungsfähig)* fit; *Unternehmen, Politik auch* sound. ~ **und munter** hale and hearty; **ich fühle mich nicht ganz** ~ I don't feel too well; ~ **leben** to live a healthy life; **jdn** ~ **schreiben** to certify sb (as) fit; **jdn** ~ **pflegen** to nurse sb back to health; **sonst bist du** ~**?** *(iro col)* are you feeling all right? *(iro)*; **wieder** ~ **werden** to recover.
**Gesund-:** **g~beten** *vt sep* to heal through prayer; ~**beter** *m* faith-healer.
**gesunden\*** *vi aux sein (geh)* to recover *(auch fig)*, to regain one's health.
**Gesundheit** *f no pl siehe adj* health; fitness; soundness; *(von Klima, Lebensweise etc)* healthiness. **bei guter** ~ in good health; ~**!** bless you; **auf Ihre** ~**!**

your (very good) health.
**gesundheitlich** *adj* ~ **geht es mir nicht besonders** my health is not particularly good; **aus** ~**en Gründen** for health reasons.
**Gesundheits-:** ~**amt** *nt* public health department; ~**apostel** *m (iro)* health freak *(col)*; ~**attest** *nt* health certificate; ~**behörde** *f* health authorities *pl*; **g~fördernd** *adj* healthy, good for the health; ~**fürsorge** *f* health care; **g~gefährdend** *adj* **g~gefährdend sein** to be a danger to health; ~**pflege** *f* hygiene; **öffentliche** ~**pflege** public health (care); ~**schaden** *m* health defect; ~**schäden** damage to one's health; **g~schädlich** *adj* unhealthy, damaging to (one's) health; ~**wesen** *nt* health service; ~**zeugnis** *nt* health certificate; ~**zustand** *m no pl* state of health.
**gesund-:** ~**schrumpfen** *sep* **1** *vt (fig)* to trim down; **2** *vr* to be trimmed down *or* streamlined; ~**stoßen** *vr sep irreg (col)* to line one's pockets *(col)*.
**Gesundung** *f no pl (lit, fig)* recovery; *(Genesung)* convalescence, recuperation.
**gesungen** *ptp of* **singen.**
**gesunken** *ptp of* **sinken.**
**getan** *ptp of* **tun. nach** ~**er Arbeit** when the day's work is done.
**Getier** *nt no pl* **(a)** *(Tiere, esp Insekten)* creatures *pl.* **(b)** *(einzelnes)* creature.
**getigert** *adj (mit Streifen)* striped; *(mit Flecken)* piebald.
**Getöse** *nt no pl* din, racket; *(von Auto, Beifall etc)* roar. **mit** ~ with a din.
**getragen** *adj* **(a)** *Kleidung* second-hand. **(b)** *(fig) Melodie, Tempo etc* stately *no adv.*
**Getrampel** *nt no pl* trampling; *(Beifalls~, Protest~)* stamping.
**Getränk** *nt* -e drink, beverage *(form)*.
**Getränke-:** ~**automat** *m* drinks machine *or* dispenser; ~**dose** *f* drinks can; ~**karte** *f (in Café)* list of beverages; *(in Restaurant)* wine list; ~**markt** *m* drinks cash-and-carry; ~**steuer** *f* alcohol tax.
**getrauen\*** *vr* to dare. **getraust du dich das?** do you dare do that?
**Getreide** *nt* - grain, cereal.
**Getreide-:** ~**(an)bau** *m* cultivation of grain *or* cereals; ~**ernte** *f* grain harvest; ~**feld** *nt* grain field, cornfield *(Brit)*; ~**pflanze** *f* cereal (plant); ~**speicher** *m* granary; *(~silo)* grain silo.
**getrennt** *adj* separate. ~ **leben** to be separated, to live apart; ~ **schlafen** not to sleep together.
**getreten** *ptp of* **treten.**
**getreu** *adj* **(a)** *(genau, entsprechend)* faithful, true *no adv.* **(b)** *pred +dat* true to.
**Getriebe** *nt* - **(a)** *(Tech)* gears *pl*; *(Kraftübertragung)* transmission; *(~kasten)* gearbox *(Brit)*, transmission *(US)*; *(Antrieb)* drive; *(von Uhr)* movement, works *pl.* **(b)** *(lebhaftes Treiben)* bustle, hurly-burly.
**getrieben** *ptp of* **treiben.**
**Getriebeschaden** *m* gearbox *(Brit) or* transmission *(US)* trouble *no indef art.*
**getroffen** *ptp of* **treffen.**
**getrogen** *ptp of* **trügen.**
**getrost** *adv* with confidence. **du kannst dich** ~ **auf ihn verlassen** you need have no fears about relying on him.
**getrübt** *adj (lit)* cloudy; *(fig) Verhältnis* disturbed.
**getrunken** *ptp of* **trinken.**
**Getto** *nt* -s ghetto.
**Getue** [gə'tuːə] *nt no pl (pej)* to-do *(col)*, fuss. **ein** ~ **machen** to make a to-do *(col) or* fuss.
**Getümmel** *nt no pl* turmoil. **sich ins** ~ **stürzen** to plunge into the tumult *or* hurly-burly.

**getupft** adj Stoff, Kleid spotted.

**Getuschel** nt no pl whispering.

**ge|übt** adj Auge, Ohr, Griff practised (Brit), practiced (US); Fahrer, Segler etc proficient. **im Reden ~ sein** to be a proficient talker.

**GEW** [geː|eːˈveː] f = **Gewerkschaft Erziehung und Wissenschaft** ≃ NUT (Brit).

**Gewächs** nt -e (a) (Pflanze) plant. (b) (Med) growth.

**gewachsen 1** ptp of **wachsen¹**. **2** adj (a) (von allein entstanden) evolved. (b) **einer Sache** (dat) **~ sein** to be up to sth; **er ist seinem Bruder (an Stärke/Intelligenz) durchaus ~** he is his brother's equal in strength/intelligence.

**Gewächshaus** nt greenhouse; (Treibhaus) hothouse.

**gewagt** adj (a) (kühn) daring; (gefährlich) risky. (b) (moralisch bedenklich) risqué.

**gewählt** adj Sprache refined no adv, elegant.

**gewahr** adj pred **eine(r) Sache ~ werden** to become aware of sth.

**Gewähr** f no pl guarantee. **dadurch ist die ~ gegeben, daß ...** that guarantees that ...; **die Angabe erfolgt ohne ~** we accept no liability for the accuracy of this information; **„ohne ~"** (auf Fahrplan, Preisliste) "subject to alteration"; (bei Lottozahlen) "no liability assumed".

**gewähren\*** vt to grant; Rabatt, Vorteile to give; Sicherheit, Schutz to afford, to give. **jdm Unterstützung ~** to provide sb with support; **jdn ~ lassen** (geh) to let sb do as they like.

**gewährleisten\*** vt insep to ensure (jdm etw sb sth); (garantieren) to guarantee (jdm etw sb sth).

**Gewährleistung** f guarantee. **zur ~ der Sicherheit** to ensure safety.

**Gewahrsam** m no pl (a) (Verwahrung) safekeeping. **etw in ~ nehmen** to take sth into safekeeping. (b) (Haft) custody. **jdn in ~ nehmen** to take sb into custody.

**Gewährsmann** m, pl **-männer** or **-leute** source.

**Gewährung** f no pl siehe vt granting; giving; affording.

**Gewalt** f **-en** (a) (Macht, Herrschaft) power. **die ausübende/gesetzgebende/richterliche ~** the executive/legislature/judiciary; **elterliche ~** parental authority; **jdn/etw in seine ~ bringen** to gain control of sb/sth; **unter jds ~** (dat) **stehen** to be under sb's control. (b) no pl (Zwang) force; (~tätigkeit) violence. **~ anwenden** to use force; **höhere ~** acts/an act of God; **nackte ~** brute force; **mit ~** by force; **etw mit aller ~ wollen** (col) to want sth desperately; **jdm/einer Sache ~ antun** to do violence to sb/sth; **einer Frau ~ antun** to violate a woman. (c) no pl (Heftigkeit, Wucht) force; (elementare Kraft auch) power.

**Gewalt-:** **~akt** m act of violence; **~androhung** f threat of violence; **~anwendung** f use of force or violence.

**Gewaltenteilung** f separation of powers.

**Gewalt-:** **~herrschaft** f no pl tyranny; **~herrscher** m tyrant.

**gewaltig** adj (a) (heftig) Sturm etc violent. (b) (groß, riesig) colossal, immense; Anblick tremendous; Stimme powerful; (col: sehr groß) Unterschied, Hitze etc tremendous, colossal (col). **sich ~ irren** to be very much mistaken.

**Gewalt-:** **g~los 1** adj non-violent; **2** adv without force/violence; **~losigkeit** f no pl non-violence; **~marsch** m forced march; (fig) marathon; **~maßnahme** f (fig) drastic measure; **g~sam 1** adj forcible; Tod violent; **2** adv forcibly, by force; **~tat** f act of violence; **~täter** m violent criminal;

**g~tätig** adj violent; **~tätigkeit** f (no pl: Brutalität) violence; (Handlung) act of violence; **~verbrechen** nt crime of violence; **~verbrecher** m violent criminal; **~verzicht** m non-aggression.

**Gewand** nt ⁼er (geh: Kleidungsstück) garment; (weites, langes) robe, gown; (Eccl) vestment, robe; (fig: Äußeres) look; (fig: Maske) guise.

**gewandt 1** ptp of **wenden**. **2** adj skilful (Brit), skillful (US); (körperlich) nimble; Auftreten, Stil elegant.

**Gewandtheit** f no pl siehe adj skilfulness; nimbleness; elegance.

**gewann** pret of **gewinnen**.

**Gewäsch** nt no pl (pej col) twaddle (col).

**gewaschen** ptp of **waschen**.

**Gewässer** nt - stretch of water. **~ pl** inshore waters pl, lakes, rivers and canals pl; **ein fließendes/stehendes ~** a stretch of running/standing water.

**Gewässerschutz** m prevention of water pollution.

**Gewebe** nt - (Stoff) fabric, material; (~art) weave; (Biol) tissue; (fig) web.

**Gewehr** nt -e (Flinte) rifle; (Schrotbüchse) shotgun. **~ ab!** (Mil) order arms!; **das ~ über!** (Mil) shoulder arms!; **präsentiert das ~!** (Mil) present arms!; **~ bei Fuß stehen** (Mil) to stand at order arms; (fig col) to be at the ready; **ran an die ~e!** (dated col) let's get started.

**Gewehr-:** **~kolben** m rifle butt; **~kugel** f rifle bullet; **~lauf** m rifle barrel; barrel of a shotgun.

**Geweih** nt -e (set of sing) antlers pl.

**Gewerbe** nt - trade. **Handel und ~** trade and industry; **das älteste ~ der Welt** (hum) the oldest profession in the world (hum); **ein ~ (be)treiben** to carry on a trade.

**Gewerbe-:** **~aufsichtsamt** nt ≃ health and safety inspectorate; **~betrieb** m commercial enterprise; **~gebiet** nt industrial area or district; (eigens angelegt) trading estate; **~ordnung** f trading regulations pl; **~schein** m trading licence (Brit) or license (US); **~steuer** f trade tax; **~treibende(r)** mf decl as adj trader.

**gewerblich** adj commercial; (industriell) industrial. **die ~e Wirtschaft** industry; **diese Räume dürfen nicht ~ genutzt werden** these rooms are not to be used for commercial purposes.

**gewerbsmäßig 1** adj professional. **~e Unzucht** (form) prostitution. **2** adv professionally, for gain.

**Gewerkschaft** f (trade or labor US) union.

**Gewerkschaft(l)er(in** f) m - trade or labor (US) unionist.

**gewerkschaftlich** adj (trade or labor US) union attr. **wir haben uns ~ organisiert** we organized ourselves into a union.

**Gewerkschafts-** in cpds (trade or labor US) union; **~bewegung** f (trade or labor US) union movement; **~bund** m federation of trade or labor (US) unions, ≃ Trades Union Congress (Brit), ≃ Federation of Labor (US); **~führer** m trade or labor (US) union leader; **~mitglied** nt (trade or labor US) union member; **~tag** m trade or labor (US) union conference.

**gewesen 1** ptp of **sein¹**. **2** adj attr former.

**gewichen** ptp of **weichen²**.

**gewichst** [gəˈvɪkst] adj (col) fly (col), crafty.

**Gewicht** nt -e no pl (lit, fig) weight. **dieser Stein hat ein ~ von 100 kg** this rock weighs 2 cwt; **spezifisches ~** specific gravity; **~ haben** (lit) to be heavy; (fig) to carry weight; **ins ~ fallen** to be crucial; **nicht ins ~ fallen** to be of no consequence; **einer Sache** (dat) **~ beimessen** to set (great) store by sth.

**gewichten\*** vi (Statistik) to weight; (fig) to evaluate.

**Gewicht-:** **~heben** nt no pl (Sport) weightlifting;

**~heber** *m* - weightlifter.
**gewichtig** *adj (fig) (wichtig)* weighty; *(einflußreich)* influential.
**Gewichts-:** **~klasse** *f (Sport)* weight (category); **~kontrolle** *f* weight check; **g~los** *adj* weightless; *(fig)* lacking substance; **~verlust** *m* weight loss; **~zunahme** *f* increase in weight.
**gewieft** *adj (col)* fly *(col)*, crafty *(in +dat* at*)*.
**gewiesen** *ptp of* weisen.
**gewillt** *adj* **~ sein, etw zu tun** to be willing to do sth; *(entschlossen)* to be determined to do sth.
**Gewimmel** *nt no pl* swarm; *(Menge)* crush, throng.
**Gewinde** *nt* - *(Tech)* thread.
**Gewinde-** *(Tech)*: **~bohrer** *m* (screw) tap; **~bolzen** *m* threaded bolt.
**Gewinn** *m* **-e** (a) *(Ertrag)* profit. **~-und-Verlust-Rechnung** profit-and-loss account; **~ abwerfen** to make a profit; **aus etw ~ schlagen** *(col)* to make a profit out of sth; **etw mit ~ verkaufen** to sell sth at a profit. (b) *(Preis, Treffer)* prize; *(bei Glücksspiel)* winnings *pl*. **jedes Los ist ein ~** every ticket wins a prize. (c) *no pl (fig: Vorteil)* gain. **das ist ein großer ~ (für mich)** that is of great benefit (to me).
**Gewinn-:** **~anteil** *m* (a) *(Comm)* dividend; (b) *(beim Wetten etc)* share; **~ausschüttung** *f* prize draw; **~beteiligung** *f (Ind)* profit-sharing; **g~bringend** *adj (lit, fig)* profitable; **~chance** *f* chance of winning; **~chancen** *(beim Wetten)* odds.
**gewinnen** *pret* **gewann**, *ptp* **gewonnen** 1 *vt* (a) to win. **jdn (für etw) ~** to win sb over (to sth); **jdn für sich ~** to win sb over (to one's side); **jdn zum Freund ~** to win sb as a friend; **den Eindruck ~, daß ...** to gain the impression that ...; **Zeit ~** to gain time; **was ist damit gewonnen?** what good is that?; **wie gewonnen, so zerronnen** *(prov)* easy come easy go *(prov)*. (b) *(als Profit)* to make (a profit of). (c) *(erzeugen)* to produce, to obtain; *Erze etc* to mine, to extract; *(aus Altmaterial)* to reclaim. 2 *vi* (a) to win *(bei, in +dat* at*)*. (b) *(profitieren)* to gain. **an Bedeutung ~** to gain (in) importance; **an Geschwindigkeit ~** to gain speed.
**gewinnend** *adj (fig)* winning, winsome.
**Gewinner(in** *f) m* - winner.
**Gewinn-:** **~schwelle** *f* break-even point; **~spanne** *f* profit margin; **~streben** *nt* pursuit of profit; **~sucht** *f* profit-seeking; **g~süchtig** *adj* profit-seeking *attr*; **g~trächtig** *adj* profitable.
**Gewinnung** *f no pl (von Kohle, Öl)* extraction; *(von Energie, Plutonium)* production.
**Gewinnzahl** *f* winning number.
**Gewirr** *nt no pl* tangle; *(fig: Durcheinander)* jumble; *(von Paragraphen, Straßen)* maze; *(von Stimmen)* confusion, babble.
**gewiß** 1 *adj* (a) *(sicher)* certain, sure *(+gen* of*)*. *(ja)* **~!** certainly, sure *(esp US)*; **ich bin dessen ~** *(geh)* I'm certain *or* sure of it. (b) *attr* certain. **ein gewisser Herr Müller** a certain Herr Müller; **in gewissem Maße** to a certain extent. 2 *adv (geh)* certainly. **ich weiß es ganz ~** I'm certain of it.
**Gewissen** *nt no pl* conscience. **ein schlechtes ~** a guilty *or* bad conscience; **jdn/etw auf dem ~ haben** to have sb/sth on one's conscience; **jdm ins ~ reden** to have a serious talk with sb; **das mußt du vor deinem ~ verantworten** you'll have to answer to your own conscience for that.
**Gewissen-:** **g~haft** *adj* conscientious; **~haftigkeit** *f no pl* conscientiousness; **g~los** *adj* unprincipled; **g~los sein** to have no conscience; **~losigkeit** *f* lack of principle.
**Gewissens-:** **~bisse** *pl* pangs of conscience *pl*; **mach dir deswegen keine ~bisse!** there's nothing

for you to feel guilty about; **~bisse bekommen** to get a guilty conscience; **~entscheidung, ~frage** *f* matter of conscience; **~freiheit** *f* freedom of conscience; **~gründe** *pl* reasons of conscience *pl*; **~konflikt** *m* moral conflict; **~not** *f* moral dilemma.
**gewissermaßen** *adv (sozusagen)* so to speak, as it were; *(auf gewisse Weise)* in a way, to an extent.
**Gewißheit** *f* certainty. **mit ~** with certainty; **wissen für certain** *or* sure; **sich (dat) ~ verschaffen** to find out for certain.
**Gewitter** *nt* - thunderstorm; *(fig)* storm.
**Gewitterluft** *f* thundery atmosphere.
**gewittern*** *vi impers* **es gewittert** it's thundering.
**Gewitter-:** **~regen**, **~schauer** *m* thundery shower; **~wolke** *f* thundercloud; *(fig col)* stormcloud.
**gewittrig** *adj* thundery.
**gewitzt** *adj* crafty, cunning.
**gewoben** *ptp of* weben.
**gewogen** 1 *ptp of* wiegen². 2 *adj (geh)* well-disposed *(+dat* towards*)*.
**gewöhnen*** 1 *vt* **jdn an etw** *(acc)* **~** to accustom sb to sth; **an jdn/etw gewöhnt sein**, **jdn/etw gewöhnt sein** *(col)* to be used to sb/sth; **daran gewöhnt sein, etw zu tun** to be used to doing sth. 2 *vr* **sich an jdn/etw ~** to get used to sb/sth; **sich daran ~, etw zu tun** to get used *or* accustomed to doing sth.
**Gewohnheit** *f* habit. **aus (lauter) ~** from (sheer) force of habit; **die ~ haben, etw zu tun** to have a habit of doing sth; **das ist ihm zur ~ geworden** it's become a habit with him; **sich (dat) etw zur ~ machen** to make a habit of sth.
**Gewohnheits-:** **g~mäßig** 1 *adj* habitual; 2 *adv (ohne nachzudenken)* automatically; **~mensch** *m* creature of habit; **~recht** *nt (Jur)* common law; **~tier** *nt (col)* creature of habit; **~trinker** *m* habitual drinker; **~verbrecher** *m* persistent offender.
**gewöhnlich** 1 *adj* (a) *attr (allgemein, üblich)* usual; *(normal)* normal; *(alltäglich)* everyday. **ein ~er Sterblicher** an ordinary mortal. (b) *(pej: ordinär)* common. 2 *adv* normally, usually. **wie ~** as usual.
**Gewöhnlichkeit** *f (pej)* commonness.
**gewohnt** *adj* usual. **etw** *(acc)* **~ sein** to be used to sth.
**gewohntermaßen** *adv* usually.
**Gewöhnung** *f no pl (das Sich-Gewöhnen)* habituation *(Sucht)* habit, addiction *(form)*; **die ~ an etw** getting used to sth.
**Gewölbe** *nt* - *(Decken~)* vault; *(Keller~ auch)* vaults *pl*.
**gewölbt** *adj Stirn* domed; *Himmel, Decke* vaulted.
**gewollt** *adj* forced, artificial.
**gewonnen** *ptp of* gewinnen.
**geworben** *ptp of* werben.
**geworden** *ptp of* werden.
**geworfen** *ptp of* werfen.
**gewrungen** *ptp of* wringen.
**Gewühl** *nt no pl (Gedränge)* crowd, throng; *(Verkehrs~)* chaos, snarl-up *(col)*.
**gewunden** 1 *ptp of* winden. 2 *adj Weg, Fluß etc* winding; *Erklärung* roundabout *no adv*, tortuous.
**gewunken** *(dial) ptp of* winken.
**gewürfelt** *adj* check(ed).
**Gewürz** *nt* **-e** spice; *(Kräutersorte)* herb; *(Pfeffer, Salz)* seasoning.
**Gewürz-:** **~bord** *nt* spice rack; **~gurke** *f* pickled gherkin; **~nelke** *f* clove; **~regal** *nt* spice rack; **~ständer** *m* cruet (set).
**gewußt** *ptp of* wissen.

**Geysir** ['gaizɪr] *m* **-e** geyser.
**gez.** = **gezeichnet** sgd.
**gezackt** *adj Fels* jagged; *Blatt* serrated.
**gezähnt** *adj* serrated; *(Tech)* cogged; *Briefmarke* perforated.
**gezeichnet** *adj* marked; *(als Straffälliger auch)* branded. **vom Tode** ~ **sein** to have the mark of death on one.
**Gezeiten** *pl* tides *pl.*
**Gezeiten-:** ~**kraftwerk** *nt* tidal power station; ~**wechsel** *m* turn of the tide.
**Gezeter** *nt no pl (col: Schimpfen)* nagging.
**gezielt** *adj* purposeful; *Schuß* well-aimed; *Frage, Maßnahme etc* specific; *Werbung* selective, targetted; *Hilfe* well-directed. ~ **schießen** to shoot to kill.
**geziemend** *adj* proper.
**geziert** *adj* affected.
**Geziertheit** *f* affectedness.
**gezogen** *ptp of* **ziehen.**
**Gezwitscher** *nt no pl* chirruping, twitter(ing).
**gezwungen 1** *ptp of* **zwingen. 2** *adj (nicht entspannt)* forced; *Atmosphäre* strained; *Stil, Benehmen* stiff.
**gezwungenermaßen** *adv* of necessity. **etw** ~ **tun** to be forced to do sth, to do sth of necessity.
**GG** = **Grundgesetz.**
**ggf.** = **gegebenenfalls.**
**Ghana** *nt* Ghana.
**Ghanaer(in** *f)* *m* - Ghanaian.
**ghanaisch** *adj* Ghanaian.
**Gicht** *f no pl (Med)* gout.
**Giebel** *m* - gable; *(Tür~, Fenster~)* pediment.
**Giebel-:** ~**dach** *nt* gabled roof; ~**fenster** *nt* gable window; ~**haus** *nt* gabled house; ~**wand** *f* gable end *or* wall.
**Gier** *f no pl (nach* for*)* greed; *(Lüsternheit)* lust.
**gierig** *adj* greedy; *(nach Geld)* avaricious; *(lüstern)* lustful. ~ **nach etw sein** to be greedy for sth; *(nach Macht auch, sexuell)* to lust for sth.
**Gießbach** *m* (mountain) torrent.
**gießen** *pret* **goß,** *ptp* **gegossen 1** *vt* **(a)** to pour; *(verschütten)* to spill; *Pflanzen* to water. **(b)** *Metall* to cast *(zu* into*).* **2** *vi impers* to pour. **es gießt in Strömen** it's pouring down.
**Gießer** *m* - *(Metall)* caster, founder.
**Gießerei** *f (Werkstatt)* foundry.
**Gieß-:** ~**kanne** *f* watering can; ~**kannenprinzip** *nt no pl (col)* principle of indiscriminate all-round distribution.
**Gift** *nt* **-e** *(lit, fig)* poison; *(Schlangen~, fig: Bosheit)* venom. ~ **nehmen** to poison oneself; **das ist** ~ **für ihn** *(col)* that is very bad for him; **darauf kannst du** ~ **nehmen** *(col)* you can bet your life on it *(col)*; ~ **und Galle spucken** *(col)* to be fuming.
**giften** *vi (col)* to be vitriolic *(gegen* about*).*
**Gift-:** **g**~**frei** *adj* non-toxic; ~**gas** *nt* poison gas; **g**~**grün** *adj* bilious green; **g**~**haltig** *adj* poisonous, toxic.
**giftig** *adj* **(a)** *(Gift enthaltend)* poisonous; *Chemikalien etc auch* toxic. **(b)** *(fig) (boshaft)* venomous; *(zornig)* vitriolic. **(c)** *(grell)* bilious.
**Gift-:** ~**mischer(in** *f)* *m* - preparer of poison; *(fig)* troublemaker; ~**müll** *m* toxic waste; ~**pfeil** *m* poisoned arrow; ~**pilz** *m* poisonous toadstool; ~**schlange** *f* poisonous snake; ~**stoff** *m* toxic substance; ~**wolke** *f* poisonous cloud; ~**zahn** *m* fang; ~**zwerg** *m (col)* spiteful little devil *(col).*
**Giga-** *pref* giga-.
**Gigant** *m* giant.
**gigantisch** *adj* gigantic, colossal.

**Gilde** *f* **-n** guild.
**Gin** [dʒɪn] *m* **-s** gin. ~ **tonic** gin and tonic.
**ging** *pret of* **gehen.**
**Ginseng** ['gɪnzɛŋ, 'ʒɪnzɛŋ] *m* **-s** ginseng.
**Ginster** *m* - *(Bot)* broom; *(Stech~)* gorse.
**Gipfel** *m* - **(a)** *(Berg~)* summit; *(Spitze)* peak. **(b)** *(fig: Höhepunkt)* height; *(des Ruhms, der Karriere auch)* peak. **das ist der** ~! *(col)* that's the limit. **(c)** *(~konferenz)* summit.
**Gipfel-:** ~**konferenz** *f (Pol)* summit conference; ~**leistung** *f* crowning achievement.
**gipfeln** *vi* to culminate *(in* +*dat* in*).*
**Gipfel-:** ~**punkt** *m (lit)* zenith; *(fig)* high point; ~**stürmer** *m (liter)* conqueror of a/the peak; ~**treffen** *nt (Pol)* summit (meeting).
**Gips** *m* **-e** plaster. **einen Arm in** ~ **legen** to put an arm in plaster.
**Gips-** *in cpds* plaster; ~**abdruck,** ~**abguß** *m* plaster cast; ~**bein** *nt (col)* leg in plaster.
**gipsen** *vt* to plaster; *Arm, Bein* to put in plaster.
**Gipser** *m* - plasterer.
**Gips-:** ~**figur** *f* plaster (of Paris) figure; ~**verband** *m (Med)* plaster cast.
**Giraffe** *f* **-n** giraffe.
**Girlande** *f* **-n** garland *(aus* of*).*
**Giro** ['ʒiːro] *nt* **-s** *(Fin)* (bank) giro; *(Indossament)* endorsement. **durch** ~ by giro.
**Giro-:** ~**bank** *f* giro bank; ~**konto** *nt* current *(Brit)* or checking *(US)* account; ~**verkehr** *m* giro system; *(~geschäft)* giro transfer (business).
**girren** *vi (lit, fig)* to coo.
**Gis** *nt* - *(Mus)* G sharp.
**Gischt** *m* **-e** *or f* **-en** spray.
**Gitarre** *f* **-n** guitar.
**Gitarrespieler(in** *f)* *m,* **Gitarrist(in** *f)* *m* guitarist.
**Gitter** *nt* - bars *pl; (vor Schaufenstern etc)* grille; *(in Fußboden, Straßendecke)* grid, grating; *(feines Draht~)* (wire) mesh.
**Gitter-:** ~**bett** *nt* cot *(Brit),* crib *(US);* ~**fenster** *nt* barred window; ~**stab** *m* bar; ~**zaun** *m* paling; *(mit gekreuzten Stäben)* lattice fence.
**Glacéhandschuh** [gla'seː-] *m* kid glove. **jdn mit** ~**en anfassen** to handle sb with kid gloves.
**Gladiator** *m* gladiator.
**Gladiole** *f* **-n** *(Bot)* gladiolus.
**Glanz** *m no pl* gleam; *(von Oberfläche auch)* shine; *(Funkeln, von Augen)* sparkle; *(von Haaren, Seide)* sheen; *(von Farbe)* gloss; *(blendend: von Sonne)* glare; *(fig) (der Schönheit, Jugend)* radiance; *(von Ruhm)* glory; *(Pracht)* splendour *(Brit),* splendor *(US).* **mit** ~ **und Gloria** *(iro col)* in grand style; **eine Prüfung mit** ~ **bestehen** *(col)* to pass an exam with flying colours *(Brit)* or colors *(US).*
**Glanz|abzug** *m (Phot)* glossy or gloss print.
**glänzen** *vi (lit, fig)* to shine; *(glitzern)* to glisten; *(funkeln)* to sparkle; *(blenden)* to glare; *(Nase)* to be shiny. **vor jdm** ~ **wollen** to want to shine in front of sb; **durch Abwesenheit** ~ *(iro)* to be conspicuous by one's absence.
**glänzend** *adj* shining; *(strahlend)* radiant; *(blendend)* dazzling; *(glitzernd)* glistening; *(funkelnd)* sparkling; *Papier* glossy, shiny; *Stoff, Nase* shiny; *(fig)* brilliant; *Aussehen, Fest* dazzling; *(erstklassig)* splendid. ~ **in Form** *(col)* in splendid form; **wir haben uns** ~ **amüsiert** we had a wonderful time; **mir geht es** ~ I'm just fine.
**Glanz-:** ~**lack** *m* gloss (paint); ~**leistung** *f* brilliant achievement; **g**~**los** *adj (lit, fig)* dull; *Lack, Oberfläche* matt; ~**nummer** *f* big number, pièce de résistance; ~**papier** *nt* glossy paper; ~**punkt** *m (fig)* highlight, high spot; ~**stück** *nt* pièce de résist-

ance; **g~voll** *adj (fig)* brilliant; *(prachtvoll)* glittering; **~zeit** *f* heyday.

**Glas** *nt* ⁼**er** *or (als Maßangabe)* - **(a)** *(Stoff, Gefäß)* glass; *(Konserven~)* jar. **ein ~ Milch** a glass of milk; **ein ~ Marmelade** a jar of jam; **zwei ~ Wein** two glasses of wine; **zu tief ins ~ schauen** *(col)* to have one too many. **(b)** *(Brillen~)* lens *sing*; *(Fern~)* binoculars *pl*.

**Glas-** *in cpds* glass; **~bläser** *m* glassblower; **~bruch** *m* broken glass.

**Gläschen** ['glɛːsçən] *nt dim of* **Glas** *(Getränk)* little drink.

**Glascontainer** *m* bottle bank.

**Glaser** *m* - glazier.

**Glaserei** *f* **(a)** *no pl (Handwerk)* glasswork. **(b)** *(Werkstatt)* glazier's workshop.

**gläsern** *adj* glass; *(fig: durchschaubar)* transparent.

**Gläsertuch** *nt* glasscloth.

**Glas-:** **~fabrik** *f* glassworks *sing or pl*; **~faser** *f* fibreglass *(Brit)*, fiberglass *(US)*; **~faserkabel** *nt* optical fibre *(Brit)* or fiber *(US)* cable; **~faseroptik** *f* fibre *(Brit)* or fiber *(US)* optics; **~fenster** *nt* glass window; **~fiber** *f* = **~faser**; **~fiberstab** *m (Sport)* fibreglass *(Brit)* or fiberglass *(US)* pole; **~form** *f* glass mould; *(Backform)* glass *or* Pyrex ® dish; **~geschirr** *nt* glassware; **~haus** *nt* greenhouse; *(in botanischen Gärten etc)* glasshouse; **wer (selbst) im ~haus sitzt, soll nicht mit Steinen werfen** *(Prov)* people who live in glass houses shouldn't throw stones *(Prov)*.

**glasieren\*** *vt* to glaze; *Kuchen* to ice, to frost *(US)*.

**glasig** *adj Blick* glassy; *(Cook) Kartoffeln* waxy; *Speck, Zwiebeln* transparent.

**Glas-:** **~kasten** *m* glass case; *(in Fabrik, Büro)* glass box; **g~klar** *adj (lit)* clear as glass; *(fig)* crystal-clear; **~kugel** *f* glass ball; *(Murmel)* marble.

**Glasnost** *f no pl* glasnost.

**Glas-:** **~perle** *f* glass bead; **~platte** *f* glass top; **~scheibe** *f* sheet of glass; *(Fenster~)* pane of glass; **~scherbe** *f* piece of broken glass; **~scherben** broken glass; **~schneider** *m* glass cutter; **~schrank** *m* glass-fronted cupboard; **~splitter** *m* splinter of glass.

**Glasur** *f* glaze; *(Metall)* enamel; *(Zuckerguß)* icing, frosting *(US)*.

**Glas-:** **~waren** *pl* glassware *sing*; **~wolle** *f* glass wool.

**glatt** *comp* **-er** *or* ⁼**er**, *superl* **-este(r, s)** *or* ⁼**este(r, s)** *or (adv)* **am -esten** *or* ⁼**esten 1** *adj* **(a)** *(eben)* smooth; *Haar* straight; *(Med) Bruch* clean; *(faltenlos) Stoff* uncreased. **(b)** *(schlüpfrig)* slippery. **(c)** *(fig) Landung, Ablauf* smooth. **(d)** *attr (col: klar, eindeutig)* outright; *Lüge, Unsinn etc auch* downright. **(e)** *(pej: allzu gewandt)* smooth, slick. **2** *adv* **(a)** smoothly. **er hat sich ~ aus der Affäre gezogen** he wriggled neatly out of the whole affair. **(b)** *(ganz, völlig)* completely; *leugnen, ablehnen* flatly. **die Rechnung ist ~ aufgegangen** the sum works out exactly.

**Glätte** *f no pl* smoothness *(auch fig)*; *(von Haar)* sleekness; *(Schlüpfrigkeit)* slipperiness.

**Glatt|eis** *nt* ice. **„Vorsicht ~!"** "danger, black ice"; **sich auf ~ begeben** *(fig)* to be skating on thin ice; **jdn aufs ~ führen** *(fig)* to take sb for a ride *(col)*.

**glätten 1** *vt (glattmachen)* to smooth out; *(glattstreichen) Haar, Tuch* to smooth. **2** *vr* to smooth out; *(Wellen, Erg)* to subside.

**glatt-:** **~gehen** *vi sep irreg aux sein* to go smoothly; **~hobeln** *vt sep* to plane smooth; **~kämmen** *vt sep* to comb straight; **~rasiert** *adj Mann, Kinn* clean-shaven; *Beine* shaved; **~schleifen** *vt sep ir-*

*reg* to rub smooth; *Diamanten etc* to grind smooth; **~schneiden** *vt sep irreg* to cut straight; **~streichen** *vt sep irreg* to smooth out; *Haare* to smooth (down); **~weg** ['glatvɛk] *adv (col)* simply, just; **das ist ~weg erlogen** that's a blatant lie.

**Glatze** *f* **-n** bald head. **eine ~ bekommen/haben** to go/be bald.

**Glatz-:** **~kopf** *m* bald head; *(col: Mann mit Glatze)* baldie *(col)*; **g~köpfig** *adj* bald(-headed).

**Glaube(n)** *m no pl (Vertrauen, Rel)* faith *(an +acc* in); *(Überzeugung)* belief *(an +acc* in). **in gutem ~n** in good faith; **(bei jdm) ~n finden** to be believed *(by* sb); **den ~n an jdn/etw verlieren** to lose faith in sb/ sth; **jdm ~n schenken** to give credence to sb.

**glauben** *vti* to believe *(an +acc* in); *(meinen, vermuten)* to think. **jdm ~** to believe sb; **das glaube ich dir nicht** I don't believe you; **glaube es mir** believe me; **jdm (etw) aufs Wort ~** to take sb's word (for sth); **d(a)ran ~ müssen** *(col)* to cop it *(col)*; *(sterben auch)* to buy it *(col)*; *(etw Unangenehmes machen müssen)* to draw the short straw; **das glaubst du doch selbst nicht!** you can't be serious; **ob du es glaubst oder nicht, ...** believe it or not ...; **wer's glaubt, wird selig** *(iro)* a likely story *(iro)*; **wer hätte das je geglaubt!** who would have thought it?; **er glaubte sich unbeobachtet** he thought nobody was watching him; **es ist nicht zu ~** it's incredible *or* unbelievable; **ich glaube, ja** I think so; **ich glaube, nein** I don't think so.

**Glaubens-:** **~bekenntnis** *nt* creed; **~eifer** *m* religious zeal; **~frage** *f* question of faith; **~freiheit** *f* religious freedom; **~gemeinschaft** *f* religious sect; *(christliche auch)* denomination; **~kampf** *m* religious battle; **~satz** *m* dogma, doctrine; **~streit** *m* religious controversy.

**glaubhaft** *adj* credible, believable; *(einleuchtend)* plausible. **(jdm) etw ~ machen** to satisfy sb of sth.

**Glaubhaftigkeit** *f no pl* credibility; *(Evidenz)* plausibility.

**gläubig** *adj* religious; *(vertrauensvoll)* trusting.

**Gläubige(r)** *mf decl as adj* believer. **die ~n** the faithful.

**Gläubiger(in** *f)* *m* - *(Comm)* creditor.

**glaublich** *adj:* **kaum ~** scarcely credible.

**glaubwürdig** *adj* credible. **~e Quellen** reliable sources.

**Glaubwürdigkeit** *f no pl* credibility.

**Glaukom** *nt* **-e** *(Med)* glaucoma.

**gleich 1** *adj (identisch, ähnlich)* same; *(~wertig, ~berechtigt, Math)* equal. **die/das ~e ... wie** the same ... as; **in ~em Abstand** at an equal distance; **zu ~en Teilen** in equal parts; **in ~er Weise** in the same way; **mit ~er Post** with the same post; **das ~e, aber nicht dasselbe Auto** the same (type of) car, but not the identical one; **wir wollten alle das ~e** we all wanted the same thing; **es waren die ~en, die ...** it was the same ones who/which ...; **zwei mal zwei (ist) ~ vier** two times two equals *or* is four; **jdm (an etw dat) ~ sein** to be sb's equal (in sth); **ihr Männer seid doch alle ~!** you men are all the same!; **es ist mir (alles *or* ganz) ~** it's all the same to me; **ganz ~ wer/was etc** no matter who/ what *etc*; **G~es mit G~em vergelten** to repay like with like; **~ und ~ gesellt sich gern** *(Prov)* birds of a feather flock together *(Prov)*.

**2** *adv* **(a)** *(ebenso)* equally; *(auf ~e Weise)* alike, the same. **sie sind ~ groß/alt** they are the same size/age.

**(b)** *(räumlich)* immediately, just. **~ hinter dem Haus** just behind the house.

**(c)** *(sofort)* immediately, right away; *(bald)* in a

minute. ~ **zu** or **am Anfang** at the very beginning; ~ **danach** right after(wards); **ich komme** ~ I'm just coming; **es ist** ~ **drei Uhr** it's very nearly three o'clock; **das habe ich mir** ~ **gedacht** I thought that straight away; **warum nicht** ~ **so?** why didn't you say/do that in the first place?; **wann machst du das?** — ~**!** when are you going to do it? — in just a moment; **so wirkt das Bild** ~ **ganz anders** that immediately makes the picture look quite different; **er ging** ~ **in die Küche** he went straight into the kitchen; **bis** ~**!** see you in a while.
  (d) (in Fragesätzen) again. **wie war doch** ~ **Ihr Name?** what was your name again?

**Gleich-:** g~**altrig** adj (of) the same age; g~**artig 1** adj of the same kind (+dat as); (ähnlich) similar (+dat to); **2** adv in the same way; similarly; ~**artigkeit** f similarity; g~**auf** adv (esp Sport) equal; g~**auf liegen** to be lying equal; g~**bedeutend** adj synonymous (mit with); (so gut wie) tantamount (mit to); ~**behandlung** f equal treatment; g~**berechtigt** adj with equal rights; g~**berechtigt sein** to have equal rights; ~**berechtigung** f equal rights sing or pl, equality (+gen, von for); g~**bleiben** sep irreg aux sein **1** vi to remain the same; **2** vr **sich** (dat) g~**bleiben** (Mensch) to remain the same; **das bleibt sich g~** it doesn't matter; **g~bleibend** adj constant, steady; **bei g~bleibendem Gehalt** when one's salary stays the same; **g~bleibend gute Qualität** consistent(ly) good quality.

**gleichen** pret **glich**, ptp **geglichen** vi **jdm/einer Sache** ~ to be like sb/sth; **sich** ~ to be alike.

**gleichermaßen** adv equally.

**Gleich-:** g~**falls** adv (ebenfalls) likewise; (auch) also; **danke g~falls!** thank you, (and) the same to you; g~**farbig** adj (of) the same colour (Brit) or color (US); g~**förmig** adj (einheitlich, fig: eintönig) uniform (auch Phys); ~**förmigkeit** f uniformity; g~**geschlechtig** adj (Biol, Zool) of the same sex, same-sex attr; g~**geschlechtlich** adj (a) homosexual; (b) = g~**geschlechtig**; g~**gesinnt** adj likeminded; g~**gestellt** adj equal (+dat to, with), on a par (+dat with); **rechtlich g~gestellt** equal in law.

**Gleichgewicht** nt no pl (lit, fig) balance, equilibrium. **das** ~ **verlieren** to lose one's balance; (fig) to be thrown off balance; **das** ~ **(be)halten** (lit) to keep one's balance; (fig) to retain one's equilibrium; **jdn aus dem** ~ **bringen** to throw sb off balance.

**gleichgewichtig** adj balanced.

**Gleichgewichts-:** ~**organ** nt organ of equilibrium; ~**sinn** m sense of balance; ~**störung** f impaired balance.

**gleichgültig** adj indifferent (gegenüber to, towards); (uninteressiert) apathetic (gegenüber towards); (unwesentlich) trivial. **Politik ist ihm** ~ he doesn't care about politics; ~, **was er tut** no matter what he does; **er war ihr nicht** ~ **geblieben** he did mean something to her.

**Gleichgültigkeit** f indifference (gegenüber to, towards); (Desinteresse) apathy (gegenüber towards).

**Gleichheit** f (a) no pl (gleiche Stellung) equality; (Identität) identity; (Übereinstimmung) uniformity; (Ind) parity. (b) (Ähnlichkeit) similarity.

**Gleichheits-:** ~**grundsatz** m, ~**prinzip** nt principle of equality; ~**zeichen** nt (Math) equals sign.

**Gleich-:** ~**klang** m (fig) harmony, accord; g~**kommen** vi sep irreg aux sein +dat (a) **niemand kommt ihm an Dummheit g~** no-one can equal him for stupidity; (b) (g~bedeutend sein mit) to be tantamount or equivalent to; ~**lauf** m no pl (Tech) synchronization; g~**laufend** adj parallel (mit to);

(Tech) synchronized; g~**lautend** adj identical; ~**macherei** f (pej) levelling down (pej), egalitarianism; ~**maß** nt no pl (a) (Ebenmaß) evenness; (von Proportionen) symmetry; (b) (Eintönigkeit) monotony (pej), regularity; g~**mäßig** adj even, regular; **Puls auch** steady; **Abstände** regular; **etw g~mäßig verteilen** to distribute sth equally; **die Farbe g~mäßig auftragen** to apply the paint evenly; ~**mäßigkeit** f siehe adj evenness, regularity; steadiness; regularity; ~**mut** m equanimity, serenity.

**Gleichnis** nt (a) (Liter) simile. (b) (Allegorie) allegory; (Bibl) parable.

**Gleich-:** g~**rangig** adj **Beamte etc** equal in rank (mit to), at the same level (mit as); **Probleme etc** equally important; g~**richten** vt sep (Elec) to rectify; ~**richter** m (Elec) rectifier.

**gleichsam** adv (geh) as it were. ~, **als ob** just as if.

**Gleich-:** g~**schalten** vt sep (pej) to bring into line; ~**schaltung** f (pej) bringing into line; g~**schenk(e)lig** adj **Dreieck** isosceles; ~**schritt** m no pl (Mil) marching in step; **im** ~**schritt** (lit, fig) in step; **im** ~**schritt, marsch!** forward march!; g~**seitig** adj **Dreieck** equilateral; g~**setzen** vt sep (als dasselbe ansehen) to equate (mit with); (als gleichwertig ansehen) to treat as equivalent (mit to); ~**stand** m no pl (a) (Sport) **den** ~**stand erzielen** to draw level; **das Spiel wurde beim** ~**stand von 4:4 beendet** the game ended in a four-all draw; (b) (Pol) equal stage of development; g~**stellen** vt sep (a) (rechtlich etc) to treat as equal; **siehe gleichgestellt**; (b) = g~**setzen**; ~**stellung** f no pl (rechtlich etc) equality (+gen of, for), equal status (+gen or of; for); ~**strom** m (Elec) direct current, DC; g~**tun** vt impers sep irreg **es jdm g~tun** to equal or match sb.

**Gleichung** f equation.

**Gleich-:** g~**viel** adv (geh) nonetheless; g~**viel ob** no matter whether; g~**wertig** adj of the same value; (gleich zu bewerten) Leistung, Qualität equal (+dat to); **Gegner** evenly matched; g~**wohl** (geh) adv nevertheless, nonetheless; g~**zeitig** adj simultaneous; **ihr sollt nicht alle g~zeitig reden** you mustn't all speak at the same time; ~**zeitigkeit** f simultaneity; g~**ziehen** vi sep irreg (col) to catch up (mit with).

**Gleis** nt -e (Rail) line, track; (einzelne Schiene) rail; (Bahnsteig) platform. ~ **6** platform or track (US) 6; **aus dem** ~ **springen** to jump the rails; **aus dem** ~ **kommen** (fig) to go off the rails (col); **jdn aus dem** ~ **bringen** (fig) to put sb off his/her stroke; **wieder ins richtige** ~ **kommen** (fig) to get back on the rails (col); **in ausgefahrenen** ~**en** (fig) in a rut.

**Gleis-:** ~**arbeiten** pl work on the line; ~**bau** m no pl railway (Brit) or railroad (US) construction; ~**kettenfahrzeug** nt caterpillar vehicle; ~**körper** m railway (Brit) or railroad (US) track.

**gleißen** vi (liter) to gleam, to glisten.

**gleiten** pret **glitt**, ptp **geglitten** vi aux sein (a) to glide; (Blick) to pass; (Hand auch) to slide. **ein Lächeln glitt über ihr Gesicht** a smile flickered across her face. (b) (rutschen) to slide; (Auto) to skid; (ent~: Gegenstand) to slip. **ins G~ kommen** to start to slide or slip.

**gleitend** adj ~**e Löhne** sliding wage scale; ~**e Arbeitszeit** flexible working hours pl, flex(i)time.

**Gleit-:** ~**flug** m glide; **im** ~**flug niedergehen** to glide down; ~**klausel** f (Comm) escalator clause; ~**komma** nt (Maths) floating point; ~**schirm** m hang-glider; ~**zeit** f flex(i)time.

**Gletscher** m - glacier.

**Gletscher-:** ~**bach** *m* glacial stream; ~**spalte** *f* crevasse; ~**wasser** *nt* glacier water.

**glich** *pret of* **gleichen.**

**Glied** *nt* **-er (a)** *(Körperteil)* limb; *(Finger~, Zehen~)* joint. **seine ~er recken** to stretch (oneself); **das steckt ihr noch in den ~ern** she still hasn't got over it. **(b)** *(Penis)* penis. **(c)** *(Ketten~, fig)* link. **(d)** *(Teil)* section, part. **(e)** *(Mil)* rank. **ins ~ zurücktreten** to step back into the ranks.

**gliedern 1** *vt* **(a)** *(ordnen)* to order, to organize. **(b)** *(unterteilen)* to (sub)divide *(in +acc into)*. **2** *vr* **sich ~ in** *(+acc)* to (sub)divide into.

**Glieder-:** ~**puppe** *f* jointed doll; *(Marionette)* (string) puppet, marionette; ~**reißen** *nt,* ~**schmerz** *m* rheumatic pains *pl.*

**Gliederung** *f* **(a)** *(das Gliedern)* organization; *(das Unterteilen)* subdivision. **(b)** *(Aufbau)* structure.

**Glied-:** ~**maßen** *pl* limbs *pl*; ~**satz** *m (Ling)* subordinate clause; ~**staat** *m* member state.

**glimmen** *pret* **glomm** *ptp* **geglommen** *vi* to glow.

**Glimmstengel** *m (hum col)* fag *(Brit col)*, cigarette, butt *(US col)*.

**glimpflich** *adj (mild)* mild, light. ~ **davonkommen** to get off lightly; ~ **ablaufen** *or* **verlaufen** to pass off without serious consequences.

**glitschen** *vi aux sein (col)* to slip *(aus out of)*.

**glitschig** *adj (col)* slippery, slippy *(col)*.

**glitt** *pret of* **gleiten.**

**glitzern** *vi* to glitter; *(Stern auch)* to twinkle.

**global** *adj* **(a)** *(weltweit)* global, worldwide. **(b)** *(ungefähr, pauschal)* general.

**Globetrotter** *m* - globetrotter.

**Globus** *m, pl* **Globen** *or* **-se** globe; *(col: Kopf)* nut *(col).*

**Glöckchen** *nt* (little) bell.

**Glocke** *f* **-n** *(auch Blüte)* bell; *(Käse~ etc)* cover; *(Taucher~)* (diving) bell. **etw an die große ~ hängen** *(col)* to shout sth from the rooftops.

**Glocken-:** ~**blume** *f* bellflower, campanula; **g~förmig** *adj* bell-shaped; ~**geläut(e)** *nt* (peal of) bells; ~**klöppel** *m* clapper; ~**läuten** *nt* (peal of) bells; ~**schlag** *m* stroke (of a/the bell); *(von Uhr auch)* chime; ~**spiel** *nt (in Turm)* carillon; *(automatisch auch)* chimes *pl*; *(Instrument)* glockenspiel; ~**strang** *m* bell rope; ~**stuhl** *m* bell cage; ~**ton** *m* sound of a/the bell; ~**turm** *m* belfry.

**Glöckner** *m* - bellringer.

**glomm** *pret of* **glimmen.**

**glorifizieren\*** *vt* to glorify.

**Glorifizierung** *f* glorification.

**glorreich** *adj* glorious. **seine Laufbahn ~ beenden** to bring one's career to a glorious conclusion.

**Glossar** *nt* **-e** glossary.

**Glosse** *f* **-n (a)** *(Press, Rad etc)* satirical commentary. **(b)** *(col)* **seine ~n über jdn/etw machen** *(col)* to make snide comments about sb/sth *(col).*

**glossieren\*** *vt (Press, Rad etc)* to do a satirical commentary on.

**Glotzaugen** *pl (col)* goggle eyes. ~ **machen** to stare (goggle-eyed), to gawp.

**Glotze** *f* **-n** *(col)* goggle-box *(col).*

**glotzen** *vi (pej col)* to gape *(auf, in +acc at).*

**Glück** *nt no pl* **(a)** luck. **ein ~!** how lucky!, what a stroke of luck!; ~/**kein ~ haben** to be lucky/ unlucky; **er hat das ~ gehabt, zu** ... he was lucky enough to ...; **auf gut ~** *(aufs Geratewohl)* on the off-chance; *(unvorbereitet)* trusting to luck; *(wahllos)* at random; **du hast ~ im Unglück gehabt** it could have been a great deal worse (for you); **viel ~ (bei...)!** good luck *or* the best of luck (with ...)!; ~ **bei Frauen haben** to be successful with women;

**jdm zum Geburtstag ~ wünschen** to wish sb (a) happy birthday; **zum ~** luckily, fortunately; **das ist dein ~!** that's lucky for you!; **mehr ~ als Verstand haben** to have more luck than brains; **sie weiß noch nichts von ihrem ~** *(iro)* she doesn't know what she's in for; **damit wirst du bei ihr kein ~ haben** you won't have any joy with her (with that) *(col)*; **sein ~ machen** to make one's fortune; **sein ~ probieren** to try one's luck; **er kann von ~ sagen, daß** ... he can count himself lucky that ...; **das hat mir gerade noch zu meinem ~ gefehlt!** *(iro)* that was all I wanted; **manche Leute muß man zu ihrem Glück zwingen** some people need persuading of their own luck; **man kann niemanden zu seinem ~ zwingen** *(prov)* you can lead a horse to water but you can't make him drink *(prov).*

**(b)** *(Freude)* happiness. **eheliches ~** wedded *or* marital bliss; **er ist ihr ganzes ~** he means the world to her.

**Glück-:** ~**auf** *nt no pl* (cry of) "good luck"; **g~bringend** *adj* lucky, propitious *(form).*

**Glucke** *f* **-n** *(Bruthenne)* broody hen; *(mit Jungen)* mother hen.

**glucken** *vi (brüten)* to brood; *(fig col)* to sit around.

**glücken** *vi aux sein* to be successful. **nicht ~** to be a failure; **ihm glückt alles/nichts** everything/nothing goes right for him; **es wollte nicht ~** it wouldn't go right.

**gluckern** *vi* to glug.

**glücklich 1** *adj* **(a)** *(froh)* happy. **ein ~es Ende** a happy ending; ~ **machen** to bring happiness. **(b)** *(erfolgreich, vom Glück begünstigt)* lucky, fortunate; *(vorteilhaft, erfreulich)* happy. ~**e Reise!** have a pleasant journey! **2** *adv* **(a)** *(froh, selig)* happily. **(b)** *(mit Glück)* by luck; *(vorteilhaft, erfreulich)* happily. **(c)** *(col: endlich, zu guter Letzt)* finally, eventually.

**glücklicherweise** *adv* luckily, fortunately.

**glücklos** *adj* hapless, luckless.

**Glücks-:** ~**bote** *m* bearer of (the) glad tidings; ~**bringer** *m* - *(Talisman)* lucky charm.

**glückselig** *adj* blissful.

**Glückseligkeit** *f* bliss, rapture.

**glucksen** *vi* **(a)** *(Kleinkind)* to gurgle; *(Erwachsener)* to chortle. **(b)** *(gluckern)* to glug.

**Glücks-:** ~**fall** *m* stroke of luck; **durch einen ~fall** by a lucky chance; ~**gefühl** *nt* feeling of happiness; ~**kind** *nt* lucky person, child of fortune *(liter)*; ~**klee** *m* four-leaf clover; ~**pilz** *m* lucky beggar *(col)*; ~**rad** *nt* wheel of fortune; ~**ritter** *m* adventurer; ~**sache** *f* **das ist ~sache** it's a matter of luck; **das war reine ~sache** it was pure luck *or* a pure fluke *(col)*; ~**spiel** *nt* game of chance; ~**spieler** *m* gambler; ~**stern** *m* lucky star; ~**strähne** *f* lucky streak; ~**tag** *m* lucky day.

**glückstrahlend** *adj* beaming (with happiness).

**Glücks-:** ~**treffer** *m* stroke of luck; *(beim Schießen, Ftbl)* lucky shot, fluke *(col)*; ~**zahl** *f* lucky number.

**Glückwunsch** *m* ⁼**e** congratulations *pl (zu on).* **herzlichen ~** congratulations; **herzlichen ~ zum Geburtstag!** happy birthday, many happy returns (of the day).

**Glüh-** *(Elec)*: ~**birne** *f* (electric) light bulb; ~**draht** *m* filament.

**glühen 1** *vi* to glow. **vor Fieber ~** to be flushed with fever. **2** *vt* to heat until red-hot.

**glühend** *adj* glowing; *(heiß~) Metall* red-hot; *Hitze* blazing; *(fig: leidenschaftlich)* ardent; *Haß* burning; *Wangen* flushed, burning.

**Glüh-:** ~**faden** *m (Elec)* filament; ~**lampe** *f (form)* electric light bulb; ~**wein** *m* glühwein, mulled wine; ~**würmchen** *nt* glow-worm; *(fliegend)* firefly.

**Glukose** f -n glucose.

**Glut** f -en (a) *(glühende Masse, Kohle)* embers pl; *(Tabaks~)* burning ash; *(Hitze)* heat. (b) *(fig liter) (glühende Farbe, Hitze)* glow; *(Leidenschaft)* ardour *(Brit)*, ardor *(US)*.

**Glut-:** ~**hitze** f sweltering heat; **g~rot** adj *(liter)* fiery red.

**Glyzerin** nt no pl *(Chem)* glycerin(e).

**Glyzine** [-iə] f wisteria.

**GmbH** [ge:|ɛmbe:'ha:] f -s = **Gesellschaft mit beschränkter Haftung** limited company, Ltd *(Brit)*, Inc *(US)*.

**Gnade** f -n *(Barmherzigkeit)* mercy; *(Rel)* grace; *(Gunst)* favour *(Brit)*, favor *(US)*; *(Verzeihung)* pardon. **um ~ bitten** to ask for mercy; **bei jdm ~ finden** to find favour with sb; **~ vor Recht ergehen lassen** to temper justice with mercy; **ohne ~** without mercy; **~!** mercy!; **Euer ~n!** *(Hist)* Your Grace; **die ~ haben, etw zu tun** *(iro)* to graciously consent to do sth.

**gnaden** vi: **(dann) gnade dir Gott!** (then) God or heaven help you!

**Gnaden-:** ~**akt** m act of mercy; ~**brot** nt no pl **jdm/einem Tier das ~brot geben** to keep sb/an animal in his/her/its old age; **einem Pferd das ~brot geben** to put a horse out to grass; ~**frist** f (temporary) reprieve; **eine ~frist von 24 Stunden** 24 hours' grace; ~**gesuch** nt plea for clemency; **g~los** adj merciless; ~**losigkeit** f mercilessness; ~**schuß** m **einem Tier den ~schuß geben** to put an animal out of its misery; ~**stoß** m coup de grâce *(with sword etc, fig)*; ~**tod** m *(geh)* mercy killing, euthanasia.

**gnädig** adj *(barmherzig)* merciful; *(herablassend)* gracious; *Strafe* lenient; *(freundlich)* kind. ~**es Fräulein** *(dated)* madam; *(jüngere Dame)* miss; ~**e Frau** *(form)* madam, ma'am; ~**er Gott!** *(col)* merciful heavens! *(col)*; **Gott sei uns ~!** *(geh)* Lord preserve us; **sei doch so ~, und mach mal Platz!** *(iro)* would you be so good as to make some room?; **es ~ machen** to show leniency.

**Gnom** m *(wk)* -en, -en gnome.

**Gnu** nt -s *(Zool)* gnu.

**Gobelin** [gobə'lɛ̃:] m -s tapestry, Gobelin.

**Gockel** m - *(esp SGer)* cock; *(fig)* old goat *(col)*.

**Go-Kart** m -s kart, go-cart.

**Gold** nt no pl *(lit, fig)* gold. **nicht mit ~ zu bezahlen** or **aufzuwiegen sein** to be worth one's weight in gold; **ein Herz aus ~** a heart of gold; **er hat ~ in der Kehle** he has a golden voice; **es ist nicht alles ~, was glänzt** *(Prov)* all that glitters is not gold *(Prov)*.

**Gold-** in cpds gold; *(von Farbe)* golden; ~**ader** f vein of gold; ~**barren** m gold ingot; ~**barsch** m *(Rotbarsch)* rosefish; **g~blond** golden blond.

**golden** adj attr *(lit, fig)* golden; *(aus Gold)* gold. ~**e Schallplatte** gold disc; ~**er Humor** irrepressible sense of humour; ~**e Worte** words of wisdom; **ein ~es Herz haben** to have a heart of gold; **die ~e Mitte wählen** to strike a happy medium; ~**e Hochzeit** golden wedding (anniversary); **das G~e Zeitalter** *(Myth, fig)* the golden age; **der Tanz ums G~e Kalb** *(fig)* the worship of Mammon.

**Gold-:** **g~farben, g~farbig** adj golden, gold-coloured *(Brit)*, gold-colored *(US)*; ~**fisch** m goldfish; ~**gräber(in** f) m gold-digger; ~**grube** f *(lit, fig)* goldmine; ~**hamster** m (golden) hamster.

**goldig** adj *(fig col: allerliebst)* sweet, cute *(col)*. **du bist vielleicht ~!** *(iro)* the ideas you get!

**Gold-:** ~**junge** m *(col)* golden boy *(col)*; ~**klumpen** m gold nugget; ~**lack** m (a) *(Bot)* wallflower; (b)

*(Glanzlack)* gold lacquer.

**Goldmedaille** f gold medal.

**Goldmedaillengewinner** m gold medallist *(Brit)* or medalist *(US)*.

**Gold-:** ~**mine** f gold mine; ~**rausch** m gold fever; ~**regen** m *(Bot)* laburnum; *(Feuerwerkskörper)* Roman candle; *(fig)* riches pl; ~**reserve** f *(Fin)* gold reserves pl; **g~richtig** adj *(col)* absolutely or dead *(col)* right; *Mensch* all right *(col)*; ~**schatz** m gold treasure; *(von Geld)* hoard of gold; ~**schmied** m goldsmith; ~**schnitt** m no pl gilt edging; ~**stück** nt piece of gold; *(fig col)* treasure; ~**sucher(in** f) m gold-hunter; ~**waage** f gold or bullion balance; **jedes Wort auf die ~waage legen** *(sich vorsichtig ausdrücken)* to weigh one's words; *(überempfindlich sein)* to be hypersensitive; ~**währung** f gold standard; ~**zahn** m gold tooth.

**Golf¹** m -e *(Meerbusen)* gulf.

**Golf²** nt no pl *(Sport)* golf.

**Golfer(in** f) m - *(col)* golfer.

**Golf-** in cpds *(Sport)* golf; ~**krieg** m Gulf War; ~**platz** m golf course; ~**schläger** m golf club; ~**spieler** m golfer; ~**staaten** pl **die ~staaten** the Gulf States pl; ~**strom** m *(Geog)* Gulf Stream.

**Gondel** f -n gondola.

**gondeln** vi aux sein *(col)* *(reisen)* to travel around; *(herumfahren)* to drive around. **durch die Welt ~** to go globetrotting *(col)*.

**Gondoliere** [gɔndo'lieːrə] m, pl **Gondolieri** gondolier.

**Gong** m -s gong; *(bei Boxkampf etc)* bell.

**Gongschlag** m stroke of the gong.

**gönnen** vt **jdm etw ~** not to begrudge sb sth; *(zuteil werden lassen)* to allow sb sth; **jdm etw nicht ~** to begrudge sb sth; not to allow sb sth; **sich** *(dat)* **etw ~** to allow oneself sth; **er gönnte mir keinen Blick** he didn't spare me a single glance; **ich gönne ihm diesen Erfolg von ganzem Herzen** I'm delighted for him that he's had this success; **das sei ihm gegönnt** I don't begrudge him that.

**Gönner(in** f) m - patron.

**Gönner-:** **g~haft** adj *(pej)* patronizing; **g~haft tun** to play the big benefactor; ~**miene** f *(pej)* patronizing air.

**gor** pret of **gären**.

**Gör** nt -en *(NGer col)* (a) *(kleines Kind)* brat *(pej col)*, kid *(col)*. (b) *(auch Göre: Mädchen)* (cheeky or saucy) little miss.

**Gorilla** m -s gorilla; *(col: Leibwächter)* heavy *(col)*.

**Gosche** f -n *(esp SGer pej)* gob *(col)*, mouth. **halt die ~!** shut your mouth or gob *(col)*.

**goß** pret of **gießen**.

**Gosse** f -n *(Rinnstein, fig)* gutter. **in der ~ enden** or **landen** to end up in the gutter.

**Gossensprache** f gutter language.

**Gote** m *(wk)* -n, -n, **Gotin** f Goth.

**Gotik** f no pl *(Art)* Gothic (style); *(Epoche)* Gothic period.

**gotisch** adj Gothic.

**Gott** m ⁼er (a) god; *(als Name)* God. **~ der Herr** the Lord God; **~ der Allmächtige** Almighty God; **der liebe ~** the dear Lord; **er ist ihr ~** she worships him like a god; **bei ~ schwören** to swear by Almighty God.

(b) **dein Schicksal liegt in ~es Hand** your fate is in God's hands; **dem lieben ~ den Tag stehlen** to laze the day(s) away; **den lieben ~ einen guten Mann sein lassen** *(col)* to take things as they come; **wie ~ ihn geschaffen hat** *(hum col)* as naked as the day he was born; **ein Bild für die ~er** *(hum col)* a sight for sore eyes; **das wissen die ~er** *(col)* God (only) knows; **ich bin weiß ~ nicht prüde, aber ...** God knows I'm no prude but ...; **so ~ will** *(geh)* God willing, D.V.; **~ und die Welt** *(fig)* everybody; **über ~ und die Welt reden** *(fig)* to talk about everything under the sun; **leider ~es** alas; **wie ~ in Frankreich leben** *(col)* to be in clover.

(c) **grüß ~!** *(esp SGer, Aus)* hello, good morning/afternoon/evening; **~ hab' ihn selig!** God have mercy on his soul; **in ~es Namen!** for heaven's sake!; **ach (du lieber) ~!** *(col)* oh Lord! *(col)*; **großer ~!** good God!; **bei ~!** by God!; **~ behüte** *or* **bewahre!, da sei ~ vor!** God *or* Heaven forbid!; **um ~es willen!** for heaven's *or* God's sake!; **~ sei Dank!** thank God!

**Gott|erbarmen** *nt* **zum ~** *(col)* pitiful(ly), pathetic(ally) *(col)*.

**Götter-:** **g~gleich** *adj* godlike; **~speise** *f (Cook)* jelly *(Brit)*, jello *(US)*.

**Gottes-:** **~anbeterin** *f (Zool)* praying mantis; **~beweis** *m* proof of the existence of God; **~dienst** *m* service; **zum ~dienst gehen** to go to church; **g~fürchtig** *adj* God-fearing; **~gabe** *f* gift from God; **~haus** *nt* place of worship; **~lästerer** *m* blasphemer; **~lästerung** *f* blasphemy; **~lohn** *m* **no** *pl* **etw für einen ~lohn tun** to do sth for love; **~mutter** *f* Mother of God; **~sohn** *m* Son of God; **~urteil** *nt* trial by ordeal.

**gott-:** **~gegeben** *adj* god-given; **~gewollt** *adj* willed by God.

**Gottheit** *f (Göttergestalt)* deity. **jdn wie eine ~ verehren** to worship sb like a god.

**Göttin** *f* goddess.

**göttlich** *adj (lit, fig)* divine.

**Gott-:** **g~lob** *interj* thank heavens; **g~los** *adj* godless; *(verwerflich)* ungodly; **~losigkeit** *f no pl* godlessness; **~vater** *m no pl* God the Father; **g~verdammt** *adj attr (col!)* goddamn(ed) *(col!)*, damn(ed) *(col!)*; **g~verlassen** *adj* godforsaken; **~vertrauen** *nt* trust in God.

**Götze** *m (wk)* **-n, -n** *(lit, fig)* idol.

**Götzen-:** **~bild** *nt* idol, graven image *(Bibl)*; **~dienst** *m,* **~verehrung** *f* idolatry.

**Götzzitat** *nt* **das ~** ≃ the V-sign *(Brit)*, the finger *(US)*.

**Goulasch** ['gula∫] *m or nt* = **Gulasch.**

**Gourmet** [gur'meː] *m* **-s** gourmet.

**Gouvernante** [guvɛr'nantə] *f* **-n** *(dated)* governess.

**Gouverneur(in** *f)* [guvɛr'nøːɐ, -'nøːrin] *m* governor.

**Grab** *nt* ∹er grave; *(Gruft)* tomb; *(fig: Untergang)* end, ruination. **jdn zu ~e tragen** to bear sb to his grave; **ein Geheimnis mit ins ~ nehmen** to take a secret with one to the grave; **verschwiegen wie ein ~ (as)** silent as the grave; **er würde sich im ~ umdrehen, wenn ...** he would turn in his grave if ...; **du bringst mich noch ins ~!** you'll send me to an early grave!; **sich** *(dat)* **sein eigenes ~ schaufeln** *(fig)* to dig one's own grave; **seine Hoffnungen** *etc* **zu ~e tragen** *(geh)* to abandon one's hopes *etc*.

**graben** *pret* **grub,** *ptp* **gegraben 1** *vti* to dig. **nach Gold/Erz ~** to dig for gold/ore. **2** *vr* **sich in etw** *(acc)* **~** *(Zähne, Krallen)* to sink into sth; **das hat sich mir tief ins Gedächtnis gegraben** *(geh)* it has imprinted itself firmly on my memory.

**Graben** *m* ∹ ditch; *(trockener ~, Mil)* trench; *(Sport)* ditch; *(Sport: Wasser~)* water-jump. **im ~ liegen** *(Mil)* to be in the trenches.

**Grabenkrieg** *m (Mil)* trench warfare.

**Gräber** *pl of* **Grab.**

**Gräberfeld** *nt* cemetery, burial ground.

**Grabes-** *(liter)*: **~stille** *f* deathly hush; **~stimme** *f* sepulchral voice.

**Grab-:** **~inschrift** *f* epitaph, inscription *(on gravestone etc)*; **~kammer** *f* burial chamber; **~legung** *f* burial; **~mal** *nt, pl* **-mäler** *or (geh)* **-e** monument; *(~stein)* gravestone; **~platte** *f* memorial slab; **~rede** *f* funeral oration; **~schänder(in** *f) m* - defiler of the grave(s)/of graves; **~schändung** *f* defilement of graves; **~stätte** *f* grave; *(Gruft)* tomb; **~stein** *m* gravestone, tombstone; **~stelle** *f* (burial) plot.

**Grabung** *f (Archeol)* excavation.

**Gracht** *f* **-en** canal *(in a Dutch town)*.

**Grad** *m* **-e** *(Sci, Univ, fig)* degree; *(Mil)* rank. **ein Winkel von 45 ~** an angle of 45 degrees; **auf dem 32. ~ nördlicher Breite** latitude 32 degrees north; **null ~** zero; **es kocht bei 100 ~** boiling occurs at 100 degrees; **ein Verwandter zweiten/dritten ~es** a relative once/twice removed; **Verbrennungen ersten ~es** *(Med)* first-degree burns; **bis zu einem gewissen ~e** to a certain degree *or* extent; **in hohem ~(e)** to a large extent; **im höchsten ~(e)** extremely.

**Grad-, grad-** = **Gerad-, gerade-.**

**grad(e)** *adj (col)* = **gerade.**

**Grad-:** **~einteilung** *f* calibration, graduation; **~messer** *m (fig)* gauge *(gen, für of)*; **~netz** *nt (Geog)* latitude and longitude grid.

**graduell** *adj (allmählich)* gradual; *(gering)* slight.

**graduieren* 1** *vi (Univ)* to graduate. **graduierter Ingenieur** engineering graduate. **2** *vt (in Grade einteilen)* to calibrate, to graduate.

**Graduierte(r)** *mf decl as adj* graduate.

**Graf** *m (wk)* **-en, -en** count; *(als Titel)* Count; *(britischer ~)* earl; *(als Titel)* Earl.

**Grafengeschlecht** *nt* dynasty of counts *(Brit)* earls.

**Graffiti** *nt* = **-s** graffiti.

**Grafik** *f* **(a)** *no pl (Art)* graphic arts *pl*; *(Technik, Comp)* graphics. **(b)** *(Art: Darstellung)* graphic; *(Druck)* print; *(Schaubild)* illustration; *(technisches Schaubild)* diagram.

**Grafiker(in** *f) m* - graphic artist; *(Illustrator)* illustrator.

**Gräfin** *f* countess.

**grafisch** *adj* graphic; *(schematisch)* diagrammatic, schematic.

**gräflich** *adj* count's; *(Brit)* earl's.

**Grafschaft** *f* land of a count; *(Brit)* earldom; *(Admin)* county.

**Grahambrot** *nt* (type of) wholemeal *(Brit)* or wholewheat *(US)* bread.

**Gralshüter** *m (fig)* guardian.

**Gram** *m no pl (geh)* grief, sorrow. **vom ~ gebeugt** bowed down with grief *or* sorrow.

**grämen 1** *vr* **sich über jdn/etw ~** to grieve over sb/sth; **sich zu Tode ~** to die of grief *or* sorrow. **2** *vt* to grieve.

**grämlich** *adj* morose.

**Gramm** *nt* **-e** *or (nach Zahlenangabe)* - gram. **100 ~ Mehl** 100 grams of flour.

**Grammatik** *f* grammar.

**grammatikalisch** *adj* grammatical.

**grammatisch** *adj* grammatical.

**Grammophon** ® [gramo'foːn] *nt* **-e** gramophone.

**Granat** *m* **-e** *(Miner)* garnet.

**Granatapfel** *m* pomegranate.

**Granate** *f* **-n** *(Mil) (Geschoß)* shell; *(Hand~)* grenade; *(Ftbl sl: Schuß aufs Tor)* cannonball shot *(col)*.

**Granat-:** **~feuer** *nt* shelling, shellfire; **~splitter** *m* shell/grenade splinter; **~trichter** *m* shell crater; **~werfer** *m* mortar.

**grandios** *adj* magnificent, superb.

**Granit** *m* **-e** granite. **auf ~ beißen (bei ...)** to bang one's head against a brick wall (with ...).

**grell**

**grantig** *adj (col)* grumpy.
**Granulat** *nt* granules *pl.*
**Grapefruit** ['greːpfruːt] *f* **-s** grapefruit.
**Graphik** = **Grafik**.
**graphisch** = **grafisch**.
**Grapho-**: ~**loge** *m,* ~**login** *f* graphologist; ~**logie** *f* graphology.
**grapschen** *(col)* **1** *vt* **(sich** *dat)* **etw** ~ to grab sth. **2** *vi* **nach etw** ~ to make a grab at sth.
**Gras** *nt* ≐er **(a)** grass. **ins** ~ **beißen** *(col)* to bite the dust *(col)*; **das** ~ **wachsen hören** *(zuviel hineindeuten)* to read too much into things; **über etw** *(acc)* ~ **wachsen lassen** *(fig)* to let the dust settle on sth; **wo er zuschlägt, wächst kein** ~ **mehr** *(col)* he packs quite a punch. **(b)** *gen* **-**, *no pl (Drogen sl: Marihuana)* grass.
**Gras-** *in cpds* grass; **g~bewachsen** *adj* grassy, grass-covered; ~**büschel** *nt* tuft of grass.
**grasen** *vi* to graze.
**Gras-**: ~**fläche** *f* grassland; *(Rasen)* patch of grass; **g~grün** *adj* grass-green; ~**halm** *m* blade of grass; ~**hüpfer** *m* **-** *(col)* grasshopper; ~**land** *nt no pl* grassland; ~**mücke** *f (Orn)* warbler; ~**narbe** *f* turf; ~**samen** *m* grass seed.
**grassieren*** *vi* to be rife.
**gräßlich** *adj* **(a)** hideous. **(b)** *(intensiv, unangenehm)* dreadful; *Mensch* horrible.
**Gräßlichkeit** *f* **(a)** hideousness. **(b)** *(gräßliche Tat etc)* atrocity.
**Grat** *m* **-e** *(Berg~)* ridge; *(Archit)* hip *(of roof)*; *(fig)* (dividing) line, border.
**Gräte** *f* **-n** (fish-)bone. **ich brech' dir alle** ~**n einzeln!** *(col)* I'll break every bone in your body.
**Gratifikation** *f* bonus.
**gratis** *adv* free; *(Comm)* free (of charge).
**Gratis-** *in cpds* free; ~**probe** *f* free sample.
**Grätsche** *f* **-n** *(Sport)* straddle.
**grätschen 1** *vi aux sein* to do a straddle (vault). **2** *vt Beine* to straddle, to put apart.
**Gratulant(in** *f)* *m* well-wisher.
**Gratulation** *f* congratulations *pl.*
**Gratulations-**: ~**cour** [-kuːɐ] *f* congratulatory reception; ~**schreiben** *nt* letter of congratulation.
**gratulieren*** *vi* **jdm (zu einer Sache)** ~ to congratulate sb (on sth); **jdm zum Geburtstag** ~ to wish sb many happy returns (of the day); **(ich) gratuliere!** congratulations!
**Gratwanderung** *f (fig)* tightrope walk.
**grau** *adj* grey *(Brit)*, gray *(US)*; *(trostlos)* bleak. ~**e Haare bekommen,** ~ **werden** *(col)* to go grey; **er malte die Lage** ~ **in** ~ *(fig)* he painted a bleak picture of the situation; ~**e Eminenz** éminence grise; **die (kleinen)** ~**n Zellen** *(hum)* the little grey cells; **der** ~**e Alltag** drab reality; **in** ~**er Vorzeit** *(fig)* in the dim and distant past; **das ist bloß** ~**e Theorie** that's all very well in theory.
**Grau** *nt* **-(s)** grey *(Brit)*, gray *(US)*; *(fig)* dullness, drabness.
**Grau-**: **g~äugig** *adj* grey-eyed *(Brit)*, gray-eyed *(US)*; **g~blau** *adj* grey-blue *(Brit)*, gray-blue *(US)*; **g~braun** *adj* greyish *(Brit)* or grayish *(US)* brown; ~**brot** *nt siehe* **Mischbrot**.
**grauen** *vi impers* **mir graut vor etw** *(dat)* I dread sth; **mir graut vor ihm** I'm terrified of him.
**Grauen** *nt no pl* **(a)** horror *(vor of)*. **(b)** *(grauenhaftes Ereignis)* horror.
**grauen-**: ~**haft,** ~**voll** *adj* terrible, atrocious.
**Grau-**: ~**gans** *f* grey(lag) *(Brit)* or gray(lag) *(US)* goose; **g~grün** *adj* grey-green *(Brit)*, gray-green *(US)*; **g~haarig** *adj* grey-haired *(Brit)*, gray-haired *(US)*; **g~meliert** *adj attr* greying *(Brit)*, graying

*(US).*
**Graupe** *f* **-n** *usu pl* grain of pearl barley. ~**n** pearl barley *sing.*
**Graupel** *f* **-n** (small) hailstone. ~**n** soft hail *sing.*
**Graupel-**: ~**regen** *m,* ~**schauer** *m* sleet.
**Graupensuppe** *f* barley broth *or* soup.
**Graus** *m no pl (old)* horror. **es war ein** ~ **zu sehen, wie ...** it was terrible to see how ...
**grausam** *adj (gefühllos, roh)* cruel *(gegen, zu* to). **sich** ~ **für etw rächen** to take (a) cruel revenge for sth.
**Grausamkeit** *f* **(a)** *no pl* cruelty. **(b)** *(grausame Tat)* (act of) cruelty; *(stärker)* atrocity.
**Grauschimmel** *m (Pferd)* grey *(Brit)* or gray *(US)* (horse).
**grausen** *vi impers siehe* **grauen**.
**Grausen** *nt no pl* horror *(vor of)*. **da kann man das kalte** ~ **kriegen** *(col)* it's enough to give you the creeps *(col)*.
**grausig** *adj* terrible, atrocious.
**Grau-**: ~**stufe** *f* shade of grey *(Brit)* or gray *(US)*; ~**ton** *m* grey colour *(Brit)*, gray color *(US)*; ~**zone** *f (fig)* grey *(Brit)* or gray *(US)* area.
**Graveur(in** *f)* [graˈvøːɐ, -øːrɪn] *m* engraver.
**gravieren*** [graˈviːrən] *vt* to engrave.
**gravierend** [graˈviːrənt] *adj* serious, grave.
**Gravitation** [gravitaˈtsioːn] *f* gravitation.
**gravitätisch** [graviˈtɛːtɪʃ] *adj* grave, solemn.
**Gravur** [graˈvuːɐ] *f* engraving.
**Grazie** [-iə] *f no pl (Liebreiz)* grace(fulness).
**grazil** *adj* (delicately) slender. ~ **gebaut sein** to have a delicate figure.
**graziös** *adj* graceful; *(lieblich)* charming.
**Gregorianisch** *adj* Gregorian. **G~er Gesang** Gregorian chant, plainsong.
**greifbar** *adj (konkret)* tangible, concrete; *(erreichbar)* ready to hand; *(verfügbar)* available; *Ware* available, in stock *pred.* **in g~barer Nähe** within easy reach.
**greifen** *pret* **griff,** *ptp* **gegriffen 1** *vt (nehmen, packen)* to take hold of, to grasp; *(grapschen)* to seize, to grab; *(fangen)* to catch; *Akkord* to strike. **diese Zahl ist zu niedrig gegriffen** *(fig)* this figure is too low; **zum G~ nahe sein** *(Sieg)* to be within reach; **die Gipfel waren zum G~ nahe** you could almost touch the peaks; **aus dem Leben gegriffen** taken from life; **sich** *(dat)* **jdn/etw** ~ to grab sb/sth.
**2** *vi* **(a)** **um sich** ~ *(fig)* to spread, to gain ground; **unter etw** *(acc)* ~ to reach under sth; **nach einer Sache** ~ to reach for sth; *(um zu halten)* to clutch *or (hastig)* grab at sth; **an etw** *(acc)* ~ *(fassen)* to grasp sth; *(berühren)* to touch sth; **zu etw** ~ to reach for sth; *(zu Methoden, Mitteln* to resort to sth; **in die Saiten/Tasten** ~ to strike up a tune; **zu den Waffen** ~ to take up arms; **zum Äußersten** ~ to resort to extremes; **nach der Macht** ~ to try to seize power. **(b)** *(nicht rutschen, einrasten)* to grip. **(c)** *(fig) (wirksam werden)* to take effect; *(zum Ziel führen)* to achieve its ends; *(Vergleich)* to hold.
**Greifer** *m* **-** *(Tech)* grab.
**Greifvogel** *m* bird of prey.
**Greis** *m* **-e** old man.
**greis** *adj* aged; *(ehrwürdig)* venerable; *(altersgrau)* grey *(Brit)*, gray *(US)*, hoary *(liter, hum)*. **sein** ~**es Haupt schütteln** *(usu iro)* to shake one's wise old head.
**Greisen-**: ~**alter** *nt* extreme old age; **g~haft** *adj* very old, aged *attr; (von jüngerem Menschen)* like an old man/woman.
**Greisin** *f* old lady.
**grell** *adj Stimme, Ton* shrill, piercing; *Licht* glaring;

*Farbe* garish, loud; *Gegensatz* sharp; *(stärker)* glaring; *(fig) Szene* lurid.

**Gremium** *nt* body; *(Ausschuß)* committee.

**Grenada** *nt* Grenada.

**Grenader(in** *f)* *m* Grenadian.

**Grenadier** *m* **-e** *(Mil: Infanterist)* infantryman.

**grenadisch** *adj* Grenadian.

**Grenz-** *in cpds* border, frontier; **~beamte(r)** *m* border official; **~bereich** *m* frontier *or* border zone *or* area; *(fig)* limits *pl;* **im ~bereich liegen** *(fig)* to lie at the limits.

**Grenze** *f* **-n** border; *(Landes~ auch)* frontier; *(Stadt~, zwischen Grundstücken)* boundary; *(fig: zwischen Begriffen)* dividing line, boundary; *(fig: äußerstes Maß)* limits *pl,* bounds *pl.* **die ~ zwischen Spanien und Frankreich** the Spanish-French border *or* frontier; **die ~ zu Österreich** the Austrian border; **über die ~ gehen/fahren** to cross the border; **einer Sache** *(dat)* **~n setzen** to set a limit *or* limits to sth; **keine ~n kennen** *(fig)* to know no bounds; **seine ~n kennen** to know one's limitations; **seiner Großzügigkeit sind keine ~n gesetzt** there is no limit to his generosity; **hart an der ~ des Erlaubten** bordering on the limits of what is permitted; **sich in ~n halten** *(fig)* to be limited; **die oberste/unterste ~** *(fig)* the upper/lower limit; **alles hat seine ~n** there are limits to everything.

**grenzen** *vi* **an etw** *(acc)* **~** *(lit)* to border (on) sth; *(fig)* to border *or* verge on sth.

**Grenzen-:** **g~los 1** *adj (lit, fig)* boundless; **2** *adv* boundlessly; *(fig)* immensely; **~losigkeit** *f* boundlessness; *(fig)* immensity.

**Grenzer** *m* - *(col) (Zöllner)* customs man; *(Grenzsoldat)* border *or* frontier guard.

**Grenz-** *in cpds* border, frontier; **~fall** *m* borderline case; **~gänger** *m* - *(Arbeiter)* international commuter *(across a local border)*; **~gebiet** *nt (lit, fig)* border area; **~konflikt** *m* border *or* frontier dispute; **~kontrolle** *f* border *or* frontier control; **~linie** *f* border; *(Sport)* line; **~situation** *f* borderline situation; **~stadt** *f* border town; **~stein** *m* boundary stone; **~streitigkeit** *f* boundary dispute; *(Pol)* border *or* frontier dispute; **~übergang** *m* **(a)** border *or* frontier crossing(-point); **(b)** = **~übertritt;** **g~überschreitend** *adj* cross-border; **~übertritt** *m* crossing of the border; **~verkehr** *m* border *or* frontier traffic; **~verlauf** *m* boundary line *(between countries)*; **~wert** *m* limit; **~zwischenfall** *m* border incident.

**Gretchenfrage** *f (fig)* crunch question *(col)*, sixty-four-thousand-dollar-question *(col)*.

**Greuel** *m* - *(no pl: Abscheu)* horror; *(~tat)* atrocity. **~ vor etw haben** to have a horror of sth; **er/es ist mir ein ~** I loathe *or* detest him/it; **die Prüfung ist mir ein ~** I'm really dreading the exam.

**Greuel-:** **~märchen** *nt* horror story; **~propaganda** *f* atrocity propaganda; **~tat** *f* atrocity.

**greulich** *adj siehe* **gräßlich.**

**Griebe** *f* **-n** *usu pl* ≃ crackling *no indef art, no pl.*

**Griebenschmalz** *nt dripping with greaves or crackling.*

**Grieche** *m (wk)* **-n, -n, Griechin** *f* Greek.

**Griechenland** *nt* Greece.

**griechisch** *adj* Greek; *Architektur, Vase, Stil auch* Grecian. **die ~e Tragödie** Greek tragedy; **~-orthodox** Greek Orthodox. **~-römisch** Graeco-Roman.

**Griechisch(e)** *nt* Greek; *siehe* **Deutsch(e).**

**Griesgram** *m* **-e** grouch *(col)*, misery.

**griesgrämig** *adj* grumpy, grouchy *(col)*.

**Grieß** *m* **-e** *(Cook)* semolina.

**Grieß-:** **~brei** *m* semolina; **~pudding** *m* semolina pudding.

**Griff** *m* **-e** **(a)** *(das Greifen)* der **~ nach etw** reaching for sth; **einen tiefen ~ in den Geldbeutel tun** *(fig)* to dig deep in one's pocket; **der ~ nach der Flasche** taking to the bottle; **der ~ nach der Macht** the bid for power. **(b)** *(Handgriff)* grip, grasp; *(beim Ringen etc)* hold. **mit festem ~** firmly; **jdn/etw in den ~ bekommen** *(fig)* to gain control of sb/sth; *(geistig)* to get a grasp of sth; **(mit jdm/etw) einen guten** *or* **glücklichen ~ tun** to make a wise choice (with sb/sth). **(c)** *(Stiel, Knauf)* handle; *(Pistolen~)* butt; *(Schwert~)* hilt; *(an Saiteninstrumenten)* neck. **(d)** *usu pl (Hunt: Kralle)* talon.

**griff** *pret of* **greifen.**

**griffbereit** *adj* ready to hand, handy.

**Griffel** *m* - *(Schreibstift)* slate pencil; *(Bot)* style.

**griffig** *adj Fahrbahn etc* giving a good grip; *(fig) Ausdruck* useful, handy; *Slogan auch* catchy.

**Grill** *m* **-s** grill; *(Aut: Kühler~)* grille.

**Grille** *f* **-n** **(a)** *(Zool)* cricket. **(b)** *(dated col: Laune)* silly notion *or* idea.

**grillen 1** *vt* to grill. **2** *vr* **sich (in der Sonne) ~ (lassen)** *(col)* to roast (in the sun). **3** *vi* to have a barbecue.

**Grillfest** *nt* barbecue party.

**Grimasse** *f* **-n** grimace. **~n schneiden** to make faces.

**grimmig** *adj* **(a)** *(zornig)* furious. **~ lächeln** to smile grimly; **~er Humor** grim humour. **(b)** *(sehr groß, heftig) Kälte etc* severe.

**Grind** *m* **-e** *(Schorf)* scab.

**grinsen** *vi* to grin; *(höhnisch auch)* to smirk.

**Grinsen** *nt no pl siehe vi* grin; smirk.

**Grippe** *f* **-n** influenza *(form)*, flu *(col)*; *(Erkältung)* cold.

**Grippe-** *in cpds* influenza (form), flu *(col)*; **~welle** *f* wave of flu.

**Grips** *m* **-e** *(col)* nous *(Brit col)*, sense. **nun strengt mal euren ~ an** use your common sense.

**Grislybär, Grizzlybär** ['grɪsli-] *m* grizzly (bear).

**grob** *adj comp* **⁼er,** *superl* **⁼ste(r, s)** *or (adv)* **am ⁼sten (a)** *(nicht fein) Arbeit* dirty *attr.* **(b)** *(ungefähr)* rough. **~ geschätzt** at a rough estimate. **(c)** *(schlimm)* gross *(auch Jur).* **den ⁼sten Schmutz habe ich schon weggeputzt** I have already cleaned off the worst of the dirt; **ein ~er Fehler** a bad mistake; **wir sind aus dem G⁓sten heraus** we're out of the woods (now). **(d)** *(brutal, derb)* rough; *(fig: derb)* coarse; *(unhöflich)* ill-mannered. **~ gegen jdn werden** to become offensive (towards sb).

**Grobe(s)** *nt (fig)* dirty work. **ein Mann fürs ~** *(col)* someone to do the dirty work.

**Grob-** *in cpds* coarse; **g~gemahlen** *adj attr* coarse-ground; **~heit** *f* **(a)** *no pl (lit, fig)* coarseness; *(Brutalität)* roughness; *(fig: Unhöflichkeit)* ill-manneredness; **(b)** *(Beschimpfung)* foul language *no pl, no indef art.*

**Grobian** *m* **-e** brute.

**grobkörnig** *adj* coarse-grained.

**gröblich** *adj (geh)* gross. **jdn ~ beschimpfen** to call sb rude names.

**Grob-:** **g~maschig** *adj* large-meshed; *(~gestrickt)* loose-knit *attr;* **g~schlächtig** *adj* coarse; *Mensch* heavily built; **~schnitt** *m (Tabak)* coarse cut.

**Grog** *m* **-s** grog.

**groggy** ['grɔgi] *adj pred (Boxen)* groggy; *(col: erschöpft)* all-in *(col).*

**grölen** *vti (pej)* to bawl. **~de Menge** raucous crowd.

**Groll** *m no pl (geh: Zorn)* anger, wrath *(liter)*; *(Erbitterung)* resentment. **einen ~ gegen jdn hegen** to

harbour *(Brit)* or harbor *(US)* a grudge against sb.
**grollen** *vi (geh)* **(a)** *(Donner etc)* to rumble, to roll.
**(b) (jdm)** ~ *(old)* to be filled with wrath (against sb) *(liter)*.
**Grönland** *nt* Greenland.
**Grönländer(in** *f) m* - Greenlander.
**grönländisch** *adj* Greenland *attr*.
**Gros** [groː] *nt* - [groːs] greater part, bulk.
**Groschen** *m (col)* 10-pfennig piece; *(Aus)* groschen; *(fig)* penny, cent *(US)*. **der** ~ **ist gefallen** *(hum col)* the penny has dropped *(col)*.
**Groschen-:** ~**grab** *nt (hum) (Spielautomat)* one-armed bandit; **diese Parkuhr ist ein richtiges**~**grab** this parking meter just swallows up your money; ~**heft** *nt (pej)* pulp magazine; *(Krimi auch)* penny dreadful *(dated)*; ~**roman** *m (pej)* cheap or dime *(US)* novel.

**groß** *comp* ⁼**er**, *superl* ⁼**te(r, s)** or *(adv)* **am** ⁼**ten 1** *adj* big; *Fläche, Haus, Hände, Summe auch, Dose, Packung etc* large; *Erfolg, Interesse, Schreck, Hoffnung auch, Freude, Leid, Höhe, Breite* great; *Buchstabe auch* capital; *Pause, Rede auch* long; *(hoch, hochgewachsen)* tall; *(bedeutend) Werk, Persönlichkeit etc* great; *Lärm* a lot of; *Geschwindigkeit* high. **wie** ~ **bist du?** how tall are you?; **du bist** ~ **geworden** you've grown; **ein ganz** ~**es Haus/Buch** a great big house/book; **die Wiese ist 10.000 m²** ~ the field is 10,000 square metres in area; **die** ~**e Masse** *(fig)* the vast majority; **ich habe nur** ~**es Geld** I haven't any change on me; **im** ~**en und ganzen (gesehen)** (taken) by and large; **die** ~**en Ferien** the long holidays; **die G**~**en** *(Erwachsene)* the grown-ups; **mit etw** ~ **geworden sein** to have grown up with sth; ~ **und klein** young and old (alike); ~**e Worte machen** to use big words; ~**en Hunger haben** to be very hungry; **eine der** ⁼**eren Firmen** one of the major companies; **ich habe** ~**e Lust zu etw** I would really like sth; **ich habe keine** ~**e Lust** I don't particularly want to; ~**e Mode sein** to be all the fashion; **er ist kein** ~**er Esser** *(col)* he's not a big eater; **ich bin kein** ~**er Redner** *(col)* I'm no great speaker; **jds** ~**e Stunde** sb's big moment; **einen** ~**en Namen haben** to be a big name; **er hat G**~**es geleistet** he has achieved great things; **Friedrich der G**~**e** Frederick the Great; **G**~**-Paris** Greater Paris; **der G**~**e Ozean** the Pacific; **die G**~**en Seen** *pl* the Great Lakes *pl*.

**2** *adv* **jdn** ~ **anblicken** to give sb a hard stare; **was soll man da schon** ~ **machen/sagen?** *(col)* you can't really do/say anything, can you?; ~ **daherreden** *(col)* to talk big *(col)*; ~ **und breit** *(fig col)* at great or enormous length; ~ **machen** *(baby-talk)* to do number two *(baby-talk)*; **ein Wort** ~ **schreiben** to write a word with a capital; **ganz** ~ **rauskommen** *(col)* to make the big time *(col)*.
**Groß-** *pref* Great; *(vor Städtenamen)* Greater.
**Groß-:** ~**abnehmer** *m (Comm)* bulk buyer; ~**aktionär** *m* major or principal shareholder; ~**alarm** *m* red alert; **g**~**angelegt** *adj attr* large-scale, on a large scale; ~**angriff** *m* large-scale attack; **g**~**artig** *adj* tremendous; *(prächtig) Bauwerk etc* magnificent; **er hat** ~**artiges geleistet** he has achieved great things; ~**artigkeit** *f (Pracht)* magnificence; ~**aufnahme** *f (Phot, Film)* close-up; ~**bank** *f* big bank; ~**betrieb** *m* large concern; *(Agr)* big farm; ~**brand** *m* major fire; ~**britannien** *nt* (Great) Britain; ~**buchstabe** *m* capital (letter), upper case letter *(Typ)*; ~**computer** *m* = ~**rechner**; ~**demonstration** *f* big demonstration; ~**druck** *m* large print.
**Größe** *f* -**n (a)** size. **nach der** ~ according to size. **(b)** *no pl (Höhe, Körper*~*)* height; *(Flächeninhalt)*

area; *(Maße)* dimensions *pl*; *(Math, Phys)* quantity. **eine unbekannte** ~ *(lit, fig)* an unknown quantity. **(c)** *no pl (Ausmaß)* extent; *(Bedeutsamkeit)* significance. **(d)** *no pl (Erhabenheit)* greatness. **(e)** *(bedeutender Mensch)* important figure.
**Groß-:** ~**einkauf** *m* bulk purchase; ~**einsatz** *m* ~**einsatz der Polizei** *etc* large-scale operation by the police *etc*; ~**eltern** *pl* grandparents *pl*; ~**enkel** *m* great-grandchild; *(Junge)* great-grandson; ~**enkelin** *f* great-granddaughter.
**Größen-:** ~**klasse** *f (Comm)* (size) class; ~**ordnung** *f* scale; *(Größe)* magnitude; *(Math)* order (of magnitude); **in dieser** ~**ordnung** of this magnitude or order.
**großenteils** *adv* for the most part.
**Größen-:** ~**unterschied** *m (im Format)* difference in size; *(in der Höhe)* difference in height; ~**verhältnis** *nt* proportions *pl (gen* between*)*; *(Maßstab)* scale; **im** ~**verhältnis 1:100** on the scale 1:100; ~**wahn(sinn)** *m* megalomania, delusions *pl* of grandeur; **g**~**wahnsinnig** *adj* megalomaniac; **g**~**wahnsinnig sein** to be a megalomaniac.
**größer** *comp of* **groß**.
**Groß-:** ~**fahndung** *f* large-scale manhunt; ~**familie** *f* extended family; ~**feuer** *nt* major fire; **g**~**flächig** *adj* extensive; ~**format** *nt* large size; *(bei Büchern, Fotos auch)* large format; **g**~**formatig** *adj* large-size; *Bücher, Fotos auch* large-format; ~**grundbesitzer** *m* big landowner.
**Großhandel** *m* wholesale trade *no art*. **etw im** ~ **kaufen** to buy sth wholesale.
**Großhandels-** *in cpds* wholesale.
**Groß-:** ~**händler** *m* wholesaler; ~**handlung** *f* wholesale business; **g**~**herzig** *adj* generous, magnanimous; ~**herzigkeit** *f* generosity, magnanimity; ~**hirn** *nt* cerebrum; ~**industrielle(r)** *mf* major industrialist.
**Grossist** *m* wholesaler.
**Groß-:** **g**~**jährig** *adj (dated)* of age; **g**~**jährig werden** to come of age; ~**kapital** *nt das* ~**kapital** big business; ~**kapitalist** *m* business tycoon; ~**konzern** *m* large combine; **g**~**kotzig** *adj (pej col)* swanky *(col)*; ~**küche** *f* canteen kitchen; ~**kundgebung** *f* mass rally.
**Großmacht** *f (Pol)* big or great power.
**Großmachtpolitik** *f* power politics.
**Groß-:** ~**mannssucht** *f no pl (pej)* craving for status; ~**markt** *m* hypermarket; **g**~**maschig** *adj* = **grobmaschig**; ~**maul** *nt (pej col)* big-mouth *(col)*; **g**~**mäulig** *adj (pej col)* big-mouthed *attr (col)*; ~**mut** *f* magnanimity; **g**~**mütig** *adj* magnanimous; ~**mutter** *f* grandmother; **das kannst du deiner** ~**mutter erzählen!** *(col)* who do you think you're kidding? *(col)*; **g**~**mütterlich** *adj attr* **(a)** *(von der* ~*mutter)* of one's grandmother; **im g**~**mütterlichen Haus wohnen** to live in one's grandmother's house; **(b)** *(in der Art einer* ~*mutter)* grandmotherly; ~**offensive** *f (Mil)* major offensive; ~**onkel** *m* great-uncle; ~**produktion** *f* large-scale production.
**Großraum** *m (einer Stadt)* **der** ~ **München** the Munich area or conurbation, Greater Munich.
**Großraum-:** ~**abteil** *nt (Rail)* open-plan carriage; ~**büro** *nt* open-plan office.
**Groß-:** **g**~**räumig** *adj* **(a)** *(geräumig)* roomy, spacious; **(b)** *(über g*~*e Flächen)* extensive; **(c)** *(im g*~*en Umkreis)* **g**~**räumig Umfahren eines Gebietes** making a large detour around an area; ~**razzia** *f* large-scale raid; ~**rechner** *m (Comp)* mainframe; ~**reinemachen** *nt* thorough cleaning, ≈ spring-cleaning; **g**~**schnäuzig** *adj (pej col)* big-

mouthed *attr (col)*; **g~schreiben** *vt sep irreg* **g~geschrieben werden** *(fig col)* to be stressed; **~schreibung** *f* capitalization; **g~sprecherisch** *adj (pej)* boastful; **g~spurig** *adj (pej)* flashy *(col)*.

**Großstadt** *f* city.

**Großstädter** *m* city-dweller.

**großstädtisch** *adj* big-city *attr.*

**Großstadt-** *in cpds* city; **~mensch** *m* city-dweller.

**Groß-:** **~tante** *f* great-aunt; **~tat** *f* great feat; **~teil** *m* large part; **zum ~teil** for the most part.

**größtenteils** *adv* in the main, for the most part.

**größte(r, s)** *superl of* **groß**.

**Größt-:** **~maß** *nt* maximum amount *(an +dat of)*; **g~möglich** *adj attr* greatest possible.

**Groß-:** **g~tuerisch** [-tuːərɪʃ] *adj (pej)* boastful, bragging; **g~tun** *sep irreg (pej) vi* to boast, to show off; **~unternehmen** *nt* large concern.

**Großvater** *m* grandfather.

**großväterlich** *adj* **(a)** *(vom Großvater)* of one's grandfather. **das ~e Erbe** one's inheritance from one's grandfather. **(b)** *(in der Art eines Großvaters)* grandfatherly.

**Groß-:** **~veranstaltung** *f* big event; *(~kundgebung)* mass rally; **~verbraucher** *m* large-scale consumer; **~verdiener** *m* big earner.

**Großwild** *nt* big game.

**Großwild-:** **~jagd** *f* big-game hunting; **eine ~jagd** a big-game hunt; **~jäger** *m* big-game hunter.

**Groß-:** **g~ziehen** *vt sep irreg* to raise; *Tier* to rear; **g~zügig** *adj* generous; *(weiträumig)* spacious; *Plan* large-scale, ambitious; **g~zügigkeit** *f siehe adj* generosity; spaciousness; (large) scale, ambitiousness.

**grotesk** *adj* grotesque.

**Groteske** *f* **-n** grotesque; grotesque play/novel.

**Grotte** *f* **-n** grotto.

**grub** *pret of* **graben**.

**Grübchen** *nt* dimple.

**Grube** *f* **-n** *(auch Min)* pit; *(kleine)* hole, hollow. **wer andern eine ~ gräbt(, fällt selbst hinein)** *(Prov)* you can easily fall into your own trap.

**Grübelei** *f* brooding *no pl.*

**grübeln** *vi* to brood *(über +acc* about, over*)*.

**Gruben-:** **~arbeiter** *m* miner, mineworker; **~gas** *nt* firedamp; **~unglück** *nt* pit *or* mine disaster.

**Grübler(in** *f) m* - brooder, brooding type.

**grüblerisch** *adj* pensive, brooding.

**Gruft** *f* ⁼e tomb, vault; *(in Kirchen)* crypt.

**grün** *adj* green; *(Pol auch)* ecologist. **~e Heringe** fresh herrings; **~er Salat** lettuce; **die G~e Insel** the Emerald Isle; **ein ~er Junge** *(col)* a greenhorn *(col)*; **~es Licht (für etw) geben** *(fig)* to give the go-ahead *or* green light (for sth); **vom ~en Tisch aus** from a bureaucratic ivory tower; **~e Minna** *(col)* police van, ≈ Black Maria *(Brit col)*, paddy wagon *(US col)*; **sich ~ und blau** *or* **gelb ärgern** *(col)* to be furious; **jdn ~ und blau schlagen** *(col)* to beat sb black and blue; **G~e Karte** *(Mot Insur)* green card; **der ~e Punkt** *symbol indicating recyclability of packaging*; **~e Welle** phased traffic lights; **~e Welle bei 60 km/h** traffic lights phased for 37 mph; **auf keinen ~en Zweig kommen** *(fig col)* to get nowhere; **die beiden sind sich gar nicht ~** *(col)* there's no love lost between them.

**Grün** *nt* - *or (col)* **~s** green; *(~flächen)* green spaces. **das ist dasselbe in G~** *(col)* it's the same thing; *siehe auch* **Grüne(r), Grüne(s)**.

**Grün-** *in cpds* green; **~anlage** *f* green space *or* area; **g~äugig** *adj* green-eyed; **g~blau** *adj* greenish blue.

**Grund** *m* ⁼e **(a)** *no pl (Erdboden, ~fläche)* ground. **~**

**und Boden** land; **in ~ und Boden** *(fig)* sich blamieren, schämen utterly; *verdammen* outright; **bis auf den ~ zerstören** to raze to the ground.

**(b)** *no pl (von Gefäßen, Becken etc)* bottom. **auf ~ laufen** *(Naut)* to run aground; **das Glas bis auf den ~ leeren** to drain the glass.

**(c)** *no pl (lit, fig: Fundament)* foundation(s *pl*); *(das Innerste)* depths *pl*. **von ~ auf** entirely, completely; **von ~ auf neu gebaut** rebuilt from scratch; **einer Sache** *(dat)* **auf den ~ gehen** *(fig)* to get to the bottom of sth; **im ~e (genommen)** basically, fundamentally.

**(d)** *(Ursache)* reason; *(Beweg~ auch)* grounds *pl*. **aus gesundheitlichen** *etc* **~en** for health *etc* reasons; **ohne ~** without reason; **auf ~ von** on the basis of; **auf ~ von Zeugenaussagen** on the strength of the witnesses' testimonies; **auf ~ einer Verwechslung** owing to a mistake; **ich habe ~ zu der Annahme, daß ...** I have reason to believe that ...; **einen ~ zum Feiern haben** to have good cause for (a) celebration; **du hast keinen ~ zum Klagen** you have no cause for complaint; **ich habe berechtigten ~ zu glauben, daß ...** I have good reason to believe that ...; **aus diesem ~** for this reason; **mit gutem ~** with good reason; **aus ~en** *(+gen)* for reasons (of).

**Grund-** *in cpds* basic; **~anstrich** *m* first coat; **~begriff** *m* basic concept; **~besitz** *m* land, property; *(das Besitzen)* ownership of land *or* property; **~besitzer** *m* landowner; **~buch** *nt* land register; **g~ehrlich** *adj* thoroughly honest; **~eigentum** *nt* = **~besitz**.

**gründen 1** *vt* to found; *Argument etc* to base *(auf +acc* on*)*; *Geschäft* to set up. **gegründet 1857** established *or* founded in 1857; **eine Familie ~** to get married (and have a family). **2** *vi* to be based *or* founded *(in +dat* on*)*. **3** *vr* **sich auf etw** *(acc)* **~** to be based *or* founded on sth.

**Gründer(in** *f) m* - founder.

**Grund-:** **g~falsch** *adj* utterly wrong; **~farbe** *f* primary colour *(Brit)* or color *(US)*; *(Grundton)* ground colour *(Brit)* or color *(US)*; **~festen** *pl (fig)* foundations *pl*; **etw bis in die ~festen erschüttern** to shake sth to its very foundations; **~fläche** *f (Math)* base; **~form** *f* basic form; *(Gram)* infinitive; **~freibetrag** *m* tax-free allowance; **~gebühr** *f* basic charge; **~gedanke** *m* basic idea.

**Grundgesetz** *nt (BRD Pol)* **das ~** the Constitution.

**grundgesetzwidrig** *adj* contrary to the Constitution, unconstitutional.

**Grundhaltung** *f* basic position.

**grundieren\*** *vt* to undercoat.

**Grundierung** *f* **(a)** *no pl (das Grundieren)* undercoating. **(b)** *(Farbe, Fläche)* undercoat.

**Grund-:** **~kapital** *nt* share capital; *(Anfangskapital)* initial capital; **~kenntnisse** *pl* basic knowledge *(in +dat* of*)*; **~kurs** *m* basic course; **~lage** *f* basis; **als ~lage für etw dienen** to serve as a basis for sth; **auf der ~lage** *+gen or* **von** on the basis of; **die ~lagen einer Wissenschaft** the fundamental principles of a science; **jeder ~lage entbehren** to be completely unfounded; **g~legend** *adj* fundamental, basic *(für* to*)*; *Werk* standard.

**gründlich 1** *adj* thorough; *Arbeit auch* painstaking. **2** *adv* thoroughly. **jdm ~ die Meinung sagen** to give sb a piece of one's mind; **da haben Sie sich ~ getäuscht** you're completely mistaken there.

**Gründlichkeit** *f no pl* thoroughness.

**Grund-:** **~linie** *f (Math, Sport)* baseline; **g~los 1** *adj* **(a)** *Tiefe etc* bottomless; **(b)** *(fig: unbegründet)* groundless, unfounded; **2** *adv (fig)* without reason; **~mauer** *f* foundation wall; **bis auf die ~mauern**

**niederbrennen** to be gutted; **~nahrungsmittel** *nt* basic food(stuff).

**Gründonnerstag** [gry:n-] *m* Maundy Thursday.

**Grund-**: **~ordnung** *f* basic order; **~pfeiler** *m* (*Archit*) supporting pier; *(fig)* cornerstone, keystone; **~rechenart** *f* basic arithmetical operation; **~recht** *nt* basic *or* constitutional right; **~regeln** *pl* ground rules *pl*; **~riß** *m* (*von Gebäude*) ground plan; *(Abriß)* outline, sketch.

**Grundsatz** *m* principle. **aus ~** on principle; **ein Mann mit Grundsätzen** a man of principle.

**grundsätzlich 1** *adj* fundamental; *Frage* of principle. **2** *adv* (*allgemein, im Prinzip*) in principle; *(aus Prinzip)* on principle; *(immer)* always. **ihre Meinungen sind ~ verschieden** their views are fundamentally different; **das ist ~ verboten** it is absolutely forbidden.

**Grundsatz|urteil** *nt* judgement that establishes a principle.

**Grund-**: **~schuld** *f* mortgage; **~schule** *f* primary (*Brit*) *or* elementary school; **~schüler** *m* primary (*Brit*) *or* elementary(-school) pupil; **~schullehrer** *m* primary (*Brit*) *or* elementary(-school) teacher; **~stein** *m* (*lit, fig*) foundation stone; **den ~stein zu etw legen** *(lit)* to lay the foundation stone of sth; *(fig)* to lay the foundations for sth; **~stellung** *f* (*Turnen, Chess*) starting position; **~steuer** *f* (local) property tax, ≈ council tax (*Brit*); **~stimmung** *f* prevailing mood; **~stock** *m* basis, foundation; **~stoff** *m* (*Rohstoff*) raw material; *(Chem)* element.

**Grundstück** *nt* plot (of land); *(Anwesen)* estate; *(Bau~ auch)* site; *(bebaut)* property.

**Grundstücksmakler** *m* estate agent (*Brit*), realtor (*US*).

**Grund-**: **~studium** *nt* (*Univ*) basic course; **~stufe** *f* first stage; *(Sch)* ≈ junior (*Brit*) *or* grade (*US*) school; **~ton** *m* (*Mus*) (*eines Akkords*) root; *(einer Tonleiter)* tonic keynote; *(~farbe)* ground colour (*Brit*) *or* color (*US*).

**Gründung** *f* founding, foundation; *(von Heim, Geschäft)* setting up. **die ~ einer Familie** starting a family.

**Grund-**: **g~verkehrt** *adj* completely wrong; **g~verschieden** *adj* totally *or* entirely different; **~wasser** *nt* ground water; **~wasserspiegel** *m* water table, ground-water level; **~wehrdienst** *m* national (*Brit*) *or* selective (*US*) service; **~wert** *m* (*Philos*) fundamental value; **~zug** *m* essential feature *or* trait; **etw in seinen ~zügen darstellen** to outline (the essentials of) sth.

**grünen** *vi* (*geh*) to turn green; *(fig: Liebe, Hoffnung)* to blossom (forth).

**Grüne(r)** *m decl as adj* (**a**) *(Pol)* ecologist, Green. **die ~n** *(als Partei)* the Greens, the Green Party. (**b**) *(dated col: Polizist)* cop *(col)*.

**Grüne(s)** *nt decl as adj* (*Gemüse*) greens *pl*, green vegetables *pl*. **ins ~ fahren** to go to the country.

**Grün-**: **~fläche** *f* green space *or* area; **~futter** *nt* green fodder, greenstuff; **g~gelb** *adj* greenish yellow; **~gürtel** *m* green belt; **~kohl** *m* (curly) kale; **g~lich** *adj* greenish; **~schnabel** *m* (*col*) (little) whippersnapper *(col)*; *(Neuling)* greenhorn *(col)*; **~span** *m no pl* verdigris; **~streifen** *m* central reservation (*Brit*), median (strip) (*US*); *(am Straßenrand)* grass verge.

**grunzen** *vti* to grunt.

**Gruppe** *f* **-n** group; *(von Mitarbeitern auch)* team; *(Mil)* ≈ squad; *(Klasse, Kategorie auch)* class.

**Gruppen-** *in cpds* group; **~arbeit** *f* teamwork; **~bild** *nt* group portrait; **~führer** *m* group leader; *(Mil)* squad leader; **~reise** *f* group travel *no pl*;

**~sex** *m* group sex; **~sieg** *m* (*Sport*) **den ~sieg erringen** to win in one's group; **~sieger** *m* (*Sport*) group winnner; **g~spezifisch** *adj* group specific; **~therapie** *f* group therapy; **g~weise** *adv* in groups; *(Ind, Comm, Sport auch)* in teams; *(Mil)* in squads.

**gruppieren*** *vtr* to group.

**Gruppierung** *f* grouping; *(Gruppe)* group; *(Pol auch)* faction.

**Gruselfilm** *m* horror film.

**grus(e)lig** *adj* horrifying, gruesome.

**gruseln 1** *vti impers* **mich** *or* **mir gruselt auf Friedhöfen** cemeteries give me the creeps. **2** *vr* **hier würde ich mich ~** a place like this would give me the creeps.

**Gruß** *m* ⁓e (**a**) greeting; *(~geste, Mil)* salute. **er ging ohne ~ an mir vorbei** he walked past me without saying hello; **viele ~e** best wishes *(an +acc to)*; **sag ihm einen schönen ~** say hello to him (from me); **einen (schönen) ~ an Ihre Gattin!** my regards to your wife. (**b**) *(als Briefformel)* **mit bestem ~** *or* **besten ~en** yours; **mit freundlichem ~** *or* **freundlichen ~en** *(bei Anrede Mr/Mrs/Miss/Ms X)* Yours sincerely, Yours truly *(esp US)*; *(bei Anrede Sir(s)/ Madam)* Yours faithfully, Yours truly *(esp US)*.

**Gruß-**: **~adresse, ~botschaft** *f* message of greeting.

**grüßen 1** *vt* (**a**) to greet; *(Mil)* to salute. **grüß dich!** *(col)* hello there!, hi! *(col)*. (**b**) *(Grüße übermitteln)* **~ Sie ihn von mir** give him my regards; **grüß dich (schön) ~** Otto sends his regards. **2** *vi* to say hello; *(Mil)* to salute. **Otto läßt ~** Otto sends his regards.

**Gruß-**: **~formel** *f* form of greeting; *(am Briefanfang)* salutation; *(am Briefende)* complimentary close, ending; **~telegramm** *nt* greetings telegram; *(Pol)* goodwill telegram; **~wort** *nt* greeting.

**Grütze** *f* **-n** (**a**) groats *pl*, grits (*US*); *(Brei)* gruel. **rote ~** (type of) red fruit jelly. (**b**) *no pl (col: Verstand)* brains *(col)*.

**Guatemala** *nt* Guatemala.

**Guatemalteke** *m*, **Guatemaltekin** *f* Guatemalan.

**guatemaltekisch** *adj* Guatemalan.

**gucken** ['gʊkn, (*NGer*) 'kʊkn] **1** *vi* (*sehen*) to look *(zu* at*)*; *(heimlich auch)* to peep, to peek; *(hervorschauen)* to peep *(aus* out of*)*. **laß mal ~!** let's have a look. **2** *vt (col)* **Fernsehen ~** to watch television *or* telly (*Brit col*).

**Gucker** *m* **-** *(col)* (**a**) *(Fernglas)* telescope; *(Opernglas)* opera glass(es). (**b**) *pl (Augen)* optics *(col)*, peepers *(col)*.

**Guck-**: **~kasten** *m* (*col: Fernseher*) telly (*Brit col*), tube (*US col*); **~loch** *nt* peephole.

**Guerilla¹** [geˈrɪlja] *f* **-s** (**a**) *(~krieg)* guerilla warfare. (**b**) *(~einheit)* guerilla unit.

**Guerilla²** [geˈrɪlja] *m* **-s** *(~kämpfer)* guerilla.

**Guerillero** [gerilˈjeːro] *m* **-s** guerilla fighter.

**Guinea** [giˈneːa] *nt* Guinea.

**Gulasch** *nt or m or -e or -s* goulash.

**Gulasch-**: **~kanone** *f (Mil sl)* field kitchen; **~suppe** *f* goulash soup.

**Gulden** *m* **-** *(niederländisch)* g(u)ilder, gulden.

**Gully** ['gʊli] *m or nt* **-s** drain.

**gültig** *adj* valid. **nach den ~en Bestimmungen** according to current regulations; **ab wann ist der Fahrplan ~?** when does the timetable come into force?; **~ werden** to become valid; *(Gesetz, Vertrag)* to come into effect; *(Münze)* to become legal tender.

**Gültigkeit** *f no pl* validity; *(von Gesetz)* legal force. **das Fünfmarkstück verliert im Herbst seine ~** the five mark piece ceases to be legal tender in the autumn.

**Gummi** *nt or m* **-s** *(Material)* rubber; *(Radier~)* rubber *(Brit)*, eraser; *(~band)* rubber *or* elastic *(Brit)* band; *(in Kleidung etc)* elastic; *(col: Kondom)* rubber *(col)*, Durex ®.

**Gummi-** *in cpds* rubber; **g~artig 1** *adj* rubbery; **2** *adv* like rubber; **~band** *nt* rubber *or* elastic *(Brit)* band; *(in Kleidung)* elastic; **~bärchen** *nt* jelly baby; **~baum** *m* rubber plant; **~boot** *nt* rubber dinghy.

**gummieren\*** *vt* to gum.

**Gummierung** *f (gummierte Fläche)* gum.

**Gummi-:** **~geschoß** *nt* rubber bullet; **~knüppel** *m* rubber truncheon *(Brit) or* billy *(US)*; **~linse** *f* *(Phot)* zoom lens; **~paragraph** *m (col)* ambiguous clause; **~reifen** *m* rubber tyre *(Brit) or* tire *(US)*; **~schlauch** *m* rubber hose; *(bei Fahrrad etc)* inner tube; **~stiefel** *m* rubber boot, wellington (boot) *(Brit)*; **~strumpf** *m* elastic stocking; **~wuchtgeschoß** *nt* rubber bullet; **~zelle** *f* padded cell; **~zug** *m* (piece of) elastic.

**Gunst** *f no pl* favour *(Brit)*, favor *(US)*; *(Wohlwollen auch)* goodwill; *(des Schicksals etc)* benevolence. **zu meinen/deinen ~en** in my/your favour; **jdm eine ~ erweisen** *(geh)* to do sb a kindness; **in jds ~** *(dat)* **stehen** to be in favour with sb.

**günstig** *adj* favourable *(Brit)*, favorable *(US)*; *(zeitlich, bei Reisen etc)* convenient; *Angebot, Preis etc* reasonable, good. **jdm/einer Sache ~ gesinnt sein** *(geh)* to be favourably disposed towards sb/sth; **bei ~er Witterung** weather permitting; **die Stadt liegt ~ (für)** the town is well situated (for); **wie komme ich am ~sten nach ...?** what's the best *or* easiest way to get to ...?; **im ~sten Fall(e)** at best; **etw ~ kaufen/verkaufen** to buy/sell sth for a good price; **DM 30?, das war aber ~ 30** marks?, that was a bargain.

**günstigstenfalls** *adv* at the very best.

**Günstling** *m (pej)* favourite *(Brit)*, favorite *(US)*.

**Günstlingswirtschaft** *f (pej)* favouritism *(Brit)*, favoritism *(US)*.

**Gurgel** *f* **-n** throat; *(Schlund)* gullet. **jdm die ~ zudrücken** *or* **abschnüren** *(lit, fig)* to strangle sb; **dann springt sie mir an die ~!** *(col)* she'll kill me for that *(col)*.

**gurgeln** *vi* **(a)** *(den Rachen spülen)* to gargle. **(b)** *(Wasser, Laut)* to gurgle.

**Gurke** *f* **-n (a)** cucumber; *(Essig~)* gherkin. **saure ~n** pickled gherkins. **(b)** *(hum col: Nase)* hooter *(col)*.

**Gurken-:** **~hobel** *m* slicer; **~salat** *m* cucumber salad.

**gurren** *vi (lit, fig)* to coo.

**Gurt** *m* **-e** *(Gürtel, Sicherheits~)* belt; *(Riemen)* strap.

**Gürtel** *m* **-** belt. **den ~ enger schnallen** *(lit, fig)* to tighten one's belt.

**Gürtel-:** **~linie** *f* waist; **ein Schlag unter die ~linie** *(lit)* a punch/blow below the belt; **das war ein Schlag unter die ~linie** *(fig)* that really was below the belt; **~reifen** *m* radial (tyre *(Brit)* or tire *US)*; **~rose** *f (Med)* shingles *sing or pl*; **~tier** *nt* armadillo.

**Guru** *m* **-s** *(lit, fig)* guru.

**GUS** [ge:|u:'|ɛs] *f* = **Gemeinschaft Unabhängiger Staaten** CIS.

**Guß** *m, pl* **Güsse (a)** *(Metal)* casting, founding; *(~stück)* cast. **(wie) aus einem ~ sein** *(fig)* to be a unified whole. **(b)** *(Strahl)* stream, gush; *(col: Regen~)* cloudburst, downpour. **(c)** *(Zucker~)* icing, frosting *(US)*; *(durchsichtig)* glaze.

**Guß-:** **~eisen** *nt* cast iron; **g~eisern** *adj* cast-iron; **~form** *f* mould *(Brit)*, mold *(US)*.

**gut** *comp* **besser,** *superl* **beste(r, s)** *or (adv)* **am besten 1** *adj* good. **probieren Sie unsere ~en Weine/Speisen!** try our fine wines/food; **er ist in der Schule/in Spanisch sehr ~** he's very good at school/Spanish; **das ist ~ gegen** *or* **für** *(col)* **Husten** it's good for coughs; **wozu ist das ~?** *(col)* what's that for?; **sei so ~ (und) gib mir das** would you mind giving me that; **dafür ist er sich zu ~** he wouldn't stoop to that sort of thing; **sind die Bilder ~ geworden?** did the pictures turn out all right?; **es wird alles wieder ~!** everything will be all right; **wie ~, daß ...** how fortunate that ...; **~, daß du das endlich einsiehst** it's a good thing you realize it at last; **ich will es damit ~ sein lassen** I'll leave it at that; **laß mal ~ sein!** that'll do; **jetzt ist aber ~!** *(col)* that's enough; **das ist ja alles ~ und schön, aber ...** that's all very well but ...; **ein ~es Pfund Reis** a good pound of rice; **~!** good; *(in Ordnung)* (all) right, OK; **also ~!** all right *or* OK then; **du bist ~!** *(col)* you're a fine one!

**2** *adv* well. **~ schmecken/riechen** to taste/smell good; **sie spricht ~ Schwedisch** she speaks good Swedish; **er hat es in seiner Jugend nicht ~ gehabt** he had a hard time (of it) when he was young; **du hast es ~!** you've got it made; **das kann ~ sein** that may well be; **so ~ wie nichts** next to nothing; **so ~ wie nicht** hardly, scarcely; **so ~ wie verloren** as good as lost; **so ~ ich kann** as well as I can; **es dauert ~ drei Stunden** it lasts a good three hours; **~ und gern** easily; **paß ~ auf!** be very careful; **ich kann ihn jetzt nicht ~ im Stich lassen** I can't very well let him down now.

**Gut** *nt* **~er (a)** *(Eigentum)* property; *(lit, fig: Besitztum)* possession. **irdische ~er** worldly goods. **(b)** *no pl (das Gute)* good. **~ und Böse** good and evil. **(c)** *(Ware, Fracht~)* item. **~er** goods; *(Fracht~)* freight *sing*, goods *(esp Brit)*. **(d)** *(Land~)* estate.

**Gut-:** **~achten** *nt* - expert opinion, report; **~achter(in** *f)* *m* - expert; *(Schätzer auch)* valuer, valuator; *(Jur: Prozeß)* expert witness; **g~artig** *adj* *Kind, Hund etc* good-natured; *Geschwür* benign; **g~aussehend** *adj* good-looking; **g~bezahlt** *adj attr* well-paid; **g~bürgerlich** *adj* solid middle-class; *Küche* homely, good plain; **~dünken** *nt no pl* discretion; **nach (eigenem) ~dünken** at one's own discretion.

**Güte** *f no pl* **(a)** *(Herzens~, Freundlichkeit)* goodness, kindness. **würden Sie die ~ haben, zu ...** *(form, iro)* would you have the goodness *or* kindness to ...; **ein Vorschlag zur ~** a conciliatory proposal; **ach du liebe** *or* **meine ~!** *(col)* goodness me! **(b)** *(einer Ware)* quality.

**Güteklasse** *f (Comm)* grade.

**Gute(r)** *mf decl as adj* **der/die ~** the dear kind soul; *(mitleidig)* the poor soul; **die ~n und die Bösen** the good and the bad; *(col: in Filmen etc)* the goodies and the baddies *(col)*.

**Güter-:** **~abfertigung** *f* **(a)** *no pl* dispatch of freight *or* goods *(esp Brit)*; **(b)** *(Abfertigungsstelle)* freight *or* goods *(esp Brit)* office; **~bahnhof** *m* freight *or* goods *(esp Brit)* depot; **~fernverkehr** *m* long-distance haulage; **~trennung** *f (Jur)* separation of property; **in ~trennung leben** to have separation of property; **~verkehr** *m* freight *or* goods *(esp Brit)* traffic; **~wagen** *m (Rail)* freight car *(US)*, goods truck *(Brit)*; **~zug** *m* freight *or* goods *(esp Brit)* train.

**Gute(s)** *nt decl as adj* **~s tun** to do good; **alles ~!** all the best!; **das führt zu nichts ~m** it'll lead to no good; **das ist des ~n zuviel** that is too much of a good thing; **das ~ daran** the good thing about it;

das ~ **im Menschen** the good in man; **sich im g~n einigen** to reach an amicable agreement; **ich sage es dir noch einmal im g~n** I'm telling you this just once more.

**Güte-: ~siegel** *nt (Comm)* stamp of quality; **~zeichen** *nt* mark of quality; *(fig auch)* hallmark.

**Gut-: g~gehen** *sep irreg aux sein* **1** *vi impers* **es geht ihm g~** he is doing well *or* nicely; *(er ist gesund)* he is well; **sonst geht's dir g~!** *(iro)* are you in your right mind?; **2** *vi* to go (off) well; **das ist noch einmal g~gegangen** it turned out all right; **g~gehend** *adj attr* thriving; **g~gelaunt** *adj* cheerful, in a good mood; **g~gemeint** *adj attr* well-meant; **g~gläubig** *adj* trusting; *(vertrauensselig auch)* credulous; **~gläubigkeit** *f siehe adj* trusting nature; credulity; **g~haben** *vt sep irreg* **etw g~haben** to have sth coming (to one) *(col) (bei from)*; **~haben** *nt* - *(Fin, Bank~)* credit; **auf meinem Konto ist ein ~haben von DM500** my account is 500 marks in credit; **g~heißen** *vt sep irreg* to approve of; *(genehmigen)* to approve; **g~herzig** *adj* kind-hearted; **~herzigkeit** *f* kind-heartedness.

**gütig** *adj* kind; *(edelmütig)* gracious.

**gütlich** *adj* amicable. **sich an etw** *(dat)* **~ tun** to make free with sth.

**Gut-: g~machen** *vt sep* **(a)** *(in Ordnung bringen) Fehler* to put right, to correct; *Schaden* to make good; **(b)** *(gewinnen)* to make *(bei* out of, on*)*; **g~mütig** *adj* good-natured; **~mütigkeit** *f* good-naturedness; **g~nachbarlich** **1** *adj* neighbourly*(Brit)*, neighborly *(US)*; **2** *adv* as good neighbours *(Brit)* or neighbors *(US)*.

**Gutsbesitzer(in** *f) m* lord of the manor; *(als Klasse)* landowner.

**Gut-: ~schein** *m* voucher, coupon; *(für Umtausch)* credit note; **g~schreiben** *vt sep irreg* to credit *(dat to)*; **~schrift** *f (Bescheinigung)* credit note; *(Betrag)* credit (item).

**Guts-: ~haus** *nt* manor (house); **~herr** *m* squire, lord of the manor; **~herrin** *f* lady of the manor; **~hof** *m* estate.

**gut-: ~situiert** *adj attr* well-off; **~tun** *vi sep irreg* **jdm ~tun** to do sb good; **das tut ~** that's good; **~unterrichtet** *adj attr* well-informed; **~verdienend** *adj attr* with a good salary, high-income; **~willig** *adj* willing; *(nicht böswillig)* well-meaning.

**Guyana** *nt* Guyana.

**Gymnasiallehrer** ≃ grammar school teacher *(Brit)*, high school teacher *(US)*.

**Gymnasiast(in** *f) m (wk)* **-en, -en** ≃ grammar school pupil *(Brit)*, high school student *(US)*.

**Gymnasium** *nt (Sch)* ≃ grammar school *(Brit)*, high school *(US)*.

**Gymnastik** *f* keep-fit exercises *pl*; *(Turnen)* gymnastics *sing.* **~ machen** to do keep-fit (exercises)/gymnastics.

**Gymnastikanzug** *m* leotard.

**gymnastisch** *adj* gymnastic.

**Gynäkologe** *m*, **Gynäkologin** *f* gynaecologist *(Brit)*, gynecologist *(US)*.

**Gynäkologie** *f* gynaecology *(Brit)*, gynecology *(US)*.

**gynäkologisch** *adj* gynaecological *(Brit)*, gynecological *(US)*.

**Gyros** ['giros] *nt no pl* ≃ doner kebab.

# H

**H, h** [haː] *nt* -, - H, h; *(Mus)* B. **H wie Heinrich** ≃ H for Harry, H for How *(US)*.

**h** = **hora/horae** *(Stunde/Stunden)* h.

**ha** = **Hektar** hectare.

**Haag** *m:* **Den ~** The Hague.

**Haar** *nt* -e hair. **sie hat schönes ~ or schöne ~e** she has nice hair; **~e auf den Zähnen haben** to be a tough customer *(Brit)* or cookie *(US)*; **~e lassen (müssen)** to come off badly; **jdm kein ~ krümmen** not to harm a hair of sb's head; **darüber laß dir keine grauen ~e wachsen** don't lose any sleep over it; **jdm aufs ~ gleichen** to be the spitting image of sb; **das ist an den ~en herbeigezogen** that's rather far-fetched; **an jdm kein gutes ~ lassen** to pull sb to pieces; **sich** *(dat)* **in die ~e kriegen** *(col)* to quarrel; **sich** *(dat)* **in den ~en liegen** to be at loggerheads; **jdm die ~e vom Kopf fressen** *(col)* to eat sb out of house and home; **um ein ~** very nearly.

**Haar-:** **~ansatz** *m* hairline; **~ausfall** *m* hair loss; **~breit** *nt:* **um kein ~breit** not an inch; **~bürste** *f* hairbrush; **~büschel** *nt* tuft of hair.

**haaren** *vi (auch vr: Tier)* to moult *(Brit)*, to molt *(US)*; *(Pelz, Teppich)* to shed.

**Haar|ersatz** *m (form)* hairpiece; *(Perücke)* wig.

**Haaresbreite** *f inv* **um ~** almost, very nearly; **verfehlen** by a hair's breadth; **er wich nicht um ~ von seiner Meinung ab** he did not change his opinion one iota.

**Haar-:** **~farbe** *f* hair colour; **~festiger** *m* - (hair) setting lotion; **h~genau** *adj* exact; **jdm etw h~genau erklären** to explain sth to sb in great detail; **das trifft h~genau zu** that's absolutely right.

**haarig** *adj* hairy; *(col) (heikel)* tricky; *(gefährlich)* hairy *(col)*; *(schwierig)* nasty.

**Haar-:** **~klammer** *f* hairgrip *(Brit)*, barrette *(US)*; **h~klein** *adv* in minute detail; **~klemme** *f* = **~klammer**; **~mode** *f* hairstyle; **~nadel** *f* hairpin; **~nadelkurve** *f* hairpin bend; **~netz** *nt* hairnet; **~pflege** *f* hair care; **h~scharf** *adj Beschreibung* exact; **das hat ihn h~scharf verfehlt** it only missed him by a hair's breadth; **~schleife** *f* bow, hair ribbon; **~schnitt** *m* haircut; **~schopf** *m* mop or shock of hair; **~sieb** *nt* fine sieve; **~spalter(in** *f)* *m* - pedant, hairsplitter; **~spalterei** *f* splitting hairs *no indef art, no pl*; **h~spalterisch** *adj* hairsplitting; **~spange** *f* hair slide, barrette *(US)*; **~spitze** *f* end (of a hair); **~spray** *nt or m* hair spray; **~strähne** *f* strand or *(dünner)* wisp of hair; **h~sträubend** *adj* hair-raising; *(unglaublich)* Frechheit incredible; **~teil** *nt* hairpiece; **~töner** *m* - hair-tinting lotion; **~trockner** *m* - hair dryer; **~waschmittel** *nt* shampoo; **~wasser** *nt* hair lotion; **~wuchs** *m* growth of hair; **einen kräftigen ~wuchs haben** to have a thick head of hair; **~wuchsmittel** *nt* hair restorer.

**Hab** *nt:* **~ und Gut** *sing* possessions *pl*, belongings *pl*, worldly goods *pl*.

**Habe** *f no pl (geh)* possessions *pl*, belongings *pl*.

**haben** *pret* **hatte**, *ptp* **gehabt 1** *vt* to have, to have got *(esp Brit)*. **ich habe eine Idee** I have or I've got *(esp Brit)* an idea; **ein Meter hat 100 cm** there are 100 cm in a metre; **da hast du 10 Mark** there's 10 marks; **die ~'s (ja)** *(col)* they can afford it; **wie hätten Sie es gern?** how would you like it?; **ich kann das nicht ~** *(col)* I can't stand it; **Ferien ~** to be on holiday; **Hunger/Angst/Sorgen ~** to be hungry/afraid/worried; **was hat er denn?** what's the matter with him?; **hast du was?** are you all right?, is (there) something the matter with you?; **was ~ wir heute für ein Wetter?** what's the weather like today?; **heute ~ wir 10°** it's 10° today; **es gut/schön ~** to have it good/nice; **sie hat es warm in ihrem Zimmer** it's warm in her room; **er hat es nicht leicht mit ihr** he has a hard time (of it) with her; **es am Herzen ~** *(col)* to have heart trouble; **es in den Beinen ~** *(col)* to have trouble with one's legs; **er hat es mit dem Malen** *(col)* he has a thing about painting *(col)*; **du hast zu gehorchen** *(müssen)* you must obey; **ich habe zu tun** I'm busy; **etw auf dem Boden liegen ~** to have sth lying on the floor; **etw ist zu ~** *(erhältlich)* sth is to be had; **er/sie ist zu ~** *(col) (nicht verheiratet)* he/she is single; *(sexuell)* he/she is available; **für etw zu ~ sein** to be keen on sth; **er/ein gutes Essen ist er immer zu ~** he's always willing to have a good meal; **ich hab's** *(col)* I've got it, I know; **du kannst mich gern ~!** *(col)* get lost! *(col)*; **da hast du's/~ wir's!** *(col)* there you/we are; **woher hast du denn das?** where did you get that from?; **wie gehabt!** *(wie gewöhnlich)* as usual; **wie gehabt!** some things don't change; **sie hat eine nette Art an sich** *(dat)* she has a nice way with her; **sie werden schon merken, was sie an ihm ~** they'll see how valuable he is; **etwas mit jdm ~** *(col)* to have a thing with sb *(col)*; **das hast du jetzt davon** now see what's happened (as a result); **etwas/nichts von etw ~** *(col)* to get something/nothing out of sth; **nichts von etw ~** *(col)* to get nothing out of sth; **die blonden Haare hat sie von ihrem Vater** she gets her blond hair from her father; **er hat etwas von einem Charmeur (an sich** *dat)* there's something of the charmer about him; **dieses Werk von Braque hat viel von Picasso** this work by Braque owes much to Picasso.

**2** *vr (col: sich anstellen)* to make a fuss. **was hast du dich denn so?** what are you making such a fuss about?

**3** *vr impers (col)* **und damit hat es sich** and that's that; **die Sache hat sich** *(ist erledigt)* that's done.

**4** *aux* **ich habe/hatte gerufen** I have/had called, I've/I'd called; **ich habe gestern angerufen** I called yesterday; **du hättest den Brief früher schreiben können** you could have written the letter earlier; **etw getan ~** to have done sth.

**Haben** *nt no pl* credit. **im ~ stehen** to be on the credit side.

**Habenichts** *m* -e *(pej)* have-not.

**Haben-:** ~**seite** f credit side; ~**zinsen** pl interest on credit sing.

**Hab-:** ~**gier** f greed, acquisitiveness; **h~gierig** adj greedy, acquisitive; **h~haft** adj (geh) jds/einer Sache **h~haft werden** to get hold of sb/sth.

**Habicht** m -e hawk.

**Habilitation** f (Lehrberechtigung) postdoctoral lecturing qualification.

**habilitieren*** vr to qualify as a university lecturer.

**Habit** nt or m -e (Ordenskleid) habit.

**Hab-:** ~**schaft** f, ~**seligkeiten** pl belongings pl; ~**sucht** f greed, acquisitiveness; **h~süchtig** adj greedy, acquisitive.

**Hachse** ['haksə] f -n = **Haxe**.

**Hack-:** ~**beil** nt chopper, cleaver; ~**block** m chopping block; ~**braten** m meat loaf; ~**brett** nt (a) chopping board; **(b)** (Mus) dulcimer.

**Hacke¹** f -n (Ferse, Absatz) heel.

**Hacke²** f -n (Pickel) pickaxe (Brit), pickax (US); (Garten~) hoe.

**hacken 1** vt (zerkleinern) to chop; (im Fleischwolf) to mince (Brit), to grind (US); Garten to hoe; Loch to hack; (Vogel) to peck. **2** vi **(a)** to hack (nach at); (Vogel) to peck (nach at); (im Garten) to hoe. **(b)** (Comp) to hack (in +acc into).

**Hacker** m - (Comp) hacker.

**Hack-:** ~**fleisch** nt mince (Brit), minced (Brit) or ground (US) meat; **aus jdm ~fleisch machen** (col) to make mincemeat of sb (col); ~**klotz** m chopping block; ~**ordnung** f (lit, fig) pecking order.

**Häcksel** nt or m no pl chaff.

**hadern** vi (dated, geh) (streiten) to quarrel; (unzufrieden sein) to be at odds.

**Hafen** m ꞊ **(a)** harbour (Brit), harbor (US); (Handels~) port; (~anlagen) docks pl. **in den ~ einlaufen** to put into harbour/port. **(b)** (fig) haven. **in den ~ der Ehe einlaufen** to enter the state of matrimony.

**Hafen-** in cpds harbour (Brit), harbor (US); port; ~**anlagen** pl docks pl; ~**arbeiter** m dockworker, docker; ~**gebühren** pl harbour (Brit) or harbor (US) dues pl; ~**polizei** f harbour (Brit) or harbor (US) police; ~**rundfahrt** f (boat-)trip round the harbour (Brit) or harbor (US); ~**stadt** f port; (am Meer auch) seaport; ~**viertel** nt dock area.

**Hafer** m - oats pl. **ihn sticht der ~** (col) he's feeling his oats (col).

**Hafer-:** ~ **brei** m porridge; ~**flocken** pl rolled oats pl; ~**korn** nt (oat) grain; ~**mehl** nt oatmeal; ~**schleim** m gruel.

**Haff** nt -s or -e lagoon.

**Haft** f no pl (vor dem Prozeß) custody; (~strafe) imprisonment; (~zeit) prison sentence; (politisch) detention. **sich in ~ befinden** to be in custody/prison/detention; **eine schwere ~ verhängen** to impose a long term of imprisonment; **in ~ nehmen** to take into custody, to detain.

**Haft-:** ~**anstalt** f detention centre (Brit) or center (US); **h~bar** adj (für jdn) legally responsible; (für etw) (legally) liable; ~**befehl** m warrant; **einen ~befehl gegen jdn ausstellen** to issue a warrant for sb's arrest; ~**dauer** f term of imprisonment.

**haften¹** vi (Jur) **für jdn ~** to be (legally) responsible for sb; **für etw ~** to be (legally) liable for sth; **die Versicherung hat für den Schaden nicht gehaftet** the insurance company did not accept liability (for the damage); **für Garderobe kann nicht gehaftet werden** all articles are left at owner's risk.

**haften²** vi (lit, fig) to stick (an +dat to); (Reifen, Phys) to adhere (an +dat to); (Rauch, Geruch) to cling (an +dat to); (Blick) to become fixed.

**haftenbleiben** vi sep irreg aux sein (lit, fig) to stick

(an or auf +dat to); (Geruch) to cling; (Phys) to adhere.

**Häftling** m prisoner; (politisch auch) detainee.

**Haft-:** ~**pflicht** f (Schadenersatzpflicht) (legal) liability; **h~pflichtig** adj liable; **h~pflichtversichert** adj **h~pflichtversichert sein** to have personal or public (US) liability insurance; (Aut) ꞊ to have third-party insurance; ~**pflichtversicherung** f personal or public (US) liability insurance no indef art; (Aut) ꞊ third-party insurance; ~**richter** m magistrate; ~**schalen** pl contact lenses pl; ~**strafe** f prison sentence; **h~unfähig** adj (Jur) not fit enough to be kept in prison.

**Haftung** f **(a)** (Jur) (legal) liability; (für Personen) (legal) responsibility. **(b)** (Tech, Phys, von Reifen) adhesion.

**Hage-:** ~**butte** f -n rose hip; ~**dorn** m hawthorn.

**Hagel** m no pl (lit, fig) hail.

**Hagelkorn** nt hailstone.

**hageln 1** vi impers **es hagelt** it's hailing. **2** vi etw hagelt auf jdn (lit, fig) sth hails down on sb. **3** vt impers (lit) to hail (down). **es hagelte etw** (fig) sth hailed down.

**Hagel-:** ~**schauer** m (short) hailstorm; ~**schlag** m (Met) hail; ~**sturm** m hailstorm.

**hager** adj gaunt, thin.

**Häher** m - jay.

**Hahn** m ꞊e **(a)** (männlicher Vogel) cock; (jünger) cockerel. **~ im Korb sein** (col) to be cock of the walk; **danach kräht kein ~ mehr** (col) no one cares two hoots about that any more (col). **(b)** pl auch -en (Tech) tap, faucet (US). **(c)** (Abzug) trigger.

**Hähnchen** nt (Cook) chicken.

**Hahnen-:** ~**fuß** m (Bot) buttercup; ~**schrei** m cockcrow; **beim ersten ~schrei** (fig) at cockcrow.

**Hai(fisch)** m -e (lit, fig) shark.

**Hain** m -(e)s, -e (poet, geh) grove (liter).

**Haiti** [ha'i:ti] nt Haiti.

**Häkchen** nt **(a)** (Sew) (small) hook. **(b)** (Zeichen) tick, check (US).

**häkeln** vti to crochet.

**Häkelnadel** f crochet hook.

**haken 1** vi (klemmen) to stick. **es hakt** (fig) there's a hold-up; **es hakt (bei jdm)** (col: nicht verstehen) sb is stuck. **2** vt (befestigen) to hook (an +acc to).

**Haken** m - **(a)** hook (auch Boxen). **die Sache hat einen ~** (col) there's a snag or a catch; **einen ~ schlagen** to dart sideways. **(b)** (Zeichen) tick, check (US).

**Haken-:** ~**kreuz** nt swastika; ~**nase** f hooked nose; **h~nasig** adj hook-nosed.

**halb 1** adj half. **ein ~er Meter** etc half a metre etc; **der ~e Tag** etc half the day etc; **eine ~e Stunde** half an hour; **alle ~e Stunde** every half hour; **ein ~es Jahr** six months pl; **auf ~em Wege** or ~**er Strecke** halfway; **zum ~en Preis** (at) half price; **Kleid mit ~em Arm** dress with half-length sleeves; **eine ~e Note** (Mus) a minim (Brit), a half-note (US); **ein ~er Ton** (Mus) a semitone; ~**e Pause** (Mus) minim/half-note rest; **~ zehn** half past nine, half nine (col); **fünf (Minuten) vor/nach ~ zwei** twenty-five (minutes) past one/to two; ~**e Arbeit leisten** to do a bad job; **die ~e Wahrheit** half of the truth; **nichts H~es und nichts Ganzes** neither one thing nor the other; **mit ~em Ohr** with half an ear; **sich nur wie ein ~er Mensch fühlen** to feel only half a person; **keine ~en Sachen machen** not to do things by halves; **die ~e Stadt/Welt** half the town/world; **sie ist schon eine ~e Schottin** she is already half Scottish; **(noch) ein ~es Kind sein** to be scarcely more than a child.

**2** adv half; (beinahe) almost. **die Zeit ist ~ vorbei**

half the time has already gone; ~ **so gut** half as good; **etw nur ~ verstehen** to only half understand something; **ich hörte nur ~ zu** I was only half listening; **das ist ~ so schlimm** it's not as bad as all that; *(Zukünftiges)* that won't be too bad; **etw nur ~ machen** to only half do sth *(col)*; **wir haben uns ~ totgelacht** we almost died laughing; **mit jdm ~e-~e machen** *(col)* to go halves with sb; **gefällt es dir? — ~ und ~** do you like it? — sort of *(col)*.

**Halb-** *in cpds* half; **h~amtlich** *adj* semi-official; **~bildung** *f* smattering of knowledge *(pej)*; **h~bitter** *adj Schokolade* semi-sweet; **~blut** *nt no pl (Mensch)* half-breed; *(Tier)* crossbreed; **~bruder** *m* half-brother; **~dunkel** *nt* semi-darkness; *(Dämmerung)* twilight; **~edelstein** *m* semi-precious stone.

**Halbe(r)** *m or f decl as adj (col)* half a litre *(Brit)* or liter *(US)* (of beer).

**halber** *prep +gen (nachgestellt) (dated, geh) (wegen)* on account of; *(um ... willen)* for the sake of.

**Halb-:** **h~fertig** *adj attr* half-finished; *(fig)* immature; **h~fest** *adj attr Zustand, Materie* semi-solid; *Gelee* half-set; **h~fett** *adj* **(a)** *(Typ)* semibold, secondary bold; **(b)** *Käse* medium-fat; **~finale** *nt* semi-final; **h~gar** *adj attr* half-cooked; **~gott** *m (Myth, fig)* demigod; **~götter in Weiß** *(iro)* doctors; **~heit** *f (pej)* half-measure; **er ist nicht für ~heiten** he is not one for half-measures; **h~herzig** *adj* half-hearted.

**halbieren\*** *vt* to halve; *(schneiden)* to cut in half.

**Halbierung** *f* halving.

**Halb-:** **~insel** *f* peninsula; **~jahr** *nt* half-year *(auch Comm)*, six months; **h~jährig** *adj attr Kind* six-month-old; *Lehrgang etc* six-month; **h~jährlich 1** *adj* half-yearly *(auch Comm)*, six-monthly; **2** *adv* every six months, twice yearly; **~kreis** *m* semicircle; **~kugel** *f* hemisphere; **nördliche/südliche ~kugel** northern/southern hemisphere; **h~lang** *adj Rock* mid-calf length; *Haar* chin-length; **(nun) mach mal h~lang!** *(col)* now wait a minute!; **h~laut 1** *adj* low; **2** *adv* in a low voice; **h~leer** *adj* half-empty; **h~leinen** *adj attr Stoff* fifty per cent linen; **~leiter** *m (Phys)* semiconductor; **h~links** *adv (Sport) spielen* (at) inside left; **h~links abbiegen** to fork left; **das Auto kam von h~links** the car came at an angle from the left; **h~mast** *adv* at half-mast; **h~matt** *adj (Phot)* semimatt; **~messer** *m* radius; **~metall** *nt* semi-metal; **h~mond** *m* half-moon; *(Symbol)* crescent; **wir haben ~mond** there's a half-moon; **h~nackt** *adj attr* half-naked; **h~offen** *adj attr* half-open; **~pension** *f* half-board *(Brit)*, European plan *(US)*; **h~rechts** *adv (Sport) spielen* (at) inside right; **h~rechts abbiegen** to fork right; **das Auto kam von h~rechts** the car came at an angle from the right; **h~reif** *adj attr* half-ripe; **h~rund** *adj attr* semicircular; **~rund** *nt* semicircle, half circle; **im ~rund** in a semicircle; **~schatten** *m* half shadow; **~schlaf** *m* light sleep, doze; **im ~schlaf sein** to be half asleep; **~schuh** *m* shoe; **~schwergewichtler** *m* light-heavyweight; **~schwester** *f* half-sister; **~seide** *f* fifty per cent silk; **h~seiden** *adj (lit)* fifty per cent silk; *(fig) Dame* fast; *(homosexuell)* gay; **h~seidenes Milieu** demimonde; **h~seitig** *adj Anzeige* half-page; **h~seitig gelähmt** hemiplegic; **~starke(r)** *m decl as adj* hooligan, rowdy; **h~stündlich** *adj, adv* half-hourly; **h~tags** *adv* in the mornings/afternoons; **h~tags arbeiten** to work part-time.

**Halbtags-:** **~arbeit**, **~beschäftigung** *f* part-time job; **~kraft** *f* part-time employee.

**Halb-:** **~ton** *m* half-tone; *(Mus)* semitone;

**h~trocken** *adj Wein* medium dry; **h~voll** *adj attr* half-filled, *Behälter auch* half-full; **h~wach** *adj attr* half awake; **in h~wachem Zustand** half awake; **~wahrheit** *f* half truth; **~waise** *f child/person who has lost one parent*; **h~wegs** *adv* partly; *gut* reasonably; *annehmbar* halfway; **wenn es dir wieder h~wegs besser geht** when you're feeling a bit better; **~welt** *f* demimonde; **~wert(s)zeit** *f* half-life; **~wissen** *nt (pej)* superficial knowledge; **h~wüchsig** *adj* adolescent; **~wüchsige(r)** *mf decl as adj* adolescent; **~zeit** *f (Sport) (Hälfte)* half; *(Pause)* half-time.

**Halde** *f -n* **(a)** *(Abfall~)* mound, heap; *(Min: Abbau~)* slagheap. **etw auf ~ legen** *Ware, Vorräte* to stockpile sth. **(b)** *(geh: Abhang)* slope.

**half** *pret of* **helfen.**

**Hälfte** *f -n* half. **die ~ der Kinder war abwesend** half the children were absent; **die ~ von etw** half (of) sth; **die ~ ist gelogen** half of it is lies; **Rentner zahlen die ~** pensioners pay half price; **um die ~ steigen** to increase by half; **es ist zur ~ fertig** it is half finished; **das werde ich zur ~ bezahlen** I will pay half (of it); **meine bessere ~** *(hum col)* my better half *(hum col)*; **auf der ~ des Weges** halfway.

**Halfter¹** *m or nt - (für Tiere)* halter.

**Halfter²** *f -n or nt - (Pistolen~)* holster.

**Hall** *m -e* echo.

**Halle** *f -n* hall; *(Hotel~)* lobby; *(Fabrik~)* shed; *(Sport~)* (sports) hall, gym(nasium); *(Flugzeug~)* hangar. **Fußball in der ~** indoor football.

**halleluja(h)** *interj* halleluja(h).

**hallen** *vi* to reverberate, to echo *(auch fig)*.

**Hallen-** *in cpds (Sport)* indoor; **~(schwimm)bad** *nt* indoor swimming pool.

**hallo** ['halo, ha'lo:] *interj* hello.

**Hallo** *nt* cheer *usu pl*; *(Gruß)* hello. **mit großem ~** with loud cheering.

**Halluzination** *f* hallucination.

**Halm** *m -e* stalk, stem; *(Gras~)* blade of grass; *(Stroh~, zum Trinken)* straw.

**Halogen** *nt -e* halogen.

**Halogenscheinwerfer** *m* halogen headlamp.

**Hals** *m ⸚e* **(a)** neck. **sich** *(dat)* **nach jdm/etw den ~ verrenken** *(col)* to crane one's neck to see sb/sth; **jdm um den ~ fallen** to fling one's arms around sb's neck; **sich jdm an den ~ werfen** *(fig col)* to throw oneself at sb; **das wird ihm noch den ~ brechen** *(col)* it'll ruin him; **~ über Kopf abreisen** to leave in a rush; **ihm steht das Wasser bis zum ~** *(fig)* he is up to his neck in it *(col)*; **jdn auf dem** *or* **am ~ haben** *(col)* to be lumbered *or* saddled with sb *(col)*; **jdn jdm auf den ~ hetzen** *(col)* to put sb onto sb; **jdm mit etw vom ~(e) bleiben** *(col)* not to bother sb with sth *(col)*; **sich jdn/etw vom ~e schaffen** *(col)* to get sb/sth off one's back *(col)*.

**(b)** *(Kehle, Rachen)* throat. **sie hat es im ~** *(col)* she has a sore throat; **aus vollem ~(e)** at the top of one's voice; **es hängt mir zum ~ heraus** *(col)* I'm sick and tired of it; **sie hat es in den falschen ~ bekommen** *(col) (sich verschlucken)* it went down the wrong way; *(falsch verstehen)* she took it wrongly; **etw bleibt jdm im ~ stecken** *(lit, fig)* sth sticks in sb's throat; **er kann den ~ nicht voll (genug) kriegen** *(fig col)* he is never satisfied.

**Hals-:** **~abschneider** *m - (pej col)* shark *(col)*; **h~abschneiderisch** *adj (pej col) Preise* extortionate; *Mensch* cutthroat *(col)*; **~ausschnitt** *m* neck(line); **~band** *nt (Hunde~)* collar; **h~brecherisch** *adj* dangerous; *Tempo* breakneck; *Fahrt* hair-raising; **~entzündung** *f* sore throat; **~kette** *f (Schmuck)* necklace; **~krause** *f* ruff.

**Hals-Nasen-Ohren-Arzt** *m* ear, nose and throat specialist.

**Hals-:** ~**schlagader** *f* carotid (artery); ~**schmerzen** *pl* sore throat *sing*; **h~starrig** *adj* stubborn; ~**starrigkeit** *f* stubbornness; ~**tuch** *nt* scarf; ~**- und Beinbruch** *interj* good luck; ~**weh** *nt* sore throat; ~**weite** *f* neck size; ~**wirbel** *m* cervical vertebra.

**Halt** *m* **-e** (a) *(für Füße, Hände)* hold; *(lit, fig: Stütze)* support; *(fig: innerer ~)* security *no art.* ~ **haben** *(Ding)* to hold; **jdm/einer Sache** ~ **geben** to support sb/sth; **keinen** ~ **haben** to have no hold/support; to be insecure; **ohne inneren** ~ insecure. (b) *(geh: Anhalten)* stop.

**halt**[1] *interj* stop.

**halt**[2] *adv (dial) siehe* **eben 2 (b).**

**haltbar** *adj* (a) ~ **sein** to keep (well); ~**e Lebensmittel** food which keeps (well); **etw** ~ **machen** to preserve sth; ~ **bis 6.11.** use by 6 Nov. (b) *(widerstandsfähig)* durable; *Stoff, Kleider* hard-wearing. (c) *Theorie* tenable.

**Haltbarkeit** *f* (a) *(von Lebensmitteln)* **eine längere** ~ **haben** to keep longer; **Lebensmittel von kurzer** ~ perishable food. (b) *siehe adj (b)* durability; hard-wearing quality.

**Haltbarkeitsdatum** *nt* best-before date.

**Haltegriff** *m* (grab) handle; *(in Bus)* strap; *(an Badewanne)* handgrip.

**halten** *pret* **hielt,** *ptp* **gehalten 1** *vt* (a) *(festhalten)* to hold; *(zurückhalten)* to stop; *(behalten, besitzen)* Haustier, Vorsprung, Versprechen to keep; Rekord, Kurs, Position to hold; Auto to run; *(beibehalten)* Temperatur, Tempo to keep up. **den Mund** ~ *(col)* to keep one's mouth shut *(col)*; **einen Fuß ins Wasser** ~ to put one's foot into the water; **ich konnte ihn/es gerade noch** ~ I just managed to grab hold of him/it; **sie ist nicht zu** ~ *(fig)* there's no holding her; **es hält mich hier nichts mehr** there's nothing to keep me here any more; **es hält dich niemand** nobody's stopping you; **die Wärme** ~ to retain heat; **sich** *(dat)* **jdn/etw** ~ to keep sb/sth; **den Ton** ~ to stay in tune; **die These läßt sich nicht länger** ~ this thesis is no longer tenable; **(mit jdm) Verbindung** ~ to keep in touch (with sb).

(b) *(abhalten)* Vorlesung to give; Rede auch to make; Gottesdienst to hold; Wache to keep. **Mittagsschlaf** ~ to have an afternoon nap.

(c) *(Sport)* Ball to save.

(d) **er hält seine Kinder sehr streng** he's very strict with his children; **es mit etw so/anders** ~ to handle sth like this/differently; **das kannst du** ~ **wie du willst** that's completely up to you; **etw einfach** ~ to keep sth simple; **der Film hält nicht, was er verspricht** the film doesn't live up to expectations; **jdn/etw für jdn/etw** ~ to take sb/sth for sb/sth; **jdn für ehrlich** ~ to think *or* consider sb is honest; **wofür** ~ **Sie mich?** what do you take me for?; **etw von jdm/etw** ~ to think sth of sb/sth; **ich halte nichts davon, das zu tun** I don't think much of the idea of doing that; **nicht viel vom Sparen** ~ not to be a great one for saving *(col)*; **etw für nötig/ratsam** ~ to judge sth to be necessary/advisable.

**2** *vi* (a) *(festhalten, zusammenhalten)* to hold. **kannst du mal 'n Moment** ~**?** can you just hold that (for) a moment? (b) *(bestehenbleiben, haltbar sein)* to last; *(Stoff)* to wear well. (c) *(stehenbleiben, anhalten)* to stop. **zum H~ bringen** to bring to a stop *or* standstill. (d) *(Sport)* to make a save. (e) **Sport hält jung** sport keeps you young; **auf etw** *(acc)* ~ *(zielen)* to aim at sth; *(steuern)* to head for sth; **etwas mehr nach links** ~ to keep more to the left; *(zielen)* to aim

more to the left; **zu jdm** ~ to stand *or* stick by sb; **(sehr) auf etw** *(acc)* ~ *(Wert legen)* to attach (a lot of) importance to sth; **auf sich** *(acc)* ~ *(auf Äußeres achten)* to take a pride in oneself.

**3** *vr* (a) *(sich festhalten)* to hold on *(an +dat -to)*. (b) *(sich nicht verändern)* to keep; *(Wetter)* to last; *(Preise)* to hold; *(nicht verschwinden)* to last; *(Geruch etc)* to stay; *(seine Position behaupten)* to hold on. **er hat sich gut gehalten** *(col)* he's well-preserved; **sich auf den Beinen** ~ to stay on one's feet; **sich gut** ~ *(in Prüfung, Spiel etc)* to make a good showing, to do well; **er hält sich sehr aufrecht** he holds *or* carries himself very erect; **der Autofahrer hielt sich ganz rechts** the driver kept to the right; **sich an ein Versprechen** ~ to keep a promise; **sich an den Text** ~ to keep *or* stick to the text; **sich an jdn** ~ *(sich wenden an)* to ask sb; **sich an jdn/etw** ~ *(bleiben bei)* to stick with sb/sth; *(sich richten nach)* to follow sb/sth; **sich nicht** ~ **können** to be unable to control oneself. (c) **er hält sich für besonders klug** he thinks he's very clever.

**Halter** *m* **-** (a) *(Haltevorrichtung)* holder. (b) *(Jur: Tier~)* owner; *(Fahrzeug~)* keeper.

**Halterin** *f* **= Halter (b).**

**Halterung** *f* mounting; *(für Regal etc)* support.

**Halte-:** ~**schild** *nt* stop *or* halt sign; ~**signal** *nt* *(Rail)* stop signal; ~**stelle** *f* stop; ~**verbot** *nt* (absolutes) ~**verbot** no stopping; *(Bereich)* no stopping zone; **eingeschränktes** ~**verbot** no waiting; *(Bereich)* no waiting zone.

**Halt-:** **h~los** *adj (schwach)* insecure; *(hemmungslos)* unrestrained; *(unbegründet)* groundless; ~**losigkeit** *f siehe adj* lack of security; uninhibitedness; groundlessness; **h~machen** *vi sep* to stop; **vor nichts h~machen** *(fig)* to stop at nothing; **vor niemandem h~machen** *(fig)* to spare no-one.

**Haltung** *f* (a) *(Körper~)* posture; *(Stellung)* position. ~ **annehmen** *(esp Mil)* to stand to attention. (b) *(fig) (Auftreten)* manner; *(Einstellung)* attitude. (c) *no pl (Beherrschtheit)* composure. ~ **bewahren** to keep one's composure. (d) *no pl (von Tieren, Fahrzeugen)* keeping.

**Halunke** *m (wk)* **-n, -n** scoundrel.

**Hamburg** *nt* Hamburg.

**Hamburger(in** *f)* *m* **-** native of Hamburg.

**hämisch** *adj* malicious, spiteful. **er hat sich** ~ **gefreut** he gloated.

**Hammel** *m* **-** (a) *(Zool)* wether. (b) *no pl (Cook)* mutton. (c) *(fig pej)* ass, donkey.

**Hammel-:** ~**beine** *pl*: **jdm die** ~**beine langziehen** *(hum col)* to give sb a dressing-down; ~**fleisch** *nt* mutton; ~**keule** *f (Cook)* leg of mutton; ~**sprung** *m (Parl)* division.

**Hammer** *m* **-** hammer. **das ist ein** ~**!** *(col) (unerhört)* that's absurd!; *(prima)* that's fantastic! *(col)*.

**hämmern 1** *vi (lit, fig)* to hammer; *(col: beim Klavierspielen etc)* to pound. **2** *vt* to hammer; *Metallgefäße, Schmuck etc* to beat. **jdm etw ins Bewußtsein** ~ *(col)* to hammer sth into sb's head *(col)*.

**Hammerwerfen** *nt no pl* hammer(-throwing).

**Hammond|orgel** ['hæmənd-] *f* electric organ.

**Hämoglobin** *nt no pl* haemoglobin, hemoglobin *(US)*.

**Hämorrhoiden** [hɛmɔro'iːdən] *pl* piles *pl*, haemorrhoids *(Brit) pl*, hemorrhoids *(US) pl*.

**Hampelmann** *m, pl* **-männer** (a) jumping jack. (b) *(col: willenloser Mensch)* **er ist nur ein** ~ he just lets people walk all over him.

**hampeln** *vi* to jump about; *(zappeln)* to fidget.

**Hamster** *m* **-** hamster.

**Hamsterer(in** *f)* *m* **-** *(col)* hoarder.

**Hamsterkauf** *m* panic-buying *no pl.* **Hamsterkäufe machen** to buy in order to hoard; *(bei Knappheit)* to panic-buy.

**hamstern** *vti (speichern)* to hoard; *(Hamsterkäufe machen)* to panic-buy.

**Hand** *f* ∸e **(a)** hand. **jdm die ~ geben** to give sb one's hand; **jdn an die** *or* **bei der ~ nehmen** to take sb by the hand; **jdm etw aus der ~ nehmen** to take sth off sb *(auch fig)*; **mit der ~, von ~** by hand; **von ~ geschrieben/genäht** handwritten/handsewn.

**(b)** *no pl (Sport: ~spiel)* handball.

**(c)** *(Besitz, Obhut)* possession, hands. **aus privater ~** privately; **etw aus der ~ geben** to let sth out of one's sight; **etw geht in jds ∸e über** sth passes into sb's hands; **zu ∸en von jdm** for the attention of sb.

**(d)** ∸e **hoch!** hands up!; ∸e **weg!** hands off!; ~ **aufs Herz** cross your/my heart; **eine ~ wäscht die andere** *(Prov)* if you scratch my back I'll scratch yours; **ich wasche meine ∸e in Unschuld** *(geh)* I wash my hands of it; **bei etw die** *or* **seine ~ im Spiel haben** to have a hand in sth; **er hat überall seine ~ im Spiel** he has a finger in every pie; **etw hat weder ~ noch Fuß** sth doesn't make sense; **sich mit ∸en und Füßen gegen etw wehren** to fight sth tooth and nail; **rechter/linker ~** on the right-/left-hand side; **eine ruhige/sichere ~** a steady hand; **eine lockere ~ haben** *(hum col)* to let fly at the slightest provocation; **bei etw eine glückliche ~ haben** to have a lucky touch with sth; **in festen ∸en** to be spoken for; **mit leeren/vollen ∸en** empty-handed/open-handedly; **alle ∸e voll zu tun haben** to have one's hands full; **sich die ~ fürs Leben reichen** *(geh)* to tie the knot; **die ~ für jdn ins Feuer legen** to vouch for sb; **jdn auf ∸en tragen** to cherish sb; **(bei etw) mit ~ anlegen** to lend a hand (with sth); **~ an jdn legen** *(geh)* to lay a hand on sb; **die ~ auf etw** *(dat)* **halten** to keep a tight rein on sth; **das liegt auf der ~** *(col)* that's obvious; **an ~ eines Beispiels** by means of an example; **an ~ dieses Berichts** from this report; **aus erster/zweiter ~** first/second-hand; **etw zur ~ haben** to have sth to hand; *Ausrede, Erklärung* to have sth ready; **mit etw schnell bei der ~ sein** *(col)* to be ready with sth; **jdm in die ∸e arbeiten** to play into sb's hands; **jdm in die ∸e fallen** *or* **geraten** to fall into sb's hands; **jdn/etw in die ∸e kriegen** *or* **bekommen** to get one's hands on sb/sth; **jdn (fest) in der ~ haben** to have sb (well) in hand; **von der ~ in den Mund leben** to live from hand to mouth; **ich habe diese Entscheidung nicht in der ~** this isn't for me to decide; **etwas gegen jdn in der ~ haben** to have some hold on sb; **in jds ~ sein** to be in sb's hands; **etw in die ~ nehmen** to pick sth up; *(fig)* to take sth in hand; **jdm etw in die ∸e spielen** to pass sth on to sb; **hinter vorgehaltener ~** on the quiet; **etw geht jdm flott/leicht von der ~** sb does sth quickly/finds sth easy; **es ist nicht von der ~ zu weisen** it cannot be denied; **zur ~ sein** to be at hand; **jdm zur ~ gehen** to lend sb a helping hand.

**Hand|arbeit** *f* work done by hand; *(Gegenstand)* handmade article; *(körperliche Arbeit)* manual work; *(Nähen, Sticken etc, als Schulfach)* needlework *no pl*; *(Stricken)* knitting *no pl*; *(Häkeln)* crochet(ing) *no pl.* **etw in ~ herstellen** to make sth by hand; **diese Tischdecke ist ~** this tablecloth is handmade.

**hand|arbeiten** *vi insep* to do needlework/knitting/crocheting.

**Hand|arbeitsgeschäft** *nt* needlework and wool shop *(Brit)* or store *(US)*.

**Hand-:** **~auflegen** *nt no pl* laying on of hands; **~ausgabe** *f (Buch)* concise edition; **~ball** *m or*

*(col) nt (Spiel)* handball; **~bedienung** *f* **(a)** *(Geräte)* hand controls *pl*; **(b)** = **~betrieb**; **~besen** *m* hand brush; **~betrieb** *m* manual operation; **mit ~betrieb** hand-operated; **~bewegung** *f (Geste, Zeichen)* gesture; **~bibliothek** *f* reference library *(with open shelves)*; **~bohrer** *m* gimlet; **~bohrmaschine** *f* (hand) drill; **~breit** *f* - **eine ~breit** ≃ four inches; **~bremse** *f* brake; *(Aut)* handbrake *(Brit)*, parking brake *(US)*; **~buch** *nt* handbook; *(technisch)* manual; **~creme** *f* hand cream.

**Hände-:** **~druck** *m* handshake; **~klatschen** *nt* clapping.

**Handel¹** *m no pl (das Handeln)* trade; *(esp illegal)* traffic; *(Wirtschaftszweig auch)* commerce; *(Warenmarkt)* market; *(Abmachung)* deal. ~ **mit etw** trade in sth; **im ~ sein** to be on the market; **etw in den ~ bringen/aus dem ~ ziehen** to put sth on/take sth off the market; **(mit jdm) ~ treiben** to trade (with sb).

**Handel²** *m* ∸ *usu pl* quarrel, argument.

**handeln 1** *vi* **(a)** to trade. **er handelt mit Gemüse** he trades *or* deals in vegetables; **er handelt mit Drogen** he traffics in drugs. **(b)** *(feilschen)* to bargain, to haggle *(um* about, over*)*; **ich lasse mit mir ~** I'm open to persuasion; *(in bezug auf Preis)* I'm open to offers. **(c)** *(tätig werden)* to act. **(d) von etw ~** to be about sth. **2** *vr impers* **es handelt sich dabei um ein Versehen** this is an error; **sich um etw ~** to be about sth, to concern sth; **es handelt sich nur ums Überleben** it's simply a question of survival. **3** *vt* to sell *(für* at, for*)*; *(an der Börse)* to trade.

**Handeln** *nt no pl* **(a)** *(Feilschen)* bargaining, haggling. **(b)** *(das Handeltreiben)* trading. **(c)** *(Verhalten)* behaviour *(Brit)*, behavior *(US)*. **(d)** *(das Tätigwerden)* action.

**handelnd** *adj* **die ~en Personen in einem Drama** the characters in a drama.

**Handels-:** **~abkommen** *nt* trade agreement; **~bank** *f* merchant bank *(Brit)*, commercial bank; **~beziehungen** *pl* trade relations *pl*; **~bilanz** *f* balance of trade; **aktive/passive ~bilanz** balance of trade surplus/deficit; **~brauch** *m* commercial practice; **~defizit** *nt* trade deficit; **h~einig** *adj pred* **h~einig werden** to agree terms; **~flagge** *f (Naut)* merchant flag; **~flotte** *f* merchant fleet; **~gesellschaft** *f* commercial company; **~gesetz** *nt* commercial law; **~gewerbe** *nt* commerce *no art*; **~gut** *nt* commodity; **~hafen** *m* trading port; **~kammer** *f* chamber of commerce; **~klasse** *f* grade; **~krieg** *m* trade war; **~marine** *f* merchant navy, merchant marine *(US)*; **~marke** *f* trade name; **~minister** *m* ≃ Trade Secretary *(Brit)*, Secretary of Commerce *(US)*; **~mission** *f* trade mission; **~name** *m* trade name; **~niederlassung** *f* branch; **~organisation** *f* trading organization; **~partner** *m* trading partner; **~politik** *f* trade *or* commercial policy; **~recht** *nt* commercial law *no def art*; **h~rechtlich 1** *adj* of/about commercial law; **2** *adv* according to commercial law; **~register** *nt* register of companies; **~reisende(r)** *mf decl as adj* commercial traveller *(Brit)* or traveler *(US)*; **~schiffahrt** *f* merchant shipping *no def art*; **~schranke** *f usu pl* trade barrier; **~schule** *f* commercial college; **~spanne** *f* profit margin; **~sperre** *f* trade embargo *(gegen* on*)*; **~straße** *f (Hist)* trade route; **h~üblich** *adj* customary; **~unternehmen** *nt* commercial enterprise; **~verkehr** *m* trade; **~vertrag** *m* trade agreement; **~vertreter** *m* commercial traveller *(Brit)* or traveler *(US)*; **~vertretung** *f* trade mission; **~ware** *f* commodity; **„keine ~ware"** ''no commercial value"; ~**waren** *pl* commodities *pl,* merchandise *sing*; ~**wert** *m* market value; ~**zweig** *m* branch.

**handeltreibend** *adj attr* trading.

**Hände-**: **h**~**ringend** *adv* wringing one's hands; *(fig)* imploringly; ~**schütteln** *nt no pl* handshaking; **mit** ~**schütteln** with a handshake; ~**trockner** *m* hand dryer.

**Hand-**: ~**feger** *m* hand brush; ~**fertigkeit** *f* dexterity; **h**~**fest** *adj* **(a)** *(kräftig) Mensch* sturdy, robust; *Essen* substantial; **(b)** *(fig) Schlägerei* violent; *Skandal* huge; *Beweis* solid, tangible; *Lüge, Betrug* flagrant, blatant; ~**fläche** *f* palm *or* flat (of the/one's hand); **h**~**gearbeitet, h**~**gefertigt** *adj* handmade; *Stickerei etc* handworked; ~**gelenk** *nt* wrist; **aus dem** ~**gelenk** *(col) (ohne Mühe)* effortlessly; *(improvisiert)* off the cuff; **h**~**gemacht** *adj* handmade; **h**~**gemalt** *adj* hand-painted; ~**gemenge** *nt* scuffle, fight; **h**~**genäht** *adj* handsewn; ~**gepäck** *nt* hand baggage *no pl*; **h**~**geschrieben** *adj* handwritten; **h**~**gesteuert** *adj (Tech)* hand-operated; ~**gestrickt** *adj* hand-knitted; *(fig)* homespun; ~**granate** *f* hand grenade; **h**~**greiflich** *adj Streit* violent; **h**~**greiflich werden** to become violent; ~**greiflichkeit** *f usu pl* violence *no pl*; ~**griff** *m* **(a)** *(Bewegung)* movement; **mit einem** ~**griff** with one flick of the wrist; *(schnell)* in no time; **(b)** *(an Gegenstand)* handle; ~**habe** *f (fig)* **ich habe gegen ihn keine** ~**habe** I have no hold on him; **etw als** ~**habe (gegen jdn) benutzen** to use sth as a lever (against sb); **h**~**haben*** *vt insep* to handle; *Maschine auch* to operate; *Gesetz* to implement; ~**habung** *f siehe vt* handling; operation; implementation.

**Handikap** ['hɛndikɛp] *nt* **-s** *(Sport, fig)* handicap.

**Hand-**: ~**kante** *f* side of the/one's hand; ~**kantenschlag** *m* karate chop; ~**käse** *m strong-smelling round German cheese*; ~**koffer** *m* (small) suitcase; ~**kuß** *m* kiss on the hand; **mit** ~**kuß** *(fig col)* with pleasure; ~**langer** *m* - odd-job man, handyman; *(fig: Untergeordneter)* dogsbody *(col)*; *(fig pej: Gehilfe)* henchman; ~**langerarbeit** *f (pej)* donkey work *no pl.*

**Händler(in** *f)* *m* - trader, dealer; *(Ladenbesitzer)* shopkeeper, store owner *(US).* **fliegender** ~ street trader.

**Händler-**: ~**preis** *m* trade price; ~**rabatt** *m* trade discount.

**handlich** *adj Gerät, Form* handy; *Gepäckstück* manageable.

**Handlichkeit** *f no pl* handiness; manageability.

**Handliniendeutung** *f* **(die)** ~ palmistry.

**Handlung** *f* action; *(Tat)* act; *(von Drama)* plot. **der Ort der** ~ the scene of the action.

**Handlungs-**: ~**ablauf** *m* plot; ~**bedarf** *m* need for action; ~**bevollmächtigte(r)** *mf* authorized agent, proxy; **h**~**fähig** *adj Regierung* able to act; *(Jur)* empowered to act; **eine h**~**fähige Mehrheit** a working majority; ~**fähigkeit** *f (von Regierung)* ability to act; *(Jur)* power to act; ~**freiheit** *f* freedom of action; ~**reisende(r)** *m (Comm)* commercial traveller, traveling salesman *(US)*; ~**spielraum** *m* scope (for action); **h**~**unfähig** *adj Regierung* unable to act; *(Jur)* without power to act; ~**unfähigkeit** *f (von Regierung)* inability to act; *(Jur)* lack of power to act; ~**vollmacht** *f* proxy; ~**weise** *f* way of behaving; **eine selbstlose** ~**weise** unselfish behaviour *(Brit)* or behavior *(US).*

**Hand-**: ~**pflege** *f* care of one's hands; ~**puppe** *f* glove puppet; ~**puppenspiel** *nt (Stück)* glove puppet show; ~**rücken** *m* back of the/one's hand;

~**säge** *f* hand-saw; ~**schelle** *f usu pl* handcuff; **jdm** ~**schellen anlegen** to handcuff sb; ~**schlag** *m* **(a)** *(Händedruck)* handshake; **ein Geschäft durch** ~**schlag abschließen** to shake on a deal; **(b) keinen** ~**schlag tun** not to do a stroke (of work); ~**schrift** *f* **(a)** handwriting; *(fig)* (trade)mark; **etw trägt/ verrät jds** ~**schrift** *(fig)* sth bears *or* has sb's (trade)mark *or* stamp; **(b)** *(Hist: Text)* manuscript; **h**~**schriftlich 1** *adj* handwritten; **2** *adv korrigieren, einfügen* by hand.

**Handschuh** *m (Finger~)* glove; *(Faust~)* mitten.

**Handschuhfach** *nt (Aut)* glove compartment.

**Hand-**: **h**~**signiert** *adj* signed; ~**spiel** *nt no pl (Sport)* handball; ~**stand** *m (Sport)* handstand; ~**steuerung** *f* manual control; ~**streich** *m* **im** ~**streich** in a surprise coup; ~**tasche** *f* handbag, purse *(US)*; ~**teller** *m* palm (of the/one's hand); ~**tuch** *nt* towel; **das** ~**tuch werfen** *(fig)* to throw in the towel; ~**umdrehen** *nt (fig)*: **im** ~**umdrehen** in the twinkling of an eye; ~**voll** *f* - *(lit, fig)* handful; ~**wagen** *m* handcart; ~**wäsche** *f* washing by hand; *(Wäschestücke)* hand wash.

**Handwerk** *nt* trade; *(Kunst~)* craft; *(fig: Tätigkeit)* business. **sein** ~ **verstehen** *(fig)* to know one's job; **jdm ins** ~ **pfuschen** *(fig)* to interfere in sb's job; **jdm das** ~ **legen** *(fig)* to put a stop to sb's game *(col).*

**Handwerker(in** *f)* *m* - (skilled) manual worker; *(Kunst~)* craftsman; craftswoman. **wir haben seit Wochen die** ~ **im Haus** we've had workmen in the house for weeks.

**handwerklich** *adj Ausbildung* as a manual worker/ craftsman; *(fig)* technical. ~**er Beruf** skilled trade; ~**es Können** craftsmanship; ~**e Fähigkeiten** manual skills.

**Handwerks-**: ~**beruf** *m* skilled trade; ~**betrieb** *m* workshop; ~**kammer** *f* trade corporation; ~**zeug** *nt no pl* tools *pl*; *(fig)* tools of the trade *pl.*

**Hand-**: ~**wörterbuch** *nt* concise dictionary; ~**zeichen** *nt* signal; *(Geste auch)* sign; *(bei Abstimmung)* show of hands; **durch** ~**zeichen** by a show of hands; ~**zettel** *m* leaflet, handbill.

**hanebüchen** *adj (dated, geh)* outrageous.

**Hanf** *m no pl (Pflanze, Faser)* hemp.

**Hang** *m* ⁼**e** **(a)** *(Abhang)* slope. **(b)** *no pl (Neigung)* tendency.

**Hangar** ['hangaːɐ] *m* **-s** hangar.

**Hänge-**: ~**bauch** *m* paunch, drooping belly *(col)*; ~**brücke** *f* suspension bridge; ~**gleiter** *m (Sport)* hang-glider; ~**lampe** *f* drop-light.

**hangeln** *vir (vi: aux sein or haben)* **er hangelte (sich) an einem Tau über den Fluß** he moved hand over hand along a rope over the river.

**Hängematte** *f* hammock.

**Hängen** *nt* **mit** ~ **und Würgen** *(col)* by the skin of one's teeth.

**hängen 1** *vi pret* **hing,** *ptp* **gehangen (a)** to hang; *(sich festhalten)* to hang on *(an +dat to)*; *(angeschlossen sein)* to be connected (up) *(an +dat to)*; *(kleben)* to be stuck *(an +dat on).* **die Gardinen** ~ **schon** the curtains are already up; **mit** ~**den Schultern** with drooping shoulders; **die Blumen ließen die Köpfe** ~ the flowers hung their heads; **den Kopf** ~ **lassen** *(fig)* to be downcast; **das Kleid hing ihr am Leib** *(col)* the dress hung on her; **das Bild hängt an der Wand** the picture is hanging on the wall; **sie hing ihm am Hals** she hung around his neck; **der Patient hängt an der künstlichen Niere/am Tropf** the patient is on the kidney machine/on the drip; **ihre Blicke hingen an dem Sänger** her eyes were fixed on the singer; **sie hängt dauernd am Telefon** *(col)* she's always on the phone; **er hängt den ganzen Tag**

**vorm Fernseher** *(col)* he spends all day in front of the telly *(col)*.
**(b)** *(lieben)* **an jdm/etw** ~ to be very attached to sb/sth; **er hängt am Leben** he clings to life.
**(c) daran hängt viel Arbeit** there's a lot of work involved in that; **der Schrank hängt voller Kleider** the cupboard is full of clothes; **der Baum hängt voller Früchte** the tree is laden with fruit; **die ganze Sache hängt an ihm** it all depends on him.
**2** *vt pret* **hängte,** *ptp* **gehängt** *(aufhängen, henken)* to hang; *(anschließen)* to connect *(an +acc* to); *(befestigen) Wohnwagen etc* to hitch up. **er hängte den Telefonhörer in die Gabel** he hung up.
**3** *vr pret* **hängte,** *ptp* **gehängt sich an etw** *(acc)* ~ to hang on to sth; **er hängte sich ans Telefon** he got on the phone; **sich an jdn** ~ *(sich anschließen)* to latch on to sb *(col)*; *(gefühlsmäßig binden)* to become attached to sb; *(verfolgen)* to pursue sb; *(Polizist)* to tail sb.
**hängenbleiben** *vi sep irreg aux sein* **(a)** to get caught *(an +dat* on*)*. **(b)** *(Sport) (zurückbleiben)* to get left behind; *(nicht durch-, weiterkommen)* not to get through. **(c)** *(Sch col: nicht versetzt werden)* to stay down. **(d)** *(sich aufhalten)* to stay on. **bei einer Nebensächlichkeit** ~ to get bogged down with a side issue. **(e)** *(haftenbleiben)* to get stuck *or* caught *(in, an +dat* on*)*. **es bleibt ja doch alles an mir hängen** *(fig col)* (in the end) it's all down to me anyhow *(col)*; **der Verdacht ist an ihm hängengeblieben** suspicion rested on him; **vom Lateinunterricht ist bei ihm nicht viel hängengeblieben** *(fig col)* not much of his Latin stuck *(col)*.
**hängend** *adj* hanging. **mit** ~**em Kopf** *(fig)* in low spirits; **mit** ~**er Zunge kam er angelaufen** *(fig)* he came running up panting.
**hängenlassen** *sep irreg, ptp* **hängen(ge)lassen 1** *vt* **(a)** *(vergessen)* to leave behind. **(b)** *(col: im Stich lassen)* to let down. **2** *vr* to let oneself go.
**Hänge-:** ~**pflanze** *f* trailing plant; ~**schloß** *nt* padlock; ~**schrank** *m* wall-cupboard.
**Hanglage** *f* sloping site. **in** ~ situated on a slope.
**Hannover** [haˈnoːfɐ] *nt* Hanover.
**Hannoveraner(in** *f)* [hanovəˈraːnɐ, -ərɪn] *m* - Hanoverian.
**hannoverisch** [haˈnoːfərɪʃ] *adj* Hanoverian.
**Hansdampf** *m* -e Jack-of-all-trades (and master of none). **er ist ein** ~ **in allen Gassen** he knows everybody and everything.
**Hanse** *f no pl (Hist),* **Hansebund** *m (Hist)* Hanseatic League.
**Hänselei** *f* teasing *no pl.*
**hänseln** *vt* to tease.
**Hansestadt** *f* Hanseatic *or* Hanse town.
**Hanswurst** *m* -e *or (hum)* ≠e clown.
**Hantel** *f* -n *(Sport)* dumb-bell.
**hantieren\*** *vi* **(a)** *(arbeiten)* to be busy. **(b)** *(umgehen mit)* **mit etw** ~ to handle sth. **(c)** *(herum~)* to tinker about *(an +dat* with, on*)*.
**hapern** *vi impers (col)* **es hapert an etw** *(dat) (fehlt)* there is a lack of sth; **es hapert bei jdm mit etw** *(fehlt)* sb is short of sth; **mit der Grammatik hapert es bei ihm** he's poor at grammar.
**Häppchen** *nt dim of* **Happen** morsel; *(Appetithappen)* titbit.
**häppchenweise** *adv (col: lit, fig)* bit by bit.
**Happen** *m - (col)* mouthful, morsel; *(kleine Mahlzeit)* bite. **ein fetter** ~ *(fig)* a good catch; **ich habe heute noch keinen** ~ **gegessen** I haven't had a bite to eat all day.
**happig** *adj (col)* steep *(col)*.
**Hardware** [ˈhaːdwɛə] *f (Comp)* hardware.

**Harem** *m* -s *(auch hum col)* harem.
**Harfe** *f* -n harp.
**Harfenist(in** *f) m,* **Harfenspieler** *m* harpist.
**Harke** *f* -n *(esp N Ger)* rake. **jdm zeigen, was eine** ~ **ist** *(fig col)* to show sb what's what *(col)*.
**harken** *vti (esp N Ger)* to rake.
**harmlos** *adj* **(a)** *(ungefährlich)* harmless; *Berg, Piste* easy; *Schnupfen, Entzündung etc* slight. **(b)** *(arglos)* innocent; *(friedlich)* harmless. **er ist ein** ~**er Mensch** he's harmless (enough).
**Harmlosigkeit** *f no pl siehe adj* **(a)** harmlessness; easiness; slightness. **(b)** innocence; harmlessness. **in aller** ~ in all innocence.
**Harmonie** *f (Mus, fig)* harmony.
**harmonieren\*** *vi (Mus, fig)* to harmonize; *(farblich auch)* to match.
**Harmonika** *f* -s *or* **Harmoniken** harmonica; *(Mund~ auch)* mouth organ; *(Zieh~)* accordion.
**harmonisch** *adj* harmonious; *(Mus, Math)* harmonic.
**harmonisieren\*** *vt Musik, Steuern* to harmonize; *(fig)* to coordinate.
**Harmonium** *nt* harmonium.
**Harn** *m* -e urine. ~ **lassen** to pass water.
**Harnblase** *f* bladder.
**Harnisch** *m* -e armour *(Brit),* armor *(US).* **jdn in** ~ **bringen** *(fig)* to get sb up in arms; **wenn sie das sieht, gerät sie in** ~ it gets her hackles up when she sees that.
**Harpune** *f* -n harpoon.
**harpunieren\*** *vti* to harpoon.
**harren** *vi (geh)* **jds/einer Sache** ~, **auf jdn/etw** ~ to await sb/sth, to wait for sb/sth.
**Harsch** *m no pl* frozen snow.
**harsch** *adj* **(a)** harsh. **(b)** *Schnee* frozen.
**hart** *comp* ≠**er,** *superl* ≠**este(r, s)** *or (adv)* **am** ≠**esten 1** *adj* **(a)** hard; *Winter auch, Strafe* severe; *Gesetze, Kurs* tough; *Auseinandersetzung* violent; *Wind* strong; *Ei* hard-boiled; *(stabil) Währung* stable; *(fig) Getränk, Droge* hard; *Verlust* cruel; *Wirklichkeit* harsh. ~ **werden** to get hard, to harden; **Eier** ~ **kochen** to hard-boil eggs; **er hat einen** ~**en Schädel** *or* **Kopf** *(fig)* he's obstinate; **ein** ~**es Herz haben** *(fig)* to have a hard heart, to be hard-hearted; **in** ~**en Dollars** in hard dollars; **der** ~**e Kern einer Vereinigung** the hard core of an organization; ~ **bleiben** to stand firm; ~ **mit jdm sein** to be hard on sb; **es geht** ~ **auf** ~ it's a tough fight. **(b)** *(rauh) Spiel, Gegner* rough; *(robust)* tough. **kalte Duschen machen** ~ cold showers make you tough; **er ist** ~ **im Nehmen** he's tough, he can take it. **(c)** *(scharf) Konturen, (Phot) Negativ* sharp; *Klang, Akzent* harsh; *Gesichtszüge* hard.
**2** *adv* **(a)** hard; *(scharf) konstrastiert* sharply; *(heftig, rauh)* roughly. ~ **klingen** to sound harsh; ~ **aneinandergeraten** to get into a fierce argument; **jdn** ~ **anfahren** to bite sb's head off *(col)*; **jdm** ~ **zusetzen** to press sb hard; **etw trifft jdn** ~ *(lit, fig)* sth hits sb hard; ~ **spielen** *(Sport)* to play rough; ~ **durchgreifen** to take tough *or* rigorous action; **jdn** ~ **anfassen** to be hard on sb. **(b)** *(nahe)* close *(an +dat* to*)*. **das ist** ~ **an der Grenze** that's almost going too far; **wir fuhren** ~ **am Abgrund vorbei** *(fig)* we were on the brink of disaster.
**Härte** *f* -n *siehe adj* **(a)** hardness; severity; toughness; violence; strength; stability; cruelty; harshness. **soziale** ~**n** social hardships. **(b)** roughness; toughness. **(c)** sharpness; harshness; hardness.
**Härte-:** ~**fall** *m* case of hardship; *(col: Mensch)* hardship case; ~**grad** *m* degree of hardness; ~**klausel** *f* hardship clause.

**härten** *vtir* to harden.

**Härtetest** *m* endurance test; *(fig)* acid test.

**Hart-:** ~**faserplatte** *f* hardboard, fiberboard *(US)*; **h~gefroren** *adj attr* frozen hard *pred*; **h~gekocht** *adj attr* hard-boiled; ~**geld** *nt* hard cash; **h~gesotten** *adj (fig)* hard-boiled; **h~herzig** *adj* hard-hearted; ~**herzigkeit** *f* hard-heartedness; ~**holz** *nt* hardwood; ~**käse** *m* hard cheese; **h~näckig** *adj* stubborn; ~**näckigkeit** *f* stubbornness.

**Härtung** *f (Tech)* hardening.

**Hartwurst** *f* salami-type sausage.

**Harz**[1] *nt* -**e** resin; *(Mus)* rosin.

**Harz**[2] *m (Geog)* Harz Mountains *pl.*

**Haschee** *nt* -**s** *(Cook)* hash.

**haschen** *(dated, geh)* **1** *vt* to catch. **2** *vi* **nach Beifall/ Lob** *etc* ~ to fish for applause/praise *etc*.

**Häschen** ['hɛsçən] *nt dim of* **Hase** young hare, leveret; *(col: Kaninchen)* bunny *(col)*.

**Haschisch** *nt or m no pl* hashish.

**Hase** *m (wk)* -**n**, -**n** hare; *(dial: Kaninchen, Oster~, in Märchen)* rabbit. **falscher** ~ *(Cook)* meat loaf; **wissen, wie der** ~ **läuft** *(fig col)* to know which way the wind blows; **alter** ~ *(fig col)* old hand; **da liegt der** ~ **im Pfeffer** *(col)* that's the crux of the matter; **mein Name ist** ~**(, ich weiß von nichts)** I don't know anything about anything.

**Hasel-:** ~**maus** *f* dormouse; ~**nuß** *f* hazelnut; ~**(nuß)strauch** *m* hazel-bush.

**Hasen-:** **h~füßig** *adj (dated col)* chicken-hearted *(col)*; ~**pfeffer** *m (Cook)* ≏ jugged hare; ~**scharte** *f (Med)* hare-lip.

**Haspel** *f* -**n** **(a)** *(Förderwinde)* windlass. **(b)** *(Garn~)* reel.

**Haß** *m no pl* **(a)** hatred, hate *(auf +acc, gegen* of*)*. **(b)** *(col: Wut)* **einen** ~ **(auf jdn) haben** *(col)* to be really mad (with sb) *(col)*.

**hassen** *vti* to hate. **etw** ~ **wie die Pest** *(col)* to detest sth.

**hassenswert** *adj* hateful, odious.

**haß|erfüllt** *adj* full of hate *or* hatred.

**häßlich** *adj* **(a)** *(auch Vorfall etc)* ugly. ~ **wie die Nacht** (as) ugly as sin. **(b)** *(gemein)* nasty, mean. ~ **über jdn sprechen** to be nasty *or* mean about sb.

**Häßlichkeit** *f siehe adj* **(a)** ugliness *no pl.* **(b)** nastiness *no pl*, meanness *no pl*; *(Bemerkung)* nasty remark.

**Haßliebe** *f* love-hate relationship *(für* with*)*.

**Hast** *f no pl* haste. **ohne** ~ without haste, without rushing; **mit einer solchen** ~ in such a hurry *or* rush.

**haste** *(col)* = **hast du. (was)** ~ **was kannste** as quick *or* fast as possible; ~ **was, biste was** *(prov)* money brings status.

**hasten** *vi aux sein (geh)* to hasten *(form)*, to hurry.

**hastig** *adj* hasty; *Essen auch, Worte* hurried. **nicht so** ~! not so fast!

**hätscheln** *vt (liebkosen)* to pet, to fondle; *(zu weich behandeln)* to mollycoddle; *(bevorzugen)* to pamper.

**hatschi** *interj* atishoo.

**hatte** *pret of* **haben.**

**Hatz** *f* -**en** **(a)** *(Hunt, fig)* hunt. **(b)** *(fig, esp S Ger, Aus)* rush.

**Haube** *f* -**n** **(a)** bonnet; *(von Krankenschwester etc)* cap. **jdn unter die** ~ **bringen** *(hum)* to marry sb off; **unter der** ~ **sein/unter die** ~ **kommen** *(hum)* to be/ get married. **(b)** *(bei Vögeln)* crest. **(c)** *(Bedeckung)* cover; *(Trocken~)* (hair) dryer, drying hood *(US)*; *(für Kaffee-, Teekanne)* cosy; *(Motor~)* bonnet *(Brit)*, hood *(US)*.

**Haubitze** *f* -**n** howitzer.

**Hauch** *m* -**e** **(a)** *(geh, poet)* *(Atem)* breath. **(b)** *(Luftzug)* breath of air, breeze. **(c)** *(Duft)* smell. **(d)** *(Andeutung)* hint, touch.

**hauchdünn** *adj* extremely thin; *Scheiben* wafer-thin; *Strümpfe* sheer; *(fig)* *Mehrheit* extremely narrow.

**hauchen** *vti* to breathe. **jdm etw** *(acc)* **ins Ohr** ~ *(liter)* to whisper sth in sb's ear.

**hauch-:** ~**fein** *adj* extremely fine; ~**zart** *adj* very delicate.

**Haudegen** *m (fig)* old campaigner.

**Haue** *f no pl (col: Prügel)* (good) hiding *(col)*.

**hauen** *pret* **haute,** *ptp* **gehauen 1** *vt* **(a)** *(col) (schlagen)* to hit, to clout *(col)*; *(verprügeln)* to hit, to thump *(col)*. **hau(t) ihn!** let him have it! *(col)*. **(b)** *(meißeln)* *Figur* to carve; *Stufen, Loch* to cut. **(c)** *(col: stoßen)* *jdn, Gegenstand* to shove *(col)*; *Körperteil* to bang, to knock *(an +acc* on, against*)*. **das haut einen vom Stuhl** it really knocks you sideways *(col)*. **(d)** *(col: werfen)* to chuck *(col)*, to fling. **(e)** *(dial)* *Baum* to chop (down); *Holz, Fleisch* to chop (up). **2** *vi* **(a)** *(col: schlagen)* to hit. **jdm auf die Schulter** ~ to slap sb on the shoulder. **3** *vr (col)* **(a)** *(sich prügeln)* to scrap, to fight. **(b)** *(sich setzen, legen)* to fling oneself.

**Hauer** *m* - **(a)** *(Min)* face-worker. **(b)** *(Zool)* tusk; *(hum: großer Zahn)* fang.

**Häufchen** *nt dim of* **Haufen** small pile. **ein** ~ **Unglück** *or* **Elend** a picture of misery.

**Haufen** *m* - **(a)** heap, pile. **jdn über den** ~ **rennen/ fahren** *etc (col)* to knock sb down; **etw** *(acc)* **über den** ~ **werfen** *(col) (verwerfen)* to chuck sth out *(col)*; *(durchkreuzen)* to mess sth up *(col)*; **soviel Geld habe ich noch nie auf einem** ~ **gesehen** I've never seen so much money in one place before. **(b)** *(col)* **ein** ~ **Arbeit/Geld** a load *or* heap of work/money, piles *or* loads of work/money *(all col)*; **ein** ~ **Unsinn** a load of nonsense *(col)*; **er hat einen ganzen** ~ **Freunde** he has loads of friends *(col)*. **(c)** *(Schar)* crowd. **dem** ~ **folgen** *(pej)* to follow the crowd; **der große** ~ *(pej)* the common herd.

**häufen 1** *vt* to pile up, to heap up. **ein gehäufter Teelöffel Salz** a heaped teaspoonful of salt. **2** *vr (lit, fig: sich ansammeln)* to mount up; *(zahlreicher werden: Unfälle, Fehler etc)* to occur increasingly often. **das kann schon mal vorkommen, es darf sich nur nicht** ~ these things happen, just as long as they don't happen too often.

**haufenweise** *adv (col)* **etw** ~ **haben** to have piles *or* heaps *or* loads of sth *(all col)*.

**häufig 1** *adj* frequent. **2** *adv* often, frequently.

**Häufigkeit** *f* frequency.

**Häufung** *f* **(a)** *(fig: das Anhäufen)* accumulation. **(b)** *(das Sich-Häufen)* increasing number.

**Haupt** *nt, pl* **Häupter (a)** *(geh: Kopf)* head. **entblößten** ~**es** bareheaded; **gesenkten/erhobenen** ~**es** with one's head bowed/raised. **(b)** *(zentrale Figur)* head.

**Haupt-** *in cpds* main, principal, chief; ~**akteur** *m (lit, fig)* leading light; *(pej)* main figure; ~**aktionär** *m* principal *or* main shareholder; ~**akzent** *m (fig)* **auf etw** *(acc)* **den** ~**akzent legen** to put the main emphasis on sth; **h~amtlich 1** *adj* full-time; **2** *adv* (on a) full-time (basis); ~**anteil** *m* main part; ~**bahnhof** *m* main *or* central station; ~**beruf** *m* main occupation; **h~beruflich 1** *adj* *Lehrer, Gärtner etc* full-time; **2** *adv* full-time; **er ist h~beruflich als Lehrer tätig** his main occupation is teaching; ~**beschäftigung** *f* main occupation; ~**betrieb** *m* **(a)** headquarters *sing or pl*; **(b)** *(geschäftigste Zeit)* peak period; ~**buch** *nt (Comm)* ledger; ~**darsteller(in** *f)* *m* principal actor/actress, leading man/lady; ~**eingang** *m* main entrance; ~**fach** *nt (Sch, Univ)* main subject, major *(US)*; **etw im** ~**fach studieren** to study sth as one's main subject, to major in sth *(US)*; ~**figur** *f (Liter)* central character; *(fig)* central figure; ~**film** *m* main film; ~**gericht** *nt* main course.

**Hauptgeschäft** *nt* (a) *(Zentrale)* head office, headquarters *sing or pl.* (b) *(Hauptverdienst)* major part of one's business.

**Hauptgeschäfts-**: ~**führer** *m* general manager; ~**stelle** *f* head office, headquarters *sing or pl*; ~**straße** *f* main shopping street; ~**zeit** *f* peak (shopping) period.

**Haupt-**: ~**gewicht** *nt (fig)* main emphasis; ~**gewinn** *m* first prize; ~**grund** *m* main reason; ~**hahn** *m* mains cock; ~**last** *f* main load; *(fig)* main burden; ~**leitung** *f* mains *pl.*

**Häuptling** *m* chief(tain); *(esp von Dorf)* headman.

**Haupt-**: ~**mahlzeit** *f* main meal; ~**mann** *m, pl* -**leute** *(Mil)* captain; ~**merkmal** *nt* main feature; ~**motiv** *nt* (a) *(Beweggrund)* primary *or* main motive; (b) *(Art, Liter, Mus)* main *or* principal motif; ~**nahrungsmittel** *nt* staple food; ~**niederlassung** *f* head office, headquarters *sing or pl*; ~**person** *f (lit, fig)* central figure; ~**platine** *f (Comp)* motherboard; ~**post** *f (col)*, ~**postamt** *nt* main post office; ~**quartier** *nt (Mil, fig)* headquarters *sing or pl*; ~**reisezeit** *f* peak travelling *(Brit) or* traveling *(US)* time(s *pl*); ~**rolle** *f (Film, Theat)* main role, lead; **die** ~**rolle spielen** *(fig)* to be all-important; *(wichtigste Person sein)* to play the main role; ~**sache** *f* main thing; *(in Brief, Rede etc)* main point; **in der** ~**sache** in the main, mainly; ~**sache, es klappt** the main thing is that it works; **h**~**sächlich 1** *adv* mainly, principally; **2** *adj* main, principal; ~**saison** *f* peak *or* high season; ~**satz** *m (Gram)* main clause; ~**schalter** *m (Elec)* master switch; ~**schlagader** *f* aorta; ~**schlüssel** *m* master key; ~**schuld** *f* main blame, main guilt *(esp Jur)*; ~**schuldige(r)** *mf* person mainly to blame, main offender *(esp Jur)*; ~**schule** *f* ≈ secondary modern (school) *(Brit)*, junior high (school) *(US)*; ~**sendezeit** *f (TV)* prime time; ~**sicherung** *f (Elec)* main fuse; ~**sitz** *m* head office, headquarters *sing or pl*; ~**speicher** *m (Comp)* main memory; ~**stadt** *f* capital (city); ~**straße** *f* main *or* major road; *(im Stadtzentrum etc)* main street; ~**teil** *m* main part; *(größter Teil auch)* major part; ~**thema** *nt* main topic; *(Mus, Liter)* main theme; ~**tribüne** *f* main stand; *(Sport auch)* grandstand.

**Hauptverkehrs-**: ~**straße** *f (in Stadt)* main street; *(Durchgangsstraße)* main thoroughfare; *(zwischen Städten)* main highway, trunk road *(Brit)*; ~**zeit** *f* peak traffic times *pl*; *(in Stadt, bei Pendlern auch)* rush hour.

**Haupt-**: ~**versammlung** *f* general meeting; ~**wäsche** *f*, ~**waschgang** *m* main wash; ~**wohnsitz** *m* main place of residence; ~**wort** *nt (Gram)* noun.

**hau ruck** *interj* heave-ho.

**Haus** *nt, pl* **Häuser** (a) *(Wohn~)* house; *(Firmengebäude)* building. **ins/im** ~ indoors; **mit jdm** ~ **an** ~ **wohnen** to live next door to sb; **von** ~ **zu** ~ **gehen** to go from door to door *or* from house to house; **vor vollem** ~ **spielen** to play to a full house.

(b) *(Zuhause, Heim)* home. ~ **und Hof** *(fig)* house and home; **etw ins/frei** ~ **liefern** *(Comm)* to deliver sth to the door/to deliver sth carriage paid; **wir liefern frei** ~ we offer free delivery; **jdm das** ~ **verbie-**

**ten** not to allow sb in the house; **aus dem** ~ **sein** to be away from home; **außer** ~ **essen** to eat out; **ins** ~ **stehen** *(fig)* to be coming up, to be forthcoming; **jdm steht etw ins** ~ *(fig)* sth is in store for sb; **nach** ~**e** *(lit, fig)* home; **zu** ~**e** at home *(auch Sport)*; **bei jdm zu** ~**e** at sb's (place), in sb's house *or* home; **bei uns zu** ~**e** at home; **für niemanden zu** ~**e sein** to be at home to nobody; **irgendwo zu** ~**e sein** *(Mensch, Tier)* to live somewhere; *(sich heimisch fühlen)* to be at home somewhere; **sich wie zu** ~**e fühlen** to feel at home; **fühl dich wie zu** ~**e!** make yourself at home!

(c) *(Bewohnerschaft eines* ~*es)* household. **ein Freund des** ~**es** a friend of the family; **der Herr/die Dame des** ~**es** *(form)* the master/the lady of the house.

(d) *(geh: Herkunft)* **aus gutem/bürgerlichem** ~**(e)** from a good/middle-class family; **von** ~**e aus** *(ursprünglich)* originally; *(von Natur aus)* naturally.

(e) **das** ~ **Windsor/Siemens** the house of Windsor/Siemens; **das erste** ~ **am Platze** the best hotel in town; *(Kaufhaus)* the best store in town; **Hohes** ~**!** *(form)* ≈ honourable members (of the House)!; **dieses hohe** ~ the *or* this House.

(f) *(von Schnecke)* shell, house *(col)*.

(g) **grüß dich, altes** ~**!** *(col)* hallo, old chap *(col)*.

**Haus-**: ~**angestellte(r)** *mf* domestic servant; ~**anzug** *m* leisure suit; ~**apotheke** *f* medicine chest; ~**arbeit** *f* (a) housework *no pl*; (b) *(Sch)* homework *no indef art, no pl*; ~**arrest** *m (im Internat)* detention; *(Jur)* house arrest; **Fritz hat heute** ~**arrest** Fritz is being kept in (by his parents) today; ~**arzt** *m* family doctor, GP; ~**aufgaben** *pl* homework *no indef art, no pl*; **seine** ~**aufgaben machen** *(auch fig)* to do one's homework; **h**~**backen** *adj (fig)* drab, homely *(US)*; ~**bau** *m* house building; *(das Bauen)* building of a/the house; ~**besetzer** *m* squatter; ~**besetzung** *f* squat; ~**besitzer(in** *f)* *m* home-owner; *(Hauswirt)* landlord/landlady; ~**besuch** *m* home visit; *(von Arzt)* house call; ~**bewohner** *m* (house) occupant *or* occupier; ~**boot** *nt* houseboat.

**Häuschen** ['hɔysçən] *nt* (a) *dim of* **Haus.** (b) *(fig col)* **ganz aus dem** ~ **sein** to be out of one's mind (with excitement/fear *etc) (col)*.

**Haus-**: **h**~**eigen** *adj* belonging to a/the hotel/firm *etc*; ~**eigentümer** *m* home-owner; *(Hauswirt)* landlord/landlady.

**hausen** *vi* (a) *(pej: wohnen)* to live. (b) *(wüten)* **(übel** *or* **schlimm)** ~ to wreak *or* create havoc; **wie die Wandalen** ~ to act like vandals.

**Häuser-**: ~**block** *m* block (of houses); ~**front** *f* front of a row of houses; ~**makler** *m* estate agent *(Brit)*, realtor *(US)*; ~**reihe**, ~**zeile** *f* row of houses; *(aneinandergebaut)* terrace.

**Hausflur** *m* (entrance) hall.

**Hausfrau** *f* housewife.

**Hausfrauenart** *f* **Wurst** *etc* **nach** ~ sausage *etc* (in) home-made style.

**hausfraulich** *adj* housewifely.

**Haus-**: ~**freund** *m* (a) friend of the family; (b) *(euph col)* man friend; ~**friede(n)** *m* domestic peace; ~**friedensbruch** *m (Jur)* trespass *(in sb's house)*; ~**gebrauch** *m* **für den** ~**gebrauch** *(Gerät)* for domestic *or* household use; **sein Französisch reicht für den** ~**gebrauch** *(col)* his French is good enough to get by; ~**geburt** *f* home birth; ~**gehilfin** *f* home help; **h**~**gemacht** *adj* home-made; ~**gemeinschaft** *f* household.

**Haushalt** *m* -**e** (a) household; *(~sführung)* housekeeping. **den** ~ **führen** to run the household; **jdm**

den ~ **führen** to keep house for sb. **(b)** *(fig: Biol etc)* balance. **(c)** *(Etat)* budget.

**haushalten** *vi sep irreg* **(a)** mit etw ~ to be economical with sth. **(b)** *(den Haushalt führen)* to keep house.

**Haushälter(in** *f)* *m* - housekeeper.

**Haushalts-** *in cpds* household; *(Pol)* budget; ~**artikel** *m* household article; ~**buch** *nt* housekeeping book; ~**debatte** *f (Parl)* budget debate; ~**defizit** *nt (Pol)* budget deficit; ~**führung** *f* housekeeping; ~**geld** *nt* housekeeping money; ~**gerät** *nt* household appliance; ~**hilfe** *f* domestic *or* home help; ~**jahr** *nt (Pol, Econ)* financial *or* fiscal year; ~**kasse** *f* household budget; ~**mittel** *pl (Pol)* budgetary funds *pl*; ~**plan** *m (Pol)* budget; ~**politik** *f (Pol)* budgetary policy; **h~politisch** *adj* concerning budgetary policy; ~**waren** *pl* household goods *pl*.

**Haus-:** ~**haltung** *f (das Haushaltführen)* housekeeping; ~**herr** *m* **(a)** head of the household; *(Gastgeber)* host; **(b)** *(Jur)* householder; ~**herrin** *f* lady of the house; *(Gastgeberin)* hostess; **h~hoch 1** *adj* (as) high as a house/houses; *(fig) Sieg* crushing; **der h~hohe Favorit** the hot favourite *(col)*; **2** *adv* high (in the sky); **h~hoch gewinnen** to win hands down *or* by miles *(col)*; **jdm h~hoch überlegen sein** to be head and shoulders above sb; **h~hohe(r, s)** *adj siehe* **h~hoch.**

**hausieren*** *vi* to hawk, to peddle *(mit etw sth)*. **mit etw ~ gehen** *(fig) mit Plänen* to hawk sth about.

**Hausierer(in** *f)* *m* - hawker, peddler.

**Haus-:** **h~intern** *adj* in-house ~**kleid** *nt* house dress; ~**lehrer(in** *f)* *m* (private) tutor.

**häuslich** *adj* domestic; *Mensch* domesticated; *(das Zuhause liebend)* home-loving. **der ~e Herd** the family home; **sich ~ einrichten** *or* **niederlassen** to settle in.

**Häuslichkeit** *f* domesticity.

**Hausmacherart** *f* **Wurst** *etc* **nach ~** sausage *etc* (in) home-made-style.

**Haus-:** ~**mann** *m*, *pl* ~**männer** *(den Haushalt versorgender Mann)* househusband; ~**mannskost** *f* plain cooking; ~**marke** *f (eigene Marke)* own brand; *(bevorzugte Marke)* favourite *(Brit) or* favorite *(US)* brand; ~**meister** *m* caretaker, janitor; ~**mitteilung** *f* internal memo; ~**mittel** *nt* household remedy; ~**müll** *m* domestic waste; ~**musik** *f* home music-making; ~**nummer** *f* house number; ~**ordnung** *f* house rules *pl*; ~**putz** *m* house cleaning; ~**putz machen** to clean the house; ~**rat** *m* no *pl* household equipment; ~**ratsversicherung** *f* (household) contents insurance; ~**recht** *nt* right(s *pl*) as a householder *(to forbid sb entrance)*; ~**sammlung** *f* house-to-house *or* door-to-door collection; ~**schlüssel** *m* front-door key, house key; ~**schuh** *m* slipper; ~**schwamm** *m* dry rot.

**Hausse** ['hoːs(ə)] *f* **-n** *(Econ)* boom *(an +dat* in); *(St Ex)* bull market.

**Haus-:** ~**segen** *m* **bei ihnen hängt der ~segen schief** *(hum)* they're a bit short on domestic bliss *(col)*; ~**stand** *m* household, home; **einen ~stand gründen** to set up house *or* home; ~**suchung** *f* house search; ~**suchungsbefehl** *m* search warrant; ~**tier** *nt* domestic animal; *(aus Liebhaberei gehalten)* pet; ~**tür** *f* front door; **gleich vor der ~tür** *(fig col)* right on one's doorstep; ~**verbot** *nt* **jdm ~verbot erteilen** to ban sb from the house; **in einem Lokal ~verbot haben** to be barred *or* banned from a bar; ~**verwalter** *m* (house) supervisor; ~**verwaltung** *f* property management; ~**wirt** *m* landlord; ~**wirtin** *f* landlady.

**Hauswirtschaft** *f* **(a)** housekeeping. **(b)** *(Sch)* home economics *sing*.

**hauswirtschaftlich** *adj* domestic.

**Hauswirtschafts-:** ~**raum** *m* utility room; ~**schule** *f* domestic science college.

**Haut** *f*, *pl* **Häute** skin; *(dick, esp von größerem Tier)* hide. **naß bis auf die ~** soaked to the skin; **nur ~ und Knochen sein** to be nothing but skin and bones; **mit ~ und Haar(en)** *(col)* completely; **das geht unter die ~** *(col)* that gets under your skin; **in seiner ~ möchte ich nicht stecken** *(col)* I wouldn't like to be in his shoes; **ihm ist nicht wohl in seiner ~** *(col) (unzufrieden)* he's (feeling) rather unsettled; *(unbehaglich)* he feels uneasy; **er kann nicht aus seiner ~ heraus** *(col)* he can't change the way he is, a leopard can't change its spots *(prov)*; **aus der ~ fahren** *(col)* to go through the roof *(col)*; **sich auf die faule ~ legen** *(col)* to sit back and do nothing; **seine ~ zu Markte tragen** *(col)* to risk one's neck; **seine eigene ~ retten** *(col)* to save one's own skin; **sich seiner ~ wehren** *(col)* to defend oneself.

**Haut-** *in cpds* skin; ~**abschürfung** *f* graze; ~**arzt** *m* skin specialist, dermatologist; ~**ausschlag** *m* (skin) rash.

**Häutchen** *nt* - *dim of* **Haut** *(auf Flüssigkeit)* skin; *(Anat, Bot)* membrane.

**Hautcreme** [-kreːm] *f* skin cream.

**häuten 1** *vt Tiere* to skin. **2** *vr (Tier)* to shed its skin; *(hum: Mensch)* to peel.

**haut|eng** *adj* skintight.

**Hautevolee** [(h)oːtvoˈleː] *f no pl* upper crust, glitterati *pl*.

**Haut-:** ~**farbe** *f* skin colour *(Brit)* or color *(US)*; *(Teint)* complexion; **h~farben** *adj* flesh-coloured *(Brit)*, flesh-colored *(US)*; ~**krebs** *m* skin cancer; **h~nah** *adj* (very) close; *Schilderung, Szene* vivid, graphic; ~**pflege** *f* skin care; ~**wunde** *f* skin wound.

**Havanna** *nt* Havana.

**Havarie** [havaˈriː] *f (Naut, Aviat) (Unfall)* accident; *(Schaden)* damage *no indef art, no pl*.

**havarieren*** *vi* **(a)** to be damaged. **(b)** *(Aus: Fahrzeug)* to crash.

**Hawaii** [haˈvaii] *nt* Hawaii.

**Haxe** *f* **-n** *(Cook)* leg (joint); *(S Ger col) (Fuß)* foot; *(Bein)* leg.

**Hbf** = **Hauptbahnhof.**

**H-Bombe** ['haː-] *f* H-bomb.

**h.c.** [haːˈtseː] = **honoris causa. Dr. ~** honorary doctor.

**he** *interj* hey; *(fragend)* eh.

**Hebamme** *f* - *m* midwife.

**Hebe-:** ~**balken** *m* lever; ~**bühne** *f* hydraulic ramp.

**Hebel** *m* - lever. **den ~ ansetzen** to position the lever; *(fig col)* to tackle it; **alle ~ in Bewegung setzen** *(col)* to move heaven and earth; **am längeren ~ sitzen** *(col)* to have the whip hand.

**Hebel-:** ~**kraft**, ~**wirkung** *f* leverage.

**heben** *pret* **hob**, *ptp* **gehoben 1** *vt* **(a)** to lift; *Arm, Fernglas auch, Augenbraue, Wrack* to raise; *Schatz* to dig up. **die Stimme ~** to raise one's voice; **einen ~ gehen** *(col)* to go for a drink; **er hebt gern einen** *(col)* he likes a drink; **heb deine Füße!** pick your feet up!; *siehe* **gehoben. (b)** *(steigern)* to increase; *Stimmung, Wohlstand* to improve; *Geschmack, jds Ansehen* to enhance. **das hebt den Mut** it's good for morale. **2** *vr* **(a)** to rise; *(Nebel, Deckel)* to lift. **(b)** *(verbessern, steigern)* to improve. **da hob sich seine Stimmung** that cheered him up. **3** *vi (Sport)* to do weightlifting.

**Hebräer(in** *f*) *m* - Hebrew.
**hebräisch** *adj* Hebrew.
**Hebung** *f* **(a)** *(von Schatz, Wrack etc)* recovery, raising. **(b)** *no pl (fig: Verbesserung)* improvement;
*(von Effekt, Selbstbewußtsein)* heightening; *(von Lebensstandard, Niveau)* rise.
**hecheln** *vi (keuchen)* to pant.
**Hecht** *m* **-e** *(Zool)* pike; *(col: Bursche)* guy *(col)*. **er
ist (wie) ein** ~ **im Karpfenteich** *(fig) (sehr aktiv)* he
certainly shakes people up; *(sorgt für Unruhe)* he's
a stirrer *(col)*.
**hechten** *vi aux sein (col)* to dive.
**Hechtsprung** *m (beim Schwimmen)* racing dive;
*(beim Turnen)* forward dive; *(Ftbl col)* dive.
**Heck** *nt* **-e** *or* **-s** *(Naut)* stern; *(Aviat)* tail, rear; *(Aut)*
rear, back.
**Heck|antrieb** *m (Aut)* rear-wheel drive.
**Hecke** *f* **-n** hedge; *(am Wegrand)* hedgerow.
**Hecken-:** ~**rose** *f* dogrose, wild rose; ~**schere** *f*
garden shears; *(elektrisch)* hedge-trimmer;
~**schütze** *m* sniper.
**Heck-:** *(Aut)* ~**fenster** *nt* rear window; ~**flosse** *f*
tail fin; ~**klappe** *f* tailgate.
**Heckmeck** *m no pl (col) (dummes Gerede)* nonsense,
rubbish; *(Umstände)* fuss, palaver *(col)*.
**Heck-:** ~**motor** *m (Aut)* rear engine; ~**scheibe** *f
(Aut)* rear window; ~**tür** *f (Aut)* tailgate.
**Hedonismus** *m* hedonism.
**Hedonist(in** *f*) *m* hedonist.
**hedonistisch** *adj* hedonistic.
**Heer** *nt* **-e** *(lit, fig)* army. **beim** ~ in the army.
**Heeresleitung** *f* command.
**Hefe** *f* **-n** yeast.
**Hefe-:** ~**gebäck** *nt* yeast-risen pastry; ~**pilz** *m*
yeast plant; ~**teig** *m* yeast dough.
**Heft**[1] *nt* **-e** *(von Werkzeug, Messer)* handle; *(von
Dolch, Schwert)* hilt. **das** ~ **in der Hand haben** *(fig)* to
hold the reins; **jdm das** ~ **aus der Hand nehmen**
*(fig)* to seize control/power from sb.
**Heft**[2] *nt* **-e** *(Schreib~)* exercise book; *(Zeitschrift)* magazine; *(Comic~)* comic; *(Nummer)* number, issue;
*(geheftetes Büchlein)* booklet.
**Heftchen** *nt* **(a)** *dim of* **Heft**[2]. **(b)** *(pej) (billiger Roman)* cheap novel *(in magazine format)*; *(Comic~)*
rag *(pej col)*. **(c)** *(Fahrkarten~, Briefmarken~)* book
of tickets/stamps.
**heften 1** *vt* **(a)** *(nähen) Saum* to tack (up); *Buch* to
sew, to stitch; *(klammern)* to clip *(an +acc to)*; *(mit
Heftmaschine auch)* to staple *(an +acc to)*. **(b)** *(befestigen)* to pin, to fix. **den Blick auf jdn/etw** ~ to
stare at sb/sth. **2** *vr* **sich an jds Fersen** *or* **Sohlen** ~
*(fig)* to dog sb's heels.
**Hefter** *m* - (loose-leaf) file.
**heftig** *adj* violent; *Schmerz, Liebe* intense; *Erkältung,
Fieber* severe; *Weinen* bitter; *Kampf, Wind, Widerstand* fierce; *Regen, Frost* heavy. **ein** ~**er Regenguß**
a downpour; **er hat sich** ~ **in sie verliebt** he has fall-
en passionately in love with her; ~ **nicken/rühren**
to nod/stir vigorously.
**Heftigkeit** *f no pl siehe adj* violence; intensity; severity; bitterness; ferocity; heaviness.
**Heft-:** ~**klammer** *f* staple; ~**maschine** *f* stapler;
~**pflaster** *nt* (sticking) plaster, adhesive tape
*(US)*; ~**roman** *m* cheap paperback novel, dime
novel *(US)*; ~**zwecke** *f* drawing pin *(Brit)*, thumb
tack *(US)*.
**hegen** *vt* **(a)** *Wild, Pflanzen* to care for, to tend. **jdn**
~ **und pflegen** to lavish care and attention on sb.
**(b)** *Groll, Verdacht* to harbour *(Brit)*, to harbor *(US)*;
*Mißtrauen, Abneigung* to feel; *Zweifel* to entertain;
*Hoffnung, Wunsch* to cherish. **ich hege den starken**

**Verdacht, daß** ... I have a strong suspicion that ...
**Hehl** *nt or m:* **kein** *or* **keinen** ~ **aus etw machen** to
make no secret of sth.
**Hehler(in** *f*) *m* - receiver (of stolen goods), fence
*(col)*.
**Hehlerei** *f no pl* receiving (stolen goods).
**hehr** *adj (liter)* noble, sublime.
**Heia** *f no pl (baby-talk)* **ab in die** ~ off to bye-byes
*(baby-talk)*; **h**~ **machen** to have a little nap.
**Heide**[1] *m (wk)* **-n, -n, Heidin** *f* heathen, pagan.
**Heide**[2] *f* **-n** moor, heath.
**Heide-:** ~**kraut** *nt* heather; ~**land** *nt* moorland,
heathland.
**Heidelbeere** *f* bilberry, blueberry *(esp US)*.
**Heiden-** *(col)*: ~**angst** *f:* **eine** ~**angst vor etw** *(dat)*
**haben** to be scared stiff of sth *(col)*; ~**arbeit** *f* real
slog *(col)*; ~**geld** *nt* packet *(col)*; ~**krach**, ~**lärm** *m*
unholy din *(col)*; ~**respekt** *m* healthy respect;
~**spaß** *m* terrific fun; **einen** ~**spaß haben** to have a
whale of a time *(col)*; ~**spektakel** *m* awful row;
*(Schimpfen)* awful fuss.
**Heidentum** *nt no pl* paganism.
**Heidin** *f siehe* **Heide**[1].
**heidnisch** *adj* heathen, pagan.
**heikel** *adj* **(a)** *Situation, Thema* tricky, delicate. **(b)**
*(dial) Mensch* particular, pernickety *(col)*, persnickety *(US col) (in bezug auf +acc* about*)*.
**heil** *adj* **(a)** *(unverletzt) Mensch* unhurt; *Glieder* unbroken; *Haut* undamaged. **wieder** ~ **sein/werden**
*(wieder gesund)* to be/get better again; *(Wunde)* to
have healed/to heal up; ~ **nach Hause kommen** to
get home safe and sound; **etw** ~ **überstehen** *Unfall*
to come through sth without a scratch; *Prüfung* to
get through sth; **mit** ~**er Haut davonkommen** to escape unscathed. **(b)** *(col: ganz)* intact; *Kleidungsstück* decent *(col)*. **eine** ~**e Welt** an ideal world
*(without problems etc)*.
**Heil 1** *nt no pl* **(a)** *(Wohlergehen)* well-being, good.
**(b)** *(Eccl, fig)* salvation. **sein** ~ **in der Flucht suchen**
to flee for one's life. **2** *interj* **Ski/Petri** ~! good
skiing/fishing!
**Heiland** *m* **-e** *(Rel)* Saviour, Redeemer.
**Heil-:** ~**anstalt** *f* nursing home; *(für Sucht- oder Gei-
steskranke)* home; ~**bad** *nt (Bad)* medicinal bath;
*(Ort)* spa; **h**~**bar** *adj* curable; **h**~**bringend** *adj
(Rel)* redeeming; *Wirkung* beneficial; *Kräuter* medicinal.
**Heilbutt** *m* **-e** halibut.
**heilen 1** *vi aux sein* to heal (up). **2** *vt* to cure; *Wunde, (Rel)* to heal. **als geheilt entlassen werden** to be
discharged with a clean bill of health; **jdn von etw**
~ *(lit, fig)* to cure sb of sth; **von jdm/etw geheilt
sein** *(fig)* to have got over sb/sth.
**heilend** *adj* healing.
**heilfroh** *adj pred (col)* jolly glad *(col)*.
**heilig** *adj* **(a)** holy; *(bei Namen von Heiligen)* Saint;
**jdm** ~ **sein** *(lit, fig)* to be sacred to sb; **H**~**er Abend**
Christmas Eve; **H**~**e Maria** Holy Mary; **der H**~**e
Geist** the Holy Spirit *or* Ghost; **der H**~**e Stuhl** the
Holy See; **die H**~**en Drei Könige** the Three Wise
Men; **die H**~**e Schrift** the Holy Scriptures *pl*. **(b)**
*Pflicht* sacred; *Zorn* righteous; *Stille, Schauer* awed.
**es ist mein** ~**er Ernst** I am deadly serious. **(c)** *(col:
groß)* incredible *(col)*; *Respekt auch* healthy.
**Heilig|abend** *m* Christmas Eve.
**heiligen** *vt* to hallow; *Sonntag etc* to keep holy. **der
Zweck heiligt die Mittel** the end justifies the means.
**Heiligen-:** ~**bild** *nt* holy picture; ~**schein** *m* halo;
**jdn mit einem** ~**schein umgeben** *(fig)* to put sb on a
pedestal.
**Heilige(r)** *mf decl as adj (lit, fig)* saint. **ein sonder-**

**barer** ~**r** *(col)* a queer fish *(col)*.
**Heilig-**: ~**keit** *f* holiness; **Seine** ~**keit** his Holiness; **h**~**sprechen** *vt sep irreg* to canonize; ~**sprechung** *f* canonization; ~**tum** *nt (Stätte)* shrine; *(Gegenstand)* (holy) relic; **jds** ~**tum sein** *(col) (Zimmer)* to be sb's sanctum; *(Gegenstand etc)* to be sacrosanct (to sb).
**Heil-**: ~**kraft** *f* healing power; **h**~**kräftig** *adj Pflanze, Tee* medicinal; ~**kraut** *nt usu pl* medicinal herb; ~**kunde** *f* medicine; ~**kundige(r)** *mf decl as adj* healer; **h**~**los** *adj* unholy *(col)*; *Schreck* terrible; ~**methode** *f* cure; ~**mittel** *nt (lit, fig)* remedy, cure; *(Medikament)* medicine; ~**pflanze** *f* medicinal plant; ~**praktiker** *m* non-medical practitioner; ~**quelle** *f* medicinal spring; **h**~**sam** *adj Erfahrung, Strafe* salutary; *Wirkung* beneficial; *(dated: heilend)* healing.
**Heils\|armee** *f* Salvation Army.
**Heilung** *f (von Wunde)* healing; *(von Krankheit, Kranken)* curing.
**Heilungsprozeß** *m* healing process.
**heim** *adv* home.
**Heim** *nt* **-e** home; *(Studentenwohn~)* hall of residence, hostel.
**Heim-** *in cpds* home; ~**arbeit** *f (Ind)* homework, outwork *both no indef art*; ~**arbeiter** *m (Ind)* homeworker.
**Heimat** *f* **-en** home. **die** ~ **verlassen** to leave one's home.
**Heimat-** *in cpds* home; ~**dichter** *m* regional writer; ~**erde** *f* native soil; ~**film** *m sentimental film in idealized regional setting*; ~**kunde** *f (Sch)* local history; ~**land** *nt* native country; **h**~**lich** *adj* native; *Bräuche, Dialekt* local; *Gefühle* nostalgic; *Klänge* of home; **h**~**los** *adj* homeless; ~**lose(r)** *mf decl as adj* homeless person; ~**museum** *nt* local history museum; ~**ort** *m* home town/village; ~**vertriebene(r)** *mf decl as adj* displaced person.
**heim-**: ~**begeben*** *vr sep irreg* to make one's way home; ~**begleiten*** *vt sep jdn* ~**begleiten** to see sb home; ~**bringen** *vt sep irreg (nach Hause bringen)* to bring home; *(~begleiten)* to take home.
**Heimchen** *nt* ~ **(am Herd)** *(pej: Frau)* housewife.
**Heimcomputer** *m* home computer.
**heimelig** *adj* cosy, homely.
**Heim-**: **h**~**fahren** *vti sep irreg (vi: aux sein)* to drive home; ~**fahrt** *f* journey home; *(Naut)* return voyage; **h**~**finden** *vi sep irreg* to find one's way home; **h**~**gehen** *vi sep irreg aux sein* to go home; **h**~**holen** *vt sep* to fetch home; **Gott hat ihn h**~**geholt** he has been called to his Maker.
**heimisch** *adj* **(a)** *(einheimisch)* indigenous, native *(in +dat to)*; *(national)* home; *(ortsansässig)* local; *(regional)* regional. **(b)** *(vertraut)* familiar. **sich** ~ **fühlen** to feel at home; ~ **werden** to become acclimatized *(an, in +dat to)*.
**Heim-**: ~**kehr** *f no pl* homecoming; **h**~**kehren** *vi sep aux sein* to return home *(aus from)*; ~**kehrer(in** *f)* *m* homecomer; ~**kind** *nt* child brought up in a home; **h**~**kommen** *vi sep irreg aux sein* to come home; ~**leiter** *m* warden of a/the home/ hostel; **h**~**leuchten** *vi sep (fig col)* **jdm h**~**leuchten** to give sb a piece of one's mind.
**heimlich** **1** *adj* secret. **2** *adv* secretly; *lachen* inwardly. **er blickte sie** ~ **an** he stole a glance at her; **sich** ~ **entfernen** to sneak away; ~**, still und leise** *(col)* quietly, on the quiet.
**Heimlichkeit** *f* secrecy; *(Geheimnis)* secret. **in aller** ~ secretly, in secret.
**Heimlich-**: ~**tuer(in** *f)* *m* - secretive person; ~**tuerei** *f* secrecy; **h**~**tun** *vi sep irreg* to be secre-

tive *(mit* about*)*.
**Heim-**: ~**reise** *f* homeward journey; *(Naut)* homeward voyage; **h**~**reisen** *vi sep aux sein* to travel home; **h**~**schicken** *vt sep* to send home; ~**spiel** *nt (Sport)* home match; ~**statt** *f* home.
**heimsuchen** *vt sep* to strike; *(für längere Zeit)* to plague; *(Gespenst)* to haunt; *(Krankheit, Alpträume)* to afflict; *(col: besuchen)* to descend on *(col)*. **von Dürre/Krieg heimgesucht** drought-stricken/war-torn.
**Heimtrainer** *m* exercise machine; *(Trimmrad)* exercise bike.
**heimtückisch** *adj* insidious; *(boshaft)* malicious; *Glatteis, Maschine* treacherous.
**Heim-**: **h**~**wärts** *adv* homewards; ~**weg** *m* way home; **sich auf den** ~**weg machen** to head for home; ~**weh** *nt* homesickness *no art*; ~**weh haben** to be homesick *(nach* for*)*; ~**werker** *m* handyman; **h**~**zahlen** *vt sep* **jdm etw h**~**zahlen** to pay sb back for sth.
**Heini** *m* **-s** *(pej col)* guy *(col)*. **blöder** ~ silly idiot.
**Heinzelmännchen** *nt* **die** ~ the little people.
**Heirat** *f* **-en** marriage.
**heiraten** **1** *vt* to marry. **2** *vi* to get married, to marry. **in eine reiche Familie** ~ to marry into a rich family.
**Heirats-**: ~**annonce** *f* = ~**anzeige (b)**; ~**antrag** *m* proposal (of marriage); **jdm einen** ~**antrag machen** to propose to sb; ~**anzeige** *f* **(a)** *(Bekanntgabe)* announcement of a forthcoming marriage; **(b)** *(zur Partnersuche)* advertisement for a marriage partner; **h**~**fähig** *adj* marriageable; ~**schwindler** *m person who makes a marriage proposal in order to obtain money*; ~**urkunde** *f* marriage certificate; ~**vermittler** *m* marriage broker; ~**vermittlung** *f* matchmaking *no pl*; *(Büro)* marriage bureau.
**heiser** *adj* hoarse.
**Heiserkeit** *f* hoarseness.
**heiß** *adj (lit, fig)* hot; *Zone* torrid; *Thema* hotly disputed; *Diskussion, Kampf* heated, fierce; *Begierde, Liebe, Wunsch* burning. **jdm wird** ~ sb is getting hot; **sie hat einen** ~**en Kopf** she has a burning forehead; **etw** ~ **machen** to heat sth up; **es wird nichts so** ~ **gegessen, wie es gekocht wird** *(prov)* things are never as bad as they seem; **es ging** ~ **her** things got heated; **die Stadt ist** ~ **umkämpft** the town is being fiercely fought over; **jdn/etw** ~ **und innig lieben** to love sb/sth madly; ~**e Tränen weinen** to cry one's heart out; **sich** *(dat)* **die Köpfe** ~ **reden** to talk till one is blue in the face; **jdn** ~ **machen** *(col)* to turn sb on *(col)*; **ein** ~**es Eisen** a hot potato *(fig col)*; **ein** ~**es Eisen anfassen** *(col)* to grasp the nettle *(fig)*; ~**er Draht** hot line; ~**e Spur** firm lead.
**heißblütig** *adj* hot-blooded.
**heißen** *pret* **hieß**, *ptp* **geheißen 1** *vi* **(a)** to be called *(Brit)* or named. **wie** ~ **Sie/heißt die Straße?** what's your name/the name of the street?; **ich heiße Müller** I'm called *or* my name is Müller; **sie heißt jetzt anders** she has changed her name; **eigentlich heißt es richtig X** actually the correct word is X; **... und wie sie alle** ~ ... and the rest of them. **(b)** *(bestimmte Bedeutung haben)* to mean. **was heißt „gut" auf englisch?** what is the English for "gut"?; **soll/will** ~ *(am Satzanfang)* in other words; **was soll das** ~**?** what does that mean?; **das will schon etwas** ~ that's quite something. **(c) das heißt** that is; *(in anderen Worten)* that is to say.
**2** *vt (geh)* **(a)** *(nennen)* to call. **(b)** *(auffordern)* to tell. **jdn willkommen** ~ to bid sb welcome.
**3** *vi impers* **es heißt, daß ...** they say that ...; **in der Bibel/in seinem Brief heißt es, daß ...** the Bible/ his letter says that ...; **es heißt hier ...** it says

here ...; **nun heißt es handeln** now we must do something.

**Heiß-: h~ersehnt** *adj attr* much longed for; **h~geliebt** *adj* dearly beloved; **~hunger** *m* voracious appetite; **etw mit ~hunger verschlingen** *(lit, fig)* to devour sth; **h~hungrig** *adj* ravenous, voracious; **h~laufen** *vi sep irreg aux sein (Motor)* to run hot; **~luft** *f* hot air; **~luftballon** *m* hot-air balloon; **~luftherd** *m* fan(-assisted) oven; **~mangel** *f (Gerät)* rotary iron; *(Geschäft) laundry specializing in ironing sheets etc*; **h~umkämpft** *adj attr* hotly disputed; **h~umstritten** *adj attr* hotly debated; **~wasserbereiter** *m* water-heater.

**heiter** *adj (fröhlich)* cheerful; *(ausgeglichen)* serene; *(amüsant) Geschichte* amusing; *(hell, klar) Farbe, Himmel, Tag* bright; *Wetter* fine; *(Met)* fair. **~ werden** to become cheerful; *(Wetter)* to clear up; **das kann ja ~ werden!** *(iro)* that sounds great *(iro)*; **aus ~em Himmel** *(fig)* out of the blue.

**Heiterkeit** *f no pl siehe adj* cheerfulness; serenity; amusingness; brightness, fineness; *(heitere Stimmung)* merriment.

**Heiz-: h~bar** *adj* heated; **schwer h~bar** difficult to heat; **~(bett)decke** *f* electric blanket.

**heizen 1** *vi* to have the heating on. **der Ofen heizt gut** the stove gives off a good heat; **mit Holz/Strom ~** to use wood/electricity for heating. **2** *vt (warm machen)* to heat; *(verbrennen)* to burn.

**Heizer** *m* - *(von Hochofen)* boilerman; *(von Lokomotive, Schiff)* stoker.

**Heiz-: ~gerät** *nt* heater; **~kissen** *nt* electric heat pad; **~körper** *m (Gerät)* heater; *(von Zentralheizung)* radiator; **~kosten** *pl* heating costs *pl*; **~lüfter** *m* fan heater; **~material** *nt* (heating) fuel; **~ofen** *m* heater; **~öl** *nt* heating *or* fuel oil; **~sonne** *f* electric fire.

**Heizung** *f* heating; *(Heizkörper)* heater.

**Heizungs-: ~anlage** *f* heating system; **~keller** *m* boiler room; **~monteur** *m* heating engineer; **~rohr** *nt* heating pipe.

**Hektar** *nt or m* -e hectare.

**Hektik** *f no pl* hectic rush; *(von Großstadt etc)* hustle and bustle; *(von Leben etc)* hectic pace. **sie arbeitet mit einer solchen ~** she works at such a hectic pace; **nur keine ~** take it easy.

**hektisch** *adj* hectic.

**Hektoliter** *m or nt* hectolitre *(Brit)*, hectoliter *(US)*.

**Held** *m (wk)* -en, -en hero. **der ~ des Tages** the hero of the hour; **kein ~ in etw** *(dat)* **sein** not to be very brave about sth; *(in Schulfach etc)* to be no great shakes at sth *(col)*; **du bist mir ein schöner ~!** *(iro)* some hero you are!

**Helden-: ~dichtung** *f* heroic poetry; **h~haft, h~mütig** *adj* heroic; **~tat** *f* heroic deed; **~tum** *nt no pl* heroism.

**Heldin** *f* heroine.

**helfen** *pret* **half,** *ptp* **geholfen** *vi* to help *(jdm sb)*. **jdm bei etw ~** to help sb with sth, to lend sb a hand with sth; **ihm ist nicht zu ~** *(fig)* he is beyond help; **ich kann mir nicht ~, ich muß es tun** I can't help doing it; **ich werd' ihm (schon) ~!** I'll give him what for *(col)*; **ich werde dir ~, die Tapeten zu beschmieren** I'll teach you to mess up the wallpaper; **sich** *(dat)* **zu ~ wissen** to be resourceful; **man muß sich** *(dat)* **nur zu ~ wissen** *(prov)* you just have to use your brains; **er weiß sich** *(dat)* **nicht mehr zu ~** he is at his wits' end; **diese Arznei hilft gegen** *or* **bei Kopfweh** this medicine is good for headaches; **es hilft nichts** it's no use *or* no good; **da hilft alles nichts ...** there's nothing for it ...; **was hilft's?** what's the use?

**Helfer(in** *f)* *m* - helper; *(Mitarbeiter)* assistant; *(von Verbrecher)* accomplice. **ein ~ in der Not** a friend in need.

**Helfershelfer** *m* accomplice.

**Helgoland** *nt* Heligoland.

**hell** *adj* **(a)** *(optisch)* light; *Licht, Himmel* bright; *Haar, Haut* fair. **es wird ~** it's getting light; **~ bleiben** to stay light; **am ~en Tage** in broad daylight; **in ~en Flammen** in flames, ablaze; **~es Bier** ≃ lager. **(b)** *Ton etc* high(-pitched). **(c)** *(col: klug)* bright; *Augenblicke* lucid. **er ist ein ~er Kopf** he has brains. **(d)** *attr (stark, groß)* great; *Verzweiflung, Unsinn* sheer, utter; *Neid* pure. **von etw ~ begeistert sein** to be very enthusiastic about sth; **in ~en Scharen** in great numbers.

**hell-** *in cpds (esp auf Farben bezüglich)* light; **~auf** *adv* completely, utterly; **~blond** *adj* very fair, blonde.

**Helle** *f no pl* = **Helligkeit.**

**helle** *adj pred (col)* bright, clever.

**Heller** *m* - **darauf geb ich keinen (roten) ~** I wouldn't give you tuppence *(Brit) or* a red cent *(US)* for it; **auf ~ und Pfennig** to the last penny.

**Helle(s)** *nt decl as adj* ≃ lager.

**hell-: ~haarig** *adj* fair-haired; **~häutig** *adj* fair-skinned; **~hörig** *adj (Archit)* poorly sound proofed; **~hörig sein** *(fig: Mensch)* to have sharp ears; **jdn ~hörig machen** to make sb prick up their ears.

**hellicht** *adj*: **am ~en Tage** in broad daylight.

**Helligkeit** *f no pl siehe* **hell (a)** lightness; brightness; fairness; *(helles Licht)* light; *(Phys, Astron)* luminosity.

**hell-: ~sehen** *vi infin only* **~sehen können** to be clairvoyant; **H~seher(in** *f)* *m (lit, fig)* clairvoyant; **~seherisch** *adj attr* clairvoyant; **~wach** *adj (lit, fig)* wide-awake; **H~werden** *nt no pl* daybreak.

**Helm** *m* -e helmet.

**Helsinki** *nt* Helsinki.

**Hemd** *nt* -en shirt; *(Unter~)* vest *(Brit)*, undershirt *(US)*. **etw wie sein ~ wechseln** *(fig)* to change sth with monotonous regularity; **für dich gebe ich mein letztes ~ her** *(col)* I'd give you the shirt off my back *(col)*; **naß bis aufs ~** wet through; **jdn bis aufs ~ ausziehen** *(fig col)* to have the shirt off sb's back *(col)*.

**Hemdbluse** *f* shirt(-blouse), shirtwaist *(US)*.

**Hemds-: ~ärmel** *m* **in ~ärmeln** in one's shirt sleeves; **h~ärmelig** *adj* shirt-sleeved; *(fig col: salopp)* pally *(col)*; *Ausdrucksweise* casual.

**Hemisphäre** *f* -n hemisphere.

**hemmen** *vt Entwicklung* to hinder; *Lauf der Dinge, Maschine* to check; *(verlangsamen)* to slow down; *Wasserlauf* to stem; *(Psych)* to inhibit.

**Hemmnis** *nt* hindrance, impediment *(für to)*.

**Hemm-: ~schuh** *m (fig)* hindrance, impediment *(für to)*; **~schwelle** *f (Psych)* inhibition threshold.

**Hemmung** *f* **(a)** *(Psych)* inhibition; *(Bedenken)* scruple. **da habe ich ~en** I've got scruples about that; **keine ~en kennen** to have no inhibitions; **nur keine ~en** don't feel inhibited. **(b)** *siehe vt* hindering; check *(gen to)*; slowing down; stemming.

**Hemmungs-: h~los** *adj (rückhaltlos)* unrestrained; *(skrupellos)* unscrupulous; **~losigkeit** *f siehe adj* lack of restraint; unscrupulousness.

**Hengst** *m* -e stallion; *(Kamel~, Esel~)* male.

**Hengst-: ~fohlen, ~füllen** *nt* (male) foal, colt.

**Henkel** *m* - handle.

**Henkel-** *in cpds* with a handle; **~mann** *m, pl* **~männer** *(col)* canteen.

**henken** *vt (dated)* to hang.

**Henker** *m* - hangman; *(Scharfrichter)* executioner.

**was zum ~** *(col)* what the devil *(col)*; **scher dich zum ~!** *(col)* go to the devil! *(col)*.

**Henkersmahl(zeit** *f)* *nt* last meal before one's execution; *(hum col)* last slap-up meal *(before an examination etc)*.

**Henna** *nt no pl* henna. **mit ~ färben** to henna.

**Henne** *f* **-n** hen.

**Hepatitis** *f, pl* **Hepatitiden** hepatitis.

**her** *adv* **(a)** **von Frankreich/dem Meer ~** from France/the sea; **~ zu mir!** *(col)* come here (to me); **um mich ~** (all) around me; **von weit ~** from a long way off; **~ damit!** *(col)* give me that; **immer ~ damit!** *(col)* let's have it/them (then). **(b)** **von der Idee/Form ~** as far as the idea/form goes; **vom finanziellen Standpunkt ~** from the financial point of view. **(c)** *(zeitlich)* **ich kenne ihn von früher ~** I know him from before; **von der Schule/meiner Kindheit ~** since school/my childhood; *siehe* **hersein (a)**.

**herab** *adv* down. **die Treppe ~** down the stairs; **von oben ~** from above.

**herab-** *pref* down; **~blicken** *vi sep (lit, fig)* to look down *(auf +acc* on); **~hängen** *vi sep irreg* to hang down; **~lassen** *sep irreg* **1** *vt* to let down, to lower; **2** *vr (lit, fig)* to lower oneself; **sich zu etw ~ lassen** to condescend *or* deign to do sth; **~lassend** *adj* condescending; **H~lassung** *f* condescension; **~mindern** *vt sep (schlechtmachen)* Leistung *etc* to belittle; *(reduzieren)* Geschwindigkeit, Niveau to reduce; **~sehen** *vi sep irreg (lit, fig)* to look down *(auf +acc* on); **~setzen** *vt sep* Ware, Preise to reduce; Niveau to lower; *(schlechtmachen)* Leistungen, jdn to belittle; **zu stark ~gesetzten Preisen** at greatly reduced prices; **~sinken** *vi sep irreg aux sein* to sink (down); **~stürzen** *sep* **1** *vt* to push off *(von etw* sth*)*; **2** *vi aux sein* to fall off *(von etw* sth*)*; *(Felsbrocken)* to fall down *(von* from*)*; **3** *vr* to jump off *(von etw* sth*)*; **~würdigen** *sep* **1** *vt* to disparage; **2** *vr* to lower oneself.

**heran** *adv* **bis an etw** *(acc)* **~** right beside sth; *(mit Bewegungsverb)* right up to sth.

**heran-:** **~bilden** *vt sep* to train (up); *(in der Schule)* to educate; **~bringen** *vt sep irreg (herbringen)* to bring over; **die Schüler an diese Probleme ~bringen** to introduce the pupils to these problems; **~eilen** *vi sep aux sein* to hurry over; **~fahren** *vti sep irreg aux sein* to drive up *(an +acc* to*)*; **~führen** *sep* **1** *vt* jdn to lead up; **jdn an etw** *(acc)* **~führen** to introduce sb to sth; **2** *vi* **an etw** *(acc)* **~führen** *(lit, fig)* to lead to sth; **~gehen** *vi sep irreg aux sein* to go up *(an +acc* to*)*; **ich würde nicht näher ~gehen** I wouldn't go any nearer; **an etw ~gehen** *an Problem, Aufgabe* to tackle sth; **~kommen** *vi sep irreg aux sein* **(a)** to draw near *(an +acc* to*)*, to approach *(an etw* *(acc))* sth); **auf 1:3 ~kommen** to pull back to 1-3; **er läßt alle Probleme an sich ~kommen** he always adopts a wait-and-see attitude; **an den Chef/Motor kommt man nicht ~** you can't get hold of the boss/get at the engine; **(b)** *(sich messen können)* **an jdn/etw ~kommen** to be up to the standard of sb/sth; **~lassen** *vt sep irreg* **jdn an etw** *(acc)* **~lassen** to let sb near sth; **er läßt keinen an sich ~** he won't let anyone near him; **~machen** *vr sep (col)* **sich an etw** *(acc)* **~machen** to get down to sth; **sich an jdn ~machen** to approach sb; **an Frau** to chat sb up *(col)*; **~nahen** *vi sep aux sein (geh)* to approach; **~reichen** *vi sep* **an jdn/etw ~reichen** *(lit)* to reach sb/sth; *(fig: sich messen können)* to come near sb/sth; **~reifen** *vi sep aux sein (geh)* to ripen; *(fig)* to mature; **~rücken** *sep* **1** *vi aux sein (sich nähern)* to approach *(an etw* *(acc)* sth*)*; *(dicht aufrücken)* to

come/go nearer *(an +acc* to*)*; **2** *vt* to pull/push up *(an +acc* to*)*; **~tragen** *vt sep irreg* to bring (over); **etw an jdn ~tragen** *(fig)* to take/bring sth to sb; **~treten** *vi sep irreg aux sein (lit)* to come/go up *(an +acc* to*)*; **näher ~treten** to come/go nearer; **mit etw an jdn ~treten** *(sich wenden an)* to approach sb with sth; **~wachsen** *vi sep irreg aux sein (geh)* to grow; *(Kind)* to grow up; **die ~wachsende Generation** the rising generation; **H~wachsende(r)** *mf decl as adj* adolescent; **~wagen** *vr sep* to venture near; **sich an etw** *(acc)* **~wagen** to venture to tackle sth; **~winken** *vt sep* to beckon *or* wave over; Taxi to hail; **~ziehen** *vt sep irreg* **(a)** to draw near *(an +acc* to*)*; **(b)** *(zu Hilfe holen)* to call in; Literatur to consult; **etw zum Vergleich ~ziehen** to use sth by way of comparison; **(c)** *Arbeitskräfte, Kapital* to bring in.

**herauf 1** *adv* up. **vom Tal ~** up from the valley; **von unten ~** up from below. **2** *prep +acc* up. **den Berg/die Treppe ~** up the mountain/stairs.

**herauf-** *pref* up; **~arbeiten** *vr sep (lit, fig)* to work one's way up; **~beschwören\*** *vt sep irreg* Vergangenheit to evoke; Unglück, Krise to cause; **~bringen** *vt sep irreg* to bring up; **~führen** *sep* **1** *vt* Pferd *etc* to lead up; jdn to show up; **2** *vi (Weg etc)* to lead up; **~kommen** *vi sep irreg aux sein* to come up; **~setzen** *vt sep* Preise *etc* to increase; **~steigen** *vi sep irreg aux sein* to climb up; *(Rauch)* to rise; *(Erinnerungen)* to well up *(in jdm* in sb*)*; **~ziehen** *sep irreg* **1** *vt* to pull up; **2** *vi aux sein (Gewitter, Unheil etc)* to approach.

**heraus** *adv* out. **~ damit!** *(col: gib her)* hand it over!; **~ mit der Sprache** out with it! *(col)*; **zum Fenster ~** out of the window; **nach vorn ~ wohnen** to live at the front; **aus dem Wunsch ~ ...** out of a desire to ...

**heraus-** *pref* out; **~arbeiten** *vt sep (aus Stein, Holz)* to carve *(aus* out of*)*; *(fig)* to bring out; **~bekommen\*** *vt sep irreg* **(a)** Fleck, Nagel *etc* to get out *(aus* of*)*; **(b)** *(ermitteln)* Täter, Geheimnis to find out *(aus jdm* from sb*)*; Lösung, Aufgabe to work out; **(c)** Wechselgeld to get back; **~bilden** *vr sep* to form, to develop *(aus* out of*)*; **~boxen** *vt sep (aus* of*)* Ball to punch out; *(col)* jdn to bail out *(col)*; **~bringen** *vt sep irreg* **(a)** to bring out *(aus* of*)*; **(b)** = **~bekommen (a, b)**; **(c)** *(auf den Markt bringen)* to bring out; **jdn/etw ganz groß ~bringen** *(col)* to give sb/sth a big build-up; **(d)** *(col: hervorbringen)* Worte to say; **aus ihm war kein Wort ~zubringen** they couldn't get a single word out of him; **~drehen** *vt sep* Birne, Schraube to unscrew *(aus* from*)*; **~drücken** *vt sep* to squeeze out *(aus* of*)*; **~fahren** *sep irreg* **1** *vi aux sein* to come out *(aus* of*)*; **2** *vt* **(a)** Auto to drive out *(aus* of*)*; **(b)** *(Sport)* **eine gute Zeit ~fahren** to record a good time; **~finden** *sep irreg* **1** *vt* Fehler, Täter *etc* to find out; *(~lesen)* Gesuchtes to pick out *(aus* from*)*; **2** *vir* to find one's way out *(aus* of*)*.

**Herausforderer** *m* - challenger.

**herausfordern** *sep* **1** *vt* to challenge *(zu* to*)*; *(provozieren)* to provoke *(zu etw* to do sth*)*; Kritik, Protest to invite; Gefahr, Unglück to court. **das Schicksal ~** to tempt providence. **2** *vi* **zu etw ~** *(provozieren)* to invite sth.

**herausfordernd** *adj* provocative; *(Auseinandersetzung suchend)* Haltung, Blick challenging.

**Herausforderung** *f* challenge; *(Provokation)* provocation.

**Herausgabe** *f* **(a)** return; *(von Personen)* handing over. **(b)** *(von Buch etc)* publication.

**herausgeben** *sep irreg* **1** *vt* **(a)** *(zurückgeben)* to return, to give back; *Gefangene etc* to hand over. **(b)** *(veröffentlichen)* to issue; *Buch, Zeitung* to publish; *(bearbeiten)* to edit. **(c)** *(Wechselgeld geben) Betrag* to give as change. **wieviel hat er dir herausgegeben?** how much change did he give you? **(d)** *(herausreichen)* to hand out *(aus of)*. **2** *vi (Wechselgeld geben)* to give change *(auf +acc for)*. **können Sie (mir) ~?** can you give me change?; **falsch ~** to give the wrong change.

**Herausgeber(in** *f)* *m (Verleger)* publisher; *(Redakteur)* editor.

**heraus-:** **~gehen** *vi sep irreg aux sein (aus of)* to go out; *(Fleck, Korken etc)* to come out; **aus sich ~gehen** *(fig)* to come out of one's shell; **~greifen** *vt sep irreg* to pick out *(aus of)*; *Beispiel* to take; **~haben** *vt sep irreg (col)* **(a) ich will ihn aus der Firma ~haben** I want him out of the firm; **(b)** *Rätsel, Aufgabe* to have solved; *Geheimnis* to have found out; **~halten** *sep irreg* **1** *vt* **(a)** *Hand, Gegenstand* to put out *(aus of)*; **(b)** *(fernhalten) Tiere, Eindringlinge* to keep out *(aus of)*; **2** *vr* to keep out of it; **sich aus etw ~halten** to keep out of sth; **~hängen** *vti sep irreg* to hang out *(aus of)*; **~heben** *sep irreg* **1** *vt* to lift out *(aus of)*; *(fig: betonen)* to bring out; **2** *vr* to stand out; **~holen** *vt sep* **(a)** *(aus of)* to get out; *(~bringen)* to bring out; **(b)** *(fig col) Antwort, Geheimnis* to get out *(aus of)*; *Vorteil, Sieg* to gain *(aus from)*; *Zeit* to make up; *Ergebnis* to get; **~hören** *vt sep (wahrnehmen)* to hear; *(fühlen)* to detect *(aus in)*; **~kehren** *vt sep (lit)* to sweep out *(aus of)*; *(fig: betonen)* to parade; **den Vorgesetzten ~kehren** to act the boss.

**herauskommen** *vi sep irreg aux sein* **(a)** *(lit, fig)* to come out *(aus of)*; *(Schwindel etc)* to come to light. **er ist nie aus seinem Dorf herausgekommen** he has never been out of his village; **aus sich ~** to come out of one's shell; **er kam aus dem Staunen nicht heraus** he couldn't get over his astonishment; **aus einer schwierigen Lage ~** to get out of a difficult situation; **aus seinen Schwierigkeiten ~** to get over one's difficulties. **(b)** *(Resultat haben)* **bei etw ~** to come of sth; **und was soll dabei ~?** and what is that supposed to achieve?, and where is that supposed to get us?; **es kommt auf dasselbe heraus** it comes (down) to the same thing. **(c)** *(Cards)* to lead.

**heraus-:** **~kriegen** *vt sep (col)* = **~bekommen;** **~lesen** *vt sep irreg (erkennen)* to gather *(aus from)*; **~locken** *vt sep* to entice out *(aus of)*; **etw aus jdm ~locken** *(ablisten)* to get sth out of sb; **~machen** *sep (col)* **1** *vt (aus of)* to take out; *Fleck* to get out; **2** *vr (sich gut entwickeln)* to come on (well); *(nach Krankheit)* to pick up; **~nehmbar** *adj* removable; **~nehmen** *vt sep irreg* **(a)** to take out *(aus of)*; *Kind (aus der Schule etc)* to take away *(aus from)*; **sich** *(dat)* **die Mandeln ~nehmen lassen** to have one's tonsils out; **den Gang ~nehmen** *(Aut)* to put the car into neutral; **(b)** *(col: sich erlauben)* **sich** *(dat)* **Freiheiten ~nehmen** to take liberties; **Sie nehmen sich zuviel ~** you're going too far; **~platzen** *vi sep aux sein (col) (spontan sagen)* to blurt it out; *(lachen)* to burst out laughing; **~putzen** *vt sep jdn* to dress up; *Stadt, Wohnung etc* to deck out; **sich ~putzen** to get dressed up; **~ragen** *vi sep siehe* **hervorragen;** **~reden** *vr sep* to talk one's way out of it *(col)*; **~reißen** *vt sep irreg* **(a)** *(lit) (aus of)* to tear out; *Zahn, Baum* to pull out; **(b)** **jdn aus etw ~reißen** *(aus Umgebung)* to tear sb away from sth; *(aus Schlaf)* to startle sb out of sth; *(col: aus Schwierigkeiten)* to get sb out of sth *(col)*; **~rücken** *sep* **1** *vt* to push out *(aus of)*; *(col: hergeben) Geld* to cough up *(col)*; *Beute, Gegenstand* to hand over; **2** *vi aux*

*sein* **(a)** *(lit)* to move out; **(b)** *(col: hergeben)* **mit etw ~rücken** *(mit Geld)* to cough sth up *(col)*; *(mit Beute)* to hand sth over; *(col: aussprechen)* to come out with sth; **~rutschen** *vi sep aux sein (lit, fig)* to slip out *(aus of)*; **das ist mir nur so ~gerutscht** it just slipped out somehow; **~schauen** *vi sep (dial)* **(a)** *(Mensch)* to look out *(aus, zu of)*; **(b)** *(zu sehen sein)* to show; **(c)** *(col)* = **springen (c); ~schinden** *vt sep irreg (col)* = **~schlagen 1 (b); ~schlagen** *sep irreg* **1** *vt* **(a)** *(lit)* to knock out *(aus of)*; **(b)** *(col) Geld* to make; *Gewinn, Vorteil* to get; *Zeit* to gain; **2** *vi aux sein (Flammen)* to shoot out; **~schleudern** *vt sep (werfen)* to hurl out *(aus of)*; *Piloten* to eject; *(fig) Fragen, Vorwürfe* to burst out with; **~schmecken** *vt sep* to detect the taste of, to taste; **~schmeißen** *vt sep irreg (col: lit, fig)* to chuck out *(aus of) (col)*.

**heraussein** *vi sep irreg aux sein (col)* to be out; *(bekannt sein)* to be known; *(entschieden sein)* to have been settled; *(Gesetz)* to be in force. **aus dem Gröbsten ~** to be over the worst.

**heraus-:** **~springen** *vi sep irreg aux sein (aus of)* **(a)** *(lit)* to jump *or* leap out; **(b)** *(sich lösen)* to come out; **(c)** *(col)* **was springt für mich dabei ~?** what's in it for me?; **~stellen** *sep* **1** *vt* **(a)** *(lit)* to put outside; **(b)** *(fig: hervorheben)* to emphasize, to underline; *jdn* to give prominence to; **2** *vr (Wahrheit)* to come to light; **sich als falsch/richtig ~stellen** to prove to be wrong/correct; **es stellte sich ~, daß ...** it turned out *or* emerged that ...; **das muß sich erst ~stellen** that remains to be seen; **~strecken** *vt sep* to stick out *(zu, aus of)*; **~streichen** *vt sep irreg* **(a)** *Fehler etc* to cross out, to delete *(aus in)*; **(b)** *(betonen) Verdienste etc* to stress; **~stürzen** *vi sep aux sein (eilen)* to rush out *(aus of)*; **~suchen** *vt sep* to pick out; **~treten** *vi sep irreg aux sein* to come out *(aus of)*, to emerge *(aus from)*; *(Adern etc)* to stand out; **~wachsen** *vi sep irreg aux sein* to grow out *(aus of)*; **~winden** *vr sep irreg (fig)* **sich aus etw ~winden** to wriggle out of sth; **~wirtschaften** *vt sep* to make *(aus* out of*)*; **~wollen** *vi sep* to want to get out *(aus of)*; **nicht mit etw ~wollen** *(col: sagen wollen)* not to want to come out with sth *(col)*; **~ziehen** *vt sep irreg* to pull out *(aus of)*; *(~schleppen)* to drag out *(aus of)*.

**herb** *adj Geruch* sharp; *Parfüm* tangy; *Wein* dry; *Enttäuschung, Verlust* bitter; *Worte, Kritik* harsh.

**herbei-:** **~bringen** *vt sep irreg* to bring over; **~eilen** *vi sep aux sein* to hurry *or* rush over; **~führen** *vt sep* to bring about; **~holen** *vt sep* to bring; *Arzt, Polizisten* to fetch; **~laufen** *vi sep irreg aux sein* to come running up; **~rufen** *vt sep* to call over; *Verstärkung* to call in; *Arzt, Polizei* to call; **~schaffen** *vt sep* to bring; *Geld* to get hold of; *Beweise* to produce; **~sehnen** *vt sep* to long for; **~strömen** *vi sep aux sein* to come flocking.

**herbemühen\*** *sep (geh)* **1** *vt* **jdn ~** to trouble sb to come here. **2** *vr* to take the trouble to come here.

**Herberge** *f* **-n (a)** *no pl* lodging *no indef art*. **(b)** *(Jugend~)* (youth) hostel.

**Herbergs-:** **~mutter** *f,* **~vater** *m* (youth hostel) warden.

**her-:** **~bestellen\*** *vt sep (col)* to send for; **~bitten** *vt sep irreg* to ask to come; **~bringen** *vt sep irreg* to bring (here).

**Herbst** *m* **-e** autumn, fall *(US)*. **im ~** in autumn, in the fall *(US)*.

**Herbst-** *in cpds* autumn, fall *(US)*; **~anfang** *m* beginning of autumn *or* fall *(US)*; **~ferien** *pl* autumn *or* fall *(US)* holiday(s); *(Sch)* half-term holiday(s); **h~lich** *adj* autumn *attr*, fall *attr (US)*; *(wie im*

*Herbst auch)* autumnal; **das Wetter ist h~lich kühl** there's an autumnal chill in the air.

**Herd** *m* **-e** (a) *(Küchen~)* cooker, stove; *(Kohle~)* range. (b) *(Krankheits~)* focus; *(von Erdbeben)* epicentre *(Brit)*, epicenter *(US)*; *(fig: von Rebellion etc)* seat.

**Herde** *f* **-n** *(lit)* herd; *(von Schafen)* flock. **der ~ folgen** *(pej)* to follow the herd.

**Herden-**: **~tier** *nt* gregarious animal; **~trieb** *m (lit, fig pej)* herd instinct.

**Herdplatte** *f (von Elektroherd)* hotplate.

**herein** *adv* in. **~!** come in!; **hier ~!** in here!; **von (dr)außen ~** from outside.

**herein-** *pref* in; **~bekommen** *vt sep irreg (col)* Waren to get in; *Radiosender* to receive; *Unkosten etc* to recover; **~bitten** *vt sep irreg* to ask (to come) in; **~brechen** *vi sep irreg aux sein (Wasser, Flut)* to gush in; **das Unglück brach über ihn ~** misfortune overtook him; **~bringen** *vt sep irreg* (a) to bring in; (b) *(col) Geldverlust* to make good; *Zeit-, Produktionsverlust* to make up for; **~drängen** *vir sep* to push one's way in; **~dringen** *vi sep irreg aux sein (Licht, Wasser)* to come in *(in +acc -to)*; **ein Geräusch drang ins Zimmer ~** a sound was heard in the room; **~dürfen** *vi sep irreg (col)* to be allowed in; **~fallen** *vi sep irreg aux sein* (a) to fall in *(in +acc -to)*; (b) *(col)* to fall for it *(col)*; *(betrogen werden)* to be had *(col)*; **auf jdn/etw ~fallen** to be taken in by sb/sth; **mit jdm/etw ~fallen** to have a bad deal with sb/sth; **~führen** *vt sep* to show in; **~holen** *vt sep* to bring in *(in +acc -to)*; **~kommen** *vi sep irreg aux sein* to come in *(in +acc -to)*; **wie ist er ~gekommen?** how did he get in?; **~lassen** *vt sep irreg* to let in *(in +acc -to)*; **~legen** *vt sep (col)* **jdn ~legen** to take sb for a ride *(col)*; **~platzen** *vi sep aux sein (col)* to burst in *(in +acc -to)*; **bei jdm ~platzen** to burst in on sb; **~regnen** *vi impers sep* **es regnet ~** the rain is coming in; **~schauen** *vi sep (dial)* **=** **~sehen**; **~schneien** *sep* **1** *vi impers* **es schneit ~** the snow's coming in; **2** *vi aux sein (col)* to drop in *(col)*; **~sehen** *vi sep irreg* to look in *(in +acc -to)*; **bei jdm ~sehen** *(col)* to look sb up; **~spazieren\*** *vi sep aux sein* to breeze in *(in +acc -to)*; **~spaziert!** come right in!; *(Schausteller)* walk up! **~strömen** *vi sep aux sein (in +acc -to)* to stream in; **~stürmen** *vi sep aux sein* to storm in *(in +acc -to)*; **~stürzen** *vi sep aux sein* to rush in *(in +acc -to)*.

**Her-**: **h~fahren** *sep irreg* **1** *vi aux sein* to come here; **hinter jdm h~fahren** to drive along behind sb; **2** *vt* to drive here; **~fahrt** *f* journey here; **h~fallen** *vi sep irreg aux sein* **über jdn h~fallen** to attack sb; *(kritisieren)* to pull sb to pieces; **über etw (acc) h~fallen** to descend upon sth; *über Eßbares etc* to pounce upon sth; **h~finden** *vi sep irreg (col)* to find one's way here.

**Hergang** *m no pl (von Ereignissen)* course. **der ~ des Unfalls** the way the accident happened.

**her-**: **~geben** *sep irreg* **1** *vt (weggeben)* to give away; *(aushändigen)* to hand over; *(zurückgeben)* to give back; **gib das ~!** give me that!; **viel/wenig ~geben** *(col: erbringen)* to be a lot of use/not to be much use; **das Thema gibt viel/nichts ~** there's a lot/nothing to this topic; **was seine Beine ~gaben** as fast as his legs would carry him; **seinen Namen für etw ~geben** to lend one's name to sth; **2** *vr* **sich zu etw ~geben** to be a party to sth; **~gebracht** *adj* in **~gebrachter Weise** in the traditional way; **~gehen** *sep irreg aux sein* **1** *vi* (a) **hinter/neben jdm ~gehen** to walk along behind/beside sb; (b) **~gehen und etw tun** *(einfach tun)* just to go and do sth; **2** *vi im-*

*pers (col: zugehen)* **es ging heiß ~** things got heated; **hier geht es hoch ~** there's plenty going on here; **~gehören\*** *vi sep* to belong here; **~gelaufen** *adj attr (pej) siehe* **dahergelaufen**; **~haben** *vt sep irreg (col)* **wo hat er das ~?** where did he get that from?; **~halten** *vi sep irreg* **für etw ~halten** to pay for sth; **als Entschuldigung für etw ~halten** to be used as an excuse for sth; **~holen** *vt sep (col)* to fetch; **~holen lassen** to send for; **weit ~geholt sein** *(fig)* to be far-fetched; **~hören** *vi sep (col)* to listen; **alle mal ~hören!** everybody listen.

**Hering** *m* **-e** (a) herring; *(fig col: Schwächling)* weakling. **wie die ~e zusammengedrängt** packed in like sardines. (b) *(Zeltpflock)* (tent) peg *(Brit)* or stake *(US)*.

**her-**: **~kommen** *vi sep irreg aux sein* to come here; *(sich nähern)* to come, to approach; *(~stammen)* to come from; **~kömmlich** *adj* conventional.

**Herkunft** *f no pl* origin; *(soziale)* background. **er ist britischer** *(gen)* **~** he is of British origin.

**Herkunftsland** *nt (Comm)* country of origin.

**her-**: **~laufen** *vi sep irreg aux sein* to come running; **hinter jdm ~laufen** *(lit, fig)* to run after sb; **~leiten** *sep* **1** *vt (folgern)* to derive *(aus from)*; **2** *vr* **sich von etw ~leiten** to be derived from sth; **~locken** *vt sep* to entice, to lure; **~machen** *sep (col)* **1** *vr* **sich über etw (acc) ~machen** *(in Angriff nehmen)* Arbeit, Essen to get stuck into sth *(col)*; *(Besitz ergreifen)* to pounce (up)on sth; **sich über jdn ~machen** to lay into sb *(col)*; **2** *vt* **viel ~machen** to look impressive.

**Hermelin** *m* **-e** *(Pelz)* ermine.

**hermetisch** *adj* hermetic. **~ abgeriegelt** completely sealed off.

**her-**: **~müssen** *vi sep irreg (col)* (a) **das muß ~** I/we have to have it; (b) *(kommen müssen)* to have to come (here); **hinter jdm ~müssen** to have to go after sb; **~nehmen** *vt sep irreg (beschaffen)* to get, to find. **wo soll ich das ~nehmen?** where am I supposed to get that from?

**Heroin** [hero'iːn] *nt no pl* heroin.

**heroisch** [he'roːɪʃ] *adj (geh)* heroic.

**Herold** *m* **-e** *(Hist)* herald.

**Herpes** *m no pl (Med)* herpes.

**Herr** *m (wk)* **-(e)n, -en** (a) *(Gebieter)* lord, master; *(Herrscher)* ruler *(über +acc of)*; *(von Hund)* master. **die ~en der Schöpfung** *(hum: Männer)* the gentlemen; **sein eigener ~ sein** to be one's own master or boss; **~ der Lage bleiben** to remain master of the situation; **über jdn/etw ~ werden** to master sb/sth; **niemand kann zwei ~en dienen** *(prov)* no man can serve two masters *(prov)*. (b) *(Gott, Christus)* Lord. **Gott, der ~** the Lord God. (c) *(feiner ~, Mann)* gentleman. **„~en"** *(Toilette)* "gentlemen" *(Brit)*, "men's room" *(US)*. (d) *(vor Eigennamen)* Mr. **mein ~!** sir!; **der ~ wünscht?** what can I do for you, sir?; **ja, ~ Doktor/Professor** yes, Doctor/Professor; **~ Präsident/Vorsitzender** Mr President/Chairman; **der ~ Präsident/Vorsitzende** the President/Chairman; **lieber ~ A, sehr geehrter ~ A** *(in Brief)* Dear Mr A; **sehr geehrte ~en** *(in Brief)* Dear Sirs.

**Herrchen** *nt (col: von Hund)* master.

**Herren-** *in cpds* men's; *(auf einzelnes Exemplar bezüglich)* man's; **~abend** *m* stag night; **~ausstatter** *m* - men's outfitter; **~begleitung** *f* in **~begleitung** in the company of a gentleman; **~bekanntschaft** *f* male acquaintance; **eine ~bekanntschaft machen** to get to know a man; **~bekleidung** *f* menswear; **~besuch** *m* male visitor/visitors; **~friseur** *m* men's hairdresser, barber; **~haus** *nt* manor house; **h~los** *adj* abandoned; *Hund etc* stray; **~salon** *m* barber's;

**~toilette** *f* men's room *(US)*, gents *sing (Brit)*.

**Herrgott** *m (dated col) (Anrede)* God, Lord. **der ~** the Lord (God); **~ noch mal!** *(col)* damn it all! *(col)*.

**Herrgottsfrüh(e)** *f:* **in aller ~** *(col)* at the crack of dawn.

**herrichten** *sep* **1** *vt* **(a)** *(vorbereiten)* to get ready *(dat, für* for*)*; *Bett* to make; *Tisch* to set. **(b)** *(instand setzen)* to do up *(col)*. **2** *vr (dial)* to get dressed up.

**Herrin** *f (Hist)* female ruler; *(von Hund)* mistress.

**herrisch** *adj* overbearing, imperious.

**herrje, herrjemine** *interj* goodness gracious.

**herrlich** *adj* marvellous *(Brit)*, marvelous *(US)*; *Kleid* gorgeous, lovely. **wir haben uns ~ amüsiert** we had marvellous fun.

**Herrlichkeit** *f* **(a)** *no pl (Pracht)* magnificence, splendour *(Brit)*, splendor *(US)*. **die ~ Gottes** the glory of God. **(b)** *usu pl (Gegenstand)* treasure.

**Herrschaft** *f* **(a)** *(Macht)* power; *(Staatsgewalt)* rule; *(Kontrolle)* control. **sich der ~ bemächtigen** to seize power; **unter der ~** under the rule *(gen, von* of*)*; **während der ~** *(+gen)* in the reign of; **er verlor die ~ über sein Auto** he lost control of his car. **(b) die ~en** *(Damen und Herren)* the ladies and gentlemen; **(meine) ~en!** ladies and gentlemen.

**herrschaftlich** *adj (vornehm)* grand.

**Herrschafts-:** **~anspruch** *m* claim to power; **~bereich** *m* territory; **~form** *f* form *or* type of rule; **~system** *nt* system of rule.

**herrschen 1** *vi* **(a)** *(über etw (acc)* sth*)* to rule; *(König)* to reign; *(fig: Mensch)* to dominate. **(b)** *(vor~)* *(Angst, Ungewißheit)* to prevail; *(Krankheit)* to be rampant. **überall herrschte Freude** there was joy everywhere; **im Zimmer herrschte bedrückende Stille** it was oppressively quiet in the room; **hier ~ ja Zustände!** things are in a pretty state around here! **2** *vi impers* **es herrscht schlechtes Wetter** we're having bad weather; **es herrscht Ungewißheit darüber, ob ...** there is uncertainty about whether ...

**herrschend** *adj Partei, Klasse* ruling; *König* reigning; *Verhältnisse, Meinungen* prevailing; *Mode* current.

**Herrscher(in** *f)* *m* - ruler *(über +acc* of*)*.

**Herrscher-:** **~geschlecht** *nt* ruling dynasty; **~haus** *nt* ruling house.

**Herrschsucht** *f* domineering nature.

**herrschsüchtig** *adj* domineering.

**her-:** **~rufen** *vt sep irreg* to call (over); **~rühren** *vi sep von etw* **~rühren** to be due to sth, to stem from sth; **~sagen** *vt sep* to recite; **~sehen** *vi sep irreg* **(a)** to look this way; **(b) hinter jdm/etw ~sehen** to follow sb with one's eyes; **~sein** *vi sep irreg aux sein* **(a) das ist schon 5 Jahre ~** that was 5 years ago; **wie lange ist es ~?** how long ago was it?; **(b)** *(~stammen)* to come from; **mit jdm/etw ist es nicht weit ~** *(col)* sb/sth is not up to much *(col)*; **(c) hinter jdm/etw ~sein** to be after sb/sth; **~stammen** *vi sep* **(a) wo stammst du ~?** where do you come from?; **(b)** *(~rühren)* **von etw ~stammen** to stem from sth.

**herstellen** *vt sep* **(a)** *(erzeugen)* to produce; *(industriell auch)* to manufacture. **in Deutschland hergestellt** made in Germany. **(b)** *(zustande bringen)* to establish; *(Telec)* *Verbindung* to make; *Stromkreis* to complete. **(c)** *(gesundheitlich)* jdn to restore to health. **er ist wieder ganz hergestellt** he has quite recovered.

**Hersteller(in** *f)* *m* - *(Produzent)* manufacturer.

**Herstellung** *f no pl siehe vt* **(a)** production; manufacture. **(b)** establishment; making; completion.

**Herstellungs-:** **~kosten** *pl* manufacturing *or* production costs *pl*; **~land** *nt* country of manufacture.

**hertragen** *vt sep irreg (col) (an bestimmten Ort)* to carry here. **etw hinter jdm ~** to carry sth behind sb.

**herüber** *adv (hierher)* over here; *(über Straße, Grenze)* across.

**herüber-** *pref* over; *(über Straße, Grenze)* across; *siehe auch* **hinüber-**; **~fahren** *sep irreg* **1** *vi aux sein* **er ist gestern ~gefahren** he came *or (mit Auto)* drove across yesterday; **2** *vt Fahrgast, Güter* to take over/across; **~holen** *vt sep* to fetch; **~kommen** *vi sep irreg aux sein* to come over/across *(über etw (acc)* sth*)*; *(col: zu Nachbarn)* to pop round *(col)*; **~reichen** *sep* **1** *vt* to pass *(über +acc* over*)*; **2** *vi* to reach across *(über etw (acc)* sth*)*; **~retten** *vt sep* **etw in die Gegenwart ~retten** to preserve sth; **~wechseln** *vi sep aux sein or haben* **in unsere Partei ~wechseln** to swap over to our party; **~ziehen** *sep irreg (über etw (acc)* sth*)* **1** *vt* to pull over/across; *(fig)* to win over; **2** *vi aux sein (Truppen, Wolken)* to move over/across.

**herum** *adv* **um Ulm ~** around Ulm; **um 50 ~** around 50; **links/rechts ~** around to the left/right; **hier/dort ~** around here/there; **oben ~** *(über Gegenstand, Berg)* over the top; *(in bezug auf Körper)* around the top; **unten ~** *(unter Gegenstand)* underneath; *(um Berg, in bezug auf Körper)* around the bottom.

**herum-** *pref* around; *siehe auch* **umher-**; **~albern** *vi sep (col)* to fool or lark *(col)* around; **~ärgern** *vr sep (col)* **sich mit jdm/etw ~ärgern** to keep struggling with sb/sth; **~basteln** *vi sep (col)* to tinker about *(an +dat* with*)*; **~bekommen** *vt sep irreg (col)* jdn to talk round; **~blättern** *vi sep* **(in einem Buch)** to browse through a book; **~bummeln** *vi sep (col)* **(a)** *(trödeln)* to mess about *(col)*; **(b)** *aux sein (spazieren)* to stroll around *(in etw (dat)* sth*)*; **~doktern** *vi sep (col)* **an jdm/einer Krankheit ~doktern** to try to cure sb/an illness; **an etw** *(dat)* **~doktern** *(fig)* to fiddle *or* tinker *(about)* with sth; **~drehen** *sep* **1** *vt* to turn; **jdm das Wort im Mund ~drehen** to twist sb's words; **2** *vr* to turn around; *(im Liegen)* to turn over; **3** *vi (col)* **an etw** *(dat)* **~drehen** to fiddle about with sth; **~drücken** *vr sep* **(a)** *(sich aufhalten)* to hang around *(col) (um etw* sth*)*; **(b)** *(vermeiden)* **sich um etw ~drücken** to dodge sth; **~drucksen** *vi sep (col)* to hum and haw *(col)*; **~erzählen\*** *vt sep* **erzähl das nicht ~** don't spread it around; **~fahren** *sep irreg* **1** *vi (col)* **(a)** to travel *or (mit Auto)* drive around; **(b)** *(sich rasch umdrehen)* to spin around; **2** *vt* to drive around; **~fragen** *vi sep (col)* to ask around *(bei* among*)*; **~fuchteln** *vi sep (col)* **(mit den Händen)** **~fuchteln** to wave one's hands around; **~führen** *sep* **1** *vt* to lead around *(um etw* sth*)*; *(bei Besichtigung)* to take *or* show around; **2** *vi* **um etw ~führen** to go around sth; **~fuhrwerken** *vi sep (col)* to bustle about; **~fummeln** *vi sep (col) (an +dat* with*)* to fiddle about; *(basteln)* to tinker *(about)*; **~gammeln** *vi sep (col)* to bum around *(col)*; **~gehen** *vi sep irreg aux sein (col)* **(a)** to go around *(um etw* sth*)*; **(b)** *(ziellos)* to wander around *(in etw (dat)* sth*)*; **es ging ihm im Kopf ~** it went round and round in his head; **(c)** *(~gereicht werden)* to be passed around; **etw ~gehen lassen** to circulate sth; **(d)** *Zeit* to pass; **~geistern** *vi sep aux sein (col) (Gespenster etc)* to haunt *(in etw (dat)* sth*)*; *(Mensch)* to wander around; **~hacken** *vi sep (col)* **auf jdm ~hacken** to pick on sb *(col)*; **~hängen** *vi sep irreg (col)* **(a)** to hang around; **(b)** *(sich lümmeln)* to loll about; **(c)** *(ständig zu finden sein)* to hang out *(col)*; **~irren** *vi sep aux sein* to wander around;

~**kommandieren\*** vt sep (col) to order about, to boss about or around (col); ~**kommen** vi sep irreg aux sein (col) (a) (um eine Ecke etc) to come around (um etw sth); (b) (~gehen können) to get around (um etw sth); (c) (vermeiden können) um etw ~**kommen** to get out of sth; (d) er ist viel ~**gekommen** he has been around a lot; ~**kriegen** vt sep (col) jdn to talk round; ~**laufen** vi sep irreg aux sein (col) to run or (gehen) walk around (um etw sth); ~**liegen** vi sep irreg (col) to lie around or about; ~**lungern** vi sep (col) to hang around; ~**machen** sep (col) 1 vi an etw (dat) ~**machen** (sich beschäftigen) to fuss about sth; (~fingern) to pick at sth; 2 vt to put around (um etw sth); ~**nörgeln** vi sep an jdm/etw ~**nörgeln** to find fault with sb/sth; ~**quälen** vr sep (col) to struggle; **sich mit Rheuma** ~**quälen** to be plagued by rheumatism; ~**reden** vi sep (col) to chat away; **um etw** ~**reden** (ausweichend) to talk around sth; ~**reichen** vt sep to pass round; ~**reißen** vt sep irreg to swing around (hard); **das Steuer** ~**reißen** (fig) to change course; ~**reiten** vi sep irreg (fig col) **auf jdm/etw** ~**reiten** to keep on at sb/about sth; ~**schlagen** sep irreg 1 vt Papier, Tuch to wrap around (um etw sth); 2 vr (col) **sich mit jdm/etw** ~**schlagen** (fig) to struggle with sb/sth; ~**schleppen** vt sep (col) Sachen to lug around (col); jdn to drag around; **etw mit sich** ~**schleppen** Sorge, Problem to be troubled by sth; Krankheit to have sth; ~**schnüffeln** vi sep (col) to sniff around (in etw (dat) sth); (fig) to snoop around (in +dat in); ~**schreien** vi sep irreg (col) to shout out loud; ~**sein** vi sep irreg aux sein (col) (a) (vorüber sein) to be past or over; (b) (in jds Nähe sein) **um jdn** ~**sein** to be around sb; ~**sitzen** vi sep irreg aux haben or sein to sit around (um jdn/etw sb/sth); ~**sprechen** vr sep irreg to get about; ~**stehen** vi sep irreg aux haben or sein (Sachen) to be lying around; (Menschen) to stand around (um jdn/etw sb/sth); ~**stochern** vi sep (col) to poke about; **im Essen** ~**stochern** to pick at one's food; ~**streiten** vr sep irreg (col) to squabble; ~**toben** vi sep aux haben or sein (col) to romp around or about; ~**tragen** vt sep irreg (col) (a) to carry about; **Sorgen mit sich** ~**tragen** to have worries; (b) (weitererzählen) to spread around; ~**treiben** vr sep irreg (col) (sich aufhalten) to hang around (in +dat in) (col); (liederlich leben) to hang around in bad places/company.

**Herumtreiber(in** f) m - (pej) tramp.
**herum-:** ~**wälzen** vr sep to roll around; **sich (schlaflos) im Bett** ~**wälzen** to toss and turn; ~**werfen** sep irreg 1 vt (a) (col) to throw around (in etw (dat) sth); (b) Kopf to turn (quickly); Steuer to throw around; 2 vr sich (im Bett) ~**werfen** to toss and turn (in bed); ~**wursteln** vi sep (col) to fiddle around (an +dat with) (col); ~**ziehen** sep irreg 1 vi aux sein to move around; **in der Welt** ~**ziehen** to roam the world; 2 vt **etw mit sich** ~**ziehen** to take sth around with one.

**herunter 1** adv down. ~! get down!; ~ **mit ihm** get him down; ~ **damit** get it down; (in bezug auf Kleider) get it off. 2 prep +acc **den Berg** ~ down the mountain.

**herunter-** pref down; siehe auch **herab-**; ~**bekommen** vt sep irreg = ~**kriegen**; ~**bringen** vt sep irreg (a) to bring down; (b) (col) = ~**kriegen**; ~**drücken** vt sep to press down; Preise to force down; Niveau to lower; ~**fallen** vi sep irreg aux sein to fall down; **von etw** ~**fallen** to fall off sth; ~**gehen** vi sep irreg aux sein to go down; (Temperatur, Preise auch) to drop; **mit den Preisen** ~**gehen** to lower one's prices; ~**gekommen** adj

Haus dilapidated; Stadt run-down; Mensch down-at-heel; ~**handeln** vt sep (col) Preis to beat down; **etw um 20 Mark** ~**handeln** to get 20 marks knocked off sth; ~**hängen** vi sep irreg to hang down; ~**hauen** vt sep irreg (col) **jdm eine** ~**hauen** to give sb a clip around the ear (col); ~**holen** vt sep to fetch down; (col) Vogel, Flugzeug to bring down; ~**klappen** vt sep Kragen to turn down; Sitz to fold down; Deckel to close; ~**kommen** vi sep irreg aux sein (a) to come down; (b) (fig col: verfallen) (Stadt, Firma, Wirtschaft) to go downhill; (gesundheitlich) to become run-down; siehe ~**gekommen**; ~**können** vi sep irreg to be able to get down; ~**kriegen** vt sep (col) (~holen, schlucken können) to get down; (abmachen können) to get off; ~**lassen** sep irreg vt Gegenstand to let down; Rolladen, Ladung etc to lower; Hose to take down; ~**leiern** vt sep (col) to reel off; ~**machen** vt sep (col) (a) (schlechtmachen) to run down, to knock (col); (b) (zurechtweisen) to tell off; (c) (abmachen) to take down; Farbe, Dreck to take off; ~**nehmen** vt sep irreg to take down; (col: von Schule) to take away; ~**putzen** vt sep (col) **jdn** ~**putzen** to tear sb off a strip (col); ~**rasseln** vt sep (col) to rattle off; ~**reißen** vt sep irreg (col) (a) to pull down; (b) (abreißen) to pull off; ~**schlucken** vt sep to swallow; ~**schrauben** vt sep (lit) Deckel to screw off; (fig) Ansprüche, Niveau to lower; ~**sehen** vi sep irreg (lit, fig) to look down (auf +acc on); ~**sein** vi sep irreg aux sein (col) (a) to be down; (abgeschnitten sein) to be (cut) off; (b) **mit den Nerven/der Gesundheit** ~**sein** to be at the end of one's tether/to be run-down; ~**setzen** vt sep (col) siehe **herabsetzen**; ~**spielen** vt sep (col) Problem, Vorfall to play down; ~**wirtschaften** vt sep (col) to bring to the brink of ruin; ~**wollen** vi sep (col) to want to get down; ~**ziehen** vt sep irreg to pull down.

**hervor** adv aus etw ~ out of sth; **hinter dem Tisch** ~ out from behind the table.

**hervor-:** ~**bringen** vt sep irreg (a) Blüten to produce; Worte to utter; (b) (verursachen) to create; ~**gehen** vi sep irreg aux sein (a) (geh: entstammen) to come (aus from); (b) **daraus geht** ~, **daß** ... from this it follows that ...; (c) **als Sieger** ~**gehen** to emerge victorious; ~**heben** vt sep irreg to emphasize; ~**ragen** vi sep to jut out, to project; (fig: sich auszeichnen) to stand out; ~**ragend** adj (ausgezeichnet) outstanding; **er hat H~ragendes geleistet** his achievement was outstanding; **das hat** ~**ragend geklappt** it worked beautifully; ~**rufen** vt sep irreg (a) **jdn** ~**rufen** to call sb out; (Theat etc) to call for sb; (b) (bewirken) Bewunderung to arouse; Reaktion, Krankheit to cause; Eindruck to create; ~**stechen** vi sep irreg aux sein (lit, fig) to stand out; ~**stechend** adj striking; ~**stehen** vi sep irreg aux sein to project; (Nase, Ohren etc) to stick out; ~**stoßen** vt sep irreg Worte to gasp (out); ~**treten** vi sep irreg aux sein (a) (heraustreten) to emerge (hinter +dat from behind); (Backenknochen) to protrude; (Adern) to bulge; (b) (sichtbar werden) to stand out; ~**tun** vr sep irreg to distinguish oneself; (col: sich wichtig tun) to show off (mit with); ~**wagen** vr sep to dare to come out; ~**zaubern** vt sep (lit, fig) to conjure up; ~**ziehen** vt sep irreg to pull out (unter +dat from under).

**Herweg** m way here.

**Herz** nt -ens, -en (a) (lit, fig) heart. **mir schlug das** ~ **bis zum Hals** my heart was pounding; **die** ~**en höher schlagen lassen** to make people's hearts beat faster; **ein goldenes** ~ a heart of gold; **schweren** ~**ens** with a heavy heart; **es gab mir einen Stich ins**

~ it hurt me; **seinem ~en Luft machen** to give vent to one's feelings; **sich** *(dat)* **etw vom ~en reden** to get sth off one's chest; **du sprichst mir aus dem ~en** that's just what I feel; **jdm das ~ schwer machen** to sadden sb; **im Grund seines ~ens** in his heart of hearts; **aus tiefstem ~en** from the bottom of one's heart; **mit ganzem ~en** wholeheartedly; **ich weiß, wie es dir ums ~ ist** I know how you feel; **jdm sein ~ schenken** to give sb one's heart; **dieser alte Hund ist mir ans ~ gewachsen** I have grown fond of this old dog; **er hat sie in sein ~ geschlossen** he has grown fond of her; **ein ~ für jdn/etw haben** to be fond of sb/sth; **sein ~ an jdn/etw hängen** to commit oneself heart and soul to sb/sth; **sich** *(dat)* **ein ~ fassen** to take heart; **ihm rutschte das ~ in die Hose** *(col)* his heart sank; **ein ~ und eine Seele sein** to be bosom friends; **alles, was das ~ begehrt** everything one's heart desires; **er hat das ~ auf dem rechten Fleck** his heart is in the right place; **es liegt mir am ~en** I am very concerned about it; **jdm etw ans ~ legen** to entrust sth to sb; **etw auf dem ~en haben** to have sth on one's mind; **jdn/etw auf ~ und Nieren prüfen** to examine sb/sth very thoroughly; **eine schwere Last fiel ihr vom ~en** a heavy load was lifted from her mind; **von ~en** with all one's heart; **etw von ~en gern tun** to love doing sth; **von ~en kommend** heartfelt; **sich** *(dat)* **etw zu ~en nehmen** to take sth to heart.

(b) *pl* - *(Cards) (no pl: Farbe)* hearts *pl*; *(Karte)* heart.

**Herz-** *in cpds (Anat, Med)* cardiac; **~anfall** *m* heart attack; **h~beklemmend** *adj* oppressive; **~beschwerden** *pl* heart trouble *sing*; **h~bewegend** *adj* heart-rending.

**Herzchen** *nt (col: Kosewort)* darling.

**Herzegowina** *nt* Herzegovina.

**herzeigen** *vt sep* to show. **zeig** *(mal)* **her!** let's see; **das kann man ~** that's worth showing off.

**herzen** *vt (dated)* to hug.

**Herzens-:** **~bedürfnis** *nt (dated)* **es ist mir ein ~bedürfnis** it is a matter dear to my heart; **~brecher** *m* - *(fig col)* heartbreaker; **h~gut** *adj* good-hearted; **~lust** *f* **nach ~lust** to one's heart's content; **~wunsch** *m* dearest wish.

**Herz-:** **h~erfrischend** *adj* refreshing; **h~ergreifend, h~erweichend** *adj* heart-rending; **~fehler** *m* heart defect; **h~förmig** *adj* heart-shaped; **h~haft** *adj (kräftig)* hearty; *Hände-druck,Griff* firm; *Geschmack* strong; **alle langten h~haft zu** everyone got stuck in *(col)*; **das schmeckt h~haft** that's tasty.

**herziehen** *sep irreg* **1** *vt* to pull closer. **jdn/etw hinter sich** *(dat)* **~** to pull sb/sth (along) behind one. **2** *vi aux sein* **(a) hinter jdm ~** to march along behind sb. **(b) über jdn/etw ~** *(col)* to pull sb/sth to pieces *(col)*.

**herzig** *adj* adorable, sweet.

**Herz-:** **~infarkt** *m* heart attack; **~kammer** *f* ventricle; **~klappe** *f* (heart) valve; **~klopfen** *nt no pl* **ich hatte/bekam ~klopfen** my heart was/started pounding; *(durch Kaffee etc)* I had/got palpitations; **mit ~klopfen** with a pounding heart; **h~krank** *adj* suffering from a heart condition; **~kranzgefäß** *nt usu pl* coronary (blood) vessel; **~leiden** *nt* heart condition.

**herzlich 1** *adj Empfang, Mensch* warm; *Lachen* hearty; *Bitte* sincere. **~e Grüße an ...** remember me to ...; **mit ~en Grüßen** best wishes; **~en Dank!** thank you very much; **~es Beileid!** you have my deepest sympathy. **2** *adv (sehr)* **~ gern!** with the greatest of pleasure!; **~ schlecht** pretty awful; **~**

**wenig** precious little; **ich habe es ~ satt** I'm sick and tired of it.

**Herzlichkeit** *f siehe adj* warmth; heartiness; sincerity.

**Herz-:** **h~los** *adj* heartless; **~losigkeit** *f* heartlessness *no pl*; **~mittel** *nt* cardiac drug.

**Herzog** ['hɛrtsoːk] *m* ⁼e duke.

**Herzogin** ['hɛrtsoːgɪn] *f* duchess.

**Herzogtum** *nt* dukedom, duchy.

**Herz-:** **~schlag** *m (einzelner)* heartbeat; *(~tätigkeit)* heart rate; *(~stillstand)* heart failure *no indef art*; **~schrittmacher** *m* pacemaker; **~schwäche** *f* **an ~schwäche leiden** to have a weak heart; **h~stärkend** *adj* **ein h~stärkendes Mittel** a cardiac stimulant; **~stillstand** *m* cardiac arrest; **~stück** *nt (fig)* heart, core; **~versagen** *nt* heart failure; **h~zerreißend** *adj* heartbreaking.

**Hesse** *m (wk)* **-n, -n Hessin** *f* Hessian.

**Hessen** *nt* Hesse.

**hessisch** *adj* Hessian.

**hetero-:** **~gen** *adj (geh)* heterogeneous; **~sexuell** *adj* heterosexual; **H~sexuelle(r)** *mf decl as adj* heterosexual.

**Hetze** *f no pl* **(a)** *(Hast)* (mad) rush, hurry. **(b)** *(pej: Hetzkampagne)* smear campaign.

**hetzen 1** *vt* **(a)** *(lit, fig: jagen)* to hound. **die Hunde auf jdn ~** to set the dogs on sb. **(b)** *(col: antreiben)* to rush, to hurry. **2** *vr* to hurry oneself. **3** *vi* **(a)** *auch aux sein* to rush. **(b)** *(pej: Haß schüren)* to stir up hatred *(gegen against)*; *(col: lästern)* to say malicious things. **bei jdm gegen jdn ~** to try to set sb against sb.

**Hetzer(in** *f)* *m* - rabble-rouser, agitator.

**Hetzerei** *f* **(a)** *no pl (Hast)* (mad) rush. **(b)** *(das Haß-schüren)* rabble-rousing, agitation.

**Hetz-:** **~jagd** *f (lit, fig)* hounding *(auf +acc of)*; **~kampagne** *f* smear campaign.

**Heu** *nt no pl* hay. **Geld wie ~ haben** *(col)* to have pots of money *(col)*.

**Heuboden** *m* hayloft.

**Heuchelei** *f* hypocrisy.

**heucheln 1** *vi* to be a hypocrite. **2** *vt Mitleid etc* to feign.

**Heuchler(in** *f)* *m* - hypocrite.

**heuchlerisch** *adj* hypocritical.

**heuer** *adv (S Ger, Aus, Sw)* this year.

**Heuer** *f* **-n** *(Naut)* pay.

**heuern** *vt* to sign on, to hire.

**Heu-:** **~gabel** *f* pitchfork, hayfork; **~haufen** *m* haystack.

**heulen** *vi* to howl; *(Motor)* to roar; *(Sirene)* to wail. **ich hätte ~ können** I could have wept; **es ist einfach zum H~** it's enough to make you weep.

**Heulen** *nt no pl siehe vi* howling; roaring; wailing.

**Heul-:** *(col)* **~peter** *m*, **~suse** *f* cry-baby *(col)*; **~ton** *m (von Sirene)* wail.

**heureka** *interj* eureka.

**heurig** *adj attr (S Ger, Aus)* this year's.

**Heurige(r)** *m decl as adj (esp Aus)* new wine.

**Heu-:** **~schnupfen** *m* hay fever; **~schober** *m (S Ger, Aus)* haystack; **~schrecke** *f* **-n** grasshopper; *(in heißen Ländern)* locust; **~speicher** *m* barn.

**heute** *adv* today. **~ morgen** this morning; **~ abend** this evening, tonight; **~ früh** this morning; **~ nacht** tonight; **bis ~** *(bisher)* to this day; **~ in einer Woche** a week today, today week; **lieber ~ als morgen** the sooner the better; **von ~ auf morgen** *(fig: plötzlich)* overnight, from one day to the next; **der Mensch von ~** modern man.

**heutig** *adj attr* today's; *(gegenwärtig)* modern, contemporary. **am ~en Abend** this evening; **unser ~es**

**Schreiben** *(Comm)* our letter of today('s date); **bis zum ~en Tage** to this day.

**heutzutage** *adv* nowadays.

**Hexa-** ['hɛksa-] *in cpds* hexa-.

**Hexe** *f* **-n** witch; *(col: altes Weib)* old hag.

**hexen** *vi* to do witchcraft. **ich kann doch nicht ~** *(col)* I'm not a magician.

**Hexen-:** **~häuschen** *nt* gingerbread house; **~jagd** *f* witch hunt; **~kessel** *m (fig)* pandemonium *no indef art*; **~meister** *m* sorcerer; **~schuß** *m (Med)* lumbago.

**Hexerei** *f* witchcraft *no pl*; *(Zaubertricks)* magic *no pl*.

**HG** = **Handelsgesellschaft.**

**hg.** = **herausgegeben** ed.

**hibbelig** *adj (dial)* jittery.

**Hickhack** *m or nt* **-s** *(col)* squabbling *no pl*.

**Hieb** *m* **-e** **(a)** *(Schlag)* stroke, blow; *(Peitschen~)* lash; *(Fechten)* cut. **(b)** *(~wunde)* gash, slash. **(c)** **~e** *pl (col: Prügel)* **~e bekommen** to get a hiding.

**hieb- und stichfest** *adj (fig)* watertight.

**hielt** *pret of* **halten.**

**hier** *adv* here. **dieser ~** this one (here); **~ draußen** out here; **~ herum** hereabouts, around here; **er ist von ~** he's a local (man); **Tag Klaus, ~ (spricht) Hans** *(Telec)* hello Klaus, it's Hans; **~ spricht Dr. Müller** *(Telec)* this is Dr Müller (speaking); **~ und da** (every) now and then.

**hieran** *adv* here. **~ erkenne ich es** I recognize it by this.

**Hierarchie** *f* hierarchy.

**hierarchisch** *adj* hierarchical.

**hier-:** **~auf** *adv* on this; *(daraufhin)* hereupon; **~aufhin** *adv* hereupon; **~aus** *adv* out of/from this, from here; **~aus folgt daß** ... from this it follows that ...; **~behalten** *vt sep irreg* to keep here; **~bei** *adv (bei dieser Gelegenheit)* on this occasion; *(in diesem Zusammenhang)* in this connection; **~bleiben** *vi sep irreg aux sein* to stay here; **~geblieben!** stop!; **~durch** *adv (lit)* through here; *(fig)* through this; **~durch teilen wir Ihnen mit, daß** ... we hereby inform you that ...; **~für** *adv* for this; **~her** *adv* here.

**hierhergehören*** *vi sep* to belong here; *(fig: relevant sein)* to be relevant. **nicht ~de Bemerkungen** irrelevant remarks.

**hier-:** **~hin** *adv* here; **bis ~hin** up to here; **~in** *adv (lit, fig)* in this; **~lassen** *vt sep irreg* to leave here; **~mit** *adv* with this, herewith *(form)*; **~mit ist der Fall erledigt** this settles the matter; **~mit erkläre ich** ... *(form)* I hereby declare ... *(form)*; **~nach** *adv* after this, thereafter; *(daraus folgend)* according to this; **~sein** *vi sep irreg aux sein* to be here; **während meines H~seins** during my stay; **~über** *adv (fig)* about this; **~über ärgere ich mich** this makes me angry; **~um** *adv (fig)* about *or* concerning this; **~um handelt es sich nicht** this isn't the issue; **~unter** *adv (lit)* under this *or* here; *(fig)* by this *or* that; *(in dieser Kategorie)* among these; **~unter fallen auch die Sonntage** this includes Sundays; **~von** *adv* from this; **~von habe ich nichts gewußt** I knew nothing about this; **~von abgesehen** apart from this; **~vor** *adv* in front of this *or* here; **~vor ekele ich mich** it revolts me; **~vor hat er großen Respekt** he has a great respect for this; **~zu** *adv (dafür)* for this; *(dazu)* with this; *(außerdem)* in addition to this, moreover; *(zu diesem Punkt)* about this; **~zu gehören auch die Katzen** this also includes the cats; **~zulande** *adv* in these parts; *(in diesem Land)* in this country.

**hiesig** *adj attr* local. **meine ~en Verwandten** my rela-

tives here; **er ist kein H~er** he is not a local (man).

**hieß** *pret of* **heißen.**

**Hi-Fi-Anlage** ['haifi-] *f* hi-fi system.

**Highlife** ['hailaif] *nt no pl* high life. **~ machen** *(col)* to live it up *(col)*.

**High-Tech-** [haɪ'tek] *in cpds* high-tech.

**hihi** *interj* heehee.

**Hilfe** *f* **-n** **(a)** *no pl* help; *(für Notleidende)* aid, relief. **(zu) ~!** help!; **jdm zu ~ kommen** to come to sb's aid *or* assistance; **jdm ~ leisten** to help sb; **bei jdm ~ suchen** to seek sb's help *or* assistance; **mit ~** with the help *or* aid *(gen* of*)*; **etw zu ~ nehmen** to use sth; **ohne fremde ~ gehen** to walk unaided. **(b)** *(Hilfsmittel)* aid. **du bist mir eine schöne ~!** *(iro)* a fine help *you* are!

**Hilfe-:** **~leistung** *f* aid, assistance; **unterlassene ~leistung** *(Jur)* denial of assistance; **~ruf** *m* call for help; **~stellung** *f (Sport, fig)* support; **h~suchend** *adj* seeking help; **Blick** beseeching.

**Hilf-:** **h~los** *adj* helpless; **~losigkeit** *f* helplessness; **h~reich** *adj* helpful.

**Hilfs-:** **~aktion** *f* relief action; **~arbeiter** *m* labourer *(Brit)*, laborer *(US)*; *(in Fabrik)* unskilled worker; **h~bedürftig** *adj* in need of help; *(notleidend)* needy, in need *pred*; **h~bereit** *adj* helpful, ready to help *pred*; **~bereitschaft** *f* helpfulness, readiness to help; **~dienst** *m* emergency service; **~kraft** *f* assistant; *(Aushilfe)* temporary worker; **~maßnahme** *f* relief action *no pl*; *(zur Rettung)* rescue action *no pl*; **~mittel** *nt* aid; **~organisation** *f* relief organization; **~programm** *nt* relief programme *(Brit)* or program *(US)*; **~schule** *f (dated)* school for backward children; **~verb** *nt* auxiliary (verb); **~werk** *nt* relief organization.

**Himalaja** *m* **der ~** the Himalayas *pl*.

**Himbeere** *f* raspberry.

**Himmel** *m* **-** **(a)** sky. **am ~** in the sky; **zwischen ~ und Erde** in midair; **jdn/etw in den ~ heben** *or* **loben** to praise sb/sth to the skies; **ihr hängt der ~ voller Geigen** everything in the garden is lovely for her; **so was fällt nicht einfach vom ~** things like that don't grow on trees. **(b)** *(Rel)* heaven. **im ~** in heaven; **in den ~ kommen** to go to heaven; **das schreit zum ~** it's a scandal; **es stinkt zum ~** *(col)* it stinks to high heaven *(col)*; **(ach) du lieber ~!** *(col)* good Heavens! *(col)*; **um ~s willen** *(col)* for Heaven's sake *(col)*.

**Himmel-:** **~bett** *nt* four-poster (bed); **h~blau** *adj* sky-blue.

**Himmelfahrt** *f* **(a)** **Christi ~** the Ascension of Christ; **Mariä ~** the Assumption of the Virgin Mary. **(b)** *(no art: Feiertag)* Ascension Day.

**Himmelfahrts-:** **~kommando** *nt (Mil col)* suicide squad; *(Unternehmen)* suicide mission; **~tag** *m* Ascension Day.

**Himmel-:** **h~hoch 1** *adj* sky-high; **2** *adv* high into the sky; **h~hoch jauchzend, zu Tode betrübt** up one minute and down the next; **~reich** *nt no pl (Rel)* Kingdom of Heaven; **h~schreiend** *adj* outrageous, appalling.

**Himmels-:** **~karte** *f* star map *or* chart; **~körper** *m* heavenly *or* celestial body; **~richtung** *f* direction; **die vier ~richtungen** the four points of the compass.

**himmelweit** *adj* **ein ~er Unterschied** a world of difference; **wir sind noch ~ davon entfernt** we're still nowhere near it.

**himmlisch** *adj (lit, fig)* heavenly; **Geduld** infinite. **der ~e Vater** our Heavenly Father.

**hin** *adv* **(a)** *(räumlich)* **nach außen ~** *(fig)* outwardly; **~ fahre ich mit dem Zug, zurück** ... on the way out

I'll take the train, coming back ...; **~ und her** *(räumlich)* to and fro, back and forth; **etw ~ und her überlegen** to agonize over sth; **das H~ und Her** the comings and goings *pl*; **nach langem H~und Her** eventually; **Feiertag ~, Feiertag her** holiday or no holiday, whether it's a holiday or not; **~ und zurück** there and back; **einmal London ~ und zurück** a return to London *(Brit)*, a roundtrip ticket to London *(US)*; **~ und wieder** (every) now and again.

(b) *(zeitlich)* **es sind nur noch drei Tage ~** it's only three days from now; **gegen Mittag ~** towards midday; **über die Jahre ~** over the years.

(c) **auf meine Bitte/meinen Vorschlag ~** at my request/suggestion; **auf meinen Brief ~** as a result of my letter; **auf sein Versprechen/seinen Rat ~** on the basis of his promise/his advice; **etw auf etw** *(acc)* **~ untersuchen** to inspect sth for sth; **nichts wie ~** *(col)* let's go then!; **wo ist es/sie ~?** where has it/she gone?

**hinab** *adv, pref siehe* **hinunter.**

**hin|arbeiten** *vi sep*: **auf etw** *(acc)* **~ (auf Ziel)** to work towards sth.

**hinauf** *adv* up. **den Berg ~** up the mountain.

**hinauf-** *pref* up; **~arbeiten** *vr sep (lit, fig)* to work one's way up; **~führen** *vti sep* to lead up; **~gehen** *vi sep irreg aux sein* to go up; **mit dem Preis ~gehen** to put up the price; **~reichen** *sep* **1** *vi* to reach up; **2** *vt* to pass up; **~steigen** *vi sep irreg aux sein* to climb up; **~ziehen** *vt sep irreg* to pull up.

**hinaus** *adv* (a) *(räumlich)* out. **~ (mit dir)!** (get) out!, out you go!; **über** *(+acc)* **~** beyond, over; **hier/dort ~** this/that way out; **hinten/vorn ~** at the back/front; **zur Straße ~** facing the street. (b) *(zeitlich)* **auf Jahre ~** for years to come; **bis weit über die Siebzig ~** until well over seventy; **über Mittwoch ~** until after Wednesday. (c) *(fig)* **über** *(+acc)* ... **~** over and above ...; **darüber ~** over and above this.

**hinaus-** *pref out; siehe auch* **heraus-;** **~befördern\*** *vt sep (col) jdn* to kick out *(col) (aus of)*; **~drängen** *sep (aus of)* **1** *vt* to force out; *(eilig)* to hustle out; **2** *vi aux sein* to push one's way out; **~fahren** *sep irreg* **1** *vi aux sein* (a) **aus etw ~fahren** to go out of sth, to leave sth; (b) *(reisen)* to go out; **aufs Meer ~fahren** to put out to sea; **2** *vt Wagen* to drive out *(aus of)*; **~finden** *vi sep irreg* to find the way out *(aus of)*; **~fliegen** *vi sep irreg aux sein* (a) to fly out *(aus of)*; (b) *(col: ~geworfen werden)* to get kicked out *(col)*; **~führen** *sep* **1** *vi* (a) to lead out *(aus of)*; (b) **über etw** *(acc)* **~führen** *(lit, fig)* to go beyond sth; **2** *vt* to lead out *(aus of)*; *(Weg, Reise)* to take *(über +acc beyond)*; **~gehen** *sep irreg aux sein* **1** *vi* (a) to go out(side); (b) **auf etw** *(acc)* **~gehen** *(Tür)* to open onto sth; *(Fenster auch)* to look onto sth; (c) *(fig: überschreiten)* **über etw** *(acc)* **~gehen** to go beyond sth; **das geht über meine Kräfte ~** it's too much for me; **2** *vi impers* **wo geht es ~?** where's the way out?; **~kommen** *vi sep irreg aux sein* (a) to come out(side); (b) *(fig: ~laufen)* **das kommt auf dasselbe ~** it boils down to *or* comes to the same thing; **~komplimentieren\*** *vt sep (hum)* to usher out *(aus of)*; **~laufen** *vi sep irreg aux sein* (a) *(lit)* to run out; (b) *(fig)* **es läuft auf dasselbe ~** it amounts *or* comes to the same thing; **~lehnen** *vr sep* to lean out *(aus of)*; **~nehmen** *vt sep irreg* to take out *(aus of)*; **~ragen** *vi sep aux sein* to jut out *(über +acc beyond)*; **über jdn/etw ~ragen** *(fig)* to tower above sb/sth; **~schaffen** *vt sep* to take out *(aus of)*; **~schieben** *vt sep irreg* (a) *Gegenstand* to push out *(aus of)*; (b) *(fig)* to put off, to postpone; **~schießen** *vi sep irreg aux sein (~rennen)* to shoot out *(aus of)*; **über das Ziel ~schießen** *(fig)* to over-

shoot the mark; **~schmeißen** *vt sep irreg (col)* to kick *or* chuck out *(col) (aus of)*; **~sehen** *vi sep irreg* to look out *(aus of)*; **~sein** *vi sep irreg aux sein* **über etw** *(acc)* **~sein** *über Kindereien, ein Alter* to be past sth; *über Enttäuschungen* to have got over sth; **~setzen** *vt sep* to put out(side); **jdn ~setzen** *(col)* to kick sb out *(col)*; **~stellen** *vt sep* to put out(side); *Sportler* to send off; **~strecken** *vt sep* to stick *or* put out *(aus of)*; **~stürzen** *vi sep aux sein (aus of)* (a) *(~fallen)* to fall out; (b) *(~eilen)* to rush out; **~tragen** *vt sep irreg* (a) to carry out *(aus of)*; (b) **etw in alle Welt ~tragen** to spread sth abroad; **~wachsen** *vi sep irreg aux sein* **über etw** *(acc)* **~wachsen** *(fig)* to outgrow sth; **er wuchs über sich selbst ~** he surpassed himself; **~weisen** *sep irreg* **1** *vt jdn* **~weisen** to show sb the door; **2** *vi* to point out(wards); **~werfen** *vt sep irreg (aus of)* (a) to throw out; **einen Blick ~werfen** to take a look out(side); (b) *(col: entfernen)* to chuck *or* kick out *(col)*; **~wollen** *vi sep* to want to get out *(aus of)*; **worauf willst du ~?** *(fig)* what are you getting *or* driving at?; **hoch ~wollen** to aim high; **~ziehen** *sep irreg* **1** *vt* (a) *(nach draußen ziehen)* to pull out *(aus of)*; (b) *(fig)* *Verhandlungen etc* to protract, to drag out; *Urlaub etc* to prolong; **2** *vi aux sein* to go out *(aus of)*; **aufs Land ~ziehen** to move out into the country; **3** *vr (Verhandlungen etc)* to drag on; *(Abfahrt etc)* to be delayed; **~zögern** *sep* **1** *vt* to delay, to put off; **2** *vr* to be delayed, to be put off.

**hin-:** **~bekommen\*** *vt sep irreg (col)* = **~kriegen;** **~biegen** *vt sep irreg (fig col)* **das/ihn werden wir schon ~biegen** we'll sort it out somehow/lick him into shape *(col)*; **~blättern** *vt sep (col) Geld* to fork out *(col)*; **H~blick** *m*: **im** *or* **in H~blick auf** *(+acc) (angesichts)* in view of; *(mit Bezug auf)* with regard to; **~blicken** *vi sep* to look *(auf +acc, nach* at, towards*)*; **~bringen** *vt sep irreg* (a) to take there; (b) *(fig) Zeit* to spend; (c) = **~kriegen;** **~denken** *vi sep irreg* **wo denkst du ~?** whatever are you thinking of!

**hinderlich** *adj* **~ sein** to be in the way; **jds Karriere** *(dat)* **~ sein** to be a hindrance to sb's career; **jdm ~ sein** to get in sb's way.

**hindern** **1** *vt* (a) *Wachstum* to impede; *jdn* to hinder *(bei* in*)*. (b) *(abhalten von)* to prevent *(an +dat* from*)*, to stop. **ich will Sie nicht ~** I shan't stand in your way. **2** *vi* to be a hindrance *(bei* to*)*.

**Hindernis** *nt* (a) *(lit, fig)* obstacle; *(beim Sprechen)* impediment. **sie empfand das Kind als ~ für ihre Karriere** she saw the child as a hindrance to her career. (b) *(beim ~lauf)* jump.

**Hindernis-:** **~lauf** *m,* **~rennen** *nt* steeplechase; *(fig)* obstacle race; **~strecke** *f* obstacle course.

**Hinderungsgrund** *m* obstacle.

**hindeuten** *vi sep* to point *(auf +acc, zu* at*)*. **es deutet alles darauf hin, daß ...** everything indicates that ...

**Hindi** *nt* Hindi.

**hindrehen** *vt sep (fig col)* to sort out.

**Hindu** *m* **-(s), -(s)** Hindu.

**Hinduismus** *m* Hinduism.

**hinduistisch** *adj* Hindu.

**hindurch** *adv* through. **mitten ~** straight through; **das ganze Jahr ~** throughout the year; **die ganze Zeit ~** all the time; **Jahre ~** for years.

**hindurchgehen** *vi sep irreg aux sein (lit, fig)* to go through *(durch etw* sth*)*.

**hindürfen** *vi sep irreg* to be allowed to go *(zu* to*)*.

**hinein** *adv* in. **~ mit dir!** *(col)* in you go!; **in etw** *(acc)* **~** into sth; **bis tief in die Nacht ~** well into the night.

**hin<u>ei</u>n-** *pref* in; *siehe auch* **ein-, herein-**; **~bekommen\*** *vt sep irreg (col)* to get in *(in +acc* to*)*; **~blicken** *vi sep* to look in *(in +acc* -to*)*; **~bringen** *vt sep irreg (~tragen)* to bring/take in *(in +acc* -to*)*; **~denken** *vr sep irreg* **sich in ein Problem ~denken** to think oneself into a problem; **sich in jdn ~denken** to put oneself in sb's position; **~fallen** *vi sep irreg aux sein* to fall in *(in +acc* -to*)*; **~finden** *vr sep irreg (fig) (sich vertraut machen)* to find one's feet; *(sich abfinden)* to come to terms with it; **~fressen** *vt sep irreg (col)* **etw in sich** *(acc)* **~fressen** *(lit)* to wolf sth (down) *(col)*; *(fig) Kummer etc* to suppress sth; **~gehen** *vi sep irreg aux sein* **(a)** to go in; **in etw** *(acc)* **~gehen** to go into *or* enter sth; **(b)** *(~passen)* to go in *(in +acc* to*)*; **~geraten\*** *vi sep irreg aux sein* **in etw** *(acc)* **~geraten** to get involved in sth; **~knien** *vr sep (fig col)* **sich in etw** *(acc)* **~knien** to get down to sth *(col)*; **~kommen** *vi sep irreg aux sein (in +acc* -to*)* **(a)** to come in; **(b)** *(lit, fig: ~gelangen können)* to get in; **~kriegen** *vt sep (col)* to get in *(in +acc* -to*)*; **~legen** *vt sep (lit, fig)* to put in *(in +acc* -to*)*; **~lesen** *vt sep irreg* **etw in etw** *(acc)* **~lesen** to read sth into sth; **~passen** *vi sep* **in etw** *(acc)* **~passen** to fit into sth; *(fig)* to fit in with sth; **~platzen** *vi aux sein (fig col)* to burst in *(in +acc* -to*)*; **~reden** *vi sep (lit: unterbrechen)* to interrupt *(jdm* sb*)*; **jdm ~reden** *(fig: sich einmischen)* to interfere in sb's affairs; **~schlagen** *vt sep irreg (in +acc* -to*) Nagel* to knock in; **~schlingen** *vt sep irreg* **etw (gierig) in sich ~schlingen** to devour sth (greedily); **~schütten** *vt sep* to pour in *(in +acc* -to*)*; **etw in sich ~schütten** *(col)* to knock sth back *(col)*; **~setzen** *sep* **1** *vt* to put in *(in +acc* -to*)*; **2** *vr (in Fahrzeug)* to get into *(in etw (acc)* sth*)*; *(in Sessel)* to sit (oneself) down *(in +acc* in*)*; **~spielen** *vi sep (beeinflussen)* to have a part to play *(in +acc* in*)*; **~stecken** *vt sep (in +acc* -to*)* to put in; **Geld/Arbeit in etw** *(acc)* **~stecken** to put money/some work into sth; **~steigern** *vr sep* to get worked up; **sich in seinen Ärger ~steigern** to work oneself up into a temper; **sie hat sich in die Vorstellung ~gesteigert, daß** ... she has managed to convince herself that ...; **~stopfen** *vt sep* to stuff *or* cram in *(in +acc* -to*)*; **Essen in sich** *(acc)* **~stopfen** to stuff oneself with food; **~stürzen** *sep* **1** *vi aux sein* to plunge in *(in +acc* -to*)*; *(~eilen)* to rush in *(in +acc* -to*)*; **2** *vt* to throw *or* hurl in *(in +acc* -to*)*; **3** *vr* to plunge in *(in +acc* -to*)*; **sich in die Arbeit ~stürzen** to throw oneself into one's work; **sich ins Vergnügen ~stürzen** to plunge in and start enjoying oneself, to let it all hang out *(col)*; **~tun** *vt sep irreg* to put in *(in +acc* -to*)*; **einen Blick in etw** *(acc)* **~tun** to take a look in sth; **ins Buch etc** to take a look at sth; **~versetzen\*** *vr sep* **sich in jdn** *or* **in jds Lage ~versetzen** to put oneself in sb's position; **sich in eine Rolle ~versetzen** to empathize with a part; **~wachsen** *vi sep irreg aux sein* **in etw** *(acc)* **~wachsen** *(lit, fig)* to grow into sth; **~wollen** *vi sep (col)* to want to get in *(in +acc* -to*)*; **~ziehen** *vt sep irreg* to pull *or* drag in *(in +acc* -to*)*; **jdn in eine Angelegenheit ~ziehen** to drag sb into an affair.

**hin-:** **~fahren** *sep irreg* **1** *vi aux sein* to go there; *(mit Fahrzeug auch)* to drive there; **2** *vt* to drive *or* take there; **H~fahrt** *f* outward journey; *(Naut)* voyage out; **~fallen** *vi sep irreg aux sein* to fall (down).

**h<u>i</u>nfällig** *adj* **(a)** frail. **(b)** *(fig: ungültig)* invalid.

**hin-:** **~finden** *vir sep irreg (col)* to find one's way there; **~fliegen** *vi sep irreg aux sein* to fly there; *(col: ~fallen)* to fall over; **H~flug** *m* outward flight.

**h<u>i</u>nführen** *vti sep* to lead there. **wo soll das ~?** *(fig)*

where is this leading to?

**h<u>i</u>ng** *pret of* **hängen**.

**H<u>i</u>ngabe** *f no pl (fig) (Begeisterung)* dedication; *(Selbstlosigkeit)* devotion. **mit ~ tanzen/singen** *etc* to put everything into one's dancing/singing.

**h<u>i</u>ngeben** *sep irreg* **1** *vt* to give up. **2** *vr* **sich einer Sache** *(dat)* **~** *der Arbeit* to devote oneself to sth; *dem Laster, der Verzweiflung* to abandon oneself to sth; **sich Hoffnungen/einer Illusion ~** to cherish hopes/to labour *(Brit)* or labor *(US)* under an illusion; **sie gab sich ihm hin** she gave herself to him.

**h<u>i</u>ngebungsvoll** **1** *adj (selbstlos)* devoted. **2** *adv* devotedly; *(begeistert)* with abandon; *lauschen* raptly.

**hing<u>eg</u>en** *conj* however.

**hin-:** **~gehen** *vi sep irreg aux sein* **(a)** *(dorthin gehen)* to go (there); **gehst du auch ~?** are you going too?; **wo geht es hier ~?** where does this go?; **(b)** *(fig: tragbar sein)* **das geht gerade noch ~** that will just about do; **~gehören\*** *vi sep* to belong; **~gelangen\*** *vi sep aux sein* to go there; **~geraten\*** *vi sep irreg aux sein* **irgendwo ~geraten** to get somewhere; **wo bin ich denn hier ~geraten?** *(col)* what kind of place is this then?; **~gerissen** *adj* enraptured; **~gerissen lauschen** to listen with rapt attention; **ich bin ganz ~- und hergerissen** *(iro)* oh great *(iro)*; **~halten** *vt sep irreg* **(a)** *lit* to hold out *(jdm* to sb*)*; **(b)** *(fig) jdn* to put off, to stall; **H~haltetaktik** *f* stalling *or* delaying tactics.

**h<u>i</u>nhauen** *sep irreg (col)* **1** *vt* **(a)** *(nachlässig machen)* to knock off *(col)*. **(b)** *(hinwerfen)* to slam down. **2** *vi* **(a)** *(zuschlagen)* to hit hard. **(b)** *aux sein (fallen)* to fall flat. **(c)** *(gutgehen)* **das wird schon ~** it will be OK *(col)* or all right. **(d)** *(klappen)* to work. **(e)** *(ausreichen)* to do. **3** *vr (col) (sich schlafen legen)* to crash out *(col)*.

**h<u>i</u>nhören** *vi sep* to listen.

**h<u>i</u>nken** *vi* **(a)** to limp. **(b)** *(fig: Beispiel, Vergleich)* to be inappropriate.

**hin-:** **~knien** *vir sep (vi: aux sein)* to kneel (down); **~kommen** *vi sep irreg aux sein* **(a)** *(da)* **~kommen** to get there; **wie komme ich zu dir ~?** how do I get to your place?; **(b)** *(an bestimmten Platz gehören)* to go; **wo ist das Buch ~gekommen?** where has the book got to?; **wo kämen wir denn ~, wenn** ... *(col)* where would we be if ...; **(c)** *(col: auskommen)* to manage; **wir kommen (damit) ~** we'll manage; **(d)** *(col: ausreichen, stimmen)* to be right; **~kriegen** *vt sep (col)* **(a)** *(fertigbringen)* to do, to manage; **das hast du gut ~gekriegt** you've made a good job of it; **wie kriegt sie das bloß immer ~?** I don't know how she does it; **(b)** *(in Ordnung bringen)* to mend, to fix; *(gesundheitlich)* to cure; **~langen** *vi sep (col) (zupacken)* to grab him/her etc; *(anfassen)* to touch; *(zuschlagen)* to take a (good) swipe *(col)*; **~länglich** **1** *adj* adequate; **2** *adv* adequately; *(zu Genüge)* sufficiently; **~laufen** *vi sep irreg aux sein* **(a)** to run there; **(b)** *(col: nicht fahren)* to walk; **~legen** *sep* **1** *vt* **(a)** to put down; *Zettel* to leave *(jdm* for sb*)*; *Verletzten etc* to lay down; *(col: bezahlen müssen)* to fork out *(col)*; **(b)** *(col: glänzend darbieten)* to give; **2** *vr* to lie down; **sich der Länge nach ~legen** *(col: hinfallen)* to fall flat; **~machen** *vt sep* **1** *vt (anbringen)* to put on; **2** *vi (col: Notdurft verrichten)* to do one's/it's etc business *(euph)*; **~nehmen** *vt sep irreg (ertragen)* to take; **~neigen** *sep* **1** *vr (zu towards)* *(Mensch)* to lean; *(fig)* to incline; **2** *vi (fig)* **zu etw ~neigen** to incline towards sth; **~passen** *vi sep* to fit (in); *(gut aussehen)* to go (well); **~reichen** *vi sep* **(a)** *(ausreichen)* to be enough; **(b)** *(sich erstrecken)* **bis zu etw ~reichen** to stretch to sth; **~reichend** *adj (ausreichend)* adequate; *(genug)* sufficient; *(reichlich)* ample; **H~reise** *f* journey out, outward journey; *(mit Schiff)* outward voyage; **~reißen** *vt sep irreg (fig: begeistern)* to thrill; **sich ~reißen lassen** to let oneself get carried away; *siehe* **~gerissen**; **~reißend** *adj Landschaft, Anblick* enchanting; *Schönheit, Mensch* captivating; **~richten** *vt sep* to execute; **H~richtung** *f* execution; **~sagen** *vt sep* to say without thinking; **~schaffen** *vt sep* **etw zu jdm ~schaffen** to get sth to sb; **~schauen** *vi sep siehe* **~sehen**; **~schicken** *vt sep* to send; **~schleppen** *sep* **1** *vt* to carry, to lug *(col)*; *(col: mitnehmen)* to drag along; **2** *vr (Mensch)* to drag oneself along; *(fig)* to drag on; **~schmeißen** *vt sep irreg (col) (hinwerfen)* to fling down *(col)*; *(fig: aufgeben) Arbeit etc* to chuck in *(col)*, to pack in *(Brit col)*; **~schreiben** *sep irreg* **1** *vt* to write; *(flüchtig)* to scribble down *(col)*; **2** *vi (col)* to write; **~sehen** *vi sep irreg* to look; **ich kann (gar) nicht ~sehen** I can't bear to look; **bei genauerem H~sehen** on closer inspection.

**hinsein** *vi sep irreg aux sein (col)* **(a)** *(kaputt sein)* to have had it *(col)*. **(b)** *(verloren sein)* to be lost; *(Ruhe)* to be gone; *(ruiniert sein)* to be in ruins. **(c)** *(col: tot sein)* to have kicked the bucket *(col)*. **(d)** *(begeistert sein)* **(von etw) ~** to be mad about sth *(col)*. **(e) bis dahin ist es noch lange hin** it's a long time till then.

**hinsetzen** *sep* **1** *vt* to put *or* set down. **2** *vr* to sit down.

**Hinsicht** *f no pl* **in dieser ~** in this respect; **in mancher** *or* **gewisser ~** in some *or* many respects *or* ways; **in finanzieller/wirtschaftlicher ~** financially/economically; **in beruflicher ~** job-wise.

**hinsichtlich** *prep +gen (bezüglich)* with regard to; *(in Anbetracht)* in view of.

**hin-:** **~sollen** *vi sep (col)* **wo soll ich/das Buch ~?** where do I/does the book go?; **H~spiel** *nt (Sport)* first leg; **~stellen** *sep* **1** *vt* **(a)** to put down; *(col) Gebäude* to put up; *(abstellen) Fahrzeug* to put; **(b) jdn/etw als jdn/etw ~stellen** to make sb/sth out to be sb/sth; **2** *vr* to stand; *(Fahrer)* to park; **~strecken** *sep* **1** *vt Hand, Gegenstand* to hold out; **2** *vr* to stretch out.

**hint|an-:** **~setzen**, **~stellen** *vt sep (zurückstellen)* to put last; *(vernachlässigen)* to neglect.

**hinten** *adv* **(a)** behind; *(am rückwärtigen Ende)* at the back. **ein Blick nach ~** a look behind; **von weit ~** from the very back; **im Buch/auf der Liste ~** at the back of the book/at the end of the list; **sich ~ anstellen** to join the end of the queue *(Brit)* or line *(US)*; **~ im Bild** in the back of the picture; **etw ~ anfügen** to add sth at the end; **von ~** from behind; **~ im Auto** in the back of the car; **nach ~ fallen, ziehen** backwards; **ich sehe ihn am liebsten von ~** *(col)* I am always glad to see the back of him; **ein nach ~ gelegenes Zimmer** a room facing the back; **das Auto da ~** the car back there; **sie waren ziemlich weit ~** they were quite far back.

**(b)** *(fig)* **~ und vorn** betrügen left, right and centre *(Brit)* or center *(US)*; *bedienen* hand and foot; **das stimmt ~ und vorn nicht** that is absolutely untrue; **das reicht ~ und vorn nicht** that's nowhere near enough; **ich weiß nicht mehr, wo ~ und vorn ist** I don't know whether I'm coming or going.

**hinten-:** **~drạn** *adv (col)* at the back; **~herum** *adv* **(a)** from the back; **kommen Sie ~herum** come around the back; **(b)** *(fig col) (auf Umwegen)* in a roundabout way; *(illegal)* under the counter; **~über** *adv* **er fiel ~über** he fell over backwards.

**hinter** *prep +dat or (mit Bewegungsverben) +acc* **(a)** behind; *(über ... hinaus)* beyond; **~ jdm/etw her** be-

hind sb/sth; **~ die Wahrheit kommen** to get to the truth; **sich ~ jdn stellen** *(fig)* to support sb; **~ jdm/etw stehen** *(lit, fig)* to be behind sb/sth; **~ der Tür hervor** (out) from behind the door; **jdn weit ~ sich** *(dat)* **lassen** to leave sb a long way behind; **acht Kilometer ~ der Grenze** five miles the other side of the border. **(b) etw ~ sich** *(dat)* **haben** *(zurückgelegt haben)* to have got through sth; *Strecke* to have covered sth; *(überstanden haben)* to have got sth over with; *anstrengende Tage* to have had sth; *Studium* to have completed sth; **sie hat viel ~ sich** she has been through a lot; **etw ~ sich** *(acc)* **bringen** to get sth over with; *Strecke* to cover sth; *Arbeit* to get sth done.

**Hinter-:** **~achse** *f* rear axle; **~ausgang** *m* back *or* rear exit; **~backe** *f usu pl* buttock; **sich auf die ~backen setzen** *(fig col)* to get down to it; **~bänkler** *m - (Pol pej)* backbencher; **~bein** *nt* **sich auf die ~beine stellen** *or* **setzen** *(fig col: sich anstrengen)* to pull one's socks up *(col)*.

**Hinterbliẹbene(r)** *mf decl as adj* surviving dependant. **die ~n** the bereaved family.

**hinterbrịngen\*** *vt insep irreg* **jdm etw ~** to pass sth on to sb.

**hinter|einạnder** *adv* one behind the other; *(nicht gleichzeitig)* one after the other. **~ hereinkommen** to come in one by one; **zwei Tage ~** two days running; **dreimal ~** three times in a row.

**hinter|einạnder-:** **~her** *adv* behind one another; **~schalten** *vt sep (Elec)* to connect in series.

**Hinter|eingang** *m* rear entrance.

**hintere(r, s)** *adj* back; *(von Tier, Gebäude, Zug auch)* rear. **der/die/das H~** the one at the back.

**Hinter-:** **h~frạgen\*** *vt insep* to analyze; *Brauch, Recht etc* to question; **~gedanke** *m* ulterior motive; **h~gehen\*** *vt insep irreg (betrügen)* to deceive; *(umgehen) Gesetze* to circumvent.

**Hintergrund** *m (von Bild, fig)* background; *(von Saal)* back; *(Theat: Kulisse)* backcloth. **im ~** in the background; **im ~ der Bühne** at the back of the stage; **vor dem ~** *(lit, fig)* against the background; **in den ~ treten** *(fig)* to retreat into the background.

**hintergründig** *adj* cryptic, enigmatic.

**Hintergrund-:** **~information** *f* piece of background information; **~programm** *nt (Comp)* background program.

**Hinter-:** **~halt** *m* **(a)** ambush; **jdn aus dem ~halt überfallen** to ambush sb; **im ~halt lauern** to lie in wait; **(b)** *(col)* **etw im ~halt haben** to have sth in reserve; **h~hältig** *adj* underhand(ed), devious; **~hältigkeit** *f* underhandedness, deviousness.

**hinterher** *adv* behind; *(zeitlich)* afterwards.

**hinterher-:** **~hinken** *vi sep aux sein (fig)* to lag behind *(hinter etw (dat)* sth, *mit* with, in*)*; **~kommen** *vi sep irreg aux sein* **(a)** *(räumlich)* to follow (behind); *(zeitlich)* to come after; **(b)** *(als letzter kommen)* to bring up the rear; **~laufen** *vi sep irreg aux sein* to run behind *(jdm* sb*)*; **jdm ~laufen** *(fig col: sich bemühen um)* to run around after sb; **~sein** *vi sep irreg aux sein (col)* to be after *(jdm* sb*)*; **~sein, daß ...** *(fig)* to see to it that ...

**Hinter-:** **~hof** *m* backyard; **~kopf** *m* back of one's head; **etw im ~kopf haben/behalten** *(col)* to have/keep sth in the back of one's mind; **~land** *nt* hinterland; **h~lạssen\*** *vt insep irreg* to leave; *(jdm etw* sb sth*)*; **h~lassene Werke/Schriften** posthumous works; **~lạssenschaft** *f* estate; *(literarisch, fig)* legacy; **h~lẹgen\*** *vt insep* to deposit; *(als Pfand)* to leave; **~legung** *f* deposit.

**Hinterlist** *f no pl* **(a)** *siehe adj* craftiness, cunning; deceitfulness. **(b)** *(Trick, List)* ruse, trick.

**hinterlistig** adj (tückisch) crafty, cunning; (betrügerisch) deceitful.

**Hintermann** m, pl ⁼er (a) person/car behind (one). **mein** ~ the person/car behind me. **(b)** (Gewährsmann) contact. **die ~er des Skandals** the men behind the scandal.

**Hintern** m - (col) bottom, backside (col). **jdm den ~ versohlen** to smack sb's bottom; **ein paar auf den ~ bekommen** to get one's bottom smacked; **sich auf den ~ setzen** (eifrig arbeiten) to buckle down to work; **jdm in den ~ kriechen** to suck up to sb.

**Hinter-:** ~**rad** nt rear or back wheel; ~**radantrieb** m rear wheel drive; **h~rücks** adv from behind; (fig: heimtückisch) behind sb's back; ~**seite** f back; **h~sinnig** adj cryptic.

**hinterste(r, s)** adj superl of **hintere(r, s)** very back; (entlegenste) remotest.

**Hinter-:** ~**teil** nt (a) (col) backside (col); (von Tier) hindquarters pl; **(b)** auch m back or rear part; ~**treffen** nt im ~**treffen sein** to be at a disadvantage; **ins** ~**treffen geraten** to fall behind; **h~treiben*** vt insep irreg (fig) to foil, to thwart; Gesetz to block; ~**treppe** f back stairs pl; ~**tür** f back door; (fig col) loophole; **durch die** ~**tür** (fig) through the back door; **sich** (dat) **eine** ~**tür** or **ein** ~**türchen offenhalten** (fig) to leave oneself a loophole or a way out; ~**wäldler** m - (col) backwoodsman, hillbilly (esp US); ~**wäldlerisch** adj (col) backwoods attr; **h~ziehen*** vt insep irreg Steuern to evade; Material to appropriate; ~**ziehung** f siehe vt evasion; appropriation; ~**zimmer** nt back room.

**hintun** vt sep irreg (col) to put. **ich weiß nicht, wo ich ihn** ~ **soll** (fig) I can't (quite) place him.

**hinüber** adv over; (über Straße auch) across.

**hinüber-** pref across; siehe auch **herüber-**; ~**fahren** sep irreg **1** vt (über etw (acc)) sth) to take across; Auto to drive across; **2** vi aux sein to travel or go across; **über den Fluß** ~**fahren** to cross the river; ~**führen** sep **1** vt jdn (über die Straße) ~**führen** to take sb across (the street); **2** vi Straße, Brücke to go across (über etw (acc)) sth); ~**gehen** vi sep irreg aux sein to go across or over; ~**kommen** vi sep irreg aux sein (über etw (acc)) sth) to come across; (über Hindernis, zu Besuch) to come over; (~**können**) to get across/over; ~**reichen** sep **1** vt to pass across; (über Zaun etc) to pass over (jdm to sb, über etw (acc)) sth); **2** vi to reach across (über etw (acc)) sth); (fig) to extend (in +acc into); ~**sein** vi sep irreg aux sein (col) (verdorben sein) to be off (Brit) or bad; (unbrauchbar, tot sein) to have had it (col); ~**wechseln** vi sep aux haben or sein to change over (zu, in +acc to); ~**ziehen** sep irreg **1** vt to pull across (über etw (acc)) sth); (fig: umstimmen) to win over (auf +acc to); **2** vi aux sein Wolken etc to move across (über etw (acc)) sth).

**hin- und her-:** ~**bewegen** vtr sep to move to and fro; ~**fahren** sep irreg **1** vi aux sein to travel to and fro or back and forth; **2** vt to drive to and fro or back and forth.

**Hin- und Rück-:** ~**fahrt** f return journey, round trip (US); ~**flug** m return flight; ~**weg** m round trip.

**hinunter 1** adv down. **bis** ~ **zu** down to. **2** prep +acc **den Berg** ~ down the mountain.

**hinunter-** pref down; siehe auch **herunter-**; ~**bringen** vt sep irreg to take down; **das bringe ich nicht** ~ (col: schlucken) I can't get that stuff down; ~**gehen** vi sep irreg aux sein to go down; (Flugzeug) to descend (auf +acc to); ~**gießen** vt sep irreg, ~**kippen** vt sep (col) Getränke to knock back

(col); ~**schlingen** vt sep irreg (col) to gulp down; Essen to gobble down; ~**schlucken** vt sep to swallow (down); (fig) Beleidigung to swallow; Kritik to take; Ärger, Tränen to choke back; ~**spülen** vt sep (a) to flush away; **(b)** Essen, Tablette to wash down; (fig) Ärger to soothe; ~**stürzen** sep **1** vi aux sein (a) (~**fallen**) to tumble down; **(b)** (eilig ~**laufen**) to rush down; **2** vt jdn to throw or hurl down; Getränk to gulp down; **3** vr to throw or fling oneself down.

**Hinweg** m way there. **auf dem** ~ on the way there.

**hinweg** adv **(a)** (old: fort) away. **(b)** **über jdn** ~ (fig) over sb's head; **über eine Zeit/zwei Jahre** ~ over a period of time/over (a period of) two years.

**hinweg-** ~**bringen** vt sep irreg (fig) jdn **über etw** (acc) ~**bringen** to help sb to get over sth; ~**gehen** vi sep irreg aux sein **über etw** (acc) ~**gehen** (fig) to pass over sth; ~**helfen** vi sep irreg (fig) jdm **über etw** (acc) ~**helfen** to help sb get over sth; ~**kommen** vi sep irreg aux sein (fig) **über etw** (acc) ~**kommen** to get over sth; **ich komme nicht darüber** ~, **daß** ... (col) I can't get over the fact that ...; ~**sehen** vi sep irreg **über jdn/etw** ~**sehen** (fig) to ignore sb/sth; **darüber** ~**sehen, daß** ... to overlook the fact that ...; ~**setzen** vr sep (fig) **sich über etw** (acc) ~**setzen** to disregard sth; ~**täuschen** vt sep **darüber** ~**täuschen, daß** ... to hide the fact that ...; **sich nicht darüber** ~**täuschen lassen, daß** ... not to blind oneself to the fact that ...; ~**trösten** vt sep jdn **über etw** (acc) ~**trösten** to console sb about sth.

**Hinweis** m -e **(a)** (Rat) tip, piece of advice; (amtlich) notice. **darf ich mir den** ~ **erlauben, daß** ...? may I point out that ...?; ~**e für den Benutzer** notes for the user. **(b)** (Verweis) reference. **unter** ~ **auf** (+acc) with reference to. **(c)** (Anhaltspunkt) indication. **sachdienliche** ~**e** relevant information.

**hinweisen** sep irreg **1** vt jdn **auf etw** (acc) ~ to point sth out to sb. **2** vi **auf jdn/etw** ~ to point to sb/sth; (verweisen) to refer to sb/sth; **darauf** ~, **daß** ... to point out that ...; (nachdrücklich) to stress that ...; (anzeigen) to indicate that ...

**Hinweis-:** ~**schild** nt, ~**tafel** f sign.

**hin-:** ~**wenden** vtr sep irreg to turn (zu, nach towards); **H~wendung** f (fig) turn (zu toward); ~**werfen** sep irreg **1** vt **(a)** to throw down; jdm etw ~**werfen** to throw sth to sb; **(b)** Bemerkung to let fall; Wort to say casually; **eine** ~**geworfene Bemerkung** a casual remark; **(c)** (col: aufgeben) Arbeit, Stelle to chuck (in) (col); **2** vr to throw or fling oneself down; ~**wirken** vi sep **auf etw** (acc) ~**wirken** to work towards sth.

**Hinz** m: ~ **und Kunz** (col) every Tom, Dick and Harry (col).

**hin-:** ~**zaubern** vt sep (fig) to rustle or whip up (col); ~**ziehen** sep irreg **1** vt **(a)** (zu sich ziehen) to draw or pull (zu towards); (fig: anziehen) to attract (zu to); **(b)** (fig: in die Länge ziehen) to drag out; **2** vi aux sein **(a)** to move (über +acc across, zu towards); **(b)** Wolken, Rauch to drift, to move (an +dat across); **3** vr **(a)** (lange dauern) to drag on; **(b)** (sich erstrecken) to stretch, to extend; ~**zielen** vi sep **auf etw** (acc) ~**zielen** to aim at sth.

**hinzu** adv (obendrein) besides, in addition.

**hinzu-:** ~**fügen** vt sep to add (dat to); (beilegen) to enclose; **H~fügung** f addition; **unter H~fügung von etw** (form) by adding sth; ~**kommen** vi sep irreg aux sein **(a)** **sie kam gerade** ~, **als** ... she happened to come on the scene when ...; **es werden später noch mehrere** ~**kommen** more people will be joining us later; **(b)** (zusätzlich eintreten) to ensue; (beigefügt werden) to be added; **es kommt noch** ~,

**daß** ... there is also the fact that ...; **kommt sonst noch etwas ~?** will there be anything else?; **~nehmen** *vt sep irreg* to include; **~treten** *vi sep irreg aux sein* (a) *(herantreten)* to come up; **zu den anderen ~treten** to join the others; (b) *(zusätzlich eintreten)* to ensue; **~tun** *vt sep irreg (col)* to add; **~zählen** *vt sep* to add; **~ziehen** *vt sep irreg* to consult.

**Hiobsbotschaft** *f* bad news *no pl.*

**Hippie** *m* hippie, hippy.

**Hirn** *nt* **-e** (a) *(Anat)* brain. (b) *(col) (Kopf)* head; *(Verstand)* brains *pl*, mind. **sich** *(dat)* **das ~ zermartern** to rack one's brain(s); **streng einmal dein ~ an** think hard. (c) *(Cook)* brains *pl*.

**Hirn-** *siehe auch* **Gehirn-**; **h~geschädigt** *adj* brain-damaged; **~gespinst** *nt* fantasy; **~hautentzündung** *f (Med)* meningitis; **h~los** *adj* brainless, braindead *(col)*; **h~rissig** *adj* harebrained; **~tod** *nt (Med)* brain death; **h~tot** *adj* braindead; **~tumor** *m* brain tumour; **h~verbrannt** *adj* hare-brained.

**Hirsch** *m* **-e** deer; *(Rot~)* red deer; *(männlicher Rot~)* stag; *(Cook)* venison.

**Hirsch-:** **~geweih** *nt* antlers *pl*; **~käfer** *m* stagbeetle; **~kuh** *f* hind; **~leder** *nt* buckskin, deerskin.

**Hirse** *f* **-n** millet.

**Hirt** *m (wk)* **-en, -en** herdsman; *(Schaf~)* shepherd.

**Hirte** *m* **-n** (a) = **Hirt**. (b) *(Eccl)* shepherd. **der Gute ~** the Good Shepherd.

**Hirtenhund** *m* sheepdog.

**Hirtin** *f* herdswoman; *(Schaf~)* shepherdess.

**hissen** *vt* to hoist.

**Historiker(in** *f)* *m* - historian.

**historisch** *adj* historical; *(bedeutsam) Ereignis* historic. **das ist ~ belegt** there is historical evidence for this.

**Hit** *m* **-s** *(Mus, fig col)* hit.

**Hit-:** **~liste** *f* charts *pl*; **~parade** *f* hit parade.

**Hitze** *f* **-n** (a) heat; *(~welle)* heat wave. **vor ~ umkommen** to be dying of heat *or* sweltering; **bei starker/mäßiger ~ backen** *(Cook)* bake in a hot/moderate oven. (b) *(fig)* passion. **in ~/leicht in ~ geraten** to get heated/to get worked up easily; **sich in ~ reden** to get oneself all worked up; **in der ~ des Gefecht(e)s** *(fig)* in the heat of the moment.

**Hitze-:** **h~beständig** *adj* heat-resistant; **~beständigkeit** *f* heat resistance; **h~empfindlich** *adj* sensitive to heat; **h~frei** *adj* **h~frei haben** *to have time off from school on account of excessively hot weather*; **~welle** *f* heat wave.

**hitzig** *adj* (a) *Mensch* hot-headed; *Streit, Debatte* heated; *Temperament* passionate. **~ werden** *(Mensch)* to flare up; *(Debatte)* to grow heated; **nicht so ~!** don't get excited! (b) *(Zool)* on heat.

**Hitzigkeit** *f siehe adj* (a) hot-headedness; heatedness; passionateness.

**Hitz-:** **~kopf** *m* hothead; **h~köpfig** *adj* hot-headed; **~schlag** *m (Med)* heat-stroke.

**HIV** [ha:|i:'fau] = **Human Immunodeficiency Virus** HIV.

**hl.** = (a) **heilig**; (b) **Hektoliter** hl.

**Hl.** = **Heilige(r)** St.

**H-Milch** ['ha:-] *f* long-life milk, UHT milk.

**HNO-Arzt** [ha:|ɛn'|o:-] *m* ENT specialist.

**hob** *pret of* **heben**.

**Hobby** *nt* **-s** hobby.

**Hobel** *m* - *(Tech)* plane; *(Cook)* slicer.

**Hobel-:** **~bank** *f* carpenter's bench; **~maschine** *f* planer, planing machine.

**hobeln** *vt* (a) *auch vi (Tech)* to plane *(an etw (dat)* sth*)*. **wo gehobelt wird, da fallen Späne** *(Prov)* you

can't make an omelette *(Brit) or* omelet *(US)* without breaking eggs *(Prov)*. (b) *(Cook)* to slice.

**Hobelspan** *m* (wood) shaving.

**Hoch** *nt* **-s** (a) **ein ~ dem Brautpaar** here's to the bride and groom. (b) *(Met, fig)* high.

**hoch** *attr* **hohe(r, s)** *comp* **höher,** *superl* **=ste(r, s)** *or (adv)* **am =sten 1** *adj* high; *Baum, Leiter* tall; *Betrag* large; *Strafe, Gewicht* heavy; *Profit, Verlust auch, Lotteriegewinn* big; *Gut, Glück, Alter* great; *Schaden* extensive; *Persönlichkeit* distinguished; *Besuch, Feiertag* important; *Offizier* high-ranking. **das Hohe Haus** *(Parl)* the House; **ein hohes Tier** *(col)* a big fish *(col)*; **das Hohe C** top C; **ein hohes Alter erreichen** to live to a ripe old age; **das ist mir zu ~** *(col)* that's above my head; **hohe Flut** spring tide; **der hohe Norden** the far North.

**2** *adv* (a) *(nach oben)* up; *(in einiger Höhe)* high. **er sah zu uns ~** he looked up to us; **~ emporragend** towering (up); **die Nase ~ tragen** *(col)* to go around with one's nose in the air *(col)*; **~ oben** high up; **die Sonne steht ~** the sun is high in the sky; **~ werfen/wachsen** to throw high/grow tall.

(b) *verehren, versichern, begabt* highly; *verlieren* heavily; *gewinnen* handsomely; *verschuldet* deeply; *erfreut* very. **das rechne ich ihm ~ an** (I think) that is very much to his credit; **~ hinauswollen** to aim high, to be ambitious; **drei Mann ~** *(col)* three of them; **wenn es ~ kommt** *(col)* at (the) most, at the outside; **~ setzen** *or* **spielen** *(im Spiel)* to play for high stakes.

(c) *(Math)* **7 ~ 3** 7 to the power of 3, 7 to the 3rd.

(d) *(col)* **es ging ~ her** there were lively goings-on *(col)*; **~ und heilig versprechen** to promise faithfully; **~ und heilig schwören** to swear blind *(col)*.

**hoch-** *pref (in Verbindung mit Bewegungsverb)* up; *versichert, begabt etc* highly; *zufrieden, erfreut, elegant etc* very; *besteuert* heavily; *verschuldet* deeply.

**Hoch-:** **h~achten** *vt sep* to respect highly; **~achtung** *f* deep respect; **bei aller ~achtung vor jdm/etw** with all due respect to sb/sth; **mit vorzüglicher ~achtung** *(form: Briefschluß)* yours faithfully; **h~achtungsvoll** *adv (Briefschluß)* yours faithfully; **~adel** *m* high nobility; **h~aktuell** *adj* highly topical; **~amt** *nt (Eccl)* High Mass; **h~angesehen** *adj attr* highly regarded; **h~arbeiten** *vr sep* to work one's way up; **h~auflösend** *adj (Comp, TV)* high-resolution; **~bahn** *f* elevated railway *or* railroad *(US)*; **~bau** *m no pl* structural engineering; *siehe* **~- und Tiefbau**; **h~begabt** *adj attr* highly talented; **h~betagt** *adj* aged *attr*, advanced in years; **~betrieb** *m* peak period; *(im Verkehr)* rush hour; **~betrieb haben** to be at one's/its busiest; **h~bringen** *vt sep irreg (col)* (a) to bring *or* take up; (b) *(col: h~heben können)* to get up; (c) *(fig: leistungsfähig machen)* to get going; *Kranken* to get back on his etc feet; **~burg** *f (fig)* stronghold; **h~deutsch** *adj* High German; **~deutsch(e)** *nt* standard *or* High German; **h~dotiert** *adj attr Arbeit* highly paid.

**Hochdruck** *m* (a) *(Met, Phys)* high pressure. **mit ~ arbeiten** to work at full stretch. (b) *(Med)* high blood pressure. (c) *(Typ)* relief print.

**Hoch-:** **~ebene** *f* plateau; **h~empfindlich** *adj (Tech) Material, Instrumente* highly sensitive; *Film* fast; *Stoff* very delicate; **h~entwickelt** *adj attr Kultur, Land* highly developed; *Geräte, Methoden* sophisticated; **h~fahren** *sep irreg* **1** *vi aux sein* (a) to go up; *(in Auto auch)* to drive up; (b) *(erschreckt)* to jump; **2** *vt* to take up; *(in Auto auch)* to drive up; **h~fahrend** *adj (überheblich)* arrogant; **~finanz** *f* high finance; **h~fliegen** *vi sep irreg aux sein* to fly up; *(hochgeschleudert werden)* to be thrown up; **h~fliegend** *adj* ambitious; *(übertrieben)* high-flown; ~**form** *f* top form; ~**format** *nt* portrait *or* vertical format; ~**frequenz** *f* *(Elec)* high frequency; ~**gebirge** *nt* high mountains *pl*; ~**gefühl** *nt* elation; **h~gehen** *vi sep irreg aux sein* (**a**) to rise; (**b**) *(col: hinaufgehen)* to go up; (**c**) *(col: explodieren)* to blow up; *(Bombe)* to go off; **etw h~gehen lassen** to blow sth up; (**d**) *(col: wütend werden)* to go through the roof *(col)*; (**e**) *(col: gefaßt werden)* to get caught; **jdn h~gehen lassen** to bust sb *(col)*; **h~geistig** *adj* highly intellectual, highbrow *no adv*; **h~gelegen** *adj attr* **ein h~gelegener Ort** a place situated high up; ~**genuß** *m* great *or* special treat; *(großes Vergnügen)* great pleasure; **h~geschätzt** *adj attr* *Mensch* highly esteemed; *Sache* greatly valued; **h~geschlossen** *adj* *Kleid etc* high-necked; ~**geschwindigkeitszug** *m* high-speed train; **h~gespannt** *adj* *(fig)* *Erwartungen* extreme; ~**gesteckt** *adj* *(fig)* *Ziele* ambitious; **h~gestellt** *adj* (**a**) *(Typ)* superscript; (**b**) *(fig)* *Persönlichkeit* high-ranking; **h~gestochen** *adj* *Reden* high-flown; *Stil* pompous; *(eingebildet)* stuck-up; **h~gewachsen** *adj* tall; **h~gezüchtet** *adj* *Motor* souped-up *(col)*; *Geräte* fancy *(col)*; *Tiere, Pflanzen* overbred.

**Hochglanz** *m* high polish; *(Phot)* gloss. **etw auf ~ polieren** *or* **bringen** to polish sth until it shines.

**hochglänzend** *adj* very shiny; *Fotoabzug* very glossy; *Möbel* highly polished.

**Hochglanz-**: ~**papier** *nt* high gloss paper; ~**politur** *f* mirror polish *or* finish; *(Poliermittel)* (furniture) polish.

**Hoch-**: **h~gradig** *adj no pred* extreme; **h~hackig** *adj* *Schuhe* high-heeled; **h~halten** *vt sep irreg* to hold up; *(fig)* to uphold; ~**haus** *nt* high-rise *or* multi-storey building; **h~heben** *vt sep irreg* *Hand* to hold up; *Last* to lift up; **h~intelligent** *adj* highly intelligent; **h~interessant** *adj* very interesting; **h~jagen** *vt sep (col)* (**a**) *(aufscheuchen)* *Menschen* to get up; (**b**) *(sprengen)* to blow up; (**c**) *Motor* to rev up; **h~jubeln** *vt sep (col)* *Künstler, Film etc* to build up, to hype *(col)*; **h~kant** *adv* (**a**) **h~kant stellen** to put on end; (**b**) *(fig col)* **jdn h~kant hinauswerfen** to chuck sb out on his/her ear *(col)*; **h~klappen** *vt sep* *Tisch* to fold up; *Sitz* to tip up; *Deckel* to lift up; *Kragen* to turn up; **h~kommen** *vi sep irreg aux sein* (**a**) *(col)* to come up; (**b**) *(col)* **das Essen ist ihm h~gekommen** he threw up (his meal) *(col)*; (**c**) *(aufstehen können)* to (manage to) get up; *(fig: gesund werden)* to get back on one's feet; (**d**) *(col: gesellschaftlich)* to come up in the world; ~**konjunktur** *f* boom; **h~krempeln** *vt sep* to roll up; ~**kultur** *f* (very) advanced civilization; ~**land** *nt* highland; **das schottische** ~**land** the Scottish Highlands *pl*; **h~leben** *vi sep* **jdn h~leben lassen** to give three cheers for sb; **er lebe h~!** three cheers (for him)!; **h~legen** *vt sep* *Beine etc* to put up.

**Hochleistungs-** *in cpds* high-performance; ~**motor** *m* high-performance engine; ~**sport** *m* top-level sport.

**Hoch-**: **h~modern** *adj* very modern, ultra-modern; ~**moor** *nt* moor; ~**mut** *m* arrogance; **h~mütig** *adj* arrogant; **h~näsig** *adj (col)* snooty *(col)*; ~**nebel** *m* (low) stratus; **h~nehmen** *vt sep irreg* (**a**) to lift; *Kind* to pick *or* lift up; (**b**) **jdn h~nehmen** *(col) (necken)* to pull sb's leg; *(schröpfen)* to fleece sb *(col)*; *(verhaften)* to pick sb up; ~**ofen** *m* blast furnace; ~**parterre** *nt* raised ground floor; **h~prozentig** *adj* *Getränke* high-proof; *Lösung* high-

ly concentrated; **h~qualifiziert** *adj attr* highly qualified; ~**rad** *nt* penny-farthing; **h~rechnen** *vt sep* to project; ~**rechnung** *f* projection; **h~rot** *adj* bright red; **mit h~rotem Gesicht** with one's face as red as a beetroot *(Brit)*, with a bright red face; ~**ruf** *m* cheer; **h~rüsten** *vt sep* **ein Land h~rüsten** to increase the weaponry of a country; ~**saison** *f* high season; **h~schlagen** *sep irreg* **1** *vt* *Kragen* to turn up; **2** *vi aux sein* *(Wellen)* to surge up; *(Flammen)* to leap up; **h~schrauben** *vt sep (fig)* *Preise* to force up; *Erwartungen* to raise; *Forderungen* to increase.

**Hochschul-**: ~**abschluß** *m* degree; ~**absolvent** *m* graduate; ~**(aus)bildung** *f* university education.

**Hochschule** *f* college; *(Universität)* university.

**Hochschüler(in** *f)* *m* student.

**Hochschul-**: ~**lehrer** *m* college/university teacher, lecturer *(Brit)*; ~**reife** *f* **er hat (die)** ~**reife** = he's got his A-levels *(Brit)*, he's graduated from high school *(US)*; ~**studium** *nt* higher education.

**hochschwanger** *adj* very pregnant *(col)*, well advanced in pregnancy.

**Hochsee-**: ~**fischerei** *f* deep-sea fishing; ~**schiffahrt** *f* ocean-going shipping.

**Hoch-**: ~**seil** *nt* high wire, tightrope; **h~sensibel** *adj* highly sensitive; ~**sicherheitstrakt** *m* high-security wing; ~**sitz** *m* *(Hunt)* (raised) hide; ~**sommer** *m* height of the summer; **h~sommerlich** *adj* very summery.

**Hochspannung** *f* *(Elec, fig)* high tension.

**Hochspannungs-**: ~**leitung** *f* high tension line, power line; ~**mast** *m* pylon.

**Hoch-**: **h~spielen** *vt sep (fig)* to blow up; ~**sprache** *f* standard language; ~**sprung** *m* high jump.

**höchst** *adv (überaus)* highly, extremely.

**Höchst-** *in cpds (obere Grenze angebend) (mit n)* maximum; *(mit adj) siehe* **Hoch-**; *(mit adj: Intensität ausdrückend)* extremely, most; ~**alter** *nt* maximum age.

**Hoch-**: ~**stapelei** *f* *(Jur)* fraud; *(einzelner Fall)* confidence trick; **h~stapeln** *vi sep* to be fraudulent; *(fig)* to put one over *(col)*; ~**stapler** *m* - confidence trickster, con man *(col)*; *(fig)* fraud.

**Höchst-**: ~**betrag** *m* maximum amount; ~**bietende(r)** *mf decl as adj* highest bidder.

**hoch-**: ~**stecken** *vt sep* to pin up; *Haare auch* to put up; ~**stehend** *adj (gesellschaftlich)* of high standing; *(geistig)* highly intellectual; *(entwicklungsmäßig)* superior; ~**stellen** *vt sep* (**a**) *Stühle etc* to put up; (**b**) *Heizung etc, Kragen* to turn up.

**höchstenfalls** *adv* at (the) most.

**höchstens** *adv* (**a**) at the most. (**b**) *(außer)* except.

**höchste(r, s)** *adj, superl of* **hoch** highest; *Wuchs, Baum* tallest; *Betrag, Summe* largest; *Strafe, Gewicht* heaviest; *Lotteriegewinn* biggest; *Schaden* most expensive; *(maximal) Verdienst, Temperatur, Geschwindigkeit etc* maximum *attr*; *Fest* most important; *Offizier* highest-ranking; *Genuß, Glück, Freude, Ehre, Gut* greatest; *Gefahr, Wichtigkeit* utmost, greatest; *Konzentration* extreme. **zu meiner** ~**n Zufriedenheit** to my great satisfaction; **im** ~**n Grade/Maße** extremely; **im** ~**n Fall(e)** at the most; **die** ~ **Instanz** *(Jur)* the supreme court of appeal; ~ **Zeit** high time; **aufs** ~ **erfreut** *etc* extremely *or* highly pleased *etc*; **Gespräche auf** ~**r Ebene** top-level talks.

**2** *adv* **am** ~**n** highest; *schätzen, versichern* most; *besteuert, verlieren* (the) most heavily; *verschuldet* (the) most deeply; **in der Rangordnung am** ~**n stehen** to be the most senior in the hierarchy; **am** ~**n stehen** *(Kurse, Temperatur)* to be at its highest.

**Höchste(s)** *nt decl as adj (fig)* highest good. **nach dem ~n streben** to aspire to perfection.

**Höchst-:** **~fall** *m* **im ~fall** at the most; **~form** *f (Sport)* top form; **~geschwindigkeit** *f* top *or* maximum speed; **~gewicht** *nt* weight limit; **~grenze** *f* upper limit.

**Hochstimmung** *f* high spirits *pl.*

**Höchst-:** **~leistung** *f* best performance; *(bei Produktion)* maximum output; **~maß** *nt* maximum amount *(an +dat of)*; **h~persönlich** *adv* personally; **es ist der Prinz h~persönlich** it's the prince in person; **~satz** *m* maximum rate; **~stand** *m* highest level; **h~wahrscheinlich** *adv* most probably.

**Hoch-:** **~tal** *nt* high-lying valley; **~technologie** *f* high technology; **~töner** *m* tweeter; **~tour** *f* auf **~touren laufen/arbeiten** to be working flat out *(col)*; **h~tourig** *adj Motor* high-revving; **h~tourig laufen** to run at high revs; **h~trabend** *adj (pej)* pompous; **h~treiben** *vt sep irreg* to drive up; *(fig) Preise* to force up; **~- und Tiefbau** *m* structural and civil engineering; **h~verehrt** *adj attr* highly esteemed; **h~verehrter Herr Präsident!** Mr President, Sir!; **~verrat** *m* high treason; **~verräter** *m* traitor; **h~verschuldet** *adj attr* deep in debt; **~wald** *m* timber forest; **~wasser** *nt* high tide; *(in Flüssen)* high water; *(Überschwemmung)* flood; *(Wassermassen)* flood water; **~wasser haben** *(Fluß)* to be in flood; **h~wertig** *adj* high-quality; *Nahrungsmittel* highly nutritious; *Stahl* high-grade; **~würden** *m no pl (Eccl: Anrede)* Reverend Father; **~zahl** *f* exponent.

**Hochzeit** *f* **-en** wedding. **~ feiern** to get married ; **man kann nicht auf zwei ~en tanzen** *(prov)* you can't have your cake and eat it *(prov).*

**Hochzeits-** *in cpds* wedding; **~feier** *nt* wedding celebrations *pl*; *(Empfang)* wedding reception; **~fest** *nt* wedding celebrations *pl*; **~reise** *f* honeymoon; **~tag** *m* wedding day; *(Jahrestag)* wedding anniversary.

**hochziehen** *sep irreg* **1** *vt* **(a)** to pull up; *Fahne* to run up; *Augenbrauen* to raise. **(b)** *(bauen) Wand* to put up *(col)*. **2** *vr* to pull oneself up.

**Hocke** *f* **-n** squatting position; *(Übung)* squat; *(beim Turnen)* squat vault; *(beim Skilaufen)* crouch.

**hocken 1** *vi* **(a)** to squat, to crouch. **(b)** *(col: sitzen)* to sit; *(auf Hocker)* to perch. **2** *vr* **(a)** to squat. **(b)** *(col: sich setzen)* to sit down.

**Hocker** *m* - *(Stuhl)* stool.

**Höcker** *m* - *(von Kamel, col: Buckel)* hump.

**Hockey** ['hɔke] *nt no pl* hockey *(Brit)*, field hockey *(US).*

**Hoden** *m* - testicle.

**Hodensack** *m* scrotum.

**Hof** *m* ⁼e **(a)** *(Platz)* yard; *(Innen~)* courtyard. **(b)** *(Bauern~)* farm. **(c)** *(Fürsten~)* court. **bei ~e** at court; **am ~e Ludwigs XIV** at the court of Louis XIV. **(d) einem Mädchen den ~ machen** *(dated)* to court a girl *(dated)*. **(e)** *(um Sonne, Mond)* halo.

**hoffen 1** *vi* to hope. **auf jdn ~** to set one's hopes on sb; **auf etw ~** *(acc)* to hope for sth; **da bleibt nur zu ~** one can only hope; **ich will nicht ~, daß er das macht** I hope he doesn't do that. **2** *vt* to hope for. **~ wir das Beste!** let's hope for the best!; **ich hoffe es** I hope so; **das will ich (doch wohl) ~** I should hope so; **ich will es nicht ~** I hope not.

**hoffentlich** *adv* hopefully. **~!** I hope so; **~ nicht** I/ we hope not.

**Hoffnung** *f* hope; *(auf Gott)* trust *(auf +acc* in*)*. **sich** *(dat)* **~en machen** to have hopes; **sich** *(dat)* **keine ~en machen** not to hold out any hopes; **er macht sich ~en bei ihr** *(col)* he fancies his chances with

her *(col)*; **mach dir keine ~(en)!** don't build up your hopes; **jdm ~en machen** to raise sb's hopes; **jdm auf etw** *(acc)* **~en machen** to lead sb to expect sth; **die ~aufgeben/verlieren** to abandon/lose hope; **sich falschen ~en hingeben** to delude oneself; **guter ~ sein** *(euph: schwanger)* to be expecting.

**Hoffnungs-:** **h~los** *adj* hopeless; **~losigkeit** *f no pl* hopelessness; *(Verzweiflung)* despair; **~schimmer** *m* glimmer of hope; **h~voll 1** *adj* hopeful; *(vielversprechend)* promising; **2** *adv* full of hope.

**hofhalten** *vi sep irreg (lit, fig)* to hold court.

**Hofhund** *m* watchdog.

**hofieren\*** *vt* to court.

**höflich** *adj* polite.

**Höflichkeit** *f* **(a)** *no pl* politeness. **jdm etw mit aller ~ sagen** to tell sb sth very politely. **(b)** *(höfliche Bemerkung)* compliment.

**Höflichkeits-:** **~besuch** *m* courtesy visit; **~floskel** *f* polite phrase; **h~halber** *adv* out of courtesy.

**Höfling** *m* courtier.

**hohe** *adj siehe* **hoch.**

**Höhe** *f* **-n (a)** height; *(Flug~, Berg~ auch)* altitude; *(von Schnee, Wasser)* depth. **in die/der ~** (up) into/ in the air; **in einer ~ von** at a height/an altitude of; **in die ~ gehen/treiben** *(fig: Preise etc)* to go up/force up; **er geht immer gleich in die Höhe** *(col)* he always flares up.

**(b)** *(An~)* hill; *(Gipfel)* top, summit; *(fig: ~punkt, Blütezeit etc)* height. **auf der ~ sein** *(fig col) (leistungsfähig)* to be at one's best; *(gesund)* to be fighting fit *(col)*; **nicht auf der ~ sein** *(fig col)* to feel below par; **die ~n und Tiefen des Lebens** the ups and downs of life; **das ist doch die ~!** *(fig col)* that's the limit!

**(c)** *(von Preisen, Temperatur, Geschwindigkeit, Strafe)* level; *(von Summe, Gewinn, Verlust, Geldstrafe)* size; *(von Wert, Druck)* amount; *(von Schaden)* extent. **in ~ von** amounting to; **ein Betrag in ~ von** the sum of; **ein Scheck in ~ von** a cheque *(Brit)* or check *(US)* for (the sum of); **Zinsen in ~ von** interest at the rate of; **bis zu einer ~ von** up to a maximum of.

**(d)** *(Mus)* pitch; *(Rad: Ton~)* treble *no pl.*

**(e)** *(Naut, Geog: Breitenlage)* latitude. **die beiden Schwimmer liegen auf gleicher ~** the two swimmers are level with each other.

**Hoheit** *f* **(a)** *no pl (Staats~)* sovereignty *(über +acc* over*)*. **(b)** member of a/the royal family; *(als Anrede)* Highness.

**Hoheits-:** **~bereich** *m (Rechtsbereich)* jurisdiction; **~gebiet** *nt* sovereign territory; **~gewalt** *f* (national) jurisdiction; **~gewässer** *pl* territorial waters *pl*; **h~voll** *adj* majestic; **~zeichen** *nt* national emblem.

**Höhen-:** **~angabe** *f* altitude reading; *(auf Karte)* altitude mark; **~angst** *f* fear of heights; **~flug** *m* high-altitude flight; **geistiger ~flug** intellectual flight; **~krankheit** *f (Med)* altitude sickness; **~lage** *f* altitude; **~leitwerk** *nt (Aviat)* tailplane; **~luft** *f* mountain air; **~messer** *m* - *(Aviat)* altimeter; **~sonne** *f* mountain sun; *(Lampe)* sunray lamp; **~unterschied** *m* difference in altitude; **~zug** *m* range of hills.

**Hohepriester** *m* **Hohenpriesters, -** *(lit, fig)* high priest.

**Höhepunkt** *m* height, peak; *(des Tages, des Lebens, einer Veranstaltung)* high spot; *(eines Stücks, Orgasmus)* climax. **auf dem ~ ...** at the peak *(gen* of*)*; **den ~ erreichen** to reach a climax; *(Krankheit)* to reach a crisis; **den ~ überschreiten** to pass the peak.

**hohe(r, s)** *adj siehe* **hoch.**

**höher** adj comp of **hoch** (lit, fig) higher; Macht superior; Klasse upper; Auflage bigger; (Comp) Programmiersprache high-level. ~**e Schule** secondary school, high school (esp US); ~**e Gewalt** an act of God; **in ~em Maße** to a greater extent; **sich ~ versichern** to increase one's insurance; **sich zu H~em berufen fühlen** to feel called to higher things.

**höhergestellt** adj attr higher, more senior.

**hohl** adj (lit, fig) hollow; Geschwätz etc empty, shallow; Blick empty, vacant. **ein ~es Kreuz** a hollow back; **in der ~en Hand** in the hollow of one's hand.

**Höhle** f -n cave; (Hohlraum) cavity, hollow; (Tierbehausung) cave, den; (fig: schlechte Wohnung) hovel, hole (col).

**Höhlen-** in cpds cave; ~**forschung**, ~**kunde** f speleology; ~**malerei** f cave painting; ~**mensch** m caveman.

**Hohl-:** ~**kopf** m (pej) numskull (col); ~**körper** m hollow body; ~**kreuz** nt (Med) hollow back; ~**maß** nt measure of capacity; ~**raum** m hollow (space), (esp Tech) cavity; ~**saum** m (Sew) hemstitch; ~**spiegel** m concave mirror.

**Höhlung** f hollow.

**Hohn** m no pl scorn. **nur ~ und Spott ernten** to receive nothing but scorn and derision; **das ist der reine ~** it's sheer mockery.

**höhnen** vi to jeer, to scoff (über +acc at).

**Hohngelächter** nt scornful laughter.

**höhnisch** adj scornful.

**Hokuspokus** m no pl (Zauberformel) hey presto; (fig) (Täuschung) hocus-pocus (col), jiggery-pokery (col); (Drumherum) palaver (col), fuss.

**hold** adj (poet, dated) fair, sweet. **das Glück war ihm ~** fortune smiled upon him.

**holen** vt to get; (abholen) to fetch, to pick up; Sieg, Preis auch to win; Krankheit auch to catch. **gestern hat ihn die Polizei geholt** the police came to take him away yesterday; **jdn ~ lassen** to send for sb; **sich (dat) eine Erkältung ~** to catch a cold; **dabei ist nichts zu ~** (col) there's nothing in it; **bei ihm ist nichts zu ~** (col) you etc won't get anything out of him.

**Holland** nt Holland.

**Holländer¹** m - Dutchman. **die ~** the Dutch (people).

**Holländer²** m no pl Dutch cheese.

**Holländerin** f Dutchwoman, Dutch girl.

**holländisch** adj Dutch.

**Hölle** f -n hell. **die ~ auf Erden** hell on earth; **in die ~ kommen** to go to hell; **ich werde ihm die ~ heiß machen** (col) I'll give him hell (col); **es war die (reinste) ~** (col) it was (pure) hell (col).

**Höllen-** in cpds of hell, infernal; (col: groß) hellish (col), infernal (col); ~**angst** f terrible fear; **eine ~angst haben** to be scared stiff (col); ~**lärm** m infernal noise; ~**qual** f (fig col) absolute agony; ~**qualen ausstehen** to suffer agonies.

**höllisch** adj (a) attr infernal, of hell. (b) (col: groß) dreadful, hellish (col). **es tut ~ weh** it hurts like hell (col); **die Prüfung war ~ schwer** the exam was hellish(ly) difficult (col).

**Holm** m -e (a) (von Barren) bar; (von Geländer) rail; (von Leiter) side rail. (b) (Griff) shaft.

**Holocaust** ['hɔləkɔːst] m holocaust.

**Hologramm** nt hologram.

**holp(e)rig** adj Weg bumpy; Rede clumsy.

**holpern** vi to bump, to jolt.

**holterdiepolter** adv helter-skelter.

**Holunder** m - elder; (Früchte) elderberries pl.

**Holunder-:** ~**beere** f elderberry; ~**busch**, ~**strauch** m elder bush.

**Holz** nt ⁼er (a) wood; (zum Bauen, Schreinern auch) timber, lumber (US). **ein ~** a piece of wood or timber; (~art) a wood; **aus ~** made of wood, wooden; **~ fällen** to fell trees; **aus einem anderen/demselben ~ geschnitzt sein** (fig) to be cast in a different/the same mould (Brit) or mold (US); **aus hartem ~ geschnitzt sein** (fig) to be made of sterner stuff. (b) (Kegel) skittle, ninepin. **gut ~!** have a good game!

**Holz-** in cpds wood; (aus ~ auch) wooden; (Build, Comm etc) timber; ~**apfel** m crab apple; ~**bearbeitung** f woodworking; (im Sägewerk) timber processing; ~**bein** nt wooden leg; ~**bestand** m stock of wood or timber; ~**bläser** m woodwind player; ~**blasinstrument** nt woodwind instrument; ~**block** m block of wood; ~**bündel** nt bundle of wood.

**Hölzchen** nt small piece of wood; (Streichholz) match.

**holzen** vi (esp Ftbl col) to hack.

**hölzern** adj (lit, fig) wooden.

**Holz-:** ~**fällen** nt no pl tree-felling, lumbering; ~**fäller** m - woodcutter, lumberjack; ~**faserplatte** f (wood) fibreboard (Brit) or fiberboard (US); **h~frei** adj Papier wood-free; ~**hacken** nt no pl chopping wood; **h~haltig** adj Papier woody; ~**hammer** m mallet; **jdm etw mit dem ~hammer beibringen** to hammer sth into sb (col); ~**hammermethode** f (col) sledgehammer method (col); ~**haufen** m pile of wood; ~**haus** nt wooden or timber house.

**holzig** adj woody; Spargel auch stringy, tough.

**Holz-:** ~**klotz** m block of wood; (Spielzeug) wooden brick; **er saß da wie ein ~klotz** (col) he sat there like a block or lump of wood; ~**kohle** f charcoal; ~**kopf** m (fig col) blockhead (col); ~**löffel** m wooden spoon; ~**scheit** nt piece of (fire)wood, log; ~**schnitt** m woodcut; ~**schnitzer** m wood carver; ~**schnitzerei** f wood carving; ~**schuh** m wooden shoe, clog; ~**schutzmittel** nt wood preservative; ~**span** m wood chip; ~**stoß** m pile of wood; ~**verarbeitung** f wood-processing; ~**weg** m **auf dem ~weg sein** (fig col) to be on the wrong track (col); ~**wirtschaft** f timber industry; ~**wolle** f wood-wool; ~**wurm** m woodworm.

**homo-** in cpds homo; ~**gen** adj homogeneous; ~**genisieren*** vt to homogenize.

**Homöo-:** ~**path** m (wk) -en, -en homoeopath (Brit), homeopath (US); ~**pathie** f no pl homoeopathy (Brit), homeopathy (US); **h~pathisch** adj homoeopathic (Brit), homeopathic (US).

**Homo-:** ~**sexualität** f homosexuality; **h~sexuell** adj homosexual; ~**sexuelle(r)** mf decl as adj homosexual.

**Honduras** nt Honduras.

**Hongkong** nt Hong Kong.

**Honig** m no pl honey. **sie schmierte ihm ~ ums Maul** (col) she buttered him up (col).

**Honig-:** ~**biene** f honey bee; ~**kuchen** m honeycake; ~**kuchenpferd** nt (col) **grinsen wie ein ~kuchenpferd** to grin like a Cheshire cat; ~**lecken** nt (fig) **das ist kein ~lecken** it's no picnic; ~**melone** f honeydew melon; **h~süß** adj as sweet as honey; (fig) Worte, Ton honeyed; Lächeln sickly sweet; ~**wabe** f honeycomb.

**Honorar** nt -e fee; (Autoren~) royalty.

**Honoratioren** [honora'tsioːrən] pl dignitaries pl.

**honorieren*** vt (Comm) to honour (Brit), to honor (US), to meet; (fig: anerkennen) to reward. **meine Arbeit wird schlecht honoriert** my work is poorly remunerated.

**Hopfen** m - (Bot) hop; (beim Brauen) hops pl. **bei ihm ist ~ und Malz verloren** (col) he's a dead loss (col).

**hoppeln** *vi aux sein (Hase)* to lollop.
**hoppla** *interj* whoops. **~, jetzt komm' ich!** look out, here I come!
**hops** *adj pred (col)* **~ gehen** *(verlorengehen)* to get lost; *(entzweigehen)* to get broken; *(verhaftet werden)* to get nabbed *(col)*; *(sterben)* to kick the bucket *(col)*; **jdn ~ nehmen** *(verhaften)* to nab sb *(col)*; **~ sein** *(verloren)* to be lost; *(Geld)* to be down the drain *(col)*; *(entzwei)* to be kaputt *(col)*.
**hopsen** *vi aux sein (col)* to hop, to skip.
**Hopser** *m (col: kleiner Sprung)* (little) jump.
**hörbar** *adj* audible. **sich ~ machen** to speak up.
**horchen** *vi* to listen *(dat, auf +acc to)*; *(heimlich)* to eavesdrop.
**Horcher** *m* - eavesdropper.
**Horde** *f* -n *(lit, fig)* horde.
**hören** *vti* **(a)** to hear. **ich höre dich nicht** I can't hear you; **ich hörte ihn kommen** I heard him coming; **gut/schlecht ~** to have good/bad hearing; **schwer ~** to be hard of hearing; **du hörst wohl schlecht!** *(col)* you must be deaf!; **das läßt sich ~** *(fig)* that doesn't sound bad; **ich habe es sagen ~** I've heard it said; **er hört sich gern reden** he likes the sound of his own voice; **na hör mal!, na ~ Sie mal!** wait a minute!, look here!; **von etw ~** to hear about *or* of sth; **von jdm gehört haben** to have heard of sb; **von jdm ~** *(Nachricht bekommen)* to hear from sb; **Sie werden noch von mir ~** *(Drohung)* you'll be hearing from me; **man hörte nie mehr etwas von ihm** he was never heard of again; **laß mal ~!** *(col)* tell us; **etwas/nichts von sich ~ lassen** to get/not to get in touch; **lassen Sie von sich ~** keep in touch; **ich lasse von mir ~** I'll be in touch; **er kommt, wie ich höre** I hear he's coming; **man höre und staune!** would you believe it!; **ich will davon nichts gehört haben** I don't want to know anything about it.
  **(b)** *(anhören)* Vortrag, Radio to listen to; Berichte, Sänger to hear.
  **(c)** **auf jdn/etw ~** to listen to sb/sth; **er will nicht ~** he won't listen; **der Hund hört auf den Namen Joe** the dog answers to the name of Joe.
**Hören** *nt no pl* hearing; *(Radio~)* listening. **das ~ von Musik** listening to music; **es verging ihm ~ und Sehen** he didn't know whether he was coming or going *(col)*.
**Hörensagen** *nt:* **vom ~** from hearsay.
**hörenswert** *adj* worth listening to.
**Hörer(in** *f)* *m* - *(Rad)* listener; *(Univ)* student (attending lectures); *(Telec)* receiver.
**Hörerschaft** *f (Rad)* listeners *pl*, audience.
**Hör-:** **~fehler** *m (Med)* hearing defect; **das war ein ~fehler** I/he *etc* must have misheard; **~funk** *m* radio; **~gerät** *nt* hearing aid.
**hörig** *adj* enslaved; *(Hist)* in bondage. **sie ist ihm (sexuell) ~** he has (sexual) power over her.
**Horizont** *m* -e *(lit, fig)* horizon. **am ~** on the horizon; **das geht über meinen ~** *(fig)* that is beyond me; **er hat einen beschränkten ~** he has limited horizons.
**horizontal** *adj* horizontal.
**Horizontale** *f* -(n) *(Math)* horizontal (line).
**Hormon** *nt* -e hormone.
**hormonell** *adj* hormone *attr*, hormonal. **jdn ~ behandeln** to give sb hormone treatment.
**Hormonersatztherapie** *f* hormone replacement therapy.
**Hörmuschel** *f* -n *(Telec)* earpiece.
**Horn** *nt* ⁼er *(von Tieren, Mus)* horn; *(fig col: Beule)* bump. **jdn mit den ~ern aufspießen** to gore sb; **sich *(dat)* die ~er abstoßen** *(col)* to sow one's wild oats; **den Stier bei den ~ern packen** *(fig)* to take the bull by the horns; **jdm ~er aufsetzen** *(col)* to cuckold sb;

**ins gleiche/in jds ~ blasen** to chime in.
**Hornbrille** *f* horn-rimmed spectacles *pl*.
**Hörnchen** *nt* - **(a)** little horn. **(b)** *(Gebäck)* croissant. **(c)** *(Zool)* squirrel.
**Hornhaut** *f* callous; *(des Auges)* cornea.
**Hornisse** *f* -n hornet.
**Hornist** *m* horn player.
**Hornochs(e)** *m (fig col)* blockhead *(col)*, idiot.
**Horoskop** *nt* -e horoscope.
**horrend** *adj* horrendous.
**Hörrohr** *nt* ear trumpet; *(Med)* stethoscope.
**Horror** *m no pl* horror *(vor +dat of)*.
**Horror-** *in cpds* horror; **~film** *m* horror film; **~video** *nt* video nasty.
**Hör-:** **~saal** *m (Univ)* lecture theatre; **~spiel** *nt (Rad)* radio play.
**Horst** *m* -e *(Nest)* nest; *(Adler~)* eyrie.
**Hörsturz** *m* hearing loss.
**Hort** *m* -e **(a)** *(Kinder~)* day home for schoolchildren in the afternoon. **(b)** *(old, poet: Schatz)* hoard, treasure. **(c)** *(geh: Zuflucht)* refuge, shelter.
**horten** *vt* Geld, Vorräte *etc* to hoard; Rohstoffe *etc* to stockpile.
**Hortensie** [-iə] *f* hydrangea.
**Hör-:** **~vermögen** *nt* hearing; **~weite** *f* **in/außer ~weite** within/out of hearing *or* earshot.
**Höschen** ['høːsçən] *nt* **(a)** *(Kinderhose)* (pair of) trousers *or* pants. **(b)** *(Unterhose)* (pair of) panties *pl or* knickers *pl*.
**Hose** *f* -n trousers *pl*, pants *pl (esp US)*; *(Damen~ auch)* slacks *pl*; *(Bade~)* swimming trunks *pl*; *(Unter~)* underpants *pl*, pants *pl (Brit)*; **ich brauche eine neue ~** I need a new pair of trousers *or* pants, I need some new trousers *or* pants; **die ~n anhaben** *(fig col)* to wear the trousers *(Brit) or* pants *(US)*; **die ~n voll haben** to be wetting oneself *(col)*; **in die ~ gehen** *(col)* to be a complete flop *(col)*.
**Hosen-:** **~anzug** *m* trouser suit *(Brit)*, pantsuit *(US)*; **~bein** *nt* trouser leg; **~boden** *m* seat (of the trousers); **den ~boden vollkriegen** *(col)* to get a smacked bottom; **sich auf den ~boden setzen** *(col)* to get stuck in *(col)*; **~bund** *m* waistband; **~klammer** *f* cycle clip; **~rock** *m* culottes *pl*, divided skirt; **~schlitz** *m* flies *pl*, fly; **~tasche** *f* trouser pocket; **~träger** *pl* (a pair of) braces *pl (Brit) or* suspenders *pl (US)*.
**Hospital** *nt* -e *or* **Hospitäler** *(dated: Krankenhaus)* hospital.
**hospitieren*** *vi (Sch, Univ)* to sit in on lectures/classes *(bei jdm* with sb*)*.
**Hospiz** *nt* -e hospice.
**Hostess, Hosteß** *f, pl* **Hostessen** hostess.
**Hostie** ['hɔstiə] *f (Eccl)* host.
**Hotel** *nt* -s hotel.
**Hotel-** *in cpds* hotel; **~fach** *nt* hotel management; **~führer** *m* hotel guide.
**Hotel garni** *nt* bed and breakfast hotel.
**Hotelgewerbe** *nt* hotel trade *or* industry.
**Hotelier** [-'lieː] *m* hotelier.
**Hotelzimmer** *nt* hotel room.
**Hr.** = **Herr** Mr.
**Hrsg.** = **Herausgeber** ed.
**Hub** *m* ⁼e **(a)** *(Kolben~)* (piston) stroke. **(b)** *(bei Kränen: Leistung)* hoisting capacity.
**Hubbel** *m* - *(col)* bump.
**hubb(e)lig** *adj (col)* bumpy.
**hüben** *adv* over here, (on) this side. **~ und drüben** on both sides.
**Hub-:** **~kraft** *f* lifting *or* hoisting capacity; **~raum** *m (Aut)* cubic capacity.
**hübsch** *adj* pretty; Geschenk, Wohnung nice. **sich ~**

**machen** to make oneself look pretty; **er macht das schon ganz ~** he's doing it very nicely; **na, ihr beiden H~en** *(col)* well, you two; **eine ~e Geschichte/ Bescherung** *(iro)* a pretty kettle of fish; **das kann ja ~ werden** *(col)* that'll be just great; **ein ~es Vermögen** a tidy sum; **eine ~e Strecke** quite a distance; **ganz ~ viel bezahlen** to pay quite a bit; **das wirst du ~ sein lassen** *(col)* you'll do nothing of the kind; **immer ~ langsam!** *(col)* nice and easy.

**Hubschrauber** *m* - helicopter.

**Hubschrauber-:** **~flugplatz**, **~landeplatz** *m* heliport.

**Hucke** *f* **-n jdm die ~ vollhauen** *(col)* to give sb a good hiding.

**huckepack** *adv* piggyback *(auch Comp)*, **jdm ~ nehmen** to give sb a piggyback.

**Huf** *m* **-e** hoof. **einem Pferd die ~e beschlagen** to shoe a horse.

**Huf-:** **~eisen** *nt* horseshoe; **~nagel** *m* horseshoe nail; **~schmied** *m* blacksmith.

**Hüft-:** **~bein** *nt* hip-bone; **~bruch** *m* fractured hip.

**Hüfte** *f* **-n** hip; *(von Tieren)* haunch. **bis an die ~n reichen** to come up to the waist.

**Hüft-:** **~gelenk** *nt* hip joint; **~gürtel**, **~halter** *m* girdle, garter belt *(US)*; **h~hoch** *adj Pflanzen etc* waist-high; *Wasser etc* waist-deep.

**Huftier** *nt* hoofed animal.

**Hüft-:** **~knochen** *m* hip-bone; **~schmerz** *m* pain in the hip; **~weite** *f* hip size.

**Hügel** *m* - hill; *(Erdhaufen)* mound.

**hüg(e)lig** *adj* hilly.

**Hügel-:** **~kette** *f* range *or* chain of hills; **~land** *nt* hilly country.

**Huhn** *nt* **≐er** chicken *(auch Cook)*; *(Henne auch)* hen; *(Gattung)* fowl. **da lachen ja die ~er** *(col)* it's enough to make a cat laugh *(col)*; **sie sah aus wie ein gerupftes ~** *(col)* she looked as though she'd been dragged through a hedge backwards *(col)*; **ein verrücktes ~** a queer fish *(col)*; **ein dummes** *(col)* **~** a silly goose.

**Hühnchen** *nt* (young) chicken, pullet. **mit jdm ein ~ zu rupfen haben** *(col)* to have a bone to pick with sb *(col)*.

**Hühner-:** **~auge** *nt (Med)* corn; **~brühe** *f* (clear) chicken broth; **~ei** *nt* hen's egg; **~futter** *nt* chicken feed; **~klein** *nt no pl (Cook)* chicken trimmings *pl*; **~stall** *m* henhouse, hen coop; **~stange** *f* perch, (chicken) roost; **~suppe** *f* chicken soup.

**huldigen** *vi* +*dat (geh)* **einem Künstler** to pay homage to; *einer Ansicht* to subscribe to; *einem Glauben* to embrace; *einem Laster* to indulge in.

**Huldigung** *f* homage.

**Hülle** *f* **-n** cover; *(für Ausweiskarten etc auch)* holder; *(Cellophan~)* wrapping; *(liter, hum: Kleidung)* clothes *pl*, piece of clothing. **die ~ fallen lassen** to strip off; **die sterbliche ~** the mortal remains *pl*; **in ~ und Fülle** in abundance; **Whisky/Sorgen in ~ und Fülle** whisky/worries galore.

**hüllen** *vt (geh)* to wrap. **in Nebel gehüllt** shrouded in mist; **sich in seinen Mantel ~** to wrap oneself up in one's coat; **sich (über etw** *acc***) in Schweigen ~** to remain silent (about sth).

**hüllenlos** *adj* unclothed.

**Hülse** *f* **-n (a)** *(Schale)* hull, husk; *(Schote)* pod. **(b)** *(Kapsel)* case; *(für Film)* cartridge.

**Hülsenfrucht** *f usu pl* pulse.

**human** *adj* humane; *(verständnisvoll auch)* considerate.

**Humanismus** *m* humanism.

**Humanist(in** *f)* *m* humanist; *(Altsprachler)* classicist.

**humanistisch** *adj siehe n* humanist(ic); classical. **~ gebildet** educated in the classics *or* humanities; **~es Gymnasium** *secondary school with bias on Latin and Greek*; ≈ grammar school *(Brit)*.

**humanitär** *adj* humanitarian.

**Humanität** *f no pl* humaneness, humanity.

**Humanmedizin** *f* (human) medicine.

**Humbug** *m no pl (col)* humbug *(col)*.

**Hummel** *f* **-n** bumble-bee.

**Hummer** *m* - lobster.

**Humor** *m* - humour *(Brit)*, humor *(US)*; *(Sinn für ~)* sense of humour. **er hat keinen (Sinn für) ~** he has no sense of humour; **er nahm die Bemerkung mit ~ auf** he took the remark in good humour; **er hat einen eigenartigen ~** he has a strange sense of humour; **er verliert nie den ~** he never loses his sense of humour.

**humorig** *adj (geh)* humorous, genial.

**Humorist(in** *f)* *m* humourist *(Brit)*, humorist *(US)*; *(Komiker)* comedian.

**humoristisch** *adj* humorous.

**Humor-:** **h~los** *adj* humourless *(Brit)*, humorless *(US)*; **h~voll** *adj* humorous, amusing; **er kann sehr h~voll erzählen** he is a very amusing talker.

**humpeln** *vi* **(a)** *aux sein* to hobble. **(b)** *(ständig hinken)* to have a limp.

**Humpen** *m* - tankard, mug; *(aus Ton)* stein.

**Humus** *m* -, *no pl* humus.

**Hund** *m* **-e** dog; *(Jagd~ auch)* hound; *(col!: Schurke)* bastard *(col!)*. **junger ~** puppy, pup; **~e, die bellen, beißen nicht** empty vessels make most noise *(Prov)*; **wie ~ und Katze leben** to live like cat and dog; **damit kann man keinen ~ hinterm Ofen hervorlocken** *(col)* that's not going to tempt anybody; **er ist bekannt wie ein bunter ~** *(col)* everybody knows him; **da liegt der ~ begraben** *(col)* that's the problem; **er ist ein armer ~** he's a poor devil *(col)*; **er ist völlig auf dem ~** *(col)* he's really gone to the dogs *(col)*; **auf den ~ kommen** *(col)* to go to the dogs *(col)*; **vor die ~e gehen** *(col)* to go to the dogs *(col)*; *(sterben)* to die a miserable death.

**Hunde-:** **~arbeit** *f (fig col)* **eine ~arbeit** an awful job; **h~elend** *adj (col)* **mir ist h~elend** I feel lousy *(col)*; **~futter** *nt* dog food; **~halsband** *nt* dog collar; **~halter(in** *f)* *m (form)* dog owner; **~hütte** *f (lit, fig)* (dog) kennel; **h~kalt** *adj (col)* freezing cold; **~kuchen** *m* dog biscuit; **~leben** *nt (col)* dog's life *(col)*; **~leine** *f* dog lead *or* leash; **~marke** *f* dog licence disc *(Brit)*, dog tag *(US)*; **h~müde** *adj pred, adv (col)* dog-tired; **~narr** *m (col)* fanatical dog lover, dog freak *(col)*; **~rasse** *f* breed (of dog); **~rennen** *nt* greyhound *or* dog racing *no art*.

**hundert** *num* a *or* one hundred. **einige ~ Menschen** a few hundred people.

**Hundert** *nt* **-e** hundred. **es geht in die ~e** it runs into the hundreds; **einer unter ~en** one out of hundreds; **zu ~en** in (their) hundreds.

**Hunderter** *m* - hundred; *(col: Geldschein)* hundred (mark *etc* note).

**Hundert-:** **h~fach 1** *adj* hundredfold; **die h~fache Menge** a hundred times the amount; **2** *adv* a hundred times; **h~fünfzigprozentig** *adj (iro)* fanatical; **~jahrfeier** *f* centenary, centennial *(US)*; **h~jährig** *adj attr* (one-)hundred-year-old; **h~mal** *adv* a hundred times; **~meterlauf** *m (Sport)* **der/ ein ~meterlauf** the/a 100 metres *(Brit)* *or* meters *(US) sing*; **h~prozentig** *adj* (a *or* one) hundred per cent; *Alkohol* pure; **ein h~prozentiger Konservativer** *etc* an out-and-out conservative *etc*; **Sie haben h~prozentig recht** you're absolutely right.

**Hundertstel** *nt* - hundredth.
**hundertste(r, s)** *adj* hundredth. **vom H~n ins Tausendste kommen** *(fig)* to get carried away.
**hunderttausend** *num* a *or* one hundred thousand. **H~e von Menschen** hundreds of thousands of people.
**Hunde-:** ~**salon** *m* dog parlour *(Brit)* or parlor *(US)*; ~**sohn** *m (pej liter)* cur; ~**steuer** *f* dog licence *(Brit)* or license *(US)* fee; ~**wetter** *nt (col)* filthy weather; ~**zucht** *f* dog breeding.
**Hündin** *f* bitch.
**Hunds-:** **h~gemein** *adj (col)* mean; *(schwierig)* fiendishly difficult; **es tut h~gemein weh** it hurts like hell *(col)*; **h~miserabel** *adj (col)* lousy *(col)*; ~**tage** *pl* dog days *pl*.
**Hüne** *m (wk)* **-n, -n** giant. **ein ~ von Mensch** a giant of a man.
**Hünen-:** ~**grab** *nt* megalithic grave; **h~haft** *adj* gigantic.
**Hunger** *m no pl (lit, fig)* hunger *(nach for)*; *(Hungersnot auch)* famine; *(nach Sonne etc)* yearning. ~ **bekommen/haben** to get/be hungry; ~ **auf etw** *(acc)* **haben** to feel like (eating) sth; **ich habe ~ wie ein Wolf** *or* **Bär** *(col)* I could eat a horse *(col)*; **vor ~ sterben** to die of hunger *or* starvation, to starve to death; **ich sterbe vor ~** *(col)* I'm starving *(col)*.
**Hunger-:** ~**gefühl** *nt* hungry feeling; ~**künstler** *m* **ich bin doch kein** ~**künstler** I'm not on a starvation diet; ~**kur** *f* starvation diet; ~**lohn** *m (fig)* pittance.
**hungern 1** *vi* **(a)** to go hungry, to starve. **jdn ~ lassen** to let sb go hungry. **(b)** *(fasten)* to go without food. **(c)** *(fig geh: verlangen)* to hunger *(nach for)*. **2** *vr* **sich zu Tode ~** to starve oneself to death; **sich schlank ~** to go on a starvation diet.
**hungernd** *adj, no comp* hungry, starving.
**Hungersnot** *f* famine.
**Hunger-:** ~**streik** *m* hunger strike; ~**tod** *m* death from starvation; ~**tuch** *nt* **am** ~**tuch nagen** *(fig)* to be starving.
**hungrig** *adj (lit, fig)* hungry *(nach for)*. ~ **nach** *or* **auf** *(acc)* **etw sein** to feel like (eating) sth.
**Hupe** *f* **-n** horn. **auf die ~ drücken** to press/sound the horn.
**hupen** *vi* to sound the horn, to hoot.
**hüpfen** *vi aux sein* to hop; *(Ball)* to bounce. **vor Freude ~** to jump for joy; **das ist gehüpft wie gesprungen** *(col)* it's six of one and half a dozen of the other *(col)*; **H~ spielen** to play hopscotch.
**Hup-:** ~**konzert** *nt (col)* barrage of hooting *(of car horns)*; ~**signal,** ~**zeichen** *nt (Aut)* hoot.
**Hürde** *f* **-n** **(a)** *(Sport, fig)* hurdle. **eine ~ nehmen** to take a hurdle. **(b)** *(Viehzaun)* fold, pen.
**Hürdenlauf** *m (Sportart)* hurdling; *(Wettkampf)* hurdles *pl or sing*.
**Hure** *f* **-n** whore.
**huren** *vi (col)* to go whoring.
**Hurensohn** *m (pej col!)* bastard *(col!)*, son of a bitch *(US col!)*.
**hurra** [hʊ'raː, 'hʊra] *interj* hurray, hurrah.
**Hurra** *nt* **-s** cheers *pl*.
**Hurra-:** ~**geschrei** *nt* cheering; ~**patriotismus** *m* jingoism, chauvinism; ~**ruf** *m* cheer.
**Hurrikan** *m* **-e** *or* **-s** hurricane.
**hurtig** *adj* nimble; *(schnell)* quick.
**husch** *interj (aufscheuchend)* shoo; *(schnell)* quick, quickly now. **und ~, weg war er** and whoosh! he was gone.
**huschen** *vi aux sein* to dart; *(Mäuse etc auch)* to scurry; *(Lächeln)* to flash.

**hüsteln** *vi* to give a little cough.
**husten 1** *vi* to cough. **auf etw** *(acc)* ~ *(col)* not to give a damn for sth *(col)*. **2** *vt* to cough (up). **denen werde ich was ~** *(col)* I'll tell them where they can get off *(col)*.
**Husten** *m no pl* cough. ~ **haben** to have a cough.
**Husten-:** ~**anfall** *m* coughing fit; ~**bonbon** *m or nt* cough drop; ~**mittel** *nt* cough medicine/drop; ~**reiz** *m* irritation of the throat; ~**saft** *m* cough mixture; **h~stillend** *adj* **das wirkt h~stillend** it relieves coughs; ~**tropfen** *pl* cough drops *pl*.
**Hut**[1] *m* ⁼e hat. **den ~ aufsetzen/abnehmen** *(geh)* to put on/take off one's hat; **vor jdm den ~ abnehmen** *(fig)* to take off one's hat to sb; ~ **ab vor solcher Leistung!** I take my hat off to that; **das kannst du dir an den ~ stecken!** *(col)* you can keep it; **unter einen ~ bringen** *(col)* to reconcile; *Termine* to fit in; **da geht einem der ~ hoch** *(col)* it's enough to make you blow your top *(col)*; **seinen ~ nehmen (müssen)** *(col)* to (have to) go; **das ist doch ein alter ~!** *(col)* that's old hat! *(col)*; **damit/mit ihm habe ich nichts am ~** *(col)* I don't want to have anything to do with that/him.
**Hut**[2] *f no pl* **(a)** *(geh)* protection, keeping. **unter** *or* **in meiner ~** in my keeping; *(Kinder)* in my care. **(b)** **auf der ~ sein** to be on one's guard *(vor +dat* against*)*.
**hüten 1** *vt* to look after, to mind; *Geheimnisse* to keep. **das Bett/Haus ~** to stay in bed/indoors; **hüte deine Zunge!** *(geh)* watch your tongue! **2** *vr* to guard *(vor +dat* against*)*, to beware *(vor +dat* of*)*. **sich ~, etw zu tun** to take care not to do sth; **ich werde mich ~!** not likely!; **ich werde mich ~, ihm das zu erzählen** there's no chance of me telling him that.
**Hüter(in** *f)* *m* - guardian, keeper.
**Hut-:** ~**krempe** *f* brim (of a hat); ~**macher(in** *f)* *m* hatter; *(für Damen auch)* milliner; ~**nadel** *f* hat pin; ~**schachtel** *f* hatbox; ~**schnur** *f* **das geht mir über die ~schnur** *(col)* that's going too far; ~**ständer** *m* hatstand.
**Hütte** *f* **-n** **(a)** hut; *(schäbiges Häuschen auch)* shack; *(Holz~, Block~)* cabin. **(b)** *(Tech: Hüttenwerk)* iron and steel works *pl or sing*.
**Hütten-:** ~**arbeiter** *m* worker in an iron and steel works; ~**industrie** *f* iron and steel industry; ~**käse** *m* cottage cheese; ~**schuh** *m* slipper-sock; ~**werk** *nt siehe* **Hütte (b)**.
**hutz(e)lig** *adj Obst* dried; *Mensch* wizened.
**Hyäne** *f* **-n** hyena; *(fig)* wildcat.
**Hyazinthe** [hya'tsɪntə] *f* **-n** hyacinth.
**Hydrant** *m* hydrant.
**Hydraulik** *f* hydraulics *sing*; *(Antrieb, Anlage)* hydraulics *pl*.
**hydraulisch** *adj* hydraulic.
**Hydro-:** ~**kultur** *f (Bot)* hydroculture; ~**meter** *nt* hydrometer.
**Hygiene** [hy'giːnə] *f no pl* hygiene.
**hygienisch** [hy'giːnɪʃ] *adj* hygienic.
**Hymne** ['hymnə] *f* **-n** hymn; *(National~)* (national) anthem.
**hyper-:** ~**modern** *adj (col)* ultramodern; ~**sensibel** *adj* hypersensitive.
**Hypnose** *f* **-n** hypnosis. **jdn in ~ versetzen** to put sb under hypnosis.
**hypnotisch** *adj* hypnotic.
**Hypnotiseur** [hypnoti'zøːɐ] *m* hypnotist.
**hypnotisieren\*** *vt* to hypnotize.
**Hypothek** *f* **-en** mortgage; *(fig: Belastung)* burden of guilt. **eine ~ aufnehmen** to raise a mortgage; **etw mit einer ~ belasten** to mortgage sth.

**Hypotheken-:** ~**bank** f *bank specializing in mortgages*; ~**brief** m mortgage certificate; ~**darlehen** nt mortgage (loan); **h**~**frei** adj unmortgaged; ~**zahlung** f mortgage repayment.
**Hypothese** f -n hypothesis.
**hypothetisch** adj hypothetical.

**Hysterektomie** f hysterectomy.
**Hysterie** f hysteria.
**Hysteriker(in** f) m - hysterical person.
**hysterisch** adj hysterical. **einen** ~**en Anfall bekommen** *(fig)* to have hysterics.
**Hz** = **Hertz** Hz.

# I

**I, i** [iː] *nt* -, - I, i. **das Tüpfelchen auf dem** ~ *(fig)* the final touch; **I wie Ida** ≃ I for Isaac, I for Item *(US)*.

**i** [iː] *interj (col)* ugh *(col)*.

**i.A.** = **im Auftrag** pp.

**IAO** [iːaːˈoː] *f* = **Internationale Arbeitsorganisation** ILO.

**ib(d)** = **ibidem** ibid.

**iberisch** *adj* Iberian. **die I~e Halbinsel** the Iberian Peninsula.

**IC** [iːˈtseː] *m* -s = **Intercity-Zug**.

**ICE** [iːtseːˈʔeː] *m* -s = **Intercity-Express-Zug** high-speed train.

**ich** *pers pron* I. **ich bin's!** it's me!; **immer ~!** it's always me!; ~ **Idiot!** what an idiot I am!; **und ~ Idiot habe es gemacht** and idiot that I am, I did it; ~ **nicht!** not me!; ~ **selbst** I myself; **wer hat gerufen?** — ~! who called? — (it was) me, I did.

**Ich** *nt* **-(s)** self; *(Psych)* ego. **das eigene** ~ one's (own) self/ego; **mein zweites** ~ *(selbst)* my other self; *(andere Person)* my alter ego.

**Ich-:** **i~bezogen** *adj* egocentric; **~form** *f* first person; **~-Roman** *m* novel in the first person.

**ideal** *adj* ideal.

**Ideal** *nt* -e ideal. **sie ist mein** ~ **einer Frau** she's my ideal woman.

**Ideal-** *in cpds* ideal; **~bild** *nt* ideal; **~fall** *m* ideal case; **im ~fall** ideally, in an ideal world; **~gewicht** *nt* ideal weight.

**idealisieren\*** *vt* to idealize.

**Idealismus** *m* idealism.

**Idealist(in** *f)* *m* idealist.

**idealistisch** *adj* idealistic.

**Ideal-:** **~typ(us)** *m* *(Sociol)* ideal type; **~vorstellung** *f* ideal.

**Idee** *f* -n [iˈdeːən] **(a)** idea. **die** ~ **zu etw** the idea for sth; **wie kommst du denn auf die** ~? whatever gave you that idea?; **ich kam auf die** ~, **Andrea zu fragen** I hit on the idea of asking Andrea; **jdn auf die** ~ **bringen, etw zu tun** to give sb the idea of doing sth. **(b)** *(ein wenig)* shade, trifle. **eine** ~ **Salz** a touch of salt; **keine** ~ **besser** not a whit better.

**ideell** *adj* Wert, Ziele non-material; *Bedürfnisse, Unterstützung* spiritual.

**ideen-** [iˈdeːən-]: **~arm** *adj* lacking in ideas; **~los** *adj* devoid of ideas; **~reich** *adj* full of ideas.

**Identifikation** *f* identification.

**Identifikationsfigur** *f* role model.

**identifizieren\*** **1** *vt* to identify. **2** *vr* **sich** ~ **mit** to identify with.

**Identifizierung** *f* identification.

**identisch** *adj* identical *(mit* with).

**Identität** *f* identity.

**Ideologe** *m*, **Ideologin** *f* ideologist.

**Ideologie** *f* ideology.

**ideologisch** *adj* ideological.

**Idiom** *nt* -e idiom.

**idiomatisch** *adj* idiomatic.

**Idiot** *m (wk)* **-en, -en** idiot.

**Idioten-:** **~hügel** *m (hum col)* beginners' *or* nursery *(Brit)* slope; **i~sicher** *adj (col)* foolproof *no adv*.

**Idiotie** *f* idiocy.

**Idiotin** *f* idiot.

**idiotisch** *adj* idiotic.

**Idol** *nt* -e idol.

**Idylle** *f* -n idyll.

**idyllisch** *adj* idyllic.

**IG** [iːˈgeː] *f* -s = **Industriegewerkschaft**.

**IGB** [iːgeːˈbeː] *m* = **Internationaler Gewerkschaftsbund** International Trades Union Congress.

**Igel** *m* - *(Zool)* hedgehog.

**igitt(igitt)!** *interj* ugh! *(col)*.

**Iglu** [ˈiːglu] *m or nt* -s igloo.

**Ignorant** *m* ignoramus.

**Ignoranz** *f* ignorance.

**ignorieren\*** *vt* to ignore.

**IHK** [iːhaːˈkaː] *f* = **Industrie- und Handelskammer**.

**ihm** *pers pron dat of* **er, es** *(bei Personen)* to him; *(bei Tieren und Dingen)* to it; *(nach Präpositionen)* him/it. **ich gab es** ~ I gave it (to) him/it; **es war** ~, **als ob er träumte** he felt as though he were dreaming; **es ist** ~ **nicht gut** he doesn't feel well; **sie schnitt** ~ **die Haare** she cut his hair (for him); **ein Freund von** ~ a friend of his, one of his friends; **wir gingen zu** ~ *(nach Hause)* we went to his place; **sie hat** ~ **einen Pulli gestrickt** she knitted him a sweater.

**ihn** *pers pron acc of* **er** him; *(bei Tieren, Dingen)* it.

**ihnen** *pers pron dat of* **sie** *pl* to them; *(nach Präpositionen)* them; *siehe* **ihm**.

**Ihnen** *pers pron dat of* **Sie** to you; *(nach Präpositionen)* you; *siehe* **ihm**.

**ihr 1** *pers pron* **(a)** 2. *pers pl nom* you. **(b)** *dat of* **sie** *sing (bei Personen)* to her; *(bei Tieren und Dingen)* to it; *(nach Präpositionen)* her/it; *siehe* **ihm. 2** *poss pron* **(a)** *(einer Person)* her; *(eines Tiers, Dings)* its. **(b)** *(von mehreren)* their.

**Ihr** *poss pron* your. ~ **Franz Müller** *(Briefschluß)* yours, Franz Müller.

**ihrer** *pers pron* **(a)** *gen of* **sie** *sing (bei Personen)* of her. **wir werden** ~ **gedenken** *(geh)* we will remember her. **(b)** *gen of* **sie** *pl* of them.

**Ihrer** *pers pron gen of* **Sie** of you.

**ihre(r, s)** *poss pron (substantivisch)* **(a)** *(einer Person)* hers; *(eines Tiers)* its. **I~ Majestät** Her Majesty; **sie und die I~n** *(geh: Familie)* she and her family. **(b)** *(von mehreren)* theirs. **sie taten das** ~ *(geh)* they did their bit.

**Ihre(r, s)** *poss pron sing and pl (substantivisch)* yours. **tun Sie das** ~ *(geh)* you do your bit.

**ihrerseits** *adv (bei einer Person)* for her part; *(bei mehreren)* for their part; *(von ihrer Seite)* on her/their part.

**Ihrerseits** *adv* for your part; *(von Ihrer Seite)* on your part.

**ihresgleichen** *pron inv (von einer Person)* people

like her; *(von mehreren)* people like them; *(von Dingen)* others like it. **eine Frechheit, die ~ sucht!** an incredible cheek!

**Ihresgleichen** *pron inv* people like you.

**ihret-:** **~halben** *(dated),* **~wegen, ~willen** *adv (bei Personen) (wegen ihr/ihnen) (sing)* because of her; *(pl)* because of them; *(für sie)* on her/their behalf; *(bei Dingen und Tieren) (sing)* because of it; *(pl)* because of them; **sie sagte, ~wegen könnten wir gehen** she said that, as far as she was concerned, we could go.

**Ihret-:** **~halben** *(dated),* **~wegen, ~willen** *adv* because of you; *(für Sie)* on your behalf.

**ihrige** *poss pron (old, geh)* **der/die/das ~** *(von einer Person)* hers; *(von mehreren)* theirs.

**Ihrige** *poss pron* **der/die/das ~** yours.

**i.J.** = **im Jahre.**

**Ikon** *nt* **-e** *(Comp)* icon.

**Ikone** *f* **-n** icon.

**illegal** *adj* illegal.

**Illegalität** *f* illegality.

**illegitim** *adj* illegitimate.

**Illusion** *f* illusion. **sich** *(dat)* **~en machen** to delude oneself; **darüber macht er sich keine ~en** he doesn't have any illusions about it.

**illusionär** *adj* illusionary.

**illusorisch** *adj* illusory. **es ist völlig ~, zu glauben ...** it's a complete illusion to believe ...

**Illustration** *f* illustration. **zur ~ von etw** to illustrate sth.

**Illustrator** *m* illustrator.

**illustrieren*** *vt* to illustrate *(jdm etw sth for sb).*

**Illustrierte** *f (wk)* **-n, -n** magazine.

**Iltis** *m* **-se** polecat.

**im** *prep* = **in dem (a)** in the. **~ zweiten Stock** on the second floor; **~ Kino/Theater** at the cinema/theatre; **~ Bett** in bed; **~ „Faust"** in "Faust"; **~ Mai** in May; **~ Alter von 91 Jahren** at the age of 91; **~ nächsten Jahr** next year. **(b) nicht ~ geringsten** not in the slightest; **~ Kommen/Gehen sein** to be coming/going; **etw ~ Liegen/Stehen tun** to do sth lying down/standing up; **~ Trab/Laufschritt** at a trot/run.

**I.M.** = **Ihre(r) Majestät** HM.

**Image** ['ɪmɪtʃ] *nt* **-s** image.

**Imagepflege** *f* image-building.

**imaginär** *adj* imaginary.

**Imbiß** *m* **-sse** snack.

**Imbiß-:** **~halle** *f* snack bar; **~stube** *f* cafe.

**Imitation** *f* imitation.

**Imitator** *m,* **Imitatorin** *f* imitator; *(von einem Bild)* copyist.

**imitieren*** *vt* to imitate.

**Imker** *m* - beekeeper.

**immanent** *adj* inherent, intrinsic. **einer Sache** *(dat)* **~ sein** to be inherent in sth.

**Immatrikulation** *f* matriculation *(form),* registration *(at university).*

**immatrikulieren*** *vr* to matriculate *(form),* to register *(at university).*

**immens** *adj* immense.

**immer** *adv* **(a)** always. **schon ~** always; **für ~** for ever, for always; **~ diese Probleme!** all these problems!; **~, wenn ...** whenever ...; **~ mal** *(col)* from time to time; **~ geradeaus gehen** to keep going straight on; **~ und ewig** *(liter)* for ever and ever; **~ noch** still; **~ noch nicht** still not; **~ wieder** again and again; **etw ~ wieder tun** to keep on doing sth; **wie ~** as always.

**(b)** *(+comp)* **~ besser** better and better; **~ häufiger** more and more often; **~ größer werdende**

Schulden constantly increasing debts.

**(c) wer/wie/wann/wo/was (auch) ~** whoever/ however/whenever/wherever/whatever.

**(d)** *(col: jeweils)* **gib mir ~ drei Bücher auf einmal** give me three books at a time; **~ am dritten Tag** every third day.

**immer-:** **~fort** *adv* the whole time; **~grün** *adj attr (lit, fig)* evergreen; **~hin** *adv* anyhow, at any rate; *(wenigstens)* at least; *(schließlich)* after all; **~während** *adj attr* perpetual; **~zu** *adv* the whole time.

**Immigrant(in** *f) m* immigrant.

**Immigration** *f* immigration.

**immigrieren*** *vi aux sein* to immigrate.

**Immobilien** [-'biːliən] *pl* real estate *sing;* *(in Zeitungsannoncen)* property *sing.*

**Immobilien-:** **~händler** *m,* **~makler** *m* estate agent *(Brit),* realtor *(US);* **~markt** *m* property market.

**immun** *adj* immune *(gegen* to).

**immunisieren*** *vt* to immunize *(gegen* against).

**Immunisierung** *f* immunization *(gegen* against).

**Immunität** *f* immunity.

**Immun-** *(in cpds) (Med)* immune; **~schwäche** *f* immunodeficiency; **~schwächekrankheit** *f* immune deficiency syndrome; **~system** *nt* immune system.

**Imperativ** *m (Gram)* imperative.

**Imperfekt** *nt* **-e** *(Gram)* imperfect (tense).

**Imperialismus** *m* imperialism.

**Imperialist(in** *f) m* imperialist.

**imperialistisch** *adj* imperialistic.

**impfen** *vt* to vaccinate, to inoculate.

**Impf-:** **~paß** *m* vaccination card; **~pistole** *f* vaccination gun; **~schein** *m* vaccination certificate; **~schutz** *m* protection given by vaccination; **~stoff** *m* vaccine, serum.

**Impfung** *f* vaccination, inoculation.

**Impfzwang** *m* compulsory vaccination.

**Implantat** *nt* implant.

**implizieren*** *vt* to imply.

**implizit** *adv* by implication, implicitly.

**implodieren*** *vi aux sein* to implode.

**imponieren*** *vi* to impress *(jdm* sb). **das imponiert mir** it's impressive.

**imponierend** *adj* impressive.

**Imponiergehabe** *nt (Zool)* display pattern; *(fig pej)* exhibitionism.

**Import** *m* **-e** import. **der ~ sollte den Export nicht übersteigen** imports should not exceed exports.

**Importeur(in** *f) [*ɪmpɔr'tøːɐ, -'tøːrɪn] *m* importer.

**Import-** *in cpds* import; **~geschäft** *nt (Handel)* import trade; *(Firma)* import business.

**importieren*** *vt (also Comp)* to import.

**Importland** *nt* importing country.

**imposant** *adj* imposing; *Leistung* impressive.

**impotent** *adj* impotent.

**Impotenz** *f* impotence.

**imprägnieren*** *vt* to impregnate; *(wasserdicht machen)* to waterproof.

**Imprägnierung** *f* impregnation; *(von Geweben)* waterproofing.

**Impressionismus** *m* impressionism.

**Impressionist** *m* impressionist.

**impressionistisch** *adj* impressionistic.

**Impressum** *nt, pl* **Impressen** imprint; *(von Zeitung)* masthead.

**Improvisation** [ɪmproviza'tsioːn] *f* improvization.

**improvisieren*** [-'viːzirən] *vti* to improvize.

**Impuls** *m* **-e** impulse. **etw aus einem ~ heraus tun** to do sth on impulse; **einer Sache** *(dat)* **neue ~e geben**

to give sth new impetus.

**impuls<u>i</u>v** *adj* impulsive. ~ **handeln** to act impulsively.

**Impulsiv<u>i</u>tät** *f* impulsiveness.

**imst<u>a</u>nde** *adj pred* ~ **sein, etw zu tun** *(fähig)* to be capable of doing sth; *(in der Lage)* to be in a position to do sth; **er ist zu allem** ~ he's capable of anything.

**<u>i</u>n 1** *prep siehe auch* **im, ins (a)** *(räumlich) (wo?* +*dat)* in; *(wohin?* +*acc)* in, into. **sind Sie schon** ~ **Deutschland gewesen?** have you ever been to Germany?; ~ **die Schule gehen** to go to school; **er ist** ~ **der Schule** he's at *or* in school. **(b)** *(zeitlich) (wann?* +*dat)* in; *(bis* +*acc)* into. ~ **diesem Jahr** *(laufendes Jahr)* this year; *(jenes Jahr)* in that year; **heute** ~ **zwei Wochen** two weeks today; **bis** ~**s 18. Jahrhundert** into *or* up to the 18th century. **(c)** ~ **Englisch steht er sehr schwach** he's very weak in *or* at English; **das ist** ~ **Englisch** it's in English; ~ **die Hunderte gehen** to run into (the) hundreds; **es** ~ **sich haben** *(col) (Text)* to be tough; *(Whisky)* to have quite a kick; *(Torte)* to be very rich.

**2** *adj pred (col)* ~ **sein** to be in *(col)*.

**<u>i</u>n|aktiv** *adj* inactive; *Mitglied* non-active.

**In|<u>a</u>ngriffnahme** *f no pl (form)* commencement.

**In|<u>a</u>nspruchnahme** *f no pl (form)* **(a)** *(Beanspruchung)* demands *pl.* **die** ~ **durch meinen Beruf** the demands made on me by my job. **(b)** *(eines Kredits)* taking out; *(von Rechten)* exertion. **im Falle einer** ~ **der Arbeitslosenunterstützung** where unemployment benefit has been sought.

**<u>I</u>nbegriff** *m* perfect example; *(der Schönheit, des Bösen etc)* epitome.

**<u>i</u>nbegriffen** *adj pred* included.

**<u>I</u>nbetriebnahme** *f* **-n** *(form)* commissioning; *(von Gebäude, U-Bahn etc)* inauguration.

**<u>i</u>nbrünstig** *adj* fervent, ardent.

**<u>I</u>nbusschlüssel** ® *m (Tech)* Allen key ®.

**ind<u>e</u>m** *conj* **(a)** *(während)* while; *(in dem Augenblick)* as. **(b)** *(dadurch, daß)* ~ **man etw macht** by doing sth.

**<u>I</u>nder(in** *f)* *m* - Indian.

**ind<u>e</u>ssen** *adv* **(a)** *(inzwischen)* meanwhile, (in the) meantime. **(b)** *(jedoch)* however.

**<u>I</u>ndex** *m* **-e** index *(auch Comp).* **auf dem** ~ **stehen** *(fig)* to be banned.

**Indi<u>a</u>ner(in** *f)* *m* - (American) Indian.

**indi<u>a</u>nisch** *adj* (American) Indian.

**<u>I</u>ndien** ['ɪndiən] *nt* India.

**indifferent** *adj (geh)* indifferent *(gegenüber* to*).*

**indigniert** *adj (geh)* indignant.

**Indikati<u>o</u>n** *f (Med)* indication *(Jur).* **medizinische/ soziale** ~ *(Jur)* medical/social grounds for the termination of pregnancy.

**<u>I</u>ndikativ** *m (Gram)* indicative.

**<u>I</u>ndik<u>a</u>tor** *m* indicator.

**<u>I</u>ndio** *m* **-s** (Central/South American) Indian.

**indirekt** *adj* indirect.

**<u>i</u>ndisch** *adj* Indian. **I**~**er Ozean** Indian Ocean.

**<u>i</u>ndiskret** *adj* indiscreet.

**<u>I</u>ndiskreti<u>o</u>n** *f* indiscretion.

**<u>i</u>ndiskutabel** *adj* out of the question.

**<u>i</u>ndisponiert** *adj (geh)* indisposed.

**Individualismus** [ɪndividuaˈlɪsmʊs] *m* individualism.

**Individualist** [ɪndividuaˈlɪst] *m* individualist.

**individualistisch** [ɪndividuaˈlɪstɪʃ] *adj* individualistic.

**Individualität** [ɪndividualiˈtɛːt] *f no pl* individuality.

**individuell** [ɪndiviˈduɛl] *adj* individual. **etw** ~ **gestalten** to give sth a personal touch; **es ist** ~ **verschie-**

**den** it differs from person to person.

**Individuum** [ɪndiˈviːduʊm] *nt, pl* **Individuen** [ɪndiˈviːduən] individual.

**Ind<u>i</u>z** *nt* **-ien** [-iən] **(a)** *(Jur)* clue; *(als Beweismittel)* piece of circumstantial evidence. **alles beruht nur auf** ~**ien** everything rests only on circumstantial evidence. **(b)** *(Anzeichen)* sign, indication *(für* of*).*

**Ind<u>i</u>zienbeweis** *m* circumstantial evidence *no pl*; piece of circumstantial evidence.

**indiz<u>ie</u>ren*** *vt (Med)* to indicate; *(Eccl)* to put on the Index; *(Comp)* to index.

**Indoch<u>i</u>na** *nt* Indochina.

**<u>i</u>ndogerm<u>a</u>nisch** *adj* Indo-Germanic.

**<u>I</u>ndoktrinati<u>o</u>n** *f* indoctrination.

**<u>i</u>ndoktrin<u>ie</u>ren*** *vt* to indoctrinate.

**Indon<u>e</u>sien** [-iən] *nt* Indonesia.

**Indon<u>e</u>sier(in** *f)* [-iɐ, -iərɪn] *m* - Indonesian.

**indon<u>e</u>sisch** *adj* Indonesian.

**Indossam<u>e</u>nt** *nt (Comm)* endorsement.

**Indukti<u>o</u>n** *f* induction.

**industrialis<u>ie</u>ren*** *vt* to industrialize.

**Industrialis<u>ie</u>rung** *f* industrialization.

**Industr<u>ie</u>** *f* industry. **in der** ~ **arbeiten** to be in industry.

**Industr<u>ie</u>-** *in cpds* industrial; ~**anlage** *f* industrial plant; ~**betrieb** *m* industrial firm; ~**erzeugnis** *nt* industrial product; ~**gebiet** *nt* industrial area; ~**gelände** *nt* industrial estate *(Brit)*, industrial park *(US)*; ~**gewerkschaft** *f* industrial trade union *or* labor union *(US)*; ~**kaufmann** *m* industrial manager; ~**land** *nt* industrialized country.

**industriell** *adj* industrial.

**Industrielle(r)** *mf decl as adj* industrialist.

**Industr<u>ie</u>-:** ~**müll** *m* industrial waste; ~**roboter** *m* industrial robot; ~**staat** *m* industrial nation; ~- **und Handelskammer** *f* chamber of commerce; ~**zweig** *m* branch of industry.

**in|ein<u>a</u>nder** *adv* **sein, liegen** *etc* in each other; **legen, hängen** *etc* into each other. ~ **übergehen** to merge (into each other); **sich** ~ **verlieben** to fall in love with each other.

**in|ein<u>a</u>nder-:** ~**fließen** *vi sep irreg aux sein* to merge; ~**fügen** *vt sep* to fit into each other; ~**greifen** *vi sep irreg (lit)* to interlock; *(Zahnräder)* to mesh; *(fig: Ereignisse etc)* to overlap; ~**passen** *vi sep* to fit into each other.

**inf<u>a</u>m** *adj* infamous.

**Infanter<u>ie</u>** *f* infantry.

**Infanter<u>i</u>st** *m* infantryman.

**infant<u>i</u>l** *adj* infantile.

**Inf<u>a</u>rkt** *m* **-e** *(Herz~)* coronary.

**Infekti<u>o</u>n** *f* infection.

**Infekti<u>o</u>ns-:** ~**gefahr** *f* danger of infection; ~**herd** *m* focus of infection; ~**krankheit** *f* infectious disease.

**Inf<u>e</u>rno** *nt no pl (lit, fig)* inferno.

**Infiltrati<u>o</u>n** *f* infiltration.

**infiltr<u>ie</u>ren*** *vt* to infiltrate.

**<u>I</u>nfinitiv** *m* infinitive.

**infiz<u>ie</u>ren*** **1** *vt* to infect. **2** *vr* to be infected *(bei* by*).*

**in fl<u>a</u>granti** *adv* in the act, red-handed.

**Inflati<u>o</u>n** *f* inflation.

**inflation<u>ä</u>r** [ɪnflatsioˈnɛːɐ] *adj* inflationary. **sich** ~ **entwickeln** to become inflated.

**Inflati<u>o</u>ns-:** **i**~**hemmend** *adj* anti-inflationary; ~**rate** *f* rate of inflation; **i**~**sicher** *adj* inflationproof.

**inflat<u>o</u>risch** *adj* inflationary.

**<u>I</u>nfo** *nt* **-s** *(col)* leaflet.

**inf<u>o</u>lge** *prep* +*gen or von* as a result of.

**infolgedessen** adv consequently.
**Informant(in** f) m informant.
**Informatik** f information science, informatics sing.
**Informatiker(in** f) m - computer or information scientist.
**Information** f (a) information no pl (über +acc about, on). **eine** ~ (a piece of) information; **zu Ihrer** ~ for your information. (b) (~sstelle) information desk. (c) ~**en** pl (Comp) data.
**informationell** [ɪnfɔrmatsio'nɛl] adj informational.
**Informations-**: ~**abruf** m information retrieval; ~**austausch** m exchange of information; ~**blatt** nt leaflet, factsheet; ~**büro** nt information bureau; ~**fluß** m no pl flow of information; ~**material** nt informative material; ~**quelle** f source of information; ~**schalter** m information desk; ~**stand** (a) information stand; (b) no pl **nach dem neuesten** ~**stand** according to the latest information; ~**technik** f information technology; ~**theorie** f information theory; ~**verarbeitung** f information processing.
**informativ** adj informative.
**informell** adj informal.
**informieren*** 1 vt to inform (über +acc, von about). **da bist du falsch informiert** you've been misinformed. 2 vr to find out.
**Infra-**: **i**~**rot** adj infra-red; ~**rotstrahler** m - infrared lamp; ~**struktur** f infrastructure.
**Infusion** f infusion.
**Ing.** = **Ingenieur.**
**Ingenieur(in** f) [ɪnʒe'niøːɐ, -iøːrɪn] m engineer.
**Ingenieur-**: ~**büro** nt engineer's office; ~**schule** f school of engineering.
**Ingwer** m no pl ginger.
**Inh.** = **Inhaber** prop.; = **Inhalt** cont.
**Inhaber(in** f) m - (von Geschäft) owner; (von Konto, Lizenz, Rekord) holder; (von Scheck, Paß) bearer.
**inhaftieren*** vt insep to take into custody.
**Inhalationsapparat** m inhaler.
**inhalieren*** vti insep (Med, col) to inhale.
**Inhalt** m -e (a) contents pl; (von Buch, Begriff auch) content; (des Lebens) meaning. **was hatte das Gespräch zum** ~? what was the content of the discussion?; **über** ~**e diskutieren** to discuss the real issues; **ein Brief des** ~**s, daß** ... (form) a letter to the effect that ... (b) (Math) (Flächen~) area; (Raum~) volume.
**inhaltlich** adj as regards content.
**Inhalts-**: ~**angabe** f summary, précis (esp Sch); **i**~**los** adj empty; Buch, Vortrag lacking in content; **i**~**reich** adj full; ~**verzeichnis** nt list of contents; (Comp) directory.
**inhuman** adj (unmenschlich, brutal) inhuman.
**Initiale** [ini'tsiaːlə] f -n (geh) initial.
**initialisieren*** [initsiali'ziːrən] vt (Comp) to initialize.
**Initialisierung** [initsiali'ziːrʊŋ] f (Comp) initialization.
**Initiative** [initsia'tiːvə] f initiative. **aus eigener** ~ on one's own initiative; **die** ~ **ergreifen** to take the initiative.
**Initiator(in** f) [ini'tsiaːtɔr, -'toːrɪn] m (geh) initiator.
**Injektion** f injection.
**injizieren*** [ɪnji'tsiːrən] vt (form) to inject (jdm etw sb with sth).
**Inka** m -s Inca.
**Inkarnation** f incarnation.
**Inkaufnahme** f no pl (form) acceptance. **unter** ~ **finanzieller Verluste** accepting the inevitable financial losses.
**inkl.** = **inklusive** incl.
**inklusive** [-ziːvə] 1 prep +gen inclusive of. 2 adv in-

clusive.
**inkognito** adv incognito.
**inkompetent** adj incompetent.
**Inkompetenz** f incompetence.
**inkonsequent** adj inconsistent.
**inkorrekt** adj incorrect.
**Inkrafttreten** nt no pl **bei** ~ **von etw** when sth comes/came etc into effect.
**Inkubationszeit** f incubation period.
**Inland** nt no pl (a) (als Staatsgebiet) home. **im** ~ **hergestellte Waren** home-produced goods; **im In- und Ausland** at home and abroad. (b) (Inneres eines Landes) inland. **im** ~ inland.
**Inland-** in cpds (Comm) home, domestic; (Geog) inland; ~**flug** m domestic or internal flight.
**inländisch** adj home attr, domestic; (Geog) inland.
**Inlands-**: ~**gespräch** nt inland call; ~**markt** m home or domestic market; ~**porto** nt inland postage.
**inmitten** 1 prep +gen in the middle of. 2 adv ~ **von** amongst, surrounded by.
**innehaben** vt sep irreg (form) Amt etc to hold.
**innehalten** vi sep irreg to pause, to stop. **in der Rede** ~ to pause.
**innen** adv inside. ~ **und außen** inside and out(side); **nach** ~ inwards; **tief** ~ **tut es doch weh** deep down inside it really hurts; **das Band befördert die Kohle nach** ~ the conveyor belt carries the coal inside; **von** ~ from the inside.
**Innen-**: ~**antenne** f indoor aerial (Brit) or antenna (US); ~**architekt** m interior designer; ~**aufnahme** f indoor photo(graph); (Film) indoor shot; ~**ausstattung** f interior décor no pl; (das Ausstatten) interior decoration and furnishing; (von Auto) interior fittings pl; ~**bahn** f (Sport) inside lane; ~**dienst** m office duty; **im** ~**dienst sein** to work in the office; ~**einrichtung** f interior furnishing; ~**hof** m inner courtyard; ~**kurve** f inside bend; ~**leben** nt no pl (col) (a) (seelisch) emotional life; (b) (körperlich) insides pl; (c) (col: eines Geräts etc) inner workings pl; ~**leuchte** f (Aut) courtesy or interior light; ~**minister** m minister of the interior; (in GB) Home Secretary; (in den USA) Secretary of the Interior; ~**ministerium** nt ministry of the interior; (in GB) Home Office; (in den USA) Department of the Interior; ~**politik** f domestic policy/policies pl; **i**~**politisch** adj domestic, home attr; **auf i**~**politischem Gebiet** in the field of home affairs; ~**raum** m (a) inner room; (b) no pl room inside; (von Wagen auch) interior; (von Stadion) central area; **mit großem** ~**raum** with a lot of room inside; ~**seite** f inside; ~**spiegel** m (Aut) interior mirror; ~**stadt** f town/city centre (Brit) or center (US); ~**tasche** f inside pocket; ~**temperatur** f (in Gebäude) indoor temperature; ~**welt** f inner world.
**inner-**: ~**betrieblich** adj in-house; **etw** ~**betrieblich regeln** to settle sth in-house; ~**deutsch** adj (before 1990) intra-German; ~**deutscher Handel** (before 1990) trade between the two Germanies.
**Innereien** pl innards pl.
**innere(r, s)** adj inner; (im Körper befindlich, inländisch) internal. **Facharzt für** ~ **Krankheiten** internist; **eine** ~ **Uhr** (col) an internal or a biological clock; **vor meinem** ~**n Auge** in my mind's eye; ~ **Führung** (Mil) moral leadership.
**Innere(s)** nt decl as adj (a) inside; (von Wagen, Schloß auch) interior; (Mitte) middle. **das** ~ **nach außen kehren** to turn something inside out. (b) (fig: Gemüt, Geist) heart. **ich wußte, was in seinem** ~**n vorging** I knew what was going on inside him.

**innerhalb 1** *prep* +*gen* inside, within. ~ **dieser Regelung** within this ruling. **2** *adv* inside.

**innerlich** *adj* (a) *(körperlich)* internal. **dieses Medikament ist** ~ **anzuwenden** this medicine is to be taken internally. (b) *(geistig, seelisch)* inward, inner *no adv*; *Mensch* inward; *Hemmung* inner. **ein** ~ **gefestigter Mensch** a person of inner strength.

**Innerlichkeit** *f (liter)* inwardness.

**inner-:** ~**örtlich** *adj* in built-up areas; ~**parteilich** *adj* within the party; ~**parteiliche Demokratie** democracy (with)in the party structure.

**innerste(r, s)** *adj superl of* **innere(r, s)** innermost.

**Innerste(s)** *nt decl as adj (lit, fig)* heart. **bis ins** ~ **getroffen** hurt to the quick.

**innewohnen** *vi sep* +*dat* to be inherent in.

**innig** *adj Grüße, Beileid* heartfelt; *Vergnügen* deep; *Freundschaft* intimate. **mein** ~**ster Wunsch** my dearest wish; **jdn** ~ **lieben** to love sb deeply.

**Innigkeit** *f (von Empfindung)* depth; *(von Liebe)* intensity; *(von Freundschaft)* intimacy.

**Innovation** *f* innovation.

**innovativ** *adj* innovative.

**Innung** *f* (trade) guild. **du blamierst die ganze** ~ *(hum col)* you're letting the whole side down.

**in|offiziell** *adj* unofficial.

**Input** ['ɪnput] *m or nt* **-s** input.

**Inquisition** *f* Inquisition.

**ins** = **in das.** ~ **Rollen geraten** to start rolling.

**Insasse** *m (wk)* **-n, -n, Insassin** *f (eines Fahrzeuges)* passenger; *(einer Anstalt)* inmate.

**Insassenversicherung** *f* passenger insurance.

**insbesondere** *adv* particularly.

**Inschrift** *f* inscription.

**Insekt** *nt* **-en** insect.

**Insekten-:** ~**bekämpfung** *f* insect control; ~**bekämpfungsmittel,** ~**gift** *nt* insecticide; ~**plage** *f* plague of insects; ~**pulver** *nt* insect powder; ~**schutzmittel** *nt* insect repellent; ~**stich** *m (von Mücken, Flöhen)* insect bite; *(von Bienen, Wespen)* (insect) sting; ~**vertilgungsmittel** *nt* insecticide.

**Insel** *f* **-n** *(lit, fig)* island.

**Insel-:** ~**bewohner** *m* islander; ~**gruppe** *f* archipelago, group of islands; ~**staat** *m* island state; ~**volk** *nt* island race; ~**welt** *f* island world; **die** ~**welt Mittelamerikas** the world of the Central American islands.

**Inserat** *nt* advert *(Brit col)*, ad *(col)*, advertisement.

**Inserent** *m* advertiser.

**inserieren\*** *vti* to advertise.

**insgeheim** *adv* secretly, in secret.

**insgesamt** *adv (alles zusammen)* altogether; *(im großen und ganzen)* all in all. **die Kosten belaufen sich auf** ~ **1.000DM** the costs amount to a total of DM 1,000.

**Insider** ['ɪnsaɪdə] *m* - insider. **der Witz war nur für** ~ **verständlich** that was an in-joke.

**Insiderhandel** *m (Fin)* insider trading *or* dealing.

**Insignien** [ɪn'zɪgniən] *pl* insignia *pl.*

**insofern 1** *adv* in this respect. ~ **als** in so far as, inasmuch as. **2** [ɪnzo'fɛrn] *conj (wenn)* if.

**Insolvenz** ['ɪnzɔlvɛnts] *f (Comm)* insolvency.

**insoweit** [ɪn'zoːvaɪt] *adv*, [ɪnzo'vaɪt] *conj siehe* **insofern.**

**in spe** [ɪn'speː] *adj (col)* **unser Schwiegersohn** ~ our son-in-law to be, our future son-in-law.

**Inspekteur** [ɪnspɛk'tøːɐ] *m (Mil)* Chief of Staff.

**Inspektion** *f* inspection; *(Aut)* service. **ich habe mein Auto zur** ~ **gebracht** I've taken my car in for a service.

**Inspektionsreise** *f* tour of inspection.

**Inspektor(in** *f)* [ɪn'spɛktɔr, -'toːrɪn] *m* inspector.

**Inspiration** [ɪnspira'tsioːn] *f* inspiration.

**inspirieren\*** [ɪnspi'riːrən] *vt* to inspire. **sich von etw** ~ **lassen** to get one's inspiration from sth.

**Inspizient(in** *f)* [ɪnspi'tsiɛnt, -ɪn] *m (Theat)* stage manager.

**inspizieren\*** [ɪnspi'tsiːrən] *vt* to inspect.

**instabil** ['ɪnstabiːl] *adj* unstable.

**Installateur** [ɪnstala'tøːɐ] *m* plumber; *(Elektro~)* electrician; *(Gas~)* gas-fitter.

**Installation** [ɪnstala'tsioːn] *f* installation.

**installieren\*** [ɪnsta'liːrən] *vt* to install *(auch fig, Comp)*.

**instand** *adj* **etw** ~ **halten** to keep sth in good condition; **etw** ~ **setzen** to get sth into good condition; *(funktionsfähig)* to get sth into working order; *(restaurieren)* to restore.

**instandbesetzen\*** *vt sep (col)* **ein Haus** ~ to squat in a house (and do it up).

**Instandhaltung** *f* maintenance.

**inständig** *adj* urgent. ~ **bitten** to beg; ~ **hoffen** to hope fervently.

**Instandsetzung** *f (von Gerät)* overhaul; *(von Gebäude)* restoration.

**Instanz** [ɪn'stants] *f* (a) *(Behörde)* authority. (b) *(Jur)* court. **Verhandlung in erster/zweiter** ~ hearing in a lower/higher court; **er ging von einer** ~ **zur anderen** he went through all the courts.

**Instinkt** [ɪn'stɪŋkt] *m* **-e** *(lit, fig)* instinct.

**instinktiv** [ɪnstɪŋk'tiːf] *adj* instinctive.

**instinktlos** *adj* insensitive.

**Institut** [ɪnsti'tuːt] *nt* **-e** institute.

**Institution** [ɪnstitu'tsioːn] *f* institution.

**institutionalisieren\*** [ɪnstitutsio-] *vt* to institutionalize.

**instruieren\*** [ɪnstru'iːrən] *vt* to instruct; *(über Unternehmen, Plan etc)* to brief.

**Instruktion** [ɪnstrʊk'tsioːn] *f* instruction.

**Instrument** [ɪnstru'mɛnt] *nt* instrument.

**instrumental** [ɪnstrumɛn'taːl] *adj (Mus)* instrumental.

**Instrumental-** *in cpds* instrumental.

**Instrumentarium** [ɪnstrumɛn'taːriʊm] *nt* instruments *pl*; *(fig)* apparatus.

**Instrumentenflug** *m* instrument flight; *(das Fliegen auch)* flying on instruments.

**Insulaner(in** *f)* *m* - *(usu hum)* islander.

**Insulin** *nt no pl* insulin.

**inszenieren\*** *vt* (a) *(Theat)* to direct; *(TV)* to produce. (b) *(fig)* to stage-manage. **einen Streit** ~ to start an argument.

**Inszenierung** *f* production.

**intakt** *adj* intact.

**integer** *adj (geh)* **ein integrer Mensch** a person of integrity.

**Integral-:** ~**helm** *m* full-face helmet; ~**rechnung** *f* integral calculus.

**Integration** *f* integration.

**integrieren\*** *vt* to integrate *(auch Math)*.

**integriert** *adj* integrated. ~**e Schaltung** integrated circuit; ~**e Gesamtschule** comprehensive school *(Brit)*.

**Integrität** *f* integrity.

**Intellekt** *m no pl* intellect.

**intellektuell** *adj* intellectual.

**Intellektuelle(r)** *mf decl as adj* intellectual.

**intelligent** *adj* intelligent.

**Intelligenz** *f* intelligence; *(Personengruppe)* intelligentsia *pl.*

**Intelligenz-:** ~**bestie** *f (pej col)* egghead *(col)*; ~**leistung** *f* display of intelligence; ~**quotient** *m*

IQ; ~test m intelligence test; einen ~test mit jdm machen to test sb's IQ.

Intendant m director; theatre manager (Brit), theater manager (US).

intendieren* vt (geh) to intend.

Intensität f intensity.

intensiv adj Arbeit, Forschung intensive; Farbe, Gefühl intense; Geruch powerful.

intensivieren* [-'vi:rən] vt to intensify.

Intensivierung f intensification.

Intensiv-: ~kurs m intensive course; ~station f intensive care unit; auf der ~station in intensive care.

Intention f (geh) intention.

Inter- in cpds inter-; i~aktiv adj interactive; ~city(-Zug) m inter-city (train).

interessant adj interesting. zu diesem Preis ist das nicht ~ für uns (Comm) we are not interested at that price; sich ~ machen to attract attention.

interessanterweise adv interestingly enough.

Interesse nt -n interest. ~ an jdm/etw or für jdn/etw haben to be interested in sb/sth; aus ~ out of interest; es liegt in Ihrem eigenen ~ it's in your own interest(s); sein ~ gilt ... his interest lies in ...; das ist für uns nicht von ~ that's of no interest to us.

Interesse-: i~halber adv out of interest; i~los adj indifferent; ~losigkeit f indifference.

Interessen-: ~gebiet nt field of interest; ~gegensatz m clash of interests; ~gemeinschaft f interest group; ~gruppe f pressure group; (Lobby) lobby; ~konflikt m conflict of interests.

Interessent(in f) m interested party. es haben sich mehrere ~en gemeldet several people have shown interest.

Interessenvertretung f representation of interests; (Personen) group representing one's interests.

interessieren* 1 vt to interest (für, an +dat in). das interessiert mich nicht! I'm not interested. 2 vr to be interested (für in).

interessiert adj interested (an +dat in). ~ zuhören to listen with interest; vielseitig ~ sein to have a wide range of interests; politisch ~ interested in politics.

Interims- in cpds interim; ~regierung f caretaker government.

Interjektion f interjection.

Inter-: i~konfessionell adj interdenominational; ~kontinentalrakete f intercontinental (ballistic) missile.

Intermezzo [-'mɛtso] nt -s or Intermezzi (Mus) intermezzo; (fig) interlude.

intern adj internal. diese Maßnahmen müssen ~ bleiben these measures must be kept private.

Internat nt boarding school.

international [ɪntɐnatsio'na:l] adj international. I~er Währungsfonds International Monetary Fund.

Internationale [ɪntɐnatsio'na:lə] f -n Internationale.

Internatsschüler m boarder.

internieren* vt to intern.

Internierte(r) mf decl as adj internee.

Internierung f internment.

Internierungslager nt internment camp.

Internist(in f) m internist.

Internspeicher m (Comp) (internal) memory.

Interpol f Interpol.

Interpret m (wk) -en, -en interpreter (of music, art etc). Lieder verschiedener ~en songs interpreted by various singers.

Interpretation f interpretation.

interpretieren* vt to interpret. etw falsch ~ to misinterpret sth.

Interpretin f siehe Interpret.

Interpunktion f punctuation.

interrogativ adj interrogative.

Interrogativ- in cpds interrogative.

Intershop ['ɪntɐʃɔp] m -s (DDR) international shop.

Intervall [-'val] nt -e interval.

intervenieren* [-ve'ni:rən] vi to intervene.

Intervention [-vɛn'tsio:n] f intervention.

Interview ['ɪntɐvju:] nt -s interview.

interviewen* [-'vju:ən] vt to interview (jdn zu etw sb about sth).

Interviewer(in f) [-'vju:ɐ, -vju:ərɪn] m - interviewer.

intim adj intimate. ~e Beziehungen (euph: sexuell) intimate relations; ein ~er Kenner von etw sein to have an intimate knowledge of sth.

Intim-: ~bereich m (Anat) genital area; ~feind m best enemy; ~hygiene f personal hygiene.

Intimität f intimacy. zwischen den beiden kam es zu ~en they became intimate with each other.

Intim-: ~sphäre f private life; jds ~sphäre verletzen to invade sb's privacy; ~verkehr m intimacy; ~verkehr mit jdm haben to be intimate with sb.

intolerant adj intolerant (jdm/einer Sache gegenüber of sb/sth).

Intoleranz f intolerance.

Intonation f intonation.

intonieren* vt (a) einen Satz falsch ~ to give a sentence the wrong intonation. (b) (Mus) Melodie to sing; (Kapelle) to play; Ton to give.

intransitiv adj intransitive.

Intrigant(in f) m schemer, intriguer.

Intrige f -n intrigue.

intrigieren* vi to intrigue, to scheme.

introvertiert [-vɛr'ti:ɐt] adj introverted. ~ sein to be an introvert.

Intuition [ɪntui'tsio:n] f intuition.

intuitiv [ɪntui'ti:f] adj intuitive.

intus adj (col) etw ~ haben (wissen) to have got sth into one's head (col); Essen, Alkohol to have sth down one (col).

Invalide [ɪnva'li:də] m (wk) -n, -n disabled person, invalid.

Invalidenrente f disability pension.

Invalidität [ɪnvalidi'tɛ:t] f disability.

Invasion [ɪnva:'zio:n] f (lit, fig) invasion.

Inventar [ɪnvɛnta:ɐ] nt -e (a) (Einrichtung) fittings pl; (Maschinen) equipment no pl, plant no pl. (b) (Verzeichnis) inventory; (Comm) assets and liabilities pl. er gehört schon zum ~ (hum) he's part of the furniture.

Inventur [ɪnvɛn'tu:ɐ] f stocktaking. ~ machen to stocktake.

investieren* [ɪnvɛs'ti:rən] vti (Comm, fig) to invest. Gefühle in jdn ~ (col) to become emotionally involved with sb.

Investition [ɪnvɛst-] f investment.

Investitions-: ~anreiz m investment incentive; ~güter pl items of capital expenditure.

Investment [ɪn'vɛstmənt] nt -s investment.

inwendig adj inside. jdn/etw in- und auswendig kennen (col) to know sb/sth inside out.

inwiefern, inwieweit adv to what extent. ~? in what way?

Inzest m -e incest no pl.

inzestuös adj incestuous.

Inzucht f inbreeding.

inzwischen adv in the meantime, meanwhile. er ist ~ 18 geworden he's now 18.

IOK [i:|o:'ka:] nt = Internationales Olympisches

**Komitee** IOC.
**Ion** [ˈioːn] *nt* **-en** ion.
**ionisch** [ˈioːnɪʃ] *adj* **l~es Meer** Ionian Sea.
**IQ** = **Intelligenzquotient** IQ.
**i.R.** [iːˈɛr] = **im Ruhestand** retd.
**IRA** [iːˈɛrˈaː] *f* = **Irisch-Republikanische Armee** IRA.
**Irak** [iˈraːk, ˈiːrak] *m* **(der)** ~ Iraq.
**Iraker(in** *f*) *m* - Iraqi.
**irakisch** *adj* Iraqi.
**Iran** *m* **(der)** ~ Iran.
**Iraner(in** *f*) *m* - Iranian.
**iranisch** *adj* Iranian.
**irden** *adj* earthenware, earthen.
**irdisch** *adj* earthly *no adv.* **den Weg alles l~en gehen** to go the way of all flesh.
**Ire** *m* *(wk)* **-n, -n** Irishman; Irish boy. **die ~n** the Irish; **er ist** ~ he is Irish.
**irgend 1** *adv* **wenn** ~ **möglich** if it's at all possible; **was ich** ~ **kann** whatever I can; **wer (es)** ~ **kann** whoever can; **so lange ich** ~ **kann** as long as I possibly can; **wo es** ~ **geht** wherever possible. **2** *mit indef pron* ~ **jemand** somebody; *(fragend, verneinend, bedingend)* anybody; **ich bin nicht** ~ **jemand** I'm not just anybody; ~ **etwas** something; *(fragend, verneinend, bedingend)* anything; **was zieh' ich an?** — ~ **etwas** what shall I wear? — anything, any old thing *(col)*; ~ **so ein Tier** some animal.
**irgend|ein** *indef pron* some; *(fragend, verneinend, bedingend)* any. **haben Sie noch ~en Wunsch?** is there anything else you would like?; **das kann** ~ **anderer machen** someone else can do it.
**irgend|eine(r, s)** *indef pron (nominal) (bei Personen)* somebody; *(bei Dingen)* something; *(fragend, verneinend, bedingend)* anybody/anything. **welchen wollen Sie?** — ~**n** which one do you want? — any one, any old one *(col)*.
**irgend|einmal** *adv* sometime; *(fragend, bedingend)* ever.
**irgendwann** *adv* sometime. ~ **einmal** some time; *(fragend, bedingend)* ever.
**irgendwas** *indef pron (col) siehe* **irgend 2.**
**irgendwelche(r, s)** *indef pron* some; *(fragend, verneinend, bedingend, jede beliebige)* any.
**irgendwer** *indef pron (col) siehe* **irgend 2.**
**irgendwie** *adv* somehow (or other). **ist es** ~ **möglich?** is it at all possible?
**irgendwo** *adv* somewhere; *(fragend, verneinend, bedingend)* anywhere.
**irgendwoher** *adv* from somewhere; *(fragend, verneinend, bedingend)* from anywhere.
**irgendwohin** *adv* somewhere; *(fragend, verneinend, bedingend)* anywhere.
**Irin** *f* Irishwoman; Irish girl. **sie ist** ~ she is Irish.
**Iris** *f* - iris.
**irisch** *adj* Irish. **l~e See** Irish Sea.
**IRK** [iːˈɛrˈkaː] *nt* = **Internationales Rotes Kreuz** International Red Cross.
**Irland** *nt* Ireland; *(Republik ~)* Eire.
**Irländer(in** *f*) *m* - *siehe* **Ire, Irin.**
**Ironie** *f* irony.
**ironisch** *adj* ironic, ironical.
**ironisieren*** *vt* to treat ironically.
**irrational** [ˈɪratsionaːl] *adj* irrational.
**irr(e) 1** *adj* **(a)** *(geistesgestört)* crazy, insane. **das macht mich ganz** ~ it's driving me crazy; **wie** ~ *(fig col)* like crazy *(col)*. **(b)** *(pred (verwirrt, unsicher)* confused. **(c)** *(col) Party, Hut* wild *(col)*, crazy *(col)*. **2** *adv (verrückt)* insanely; *(col: sehr)* incredibly *(col)*. ~ **gut** *(col)* brilliant *(col)*.
**Irre** *f*: **jdn in die** ~ **führen** *(lit, fig)* to lead sb astray.

**irreal** *adj* unreal.
**Irre-:** **i~führen** *vt sep* to mislead; **sich i~führen lassen** to be misled; **i~führend** *adj* misleading; ~**führung** *f* misleading.
**irregulär** *adj* irregular.
**irrelevant** [ˈɪrelevant] *adj* irrelevant *(für* for, to*)*.
**irremachen** *vt sep* to confuse, to muddle.
**irren 1** *vi aux sein (umher~)* to wander. **2** *vir* to be mistaken *or* wrong. **I~ ist menschlich** *(Prov)* to err is human *(Prov)*; **jeder kann sich mal** ~ anyone can make a mistake; **wenn ich mich nicht sehr irre ...** unless I'm very much mistaken ...
**Irren-:** ~**anstalt** *f (dated)*, ~**haus** *nt (dated, pej)* lunatic asylum *(dated)*; **hier geht es zu wie im ~haus** *(col)* this place is an absolute madhouse.
**irreparabel** *adj* irreparable.
**Irre(r)** *mf decl as adj* lunatic; *(col auch)* madman. **ein armer ~r** *(hum col)* a poor fool.
**Irr-:** ~**fahrt** *f* wandering; ~**garten** *m* maze; ~**glaube(n)** *m (Rel, fig)* heresy; *(irrige Ansicht)* mistaken belief.
**irrig** *adj* incorrect, wrong.
**irritieren*** *vt (verwirren)* to confuse, to muddle; *(ärgern)* to irritate.
**Irr-:** ~**lehre** *f* heresy; ~**licht** *nt* will-o'-the-wisp.
**Irrsinn** *m no pl* madness, insanity. **so ein ~!** that's madness!
**irrsinnig** *adj* mad, crazy. **wie ein l~er** like a madman; **ein ~er Verkehr** *(col)* an incredible amount of traffic; ~ **komisch** incredibly funny.
**Irrtum** *m* mistake, error. **ein** ~ **von ihm** a mistake on his part; **im** ~ **sein** to be wrong *or* mistaken; ~**!** wrong!; ~ **vorbehalten** errors excepted.
**irrtümlich 1** *adj attr* mistaken, erroneous. **2** *adv* mistakenly; *(aus Versehen)* by mistake.
**irrtümlicherweise** *adv* mistakenly; *(aus Versehen)* by mistake.
**Irrweg** *m (fig)* **auf dem** ~ **sein** to be on the wrong track; **zu studieren erwies sich für ihn als** ~ going to university proved to be a mistake for him.
**ISBN** [iːˈɛsbeːˈɛn] *f* = **Internationale Standard-Buchnummer** ISBN.
**Ischias** *m or nt no pl* sciatica.
**Ischiasnerv** *m* sciatic nerve.
**Islam** *m no pl* Islam.
**islamisch** *adj* Islamic.
**Island** *nt* Iceland.
**Isländer(in** *f*) *m* - Icelander.
**isländisch** *adj* Icelandic.
**Isländisch(e)** *nt* Icelandic; *siehe* **Deutsch(e).**
**Isobare** *f* **-n** isobar.
**Isolation** *f* **(a)** isolation; *(von Häftlingen)* solitary confinement. **(b)** *(Elec, gegen Lärm, Kälte etc)* insulation.
**Isolationismus** *m* isolationism.
**Isolations-:** ~**folter** *(pej)*, ~**haft** *f* solitary confinement.
**Isolator** *m* insulator.
**Isolierband** *nt* insulating tape *(Brit)*, friction tape *(US)*.
**isolieren*** **1** *vt* **(a)** to isolate. **völlig isoliert leben** to live in complete isolation. **(b)** *(elektrische Leitungen, Häuser, Fenster)* to insulate. **2** *vr* to isolate oneself (from the world).
**Isolier-:** ~**haft** *f* solitary confinement; ~**kanne** *f* thermos ® flask; ~**station** *f* isolation ward.
**Isolierung** *f* = **Isolation.**
**Israel** [ˈɪsraɛl] *nt* Israel.
**Israeli** *m* **-(s)** Israeli.
**israelisch** *adj* Israeli.
**iß** *imper sing of* **essen.**

**ist** *3. pers sing pres of* **sein¹** is.
**Istanbul** *nt* Istanbul.
**Ist-:** ~**-Bestand** *m (Geld)* cash in hand; *(Waren)* ac-
tual stock; ~**-Stärke** *f (Mil)* effective strength, ~**-**
**Wert** *m* actual value.
**Italien** [-iən] *nt* Italy.
**Italiener(in** *f)* [-'lieːnɐ, -ərɪn] *m* - Italian.

**italienisch** [-'lieːnɪʃ] *adj* Italian. **die** ~**e Schweiz**
Italian-speaking Switzerland.
**Italienisch(e)** [-'lieːnɪʃ(ə)] *nt* Italian; *siehe* **Deut-**
**sch(e).**
**i.V.** = **in Vertretung** pp.
**IWF** [iːveːˈɛf] *m* = **Internationaler Währungs-**
**fonds** IMF.

# J

**J, j** [jɔt] *nt* -, - J, j. **J wie Julius** J for Jack, J for Jig *(US)*.

**ja** *adv* **(a)** yes; *(bei Trauung)* I do. **kommst du morgen?** — ~ are you coming tomorrow? — yes(, I am); **haben Sie das gesehen?** — ~ did you see it? — yes(, I did); **ich glaube** ~ (yes) I think so; ~ **und amen zu allem sagen** *(col)* to accept everything without question.

**(b)** *(fragend, zweifelnd)* ~? really?; **ich habe gekündigt** — ~? I've given my notice — have you?

**(c)** **aber** ~! yes, of course; **das ist also abgemacht,** ~? that's agreed then, OK?; **ach** ~! oh yes; **nun** ~ oh well; ~ **doch** yes, of course; **kann ich reinkommen?** — ~ **bitte** can I come in? — yes, do; **sei** ~ **vorsichtig!** do be careful; **vergessen Sie es *ja* nicht!** don't forget, whatever you do!; **sie ist** ~ **erst fünf** (after all) she's only five; **das ist** ~ **richtig, aber ...** that's (certainly) right, but ...; **das ist gut,** ~ **sogar sehr gut** it's good, in fact it's (even) very good; **da haben wir's** ~ there you are (then); **da kommt er** ~ here he comes; **das sag' ich** ~! that's just what I'm saying; **das wissen wir** ~ **alle** we all know that (anyway); **Sie wissen** ~, **daß ...** as you know ...; **Sie wissen** ~, **wie das so ist** you know how it is; **das ist** ~ **fürchterlich** that's (really) terrible.

**Ja** *nt* **-(s)** yes. **mit** ~ **antworten/stimmen** to answer/vote yes; **ein** ~ **zum Kind/Frieden** a positive attitude to children/a vote for peace.

**Jacht** *f* **-en** yacht.

**Jachthafen** *m* yacht harbour, marina.

**Jacke** *f* **-n** jacket, coat *(esp US)*; *(Woll~)* cardigan. **das ist** ~ **wie Hose** *(col)* it's six of one and half a dozen of the other *(col)*.

**Jacken-:** ~**kleid** *nt* *(Kleid und Jacke)* two-piece; ~**tasche** *f* jacket *or* coat *(esp US)* pocket.

**Jacketkrone** ['dʒɛkɪt-] *f* *(Zahnheilkunde)* jacket crown.

**Jackett** [ʒaˈkɛt] *nt* **-s** jacket, coat *(esp US)*.

**Jade** *m or f no pl* jade.

**Jagd** *f* **-en** hunt; *(Ausführung der ~)* hunting; *(fig: Verfolgung)* hunt *(nach* for), chase *(nach* after); *(Wettlauf)* race. **die** ~ **auf Rotwild** deer-hunting; **auf die** ~ **(nach etw) gehen** *(lit, fig)* to go hunting (for sth); **auf jdn/etw** ~ **machen** *(lit, fig)* to hunt for sb/sth; **die** ~ **nach Geld** the pursuit of money.

**Jagd-:** **j~bar** *adj ...* **sind j~bar ...** may be hunted, ... are fair game; ~**beute** *f* bag; ~**bomber** *m* *(Mil)* fighter-bomber; ~**flieger** *m* *(Mil)* fighter pilot; ~**flugzeug** *nt* *(Mil)* fighter aircraft; ~**gebiet** *nt* hunting ground; ~**gesellschaft** *f* hunting party; ~**gewehr** *nt* hunting rifle; ~**horn** *nt* hunting horn; ~**hund** *m* hunting dog; ~**revier** *nt* shoot; ~**schein** *m* hunting licence *(Brit)* or license *(US)*; **einen** ~**schein haben** *(hum col)* to be certified *(col)*; ~**wild** *nt* game; ~**wurst** *f* smoked sausage; ~**zeit** *f* hunting season.

**jagen** **1** *vt* to hunt; *(hetzen)* to chase, to drive. **jdn in die Flucht** ~ to put sb to flight; **ein Unglück jagte** das andere one misfortune followed on the other; **mit diesem Essen kannst du mich** ~ *(col)* I wouldn't eat this if you paid me. **2** *vi* **(a)** *(auf die Jagd gehen)* to hunt, to go hunting. **(b)** *aux sein (rasen)* to race. **nach etw** ~ to chase after sth.

**Jäger** *m* - **(a)** hunter, huntsman. **(b)** *(Mil: Flugzeug)* fighter.

**Jägerei** *f no pl* hunting.

**Jägerin** *f* huntress, huntswoman.

**Jäger-:** ~**latein** *nt* *(col)* hunters' tales *pl*; ~**schnitzel** *nt* *(Cook)* cutlet served with mushroom sauce; ~**zaun** *m* (rustic) lattice fence.

**Jaguar** *m* **-e** jaguar.

**jäh** *adj (geh)* **(a)** *(plötzlich)* sudden. **(b)** *(steil)* sheer. **der Abhang fällt** ~ **herab** the slope falls sharply.

**Jahr** *nt* **-e** year. **ein halbes** ~ six months *sing or pl*; **ein dreiviertel** ~ nine months *sing or pl*; **anderthalb** ~**e** one and a half years *sing,* eighteen months *sing or pl*; **zwei** ~**e Garantie** a two-year guarantee; **im** ~**(e) 1066** in (the year) 1066; **die sechziger** ~**e** the sixties *sing or pl*; **alle zehn** ~**e** every ten years; **auf** ~**e hinaus** for years ahead; **auf** ~ **und Tag** to the very day; **einmal im** ~**(e)** once a year; **das Buch des** ~**es** the book of the year; **nach** ~ **und Tag** after (many) years; **mit den** ~**en** as the years go by; **zwischen den** ~**en** *(col)* between Christmas and New Year; **er ist zehn** ~**e (alt)** he is ten years old; **mit dreißig** ~**en** at the age of thirty; **in die** ~**e kommen** *(col)* to be getting on (in years); **in den besten** ~**en sein** to be in the prime of one's life.

**jahr|aus** *adv:* ~, **jahrein** year in, year out.

**Jahrbuch** *nt* yearbook; *(Kalender)* almanac.

**jahrelang** **1** *adj attr* lasting for years. ~**es Warten/** ~**e Forschungen** years of waiting/research. **2** *adv* for years. **und dann dauerte es noch** ~, **bevor ...** and then it took years until ...

**jähren** *vr* **heute jährt sich der Tag, an dem ...** it's a year ago today that ...

**Jahres-** *in cpds* annual, yearly; ~**abonnement** *nt* annual subscription; ~**abschluß** *m* *(Comm)* annual accounts *pl*; ~**beginn** *m* beginning of a/the new year; ~**beitrag** *m* annual subscription; ~**bericht** *m* annual report; ~**bestzeit** *f* *(Sport)* best time of the year; ~**bilanz** *f* *(Comm)* annual balance sheet; ~**einkommen** *nt* annual income; ~**ende** *nt* end of the year; ~**frist** *f* **binnen/nach** ~**frist** within/after (a period of) one year; ~**gehalt** *nt* annual salary; ~**hauptversammlung** *f* *(Comm)* annual general meeting, AGM; ~**karte** *f* annual season ticket; ~**ring** *m* *(an Baum)* (annual) ring; ~**tag** *m* anniversary; ~**umsatz** *m* *(Comm)* yearly turnover; ~**urlaub** *m* annual holiday *or* leave; ~**wagen** *m* one-year-old car; ~**wechsel** *m* new year; ~**wende** *f* new year; ~**zahl** *f* date, year; ~**zeit** *f* season.

**Jahr-:** ~**gang** *m* **(a)** *(Sch, Univ)* year; **er ist** ~**gang 1950** he was born in 1950; **(b)** *(einer Zeitschrift)* year's issues *pl*; **(c)** *(von Wein)* vintage, year; ~**hundert** *nt* **-e** century.

**jeweilig**

jahrhunderte-: ~alt *adj* centuries-old; ~lang 1 *adj* lasting for centuries; 2 *adv* for centuries.

Jahrhundert-: ~feier *f* centenary; *(Feierlichkeiten)* centenary celebrations; ~wende *f* turn of the century.

jährlich 1 *adj* annual, yearly. 2 *adv* annually, yearly; *(Comm)* per annum. zweimal ~ twice a year.

Jahrmarkt *m* fair, funfair *(Brit)*.

Jahr-: ~tausend *nt* -e millennium, a thousand years; ~tausende thousands of years; ~zehnt *nt* -e decade; j~zehntelang 1 *adj* lasting for decades; 2 *adv* for decades.

Jähzorn *m* violent temper.

jähzornig *adj* bad-tempered.

Jakarta [dʒaˈkaːta] *nt* Djakarta.

Jakob *m* ≈ James.

Jalousie [ʒaluˈziː] *f* venetian blind.

Jamaika *nt* Jamaica.

Jamaikaner(in *f*) *m* - Jamaican.

jamaikanisch *adj* Jamaican.

Jammer *m no pl (Elend)* misery, wretchedness; *(Klage)* wailing, lamentation. es wäre ein ~, wenn ... *(col)* it would be a crying shame if ... *(col)*.

Jammer-: ~bild *nt* picture of misery; ~gestalt *f* wretched figure; ~lappen *m (pej col)* wet *(col)*.

jämmerlich 1 *adj* wretched; *Zustand auch* deplorable. 2 *adv (col: sehr)* terribly *(col)*.

jammern *vi* to wail *(über +acc over)*; *(sich beklagen auch)* to moan.

jammer-: ~schade *adj* es ist ~schade *(col)* it's a crying shame *(col)*; ~voll *adj* = jämmerlich.

Jan. = Januar Jan.

Januar *m* -e January; *siehe* März.

Japan *nt* Japan.

Japaner(in *f*) *m* - Japanese.

japanisch *adj* Japanese; *siehe* deutsch.

Japanisch(e) *nt* Japanese; *siehe* Deutsch(e).

japsen *vi (col)* to pant.

Jargon [ʒarˈgõː] *m* -s jargon.

Jasager *m* - *(pej)* yes-man.

Jasmin *m* -e jasmine.

Jastimme *f* vote in favour (of); *(Parl auch)* aye *(Brit)*, yea *(US)*.

jäten *vti* to weed. Unkraut ~ to weed.

Jauche *f* -n liquid manure; *(pej col) (Getränk)* piss *(col!)*; *(Abwasser)* sewage.

Jauchegrube *f* cesspool, cesspit.

jauchzen *vi (geh)* to rejoice *(liter)*; *(Publikum)* to cheer.

Jauchzer *m* - jubilant cheer *or* shout.

jaulen *vi (lit, fig)* to howl.

Jause *f* -n *(Aus)* break (for a snack); *(Proviant)* snack.

Java [ˈjaːva] *nt* Java.

jawohl, jawoll *(hum col) adv* yes; *(Mil)* yes, sir; *(Naut)* aye, aye, sir.

Jawort *nt* jdm das ~ geben to consent to marry sb; *(bei Trauung)* to say "I do".

Jazz [dʒæz, jats] *m no pl* jazz.

Jazzkeller *m* jazz club.

je 1 *adv* (a) *(jemals)* ever. (b) *(jeweils)* every, each. für ~ drei Stück zahlst du eine Mark you pay one mark for (every) three; ~ zwei Schüler aus jeder Klasse two children from each class; sie zahlten ~ eine Mark they paid one mark each. 2 *prep +acc (pro)* per. ~ Person zwei Stück two per person. 3 *conj* (a) ~ eher, desto *or* um so besser the sooner the better; ~ länger, ~ lieber the longer the better. (b) ~ nach depending on; ~ nachdem it all depends; ~ nachdem, wie/ob ... depending on how/

whether ...

Jeans [dʒiːnz] *pl* jeans.

Jeans- *in cpds* denim; ~anzug *m* denim suit; ~hose *f* pair of jeans; ~stoff *m* denim.

jedenfalls *adv* anyhow, in any case; *(zumindest)* at least, at any rate. er ist nicht reif zum Studieren, ~ jetzt noch nicht he's not mature enough to go to university, at least not yet.

jede(r, s) *indef pron* (a) *(adjektivisch) (einzeln)* each; *(von zweien auch)* either; *(~r von allen)* every; *(~r beliebige)* any. ohne ~ Anstrengung without any effort; es kann ~n Augenblick passieren it might happen any minute; fern von ~r Kultur far from all civilization. (b) *(substantivisch) (einzeln)* each (one); *(~ Person)* everyone, everybody; *(~ beliebige Person)* anyone, anybody. ~r von uns each (one)/every one/any one of us; ~r zweite every other one; ~r für sich everyone for himself; das kann nicht ~r not everyone can do that; er spricht nicht mit ~m he doesn't speak to just anybody.

jedermann *indef pron* everyone, everybody; *(jeder beliebige auch)* anyone, anybody. das ist nicht ~s Sache it's not everyone's cup of tea *(col)*.

jederzeit *adv* at any time. du kannst ~ kommen you can come any time (you like).

jedesmal *adv* every *or* each time. ~, wenn sie ... every time she ..., whenever she ...

jedoch *conj, adv* however. er verlor ~ die Nerven he lost his nerve however.

Jeep ® [dʒiːp] *m* -s jeep ®.

jegliche(r, s) *indef pron (adjektivisch)* any.

jeher [ˈjeːheːɐ] *adv:* von *or* seit ~ always; das ist schon seit ~ so it has always been like that.

jein *adv (hum)* yes and no.

jemals *adv* ever.

jemand *indef pron* somebody, someone; *(bei Fragen, bedingenden Sätzen auch, Negation)* anybody, anyone. ist da ~? is anybody *or* somebody there?; ohne ~en zu fragen without asking anyone; ~ anders/Neues somebody else/new.

Jemen *m (der)* ~ (the) Yemen.

Jemenit(in *f*) *m* Yemeni.

jemenitisch *adj* Yemeni.

Jenaer Glas ® [ˈjeːnaɐ-] *nt* Pyrex ®, heatproof glass.

jene(r, s) *dem pron (geh)* (a) *(adjektivisch)* that; *pl* those; *(der Vorherige, die Vorherigen)* the former. in ~r Zeit at that time. (b) *(substantivisch)* that one; *pl* those (ones); *(der Vorherige, die Vorherigen)* the former; *siehe* diese(r, s).

jenseitig *adj attr* Ufer opposite. das ~e Leben the life after death.

jenseits 1 *prep +gen* on the other side of. 2 km ~ der Grenze 2 kms beyond the border. 2 *adv* ~ von on the other side of; ~ von Gut und Böse beyond good and evil; *(hum col)* past it *(col)*.

Jenseits *nt no pl* hereafter. jdn ins ~ befördern *(col)* to send sb to kingdom come *(col)*.

Jerusalem *nt* Jerusalem.

Jesuit *m (wk)* -en, -en Jesuit.

Jesus *m gen* Jesu Jesus. ~ Christus Jesus Christ.

Jet [dʒɛt] *m* -s *(col)* jet.

Jeton [ʒəˈtõː] *m* -s chip.

jetten [ˈdʒɛtn] *vi aux sein (col)* to fly, to jet *(col)*.

jetzig *adj attr* present *attr*, current. in der ~en Zeit in our times.

jetzt *adv* now; *(heutzutage auch)* nowadays. bis ~ so far; ich bin ~ (schon) fünf Tage hier I have been here five days now; ~ gleich right now; ~ schon? already?

jeweilig *adj attr* respective; *(vorherrschend)* Verhält-

*nisse* prevailing. **die ~e Regierung** the government of the day.

**jeweils** *adv* at any one time; *(jedesmal)* each time; *(jeder einzelne)* each. **~ zwei zusammen** two at a time; **~ am Monatsletzten** on the last day of each month; **die ~ größten aus einer Gruppe** the biggest from each group.

**Jg.** = **Jahrgang**.

**Jh.** = **Jahrhundert** c.

**jiddisch** *adj* Yiddish.

**Job** [dʒɔp] *m* **-s** *(col, Comp)* job.

**jobben** ['dʒɔbn] *vi (col)* to take a job; *(mehrere Arbeiten)* to do odd jobs.

**Joch** *nt* **-e** *(lit, fig)* yoke.

**Jochbein** *nt* cheekbone.

**Jockei** ['jʒɔke], **Jockey** ['dʒɔki] *m* **-s** jockey.

**Jod** *nt no pl* iodine.

**jodeln** *vti* to yodel.

**Jodler(in** *f)* *m* - yodeller *(Brit)*, yodeler *(US)*.

**Joga** *m or nt no pl* yoga.

**joggen** ['dʒɔgn] *vi* to jog.

**Jogger(in** *f)* ['dʒɔgɐ, -ərɪn] *m* - jogger.

**Jogging** ['dʒɔgɪŋ] *nt no pl* jogging.

**Jogging-** *in cpds* jogging; **~anzug** *m* tracksuit.

**Joghurt** *m or nt* **-(s)** yog(h)urt.

**Johann, Johannes** *m* = John.

**Johannis-:** **~beere** *f* rote/schwarze **~beere** redcurrant/blackcurrant; **~brot** *nt* carob; **~nacht** *f* Midsummer's Eve.

**johlen** *vi* to howl.

**Joint** [dʒɔɪnt] *m* **-s** *(col)* joint *(col)*.

**Jojo** *nt* **-s** yo-yo.

**Joker** ['jʒɔːkɐ, 'dʒɔːkɐ] *m* - *(Cards)* joker.

**Jolle** *f* **-n** *(Naut)* jolly-boat, dinghy.

**Jongleur** [ʒõ'gløːɐ] *m* juggler.

**jonglieren*** [ʒõ'gliːrən] *vi (lit, fig)* to juggle.

**Jordanien** [-iən] *nt* Jordan.

**Jordanier(in** *f)* [-iɐ, -iərɪn] *m* - Jordanian.

**jordanisch** *adj* Jordanian.

**Jota** *nt* **-s** iota. **kein ~** not a jot *or* one iota.

**Joule** [dʒuːl] *nt* - joule.

**Journal** [ʒʊr'naːl] *nt* **-e** journal; *(dated: Zeitschrift)* magazine.

**Journalismus** [ʒʊrna'lɪsmʊs] *m no pl* journalism.

**Journalist(in** *f)* [ʒʊrna'lɪst, -ɪstɪn] *m* journalist.

**journalistisch** [ʒʊrna'lɪstɪʃ] *adj* journalistic.

**jovial** [jo'viaːl] *adj* jovial.

**jr.** = **junior** jnr., jr.

**Jubel** *m no pl* jubilation; *(~rufe auch)* cheering. **~, Trubel, Heiterkeit** laughter and merriment.

**Jubeljahr** *nt* **alle ~e (einmal)** *(col)* once in a blue moon *(col)*.

**jubeln** *vi* to cheer. **vor Freude ~** to shout with joy.

**Jubel-:** **~paar** *nt couple celebrating a special anniversary*; **~ruf** *m* (triumphant) cheer.

**Jubilar(in** *f)* *m person celebrating an anniversary*.

**Jubiläum** *nt, pl* **Jubiläen** jubilee; *(Jahrestag)* anniversary.

**Jubiläums-** *in cpds* jubilee.

**juchhe** *interj* hurrah, whoopee.

**juchzen** *vi* to shriek with delight.

**jucken 1** *vti* to itch. **der Rücken juckt mir** my back itches; **der Stoff juckt mich** this material makes me itch; **es juckt mich, das zu tun** *(col)* I'm itching to do it *(col)*; **das juckt mich doch nicht** *(col)* I don't care; **ihm juckt das Fell** *(col)* he's asking for a good hiding. **2** *vt (kratzen)* to scratch.

**Juck-:** **~pulver** *nt* itching powder; **~reiz** *m* itching.

**Judas** *m* **-, -se** *(fig liter)* Judas.

**Judaslohn** *m (liter)* blood money.

**Jude** *m (wk)* **-n, -n** Jew. **er ist ~** he is a Jew, he is

Jewish.

**Juden-:** **j~feindlich** *adj* anti-Semitic; **~stern** *m* star of David; **~tum** *nt (Gesamtheit der ~)* Jews *pl*, Jewry *no art*; *(jüdisches Wesen)* Jewishness; **~verfolgung** *f* persecution of the Jews.

**Jüdin** *f* Jew, Jewish woman.

**jüdisch** *adj* Jewish.

**Judo** *nt no pl* judo.

**Jugend** *f no pl* **(a)** *(~zeit)* youth. **frühe ~** early youth, adolescence; **von ~ an** *or* **auf** from one's youth. **(b)** *(junge Menschen)* youth, young people *pl*. **die heutige ~** the youth of today.

**Jugend-:** **~alter** *nt* adolescence; **~amt** *nt* youth welfare department; **~arbeit** *f no pl (~fürsorge)* youth work; **~arbeitslosigkeit** *f* youth unemployment; **~arrest** *m (Jur)* youth custody *(up to four weeks)*; **~bild** *nt* portrait (of sb) as a young man/woman; **~bilder Churchills** pictures of the young Churchill; **~buch** *nt* book for the younger reader; **~erinnerung** *f* youthful memory; **j~frei** *adj* suitable for young people; *Film* U(-certificate), G *(US)*; **~freund** *m* friend of one's youth; **~fürsorge** *f* youth welfare; **j~gefährdend** *adj* liable to corrupt the young; **~gericht** *nt* juvenile court; **~gruppe** *f* youth group; **~herberge** *f* youth hostel; **~hilfe** *f (Admin)* = **~fürsorge**; **~jahre** *pl* days of one's youth *pl*; **~klub** *m* youth club; **~kriminalität** *f* juvenile crime *or* delinquency.

**jugendlich** *adj (jung)* young; *(jung wirkend)* youthful. **er kleidet sich immer sehr ~** he always wears very youthful clothes; **~e Banden** gangs of youths; **ein ~er Täter** a young offender.

**Jugendliche(r)** *mf decl as adj* young person; *(männlicher ~ auch)* youth.

**Jugendlichkeit** *f* youthfulness.

**Jugend-:** **~liebe** *f (Geliebter)* love of one's youth; **~literatur** *f* literature for younger readers; **~mannschaft** *f* youth team; **~organisation** *f* youth organization; **~pflege** *f* youth welfare; **~pfleger** *m* youth (welfare) worker; **~recht** *nt* law relating to young persons; **~richter** *m (Jur)* magistrate *in a juvenile court*; **~schutz** *m* protection of children and young people; **~stil** *m (Art)* Art Nouveau; **~strafanstalt** *f (form)* youth custody centre; **~strafe** *f* youth custody; **~sünde** *f* youthful misdeed; **~traum** *m* youthful dream; **~verband** *m* youth organization; **~verbot** *nt* für einen Film **~verbot aussprechen** to ban a film for young people; **~zeit** *f* younger days *pl*; **~zentrum** *nt* youth centre *(Brit)* or center *(US)*.

**Jugoslawe** *m (wk)* **-n, -n, Jugoslawin** *f (Hist)* Yugoslav.

**Jugoslawien** [-iən] *nt (Hist)* Yugoslavia.

**jugoslawisch** *adj (Hist)* Yugoslav(ian).

**Jul.** = **Juli** Jul.

**Juli** *m* **-s** July; *siehe* **März.**

**Jun.** = **Juni** Jun.

**jun.** = **junior** jun.

**jung** *adj, comp* **=er**, *superl* **=ste(r, s)** *or (adv)* am **=sten** *(lit, fig)* young. **~ und alt** (both) young and old; **von ~ auf** from one's youth; **sie ist 18 Jahre ~** *(hum)* she's 18 years young *(hum)*; **~ heiraten/sterben** to marry/die young.

**Junge** *m (wk)* **-n, -n** *or (col)* **Jungs** boy; *(Cards col)* jack, knave. **~, ~!** *(col)* boy oh boy *(col)*; **alter ~** *(col)* my old pal *(col)*; **unsere Jungs haben gewonnen** our lads won.

**Jungen-:** **j~haft** *adj* boyish; **sie ist ein j~haftes Mädchen** she's a bit of a tomboy; **~schule** *f* boys' school; **~streich** *m* boyish prank.

**jünger** *adj* **(a)** *comp of* **jung** younger. **sie ist eine ~e**

**Frau** she's a fairly young woman; **Holbein der J~e** the younger Holbein. **(b)** *Geschichte etc* recent.

**Jünger** *m* - *(Bibl, fig)* disciple.

**Jüngerin** *f* (female) disciple.

**Junge(s)** *nt decl as adj (Zool)* young one; *(von Hund)* pup(py); *(von Katze)* kitten; *(von Wolf, Löwe, Bär)* cub; *(von Vogel)* young bird. **die ~n** the young.

**Jungfer** *f* **-n** *(old, hum: ledige Frau)* spinster. **eine alte ~** an old maid.

**Jungfern-:** **~fahrt** *f* maiden voyage; **~flug** *m* maiden flight; **~häutchen** *nt (Anat)* hymen, maidenhead; **~inseln** *pl* **die ~inseln** the Virgin Islands *pl*; **~rede** *f (Parl)* maiden speech.

**Jungfrau** *f* virgin; *(Astrol)* Virgo *no art.* **ich bin ~** I am a virgin; *(Astrol)* I am (a) Virgo; **die ~ Maria** the Virgin Mary; **dazu bin ich gekommen wie die ~ zum Kind(e)** it just fell into my hands.

**jungfräulich** *adj* virgin; *(liter) Seele* pure.

**Jungfräulichkeit** *f siehe adj* virginity; purity.

**Junggeselle** *m* bachelor.

**Junggesellen-:** **~bude** *f (col)* bachelor pad *(col)*; **~wohnung** *f* bachelor flat *(Brit)* or apartment *(US)*; **~zeit** *f* bachelor days *pl.*

**Junggesellin** *f* single woman.

**Junglehrer** *m* student teacher.

**Jüngling** *m (liter, hum)* youth.

**Jungsozialist** *m (BRD Pol)* Young Socialist.

**jüngst** *adv (geh)* recently, lately.

**jüngste(r, s)** *adj* **(a)** *superl of* **jung** youngest. **(b)** *Werk, Ereignis* latest, (most) recent; *Zeit, Vergangenheit* recent. **in der ~n Zeit** recently; **das J~ Gericht** the Last Judgement; **der J~ Tag** Doomsday, the Day of Judgement; **sie ist auch nicht mehr die J~** she's no chicken *(col)*.

**Jung-:** **~verheiratete(r)** *mf decl as adj* newly-wed; **~wähler** *m* young voter.

**Juni** *m* **-s** June; *siehe* **März.**

**junior** *adj* **Franz Schulz ~** Franz Schulz, Junior.

**Junior** *m* **(a)** *(usu hum: Sohn)* junior. **(b)** *(Comm:* *auch* **~chef)** son of the chairman/boss. **(c)** *usu pl (Sport)* junior.

**Juniorin** *f* = **Junior (c).**

**Junta** ['xʊnta, 'jʊnta] *f, pl* **Junten** *(Pol)* junta.

**Jupiter** *m* Jupiter.

**Jura** *no art (Univ)* law; *(science)* jurisprudence.

**Jurastudium** *nt* study of law.

**Jurist(in** *f)* *m* lawyer; *(Student)* law student.

**Juristen-:** **~deutsch** *nt,* **~sprache** *f no pl* legalese *(pej)*, legal jargon.

**juristisch** *adj* legal. **die J~e Fakultät** the Faculty of Law; **eine ~e Person** a legal entity.

**Juror(in** *f)* ['juːrɔr, -'roːrɪn] *m* juror; *(bei Wettbewerb)* judge.

**Jury** [ʒy'riː, 'ʒyːriː] *f* **-s** jury *sing or pl; (bei Wettbewerb auch)* judges *pl.*

**Juso** *m* **-s** *(BRD Pol)* = **Jungsozialist.**

**just** *adv (old, hum)* precisely, just.

**justieren\*** *vt Waage* to adjust; *(Typ, Comp)* to justify.

**Justiz** [jʊs'tiːts] *f no pl (als Prinzip)* justice; *(als Institution)* judiciary; *(die Gerichte)* courts *pl.*

**Justiz-:** **~beamte(r)** *m* judicial officer; **~irrtum** *m* miscarriage of justice; **~minister** *m* minister of justice, ≃ Attorney General *(US),* ≃ Lord (High) Chancellor *(Brit)*; **~ministerium** *nt* ministry of justice, ≃ Department of Justice *(US)*; **~mord** *m* judicial murder; **~vollzugsanstalt** *f (form)* place of detention.

**Jute** *f no pl* jute.

**Juwel** [ju'veːl] *nt* **-en** *or (fig)* **-e** jewel, gem.

**Juwelier** *m* **-e** jeweller *(Brit)*, jeweler *(US)*.

**Juwelier-:** **~geschäft** *nt,* **~laden** *m* jeweller's (shop), jewelry store *(US)*.

**Jux** *m* **-e** *(col)* **etw aus ~ tun/sagen** to do/say sth in fun; **sich** *(dat)* **einen ~ aus etw machen** to make a joke (out) of sth.

**juxen** *vi (col)* to joke.

**jwd** [jɔtveːˈdeː] *adv (hum)* in the back of beyond.

# K

**K, k** [kaː] nt -, - K, k. **K wie Kaufmann** ≃ K for King.

**Kabarętt** nt -e or -s cabaret. **ein politisches ~** a satirical political revue.

**Kabarettịst(in** f) m cabaret artist.

**kabarettịstisch** adj Darbietung cabaret; Stil revue attr.

**Kabbelẹi** f (col) bickering, squabbling.

**kạbbeln** vir (col) to bicker, to squabble.

**Kạbel** nt - cable; (Draht) wire; (Telefon~) flex, cord.

**Kabel-:** **~anschluß** m (TV) cable connection; **~anschluß haben** to have cable TV; **~fernsehen** nt cable television.

**Kạbeljau** m -e or -s cod.

**kạbeln** vti to cable.

**Kabịne** f cabin; (Umkleide~, Dusch~) cubicle; (Telec) booth; (Seilbahn~) car.

**Kabinẹtt¹** nt -e (Pol) cabinet.

**Kabinẹtt²** m -e high quality German white wine.

**Kabinẹtts-:** **~beschluß** m cabinet decision; **~mitglied** nt cabinet member; **~sitzung** f cabinet meeting; **~umbildung** f cabinet reshuffle.

**Kabinẹttstück** nt (old: einer Sammlung) pièce de résistance; (fig) masterstroke.

**Kạbrio** nt -s (col), **Kabriolett** [kabrio'lɛt, (Aus, S Ger) kabrio'leː] nt -s (Aut) convertible.

**Kạchel** f -n (glazed) tile.

**kạcheln** vt to tile.

**Kạchel|ofen** m tiled stove.

**Kạcke** f no pl (col!) crap (col!).

**kạcken** vi (col!) to crap (col!).

**Kadaver** [ka'daːvɐ] m - carcass.

**Kadạvergehorsam** m (pej) blind obedience.

**Kadẹnz** f cadence; (Improvisation) cadenza.

**Kạder** m - (Mil, Pol) cadre; (Sport) squad; (DDR, Sw: Fachleute) group of specialists.

**Kạderschmiede** f no pl (pej) élite school.

**Kadẹtt** m (wk) -en, -en (Mil) cadet.

**Kadẹttenanstalt** f cadet school.

**Kạdi** m -s (col) beak (col). **jdn vor den ~ schleppen** to take sb to court.

**Kạdmium** nt cadmium.

**Käfer** m - (auch col: VW) beetle.

**Kạff** nt -s or -e (col) dump (col), hole (col).

**Kạffee** [or ka'feː] m -s (a) coffee. **zwei ~, bitte!** two coffees please; **~ mit Milch** white coffee (Brit), coffee with milk; **~ kochen** to make coffee; **das ist kalter ~** (col) that's old hat (col). **(b)** no pl (Nachmittags~) afternoon coffee. **~ und Kuchen** (afternoon) coffee and cakes.

**Kaffee-:** **~bohne** f coffee bean; **~-Extrakt** m coffee essence; **~fahrt** f day trip; (Verkaufsfahrt) promotional trip; **~filter** m coffee filter; (col: Filterpapier) filter (paper); **~geschirr** nt coffee set; **~haus** nt coffee house, café; **~kanne** f coffeepot; **~klatsch** (col) m no pl, **~kränzchen** nt coffee circle, coffee klatsch (US); **~löffel** m coffee spoon; **~maschine** f coffee maker; **~mühle** f coffee grinder; **~pause** f coffee break; **~satz** m coffee

grounds pl; **aus dem ~satz lesen** to tell fortunes from the coffee grounds; **~service** nt coffee set; **~strauch** m coffee tree; **~tante** f (hum) coffee addict; (in Café) old biddy; **~tasse** f coffee cup; **~tisch** m (Frühstückstisch) breakfast table; (nachmittags) (afternoon) tea table; **~wärmer** m - cosy (for coffee pot).

**Käfig** m -e cage.

**Kạftan** m -e caftan.

**kahl** adj Mensch, Kopf bald; (~geschoren) shaven, shorn; Wand, Raum, Baum bare; Landschaft barren. **eine ~e Stelle** a bald patch; **~ werden** (Mensch) to go bald; (Baum) to lose its leaves.

**Kahl-:** **k~fressen** vt sep irreg to strip bare; **k~geschoren** adj Kopf shaven; **~heit** f siehe adj baldness; bareness; barrenness; **~kopf** m bald head; (Mensch) bald person; **k~köpfig** adj bald(-headed); **~schlag** m (Forest) clearing.

**Kahn** m ̈e (a) (small) boat. **~ fahren** to go for a row. **(b)** (Lastschiff) barge. **ein alter ~** (col) an old tub (col).

**Kahnfahrt** f row.

**Kai** m -e or -s quay; (Uferdamm auch) waterfront.

**Kai|anlage** f quayside.

**Kaimauer** f quay wall.

**Kairo** nt Cairo.

**Kaiser** m - emperor. **sich um des ~s Bart streiten** (fig) to split hairs.

**Kaiserin** f empress.

**kaiserlich** adj imperial.

**Kaiser-:** **~reich** nt empire; **~schmạrr(e)n** m - (Cook) sugared, cut-up pancake with raisins; **~schnitt** m Caesarean or Cesarean (US) (section).

**Kajak** m or nt -s kayak.

**Kajüte** f -n cabin; (größer auch) stateroom.

**Kạkadu** m -s cockatoo.

**Kakao** [auch ka'kau] m -s cocoa. **jdn/etw durch den ~ ziehen** (col) (veralbern) to make fun of sb/sth; (boshaft reden) to run sb/sth down.

**Kạkerlak** m -en cockroach.

**Kaktee** f -n [-eːən], **Kạktus** m -, **Kakteen** [-eːən] or (col) -se cactus.

**Kalauer** m - corny joke; (Wortspiel) corny pun.

**kalauern** vi (col) to joke; to pun.

**Kạlb** nt ̈er calf; (von Rehwild auch) fawn.

**kạlben** vi (Kuh) to calve.

**Kạlbfleisch** nt veal.

**Kạlbs-:** **~braten** m roast veal; **~hachse**, **~haxe** f (Cook) knuckle of veal; **~leber** f calves' liver; **~leder** nt calfskin; **~schnitzel** nt veal cutlet.

**Kaleidoskop** nt -e kaleidoscope.

**Kalẹnder** m - calendar; (Taschen~) diary.

**Kalẹnder-:** **~blatt** nt page of a/the calendar; **~jahr** nt calendar year; **~monat** m calendar month; **~spruch** m calendar motto.

**Kạli** nt -s potash.

**Kaliber** nt - (lit, fig) calibre (Brit), caliber (US).

**Kalifọrnien** [-iən] nt -s California.

**Kalifornier(in** *f)* *m* Californian.
**kalifornisch** *adj* Californian.
**Kalium** *nt no pl* potassium.
**Kalk** *m* **-e** lime; *(zum Tünchen)* whitewash; *(Anat)* calcium. **gebrannter/gelöschter** ~ quicklime/slaked lime; **bei ihm rieselt schon der** ~ *(col)* he's going a bit gaga *(col)*.
**kalken** *vt (tünchen)* to whitewash; *(Agr)* to lime.
**Kalk-:** ~**grube** *f* lime pit; **k**~**haltig** *adj Boden* chalky; *Wasser* hard; ~**mangel** *m (Med)* calcium deficiency; *(von Boden)* lime deficiency; ~**ofen** *m* lime kiln; ~**stein** *m* limestone.
**Kalkül** *m or nt* **-e** *(geh)* calculation *usu pl.*
**Kalkulation** *f* calculation; *(Kostenrechnung)* costing.
**kalkulieren**\* *vt* to calculate. **ein kalkuliertes Risiko eingehen** to take a calculated risk.
**Kalkutta** *nt* Calcutta.
**Kalorie** *f* calorie.
**Kalorien-** [-iən]: **k**~**arm** *adj* low-calorie; **k**~**bewußt** *adj* calorie-conscious; ~**bombe** *f (col)* mass of calories; ~**gehalt** *m* calorie content; **k**~**reich** *adj* high-calorie.
**kalt** *adj comp* ⸚**er,** *superl* ⸚**este(r, s)** *or (adv)* **am** ⸚**esten** cold. **mir ist/wird** ~ I am/I'm getting cold; **im K**~**en** in the cold; ~**e Platte** cold meal; **abends essen wir** ~ we have a cold meal in the evening; **etw** ~ **stellen** to put sth to chill; **die Wohnung kostet** ~ **480 DM** the flat costs 480 marks without heating; **jdm die** ~**e Schulter zeigen** to give sb the cold shoulder, to cold-shoulder sb; **da kann ich nur** ~ **lächeln** *(col)* that makes me laugh; **es überlief ihn** ~ cold shivers ran through him; **der** ~**e Krieg** the Cold War; **ein** ~**er Staatsstreich** a bloodless coup.
**Kalt-:** **k**~**herzig** *adj* cold-hearted; **k**~**bleiben** *vi sep irreg aux sein (fig)* to remain unmoved; ~**blüter** *m* - *(Zool)* cold-blooded animal; **k**~**blütig** *adj (Zool, fig)* cold-blooded; *(gelassen)* cool; ~**blütigkeit** *f siehe adj* cold-bloodedness; cool(ness).
**Kälte** *f no pl* coldness; *(Wetter)* cold; *(~periode)* cold spell. **5 Grad** ~ 5 degrees below freezing; **vor** ~ **zittern** to shiver with cold; **bei dieser** ~ in this cold.
**Kälte-:** **k**~**beständig** *adj* cold-resistant; ~**einbruch** *m* cold spell; **k**~**empfindlich** *adj* sensitive to cold; ~**grad** *m* degree of frost; ~**technik** *f* refrigeration technology; ~**welle** *f* cold spell.
**Kalt-:** **k**~**herzig** *adj* cold-hearted; **k**~**lächelnd** *adv (iro)* cool as you please; **k**~**lassen** *vt sep irreg (fig)* **jdn k**~**lassen** to leave sb cold; ~**luft** *f (Met)* cold air; **k**~**machen** *vt sep (col)* to do in *(col)*; ~**miete** *f* rent exclusive of heating; ~**schale** *f (Cook) cold sweet soup*; **k**~**schnäuzig** *adj (col) (gefühllos)* cold, callous; *(unverschämt)* insolent; **k**~**stellen** *vt sep (col)* jdn to put out of harm's way *(col)*.
**Kalzium** *nt no pl* calcium.
**kam** *pret of* **kommen.**
**Kambodscha** *nt* Cambodia.
**Kambodschaner(in** *f)* *m* Cambodian.
**kambodschanisch** *adj* Cambodian.
**Kamel** *nt* **-e (a)** camel. **(b)** *(col)* clot *(col)*. **ich** ~**!** silly me!
**Kamelhaar** *nt (Tex)* camel hair.
**Kamelie** [-iə] *f* camellia.
**Kameltreiber** *m* camel driver; *(pej: Orientale)* wog *(pej)*.
**Kamera** *f* **-s** camera.
**Kamerad(in** *f)* *m (wk)* **-en, -en** *(Mil etc)* comrade; *(Freund)* friend.
**Kameradschaft** *f* comradeship, camaraderie.
**kameradschaftlich** *adj* comradely.
**Kamera-:** ~**einstellung** *f* take; ~**frau** *f* camera-

woman; ~**führung** *f* camera work; ~**mann** *m, pl* ~**männer** cameraman; ~**team** *nt* film crew.
**Kamerun** *nt* the Cameroons *pl.*
**Kamille** *f* **-n** camomile.
**Kamillentee** *m* camomile tea.
**Kamin** *m* **-e** *(Schornstein)* chimney; *(Abzugsschacht)* flue; *(offene Feuerstelle)* fireplace. **wir saßen am** ~ we sat in front of the fire.
**Kamin-:** ~**feger** *m* - *(dial)* chimney sweep; ~**feuer** *nt* open fire; ~**kehrer** *m* - *(dial)* chimney sweep; ~**sims** *m or nt* mantelpiece.
**Kamm** *m* ⸚**e (a)** comb. **alle/alles über einen** ~ **scheren** *(fig)* to lump everyone/everything together. **(b)** *(von Vogel)* comb. **(c)** *(Cook)* neck. **(d)** *(Gebirgs~, Wellen~)* crest.
**kämmen 1** *vt* to comb. **2** *vr* to comb one's hair.
**Kammer** *f* **-n (a)** chamber; *(Parl auch)* house; *(Ärzte~, Anwalts~)* professional association; *(Herz~)* ventricle. **(b)** *(Zimmer)* small room.
**Kammer-:** ~**diener** *m* valet; ~**gericht** *nt* ≃ Supreme Court; ~**jäger** *m (Schädlingsbekämpfer)* pest controller; ~**konzert** *nt* chamber concert.
**Kämmerlein** *nt* chamber. **im stillen** ~ in private.
**Kammer-:** ~**musik** *f* chamber music; ~**orchester** *nt* chamber orchestra; ~**spiele** *pl* studio theatre *(Brit) or* theater *(US)*; ~**ton** *m* concert pitch; ~**zofe** *f* chambermaid.
**Kamm-:** ~**garn** *nt* worsted; ~**stück** *nt (Cook)* shoulder.
**Kampagne** [kam'panjə] *f* **-n** campaign.
**Kampf** *m* ⸚**e** fight, struggle *(um* for*)*; *(Gefecht)* battle; *(Box~)* fight, contest. **jdm/einer Sache den** ~ **ansagen** *(fig)* to declare war on sb/sth; **es kam zum** ~ fighting broke out; **auf in den** ~! *(hum)* once more unto the breach! *(hum)*; **er ist im** ~ **gefallen** he fell in action *or* battle; **der** ~ **ums Dasein** the struggle for existence; **der** ~ **um die Macht** the battle *or* struggle for power; **ein** ~ **auf Leben und Tod** a fight to the death; **innere** ~̃**e** inner conflicts.
**Kampf-:** ~**abstimmung** *f* vote; **es kam zur** ~**abstimmung** they put it to the vote; ~**ansage** *f* declaration of war; *(Sport)* announcement; ~**bahn** *f* sports stadium, arena; **k**~**bereit** *adj* ready for battle.
**kämpfen 1** *vi* to fight, to struggle *(um, für* for*)*. **gegen etw** ~ to fight (against) sth; **mit den Tränen** ~ to fight back one's tears; **ich habe lange mit mir** ~ **müssen, ehe ...** I had a long battle with myself before ... **2** *vt (usu fig) Kampf* to fight.
**Kampfer** *m no pl* camphor.
**Kämpfer(in** *f)* *m* - fighter.
**kämpferisch** *adj* aggressive.
**Kampf-:** **k**~**erprobt** *adj* battle-tried; **k**~**fähig** *adj (Mil)* fit for action; *Boxer* fit to fight; ~**flugzeug** *nt* fighter-bomber; ~**gas** *nt* poison gas; ~**geist** *m* fighting spirit; ~**handlung** *f usu pl* clash *usu pl*; ~**kraft** *f* fighting strength; **k**~**los** *adj* sich **k**~**los ergeben** to surrender without a fight; **k**~**lustig** *adj* belligerent, pugnacious; ~**maßnahme** *f* offensive measure; ~**maßnahmen ergreifen** to go onto the offensive; ~**platz** *m* battlefield; *(Sport)* arena, stadium; ~**richter** *m (Sport)* referee; ~**schrift** *f* broadsheet; ~**sport** *m* combat sport; ~**stärke** *f (Mil)* combat strength; ~**stoff** *m* nuclear, chemical or biological weapon; **k**~**unfähig** *adj (Mil)* unfit for battle; *(Sport)* unfit; **ein Schiff k**~**unfähig machen** to put a ship out of action.
**kampieren**\* *vi* to camp (out). **im Wohnzimmer** ~ *(col)* to doss down in the sitting room *(col)*.
**Kampuchea** *nt* Kampuchea.
**Kanada** *nt* Canada.

**Kanadier** [-iɐ] *m* - Canadian; *(Sport)* Canadian canoe.
**Kanadierin** [-iərɪn] *f* Canadian (woman/girl).
**kanadisch** *adj* Canadian.
**Kanake** *m* -n *(pej: Ausländer)* wop *(pej)*.
**Kanal** *m, pl* **Kanäle** **(a)** *(Schiffahrtsweg)* canal; *(Wasserlauf)* channel; *(zur Entwässerung)* drain; *(für Abwässer)* sewer. **der (Ärmel)~** the (English) Channel; **den ~ voll haben** *(col) (betrunken sein)* to be canned *(col)*; *(es satt haben)* to have had a bellyful *(col!)*. **(b)** *(Radio, TV, fig: Weg)* channel. **dunkle Kanäle** dubious channels.
**Kanal-:** **~arbeiter** *m* sewerage worker; **~deckel** *m* drain cover; **~fähre** *f* cross-channel ferry; **~inseln** *pl* Channel Islands.
**Kanalisation** *f (Abwasserkanäle)* sewerage system, sewers *pl*.
**kanalisieren\*** **1** *vt (fig) Energie etc* to channel. **2** *vti* to lay sewers (in).
**Kanaltunnel** *m* Channel Tunnel.
**Kanapee** *nt* -s *(old, hum)* sofa, settee.
**Kanarienvogel** [-iən-] *m* canary.
**Kanarische Inseln** *pl* Canaries *pl*, Canary Islands *pl*.
**Kandare** *f* -n (curb) bit. **jdn an die ~ nehmen** *(fig)* to take sb in hand.
**Kandidat(in** *f*) *m (wk)* **-en, -en** candidate; *(bei Bewerbung auch)* applicant. **jdn als ~en aufstellen** to nominate sb.
**Kandidatur** *f* candidature, candidacy.
**kandidieren\*** *vi (Pol)* to stand, to run *(für* for*)*.
**kandiert** *adj Frucht* candied.
**Kandis(zucker)** *m* rock candy.
**Känguruh** ['kɛŋguru] *nt* -s kangaroo.
**Kaninchen** *nt* rabbit.
**Kaninchen-:** **~bau** *m* rabbit warren; **~stall** *m* rabbit hutch.
**Kanister** *m* - can.
**Kännchen** *nt* pot; *(für Milch)* jug.
**Kanne** *f* -n can; *(Tee~, Kaffee~)* pot; *(Milch~)* churn; *(Gieß~)* watering can.
**kanneliert** *adj (Archit)* fluted.
**Kannibale** *m (wk)* **-n, -n, Kannibalin** *f* cannibal.
**kannibalisch** *adj* cannibalistic; *(brutal)* brutal.
**Kannibalismus** *m* cannibalism.
**kannte** *pret of* **kennen**.
**Kanon** *m* -s canon.
**Kanonade** *f (Mil)* barrage; *(fig auch)* tirade.
**Kanone** *f* -n **(a)** gun; *(Hist)* cannon; *(col: Pistole)* shooter *(col)*. **mit ~n auf Spatzen schießen** *(col)* to take a sledgehammer to crack a nut. **(b)** *(fig col: Könner)* ace *(col)*. **(c)** *(col)* **das ist unter aller ~** that defies description.
**Kanonen-:** **~boot** *nt* gunboat; **~donner** *m* rumbling of guns; **~futter** *nt (col)* cannon fodder; **~kugel** *f* cannon ball; **~rohr** *nt* gun barrel; **heiliges ~rohr!** *(col)* good grief *(col)*.
**Kantate** *f* -n *(Mus)* cantata.
**Kante** *f* -n *(Ecke)* edge; *(Rand, Borte)* border; *(Web~)* selvedge. **Geld auf die hohe ~ legen** *(col)* to put money by.
**kantig** *adj Holz* edged; *Gesicht* angular.
**Kantine** *f* canteen.
**Kanton** *m* -e canton.
**Kantor** *m* choirmaster.
**Kanu** *nt* -s canoe.
**Kanusport** *m* canoeing.
**Kanute** *m* -n canoeist.
**Kanzel** *f* -n **(a)** pulpit. **(b)** *(Aviat)* cockpit.
**Kanzlei** *f (Dienststelle)* office; *(Büro eines Notars etc)* chambers *pl*.

**Kanzler** *m* - chancellor.
**Kanzler-:** **~amt** *nt* chancellery; *(Posten auch)* chancellorship; **~kandidat** *m* candidate for the chancellorship.
**Kap** *nt* -s cape. **das ~ der guten Hoffnung** the Cape of Good Hope; **~ Hoorn** Cape Horn.
**Kap.** = **Kapitel** ch.
**Kapazität** *f* capacity; *(fig: Experte)* expert, authority.
**Kapelle** *f* **(a)** *(Kirche)* chapel. **(b)** *(Mus)* band, orchestra.
**Kapellmeister** *m* director of music; *(Mil, von Tanzkapelle etc)* bandmaster, bandleader.
**Kaper** *f* -n *(Bot, Cook)* caper.
**kapern** *vt (Naut)* to seize; *(fig col)* to grab.
**kapieren\*** *vti (col)* to get *(col)*, to understand. **kapiert?** got it? *(col)*; **er hat schnell kapiert** he caught on quick *(col)*.
**Kapital** *nt* -e *or* -ien [-iən] **(a)** *(Fin)* capital *no pl*; *(pl: angelegtes ~)* capital investments *pl*. **(b)** *(fig)* asset. **aus etw ~ schlagen** *(pej: lit, fig)* to make capital out of sth.
**Kapital-:** **~anlage** *f* capital investment; **~anlagegesellschaft** *f* investment fund; **~aufwand** *m* capital expenditure; **~einlage** *f* capital contribution; **~ertrag** *m* capital gains; **~ertragssteuer** *f* capital gains tax; **~flucht** *f* flight of capital; **~gesellschaft** *f (Comm)* joint-stock company; **k~intensiv** *adj* capital-intensive.
**Kapitalismus** *m* capitalism.
**Kapitalist** *m* capitalist.
**kapitalistisch** *adj* capitalist.
**Kapital-:** **k~kräftig** *adj* wealthy; **~markt** *m* money market; **~verbrechen** *nt* serious crime; *(mit Todesstrafe)* capital crime; **~vermögen** *nt* capital assets *pl*.
**Kapitän** *m* -e captain. **~ zur See** Captain.
**Kapitel** *nt* - **(a)** chapter; *(fig auch)* period; *(Angelegenheit)* chapter of events, story. **ein trauriges ~** a sad story; **das ist ein anderes ~** that's another story. **(b)** *(Eccl: Dom~)* chapter.
**Kapitulation** *f* surrender, capitulation *(auch fig)* *(vor +dat* to*)*.
**kapitulieren\*** *vi* to capitulate; *(Mil also)* to surrender. **ich kapituliere, das ist zu schwierig** I give up, it's too difficult.
**Kaplan** *m, pl* **Kapläne** *(in Pfarrei)* curate; *(mit besonderen Aufgaben)* chaplain.
**Kappe** *f* -n cap; *(von Flasche etc)* top. **das nehme ich auf meine ~** *(fig col)* I'll take the responsibility for that.
**kappen** *vt (Naut) Tau, Leine* to cut.
**Käppi** *nt* -s cap.
**Kapriole** *f* -n *(fig)* caper. **~n machen** to cut capers.
**kapriziös** *adj (geh)* capricious.
**Kapsel** *f* -n capsule; *(Etui)* container; *(an Flasche)* cap, top.
**Kapstadt** *nt* Cape Town.
**kaputt** *adj (col)* broken; *Maschine, Auto* broken down; *Maschine auch, Glühbirne etc* kaput *(col)*; *(erschöpft) Mensch, Nerven* shattered *(col)*; *Beziehungen, Gesundheit* ruined; *Firma* bust *pred (col)*. **irgend etwas muß an deinem Auto ~ sein** something must be wrong with your car; **der Fernseher ist ~** the TV's not working; **meine Hose ist ~** my trousers have had it *(col)*; **ein ~er Typ** *(col)* a wreck *(col)*.
**kaputt-:** **~fahren** *vt sep irreg (col) Auto* to drive into the ground; *(durch Unfall)* to smash up; **~gehen** *vi sep irreg aux sein (col)* to break; *(esp Maschine)* to break down; *(Ehe)* to break up *(an +dat* because

of); (Beziehungen, Nerven) to be ruined; (Firma) to go bust (col); (Kleidung) to come to pieces; (zerrissen werden) to tear; (Blumen) to die off; **er ist am Alkohol** ~**gegangen** alcohol was his downfall; ~**kriegen** vt sep (col) **das Auto ist nicht** ~**zukriegen** this car just goes on for ever; **wie hast du denn das** ~**gekriegt?** how did you manage to break it?; ~**lachen** vr sep (col) to die laughing (col); ~**machen** sep (col) **1** vt to ruin; Zerbrechliches to break; Brücke, Sandburg to knock down; (erschöpfen) jdn to wear out; **diese Arbeit macht mich** ~ this job will be the death of me (col); **2** vr (sich überanstrengen) to wear oneself out; ~**schlagen** vt sep irreg (col) to smash.

**Kapuze** f -n hood; (Mönchs~) cowl.

**Kapuziner(kresse** f) m - (Bot) nasturtium.

**Karabiner** m - (Gewehr) carbine.

**Karacho** nt no pl: **mit** ~ (col) hell for leather (col).

**Karaffe** f -n carafe; (mit Stöpsel) decanter.

**Karambolage** [karambo'la:ʒə] f -n (Aut) collision, crash; (Billard) cannon.

**Karamel** m no pl caramel no pl.

**Karamelbonbon** nt, **Karamelle** f caramel (toffee).

**Karat** nt -e or (bei Zahlenangabe) - carat.

**Karate** nt no pl karate.

**Karatehieb** m karate chop.

**Karawane** f -n caravan.

**Kardan-**: ~**gelenk** nt universal joint; ~**welle** f (Aut) prop(eller) shaft.

**Kardinal** m, pl **Kardinäle** (Eccl) cardinal.

**Kardinal-**: ~**fehler** m cardinal error; ~**tugend** f (Philos, Rel) cardinal virtue; ~**zahl** f cardinal (number).

**Kardio-**: ~**gramm** nt cardiogram; ~**logie** f cardiology; **k**~**logisch** adj cardiological.

**Karenz-**: ~**tag** m unpaid day of sick leave; ~**zeit** f waiting period.

**Karfiol** m no pl (Aus) cauliflower.

**Karfreitag** m Good Friday.

**karg** adj Vorrat, Gehalt meagre (Brit), meager (US). **etw** ~ **bemessen** to be mean with sth.

**Kargheit** f meagreness (Brit), meagerness (US).

**kärglich** adj meagre (Brit), meager (US); Mahl frugal.

**Kargo** m -s cargo.

**Karibik** f **die** ~ the Caribbean.

**karibisch** adj Caribbean. **das K**~**e Meer** the Caribbean Sea.

**kariert** adj Stoff, Muster checked, checkered (esp US); Papier squared.

**Karies** ['ka:ri̯ɛs] f no pl caries.

**Karikatur** f caricature.

**Karikaturist(in** f) m cartoonist.

**karikieren**\* vt to caricature.

**kariös** adj Zahn decayed.

**Karitas** f no pl charity.

**karitativ** adj charitable.

**Karl** m ≈ Charles. ~ **der Große** Charlemagne.

**karmin(rot)** adj carmine (red).

**Karneval** ['karnəval] m -e or -s carnival.

**Karnevalszug** m carnival procession.

**Karnickel** nt - (col) rabbit.

**Karo** nt -s (Quadrat) square; (auf der Spitze stehend) diamond, lozenge; (Muster) check; (diagonal) diamond; (Cards) (Farbe) diamonds pl; (Karte) diamond.

**Karomuster** nt checked or checkered (esp US) pattern.

**Karosse** f -n (Prachtkutsche) (state) coach.

**Karosserie** f (Aut) bodywork.

**Karosserie-**: ~**bauer** m coachbuilder; ~**schaden** m damage to the bodywork; ~**werkstatt** f body (repair) shop.

**Karotte** f -n carrot.

**Karpaten** pl Carpathians pl.

**Karpfen** m - carp.

**Karre** f -n **(a)** siehe **Karren**. **(b)** (col: Auto) (old) crate (col).

**Karree** nt -s square; (Häuserblock) block. **einmal ums** ~ **gehen** to walk around the block.

**Karren** m - **(a)** (Wagen) cart; (esp für Garten, Baustelle) (wheel)barrow; (für Gepäck etc) trolley (Brit), cart (US). **(b)** (fig col) **jdm an den** ~ **fahren** to take sb to task; **jdn vor seinen** ~ **spannen** to use sb; **den** ~ **in den Dreck fahren** to get things in a mess; **den** ~ **aus dem Dreck ziehen** to get things sorted out.

**karren** vt to cart.

**Karriere** f -n (Laufbahn) career. ~ **machen** to make a career for oneself.

**Karriere-**: ~**frau** f career woman; ~**macher** m careerist.

**Karsamstag** m Easter Saturday.

**Karst** m -e (Geog, Geol) karst, barren landscape.

**Karte** f -n **(a)** card. **jdm die** ~**n lesen** to tell sb's fortune from the cards; **mit offenen** ~**n spielen** (fig) to put one's cards on the table; **er spielt mit verdeckten** ~**n** (fig) he's playing his cards very close to his chest; **alle** ~**n in der Hand halten** (fig) to hold all the cards; **es ist unmöglich, ihm in die** ~**n zu sehen** (fig) it's impossible to know what he's up to; **alles auf eine** ~ **setzen** to put all one's eggs in one basket (prov); **schlechte/gute** ~**n haben** to have a bad/good hand; (fig) to be in a difficult/strong position. **(b)** (Fahr~, Eintritts~) ticket; (Einladungs~) invitation (card). **die** ~**n, bitte!** tickets, please! **(c)** (Land~) map; (See~) chart. **(d)** (Speise~) menu; (Wein~) wine list.

**Kartei** f card index.

**Kartei-**: ~**karte** f file or index card; ~**kasten** m file-card box; ~**leiche** f (col) non-active member; ~**schrank** m filing cabinet.

**Kartell** nt -e cartel.

**Kartell-**: ~**amt** nt monopolies commission; ~**gesetzgebung** f anti-trust legislation.

**Karten-**: ~**haus** nt **(a)** house of cards; **wie ein** ~**haus (in sich) zusammenfallen** to collapse like a house of cards; **(b)** (Naut) chart room; ~**kunststück** nt card trick; ~**legen** nt fortune-telling (using cards); ~**spiel** nt **(a)** card-playing; (ein Spiel) card game; **beim** ~**spiel** when playing cards; **(b)** (Karten) pack or deck (of cards); ~**telefon** nt card phone; ~**vorverkauf** m advance sale of tickets.

**Kartoffel** f -n potato. **rein in die** ~**n, raus aus den** ~**n** (col) first it's one thing, then it's another; **jdn/etw fallenlassen wie eine heiße** ~ (col) to drop sb/sth like a hot brick (col).

**Kartoffel-** in cpds potato; ~**brei** m mashed potatoes pl; ~**chips** pl potato crisps pl (Brit), potato chips pl (US); ~**käfer** m Colorado beetle; ~**puffer** m potato fritter; ~**püree** nt mashed potatoes pl; ~**salat** m potato salad; ~**schalen** pl potato peel(ings); ~**schäler** m potato peeler.

**Kartograph(in** f) m cartographer.

**Karton** [kar'tɔŋ, kar'tõ:] m -s **(a)** (Pappe) card, cardboard. **(b)** (Schachtel) cardboard box.

**kartoniert** adj Bücher hardback.

**Karussell** nt -s or -e merry-go-round, roundabout (Brit). ~ **fahren** to have a ride on the merry-go-round or (Brit) roundabout.

**Karwoche** f (Eccl) Holy Week.

**Karzinogen** *nt* **-e** carcinogen.
**karzinogen** *adj (Med)* carcinogenic.
**Karzinom** *nt* **-e** *(Med)* carcinoma.
**kaschieren\*** *vt* to conceal.
**Kaschmir¹** *nt (Geog)* Kashmir.
**Kaschmir²** *m* **-e** *(Tex)* cashmere.
**Käse** *m* **- (a)** cheese. **(b)** *(col: Unsinn)* rubbish, twaddle *(col)*.
**Käse-** *in cpds* cheese; **~blatt** *nt (col)* rag *(col)*; **~brot** *nt* bread and cheese; **~gebäck** *nt* cheese savouries *(Brit)* or savories *(US) pl*; **~glocke** *f* cheese cover; **~kuchen** *m* cheesecake; **~platte** *f* cheeseboard.
**Kaserne** *f* **-n** barracks *pl*.
**Kasernenhof** *m* barrack square.
**kasernieren\*** *vt Truppen* to quarter in barracks.
**Käse-:** **~torte** *f* cheesecake; **k~weiß** *adj (col)* white (as a sheet).
**käsig** *adj* **(a)** *(fig col) Gesicht, Haut* pasty, pale; *(vor Schreck)* white. **(b)** *(lit)* cheesy.
**Kasino** *nt* **-s (a)** *(Spielbank)* casino. **(b)** *(Offiziers~)* (officers') mess; *(Speiseraum)* dining room.
**Kaskade** *f* cascade.
**Kaskoversicherung** *f (Aut)* comprehensive insurance.
**Kasper** *m* **-** *(im Puppenspiel)* Punch; *(col)* clown *(col)*.
**Kasperl(e)-:** **~figur** *f* glove puppet; **~theater** *nt* Punch and Judy (show).
**Kaspisches Meer** *nt* Caspian Sea.
**Kassandraruf** *m* gloomy prediction.
**Kasse** *f* **-n (a)** cashdesk, cash point; *(in Supermarkt auch)* checkout; *(Zahlraum)* cashier's office; *(Theat etc)* box office. **an der ~** *(in Geschäft)* at the desk. **(b)** *(Geldkasten)* cashbox; *(in Läden)* cash register, till; *(bei Spielen)* kitty; *(in einer Spielbank)* bank. **die ~n klingeln** the money is really rolling in; **unsere ~ ist leer** the coffers are empty. **(c)** *(Bargeld)* cash. **bei ~ sein** *(col)* to be flush *(col)*; **knapp/gut/ schlecht bei ~ sein** *(col)* to be short of cash/well off/ badly off; **~ machen** to cash up; *(col: gut verdienen)* to make a bomb *(col)*; **die ~ führen** to be in charge of the money; **die ~ stimmt!** *(col)* the money's OK *(col)*; **zur ~ bitten** to ask for money; **jdn zur ~ bitten** to ask sb to pay up.
**Kasseler** *nt* **-** *lightly smoked pork loin.*
**Kassen-:** **~arzt** *m* ≃ National Health doctor *(Brit)*, panel doctor *(US)*; **~beleg** *m* sales receipt *or* check *(US)*; **~bericht** *m* financial report; **~bestand** *m* cash in hand; **~bon** *m* sales slip; **~buch** *nt* cashbook; **~erfolg, ~füller** *m (Theat etc)* box-office hit; **~magnet** *m (Theat etc)* big draw; **~patient** *m* ≃ National Health patient *(Brit)*; **~preis** *m* cash price; **~prüfung** *f* audit; **~schlager** *m (col) (Theat etc)* box-office hit; *(Ware)* big seller; **~stunden** *pl* hours of business; **~sturz** *m (Comm)* cashing-up; **~sturz machen** to check one's finances; *(Comm)* to cash up; **~wart** *m* **-e** treasurer; **~zettel** *m* sales slip.
**Kasserolle** *f* **-n** saucepan; *(mit Henkeln)* casserole.
**Kassette** *f* **(a)** cassette. **(b)** *(Kästchen)* case, box; *(Geschenk~)* gift set.
**Kassetten-:** **~deck** *nt* cassette deck; **~recorder** *m* cassette recorder.
**Kassiber** *m* **-** secret message.
**kassieren\*** **1** *vt* **(a)** *Gelder etc* to collect; *(col) Abfindung, Finderlohn* to pick up *(col)*; *Summe* to make. **(b)** *(col: wegnehmen)* to take away, to confiscate. **2** *vi* **bei jdm ~** to collect the money from sb; **darf ich ~, bitte?** would you like to pay now?; **bei diesem Geschäft hat er ganz schön kassiert** he

made a packet on the deal *(col)*.
**Kassierer(in** *f) m* **-** cashier; *(Bank~)* clerk; *(eines Klubs)* treasurer.
**Kastagnette** [kastan'jɛtə] *f* castanet.
**Kastanie** [-iə] *f* chestnut. **für jdn die ~n aus dem Feuer holen** *(fig)* to pull sb's chestnuts out of the fire.
**Kastanien-** [-iən]: **~baum** *m* chestnut tree; **k~braun** *adj* maroon; *Pferd, Haar* chestnut.
**Kästchen** *nt* **(a)** small box; *(für Schmuck)* case, casket. **(b)** *(auf kariertem Papier)* square.
**Kaste** *f* **-n** caste.
**Kasten** *m* ⸗ **(a)** box *(auch Sport)*; *(Kiste)* crate; *(Brief~)* postbox, letterbox; *(Brot~)* breadbin. **(b)** *(col) (Gebäude)* barn *(col)*; *(Auto)* crate *(col)*; *(Schiff)* tub *(col)*; *(Fernseher)* box *(Brit col)*, tube *(US col)*; *(Ftbl: Tor)* goal. **er hat was auf dem ~** *(col)* he's brainy *(col)*.
**Kasten-:** **~drachen** *m* box kite; **~form** *f (Cook)* (square) baking tin; **~wagen** *m (Aut)* van, panel truck *(US)*.
**Kastilien** [-iən] *nt* Castile.
**Kastrat** *m (wk)* **-en, -en** eunuch; *(Mus)* castrato.
**Kastration** *f* castration.
**kastrieren\*** *vt (lit, fig)* to castrate.
**Kasus** *m* **-, -** *(Gram)* case.
**Kat** *m* = **Katalysator.**
**Katakombe** *f* **-n** catacomb.
**Katalog** *m* **-e** catalogue.
**katalogisieren\*** *vt* to catalogue.
**Katalysator** *m (lit, fig)* catalyst; *(Aut)* catalytic converter.
**Katalysator-:** **~auto** *nt* car fitted with a catalytic converter; **~modell** *nt* model with a catalytic converter.
**Katamaran** *m* **-e** catamaran.
**Katapult** *nt or m* **-e** catapult.
**katapultieren\*** **1** *vr* to catapult. **2** *vr* to catapult oneself; *(Pilot)* to eject.
**Katapultsitz** *m* ejector seat.
**Katar** *nt* Qatar.
**Katarrh** *m* **-e** catarrh.
**Kataster** *m or nt* **-** land register.
**Kataster|amt** *nt* land registry.
**katastrophal** *adj* disastrous, catastrophic. **das sind ja ~e Zustände** it's a terrible state of affairs.
**Katastrophe** *f* **-n** disaster, catastrophe.
**Katastrophen-:** **~alarm** *m* emergency alert; **~dienst** *m* emergency service; **~einsatz** *m* im **~einsatz** on emergency duty; **~gebiet** *nt* disaster area; **~schutz** *m* emergency services; *(vorbeugend)* disaster prevention.
**Kate** *f* **-n** *(N Ger)* cottage.
**Katechismus** *m* catechism.
**Kategorie** *f* category. **er gehört zur ~ derer, die ...** he's one of those who ...
**kategorisch** *adj* categorical, absolute; *Ablehnung auch* flat.
**kategorisieren\*** *vt* to categorize.
**Kater** *m* **- (a)** tom(cat). **wie ein verliebter ~** like an amorous tomcat. **(b)** *(col: Katzenjammer)* hangover.
**Kater-:** **~frühstück** *nt breakfast (of pickled herring etc) to cure a hangover*; **~stimmung** *f* depression, the blues *pl (col)*.
**kath.** = **katholisch.**
**Katheder** *m or nt* **-** *(in Schule)* teacher's desk; *(in Universität)* lectern.
**Kathedrale** *f* **-n** cathedral.
**Katheter** *m* **-** *(Med)* catheter.
**Kathode** *f* **-n** *(Phys)* cathode.
**Kathoden-:** **~strahlen** *pl (Phys)* cathode rays *pl*;

~**strahlröhre** *f (TV etc)* cathode ray tube.
**Katholik(in** *f) m (wk)* **-en, -en** (Roman) Catholic.
**katholisch** *adj* (Roman) Catholic. **sie ist streng** ~ she's a strict Catholic.
**Katholizismus** *m* (Roman) Catholicism.
**Kattun** *m* **-e** *(old)* calico.
**katzbuckeln** *vi (pej col)* to bow and scrape.
**Kätzchen** *nt* **(a)** kitten. **(b)** *(Bot)* catkin.
**Katze** *f* **-n** cat. **sie ist eine falsche** ~ she's two-faced; **meine Arbeit war für die Katz** *(fig)* my work was a waste of time; **Katz und Maus mit jdm spielen** to play cat and mouse with sb; **die** ~ **aus dem Sack lassen** *(col)* to let the cat out of the bag; **die** ~ **im Sack kaufen** to buy a pig in a poke *(prov)*; **die** ~ **läßt das Mausen nicht** *(Prov)* the leopard cannot change its spots *(Prov)*; **bei Nacht sind alle** ~**n grau** everything looks the same in the dark.
**Katzen-:** ~**auge** *nt (Rückstrahler)* reflector; **k**~**haft** *adj* catlike, feline; ~**hai** *m* dogfish; ~**jammer** *m (col) (Kater)* hangover; *(jämmerliche Stimmung)* depression, the blues *pl (col)*; ~**musik** *f (fig)* caterwauling; ~**sprung** *m (col)* stone's throw; ~**streu** *f* cat litter; ~**tisch** *m (hum)* children's table; ~**wäsche** *f (hum col)* a lick and a promise *(col)*.
**Kauderwelsch** *nt no pl (pej)* gibberish, double Dutch *(Brit col)*.
**kauen** *vti* to chew; *Nägel* to bite. **an etw** *(dat)* ~ to chew (on) sth; **an den Nägeln** ~ to bite one's nails; **daran hatte ich lange zu** ~ *(fig)* it took me a long time to get over it.
**kauern** *vir (vi auch aux sein)* to crouch (down); *(ängstlich)* to cower.
**Kauf** *m, pl* **Käufe** purchase. **das war ein günstiger** ~ that was a good buy; **beim** ~ **eines Autos** when buying a car; **etw zum** ~ **anbieten** to offer sth for sale; **einen** ~ **tätigen** *(form)* to complete a purchase; **etw in** ~ **nehmen** *(fig)* to accept sth.
**kaufen** **1** *vt* **(a)** *(auch sich (dat)* ~**)** to buy, to purchase *(esp form)*. **ich habe (mir) einen neuen Anzug gekauft** I bought (myself) a new suit; **etw für teures Geld** ~ *(col)* to pay a lot (of money) for sth; **diese Zigaretten werden viel/nicht gekauft** a lot of people buy/nobody buys these cigarettes; **dafür kann ich mir nichts** ~ *(iro)* what use is that to me! **(b)** *(bestechen)* jdn ~ to bribe, to buy off; *Stimmen* to buy. **der Sieg war gekauft** it was fixed. **(c)** **sich** *(dat)* **jdn** ~ *(col)* to give sb a piece of one's mind *(col)*; *(tätlich)* to fix sb *(col)*. **2** *vi* to buy; *(Einkäufe machen)* to shop.
**Käufer(in** *f) m* **-** buyer, purchaser *(esp form)*; *(Kunde)* customer, shopper.
**Kauf-:** ~**frau** *f* businesswoman; ~**haus** *nt* department store; ~**kraft** *f* purchasing power; **k**~**kräftig** *adj Währung* with good purchasing power; *Kunde* with money to spend; ~**laden** *m (Spielzeug)* play shop.
**käuflich** *adj* **(a)** for sale. **Glück ist nicht** ~ happiness cannot be bought; **etw** ~ **erwerben** *(form)* to purchase sth. **(b)** *(fig)* venal. ~ **sein** *(Mensch)* to be open to bribery; **ich bin nicht** ~ you can't buy me!; ~**e Liebe** *(geh)* prostitution.
**Käuflichkeit** *f (fig)* corruptibility.
**Kauf-:** ~**lust** *f* desire to buy things; *(St Ex)* buying; **k**~**lustig** *adj* in a buying mood; **in den Straßen drängten sich die** ~**lustigen** the streets were thronged with shoppers.
**Kaufmann** *m, pl* **-leute** **(a)** businessman; *(Händler)* trader. **(b)** *(dated: Einzelhandels*~*)* small shopkeeper, grocer *(dated)*. **zum** ~ **gehen** to go to the grocer's *(Brit)* or grocer.
**kaufmännisch** *adj* commercial, business *attr*. ~**er**

**Angestellter** business employee; ~**e Lehre** commercial training; **er wollte einen** ~**en Beruf ergreifen** he wanted to make a career in business; **er übt einen** ~**en Beruf aus** he is in business; ~ **denken** to think in business terms; **sie ist** ~ **tätig** she is in business *or* is a businesswoman.
**Kauf-:** ~**preis** *m* purchase price; ~**rausch** *m* spending spree; **im** ~**rausch sein** to be on a spending spree; ~**vertrag** *m* bill of sale; ~**wert** *m* market value; ~**zwang** *m* obligation to buy; **kein/ohne** ~**zwang** no/without obligation.
**Kaugummi** *m* chewing gum.
**Kaukasier(in** *f)* [-iɐ, -iərın] *m* **-** Caucasian.
**kaukasisch** *adj* Caucasian.
**Kaukasus** *m* **der** ~ (the) Caucasus.
**Kaulquappe** *f* tadpole.
**kaum** **1** *adv* hardly, scarcely. ~ **jemand/jemals** hardly *or* scarcely anyone/ever; **wir hatten** ~ **noch Benzin** we had hardly any petrol left; **wohl** ~**/ich glaube** ~ I hardly think so; **das wird wohl** ~ **stimmen** surely that can't be right; **das wird** ~ **passieren** that's hardly likely to happen. **2** *conj* hardly, scarcely. ~ **hatte er das gesagt, da** ... hardly had he said that when ...
**Kaumuskel** *m* jaw muscle.
**kausal** *adj* causal.
**Kausalzusammenhang** *m* causal connection.
**Kautabak** *m* chewing tobacco.
**Kaution** *f* **(a)** *(Jur)* bail. **er stellte 1000 Mark** ~ he put up 1000 marks (as) bail; **gegen** ~ on bail; **jdn gegen** ~ **freibekommen** to bail sb out. **(b)** *(Comm)* security. **(c)** *(für Miete)* deposit.
**Kautschuk** *m* **-e** (india)rubber.
**Kauz** *m, pl* **Käuze** **(a)** screech owl. **(b)** *(Sonderling)* oddball *(col)*. **ein komischer** ~ an odd bird.
**Käuzchen** *nt dim of* **Kauz** **(a)**.
**kauzig** *adj* odd, cranky.
**Kavalier** [kava'liːɐ] *m* **-e** gentleman. **er ist immer** ~ he's always a gentleman.
**Kavaliersdelikt** *nt* trivial offence.
**Kavalkade** [kaval'kɑːdə] *f* cavalcade.
**Kavallerie** [kavalə'riː] *f (Mil)* cavalry.
**Kaviar** ['kɑːviar] *m* **-e** caviar.
**KB** [kaːˈbeː] *n* **-(s)** = **Kilobyte** K.
**Kcal** = **Kilokalorie**.
**keck** *adj (dated)* **(a)** *(frech)* cheeky, saucy. **(b)** *(flott)* pert, saucy. **(c)** *(kühn)* bold.
**Kefir** *m no pl* kefir, *milk product similar to* yoghurt.
**Kegel** *m* **- (a)** *(Spielfigur)* skittle; *(bei Bowling)* pin. **(b)** *(Geometrie)* cone; *(Berg*~*)* peak. **(c)** *(Licht*~*)* beam (of light).
**Kegel-:** ~**bahn** *f* (bowling) lane; *(Anlage)* skittle-alley; *(automatisch)* bowling alley; ~**bruder** *m (col)* member of a skittle/bowling club; **k**~**förmig** *adj* conical; ~**klub** *m* skittle club; *(für Bowling)* bowling club.
**kegeln** *vi* ~ **(gehen)** to play skittles; *(bei Bowling)* to go bowling.
**Kegelschwester** *f (col)* (female) member of a skittle/bowling club.
**Kegler(in** *f) m* **-** skittle-player; *(bei Bowling)* bowler.
**Kehle** *f* **-n** *(Gurgel)* throat. **er hat das in die falsche** ~ **bekommen** *(lit)* it went down the wrong way; *(fig)* he took it the wrong way; **eine trockene** ~ **haben** to be dry; **er hat Gold in der** ~ *(col)* his voice is/could be a real gold mine; **aus voller** ~ at the top of one's voice.
**kehlig** *adj Sprechweise* guttural; *Lachen etc* throaty.
**Kehlkopf** *m* larynx.
**Kehlkopf-:** ~**entzündung** *f* laryngitis; ~**krebs** *m* cancer of the throat.

**Kehllaut** *m* guttural (sound).

**Kehr-:** ~**aus** *m* -, *no pl* last dance; *(fig: Abschiedsfeier)* farewell celebration; ~**besen** *m* broom; ~**blech** *nt* shovel.

**Kehre** *f* -**n** (sharp) bend.

**kehren**[1] *vt* to turn. **in sich** *(acc)* **gekehrt** *(versunken)* pensive; *(verschlossen)* introspective, introverted.

**kehren**[2] *vti (fegen)* to sweep. **jeder kehre vor seiner Tür!** *(Prov)* everyone should first put his own house in order.

**Kehricht** *m or nt no pl (old, form)* sweepings *pl*.

**Kehr-:** ~**maschine** *f (Straßen~)* roadsweeper; *(Teppich~)* carpet-sweeper; ~**reim** *m* chorus, refrain; ~**schaufel** *f* shovel; ~**seite** *f (von Münze)* reverse; *(col: Rücken)* back; *(hum: Gesäß)* backside *(col)*; *(fig: Nachteil)* drawback; *(fig: Schattenseite)* other side; **die** ~**seite der Medaille** the other side of the coin.

**kehrt** *interj (Mil)* about turn!

**Kehrt-:** **k**~**machen** *vi sep* to do an about-turn; *(zurückgehen)* to turn back; ~**wendung** *f* about-turn.

**keifen** *vi* to bicker.

**Keil** *m* -**e** *(lit, fig)* wedge.

**Keile** *pl (col)* thrashing, hiding.

**Keiler** *m* - (male) wild boar.

**Keilerei** *f (col)* punch-up *(col)*.

**Keil-:** **k**~**förmig** *adj* wedge-shaped; ~**hosen** *pl* (tapering) slacks *pl*, ski pants *pl*; ~**riemen** *m (Aut)* V-belt.

**Keim** *m* -**e** shoot, sprout; *(Embryo, fig)* embryo; *(Krankheits~)* germ; *(fig: des Hasses etc)* seed *usu pl*. **etw im** ~ **ersticken** to nip sth in the bud; **den** ~ **zu etw legen** to sow the seeds of sth.

**keimen** *vi* to germinate; *(fig: Verdacht)* to be aroused.

**Keim-:** **k**~**frei** *adj* germ-free; *(Med auch, fig)* sterile; **k**~**frei machen** to sterilize; **k**~**tötend** *adj* germicidal; ~**zelle** *f* germ cell; *(fig)* nucleus.

**kein, keine, kein** *indef pron* (**a**) *(adjektivisch)* no. ~ **Mann/~e Häuser/~ Whisky** no man/houses/whisky; **ich sehe da** ~**en Unterschied** I see no difference, I don't see any difference; **da sind** ~**e Häuser** there are no houses there, there aren't any houses there; ~**e schlechte Idee** not a bad idea; **das ist** ~**e Antwort auf unsere Frage** that's not an answer to our question; ~ **bißchen** not a bit; **ich habe** ~ **bißchen Lust** I've absolutely no desire to; **ich bin doch** ~ **Kind mehr!** I am not a child any longer; **in** ~**ster Weise** *(col)* not in the least. (**b**) *(nicht einmal)* ~ **Stunde/drei Monate** less than an hour/three months.

**keine(r, s)** *indef pron (niemand)* nobody, no-one; *(von Gegenstand)* not one, none. **es war** ~**r da** there was nobody there, there wasn't anybody there; *(Gegenstand)* there wasn't one there; **es waren** ~ **da** *(Gegenstände)* there weren't any there, there were none there; **ich habe** ~**s** I haven't got one; ~**r von uns/von uns (beiden)** none/neither of us; *(betont)* not one of us; ~**s der (beiden) Kinder** neither of the children; ~**s der sechs Kinder** none of the six children; *(betont)* not one of the six children; **ist Bier da?** — **nein, ich habe** ~**s gekauft** is there any beer? — no, I didn't buy any.

**keinerlei** *adj attr inv* no ... whatever.

**keinesfalls** *adv* under no circumstances.

**keineswegs** *adv* not at all.

**keinmal** *adv* never once, not once.

**keins** = **keines** *siehe* **keine(r, s)**.

**Keks** *m* -**e** biscuit *(Brit)*, cookie *(US)*. **jdm auf den** ~ **gehen** *(col)* to get on sb's nerves.

**Kelch** *m* -**e** (**a**) goblet; *(liter)* cup. (**b**) *(Bot)* calyx.

**Kelle** *f* -**n** *(Suppen~ etc)* ladle; *(Schaumlöffel)* strainer; *(Maurer~)* trowel; *(Signalstab)* signalling disc.

**Keller** *m* - cellar; *(Geschoß)* basement.

**Keller|assel** *f* woodlouse.

**Kellerei** *f* wine cellars *pl*; *(Firma)* wine producer.

**Keller-:** ~**geschoß** *nt* basement; ~**gewölbe** *nt (Keller)* cellars *pl*; ~**lokal** *nt* cellar bar; ~**wohnung** *f* basement flat *(Brit) or* apartment.

**Kellner** *m* - waiter.

**Kellnerin** *f* waitress.

**kellnern** *vi (col)* to work as a waiter/waitress.

**Kelte** *m (wk)* -**n**, -**n**, **Keltin** *f* Celt.

**Kelter** *f* -**n** winepress; *(Obst~)* press.

**keltern** *vt Trauben, Wein* to press.

**keltisch** *adj* Celtic.

**Kenia** *nt* Kenya.

**Kenianer(in** *f)* *m* - Kenyan.

**kenianisch** *adj* Kenyan.

**kennen** *pret* **kannte,** *ptp* **gekannt** *vt* to know; *(geh: er~)* to recognize. **er kennt keine Müdigkeit** he doesn't know what tiredness is; **kein Erbarmen/Mitleid** *etc* ~ to know no mercy/pity *etc*; **so was** ~ **wir hier nicht!** we don't have that sort of thing here; **das** ~ **wir gar nicht anders** it's always been like that; **jdn als etw** ~ to know sb to be sth; ~ **Sie sich schon?** do you know each other (already)?; ~ **Sie den (schon)?** *(Witz)* have you heard this one?; **kennst du mich noch?** do you remember me?; **wie ich ihn kenne** ... if I know him (at all) ...; **da kennst du mich aber schlecht** you don't know me.

**kennenlernen** *vt sep* to get to know; *(zum ersten Mal treffen)* to meet. **sich** ~ to get to know each other; to meet each other; **ich freue mich, Sie kennenzulernen** *(form)* (I am) pleased to meet you *or* to make your acquaintance *(form)*; **der wird mich noch** ~ *(col)* he'll have me to reckon with *(col)*; **bei näherem K**~ **erwies er sich als** ... on closer acquaintance he proved to be ...

**Kenner(in** *f)* *m* - expert *(von or gen on)*, authority *(von or gen on)*; *(Wein~ etc)* connoisseur.

**Kennerblick** *m* expert's eye.

**kennerhaft** *adj* **mit** ~**em Blick/Griff** with an expert eye/touch.

**Kennermiene** *f* connoisseur's expression. **mit** ~ **betrachtete er** ... he looked at ... like a connoisseur.

**kenntlich** *adj (zu erkennen)* recognizable *(an +dat* by)*; *(deutlich)* clear. **etw** ~ **machen** to identify sth (clearly).

**Kenntnis** *f* (**a**) *(Wissen)* knowledge *no pl*. **über** ~**se von etw verfügen** to have a knowledge of sth; **gute** ~**se in Mathematik haben** to have a good knowledge of mathematics. (**b**) *no pl (form)* **etw zur** ~ **nehmen** to take note of sth; **jdn von etw in** ~ **setzen** to inform *or* advise *(Comm, form)* sb about sth.

**Kenntnis-:** ~**nahme** *f no pl (form)* **zur** ~**nahme an** ... for the attention of ...; ~**stand** *m no pl* **nach dem neuesten** ~ according to the latest information.

**Kenn-:** ~**wort** *nt, pl* ~**wörter** *(Chiffre)* code name; *(Losungswort)* password, code word; ~**zeichen** *nt* (**a**) *(Aut)* **(amtliches/polizeiliches)** ~**zeichen** registration number *(Brit)*, license number *(US)*; (**b**) *(Markierung, Erkennungszeichen)* mark, sign; *(Eigenart)* characteristic *(für, gen* of)*; *(für Qualität)* hallmark; **unveränderliche** ~**zeichen** distinguishing marks; **k**~**zeichnen** *vt insep* (**a**) to mark; *(durch Etikett auch)* to label; (**b**) *(charakterisieren)* to characterize; **jdn als etw k**~**zeichnen** to show sb to be sth; **k**~**zeichnend** *adj* typical, characteristic *(für* of)*; ~**ziffer** *f* (code) number; *(Comm)* reference number.

**kentern** vi aux sein (Schiff) to capsize.
**Keramik** f (a) no pl (Art) ceramics pl; (Gebrauchsgegenstände auch) pottery. (b) (Kunstgegenstand) ceramic.
**keramisch** adj ceramic.
**Kerbe** f -n notch. **in die gleiche ~ hauen** or **schlagen** (fig col) to take the same line.
**Kerbholz** nt: **etwas auf dem ~ haben** (col) to have done something bad.
**Kerker** m (Hist, geh) dungeon; (Strafe) imprisonment.
**Kerl** m -e or -s (col) fellow (col), guy (col); (pej) character. **du gemeiner ~!** you swine (col); **ein ganzer ~** a real man; **sie ist ein netter ~** she's a nice girl.
**Kern** m -e (von Obst) pip, seed; (von Steinobst) stone; (Nuß~) kernel; (Phys, Biol) nucleus; (von Reaktor) core; (fig) crux, core; (von Stadt) centre (Brit), center (US). **der harte ~** (fig) the hard core.
**Kern-** in cpds (Nuklear-) nuclear; ~**arbeitszeit** f core time; ~**energie** f nuclear energy; ~**fach** nt (Sch) core subject; ~**forschung** f nuclear research; ~**frage** f central question; ~**fusion** f nuclear fusion; ~**gedanke** m central idea; ~**gehäuse** nt core; **k~gesund** adj as fit as a fiddle.
**kernig** adj (fig) Ausspruch pithy; (urwüchsig) earthy; (kraftvoll) robust, powerful.
**Kernkraft** f no pl nuclear power.
**Kernkraft-**: in cpds nuclear power; ~**werk** nt nuclear power station.
**Kern-**: ~**land** nt heartland; **k~los** adj seedless, pipless; ~**obst** nt fruit with core and pips such as apples; ~**physik** f nuclear physics; ~**problem** nt central problem; ~**punkt** m central point, crux; ~**reaktor** m nuclear reactor; ~**satz** m key sentence, key phrase; ~**schmelze** f meltdown; ~**seife** f washing soap; ~**spaltung** f nuclear fission; **die erste ~spaltung** the first splitting of the atom; ~**stück** nt (fig) main item; (von Theorie etc) central part, core; **k~technisch** adj **k~technische Anlage** nuclear plant; ~**waffe** f nuclear weapon; **k~waffenfrei** adj nuclear-free; ~**zeit** f core time.
**Kerze** f -n (Wachs~) candle; (Aut) (spark) plug; (Turnen) shoulder-stand.
**Kerzen-**: ~**beleuchtung** f candlelight; **k~gerade** adj (as) straight as a die; ~**halter**, ~**leuchter** m candlestick; ~**licht** nt no pl, ~**schein** m candlelight; ~**schlüssel** m (spark) plug spanner.
**Kescher** m - fishing-net.
**keß** adj saucy.
**Kessel** m - (a) (Tee~) kettle; (für offenes Feuer) cauldron; (esp in Brauerei) vat; (Dampf~) boiler; (Behälter für Flüssigkeiten etc) tank. (b) (Mulde) basin.
**Kessel-**: ~**haus** nt boiler house; ~**pauke** f kettledrum; ~**stein** m scale, fur; ~**treiben** nt (fig) witchhunt.
**Ketchup** ['kɛtʃap] m or nt -s ketchup.
**Kette** f -n (lit, fig) chain; (an Kettenfahrzeug) chain track; (von Truppen, Fahrzeugen) line; (Tex) warp. **eine ~ aus Perlen** etc a string of pearls etc; **einen Hund an die ~ legen** to chain up a dog; **seine ~n sprengen** (fig) to throw off one's chains.
**ketten** vt to chain (an +acc to). **jdn an sich ~** (fig) to bind sb to oneself.
**Ketten-**: ~**antrieb** m chain drive; ~**fahrzeug** nt tracked vehicle; ~**glied** nt (chain-)link; ~**hund** m guard-dog; ~**karussell** nt merry-go-round (with gondolas suspended on chains); ~**rad** nt sprocket(wheel); ~**raucher** m chain-smoker; ~**reaktion** f chain reaction; ~**säge** f chainsaw; ~**schaltung** f dérailleur gear; ~**schutz** m chain guard; ~**stich**

m (Sew) chain stitch.
**Ketzer(in** f) m - (Eccl, fig) heretic.
**Ketzerei** f heresy.
**ketzerisch** adj heretical.
**keuchen** vi to pant, to puff; (Asthmatiker etc) to wheeze.
**Keuchhusten** m whooping cough.
**Keule** f -n club; (Sport) (Indian) club; (Cook) leg.
**Keulen-**: ~**hieb**, ~**schlag** m blow with a club; **es traf ihn wie ein ~schlag** (fig) it hit him like a thunderbolt.
**keusch** adj (lit, fig) chaste.
**Keuschheit** f chastity.
**kfm** = **kaufmännisch**.
**Kfz** [kaɛf'tsɛt] nt -(s) (form) = **Kraftfahrzeug** motor vehicle.
**kg** = **Kilogramm** kg.
**KG** [ka'geː] f -s = **Kommanditgesellschaft** limited partnership.
**khaki** adj pred khaki.
**KHz** = **Kilohertz** kHz.
**Kibbuz** m, pl **Kibbuzim** or -e kibbutz.
**Kicher|erbse** f chickpea.
**kichern** vi to giggle.
**kicken** (Ftbl) **1** vt to kick. **2** vi to play football; (den Ball ~) to kick.
**Kicker** m - (Ftbl sl) player.
**kidnappen** ['kɪtnɛpn] vt insep to kidnap.
**Kidnapper(in** f) ['kɪtnɛpɐ, -ərɪn] m - kidnapper.
**Kidnapping** ['kɪtnɛpɪŋ] nt -s kidnapping.
**Kiebitz** m -e (Orn) lapwing.
**Kiefer¹** f -n pine (tree); (Holz) pine(wood).
**Kiefer²** m - jaw; (~knochen) jawbone.
**Kiefern-**: ~**holz** nt pine(wood); ~**nadel** f pine needle; ~**zapfen** m pinecone.
**Kieferorthopäde** m orthodontist.
**Kieker** m **jdn auf dem ~ haben** (col) to have it in for sb (col).
**Kiel** m -e (Schiffs~) keel; (Feder~) quill. **ein Schiff auf ~ legen** to lay down a ship.
**Kielwasser** nt wake, wash. **in jds ~ segeln** (fig) to follow in sb's wake.
**Kieme** f -n gill.
**Kies** m -e gravel; (am Strand) shingle.
**Kiesel** m -, **Kieselstein** m pebble.
**Kies-**: ~**grube** f gravel pit; ~**weg** m gravel path.
**Kiew** ['kiːɛf] nt Kiev.
**kiffen** vi (col) to smoke pot (col) or grass (col).
**kikeriki** interj cock-a-doodle-do.
**Killer(in** f) m - (col) killer, murderer; (gedungener) hit man (col).
**Kilo** nt -(s) kilo.
**Kilo-** in cpds kilo-; ~**byte** [-'baɪt] nt (Comp) kilobyte; ~**gramm** nt kilogram(me); ~**hertz** nt kilohertz.
**Kilometer** m kilometre (Brit), kilometer (US). **80 ~ fahren** (col) to be doing 50 (mph).
**Kilometer-**: ~**fresser** m (col) long-haul driver; ~**geld** nt mileage allowance; **k~lang 1** adj miles long; **ein k~langer Stau** a hold-up several miles/ kilometres long; **2** adv for miles (and miles), for miles on end; ~**pauschale** f mileage allowance (against tax); ~**stand** m ≈ mileage; ~**stein** m ≈ milestone; **k~weit 1** adj miles long; **2** adv for miles (and miles); ~**zähler** m ≈ mileometer (Brit), odometer (US).
**Kilo-**: ~**watt** nt kilowatt; ~**wattstunde** f kilowatt hour.
**Kimme** f -n (von Gewehr) back sight.
**Kimono** m -s kimono.
**Kind** nt -er child, kid (col); (Kleinkind) baby; (esp Psych, Med) infant. **ein ~ erwarten/bekommen** to be

expecting a baby/to have a baby *or* child; **von ~ auf** from childhood; **ein ~ seiner Zeit sein** to be a child of one's time; **sich freuen wie ein ~** to be as pleased as Punch; **das weiß doch jedes ~!** any five-year-old would tell you that!; **das ist nichts für kleine ~er** *(fig col)* that's not for your ears/eyes; **mit ~ und Kegel** *(hum col)* with the whole family; **das ~ mit dem Bade ausschütten** to throw out the baby with the bathwater *(prov)*; **~er, ~er!** good heavens!
**Kindbett** *nt* **im ~** in confinement.
**Kinder-:** **~arbeit** *f* child labour *(Brit)* or labor *(US)*; **~arzt** *m* paediatrician *(Brit)*, pediatrician *(US)*; **~bekleidung** *f* children's wear; **~besteck** *nt* child's cutlery; **~bett** *nt* child's bed; **~buch** *nt* children's book; **~chor** *m* children's choir.
**Kinderei** *f* childishness *no pl.*
**Kinder-:** **~erziehung** *f* bringing up of children; *(durch Schule)* education of children; **~fahrkarte** *f* child's ticket; **k~feindlich** *adj* hostile to children, anti-children; *Architektur, Planung* not catering for children; **~feindlichkeit** *f* anti-children attitude; *(von Architektur)* failure to cater for children; **~freibetrag** *m* child allowance; **k~freundlich 1** *adj Mensch* fond of children; *Gesellschaft* child-orientated; *Möbel, Architektur etc* child-friendly; **2** *adv* with children in mind; **~funk** *m* children's radio; **~garten** *m* kindergarten; **~gärtner(in** *f***)** *m* kindergarten teacher; **~geld** *nt* child allowance *or* benefit; **~gesicht** *nt* baby face; **~heim** *nt* children's home; **~hort** *m* day nursery *(Brit)*, daycare center *(US)*; **~kleidung** *f* children's clothes *pl*; **~klinik** *f* children's clinic; **~krankenhaus** *nt* children's hospital; **~krankheit** *f* children's disease; *(fig)* teething troubles *pl*; **~kriegen** *nt no pl* having children; **~krippe** *f* crèche; **~laden** *m* (alternative) playgroup; **~lähmung** *f* poliomyelitis, polio; **k~leicht** *adj* childishly simple, dead easy *(col)*; **es ist k~leicht** it's child's play; **k~lieb** *adj* fond of children; **~lied** *nt* nursery rhyme; **k~los** *adj* childless; **~losigkeit** *f* childlessness; **~mädchen** *nt* nanny; **~mund** *m (fig)* children's talk; **~narr** *m* **er ist ein ~narr** he adores children; **~pflegerin** *f* child minder; **k~reich** *adj* with many children; *Familie* large; **~reichtum** *m* an abundance of children; **~reim** *m* nursery rhyme; **~sachen** *pl (Kleidung)* children's clothes *pl*; *(Spielsachen)* toys *pl*; **~schreck** *m* bog(e)yman; **~schuh** *m* child's shoe; **etw steckt noch in den ~schuhen** *(fig)* sth is still in its infancy; **den ~schuhen entwachsen sein** *(fig) (Mensch)* to have grown up; *(Technik etc)* to be no longer in its infancy; **~schutz** *m* protection of children; **~schutzbund** *m* child protection league; **~schwester** *f* children's nurse; **k~sicher** *adj* childproof; **~sitz** *m* child's seat; **~spiel** *nt* children's game; *(fig)* child's play *no art*; **~spielplatz** *m* children's playground; **~spielzeug** *nt* (children's) toys *pl*; **~sprache** *f* children's language; *(verniedlichend von Erwachsenen)* baby talk *no art*; **~sterblichkeit** *f* infant mortality; **~stube** *f (fig)* upbringing; **~stuhl** *m* child's chair; *(Hochstuhl)* high chair; **~tagesstätte** *f* day nursery *(Brit)*, daycare center *(US)*; **~teller** *m (in Restaurant)* children's dish; **~wagen** *m* pram *(Brit)*, baby carriage *(US)*; *(Sportwagen)* pushchair *(Brit)*, stroller *(US)*; **~zimmer** *nt* child's/children's room; *(esp für Kleinkinder)* nursery; **~zulage** *f*, **~zuschlag** *m* child allowance.
**Kindes-:** **~alter** *nt* childhood; **seit frühestem ~alter** from infancy; **~annahme** *f* adoption; **~beine** *pl*: **von ~beinen an** from childhood; **~entführung** *f*

kidnapping (of a child/children); **~mißhandlung** *f* child abuse.
**kindgemäß** *adj* suitable for a child/children.
**Kindheit** *f* childhood; *(früheste ~heit)* infancy.
**Kindheits-:** **~erinnerung** *f* childhood memory; **~traum** *m* childhood dream.
**kindisch** *adj (pej)* childish. **sich ~ über etw** *(acc)* **freuen** to be as pleased as Punch about sth.
**kindlich 1** *adj* childlike; *(pej)* childish. **2** *adv* like a child.
**Kinds-** *in cpds siehe* **Kindes-**; **~kopf** *m (col)* big kid *(col)*.
**Kinkerlitzchen** *pl (col)* knicknacks *pl (col)*; *(dumme Streiche)* tomfoolery *sing (col)*.
**Kinn** *nt* **-e** chin.
**Kinn-:** **~haken** *m* hook to the chin; **~lade** *f* jaw(bone); **~riemen** *m* chinstrap.
**Kino** *nt* **-s** cinema *(Brit)*, movie theater *(US)*. **ins ~ gehen** to go to the cinema *or* pictures *(Brit)* or movies *(esp US)*; **das ~ der zwanziger Jahre** the cinema *(Brit)* or movies *(esp US)* of the twenties.
**Kino-** *in cpds* cinema *(Brit)*, movie *(esp US)*; **~besucher**, **~gänger** *m* cinemagoer *(Brit)*, moviegoer *(US)*; **~karte** *f* cinema *(Brit)* or movie theater *(US)* ticket; **~kasse** *f* cinema *(Brit)* or movie theater *(US)* box office; **~programm** *nt* film programme; *(Übersicht)* film guide.
**Kintopp** *m or nt (dated)* cinema *(Brit)*, movie theater *(US)*.
**Kiosk** *m* **-e** kiosk.
**Kippe** *f* **-n** **(a)** **auf der ~ stehen** *(Gegenstand)* to be balanced precariously; **sie steht auf der ~** *(fig)* it's touch and go with her. **(b)** *(col: Zigarettenstummel)* cigarette stub, fag end *(Brit col)*. **(c)** *(Müll~, Min)* tip.
**kippen 1** *vt* **(a)** *Behälter, Fenster* to tilt; *Ladefläche, Tisch* to tip *or* tilt (up). **„bitte nicht ~"** "please do not tilt". **(b)** *(schütten)* to tip. **2** *vi aux sein* to tip over, to topple over. **aus den Latschen ~** *(fig col)* *(überrascht sein)* to fall through the floor *(col)*; *(ohnmächtig werden)* to pass out.
**Kipper** *m* **-** *(Aut)* tipper, dump(er) truck.
**Kipp-:** **~fenster** *nt* tilt window; **~lore** *f* tipper wagon; **~schalter** *m* toggle switch.
**Kirche** *f* **-n** church. **in die** *or* **zur ~ gehen** to go to church; **die ~ im Dorf lassen** not to get carried away.
**Kirchen-** *in cpds* church; **~austritt** *m* leaving the Church *no art*; **~bank** *f* pew; **~besuch** *m* church attendance; **~buch** *nt* parish register; **~chor** *m* church choir; **k~feindlich** *adj* anticlerical; **~fest** *nt* religious *or* church festival; **~gemeinde** *f* parish; **~jahr** *nt* church *or* ecclesiastical year; **~licht** *nt*: **kein (großes) ~licht sein** *(fig col)* to be not very bright; **~lied** *nt* hymn; **~maus** *f*: **arm wie eine ~maus** poor as a church mouse; **~recht** *nt* canon law; **k~rechtlich** *adj* canonical; **~schiff** *nt (Längsschiff)* nave; *(Querschiff)* transept; **~steuer** *f* church tax; **~tag** *m* church congress.
**Kirch-:** **~gang** *m* going to church *no art*; **~gänger(in** *f***)** *m* **-** churchgoer; **~hof** *m* churchyard; *(Friedhof)* graveyard.
**kirchlich** *adj* church *attr*; *Zustimmung, Mißbilligung* by the church; *Gebot, Gericht* ecclesiastical. **sich ~ trauen lassen** to have a church wedding; **~ bestattet werden** to have a religious funeral.
**Kirch-:** **~turm** *m* church tower; *(mit Turmspitze)* church steeple; **~turmspitze** *f* church spire; **~weih** *f* **-en** fair, kermis *(US)*.
**Kirmes** *f* **-sen** *(dial)* fair, kermis *(US)*.
**Kirsch** *m* **-** kirsch.

**Kirsch-** *in cpds* cherry; **~baum** *m* cherry tree; *(Holz)* cherry (wood); **~blüte** *f* cherry blossom.

**Kirsche** *f* **-n** cherry. **mit ihm ist nicht gut ~n essen** *(col)* it's best not to tangle with him.

**Kirsch-:** **~kern** *m* cherry stone; **~likör** *m* cherry brandy; **k~rot** *adj* cherry red; **~torte** *f*: Schwarzwälder **~torte** Black Forest gateau; **~wasser** *nt* kirsch.

**Kissen** *nt* - cushion; *(Kopf~)* pillow; *(Stempel~, an Heftpflaster)* pad.

**Kissen-:** **~bezug** *m* cushion cover; *(Kopf~)* pillow case; **~schlacht** *f* pillow fight.

**Kiste** *f* **-n** **(a)** box; *(für Wein etc)* case; *(Latten~)* crate; *(Truhe)* chest; *(col: Auto)* crate *(col)*; *(col: Fernsehen)* box *(Brit col)*, tube *(US col)*. **in die ~ gehen** *(col: Bett)* to hit the hay *(col)*. **(b)** *(col: Angelegenheit)* affair.

**kistenweise** *adv* by the box/case *etc*.

**Kita** *f* = **Kindertagesstätte**.

**Kitsch** *m no pl* kitsch.

**kitschig** *adj* kitschy.

**Kitt** *m* **-e** *(Fenster~)* putty; *(für Porzellan, Stein etc)* cement; *(fig)* bond.

**Kittchen** *nt (col)* clink *(col)*.

**Kittel** *m* - *(Arbeits~)* overall; *(von Arzt, Laborant etc)* (white) coat; *(blusenartig)* smock.

**kitten** *vt* to cement; *Fenster* to putty; *(füllen)* to fill; *(fig)* to patch up.

**Kitz** *nt* **-e** kid; *(Reh~)* fawn.

**Kitzel** *m* - tickle; *(fig)* thrill.

**kitz(e)lig** *adj (lit, fig)* ticklish.

**kitzeln** *vti (lit, fig)* to tickle.

**Kiwi¹** *f* **-s** kiwi (fruit).

**Kiwi²** *m* **-s** *(Orn)* kiwi.

**KKW** [ka:ka:'ve:] *nt* **-s** = **Kernkraftwerk**.

**Klacks** *m* **-e** *(col) (von Kartoffelbrei, Sahne etc)* dollop *(col)*; *(von Senf, Farbe etc)* blob *(col)*. **das ist ein ~** that's nothing *(col)*.

**klacksen** *(col) vt Sahne etc* to dollop *(col)*; *Farbe* to splash.

**Kladde** *f* **-n** *(Sch)* rough book; *(Notizbuch)* notebook; *(Block)* scribbling pad.

**klaffen** *vi* to gape. **da klafft eine Wunde** there is a gaping wound; **zwischen uns beiden klafft ein Abgrund** *(fig)* we are poles apart.

**kläffen** *vi (pej, fig)* to yap.

**klaffend** *adj* gaping; *(fig)* irreconcilable; *Widerspruch* blatant.

**Kläffer** *m* - *(lit, fig: pej)* yapper.

**Klage** *f* **-n** **(a)** *(Beschwerde)* complaint. **(bei jdm) über jdn/etw ~ führen** to lodge a complaint (with sb) about sb/sth; **~n (über jdn/etw) vorbringen** to make complaints (about sb/sth); **Grund zur ~** reason for complaint. **(b)** *(in Trauer)* lament(ation) *(um, über +acc for)*; *(~laut)* plaintive cry. **(c)** *(Jur)* action, suit; *(Scheidungs~ auch)* petition; *(~schrift)* charge. **eine ~ gegen jdn einreichen/erheben** to institute proceedings against sb.

**Klage-:** **~erhebung** *f (Jur)* institution of proceedings; **~frist** *f (Jur)* period for instituting proceedings; **~laut** *m* plaintive cry; **~lied** *nt* lament; **ein ~lied über jdn/etw anstimmen** *(fig)* to complain about sb/sth; **~mauer** *f* **die ~mauer** The Wailing Wall.

**klagen** **1** *vi* **(a)** *(jammern)* to moan, to wail; *(Tiere)* to cry; *(Trauer äußern)* to lament *(um jdn/etw sb/ sth)*. **(b)** *(sich beklagen)* to complain *(über +acc about)*. **ohne zu ~** without complaining; **ich kann nicht ~** *(col)* I can't complain, (I) mustn't grumble *(col)*. **(c)** *(Jur)* to sue *(auf +acc for)*. **2** *vt* **jdm sein Leid/seine Not ~** to pour out one's sorrow/distress

to sb.

**klagend** *adj* lamenting; *Blick, Ton* plaintive; *Gesicht* sorrowful; *(jammernd)* complaining.

**Kläger(in** *f)* *m* - *(Jur) (im Zivilrecht)* plaintiff; *(in Scheidung)* petitioner; *(im Strafrecht auch)* prosecuting party.

**Klage-:** **~ruf** *m* plaintive cry; **~schrift** *f (Jur)* charge; *(bei Scheidung)* petition; **~weg** *m (Jur)* **auf dem ~weg(e)** by legal action; **den ~weg beschreiten** to take legal action.

**kläglich** **1** *adj* pitiful; *Rest* miserable; *Niederlage, Verhalten* despicable; *(pej: dürftig)* pathetic. **2** *adv (in beschämender Weise)* miserably.

**klaglos** *adv* uncomplainingly.

**Klamauk** *m no pl (col) (Albernei)* tomfoolery; *(Theater)* slapstick. **~ machen** to fool about.

**klamm** *adj (steif vor Kälte)* numb; *(naß und kalt)* clammy.

**Klamm** *f* **-en** gorge.

**Klammer** *f* **-n** **(a)** *(Wäsche~)* peg *(Brit)*, pin *(US)*; *(Hosen~, Med)* clip; *(Büro~)* paperclip; *(Heft~)* staple; *(Haar~)* (hair)grip *(Brit)*, barrette *(US)*; *(für Zähne)* brace; *(Bau~)* clamp. **(b)** *(in Text)* bracket. **~ auf/zu** open/close brackets; **in ~n** in brackets.

**klammern** **1** *vt (an +acc to) Papier etc* to staple; *(Tech)* to clamp; *(Med) Wunde* to clip; *Zähne* to brace. **2** *vr* **sich an jdn/etw ~** *(lit, fig)* to cling to sb/sth. **3** *vi (Sport)* to clinch.

**klammheimlich** *(col)* **1** *adj* secret. **2** *adv* on the quiet. **~ aus dem Haus gehen** to sneak out of the house.

**Klamotte** *f* **-n** **(a)** **~n** *pl (col) (Kleidung)* clothes *pl*, togs *pl (col); (Zeug)* clobber *(Brit col)*, stuff *no pl*. **(b)** *(pej: Film etc)* rubbishy old film *etc*. **das sind doch alte ~n** *(col)* that's old hat *(col)*.

**Klampfe** *f* **-n** *(col)* guitar.

**klang** *pret of* **klingen**.

**Klang** *m* **⸚e** sound; *(Tonqualität)* tone. **~e** *(Musik)* sounds, tones.

**Klang-:** **~farbe** *f* tone colour *(Brit)* or color *(US)*; **k~lich** **1** *adj* **k~liche Unterschiede** differences in sound; *(von Tonqualität)* tonal difference; **2** *adv* **k~lich gut sein** *(Musik, Stimme)* to sound good; *(Instrument, Gerät)* to have a good tone; **~regler** *m (Rad etc)* tone control; **k~treu** *adj Wiedergabe* faithful; *Empfänger* high-fidelity; *Ton* true; **k~voll** *adj Stimme* sonorous; *(fig) Titel, Name* fine-sounding.

**Klappbett** *nt* folding bed.

**Klappe** *f* **-n** **(a)** flap; *(an Lastwagen)* tailboard; *(seitlich)* sidegate; *(an Kombiwagen)* tailgate; *(von Tisch)* leaf; *(von Ofen)* shutter, flap; *(Klappdeckel)* (hinged) lid; *(an Oboe etc)* key; *(Falltür)* trapdoor; *(Film)* clapperboard; *(Herz~)* valve. **(b)** *(Schulter~)* strap; *(Hosen~, an Tasche)* flap; *(Augen~)* patch. **(c)** *(Fliegen~)* (fly) swat. **(d)** *(col: Mund)* **die ~ halten** to shut one's trap *(col)*; **eine große ~ haben** to have a big mouth *(col)*.

**klappen** **1** *vt* **etw nach oben/unten ~** *Sitz, Bett* to fold sth up/down; *Kragen* to turn sth up/down; *Deckel* to lift sth/to lower sth; **etw nach vorn/hinten ~** *Sitz* to tip sth forward/back; *Deckel* to lift sth forward/back. **2** *vi* **(a)** to bang. **(b)** *(fig col)* to work; *(Aufführung, Abend)* to go smoothly. **hat es mit den Karten/dem Job geklappt?** did you get the tickets/job OK *(col)*?

**Klappentext** *m (Typ)* (jacket) blurb.

**Klapper** *f* **-n** rattle.

**Klapperkiste** *f (pej)* rattletrap *(hum col)*, clunker *(US col)*.

**klappern** *vi* to clatter; *(Klapperschlange, Fenster)* to rattle. **er klapperte vor Kälte mit den Zähnen** his teeth were chattering with cold.

**Klapper-:** ~**schlange** f _(Zool)_ rattlesnake; ~**storch** m stork; **er glaubt noch an den** ~**storch** ≃ he still thinks babies are found under the gooseberry bush.

**Klapp-:** -**fahrrad** nt folding bicycle; ~**messer** nt flick knife; ~**rad** nt folding bike.

**klapprig** adj shaky; _Auto etc_ ramshackle.

**Klapp-:** ~**sitz** m folding seat; ~**stuhl** m folding chair; ~**tisch** m folding table.

**Klaps** m -e _(Schlag)_ smack, slap. **einen** ~ **haben** _(col)_ to have a screw loose _(col)_.

**Klapsmühle** f _(pej col)_ loony bin _(col)_.

**klar** adj clear; _(fertig)_ ready. ~ **zum Gefecht** _(Mil)_ ready for action; ~ **Schiff machen** _(lit, fig)_ to clear the decks; ~**er Fall!** _(col)_ sure thing _(col)_; **alles** ~? everything OK? _(col)_; **jetzt ist mir alles** ~! now I understand; **bei** ~**em Verstand sein** to be in full possession of one's faculties; **etw** ~ **und deutlich sagen** to spell sth out; **jdm etw** ~ **und deutlich sagen** to tell sb sth straight _(col)_; **etw** ~ **zum Ausdruck bringen** to make sth clear; ~ **zutage treten** to become obvious; **sich** _(dat)_ **über etw** _(acc)_ **im** ~**en sein** to be aware of sth; **sich** _(dat)_ **darüber im** ~**en sein, daß ...** to realize that ...; **ins** ~**e kommen** to get things straight.

**Klär|anlage** f sewage plant; _(von Fabrik)_ purification plant.

**klären 1** vt to clear; _Wasser, Luft_ to purify; _Abwasser_ to treat; _Fall_ to clarify, to clear up; _Frage_ to settle. **2** vi _(Sport)_ to clear (the ball). **3** vr _(Wasser, Himmel)_ to clear; _(Wetter)_ to clear up; _(Meinungen, Sachlage)_ to become clear; _(Streitpunkte)_ to be clarified; _(Frage)_ to be settled.

**Klare(r)** m decl as adj _(col)_ schnaps.

**klargehen** vi sep irreg aux sein _(col)_ to be all right or OK _(col)_.

**Klarheit** f _(lit: Reinheit)_ clearness; _(fig: Deutlichkeit)_ clarity; _(geistige ~)_ lucidity. **sich** _(dat)_ **über etw** _(acc)_ **verschaffen** to get sth straight, to get sth clear in one's mind.

**Klarinette** f clarinet.

**Klarinettist(in** f) m clarinettist.

**Klar-:** **k**~**kommen** vi sep irreg aux sein _(col)_ to manage, to get by; **mit jdm/etw k**~**kommen** to be able to cope with sb/sth; **k**~**kriegen** vt sep _(col)_ to sort out; **k**~**legen** vt sep to make clear; **k**~**machen** sep **1** vt to make clear; _Flugzeug_ to clear; **jdm etw k**~**machen** to make sth clear to sb; **sich** _(dat)_ **etw k**~**machen** to get sth clear in one's mind; **2** vi _(Naut)_ to make ready; **zum Gefecht k**~**machen** to clear the decks for action; ~**schriftleser** m (**optischer**) ~ optical character reader; **k**~**sehen** vi sep irreg to see clearly; **in etw** _(dat)_ **k**~**sehen** to have understood sth; ~**sichtfolie** f transparent film; ~**sichtpackung** f see-through pack; **k**~**stellen** vt sep _(klären)_ to clear up, to clarify; **ich möchte k**~**stellen, daß ...** I want to make it clear that ...; ~**stellung** f clarification; ~**text** m **im** ~**text** in clear; _(fig col)_ in plain English.

**Klärung** f _(lit)_ purification; _(fig)_ clarification.

**klarwerden** sep irreg aux sein vr **sich** _(dat)_ (**über etw** acc) ~ to get (sth) clear in one's mind. **2** vi **jetzt wird mir das klar** now it's clear, now I see.

**klasse** adj inv _(col)_ great _(col)_.

**Klasse** f -n _(col)_ class; _(Spiel~)_ league; _(Steuer~ auch)_ bracket; _(Güter~)_ grade; _(Sch: ~nzimmer)_ classroom. **ein Fahrschein erster/zweiter** ~ a first-/second-class ticket; **das ist (große)** ~! _(col)_ that's great _(col)_.

**Klasse-** in cpds _(col)_ top-class; ~**frau** f fantastic woman.

**Klassen-** in cpds class; ~**arbeit** f (written) class test; ~**beste(r)** mf **er ist** ~**beste(r)** he is top of the class; ~**bewußtsein** nt class consciousness; ~**buch** nt (class-) register; ~**feind** m _(Pol)_ class enemy; ~**gegensatz** m usu pl _(Sociol)_ class difference; ~**gesellschaft** f class society; ~**haß** m _(Sociol)_ class hatred; ~**justiz** f _(Pol)_ legal system with class bias; ~**kamerad** m classmate; ~**kampf** m class struggle; ~**krieg** m class warfare; ~**lehrer,** ~**leiter** m class or form teacher; **k**~**los** adj Gesellschaft classless; _Krankenhaus_ one-class; ~**sprecher(in** f) m _(Sch)_ class spokesperson; ~**treffen** nt _(Sch)_ class reunion; ~**unterschied** m class difference; ~**ziel** nt _(Sch)_ **das** ~**ziel nicht erreichen** not to reach the required standard (for the year); _(fig)_ not to make the grade; ~**zimmer** nt classroom.

**klassifizieren\*** vt to classify.

**Klassifizierung** f classification.

**Klassik** f no pl classical period.

**Klassiker(in** f) m - classic. **ein** ~ **des Jazz** a jazz classic; **die antiken** ~ the classics.

**klassisch** adj classical; _(typisch, zeitlos)_ classic.

**Klassizismus** m classicism.

**Klatsch** m -e (**a**) splash; _(bei Schlag, Aufprall)_ smack. (**b**) no pl _(pej col: Tratsch)_ gossip.

**Klatsch-:** ~**base** f _(pej col)_ gossip; ~**blatt** nt _(col)_ gossipy magazine.

**klatschen 1** vi (**a**) to clap. **in die Hände** ~ to clap one's hands. (**b**) _(einen Klaps geben)_ to slap. **sich** _(dat)_ **auf die Schenkel** ~ to slap one's thighs. (**c**) aux sein _(aufschlagen)_ _(harte Gegenstände)_ to go smack; _(Flüssigkeiten)_ to splash. (**d**) _(pej col: tratschen)_ **über jdn/etw** ~ to gossip about sb/sth. **2** vt (**a**) to clap. **jdm Beifall** ~ to applaud or clap sb. (**b**) _(knallen)_ to smack, to slap; _(werfen)_ to throw.

**Klatschen** nt no pl _(Beifall~)_ applause; _(col: Tratschen)_ gossiping.

**Klatsch-:** ~**mohn** m (corn) poppy; **k**~**naß** adj _(col)_ sopping wet _(col)_; ~**spalte** f _(col)_ gossip column; ~**sucht** f passion for gossip; **k**~**süchtig** adj **ein k**~**süchtiger Mensch** a compulsive gossip; ~**tante** f _(pej col)_, ~**weib** nt _(pej col)_ gossip(monger).

**Klaue** f -n (**a**) claw. **in den** ~**n der Verbrecher** etc in the clutches of the criminals etc. (**b**) _(pej col: Schrift)_ scrawl _(pej)_.

**klauen** _(col)_ **1** vt to pinch _(col)_ _(jdm etw_ sth from sb). **2** vi to steal, to pinch things _(col)_.

**Klausel** f -n clause; _(Vorbehalt)_ proviso.

**Klausur** f (**a**) _(Univ)_ exam, paper. (**b**) no pl _(Abgeschlossenheit)_ seclusion. **eine Arbeit in** ~ **schreiben** to write a piece of work under examination conditions.

**Klausur-:** ~**arbeit** f examination paper; ~**tagung** f convention, conference.

**Klaviatur** [klavia'tu:ɐ] f keyboard.

**Klavier** [-'vi:ɐ] nt -e piano.

**Klavier-** in cpds piano; ~**auszug** m piano score; ~**begleitung** f piano accompaniment; ~**spieler** m pianist; ~**stimmer** m piano tuner.

**Klebe-:** ~**band** nt adhesive tape _(Brit)_, sticky tape; ~**etikett** nt adhesive label; ~**mittel** nt adhesive.

**kleben 1** vi to stick. **an etw** _(dat)_ ~ _(lit)_ to stick to sth; **an seinen Händen klebt Blut** _(fig)_ he has blood on his hands. **2** vt to stick; _(mit Klebstoff auch)_ to glue; _Film, Tonband_ to splice. **Marken** ~ _(col: Insur)_ to pay stamps; **jdm eine** ~ _(col)_ to belt sb one _(col)_.

**klebenbleiben** vi sep irreg aux sein to stick _(an +dat_ to); _(fig col: nicht wegkommen)_ to get stuck.

**Klebepflaster** nt sticking plaster.

**Kleber** m - _(im Mehl)_ gluten; _(col: Klebstoff)_ glue.

**Klebe-**: ~**stelle** f join; *(an Film)* splice; ~**streifen** m adhesive tape; ~**zettel** m gummed label.
**klebrig** adj sticky; *(klebfähig)* adhesive.
**Kleb-**: ~**stoff** m adhesive; ~**streifen** m adhesive tape.
**kleckern 1** vt to spill. **2** vi **(a)** to make a mess. **(b)** *(tropfen)* to spill. **(c)** *(col: stückchenweise arbeiten)* to fiddle about. **nicht** ~, **sondern klotzen** *(col)* to do things in a big way *(col)*.
**kleckerweise** adv in dribs and drabs.
**Klecks** m **-e** *(Tinten~)* (ink)blot; *(Farb~)* blob.
**klecksen** vi *(mit Tinte)* to make blots/a blob.
**Klee** m no pl clover. **jdn/etw über den grünen ~ loben** to praise sb/sth to the skies.
**Kleeblatt** nt cloverleaf; *(fig: Menschen)* threesome, trio. **vierblättriges ~** four-leaf clover.
**Kleid** nt **-er** **(a)** *(Damen~)* dress. **ein zweiteiliges ~** a two-piece (suit). **(b)** ~**er** pl *(Kleidung)* clothes pl; ~**er machen Leute** *(Prov)* fine feathers make fine birds *(Prov)*. **(c)** *(liter)* *(Feder~)* plumage; *(Pelz)* coat; *(fig: von Natur, Bäumen etc)* mantle *(liter)*.
**kleiden 1** vr to dress. **2** vt **(a)** *(lit, fig)* to clothe. **etw in schöne Worte ~** to dress sth up in fancy words. **(b) jdn ~** *(jdm stehen)* to suit sb.
**Kleider-**: ~**bügel** m coathanger; ~**bürste** f clothes brush; ~**haken** m coat hook; ~**schrank** m wardrobe; ~**ständer** m coat-stand.
**kleidsam** adj flattering.
**Kleidung** f no pl clothes pl, clothing.
**Kleidungsstück** nt garment. ~**e** pl clothes pl.
**Kleie** f no pl bran.
**klein** adj **(a)** little, small; *Finger* little; *Format, Gehalt, Zahl, (Hand)schrift, Buchstabe* small; *Pause, Vortrag* short; *(Mus)* Terz minor. **der K~e Bär** the Little Bear, Ursa Minor; **haben Sie es nicht ~er?** haven't you got anything smaller?; **ein ~ bißchen** or **wenig** a little (bit); **ein ~ bißchen** or **wenig Salat** a little (bit of) salad; **ein ~es Bier, ein K~es** *(col)* ≈ half a pint, a half; **mein ~er Bruder** my little brother; **er ist ~er als sein Bruder** he's smaller than his brother; **er schreibt sehr ~** his writing is very small; **sich ~ machen** to bend down low; to curl up tight; **macht euch ein bißchen ~er!** squeeze up closer; ~, **aber oho!** *(col)* good things come in small packages; ~, **aber fein!** small is beautiful; **ein Wort ~ schreiben** to write a word with small initial letters; **im ~en** in miniature; **bis ins ~ste** in minute detail; **von ~ an** or **auf** *(von Kindheit an)* from his/her childhood; *(von Anfang an)* from the very beginning; ~**en Augenblick, bitte!** just one moment, please; **einen Kopf ~er als jd sein** to be a head shorter than sb; **beim ~sten Schreck** at the slightest or smallest shock; **das ~ere Übel** the lesser evil; **ein paar ~ere Fehler** a few minor mistakes.
**(b)** *(unbedeutend)* petty* *(pej)*; *Leute* ordinary; *(armselig)* Verhältnisse humble. **er ist ein ~er Geist** he is small-minded; **der ~e Mann** the ordinary citizen, the man in the street; **ein ~er Ganove** a small-time crook; **sein Vater war (ein) ~er Beamter** his father was a minor civil servant; ~ **anfangen** to start off in a small way.
**Klein-**: ~**anzeige** f small ad *(Brit col)*, classified ad; ~**arbeit** f detailed work; **in zäher/mühseliger** ~**arbeit** with rigorous/painstaking attention to detail; ~**asien** nt Asia Minor; ~**bauer** m small farmer, smallholder; ~**betrieb** m small business; ~**bildkamera** f 35mm camera; ~**buchstabe** m small letter; ~**bürger** m petty bourgeois; **k~bürgerlich** adj lower middle-class, petty bourgeois *(pej)*; ~**bürgertum** nt *(Sociol)* lower middle class, petty bourgeoisie; ~**bus** m minibus.

**Kleine(r)** mf decl as adj **(a)** little one; little boy/girl; baby. **unser ~r** *(Jüngster)* our youngest (child); **die lieben ~n** *(iro)* the dear little things. **(b)** *(col: auch* ~**s**: *Liebling)* baby *(col)*.
**Klein-**: ~**familie** f small family, nuclear family *(Sociol)*; ~**format** nt small format; **im** ~**format** in miniature; ~**garten** m allotment *(Brit)*; ~**gärtner** m allotment holder *(Brit)*; **k~gedruckt** adj attr in small print; ~**gedruckte(s)** nt small print; ~**geld** nt (small) change; **das nötige ~ geld haben** *(col)* to have the necessary or the wherewithal *(col)*; **k~gemustert** adj small-patterned; **k~gewachsen** adj short, small; *Baum* small; **k~gläubig** adj *(zweiflerisch)* timid; **k~gläubig sein** to lack conviction; **k~hacken** vt sep to chop up small; ~**heit** f smallness, small size; ~**holz** nt no pl firewood; **aus etw** ~**holz machen** *(hum col)* to smash sth to pieces; ~**holz aus jdm machen** *(col)* to make mincemeat of sb *(col)*.
**Kleinigkeit** f **(a)** little or small thing; *(Bagatelle)* trivial matter, trifle; *(Einzelheit)* minor detail. **ich habe noch ein paar ~en in der Stadt zu erledigen** I still have a few little things to attend to in town; **es war nur eine ~ zu reparieren** there was only something minor to be repaired; **die Reparatur/Prüfung war eine ~** the repair job/exam was no trouble at all; **eine ~ essen** to have a bite to eat; **wegen** or **bei jeder ~** for the slightest reason; **großen Wert auf** ~**en legen** to be a stickler for detail(s). **(b)** *(ein bißchen)* **eine ~** a little (bit), a trifle; **eine ~ zu groß** a little (bit) etc too big.
**Kleinigkeitskrämer** m *(pej)* pedant.
**Klein-**: ~**kaliber** nt small bore; **k~kariert** adj *(fig)* small-time *(col)*; **k~kariert denken** to think small; ~**kind** nt small child, infant *(Psych)*; ~**kram** m *(col)* odds and ends pl; *(Trivialitäten)* trivia pl; ~**kredit** m personal loan; ~**krieg** m *(fig)* **ein ständiger** ~**krieg** a constant battle; **einen** ~**krieg mit jdm führen** to be fighting a running battle with sb.
**kleinkriegen** vt sep **(a)** *(lit)* Holz to chop (up); *Nuß* to break. **(b)** *(col: kaputtmachen)* to smash, to break. **(c)** *(col)* *(gefügig machen)* to bring into line *(col)*; *(unterkriegen)* to get down; *(körperlich)* to tire out. **er ist einfach nicht kleinzukriegen** he refuses to be beaten.
**Klein-**: ~**kunst** f cabaret; **k~laut** adj subdued; **dann wurde er ganz k~laut** that made him shut up; **k~laut um Verzeihung bitten** to apologize rather sheepishly.
**kleinlich** adj petty; *(knauserig)* mean, stingy *(col)*; *(engstirnig)* narrow-minded.
**Kleinlichkeit** f *siehe* adj pettiness; meanness, stinginess *(col)*; narrow-mindedness.
**kleinmachen** vt sep **(a)** to chop or cut up. **(b)** *(col)* Geld to change.
**Klein-**: ~**mut** m faintheartedness, timidity; **k~mütig** adj fainthearted, timid; **k~schneiden** vt sep irreg to cut up small; **k~schreiben** vt sep irreg *(fig)* **k~geschrieben werden** to count for (very) little; ~**schreibung** f use of small initial letters; ~**staat** m small state; ~**stadt** f small town; **k~städtisch** adj provincial, small-town attr.
**kleinste(r, s)** superl of **klein**.
**kleinstmöglich** adj smallest possible.
**Klein-**: ~**tier** nt small animal; ~**vieh** nt: ~**vieh macht auch Mist** *(prov)* every little helps; ~**wagen** m small car.
**Kleister** m **-** *(Klebstoff)* paste.
**kleistern** vti *(zusammenkleben)* to paste.
**Klematis** f **-** clematis.
**Klementine** f clementine.

**Klemme** f -n **(a)** *(Haar~, für Papiere etc)* clip; *(Elec)* crocodile clamp; *(Med)* clamp. **(b)** *(fig col)* in der ~ sitzen *or* sein to be in a fix *(col)*; jdm aus der ~ helfen to help sb out of a fix *(col)*.

**klemmen 1** *vt Draht etc* to clamp, to clip; *(in Spalt)* to wedge, to jam. **sich** *(dat)* **den Finger (in etw** *dat)* ~ to catch one's finger (in sth); **sich** *(dat)* **etw unter den Arm** ~ to tuck sth under one's arm. **2** *vr* to catch oneself *(in +dat* in). **sich hinter etw** *(acc)* ~ *(col)* to get stuck into sth *(col)*; **sich hinter jdn** ~ *(col)* to get to work on sb. **3** *vi (Tür, Schloß etc)* to stick, to jam.

**Klempner** m - plumber.

**Klempnerei** f **(a)** *no pl* plumbing. **(b)** *(Werkstatt)* plumber's workshop.

**Kleptomane** m, **Kleptomanin** f kleptomaniac.

**Kleriker** m - cleric.

**Klerus** m -, *no pl* clergy.

**Klette** f -n *(Bot)* burdock; *(Blütenkopf)* bur(r); *(pej: lästiger Mensch)* nuisance. **sich wie eine** ~ **an jdn hängen** to cling to sb like a limpet.

**Kletterer** m - climber.

**Klettergerüst** nt climbing frame.

**klettern** *vi aux sein* to climb; *(mühsam)* to clamber. **auf Bäume** ~ to climb trees.

**Kletter-:** ~**partie** f climbing trip; ~**pflanze** f climbing plant; ~**rose** f rambling rose; ~**tour** f = ~**partie**.

**Klettverschluß** m Velcro ® fastener.

**klicken** *vi* to click.

**Klient(in** *f)* [kli'ɛnt(ɪn)] m *(wk)* -en, -en client.

**Klima** nt -s *or* -te [kli'maːtə] *(lit, fig)* climate.

**Klima|anlage** f air conditioning. **mit** ~ air-conditioned.

**klimatisch** *adj no pred* climatic.

**klimatisieren*** *vt* to air-condition.

**klimatisiert** *adj* air-conditioned.

**Klima-:** ~**wechsel** m *(lit, fig)* change in the climate; ~**zone** f (climatic) zone.

**Klimbim** m *no pl (col)* odds and ends pl; *(Umstände)* fuss.

**Klimmzug** m *(Sport)* pull-up.

**klimpern** *vi* to tinkle; *(stümperhaft)* to plonk away *(col)*; *(auf Banjo)* to twang; *(Münzen)* to jingle.

**Klinge** f -n blade.

**Klingel** f -n bell.

**Klingelknopf** m bell push.

**klingeln** *vi* to ring *(nach* for*)*; *(Motor)* to pink, to knock. **es hat schon geklingelt** *(in Schule)* the bell has already gone; **es hat geklingelt** *(an Tür)* somebody just rang the doorbell; **immer wenn es an der Tür klingelt** ... whenever the doorbell rings ...

**klingen** *pret* **klang,** *ptp* **geklungen** *vi* to sound; *(Glocke, Ohr)* to ring; *(Glas)* to clink; *(Metall)* to clang. **nach etw** ~ to sound like sth.

**Klinik** f -en clinic; *(Universitäts~)* (university) hospital.

**klinisch** *adj* clinical. ~ **tot** clinically dead.

**Klinke** f -n *(Tür~)* (door) handle.

**Klinkenputzer** m *(col) (Hausierer)* hawker; *(Vertreter)* door-to-door salesman.

**Klinker** m - *(Ziegelstein)* clinker (brick).

**klipp** *adv:* ~ **und klar** clearly; *(offen)* frankly.

**Klippe** f -n *(Fels~)* cliff; *(im Meer)* rock; *(fig)* obstacle. ~**n umschiffen** *(lit, fig)* to negotiate obstacles.

**Klips** m -e = Clip.

**klirren** *vi* to clink; *(Fensterscheiben)* to rattle; *(Lautsprecher, Mikrofon)* to crackle; *(Eis)* to crunch. ~**de Kälte** *(liter)* crisp cold.

**Klischee** nt -s *(Typ)* plate; *(fig: Phrase)* cliché.

**Klischeevorstellung** f cliché, stereotype.

**Klitoris** f - clitoris.

**klitzeklein** *adj (col)* teeny-weeny *(col)*.

**Klo** nt -s *(col)* loo *(Brit col)*, john *(US col)*.

**Klo-** *in cpds* toilet, loo *(Brit col); siehe auch* **Klosett-**.

**Kloake** f -n sewer.

**klobig** *adj* hefty *(col); Mensch* hulking great *(col)*.

**Klon** m -e clone.

**klonen** *vti* to clone.

**Klopapier** nt *(col)* toilet *or* loo *(Brit col)* paper.

**klopfen 1** *vt* to knock; *Fleisch, Teppich* to beat; *Steine* to knock down. **den Takt** ~ to beat time. **2** *vi* to knock; *(Herz)* to beat; *(vor Aufregung, Anstrengung auch)* to pound; *(Puls)* to throb; *(Motor)* to knock, to pink *(Brit)*. **es hat geklopft** there's someone knocking at the door; **jdm auf die Schulter/den Rücken** ~ to tap sb on the shoulder/to pat sb on the back; *(heftig)* to slap sb on the shoulder/back; **jdm auf die Finger** ~ *(lit, fig)* to rap sb on the knuckles; **mit** ~**dem Herzen** with beating *or* pounding heart.

**Klopfer** m - *(Tür~)* (door) knocker; *(Fleisch~)* (meat) mallet; *(Teppich~)* carpet beater.

**Klöppel** m - *(Glocken~)* clapper; *(Spitzen~)* bobbin; *(Trommel~)* stick.

**Klöppelei** f (pillow) lace making.

**klöppeln** *vi* to make (pillow) lace.

**Klöppelspitze** f pillow lace.

**Klops** m -e *(Cook)* meatball.

**Klosett** nt -e *or* -s lavatory.

**Klosett-:** ~**brille** f toilet seat. ~**bürste** f lavatory brush; ~**deckel** m lavatory seat lid; ~**frau** f lavatory attendant; ~**papier** nt toilet paper.

**Kloß** m -̈e dumpling; *(Fleisch~)* meatball; *(Bulette)* rissole. **einen** ~ **im Hals haben** *(fig)* to have a lump in one's throat.

**Kloßbrühe** f: **klar wie** ~ as clear as day; *(iro)* as clear as mud.

**Kloster** nt -̈ cloister; *(Mönchs~ auch)* monastery; *(Nonnen~ auch)* convent. **ins** ~ **gehen** to become a monk/nun.

**Klosterschule** f monastic/convent school.

**Klotz** m -̈e *(Holz~)* block (of wood); *(pej: Beton~)* concrete block; *(col: Person)* great lump *(col)*. **jdm ein** ~ **am Bein sein** to be a hindrance to sb.

**klotzen** *vi (col: protzig auftreten)* to show off; *siehe* **kleckern**.

**klotzig** *adj (col)* huge, massive.

**Klub** m -s club.

**Klub-:** ~**abend** m club night; ~**garnitur** f (three-piece) suite; ~**jacke** f blazer; ~**sessel** m club-chair.

**Kluft** f -̈e **(a)** *(Erdspalte)* cleft; *(in Bergen)* crevasse; *(Abgrund)* chasm. **(b)** *(fig)* gulf, gap. **in der Partei tat sich eine tiefe** ~ **auf** a deep rift opened up in the party. **(c)** *no pl (Uniform)* uniform; *(col: Kleidung)* gear *(col)*.

**klug** *adj, comp* -̈**er,** *superl* -̈**ste(r, s)** clever, intelligent; *(vernünftig)* Entscheidung, Rat sound; *Überlegung* prudent; *Geschäftsmann* shrewd. **es wird am** ~**sten sein, wenn** ... it would be most sensible if ...; **es wäre politisch** ~ ... it would make good political sense ...; **ein** ~**er Kopf** a capable person; **in** ~**er Voraussicht** shrewdly; **ich werde daraus nicht** ~ I can't make head or tail of it; **aus ihm werde ich nicht** ~ I can't make him out; ~**e Reden halten** *(iro)* to make fine-sounding speeches; ~**e Bemerkungen/ Ratschläge** *(iro)* clever *or* helpful remarks/advice *(iro)*; **nun bin ich genau so** ~ **wie vorher** I am still none the wiser.

**klugerweise** *adv* (very) cleverly, (very) wisely.

**Klugheit** f *siehe adj* cleverness, intelligence; soundness; prudence; shrewdness. **aus** ~ (very) wisely.

**Klug-:** ~**redner** m know-all, know-it-all *(US)*; ~**scheißer** m *(col!)* smart-ass *(col!)*.
**Klumpen** m - lump; *(Gold~)* nugget; *(Blut~)* clot. ~ **bilden** *(Mehl etc)* to go lumpy.
**klumpen** vi *(Sauce etc)* to go lumpy.
**Klumpfuß** m club foot.
**klumpig** adj lumpy.
**Klüngel** m - *(col: clique)* clique.
**Klunker** m - *(col: Edelstein)* rock *(col)*.
**km** = **Kilometer** km.
**km/h** = **Kilometer pro Stunde** kph.
**knabbern** vti to nibble. **nichts zu** ~ **haben** *(col)* to have nothing to eat.
**Knabe** m *(wk)* **-n, -n** *(liter)* boy, lad.
**Knaben-:** ~**chor** m boys' choir; **k~haft** adj boyish.
**Knäckebrot** nt crispbread.
**knacken 1** vt *(lit, fig)* to crack; *(col)* Auto to break into. **2** vi *(brechen)* to crack; *(Dielen, Stuhl)* to creak; *(knistern: Holz)* to crackle. **daran wird er zu** ~ **haben** *(col)* that'll give him something to think about; *(darüber hinwegkommen)* he'll have a rough time getting over it.
**Knacker** m **(a)** *type of frankfurter.* **(b)** *(pej col)* **alter** ~ old fog(e)y *(col)*.
**knackig** adj crisp; *(col)* Mädchen luscious *(col)*.
**Knacklaut** m glottal stop.
**Knacks** m **-e** *(Sprung)* crack. **der Fernseher hat einen** ~ *(col)* there is something wrong with the television.
**Knackwurst** f *type of frankfurter.*
**Knall** m **-e** bang; *(mit Peitsche)* crack; *(von Korken)* pop; *(col: Krach)* trouble. ~ **auf Fall** *(col)* just like that *(col)*; **einen** ~ **haben** *(col)* to be crazy *(col)* or crackers *(Brit col)*.
**Knall|effekt** m *(col)* bombshell *(col)*.
**knallen 1** vi **(a)** to bang, to explode; *(Schuß)* to ring out; *(Pfropfen)* to (go) pop; *(Peitsche)* to crack; *(Tür etc)* to bang, to slam; *(Auspuff)* to backfire; *(aux sein: auftreffen)* to bang. **mit der Tür** ~ to bang or slam the door; **draußen knallte es** there was a shot/were shots outside; **sei nicht so frech, sonst knallt's** *(col)* don't be so cheeky, or there'll be trouble. **(b)** *(col: Sonne)* to blaze down. **2** vt to bang; Tür, Buch auch to slam; Schüsse to fire (off); Peitsche to crack. **den Hörer auf die Gabel** ~ *(col)* to slam or bang down the receiver; **jdm eine** ~ *(col)* to clout sb *(col)*.
**Knall-:** ~**frosch** m jumping jack; **k~gelb** adj *(col)* bright yellow; **k~hart** adj *(col)* really hard; Film brutal; Porno hard-core; Job, Truppen, Mensch really tough; Schuß, Schlag really hard.
**knallig** adj *(col)* Farben loud, gaudy.
**Knall-:** ~**kopf** m *(col)* dickhead *(col)*; ~**körper** m fire-cracker; **k~rot** adj *(col)* bright red.
**knapp** adj **(a)** *(nicht ausreichend)* scarce, in short supply; Gehalt low. **mein Geld ist** ~ I'm short of money; **mein Geld wird** ~ I am running short of money; **das Essen wird** ~ we/they etc are running short of food; **mein Geld/meine Zeit ist** ~ **bemessen** I am short of money/time. **(b)** *(gerade noch ausreichend)* Zeit, Geld just enough; Mehrheit, Sieg narrow; Kleidungsstück etc *(eng)* tight; *(kurz)* short; Bikini scanty. **eine** ~**e Sache** a close-run thing; **wir haben** ~ **verloren/gewonnen** we only just lost/won. **(c)** *(nicht ganz)* almost. **ein** ~**es Pfund Mehl** just under a pound of flour. **(d)** Stil, Worte concise; Geste terse; Antwort pithy. **(e)** *(gerade so eben)* just. **mit** ~**er Not** only just.
**knapphalten** vt sep irreg jdn ~ to keep sb short *(mit of)*.
**Knappheit** f shortage; *(fig: des Ausdrucks)* concise-

ness.
**Knarre** f **-n** *(col: Gewehr)* gun, shooter *(col)*.
**knarren** vi to creak. **eine** ~**de Stimme** a grating voice.
**Knast** m no pl *(col)* clink *(col)*, can *(US col)*.
**Knatsch** m no pl *(col)* trouble.
**knatschig** adj *(col)* whingeing *(col)*.
**knattern** vi *(Motorrad)* to bang away; *(Preßlufthammer)* to hammer; *(Maschinengewehr)* to rattle; *(Schüsse)* to rattle out.
**Knäuel** m or nt - ball; *(wirres)* tangle; *(von Menschen)* group, knot.
**Knauf** m, pl **Knäufe** *(Tür~)* knob.
**knauserig** adj *(col)* mean, stingy *(col)*.
**knausern** vi *(col)* to be mean or stingy *(col)* *(mit with)*.
**knautschen** vti *(col)* to crumple (up).
**Knautschzone** f *(Aut)* crumple zone.
**Knebel** m - *(Mund~)* gag; *(Paket~)* (wooden) handle; *(an Mänteln)* toggle.
**knebeln** vt jdn, Presse to gag.
**Kneb(e)lung** f no pl *(lit, fig)* gagging.
**Knecht** m **-e** servant; *(beim Bauern)* (farm)worker; *(Stall~)* stableboy; *(fig: Sklave)* slave *(gen to)*.
**knechten** vt *(geh)* to subjugate, to oppress.
**Knechtschaft** f slavery.
**kneifen** pret **kniff**, ptp **gekniffen 1** vti to pinch. **jdn** or **jdm in den Arm** ~ to pinch sb's arm. **2** vi *(col: ausweichen)* to back out *(vor +dat of)*.
**Kneifer** m - *(Brille)* pince-nez.
**Kneifzange** f pliers pl; *(kleine)* pincers pl. **eine** ~ (a pair of) pliers/(a pair of) pincers.
**Kneipe** f **-n** *(col: Lokal)* pub *(Brit)*, bar.
**Kneipen-:** ~**bummel** m pub crawl *(Brit)*, bar hop *(US)*; ~**wirt** m *(col)* landlord *(Brit)*, barkeeper *(US)*.
**Kneippkur** f Kneipp cure, *type of hydropathic treatment combined with diet, rest etc.*
**Knete** f no pl *(col)* dough *(col)*.
**kneten** vt to knead; Ton to work; Figuren to model.
**Knet-:** ~**gummi** m or nt plasticine ®; ~**masse** f modelling *(Brit)* or modeling *(US)* clay.
**Knick** m **-e** or **-s** *(Falte)* crease; *(Biegung)* (sharp) bend; *(bei Draht)* kink. **einen** ~ **machen** to bend sharply.
**knicken** vti *(vi: aux sein)* to snap; Papier to fold. „**nicht** ~**!**" "do not bend".
**knick(e)rig** adj *(col)* stingy *(col)*, mean.
**Knicks** m **-e** bob; *(tiefer)* curts(e)y. **einen** ~ **machen** to curts(e)y *(vor +dat to)*.
**knicksen** vi to curts(e)y *(vor +dat to)*.
**Knie** nt - **(a)** knee. **auf** ~**n** on bended knee; **auf die** ~ **fallen** to drop to one's knees; **jdm auf** ~**n danken** to go down on one's knees and thank sb; **in die** ~ **gehen** to kneel; *(fig)* to be brought to one's knees; **jdn in** or **auf die** ~ **zwingen** to force sb to his knees; **jdn übers** ~ **legen** *(col)* to put sb across one's knee; **etw übers** ~ **brechen** *(fig)* to rush sth. **(b)** *(Fluß~)* sharp bend; *(in Rohr)* elbow.
**Knie-:** ~**beuge** f *(Sport)* knee bend; ~**bundhose** f knee breeches; ~**fall** m **einen** ~**fall vor jdm machen** *(lit, fig)* to kneel before sb; ~**gelenk** nt knee joint; ~**hose** f knee breeches pl; ~**kehle** f back of the knee; **k~lang** adj knee-length.
**knien** [kniːn, ˈkniːən] **1** vi to kneel. **im K~** kneeling. **2** vr to kneel (down). **sich in die Arbeit** ~ *(fig)* to get down to one's work.
**Knie-:** ~**scheibe** f kneecap; ~**schützer** m - knee-pad; ~**strumpf** m knee-length sock; **k~tief** adj knee-deep.
**kniff** pret of **kneifen**.
**Kniff** m **-e (a)** *(col)* trick. **den** ~ **bei etw heraushaben**

to have the knack of sth *(col)*. **(b)** *(Falte)* crease, fold.

**kniff(e)lig** *adj (col)* fiddly; *(heikel)* tricky.

**knipsen 1** *vt* **(a)** *(Phot col)* to snap *(col)*. **(b)** *Fahrschein* to punch, to clip. **2** *vi* **(a)** *(Phot col)* to take pictures. **(b) mit den Fingern** ~ to snap one's fingers.

**Knirps** *m* **-e (a)** *(Junge)* whippersnapper. **(b)** ® ≃ telescopic umbrella.

**knirschen** *vi (Sand, Schnee)* to crunch; *(Getriebe)* to grind. **mit den Zähnen** ~ to grind one's teeth.

**knistern** *vi (Feuer)* to crackle; *(Papier, Seide)* to rustle. **mit Papier** *etc* ~ to rustle paper *etc*.

**knitterfrei** *adj Stoff, Kleid* crease-resistant.

**knittern** *vti* to crease, to crush.

**knobeln** *vi (würfeln)* to play dice; *(um eine Entscheidung)* to toss for it *(col)*.

**Knoblauch** *m no pl* garlic.

**Knoblauch-:** *in cpds* garlic; **~presse** *f* garlic press; **~zehe** *f* clove of garlic.

**Knöchel** *m* **- (a)** *(Fuß~)* ankle. **bis über die** ~ up to the ankles. **(b)** *(Finger~)* knuckle.

**knöcheltief** *adj* ankle-deep.

**Knochen** *m* **-** bone. **Fleisch mit/ohne** ~ meat on/off the bone; **er ist bis auf die** ~ **abgemagert** he is just skin and bones; **ihm steckt die Grippe/Angst in den** ~ *(col)* he's got flu/he's scared stiff *(col)*; **naß bis auf die** ~ *(col)* soaked to the skin; **der Schreck fuhr ihm in die** ~ he was paralyzed with fright; **sich bis auf die** ~ **blamieren** *(col)* to make a proper fool of oneself *(col)*.

**Knochen-:** **~arbeit** *f* hard graft; **~bau** *m* bone structure; **~bruch** *m* fracture; **~gerüst** *nt* skeleton; **k~hart** *adj (col)* rock-hard; **~mark** *nt* bone marrow; **~mehl** *nt* bone meal; **~schinken** *m* ham on the bone; **k~trocken** *adj (col)* bone dry; *(fig) Humor etc* very dry.

**knöchern** *adj (aus Knochen)* bone.

**knochig** *adj* bony.

**Knödel** *m* **-** dumpling.

**Knöllchen** *nt (col: Strafzettel)* (parking) ticket.

**Knolle** *f* **-n** *(Bot)* tubercule; *(von Kartoffel)* tuber.

**knollig** *adj Wurzel* tuberous; *Auswuchs* knobbly; *Nase* bulbous.

**Knopf** *m* **-e (a)** button. **das kannst du an den ~en abzählen** you might as well toss a coin for it. **(b)** *(an Tür, Stock)* knob; *(Sattel~, Degen~)* pommel. **(c)** *(col) (Kind)* little chap/little lass; *(Kerl)* chap, fellow.

**Knopfdruck** *m* touch of a button.

**knöpfen** *vt* to button (up).

**Knopfloch** *nt* buttonhole.

**Knorpel** *m* **-** *(Anat)* cartilage; *(Cook)* gristle.

**knorpelig** *adj (Anat)* cartilaginous; *Fleisch* gristly.

**knorrig** *adj Baum* gnarled; *Holz* knotty; *(fig) alter Mann* rugged; *(eigenwillig) Mensch* surly, gruff.

**Knospe** *f* **-n** bud. **~n ansetzen** to bud.

**knospen** *vi* to bud. **~d** *(lit, fig liter)* budding.

**Knoten** *m* **-** knot *(auch Naut)*; *(Med: Geschwulst)* lump; *(Haar auch)* bun.

**knoten** *vt Seil etc* to tie a knot in. **etw an etw** ~ to tie sth to sth.

**Knotenpunkt** *m (Mot)* (road) junction *(Brit)*, intersection; *(Rail)* junction; *(fig)* centre *(Brit)*, center *(US)*.

**knotig** *adj* knotted, full of knots; *Äste, Finger* gnarled.

**knuffen** *vti (col)* to poke *(col)*; *(mit Ellbogen)* to nudge.

**knüllen** *vti* to crumple, to crease (up).

**Knüller** *m* **-** *(col)* sensation; *(Press)* scoop.

**knüpfen 1** *vt Knoten, Band* to tie; *Teppich* to knot;

*Netz* to mesh; *Freundschaft* to form. **jdn an den Galgen** ~ *(col)* to string sb up *(col)*; **große Erwartungen an etw** *(acc)* ~ to have great expectations of sth. **2** *vr* **sich an etw** *(acc)* ~ to be linked to sth.

**Knüppel** *m* **- (a)** stick; *(Waffe)* cudgel, club; *(Polizei~)* truncheon *(Brit)*, night stick *(US)*. **jdm** ~ **zwischen die Beine werfen** *(fig)* to put a spoke in sb's wheel. **(b)** *(Aviat)* joystick; *(Aut)* gear lever *(Brit)*, gearshift *(US)*.

**Knüppel-:** **k~dick** *(col)* **1** *adj Steak, Schicht* very thick; **2** *adv* **bei ihm kam es k~dick** he had one problem after the other; **~schaltung** *f (Aut)* floormounted gear lever *(Brit)* or gearshift *(US)*; **k~voll** *adj (col)* jam-packed.

**knurren 1** *vi (Hund etc)* to growl; *(Magen)* to rumble; *(fig: sich beklagen)* to groan *(über +acc* about). **2** *vti (mürrisch sagen)* to growl.

**Knurren** *nt no pl siehe vi* growl(ing); rumbling; groaning.

**knurrig** *adj* grumpy; *Angestellte etc* disgruntled.

**knusprig** *adj Braten* crisp; *Gebäck auch* crunchy; *(fig) Mädchen* scrumptious *(col)*.

**Knute** *f* **-n unter jds** ~ *(dat)* **stehen** to be completely dominated by sb.

**knutschen** *(col)* **1** *vt* to neck with *(col)*. **2** *vir* to neck *(col)*.

**k. o.** [kaː'|oː] *adj pred (Sport)* knocked out; *(fig col)* whacked *(col)*. **jdn** ~ **schlagen** to knock sb out.

**Koala, Koalabär** *m* koala (bear).

**koalieren\*** *vi (esp Pol)* to form a coalition.

**Koalition** *f (esp Pol)* coalition.

**Koalitions-** *in cpds* coalition; **~partner** *m* coalition partner; **~regierung** *f* coalition government.

**Kobalt** *nt no pl* cobalt.

**Kobold** *m* **-e** goblin, imp.

**Kobra** *f* **-s** cobra.

**Koch** *m* **-̈e** cook; *(von Restaurant auch)* chef. **viele ~̈e verderben den Brei** *(Prov)* too many cooks spoil the broth *(Prov)*.

**Koch-:** **~apfel** *m* cooking apple; **~buch** *nt* cookery book, cookbook; **k~echt** *adj Farbe* fast; *Wäsche etc* that may be boiled.

**kochen 1** *vi* **(a)** *(Flüssigkeit, Speise)* to boil. **etw zum K~ bringen** to bring sth to the boil; **jdn zum K~ bringen** *(fig col)* to make sb's blood boil; **das Auto kocht** *(col)* the car is overheating; **er kochte vor Wut** *(col)* he was seething. **(b)** *(Speisen zubereiten)* to cook; *(als Koch fungieren)* to do the cooking. **er kocht gut** he's a good cook; **er kocht scharf/pikant** his cooking is highly seasoned/spiced. **2** *vt* **(a)** *Nahrungsmittel, Wäsche* to boil. **etw auf kleiner Flamme** ~ to simmer sth over a low heat. **(b)** *(zubereiten) Essen* to cook; *Kaffee, Tee* to make. **etw gar/weich** ~ to cook sth until it is done/soft; **Eier weich/hart** ~ to soft-boil/hard-boil eggs.

**kochend** *adj* boiling. ~ **heiß sein** to be boiling hot; *(Suppe etc)* to be piping hot.

**kochendheiß** *adj attr* boiling hot; *Suppe etc* piping hot.

**Kocher** *m* **-** *(Herd)* cooker, stove.

**Köcher** *m* **-** *(für Pfeile)* quiver.

**Koch-:** **~feld** *nt* ceramic hob; **k~fertig** *adj* ready-to-cook; **~gelegenheit** *f* cooking facilities *pl*; **~herd** *m* cooker.

**Köchin** *f* cook; *(von Restaurant auch)* chef.

**Koch-:** **~kunst** *f* cooking; *(Gastronomie)* cuisine; **~kurs(us)** *m* cookery course; **~löffel** *m* cooking spoon; **~nische** *f* kitchenette; **~platte** *f (Herdplatte)* hotplate; **~rezept** *nt* recipe; **~salz** *nt* cooking salt; **~topf** *m* (cooking) pot; *(mit Stiel)* saucepan; **~wäsche** *f* washing that can be boiled; **~zeit** *f*

cooking time.
**Kode** [koːt, 'koːdə] *m* **-s** code.
**Köder** *m* - bait; *(fig auch)* lure.
**ködern** *vt (lit)* to lure; *(fig)* to tempt. **jdn zu ~ versuchen** to woo sb; **jdn für etw ~** to rope sb in for sth *(col)*; **sich von jdm/etw nicht ~ lassen** not to be tempted by sb/sth.
**Kodewort** *nt* code word.
**kodieren\*** *vt* to encode.
**Kodierer** *m* -, **Kodiergerät** *nt* encoder.
**Ko|edukation** *f* co-education.
**Ko|existenz** *f* coexistence.
**Koffein** *nt no pl* caffeine.
**koffeinfrei** *adj* decaffeinated.
**Koffer** *m* - (suit)case, bag; *(Schrank~)* trunk; *(Arzt~)* bag; *(für Schreibmaschine, Kosmetika etc)* case. **die ~** *pl (Gepäck)* the luggage *or* baggage *or* bags *pl*; **die ~ packen** *(lit, fig)* to pack one's bags.
**Koffer-:** **~gerät** *nt* portable (set); **~kuli** *m* (luggage) trolley *(Brit)*, cart *(US)*; **~radio** *nt* portable radio; **~raum** *m (Aut)* boot *(Brit)*, trunk *(US)*; *(Volumen)* luggage space.
**Kognak** ['kɔnjak] *m* **-s** *or* **-e** brandy.
**Kohl** *m* **-e (a)** cabbage. **das macht den ~ auch nicht fett** *(col)* that's not much help. **(b)** *(col: Unsinn)* nonsense.
**Kohldampf** *m no pl (col)* **~ haben** to be famished.
**Kohle** *f* **-n (a)** coal; *(Stück ~)* (lump of) coal. **wir haben keine ~n mehr** we have no coal left; **zwei ~n** two lumps of coal; **(wie) auf glühenden** *or* **heißen ~n sitzen** to be like a cat on hot bricks. **(b)** *(Verkohltes, Holz~, Art)* charcoal. **(c)** *(Tech)* carbon. **(d)** *(col: Geld)* dough *(col)*, cash *(col)*. **die ~n stimmen** the money's right.
**Kohle-:** **~filter** *m* charcoal filter; **~hydrat** *nt* carbohydrate; **~kraftwerk** *nt* coal-fired power station.
**Kohlen-** *in cpds* coal; **~bergbau** *m* coal-mining; **~bergwerk** *nt* coalmine, pit, colliery; **~dioxid, ~dioxyd** *nt* carbon dioxide; **~grube** *f* coalmine, pit; **~halde** *f* pile of coal; **~händler** *m* coal merchant; **~heizung** *f* coal heating; **~herd** *m* range; **~kasten** *m* coal-box; **~keller** *m* coal cellar; **~lager** *nt (Vorrat)* coal depot; *(im Stollen, Berg)* coal seam; **~monoxid, ~monoxyd** *nt* carbon monoxide; **~ofen** *m* (coal-burning) stove; **~säure** *f (Chem)* carbonic acid; **ein Getränk ohne ~säure** a non-fizzy *or* still drink; **~schaufel** *f* coal shovel; **~stoff** *m* carbon; **~wasserstoff** *m* hydrocarbon.
**Kohle-:** **~papier** *nt* carbon paper; **~stift** *m (Art)* (piece of) charcoal; **~tablette** *f (Med)* charcoal tablet; **~zeichnung** *f* charcoal drawing.
**Kohl-:** **~kopf** *m* cabbage; **~meise** *f* great tit; **k~(pech)rabenschwarz** *adj Haar* jet black; *Nacht* pitch-black; **~rabi** *m* **-(s)** kohlrabi; **~rübe** *f* turnip; **k~schwarz** *adj Haare, Augen* jet black; *Gesicht, Hände* black as coal.
**Koitus** ['koːitus] *m* -, - *or* **-se** coitus.
**Koje** *f* **-n** *(esp Naut)* bunk; *(col: Bett)* bed.
**Kokain** *nt no pl* cocaine.
**kokett** *adj* coquettish, flirtatious.
**kokettieren\*** *vi* to flirt. **mit seinem Alter ~** to play on one's age; **mit einem Gedanken ~** to toy with an idea.
**Kokos-** *in cpds* coconut; **~flocken** *pl* desiccated coconut; **~milch** *f* coconut milk; **~nuß** *f* coconut; **~palme** *f* coconut palm.
**Koks** *m* **-e** coke.
**Koksheizung** *f* coke heating.
**Kolben** *m* - *(Tech)* piston; *(Gewehr~)* butt; *(Chem: Destillier~)* retort; *(von Lötapparat)* bit.

**Kolben-:** **k~förmig** *adj* club-shaped; **~ring** *m* piston ring.
**Kolibri** *m* **-s** humming bird.
**Kolik** *f* **-en** colic.
**Kollaborateur(in** *f)* [-'tøːɐ, -'tøːrɪn] *m (Pol)* collaborator.
**Kollage** [kɔ'laːʒə] *f* **-n** *(Art, fig)* collage.
**Kollaps** *m* **-e** *(Med)* collapse.
**Kolleg** *nt* **-s** *or* **-ien** [-iən] *(Univ: Vorlesung)* lecture; *(Vorlesungsreihe)* (course of) lectures.
**Kollege** *m (wk)* **-n,** **-n, Kollegin** *f* colleague. **seine ~n vom Fach** his professional colleagues, his fellow doctors/teachers *etc*; **meine ~n** the people I work with; **Herr ~!** Mr X/Y.
**kollegial** *adj* cooperative. **sich ~ verhalten** to be cooperative.
**Kollegialität** *f* cooperativeness.
**Kollegin** *siehe* **Kollege**.
**Kollegium** *nt (Lehrer~ etc)* staff; *(Ausschuß)* working party.
**Kollegmappe** *f* document case.
**Kollekte** *f* **-n** *(Eccl)* collection.
**Kollektion** *f* collection; *(Sortiment)* range.
**kollektiv** *adj* collective.
**Kollektiv** *nt* collective.
**Kollektiv-:** **~schuld** *f* collective guilt; **~strafe** *f* collective punishment; **~wirtschaft** *f (Econ)* collective economy.
**Koller** *m* - *(col) (Anfall)* funny mood; *(Wutanfall)* rage; *(Tropen~, Gefängnis~)* tropical/prison madness. **seinen ~ bekommen/haben** to get into/to be in one of one's silly *or* funny moods; **einen ~ haben/bekommen** to be in/fly into a rage.
**kollidieren\*** *vi (geh)* **(a)** *aux sein (Fahrzeuge)* to collide. **(b)** *aux sein or haben (fig)* to clash.
**Kollier** [kɔ'lieː] **-s** necklace.
**Kollision** *f (geh) (Zusammenstoß)* collision; *(Streit)* conflict, clash.
**Kollisionskurs** *m* **auf ~ gehen** *(fig)* to be heading for trouble.
**Kolloquium** *nt* colloquium.
**Köln** *nt* Cologne.
**Kölner** *adj attr* Cologne.
**kölnisch** *adj* Cologne.
**Kölnischwasser, Kölnisch Wasser** *nt* eau de Cologne, cologne.
**Kolonialismus** *m no pl* colonialism.
**Kolonial-:** **~macht** *f* colonial power; **~warenhändler** *m (dated)* grocer *(dated)*; **~zeit** *f* colonial era.
**Kolonie** *f* colony; *(Ferien~)* camp.
**kolonisieren\*** *vt Land* to colonize.
**Kolonnade** *f* colonnade.
**Kolonne** *f* **-n** column; *(Autoschlange)* queue *(Brit)*, line; *(Arbeits~)* gang. **„Achtung ~!"** "convoy"; **~ fahren** to drive in (a) convoy.
**Koloß** *m* **-sse** colossus.
**kolossal 1** *adj* colossal, enormous. **2** *adv (col)* enormously.
**Kolumbianer(in** *f)* *m* - Colombian.
**kolumbianisch** *adj* Colombian.
**Kolumbien** [-iən] *nt* Colombia.
**Kolumne** *f* **-n** *(Typ, Press)* column.
**Koma** *nt* **-s** *or* **-ta** *(Med)* coma.
**Kombi** *m* **-s** *(Aut)* estate (car) *(Brit)*, station wagon *(esp US)*.
**Kombination** *f* **(a)** *(Verbindung, Zahlen~)* combination; *(Sport: Zusammenspiel)* (piece of) team work. **(b)** *(Schlußfolgerung)* deduction; *(Vermutung)* conjecture. **(c)** *(Kleidung)* suit, ensemble; *(Hemdhose)* combinations *pl*; *(Arbeitsanzug)* overalls *pl*, boiler-

suit *(Brit)*; *(Flieger~)* flying suit.
**Kombinationsschloß** *nt* combination lock.
**kombinieren\* 1** *vt* to combine. **2** *vi (folgern)* to deduce; *(vermuten)* to suppose. **gut ~ können** to be good at deduction.
**Kombi-:** **~wagen** *m* estate (car) *(Brit)*, station wagon *(esp US)*; **~zange** *f* combination pliers *pl.*
**Komet** *m (wk)* **-en, -en** comet; *(fig)* meteor.
**kometenhaft** *adj (fig) Aufstieg* meteoric.
**Komfort** [kɔmˈfoːɐ] *m no pl (von Hotel etc)* luxury; *(von Möbel etc)* comfort; *(von Auto)* luxury features *pl*; *(von Gerät)* extras *pl*; *(von Wohnung)* amenities *pl.*
**komfortabel** *adj* luxurious, luxury *attr*; *(bequem) Sessel, Bett* comfortable.
**Komik** *f no pl (das Komische)* comic; *(komische Wirkung)* comic effect; *(lustiges Element)* comic element.
**Komiker** *m - (lit, fig)* comedian, comic.
**komisch** *adj* **(a)** *(spaßig)* funny, comical; *(Theat)* comic. **(b)** *(seltsam)* funny, strange, odd. **das K~e daran ist ...** the funny *or* strange *or* odd thing about it is ...; **mir ist so ~** *(col)* I feel funny.
**komischerweise** *adv* funnily enough.
**Komitee** *nt* **-s** committee.
**Komma** *nt* **-s** *or* **-ta** comma; *(Math)* decimal point. **fünf ~ drei** five point three.
**Kommandant** *m (Mil)* commanding officer; *(Naut)* captain; *(von Stadt)* commandant.
**Kommandeur** [kɔmanˈdøːɐ] *m* commander.
**kommandieren\* 1** *vt* **(a)** *(befehligen)* to command, to be in command of. **(b)** *(befehlen)* **jdn an einen Ort ~** to order sb to a place. **2** *vi* **(a)** *(Befehlsgewalt haben)* to be in command. **~der General** commanding general. **(b)** *(Befehle geben)* to give orders.
**Kommanditgesellschaft** *f* limited partnership.
**Kommando** *nt* **-s** **(a)** *(Befehl)* command, order. **das ~ zum Schießen geben** to give the command *or* order to fire; **auf ~ schreit ihr alle ...** on the command (you) all shout ...; **ich kann doch nicht auf ~ lustig sein** I can't be cheerful to order; **wie auf ~ stehenbleiben** to stand still as if by command. **(b)** *(Befehlsgewalt)* command. **das ~ haben** to be in command *(über +acc of)*. **(c)** *(Mil) (Behörde)* command; *(Abteilung)* commando.
**Kommando-:** **~brücke** *f (Naut)* bridge; **~wirtschaft** *f* command economy.
**kommen** *pret* **kam**, *ptp* **gekommen** *aux sein* **1** *vi* **(a)** to come; *(an~ auch)* to arrive; *(her~)* to come over; *(hervor~) (Blüten, Sonne)* to come out; *(Zähne auch)* to come through; *(sich entwickeln: Pflanzen)* to come on. **ich komme (schon)** I'm just coming; **er wird gleich ~** he'll be here right away; **der Nachtisch kommt gleich** dessert is coming straight away; **wann soll der Zug/das Baby ~?** when is the train/baby due?; **nach Hause ~** to come *or* get home; **der Wagen kommt in 16 Sekunden auf 100 km/h** the car reaches 62 mph in 16 seconds; **das Schlimmste kommt noch** the worst is yet to come; **ich komme zuerst an die Reihe** I'm first; **jetzt kommt's** here it comes, wait for it! *(col)*; **bohren, bis Öl/Grundwasser kommt** to drill until one strikes oil/finds water; **jetzt muß bald die Grenze/Hannover ~** we should soon be at the border/in Hanover; **wie sie (gerade) ~** just as they come; **bitte kommen!** *(Telec)* come in please; **daher kommt es, daß...** that's why ...; **das kommt davon, daß ...** that's because ...; **das kommt daher, daß es soviel geregnet hat** that's because of *or* that comes from all the rain we've had; **das kommt davon!** see what happens?

**(b)** *(stattfinden, sich zutragen)* to happen; *(TV, Rad, etc: gegeben werden)* to be on. **ich glaube, es kommt ein Unwetter** I think there's some bad weather on the way; **was kommt diese Woche im Kino?** what's on at the cinema this week?; **egal, was kommt, ich bleibe fröhlich** whatever happens, I shall remain cheerful; **komme, was da wolle** come what may; **so mußte es ja ~** it had to happen; **das hätte nicht ~ dürfen** that should never have happened.
**(c)** *(kosten, sich belaufen)* **das kommt zusammen auf 20 DM** that comes to 20 marks altogether.
**(d)** *(gelangen)* to get; *(mit Hand etc erreichen können)* to reach. **wie komme ich nach London?** how do I get to London?; **ich komme zur Zeit nicht aus dem Haus** at the moment I never get out of the house; **durch den Zoll/die Prüfung ~** to get through customs/the exam; **zu einem Entschluß/einer Einigung ~** to come to a conclusion/an agreement; **in das Alter ~, wo ...** to reach the age when ...
**(e)** *(hingehören, gebracht werden)* to go. **das Buch kommt ins oberste Fach** the book goes on the top shelf; **in die Ecke kommt noch ein Schrank** another cupboard is to go in that corner; **ins Gefängnis ~** to go to prison; **in die Schule ~** to start school; **ins Krankenhaus ~** to go into hospital.
**(f)** **komm, wir gehen** come along, we're going; **ach komm!** come on!; **komm, fang bloß nicht wieder damit an** come on, don't start that again; **ihm kamen Zweifel** he started to have doubts; **jdm kommen die Tränen** tears come to sb's eyes; **ihm kam das Grausen** terror seized him; **mir kommt eine Idee** I just had an idea; **du kommst mir gerade recht** *(iro)* you're just what I need; **das kommt mir gerade recht** that's just fine; **jdm frech/dumm ~** to be cheeky to sb/to act stupid; **angelaufen ~** to come running along *or (auf einen zu)* up; **kommt essen!** come and eat!; **jdn besuchen ~** to come and visit sb; **neben jdm zu sitzen ~** to end up sitting next to sb; **jdn ~ sehen** to see sb coming; **ich habe es ~ sehen** I saw it coming; **die Zeit für gekommen halten** to think the time has come; **jdn ~ lassen** *Arzt, Polizei, Schüler, Sekretärin* to send for sb; **etw ~ lassen** *Mahlzeit, Taxi* to order; *Kupplung* to let in; *Seil* to let come; *Motor* to start up; **in Bewegung ~** to start moving; **ins Erzählen ~** to get talking; **zum Blühen/Wachsen etc ~** to start flowering/growing; **zum Stehen/Stillstand ~** to come to a halt/standstill; **kommt Zeit, kommt Rat** *(Prov)* things have a way of working themselves out; **wer zuerst kommt, mahlt zuerst** *(Prov)* first come first served.
**(g)** **an etw** *(acc)* **~** *(berühren)* to touch sth; *(sich verschaffen)* to get hold of sth; **auf etw** *(acc)* **~** *(sich erinnern)* to think of sth; *(sprechen über)* to get onto sth; **auf einen Gedanken ~** to have a thought; **das kommt auf die Rechnung** that goes onto the bill; **auf ihn/darauf lasse ich nichts ~** *(col)* I won't hear a word against him/it; **auf jeden ~ fünf Mark** there are five marks (for) each; **wie kommst du darauf?** what makes you think that?; **darauf bin ich nicht gekommen** I didn't think of that; **ich komme im Moment nicht auf seinen Namen** his name escapes me for the moment; **hinter etw** *(acc)* **~** *(herausfinden)* to find sth out; **mit einem Anliegen ~** to have a request (to make); **um etw ~** *(verlieren)* um Besitz, Leben to lose sth; *um Essen, Schlaf* to (have to) go without sth; **zu etw ~** *(Zeit finden für)* to get around to sth; *(erhalten)* to come by sth; *(erben)* to come into sth; **wie komme ich zu der Ehre?** to what do I owe this honour?; **hierzu kommt noch seine Kurzsichtigkeit** then there's his shortsightedness on top

of that; **zu sich** ~ to come to; *(sich fassen)* to recover; *(sich finden)* to sort oneself out.

    **2** *vi impers* **es** ~ **jetzt die Nachrichten** and now the news; **es werden viele Leute** ~ a lot of people will come; **es kommt noch einmal so weit** *or* **dahin, daß** ... it will get to the point where ...; **so weit kommt es (noch)** that'll be the day *(col)*; **wie kommt es, daß du ...?** how is it that you ...?; **ich wußte, daß es so** ~ **würde** I knew that would happen; **dazu kam es gar nicht mehr** it didn't come to that; **es kam zum Streit** there was a quarrel; **es kam eins zum anderen** one thing led to another; **und so kam es, daß ...** and that is how it happened that ...; **es kam ganz plötzlich** it happened very suddenly; **es kam, wie es** ~ **mußte** the inevitable happened; **es kommt immer anders, als man denkt** *(prov)* things never turn out the way you expect; **es mag** ~**, wie es** ~ **will** whatever happens.

    **3** *vt (col: kosten)* to cost.

**Kommen** *nt no pl* coming. **ein einziges** ~ **und Gehen** a constant coming and going; **jd ist im** ~ *(fig)* sb is on his/her way up.

**kommend** *adj Jahr, Woche, Generation* coming; *Ereignisse, Mode* future. **der** ~**e Meister** the future champion; **(am)** ~**en Montag** next Monday.

**Kommentar** *m (Bemerkung, Stellungnahme)* comment; *(Press, Jur, Liter)* commentary. **kein** ~**!** no comment; **einen** ~ **(zu etw) (ab)geben** to comment on sth.

**kommentarlos** *adj* without comment.

**Kommentator** *m*, **Kommentatorin** *f* commentator.

**kommentieren\*** *vt (Press etc)* to comment on; **kommentierte Ausgabe** annotated edition.

**kommerzialisieren\*** *vt* to commercialize.

**kommerziell** *adj* commercial.

**Kommilitone** *m (wk)* **-n, -n, Kommilitonin** *f* fellow student.

**Kommissar** *m (Polizei~)* inspector; *(ranghöher)* (police) superintendent.

**Kommissariat** *nt (Polizei) (Amt)* office of inspector or *(ranghöher)* superintendent; *(Dienststelle)* superintendent's department.

**kommissarisch 1** *adj* temporary. **2** *adv* on a temporary basis.

**Kommission** *f* **(a)** *(Ausschuß)* committee; *(zur Untersuchung)* commission. **(b)** *(Comm)* commission. **etw in** ~ **geben** to give (to a dealer) for sale on commission; **etw in** ~ **nehmen/haben** to take/have sth on commission.

**Kommode** *f* **-n** chest of drawers; *(hohe)* tallboy *(Brit)*, highboy *(US)*.

**kommunal** *adj* local; *(von Stadt auch)* municipal.

**Kommunal-:** ~**abgaben** *pl* local rates and taxes *pl*; ~**politik** *f* local government politics; ~**verwaltung** *f* local government; ~**wahlen** *pl* local (government) elections *pl*.

**Kommune** *f* **-n (a)** *(Gemeinde)* community. **(b)** *(Wohngemeinschaft)* commune.

**Kommunikation** *f* communication.

**Kommunion** *f (Eccl)* (Holy) Communion.

**Kommuniqué** [kɔmyniˈkeː] *nt* **-s** communiqué.

**Kommunismus** *m* communism.

**Kommunist(in** *f)* *m* Communist.

**kommunistisch** *adj* communist; *(Partei, Manifest etc)* Communist.

**kommunizieren\*** *vi* **(a)** to communicate. **(b)** *(Eccl)* to receive (Holy) Communion.

**Komödie** [-iə] *f* comedy; *(fig: heiteres Ereignis)* farce. ~ **spielen** *(fig)* to put on an act.

**Kompagnon** [ˈkɔmpanjõ] *m* **-s** *(Comm)* partner, associate.

**kompakt** *adj* compact.

**Kompakt|anlage** *f (Rad)* compact audio system.

**Kompanie** *f (Mil)* company.

**Komparativ** *m (Gram)* comparative.

**Komparse** *m (wk)* **-n, -n, Komparsin** *f (Film)* extra; *(Theat)* supernumerary.

**Kompaß** *m* **-sse** compass. **nach dem** ~ by the compass.

**Kompaßnadel** *f* compass needle.

**kompatibel** *adj (Tech)* compatible.

**Kompatibilität** *f* compatibility.

**Kompensation** *f* compensation.

**kompensieren\*** *vt* to compensate for, to offset.

**kompetent** *adj* competent; *(befugt)* authorized.

**Kompetenz** *f* (area of) authority *or* competence; *(eines Gerichts)* jurisdiction, competence. **da hat er ganz eindeutig seine** ~**en überschritten** he has clearly exceeded his authority here; **das fällt in die** ~ **dieses Amtes** that's the responsibility of this office; **seine mangelnde** ~ **in dieser Frage** his lack of competence in this issue.

**Kompetenzstreitigkeiten** *pl* dispute over respective areas of responsibility.

**komplementär** *adj* complementary.

**komplett 1** *adj* complete. **2** *adv* completely.

**Komplex** *m* **-e** complex.

**komplex** *adj* complex.

**Komplikation** *f* complication.

**Kompliment** *nt* compliment. **jdm** ~**e machen** to pay sb compliments *(wegen* on*)*.

**Komplize** *m (wk)* **-n, -n, Komplizin** *f* accomplice.

**komplizieren\*** *vt* to complicate.

**kompliziert** *adj* complicated; *(Med) Bruch* compound.

**Komplott** *nt* **-e** plot, conspiracy. **ein** ~ **schmieden** to hatch a plot.

**Komponente** *f* **-n** component.

**komponieren\*** *vti* to compose.

**Komponist(in** *f)* *m* composer.

**Komposition** *f* composition.

**Kompositum** *nt, pl* **Komposita** *(Gram, Chem)* compound.

**Kompost** *m* **-e** compost.

**Komposthaufen** *m* compost heap.

**Kompott** *nt* **-e** stewed fruit.

**Kompresse** *f* compress.

**Kompression** *f (Tech)* compression.

**Kompressor** *m* compressor.

**komprimieren\*** *vt* to compress; *(fig)* to condense.

**Kompromiß** *m* **-sse** compromise. **einen** ~ **schließen** to compromise.

**Kompromiß-:** **k**~**bereit** *adj* willing to compromise; ~**bereitschaft** *f* willingness to compromise; **k**~**los** *adj* uncompromising; ~**lösung** *f* compromise solution.

**kompromittieren\* 1** *vt* to compromise. **2** *vr* to compromise oneself.

**Kondensation** *f (Chem, Phys)* condensation.

**Kondensator** *m (Aut, Chem)* condenser; *(Elec auch)* capacitor.

**kondensieren\*** *vti (lit, fig)* to condense; *(fig auch)* to distil *(Brit)*, to distill *(US)*.

**Kondens-:** ~**milch** *f* evaporated milk; ~**streifen** *m* vapour *(Brit)* or vapor *(US)* trail; ~**wasser** *nt* condensation.

**Kondition** *f* condition, shape; *(Durchhaltevermögen)* stamina. **eine gute/schlechte** ~ **haben** to be in good/bad shape; **wie ist seine** ~**?** what sort of condition is he in?; **er hat überhaupt keine** ~ he is completely unfit; *(fig)* he has absolutely no stamina.

**Konditions-**: ~**schwäche** f lack of fitness *no pl*; ~**training** *nt* fitness training.
**Konditor** *m*, **Konditorin** f pastrycook.
**Konditorei** f cake shop; *(mit Café)* café.
**Kondolenz-** *in cpds* of condolence.
**kondolieren*** *vi* (jdm) ~ to offer one's condolences (to sb).
**Kondom** *m or nt* -**e** condom.
**Konfekt** *nt* -**e** confectionery.
**Konfektion** f *(Herstellung)* manufacture of ready-to-wear clothing; *(Bekleidung)* ready-to-wear clothes *pl or* clothing.
**Konfektions-** *in cpds* ready-to-wear; ~**größe** f standard size.
**Konferenz** f conference; *(Besprechung)* meeting.
**Konferenz-** *in cpds* conference; ~**schaltung** f *(Telec)* conference circuit; *(Rad, TV)* (television/radio) link-up.
**konferieren*** *vi* to confer *(über +acc* on *or* about).
**Konfession** f (religious) denomination.
**konfessionell** *adj* denominational.
**Konfessions-**: k~**los** *adj* non-denominational; ~**schule** f denominational school.
**Konfetti** *nt no pl* confetti.
**Konfiguration** f *(auch Comp)* configuration.
**Konfirmand(in** f) *m* (wk) -**en**, -**en** *(Eccl)* confirmation candidate.
**Konfirmation** f *(Eccl)* confirmation.
**konfiszieren*** *vt* to confiscate.
**Konfitüre** f -**n** jam.
**Konflikt** *m* -**e** conflict. **bewaffneter** ~ armed conflict; **er befindet sich in einem (inneren)** ~ he is in a state of inner conflict.
**Konflikt-**: ~**fall** *m* **im** ~**fall** in case of conflict; **k~freudig** *adj* combative; ~**herd** *m* *(esp Pol)* centre *(Brit) or* center *(US)* of conflict; ~**situation** f conflict situation; ~**stoff** *m* cause for conflict.
**konform** *adj* Ansichten *etc* concurring. **mit jdm** ~ **gehen** to be in agreement with sb *(in +dat* about*)*.
**Konformist(in** f) *m* *(pej)* conformist.
**konformistisch** *adj* conformist, conforming.
**Konfrontation** f confrontation.
**konfrontieren*** *vt* to confront *(mit* with*)*.
**konfus** *adj* confused, muddled.
**Kongo** *m* Congo.
**Kongolese** *m* (wk) -**n**, -**n**, **Kongolesin** f Congolese.
**kongolesisch** *adj* Congolese.
**Kongreß** *m* -**sse** *(Pol)* congress; *(US Pol)* Congress; *(fachlich)* convention, conference.
**Kongreß-**: ~**mitglied** *nt* *(US Pol)* Congressman/-woman; ~**teilnehmer** *m* person attending a congress/conference *or* convention; ~**zentrum** *nt* conference centre.
**kongruent** *adj* *(Math)* congruent.
**König** *m* -**e** king.
**Königin** f *(auch Zool)* queen.
**Königinpastete** f vol-au-vent.
**königlich 1** *adj* royal. **2** *adv* **sich** ~ **amüsieren** *(col)* to have the time of one's life *(col)*.
**Königreich** *nt* kingdom, realm *(poet)*.
**Königs-**: k~**blau** *adj* royal blue; ~**krone** f royal crown; ~**paar** *nt* royal couple; k~**treu** *adj* royalist.
**konisch** *adj* conical.
**Konjugation** f conjugation.
**konjugieren*** *vt* to conjugate.
**Konjunktion** f *(Astron, Gram)* conjunction.
**Konjunktiv** *m* *(Gram)* subjunctive.
**Konjunktur** f economic situation; *(Hoch~)* boom. **steigende/fallende** ~ upward/downward economic trend.

**Konjunktur-**: ~**abschwung** *m* economic downturn; ~**aufschwung** *m* economic upturn; ~**einbruch** *m* slump.
**konjunkturell** *adj* economic. ~ **bedingt** caused by economic factors.
**Konjunkturpolitik** f *policies aimed at preventing economic fluctuation.*
**konkav** *adj* concave.
**konkret** *adj* concrete. **ich kann dir nichts K~es sagen** I can't tell you anything definite.
**konkretisieren*** *vt* to put in concrete form *or* terms.
**Konkurrent(in** f) *m* rival; *(Comm auch)* competitor.
**Konkurrenz** f *(Wettbewerb)* rivalry; *(~betrieb)* competitors *pl*; *(Gesamtheit der Konkurrenten)* competition, competitors *pl*. **die** ~ **auf diesem Gebiet ist größer geworden** the competition in this field has increased; **jdm** ~ **machen** *(Comm, fig)* to compete with sb; *(Comm)* to be in/enter into competition with sb.
**Konkurrenz-**: ~**druck** *m* pressure of competition; k~**fähig** *adj* competitive; ~**kampf** *m* competition; *(zwischen zwei Menschen auch)* rivalry; **ein** ~**kampf, bei dem wir uns durchgesetzt haben** a competitive situation in which we came out on top; k~**los** *adj* without competition.
**konkurrieren*** *vi* to compete.
**Konkurs** *m* -**e** bankruptcy. **in** ~ **gehen**, ~ **machen** *(col)* to go bankrupt.
**Konkurs-**: ~**masse** f bankrupt's estate; ~**verfahren** *nt* bankruptcy proceedings *pl*; ~**verwalter** *m* receiver; *(von Gläubigern bevollmächtigt)* trustee.
**können** *pret* **konnte**, *ptp* **gekonnt** *or (bei modal aux)* ~ *vti, modal aux* **(a)** *(vermögen)* to be able to. **ich kann es machen** I can do it, I am able to do it; **ich kann es nicht machen** I can't do it; **man konnte ihn retten** they managed to save him; **man konnte ihn nicht retten** they couldn't save him; **ich konnte es nicht verstehen** I couldn't *or* was unable to understand it; **ich habe es sehen** ~ I could see it; **er hat es gekonnt** he was able to do it; **morgen kann ich nicht** I can't (manage) tomorrow; **das hättest du gleich sagen** ~ you could *or* might have said that straight away; **ich kann das nicht mehr sehen** I can't stand the sight of it any more; **ich kann nicht mehr** I can't go on; *(ertragen)* I can't take any more; *(essen)* I can't eat any more; **so schnell er konnte** as fast as he could.
**(b)** *(beherrschen)* Sprache to know, to be able to speak; Schach to be able to play; Klavier spielen, lesen, schwimmen, Skilaufen *etc* to be able to, to know how to. **was** ~ **Sie?** what can you do?; **was du alles kannst!** the things you can do!; **er kann was** he's very capable; ~ **Sie Deutsch?** do you speak German?; **er kann gut Englisch** he speaks English well; **er kann keine Grammatik** he has no idea of grammar.
**(c)** *(dürfen)* to be allowed to. **kann ich jetzt gehen?** can I go now?; **könnte ich ...?** could I ...?; **er kann sich nicht beklagen** he can't complain; **man kann wohl sagen, daß ...** one could well say that ...; **du kannst mich (mal)!** *(col)* get lost! *(col)*; **kann ich mit?** *(col)* can I come with you?
**(d)** *(möglich sein)* **Sie könnten recht haben** you may be right; **er kann jeden Augenblick kommen** he might come any minute; **das kann nur er gewesen sein** it can only have been him; **wer könnte das gewesen sein?** who could it have been?; **das kann nicht sein** that can't be true; **es kann sein/es kann nicht sein, daß er da war** he may have been there/

**Kontrolle**

he couldn't have been there; **kann sein** maybe.
(e) **für etw** ~ to be responsible for sth; **ich kann nichts dafür** it's not my fault.
**Können** nt no pl ability, skill.
**Könner** m - expert.
**konnte** pret of **können**.
**Konsens** m **-e** agreement, consent.
**konsequent** adj consistent. **die Bestimmungen** ~ **einhalten** to observe the regulations strictly; **wir werden** ~ **durchgreifen** we will take rigorous action; **~e Weiterentwicklung eines Stils** logically consistent development of a style; **wenn du das** ~ **durchdenkst** if you follow it through to its logical conclusion; **ein Ziel** ~ **verfolgen** to pursue an objective single-mindedly.
**Konsequenz** f (a) (Schlußfolgerung) consequence. **die ~en tragen** to take the consequences; **(aus etw) die ~en ziehen** to draw the logical conclusion (from sth). (b) (Beharrlichkeit) consistency; (bei Maßnahmen) rigorousness. **die ~, mit der er sein Ziel verfolgte** the single-mindedness with which he pursued his aim.
**konservativ** [-va-] adj conservative; (Brit Pol) Conservative, Tory.
**Konservative(r)** [-va-] mf decl as adj conservative; (Brit Pol) Conservative, Tory.
**Konservatorium** [-va-] nt conservatory.
**Konserve** [kɔn'zɛrvə] f **-n** preserved food; (in Dosen) tinned (Brit) or canned food; (~ndose) tin (Brit), can; (Med: Blut~) unit of stored blood. **sich von ~n ernähren** to live out of cans.
**Konserven-**: **~büchse**, **~dose** f tin (Brit), can.
**konservieren*** [kɔnzɛr'viːrən] vt to preserve.
**Konservierung** f preservation.
**Konservierungs-**: **~mittel** nt, **~stoff** m preservative.
**Konsistenz** f consistency.
**konsolidieren*** vt to consolidate.
**Konsolidierung** f consolidation.
**Konsonant** m consonant.
**Konsorten** pl (pej col) gang (col), mob (col). **X und** ~ **X** and his gang or mob.
**Konsortium** [kɔn'zɔrtsiʊm] nt consortium.
**Konspiration** [kɔnspira'tsioːn] f conspiracy, plot.
**konspirativ** [kɔnspira'tiːf] adj **~e Wohnung** safe house (used by terrorists).
**konspirieren*** [kɔnspi'riːrən] vi to conspire, to plot.
**konstant** [kɔn'stant] adj constant.
**Konstante** [kɔn'stantə] f **-n** constant.
**konstatieren*** [kɔnsta'tiːrən] vt (geh) to see, to notice; (sagen) to state.
**Konstellation** [kɔnstɛla'tsioːn] f constellation; (fig) line-up; (von Faktoren etc) combination.
**konsterniert** adj filled with consternation.
**Konstitution** [kɔnstitu'tsioːn] f (Pol, Med) constitution.
**konstitutionell** [kɔnstitutsio'nɛl] adj constitutional.
**konstruieren*** [kɔnstru'iːrən] vt to construct; (Gram auch) to construe. **ein konstruierter Fall** a hypothetical case.
**Konstrukteur(in** f) [kɔnstrʊk'tøːɐ, -tøːrɪn] m designer.
**Konstruktion** [kɔnstrʊk'tsioːn] f construction; (Entwurf, Bauart auch) design.
**Konstruktionsfehler** m (im Entwurf) design fault; (im Aufbau) structural defect.
**konstruktiv** [kɔnstrʊk'tiːf] adj constructive.
**Konsul** m **-n** consul.
**Konsulat** nt consulate.
**Konsultation** f (form) consultation.

**konsultieren*** vt (form) to consult.
**Konsum** m **-s** (a) [kɔn'zuːm] no pl (Verbrauch) consumption. (b) ['kɔnzuːm, 'kɔnzʊm] (Genossenschaft) cooperative society; (Laden) cooperative store, co-op (col).
**Konsum-**: **~artikel** m consumer item; **~artikel** pl consumer goods pl; **~denken** nt consumerism.
**Konsument(in** f) m consumer.
**Konsum-**: **~gesellschaft** f consumer society; **~güter** pl consumer goods pl.
**konsumieren*** vt to consume.
**Konsum-**: **~terror** m (pej) pressures pl of a materialistic society; **~zwang** m (Sociol) compulsion to buy.
**Kontakt** m **-e** contact; (pl: Aut) contacts, points pl. **mit jdm in** ~ **kommen** to come into contact with sb; **zu jdm** ~ **finden** to get to know sb; **mit jdm** ~ **aufnehmen/in** ~ **stehen** to get/be in touch with sb; ~ **herstellen** to make contact; **den** ~ **unterbrechen** to break contact; **keinen** ~ **mehr haben, den** ~ **verloren haben** to be out of touch.
**Kontakt-**: **~anzeigen** pl personal column; **k~arm** adj **er ist k~arm** he finds it difficult to make friends; **~bildschirm** m touch-sensitive screen; **k~freudig** adj sociable; **~linse** f contact lens; **~mann** m, pl **~männer** (Agent) contact; **~person** f contact; **~sperre** f (für Gefangene) ban on visits and letters.
**Konten** pl of **Konto**.
**kontern** vti Schlag, Angriff to counter.
**Kontext** m **-e** context.
**Kontinent** m **-e** continent.
**kontinental** adj continental.
**Kontingent** [kɔntɪŋ'gɛnt] nt **-e** (Comm) quota, share; (Zuteilung) allocation.
**kontinuierlich** adj continuous.
**Kontinuität** [kɔntinui'tɛːt] f continuity.
**Konto** nt, pl **-s** or **Konten** account. **auf meinem/ mein** ~ in my/into my account; **das geht auf mein** ~ (col) (ich bin schuldig) I am to blame for this; (ich zahle) this is on me (col).
**Konto-**: **~auszug** m (bank) statement; **~führungsgebühr** f bank charge; **~inhaber** m account holder; **~nummer** f account number; **~stand** m balance.
**kontra** prep +acc against; (Jur) versus.
**Kontra** nt **-s** (Cards) double. **jdm** ~ **geben** (fig) to contradict sb.
**Kontrabaß** m double-bass.
**Kontrahent** [kɔntra'hɛnt] m (bei Vertrag) contracting party; (Gegner) opponent, adversary.
**Kontra|indikation** f (Med) contra-indication.
**Kontrakt** m **-e** contract.
**Kontrapunkt** m (Mus) counterpoint.
**konträr** adj (geh) Meinungen contrary, opposite.
**Kontrast** m **-e** contrast.
**Kontrast-**: **~brei** m (Med) barium meal; **~farbe** f contrasting colour (Brit) or color (US).
**kontrastieren*** vi to contrast.
**Kontroll|abschnitt** m (Comm) counterfoil (Brit), stub.
**Kontrollampe** f pilot lamp; (Aut: für Ölstand etc) warning light.
**Kontrollbeamte(r)** m inspector; (an der Grenze) frontier guard; (zur Paßkontrolle) passport officer; (zur Zollkontrolle) customs officer; (zur Überwachung) security officer.
**Kontrolle** f **-n** (a) (Beherrschung, Regulierung) control. **über jdn/etw die** ~ **verlieren** to lose control of sb/sth; **jdn/etw unter** ~ **haben/halten** to have/keep sb/sth under control. (b) (Nachprüfung) check (gen

on*)*; *(Aufsicht)* supervision; *(Paß~)* passport control; *(Zoll~)* customs examination. **zur ~ haben wir noch einmal alles nachgerechnet** we went over all the figures again to check; **die ~ von Lebensmitteln** the inspection of foodstuffs. **(c)** *(Stelle) (für Nach-/ Überprüfung, Verkehr)* checkpoint; *(Paß~/Zoll~)* passport control/customs; *(vor Fabrik)* gatehouse; *(an der Grenze)* border post.

**Kontrolleur** [kɔntrɔ'løːɐ] *m* inspector.

**kontrollieren*** *vt* **(a)** *(regulieren, beherrschen)* to control. **(b)** *(nachprüfen, überwachen)* to check; *(Aufsicht haben über)* to supervise; *Paß, Fahrkarte etc* to inspect, to check. **die Qualität der Waren muß streng kontrolliert werden** a strict check must be kept on the quality of the goods; **jdn/etw nach etw ~** to check sb/sth for sth.

**Kontrolliste** *f* check-list.

**Kontroll-:** **~kommission** *f* control commission; **~punkt** *m*, **~stelle** *f* checkpoint; **~turm** *m* control tower; **~uhr** *f* time clock; **~versuch** *m* control experiment; **~zentrum** *nt* *(Space)* control centre *(Brit)* or center *(US)*.

**kontrovers** [kɔntro'vɛrs] *adj* controversial.

**Kontroverse** [kɔntro'vɛrzə] *f* **-n** controversy.

**Kontur** *f* **-en** outline, contour.

**Konvention** [kɔnvɛn'tsioːn] *f* convention. **sich über die ~en hinwegsetzen** to ignore conventions.

**Konventionalstrafe** [kɔnvɛntsio'naːl-] *f* penalty or fine (for breach of contract).

**konventionell** [kɔnvɛntsio'nɛl] *adj* conventional.

**Konversation** [kɔnvɛrza'tsioːn] *f* conversation. **~ machen** to make conversation.

**Konversationslexikon** *nt* encyclopaedia *(Brit)*, encyclopedia *(US)*.

**konvertieren*** [kɔnvɛr'tiːrən] *vt* to convert *(in +acc* into*)*.

**konvex** [kɔn'vɛks] *adj* convex.

**Konvoi** ['kɔnvɔy, -'-] *m* **-s** convoy. **im ~ fahren** to drive in convoy.

**Konzentrat** *nt* concentrate.

**Konzentration** *f* concentration *(auf +acc* on*)*.

**Konzentrations-:** **~fähigkeit** *f* powers of concentration *pl*; **~lager** *nt* concentration camp; **~schwäche** *f* poor concentration.

**konzentrieren*** **1** *vt* to concentrate *(auf +acc* on*)*; *Truppen auch* to mass. **2** *vr* to concentrate *(auf +acc* on*)*; *(Untersuchung, Arbeit etc)* to be concentrated *(auf +acc* on*)*.

**konzentriert** *adj* **(a)** *(Chem)* concentrated. **(b)** **mit ~er Aufmerksamkeit** with all one's concentration; **~ arbeiten/zuhören** to work/listen with concentration; **~ nachdenken** to concentrate.

**konzentrisch** *adj* concentric.

**Konzept** *nt* **-e** *(Rohentwurf)* draft, notes *pl*; *(Plan, Programm)* plan; *(Begriff, Vorstellung)* concept. **jdn aus dem ~ bringen** to break sb's train of thought; *(col: aus dem Gleichgewicht)* to throw sb *(col)*; **das paßt mir nicht ins ~** that doesn't fit in with my plans; *(gefällt mir nicht)* I don't like the idea.

**Konzeption** *f* *(geh)* conception.

**konzeptionslos** *adj* without a definite line.

**Konzeptpapier** *nt* rough paper.

**Konzern** *m* **-e** combine, group (of companies). **die ~e haben zuviel Macht** the big companies have too much power.

**Konzert** *nt* **-e** concert; *(Komposition)* concerto.

**Konzert-:** **~besucher** *m* concertgoer; **~flügel** *m* concert grand.

**konzertiert** *adj* **~e Aktion** *(Fin, Pol)* concerted action.

**Konzertina** *f, pl* **Konzertinen** concertina.

**Konzert-:** **~meister** *m* leader, concertmaster *(US)*; **~pianist** *m* concert pianist; **~saal** *m* concert hall.

**Konzession** *f* **(a)** *(Gewerbeerlaubnis)* concession, licence *(Brit)*, license *(US)*. **(b)** *(Zugeständnis)* concession *(an +acc* to*)*.

**konzessionsbereit** *adj* willing to make concessions.

**Konzil** *nt* **-e** or **-ien** [-iən] *(Eccl, Univ)* council.

**konzipieren*** *vt* to conceive; *(entwerfen auch)* to design.

**Ko|operation** *f* cooperation.

**ko|operativ** *adj* cooperative.

**ko|operieren*** *vi* to cooperate.

**Ko|ordinate** *f* **-en** *(Math)* coordinate.

**Ko|ordination** *f* coordination.

**Ko|ordinator** *m*, **Ko|ordinatorin** *f* coordinator.

**ko|ordinieren*** *vt* to coordinate.

**Ko|ordinierung** *f* coordination.

**Kopenhagen** *nt* Copenhagen.

**Köper** *m no pl (Tex)* twill.

**Kopf** *m* **ːe (a)** head. **mit bloßem ~** bareheaded; **~ an ~** shoulder to shoulder; *(Pferderennen, Sport)* neck and neck; **bis über den ~** *(im Wasser)* up to one's neck; *(in Schulden)* up to one's ears; **~ hoch!** chin up!; **auf dem ~ stehen** to stand on one's head; **jdm den ~ waschen** *(col)* to give sb a piece of one's mind *(col)*; **den ~ oben behalten** to keep one's chin up; **jds ~ fordern** *(lit, fig)* to demand sb's head; **von ~ bis Fuß** from head to foot; **sich *(dat)* an den ~ fassen** *(fig)* to be speechless; **da kann man sich nur an den ~ fassen** it makes you despair; **die ~e zusammenstecken** to put their heads together; *(heimlich)* to go into a huddle *(col)*; **einen schweren ~ haben** to have a thick head; **Geld** *etc* **auf den ~ hauen** *(col)* to blow one's money *etc (col)*; **jdm über den ~ wachsen** *(lit)* to outgrow sb; *(fig: Sorgen etc)* to be more than sb can cope with; **den ~ für jdn/etw hinhalten** *(col)* to take the blame for sb/sth; **etw auf den ~ stellen** *(lit, fig: durchsuchen)* to turn sth upside-down; **Tatsachen auf den ~ stellen** to stand facts on their heads; **und wenn du dich auf den ~ stellst, ...** *(col)* no matter what you say/do ...; **jdn den ~ kosten** *(lit)* to cost sb his head; *(fig)* to cost sb his career or job; **~ und Kragen riskieren** *(col)* to risk one's neck; **auf jds ~** *(acc)* **eine Belohnung aussetzen** to put a reward on sb's head; **er ist nicht auf den ~ gefallen** he's no fool; **jdm Beleidigungen an den ~ werfen** *(col)* to hurl insults at sb; **jdm etw auf den ~ zusagen** to say sth straight out to sb; **den ~ hängenlassen** *(fig)* to be downcast or despondent; **jdn vor den ~ stoßen** to antagonize sb; **jdm den ~ zurechtrücken** to bring sb to his/her senses; **mit dem ~ durch die Wand wollen** *(col)* to be determined to get one's own way regardless; **(jdm) zu ~(e) steigen** to go to sb's head; **ich war wie vor den ~ geschlagen** I was dumbfounded; **über jds ~** *(acc)* **hinweg** over sb's head; **ein ~ Salat/Kohl** a head of lettuce/cabbage; **~ oder Zahl?** heads or tails?

**(b)** *(Einzelperson)* person. **pro ~** per person or head; **das Einkommen pro ~** the per capita income.

**(c)** *(fig) (Verstand)* head; *(Denker)* thinker; *(leitende Persönlichkeit)* leader; *(Bandenführer)* brains *sing.* **sich** *(dat)* **über etw** *(acc)* **den ~ zerbrechen** to rack one's brains over sth; **er ist nicht ganz richtig im ~** *(col)* he is not quite right in the head; **ein kluger ~** an intelligent person; **er ist ein fähiger ~** he has a good head on his shoulders; **die besten ~e** the best brains or minds.

**(d)** *(Sinn)* head, mind. **sich** *(dat)* **etw durch den ~ gehen lassen** to think about sth; **nichts als Tanzen/ Fußball im ~ haben** to think of nothing but dancing/

football; **andere Dinge im ~ haben** to have other things on one's mind; **ich weiß kaum, wo mir der ~ steht** I scarcely know whether I'm coming or going; **den ~ verlieren** to lose one's head; **sich** *(dat)* **etw aus dem ~ schlagen** to put sth out of one's mind; **jdm den ~ verdrehen** to turn sb's head; **der Gedanke will mir nicht aus dem ~** I can't get the thought out of my head *or* mind; **das will mir nicht in den ~ hinein** I just can't grasp it; **im ~** in one's head; **etw im ~ rechnen** to work sth out in one's head; **aus dem ~** from memory; **sie hat es sich** *(dat)* **in den ~ gesetzt, das zu tun** she has taken it into her head to do that; **seinen ~ durchsetzen** to get one's own way.

**Kopf-: ~-an-~-Rennen** *nt* neck-and-neck race; **~arbeit** *f* brain-work; **~bahnhof** *m* terminus (station); **~ball** *m (Ftbl)* header; **~bedeckung** *f* headgear; **ohne ~bedeckung** without a hat.

**Köpfchen** *nt dim of* **Kopf** little head; *(fig hum)* brains. **~ haben** to be brainy *(col)*.

**köpfen** *vti* **(a)** *jdn* to behead; *(hum)* *Flasche Wein* to crack (open). **(b)** *(Ftbl)* to head. **ins Tor ~** to head the ball in.

**Kopf-: ~ende** *nt* head; **~geld** *nt* head money; **~grippe** *f* flu (and headache); **~haut** *f* scalp; **~hörer** *m* headphone; **~jäger** *m* head-hunter; **~kissen** *nt* pillow; **~kissenbezug** *m* pillow case; **~lage** *f (Med)* head presentation; **~länge** *f* **um eine ~länge** by a head; **k~lastig** *adj (lit, fig)* top-heavy; *Flugzeug* nose-heavy; **k~los** *adj (fig)* in a panic; *(lit)* headless; **k~los werden** to get into a flap *(col)*; **~losigkeit** *f (fig)* panickiness; **~nicken** *nt no pl* nod (of the head); **~prämie** *f* reward; **~rechnen** *nt* mental arithmetic; **~salat** *m* lettuce; **k~scheu** *adj* **jdn k~scheu machen** to intimidate sb; **~schmerz** *m usu pl* headache; **~schmerzen haben** to have a headache; **sich** *(dat)* **wegen etw ~schmerzen machen** *(fig)* to worry about sth; **~schmerztablette** *f* headache tablet; **~schuß** *m* shot in the head; **~schutz** *m* protection for the head; *(~schützer)* headguard; **~seite** *f (von Münze)* head, face side; **~sprung** *m* header, dive; **einen ~sprung machen** to dive (headfirst); **~stand** *m* headstand; **einen ~stand machen** to stand on one's head; **k~stehen** *vi sep irreg aux sein* **(a)** *(lit)* to stand on one's head; **(b)** *(fig) (vor Ausgelassenheit)* to go wild (with excitement); *(durcheinander sein)* to be all topsy-turvy *(col)*; **~steinpflaster** *nt* cobblestones *pl*; **eine Straße mit ~steinpflaster** a cobbled street; **~steuer** *f* poll tax; **~stütze** *f* head-rest; *(Aut)* head restraint; **~tuch** *nt* (head)scarf; **k~über** *adv (lit, fig)* headfirst, headlong; **~verletzung** *f* head injury; **~wäsche** *f* shampoo, hair-wash; **~weh** *nt siehe* **~schmerz**; **~zerbrechen** *nt* **sich** *(dat)* **über etw** *(acc)* **~zerbrechen machen** to worry about sth.

**Kopie** *f* copy; *(fig)* carbon copy; *(Durchschlag auch)* carbon (copy); *(Ablichtung)* photocopy; *(Phot)* print.

**kopieren*** *vti (lit, fig)* to copy; *(nachahmen)* to imitate; *(ablichten)* to photocopy; *(durchpausen)* to trace; *(Phot, Film)* to print.

**Kopierer** *m* copier.

**Kopier-: ~gerät** *nt* photocopier; **~papier** *nt* photocopy paper; **~schutz** *m (Comp)* copy protection; **mit ~schutz** copy-protected; **~stift** *m* indelible pencil.

**Kopilot(in** *f)* *m* co-pilot.

**Koppel** *f -n (Weide)* paddock, enclosure. **auf der ~** in the paddock *etc.*

**koppeln** *vt* **(a)** *(zusammenbinden)* to tie together.

**(b)** *(verbinden)* to couple, to join *(etw an etw (acc)* sth to sth)*; *zwei Dinge* to couple *or* join together; *(fig)* to link, to couple; *(als Bedingung)* to tie; *Ziele, Zwecke* to combine. **eine Dienstreise mit einem Urlaub ~** to combine a business trip with a holiday. **(c)** *(Elec)* to couple.

**Kopp(e)lung** *f no pl* **(a)** *(Elec)* coupling. **(b)** *(Verbindung) (lit)* coupling, joining; *(fig, von Raumschiffen)* link-up.

**Koproduktion** *f* co-production.

**Koproduzent** *m* co-producer.

**Kopulation** *f (Biol)* copulation, coupling.

**kopulieren*** *vi (koitieren)* to copulate.

**Koralle** *f -n* coral.

**Korallen-: ~bank** *f* coral reef; **~kette** *f* coral necklace; **~meer** *nt* Coral Sea; **~riff** *nt* coral reef.

**Koran** *m no pl* Koran.

**Korb** *m ⸚e* **(a)** basket; *(Fisch~ auch)* creel; *(Bienen~)* hive; *(Förder~)* cage. **ein ~ Äpfel** a basket of apples. **(b)** *(~geflecht)* wicker. **ein Sessel aus ~** a wicker(work) chair. **(c)** *(col: Abweisung)* refusal, rebuff. **einen ~ bekommen, sich** *(dat)* **einen ~ holen** to be turned down; **jdm einen ~ geben** to turn sb down.

**Korbball** *m* basketball.

**Körbchen** *nt* **(a)** *dim of* **Korb. ins ~!** *(baby-talk)* off to bye-byes *(baby-talk)*. **(b)** *(von Büstenhalter)* cup.

**Korb-: ~geflecht** *nt* basketwork, wickerwork; **~möbel** *pl* wicker(work) furniture; **~sessel, ~stuhl** *m* wicker(work) chair.

**Kord** *m -e* = **Cord.**

**Kordel** *f -n* cord.

**Korea** *nt* Korea.

**Koreaner(in** *f)* *m -* Korean.

**koreanisch** *adj* Korean.

**Koriander** *m no pl* coriander.

**Korinthe** *f -n* currant.

**Kork** *m -e* cork.

**Korken** *m -* cork; *(aus Plastik)* stopper.

**Korkenzieher** *m -* corkscrew.

**Kormoran** [kɔrmo'raːn] *m -e* cormorant.

**Korn¹** *nt -er* **(a)** *(Samen~)* seed, grain; *(Pfeffer~)* corn; *(Salz~, Sand~, Phot)* grain; *(Hagel~)* stone. **(b)** *no pl (Getreide)* grain, corn *(Brit)*.

**Korn²** *m - or -s (Kornbranntwein)* corn schnaps.

**Korn³** *nt -e (am Gewehr)* front sight, bead. **jdn/etw aufs ~ nehmen** *(fig col)* to keep tabs on sb *(col)*/to hit out at sth.

**Kornblume** *f* cornflower.

**Körnchen** *nt* **ein ~ Wahrheit** a grain of truth.

**körnig** *adj* granular, grainy.

**Körnung** *f (Tech)* grain size; *(Phot)* granularity.

**Körper** *m -* body; *(Schiffs~)* hull. **~ und Geist** mind and body; **am ganzen ~ zittern/frieren** to tremble/to be cold all over.

**Körper-: ~bau** *m* physique, build; **~beherrschung** *f* physical control; **k~behindert** *adj* physically handicapped, disabled; **~behinderte(r)** *mf* disabled person; **die ~behinderten** the disabled; **~geruch** *m* body odour *(Brit)* or odor *(US)*, BO *(col)*; **~gewicht** *nt* weight; **~größe** *f* height; **~haltung** *f* posture; **~kontakt** *m* physical contact; **~kraft** *f* physical strength.

**körperlich** *adj* physical; *(stofflich)* material, corporeal. **~e Arbeit** manual work; **~e Züchtigung** corporal punishment.

**Körper-: k~los** *adj* bodiless, incorporeal; **~maße** *pl* measurements *pl*; **~pflege** *f* personal hygiene; **~puder** *m or nt* body powder.

**Körperschaft** *f* corporation, (corporate) body. **gesetzgebende ~** legislative body; **~ des öffentlichen**

**Rechts** public corporation *or* body.
**Körper-:** ~**schwäche** f physical weakness; ~**sprache** f body language; ~**teil** m part of the body; ~**temperatur** f body temperature; ~**verletzung** f *(Jur)* physical injury; **fahrlässige** ~**verletzung** physical injury resulting from negligence; **schwere** ~**verletzung** grievous bodily harm; ~**wärme** f body heat.
**Korporal** m -e *or* **Korporäle** corporal.
**Korps** [koːɐ] nt - [koːɐ(s)], - [koːɐs] *(Mil)* corps; *(Univ)* (duelling) corps.
**korpulent** adj corpulent.
**Korpulenz** f no pl corpulence.
**korrekt** adj correct.
**Korrektheit** f correctness.
**Korrektor** m, **Korrektorin** f *(Typ)* proofreader.
**Korrektur** f correction; *(Typ) (Vorgang)* proofreading; *(Verbesserung)* proof correction; ~ **lesen** to proofread *(bei etw* sth*)*.
**Korrektur-:** ~**abzug** m galley (proof); ~**band** nt correction tape; ~**fahne** f galley (proof); ~**taste** f correction key; ~**zeichen** nt proofreader's mark.
**Korrespondent(in** f) m correspondent.
**Korrespondenz** f correspondence. **mit jdm in** ~ **stehen** to be in correspondence with sb.
**korrespondieren\*** vi to correspond.
**Korridor** m -e *(auch Luft~ etc)* corridor; *(Flur)* hall.
**korrigieren\*** vt *(berichtigen)* to correct; *Aufsätze etc* auch to mark; *Meinung, Einstellung* to change.
**Korrosion** f corrosion.
**Korrosionsschutz** m corrosion prevention.
**korrumpieren\*** vt to corrupt.
**Korrumpierung** f *(Comp)* corruption.
**korrupt** adj corrupt.
**Korruption** f no pl corruption.
**Korse** m *(wk)* -n, -n Corsican.
**Korsett** nt -s *or* -e corset(s pl).
**Korsika** nt Corsica.
**Korsin** f Corsican.
**korsisch** adj Corsican.
**Korvette** [kɔr'vɛtə] f *(Naut)* corvette.
**Korvettenkapitän** m lieutenant commander.
**Kosak** m *(wk)* -en, -en Cossack.
**koscher** adj *(Rel, fig col)* kosher.
**Kose-:** ~**form** f affectionate form *(of a name)*; ~**name** m pet name; ~**wort** nt term of endearment.
**K.-o.-Sieg** [kaːˈ|oː-] m win by a knockout.
**Kosinus** m - *or* -se *(Math)* cosine.
**Kosmetik** f no pl beauty culture; *(Kosmetika, fig)* cos- metics pl.
**Kosmetiker(in** f) m - beautician.
**Kosmetikkoffer** m vanity case.
**Kosmetikum** nt, pl **Kosmetika** cosmetic.
**kosmetisch** adj cosmetic. **ein** ~**es Mittel** a cosmetic.
**kosmisch** adj cosmic. ~ **beeinflußt werden** to be influenced by the stars.
**Kosmo-:** ~**naut(in** f) m *(wk)* -en, -en cosmonaut; ~**polit(in** f) m *(wk)* -en, -en cosmopolitan; **k~politisch** adj cosmopolitan.
**Kosmos** m no pl cosmos.
**Kost** f no pl *(Nahrung, Essen)* food, fare. **vegetarische/fleischlose** ~ vegetarian/meatless diet; **geistige** ~ *(fig)* intellectual fare; **leichte/schwere** ~ **sein** *(fig)* to be easy/heavy going *(col)*; ~ **und Logis** board and lodging.
**kostbar** adj *(wertvoll)* valuable, precious.
**Kostbarkeit** f (a) value, preciousness. (b) *(Gegenstand)* treasure, precious object; *(Leckerbissen)* delicacy.

**Kosten** pl cost(s); *(Jur)* costs pl; *(Un~)* expenses pl; *(Auslagen auch)* outlay. **die** ~ **tragen** to bear the cost(s); **auf** ~ **von** *or* +gen *(fig)* at the expense of; **auf meine** ~ *(lit, fig)* at my expense; **auf seine** ~ **kommen** *(fig)* to get one's money's worth.
**kosten**[1] vti *(lit, fig)* to cost; *Zeit, Geduld etc* to take. **was kostet das?** how much does it cost?, how much is it?; **koste es, was es wolle** whatever the cost; **das lasse ich mich etwas** ~ I don't mind spending a bit of money on it; **jdn sein Leben/den Sieg** ~ to cost sb his life/the victory.
**kosten**[2] vti *(lit, fig: probieren)* to taste. **von etw** ~ to taste sth.
**Kosten-:** ~**aufwand** m expense; **k~deckend** adj cost-effective; ~**ersparnis** f cost saving; ~**erstattung** f reimbursement of expenses; ~**frage** f question of cost(s); **k~günstig** adj economical; **k~los** adj, adv free (of charge); **k~pflichtig** adj **das ist k~pflichtig** there is a charge (on it); **ein Kfz k~pflichtig abschleppen** to tow away a vehicle at the owner's expense; ~**planung** f costing; ~**punkt** m cost question; ~**punkt?** *(col)* what'll it cost?; ~**satz** m rate; **k~sparend** adj cost-saving; ~**stelle** f cost centre *(Brit)* or center *(US)*; ~**voranschlag** m (costs) estimate.
**köstlich** adj (a) *Wein, Speise* exquisite. (b) *(amüsant)* priceless. **sich** ~ **amüsieren** to have a great time.
**Köstlichkeit** f (a) no pl exquisiteness. (b) *(Leckerbissen etc)* (culinary) delicacy.
**Kost-:** ~**probe** f *(von Wein, Käse)* taste; *(fig)* sample; **k~spielig** adj expensive.
**Kostüm** nt -e (a) *(Theat: Tracht)* costume. (b) *(Schneider~)* costume *(dated)*, suit. (c) *(Masken~)* fancy dress.
**Kostüm-:** ~**ball** m fancy-dress ball; ~**bildner(in** f) m costume designer; ~**fest** nt fancy-dress party.
**kostümieren\*** vr to dress up.
**Kostüm-:** ~**probe** f *(Theat)* dress rehearsal; ~**verleih** m (theatrical) costume agency.
**Kot** m no pl *(form)* excrement, faeces *(form)* pl.
**Kotelett** [ˈkɔtlɛt, kɔtˈlɛt] nt -s chop, cutlet.
**Kotelette** f usu pl (side)whisker, sideburn *(US)*.
**Köter** m - *(pej)* cur.
**Kotflügel** m *(Aut)* wing *(Brit)*, fender *(US)*.
**kotzen** vi *(col!)* to throw up *(col)*, to puke *(col!)*. **das ist zum K~** it makes you sick.
**kotzübel** adj *(col!)* **mir ist** ~ I feel like throwing up *(col)*.
**Kotz- und Freßsucht** f *(col)* bulimia.
**KP** [kaːˈpeː] f = **Kommunistische Partei**.
**Krabbe** f -n *(Zool) (klein)* shrimp; *(größer)* prawn.
**Krabbel|alter** nt crawling stage *(of a baby)*.
**krabbeln 1** vi aux sein to crawl. **2** vt *(kitzeln)* to tickle.
**Krach** m ⁼e (a) no pl *(Lärm)* noise, din *(col)*; *(Schlag)* crash. ~ **machen** to make a noise. (b) *(col: Streit)* row, quarrel. **mit jdm** ~ **haben** to (have a) row with sb; **mit jdm** ~ **kriegen** to get into trouble with sb; ~ **schlagen** to make a fuss.
**krachen** vi (a) *(Lärm machen)* to crash, to bang; *(Holz)* to creak; *(Schuß)* to ring out; *(Donner)* to crash. ~**d fallen** etc to fall etc with a crash; ..., **daß es nur so krachte** *(lit)* with a crash; *(fig)* with a vengeance. (b) aux sein *(col: aufplatzen)* to rip (open), to split.
**Kracher** m - banger *(Brit)*, firecracker *(esp US)*.
**Krächzen** nt no pl croak(ing); *(von Vogel)* caw(ing).
**krächzen** vi to croak; *(Vogel)* to caw.
**Kräcker** m - *(Cook)* cracker.

**Kraft** f ⁼e **(a)** *(körperlich, sittlich)* strength *no pl*; *(geistig, schöpferisch)* powers *pl*; *(von Prosa, Stimme)* power, force; *(Energie)* energy, energies *pl.* **die ~e (mit jdm) messen** to pit one's strength (against sb); *(fig)* to pit oneself against sb; **seine ~e sammeln** to build up one's strength; **mit frischer ~** with renewed strength; **mit letzter ~** with one's last ounce of strength; **die ~ aufbringen, etw zu tun** to find the strength to do sth; **mit vereinten ~en werden wir ...** if we combine our efforts we will ...; **mit seinen ~en haushalten** to conserve one's energy; **das geht über meine ~e** it's more than I can take; **mit aller** *or* **voller ~** with all one's might; **er will mit aller ~ durchsetzen, daß ...** he will do his utmost to ensure that ...; **aus eigener ~** by himself/myself *etc*; **nach (besten) ~en** to the best of one's ability; **er tat, was in seinen ~en stand** he did everything (with)in his power; **nicht/wieder bei ~en sein** not to be in very good shape/to have (got) one's strength back; **wieder zu ~en kommen** to regain one's strength.

**(b)** *(Macht, der Sonne)* power; *(Phys)* force. **die treibende ~** *(fig)* the driving force; **das Gleichgewicht der ~e** *(Pol)* the balance of power; **halbe/volle ~ voraus!** half/full speed ahead.

**(c)** *(usu pl: in Wirtschaft, Politik etc)* force.

**(d)** *no pl (Jur: Geltung)* force. **in ~ sein/treten** to be in/come into force; **außer ~ sein** to be no longer in force; **außer ~ treten** to cease to be in force; **außer ~ setzen** to annul.

**(e)** *(Arbeits~)* employee, worker. **~e** staff, personnel *no pl.*

**kraft** *prep +gen (form)* by virtue of; *(mittels)* by use of. **~ meines Amtes** by virtue of my office.

**Kraft-:** **~akt** *m (fig)* show of strength; **~aufwand** *m* effort; **~ausdruck** *m* swearword; **~brühe** *f* beef tea.

**Kräfteverhältnis** *nt (Pol)* balance of power; *(von Mannschaften etc)* relative strength.

**Kraftfahrer(in** *f)* *m (form)* motorist, driver; *(als Beruf)* driver.

**Kraftfahrzeug** *nt* motor vehicle.

**Kraftfahrzeug-:** **~brief** *m* (vehicle) registration document, logbook *(Brit)*; **~kennzeichen** *nt* (vehicle) registration; **~mechaniker** *m* motor mechanic; **~schein** *m* (vehicle) registration document; **~steuer** *f* motor vehicle tax, road tax *(Brit)*; **~versicherung** *f* motor insurance.

**kräftig 1** *adj* strong; *Muskel, Stimme auch* powerful; *Ausdrucksweise auch* forceful; *Haarwuchs, Pflanze auch* healthy; *Schlag* hard, powerful, hefty *(col)*; *Händedruck* firm; *Fluch* violent; *Suppe, Essen* nourishing; *(groß)* Portion, Preiserhöhung huge; *Beifall* loud. **einen ~en Schluck nehmen** to take a good swig.

**2** *adv* **gebaut** powerfully; *zuschlagen, treten, pressen* hard; *klatschen* loudly; *lachen, mitsingen* heartily; *fluchen, niesen* violently. **etw ~ schütteln** to give sth a good shake; **jdn ~ verprügeln** to give sb a good beating; **er hat sich ~ gewehrt** he objected most strongly; *(körperlich)* he put up a strong resistance; **es hat ~ geregnet/geschneit** it rained/snowed heavily; **die Preise sind ~ gestiegen** prices have gone up a lot; **jdn ~ ausschimpfen** to give sb a good bawling out *(col)*.

**kräftigen** *vt (geh)* **jdn ~** to build up sb's strength; *(Luft, Bad etc)* to invigorate sb; *(Essen, Mittel etc)* to fortify sb; **ein ~des Mittel** a tonic.

**Kräftigung** *f (geh) siehe vt* strengthening; invigoration; fortification.

**kraftlos** *adj (schwach)* feeble, weak; *(schlaff)* limp; *(machtlos)* powerless; *(Jur)* invalid.

**Kraft-:** **~meier** *m (col)* muscleman *(col)*; *(fig)* strong-man; **~meierei** *f* strongarm tactics *pl*; **~probe** *f* test of strength; *(zwischen zwei Gruppen etc)* trial of strength; **~protz** *m (col)* muscle man *(col)*; **~rad** *nt* motorcycle; **~stoff** *m* fuel; **~stoffverbrauch** *m* fuel consumption; **k~strotzend** *adj* exuding vitality; *Pflanze* healthy-looking; *(muskulös)* with bulging muscles; **~übertragung** *f* power transmission; **k~voll** *adj Stimme* powerful; **~wagen** *m* motor vehicle; **~werk** *nt* power station.

**Kragen** *m* - collar. **jdn am** *or* **beim ~ packen** to grab sb by the collar; *(fig col)* to collar sb; **mir platzte der ~** *(col)* I blew my top *(col)*; **jetzt platzt mir aber der ~!** this is the last straw!; **jdn** *or* **jdm den ~ kosten** *(fig)* to be sb's downfall; *(umbringen)* to be the end of sb; **es geht ihm jetzt an den ~** *(col)* he's in for it now *(col)*.

**Kragenweite** *f (lit)* collar size. **das ist nicht meine ~** *(fig col)* that's not my cup of tea *(col)*.

**Krähe** *f* **-n** crow. **eine ~ hackt der anderen kein Auge aus** *(Prov)* birds of a feather stick together *(Prov)*.

**krähen** *vi* to crow.

**Krake** *m (wk)* **-n, -n** octopus.

**krakeelen\*** *vi (col)* to make a row *or* racket *(col)*.

**krakelig** *adj* scrawly.

**krakeln** *vti* to scrawl, to scribble.

**Kralle** *f* **-n** claw; *(von Raubvogel auch)* talon; *(pej: Fingernagel)* claw; *(col: Hand)* paw *(col)*; *(Park~)* wheel clamp. **jdn/etw in seinen ~n haben** *(fig col)* to have sb/sth in one's clutches.

**krallen 1** *vr* **sich an jdn/etw ~** *(lit, fig)* to cling to sb/sth; *(Katze)* to dig its claws into sb/sth; **sich in etw** *(acc)* **~** to sink its claws into sth; *(mit Fingern)* to dig one's fingers into sth; **sich** *(dat)* **jdn/etw ~** *(col)* to get a hold of sb/to pinch sth. **2** *vt* **(a) die Finger in etw** *(acc)***/um etw ~** to dig one's fingers into sth. **(b)** *(col)* to pinch *(col)*. **(c)** *(Aut)* to clamp. **3** *vi* to claw *(an +dat at)*.

**Kram** *m no pl (col) (Gerümpel)* junk; *(Zeug)* things *pl*, stuff *(col)*; *(Angelegenheit)* business. **den ~ hinschmeißen** to chuck the whole thing *(col)*.

**kramen 1** *vi* to rummage about *(in +dat* in, *nach* for*)*. **2** *vt* **etw aus etw ~** to fish sth out of sth.

**Kramladen** *m (pej col)* tatty little shop *(col)*.

**Krampf** *m* ⁼e **(a)** *(Zustand)* cramp; *(Verkrampfung)* spasm; *(wiederholt)* convulsion(s *pl*). **(b)** *no pl (col) (Getue)* palaver *(col)*; *(Unsinn)* rubbish.

**Krampf-:** **~ader** *f* varicose vein; **k~artig** *adj* convulsive.

**krampfen 1** *vt Finger, Hand* to clench *(um etw* around sth*)*. **2** *vr* **sich um etw ~** to clench sth.

**krampfhaft** *adj Zuckung* convulsive; *(col: angestrengt, verzweifelt)* frantic, desperate; *Lachen* forced *no adv.* **sich ~ an etw** *(dat)* **festhalten** *(lit, fig col)* to cling desperately to sth.

**Kran** *m* ⁼e **(a)** crane. **(b)** *(Hahn)* tap, faucet *(US)*.

**Kranführer** *m* crane driver.

**Kranich** *m* **-e** *(Orn)* crane.

**krank** *adj comp* ⁼**er,** *superl* ⁼**ste(r, s)** *or (adv)* **am** ⁼**sten** ill *usu pred*, sick *(auch fig)*, not well; *(leidend)* invalid; *Pflanze, Organ* diseased; *Zahn, Bein* bad; *Wirtschaft* ailing. **~ werden** to fall ill; **schwer ~** seriously ill; **vor Aufregung/Angst ~** sick with excitement/fear; **sich ~ melden** to let one's boss *etc* know that one is ill; *(telefonisch)* to phone in sick; *(esp Mil)* to report sick; **jdn ~ schreiben** to give sb a medical certificate; *(esp Mil)* to put sb on the sick-list; **er ist schon seit einem halben Jahr ~ geschrieben** he's been off sick for six months; **sich ~ stellen** to pretend to be ill, to malinger; **das macht mich ~!**

*(col)* it gets on my nerves! *(col)*, it drives me round the bend! *(Brit col)*.

**kränkeln** *vi* to be ailing *(auch Wirtschaft)*, to be sickly, to be in poor health.

**kranken** *vi* to suffer *(an +dat* from*)*. **das krankt daran, daß ...** *(fig)* it suffers from the fact that ...

**kränken** *vt* jdn ~ to hurt sb('s feelings); **sie war sehr gekränkt** she was very hurt; **jdn in seiner Ehre** ~ to offend sb's pride; **~d** hurtful.

**Kranken-:** **~akte** *f* medical file; **~bericht** *m* medical report; **~besuch** *m* visit (to a sick person); *(von Arzt)* house call; **~bett** *nt* sickbed; **~geld** *nt* sickness benefit; *(von Firma)* sick pay; **~geschichte** *f* medical history; **~gymnastik** *f* physiotherapy; **~gymnast(in** *f)* *m* physiotherapist.

**Krankenhaus** *nt* hospital. **ins** ~ **gehen** *(als Patient)* to go into (the *US)* hospital; **im** ~ **liegen** to be in (the *US)* hospital.

**Krankenhaus-** *in cpds* hospital; **~aufenthalt** *m* stay in hospital; **~kosten** *pl* hospital charges *pl*.

**Kranken-:** **~kasse** *f (Versicherung)* medical *or* health insurance; *(Gesellschaft)* medical *or* health insurance company; **er ist in keiner ~kasse** he has no medical insurance; **~pflege** *f* nursing; **~pfleger** *m* orderly; *(mit Schwesternausbildung)* male nurse; **~pflegerin** *f* nurse; **~schein** *m* medical insurance certificate; **~schwester** *f* nurse; **~versicherung** *f* medical *or* health insurance; **soziale/private ~versicherung** state *or* national/private health insurance; **~wagen** *m* ambulance; **~zimmer** *nt* sickroom; *(im Krankenhaus)* hospital room.

**Kranke(r)** *mf decl as adj* sick person, invalid; *(Patient)* patient. **die ~n** the sick.

**krankfeiern** *vi sep (col)* to be off sick; *(vortäuschend)* to skive *(Brit col)*.

**krankhaft** *adj* (a) *Stelle, Zelle* diseased; *Vergrößerung, Zustand* morbid; *Aussehen* sickly. **~e Veränderung** affection. (b) *(seelisch)* pathological. **sein Geiz ist schon** ~ his meanness is positively pathological.

**Krankheit** *f (lit, fig)* illness, sickness; *(eine bestimmte* ~ *wie Krebs, Masern etc auch, von Pflanzen)* disease. **wegen** ~ due to illness; **sich** *(dat)* **eine** ~ **zuziehen** to contract an illness *(form)*; **nach langer schwerer** ~ after a long serious illness; **während meiner** ~ during my illness.

**Krankheits|erreger** *m* disease-causing agent.

**kränklich** *adj* sickly, in poor health.

**Krankmeldung** *f* notification of illness.

**Kränkung** *f* insult. **etw als** ~ **empfinden** to take offence *(Brit)* or offense *(US)* at sth; **das war eine** ~ **seiner Gefühle** that hurt his feelings.

**Kranz** *m* ⁼e (a) wreath; *(Sieger~, Braut~ auch)* garland; *(fig: von Geschichten etc)* cycle. (b) *(Tech: Rad~)* rim; *(von Glocke auch)* lip.

**Kränzchen** *nt* small wreath/garland; *(fig: Kaffee~)* coffee circle.

**Kranzgefäß** *nt (Anat)* coronary artery.

**Kräpfen** *m - (dial Cook)* ≈ doughnut.

**kraß** *adj Gegensatz, Worte, Stil* stark; *Farben* garish; *Unterschied, Fall, Haltung* extreme; *Ungerechtigkeit, Lüge* blatant; *Materialist, Unkenntnis* crass; *Egoist* out-and-out; *Außenseiter* rank.

**Krater** *m -* crater.

**Krätz-:** **~bürste** *f* wire brush; *(col)* prickly character; **k~bürstig** *adj (col)* prickly.

**Krätze** *f no pl (Med)* scabies.

**kratzen 1** *vti* (a) to scratch; *(ab~ auch)* to scrape *(von off)*. **der Rauch kratzt (mich) im Hals** the smoke irritates my throat. (b) *(col: stören)* to bother. **das**

**kratzt mich nicht** *(col)* I couldn't care less (about that). **2** *vr* to scratch oneself.

**Kratzer** *m - (Schramme)* scratch; *(Werkzeug)* scraper.

**kratzig** *adj (col)* scratchy *(col)*.

**Kraul** *nt no pl (Schwimmen)* crawl. **(im)** ~ **schwimmen** to do the crawl.

**kraulen¹** *(Schwimmen) aux haben or sein* **1** *vi* to do the crawl. **2** *vt* **er hat** *or* **ist 100 m gekrault** he did a 100 metre crawl.

**kraulen²** *vt* to fondle. **jdn am Kinn** ~ to chuck sb under the chin.

**kraus** *adj* crinkly; *Haar, Kopf* frizzy; *Stirn* furrowed; *(fig: verworren)* muddled, confused. **die Stirn** ~ **ziehen** to knit one's brow; *(mißbilligend)* to frown.

**Krause** *f -n* (a) *(Hals~)* ruff; *(an Ärmeln etc)* ruffle, frill. (b) *(col: Frisur)* frizzy hair.

**kräuseln 1** *vt Haar* to make frizzy; *(Sew)* to gather *(in small folds)*; *(Tex)* to crimp; *Stirn* to knit; *Wasseroberfläche* to ripple. **2** *vr (Haare)* to go frizzy; *(Stoff)* to go crinkly; *(Stirn)* to wrinkle up; *(Wasser)* to ripple.

**Kraus-:** **k~haarig** *adj* frizzy-haired; **~kopf** *m (Frisur)* frizzy hair; *(Mensch)* curly-head.

**Kraut** *nt, pl* **Kräuter** (a) herb. **dagegen ist kein** ~ **gewachsen** *(fig)* there's nothing anyone can do about that. (b) *no pl (grüne Teile von Pflanzen)* foliage, stems and leaves *pl*; *(von Gemüse)* tops *pl*. **wie** ~ **und Rüben durcheinanderliegen** *(col)* to lie (about) all over the place *(col)*; **ins** ~ **schießen** *(lit)* to run to seed; *(fig)* to get out of control. (c) *no pl (Rot~, Weiß~)* cabbage.

**Kräuter-:** **~butter** *f* herb butter; **~käse** *m* herb cheese; **~likör** *m* herbal liqueur; **~tee** *m* herb(al) tea.

**Krautsalat** *m* ≈ coleslaw.

**Krawall** *m -e (Aufruhr)* riot; *(col: Lärm)* racket *(col)*, din *(col)*. ~ **machen** *(col)* to kick up a row; *(randalieren)* to go on the rampage; *(sich beschweren)* to kick up a fuss.

**Krawallmacher** *m (col)* hooligan.

**Krawatte** *f -n* tie, necktie *(esp US)*.

**Krawattennadel** *f* tiepin.

**kraxeln** *vi aux sein (SGer)* to clamber (up).

**Kreation** *f (Fashion etc)* creation.

**kreativ** *adj* creative.

**Kreativität** [kreativi'tɛːt] *f* creativity.

**Kreatur** *f* (a) *(lit, fig, pej)* creature. (b) *no pl (alle Lebewesen)* creation. **die** ~ all creation.

**Krebs** *m -e* (a) crab; *(Fluß~)* crayfish, crawfish *(US)*. **rot wie ein** ~ red as a lobster. (b) *(Astrol)* Cancer. (c) *(Med)* cancer; *(Bot)* canker.

**Krebs-:** **k~artig** *adj (Med)* cancerous; **k~erregend** *adj* carcinogenic; **k~erregend wirken** to cause cancer; **~forschung** *f* cancer research; **~geschwulst** *f (Med)* cancerous tumour *or* growth; **k~krank** *adj* suffering from cancer; **k~krank sein** to have cancer; **~kranke(r)** *mf* cancer victim; *(Patient)* cancer patient; **k~rot** *adj* red as a lobster; **~tiere** *pl* crustaceans *pl*.

**Kredit** *m -e* credit; *(Darlehen)* loan; *(fig auch)* standing. **auf** ~ on credit; **er hat bei der Bank** ~ his credit is good with the bank; ~ **haben** *(fig)* to have standing.

**Kredit-:** **~anstalt** *f* credit institution; **~aufnahme** *f* borrowing; **~brief** *m* letter of credit; **k~fähig** *adj* credit-worthy; **~geber(in** *f)* *m* creditor; **~grenze** *f* credit limit; **~hai** *m (col)* loanshark; **~institut** *nt* credit institution; **~karte** *f* credit card; **~konto** *nt* credit account; **~nehmer(in** *f)* *m* borrower; **~politik** *f* lending policy; **k~würdig** *adj* credit-worthy.

**Kredo** *nt* -s *(lit, fig)* creed.

**Kreide** *f* -n chalk. **eine ~** a piece of chalk; **bei jdm (tief) in der ~ stehen** to be (deep) in debt to sb.

**Kreide-:** **k~bleich** *adj* (as) white as a sheet; **~felsen** *m* chalk cliff; **~zeichnung** *f* chalk drawing.

**kreieren\*** [kre'iːrən] *vt* to create.

**Kreis** *m* -e (**a**) circle. **einen ~ ziehen** to describe a circle; **einen ~ um jdn bilden** to make a circle around sb; **im ~ (sitzen)** (to sit) in a circle; **(weite) ~e ziehen** *(fig)* to have (wide) repercussions; **sich im ~ drehen** *(lit)* to go around in a circle; *(fig)* to go around in circles; **der ~ schließt sich** *(fig)* the wheel turns full circle; **der ~ seiner Leser** his readers *pl*; **weite ~e der Bevölkerung** wide sections of the population; **im ~e von Freunden** among friends; **eine Feier im kleinen ~e** a celebration for a few close friends and relatives; **das kommt auch in den besten ~en vor** that happens even in the best of circles. (**b**) *(Elec: Strom~)* circuit. (**c**) *(Bereich: von Interessen etc)* sphere. (**d**) *(Stadt~, Land~)* district. **~ Bonn** Bonn District.

**Kreis-:** **~abschnitt** *m* segment; **~ausschnitt** *m* sector; **~bahn** *f (Astron, Space)* orbit.

**kreischen** *vi* to screech; *(Mensch auch)* to shriek.

**Kreisel** *m* - *(Tech)* gyroscope; *(Spielzeug)* (spinning) top.

**kreisen** *vi aux sein or haben* to circle *(um* around, *über* +*dat* over); *(um eine Achse)* to revolve *(um* around*)*; *(Satellit, Planet auch)* to orbit *(um etw* sth); *(fig: Gedanken, Gespräch)* to revolve *(um* around*)*. **die Arme ~ lassen** to swing one's arms around (in a circle).

**kreisförmig** *adj* circular.

**Kreislauf** *m (Blut~, Öl~, von Geld)* circulation; *(der Natur, des Wassers)* cycle.

**Kreislauf-:** **~kollaps** *m* circulatory collapse; **~mittel** *nt* cardiac stimulant; **~störungen** *pl* circulation trouble *sing*.

**Kreis-:** **k~rund** *adj* (perfectly) circular; **~säge** *f* circular saw.

**Kreißsaal** *m* delivery room.

**Kreis-:** **~stadt** *f* district town, ≈ county town *(Brit)*; **~tag** *m* district assembly, ≈ county council *(Brit)*; **~verkehr** *m* roundabout *(Brit)*, traffic circle *(US)*; **~wehrersatzamt** *nt* district recruiting office.

**Krematorium** *nt* crematorium.

**kremig** *adj* creamy.

**Kreml** *m* **der ~** the Kremlin.

**Krempe** *f* -n *(Hut~)* brim.

**Krempel** *m* no pl *(col) (Sachen)* stuff *(col)*; *(wertloses Zeug)* junk.

**krepieren\*** *vi aux sein* (**a**) *(Mil sl: Bombe etc)* to explode. (**b**) *(col!: sterben)* to snuff it *(col)*; *(col: elend sterben)* to die a wretched death.

**Krepp** *m* -e *or* -s crepe.

**Kreppapier** *nt* crepe paper.

**Kreppsohle** *f* crepe sole.

**Kresse** *f no pl* cress.

**Kreta** *nt* Crete.

**Kreter(in** *f)* *m* - Cretan.

**kretisch** *adj* Cretan.

**Kreuz** *nt* -e (**a**) cross; *(als Anhänger etc)* crucifix. **ein ~ schlagen** *or* **machen** to make the sign of the cross; *(sich bekreuzigen auch)* to cross oneself; **mit jdm über ~ sein** *(fig)* to be on bad terms with sb; **sein ~ geduldig tragen** *(geh)* to bear one's cross with patience; **es ist ein ~ mit ihm/damit** he's/it's an awful problem; **ich mache drei ~e, wenn er geht** *(col)* it'll be such a relief when he has gone; **zu ~e**

**kriechen** *(fig)* to eat humble pie, to eat crow *(US)*. (**b**) *(Anat)* small of the back; *(von Tier)* back. **ich hab's im ~** *(col)* I have back trouble; **aufs ~ fallen** to fall on one's back; *(fig col)* to be staggered *(col)*; **jdn aufs ~ legen** to throw sb on his back; *(fig col)* to take sb for a ride *(col)*. (**c**) *(Mus)* sharp. (**d**) *(Autobahn~)* intersection. (**e**) *(Cards) (Farbe)* clubs *pl*; *(Karte)* club. **die ~-Dame** the Queen of Clubs.

**kreuz** *adj:* **~ und quer** all over; **sie lagen ~ und quer durcheinander** they were lying all over the place.

**Kreuz-:** **~bein** *nt (Anat)* sacrum; **k~brav** *adj Kind* as good as gold; **~flug** *m* cruise flight.

**kreuzen** **1** *vt* to cross *(auch Biol)*. **die Arme ~** to fold one's arms. **2** *vr* to cross; *(Meinungen etc)* to clash. **3** *vi aux haben or sein (Naut)* to cruise.

**Kreuzer** *m* - *(Naut)* cruiser.

**Kreuz-:** **~fahrer** *m (Hist)* crusader; **~fahrt** *f (Naut)* cruise; **eine ~fahrt machen** to go on a cruise; **~feuer** *nt (Mil, fig)* crossfire; **ins ~feuer (der Kritik) geraten** *(fig)* to come under fire; **k~förmig** *adj* cross-shaped; **~gang** *m* cloister.

**kreuzigen** *vt* to crucify.

**Kreuzigung** *f* crucifixion.

**Kreuz-:** **~otter** *f (Zool)* adder, viper; **~ritter** *m (Hist)* crusader; **~schlitzschraube** *f* cross-head screw, Phillips screw ®; **~schlüssel** *m* wheelbrace; **~schmerzen** *pl* backache *sing*; **~spinne** *f (Zool)* garden *or* cross spider.

**Kreuzung** *f* (**a**) *(Straßen~)* crossroads *sing or pl*, intersection *(esp US)*. (**b**) *(das Kreuzen)* crossing; *(von Tieren auch)* cross-breeding. (**c**) *(Rasse)* hybrid; *(Tiere auch)* cross(-breed).

**Kreuz-:** **k~unglücklich** *adj* absolutely miserable; **~verhör** *nt* cross-examination; **jdn ins ~verhör nehmen** to cross-examine sb; **~weg** *m (fig)* crossroads *sing*; **k~weise** *adv* crosswise; **du kannst mich k~weise!** *(col!)* get stuffed! *(col!)*; **~worträtsel** *nt* crossword puzzle; **~zeichen** *nt* sign of the cross; **~zug** *m (lit, fig)* crusade.

**Krevette** [kre'vɛtə] *f* shrimp.

**kribb(e)lig** *adj (col)* fidgety *(col)*; *(kribbelnd)* tingly *(col)*.

**kribbeln** *vi* (**a**) *(jucken)* to itch; *(prickeln)* to tingle. **auf der Haut ~** to cause a prickling sensation; *(angenehm)* to make the skin tingle; **es kribbelt mir im Fuß** *(lit)* I have pins and needles in my foot; **es kribbelt mir in den Fingern, etw zu tun** *(col)* I'm itching to do sth. (**b**) *aux sein (Insekten)* **es kribbelt von Ameisen** the place is crawling with ants.

**Cricket** *nt* -s *(Sport)* cricket.

**kriechen** *pret* **kroch**, *ptp* **gekrochen** *vi aux sein* to creep, to crawl *(auch Schlange)*; *(fig: Zeit)* to creep by; *(fig: unterwürfig sein)* to grovel *(vor* +*dat* before*)*.

**Kriecher** *m* - crawler *(col)*.

**kriecherisch** *adj* grovelling *(Brit)*, groveling *(US)*, servile.

**Kriech-:** **~spur** *f* crawler lane; **~tier** *nt (Zool)* reptile.

**Krieg** *m* -e war; *(Art der Kriegsführung)* warfare. **~ anfangen mit** to start a war with; **einer Partei etc den ~ erklären** *(fig)* to declare war on a party etc; **~ führen (mit** *or* **gegen)** to wage war (on); **im ~ sein (mit)** to be at war (with); **im ~e fallen** to be killed in action; **in den ~ ziehen** to go to war.

**kriegen** *vt (col)* to get; *Bus, Schnupfen, Dieb etc auch* to catch; *Schlaganfall, eine Spritze, Besuch auch* to have; *Junge, ein Kind* to have. **sie kriegt ein Kind** she's going to have a baby; **graue Haare/eine Glatze ~** to go grey/bald; **sie** *or* **es ~** *(col: Prügel)* to get a hiding; **es mit jdm zu tun ~** to be in trouble with

sb; **sie** ~ **sich** *(in Kitschroman)* boy gets girl; **dann kriege ich zuviel** then it gets too much for me; **ich kriege ein Steak** *(in Restaurant)* I'll have a steak; **jdn dazu** ~, **etw zu tun** to get sb to do sth; **etw gemacht** ~ to get sth done.
**Krieger** *m* - warrior.
**Kriegerdenkmal** *nt* war memorial.
**kriegerisch** *adj* warlike *no adv*; *Haltung auch* belligerent. ~**e Auseinandersetzung** military conflict.
**Krieg-: k**~**führend** *adj* warring; ~**führung** *f* warfare *no art*; *(eines Feldherrn)* conduct of the war.
**Kriegs-:** ~**ausbruch** *m* outbreak of war; **k**~**bedingt** *adj* caused by war; ~**beginn** *m* start of the war; ~**beil** *nt* tomahawk; **das** ~**beil begraben** *(fig)* to bury the hatchet; ~**bemalung** *f* *(lit, hum)* warpaint; **k**~**beschädigt** *adj* war-disabled; ~**beschädigte(r)** *mf decl as adj* war-disabled (ex-serviceman/-woman); ~**dienst** *m* *(old, form)* military service; ~**dienstverweigerer** *m* - conscientious objector; ~**ende** *nt* end of the war; ~**erklärung** *f* declaration of war; ~**erlebnis** *nt* war-time experience; ~**fall** *m* **im** ~**fall** in the event of war; ~**folge** *f* consequence of (a/the) war; ~**fuß** *m* *(col)*: **mit jdm/etw auf** ~**fuß stehen** to be at loggerheads with sb/not to get on with sth; ~**gebiet** *nt* war-zone; ~**gefahr** *f* danger of war; ~**gefangene(r)** *mf* prisoner of war, P.O.W.; ~**gefangenschaft** *f* captivity; **in** ~**gefangenschaft sein** to be a prisoner of war; ~**gericht** *nt* court-martial; **jdn vor ein** ~**gericht stellen** to court-martial sb; ~**herr** *m* **oberster** ~**herr** commander-in-chief; ~**hetze** *f* warmongering; ~**hetzer** *m* - *(pej)* warmonger; ~**jahr** *nt* year of war; **die** ~**jahre** the war years; **im** ~**jahr 1945** (during the war) in 1945; ~**kamerad** *m* war-time comrade; ~**kosten** *pl* cost of the war *sing*; ~**list** *f* *(old, liter)* stratagem; ~**marine** *f* navy; **k**~**mäßig** *adj* for war; **k**~**müde** *adj* war-weary; ~**opfer** *nt* war victim; ~**pfad** *m* *(liter)*: **auf dem** ~**pfad** on the warpath; ~**rat** *m* council of war; ~**rat halten** *(fig)* to have a pow-wow *(col)*; ~**recht** *nt* *(Mil)* martial law; ~**schäden** *pl* war damage; ~**schauplatz** *m* theatre *(Brit)* or theater *(US)* of war; ~**schiff** *nt* warship; ~**spiel** *nt* war game; ~**spielzeug** *nt* war toy; ~**teilnehmer** *m* combatant; *(ehemaliger Soldat)* ex-serviceman; ~**verbrechen** *nt* war crime; ~**verbrecher** *m* war criminal; ~**verletzung** *f* war wound; ~**zeit** *f* wartime; **in** ~**zeiten** in times of war; ~**zustand** *m* state of war; **im** ~**zustand** at war.
**Krim** *f* **die** ~ the Crimea.
**Krimi** *m* **-s** *(col)* **(a)** (crime) thriller; *(mit Detektiv als Held)* detective novel; *(von Mord handelnd)* murder mystery. **(b)** *(Film)* crime film or movie *(esp US)*; *(Fernsehserie)* detective series.
**Kriminal-:** ~**beamte(r)** *m* CID officer; ~**film** *m* crime film or movie *(esp US)*.
**kriminalisieren*** *vt* to criminalize.
**Kriminalistik** *f* criminology.
**Kriminalität** *f* crime; *(Ziffer)* crime rate.
**Kriminal-:** ~**kommissar** *m* detective superintendent; ~**komödie** *f* comedy thriller; ~**polizei** *f* criminal investigation department; ~**polizist** *m* detective, CID officer; ~**roman** *m* *siehe* **Krimi (a)**.
**kriminell** *adj* *(lit, fig col)* criminal. ~ **werden** to turn to crime.
**Kriminelle(r)** *mf decl as adj* criminal.
**Kriminologie** *f* criminology.
**Krimskrams** *m no pl* *(col)* odds and ends *pl*.
**Kringel** *m* - *(der Schrift)* squiggle; *(Cook)* ring.
**kringelig** *adj* crinkly. **sich** ~ **lachen** *(col)* to kill one-

self (laughing) *(col)*.
**kringeln** *vr* to go frizzy. **sich** ~ **vor Lachen** *(col)* to kill oneself (laughing) *(col)*.
**Kripo** *f* **-s** *(col)* = **Kriminalpolizei. die** ~ the cops *(col) pl*, the CID.
**Kripo-** *in cpds (col)* police.
**Krippe** *f* **-n (a)** *(Futter~)* (hay)box. **(b)** *(Weihnachts~)* crib; *(Bibl auch)* manger. **(c)** *(Kinderhort)* crèche.
**Krippen-:** ~**spiel** *nt* nativity play; ~**tod** *m* cot death.
**Krise** *f* **-n** crisis.
**kriseln** *vi impers* *(col)* **es kriselt** there is trouble brewing.
**Krisen-: k**~**fest** *adj* stable; ~**gebiet** *nt* crisis area; ~**herd** *m* flash point; ~**sitzung** *f* emergency session; ~**stab** *m* action or crisis committee.
**Kristall¹** *m* **-e** crystal.
**Kristall²** *nt no pl* crystal.
**Kristallglas** *nt* crystal glass.
**Kristallisation** *f* crystallization.
**kristallisieren*** *vir (lit, fig)* to crystallize.
**Kristall-: k**~**klar** *adj* crystal-clear; ~**zucker** *m* refined sugar (in) crystals.
**Kriterium** *nt (Merkmal)* criterion.
**Kritik** *f* **-en (a)** *no pl* criticism *(an +dat of)*. **an jdm/etw** ~ **üben** to criticize sb/sth; **unter aller** ~ **sein** *(col)* to be beneath contempt. **(b)** *(Rezensieren)* criticism; *(Rezension auch)* review. **eine gute** ~ **haben** to get good reviews. **(c)** *no pl (die Kritiker)* critics *pl*. **(d)** *no pl (Urteilsfähigkeit)* discrimination. **ohne jede** ~ uncritically.
**Kritiker(in** *f)* *m* - critic.
**kritiklos** *adj* uncritical.
**kritisch** *adj* critical. **jdm/einer Sache** ~ **gegenüberstehen** to be critical of sb/sth.
**kritisieren*** *vti* to criticize.
**Krittelei** *f* fault-finding *no pl*.
**kritteln** *vi* to find fault *(an +dat, über +acc with)*.
**Kritzelei** *f* scribble; *(das Kritzeln)* scribbling; *(an Wänden)* graffiti.
**kritzeln** *vti* to scribble.
**Kroate** *m* **-n, -n, Kroatin** *f* Croat, Croatian.
**Kroatien** [kro'a:tsiən] *nt* Croatia.
**kroatisch** *adj* Croat, Croatian.
**Kroatisch(e)** *nt* Croatian; *siehe* **Deutsch(e)**.
**kroch** *pret of* **kriechen**.
**Krokant** *m no pl (Cook)* cracknel.
**Krokette** *f (Cook)* croquette.
**Kroko** *nt no pl* crocodile (leather).
**Krokodil** *nt* **-e** crocodile.
**Krokodilleder** *nt* crocodile leather.
**Krokodilstränen** *pl* crocodile tears *pl*.
**Krokus** *m* - or **-se** crocus.
**Krone** *f* **-n (a)** crown. **die** ~ *(fig)* the Crown. **(b)** *(Mauer~)* coping; *(Schaum~)* crest; *(Zahn~)* crown; *(Baum~)* top. **die** ~ **der Schöpfung** the pride of creation; **das setzt der Dummheit die** ~ **auf** *(col)* that beats everything for stupidity; **einen in der** ~ **haben** *(col)* to be tipsy; **dabei fällt dir kein Stein** or **Zacken aus der** ~ *(col)* it won't hurt you. **(c)** *(Währungseinheit)* crown.
**krönen** *vt (lit, fig)* to crown. **jdn zum König** ~ to crown sb king; **von Erfolg gekrönt sein/werden** to be crowned with success; **der** ~**de Abschluß** the culmination.
**Kronenkorken** *m* crown cap.
**Kron-:** ~**juwelen** *pl* crown jewels; ~**korken** *m* crown cap; ~**leuchter** *m* chandelier; ~**prinz** *m* crown prince; *(in Großbritannien)* Prince of Wales; *(fig)* heir apparent; ~**prinzessin** *f* crown princess.

**Krönung** f coronation; (fig) culmination.

**Kronzeuge** m (Jur) person who turns King's/ Queen's evidence or (US) State's evidence; (Hauptzeuge) principal witness. ~ **sein, als** ~ **auftreten** to turn King's/Queen's/State's evidence; to appear as principal witness.

**Kropf** m ⁼e (a) (von Vogel) crop. (b) (Med) goitre.

**kroß** adj (NGer) crisp; Brötchen auch crusty.

**Krösus** m -se **ich bin doch kein** ~ (col) I'm not made of money (col).

**Kröte** f -n (a) (Zool) toad. **eine freche (kleine)** ~ (col) a cheeky (little) minx (col). (b) ~**n** pl (col: Geld) pennies (col).

**Krücke** f -n (a) crutch; (fig) prop. **an** ~**n** (dat) **gehen** to walk on crutches. (b) (Schirm~) crook.

**Krückstock** m walking stick.

**Krug** m ⁼e jug; (Bier~) (beer-)mug.

**Krume** f -n (geh) (a) (Brot~) crumb. (b) (liter: Acker~) (top)soil.

**Krümel** m - (a) (Brot~ etc) crumb. (b) (col: Kind) tiny tot (col).

**krümelig** adj crumbly.

**krümeln** vti to crumble; (beim Essen) to make crumbs.

**krumm** adj (a) crooked; (verbogen auch) bent; (hakenförmig) hooked; Beine auch bandy; Rücken hunched. ~**e Nase** hook(ed) nose; ~ **gewachsen** crooked; **etw** ~ **biegen** to bend sth; ~ **und schief** askew; **sich** ~ **und schief lachen** (col) to fall about laughing (col); **keinen Finger** ~ **machen** (col) not to lift a finger; **steh/sitz nicht so** ~ **da!** stand/sit up straight. (b) (col: unehrlich) crooked (col). ~**er Hund** (pej) crooked swine; **ein** ~**es Ding drehen** (col) to do something crooked; **etw auf die** ~**e Tour versuchen** to try to wangle sth (col).

**krümmen 1** vt to bend. **die Katze krümmte den Buckel** the cat arched its back. **2** vr to bend; (Fluß) to wind; (Straße) to curve; (Wurm) to writhe. **sich vor Lachen** ~ to double up with laughter; **sich vor Schmerzen** (dat) ~ to writhe with pain.

**krumm-:** ~**lachen** vr sep (col) to double up laughing; ~**legen** vr sep (col) to pinch and scrape (col); ~**nehmen** vt sep irreg (col) (jdm) **etw** ~**nehmen** to take sth amiss.

**Krümmung** f (von Weg, Fluß) curve; (Math, Med, Opt) curvature.

**Krüppel** m - cripple. **zum** ~ **werden** to be crippled; **jdn zum** ~ **schlagen** to cripple sb.

**Kruste** f -n crust; (von Schweinebraten) crackling; (von Braten) crisped outside.

**krustig** adj crusty.

**Kruzifix** nt -e crucifix.

**KSZE** [kaː|ɛstsɛt'eː] f = **Konferenz über Sicherheit und Zusammenarbeit in Europa** CSCE.

**Kt** = (a) **Karat** ct. (b) **Kanton**.

**Kto** = **Konto** acct.

**Kuba** nt Cuba.

**Kubaner(in** f) m - Cuban.

**kubanisch** adj Cuban.

**Kübel** m - bucket; (für Jauche etc) container; (für Pflanzen) tub. **es regnet (wie) aus** ~**n** it's bucketing down.

**Kubik** nt - (Aut col: Hubraum) cc.

**Kubik-:** ~**meter** m or nt cubic metre (Brit) or meter (US); ~**zentimeter** m or nt cubic centimetre (Brit) or centimeter (US), cc.

**kubisch** adj cubic.

**Kubismus** m (Art) cubism.

**Küche** f -n (a) kitchen; (klein) kitchenette. (b) (Kochkunst) **gutbürgerliche** ~ good home cooking; **französische** ~ French cooking or cuisine. (c) (Spei-sen) **warme/kalte** ~ hot/cold food.

**Kuchen** m - cake; (Torte auch) gateau; (mit Obst gedeckt) (fruit) flan (Brit), tart.

**Küchen\abfälle** pl kitchen scraps pl.

**Kuchenblech** nt baking sheet or tin.

**Küchenchef** m chef.

**Kuchen-:** ~**form** f cake tin; ~**gabel** f pastry fork.

**Küchen-:** ~**gerät** nt kitchen utensil; (kollektiv) kitchen utensils pl; (elektrisch) kitchen appliance; ~**geschirr** nt kitchenware no pl; ~**herd** m (electric/gas) cooker; ~**maschine** f food processor; ~**meister** m chef; ~**messer** nt kitchen knife; ~**schabe** f (Zool) cockroach; ~**schrank** m (kitchen) cupboard; (in Einbauküche) kitchen unit.

**Kuchenteig** m cake mixture; (Hefeteig) dough.

**Küchen-:** ~**tisch** m kitchen table; ~**waage** f kitchen scales pl; ~**zettel** m menu.

**Kuckuck** m -e (a) cuckoo. (b) (col: Siegel des Gerichtsvollziehers) bailiff's seal (for distraint of goods). (c) (col) **zum** ~ **(noch mal)!** hell's bells! (col); **hol's der** ~**!** botheration! (col); **geh zum** ~ go to blazes (col); **das weiß der** ~ heaven (only) knows (col).

**Kuckucks-:** ~**ei** nt cuckoo's egg; **man hat uns ein** ~**ei untergeschoben** (col) we've been left holding the baby (col); ~**uhr** f cuckoo clock.

**Kuddelmuddel** m or nt no pl (col) mess.

**Kufe** f -n (von Schlitten etc) runner; (von Flugzeug) skid.

**Kugel** f -n ball; (geometrische Figur) sphere; (Erd~) sphere, globe; (Kegel~) bowl; (Gewehr~) bullet; (für Luftgewehr) pellet; (Kanonen~) (cannon)ball; (beim ~stoßen) shot; (Murmel) marble. **eine ruhige** ~ **schieben** (col) to have a cushy number (col); (aus Faulheit) to swing the lead (col); **rund wie eine** ~ (col) like a barrel.

**Kugel-:** ~**blitz** m (Met) ball lightning; **k~förmig** adj spherical; ~**gelenk** nt (Anat, Tech) ball-and-socket joint; ~**hagel** m hail of bullets; ~**kopf** m golf ball; ~**kopfschreibmaschine** f golf-ball typewriter; ~**lager** nt ball-bearing.

**kugeln 1** vi aux sein (rollen, fallen) to roll. **2** vr to roll (about). **sich (vor Lachen)** ~ (col) to double up (laughing).

**Kugel-:** **k~rund** adj as round as a ball; (col) Mensch tubby (col); ~**schreiber** m ballpoint (pen), biro ®; **k~sicher** adj bullet-proof; ~**stoßen** nt no pl shotputting; ~**stoßer(in** f) m - shot-putter; ~**wechsel** m exchange of shots.

**Kuh** f ⁼e cow. **heilige** ~ (lit, fig) sacred cow.

**Kuh-:** ~**dorf** nt (pej col) one-horse town (col); ~**fladen** m cowpat; ~**glocke** f cowbell; ~**handel** m (pej col) horse-trading (col) no pl; ~**haut** f **das geht auf keine** ~**haut** (col) that's absolutely incredible; ~**herde** f herd of cows.

**kühl** adj (lit, fig) cool; (abweisend) cold. **mir wird etwas** ~ I'm getting rather chilly; **etw** ~ **lagern** to store sth in a cool place; **einen** ~**en Kopf bewahren** to keep a cool head, to keep one's cool (col).

**Kühl\anlage** f refrigeration plant.

**Kühle** f no pl (lit) cool(ness); (fig) coolness; (Abweisung) coldness.

**kühlen 1** vt to cool; (auf Eis) to chill. **2** vi to have a cooling effect.

**Kühler** m - (Tech) cooler; (Aut) radiator; (col: ~haube) bonnet (Brit), hood (US); (Sekt~) ice bucket.

**Kühler-:** ~**figur** f (Aut) radiator mascot; ~**haube** f (Aut) bonnet (Brit), hood (US).

**Kühl-:** ~**fach** nt freezer compartment; ~**flüssigkeit** f coolant; ~**haus** nt cold-storage depot; ~**mittel** nt

*(Tech)* coolant; **~raum** *m* cold storage room; **~schrank** *m* refrigerator, fridge *(Brit col)*; **~tasche** *f* cold bag; **~truhe** *f* (chest) freezer, deep freeze *(Brit)*; **~turm** *m (Tech)* cooling tower.

**Kühlung** *f (das Kühlen)* cooling; *(Kühle)* coolness. **zur ~ des Motors** to cool the engine.

**Kühl-:** **~wagen** *m* **(a)** *(Rail)* refrigerator van *or* car *(US)*; **(b)** *(Lastwagen)* refrigerator truck; **~wasser** *nt* coolant.

**Kuh-:** **~milch** *f* cow's milk; **~mist** *m* cow dung.

**kühn** *adj (lit, fig)* bold. **das übertrifft meine ~sten Erwartungen** it's beyond my wildest dreams.

**Kühnheit** *f* boldness.

**Kuh-:** **~stall** *m* cow shed; **~weide** *f* pasture.

**k.u.k.** ['ka:|ont'ka:] = **kaiserlich und königlich** imperial and royal.

**Küken** *nt* - *(Huhn)* chick; *(col: Nesthäkchen)* baby of the family *(col)*; *(jüngste Person)* baby.

**kulant** *adj* accommodating; *Bedingungen* generous.

**Kulanz** *f no pl siehe adj* accommodating attitude; generousness. **aus ~** out of good will.

**Kuli** *m* **-s** **(a)** *(Lastträger)* coolie; *(fig)* slave. **(b)** *(col: Kugelschreiber)* ballpoint, biro ®.

**kulinarisch** *adj* culinary.

**Kulisse** *f* **-n** scenery *no pl*; *(fig: Hintergrund)* background, backdrop. **das ist alles nur ~** *(fig)* that is only a façade; **einen Blick hinter die ~n werfen** *(fig)* to have a glimpse behind the scenes.

**Kulissenschieber(in** *f)* *m* - stagehand.

**Kulleraugen** *pl (col)* big/wide eyes *pl*.

**kullern** *vti (vi: aux sein) (col)* to roll.

**Kult** *m* **-e** cult; *(Verehrung)* worship. **einen ~ mit jdm/etw treiben** to make a cult out of sb/sth.

**Kult-:** **~figur** *f* cult figure; **~film** *m* cult film; **~handlung** *f* ritual(istic) act.

**kultisch** *adj* ritual(istic).

**kultivieren\*** [kulti'vi:rən] *vt (lit, fig)* to cultivate.

**kultiviert** *adj Mensch* cultured, refined; *Geschmack, Unterhaltung* cultivated. **wenn Sie ~ reisen wollen** if you want to travel in style; **Kerzen beim Essen, das ist sehr ~** meals by candlelight, very civilized.

**Kultivierung** [kulti'vi:ruŋ] *f (lit, fig)* cultivation.

**Kultstätte** *f* place of worship.

**Kultur** *f* **(a)** *(no pl: Kunst und Wissenschaft)* culture. **er hat keine ~** he is uncultured. **(b)** *(Lebensform)* civilization. **dort leben verschiedene ~en harmonisch zusammen** different cultures live harmoniously together there. **(c)** *(Bakterien~, Pilz~ etc)* culture; *(Bestand angebauter Pflanzen)* plantation.

**Kultur-:** **~austausch** *m* cultural exchange; **~banause** *m (col)* philistine; **~beutel** *m* toilet bag *(Brit)*, washbag.

**kulturell** *adj* cultural.

**Kultur-:** **~film** *m* documentary film; **~geschichte** *f* history of civilization; **~gut** *nt* cultural assets *pl*; **~kreis** *m* culture group; **~leben** *nt* cultural life; **k~los** *adj* uncultured; **~losigkeit** *f* lack of culture; **~pessimismus** *m* despair of civilization; **~politik** *f* cultural and educational policy; **~revolution** *f* cultural revolution; **~shock** *m* culture shock; **~stätte** *f* place of cultural interest; **~stufe** *f* level of civilization; **~teil** *m (von Zeitung)* arts section; **~volk** *nt* civilized nation; **~zentrum** *nt* **(a)** *(Stadt)* cultural centre *(Brit)* or center *(US)*; **(b)** *(Anlage)* arts centre *(Brit)* or center *(US)*.

**Kultus-:** **~minister** *m* minister of education and the arts; **~ministerium** *nt* ministry of education and the arts.

**Kümmel** *m* - **(a)** *no pl (Gewürz)* caraway (seed). **(b)** *(col: Schnaps)* kümmel.

**Kummer** *m no pl (Betrübtheit)* grief, sorrow; *(Unan-*

*nehmlichkeit)* trouble. **hast du ~?** have you got problems?; **aus** *or* **vor ~ sterben** to die of grief; **vor ~ vergehen** to be pining away with sorrow; **er fand vor ~ keinen Schlaf mehr** he was so griefstricken that he could no longer sleep; **wir sind (an) ~ gewöhnt** *(col)* we're used to that sort of thing.

**kümmerlich** *adj* **(a)** *(karg, armselig)* wretched, miserable; *Lohn, Rente auch* paltry; *Mahlzeit auch* meagre *(Brit)*, meager *(US)*. **(b)** *(schwächlich)* puny.

**kümmern 1** *vt* to concern. **was kümmert Sie das?** what business is that of yours?; **was kümmert mich das?** what's that to me? **2** *vr* **sich um jdn/etw ~** to look after sb/sth; **sich darum ~, daß ...** to see to it that ...; **kümmere dich gefälligst um deine eigenen Angelegenheiten!** mind your own business!; **er kümmert sich nicht darum, was die Leute denken** he doesn't care what people think.

**Kumpan(in** *f)* *m* **-e** *(dated col)* mate *(Brit col)*, buddy *(esp US col)*.

**Kumpel** *m* - *or (col)* **-s (a)** *(Min: Bergmann)* miner. **(b)** *(col: Kollege, Freund)* mate *(Brit col)*, buddy *(esp US col)*.

**kumpelhaft** *adj* chummy, matey *(Brit col)*.

**kündbar** *adj Vertrag* terminable; *Anleihe* redeemable. **Beamte sind nicht ohne weiteres ~** civil servants cannot be dismissed without good cause.

**Kündbarkeit** *f (von Vertrag)* terminability; *(von Anleihe)* redeemability.

**Kunde¹** *f no pl (geh)* news *sing*, tidings *pl (old)*.

**Kunde²** *m* **-n, -n** *(auch pej col)* customer.

**künden** *vi (geh)* **von etw ~** to tell of sth.

**Kunden-:** **~beratung** *f* customer advisory service; **~dienst** *m* customer service; **~fang** *m (pej)* **auf ~fang sein** to be touting for customers; **ein Vertreter auf ~fang** a salesman chasing up some business; **~(kredit)karte** *f* charge card; **~(kredit)konto** *nt* charge account; **~kreis** *m* customers *pl*, clientèle; **~werbung** *f* publicity (aimed at attracting custom *or* customers).

**kundgeben** *vt sep irreg (dated)* **etw ~** to announce sth *(jdm to sb)*; *Gefühle etc* to express sth.

**Kundgebung** *f (Versammlung)* rally.

**kundig** *adj (geh)* knowledgeable; *(sach~)* expert. **einer Sache** *(gen)* **~ sein** to have a knowledge of sth.

**kündigen 1** *vt Stellung* to hand in one's notice for; *Abonnement, Mitgliedschaft* to cancel; *Vertrag* to terminate; *Tarife* to discontinue; *(col) jdn* to dismiss. **jdm die Wohnung ~** to give sb notice to quit his flat; **ich habe meine Wohnung gekündigt** I've given in notice that I'm leaving my flat; **die Stellung ~** to hand in one's notice; **jdm die Stellung ~** to give sb his/her notice; **sie hat ihm die Freundschaft gekündigt** she has broken off their friendship. **2** *vi (Arbeitnehmer)* to give in one's notice; *(Mieter)* to give notice. **jdm ~** *(Arbeitgeber)* to give sb his notice; *(Vermieter)* to give sb notice to quit; **zum 1. April ~** to give one's notice for April 1st; *(Mieter)* to give notice for April 1st; *(bei Mitgliedschaft)* to cancel one's membership as of April 1st.

**Kündigung** *f* **(a)** *(Mitteilung) (von Vermieter)* notice to quit; *(von Mieter, von Stellung)* notice; *(von Vertrag)* termination. **(b)** *(das Kündigen) (von Arbeitgeber)* dismissal; *(von Arbeitnehmer)* giving in one's notice; *(von Vertrag)* termination; *(von Mitgliedschaft, Abonnement)* cancellation.

**Kündigungs-:** **~frist** *f* period of notice; **vierteljährliche ~frist haben** to have (to give) three months' notice; **~geld** *nt (Fin)* deposits *pl* at notice; **~grund** *m* grounds *pl* for giving notice; *(von Arbeitgeber auch)* grounds *pl* for dismissal; **~schreiben** *nt* written notice; **~schutz** *m* protection against

wrongful dismissal.
**Kundin** f customer.
**Kundschaft** f customers pl.
**Kundschafter** m - spy; (Mil) scout.
**kundtun** vt sep irreg (geh) to make known.
**künftig 1** adj future. **2** adv in future.
**Kunst** f ≃e **(a)** art. **die schönen** ~e the fine arts; (als Gesamtheit) fine art sing. **(b)** (Können, Fertigkeit) art, skill; (Kunststück) trick. **mit seiner** ~ **am Ende sein** to be at one's wits' end; **ärztliche** ~ medical skill; **das ist keine** ~! it's like taking candy from a baby (col); (ein Kinderspiel) it's a piece of cake (col); **das ist eine brotlose** ~ there's no money in that; **was macht die** ~? (col) how's tricks? (col).
**Kunst-** in cpds (Art) art; (künstlich) artificial; ~**akademie** f college of art; ~**ausstellung** f art exhibition; ~**banause** m (pej) philistine; ~**druck** m art print; ~**druckpapier** nt art paper; ~**dünger** m artificial fertilizer; ~**erzieher** m art teacher; ~**erziehung** f (Sch) art; ~**faser** f man-made fibre (Brit) or fiber (US); ~**fehler** m professional error; (weniger ernst) slip; **k**~**fertig** adj (geh) skilful (Brit), skillful (US); ~**fertigkeit** f skill; ~**flieger** m stunt flyer; ~**flug** m aerobatics sing; ~**gegenstand** m art object; **k**~**gerecht** adj (fachmännisch) skilful (Brit), skillful (US); ~**geschichte** f history of art, art history; ~**gewerbe** nt arts and crafts pl; ~**gewerbler(in** f) m - craftsman/-woman; **k**~**gewerblich** adj **k**~**gewerbliche Gegenstände** craft objects; ~**griff** m trick, dodge (col); ~**handel** m art trade; ~**händler** m art dealer; ~**handwerk** nt craft industry; ~**hochschule** f art college; ~**kenner** m art connoisseur; ~**kritik** f no pl art criticism; (die Kritiker) art critics pl; (Rezension) art review; ~**kritiker** m art critic; ~**leder** nt artificial or imitation leather.
**Künstler(in** f) m - **(a)** artist; (Unterhaltungs~) artiste. **bildender** ~ visual artist. **(b)** (Könner) genius (in +dat at).
**künstlerisch** adj artistic.
**Künstler-**: ~**name** m pseudonym; (von Schriftsteller auch) pen name; (von Schauspieler auch) stage name; ~**pech** nt (col) hard luck.
**künstlich** adj artificial; Zähne, Wimpern, Fingernägel false; Faserstoffe synthetic; Diamanten imitation, fake (col). ~**e Intelligenz** artificial intelligence; **jdn** ~ **ernähren** (Med) to feed sb artificially; **sich** ~ **aufregen** (col) to get all worked up about nothing (col).
**Kunst-**: **k**~**los** adj unsophisticated; ~**maler** m artist, painter; ~**pause** f pause for effect; (iro) awkward pause; ~**sammlung** f art collection; ~**schätze** pl art treasures pl; ~**seide** f artificial silk; ~**springen** nt diving; ~**stoff** m man-made material; ~**stopfen** nt invisible mending; ~**stück** nt trick; ~**stück!** (iro) no wonder!; **das ist kein** ~**stück** (fig) there's nothing to it; ~**turnen** nt gymnastics sing; ~**verstand** m appreciation of art; **k**~**voll** adj artistic; ~**werk** nt work of art.
**kunterbunt** adj Sammlung, Gruppe etc motley attr; (vielfarbig auch) multi-coloured (Brit), multi-colored (US); Programm varied. ~ **durcheinander** higgledy-piggledy (col).
**Kupfer** nt no pl copper.
**Kupfergeld** nt coppers pl, copper coins pl.
**kupfern** adj copper.
**Kupfer-**: **k**~**rot** adj copper-coloured (Brit), copper-colored (US); ~**stecher** m - copper(plate) engraver; ~**stich** m copperplate (engraving or etching).
**kupieren\*** vt Schwanz, Ohren to dock.
**Kupon** [ku'põ:] m -s coupon.
**Kuppe** f -n (Berg~) (rounded) hilltop; (Finger~) tip.

**Kuppel** f -n dome, cupola.
**Kuppeldach** nt dome-shaped roof.
**Kuppelei** f (Jur) procuring.
**kuppeln 1** vt (Tech) to couple; (fig auch) to link. **2** vi (Aut) to operate the clutch.
**Kuppler(in** f) m - (Jur) procurer/procuress.
**Kupplung** f (Tech) coupling; (Aut etc) clutch. **die** ~ **(durch)treten** to disengage the clutch; **die** ~ **kommen lassen** (Aut) to let the clutch in.
**Kupplungs-** in cpds (Aut) clutch; ~**pedal** nt clutch pedal.
**Kur** f -en (in Badeort) (health) cure; (Haar~ etc) treatment no pl; (Schlankheits~, Diät~) diet. **zur** ~ **fahren** to go to a health resort (to take a cure); **eine** ~ **machen** to take a cure; (Schlankheits~) to diet; **jdn zur** ~ **schicken** to send sb to a health resort (for a cure).
**Kür** f -en **(a)** (Sport) free (skating) programme (Brit) or program US). **eine** ~ **laufen** to perform one's free programme. **(b)** (old: Wahl) election.
**Kuratorium** nt (Vereinigung) committee.
**Kurbel** f -n crank.
**kurbeln** vti to turn, to wind.
**Kurbelwelle** f crankshaft.
**Kürbis** m -se pumpkin; (col: Kopf) nut (col).
**Kurde** m (wk) -n, -n **Kurdin** f Kurd.
**kurdisch** adj Kurdish.
**küren** vt (old, geh) to choose, to elect (zu as).
**Kur-**: ~**fürst** m Elector, electoral prince; ~**gast** m patient at a health resort or spa.
**Kurier** m -e courier, messenger.
**Kurierdienst** m courier or messenger service.
**kurieren\*** vt (lit, fig) to cure (von of). **von ihm bin ich kuriert** I've gone right off him.
**kurios** adj (merkwürdig) curious, strange, odd.
**Kuriosität** f **(a)** (Gegenstand) curio(sity). **(b)** (Eigenart) peculiarity.
**Kurkonzert** nt spa concert.
**Kürlauf(en** nt) m free (skating) programme (Brit) or program (US).
**Kur-**: ~**ort** m health resort; (Heilbad) spa; ~**pfuscher** m (pej col) quack (doctor); ~**pfuscherei** f (pej col) quackery.
**Kurs** m -e **(a)** (Naut, Aviat, fig) course; (Pol, Richtung auch) line. **harter/weicher** ~ (Pol) hard/soft line; **den** ~ **ändern/beibehalten** (lit, fig) to alter/hold (one's) course; ~ **nehmen auf** (+acc) to set course for; ~ **haben auf** (+acc) to be heading for. **(b)** (Fin: Wechsel~) exchange rate; (Aktien~) (going) rate; (Marktpreis) market value. **zum** ~ **von** at the rate of; **hoch im** ~ **stehen** (Aktien) to be high; (fig) to be popular (bei with). **(c)** (Lehrgang) course (in +dat, für in). **einen** ~ **besuchen** or **mitmachen** to attend a course.
**Kurs-**: ~**änderung** f (lit, fig) change of course; ~**buch** nt (Rail) timetable (Brit), schedule (US).
**Kürschner(in** f) m - furrier.
**kursieren\*** vi aux haben or sein to be in circulation; (fig) to circulate.
**kursiv** adj italic. **etw** ~ **drucken** to italicize sth.
**Kursivschrift** f italics pl.
**Kurs-**: ~**korrektur** f (lit, fig) course correction; ~**rückgang** m fall in prices; ~**schwankung** f fluctuation in exchange rates; (St Ex) fluctuation in market rates.
**Kursus** m, pl **Kurse** (geh: Lehrgang) course.
**Kurs-**: ~**wagen** m (Rail) through car; ~**wechsel** m change of direction; ~**wert** m (Fin) market value.
**Kurtaxe** f -n visitor's tax (at health resort or spa).
**Kurve** ['kʊrvə] f -n (Math, col: Körperrundung) curve; (Biegung, Straßen~ auch) bend; (schärfer auch) cor-

ner; *(statistisch, Fieber~ etc)* graph. **die Straße macht eine** ~ the road bends; **die** ~ **kratzen** *(col: schnell weggehen)* to make tracks *(col)*; **die** ~ **nicht kriegen** *(col)* not to get around to it.
**kurven** ['kʊrvn] *vi aux sein (col) (Aviat)* to circle. **durch Italien** ~ to drive around Italy.
**kurvenreich** *adj Straße* winding; *(col) Frau* curvaceous, shapely. **„~e Strecke"** "bends".
**Kurverwaltung** f spa authorities *pl*.
**kurvig** ['kʊrvɪç] *adj* winding, twisting.
**kurz** *comp* ⁼**er**, *superl* ⁼**ste(r, s)** *or (adv)* **am** ⁼**esten**
**1** *adj* short; *Zeit, Aufenthalt, Bericht, Antwort etc auch* brief; *Blick, Folge* quick; *Gedächtnis auch* short-lived. **etw** ~**er machen** to shorten sth; **mach's** ~**!** make it quick; **den** ~**eren ziehen** *(fig col)* to get the worst of it; **mit ein paar** ~**en Worten** in a few brief words; **ein** ~**erer Weg** a shorter way; **in** ~**ester Frist** before very long.
  **2** *adv* **(a)** ~ **atmen** to take short breaths; **eine Sache** ~ **abtun** to dismiss sth out of hand; **zu** ~ **kommen** to get a raw deal *(col)*; ~ **entschlossen** without a moment's hesitation; ~ **gesagt** in a word; **sich** ~ **fassen** to be brief; ~ **und bündig** concisely; ~ **und gut** in short; ~ **und schmerzlos** *(col)* short and sweet; **jdn/etw** ~ **und klein schlagen** to beat sb up/ to smash sth to pieces.
  **(b)** *(für eine* ~*e Zeit)* briefly. **ich habe ihn nur** ~ **gesehen** I only saw him briefly; **ich bleibe nur** ~ I'll only stay for a short while; **darf ich mal** ~ **stören?** could I just interrupt for a moment?
  **(c)** *(zeitlich, räumlich: nicht lang)* shortly, just. ~ **vor Köln/Ostern** shortly *or* just before Cologne/ Easter; **er hat den Wagen erst seit** ~**em** he's only had the car for a short while; **seit** ~**em gibt es Bier in der Kantine** they've recently started serving beer in the canteen; **über** ~ **oder lang** sooner or later; **(bis) vor** ~**em** (until) recently; ~ **nacheinander** shortly after each other.
**Kurz-:** ~**arbeit** f short-time (working); **k~arbeiten** *vi sep* to be on short time; ~**arbeiter** *m* short-time worker; **k~ärm(e)lig** *adj* short-sleeved; **k~atmig** *adj (fig)* feeble, lame; *(Med)* short-winded; ~**ausbildung** f short training course.
**Kürze** f *no pl* shortness; *(von Besuch, Bericht etc auch)* brevity; *(fig: Bündigkeit)* conciseness; **in** ~ shortly; **in aller** ~ very briefly; **in der** ~ **liegt die Würze** *(Prov)* brevity is the soul of wit *(prov)*.
**Kürzel** *nt* - *(stenographisches Zeichen)* shorthand symbol; *(Kurzwort)* contraction.
**kürzen** *vt* to shorten; *(Math) Bruch* to cancel (down); *Gehalt, Etat, Produktion* to cut (back). **jdm das Gehalt etc** ~ to cut back sb's salary *etc*.
**Kurze(r)¹** *m decl as adj (col)* **(a)** *(Schnaps)* short. **(b)** *(Kurzschluß)* short (circuit).
**Kurze(r)²** *mf decl as adj (col)* small child.
**kurzerhand** *adv* without further ado; *entlassen* on the spot.
**Kurz-:** ~**fassung** f abridged version; ~**film** *m* short (film); **k~fristig 1** *adj* short-term; *Wettervorhersage* short-range; **2** *adv (auf kurze Sicht)* for the short term; *(für kurze Zeit)* for a short time; **k~fristig seine Pläne ändern** to change one's plans at short notice; **k~gefaßt** *adj* concise; ~**geschichte** f short story; **k~haarig** *adj* short-haired; **k~halten** *vt sep irreg* **jdn k~halten** to keep sb short; **k~lebig** *adj*

short-lived, ephemeral.
**kürzlich** *adv* recently, lately. **erst** ~ just recently.
**Kurz-:** ~**meldung** f news flash; ~**nachrichten** *pl* news headlines *pl*; *(in Zeitung auch)* news in brief; ~**parken** *nt* short-stay parking; ~**parker** *m* short-term parker; ~**reise** f short trip; ~**schließen** *sep irreg* **1** *vt* to short circuit; **2** *vr (in Verbindung treten)* to get in contact *(mit* with*)*; ~**schluß** *m* **(a)** short circuit; **(b)** *(fig: auch* ~**schlußhandlung)** rash action; ~**schlußreaktion** f reaction in the heat of the moment; ~**schrift** f shorthand; **k~sichtig** *adj (lit, fig)* short-sighted; ~**sichtigkeit** f *(lit, fig)* short-sightedness.
**Kurzstrecken-** *in cpds* short-range; ~**flugzeug** *nt* short-haul aircraft; ~**läufer** *m (Sport)* sprinter; ~**rakete** f short-range missile.
**kurz-:** ~**treten** *vi sep irreg (fig col)* to go easy; ~**um** *adv* in a word.
**Kürzung** f shortening; *(eines Buchs)* abridgement; *(von Gehältern, der Produktion)* cut *(gen* in*)*.
**Kurz-:** ~**urlaub** *m* short holiday *(Brit)* or vacation *(US)*; *(Mil)* short leave; ~**waren** *pl* haberdashery *(Brit)*, notions *pl (US)*; **k~weilig** *adj* entertaining; ~**welle** f *(Rad)* short wave.
**Kurzzeit-** *in cpds* short-term.
**kuschelig** *adj (col)* cosy, snug.
**kuscheln** *vr* **sich an jdn** ~ to snuggle up to sb; **sich in etw** *(acc)* ~ to snuggle up in sth.
**kuschen** *vir (Hund etc)* to get down; *(fig)* to knuckle under.
**Kusine** f (female) cousin.
**Kuß** *m* ⁼**sse** kiss.
**Küßchen** *nt* peck *(col)*. **gib** ~ give us a kiss.
**küssen 1** *vti* to kiss. **jdm die Hand** ~ to kiss sb's hand. **2** *vr* to kiss (each other).
**Kußhand** f **jdm eine** ~ **zuwerfen** to blow sb a kiss; **jdn/etw mit** ~ **nehmen** *(col)* to be only too glad to take sb/sth.
**Küste** f **-n** coast; *(Ufer)* shore.
**Küsten-** *in cpds* coastal; ~**fischerei** f inshore fishing; ~**gebiet** *nt* coastal area; ~**gewässer** *pl* coastal waters *pl*; ~**nebel** *m* sea mist; ~**schiffahrt** f coastal shipping; ~**wache**, ~**wacht** f coastguard.
**Küster** *m* - verger, sexton.
**Kutsche** f **-n** coach, carriage; *(col: Auto)* jalopy *(col)*.
**Kutscher** *m* - coachman, driver.
**kutschieren\* 1** *vi aux sein* to drive, to ride. **durch die Gegend** ~ *(col)* to drive around. **2** *vt* to drive.
**Kutte** f **-n** *(monk's)* habit.
**Kutter** *m* - *(Naut)* cutter.
**Kuvert** [ku'veːɐ, ku'veːr] *nt* **-s** *(Brief~)* envelope.
**Kuvertüre** [kuver'tyːrə] f **-n** *(Cook)* (chocolate) coating.
**k.u.w.** = **kalt und warm** h & c.
**Kuwait** *nt* Kuwait.
**Kuwaiter(in** f**)** *m* - Kuwaiti.
**Kuwaiti** *m* Kuwaiti.
**kuwaitisch** *adj* Kuwaiti.
**kW** = **Kilowatt** KW.
**KW** = **Kurzwelle** SW.
**Kybernetik** f cybernetics *sing*.
**kyrillisch** *adj* Cyrillic.
**KZ** [kaːˈtsɛt] *nt* **-s** = **Konzentrationslager**.

# L

**L, l** [ɛl] *nt* -, - L, l. **L wie Ludwig** ≃ L for Lucy *(Brit)*, L for Love *(US)*.
**l** = **(a)** **links** l. **(b)** **Liter** l.
**labb(e)rig** *adj (col)* Bier, Suppe watery; *Kaffee, Tee auch* weak; *Essen* mushy.
**laben** *vr (liter)* to feast (oneself) *(an +dat on)*; *(an Quelle etc)* to refresh oneself *(mit, an +dat with)*.
**labern** *(col)* **1** *vi* to prattle on *(col)*. **2** *vt* to talk. **was laberst du denn da?** what are you prattling on about? *(col)*.
**labil** *adj (physisch)* Gesundheit delicate; *Kreislauf* poor; *Patient* frail; *(psychisch)* unstable.
**Labilität** *f siehe adj* delicateness; poorness; frailty; weakness.
**Labor** *nt* -s *or* -e laboratory, lab *(col)*.
**Laborant(in** *f)* *m* lab(oratory) technician.
**Laboratorium** *nt* laboratory.
**laborieren*** *vi* to labour *(Brit)*, to labor *(US)* *(an +dat at)*; *(leiden)* to be plagued *(an +dat by)*.
**Labyrinth** *nt* -e labyrinth; *(fig auch)* maze.
**Lach|anfall** *m* laughing fit.
**Lache¹** ['laxə, 'la:xə] *f* -n puddle; *(von Benzin, Blut auch)* pool.
**Lache²** *f* -n *(col)* laugh.
**lächeln** *vi* to smile. **verlegen/freundlich** ~ to give an embarrassed/a friendly smile.
**Lächeln** *nt no pl* smile.
**lachen 1** *vi* to laugh *(über +acc at)*. **jdn zum L~ bringen** to make sb laugh; **zum L~ sein** *(lustig)* to be hilarious; *(lächerlich)* to be laughable; **mir ist nicht zum L~ (zumute)** I'm in no laughing mood; **daß ich nicht lache!** *(col)* don't make me laugh! *(col)*; **da kann ich doch nur** ~ I can't help laughing (at that); **du hast gut** ~**!** it's all right for you to laugh!; **gezwungen/verlegen** ~ to give a forced/an embarrassed laugh; **wer zuletzt lacht, lacht am besten** *(Prov)* he who laughs last, laughs longest *(Prov)*; **die Sonne lacht** the sun is shining brightly; **ihm lachte das Glück** Fortune smiled on him.
**2** *vt* **da gibt es gar nichts zu** ~ that's nothing to laugh about; *(es ist etwas Ernstes auch)* that's not funny; **er hat bei seiner Frau nichts zu** ~ *(col)* he has a hard time of it with his wife; **das wäre doch gelacht, wenn ...** it would be ridiculous if ...; **das wäre doch gelacht!** that's dead easy *(col)*; **sich schief** ~ *(col)* to split one's sides (laughing) *(col)*.
**Lachen** *nt no pl* laughter, laughing; *(Art des* ~*s)* laugh. **dir wird das** ~ **schon noch vergehen!** you'll soon be laughing on the other side of your face.
**Lacher** *m* - **die** ~ **auf seiner Seite haben** to have the last laugh; *(einen Lacherfolg verbuchen)* to get a laugh.
**Lach|erfolg** *m* **ein** ~ **sein, einen** ~ **erzielen** to make everybody laugh.
**lächerlich** *adj* **(a)** ridiculous, absurd. **jdn/etw** ~ **machen** to make sb/sth look silly *(vor jdm* in front of sb)*; **jdn/sich** ~ **machen** to make a fool of sb/oneself *(vor jdm* in front of sb)*; **etw ins L~e ziehen** to make fun of sth. **(b)** *(geringfügig)* Anlaß trivial, petty.
**Lächerlichkeit** *f* **(a)** *no pl* ridiculousness; *(von Argument etc auch)* absurdity. **jdn der** ~ **preisgeben** to make a laughing stock of sb. **(b)** *(Geringfügigkeit)* triviality.
**Lach-:** ~**gas** *nt* laughing gas; **l~haft** *adj* ludicrous; *Argument auch* laughable; ~**krampf** *m* **einen** ~**krampf bekommen** to go into fits of laughter.
**Lachs** [laks] *m* -e salmon.
**Lachsalve** *f* burst *or* roar of laughter.
**Lachs-:** **l~farben** *adj* salmon pink; ~**forelle** *f* salmon *or* sea trout; ~**schinken** *m* smoked, rolled fillet of ham.
**Lack** *m* -e *(Holz~, Nagel~)* varnish; *(Auto~)* paint.
**Lack-:** ~**affe** *m (pej col)* flash Harry *(col)*; ~**farbe** *f* gloss paint.
**lackieren*** *vt Holz* to varnish; *Fingernägel auch* to paint; *Auto* to spray.
**Lackierung** *f* **(a)** *(das Lackieren) (von Autos)* spraying; *(von Möbeln)* varnishing. **(b)** *(der Lack) (von Auto)* paintwork; *(Holz~)* varnish.
**Lackleder** *nt* patent leather.
**Lackmuspapier** *nt* litmus paper.
**Lack-:** ~**schaden** *m* damage to paintwork; ~**schuh** *m* patent-leather shoe.
**Lade** *f* -n chest; *(col: Schub~)* drawer.
**Lade-:** ~**baum** *m* derrick; ~**bühne** *f* loading ramp; ~**fläche** *f* load area; ~**gerät** *nt* battery charger; ~**gewicht** *nt* load capacity; ~**hemmung** *f* **das Gewehr hat** ~**hemmung** the gun is jammed.
**laden¹** *pret* **lud**, *ptp* **geladen** *vti* to load; *(Comp auch)* to download; *(Phys)* to charge. **das Schiff hat Autos geladen** the ship has a cargo of cars; **der Lkw hat zuviel geladen** the lorry is overloaded; **Verantwortung/Schulden auf sich** *(acc)* ~ to saddle oneself with responsibility/debts; **eine schwere Schuld auf sich** *(acc)* ~ to place oneself under a heavy burden of guilt; **er hatte schon ganz schön geladen** *(col)* he was already pretty tanked up *(col)*; **mit Spannung geladen** charged with tension; *siehe* **geladen**.
**laden²** *pret* **lud**, *ptp* **geladen** *vt (liter: einladen)* to invite; *(form: vor Gericht)* to summon. **nur für geladene Gäste** by invitation only.
**Laden¹** *m* ⁼ shop *(esp Brit)*, store *(US)*; *(col: Betrieb)* outfit *(col)*. **der** ~ **läuft** *(col)* business is good; **den** ~ **schmeißen** *(col)* to run the show; *(zurechtkommen)* to manage; **den (ganzen)** ~ **hinschmeißen** *(col)* to chuck the whole thing in *(col)*.
**Laden²** *m* ⁼ *or* - *(Fenster~)* shutter.
**Laden-:** ~**besitzer** *m* shopowner *(esp Brit)*, shopkeeper *(esp Brit)*, storekeeper *(US)*; ~**dieb** *m* shoplifter; ~**diebstahl** *m* shoplifting; ~**hüter** *m* nonseller; ~**kasse** *f* till; ~**kette** *f* chain of shops *or* stores; ~**preis** *m* shop price; ~**schluß** *m* **nach/vor** ~**schluß** after/before the shops *(esp Brit)* or stores *(US)* shut; **um fünf Uhr ist** ~**schluß** the shops/stores shut at five o'clock; ~**tisch** *m* shop counter; **über**

**den/unter dem ~tisch** over/under the counter.
**Lade-:** **~rampe** *f* loading ramp; **~raum** *m* load room; *(Aviat, Naut)* hold.
**lädieren*** *vt* to damage. **lädiert sein/aussehen** *(hum)* to be/look the worse for wear.
**Ladung** *f* **(a)** load; *(von Sprengstoff)* charge. **eine geballte ~ Schnee/Dreck** *(col)* a whole lot of snow/mud; **eine geballte ~ von Schimpfwörtern** a whole torrent of abuse. **(b)** *(Vorladung)* summons *sing.*
**Lafette** *f (Mil)* (gun)carriage.
**lag** *pret of* **liegen.**
**Lage** *f* **-n (a)** *(geographische ~)* situation, location. **in günstiger ~** well-situated; **eine gute/ruhige ~ haben** to be in a good/quiet location. **(b)** *(Art des Liegens)* position. **(c)** *(Situation)* situation. **dazu bin ich nicht in der ~** I'm not in a position to do that; **in der glücklichen ~ sein, etw zu tun** to be in the happy position of doing sth; **Herr der ~ sein** to be in control of the situation; **die ~ der Dinge erfordert es, daß ...** the situation requires that ... **(d)** *(Schicht)* layer. **(e)** *(Mus)* *(Stimm~)* register; *(Ton~)* pitch. **(f)** *(Runde)* round. **eine ~ schmeißen** *(col)* to stand a round.
**Lage-:** **~bericht** *m* report; *(Mil)* situation report; **~besprechung** *f:* **eine ~besprechung abhalten** to discuss the situation; **~plan** *m* ground plan.
**Lager** *nt -* **(a)** *(Unterkunft)* camp; *(liter: Schlafstätte)* bed. **(b)** *(fig: Partei)* camp; *(von Staaten)* bloc. **ins andere ~ überwechseln** to change camps. **(c)** *pl auch ⸗* *(Vorratsraum)* store(room); *(von Laden)* stockroom; *(~halle)* warehouse; *(Vorrat)* stock. **etw auf ~ haben** to have sth in stock; *(fig) Witz etc* to have sth at the ready. **(d)** *(Tech)* bearing. **(e)** *(Geol)* bed.
**Lager-:** **~bestand** *m* stock; **~feuer** *nt* campfire; **~halle** *f,* **~haus** *nt* warehouse.
**Lagerist(in** *f)* *m* storeman/storewoman.
**lagern 1** *vt* **(a)** *(aufbewahren)* to store. **kühl ~!** store in a cool place. **(b)** *(hinlegen)* **jdn** to lay down; *Bein etc* to rest. **einen Kranken weich ~** to lay an invalid on something soft; **das Bein hoch ~** to put one's leg up; *siehe* **gelagert. 2** *vi* **(a)** *(Lebensmittel etc)* to be stored. **(b)** *(liegen)* to lie. **(c)** *(von Truppen)* to camp, to be encamped.
**Lager-:** **~raum** *m* storeroom; *(in Geschäft)* stockroom; **~stätte** *f* **(a)** *(old liter)* bed, couch *(liter);* **(b)** *(Geol)* deposit.
**Lagerung** *f* storage; *(das Lagern auch)* storing.
**Lagune** *f* **-n** lagoon.
**lahm** *adj* **(a)** *(gelähmt) Bein, Mensch* lame; *(col: steif)* stiff. **er hat ein ~es Bein** he is lame in one leg. **(b)** *(col: langsam, langweilig)* dreary, dull; *Geschäftsgang* slow, sluggish. **eine ~e Ente sein** *(col)* to have no zip *(col).*
**lahmen** *vi* to be lame *(auf + dat in).*
**lähmen** *vt* to paralyze; *(fig) Industrie auch* to cripple; *Verhandlungen, Verkehr* to hold up. **er ist an beiden Beinen gelähmt** he is paralyzed in both legs; **vor Angst wie gelähmt sein** to be petrified.
**Lahme(r)** *mf decl as adj (old)* cripple.
**lahmlegen** *vt sep Verkehr, Produktion* to bring to a standstill; *Industrie auch* to paralyze.
**Lähmung** *f (lit)* paralysis; *(fig)* immobilization.
**Laib** *m* **-e** loaf.
**laichen** *vi* to spawn.
**Laie** *m (wk)* **-n, -n** layman, layperson; *(fig also, Theat)* amateur. **die ~n** *(Eccl)* the laity; **da staunt der ~, der Fachmann wundert sich** *(hum col)* that's a real turn-up for the books *(col).*
**Laien-:** **~darsteller** *m* amateur actor; **l~haft** *adj Arbeit* amateurish; *Urteil, Meinung* lay *attr only;*

**~prediger** *m* lay preacher; **~spiel** *nt* **(a)** amateur drama *no pl;* **(b)** *(Stück)* play for amateurs; **~theater** *nt* amateur theatre *(Brit)* or theater *(US);* *(Ensemble)* amateur theatre *(Brit)* or theater *(US)* group.
**Lakai** *m (wk)* **-en, -en** *(lit, fig)* lackey.
**Lake** *f* **-n** brine.
**Laken** *nt -* sheet.
**lakonisch** *adj* laconic.
**Lakritz** *m* **-e** *(dial),* **Lakritze** *f* **-n** liquorice *(Brit),* licorice *(US).*
**lala** *adv (col):* **so ~** so-so *(col),* not too bad *(col).*
**lallen** *vti* to babble; *(Betrunkener)* to mumble.
**Lama** *nt* **-s** llama.
**Lamelle** *f* **(a)** *(Biol)* lamella. **(b)** *(von Jalousien)* slat; *(von Heizkörper)* rib.
**Lamellentür** *f* louvre door.
**lamentieren*** *vi* to moan, to complain.
**Lametta** *nt no pl* lametta.
**Lamm** *nt* **⸗er** lamb. **wie das ~ zur Schlachtbank** like a lamb to the slaughter.
**Lamm-:** **~braten** *m* roast lamb; **~fell** *nt* lambskin; **~fleisch** *nt* lamb; **l~fromm** *adj Gesicht, Miene* innocent; **l~fromm sein** to be like a (little) lamb; **~kotelett** *nt* lamb chop; **~wolle** *f* lambswool.
**Lampe** *f* **-n** light; *(Öl~, Steh~, Tisch~)* lamp; *(Glüh~)* bulb.
**Lampen-:** **~fieber** *nt* stage fright; **~schirm** *m* lampshade.
**Lampion** [lamˈpioː, lamˈpioŋ] *m* **-s** Chinese lantern.
**lancieren*** [lãˈsiːrən] *vt Produkt, Künstler* to launch; *Nachricht* to put out. **jdn/etw in etw** *(acc)* **~** to get sb/sth into sth.
**Land** *nt* **⸗er (a)** *(Gelände, Festland)* land. **ein Stück ~** a plot of land; **~ bestellen/bebauen** to till the soil/to cultivate the land; **an ~ gehen/schwimmen** to go/swim ashore; **~ sehen** *(lit)* to sight land; **endlich sehe ich ~** *(fig)* at last I can see the light at the end of the tunnel; **etw an ~ ziehen** to pull sth ashore; **einen Auftrag an ~ ziehen** *(col)* to land an order; **~ in Sicht!** land ahoy!; **~ unter!** land submerged!
  **(b)** *(ländliches Gebiet)* country. **auf dem ~(e)** in the country.
  **(c)** *(Staat)* country, land *(esp liter); (Bundes~)* *(in BRD)* Land, state; *(in Österreich)* province. **das ~ Hessen/Tirol** the state of Hesse/the province of Tyrol; **die neuen ̃er** *(BRD)* former East Germany; **außer ̃es sein** to be out of the country; **~ und Leute kennenlernen** to get to know the country and its inhabitants; **aus aller Herren ̃er** from all over the world.
**Land-:** **~adel** *m* landed gentry; **~arbeit** *f* agricultural work; **~arbeiter** *m* agricultural farmworker; **l~auf** *adv:* **l~auf, l~ab** the length and breadth of the country; **~besitz** *m* **~besitz haben** to be a landowner; **~besitzer** *m* landowner; **~bevölkerung** *f* rural population.
**Lande-:** **~anflug** *m* approach; **~bahn** *f* runway; **~erlaubnis** *f* landing permission; **~fähre** *f (Space)* landing module.
**landeinwärts** *adv* inland.
**landen** *vti (vi: aux sein)* to land. **weich ~** to make a soft landing; **im Gefängnis ~** to land or end up in prison; **mit deinen Komplimenten kannst du bei mir nicht ~** your compliments won't get you anywhere with me.
**Land|enge** *f* isthmus.
**Lande-:** **~piste** *f* landing strip; **~platz** *m (für Flugzeuge)* landing strip; *(für Hubschrauber)* landing pad; *(für Schiffe)* landing place.
**Ländereien** *pl* estates *pl.*

**Länderspiel** nt international (match).
**Landes-:** ~**grenze** f (von Staat) (national) frontier; (von Bundesland) state/provincial boundary; ~**hauptstadt** f capital of the Land/province; ~**innere(s)** nt interior; ~**kunde** f regional studies pl; l~**kundig** adj l~**kundiger Reiseleiter** courier who knows the country; l~**kundlich** adj Themen, Aspekte regional; ~**liste** f (Parl) regional list of parliamentary candidates for election to the Federal parliament; ~**meister** m (Sport) regional champion; ~**regierung** f government of a Land/provincial government; ~**sprache** f national language; **der** ~**sprache unkundig sein** not to know the language.
**Landesteg** m jetty, landing stage (Brit).
**Landes-:** ~**teil** m region, area; ~**tracht** f national dress or costume; l~**üblich** adj customary; **das ist dort l~üblich** that's the custom there; ~**verrat** m treason; ~**verteidigung** f national defence (Brit) or defense (US); ~**währung** f currency of the country.
**Landeverbot** nt refusal of permission to land; ~ **erhalten** to be refused permission to land.
**Land-:** ~**flucht** f emigration to the cities; ~**friedensbruch** m (Jur) breach of the peace; ~**funk** m farming (radio) programme (Brit) or program (US); ~**gang** m shore leave; ~**gericht** nt district court; l~**gestützt** adj Raketen land-based; ~**gut** nt estate; ~**haus** nt country house; ~**heer** nt army; ~**jäger** m (Wurst) pressed smoked sausage; ~**karte** f map; ~**klima** nt continental climate; ~**kreis** m administrative district; ~**krieg** m land warfare; l~**läufig** adj popular, common; **entgegen der l~läufigen Meinung** contrary to popular opinion; ~**leben** nt country life.
**ländlich** adj rural; Tracht country attr; Tanz country attr, folk attr; Idylle pastoral.
**Land-:** ~**luft** f country air; ~**macht** f land power; ~**plage** f plague; (fig col) pest; ~**ratte** f (hum) landlubber; ~**regen** m steady rain.
**Landschaft**f scenery no pl; (einer bestimmten Gegend auch) landscape; (ländliche Gegend) countryside. **eine öde** ~ a barren landscape; **die** ~ **um London** the countryside around London; **die** ~**en Italiens** the regions of Italy; **wir sahen eine reizvolle** ~ we saw some delightful scenery; **in der** ~ **herumstehen** (col) to stand around; **die politische/kulturelle** ~ the political/cultural scene.
**landschaftlich** adj Schönheiten etc scenic; Besonderheiten regional. **diese Gegend ist** ~ **ausgesprochen reizvoll** the scenery in this area is particularly delightful; **das ist** ~ **unterschiedlich** it differs from one part of the country to another.
**Landschafts-:** ~**malerei** f landscape painting; ~**schutz** m protection of the countryside; ~**schutzgebiet** nt nature reserve.
**Landsitz** m country seat.
**Landsmann** m, **Landsmännin** f, pl ~**leute** fellow countryman/-woman.
**Land-:** ~**straße** f country road; (Straße zweiter Ordnung) secondary road; ~**streicher(in** f) m - (pej) tramp, hobo (US); ~**streicherei** f vagrancy; ~**streitkräfte** pl land forces pl; ~**strich** m area; **ein flacher** ~**strich** a flat belt of land; ~**tag** m Landtag (state parliament).
**Landung** f (von Flugzeug, Truppen etc) landing. **zur** ~ **gezwungen werden** to be forced down.
**Landungs-:** ~**boot** nt landing craft; ~**brücke** f jetty, landing stage; ~**steg** m landing stage (Brit), jetty.
**Land-:** ~**urlaub** m shore leave; ~**vermesser** m land surveyor; ~**vermessung** f land surveying;

~**weg** m **auf dem** ~**weg** by land, overland; ~**wein** m vin ordinaire; ~**wirt** m farmer.
**Landwirtschaft** f agriculture, farming; (Betrieb) farm. ~ **betreiben** to farm.
**landwirtschaftlich** adj agricultural.
**Landwirtschafts-** in cpds agricultural; ~**ausstellung** f agricultural show; ~**ministerium** nt ministry of agriculture; ~**schule** f agricultural college.
**Landzunge** f spit (of land), promontory.
**lang** comp ≈**er**, superl ≈**ste(r, s)** or (adv) **am ≈sten 1** adj **(a)** long; Film, Roman, Aufenthalt, Rede auch lengthy. **das war seit** ~**em geplant** that was planned a long time ago; **ich habe seit** ~**em nichts von ihm gehört** I haven't heard from him for a long time; **vor** ~**er Zeit** a long time ago; **hier wird mir die Zeit nicht** ~ I won't get bored here; **etw** ~**er machen** to lengthen sth; **er machte ein** ~**es Gesicht** his face fell; **man sah überall nur** ~**e Gesichter** you saw nothing but long faces; **etw von** ~**er Hand vorbereiten** to prepare sth over a long period; **einen** ~**en Hals machen** (col) to crane one's neck. **(b)** (col: groß) Mensch tall.
**2** adv **der** ~ **erwartete Regen** the long-awaited rain; **der** ~ **ersehnte Urlaub** the longed-for holiday; ~ **anhaltender Beifall** prolonged applause; **zwei Stunden** ~ for two hours; **mein ganzes Leben** ~ my whole life; ~ **und breit** at great length; siehe **entlang**.
**lang-:** ~**ärm(e)lig** adj long-sleeved; ~**atmig** adj long-winded; ~**beinig** adj long-legged.
**lang(e)** adv comp ≈**er**, superl **am längsten (a)** (zeitlich) a long time; (in Fragen, Negativsätzen) long. **die Sitzung hat heute** ~ **gedauert** the meeting went on (for) a long time today; **wie** ~ **lernst du schon Deutsch?** how long have you been learning German (for)?; **es ist noch gar nicht** ~ **her, daß wir diese Frage diskutiert haben** it's not long since we discussed this question; **bis Weihnachten ist es ja noch** ~ **hin** it's still a long time till Christmas, we're a long way from Christmas. **(b)** (col: längst) **noch** ~ **nicht** not by any means; ~ **nicht so** ... not nearly as ...; **wenn der das schafft, kannst du das schon** ~ if he can do it, you can do it easily.
**Länge** f -n **(a)** length; (col: von Mensch) height. **ein Seil von 10 Meter** ~ a rope 10 metres long; **ein Vortrag/eine Fahrt von einer Stunde** ~ an hour-long lecture/an hour's journey; **etw der** ~ **nach falten** to fold sth lengthways; **der** ~ **nach hinfallen** to fall full length, to go sprawling; **in die** ~ **gehen** (Kleidungsstücke) to stretch; **etw in die** ~ **ziehen** to drag sth out (col); **sich in die** ~ **ziehen** to go on and on; **der** ~ **nach hinfallen** to fall flat (on one's face); **mit einer** ~ **gewinnen** (Sport) to win by a length. **(b)** (Geog) longitude. **der Ort liegt auf 20 Grad östlicher** ~ the town has a longitude of 20 degrees east.
**langen** (col) **1** vi **(a)** (sich erstrecken, greifen) to reach (nach for, in +acc in, into). **(b)** (ausreichen) to be enough; (auskommen) to get by, to manage. **jetzt langt's mir aber!** I've had just about enough! **2** vt (reichen) **jdm etw** ~ to hand sb sth; **jdm eine** ~ to give sb a clip on the ear (col).
**Längen-:** ~**grad** m degree of longitude; ~**maß** nt measure of length.
**lang**|**ersehnt** adj attr longed-for.
**Langeweile** f no pl boredom. ~ **haben** to be bored.
**lang-:** ~**finger** m (hum) pickpocket; l~**fristig 1** adj long-term; **2** adv in the long term; planen for the long term; l~**gehen** vi sep irreg (col) **(a)** (Weg etc) **wo geht's hier** ~? where does this road/path go? **(b)** (fig) **sie weiß, wo es l~geht** she knows what's what;

**l~haarig** *adj* long-haired; **l~jährig 1** *adj Freundschaft, Gewohnheit* long-standing; *Erfahrung, Verhandlungen* many years of; *Mitarbeiter* of many years' standing; **2** *adv* for many years; **~lauf** *m (Ski)* cross-country skiing; **~läufer** *m (Ski)* cross-country skier; **~laufski** *m* cross-country ski; **l~lebig** *adj* long-lasting; *Gerücht, Mensch, Tier* long-lived; **l~lebige Gebrauchsgüter** *pl* consumer durables *pl*; **~lebigkeit** *f (von Tieren, Menschen)* longevity; **l~legen** *vr sep* to have a lie-down.

**länglich** *adj* long, elongated.

**Lang-:** **~mut** *f no pl* patience, forbearance; **l~mütig** *adj* patient, forbearing.

**längs 1** *adv* lengthways, lengthwise. **2** *prep +gen* along. **~ der Straße stehen Kastanien** chestnut trees line the road.

**Längs|achse** *f* longitudinal axis.

**langsam 1** *adj* slow. **2** *adv* **(a)** slowly. **fahr/sprich ~er!** slow down!, drive/speak (a bit) more slowly!; **immer schön ~!** *(col)* easy does it!; **~ aber sicher** slowly but surely. **(b)** *(allmählich)* **es wird ~ Zeit, daß ...** it's getting about time that ...; **ich muß jetzt ~ gehen** I must be getting on my way; **~ (aber sicher) reicht es mir** I've just about had enough.

**Langsamkeit** *f* slowness.

**Langschläfer** *m* late riser.

**Langspielplatte** *f* long-playing record.

**Längs-:** **~schnitt** *m* longitudinal section; **~seite** *f* long side; *(Naut)* broadside; **l~seit(s)** *adv, prep +gen* alongside.

**längst** *adv* **(a)** *(seit langem, schon lange)* for a long time. **das ist ~ nicht mehr so** it hasn't been like that for a long time; **als wir ankamen, war der Zug ~ weg** when we arrived the train had long since gone. **(b)** *siehe* **lange (b).**

**längstens** *adv* **(a)** *(höchstens)* at the most. **(b)** *(spätestens)* at the latest.

**Langstrecken-** *in cpds* long-range; **~flugzeug** *nt* long-range aircraft; **~lauf** *m (Disziplin)* distance running; *(Wettkampf)* long-distance race; **~läufer** *m* distance runner; **~rakete** *f* long-range missile.

**Languste** [laŋˈgʊstə] *f* -n crayfish, crawfish *(US)*.

**langweilen** *insep* **1** *vt* to bore. **2** *vi* to be boring. **3** *vr* to be/get bored.

**Langweiler** *m* - bore.

**langweilig** *adj* **(a)** boring. **(b)** *(col: langsam)* slow.

**Lang-:** **~welle** *f* long wave; **l~wierig** *adj* long, lengthy; *Verhandlungen, Krankheit auch* prolonged; **~wierigkeit** *f* lengthiness.

**Langzeit-** *in cpds* long-term.

**Lanolin** *nt no pl* lanolin(e).

**Lanze** *f* -n lance; *(zum Werfen)* spear. **für jdn eine ~ brechen** *(fig)* to take up the cudgels for sb, to go to bat for sb *(esp US)*.

**Lanzette** *f (Med)* lancet.

**Laos** *nt* Laos.

**Laote** *m (wk)* -n, -n, **Laotin** *f* Laotian.

**laotisch** *adj* Laotian.

**lapidar** *adj* succinct.

**Lappalie** [-iə] *f* trifle, petty little matter.

**Lappe** *m (wk)* -n, -n, **Lappin** *f* Lapp, Laplander.

**Lappen** *m* - **(a)** *(Stück Stoff)* cloth; *(Wasch~)* face cloth. **(b)** *(col: Geldschein)* note *(Brit)*, bill *(US)*. **(c)** *(col)* **jdm durch die ~ gehen** to slip through sb's fingers.

**läppern** *vr impers (col)* **es läppert sich** it (all) mounts up.

**läppisch** *adj* silly. **wegen ~en zwei Mark macht er so ein Theater** *(col)* he makes such a fuss about a mere two marks.

**Lappland** *nt* Lapland.

**Lappländer(in** *f)* *m* - = **Lappe**.

**lappländisch** *adj* Lapp.

**Lapsus** *m* -, - mistake, slip; *(gesellschaftlich, diplomatisch)* faux pas.

**Laptop** [ˈlɛptɔp] *m* -s *(Comp)* laptop.

**Lärche** *f* -n larch.

**Larifari** *nt no pl (col)* nonsense.

**Lärm** *m no pl* noise; *(Geräuschbelästigung auch)* din, racket; *(Aufsehen)* fuss. **viel ~ um jdn/etw machen** to make a big fuss about sb/sth.

**Lärm-:** **~bekämpfung** *f* noise abatement; **~belästigung** *f* noise pollution; **l~empfindlich** *adj* sensitive to noise.

**lärmen** *vi* to make a noise. **~d** noisy.

**Lärmschutz** *m* noise abatement.

**Lärmschutz-:** **~wall** *m*, **~wand** *f* sound *or* noise barrier.

**Larve** [ˈlarfə] *f* -n *(Tier~)* larva.

**las** *pret of* **lesen.**

**lasch** *adj (col)* **(a)** *(schlaff) Bewegungen* feeble. **(b)** *Erziehung, Polizei* lax.

**Lasche** *f* -n *(Schlaufe)* loop; *(Schuh~)* tongue; *(als Verschluß)* tab, flap; *(Tech)* splicing plate.

**Laser** [ˈleːzɐ, ˈlaːzɐ] *m* - laser.

**Laser-** *in cpds* laser; **~drucker** *m* laser printer; **~strahl** *m* laser beam; **~technik** *f no pl* laser technology.

**lasieren\*** *vt Bild, Holz* to varnish; *Glas* to glaze.

**lassen** *pret* **ließ**, *ptp* **gelassen 1** *vt* **(a)** *(unter~)* to stop; *(momentan aufhören)* to leave. **laß das (sein)!** don't (do it)!; *(hör auf)* stop it!; **laß diese Bemerkungen!** that's enough of that kind of remark!; **~ wir das!** let's leave it *or* that!; **er kann das Trinken nicht ~** he can't stop drinking; **er kann es nicht ~!** he will keep on doing it!; **dann ~ wir es eben** let's drop the whole idea!; **wenn du nicht willst, dann laß es doch** if you don't want to, then don't; **tu, was du nicht ~ kannst!** if you must, you must!

**(b)** *(zurück~, be~)* to leave. **jdn allein ~** to leave sb alone; **etw ~, wie es ist** to leave sth (just) as it is.

**(c)** *(über~)* **jdm etw ~** to let sb have sth; *(behalten ~)* to let sb keep sth; **das muß man ihr ~** *(zugestehen)* you've got to grant her that.

**(d)** *(hinein~, hinaus~)* to let *(in +acc* into, *aus* out of); *(col: los~)* to let go; *(in Ruhe ~)* to let be. **Wasser in die Badewanne (laufen) ~** to run water into the bath.

**2** *modal aux ptp* **~ (a)** *(veranlassen)* **etw tun ~** to have *or* get sth done; **sich** *(dat)* **etw schicken ~** to have sth sent to one; **jdm ausrichten ~, daß ...** to leave a message for sb that ...; **jdn kommen ~** to send for sb; **mein Vater wollte mich studieren ~** my father wanted me to study.

**(b)** *(zu~)* **jdn etw wissen/sehen ~** to let sb know/ see sth; **sie hat mich nichts merken ~** she didn't show it/anything; **sich** *(dat)* **einen Bart wachsen ~** to grow a beard; **den Tee ziehen ~** to let the tea draw; **das Licht brennen ~** to leave the light on; **jdn warten ~** to keep sb waiting; **er hat sich überreden ~** he let himself be persuaded; **ich lasse mich nicht zwingen** I won't be coerced; **das Fenster läßt sich nicht öffnen** *(grundsätzlich nicht)* the window doesn't open; *(momentan nicht)* the window won't open; **das Wort läßt sich nicht übersetzen** the word is untranslatable; **das läßt sich machen** that can be done; **es ließ sich nicht ändern** it couldn't be changed; **daraus läßt sich schließen, daß ...** one can conclude from this that ...

**(c)** *(als Imperativ)* **laß uns gehen!** let's go!; **laß es dir gutgehen!** take care of yourself!; **laß dir das ge-**

sagt sein! let me tell you this!
  3 vi (a) laß mal, ich mache das schon leave it, I'll do it. (b) (ab~) von jdm/etw ~ to give sb/sth up.
lässig adj (ungezwungen) casual. das hat er ganz ~ hingekriegt (col) pretty cool, the way he did that (col).
Lässigkeit f casualness.
läßlich adj (Eccl) Sünde venial, pardonable.
Lasso m or nt -s lasso.
Last f -en (a) load; (Trag~ auch) burden; (lit, fig: Gewicht) weight. (b) (fig: Bürde) burden. jdm zur ~ fallen/werden to be/become a burden on sb; die ~ der Verantwortung/des Amtes the burden of responsibility/the weight of office; jdm eine ~ abnehmen to take a load off sb's shoulders; jdm etw zur ~ legen to accuse sb of sth. (c) ~en (Kosten) costs; (des Steuerzahlers) charges; soziale ~en welfare costs or charges; zu jds ~en gehen to be chargeable to sb.
Last|auto nt van (Brit), panel truck (US).
lasten vi to weigh heavily (auf +dat on). auf dem Haus lastet noch eine Hypothek the house is still encumbered (with a mortgage) (form); auf ihm lastet die ganze Verantwortung all the responsibility rests on him.
Lasten|aufzug m hoist, goods lift (Brit) or elevator (US).
Laster¹ m - (col) lorry (Brit), truck.
Laster² nt - vice.
Lästerei f (col) (a) no pl (das Lästern) running down (über +acc of). (b) (Lästerwort) malicious remark.
lasterhaft adj depraved.
Lasterhöhle f den of vice or iniquity.
lästerlich adj malicious; (gottes~) blasphemous.
lästern 1 vi über jdn/etw ~ to make malicious remarks about sb/sth. 2 vt Gott to blaspheme against.
lästig adj tiresome; (ärgerlich auch) irksome, aggravating; Husten etc troublesome. wie ~! what a nuisance!; jdm ~ sein to bother sb; dieser Verband ist mir ~ this bandage is bothering me; jdm ~ werden to become a nuisance (to sb); (zum Ärgernis werden) to get annoying (to sb).
Last-: ~kahn m barge; ~kraftwagen m (form) heavy goods vehicle; ~schiff nt cargo ship; ~schrift f debit; (Eintrag) debit entry; ~tier nt beast of burden; ~wagen m lorry (Brit), truck; ~wagenfahrer m lorry (Brit) or truck driver; ~zug m truck-trailer.
Lasur f (auf Holz, Bild) varnish; (auf Glas, Email) glaze.
Latein nt Latin. mit seinem ~ am Ende sein (col) to be stumped (col).
Latein-: ~amerika nt Latin America; ~amerikaner(in f) m Latin American; l~amerikanisch adj Latin-American.
lateinisch adj Latin.
latent adj latent; Selbstmörder, Gefahr potential. ~ vorhanden sein to be latent.
Laterne f -n lantern; (Straßen~) streetlamp.
Laternenpfahl m lamp post.
Latinum nt no pl kleines/großes ~ qualification in Latin gained after 3/6 years of study.
Latrine f latrine.
Latschen m - (col) (Hausschuh) slipper; (pej: Schuh) worn-out shoe.
latschen vi aux sein (col) to wander; (durch die Stadt etc) to traipse; (schlurfend) to slouch along.
Latte f -n (a) (schmales Brett) slat. nicht alle auf der ~ haben (col) to have a screw loose (col). (b) (Sport) bar; (Ftbl) (cross)bar. (c) (col: Liste) eine (ganze) ~ von Vorstrafen a whole string of previous convic-

tions.
Latten-: ~rost m duckboards pl; (in Bett) slatted frame; ~schuß m (Ftbl) shot against the bar; ~zaun m wooden fence.
Latz m ⁼e (Lätzchen, bei Kleidung) bib; (Hosen~) (front) flap. jdm eins vor den ~ knallen (col) to sock sb one (col).
Lätzchen nt bib.
Latzhose f (pair of) dungarees pl.
lau adj (a) Wind, Abend mild. (b) Flüssigkeit tepid, lukewarm; (fig) Haltung lukewarm.
Laub nt no pl leaves pl; (an Bäumen etc auch) foliage.
Laubbaum m deciduous tree.
Laube f -n (a) (Gartenhäuschen) summerhouse. (b) (Gang) pergola; (Arkade) arcade.
Laub-: ~frosch m (European) tree frog; ~säge f fretsaw; ~wald m deciduous forest.
Lauch m (esp SGer: Porree) leek.
Lauer f no pl: auf der ~ sein or liegen to lie in wait.
lauern vi (lit, fig) to lurk, to lie in wait (auf +acc for); (col) to wait (auf +acc for). ein ~der Blick a furtive glance.
Lauf m, pl Läufe (a) (schneller Schritt) run; (Wett~) race. sein ~ wurde immer schneller he ran faster and faster. (b) (Verlauf) course. im ~ der Jahre through the years; im ~e des Gesprächs in the course of the conversation; sie ließ ihren Gefühlen freien ~ she gave way to her feelings; den Dingen ihren ~ lassen to let matters take their course. (c) (Gang, Arbeit) running, operation; (Comp) run. (d) (Fluß~, Astron) course. der obere/untere ~ der Donau the upper/lower reaches of the Danube. (e) (Gewehr~) barrel. (f) (Hunt: Bein) leg.
Laufbahn f career. eine ~ einschlagen to embark on a career.
Laufbursche m errand-boy, messenger boy.
laufen pret lief, ptp gelaufen 1 vi aux sein (a) to run. es lief mir eiskalt über den Rücken a chill ran up my spine.
  (b) (col: gehen) to go; (zu Fuß gehen) to walk. das Kind läuft schon the child is already walking; das L~ lernen to learn to walk; es sind nur 10 Minuten zu ~ it's only 10 minutes' walk; er läuft dauernd zum Arzt he's always running to the doctor.
  (c) (fließen) to run; (schmelzen: Käse, Butter) to melt; (undicht sein) (Gefäß, Wasserhahn) to leak; (Nase, Wunde) to run. in Strömen ~ to stream or pour (in/out/down etc); Wasser in die Badewanne ~ lassen to run water into the bath; ihm läuft die Nase he's got a runny nose.
  (d) (in Betrieb sein) to run, to go; (Comp) to run; (Uhr) to go; (Elektrogerät) (eingeschaltet sein) to be on; (funktionieren) to work. ein Programm ~ lassen (Comp) to run a program.
  (e) (fig: im Gange sein) (Prozeß, Verhandlung) to go on, to be in progress; (Bewerbung, Antrag) to be under consideration; (gezeigt werden) (Film, Stück) to be on. der Film lief schon, als wir ankamen the film had already started when we arrived; der Film läuft über drei Stunden the film goes on for three hours; etw läuft gut/schlecht sth is going well/badly; mal sehen, wie die Sache läuft let's see how things go; die Dinge ~ lassen to let things slide; die Sache ist gelaufen (col) it's in the bag (col); es ist zu spät, die Sache ist schon gelaufen (col) it's too late now, it's all finished with.
  (f) das Auto läuft auf meinen Namen the car is in my name; das läuft unter „Sonderausgaben" that comes under "special expenses".
  2 vt aux sein (a) auch aux haben (Sport) Rekordzeit

to run; *Rekord* to set. **Ski/Schlittschuh/Rollschuh** *etc*
~ to ski/skate/rollerskate *etc*. **(b)** *(fahren: Auto etc)*
*Geschwindigkeit, Strecke* to do. **(c)** *(zu Fuß gehen)* to
walk; *(schnell)* to run.

  **3** *vr* **sich warm** ~ to warm up; **sich müde** ~ to
tire oneself out; **in den Schuhen läuft es sich gut**
these shoes are good for walking/running in.

**laufend 1** *adj attr Arbeiten, Ausgaben* regular; *Monat, Jahr* current. **10 DM der** ~**e Meter** 10 marks per
metre; ~**e Nummer** serial number; *(von Konto)*
number; **auf dem** ~**en bleiben/sein** to keep
(oneself)/be up-to-date; **jdn auf dem** ~**en halten** to
keep sb posted. **2** *adv* continually, constantly.

**laufenlassen** *vt sep irreg (col)* **jdn** ~ to let sb go.

**Läufer** *m* - **(a)** *(Sport)* runner; *(Hürden~)* hurdler;
*(Ftbl)* halfback; *(Chess)* bishop. **rechter/linker** ~
*(Ftbl)* right/left half. **(b)** *(Teppich)* rug; *(Treppen~,
Tisch~)* runner.

**Lauferei** *f (col)* running about *no pl*.

**Läuferin** *f (Sport)* runner; *(Hürden~)* hurdler.

**Lauf-:** ~**feuer** *nt:* **sich wie ein** ~ **feuer verbreiten** to
spread like wildfire; ~**gitter** *nt* playpen.

**läufig** *adj* on heat.

**Lauf-:** ~**junge** *m* errand-boy; ~**kunde** *m* casual
customer; ~**kundschaft** *f* casual custom;
~**masche** *f* ladder *(Brit)*, run; ~**paß** *m:* **jdm den**
~**paß geben** *(col)* to give sb his/her marching orders *(col)*; ~**schritt** *m* trot; *(Mil)* quick march at
the double; **im** ~**schritt** *(Mil)* at the double; ~**stall**
*m* playpen; ~**steg** *m* catwalk; ~**werk** *nt (Mech)*
running gear; *(von Uhr)* movement; *(Comp)* drive;
~**zeit** *f* **(a)** *(von Wechsel, Vertrag)* period of validity; *(von Kredit)* period; **(b)** *(von Maschine)* life;
~**zettel** *m (an Akten, Maschinen)* docket.

**Lauge** *f* -**n** *(Chem)* alkaline solution; *(Seifen~)* soapy
water.

**Laune** *f* -**n** **(a)** *(Stimmung)* mood. **(je) nach (Lust und)**
~ just as the mood takes one; **gute/schlechte** ~ **haben** to be in a good/bad mood. **(b)** *(Einfall)* whim.
**etw aus einer** ~ **heraus tun** to do sth on a whim.

**launenhaft, launisch** *adj* moody; *(unberechenbar)*
capricious.

**Laus** *f, pl* **Läuse** louse. **ihm ist (wohl) eine** ~ **über die
Leber gelaufen** *(col)* something's biting him *(col)*.

**Lausbub** *m (hum)* rascal, scamp.

**Lausch\angriff** *m* bugging operation *(gegen* on*)*.

**lauschen** *vi* **(a)** *(geh)* to listen *(dat, auf +acc* to*)*. **(b)**
*(heimlich)* to eavesdrop.

**Lauscher(in** *f) m* - eavesdropper.

**lauschig** *adj Plätzchen* cosy, snug; *(im Freien)* secluded.

**Lausejunge** *m (col)* little devil *(col)*; *(wohlwollend)*
rascal.

**lausen** *vt* to delouse. **ich denk', mich laust der Affe!**
*(col)* well blow me down! *(col)*.

**lausig** *(col)* **1** *adj* lousy *(col)*; *Kälte* perishing. **2** *adv*
awfully.

**laut**[1] *adj* **(a)** loud. ~**er sprechen** to speak up; ~ **auflachen** to burst out laughing; **etw** ~**(er) stellen** to
turn sth up (loud). **(b)** *(lärmend)* noisy; *(aufdringlich) Mensch* loudmouthed; *Farbe etc* loud. **(c)** *(hörbar)* aloud *pred, adv*. **etw** ~ **sagen** *(lit)* to say sth out
loud; *(fig)* to shout sth from the rooftops; **das
kannst du** ~ **sagen** you can say that again; ~ **werden** *(bekannt)* to become known.

**laut**[2] *prep +gen or dat* according to.

**Laut** *m* -**e** sound. **keinen** ~ **von sich** *(dat)* **geben** not
to utter a sound.

**Laute** *f* -**n** lute.

**lauten** *vi* to be; *(Rede)* to go; *(Schriftstück)* to read.
**auf den Namen ...** ~ *(Paß)* to be in the name of ...;

*(Scheck)* to be made out to ...

**läuten** *vti* to ring. **es hat geläutet** the bell rang; **er
hat davon (etwas)** ~ **hören** *(col)* he has heard something about it.

**lauter 1** *adj (geh) Absichten* honourable *(Brit)*, honorable *(US)*; *Wahrheit* honest. **2** *adv (nur)* nothing/
nobody but. ~ **Unsinn** sheer nonsense; **vor** ~ **Rauch
kann man nichts sehen** you can't see anything for
all the smoke.

**läutern** *vt (liter)* to purify; *(fig)* to reform.

**lauthals** *adv* at the top of one's voice.

**Laut-:** ~**lehre** *f* phonetics *sing*; **l~lich** *adj* phonetic;
**l~los** *adj* noiseless; *(wortlos)* silent; ~**losigkeit** *f
siehe adj* noiselessness; silence; **l~malend** *adj*
onomatopoeic; ~**malerei** *f* onomatopoeia; ~**schrift**
*f* phonetics *pl*; *(Umschrift)* phonetic transcription;
*(Zeichen)* phonetic alphabet.

**Lautsprecher** *m* (loud)speaker.

**Lautsprecher-:** ~**anlage** *f* öffentliche ~**anlage** public address *or* PA system; ~**box** *f* speaker enclosure; ~**wagen** *m* loudspeaker car/van.

**Laut-:** **l~stark** *adj* loud; *(Rad, TV etc)* high-volume;
*Protest* vociferous; ~**stärke** *f siehe adj* loudness;
volume; vociferousness; **ein Radio in voller** ~**stärke
spielen lassen** to have a radio on full volume.

**lauwarm** *adj (lit, fig)* lukewarm.

**Lava** ['laːva] *f, pl* **Laven** ['laːvn] lava.

**Lavendel** [la'vɛndl] *m* - lavender.

**lavieren*** [la'viːrən] *vi* **(a)** *(Naut)* to tack. **(b)** *(fig)* to
manoeuvre *(Brit)*, to maneuver *(US)*.

**Lawine** *f (lit, fig)* avalanche.

**Lawinen-:** **l~artig** *adj* like an avalanche; **l~artig
anwachsen** to snowball; ~**gefahr** *f* danger of ava-
lanches.

**Layout** ['leːˌaut] *nt* -**s** layout.

**Lazarett** *nt* -**e** *(Mil)* sickbay; *(Krankenhaus)* hospital.

**Lazarettschiff** *nt* hospital ship.

**LCD-** [ɛltseː'deː] *in cpds* LCD; ~**-Anzeige** *f* LCD display.

**leasen** ['liːzn] *vt (Comm)* to lease.

**Leasing** ['liːzɪŋ] *nt* -**s** *(Comm)* leasing *no art, no pl*.

**Leben** *nt* - life. **das** ~ life; **am** ~ **sein/bleiben** to be/
stay alive; **solange ich am** ~ **bin** as long as I live;
**jdm das** ~ **retten** to save sb's life; **ein glückliches
etc** ~ **führen** to live a happy *etc* life; **mit dem** ~ **davonkommen** to escape with one's life; **sein** ~ **aufs
Spiel setzen** to take one's life in one's hands; **mit
dem** ~ **abschließen** to prepare for death; **etw ins** ~
**rufen** to bring sth into being; **seines** ~**s nicht mehr
sicher sein** to fear for one's life; **ums** ~ **kommen** to
die; **sein** ~ **lassen (müssen)** to lose one's life; **jdn
am** ~ **lassen** to spare sb's life; **sich** *(dat)* **das** ~ **nehmen** to take one's (own) life; **jdn wieder ins** ~ **zurückrufen** to bring sb back to life; *Bewußtlosen* to
revive sb; **der Mann/die Frau meines** ~**s** my ideal
man/woman; **etw für sein** ~ **gern tun** to love doing
sth; **jdn künstlich am** ~ **erhalten** to keep sb alive artificially; **er hat es nie leicht gehabt im** ~ he has
never had an easy life; **ein** ~ **lang** one's whole
life (long); **mein** ~ **lang** all my life; **ich habe noch
nie im** ~ **geraucht** I have never smoked in all my
life; **nie im** ~**!** never!; **im** ~ **ist das ganz anders** in
real life it's very different; **ein Film nach dem** ~ a
film from real life; **so ist das** ~ *(eben)* that's life;
**auf dem Markt herrscht reges** ~ the market is a
hive of activity; ~ **in etw** *(acc)* **bringen** *(col)* to liven
sth up.

**leben** *vi* to live; *(am Leben sein)* to be alive; *(wei-
ter~)* to live on. **ich möchte nicht mehr** ~ I don't
want to go on living; **er wird nicht mehr lange zu** ~
**haben** he won't live much longer; **von etw** ~ to live

on sth; **lebst du noch?** *(hum col)* are you still in the land of the living? *(hum)*; **zum L~ zu wenig, zum Sterben zuviel** it's barely enough to keep body and soul together; **einsam ~** to lead a lonely life; **hier läßt es sich (gut) ~** it's a good life here.

**lebend** *adj* live *attr*, alive *pred*; *Wesen, Beispiel, Sprache* living. **ein Tier ~ fangen** to catch an animal alive; **~es Inventar** livestock.

**Lebend-:** **~geburt** *f* live birth; **~gewicht** *nt* live weight.

**lebendig** *adj* **(a)** *(nicht tot)* live *attr*, alive *pred*; *Wesen* living. **jdn bei ~em Leibe verbrennen** to burn sb alive. **(b)** *(fig: lebhaft)* lively *no adv; Darstellung, Bild auch* vivid; *Glaube* fervent.

**Lebendigkeit** *f no pl (fig) siehe adj (b)* liveliness; vividness; fervour.

**Lebens-:** **~abend** *m* old age; **~abschnitt** *m* phase in one's life; **~alter** *nt* age; **ein hohes ~alter erreichen** to have a long life; **~angst** *f* angst; **~anschauung** *f* philosophy of life; **~arbeitszeit** *f* working life; **~art** *f no pl* **(a)** way of life; **(b)** *(Manieren)* manners *pl; (Stil)* style; **~auffassung** *f* attitude to life; **~bedingungen** *pl* living conditions *pl;* **l~bedrohend** *adj* life-threatening; **l~bejahend** *adj* **eine l~bejahende Einstellung** a positive approach to life; **~bereich** *m* area of life; **~dauer** *f* life(span); *(von Maschine)* life; **l~echt** *adj* true-to-life; **~elixier** *nt* **das ist sein ~elixier** *(fig)* he thrives on it; **~ende** *nt* **bis an mein/sein** *etc* **~ende** until the end of my/his *etc* life *or* days; **~erfahrung** *f* experience of life; **~erinnerungen** *pl* memoirs *pl;* **~erwartung** *f* life expectancy; **l~fähig** *adj (lit, fig)* viable; **~form** *f (Biol)* life-form; *(Form des Zusammenlebens)* way of life; **~frage** *f* vital matter; **l~fremd** *adj* out of touch with life; **~freude** *f* joie de vivre; **l~froh** *adj* full of the joys of life; **~führung** *f* lifestyle; **~gefahr** *f* (mortal) danger; **„~gefahr!"** "danger"; **er schwebt in ~gefahr** his life is in danger; **außer ~gefahr sein** to be out of danger; **etw unter ~gefahr** *(dat)* **tun** to risk one's life doing sth; **l~gefährlich** *adj* highly dangerous; *Verletzung* critical; **~gefährte** *m,* **~gefährtin** *f* longtime companion; **ihr ~gefährte** the man she lives with; **~gemeinschaft** *f* long-term relationship; *(Biol, Zool)* symbiosis; **~geschichte** *f* life-story; **~gewohnheit** *f* habit; **l~groß** *adj* lifesize; **~größe** *f* **eine Figur in ~größe** a lifesize figure; **~haltungskosten** *pl* cost of living *sing;* **~hilfe** *f* counselling *(Brit)*, counseling *(US);* **l~hungrig** *adj* thirsty for life; **~inhalt** *m* purpose in life; **etw zu seinem ~inhalt machen** to devote oneself to sth; **~jahr** *nt* year of (one's) life; **nach Vollendung des 18. ~jahres** on attaining the age of 18; **~kraft** *f* vitality; **~künstler** *m* master in the art of living; **er ist ein echter ~künstler** he really knows how to live; **~lage** *f* situation; **l~lang** *adj* lifelong; *Haft* life *attr,* for life; **l~länglich** *adj* Rente, Strafe for life; **sie hat ~länglich bekommen** *(col)* she got life *(col);* **~lauf** *m* curriculum vitae, résumé *(US);* **~lust** *f* zest for life; **l~lustig** *adj* in love with life.

**Lebensmittel** *pl* food *sing*, groceries *pl.*

**Lebensmittel-:** **~abteilung** *f* food department; **~geschäft** *nt* food shop *(Brit)*, food store *(esp US);* **~gesetz** *nt* food law; **~händler** *m* grocer; **~karte** *f* food ration card; **~karten** *pl* ≃ ration book; **~vergiftung** *f* food poisoning.

**Lebens-:** **l~müde** *adj* tired of life; **ein ~müder** a potential suicide; **l~nah** *adj* true-to-life; **l~notwendig** *adj* essential; *Organ* vital (for life); **~qualität** *f* quality of life; **~raum** *m (Biol)* biosphere; **~regel** *f* rule (of life); **~retter** *m* rescuer,

lifesaver; **~standard** *m* standard of living; **~stellung** *f* job for life; **~stil** *m* lifestyle; **l~tüchtig** *adj* able to cope with life; **~umstände** *pl* circumstances *pl;* **~unterhalt** *m* **seinen ~unterhalt verdienen** to earn one's living; **für jds ~unterhalt sorgen** to support sb; **l~untüchtig** *adj* unable to cope with life; **l~verlängernd** *adj* Maßnahme life-prolonging; **~versicherung** *f* life insurance; **eine ~versicherung abschließen** to take out life insurance; **~wandel** *m* way of life; **einen einwandfreien ~wandel führen** to lead an irreproachable life; **~weg** *m* journey through life; **alles Gute für den weiteren ~weg** every good wish for the future; **~weise** *f* way of life; **~weisheit** *f* maxim; *(~erfahrung)* wisdom; **~werk** *nt* life's work; **l~wert** *adj* worth living; **l~wichtig** *adj* vital; **~wille** *m* will to live; **~zeichen** *nt* sign of life; **kein ~zeichen mehr von sich geben** to show no sign(s) of life; **~zeit** *f* life(time); **auf ~zeit** for life; **Beamter auf ~zeit** permanent civil servant; **~ziel** *nt* aim in life.

**Leber** *f* **-n** liver. **ich habe es an der ~** *(col)* I've got liver trouble; **frei** *or* **frisch von der ~ weg reden** *(col)* to speak frankly.

**Leber-:** **~entzündung** *f* hepatitis; **~fleck** *m* mole; *(Hautfärbung)* liver spot; **~käse** *m no pl* ≃ meat loaf; **~knödel** *m* liver dumpling; **~krebs** *m* cancer of the liver; **~leiden** *nt* liver disorder; **~pastete** *f* liver pâté; **~tran** *m* cod-liver oil; **~wurst** *f* liver sausage.

**Lebewesen** *nt* living thing. **kleinste ~** microorganisms.

**Lebewohl** *nt no pl (liter)* farewell *(liter).*

**Leb-:** **l~haft** *adj* lively *no adv; Verkehr* brisk; *(deutlich) Erinnerung* vivid. **es geht l~haft zu** things are lively; **ich kann mir l~haft vorstellen, daß ...** I can (very) well imagine that ...; **etw in l~er Erinnerung haben** to remember sth vividly; **~haftigkeit** *f* liveliness; **~kuchen** *m* gingerbread; **l~los** *adj Körper* lifeless; **l~loser Gegenstand** inanimate object; **~tag** *m (col)* **mein/dein** *etc* **~tag** all my/your *etc* life; **das werde ich mein ~tag nicht vergessen** I'll never forget that as long as I live; **~zeiten** *pl* **zu jds ~zeiten** *(Leben)* in sb's lifetime; *(Zeit)* in sb's day.

**lechzen** *vi (geh)* **nach etw ~** to thirst for sth.

**leck** *adj* leaky. **~ sein** to leak; **~ schlagen** to hole.

**Leck** *nt* **-s** leak.

**lecken[1]** *vi (undicht sein)* to leak.

**lecken[2]** *vti* to lick. **an jdm/etw ~** to lick sb/sth.

**lecker** *adj Speisen* delicious.

**Leckerbissen** *m (Speise)* delicacy; *(fig)* gem.

**Leckerei** *f* delicacy.

**Leckermaul** *nt (col)* sweet-toothed child/person *etc.* **ein ~ sein** to have a sweet tooth.

**LED** [ɛlleːˈdeː] *f* **-s** LED.

**led.** = **ledig**.

**Leder** *nt* **- (a)** leather; *(Wild~)* suede. **in ~ gebunden** leather-bound; **zäh wie ~** as tough as old boots *(col).* **(b)** *(col: Fußball)* ball. **am ~ bleiben** to stick with the ball.

**Leder-** *in cpds* leather; **~hose** *f* leather trousers *pl; (von Tracht)* leather shorts *pl;* **~jacke** *f* leather jacket; **~mantel** *m* leather coat.

**ledern** *adj* leather; *(zäh) Fleisch* leathery.

**Leder-:** **~waren** *pl* leather goods *pl;* **~zeug** *nt* leather gear.

**ledig** *adj* **(a)** single; *Mutter* unmarried. **(b)** *(geh: frei)* free. **(los und) ~ sein** to be footloose and fancy free; **aller Pflichten** *(Gen)* **~ sein** to be free of all commitments.

**Ledige(r)** *mf decl as adj* single person.
**lediglich** *adv* merely, simply.
**Lee** *f no pl (Naut)* lee.
**leer** *adj* empty; *Blick* blank. **eine ~e Stelle** an empty space; **ins L~e greifen** to clutch at thin air; **mit ~en Händen** *(fig)* empty-handed; **~ laufen** *(Motor)* to idle; **etw ~ machen** to empty sth; **den Teller ~ essen** to eat everything on the plate; **~ stehen** to stand empty.
**Leere** *f no pl (lit, fig)* emptiness. **(eine) geistige ~** a mental vacuum; **(eine) gähnende ~** a gaping void.
**leeren** *vt* to empty.
**Leer-:** **l~gefegt** *adj* **wie l~gefegt** deserted; **~gewicht** *nt* unladen weight; **~gut** *nt* empties *pl*; **~lauf** *m* **(a)** neutral; *(von Fahrrad)* freewheel; **im ~lauf fahren** to coast; **(b)** *(fig)* slack; **l~laufen** *vi sep irreg aux sein (Faß etc)* to run dry; **l~laufen lassen** to drain; **l~stehend** *adj* empty; **~taste** *f* space-bar.
**Leerung** *f* emptying. **nächste ~: 18 Uhr** *(an Briefkasten)* next collection: 6 p.m.
**Lefze** *f -n usu pl* chaps *pl*; *(von Pferd)* lip.
**legal** *adj* legal, lawful.
**legalisieren*** *vt* to legalize.
**Legalität** *f* legality. **(etwas) außerhalb der ~** *(euph)* (slightly) outside the law.
**Legasthenie** *f* dyslexia.
**Legastheniker(in** *f) m -* dyslexic.
**legasthenisch** *adj* dyslexic.
**Legebatterie** *f* hen battery.
**Leg(e)henne** *f* layer, laying hen.
**legen 1** *vt* **(a)** *(hin~)* to lay down; *(mit adv)* to lay; *(mit Raumangabe)* to put, to place; *(Sport sl)* to bring down. **etw beiseite ~** to put sth aside; **etw in Essig etc ~** to preserve sth in vinegar etc. **(b)** *(verlegen) Fliesen, Leitungen, Schienen* to lay, to put down. **sich** *(dat)* **die Haare ~ lassen** to have one's hair set. **(c)** *auch vi Eier* to lay. **2** *vr* **(a)** *(hin~)* to lie down *(auf +acc on)*. **sich ins Bett ~** to go to bed; **sich zu jdm ~** to lie down beside sb; **sich in die Sonne ~** to lie in the sun. **(b)** *(mit Ortsangabe) (nieder~: Nebel, Rauch)* to settle *(auf +acc on)*. **sich auf die Seite ~** to lie on one's side; *(Boot)* to heel over; **sich in die Kurve ~** to lean into the corner. **(c)** *(nachlassen)* to die down; *(Rauch, Nebel)* to clear.
**legendär** *adj* legendary.
**Legende** *f -n* legend.
**leger** [leˈʒeːɐ] *adj* casual, informal.
**Legierung** *f* alloy.
**Legion** *f* legion.
**Legionär** *m* legionary, legionnaire.
**Legionärskrankheit** *f* legionnaire's disease.
**legislativ** *adj* legislative.
**Legislative** *f* legislature, legislative assembly.
**Legislaturperiode** *f* parliamentary term.
**legitim** *adj* legitimate.
**Legitimation** *f* identification; *(Berechtigung)* authorization; *(eines Kindes)* legitimation.
**legitimieren*** **1** *vt* to legitimize; *(berechtigen)* to entitle. **2** *vr* to show (proof of) authorization; *(sich ausweisen)* to identify oneself.
**Legitimität** *f no pl* legitimacy.
**Lehm** *m -e* clay; *(Boden)* loam.
**Lehm-:** **~boden** *m* clay soil; **~hütte** *f* mud hut.
**lehmig** *adj* loamy; *(tonartig)* clayey.
**Lehm-:** **~packung** *f* mudpack; **~ziegel** *m* clay brick.
**Lehne** *f* **-n** *(Arm~)* arm(rest); *(Rücken~)* back(rest).
**lehnen 1** *vtr* to lean *(an +acc against)*. **2** *vi* to be leaning *(an +dat against)*.

**Lehnstuhl** *m* easy chair.
**Lehr-:** **~amt** *nt* das **~amt** the teaching profession; **~auftrag** *m (als Sonderlehrer)* special teaching post; **einen ~auftrag für etw haben** *(Univ)* to give (a series of) lectures on sth; **~befähigung** *f* teaching qualification; **~beruf** *m* **(a)** *(als Lehrer)* teaching profession; **den ~beruf ergreifen** to go into teaching; **(b)** *(dated: Beruf mit ~zeit)* trade requiring an apprenticeship; **~brief** *m (Hist)* apprenticeship certificate; **~buch** *nt* textbook.
**Lehre** *f* **-n** **(a)** *(dated: Ausbildung)* training; *(im Handwerk)* apprenticeship. **bei jdm in die ~ gehen** to serve one's apprenticeship with sb. **(b)** *(von Christus, Marx etc)* teachings *pl*; *(von Kant, Freud etc)* theory; *(von Schall, Leben etc)* science. **die christliche ~** Christian doctrine. **(c)** *(Erfahrung)* lesson; *(einer Geschichte)* moral. **seine ~(n) aus etw ziehen** to learn a lesson from sth; **laß dir das eine ~ sein!** let that be a lesson to you!
**lehren** *vti* to teach. **jdn lesen** *etc* **~** to teach sb to read *etc*.
**Lehrer(in** *f) m -* teacher; *(Flug~, Fahr~ etc)* instructor/instructress. **er ist ~** he's a teacher; **~ für Naturwissenschaften** science teacher.
**Lehrer-:** **~ausbildung** *f* teacher training; **~kollegium** *nt* teaching staff; **~zimmer** *nt* staff *(esp Brit)* or teachers' room.
**Lehr-:** **~gang** *m* course *(für* in*)*; **~geld** *nt* **~geld für etw zahlen müssen** *(fig)* to pay dearly for sth; **laß dir dein ~geld zurückgeben!** *(hum col)* go to the bottom of the class! *(hum col)*; **l~haft** *adj* didactic; **~herr** *m (dated)* master (of an apprentice); **~jahr** *nt* year as an apprentice; **~kraft** *f (form)* teacher.
**Lehrling** *m (dated: Auszubildender)* trainee; *(im Handwerk)* apprentice.
**Lehrlings|ausbildung** *f (dated)* training of trainees/apprentices.
**Lehr-:** **~meister** *m* master; **~methode** *f* teaching method; **~mittel** *nt* teaching aid; **~plan** *m* curriculum; **~probe** *f* demonstration lesson, crit *(col)*; **~programm** *nt* teaching programme *(Brit)* or program *(US)*; **l~reich** *adj (informativ)* instructive; **~satz** *m (Math, Philos)* theorem; *(Eccl)* dogma; **~stelle** *f* place; **dort sind noch zwei ~stellen frei** there are two vacancies for trainees/apprentices; **~stoff** *m* subject; *(eines Jahres)* syllabus; **~stuhl** *m (Univ)* chair *(für* of*)*; **~werkstatt** *f* training workshop; **~zeit** *f* apprenticeship.
**Leib** *m* **-er (a)** *(Körper)* body. **Gefahr für ~ und Leben** *(geh)* danger to life and limb; **mit ~ und Seele** heart and soul; **etw am eigenen ~(e) spüren** to experience sth for oneself; **kein Hemd mehr am ~ haben** to be completely destitute; **sich** *(dat)* **jdn/etw vom ~e halten** to keep sb/sth at bay; **halt ihn mir vom ~** keep him away from me. **(b)** *(old, dial: Bauch)* stomach; *(Mutter~)* womb.
**Leib|eigenschaft** *f* serfdom; *(fig)* bondage.
**leiben** *vi*: **wie er/sie lebt und lebt** to a T *(col)*.
**Leibes-:** **~erziehung** *f* physical education; **~frucht** *f (geh)* unborn child; **~kraft** *f*: **aus ~kräften schreien** *etc* to shout *etc* with all one's might; **~übung** *f* (physical) exercise; **~übungen** *(Schulfach)* physical education *no pl*; **~visitation** *f* body check.
**Leibgericht** *nt* favourite *(Brit)* or favorite *(US)* dish.
**leibhaftig** *adj* personified. **die ~e Güte** *etc* goodness *etc* personified.
**leiblich** *adj Mutter, Vater* natural; *Kind* by birth; *Bruder, Schwester* full.
**Leib-:** **~rente** *f* life annuity; **~wache** *f*, **~wächter** *m* bodyguard; **~wäsche** *f* underwear.

**Leiche** f -n corpse. **wie eine lebende** or **wandelnde ~ aussehen** to look like death (warmed up col); **er geht über ~n** (col) he'd stick at nothing; **nur über meine ~!** (col) over my dead body!

**Leichen-:** **~beschauer** m - doctor conducting a post-mortem; **I~blaß** adj deathly pale; **~halle** f mortuary; **~hemd** nt shroud; **~rede** f funeral address; **~schändung** f desecration of corpses; **~schau** f post-mortem (examination); **~schauhaus** nt morgue; **~schmaus** m funeral meal; **~tuch** nt shroud; **~verbrennung** f cremation; **~wagen** m hearse; **~zug** m funeral procession.

**Leichnam** m -e (form) body.

**leicht** 1 adj (a) light; (aus ~em Material) lightweight; (schwach, gering) slight; (Jur) Diebstahl, Vergehen etc minor, petty. **~e Musik/~es Essen** light music/food; **er hat einen leichten Schlaf** he's a light sleeper; **~es Mädchen** tart (col); **mir ist so ~ ums Herz** my heart is so light; **nimm das nicht zu ~** don't take it too lightly. (b) (ohne Schwierigkeiten, einfach) easy. **du hast es ~** it's easy for you; **mit dem werden wir (ein) ~es Spiel haben** he'll be no problem; **keinen ~en Stand haben** not to have an easy time (of it) (bei, mit with); **nichts ~er als das!** nothing (could be) simpler; **die Aufgabe ist ~ zu lösen** the exercise is easy to do.

  2 adv (a) (schnell, unversehens) easily. **er wird ~ böse** he gets angry easily; **~ zerbrechlich** very fragile; **man kann einen Fehler ~ übersehen** it's easy to miss a mistake; **das ist ~ möglich** that's quite possible; **~ begreifen** to understand quickly; **das ist ~er gesagt als getan** that's easier said than done; **das passiert mir so ~ nicht wieder** I won't let that happen again in a hurry (col). (b) (etwas) slightly. **~ gewürzt** lightly seasoned; **~ bekleidet** scantily clad; **das ist ~ übertrieben** it's slightly exaggerated.

**Leicht-:** **~athlet** m (track and field) athlete; **~athletik** f (track and field) athletics; **~bau(weise** f) m lightweight construction; **I~bewaffnet** adj attr lightly armed; **I~fallen** vi sep irreg aux sein to be easy (jdm for sb); **Sprachen sind mir schon immer I~gefallen** I've always found languages easy; **I~fertig** adj thoughtless; **etw I~fertig aufs Spiel setzen** to risk sth heedlessly; **~fertigkeit** f thoughtlessness; **~gewicht** nt (Sport, fig) lightweight; **Weltmeister im ~gewicht** world lightweight champion; **I~gläubig** adj credulous; (leicht zu täuschen) gullible; **~gläubigkeit** f siehe adj credulity; gullibility.

**leichthin** adv lightly.

**Leichtigkeit** f ease. **mit ~** with no trouble.

**Leicht-:** **~industrie** f light industry; **I~lebig** adj easygoing; **es sich** (dat) **I~machen** (nicht gewissenhaft sein) to make things easy for oneself; **~matrose** m ordinary seaman; **~metall** nt light alloy.

**Leichtsinn** m thoughtlessness. **sträflicher ~** criminal negligence.

**leichtsinnig** adj thoughtless. **~ mit etw umgehen** to be careless with sth.

**Leicht-:** **I~verdaulich** adj attr easily digestible; **I~verderblich** adj attr perishable; **I~verletzt** adj attr slightly injured; **~verletzte(r)** mf decl as adj slightly injured person; **I~verständlich** adj attr readily understandable.

**leid** adj pred (a) **es tut mir ~, daß ich so spät gekommen bin** I'm sorry for coming so late; **tut mir ~!** (I'm) sorry!; **er/sie tut mir ~** I'm sorry for him/her; **sie kann einem ~ tun** you can't help feeling

sorry for her; **das wird dir noch ~ tun** you'll regret it, you'll be sorry. (b) (überdrüssig) **jdn/etw ~ sein** to be tired of sb/sth.

**Leid** nt no pl sorrow no indef art; (Unglück) misfortune; (Böses, Schaden) harm. **es soll dir kein ~ geschehen** you will come to no harm; **jdm sein ~ klagen** to tell sb one's troubles.

**leiden** pret **litt**, ptp **gelitten** 1 vt (a) Hunger, Schmerz etc to suffer. (b) **ich kann** or **mag ihn/es (gut) ~** I like him/it (very much); **ich kann ihn/es nicht (gut) ~** I don't like him/it (very much); **er kann es nicht ~, wenn man ihn kritisiert** he can't stand being criticized. 2 vi to suffer (an +dat, unter +dat from).

**Leiden** nt - (a) suffering. (b) (Krankheit) illness; (Beschwerden) complaint.

**leidend** adj ailing; (col) Miene long-suffering. **~ aussehen** to look ill.

**Leidenschaft** f passion. **ich koche mit großer ~** cooking is a great passion of mine.

**leidenschaftlich** adj passionate. **etw ~ gern tun** to absolutely love doing sth.

**Leidens-:** **~druck** m no pl mental trauma; **~genosse** m, **~genossin** f fellow-sufferer; **~geschichte** f tale of woe; **die ~geschichte (Christi)** (Bibl) Christ's Passion; **~miene** f (hum col) (long-)suffering expression.

**leider** adv unfortunately. **ja, ~!** I'm afraid so; **~ nein** or **nicht** unfortunately not, I'm afraid not.

**leidig** adj attr tiresome.

**leidlich** 1 adj fair. 2 adv reasonably. **wie geht's — danke, ~!** how are you? — not too bad, thanks.

**Leidtragende(r)** mf decl as adj (a) (Hinterbliebener) bereaved. (b) (Benachteiligter) **der/die ~** the sufferer.

**Leidwesen** nt: **zu jds ~** (much) to sb's disappointment.

**Leier** f -n (Mus) lyre; (Dreh~) hurdy-gurdy. **es ist immer die gleiche ~** (col) it's always the same old story.

**Leierkasten** m barrel organ.

**leiern** vti (col) Gedicht to drone.

**Leih-:** **~arbeit** f no pl subcontracted labour; **~auto** nt hire(d) (Brit) or rental (US) car; **~bücherei** f lending library.

**leihen** pret **lieh**, ptp **geliehen** vt (ver~) to lend; (ent~) to borrow; (mieten, aus~) to hire (esp Brit), to rent. **sich** (dat) **etw ~** to borrow/hire/rent sth.

**Leih-:** **~flasche** f returnable bottle; **~gabe** f loan; **~gebühr** f hire charge; (für Buch) lending charge; **~haus** nt pawnshop; **~mutter** f surrogate mother; **~stimme** f (Pol) tactical vote; **~wagen** m hire(d) (Brit) or rental (US) car; **I~weise** adv on loan.

**Leim** m -e glue. **jdm auf den ~ gehen** to be taken in by sb; **aus dem ~ gehen** (col: Sache) to fall apart.

**leimen** vt to glue. **jdn ~** (col) to take sb for a ride (col); **der Geleimte** the mug (col).

**Leine** f -n cord; (Tau, Zelt~) rope; (Schnur) string; (Angel~, Wäsche~) line; (Hunde~) leash. **Hunde bitte an der ~ führen!** dogs should be kept on a leash; **den Hund an die ~ nehmen** to put the dog on a lead; **~ ziehen** (col) to clear out (col).

**leinen** adj siehe **Leinen** linen; canvas; cloth.

**Leinen** nt - linen; (grob, segeltuchartig) canvas; (als Bucheinband) cloth.

**Leinen-** in cpds linen; canvas; cloth; **~band** m cloth(-bound) volume; **~tuch** nt linen (cloth); (grob) canvas; **~zeug** nt linen.

**Lein-:** **~öl** nt linseed oil; **~samen** m linseed.

**Leinwand** f no pl canvas; (Film, für Dias) screen.

**leise** adj (a) quiet; Musik soft; Radio auch low. **das**

**Radio** ~r **stellen** to turn the radio down; **mit** ~r **Stimme** in a low voice; **sprich doch** ~r! keep your voice down a bit. **(b)** *(gering, schwach)* slight, faint; *Schlaf, Regen, Berührung* light; *Wind, Seegang* gentle. **nicht die** ~**ste Ahnung haben** not to have the slightest (idea).

**Leisetreter** m - *(pej col)* pussyfoot(er) *(pej col)*.

**Leiste** f -n **(a)** *(Holz~ etc)* strip (of wood/metal *etc)*; *(Zier~)* trim; *(Umrandung)* border; *(zur Bilderaufhängung)* rail. **(b)** *(Anat)* groin.

**leisten** vt **(a)** to achieve; *Überstunden* to do; *(Maschine)* to manage. **etwas** ~ *(arbeiten)* to do something; *(Motor etc)* to be quite powerful; **gute Arbeit** ~ to do a good job. **(b) sich** *(dat)* **etw** ~ to allow oneself sth; *(sich gönnen)* to treat oneself to sth; **sich** *(dat)* **etw** ~ **können** to be able to afford sth; **sich** *(dat)* **eine Frechheit/Frechheiten** ~ to be cheeky or impudent; **da hast du dir ja was geleistet** *(iro)* you've really done it now; **er hat sich tolle Sachen geleistet** he got up to the craziest things.

**Leisten** m - *(Schuh~)* last. **er schlägt alles über einen** ~ he doesn't make distinctions.

**Leistenbruch** m *(Med)* hernia, rupture.

**Leistung** f **(a)** performance; *(großartige, gute, Soziol)* achievement; *(Ergebnis)* result(s); *(geleistete Arbeit)* work no pl; *(Produktion: von Fabrik)* output. **das ist eine** ~! that's quite an achievement; **das ist keine besondere** ~ that's nothing special; **nach** ~ **bezahlt werden** to be paid on results; **seine schulischen** ~**en haben nachgelassen** his schoolwork has deteriorated. **(b)** *(~sfähigkeit)* capacity; *(eines Motors)* power (output). **(c)** *(von Krankenkasse etc, sozial)* benefit; *(Zahlung)* payment; *(Dienst~)* service. **die** ~**en des Reiseveranstalters** what the travel company offers.

**Leistungs-:** ~**abfall** m *(in bezug auf Qualität)* drop in performance; *(in bezug auf Quantität)* drop in productivity; ~**druck** m pressure (to do well); ~**fach** nt *(Sch)* special subject; **l**~**fähig** adj efficient; *Motor* powerful; ~**fähigkeit** f efficiency; *(von Motor)* power; **l**~**fördernd** adj conducive to efficiency; *(in Schule, Universität etc)* conducive to learning; ~**gesellschaft** f meritocracy; ~**klasse** f *(Sport)* class; ~**kontrolle** f *(Sch, Univ)* assessment; *(in der Fabrik)* productivity check; ~**kraft** f power; ~**kurs** m *(Sch)* set; ~**kurve** f productivity curve; **l**~**orientiert** adj achievement-orientated; ~**prämie** f productivity bonus; ~**prinzip** nt achievement principle; ~**sport** m competitive sport; ~**wille** m motivation; ~**zulage** f productivity bonus.

**Leit-:** ~**artikel** m leader; ~**bild** nt model.

**leiten 1** vt **(a)** to lead; *Verkehr* to route; *Gas, Wasser, (Phys)* to conduct. **etw an die zuständige Stelle** ~ to pass sth on to the proper authority; **sich von jdm/etw** ~ **lassen** *(lit, fig)* to (let oneself) be guided by sb/sth. **(b)** *(verantwortlich sein für)* to be in charge of; *Orchester, Theatergruppe etc* to direct; *Expedition, Sitzung, Verhandlungen* to lead; *(als Vorsitzender)* to chair. **2** vi *(Phys)* to conduct. **gut** ~ to be a good conductor.

**leitend** adj leading; *Gedanke, Idee* dominant; *Stellung, Position* managerial; *Ingenieur, Beamter* in charge; *(Phys)* conductive. **nicht** ~ *(Phys)* non-conductive; ~**e(r) Angestellte(r)** executive.

**Leiter**[1] f -n *(lit, fig)* ladder; *(Steh~)* stepladder.

**Leiter**[2] m - **(a)** leader; *(von Hotel, Geschäft)* manager; *(Abteilungs~)* head; *(von Chor, Theatergruppe etc)* director. **kaufmännischer** ~ sales director. **(b)** *(Phys)* conductor.

**Leiterin** f = **Leiter**[2] **(a)**.

**Leiterplatte** f *(Comp)* circuit board.

**Leit-:** ~**faden** m *(fig)* connecting thread; *(Fachbuch)* introduction; *(Gebrauchsanleitung)* manual; ~**gedanke** m central idea; ~**hammel** m *(fig col)* leader; ~**linie** f *(fig)* broad outline; *(Bestimmung)* guideline; ~**motiv** nt *(Mus, Liter, fig)* leitmotif; ~**planke** f crash barrier; ~**satz** m basic principle; ~**spruch** m motto; ~**stelle** f regional headquarters pl.

**Leitung** f **(a)** no pl siehe vt **(a)** leading; routing; conducting. **(b)** no pl *(von Organisationen etc)* running; *(von Orchester etc)* direction; *(von Expedition)* leadership. **die** ~ **einer Abteilung haben** to be in charge of a department; **die** ~ **des Gesprächs hat Horst Bauer** Horst Bauer is leading or *(als Vorsitzender)* chairing the discussion. **(c)** *(die Leitenden)* leaders pl; *(eines Betriebes etc)* management sing or pl; *(einer Schule)* head teachers pl. **(d)** *(für Gas, Wasser)* main; *(im Haus)* pipe; *(Elec)* main; *(im Haus)* wire; *(dicker)* cable; *(Überlandleitung)* line; *(Telefon~)* *(Draht)* wire; *(Verbindung)* line. **da ist jemand in der** ~ *(col)* there's somebody else on the line; **eine lange** ~ **haben** *(hum col)* to be slow on the uptake.

**Leitungs-:** ~**draht** m wire; ~**mast** m *(Elec)* (electricity) pylon; ~**rohr** nt main; *(im Haus)* (supply) pipe; ~**wasser** nt tapwater.

**Leit-:** ~**werk** nt *(Aviat)* tail unit; ~**wort** nt motto; ~**zins** m base rate.

**Lektion** f lesson. **jdm eine** ~ **erteilen** *(fig)* to teach sb a lesson.

**Lektor** m, **Lektorin** f *(Univ)* teaching assistant; *(Verlags~)* editor.

**Lektorat** nt *(im Verlag)* editorial office.

**Lektüre** f -n *(no pl: das Lesen)* reading; *(Lesestoff)* reading matter. **das wird zur** ~ **empfohlen** that is recommended reading; **das ist eine gute** etc ~ it makes good etc reading.

**Lemming** m lemming.

**Lende** f -n *(Anat, Cook)* loin.

**Lenden-:** ~**schurz** m loincloth; ~**stück** nt fillet.

**Leninismus** m Leninism.

**lenkbar** adj *(Tech)* steerable; *Kind* tractable; *Rakete* guided. **leicht/schwer** ~ **sein** to be easy/difficult to steer.

**lenken** vt **(a)** *(steuern)* to steer; *(führen, leiten)* to guide. **gelenkte Wirtschaft** planned economy. **(b)** *(fig) Schritte, Gedanken, Aufmerksamkeit, Blick* to direct *(auf +acc to)*; *Verdacht* to throw *(auf +acc onto)*; *Gespräch* to lead; *Schicksal* to guide.

**Lenker** m - **(a)** *(Fahrrad~ etc)* handlebars pl. **(b)** *(Tech, fig)* guide.

**Lenk-:** ~**rad** nt (steering) wheel; ~**radschloß** nt *(Aut)* steering lock; ~**stange** f *(von Fahrrad etc)* handlebars pl.

**Lenkung** f **(a)** siehe vt steering; guidance; *(fig)* direction. **(b)** *(Tech: Lenkeinrichtung)* steering.

**Lenkwaffe** f guided missile.

**Lenz** m -e *(liter: Frühling)* spring(time). **einen** ~ **schieben** *(col)*, **sich** *(dat)* **einen (fauden)** ~ **machen** *(col)* to laze about, to swing the lead *(col)*.

**Leopard** m *(wk)* -en, -en leopard.

**Lepra** f no pl leprosy.

**Leprakranke(r), Lepröse(r)** mf decl as adj leper.

**Lerche** f -n lark.

**Lern-:** **l**~**bar** adj learnable; **l**~**begierig** adj eager to learn; **l**~**behindert** adj educationally handicapped; ~**eifer** m eagerness to learn; **l**~**eifrig** adj eager to learn.

**lernen 1** vt to learn; *Bäcker, Schlosser etc* to train as. **lesen/schwimmen** etc ~ to learn to read/swim etc; **Schreibmaschine** ~ to learn typing; **etw von/**

**bei jdm** ~ to learn sth from sb; **er lernt's nie** he never learns. **2** *vi* to learn; *(arbeiten)* to study; *(als Berufsausbildung)* to train. **lerne fleißig in der Schule** work hard at school; **von ihm kannst du noch** ~! you could learn a thing or two from him; **er lernt bei der Firma Braun** he's training at Braun's.

**Lern-:** ~**hilfe** *f* educational aid; ~**mittel** *pl* schoolbooks and equipment *pl*; ~**prozeß** *m* learning process; ~**ziel** *nt* learning target.

**Les-:** ~**art** *f (lit, fig)* version; **l~bar** *adj* legible; *Buch* readable; ~**barkeit** *f* legibility.

**Lesbe** *f* -**n** *(col)* lesbian, dyke *(col)*.

**Lesbierin** ['lɛsbiərɪn] *f* lesbian.

**lesbisch** *adj* lesbian.

**Lese** *f* -**n** *(Wein~)* vintage.

**Lese-:** ~**brille** *f* reading glasses *pl*; ~**buch** *nt* reader; ~**kopf** *m (Comp)* read head; ~**lampe** *f* reading lamp.

**lesen¹** *pret* **las**, *ptp* **gelesen** *vti* **(a)** *(auch Comp)* to read; *(Eccl) Messe* to say. **(b)** *(deuten) Gedanken* to read. **jdm (sein Schicksal) aus der Hand** ~ to read sb's palm. **2** *vi (Univ)* to lecture *(über +acc on)*.

**lesen²** *pret* **las**, *ptp* **gelesen** *vt* **(a)** *(sammeln) Trauben, Beeren* to pick. **(b)** *(ver~) Erbsen, Linsen etc* to sort; *Salat* to clean.

**lesenswert** *adj* worth reading.

**Lese-:** ~**probe** *f* **(a)** *(Theat)* reading; **(b)** *(Ausschnitt aus Buch)* excerpt; ~**pult** *nt* lectern.

**Leser(in** *f)* *m* - reader.

**Leseratte** *f (col)* bookworm *(col)*.

**Leser-:** ~**brief** *m* (reader's) letter; „~**briefe"** "letters to the editor"; ~**kreis** *m* readership; **l~lich** *adj* legible; ~**schaft** *f* readership; ~**zuschrift** *f* = ~**brief**.

**Lese-:** ~**saal** *m* reading room; ~**speicher** *m (Comp)* read-only memory, ROM; ~**stift** *m (für Strichcodes)* wand; ~**stoff** *m* reading material; ~**zeichen** *nt* bookmark; ~**zirkel** *m* magazine subscription club.

**Lesung** *f (auch Parl)* reading.

**Lethargie** *f (Med, fig)* lethargy.

**lethargisch** *adj (Med, fig)* lethargic.

**Lette** *m (wk)* -**n**, -**n**, **Lettin** *f* Latvian.

**lettisch** *adj* Latvian.

**Lettisch(e)** *nt* Latvian; *siehe auch* **Deutsch(e)**.

**Lettland** *nt* Latvia.

**Letzt** *f:* **zu guter** ~ finally, in the end.

**letztemal** *adv* **das** ~ (the) last time; **zum letztenmal** (for) the last time.

**letztens** *adv* recently.

**letzte(r, s)** *adj* **(a)** *(örtlich, zeitlich)* last; *(restlich)* last (remaining). ~**(r) werden** to be last; **als** ~**(r) (an)kommen** to be the last to arrive, to arrive last; **auf dem** ~**n Platz liegen** to be last; **den** ~**n beißen die Hunde** *(Prov)* (the) devil take the hindmost *(prov)*; **er wäre der** ~, **den ich** ... he would be the last person I'd ...; **mein** ~**s Geld** the last of my money; **in** ~**r Zeit** recently; **zum** ~**n Mittel greifen** to resort to drastic methods; **der L~ Wille** the last will and testament; **zum** ~**en Mal** for the last time; **bis ins** ~ (right) down to the last detail; **bis zum** ~**n** to the utmost. **(b)** *(neueste) Mode, Nachricht, Neuigkeit etc* latest. **(c)** *(schlechteste)* most terrible. **das ist der** ~ **Dreck** that's absolute trash; **jdn wie den** ~**n Dreck behandeln** to treat sb like dirt.

**Letzte(r)** *mf decl as adj* last; *(dem Rang nach)* lowest. **der** ~ **des Monats** the last (day) of the month; **der/die** ~ **in der Klasse sein** to be bottom of the class.

**letztere(r, s)** *adj* the latter.

**Letzte(s)** *nt decl as adj* last thing. **sein** ~**s geben** to do one's utmost; **das ist ja das** ~! *(col)* that really is the limit.

**Letzt-:** **l~genannt** *adj* last-mentioned; **l~lich** *adv* in the end; **l~möglich** *adj attr* last possible; ~**nummernspeicher** *m (Telec)* last number redial.

**Leucht-:** ~**anzeige** *f* illuminated display; ~**diodenanzeige** *f* LED display.

**Leuchte** *f* -**n** light; *(col: Mensch)* genius.

**leuchten** *vi* **(a)** to shine; *(Feuer, Zifferblatt)* to glow; *(auf~)* to flash. **(b)** *(Mensch)* **mit einer Lampe in/auf etw** *(acc)* ~ to shine a lamp into/onto sth; **leuchte mal hierher!** shine some light over here.

**leuchtend** *adj (lit, fig)* shining; *Farbe* bright. **etw in den** ~**sten Farben schildern** to paint sth in glowing colours *(Brit)* or colors *(US)*.

**Leuchter** *m* - *(Kerzen~)* candlestick; *(Kron~)* chandelier.

**Leucht-:** ~**farbe** *f* fluorescent paint; ~**feuer** *nt* navigational light; ~**gas** *nt* town gas; ~**geschoß** *nt* flare; ~**käfer** *m* glow-worm; ~**kugel**, ~**patrone** *f* flare; ~**pistole** *f* flare pistol; ~**rakete** *f* signal rocket; ~**reklame** *f* neon sign; ~**röhre** *f* fluorescent tube; ~**schrift** *f* neon writing; **eine** ~**schrift** a neon sign; ~**spurgeschoß** *nt (Mil)* tracer bullet; ~**stift** *m* highlighter; ~**turm** *m* lighthouse; ~**zifferblatt** *nt* luminous dial.

**leugnen 1** *vt* to deny. ~, **etw getan zu haben** to deny having done sth; **es ist nicht zu** ~, **daß** ... it cannot be denied that ... **2** *vi* to deny everything.

**Leugnung** *f* denial.

**Leukämie** *f* leukaemia *(Brit)*, leukernia *(US)*.

**Leukoplast** ® *nt* -**e** sticking plaster ≃ elastoplast ® *(Brit)*, Bandaid ® *(US)*.

**Leumund** *m no pl* reputation, name.

**Leute** *pl* **(a)** people *pl*. **alle** ~ everybody; **kleine** ~ *(fig)* ordinary people; **es ist nicht wie bei armen** ~**n** *(hum col)* we're not on the breadline yet *(hum col)*; **etw unter die** ~ **bringen** *(col)* Gerücht *etc* to spread sth around; **unter die** ~ **kommen** *(col) (Mensch)* to meet people; *(Gerüchte etc)* to go around. **(b)** *(Mannschaft, Arbeiter etc)* **der Offizier ließ seine** ~ **antreten** the officer ordered his men to fall in; **dafür brauchen wir mehr** ~ we need more people/ staff/workers for that.

**Leutnant** *m* -**s** *or* -**e** (second) lieutenant. ~ **zur See** sublieutenant *(Brit)*, lieutenant junior grade *(US)*.

**leutselig** *adj (umgänglich)* affable.

**Leutseligkeit** *f* affability.

**Leviten** [le'vi:tən] *pl*: **jdm die** ~ **lesen** *(col)* to haul sb over the coals *(col)*.

**Lexikograph(in** *f)* *m (wk)* -**en**, -**en** lexicographer.

**Lexikographie** *f* lexicography.

**Lexikon** *nt, pl* **Lexika** encyclopedia; *(Wörterbuch)* dictionary.

**Liaison** [liɛ'zõ:] *f* -, -**s** liaison.

**Liane** *f* -**n** liana.

**Libanese** *m (wk)* -**n**, -**n**, **Libanesin** *f* Lebanese.

**libanesisch** *adj* Lebanese.

**Libanon** *m* -**(s) der** ~ *(Land)* the Lebanon.

**Libelle** *f (Zool)* dragonfly.

**liberal** *adj* liberal.

**Liberale(r)** *mf decl as adj (Pol)* Liberal.

**liberalisieren*** *vt* to liberalize.

**Liberalisierung** *f* liberalization.

**Liberalismus** *m* liberalism.

**Liberia** *nt* Liberia.

**Liberianer(in** *f)* *m* - Liberian.

**liberianisch** *adj* Liberian.

**Libero** *m* -**s** *(Ftbl)* sweeper.

**Libretto** *nt* -**s** *or* **Libretti** libretto.

**Libyen** ['li:byən] *nt* -**s** Libya.

**Libyer(in** *f*) ['liːbyɪɐ, -ərɪn] *m* - Libyan.
**libysch** ['liːbyʃ] *adj* Libyan.
**Licht** *nt* **-er** **(a)** light. ~ **machen** *(anschalten)* to turn
on the lights; *(anzünden)* to light a candle *etc*; **etw**
**gegen das** ~ **halten** to hold sth up to the light;
**gegen das** ~ **fotographieren** to take a photograph
against *or* into the light; **bei** ~**e besehen** *(fig)* in the
cold light of day; **jdm im** ~ **stehen** *(lit)* to stand in
sb's light; **das** ~ **der Welt erblicken** *(geh)* to see the
light of day. **(b)** *(fig)* light; *(Könner)* genius. ~ **in**
**eine (dunkle) Sache bringen** to shed some light on a
matter; **etw ans** ~ **bringen** to bring sth out into the
open; **ans** ~ **kommen** to come to light; **jdn hinters**
~ **führen** to lead sb up the garden path; **mir geht**
**ein** ~ **auf** it's dawned on me; **kein gutes** ~ **auf jdn/**
**etw werfen** to show sb/sth in a bad light; **etw ins**
**rechte** ~ **rücken** to show sth in its true light.
**licht** *adj* **(a)** *(hell)* light. **(b)** *Wald* sparse. **(c)** *(Tech)*
~**e Höhe/Weite** headroom/internal width.
**Licht-:** ~**anlage** *f* lights *pl*; **l~beständig** *adj* Farben, Stoff non-fade; ~**bild** *nt* photograph; *(Dia)*
slide; ~**bildervortrag** *m* illustrated talk; ~**blick** *m*
*(fig)* ray of hope; ~**bogen** *m* *(Elec)* arc;
**l~durchlässig** *adj* pervious to light; *(durchsichtig)*
transparent; *(durchscheinend)* translucent; **l~echt**
*adj* non-fade; **l~empfindlich** *adj* sensitive to light;
~**empfindlichkeit** *f* sensitivity to light; *(Phot)* film
speed.
**lichten¹ 1** *vt Wald* to thin (out). **2** *vr (Reihen, Wald,*
*Haare)* to thin (out); *(Nebel)* to clear.
**lichten²** *vt Anker* to weigh.
**Lichter-:** ~**kette** *f (fig)* candlelight demonstration;
**l~loh** *adv* **l~loh brennen** *(lit)* to be ablaze; *(fig:*
*Herz)* to be aflame; ~**meer** *nt (liter)* sea of light.
**Licht-:** ~**geschwindigkeit** *f* speed of light; ~**griffel**
*m (Comp)* light pen; ~**hupe** *f (Aut)* flash (of the
headlights); **die** ~**hupe benutzen** to flash one's
lights; ~**jahr** *nt* light year; ~**kegel** *m (Phys)* cone
of light; *(von Scheinwerfer)* beam (of light);
~**leiter** *m*, ~**leitfaser** *f* optic fibre *(Brit)* or fiber
*(US)*; ~**leitung** *f* lighting wire; **l~los** *adj* dark;
~**maschine** *f* dynamo; *(für Drehstrom)* alternator;
~**mast** *m* lamppost; ~**pause** *f* photocopy; *(bei*
*Blaupausverfahren)* blueprint; ~**punkt** *m* point of
light; ~**quelle** *f* source of light; ~**schacht** *m* air
shaft; ~**schalter** *m* light switch; ~**schein** *m*
gleam of light; **l~scheu** *adj* averse to light; *(fig)*
*Gesindel* shady; ~**schranke** *f* photoelectric barrier; ~**schutzfaktor** *m* (protection) factor *(of sun-*
*tan lotion)*; ~**signal** *nt* light signal; ~**spielhaus** *nt*
cinema; ~**stift** *m (Comp)* light pen; ~**strahl** *m*
beam of light; **l~undurchlässig** *adj* opaque.
**Lichtung** *f* clearing, glade.
**Lichtverhältnisse** *pl* lighting conditions *pl*.
**Lid** *nt* **-er** eyelid.
**Lid-:** ~**schatten** *m* eye shadow; ~**strich** *m* eyeliner.
**lieb** *adj* **(a)** kind; *(nett)* nice; *(artig) Kind* good; *Gast*
pleasant. **(viele)** ~**e Grüße Deine Silvia** love Silvia;
**sich** ~ **um jdn kümmern** to be very kind to sb; **wür-**
**dest du (bitte) so** ~ **sein und das Fenster aufmachen**
would you be so kind as to open the window; **sich**
**bei jdm** ~ **Kind machen** *(pej)* to suck up to sb. **(b)**
*(angenehm)* **etw ist jdm** ~ sb likes sth; **es wäre mir**
~, **wenn** ... I'd be glad if ...; **es wäre ihm** ~**er** he
would prefer it; *siehe auch* **lieber 2, liebste(r, s)**
**2. (c)** *(geliebt, in Anrede)* dear. ~**ste(r, s)** favourite
*(Brit)*, favorite *(US)*; **der** ~**e Gott** the Good Lord;
~**er Gott** *(Anrede)* dear God; **L~e Anna, ~er Klaus!**
... Dear Anna and Klaus, ...; **den** ~**en langen Tag**
*(col)* the whole livelong day; **(ach) du** ~**er Himmel/**

~**er Gott/~e Zeit** good heavens *or* Lord!
**lieb|äugeln** *vi insep* ~ **mit** to have one's eye on;
*(mit Gedanken)* to be toying with.
**Liebe** *f no pl* **(a)** love *(zu jdm, für jdn* for *or* of sb, *zu*
*etw* of sth). **die große** ~ the love of one's life; **aus**
~ **zu jdm/einer Sache** for the love of sb/sth; **etw mit**
**viel** ~ **tun** to do sth with loving care; **in** ~ with
love; **sie/er ist gut in der** ~ *(col)* she/he is good at
making love. **(b)** *(col: Gefälligkeit)* favour. **tu mir die**
~ **und** ... would you do me a favour and .... **(c)** *(Ge-*
*liebter)* love. **eine alte** ~ **von mir** an old flame of
mine.
**liebebedürftig** *adj* ~ **sein** to need a lot of affection.
**Liebelei** *f (col)* flirtation; affair.
**lieben** *vti* to love; *(als Liebesakt)* to make love *(jdn* to
sb). **etw nicht** ~ not to like sth; **etw** ~**d gern tun** to
love to do sth.
**Liebende(r)** *mf decl as adj* lover.
**liebenswert** *adj* lovable, endearing.
**liebenswürdig** *adj* kind. **würden Sie so** ~ **sein und**
**die Tür schließen?** would you be so kind as to shut
the door?
**liebenswürdigerweise** *adv* kindly.
**Liebenswürdigkeit** *f* *(Höflichkeit)* politeness;
*(Freundlichkeit)* kindness.
**Liebe(r)** *mf decl as adj* dear. **meine** ~**n** my dears.
**lieber 1** *adj comp of* **lieb. 2** *adv comp of* **gern** **(a)**
*(vorzugsweise)* rather. **das tue ich** ~ *(im Augenblick)*
I'd rather do that; *(grundsätzlich)* I prefer doing
that; **das würde ich** ~ **tun** I would prefer to do that;
**ich trinke** ~ **Wein als Bier** I prefer wine to beer;
**(das möchte ich)** ~ **nicht!** I'd rather not. **(b)** *(besser)*
better. **bleibe** ~ **im Bett** you'd better stay in bed;
**ich hätte** ~ **nachgeben sollen** I'd have done better to
give in; **nichts** ~ **als das** there's nothing I'd rather
do/have.
**Liebes-** *in cpds* love; ~**abenteuer** *nt* amorous adventure; ~**affäre** *f* (love) affair; ~**akt** *m* sex act;
~**beziehung** *f* romantic attachment; (sexual) relationship; ~**brief** *m* love letter; ~**dienst** *m (fig:*
*Gefallen)* favour; ~**entzug** *m no pl* withdrawal of
affection; ~**erklärung** *f* declaration of love;
~**geschichte** *f* **(a)** *(Liter)* love story; **(b)** *(col:*
*Liebschaft)* love affair; ~**heirat** *f* love match;
~**kummer** *m* lovesickness; ~**kummer haben** to be
lovesick; ~**leben** *nt* love life; ~**lied** *nt* love song;
~**müh(e)** *f*: **das ist vergebliche** ~**müh(e)** that is futile; ~**paar** *nt* lovers *pl*; ~**roman** *m* romantic
novel; ~**spiel** *nt* loveplay; ~**szene** *f* love scene;
~**verhältnis** *nt* (sexual) relationship.
**liebevoll** *adj* loving.
**lieb-:** ~**gewinnen*** *vt sep irreg* to grow fond of;
~**geworden** *adj attr* well-loved; *Brauch* favourite
*(Brit)*, favorite *(US)*; ~**haben** *vt sep irreg* to love;
*(weniger stark)* to be (very) fond of.
**Liebhaber(in** *f*) *m* - **(a)** lover. **(b)** *(Interessent)* enthusiast *(von* for*)*; *(Sammler)* collector *(von* of*)*.
**Liebhaberei** *f (fig)* hobby. **etw aus** ~ **tun** to do sth
as a hobby.
**Liebhaber-:** ~**preis** *m* collector's price; ~**stück** *nt*
collector's item.
**liebkosen*** *vt insep (liter)* to caress.
**Liebkosung** *f (liter)* caress.
**lieblich** *adj* delightful; *Duft, Wein* sweet.
**Liebling** *m* darling; *(bevorzugter Mensch)* favourite
*(Brit)*, favorite *(US)*.
**Lieblings-** *in cpds* favourite *(Brit)*, favorite *(US)*.
**Lieb-:** **l~los** *adj* unloving; *Bemerkung* unkind; *Be-*
*nehmen* inconsiderate; ~**losigkeit** *f* **(a)** *siehe adj*
coldness; unkindness; inconsiderateness; **(b)**
*(Äußerung)* unkind remark; **(c)** *(Tat)* unkind act;

**~schaft** f affair.
**Liebste(r)** mf decl as adj sweetheart.
**liebste(r, s) 1** adj superl of **lieb. 2** adv superl of
**gern: am ~n** best; **am ~n hätte ich ...** what I'd like
most would be ...; **am ~n lese ich Krimis** best of all
I like reading detective novels; **am ~n hätte ich
ihm eine geklebt!** (col) I could have belted him one
(col).
**Liechtenstein** ['lıçtnʃtain] nt Liechtenstein.
**Liechtensteiner(in** f) ['lıçtn-] m - Liechtensteiner.
**liechtensteinisch** ['lıçtn-] adj Liechtenstein.
**Lied** nt **-er** song; (Kirchen~) hymn. **das Ende vom ~**
(fig col) the outcome (of all this); **davon kann ich
ein ~ singen** I could tell you a thing or two about
that (col).
**Lieder-: ~abend** m song recital; **~buch** nt songbook; (mit Kirchen~n) hymnbook.
**liederlich** adj (schlampig) slovenly attr, pred; (unmoralisch) Leben, Mann dissolute; Frau, Mädchen
loose. **ein ~es Frauenzimmer** (pej) a slut.
**Lieder-: ~macher(in** f) m singer-songwriter;
**~zyklus** m song cycle.
**lief** pret of **laufen.**
**Lieferant** m supplier; (Auslieferer) delivery man.
**Lieferanteneingang** m tradesmen's entrance;
(von Warenhaus etc) goods entrance.
**Liefer-: l~bar** adj (vorrätig) available; **die Ware ist
sofort l~bar** the article can be delivered at once;
**~firma** f supplier; (Zusteller) delivery firm; **~frist**
f delivery period; **die ~frist einhalten** to meet the
delivery date.
**liefern** vti to supply; Beweise, Informationen auch to
furnish; Ertrag to yield; (col: stellen) to provide;
(zustellen) to deliver (an +acc to). **jdm etw ~** to supply sb with sth/provide sb with sth/deliver sth to
sb; **wir ~ nicht ins Ausland** we don't supply the foreign market; siehe **geliefert.**
**Liefer-: ~schein** m delivery note; **~termin** m delivery date.
**Lieferung** f delivery; (Versorgung) supply. **bei ~ zu
bezahlen** payable on delivery.
**Liefer-: ~vertrag** m sale contract; **~wagen** m (delivery) van, panel truck (US); (offen) pick-up;
**~zeit** f delivery (period), lead time (Comm);
**~zettel** m delivery order.
**Liege** f **-n** couch; (Camping~) camp bed (Brit), cot
(US).
**liegen** pret **lag,** ptp **gelegen** vi **(a)** to lie. **hart/weich
~** to lie on a hard/soft bed etc; **unbequem ~** to lie
uncomfortably; **auf den Knien ~** to be kneeling; **im
Krankenhaus ~** to be in hospital; **der Kranke muß
unbedingt ~** the patient must stay lying down; **der
Schnee liegt 50 cm hoch** the snow is 50 cm deep;
**der Schnee bleibt nicht ~** the snow isn't lying; **etw
~ lassen** to leave sth.
   **(b)** (sich befinden, sein) to be; (Haus, Stadt etc
auch) to be situated, to lie. **Paris liegt an der Seine**
Paris is (situated) on the Seine; **nach Süden/der
Straße ~** to face south/the road; **verstreut ~** to lie
scattered; **das Haus liegt ganz ruhig** the house is in
a very quiet location; **das liegt doch auf dem Weg/
ganz in der Nähe** it's on the way/quite nearby; **das
Schiff liegt am Kai** the ship is (tied up) alongside
the quay; **die Betonung liegt auf der zweiten Silbe**
the stress is on the second syllable; **so, wie die Dinge jetzt ~** as things stand at the moment; **damit
liegst du (gold)richtig** (col) you're right there; **an der
Spitze ~** to be right out in front; **der zweite Läufer
liegt weit hinter dem ersten** the second runner is
lying a long way behind the first; **die Preise ~ zwischen 60 und 80 Mark** the prices are between 60 and
80 marks.
   **(c)** (wichtig sein) **es liegt mir wenig daran** that
isn't very important to me; **mir liegt an guten Beziehungen** I am concerned that there should be
good relations.
   **(d)** (begründet sein) **an jdm/etw ~** to be because
of sb/sth; **woran liegt es?** why is that?; **das liegt
daran, daß ...** that is because ...; **an mir soll es nicht
~, wenn die Sache schiefgeht** it won't be my fault if
things go wrong; **das liegt ganz bei dir** that is entirely up to you; **die Entscheidung liegt bei Ihnen**
the decision rests with you.
   **(e)** (geeignet sein, passen) **jdm liegt etw nicht** sth
doesn't suit sb; (Mathematik etc) sb has no aptitude
for sth; **Krankenschwester liegt mir nicht** (col) nursing doesn't appeal to me.
**liegenbleiben** vi sep irreg aux sein **(a)** (nicht aufstehen) to remain lying (down). **(im Bett) ~** to stay in
bed; **bleib liegen!** don't get up! **(b)** (vergessen werden) to get left behind; (nicht verkauft werden) to be
left unsold; (nicht ausgeführt werden) to be left (undone).
**liegend** adj (Art) reclining. **~ aufbewahren** to store
flat.
**liegenlassen** vt sep irreg, ptp ~ or **liegengelassen**
(nicht erledigen) to leave; (vergessen) to leave (behind); (herum~) to leave lying about.
**Liegenschaft(en** pl) f real estate sing, property
sing.
**Liege-: ~platz** m place to lie; (Ankerplatz) moorings
pl; **~sitz** m reclining seat; (auf Boot) couchette;
**~stuhl** m (mit Holzgestell) deck chair; (mit Metall-
gestell) lounger; **~stütz** m (Sport) press-up;
**~wagen** m (Rail) couchette coach or car (esp US);
**~wiese** f lawn (for sunbathing).
**lieh** pret of **leihen.**
**ließ** pret of **lassen.**
**Lift** m **-e** or **-s** (Personen~) lift (Brit), elevator (esp
US); (Ski~) ski lift.
**Liga** f, pl **Ligen** league.
**liieren*** vt to bring or get together. **liiert sein** to have
joined forces; (Firmen etc) to be working together;
(Pol) to be allied; (ein Verhältnis haben) to have a
relationship.
**Likör** m **-e** liqueur.
**lila** adj inv purple.
**Lilie** [-iə] f lily.
**Liliput-** in cpds miniature.
**Liliputaner(in** f) m - midget.
**Limit** nt **-s** limit; (Fin) ceiling.
**limitieren*** vt (form) to limit; (Fin) to put a ceiling
on.
**Limo** f **-s** (col), **Limonade** f lemonade.
**Limone** f **-n** lime.
**Limousine** [limu'zi:nə] f saloon (Brit), sedan (US).
**lind** adj (liter) balmy; Regen gentle.
**Linde** f **-n** linden or lime (tree); (~nholz) limewood.
**Lindenblütentee** m lime blossom tea.
**lindern** vt to ease, to relieve.
**Linderung** f easing, relief.
**lindgrün** adj lime green.
**Lineal** nt **-e** ruler.
**linear** adj linear.
**Linguist(in** f) m linguist.
**Linguistik** f linguistics sing.
**linguistisch** adj linguistic.
**Linie** [-iə] f **(a)** line. **ein Schreibblock mit ~n** a ruled
notepad; **in einer ~ stehen** to be in a line; **sich in
einer ~ aufstellen** to line up; **einer Sache** (dat) **fehlt
die klare ~** there's no clear line to sth; **eine ~ ziehen zwischen ...** (+dat) (fig) to draw a line between

...; **auf der ganzen** ~ *(fig)* all along the line; **auf** ~ **bleiben** *(fig)* to toe the line; **auf die** ~ **achten** to watch one's figure; **in erster** ~ first and foremost. **(b)** *(Verkehrsverbindung)* route. **fahren Sie mit der** ~ **2** take a *or* the 2; **die** ~ **Köln-Bonn** the Cologne-Bonn line.

**Linien-** [-iən]: ~**bus** *m* regular bus; ~**flug** *m*, ~**maschine** *f* scheduled flight; ~**papier** *nt* lined paper; ~**richter** *m (Sport)* linesman; *(Tennis)* line judge; ~**schiff** *nt* regular service ship; l~**treu** *adj* loyal to the party line; l~**treu sein** to toe the party line; ~**verkehr** *m* regular traffic; *(Aviat)* scheduled traffic; **im** ~**verkehr fahren** to operate on regular services.

**linieren\*** *vt* to rule, to draw lines on. **liniert** lined.

**link** *adj (pej col) Typ* underhanded; **komm mir nicht so** ~ **stop** trying to put one over on me *(col)*; **ein ganz** ~**er Hund** a two-faced bastard *(pej col)*; **eine ganz** ~**e Masche** *or* **Tour** a real con *(col)*.

**Linke** *f (wk)* **-n**, **-n (a)** *(Hand)* left hand; *(Seite)* left side; *(Boxen)* left. **zu seiner** ~**n** to his left. **(b)** *(Pol)* Left.

**linken** *vt (col: hereinlegen)* to con *(col)*.

**Linke(r)** *mf decl as adj (Pol)* left-winger, leftist *(pej)*.

**linke(r, s)** *adj attr* **(a)** left. **die** ~ **Seite** the left(-hand) side; *(von Stoff)* the wrong side; ~**e Masche** purl (stitch); **eine** ~**e Masche stricken** to purl one; **das mache ich mit der** ~**n Hand** *(col)* I can do that with my eyes shut *(col)*; **er ist heute mit dem** ~**n Bein zuerst aufgestanden** *(col)* he got out of bed on the wrong side this morning *(col)*. **(b)** *(Pol)* left-wing; *Flügel* left.

**linkisch** *adj* clumsy, awkward.

**links 1** *adv* **(a)** on the left; *schauen, abbiegen* left. **nach** ~ (to the) left; **von** ~ from the left; ~ **von etw** left of sth; **sich** ~ **halten** to keep to the left; **weiter** ~ further to the left; **sich** ~ **einordnen** to move into the left-hand lane; **jdn** ~ **liegenlassen** *(fig col)* to ignore sb; **das mache ich mit** ~ *(col)* I can do that with my eyes shut *(col)*; ~ **von der Mitte** *(Pol)* left of centre; ~ **stehen** *(Pol)* to be left-wing. **(b)** *(verkehrt) bügeln* on the reverse; *tragen* inside out; ~ **stricken** to purl. **2** *prep* +*gen* on *or* to the left of.

**Links-:** ~**abbieger** *m* motorist/vehicle turning left; ~**außen** *m* - *(Ftbl)* outside left; *(Pol)* extreme left-winger; l~**bündig** *adj (Typ)* ranged *or* flush left; ~**drall** *m (von Billardball)* spin to the left; *(von Auto, Pferd)* pull to the left; *(Pol col)* leaning to the left; ~**extremismus** *m* left-wing extremism; ~**extremist** *m* left-wing extremist; l~**gerichtet** *adj (Pol)* left-wing *no adv*; ~**händer(in** *f)* *m* - left-hander; ~**händer sein** to be left-handed; l~**händig** *adj, adv* left-handed; l~**herum** *adv* (around) to the left; ~**intellektuelle(r)** *mf* left-wing intellectual; ~**kurve** *f (von Straße)* left-hand bend; l~**lastig** *adj* listing to the left; *(fig)* leftist *(pej)*, leaning to the left; l~**radikal** *adj (Pol)* radically left-wing; **die** ~**radikalen** the left-wing radicals; ~**radikalismus** *m (Pol)* left-wing radicalism; l~**rheinisch** *adj* to *or* on the left of the Rhine; ~**ruck**, ~**rutsch** *m (Pol)* swing to the left; l~**seitig** *adj* on the left(-hand) side; l~**seitig gelähmt** paralyzed in the left side; ~**verkehr** *m no pl* left-hand rule of the road; **in Großbritannien ist** ~**verkehr** you have to drive on the left in Britain.

**Linoleum** [li'no:leυm] *nt no pl* linoleum, lino *(Brit)*.

**Linolschnitt** *m (Art)* linocut.

**Linse** *f* **-n (a)** *(Bot, Cook)* lentil. **(b)** *(Opt)* lens.

**linsen** *vi (col)* to peek *(col)*.

**Lippe** *f* **-n** lip. **es soll kein Wort über meine** ~**n kommen** not a word shall pass my lips; **er brachte kein**

**Wort über die** ~**n** he couldn't say *or* utter a word; **eine (große** *or* **dicke)** ~ **riskieren** *(col)* to talk big *(col)*.

**Lippen-:** ~**bekenntnis** *nt* lip service; ~**pflegestift** *m* lip salve (stick); ~**stift** *m* lipstick.

**Liquidation** *f (form)* liquidation. **in** ~ **treten** to go into liquidation.

**liquid(e)** *adj (Econ) Firma* solvent.

**liquidieren\*** *vt Firma* to liquidate; *jdm* to eliminate.

**Liquidität** *f (Econ)* liquidity.

**lispeln** *vti* to lisp. **das Kind lispelt** the child has a lisp.

**Lissabon** *nt* Lisbon.

**List** *f* **-en** *(Täuschung)* cunning; *(Plan)* trick. **mit** ~ **und Tücke** *(col)* with a lot of coaxing.

**Liste** *f* **-n** *(Aufstellung)* list; *(Wähler~)* register. **sich in eine** ~ **eintragen** to put one's name on a list.

**Listen-:** ~**platz** *m (Pol)* place on the list of candidates; ~**preis** *m* list price.

**listig** *adj* cunning, wily *no adv*.

**Litanei** *f (Eccl, fig)* litany. **eine** ~ **von Klagen** a long list of complaints.

**Litauen** *nt* **-s** Lithuania.

**Litauer(in** *f)* *m* - Lithuanian.

**litauisch** *adj* Lithuanian.

**Liter** *m or nt* - litre *(Brit)*, liter *(US)*.

**literarisch** *adj* literary.

**Literatur** *f* literature.

**Literatur-:** ~**angabe** *f* bibliographical reference; ~**gattung** *f* literary genre; ~**geschichte** *f* history of literature; ~**kritik** *f* literary criticism; ~**kritiker** *m* literary critic; ~**verzeichnis** *nt* bibliography; ~**wissenschaft** *f* literary studies *pl*.

**Literflasche** *f* litre *(Brit)* or liter *(US)* bottle.

**literweise** *adv (lit)* by the litre *(Brit)* or liter *(US)*; *(fig)* by the gallon.

**Litfaßsäule** *f* advertising column.

**Litho-:** ~**graph** *m* lithographer; ~**graphie** *f* **(a)** *(Verfahren)* lithography; **(b)** *(Druck)* lithograph.

**litt** *ptp of* **leiden.**

**Liturgie** *f* liturgy.

**liturgisch** *adj* liturgical.

**Litze** *f* **-n** braid; *(Elec)* flex.

**live** [laif] *adj pred, adv (Rad, TV)* live.

**Live-Sendung** [laif-] *f* live broadcast.

**Livree** [li'vre:] *f* **-n** [-e:ən] livery.

**Lizenz** *f* licence *(Brit)*, license *(US)*. **etw in** ~ **herstellen** to manufacture sth under licence.

**Lizenz-:** ~**ausgabe** *f* licensed edition; ~**geber** *m* licenser; *(Behörde)* licensing authority; ~**gebühr** *f* licence fee *(Brit)*, license fee *(US)*; ~**inhaber** *m* licensee; **er ist** ~**inhaber** he has a licence *(Brit)* or license *(US)*; ~**spieler** *m (Ftbl)* professional player.

**Lkw** [ɛlka:'ve:] *m* **-(s)** = **Lastkraftwagen** ≃ HGV.

**Lob** *nt no pl* praise. **(viel)** ~ **für etw bekommen** to come in for (a lot of) praise for sth; **jdm** ~ **spenden** *or* **zollen** to praise sb.

**loben** *vt* to praise. **jdn/etw** ~**d erwähnen** to commend sb/sth; **das lob ich mir** that's what I like (to see/hear *etc*).

**lobenswert** *adj* laudable.

**Lobeshymne** *f (fig)* hymn of praise.

**Lobhudelei** *f (pej)* gushing praise.

**löblich** *adj (dated, iro)* commendable.

**Lob-:** ~**lied** *nt* song of praise; **ein** ~**lied auf jdn/etw anstimmen** *(fig)* to sing sb's/sth's praises; ~**rede** *f* eulogy; **eine** ~**rede auf jdn halten** *(lit)* to make a speech in sb's honour *(Brit)* or honor *(US)*; *(fig)* to eulogize sb.

**Loch** *nt* ⁼**er** hole; *(Luft~)* gap; *(fig col: elende Wohnung)* dump *(col)*, hole *(col)*. **sich** *(dat)* **ein** ~ **in den**

**Kopf schlagen** to gash one's head; **~er in die Luft gucken** to gaze into space; **ein großes ~ in jds Geldbeutel** *(acc)* **reißen** *(col)* to make a big hole in sb's pocket.

**lochen** *vt* to punch holes/a hole in; *Fahrkarte* to punch.

**Locher** *m* - (a) punch. (b) *(Mensch)* punch-card operator.

**löcherig** *adj* full of holes.

**löchern** *vt (col)* to pester (to death) with questions.

**Loch-:** **~karte** *f* punch card; **~streifen** *m* (punched) paper tape.

**Lochung** *f* punching; *(Stelle)* perforation.

**Lochzange** *f* punch.

**Locke** *f* -n *(Haar)* curl. **~n haben** to have curly hair.

**locken¹** *vtr Haar* to curl. **gelocktes Haar** curly hair.

**locken²** *vt* to lure. **jdn in einen Hinterhalt ~** to lure sb into a trap; **die Henne lockte ihre Küken** the hen called to its chicks.

**lockend** *adj* tempting.

**Locken-:** **~kopf** *m* curly hairstyle; *(Mensch)* curly-head; **~wickler** *m* - (hair-)curler.

**locker** *adj (lit, fig)* loose; *Kuchen, Schaum* light; *(nicht gespannt)* slack; *Haltung, Sitzweise* relaxed; *(col)* cool *(col)*. **~ werden** *(lit, fig)* to get loose; *(Muskeln, Mensch)* to loosen up; **etw ~ machen** to loosen sth/make sth light/slacken sth; **etw ~ lassen** to slacken sth off; *Bremse* to let sth off; **~ sitzen** *(Ziegel, Schraube etc)* to be loose; **bei ihr sitzt die Hand ziemlich ~** she's quick to lash out; **bei ihm sitzt der Revolver ~** he's trigger-happy; **das mache ich ganz ~** *(col)* I can do it just like that *(col)*.

**locker-:** **~lassen** *vi sep irreg (col)* **nicht ~lassen** not to let up; **~machen** *vt sep (col) Geld* to shell out *(col)*.

**lockern 1** *vt* (a) *(locker machen)* to loosen; *Seil, (lit, fig) Zügel* to slacken. (b) *(entspannen) Muskeln* to loosen up; *(fig) Vorschriften* to relax. **2** *vr* to work itself loose; *(Sport)* to loosen up; *(Verkrampfung)* to ease off; *(Atmosphäre)* to get more relaxed.

**Lockerungsübung** *f* loosening-up exercise; *(zum Warmwerden)* limbering-up exercise.

**lockig** *adj Haar* curly; *Mensch* curly-headed.

**Lock-:** **~mittel** *nt* lure; **~ruf** *m* call.

**Lockung** *f* lure; *(Versuchung)* temptation.

**Lockvogel** *m (lit, fig)* decoy.

**Lockvogel|angebot** *nt* tempting offer, loss leader *(Comm)*.

**Loden** *m* - loden (cloth).

**Lodenmantel** *m* loden (coat).

**lodern** *vi (lit, fig)* to blaze.

**Löffel** *m* - spoon; *(als Maß)* spoonful; *(von Bagger)* bucket. **den ~ abgeben** *(col)* to kick the bucket *(col)*; **jdm ein paar hinter die ~ geben** to give sb a clout around the ear(s).

**löffeln** *vt* to spoon.

**löffelweise** *adv* by the spoonful.

**log** *pret of* **lügen**.

**Logarithmentafel** *f* log table.

**Logarithmus** *m* logarithm.

**Logbuch** *nt* log(book).

**Loge** *f* -n (a) *(Theat)* box; *(Pförtner~)* lodge. (b) *(Freimaurer~)* lodge.

**Logenplatz** ['lo:ʒən-] *m (Theat)* seat in a box.

**logieren*** [lo'ʒi:rən] *vi (dated)* to stay.

**Loggia** ['lɔdʒa] *f, pl* **Loggien** [-iən] balcony.

**Logik** *f* logic.

**Logiker(in** *f)* *m* - logician.

**Logis** [lo'ʒi:] *nt* - **Kost und ~** board and lodging.

**logisch** *adj* logical; *(col: selbstverständlich)* natural. **gehst du auch hin?** — **~** are you going too? — of course.

**logischerweise** *adv* logically.

**Logistik** *f* (a) *(Math)* logic. (b) *(Mil)* logistics *sing*.

**Logo** *nt* -s *(Firmen~)* logo.

**logo** *interj (col)* you bet *(col)*.

**Logopäde** *m (wk)* -n, -n, **Logopädin** *f* speech therapist.

**Logopädie** *f* speech therapy.

**Lohn** *m* ⁼e (a) *(Arbeitsentgelt)* wage(s), pay *no pl, no indef art*. **bei jdm in ~ und Brot stehen** *(geh)* to be in sb's employ *(form)*. (b) *(fig: Belohnung)* reward; *(Strafe)* punishment. **zum ~ für ... as a reward/punishment for ...;** **das ist nun der ~ für meine Mühe!** *(iro)* that's what I get for my trouble.

**Lohn-:** **l~abhängig** *adj* on a payroll; **~abhängige(r)** *mf* worker (on a payroll); **~abrechnung** *f* wages slip; **~arbeit** *f* waged labour *(Brit)* or labor *(US)*; **~ausfall** *m* loss of earnings; **~ausgleich** *m* wage adjustment; **bei vollem ~ausgleich** with full pay; **~buchhalter** *m* wages clerk; **~büro** *nt* wages office; **~empfänger** *m* wage earner, wage worker *(US)*.

**lohnen 1** *vir* to be worth it. **es lohnt (sich), etw zu tun** it is worth doing sth; **die Mühe lohnt sich** it is worth the effort; **das lohnt sich nicht für mich** it's not worth my while. **2** *vt* **jdm etw ~** to reward sb for sth; **er hat mir meine Mühe schlecht gelohnt** he gave me poor thanks for my efforts.

**löhnen** *vti (col: bezahlen)* to shell out *(col)*.

**lohnend** *adj* rewarding; *(nutzbringend)* worthwhile; *(einträglich)* profitable.

**lohnenswert** *adj* worthwhile.

**Lohn-:** **~erhöhung** *f* pay rise; **~forderung** *f* pay claim; **~fortzahlung** *f* continued payment of wages; **~gefälle** *nt* wage differential; **~gruppe** *f* wage group; **~kosten** *pl* wage costs *pl*; **~kürzung** *f* wage cut; **~liste** *f* payroll; **~politik** *f* pay policy; **~runde** *f* pay round; **~skala** *f* pay scale; **~steuer** *f* income tax.

**Lohnsteuer-:** **~jahresausgleich** *m* income tax return; **~karte** *f* (income) tax card.

**Lohn-:** **~stopp** *m* pay freeze; **~streifen** pay slip; **~tarif** *m* wage rate; **~tüte** *f* pay packet *(Brit)* or envelope *(US)*; **~verhandlung** *f* pay negotiations *pl*; **~zahlung** *f* payment of wages.

**Loipe** *f* -n cross-country ski run.

**Lok** *f* -s = **Lokomotive** engine.

**lokal** *adj (örtlich)* local.

**Lokal** *nt* -e *(Gaststätte)* ≃ pub *(esp Brit)*, bar; *(Restaurant)* restaurant.

**Lokal-** *in cpds* local; **~anästhesie** *f (Med)* local anaesthetic *(Brit)* or anesthetic *(US)*; **~blatt** *nt* local paper.

**lokalisieren*** *vt* (a) *(Ort feststellen)* to locate. (b) *(Med)* to localize.

**Lokalität** *f* locality; *(innen)* premises *pl*.

**Lokal-:** **~kolorit** *nt* local colour *(Brit)* or color *(US)*; **~nachrichten** *pl* local news *sing*; **~patriotismus** *m* local patriotism; **~teil** *m* local section; **~termin** *m (Jur)* visit to the scene of the crime; **~verbot** *nt* **~verbot haben** to be barred or banned from a pub *(Brit)* or bar; **~zeitung** *f* local newspaper.

**Lokomotive** *f* locomotive, (railway) engine.

**Lokomotivführer** *m* engine driver, engineer *(US)*.

**Lombard-** *(Fin):* **~geschäft** *nt* loan on security; **~satz** *m* rate for loans on security.

**London** *nt* London.

**Londoner** *adj attr* London.

**Londoner(in** *f)* *m* - Londoner.

**Looping** ['lu:pɪŋ] *m or nt* -s *(Aviat)* looping the loop. **einen ~ machen** to loop the loop.

**Lorbeer** *m* **-en** *(lit: Gewächs)* laurel; *(als Gewürz)* bayleaf; *(~kranz)* laurel wreath. **sich auf seinen ~en ausruhen** *(fig col)* to rest on one's laurels.

**Lorbeer-:** **~baum** *m* laurel (tree); **~blatt** *nt* bayleaf; **~kranz** *m* laurel wreath.

**Los** *nt* **-e (a)** *(für Entscheidung)* lot; *(in der Lotterie)* (lottery) ticket. **das Große ~ ziehen** *(lit, fig)* to hit the jackpot; **etw durch das ~ entscheiden** to decide sth by drawing lots; **jdn durch das ~ bestimmen** to pick sb by drawing lots; **das ~ fiel auf mich** it fell to my lot. **(b)** *no pl (Schicksal)* lot. **er hat ein hartes ~** his is a hard lot.

**los 1** *adj pred* **(a)** *(nicht befestigt)* loose. **der Hund ist von der Leine ~** the dog is off the lead. **(b)** *(frei)* **jdn/etw ~ sein** *(col)* to be rid of sb/sth; **ich bin mein ganzes Geld ~** *(col)* I'm cleaned out *(col)*. **(c)** *(col)* **etwas ~ machen** *(col)* to make sth happen; **was ist denn hier ~?** what's going on here?; **was ist ~?** what's the matter?; **irgendwas ist mit ihm ~** there's something wrong with him; **mit dem ist doch nichts mehr ~** he isn't up to much any more; **da war was ~** there was plenty of action; *(Schlägerei etc)* all hell was let loose; **ist hier abends nichts ~?** isn't there anything to do here in the evenings?

**2** *adv* **(a)** *(Aufforderung)* **~!** come on!; **nichts wie ~!** let's get going; **(na) ~, mach schon!** (come on,) get on with it; **~, fahr doch endlich** come on, start driving; **auf die Plätze, fertig, ~** on your marks, get set, go! **(b)** *(weg)* **wir wollen früh ~** we want to be off early.

**lösbar** *adj Problem etc* soluble.

**los-:** **~binden** *vt sep irreg* to untie *(von from)*; **~brechen** *sep irreg* **1** *vt* to break off; **2** *vi aux sein (Gelächter etc)* to break out; *(Sturm, Gewitter)* to break.

**Löschblatt** *nt* sheet of blotting paper.

**löschen** *vt* **(a)** *Feuer, Kerze* to put out, to extinguish; *Durst* to quench; *Tonband* to erase; *Schuld* to pay off; *Eintragung, Zeile* to delete; *Konto* to close; *(aufsaugen) Tinte* to blot; *(Comp) Speicher, Bildschirm* to clear; *Daten, Information* to erase, to delete. **(b)** *(Naut) Ladung* to unload.

**Lösch-:** **~fahrzeug** *nt* fire engine; **~mittel** *nt* (fire-)extinguishing agent; **~papier** *nt* (piece of) blotting paper; **~taste** *f (Comp)* delete key; **~zug** *m* set of fire-fighting appliances.

**lose** *adj (lit, fig)* loose; *(nicht gespannt) Seil* slack. **etw ~ verkaufen** to sell sth loose.

**Lösegeld** *nt* ransom (money).

**los|eisen** *vtr sep (col)* **etw bei jdm ~** to get sth out of sb; **sich/jdn von jdm ~** to get away from sb/sb away from sb.

**losen** *vi* to draw lots *(um for)*.

**lösen 1** *vt* **(a)** *(losmachen)* to remove *(von from)*; *Boot* to cast off *(von from)*; *(aufbinden)* to undo; *Hände* to unclasp; *Handbremse* to release; *Husten, Krampf* to ease; *Muskeln* to loosen up; *(lit, fig: lockern)* to loosen; **siehe gelöst. (b)** *(klären)* to solve; *Konflikt* to resolve. **(c)** *(annullieren) Vertrag* to cancel; *Verlobung* to break off; *Verbindung* to sever; *Ehe* to dissolve. **(d)** *(kaufen) Fahrkarte* to buy, to get.

**2** *vr* **(a)** *(sich losmachen)* to detach oneself *(von from)*; *(sich ab~)* to come off *(von etw sth)*; *(Knoten, Haare)* to come undone; *(Schuß)* to go off; *(Husten, Krampf)* to ease; *(Muskeln)* to loosen up; *(lit, fig: sich lockern)* to (be)come loose. **sich von jdm ~** to break away from sb; **sich von etw ~** *von Vorurteilen etc* to rid oneself of sth.

**(b)** *(sich aufklären)* to be solved. **sich von selbst ~** *(Mordfall)* to solve itself. **(c)** *(in Flüssigkeit)* to dis-

solve *(in +dat in)*.

**los-:** **~fahren** *vi sep irreg aux sein (abfahren)* to set off; *(Fahrzeug)* to move off; *(Auto)* to drive off; **~gehen** *vi sep irreg aux sein* **(a)** *(weggehen)* to set off; *(Schuß etc)* to go off; **nach hinten ~gehen** *(col)* to backfire; **(mit dem Messer) auf jdn ~gehen** to go for sb (with a knife); **(b)** *(col: anfangen)* to start; **gleich geht's ~** it's just about to start; **jetzt geht's ~!** here we go!; *(Reise, Bewegung)* we're/you're off!; **(c)** *(col: abgehen)* to come off; **~heulen** *vi sep (col: weinen)* to burst out crying; **~kommen** *vi sep irreg aux sein (Mensch)* to get away *(von from)*; *(sich befreien)* to free oneself *(von from)*; **~kriegen** *vt sep (col: ablösen)* to get off; **~lachen** *vi sep* to burst out laughing; **~lassen** *vt sep irreg* **(a)** to let go of; **der Gedanke läßt mich nicht mehr ~** the thought haunts me; **(b)** *(col: abfeuern) Feuerwerk* to let off; **(c) jdn (auf jdn) ~lassen** *(fig col)* to let sb loose (on sb); **die Hunde auf jdn ~lassen** to set the dogs on(to) sb; **~laufen** *vi sep irreg aux sein* to start to run; **~legen** *vi sep (col)* to get going; **nun leg mal ~ und erzähle ...** now come on and tell me/us ...

**löslich** *adj* soluble. **leicht/schwer ~** readily/not readily soluble.

**los-:** **~lösen** *sep* **1** *vt* to remove *(von from)*; *(ablösen auch)* to take off *(von etw sth)*; *(lockern)* to loosen; **2** *vr* to detach oneself *(von from)*; *(sich ablösen auch)* to come off *(von etw sth)*; *(lockern)* to become loose; **sich von jdm ~lösen** to break away from sb; **~machen** *sep* **1** *vt* **(a)** to free; *(~binden)* to untie; **(b) einen** *or* **was ~machen** *(col)* to have some action *(col)*; **2** *vi (col: sich beeilen)* to step on it *(col)*; **3** *vr* to get away *(von from)*; **~müssen** *vi sep irreg (col)* to have to go.

**Losnummer** *f* (lottery) ticket number.

**los-:** **~reißen** *sep irreg* **1** *vt* to tear off *(von etw sth)*; **2** *vr* **sich (von etw) ~reißen** *(Hund etc)* to break free (from sth); *(fig)* to tear oneself away (from sth); **~rennen** *vi sep irreg aux sein (col)* to run off; *(anfangen zu laufen)* to start to run; **~sagen** *vr sep* **sich von etw ~sagen** to renounce sth; **~schicken** *vt sep* to send off; **~schießen** *vi sep irreg* **schieß ~!** *(fig col)* fire away! *(col)*; **~schlagen** *vi sep irreg* to hit out; **auf jdn ~schlagen** to go for sb; **~schnallen** *vt sep* to unbuckle; **~schrauben** *vt sep* to unscrew; *(lockern auch)* to loosen; **~sprechen** *vt sep irreg* to absolve; **~stürzen** *vi sep aux sein* to rush off; **auf jdn/etw ~stürzen** to pounce on sb/sth.

**Lostrommel** *f* drum (for lottery draw), tombola drum.

**Losung** *f* **(a)** motto. **(b)** *(Kennwort)* password.

**Lösung** *f* **(a)** solution *(gen to)*; *(das Lösen)* solution *(gen of)*; *(eines Konfliktes)* resolving. **(b)** *(Chem)* solution.

**Lösungs-:** **~mittel** *nt* solvent; **~vorschlag** *m* proposed solution; **einen ~vorschlag machen** to propose a solution.

**loswerden** *vt sep irreg aux sein* to get rid of; *Gedanken* to get away from; *Geld (ausgeben)* to spend.

**losziehen** *vi sep irreg aux sein (aufbrechen)* to set out *(in +acc, nach for)*.

**Lot** *nt* **-e (a)** *(Senkblei)* plumbline. **im ~ sein** to be in plumb; **die Sache ist wieder im ~** things have been straightened out. **(b)** *(Math)* perpendicular. **das ~ fällen** to drop a perpendicular.

**loten** *vt* to plumb.

**löten** *vti* to solder.

**Lothringen** *nt* Lorraine.

**Lothringer(in** *f) m* Lorrainer.
**lothringisch** *adj* of Lorraine, Lorrainese.
**Lotion** *f* lotion.
**Löt-:** ~**kolben** *m* soldering iron; ~**lampe** *f* blow-lamp; ~**metall** *nt* solder.
**Lotos-:** ~**blume** *f* lotus (flower); ~**sitz** *m* lotus position.
**lotrecht** *adj (Math)* perpendicular.
**Lotse** *m (wk)* **-n, -n** *(Naut)* pilot; *(Flug~)* air-traffic controller; *(fig)* guide.
**lotsen** *vt* to guide. **jdn irgendwohin** ~ *(col)* to drag sb somewhere *(col)*.
**Lotterie** *f* lottery; *(Tombola)* raffle.
**Lotterie-:** ~**gewinn** *m* lottery/raffle prize *or (Geld)* winnings *pl*; ~**los** *nt* lottery/raffle ticket.
**lott(e)rig** *adj (col)* slovenly *no adv*.
**Lotterleben** *nt (col)* dissolute life.
**Lotto** *nt* **-s** national lottery. **(im)** ~ **spielen** to do the national lottery; **du hast wohl im** ~ **gewonnen** you must have won the pools *(Brit)*.
**Lotto-:** ~**gewinn** *m* Lotto win; *(Geld)* Lotto winnings *pl*; ~**schein** *m* Lotto coupon; ~**zahlen** *pl* winning Lotto numbers *pl*.
**Löwe** *m (wk)* **-n, -n** lion; *(Astron, Astrol)* Leo.
**Löwen-:** ~**anteil** *m (col)* lion's share; ~**bändiger** *m* lion-tamer; ~**jagd** *f* lion hunt; ~**maul**, ~**mäulchen** *nt* snapdragon, antirrhinum; ~**zahn** *m* dandelion.
**Löwin** *f* lioness.
**loyal** [loa'ja:l] *adj* loyal *(jdm gegenüber* to sb).
**Loyalität** [loajali:'tɛ:t] *f* loyalty.
**LP** [ɛl'pe:] *f* **-s = Langspielplatte** LP.
**LSD** [ɛl|ɛs'de:] *nt no pl* LSD.
**lt. = laut²**.
**Luchs** [lʊks] *m* **-e** lynx. **Augen wie ein** ~ **haben** *(col)* to have eyes like a hawk.
**Luchs|augen** *pl (col)* eagle eyes *pl*.
**Lücke** *f* **-n** *(lit, fig)* gap; *(Gesetzes~)* loophole; *(in Versorgung)* break.
**Lücken-:** ~**büßer**, ~**füller** *m* stopgap; l~**haft** *adj* full of gaps; *Versorgung* deficient; *Gesetz, Alibi* full of holes; **sein Wissen ist sehr l~haft** there are great gaps in his knowledge; l~**los** *adj* complete; *Kenntnisse* perfect; *Versorgung, Überlieferung* unbroken.
**lud** *pret of* **laden¹, laden²**.
**Luder** *nt* **-** *(col)* minx. **armes/dummes** ~ poor/stupid creature.
**Luft** *f* **(a)** air *no pl*. **im Zimmer ist schlechte** ~ the air is stuffy in the room; **dicke** ~ *(col)* a bad atmosphere; **(frische)** ~ **schnappen** *(col)* to get some fresh air; **die** ~ **ist rein** *(col)* the coast is clear; **aus der** ~ from the air; **jdn an die (frische)** ~ **setzen** *(col)* to show sb the door; **in die** ~ **fliegen** *(col)* to explode; **etw in die** ~ **jagen** *(col)* to blow sth up; **leicht in die** ~ **gehen** *(fig)* to be quick to blow one's top *(col)*; **es liegt etwas in der** ~ there's something in the air; **in die** ~ **gucken** to stare into space; **jdn/etw in der** ~ **zerreißen** *(col)* to tear sb/sth to pieces; **das kann sich doch nicht in** ~ **aufgelöst haben** it can't have vanished into thin air; **die Behauptung ist aus der** ~ **gegriffen** this statement is pure invention; **vor Freude in die** ~ **springen** to jump for joy; **von** ~ **und Liebe leben** to live on love; **er ist** ~ **für mich** I'm not speaking to him.
  **(b)** *(Atem~)* breath. **der Kragen schnürt mir die** ~ **ab** this collar is choking me; **nach** ~ **schnappen** to gasp for breath; **die** ~ **anhalten** *(lit)* to hold one's breath; **nun halt mal die** ~ **an!** *(col) (rede nicht)* hold your tongue!; *(übertreibe nicht)* come off it! *(col)*; **keine** ~ **mehr kriegen** not to be able to breathe; ~ **holen** to catch one's breath; **tief** ~ **holen** *(lit, fig)* to

take a deep breath; **mir blieb vor Schreck die** ~ **weg** the shock took my breath away; **wieder** ~ **bekommen** *(nach Sport etc)* to get one's breath back; *(fig)* to get a chance to catch one's breath; **seinem Herzen** ~ **machen** to get everything off one's chest; **seinem Zorn** *etc* ~ **machen** to give vent to one's anger *etc*.
  **(c)** *(fig: Spielraum)* space, room.
**Luft-:** ~**abwehr** *f (Mil)* anti-aircraft defence *(Brit)* or defense *(US)*; ~**angriff** *m* airraid *(auf +acc* on); ~**aufnahme** *f* aerial photograph; ~**ballon** *m* balloon; ~**belastung** *f no pl* air pollution; ~**bild** *nt* aerial photograph; ~**blase** *f* air bubble; ~**brücke** *f* airlift.
**Lüftchen** *nt* breeze.
**Luft-:** l~**dicht** *adj* airtight *no adv;* **die Ware ist** l~**dicht verpackt** the article is in airtight packaging; ~**druck** *m* air pressure; l~**durchlässig** *adj* pervious to air.
**lüften 1** *vt* **(a)** to air. **(b)** *Schleier* to raise. **2** *vi (Luft hereinlassen)* to let some air in.
**Lüfter** *m* **-** fan.
**Luft-:** ~**fahrt** *f* aviation *no art;* ~**fahrtgesellschaft** *f* airline (company); ~**fahrzeug** *nt* aircraft; ~**feuchtigkeit** *f* humidity; ~**fracht** *f* air freight; l~**gekühlt** *adj* air-cooled; l~**getrocknet** *adj* airdried; ~**gewehr** *nt* air rifle; ~**herrschaft** *f* air supremacy; ~**hoheit** *f* air sovereignty.
**luftig** *adj Zimmer* airy; *Kleidung* light.
**Luft-:** ~**kampf** *m* air battle; *(Duell)* dogfight; ~**kissen** *nt* air cushion; ~**kissenboot**, ~**kissenfahrzeug** *nt* hovercraft; ~**krieg** *m* aerial warfare; ~**kühlung** *f* air-cooling; ~**kurort** *m* health resort; ~**landetruppe** *f* airborne troops *pl;* l~**leer** *adj (völlig)* l~**leer sein** to be a vacuum; l~**leerer Raum** vacuum; ~**linie** *f* 200 km ~**linie** 125 miles as the crow flies; ~**loch** *nt* airhole; *(Aviat)* air pocket; ~**matratze** *f* airbed; ~**pirat** *m* hijacker; ~**post** *f* airmail; **mit** ~**post** by airmail; ~**pumpe** *f (für Fahrrad)* (bicycle) pump; ~**raum** *m* airspace; ~**reinhaltung** *f* prevention of air pollution; ~**röhre** *f (Anat)* windpipe; ~**sack** *m (Aut)* air bag; ~**schacht** *m* ventilation shaft; ~**schicht** *f (Met)* layer of air; ~**schiff** *nt* airship; ~**schiffahrt** *f* aeronautics *sing;* ~**schlacht** *f* air battle; ~**schlange** *f* (paper) streamer; ~**schloß** *nt (fig)* castle in the air; ~**schneise** *f* air lane.
**Luftschutz** *m* anti-aircraft defence *(Brit)* or defense *(US)*.
**Luftschutz-:** ~**bunker**, ~**keller** *m* air-raid shelter; ~**übung** *f* air-raid drill.
**Luft-:** ~**spiegelung** *f* mirage; ~**sprung** *m* jump in the air; **vor Freude einen** ~**sprung machen** to jump for joy; ~**straße** *f* air route; ~**streitkräfte** *pl* air force *sing;* ~**strom** *m* stream of air; ~**strömung** *f* current of air; ~**stützpunkt** *m* airbase; ~**temperatur** *f* air temperature.
**Lüftung** *f* airing; *(ständig, systematisch)* ventilation.
**Luft-:** ~**unterstützung** *f (Mil)* air support *or* cover; ~**veränderung** *f* change of air; ~**verkehr** *m* air traffic; ~**verschmutzung** *f* air pollution; ~**versorgung** *f* air supplies *pl;* ~**verteidigung** *f* air defence *(Brit)* or defense *(US)*; ~**waffe** *f (Mil)* air force; ~**waffenstützpunkt** *m* air force base; ~**weg** *m* **etw auf dem** ~**weg befördern** to transport sth by air; ~**widerstand** *m* air resistance; ~**zufuhr** *f* air supply; ~**zug** *m* (mild) breeze; *(in Gebäude)* draught *(Brit)*, draft *(US)*.
**Lug** *m:* ~ **und Trug** lies *pl* (and deception).
**Lüge** *f* **-n** lie. **das ist alles** ~ that's all lies; **jdn/etw** ~**n strafen** to give the lie to sb/sth.

**lügen** *pret* **log,** *ptp* **gelogen** *vi* to lie. **ich müßte ~, wenn ...** I would be lying if ...; **das ist gelogen!** *(col)* that's a lie!

**Lügen-:** **~detektor** *m* lie detector; **~geschichte** *f* pack of lies; **~märchen** *nt* tall story; **~maul** *nt* *(pej col)* liar; **~propaganda** *f* propagandist lies *pl.*

**Lügner(in** *f)* *m* - liar.

**lügnerisch** *adj Mensch* lying *attr,* untruthful.

**Lukas** *m* Luke.

**Luke** *f* **-n** hatch; *(Dach~)* skylight.

**lukrativ** *adj* lucrative.

**Lulatsch** *m* **-(es), -e** *(hum col)* **langer ~** beanpole *(col).*

**Lümmel** *m* - *(pej)* lout, oaf.

**lümmelhaft** *adj (pej)* ill-mannered.

**lümmeln** *vr (col)* to sprawl; *(sich hin~)* to flop down.

**Lump** *m (wk)* **-en, -en** *(pej)* rogue.

**lumpen** *vt (col)* **er ließ sich nicht ~** he was very generous.

**Lumpen** *m* - rag.

**Lumpen-:** **~gesindel, ~pack** *nt (pej)* rabble *pl (pej);* **~sammler** *m* rag-and-bone man.

**lumpig** *adj* **(a)** *Gesinnung, Tat* shabby, mean. **(b)** **~e 10 Mark** a measly 10 marks *(col).*

**Lunge** *f* **-n** lung. **(auf) ~ rauchen** to inhale; **sich** *(dat)* **die ~ aus dem Hals schreien** *(col)* to yell till one is blue in the face *(col).*

**Lungen-:** **~embolie** *f* pulmonary embolism *(spec);* **~entzündung** *f* pneumonia; **~flügel** *m* lung; **l~krank** *adj* suffering from a lung disease; **~krankheit** *f* lung disease; **~krebs** *m* lung cancer; **~zug** *m* inhalation; **einen ~zug machen** to inhale.

**Lunte** *f* **-n** **~ riechen** *(Verdacht schöpfen)* to smell a rat *(col);* *(Gefahr wittern)* to sense danger.

**Lupe** *f* **-n** magnifying glass. **solche Leute kannst du mit der ~ suchen** people like that are few and far between; **jdn/etw unter die ~ nehmen** *(col)* to take a close look at sb/sth, to investigate sb/sth.

**lupenrein** *adj (lit) Edelstein* flawless; *(fig) Gentleman, Intellektueller* through and through *pred.*

**Lupine** *f* lupin.

**Lurch** *m* **-e** amphibian.

**Lusche** *f* **-n** *(Cards)* low card; *(fig col: Versager)* dead loss *(col).*

**Lust** *f* **-ë (a)** *no pl (Freude)* pleasure, joy. **er hat die ~ daran verloren** he has lost all interest in it; **da kann einem alle ~ vergehen** it puts you off; **jdm die ~ an etw** *(dat)* **nehmen** to take all the fun out of sth for sb. **(b)** *no pl (Neigung)* inclination. **zu etw ~ haben** to feel like sth; **ich habe keine ~ zu arbeiten** I don't feel like working; **ich habe jetzt keine ~** I'm not in the mood just now; **ich hätte ~ dazu** I'd like to; **hast du ~?** how about it?; **auf etw** *(acc)* **~ haben** to fancy sth; **er kann bleiben, so lange er ~ hat** he can stay as long as he likes. **(c)** *(sinnliche Begierde)* desire; *(sexuell auch)* lust *(usu pej).* **~ haben** to feel desire.

**Lüster** *m* - **(a)** *(Leuchter)* chandelier. **(b)** *(Stoff, Glanzüberzug)* lustre *(Brit),* luster *(US).*

**lüstern** *adj* lecherous.

**Lüsternheit** *f* lechery, lecherousness.

**Lust-:** **~gefühl** *nt* feeling of pleasure; **~gewinn** *m* pleasure.

**lustig** *adj Leute, Abend* cheerful. **die Party war sehr ~** the party was great fun; **er ist ein sehr ~er Typ** he's great fun; **so lange du ~ bist** *(col)* as long as you like; **es wurde ~** things got quite merry; **das kann ja ~ werden!** *(iro)* that's going to be fun *(iro);* **sich über jdn/etw ~ machen** to make fun of sb/sth.

**Lüstling** *m* lecher.

**Lust-:** **l~los** *adj* unenthusiastic; *(Fin) Börse* slack; **~molch** *m (hum col)* sex maniac *(col);* **~mord** *m* sex murder; **~objekt** *nt* sex object; **~prinzip** *nt (Psych)* pleasure principle; **~schloß** *nt* summer residence; **~spiel** *nt* comedy; **l~voll 1** *adj* full of relish; **2** *adv* with relish; **l~wandeln** *vi insep aux* sein *sein or haben (liter)* to (take a) stroll.

**Lutheraner(in** *f)* *m* - Lutheran.

**lutherisch** *adj* Lutheran.

**lutschen** *vti* to suck *(an etw (dat)* sth).

**Lutscher** *m* - lollipop.

**Lüttich** *nt* Liège.

**Luv** [lu:f] *f no pl (Naut)* windward.

**Luxemburg** *nt* Luxembourg.

**Luxemburger(in** *f)* *m* - Luxembourger.

**luxemburgisch** *adj* Luxembourgian.

**luxuriös** *adj* luxurious. **ein ~es Leben** a life of luxury.

**Luxus** *m no pl* luxury; *(pej: Verschwendung)* extravagance. **im ~ leben** to live in luxury.

**Luxus-** *in cpds* luxury; **~ausführung** *f* de luxe model; **~dampfer** *m* luxury liner; **~limousine** *f* limousine; **~restaurant** *nt* first-class restaurant.

**Luzern** *nt* Lucerne.

**LW** = **Langwelle** LW.

**Lycra** ® ['laikra] *nt* **-(s)** Lycra ®.

**Lymphdrüse** *f* lymph gland.

**Lymphe** ['lymfə] *f* **-n** lymph.

**Lymphknoten** *m* lymph node *or* gland.

**lynchen** ['lynçn, 'linçn] *vt (lit)* to lynch; *(fig)* to kill.

**Lynch-** ['lynç-]: **~justiz** *f* lynch law; **~mord** *m* lynching.

**Lyrik** *f no pl* lyric poetry *or* verse.

**Lyriker(in** *f)* *m* - lyric poet, lyricist.

**lyrisch** *adj (lit, fig)* lyrical; *Dichtung, Dichter* lyric.

# M

**M, m** [ɛm] *nt* -, - **M, m. M wie Martha** ≃ M for Mary, M for Mike *(US)*.

**m = Meter** *m*.

**Maat** *m* -e *or* -en *(Naut)* (ship's) mate.

**Mach|art** *f* make; *(Muster)* design; *(lit, fig: Stil)* style.

**machbar** *adj* feasible, possible.

**Mache** *f no pl (col)* **reine ~ sein** to be (a) sham; **etw in der ~ haben** *(col)* to be working on sth; **in der ~ sein** *(col)* to be in the making; **jdn in der ~ haben** *(col)* to be having a go at sb *(col)*; *(verprügeln)* to be working sb over *(col)*.

**machen 1** *vt* **(a)** to do; *(herstellen, bilden, formen, zubereiten)* to make. **was ~ Sie (beruflich)?** what do you do for a living?; **was habe ich nur falsch gemacht?** what have I done wrong?; **gut, wird gemacht** right, I'll get that done *or* will be done *(col)*; **das ist zu/nicht zu ~** that can/can't be done; **(da ist) nichts zu ~** *(geht nicht)* (there's) nothing to be done; *(kommt nicht in Frage)* nothing doing; **wie man's macht, ist's verkehrt** whatever you do it's bound to be wrong; **was machst du da?** what are you doing (there)?; **was machst du denn hier?** what (on earth) are you doing here?; **ich muß noch so viel ~** I still have so much to do; **ich kann da auch nichts ~** I can't do anything about it either; **so etwas macht man nicht** that sort of thing just isn't done; **wie ~ Sie das nur?** how do you do it?; **sich/jdm etw ~ lassen** to have sth made for oneself/sb; **Bilder** *or* **Fotos ~** to take photos; **er ist für den Beruf wie gemacht** he's made for the job; **Bier wird aus Gerste gemacht** beer is made from barley; **aus Holz gemacht** made of wood; **das Essen ~** to get the meal; *siehe* **gemacht.**

**(b)** *(verursachen)* Schwierigkeiten, Arbeit to make *(jdm for sb)*; Mühe, Schmerzen to cause *(jdm for sb)*. **jdm Angst/Freude ~** to make sb afraid/happy; **jdm Kopfschmerzen ~** to give sb a headache; **das macht Hunger** that makes you hungry.

**(c)** *(bewirken)* to do; *(+infin)* to make. **das macht die Kälte** it's the cold that does that; **jdn lachen/etw vergessen ~** to make sb laugh/forget sth; **~, daß etw geschieht** to make sth happen; **(viel) von sich reden ~** to be much talked about; **mach, daß du hier verschwindest!** (you just) get out of here!

**(d)** *(veranstalten)* Fest to have, to give; *(teilnehmen an)* Lehrgang to do.

**(e)** *(ausmachen, schaden)* to matter. **macht nichts!** (it) doesn't matter; **macht das was?** does that matter?; **das macht mir doch nichts!** that doesn't matter to me; **die Kälte macht mir nichts** I don't mind the cold; **die Kälte macht dem Motor nichts** the cold doesn't harm the engine.

**(f)** *(erzielen)* Punkte, Preis to get, to win; *Doktor, Diplom etc* to do; *Gewinn, Verlust* to make.

**(g)** *(col: ergeben)* to make; *(kosten, Math)* to be. **drei und fünf macht acht** three and five is *or* are eight; **100 cm ~ einen Meter** there are 100 cm in a metre; **wieviel macht das (alles zusammen)?** how much does that come to *or* what does that make altogether?

**(h)** **was macht die Arbeit?** how's the work going?; **was macht dein Bruder?** how is your brother doing?; **mach's kurz!** make it brief; **mach's gut!** take care, all the best; **er wird's nicht mehr lange ~** *(col)* he won't last long; **mit mir kann man's ja ~!** *(col)* the things I put up with! *(col)*; **das läßt er nicht mit sich ~** he won't stand for that; **jdn unglücklich ~** to make sb unhappy; **etw sauber/schmutzig ~** to get sth clean/dirty; **jdn alt/jung ~** *(aussehen lassen)* to make sb look old/young; **mach's dir doch bequem** make yourself comfortable; **mach es ihm nicht noch schwerer** don't make it harder for him; **er macht es sich** *(dat)* **nicht leicht** he doesn't make it easy for himself; **etw aus jdm/etw ~** *(darstellen, interpretieren als)* to make sth of sb/sth; *(verwandeln in)* to make sth (out) of sb/out of sth, to make sb/sth into sth; **jdn zu etw** *(dat)* **~** *(verwandeln in)* to turn sb into sth; *(Rolle, Image, Status geben)* to make sb sth; **jdm etw zur Hölle/Qual** *etc* **~** to make sth hell/a misery *etc* for sb; **jdn zu seiner Frau ~** to make sb one's wife; **Halt ~** to call a halt; **das Geschirr ~** to do the dishes; **eine Prüfung ~** to take an exam; **ein Spiel ~** to play a game; **das Auto/den Kühlschrank ~ lassen** to have the car/refrigerator seen to; **er macht mir die Haare/Zähne** *(col)* he does my hair/teeth; **das Bett ~** to make the bed; **den Ghostwriter für jdn ~** *(col)* to act as sb's ghostwriter; **groß/klein ~** *(col: Notdurft)* to do a big/little job *(baby-talk)*.

**2** *vi* **(a)** **mach schon/schneller!** *(col)* get a move on! *(col)*, hurry up; **ich mach ja schon!** *(col)* I am hurrying; **sie machten, daß sie nach Hause kamen** they hurried home; **er macht in Politik/Malerei** *(col)* he's in politics/doing some painting; **jetzt macht sie auf große Dame** *(col)* she's playing the lady now; **sie macht auf gebildet** *(col)* she's doing her cultured bit *(col)*; **jetzt macht er auf beleidigt** *(col)* now he's playing the injured innocent; **er macht auf Schau** *(col)* he's out for effect *(col)*; **laß ihn nur ~** *(verlaß dich auf ihn)* just leave it to him; **laß mich mal ~** let me do it; *(ich bringe das in Ordnung)* let me see to that; **gut, mache ich** right, I'll do that; **das macht müde** that makes you tired; **das Kleid macht schlank** that dress makes you look slim.

**(b)** *(col: Notdurft verrichten)* to go to the toilet; *(Hund etc)* to do its business *(euph)*. **(sich** *dat***) in die Hosen ~** *(lit, fig)* to wet oneself; **ins Bett ~** to wet the bed.

**3** *vr* **wie macht sich der Garten?** how is the garden coming along?; **er macht sich** he's doing well; **der Schal macht sich sehr hübsch zu dem Kleid** the scarf looks very pretty with that dress; **sich an etw** *(acc)* **~** to get down to sth/doing sth; **sich auf den Weg ~** to get going; **sich verständlich/wichtig ~** to make oneself understood/important; **sich bei jdm beliebt/**

**verhaßt** ~ to make oneself popular with/hated by sb; **sich** *(dat)* **viel aus jdm/etw** ~ to like sb/sth; **sich** *(dat)* **wenig aus jdm/etw** ~ not to be very keen on sb/sth; **mach dir nichts daraus** don't let it bother you; **sich** *(dat)* **einen schönen Abend** ~ to have a nice evening; **sich** *(dat)* **jdn zum Freund** ~ to make sb one's friend; **sich zum Sprecher** ~ to make oneself spokesman.

**Machenschaften** *pl* wheelings and dealings *pl.*

**Macher** *m* - *(col)* doer, man of action.

**Machete** *f* **-n** machete.

**Macho** ['matʃo] *m* **-s** macho type *(col)*.

**Macht** *f* ≠e **(a)** *no pl* power; *(Stärke auch)* might. **die** ~ **der Gewohnheit/des Schicksals** the force of habit/destiny; **alles in unserer** ~ **Stehende** everything in our power; **mit aller** ~ with all one's might; **die** ~ **ergreifen/erringen** to seize/gain power; **an die** ~ **kommen** to come to power; **an der** ~ **sein** to be in power; **die** ~ **übernehmen** to assume power. **(b)** *(Staat)* power. **böse/himmlische** ~e evil forces/heavenly powers.

**Macht-:** ~**anspruch** *m* claim to power; ~**befugnis** *f* power, authority *no pl*; ~**bereich** *m* sphere of influence; ~**ergreifung** *f* seizure of power; ~**gier** *f* lust for power; ~**haber** *m* - ruler; *(pej)* dictator.

**mächtig 1** *adj* **(a)** *(einflußreich)* powerful. **die M~en (dieser Erde)** the wielders of power. **(b)** *(sehr groß)* mighty; *Felsen auch, Körper* massive; *Stimme, Schlag auch* powerful; *Essen* heavy; *(col: enorm) Hunger, Durst* terrific *(col)*, tremendous. ~**e Angst haben** *(col)* to be scared stiff. **(c)** *(liter)* **einer Sprache** *(gen)* ~ **sein** to have a good command of a language. **2** *adv (col: sehr)* terrifically *(col)*, tremendously; *schneien, sich beeilen* like mad *(col)*. **sich** ~ **anstrengen** to make a tremendous effort.

**Mächtigkeit** *f (Größe)* mightiness.

**Macht-:** ~**kampf** power struggle; **m~los** *adj* powerless; *(hilflos)* helpless; ~**losigkeit** *f no pl* powerlessness; helplessness; ~**mißbrauch** *m* misuse of power; ~**politik** *f* power politics *pl*; ~**position** *f* position of power; ~**probe** *f* trial of strength; ~**übernahme** *f* takeover *(durch by)*; ~**verhältnisse** *pl* balance of power *sing*; **m~voll** *adj* powerful; ~**wechsel** *m* changeover of power; ~**wort** *nt* **ein** ~**wort sprechen** to exercise one's authority.

**Machwerk** *nt (pej)* sorry effort. **ein elendes** ~ a pathetic attempt; **das ist ein** ~ **des Teufels** that is the work of the devil.

**Macke** *f* **-n** *(col)* **(a)** *(Tick, Knall)* quirk. **eine** ~ **haben** *(col)* to have a screw loose *(col)*. **(b)** *(Fehler, Schadstelle)* fault.

**Macker** *m* - *(col)* fellow *(col)*, guy *(col)*. **spiel hier nicht den** ~ don't come the tough guy here *(col)*.

**MAD** [ɛm|aː'deː] *m* = **Militärischer Abschirmdienst** ≃ MI5 *(Brit)*, CIA *(US)*.

**Madagaskar** *nt* Madagascar.

**Madagasse** *m (wk)* **-n, -n, Madagassin** *f* Madagascan.

**madagassisch** *adj* Madagascan.

**Mädchen** *nt* girl; *(Tochter auch)* daughter. **ein** ~ **für alles** *(col)* a dogsbody; *(im Haushalt auch)* a maid-of-all-work.

**Mädchen-:** ~**buch** *nt* book for girls; **m~haft** *adj* girlish; *aussehen, sich kleiden* like a girl; ~**handel** *m* white slave trade; ~**klasse** *f* girls' class; ~**kleidung** *f* girls' clothing; ~**name** *m* **(a)** girl's name; **(b)** *(von verheirateter Frau)* maiden name; ~**schule** *f* girls' school.

**Made** *f* **-n** maggot. **wie die** ~ **im Speck leben** *(col)* to live in luxury.

**Mädel** *nt* **-(s)** *(dial)* lass *(dial)*, girl.

**madig** *adj* maggoty; *Obst auch* worm-eaten. **jdm etw** ~ **machen** *(col)* to put sb off sth.

**Madonna** *f, pl* **Madonnen** Madonna.

**Madrid** *nt* Madrid.

**Maf(f)ia** *f no pl* Mafia.

**Magazin** *nt* **-e (a)** *(Lager)* storeroom; *(Bibliotheks~)* stockroom. **(b)** *(am Gewehr)* magazine. **(c)** *(Zeitschrift)* magazine, journal; *(TV, Rad)* magazine programme *(Brit)* or program *(US)*.

**Magd** *f* ≠e *(old)* maid; *(Landarbeiterin)* farm girl.

**Magen** *m* ≠ *or* - stomach. **(die) Liebe geht durch den** ~ *(Prov)* the way to a man's heart is through his stomach *(prov)*; **etw liegt jdm im** ~ *(col)* sth lies heavily on sb's stomach; *(fig)* sth preys on sb's mind; **jdm auf den** ~ **schlagen** *(col)* to upset sb's stomach; *(fig)* to upset sb; **sich** *(dat)* **den** ~ **verderben** to upset one's stomach; **dabei dreht sich mir der** ~ **um** *(col)* it turns my stomach.

**Magen-:** ~**beschwerden** *pl* stomach trouble *sing*; ~**bitter** *m* bitters *pl*; ~**geschwür** *nt* stomach ulcer; ~**knurren** *nt no pl* tummy rumbles *pl (col)*; **m~krank** *adj* **m~krank sein** to have stomach trouble; ~**krebs** *m* cancer of the stomach; ~**leiden** *nt* stomach disorder; ~**säure** *f* gastric acid; ~**schmerzen** *pl* stomach ache *sing*, tummy ache *sing (col)*; ~**verstimmung** *f* stomach upset.

**mager** *adj* **(a)** *(fettarm) Fleisch* lean; *Kost* low-fat. ~ **essen** to be on a low-fat diet. **(b)** *(dünn)* thin, skinny *(col)*; *(abgemagert)* emaciated; *(Typ) Druck* roman. **(c)** *Boden, Felder* poor, infertile. **(d)** *(dürftig)* meagre *(Brit)*, meager *(US)*; *Ergebnis* poor. **die sieben** ~**en Jahre** the seven lean years.

**Mager-:** ~**käse** *m* low-fat cheese; ~**milch** *f* skimmed milk; ~**motor** *m (Aut)* lean-burn engine; ~**quark** *m* low-fat curd cheese; ~**sucht** *f (Med)* anorexia.

**Magie** *f no pl* magic.

**Magier** ['maːgiɐ] *m* - magician.

**magisch** *adj* magic(al); *Quadrat, (Tech) Auge* magic. **mit** ~**er Gewalt** with magical force; *(fig)* as if by magic.

**Magister** *m* - *(Univ)* M.A., Master of Arts.

**Magistrat** *m* **-e** municipal authorities *pl.*

**Magnat** *m (wk)* **-en, en** magnate *(auch Hist)*.

**Magnet** *m* **-s** *or* **-en, -e(n)** *(lit, fig)* magnet.

**Magnet-** *in cpds* magnetic; ~**bahn** *f* magnetic railway; ~**band** *nt* magnetic tape; ~**feld** *nt* magnetic field.

**magnetisch** *adj (lit, fig)* magnetic.

**magnetisieren\*** *vt Metall* to magnetize.

**Magnetismus** *m no pl* magnetism.

**Magnet-:** ~**karte** *f* magnetic card; *(Bank etc auch)* cashpoint card; ~**nadel** *f* magnetic needle; ~**platte** *f* magnetic disk; ~**schwebebahn** *f* magnetic railway; ~**streifen** *m* magnetic strip; ~**zündung** *f (Aut)* magneto ignition.

**Magnolie** [mag'noːliə] *f* magnolia.

**Mahagoni** *nt no pl* mahogany.

**Maharadscha** *m* **-s** maharajah.

**Mähdrescher** *m* combine (harvester).

**mähen**[1] **1** *vt Gras* to cut; *Getreide auch* to reap; *Rasen* to mow. **2** *vi* to reap; *(Rasen~)* to mow.

**mähen**[2] *vi (Schaf)* to bleat.

**Mahl** *nt* **-e** *(geh)* meal, repast *(form)*; *(Gast~)* banquet.

**mahlen** *pret* **mahlte**, *ptp* **gemahlen** *vti* to grind.

**Mahlzeit** *f* meal. ~**!** *(col) greeting used around mealtimes*; *(guten Appetit)* enjoy your meal; **(prost)** ~**!** *(iro col)* that's just great *(col)* or swell *(esp US col)*.

**Mähmaschine** f mower; *(Getreide~)* reaper.
**Mahn-**: ~**bescheid**, ~**brief** m reminder (letter).
**Mähne** f -n *(lit, fig)* mane.
**mahnen 1** vt (a) *(erinnern)* to remind *(wegen* of*)*; *(warnend)* to admonish *(wegen* on account of*)*. **gemahnt werden** *(Schuldner)* to receive a reminder. (b) *(auffordern)* **jdn zur Eile/Geduld** *etc* ~ to urge sb to hurry/be patient *etc*. **2** vi (a) *(wegen Schulden etc)* to send a reminder. (b) **zur Eile/Geduld** ~ to urge haste/patience; **der Lehrer mahnte zur Ruhe** the teacher called for quiet.
**Mahn-**: ~**gebühr** f reminder fee; ~**mal** nt memorial; ~**schreiben** nt reminder (letter).
**Mahnung** f (a) *(Ermahnung)* exhortation; *(warnend)* admonition. (b) *(Mahnbrief)* reminder.
**Mai** m -e May. **der Erste** ~ May Day; *siehe* **März.**
**Mai-** *in cpds* May; *(Pol)* May Day; ~**baum** m maypole; ~**bowle** f white wine punch *(flavoured with woodruff)*; ~**feier** f May Day celebrations *pl*; ~**feiertag** m *(form)* May Day *no art*; ~**glöckchen** nt lily of the valley; ~**käfer** m cockchafer.
**Mailand** nt Milan.
**Mais** m no pl maize, (Indian) corn *(esp US)*.
**Mais-**: ~**kolben** m corn cob; *(Gericht)* corn on the cob; ~**korn** nt grain of maize or corn *(esp US)*; ~**mehl** nt maize or corn *(esp US)* meal; ~**stärke** f cornflour, cornstarch *(US)*.
**Majestät** f (a) *(Titel)* Majesty. **Seine/Ihre/Eure** ~ His/Her/Your Majesty. (b) *(liter)* majesty.
**majestätisch** adj majestic.
**Majestätsbeleidigung** f lèse-majesté.
**Major** m -e *(Mil)* major; *(in Luftwaffe)* squadron leader *(Brit)*, major *(US)*.
**Majoran** m -e marjoram.
**majorisieren*** vt to outvote.
**Majorität** f majority.
**MAK** = **maximale Arbeitsplatzkonzentration** *maximum permitted pollution level at work.*
**makaber** adj macabre; *Witz, Geschichte* sick.
**Makel** m - (a) *(Schandfleck)* stigma. **ohne** ~ without a stain on one's reputation; **mit einem** ~ **behaftet sein** *(liter)* to bear a stigma. (b) *(Fehler)* blemish; *(bei Waren)* defect. **ohne** ~ flawless.
**Mäkelei** f carping no pl, fault-finding no pl *(an +dat, über +acc* about, over*)*.
**makellos** adj *Reinheit, Frische* spotless; *Charakter* unimpeachable; *Figur, Haut* flawless; *Kleidung* immaculate; *Alibi* watertight.
**Makellosigkeit** f *(Reinheit)* spotlessness; *(von Haut)* flawlessness; *(von Kleidung)* immaculateness.
**mäkeln** vi *(col: nörgeln)* to carp *(an +dat* at*)*.
**Make-up** [meːkˈʔap] nt -s make-up; *(flüssig)* foundation.
**Makkaroni** pl macaroni *sing.*
**Makler(in** f*)* m - broker; *(Grundstücks~)* estate agent *(Brit)*, realtor *(US)*.
**Maklergebühr** f broker's commission, brokerage.
**Makrele** f -n mackerel.
**Makro** nt -s *(Comp)* macro.
**Makro-** *in cpds* macro-; ~**befehl** m *(Comp)* macro command; **m~biotisch** adj macrobiotic; ~**kosmos** m macrocosm.
**Makrone** f -n macaroon.
**Makulatur** f *(Typ)* wastepaper; *(fig pej)* rubbish.
**Mal¹** nt -e (a) *(lit, fig: Fleck)* mark. (b) *pl auch* ⸚**er** *(liter: Ehren~)* memorial, monument. (c) *(Schlagball)* base.
**Mal²** nt -e time. **(nur) dieses eine** ~ *(just)* this once; **das eine oder andere** ~ now and then *or* again; **kein einziges** ~ not once; **wenn du bloß ein einziges** ~ **auf mich hören würdest** if you would only listen to

me for once; **ein für alle** ~**e** once and for all; **das vorige** ~ the time before; **ein letztes** ~ *(liter)* one last time; **als ich das letzte** ~ **in London war** (the) last time I was in London; **beim ersten/letzten** ~ the first/last time; **zum ersten/letzten** ~ for the first/last time; **von** ~ **zu** ~ each *or* every time; **für dieses** ~ for the time being; **mit einem** ~**e** all of a sudden.
**mal¹** adv *(Math)* times; *(bei Flächenangaben)* by.
**mal²** adv *(col) siehe* **einmal.**
**Malaie** [maˈlaiə] m *(wk)* -n, -n, **Malaiin** [maˈlaiɪn] f Malayan, Malay.
**malaiisch** [maˈlaiʃ] adj Malayan, Malay *attr.*
**Malaiisch(e)** [maˈlaiʃ(ə)] nt Malay; *siehe* **Deutsch(e).**
**Malaria** f no pl malaria.
**Malawi** nt Malawi.
**Malawier(in** f*)* [-iɐ, -iərɪn] m - Malawian.
**malawisch** adj Malawian, Malawi *attr.*
**Malaya** [maˈlaia] nt Malaya.
**Malaysia** [maˈlaizia] nt Malaysia.
**Malaysier(in** f*)* [maˈlaiziɐ, -iərɪn] m - Malaysian.
**malaysisch** [maˈlaizɪʃ] adj Malaysian.
**Malbuch** nt colouring *(Brit)* or coloring *(US)* book.
**Malediven** [maleˈdiːvn] pl **die** ~ the Maldive Islands.
**malen** vti to paint; *(col: zeichnen)* to draw. **sich** ~ **lassen** to have one's portrait painted; **etw rosig/schwarz** *etc* ~ *(fig)* to paint a rosy/black *etc* picture of sth.
**Maler(in** f*)* m - painter; *(Kunst~ auch)* artist.
**Malerei** f *(no pl: Malkunst)* art; *(Bild)* painting; *(Zeichnung)* drawing.
**malerisch** adj (a) picturesque; *Landschaft auch* scenic. (b) *(bildnerisch)* in painting; *Talent* as a painter.
**Malermeister** m (master) painter.
**Malheur** [maˈløːɐ] nt -s *or* -e mishap. **das ist doch kein** ~! it's not serious.
**Malkasten** m paintbox.
**Mallorca** nt Majorca, Mallorca.
**malnehmen** vti sep irreg to multiply *(mit* by*)*.
**Maloche** f no pl *(col)* graft *(col)*. **du mußt zur** ~ you've got to go to work.
**malochen*** vi *(col)* to graft *(col)*, to sweat away *(col)*.
**Malstift** m crayon.
**Malta** nt Malta.
**Maltechnik** f painting technique.
**Malteser(in** f*)* m - Maltese.
**Malteser-**: ~**-Hilfsdienst** m ≈ St. John's Ambulance Brigade *(Brit)*; ~**kreuz** nt Maltese cross.
**maltesisch** adj Maltese.
**malträtieren*** vt to ill-treat, to maltreat.
**Malve** [ˈmalvə] f -n *(Bot)* mallow.
**Malz** nt no pl malt.
**Malz-**: ~**bier** nt malt beer; ~**bonbon** nt or m malt lozenge; ~**kaffee** m *coffee substitute made from barley malt.*
**Mama, Mami** f -s *(col)* mummy, mommy *(US)*.
**Mammographie** f no pl breast screening, mammography *(spec)*.
**Mammut-** *in cpds (lit, fig)* mammoth; *(lange dauernd)* marathon; ~**baum** m sequoia, giant redwood.
**mampfen** vti *(col)* to munch, to chomp *(col)*.
**man** indef pron (a) you, one; *(ich)* one; *(wir)* we. ~ **kann nie wissen** you *or* one can never tell; **das tut** ~ **nicht** that's not done. (b) *(jemand)* somebody, someone. ~ **hat mir gesagt** ... I was told ...; ~ **hat festgestellt, daß** ... it has been established that ...

**(c)** *(die Leute)* they *pl,* people *pl.* **früher glaubte ~ people used to believe; ~ will die alten Häuser niederreißen** they want to pull down the old houses. **(d)** ~ **nehme ...** take ...

**Management** ['mɛnɪdʒmənt] *nt* **-s** management.

**managen** ['mɛnɪdʒn] *vt* to manage. **ich manage das schon!** *(col)* OK, I can deal with it.

**Manager(in** *f)* ['mɛnɪdʒɐ, -ərɪn] *m* - manager.

**manch** *indef pron* ~ **eine(r)** many a person; ~ **einem kann man nie Vernunft beibringen** some people never learn; ~ **anderer** many another; **~er, der ...** many a person who ...; **~es Schöne** quite a few beautiful things; **(so) ~es** a good many things; **in ~em hat er recht** he's right about some things.

**mancherlei** *adj inv (adjektivisch mit pl n)* various; *(substantivisch)* various things *pl.*

**manchmal** *adv* sometimes.

**Mandant(in** *f) m (Jur)* client.

**Mandarine** *f* mandarin (orange), tangerine.

**Mandat** *nt (Auftrag, Vollmacht)* mandate *(auch Pol)*, authorization *(gen* from*)*; *(Parl: Abgeordnetensitz)* seat. **sein ~ niederlegen** *(Parl)* to resign one's seat.

**Mandats-: ~gebiet** *nt (Hist)* mandate; **~träger** *m* (parliamentary) representative; **~verlust** *m* loss (of a seat).

**Mandel** *f* **-n (a)** almond. **(b)** *(Anat)* tonsil.

**Mandel-: m~äugig** *adj (poet)* almond-eyed; **~baum** *m* almond tree; **~entzündung** *f* tonsillitis; **~operation** *f* tonsillectomy.

**Mandoline** *f* mandolin.

**Manege** [ma'ne:ʒə] *f* **-n** ring, arena.

**Mangel¹** *f* **-n** mangle; *(Heiß~)* rotary iron. **jdn durch die ~ drehen** *(fig col)* to put sb through it *(col)*; *Prüfling etc auch* to put sb through the mill.

**Mangel²** *m* **=̈ (a)** *(Fehler)* fault; *(bei Maschine auch)* defect; *(Charakter~)* flaw. **(b)** *no pl (das Fehlen)* lack *(an +dat* of*)*; *(Knappheit auch)* shortage *(an +dat* of*)*; *(Med auch)* deficiency *(an +dat* of*)*. **aus ~ an** *(+dat)* for lack of; **wegen ~s an Beweisen** for lack of evidence; **es herrscht ~ an etw** *(dat)* there is a shortage of sth.

**Mängelbericht** *m* list of faults.

**Mangel-: ~beruf** *m* understaffed profession; **~erscheinung** *f (Med)* deficiency symptom.

**mangelhaft** *adj (unzulänglich)* poor; *Ausrüstung auch* inadequate; *Informationen, Interesse* insufficient; *(fehlerhaft)* Ware faulty; *(Schulnote auch)* unsatisfactory.

**Mangelkrankheit** *f* deficiency disease.

**mangeln** *vi impers* **es mangelt an etw** *(dat)* there is a lack of sth; *(unzureichend vorhanden auch)* there is a shortage of sth; **es mangelt jdm an etw** *(dat)* sb lacks sth; **~des Verständnis** *etc* a lack of understanding *etc*; **wegen ~der Aufmerksamkeit** through not paying attention.

**mangels** *prep +gen* for lack of.

**Mangelware** *f* scarce commodity. **~ sein** *(fig)* to be a rare thing; *(gute Ärzte, Lehrer etc)* not to grow on trees *(col)*.

**Mango** ['mango] *f* **-s** mango.

**Manie** *f (Med, fig)* mania; *(fig auch)* obsession.

**Manier** *f* **-en (a)** *no pl (Art und Weise)* manner; *(eines Künstlers etc)* style. **in überzeugender ~** in a most convincing manner. **(b) ~en** *pl (Umgangsformen)* manners; **was sind das für ~en** *(col)* that's no way to behave.

**maniert** *adj* affected; *Benehmen auch* mannered.

**manierlich 1** *adj Kind* well-mannered; *Benehmen* good; *Aussehen* respectable. **2** *adv essen* politely; *sich benehmen* properly; *sich kleiden* respectably.

**Manifest** *nt* **-e** *(Pol)* manifesto.

**Maniküre** *f* **-n (a)** *(Handpflege)* manicure. **(b)** *(Handpflegerin)* manicurist.

**maniküren\*** *vt* to manicure.

**Manipulation** *f* manipulation; *(Trick)* manoeuvre *(Brit)*, maneuver *(US)*.

**manipulierbar** *adj* manipulable. **leicht/schwer ~** easily manipulated/difficult to manipulate.

**manipulieren\*** *vt* to manipulate.

**manisch** *adj* manic.

**manisch-depressiv** *adj* manic-depressive.

**Manko** *nt* **-s (a)** *(Comm: Fehlbetrag)* deficit. **~ machen** *(col: bei Verkauf)* to make a loss. **(b)** *(fig: Nachteil)* shortcoming.

**Mann** *m* **=̈er (a)** man. **ein feiner ~** a (perfect) gentleman; **ein ~ aus dem Volk(e)** a man of the people; **der ~ im Mond** the man in the moon; **ein ~ der Wissenschaft** a man of science; **er ist nicht der ~ dafür** he's not the man for that; *(nicht seine Art)* he's not the sort; **wie ein ~** as one man; **etw an den ~ bringen** *(col)* to get rid of sth; **seinen ~ stehen** to hold one's own; **einen kleinen ~ im Ohr haben** *(hum col)* to be crazy *(col)*; **und ein ~, ein Wort, er hat's auch gemacht** and, as good as his word, he did it; **~ für ~** *(allesamt)* every single one; **~ gegen ~** man against man; **pro ~** per head; **ein Gespräch von ~ zu ~** a man-to-man talk.

**(b)** *(Ehe~)* husband. **~ und Frau werden** to become man and wife.

**(c)** *pl* **Leute** *(Besatzungsmitglied)* hand, man; *(Sport, Cards)* player, man. **20 ~** 20 hands *or* men; **mit ~ und Maus untergehen** to go down with all hands; *(Passagierschiff)* to go down with no survivors.

**(d)** *(col: als Interjektion)* (my) God *(col)*; *(bewundernd, erstaunt auch)* hey. **mach schnell, ~!** hurry up, man!; **~, oh ~!** oh boy! *(col)*.

**Männchen** *nt dim of* **Mann (a)** little man; *(Zwerg)* man(n)ikin. **~ malen** to draw (little) matchstick men, ≈ to doodle. **(b)** *(Biol)* male; *(Vogel~ auch)* cock. **(c)** ~ **machen** *(Hund)* to (sit up and) beg.

**Mannequin** ['manəkɛ̃] *nt* **-s** (fashion) model.

**Männer** *pl of* **Mann**.

**Männer-: ~bekanntschaft** *f usu pl* man friend; **~beruf** *m* male profession; **~chor** *m* male-voice choir; **~fang** *m (hum)* **auf ~fang ausgehen** to go looking for a man/for men; **~gesangverein** *m* male choral society; **~gesellschaft** *f (Sociol)* male-dominated society; **m~mordend** *adj (hum)* man-eating; **~sache** *f (Angelegenheit)* man's business; *(Arbeit)* man's job; **Fußball war früher ~sache** football used to be a male preserve; **~stimme** *f* man's voice; *(Mus)* male voice.

**Mannes-: ~alter** *nt* manhood *no art*; **im besten ~alter sein** to be in the prime of (one's) life; **~kraft** *f (dated, hum)* virility.

**mannhaft** *adj* manly *no adv*; *(tapfer)* manful, valiant; *(entschlossen)* resolute; *Widerstand* stout.

**mannigfach** *adj attr* manifold, multifarious.

**mannigfaltig** *adj (geh)* diverse, varied.

**Mannigfaltigkeit** *f* diversity, variety.

**männlich** *adj* **(a)** male; *Wort* masculine. **(b)** *(fig: mannhaft)* Mut, Entschluß manly; *Frau* mannish.

**Männlichkeit** *f (fig)* masculinity, manliness; *(von Frau)* mannishness.

**Mannsbild** *nt (dated pej)* fellow.

**Mannschaft** *f (Sport, fig)* team; *(Naut, Aviat)* crew. **~(en)** *(Mil)* men *pl.*

**Mannschafts-** *in cpds (Sport)* team; **~aufstellung** *f* team line-up; *(das Aufstellen)* selection of the team; **~geist** *m* team spirit; **~raum** *m (Sport)* team quarters *pl*; *(Naut)* crew's quarters *pl.*

**manns-**: ~**hoch** adj as high as a man; **der Schnee liegt** ~**hoch** the snow is six feet deep; ~**toll** adj nympho (col).

**Mannweib** nt (pej) mannish woman.

**Manometer** nt (Tech) pressure gauge. ~! (col) wow! (col).

**Manöver** [ma'nøːvɐ] nt - (lit, fig) manoeuvre (Brit), maneuver (US).

**Manöverkritik** f (fig) inquest, post-mortem (fig).

**manövrieren*** [manøˈvriːrən] vti (lit, fig) to manoeuvre (Brit), to maneuver (US).

**Manövrier-** [manøˈvriːɐ]: **m**~**fähig** adj manoeuvrable (Brit), maneuverable (US); ~**fähigkeit** f manoeuvrability (Brit), maneuverability (US); **m**~**unfähig** adj disabled.

**Mansarde** f -n garret; (Boden) attic.

**Manschette** f (Ärmelaufschlag) cuff. ~**n haben** (col) to be scared silly (col).

**Manschettenknopf** m cufflink.

**Mantel** m ⸚ (a) coat; (fig) cloak, mantle. (b) (Tech) casing; (Rohr~) jacket.

**Mantel-** in cpds (Tex) coat; ~**stoff** m coat fabric; ~**tarifvertrag** m general agreement on conditions of employment.

**manuell** adj Arbeit manual. **etw** ~ **bedienen** to operate sth manually.

**Manuskript** nt -e manuscript; (Rad, Film, TV) script.

**maoistisch** adj Maoist.

**Maori** m -(s), -(s) Maori.

**Mappe** f -n (Aktenhefter) folder, file; (Aktentasche) briefcase; (Schul~) (school) bag; (Feder~, Bleistift~) pencil case.

**Maracuja** f -s passion fruit.

**Marathon¹** m marathon.

**Marathon²** nt (fig) marathon.

**Marathon-** in cpds marathon; ~**lauf** m marathon; ~**läufer** m marathon runner.

**Märchen** nt - fairy story; (col) tall story.

**Märchen-** in cpds fairytale; ~**buch** nt book of fairytales; ~**erzähler** m teller of fairytales; (fig) storyteller; **m**~**haft** adj fairytale attr; (fig) fabulous; ~**land** nt fairyland; ~**prinz** m Prince Charming.

**Marder** m - marten.

**Margarine** f margarine.

**Marge** ['marʒə] f -n (Comm) margin.

**Margerite** f -n daisy, marguerite.

**Maria** f - Mary. **die Mutter** ~ the Virgin Mary.

**Marien-** [-iːən]: ~**bild** nt picture of the Virgin Mary; ~**käfer** m ladybird.

**Marihuana** [mariˈhuaːna] nt no pl marijuana.

**Marinade** f (Cook) marinade; (Soße) mayonnaise-based sauce.

**Marine** f navy.

**Marine-** in cpds naval; **m**~**blau** adj navy blue; ~**soldat** m marine.

**marinieren*** vt Fisch, Fleisch to marinate.

**Marionette** f marionette, puppet; (fig) puppet.

**Marionetten-** in cpds puppet; ~**spieler** m puppeteer; ~**theater** nt puppet theatre (Brit) or theater (US).

**Mark¹** nt no pl (Knochen~) marrow; (Bot: Gewebe~) medulla, pith. **bis ins** ~ (fig) to the core; **jdn bis ins** ~ **treffen** (fig) to cut sb to the quick; **es geht mir durch** ~ **und Bein** (col) it goes right through me; **kein** ~ **in den Knochen haben** (fig) to have no backbone.

**Mark²** f - or (hum) ⸚**er** mark. **Deutsche** ~ German mark, deutschmark; **vier** ~ **zwanzig** four marks

twenty (pfennigs); **mit jeder** ~ **rechnen müssen** to have to count every penny.

**markant** adj (ausgeprägt) clear-cut; Schriftzüge clearly defined.

**Marke** f -n (a) (bei Lebens- und Genußmitteln) brand; (bei Industriegütern) make. **du bist (vielleicht) eine** ~! (col) you're a fine one (col). (b) (Brief~) stamp; (Essen~) voucher; (Rabatt~) (trading) stamp; (Lebensmittel~) coupon. (c) (Erkennungs~) disc, tag; (Garderoben~) ticket, check (US); (Polizei~) badge; (Spiel~) chip; (Pfand~ etc) token.

**Marken-**: ~**artikel** m proprietary article; ~**butter** f best quality butter; ~**erzeugnis**, ~**fabrikat** nt proprietary article; ~**name** m brand name; ~**treue** f brand loyalty; ~**ware** f branded goods pl; ~**zeichen** nt trademark.

**Marketing** nt no pl marketing.

**markieren*** vt (lit, fig, Sport) to mark; (col: vortäuschen) to play. **den starken Mann** ~ (col) to come the strong man (col).

**Markierstift** m marker pen.

**Markierung** f marking; (Zeichen) mark.

**markig** adj (kraftvoll) vigorous, pithy.

**Markise** f -n awning.

**Mark-**: ~**knochen** m (Cook) marrowbone; ~**stein** m (lit, fig) milestone; ~**stück** nt (one-)mark piece.

**Markt** m ⸚**e** (a) market; (~platz) marketplace; (Jahr~) fair. ~ **abhalten** to hold a market; **dienstags ist** ~ there is a market every Tuesday. (b) (Comm) market; (Warenverkehr) trade. **auf dem** ~ on the market; **auf den** ~ **bringen** to put on the market.

**Markt-** in cpds market; ~**analyse** f market analysis; ~**anteil** m market share, share of the market; **m**~**beherrschend** adj **m**~**beherrschend sein** to dominate the market; ~**bude** f market stall; ~**fähigkeit** f marketability; ~**flecken** m small market town; ~**forschung** f market research; ~**frau** f market woman; ~**führer** m market leader; **m**~**gerecht** adj geared to market requirements; ~**halle** f covered market; ~**lage** f state of the market; ~**lücke** f gap in the market; ~**platz** m marketplace; **am/auf dem** ~**platz** on/in the marketplace; ~**preis** m market price; ~**schreier** m market crier; **m**~**schreierisch** adj loud and vociferous; (fig) blatant; ~**stand** m market stall; ~**studie** f market survey; ~**tag** m market day; ~**weib** nt (pej) market woman; (fig) fish-wife; ~**wert** m market value; ~**wirtschaft** f market economy; **m**~**wirtschaftlich** adj attr free enterprise.

**Markus** m ≈ Mark.

**Marmelade** f jam; (Orangen~) marmalade.

**Marmeladenglas** nt jam-jar.

**Marmor** m -e marble.

**marmorieren*** vt to marble. **marmoriert** marbled.

**Marmorkuchen** m marble cake.

**marmorn** adj marble.

**Marokkaner(in** f) m - Moroccan.

**marokkanisch** adj Moroccan.

**Marokko** nt Morocco.

**Marone** f -n (sweet or Spanish) chestnut.

**Marotte** f -n quirk.

**Mars** m no pl (Myth, Astron) Mars.

**marsch** interj (a) (Mil) march. **vorwärts** ~! forward march! (b) (col) off with you. ~ **ins Bett!** off to bed with you!

**Marsch¹** m ⸚**e** (a) (das Marschieren) march; (Wanderung) hike. **sich in** ~ **setzen** to move off. (b) (~musik) march. **jdm den** ~ **blasen** (col) to give sb a rocket (col).

**Marsch**[2] *f* **-en** marsh, fen.
**Marschall** *m, pl* **Marschälle** (field) marshal.
**Marsch-:** ~**befehl** *m* *(Mil)* *(für Truppen)* marching orders *pl*; *(für einzelnen)* travel orders *pl*; **m~bereit** *adj* ready to move; ~**flugkörper** *m* cruise missile; ~**gepäck** *nt* pack.
**marschieren*** *vi aux sein* to march; *(fig)* to march off.
**Marsch-:** ~**land** *nt* marsh(land), fen; ~**musik** *f* military marches *pl*; ~**ordnung** *f* marching order; ~**richtung** *f* *(lit)* route of march; *(fig)* line of approach; ~**verpflegung** *f* rations *pl*; *(Mil)* field rations *pl*.
**Marsmensch** *m* Martian.
**Marter** *f* **-n** *(liter)* torment.
**martern** *(liter)* *vt* to torture, to torment.
**Marterpfahl** *m* stake.
**martialisch** [mar'tsia:lɪʃ] *adj (geh)* martial, warlike.
**Martinshorn** *nt* siren *(of police etc)*. **mit** ~ with its siren blaring *or* going.
**Märtyrer(in** *f) m* **-** *(Eccl, fig)* martyr.
**Martyrium** *nt (fig)* ordeal.
**Marxismus** *m* Marxism.
**Marxist(in** *f) m* Marxist.
**marxistisch** *adj* Marxist.
**März** *m* **-e** March. **im** ~ in March; **im Monat** ~ in the month of March; **heute ist der zweite** ~ today is the second of March *or* March second *(US)*; *(geschrieben)* today is 2nd March; **am ersten** ~ **fahren wir nach ...** on the first of March we are going to ...; **in diesem** ~ this March; **im Laufe des** ~ during March; **der** ~ **war sehr warm** March was very warm; **Anfang/Ende/Mitte** ~ at the beginning/end/in the middle of March; **den 4.** ~ **1987** March 4th 1987.
**Marzipan** [martsi'pa:n] *nt* **-e** marzipan.
**Masche** *f* **-n** **(a)** *(Strick~, Häkel~)* stitch; *(von Netz)* hole. **die** ~**n eines Netzes** the mesh of a net; **durch die** ~**n schlüpfen** to slip through the net. **(b)** *(col: Trick)* trick, dodge *(col)*. **die** ~ **raushaben** to know how to do it; **das ist seine neueste** ~ that's his latest (fad).
**Maschendraht** *m* wire netting.
**Maschine** *f* machine; *(Motor)* engine; *(col: Motorrad)* bike; *(Schreib~)* typewriter; *(Flugzeug)* plane. **etw mit der** ~ **schreiben** to type sth.
**maschinell 1** *adj Herstellung* mechanical, machine *attr.* ~**e Übersetzung** machine translation. **2** *adv* mechanically, by machine.
**Maschinen-:** ~**bau** *m* mechanical engineering; ~**bauingenieur** *m* mechanical engineer; ~**fabrik** *f* engineering works *sing or pl*; **m~geschrieben** *adj* typewritten; ~**gewehr** *nt* machine gun; **mit** ~**gewehr(en) beschießen** to machine-gun; ~**haus** *nt* machine room; **m~lesbar** *adj* machine-readable; ~**öl** *nt* lubricating oil; ~**park** *m* plant; ~**pistole** *f* submachine gun; ~**raum** *m* plant room; *(Naut)* engine room; ~**schaden** *m* mechanical failure *or (Defekt)* fault; *(Aviat etc)* engine trouble; ~**schlosser** *m* engine fitter; ~**schrift** *f* typescript, typing; *(Schriftart)* typeface; **m~schriftlich** *adj* typewritten *no adv*; ~**sprache** *f* machine language; ~**stürmer** *m* **-** machine wrecker; *(Hist)* Luddite; ~**teil** *nt* machine part.
**Maschinerie** *f (fig)* machinery.
**maschineschreiben** *vi sep irreg* to type. **sie schreibt Maschine** she types.
**Maschinist(in** *f) m* machine operative; *(Schiffs~)* engineer.
**Maser** *f* **-n** *(von Holz)* vein.
**Masern** *pl* measles *sing*.

**Maserung** *f* grain.
**Maske** *f* **-n** *(lit, fig, Typ, Comp, Sport, Med)* mask. **die** ~ **fallen lassen** *(fig)* to throw off one's mask; **jdm die** ~ **herunterreißen** *(fig)* to unmask sb; **ohne** ~ *(fig)* undisguised; **unter der** ~ **von etw** *(fig)* under the guise of sth; **das ist alles nur** ~ that's all just pretence *(Brit)* or pretense *(US)*.
**Masken-:** ~**ball** *m* masked ball; ~**bildner(in** *f) m* make-up artist.
**Maskerade** *f (Verkleidung)* costume; *(fig)* masquerade.
**maskieren*** **1** *vt* **(a)** *(verkleiden)* to dress up; *(unkenntlich machen)* to disguise. **(b)** *(verbergen)* to mask. **2** *vr* to dress up; *(sich unkenntlich machen)* to disguise oneself.
**maskiert** *adj* masked.
**Maskierung** *f (Verkleidung)* fancy-dress costume; *(von Spion etc)* disguise; *(Verhüllung)* masking.
**Maskottchen** *nt* (lucky) mascot.
**maskulin** *adj* masculine.
**Maskulinum** *nt, pl* **Maskulina** masculine noun.
**Masochismus** *m no pl* masochism.
**Masochist(in** *f) m* masochist.
**masochistisch** *adj* masochist.
**maß** *pret of* **messen**.
**Maß**[1] *nt* **-e (a)** *(~einheit)* measure *(für of)*; *(Zollstock)* rule; *(Bandmaß)* tape measure. ~**e und Gewichte** weights and measures; **das** ~ **aller Dinge** *(fig)* the measure of all things; **mit zweierlei** ~ **messen** *(fig)* to operate a double standard; **das** ~ **ist voll** *(fig)* enough is enough; **in reichem** ~**(e)** abundantly; **über das übliche** ~ **hinausgehen** to overstep the mark; **weder** ~ **noch Ziel kennen** to know no bounds.
  **(b)** *(Meßgröße)* measurement; *(von Zimmer, Möbelstück auch)* dimension. **sich** *(dat)* **etw nach** ~ **anfertigen lassen** to have sth made to measure *or* order *(US)*; ~ **nehmen** to measure up; **bei jdm** ~ **nehmen** to take sb's measurements.
  **(c)** *(Ausmaß)* extent, degree. **ein gewisses** ~ **an ...** a certain degree of ...; **in hohem** ~**(e)** to a high degree; **in solchem** ~**(e), daß ...** to such an extent that ...; **in großem** ~**e** to a great extent; **in vollem** ~**e** fully; **in besonderem** ~**e** especially; **in höchstem** ~**e** extremely; **über alle** ~**en** *(liter)* extremely, beyond measure.
**Maß**[2] *f (S Ger, Aus)* litre *(Brit)* or liter *(US)* of beer.
**Massage** [ma'sa:ʒə] *f* **-n** massage.
**Massagesalon** *m (euph)* massage parlour *(Brit)* or parlor *(US)*.
**Massaker** *nt* **-** massacre.
**massakrieren*** *vt* to massacre.
**Maß-:** ~**anzug** *m* made-to-measure *or* made-to-order *(US)* suit; ~**arbeit** *f (col)* **das war** ~**arbeit** that was a neat bit of work.
**Masse** *f* **-n (a)** *(Stoff, Phys)* mass; *(Cook)* mixture. **(b)** *(große Menge)* heaps *pl (col)*; *(von Besuchern etc)* host. **die (breite)** ~ **der Bevölkerung** *etc* the bulk of the population *etc*; **eine ganze** ~ *(col)* a great deal; **die** ~ **muß es bringen** *(Comm)* the profit only comes with quantity. **(c)** *(Menschenmenge)* crowd. **(d)** *(Bevölkerungs~)* masses *pl (auch pej)*. **die breite** ~ the masses *pl*.
**Maßeinheit** *f* unit of measurement.
**Massel** *m no pl (col)* ~ **haben** to be dead lucky *(col)*.
**Massen-** *in cpds* mass; ~**andrang** *m* crush; ~**arbeitslosigkeit** *f* mass unemployment; ~**artikel** *m* mass-produced article; ~**auflauf** *m no pl* crowds *pl* of people; ~**bedarfsgüter** *pl* basic consumer goods *pl*; ~**entlassung** *f* mass redundancy; ~**grab** *nt* mass grave; ~**güter** *pl* bulk goods *pl*; **m~haft** *adj* on a huge *or* massive scale;

m~haft **Sekt** etc (col) masses of champagne etc (col); **~karambolage** f multiple (car) crash, pile-up (col); **~medien** pl mass media pl; **~mord** m mass murder; **~mörder** m mass murderer; **~produktion** f mass production; **~psychose** f mass hysteria; **~szene** f crowd scene; **~tierhaltung** f intensive livestock farming; **~vernichtungswaffe** f weapon of mass destruction; **~ware** f mass-produced article; **m~weise** adj siehe **m~haft**.

**Masseur** [ma'søːɐ] m masseur.

**Masseurin** [-'søːrɪn] f (Berufsbezeichnung) masseuse.

**Masseuse** [-'søːzə] f (euph) masseuse.

**maßgebend, maßgeblich** adj (entscheidend) Einfluß decisive; Meinung definitive; Text definitive, authoritative; Fachmann authoritative; (wichtig) Persönlichkeit leading; Beteiligung substantial; (zuständig) competent. **~e Kreise** influential circles; **das war für mich nicht ~** that didn't weigh with me.

**maßgeschneidert** adj Anzug made-to-measure, made-to-order (US), custom attr (US).

**maßhalten** vi sep irreg to practise (Brit) or practice (US) moderation.

**Maßhalteparole** f appeal for moderation.

**massieren**¹* vt to massage.

**massieren**²* vt Truppen to mass.

**massig** 1 adj massive, huge. 2 adv (col: sehr viel) **~ Geld** etc stacks of money etc (col).

**mäßig** adj (a) moderate. **~ essen** to eat with moderation; **~ rauchen** to smoke in moderation; **~, aber regelmäßig** in moderation but regularly. (b) (schwach) Leistung etc mediocre; Begabung, Beifall moderate.

**mäßigen** 1 vt (mildern) Anforderungen to moderate; Sprache auch to tone down; Zorn, Ungeduld to curb. **sein Tempo ~** to slacken one's pace; siehe **gemäßigt**. 2 vr (im Essen, Trinken, Temperament) to restrain oneself. **~ Sie sich in Ihren Worten!** tone down your language!

**Mäßigkeit** f (beim Essen, Trinken) moderation; (von Forderungen etc) moderateness.

**Mäßigung** f restraint.

**massiv** adj (a) (pur, stabil) solid. (b) (heftig) Beleidigung gross; Drohung, Kritik heavy; Anschuldigung severe. **~ werden** (col) to turn nasty.

**Massiv** nt -e (Geol) massif.

**Maßkrug** m litre (Brit) or liter (US) beer mug; (Steinkrug) stein.

**maßlos** 1 adj extreme; Forderungen auch excessive; Freude, Ehrgeiz auch boundless; Mensch (in Essen etc) immoderate. **er raucht/trinkt ~** he smokes/drinks to excess. 2 adv (äußerst) extremely; übertreiben grossly, hugely.

**Maßlosigkeit** f siehe adj extremeness; excessiveness; boundlessness; lack of moderation.

**Maßnahme** f -n measure. **~n treffen, um etw zu tun** to take steps to do sth.

**maßregeln** vt insep (zurechtweisen) to reprimand; (bestrafen) to discipline.

**Maßreg(e)lung** f (a) no pl siehe vt reprimanding; disciplining. (b) (Rüge) reprimand.

**Maßstab** m (a) (Karten~) scale. **im ~ 1:1000** on a scale of 1:1000. (b) (fig: Richtlinie, Kriterium) standard. **einen strengen ~ anlegen** to apply a strict standard (an +acc to); **als ~ dienen** to serve as a model; **sich (dat) etw zum ~ nehmen** to take sth as a yardstick.

**maßstab(s)getreu** adj (true) to scale. **eine ~e Karte** an accurate scale map.

**maßvoll** adj moderate.

**Mast**¹ m -en or -e (Naut, Rad, TV) mast; (Stange) pole; (Elec) pylon.

**Mast**² f -en (das Mästen) fattening.

**Mastdarm** m rectum.

**mästen** 1 vt to fatten. 2 vr (col) to gorge oneself.

**Mast-** in cpds (zu mästen) feeder; (gemästet) fattened; **~futter** nt (fattening) feed; (für Schweine) mast; **~korb** m (Naut) crow's nest; **~schwein** nt (zu mästen) porker; (gemästet) fattened pig.

**Masturbation** f masturbation.

**masturbieren*** vtir to masturbate.

**Matador** m -e (Stierkampf) matador; (fig) kingpin.

**Matchball** m (Tennis) match point.

**Material** nt -ien [-iən] material; (Bau~, Gerät~) materials pl; (Beweis~) evidence.

**Materialfehler** m defect in the material.

**Materialismus** m materialism.

**Materialist(in** f) m materialist.

**materialistisch** adj materialist(ic); (pej) materialistic.

**Material-:** **~kosten** pl cost of materials sing; **~schaden** m material defect.

**Materie** [-iə] f (a) no pl (Phys, Philos) matter no art. (b) (Stoff, Thema) subject matter no indef art.

**materiell** adj (a) (Philos) material, physical. (b) (wirtschaftlich) financial; Vorteile auch material; (gewinnsüchtig) materialistic. **~ eingestellt sein** to be materialistic.

**Mathe** f no pl (Sch col) maths sing (Brit col), math (US col).

**Mathematik** f mathematics sing no art.

**Mathematiker(in** f) m mathematician.

**mathematisch** adj mathematical.

**Matinee** f -n [-eːən] matinée.

**Matjes** m -, -, **Matjeshering** m (col) young herring.

**Matratze** f -n mattress.

**Mätresse** f (dated pej) mistress.

**Matriarchat** nt matriarchy.

**Matrikel** f -n (Univ) matriculation register.

**Matrixdrucker** m dot-matrix printer.

**Matrize** f -n (Typ) matrix, mould (Brit), mold (US); (für Schreibmaschine) stencil. **etw auf ~ schreiben** to stencil sth.

**Matrone** f -n matron.

**Matrose** m (wk) -n, -n sailor; (als Rang) rating (Brit), ordinary seaman.

**Matrosenanzug** m sailor suit.

**Matsch** m no pl (col) (breiige Masse) mush; (Schlamm) mud; (Schnee~) slush.

**matschig** adj (col) (breiig) gooey (col), mushy; (schlammig) muddy; Schnee slushy.

**matt** adj (a) (schwach) Kranker weak. **sich ~ fühlen** to have no energy. (b) (glanzlos) Augen, Farbe dull; (nicht glänzend) Farbe, Papier matt; Licht dim; Glühbirne opal, pearl; Spiegel cloudy, dull. (c) (fig) Ausdruck, Rede lame, feeble. (d) (Chess) (check)mate. **jdn ~ setzen** to checkmate sb (auch fig).

**Matt** nt -s (Chess) (check)mate.

**Matte** f -n mat. **auf der ~ stehen** (col) to be on the doorstep (col); (bereit sein) to be (there and) ready for action; (am Arbeitsplatz etc) to be in.

**Mattglas** nt frosted glass.

**Matthäus** [ma'tɛːʊs] m, **Matthäi** [ma'tɛːi] ≈ Matthew.

**Mattigkeit** f weariness; (von Kranken) weakness.

**Mattlack** m mat(t) varnish.

**Mattscheibe** f (Phot) focus(s)ing screen; (col: Fernseher) telly (Brit col), tube (US col). **(eine) ~ haben** (col: dumm sein) to be soft in the head (col); (nicht klar denken können) to have a mental block.

**Matura** *f no pl (Aus, Sw)* = **Abitur.**
**Mätzchen** *nt (col)* antic. ~ **machen** to fool a-round *(col)*.
**mau** *adj pred (col)* poor, bad. **mir ist** ~ I feel poorly *(col)*.
**Mauer** *f* -**n** *(lit, fig)* wall. **etw mit einer** ~ **umgeben** to wall sth in; **die** ~**n einreißen** *(fig)* to tear down the barriers.
**Mauerblümchen** *nt (fig col)* wallflower.
**mauern 1** *vi* (a) to build, to lay bricks. (b) *(Ftbl sl)* to stonewall *(Ftbl sl)*, to play defensively; *(fig)* to stonewall *(esp Parl)*. **2** *vt* to build.
**Mauer-:** ~**schwalbe** *f,* ~**segler** *m* swift; ~**vorsprung** *m* projection on a/the wall; ~**werk** *nt* (a) *(Steinmauer)* stonework, masonry; *(Ziegelmauer)* brickwork; (b) *(die Mauern)* walls *pl*.
**Maul** *nt, pl* **Mäuler** mouth; *(von Löwe etc)* jaws *pl*; *(pej: von Mensch)* gob *(col!)*. **ein loses** *or* **lockeres** ~ **haben** *(col) (frech sein)* to be an impudent so-and-so *(col)*; *(indiskret sein)* to be a blabbermouth *(col!)*; **das** ~ **zu weit aufreißen** *(col!)* to be too cocksure *(col)*; **ein großes** ~ **haben** *(col!)* to be a big-mouth *(col)*; **darüber werden sich die Leute das** ~ **zerreißen** *(col)* that will start people's tongues wagging; **dem Volk** *or* **den Leuten aufs** ~ **schauen** *(col)* to listen to what people really say; **halt's** ~**!** *(col!)* shut your face *(col!)*; **jdm das** ~ **stopfen** *(col!)* to shut sb up *(col)*.
**maulen** *vi (col)* to moan.
**Maul-:** ~**esel** *m* mule; **m**~**faul** *adj (col)* uncommunicative; ~**held** *m (pej)* loud-mouth *(col)*; ~**korb** *m (lit, fig)* muzzle; ~**tasche** *f (Cook)* filled pasta square; ~**tier** *nt* mule; ~**- und Klauenseuche** *f (Vet)* foot-and-mouth disease; ~**werk** *nt (col)* siehe **Mundwerk.**
**Maulwurf** *m, pl* **Maulwürfe** *(auch fig)* mole.
**Maulwurfs-:** ~**haufen,** ~**hügel** *m* molehill.
**Maurer(in** *f)* *m* - bricklayer. **pünktlich wie die** ~ *(hum)* super-punctual.
**Maurer-:** ~**arbeit** *f* bricklaying (work) *no pl*; ~**kelle** *f* (bricklayer's) trowel; ~**meister** *m* master builder.
**Mauretanien** *nt* Mauritania.
**Mauritius** [mau'ri:tsiʊs] *nt* Mauritius.
**Maus** *f, pl* **Mäuse** (a) *(auch Comp)* mouse. **weiße** ~ *(fig col)* traffic cop *(col)*; **weiße Mäuse sehen** *(fig col)* to see pink elephants *(col)*; **eine graue** ~ *(col)* a mouse *(col)*. (b) **Mäuse** *pl (col: Geld)* bread *(col)*, dough *(col)*.
**Mauschelei** *f (col: Korruption)* fiddle *(col)*.
**mauscheln** *vti (manipulieren)* to fiddle *(col)*.
**Mäuschen** ['mɔʏsçən] *nt* (a) little mouse. **da möchte ich mal** ~ **sein** *(col)* I'd like to be a fly on the wall. (b) *(fig)* sweetheart *(col)*.
**mäuschenstill** ['mɔʏsçən-] *adj* dead quiet; *(reglos)* stock-still.
**Mause-:** ~**falle** *f* mousetrap; ~**loch** *nt* mousehole; **sich in ein** ~**loch verkriechen** *(fig)* to crawl into a hole in the ground.
**mausen** *vt (dated col)* to pinch *(col)*.
**Mauser** *f no pl (Orn)* moult *(Brit)*, molt *(US)*. **in der** ~ **sein** to be moulting *(Brit)* or molting *(US)*.
**mausern** *vr (Orn)* to moult *(Brit)*, to molt *(US)*.
**mausetot** *adj (col)* stone-dead.
**mausgrau** *adj* (a) *(~farben)* mouse-grey *(Brit)*, mouse-gray *(US)*. (b) *(unauffällig)* mousy.
**mausig** *adj:* **sich** ~ **machen** *(col)* to get uppish *(col)*.
**Mausoleum** [-'le:ʊm] *nt, pl* **Mausoleen** [-'le:ən] mausoleum.
**Maussteuerung** *f (Comp)* mouse control.
**Maut** *f* -**en** *(S Ger, Aus)* toll.
**max.** = **maximal** max.

**Maxi-** *in cpds* maxi-.
**maximal 1** *adj* maximum. **2** *adv (höchstens)* at most. **bis zu** ~ **$100** up to a maximum of $100.
**Maximal-** *in cpds* maximum.
**Maxime** *f* -**n** *(liter, Philos)* maxim.
**maximieren*** *vt (Econ)* to maximize.
**Maximierung** *f (Econ)* maximization.
**Maximum** *nt, pl* **Maxima** maximum *(an +dat of)*.
**Mayonnaise** [majo'nɛːzə] *f* -**n** mayonnaise.
**Mazedonien** [-iən] *nt* Macedonian.
**Mazedonier(in** *f)* *m* Macedonian.
**mazedonisch** *adj* Macedonian.
**Mäzen** *m* -**e** patron.
**M-Bahn** *f* = **Magnetbahn.**
**MdB** [ɛm'deː'beː] *m* -**s** = **Mitglied des Bundestages** Member of the Bundestag, ≃ MP.
**MdL** [ɛm'deː'ɛl] *m* -**s** = **Mitglied des Landtages** Member of the Landtag.
**m.E.** = **meines Erachtens** in my opinion.
**Mechanik** *f* (a) *no pl (Phys)* mechanics *sing.* (b) *(Mechanismus)* mechanism.
**Mechaniker(in** *f)* *m* - mechanic.
**mechanisch** *adj* mechanical.
**mechanisieren*** *vt* to mechanize.
**Mechanisierung** *f* mechanization.
**Mechanismus** *m* mechanism.
**Meckerei** *f (col)* grumbling.
**Meckerer** *m* - *(col)* grumbler.
**meckern** *vi (Ziege)* to bleat; *(col: Mensch)* to moan, to bitch *(col)*.
**Meckerziege** *f (pej col)* sourpuss *(col)*.
**Mecklenburg-Vorpommern** *nt* Mecklenburg-Vorpommern.
**Medaille** [me'daljə] *f* -**n** *(bei Wettbewerben)* medal.
**Medaillengewinner** [me'daljən-] *m* medallist *(Brit)*, medalist *(US)*.
**Medaillon** [medal'jõː] *nt* -**s** *(Bildchen)* medallion; *(Schmuckkapsel)* locket.
**Medien** ['meːdiən] *pl* media *pl*.
**Medien-:** ~**berater** *m* press adviser; ~**konzern** *m* media group; ~**rummel** *m* media hype.
**Medikament** *nt* medicine.
**medikamentös** *adj* medicinal.
**Meditation** *f* meditation.
**meditieren*** *vi* to meditate.
**Medium** *nt* medium.
**Medizin** *f* -**en** (a) *no pl (Heilkunde)* medicine. (b) *(col: Heilmittel)* medicine.
**Medizinball** *m (Sport)* medicine ball.
**Mediziner(in** *f)* *m* - doctor; *(Univ)* medic *(col)*.
**medizinisch** *adj* (a) *(ärztlich)* medical. **M**~**e Fakultät** school *or* faculty of medicine; ~**-technische Assistentin,** ~**-technischer Assistent** medical technician. (b) *(heilend)* Bäder medicinal; Shampoo medicated.
**Medizin-:** ~**mann** *m, pl* -**männer** medicine man; *(hum: Arzt)* quack *(col)*, medico *(US col)*; ~**student** *m* medical student; ~**studium** *nt* medical studies *pl*.
**Meer** *nt* -**e** sea; *(Welt*~*)* ocean. **am** ~**(e)** by the sea; **übers** ~ **fahren** to travel (across) the seas; **ans** ~ **fahren** to go to the sea(side); **über dem** ~ above sea level.
**Meer-:** ~**busen** *m* gulf, bay; ~**enge** *f* straits *pl*, strait.
**Meeres-:** ~**arm** *m* arm of the sea, inlet; ~**biologie** *f* marine biology; ~**boden** *m* seabed; ~**früchte** *pl* seafood *sing*; ~**grund** *m* seabed; ~**klima** *nt* maritime climate; ~**kunde** *f* oceanography; ~**oberfläche** *f* surface of the sea; ~**spiegel** *m* sea level; **über/unter dem** ~**spiegel** above/below sea level; ~**tier** *nt* marine creature.

**Meer-**: ~**gott** m (Myth) seagod; ~**göttin** f seagoddess; **m**~**grün** adj sea-green; ~**jungfrau** f mermaid; ~**rettich** m horseradish; ~**salz** nt sea salt; ~**schweinchen** nt guinea-pig; ~**wasser** nt sea water.

**Mega-** in cpds mega-; ~**byte** [-'baɪt] nt (Comp) megabyte; ~**phon** nt megaphone; ~**tonne** f megaton; ~**watt** nt megawatt.

**Mehl** nt -e flour; (grober) meal; (Pulver) powder.

**mehlig** adj Äpfel, Kartoffeln mealy.

**Mehl-**: ~**sack** m flour bag; ~**schwitze** f (Cook) roux; ~**speise** f (Aus) (Nachspeise) sweet, dessert; (Kuchen) pastry; ~**tau** m (Bot) mildew.

**mehr 1** indef pron inv comp of **viel, sehr** more. **was wollen Sie ~?** what more do you want?; **~ will er nicht bezahlen** he doesn't want to pay (any) more; **ist das alles, ~ kostet das nicht?** is that all it costs?
  **2** adv **(a)** (in höherem Maße) more. **immer ~** more and more; **~ oder weniger** more or less; **~ Geschäftsmann als Arzt** more (of) a businessman than a doctor; **~ ein juristisches Problem** more (of) a legal problem. **(b)** (+neg: sonst, länger) **ich habe kein Geld ~** I haven't any more money; **du bist doch kein Kind ~!** you're no longer a child!; **es besteht keine Hoffnung ~** there's no hope left; **kein Wort ~!** not another word!; **es war niemand ~ da** there was no one left; **wenn niemand ~ einsteigt, ...** if nobody else gets in ...; **das benutzt man nicht ~** it's no longer used; **das darf nicht ~ vorkommen** that must not happen again; **nicht ~ lange** not much longer; **nichts ~** nothing more; **nie ~** never again, nevermore (liter); **ich will dich nie ~ wiedersehen** I don't ever want to see you again.

**Mehr** nt no pl (Zuwachs) increase.

**Mehr-**: ~**arbeit** f extra time or work; ~**aufwand** m additional expenditure; ~**bedarf** m greater need (an +dat of, for); (Comm) increased demand (an +dat for); ~**belastung** f excess load; (fig) additional burden; **m**~**deutig** adj ambiguous; ~**einnahme** f additional revenue.

**mehren 1** vt (liter: vergrößern) to augment. **2** vr (geh: sich vermehren) to multiply.

**mehrere** indef pron several; (verschiedene auch) various.

**mehrfach 1** adj multiple; (zahlreich) numerous; (wiederholt) repeated. **ein ~er Millionär** a multimillionaire; **der ~e Meister im 100-m-Lauf** the several times 100 metres champion; **die Unterlagen in ~er Ausfertigung einsenden** to send in several copies of the documents. **2** adv (öfter) many or several times; (wiederholt) repeatedly.

**Mehrfach-**: ~**stecker** m (Elec) multiple adaptor; ~**täter** m repeat offender.

**Mehr-**: ~**familienhaus** nt multiple dwelling (form); **m**~**farbig** adj multicoloured (Brit), multicolored (US).

**Mehrheit** f majority. **die ~ besitzen/erringen** to have/gain a majority; **die ~ verlieren** to lose one's majority; **mit zwei Stimmen ~** with a majority of two.

**mehrheitlich** adj **wir sind ~ der Ansicht, daß ...** the majority of us think(s) that ...; **~ beschließen, daß ...** to reach a majority decision that ...

**Mehrheits-**: ~**beschluß** m, ~**entscheidung** f majority decision; **m**~**fähig** adj capable of winning a majority; ~**prinzip** nt principle of majority rule; ~**wahlrecht** nt majority vote system, first-past-the-post system.

**Mehr-**: **m**~**jährig** adj attr of several years; **m**~**jährige Erfahrung** several years of experience; ~**kosten** pl additional costs pl; **m**~**malig** adj attr

repeated; **m**~**mals** adv several times; ~**parteiensystem** nt multi-party system; ~**platzrechner** m (Comp) multi-user or multi-access system; **m**~**sprachig** adj multilingual; **m**~**sprachig aufwachsen** to grow up multilingual; **m**~**stimmig** adj (Mus) for several voices; **m**~**stimmiger Gesang** part-singing; **m**~**stimmig singen** to sing in harmony or in several parts; **m**~**stöckig** adj multistorey (Brit), multilevel (US); **m**~**stündig** adj attr lasting several hours; **mit m**~**stündiger Verspätung eintreffen** to arrive several hours late; **m**~**tägig** adj attr Konferenz lasting several days; **m**~**teilig** adj in several parts.

**Mehrweg-** in cpds reusable; ~**flasche** f returnable bottle.

**Mehr-**: ~**wert** m (Econ) added value; ~**wertsteuer** f value added tax, VAT; ~**zahl** f no pl **(a)** (Gram) plural; **(b)** (Mehrheit) majority.

**Mehrzweck-** in cpds multipurpose.

**meiden** pret **mied**, ptp **gemieden** vt to avoid.

**Meile** f -n mile. **das riecht man drei ~n gegen den Wind** (col) you can smell that a mile off (col).

**Meilen-**: ~**stein** m (lit, fig) milestone; **m**~**weit** adv for miles; **m**~**weit entfernt** (lit, fig) miles away.

**Meiler** m - (Kohlen~) charcoal kiln; (Atom~) (atomic) pile.

**mein** poss pron **(a)** (adjektivisch) my. **(b)** (old: substantivisch) mine.

**Mein|eid** m perjury no indef art. **einen ~ leisten** to commit perjury.

**meinen 1** vi (denken, glauben) to think. **ich meine, ...** I think ...; **~ Sie?** (do) you think so?; **wie Sie ~!** as you wish; (drohend auch) have it your own way; **wenn du meinst!** if you like; **man sollte ~** one would have thought. **2** vt (der Ansicht sein) to think; (sagen wollen) to mean; (col: sagen) to say. **was ~ Sie dazu?** what do you think or say?; **~ Sie das im Ernst?** are you serious about that?; **das will ich ~!** I quite agree!; **wie ~ Sie das?** how do you mean?; **damit bin ich gemeint** that refers to me; (Anspielung) that was aimed at me; **sie meint es gut** she means well; **sie meint es nicht böse** she means no harm.

**meiner** pers pron gen of **ich** of me.

**meine(r, s)** poss pron (substantivisch) mine. **der/die/das ~** (geh) mine; **ich tue das M~** (geh) I'll do my bit.

**meinerseits** adv for my part. **Vorschläge ~** suggestions from me.

**meines-**: ~**gleichen** pron inv (meiner Art) people like myself; ~**teils** adv for my part.

**meinet-**: ~**halben** (dated), ~**wegen** adv **(a)** (wegen mir) on my account; **(b)** (von mir aus) as far as I'm concerned; ~**wegen!** if you like; ~**willen** adv: **um ~willen** for my sake.

**meinige** poss pron **der/die/das ~** (form, old) mine.

**meins** poss pron mine.

**Meinung** f opinion; (Anschauung auch) view. **meiner ~ nach** in my opinion; **ich bin der ~, daß ...** I take the view that ...; **seine ~ ändern** to change one's opinion or mind; **einer ~ sein** to think the same; **das ist auch meine ~!** that's just what I think; **jdm die ~ sagen** (col) to give sb a piece of one's mind (col).

**Meinungs-**: ~**äußerung** f (expression of) opinion; ~**austausch** m exchange of views (über +acc on, about/; ~**forscher** m (opinion) pollster; ~**forschung** f (public) opinion polling; ~**forschungsinstitut** nt opinion research institute; ~**freiheit** f freedom of speech; ~**mache** f (pej col) propaganda; ~**macher** m (col) opinion-maker;

**~umfrage** f opinion poll; **~umschwung** m swing of opinion; **~verschiedenheit** f difference of opinion.

**Meise** f **-n** titmouse. **eine ~ haben** *(col)* to be crackers *(Brit col)* or crazy.

**Meißel** m - chisel.

**meißeln** vti to chisel.

**Meiß(e)ner** adj **~ Porzellan** Dresden china.

**meist** adv siehe **meistens**.

**meistbietend** adj highest bidding; **~ versteigern** to auction to the highest bidder.

**meisten: am ~** adv superl of **viel**, **sehr** the most, most of all.

**meistens** adv mostly; *(zum größten Teil)* for the most part.

**meistenteils** adv siehe **meistens**.

**Meister** m - (a) *(Handwerks~)* master (craftsman); *(Sport)* champion; *(Mannschaft)* champions pl. **seinen ~ machen** to take one's master craftsman's diploma. (b) *(Lehr~, Künstler)* master *(auch fig)*. **er hat seinen ~ gefunden** *(fig)* he's met his match; **es ist noch kein ~ vom Himmel gefallen** *(Prov)* no one is born an expert.

**meiste(r, s)** indef pron superl of **viel** (a) *(adjektivisch)* **die ~n Leute** most people; **die ~n Gläser gingen kaputt** most of the glasses were broken; **die ~e Zeit** most of the time; **du hast die ~e Zeit** you have (the) most time. (b) *(substantivisch)* **die ~n (von ihnen)** most (of them).

**Meister-** in cpds master; **~brief** m master craftsman's diploma; **m~haft 1** adj masterly; **2** adv in a masterly manner; **er versteht es m~haft, zu lügen** he is brilliant at lying; **~hand** f: **von ~hand** by a master hand.

**Meisterin** f *(Handwerks~)* master craftswoman; *(Sport)* champion.

**Meisterleistung** f masterly performance; *(iro)* brilliant achievement, masterstroke.

**meistern** vt to master; **Schwierigkeiten** to overcome. **sein Schicksal ~** to become master of one's fate.

**Meisterprüfung** f examination for master craftsman's diploma.

**Meisterschaft** f (a) *(Sport)* championship; *(Veranstaltung)* championships pl. (b) no pl *(Können)* mastery.

**Meisterschaftsspiel** nt *(Sport)* championship match; *(Ligaspiel)* league match.

**Meister-:** **~stück** nt *(von Handwerker)* work done to qualify as master craftsman; *(fig)* masterpiece; *(geniale Tat)* masterstroke; **~werk** nt masterpiece.

**meist-:** **~gekauft** adj attr best-selling; **~genannt** adj attr most frequently mentioned.

**Mekka** nt *(Geog, fig)* Mecca.

**Melancholie** [melaŋkoˈliː] f melancholy.

**melancholisch** [melaŋˈkoːlɪʃ] adj melancholy.

**Melasse** f **-n** molasses.

**Melde-:** **~amt** nt registration office; **~behörde** f registration authorities pl; **~frist** f registration period.

**melden 1** vt to report; *(registrieren)* to register; *(ankündigen)* to announce. **Änderungen der Behörde** *(dat)* **~** to notify the authorities of changes; **wie soeben gemeldet wird** *(Rad, TV)* according to reports just coming in; **nichts zu ~ haben** *(col)* to have no say; **wen darf ich ~?** who(m) shall I say (is here)?

**2** vr (a) to report *(zu for)*. **sich für etw ~** *(esp Mil)* to sign up for sth; *(für Lehrgang)* to enrol for sth; **sich krank/zum Dienst ~** to report sick/for work; **sich auf eine Anzeige ~** to answer an advertisement. (b) *(fig: sich ankündigen)* to announce one's presence; *(Sport, zur Prüfung)* to enter (one's name) *(zu for)*; *(durch Handaufheben)* to put one's hand up. (c) *(esp Telec: antworten)* to answer. **es meldet sich niemand** there's no answer. (d) *(von sich hören lassen)* to get in touch *(bei with)*. **seitdem hat er sich nicht mehr gemeldet** he hasn't been heard of since; **wenn du was brauchst, melde dich** if you need anything give a shout *(col)*.

**Melde-:** **~pflicht** f *(beim Ordnungsamt)* obligation to register *(when moving house)*; **polizeiliche ~pflicht** obligation to register with the police; **m~pflichtig** adj (a) obliged to register; (b) *Krankheit* notifiable; **~stelle** f place of registration.

**Meldung** f (a) *(Mitteilung)* announcement; *(Press, Rad, TV)* report *(über +acc* on, about*)*. **~en vom Sport** sports news sing. (b) *(dienstlich, bei der Polizei)* report. **(eine) ~ machen** to make a report. (c) *(Sport, Examens~)* entry. (d) *(Comp)* (on-screen) message.

**meliert** adj *Haar* streaked with grey *(Brit)* or gray *(US)*; *Wolle* flecked.

**Melisse** f **-n** *(Bot)* balm.

**melken** pret **melkte** ptp **gemolken** vti (a) to milk. **frisch gemolkene Milch** milk fresh from the cow. (b) *(fig col)* to milk *(col)*, to fleece *(col)*.

**Melodie** f melody; *(Weise auch)* tune.

**melodiös** adj *(geh)* melodious.

**melodisch** adj melodic, tuneful.

**melodramatisch** adj melodramatic *(auch fig)*.

**Melone** f **-n** (a) melon. (b) *(Hut)* bowler *(Brit)*, derby *(US)*.

**Membran** f **-en** (a) *(Anat)* membrane. (b) *(Phys, Tech)* diaphragm.

**Memme** f **-n** *(col)* cissy *(col)*, yellow-belly *(col)*.

**Memoiren** [meˈmoaːrən] pl memoirs pl.

**Memorandum** nt, pl **Memoranden** or **Memoranda** *(Pol)* memorandum.

**Menge** f **-n** (a) *(Quantum)* amount, quantity. (b) *(col)* *(große Anzahl)* lot, load *(col)*; *(Haufen auch)* pile *(col)*, heap *(col)*. **eine ~ Zeit/Häuser** lots *(col)* of time/houses; **jede ~ masses** pl *(col)*, loads pl *(col)*; **wir haben jede ~ getrunken** we drank a hell of a lot *(col)*; **eine ganze ~** quite a lot. (c) *(Menschen~)* crowd; *(geh: Masse)* mass; *(pej: Pöbel)* mob.

**mengen 1** vt *(geh)* to mix *(unter +acc* with*)*. **2** vr to mingle *(unter +acc* with*)*.

**Mengen-:** **~einkauf** m bulk buying; **~lehre** f *(Math)* set theory; **m~mäßig** adj as far as quantity is concerned; **~rabatt** m bulk discount.

**Meniskus** m, pl **Menisken** *(Anat, Phys)* meniscus.

**Menorca** nt Minorca.

**Mensa** f, pl **Mensen** *(Univ)* refectory *(Brit)*, commons *(US)*.

**Mensch** m *(wk)* **-en**, **-en** (a) *(Person)* person, man/woman. **von ~ zu ~** man to man/woman to woman; **es war kein ~ da** there was not a soul there; **als ~** as a person; **das konnte kein ~ ahnen!** no one could have foreseen that! (b) *(als Gattung)* **der ~** man; **die ~en** man sing, human beings pl, people pl; **ein Tier, das keine ~en mag** an animal that doesn't like people; **ich bin auch nur ein ~!** I'm only human; **~ und Tier** man and beast. (c) *(die Menschheit)* **die ~en** mankind, man; **alle ~en** everyone. (d) *(col: als Interjektion)* hey. **~, das habe ich ganz vergessen** damn *(col)*, I completely forgot; **~ Meier!** golly! *(col)*, gosh! *(col)*.

**Mensch ärgere dich nicht** nt no pl *(Spiel)* ludo *(Brit)*, aggravation *(US)*.

**Menschen-** in cpds human; **~affe** m ape; **~alter** nt (a) *(30 Jahre)* generation; (b) *(Lebensdauer)* life-

time; ~**ansammlung** f gathering (of people);
~**auflauf** m crowd (of people); ~**feind** m misanthropist; **m~feindlich** adj Mensch misanthropic;
Landschaft hostile to man; ~**fleisch** nt human
flesh; ~**fresser(in** f) m - (col: Kannibale) cannibal;
~**freund** m philanthropist; **m~freundlich** adj
Mensch philanthropic; Gegend hospitable;
~**führung** f leadership; ~**gedenken** nt der kälteste Winter seit ~**gedenken** the coldest winter in living memory; ~**gestalt** f human form; ~**hai** m
man-eating shark; ~**hand** f human hand; **von**
~**hand geschaffen** fashioned by the hand of man;
~**handel** m slave trade; (Jur) trafficking in human
beings; ~**händler** m slave trader; (Jur) trafficker
in human beings; ~**kenner** m judge of character;
~**kenntnis** f no pl knowledge of human nature;
~**kenntnis haben** to know human nature; ~**kette** f
human chain; ~**leben** nt human life; **ein** ~**leben**
**lang** a whole lifetime; ~**leben waren nicht zu beklagen** there was no loss of life; **das Unglück hat zwei**
~**leben gefordert** the accident claimed two lives;
**m~leer** adj deserted; ~**masse,** ~ **menge** f crowd
(of people); **m~möglich** adj humanly possible;
**das m~mögliche tun** to do all that is humanly possible; ~**raub** m (Jur) kidnapping.
**Menschenrecht** nt human right.
**Menschenrechts-**: ~**konvention** f Human Rights
Convention; ~**verletzung** f violation of human
rights.
**Menschen-**: ~**scheu** f fear of people; **m~scheu**
adj afraid of people; ~**schlag** m (col) kind of
people; ~**seele** f human soul; **keine** ~**seele** (fig) not
a soul.
**Menschenskind** interj good heavens.
**Menschen-**: **m~unwürdig** adj beneath human dignity; Behandlung inhumane; Behausung unfit for
human habitation; **m~verachtend** adj inhuman;
~**verachtung** f contempt for mankind; ~**verstand**
m gesunder ~**verstand** common sense; ~**würde** f
human dignity no art; **m~würdig** adj Behandlung
humane; Unterkunft fit for human habitation.
**Menschheit** f die ~ mankind, humanity.
**menschlich** adj (a) human. **das** ~**e Leben** human
life; **der** ~**e Körper/Geist** the human body/mind; **die**
~**e Gemeinschaft** human society; **er ist mir** ~ **sympathisch** I like him as a person; **(einigermaßen)** ~
**aussehen** (col) to look more or less human. **(b)**
(menschenwürdig) Behandlung etc humane.
**Menschlichkeit** f no pl humanity no art. **aus reiner**
~ on purely humanitarian grounds.
**Menschwerdung** f (Bibl) incarnation.
**Mensen** pl of **Mensa**.
**Mensur** f (Univ) (students') fencing bout.
**Mentalität** f mentality.
**Menthol** nt -e menthol.
**Mentor** m (dated, geh) mentor.
**Menü** nt -s (a) (Tages~) set meal or menu. **(b)**
(Comp) menu.
**Menü-** (Comp) in cpds menu.
**Menuett** nt -e (Tanz, Mus) minuet.
**menügesteuert** adj menu-driven.
**Meridian** m -e (Astron, Geog) meridian.
**Merk-**: **m~bar** adj (wahrnehmbar) noticeable;
~**blatt** nt leaflet; (mit Anweisungen auch) instructions pl.
**merken 1** vt (entdecken) to notice; (spüren) to feel;
(erkennen) to realize. **davon habe ich nichts gemerkt**
I didn't notice anything; **jdn etw** ~ **lassen** to make
sb feel sth; **woran hast du das gemerkt?** how could
you tell that?; **du merkst auch alles!** (iro) nothing
escapes you, does it?; **das merkt keiner!** nobody

will notice; **ich merke keinen Unterschied** I can't
tell the difference. **2** vr sich (dat) **jdn/etw** ~ to remember sb/sth; **das werde ich mir** ~! I won't forget
that; **merk dir das!** mark my words!; **sich** (dat) **eine**
**Autonummer** ~ to memorize a licence number; **diesen Schriftsteller wird man sich** (dat) ~ **müssen** this
author is someone to take note of.
**merklich** adj noticeable. **kein** ~**er Unterschied** no noticeable difference.
**Merkmal** nt -e characteristic, feature.
**Merksatz** m mnemonic.
**Merkur** m no pl (Myth, Astron) Mercury.
**Merk-**: **m~würdig** adj strange, odd; **er hat sich**
**ganz m~würdig verändert** he has undergone a curious change; **m~würdigerweise** adv strangely
enough; ~**würdigkeit** f no pl strangeness, oddness.
**meschugge** adj (col) nuts (col), bonkers (Brit col).
**Meß-**: ~**band** nt tape measure; **m~bar** adj
measurable; ~**becher** m (Cook) measuring jug;
~**daten** pl readings pl; ~**diener** m (Eccl) server,
acolyte (form).
**Messe** f -n (a) (Eccl, Mus) mass. **zur** ~ **gehen** to go
to mass. **(b)** (Ausstellung) (trade) fair. **auf der** ~ at
the fair. **(c)** (Naut, Mil) mess.
**Messe-** in cpds fair; ~**gelände** nt exhibition centre
(Brit) or center (US); ~**halle** f fair pavilion.
**messen** pret **maß,** ptp **gemessen 1** vti to measure; (zeitlich) to time; (abschätzen) Entfernung etc to
judge. **jds Blutdruck** ~ (Arzt etc) to take sb's blood
pressure; **während ich lief, maß er die Zeit** I ran
and he timed me; **seine Kräfte mit jdm** ~ to match
one's strength against sb's; **etw an etw** (dat) ~
(ausprobieren) to try sth out on sth; (vergleichen) to
compare sth with sth. **2** vr (geh: in Wettkampf etc)
to compete (mit against). **sich mit jdm/etw nicht** ~
**können** to be no match for sb/sth.
**Messer** nt - knife; (Tech auch) cutter, blade; (Rasier~) (cutthroat) razor. **unter dem** ~ **sein** (Med col)
to be under the knife; **jdm das** ~ **an die Kehle setzen** (lit, fig) to hold a knife to sb's throat; **ins (offene)** ~ **laufen** (fig) to walk straight into the trap; **die**
~ **wetzen** (fig) to prepare for the kill; **damit würden**
**wir ihn ans** ~ **liefern** (fig) that would be putting his
head on the block; **ein Kampf bis aufs** ~ (fig) a fight
to the finish; **auf des** ~**s Schneide stehen** (fig) to
hang in the balance.
**Messer-** in cpds knife; **m~scharf** adj (lit, fig) razorsharp; **m~scharf schließen** (iro) to conclude with
brilliant logic (iro); ~**spitze** f knife point; **eine**
~**spitze (voll)** (Cook) a pinch; ~**stecher(in** f) m -
knifer (col); ~**stecherei** f knife fight; ~**stich** m
knife thrust; (Wunde) stab wound; ~**werfer** m
knife-thrower.
**Messe-**: ~**stadt** f (town with an) exhibition centre
(Brit) or center (US); ~**stand** m stand (at a fair).
**Meßgerät** nt (für Öl, Druck etc) measuring instrument, gauge.
**Messias** m, gen - (Rel, fig) Messiah.
**Messing** nt no pl brass.
**Meß-**: ~**instrument** nt gauge; ~**schraube** f micrometer; ~**stab** m (Aut: Ölmeßstab etc) dipstick;
~**technik** f measurement technology.
**Messung** f (a) (das Messen) measuring; (das Ablesen) reading; (von Blutdruck) taking. **(b)** (Meßergebnis) measurement; (Ableseergebnis) reading.
**Meßwert** m measurement; (Ableseergebnis) reading.
**Metall** nt -e metal.
**Metall-** in cpds metal-; ~**arbeiter** m metalworker;
**m~haltig** adj containing metal; ~**industrie** f

metalworking industry.
**metallisch** *adj* metal; *(metallartig, fig)* Stimme, Klang metallic. ~ **glänzen** to gleam like metal.
**Metallurgie** *f* metallurgy.
**Metall-: m~verarbeitend** *adj* die m~verarbeitende **Industrie** the metal-processing industry; ~**verarbeitung** *f* metal processing.
**Metamorphose** [-'foːzə] *f* **-n** metamorphosis.
**Metapher** [me'tafɛ] *f* **-n** *(Liter, Poet)* metaphor.
**metaphorisch** *adj (Liter, Poet)* metaphoric(al).
**Metaphysik** *f* metaphysics *sing*.
**metaphysisch** *adj* metaphysical.
**Metastase** [meta'staːzə] *f* **-n** *(Med)* secondary growth.
**Meteor** *m* **-e** meteor.
**Meteorit** *m (wk)* **-en, -en** meteorite.
**Meteorologe** *m*, **Meteorologin** *f* meteorologist; *(im Wetterdienst)* weather forecaster.
**Meteorologie** *f* meteorology.
**meteorologisch** *adj* meteorological.
**Meter** *m or nt* - metre *(Brit)*, meter *(US)*. **in 500 ~ Höhe** at a height of 500 metres; **nach ~n** by the metre.
**Meter-: m~hoch** *adj* Wellen *etc* enormous; ~**maß** *nt* **(a)** *(Bandmaß)* measuring tape; **(b)** *(Stab)* metre *(Brit)* or meter *(US)* rule; ~**ware** *f (Tex)* material or fabric sold by the metre *(Brit)* or meter *(US)*; **m~weise** *adv* by the metre *(Brit)* or meter *(US)*.
**Methadon** *nt no pl* methadone.
**Methan** *nt no pl* methane.
**Methode** *f* **-n** **(a)** method. **etw mit ~ machen** to do sth methodically; **das ist auch eine ~** *(iro)* that's one way of doing it. **(b)** ~**n** *pl (Sitten)* behaviour *(Brit)*, behavior *(US)*; **was sind denn das für ~n?** what sort of way is that to behave?
**Methodik** *f* methodology.
**methodisch** *adj* methodical.
**Methodist(in** *f*) *m* Methodist.
**Methusalem** *m* alt wie ~ old as Methuselah.
**Metier** [me'tieː] *nt* **-s** *(hum)* job, profession.
**Metrik** *f (Poet, Mus)* metrics *sing*.
**metrisch** *adj (Sci)* metric; *(Poet, Mus auch)* metrical.
**Metronom** *nt* **-e** *(Mus)* metronome.
**Metropole** *f* **-n** **(a)** *(größte Stadt)* metropolis. **(b)** *(Zentrum)* capital.
**Mett** *nt no pl (Cook)* minced *(Brit)* or ground *(US)* pork.
**Mette** *f* **-n** *(Eccl)* matins *sing*; *(Abend~)* vespers *sing*.
**Mettwurst** *f* (smoked) pork/beef sausage.
**Metzger(in** *f*) *m* - butcher.
**Metzger-** *siehe* **Fleischer-**.
**Metzgerei** *f* butcher's (shop) *(Brit)*, butcher *(US)*.
**Meuchel-:** ~**mord** *m* (treacherous) murder; ~**mörder** *m* (treacherous) assassin.
**Meute** *f* **-n** pack (of hounds); *(fig pej)* mob.
**Meuterei** *f* mutiny; *(fig auch)* rebellion.
**Meuterer** *m* - mutineer; *(fig)* rebel.
**meutern** *vi* to mutiny; *(col auch)* to rebel. **die ~den Soldaten** the mutinous soldiers.
**Mexikaner(in** *f*) *m* - Mexican.
**mexikanisch** *adj* Mexican.
**Mexiko** *nt* Mexico. ~ **City**, ~**-Stadt** Mexico City.
**MEZ** = **mitteleuropäische Zeit** CET.
**Mezzosopran** *m* mezzo-soprano.
**MFG** [ɛmɛf'geː] *f* = **Mitfahrgelegenheit**.
**MG** [ɛm'geː] *nt* **-(s)** = **Maschinengewehr**.
**mg** = **Milligramm** mg.
**MHz** = **Megahertz** MHz.
**Mi** = **Mittwoch** Wed.

**miau** *interj* miaow.
**miauen*** *vi* to miaow.
**mich 1** *pers pron acc of* **ich** me. **2** *reflexive pron* myself. **ich fühle ~ wohl** I feel fine.
**mick(e)rig** *adj (col)* pathetic; *Betrag auch* paltry; *altes Männchen* puny.
**Midi-** *in cpds* midi; ~**-Anlage** *f*, ~**-System** *nt* midi (system).
**mied** *pret of* **meiden**.
**Mieder** *nt* - *(Leibchen)* bodice.
**Miederwaren** *pl* corsetry *sing*.
**Mief** *m no pl (col)* fug; *(muffig)* stale air; *(Gestank)* stink, pong *(Brit col)*. **im Büro ist so ein ~** the air in the office is so stale.
**miefen** *vi (col)* to stink, to pong *(Brit col)*. **hier mieft es** there's a pong in here.
**Miene** *f* **-n** *(Gesichtsausdruck)* expression. **eine finstere ~ machen** to look grim; **gute ~ zum bösen Spiel machen** to grin and bear it.
**Mienenspiel** *nt* facial expressions *pl*.
**mies** *adj (col)* rotten *(col)*, lousy *(col)*. **jdn/etw ~ machen** to run sb/sth down; **in den M~en sein** *(col)* to be in the red.
**Miesepeter** *m* - *(col)* grumble-guts *(col)*.
**miesepet(e)rig** *adj (col)* grouchy *(col)*.
**Miesmacher** *m (col)* killjoy.
**Miesmuschel** *f* mussel.
**Miet|auto** *nt* hire(d) car *(Brit)*, rental car *(US)*.
**Miete** *f* **-n** *(für Wohnung)* rent; *(für Gegenstände)* rental. **zur ~ wohnen** to live in rented accommodation *(Brit)* or accommodations *(US)*.
**mieten** *vt* to rent; *Boot, Auto auch* to hire *(Brit)*.
**Mieter(in** *f*) *m* - tenant; *(Untermieter)* lodger.
**Miet|erhöhung** *f* rent increase.
**Mieterschutz** *m* rent control.
**Miet-: m~frei** *adj* rent-free; ~**partei** *f* tenant (and family); ~**recht** *nt* rent law.
**Miets-:** ~**haus** *nt* block of (rented) flats *(Brit)*, apartment house *(US)*; ~**kaserne** *f (pej)* tenement house.
**Miet-:** ~**spiegel** *m* rent level; ~**verhältnis** *nt* tenancy; ~**vertrag** *m* lease; *(von Auto)* rental agreement; ~**wagen** *m* hire car *(Brit)*, rental car *(US)*; ~**wohnung** *f* rented flat *(Brit)* or apartment; ~**wucher** *m* ~**wucher ist strafbar** charging exorbitant rent(s) is a punishable offence.
**Mieze** *f* **-n** *(col)* **(a)** *(Katze)* pussy *(col)*. **(b)** *(Mädchen)* chick *(col)*, bird *(Brit col)*.
**Migräne** *f no pl* migraine.
**Mikado** *nt* **-s** *(Spiel)* pick-a-stick.
**Mikro** *nt* **-s** *(col)* = **Mikrofon** mike.
**Mikro-** *in cpds* micro-.
**Mikrobe** *f* **-n** microbe.
**Mikro-:** ~**chirurgie** *f* microsurgery; ~**computer** *m* micro(computer); ~**elektronik** *f* microelectronics *sing*; ~**fiche** [-fiːʃ] *m or nt* **-s** microfiche.
**Mikrofon** *nt* **-e** microphone.
**Mikrokosmos** *m* microcosm.
**Mikroprozessor** *m* microprocessor.
**Mikroskop** *nt* **-e** microscope.
**mikroskopisch** *adj* microscopic. **etw ~ untersuchen** to examine sth under the microscope.
**Mikrowelle** *f* microwave.
**Mikrowellenherd** *m* microwave oven.
**Milbe** *f* **-n** mite.
**Milch** *f no pl* milk; *(Fischsamen)* soft roe. ~ **geben** *(Kuh)* to yield milk.
**Milch-** *in cpds* milk; ~**bart** *m (col)* fluffy beard; *(fig pej: Jüngling)* milksop; ~**brötchen** *nt* roll made with milk and sugar; ~**drüse** *f* mammary gland; ~**flasche** *f* milk bottle; ~**frau** *f (col)* dairywoman;

~**gebiß** *nt* milk teeth *pl*; ~**geschäft** *nt* dairy; ~**gesicht** *nt (col)* baby face; ~**glas** *nt* milk glass.
**milchig** *adj* milky.
**Milch-**: ~**kaffee** *m* milky coffee; ~**kännchen** *nt* small milk jug; ~**kanne** *f* milk can; *(größer)* milk churn; ~**mädchenrechnung** *f (col)* naive fallacy; ~**mann** *m, pl* -**männer** milkman; ~**mixgetränk** *nt* milk shake; ~**produkt** *nt* milk product; ~**pulver** *nt* dried milk; ~**reis** *m* round-grain rice; *(gekocht)* rice pudding; ~**straße** *f* Milky Way; ~**tüte** *f* milk carton; ~**wirtschaft** *f* dairy farming; ~**zahn** *m* milk tooth.
**mild(e)** *adj* mild; *Seife auch* gentle; *(nachsichtig) Behandlung, Richter, Urteil* lenient. **jdn** ~ **stimmen** to put sb in a lenient mood; **eine** ~**e Gabe** alms *pl*; ~ **gesagt** to put it mildly.
**Milde** *f no pl siehe adj* (a) mildness. (b) leniency. ~ **walten lassen** to be lenient.
**mildern** *vt (geh) Schmerz* to ease; *Furcht* to calm; *Urteil, Zorn, Worte* to moderate; *Gegensätze* to make less crass. ~**de Umstände** *(Jur)* extenuating circumstances.
**Milderung** *f no pl (von Schmerz)* easing; *(von Ausdruck, Strafe, des Klimas)* moderation.
**mildtätig** *adj (geh)* charitable.
**Mildtätigkeit** *f (geh)* charity.
**Milieu** [mi'liø:] *nt* -**s** *(Umwelt)* environment, milieu.
**militant** *adj* militant.
**Militanz** *f no pl* militancy.
**Militär**[1] *nt no pl* military, armed forces *pl*. **beim** ~ **sein** *(col)* to be in the forces; **zum** ~ **gehen** to join up.
**Militär**[2] *m* -**s** (army) officer.
**Militär-** *in cpds* military; ~**dienst** *m* military service; **(seinen)** ~**dienst ableisten** to do one's military service; ~**gericht** *nt* court martial; **vor ein** ~**gericht gestellt werden** to be court-martialled; ~**hilfe** *f* military aid.
**militärisch** *adj* military. ~ **grüßen** to salute.
**Militarismus** *m no pl* militarism.
**Militarist(in** *f)* *m* militarist.
**militaristisch** *adj* militaristic.
**Military** ['mɪlɪtərɪ] *f* -**s** *(Reiten)* three-day event; *(als Sportart)* eventing.
**Miliz** *f* -**en** militia; *(Polizei)* police.
**Mill.** = **Million(en)** m.
**Milliardär(in** *f)* *m* multi-millionaire, billionaire.
**Milliarde** *f* -**n** thousand millions *(Brit)*, billion *(US)*.
**Milli-** *in cpds* milli-; ~**bar** *nt* - millibar; ~**gramm** *nt* milligramme *(Brit)*, milligram *(US)*; ~**liter** *m or nt* millilitre *(Brit)*, milliliter *(US)*; ~**meter** *m or nt* millimetre *(Brit)*, millimeter *(US)*; ~**meterpapier** *nt* graph paper.
**Million** *f* million. **zwei** ~**en Einwohner** two million inhabitants.
**Millionär(in** *f)* *m* millionaire(ss). **es zum** ~ **bringen** to make a million.
**Millionen-**: ~**auflage** *f* edition of a million copies *pl*; ~**erbe** *m*, ~**erbin** *f* inheritor of millions; **m**~**fach 1** *adj* millionfold; **2** *adv* a million times; **m**~**schwer** *adj (col)* worth a few million; ~**stadt** *f* town with over a million inhabitants.
**Millionstel** *nt* millionth.
**Milz** *f* -**en** spleen.
**Milzbrand** *m (Med, Vet)* anthrax.
**mimen** *(old)* **1** *vt* to mime. **er mimt den Unschuldigen** *(col)* he's acting the innocent. **2** *vi* to play-act.
**Mimik** *f no pl* facial expression.
**mimisch** *adj* mimic.
**Mimose** *f* -**n** mimosa. **empfindlich wie eine** ~ **sein** to be oversensitive.

**Min., min.** = **Minute(n)** m, min.
**Minarett** *nt* -**e** minaret.
**minder** *adv* less. **und das nicht** ~ and no less so.
**minder-**: ~**begabt** *adj* less gifted; ~**bemittelt** *adj (dated)* less well off; **geistig** ~**bemittelt** *(iro)* mentally less gifted.
**mindere(r, s)** *adj attr* lesser; *Qualität* inferior.
**Minderheit** *f* minority.
**Minderheitsregierung** *f* minority government.
**Minder-**: **m**~**jährig** *adj* who is (still) a minor; ~**jährige(r)** *mf decl as adj* minor; ~**jährigkeit** *f* minority.
**mindern 1** *vt (herabsetzen) Würde, Verdienste* to diminish; *(verringern) Wert, Qualität* to reduce. **2** *vr* to diminish.
**Minderung** *f siehe vb* diminishing *no indef art*; reduction *(gen in)*.
**minderwertig** *adj* inferior; *Waren, Material, Arbeit auch* poor-quality; *Qualität auch* low.
**Minderwertigkeit** *f* inferiority.
**Minderwertigkeits-**: ~**gefühl** *nt* feeling of inferiority; ~**komplex** *m* inferiority complex.
**Minderzahl** *f* minority. **in der** ~ in the minority.
**Mindest-** *in cpds* minimum; ~**alter** *nt* minimum age; ~**betrag** *m* minimum amount.
**mindeste(r, s) 1** *adj attr* least, slightest. **das** ~ **the** (very) least; **ich verstehe nicht das** ~ **von (der) Kunst** I don't know the slightest thing about art. **2** *adv* **zum** ~**n** at the very least; **(nicht) im** ~**n** (not) in the least.
**mindestens** *adv* at least.
**Mindest-**: ~**größe** *f* minimum size; *(von Menschen)* minimum height; ~**lohn** *m* minimum wage; ~**maß** *nt* minimum amount *(an +dat of)*; ~**umtausch** *m* minimum obligatory exchange.
**Mine** *f* -**n** (a) *(Min)* mine. (b) *(Mil)* mine. **auf eine** ~ **laufen** to hit a mine. (c) *(Bleistift~)* lead; *(Kugelschreiber~, Filzstift~)* refill.
**Minen-**: ~**feld** *nt (Mil)* minefield; ~**leger** *m* - *(Mil, Naut)* minelayer; ~**suchboot** *nt* minesweeper.
**Mineral** *nt* -**e** *or* -**ien** [-iən] mineral.
**mineralisch** *adj* mineral.
**Mineral-**: ~**öl** *nt* (mineral) oil; ~**ölsteuer** *f* tax on oil; ~**quelle** *f* mineral spring; ~**wasser** *nt* mineral water.
**Mini-** *in cpds* mini-.
**Miniatur** *f (Art)* miniature.
**Miniatur-** *in cpds* miniature; ~**ausgabe** *f* miniature version; *(Buch)* miniature edition.
**Minigolf** *nt* crazy golf, minigolf.
**minimal** *adj* minimal. **mit** ~**er Anstrengung** with a minimum of effort.
**Minimal-** *in cpds* minimum.
**Minimum** *nt, pl* **Minima** minimum *(an +dat of)*.
**Minirock** *m* miniskirt.
**Minister(in** *f)* *m* - *(Pol)* minister *(Brit) (für* of*)*, secretary *(für* for*)*.
**Ministerialbeamte(r)** *m* ministry official.
**ministeriell** *adj attr* ministerial.
**Ministerium** *nt* ministry *(Brit)*, department.
**Ministerpräsident** *m* prime minister; *(eines Bundeslandes)* chief minister of a Federal German state.
**Minna** *f no pl* **jdn zur** ~ **machen** *(col)* to give sb a piece of one's mind.
**Minne-**: ~**sang** *m* minnesong; ~**sänger** *m* minnesinger.
**Minorität** *f* = **Minderheit**.
**minus 1** *prep +gen* minus, less; *(Math)* minus. **2** *adv* minus; *(Elec)* negative. **10 Grad** ~ 10 degrees below zero; ~ **machen** *(col)* to make a loss.

**Minus** *nt* -, - *(Fehlbetrag)* deficit; *(auf Konto)* overdraft; *(fig: Nachteil)* bad point; *(in Beruf etc)* disadvantage.

**Minus-:** ~**pol** *m* negative pole; ~**punkt** *m* penalty point; *(fig)* minus point; ~**zeichen** *nt* minus sign.

**Minute** *f* -**n** minute. **auf die** ~ **(genau/pünktlich)** (right) on the dot; **in letzter** ~ at the last minute; **es vergeht keine** ~, **ohne daß** ... not a moment goes by without ...

**Minuten-:** **m**~**lang 1** *adj attr* several minutes of; **2** *adv* for several minutes; ~**zeiger** *m* minute hand.

**minuziös** *adj (geh)* meticulous.

**Minze** *f* -**n** *(Bot)* mint.

**Mio.** = **Million(en)** m.

**mir** *pers pron dat of* **ich** to me; *(nach Präpositionen)* me. **ein Freund von** ~ a friend of mine; **von** ~ **aus!** *(col)* I don't mind, fair enough; ~ **nichts, dir nichts** *(col)* just like that; *(unhöflich)* without so much as a by-your-leave; **es war** ~ **nichts, dir nichts weg** the next thing I knew it had gone; **wie du** ~, **so ich dir** *(prov)* tit for tat *(col)*; *(als Drohung)* I'll get my own back.

**Mirabelle** *f* mirabelle, *small yellow plum.*

**Misch-:** ~**batterie** *f* mixer tap; ~**brot** *nt* bread *made from more than one kind of flour*; ~**ehe** *f* mixed marriage.

**mischen 1** *vt* to mix; *Karten* to shuffle; *(Comp)* Dateien to merge. **2** *vr* to mix. **sich unter die Menge** ~ to mix with the crowd; **sich in etw** *(acc)* ~ to meddle in sth; **sich in das Gespräch** ~ to butt into the conversation.

**Misch-:** ~**farbe** *f* mixed *or* blended colour *(Brit)* or color *(US)*; *(Phys)* secondary colour; ~**form** *f* mixture; *(von zwei Elementen auch)* hybrid (form); ~**gewebe** *nt* mixed fibres *pl*; ~**konzern** *m* conglomerate; ~**ling** *m (Mensch)* half-caste; *(Zool)* half-breed; ~**masch** *m* -**e** *(col)* hotchpotch; *(Essen auch)* concoction; ~**maschine** *f* cement-mixer; ~**pult** *nt (Rad, TV)* mixing desk, mixer.

**Mischung** *f* **(a)** *(das Mischen)* mixing. **(b)** *(lit, fig: Gemischtes)* mixture; *(von Tee etc auch)* blend.

**Mischwald** *m* mixed (deciduous and coniferous) woodland.

**miserabel** *adj (col)* lousy *(col)*; *Gesundheit* wretched; *Benehmen* dreadful.

**Misere** *f* -**n** *(von Leuten, Wirtschaft etc)* plight; *(von Hunger, Krieg etc)* misery, miseries *pl*. **in einer** ~ **stecken** to be in a dreadful state; *(Mensch)* to be in a mess.

**miß|achten*** *vt insep (ignorieren)* to disregard.

**Miß|achtung** *f* **(a)** disregard. **(b)** *(Geringschätzung)* disrespect *(gen for)*.

**Mißbehagen** *nt (geh) (Unbehagen)* uneasiness; *(Mißfallen)* discontent(ment).

**mißbilden** *ptp* **mißgebildet** *vt insep* to deform.

**Mißbildung** *f* deformity, malformation.

**mißbilligen*** *vt insep* to disapprove of.

**Mißbilligung** *f* disapproval.

**Mißbrauch** *m* abuse; *(falsche Anwendung)* misuse; *(von Notbremse, Feuerlöscher etc)* improper use. **unter** ~ **seines Amtes** in abuse of his office.

**mißbrauchen*** *vt insep* to abuse; *(geh: vergewaltigen)* to assault. **jdn zu etw** ~ to take advantage of sb for sth *or* to do sth.

**mißbräuchlich** *adj (form)* improper.

**mißdeuten*** *vt insep* to misinterpret.

**Mißdeutung** *f* misinterpretation.

**missen** *vt (geh)* to do without. **das möchte ich nicht** ~ I wouldn't do without it (for the world).

**Miß|erfolg** *m* failure; *(Theat, Buch etc auch)* flop *(col)*.

**Miß|ernte** *f* crop failure.

**Missetat** *f (old, liter)* misdeed.

**Missetäter** *m (old, liter)* culprit.

**mißfallen*** *vi insep irreg* +*dat* to displease. **es mißfällt mir, wie er** ... I dislike the way he ...

**Mißfallen** *nt no pl* displeasure *(über* +*acc* at*)*. **jds** ~ **erregen** to incur sb's displeasure.

**Mißfallens-:** ~**äußerung** *f* expression of displeasure; ~**bekundung**, ~**kundgebung** *f* demonstration of displeasure.

**mißfällig** *adj Bemerkung* deprecatory.

**Mißgeburt** *f* deformed person/animal; *(fig col)* failure.

**Mißgeschick** *nt* mishap; *(Pech, Unglück)* misfortune.

**mißglücken*** *vi insep aux sein* to be unsuccessful. **mißglückt** unsuccessful; **der Versuch ist (ihm) mißglückt** the/his attempt was a failure.

**mißgönnen*** *vt insep* **jdm etw** ~ to (be)grudge sb sth.

**Mißgriff** *m* mistake.

**Mißgunst** *f* resentment (at).

**mißgünstig** *adj* resentful *(auf* +*acc* towards*)*.

**mißhandeln*** *vt insep* to ill-treat, to maltreat.

**Mißhandlung** *f* ill-treatment, maltreatment.

**Mission** *f (Eccl, Pol, fig)* mission; *(diplomatische Vertretung)* legation, mission *(US)*; *(Gruppe)* delegation.

**Missionar(in** *f)* *m* missionary.

**missionarisch** *adj* missionary.

**missionieren*** **1** *vi* to do missionary work; *(fig)* to preach. **2** *vt* to convert.

**Mißklang** *m* discord *(auch Mus)*, dissonance; *(Mißton, fig)* discordant note.

**Mißkredit** *m no pl* discredit. **jdn/etw in** ~ **bringen** to bring sb/sth into discredit.

**mißlang** *pret of* **mißlingen**.

**mißlich** *adj (geh)* awkward, difficult.

**mißliebig** *adj* unpopular.

**Mißlingen** *nt no pl* failure.

**mißlingen** *pret* **mißlang**, *ptp* **mißlungen** *vi aux sein* to be unsuccessful. **ein mißlungener Versuch** an unsuccessful attempt.

**Mißmut** *m* sullenness; *(Unzufriedenheit)* displeasure.

**mißmutig** *adj* sullen; *(unzufrieden)* discontented; *Äußerung, Aussehen* disgruntled.

**mißraten*** **1** *vi insep irreg aux sein* to go wrong. **der Kuchen ist mir** ~ my cake was a failure. **2** *adj Kind* wayward.

**Mißstand** *m* anomaly; *(allgemeiner Zustand)* deplorable state of affairs *no pl*; *(Ungerechtigkeit)* abuse; *(Mangel)* defect.

**Mißstimmung** *f* **(a)** *(Uneinigkeit)* discord. **eine** ~ a note of discord. **(b)** *(schlechte Laune)* bad mood; *(Unzufriedenheit)* discontent *no pl*.

**Mißton** *m* discord; *(fig)* discordant note. ~**e** *(Klang)* dissonance; *(fig)* discord.

**mißtrauen*** *vi insep* +*dat* to mistrust.

**Mißtrauen** *nt no pl* mistrust *(gegenüber* of*)*. ~ **gegen jdn/etw haben** to be suspicious of sb/sth.

**Mißtrauens-:** ~**antrag** *m* motion of no confidence; ~**votum** *nt* vote of no confidence.

**mißtrauisch** *adj* distrustful; *(argwöhnisch)* suspicious.

**Mißverhältnis** *nt* discrepancy.

**mißverständlich** *adj* unclear.

**Mißverständnis** *nt* misunderstanding.

**mißverstehen*** *vt insep irreg* to misunderstand.

**Mißwahl, Misswahl** *f* beauty contest.

**Mißwirtschaft** *f* mismanagement.

**Mist** m no pl (**a**) *(Tierkot)* droppings pl; *(Pferde~, Kuh~ etc)* dung; *(Dünger)* manure. **das ist nicht auf seinem ~ gewachsen** *(col)* he didn't think that up himself. (**b**) *(col) (Unsinn)* nonsense; *(Schund)* rubbish. **~! blast!** *(col)*; **da hat er ~ gemacht** or **gebaut** he really messed that up *(col)*; **mach keinen ~!** don't be a fool!

**Mistel** f **-n** mistletoe no pl.

**Mist-:** **~fink** m *(col)* dirty-minded character; *(Journalist etc)* muck-raker *(col)*; **~gabel** f pitchfork *(used for shifting manure)*; **~haufen** m manure heap; **~käfer** m dung beetle; **~stück**, **~vieh** nt *(col!) (Mann)* bastard *(col!)*; *(Frau auch)* bitch *(col!)*; **~wetter** nt *(col)* lousy weather *(col)*.

**mit 1** prep +dat with. **~ dem Hut in der Hand** (with) his hat in his hand; **ein Topf ~ Suppe** a pot of soup; **wie wär's ~ einem Bier?** *(col)* how about a beer?; **~ der Bahn/dem Bus/dem Auto** by train/bus/car; **~ Gewalt** by force; **~ Bleistift schreiben** to write in pencil; **~ dem nächsten Flugzeug/Bus kommen** to come on the next plane/bus; **~ einem Wort** in a word; **~ achtzehn Jahren** at (the age of) eighteen; **es wird ~ jedem Tag schlimmer** it's getting worse every day; **~ der Zeit** in time; **etw ~ DM 50.000 versichern** to insure sth for 50,000 marks; **~ 80 km/ h** at 50 mph; **~ 4:2 gewinnen** to win 4-2; **~ mir waren es 5** there were 5 including me; **du ~ deinen dummen Ideen** *(col)* you and your stupid ideas; **~ lauter Stimme** in a loud voice; **~ Verlust** at a loss.

**2** adv **er wollte ~** *(col)* he wanted to come too; **er war ~ dabei** he was there too; **er ist ~ der Beste der Gruppe** he is among the best in the group; **das gehört ~ dazu** that's part and parcel of it; **etw ~ in Betracht ziehen** to consider sth as well.

**Mit|angeklagte(r)** mf co-defendant.

**Mit|arbeit** f collaboration; *(Hilfe auch)* assistance; *(Teilnahme)* participation *(auch Sch)*. **unter ~ von** in collaboration with.

**mit|arbeiten** vi sep to collaborate. **er hat beim Bau des Hauses mitgearbeitet** he helped build the house; **beim Unterricht ~** to take an active part in lessons; **seine Frau arbeitet mit** *(col)* his wife works too.

**Mit|arbeiter(in** f) m *(Betriebsangehöriger)* employee; *(Kollege)* colleague; *(an Projekt etc)* collaborator. **freier ~** freelance.

**Mit|arbeiterstab** m staff.

**Mitbegründer** m co-founder; *(bei einem Verein)* founding member.

**mitbekommen*** vt sep irreg (**a**) to get or be given sth. (**b**) *(col: verstehen)* to get *(col)*.

**mitbenutzen*** vt sep to share (the use of).

**Mitbenutzung** f joint use.

**Mitbesitzer** m joint owner.

**mitbestimmen*** sep **1** vi to have a say *(bei in)*; to participate *(bei in)*. **~d sein** to have an influence *(bei, für on)*. **2** vt to have an influence on.

**Mitbestimmung** f co-determination, participation *(bei in)*. **~ am Arbeitsplatz** worker participation.

**Mitbewerber** m (fellow) competitor. **meine ~** *(für Stelle)* the other applicants.

**Mitbewohner** m (fellow) occupant.

**mitbringen** vt sep irreg (**a**) to bring; *Freund, Begleiter* to bring along. **jdm etw aus der Stadt/vom Bäcker ~** to bring sb sth back from town/the baker's; **was sollen wir der Gastgeberin ~?** what should we take to our hostess? (**b**) *Mitgift, Kinder* to bring with one. **etw in die Ehe ~** to have sth when one gets married. (**c**) *(fig) Befähigung etc* to have, to possess.

**Mitbringsel** nt *(Geschenk)* small present; *(Andenken)* souvenir.

**Mitbürger** m fellow citizen.

**mitdenken** vi sep irreg to follow (sb's train of thought/line of argument).

**mitdürfen** vi sep irreg **wir durften nicht mit** we weren't allowed to go along.

**Mit|eigentümer** m joint-owner.

**Mit|einander** nt no pl living and/or working together.

**mit|einander** adv with one another; *(gemeinsam)* together. **wir haben lange ~ geredet** we had a long talk.

**mit|empfinden*** sep irreg **1** vt to share. **2** vi **mit jdm ~** to sympathize with sb.

**mit|erleben*** vt sep Krieg to live through; *(im Fernsehen)* to watch.

**mit|essen** vt sep irreg Schale etc to eat as well.

**Mit|esser** m - blackhead.

**mitfahren** vi sep irreg aux sein to go (with sb). **sie fährt mit** she is going too; **(mit jdm) ~** to go with sb; *(auf Reise auch)* to travel with sb; **kann ich (mit Ihnen) ~?** can you give me a lift?

**Mitfahrer** m passenger (receiving a lift).

**Mitfahrerzentrale** f agency for arranging lifts.

**Mitfahrgelegenheit** f lift.

**mitfühlen** vi sep = **mitempfinden**.

**mitfühlend** adj compassionate.

**mitführen** vt sep Papiere, Ware etc to carry (with one); *(Fluß)* to carry along.

**mitgeben** vt sep irreg **jdm etw ~** to give sb sth to take with him/her; Rat, Erziehung to give sb sth.

**Mitgefühl** nt sympathy.

**mitgehen** vi sep irreg aux sein (**a**) to go too or along. **mit jdm ~** to go with sb. (**b**) *(fig: Publikum etc)* to respond (favourably) *(mit to)*. (**c**) *(col)* etw **~ lassen** to pinch sth *(col)*.

**Mitgift** f **-en** dowry.

**Mitgiftjäger** m *(col)* dowry-hunter.

**Mitglied** nt member *(gen, bei, in +dat* of*)*.

**Mitglieds-:** **~ausweis** m membership card; **~beitrag** m membership subscription.

**Mitgliedschaft** f membership.

**Mitglied(s)staat** m member state.

**mithaben** vt sep irreg **etw ~** to have sth (with one); **hast du alles mit?** have you got everything?

**mithalten** vi sep irreg *(bei Tempo etc)* to keep pace *(mit* with*)*. **bei einer Diskussion ~ können** to be able to hold one's own in a discussion.

**mithelfen** vi sep irreg to help. **beim Bau des Hauses ~** to help build the house.

**Mithilfe** f assistance, aid.

**mithören** sep **1** vt to listen to (too); *Gespräch* to overhear; *(heimlich)* to listen in on. **ich habe alles mitgehört** I heard everything. **2** vi to listen in *(bei on)*; *(zufällig)* to overhear.

**Mit|inhaber** m joint owner.

**mitklingen** vi sep irreg *(Ton, Saite)* to sound, to resonate. **in ihrer Äußerung klang ein leichter Vorwurf mit** there was a slight note of reproach in her remark.

**mitkommen** vi sep irreg aux sein (**a**) to come along *(mit* with*)*. **ich kann nicht ~** I can't come; **komm doch mit!** why don't you come too? (**b**) *(col) (mithalten)* to keep up; *(verstehen)* to follow. **da komme ich nicht mit** I don't get it *(col)*; *(es ist mir zu hoch)* that's beyond me; **sie kommt in der Schule gut mit** she is getting on well at school.

**mitkriegen** vt sep *(col)* = **mitbekommen**.

**mitlaufen** vi sep irreg aux sein to run *(mit* with*)*.

**Mitläufer** m hanger-on; *(Pol, pej)* fellow traveller *(Brit)* or traveler *(US)*.

**Mitlaut** m consonant.

**Mitleid** *nt no pl* pity, compassion *(mit* for*)*; *(Mitgefühl)* sympathy *(mit* with, for*)*.

**Mitleidenschaft** *f:* **jdn/etw in ~ ziehen** to affect sb/sth (detrimentally).

**mitleid|erregend** *adj* pitiful.

**mitleidig** *adj* pitying; *(mitfühlend)* sympathetic; *Mensch auch* compassionate. **~ lächeln** to smile pityingly.

**mitleid(s)-:** **~los** *adj* heartless; **~voll** *adj* compassionate.

**mitmachen** *vti sep* **(a)** *(teilnehmen) Spiel, Singen etc* to join in; *Reise* to go on; *Kurs* to do; *Mode* to follow. **etw** *(acc) or* **bei etw** *(dat)* **~** to join in sth; **meine Beine machen nicht mehr mit** my legs are giving up. **(b)** *(col: einverstanden sein)* **da macht mein Chef nicht mit** my boss won't go along with that; **ich mache das nicht mehr lange mit** I won't put up with that much longer. **(c)** *(erleben)* to live through; *(erleiden)* to go through.

**Mitmensch** *m* fellow man.

**mitmenschlich** *adj Kontakte etc* human.

**mitmischen** *vi sep (col) (sich beteiligen)* to be involved *(in +dat, bei* in*)*; *(sich einmischen)* to interfere *(in +dat, bei* in sth*)*.

**mitnehmen** *vt sep irreg* **(a)** to take (with one); *(ausleihen)* to borrow; *(kaufen)* to take. **jdn (im Auto) ~** to give sb a lift; **einen Hamburger zum M~** a hamburger to take away *(Brit) or* to go *(US)*. **(b)** *(erschöpfen) jdn* to exhaust, to weaken; *(beschädigen)* to be bad for. **mitgenommen aussehen** to look the worse for wear. **(c)** *(stehlen)* to walk off with. **(d)** *(col) Sehenswürdigkeit etc* to take in.

**Mitrauchen** *nt* passive smoking.

**mitrechnen** *vt sep* to count; *Betrag* to count in.

**mitreden** *sep* **1** *vi (Meinung äußern)* to join in *(bei etw* sth*)*; *(mitbestimmen)* to have a say *(bei* in*)*. **da kann er nicht ~** he wouldn't know anything about that. **2** *vt* **Sie haben hier nichts mitzureden** this is none of your concern.

**mitreisen** *vi sep aux sein* to go/travel too. **mit jdm ~** to go/travel with sb.

**Mitreisende(r)** *mf* fellow traveller *(Brit) or* traveler *(US)*.

**mitreißen** *vt sep irreg (Fluß, Lawine)* to sweep away. **seine Rede hat alle mitgerissen** everyone was carried away by his speech.

**mitreißend** *adj Rhythmus* infectious; *Reden* rousing; *Film, Fußballspiel* thrilling, exciting.

**mitsamt** *prep +dat* together with.

**mitschicken** *vt sep (in Brief etc)* to enclose.

**mitschneiden** *vt sep irreg (Rad, TV)* to record.

**Mitschnitt** *m (Rad, TV)* recording.

**mitschreiben** *sep irreg* **1** *vt* **etw ~** to write *or* take sth down. **2** *vi* to take notes.

**Mitschrift** *f* record; *(von Vorlesung etc)* notes *pl*.

**Mitschuld** *f* share of the blame *(an +dat* for*)*; *(an einem Verbrechen)* complicity *(an +dat* in*)*.

**mitschuldig** *adj (an Verbrechen)* implicated *(an +dat* in*)*; *(an Unfall)* partly responsible *(an +dat* for*)*.

**Mitschuldige(r)** *mf* accomplice.

**Mitschüler** *m* schoolfriend; *(in derselben Klasse)* classmate.

**mitsingen** *sep irreg* **1** *vt* to join in (singing). **2** *vi* to sing along. **in einem Chor ~** to sing in a choir.

**mitspielen** *vi sep* **(a)** to play too; *(in Team etc)* to play *(bei* in*)*. **in einem Film ~** to be in a film. **(b)** *(Gründe, Motive)* to play a part *(bei* in*)*, to be involved *(bei* in*)*. **(c)** *(Schaden zufügen)* **er hat ihr übel/hart mitgespielt** he has treated her badly.

**Mitspieler** *m (Sport)* player; *(Theat)* member of the

cast.

**Mitsprache** *f* a say.

**Mitspracherecht** *nt* right to a say in a matter. **jdm ein ~ einräumen** to allow sb a say *(bei* in*)*.

**mitsprechen** *sep irreg* **1** *vt Gebet* to join in (saying). **2** *vi (mitbestimmen)* to have a say in sth.

**Mitstreiter** *m (geh)* comrade-in-arms.

**mittag** *adv* **gestern/heute ~** at midday yesterday/today, yesterday/today lunchtime.

**Mittag** *m* **-e (a)** midday. **jeden ~** every day at midday, every lunchtime; **zu ~ essen** to have lunch. **(b)** *(col: ~spause)* lunch hour, lunch break. **~ machen** to take one's lunch hour.

**Mittag|essen** *nt* midday meal. **er kam zum ~** he came to lunch.

**mittäglich** *adj attr* midday, lunchtime.

**mittags** *adv* at lunchtime. **~ um 12 Uhr** at 12 noon; **sonnabends ~** Saturday lunchtime.

**Mittags-:** **~hitze** *f* midday heat; **~pause** *f* lunch hour, lunch break; **~pause machen/haben** to take/have one's lunch hour *etc*; *(Geschäft etc)* to close at lunchtime; **~ruhe** *f* period of quiet (after lunch); *(in Geschäft)* midday closing; **~schlaf** *m* siesta, early afternoon nap; **~stunde** *f* midday; **um die ~stunde** around midday; **~tisch** *m* lunch table; **am ~tisch sitzen** to be sitting (at the table) having lunch; **~zeit** *f* lunchtime; **während** *or* **in der ~zeit** at lunchtime.

**Mittäter** *m* accomplice.

**Mitte** *f* **-n** middle; *(fig auch, von Kreis, Kugel etc, Pol)* centre *(Brit)*, center *(US)*. **das Reich der ~** *(liter)* the Middle Kingdom; **~ August** in the middle of August, in mid August; **er ist ~ vierzig** he's in his mid-forties; **die goldene ~** the golden mean; **in der ~ in the middle**; *(zwischen zwei Menschen)* in between (them/us *etc)*; *(zwischen Ortschaften)* halfway, midway; **einer aus unserer ~** one of our number; **in unserer ~** in our midst.

**mitteilen** *sep irreg* **1** *vt* **jdm etw ~** to tell sb sth; *(benachrichtigen)* to inform sb about sth; *(bekanntgeben)* to announce (sth) to sb; *(Comm, Admin)* to notify sb of sth. **2** *vr* to communicate *(jdm* with sb*)*. **er kann sich gut/schlecht ~** he finds it easy/difficult to communicate.

**mitteilsam** *adj* communicative; *(gesprächig)* talkative.

**Mitteilung** *f (Bekanntgabe)* announcement; *(Benachrichtigung)* notification; *(Comm, Admin)* communication; *(an Mitarbeiter etc)* memo. **jdm (eine) ~ (von etw) machen** *(form)* to inform sb (of sth); *(bekanntgeben)* to announce (sth) to sb; *(benachrichtigen)* to inform sb (of sth).

**Mitteilungsbedürfnis** *nt* need to communicate.

**Mittel** *nt* **- (a)** *(~ zum Zweck)* means *sing*; *(Maßnahme, Methode)* way, method. **~ und Wege finden** to find ways and means; **~ zum Zweck** a means to an end; **kein ~ unversucht lassen** to try everything; **als letztes ~** as a last resort; **ihm ist jedes ~ recht** he will do anything (to achieve his ends); **etw mit allen ~n verhindern** to do one's utmost to prevent sth. **(b)** *pl (Geld~)* funds *pl*, means *pl*. **(c)** *(Medikament, kosmetisch)* preparation; *(Medizin)* medicine; *(Putz~)* cleaning agent; *(Wasch~)* detergent. **welches ~ nimmst du?** *(Med: einnehmen)* what do you take?; **das ist ein ~ gegen Schuppen** that is for dandruff; **sich** *(dat)* **ein ~ verschreiben lassen** to get the doctor to prescribe something; **das beste ~ gegen etw** the best cure for sth. **(d)** *(Math: Durchschnitt)* average. **arithmetisches ~** arithmetical mean.

**Mittel-:** **~alter** *nt* Middle Ages *pl*; **im finsteren**

~**alter** in the Dark Ages; **m~alterlich** *adj* medieval; ~**amerika** *nt* Central America (and the Caribbean); **m~amerikanisch** *adj* Central American; **m~bar** *adj* indirect *(auch Jur)*; **m~deutsch** *adj (Geog, Ling)* Central German; ~**ding** *nt (Mischung)* cross; **ein** ~**ding** *(weder das eine noch das andere)* something in between; ~**europa** *nt* Central Europe; ~**europäer** *m* Central European; **m~europäisch** *adj* Central European; ~**feld** *nt (Sport)* midfield; ~**finger** *m* middle finger; **m~fristig** *adj Finanzplanung, Politik* medium-term; ~**gebirge** *nt* low mountain range; ~**gewicht** *nt* middleweight; **m~groß** *adj* medium-sized; ~**hochdeutsch(e)** *nt* Middle High German; ~**klasse** *f* **(a)** *(Comm)* middle of the market; **(b)** *(Sociol)* middle classes *pl*; ~**klassewagen** *m* mid-range car; ~**linie** *f* centre *(Brit)* or center *(US)* line; **m~los** *adj* without means; *(arm)* impoverished; ~**losigkeit** *f* lack of means; *(Armut)* impoverishment; ~**maß** *nt* mediocrity *no art*; **das (gesunde)** ~**maß** the happy medium; **m~mäßig 1** *adj* mediocre; *Schriftsteller, Spieler etc auch* indifferent; **2** *adv* indifferently; **wie gefällt es dir hier? — so m~mäßig** how do you like it here? — so-so; ~**mäßigkeit** *f* mediocrity.

**Mittelmeer** *nt* Mediterranean (Sea).

**Mittelmeer-** *in cpds* Mediterranean.

**Mittelmeerraum** *m* Mediterranean (region).

**Mittel-:** **m~prächtig** *adj (hum col)* not bad *pred,* so-so *pred (col)*; ~**punkt** *m (Math, räumlich)* centre *(Brit)*, center *(US)*; *(fig: visuell)* focal point; **er steht im ~punkt des Interesses** he is the centre of attention; ~**scheitel** *m* centre parting *(Brit)*, center part *(US)*; ~**schicht** *f (Sociol)* middle class.

**Mittelsmann** *m, pl* **-männer** or **-leute** intermediary.

**Mittel-:** ~**stand** *m* middle classes *pl*; **m~ständisch** *adj* **(a)** middle-class; **(b)** *(Betrieb)* medium-sized.

**Mittelstrecken-:** ~**flugzeug** *nt* medium-range aircraft; ~**lauf** *m* middle-distance race; ~**läufer** *m* middle-distance runner; ~**rakete** *f* intermediate-range *or* medium-range missile.

**Mittel-:** ~**streifen** *m* central reservation *(Brit)*, median (strip) *(US)*; ~**stück** *nt* middle part; ~**stufe** *f (Sch)* middle school *(Brit)*, junior high *(US)*; ~**stürmer** *m (Sport)* centre forward; ~**weg** *m* middle course; **der goldene** ~**weg** the happy medium, the golden mean; ~**welle** *f (Rad)* medium wave(band); ~**wert** *m* mean.

**mitten** *adv* ~ **in/auf etw** (right) in the middle of sth; ~ **aus etw** (right) from the middle of sth; ~ **durch etw** (right) through the middle of sth; ~ **im Urwald** in the depths of the jungle; ~ **ins Gesicht** right in the face; ~ **unter uns** (right) in our midst.

**mitten-:** ~**drin** *adv* (right) in the middle of it; ~**durch** *adv* (right) through the middle.

**Mitternacht** *f* midnight *no art*.

**mitternächtlich** *adj attr* midnight. **zu** ~**er Stunde** *(geh)* at the midnight hour.

**Mittler** *m* - mediator.

**mittlere(r, s)** *adj attr* **(a)** *(dazwischenliegend)* middle. **der/die/das** ~ the middle one; **der M~ Osten** the Middle East. **(b)** *(den Mittelwert bildend)* medium; *(mittelschwer)* Kursus, Aufgabe intermediate; *(durchschnittlich)* average; *(Math)* mean. ~**n Alters** middle-aged; ~ **Preislage** medium price range.

**mittlerweile** *adv* in the meantime.

**Mitt-:** ~**woch** *m* -e Wednesday; *siehe* **Dienstag**; **m~wochs** *adv* on Wednesdays.

**mit|unter** *adv* now and again, once in a while.

**mitver|antwortlich** *adj* jointly responsible *pred*.

**Mitver|antwortung** *f* share of the responsibility.

**mitverdienen\*** *vi sep* to (go out to) work as well.

**Mitverfasser** *m* co-author.

**Mitverschulden** *nt* **ihn trifft ein** ~ **an diesem Vorfall** he was partly to blame for this incident.

**mitversichern\*** *vt sep* to include in the insurance.

**mitwirken** *vi sep (an +dat, bei in)* to play a part; *(beteiligt sein)* to be involved; *(Theat, in Diskussion)* to take part; *(in Film)* to appear.

**Mitwirkende(r)** *mf decl as adj* participant *(an +dat, bei* in*)*. **die** ~**n** *(Theat)* the cast *pl*.

**Mitwirkung** *f (Beteiligung)* involvement *(an +dat, bei* in*)*; *(an Buch, Film)* collaboration *(an +dat, bei* on*)*; *(Teilnahme) (an Diskussion, Projekt)* participation *(an +dat, bei* in*)*; *(von Schauspieler)* appearance *(an +dat, bei* in*)*. **unter** ~ **von** with the participation of.

**Mitwisser(in** *f)* *m* - *(Jur)* accessory *(gen* to*)*. ~ **einer Sache** *(gen)* **sein** to know about sth.

**mitzählen** *vti sep* to count; *Betrag* to count in.

**mitziehen** *vi sep irreg aux sein (fig col)* to go along with it.

**Mixbecher** *m* (cocktail) shaker.

**mixen** *vt Getränke, (Rad, TV)* to mix.

**Mixer** *m* - **(a)** *(Bar~)* barman, bartender *(US)*. **(b)** *(Küchen~)* blender; *(Rührmaschine)* mixer. **(c)** *(Film, Rad, TV)* mixer.

**Mixgetränk** *nt* mixed drink; *(alkoholisch)* cocktail.

**Mixtur** *f (Pharm, Mus, fig)* mixture.

**ml** = **Milliliter** ml.

**mm** = **Millimeter** mm.

**Mo.** = **Montag** Mon.

**Mob** *m no pl (pej)* mob.

**Möbel** *nt* - *(~stück)* piece of furniture. ~ *pl* furniture *sing*.

**Möbel-** *in cpds* furniture; ~**haus** *nt* furniture store; ~**lager** *nt* furniture showroom; ~**packer** *m* removal man; ~**spedition** *f* removal firm; ~**stoff** *m* furnishing fabric; ~**stück** *nt* piece of furniture; ~**wagen** *m* removal van *(Brit)*, moving van *(US)*.

**mobil** *adj* **(a)** mobile. ~ **machen** *(Mil)* to mobilize. **(b)** *(col: flink, munter)* lively.

**Mobile** ['moːbilə] *nt* **-s** mobile.

**Mobiliar** *nt no pl* furnishings *pl*.

**mobilisieren\*** *vt (Mil, fig)* to mobilize.

**Mobilisierung** *f* mobilization.

**Mobilität** *f* mobility.

**Mobil-:** ~**machung** *f (Mil)* mobilization; ~**telefon** *nt* portable telephone.

**möbl.** = **möbliert** furnished.

**möblieren\*** *vt* to furnish. **ein möbliertes Zimmer** a furnished room; **möbliert wohnen** to live in furnished accommodation *(Brit)* or accommodations *(US)*.

**mochte** *pret of* **mögen**.

**Möchtegern-** *in cpds (iro)* would-be.

**Modalität** *f usu pl (von Plan, Vertrag etc)* arrangement; *(von Verfahren, Arbeit)* procedure.

**Mode** *f* **-n** fashion; *(Sitte)* custom. ~ **sein** to be the fashion; *(Sitte)* to be the custom; **in** ~**/aus der** ~ **kommen** to come into/go out of fashion.

**Mode-:** ~**artikel** *m* fashion accessory; **m~bewußt** *adj* fashion-conscious; ~**farbe** *f* fashionable colour *(Brit)* or color *(US)*; ~**geschäft** *nt* fashion shop *(Brit)* or store *(US)*; ~**heft**, ~**journal** *nt* fashion magazine.

**Modell** *nt* -e model. **zu etw** ~ **stehen** to be the model for sth.

**Modell-:** ~**eisenbahn** *f* model railway; *(als Spielzeug)* train set; ~**flugzeug** *nt* model aircraft.

**modellieren\*** *vti* to model.
**Modell-:** ~**kleid** *nt* model (dress); ~**versuch** *m* *(esp Sch)* pilot scheme.
**Modem** *m* -**s** modem.
**Modenschau** *f* fashion show.
**Moder** *m no pl* mustiness; *(Schimmel)* mildew. **es riecht nach** ~ it smells musty.
**Moderation** *f (Rad, TV)* presentation.
**Moderator** *m,* **Moderatorin** *f* presenter.
**Modergeruch** *m* musty smell.
**moderieren\*** *vti (Rad, TV)* to present.
**mod(e)rig** *adj Geruch* musty.
**modern**[1] *vi aux sein or haben* to rot.
**modern**[2] *adj* modern *no adv; (modisch)* fashionable; *Ansichten, Eltern, Lehrer* progressive.
**Moderne** *f no pl (geh)* modern age.
**modernisieren\*** *vt Gebäude* to modernize; *Kleidung* to make more fashionable.
**Modernisierung** *f* modernization.
**Modernismus** *m* modernism.
**modernistisch** *adj* modernistic.
**Modernität** *f (geh)* modernity.
**Mode-:** ~**schmuck** *m* costume jewellery *(Brit)* or jewelry *(US)*; ~**schöpfer(in** *f)* *m* fashion designer; ~**tanz** *m* popular dance; ~**wort** *nt* trendy *or* buzz word; ~**zeitschrift** *f* fashion magazine.
**Modifikation** *f* modification.
**modifizieren\*** *vt* to modify.
**modisch** *adj* stylish, fashionable.
**Modistin** *f* milliner.
**Modul** *nt* -**e** *(Comp)* module.
**modular** *adj (Comp)* modular.
**modulieren\*** *vt* to modulate.
**Modus** *m* -, **Modi (a)** way. **(b)** *(Gram)* mood. **(c)** *(Comp)* mode.
**Mofa** *nt* -**s** small moped.
**Mogadischu** *nt* Mogadischu.
**Mogelei** *f* cheating *no pl.*
**mogeln** *vi* to cheat.
**mögen** *pret* **mochte,** *ptp* **gemocht 1** *vt* to like. ~ **Sie ihn?** do you like him?; **was möchten Sie, bitte?** what would you like?; *(Verkäufer)* what can I do for you?; **nein danke, ich möchte lieber Tee** no thank you, I would rather have tea.
  **2** *vi (etw tun* ~*)* to like to. **ich mag nicht mehr** I've had enough; *(bin am Ende)* I can't take any more; **kommen Sie mit?** — **ich möchte gern, aber ...** are you coming too? — I'd like to, but ...; **ich möchte lieber in die Stadt** I would prefer to go into town.
  **3** *ptp* ~ *modal aux* **(a)** to like to *+infin; (wollen)* to want. **möchten Sie etwas essen?** would you like something to eat?; **hier möchte ich nicht wohnen** *(würde nicht gern)* I wouldn't like to live here; *(will nicht)* I don't want to live here; **ich hätte gern dabeisein** ~ I would like to have been there; **man möchte meinen, daß ...** you would think that ...; **sie mag nicht bleiben** she doesn't want to stay.
  **(b) es mag wohl sein, daß er recht hat, aber ...** he may well be right, but ...; **wie dem auch sein mag** however that may be; **mag kommen was da will** come what may; **es mochten etwa fünf Stunden vergangen sein** about five hours must have passed; **wie alt mag sie sein?** how old is she, I wonder?; **was mag das wohl heißen?** what might that mean?
  **(c)** *(Aufforderung, indirekte Rede)* **(sagen Sie ihm,) er möchte zu mir kommen** would you tell him to come and see me; **Sie möchten zu Hause anrufen** you should call home.
**Mogler(in** *f)* *m* - cheat.
**möglich** *adj* possible; *(attr: eventuell auch)* potential. **alles** ~**e** everything you can think of; **alles M**~**e tun**

to do everything possible; **er hat allen** ~**en Blödsinn gemacht** he did all sorts of stupid things; **so viel/bald wie** ~ as much/soon as possible; **es war mir nicht** ~ **mitzukommen** I couldn't manage to come; **nicht** ~**!** never!; **er tat sein** ~**stes** he did his utmost.
**möglicherweise** *adv* possibly. ~ **kommt er morgen** he may (possibly) come tomorrow.
**Möglichkeit** *f* **(a)** possibility. **es besteht die** ~**, daß ...** there is a possibility that ...; **nach** ~ if possible; **ist denn das die** ~**?** *(col)* I don't believe it! **(b)** *(Aussicht)* chance; *(Gelegenheit auch)* opportunity. **er hatte keine andere** ~ he had no other choice.
**möglichst** *adv* ~ **schnell/oft** as quickly/often as possible; **in** ~ **kurzer Zeit** as quickly as possible.
**Mohair** [mo'hɛːɐ] *m* -**e** *(Tex)* mohair.
**Mohammed** *m* Mohammed.
**Mohammedaner(in** *f)* [mohame'daːnɐ, -ərɪn] *m* - Mohammedan.
**mohammedanisch** [mohame'daːnɪʃ] *adj* Mohammedan.
**Mohikaner** [mohi'kaːnɐ] *m* - Mohican. **der letzte** ~ *(hum col)* the very last one.
**Mohn** *m* -**e (a)** poppy. **(b)** *(~samen)* poppy seed.
**Mohn-** *in cpds* poppy; *(Cook)* poppy-seed; ~**blume** *f* poppy; ~**kuchen** *m* poppy-seed cake.
**Möhre** *f* -**n** carrot.
**Mohrenkopf** *m* chocolate-covered marshmallow.
**Mohrrübe** *f* carrot.
**mokieren\*** *vr* to sneer *(über* +*acc* at*)*.
**Mokka** *m* -**s** mocha, *strong coffee.*
**Molch** *m* -**e** salamander.
**Moldau** *f (Fluß)* Vltava.
**Moldawien** [-iən] *nt* Moldavia.
**Mole** *f* -**n** *(Naut)* mole.
**Molekül** *nt* -**e** molecule.
**molekular** *adj* molecular.
**molk** *pret of* **melken.**
**Molke** *f no pl* whey.
**Molkerei** *f* dairy.
**Molkerei-:** ~**butter** *f* blended butter; ~**produkt** *nt* dairy product.
**Moll** *nt* -, - *(Mus)* minor (key). **a-**~ A minor.
**mollig** *adj (col)* **(a)** cosy *(Brit)*, cozy *(US)*. **(b)** *(rundlich)* plump.
**Molltonleiter** *f* minor scale.
**Moment**[1] *m* -**e** moment. **jeden** ~ any moment; ~ **mal!** just a minute!; **im** ~ at the moment; **im ersten** ~ for a moment.
**Moment**[2] *nt* -**e** *(Umstand)* fact; *(Faktor)* factor; *(Bestandteil)* element.
**momentan 1** *adj (vorübergehend)* momentary; *(augenblicklich)* present *attr.* **2** *adv (vorübergehend)* momentarily; *(augenblicklich)* at present.
**Monaco** ['moːnako, mo'nako] *nt* Monaco.
**Monarch(in** *f)* *m (wk)* -**en,** -**en** monarch.
**Monarchie** *f* monarchy.
**Monarchist(in** *f)* *m* monarchist.
**monarchistisch** *adj* monarchistic.
**Monat** *m* -**e** month. **der** ~ **Mai** the month of May; **sie ist im sechsten** ~ **(schwanger)** she's five months pregnant; **was verdient er im** ~**?** how much does he earn a month?; **am 12. dieses** ~**s** on the 12th (of this month).
**monatelang 1** *adj attr Verhandlungen, Kämpfe* which go/went *etc* on for months. **nach** ~**em Warten** after months of waiting; **mit** ~**er Verspätung** months late. **2** *adv* for months.
**monatlich** *adj* monthly. ~ **stattfinden** to take place every month.
**Monats-:** ~**anfang** *m* beginning of the month; ~**blutung** *f* menstrual period; ~**einkommen** *nt*

monthly income; ~**ende** *nt* end of the month; ~**erste(r)** *m decl as adj* first (day) of the month; ~**gehalt** *nt* monthly salary; **zwei** ~**gehälter** two months' salary; ~**karte** *f* monthly season (ticket); ~**lohn** *m* monthly wage; ~**rate** *f* monthly instalment *(Brit)* or installment *(US)*.

**Mönch** *m* -e monk; *(Bettel~ auch)* friar.

**Mond** *m* -e moon. **auf** *or* **hinter dem** ~ **leben** *(col)* to be behind the times; **in den** ~ **gucken** *(col)* to go empty-handed; **deine Uhr geht nach dem** ~ *(col)* your watch/clock is way out *(col)*.

**mondän** *adj* chic.

**Mond-:** ~**aufgang** *m* moonrise; ~**bahn** *f* lunar orbit; ~**finsternis** *f* lunar eclipse; ~**gesicht** *nt* moonface; **m**~**hell** *adj* moonlit; ~**(lande)fähre** *f (Space)* lunar module; ~**landschaft** *f* lunar landscape; ~**landung** *f* moon landing; ~**licht** *nt* moonlight; **m**~**los** *adj* moonless; ~**nacht** *f (geh)* moonlit night; ~**schein** *m* moonlight; ~**sonde** *f (Space)* lunar probe; **m**~**süchtig** *adj* **m**~**süchtig sein** to sleepwalk; ~**untergang** *m* moonset.

**Monegasse** *m (wk)* -n, -n, **Monegassin** *f* Monegasque.

**monegassisch** *adj* Monegasque.

**Monetarismus** *m (Econ)* monetarism.

**Monetarist(in** *f) m (Econ)* monetarist.

**Moneten** *pl (col)* bread *(col)*, dough *(col)*.

**Mongole** *m (wk)* -n, -n, **Mongolin** *f* Mongolian, Mongol.

**Mongolei** *f* **die** ~ Mongolia.

**mongolisch** *adj* Mongolian, Mongol.

**Mongolismus** *m (Med)* mongolism.

**mongoloid** *adj (Med)* mongoloid.

**monieren\* 1** *vt* to complain about. **2** *vi* to complain.

**Monitor** *m (TV, Phys)* monitor.

**Mono-, mono-** *in cpds* mono-.

**Mono-:** **m**~**chrom** [mono'kro:m] *adj* monochrome; **m**~**gam** *adj* monogamous; ~**gamie** *f* monogamy; ~**gramm** *nt* monogram.

**Monokel** *nt* - monocle.

**Monolith** *m (wk)* -en, e(n) monolith.

**monolithisch** *adj (auch fig)* monolithic.

**Monolog** *m* -e *(Liter, fig)* monologue; *(Selbstgespräch)* soliloquy. **einen** ~ **halten** *(fig)* to hold a monologue, to talk on and on.

**Monopol** *nt* -e monopoly *(auf +acc, für on)*.

**monopolisieren\*** *vt (lit, fig)* to monopolize.

**Monopol-:** ~**kapital** *nt (Kapital)* monopoly capital; *(Kapitalisten)* monopoly capitalism; ~**stellung** *f* monopoly.

**monoton** *adj* monotonous.

**Monotonie** *f* monotony.

**Monster** *nt* - *(col)* monster.

**Monster-** *in cpds (usu pej)* mammoth, monster; ~**film** *m* mammoth (film) production.

**Monstranz** *f (Eccl)* monstrance.

**monströs** *adj* monstrous; *(riesig groß)* monster.

**Monstrum** *nt, pl* **Monstren** *(lit, fig)* monster.

**Monsun** *m* -e monsoon.

**Montag** *m* Monday; *siehe* **Dienstag**.

**Montage** [mɔn'ta:ʒə] *f* -n **(a)** *(Tech) (Aufstellung)* installation; *(von Gerüst)* erection; *(Zusammenbau)* assembly. **(b)** *(Art)* montage; *(Film)* editing.

**Montage-:** ~**band** *nt* assembly line; ~**halle** *f* assembly shop.

**montags** *adv* on Mondays.

**Montan|industrie** *f* coal and steel industry.

**Monteur(in** *f)* [mɔn'tø:ɐ, -'tø:rɪn] *m (Tech)* fitter; *(Aut)* mechanic.

**montieren\*** *vt (Tech)* to install; *(zusammenbauen)*

to assemble; *(befestigen)* to fit *(auf or an +acc to)*; *(aufstellen) Gerüst* to erect.

**Montur** *f (col: Spezialkleidung)* gear *(col)*, rig-out *(col)*.

**Monument** *nt* monument.

**monumental** *adj* monumental.

**Moor** *nt* -e bog; *(Hoch~)* moor.

**Moor-:** ~**bad** *nt* mud bath; ~**huhn** *nt* grouse.

**moorig** *adj* boggy.

**Moos** *nt* -e **(a)** moss. ~ **ansetzen** to become covered with moss. **(b)** *no pl (col: Geld)* bread *(col)*, dough *(col)*.

**moos-:** ~**bedeckt** *adj* moss-covered; ~**grün** *adj* moss-green.

**moosig** *adj* mossy.

**Mop** *m* -s mop.

**Moped** *nt* -s moped.

**Mopedfahrer** *m* moped rider.

**Mops** *m* ̈e **(a)** *(Hund)* pug (dog). **(b)** *(Dickwanst)* roly-poly *(col)*. **(c)** ̃e *pl (col: Geld)* bread *sing (col)*, dough *sing (col)*.

**mopsen** *vt (col: stehlen)* to pinch *(col)*.

**mopsig** *adj (col: frech)* **sich** ~ **machen**, ~ **werden** to get cheeky *(esp Brit)* or fresh *(esp US)*.

**Moral** *f no pl* **(a)** *(Sittlichkeit)* morals *pl*. **eine hohe** ~ **haben** to have high moral standards; **die bürgerliche** ~ bourgeois morality; **eine doppelte** ~ double standards *pl*. **(b)** *(Lehre)* moral. **und die** ~ **von der Geschicht'** and the moral of this story. **(c)** *(Disziplin: von Volk, Soldaten)* morale. **die** ~ **sinkt** morale is getting low.

**Moral-** *in cpds* moral; ~**apostel** *m (pej)* upholder of moral standards.

**moralisch** *adj* moral. **das war eine** ~**e Ohrfeige für die Regierung** that was one in the eye for the government *(col)*; **einen M**~**en haben** *(col)* to have (a fit of) the blues *(col)*.

**Moralist(in** *f) m* moralist.

**Moralpredigt** *f* homily, sermon. ~**en halten** to moralize.

**Morast** *m* -e *(lit, fig)* mire; *(Sumpf auch)* morass.

**morastig** *adj* marshy; *(schlammig)* muddy.

**Morchel** *f* -n *(Bot)* morel.

**Mord** *m* -e murder, homicide *(US) (an +dat of)*; *(an Politiker etc)* assassination *(an +dat of)*. **wegen** ~**es** for murder *or* homicide *(US)*; **politischer** ~ political killing; **dann gibt es** ~ **und Totschlag** *(col)* there'll be hell to pay *(col)*.

**Mord-:** ~**anschlag** *m* murderous attack *(auf +acc on)*; *(Attentat)* assassination attempt *(auf +acc on)*; **einen** ~**anschlag auf jdn verüben** to make an attempt on sb's life; ~**drohung** *f* threat on one's life.

**morden** *vti (liter)* to murder, to slay *(liter)*.

**Mörder(in** *f) m* - murderer *(auch Jur)*, killer; *(Attentäter)* assassin.

**Mörder-:** ~**bande** *f* gang of killers; ~**grube** *f*: **aus seinem Herzen keine** ~**grube machen** to speak frankly.

**mörderisch 1** *adj (fig) (schrecklich)* dreadful, terrible; *Tempo* gruelling; *Preise* iniquitous; *Konkurrenzkampf* cut-throat. **2** *adv (col: entsetzlich)* dreadfully, terribly. ~ **schreien** to scream blue murder *(col)*.

**Mord-:** ~**fall** *m* murder *or* homicide *(US)* (case); ~**kommission** *f* murder squad, homicide squad *or* division *(US)*; ~**prozeß** *m* murder trial.

**Mords-** *in cpds (col)* terrible, awful; *(toll, prima)* hell of a *(col)*; ~**ding** *nt (col)* whopper *(col)*; ~**glück** *nt (col)* tremendous stroke of luck; ~**lärm** *m (col)* hell of a noise *(col)*; **m**~**mäßig** *(col)* **1** *adj* incredible; **2** *adv (+vb)* terribly, awfully.

**Mord-:** ~**verdacht** *m* suspicion of murder; **unter** ~**verdacht** *(dat)* **stehen** to be suspected of murder; ~**versuch** *m* attempted murder; ~**waffe** *f* murder weapon.

**Morgen** *m* - **(a)** *(Tagesanfang)* morning. **am** ~ in the morning; **bis in den** ~ **(hinein)** into the early hours; **eines** ~**s** one morning; **es wird** ~ day is breaking; **guten** ~! good morning; ~! *(col)* morning. **(b)** *(Measure)* ≃ acre. **drei** ~ **Land** three acres of land.

**morgen** *adv* **(a)** tomorrow. ~ **früh** tomorrow morning; ~ **in acht Tagen** a week (from) tomorrow; ~ **um diese Zeit** this time tomorrow; **bis** ~! see you tomorrow; ~ **ist auch (noch) ein Tag!** *(Prov)* there's always tomorrow; **die Technik von** ~ the technology of tomorrow. **(b) gestern** ~ yesterday morning; **heute** ~ this morning.

**Morgen-** *in cpds* morning; ~**andacht** *f* morning service; ~**ausgabe** *f* morning edition; ~**dämmerung** *f* = ~**grauen**.

**morgendlich** *adj* morning *attr*; *(früh~)* early morning *attr*.

**Morgen-:** ~**grauen** *nt* - dawn, daybreak; ~**gymnastik** *f* morning exercises *pl*; ~**land** *nt* *(old, liter)* Orient; ~**luft** *f* early morning air; ~**luft wittern** *(fig col)* to see one's chance; ~**mantel** *m* dressing-gown; ~**muffel** *m* *(col)* **er ist ein schrecklicher** ~**muffel** he's terribly grumpy in the mornings *(col)*; ~**rock** *m* dressing-gown; ~**rot** *nt no pl* sunrise; *(fig)* dawn(ing).

**morgens** *adv* in the morning. **(um) drei Uhr** ~ at three a.m.; **von** ~ **bis abends** from morning to night; **Freitag** ~ on Friday morning; *(regelmäßig)* on Friday mornings.

**Morgen-:** ~**stern** *m* morning star; ~**stunde** *f* morning hour; **bis in die frühen** ~**stunden** into the early hours (of the morning); ~**stund(e) hat Gold im Mund(e)** *(Prov)* the early bird catches the worm *(Prov)*.

**morgig** *adj attr* tomorrow's. **der** ~**e Tag** tomorrow.

**Mormone** *m* *(wk)* -**n**, -**n**, **Mormonin** *f* Mormon.

**Morphium** ['mɔrfiʊm] *nt no pl* morphine.

**morsch** *adj (lit, fig)* rotten; *Knochen* brittle; *Gebäude* ramshackle.

**Morse|alphabet** *nt* Morse (code).

**morsen 1** *vi* to send a message in Morse (code). **2** *vt* to send in Morse (code).

**Mörser** *m* - mortar *(auch Mil)*.

**Morsezeichen** *nt* Morse signal.

**Mörtel** *m* - *(zum Mauern)* mortar; *(Putz)* stucco.

**Mosaik** *nt* -**e(n)** *(lit, fig)* mosaic.

**Mosambik** [mosam'bɪk, -'biːk] *nt* Mozambique.

**Moschee** *f* -**n** [-'eːən] mosque.

**Moschus** *m no pl* musk.

**Möse** *f* -**n** *(col!!)* cunt *(col!!)*.

**Mosel**[1] *f (Geog)* Moselle.

**Mosel**[2] *m* -, **Moselwein** *m* Moselle (wine).

**mosern** *vi (col)* to gripe *(col)*, to belly-ache *(col)*.

**Moskau** *nt* Moscow.

**Moskauer** *adj attr* Moscow attr.

**Moskauer(in** *f)* *m* - Muscovite.

**Moskito** *m* -**s** mosquito.

**Moslem** *m* -**s**, **Moslime** *f* Muslim.

**moslemisch** *adj attr* Muslim.

**Most** *m no pl* **(a)** unfermented fruit juice; *(für Wein)* must. **(b)** *(SGer, Sw: Obstwein)* fruit wine; *(Apfel~)* ≃ cider.

**Most|apfel** *m* ≃ cider apple.

**Motel** *nt* -**s** motel.

**Motiv** *nt* -**e** **(a)** *(Psych, Jur, fig)* motive. **das** ~ **einer Tat** the motive for a deed. **(b)** *(Art, Liter)* subject; *(Leit~, Mus)* motif.

**Motivation** [-va'tsioːn] *f* motivation.

**motivieren\*** [moti'viːrən] *vt* **(a)** *(begründen)* **etw (jdm gegenüber)** ~ to give (sb) reasons for sth. **(b)** *(anregen)* to motivate.

**Motivierung** *f* motivation.

**Motor** *m* -**en** [mo'toːrən] engine; *(Elektro~)* motor; *(fig)* driving force *(gen in)*.

**Motor-:** ~**antrieb** *m* **mit** ~**antrieb** powered (by an engine); ~**boot** *nt* motorboat; ~**geräusch** *nt* engine noise; ~**haube** *f* bonnet *(Brit)*, hood *(US)*; *(Aviat)* engine cowling.

**motorisch** *adj (Physiol)* motor attr.

**motorisiert\*** *adj* motorized.

**Motor-:** ~**jacht** *f* motor yacht; ~**leistung** *f* engine power; ~**öl** *nt* engine oil.

**Motorrad** *nt* motorcycle.

**Motorradfahrer** *m* motorcyclist.

**Motor-:** ~**raum** *m* engine compartment; ~**roller** *m* (motor) scooter; ~**säge** *f* power saw; ~**schaden** *m* engine trouble *no pl*; ~**sport** *m* motor sport.

**Motte** *f* -**n** moth. **von** ~**n zerfressen** moth-eaten; **du kriegst die** ~**n!** *(col)* blow me! *(col)*.

**Motten-:** **m**~**fest** *adj* mothproof; ~**kiste** *f (fig)* **etw aus der** ~**kiste hervorholen** to dig sth out; ~**kugel** *f* mothball.

**Motto** *nt* -**s** *(Wahlspruch)* motto.

**motzen** *vi (col)* to beef *(col)*, to grouse *(col)*.

**Möwe** *f* -**n** seagull, gull.

**MP** [ɛm'piː] = **Maschinenpistole**.

**Mrd.** = **Milliarde**.

**Mrz.** = **März** Mar.

**MS** [ɛm'ɛs] = **Multiple Sklerose** MS.

**Ms., Mskr.** = **Manuskript** MS.

**MTA** [ɛmteː'|aː] *mf* = **medizinisch-technische Assistentin, medizinisch-technischer Assistent**.

**mtl.** = **monatlich**.

**Mücke** *f* -**n** *(Insekt)* mosquito; *(kleiner)* gnat; *(winzig)* midge. **aus einer** ~ **einen Elefanten machen** *(col)* to make a mountain out of a molehill.

**Muckefuck** *m no pl (col)* coffee substitute.

**mucken 1** *vi (col)* to mutter. **ohne zu** ~ without a murmur. **2** *vr* to utter a sound.

**Mucken** *pl (col)* moods *pl*. **(seine)** ~ **haben** to be moody; *(Sache)* to be temperamental.

**Mückenstich** *m* mosquito/gnat/midge bite.

**Mucks** *m* -**e** *(col)* sound. **keinen** ~ **sagen** not to make a sound; *(nicht widersprechen)* not to say a word.

**mucksen** *vr (col)* **sich nicht** ~ not to move (a muscle); *(sich nicht äußern)* not to utter a sound.

**mucksmäuschenstill** [-'mɔysçən-] *adj (col)* (as) quiet as a mouse.

**müde** *adj* tired; *Haupt* weary. **sie wird nicht** ~, **das zu tun** she never wearies of doing that; **keine** ~ **Mark** *(col)* not a single penny.

**Müdigkeit** *f (Schlafbedürfnis)* tiredness; *(Schläfrigkeit)* sleepiness. **vor** ~ *(dat)* **umfallen** to drop from exhaustion; **nur keine** ~ **vorschützen!** *(col)* don't (you) tell me you're tired.

**Muff**[1] *m no pl (N Ger: Modergeruch)* musty smell.

**Muff**[2] *m* -**e** muff.

**Muffel** *m* - *(col: Murrkopf)* grouch, grouser.

**muff(e)lig** *adj (col)* grumpy.

**Muffensausen** *nt (col):* ~ **kriegen/haben** to be/get scared stiff *(col)*.

**muffig** *adj (dial) Geruch* musty.

**muh** *interj* moo.

**Mühe** *f* -**n** trouble; *(Anstrengung auch)* effort; *(Arbeitsaufwand auch)* bother. **ohne** ~ without any bother; **nur mit** ~ only just; **mit Müh(e) und Not** *(col)* with great difficulty; **wenig/keine** ~ **haben** not to have much bother *(etw zu tun* doing sth*)*; **es ist der** *(gen)* ~ **wert** it's worth the trouble *(etw zu tun* of doing sth*)*; **sich** *(dat)* **keine** ~ **geben** to take no trouble; **gib dir keine** ~! *(hör auf)* don't bother, save yourself the trouble; **sich** *(dat)* **die** ~ **machen, etw zu tun** to take the trouble to do sth; **jdm** ~ **machen** to give sb some bother; **verlorene** ~ a waste of effort.

**mühelos** *adj* effortless; *Sieg, Aufstieg auch* easy.

**Mühelosigkeit** *f siehe adj* effortlessness; ease.

**muhen** *vi* to moo, to low.

**mühen** *vr (geh)* to strive *(um for)*.

**mühevoll** *adj* laborious, arduous; *Leben* arduous.

**Mühle** *f* **-n (a)** mill; *(Kaffee~)* grinder. **(b)** *(fig: Routine)* treadmill. **(c)** *(~spiel)* nine men's morris. **(d)** *(col)* *(Auto)* crate *(col)*, banger *(col)*, jalopy *(col)*; *(Fahrrad)* boneshaker *(col)*.

**Mühl-:** ~**rad** *nt* millwheel; ~**stein** *m* millstone.

**Mühsal** ['myːzaːl] *f* **-e** *(geh)* tribulation; *(Strapaze)* toil.

**mühsam** ['myːzam] **1** *adj* arduous. **2** *adv* with difficulty. ~ **verdientes Geld** hard-earned money.

**mühselig** ['myːzeːlɪç] *adj* arduous.

**Mulatte** *m (wk)* **-n, -n, Mulattin** *f* mulatto.

**Mulde** *f* **-n** *(Geländesenkung)* hollow.

**Mull** *m (Gewebe)* muslin; *(Med)* gauze.

**Müll** *m no pl (Haushalts~)* rubbish, garbage *(esp US)*, refuse *(form)*; *(Gerümpel)* rubbish; *(Industrie~)* waste.

**Müll-:** ~**abfuhr** *f* refuse *or* garbage *(US)* collection; *(Stadtreinigung)* refuse *etc* collection department; ~**abladeplatz** *m* rubbish *or* garbage *(US)* dump; ~**beutel** *m* bin liner *(Brit)*, trashcan liner *(US)*.

**Mullbinde** *f* gauze bandage.

**Müll-:** ~**deponie** *f* waste disposal site, sanitary (land)fill *(US form)*; ~**eimer** *m* rubbish bin *(Brit)*, garbage can *(US)*.

**Müller** *m* **-** miller.

**Müll-:** ~**halde, ~kippe** *f* rubbish *or* garbage *(US)* dump; ~**mann** *m, pl* ~**männer** *(col)* dustman *(Brit)*, trash collector *(US)*; ~**sack** *m* rubbish *or* garbage *(US)* bag; ~**schlucker** *m* **-** refuse chute; ~**sortierung** *f no pl* separation of waste; ~**tonne** *f* dustbin *(Brit)*, trashcan *(US)*; ~**tüte** *f* = ~**beutel**; ~**verbrennungsanlage** *f* incinerator, incinerating plant; ~**wagen** *m* dustcart *(Brit)*, garbage truck *(US)*.

**mulmig** *adj* uncomfortable. **mir war** ~ **zumute** *(lit)* I felt queasy; *(fig)* I had butterflies *(col)*.

**Multi** *m* **-s** *(col)* multinational (organization).

**Multi-** *in cpds* multi-; **m~lateral** *adj* multilateral; ~**millionär** *m* multimillionaire; **m~national** *adj* multinational.

**multipel** *adj* multiple. **multiple Sklerose** multiple sclerosis.

**Multiplikation** *f* multiplication.

**multiplizieren*** **1** *vt (lit, fig)* to multiply *(mit by)*. **2** *vr (fig)* to multiply.

**Mumie** ['muːmiə] *f* mummy.

**mumifizieren*** *vt* to mummify.

**Mumm** *m no pl (col: Mut)* spunk *(dated col)*, guts *pl (col)*.

**mümmeln** *vi (col)* to nibble.

**Mumpitz** *m no pl (col)* balderdash *(dated col)*.

**Mumps** *m or (col)* *f* **-,** *no pl* (the) mumps *sing*.

**München** *nt* Munich.

**Mund** *m* **-er** *(col: Mundwerk)* tongue. **etw in den** ~ **nehmen** to put sth in one's mouth; **dieses Wort nehme ich nicht in den** ~ I never use that word; **den** ~ **aufmachen** *(fig: seine Meinung sagen)* to speak up; **einen großen** ~ **haben** *(fig) (aufschnei-*

*den)* to talk big *(col)*; *(frech sein)* to be cheeky *(esp Brit)* or fresh *(esp US)*; **jdm den** ~ **verbieten** to order sb to be quiet; **halt den** ~! shut up! *(col)*; **er kann den** ~ **einfach nicht halten** *(col)* he can't keep his big mouth shut *(col)*; **jdm über den** ~ **fahren** to cut sb short; **jdm den** ~ **stopfen** *(col)* to shut sb up *(col)*; **in aller** ~**e sein** to be on everyone's lips; **Sie nehmen mir das Wort aus dem** ~ you've taken the (very) words out of my mouth; **jdm nach dem** ~ **reden** *(col)* to say what sb wants to hear; **sie ist nicht auf den** ~ **gefallen** *(col)* she's never at a loss for words; **den** ~ **(zu) voll nehmen** *(col)* to talk (too) big *(col)*.

**Mund|art** *f* dialect.

**mund|artlich** *adj* dialect(al).

**Munddusche** *f* water jet ®.

**Mündel** *nt or (Jur) m* **-** ward.

**munden** *vi (liter)* **jdm köstlich** ~ to taste delicious to sb; **sich** *(dat)* **etw** ~ **lassen** to savour *(Brit)* or savor *(US)* sth.

**münden** *vi aux sein or haben (Fluß)* to flow *(in +acc* into*)*; *(Straße)* to lead *(in +acc, auf +acc* into*)*.

**Mund-:** **m~faul** *adj (col)* uncommunicative; **sei doch nicht so m~faul!** make an effort and say something!; **m~gerecht** *adj* bite-sized; ~**geruch** *m* bad breath; ~**harmonika** *f* mouth organ.

**mündig** *adj* of age; *(fig)* mature.

**Mündigkeit** *f* majority; *(fig)* maturity.

**mündlich** *adj* verbal; *Prüfung, Leistung* oral. ~**e Verhandlung** *(Jur)* hearing; **die** ~**e Prüfung, das M~e** *(col)* *(Sch, Univ)* the oral; *(bei Dissertation etc)* the viva (voce); **alles weitere** ~! let's talk about it more when I see you.

**Mund-:** ~**propaganda** *f* verbal propaganda; ~**raub** *m (Jur)* theft of food for personal consumption; ~**schutz** *m* mask (over one's mouth); ~**stück** *nt (von Pfeife, Blasinstrument)* mouthpiece; *(von Zigarette)* (filter-)tip; **m~tot** *adj (col)* **jdn m~tot machen** to silence sb.

**Mündung** *f (von Fluß, Rohr etc)* mouth; *(Trichter~)* estuary; *(Gewehr~)* muzzle.

**Mund-:** ~**wasser** *nt* mouthwash; ~**werk** *nt (col)* **ein freches/großes/lockeres** ~**werk haben** to be cheeky *(esp Brit)* or fresh *(esp US)*/talk big *(col)*/talk too much; **ihr** ~**werk steht nie still** her tongue never stops wagging *(col)*; ~**winkel** *m* corner of one's mouth; ~**-zu-~-Beatmung** *f* mouth-to-mouth resuscitation.

**Munition** *f* ammunition.

**Munitions-:** ~**depot** *nt* munitions dump; ~**fabrik** *f* munitions factory; ~**lager** *nt* munitions dump.

**munkeln** *vti* **man munkelt, daß ...** there's a rumour *(Brit)* or rumor *(US)* that ...

**Münster** *nt* **-** minster, cathedral.

**munter** *adj* **(a)** *(lebhaft)* lively *no adv*; *(fröhlich)* cheerful, merry. ~ **und vergnügt** bright and cheery; ~ **drauflos reden** to prattle away merrily. **(b)** *(wach)* awake; *(aufgestanden)* up and about.

**Munterkeit** *f (Lebhaftigkeit)* liveliness; *(Fröhlichkeit)* cheerfulness, merriness.

**Münz|automat** *m* slot machine.

**Münze** *f* **-n** coin. **jdm etw mit gleicher** ~ **heimzahlen** *(fig)* to pay sb back in his own coin for sth.

**münzen** *vt* to mint, to coin. **das war auf ihn gemünzt** *(fig)* that was aimed at him.

**Münz-:** ~**fernsprecher** *m (form)* payphone; ~**tankstelle** *f* coin-operated petrol *(Brit)* or gas(oline) *(US)* station; ~**telefon** *nt* payphone; ~**wechsler** *m* change machine.

**mürb(e)** *adj* crumbly; *(zerbröckelnd)* crumbling; *Fleisch* tender; *Obst* soft. **jdn** ~ **machen/kriegen** *(fig: zermürbt)* to wear sb down/to break sb.

**Mürb(e)teig** *m* short (crust) pastry.
**Murks** *m no pl (col)* ~ **machen** to bungle things *(col)*; **das ist** ~! that's a botch-up *(col)*.
**Murmel** *f* **-n** marble.
**murmeln** *vti* to murmur; *(undeutlich)* to mumble; *(brummeln)* to mutter. **etw vor sich** *(acc)* **hin** ~ to mutter sth to oneself.
**Murmeltier** *nt* marmot. **schlafen wie ein** ~ to sleep like a log.
**murren** *vi* to grumble *(über +acc about)*.
**mürrisch** *adj (abweisend)* sullen, morose; *(schlechtgelaunt)* grumpy.
**Mus** *nt* **-e** mush. **jdn zu** ~ **schlagen** *(col)* to make mincemeat of sb.
**Muschel** *f* **-n** **(a)** mussel *(auch Cook)*, bivalve; *(Schale)* shell. **(b)** *(Ohr~)* external ear. **(c)** *(Telec)* *(Sprech~)* mouthpiece; *(Hör~)* earpiece.
**Muse** *f* **-n** *(Myth)* Muse. **die leichte** ~ *(fig)* light entertainment; **von der** ~ **geküßt werden** *(fig)* to be inspired.
**Museum** [mu'zeːʊm] *nt, pl* **Museen** [mu'zeːən] museum.
**Museums-:** ~**führer** *m* museum guide; **m~reif** *adj (hum)* antique; **m~reif sein** to belong in a museum; ~**stück** *nt* museum piece.
**Musical** ['mjuːzɪkl] *nt* **-s** musical.
**Musik** *f* **-en** music. **das ist** ~ **in meinen Ohren** *(fig)* that's music to my ears.
**musikalisch** *adj* musical.
**Musikant(in** *f)* *m* musician, minstrel *(old)*.
**Musik-:** ~**begleitung** *f* musical accompaniment; ~**box** *f* jukebox.
**Musiker(in** *f)* *m* - musician.
**Musik-:** ~**hochschule** *f* college of music; ~**instrument** *nt* musical instrument; ~**kapelle** *f* band; ~**kassette** *f* music cassette; ~**korps** *nt* music corps *sing*; ~**lehrer** *m* music teacher; ~**liebhaber** *m* music-lover; ~**saal** *m* music room; ~**sendung** *f* music programme *(Brit)* or program *(US)*; ~**stück** *nt* piece of music; ~**stunde** *f* music lesson.
**musisch** *adj* Fächer (fine) arts *attr*; Begabung for the arts; Veranlagung, Mensch artistic.
**musizieren*** *vi* to play. **sie saßen auf dem Marktplatz und musizierten** they sat in the market place playing their instruments.
**Muskat** *m* **-e, Muskatnuß** *f* nutmeg.
**Muskel** *m* **-n** muscle. ~**n haben** to be muscular; **seine** ~**n spielen lassen** *(lit, fig)* to flex one's muscles.
**Muskel-:** ~**dystrophie** *f* muscular dystrophy; ~**faser** *f* muscle fibre; ~**kater** *m* aching muscles *pl*; ~**kater haben** to be stiff; ~**kraft** *f* physical strength; ~**krampf** *m* muscle cramp *no indef art*; ~**paket** *nt, (col)* ~**protz** *m (col)* muscleman *(col)*; ~**riß** *m* torn muscle; ~**schwund** *m* muscular atrophy *or* wasting; ~**zerrung** *f* pulled muscle.
**Musketier** *m* **-e** musketeer.
**Muskulatur** *f* muscular system.
**muskulös** *adj* muscular. ~ **gebaut sein** to have a muscular build.
**Müsli** *nt* **-s** muesli.
**Muslim** *m* **-e, Muslime** *f* Muslim.
**muslimisch** *adj* Muslim.
**Muß** *nt no pl* **es ist ein/kein** ~ it's/it's not a must.
**Muße** *f no pl* leisure. **dafür fehlt mir die** ~ I don't have the time; **etw mit** ~ **tun** to do sth in a leisurely way.
**Muß|ehe** *f (col)* shotgun wedding *(col)*.
**Musselin** *m* **-e** muslin.
**müssen 1** *modal aux pret* **mußte,** *ptp* ~ **(a)** *(Zwang)* to have to; *(Notwendigkeit auch)* to need to. **ich muß** *(Zwang)* I have to, I must *nur pres,* I've got to *(esp Brit)*; *(Notwendigkeit auch)* I need to; **ich muß nicht** *(Zwang)* I don't have to, I haven't got to *(esp Brit)*; *(Notwendigkeit auch)* I don't need to, I needn't; **muß er?** must he?, does he have to?, has he got to? *(esp Brit)*; **mußtest du?** did you have to?; **das muß irgendwann mal gemacht werden** it will have to be done some time; **er sagte, er müsse bald gehen** he said he would have to go soon; **man mußte lachen/weinen** *etc* you couldn't help laughing/crying *etc*; **wenn es (unbedingt) sein muß** if it's absolutely necessary; **das muß man sich** *(dat)* **mal vorstellen!** (just) imagine that!; **was habe ich da hören** ~? what's this I hear?

**(b)** *(sollen)* **das müßtest du eigentlich wissen** you ought to *or* you should know that; **das mußt du nicht tun!** you oughtn't to *or* shouldn't do that.

**(c)** **es muß geregnet haben** it must have rained; **es muß wahr sein** it must be true; **es muß nicht wahr sein** it needn't be true; **es müssen zehntausend Zuschauer im Stadion gewesen sein** there must have been ten thousand spectators in the stadium; **er müßte schon da sein** he should be there by now; **so muß es gewesen sein** that's how it must have been; **man müßte noch mal von vorn anfangen können!** if only one could begin again!

**2** *vi pret* **mußte,** *ptp* **gemußt wann müßt ihr zur Schule?** when do you have to go to school?; **der Brief muß heute noch zur Post** the letter must be mailed today; **ich muß mal** *(col)* I need to go to the loo *(Brit col)* or bathroom *(esp US)*.
**Mußestunde** *f* hour of leisure.
**Mußheirat** *f (col)* = **Mußehe.**
**müßig** *adj (untätig)* idle; Leben, Stunden of leisure; *(unnütz)* futile.
**Müßig-:** ~**gang** *m (liter)* idleness; ~**gang ist aller Laster Anfang** *(Prov)* the devil finds work for idle hands *(Prov)*; ~**gänger(in** *f)* *m* - idler.
**mußte** *pret of* **müssen.**
**Mustang** *m* mustang.
**Muster** *nt* - **(a)** *(Vorlage)* pattern; *(für Brief, Bewerbung etc)* specimen. **nach einem** ~ **stricken** *etc* to knit *etc* from a pattern. **(b)** *(Probestück)* sample; *(Buch etc)* specimen. ~ **ohne Wert** sample of no commercial value. **(c)** *(fig: Vorbild)* model *(an +dat* of*)*. **als** ~ **dienen** to serve as a model; **ein** ~ **an Tugend** a paragon of virtue.
**Muster-** *in cpds* model; ~**beispiel** *nt* classic example; **m~gültig, m~haft** *adj* exemplary; **er hat sich m~haft verhalten** his conduct was exemplary; ~**haus** *nt* show house; ~**knabe** *m (iro)* paragon.
**mustern** *vt* **(a)** *(betrachten)* to scrutinize. **(b)** *(Mil: inspizieren)* to inspect, to review. **(c)** *(Mil: für Wehrdienst)* **jdn** ~ to give sb his/her medical. **(d)** Stoff *siehe* **gemustert.**
**Muster-:** ~**prozeß** *m* test case; ~**schüler** *m* model pupil; *(fig)* star pupil.
**Musterung** *f* **(a)** pattern. **(b)** *(Mil) (von Truppen)* inspection, review; *(von Rekruten)* medical (examination). **(c)** *(durch Blicke)* scrutiny.
**Mut** *m no pl* courage, pluck *(col)*; *(Zuversicht)* heart. ~ **fassen** to pluck up courage; **mit frischem** ~ with new heart; **nur** ~! cheer up!, keep your pecker up! *(Brit col)*; **jdm den** ~ **nehmen** to discourage sb; **den** ~ **verlieren** to lose heart; **jdm** ~ **machen** to encourage sb; **das gab ihr wieder neuen** ~ that gave her new heart; **mit dem** ~ **der Verzweiflung** with courage born of desperation; **frohen/guten** ~**es sein** *(geh)* to be in good spirits.
**Mutation** *f* mutation.
**Mütchen** *nt:* **sein** ~ **an jdm kühlen** *(col)* to take it out

on sb *(col)*.

**mutieren\*** *vi* to mutate.

**mutig** *adj (tapfer)* courageous, brave.

**Mut-: m~los** *adj* disheartened *no adv*; *(bedrückt)* despondent; **jdn m~los machen** to make sb lose heart; **~losigkeit** *f* despondency.

**mutmaßen** *vti insep* to conjecture.

**mutmaßlich 1** *adj attr Vater* presumed; *Täter, Terrorist* suspected. **2** *adv* **~ soll er der Vater sein** he is presumed to be the father.

**Mutmaßung** *f* conjecture.

**Mutprobe** *f* test of courage.

**Mutter¹** *f* ⸚ mother. **sie ist jetzt ~** she's a mother now; **sie ist ~ von drei Kindern** she's a mother of three; **~ Natur/Erde** *(liter)* Mother Nature/Earth; **wie bei ~n** *(col)* just like (at) home; *(Essen)* just like mother makes/used to make.

**Mutter²** *f* **-n** *(Tech)* nut.

**Mutterboden** *m* topsoil.

**Mütterchen** *nt* (**a**) *dim of* **Mutter¹** mummy *(col)*, mommy *(US col)*. (**b**) *(alte Frau)* grandma.

**Mutter-: ~erde** *f* topsoil; **~freuden** *pl* the joys of motherhood *pl*; **~gesellschaft** *f (Comm)* parent company; **~instinkt** *m* maternal instinct; **~kuchen** *m (Anat)* placenta; **~land** *nt* mother country; **~leib** *m* womb.

**mütterlich** *adj* (**a**) maternal. **die ~en Pflichten** one's duties as a mother. (**b**) *(liebevoll besorgt)* motherly *no adv.* **jdn ~ umsorgen** to mother sb.

**mütterlicherseits** *adv* on his/her *etc* mother's side. **sein Großvater ~** his maternal grandfather.

**Mütterlichkeit** *f* motherliness.

**Mutter-: ~liebe** *f* motherly love; **m~los** *adj* motherless; **~mal** *nt* birthmark; **~milch** *f*

mother's milk; **~mord** *m* matricide; **~mund** *m (Anat)* cervix.

**Mutterschaft** *f* motherhood.

**Mutterschafts-: ~geld** *nt* maternity grant; **~urlaub** *m* maternity leave.

**Mutter-: ~schutz** *m* legal protection of expectant and nursing mothers; **m~seelenallein** *adj, adv* all on one's own; **~söhnchen** *nt (pej)* mummy's boy; **~sprache** *f* native language, mother tongue; **~sprachler(in** *f)* *m* native speaker; **~stelle** *f* **bei jdm ~stelle vertreten** to take the place of sb's mother; **~tag** *m* Mother's Day; **~tier** *nt* mother (animal); *(Zuchttier)* brood animal; **~witz** *m (Schläue)* mother wit; *(Humor)* natural wit.

**Mutti** *f* **-s** *(col)* mummy, mum, mommy *(US)*.

**Mutwille** *m* **-ns**, *no pl (böse Absicht)* malice. **etw aus ~n tun** to do sth out of malice.

**mutwillig 1** *adj (böswillig)* malicious; *Zerstörung auch* wilful. **2** *adv (absichtlich)* wilfully.

**Mütze** *f* **-n** cap.

**MW** = **Mittelwelle** MW.

**MWSt.** = **Mehrwertsteuer** VAT.

**Mysterienspiel** *nt (Theat)* mystery play.

**mysteriös** *adj* mysterious.

**Mysterium** *nt* mystery.

**Mystik** *f* mysticism *no art.*

**Mystiker(in** *f)* *m* - mystic.

**mystisch** *adj* mystic(al); *(fig: geheimnisvoll)* mysterious.

**mythisch** *adj* mythical.

**Mythologie** *f* mythology.

**mythologisch** *adj* mythologic(al).

**Mythos** *m* **-**, **Mythen** *(lit, fig)* myth.

# N

**N, n** [ɛn] *nt* -, - N, n. **N wie Nordpol** N for Nellie, N for Nan *(US)*.

**N** = **Norden** N.

**na** *interj (col)* **(a)** well. ~, **kommst du mit?** are you coming then?; ~ **ja** well; ~ **gut,** ~ **schön** all right, OK *(col)*; ~ **also!,** ~ **eben!** (well,) there you are (then)!; ~ **und ob!** *(auf jeden Fall)* you bet! *(col)*; *(und wie)* and how! *(col)*. **(b)** *(Ermahnung)* now; *(Zurückweisung)* well. ~ **(~)!** now then!; ~ **warte!** just you wait!; ~ **so was!** well, I never!; ~ **und?** so what?

**Nabe** *f* **-n** hub.

**Nabel** *m* - *(Anat)* navel, umbilicus *(spec)*. **der ~ der Welt** *(fig)* the hub of the universe.

**Nabelschnur** *f (Anat)* umbilical cord.

**nach 1** *prep* +*dat* **(a)** *(örtlich)* to. **ich fuhr mit dem Zug ~ Mailand** I took the train to Milan; **er ist schon ~ London abgefahren** he has already left for London; ~ **Osten/Westen** eastward(s)/westward(s); ~ **links/rechts** (to the) left/right; ~ **hinten/vorn** to the back/front; ~ **Norden zu** *or* **hin** to *or* towards *(esp Brit) or* toward *(esp US)* the north.

**(b)** *(zeitlich, Reihenfolge)* after. **fünf (Minuten) ~ drei** five (minutes) past *or* after *(US)* three; **sie kam ~ zehn Minuten** she came ten minutes later; ~ **Empfang** *or* **Erhalt** on receipt; **drei Tage ~ Empfang** three days after receipt; **eine(r, s) ~ dem/der anderen** one after another; **(bitte) ~ Ihnen!** after you!; ~ **„mit" steht der Dativ** "mit" takes the dative.

**(c)** *(entsprechend)* according to; *(im Einklang mit)* in accordance with. ~ **dem Gesetz** according to the law; ~ **Artikel 142c** under article 142c; **etw ~ Gewicht kaufen** to buy sth by weight; ~ **Verfassern in** order of authors; **die Uhr ~ dem Radio stellen** to put a clock right by the radio; **ihrer Sprache ~ (zu urteilen)** judging by her language; ~ **dem, was er gesagt hat** according to what he's said; ~ **allem, was ich weiß** as far as I know; ~ **einem Gedicht von Schiller** after a poem by Schiller; **er wurde ~ seinem Großvater genannt** he was called after *or* for *(US)* his grandfather.

**2** *adv* **(a)** *(räumlich)* **mir ~!** *(liter, hum)* follow me! **(b)** *(zeitlich)* ~ **und** ~ little by little; ~ **wie vor** still.

**nach|äffen** *vt sep (pej) Moden, Ideen* to ape; *jdn* to mimic.

**nach|ahmen** *vt sep* to imitate; *(karikieren)* to mimic; *(kopieren)* to copy.

**nach|ahmenswert** *adj* exemplary.

**Nach|ahmer(in** *f) m* - imitator.

**Nach|ahmung** *f siehe vt* **(a)** *(das Imitieren)* imitation; mimicking; copying. **etw zur ~ empfehlen** to recommend sth as an example to follow. **(b)** *(die Imitation)* imitation; impression; copy.

**nach|arbeiten** *sep* **1** *vt* **(a)** *(aufholen)* versäumte Stunden to make up for. **(b)** *(überarbeiten)* to work over. **(c)** *(nachbilden)* to copy, to reproduce. **2** *vi* **wir müssen morgen ~** we'll have to make up for the missed time tomorrow.

**Nachbar(in** *f) m (wk)* **-n, -n** neighbour *(Brit)*, neighbor *(US)*. **Herr X war beim Konzert mein ~** Mr X sat next to me at the concert; ~**s Garten** the next-door garden.

**Nachbar-:** ~**dorf** *nt* neighbouring village; ~**haus** *nt* house next door; ~**land** *nt* neighbouring country.

**nachbarlich** *adj (freundlich)* neighbourly *no adv (Brit)*, neighborly *no adv (US)*; *(benachbart)* neighbouring *no adv (Brit)*, neighboring *no adv (US)*.

**Nachbarschaft** *f (Gegend)* neighbourhood *(Brit)*, neighborhood *(US)*; *(Nachbarn)* neighbours *pl (Brit)*, neighbors *pl (US)*; *(Nähe)* vicinity.

**Nachbeben** *nt* aftershock.

**nachbehandeln\*** *vt sep (Med)* jdn/etw ~ to give sb follow-up treatment.

**Nachbehandlung** *f (Med)* follow-up treatment.

**nachbessern** *sep* **1** *vt* to retouch. **2** *vi* to make improvements.

**nachbestellen\*** *vt sep* to order some more; *(Comm)* to reorder.

**Nachbestellung** *f (gen for)* repeat order.

**nachbeten** *vt sep (pej col)* to repeat parrot-fashion.

**nachbezahlen\*** *sep* **1** *vt* to pay; *(später)* to pay later. **Steuern ~** to pay back-tax. **2** *vi* to pay the rest.

**nachbilden** *vt sep* to copy; *(exakt)* to reproduce.

**Nachbildung** *f* copy; *(exakt)* reproduction.

**nachblicken** *vi sep* = **nachsehen 1.**

**Nachbrenner** *m (Aviat)* afterburner.

**nachdatieren\*** *vt sep* to postdate.

**nachdem** *conj (zeitlich)* after.

**nachdenken** *vi sep irreg* to think *(über* +*acc* about). **darüber darf man gar nicht ~** it doesn't bear thinking about; **laut ~** to think aloud; **denk doch mal nach!** think about it!

**Nachdenken** *nt* thought, reflection. **nach langem ~** after (giving the matter) considerable thought; **gib mir ein bißchen Zeit zum ~** give me a bit of time to think (about it).

**nachdenklich** *adj Mensch, Miene* thoughtful, pensive. **jdn ~ stimmen** to set sb thinking; ~ **gestimmt sein** to be in a thoughtful mood.

**Nachdenklichkeit** *f no pl* thoughtfulness, pensiveness.

**Nachdichtung** *f (Liter)* free rendering.

**Nachdruck** *m* **(a)** *no pl (Betonung)* stress, emphasis. **besonderen ~ darauf legen, daß ...** to stress *or* emphasize particularly that ...; **etw mit ~ betreiben** to pursue sth energetically. **(b)** *(das Nachdrucken)* reprinting; *(das Nachgedruckte)* reprint.

**nachdrucken** *vt sep* to reprint.

**nachdrücklich** *adj* emphatic. ~ **auf etw** *(dat)* **bestehen** to insist firmly on sth; **jdm ~ raten, etw zu tun** to urge sb to do sth; **jdn ~ warnen** to give sb a firm warning.

**Nachdurst** *m (nach Alkoholgenuß)* dehydration. **er hat wohl ~** he must be pretty dehydrated after all that drinking.

**nach|eifern** *vi sep* **jdm/einer Sache** ~ to emulate sb/sth.

**nach|einander** *adv (räumlich)* one after the other; *(zeitlich auch)* in succession. **zweimal** ~ twice running; **kurz** ~ shortly after each other; **drei Tage** ~ three days running, three days on the trot *(col)*.

**nach|empfinden\*** *vt sep irreg* **(a)** *Stimmung* to feel. **das kann ich ihr** ~ I can understand her feelings. **(b)** *(nachgestalten)* to adapt *(dat from)*.

**nach|erzählen\*** *vt sep* to retell.

**Nach|erzählung** *f* retelling; *(Sch)* (story) reproduction.

**Nachf.** = **Nachfolger.**

**Nachfahr** *m* **-en** *(liter)* descendant.

**nachfahren** *vi sep irreg aux sein* to follow (on). **jdm** ~ to follow sb.

**nachfassen** *vi sep* **(a)** *(noch einmal zufassen)* to regain one's grip. **(b)** *(col: nachforschen)* to probe a bit deeper.

**nachfeiern** *vti sep (später feiern)* to celebrate later.

**nachfinanzieren\*** *vt sep* to find additional finance for.

**Nachfolge** *f no pl* succession. **jds/die** ~ **antreten** to succeed sb/to succeed.

**Nachfolge-** *in cpds* follow-up; ~**modell** *nt (von Produkt, Auto)* successor, follow-up model *(gen to)*.

**nachfolgen** *vi sep aux sein (hinterherkommen)* to follow (on). **jdm** ~ to follow sb; **jdm im Amt** ~ to succeed sb in office.

**nachfolgend** *adj* following. **das N~e** the following.

**Nachfolge|organisation** *f* successor organization.

**Nachfolger(in** *f)* *m* - *(im Amt etc)* successor. **Friedrich Reißnagel** ~ successors to Friedrich Reißnagel.

**Nachforderung** *f* subsequent demand.

**nachforschen** *vi sep* to try to find out; *(polizeilich etc)* to carry out an investigation *(dat into)*; *(amtlich etc)* to make inquiries *(dat into)*.

**Nachforschung** *f* inquiry; *(polizeilich etc)* investigation. ~**en anstellen** to make inquiries.

**Nachfrage** *f* **(a)** *(Comm)* demand *(nach, in +dat for)*. **danach besteht eine rege** ~ there is a great demand for it. **(b)** *(Erkundigung)* inquiry. **danke der** ~ *(form)* thank you for your concern; *(col)* nice of you to ask.

**nachfragen** *vi sep* to ask, to inquire.

**nachfühlen** *vt sep* = **nachempfinden.**

**nachfüllen** *vt sep leeres Glas etc* to refill; *halbleeres Glas, Batterie etc* to top up.

**Nachfüllpackung** *f* refill pack.

**nachgeben** *sep irreg* **1** *vi* **(a)** to give way *(dat to)*; *(federn)* to give; *(fig: Mensch)* to give in *(dat to)*. **(b)** *(Comm: Preise, Kurse)* to drop, to fall. **2** *vt (noch mehr geben)* **darf ich Ihnen noch etwas Gemüse** ~? may I give you a few more vegetables?

**Nachgebühr** *f* excess (postage).

**Nachgeburt** *f* afterbirth; *(Vorgang)* expulsion of the afterbirth.

**nachgehen** *vi sep irreg aux sein* **(a)** +*dat (hinterhergehen)* to follow; **jdm** *auch* to go after. **(b)** *(Uhr)* to be slow. **deine Uhr geht fünf Minuten nach** your clock is five minutes slow. **(c)** +*dat (ausüben)* Beruf to practise *(Brit)*, to practice *(US)*; *Studium, Vergnügungen, Interessen etc* to pursue; *Geschäften* to go about. **einer geregelten Arbeit** ~ to have a steady job. **(d)** +*dat (erforschen)* to investigate, to look into.

**nachgelassen** *adj Werke, Papiere* posthumous.

**nachgemacht** *adj Gold, Leder etc* imitation; *Geld* counterfeit.

**nachgerade** *adv (geradezu)* practically, virtually.

**Nachgeschmack** *m (lit, fig)* aftertaste. **einen üblen** ~ **hinterlassen** *(fig)* to leave a bad taste in the mouth.

**nachgestellt** *adj (Gram)* postpositive.

**nachgiebig** *adj* **(a)** *Material* pliable; *Boden etc* yielding, soft. ~ **sein** to give. **(b)** *(fig) Mensch, Haltung* soft; *(entgegenkommend)* compliant. **sie behandelt die Kinder zu** ~ she's too soft with the children.

**Nachgiebigkeit** *f siehe adj* **(a)** pliability; softness. **(b)** softness; compliance.

**nachgießen** *vti sep irreg Wasser, Milch* to add. **darf ich Ihnen (noch etwas Wein)** ~? would you like some more (wine)?

**nachgrübeln** *vi sep* to think *(über +acc about)*; *(sich Gedanken machen)* to ponder *(über +acc on)*.

**nachgucken** *vti sep siehe* **nachsehen.**

**nachhaken** *vi sep (col)* to dig deeper.

**Nachhall** *m* reverberation; *(fig)* echo.

**nachhallen** *vi sep* to reverberate.

**nachhaltig** *adj* lasting *no adv.* **ihre Gesundheit hat sich** ~ **gebessert** there has been a lasting improvement in her health.

**nachhängen** *vi sep irreg* +*dat* to give oneself up to. **seinen Erinnerungen** ~ to lose oneself in one's memories.

**Nachhauseweg** *m* way home.

**nachhelfen** *vi sep irreg* to help. **er hat dem Glück ein bißchen nachgeholfen** he engineered himself a little luck.

**nachher** *adv* **(a)** *(danach)* afterwards; *(später auch)* later. **bis** ~ see you later! **(b)** *(col: womöglich)* ~ **stimmt das gar nicht** that might not be true at all.

**Nachhilfe** *f (Sch)* private tuition *or* tutoring *(US)*.

**Nachhilfe-:** ~**lehrer** *m* private tutor; ~**stunde** *f* private lesson; ~**unterricht** *m* private tuition *or* tutoring *(US)*.

**nachhinein** *adv:* **im** ~ afterwards; *(rückblickend)* in retrospect.

**nachhinken** *vi sep aux sein (fig col)* to lag behind.

**Nachholbedarf** *m* **einen** ~ **an etw** *(dat)* **haben** to have a lot of sth to catch up on.

**nachholen** *vt sep* **(a)** *(aufholen)* to make up (for). **(b)** **jdn** ~ *(nachkommen lassen)* to get sb to join one.

**Nachhut** *f* **-en** *(Mil)* rearguard. **bei der** ~ in the rearguard.

**Nach|impfung** *f* booster.

**nachjagen** *vi sep aux sein* +*dat* to chase (after).

**nachklingen** *vi sep irreg aux sein (Ton, Echo)* to go on sounding; *(Worte, Erinnerung)* to linger on.

**Nachkomme** *m (wk)* **-n, -n** descendant.

**nachkommen** *vi sep irreg aux sein* **(a)** *(später kommen)* to follow later. **Sie können Ihr Gepäck** ~ **lassen** you can have your luggage sent on (after). **(b)** *(Schritt halten)* to keep up. **(c)** +*dat (erfüllen)* einer Pflicht to carry out; *einer Forderung, einem Wunsch* to comply with.

**Nachkommenschaft** *f* descendants *pl.*

**Nachkömmling** *m (Kind)* afterthought *(hum)*.

**Nachkriegs-** *in cpds* postwar; ~**zeit** *f* postwar period.

**Nachlaß** *m* **-lasse** *or* **-lässe** **(a)** *(Preis~)* discount *(auf +acc on)*. **(b)** *(Erbschaft)* estate. **literarischer** ~ unpublished works *pl.*

**nachlassen** *sep irreg* **1** *vt* **(a)** **die Hälfte des Preises** ~ to take 50% off the price; **10% vom Preis** ~ to give a 10% discount. **(b)** *(locker lassen) Seil* to slacken. **(c)** *siehe* **nachgelassen. 2** *vi* to decrease, to diminish; *(Interesse auch)* to flag, to wane; *(Regen, Nasenbluten)* to ease off; *(Leistung, Geschäfte)* to fall off; *(Preise)* to fall. **er hat in letzter Zeit sehr**

**nachgelassen** he hasn't performed nearly as well recently.

**nachlässig** *adj* careless; *(unachtsam)* thoughtless.

**Nachlässigkeit** *f siehe adj* carelessness; thoughtlessness.

**Nachlaßverwalter** *m* executor.

**nachlaufen** *vi sep irreg aux sein* +*dat* **jdm/einer Sache** ~ to run after sb/sth; **den Mädchen** ~ to chase girls.

**nachlegen** *vt sep* **noch Kohlen/Holz** ~ to put some more coal/wood on (the fire).

**Nachlese** *f* second harvest; *(Ertrag)* gleanings *pl*.

**nachlesen** *sep irreg* **1** *vt (in einem Buch)* to read; *(nachschlagen)* to look up. **man kann das in der Bibel** ~ it says so in the Bible. **2** *vi* to have a second harvest; *(Ähren* ~*)* to glean.

**nachliefern** *vt sep (später liefern)* to deliver at a later date; *(zuzüglich liefern)* to make a further delivery of.

**nachlösen** *vi sep* to pay on the train/when one gets off; *(zur Weiterfahrt)* to pay the extra.

**nachmachen** *vt sep* **(a)** to copy; *(nachäffen)* to mimic; *(fälschen)* to forge. **sie macht mir alles nach** she copies everything I do; **das soll erst mal einer** ~! I'd like to see anyone else do that!; *siehe* **nachgemacht. (b)** *(col: nachholen)* to make up.

**nachmessen** *vti sep irreg (prüfend messen)* to check.

**Nachmieter** *m* **unser** ~ the tenant after us; **wir müssen einen** ~ **finden** we have to find someone to take over the flat *etc*.

**nachmittag** *adv* **gestern/heute** ~ yesterday/this afternoon.

**Nachmittag** *m* afternoon. **am** ~ in the afternoon; **am heutigen** ~ this afternoon.

**nachmittäglich** *adj no pred* afternoon *attr*.

**nachmittags** *adv* in the afternoon. **dienstags** ~ on Tuesday afternoons.

**Nachmittags-:** ~**schlaf** *m* ~**schlaf halten** to have a sleep after lunch; ~**vorstellung** *f* matinée (performance).

**Nachnahme** *f* -n cash *or* collect *(US)* on delivery, COD; *(col:* ~**sendung)** COD parcel. **etw per** ~ **schicken** to send sth COD.

**Nachnahme-:** ~**gebühr** *f* COD charge; ~**sendung** *f* COD parcel.

**Nachname** *m* surname, family *or* last name.

**nachplappern** *vt sep* to repeat parrot-fashion.

**Nachporto** *nt* excess (postage).

**nachprüfbar** *adj* verifiable.

**Nachprüfbarkeit** *f* verifiability.

**nachprüfen** *vti sep* to verify, to check.

**Nachprüfung** *f (von Aussagen etc)* check *(gen* on*)*.

**nachrechnen** *vti sep* to check.

**Nachrede** *f* **(a)** *(Verunglimpfung)* **üble** ~ *(Jur)* defamation of character; **üble** ~**n über jdn verbreiten** to cast aspersions on sb's character. **(b)** *(Epilog)* epilogue.

**nachreden** *vt sep* **(a)** *(wiederholen)* to repeat. **(b)** **jdm (etwas) Schlechtes** ~ to speak badly of sb.

**nachreichen** *vt sep* to hand in later.

**nachreisen** *vi sep aux sein* **jdm** ~ to follow sb.

**Nachricht** *f* -en (piece of) news; *(Botschaft)* message. **eine** ~ a piece of news; a message; **die** ~**en** the news *sing (auch Rad, TV)*; **schlechte** ~**en** bad news; ~ **erhalten, daß ...** to receive (the) news that ...; **wir geben Ihnen** ~ we'll let you know.

**Nachrichten-:** ~**agentur** *f* news agency; ~**dienst** *m* **(a)** *(Rad, TV)* news service; **(b)** *(Pol, Mil)* intelligence (service); ~**magazin** *nt* news magazine; ~**satellit** *m* (tele)communications satellite;

~**sperre** *f* news blackout; ~**sprecher** *m* newsreader; ~**technik** *f* telecommunications *sing*.

**nachrücken** *vi sep aux sein* to move up; *(auf Posten, Stelle)* to succeed; *(Mil)* to advance.

**Nachruf** *m* obituary.

**Nachruhm** *m* fame after death.

**nachrüsten** *sep* **1** *vi (Mil)* to deploy new arms; *(modernisieren)* to modernize. **2** *vt* Kraftwerk *etc* to modernize; Auto *etc* to equip (with accessories).

**Nachrüstung** *f* **(a)** *(Mil)* deployment of new arms; *(Modernisierung)* arms modernization. **(b)** *(Tech)* *(von Kraftwerk etc)* modernization; *(von Auto etc)* equipping (with new accessories).

**nachsagen** *vt sep* **(a)** *(wiederholen)* to repeat. **(b)** **jdm etw** ~ to accuse sb of sth; **jdm Schlechtes** ~ to speak ill of sb; **ihm wird nachgesagt, daß ...** it's said that he ...; **das lasse ich mir nicht** ~! I'm not having that said of me!

**Nachsaison** *f* off-season.

**nachschauen** *vti sep siehe* **nachsehen 1, 2 (a)**.

**nachschenken** *vti sep* **darf ich Ihnen (etwas)** ~? may I top up your glass?

**nachschicken** *vt sep* to send on, to forward.

**nachschieben** *vt sep irreg* Erklärung, Begründung *etc* to provide afterwards. **nachgeschobene Gründe** rationalizations.

**Nachschlag** *m (col)* second helping.

**nachschlagen** *sep irreg* **1** *vt* Stelle, Zitat to look up. **2** *vi (in Lexikon etc)* to look.

**Nachschlagewerk** *nt* reference book *or* work.

**nachschleichen** *vi sep irreg aux sein* +*dat* to creep after.

**Nachschlüssel** *m* duplicate key; *(Dietrich)* skeleton key.

**nachschmeißen** *vt sep irreg (col)* **jdm etw** ~ to fling sth after sb; **das ist ja nachgeschmissen!** it's a real bargain.

**nachschnüffeln** *vi sep (col)* **jdm** ~ to spy on sb.

**Nachschrift** *f (Zugefügtes)* postscript.

**Nachschub** ['naːxʃuːp] *m* supplies *pl (an* +*dat* of*)*.

**Nachschub-** *(Mil)*: ~**linie** *f* supply line; ~**weg** *m* supply route.

**nachsehen** *sep irreg* **1** *vi* to have a look; *(prüfen)* to check. **jdm/einer Sache** ~ *(hinterherschauen)* to gaze after sb/sth. **2** *vt* **(a)** *(prüfen)* to check; Schulaufgaben *etc* to mark; *(nachschlagen)* to look up. **(b)** *(verzeihen)* **jdm etw** ~ to forgive sb (for) sth.

**Nachsehen** *nt:* **das** ~ **haben** to be left standing; *(nichts bekommen)* to be left empty-handed.

**nachsenden** *vt sep irreg* to forward.

**nachsetzen** *sep* **1** *vi* **jdm** ~ to pursue sb. **2** *vt* Fuß to drag.

**Nachsicht** *f no pl (Milde)* leniency; *(Geduld)* forbearance. **er kennt keine** ~ he knows no mercy; ~ **haben** to be lenient.

**nachsichtig** *adj (milde)* lenient; *(geduldig)* forbearing *(gegen, mit* with*)*.

**Nachsilbe** *f* suffix.

**nachsinnen** *vi sep irreg* to ponder *(über* +*acc* over, about*)*.

**nachsitzen** *vi sep irreg (Sch)* ~ **(müssen)** to be kept in; **jdn** ~ **lassen** to keep sb in.

**Nachsommer** *m* Indian summer.

**Nachsorge** *f (Med)* after-care.

**Nachspann** *m* -e credits *pl*.

**Nachspeise** *f* dessert, sweet *(Brit)*.

**Nachspiel** *nt (Theat)* epilogue; *(Mus)* closing section; *(fig)* sequel. **das geht nicht ohne** ~ **ab** that's bound to have repercussions; **ein gerichtliches** ~ **haben** to have legal repercussions.

**nachspielen** *sep* **1** *vt* to play. **2** *vi (Sport)* to play extra time *(Brit)* or overtime *(US)*. **der Schiedsrichter ließ** ~ the referee allowed extra time.

**nachspionieren\*** *vi sep (col)* **jdm** ~ to spy on sb.

**nachsprechen** *vt sep irreg* to repeat. **jdm etw** ~ to repeat sth after sb.

**nächstbeste** *adj attr* **der/die/das** ~ ... the first ... I/you *etc* see; **der** ~ **Zug/Job** the first train/job that comes along.

**nachstehen** *vi sep irreg* **jdm** ~ to take second place to sb; **jdm in nichts** *(dat)* ~ to be sb's equal in every way.

**nachstehend** *adj attr* following. ~**es müssen Sie beachten** you must take note of the following.

**nachsteigen** *vi sep irreg aux sein* **jdm** ~ *(fig col)* to run after sb.

**nachstellen** *sep* **1** *vt* **(a)** *(Tech) (neu einstellen)* to adjust; *(zurückstellen)* to put back. **(b) einen Vorfall/den Unfallhergang** ~ to reconstruct an incident/the accident. **2** *vi* **jdm** ~ to follow sb; *(aufdringlich umwerben)* to pester sb.

**Nächstenliebe** *f* brotherly love; *(Barmherzigkeit)* compassion.

**nächstens** *adv* **(a)** *(das nächste Mal)* (the) next time; *(bald einmal)* some time soon. **(b)** *(col: am Ende)* next.

**nächste(r, s)** *adj superl of* **nah(e)** **(a)** *(räumlich)* nearest. **das** ~ **Telefon** the nearest telephone; **ist dies der** ~ **Weg zum Bahnhof?** is this the quickest way to the station?; **in** ~**r Nähe** in the immediate vicinity; **aus** ~**r Nähe** from close by; *betrachten* at close quarters; *schießen* at close range; **im** ~**n Haus** next door. **(b)** *(zeitlich)* next. ~**s Mal** next time; **Ende** ~**n Monats** at the end of next month; **am** ~**n Tag** (the) next day; **in den** ~**n Tagen** in the next few days; **bei** ~**r Gelegenheit** at the earliest opportunity; **in** ~**r Zeit** some time soon. **(c) die** ~**n Verwandten** the immediate family; **der** ~ **Angehörige** the next of kin; **fürs** ~ for the time being.

**Nächste(r)** *mf decl as adj* **(a)** next one. **der** ~, **bitte** next please, first please *(US, Scot)*. **(b)** *(Mitmensch)* neighbour *(Brit)*, neighbor *(US)*. **jeder ist sich selbst der** ~ *(Prov)* it's every man for himself.

**Nächste(s)** *nt decl as adj* **das** ~ the next thing; *(das erste)* the first thing; **als** ~**s** next/first.

**nächst-:** ~**folgend** *adj attr* next; ~**gelegen** *adj attr* nearest; ~**höher** *adj attr* one higher; **die** ~**höhere Klasse** one class higher; ~**jährig** *adj attr* next year's; ~**liegend** *adj attr (lit)* nearest; *(fig)* most obvious; **das N**~**liegende** the most obvious thing (to do); ~**möglich** *adj attr* next possible.

**nachsuchen** *vi sep* **(a)** to look. **(b)** *(form: beantragen)* **um etw** ~ to request sth *(bei jdm* of sb).

**nacht** *adv* **heute** ~ tonight; *(letzte* ~) last night; **Dienstag** ~ (on) Tuesday night.

**Nacht** *f* ⁼e *(lit, fig)* night. **es wird/ist** ~ it's getting/it is dark; **in der** ~ at night; **in der** ~ **vom 12. zum 13. April** during the night of April 12th to 13th; **in der** ~ **auf Dienstag** during Monday night; **diese** ~ tonight; **des** ~**s** *(geh)* at night; **bis tief in die** ~ **arbeiten** to work far into the night; **über** ~ *(lit, fig)* overnight; **sich** *(dat)* **die** ~ **um die Ohren schlagen** *(col)*, **die** ~ **zum Tage machen** to stay up all night (working *etc)*; *(mit Feiern)* to make a night of it; **gute** ~! good night!; **na, dann gute** ~! *(col)* what a prospect!; **bei** ~ **und Nebel** *(col)* at dead of night.

**Nacht-:** *in cpds* night; ~**arbeit** *f* night work; ~**ausgabe** *f* late final (edition); ~**blindheit** *f* night blindness; ~**dienst** *m* night duty; *(von Apotheke)* all-night service; ~**dienst haben** to be on night duty; *(Apotheke)* to be open all night.

**Nachteil** *m* -e disadvantage. ~**e durch etw haben** to

lose by sth; **im** ~ **sein** to be at a disadvantage *(jdm gegenüber* with sb*)*; **der** ~, **allein zu leben** the disadvantage of living alone.

**nachteilig** *adj (ungünstig)* disadvantageous; *(schädlich)* detrimental. **er hat sich sehr** ~ **über mich geäußert** he spoke very unfavourably *(Brit)* or unfavorably *(US)* about me.

**nächtelang** *adv* for nights (on end).

**Nacht-:** ~**eule** *f (fig col)* night owl; ~**falter** *m* moth; ~**flug** *m* night flight; ~**flugverbot** *nt* ban on night flights; ~**frost** *m* night frost; ~**gebet** *nt* evening prayer; ~**hemd** *nt (für Damen)* nightdress *(Brit)*, nightgown; *(für Herren)* nightshirt.

**Nachtigall** *f* -en nightingale.

**nächtigen** *vi (geh)* to spend the night.

**Nachtisch** *m* dessert, sweet *(Brit)*, pudding.

**Nachtleben** *nt* night life.

**nächtlich** *adj attr* night. **die** ~**e Stadt** the town at night; **zu** ~**er Stunde** at a late hour.

**Nacht-:** ~**lokal** *nt* night club; ~**mensch** *m* night person; ~**portier** *m* night porter; ~**programm** *nt* late-night programme *(Brit)* or program *(US)*.

**Nachtrag** *m, pl* **Nachträge** postscript; *(zu einem Buch)* supplement.

**nachtragen** *vt sep irreg* **(a) jdm etw** ~ *(lit)* to go after sb with sth; *(fig)* to bear sb a grudge for sth. **(b)** *(hinzufügen)* to add.

**nachtragend** *adj* unforgiving.

**nachträglich** *adj (später)* later; *(verspätet)* belated; *(nach dem Tod)* posthumous.

**nachtrauern** *vi sep +dat* **jdm/etw** ~ to mourn the loss of sb/sth.

**Nachtruhe** *f* night's rest; *(in Anstalten)* lights-out.

**nachts** *adv* at night. **dienstags** ~ (on) Tuesday nights.

**Nacht-:** ~**schalter** *m* night desk; ~**schicht** *f* night shift; ~**schicht haben** to be on nights; **n**~**schlafend** *adj*: **zu n**~**schlafender Zeit** in the middle of the night; ~**schwärmer** *m (fig hum)* night owl; ~**schwester** *f* night nurse; ~**speicherofen** *m* storage heater; ~**strom** *m* off-peak electricity.

**nachtsüber** *adv* by night.

**Nacht-:** ~**tarif** *m* off-peak rate; ~**tisch** *m* bedside table; ~**tischlampe** *f* bedside lamp; ~**topf** *m* chamber pot.

**nachtun** *vt sep irreg* **es jdm** ~ to copy sb.

**Nacht-:** ~**-und-Nebel-Aktion** *f* cloak-and-dagger operation; ~**vorstellung** *f* late-night performance; ~**wache** *f* night watch; *(im Krankenhaus)* night duty; ~**wache haben** to be on night duty; ~**wächter** *m (in Betrieben etc)* night watchman; **n**~**wandeln** *vi insep aux sein or haben* to sleepwalk, to walk in one's sleep; ~**zeug** *nt* night things *pl*; ~**zug** *m* night train; ~**zuschlag** *m* night supplement.

**Nachuntersuchung** *f (weitere Untersuchung)* further examination; *(spätere Untersuchung)* check-up.

**nachvollziehbar** *adj* comprehensible.

**nachvollziehen\*** *vt sep irreg* to understand, to comprehend.

**nachwachsen** *vi sep irreg aux sein* to grow again.

**Nachwahl** *f (Pol)* ≈ by-election *(esp Brit)*.

**Nachwehen** *pl* after-pains *pl*; *(fig)* painful aftermath *sing*.

**nachweinen** *vi sep +dat* to mourn. **dieser Sache weine ich keine Träne nach** I won't shed any tears over that.

**Nachweis** *m* -e *(Beweis)* proof *(gen, für, über +acc* of*)*; *(Zeugnis)* certificate. **den** ~ **für etw erbringen** or **liefern** to furnish proof of sth.

**nachweisbar** *adj (beweisbar)* provable; *Fehler* demonstrable; *(Tech)* detectable.

**nachweisen** *vt sep irreg (beweisen)* to prove; *(Tech)* to detect. **dem Angeklagten konnte seine Schuld nicht nachgewiesen werden** the accused's guilt could not be proved.

**nachweislich** *adj* provable; *Fehler* demonstrable. **er war ~ in London** it can be proved that he was in London.

**Nachwelt** *f* **die ~** posterity.

**nachwerfen** *vt sep irreg* **jdm etw ~** *(lit)* to throw sth after *or* at sb; **das ist nachgeworfen** *(col)* that's a gift.

**nachwinken** *vi sep* **jdm ~** to wave (goodbye) to sb.

**Nachwirkung** *f* after-effect; *(fig)* consequence.

**Nachwort** *nt* epilogue.

**Nachwuchs** *m* **(a)** *(fig: junge Kräfte)* young people *pl* (in the profession/sport *etc*). **der schauspielerische ~** the up and coming actors. **(b)** *(hum: Nachkommen)* offspring *pl.*

**Nachwuchs-:** **~kraft** *f* junior member of the staff; **~schauspieler** *m* talented young actor; **~sorgen** *pl* recruitment problems *pl*; **~spieler** *m (Sport)* junior.

**nachzahlen** *vti sep siehe* **nachbezahlen.**

**nachzählen** *vti sep* to check.

**Nachzahlung** *f (nachträglich)* back-payment; *(zusätzlich)* additional payment.

**nachziehen** *sep irreg* **1** *vt* **(a)** *(hinterherziehen)* **etw ~** to drag sth behind one; **das rechte Bein ~** to drag one's right leg. **(b)** *Linie* to go over; *Lippen* to paint; *Augenbrauen* to pencil in. **(c)** *Schraube, Seil* to tighten (up). **2** *vi* **(a)** *aux sein +dat (folgen)* to follow. **(b)** *(col: gleichtun)* to follow suit.

**Nachzügler(in** *f)* ['na:xtsy:klɐ, -ərin] *m* - latecomer *(auch fig).*

**Nackedei** *m* **-e** *or* **-s** *(hum col)* naked person; *(Kind)* little bare monkey *(hum col).*

**Nacken** *m* - (nape of the) neck. **jdn im ~ haben** *(col)* to have sb on one's tail; **jdm im ~ sitzen** *(col)* to breathe down sb's neck; **ihm sitzt die Furcht im ~** he's frightened out of his wits *(col).*

**nackt** *adj (lit, fig)* naked; *Haut, Wand, Tatsachen* bare; *Wirklichkeit* stark. **~ baden/schlafen** to bathe/ sleep in the nude; **das ~e Leben retten** to escape with one's bare life.

**Nackt-:** **~baden** *nt* nude bathing; **~badestrand** *m* nudist beach; **~heit** *f* nakedness; *(von Mensch auch)* nudity; *(Kahlheit)* bareness; **~kultur** *f* nudism.

**Nadel** *f* **-n** needle; *(Steck~, Haar~, Comp: von Drucker)* pin; *(Häkel~)* hook.

**Nadel-:** **~baum** *m* conifer; **~drucker** *m* dot-matrix printer; **~hölzer** *pl* conifers *pl*; **~kissen** *nt* pincushion; **~kopf** *m* pin-head.

**nadeln** *vi (Baum)* to shed (its needles).

**Nadel-:** **~öhr** *nt* eye of a needle; **~stich** *m* prick; *(beim Nähen, Med)* stitch; **~streifen** *pl* pinstripes *pl*; **~streifenanzug** *m* pinstripe(d) suit; **~wald** *m* coniferous forest.

**Nadir** *m* *no pl* nadir.

**Nagel** *m* ⁼ nail *(auch Anat)*; *(Zwecke)* tack; *(an Schuhen)* hobnail, stud; *(Med)* pin. **sich** *(dat)* **etw unter den ~ reißen** *(col)* to pinch sth *(col)*; **etw an den ~ hängen** *(fig)* to chuck sth in *(col)*; **den ~ auf den Kopf treffen** *(fig)* to hit the nail on the head; **~ mit Köpfen machen** *(col)* to do the job properly.

**Nagel-:** **~bett** *nt (Anat)* bed of the nail; **~brett** *nt (von Fakir)* bed of nails; **~bürste** *f* nailbrush; **~feile** *f* nailfile; **~haut** *f* cuticle.

**Nägelkauen** *nt* nail-biting.

**Nagel-:** **~lack** *m* nail varnish *(Brit)* or polish; **~lackentferner** *m* nail varnish *(Brit)* or polish remover.

**nageln** *vt* to nail *(an +acc* to*)*; *(Med)* to pin.

**Nagel-:** **n~neu** *adj (col)* brand-new; **~pflege** *f* nail care; **~probe** *f (fig)* acid test; **~schere** *f* (pair of) nail scissors *pl.*

**nagen 1** *vi (lit, fig)* to gnaw *(an +dat* at*)*; *(knabbern)* to nibble *(an +dat* at*)*; *(Rost)* to eat *(an +dat* into*).* **2** *vt* to gnaw.

**nagend** *adj Hunger* gnawing; *Zweifel etc* nagging.

**Nager** *m* -, **Nagetier** *nt* rodent.

**Nah|aufnahme** *f (Phot)* close-up.

**nah(e)** *comp* **näher,** *superl* **nächste(r, s)** *or (adv)* **am nächsten 1** *adj* **(a)** *(örtlich)* near *pred,* nearby. **der N~e Osten** the Middle East; **von ~em** at close quarters; **jdm ~ sein** to be near (to) sb. **(b)** *(zeitlich)* near *pred,* approaching. **(c)** *(eng) Freund etc* close. **2** *adv* **(a)** *(örtlich)* near. **~e an** near *or* close to; **~e bei** close by, near; **~ vor** right in front of; **von ~ und fern** from near and far; **jdm zu ~(e) treten** *(fig)* to offend sb. **(b)** *(zeitlich)* **~ bevorstehend** approaching; **sie ist ~ an (die) achtzig** she's nearing eighty. **(c)** *(eng)* closely. **mit jdm ~ verwandt sein** to be closely related to sb. **3** *prep +dat* near (to). **dem Wahnsinn ~e sein** to be on the verge of madness.

**Nähe** *f no pl* **(a)** *(örtlich) (Nahesein)* nearness, proximity; *(Nachbarschaft)* vicinity. **in meiner ~** near me; **aus der ~** from close to. **(b)** *(zeitlich)* closeness.

**nahebei** *adv* nearby.

**nahebringen** *vt sep irreg +dat (fig)* **jdm etw ~** to bring sth home to sb.

**nahegehen** *vi sep irreg aux sein +dat (fig)* to upset.

**nahekommen** *vi sep irreg aux sein +dat (fig)* **jdm ~** *(vertraut werden)* to get on close terms with sb; **das kommt der Wahrheit schon eher nahe** that is getting nearer the truth.

**nahelegen** *vt sep (fig)* **jdm etw ~** to suggest sth to sb; **jdm ~, etw zu tun** to advise sb to do sth.

**naheliegen** *vi sep irreg (fig: Idee, Frage, Lösung)* to suggest itself. **der Verdacht liegt nahe, daß ...** it seems reasonable to suspect that ...

**naheliegend** *adj Gedanke* which suggests itself; *Vermutung* natural. **aus ~en Gründen** for obvious reasons.

**nahen** *vir aux sein (liter)* to approach *(jdm/einer Sache* sb/sth*)*, to draw near *or* nigh *(liter) (jdm/einer Sache* sb/sth*).*

**nähen 1** *vt* to sew; *Kleid* to make; *Wunde* to stitch (up), to suture *(spec).* **2** *vi* to sew.

**näher** *comp of* **nah(e) 1** *adj* **(a)** *(örtlich)* nearer. **dieser Weg ist ~** this way is shorter; **die ~e Umgebung** the immediate vicinity. **(b)** *(zeitlich)* closer, sooner *pred.* **(c)** *(genauer) Auskünfte* further *attr,* more detailed. **(d)** *(enger) Verwandter, Beziehungen* closer. **die ~e Verwandtschaft** the immediate family. **2** *adv* **(a)** *(örtlich, zeitlich)* nearer. **(b)** *(genauer)* more closely; *ausführen* in more detail. **jdn ~ kennenlernen** to get to know sb better; **ich kenne ihn nicht ~** I don't know him well.

**näherbringen** *vt sep irreg +dat* **jdm etw ~** to give sb an understanding of sth.

**Nähere(s)** *nt decl as adj* further details *pl.*

**Nah|erholungsgebiet** *nt* recreational area (close to a town).

**Näherin** *f* seamstress.

**näherkommen** *vi sep irreg aux sein (fig)* **jdm ~** to get closer to sb.

**näherliegen** *vi sep irreg (fig)* to be more obvious.

**nähern** *vr* **sich (jdm/einer Sache) ~** to approach (sb/ sth), to draw nearer (to sb/sth).

**Näherungswert** *m* approximate value.
**nahestehen** *vi sep irreg +dat (fig)* to be close to; *(Pol)* to sympathize with. **sich** ~ *(Menschen, Ideen)* to be close; **eine den Konservativen ~de Zeitung** a paper with Conservative sympathies.
**nahezu** *adv* nearly, almost, virtually.
**Nähgarn** *nt* (sewing) cotton *or* thread.
**Nahkampf** *m (Mil)* hand-to-hand fighting.
**Näh-:** ~**kästchen** *nt,* ~**kasten** *nt* workbox, sewing box; **aus dem ~kästchen plaudern** *(col)* to give away private details.
**nahm** *pret of* **nehmen**.
**Näh-:** ~**maschine** *f* sewing machine; ~**nadel** *f* needle.
**Nah|ost** *m* in/aus ~ in/from the Middle East.
**nah|östlich** *adj attr* Middle East(ern).
**Nährboden** *m (lit)* fertile soil; *(für Bakterien)* culture medium; *(fig)* breeding-ground.
**nähren** *vt (geh)* to feed; *(fig) (steigern)* to increase, to feed; *(haben) Hoffnungen* to nurse. **er sieht gut genährt aus** he looks well-fed.
**nahrhaft** *adj Kost* nourishing; *Boden* fertile.
**Nähr-:** ~**mittel** *pl* cereal products *pl;* ~**stoff** *m usu pl* nutrient.
**Nahrung** *f no pl* food. **flüssige/feste** ~ liquids/solids *pl;* **geistige** ~ intellectual stimulation; **einer Sache** *(dat)* **(neue)** ~ **geben** to reinforce sth.
**Nahrungs-:** ~**aufnahme** *f* ingestion (of food) *(form);* **die ~aufnahme verweigern** to refuse food; ~**kette** *f (Biol)* food chain; ~**mittel** *nt* food(stuff); ~**suche** *f* search for food.
**Nährwert** *m* nutritional value.
**Nähseide** *f* sewing silk.
**Naht** *f* ⸚**e** seam; *(Med)* stitches *pl,* suture *(spec); (Anat)* suture. **aus allen** ⸚**en platzen** to be bursting at the seams.
**nahtlos** *adj (lit) Teil, Anzug* seamless; *(fig) Übergang* smooth.
**Nahtstelle** *f* **(a)** *(lit)* seam. **(b)** *(fig)* link.
**Nahverkehr** *m* local traffic. **der öffentliche** ~ local public transport.
**Nahverkehrs-:** ~**mittel** *pl* means of local transport *pl;* ~**zug** *m* local train.
**Nähzeug** *nt* sewing kit, sewing things *pl.*
**Nahziel** *nt* immediate aim *or* objective.
**naiv** *adj* naive.
**Naivität** [naivi'tɛːt] *f* naivety.
**Name** *m* -**ns,** -**n** name; *(fig: Ruf auch)* reputation. **mit** ~**n** by the name of; **dem** ~**n nach** by name; **ich kenne das Stück nur dem** ~**n nach** I've heard of the play but that's all; **dem** ~**n nach müßte sie Deutsche sein** judging by her name she must be German; **auf jds** ~**n** *(acc)* in sb's name; **unter dem** ~**n** under the name of; **er nannte seinen** ~**n** he gave his name; **einen** ~**n haben** *(fig)* to have a name; **sich** *(dat)* **einen** ~**n machen** to make a name for oneself; **die Dinge beim** ~**n nennen** to call a spade a spade; **im** ~**n** *(+gen)* on *or* in *(US)* behalf of; **im** ~**n des Volkes** in the name of the people.
**namenlos** *adj* **(a)** nameless *(auch fig),* unnamed; *Helfer* anonymous. **(b)** *(geh: unsäglich)* unspeakable.
**namens 1** *adv (mit Namen)* by the name of. **2** *prep +gen (form: im Auftrag)* in the name of.
**Namen(s)-** *in cpds* name; ~**änderung** *f* change of name; ~**schild** *nt* nameplate; ~**tag** *m* name day, saint's day; ~**vetter** *m* namesake; ~**zeichen** *nt* initials *pl;* ~**zug** *m* signature.
**namentlich 1** *adj* by name. ~**e Abstimmung** roll call vote; ~**er Aufruf** roll call. **2** *adv* in particular.
**namhaft** *adj* **(a)** *(bekannt)* famous. ~ **machen** *(form)*

to identify. **(b)** *(beträchtlich)* considerable.
**Namibia** *nt* Namibia.
**Namibier(in** *f***)** *m* - Namibian.
**namibisch** *adj* Namibian.
**nämlich** *adv* **(a)** namely. **(b)** *(denn)* **wir haben uns verspätet, wir haben** ~ **einen Umweg machen müssen** we were late since we had to make a detour.
**nannte** *pret of* **nennen**.
**Nano-** *in cpds* nano-.
**nanu** *interj* well I never. ~**, wer ist das denn?** hello (hello), who's this?
**Napalm** *nt no pl* napalm.
**Napf** *m* ⸚**e** bowl.
**Napfkuchen** *m* ≈ ring-shaped poundcake.
**Narbe** *f* -**n** **(a)** *(lit, fig)* scar. **(b)** *(Bot)* stigma. **(c)** *(Gras~)* turf.
**narbig** *adj* scarred.
**Narkose** *f* -**n** **jdm eine** ~ **geben** to give sb an anaesthetic *(Brit) or* anesthetic *(US);* **aus der** ~ **aufwachen** to come to from an/the anaesthetic.
**Narkose|arzt** *m* anaesthetist *(Brit),* anesthetist *(US).*
**Narkotikum** *nt, pl* **Narkotika** *(Med)* narcotic.
**narkotisch** *adj* narcotic; *Düfte* overpowering.
**Narr** *m (wk)* -**en,** -**en** fool. **jdn zum** ~**en halten** to make a fool of sb.
**narren** *vt (geh)* **jdn** ~ *(zum besten haben)* to make a fool of sb; *(täuschen)* to dupe sb.
**Narren-:** ~**freiheit** *f* freedom to do whatever one wants; **sie hat bei ihm** ~**freiheit** he gives her (a) free rein; ~**kappe** *f* jester's cap; **n**~**sicher** *adj* foolproof.
**Narrheit** *f* **(a)** *no pl* folly. **(b)** *(Streich)* prank.
**Närrin** *f* fool.
**närrisch** *adj* foolish; *(verrückt)* mad; *(col: sehr)* madly. **die** ~**en Tage** *Fasching and the period leading up to it;* **ganz** ~ **auf etw sein** *(col)* to be crazy about sth *(col).*
**Narzisse** *f* -**n** narcissus.
**narzißtisch** *adj* narcissistic.
**NASA, Nasa** ['naːza] *f* NASA.
**Nasal** *m* -**e** nasal.
**nasal** *adj* nasal. ~**er Ton** nasal twang.
**naschen 1** *vi* to eat sweet things; *(heimlich kosten)* to pinch a bit *(col).* **darf ich mal** ~**?** can I try a bit?; **die Kinder haben den ganzen Tag nur genascht** the children have been nibbling all day. **2** *vt* to nibble. **hast du was zum N**~**?** have you something for my sweet tooth?
**Nascherei** *f no pl* nibbling; *(von Süßigkeiten)* eating sweets *(Brit) or* candy *(US).*
**Nasch-:** **n**~**haft** *adj* fond of sweet things; ~**katze** *f (col)* guzzler; **ich bin halt so eine alte** ~**katze** I've got such a sweet tooth.
**Nase** *f* -**n** **(a)** nose. **sich die** ~ **putzen** to wipe one's nose; *(sich schnäuzen)* to blow one's nose; **pro** ~ *(hum)* per head; **(immer) der** ~ **nachgehen** *(col)* to follow one's nose; **die richtige** ~ **für etw haben** *(col)* to have a nose for sth; **faß dich an deine eigene** ~**!** *(col)* you can *or* can't talk!; **jdm etw unter die** ~ **reiben** *(col)* to rub sb's nose in sth *(col);* **jdm auf der** ~ **herumtanzen** *(col)* to play sb up *(col);* **seine** ~ **gefällt mir nicht** *(col)* I don't like his face; **es muß nicht immer nach deiner** ~ **gehen** *(col)* you can't always have it your way; **ich sah es ihm an der** ~ **an** *(col)* I could see it on his face *(col);* **auf der** ~ **liegen** *(col) (krank sein)* to be laid up; *(hingefallen sein)* to be flat on one's face *(col);* **steck deine** ~ **ins Buch!** *(col)* get on with your book; **auf die** ~ **fallen** *(lit, fig)* to fall flat on one's face; **jdm etw vor der** ~ **wegschnappen** *(col)* to just beat sb to sth; **jdm die Tür vor der** ~ **zuschlagen** *(col)* to slam the door in sb's face; **jdm**

**etw unter die ~ halten** to shove sth right under sb's nose *(col)*; **jdm eins auf die ~ geben** *(lit)* to punch sb on the nose; *(fig)* to put sb in his/her place; **die ~ voll haben** *(col)* to have had enough; **jdn an der ~ herumführen** *(als Täuschung)* to lead sb by the nose; *(als Scherz)* to pull sb's leg; **jdm etw auf die ~ binden** *(col)* to tell sb all about sth; **er steckt seine ~ in alles (hinein)** *(col)* he pokes his nose into everything. **(b)** *(col: Farbtropfen)* run.

**naselang** *adv:* **alle ~** all the time, again and again.

**näseln** *vi* to talk *or* speak through one's nose.

**Nasen-:** **~bein** *nt* nose bone; **~bluten** *nt* a nosebleed; **ein Mittel gegen ~bluten** something for nosebleeds; **ich habe ~bluten** my nose is bleeding; **~flügel** *m* side of the nose; **~höhle** *f* nasal cavity; **~länge** *f (fig)* **mit einer** *or* **um eine ~länge gewinnen** to win by a head; **jdm eine ~länge voraus sein** to be a hair's breadth ahead of sb; **~loch** *nt* nostril; **~rücken** *m* bridge of the nose; **~spitze** *f* tip of the/sb's nose; **ich seh es dir an der ~spitze an** I can tell by your face; **~stüber** *m* - bump on the nose; **jdm einen ~stüber versetzen** *(lit)* to bop *(col)* sb on the nose; *(fig)* to tick *or* tell sb off; **~tropfen** *pl* nose drops.

**Nase-:** **n~rümpfend** *adj* **er sagte n~rümpfend** wrinkling his nose, he said; **n~weis** *adj* cheeky; *(vorlaut)* precocious; **~weis** *m* **-e** *(Vorlauter)* cheeky *(esp Brit)* or precocious brat *(col)*; *(Überschlauer)* know-all *(col)*, wiseguy *(col)*.

**Nashorn** *nt* rhinoceros, rhino.

**naß** *adj* wet. **etw ~ machen** to make sth wet; *(für bestimmten Zweck)* to wet sth; **sich ~ machen** *(col)* to wet oneself; **mit nassen Augen** with moist eyes; **wie ein nasser Sack** *(col)* like a wet rag *(col)*.

**Nassauer** *m* - *(col)* scrounger.

**Nässe** *f no pl* wetness, moisture. **„vor ~ schützen"** "keep dry"; **vor ~ triefen** to be dripping wet.

**nässen 1** *vi (Wunde)* to discharge. **2** *vt Bett* to wet.

**Naß-:** **n~forsch** *adj (col)* brash; **n~kalt** *adj* chilly and damp, raw; **~rasur** *f* **die ~rasur** wet shaving; **eine ~rasur** a wet shave.

**Natal** *nt* Natal.

**Nation** *f* nation.

**national** [natsio'naːl] *adj* national; *(patriotisch)* nationalist(ic).

**National-** *in cpds* national; **n~bewußt** *adj* nationally conscious; **~bewußtsein** *nt* national consciousness; **~elf** *f* international (football) team; **~feiertag** *m* national holiday; **~flagge** *f* national flag; **~garde** *f* National Guard; **~gefühl** *nt* national feeling; **~gericht** *nt* national dish; **~hymne** *f* national anthem.

**nationalisieren\*** *vt (verstaatlichen)* to nationalize.

**Nationalisierung** *f (Verstaatlichung)* nationalization.

**Nationalismus** *m* nationalism.

**Nationalist(in** *f)* *m* nationalist.

**nationalistisch** *adj* nationalist(ic).

**Nationalität** *f* nationality.

**National-:** **~mannschaft** *f* international team; **er spielt in der schottischen ~mannschaft** he plays for Scotland; **~ökonomie** *f* economics *sing*; **~sozialismus** *m* National Socialism; **~sozialist** *m* National Socialist; **~spieler** *m* international (footballer *etc)*.

**NATO, Nato** ['naːto] *f* **die ~** NATO.

**Natrium** *nt no pl* sodium.

**Natron** *nt no pl* sodium compound, esp bicarbonate of soda.

**Natter** *f* **-n** adder, viper; *(fig)* snake.

**Natur** *f* **(a)** *no pl* nature. **gegen die ~** against nature; **ich bin von ~ aus schüchtern** I am shy by nature; **sein Haar ist von ~ aus blond** his hair is naturally blond. **(b)** *no pl (freies Land)* countryside; **in der freien ~** in the open countryside. **(c)** *(Wesensart)* nature; *(Mensch)* type. **es liegt in der ~ der Sache** *or* **der Dinge** it is in the nature of things; **das geht gegen meine ~** it goes against the grain; **eine Frage allgemeiner ~** a question of a general nature; **das ist ihm zur zweiten ~ geworden** it's become second nature to him.

**Naturalien** [-iən] *pl* natural produce *sing*. **in ~ bezahlen** to pay in kind.

**Naturalismus** *m* naturalism.

**Naturalist(in** *f)* *m* naturalist.

**naturalistisch** *adj* naturalistic.

**Natur-:** **~beschreibung** *f* description of nature; **~bursche** *m* nature-boy *(col)*.

**Naturell** *nt* **-e** temperament, disposition.

**Natur-:** **~ereignis** *nt,* **~erscheinung** *f* natural phenomenon; **~faser** *f* natural fibre *(Brit)* or fiber *(US)*; **~forscher** *m* natural scientist; **~freund** *m* nature-lover; **n~gegeben** *adj (lit, fig)* natural; **n~gemäß** *adj* natural; **~geschichte** *f* natural history; **~gesetz** *nt* law of nature; **n~getreu** *adj* true to life; *(in Lebensgröße)* life-size; **~heilkunde** *f* nature healing; **~heilverfahren** *nt* natural cure; **~katastrophe** *f* natural disaster; **~kostladen** *m* health food shop; **~kunde** *f* natural history; **~lehrpfad** *m* nature trail.

**natürlich 1** *adj* natural. **in seiner ~en Größe** life-size; **eines ~en Todes sterben** to die of natural causes. **2** *adv* naturally. **die Krankheit verlief ganz ~** the illness took its natural course. **~!** naturally!, of course!, sure! *(esp US)*.

**natürlicherweise** *adv* naturally.

**Natürlichkeit** *f* naturalness.

**Natur-:** **~notwendigkeit** *f* physical inevitability; **~produkt** *nt* natural product; **~produkte** natural produce *sing*; **n~rein** *adj* pure, unadulterated; **~schutz** *m* nature conservancy; **unter ~schutz stehen** to be legally protected; **~schutzgebiet** *nt* nature reserve; **~talent** *nt* natural prodigy; **sie ist ein ~talent** she is a natural; **~trieb** *m* (natural) instinct; **n~verbunden** *adj* nature-loving; **~ˈwissenschaft** *f* natural sciences *pl*; *(Zweig)* natural science; **~wissenschaftler** *m* (natural) scientist; **n~wissenschaftlich** *adj* scientific; **~zustand** *m* natural state.

**Nautik** *f no pl* nautical science, navigation.

**nautisch** *adj* navigational. **~e Meile** nautical mile.

**Navigation** [naviga'tsioːn] *f* navigation.

**Navigations-:** **~fehler** *m* navigational error; **~raum** *m* charthouse.

**Nazi** *m* **-s** *(pej)* Nazi.

**Nazismus** *m (pej: Nationalsozialismus)* Nazism.

**nazistisch** *adj (pej)* Nazi.

**Nazizeit** *f* Nazi period.

**NB** [ɛn'beː] = **nota bene** NB.

**NC** [ɛn'tseː] = **Numerus clausus**.

**n.Chr.** = **nach Christus** AD.

**NDR** [ɛndeː'ʔɛr] *m* = **Norddeutscher Rundfunk**.

**ne** *adv (col)* no, nope *(col)*.

**Neandertaler** *m* - Neanderthal man.

**Neapel** *nt* Naples.

**Neapolitaner(in** *f)* *m* - Neapolitan.

**neapolitanisch** *adj* Neapolitan.

**Nebel** *m* - mist; *(dichter)* fog; *(Mil: künstlich)* smoke; *(fig)* mist, haze. **bei ~** in mist/fog; **das fällt wegen ~(s) aus** *(hum col)* it's all off.

**Nebel-:** **~bank** *f* fog bank; **n~haft** *adj (fig)* nebulous; **~horn** *nt (Naut)* foghorn.

**neb(e)lig** adj misty; (bei dichterem Nebel) foggy.
**Nebel-:** ~**scheinwerfer** m (Aut) fog light; ~**schleier** m (geh) veil of mist; ~**(schluß)leuchte** f (Aut) rear fog light; ~**wand** f wall of fog; (Mil) smokescreen.
**neben** prep (a) (örtlich: +dat/acc) beside, next to. (b) (außer: +dat) apart from, aside from (esp US). (c) (verglichen mit: +dat) compared with.
**nebenamtlich** adj Tätigkeit secondary, additional. das macht er nur ~ he does that just as a secondary occupation.
**neben|an** adv next door. die Tür ~ the next door.
**Neben|anschluß** m (Telec) extension.
**nebenbei** adv (a) (gleichzeitig) at the same time. etw ~ machen to do sth on the side. (b) (außerdem) additionally, in addition. (c) (beiläufig) incidentally. ~ bemerkt or gesagt by the way, incidentally.
**Neben-:** ~**beruf** m extra job; er ist im ~**beruf** Nachtwächter he has a second job as a night watchman; **n~beruflich 1** adj extra, supplementary; **2** adv as a second job, as a sideline (col); er verdient **n~beruflich** mehr als hauptberuflich he earns more from his second job than he does from his main job; ~**beschäftigung** f (Zweitberuf) extra job; ~**buhler(in** f) m rival; ~**darsteller(in** f) m supporting actor/actress.
**neben|einander** adv (a) (räumlich) side by side; (bei Rennen) neck and neck. (b) (zeitlich) at the same time.
**neben|einanderher** adv side by side. sie leben nur noch ~ (Ehepaar etc) they're just two people living in the same house.
**neben|einander-:** ~**legen** vt sep to lay side by side; ~**stellen** vt sep to place side by side; (fig: vergleichen) to compare.
**Neben-:** ~**eingang** m side entrance; ~**einkünfte**, ~**einnahmen** pl supplementary income; ~**erwerb** m second occupation; ~**fach** nt (Sch, Univ) subsidiary (subject), minor (US); ~**fluß** m tributary; ~**frage** f side issue; ~**gebäude** nt (a) (Zusatzgebäude) annexe, (small) outhouse; (b) (Nachbargebäude) adjacent building; ~**gedanke** m ulterior motive; ~**geräusch** nt (Rad, Telec) interference; ~**handlung** f (Liter) subplot; ~**haus** nt house next door.
**nebenher** adv (a) (zusätzlich) in addition. (b) (gleichzeitig) at the same time.
**nebenhin** adv (beiläufig) in passing, casually.
**Neben-:** ~**höhle** f (Physiol) sinus (of the nose); ~**kläger** m (Jur) joint plaintiff; ~**kosten** pl additional costs pl; ~**mann** m, pl ~**männer** Ihr ~**mann** the person next to you; ~**produkt** nt byproduct; ~**raum** m (benachbart) adjoining room; (weniger wichtig) side room; ~**rolle** f supporting role; (fig) minor role; das spielt für mich nur eine ~**rolle** that's only of minor concern to me; ~**sache** f trifle, triviality; das ist ~**sache** that's irrelevant; **n~sächlich** adj minor, peripheral; ~**sächlichkeit** f triviality; ~**saison** f low season; ~**satz** m (Gram) subordinate clause; **n~stehend** adj **n~stehende Erklärungen** explanations in the margin; **n~stehende Abbildung** illustration opposite; ~**stelle** f (Telec) extension; (Comm) branch; (Post) sub-post office; ~**straße** f (in der Stadt) side street; (Landstraße) minor road; ~**strecke** f (Rail) branch or local line; ~**tisch** m adjacent table; am ~**tisch** at the next table; ~**verdienst** m secondary income; ~**wirkung** f side effect; ~**zimmer** nt adjoining room; ~**zweck** m secondary aim.
**neblig** adj = neb(e)lig.
**Necessaire** [nɛsɛˈsɛːɐ] nt -s (Kulturbeutel) vanity

bag; (zur Nagelpflege) manicure case; (Nähzeug) sewing bag.
**necken** vt to tease.
**Neckerei** f teasing no pl.
**neckisch** adj (scherzhaft) merry, teasing; (col: kokett, keß) Kleid, Frisur saucy; Spielchen mischievous.
**nee** adv (col) no, nope (col).
**Neffe** m (wk) -n, -n nephew.
**Negation** f negation.
**Negativ** nt (Phot) negative.
**negativ** adj negative. jdm auf eine Frage ~ antworten to answer sb's question in the negative; sich ~ zu etw äußern to speak negatively about sth.
**Neger** m - Negro.
**Negerin** f Negress, Negro woman.
**Negerkuß** m chocolate-covered marshmallow.
**negieren*** vt (bestreiten) Tatsache to deny.
**Negligé** [negliˈʒeː] nt -s negligee.
**nehmen** pret **nahm**, ptp **genommen** vti to take; (verwenden) to use. etw an sich (acc) ~ (aufbewahren) to take charge of sth; (sich aneignen) to take sth (for oneself); jdm etw ~ to take sth (away) from sb; jdm die Hoffnung ~ to deprive sb of his/ her hope; die Mauer nimmt einem die ganze Sicht the wall blocks the whole view; er ließ es sich (dat) nicht ~, mich persönlich hinauszubegleiten he insisted on showing me out himself; diesen Erfolg lasse ich mir nicht ~ I won't be robbed of this success; sie ~ sich (dat) nichts (col) there's nothing to choose between them; man nehme ... (Cook) take ...; ~ Sie sich doch bitte! please help yourself; jdn zu sich ~ to take sb in; etw ~, wie es kommt to take sth as it comes; jdn ~, wie er ist to take sb as he is; etw auf sich (acc) ~ to take sth upon oneself; etw zu sich ~ to take sth, to partake of sth (liter); wie man's nimmt (col) depending on your point of view.
**Nehrung** f spit (of land).
**Neid** m no pl envy. aus ~ out of envy; grün (und gelb) vor ~ (col) green with envy; das muß ihm der ~ lassen (col) give the devil his due.
**neiden** vt jdm etw ~ to envy sb (for) sth.
**Neider** m - envious person. reiche Leute haben viele ~ rich people are much envied.
**Neidhammel** m (col) envious person.
**neidisch** adj envious. auf jdn/etw ~ sein to be envious of sb/sth.
**neidlos** adj ungrudging, without envy.
**Neige** f -n (a) (liter) das Glas bis zur ~ leeren to drain the cup to the dregs. (b) no pl (geh: Ende) zur ~ gehen to draw to a close; die Vorräte gehen zur ~ the provisions are fast becoming exhausted.
**neigen 1** vt Kopf, Körper to bend; Glas to tip. **2** vr (Ebene) to slope; (Mensch) to bend; (unter Last: Bäume etc) to bow; (Gebäude etc) to lean; (kippen) to tip (up), to tilt (up). **3** vi zu etw ~ to have a tendency to sth; (für etw anfällig sein) to be prone to sth; zu der Ansicht ~, daß ... to be inclined to take the view that ...; siehe geneigt.
**Neigung** f (a) (das Neigen) inclination; (Gefälle auch) incline, gradient (esp Rail). (b) (Tendenz) tendency; (Veranlagung) leaning usu pl; (Hang, Lust) inclination. künstlerische/politische ~ en artistic/ political leanings; etw aus ~ tun to do sth by inclination; keine ~ verspüren, etw zu tun to have no inclination to do sth.
**Neigungs-:** ~**ehe** f love match; ~**winkel** m angle of inclination.
**nein** adv no. kommt er? — ~ is he coming? — no, (he isn't); ich sage nicht ~ I wouldn't say no; Hunderte, ~ Tausende hundreds, no thousands; ~, so

**was!** well I never!

**Nein** *nt no pl* no. **bei seinem** ~ **bleiben** to stick to one's refusal.

**Nein-:** ~**sager(in** *f) m -* **er ist ein ewiger** ~**sager** he always says no; ~**stimme** *f (Pol)* no(-vote), nay *(US).*

**Nektar** *m no pl (Myth, Bot, Frucht~)* nectar.

**Nektarine** *f* nectarine.

**Nelke** *f* -**n** (a) carnation. (b) *(Gewürz)* clove.

**nennen** *pret* **nannte,** *ptp* **genannt 1** *vt* (a) *(bezeichnen)* to call. **jdn nach jdm** ~ to name sb after *or* for *(US)* sb; **das nenne ich Mut!** that's what I call courage!; **das nennst du schön?** you call that beautiful? (b) *(angeben, aufzählen)* to name; *(erwähnen)* to mention. **die genannten Namen** the names mentioned; **können Sie mir einen guten Anwalt** ~? could you give me the name of a good lawyer?; **das genannte Schloß** the castle referred to. **2** *vr* to call oneself; *(heißen)* to be called *(Brit)* or named. **und so was nennt sich Liebe** *(col)* and that's supposed to be love!

**nennenswert** *adj* considerable. **nicht** ~ not worth mentioning; **nichts N~es** nothing worth mentioning.

**Nenner** *m - (Math)* denominator. **etw auf einen** ~ **bringen** *(lit, fig)* to reduce sth to a common denominator.

**Nennung** *f (das Nennen)* naming; *(Sport)* entry.

**Nennwert** *m (Fin)* nominal *or* par value; **zum** ~ at par.

**neo-, Neo-** *in cpds* neo-.

**Neon** *nt no pl* neon.

**Neo-:** ~**nazi** *m* neo-Nazi; ~**nazismus** *m* neo-Nazism; **n~nazistisch** *adj* neo-Nazi.

**Neon-:** ~**licht** *nt* neon light; ~**reklame** *f* neon sign; ~**röhre** *f* neon tube.

**Nepal** *nt* Nepal.

**Nepp** *m no pl (col)* **der reinste** ~ daylight robbery *(col)*, a pure rip-off *(col).*

**neppen** *vt (col)* to fleece *(col)*, to rip off *(col).*

**Nepplokal** *nt (col)* clipjoint *(col).*

**Neptun** *m* Neptune.

**Nerv** [nɛrf] *m* -**en** nerve. **leicht die** ~**en verlieren** to scare easily; **die** ~**en sind mit ihm durchgegangen** he lost his self-control, something in him snapped *(col)*; **der hat (vielleicht)** ~**en!** *(col)* he's got a nerve! *(col)*; **es geht mir auf die** ~**en** *(col)* it gets on my nerves.

**nerven** ['nɛrfn] *(col)* **1** *vt* **jdn** ~ to get on sb's nerves. **2** *vi* **das nervt** it gets on your nerves.

**Nerven-** ['nɛrfn-]: ~**arzt** *m* neurologist; **n~aufreibend** *adj* nerve-racking; ~**belastung** *f* strain on the nerves; ~**bündel** *nt (fig col)* bundle of nerves *(col)*; ~**gas** *nt (Mil)* nerve gas; ~**gift** *nt* neurotoxin; ~**heilanstalt** *f* mental hospital; ~**heilkunde** *f* neurology; ~**kitzel** *m (fig)* thrill; ~**klinik** *f* psychiatric clinic; ~**kostüm** *nt (hum)* **ein starkes/schwaches** ~**kostüm haben** to have strong/weak nerves; **n~krank** *adj* suffering from a nervous disease; ~**krankheit** *f* nervous disorder; ~**krieg** *m (fig)* war of nerves; ~**leiden** *nt* nervous complaint; ~**probe** *f* trial; ~**sache** *f (col)* question of nerves; ~**säge** *f (col)* pain (in the neck) *(col)*; ~**system** *nt* nervous system; ~**zentrum** *nt (Physiol, fig)* nerve centre; ~**zusammenbruch** *m* nervous breakdown.

**nervig** *adj (col) Musik, Lärm* irritating. **der ist vielleicht** ~ he gets on your nerves.

**nervlich** ['nɛrflɪç] *adj* **der** ~**e Zustand des Patienten** the state of the patient's nerves; ~ **bedingt** nervous.

**nervös** [nɛr'vøːs] *adj* nervous; *(aufgeregt auch)* jumpy *(col)*, on edge *pred.*

**Nervosität** [nɛrvozi'tɛːt] *f* nervousness.

**nervtötend** ['nɛrf-] *adj (col)* nerve-racking; *Arbeit* soul-destroying.

**Nerz** *m* -**e** mink.

**Nerzmantel** *m* mink coat.

**Nessel**[1] *f* -**n** *(Bot)* nettle. **sich in die** ~**n setzen** *(col)* to put oneself in a spot *(col).*

**Nessel**[2] *m - (Tex)* (untreated) cotton.

**Nessel-:** ~**ausschlag** *m*, ~**fieber** *nt* nettle rash.

**Nest** *nt* -**er** (a) *(Brutstätte)* nest. (b) *(fig: Schlupfwinkel)* hideout, lair. (c) *(fig: Heim)* nest, home. **sein eigenes** ~ **beschmutzen** to foul one's own nest; **da hat er sich ins warme** ~ **gesetzt** *(col)* he's got it made *(col)*. (d) *(fig: Bett)* bed. (e) *(pej col: Ort)* one-horse town *(col)*. **gottverlassenes** ~ godforsaken hole *(col).*

**Nest-:** ~**beschmutzer** *m (pej)* denigrator of one's family *or* country; ~**beschmutzung** *f (pej)* denigration of one's family *or* country.

**nesteln** *vi an etw (dat)* ~ to fumble with sth.

**Nest-:** ~**häkchen** *nt* baby of the family; ~**wärme** *f (fig)* happy home life.

**nett** *adj* nice; *(hübsch auch)* pretty. **das kann ja** ~ **werden!** *(iro)* that'll be nice (I don't think!) *(col)*; **sei so** ~ **und räum' auf!** would you mind clearing up?; ~, **daß Sie gekommen sind!** nice of you to come.

**netterweise** *adv* kindly.

**Nettigkeit** *f* (a) *no pl (nette Art)* kindness, goodness. (b) *(nette Worte)* ~**en** kind words.

**netto** *adv (Comm)* net.

**Netto-** *in cpds* net; ~**lohn** *m* take-home pay.

**Netz** *nt* -**e** (a) net; *(Spinnen~, fig: von Lügen etc)* web; *(Haar~)* (hair)net; *(Einkaufs~)* net bag; *(Gepäck~)* (luggage) rack. **ins** ~ **gehen** *(Ftbl)* to go into the net; **jdm ins** ~ **gehen** *(fig)* to fall into sb's trap; **jdm durchs** ~ **gehen** *(fig)* to give sb the slip. (b) *(System, Comp)* network; *(Strom~)* mains *sing or pl.* **das soziale** ~ the social security net. (c) *(Math)* net; *(Kartengitter)* grid.

**Netz-:** ~**anschluß** *m (Elec)* mains connection; ~**ball** *m (Tennis etc)* netball; ~**gerät** *nt* mains receiver; ~**haut** *f* retina; ~**hemd** *nt* string vest *(Brit)* or undershirt *(US)*; ~**karte** *f (Rail)* unlimited travel ticket; ~**spannung** *f* mains voltage; ~**strümpfe** *pl* fish-net stockings *pl*; ~**teil** *nt* mains adapter; ~**werk** *nt (Elec, Comp, fig)* network; *(aus Draht)* netting.

**neu** *adj* new; *Kräfte, Hoffnung auch* fresh; *(kürzlich entstanden auch)* recent; *Wäsche* clean; *Wein* young. **das N~e Testament** the New Testament; **die N~e Welt** the New World; **ein** ~**er Anfang** a new *or* fresh start; ~**eren Datums** of (more) recent date; **die** ~**(e)ste Mode** the latest fashion; **die** ~**esten Nachrichten** the latest news; **ein ganz** ~**er Wagen** a brand-new car; **das ist mir** ~! that's news to me; **in** ~**erer Zeit** in modern times; **erst in** ~**erer Zeit** only recently; **die** ~**eren Sprachen** modern languages; **seit** ~**(e)stem gibt es ...** since recently there has been ...; **aufs** ~**e** *(geh)* afresh; **auf ein** ~**es!** *(Aufmunterung)* let's try again; **der/die N~e** the newcomer, the new guy *(col)*; **was ist das N~e an dem Buch?** what's new about the book?; **weißt du schon das N~(e)ste?** have you heard the latest?; **was gibt's N~es?** *(col)* what's the latest?; **von** ~**em** *(von vorn)* from the beginning; *(wieder)* again; ~ **beginnen** to make a fresh start, to start again; **er ist** ~ **hinzugekommen** he's joined (him/them) recently; **ein Zimmer** ~ **einrichten** to refurnish a room.

**Neu-:** ~**ankömmling** *m* newcomer; ~**anschaffung**

*f* new acquisition; **n~artig** *adj* new; **ein n~artiges Wörterbuch** a new type of dictionary; **~auflage** *f* reprint; **~ausgabe** *f* new edition.

**Neubau** *m* new house/building.

**Neubau-:** **~gebiet** *nt* development area; **~siedlung** *f* new housing estate *(Brit)* or development; **~wohnung** *f* newly-built flat.

**Neu-:** **~bearbeitung** *f* revised edition; *(von Oper etc)* new version; *(das ~bearbeiten)* revision; reworking; **~beginn** *m* new beginning(s); **~druck** *m* reprint; **~einstellung** *f* new appointment; **~entdeckung** *f* rediscovery; *(Mensch)* new discovery; **n~entwickelt** *adj attr* newly developed; **~entwicklung** *f* new development.

**neuerdings** *adv* recently. **~ raucht er wieder** now he's started smoking again.

**Neuerer** *m* - innovator.

**Neu-:** **n~eröffnet** *adj attr* newly opened; *(wieder-eröffnet)* reopened; **~eröffnung** *f* *(Wiedereröffnung)* reopening; **die ~eröffnung der Fluglinie** the opening of the new airline; **~erscheinung** *f* *(Buch)* new publication; *(CD etc)* new release.

**Neuerung** *f* innovation; *(Reform)* reform.

**Neu|erwerbung** *f* new acquisition.

**neu(e)stens** *adv* lately, recently.

**Neu-:** **~fassung** *f* revised version; **~fundland** *nt* Newfoundland; **~fundländer** *m* - *(Hund)* Newfoundland (dog); **n~geboren** *adj* newborn; **sich wie n~geboren fühlen** to feel (like) a new man/woman; **~geborene(s)** *nt decl as adj* newborn child; **n~gewählt** *adj attr* newly elected.

**Neugier(de)** *f no pl* curiosity, inquisitiveness; *(pej auch)* nosiness *(col)*. **aus ~** out of curiosity.

**neugierig** *adj* inqisitive, curious *(auf +acc about)*; *(pej)* nosy *(col)*; *(gespannt)* longing to know. **ein N~er** an inquisitive person; *(pej auch)* a nosy parker *(col)*; **jdn ~ machen** to arouse sb's curiosity; **ich bin ~, ob** I wonder if; **da bin ich aber ~!** I can hardly wait *(col)*.

**Neu-:** **n~griechisch** *adj* Modern Greek; **~griechisch(e)** *nt* Modern Greek; *siehe* **Deutsch(e)**; **~gründung** *f* *(Wiederbegründung)* re-establishment; **die ~gründung von Universitäten** the founding of new universities; **~guinea** *nt* New Guinea.

**Neuheit** *f* **(a)** *no pl* novelty. **(b)** new thing/idea.

**Neuigkeit** *f* piece of news. **~en** news *sing*.

**Neujahr** *nt* New Year.

**Neujahrs-:** **~abend** *m* New Year's Eve, Hogmanay *(Scot)*; **~tag** *m* New Year's Day.

**Neuland** *nt no pl* virgin land; *(fig)* new ground.

**neulich** *adv* recently, the other day. **~ abend(s)** the other evening.

**Neuling** *m* newcomer.

**neumodisch** *adj* fashionable; *(pej)* new-fangled *(pej)*.

**Neumond** *m* new moon. **bei ~** at new moon; **heute ist ~** there's a new moon today.

**Neun** *f* **-en** nine. **ach du grüne ~e!** *(col)* well I'm blowed! *(col)*; *siehe* **Vier**.

**neun** *num* nine. **alle ~e!** *(beim Kegeln)* strike!; *siehe* **vier**.

**Neun-:** **n~hundert** *num* nine hundred; **n~mal** *adv* nine times; *siehe* **viermal**; **n~malklug** *adj (iro)* smart-aleck *attr (col)*.

**Neuntel** *nt* - ninth; *siehe* **Viertel¹**.

**neuntens** *adv* ninth(ly), in the ninth place.

**neunte(r, s)** *adj* ninth; *siehe* **vierte(r, s)**.

**neunzehn** *num* nineteen; *siehe* **vierzehn**.

**neunzig** *num* ninety; *siehe* **vierzig**.

**Neu-:** **~ordnung** *f* reorganization; *(Reform)* re-

form; **~philologe** *m* modern linguist.

**Neuralgie** *f* neuralgia.

**Neu-:** **~reg(e)lung** *f* adjustment; **n~reich** *adj (pej)* nouveau riche; **~reiche(r)** *mf (pej)* nouveau riche.

**Neuro-** *in cpds* neuro-; **~loge** *m*, **~login** *f* neurologist; **~logie** *f* neurology.

**Neurose** *f* **-n** neurosis.

**Neurotiker(in** *f)* *m* - neurotic.

**neurotisch** *adj* neurotic.

**Neu-:** **~schnee** *m* fresh snow; **~seeland** *nt* New Zealand; **~seeländer(in** *f)* *m* New Zealander; **n~seeländisch** *adj* New Zealand; **~silber** *nt* nickel silver; **n~sprachlich** *adj* modern language; **n~sprachliches Gymnasium** ≃ grammar school *(Brit)*, high school *(esp US, Scot)* stressing modern *languages*; **~stadt** *f* new town.

**neutral** *adj* neutral.

**neutralisieren\*** *vt* to neutralize.

**Neutralität** *f* neutrality.

**Neutron** *nt* **-en** [nɔy'troːnən] neutron.

**Neutronen-** *in cpds* neutron; **~bombe** *f* neutron bomb.

**Neutrum** *nt, pl* **Neutra** *(Gram, fig)* neuter.

**Neu-:** **~verschuldung** *f* new borrowings *pl*; **~wagen** *m* new car; **~wahl** *f* *(Pol)* new election; **~wert** *m* value when new; **n~wertig** *adj* as new; **~zeit** *f* modern times *pl*; **Literatur der ~zeit** modern literature; **n~zeitlich** *adj* modern; **~zugang** *m* new arrival; *(Mil, bei Firma)* new recruit; **~zulassung** *f* *(Aut)* ≃ registration of a new vehicle.

**New York** ['njuː'jɔːk] *nt* New York.

**Nicaragua** *nt* Nicaragua.

**Nicaraguaner(in** *f)* *m* - Nicaraguan.

**nicaraguanisch** *adj* Nicaraguan.

**nicht** *adv* **(a)** *(Verneinung)* not. **er raucht ~** *(augenblicklich)* he isn't smoking; *(gewöhnlich)* he doesn't smoke; **kommst du? – nein, ich komme ~** are you coming? – no, I'm not (coming); **ich kann das ~ – ich auch ~** I can't do it – neither *or* nor can I; **~ mehr als** no more than; **~ heute und ~ morgen** neither today nor tomorrow; **er ~!** not him. **(b)** *(Bitte, Verbot)* **~ berühren!** do not touch; *(gesprochen)* don't touch; **~!** don't!, no!; **tu's ~!** don't do it!; **~ doch!** stop it!; **bitte ~!** please don't. **(c)** *(rhetorisch)* **er kommt, ~ (wahr)?** he's coming, isn't he?; **er kommt ~, ~ wahr?** he isn't coming, is he?; **das ist schön, ~ (wahr)?** it's nice, isn't it?; **jetzt wollen wir Schluß machen, ~?** let's leave it now, OK?

**Nicht-, nicht-** *pref* non-.

**Nicht-:** **~achtung** *f* *(+gen* for*)* disregard; **n~amtlich** *adj* unofficial; **~angriffspakt** *m* non-aggression pact; **~beachtung** *f* non-observance; **n~christlich** *adj* non-Christian.

**Nichte** *f* **-n** niece.

**Nicht-:** **~einhaltung** *f* non-compliance *(+gen* with*)*; **~einmischung** *f* *(Pol)* non-intervention; **~erscheinen** *nt* non-appearance; **n~flüchtig** *adj* *(Chem, Comp)* non-volatile; **~gefallen** *nt:* **bei ~gefallen** if not satisfied.

**nichtig** *adj* **(a)** *(Jur: ungültig)* void. **(b)** *(unbedeutend)* trivial.

**Nichtigkeit** *f* **(a)** *(Jur: Ungültigkeit)* invalidity, nullity. **(b)** *no pl (Bedeutungslosigkeit)* vainness, emptiness. **(c)** *usu pl (Kleinigkeit)* triviality, trivia *pl*.

**Nicht-:** **~mitglied** *nt* non-member; **n~öffentlich** *adj attr* not open to the public; **n~öffentliche Sitzung** meeting in camera *(Jur)* or behind closed doors; **~raucher** *m* *(auch Rail)* non-smoker; **ich bin ~raucher** I don't smoke; **~raucherabteil** *nt* no-smoking compartment; **n~rostend** *adj attr* rustproof.

**Nichts** *nt* **(a)** *no pl (Philos)* nothingness; *(Leere)* emptiness, void. **etw aus dem ~ aufbauen** to build sth up from nothing; **vor dem ~ stehen** to be left with nothing. **(b)** *pl* **-e** *(Mensch)* nonentity.

**nichts** *indef pron inv* nothing. **ich weiß ~** I don't know anything, I know nothing; **~ als** nothing but; **~ (anderes) als** nothing but; **~ von Bedeutung** nothing of (any) importance; **~ Besseres/Neues** *etc* nothing better/new *etc*; **~ da!** *(col) (weg da)* no you don't!; *(ausgeschlossen)* nothing doing *(col)*; **das ist ~ für mich** that's not my cup of tea *(col)*; **für ~ und wieder ~** *(col)* for nothing at all; **(es war) ~ mehr zu machen** there was nothing more that could be done; **ich weiß ~ Genaues** I don't know any details; **~ wie raus/hin** *etc (col)* let's get out/over there *etc* (on the double).

**nichts|ahnend** *adj* unsuspecting.

**Nicht-:** **~schwimmer** *m* non-swimmer; **sie ist ~schwimmer** she's a non-swimmer; **~\*schwimmerbecken** *nt* pool for non-swimmers.

**nichts-:** **~destotrotz** *adv* notwithstanding *(form)*, nonetheless; **~destoweniger** *adv* nevertheless.

**Nichtseßhafte(r)** *mf decl as adj (form)* person of no fixed abode *(form)*.

**Nichts-:** **~könner** *m* incompetent person; **~nutz** *m* **-e** good-for-nothing; **n~nutzig** *adj* useless; *(unartig)* good-for-nothing; **n~sagend** *adj Buch, Worte* meaningless; *Mensch* insignificant; *Gesichtsausdruck* blank; **~tuer(in** *f) m* - idler; **~tun** *nt* idleness; *(Muße)* leisure; **viel Zeit mit ~tun verbringen** to spend a lot of time doing nothing.

**Nicht-:** **~tänzer** *m* non-dancer; **ich bin ~tänzer** I don't dance; **~trinker** *m* non-drinker; **er ist ~trinker** he doesn't drink; **~verbreitung** *f (von Kernwaffen)* non-proliferation; **~vorhandensein** *nt* absence; **~wissen** *nt* ignorance; **~zutreffende(s)** *nt decl as adj* **(etwas)** **~zutreffendes** something incorrect; **~zutreffendes (bitte) streichen!** (please) delete as applicable.

**Nickel** *nt no pl* nickel.

**Nickelbrille** *f* metal-rimmed spectacles *pl.*

**nicken** *vi* to nod. **mit dem Kopf ~** to nod one's head.

**Nickerchen** *nt (col)* forty winks *(col)*. **ein ~ machen** to have forty winks.

**Nicki** *m* **-s** velour pullover.

**nie** *adv* never. **~ im Leben, ~ und nimmer** never ever; **~ wieder** *or* **mehr** never again; **fast ~** hardly ever.

**nieder 1** *adj attr* low; *(weniger bedeutend) Klasse, Stand* lower; *(geringer) Geburt, Herkunft* lowly; *Volk* common; *Arbeit* menial; *(Comp) Programmiersprache* low-level. **2** *adv* down.

**Nieder-** *pref (Geog)* lower; **n~beugen** *sep* **1** *vt (lit, fig)* to bow down; **2** *vr* to bend down; **n~brennen** *vti sep irreg (vi: aux sein)* to burn down; **n~brüllen** *vt sep Redner* to shout down; **n~deutsch** *adj (Ling)* Low German; **~druck** *m (Tech)* low pressure; **n~drücken** *vt sep (lit)* to press down; *(fig: bedrücken)* **jdn n~drücken** to depress sb, to get sb down *(col)*; **~gang** *m (fig: Verfall)* decline; **n~gehen** *vi sep irreg aux sein* to descend; *(Regen)* to fall; *(Gewitter)* to break *(auch fig)*; *(Boxer)* to go down; **n~geschlagen** *adj* dejected, despondent; **~geschlagenheit** *f* dejection, despondency; **n~halten** *vt sep irreg* to hold *or* keep down; *Volk* to oppress; *(Mil)* to pin down; **n~kämpfen** *vt sep Feuer* to fight down; *Feind* to overcome; *Tränen* to fight back; **n~knien** *vi sep aux sein* to kneel down; **n~kommen** *vi sep irreg aux sein (old)* to be delivered *(old) (mit* of*)*; **~kunft** *f* **-e** *(old)* delivery;

**~lage** *f* defeat; **jdm eine ~lage beibringen** to inflict a defeat on sb.

**Niederlande** *pl* **die ~** the Netherlands *sing or pl*, the Low Countries *pl.*

**Niederländer(in** *f) m* - Dutchman/Dutchwoman. **die ~** the Dutch.

**niederländisch** *adj* Dutch, Netherlands.

**Niederländisch(e)** *nt* Dutch; *siehe* **Deutsch(e).**

**niederlassen** *vr sep irreg* **(a)** *(geh)* to sit down; *(Vögel)* to alight. **(b)** *(Praxis, Geschäft eröffnen)* to establish oneself. **sich als Arzt/Rechtsanwalt ~** to set up as a doctor/lawyer; **die niedergelassenen Ärzte** general practitioners, GPs.

**Niederlassung** *f* **(a)** *no pl (das Niederlassen)* settlement; *(eines Arztes etc)* setting-up. **(b)** *(Siedlung)* settlement. **(c)** *(Comm)* registered office; *(Zweigstelle)* branch.

**niederlegen** *sep* **1** *vt* **(a)** to lay *or* put down; *Waffen* to lay down. **(b)** *(aufgeben) Amt, Mandat* to resign (from), to give up; *Führung* to renounce, to give up. **die Arbeit ~** *(aufhören, streiken)* to stop work. **(c)** *(schriftlich festlegen)* to write down. **2** *vr* to lie down.

**Niederlegung** *f* **(a)** *(von Kranz)* laying. **(b)** *(von Amt, Mandat)* resignation (from). **~ der Arbeit** industrial action. **(c)** *(schriftlich)* setting-out.

**Nieder-:** **n~machen, n~metzeln** *vt sep* to massacre, to butcher; **n~prasseln** *vi sep aux sein (Regen etc)* to beat down; *(fig: Beschimpfungen)* to rain down; **n~reißen** *vt sep irreg* to pull down; *(fig) Schranken* to tear down; **~rhein** *m* Lower Rhine; **n~rheinisch** *adj* Lower Rhine; **~sachsen** *nt* Lower Saxony; **n~schießen** *vt sep irreg* to shoot down.

**Niederschlag** *m* **(a)** *(Met)* precipitation *(form)*; *(Chem)* precipitate; *(Bodensatz)* sediment, dregs *pl.* **radioaktiver ~** (radioactive) fallout; **für morgen sind heftige ~e gemeldet** tomorrow there will be heavy rain/hail/snow. **(b)** *(Boxen)* knock-down blow.

**niederschlagen** *sep irreg* **1** *vt* **(a)** *jdn* to knock down; *Aufstand, Revolte* to put down; *Augen* to lower, to cast down *(liter)*; *siehe* **niedergeschlagen.** **(b)** *(Chem)* to precipitate. **2** *vr (Flüssigkeit)* to condense; *(Bodensatz)* to settle; *(Chem)* to precipitate. **sich in etw** *(dat)* **~** *(Erfahrungen etc)* to find expression in sth.

**Niederschlags-:** **n~frei** *adj* dry, without precipitation *(form)*; **~menge** *f* rainfall/snowfall, precipitation *(form)*.

**Nieder-:** **~schlagung** *f (eines Aufstands)* suppression; **n~schmettern** *vt sep* to batter down; *(fig)* to shatter; **n~schmetternd** *adj Nachricht, Ergebnis* shattering; **n~schreiben** *vt sep irreg* to write down; **~schrift** *f (das ~schreiben)* writing down; *(~geschriebenes)* notes *pl*; *(Protokoll) (einer Sitzung)* minutes *pl*; *(Jur)* record; *(von Bandaufzeichnung)* transcript; **n~setzen** *sep* **1** *vt Kind, Glas* to put down; **2** *vr* to sit down; **~spannung** *f (Elec)* low voltage *or* tension; **n~stimmen** *vt sep* to vote down; **n~strecken** *vt sep (geh)* to lay low; **n~stürzen** *vi sep aux sein* to crash down; **n~tourig** [-tu:rɪç] *adj* low-revving; **n~tourig fahren** to keep the revs down.

**Niedertracht** *f =* **Niederträchtigkeit.**

**niederträchtig** *adj Person* malicious, spiteful; *Tat* despicable **jdn ~ verraten** to betray sb in a despicable way.

**Niederträchtigkeit** *f* **(a)** *no pl* **so viel ~ hätte ich ihm nicht zugetraut** I would not have believed him capable of such despicable behaviour. **(b)** *(Tat)* despicable act.

**niedertreten** *vt sep irreg* to trample down.

**Niederung** f low-lying area; *(Senke)* depression.
**Nieder-:** n~**werfen** *sep irreg* **1** *vt* to throw or cast *(liter)* down; *Aufstand* to suppress; *Gegner (lit)* to floor; *(fig)* to overcome; **er wurde von einer Krankheit** n~**geworfen** he was laid low by an illness; **2** *vr* to prostrate oneself; ~**werfung** f *(von Aufstand)* suppression.
**niedlich** *adj* sweet, cute, pretty little *attr.*
**Niedlichkeit** f sweetness, cuteness.
**niedrig** *adj* low. ~ **fliegen** to fly low; ~**ste Preise** rock-bottom prices; **ich schätze seine Chancen sehr** ~ **ein** I don't think much of his chances.
**Niedrig-:** n~**stehend** *adj Volk, Kultur* primitive; ~**wasser** nt *(Naut)* low water.
**niemals** *adv* never.
**niemand** *indef pron* nobody, no one. **es war** ~ **zu Hause** there was nobody at home, there wasn't anyone at home; ~ **anders kam** nobody else came; **ich habe** ~ **anders gesehen** I didn't see anybody else; **sag das** ~**(em)!** don't tell anybody.
**Niemand** m *no pl* **er ist ein** ~ he's a nobody.
**Niemandsland** nt no man's land.
**Niere** f -n kidney. **künstliche** ~ kidney machine; **es geht mir an die** ~**n** *(col)* it gets me down.
**Nieren-** *in cpds (Anat)* renal; ~**entzündung** f kidney infection, nephritis *(spec)*; n~**förmig** *adj* kidney-shaped; ~**leiden** nt kidney disease; ~**schützer** m kidney belt; ~**stein** m kidney stone, renal calculus *(spec)*; ~**tisch** m kidney-shaped table.
**nieseln** *vi impers* to drizzle.
**Nieselregen** m drizzle.
**niesen** *vi* to sneeze.
**Niespulver** nt sneezing powder.
**Niet** m -e *(spec)*, **Niete**[1] f -n rivet; *(auf Kleidung)* stud.
**Niete**[2] f -n *(Los)* blank; *(col: Mensch)* dead loss *(col)*.
**nieten** *vt* to rivet.
**Nietenhose** f (pair of) studded jeans *pl.*
**niet- und nagelfest** *adj (col)* nailed down.
**Niger** nt Niger.
**Nigeria** nt Nigeria.
**Nigerianer(in** f) m - Nigerian.
**nigerianisch** *adj* Nigerian.
**Nihilismus** [nihi'lɪsmʊs] m nihilism.
**Nihilist** [nihi'lɪst] m nihilist.
**nihilistisch** [nihi'lɪstɪʃ] *adj* nihilistic.
**Nikolaus** m -, -e *or (hum col)* **Nikoläuse** St Nicholas; *(~tag)* St Nicholas' Day.
**Nikotin** nt *no pl* nicotine.
**Nikotin-:** n~**arm** *adj* low-nicotine; n~**frei** *adj* nicotine-free; ~**gehalt** m nicotine content; n~**haltig** *adj* containing nicotine; ~**vergiftung** f nicotine poisoning.
**Nil** m Nile.
**Nilpferd** nt hippopotamus, hippo.
**Nimbus** m -, -se *(Heiligenschein)* halo; *(fig)* aura.
**Nimmer-:** n~**mehr** *adv (liter)* nevermore *(liter)*, never again; n~**müde** *adj attr* tireless, untiring; ~**satt** m -e glutton; **ein** ~**satt sein** to be insatiable; n~**satt** *adj* insatiable; ~**wiedersehen** nt *(col)* **auf** ~**wiedersehen!** I never want to see you again; **auf** ~**wiedersehen verschwinden** to disappear never to be seen again.
**nippen** *vti* to nip *(an +dat at)*. **am Wein** ~ to sip (at) the wine.
**Nippes, Nippsachen** *pl* knick-knacks *pl*, bric-à-brac *sing.*
**Nippon** nt Japan.
**nirgends, nirgendwo** *adv* nowhere, not ... anywhere. **ihm gefällt es** ~ he doesn't like it anywhere;

**überall und** ~ here, there and everywhere.
**nirgendwohin** *adv* nowhere, not ... anywhere.
**Nische** f -n alcove; *(Koch~ etc)* corner.
**nisten** *vi* to nest.
**Nist-:** ~**kasten** m nesting box; ~**platz** m nesting place; ~**zeit** f (the) nesting season.
**Nitrat** nt nitrate.
**Nitroglyzerin** nt nitroglycerine.
**Niveau** [ni'voː] nt -s *(lit, fig)* level. **auf gleichem** ~ **liegen** to be on the same level; **diese Schule hat ein hohes** ~ this school has high standards; **unter** ~ below par; **unter meinem** ~ beneath me; **ein Hotel mit** ~ a hotel with class.
**niveau-** [ni'voː]: ~**los** *adj* mediocre; ~**voll** *adj* high-class.
**nivellieren** [nivɛ'liːrən] *vt (lit, fig)* to level out.
**Nivellierung** [nivɛ'liːrʊŋ] f *(Ausgleichung)* levelling out.
**nix** *indef pron (col)* = **nichts.**
**Nixe** f -n water sprite; *(mit Fischschwanz)* mermaid.
**Nizza** nt Nice.
**n.J.** = **nächsten Jahres.**
**n.M.** = **nächsten Monats.**
**NN, N.N.** = **Normalnull** msl.
**NO** = **Nordosten** NE.
**no.** = **netto** net.
**nobel** *adj (edelmütig)* noble; *(col) (großzügig)* generous; *(kostspielig)* extravagant; *(elegant)* posh *(col)*. **sich** ~ **zeigen** *(col)* to be generous.
**Nobelpreis** m Nobel prize.
**Nobelpreisträger** m Nobel prize winner.
**noch 1** *adv* **(a)** *(weiterhin, bis jetzt)* still. ~ **nicht** still not, not yet; **bist du fertig?** – ~ **nicht** are you ready? – not yet; ~ **immer** still; ~ **nie** never; **ich gehe kaum** ~ **aus** I hardly go out any more; **ich möchte gerne** ~ **bleiben** I'd like to stay on longer.
  **(b)** *(irgendwann)* some time. **er wird sich (schon)** ~ **daran gewöhnen** he'll get used to it (one day); **das kann** ~ **passieren** that might still happen; **er wird** ~ **kommen** he'll come (yet).
  **(c)** *(eben, nicht später als)* **ich habe ihn** ~ **vor zwei Tagen gesehen** I saw him only two days ago; **er ist** ~ **am selben Tag gestorben** he died the very same day; ~ **im 18. Jahrhundert** as late as the 18th century; **können Sie das heute** ~ **erledigen?** can you do it (for) today?
  **(d)** *(einschränkend)* (only) just. **(gerade)** ~ **gut genug** (only) just good enough.
  **(e)** *(außerdem, zusätzlich)* **wer war** ~ **da?** who else was there?; ~ **etwas Fleisch** some more meat; ~ **einer** another (one); ~ **einmal** once more; **und es regnete auch** ~ and on top of that it was raining.
  **(f)** *(bei Vergleichen)* even, still, yet. ~ **größer** even bigger; **das ist** ~ **besser** that's better still; **seien sie auch** ~ **so klein** however small they might be.
  **(g)** *(col)* **Geld** ~ **und** ~ *or (hum col)* ~**er** heaps and heaps of money *(col)*; **sie hat** ~ **und** ~ **versucht, ...** she tried again and again to ...
  **2** *conj* **weder X** ~ **Y** neither X nor Y.
**nochmalig** *adj attr* renewed. **eine** ~**e Überprüfung** a further check.
**nochmals** *adv* again.
**Nockenwelle** f camshaft.
**NOK** [enloː'ka] nt = **Nationales Olympisches Komitee.**
**Nom.** = **Nominativ.**
**Nomade** m *(wk)* -n, -n *(lit, fig)* nomad.
**Nomaden-** *in cpds* nomadic; ~**tum** nt nomadism.
**Nomadin** f *(lit, fig)* nomad.
**Nomen** nt, *pl* **Nomina** *(Gram)* noun.
**nominal** *adj* nominal.

**Nominal-** *in cpds (Gram, Fin)* nominal; **~wert** *m*
*(Fin)* nominal *or* par value.
**Nominativ** *m* nominative.
**nominell** *adj* nominal.
**nominieren*** *vt* to nominate.
**Nonkonformist(in** *f)* *m* nonconformist.
**nonkonformistisch** *adj* nonconformist.
**Nonne** *f* **-n** nun.
**Nonnenkloster** *nt* convent, nunnery *(old, hum)*.
**Nonplus|ultra** *nt no pl (geh)* ultimate.
**Nonsens** *m no pl* nonsense.
**nonstop** [nɔn'ʃtɔp, nɔn'stɔp] *adv* non-stop.
**Nonstop-** *in cpds* non-stop.
**nonverbal** *adj* non-verbal.
**Noppe** *f* **-n** *(Gummi~)* nipple, knob; *(Knoten)* burl;
*(Schlinge)* loop.
**Nord** *no art no pl (Naut, Met, liter)* north.
**Nord-** *in cpds (Geog)* North; **~afrika** *nt* North Africa; **~amerika** *nt* North America; **~atlantikpakt**
*m* North Atlantic Treaty; **n~atlantisches Vertei-**
**digungsbündnis** *nt* NATO alliance; **n~deutsch**
*adj* North German; **~deutschland** *nt* North(ern)
Germany.
**Norden** *m no pl* north; *(von Land)* North. **von ~ her**
from the north; **nach ~** north(wards), to the north;
**der Balkon liegt nach ~** the balcony faces
north(wards).
**Nord-:** **~england** *nt* the North of England; **~irland**
*nt* Northern Ireland, Ulster.
**nordisch** *adj* Wälder northern; *Völker, Sprache* nordic. **~e Kombination** *(Ski)* nordic combined.
**Nord-:** **~kap** *nt* North Cape; **~korea** *nt* North Korea; **~küste** *f* north(ern) coast; **~länder(in** *f)* *m* -
Scandinavian.
**nördlich 1** *adj* northern; *Wind, Richtung* northerly.
**der ~e Polarkreis** the Arctic Circle; **N~es Eismeer**
Arctic Ocean; **52 Grad ~er Breite** 52 degrees north.
**2** *adv* (to the) north. **~ von Köln (gelegen)** north of
Cologne. **3** *prep* +*gen* (to the) north of.
**Nordlicht** *nt* northern lights *pl*, aurora borealis.
**Nordost** *m* north-east. **aus ~** from the north-east.
**Nordosten** *m* north-east; *(von Land)* North East.
**nord|östlich 1** *adj* Gegend north-eastern; *Wind*
north-east(erly). **2** *adv* (to the) north-east. **3** *prep*
+*gen* (to the) north-east of.
**Nord-Ostsee-Kanal** *m* Kiel Canal.
**Nordpol** *m* North Pole.
**Nordpolargebiet** *nt* Arctic (Zone).
**Nordrhein-Westfalen** *nt* North Rhine-Westphalia.
**Nordsee** *f* North Sea.
**Nord-:** **~seite** *f* north(ern) side; *(von Berg)*
north(ern) face; **~staaten** *pl (Hist)* northern states
*pl*, Union; **~stern** *m* North Star, Polar Star;
**~-Süd-Gefälle** *nt* north-south divide; **~wand** *f*
*(von Berg)* north face.
**Nordwest** *m* north-west. **aus ~** from the north-
west.
**Nordwesten** *m* north-west; *(von Land)* North-West.
**nordwestlich 1** *adj* Gegend north-western; *Wind*
north-west(erly). **2** *adv* (to the) north-west. **3** *prep*
+*gen* (to the) north-west of.
**Nordwind** *m* north wind.
**Nörgelei** *f* carping, niggling.
**nörgeln** *vi (an* +*dat* about) to carp, to niggle.
**Nörgler(in** *f)* *m* - carper, niggler.
**Norm** *f* **-en (a)** norm; *(Größenvorschrift)* standard
(specification). **die ~ sein** to be (considered) normal. **(b)** *(Leistungssoll)* quota, norm. **die ~ erreichen**
to achieve one's quota.
**normal** *adj* normal; *Format, Maß, Gewicht* standard.
**bist du noch ~?** *(col)* have you gone mad?

**Normal-** *in cpds (üblich)* normal; *(genormt)* standard; **~benzin** *nt* two-star (petrol) *(Brit old)*, regular (gas) *(US)*.
**normalerweise** *adv* normally, usually.
**Normal-:** **~fall** *m* normal case; **im ~fall** normally;
**~gewicht** *nt* normal weight; *(genormt)* standard
weight.
**normalisieren*** **1** *vt* to normalize. **2** *vr* to return to
normal.
**Normalisierung** *f* normalization.
**Normalität** *f* normality, normalcy.
**Normal-:** **~maß** *nt* standard (measure); **~null** *nt*
(mean) sea level; **~verbraucher** *m* average consumer; **Otto ~verbraucher** *(col)* your average punter *(col)*, John Doe *(US)*; **~zeit** *f* standard time.
**Normandie** *f* Normandy.
**normen, normieren*** *vt* to standardize.
**Normierung, Normung** *f* standardization.
**Norwegen** *nt* Norway.
**Norweger(in** *f)* *m* - Norwegian.
**norwegisch** *adj* Norwegian.
**Norwegisch(e)** *nt* Norwegian; *siehe* **Deutsch(e)**.
**Nostalgie** *f* nostalgia.
**nostalgisch** *adj* nostalgic.
**Not** *f* **=e (a)** *no pl (Mangel, Elend)* need(iness), poverty. **eine Zeit der ~** a time of need; **aus ~** out of
poverty; **~ leiden** to suffer deprivation; **in ~ leben**
to live in poverty; **wenn ~ am Mann ist** if you/they
*etc* are short *(col)*; *(im Notfall)* in an emergency; **~**
**macht erfinderisch** *(Prov)* necessity is the mother of
invention *(Prov)*.
   **(b)** *(Bedrängnis)* distress *no pl*; *(Problem)*
problem. **in seiner ~** in his hour of need; **in unserer**
**~ blieb uns nichts anderes übrig** in this emergency
we had no choice; **jdm seine ~ klagen** to tell sb
one's troubles; **in ~ sein** to be in distress; **in ~ ge-**
**raten** to get into serious difficulties.
   **(c)** *no pl (Sorge, Mühe)* difficulty, trouble. **er hat**
**seine liebe ~ mit ihr/damit** he really has problems
with her/it.
   **(d)** *(Zwang, Notwendigkeit)* necessity. **etw ohne ~**
**tun** to do sth without having to; **zur ~** if need(s)
be; *(gerade noch)* at a pinch; **aus der ~ eine Tugend**
**machen** to make a virtue (out) of necessity.
**not** *adj (geh)* **~ tun** to be necessary.
**Notar(in** *f)* *m* notary public.
**Notariat** *nt* notary's office.
**notariell** *adj* notarial. **~ beglaubigt** legally certified
by a notary.
**Not-:** **~arzt** *m* doctor on call, casualty officer;
**~aufnahme** *f* casualty unit; **~ausgang** *m* emergency exit; **~behelf** *m* stopgap (measure),
makeshift; **~bremse** *f* emergency brake, communication cord *(Brit)*; **die ~bremse ziehen** to pull the
emergency brake; *(Ftbl sl: foulen)* to commit a blatant foul; **~bremsung** *f* emergency stop; **~dienst**
*m* **~dienst haben** *(Apotheke)* to be open 24 hours;
*(Arzt)* to be on call.
**Notdurft** *f* *no pl (euph geh)* call of nature *(euph)*.
**seine ~ verrichten** to relieve oneself.
**notdürftig** *adj (kaum ausreichend)* meagre *(Brit)*,
meager *(US)*; *Kleidung* scanty; *(behelfsmäßig)*
makeshift *no adv*, rough and ready *no adv*. **damit**
**Sie sich wenigstens ~ verständigen können** so that
you can at least communicate to some extent; **ei-**
**nen Reifen ~ flicken** to patch up a tyre *(Brit) or* tire
*(US)*.
**Note** *f* **-n (a)** *(Mus)* note. **~n** *pl* music; **~n lesen** to
read music; **nach ~n spielen** to play from music.
**(b)** *(Sch)* mark. **(c)** *(Pol)* note. **(d)** *(Bank~)*
(bank)note *(Brit)*, bill *(US)*. **(e)** *no pl (Eigenart)* (in

bezug auf Gespräch, Brief etc) note; (in bezug auf Atmosphäre) tone, character. **einer Sache** (dat) **eine persönliche ~ verleihen** to give sth a personal touch.

**Noten-:** ~**bank** f issuing bank; ~**blatt** nt sheet of music; ~**papier** nt manuscript paper; ~**presse** f money press; ~**schlüssel** m clef; ~**schrift** f musical notation; ~**ständer** m music stand.

**Notfall** m emergency. **für den ~ nehme ich einen Schirm mit** I'll take an umbrella (just) in case; **im ~** if need be; **bei einem ~** in case of emergency.

**notfalls** adv if necessary, if need be.

**notgedrungen** adv of necessity. **ich muß mich ~ dazu bereit erklären** I've no choice but to agree.

**Notgroschen** m nest egg.

**notieren*** **1** vt **(a)** (Notizen machen) to make a note of; (schnell) to jot down. **(b)** (vormerken) (Comm) Auftrag to note, to book. **jdn ~** to put sb's name down. **(c)** (St Ex: festlegen) to quote (mit at). **2** vi (St Ex: wert sein) to be quoted (auf +acc at).

**Notierung** f (Comm) note; (St Ex) quotation.

**nötig 1** adj necessary. **es ist nicht ~, daß er kommt** it's not necessary for him to come, there's no need for him to come; **wenn ~** if necessary, if need be; **etw ~ haben** to need sth; **er hat das natürlich nicht ~** (iro) but, of course, he's different; **ich habe es nicht ~, mich von dir anschreien zu lassen** I don't have to let you shout at me; **du hast es gerade ~, so zu reden** (col) you're a fine one to talk (col); **das habe ich nicht ~!** I can do without that; **das N~ste** the (bare) necessities. **2** adv (dringend) **etw ~ brauchen** to need something urgently.

**nötigen** vt (geh: zwingen) to compel; (Jur) to coerce; (auffordern) to urge. **sich ~ lassen** to need urging; **lassen Sie sich nicht (erst) ~!** don't wait to be asked; siehe **genötigt**.

**nötigenfalls** adv (form) if necessary.

**Nötigung** f (Zwang) compulsion; (Jur) coercion.

**Notiz** f -en **(a)** (Vermerk) note; (Zeitungs~) item. **sich** (dat) ~**en machen** to make notes. **(b)** ~ **nehmen von** to take notice of; **keine ~ nehmen von** to ignore.

**Notiz-:** ~**block** m notepad, scratchpad (US, Comp); ~**buch** nt notebook.

**Notlage** f crisis; (Elend) plight. **jds ~** (acc) **ausnützen** to exploit sb's difficulties; **in eine ~ geraten** to get into serious difficulties.

**notlanden** pret **notlandete**, ptp **notgelandet** vi aux sein to make an emergency landing.

**Notlandung** f emergency landing.

**notleidend** adj needy. **die N~en** the needy.

**Not-:** ~**lösung** f compromise solution; (provisorisch) temporary solution; ~**lüge** f white lie.

**notorisch** adj notorious.

**Not-:** ~**ruf** m (Telec) (Gespräch) emergency call; (Nummer) emergency number; ~**rufsäule** f emergency telephone; **n~schlachten** pret **n~schlachtete**, ptp **n~geschlachtet** vt to destroy, to put down; ~**schlachtung** f putting down; ~**signal** nt distress signal; ~**situation** f emergency; ~**sitz** m foldaway seat.

**Notstand** m crisis; (Pol) state of emergency; (Jur) emergency.

**Notstands-:** ~**gebiet** nt (wirtschaftlich) depressed area; (bei Katastrophen) disaster area; ~**gesetze** pl (Pol) emergency laws pl.

**Not-:** ~**stromaggregat** nt emergency power generator; ~**unterkunft** f emergency accommodation; ~**verband** m emergency or first-aid dressing; ~**verpflegung** f emergency rations.

**notwassern** pret **notwasserte**, ptp **notgewassert**

vi to ditch (Aviat sl).

**Notwehr** f no pl self-defence (Brit), self-defense (US). **aus/in ~** in self-defence.

**notwendig** adj necessary. **~ brauchen** to need urgently; **das N~ste** the (bare) essentials.

**notwendigerweise** adv of necessity, inevitably.

**Notwendigkeit** f necessity. **die ~, etw zu tun** the necessity of doing sth.

**Notzucht** f (Jur) rape.

**Nougat** ['nu:gat] m or nt -s nougat.

**Nov.** = **November** Nov.

**Novelle** [no'vɛlə] f **(a)** long short story, novella. **(b)** (Pol) amendment.

**novellieren*** [novɛ'li:rən] vt (Pol) to amend.

**November** [no'vɛmbɐ] m - November; siehe **März**.

**Novize** [no'vi:tsə] m (wk) -n, -n, **Novizin** f novice.

**Novum** ['no:vʊm] nt, pl **Nova** ['no:va] novelty.

**NPD** [ɛnpe:'de:] f = **Nationaldemokratische Partei Deutschlands**.

**Nr.** = **Nummer** No.

**NRW** = **Nordrhein-Westfalen**.

**NS-** [ɛn'|ɛs-] in cpds Nazi.

**NT** = **Neues Testament** NT.

**n-te** ['ɛntə] adj (Math) nth.

**Nu** m: **im ~** in no time, in a flash or trice.

**Nuance** [ny'ã:sə] f -n nuance; (Kleinigkeit) shade. **um eine ~ zu laut** a shade too loud.

**nüchtern** adj **(a)** (ohne Essen) **eine Medizin ~ einnehmen** to take a medicine on an empty stomach; **mit ~em/auf ~en Magen** with/on an empty stomach. **(b)** (nicht betrunken) sober. **wieder ~ werden** to sober up. **(c)** (schmucklos) sober; (sachlich) down-to-earth no adv, rational; Zahlen, Tatsachen bare, plain.

**Nüchternheit** f **(a)** (Unbetrunkenheit) soberness, sobriety. **(b)** (Schmucklosigkeit) soberness; (Sachlichkeit) rationality.

**nuckeln** vi (col) (Mensch) to suck (an +dat at); (Tier) to suckle (an +dat from). **am Daumen ~** to suck one's thumb.

**Nudel** f -n usu pl **(a)** (als Beilage) pasta no pl; (als Suppeneinlage) noodle. **(b)** (col: Mensch) (dick) dumpling (col); (komisch) character.

**Nudel-:** ~**brett** nt pastryboard; ~**holz** nt rolling pin; ~**suppe** f noodle soup.

**Nudismus** m nudism.

**Nudist(in** f) m nudist.

**Nugat** m or nt -s nougat.

**nuklear** adj attr nuclear.

**Nuklear-:** in cpds nuclear; ~**macht** f nuclear power; ~**test** m nuclear test; ~**waffe** f nuclear weapon.

**Null** f -en **(a)** (Zahl) nought, zero; (Gefrierpunkt) zero. **die ~** the figure nought, zero; **gleich ~ sein** to be absolutely nil; **in ~ Komma nichts** (col) in less than no time; **seine Stimmung sank auf ~** (col) his mood sank; **im Jahre ~** in the year nought; **die Stunde ~** the new starting point. **(b)** (col: Mensch) dead loss (col).

**null** num zero; (Telec) O [əʊ] (Brit), zero (US); (Sport) nil; (Tennis) love. **~ Komma eins** (nought) point one; **es ist ~ Uhr zehn** it's ten past midnight; **~ Grad** zero, freezing point; **~ Fehler** no or zero (col) mistakes; **es steht ~ zu ~** it's nil-nil; **das Spiel wurde ~ zu ~ beendet** the game was a goalless draw; **~ und nichtig** (Jur) null and void.

**null|achtfünfzehn** (col) **1** adj pred run-of-the-mill (col). **2** adv in a run-of-the-mill way.

**Null|achtfünfzehn-** in cpds (col) run-of-the-mill.

**Null-Bock-** in cpds apathetic; ~-**Generation** f "couldn't care less" generation.

**Nulldiät** *f* starvation diet.
**Nullösung** *f (Pol)* zero option.
**Nullpunkt** *m* zero. **die Stimmung sank unter den ~** the atmosphere became icy; **auf dem ~ angekommen sein** *(fig)* to have reached rock-bottom.
**Null-:** ~**stellung** *f* zero position; **in der** ~**stellung sein** to be on zero; ~**tarif** *m (für Verkehrsmittel)* free travel; **zum** ~**tarif** *(hum)* free of charge; ~**wachstum** *nt (Econ)* zero growth.
**numerieren*** *vt* to number.
**numerisch** *adj* numeric(al).
**Numerus** *m, pl* **Numeri** *(Gram)* number. **~ clausus** *(Univ)* restricted entry.
**Nummer** *f* **-n** number; *(Größe)* size; *(col: Mensch)* character; *(col!: Koitus)* screw *(col!)*. **unser Haus hat die ~ 25** our house is number 25; **nur eine ~ unter vielen sein** *(fig)* to be a cog (in the machine); **auf ~ Sicher gehen** *(col)* to play (it) safe; **eine ~ abziehen** *(col)* to put on an act.
**Nummern-:** ~**konto** *nt* numbered bank account; ~**schild** *nt (Aut)* number plate *(Brit)*, license plate *(US)*.
**nun** *adv* **(a)** *(jetzt)* now. **von ~ an** from now on, from here on in *(US)*; **~ erst** only now; **~ endlich** (now) at last; **was ~?** what now?; **was ~ (schon wieder)?** what (is it) now? **(b) er will ~ mal nicht** he simply doesn't want to; **~, wenn's unbedingt sein muß** well, if I/you *etc* really must; **das ist ~ (ein)mal so** that's just the way things are; **~ ja, aber ...** OK *(col)*, but ...; **~ ja** well yes; **~ gut** (well) all right, (well) OK *(col)*; **~ erst recht!** that makes me all the more determined! **(c)** *(bei Fragen)* **~?** well?; **~, wird's bald?** *(col)* come on then.
**nunmehr** *adv* *(geh)* *(jetzt)* now, at this point; *(von jetzt an)* henceforth *(form)*, from now on.
**nur** *adv* **(a)** *(einschränkend)* only, just. **ich habe ~ ein Stück Brot gegessen** I've only eaten a piece of bread; **alle, ~ ich nicht** everyone but me; **~ schade, daß ...** it's just a pity that ...; **~ daß** it's just that; **~ noch zwei Minuten** just another two minutes; **nicht ~ ..., sondern auch** not only ... but also; **alles, ~ das nicht!** anything but that!; **warum möchtest du das denn wissen? — ach, ~ so!** why do you want to know? — oh no special reason; **ich hab' das ~ so gesagt** I was just talking.
  **(b)** *(mit Fragepronomen)* -ever. **warum sie ~ dahin geht?** whyever does she go there?; **wie kannst du ~ (so etwas sagen)?** how could you (say such a thing)?; **sie bekommt alles, was sie ~ will** she gets whatever she wants.
  **(c) wenn (...) ~** if only; **wenn er ~ (erst) käme** if only he would come; **es wird klappen, wenn er ~ nicht die Nerven verliert** it will be all right as long as he doesn't lose his nerve.
  **(d) sagen Sie das ~ nicht Ihrer Frau!** don't tell your wife (whatever you do); **geh ~!** go on; **~ zu!** go on; **sieh ~** just look; **~ her damit!** *(col)* let's have it; **Sie brauchen es ~ zu sagen** just say (the word); **er soll ~ lachen!** let him laugh.
**Nürnberg** *nt* Nuremberg.

**nuscheln** *vti (col)* to mutter, to mumble.
**Nuß** *f, pl* **Nüsse (a)** nut. **(b)** *(col: Mensch)* **eine taube ~** a dead loss *(col)*; **eine doofe ~** a stupid twit *(Brit col)* or clown *(col)*.
**Nuß-:** ~**baum** *m (Baum)* walnut tree; *(Holz)* walnut; ~**knacker** *m* nutcracker; ~**schale** *f* nutshell; *(fig: Boot)* cockleshell.
**Nüster** *f* **-n** nostril.
**Nut** *f* **-en** *(spec)*, **Nute** *f* **-n** groove.
**Nutte** *f* **-n** *(pej, col!)* tart *(col)*, hooker *(esp US col)*.
**nutzbar** *adj* usable; *Bodenschätze* exploitable. **~ machen** to make usable; *Sonnenenergie* to harness; *Bodenschätze* to exploit.
**Nutzbarmachung** *f* utilization; *(von Bodenschätzen)* exploitation.
**nutzbringend** *adj* profitable. **etw ~ anwenden** to use sth to good effect, to put sth to good use.
**nütze** *adj pred* **zu etw/nichts ~ sein** to be useful for sth/to be no use for anything.
**Nutzen** *m* **-** **(a)** use; *(Nützlichkeit)* usefulness. **zum ~ der Öffentlichkeit** for the benefit of the public; **jdm von ~ sein** to be of use to sb. **(b)** *(Vorteil)* advantage, benefit; *(Gewinn)* profit. **jdm ~ bringen** *(Vorteil)* to be of advantage to sb; *(Gewinn)* to bring sb profit; **von etw ~ haben** to profit by sth.
**nutzen, nützen 1** *vi* to be of use *(jdm zu etw* to sb for sth*)*. **die Ermahnungen haben genützt/nichts genützt** the warnings had the desired effect/didn't do any good; **da nützt alles nichts** there's nothing to be done; **das nützt (mir/dir) nichts** that won't help (me/you); **wozu soll das alles ~?** what's the point of that? **2** *vt* to make use of; *Gelegenheit* to take advantage of.
**Nutzer(in** *f)* *m* **-** user.
**Nutz-:** ~**fahrzeug** *nt* farm vehicle; military vehicle *etc*; *(Comm)* commercial vehicle; ~**fläche** *f* usable floor space; *(Agr)* (agriculturally) productive land; ~**last** *f* payload.
**nützlich** *adj* useful; *Hinweis, Buch auch* helpful. **~ für die Gesundheit** beneficial to one's health; **sich ~ machen** to make oneself useful.
**Nützlichkeit** *f* usefulness, utility *(form)*.
**nutzlos** *adj* **(a)** useless; *(vergeblich)* futile, vain *attr*, in vain *pred*. **es ist völlig ~, das zu tun** it's absolutely pointless doing that. **(b)** *(unnötig)* needless. **sein Leben ~ aufs Spiel setzen** to risk one's life needlessly *or* unnecessarily.
**Nutzlosigkeit** *f* uselessness; *(Vergeblichkeit)* futility.
**Nutznießer(in** *f)* *m* **-** beneficiary.
**Nutzung** *f (Gebrauch)* use; *(das Ausnutzen)* exploitation. **ich habe ihm meinen Garten zur ~ überlassen** I gave him the use of my garden.
**Nutzungsrecht** *nt (Jur)* usufruct.
**NW** = **Nordwesten** NW.
**Nylon** ® ['nailɔn] *nt no pl* nylon.
**Nylonstrumpf** ['nailɔn-] *m* nylon (stocking).
**Nymphe** ['nʏmfə] *f* **-n** nymph.
**Nymphomanin** [nʏmfo-] *f* nymphomaniac, nympho *(col)*.

# O

**O, o** [o:] *nt* -, - O, o. **O wie Otto** O for Oliver, O for oboe *(US)*.

**O** = **Osten** E.

**ọ** *interj* oh.

**o. ä.** = **oder ähnliche(s).**

**O**|**ase** *f* **-n, -n** oasis; *(fig)* haven, oasis.

**ọb** *conj* **(a)** *(indirekte Frage)* if, whether. **Sie müssen kommen, ~ Sie (nun) wollen oder nicht** whether you like it or not, you have to come; **~ er (wohl) morgen kommt?** I wonder if he'll come tomorrow; **~ wir jetzt Pause machen?** shall we have a break now?; **~ ich nicht lieber gehe?** maybe I'd better go; **~ Sie mir wohl mal helfen können?** I wonder if you could help me. **(b)** *(verstärkend)* **und ~** *(col)* you bet *(col)*; **und ~ ich das gesehen habe!** of course I saw it! **(c)** *(vergleichend)* **als ~** as if; **(so) tun als ~** *(col)* to pretend; **tu nicht so als ~!** stop pretending!

**OB** [o:'be:] *m* **-s** = **Oberbürgermeister.**

**o.B.** = **ohne Befund.**

**Ọbacht** *f no pl (esp S Ger)* **~!** watch out!, careful!; **~ geben auf** *(+acc) (aufmerken)* to pay attention to; *(bewachen)* to keep an eye on.

**Ọbdach** *nt no pl (geh)* shelter. **jdm ~ gewähren** to offer sb shelter; **kein ~ haben** to be homeless.

**Ọbdach-:** **o~los** *adj* homeless; **o~los werden** to be made homeless; **~lose(r)** *mf decl as adj* homeless person; **die ~losen** the homeless.

**Ọbdachlosen-:** **~asyl, ~heim** *nt* hostel *or* shelter for the homeless; **~siedlung** *f* settlement for the homeless.

**Ọbdachlosigkeit** *f* homelessness.

**Obduktion** *f* post-mortem, autopsy.

**obduzieren\*** *vt* to do a post-mortem *or* autopsy on.

**O-Beine** *pl (col)* bow *or* bandy legs *pl*.

**Obelisk** *m* **-en, -en** obelisk.

**ọben** *adv* **(a)** *(am oberen Ende)* at the top; *(an der Oberfläche)* on the surface; *(im Hause)* upstairs; *(in der Höhe)* up. **~ und unten (von etw) verwechseln** to get sth upside down; **wo ist ~ (bei dem Bild)?** which is the right way up (for the picture)?; **wir wohnen rechts ~** *or* **~ rechts** we live on the top floor to the right; **die Abbildung ~ links** *or* **links ~** the illustration in the top left-hand corner; **der ist ~ nicht ganz richtig** *(col)* he's not quite right up top *(col)*; **~ ohne gehen** *or* **tragen** *(col)* to be topless; **ganz ~** right at the top; **hier/dort ~** up here/there; **die ganze Sache steht mir bis hier ~** *(col)* I'm fed up to the back teeth with the whole thing *(col)*; **bis ~ (hin)** to the top; **hoch ~** high (up) above; **weiter ~** nearer the top; **~ auf dem Berg/der Leiter/dem Dach** on top of the mountain/ladder/roof; **~ am Himmel/im Norden** up in the sky/north; **nach ~** up, upwards; *(im Hause)* upstairs; **der Fahrstuhl fährt nach ~** the lift is going up; **der Weg nach ~** *(fig)* the road to the top; **endlich hat sie den Weg nach ~ geschafft** *(fig)* she finally made it (to the top); **nach ~ zu** *or* **hin** towards the top; **von ~ hat man eine schöne Aussicht** there's a nice view from the top; **von ~ bis unten** from top to bottom; *(von Mensch)* from top to toe; **jdn von ~ bis unten mustern** to look sb up and down; **jdn von ~ herab behandeln** to treat sb condescendingly; **weiter ~** further up.

**(b)** *(col: die Vorgesetzten)* **die da ~** the powers that be *(col)*; **das wird ~ entschieden** that's decided higher up; **etw nach ~ (weiter)melden** to report sth to a superior; **der Befehl kommt von ~** it's orders from above.

**(c)** *(vorher)* above. **siehe ~** see above; **wie ~ erwähnt** as mentioned above; **der weiter ~ erwähnte Fall** the case referred to above.

**ọben-:** **~an** *adv* at the top *or* on (the) top; **~auf** *adv* on (the) top; **gestern war er krank, aber heute ist er wieder ~auf** *(col)* he wasn't well yesterday, but he's back on form today; **~drauf** *adv (col)* on top; **~drein** *adv (col)* on top of everything *(col)*; **~erwähnt, ~genannt** *adj attr* above-mentioned; **~hin** *adv* **etw nur so ~hin sagen** to say sth in an offhand way; **~-ohne** *adj attr* topless; **~stehend** *adj attr* above-mentioned.

**Ober** *m* - *(Kellner)* waiter. **Herr ~!** waiter!

**Ober-:** **~arm** *m* upper arm; **~arzt** *m* senior physician; **~aufseher** *m* (head) supervisor; *(im Gefängnis)* head warden *(Brit)* or guard *(US)*; **~aufsicht** *f* supervision; **die ~aufsicht haben** to have overall control *(über +acc of)*; **~bayern** *nt* Upper Bavaria; **~befehl** *m (Mil)* **den ~befehl haben** to be in supreme command *(über +acc of)*; **~befehlshaber** *m (Mil)* commander-in-chief; **~begriff** *m* generic term; **~bekleidung** *f* outer clothing; **~bett** *nt* quilt; **~bürgermeister** *m* mayor; **~deck** *nt* upper *or* top deck.

**ọbere(r, s)** *adj attr* Ende, Stockwerke, (Schul)klassen upper, top. **die O~n** *(col)* the bosses; **die ~en Zehntausend** *(col)* high society.

**Oberfläche** *f* surface; *(Tech, Math)* surface area. **an die ~ kommen** *(lit)* to surface; *(fig)* to emerge; **an der ~ bleiben** *(lit)* to remain on the surface; **sein Referat blieb völlig an der ~** his paper was purely superficial.

**oberflächlich** *adj* superficial. **~e Verletzung** surface wound; **bei ~er Betrachtung** at a quick glance; **seine Kenntnisse sind nur ~** his knowledge has no depth; **~ arbeiten** to work superficially; **etw ~ lesen** to skim through sth; **jdn (nur) ~ kennen** to know sb (only) slightly; **nach ~er Schätzung** at a rough guess.

**Oberflächlichkeit** *f* superficiality.

**Ọber-:** **o~gärig** *adj* Bier top-fermented; **~geschoß** *nt* top floor; **im zweiten ~geschoß** on the second *(Brit)* or third *(US)* floor; **o~halb 1** *prep +gen* above; **2** *adv* above; **o~halb von Basel** above Basel; **weiter o~halb** further *or* higher up; **~hand** *f (fig)* upper hand; **die ~hand haben/gewinnen** to have/get the upper hand *(über +acc over)*; **~haupt** *nt (Repräsentant)* head; *(Anführer)* leader; **~haus** *nt (Pol)* upper house; *(in GB)* House of Lords; **~hemd**

*nt* shirt; ~**herrschaft**, ~**hoheit** *f* sovereignty.
**Oberin** *f* (a) *(im Krankenhaus)* = **Oberschwester**. (b) *(Eccl)* Mother Superior.
**Ober-: o**~**irdisch** *adj* above ground; ~**italien** *nt* Northern Italy; ~**kellner** *m* head waiter; ~**kiefer** *m* upper jaw; ~**kommando** *nt (~befehl)* Supreme Command; *(Befehlsstab)* headquarters *pl*; ~**körper** *m* upper part of the body; **mit bloßem** *or* **nacktem** ~**körper** stripped to the waist; ~**lauf** *m* **am** ~**lauf des Rheins** in the upper reaches of the Rhine; ~**leder** *nt* (leather) uppers *pl*; ~**leitung** *f (Elec)* overhead cable; ~**leutnant** *m* lieutenant *(Brit)*, first lieutenant *(US)*; *(Luftwaffe)* flying officer *(Brit)*, first lieutenant *(US)*; ~**licht** *nt (hochgelegenes Fenster)* small, high window; *(Lüftungsklappe, über einer Tür)* fanlight, transom (window); ~**liga** *f (Sport)* top *or* first league; ~**lippe** *f* upper lip; ~**material** *nt (von Schuh)* upper; ~**schenkel** *m* thigh; ~**schicht** *f* top layer; *(Sociol)* upper strata (of society) *pl*; ~**schule** *f (old: Gymnasium)* ≈ grammar school *(Brit)*, high school *(US)*; ~**schwester** *f* senior nursing officer; *(von Station)* sister; ~**seite** *f* top (side).
**Oberst** *m (wk)* **-en, -e(n)** (a) *(Heer)* colonel. (b) *(Luftwaffe)* group captain *(Brit)*, colonel *(US)*.
**Oberstaatsanwalt** *m* public prosecutor, district attorney *(US)*.
**oberste(r, s)** *adj* (a) *(ganz oben) Stockwerk, Schicht* uppermost, very top. (b) *Gesetz, Prinzip* supreme; *Dienstgrad* most senior. **O**~**er Gerichtshof** supreme court; *(in GB)* High Court (of Justice); *(in USA)* Supreme Court.
**Oberstimme** *f* soprano; *(Knaben~)* treble; *(Diskant)* descant.
**Oberstleutnant** *m* (a) *(Heer)* lieutenant colonel. (b) *(Luftwaffe)* wing commander *(Brit)*, lieutenant colonel *(US)*.
**Ober-:** ~**stübchen** *nt (col)*: **er ist nicht ganz richtig im** ~**stübchen** he's not quite right in the head *(col)*; ~**studiendirektor** *m* headmaster *(Brit)*, principal *(US)*; ~**studienrat** *m* senior teacher; ~**stufe** *f* upper school; *(Univ)* advanced level; ~**stufenkolleg** *nt* ≈ sixth-form college *(Brit)*; ~**teil** *nt or m* upper part, top; ~**trottel** *m (col)* prize idiot; ~**verwaltungsgericht** *nt* Higher Administrative Court; ~**wasser** *nt (fig col)* **wieder** ~**wasser bekommen** to get back into one's stride; **sobald sein älterer Bruder dabei ist, hat er** ~**wasser** as soon as his elder brother is there he opens up; ~**weite** *f* bust measurement.
**obgleich** *conj* although, (even) though.
**Obhut** *f no pl (geh)* care. **jdn/etw jds** ~ *(dat)* **anvertrauen** to place sb/sth in sb's care.
**obige(r, s)** *adj attr* above. **der O**~ *(form)* the above *(form)*.
**Objekt** *nt* **-e** *(auch Gram)* object; *(Comm: Grundstück)* property; *(Phot)* subject. **das** ~ **der Untersuchung** the object under examination.
**objektiv** *adj* objective. ~ **über etw** *(acc)* **urteilen** to judge sth objectively.
**Objektiv** *nt* lens.
**Objektivität** *f* objectivity. **sich um größte** ~ **bemühen** to try to be as objective as possible.
**Objekt-:** ~**satz** *m* object clause; ~**schutz** *m* protection of property.
**Oblate** *f* **-n** wafer; *(Eccl)* host.
**Obligation** *f (auch Fin)* obligation.
**obligatorisch** *adj* obligatory; *Fächer, Vorlesung* compulsory; *Qualifikationen* necessary.
**Oboe** [o'bo:ə] *f* **-n** oboe.
**Oboist(in** *f)* [obo'ɪst(ɪn)] *m (wk)* oboist.

**Obolus** *m* **-se** contribution.
**Obrigkeit** *f* (a) *(als Begriff)* authority. (b) *(Behörden)* **die** ~ the authorities *pl*.
**Obrigkeits-:** ~**denken** *nt* acceptance of authority; ~**staat** *m* authoritarian state.
**Obrist** *m (wk)* colonel.
**obschon** *conj (liter)* although.
**Observatorium** [ɔpzɛrva'to:riʊm] *nt* observatory.
**obskur** *adj* obscure; *(fragwürdig)* suspect, dubious.
**Obst** *nt no pl* fruit.
**Obst-:** ~**(an)bau** *m* fruit-growing; ~**baum** *m* fruit-tree; ~**garten** *m* orchard; ~**händler** *m* fruit merchant; ~**kuchen** *m* fruit flan.
**Obstler** *m* - *(dial)* fruit schnaps.
**Obstmesser** *nt* fruit knife.
**Obstruktion** *f (Pol)* obstruction, filibuster. ~ **betreiben** to obstruct, to filibuster.
**Obst-:** ~**saft** *m* fruit juice; ~**salat** *m* fruit salad; ~**torte** *f* fruit flan; ~**wasser** *nt* fruit schnaps.
**obszön** *adj* obscene.
**Obszönität** *f* obscenity.
**Obus** *m* **-se** *(col)* trolley bus.
**obwohl** *conj* although, (even) though.
**Ochse** ['ɔksə] *m (wk)* **-n, -n** (a) ox, bullock. ~ **am Spieß** roast ox; **er stand da wie der** ~ **vorm Berg** *(col)* he stood there utterly bewildered. (b) *(col: Dummkopf)* twit *(Brit col)*, clown *(col)*.
**ochsen** ['ɔksn] *vti (Sch sl)* to mug up *(col)*.
**Ochsen-** ['ɔksn-]: ~**schwanzsuppe** *f* oxtail soup; ~**tour** *f (col: Schinderei)* slog *(col)*; ~**zunge** *f* ox tongue.
**Ocker** *m or nt* - ochre *(Brit)*, ocher *(US)*.
**ocker-:** ~**braun**, ~**gelb** *adj* ochre *(Brit)*, ocher *(US)*.
**OCR-Schrift** [o:tse:'|ɛr-] *f* OCR font.
**od.** = **oder**.
**Ode** *f* **-n** ode.
**öd(e)** *adj* (a) *(verlassen) Stadt, Strand* deserted, empty; *(unbewohnt)* desolate, bleak; *(unbebaut)* waste. **öd und leer** dreary and desolate. (b) *(fig: fade)* dreary, tedious; *Dasein* barren.
**Öde** *f* **-n** *(liter)* (a) *(einsame Gegend)* wasteland. (b) *(Langeweile)* dreariness, monotony.
**oder** *conj* (a) or. ~ **aber** or else; ~ **auch** or even; **eins** ~ **das andere** one or the other; **entweder ...** ~ either ... or. (b) *(in Fragen)* **so war's doch,** ~ **nicht?** that was what happened, wasn't it?; **du kommst doch,** ~**?** you're coming, aren't you?; **lassen wir es so,** ~**?** let's leave it at that, OK?
**Oder** *f* Oder. ~**-Neiße-Linie** Oder-Neisse-line.
**Ödipuskomplex** *m* Oedipus complex.
**Odyssee** *f* **-n** [-e:ən] *(Liter)* Odyssey; *(fig)* odyssey.
**OECD** [o:|e:tse:'de:] *f* OECD. ~**-Land** OECD member country.
**OEZ** [o:|e:'tsɛt] *f* = **osteuropäische Zeit** EET.
**Ofen** *m* ⁼ (a) *(Heiz~)* heater; *(Elektro~, Gas~ auch)* fire; *(Kohle~)* stove. **hinter dem** ~ **hocken** to be a stay-at-home; **jetzt ist der** ~ **aus** *(col)* that does it *(col)*. (b) *(Herd)* oven, stove; *(Back~)* oven. (c) *(Tech)* furnace, oven; *(Brenn~)* kiln; *(Hoch~)* blast furnace.
**Ofen-:** **o**~**fertig** *adj Gericht* oven ready; **o**~**frisch** *adj Brot* oven fresh; ~**heizung** *f* stove heating; ~**rohr** *nt* stovepipe; ~**schirm** *m* firescreen.
**offen** *adj (lit, fig)* open; *Bein* ulcerated; *Flamme* naked; *Stelle* vacant; *Rechnung* outstanding. **ein** ~**er Brief** an open letter; **die Haare** ~ **tragen** to wear one's hair loose; **der Laden hat bis 7 Uhr** ~ the shop stays open until 7 o'clock; ~**er Wein** wine by the carafe/glass; *(vom Faß)* wine on draught *(Brit)* or draft *(US)*; **auf** ~**er Strecke** *(Straße)* on the open road; *(Rail)* between stations; **auf** ~**er Straße** in the

middle of the street; *(Landstraße)* on the open road; **auf ~er See** on the open sea; **Beifall auf ~er Szene** a spontaneous burst of applause; **mit ~em Munde dastehen** *(fig)* to stand gaping; **~e Türen einrennen** *(fig)* to kick at an open door; **Tag der ~en Tür** open day; **jdn mit ~en Armen empfangen** to welcome sb with open arms; **allem Neuen gegenüber ~ sein** to be receptive *or* open to (all) new ideas; **~e Handelsgesellschaft** general *or (US)* ordinary partnership; **~e Stellen** vacancies; **die Entscheidung ist noch ~** nothing has been decided yet; **~ gestanden** *or* **gesagt** quite honestly; **etw ~ zugeben** to admit sth frankly; **seine Meinung ~ sagen** to speak one's mind; **~ mit jdm reden** to be frank with sb; **ein ~es Wort mit jdm reden** to have a frank talk with sb.

**offenbar 1** *adj* obvious. **sein Zögern machte ~, daß ...** it was obvious from the way he hesitated that ...; **~ werden** to become obvious. **2** *adv (vermutlich)* apparently. **er hat ~ den Zug verpaßt** he must have missed the train; **da haben Sie sich ~ geirrt** you seem to have made a mistake.

**offenbaren* 1** *vt* to reveal. **2** *vr* to reveal itself/oneself. **sich als etw ~** to show oneself to be sth; **sich jdm ~** to reveal oneself to sb.

**Offenbarung** *f* revelation.

**Offenbarungs|eid** *m (Jur)* oath of disclosure, *sworn statement in bankruptcy cases.* **den ~ leisten** *(lit)* to swear an oath of disclosure.

**offen-: ~bleiben** *vi sep irreg aux sein* to remain open; **alle ~gebliebenen Probleme** all unsolved problems; **~halten** *vt sep irreg* to keep open.

**Offenheit** *f* openness, frankness.

**offen-: ~herzig** *adj* open, frank; *(hum col)* **Kleid** revealing; **O~herzigkeit** *f* openness, frankness; **~kundig** *adj* obvious; **Beweise** clear; **~lassen** *vt sep irreg* to leave open; **~sichtlich** *adj* obvious; *Irrtum, Lüge auch* blatant.

**offensiv** *adj* offensive.

**Offensive** *f* offensive. **in die ~ gehen** to go onto the offensive.

**Offensiv-: ~rakete** *f* offensive missile; **~waffe** *f* offensive weapon.

**offenstehen** *vi sep irreg* **(a)** *(Tür, Fenster)* to be open. **(b)** *(Comm: Rechnung, Betrag)* to be outstanding. **(c) jdm ~** *(fig: zugänglich sein)* to be open to sb; **die (ganze) Welt steht ihm offen** he has the (whole) world at his feet; **es steht ihr offen, sich uns anzuschließen** she's free to join us.

**öffentlich** *adj* public. **etw ~ bekanntmachen** to make sth public; **eine Persönlichkeit des ~en Lebens** a person in public life; **jdn ~ beschuldigen** to accuse sb publicly; **die ~e Meinung/Moral** public opinion/morality; **die ~e Ordnung** law and order; **~er Dienst** civil service; **~es Recht** *(Jur)* public law; **Anstalt des ~en Rechts** public institution; **~e Schule** state school, public school *(US)*; **die ~e Hand** (central/local) government; **Ausgaben der ~en Hand** public spending.

**Öffentlichkeit** *f* **(a)** *(Allgemeinheit)* the (general) public. **die ~ scheuen** to shun publicity; **in aller ~** in public; **unter Ausschluß der ~** *(Jur)* in private; **im camera; als er das erstemal vor die ~ trat** when he made his first public appearance; **etw vor die ~ bringen** to bring sth before the public; **an die ~ gelangen** to become known. **(b)** *(einer Versammlung etc)* public nature. **die ~ einer Versammlung herstellen** to make a meeting public.

**Öffentlichkeits|arbeit** *f* public relations *or* PR work.

**öffentlich-rechtlich** *adj attr* (under) public law.

**offerieren*** *vt (Comm, form)* to offer.

**Offerte** *f* **-n** *(Comm)* offer; *(für Auftrag)* tender.

**offiziell** *adj* official. **wie von ~er Seite verlautet** according to official sources.

**Offizier** *m* **-e** officer.

**Offiziers-: ~anwärter** *m* officer cadet; **~kasino** *nt* officers' mess; **~korps** *nt* officer corps; **~messe** *f* officers' mess.

**Off-Line-Betrieb** [ɔf'lain-] *m (Comp)* off-line mode. **im ~ arbeiten** to operate off-line.

**öffnen 1** *vti* to open. **jdm (die Tür) ~** to open the door for sb; **jdm den Blick für etw ~** to open sb's eyes to sth; **es hat geklingelt, könnten Sie mal ~?** that was the doorbell, would you answer it?; **eine Datei ~** *(Comp)* to open a file. **2** *vr (Tür, Blume, Augen)* to open; *(weiter werden)* to open out. **das Tal öffnet sich nach Süden** the valley opens to the south.

**Öffner** *m* **-** opener.

**Öffnung** *f* opening. **~ der Leiche** post-mortem; **eine Politik der ~** a policy of openness.

**Öffnungszeiten** *pl* opening hours *pl*; *(von Geschäft)* hours of business *pl*.

**Offsetdruck** ['ɔfset-] *m* offset (printing).

**oft** *adv comp* **=er**, *superl* **am =esten** *(häufig)* often, frequently. **schon so ~, ~ genug** often enough; **wie ~ fährt der Bus?** how often does the bus go?; **wie ~ warst du schon in Deutschland?** how many times have you been to Germany?; **des ~eren** quite frequently; **je ~er ...** the more often ...

**öfter(s)** *adv* (every) now and then. **~ mal was Neues** *(col)* variety is the spice of life *(prov)*.

**oftmals** *adv (geh)* often, oft *(poet)*.

**OG** = **Obergeschoß.**

**o.G.** = **ohne Gewähr.**

**oh** *interj* oh.

**OHG** = **offene Handelsgesellschaft.**

**ohne 1** *prep +acc* **(a)** without. **~ Auto** without a car; **~ (die) Vororte hat die Stadt 100.000 Einwohner** the city has 100,000 inhabitants not counting the suburbs; **~ mich!** count me out!; **er ist nicht ~** *(col)* there's more to him than meets the eye; **die Sache ist (gar) nicht (so) ~** *(col) (interessant)* it's not at all bad; *(schwierig)* it's not that easy *(col)*.

**(b) ich hätte das ~ weiteres getan** I'd have done it without a second thought; **ja, das kann man ~ weiteres sagen** yes, that's very true; **ich würde ~ weiteres sagen, daß ...** I would not hesitate to say that ...; **das Darlehen ist ~ weiteres bewilligt worden** the loan was granted without any problem; **ihm können Sie ~ weiteres vertrauen** you can trust him implicitly; **das läßt sich ~ weiteres arrangieren** that can easily be arranged; **das kann man nicht ~ weiteres voraussetzen** you can't just assume that automatically.

**2** *conj* **~ zu zögern** without hesitating; **~ daß ich ihn darum gebeten hätte** without my *or* me asking him.

**ohne-: ~dies** *adv siehe* **~hin; ~einander** *adv* without each other; **~gleichen** *adj inv* unparalleled; **ein Erfolg ~gleichen** an unparalleled success; **diese Frechheit ist ~gleichen!** I've never known such a cheek!; **~hin** *adv* anyway; **wir sind ~hin zu viel Leute** there are too many of us as it is; **es ist ~hin schon spät** it's late enough already.

**Ohnmacht** *f* **-en** *(Med)* faint; *(Machtlosigkeit)* helplessness. **in ~ fallen** to faint.

**ohnmächtig** *adj (bewußtlos)* unconscious; *(machtlos)* powerless, helpless. **~ werden** to faint, to pass out; **~ sein** to have fainted *or* passed out; **~e Wut, ~er Zorn** helpless rage; **einer Sache** *(dat)* **~ gegenüberstehen** to be helpless in the face of sth; **~ zuse-**

**hen müssen** to look on helplessly.
**Ohnmachts|anfall** m (lit, fig) fainting fit. **als ich das hörte, habe ich fast einen ~ bekommen** (col) when I heard that I was flabbergasted or gobsmacked (Brit col).
**oho** interj oho, hello.
**Ohr** nt **-en** ear. **seine ~en sind nicht mehr so gut** his hearing isn't too good any more; **auf einem ~ taub sein** to be deaf in one ear; **auf dem ~ bin ich taub** (fig) nothing doing (col); **bei jdm ein offenes ~ finden** to find sb a sympathetic listener; **die ~en anlegen** (Hund) to put its ears back; (fig col) to brace oneself; **mach** or **sperr die ~en auf!** (col) clean your ears out (col); **jdm die ~en volljammern** (col) to keep moaning at sb; **ganz ~ sein** (hum) to be all ears; **sich aufs ~ legen** or **hauen** (col) to kip down (col); **sitzt er auf seinen ~en?** (col) is he deaf or something?; **jdm die ~en langziehen** (col) to tweak sb's ear(s); **jdm etw um die ~en hauen** (col) to hit sb over the head with sth; **schreib es dir hinter die ~en** (col) will you (finally) get that into your (thick) head (col); **noch nicht trocken hinter den ~en sein** to be still wet behind the ears; **die Melodie geht ins ~** the tune is very catchy; **du hast wohl Watte in den ~en!** (col) are you deaf or something?; **ich habe seine Worte noch deutlich im ~** I can still hear his words clearly; **jdm in den ~en liegen** to keep on at sb (col); **jdn übers ~ hauen** to pull a fast one on sb (col); **bis über die** or **beide ~en verliebt sein** to be head over heels in love; **viel um die ~en haben** (col) to have a lot on (one's plate) (col); **es ist mir zu ~en gekommen** it has come to my ears (form); **das geht zum einen ~ hinein und zum anderen wieder hinaus** (col) it goes in one ear and out the other (col); **halt die ~en steif!** take care; **dein Wort in Gottes ~** God willing.
**Öhr** nt **-e** eye.
**Ohren-**: **~arzt** m ear specialist; **o~betäubend** adj (fig) earsplitting; **~sausen** nt (Med) buzzing in one's ears; **~schmalz** nt earwax; **~schmaus** m **das Konzert war ein richtiger ~schmaus** the concert was a feast for the ears; **~schmerzen** pl earache; **~schützer** pl earmuffs pl; **~sessel** m wing chair; **~stöpsel** m ear plug.
**Ohrfeige** f **-n** slap (on or around the face); (als Strafe) box on the ears. **jdm eine ~ geben** or **verabreichen** to slap sb's face; **eine ~ bekommen** to get a slap around the face.
**ohrfeigen** vt insep **jdn ~** to box sb's ears; **ich könnte mich selbst ~, daß ich das gemacht habe** I could kick myself for doing it.
**Ohr-**: **~läppchen** nt (ear) lobe; **~muschel** f (outer) ear; **~ring** m earring; **~stecker** m stud earring; **~wurm** m earwig; **der Song ist ein richtiger ~wurm** (col) that's a really catchy song (col).
**oje, ojemine** interj oh dear.
**okay** [o'ke:] interj okay, OK.
**Okkultismus** m occultism.
**Okkupation** f occupation.
**okkupieren*** vt to occupy.
**Öko-** in cpds eco-, ecological; (Umwelt betreffend auch) environmental; **~bauer** m (col) ecologically-minded farmer; **~laden** m wholefood shop.
**Ökologe** m, **Ökologin** f ecologist.
**Ökologie** f ecology.
**ökologisch** adj ecological, environmental.
**Ökonomie** f economy; (als Wissenschaft) economics sing. **politische ~ studieren** to study political economy.
**ökonomisch** adj economic; (sparsam) economical.
**Ökosystem** nt ecosystem.

**Okt.** = **Oktober** Oct.
**Oktanzahl** f octane rating. **Benzin mit einer hohen ~** high octane petrol.
**Oktave** [ɔk'ta:və] f **-n** octave.
**Oktett** nt **-e** octet.
**Oktober** m **-** October; siehe **März**.
**ökumenisch** adj ecumenical.
**Öl** nt **-e** oil. **auf ~ stoßen** to strike oil; **~ fördern** to extract oil; **in ~ malen** to paint in oils; **~ ins Feuer gießen** (prov) to add fuel to the fire (prov).
**Öl-**: **~baum** m olive tree; **~bild** nt oil painting, oil; **~bohrung** f oil drilling.
**Oldie** ['ouldi] m **-s** (col: Schlager) (golden) oldie (col).
**Oldtimer** ['ouldtaimɐ] m **-** (Auto) old car, oldie (col); (aus den 20er Jahren) vintage car.
**ölen** vt to oil. **wie geölt** (col) like clockwork (col); **wie ein geölter Blitz** (col) like greased lightning (col).
**Öl-**: **~farbe** f oil-based paint; (Art) oil (paint); **mit ~farben malen** to paint in oils; **~feld** nt oil field; **~film** m film of oil; **~gemälde** nt oil painting; **~götze** m (col) **wie ein ~götze** like a tailor's dummy (col); **~heizung** f oil-fired central heating.
**ölig** adj oily; (fig auch) greasy.
**Oligarchie** f oligarchy.
**Öl|industrie** f oil industry.
**oliv** adj pred olive(-green).
**Olive** [o'li:və] f **-n** olive.
**Oliven-**: **~baum** m olive tree; **~öl** nt olive oil.
**olivgrün** adj olive-green.
**Öl-**: **~jacke** f oilskin jacket; **~kännchen** nt, **~kanne** f oil can; **~konzern** m oil company; **~krise** f oil crisis.
**oll** adj (NGer col) old. **das sind ~e Kamellen** (col) that's old hat (col).
**Öl-**: **~malerei** f oil painting; **~meßstab** m (Aut) dipstick; **~ofen** m oil heater; **~pest** f oil pollution; **~plattform** f oil-rig; **ö~reich** adj oil-rich; **~sardine** f sardine; **wie die ~sardinen** (col) crammed in like sardines (col); **~scheich** m oil sheik; **~spur** f patch of oil; **~stand** m oil level; **~standsanzeiger** m oil-level gauge; **~tanker** m oil tanker; **~teppich** m oil slick.
**Ölung** f oiling. **Letzte ~** (Eccl) extreme unction, last rites.
**Öl-**: **~vorkommen** nt oil deposit; **~wanne** f (Aut) sump (Brit), oil pan (US); **~wechsel** m oil change; **den ~wechsel machen** to change the oil.
**Olymp** m (Berg) Mount Olympus.
**Olympiade** f (Olympische Spiele) Olympic Games pl, Olympics pl.
**Olympia-**: **~medaille** f Olympic medal; **~sieger** m Olympic champion; **~stadion** nt Olympic stadium.
**olympisch** adj (die Olympiade betreffend) Olympic. **die O~en Spiele** the Olympic Games.
**Öl-**: **~zeug** nt oilskins pl; **~zweig** m (lit, fig) olive-branch.
**Oma** f **-s** (col) granny (col), grandma (col).
**Oman** nt Oman.
**Omaner(in** f) m **-** Omani.
**omanisch** adj Omani.
**Ombudsmann** m, pl **-männer** ombudsman.
**Omelett** [ɔm(ə)'lɛt] nt **-e** or **-s** omelette (Brit), omelet (US).
**Omen** nt **-** omen.
**ominös** adj (geh) ominous, sinister.
**Omnibus** m bus.
**Omnibuslinie** f bus route.
**Onanie** f masturbation, onanism.
**onanieren*** vi to masturbate.
**ondulieren*** vtr to crimp.

Onkel *m* - uncle.
On-line-Betrieb [ɔn'lain-] *m (Comp)* on-line mode. im ~ arbeiten to operate on-line.
Onyx *m* -e onyx.
OP [oː'peː] *m* -s = Operationssaal.
Opa *m* -s *(col)* grandpa *(col)*, grandad *(col)*.
Opal *m* -e opal.
OPEC ['oːpɛk] *f* die ~ OPEC.
Oper *f* -n opera; *(Ensemble)* Opera; *(Opernhaus)* Opera, Opera House. in die ~ gehen to go to the opera; zur ~ gehen to become an opera singer.
Operation *f* operation.
Operations-: ~saal *m* operating theatre *(Brit)* or room *(US)*; ~schwester *f* theatre sister *(Brit)*, operating room nurse *(US)*.
operativ *adj (Med)* surgical. eine Geschwulst ~ entfernen to remove a growth by surgery.
Operette *f* operetta.
operieren* 1 *vt Patienten, Krebs, Magen* to operate on. jdn am Magen ~ to operate on sb's stomach. 2 *vi* to operate *(an jdm/etw* on sb/sth*).* sich ~ lassen to have an operation.
Opern-: ~arie *f* (operatic) aria; ~ball *m* opera ball; ~glas *nt* opera glasses *pl*; o~haft *adj* operatic; ~haus *nt* opera house; ~sänger *m* opera singer; ~text *m* libretto.
Opfer *nt* - (a) *(~gabe)* sacrifice *(auch fig)*. für ihre Kinder scheut sie keine ~ she sacrifices everything for her children; wir müssen alle ~ bringen we must all make sacrifices. (b) *(geschädigte Person)* victim. jdm/einer Sache zum ~ fallen to be (the) victim of sb/sth; ein ~ einer Sache *(gen)* werden to be a victim of sth, to fall victim to sth; das Erdbeben forderte viele ~ the earthquake claimed many victims.
Opfer-: o~bereit *adj* willing to make sacrifices; ~bereitschaft *f* readiness to make sacrifices; ~gabe *f (liter)* sacrificial offering; *(Eccl)* offering; ~lamm *nt (lit, fig)* sacrificial lamb; ~mut *m* self-sacrifice.
opfern 1 *vt (lit, fig)* to sacrifice; *Feldfrüchte etc* to offer (up). sein Leben ~ to sacrifice one's life. 2 *vr* (a) *(sein Leben hingeben)* to sacrifice one's life. (b) *(col: sich bereit erklären)* to be a martyr *(col)*. wer opfert sich, die Reste aufzuessen? who's going to volunteer to eat up the remains?
Opfer-: ~stätte *f* sacrificial altar; ~stock *m* offertory box; ~tier *nt* sacrificial animal.
Opferung *f (das Opfern)* sacrifice; *(Eccl)* offertory.
Opiat *nt* opiate.
Opium *nt no pl* opium.
opponieren* *vi* to oppose *(gegen jdn/etw* sb/sth*)*, to offer opposition *(gegen* to*)*.
opportun *adj (geh)* opportune.
Opportunismus *m* opportunism.
Opportunist(in *f)* *m* opportunist.
opportunistisch *adj* opportunistic, opportunist. ~ handeln to act in an opportunist fashion.
Opposition *f* opposition. etw aus lauter *or* reiner ~ tun to do sth out of sheer contrariness.
oppositionell *adj Gruppen, Kräfte* opposition.
Oppositionsführer *m* leader of the opposition.
optieren* *vi (Pol form)* ~ für to opt for.
Optik *f* (a) *(Phys)* optics. (b) *(Phot)* lens system. du hast wohl einen Knick in der ~! *(col)* can't you see straight? *(col)*; das ist eine Frage der ~ *(fig)* it depends on your point of view; in *or* aus seiner ~ in his eyes. (c) *(Mode, Aussehen)* look; *(Schein)* appearances *pl*. das ist nur hier wegen der ~ *(fig)* it's just here for visual effect.
Optiker(in *f)* *m* - optician.

optimal *adj* optimal, optimum *attr*.
Optimismus *m* optimism.
Optimist(in *f)* *m (wk)* optimist.
optimistisch *adj* optimistic.
Option [ɔp'tsioːn] *f* option.
optisch *adj* visual; *Gesetze, Instrumente* optical. ~e Täuschung optical illusion; ~ größer wirken to look larger (than it is).
opulent *adj* lavish; *Mahl auch* sumptuous.
Orakel *nt* - oracle.
orakeln* *vi (col)* (a) *(rätseln)* wir haben lange orakelt, was der Satz bedeuten sollte we spent a long time trying to decipher the sentence. (b) *(weissagen)* to prognosticate *(hum)*.
oral *adj* oral.
Orange¹ [o'rãːʒə] *f* -n *(Frucht)* orange.
Orange² [o'rãːʒə] *nt* -, - *or (col)* -s orange.
orange- [o'rãːʒə-]: ~farben, ~farbig *adj* orange.
orange(n) [o'rãːʒə(n)] *adj* orange.
Orangeat [orãːʒaːt] *nt* candied (orange) peel.
Orangen- [o'rãːʒən-]: ~baum *m* orange (tree); ~marmelade *f* orange marmalade; ~saft *m* orange juice; ~schale *f* orange peel.
Orangerie [orãːʒə'riː] *f* orangery.
Orang-Utan *m* -s orang-utan, orang-outang.
Oratorium *nt* (a) *(Mus)* oratorio. (b) *(Betraum)* oratory.
Orchester [ɔr'kɛstɐ] *nt* - orchestra.
orchestrieren* [ɔrkɛs'triːrən] *vt* to orchestrate.
Orchestrierung *f* orchestration.
Orchidee *f* -n [-'deːən] orchid.
Orden *m* - (a) *(Ehrenzeichen)* decoration; *(Mil auch)* medal. ~ tragen to wear one's decorations; jdm einen ~ *(für etw)* verleihen to decorate sb (for sth). (b) *(Gemeinschaft)* (holy) order. in einen ~ eintreten, einem ~ beitreten to become a member of an order.
Ordens-: ~bruder *m (Eccl)* monk; ~gemeinschaft *f* religious order; ~schwester *f* sister, nun.
ordentlich *adj* (a) *Mensch, Zimmer* tidy, neat. bei ihr sieht es immer ~ aus her house always looks neat and tidy; ~ arbeiten to be a thorough and precise worker. (b) *(ordnungsgemäß)* ~es Gericht law court; ~es Mitglied full member; ~er Professor (full) professor. (c) *(anständig)* respectable. sich ~ benehmen to behave properly; etwas O~es lernen to learn a proper trade. (d) *(col: tüchtig, richtig)* ~ essen/trinken to eat/drink (really) well; ein ~es Frühstück a proper breakfast; wir haben ~ gearbeitet we really got down to it; jetzt hab' ich aber ~ Appetit I'm really hungry now; eine ~e Tracht Prügel a proper hiding. (e) *(annehmbar, ganz gut) Preis, Leistung* reasonable.
Order *f* -s *or* -n (a) *(Comm: Auftrag)* order. (b) *(Anweisung)* order. sich an eine ~ halten to keep to one's orders.
ordern *vt (Comm)* to order.
Ordinalzahl *f* ordinal number.
ordinär *adj* (a) *(gemein, unfein)* vulgar, common. (b) *(alltäglich)* ordinary.
Ordinarius *m, pl* Ordinarien [-iən] *(Univ)* professor *(für* of*)*.
ordnen 1 *vt Gedanken, Material* to order, to organize; *Finanzen, Privatleben* to put in order, to straighten out; *siehe* geordnet. 2 *vr* to get into order. die Menge ordnete sich zu einem Festzug the crowd itself into a procession.
Ordner *m* - (a) steward; *(bei Demonstration auch)* marshal. (b) *(Akten~)* file.
Ordnung *f* (a) *(geordneter Zustand)* order. ~ halten to keep things tidy; ~ schaffen, für ~ sorgen to put

things in order, to tidy things up; **Sie müssen für mehr ~ in Ihrer Klasse sorgen** you'll have to keep your class in better order; **etw in ~ halten** to keep sth in order; *Garten, Haus etc auch* to keep sth tidy; **etw in ~ bringen** *(reparieren)* to fix sth; *(herrichten)* to put sth in order; *(bereinigen)* to sort sth out; **ich finde es (ganz) in ~, daß** ... I find it quite right that ...; **(das ist) in ~!** *(col)* (that's) OK *(col)* or all right!; **geht in ~** *(col)* that's all right or OK *(col)*; **Ihre Bestellung geht in ~** we'll put your order through; **der ist in ~** *(col)* he's OK *(col)* or all right *(col)*; **mit ihm/der Maschine ist etwas nicht in ~** there's something the matter with him/the machine; **es ist alles in bester ~** things couldn't be better; **jdn zur ~ rufen** to call sb to order; **bei ihm muß alles seine ~ haben** *(räumlich)* he has to have everything in its proper place; *(zeitlich)* he does everything according to a fixed schedule; **das Kind braucht seine ~** the child needs a routine.

**(b)** *(Vorschrift)* rules *pl.* **sich an eine ~ halten** to keep to the rules; **ich frage nur der ~ halber** it's only a routine question.

**(c)** *(Rang, Biol)* order. **Straße erster ~** first-class road; **das war ein Fauxpas erster ~** *(col)* that was a faux-pas of the first order or a real clanger *(col)*.

**Ordnungs-:** **~amt** *nt* ≃ town clerk's office; **~fanatiker** *m* fanatic for order; **o~gemäß** *adj* in accordance with the rules, proper; **o~halber** *adv* as a matter of form; **~hüter** *m (hum)* custodian of the law *(hum)*; **~liebe** *f* love of order; **o~liebend** *adj* tidy-minded, orderly; **~ruf** *m* call to order; **der Präsident mußte mehrere ~rufe erteilen** the chairman had to call the meeting to order several times; **~sinn** *m* sense of order; **~strafe** *f* fine; **jdn mit einer ~strafe belegen** to fine sb; **o~widrig** *adj* irregular; *Parken, Verhalten (im Straßenverkehr)* illegal; **o~widrig handeln** to infringe rules or regulations; **~widrigkeit** *f* infringement *(of law or rule)*; **~zahl** *f* ordinal number.

**ORF** [oː|ɛr|ɛf, *(col)* ɔrf] *m* = **Österreichischer Rundfunk.**

**Organ** *nt* **-s, -e (a)** *(Med, Biol, fig)* organ. **(b)** *(col: Stimme)* voice.

**Organisation** *f* organization.

**Organisationstalent** *nt* talent for organization. **er ist ein ~** he has a talent for organization.

**Organisator** *m*, **Organisatorin** *f* organizer.

**organisatorisch** *adj* organizational. **eine ~e Höchstleistung** a masterpiece of organization.

**organisch** *adj Chemie, Verbindung, Salz* organic; *Erkrankung, Leiden* physical. **sich ~ einfügen** to merge, to blend *(in +acc* with, into*)*.

**organisieren*** **1** *vti* **(a)** to organize. **er kann ausgezeichnet ~** he's excellent at organizing. **(b)** *(col: stehlen)* to lift *(col)*, to get hold of. **2** *vr* to get organized; *(gewerkschaftlich auch)* to organize.

**Organismus** *m* organism.

**Organist(in** *f)* *m (wk)* organist.

**Organ-:** **~spender** *m* donor *(of an organ)*; **~spenderausweis** *m* donor card; **~verpflanzung** *f* transplant(ation) *(of organs)*.

**Orgasmus** *m* orgasm.

**Orgel** *f* **-n** organ.

**Orgel-** *in cpds* organ; **~pfeife** *f* organ pipe; **die Kinder standen da wie die ~pfeifen** *(hum)* the children were standing in order of height.

**Orgie** [-iə] *f* orgy. **~n feiern** *(lit)* to have orgies/an orgy; *(fig)* to go wild.

**Orient** ['oːriɛnt, oˈriɛnt] *m no pl (liter)* Orient. **der Vordere ~** the Near East.

**Orientale** [oriɛnˈtaːlə] *m (wk)* **-n, -n, Orientalin** *f*

Oriental. **er ist ~** he is an Oriental.

**orientalisch** [oriɛnˈtaːlɪʃ] *adj* oriental.

**orientieren*** [oriɛnˈtiːrən] **1** *vt* **(a)** *(unterrichten)* to put in the picture *(über +acc* about*)*. **gut/falsch orientiert** well/wrongly informed. **(b)** *(ausrichten) (lit, fig)* to orient, to orientate *(nach, auf* to, towards*)*. **links orientiert sein** to tend to the left; **links orientierte Gruppen** left-wing groups. **2** *vr* **(a)** *(sich unterrichten)* to inform oneself *(über +acc* about or on*)*. **(b)** *(sich zurechtfinden)* to orientate oneself *(an +dat,* nach by*)*, to get one's bearings. **in einer fremden Stadt kann ich mich nicht ~** I can't find my way around in a strange city. **(c)** *(sich ausrichten)* to adapt or orientate (oneself) *(an +dat* to*)*.

**Orientierung** [oriɛnˈtiːrʊŋ] *f* orientation; *(Unterrichtung)* information. **die ~ verlieren** to lose one's bearings; **zu Ihrer ~** for your information.

**Orientierungs-:** **~punkt** *m* point of reference; **~sinn** *m* sense of direction; **~stufe** *f (Sch) period during which pupils are selected to attend different schools.*

**Original** *nt* **-e (a)** original. **(b)** *(Mensch)* character. **(c)** *(Comp)* master (copy).

**original** *adj* original. **~ Meißener Porzellan** genuine Dresden china.

**Original-:** **~ausgabe** *f* first edition; **~fassung** *f* original (version); **o~getreu** *adj* true to the original.

**Originalität** *f no pl* **(a)** *(Echtheit)* authenticity, genuineness. **(b)** *(Urtümlichkeit)* originality.

**Originalton** *m* original soundtrack. *(fig)* **im ~ Kohl** in Kohl's own words.

**originell** *adj (selbständig)* Idee, Argumentation original; *(neu)* novel; *(geistreich)* witty. **das finde ich ~ (von ihm)** that's pretty original/witty.

**Orkan** *m* **-e** hurricane.

**Orkan-:** **o~artig** *adj* Wind gale-force; *Beifall* thunderous; **~stärke** *f* hurricane force.

**Ornament** *nt* decoration, ornament.

**Ornat** *m* **-e** regalia *pl*; *(Eccl)* vestments *pl*; *(Jur)* official robes *pl.* **in vollem ~** *(col)* dressed up to the nines *(col)*.

**Ornithologe** *m (wk)*, **Ornithologin** *f* ornithologist.

**Ort[1]** *m* **-e** place. **~ der Handlung** *(Theat)* scene of the action; **an den ~ der Tat** or **des Verbrechens zurückkehren** to return to the scene of the crime; **der Stuhl steht wieder an seinem ~** the chair is back in (its) place again; **am angegebenen ~** in the place quoted, loc. cit. *abbr*; **an ~ und Stelle** on the spot, there and then; **an ~ und Stelle ankommen** to arrive (at one's destination); **das ist höheren ~s entschieden worden** *(hum, form)* the decision came from above; **in einem kleinen ~ in Cornwall** in a little place in Cornwall; **~e über 100.000 Einwohner** places with over 100,000 inhabitants; **am ~** in the place; **das beste Hotel am ~** the best hotel in town; **wir haben keinen Arzt am ~** we have no resident doctor; **am ~ wohnen** to live locally; **mitten im ~** in the centre (of the place/town); **der nächste ~** the next village/town *etc*; **von ~ zu ~** from place to place.

**Ort[2]** *m* **ⁿer** *(Min)* coal face, (working) face. **vor ~** at the (coal) face; *(fig)* on the spot.

**Örtchen** *nt (col)* loo *(Brit col)*, john *(US col)*.

**orten** *vt* to locate, to get a fix on.

**orthodox** *adj (lit, fig)* orthodox.

**Orthographie** *f* orthography.

**orthographisch** *adj* orthographic(al). **ein ~er Fehler** a spelling mistake.

**Orthopäde** *m (wk)* **-n, -n, Orthopädin** *f* orthopaedic *(Brit)* or orthopedic *(US)* specialist.

**Orthopädie** *f* orthopaedics *sing (Brit)*, orthopedics

sing *(US)*.
**orthopädisch** *adj* orthopaedic *(Brit)*, orthopedic *(US)*.
**örtlich** *adj* local. **das ist ~ verschieden** it varies from place to place; **jdn/etw ~ betäuben** to give sb/sth a local anaesthetic.
**Örtlichkeit** *f* locality. **sich mit den ~en vertraut machen** to get to know the place; **die ~en** *(euph)* the cloakroom *(Brit euph)*, the comfort station *(US euph)*.
**Orts-: ~angabe** *f (bei Anschriften)* (name of the) town; **ohne ~angabe** *(von Buch)* no place of publication indicated; **o~ansässig** *adj* local; **die ~ansässigen** the local residents.
**Ortschaft** *f* **-en** *(Dorf)* village; *(Stadt)* town. **geschlossene ~** built-up area.
**Orts-: o~fremd** *adj* non-local; **ich bin hier o~fremd** I'm a stranger here; **~gespräch** *nt (Telec)* local call; **~gruppe** *f* local branch *or* group; **~kenntnis** *f* local knowledge; **(gute) ~kenntnisse haben** to know one's way around (well); **~krankenkasse** *f* **Allgemeine ~krankenkasse** *compulsory medical insurance organization*; **o~kundig** *adj* **ein ~kundiger** somebody who knows the place; **~mitte** *f* centre; **~name** *m* place name; **~netz** *nt (Telec)* local (telephone) exchange area; *(Elec)* local grid; **~netzkennzahl** *f (Telec form)* dialling *(Brit) or* area code; **~schild** *nt* place name sign; **~sinn** *m* sense of direction; **~tarif** *m (Telec)* charge for local phone-calls; **o~üblich** *adj* local; **das ist hier o~üblich** it's a local custom here; **o~übliche Mieten** standard local rents; **~verkehr** *m* local traffic; **Gebühren im ~verkehr** *(Telec)* charges for local (phone) calls; **~zeit** *f* local time; **~zuschlag** *m* (local) weighting allowance.
**Ortung** *f* locating.
**Öse** *f* **-n** loop; *(an Kleidung)* eye.
**Oslo** *nt* Oslo.
**Osmose** *f no pl* osmosis.
**Ossi** *m* **-s** *(col)* East German.
**Ost** *m no pl (liter)* East.
**Ost-** *in cpds* East; *(geographisch auch)* Eastern, the East of ...; **~afrika** *nt* East Africa; **~asien** *nt* Eastern Asia; **~block** *m (Hist)* Eastern bloc; **o~deutsch** *adj (Hist Pol)* East German; *(Geog)* Eastern German; **~deutsche(r)** *mf (Hist Pol)* East German; *(Geog)* Eastern German; **~deutschland** *nt (Hist Pol)* East Germany; *(Geog)* Eastern Germany.
**Osten** *m no pl* east; *(von Land)* East. **der ~** *(Hist Pol)* the East; **der Ferne ~** the Far East; **der Nahe ~** the Middle East, the Near East; **im ~** in the East; **nach ~** to the East; **von ~, aus dem ~** from the East.
**ostentativ** *adj (geh)* pointed.
**Oster-: ~ei** *nt* Easter egg; **~fest** *nt* Easter; **~glocke** *f* daffodil; **~hase** *m* Easter bunny;

**~insel** *f* Easter Island.
**österlich** *adj* Easter.
**Oster-: ~marsch** *m* Easter peace march; **~montag** *m* Easter Monday.
**Ostern** *nt* - Easter. **frohe** *or* **fröhliche ~!** Happy Easter!; **zu ~** at Easter.
**Österreich** *nt* Austria.
**Österreicher(in** *f)* *m* - Austrian.
**österreichisch** *adj* Austrian. **~-ungarisch** *(Hist)* Austro-Hungarian; **das Ö~e** *(Ling)* Austrian.
**Ostersonntag** *m* Easter Sunday.
**Ost-: ~europa** *nt* East(ern) Europe; **o~europäisch** *adj* East European; **~friesische Inseln** *pl* East Frisian Islands; **~friesland** *nt* East Frisia; **~küste** *f* East coast.
**östlich 1** *adj Richtung, Winde* easterly; *Gebiete* eastern. **30° ~er Länge** 30° (longitude) east. **2** *adv* **~ von Hamburg/des Rheins** (to the) east of Hamburg/the Rhine. **3** *prep +gen* (to the) east of.
**Ostpolitik** *f* Ostpolitik, *foreign policy towards the former Eastern bloc.*
**Östrogen** [œstroˈgeːn] *nt* **-e** oestrogen *(Brit)*, estrogen *(US)*.
**Ostsee** *f* **die ~** the Baltic (Sea).
**Ost-: ~staaten** *pl (in USA)* the Eastern *or* East coast states; **o~wärts** *adv* eastwards; **~-West-Verhandlungen** *pl (Hist)* East-West negotiations; **~wind** *m* east *or* easterly wind.
**oszillieren*** *vi* to oscillate.
**O-Ton** *m* = Originalton.
**Otter¹** *m* - otter.
**Otter²** *f* **-n** viper, adder.
**Ottomotor** *m* four-stroke internal combustion petrol engine, Otto engine.
**ÖTV** [øːteːˈfau] *f* = **Gewerkschaft Öffentliche Dienste, Transport und Verkehr** ≃ TGWU *(Brit)*.
**Ouvertüre** [uverˈtyːrə] *f* **-n** overture.
**oval** [oˈvaːl] *adj* oval.
**Oval** [oˈvaːl] *nt* **-e** oval.
**Ovation** [ovaˈtsioːn] *f* ovation. **jdm eine ~** *or* **~en darbringen** to give sb an ovation.
**Overall** [ˈoʊvərɔːl] *m* **-s** *(Schutzanzug)* overalls *pl*.
**ÖVP** [øːfauˈpeː] *f* = **Österreichische Volkspartei.**
**Oxid, Oxyd** *nt* **-e** oxide.
**Oxidation, Oxydation** *f* oxidation.
**oxidieren*, oxydieren*** *vti (vi: aux sein or haben)* to oxidize.
**Ozean** *m* **-e** ocean.
**Ozeandampfer** *m* ocean liner.
**Ozeanien** [-iən] *nt* Oceania.
**ozeanisch** *adj Flora* oceanic; *Sprachen* Oceanic.
**Ozeanriese** *m (col)* ocean liner.
**Ozelot** *m* **-e** ocelot.
**Ozon** *nt or (col)* *m no pl* ozone.
**Ozon-** *in cpds* ozone; **~hülle** *f* ozone layer; **~loch** *nt* hole in the ozone layer; **~schicht** *f* ozone layer.

# P

**P, p** [peː] *nt* -, - P, p. **P wie Peter** ≃ P for Peter.
**p** *(Mus)* = **piano** *p*.
**Paar** *nt* -e pair; *(Mann und Frau auch)* couple. **zwei ~ Socken** two pairs of socks; **ein ~ Würstchen** a couple of *or* two sausages.
**paar** *adj inv* **ein ~** a few; *(zwei oder drei auch)* a couple of; **alle ~ Minuten/Wochen** every few minutes/weeks.
**paaren 1** *vt Tiere* to mate, to pair; *(Sport)* to match. **2** *vr (Tiere)* to mate; *(fig)* to be coupled.
**Paar-:** **~hufer** *pl (Zool)* cloven-hoofed animals *pl*; **~lauf** *m*, **~laufen** *nt* pair-skating, pairs *pl*.
**paarmal** *adv* **ein ~** a few times; *(zwei- oder dreimal auch)* a couple of times.
**Paarung** *f* **(a)** *(Sport, fig liter)* combination; *(Sport: Begegnung)* draw, match. **(b)** *(Kopulation)* mating; *(Kreuzung)* crossing.
**Paarungszeit** *f* mating season.
**paarweise** *adv* in pairs, in twos.
**Pacht** *f* -en lease; *(Entgelt)* rent. **etw in ~ geben** to lease sth (out); **etw in ~ haben** to have sth on lease.
**Pachtbrief** *m* lease.
**pachten** *vt* to lease. **du hast das Sofa doch nicht für dich gepachtet** *(col)* don't hog the sofa *(col)*.
**Pächter(in** *f)* *m* leaseholder.
**Pacht-:** **~grundstück** *nt* leasehold property; **~gut** *nt*, **~hof** *m* smallholding; **~verhältnis** *nt* tenancy; **~vertrag** *m* lease; **~zins** *m* rent.
**Pack¹** *m (von Büchern, Wäsche)* pile; *(zusammengeschnürt)* bundle.
**Pack²** *nt no pl (pej)* rabble *pl (pej)*.
**Päckchen** *nt* package, (small) parcel; *(Post)* small packet; *(Packung)* packet, pack. **ein ~ Zigaretten** a packet *or* pack *(esp US)* of cigarettes; **jeder hat sein ~ zu tragen** *(fig col)* we all have our cross to bear.
**Pack|eis** *nt* pack ice.
**packen 1** *vti* **(a)** *Koffer* to pack; *(verstauen)* to pack (away). **etw in Watte ~** wrap sth (up) in cotton wool; **jdn ins Bett ~** *(col)* to tuck sb up (in bed). **(b)** *(fassen)* to grab (hold of); *(Gefühle)* to grip. **jdn am** *or* **beim Kragen ~** *(col)* to grab sb by the collar; **das Theaterstück hat mich gepackt** I was really gripped by the play. **(c)** *(col: schaffen)* to manage. **hast du die Prüfung gepackt?** did you (manage to) get through the exam? **(d)** *(col: gehen)* **~ wir's!** let's go. **(e)** *(col: kapieren)* to get *(col)*. **er packt es nie** he'll never get it *(col)*. **2** *vr (col)* to clear off.
**Packen** *m* - pile; *(Bündel)* bundle.
**Packer(in** *f)* *m* - packer.
**Pack-:** **~esel** *m (fig)* packhorse; **~papier** *nt* wrapping *or* brown paper.
**Packung** *f* **(a)** *(Schachtel)* packet, pack. **eine ~ Zigaretten** a packet *or* pack *(esp US)* of cigarettes. **(b)** *(Med)* pack; *(Kosmetik)* beauty pack. **(c)** *(col: Niederlage)* hammering *(col)*.
**Packzettel** *m* packing slip.
**Pädagoge** *m*, **Pädagogin** *f* educationalist.

**Pädagogik** *f* educational theory.
**pädagogisch** *adj* educational. **P~e Hochschule** college of education; **seine ~en Fähigkeiten** his teaching ability.
**Paddel** *nt* - paddle.
**Paddelboot** *nt* canoe.
**paddeln** *vi aux sein or haben* to paddle (a canoe); *(als Sport)* to canoe.
**Pädiatrie** *f* paediatrics *sing (Brit)*, pediatrics *sing (US)*.
**Pädophilie** *f* paedophilia *(Brit)*, pedophilia *(US)*.
**paffen 1** *vi (col: rauchen)* to puff away; *(nicht inhalieren)* to puff. **2** *vt* to puff (away) at.
**Page** ['paːʒə] *m (wk)* **-n, -n** *(Hotel~)* page(boy), bellhop *(US)*.
**Pagen-:** **~frisur** *f*, **~kopf** *m* pageboy (hairstyle).
**paginieren\*** *vt* to paginate.
**Paginierung** *f* pagination.
**Pagode** *f* -n pagoda.
**Paillette** [pai'jɛtə] *f* sequin.
**Paket** *nt* -e *(Post)* parcel; *(Packung)* packet; *(fig, Comp)* package.
**Paket-:** **~adresse** *f* stick-on address label; **~annahme/~ausgabe** *f* parcels office; **~bombe** *f* parcel *(Brit)* or package *(US)* bomb; **~karte** *f* dispatch form; **~post** *f* parcel post; **~schalter** *m* parcels counter.
**Pakistan** *nt* Pakistan.
**Pakistaner(in** *f)* *m* -, **Pakistani** *m* -(s) Pakistani.
**pakistanisch** *adj* Pakistani.
**Pakt** *m* pact. **einem ~ beitreten** to enter into an agreement.
**Palast** *m*, *pl* **Paläste** *(lit, fig)* palace.
**Palästina** *nt* Palestine.
**Palästinenser(in** *f)* *m* - Palestinian.
**palästinensisch** *adj* Palestinian.
**Palaver** [pa'laːvɐ] *nt* - *(col)* unending discussion.
**palavern\*** [pa'laːvɐn] *vi (col)* to ramble on.
**Palette** *f* **(a)** *(Malerei)* palette; *(fig)* range. **(b)** *(Stapelplatte)* pallet.
**Palisade** *f* palisade.
**Palisander(holz** *nt)* *m* - jacaranda.
**Palme** *f* -n palm (tree). **jdn auf die ~ bringen** *(col)* to make sb see red *(col)*.
**Palm-:** **~lilie** *f* yucca; **~sonntag** *m* Palm Sunday; **~wedel** *m* palm frond.
**Pampas** *pl* pampas *pl*.
**Pampasgras** *nt* pampas grass.
**Pampe** *f no pl (col)* mush *(col)*.
**Pampelmuse** *f* -n grapefruit.
**Pamphlet** *nt* -e lampoon.
**pampig** *adj (col)* **(a)** *(breiig)* gooey *(col)*. **(b)** *(frech)* stroppy *(col)*.
**pan-** *pref* pan-; **~amerikanisch** pan-American.
**Panama** *nt* Panama.
**Panamakanal** *m* Panama Canal.
**Paneel** *nt* -e *(einzeln)* panel; *(Täfelung)* panelling *(Brit)*, paneling *(US)*, wainscoting.

**paramilitärisch**

**Panflöte** f panpipes pl.
**panieren\*** vt to bread, to coat with breadcrumbs. **paniert** in breadcrumbs.
**Paniermehl** nt breadcrumbs pl.
**Panik** f -en panic. **in ~ ausbrechen** to panic; **von ~ ergriffen** panic-stricken; **nur keine ~!** don't panic!
**Panik-:** ~**kauf** m (Comm) panic buying; ~**mache** f (col) panicmongering.
**panisch** adj no pred panic-stricken. **er hatte eine ~e Angst zu ertrinken** he was terrified of drowning; **sich ~ fürchten (vor)** to be petrified (of); **sie rannten ~ durcheinander** they ran about in panic.
**Panne** f -n **(a)** (Störung) breakdown. **mein Auto hatte eine ~** my car broke down. **(b)** (fig col) boob (Brit col), goof (US col). **mit jdm/etw eine ~ erleben** to have (a bit of) trouble with sb/sth; **uns ist eine ~ passiert** we've boobed (Brit col) or goofed (US col); **da ist eine ~ passiert mit dem Brief** something has gone wrong with the letter.
**Pannen-:** ~**dienst** m, ~**hilfe** f breakdown service (Brit), emergency road service (US).
**Panorama** nt, pl **Panoramen** panorama.
**panschen 1** vt to adulterate; (verdünnen) to water down. **2** vi (col) to splash (about).
**Panther** m - panther.
**Pantoffel** m -n slipper. **unterm ~ stehen** (col) to be henpecked.
**Pantoffel-:** ~**held** m (col) henpecked husband; ~**kino** nt (col) telly (Brit col), tube (US col).
**Pantomime[1]** f -n mime.
**Pantomime[2]** m (wk) -n, -n mime (artist).
**pantschen** vti = **panschen**.
**Panzer** m - **(a)** (Mil) tank. **(b)** (Hist: Rüstung) armour (Brit), armor (US) no indef art, suit of armour (Brit) or armor (US). **(c)** (Panzerung) armour (Brit) or armor (US) plate. **(d)** (Zool) shell; (dicke Haut) armour (Brit), armor (US). **(e)** (fig) shield.
**Panzer-:** ~**abwehr** f anti-tank defence (Brit) or defense (US); (Truppe) anti-tank unit; ~**abwehrkanone** f anti-tank gun; ~**faust** f bazooka; ~**glas** nt bulletproof glass; ~**grenadier** m armoured (Brit) or armored (US) infantryman; ~**kampfwagen** m armoured (Brit) or armored (US) vehicle; ~**kette** f tank-track.
**panzern 1** vt to armour-plate (Brit), to armor-plate (US). **gepanzerte Fahrzeuge** armoured (Brit) or armored (US) vehicles. **2** vr (fig) to arm oneself.
**Panzer-:** ~**schrank** m safe; ~**truppe** f tank division.
**Panzerung** f armour (Brit) or armor (US) plating; (fig) shield.
**Panzerwagen** m armoured (Brit) or armored (US) car.
**Papa** m -s (col) daddy (col), pa (US col).
**Papagei** m -en parrot. **er plappert alles wie ein ~ nach** he repeats everything parrot fashion.
**Papi** m -s (col) daddy (col).
**Papier** nt -e **(a)** no pl paper. **ein Blatt ~** a sheet of paper; **das steht nur auf dem ~** that's only in theory. **(b)** (Schriftstück) paper. ~**e** pl (identity) papers pl; (Urkunden) documents pl; **er hatte keine ~e bei sich** he had no means of identification with him; **seine ~e bekommen** (entlassen werden) to get one's cards. **(c)** (Fin, Wert~) security.
**Papier-:** ~**deutsch** nt officialese; ~**einzug** m paper feed; ~**fabrik** f paper mill; ~**geld** nt paper money; ~**handtuch** nt paper towel; ~**korb** m wastepaper basket; ~**kram** m (col) bumf (Brit col), paperwork; ~**krieg** m (col) **vor lauter ~krieg kommen wir nicht zur Forschung** there's so much paperwork we can't get on with our research; **erst nach**

einem langen ~**krieg** after going through a lot of red tape; ~**serviette** f paper napkin; ~**taschentuch** nt tissue, paper handkerchief; ~**tiger** m (fig) paper tiger; ~**vorschub** m (Comp) form or paper feed; ~**zuführung** f (Comp) sheet feed.
**Papp-:** ~**becher** m paper cup; ~**deckel** m (thin) cardboard.
**Pappe** f -n (Pappdeckel) cardboard; (Dach~) roofing felt. **das ist nicht von ~** (col) that is really something.
**Pappel** f -n poplar.
**pappen** (col) **1** vt to stick (an or auf +acc on). **2** vi (col) (klebrig sein) to be sticky; (Schnee) to pack.
**Pappen-:** ~**deckel** m (thin) cardboard; ~**heimer** pl: **ich kenne meine ~heimer** (col) I know you lot/ that lot (inside out) (col); ~**stiel** m (fig col): **5.000 Mark sind kein ~stiel** 5,000 marks isn't peanuts (col); **das habe ich für einen ~stiel gekauft** I bought it for a song.
**papperlapapp** interj (col) (stuff and) nonsense.
**pappig** adj (col) sticky.
**Papp-:** ~**karton** m (Schachtel) cardboard box; (Material) cardboard; ~**maché** [-ma'ʃe:] nt -s papiermâché; ~**schnee** m wet snow; ~**teller** m paper plate.
**Paprika** m -(s) (no pl: Gewürz) paprika; (~schote) pepper.
**Paprikaschote** f pepper. **gefüllte ~n** stuffed peppers.
**Papst** m ⸚e pope; (fig) high priest.
**päpstlich** adj papal; (fig pej) pontifical. ~**er als der Papst sein** to be more Catholic than the Pope.
**Papua** m -(s), -(s) Papuan.
**Papua-Neuguinea** [-gi'ne:a] nt Papua New Guinea.
**Parabel** f -n **(a)** (Liter) parable. **(b)** (Math) parabola, parabolic curve.
**Parabol-:** ~**antenne** f satellite dish; ~**spiegel** m parabolic reflector.
**Parade** f **(a)** (Mil) review. **die ~ abnehmen** to take the salute. **(b)** (Sport: Fechten, Boxen) parry; (Ballspiele) save; (Reiten) check. **jdm in die ~ fahren** (fig) to cut sb off short.
**Parade-:** ~**beispiel** nt prime example; ~**marsch** m parade step; (Stechschritt) goose-step; ~**stück** nt (fig) showpiece; (Gegenstand auch) pièce de résistance.
**Paradies** nt -e (lit, fig) paradise. **das ~ auf Erden** heaven on earth.
**paradiesisch** adj (fig) heavenly. **hier ist es ~ schön** this is paradise; ~ **leere Strände** blissfully empty beaches.
**Paradiesvogel** m bird of paradise.
**paradox** adj paradoxical.
**Paradox** nt -e paradox.
**paradoxerweise** adv paradoxically.
**Paraffin** nt -e (Chem) (~öl) paraffin (Brit), kerosene (US); (~wachs) paraffin wax.
**Paragraph** m (Jur) section; (Abschnitt) paragraph.
**Paragraphenreiter** m (col) pedant.
**Paraguay** nt Paraguay.
**Paraguayer(in** f) m - Paraguayan.
**paraguayisch** adj Paraguayan.
**parallel** adj parallel. ~ **laufen** to run parallel; ~ **schalten** (Elec) to connect in parallel.
**Parallele** f -n parallel (line); (fig) parallel. **eine ~ zu etw ziehen** (fig) to draw a parallel to sth.
**Parallelogramm** nt -e parallelogram.
**Parallel-:** ~**schaltung** f parallel connection; ~**schwung** m (Ski) parallel turn.
**Parameter** m parameter.
**paramilitärisch** adj paramilitary.

**Paranoia** [para'nɔya] *f no pl* paranoia.
**paranoid** [parano'iːt] *adj* paranoid.
**Paranuß** *f (Bot)* Brazil nut.
**paraphieren\*** *vt (Pol)* to initial.
**Paraphrase** *f* paraphrase; *(Mus)* variation.
**Parapsychologie** *f* parapsychology.
**Parasit** *m (wk)* **-en, -en** *(Biol, fig)* parasite.
**parasitär** *adj (Biol, fig)* parasitic(al).
**parat** *adj* prepared; *Werkzeug etc* handy. **er hatte immer eine Ausrede** ~ he was always ready with an excuse.
**Pärchen** *nt* (courting) couple.
**Parcours** [par'kuːɐ] *m* **-,** **-** show-jumping course; *(Sportart)* show-jumping.
**Pardon** [par'dõː] *m or nt no pl* **(a)** *(dated)* pardon. **(b)** *(col)* ~! *(Verzeihung)* sorry; **kein** ~ **kennen** to be ruthless; **das Zeug räumst du auf, da gibt's kein** ~ you'll clear that stuff up and that's that! *(col)*.
**Parfum** [par'fœ̃ː] *nt* **-s, Parfüm** *nt* **-e** *or* **-s** perfume, scent.
**Parfümerie** *f* perfumery.
**parfümieren\*** **1** *vt* to scent. **2** *vr* to put scent on.
**parieren\*** **1** *vt* **(a)** *(Fechten, fig)* to parry; *(Ftbl)* to deflect. **(b)** *(Reiten)* to rein in. **2** *vi* to obey. **aufs Wort** ~ to jump to it.
**Paris** *nt* **-** Paris.
**Pariser**[1] *m* **-** **(a)** Parisian. **(b)** *(col: Kondom)* French letter *(col)*.
**Pariser**[2] *adj attr* Parisian.
**Pariserin** *f* Parisienne.
**Parität** *f (Fin, Sci, Comp)* parity.
**paritätisch** *adj* equal. ~**e Mitbestimmung** equal representation.
**Park** *m* **-s** park; *(von Schloß)* grounds *pl*.
**Parka** *m* **-s** parka.
**Park-and-ride System** ['paːkənd'raɪd-] *nt* park and ride (system).
**Park-:** ~**anlage** *f* park; ~**bucht** *f* parking bay; ~**deck** *nt* parking level.
**parken** *vti* to park. „**P**~ **verboten!"** "No parking"; **ein** ~**des Auto** a parked car.
**Parkett** *nt* **-e** **(a)** *(Fußboden)* parquet (flooring). **sich auf jedem** ~ **bewegen können** *(fig)* to be able to move in any society. **(b)** *(Tanzfläche)* (dance) floor. **eine tolle Nummer aufs** ~ **legen** *(col)* to put on a great show. **(c)** *(Theat)* stalls *pl*, parquet *(US)*. **wir sitzen** ~ we sit in the stalls.
**Parkett-:** ~**platz**, ~**sitz** *m (Theat)* seat in the stalls *or* parquet *(US)*.
**Park-:** ~**gebühr** *f* parking fee; ~**haus** *nt* multistorey car park *(Brit)*, multilevel parking garage *(US)*.
**Parkinsonsche Krankheit** *f* Parkinson's disease.
**Park-:** ~**kralle** *f* wheel clamp; ~**landschaft** *f* parkland; ~**lücke** *f* parking space; ~**platz** *m* car park *(Brit)*, parking lot *(US)*; *(für Einzelwagen)* (parking) space; ~**scheibe** *f* parking disc; ~**schein** *m* car park ticket; ~**uhr** *f* parking meter; ~**verbot** *nt* parking ban; **hier ist** ~**verbot** there's no parking here; **im** ~**verbot stehen** to be parked illegally.
**Parlament** *nt* parliament.
**Parlamentarier(in** *f)* [-iɐ, -iərɪn] *m* **-** parliamentarian.
**parlamentarisch** *adj* parliamentary.
**Parlaments-:** ~**ausschuß** *m* parliamentary committee; ~**beschluß** *m* decision of parliament; ~**ferien** *pl* recess; ~**gebäude** *nt* parliamentary building(s); ~**mitglied** *nt* member of parliament, MP *(Brit)*; *(in USA)* Congressman/-woman; ~**sitzung** *f* sitting (of parliament); ~**wahl** *f usu pl* parliamentary election(s).

**Parmesan(käse)** *m no pl* Parmesan (cheese).
**Parodie** *f* parody *(auf +acc* on, *zu* of*)*.
**parodieren\*** *vt* to parody.
**Parodontose** *f* **-n** shrinking gums.
**Parole** *f* **-n** **(a)** *(Mil)* password. **(b)** *(fig: Wahlspruch)* motto; *(Pol)* slogan.
**Paroli** *nt:* **jdm** ~ **bieten** *(geh)* to defy sb.
**Parser** *m* **-** *(Comp)* parser.
**Part** *m* **-e** **(a)** *(Anteil)* share. **(b)** *(Theat, Mus)* part.
**Partei** *f* **(a)** *(Pol, Jur)* party. **die** ~ **wechseln** to change parties; **die streitenden** ~**en** *(Jur)* the disputing parties; **für jdn** ~ **ergreifen** to side with sb; **gegen jdn** ~ **ergreifen** to take sides against sb; **ein Richter sollte über den** ~**en stehen** a judge should be impartial. **(b)** *(im Mietshaus)* tenant, party *(form)*.
**Partei-:** ~**anhänger** *m* party supporter; ~**buch** *nt* party membership card; **das falsche** ~**buch haben** to belong to the wrong party; ~**chef** *m* party leader; ~**führung** *f* leadership of a party; *(Vorstand)* party executive; ~**genosse** *m* party member; **p**~**intern** *adj* internal party; **etw p**~**intern lösen** to solve sth within the party.
**parteiisch** *adj* biased, partial.
**Parteilichkeit** *f* bias, partiality.
**Partei-:** ~**linie** *f* party line; **auf die** ~**linie einschwenken** to toe the party line; **p**~**los** *adj* independent, non-party; ~**lose(r)** *mf decl as adj* independent; ~**mitglied** *nt* party member; ~**nahme** *f* **-n** partisanship; ~**politik** *f* party politics *pl*; ~**politisch** *adj* party political; ~**programm** *nt* (party) manifesto; ~**spende** *f* party donation; ~**tag** *m* party conference *or* convention; ~**versammlung** *f* party meeting; ~**vorsitzende(r)** *mf* party leader; ~**vorstand** *m* party executive; ~**zugehörigkeit** *f* party membership.
**Parterre** [par'tɛr(ə)] *nt* **-s** *(von Gebäude)* ground floor *(Brit)*, first floor *(US)*. **im** ~ **wohnen** to live on the ground floor.
**Parterrewohnung** *f* ground-floor flat *(Brit)*, first-floor apartment *(US)*.
**Partie** *f* **(a)** *(Teil, Theat, Mus)* part. **(b)** *(Sport)* game; *(Fechten)* round. **eine** ~ **Schach spielen** to play a game of chess. **(c)** *(Comm)* lot, batch. **(d)** *(col)* catch. **eine gute** ~ **(für jdn) sein** to be a good catch (for sb); **eine gute** ~ **(mit jdm) machen** to marry (into) money. **(e) mit von der** ~ **sein** to be in on it; **da bin ich mit von der** ~ **count me in.
**partiell** [par'tsiɛl] *adj* partial.
**Partikel** *f* **-n** *(Gram, Phys)* particle.
**Partisan(in** *f)* *m* **-en** partisan.
**Partisanenkrieg** *m* partisan war; *(Art des Krieges)* guerrilla warfare.
**Partitur** *f (Mus)* score.
**Partizip** *nt* **-ien** [-iən] *(Gram)* participle. ~ **Präsens/Perfekt** present/past participle.
**Partner(in** *f)* *m* **-** partner; *(Film)* co-star. **als jds** ~ **spielen** *(in Film)* to play opposite sb; *(Sport)* to be partnered by sb.
**Partnerschaft** *f* partnership; *(Städte~)* twinning.
**partnerschaftlich** *adj* ~**es Verhältnis** (relationship based on) partnership; ~**e Zusammenarbeit** working together as partners.
**Partner-:** ~**stadt** *f* twin town *(Brit)*; ~**tausch** *m (Tanz, Tennis)* change of partners; *(sexuell)* partner-swopping.
**partout** [par'tuː] *adv* **er will** ~ **ins Kino gehen** he insists on going to the cinema; **sie will** ~ **nicht nach Hause gehen** she just doesn't want to go home.
**Party** ['paːɐti] *f* **-s** party. **eine** ~ **geben** *or* **veranstalten** to give *or* have a party; **bei** *or* **auf einer** ~ at a

party.
**Partymuffel** m party pooper *(col)*.
**Pasch** m -e or ̈e *(beim Würfelspiel)* doublets *pl*.
**Pascha** m - pasha. **wie ein** ~ like Lord Muck *(col)*.
**Paß** m, pl **Pässe** (a) passport. (b) *(im Gebirge etc)* pass. (c) *(Ballspiele)* pass.
**passabel** adj passable, reasonable.
**Passage** [pa'sa:ʒə] f -n passage; *(Ladenstraße)* arcade.
**Passagier** [pasa'ʒiːɐ] m passenger.
**Passagier-:** ~**dampfer** m passenger steamer; ~**flugzeug** nt air-liner; ~**schiff** nt passenger liner.
**Passah(fest)** nt (Feast of the) Passover.
**Paß|amt** nt passport office.
**Passant(in** f) m *(wk)* passer-by.
**Passat(wind)** m -e trade wind.
**Paßbild** nt passport photo(graph).
**passé** [pa'seː] adj pred **diese Mode ist längst** ~ this fashion went out long ago; **die Sache ist längst** ~ that's all in the past.
**passen¹** vi (a) to fit. **die Schuhe** ~ **(mir) gut** the shoes fit (me) nicely *or* are a good fit (for me); **der Deckel paßt nicht auf das Glas** the lid won't go on the jar.
  (b) *(harmonieren)* **zu etw** ~ to go with sth; *(ähnlich sein)* to match sth; **zu jdm** ~ *(Mensch)* to suit sb; **zueinander** ~ to go together; *(Menschen auch)* to be well matched; **das paßt zu ihm, so etwas zu sagen** that's just like him to say that; **es paßt nicht zu dir, Bier zu trinken** you don't look right drinking beer; **das Rot paßt da nicht** the red is all wrong there; **er paßt nicht in dieses Team** he is out of place in this team.
  (c) *(genehm sein)* to suit. **er paßt mir einfach nicht** I just don't like him; **Sonntag paßt uns nicht** Sunday is no good for us; **das paßt mir gar nicht** *(kommt ungelegen)* that isn't at all convenient; *(gefällt mir nicht)* I don't like that at all; **das könnte dir so** ~**!** *(col)* you'd like that, wouldn't you?
**passen²** vi *(Cards)* to pass. **(ich) passe!** (I) pass!; **bei dieser Frage muß ich** ~ *(fig)* I'll have to pass on this question.
**passend** adj (a) *(in Größe, Form)* **gut/schlecht** ~ well-/ill-fitting. (b) *(in Farbe, Stil)* matching. **etwas dazu P**~**es** something to match (it). (c) *(genehm)* Zeit, Termin convenient; *(angemessen)* Bemerkung, Kleidung suitable; Wort right. **er findet immer das** ~**e Wort** he always knows the right thing to say. (d) Geld exact. **haben Sie es** ~**?** have you got the right money?
**Paß-:** ~**form** f fit; **eine gute** ~**form haben** to be a good fit; ~**foto** nt passport photo(graph); ~**höhe** f top of the pass.
**passierbar** adj passable; Fluß, Kanal negotiable.
**passieren*** 1 vt (a) auch vi to pass. **die Grenze** ~ to cross the border; **die Zensur** ~ to be passed by the censor. (b) *(Cook)* to strain. 2 vi aux sein *(sich ereignen)* to happen *(mit to)*. **ist ihm etwas passiert?** has anything happened to him?; **beim Sturz ist ihm nichts passiert** he wasn't hurt in the fall; **es ist ein Unfall passiert** there has been an accident; **das kann auch nur mir** ~**!** just my luck!
**Passierschein** m pass, permit.
**Passion** f passion; *(religiös)* Passion. **er ist Jäger aus** ~ he has a passion for hunting.
**passioniert** adj enthusiastic, passionate.
**Passions-:** ~**blume** f passion flower; ~**spiel** nt Passion play; ~**zeit** f Lent.
**passiv** adj passive. **sich** ~ **verhalten** to be passive; ~**es Mitglied** non-active member; ~**e Handelsbilanz** *(Comm)* adverse trade balance.

**Passiv** nt -e *(Gram)* passive (voice).
**Passiva** [pa'si:va] pl *(Comm)* liabilities pl.
**Passivität** [pasivi'tɛːt] f passivity.
**Passiv-:** ~**posten** m *(Comm)* debit entry; ~**rauchen** nt passive smoking; ~**saldo** m *(Comm)* debit account; ~**seite** f *(Comm)* debit side.
**Paß-:** ~**kontrolle** f passport control; ~**photo** nt = ~**foto**; ~**straße** f (mountain) pass; ~**wort** nt *(Comp)* password.
**Paste** f -n paste.
**Pastell** nt -e pastel (drawing).
**Pastell-:** ~**farbe** f pastel (crayon); *(Farbton)* pastel; p~**farben** adj pastel; ~**ton** m pastel shade.
**Pastete** f -n (a) *(Schüssel~)* pie; *(Pastetchen)* vol-au-vent; *(ungefüllt)* vol-au-vent case. (b) *(Leber~ etc)* pâté.
**pasteurisieren*** [pastøri'ziːrən] vt to pasteurize.
**Pastille** f -n pastille.
**Pastor** m, **Pastorin** f = Pfarrer(in).
**pastoral** adj pastoral.
**Pate** m -n godfather, godparent. **bei einem Kind** ~ **stehen** to be a child's godparent; **bei etw** ~ **gestanden haben** *(fig)* to be the force behind *or* *(Vorbild)* model for sth.
**Paten-:** ~**kind** nt godchild; godson; goddaughter; ~**onkel** m godfather; ~**schaft** f duties pl as a godparent; **die** ~**schaft für jdn übernehmen** *(fig)* to adopt sb; ~**stadt** f twin(ned) town *(Brit)*.
**patent** adj *(col)* ingenious, clever. **ein** ~**er Kerl** a great guy/girl *(col)*.
**Patent** nt -e *(Erfindung, Urkunde)* patent. **etw als** *or* **zum** ~ **anmelden** to apply for a patent for sth.
**Patent|amt** nt patent office.
**Patentante** f godmother.
**Patent|anwalt** m patent agent *or* attorney.
**patentieren*** vt to patent. **sich** *(dat)* **etw** ~ **lassen** to have sth patented.
**Patent-:** ~**inhaber** m patentee; ~**lösung** f *(fig)* patent remedy; ~**schrift** f patent specification; ~**schutz** m patent protection; ~**urkunde** f letters patent pl.
**Pater** m, pl - or **Patres** *(Eccl)* Father.
**Paternoster** m - *(Aufzug)* paternoster lift.
**pathetisch** adj emotional; Rede, Stil auch emotive; Gehabe auch histrionic.
**Pathologe** m, **Pathologin** f pathologist.
**Pathologie** f pathology.
**pathologisch** adj pathological.
**Pathos** nt no pl emotiveness, emotionalism. **ein Gedicht mit** ~ **vortragen** to read a poem with feeling.
**Patience** [pa'siãːs] f -n patience no pl. ~**n legen** to play patience.
**Patient(in** f) [pa'tsiɛnt(ɪn)] m *(wk)* -en, -en patient.
**Patin** f godmother, godparent.
**Patina** f no pl *(lit, fig)* patina.
**Patriarch** m *(wk)* -en, -en *(lit, fig)* patriarch.
**patriarchalisch** adj *(lit, fig)* patriarchal.
**Patriot(in** f) m *(wk)* -en, -en patriot.
**patriotisch** adj patriotic.
**Patriotismus** m patriotism.
**Patron(in** f) m -e *(Eccl)* patron saint.
**Patrone** f -n *(Film, Mil, von Füller)* cartridge.
**Patronen-:** ~**gürtel** m cartridge belt; ~**hülse** f cartridge case.
**Patrouille** [pa'trʊljə] f -n patrol. ~ **gehen** to patrol.
**patrouillieren*** [patrʊl'jiːrən] vi to patrol. **an der Grenze** ~ to patrol the border.
**Patsch** interj splash, splat.
**Patsche** f -n *(col)* (tight) spot *(col)*. **in der** ~ **sitzen** to be in a jam *(col)*; **jdm aus der** ~ **helfen** to get sb out of a jam *(col)*.

**patschen** *vi (im Wasser)* to splash. **die Kinder ~ mit den Händen** *(col)* the children clap their hands (together).

**Patsch-:** ~**händchen** *nt (col)* paw *(col)*; **p~naß** *adj (col)* dripping wet.

**Patt** *nt* -s *(lit, fig)* stalemate.

**patzen** *vi (col)* to boob *(Brit col)*, to goof *(US col)*.

**Patzer** *m* - *(col: Fehler)* boob *(Brit col)*, goof *(US col)*.

**patzig** *adj (col)* snotty *(col)*, insolent.

**Pauke** *f* -n *(Mus)* kettledrum. ~**n** timpani *pl*; **mit ~n und Trompeten durchfallen** *(col)* to fail dismally; **auf die ~ hauen** *(col) (angeben)* to brag; *(feiern)* to paint the town red *(col)*.

**pauken 1** *vi (col: lernen)* to swot *(col)*. **2** *vt* to swot up *(col)*.

**Paukenschlag** *m* drum beat. **wie ein ~** *(fig)* like a thunderbolt.

**Pauker** *m* - *(Sch col: Lehrer)* teacher.

**Paukerei** *f (Sch col)* swotting *(col)*.

**Paulus** *m (Bibl)* ≈ Paul.

**Pausbacken** *pl* chubby cheeks *pl*.

**pausbäckig** *adj* chubby-cheeked.

**pauschal** *adj (einheitlich)* flat-rate *attr only*; *(inklusiv)* inclusive. **die Werkstatt berechnet ~ pro Inspektion 250 DM** the garage has a flat rate of 250 marks for a service; **die Gebühren werden ~ bezahlt** the charges are paid in a lump sum; **die Reisekosten verstehen sich ~** the travelling costs are inclusive; **so ~ kann man das nicht sagen** *(fig)* that's much too sweeping a statement.

**Pauschale** *f* -n *(Einheitspreis)* flat rate; *(vorläufig geschätzer Betrag)* estimated amount.

**Pauschal-:** ~**gebühr** *f* flat rate (charge); ~**preis** *m (Einheitspreis)* flat rate; *(Inklusivpreis)* all-in price; ~**reise** *f* package holiday *or* tour; ~**summe** *f* lump sum; ~**urteil** *nt* sweeping statement; ~**versicherung** *f* comprehensive insurance *no pl*.

**Pauschbetrag** *m* flat rate.

**Pause** *f* -n **(a)** break; *(das Innehalten)* pause; *(Theat)* interval, intermission; *(Sch)* break *(Brit)*, recess *(US)*. **(eine) ~ machen, eine ~ einlegen** *(sich entspannen)* to have a break; *(rasten)* to take a rest; *(innehalten)* to pause; **nach einer langen ~ sagte er ...** after a long silence he said ... **(b)** *(Mus)* rest. **(c)** *(Durchzeichnung)* tracing.

**pausen** *vt* to trace.

**Pausen-:** ~**brot** *nt (Sch)* sandwich *to eat at break (Brit) or in the recess (US)*; ~**hof** *m* playground, schoolyard; **p~los** *adj no pred* continuous; **er arbeitet p~los** he works non-stop; ~**zeichen** *nt (Mus)* rest; *(Rad)* call sign.

**pausieren\*** *vi* to (take a) break.

**Pauspapier** *nt* tracing paper; *(Kohlepapier)* carbon paper.

**Pavian** ['pa:via:n] *m* -e baboon.

**Pavillon** [pavɪl'jõ:] *m* -s pavilion.

**Pazifik** *m* Pacific. **eine Insel im ~** a Pacific island.

**pazifisch** *adj* Pacific. **der P~e Ozean** the Pacific (Ocean).

**Pazifismus** *m* pacifism.

**Pazifist(in** *f)* *m* pacifist.

**pazifistisch** *adj* pacifist.

**PC** [pe:'tse:] *m* -s = **Personalcomputer** PC.

**PDS** [pe:de:'ɛs] *f* = **Partei des demokratischen Sozialismus** *German socialist party.*

**Pech** *nt* -e **(a)** *(Stoff)* pitch. **die beiden halten zusammen wie ~ und Schwefel** the two are inseparable. **(b)** *no pl (col: Mißgeschick)* bad *or* hard luck. **bei etw ~ haben** to have bad luck with sth; **~ gehabt!** tough! *(col)*; **so ein ~!** just my/our *etc* luck!

**Pech-:** **p~(raben)schwarz** *adj (col)* pitch-black; *Haar* jet-black; ~**strähne** *f (col)* bad *or* unlucky patch; ~**vogel** *m (col)* unlucky person.

**Pedal** *nt* -e pedal. **(fest) in die ~e treten** to pedal (hard).

**Pedant** *m (wk)* pedant.

**Pedanterie** *f* pedantry.

**pedantisch** *adj* pedantic.

**Peddigrohr** *nt* cane.

**Pediküre** *f* -n **(a)** *no pl (Fußpflege)* pedicure. **(b)** *(Fußpflegerin)* chiropodist *(Brit)*, podiatrist *(US)*.

**Peep-Show** ['pi:pʃo:] *f* peepshow.

**Pegel** *m* - **(a)** water depth gauge; *(Elec)* level indicator. **(b)** *(Tech: Stand)* level; *(auch ~stand)* water level.

**peilen** *vt Wassertiefe* to sound; *Sender* to take the bearings of; *Richtung* to plot; *(entdecken)* to detect. **die Lage ~** *(col)* to see how the land lies; **über den Daumen ~** *(col)* to guess roughly; **über den Daumen gepeilt** *(col)* at a rough estimate.

**Peilgerät** *nt* direction finder.

**Peilung** *f (von Wassertiefe)* sounding; *(von Sender)* locating; *(von Richtung)* plotting.

**Pein** *f no pl (geh, liter)* agony, suffering.

**peinigen** *vt (geh)* to torture; *(fig)* to torment. **von Schmerzen/Zweifeln gepeinigt** tormented by pain/ doubt.

**peinlich** *adj* **(a)** *(unangenehm)* (painfully) embarrassing; *Lage, Fragen auch* awkward. **es war ihm ~(, daß ...)** he felt embarrassed (because ...); **das ist mir ja so ~** I feel awful about it. **(b)** *(gewissenhaft)* painstaking. **~ sauber** meticulously clean; **in seinem Zimmer herrschte ~e Ordnung** his room was meticulously tidy; **der Koffer wurde ~ genau untersucht** the case was given a very thorough going-over *(col)*; **er vermied es ~st, davon zu sprechen** he was at pains not to talk about it.

**Peinlichkeit** *f (Unangenehmheit)* embarrassment.

**Peitsche** *f* -n whip.

**peitschen** *vti* to whip; *(fig)* to lash.

**Peitschen-:** ~**hieb** *m* lash; ~**knall** *m* crack of a whip.

**Pekinese** *m (wk)* -n, -n pekinese, peke *(col)*.

**Peking** *nt* Peking.

**Pektin** *nt* -e pectin.

**Pelikan** *m* -e pelican.

**Pelle** *f* -n *(col)* skin. **der Chef sitzt mir auf der ~** *(col)* I've got the boss on my back *(col)*; **er geht mir nicht von der ~** *(col)* he won't stop pestering me.

**pellen** *vtr (col)* to peel.

**Pellkartoffeln** *pl* potatoes *pl* boiled in their jackets.

**Pelz** *m* -e fur; *(nicht gegerbt auch)* hide.

**Pelz-** *in cpds* fur; ~**besatz** *m* fur trimming; ~**händler** *m* furrier.

**pelzig** *adj* furry.

**Pelz-:** ~**mantel** *m* fur coat; ~**mütze** *f* fur hat; ~**tier** *nt* animal prized for its fur; ~**waren** *pl* furs *pl*.

**Pendant** [pã'dã:] *nt* -s counterpart.

**Pendel** *nt* - pendulum.

**Pendeldiplomatie** *f* shuttle diplomacy.

**pendeln** *vi* **(a)** *(schwingen)* to swing (to and fro). **(b)** *aux sein (Zug, Fähre etc)* to shuttle; *(Mensch)* to commute; *(fig)* to fluctuate.

**Pendel-:** ~**tür** *f* swing door; ~**uhr** *f* pendulum clock; ~**verkehr** *m* shuttle service; *(Berufsverkehr)* commuter traffic.

**Pendler(in** *f)* *m* - commuter.

**penetrant** *adj* **(a)** *Geruch* penetrating. **das schmeckt ~ nach Knoblauch** it has a very strong taste of garlic. **(b)** *(fig: aufdringlich)* insistent; *Selbstsicherheit* overpowering.

**peng** *interj* bang.

**penibel** *adj* pernickety *(col)*, precise.

**Penis** *m* -, -se *or* **Penes** penis.

**Penizillin** *nt* -e penicillin.

**Pennbruder** *m (col)* tramp, hobo *(US)*.

**Penne** *f* -n (a) *(Sch sl)* school. (b) *(col: Herberge)* doss house *(col)*.

**pennen** *vi (col)* to kip *(col)*.

**Penner(in** *f) m* - *(col)* (a) tramp, hobo *(US)*. (b) *(verschlafener Mensch)* sleepyhead *(col)*.

**Pension** *[auch* pã'zio:n] *f* -en (a) *(Fremdenheim)* guest-house. (b) *no pl (Verpflegung)* board. **halbe/volle** ~ half/full board *(Brit)*, European/American plan *(US)*. (c) *(Ruhegehalt)* pension. (d) *no pl (Ruhestand)* retirement. **in** ~ **gehen** to retire; **in** ~ **sein** to be retired.

**Pensionär(in** *f) [auch* pãzio'nɛːɐ, -ɛːərɪn] *m (Pension beziehend)* pensioner; *(im Ruhestand befindlich)* retired person.

**Pensionat** [pãzio'naːt] *nt (dated)* boarding school.

**pensionieren*** *[auch* pãzio'niːrən] *vt* to retire. **sich** ~ **lassen** to retire.

**pensioniert** *adj* retired.

**Pensionierung** *f (Zustand)* retirement; *(Vorgang)* pensioning-off.

**Pensions-:** ~**alter** *nt* retiring age; ~**anspruch** *m* right to a pension; **p~berechtigt** *adj* entitled to a pension; ~**preis** *m* price for full board *(Brit)* or American plan *(US)*; **p~reif** *adj (col)* ready for retirement.

**Pensum** *nt, pl* **Pensa** *or* **Pensen** workload; *(Sch)* curriculum. **tägliches** ~ daily quota; **er hat sein** ~ **nicht geschafft** he didn't achieve his target.

**Pep** *m no pl (col)* pep *(col)*, life; *(Schwung)* oomph *(col)*.

**Peperoni** *pl* chillies *pl*.

**per** *prep* (a) *(mittels)* by. **mit jdm** ~ **du sein** *(col)* to call sb "du", ≈ to be on first-name terms with sb; ~ **pedes** *(hum)* on shanks's pony *(hum)*. (b) *(Comm) (bis)* by; *(pro)* per. ~ **Adresse** care of, c/o.

**Perestroika** *f no pl* perestroika.

**perfekt** *adj* (a) *(vollkommen)* perfect. (b) *pred (abgemacht)* settled. **die Sache** ~ **machen** to clinch the deal; **der Vertrag ist** ~ the contract is all settled.

**Perfekt** *nt* -e perfect (tense).

**Perfektion** *f* perfection.

**perfektionieren*** [pɛrfɛktsio'niːrən] *vt* to perfect.

**Perfektionismus** [pɛrfɛktsio'nɪsmʊs] *m* perfectionism.

**Perfektionist(in** *f) m* perfectionist.

**perfektionistisch** [pɛrfɛktsio'nɪstɪʃ] *adj* perfectionist.

**Perforation** *f* perforation.

**perforieren*** *vt* to perforate.

**Pergament** *nt* parchment; *(Kalbs~ auch)* vellum.

**Pergamentpapier** *nt* greaseproof paper.

**Pergola** *f, pl* **Pergolen** pergola.

**Periode** *f* -n period *(auch Physiol)*; *(von Wetter auch)* spell; *(Elec)* cycle. **0,33** ~ 0.33 recurring.

**periodisch** *adj* periodic(al); *(regelmäßig)* regular; *(Phys)* periodic.

**peripher** *adj* peripheral.

**Peripherie** *f* periphery; *(von Stadt)* outskirts *pl*. **an der** ~ **Bonns** on the outskirts of Bonn.

**Peripheriegerät** *nt (Comp)* peripheral.

**Perle** *f* -n (a) *(auch fig)* pearl. ~**n vor die Säue werfen** *(prov)* to cast pearls before swine *(prov)*. (b) *(Glas~, Holz~, von Schweiß)* bead; *(Luftbläschen)* bubble. (c) *(dated col: Hausgehilfin)* maid.

**perlen** *vi (sprudeln)* to bubble; *(fallen, rollen)* to

trickle.

**Perlen-:** ~**kette** *f,* ~**kollier** *nt* pearl necklace, string of pearls.

**Perl-:** ~**huhn** *nt* guinea fowl; ~**muschel** *f* pearl oyster; ~**mutt** *nt no pl* mother-of-pearl.

**Perlon** ® *nt no pl* ≈ nylon.

**Perlwein** *m* sparkling wine.

**permanent** *adj* permanent.

**perplex** *adj* dumbfounded, thunderstruck.

**Perser** *m* - (a) Persian. (b) *(col: Teppich)* Persian carpet.

**Perserin** *f* Persian.

**Perserteppich** *m* Persian carpet.

**Persianer** *m* - (a) *(Pelz)* Persian lamb. (b) *(auch* ~**mantel***)* Persian lamb (coat).

**Persien** [-iən] *nt* Persia.

**Persiflage** [pɛrzi'flaːʒə] *f* -n pastiche, satire *(gen, auf +acc* on, of*)*.

**persisch** *adj* Persian. **P~er Golf** Persian Gulf.

**Person** *f* -en (a) *(auch Gram)* person. ~**en** people, persons *(form)*; **eine aus sechs** ~**en bestehende Familie** a family of six; **die eigene** ~ oneself; **ich für meine** ~ ... I for my part ...; **ich hatte den Chef in** ~ **vor mir** I was talking to the boss himself; **er ist Finanz- und Außenminister in einer** ~ he's the Chancellor of the Exchequer and Foreign Secretary rolled into one; **natürliche/juristische** ~ *(Jur)* natural/legal person; **sie ist die Geduld in** ~ she's patience personified; **lassen wir seine** ~ **aus dem Spiel** let's not get personal (about him). (b) *(pej: Frau)* female. (c) *(Liter, Theat)* character.

**Personal** *nt no pl* personnel, staff. **ungenügend mit** ~ **versehen sein** to be understaffed.

**Personal-:** ~**abbau** *m* staff cuts *pl*; ~**abteilung** *f* personnel (department); ~**akte** *f* personal file; ~**angaben** *pl* particulars *pl*; ~**ausweis** *m* identity card; ~**büro** *nt* personnel (department); ~**chef** *m* personnel manager; ~**computer** *m* personal computer; ~**führung** *f* personnel management.

**Personalien** [-iən] *pl* particulars *pl*.

**Personal-:** ~**kartei** *f* personnel index; ~**leiter** *m* personnel manager; ~**mangel** *m* shortage of staff; ~**pronomen** *nt* personal pronoun; ~**rat** *m (Ausschuß)* staff council for civil servants; ~**union** *f* ... **in** ~**union** ... in one.

**personell** *adj* staff *attr*, personnel *attr*. **unsere Schwierigkeiten sind rein** ~ our difficulties are simply to do with staffing.

**Personen-:** ~**aufzug** *m* (passenger) lift *(Brit)*, elevator *(US)*; ~**beschreibung** *f* (personal) description; **p~bezogen** *adj Daten* personal; ~**gedächtnis** *nt* memory for faces; ~**gesellschaft** *f* partnership; ~**kraftwagen** *m (form)* (private) car, automobile *(US)*; ~**kreis** *m* group of people; ~**kult** *m* personality cult; ~**schaden** *m* injury to persons; ~**schutz** *m* personal security; ~**stand** *m* marital status; ~**standsregister** *nt* register of births, marriages and deaths; ~**verkehr** *m* passenger services *pl*; ~**waage** *f* pair of scales; ~**wagen** *m (Aut)* (private) car, automobile *(US)*; ~**zug** *m* passenger train; *(Gegensatz: Schnellzug)* slow train.

**Personifikation** *f* personification.

**personifizieren*** *vt* to personify.

**persönlich 1** *adj* personal; *Atmosphäre* friendly. ~ **werden** to get personal. **2** *adv* personally; *(auf Briefen)* private (and confidential). **etw** ~ **meinen/ nehmen** to mean/take sth personally; **Sie müssen** ~ **erscheinen** you are required to appear in person; ~ **haften** *(Comm)* to be personally liable.

**Persönlichkeit** *f* personality. **er besitzt wenig** ~ he hasn't got much personality; **er ist eine** ~ he's quite a personality; ~**en des öffentlichen Lebens** public figures.

**Perspektive** [-'tiːvə] *f (Art, Opt)* perspective; *(Blickpunkt)* angle; *(fig: Zukunftsausblick)* prospects *pl.* **das eröffnet ganz neue** ~**n für uns** that opens new horizons for us.

**perspektivisch** [-'tiːvɪʃ] *adj* perspective *attr*, in perspective. **die Zeichnung ist nicht** ~ the drawing is not in perspective; ~**e Verkürzung** foreshortening.

**Peru** *nt* Peru.

**Peruaner(in** *f) m* - Peruvian.

**peruanisch** *adj* Peruvian.

**Perücke** *f* -n wig.

**pervers** [pɛr'vɛrs] *adj* perverted. **ein** ~**er Mensch** a pervert.

**Perversion** [pɛrvɛr'zioːn] *f* perversion.

**Perversität** [pɛrvɛrzi'tɛːt] *f* perversion.

**pervertieren\*** [pɛrvɛr'tiːrən] **1** *vt* to pervert. **2** *vi aux sein* to become perverted.

**pervertiert** [pɛrvɛr'tiːɐt] *adj* perverted.

**Pessar** *nt* -e pessary; *(zur Empfängnisverhütung)* cap, diaphragm.

**Pessimismus** *m* pessimism.

**Pessimist(in** *f) m* pessimist.

**pessimistisch** *adj* pessimistic.

**Pest** *f no pl (Hist, Med)* plague. **jdn/etw wie die** ~ **hassen** *(col)* to detest sb/sth; **jdn wie die** ~ **meiden** *(col)* to avoid sb like the plague; **wie die** ~ **stinken** *(col)* to stink to high heaven *(col)*.

**Petersilie** [-iə] *f* parsley.

**Petition** *f* petition.

**Petrochemie** *f* petrochemistry.

**Petroleum** [pe'troːleʊm] *nt no pl* paraffin (oil) *(Brit)*, kerosene *(US)*.

**Petrus** *m (Bibl)* ≈ Peter.

**Petunie** [-iə] *f* petunia.

**Petze** *f* -n, **Petzer** *m* - *(Sch sl)* sneak *(Sch sl)*.

**petzen** *(col)* **1** *vt* **der petzt alles** he always tells; **er hat's dem Lehrer gepetzt** he told sir *(Brit Sch sl)*. **2** *vi* to tell (tales).

**Pf** = **Pfennig.**

**Pfad** *m* -e path *(also Comp)*, track.

**Pfadfinder** *m* - (boy) scout. **er ist bei den** ~**n** he's in the (Boy) Scouts.

**Pfadfinderin** *f* girl guide *(Brit)*, girl scout *(US)*.

**Pfaffe** *m (wk)* -n, -n *(pej)* cleric *(pej)*.

**Pfahl** *m* ⁼e post; *(Zaun~ auch, Marter~)* stake; *(Brücken~)* pile.

**Pfahlbau** *m* -ten **(a)** *no pl (Bauweise)* building on stilts. **(b)** *(Haus)* pile dwelling.

**Pfalz** *f (Geog)* Palatinate.

**Pfälzer(in** *f) m* - **(a)** person from the Palatinate, Palatinate. **(b)** *(Wein)* wine from the Rhine Palatinate.

**pfälzisch** *adj* Palatine.

**Pfand** *nt* ⁼er security; *(beim Pfänderspiel)* forfeit; *(Flaschen~)* deposit; *(fig geh)* pledge. **etw als** ~ **geben** *(lit, fig)* to pledge sth; *(beim Pfänderspiel)* to pay sth as a forfeit; **auf der Flasche ist 30 Pf** ~ there's 30 Pf (back) on the bottle *(col)*; **ein** ~ **einlösen** to redeem a pledge; **etw als** ~ **behalten** to keep sth as (a) security.

**Pfandbrief** *m* bond, debenture.

**pfänden** *vt (Jur)* to impound. **man hat ihm die Möbel gepfändet** they took away his furniture; **jdn** ~ **lassen** to get the bailiffs onto sb.

**Pfänderspiel** *nt* (game of) forfeits.

**Pfand-:** ~**flasche** *f* returnable bottle; ~**haus** *nt*, ~**leihe** *f* pawnshop; ~**leiher** *m* - pawnbroker; ~**schein** *m* pawn ticket.

**Pfändung** *f* seizure, distraint *(form)*.

**Pfanne** *f* -n *(Cook)* pan. **jdn in die** ~ **hauen** *(col)* to tear a strip off sb *(col)*.

**Pfannkuchen** *m* pancake. **Berliner** ~ (jam) doughnut.

**Pfarr|amt** *nt* parish office.

**Pfarrei** *f (Gemeinde)* parish; *(Amtsräume)* parish office.

**Pfarrer** *m* - vicar; *(lutheranisch)* pastor; *(katholisch)* parish priest; *(von Freikirchen)* minister; *(Gefängnis~, Militär~ etc)* chaplain, padre.

**Pfarrerin** *f* vicar; *(von Freikirchen)* minister.

**Pfarr-:** ~**gemeinde** *f* parish; ~**haus** *nt* vicarage; *(katholisch)* presbytery.

**Pfau** *m* -en peacock. **aufgedonnert wie ein** ~ *(col)* dressed up to the nines *(col)*.

**Pfauen|auge** *nt (Tag~)* peacock butterfly.

**Pfeffer** *m* - pepper. **er kann bleiben, wo der** ~ **wächst!** *(col)* he can take a running jump *(col)*.

**pfeff(e)rig** *adj* peppery.

**Pfeffer-:** ~**korn** *nt* peppercorn; ~**kuchen** *m* gingerbread.

**Pfefferminz(bonbon)** *nt* -(e) peppermint.

**Pfefferminze** *f no pl* peppermint.

**Pfeffermühle** *f* pepper-mill.

**pfeffern** *vt* **(a)** *(Cook)* to pepper; *siehe* **gepfeffert.** **(b)** *(col) (heftig werfen)* to fling; *(hinauswerfen)* to sling out *(col)*. **jdm eine** ~ to clout sb one *(col)*.

**Pfeffer-:** ~**nuß** *f* gingerbread biscuit; ~**streuer** *m* pepper pot *or (US)* shaker.

**Pfeife** *f* -n **(a)** whistle; *(Quer~)* fife *(esp Mil)*; *(Orgel~)* pipe. **nach jds** ~ **tanzen** to dance to sb's tune. **(b)** *(zum Rauchen)* pipe. ~ **rauchen** to smoke a pipe.

**pfeifen** *pret* **pfiff**, *ptp* **gepfiffen** *vti* to whistle *(dat* for*)*; *(auf einer Trillerpfeife)* to blow one's whistle; *(Mus)* to pipe; *(col)* Spiel to referee. **auf dem letzten Loch** ~ *(col) (erschöpft sein)* to be on one's last legs *(col)*; *(finanziell)* to be on one's beam ends *(col)*; **ich pfeife darauf!** *(col)* I don't give a damn *(col)*; **das** ~ **ja schon die Spatzen von den Dächern** it's all over town.

**Pfeifen-:** ~**kopf** *m* bowl (of a pipe); ~**stopfer** *m* tamper; ~**tabak** *m* pipe tobacco.

**Pfeifer** *m* - piper.

**Pfeiferei** *f (col)* whistling.

**Pfeifkonzert** *nt* catcalls *pl.*

**Pfeil** *m* -e arrow; *(Wurf~)* dart. ~ **und Bogen** bow and arrow; **er schoß wie ein** ~ **davon** he was off like a shot.

**Pfeiler** *m* - *(lit, fig)* pillar; *(Brücken~ auch)* pier; *(Stütz~)* buttress.

**Pfeil-:** **p~gerade** *adj* Linie dead straight; **sie kam p~gerade auf uns zu** she headed straight for us; **p~schnell** *adj* as swift as an arrow *(liter)*; ~**spitze** *f* arrowhead; ~**taste** *f (Comp)* arrow key; ~**wurfspiel** *nt* darts *pl.*

**Pfennig** *m* -e *or (nach Zahlenangabe)* - pfennig *(one hundredth of a mark)*. **30** ~ 30 pfennigs; **er hat keinen** ~ **Geld** he hasn't got a penny to his name *or* doesn't have a dime *(US)*; **nicht für fünf** ~ *(col)* not the slightest (bit of); **er hat nicht für fünf** ~ **Verstand** *(col)* he hasn't an ounce of intelligence; **mit jedem** ~ **rechnen müssen** *(fig)* to have to count every penny; **jeden** ~ **umdrehen** *(fig col)* to think twice about every penny one spends.

**Pfennig-:** ~**absatz** *m* stiletto heel; ~**fuchser** *m* - *(col)* skinflint *(col)*; ~**stück** *nt* pfennig (piece).

**Pferch** *m* -e fold, pen.

**pferchen** *vt* to cram, to pack.

**Pferd** *nt* -e *(Tier, Turngerät)* horse; *(beim Schachspiel)* knight, horse *(US col)*. **zu** ~**e** on horseback; **aufs falsche/richtige** ~ **setzen** *(lit, fig)* to back the wrong/right horse; **wie ein ~ arbeiten** *(col)* to work like a Trojan; **keine zehn ~e brächten mich dahin** *(col)* wild horses wouldn't drag me there; **mit ihm kann man ~e stehlen** *(col)* he's a great sport *(col)*; **er ist unser bestes ~ im Stall** he's our best man; **ich glaub, mich tritt ein ~** *(col)* blow me down *(col)*.

**Pferde-**: **~äpfel** *pl* horse droppings *pl or* dung *no pl*; **~fuhrwerk** *nt* horse and cart; **~fuß** *m* **die Sache hat aber einen ~fuß** there's just one snag; **~gebiß** *nt* horsey teeth; **~haar** *nt* horsehair; **~knecht** *m* groom; **~koppel** *f* paddock; **~rennbahn** *f* race course; **~rennen** *nt (Sportart)* (horse-)racing; *(einzelnes Rennen)* (horse-)race; **~schwanz** *m* horse's tail; *(Frisur)* ponytail; **~stall** *m* stable; **~stärke** *f* horsepower *no pl*, hp *abbr*; **~wagen** *m (für Personen)* trap, horse buggy *(US)*; *(für Lasten)* horse-drawn cart; **~zucht** *f* horse breeding; *(Gestüt)* stud farm.

**pfiff** *pret of* **pfeifen.**

**Pfiff** *m* **-e (a)** whistle. **(b)** *(Reiz)* style, pizzazz *(col)*. **der Soße fehlt noch der letzte ~** the sauce still needs that extra something.

**Pfifferling** *m* chanterelle. **er kümmert sich keinen ~ darum** *(col)* he doesn't give a damn about it *(col)*; **keinen ~ wert** *(col)* not worth a thing.

**pfiffig** *adj* smart, cute.

**Pfingsten** *nt* - Whitsun, Pentecost *(Eccl)*.

**Pfingst-**: **~montag** *m* Whit Monday; **~ochse** *m*: **herausgeputzt wie ein ~ochse** *(col)* dressed up to the nines *(col)*; **~rose** *f* peony; **~sonntag** *m* Whit Sunday, Pentecost *(Eccl)*; **~zeit** *f* Whitsun(tide).

**Pfirsich** *m* **-e** peach.

**Pflanze** *f* **-n (a)** *(Gewächs)* plant. **(b)** *(col: Mensch)* **sie ist eine seltsame ~** she is an odd bird *(col)*.

**pflanzen 1** *vt* to plant. **2** *vr (col)* to plonk oneself *(col)*.

**Pflanzen-**: **~fett** *nt* vegetable fat; **~fresser** *m* herbivore; **~kunde**, **~lehre** *f* botany; **~öl** *nt* vegetable oil; **~reich** *nt* plant kingdom; **~schädling** *m* pest; **~schutz** *m* protection of plants; *(gegen Ungeziefer)* pest control; **~schutzmittel** *nt* pesticide; **~welt** *f* **die ~welt des Mittelmeers** the flora of the Mediterranean.

**Pflanzgefäß** *nt* planter.

**pflanzlich** *adj attr* vegetable.

**Pflanzung** *f (das Pflanzen)* planting; *(Plantage)* plantation.

**Pflaster** *nt* - **(a)** *(Heft~)* (sticking-)plaster. **(b)** *(Straßen~)* (road) surface; *(Kopfstein~)* cobbles *pl*. **ein teures ~** *(col)* a pricey place *(col)*; **ein gefährliches or heißes ~** *(col)* a dangerous place.

**Pflastermaler** *m* pavement artist.

**pflastern** *vt Straße* to surface; *(mit Kopfsteinpflaster)* to cobble; *(mit Steinplatten)* to pave.

**Pflasterstein** *m (Kopfstein)* cobble(stone); *(Steinplatte)* paving stone.

**Pflaume** *f* **-n (a)** plum. **getrocknete ~** prune. **(b)** *(col: Mensch)* twit *(Brit col)*, dope *(col)*.

**Pflaumen-**: **~kompott** *nt* stewed plums *pl*; **~kuchen** *m* plum flan; **~mus** *nt* plum jam.

**Pflege** *f no pl* care; *(von Kranken auch)* nursing; *(von Garten auch)* attention; *(von Beziehungen, Künsten)* cultivation; *(von Maschinen, Gebäuden)* upkeep. **jdn/etw in ~ nehmen** to look after sb/sth; **ein Kind in ~ nehmen** *(dauernd)* to foster a child; **ein Kind in ~ geben** to have a child fostered; *(von Behörden)* to foster a child out *(zu jdm* with sb*)*.

**Pflege-**: **p~bedürftig** *adj* in need of care; **~eltern** *pl* foster parents *pl*; **~fall** *m* case for nursing *or* care; **sie ist ein ~fall** she needs constant care; **~geld** *nt (für ~kinder)* boarding-out allowance; *(für*

*Kranke)* attendance allowance; **~heim** *nt* nursing home; **~kind** *nt* foster child; **p~leicht** *adj* easycare; *(fig: Person)* easy to handle; **~mutter** *f* foster mother.

**pflegen 1** *vt* to look after; *Kranke auch* to nurse; *Beziehungen, Kunst* to cultivate; *Maschinen, Gebäude* to maintain. **2** *vi (gewöhnlich tun)* to be in the habit *(zu* of*)*. **sie pflegte zu sagen** she used to say.

**Pflegepersonal** *nt* nursing staff.

**Pfleger** *m* - *(im Krankenhaus)* orderly; *(voll qualifiziert)* (male) nurse.

**Pflegerin** *f* nurse.

**Pflege-**: **~satz** *m* hospital and nursing charges *pl*; **~sohn** *m* foster son; **~spülung** *f* hair conditioner; **~station** *f* nursing ward; **~tochter** *f* foster daughter; **~vater** *m* foster father; **~versicherung** *f* geriatric care insurance.

**pfleglich** *adj* careful.

**Pflicht** *f* **-en (a)** *(Verpflichtung)* duty. **als Abteilungsleiter hat er die ~, ...** it's his responsibility as head of department ...; **Rechte und ~en** rights and responsibilities; **seine ~ erfüllen** to do one's duty; **die ~ ruft** duty calls; **das/Schulbesuch ist ~** it's/going to school is compulsory; **es ist seine (verdammte** *col***) ~ und Schuldigkeit(, das zu tun)** he damn well ought to (do it) *(col)*. **(b)** *(Sport)* compulsory section.

**Pflicht-**: **p~bewußt** *adj* conscientious; **er ist sehr p~bewußt** he takes his duties very seriously; **~bewußtsein** *nt* sense of duty; **~fach** *nt* compulsory subject; **~gefühl** *nt* sense of duty; **p~gemäß** *adj* dutiful; **~lektüre** *f* compulsory reading; *(Sch auch)* set book(s); **~übung** *f* compulsory exercise; **p~vergessen** *adj* irresponsible; **~vergessenheit, ~versäumnis** *nt* neglect of duty *no pl*; **p~versichert** *adj* compulsorily insured; **~versicherung** *f* compulsory insurance.

**Pflock** *m* ⁼e peg; *(für Tiere)* stake.

**pflücken** *vt* to pick, to pluck.

**Pflücker(in** *f* **)** *m* - picker.

**Pflug** *m* ⁼e plough *(Brit)*, plow *(US)*.

**pflügen** *vti (lit, fig)* to plough *(Brit)*, to plow *(US)*.

**Pflugschar** *f* **-en** ploughshare *(Brit)*, plowshare *(US)*.

**Pforte** *f* **-n** *(Tor)* gate; *(Geog)* gap. **die ~ zum Himalaja** the gateway to the Himalayas.

**Pförtner(in** *f* **)** *m* - porter; *(von Fabrik)* gateman; *(von Wohnhaus, Behörde)* doorman; *(von Schloß)* gatekeeper.

**Pförtnerloge** [-loːʒə] *f* porter's office; *(in Fabrik)* gatehouse; *(in Wohnhaus, Büro)* doorman's office.

**Pfosten** *m* - *(auch Ftbl)* post; *(senkrechter Balken)* upright; *(Fenster~, Tür~)* jamb; *(Stütze)* prop.

**Pfote** *f* **-n (a)** *(lit, fig col)* paw. **sich** *(dat)* **die ~n verbrennen** *(col)* to burn one's fingers. **(b)** *(col: schlechte Handschrift)* scribble, scrawl.

**Pfropf** *m* **-e** *or* ⁼e, **Pfropfen** *m* - *(Stöpsel)* stopper; *(Kork, Sekt~)* cork; *(Watte~ etc)* plug; *(von Faß)* bung; *(Med)* *(Blut~)* (blood) clot.

**pfropfen** *vt* **(a)** *Flasche* to put the stopper in. **(b)** *(col: hineinzwängen)* to cram. **gepfropft voll** crammed full.

**pfui** *interj (Ekel)* ugh, yuck; *(Mißbilligung)* tut tut; *(zu Hunden)* oy, hey; *(Buhruf)* boo. **~ Teufel!** *(col)* ugh, yuck; **~, schäm dich!** shame on you!

**Pfund** *nt* **-e** *or (nach Zahlenangabe)* - **(a)** *(Gewicht)* *(metrisches System)* 500 grams, half a kilo(gram); *(britisches System)* pound. **drei ~ Äpfel** three pounds of apples. **(b)** *(Währungseinheit)* pound. **zwanzig ~ Sterling** twenty pounds sterling; **das ~ sinkt** sterling *or* the pound is falling.

**pfundig** *adj (col)* fantastic, swell *no adv (US)*.

**Pfundskerl** *m (col)* great guy *(col).*
**pfundweise** *adv* by the pound.
**Pfusch** *m no pl (col)* = **Pfuscherei.**
**pfuschen** *vi* to bungle; *(einen Fehler machen)* to slip up.
**Pfuscher(in** *f) m* - *(col)* bungler.
**Pfuscherei** *f (das Pfuschen)* bungling *no pl*; *(gepfuschte Arbeit)* botched-up job.
**Pfütze** *f* -n puddle.
**PH** [peː'haː] *f* -s = **Pädagogische Hochschule.**
**Phallussymbol** *nt* phallic symbol.
**Phänomen** *nt* -e phenomenon.
**phänomenal** *adj* phenomenal.
**Phantasie** *f* (a) *no pl (Einbildung)* imagination. **eine schmutzige ~ haben** to have a dirty mind. (b) *usu pl (Trugbild)* fantasy.
**Phantasie-:** **p~begabt** *adj* imaginative; **~gebilde** *nt* (a) *(phantastische Form)* fantastic form; (b) *(Einbildung)* figment of the imagination; **p~los** *adj* unimaginative; **~losigkeit** *f* lack of imagination.
**phantasieren\*** **1** *vi* to fantasize *(von* about*)*; *(von Schlimmem)* to have visions *(von* of*)*; *(Med)* to be delirious; *(Mus)* to improvise. **er phantasiert von einem großen Haus auf dem Lande** he has fantasies about a big house in the country. **2** *vt Geschichte* to dream up. **was phantasierst du denn da?** *(col)* what are you (going) on about? *(col).*
**Phantasie-:** **p~voll** *adj* highly imaginative; **~vorstellung** *f* figment of the imagination.
**Phantast** *m (wk)* -en, -en dreamer, visionary.
**phantastisch** *adj* fantastic.
**Phantom** *nt* -e *(Trugbild)* phantom. **einem ~ nachjagen** *(fig)* to tilt at windmills.
**Phantombild** *nt* Identikit ® (picture).
**Pharma-** *in cpds* pharmaceutical.
**Pharmakologie** *f* pharmacology.
**Pharmazeut(in** *f) m (wk)* -en, -en pharmacist, druggist *(US).*
**pharmazeutisch** *adj* pharmaceutical.
**Pharmazie** *f* pharmacy, pharmaceutics *sing.*
**Phase** *f* -n phase.
**Philanthrop** *m* -en, -en philanthropist.
**Philanthropie** *f* philanthropy.
**philanthropisch** *adj* philanthropic (al).
**Philatelie** *f* philately.
**Philatelist(in** *f) m* philatelist.
**Philharmonie** *f (Orchester)* philharmonic (orchestra); *(Konzertsaal)* philharmonic hall.
**Philharmoniker** *m* - **die Berliner ~** the Berlin Philharmonic (Orchestra).
**Philippine** *m (wk)* -n, -n, **Philippinin** *f* Filipino.
**Philippinen** *pl* Philippines *pl.*
**philippinisch** *adj* Filipino.
**Philologe** *m,* **Philologin** *f* philologist.
**Philologie** *f* philology.
**Philosoph(in** *f) m (wk)* -en, -en philosopher.
**Philosophie** *f* philosophy.
**philosophieren\*** *vi* to philosophize *(über +acc* about*).*
**philosophisch** *adj* philosophical.
**Phlegma** *nt no pl* apathy.
**Phlegmatiker(in** *f) m* - apathetic person.
**phlegmatisch** *adj* apathetic.
**Phobie** [foˈbiː] *f* phobia *(vor +dat* about*).*
**Phonetik** *f* phonetics *sing.*
**phonetisch** *adj* phonetic.
**Phonotypistin** *f* audio-typist.
**Phosphat** [fɔsˈfaːt] *nt* phosphate.
**Phosphor** [ˈfɔsfɔr] *m no pl* phosphorus.
**phosphoreszieren\*** *vi* to phosphoresce.
**Photo** *nt* -s = **Foto.**

**Phrase** *f* -n phrase; *(pej)* hollow phrase. **das sind alles nur ~n** that's just talk; **~n dreschen** *(col)* to churn out one cliché after another.
**Phrasen-:** **~drescher** *m (pej)* windbag; **~drescherei** *f (pej)* phrase-mongering; *(Geschwafel)* hot air; **p~haft** *adj* empty.
**pH-Wert** [peːˈhaː-] *m* pH-value.
**Physik** *f no pl* physics *sing.*
**physikalisch** *adj* physical; *Experimente* physics *attr.* **das ist ~ nicht erklärbar** that cannot be explained in terms of physics.
**Physiker(in** *f) m* - physicist.
**Physikum** *nt no pl (Univ)* preliminary examination in medicine.
**Physiologe** *m,* **Physiologin** *f* physiologist.
**Physiologie** *f* physiology.
**physiologisch** *adj* physiological.
**physisch** *adj* physical.
**Pianist(in** *f) m* pianist.
**picheln** *vi (col)* to booze *(col).*
**Pickel** *m* - (a) spot, pimple. (b) *(Spitzhacke)* pick (axe *(Brit)* or ax *US*); *(Eis~)* ice axe *(Brit),* ice ax *(US).*
**pick(e)lig** *adj* spotty, pimply.
**picken** *vti* to peck *(nach* at*).*
**Picknick** *nt* -s *or* -e picnic. **~ machen** to have a picnic.
**picknicken** *vi* to (have a) picnic.
**piekfein** *adj (col)* posh *(col).*
**pieksauber** *adj (col)* spotless.
**piep** *interj* tweet (-tweet).
**Piep** *m* -e *(col)* **er sagt keinen ~** he doesn't say a (single) word; **keinen ~ mehr machen** to have had it *(col).*
**piepe, piep|egal** *adj pred* **das ist mir ~!** *(col)* it's all one to me *(col).*
**piepen, piepsen** *vi (Vogel)* to cheep; *(Kinderstimme)* to pipe; *(Maus)* to squeak; *(Funkgerät etc)* to bleep. **bei dir piept's wohl!** *(col)* are you off your head?; **es war zum P~!** *(col)* it was a scream *(col).*
**Piepmatz** *m (col: kleiner Vogel)* birdie *(col).*
**Piepser** *m* - *(col)* (a) = **Piep.** (b) *(Telec)* bleeper.
**piepsig** *adj (col)* squeaky.
**Piepsstimme** *f (col)* squeaky voice.
**Pier** *m* -s *or* -e *or f* -s jetty, pier.
**piesacken** *vt (col) (quälen)* to torment; *(belästigen)* to pester.
**Pietät** [pieˈtɛːt] *f* reverence *no pl*; *(Achtung)* respect.
**pietätlos** [pieˈtɛːt-] *adj* irreverent.
**Pietätlosigkeit** [pieˈtɛːt-] *f* irreverence.
**Pigment** *nt* pigment.
**Pigmentfleck** *m* pigmentation mark.
**Pik¹** *m (col)* **einen ~ auf jdn haben** to have a grudge against sb.
**Pik²** *nt* -s *(Cards) (Farbe)* spades *pl*; *(Karte)* spade. **~-As** ace of spades.
**pikant** *adj* piquant; *Witz, Geschichte auch* racy. **~ gewürzt** appetizingly seasoned.
**Pikanterie** *f* (a) *no pl siehe adj* piquancy; raciness. (b) *(Bemerkung)* racy remark.
**Pike** *f* -n pike. **etw von der ~ auf lernen** *(fig)* to learn sth by starting from the bottom.
**piken** *vti (col)* to prick.
**pikiert** *adj (col)* peeved, piqued. **sie machte ein ~es Gesicht** she looked peeved.
**Pikkolo** *m* -s (a) *(Kellnerlehrling)* trainee waiter. (b) *(fig)* mini-version, baby; *(auch ~flasche)* quarter bottle of champagne. (c) *(Mus: auch ~flöte)* piccolo.
**pikobello** *adj (col)* spick and span.
**piksen** *vti (col)* to prick.
**Piktogramm** *nt* pictogram.
**Pilger(in** *f) m* - pilgrim.

**Pilgerfahrt** f pilgrimage.

**pilgern** vi aux sein to make a pilgrimage; (col: gehen) to wend one's way.

**Pille** f -n pill. **sie nimmt die** ~ she's on the pill; ~ **am Morgen danach** morning-after pill.

**Pilot(in** f) m (wk) -en, -en pilot.

**Pilot-:** ~**projekt** nt pilot scheme; ~**studie** f pilot study.

**Pils** nt -, -, **Pils(e)ner** nt - pils, pilsner.

**Pilz** m -e (a) fungus; (giftig) toadstool; (eßbar) mushroom; (Atom~) mushroom cloud. **wie** ~**e aus dem Boden schießen** to mushroom. (b) (Haut~) ringworm; (Fuß~) athlete's foot.

**Pilz-:** ~**krankheit** f fungal disease; ~**vergiftung** f fungus poisoning.

**Pimmel** m - (col: Penis) willie (col).

**pingelig** adj (col) finicky (col), fussy.

**Pingpong** nt -s (col) ping-pong.

**Pinguin** ['pɪŋguiːn] m -e penguin.

**Pinie** ['piːniə] f umbrella pine.

**Pinkel** m - (col) **ein feiner** or **vornehmer** ~ a swell (col).

**pinkeln** vi (col) to pee (col), to piddle (col).

**Pinnwand** f pinboard.

**Pinscher** m - pinscher.

**Pinsel** m - (a) brush. (b) (col) **ein eingebildeter** ~ a self-opinionated twerp (col).

**pinseln** vti (col) to paint; (pej: malen) to daub.

**Pinselstrich** m brush stroke.

**Pinte** f -n (col: Lokal) boozer (Brit col), bar.

**Pinzette** f (pair of) tweezers pl.

**Pionier** m -e (a) (Mil) sapper. (b) (fig) pioneer.

**Pionier|arbeit** f pioneering work.

**Pipapo** nt no pl (col) **das ganze** ~ the whole caboodle (col); **eine Party mit allem** ~ a party with all the trimmings.

**Pipette** f pipette, dropper.

**Pipi** nt or m -s (baby-talk) wee-wee (baby-talk). ~ **machen** to do a wee-wee (baby-talk), to piddle (col).

**Piranha** [pi'ranja] m -(s), -s piranha.

**Pirat** m (wk) -en, -en pirate.

**Piratensender** m pirate radio station.

**Piraterie** f (lit, fig) piracy.

**Pirsch** f no pl stalk. **auf (die)** ~ **gehen** to go stalking.

**pirschen** vi to stalk, to go stalking.

**Piß** m no pl, **Pisse** f no pl (col!) piss (col!).

**pissen** vi (col!) to (have a) piss (col!); (regnen) to piss down (col!).

**Pistazie** [pɪs'taːtsiə] f pistachio.

**Piste** f -n (Ski) piste, (ski-)run; (Rennbahn) track; (Aviat) runway; (behelfsmäßig) airstrip.

**Pistole** f -n pistol. **jdn mit vorgehaltener** ~ **zwingen** to force sb at gunpoint; **jdm die** ~ **auf die Brust setzen** (fig) to hold a pistol to sb's head; **wie aus der** ~ **geschossen** (fig) like a shot.

**pitsch(e)naß** adj (col) soaking (wet).

**pittoresk** adj picturesque.

**Pixel** nt -s (Comp) pixel.

**Pizza** f -s pizza.

**Pkw, PKW** ['peːkaːveː] m -s = **Personenkraftwagen.**

**pl., Pl.** = Plural pl.

**Placebo** [pla'tseːbo] nt -s placebo.

**placken** vr (col) to slave (away) (col).

**Plackerei** f (col) grind (col).

**plädieren\*** vi (Jur, fig) to plead (für, auf +acc for).

**Plädoyer** [plɛdoa'jeː] nt -s (Jur) summing up, summation (US); (fig) plea.

**Plage** f -n (fig) nuisance. **sie hat ihre** ~ **mit ihm** he's a trial for her; **man hat schon seine** ~ **mit dir** you are a nuisance.

**Plagegeist** m nuisance, pest.

**plagen 1** vt to torment; (mit Bitten und Fragen auch) to pester. **ein geplagter Mann** a harassed man. **2** vr (a) (leiden) to be bothered (mit by). (b) (arbeiten) to slave away (col).

**Plagiat** nt plagiarism.

**Plagiator** m plagiarist.

**Plakat** nt -e poster; (aus Pappe) placard.

**Plakatfarbe** f poster paint.

**plakatieren\*** vt to placard; (fig) to broadcast.

**plakativ** adj striking, bold.

**Plakatwand** f hoarding, billboard (US).

**Plakette** f (Abzeichen) badge; (Münze) commemorative coin; (an Wänden) plaque.

**Plan¹** m ⁼e (a) plan. **den** ~ **fassen, etw zu tun** to plan to do sth; ~**e machen** or **schmieden** to make plans; **nach** ~ **verlaufen** to go according to plan. (b) (Stadt~) (street-)map; (Grundriß, Bau~) blueprint; (Zeittafel) timetable (Brit), schedule (US).

**Plan²** m ⁼e **auf den** ~ **treten** (fig) to come on the scene; **jdn auf den** ~ **rufen** (fig) to bring sb into the arena.

**Plane** f -n tarpaulin; (von LKW) canvas cover; (Schutzdach) awning.

**planen** vti to plan.

**Planer(in** f) m - planner.

**Planet** m (wk) -en, -en planet.

**Planetarium** nt planetarium.

**Planetensystem** nt planetary system.

**plangemäß** adj = **planmäßig.**

**planieren\*** vt Boden to level (off).

**Planierraupe** f bulldozer.

**Planke** f -n plank, board; (Leit~) crash barrier.

**Plänkelei** f (fig) squabble.

**Plankton** nt no pl plankton.

**planlos** adj unsystematic; (ziellos) random.

**Planlosigkeit** f lack of planning.

**planmäßig** adj (wie geplant) as planned; (pünktlich) on schedule; (methodisch) methodical. ~**e Ankunft/ Abfahrt** scheduled time of arrival/departure.

**Planquadrat** nt grid square.

**Planschbecken** nt paddling (Brit) or wading (US) pool.

**planschen** vi to splash around.

**Plan-:** ~**soll** nt output target; ~**stelle** f post.

**Plantage** [plan'taːʒə] f -n plantation.

**Planung** f planning. **in der** ~ at the planning stage.

**Plan-:** ~**wagen** m covered wagon; ~**wirtschaft** f planned economy.

**Plappermaul** nt (col) chatterbox (col); (Schwätzer) gossip (col).

**plappern 1** vi to prattle; (Geheimnis verraten) to blab (col). **2** vt Blödsinn to talk.

**plärren** vti (col: weinen) to bawl; (Radio) to blare (out).

**Plasma** nt, pl **Plasmen** plasma.

**Plastik¹** nt -s (Kunststoff) plastic.

**Plastik²** f (Skulptur, Kunst) sculpture.

**Plastik-:** ~**beutel** m = ~**tüte;** ~**folie** f plastic film; ~**sprengstoff** m plastic explosive; ~**tüte** f plastic bag.

**plastisch** adj (a) (knetbar) malleable. (b) (dreidimensional) three-dimensional, 3-D; (fig: anschaulich) vivid. ~**e Sprache** vivid language; **das kann ich mir** ~ **vorstellen** I can just picture it. (c) (Art, Med) plastic. ~**e Chirurgie** plastic surgery.

**Plastizität** f no pl (a) (Formbarkeit) malleability. (b) (fig: Anschaulichkeit) vividness.

**Platane** f -n plane tree.

**Plateau** [pla'toː] nt -s plateau.

**Platin** nt no pl platinum.

**Platine** *f (Comp, Elec)* circuit board.
**platonisch** *adj* platonic.
**platsch** *interj* splash, splosh.
**platschen** *vi (col)* to splash; *(regnen)* to pour.
**plätschern** *vi* to splash; *(Bach auch)* to babble. **eine**
**~de Unterhaltung** light conversation.
**platschnaß** *adj (col)* soaking (wet).
**platt** *adj* **(a)** *(flach)* flat. **etw ~ drücken** to flatten sth;
**einen P~en** *(col) or* **einen ~en Reifen haben** to have
a flat (tyre *Brit or* tire *US*). **(b)** *(fig: geistlos)* dull.
**(c)** *(col: verblüfft)* **~ sein** to be flabbergasted *(col)*.
**Platt** *nt no pl (col)* Low German, Plattdeutsch.
**plattdeutsch** *adj* Low German.
**Platte** *f* **-n (a)** *(Holz~)* board; *(Glas~/Metall~/*
*Plastik~)* sheet of glass/metal/plastic; *(Beton~,*
*Stein~)* slab; *(zum Pflastern)* flagstone; *(Kachel, Flie-*
*se)* tile; *(Herd~)* hotplate; *(Tisch~)* (table-)top;
*(Phot)* plate; *(Gedenktafel)* plaque; *(Comp)* disk. **(b)**
*(Fleisch)* serving-dish; *(Torten~)* cake plate. **kalte ~**
cold dish. **(c)** *(Schall~)* record, disc. **etw auf ~ auf-**
**nehmen** to record sth on disc; **die ~ kenne ich**
**schon** *(col)* I've heard all that before *(col)*; **leg doch**
**mal eine neue ~ auf!** *(col)* can't you change the subject for once? **(d)** *(col: Glatze)* bald head; *(kahle*
*Stelle)* bald patch.
**plätten** *vt (dial)* to iron, to press; *siehe* **geplättet.**
**Platten-:** **~leger** *m* - paver; **~sammlung** *f* record
collection; **~spieler** *m* record-player; **~teller** *m*
turntable; **~wechsler** *m* - record changer.
**Platt-:** **~fisch** *m* flatfish; **~form** *f* platform; *(fig:*
*Grundlage)* basis; **~fuß** *m* flat foot; **p~füßig** *adj,*
*adv* flat-footed; **~heit** *f* **(a)** *no pl (Geistlosigkeit)*
dullness; **(b)** *usu pl (Redensart etc)* platitude.
**Platz** *m* =**e (a)** *(freier Raum)* room, space. **~ für jdn/**
**etw schaffen** to make room for sb/sth; **mehr als 10**
**Leute haben hier nicht ~** there's not room for more
than 10 people here; **jdm den (ganzen) ~ wegneh-**
**men** to take up all sb's space; **~ machen** to get out
of the way *(col)*; **~ machen für jdn/etw ~** make
a bit of room; **~ für jdn/etw bieten** to have space
for sb/sth; **~ da!** *(col)* (get) out of the way there!
*(col)*.
(b) *(Sitzplatz)* seat. **~ nehmen** to take a seat; **be-**
**halten Sie doch bitte ~!** *(form)* please remain
seated *(form)*; **der Saal hat 2.000 ~e** the hall seats
2,000; **mit jdm den ~ tauschen** to change places
with sb; **~!** *(zum Hund)* sit!
(c) *(Stelle, Ort, Rang, Arbeits~)* place. **etw (wieder)**
**an seinen ~ stellen** to put sth (back) in (its) place;
**fehl** *or* **nicht am ~e sein** to be out of place; **auf die**
**~e, fertig, los!** *(Sport)* on your marks, get set, go!;
**seinen ~ behaupten** to stand one's ground; **das**
**Buch hat einen festen ~ auf der Bestsellerliste** the
book is firmly established on the bestseller list;
**den ersten ~ einnehmen** *(fig)* to come first; **auf ~**
**zwei** in second place; **jdn auf die ~e verweisen** *(fig)*
to beat sb; **auf ~ wetten** to make a place bet; **wir**
**haben noch einen freien ~ im Büro** we've still got
one vacancy in the office; **das erste Hotel am ~** the
best hotel in the place.
(d) *(umbaute Fläche)* square. **auf dem ~** in the
square.
(e) *(Sport~)* playing field; *(Ftbl, Hockey)* pitch
*(Brit)*, field; *(Handball~, Tennis~)* court; *(Golf~)*
(golf) course. **einen Spieler vom ~ stellen** *or* **verwei-**
**sen** to send a player off.
**Platz-:** **~angst** *f (col)* claustrophobia; **~angst be-**
**kommen** to get claustrophobic; **~anweiser(in** *f) m*
- usher(ette).
**Plätzchen** *nt* **(a)** *dim of* **Platz** spot. **(b)** *(Gebäck)* biscuit *(Brit)*, cookie *(US)*.

**platzen** *vi aux sein* **(a)** *(aufreißen)* to burst; *(Naht,*
*Hose, Haut)* to split; *(explodieren)* to explode; *(einen*
*Riß bekommen)* to crack. **wir sind vor Lachen fast**
**geplatzt** we split our sides laughing; **ins Zimmer ~**
*(col)* to burst into the room; **jdm ins Haus ~** *(col)* to
descend on sb; **(vor Wut/Neid) ~** *(col)* to be bursting
(with rage/envy). **(b)** *(col: scheitern) (Geschäft)* to
fall through; *(Freundschaft)* to break up; *(Theorie,*
*Verschwörung)* to collapse; *(Wechsel)* to bounce
*(col)*. **die Verlobung ist geplatzt** the engagement is
(all) off; **etw ~ lassen** *Plan* to make sth fall
through; *Theorie* to explode sth; *Spionagering* to
smash sth; *Wechsel* to make sth bounce *(col)*.
**Platz-:** **~hirsch** *m (lit, fig)* dominant male; **~karte** *f*
*(Rail)* seat reservation (ticket); **~konzert** *nt* open-
air concert; **~mangel** *m* lack of space; **~miete** *f*
*(Theat)* season ticket; *(Sport)* ground rent;
**~patrone** *f* blank (cartridge); **~regen** *m* cloudburst; **das ist nur ein ~regen** it's only a (passing)
shower; **p~sparend** *adj* space-saving *attr*; **das ist**
**p~sparender** that saves more space; **~verweis** *m*
sending-off; **~wahl** *f* toss-up; **~wart** *m (Sport)*
groundsman; **~wechsel** *m* change of place;
*(Sport)* change of position; **~wette** *f* place bet;
**~wunde** *f* laceration.
**Plauderei** *f* chat, conversation.
**Plauderer** *m* -, **Plauderin** *f* conversationalist.
**plaudern** *vi* to chat *(über +acc, von* about*)*; *(etwas*
*verraten)* to talk. **mit ihm läßt sich gut ~** he's easy
to talk to.
**Plausch** *m* **-e** *(col)* chat.
**plauschen** *vi (col)* to have a chat.
**plausibel** *adj* plausible. **jdm etw ~ machen** to explain sth to sb.
**Plausibilität** *f* plausibility.
**Playback** ['pleɪbæk] *nt* **-s (a)** *(Bandaufnahme)* backing track. **(b)** *no pl (Verfahren) (bei Schallplatte)*
double-tracking *no pl*; *(TV)* miming *no pl*.
**plazieren\*** 1 *vt* **(a)** *(Platz anweisen)* to put; *(Tennis)*
to seed. **(b)** *(zielen) Ball* to position; *Schlag* to land.
**gut plazierte Aufschläge** well-positioned services. 2
*vr* **(a)** *(col: sich setzen, stellen)* to plant oneself *(col)*.
**(b)** *(Sport)* to be placed; *(Tennis)* to be seeded. **der**
**Läufer konnte sich gut/nicht ~** the runner was well-
placed/wasn't even placed.
**Plazierung** *f (bei Rennen)* order; *(Tennis)* seeding;
*(Platz)* place. **welche ~ hatte er?** where did he come
in?
**Plebejer(in** *f) m* - *(lit, fig)* plebeian.
**plebejisch** *adj* plebeian *no adv*.
**Plebiszit** *nt* **-(e)s, -e** plebiscite.
**pleite** *adj pred, adv (col) Mensch* broke *(col)*; *Firma*
*auch* bust *(col)*. **~ gehen** to go bust.
**Pleite** *f* **-n** *(col)* bankruptcy; *(fig)* washout *(col)*. **~**
**machen** to go bust *(col)*; **damit/mit ihm haben wir**
**eine ~ erlebt** it/he was a disaster for us.
**Pleitegeier** *m (col)* **(a)** *(drohende Pleite)* threat of
bankruptcy. **über der Firma schwebt der ~** the firm
is threatened with bankruptcy. **(b)** *(Bankrotteur)*
bankrupt.
**Plektron, Plektrum** *nt, pl* **Plektren** *or* **Plektra**
plectrum.
**plemplem** *adj pred (col)* nuts *(col)*.
**Plenar-:** **~saal** *m* assembly room; *(Parl)* chamber;
**~sitzung** *f* plenary session.
**Plenum** *nt* plenum.
**Pleuelstange** *f* connecting rod.
**Plexiglas** ® *nt* acrylic glass.
**Plissee-:** **~falte** *f* pleat; **~rock** *m* pleated skirt.
**PLO** [peː|ɛl'|oː] *f* PLO.
**Plombe** *f* **-n (a)** *(Siegel)* lead seal. **(b)** *(Zahn~)*

filling.
**plombieren\*** vt (a) (versiegeln) to seal. (b) Zahn to fill. **er hat mir zwei Zähne plombiert** he did two fillings.
**Plotter** m - (Comp) plotter.
**plötzlich 1** adj sudden. **2** adv suddenly; (auf einmal) all of a sudden. **aber etwas ~!** (col) look sharp! (col); **das kommt alles so ~** (col) this is all so sudden.
**Pluderhose** f Turkish trousers pl.
**Plumeau** [ply'moː] nt -s eiderdown, quilt.
**plump** adj Figur, Form ungainly no adv; Ausdruck clumsy; Bemerkung crass; Mittel, Lüge crude. **~e Annäherungsversuche** very obvious advances.
**plumps** interj bang; (lauter) crash.
**Plumps** m -e (col) (Fall) tumble; (Geräusch) thud. **einen ~ machen** (baby-talk) to fall; **mit einem ~ ins Wasser fallen** to fall into the water with a splash.
**plumpsen** vi aux sein (col) to tumble. **er plumpste ins Wasser** he fell into the water with a splash.
**Plumpsklo(sett)** nt (col) earth closet.
**plump-vertraulich 1** adj hail-fellow-well-met. **2** adv in a hail-fellow-well-met sort of way.
**Plunder** m no pl junk, rubbish.
**Plünd(e)rer** m - looter, plunderer.
**Plundergebäck** nt flaky pastry.
**plündern** vti to loot; (ausrauben) to raid; Obstbaum to strip.
**Plünderung** f looting, pillage.
**Plural** m -e plural. **im ~ stehen** to be in the plural.
**plus 1** prep +gen plus. **2** adv plus. **bei ~ 5 Grad** at 5 degrees (above freezing or zero); **~/minus 10** plus or minus 10; **mit ~ minus null abschließen** to break even. **3** conj (col) plus.
**Plus** nt - (a) (Phys col: ~pol) positive (pole). (b) (Comm) (Zuwachs) increase; (Gewinn) profit; (Überschuß) surplus. (c) (fig: Vorteil) plus, advantage. **das ist ein ~ für dich** that's a point in your favour (Brit) or favor (US).
**Plüsch** m -e plush.
**Plüsch-** in cpds plush; **~tier** nt ≈ soft toy.
**Plus-:** **~pol** m (Elec) positive pole; **~punkt** m (Sport) point; (Sch) extra mark; (fig) plus point, advantage; **~quamperfekt** nt pluperfect; **~zeichen** nt plus sign.
**Plutonium** nt no pl plutonium.
**PLZ** [peːɛl'tsɛt] f = **Postleitzahl.**
**pneumatisch** [pnɔy'maːtɪʃ] adj pneumatic.
**Po** m -s (col) = **Popo.**
**Pöbel** m no pl rabble, mob.
**pöbelhaft** adj uncouth, vulgar.
**pochen** vi to knock; (Herz, Blut) to pound. **auf etw** (acc) **~** (fig) to insist on sth.
**pochieren\*** [pɔ'ʃiːrən] vt Ei to poach.
**Pocken** pl smallpox.
**Pocken-:** **~narbe** f pockmark; **p~narbig** adj pockmarked; **~(schutz)impfung** f smallpox vaccination.
**Podest** nt or m -e (Sockel) pedestal (auch fig); (Podium) platform; (Treppenabsatz) landing.
**Podium** nt (lit, fig) platform; (des Dirigenten) rostrum; (bei Diskussion) panel.
**Podiumsdiskussion** f panel discussion.
**Poesie** [poe'ziː] f (lit, fig) poetry.
**Poesie|album** nt child's scrapbook containing verses written by friends.
**Poet(in** f) m (wk) -en, -en (geh) poet.
**poetisch** adj poetic.
**Pointe** ['poɛ̃ːtə] f -n (eines Witzes) punch-line; (einer Geschichte) point.
**pointiert** [poɛ̃'tiːɐt] adj trenchant, pithy.

**Pokal** m -e (zum Trinken) goblet; (Sport) cup.
**Pokal-:** **~endspiel** nt cup final; **~sieger** m cup-winners pl; **~spiel** nt cup tie.
**Pökelfleisch** nt salt meat.
**pökeln** vt Fleisch, Fisch to salt, to pickle.
**Poker** nt no pl poker.
**pokern** vi to play poker. **um etw ~** (fig) to haggle for sth.
**Pol** m -e pole. **der ruhende ~** (fig) the calming influence.
**polar** adj polar. **~e Kälte** arctic coldness; **~ entgegengesetzt** diametrically opposed.
**polarisieren\*** vtr to polarize.
**Polarisierung** f polarization.
**Polarität** f polarity.
**Polar-:** **~kreis** m polar circle; **nördlicher/südlicher ~kreis** Arctic/Antarctic Circle; **~licht** nt polar lights pl; **~stern** m Pole or North Star.
**Pole** m (wk) -n, -n Pole.
**Polemik** f polemics sing; (Streitschrift) polemic.
**polemisch** adj polemic(al).
**polemisieren\*** vi to polemicize. **~ gegen** to inveigh against.
**Polen** nt Poland.
**Polente** f no pl (dated col) cops pl (col).
**Police** [po'liːsə] f -n (insurance) policy.
**Polier** m -e site foreman.
**polieren\*** vt (lit, fig) to polish. **jdm die Fresse** or **Schnauze ~** (col!) to smash sb's face in (col).
**Polier-:** **~mittel** nt polish; **~wachs** nt wax polish.
**Poliklinik** f (Krankenhaus) clinic (for outpatients only); (Abteilung) outpatients' department.
**Polin** f Pole, Polish woman/girl.
**Politesse** f (woman) traffic warden (Brit).
**Politik** f (a) no pl politics sing; (politischer Standpunkt) politics pl. **welche ~ vertritt er?** what are his politics?; **in die ~ gehen** to go into politics. (b) (bestimmte ~) policy. **ihre gesamte ~** all their policies.
**Politiker(in** f) m - politician.
**politisch** adj political.
**politisieren\* 1** vi to talk politics, to politicize. **2** vt to politicize; jdn to make politically aware.
**Politisierung** f politicization.
**Politologe** m (wk), **Politologin** f political scientist.
**Politologie** f political science, politics sing.
**Politur** f polish.
**Polizei** f police pl; (Gebäude) police station. **auf die** or **zur ~ gehen** to go to the police; **er ist bei der ~** he's in the police (force).
**Polizei-** in cpds police; **~aufgebot** nt police presence; **~aufsicht** f **unter ~aufsicht stehen** to be under police surveillance; **~beamte(r)** m police official; (Polizist) police officer; **~chef** m chief constable, chief of police (US); **~dienststelle** f (form) police station; **~direktion** f police headquarters pl; **~funk** m police radio; **~haft** f detention; **~hund** m police dog; **~kommissar** m (police) inspector.
**polizeilich** adj no pred police attr. **~es Führungszeugnis** certificate issued by the police, stating that the holder has no criminal record; **sich ~ melden** to register with the police.
**Polizei-:** **~präsident** m chief constable, chief of police (US); **~präsidium** nt police headquarters pl; **~revier** nt (~wache) police station; **~spitzel** m (police) informer; **~staat** m police state; **~streife** f police patrol; **~stunde** f closing time; **~wache** f police station.
**Polizist** m policeman.
**Polizistin** f policewoman.
**Pollen** m - pollen.

**Pollenflug** *m* pollen count.
**polnisch** *adj* Polish.
**Polnisch(e)** *nt decl as adj* Polish; *siehe* **Deutsch(e)**.
**Polohemd** *nt* polo shirt.
**Polster** *nt* - (a) cushion; *(Polsterung)* upholstery *no pl*; *(bei Kleidung)* pad, padding *no pl.* (b) *(fig) (Fett~)* flab *no pl (col)*; *(Bauch)* spare tyre *(Brit)* or tire *(US)*; *(Geldreserve)* reserves *pl.*
**Polster-**: ~**garnitur** *f* three-piece suite; ~**möbel** *pl* upholstered furniture.
**polstern** *vt* to upholster; *Kleidung, Tür* to pad. **etw neu ~** to reupholster sth; **sie ist gut gepolstert** *(col)* she's well-padded; *(finanziell)* she's not short of the odd penny.
**Polster-**: ~**sessel** *m* armchair, easy chair; ~**stuhl** *m* upholstered chair.
**Polsterung** *f* upholstery.
**Polter|abend** *m party on the eve of a wedding with smashing of crockery*, ≈ shower *(US)*.
**Poltergeist** *m* poltergeist.
**poltern** *vi* (a) to crash about. **was hat da eben so gepoltert?** what was that crash?; **es poltert** there's a real din going on. (b) *aux sein (sich laut bewegen)* to crash, to bang. (c) *(col: schimpfen)* to rant (and rave).
**Poly-**: ~**äthylen** *nt* -e polyethylene; ~**ester** *m* - polyester; ~**gamie** *f* polygamy.
**Polynesien** [-iən] *nt* Polynesia.
**Polynesier(in** *f)* [-iɐ, -iərɪn] *m* - Polynesian.
**polynesisch** *adj* Polynesian.
**Polyp** *m (wk)* -en, -en (a) *(Zool)* polyp. (b) *(Med)* ~en adenoids. (c) *(hum col: Polizist)* cop *(col)*.
**Poly-**: ~**technikum** *nt* polytechnic, poly *(col)*; **p~technisch** *adj* polytechnic.
**Pomade** *f* hair-cream.
**Pommern** *nt* Pomerania.
**Pommes frites** [pɔm'frit(s)] *pl* chips *pl (Brit)*, French fries *pl.*
**Pomp** *m no pl* pomp.
**pompös** *adj* grandiose.
**Pontius** ['pɔntsius] *m*: **von ~ zu Pilatus** from pillar to post.
**Pony¹** ['pɔni] *nt* -s pony.
**Pony²** ['pɔni] *m* -s fringe *(Brit)*, bangs *pl (US)*.
**Ponyfrisur** *f* **sie hat eine ~** she has a fringe *(Brit)*, she has bangs *(US)*.
**Pool(billard)** ['puːl(bɪljart)] *nt* pool.
**Pop** *m no pl (Mus)* pop; *(Art)* pop-art.
**Popanz** *m* -e *(Schreckgespenst)* bogey.
**Popcorn** [-kɔːn] *nt no pl* popcorn.
**pop(e)lig** *adj (col)* (a) *(knauserig)* stingy *(col)*. (b) *(dürftig)* crummy *(col)*.
**Popelin** *m* -e, **Popeline** *f* - poplin.
**popeln** *vi (col)* **(in der Nase)** ~ to pick one's nose.
**Pop-**: ~**festival** *nt* pop festival; ~**gruppe** *f* pop group; ~**konzert** *nt* pop concert; ~**musik** *f* pop music.
**Popo** *m* -s *(col)* bottom, bum *(col)*.
**Popper** *m (col)* preppy *(col)*.
**poppig** *adj (col) (Art, Mus)* pop *no adv*; *Kleidung* trendy.
**populär** *adj* popular *(bei* with*)*.
**popularisieren\*** *vt* to popularize.
**Popularität** *f* popularity.
**populärwissenschaftlich** *adj* popular science.
**Populismus** *m (Pol)* populism.
**Populist(in** *f)* *m* populist.
**populistisch** *adj* populist.
**Pore** *f* -n pore.
**Porno** *m* -s *(col)* porn *(col)*, porno *(US col)*.
**Pornographie** *f* pornography.

**pornographisch** *adj* pornographic.
**porös** *adj (durchlässig)* porous; *(brüchig)* perished.
**Porree** ['pɔre] *m* -s leek.
**Portal** *nt* -e portal.
**Portemonnaie** [pɔrtmɔ'neː] *nt* -s purse.
**Portier** [pɔr'tieː] *m* -s porter.
**Portion** *f* (a) *(beim Essen)* portion, helping. **eine halbe ~** *(fig col)* a half-pint *(col)*; **eine zweite ~** a second helping; **eine ~ Kaffee** a pot of coffee. (b) *(fig col: Anteil)* amount. **er besitzt eine ganze ~ Frechheit** he's got a fair bit of cheek *(col)*.
**Porto** *nt, pl* -s or **Porti** postage *no pl (für* on, for*)*; *(für Kisten etc)* carriage. **~ zahlt Empfänger** postage paid *or (US)* prepaid.
**portofrei** *adj* postage paid *or (US)* prepaid.
**Portokasse** *f* ≈ petty cash.
**Porträt** [*auch* pɔr'trɛː] *nt* -s *(lit, fig)* portrait.
**porträtieren\*** *vt* **jdn ~** to paint sb's portrait; *(fig)* to portray sb.
**Portugal** *nt* Portugal.
**Portugiese** *m (wk)* -n, -n, **Portugiesin** *f* Portuguese.
**Portugiesisch(e)** *nt* Portuguese; *siehe* **Deutsch(e)**.
**portugiesisch** *adj* Portuguese.
**Portwein** *m* port.
**Porzellan** *nt* -e *(Material)* porcelain; *(Geschirr)* china.
**Porzellan-** *in cpds* china; ~**erde** *f* china clay; ~**geschirr** *nt* china, crockery; ~**manufaktur** *f* china factory.
**Posaune** *f* -n trombone; *(fig: von Engeln etc)* trumpet.
**posaunen\*** *(col)* **1** *vi* to play the trombone. **2** *vti (fig)* to bellow, to bawl. **etw in alle Welt ~** to tell sth to the whole world.
**Posaunenbläser** *m*, **Posaunist(in** *f)* *m* trombonist.
**Pose** *f* -n pose.
**posieren\*** *vi* to pose.
**Position** *f* position; *(Comm: auf Liste)* item.
**Positionslicht** *nt* navigation light.
**positiv** *adj* positive. **eine ~e Antwort** an affirmative (answer); **etw ~ wissen** to know sth for a fact; **einen ~en Eindruck haben** to be favourably *(Brit)* or favorably *(US)* impressed; **~ zu etw stehen** to be in favour *(Brit)* or favor *(US)* of sth.
**Positiv** *nt (Phot)* positive.
**Positur** *f* posture. **sich in ~ setzen/stellen** to adopt a posture.
**Posse** *f* -n farce.
**Possen** *m* - *(dated)* prank, tomfoolery *no pl.* **~ reißen** to clown around.
**Possessivpronomen** *nt* possessive pronoun.
**possierlich** *adj* comical, funny.
**Post** *f* -en post *(Brit)*, mail; *(~amt, ~wesen)* post office. **war die ~ schon da?** has the post *or* mail come yet?; **ist ~ für mich da?** are there any letters for me?; **etw mit der ~ schicken** to send sth by post *or* mail; **etw auf die ~ geben** to post *or* mail sth; **auf die** *or* **zur ~ gehen** to go to the post office; **mit getrennter ~** under separate cover.
**postalisch** *adj* postal.
**Post-**: ~**amt** *nt* post office; ~**anweisung** *f* ≈ postal *(Brit)* or money order; ~**auto** *nt* post office van; ~**beamte(r)** *m*, ~**beamtin** *f* post office official; ~**bote** *m* postman *(Brit)*, mailman *(US)*.
**Posten** *m* - (a) *(Anstellung)* post, job. (b) *(Mil: Wachmann)* guard; *(Stelle)* post. **~ stehen** to stand guard; **~ beziehen** to take up one's post. (c) **auf dem ~ sein** *(aufpassen)* to be awake; *(gesund sein)* to be fit; **nicht ganz auf dem ~ sein** to be off colour

*(Brit) or* under the weather. **(d)** *(Streik~)* picket. **(e)** *(Comm: Warenmenge)* quantity, lot. **(f)** *(Comm: im Etat)* item, entry.
**Poster** *nt* **-(s)** poster.
**Postfach** *nt* PO Box.
**Postgiro-** [-ʒiːro]: **~amt** *nt* ≈ National Giro Office *(Brit)*; **~konto** *nt* post office giro account *(Brit)*.
**posthum** *adj* posthumous.
**postieren*** **1** *vt* to position. **2** *vr* to position oneself.
**Post-**: **~karte** *f* postcard; **~kasten** *m* pillar box *(Brit)*, mailbox *(US)*; **~kutsche** *f* mail coach, stagecoach; **p~lagernd 1** *adj* to be called for; **2** *adv* poste restante *(Brit)*, general delivery *(US)*; **~leitzahl** *f* post(al) code, zip code *(US)*; **~minister** *m* ≈ postmaster general; **p~modern** *adj* postmodern; **~modernismus** *m* postmodernism; **~sache** *f* post office mail *no pl*; **~scheck** *m* post office giro cheque *(Brit)*; **~scheckamt** *nt* = **~giroamt**; **~scheckkonto** *nt* = **~girokonto**; **~sparbuch** *nt* post office savings book *(Brit)*; **~sparkasse** *f* post office savings bank; **~stempel** *m* postmark; **Datum des ~stempels** date as postmark; **~überweisung** *f* Girobank transfer.
**postulieren*** *vt* to postulate.
**postum** *adj* posthumous.
**Post-**: **p~wendend** *adv* by return (of post) *(Brit)*, by return mail; **~wertzeichen** *nt (form)* postage stamp *(form)*; **~wurfsendung** *f* direct-mail item; **~wurfsendungen** direct mail; **~zustellung** *f* mail delivery.
**potent** *adj* potent; *(fig) Phantasie* powerful.
**Potential** [potɛn'tsiaːl] *nt* **-e** potential.
**potentiell** [potɛn'tsiɛl] *adj* potential.
**Potenz** *f* **(a)** *(Med)* potency; *(fig)* ability. **(b)** *(Math)* power. **zweite/dritte** ~ square/cube.
**potenzieren*** *vt (Math)* to raise to the power of; *(col: steigern)* to multiply.
**Potpourri** ['pɔtpʊri] *nt* **-s** *(Mus)* medley *(aus of)*; *(fig)* assortment.
**Pott** *m* ÷e *(col)* pot.
**Pott-**: **~asche** *f* potash; **~wal** *m* sperm whale.
**Poularde** [pu-] *f* **-n** baby chicken.
**poussieren** [pu'siːrən] *vi (dated col: flirten)* to flirt.
**powern** ['paʊɐn] *vi (col)* to get things moving.
**prä-, prae-** *pref* pre-.
**Prä|ambel** *f* preamble *(gen to)*.
**Pracht** *f no pl (lit)* splendour *(Brit)*, splendor *(US)*. **in seiner vollen** *or* **ganzen** ~ in all its splendour; **es ist eine wahre** ~ it's (really) superb.
**Pracht-**: **~entfaltung** *f* magnificent display; **~exemplar** *nt* beauty *(col)*; *(fig: Mensch)* fine specimen.
**prächtig** *adj (prunkvoll, großartig)* splendid.
**Pracht-**: **~kerl** *m (col)* great guy *(col)*; *(~exemplar)* beauty *(col)*; **~stück** *nt* = **~exemplar**; **p~voll** *adj* = **prächtig**.
**prädestinieren*** *vt* to predestine.
**Prädikat** *nt (Gram)* predicate; *(Bewertung)* rating; *(Rangbezeichnung)* title. **Wein mit** ~ special quality wine.
**prädikativ** *adj* predicative.
**Prag** *nt* Prague.
**prägen** *vt* **(a)** to stamp; *Münzen* to mint; *Leder, Papier* to emboss; *(erfinden) Begriffe, Wörter* to coin. **(b)** *(fig: formen) Charakter* to form; *(Erlebnis, Kummer) jdn* to leave its/their mark on. **(c)** *(kennzeichnen) Stadtbild* to characterize.
**prägend** *adj Erlebnis etc* formative.
**Prägestempel** *m* die, stamp.
**Pragmatiker(in** *f)* *m* - pragmatist.

**pragmatisch** *adj* pragmatic.
**Pragmatismus** *m* pragmatism.
**prägnant** *adj* concise, terse.
**Prägnanz** *f* conciseness, terseness.
**Prägung** *f* **(a)** *siehe vt (a, b)* stamping; minting; embossing; coining; forming. **(b)** *(auf Münzen)* imprint; *(auf Leder, Papier)* embossing; *(Eigenart)* character; *(von Charakter)* mould *(Brit)*, mold *(US)*.
**prahlen** *vi* to brag *(mit about)*.
**Prahlerei** *f* bragging *no pl*.
**prahlerisch** *adj* boastful, bragging *attr*.
**Prahlhans** *m, pl* **-hänse** *(col)* show-off.
**Praktik** *f* procedure, method; *(usu pl: Kniff)* practice, trick *(col)*.
**praktikabel** *adj* practicable, practical.
**Praktikant(in** *f)* *m* trainee.
**Praktiker(in** *f)* *m* - practical man/woman.
**Praktikum** *nt, pl* **Praktika** practical training.
**praktisch 1** *adj* practical; *(nützlich auch)* handy. **~er Arzt** general practitioner; **~es Beispiel** concrete example. **2** *adv* practically; *(in der Praxis)* in practice.
**praktizieren*** **1** *vi* to practise *(Brit)*, to practice *(US)*. **2** *vt (ausführen)* to put into practice.
**Praline** *f* chocolate, chocolate candy *(US)*.
**prall** *adj* Sack, Brieftasche bulging; *Arme, Schenkel* big strong *attr*; *Sonne* blazing. ~ **gefüllt** filled to bursting.
**prallen** *vi aux sein* **gegen etw** ~ to crash into sth; *(Ball)* to bounce off sth.
**prallvoll** *adj* full to bursting; *Brieftasche* bulging.
**prämenstruell** *adj* premenstrual.
**Prämie** [-iə] *f* premium; *(Belohnung)* bonus; *(Preis)* prize.
**prämien-** [-iən]: **~begünstigt** *adj* with benefit of premiums; **~sparen** *vi sep infin, ptp only* to save in a bonus scheme.
**präm(i)ieren*** *vt (auszeichnen)* to give an award; *(belohnen)* to give a bonus. **etw mit dem ersten Preis** ~ to award sth first prize.
**Präm(i)ierung** *f* **(a)** *(das Prämieren)* **für diesen Film kommt eine** ~ **nicht in Frage** we can't possibly give this film an award. **(b)** *(Veranstaltung)* presentation.
**Pranger** *m* - stocks *pl*, pillory. **jdn/etw an den** ~ **stellen** *(fig)* to pillory sb/sth.
**Pranke** *f* **-n** *(auch col)* paw.
**Präparat** *nt* preparation.
**präparieren*** *vt* **(a)** *(konservieren)* to preserve. **(b)** *(Med: zerlegen)* to dissect.
**Präposition** *f* preposition.
**Prärie** *f* prairie.
**Präsens** *nt, pl* **Präsenzien** [-iən] present (tense).
**präsent** *adj* present. **etw** ~ **haben** to have sth at hand.
**präsentieren*** **1** *vt* to present. **jdm etw** ~ to present sb with sth. **2** *vr* to present oneself.
**Präsenzbibliothek** *f* reference library.
**Präservativ** [prɛzɛrva'tiːf] *nt* contraceptive, condom.
**Präsident(in** *f)* *m* president.
**Präsidentschaft** *f* presidency.
**Präsidentschafts-**: **~kandidat** *m* presidential candidate; **~wahl** *f* presidential election.
**präsidieren*** *vi* to preside.
**Präsidium** *nt (Vorsitz)* presidency; *(Führungsgruppe)* committee; *(Polizei~)* headquarters *pl*.
**prasseln** *vi* **(a)** *aux sein (a) Regen* to drum; *(fig)* to hail down. **(b)** *(Feuer)* to crackle.
**prassen** *vi (schlemmen)* to feast; *(in Luxus leben)* to live the high life.
**Prasserei** *f (Schlemmerei)* feasting; *(Luxusleben)*

high life.
**Präteritum** *nt, pl* **Präterita** preterite.
**präventiv** [prɛvɛn'tiːf] *adj* prevent(at)ive.
**Präventiv-**: ~**medizin** *f* preventive medicine;
~**schlag** *m (Mil)* pre-emptive strike.
**Praxis** *f, pl* **Praxen** (a) *no pl* practice; *(Erfahrung)*
experience. **in der** ~ in practice; **die** ~ **sieht anders
aus** the facts are different; **eine Idee in die** ~ **umsetzen** to put an idea into practice; **ein Beispiel aus
der** ~ an example from real life. (b) *(eines Arztes,
Rechtsanwalts)* practice. (c) *(Behandlungsräume)*
surgery *(Brit)*, doctor's office *(US)*; *(Anwaltsbüro)*
office.
**praxis-**: ~**fern,** ~**fremd** *adj* impractical; ~**nah,**
~**orientiert** *adj* practical.
**Präzedenzfall** *m* precedent.
**präzis(e)** *adj* precise.
**präzisieren\*** *vt* to state more precisely.
**Präzision** *f* precision.
**Präzisions-** *in cpds* precision; ~**arbeit** *f* precision
work; ~**arbeit leisten** to work with precision.
**predigen** *vti* to preach. **jdm etw** ~ *(fig)* to lecture sb
on sth.
**Prediger(in** *f)* *m -* preacher/woman preacher.
**Predigt** *f -en (lit, fig)* sermon. **jdm eine** ~ **über etw**
*(acc)* **halten** *(fig)* to give sb a sermon about sth.
**Preis** *m -e* (a) price *(für of)*. **zum halben** ~ half-
price; **um jeden** ~ *(fig)* at all costs; **um keinen** ~
*(fig)* not at any price. (b) *(bei Wettbewerben)* prize;
*(Auszeichnung)* award. (c) *(Belohnung)* reward. (d)
*no pl (liter: Lob)* praise *(auf +acc of)*.
**Preis-**: ~**absprache** *f* price fixing *no pl*; ~**angabe** *f*
**hier fehlt die** ~**angabe** there's no price given;
~**anstieg** *m* rise in prices; ~**ausschreiben** *nt*
competition; **p~bewußt** *adj* price-conscious;
~**bindung** *f* price fixing; ~**boxer** *m* prize-fighter;
~**brecher** *m (Firma)* undercutter; ~**disziplin** *f*
price restraint.
**Preiselbeere** *f* cranberry.
**preisen** *pret* **pries,** *ptp* **gepriesen** *vt (geh)* to praise.
**sich glücklich** ~ to count oneself lucky.
**Preis-**: ~**entwicklung** *f* price trend; ~**erhöhung** *f*
price increase; ~**frage** *f* (a) question of price; (b)
*(beim* ~**ausschreiben)* prize question *(in a competition)*; ~**gabe** *f (geh) (Aufgabe)* abandoning; *(von
Geheimnis)* betrayal.
**preisgeben** *vt sep irreg (geh)* (a) *(ausliefern)* to
leave to the mercy of. (b) *(aufgeben)* to abandon.
(c) *(verraten)* to betray.
**Preis-**: ~**gefälle** *nt* price gap; **p~gekrönt** *adj*
award-winning; ~**gericht** *nt* jury; **p~günstig** *adj*
inexpensive; **etw p~günstig bekommen** to get sth
at a good price; ~**klasse** *f* price range;
~**kontrolle** *f* price control; ~**krieg** *m* price war;
~**lage** *f* price range.
**preislich** *adj no pred* price attr, in price.
**Preis-**: ~**liste** *f* price list; ~**nachlaß** *m* discount;
**10%** ~**nachlaß bei Barbezahlung** 10% off cash sales;
~**politik** *f* prices policy; ~**rätsel** *nt* prize competition; ~**richter** *m* judge *(in a competiton)*; ~**schild**
*nt* price-tag; ~**schlager** *m* (all-time) bargain;
~**senkung** *f* price cut; **p~stabil** *adj* stable in
price; ~**stopp** *m* price freeze; ~**träger(in** *f)* *m*
prize-winner; *(Kultur~)* award-winner; ~**treiberei** *f*
forcing up of prices; *(Wucher)* profiteering;
~**verfall** *m* drop-off in prices; ~**vergleich** *m* price
comparison; **einen** ~**vergleich machen** to shop
around; ~**verleihung** *f* presentation (of prizes/
awards); **p~wert** *adj* good value *pred*; **ein
p~wertes Kleid** a dress which is good value (for
money).

**prekär** *adj (peinlich)* awkward; *(schwierig)* precarious.
**Prellbock** *m (Rail)* buffers *pl*, buffer-stop; *(fig col)*
scapegoat *(col)*, fallguy *(esp US col)*.
**prellen 1** *vt* (a) to bruise; *(anschlagen)* to hit. (b)
*(fig col: betrügen)* to swindle. **jdn um etw** ~ to swindle sb out of sth; **die Zeche** ~ to avoid paying the
bill. **2** *vr* to bruise oneself.
**Prellung** *f* bruise, contusion.
**Premiere** [prə'miːrə, pre-] *f* -**n** premiere.
**Premierminister** [prə'miː-, pre-] *m* prime minister.
**preschen** *vi aux sein (col)* to tear, to dash.
**Presse** *f* -**n** *(Mech, Zeitungen)* press. **eine gute** ~ haben to get a good press.
**Presse-**: ~**agentur** *f* news agency; ~**amt** *nt* press
office; ~**bericht** *m* press report; **die** ~**berichte** the
press coverage *(über +acc of)*; ~**erklärung** *f* press
release; ~**freiheit** *f* freedom of the press;
~**konferenz** *f* press conference; ~**meldung** *f*
press report; ~**mitteilung** *f* press release.
**pressen** *vt* to press; *Obst auch* to squeeze; *(fig:
zwingen)* to force *(in +acc into)*.
**Presse-**: ~**notiz** *f* paragraph in the press;
~**sprecher** *m* press officer; ~**stelle** *f* press office.
**pressieren\*** *vi (S Ger, Aus, Sw) (Sache)* to be urgent. **mir pressiert's** I am in a hurry.
**Preßluft** *f* compressed air.
**Preßluft-**: ~**bohrer** *m* pneumatic drill; ~**hammer**
*m* pneumatic hammer.
**Prestige** [prɛs'tiːʒə] *nt no pl* prestige.
**Preuße** *m (wk)* -**n, -n, Preußin** *f* Prussian.
**Preußen** *nt* Prussia.
**preußisch** *adj* Prussian.
**prickeln** *vi (kribbeln)* to tingle; *(kitzeln)* to tickle;
*(Bläschen bilden)* to sparkle, to bubble.
**prickelnd** *adj siehe vi* tingling; tickling; sparkling,
bubbling. **der** ~**e Reiz der Neuheit** the thrill of
novelty.
**pries** *pret of* **preisen.**
**Priester** *m -* priest.
**Priesterin** *f* priestess.
**priesterlich** *adj* priestly *no adv*.
**Priester-**: ~**seminar** *nt* seminary; ~**weihe** *f* ordination (to the priesthood).
**prima** *adj inv* (a) *(col)* fantastic *(col)*. **das hast du** ~
gemacht you did that beautifully. (b) *(Comm)* top-
quality.
**Prima** *f, pl* **Primen** *(Sch dated)* eighth and ninth year
of German secondary school.
**Primadonna** *f* -**donnen** prima donna.
**Primaner(in** *f)* *m - (Sch dated)* ≃ sixth-former *(Brit)*.
**primär** *adj* primary.
**Primas** *m* -, -**se** *(Eccl)* primate.
**Primat** *m (wk)* -**en, -en** *(Zool)* primate.
**Primel** *f* -**n** *(Wald~)* (wild) primrose; *(farbige Gar-
ten~)* primula.
**primitiv** *adj* primitive.
**Primzahl** *f* prime (number).
**Prinz** *m (wk)* -**en, -en** prince.
**Prinzessin** *f* princess.
**Prinzip** *nt* -**ien** [-iən] principle. **aus** ~ on principle;
**im** ~ in principle; **das funktioniert nach einem einfa-
chen** ~ it works on a simple principle; **ein Mann
mit** ~**ien** a man of principle.
**prinzipiell** *adj (im Prinzip)* in principle; *(aus Prinzip)*
on principle.
**prinzipienlos** *adj* unprincipled.
**Prior** *m* prior.
**Priorin** *f* prioress.
**Priorität** *f* priority. ~**en** *pl (Comm)* preference

shares *pl*, preferred stock *(US)*; ~ **vor etw** *(dat)* **haben** to take precedence over sth; **~en setzen** to establish one's priorities.

**Prise** *f* **-n** *(kleine Menge)* pinch.

**Prisma** *nt*, *pl* **Prismen** prism.

**Pritsche** *f* **-n** **(a)** *(Liegestatt)* plank bed. **(b)** *(von Lkw)* platform.

**privat** [pri'va:t] *adj* private. ~ **ist er ganz anders** he's quite different socially; **jdn** ~ **sprechen** to speak to sb privately *or* in private; **ich sagte es ihm ganz** ~ I told him in absolute confidence; **etw an P~ verkaufen** to sell sth privately; ~ **versichert sein** to be privately insured.

**Privat-** *in cpds* private; **~adresse** *f* home address; **~angelegenheit** *f* = **~sache**; **~besitz** *m* private property; **in ~besitz sein** to be privately owned; **~dozent** *m* outside lecturer *(not on the staff)*; **~eigentum** *nt* private property; **~fernsehen** *nt* commercial television; **~gespräch** *nt* private conversation; *(am Telefon)* private call.

**privatisieren\*** [privati'zi:rən] *vt* to privatize.

**Privatisierung** *f* privatization.

**Privat-**: **~leben** *nt* private life; **~patient** *m* private patient; **~person** *f* private individual; **~recht** *nt* private *or* civil law; **~sache** *f* private matter; **das ist meine ~sache** that's a private matter; **~schule** *f* private school; **~sekretär(in** *f)* *m* personal assistant, PA; **~unterricht** *m* private tuition; **~vermögen** *nt* private fortune; **~wirtschaft** *f* private industry *or* sector.

**Privileg** [privi'le:k] *nt* **-ien** [-'le:giən] privilege.

**privilegieren\*** [privile'gi:rən] *vt* to favour *(Brit)*, to favor *(US)*. **privilegiert** privileged.

**pro** *prep* per. ~ **Jahr** per annum *(form)*, a year; ~ **Kopf** per capita *(form)*; ~ **Stück** each, apiece.

**Pro** *nt* **(das)** ~ **und Kontra** the pros and cons *pl*.

**pro-** *pref* pro-; **~arabisch** *adj* pro-Arab.

**Probe** *f* **-n** **(a)** *(Prüfung)* test. **die** ~ **(auf eine Rechnung) machen** to check a calculation; **er ist auf** ~ **angestellt** he's employed for a probationary period; **jdn/etw auf** ~ **nehmen** to take sb/sth on trial; **jdn/ etw auf die** ~ **stellen** to put sb/sth to the test; **zur** ~ to try out. **(b)** *(Theat)* rehearsal. **(c)** *(Teststück, Beispiel)* sample.

**Probe-**: **~abzug** *m* proof; **~angebot** *nt* trial offer; **~bohrung** *f* test drill; **~exemplar** *nt* specimen (copy); **p~fahren** *sep irreg infin, ptp only* **1** *vt* to test-drive; **2** *vi aux sein* to go for a test drive; **~fahrt** *f* test drive; **~lauf** *m* trial run; *(Sport)* practice run.

**proben** *vti* to rehearse.

**Probe-**: **~packung** *f* trial pack; **~stück** *nt* specimen; **p~weise** *adv* on a trial basis; **~zeit** *f* trial *or* probationary period.

**probieren\*** **1** *vt* to have a try at; *(kosten) Speisen, Getränke* to sample; *(prüfen)* to test. **laß es mich mal ~**! let me have a go! **2** *vi (versuchen, kosten)* to try. **P~ geht über Studieren** *(Prov)* the proof of the pudding is in the eating *(Prov)*.

**Problem** *nt* **-e** problem. **vor einem** ~ **stehen** to be faced with a problem.

**Problematik** *f* difficulty *(gen* with*)*; *(Problembereich)* problems *pl*.

**problematisch** *adj* problematic; *(fragwürdig)* questionable.

**problemlos** *adj* problem-free. ~ **ablaufen** to go without a hitch.

**Produkt** *nt* **-e** *(lit, fig)* product.

**Produktion** *f* production.

**Produktions-** *in cpds* production; **~ausfall** *m* loss of production; **~kosten** *pl* production costs *pl*;

**~leiter** *m* production manager; **~menge** *f* output; **~mittel** *pl* means of production *pl*; **~rückgang** *m* drop in production.

**produktiv** *adj* productive.

**Produktivität** *f* productivity.

**Produzent(in** *f)* *m* producer.

**produzieren\*** **1** *vt* **(a)** *auch vi* to produce. **(b)** *(col: hervorbringen) Lärm* to make; *Entschuldigung* to come up with *(col)*; *Romane* to churn out *(col)*. **2** *vr (pej)* to show off.

**Prof.** = **Professor** Prof.

**profan** *adj (weltlich)* secular; *(gewöhnlich)* mundane.

**professionell** *adj* professional.

**Professor** *m*, **Professorin** *f* **(a)** *(Hochschul~)* professor. **(b)** *(Aus: Gymnasiallehrer)* grammar school teacher *(Brit)*, high school teacher *(US)*.

**Professur** *f* chair, professorship *(für* in, of*)*.

**Profi** *m* **-s** *(col)* pro *(col)*.

**Profifußballer** *m* professional footballer.

**Profil** *nt* **-e** **(a)** *(von Gesicht)* profile; *(fig: Ansehen)* image. **im** ~ **in** profile; **die Partei hat mehr** ~ **bekommen** the party has sharpened its image. **(b)** *(von Reifen, Schuhsohle)* tread. **(c)** *(Querschnitt)* cross-section; *(Längsschnitt)* vertical section; *(fig: Skizze)* profile.

**profilieren\*** **1** *vt (scharf umreißen)* to define. **2** *vr (sich ein Image geben)* to create a distinctive personal image for oneself. **er will sich akademisch/ politisch** ~ he wants to make his mark academically/in politics.

**profiliert** *adj (scharf umrissen)* clear-cut *no adv*; *(hervorstechend)* distinctive.

**Profilsohle** *f* sole with a tread.

**Profit** *m* **-e** profit. ~ **aus etw ziehen** *(lit)* to make a profit from sth; *(fig)* to reap the benefits from sth; **den/keinen** ~ **von etw haben** to profit/not to profit from sth; **ohne/mit** ~ **arbeiten** to work unprofitably/profitably.

**Profit-**: **p~bringend** *adj* profitable; **~denken** *nt* profit orientation; **~gier** *f* greed for profit.

**profitieren\*** *vti* to profit; *(fig auch)* to gain. **und was profitierst du dabei** *or* **davon?** what do you stand to gain by it?

**Profit-**: **~jäger**, **~macher** *m (col)* profiteer; **~macherei** *f (col)* profiteering; **~streben** *nt* profit-seeking.

**pro forma** *adv* as a matter of form.

**Pro-forma-Rechnung** *f* pro forma invoice.

**Prognose** *f* **-n** prognosis; *(Wetter~)* forecast.

**Programm** *nt* **-e** programme *(Brit)*, program *(US, Comp)*; *(Tagesordnung)* agenda; *(TV: Sender)* channel; *(Sendefolge)* programmes *(Brit) pl*, programs *(US) pl*; *(gedrucktes Radio~, TV~)* programme *(Brit) or* program *(US)* guide; *(Verlags~)* list; *(Kollektion)* range. **nach** ~ as planned; **auf dem** ~ **stehen** to be on the programme/agenda.

**Programm-**: **~fehler** *m (Comp)* bug (in the program); **p~gemäß** *adj* according to plan; **~heft** *nt* programme *(Brit)*, program *(US)*; **~hinweis** *m (Rad, TV)* programme *(Brit) or* program *(US)* announcement.

**programmierbar** *adj* programmable.

**programmieren\*** *vti* to programme *(Brit)*, to program *(US, Comp)*; *(fig auch)* to condition. **auf etw** *(acc)* **programmiert sein** *(fig)* to be geared to sth.

**Programmierer(in** *f)* *m* - programmer.

**Programmiersprache** *f* programming language.

**Programmierung** *f* programming; *(fig auch)* conditioning.

**Programm-**: **~kino** *nt* arts *or* repertory *(US)* cinema; **~vorschau** *f* preview *(für* of*)*; *(Film)* trailer;

~**zeitschrift** f *(Rad, TV)* programme *(Brit)* or program *(US)* guide.
**progressiv** *adj* progressive.
**Projekt** *nt* **-e** project.
**Projektion** f projection.
**Projektleiter** *m* project leader or *(Comm)* manager.
**Projektor** *m* projector.
**projizieren*** *vt* to project.
**proklamieren*** *vt* to proclaim.
**Pro-Kopf-Einkommen** *nt* per capita income.
**Prokura** f, *pl* **Prokuren** *(form)* general commercial power of attorney.
**Prokurist(in** f) *m* holder of a general power of attorney, ≈ company secretary *(Brit)*.
**Prolet** *m (wk)* **-en, -en** *(pej)* prole *(pej)*, pleb *(pej)*.
**Proletariat** *nt* proletariat.
**Proletarier** [-iɐ] *m* - proletarian.
**proletarisch** *adj* proletarian.
**proletenhaft** *adj (pej)* plebeian *(pej)*.
**Prolog** *m* **-e** prologue.
**Promenaden-:** ~**deck** *nt* promenade deck; ~**mischung** f *(hum)* mongrel.
**Promille** *nt* - thousandth (part); *(col: Alkoholspiegel)* alcohol level. **0,8** ~ 80 millilitres *(Brit)* or milliliters *(US)* alcohol level.
**Promille-:** ~**grenze** f legal (alcohol) limit; ~**messer** *m* Breathalyzer ®.
**prominent** *adj* prominent.
**Prominente(r)** *mf decl as adj* VIP.
**Prominenz** f VIP's *pl*.
**Promotion**[1] f *(Univ)* doctorate, PhD. **während seiner** ~ while he was doing his PhD.
**Promotion**[2] [prɔ'mouʃən] f *(Comm)* promotion.
**promovieren*** [promo'viːrən] *vi* to do a PhD; *(Doktorwürde erhalten)* to receive a doctorate.
**prompt 1** *adj* prompt. **2** *adv* promptly; *(wie erwartet)* of course.
**Pronomen** *nt* - pronoun.
**Propaganda** f *no pl* propaganda. ~ **mit etw machen** to make propaganda out of sth.
**Propagandist(in** f) *m* **(a)** propagandist. **(b)** *(Comm)* demonstrator.
**propagieren*** *vt* to propagate.
**Propangas** *nt* propane gas.
**Propeller** *m* - propeller.
**Propeller-:** ~**antrieb** *m* propeller-drive; ~**flugzeug** *nt* propeller-driven aircraft; ~**turbine** f turboprop.
**proper** *adj (col)* neat, tidy.
**Prophet** *m (wk)* **-en, -en** prophet.
**Prophetin** f prophetess.
**prophetisch** *adj* prophetic.
**prophezeien*** *vt* to prophesy.
**Prophezeiung** f prophecy.
**prophylaktisch** *adj* prophylactic *(form)*, preventive.
**Proportion** f proportion.
**proportional** [propɔrtsio'naːl] *adj* proportional.
**Proportional-:** ~**druck** *m* proportional printing; ~**schrift** f proportional spacing.
**proportioniert** [propɔrtsio'niːɐt] *adj* proportioned.
**Proporz** *m* **-e** proportional representation *no art*.
**proppe(n)voll** *adj (col)* jam-packed *(col)*.
**Prosa** f *no pl* prose.
**prosaisch** [pro'zaːɪʃ] *adj* **(a)** *(nüchtern)* prosaic. **(b)** *(Liter)* prose *attr*.
**prosit** *interj* your health. ~ **Neujahr!** happy New Year!
**Prosit** *nt* **-s** toast. **ein** ~ **der Köchin!** here's to the cook!
**Prospekt** [pro'spɛkt] *m* **-e** brochure; *(Werbezettel)*

leaflet; *(Verzeichnis)* catalogue.
**prost** *interj* cheers, cheerio.
**Prostata** f *no pl* prostate gland.
**Prostituierte** [prostitu'iːɐtə] f *(wk)* **-n, -n** prostitute.
**Prostitution** [prostitu'tsioːn] f prostitution.
**Protagonist(in** f) *m (lit, fig)* protagonist.
**protegieren*** [prote'ʒiːrən] *vt Schriftsteller, Projekt* to sponsor; *Land, Regime* to support.
**Protein** *nt* **-e** protein.
**Protektion** [protɛk'tsioːn] f *(Schutz)* protection; *(Begünstigung)* patronage.
**Protektionismus** [protɛktsio'nɪsmʊs] *m (Econ)* protectionism.
**Protektorat** *nt (Schirmherrschaft)* patronage; *(Schutzgebiet)* protectorate.
**Protest** *m* **-e** protest. **(scharfen)** ~ **gegen jdn/etw erheben** to make a (strong) protest against sb/sth; **aus** ~ in protest; **unter** ~ protesting; *(gezwungen)* under protest.
**Protestant(in** f) *m* Protestant.
**protestantisch** *adj* Protestant.
**Protest-:** ~**bewegung** f protest movement; ~**demonstration** f protest (demonstration).
**protestieren*** *vi* to protest.
**Protest-:** ~**kundgebung** f protest (rally); ~**marsch** *m* protest march; ~**schreiben** *nt* letter of protest; ~**stimme** f protest vote; ~**welle** f wave of protest.
**Prothese** f **-n** artificial limb, prosthesis *(Med, form)*; *(Gebiß)* dentures *pl*.
**Protokoll** *nt* **-e (a)** *(Niederschrift)* record; *(von Sitzung)* minutes *pl*; *(bei Polizei)* statement; *(bei Gericht)* transcript. **(das)** ~ **führen** *(bei Sitzung)* to take the minutes; *(bei Gericht)* to make a transcript of the proceedings; **etw zu** ~ **geben** to have sth put on record; *(bei Polizei)* to say sth in one's statement. **(b)** *(diplomatisch, Comp)* protocol. **(c)** *(Strafzettel)* ticket.
**Protokollant(in** f) *m* = **Protokollführer.**
**protokollarisch** *adj* **(a)** *(protokolliert)* on record; *(in Sitzung)* minuted. **(b)** *(zeremoniell)* ~**e Vorschriften** rules of protocol.
**Protokollführer** *m* secretary; *(Jur)* clerk (of the court).
**protokollieren*** **1** *vi (bei Sitzung)* to take the minutes (down); *(bei Polizei)* to take a/the statement down. **2** *vt* to take down; *Sitzung* to minute.
**Proton** *nt, pl* **Protonen** proton.
**Proto-:** ~**plasma** *nt* protoplasm; ~**typ** *m* prototype.
**protzen** *vi (col)* to show off. **mit etw** ~ to show sth off.
**protzig** *adj (col)* swanky *(col)*, showy *(col)*.
**Provence** [prɔ'vãːs] f *no pl* **die** ~ Provence.
**Proviant** [pro'viant] *m* **-e** provisions *pl*, supplies *pl (esp Mil)*; *(Reise~)* food for the journey.
**Provinz** [pro'vɪnts] f **-en** province; *(im Gegensatz zur Stadt)* provinces *pl (auch pej)*, country. **das ist finsterste** ~ *(pej)* it's a cultural backwater.
**provinziell** [provɪn'tsiɛl] *adj* provincial *(auch pej)*.
**Provision** [provi'zioːn] f commission. **auf** ~ on commission.
**provisorisch** [provi'zoːrɪʃ] *adj* temporary. **Straßen mit** ~**em Belag** roads with a temporary surface; **ich habe den Stuhl** ~ **repariert** I've fixed the chair up for the time being.
**Provisorium** *nt* provisional arrangement.
**Provokation** [provoka'tsioːn] f provocation.
**provokativ, provokatorisch** [provoka-] *adj* provocative, provoking.
**provozieren*** [provo'tsiːrən] *vti* to provoke.

**Prozedur** *f* (a) *(Vorgang)* procedure. (b) *(pej)* carry-on *(col)*.

**Prozent** *nt* -e *or (nach Zahlenangaben)* - per cent *no pl.* **fünf** ~ five per cent; **wieviel** ~? what percentage?; **zu zehn** ~ at ten per cent; **zu hohen** ~**en** at a high percentage; **dieser Whisky hat 35** ~ this whisky contains 35 per cent alcohol; ~**e bekommen** *(col)* to get a discount.

**Prozent-:** ~**rechnung** *f* percentage calculation; ~**satz** *m* percentage; *(Zins)* interest rate.

**prozentual** *adj* percentage *attr.* ~**er Anteil** percentage; **etw** ~ **ausdrücken** to express sth as a percentage; ~ **gut abschneiden** to get a good percentage.

**Prozentzeichen** *nt* percentage sign.

**Prozeß** *m* -sse (a) *(Straf~)* trial; *(Rechtsfall)* (court) case. **einen** ~ **gewinnen/verlieren** to win/lose a case; **gegen jdn einen** ~ **anstrengen** to bring an action against sb; **es zum** ~ **kommen lassen** to go to court; **jdm den** ~ **machen** *(col)* to take sb to court; **mit jdm/etw kurzen** ~ **machen** *(fig col)* to make short work of sb/sth *(col)*. (b) *(Vorgang)* process.

**Prozeß-:** **p~führend** *adj* **p~führende Partei** litigant; ~**führung** *f* handling of a/the case.

**prozessieren*** *vi* to go to court. **er prozessiert mit fünf Firmen** he's got cases going on against five firms.

**Prozession** *f* procession.

**Prozeßkosten** *pl* legal costs *pl.*

**Prozessor** *m (Comp)* processor.

**Prozeßordnung** *f* legal procedure.

**Prozeßsprache** *f (Comp)* processing language.

**prüde** *adj* prudish.

**Prüderie** *f* prudishness.

**prüfen** *vt* (a) *(auch vi) (Sch, Univ)* **jdn** to examine. **schriftlich geprüft werden** to take a written examination. (b) *(überprüfen)* to check *(auf +acc for)*; *(untersuchen)* to examine; *(durch Ausprobieren)* to test; *Geschäftsbücher* to audit, to examine; *Lebensmittel, Wein* to inspect, to test; *Beschwerde* to investigate, to look into. (c) *(erwägen)* to consider. **etw nochmals** ~ to review sth. (d) *(mustern)* to scrutinize. **ein** ~**der Blick** a searching look. (e) *(heimsuchen)* to afflict. **ein schwer geprüfter Vater** a sorely tried father.

**Prüfer(in** *f) m* - examiner; *(Wirtschafts~)* auditor.

**Prüfling** *m* examination candidate.

**Prüf-:** ~**stand** *m* test bed; **auf dem** ~**stand sein** to be on test; ~**stein** *m (fig)* touchstone *(für* or of *for)*, measure *(für* of*)*.

**Prüfung** *f siehe vt* (a) exam, examination. **eine** ~ **machen** to take an exam; **durch eine** ~ **fallen** to fail an exam. (b) check; examination; test; audit; inspection; investigation. **nach der** ~ **wird das Auto ...** after being tested the car is ...; **bei nochmaliger** ~ **der Rechnung** on rechecking the account. (c) consideration. (d) *(Heimsuchung)* test, trial.

**Prüfungs-:** ~**angst** *f* exam nerves *pl*; ~**arbeit** *f* dissertation; ~**ausschuß** *m* board of examiners; ~**kandidat** *m* (examination) candidate; ~**ordnung** *f* examination regulations *pl.*

**Prügel** *m* - (a) *(Stock)* club. (b) ~ *pl (col: Schläge)* thrashing; ~ **bekommen** to get a thrashing.

**Prügelei** *f (col)* fight, punch-up *(Brit col)*.

**Prügelknabe** *m (fig)* whipping boy.

**prügeln 1** *vti* to beat. **2** *vr* to fight. **sich mit jdm** ~ to fight sb; **sich um etw** *(acc)* ~ to fight over sth.

**Prügelstrafe** *f* corporal punishment.

**Prunk** *m no pl (Pracht)* splendour *(Brit)*, splendor *(US)*. **großen** ~ **entfalten** to put on a show of great splendour.

**Prunk-:** ~**saal** *m* palatial room; ~**stück** *nt* showpiece; **p~voll** *adj* magnificent.

**prusten** *vi (col)* to snort. **vor Lachen** ~ to snort with laughter.

**PS** [pe:'|ɛs] *nt* = **Pferdestärke** hp.

**P.S., PS** [pe:'|ɛs] *nt* -, - **Postskript(um)** PS.

**Psalm** *m* -en psalm.

**Pseudo-, pseudo-** *in cpds* pseudo.

**Pseudonym** *nt* -e pseudonym.

**Psyche** *f* -n psyche.

**Psychiater(in** *f) m* - psychiatrist.

**Psychiatrie** *f* psychiatry.

**psychiatrisch** *adj* psychiatric.

**psychisch** *adj Belastung etc* emotional, psychological; *Phänomen* psychic. ~**e Erkrankung** mental illness; ~ **gestört** emotionally *or* psychologically disturbed; **er ist** ~ **völlig am Ende** his nerves can't take any more.

**Psycho-** *in cpds* psycho-; ~**analyse** *f* psychoanalysis; ~**analytiker(in** *f) m* psychoanalyst; **p~analytisch** *adj* psychoanalytic(al); ~**krimi** *m* psychological thriller; ~**loge** *m*, ~**login** *f* psychologist; ~**logie** *f* psychology; **p~logisch** *adj* psychological; ~**path(in** *f) m* -en, -en psychopath; ~**terror** *m* psychological intimidation; ~**therapeut(in** *f) m* psychotherapist; **p~therapeutisch** *adj* psychotherapeutic; ~**therapie** *f* psychotherapy.

**PTA** [pe:te:'|a:] = **pharmazeutisch-technische Assistentin, pharmazeutisch-technischer Assistent.**

**pubertär** *adj* of puberty, adolescent.

**Pubertät** *f* puberty.

**Pubertäts-:** ~**alter** *nt* age of puberty; ~**erscheinung** *f* symptom of puberty; ~**zeit** *f* puberty (period).

**Publicity** [pʌ'blɪsɪtɪ] *f no pl* publicity.

**publik** *adj pred* public. ~ **werden** to become public knowledge; **die Sache ist längst** ~ that's long been common knowledge.

**Publikation** *f* publication.

**Publikum** *nt no pl* public; *(Zuschauer, Zuhörer)* audience; *(Sport)* crowd. **das** ~ **in dieser Bar ist sehr gemischt** you get a very mixed group of people using this bar; **sein** ~ **finden** to find a public.

**Publikums-:** ~**erfolg** *m* popular success; ~**liebling** *m* darling of the public; ~**magnet** *m* crowd puller; ~**verkehr** *m* „heute kein ~**verkehr"** "closed today for public business"; **p~wirksam** *adj* **p~wirksam sein** to have public appeal.

**publizieren** *vti* to publish.

**Publizist(in** *f) m* publicist; *(Journalist)* journalist.

**Publizistik** *f* journalism.

**Pudding** *m* -s = blancmange.

**Puddingpulver** *nt* custard powder.

**Pudel** *m* poodle. **das ist des** ~**s Kern** *(fig)* that's what it's really all about.

**Pudel-:** ~**mütze** *f* bobble hat *(col)*; **p~naß** *adj* dripping wet; **p~wohl** *adj (col)* **sich p~wohl fühlen** to feel on top of the world *(col)*.

**Puder** *m or (col) nt* - powder.

**Puderdose** *f* (powder) compact.

**pudern** *vt* to powder.

**Puder-:** ~**quaste** *f* powder puff; ~**zucker** *m* icing sugar.

**Puertoricaner(in** *f)* [puɛrtori'ka:nɐ, -ərɪn] *m* - Puerto Rican.

**puertoricanisch** [puɛrtori'ka:nɪʃ] *adj* Puerto Rican.

**Puerto Rico** [puɛrto'ri:ko] *nt* Puerto Rico.

**Puff¹** *m* ⁼e *(Stoß)* blow; *(in die Seite)* dig.

**Puff²** *m or nt* -s *(col)* brothel, cathouse *(esp US col)*.

**Puff|ärmel** *m* puff(ed) sleeve.

**puffen 1** *vt* **(a)** *(schlagen)* to thump; *(in die Seite)* to prod. **(b)** *Rauch* to puff. **2** *vi (col: puff machen)* to go bang; *(Rauch, Abgase)* to puff.

**Puffer** *m* - **(a)** *(Rail, Comp)* buffer. **(b)** *(Cook)* potato fritter.

**Puffer-:** ~**speicher** *m (Comp)* buffer (memory); ~**staat** *m* buffer state; ~**zone** *f* buffer zone.

**Puffreis** *m* puffed rice.

**puh** *interj (Abscheu)* ugh; *(Erleichterung)* phew.

**Pulk** *m* -s **(a)** *(Mil)* group. **(b)** *(Menge) (von Menschen)* throng; *(von Dingen)* pile.

**Pulle** *f* -n *(col)* bottle. **volle** ~ **fahren** *(col)* to drive flat out *(col)*.

**Pulli** *m* -s *(col)*, **Pullover** [pʊˈloːvɐ] *m* - jumper *(Brit)*, sweater.

**Pullunder** *m* - slipover.

**Puls** *m* -e *(lit, fig)* pulse. **sein** ~ **geht regelmäßig** his pulse is regular; **jdm den** ~ **fühlen** to feel *or* take sb's pulse.

**Puls|ader** *f* artery. **sich** *(dat)* **die** ~**(n) aufschneiden** to slash one's wrists.

**pulsieren\*** *vi (lit, fig)* to pulsate, to throb.

**Puls-:** ~**schlag** *m* pulse-beat; *(fig)* pulse; **den** ~**schlag der Zeit spüren** to feel life pulsing around one; ~**wärmer** *m* - wrist warmer.

**Pult** *nt* -e desk.

**Pulver** [ˈpʊlfɐ, -lvɐ] *nt* - powder. **er hat das** ~ **nicht erfunden** *(fig)* he'll never set the Thames *(Brit)* or the world on fire *(prov)*; **sein** ~ **verschossen haben** *(fig)* to have shot one's bolt.

**Pulverfaß** *nt (fig)* powder keg; **(wie) auf einem** ~ **sitzen** *(fig)* to be sitting on a volcano.

**pulv(e)rig** [ˈpʊlv(ə)rɪç] *adj* powdery *no adv*.

**pulverisieren \*** [pʊlveriˈziːrən] *vt* to pulverize.

**Pulver-:** ~**kaffee** *m (col)* instant coffee; ~**schnee** *m* powder snow.

**Puma** *m* -s puma.

**Pummelchen** *nt (col)* roly-poly *(col)*.

**pumm(e)lig** *adj (col)* chubby, plump.

**Pump** *m no pl (col)* **auf** ~ **kaufen/leben** to buy/live on tick *(Brit col)* or credit.

**Pumpe** *f* -n **(a)** pump. **(b)** *(col) (Herz)* ticker *(col)*.

**pumpen** *vti* **(a)** to pump. **(b)** *(col) (entleihen)* to borrow; *(verleihen)* to loan.

**Pumpernickel** *m* - pumpernickel.

**Pumphose** *f* knickerbockers *pl*.

**Pumps** [pœmps] *m* -, - court shoe.

**puncto** *prep +gen*: **in** ~ **X** where X is concerned.

**Punk** [paŋk] *m* -s, *no pl* punk.

**Punker(in** *f*) [ˈpaŋkɐ, -ərɪn] *m* - punk.

**Punkt** *m* -e **(a)** *(Tupfen)* spot, dot. **(b)** *(Satzzeichen)* full stop, period *(esp US)*; *(Typ)* point; *(auf dem i, Mus, Auslassungszeichen, von* ~**linie, Comp)* dot. **nun mach aber mal einen** ~**!** *(col)* that's enough of that!; **ohne** ~ **und Komma reden** *(col)* to talk nineteen to the dozen *(col)*. **(c)** *(Stelle)* point. ~ **12 Uhr** at 12 o'clock on the dot; **wir sind auf** *or* **an dem** ~ **angelangt, wo ...** we have reached the point where ... **(d)** *(Bewertungseinheit)* point, mark; *(bei Prüfung)* mark. **nach** ~**en führen/siegen** to lead/win on points. **(e)** *(bei Diskussion etc)* point. **in diesem** ~ on this point; **etw auf den** ~ **bringen** to get to the heart of sth.

**Punkt-:** **p**~**gleich** *adj (Sport)* level; ~**gleichheit** *f (Sport)* level score; **bei** ~**gleichheit** if the scores are level.

**punktieren\*** *vt* **(a)** *(Med)* to aspirate. **(b)** *(mit Punkten)* to dot. **punktierte Linie** dotted line.

**pünktlich 1** *adj* punctual. **2** *adv* on time. **er kam** ~ **um 3 Uhr** he came at 3 o'clock sharp; ~ **dasein** to be there on time.

**Pünktlichkeit** *f* punctuality.

**Punkt-:** ~**richter** *m* judge; ~**sieg** *m* points win; ~**sieger** *m* winner on points.

**punktuell** *adj* dealing with certain points. ~**e Verkehrskontrollen** spot checks on traffic.

**Punkt-:** ~**wertung** *f* points system; **in der** ~**wertung liegt er vorne** he's leading on points; ~**zahl** *f* score.

**Punsch** *m* -e (hot) punch.

**Pupille** *f* -n pupil.

**Puppe** *f* -n **(a)** *(Kinderspielzeug)* doll; *(Marionette)* puppet; *(Schaufenster*~*, Mil: Übungs*~*)* dummy; *(col: Mädchen)* doll *(col)*, bird *(esp Brit col)*. **die** ~**n tanzen lassen** *(col)* to live it up *(col)*; **bis in die** ~**n schlafen** *(col)* to sleep to all hours. **(b)** *(Zool)* pupa.

**Puppen-** *in cpds* doll's; **p**~**haft** *adj* doll-like; ~**haus** *nt* doll's house, dollhouse *(US)*; ~**spiel** *nt* puppet show; ~**spieler** *m* puppeteer; ~**stube** *f* doll's house, dollhouse *(US)*; ~**theater** *nt* puppet theatre *(Brit)* or theater *(US)*; ~**wagen** *m* doll's pram *(Brit)*, baby carriage *(US)*.

**Pups** *m* -e, **Pupser** *m* - *(col: Furz)* rude noise/smell.

**pupsen** *vi (col)* to make a rude noise/smell.

**pur** *adj (rein)* pure; *(unverdünnt)* neat; *(völlig)* sheer. ~**er Unsinn** absolute nonsense; ~**er Zufall** sheer coincidence; **Whisky** ~ neat whisky.

**Püree** *nt* -s puree; *(Kartoffel*~*)* creamed potatoes *pl*.

**pürieren\*** *vt* to puree.

**Purist(in** *f*) *m* purist.

**puritanisch** *adj (Hist)* Puritan; *(pej)* puritanical.

**Purpur** *m no pl* purple; *(sattrot)* (deep) crimson.

**Purpur-:** **p**~**farben** *adj* purple; *(sattrot)* (deep) crimson; ~**mantel** *m* purple robe; **p**~**rot** *adj* (deep) crimson.

**Purzelbaum** *m* somersault. **einen** ~ **machen** or **schlagen** to turn a somersault.

**purzeln** *vi aux sein* to tumble.

**Puste** *f no pl (col)* puff *(col)*, breath. **außer** ~ **sein** to be out of puff *(col)*, to be puffed (out) *(col)*.

**Pusteblume** *f (col)* dandelion.

**Pustekuchen** *interj (col)* fiddlesticks *(col)*.

**Pustel** *f* -n *(Pickel)* pimple; *(Med)* pustule.

**pusten** *(col)* **1** *vi (blasen)* to puff; *(keuchen)* to puff (and pant). **2** *vt (blasen)* to puff, to blow.

**Pute** *f* -n turkey (hen). **dumme** ~ *(col)* silly goose *(col)*.

**Puter** *m* - turkey (cock).

**puterrot** *adj* scarlet.

**Putsch** *m* -e coup (d'état), revolt.

**putschen** *vi* to rebel, to revolt.

**Putschist(in** *f*) *m* rebel.

**Putschversuch** *m* attempted coup (d'état).

**Pütt** *m* -s *(dial)* pit, mine.

**Putte** *f* -n *(Art)* cherub.

**Putz** *m no pl* **(a)** *(Build)* plaster; *(Rauh*~*)* roughcast. **eine Mauer mit** ~ **verkleiden** to roughcast a wall; **unter** ~ under the plaster. **(b)** **auf den** ~ **hauen** *(col)* *(angeben)* to show off; *(ausgelassen feiern)* to have a rave-up *(col)*; *(meckern)* to kick up a fuss *(col)*. **(c)** *(dated: Kleidung)* finery. **in vollem** ~ **erscheinen** to arrive dressed up in one's Sunday best.

**putzen 1** *vt* to clean; *(scheuern auch)* to scrub; *(polieren auch)* to polish; *(wischen auch)* to wipe. **die Schuhe** ~ to clean *or* polish one's shoes; **Fenster** ~ to clean the windows; **sich** *(dat)* **die Nase** ~ to wipe one's nose; *(sich schneuzen)* to blow one's nose; **sich** *(dat)* **die Zähne** ~ to brush one's teeth; **einem Baby den Hintern/die Nase** ~ to wipe a baby's bottom/nose. **2** *vr* **(a)** *(sich säubern)* to wash oneself. **(b)** *(dated: sich schmücken)* to dress oneself up.

**Putz-:** ~**fimmel** m (pej) = ~**wut**; ~**frau** f cleaning lady, charwoman (Brit).

**putzig** adj (col) (komisch) comical; (niedlich) cute.

**Putz-:** ~**kolonne** f team of cleaners; ~**lappen** m cloth; (Staubtuch) duster; ~**mann** m cleaning man; ~**mittel** nt (zum Scheuern) cleaner, cleaning agent; (zum Polieren) polish; ~**mittel** pl cleaning things pl; **p~munter** adj (col) full of beans (col); ~**teufel** m (col: Frau) maniac for housework; ~**tuch** nt (Staubtuch) duster; (Wischlappen) cloth; ~**wut** f obsession with cleaning; ~**zeug** nt cleaning things pl.

**Puzzle(spiel)** ['pazl-] nt -**s** jigsaw (puzzle).

**PVC** [peːfauˈtseː] nt -**(s)** PVC.

**Pygmäe** [pyˈgmɛːə] m (wk) -**n**, -**n** pygmy.

**Pyjama** [pyˈdʒaːma] m -**s** pyjamas pl (Brit), pajamas pl (US). **im** ~ in his pyjamas.

**Pyjamahose** f pyjama (Brit) or pajama (US) trousers pl.

**Pyramide** f -**n** pyramid.

**Pyrenäen** [pyreˈnɛːən] pl **die** ~ the Pyrenees pl.

**pyrenäisch** [pyreˈnɛːɪʃ] adj Pyrenean.

**Pyro-:** ~**mane** m (wk) -**n**, -**n**, ~**manin** f pyromaniac; ~**manie** f pyromania; ~**technik** f pyrotechnics sing; **p~technisch** adj pyrotechnic.

**Python(schlange** f) ['pyːtɔn-] m -**s** python.

# Q

**Q, q** [ku:] *nt* -, - Q, q. **Q wie Quelle** ≃ Q for Queen.
**qcm** = **Quadratzentimeter.**
**qkm** = **Quadratkilometer.**
**qm** = **Quadratmeter.**
**quabbelig** *adj (N Ger col)* jelly-like; *Pudding* wobbly.
**Quacksalber** *m* - *(pej)* quack (doctor).
**Quacksalberei** *f* quack medicine.
**Quaddel** *f* -n hives *pl*, rash; *(durch Insekten)* bite.
**Quader** *m (Math)* rectangular solid; *(Archit)* ashlar, stone block.
**Quadrat** *nt (Fläche, Potenz)* square. **vier zum** ~ four squared; **drei Meter im** ~ three metres square.
**Quadrat-** *in cpds* square.
**quadratisch** *adj Form* square; *(Math) Gleichung* quadratic.
**Quadrat-:** ~**latschen** *pl (hum) (Schuhe)* clodhoppers *(col)*; *(Füße)* huge feet; ~**meter** *m or nt* square metre *(Brit) or* meter *(US).*
**Quadratur** *f* quadrature. **das käme der** ~ **des Kreises gleich** *(geh)* that's like trying to square the circle.
**Quadrat-:** ~**wurzel** *f* square root; ~**zahl** *f* square number.
**quadrieren\*** *vt Zahl* to square.
**Quadro** *nt no pl* = **Quadrophonie.**
**quadrophon** *adj* quadraphonic.
**Quadrophonie** *f* quadraphonic sound, quadrophony.
**quak** *interj (von Frosch)* croak; *(von Ente)* quack.
**quaken** *vi (Frosch)* to croak; *(Ente)* to quack; *(col: Mensch)* to squawk *(col).*
**quäken** *vti (col)* to screech, to squawk.
**Quäker(in** *f)* *m* - Quaker.
**Qual** *f* -en *(Schmerz) (körperlich)* pain, agony; *(seelisch)* anguish. **jds** ~**en lindern** to lessen sb's suffering; **unter großen** ~**en sterben** to die in agony; **sein Leben war eine einzige** ~ he lived a life of constant suffering; **es ist eine** ~, **das mit ansehen zu müssen** it is agonizing to watch; **jeder Schritt wurde ihm zur** ~ every step was agony for him; **er machte ihr das Leben zur** ~ he made her life a misery; **die** ~**en, die sie um ihn ausgestanden hat** the suffering she has gone through because of him.
**quälen 1** *vt* to torment; *Tiere auch* to tease; *(mit Bitten etc)* to pester. **jdn zu Tode** ~ to torture sb to death; ~**de Ungewißheit** agonizing uncertainty; ~**der Durst** excruciating thirst; *siehe* **gequält. 2** *vr* **(a)** *(seelisch)* to torment oneself; *(leiden)* to be in agony. **(b)** *(sich abmühen)* to struggle. **er mußte sich** ~, **damit er das schaffte** it was a struggle for him to do it; **sich durch ein Buch** ~ to struggle through a book.
**Quälerei** *f* **(a)** *(Grausamkeit)* torture; *(seelische, nervliche Belastung)* torment. **das ist doch eine** ~ **für das Tier** that is cruel to the animal. **(b)** *(mühsame Arbeit)* struggle.
**Quälgeist** *m (col)* pest *(col).*

**Qualifikation** *f* qualification. **er hat die** ~ **zu diesem Amt** he has the qualifications for this office; **zur** ~ **fehlten ihr nur wenige Sekunden** she was only a few seconds outside the qualifying time.
**Qualifikationsspiel** *nt* qualifying game.
**qualifizieren\*** *vtr* to qualify *(für, zu* for).
**qualifiziert** *adj* **(a)** *Arbeiter, Nachwuchs* qualified; *Arbeit* professional. **(b)** *(Pol) Mehrheit* requisite.
**Qualität** *f* quality. **von ausgezeichneter** ~ (of) top quality.
**qualitativ** *adj* qualitative.
**Qualitäts-** *in cpds* quality; ~**arbeit** *f* quality work; ~**kontrolle** *f* quality check *or* control; ~**ware** *f* quality goods *pl*; ~**wein** *m wine of certified origin and quality.*
**Qualle** *f* -n jellyfish.
**Qualm** *m no pl* dense smoke; *(Tabaks~)* fug.
**qualmen 1** *vi* **(a)** to smoke. **es qualmt aus dem Schornstein** clouds of smoke are coming from the chimney. **(b)** *(col: Mensch)* to smoke. **sie qualmt einem die ganze Bude voll** she fills the whole place with smoke. **2** *vt (col) Zigarette, Pfeife* to puff away at *(col).*
**qualmig** *adj* smoky.
**qualvoll** *adj* painful; *Schmerzen* excruciating; *Gedanke* agonizing; *Anblick* harrowing.
**Quant** *nt* -en quantum.
**Quanten** *pl* **(a)** *pl of* **Quant, Quantum. (b)** *(col: Füße)* feet.
**Quanten-:** ~**physik** *f* quantum physics *sing*; ~**sprung** *m* quantum leap; ~**theorie** *f* quantum theory.
**quantifizieren\*** *vt* to quantify.
**Quantität** *f* quantity.
**quantitativ** *adj* quantitative.
**Quantum** *nt, pl* **Quanten** *(Menge)* quantity; *(Anteil)* quota *(an +dat* of).
**Quarantäne** *f* -n quarantine. **unter** ~ **stellen** to put in quarantine; **über das Gebiet wurde** ~ **verhängt** the area was placed under quarantine.
**Quarantänestation** *f* isolation ward.
**Quark** *m no pl* **(a)** quark, *soft curd cheese.* **(b)** *(col: Unsinn)* rubbish. **so ein** ~! stuff and nonsense!; **das geht ihn einen** ~ **an!** it's none of his business!
**Quark-:** ~**kuchen** *m* cheesecake; ~**tasche** *f*, ~**teilchen** *nt curd cheese turnover.*
**Quart¹** *f* -en **(a)** *(Mus: auch* ~**e)** fourth. **(b)** *(Fechten)* quarte.
**Quart²** *nt no pl (Typ)* quarto *(format).*
**Quarta** *f, pl* **Quarten** *(Sch dated) third year of German secondary school.*
**Quartal** *nt* -e quarter (year). **Kündigung zum** ~ quarterly notice date.
**Quartal(s)-:** ~**abschluß** *m* end of the quarter; ~**säufer** *m (col)* heavy drinker; **q**~**weise** *adj* quarterly.
**Quartaner(in** *f)* *m* - *(Sch dated) pupil in third year of German secondary school.*

**Quarte** f -n *(Mus)* fourth.
**Quartett** nt -e **(a)** *(Mus)* quartet. **(b)** *(Cards) (Spiel)* ≈ happy familes; *(Karten)* set of four cards.
**Quartier** nt -e **(a)** *(Unterkunft)* accommodation *(Brit)*, accommodations *(US)*. **wir sollten uns ein ~ suchen** we should look for a place to stay; **wir hatten unser ~ in einem alten Bauernhof** we stayed in an old farmhouse. **(b)** *(Mil)* quarters *pl*, billet.
**Quarz** m -e quartz.
**Quarz-**: **~lampe** f quartz lamp; **~uhr** f quartz clock/watch.
**Quasar** m -e quasar.
**quasi 1** *adv* virtually. **2** *pref* quasi.
**Quasselei** f *(col)* gabbling *(col)*, blethering *(col)*.
**quasseln** *vti* to gabble *(col)*, to blether *(col)*.
**Quasselstrippe** f *(col)* chatterbox *(col)*.
**Quaste** f -n *(Troddel)* tassle; *(von Pinsel)* bristles *pl*; *(Schwanz~)* tuft.
**Quästur** f *(Univ)* bursar's office.
**Quatsch** m no *pl (col)* **(a)** *(Unsinn)* rubbish. **das ist der größte ~, den ich je gehört habe** that is the biggest load of rubbish I have ever heard; **ach ~!** rubbish!; **so ein ~!** what rubbish. **(b)** *(Dummheiten)* nonsense. **hört doch endlich mit dem ~ auf!** stop being so stupid!; **laß den ~** cut it out! *(col)*; **~ machen** to mess about *(col)*; **mach keinen ~, sonst ...** don't try anything funny or ...
**quatschen** *(col)* **1** *vti (dummes Zeug reden)* to gab (away) *(col)*. **2** *vi* **(a)** *(plaudern)* to chatter, to natter *(Brit col)*. **ich hab' mit ihm am Telefon gequatscht** I had a good natter with him on the phone. **(b)** *(etw ausplaudern)* to squeal *(col)*, to talk.
**Quatscherei** f *(col)* blathering *(col)*, yacking *(col)*.
**Quatschkopf** m *(pej col) (Schwätzer)* windbag *(col)*; *(Dummkopf)* fool, twit *(Brit col)*.
**Quebec** [kwɪˈbɛk] nt Quebec.
**Quecksilber** nt mercury.
**Quecksilber-** *in cpds* mercury; **q~haltig** *adj* mercurial.
**Quell** m -e *(poet)* spring, source.
**Quelle** f -n **(a)** spring; *(von Fluß auch)* source; *(Erdöl~, Gas~)* well. **(b)** *(fig, für Waren)* source. **die ~ allen Übels** the root of all evil; **eine ~ der Freude** a source of pleasure; **aus zuverlässiger ~** from a reliable source; **an der ~ sitzen** *(fig)* to be close to the source (of supply/information), to be well-placed.
**quellen** *vi pret* **quoll**, *ptp* **gequollen** *aux sein* **(a)** *(herausfließen)* to pour, to stream. **(b)** *(Reis, Erbsen)* to swell. **lassen Sie die Bohnen über Nacht ~** leave the beans to soak overnight.
**Quellen-**: **~angabe** f reference; **~forschung** f source research; **~steuer** f tax at source.
**Quell-**: **~fluß** m source (river); **~programm** nt *(Comp)* source program; **~sprache** f source language; **~wasser** nt spring water.
**Quengelei** f *(col)* whining.
**queng(e)lig** *adj* whining. **die Kinder wurden ~** the children started to whine *or* grizzle *(Brit col)*.
**quengeln** *vi (col)* to whine, to grizzle *(Brit col)*.
**quer** *adv (schräg)* crosswise; *(rechtwinklig)* at right angles. **er legte sich ~ aufs Bett** he lay down across the bed; **die Loipe verläuft ~ zum Hang** the ski run runs across the slope; **die Straße/Linie verläuft ~** the road/line runs at right angles; **der Wagen stand ~ zur Fahrbahn** the car was standing sideways across the road; **~ durch etw gehen/laufen** *etc* to go through sth; **~ über etw** *(acc)* **gehen/laufen** to go across sth.
**Quer-**: **~balken** m crossbeam; *(von Türrahmen)* lintel; *(Sport)* crossbar; **q~beet** *adv (col) (wahllos)* at

random; *(~feldein)* across country; **~denker** m maverick.
**Quere** f no *pl* **jdm in die ~ kommen** to cross sb's path; **der Lastwagen kam mir in die ~** the lorry got in my way.
**Querele** f -n *usu pl (geh)* dispute, quarrel.
**querfeld|ein** *adv* across country.
**Querfeld|einrennen** nt cross-country; *(Aut)* autocross; *(mit Motorrädern)* motocross; *(Radrennen)* cyclecross.
**Quer-**: **~flöte** f (transverse) flute; **~format** nt landscape *or* oblong format; **q~gestreift** *adj attr* horizontally striped; **~kopf** m *(col)* awkward customer *(col)*; **q~köpfig** *adj* perverse; **~latte** f crossbar; **q~legen** *vr sep (fig col)* to be awkward; **~paß** m cross; **~schiff** nt transept; **~schläger** m ricochet.
**Querschnitt** m *(lit, fig)* cross-section.
**querschnittsgelähmt** *adj* paraplegic. **seit dem Autounfall ist er ~** since the car accident he has been paralyzed from the waist down.
**Querschnittslähmung** f paraplegia.
**Quer-**: **q~stellen** *vr sep (fig col)* to be awkward; **~straße** f **die ~straßen zur Königstraße** the streets crossing (the) Königstraße; **das ist eine ~straße zur Hauptstraße** this street runs at right angles to the high street; **bei** *or* **an der zweiten ~straße fahren Sie links ab** turn left at the second junction *(Brit) or* crossroads; **~streifen** m horizontal stripe; **~strich** m (horizontal) stroke *or* line; **~summe** f *(Math)* sum of digits of a number; **~treiber** m *(col)* troublemaker.
**Querulant(in** f) m grumbler.
**Quer-**: **~verbindung** f connection, link; **~verweis** m cross-reference.
**quetschen 1** *vt (drücken)* to squash, to crush; *(aus einer Tube)* to squeeze. **etw in etw** *(acc)* **~ to** squeeze sth into sth; **sich den Finger ~** to squash one's finger. **2** *vr (sich klemmen)* to be caught; *(sich zwängen)* to squeeze (oneself).
**Quetschkommode** f *(hum col)* squeeze box *(col)*.
**Quetschung, Quetschwunde** f *(Med)* bruise, contusion *(form)*.
**Queue** [køˈ] nt -s *(Billard)* cue.
**Quiche** [kiʃ] f -s quiche.
**quicklebendig** *adj (col)* Kind lively, active; *ältere Person auch* spry.
**quiek(s)en** *vi* to squeal, to squeak.
**quietschen** *vi (Tür, Schloß)* to squeak; *(Reifen, Mensch)* to squeal.
**quietschfidel, quietschvergnügt** *adj (col)* happy as a sandboy *(col)*.
**Quint** f -, -en **(a)** *(Mus)* fifth. **(b)** *(Fechten)* quinte.
**Quinta** f, *pl* **Quinten** *(Sch dated)* second year of German secondary school.
**Quintaner(in** f) m - *(Sch dated)* pupil in second year of German secondary school.
**Quinte** f -n *(Mus)* fifth.
**Quint|essenz** f *(geh)* quintessence.
**Quintett** nt -e quintet.
**Quirl** m -e **(a)** *(Cook)* whisk, beater. **(b)** *(col: Mensch)* live wire *(col)*.
**quirlen** *vt* to whisk, to beat.
**quirlig** *adj* lively.
**quitt** *adj* **~ sein (mit jdm)** to be quits (with sb); **jdn/etw ~ sein** to be rid of sb/sth.
**Quitte** f -n quince.
**quittieren\* 1** *vt* **(a)** *(bestätigen)* Betrag, Empfang to give a receipt for. **lassen Sie sich** *(dat)* **die Rechnung ~** get a receipt for the bill. **(b)** *(beantworten)* to meet. **(c)** *(verlassen)* Dienst to quit, to resign. **2** *vi*

*(bestätigen)* to sign.

**Quittung** *f* **(a)** receipt. **gegen** ~ on production of a receipt; **eine** ~ **über 500 Mark** a receipt for 500 marks. **(b)** *(fig)* **das ist die** ~ **für Ihre Unverschämtheit** that is what you get for being so insolent; **er hat seine** ~ **bekommen** he's paid the penalty *or* price.

**Quiz** [kvɪz] *nt* -, - quiz.

**Quizmaster** ['kvɪsmaːstɐ] *m* - quizmaster, question master.

**quoll** *pret of* **quellen.**

**Quorum** *nt no pl* quorum.

**Quote** *f* -n **(a)** *(Statistik) (Anteilsziffer)* proportion; *(Rate)* rate. **(b)** *(Econ, Quantum)* quota.

**Quoten-:** ~**frau** *f* token woman; ~**regelung** *f* quota system *(ensuring that women are adequately represented)*.

**Quotient** [kvoˈtsiɛnt] *m* quotient.

**Quotierung** *f (Comm)* quotation.

**Qwerty-Tastatur** ['kwɛrtɪ-] *f* Qwerty keyboard.

# R

**R, r** [ɛr] *nt* -, - R, r. **das R rollen** to roll one's r's; **R wie Richard** ≃ R for Robert, R for Roger *(US)*.
**r** = **rechts** r.
**Rabatt** *m* -e discount. **mit 10%** ~ at (a) 10% discount.
**Rabatte** *f (Beet)* (flower) border.
**Rabattmarke** *f (Comm)* (trading) stamp.
**Rabatz** *m no pl (col)* row, din.
**Rabauke** *m (wk)* -n, -n *(col)* hooligan, lout *(col)*.
**Rabbi** *m* -s, **Rabbiner** *m* - rabbi.
**Rabe** *m (wk)* -n, -n raven. **wie ein** ~/**die** ~**n stehlen** *(col)* to nick everything in sight *(col)*.
**Raben-:** ~**eltern** *pl (col)* neglectful parents *pl*; ~**mutter** *f (col)* neglectful mother; **r**~**schwarz** *adj* pitch-black; *Haare* jet-black; ~**vater** *m (col)* neglectful father.
**rabiat** *adj Kerl, Autofahrer, Umgangston* aggressive; *Geschäftsleute, Methoden* ruthless.
**Rache** *f no pl* revenge, vengeance. **das ist die** ~ **für deine Untat** this is the retribution for your misdeed *(liter)*; **(an jdm)** ~ **nehmen** *or* **üben** to take revenge (on sb); **etw aus** ~ **tun** to do sth in revenge; ~ **ist süß** *(prov)* revenge is sweet *(prov)*.
**Rache-:** ~**akt** *m* act of revenge *or* vengeance; **r**~**durstig** *adj* thirsting for revenge; ~**engel** *m* avenging angel.
**Rachen** *m* - throat, pharynx *(spec)*; *(von großen Tieren, fig)* jaws *pl*. **jdm etw in den** ~ **werfen** *(col)* to shove sth down sb's throat *(col)*.
**rächen 1** *vt jdn, Untat* to avenge *(etw an jdm* sth on sb*)*. **2** *vr (Mensch)* to get one's revenge *(an jdm für etw* on sb for sth*)*; *(Sünde)* to be avenged. **deine Faulheit wird sich** ~ you'll pay for being so lazy.
**Rächer(in** *f)* *m* - avenger.
**Rachitis** *f no pl* rickets.
**rachitisch** *adj* rickety.
**Rach-:** ~**sucht** *f* vindictiveness; **r**~**süchtig** *adj* vindictive.
**Racker** *m* - *(col: Kind)* rascal *(col)*, monkey *(col)*.
**rackern** *vir (col)* to slave (away) *(col)*.
**Rad** *nt* ⁼er (a) wheel; *(Rolle)* castor; *(Zahn*~*)* gearwheel. **ein** ~ **schlagen** *(Sport)* to do a cartwheel; **der Pfau schlägt ein** ~ the peacock is fanning out its tail; **nur ein** ~ *or* **Rädchen im Getriebe sein** *(fig)* to be only a cog in the machine; **unter die** ⁼**er kommen** *(col)* to fall into bad ways; **das fünfte** ~ **am Wagen sein** *(col)* to be de trop *or* in the way; **ein** ~ **abhaben** *(col)* to have a screw loose. **(b)** *(Fahr*~*)* bicycle, bike *(col)*. **mit dem** ~ **fahren** to go by bicycle.
**Radar** *m or nt or no pl* radar.
**Radar-:** ~**anlage** *f* radar (equipment) *no indef art*; ~**falle** *f* speed trap; ~**kontrolle** *f* radar speed check; ~**schirm** *m* radar screen.
**Radau** *m no pl (col)* din, racket *(col)*. ~ **machen** to kick up a row; *(Unruhe stiften)* to cause trouble.
**Rad|aufhängung** *f (Aut)* (wheel) suspension.
**Rädchen** *nt dim of* **Rad** small wheel; *siehe* **Rad**.
**Raddampfer** *m* paddle steamer.

**radebrechen** *vti insep* to speak broken English/ German *etc*.
**radeln** *vi aux sein (col)* to cycle.
**Rädelsführer** *m* ringleader.
**rädern** *vt (Hist)* to break on the wheel; *siehe* **gerädert**.
**Räderwerk** *nt (Zahnräder)* gears *pl*; *(einer Uhr etc)* works *pl*; *(fig)* machinery.
**radfahren** *vi sep irreg aux sein* **(a)** to cycle. **ich fahre Rad** I ride a bicycle; **kannst du** ~? can you ride a bike? **(b)** *(pej col: kriechen)* to crawl *(col)*.
**Radfahrer** *m* **(a)** cyclist. **(b)** *(pej col)* crawler *(col)*.
**Radfahrweg** *m* cycle track, cycleway.
**Radgabel** *f* fork.
**Radi** *m* - *(S Ger, Aus)* radish.
**radial** *adj* radial.
**Radiator** *m* radiator.
**radieren*** *vti* **(a)** to rub out. **(b)** *(Art)* to etch.
**Radiergummi** *m* rubber *(Brit)*, eraser *(esp US)*.
**Radierung** *f (Art)* etching.
**Radieschen** [ra'diːsçən] *nt* radish. **sich** *(dat)* **die** ~ **von unten ansehen** *(hum col)* to be pushing up the daisies *(col)*.
**radikal** *adj* radical; *Entfernen* total; *Ablehnung* flat. ~ **gegen etw vorgehen** to take radical steps against sth.
**Radikale(r)** *mf decl as adj* radical.
**radikalisieren*** *vt* to make more radical.
**Radikalisierung** *f* radicalization.
**Radikalismus** *m (Pol)* radicalism.
**Radikalkur** *f (col)* drastic remedy.
**Radio** *nt* -s radio, wireless *(esp Brit)*. ~ **hören** to listen to the radio; **im** ~ on the radio.
**Radio-** *in cpds* radio; **r**~**aktiv** *adj* radioactive; **r**~**aktiver Niederschlag** (radioactive) fallout; ~**aktivität** *f* radioactivity; ~**apparat** *m* radio (set); ~**durchsage** *f* radio announcement; ~**gerät** *nt* radio (set); ~**loge** *m*, ~**login** *f (Med)* radiologist; ~**logie** *f (Med)* radiology; ~**recorder** *m* radio-cassette recorder; ~**sender** *m (Rundfunkanstalt)* radio station; *(Sendeeinrichtung)* radio transmitter; ~**sendung** *f* radio programme *(Brit)* or program *(US)*; ~**station** *f* radio station; ~**teleskop** *nt* radio telescope; ~**wecker** *m* radio alarm (clock).
**Radium** *nt no pl* radium.
**Radius** *m, pl* **Radien** [-iən] radius.
**Rad-:** ~**kappe** *f* hub cap; ~**lager** *nt* wheel bearing.
**Radler** *m* **(a)** cyclist; **(b)** *(S Ger: Bier mit Limonade)* shandy.
**Radlerhose** *f* cycling shorts *sing*.
**Radlerin** *f* cyclist.
**Rad-:** ~**mantel** *m (Bereifung)* bicycle tyre *(Brit)* or tire *(US)*; ~**nabe** *f* (wheel) hub.
**Radon** *nt no pl* radon.
**Rad-:** ~**rennbahn** *f* cycle (racing) track; ~**rennen** *nt* cycle race; *(Sportart)* cycle racing; ~**rennfahrer** *m* racing cyclist; **r**~**schlagen** *vi sep irreg* to do cartwheels; ~**sport** *m* cycling; ~**sportler** *m* cy-

clist; ~**tour** f cycle tour; ~**wechsel** m wheel change; ~**weg** m cycle track, cycleway.

**RAF** [ɛr|aː'|ɛf] f = **Rote-Armee-Fraktion** Red Army Faction.

**raffen** vt (a) *(anhäufen)* to pile, to heap. (b) *Stoff, Gardine* to gather; *langes Kleid, Rock* to gather up. (c) *(col: verstehen)* to catch on to *(col)*. **er hat es immer noch nicht gerafft** he still hasn't got it.

**Raff-:** ~**gier** f greed, avarice; **r~gierig** adj grasping.

**Raffinade** f *(Zucker)* refined sugar.

**Raffinerie** f refinery.

**Raffinesse** f (a) *(Feinheit)* refinement no pl. (b) *(Schlauheit)* cunning no pl.

**raffinieren\*** vt Zucker, Öl to refine.

**raffiniert** adj (a) Zucker, Öl refined. (b) *(col)* Apparat fancy *(col)*; Kleidung stylish. (c) *(schlau)* cunning; *(durchtrieben auch)* crafty.

**Raffiniertheit** f *siehe adj* fanciness *(col)*; stylishness; cunning; craftiness.

**Rage** ['raːʒə] f no pl *(Wut)* rage, fury. **jdn in ~ bringen** to infuriate sb.

**ragen** vi to tower, to loom; *(heraus~)* to jut.

**Ragout** [ra'guː] nt -s ragout.

**Rahm** m no pl cream.

**rahmen** vt to frame; Dias to mount.

**Rahmen** m - (a) frame. (b) *(fig)* framework; *(Atmosphäre)* setting; *(Größe)* scale. **im ~** within the framework *(gen of)*; **im ~ des Möglichen** within the bounds of possibility; **im ~ bleiben** not to go too far; **aus dem ~ fallen** to go too far; **mußt du denn immer aus dem ~ fallen!** do you always have to show yourself up?; **ein Geschenk, das aus dem ~ des Üblichen fällt** a present with a difference; **in den ~ von etw passen** to blend in with sth; **das würde den ~ sprengen** it would be out of all proportion; **einer Feier den richtigen ~ geben** to provide the appropriate setting for a celebration; **in größerem/kleinerem ~** on a large/small scale.

**Rahmen-:** ~**handlung** f *(Liter)* background story; ~**plan** m outline plan; ~**programm** nt framework; *(von Veranstaltung etc)* supporting acts pl; ~**richtlinien** pl guidelines pl.

**rahmig** adj creamy.

**Rahmkäse** m cream cheese.

**räkeln** vr = **rekeln**.

**Rakete** f -n rocket *(auch Space)*; *(Mil auch)* missile.

**Raketen-** in cpds rocket; *(Mil auch)* missile.

**Raketen|abwehr** f antimissile defence *(Brit)* or defense *(US)*.

**Raketen|abwehr-** in cpds antimissile; ~**system** nt missile defence *(Brit)* or defense *(US)* system.

**Raketen-:** **r~getrieben** adj rocket-propelled; ~**stufe** f stage (of a rocket/missile); ~**stützpunkt** m missile base; ~**triebwerk** nt rocket engine; ~**werfer** m rocket launcher.

**Rallye** ['rali, 'rɛli] f -s rally.

**Rallyefahrer** m rally driver.

**RAM** [ram] m or nt -s *(Comp)* RAM.

**rammdösig** adj *(col)* giddy, dizzy.

**Ramme** f -n ram; *(für Pfähle)* pile-driver.

**Rammelei** f *(col: Gedränge)* crush *(col)*.

**rammeln 1** vt *siehe* **gerammelt**. **2** vi *(Hunt)* to mate; *(col!)* to have it off *(col!)*.

**rammen** vt to ram.

**Rampe** f -n (a) ramp. (b) *(Theat)* apron.

**Rampenlicht** nt *(Theat)* footlights pl. **sie möchte im ~ stehen** *(fig)* she wants to be in the limelight.

**ramponieren\*** vt *(col)* to ruin; Möbel to bash about *(col)*. **er sah ziemlich ramponiert aus** he looked the worse for wear *(col)*.

**Ramsch** m no pl *(col)* junk, rubbish.

**Ramsch-:** ~**händler** m *(pej)* junk dealer; ~**laden** m *(pej)* junk shop; ~**ware** f *(pej)* trashy goods pl, rubbish.

**ran** *(col)* **1** interj come on. **2** adv = **heran**.

**Rand** m ⁼er (a) edge; *(von Brunnen, Tasse)* rim, brim; *(von Abgrund)* brink. **voll bis zum ~** full to the brim; **am ~e erwähnen** to mention in passing; *interessieren, beteiligt sein* marginally; **am ~e des Waldes** at the edge of the forest; **am ~e der Stadt** on the outskirts of the town; **am ~e des Wahnsinns** on the verge of madness; **am ~e eines Krieges** on the brink of war; **etw am ~e miterleben** to experience sth from the sidelines; **am ~e der Gesellschaft** on the fringes of society.

(b) *(Umrandung)* border; *(Teller~)* edge, side; *(Brillen~)* rim; *(von Hut)* brim; *(Buch~, Heft~)* margin. **etw an den ~ schreiben** to write sth in the margin.

(c) *(Schmutz~)* ring. **rote ~er um die Augen haben** to have red rims around one's eyes.

(d) *(fig)* **sie waren außer ~ und Band** they were going wild; **allein komme ich damit nicht zu ~e** I can't manage (it) by myself; **halt den ~!** *(col)* shut your face *(col!)*.

**Randale** f rioting. **~ machen** to riot.

**randalieren\*** vi to rampage (about). ~**de Jugendliche** (young) hooligans; ~**de Studenten** rioting students; **die Gefangenen fingen an zu ~** the prisoners started to get violent.

**Randalierer** m - hooligan, rioter.

**Rand-:** ~**ausgleich** m *(Comp)* justification; ~**bemerkung** f marginal note; *(fig)* (passing) comment; ~**erscheinung** f matter of minor importance; *(Nebenwirkung)* side effect; ~**figur** f minor figure; ~**gebiet** nt *(Geog)* fringe; *(Pol)* border territory; *(fig)* subsidiary; ~**gruppe** f fringe group; **r~los** adj Brille rimless; Hut brimless; ~**stein** m = **Bordstein**; **r~voll** adj Glas full to the brim; ~**zone** f peripheral zone; **in der ~zone** on the periphery.

**rang** pret of **ringen**.

**Rang** m ⁼e (a) *(Mil)* rank; *(in Firma)* position; *(gesellschaftlich auch)* position. **im ~ eines Hauptmanns stehen** to have the rank of captain; **im ~ höher/tiefer stehen** to have a higher/lower rank/position, to rank higher/lower; **ein Mann ohne ~ und Namen** a man without any standing; **alles, was ~ und Namen hat** everybody who is anybody; **jdm den ~ ablaufen** *(fig)* to outstrip sb. (b) *(Qualität)* quality, class. **ein Künstler von ~** an artist of standing; **von hohem ~** high-class; **ein Essen ersten ~es** a first-rate meal. (c) *(Theat)* circle. **erster/zweiter ~** dress/upper circle; **vor leeren ~en spielen** to play to an empty house. (d) ~e pl *(Sport)* stands pl. (e) *(Gewinnklasse)* prize category; *(Platz)* place.

**Rangälteste(r)** m *(Mil)* senior officer.

**Range** f -n urchin.

**rangehen** vi sep irreg aux sein *(col)* to get stuck in *(col)*. **geh ran!** go on!; *siehe* **herangehen**.

**Rangelei** f *(col)* = **Gerangel**.

**rangeln** vi *(col)* to scrap; *(um Posten)* to wrangle *(um for)*.

**Rang-:** ~**folge** f order of rank *(esp Mil)*; ~**höchste(r)** mf decl as adj senior person; *(Mil)* highest-ranking officer.

**Rangierbahnhof** [rã'ʒiːɐ-] m marshalling yard, switchyard *(US)*.

**rangieren\*** [rã'ʒiːrən] **1** vt *(Rail)* to shunt, to switch *(US)*. **2** vi *(Rang einnehmen)* to rank. **an erster/letzter Stelle ~** to come first/last.

**Rangier-** [rãˈʒiːɐ-]: **~gleis** nt siding, sidetrack (US); **~lok(omotive)** f shunter, switcher (US).

**Rang-:** **~liste** f (Mil) active list; (Sport) rankings pl; **er steht auf der ~liste der weltbesten Boxer** he ranks among the world's top boxers; **r~mäßig** adj according to rank; **~ordnung** f hierarchy; (Mil) (order of) ranks; **~stufe** f rank.

**Rangun** nt Rangoon.

**Rang|unterschied** m social distinction; (Mil) difference of rank.

**ranhalten** vr sep irreg (col: sich beeilen) to get a move on (col).

**rank** adj (liter) **~ und schlank** slender and supple.

**Ranke** f -n tendril; (von Weinrebe) shoot.

**Ränke** pl (liter) intrigue, cabal (liter). **~ schmieden** to intrigue, to cabal (liter).

**ranken** **1** vr **sich um etw ~** (lit, fig) to have grown up around sth. **2** vi aux haben or sein **an etw** (dat) **~** to entwine itself around sth.

**Ränkeschmied** m (liter) intriguer.

**ran:-** **~klotzen** vi sep (col) to get stuck in (col); **~kommen = herankommen; ~lassen** vt irreg (col) **jdn ~lassen** to let sb have a go; **sie läßt keinen (an sich** acc) **~** (col) she won't let anybody near her.

**rann** pret of **rinnen**.

**rannte** pret of **rennen**.

**Ranzen** m - (a) (Schul~) satchel. (b) (col: Bauch) belly (col), gut (col).

**ranzig** adj rancid.

**rapid(e)** adj rapid.

**Rapier** nt -e rapier.

**Rappe** m (wk) **-n, -n** black horse.

**Rappel** m - (col) (a) (Fimmel) craze. **seinen ~ kriegen** to get one of one's crazy moods. (b) (Wutanfall) **einen ~ kriegen** to throw a fit.

**rapp(e)lig** adj (col) (a) (verrückt) crazy (col) (b) (nervös, unruhig) jumpy (col).

**rappeln** vi (col) (klappern) to rattle. **bei dir rappelt's wohl!** are you crazy?

**Rappen** m - (Sw) centime, rappen.

**Rapport** m -e report. **sich zum ~ melden** to report.

**Raps** m -e (Bot) rape.

**Raps|öl** nt rape(seed) oil.

**Rapunzel** f -n (Bot) corn salad, lamb's lettuce.

**rar** adj rare. **sich ~ machen** (col) to stay away; (sich zurückziehen) to make oneself scarce (col).

**Rarität** f rarity.

**rasant** adj (col) (a) Tempo, Spurt lightning attr (col); Auto, Fahrer fast; Karriere meteoric; Entwicklung rapid. (b) (imponierend) Leistung terrific.

**Rasanz** f no pl (col: Geschwindigkeit) speed.

**rasch** **1** adj (a) (schnell) quick; Tempo great. (b) (übereilt) hasty. **2** adv quickly.

**rascheln** vi to rustle. **es rascheln (im Laub)** there's something rustling (in the leaves); **mit etw ~** to rustle sth.

**rasen** vi (a) (wüten, toben) to rave; (Sturm) to rage. **er raste vor Schmerz/Wut** he was going wild with pain/he was mad with rage. (b) aux sein (sich schnell bewegen) to race, to tear; (Puls) to race. **das Auto raste in den Fluß** the car plunged into the river; **ras doch nicht so!** (col) don't go so fast!; **die Zeit rast** time flies.

**Rasen** m - grass no indef art, no pl; (Zier~ auch) lawn; (von Sportplatz) turf, grass; (Sportplatz) field, pitch (Brit).

**rasend** **1** adj (a) (enorm) terrific; Eile auch tearing; Hunger, Durst auch raging; Beifall auch wild, rapturous; Eifersucht burning. **~e Kopfschmerzen** a splitting headache. (b) (wütend) furious. **er macht mich noch ~** he'll drive me crazy. **2** adv (col) terrifically; weh tun, sich beeilen like mad (col) or crazy (col); verliebt, eifersüchtig sein madly (col). **~ gern!** I'd simply love to!

**Rasende(r)** mf decl as adj maniac.

**Rasen-:** **~fläche** f lawn; **~mäher** m lawn mower; **~sprenger** m - (lawn) sprinkler.

**Raser(in** f) m - (col) speed merchant (col).

**Raserei** f (a) (Wut) fury, frenzy. (b) (col: schnelles Fahren, Gehen) mad rush.

**Rasier-** in cpds shaving; **~apparat** m razor; (elektrisch auch) shaver.

**rasieren*** vtr to shave. **sich naß/trocken ~** to have a wet shave/to use an electric shaver.

**Rasier-:** **~klinge** f razor blade; **~messer** nt (open) razor; **~pinsel** m shaving brush; **~schaum** m shaving foam; **~wasser** nt aftershave; (vor der Rasur) pre-shave (lotion).

**Räson** [rɛˈzõː] f no pl **jdn zur ~ bringen** to make sb see sense.

**Raspel** f -n (a) (Holzfeile) rasp. (b) (Cook) grater.

**raspeln** vt to grate; Holz to rasp.

**Rasse** f -n (Menschen~) race; (Tier~) breed. **das Pferd/der Hund hat ~** the horse/dog has spirit.

**Rasse-:** **~hund** m thoroughbred dog; **~katze** f pedigree cat.

**Rassel** f -n rattle.

**rasseln** vi (a) to rattle. **mit etw** (dat) **~** to rattle sth. (b) aux sein (col) **durch eine Prüfung ~** to flunk an exam (col).

**Rassen-** in cpds racial; **~diskriminierung** f racial discrimination; **~haß** m race hatred; **~konflikt** m racial conflict; **~krawall** m race riot; **~trennung** f (racial) segregation; **~unruhen** pl racial disturbances pl; **~vorurteil** nt racial prejudice; **~vorurteile haben** to be racially prejudiced.

**Rassepferd** nt thoroughbred (horse).

**rassig** adj Pferd, Auto sleek; Frau vivacious; Wein spirited, lively.

**rassisch** adj racial. **jdn ~ verfolgen** to persecute sb because of his/her race.

**Rassismus** m racialism, racism.

**Rassist(in** f) m racialist, racist.

**rassistisch** adj racialist, racist.

**Rast** f no pl rest, repose (liter). **~ machen** to stop (to eat); (Mil) to make a halt; **ohne ~ und Ruh** (liter) without respite.

**Raste** f -n notch.

**rasten** vi to rest; (Mil) to make a halt. **wer rastet, der rostet** (Prov) you have to keep active.

**Raster** m - (Archit) grid; (Phot: Gitter) screen; (TV) raster; (fig) framework.

**Rasterfahndung** f computer search (for criminal).

**rastern** vt (TV) to scan.

**Rast-:** **~haus** nt (travellers' Brit or travelers' US) inn; (an Autobahn) motorway restaurant; **~hof** m (motorway) motel; (mit Tankstelle) service area; **r~los** adj (unruhig) restless; (unermüdlich) tireless; **~losigkeit** f restlessness; **~platz** m resting place; (an Autostraßen) picnic area; **~stätte** f service area, services pl.

**Rasur** f (Bart~) shave; (das Rasieren) shaving.

**Rat** m (a) pl **Ratschläge** (Empfehlung) advice no pl. **ein ~** a piece of advice; **jdm um ~ fragen** to ask sb's advice; **jdm mit ~ und Tat zur Seite stehen** to support sb in (both) word and deed; **da ist guter ~ teuer** it's hard to know what to do. (b) no pl **jdn/ etw zu ~e ziehen** to consult sb/sth; **~ (für etw) wissen** to know what to do (about sth); **sie wußte sich** (dat) **keinen ~ mehr** she was at her wits' end. (c) pl **=e** (Körperschaft) council. **der ~ der Gemeinde/Stadt ≈** the district council; **im ~ sitzen** to be on the council.

**Rate** f -n instalment *(Brit)*, installment *(US)*. **auf ~n kaufen** to buy on hire purchase *(Brit) or* on the installment plan *(US)*; **in ~n zahlen** to pay in instalments.

**raten** pret **riet**, ptp **geraten** vti **(a)** *(Ratschläge geben)* to advise. **jdm gut/schlecht ~** to give sb good/bad advice; **jdm zu etw ~** to recommend sth to sb; **jdm ~, etw nicht zu tun** to advise sb not to do sth *or* against doing sth; **das würde ich dir nicht ~** I wouldn't advise it; **das möchte ich dir auch geraten haben!** you better had *(col)*; **was** *or* **wozu ~ Sie mir?** what do you advise (me to do)? **(b)** *(erraten)* to guess; *Kreuzworträtsel etc* to solve, to do. **rate mal!** (have a) guess; **dreimal darfst du ~** I'll give you three guesses *(auch iro)*; **das rätst du nie!** you'll never guess!; **(gut) geraten!** good guess!; **falsch geraten!** wrong!

**Raten-:** **~kauf** m *(Kaufart)* hire purchase *(Brit)*, HP *(Brit col)*, the installment plan *(US)*; **r~weise** adv in instalments *(Brit) or* installments *(US)*; **~zahlung** f *(Zahlung in Raten)* payment by instalments *(Brit) or* installments *(US)*.

**Ratespiel** nt guessing game; *(TV)* quiz; *(Beruferaten etc auch)* panel game.

**Rat-:** **~geber** m adviser, counsellor *(form)*; **~haus** nt town hall; *(einer Großstadt)* city hall.

**Ratifikation** f ratification.

**ratifizieren\*** vt to ratify.

**Ratifizierung** f ratification.

**Ration** [ra'tsɪoːn] f ration.

**rational** [ratsɪo'naːl] adj rational.

**rationalisieren\*** [ratsɪonali'ziːrən] vti to rationalize.

**Rationalisierung** [ratsɪonali'ziːrʊŋ] f rationalization.

**rationell** [ratsɪo'nɛl] adj efficient.

**rationieren\*** [ratsɪo'niːrən] vt to ration.

**Rationierung** [ratsɪo'niːrʊŋ] f rationing.

**ratlos** adj at a loss. **ich bin völlig ~(, was ich tun soll)** I just don't know what to do; **sie machte ein ~es Gesicht** she looked at a loss.

**Ratlosigkeit** f perplexity. **in meiner ~ ...** being at a loss ...

**rätoromanisch** adj Rhaetian.

**Rätoromanisch(e)** nt Rhaeto-Romanic; *siehe* **Deutsch(e)**.

**ratsam** adj advisable.

**Ratschlag** m piece of advice. **ein guter ~** a good piece of advice; **Ratschläge advice**; **drei Ratschläge** three pieces of advice.

**Rätsel** nt - **(a)** riddle; *(Kreuzwort~)* crossword (puzzle); *(Silben~, Bilder~ etc)* puzzle. **jdm ein ~ aufgeben** to ask sb a riddle. **(b)** *(fig: Geheimnis)* mystery *(um of)*. **vor einem ~ stehen** to be baffled; **es ist mir ein ~, wie ...** it's a mystery to me how ...

**Rätsel-:** **~ecke** f puzzle corner; **r~haft** adj mysterious; **es ist mir r~haft** it's a mystery to me; **~heft** nt puzzle book.

**rätseln** vi to puzzle (over sth).

**Rätselraten** nt guessing game.

**Rats-:** **~herr** m councillor *(esp Brit)*, councilman *(US)*; **~sitzung** f council meeting.

**ratsuchend** adj seeking advice. **sich ~ an jdn wenden** to turn to sb for advice; **R~e** those seeking advice.

**Ratte** f -n rat.

**Ratten-:** **~gift** nt rat poison; **~schwanz** m **(a)** *(lit)* rat's tail; **(b)** *(fig col: Serie, Folge)* string.

**rattern** vi *(als Bewegungsverb: aux sein)* to clatter; *(Maschinengewehr)* to chatter.

**Raub** m no pl **(a)** *(das Rauben)* robbery. **(b)** *(Entführung)* abduction. **(c)** *(Beute)* booty, loot. **ein ~ der Flammen werden** *(liter)* to fall victim to the flames.

**Raub-:** **~bau** m no pl overexploitation (of natural resources); **~bau an etw** *(dat)* **treiben** to overexploit *etc* sth; **mit seiner Gesundheit ~bau treiben** to ruin one's health; **~druck** m pirate(d) edition.

**rauben 1** vt **(a)** *(wegnehmen)* to steal. **(b)** *(entführen)* to abduct, to carry off. **(c)** *(fig)* **jdm etw ~** to rob sb of sth; **das hat uns viel Zeit geraubt** it cost us a lot of time. **2** vi to plunder, to pillage.

**Räuber** m - robber. **~ und Gendarm** cops and robbers.

**Räuberbande** f *(pej)* bunch of thieves.

**räuberisch** adj rapacious; *(Angriff, Bande)* predatory.

**räubern** vi *(col)* to thieve. **in der Speisekammer ~** to raid the larder.

**Räuberpistole** f *(col)* far-fetched story.

**Raub-:** **~fisch** m predatory fish; **~gier** f *(liter)* rapacity; **r~gierig** adj *(liter)* rapacious; **~katze** f (predatory) big cat; **~kopie** f pirate(d) copy; **~mord** m robbery with murder; **~mörder** m robber and murderer; **~tier** nt predator, beast of prey; **~überfall** m robbery; *(auf Bank etc auch)* raid; **einen ~überfall auf jdn verüben** to hold sb up; **~vogel** m bird of prey; **~zug** m series *sing* of robberies.

**Rauch** m no pl smoke; *(giftig auch)* fumes *pl*. **sich in ~ auflösen** *(lit, fig)* to go up in smoke.

**Rauch-:** **~abzug** m smoke outlet; **~bombe** f smoke bomb.

**rauchen 1** vi *(Rauch abgeben)* to smoke. **sie sah, daß es in unserer Küche rauchte** she saw smoke coming from our kitchen; **mir raucht der Kopf** my head's spinning. **2** vti to smoke. **eine ~ to have a smoke; **hast du was zu ~?** have you got a smoke?; **„R~ verboten"** ''no smoking''; **sich** *(dat)* **das R~ an-/abgewöhnen** to take up/give up smoking; **stark ~** to be a heavy smoker.

**Raucher** m - *(auch Rail)* smoker.

**Räucheraal** m smoked eel.

**Raucherabteil** nt smoking compartment.

**Räucherhering** m = kipper.

**Raucherhusten** m smoker's cough.

**Raucherin** f (woman) smoker.

**Räucher-:** **~kerze** f incense cone; **~lachs** m smoked salmon.

**räuchern** vt to smoke.

**Räucher-:** **~schinken** m smoked ham; **~speck** m = smoked bacon; **~stäbchen** nt joss stick.

**Rauch-:** **~fang** m *(~abzug)* chimney hood; **~fleisch** nt smoked meat; **r~frei** adj smokeless; **~glocke** f pall of smoke.

**rauchig** adj smoky.

**Rauch-:** **~melder** m smoke detector; **~säule** f column of smoke; **~schleier** m veil of smoke; **~schwaden** pl drifts of smoke pl; **~signal** nt smoke signal; **~verbot** nt ban on smoking; **hier herrscht ~verbot** smoking is not allowed here; **~vergiftung** f fume poisoning; **~vorhang** m, **~wand** f smokescreen; **~waren**[1] pl tobacco (products pl); **~waren**[2] pl *(Pelze)* furs pl; **~wolke** f cloud of smoke; **~zeichen** nt smoke signal.

**Räude** f -n *(Vet)* mange.

**räudig** adj mangy.

**rauf** adv *(col)* siehe **herauf, hinauf**.

**Raufbold** m -e *(dated)* ruffian.

**raufen 1** vt Unkraut to pull up. **sich** *(dat)* **die Haare ~** to tear (at) one's hair. **2** vir to scrap.

**Rauferei** f scrap, roughhouse *(col)*.

**Rauf-:** **~lust** f pugnacity; **r~lustig** adj ready for a fight.

**rauh** adj (a) rough; *Wind* raw; *Winter, Klima* harsh; *(unwirtlich) Gebiet* bleak; *(hart) Mann* tough. **im ~en Norden** in the rugged north; **(die) ~e Wirklichkeit** harsh reality, the hard facts pl; **~, aber herzlich** bluff; *Begrüßung, Ton* rough but jovial. **(b)** *Hals, Kehle* sore; *Stimme* husky; *(heiser)* hoarse. **(c)** *(col)* **in ~en Mengen** by the ton *(col)*, galore *(col)*; **Geld in ~en Mengen** tons of money.
**Rauh-:** **~bein** nt *(col)* rough diamond; **r~beinig** adj *(col)* bluff.
**Rauheit** f no pl roughness; *(von Klima etc)* harshness; *(von Hals)* soreness; *(von Stimme)* huskiness.
**Rauh-:** **~fasertapete** f woodchip paper; **~haardackel** m wire-haired dachshund; **r~haarig** adj coarse-haired; **~putz** m roughcast; **~reif** m hoarfrost; *(gefrorener Nebel)* rime.
**Raum** m, pl **Räume** (a) room; *(no pl: Platz auch)* space; *(Gebiet, Bereich)* area; *(fig)* sphere. **auf engstem ~ leben** to live in a very confined space; **eine Frage im ~ stehen lassen** to leave a question unresolved; **der ~ Frankfurt** the Frankfurt area; **~ gewinnen** *(Mil, fig)* to gain ground. **(b)** no pl *(Phys, Space)* space no art. **der offene** or **leere ~** the void.
**Raum-:** **~anzug** m spacesuit; **~ausstatter(in** f) m - interior decorator.
**Räumboot** nt minesweeper.
**räumen** vt (a) *(verlassen) Gebäude, Gebiet* to evacuate; *(Mil: Truppen)* to withdraw from; *Wohnung* to move out of; *Sitzplatz* to vacate. **(b)** *(leeren) Gebäude, Lager* to clear *(von of)*. **(c)** *(weg~)* to shift; *Schnee, Schutt auch* to clear (away); *Minen* to clear. **räum deine Sachen in den Schrank** put your things away in the cupboard.
**Raum-:** **~fähre** f space shuttle; **~fahrer** m astronaut; *(sowjetisch)* cosmonaut.
**Raumfahrt** f space travel no art or flight no art. **das Zeitalter der ~** the space age.
**Raumfahrt-** in cpds space; **~behörde** f space authority; **~programm** nt space programme *(Brit)* or program *(US)*.
**Raumfahrzeug** nt spacecraft.
**Räumfahrzeug** nt bulldozer; *(für Schnee)* snowclearer.
**Raum-:** **~flug** m space flight; **~gewinn** m extra space gained; **~inhalt** m volume, (cubic) capacity; **~kapsel** f space capsule.
**räumlich** adj (a) *(den Raum betreffend)* spatial. **~e Verhältnisse** physical conditions; **wir wohnen ~ sehr beengt** we live in very cramped conditions; **rein ~ ist das unmöglich** there just isn't the space (for that). **(b)** *(dreidimensional)* three-dimensional. **ich kann mir das nicht ~ vorstellen** I can't really picture it.
**Räumlichkeit** f (a) no pl three-dimensionality. **(b)** **~en** pl premises pl.
**Raum-:** **~mangel** m lack of space; **~maß** nt unit of volume; **~not** f shortage of space; **~pflegerin** f cleaner, cleaning lady; **~schiff** nt spaceship; **~sonde** f space probe; **~station** f space station; **~textilien** pl soft furnishings; **~transporter** m space shuttle.
**Räumung** f clearing; *(von Wohnhaus)* vacation; *(wegen Gefahr etc)* evacuation; *(unter Zwang)* eviction; *(von Lager, Geschäft)* clearance.
**Räumungs-:** **~befehl** m eviction order; **~frist** f (period of) notice; **~klage** f action for eviction; **~verkauf** m clearance sale.
**raunen** vti *(liter)* to whisper. **es ging ein R~ durch die Menge** a murmur went through the crowd.
**Raupe** f -n (a) caterpillar. **(b)** *(Planier~)* bulldozer.
**Raupen-:** **~fahrzeug** nt caterpillar (vehicle);

**~kette** f caterpillar track; **~schlepper** m caterpillar (tractor).
**raus** adv *(col)* **~**! (get) out!; *siehe* **heraus, hinaus.**
**Rausch** m, pl **Räusche** (a) *(Trunkenheit)* intoxication; *(Drogen~)* high *(col)*. **einen ~ haben** to be drunk; **etw im ~ tun** to do sth while one is drunk; **seinen ~ ausschlafen** to sleep it off. **(b)** *(liter: Ekstase)* ecstasy, rapture; *(Blut~, Mord~ etc)* frenzy.
**rausch|arm** adj low-noise.
**rauschen** vi (a) *(Wasser, Meer, Brandung)* to roar; *(sanft, Wind)* to murmur; *(Baum, Wald)* to rustle; *(Seide)* to swish; *(Radio etc)* to hiss; *(Regen)* to pour down. **~der Beifall** thunderous applause; **~de Feste** glittering parties. **(b)** aux sein *(sich bewegen)* *(Bach)* to rush; *(Geschoß)* to whizz. **(c)** aux sein *(col: Mensch)* to sweep. **sie rauschte aus dem Zimmer** she swept out of the room.
**Rauschen** nt no pl siehe vi roaring; murmuring; rustling; swishing; hissing. **das ~ des Regens** the sound of rain.
**Rauschgift** nt drug; *(Drogen)* drugs pl, narcotics pl.
**Rauschgift-:** **~handel** m drug traffic; **~händler** m drug trafficker; **~sucht** f drug addiction; **r~süchtig** adj drug-addicted; **er ist r~süchtig** he's a drug addict; **~süchtige(r)** mf drug addict.
**raus|ekeln** vt sep *(col)* to freeze out *(col)*.
**rausfliegen** vi sep irreg aux sein *(col)* to be chucked out *(col)*.
**rauskriegen** vt sep *(col)* to get out; *(herausfinden)* to find out.
**räuspern** vr to clear one's throat.
**rausreißen** vt sep irreg *(col)* **jdn ~** to save sb's bacon *(col)*.
**rausschmeißen** vt sep irreg *(col)* to chuck out *(col)*. **das ist rausgeschmissenes Geld** that's money down the drain *(col)*.
**Rausschmeißer(in** f) m - *(col)* bouncer; *(letzter Tanz)* last dance.
**Rausschmiß** m -sse *(col)* booting out *(col)*. **man drohte uns mit dem ~** they threatened us with the push *(col)*.
**Raute** f -n (a) *(Bot)* rue. **(b)** *(Math)* rhombus.
**rautenförmig** adj rhomboid, diamond-shaped.
**Ravioli** [ravi'o:li] pl ravioli sing.
**Razzia** f, pl **Razzien** ['ratsiən] raid, swoop *(col)*.
**Re** nt -s *(Cards)* redouble.
**Reagenzglas** nt *(Chem)* test tube.
**reagieren*** vi to react *(auf +acc to)*.
**Reaktion** f (a) reaction *(auf +acc to)*. **(b)** *(Pol pej)* reactionary forces pl.
**reaktionär** [reaktsio'nɛːɐ] adj *(Pol pej)* reactionary.
**Reaktionär(in** f) m *(pej)* reactionary.
**Reaktions-:** **~fähigkeit** f reactions pl; **~geschwindigkeit** f (speed of) reaction; **r~schnell** adj with fast reactions; **r~schnell sein** to have fast reactions; **~vermögen** nt reactions pl; **~zeit** f reaction time.
**reaktivieren*** [reakti'viːrən] vt *(Sci)* to reactivate; *(fig)* to revive; *Kenntnisse* to polish up.
**Reaktor** m reactor.
**Reaktor-:** **~kern** m reactor core; **~unglück** nt nuclear accident.
**real** adj real; *(wirklichkeitsbezogen)* realistic.
**Real|einkommen** nt real income.
**Realisation** f realization; *(TV, Rad, Theat)* production.
**realisierbar** adj practicable, feasible.
**realisieren*** vt (a) *Pläne, Programm* to carry out; *(TV, Rad, Theat)* to produce. **(b)** *(Fin)* to realize.
**Realisierung** f realization.
**Realismus** m realism.

**Realist(in** *f)* *m* realist.
**realistisch** *adj* realistic.
**Realität** *f* reality. ~**en** *pl (Gegebenheiten)* facts *pl.*
**Realitäts-:** **r~fern** *adj* unrealistic; **r~fremd** *adj* out of touch with reality; **r~nah** *adj* realistic; ~**sinn** *m* sense of reality.
**Real-:** ~**lexikon** *nt* specialist dictionary; ~**lohn** *m* real wages *pl;* ~**politik** *f* political realism; ~**politiker** *m* political realist; ~**schule** *f* ≈ secondary modern school *(Brit),* high school *(US);* ~**wert** *m (Fin)* real value.
**Rebe** *f* -**n** *(Ranke)* shoot; *(Weinstock)* vine.
**Rebell(in** *f)* *m (wk)* -**en,** -**en** rebel.
**rebellieren\*** *vi* to rebel, to revolt.
**Rebellion** *f* rebellion, revolt.
**rebellisch** *adj* rebellious.
**Rebhuhn** *nt* (common) partridge.
**Reb-:** ~**laus** *f* vine pest; ~**stock** *m* vine.
**Rebus** *m or nt* -, -**se** picture puzzle.
**Rechaud** [re'ʃoː] *m or nt* -**s** tea/coffee *etc* warmer; *(für Fondue)* spirit burner.
**Rechen** *m* - *(S Ger: Harke)* rake.
**rechen** *vt (S Ger)* to rake.
**Rechen-:** ~**anlage** *f* computer; ~**art** *f* type of calculation; **die vier** ~**arten** the four arithmetical operations; ~**aufgabe** *f* arithmetical problem; ~**fehler** *m* arithmetical error; ~**geschwindigkeit** *f (Comp)* processing speed; ~**heft** *nt* arithmetic book; ~**maschine** *f* adding machine; ~**operation** *f* calculation.
**Rechenschaft** *f* account. **jdm über etw** *(acc)* ~ **ablegen** to account to sb for sth; **jdm** ~ **schulden** to be accountable to sb; **jdn (für etw) zur** ~ **ziehen** to call sb to account (for *or* over sth).
**Rechenschaftsbericht** *m* report.
**Rechen-:** ~**schieber** *m* slide rule; ~**zentrum** *nt* computer centre *(Brit) or* center *(US).*
**Recherche** [re'ʃɛrʃə] *f* -**n** investigation.
**recherchieren\*** [reʃɛr'ʃiːrən] *vti* to investigate.
**rechnen 1** *vt* (a) *(addieren etc)* to calculate. **rund gerechnet** in round figures. (**b**) *(einstufen)* to count. **jdn/etw zu etw** ~ to count sb among sth. (**c**) *(veranschlagen)* to estimate, to reckon. **wir hatten nur drei Tage gerechnet** we were only reckoning on three days; **das ist zu hoch/niedrig gerechnet** that's too high/low (an estimate). (**d**) *(einberechnen)* to take into account. **alles in allem gerechnet** taking everything into account.
  **2** *vi* (a) **falsch** ~ to go wrong (in one's calculations); **richtig** ~ to calculate correctly; **gut/schlecht** ~ **können** to be good/bad at sums *(esp Sch) or* with figures; ~ **lernen** to learn arithmetic. (**b**) *(eingestuft werden)* to count. **er rechnet noch als Kind** he still counts as a child. (**c**) *(sich verlassen)* **auf jdn/etw** ~ to count on sb/sth. (**d**) **mit jdm/etw** ~ to reckon with sb/sth; **mit allem/dem Schlimmsten** ~ to be prepared for anything/the worst; **damit** ~ **müssen, daß ...** to have to expect that ...; **du mußt damit** ~, **daß es regnet** you must expect some rain; **mit dieser Partei wird man** ~ **müssen** this party will have to be reckoned with; **damit hatte ich nicht gerechnet** I wasn't expecting that; **er rechnet mit einem Sieg** he reckons he'll win.
  **3** *vr* to pay off. **etw rechnet sich nicht** sth is not economical.
**Rechnen** *nt no pl* arithmetic; *(esp Sch)* sums *pl.*
**Rechner** *m* - (**a**) **ein guter** ~ **sein** to be good at arithmetic. (**b**) *(Elektronen~)* computer; *(Taschen~)* calculator.
**rechner-:** ~**gesteuert** *adj* computer-controlled; ~**gestützt** *adj* computer-aided.

**rechnerisch** *adj* arithmetical. **ich bin rein** ~ **überzeugt, aber ...** I'm convinced as far as the figures go but ...
**Rechnerverbund** *m* computer network.
**Rechnung** *f* (**a**) *(Berechnung)* calculation; *(als Aufgabe)* sum. **die** ~ **geht nicht auf** *(lit, fig)* it won't work (out). (**b**) *(Kostenforderung)* bill, check *(US); (von Firma auch)* invoice. **das geht auf meine** ~ I'm paying; **laut** ~ as per invoice; **auf eigene** ~ on one's own account; **(jdm) etw in** ~ **stellen** to charge (sb) for sth; **einer Sache** *(dat)* ~ **tragen** to bear sth in mind.
**Rechnungs-:** ~**betrag** *m* (total) amount of a bill *or* check *(US)/*invoice; ~**hof** *m* ≈ Auditor-General's office *(Brit),* audit division *(US);* ~**jahr** *nt* financial year; ~**prüfer** *m* auditor; ~**prüfung** *f* audit.
**Recht** *nt* -**e** (**a**) *(Rechtsordnung, sittliche Norm)* law; *(Gerechtigkeit auch)* justice. ~ **sprechen** to administer justice; **nach englischem** ~ under English law; **für das** ~ **kämpfen** to fight for justice; **von** ~**s wegen** as of right; *(col: eigentlich)* by rights *(col).* (**b**) *(Anspruch, Berechtigung)* right *(auf +acc* to*).* **sein** ~ **fordern** to demand one's rights; **sein** ~ **bekommen** to get one's rights; **zu seinem** ~ **kommen** *(lit)* to gain one's rights; *(fig)* to come into one's own; **gleiches** ~ **für alle!** equal rights for all!; **das** ~ **des Stärkeren** the law of the jungle; **mit** *or* **zu** ~ rightly; **und (das) mit** ~ and rightly so; **im** ~ **sein** to be in the right; **das ist mein gutes** ~ it's my right; **mit welchem** ~? by what right?
**recht 1** *adj* (**a**) *(richtig)* right. **es soll mir** ~ **sein** it's OK *(col)* by me; **ganz** ~! quite right; **ist schon** ~! *(col)* that's OK *(col);* **alles, was** ~ **ist** *(empört)* fair's fair; *(anerkennend)* you can't deny it; **hier geht es nicht mit** ~**en Dingen zu** there's something odd *or* not right here; **ich habe keine** ~**e Lust** I don't particularly feel like it; **nichts R~es** no good; **aus dem Jungen kann nichts R~es werden** that boy will come to no good; **er hat nichts R~es gelernt** he didn't learn any proper trade; **nach dem R~en sehen** to see that everything's OK *(col);* **es ist nicht mehr als** ~ **und billig** it's only right and proper. (**b**) ~ **haben** to be right; ~ **behalten** to be right; **er will immer** ~ **behalten** he always has to be right; **jdm** ~ **geben** to admit that sb is right.
  **2** *adv* (**a**) *(richtig)* properly; *(wirklich)* really. **verstehen Sie mich** ~ don't get me wrong *(col);* **wenn ich Sie** ~ **verstehe** if I understand you rightly; **sehe/höre ich** ~? am I seeing/hearing things?; **das geschieht ihm** ~ it serves him right; **jetzt mache ich es erst** ~ **(nicht)** now I'm definitely (not) going to do it; **du kommst gerade** ~, **um ...** you're just in time to ...; **das ist mir** ~ that suits me fine; **gehe ich** ~ **in der Annahme, daß ...?** am I correct in assuming that ...?; **hat es dir gefallen? — nicht so** ~ did you like it? — not really; **man kann ihm nichts** ~ **machen** you can't do anything right for him; **man kann es nicht allen** ~ **machen** you can't please everyone. (**b**) *(ziemlich, ganz)* quite, fairly *(col).* ~ **viel** quite a lot. (**c**) *(sehr)* very, right *(dial).* ~ **herzlichen Dank** thank you very much indeed.
**Rechte** *f (wk)* -**n,** -**n** (**a**) *(Hand)* right hand; *(Seite)* right(-hand) side; *(Boxen)* right. (**b**) *(Pol)* Right.
**Recht-:** ~**eck** *nt* rectangle; **r~eckig** *adj* rectangular.
**Rechtens** *gen of* **Recht** *(form)* **die Sache war nicht** ~ the matter was not right *or (Jur)* legal.
**Rechte(r)** *mf decl as adj (Pol)* right-winger.
**rechte(r, s)** *adj attr* (**a**) right, right-hand. **jds** ~ **Hand sein** to be sb's right-hand man. (**b**) **ein** ~**r Winkel** a right angle. (**c**) *(konservativ)* right-wing. **der** ~ **Flü-**

**gel** the right wing. **(d)** *(beim Stricken)* plain. **eine ~e Masche stricken** to knit one.

**rechtfertigen** *insep* **1** *vt* to justify. **2** *vr* to justify oneself.

**Rechtfertigung** *f* justification. **zu meiner ~** in my defence *(Brit)* or defense *(US)*.

**Recht-:** **~haber** *m* - *(pej)* know-all *(col)*; **r~haberisch** *adj* know-all *attr (col)*, self-opinionated.

**rechtlich** *adj (gesetzlich)* legal. **~ zulässig** permissible in law, legal; **~ nicht zulässig** not permissible in law, illegal.

**Recht-:** **r~los** *adj* **(a)** without rights; **(b)** *Zustand* lawless; **~losigkeit** *f* **(a)** *(von Mensch)* lack of rights; **(b)** *(in Land)* lawlessness; **r~mäßig** *adj (legitim)* legitimate; *Erben, Besitzer auch* rightful; *(dem Gesetz entsprechend)* legal; **für r~mäßig erklären** to declare legal; **~mäßigkeit** *f (Legitimität)* legitimacy; *(Legalität)* legality.

**rechts 1** *adv* **(a)** on the right. **nach ~** (to the) right; **von ~** from the right; **sich ~ einordnen** to take the right-hand lane; **sich ~ halten** to keep (to the) right; **~ stehen** *or* **sein** *(Pol)* to be right-wing. **(b)** **~ stricken** to knit (plain); **zwei ~, zwei links** *(beim Stricken)* knit two, purl two. **2** *prep* +*gen* **~ des Rheins** on the right of the Rhine.

**Rechts-** *in cpds (Pol)* right-wing; *(Jur)* legal; **~abbieger** *m* - vehicle turning right; **~abbiegerspur** *f* right-hand turn-off lane; **~anspruch** *m* legal right; **einen ~anspruch auf etw** *(acc)* **haben** to be legally entitled to sth; **~anwalt** *m* lawyer, attorney *(US)*; *(als Berater auch)* solicitor *(Brit)*; *(vor Gericht auch)* barrister *(Brit)*; **~ausleger** *m (Boxen)* southpaw; **~außen** *m -, - (Ftbl)* outside right; **~beistand,** **~berater** *m* legal adviser; **~brecher(in** *f)* *m* - lawbreaker; **r~bündig** *adj (Typ)* ranged right.

**rechtschaffen** *adj (redlich)* honest, upright.

**Rechtschaffenheit** *f* honesty, uprightness.

**Rechtschreib-:** **~fehler** *m* spelling mistake; **~prüfung** *f (Comp)* spellcheck; *(Programm)* spellchecker.

**Rechtschreibung** *f* spelling.

**Rechts-:** **~drall** *m (von Billardball)* spin to the right; *(von Auto, Pferd)* pull to the right; *(Pol col)* leaning to the right; **einen ~drall haben** to spin/pull/lean to the right; **~empfinden** *nt* sense of justice; **~extremismus** *m* right-wing extremism; **~extremist** *m* right-wing extremist; **~fall** *m* court case; **r~frei** *adj* **r~freier Raum** unlegislated area; **r~gängig** *adj (Tech)* right-hand(ed); **r~gerichtet** *adj (Pol)* right-wing; **~geschäft** *nt* legal transaction; **~geschichte** *f* legal history; **~grundsatz** *m* legal maxim; **r~gültig** *adj* legally valid; **~gültigkeit** *f* legal validity; **~händer(in** *f)* *m* - right-handed person, right-hander *(esp Sport)*; **~händer sein** to be right-handed; **r~händig** *adj, adv* right-handed; **r~herum** *adv* (around) to the right; **r~kräftig** *adj Urteil* final; *Vertrag* legally valid; **r~kundig** *adj* versed in the law; **~kurve** *f* right-hand bend; **~lage** *f* legal position; **r~lastig** *adj* listing to the right; *(fig)* leaning to the right; **r~lastig sein** to lean to the right; **~mittel** *nt* **~mittel einlegen** to lodge an appeal; **~ordnung** *f* **eine ~ordnung** a system of laws; **die ~ordnung** the law; **~partei** *f* right-wing party; **~pflege** *f* administration of justice; **~pfleger** *m official with certain judicial powers.*

**Rechtsprechung** *f* **(a)** *(Gerichtsbarkeit)* jurisdiction. **(b)** *(richterliche Tätigkeit)* dispensation of justice. **(c)** *(bisherige Urteile)* precedents *pl.*

**Rechts-:** **r~radikal** *adj* radical right-wing; **die ~radikalen** the right-wing radicals; **~radikalismus** *m* right-wing radicalism; **r~rheinisch** *adj* on the right of the Rhine; **~ruck, ~rutsch** *m (Pol)* swing to the right; **r~rum** *adv (col)* to the right; **~sache** *f* legal matter; *(Fall)* case; **~schutz** *m* legal protection; **~schutzversicherung** *f* legal costs insurance; **r~seitig** *adj* on the right(-hand) side; **r~seitig gelähmt** paralysed in the right side; **~staat** *m* state under the rule of law; **r~staatlich** *adj* **r~staatliche Ordnung** law and order; **~staatlichkeit** *f* rule of law; **r~stehend** *adj attr* right-hand, on the right; *(Pol)* right-wing; **~steuerung** *f* right-hand drive; **~streit** *m* lawsuit; **~verkehr** *m* driving on the right *no def art*; **in Deutschland ist ~verkehr** in Germany they drive on the right; **~verletzung** *f* infringement of the law; **~weg** *m* **den ~weg beschreiten** to go to law; **der ~weg ist ausgeschlossen** ≈ the judges' decision is final; **r~widrig** *adj* illegal; **~widrigkeit** *f* illegality.

**recht-:** **~winklig** *adj* right-angled; **~zeitig 1** *adj (früh genug)* timely; *(pünktlich)* punctual; **um ~zeitige Anmeldung wird gebeten** you are requested to apply in good time; **2** *adv (früh genug)* in (good) time; *(pünktlich)* on time.

**Reck** *nt* **-e** *(Sport)* horizontal bar.

**recken 1** *vt (aus-, emporstrecken)* to stretch. **den Kopf/Hals ~** to crane one's neck; **die Glieder ~** to stretch (oneself). **2** *vr* to stretch (oneself).

**Reck-:** **~stange** *f* horizontal bar; **~turnen** *nt* bar exercises *pl.*

**recyceln\*** [riːˈsaɪkəln] *vt* to recycle.

**Recycling** [riːˈsaɪklɪŋ] *nt no pl* recycling.

**Recycling-:** **~papier** *nt* recycled paper; **~werk** *nt* recycling plant.

**Redakteur(in** *f)* [-ˈtøːɐ̯, -ˈtøːrɪn] *m* editor.

**Redaktion** *f* **(a)** *no pl (das Redigieren)* editing. **(b)** *(Personal)* editorial staff. **(c)** *(~sbüro)* editorial office(s).

**redaktionell** [redaktsioˈnɛl] *adj* editorial. **etw ~ bearbeiten** to edit sth.

**Redaktionsschluß** *m* time of going to press; *(Einsendeschluß)* copy deadline.

**Rede** *f* **-n** **(a)** speech; *(Ansprache)* address. **eine ~ halten** to make a speech; **direkte/indirekte ~** direct/indirect speech *or* discourse *(US)*; **in freier ~** without (consulting) notes; **der langen ~ kurzer Sinn** *(prov)* the long and the short of it.

**(b)** *(Äußerungen)* words *pl*, language *no pl.* **seine frechen ~n** his cheek; **große ~n führen** to talk big *(col)*; **das ist meine ~!** that's what I've always said; **das ist nicht der ~ wert** it's not worth mentioning.

**(c)** *(Gespräch)* conversation, talk. **die ~ kam auf** (+*acc*) the conversation turned to; **es war von einer Gehaltserhöhung die ~** there was talk of a salary increase; **von Ihnen war eben die ~** we were just talking about you; **aber davon war doch nie die ~** but there was never any mention of that; **davon kann keine ~ sein** it's out of the question.

**(d)** **es geht die ~, daß** rumour *(Brit)* or rumor *(US)* has it that; **(jdm) für etw ~ und Antwort stehen** to account (to sb) for sth; **jdn zur ~ stellen** to take sb to task.

**Rede-:** **~duell** *nt* verbal exchange; **~fluß** *m* volubility; **er stockte plötzlich in seinem ~fluß** his flow of words suddenly stopped; **~freiheit** *f* freedom of speech; **r~gewandt** *adj* eloquent; **~gewandtheit** *f* eloquence; **~kunst** *f* **die ~kunst** rhetoric.

**reden 1** *vi* to talk, to speak. **R~ während des Unterrichts** talking in class; **mit jdm ~** to talk to sb; **so**

**lasse ich nicht mit mir** ~! I won't be spoken to like that!; **sie hat geredet und geredet** she talked and talked; **mit jdm über jdn/etw** ~ to talk to sb about sb/sth; ~ **Sie doch nicht!** *(col)* come off it! *(col)*; **(viel) von sich** ~ **machen** to become (very much) a talking point; **du hast gut** ~! it's all very well for you (to talk); **darüber läßt sich** ~ that's a possibility; *(über Preis, Bedingungen)* I think we could discuss that; **er läßt mit sich** ~ he could be persuaded; *(in bezug auf Preis)* he's open to offers; *(gesprächsbereit)* he's open to discussion; **R~ ist Silber, Schweigen ist Gold** *(Prov)* (speech is silver but) silence is golden *(Prov)*; **in so einem Dorf wird natürlich viel geredet** in a village like that naturally there is a lot of gossip; **er kann gut** ~ he is a good talker *or (als Redner)* speaker; **jdn zum R~ bringen** to get sb to talk.
  **2** *vt* to talk; *Worte* to say. **kein Wort** ~ not to say a word; **einer Sache das Wort** ~ to speak in favour *(Brit)* or favor *(US)* of sth; **Schlechtes über jdn** ~ to say bad things about sb.
  **3** *vr* **sich heiser/in Wut** ~ to talk oneself hoarse/ into a fury.

**Redens|art** *f (Redewendung)* expression, idiom; *(Sprichwort)* saying; *(Phrase)* cliché. **bloße ~en** empty talk.

**Rederei** *f (Geschwätz)* chatter *no pl,* talk *no pl*; *(Klatsch)* gossip *no pl.*

**Rede-:** **~schwall** *m* torrent of words; **~verbot** *nt* ban on speaking; **jdm ~verbot erteilen** to ban sb from speaking; **~weise** *f* manner (of speaking); **~wendung** *f* idiomatic expression.

**redigieren** * *vt* to edit.

**redlich** *adj* honest. **sich** *(dat)* **etw** ~ **verdient haben** to have really earned sth; ~ **(mit jdm) teilen** to share (things) equally (with sb).

**Redlichkeit** *f* honesty.

**Redner(in** *f)* *m* - speaker.

**rednerisch** *adj* rhetorical, oratorical. ~ **begabt sein** to be a gifted speaker.

**Rednerpult** *nt* lectern.

**redselig** *adj* talkative.

**Redseligkeit** *f* talkativeness.

**reduzieren** * **1** *vt* to reduce. **2** *vr* to decrease, to diminish.

**Reduzierung** *f* reduction.

**Reeder** *m* - ship owner.

**Reederei** *f* shipping company.

**reell** *adj* **(a)** *(ehrlich)* honest, straight; *(Comm) Geschäft* sound; *Preis* fair. **(b)** *(wirklich)* real.

**Reet-** *(N Ger)*: **~dach** *nt* thatched roof; **r~gedeckt** *adj* thatched *(with reed).*

**Referat** *nt* **(a)** *(Univ)* seminar paper. **ein** ~ **halten** to present a seminar paper. **(b)** *(Admin: Ressort)* department.

**Referendar(in** *f)* *m* trainee (in civil service); *(Studien~)* student teacher; *(Gerichts~)* articled clerk.

**Referendarzeit** *f* traineeship; *(Studien~)* teacher training.

**Referendum** *nt, pl* **Referenden** referendum.

**Referent(in** *f)* *m (Sachbearbeiter)* consultant, expert; *(Redner)* speaker; *(Univ: Gutachter)* examiner.

**Referenz** *f* reference.

**referieren** * *vi* to (give a) report *(über +acc* on).

**Reff** *nt* -e *(Naut)* reef.

**reffen** *vt (Naut)* to reef.

**reflationär** *adj (Econ)* reflationary.

**reflektieren** * **1** *vt* to reflect. **2** *vi* **(a)** *(geh: nachdenken)* to reflect, to ponder *(über +acc* (up)on*).* **(b)** *(col)* **auf etw** *(acc)* ~ to be interested in sth.

**Reflektor** *m* reflector.

**Reflex** *m* -e reflection; *(Physiol)* reflex.

**Reflexbewegung** *f* reflex action.

**Reflexion** *f (Phys, fig)* reflection.

**Reflexionswinkel** *m (Phys)* angle of reflection.

**reflexiv** *adj (Gram)* reflexive.

**Reform** *f* -en reform.

**Reformation** *f* Reformation.

**reformatorisch** *adj* reforming.

**reformbedürftig** *adj* in need of reform.

**Reformer(in** *f)* *m* - reformer.

**Reform-:** **r~freudig** *adj* avid for reform; **~haus** *nt* health food shop *(Brit)* or store *(US).*

**reformieren** * *vt* to reform.

**Reformkost** *f* health food.

**Refrain** [rə'frɛ̃ː, re-] *m* -s *(Mus)* chorus, refrain.

**Regal** *nt* -e *(Bord)* shelves *pl.*

**Regatta** *f, pl* **Regatten** regatta.

**Reg.-Bez.** = **Regierungsbezirk.**

**rege** *adj (betriebsam)* lively. **ein ~s Treiben** a busy to-and-fro; **körperlich und geistig** ~ **sein** to be physically and mentally active; **noch sehr** ~ **sein** to be very active still; ~ **Beteiligung** lively participation; *(zahlreich)* good attendance.

**Regel** *f* -n **(a)** *(Vorschrift, Norm)* rule; *(Verordnung)* regulation. **nach allen ~n der Kunst** *(fig)* thoroughly; **sie überredete ihn nach allen ~n der Kunst,** ... she used every trick in the book to persuade him ... **(b)** *(Gewohnheit)* habit, rule. **sich** *(dat)* **etw zur** ~ **machen** to make a habit of sth; **in der** ~ as a rule. **(c)** *(Monatsblutung)* period; *(Menstruation)* menstruation *no art.* **die** ~ **bekommen** to get one's period.

**Regel-:** **~arbeitszeit** *f* core working hours *pl*; **r~bar** *adj (steuerbar)* adjustable; **~fall** *m* rule; **im ~fall** as a rule; **r~los** *adj (ungeregelt)* irregular; *(unordentlich)* haphazard; **~losigkeit** *f siehe adj* irregularity; haphazardness; **r~mäßig** *adj* regular; **r~mäßig spazierengehen** to take regular walks; **er kommt r~mäßig zu spät** he's always late; **~mäßigkeit** *f* regularity.

**regeln** **1** *vt* **(a)** *(regulieren)* to control; *siehe* **geregelt.** **(b)** *(erledigen)* to see to; *(endgültig)* to settle; *Problem etc* to sort out; *(in Ordnung bringen)* to settle, to resolve. **wir haben die Sache so geregelt** ... we have arranged things like this ...; **gesetzlich geregelt sein** to be laid down by law. **2** *vr* to resolve itself; **das wird sich von selbst** ~ that will take care of itself.

**regelrecht 1** *adj* real, proper; *Betrug, Beleidigung* downright; **das Spiel artete in eine ~e Schlägerei aus** the match degenerated into a regular brawl. **2** *adv* really; *beleidigend* downright.

**Regelung** *f* **(a)** *(Regulierung)* regulation, control. **(b)** *(Erledigung)* settling; *(von Unstimmigkeiten)* resolution. **(c)** *(Abmachung)* arrangement; *(Bestimmung)* ruling.

**Regel-:** **r~widrig** *adj* against the rules; *(gegen Verordnungen verstoßend)* against the regulations; **~widrigkeit** *f* irregularity; *(Verstoß auch)* breach of the rules.

**regen 1** *vt (bewegen)* to move. **2** *vr (Mensch, Glied, Baum etc)* to move, to stir; *(Gefühl, Wind etc)* to stir. **unter den Zuhörern regte sich Widerspruch** there were mutterings of disapproval from the audience.

**Regen** *m* - rain; *(fig: von Schimpfwörtern, Blumen etc)* shower. **in den** ~ **kommen** to be caught in the rain; **ein warmer** ~ *(fig)* a windfall; **jdn im** ~ **stehenlassen** *(fig)* to leave sb out in the cold; **vom** ~ **in die Traufe kommen** *(prov)* to jump out of the frying pan into the fire *(prov).*

**regen|arm** *adj* dry, rainless.
**Regenbogen** *m* rainbow.
**Regenbogen-:** **~farben** *pl* colours *(Brit)* or colors *(US)* *pl* of the rainbow; **r~farben** *adj* rainbow-coloured *(Brit)*, rainbow-colored *(US)*; **~haut** *f* *(Anat)* iris; **~presse** *f* trashy magazines *pl.*
**regendicht** *adj* rainproof.
**Regeneration** *f* regeneration; *(fig auch)* revitalization.
**regenerieren\* 1** *vr* *(Biol)* to regenerate; *(fig)* to revitalize or regenerate oneself/itself; *(nach Anstrengung, Schock etc)* to recover. **2** *vt* *(Biol)* to regenerate; *(fig auch)* to revitalize.
**Regen-:** **~fall** *m usu pl* (fall of) rain; **tropische ~fälle** tropical rains; **r~frei** *adj* rainless; **~guß** *m* downpour; **~mantel** *m* raincoat; **r~reich** *adj* rainy; **~rinne** *f* gutter; **~schauer** *m* shower (of rain); **~schirm** *m* umbrella.
**Regent(in** *f)* *m* sovereign, reigning monarch.
**Regen-:** **~tag** *m* rainy day; **~tonne** *f* water butt; **~tropfen** *m* raindrop.
**Regentschaft** *f* reign.
**Regen-:** **~wald** *m* *(Geog)* rain forest; **~wasser** *nt* rainwater; **~wetter** *nt* rainy weather; **er macht ein Gesicht wie drei** or **sieben Tage ~wetter** *(col)* he's got a face as long as a month of Sundays *(col)*; **~wolke** *f* rain cloud; **~wurm** *m* earthworm; **~zeit** *f* rainy season.
**Regie** [re'ʒiː] *f* **(a)** *(künstlerische Leitung)* direction; *(Theat, Rad, TV auch)* production *(Brit)*. **die ~ bei etw führen** to direct/produce sth; *(fig)* to be in charge of sth; **unter der ~ von** directed/produced by. **(b)** *(Leitung, Verwaltung)* management. **etw in eigener ~ tun** to do sth on one's own initiative; **unter staatlicher ~** under state control.
**Regie-** [re'ʒiː-]: **~anweisung** *f* (stage) direction; **~assistent** *m* assistant producer/director.
**regieren\* 1** *vi* *(herrschen)* to rule; *(fig)* to reign. **2** *vt* Staat to rule (over), to govern; Markt, Fahrzeug to control; *(Gram)* to govern.
**Regierung** *f* government; *(von Monarch)* reign; *(Zeitabschnitt)* period of government. **die ~ Kohl** the Kohl government or administration; **an die ~ kommen** to come to power; *(durch Wahl auch)* to come into or take office; **die ~ antreten** to take power; *(nach Wahl auch)* to take office.
**Regierungs-:** **~antritt** *m* coming to power; **~bank** *f* government bench; **~bezirk** *m* ≈ region *(Brit)*, ≈ county *(US)*; **~bildung** *f* formation of a government; **~chef** *m* head of a/the government; **der belgische ~chef** the head of the Belgian government; **~erklärung** *f* inaugural speech; *(in GB)* King's/ueen's Speech; **~fähigkeit** *f* ability to govern; **r~feindlich** *adj* anti-government *no adv*; **~form** *f* form of government; **r~freundlich** *adj* pro-government *no adv*; **~geschäfte** *pl* government business *sing*; **~kreise** *pl* government circles *pl*; **~krise** *f* government(al) crisis; **~rat** *m* senior civil servant; **~sitz** *m* seat of government; **~sprecher** *m* government spokesman; **~system** *nt* system of government; **r~treu** *adj* loyal to the government; **~umbildung** *f* cabinet reshuffle or shake-up *(US)*; **~vorlage** *f* government bill; **~wechsel** *m* change of government; **~zeit** *f* rule; *(von Monarch)* reign; *(von Regierung)* term of office.
**Regime** [re'ʒiːm] *nt* **-s** *(pej)* regime.
**Regime-:** **~gegner** *m* opponent of the regime; **~kritiker** *m* critic of the regime.
**Regiment** *nt* **-e** or *(Mil)* **-er (a)** *(Herrschaft)* rule. **das ~ führen** *(col)* to be the boss *(col)*; **ein strenges ~ führen** *(col)* to be strict. **(b)** *(Mil)* regiment.

**Regiments-** *in cpds* regimental.
**Region** *f* region.
**regional** *adj* regional. **~ verschieden sein** to vary from one region to another.
**Regionalprogramm** *nt* *(Radio)* regional station; *(TV)* regional channel.
**Regisseur(in** *f)* [reʒɪ'søːɐ, -'søːrɪn] *m* director; *(Theat, Rad, TV auch)* producer *(Brit)*.
**Register** *nt* **-** *(Liste, Mus)* register; *(von Orgel auch)* stop; *(Stichwortverzeichnis)* index. **alle ~ ziehen** *(fig)* to pull out all the stops.
**Registertonne** *f* *(Naut)* register ton.
**Registratur** *f* registration; *(Büro)* records office; *(Aktenschrank)* filing cabinet.
**registrieren\*** *vti* to register; *(col: zur Kenntnis nehmen)* to note.
**Registrierkasse** *f* cash register.
**Registrierung** *f* registration.
**reglementieren\*** *vt* to regulate; *jdn* to regiment.
**Reglementierung** *f siehe vt* regulation; regimentation.
**Regler** *m* **-** regulator, control.
**reglos** *adj* motionless.
**regnen** *vti impers* to rain. **es regnet in Strömen** it's pouring (with rain); **es regnet Proteste** protests are pouring in; **es regnete Vorwürfe** reproaches hailed down.
**regnerisch** *adj* rainy.
**Regreß** *m* **-sse** *(Jur)* recourse, redress.
**Regreß-:** **~anspruch** *m* *(Jur)* claim for compensation; **r~pflichtig** *adj* liable for compensation.
**regsam** *adj* active, alert, lively.
**regulär** *adj* normal; *(vorschriftsmäßig)* proper, regular. **~e Truppen** regular troops.
**regulierbar** *adj* adjustable.
**regulieren\* 1** *vt* **(a)** to regulate; *(nachstellen auch)* to adjust. **(b)** Rechnung, Forderung to settle. **2** *vr* to become more regular. **sich von selbst ~** to be self-regulating.
**Regulierung** *f* regulation.
**Regung** *f* *(Bewegung)* movement; *(des Gefühls, von Mitleid)* stirring. **ohne jede ~** without a flicker (of emotion).
**regungslos** *adj* motionless.
**Regungslosigkeit** *f* motionlessness.
**Reh** *nt* **-e** deer; *(weiblich)* roe deer. **~e** deer.
**Reha-** *in cpds* = **Rehabilitations-**.
**Rehabilitation** *f* rehabilitation; *(von Ruf, Ehre)* vindication.
**Rehabilitationszentrum** *nt* rehabilitation centre.
**rehabilitieren\* 1** *vt* to rehabilitate; Ruf, Ehre to vindicate. **2** *vr* to rehabilitate *(form)* or vindicate oneself.
**Reh-:** **~bock** *m* roebuck; **~braten** *m* roast venison; **r~braun** *adj* russet; Augen hazel; **~keule** *f (Cook)* haunch of venison; **~kitz** *nt* fawn; **~rücken** *m (Cook)* saddle of venison.
**Reibach** *m no pl (col)* killing *(col)*. **einen ~ machen** *(col)* to make a killing *(col)*.
**Reibe** *f* **-n** *(Cook)* grater.
**Reib|eisen** *nt* rasp; *(Cook)* grater; *(fig: zänkische Frau)* shrew. **rauh wie ein ~** *(col)* like sandpaper.
**Reibekuchen** *m (Cook)* ≈ potato fritter.
**reiben** *pret* **rieb**, *ptp* **gerieben 1** *vti* **(a)** to rub. **etw blank ~** to rub sth till it shines; **jdm den Rücken ~** to rub sb's back. **(b)** *(zerkleinern)* to grate. **2** *vr* to rub oneself *(an +dat* on, against*)*; *(sich verletzen)* to scrape oneself *(an +dat* on*)*.
**Reiberei** *f usu pl (col)* friction *no pl.*
**Reibung** *f* **(a)** *(das Reiben)* rubbing; *(Phys)* friction. **(b)** *(fig)* friction *no pl.*

**Reibungs-:** ~**fläche** *f (fig)* source of friction; **r~los** *adj* frictionless; *(fig col)* trouble-free; **r~los verlaufen** to go off smoothly; ~**wärme** *f (Phys)* frictional heat.

**Reich** *nt* **-e** (**a**) *(Herrschaft(sgebiet), Imperium)* empire; *(König~)* kingdom. **das Deutsche ~** the German Reich; **das Dritte ~** the Third Reich; **das ~ Gottes** the Kingdom of God. (**b**) *(Bereich, Gebiet)* realm. **das ~ der Tiere/Pflanzen** the animal/ vegetable kingdom; **das ~ der Natur** the realm of nature; **das ist mein ~** *(fig)* that is my domain.

**reich** *adj* rich; *(wohlhabend auch)* wealthy; *(groß, vielfältig)* large, copious; *Auswahl, Erfahrung, Kenntnisse* wide; *Mahl* sumptuous; *Vegetation* rich. ~ **heiraten** *(col)* to marry (into) money; ~ **geschmückt** richly decorated; *Mensch* richly adorned; **eine ~ ausgestattete Bibliothek** a well stocked library; ~ **mit Vorräten ausgestattet** amply stocked up with supplies; **jdn ~ belohnen** to give sb a rich reward; **jdn ~ beschenken** to shower sb with presents; **eine mit Kindern ~ beschenkte Familie** a family blessed with many children; ~ **an etw** *(dat)* **sein** to be rich in sth; **in ~em Maße vorhanden sein** to abound; ~ **illustriert** richly illustrated.

**reichen 1** *vi* (**a**) *(sich erstrecken)* to stretch, to extend *(bis zu to)*; *(Stimme auch)* to carry *(bis zu to)*. **das Wasser reicht mir bis zum Hals** the water comes up to my neck; **jdm bis zur Schulter ~** to come up to sb's shoulder; **so weit ~ meine Beziehungen/ Fähigkeiten nicht** my connections are not that extensive/my skills are not that wide-ranging; **so weit das Auge reicht** as far as the eye can see.

   (**b**) *(langen)* to be enough, to suffice *(form)*. **der Saal reicht nicht für so viele Leute** the room isn't big enough for so many people; **reicht mein Geld noch bis zum Monatsende?** will my money last until the end of the month?; **reicht das Licht zum Lesen?** is there enough light to read by?; **dazu reicht meine Geduld nicht** I haven't got enough patience for that; **jetzt reicht's (mir aber)!** *(Schluß)* that's enough!

   **2** *vt (entgegenhalten, geben)* to hand; *(herüber~, hinüber~ auch)* to pass (over); *(anbieten)* to serve. **jdm etw ~** to hand/pass sb sth; **jdm die Hand ~** to hold out one's hand (to sb); **sich die Hände ~** to join hands; *(zur Begrüßung)* to shake hands.

**Reiche(r)** *mf decl as adj* rich *or* wealthy man/woman *etc.* **die ~n** the rich *or* wealthy.

**Reich-:** **r~geschmückt** *adj attr* richly adorned; **r~haltig** *adj* extensive; *Essen* rich; *Informationen* comprehensive; *Programm* varied; ~**haltigkeit** *f siehe adj* extensiveness; comprehensiveness; variety.

**reichlich 1** *adj* ample; *Zeit, Geld, Platz* ample, plenty of. **2** *adv* (**a**) *(sehr viel)* belohnen, sich eindecken amply; *verdienen* richly. ~ **Trinkgeld geben** to tip generously; ~ **Zeit/Geld haben** to have plenty of time/money; ~ **vorhanden sein** to abound; **mehr als ~ belohnt** more than amply rewarded; **das ist ~ gerechnet** that's a generous estimate; ~ **1.000 Mark** a good 1,000 marks. (**b**) *(col: ziemlich)* pretty.

**Reichtum** *m (lit, fig)* wealth *no pl*; *(Besitz)* riches *pl*. **zu ~ kommen** to become rich; **~̃er erwerben** to gain riches; **damit kann man keine ~̃er gewinnen** you won't get rich that way; **der ~ an Fischen** the abundance of fish.

**Reichweite** *f (von Geschoß, Sender)* range; *(greifbare Nähe)* reach; *(fig: Einflußbereich)* scope. **in ~** within range/the reach *(gen of)*; **jd ist in ~** sb is nearby; **außer ~** out of range/reach *(gen of)*.

**Reif¹** *m* **-(e)s**, *no pl* = **Rauhreif**.

**Reif²** *m* **-(e)s**, **-e** *(old, liter) (Stirn~)* circlet; *(Arm~)* bungle; *(Fingerring)* ring.

**reif** *adj* ripe; *Ei, Mensch, Arbeit* mature. **in ~(er)em Alter** in one's mature(r) years; **im ~en Alter von ...** at the ripe old age of ...; ~ **zur Veröffentlichung** ripe for publication; **die Zeit ist ~** the time is ripe; **eine ~e Leistung** *(col)* a brilliant achievement; **für etw ~ sein** *(col)* to be ready for sth.

**Reife** *f no pl (das Reifen)* ripening; *(das Reifsein)* ripeness; *(von Ei, Mensch, Arbeit)* maturity. **zur ~ kommen** to ripen; **ihm fehlt die ~** he lacks maturity; **mittlere ~** *(Sch)* first public examination in secondary school, ≈ GCSE *(Brit)*.

**reifen 1** *vt Obst* to ripen; *jdn* to mature; *siehe* **gereift. 2** *vi aux sein* (**a**) *(Obst)* to ripen; *(Ei, Mensch)* to mature. **er reifte zum Manne** he became a man. (**b**) *(fig: Plan etc)* to mature. **zur Gewißheit ~** to harden into certainty.

**Reifen** *m* **-** tyre *(Brit)*, tire *(US)*; *(Spiel~, von Faß)* hoop; *(Arm~)* bangle.

**Reifen-:** ~**druck** *m* tyre *(Brit)* or tire *(US)* pressure; ~**panne** *f* puncture, flat; ~**profil** *nt* tyre *(Brit)* or tire *(US)* tread; ~**wechsel** *m* tyre *(Brit)* or tire *(US)* change.

**Reife-:** ~**prüfung** *f (Sch)* = **Abitur;** ~**zeit** *f* ripening time; *(von Ei)* period of incubation; *(Pubertät)* puberty *no def art;* ~**zeugnis** *nt (Sch)* = **Abiturzeugnis.**

**reiflich** *adj* thorough, careful. **sich** *(dat)* **etw ~ überlegen** to consider sth carefully.

**Reifung** *f* ripening; *(von Ei)* maturation.

**Reigen** *m* **-** round dance; *(fig)* round. **ein bunter ~ von Melodien** a varied selection of melodies.

**Reihe** *f* **-n** (**a**) *(geregelte Anordnung)* row, line; *(Sitz~, Sew)* row; *(Serie, Math, Mus, fig)* series *sing.* **in Reih und Glied antreten** to line up in formation; **aus der ~ tanzen** *(fig col)* to be different; *(gegen Konventionen verstoßen)* to step out of line; **die ~n schließen** *(Mil, fig)* to close ranks; **die ~n lichten sich** *(fig)* the ranks are thinning; **in den eigenen ~n** within our/their *etc* own ranks.

   (**b**) *(Reihenfolge)* **er ist an der ~** it's his turn; **warte, bis du an die ~ kommst** wait till it's your turn; **der ~ nach** in order, in turn; **sie sollen der ~ nach hereinkommen** they are to come in one by one; **außer der ~** out of turn; *(ausnahmsweise)* out of the usual way of things; **er kommt immer außer der ~** he always comes just when he pleases.

   (**c**) *(unbestimmte Anzahl)* number. **eine ganze ~ (von)** a whole lot (of).

   (**d**) *(col: Ordnung)* **wieder in die ~ kommen** to get one's equilibrium back; *(gesundheitlich)* to get back on form; **in die ~ bringen** to put straight; **ich kriege heute nichts auf die ~** I can't get my act together today.

**reihen 1** *vt* (**a**) **Perlen auf eine Schnur ~** to string beads (on a thread). (**b**) *(Sew)* to tack. **2** *vr* **etw reiht sich an etw** *(acc)* sth follows (after) sth.

**Reihenfolge** *f* order; *(notwendige Aufeinanderfolge)* sequence. **der ~ nach** in sequence; **zeitliche ~** chronological order.

**Reihen-:** ~**haus** *nt* terraced house *(Brit)*, row house *(US)*; ~**schaltung** *f (Elec)* series connection; **in ~schaltung** in series; ~**untersuchung** *f* mass screening; **r~weise** *adv* (**a**) *(in Reihen)* in rows; (**b**) *(fig: in großer Anzahl)* by the dozen.

**Reiher** *m* **-** heron.

**reihern** *vi (col)* to puke (up) *(col!)*.

**reih|um** *adv* around. **es geht ~** everybody takes their turn; **etw ~ gehen lassen** to pass sth around.

**Reim** *m* **-e** rhyme. **ein ~ auf „Hut"** a rhyme for

"Hut"; ~e bilden to make rhymes; ~e schmieden *(hum)* to write verse; sich *(dat)* einen ~ auf etw *(acc)* machen *(col)* to make sense of sth; ich kann mir keinen ~ darauf machen *(col)* I can see no rhyme (n)or reason in it.

reimen *vtr* to rhyme *(auf +acc, mit* with*).* das reimt sich nicht *(fig)* it doesn't make sense.

Reim-: r~los *adj* unrhymed, non-rhyming; ~schema *nt* rhyme scheme; ~wort *nt, pl* -wörter rhyme.

rein¹ *adv (col)* = herein, hinein.

rein² 1 *adj* pure; *Wahrheit* plain; *Gewinn* clear; *(sauber)* clean; *Haut auch, Gewissen* clear. das ist die ~ste Freude/der ~ste Hohn *etc* it's pure *or* sheer joy/mockery *etc*; er ist der ~ste Künstler he's a real artist; die ~e Arbeit kostet ... the work alone costs ...; eine ~e Jungenklasse an all boys' class; eine ~e Industriestadt a purely industrial town; ~en Tisch machen *(fig)* to get things straight; etw ins ~e schreiben to write out a fair copy of sth; etw ins ~e bringen to clear sth up; mit sich selbst ins ~e kommen to sort things out with oneself. 2 *adv* (a) *(ausschließlich)* purely. ~ theoretisch gesprochen speaking purely theoretically. (b) *(col: ganz, völlig)* absolutely. ~ alles/unmöglich absolutely everything/impossible.

Rein(e)machefrau *f* cleaner, cleaning lady.

Reinemachen *nt no pl (col)* cleaning.

Rein-: ~erlös, ~ertrag *m* net profit(s).

rein(e)weg *adv (col)* completely, absolutely. das ist ~ erlogen it's a downright lie.

Reinfall *m (col)* disaster *(col)*; *(Pleite auch)* flop *(col)*.

reinfallen *vi sep irreg aux sein (col)* = hereinfallen, hineinfallen.

Rein-: ~gewicht *nt* net(t) weight; ~gewinn *m* net(t) profit; ~haltung *f* keeping clean; die ~haltung des Spielplatzes keeping the playground clean.

Reinheit *f* purity; *(Sauberkeit)* cleanness.

reinigen 1 *vt* to clean. etw chemisch ~ to dry-clean sth; ein ~des Gewitter *(fig col)* a row which clears/cleared the air. 2 *vr* to clean itself; *(Mensch)* to cleanse oneself.

Reiniger *m* - cleaner.

Reinigung *f* (a) cleaning. (b) *(chemische ~) (Vorgang)* dry-cleaning; *(Anstalt)* (dry-)cleaner's *(Brit)* or cleaner *(US)*.

Reinigungs-: ~creme *f* cleansing cream; ~mittel *nt* cleansing agent.

reinkriegen *vt sep (col)* = hereinbekommen, hineinbekommen.

Reinkultur *f (Biol)* cultivation of pure cultures. Kitsch in ~ *(col)* pure unadulterated kitsch.

reinlegen *vt sep (col)* = hereinlegen, hineinlegen.

reinlich *adj* cleanly; *(ordentlich)* neat, tidy; *(klar)* clear.

Reinlichkeit *f siehe adj* cleanliness; neatness, tidiness; clearness.

Rein-: r~rassig *adj* pure-blooded; *Tier* pure-bred, thoroughbred; ~rassigkeit *f* racial purity; *(von Tier)* pure breeding; r~reiten *vt sep irreg* jdn r~reiten *(col)* to get sb into a mess *(col)*; ~schrift *f (Geschriebenes)* fair copy; ~seiden *adj* pure silk; r~tun *vr (col)* sich *(dat)* etw r~tun to imagine sth; ~vermögen *nt* net assets *pl*.

re|investieren* *vti (Comm)* to reinvest.

rein-: ~waschen *sep irreg* 1 *vt (von of)* to clear; 2 *vr (fig)* to clear oneself; ~weg *adv* = rein(e)weg; ~würgen *vt (col) Essen etc* to force down; jdm einen ~würgen to do the dirty on sb *(col)*; ~ziehen *vr (col)* sich *(dat)* etw ~ziehen *Drogen* to take sth;

*Musik* to listen to sth; *Film* to watch sth; *Getränk* to knock sth back.

Reis *m* -e rice.

Reisbrei *m* ≃ creamed rice.

Reise *f* -n journey, trip; *(Schiffs~)* voyage; *(Geschäfts~)* trip. seine ~n durch Europa his travels through Europe; eine ~ mit der Eisenbahn/dem Auto a train/car journey; eine ~ zu Schiff a sea voyage; eine ~ machen to go on a journey; auf ~n sein to be away (travelling *(Brit)* or traveling *(US)*); er ist viel auf ~n he does a lot of travelling; wohin geht die ~? where are you off to?; gute ~! bon voyage!, have a good journey!

Reise-: ~andenken *nt* souvenir; ~apotheke *f* first aid kit; ~begleiter *m* (a) travelling *(Brit)* or traveling *(US)* companion; (b) = ~leiter; ~bericht *m* account of one's journey; *(Buch)* travel story; *(Film)* travelogue; ~beschränkungen *pl* travel restrictions *pl*; ~beschreibung *f* description of one's travels; travel book *or* story; *(Film)* travelogue; ~büro *nt* travel agency; ~bus *m* coach; ~erleichterungen *pl* easing of travel restrictions; r~fertig *adj* ready to leave; ~fieber *nt* vom ~fieber gepackt excited about going on a trip; ~führer *m (Buch)* guidebook; *(Person)* courier; ~gefährte *m* travelling *(Brit)* or traveling *(US)* companion; ~geld *nt* fare; ~gepäck *nt* luggage, baggage; ~gesellschaft, ~gruppe *f* (tourist) party; *(im Bus auch)* coach party *(Brit)*; *(Veranstalter)* travel company; ~koffer *m* suitcase; ~kosten *pl* travelling *(Brit)* or traveling *(US)* expenses *pl*; ~land *nt* holiday destination; ~leiter *m* courier, tour guide; ~leitung *f (das Leiten)* tour management; *(~leiter)* courier(s); ~lektüre *f* reading matter (for a journey); etw als ~lektüre mitnehmen to take sth to read on the journey; ~lust *f* wanderlust, travel bug *(col)*; r~lustig *adj* keen on travel.

reisen *vi aux sein* to travel. in etw *(dat)* ~ *(Comm)* to travel in sth.

Reisende(r) *mf decl as adj* traveller *(Brit)*, traveler *(US)*; *(Fahrgast)* passenger; *(Comm)* (commercial) traveller *(Brit)*, traveler *(US)*.

Reise-: ~paß *m* passport; ~pläne *pl* plans *pl* (for a/the journey); ~proviant *m* food for the journey; ~route *f* route, itinerary; ~scheck *m* traveller's cheque *(Brit)*, traveler's check *(US)*; ~schreibmaschine *f* portable typewriter; ~spesen *pl* travelling *(Brit)* or traveling *(US)* expenses *pl*; ~tasche *f* grip, travelling *(Brit)* or traveling *(US)* bag; ~veranstalter *m* tour operator; ~verkehr *m* holiday traffic; ~versicherung *f* travel insurance; ~vorbereitungen *pl* travel preparations *pl*; ~wecker *m* travelling (alarm) clock; ~welle *f* die ~welle nach Süden the trail of holidaymakers heading south; ~zeit *f* time for travelling *(Brit)* or traveling *(US)*; die beste ~zeit für Ägypten the best time to go to Egypt; ~ziel *nt* destination.

Reisfeld *nt* paddy field.

Reisig *nt no pl* brushwood, twigs *pl*.

Reiskorn *nt* grain of rice.

Reiß|aus *m:* ~ nehmen *(col)* to clear off *(col)*.

Reiß-: ~brett *nt* drawing board; ~brettstift *m* drawing pin *(Brit)*, thumb tack *(US)*.

reißen *pret* riß, *ptp* gerissen 1 *vt* (a) *(zer~)* to tear, to rip. (b) *(ab~, ent~)* to tear, to pull, to rip *(etw von etw* sth off sth*)*; *(mit~, zerren)* to pull, to drag. jdn zu Boden ~ to drag sb to the ground; der Fluß hat die Brücke mit sich gerissen the river swept the bridge away; jdn aus seinen Träumen ~ to wake sb from his/her dreams; hin und her gerissen sein *(fig)* to be torn between two possibilities. (c) etw an sich *(acc)* ~ to seize sth; *Unterhaltung* to monopolize sth. **(d)** *(Sport) Latte, Hürde* to knock off. **(e)** *(töten)* to take, to kill. **(f)** *(col: machen) Witze* to crack *(col)*; *Possen* to play.

**2** *vi* **(a)** *aux sein (zer~)* to tear, to rip; *(Seil)* to tear, to break, to snap; *(Risse bekommen)* to crack. **mir ist die Kette gerissen** my chain has broken *or* snapped; **wenn alle Stricke** ~ *(fig col)* if the worst comes to the worst. **(b)** *(zerren) (an +dat at)* to tug; *(wütend)* to tear. **(c)** *(Sport) (Gewichtheben)* to snatch; *(Leichtathletik)* to knock the bar off.

**3** *vr* **(a)** *(sich verletzen)* to cut oneself *(an +dat on)*. **(b)** *(sich los~)* to tear oneself/itself. **(c)** *(col)* **sich um jdn/etw** ~ to fight over sb/sth *(fig)*.

**Reißen** *nt no pl* **(a)** *(Gewichtheben: Disziplin)* snatch. **(b)** *(col: Glieder~)* ache.

**reißend** *adj Fluß* torrential, raging; *Schmerzen* searing; *Verkauf, Absatz* massive. ~**en Absatz finden** to sell like hot cakes *(col)*.

**Reißer** *m* - *(col) (Buch, Film)* thriller; *(Ware)* big seller.

**reißerisch** *adj* sensational.

**Reiß-:** **r~fest** *adj* tearproof; ~**leine** *f* ripcord; ~**nagel** *m* = ~**zwecke**; ~**verschluß** *m* zip(-fastener) *(Brit)*, zipper *(US)*; ~**wolf** *m* shredder; ~**zahn** *m* fang; ~**zeug** *nt* drawing instruments *pl*; ~**zwecke** *f* drawing pin *(Brit)*, thumb tack *(US)*.

**Reit-:** ~**anzug** *m* riding habit; ~**bahn** *f* arena.

**reiten** *pret* **ritt**, *ptp* **geritten 1** *vi aux sein* to ride. **auf etw** *(dat)* ~ to ride (on) sth; **im Schritt/Galopp** ~ to ride at a walk/gallop. **2** *vt* to ride. **ein schnelles Tempo** ~ to ride at a fast pace.

**Reiter** *m* - **(a)** rider, horseman; *(Mil)* cavalryman. **(b)** *(Kartei~)* index-tab.

**Reiterin** *f* rider, horsewoman.

**Reiterregiment** *nt* cavalry regiment.

**Reit-:** ~**gerte** *f* riding crop; ~**hose** *f* riding breeches *pl*; *(Sport)* jodhpurs *pl*; ~**peitsche** *f* riding whip; ~**pferd** *nt* saddle-horse, mount; ~**schule** *f* riding school; ~**sport** *m* (horse-)riding, equestrian sport *(form)*; ~**stall** *m* riding stable; ~**stiefel** *m* riding boot; ~**turnier** *nt* horse show; *(Geländereiten)* point-to-point; ~**weg** *m* bridle path.

**Reiz** *m* **-e (a)** *(Physiol)* stimulus. **einen** ~ **auf etw** *(acc)* **ausüben** to act as a stimulus to sth. **(b)** *(Verlockung)* attraction, appeal; *(Zauber)* charm. **der** ~ **der Neuheit/des Verbotenen** the appeal of novelty/forbidden fruits; **(auf jdn) einen** ~ **ausüben** to hold great attraction(s) (for sb); **den** ~ **verlieren** to lose all one's/its charm; **weibliche** ~**e** feminine charms.

**Reiz-:** **r~bar** *adj* *(empfindlich)* sensitive, touchy *(col)*; *(erregbar, Med)* irritable; **leicht r~bar sein** to be very sensitive/irritable; ~**barkeit** *f siehe adj* sensitivity, touchiness *(col)*; irritability.

**reizen 1** *vt* **(a)** *(Physiol)* to irritate; *(stimulieren)* to stimulate. **(b)** *(verlocken)* to appeal to. **es würde mich ja sehr** ~, **das zu tun** I'd love to do that; **Ihr Angebot reizt mich sehr** I find your offer very tempting. **(c)** *(ärgern)* to annoy; *(herausfordern)* to provoke. **jds Zorn** ~ to arouse sb's anger; *siehe* **gereizt.** **(d)** *(Cards)* to bid. **2** *vi* **(a)** *(Med)* to irritate; *(stimulieren)* to stimulate. **zum Widerspruch** ~ to invite contradiction. **(b)** *(Cards)* to bid.

**reizend** *adj* charming. **das ist ja** ~ *(iro)* (that's) charming.

**Reiz-:** ~**gas** *nt* irritant gas; ~**husten** *m* chesty cough; ~**klima** *nt* bracing climate; **r~los** *adj* dull, uninspiring; ~**mittel** *nt (Med)* stimulant; ~**stoff** *m* irritant.

**Reizung** *f* **(a)** *(Med)* stimulation; *(krankhaft)* irritation. **(b)** *(Herausforderung)* provocation.

**Reiz-:** **r~voll** *adj* charming, delightful; *Aufgabe, Beruf* attractive; **die Aussicht ist nicht gerade r~voll** the prospect is not exactly appealing; ~**wäsche** *f (col)* sexy underwear; ~**wort** *nt* emotive word.

**rekapitulieren*** *vt* to recapitulate.

**rekeln** *vr (col: sich strecken)* to stretch. **er rekelte sich in einem behaglichen Sessel** he lay sprawled in a comfy chair.

**Reklamation** *f* complaint.

**Reklame** *f* **-n (a)** advertising. ~ **für jdn/etw machen** to advertise sb/sth; **mit etw** ~ **machen** *(pej)* to show off about sth. **(b)** *(Anzeige)* advertisement, advert *(Brit col)*; *(TV, Rad auch)* commercial.

**Reklame-:** ~**schild** *nt* advertising sign; ~**sendung** *f* commercial break; ~**trommel** *f*: **die** ~**trommel für jdn/etw rühren** *(col)* to beat the (big) drum for sb/sth, to do a lot of promotion for sb/sth; ~**zettel** *m* (advertising) leaflet.

**reklamieren*** **1** *vi (Einspruch erheben)* to complain, to make a complaint. **bei jdm wegen etw** ~ to complain to sb about sth. **2** *vt* **(a)** *(bemängeln) Rechnung* to query *(etw bei jdm* sth with sb*)*. **(b)** *(beanspruchen)* **jdn/etw für sich** ~ to lay claim to sb/sth.

**rekonstruieren*** *vt* to reconstruct.

**Rekonstruktion** *f* reconstruction.

**Rekord** *m* **-e** record.

**Rekord-** *in cpds* record; ~**halter,** ~**inhaber** *m* record-holder; ~**lauf** *m* record(-breaking) run; ~**leistung** *f* record; ~**marke** *f (Sport, fig)* record; ~**versuch** *m* record attempt; ~**zeit** *f* record time.

**Rekrut** *m (wk)* **-en, -en** *(Mil)* recruit.

**rekrutieren*** **1** *vt (Mil, fig)* to recruit. **2** *vr (fig)* **sich** ~ **aus** to be drawn from.

**Rekrutierung** *f* recruitment, recruiting.

**Rektor** *m,* **Rektorin** *f (Sch)* headteacher, principal *(esp US)*; *(Univ)* vice-chancellor, rector *(US)*; *(von Fachhochschule)* principal.

**Relais** [rə'lɛː] *nt* - [rə'lɛː(s)], - [rə'lɛːs] *(Elec)* relay.

**Relation** *f* relation. **in einer/keiner** ~ **zu etw stehen** to bear some/no relation to sth.

**relativ 1** *adj* relative. ~**e Mehrheit** *(Parl)* simple majority. **2** *adv* relatively.

**relativieren*** [relati'viːrən] *vt (geh)* to qualify.

**Relativität** [relativi'tɛːt] *f* relativity.

**Relativ-:** ~**pronomen** *nt* relative pronoun; ~**satz** *m* relative clause.

**relevant** [rele'vant] *adj* relevant.

**Relevanz** [rele'vants] *f* relevance.

**Relief** [reli'ɛf] *nt* **-s** *or* **-e** relief.

**Religion** *f* religion; *(Schulfach)* religious instruction or education, RE *(Brit col)*.

**Religions-:** ~**bekenntnis** *nt* denomination; ~**freiheit** *f* freedom of worship; ~**führer** *m* religious leader; ~**gemeinschaft** *f* religious community; ~**krieg** *m* religious war; ~**lehrer** *m* teacher of religious education, RE teacher *(Brit col)*; **r~los** *adj* not religious; ~**stunde** *f* religious education *no indef art,* RE lesson *(Brit col)*; ~**unterricht** *m* religious education; ~**zugehörigkeit** *f* religion.

**religiös** *adj* religious. ~ **erzogen werden** to receive a religious upbringing.

**Religiosität** *f* religiousness.

**Relikt** *nt* **-e** relic.

**Reling** *f* **-s** *or* **-e** *(Naut)* (deck) rail.

**Reliquie** [-iə] *f* relic.

**remis** [rə'miː] *adj inv* drawn. ~ **spielen** to draw; **die Partie ist** ~ the game has ended in a draw.

**Remis** [rə'miː] *nt* - [rə'miː(s)], - [rə'miːs] *or* **-en** [rə'miːzn] *(Schach, Sport)* draw.

**Remittende** f -n *(Comm)* return.
**Remittent(in** f) m *(Fin)* payee.
**remittieren*** vt *(Comm) Waren* to return; *Geld* to remit.
**Remmidemmi** nt no pl *(col) (Krach)* shindig *(col)*, rumpus *(col)*; *(Trubel)* rave-up *(col)*.
**Rempelei** f *(col)* jostling; *(Sport: Foul)* pushing.
**rempeln** vti *(col)* to jostle, to elbow; *(im Sport)* to barge *(jdn* into sb); *(foulen)* to push.
**Ren** nt -e reindeer.
**Renaissance** [rənɛ'sãːs] f -en (a) *(Hist)* renaissance. (b) *(fig)* revival, rebirth.
**Rendezvous** [rãde'vuː] nt - [-'vuː(s)], - [-'vuːs] rendezvous *(liter, hum)*, date.
**Rendite** f -n *(Fin)* yield, return on capital.
**renitent** adj awkward, refractory.
**Renitenz** f awkwardness, refractoriness.
**Renn-** in cpds race; ~**bahn** f (race)track; ~**boot** nt (racing) powerboat.
**rennen** pret **rannte**, ptp **gerannt 1** vi aux sein to run. **um die Wette** ~ to have a race; **ins Unglück** ~ to rush headlong into disaster; **er rennt zu jedem Fußballspiel** he goes to every football match; **gegen jdn/etw** ~ to run into sb/sth; **er rannte mit dem Kopf gegen** ... he bumped his head against ... **2** vt **(a)** aux haben or sein *(Sport)* to run. **(b) jdn zu Boden** or **über den Haufen** ~ to knock sb down. **(c)** *(stoßen) Messer etc* to run.
**Rennen** nt - running; *(Sport) (Vorgang)* racing; *(Veranstaltung)* race. **totes** ~ dead heat; **gut im** ~ **liegen** *(lit, fig)* to be well placed; **das** ~ **ist gelaufen** *(lit)* the race is over; *(fig)* it's all over; **das** ~ **machen** *(lit, fig)* to win (the race).
**Renner** m - *(col)* big seller.
**Rennerei** f *(col) (lit, fig: das Herumrennen)* running around; *(Hetze)* mad chase *(col)*.
**Renn-**: ~**fahrer** m *(Rad~)* racing cyclist; *(Motorrad~)* racing motorcyclist; *(Auto~)* racing driver; ~**pferd** nt racehorse; ~**piste** f (race)track; ~**platz** m racecourse; ~**rad** nt racing bike *(col)*; ~**saison** f racing season; ~**schlitten** m bob-(sleigh); ~**schuh** m *(Sport)* running or track shoe; ~**sport** m racing; ~**stall** m *(Tiere, Zucht)* stable; ~**strecke** f racecourse; *(Ring)* racing circuit; ~**tag** m day of the race; ~**veranstaltung** f race meeting; ~**wagen** m racing car.
**Renommee** nt -s reputation, name.
**renommieren*** vi to show off.
**renommiert** adj renowned, famous *(wegen* for).
**renovieren*** [reno'viːrən] vt to renovate; *(esp tapezieren etc)* to redecorate, to do up *(col)*.
**Renovierung** [reno'viːrʊŋ] f renovation.
**rentabel** adj profitable. **es ist nicht** ~, **das reparieren zu lassen** it is not worth(while) having it repaired; **das ist eine rentable Sache** it will pay (off).
**Rentabilität** f profitability.
**Rente** f -n pension; *(aus Versicherung, Lebens~)* annuity; *(aus Vermögen)* income. **in** ~ **gehen/sein** *(col)* to start drawing one's pension/to be on a pension.
**Renten-**: ~**alter** nt retirement age; ~**anspruch** m right to a pension; ~**basis** f annuity basis; ~**empfänger** m pensioner; ~**erhöhung** f pension increase; ~**papier** nt *(Fin)* fixed-interest security; ~**versicherung** f pension scheme.
**Rentier** nt *(Zool)* reindeer.
**rentieren*** vir to be worthwhile; *(Geschäft etc auch, Maschine)* to pay. **das rentiert (sich) nicht** it's not worth it.
**Rentner(in** f) m - pensioner; *(Alters~* auch) senior citizen, old age pensioner *(Brit)*.

**re|organisieren*** vt to reorganize.
**reparabel** adj repairable.
**Reparationen** pl reparations pl.
**Reparatur** f repair. ~**en am Auto** car repairs; ~**en am Haus vornehmen** to do some repairs to the house; **in** ~ being repaired; **etw in** ~ **geben** to have sth repaired.
**Reparatur-**: **r~anfällig** adj apt to break down; **r~bedürftig** adj in need of repair; ~**kosten** pl repair costs pl; ~**werkstatt** f workshop; *(Autowerkstatt)* garage.
**reparieren*** vt to mend; *Auto* to repair.
**Repertoire** [reper'toaːɐ] nt -s repertory, repertoire *(auch fig)*.
**Replik** f -en *(fig geh)* riposte, reply.
**Report** m -e report.
**Reportage** [repɔr'taːʒə] f -n report.
**Reporter(in** f) m - reporter.
**Repräsentant(in** f) m representative.
**Repräsentantenhaus** nt *(US Pol)* House of Representatives.
**repräsentativ** adj *(stellvertretend, typisch)* representative *(für* of); *Haus, Auto* prestigious. **zu** ~**en Zwecken** for purposes of prestige; **die** ~**en Pflichten eines Botschafters** the social duties of an ambassador.
**repräsentieren*** **1** vt to represent. **2** vi to perform official duties.
**Repressalie** [-iə] f reprisal.
**Repression** f repression.
**repressiv** adj repressive.
**Reprise** f -n *(Mus)* recapitulation; *(Film, Theat)* rerun; *(nach längerer Zeit)* revival.
**Reproduktion** f reproduction.
**reproduktiv** adj reproductive.
**reproduzieren*** vt to reproduce.
**Reptil** nt -ien [-iən] reptile.
**Republik** f -en republic.
**Republikaner(in** f) m - republican. **die** ~ *(BRD Pol)* the Republicans.
**republikanisch** adj republican.
**Republik-**: ~**flucht** f *(DDR)* illegal crossing of the border; ~**flüchtling** m *(DDR)* illegal emigrant.
**Requiem** ['reːkviɛm] nt -s requiem.
**Requisit** nt -en piece of equipment, requisite *(form)*. ~**en** *(Theat)* props, properties *(form)*.
**Requisiteur(in** f) [-'tøːɐ, -'tøːrɪn] m *(Theat)* props or property manager.
**Reseda** f, pl **Reseden** *(Bot) (Gattung)* reseda; *(Garten~)* mignonette.
**Reservat** [resɛr'vaːt] nt **(a)** *(Wildpark)* reserve. **(b)** *(für Volksstämme)* reservation.
**Reserve** [re'zɛrvə] f -n **(a)** *(Vorrat)* reserve(s) *(an +dat* of); *(Geld)* savings pl; *(Mil, Sport)* reserves pl. **(b)** *(Zurückhaltung)* reserve. **jdn aus der** ~ **locken** to bring sb out of his/her shell *(col)*.
**Reserve-**: ~**bank** f *(Sport)* substitutes bench; ~**kanister** m spare can; ~**rad** nt spare wheel; ~**reifen** m spare tyre *(Brit)* or tire *(US)*; ~**spieler** m *(Sport)* reserve; ~**tank** m reserve tank; ~**truppen** pl reserves pl; ~**übung** f (army) reserve training no pl.
**reservieren*** [rezɛr'viːrən] vt to reserve.
**reserviert** adj *Platz, Mensch* reserved.
**Reserviertheit** f reserve.
**Reservierung** f reservation.
**Reservist** [rezɛr'vɪst] m reservist.
**Reservoir** [rezɛr'voaːɐ] nt -e reservoir; *(fig auch)* pool.
**Residenz** f *(Wohnung)* residence.
**residieren*** vi to reside.

**Resignation** *f (geh)* resignation.
**resignieren\*** *vi* to give up. **resigniert** resigned; ... **sagte er ~d** ... he said with resignation.
**resistent** *adj (auch Med)* resistant *(gegen* to*)*.
**resolut** *adj* determined.
**Resolution** *f (Pol) (Beschluß)* resolution; *(Bittschrift)* petition.
**Resonanz** *f* **(a)** *(Mus, Phys)* resonance. **(b)** *(fig)* response *(auf +acc* to*)*. **keine/große ~ finden** to meet with no/a good response.
**Resonanzboden** *m* sounding board.
**Resopal** ® *nt no pl* ≃ Formica ®.
**resozialisieren\*** *vt* to rehabilitate.
**Resozialisierung** *f* rehabilitation.
**Respekt** *m no pl* respect; *(Angst)* fear. **bei allem ~ (vor jdm/etw)** with all due respect (to sb/sth); **vor jdm/etw ~ haben** to have respect for sb/sth; *(Angst)* to be afraid of sb/sth.
**respektabel** *adj* respectable.
**respektieren\*** *vt* to respect; *Wechsel* to honour *(Brit)*, to honor *(US)*.
**respektive** [respɛk'tiːvə] *adv (geh, Comm)* **(a)** *siehe* **beziehungsweise.** **(b)** *(anders ausgedrückt)* or rather; *(genauer gesagt)* (or) more precisely.
**Respekt-:** **r~los** *adj* disrespectful, irreverent; **~losigkeit** *f* **(a)** *(no pl: Verhalten)* disrespect(fulness), irreverence; **(b)** *(Bemerkung)* disrespectful remark.
**Respektsperson** *f* person to be respected.
**respektvoll** *adj* respectful.
**Ressentiment** [rɛsãti'mãː, rə-] *nt* **-s** resentment *no pl (gegen* against*)*.
**Ressort** [rɛ'soːɐ] *nt* **-s** department. **in das ~ von jdm fallen** *(lit, fig)* to be sb's department.
**Rest** *m* **-e** **(a)** rest; *(Stoff~)* remnant. **die ~e einer Stadt/Kultur** the remains of a city/civilization; **der letzte ~** the last bit; **dieser kleine ~** this little bit that's left (over); **der ~ ist für Sie** *(beim Bezahlen)* keep the change; **jdm/einer Sache den ~ geben** *(col)* to finish sb/sth off. **(b)** **~e** *pl (Essens~)* left-overs *pl.*
**Restaurant** [rɛsto'rãː] *nt* **-s** restaurant.
**Restauration** *f* restoration.
**Restaurator** *m,* **Restauratorin** *f* restorer.
**restaurieren\*** *vt* to restore.
**Restaurierung** *f* restoration.
**Rest-** *in cpds* remaining; **~bestand** *m* remaining stock; **~betrag** *m* balance; **r~lich** *adj* remaining, rest of the ...; **die r~lichen** the rest; **r~los 1** *adj* complete, total; **2** *adv* completely, totally, *begeistert* wildly; **~posten** *m (Comm)* remaining stock; **ein ~posten** remaining stock; **~summe** *f* balance, amount remaining.
**Resultat** *nt* result. **zu dem ~ kommen, daß ...** to come to the conclusion that ...
**resultieren\*** *vi (geh)* to result *(in +dat* in*)*. **aus etw ~** to result from sth; **die daraus ~den** ... the resulting ...
**Resümee** *nt* **-s** *(geh)* summary, résumé.
**resümieren\*** *vti (geh)* to summarize, to sum up.
**Retorte** *f* **-n** *(Chem)* retort. **aus der ~** *(col)* synthetic.
**Retortenbaby** *nt* test-tube baby.
**retour** [re'tuːɐ] *adv (old, dial)* back.
**Retourkutsche** [re'tuːɐ-] *f (col)* riposte.
**Retrospektive** *f* retrospective.
**retten 1** *vt* to save; *(befreien)* to rescue. **jdm das Leben ~** to save sb's life; **jdn vor jdm/etw ~** to save sb from sb/sth; **ein ~der Gedanke** a bright idea that saved the situation; **bist du noch zu ~?** *(col)* are you out of your mind? *(col).* **2** *vr* to escape. **sich aus etw ~** to escape from sth; **sich vor jdm/etw ~** to escape (from) sb/sth; **sich vor etw nicht mehr ~ kön-**

**nen** *(fig)* to be swamped with sth; **rette sich, wer kann!** (it's) every man for himself!
**Retter(in** *f)* *m* - rescuer; *(Rel)* Saviour *(Brit)*, Savior *(US)*.
**Rettich** *m* **-e** radish.
**Rettung** *f* rescue, deliverance *(liter)*; *(Rel)* salvation. **die ~ kam in letzter Minute** the situation was saved in the last minute; *(für Schiffbrüchige etc)* help came in the nick of time; **auf ~ hoffen** to hope to be saved; **für den Patienten gibt es keine ~ mehr** the patient is beyond saving; **das/er war meine ~** that/ he was my salvation; **das war meine letzte ~** that was my last hope.
**Rettungs-:** **~aktion** *f* rescue operation; **~anker** *m* sheet anchor; *(fig)* anchor; **~boot** *nt* lifeboat; **~dienst** *m* rescue service; **~hubschrauber** *m* rescue helicopter; **~kommando** *nt* rescue squad; **r~los 1** *adj* beyond saving; *Lage* hopeless; **2** *adv verloren* irretrievably; **~mannschaft** *f* rescue party *or* team; **~ring** *m* lifebelt; **~schwimmer** *m* lifesaver; *(am Strand)* lifeguard; **~wagen** *m* ambulance.
**retuschieren\*** *vt (Phot)* to retouch, to touch up *(col, auch fig).*
**Reue** *f no pl* remorse *(über +acc* at, about*)*, repentance *(auch Rel) (über +acc* of*)*; *(Bedauern)* regret *(über +acc* at, about*)*.
**reuelos** *adj* unrepentant.
**reuen** *vt (liter)* **etw reut jdn** sb regrets sth.
**reuevoll, reuig** *adj (liter) siehe* **reumütig.**
**reumütig** *adj* remorseful; *Sünder* contrite. **~ gestand er ...** full of remorse he confessed ...
**Reuse** *f* **-n** fish trap.
**Revanche** [re'vãːʃ(ə)] *f* **-n** revenge; *(~partie)* return match. **du mußt ihm ~ geben!** you'll have to give him a return match.
**revanchieren\*** [revã'ʃiːrən] *vr* **(a)** to get one's own back *(bei jdm für etw* on sb for sth*)*. **(b)** *(sich erkenntlich zeigen)* to reciprocate. **sich bei jdm für eine Einladung ~** to return sb's invitation.
**Revanchismus** [revã'ʃɪsmʊs] *m* revanchism.
**revanchistisch** [revã'ʃɪstɪʃ] *adj* revanchist.
**Reverenz** [reve'rɛnts] *f (old)* **jdm seine ~ erweisen** to show one's reverence for sb.
**Revers** [re'veːɐ] *nt or m* - [re'veːɐ(s)], - [re'veːɐs] *(an Kleidung)* lapel, revers *(esp US)*.
**revidieren\*** [revi'diːrən] *vt* to revise; *(Comm)* to audit.
**Revier** [re'viːɐ] *nt* **-e** **(a)** *(Polizei~) (Dienststelle)* (police) station, station house *(US)*; *(Dienstbereich)* beat, precinct *(US)*, patch *(col).* **(b)** *(Zool: Gebiet)* territory. **die Küche ist mein ~** the kitchen is my preserve. **(c)** *(Hunt: Jagd~)* hunting ground, shoot. **(d)** *(Min: Kohlen~)* (coal)mine. **das ~** the Ruhr/ Saar coalfields.
**Revision** [revi'zioːn] *f* **(a)** *(von Meinung, Politik etc)* revision. **(b)** *(Comm: Prüfung)* audit. **(c)** *(Jur: Urteilsanfechtung)* appeal *(an +acc* to*)*.
**Revisionismus** [revizio'nɪsmʊs] *m (Pol)* revisionism.
**revisionistisch** [revizio'nɪstɪʃ] *adj (Pol)* revisionist.
**Revisions-:** **~frist** *f (Jur)* time for appeal; **~verhandlung** *f (Jur)* appeal hearing.
**Revisor** [re'viːzɔr] *m (Comm)* auditor.
**Revolte** [re'vɔltə] *f* **-n** revolt.
**revoltieren\*** [revɔl'tiːrən] *vi* to revolt, to rebel.
**Revolution** [revolu'tsioːn] *f (lit, fig)* revolution.
**revolutionär** [revolutsio'nɛːɐ] *adj (lit, fig)* revolutionary.
**Revolutionär(in** *f)* [revolutsio'nɛːɐ, -'nɛːərɪn] *m* revolutionary.
**revolutionieren\*** [revolutsio'niːrən] *vt* to revolutio-

nize.

**Revolutions-** *in cpds* revolutionary.

**Revoluzzer(in** *f)* [revo'lʊtsɐ, -ərɪn] *m* - *(pej)* would-be revolutionary.

**Revolver** [re'vɔlvɐ] *m* - revolver, gun.

**Revolver-**: ~**blatt** *nt (pej)* scandal sheet; ~**held** *m (pej)* gunslinger.

**Revue** [rə'vyː] *f* -**n** [-yːən] *(Theat)* revue. **etw** ~ **passieren lassen** *(fig)* to pass sth in review.

**Revuetänzerin** [rə'vyː-] *f* chorus girl.

**Reykjavik** ['raikjaviːk] *nt* Reykjavik.

**Rezensent(in** *f)* *m* reviewer.

**rezensieren\*** *vt* to review.

**Rezension** *f* review.

**Rezept** *nt* -**e** (a) *(Med)* prescription; *(fig)* remedy *(für, gegen* for*)*. **auf** ~ on prescription. (b) *(Cook, fig)* recipe.

**rezeptfrei 1** *adj* available without prescription. **2** *adv* over the counter.

**Rezeption** *f (von Hotel: Empfang)* reception, front desk *(US)*.

**Rezept-**: ~**pflicht** *f* prescription requirement; **r**~**pflichtig** *adj* available only on prescription.

**Rezession** *f (Econ)* recession.

**rezessiv** *adj (Biol)* recessive.

**reziprok** *adj (Math, Gram)* reciprocal.

**rezitieren\*** *vti* to recite.

**R-Gespräch** ['ɛr-] *nt* reverse charge call *(Brit)*, collect call.

**RGW** [ɛr'geː've:] *m* = **Rat für gegenseitige Wirtschaftshilfe** COMECON.

**Rh** [ɛr'haː] = **Rhesusfaktor positiv.**

**rh** [ɛr'haː] = **Rhesusfaktor negativ.**

**Rhabarber** *m no pl (auch Gemurmel)* rhubarb.

**Rhapsodie** *f* rhapsody.

**Rhein** *m* Rhine.

**Rhein-**: **r**~**ab(wärts)** *adv* down the Rhine; ~**armee** *f* British Army of the Rhine; **r**~**auf(wärts)** *adv* up the Rhine; ~**fall** *m* Rhine Falls *pl*.

**rheinisch** *adj attr* Rhenish, Rhineland.

**Rhein-**: ~**land** *nt* Rhineland; ~**länder(in** *f)* *m* - Rhinelander; **r**~**ländisch** *adj* Rhineland; ~**land-Pfalz** *nt* Rhineland-Palatinate; ~**wein** *m* Rhine wine; *(weißer auch)* hock *(Brit)*.

**Rhesus-**: ~**affe** *m* rhesus monkey; ~**faktor** *m (Med)* rhesus factor.

**Rhetorik** *f* rhetoric.

**rhetorisch** *adj* rhetorical. ~**e Frage** rhetorical question.

**Rheuma** *nt no pl* rheumatism.

**Rheumatiker(in** *f)* *m* - rheumatism sufferer.

**rheumatisch** *adj* rheumatic.

**Rheumatismus** *m* rheumatism.

**Rhinozeros** *nt* -(**ses**), -**se** rhinoceros, rhino *(col)*; *(col: Dummkopf)* fool.

**Rhodesien** [-iən] *nt (Hist)* Rhodesia.

**Rhodesier(in** *f)* [-iɐ, -iərɪn] *m* - *(Hist)* Rhodesian.

**rhodesisch** *adj (Hist)* Rhodesian.

**Rhododendron** [rodo'dɛndrɔn] *m or nt, pl* **Rhododendren** rhododendron.

**Rhodos** ['roːdɔs, 'rɔdɔs] *nt* Rhodes.

**Rhombus** *m, pl* **Rhomben** rhombus.

**rhythmisch** *adj* rhythmic (al).

**Rhythmus** *m (Mus, Poet, fig)* rhythm.

**RIAS** *m* = **Rundfunk im amerikanischen Sektor** *broadcasting station in the former American Sector (of Berlin)*.

**Richtantenne** *f* directional aerial *(esp Brit)* or antenna.

**richten 1** *vt* (a) *(lenken)* to direct *(auf +acc* towards*)*, to point *(auf +acc* at, towards*)*; *Augen, Auf-*

*merksamkeit* to turn *(auf +acc* towards*)*, to focus *(auf +acc* on*)*. (b) *(aus~)* etw **nach jdm/etw** ~ to suit sth to sb/sth; *Verhalten* to adapt sth to sb/sth. (c) *(adressieren) Briefe, Anfragen* to address *(an +acc* to*)*; *Bitten, Forderungen* to make *(an +acc* to*)*; *Kritik, Vorwurf* to direct *(gegen* at, against*)*. (d) *(esp S Ger) (zurechtmachen)* to prepare, to get ready; *(in Ordnung bringen)* to do, to fix; *(reparieren)* to fix; *Haare* to do; *Tisch* to lay *(Brit)*, to set; *Betten* to make, to do. (e) *(einstellen)* to set.

**2** *vr* (a) *(sich hinwenden)* to focus, to be focussed *(auf +acc* on*)*, to be directed *(auf +acc* towards*)*. (b) *(sich wenden)* to consult *(an jdn* sb*)*; *(Maßnahme, Vorwurf etc)* to be aimed *(gegen* at*)*. (c) *(sich anpassen)* to follow *(nach jdm/etw* sb/sth*)*. **sich nach den Vorschriften/den Sternen** ~ to go by the rules/the stars; **sich nach jds Wünschen** ~ to comply with sb's wishes; **wir** ~ **uns ganz nach unseren Kunden** we are guided entirely by our customers' wishes; **und richte dich (gefälligst) danach!** *(col)* (kindly) do as you're told. (d) *(abhängen von)* to depend *(nach* on*)*. (e) *(esp SGer: sich zurechtmachen)* to get ready.

**3** *vi (liter: urteilen)* to judge *(über jdn* sb*)*, to pass judgement *(über +acc* on*)*.

**Richter(in** *f)* *m* - judge. **jdn/etw vor den** ~ **bringen** to take sb/sth to court; **sich zum** ~ **machen** *(fig)* to set (oneself) up in judgement.

**Richter-**: **r**~**lich** *adj attr* judicial; ~**schaft** *f* judiciary, Bench.

**Richt-**: ~**fest** *nt* topping-out ceremony; ~**geschwindigkeit** *f* recommended speed.

**richtig 1** *adj* (a) right *no comp*; *(zutreffend auch)* correct. **eine** ~**e Erkenntnis** a correct realization; **ich halte es für** ~/**das** ~**ste, ...** I think it would be right/best ...; **bin ich hier** ~ **bei Müller?** *(col)* is this right for the Müllers? (b) *(wirklich, echt)* real, proper. **der** ~**e Vater/die** ~**e Mutter** the real father/mother; **ein** ~**er Idiot** *etc* a right idiot *etc (col)*.

**2** *adv* (a) *(korrekt)* correctly, right. **die Uhr geht** ~ the clock is right; **du kommst gerade** ~**!** you're just in time. (b) *(col: ganz und gar)* really, real *(esp US col)*. (c) *(wahrhaftig)* right, correct. **das ist doch Paul!** — **ach ja,** ~ that's Paul — oh yes, so it is.

**Richtige(r)** *mf decl as adj* right person/man/woman *etc*. **sechs** ~ **im Lotto** six right in the lottery.

**Richtige(s)** *nt decl as adj* right thing. **das ist genau das** ~ that's just the job *(col)*; **ich habe nichts** ~**s gegessen/gelernt** I haven't had a proper meal/I didn't really learn a proper trade; **ich habe endlich was** ~**s gefunden** at last I've found something suitable.

**richtiggehend 1** *adj attr Uhr, Waage* accurate; *(col: regelrecht)* real. **2** *adv (col)* ~ **intelligent** really intelligent.

**Richtigkeit** *f* correctness, accuracy; *(von Verhalten, einer Entscheidung)* correctness. **an der** ~ **von etw zweifeln** to doubt whether sth is right; **das hat schon seine** ~ it's right enough.

**Richtig-**: **r**~**liegen** *vi sep irreg (col) (recht haben)* to be right; *(angepaßt sein)* to fit in; **r**~**stellen** *vt sep* to correct; ~**stellung** *f* correction.

**Richt-**: ~**kranz** *m (Build) wreath used in the topping-out ceremony*; ~**linie** *f usu pl* guideline; ~**mikrofon** *nt* directional microphone; ~**platz** *m* place of execution; ~**preis** *m* recommended price; ~**schnur** *f (fig: Grundsatz)* guiding principle.

**Richtung** *f* (a) direction. **in** ~ **Hamburg** in the direction of Hamburg; **in nördliche** ~ towards the north, in a northerly direction; **die Autobahn/der Zug** ~ **Hamburg** the autobahn/train going towards Hamburg; **die ~ ändern** to change direction(s); **eine ~ nehmen** *or* **einschlagen** to head in a direction; **seine Gedanken nahmen eine neue ~** his thoughts took a new turn; **in jeder ~** each way; *(fig: in jeder Hinsicht)* in every respect. **(b)** *(Tendenz)* trend; *(die Vertreter einer ~)* movement; *(Denk~, Lehrmeinung)* school of thought.

**Richtungs-:** **~änderung** *f* change in direction; **r~los** *adj* lacking a sense of direction; **~losigkeit** *f* lack of a sense of direction; **~wechsel** *m (lit, fig)* change of direction.

**richtungweisend** *adj* pointing the way. **~ sein** to point the way (ahead).

**Richt-:** **~wert** *m* guideline; **~zahl** *f* ballpark figure.

**Ricke** *f* **-n** doe.

**rieb** *pret of* **reiben.**

**riechen** *pret* **roch,** *ptp* **gerochen 1** *vti* to smell. **gut/schlecht ~** to smell good/bad; **nach etw ~** to smell of sth; **an jdm/etw ~** to sniff (at) sb/sth; **ich rieche dieses Gewürz gern** I like the smell of this spice; **das riecht nach Betrug** *(fig col)* that smacks of deceit; **jdn nicht ~ können** *(col)* to hate sb's guts *(col)*; **das konnte ich doch nicht ~!** *(col)* how was I (supposed) to know? **2** *vi (Geruchssinn haben)* **nicht mehr ~ können** to have lost one's sense of smell. **3** *vi impers* to smell. **es riecht angebrannt/nach Gas** there's a smell of burning/gas.

**Riecher** *m* - *(col)* **einen guten** *or* **den richtigen ~ (für etw) haben** *(col)* to have a nose (for sth) *(col)*.

**Ried** *nt* **-e** *(Schilf)* reeds *pl.*

**Riedgras** *nt* sedge.

**rief** *pret of* **rufen.**

**Riege** *f* **-n** *(Sport)* team, squad.

**Riegel** *m* - **(a)** *(Verschluß)* bolt. **einer Sache** *(dat)* **einen ~ vorschieben** *(fig)* to clamp down on sth. **(b)** *(Schokolade)* bar; *(Seife auch)* cake.

**Riemen** *m* - **(a)** *(Treib~, Gürtel)* belt; *(an Kleidung, Koffer~)* strap; *(Schnürsenkel)* shoelace. **den ~ enger schnallen** *(col)* to tighten one's belt; **sich am ~ reißen** *(fig col)* to get a grip on oneself. **(b)** *(Sport)* oar.

**Riemen|antrieb** *m* belt drive.

**Riese[1]:** **das macht nach Adam ~ 3 Mark 50** *(hum col)* the way I learned it at school that makes 3 marks 50.

**Riese[2]** *m (wk)* **-n, -n** *(lit, fig)* giant; *(col: Tausendmarkschein)* 1000 mark note, big one *(esp US col)*.

**rieseln** *vi aux sein (Wasser, Sand)* to trickle; *(Regen)* to drizzle; *(Schnee)* to fall gently. **der Kalk rieselt von der Wand** lime is crumbling off the wall; **ein Schauder rieselte mir über den Rücken** a shiver went down my spine.

**Riesen-** *pref* gigantic; *(Zool, Bot etc auch)* giant; **~chance** *f* tremendous chance; **~erfolg** *m* gigantic success; *(Theat, Film)* smash hit; **~gebirge** *nt (Geog)* Sudeten Mountains *pl*; **r~groß** *adj* gigantic; **~hunger** *m (col)* enormous appetite; **~rad** *nt* big *or* Ferris wheel; **~schlange** *f* boa; **~schritt** *m* giant stride; *(fig)* quantum leap; **sich mit ~schritten nähern** *(fig)* to be drawing on apace; **~slalom** *m* giant slalom.

**riesig 1** *adj* gigantic. **2** *adv (col: sehr)* enormously.

**Riesin** *f* (female) giant.

**riet** *pret of* **raten.**

**Riff** *nt* **-e** *(Felsklippe)* reef.

**rigoros** *adj* rigorous.

**Rille** *f* **-n** groove; *(in Säule)* flute.

**Rimesse** *f (Fin)* remittance.

**Rind** *nt* **-er (a)** *(Tier)* cow. **~er** cattle *pl*; **10 ~er** 10 head of cattle. **(b)** *(col: Rindfleisch)* beef. **vom ~** beef *attr.*

**Rinde** *f* **-n** *(Baum~)* bark; *(Brot~)* crust; *(Käse~)* rind.

**Rinder-:** **~braten** *m (roh)* joint of beef; *(gebraten)* roast beef *no indef art*; **~filet** *nt* fillet of beef; **~herde** *f* herd of cattle; **~roulade** *f ≈* beef olive; **~zucht** *f* cattle farming.

**Rindfleisch** *nt* beef.

**Rindsleder** *nt* leather; *esp* cowhide, oxhide.

**Rindvieh** *nt* **(a)** *no pl* cattle *pl*. **10 Stück ~** 10 head of cattle. **(b)** *pl* **-viecher** *(col: Dummkopf)* ass *(col)*.

**Ring** *m* **-e (a)** ring; *(von Menschen auch)* circle; *(Ketten~)* link; *(Rettungs~)* lifebelt; *(~straße)* ring road. **die ~e tauschen** to exchange rings; **~e** *(Turnen)* rings; **~ frei!** *(Boxen)* seconds out! **(b)** *(Vereinigung)* circle, group; *(Bande)* ring. **(c)** *(liter: Kreislauf)* circle, cycle. **der ~ schließt sich** the wheel turns full circle.

**Ringbuch** *nt* ring binder.

**Ringel-:** **~blume** *f* marigold; **~locke** *f* ringlet.

**ringeln 1** *vt (Pflanze)* to (en)twine; *Schwanz etc auch* to curl; *siehe* **geringelt. 2** *vr* to go curly, to curl; *(Rauch)* to curl up(wards). **die Schlange ringelte sich um den Baum** the snake coiled itself around the tree.

**Ringel-:** **~natter** *f* grass snake; **~reigen, ~reihen** *m* ring-a-ring-o' roses; **~schwanz** *m* curly tail; **~taube** *f* wood pigeon.

**ringen** *pret* **rang,** *ptp* **gerungen 1** *vt* **die Hände ~** to wring one's hands; **er rang ihr das Messer aus der Hand** he wrested the knife from her hand. **2** *vi* **(a)** *(lit, fig: kämpfen)* to wrestle. **mit dem Tode ~** to wrestle with death. **(b)** *(streben)* **nach** *or* **um etw ~** to struggle for sth; **ums Überleben ~** *(liter)* to struggle to survive.

**Ringen** *nt no pl (Sport)* wrestling; *(fig)* struggle.

**Ringer(in** *f)* *m* - wrestler.

**Ring-:** **~finger** *m* ring finger; **r~förmig** *adj* ringlike; **~kampf** *m* fight; *(Sport)* wrestling match; **~kämpfer** *m* wrestler; **~ordner** *m* ring binder; **~richter** *m* referee.

**rings** *adv* (all) around.

**ringsherum** *adv* all (the way) around.

**Ringstraße** *f* ring road.

**ring|sum, rings|umher** *adv* (all) around.

**Rinne** *f* **-n** *(Rille)* groove; *(Furche, Abfluß~, Fahr~)* channel; *(Dach~, col: Rinnstein)* gutter.

**rinnen** *pret* **rann,** *ptp* **geronnen** *vi aux sein (fließen)* to run. **das Geld rinnt ihm durch die Finger** *(fig)* money slips through his fingers.

**Rinn-:** **~sal** *nt* **-e** rivulet; **~stein** *m (Gosse)* gutter.

**Rio (de Janeiro)** [ˈriːo(deʒaˈneːro)] *nt* Rio (de Janeiro).

**R.I.P.** = **requiescat in pace** R.I.P.

**Rippchen** *nt (Cook)* spare rib.

**Rippe** *f* **-n** rib; *(von Apfelsine)* segment. **er hat nichts auf den ~n** *(col)* he's just skin and bones; **... damit du was auf die ~n kriegst** *(col)* ... to put a bit of flesh on you; **ich kann es mir nicht aus den ~n schneiden** *(col)* I can't just produce it from nowhere.

**Rippen-:** **~bruch** *m* broken rib; **~fell** *nt* pleura; **~fellentzündung** *f* pleurisy; **~speer** *m or nt (Cook)* spare rib; **Kasseler ~speer** *slightly cured pork spare rib*; **~stoß** *m* dig in the ribs.

**Risiko** *nt*, *pl* **-s** *or* **Risiken** risk. **auf eigenes ~** at one's own risk; **etw ohne ~ tun** to do sth without taking a risk.

**Risiko-:** **r~freudig** *adj* prepared to take risks; **~gruppe** *f* high-risk group; **~kapital** *nt (Fin)* venture capital; **r~los** *adj* safe.

**riskant** *adj* risky, chancy *(col)*.

**riskieren\*** vt (aufs Spiel setzen) to risk; (wagen) to venture. **etwas/nichts** ~ to take chances/no chances; **seine Stellung** ~ to put one's job at risk; **in Gegenwart seiner Frau riskiert er kein Wort** when his wife is present he dare not say a word.

**Rispe** f **-n** (Bot) panicle.

**riß** pret of **reißen.**

**Riß** m, pl **Risse (a)** (in Stoff, Papier etc) tear, rip; (in Erde, Gestein) crevice, fissure; (in Wand, Behälter etc) crack; (Haut~) chap; (fig: Kluft) rift, split. **die Freundschaft hat einen** ~ **bekommen** a rift has developed in their friendship. **(b)** (Tech etc: Zeichnung) sketch, sketch plan.

**rissig** adj Boden, Leder cracked; Haut chapped.

**Rist** m **-e** (am Fuß) instep.

**Riten** pl of **Ritus.**

**ritt** pret of **reiten.**

**Ritt** m **-e** ride. **einen** ~ **machen** to go for a ride.

**Ritter** m - knight; (Kavalier) cavalier. **jdn zum** ~ **schlagen** to knight sb; **arme** ~ pl (Cook) sweet French toast soaked in milk.

**Ritter-:** ~**burg** f knight's castle; ~**kreuz** nt (Mil) Knight's Cross; ~**kreuzträger** m holder of the Knight's Cross; **r~lich** adj (lit) knightly; (fig) chivalrous; ~**lichkeit** f chivalry; ~**orden** m order of knights; ~**schlag** m **den** ~**schlag empfangen** to be knighted.

**Rittersmann** m, pl **-leute** (poet) knight.

**Ritter-:** ~**sporn** m (Bot) larkspur, delphinium; ~**stand** m knighthood.

**rittlings** adv astride (auf etw (dat) sth).

**Rittmeister** m (old Mil) cavalry captain.

**Ritual** nt **-e** or **-ien** [-iən] (lit, fig) ritual.

**rituell** adj ritual.

**Ritus** m **-,** **Riten** rite; (fig) ritual.

**Ritze** f **-n** (Riß) crack; (Fuge) gap.

**Ritzel** nt - (Tech) pinion.

**ritzen 1** vt to scratch; (einritzen) Namen etc auch to carve. **die Sache ist geritzt** (col) it's all fixed up. **2** vr to scratch oneself.

**Rivale** [ri'vaːlə] m (wk) **-n, -n, Rivalin** [ri'vaːlɪn] f rival.

**rivalisieren\*** [rivali'ziːrən] vi **mit jdm** ~ to compete with sb; **die** ~**den Parteien** the rival parties.

**Rivalität** [rivali'tɛːt] f rivalry.

**Riviera** [ri'vieːra] f - **die französische/italienische** ~ the (French)/Italian Riviera.

**Rizinus(öl** nt) m **-,** **-** or **-se** castor oil.

**rk, r.-k.** = römisch-katholisch RC.

**RNS** [ɛr|ɛn|'ɛs] f = **Ribonukleinsäure** RNA.

**Roastbeef** ['roːstbiːf] nt **-s** (roh) beef; (gebraten) roast beef.

**Robbe** f **-n** seal.

**robben** vi aux sein (Mil) to crawl.

**Robben-:** ~**fang** m seal hunting; ~**fänger** m seal hunter; ~**schlag** m cull of seals.

**Robe** f **-n (a)** (Abendkleid) evening gown. **(b)** (Amtstracht) (official) robe or robes pl.

**Roboter** m - robot.

**Robotertechnik** f robotics sing.

**robust** adj Mensch, Gesundheit robust; Material tough.

**Robustheit** f siehe adj robustness; toughness.

**roch** pret of **riechen.**

**Rochade** [rɔ'xaːdə, rɔ'ʃaːdə] f (Chess) castling. **die kleine/große** ~ castling king's side/queen's side.

**Röcheln** nt no pl groan; (Todes~) death rattle.

**röcheln** vi to groan; (Sterbender) to give the death rattle.

**Rochen** m - ray.

**Rock¹** m ⁼e **(a)** (Damen~) skirt; (Schotten~) kilt. **(b)**

(Jackett) jacket.

**Rock²** m no pl (Mus) rock.

**rocken** vi (Mus) to rock.

**Rocker** m - rocker.

**Rock-:** ~**falte** f (von Damenrock) inverted pleat; (von Jackett) vent; ~**futter** nt skirt lining.

**rockig** adj Musik rock-like.

**Rockmusik** f rock music.

**Rock-:** ~**saum** m hem of a/the skirt; ~**schoß** m coat-tail; **an jds** ~**schößen hängen** to cling to sb's coat-tails (col); ~**zipfel** m **an Mutters** ~**zipfel hängen** (col) to cling to (one's) mother's apron-strings (col).

**Rodel** m - = **Rodelschlitten.**

**Rodelbahn** f toboggan run.

**rodeln** vi aux sein or haben to toboggan (auch Sport), to sledge.

**Rodelschlitten** m toboggan, sledge.

**roden** vt Wald, Land to clear.

**Rodung** f (das Roden, Fläche) clearing.

**Rogen** m - roe.

**Roggen** m no pl rye.

**Roggen-:** ~**brot** nt rye bread; ~**brötchen** nt ryebread roll.

**roh** adj **(a)** (ungekocht) raw. **(b)** (unbearbeitet) rough; Eisen, Metall crude. **(c)** (brutal) rough. ~**e Gewalt** brute force.

**Roh-:** ~**bau** m (Bauabschnitt) shell (of a/the house); **das Haus ist im** ~**bau fertig(gestellt)** the house is structurally complete; ~**diamant** m rough or uncut diamond; ~**eisen** nt pig iron.

**Roheit** f **(a)** no pl (Eigenschaft) roughness; (Brutalität auch) brutality. **(b)** (Tat) brutality. **(c)** (ungekochter Zustand) rawness.

**Roh-:** ~**entwurf** m rough draft; ~**ertrag** m gross proceeds pl; ~**kost** f raw fruit and vegetables pl; ~**leder** nt rawhide; ~**ling** m **(a)** (Grobian) brute, ruffian; **(b)** (Tech) blank; ~**material** nt raw material; ~**öl** nt crude oil; ~**produkt** nt raw material.

**Rohr** nt **-e (a)** (Tech, Mech) pipe; (Geschütz~) (gun) barrel. **(b)** (Schilf~) reed; (Zucker~) cane; (für Stühle etc) cane, wicker no pl.

**Rohrbruch** m burst pipe.

**Röhrchen** nt tube; (Chem) test tube; (col: zur Alkoholkontrolle) breathalyzer. **ins** ~ **blasen (müssen)** (col) to be breathalyzed.

**Röhre** f **-n (a)** (Hohlkörper) tube; (Neon~) (neon) tube or strip; (Elektronen~) valve (Brit), tube (US); (fig: Fernsehgerät) telly (Brit col), tube (US col). **(b)** (Ofen~) warming oven; (Back~) oven. **in die** ~ **gucken** (col) to be left out.

**röhren** vi (Hunt) to bell; (Motorrad, Mensch) to roar.

**Röhren-:** **r~förmig** adj tubular; ~**hose** f (col) drainpipe trousers pl.

**Rohr-:** ~**flöte** f (Mus) reed pipe; ~**geflecht** nt wickerwork, basketwork; ~**krepierer** m - (Mil sl) barrel burst; **ein** ~**krepierer sein** (fig) to backfire; ~**leitung** f pipe, conduit; ~**post** f pneumatic dispatch system; ~**spatz** m **schimpfen wie ein** ~**spatz** (col) to curse and swear; ~**stock** m cane; ~**zange** f pipe wrench; ~**zucker** m cane sugar.

**Roh-:** ~**seide** f wild silk; ~**stoff** m raw material; (St Ex) commodity; ~**zucker** m unrefined sugar; ~**zustand** m unprocessed state; **das Manuskript ist noch im** ~**zustand** the manuscript is still in a fairly rough state.

**Rokoko** nt no pl Rococo period; (Stil) Rococo, rococo.

**Rolladen** m, pl **Rolläden** or - (an Fenster, Tür etc) roller shutter; (von Schreibtisch) roll-top.

**Roll-:** ~**bahn** f taxiway; ~**braten** m (Cook) roast;

~**brett** *nt* skateboard.
**Röllchen** *nt* little roll; *(von Garn)* reel.
**Rolle** *f* -n (a) *(Zusammengerolltes)* roll; *(Garn~, Zwirn~, Papier~)* reel; *(Urkunde)* scroll. **eine ~ Bindfaden** a ball of string. (b) *(walzenförmig)* roller; *(an Möbeln, Kisten)* castor; *(an Flaschenzug)* pulley. (c) *(Sport)* forward roll; *(Aviat)* roll. **die ~ rückwärts** the backward roll. (d) *(Theat, Film, fig)* role, part; *(Sociol)* role. **eine Ehe mit streng verteilten ~n** a marriage with strict allocation of roles; **jds ~ bei etw** *(fig)* sb's part in sth; **bei** *or* **in etw** *(dat)* **eine ~ spielen** to play a part in sth; *(Mensch auch)* to play a role in sth; **etw spielt eine große ~ (bei jdm)** sth is very important (to sb); **es spielt keine ~, (ob)** ... it doesn't matter (whether) ...; **bei ihm spielt Geld keine ~** with him money is no object; **aus der ~ fallen** *(fig)* to make an exhibition of oneself.
**rollen 1** *vi* (a) *aux sein* to roll; *(Flugzeug)* to taxi. **etw/den Stein ins R~ bringen** *(fig)* to start sth/the ball rolling; **es werden einige Köpfe ~** heads will roll. (b) **mit den Augen ~** to roll one's eyes. **2** *vt* to roll; *Teig* to roll out; *Teppich, Papier* to roll up. **3** *vr* to curl up.
**Rollen-:** ~**besetzung** *f (Theat, Film)* casting; ~**bild** *nt (Sociol)* role model; ~**erwartung** *f (Sociol)* role expectation; ~**fach** *nt (Theat)* type of character; **r~förmig** *adj* cylindrical; **r~spezifisch** *adj* role-specific; ~**spiel** *nt (Sociol)* role play; ~**tausch** *m* exchange of roles; *(Sociol auch)* role reversal; ~**verteilung** *f (Sociol)* role allocation.
**Roller** *m* - (a) scooter. (b) *(Walze, Naut: Welle)* roller.
**Roll-:** ~**feld** *nt* runway; ~**film** *m* roll film; ~**kommando** *nt* raiding party; ~**kragen** *m* roll *or* polo neck; ~**mops** *m* rollmops, rolled pickled herring.
**Rollo** *nt* -s (roller) blind.
**Roll-:** ~**schinken** *m* smoked ham; ~**schrank** *m* roll-fronted cupboard.
**Rollschuh** *m* roller skate. **~ laufen** to roller-skate.
**Rollschuh-:** ~**bahn** *f* roller-skating rink; ~**laufen** *nt* roller-skating; ~**läufer** *m* roller-skater.
**Roll-:** ~**splitt** *m* grit; „~**splitt**" ''loose chippings''; ~**stuhl** *m* wheelchair; ~**treppe** *f* escalator.
**ROM** [rɔm] *m or nt* -s *(Comp)* ROM.
**Rom** *nt* Rome. **~ ist auch nicht an einem Tag erbaut worden** *(prov)* Rome wasn't built in a day *(Prov)*; **viele Wege führen nach ~** *(Prov)* all roads lead to Rome *(Prov)*; **das sind Zustände wie im alten ~** *(col) (unmoralisch)* what disgraceful goings-on!; *(primitiv)* it's positively medieval *(col)*.
**Roma** *pl (Zigeuner)* Romany.
**Roman** *m* -e novel. **(jdm) einen ganzen ~ erzählen** *(col)* to give sb a long rigmarole *(col)*.
**Roman-:** ~**autor** *m* novelist; ~**figur** *f* character from a novel; **r~haft** *adj* like a novel; ~**heft** *nt* cheap pulp novel; ~**held** *m* hero of a/the novel.
**Romanik** *f (Archit, Art)* Romanesque period; *(Stil)* Romanesque (style).
**romanisch** *adj Volk, Sprache* Romance; *(Art)* Romanesque.
**Romanist(in** *f)* *m (Univ)* teacher/student/scholar of Romance languages and literature.
**Romanistik** *f (Univ)* Romance languages and literature.
**Roman-:** ~**leser** *m* novel reader; ~**schreiber** *m (col)* novel-writer; ~**schriftsteller** *m* novelist.
**Romantik** *f* (a) *(Liter, Art, Mus)* Romanticism; *(Epoche)* Romantic period. (b) *(fig)* romance.
**Romantiker(in** *f)* *m - (Liter, Art, Mus)* Romantic; *(fig)* romantic.

**romantisch** *adj* romantic; *(Liter etc)* Romantic.
**Romanze** *f* -n *(Liter, Mus, fig)* romance.
**Römer** *m* - *(Weinglas)* type of large wineglass, rummer.
**Römer(in** *f)* *m* - Roman. **die alten ~** the (ancient) Romans.
**Römer-:** ~**reich** *nt* Roman Empire; ~**topf** ® *m (Cook)* ≃ (chicken) brick.
**römisch** *adj* Roman.
**römisch-katholisch** *adj* Roman Catholic.
**röm.-kath.** = **römisch-katholisch** RC.
**Rommé** [rɔ'meː, 'rɔme] *nt no pl* rummy.
**Rondo** *nt* -s *(Mus)* rondo.
**röntgen** *vt* to X-ray. **geröntgt werden, sich ~ lassen** to have an X-ray.
**Röntgen** *nt no pl* X-raying.
**Röntgen-:** ~**apparat** *m* X-ray equipment *no indef art, no pl*; ~**assistent** *m* radiographer; ~**aufnahme** *f* X-ray (plate); ~**augen** *pl (hum)* X-ray eyes *pl (hum)*; ~**bild** *nt* X-ray picture.
**Röntgenologe** *m*, **Röntgenologin** *f* radiologist.
**Röntgenologie** *f* radiology.
**Röntgen-:** ~**strahlen** *pl* X-rays *pl*; ~**untersuchung** *f* X-ray examination.
**Rosa** *nt* pink.
**rosa** *adj inv* pink. **ein ~** *or* ~**nes** *(col)* **Kleid** a pink dress; **die Welt durch eine ~(rote) Brille sehen** to see the world through rose-coloured *(Brit)* or rose-colored *(US)* spectacles; **in ~(rotem) Licht** in a rosy light.
**rosa-:** ~**farben, ~farbig** *adj* = **rosa**; ~**rot** *adj* rose-pink; *siehe* **rosa.**
**Röschen** ['røːsçən] *nt* (little) rose.
**Rose** *f* -n *(Blume)* rose. **er ist nicht auf ~n gebettet** *(fig)* life isn't a bed of roses for him.
**Rosé** *m* -s rosé (wine).
**rosé** *adj inv* pale pink.
**Rosen-:** ~**beet** *nt* rose bed; **r~farben, r~farbig** *adj* rose-coloured *(Brit)* or rose-colored *(US)*; ~**holz** *nt* rosewood; ~**knospe** *f* rosebud; ~**kohl** *m* Brussel(s) sprouts *pl*; ~**kranz** *m (Eccl)* rosary; **den ~kranz beten** to say a rosary; ~**montag** *m Monday preceding Ash Wednesday*; ~**montagszug** *m Carnival parade which takes place on the Monday preceding Ash Wednesday*; ~**öl** *nt* attar of roses; ~**stock** *m* standard rose, rose tree; ~**strauch** *m* rosebush.
**Rosette** *f* rosette.
**Roséwein** *m* rosé wine.
**rosig** *adj (lit, fig)* rosy.
**Rosine** *f* raisin. **(große) ~n im Kopf haben** *(col)* to have big ideas; **sich** *(dat)* **die (besten) ~n herauspicken** *(col)* to take the pick of the bunch.
**Rosinenbrötchen** *nt* currant bun.
**Rosmarin** *m (Cook)* rosemary.
**Roß** *nt, pl* -**sse** *or* ⁼**sser** *(liter)* steed *(liter)*, horse. **hoch zu ~** on horseback; **auf dem hohen ~ sitzen** *(fig)* to be on one's high horse; **~ und Reiter nennen** *(fig geh)* to name names.
**Roß-:** ~**haar** *nt* horsehair; ~**kastanie** *f* horse chestnut; ~**kur** *f (col)* kill-or-cure remedy; ~**täuscher** *m (fig)* horse-trader.
**Rost¹** *m no pl (auch Bot)* rust. **~ ansetzen** to start to rust.
**Rost²** *m* -e *(Ofen~)* grill; *(Gitter~)* grating, grille. **auf dem ~ braten** *(Cook)* to barbecue, to grill on charcoal.
**Rost-:** **r~beständig** *adj* rust-resistant; ~**bildung** *f* rust formation; ~**braten** *m (Cook)* ≃ roast; ~**bratwurst** *f* barbecue sausage; **r~braun** *adj* russet; *Haar* auburn.
**Röstbrot** [*S Ger*: 'røːst-, *N Ger*: 'rœst-] *nt* toast.

**rosten** *vi aux sein or haben* to get rusty *(auch fig)*. **alte Liebe rostet nicht** *(Prov)* old love never dies.

**rösten** [*S Ger:* 'røːstɛn, *N Ger:* 'rœstɛn] *vt Kaffee* to roast; *Brot* to toast. **sich in der Sonne ~ lassen** to lie in the sun and roast.

**Rost-:** **r~farben, r~farbig** *adj siehe* **r~braun;** **~fleck** *m* patch of rust; **r~frei** *adj* rustproof; *(Stahl)* stainless.

**Rösti** [*S Ger:* 'røːsti, *N Ger:* 'rœsti] *pl fried grated potatoes.*

**rostig** *adj (lit, fig)* rusty.

**Röstkartoffeln** [*S Ger:* 'røːst-, *N Ger:* 'rœst-] *pl* fried potatoes.

**Rost-:** **~laube** *f (hum)* rust-heap *(hum)*; **r~rot** *adj* rust-coloured *(Brit)*, rust-colored *(US)*, russet; **~schutz** *m* rust protection, rustproofing; *(~schutzmittel)* rustproofing agent; **~schutzmittel** *nt* rustproofing agent.

**rot** *adj* red *(auch Pol)*. **~e Bete** beetroot; **das R~e Kreuz** the Red Cross; **der R~e Platz** Red Square; **das R~e Meer** the Red Sea; **die R~e Armee** the Red Army; **die R~en** *(pej)* the reds; **in den ~en Zahlen stecken** to be in the red; **~ werden, einen ~en Kopf bekommen** to blush, to go red; **sich** *(dat)* **etw ~ (im Kalender) anstreichen** *(col)* to make sth a red-letter day.

**Rot** *nt* -s *or* - red; *(Wangen~)* rouge. **bei ~** at red; **die Ampel stand auf ~** the lights were (at) red.

**Rot|armist** *m* soldier in the Red Army.

**Rotation** *f* rotation.

**Rotations-:** **~achse** *f* axis of rotation; **~maschine, ~presse** *f (Typ)* rotary press; **~prinzip** *nt (Pol)* rota system.

**Rot-:** **r~backig, r~bäckig** *adj* rosy-cheeked; **~barsch** *m* rosefish; **r~blond** *adj Haar* sandy; *(dunkler)* ginger; *Mann* sandy-haired/ginger-haired; *Frau* strawberry blonde; **r~braun** *adj* reddish brown; **~buche** *f* (common) beech; **~dorn** *m* hawthorn.

**Röte** *f no pl* redness, red; *(Erröten)* blush. **die ~ stieg ihr ins Gesicht** her face reddened.

**Röteln** *pl* German measles *sing*.

**röten 1** *vt (geh)* to redden, to make red; *Himmel* to turn red. **ein gerötetes Gesicht** a flushed face. **2** *vr* to turn red.

**Rot-:** **~filter** *nt or m (Phot)* red filter; **~fuchs** *m* red fox; *(Pferd)* sorrel *or* bay (horse); *(fig col)* carrot-top *(col)*; **~gardist** *m* Red Guard; **r~gerändert** *adj* red-rimmed; *adj Metall* red-hot; **r~-grün** *adj* **die r~-grüne Koalition** the coalition between the Social Democrats and the Greens; **r~haarig** *adj* red-haired; **~haut** *f (dated hum)* red-skin; **~hirsch** *m* red deer.

**rotieren*** *vi* **(a)** to rotate. **(b)** *(col)* to be in a flap. **anfangen zu ~** to get into a flap.

**Rot-:** **~käppchen** *nt (Liter)* Little Red Riding Hood; **~kehlchen** *nt* robin; **~kohl** *m*, **~kraut** *nt* red cabbage.

**Rotkreuz-** *in cpds* Red Cross.

**rötlich** *adj* reddish.

**Rotlicht** *nt* red light.

**Rotor** *m* rotor.

**Rotorflügel** *m (Aviat)* rotor blade.

**Rot-:** **r~sehen** *vi sep irreg (col)* to see red *(col)*; **~stift** *m* red pencil; **dem ~stift zum Opfer fallen** *(fig)* to be scrapped; **~tanne** *f* Norway spruce.

**Rotte** *f* -, **-n** gang; *(Mil Aviat, Mil Naut)* pair *(of planes/ships operating together)*; *(von Hunden etc)* pack; *(Hunt)* herd.

**Rottweiler** *m* - *(Hund)* Rottweiler.

**Rötung** *f* reddening.

**Rot-:** **r~wangig** *adj* rosy-cheeked; **~wein** *m* red wine; **~wild** *nt* red deer.

**Rotz** *m no pl* **(a)** *(col)* snot *(col)*. **~ und Wasser heulen** to blubber; **Graf ~** Lord Muck *(col)*; **der ganze ~** the whole bloody *(Brit)* or goddam *(US)* show *(col)*. **(b)** *(Vet)* glanders *sing*.

**rotzfrech** *adj (col)* cocky *(col)*.

**rotzig** *adj (col)* snotty *(col)*.

**Rotz-:** **~nase** *f (col)* **(a)** snotty nose *(col)*; **(b)** *(Kind)* snotty-nosed brat *(col)*; **r~näsig** *adj (col)* **(a)** snotty-nosed *(col)*; **(b)** *(frech)* snotty *(col)*.

**Rouge** [ruːʒ] *nt* -s rouge, blusher.

**Roulade** [ru'laːdə] *f (Cook)* ≈ beef olive.

**Roulett(e)** [ru'lɛt(ə)] *nt* - *or* -s roulette.

**Route** ['ruːtə] *f* -n route.

**Routine** [ru'tiːnə] *f (Erfahrung)* experience; *(Gewohnheit, Trott)* routine.

**Routine-:** **~angelegenheit** *f* routine matter; **r~mäßig 1** *adj* routine; **2** *adv* **ich gehe r~mäßig zum Zahnarzt** I make routine visits to the dentist; **das wird r~mäßig überprüft** it's checked as a matter of routine; **~sache** *f* routine matter; **~untersuchung** *f* routine examination.

**Routinier** [ruti'nieː] *m* -s old hand.

**routiniert** [ruti'niːɐt] *adj* experienced.

**Rowdy** ['raudi] *m*, *pl* -s *or* **Rowdies** hooligan; *(zerstörerisch)* vandal; *(lärmend)* rowdy (type).

**Rowdytum** ['rauditu:m] *nt no pl siehe* **Rowdy** hooliganism; vandalism; rowdyism.

**Rubbel-:** **~karte** *f* scratch card; **~lotterie** *f* scratch card lottery.

**rubbeln** *vti (col)* to rub.

**Rübe** *f* -n **(a)** turnip. **rote ~** beetroot *(Brit)*, red beet *(US)*; **weiße ~** white turnip; **gelbe ~** *(S Ger, Sw)* carrot. **(b)** *(col: Kopf)* nut *(col)*. **eins auf die ~ kriegen** to get a bash over the head *(col)*.

**Rubel** *m* - rouble, ruble *(US)*. **der ~ rollt** *(col)* the money's rolling in *(col)*.

**Rüben-:** **~kraut** *nt*, **~saft** *m* sugar beet syrup; **~zucker** *m* beet sugar.

**rüber-** *in cpds (col)* = **herüber-, hinüber-.**

**Rubin** *m* -e ruby.

**rubinrot** *adj* ruby-red, ruby.

**Rubrik** *f* **(a)** *(Kategorie)* category. **(b)** *(Zeitungs~)* section, column.

**ruch-:** **~bar** *adj:* **~bar werden** *(geh)* to become known; **~los** *adj (dated, geh)* dastardly *(liter)*.

**Ruck** *m* -e jerk, tug; *(von Fahrzeug)* jolt, jerk; *(Pol)* swing, shift. **er stand mit einem ~ auf** he sprang to his feet; **sich** *(dat)* **einen ~ geben** *(col)* to make an effort; **etw in einem ~ erledigen** to do sth at one fell swoop.

**Rück-:** **~ansicht** *f* rear view; **~antwort** *f* reply; **um ~antwort wird gebeten** please reply; **~antwortkarte** *f* reply-paid postcard.

**ruck|artig** *adj* jerky. **er stand ~ auf** he jumped to his feet.

**Rück-:** **~besinnung** *f* recollection; **r~bezüglich** *adj (Gram)* reflexive; **~bildung** *f (Biol)* degeneration; **~blende** *f* flashback; **~blick** *m* look back *(auf +acc* at*)*; **im ~blick auf etw** *(acc)* looking back on sth; **r~blickend** *adj* retrospective; **r~blickend läßt sich sagen, daß** ... in retrospect we can say that ...; **r~datieren*** *vt sep infin, ptp only* to backdate.

**rucken** *vi* **(a)** *(Fahrzeug)* to jerk, to jolt. **(b)** *(Taube)* to coo.

**Rücken** *m* - back; *(Nasen~)* ridge; *(Fuß~)* instep; *(Hügel~, Berg~)* crest; *(Buch~)* spine. **auf dem/den ~** on one's back; **den Feind im ~ haben** to have the enemy in one's rear; **den Wind im ~ haben** to have a tailwind; **er hat doch die Firma des Vaters im** ~ but he's got his father's firm behind him; **mit dem** ~ **zur Wand** *(lit, fig)* with one's back to the wall; **der verlängerte** ~ *(hum col)* one's posterior *(hum col)*; ~ **an** ~ back to back; **hinter jds** ~ *(dat) (fig)* behind sb's back; **jdm/einer Sache den** ~ **kehren** *(lit, fig)* or **zudrehen** *(lit)* to turn one's back on sb/sth; **jdm in den** ~ **fallen** *(fig)* to stab sb in the back; **sich** *(dat)* **den** ~ **freihalten** *(col)* to cover oneself; **jdm den** ~ **decken** *(fig col)* to back sb up *(col)*; **jdm den** ~ **stärken** *(fig)* to give sb encouragement.

**rücken** *vi aux sein* to move; *(Platz machen)* to move up *or (zur Seite auch)* over; *(weiter~: Zeiger)* to move on *(auf +acc to)*. **näher** ~ to move closer; *(Zeit)* to get closer; **ins Manöver/an die Front** ~ to go off on manoeuvres/to go up to the front; **an etw** *(dat)* ~ **an Uhrzeiger** to move sth; *an Krawatte* to pull sth (straight); *(schieben)* to push at sth; *(ziehen)* to pull at sth; **an jds Stelle** *(acc)* ~ to take sb's place; **jdm auf den Leib** *or* **Pelz** *(col)* or **die Pelle** *(col)* ~ *(zu nahe kommen)* to crowd sb; *(sich jdn vorknöpfen)* to have a go at sb; *(hum: besuchen)* to move in on sb; **einer Sache** *(dat)* **zu Leibe** ~ to have a go at sth.

**Rücken-:** ~**deckung** *f (fig)* backing; **jdm** ~**deckung geben** to back sb; **r~frei** *adj Kleid* backless; ~**lage** *f* supine position; **er schläft in** ~**lage** he sleeps on his back; ~**lehne** *f* back, backrest; ~**mark** *nt* spinal cord; ~**schmerz(en** *pl)* *m* backache; ~**schwimmen** *nt* backstroke; ~**stärkung** *f (fig)* moral support; ~**stütze** *f* backrest.

**Rück\entwicklung** *f* fall-off *(gen* in*)*; *(Biol)* degeneration.

**Rückenwind** *m* tailwind.

**Rück-:** **r~erstatten\*** *vt sep infin, ptp only* to refund; ~**erstattung** *f* refund; ~**fahrkarte** *f* return ticket *(Brit)*, round-trip ticket *(US)*; ~**fahrscheinwerfer** *m (Aut)* reversing light; ~**fahrt** *f* return journey; ~**fall** *m (Med, fig)* relapse; *(Jur)* subsequent offence *(Brit)* or offense *(US)*; **r~fällig** *adj (Med, fig)* relapsed; *(Jur)* recidivistic *(form)*; **r~fällig werden** *(Med, fig)* to relapse; *(Jur)* to reoffend; ~**flug** *m* return flight; ~**fluß** *m* reflux, flowing back; ~**forderung** *f* ~**forderung des Geldes** demand for the return of the money; ~**frage** *f* inquiry; **nach** ~**frage bei der Zentrale** ... after checking this with the exchange ...; **r~fragen** *vi sep infin, ptp only* to inquire; *(nachprüfen)* to check; ~**führung** *f* **(a)** *(Deduktion)* tracing back; **die** ~**führung der Probleme auf** *(+acc)* tracing the problems back to; **(b)** *(von Menschen)* repatriation, return; ~**gabe** *f* return; ~**gaberecht** *nt* right of return; ~**gang** *m* drop *(gen* in*)*; **r~gängig** *adj* **(a)** *(Comm: zurückgehend)* dropping; **(b) r~gängig machen** *(widerrufen) Bestellung, Termin* to cancel; *Verlobung* to call off; **das kann man jetzt nicht mehr r~gängig machen** what's done can't be undone; ~**gewinnung** *f* recovery; *(von Land, Gebiet)* reclaiming; *(aus verbrauchten Stoffen)* recycling.

**Rückgrat** *nt* -e spine, backbone. **er ist ein Mensch ohne** ~ *(fig)* he's got no backbone; **jdm das** ~ **stärken** *(col)* to give sb encouragement; **jdm das** ~ **brechen** to ruin sb.

**Rückgratverkrümmung** *f* curvature of the spine.

**Rück-:** ~**griff** *m* **(a) durch einen** ~**griff auf jdn/etw** by reverting to sb/sth; **(b)** *(Jur)* = **Regreß**; ~**halt** *m* **(a)** *(Unterstützung)* support, backing; **(b)** *(Einschränkung)* **ohne** ~**halt** without reservation; **r~haltlos** *adj* complete; *Unterstützung auch* unqualified; ~**hand** *f (Sport)* backhand; ~**kauf** *m* repurchase; ~**kaufoption** *f* buy-back option; ~**kehr**

*f no pl* return; **bei seiner** ~**kehr** on his return; **jdn zur** ~**kehr bewegen** to persuade sb to return; ~**koppelung** *f (Elec)* feedback; ~**lage** *f (Fin: Reserve)* reserve, reserves *pl*; *(Ersparnisse auch)* savings *pl*; ~**lauf** *m no pl (Tech)* reverse running; *(von Maschinenteil)* return travel; *(beim Tonband)* fast rewind; **r~läufig** *adj* dropping; *Tendenz* downward; **eine r~läufige Entwicklung** a decline; ~**lauftaste** *f* carriage return; ~**licht** *nt* rear light; **r~lings** *adv* *(von hinten)* from behind; *(auf dem Rücken)* on one's back; ~**marsch** *m (Mil)* march back; *(~zug)* retreat; ~**meldung** *f* **(a)** *(Univ)* re-registration; **(b)** *(Comp)* echo; ~**nahme** *f* -**n** taking back; **ich bestehe auf der** ~**nahme des Gerätes** I must insist that you take this set back; ~**nahmepreis** *m* repurchase price; ~**paß** *m (Sport)* back pass; ~**porto** *nt* return postage; ~**reise** *f* return journey; ~**reiseverkehr** *m* homebound traffic; ~**ruf** *m* *(am Telefon)* **Herr X hat angerufen und bittet um** ~**ruf** Mr X called and asked you to call back.

**Rucksack** *m* rucksack.

**Rucksacktourist(in** *f)* *m* backpacker.

**Rück-:** ~**schau** *f* reflection *(auf +acc* on*)*; *(in Medien)* review *(auf +acc* of*)*; ~**schau halten** to reminisce; **auf etw** *(acc)* ~**schau halten** to look back on sth; ~**schein** *m* ≃ recorded delivery slip; ~**schlag** *m (von Ball)* rebound; *(fig)* setback; *(bei Patient)* relapse; *(Biol)* reversion to type; ~**schluß** *m* conclusion; **den** ~**schluß ziehen, daß** ... to conclude that ...; ~**schritt** *m (fig)* retrograde step; **r~schrittlich** *adj* reactionary; *Entwicklung* retrograde; ~**seite** *f* back; *(von Buchseite, Münze)* reverse; **siehe** ~**seite** see over(leaf); ~**sendung** *f* return; **r~setzen** *vti (Comp)* to reset.

**Rücksicht** *f* -**en** *(Nachsicht)* consideration. ~**en** *pl* *(Gründe, Interessen)* considerations *pl*; **aus** *or* **mit** ~ **auf jdn/etw** out of consideration for sb/sth; **ohne** ~ **auf jdn/etw** with no consideration for sb/sth; **ohne** ~ **auf Verluste** *(col)* regardless; **auf jdn/etw** ~ **nehmen** to show consideration for sb/sth; **er kennt keine** ~ he's ruthless.

**Rücksichtnahme** *f no pl* consideration.

**Rücksichts-:** **r~los** *adj* thoughtless; *(im Verkehr)* reckless; *(unbarmherzig)* ruthless; ~**losigkeit** *f* siehe *adj* thoughtlessness *no pl*; recklessness; ruthlessness; **r~voll** *adj* considerate *(gegenüber, gegen* towards*)*.

**Rück-:** ~**sitz** *m (von Motorrad)* pillion; *(von Auto)* back seat; ~**spiegel** *m (Aut)* rear(view) mirror; *(außen)* outside mirror; ~**spiel** *nt (Sport)* return match; ~**sprache** *f* consultation; ~**sprache mit jdm nehmen** to confer with sb.

**Rückstand** *m* **(a)** *(Überrest)* remains *pl*; *(bei Verbrennung, Bodensatz)* residue. **(b)** *(Verzug)* delay; *(bei Aufträgen)* backlog. **im** ~ **sein/in** ~ **geraten** to be/fall behind; **mit 0:2 Toren im** ~ **sein** to be 2 goals to nil down. **(c)** *usu pl (Außenstände)* arrears *pl*. ~**e eintreiben** to collect arrears.

**rückständig** *adj* **(a)** *(überfällig) Betrag* overdue. **(b)** *(zurückgeblieben)* backward. ~ **denken** to have antiquated ideas.

**Rückständigkeit** *f no pl* backwardness.

**Rück-:** ~**stau** *m (von Wasser)* backwater; *(von Autos)* tailback *(Brit)*, line of cars; ~**stoß** *m* repulsion; *(bei Gewehr)* recoil; *(von Rakete)* thrust; ~**strahler** *m* - reflector; ~**strom** *m (von Menschen, Fahrzeugen)* return; **der** ~**strom der Urlauber aus Italien** the stream of holidaymakers returning from Italy; ~**taste** *f (an Schreibmaschine, Computer)* backspace key.

**Rücktritt** *m* **(a)** *(Amtsniederlegung)* resignation;

*(von König)* abdication. **(b)** *(Jur: von Vertrag)* withdrawal *(von* from*)*.

**Rücktrittbremse** *f* backpedal brake.

**Rücktritts-:** ~**drohung** *f* threat to resign/abdicate; ~**klausel** *f* withdrawal clause; ~**recht** *nt* right of withdrawal.

**Rück-:** r~**vergüten*** *vt sep infin, ptp only* to refund *(jdm etw* sb sth*)*; ~**vergütung** *f* refund; **r~versichern*** *sep* **1** *vti* to reinsure; **2** *vr* to check (up *or* back); ~**versicherung** *f* reinsurance; ~**wand** *f* back wall; *(von Möbelstück etc)* back; **r~wärtig** *adj* back; *Tür auch, (Mil)* rear.

**rückwärts** *adv* **(a)** *(zurück)* backwards. ~ **einparken** to back into a parking space. **(b)** *(esp S Ger, Aus: hinten)* behind, at the back. **von** ~ from behind.

**Rückwärts-:** ~**drehung** *f* reverse turn; ~**gang** *m* reverse gear; **den** ~**gang einlegen** to engage reverse; **im** ~**gang fahren** to reverse.

**Rückweg** *m* way back. **sich auf den** ~ **machen** to head back.

**ruckweise** *adv* jerkily. **sich** ~ **bewegen** to move jerkily.

**Rück-:** r~**wirkend** *adj (Jur)* retrospective; *Lohn-, Gehaltserhöhung* backdated; **das Gesetz tritt r~wirkend vom 1. Januar in Kraft** the law is made retrospective to 1st January; ~**wirkung** *f* repercussion; **eine Zahlung mit** ~**wirkung vom ...** a payment backdated to ...; **r~zahlbar** *adj* repayable; ~**zahlung** *f* repayment; ~**zieher** *m* - **(a)** *(col)* climbdown *(col)*; **einen** ~**zieher machen** to back out *(col)*; **(b)** *(Ftbl)* overhead kick.

**ruck, zuck** *adv* in a flash. ~! jump to it!; **das geht** ~ it won't take a second.

**Rückzug** *m (Mil)* retreat. **auf dem** ~ in the retreat; **den** ~ **antreten** *(lit, fig)* to retreat.

**Rückzugsgefecht** *nt (Mil, fig)* rearguard action.

**Rüde** *m (wk)* -**n**, -**n** *(Männchen)* dog, male; *(Hetzhund)* hound.

**rüde** *adj* impolite; *Antwort* curt, brusque.

**Rudel** *nt* - *(von Hunden, Wölfen)* pack; *(von Wildschweinen, Hirschen)* herd; *(fig dated)* horde.

**rudelweise** *adv* in packs/herds/hordes.

**Ruder** *nt* - *(von* ~*boot etc)* oar; *(Naut, Aviat: Steuer~)* rudder; *(zur: Führung)* helm. **das** ~ **fest in der Hand haben** *(fig)* to be in control of the situation; **am** ~ **sein** *(lit, fig)*/**ans** ~ **kommen** *(fig)* to be at/to take over (at) the helm; **das** ~ **herumwerfen** *(fig)* to change tack; **aus dem** ~ **laufen** *(fig)* to get out of hand.

**Ruder-:** ~**bank** *f* rowing seat; ~**blatt** *nt* (oar) blade; ~**boot** *nt* rowing boat *(Brit)*, rowboat *(US)*.

**Ruderer** *m* - oarsman.

**Ruderin** *f* oarswoman.

**rudern** **1** *vi* **(a)** *aux haben or sein* to row. **(b)** *(Schwimmvögel)* to paddle. **mit den Armen** ~ *(fig)* to flail one's arms about. **2** *vt* to row.

**Ruder-:** ~**regatta** *f* rowing regatta; ~**sport** *m* rowing *no def art*.

**Rudiment** *nt* rudiment.

**rudimentär** *adj* rudimentary.

**Ruf** *m* -**e** **(a)** *(Aus*~, *Vogel*~, *fig: Auf*~*)* call; *(lauter)* shout; *(Schrei)* cry. **dem** ~ **des Herzens folgen** *(fig)* to obey the voice of one's heart; **der** ~ **nach Freiheit** *(fig)* the call for freedom; **der** ~ **zur Ordnung** *(fig)* the call to order. **(b)** *(Ansehen, Leumund)* reputation. **einen guten** ~ **haben** to have a good reputation; **eine Firma von** ~ a firm with a good name; **von üblem** *or* **zweifelhaftem** ~ **sein** to have a bad reputation; **jdn/etw in schlechten** ~ **bringen** to give sb/sth a bad name; **sie ist besser als ihr** ~ she is better than she is made out to be. **(c)** *(Univ: Beru-*

*fung)* offer of a chair. **(d)** *(*~*nummer)* telephone number. „~": **27785"** "Tel: 27785".

**rufen** *pret* **rief**, *ptp* **gerufen** **1** *vi* to call *(nach* for*)*; *(Mensch: laut* ~*)* to shout; *(Glocke etc)* to sound *(zu* for*)*. **um Hilfe** ~ to call for help; **die Pflicht ruft** duty calls; **die Arbeit ruft** my/your *etc* work is waiting. **2** *vt* **(a)** to call; *(aus*~*)* to cry; *(Mensch: laut* ~*)* to shout. **bravo** ~ to shout hooray. **(b)** *(kommen lassen)* to send for; *Arzt, Polizei auch, Taxi* to call. ~ **Sie ihn bitte!** please send him to me; **jdn zu Hilfe** ~ to call on sb to help; **du kommst wie gerufen** you're just the person (I wanted); **das kommt mir wie gerufen** that's just what I needed; *(kommt mir gelegen)* that suits me fine *(col)*.

**Rüffel** *m* - *(col)* telling-off, ticking-off *(col)*.

**Ruf-:** ~**mord** *m* character assassination; ~**mordkampagne** *f* smear campaign; ~**name** *m* Christian name (by which one is generally known); ~**nummer** *f* telephone number; ~**säule** *f* *(für Taxi)* telephone; *(an Autobahn)* emergency telephone; ~**zeichen** *nt (von Telefon)* ringing tone.

**Rugby** ['ragbi] *nt no pl* rugby.

**Rüge** *f* -**n** *(Verweis)* reprimand, rebuke; *(Kritik)* criticism *no indef art*. **jdm eine** ~ **erteilen** to reprimand sb *(für, wegen* for*)*.

**rügen** *vt (form)* jdn to reprimand *(wegen, für* for*)*; *etw* to reprehend.

**Ruhe** *f no pl* **(a)** *(Schweigen, Stille)* quiet, silence. ~! quiet!, silence!; **gebt** ~! be quiet!; **sich** *(dat)* ~ **verschaffen** to get silence; **es herrscht** ~ all is silent; *(fig: Disziplin, Frieden)* all is quiet; ~ **halten** *(lit, fig)* to keep quiet; **die** ~ **vor dem Sturm** *(fig)* the calm before the storm.

**(b)** *(Ungestörtheit, Frieden)* peace, quiet. ~ **ausstrahlen** to radiate a sense of calm; ~ **und Frieden** peace and quiet; **in** ~ **und Frieden leben** to live a quiet life; ~ **und Ordnung** law and order; **ich brauche meine** ~ I need a bit of peace; **laß mich in** ~! leave me in peace; **vor jdm** ~ **haben wollen** to want a rest from sb; *(endgültig)* to want to be rid of sb; **jdm keine** ~ **lassen** *(Mensch)* not to give sb any peace; **das läßt ihm keine** ~ he can't stop thinking about it; **keine** ~ **geben** to keep on and on; **zur** ~ **kommen** to get some peace; *(solide werden)* to settle down; **jdn zur** ~ **kommen lassen** to give sb a chance to rest; **keine** ~ **finden (können)** to know no peace; **die letzte** ~ **finden** *(liter)* to be laid to rest *(liter)*.

**(c)** *(Erholung)* rest, repose *(liter)*; *(*~*stand)* retirement; *(Stillstand)* rest. **sich zur** ~ **begeben** *(form)* to retire (to bed) *(form)*; **angenehme** ~! sleep well!; **sich zur** ~ **setzen** to retire.

**(d)** *(Gelassenheit)* calm(ness); *(Disziplin)* quiet, order. **die** ~ **weghaben** *(col)* to be unflappable *(col)*; ~ **bewahren** to keep calm; **die** ~ **selbst sein** to be calmness itself; **jdn aus der** ~ **bringen** to throw sb *(col)*; **sich nicht aus der** ~ **bringen lassen** not to (let oneself) get worked up; **sich** *(dat)* **etw in** ~ **ansehen** to look at sth in one's own time; **immer mit der** ~ *(col)* don't panic.

**Ruhe-:** ~**bedürfnis** *nt* need for rest; **r~bedürftig** *adj* in need of rest; ~**gehalt** *nt (form)* superannuation; ~**geld** *nt (form)* pension; ~**lage** *f (von Mensch)* reclining position; *(Med: bei Bruch)* immobile position; **r~los** *adj* restless; **eine r~lose Zeit** a time of unrest; ~**losigkeit** *f* restlessness.

**ruhen** *vi* **(a)** *(aus*~, *geh: liegen)* to rest; *(liter: schlafen)* to sleep. **nicht (eher)** ~, **bis ...** *(fig)* not to rest until ... **(b)** *(stillstehen)* to stop; *(Maschinen)* to stand idle; *(Arbeit auch, Verkehr)* to cease; *(Waffen)* to be laid down. **(c)** *(begraben sein)* to lie, to be buried. **„hier ruht ..."** "here lies ..."; **„ruhe sanft!"** "rest eternal".

**Ruhe-:** ~**pause** *f* break; **eine** ~**pause einlegen** to take a break; ~**platz** *m* resting place; ~**punkt** *m* place of rest; ~**stand** *m* retirement; **im** ~**stand sein/leben** to be retired; **er ist Bankdirektor im** ~**stand** he is a retired bank director; **in den** ~**stand treten** to retire; **jdn in den** ~**stand versetzen** to retire sb; ~**ständler** *m* - retired person; ~**stätte** *f* resting place; **letzte** ~**stätte** last *or* final resting place; ~**stellung** *f (von Körper)* resting position; *(von Gegenstand)* resting point; *(von Maschinen)* off position; **r**~**störend** *adj* **r**~**störender Lärm** *(Jur)* disturbance of the peace; ~**störer** *m* disturber of the peace; ~**störung** *f (Jur)* disturbance of the peace; ~**tag** *m* day off; *(von Geschäft etc)* closing day; **„Mittwoch** ~**tag"** "closed (on) Wednesdays".

**ruhig 1** *adj* **(a)** *(still, geruhsam)* quiet; *Wetter, Meer* calm; *Überfahrt, Verlauf* smooth. **seid** ~**!** be quiet!; **sitz doch** ~**!** sit still!; **gegen 6 Uhr wird es** ~**er** it quietens down around 6 o'clock; **sie hat keine** ~**e Minute** she doesn't have a moment's peace. **(b)** *(gelassen)* calm; *Gewissen* easy; *(sicher) Hand, Blick* steady. **nur** ~ **(Blut)!** take it easy *(col)*; **bei** ~**er Überlegung** on (mature) consideration; **du kannst/ Sie können ganz** ~ **sein** I can assure you; **etw** ~ **mitansehen** *(gleichgültig)* to stand by and watch sth. **2** *adv* **du kannst** ~ **hierbleiben** feel free to stay here; **ihr könnt** ~ **gehen, ich passe schon auf** you just go and I'll look after things; **man kann** ~ **behaupten, daß ...** *(mit Recht)* one may well assert that ...; **du könntest** ~ **mal etwas für mich tun!** it's about time you did something for me!

**Ruhm** *m no pl* glory; *(Berühmtheit)* fame. **sich in seinem** ~ **sonnen** to rest on one's laurels.

**rühmen 1** *vt (preisen, empfehlen)* to praise *(jdn wegen etw* sb for sth*)*. **2** *vr* **sich einer Sache** *(gen)* ~ *(prahlen)* to boast about sth; *(stolz sein)* to pride oneself on sth; **ohne mich zu** ~ without wishing to boast.

**Ruhmes-:** ~**blatt** *nt (fig)* glorious chapter; ~**tat** *f* glorious deed.

**rühmlich** *adj* praiseworthy; *Ausnahme* notable.

**ruhm-:** ~**los** *adj* inglorious; **r**~**reich** *adj (liter)*, **r**~**voll** *adj* glorious.

**Ruhr** *f no pl (Krankheit)* dysentery.

**Rühr|ei** *nt* scrambled eggs *pl.*

**rühren 1** *vi* **(a)** *(um~)* to stir. **(b) an etw** *(acc)* ~ *(anfassen)* to touch sth; *(fig: erwähnen)* to touch on sth; **von etw** ~ to stem from sth; **das rührt daher, daß ...** that is because ... **2** *vt* **(a)** *(um~)* Teig, Farbe to stir; *(schlagen)* Eier to beat. **(b)** *(lit, fig: bewegen)* to move; *Herz* to stir. **er rührte keinen Finger, um mir zu helfen** *(col)* he didn't lift a finger to help me *(col)*; **das kann mich nicht** ~**!** that leaves me cold; **jdn zu Tränen** ~ to move sb to tears. **3** *vr* **(a)** to move; *(Blatt etc)* to stir; *(aktiv sein)* to buck up *(col)*; *(sich beeilen)* to get a move on *(col)*. **rührt euch!** *(Mil)* at ease!; **kein Lüftchen rührte sich** the air was still; **nichts hat sich gerührt** nothing happened. **(b)** *(Gewissen etc)* to be awakened.

**rührend** *adj* touching. **das ist** ~ **von Ihnen** that is sweet of you.

**Ruhrgebiet** *nt* Ruhr (area).

**rührig** *adj* active.

**Rühr-:** ~**löffel** *m* mixing spoon; **r**~**selig** *adj (pej)* tear-jerking *(pej col)*; ~**seligkeit** *f no pl* sentimentality; ~**stück** *nt (Theat)* melodrama; ~**teig** *m* sponge mixture.

**Rührung** *f no pl* emotion. **von** ~ **ergriffen** moved; **vor** ~ **nicht sprechen können** to be choked with emotion.

**Ruin** *m no pl* ruin. **vor dem** ~ **stehen** to be on the verge of ruin; **du bist noch mein** ~**!** *(hum col)* you'll be the ruin of me.

**Ruine** *f* -n *(lit, fig)* ruin.

**ruinieren\*** *vt* to ruin. **sich** ~ to ruin oneself.

**ruinös** *adj* ruinous.

**rülpsen** *vi* to belch.

**Rülpser** *m* - *(col)* belch.

**rum** *adv (col)* = **herum.**

**Rum** *m* -s rum.

**Rumäne** *m (wk)* -n, -n, **Rumänin** *f* Romanian.

**Rumänien** [-iən] *nt* Romania.

**rumänisch** *adj* Romanian.

**Rumänisch(e)** *nt* Romanian; *siehe* **Deutsch(e).**

**rum-:** ~**flachsen** *vi sep (col)* to kid around; ~**kriegen** *vt sep (col)* **jdn** ~**kriegen** to talk sb round.

**Rummel** *m no pl* **(a)** *(col) (Betrieb)* (hustle and) bustle; *(Getöse)* racket *(col)*; *(Aufheben)* fuss *(col)*. **der ganze** ~ the whole carry-on *(col)*. **(b)** *(Jahrmarkt)* fair.

**Rummelplatz** *m (col)* fairground.

**rumoren\* 1** *vi* to make a noise; *(Mensch)* to bang about; *(Bauch)* to rumble. **2** *vi impers* **es rumort in meinem Bauch** my stomach's rumbling; **es rumort im Volk** *(fig)* there is growing unrest among the people.

**Rumpelkammer** *f (col)* junk room *(col)*.

**rumpeln** *vi aux sein (sich polternd bewegen)* to rumble; *(Mensch)* to clatter.

**Rumpf** *m* ⁼e trunk; *(Sport)* body; *(Statue)* torso; *(von Schiff)* hull; *(von Flugzeug)* fuselage.

**rümpfen** *vt* **die Nase** ~ to turn up one's nose *(über +acc* at*)*.

**Rumpsteak** ['rʊmpsteːk] *nt* rump steak.

**rums** *interj* bang.

**Rum-:** ~**topf** *m* soft fruit in rum; ~**verschnitt** *m* blended rum.

**Run** [ran] *m* -s *(Comm, Fin)* run *(auf +acc* on*)*.

**rund 1** *adj* round; *Figur, Arme* plump; *Klang* full. ~**e 50 Jahre/2.000 Mark** a good 50 years/2,000 marks; **ein** ~**es Dutzend Leute** a dozen or more people; **Konferenz am** ~**en Tisch** round-table talks *pl*; **die Sache wird** ~ it's all working out nicely. **2** *adv* **(a)** *(herum)* (a) round. ~ **um die Uhr** right (a) round the clock. **(b)** *(ungefähr)* (round) about, roughly. **(c)** *(fig: glattweg)* ablehnen flatly. **(d)** *(Aut)* **der Motor läuft** ~ the engine is running smoothly.

**Rund-:** ~**blick** *m* panorama; ~**brief** *m* circular.

**Runde** *f* -n **(a)** *(Gesellschaft)* company. **sich zu einer gemütlichen** ~ **treffen** to meet informally. **(b)** *(Rundgang)* walk, turn; *(von Wachmann)* rounds *pl*; *(von Briefträger etc)* round. **die** ~ **machen** to do the rounds; *(herumgegeben werden)* to be passed round; **eine** ~ **machen** to go for a walk; *(mit Fahrzeug)* to go for a ride *or* run. **(c)** *(Sport) (bei Rennen)* lap; *(Boxen etc, Gesprächs~)* round. **über die** ~**n kommen** *(Sport, fig)* to pull through. **(d)** *(von Getränken)* round. **eine** ~ **spendieren** *or* **schmeißen** *(col)* to stand a round.

**runden 1** *vt* Lippen to round. **2** *vr (lit: rund werden)* to become round; *(Lippen)* to grow round. **sich zu etw** ~ *(fig)* to develop into sth.

**Rund-:** **r**~**erneuern\*** *vt sep infin, ptp only* to remould *(Brit)*, to remold *(US)*; **r**~**erneuerter Reifen** remould *(Brit)*, remold *(US)*; ~**fahrt** *f* tour; **eine** ~**fahrt machen** to go on a tour; ~**frage** *f* survey *(an +acc, unter +dat* of*)*.

**Rundfunk** *m* broadcasting; *(besonders Hörfunk)* radio. **im** ~ on the radio; ~ **hören** to listen to the radio; **beim** ~ **arbeiten** to be in broadcasting.

**Rundfunk-** *in cpds* radio; **~anstalt** *f* broadcasting corporation; **~gebühr** *f* radio licence *(Brit) or* license *(US)* fee; **~gerät** *nt* radio set; **~gesellschaft** *f* broadcasting company; *(Sendeanstalt)* radio station; **~programm** *nt* radio programme *(Brit) or* program *(US)*; *(gedruckt)* radio programme *(Brit) or* program *(US)* guide; **~sender** *m* radio station; *(Sendeanlage)* radio transmitter; **~sendung** *f* radio programme *(Brit) or* program *(US)*; **~techniker** *m* radio engineer; **~übertragung** *f* radio broadcast; **~zeitschrift** *f* radio programme *(Brit) or* program *(US)* guide.

**Rund-:** **~gang** *m (Spaziergang)* walk; *(zur Besichtigung)* tour *(durch of)*; *(von Wachmann)* rounds *pl*; *(von Briefträger etc)* round; **r~gehen** *vi sep irreg (col)* **(a)** **jetzt geht's r~** this is where the fun starts *(col)*; **wenn er das erfährt, geht's r~** there'll be all hell let loose when he finds out *(col)*; **es geht r~ im Büro** it's all go at the office; **(b)** *(herumgehen)* to do the rounds; **~heit** *f* roundness; **r~heraus** *adv* straight out; **r~heraus gesagt** frankly; **r~herum** *adv* all around; *(fig col: völlig)* totally; **r~lich** *adj* plump; **~reise** *f* tour *(durch of)*; **~schreiben** *nt* circular; **r~um** *adv* all around; *(fig)* completely; **~umschlag** *m (lit, fig)* sweeping blow.

**Rundung** *f* curve.

**Rund-:** **~(wander)weg** *m* circular walk *or* hike; **r~weg** *adv* straight out.

**Rune** *f* -n rune.

**Runkelrübe** *f* mangel-wurzel.

**runter** *adv (col)* = **herunter, hinunter.** **~!** down!

**runter-** *pref (col)* down; *siehe* **herunter-, hinunter-;** **~hauen** *vt sep* **jdm eine ~hauen** to give sb a clip round the ear; **~sein** *vi sep aux sein* to be run down; **mit den Nerven ~sein** to be a nervous wreck.

**Runzel** *f* -n wrinkle.

**runz(e)lig** *adj* wrinkled.

**runzeln 1** *vt Stirn* to wrinkle, to crease. **2** *vr* to become wrinkled.

**Rüpel** *m* - lout, yob(bo) *(Brit col)*.

**rüpelhaft** *adj* loutish.

**Rupfen** *m* - hessian.

**rupfen** *vt Gänse, Hühner* to pluck; *Gras, Unkraut* to pull up. **jdn ~** *(fig col)* to fleece sb *(col)*, to take sb to the cleaners *(col)*; **wie ein gerupftes Huhn aussehen** to look like a shorn sheep.

**Rupie** ['ruːpiə] *f* rupee.

**ruppig** *adj (grob)* rough; *Benehmen, Antwort* gruff; *Äußeres* scruffy.

**Rüsche** *f* -n ruche, frill.

**Ruß** *m no pl* soot; *(von Kerze)* smoke.

**Russe** *m (wk)* -n, -n Russian, Russian man/boy.

**Rüssel** *m* - snout *(auch col: Nase)*; *(Elefanten~)* trunk; *(von Insekt)* proboscis.

**rußen** *vi (Öllampe, Kerze)* to smoke; *(Ofen)* to produce soot.

**rußig** *adj* sooty.

**Russin** *f* Russian, Russian woman/girl.

**russisch** *adj* Russian. **~es Roulett** Russian roulette; **~e Eier** *(Cook)* egg(s) mayonnaise; *siehe* **deutsch.**

**Russisch(e)** *nt* Russian; *siehe* **Deutsch(e).**

**Rußland** *nt* Russia.

**rüsten 1** *vi (Mil)* to arm. **zum Kampf ~** to arm for battle; **gut/schlecht gerüstet sein** to be well/badly armed. **2** *vr* to prepare *(zu* for*)*; *(lit, fig: sich wappnen)* to arm oneself *(gegen* for*)*.

**rüstig** *adj* sprightly.

**rustikal** *adj* rustic. **sich ~ einrichten** to furnish one's home in a rustic style.

**Rüstung** *f* **(a)** *(das Rüsten)* armament; *(Waffen)* arms *pl*, weapons *pl*. **(b)** *(Ritter~)* armour *(Brit)*, armor *(US)*.

**Rüstungs-** *in cpds* arms; **~begrenzung, ~beschränkung** *f* arms limitation; **~gegner** *m* supporter of disarmament; **~industrie** *f* armaments industry; **~kontrolle** *f* arms control; **~stopp** *m* arms freeze; **~wettlauf** *m* arms race.

**Rüstzeug** *nt no pl (fig)* qualifications *pl*.

**Rute** *f* -n **(a)** *(Gerte)* switch; *(esp Stock zum Züchtigen)* cane, rod; *(Birken~)* birch (rod). **(b)** *(Angel~)* (fishing) rod. **(c)** *(Hunt: Schwanz)* tail.

**Rutsch** *m* -e slip, slide; *(Erd~)* landslide; *(von Steinen)* rockfall; *(fig Pol)* shift, swing; *(col: Ausflug)* trip, outing. **guten ~!** *(col)* have a good new year; **in einem ~** in one go.

**Rutschbahn, Rutsche** *f (Kinder~)* slide; *(Mech)* chute.

**rutschen** *vi aux sein* **(a)** *(gleiten)* to slide; *(aus~, entgleiten)* to slip; *(Aut)* to skid; *(fig: Preise, Kurse)* to slip. **auf dem Stuhl hin und her ~** to fidget around on one's chair. **(b)** *(col: rücken)* to move up. **zur Seite ~** to move over. **(c)** *(~d kriechen)* to crawl.

**rutschfest** *adj* non-slip.

**rutschig** *adj* slippery, slippy *(col)*.

**rütteln 1** *vt* to shake (about). **2** *vi* to shake; *(Fahrzeug)* to jolt. **an etw** *(dat)* **~** *an Tür, Fenster etc* to rattle (at) sth; *(fig) an Grundsätzen etc* to shake sth.

# S

**S, s** [ɛs] *nt, -, -* S, s. **S wie Samuel** ≃S for Sugar.
**S** = **Süden** S.
**S.** = **Seite** p.
**s** = **Sekunde** sec.
**s.** = **siehe** see.
**Sa.** = **Samstag** Sat.
**s. a.** = **siehe auch** see also.
**Saal** *m, pl* **Säle** hall; *(für Sitzungen etc)* room; *(Tanz~)* ballroom; *(Theater~)* auditorium.
**Saal|ordner** *m* usher.
**Saarland** *nt* Saarland.
**Saat** *f* **-en (a)** *(das Säen)* sowing. **(b)** *(Samen, ~gut)* seed(s) *(auch fig)*. **wenn die ~ aufgeht** *(lit)* when the seed begins to grow; *(fig)* when the seeds bear fruit; **die ~ für etw legen** *(fig)* to sow the seed(s) of sth. **(c)** *(junges Getreide)* young crop(s), seedlings *pl*.
**Saat-:** **~gut** *nt no pl* seed(s); **~kartoffel** *f* seed potato; **~korn** *nt* seed corn; **~zeit** *f* sowing time.
**Sabbat** *m* **-e** Sabbath.
**sabbeln** *(dial)*, **sabbern** *(col)* **1** *vi* to slobber. **vor sich hin ~** *(fig)* to mutter away to oneself. **2** *vt* to blather *(col)*. **dummes Zeug ~** to talk drivel *(col)*.
**Säbel** *m* - sabre *(Brit)*, saber *(US)*. **mit dem ~ rasseln** *(fig)* to rattle the sabre.
**Säbel-:** **~fechten** *nt* sabre *(Brit)* or saber *(US)* fencing; **~hieb** *m* stroke of one's sabre *(Brit)* or saber *(US)*.
**säbeln** *(col)* **1** *vt* to saw away at. **2** *vi* to saw away *(an +dat* at*)*.
**Säbel-:** **~rasseln** *nt no pl* sabre-rattling *(Brit)*, saber rattling *(US)*; **s~rasselnd** *adj* sabre-rattling *(Brit)*, saber-rattling *(US)*.
**Sabotage** [zabo'taːʒə] *f* **-n** sabotage. **~ treiben** to perform acts of sabotage.
**Sabotage|akt** *m* act of sabotage.
**Saboteur(in** *f)* [-'tøːɐ, -'tøːrɪn] *m* saboteur.
**sabotieren\*** *vt* to sabotage.
**Sa(c)charin** *nt no pl* saccharin.
**Sach-:** **~bearbeiter** *m* *(Beamter)* official in charge *(für* of*)*; **der zuständige ~bearbeiter** the person dealing with the matter; **~bereich** *m* (specialist) area; **~beschädigung** *f* damage to property; **s~bezogen** *adj Wissen, Fragen* relevant, pertinent; **~buch** *nt* non-fiction book; **s~dienlich** *adj* useful; **s~dienliche Hinweise** helpful information.
**Sache** *f* **-n (a)** thing; *(Gegenstand auch)* object. **~n** *pl (col: Zeug)* things *pl*; *(Jur)* property; **das liegt in der Natur der ~** that's in the nature of things.
**(b)** *(Angelegenheit)* matter; *(Frage auch)* question; *(Thema)* subject; *(Jur)* case; *(Aufgabe)* job; *(Vorfall)* business, affair; *(no pl: Ideal)* cause. **eine ~ der Polizei** a matter for the police; **das ist eine ganz tolle ~** it's really fantastic; **ich habe mir die ~ anders vorgestellt** I had imagined things differently; **das ist eine andere ~** that's a different matter; **das ist meine/seine ~** that's my/his business; **in ~n A gegen B** *(Jur)* in the case (of) A versus B; **er ver-**

steht seine ~ he knows what he's doing; **er macht seine ~ gut** he's doing very well; *(beruflich)* he's doing a good job; **diese Frage können wir nicht hier mitbesprechen, das ist eine ~ für sich** we can't discuss this question now, it's a separate issue; **das ist so eine ~** *(col)* it's a bit tricky; **solche ~n liegen mir nicht** I don't like things like that; **wann ist die ~ passiert?** when did it (all) happen?; **was hat die Polizei zu der ~ gesagt?** what did the police say about it?; **das ist (eine) beschlossene ~** it's (all) settled; **mach keine ~n!** *(col)* don't be daft! *(col)*; **eine ~ des Geschmacks** a question of taste; **zur ~!** let's get on with it; *(Parl, Jur etc)* come to the point!; **das tut nichts zur ~** that's got nothing to do with it; **bei der ~ sein** to be with it *(col)*; **bei der ~ bleiben** to keep one's mind on the job; *(bei Diskussion)* to keep to the point; **so steht die ~ also** so that's the way things are; **jdm sagen, was ~ ist** *(col)* to tell sb what's what; **für eine gerechte ~ kämpfen** to fight for a just cause.
**(c)** *(Tempo)* **mit 80/160 ~n** *(col)* at 50/100 (mph).
**Sachertorte** *f a rich chocolate cake*, sachertorte.
**Sach-:** **~frage** *f* factual question; **~gebiet** *nt* subject area; **s~gemäß**, **s~gerecht** *adj* proper; **bei s~gemäßer Anwendung** if used properly; **~kenntnis** *f (in bezug auf Wissensgebiet)* expertise; *(in bezug auf ~lage)* knowledge of the facts; **~kunde** *f (Schulfach)* general knowledge; **s~kundig** *adj* (well-)informed *no adv*; **s~kundig antworten** to give an informed answer; **sich s~kundig machen** to inform oneself; **~lage** *f* state of affairs; **~leistung** *f* payment in kind.
**sachlich** *adj* **(a)** *(faktisch)* Irrtum, Angaben factual; Grund, Einwand practical; *(sachbezogen)* Frage, Wissen relevant. **rein ~ hast du recht** from a purely factual point of view you are right. **(b)** *(objektiv)* Kritik etc objective; *(unemotional)* matter-of-fact. **bleiben Sie mal ~** don't get carried away; *(nicht persönlich werden)* stay objective. **(c)** *(schmucklos)* functional, businesslike.
**sächlich** *adj (Gram)* neuter.
**Sachlichkeit** *f* **(a)** siehe adj (b) objectivity; matter-of-factness. **(b)** *(Schmucklosigkeit)* functionality.
**Sach-:** **~register** *nt* subject index; **~schaden** *m* damage (to property).
**Sachse** ['zaksə] *m (wk)* **-n, -n**, **Sächsin** ['zɛksɪn] *f* Saxon.
**Sachsen** ['zaksn] *nt* Saxony. **~-Anhalt** Saxony-Anhalt.
**sächsisch** ['zɛksɪʃ] *adj* Saxon.
**sacht(e)** *adj (leise)* soft; *(sanft)* gentle; *(vorsichtig)* cautious, careful; *(allmählich)* gentle, gradual. **~, ~!** *(col)* take it easy!
**Sach-:** **~verhalt** *m* **-e** facts *pl* (of the case); **~verstand** *m* expertise; **s~verständig** *adj* knowledgeable; Meinung, Urteil expert; **~verständige(r)** *mf decl as adj* expert, specialist; *(Jur)* expert witness; **~wert** *m* real value; **~werte** *pl* ma-

terial assets *pl*; ~**wissen** *nt* specialist knowledge; ~**wörterbuch** *nt* specialist dictionary; ~**zwang** *m* practical constraint.

**Sack** *m* ⁼e (a) sack; *(aus Papier, Plastik)* bag. **drei** ~ **Kohlen** three sacks of coal; **mit** ~ **und Pack** *(col)* with bag and baggage; **jdn in den** ~ **stecken** *(fig col)* to put sb in the shade. (b) *(Anat, Zool)* sac. (c) *(col!: Hoden)* balls *pl (col!)*. (d) *(col!: Kerl, Bursche)* bastard *(col!)*. **fauler** ~ lazy bastard.

**Sackbahnhof** *m* terminus.

**sacken** *vi aux sein (lit, fig: sinken)* to sink. **in die Knie** ~ to sag at the knees.

**Sack-:** ~**gasse** *f* cul-de-sac *(esp Brit)*, dead end; *(fig)* dead end; **in eine** ~**gasse geraten** *(fig)* to finish up a blind alley; *(Verhandlungen)* to reach an impasse; ~**hüpfen** *nt no pl* sack race; ~**karre** *f* handcart; ~**leinen** *nt*, ~**leinwand** *f* sacking, burlap *(US)*.

**Sadismus** *m no pl* sadism.

**Sadist(in** *f)* *m* sadist.

**sadistisch** *adj* sadistic.

**säen** *vti* to sow; *(fig)* to sow (the seeds of). **dünn gesät** *(fig)* thin on the ground, few and far between.

**Safari** *f* -s safari. **eine** ~ **machen** to go on safari.

**Saffian** *m no pl*, **Saffianleder** *nt* morocco (leather).

**Safran** *m* -e saffron.

**Saft** *m* ⁼e *(Obst~)* (fruit) juice; *(Pflanzen~)* sap; *(Fleisch~)* juice; *(Husten~ etc)* syrup; *(col: Strom, Benzin)* juice *(col)*. **ohne** ~ **und Kraft** *(fig)* wishywashy *(col)*, feeble.

**saftig** *adj* (a) *(voll Saft)* Obst, Fleisch juicy; *Wiese, Grün* lush. (b) *(col: kräftig)* Witz juicy *(col)*; *Rechnung, Ohrfeige* hefty *(col)*; *Brief, Antwort* hardhitting.

**Saftigkeit** *f (von Obst, Witz)* juiciness; *(von Wiese etc)* lushness.

**Saft-:** ~**laden** *m (pej col)* useless outfit *(pej col)*; **s~los** *adj* not juicy; ~**presse** *f* fruit press; ~**sack** *m (col!)* stupid bastard *(col!)*.

**saft- und kraftlos** *adj* wishy-washy *(col)*, feeble.

**Sage** *f* -n legend; *(altnordische)* saga. **es geht die** ~, **daß** ... legend has it that ...; *(Gerücht)* rumour *(Brit)* or rumor *(US)* has it that ...

**Säge** *f* -n *(Werkzeug)* saw.

**Säge-:** ~**blatt** *nt* saw blade; ~**maschine** *f* mechanical saw; ~**mehl** *nt* sawdust; ~**messer** *nt* serrated knife; ~**mühle** *f* sawmill.

**sagen** *vt* (a) to say. **jdm etw** ~ to say sth to sb; *(mitteilen, ausrichten)* to tell sb sth; **sich** *(dat)* **etw** ~ to say sth to oneself; **unter uns gesagt** between you and me (and the gatepost *hum col*); **genauer/ deutlicher gesagt** to put it more precisely/clearly; **könnten Sie mir** ~ ...? could you tell me ...?; **ich sag's ihm** I'll tell him; **ich habe mir** ~ **lassen,** ... I've been told ...; **was ich mir von ihm nicht alles** ~ **lassen muß!** the things I have to take from him!; **das kann ich Ihnen nicht** ~ I couldn't say; **so was sagt man doch nicht!** you mustn't say things like that; *(bei Schimpfen, Fluchen)* (mind your) language!; **das sage ich nicht!** I'm not telling; **was ich noch** ~ **wollte,** ... *(col)* there's something else I wanted to say ...; **dann will ich nichts gesagt haben** in that case forget I said anything; **ich sage, wie es ist** I'm just telling you the way it is; **um nicht zu** ~ not to say; **jdm** ~, **er solle etw tun** to tell sb to do sth; **hat er im Betrieb etwas zu** ~**?** does he have a say in the firm?; **sie hat das S~** what she says, goes; **laß dir das gesagt sein** take it from me; **er läßt sich** *(dat)* **nichts** ~ he won't be told; **das laß ich mir von dir nicht** ~ I won't take that from you; **sie ließen es sich** *(dat)* **nicht zweimal** ~ they didn't need to be told twice; **ich möchte fast** ~, ... I'd almost say ...;

**wenn ich so** ~ **darf** if I may say so; **da soll noch einer** ~, ... never let it be said ...

(b) *(bedeuten, meinen)* to mean. **was will er damit** ~**?** what does he mean (by that)?; **ich will damit nicht** ~, **daß** ... I don't mean to imply that ...; **damit ist nicht gesagt, daß** ... that doesn't mean (to say) that ...; **das hat nichts zu** ~ that doesn't mean anything; **sagt dir der Name etwas?** does the name mean anything to you?

(c) ~ **Sie mal/sag mal,** ... tell me, ..., say, ...; **du, Vera, sag mal, wollen wir** ... hey, Vera, listen, shall we ...; **wem** ~ **Sie das!** you don't need to tell *me* that!; **sag bloß!** you don't say!; **was Sie nicht** ~**!** you don't say!; **das kann man wohl** ~ you can say that again!; **ich muß schon** ~ I must say; **das muß man** ~ you must admit that; **das ist nicht gesagt** that's by no means certain; **leichter gesagt als getan** easier said than done; **gesagt, getan** no sooner said than done; **wie gesagt** as I said; **wie schon gesagt** as already mentioned; **ich bin,** ~ **wir, in einer Stunde da** I'll be there in, let's say, an hour; **sage und schreibe 100 Mark** 100 marks, would you believe it.

**sägen 1** *vti* to saw. **2** *vi (hum col: schnarchen)* to snore, to saw wood *(US col)*.

**Sagen-:** ~**dichtung** *f sagas pl*; **s~haft** *adj* (a) *(nach Art einer Sage)* legendary; (b) *(col: hervorragend)* fantastic *(col)*, terrific *(col)*; **s~haft schnell** incredibly fast *(col)*; **s~umwoben** *adj* legendary; ~**welt** *f* mythology, legend.

**Säge-:** ~**späne** *pl* wood shavings *pl*; ~**werk** *nt* sawmill.

**Sago** *m no pl* sago.

**sah** *pret of* **sehen**.

**Sahara** [za'haːra, 'zaːhara] *f* Sahara (Desert).

**Sahne** *f no pl* cream.

**Sahne-:** ~**bonbon** *m or nt* toffee; ~**eis** *nt* icecream; ~**torte** *f* cream gateau.

**sahnig** *adj* creamy.

**Saison** [zɛˈzõː, zɛˈzɔŋ] *f* -s season. **außerhalb der** ~ in the off season.

**saisonal** [zɛzoˈnaːl] *adj* seasonal.

**Saison-** [zɛˈzõː] *in cpds* seasonal; ~**arbeit** *f* seasonal work; ~**arbeiter** *m* seasonal worker; **s~bedingt** *adj* seasonal; ~**beginn** *m* start of the season; **s~bereinigt** *adj* seasonally adjusted; ~**betrieb** *m (Hochsaison)* high season; *(~geschäft)* seasonal business; ~**eröffnung** *f* opening of the season; ~**geschäft** *nt* seasonal business; ~**schluß** *m* end of the season; ~**zuschlag** *m* in-season supplement.

**Saite** *f* -n (a) *(Mus, Sport)* string. (b) *(fig liter)* **eine** ~ **in jdm berühren** to strike a chord in sb; **andere** ~**n aufziehen** *(col)* to get tough.

**Saiten|instrument** *nt* string(ed) instrument.

**Sakko** *m or nt* -s jacket; *(aus Tweed etc)* sports jacket *(Brit)*, sport coat *(US)*.

**sakral** *adj* sacred, sacral.

**Sakrament** *nt* sacrament.

**Sakrileg** *nt* -e sacrilege.

**Sakristei** *f* sacristy.

**Salamander** *m* - salamander.

**Salami** *f* -s salami.

**Salamitaktik** *f (col)* policy of small steps.

**Salat** *m* -e (a) *(Pflanze, Kopf~)* lettuce. (b) *(Gericht)* salad. **da haben wir den** ~**!** *(col)* now we're in a fine mess.

**Salat-:** ~**besteck** *nt* salad servers *pl*; ~**gurke** *f* cucumber; ~**kopf** *m* (head of) lettuce; ~**öl** *nt* salad oil; ~**platte** *f* salad; ~**schleuder** *f* salad spinner; ~**schüssel** *f* salad bowl; ~**soße** *f* salad dressing.

**Salbe** *f* -n ointment.
**Salbei** *m or f no pl* sage.
**salben** *vt (liter)* to anoint.
**salbungsvoll** *adj (pej)* unctuous *(pej).*
**saldieren\*** *vt (Comm)* to balance.
**Saldo** *m, pl* -s *or* **Salden** *(Fin)* balance. **per** ~ *(lit, fig)* on balance.
**Saldo|übertrag, Saldovortrag** *m (Fin)* balance carried forward.
**Säle** *pl of* **Saal.**
**Saline** *f* saltworks *sing or pl.*
**Salmiak** *m or nt no pl* sal ammoniac, ammonium chloride.
**Salmiak-:** ~**geist** *m* (liquid) ammonia; ~**pastille** *f* *bitter-tasting liquorice and sal ammoniac lozenge*, liquorice imp.
**Salmonellen** *pl* salmonellae *pl.*
**Salmonellenvergiftung** *f* salmonella (poisoning).
**salomonisch** *adj:* **ein** ~**es Urteil** a judgement of Solomon.
**Salon** [za'lõː, za'lɔŋ] *m* -s **(a)** *(Gesellschaftszimmer)* drawing room. **(b)** *(Friseur~, Mode~ etc)* salon.
**Salon-** [za'lõː-]: **s~fähig** *adj (iro)* socially acceptable; *Leute, Aussehen* presentable; **ein nicht s~fähiger Witz** an objectionable joke; ~**löwe** *m (pej col)* social lion.
**salopp** *adj* **(a)** *(nachlässig)* sloppy, slovenly; *Manieren* slovenly; *Sprache* slangy. **(b)** *(ungezwungen)* casual.
**Salpeter** *m no pl* saltpetre *(Brit)*, saltpeter *(US).*
**Salpetersäure** *f* nitric acid.
**Salto** *m, pl* -s *or* **Salti** somersault. **ein anderthalbfacher** ~ a one-and-a-half somersault *or* turn; ~ **mortale** triple somersault.
**Salut** *m* -e *(Mil)* salute. ~ **schießen** to fire a salute; **21 Schuß** ~ 21-gun salute.
**salutieren\*** *vti (Mil)* to salute.
**Salve** ['zalvə] *f* -n salvo, volley; *(Ehren~)* salute; *(fig: von Applaus)* volley, burst.
**Salz** *nt* -e salt. **das ist das** ~ **in der Suppe** *(fig)* that's what gives it that extra something; **wie eine Suppe ohne** ~ *(fig)* like ham without eggs *(hum).*
**Salz-:** **s~arm** *adj⁻ (Cook)* low-salt; **s~arm essen** to eat a low-salt diet; ~**bergwerk** *nt* salt mine; ~**brezel** *f* pretzel.
**salzen** *pret* **salzte**, *ptp* **gesalzen** *vt* to salt; *siehe* **gesalzen.**
**Salz-:** **s~frei** *adj* salt-free; *Diät auch* no-salt *attr*; ~**gebäck** *nt* savoury biscuits *pl (Brit)*, savory cookies *pl (US)*; ~**gurke** *f* pickled gherkin; **s~haltig** *adj* salty, saline; ~**hering** *m* salted herring.
**salzig** *adj* salty, salt.
**Salz-:** ~**kartoffeln** *pl* boiled potatoes *pl*; ~**korn** *nt* grain of salt; **s~los** *adj* salt-free; **s~los essen** not to eat salt; ~**lösung** *f* saline solution; ~**säule** *f:* **zur** ~**säule erstarren** *(fig)* to stand as though rooted to the spot; ~**säure** *f* hydrochloric acid; ~**see** *m* salt lake; ~**stange** *f* pretzel stick; ~**streuer** *m* - salt cellar *or (US)* shaker; ~**wasser** *nt* salt water; ~**wüste** *f* salt flat.
**Samariter** *m (Bibl, fig)* Samaritan. **der Barmherzige** ~ the good Samaritan.
**Sambia** *nt* Zambia.
**Sambier(in** *f)* [-iɐ, -iərɪn] *m* - Zambian.
**sambisch** *adj* Zambian.
**Same** *m* -ns, -n *(liter)*, **Samen** *m* - **(a)** *(Bot, fig)* seed; *(fig auch)* seeds *pl.* **(b)** *(Menschen~, Tier~)* sperm.
**Samen-:** ~**bank** *f* sperm bank; ~**erguß** *m* ejaculation; ~**flüssigkeit** *f* seminal fluid; ~**handlung** *f* seed shop *(Brit)* or store *(US)*; ~**kapsel** *f* seed cap-

sule; ~**korn** *nt* seed; ~**leiter** *m* vas deferens *(spec)*, sperm duct; ~**spender** *m* sperm donor; ~**zelle** *f* sperm cell.
**sämig** *adj* thick, creamy.
**Sammel-:** ~**album** *nt* (collector's) album; ~**anschluß** *m (Telec)* private (branch) exchange; *(von Privathäusern)* party line; ~**band** *m* anthology; ~**becken** *nt* collecting tank; *(fig)* melting pot *(von for)*; ~**begriff** *m* collective term; ~**bestellung** *f* joint order; ~**büchse** *f* collecting box; ~**fahrschein** *m*, ~**karte** *f (für mehrere Fahrten)* multi-journey ticket; *(für mehrere Personen)* group ticket; ~**mappe** *f* file.
**sammeln 1** *vt* to collect; *Holz, Material, Erfahrungen auch* to gather; *Blumen, Pilze etc* to pick, to gather; *Truppen, Anhänger* to gather, to assemble. **neue Kräfte** ~ to build up one's energy again. **2** *vr* **(a)** to gather, to collect; *(Wasser, Geld etc)* to collect, to accumulate; *(Lichtstrahlen)* to converge, to meet. **(b)** *(fig: sich konzentrieren)* to collect one's thoughts; *siehe* **gesammelt. 3** *vi* to collect *(für for).*
**Sammel-:** ~**name** *m* collective term; ~**nummer** *f (Telec)* private exchange number, switchboard number; ~**platz** *m* **(a)** *(Treffpunkt)* assembly point; **(b)** *(Lagerplatz)* collecting point; ~**punkt** *m (Treffpunkt)* assembly point; ~**stelle** *f* = ~**punkt.**
**Sammelsurium** *nt* conglomeration.
**Sammler(in** *f)* *m* - collector.
**Sammlung** *f* **(a)** collection. **(b)** *(fig: Konzentration)* composure.
**Samowar** *m* -e samovar.
**Samstag** *m* -e Saturday; *siehe* **Dienstag.**
**samstags** *adv* on Saturdays.
**samt 1** *prep* +*dat* together with. **sie kam** ~ **Katze** *(hum)* she came complete with cat. **2** *adv* **sie waren** ~ **und sonders** ... the whole lot of them were ... *(col).*
**Samt** *m* -e velvet. **in** ~ **und Seide** *(liter)* in silks and satins.
**Samt-** *in cpds* velvet; ~**handschuh** *m* velvet glove; **jdn mit** ~**handschuhen anfassen** *(col)* to handle sb with kid gloves *(col).*
**samtig** *adj* velvety.
**sämtlich** *adj (alle)* all; *(vollständig)* complete. **Schillers** ~**e Werke** the complete works of Schiller; ~**e Anwesenden** all those present.
**samtweich** *adj* velvety.
**Sanatorium** *nt* sanatorium *(Brit)*, sanitarium *(US).*
**Sand** *m* -e sand; *(Scheuer~)* scouring powder; *(Streu~)* grit. **mit** ~ **bestreuen** to sand; **das/die gibt's wie** ~ **am Meer** *(col)* there are heaps of them *(col)*; **auf** ~ **laufen** to run aground; **auf** ~ **bauen** *(fig)* to build upon sandy ground; **jdm** ~ **in die Augen streuen** *(fig)* to throw dust in sb's eyes; ~ **ins Getriebe streuen** to throw a spanner in the works *(Brit)*, to cause problems; **im** ~**e verlaufen** *(col)* to peter out; **den Kopf in den** ~ **stecken** to bury one's head in the sand; **etw in den** ~ **setzen** *(col) Projekt, Prüfung* to blow sth *(col).*
**Sandale** *f* -n sandal.
**Sandalette** *f* high-heeled sandal.
**Sand-** *in cpds* sand; ~**bank** *f* sandbank; ~**boden** *m* sandy soil; ~**burg** *f* sandcastle.
**Sandel-:** ~**holz** *nt* sandalwood; ~**öl** *nt* sandalwood oil.
**Sand-:** **s~farben, s~farbig** *adj* sand-coloured *(Brit)*, sand-colored *(US)*; ~**haufen** *m* heap of sand.
**sandig** *adj* sandy.
**Sand-:** ~**kasten** *m* sandpit *(esp Brit)*, sandbox *(US)*; ~**kastenspiele** *pl (Mil)* sand-table exercises *pl*;

*(fig)* tactical manoeuvrings *(Brit) or* maneuverings *(US) pl*; ~**korn** *nt* grain of sand; ~**kuchen** *m (Cook) a Madeira-type cake*; ~**mann** *m*, ~**männchen** *nt (in Geschichten)* sandman; ~**papier** *nt* sandpaper; ~**sack** *m* sandbag; *(Boxen)* punchbag, punching bag *(US)*; ~**stein** *m* sandstone; **s**~**strahlen** *vti insep* to sandblast; ~**strahlgebläse** *nt* sandblasting equipment *no indef art, no pl*; ~**strand** *m* sandy beach; ~**sturm** *m* sandstorm.

**sandte** *pret of* **senden**[1].

**Sand-:** ~**uhr** *f* hourglass; *(Eieruhr)* eggtimer; ~**wüste** *f* sandy waste; *(Geog)* (sandy) desert.

**sanft** *adj* gentle; *Haut* soft; *Schlaf, Tod* peaceful. **sich** ~ **anfühlen** to feel soft; **mit** ~**er Gewalt** gently but firmly; **er ist** ~ **entschlafen** he passed away peacefully.

**Sänfte** *f* -**n** litter; *(esp im 17., 18. Jh. Europas)* sedan-chair.

**Sanftheit** *f siehe adj* gentleness; softness.

**Sanftmut** *f no pl (liter)* gentleness.

**sanftmütig** *adj (liter)* gentle.

**sang** *pret of* **singen**.

**Sang** *m* ⁼**e** *(old liter) (Gesang)* song; *(das Singen)* singing. **mit** ~ **und Klang** *(lit)* with drums drumming and pipes piping; *(fig iro) durchfallen etc* disastrously, catastrophically.

**Sänger(in** *f)* *m* - singer; *(esp Jazz*~, *Pop*~ *auch)* vocalist.

**sang- und klanglos** *adv (col)* without any ado, quietly. **sie ist** ~ **verschwunden** she simply disappeared.

**sanieren*** **1** *vt* **(a)** *Stadtteil* to redevelop; *Haus* to renovate; *Fluß* to clean up. **(b)** *(Econ) Unternehmen, Wirtschaft* to rehabilitate, to put back on its feet. **2** *vr* **(a)** *(Unternehmen, Industrie)* to get back on its feet again. **(b)** *(col: sich bereichern)* to line one's own pocket *(col)*.

**Sanierung** *f* **(a)** *siehe vt* **(a)** redevelopment; renovation; cleaning up. **(b)** *(Econ)* rehabilitation.

**Sanierungs-:** ~**gebiet** *nt* redevelopment area; ~**maßnahme** *f (für Gebiete etc)* redevelopment measure; *(Econ)* rehabilitation measure.

**sanitär** *adj no pred* sanitary. ~**e Anlagen** sanitary facilities.

**Sanitäter** *m* - first-aid attendant, paramedic; *(Mil)* (medical) orderly; *(in Krankenwagen)* ambulance man.

**Sanitäts-:** ~**auto** *nt* ambulance; ~**dienst** *m (Mil)* medical duty; *(Heeresabteilung)* medical corps; ~**kasten** *m* first-aid kit; ~**korps** *nt* medical corps; ~**offizier** *m (Mil)* Medical Officer, MO; ~**truppe** *f* medical corps; ~**wagen** *m* ambulance.

**sank** *pret of* **sinken**.

**Sankt** *adj inv* Saint.

**Sanktion** *f* sanction.

**sanktionieren*** *vt* to sanction.

**sann** *pret of* **sinnen**.

**Saphir** *m* -**e** sapphire.

**Sarde** *m (wk)* -**n**, -**n**, **Sardin** *f* Sardinian.

**Sardelle** *f* anchovy.

**Sardine** *f* sardine.

**Sardinenbüchse** *f* sardine-can. **wie in einer** ~ *(fig col)* like sardines *(col)*.

**Sardinien** [-iən] *nt* Sardinia.

**Sardinier(in** *f)* [-iɐ, -iərɪn] *m* - Sardinian.

**sardinisch, sardisch** *adj* Sardinian.

**sardonisch** *adj* sardonic.

**Sarg** *m* ⁼**e** coffin, casket *(US)*.

**Sarg-:** ~**deckel** *m* coffin lid, casket lid *(US)*; ~**nagel** *m* coffin nail; *(fig col: Zigarette)* cancer

stick *(col)*; ~**träger** *m* pallbearer.

**Sarkasmus** *m* sarcasm.

**sarkastisch** *adj* sarcastic.

**Sarkophag** *m* -**e** sarcophagus.

**saß** *pret of* **sitzen**.

**Satan** *m* -**e** *(Bibl, fig)* Satan.

**satanisch** *adj* satanic.

**Satansbraten** *m (hum col)* young devil.

**Satellit** *m (wk)* -**en**, -**en** satellite.

**Satelliten-** *in cpds* satellite; ~**antenne** *f* satellite dish; ~**bahn** *f* satellite orbit; ~**fernsehen** *nt* satellite television; ~**foto** *nt* satellite picture; ~**schüssel** *f (col)* satellite dish; ~**staat** *m* satellite state; ~**stadt** *f* satellite town; ~**station** *f* space station; ~**übertragung** *f (Rad, TV)* satellite transmission.

**Satin** [za'tɛ̃:] *m* -**s** satin.

**Satire** *f* -**n** satire *(auf +acc* on).

**Satiriker(in** *f)* *m* - satirist.

**satirisch** *adj* satirical.

**satt** *adj* **(a)** *(gesättigt) Mensch* full (up) *(col)*; *Magen, Gefühl* full. ~ **sein** to have had enough (to eat), to be full (up) *(col)*; ~ **werden** to have enough to eat; **von so was kann man doch nicht** ~ **werden** this sort of thing isn't enough to satisfy you; **das macht** ~ it's filling; **sich (an etw** *dat)* ~ **essen** to eat one's fill (of sth); **wie soll sie ihre Kinder** ~ **kriegen?** *(col)* how is she supposed to feed her children?; **er ist kaum** ~ **zu kriegen** *(col: lit, fig)* he's insatiable; **er konnte sich an ihr nicht** ~ **sehen** he could not see enough of her; **jdn/etw** ~ **haben** *or* **sein** to be fed up with sb/sth *(col)*. **(b)** *(blasiert, übersättigt)* well-fed; *(selbstgefällig)* smug. **(c)** *(kräftig, voll) Farben, Klang* rich, full. ~**e 100 Mark/10 Prozent** *(col)* a cool 100 marks/10 per cent.

**Sattel** *m* ⁼ saddle. **ohne** ~ bareback; **er ist in allen** ~**n gerecht** *or* **sicher** *(fig)* he can turn his hand to anything; **fest im** ~ **sitzen** *(fig)* to be firmly in the saddle.

**Sattel-:** ~**anhänger** *m* semitrailer, semi *(US col)*; ~**dach** *nt* pitched *or* saddle roof; ~**decke** *f* saddlecloth; **s**~**fest** *adj* **s**~**fest sein** *(Reiter)* to have a good seat; **in etw** *(dat)* **s**~**fest sein** *(fig)* to have a firm grasp of sth.

**satteln** *vt Pferd* to saddle (up). **für etw gesattelt sein** *(fig)* to be ready for sth.

**Sattel-:** ~**schlepper** *m* tractor unit; *(*~*zug)* articulated lorry *(Brit)*, rig *(US)*; ~**tasche** *f* saddlebag; *(Gepäcktasche am Fahrrad)* pannier; ~**zug** *m* articulated lorry *(Brit)*, rig *(US)*.

**Sattheit** *f* **(a)** *(Gefühl)* feeling of being full. **(b)** *(von Farben)* richness, fullness.

**sättigen** **1** *vt* **(a)** *Hunger, Neugier* to satisfy, to satiate. **ich bin gesättigt** I am replete. **(b)** *(Comm, Chem)* to saturate. **2** *vi* to be filling. **3** *vr* **sich an etw** *(dat) or* **mit etw** ~ to eat one's fill of sth.

**sättigend** *adj Essen* filling.

**Sättigung** *f* **(a)** *(geh: Sattsein)* repletion. **die** ~ **der Hungrigen** the feeding of the hungry. **(b)** *(Chem, Comm)* saturation.

**Sättigungs-:** ~**grad** *m* degree of saturation; ~**punkt** *m* saturation point.

**Sattler(in** *f)* *m* - saddler; *(Polsterer)* upholsterer.

**sattsam** *adv* amply. ~ **bekannt** only too well known.

**Saturn** *m (Astron)* Saturn.

**Satz** *m* -**es**, ⁼**e** **(a)** sentence; *(Teilsatz)* clause; *(Jur: Gesetzabschnitt)* clause. **ich kann nur ein paar** ⁼**e Italienisch** I only know a few phrases of Italian. **(b)** *(Lehr*~, *Philos)* proposition; *(Math)* theorem. **(c)** *(Typ) (das Setzen)* setting; *(das Gesetzte)* type *no pl*.

**das Buch ist im** ~ the book is being set. **(d)** *(Mus)* movement. **(e)** *(Boden~)* dregs *pl*; *(Kaffee~)* grounds *pl*. **(f)** *(Zusammengehöriges)* set. **(g)** *(Sport)* set; *(Tischtennis)* game. **(h)** *(Tarif~)* charge; *(Spesen~)* allowance. **(i)** *(Sprung)* leap, jump. **einen** ~ **machen** to leap, to jump; **mit einem** ~ in one leap *or* bound.

**Satz-:** ~**aussage** *f (Gram)* predicate; ~**ball** *m (Sport)* set point; *(Tischtennis)* game point; ~**bau** *m* sentence construction; ~**ergänzung** *f (Gram)* object; ~**gegenstand** *m (Gram)* subject; ~**glied** *nt =* ~**teil**; ~**herstellung** *f (Typ)* typesetting; ~**teil** *m* part of a/the sentence.

**Satzung** *f* constitution, statutes *pl*; *(Vereins~)* rules *pl*.

**satzungsgemäß** *adj* according to the statutes/ rules.

**Satzzeichen** *nt* punctuation mark.

**Sau** *f, pl* **Säue** *or (Hunt)* -**en** **(a)** sow; *(col: Schwein)* pig; *(Hunt)* wild boar. **die** ~ **rauslassen** *(fig col)* to let it all hang out *(col)*; *(sich äußern)* to speak out; **wie eine gesengte** ~ *(col)* like a bat out of hell *(col)*. **(b)** *(pej col: Schmutzfink)* dirty swine *(col)*; *(Frau auch)* bitch *(pej col)*. **(c)** *(fig col)* **jdn zur** ~ **machen** to bawl sb out *(col)*; **unter aller** ~ bloody *(Brit col)* or goddamn *(col)* awful.

**sauber** *adj* **(a)** *(rein, reinlich)* clean. ~ **sein** *(Hund etc)* to be house-trained; *(Kind)* to be potty-trained. **(b)** *(ordentlich)* neat, tidy; *(exact)* accurate. **(c)** *(anständig)* honest, upstanding. ~ **bleiben** to keep one's hands clean. **(d)** *(col: großartig)* fantastic, great. **du bist mir ja ein** ~**er Freund!** *(iro)* a fine friend you are! *(iro)*.

**sauberhalten** *vt sep irreg* to keep clean.

**Sauberkeit** *f* **(a)** cleanness; *(Hygiene, Ordentlichkeit)* cleanliness. **(b)** *(Anständigkeit)* honesty.

**säuberlich** *adj* neat and tidy. **fein** ~ neatly and tidily.

**saubermachen** *vt sep* to clean.

**Saubermann** *m (col)* cleanliness freak. **die Saubermänner** *(fig: moralisch)* the squeaky-clean brigade *(col)*.

**säubern** *vt* **(a)** to clean. **(b)** *(fig euph)* Partei, Buch to purge *(von of)*; Saal, *(Mil)* Gegend to clear *(von of)*.

**Säuberung** *f siehe vt* **(a)** cleaning. **(b)** purging; clearing; *(Pol: Aktion)* purge.

**Säuberungs|aktion** *f* cleaning-up operation; *(Pol)* purge.

**Sau-:** **s~blöd** *adj (col)* bloody *(Brit col)* or damn *(col)* stupid; ~**bohne** *f* broad bean.

**Sauce** ['zo:sə] *f* -**n** sauce; *(Braten~)* gravy.

**Sauciere** [zo'sie:rə, -'sie:rə] *f* -**n** sauce boat; *(für Bratensauce)* gravy boat.

**Saudi** *m* -**(s)**, -**(s)** Saudi.

**Saudi-:** ~**araber** *m* Saudi (Arabian); ~-**Arabien** *nt* Saudi Arabia; **s~arabisch** *adj* Saudi *attr*, Saudi-Arabian.

**saudumm** *adj (col)* damn stupid *(col)*. **sich** ~ **benehmen** to behave like a stupid idiot *(col)*.

**sauer** *adj* **(a)** *(nicht süß)* sour; Wein, Bonbons acid(ic), sharp. **saure Drops** acid drops. **(b)** *(verdorben)* off *pred (Brit)*, spoiled *(US)*. ~ **werden** *(Milch, Sahne)* to go sour, to turn. **(c)** Gurke, Hering pickled. **saure Sahne** soured cream. **(d)** *(Chem)* acid(ic). **saurer Regen** acid rain. **(e)** *(col: schlecht gelaunt)* *(auf +acc with)* mad *(col)*, cross. ~ **reagieren** to get annoyed. **(f)** **das habe ich mir** ~ **verdient** I got that the hard way; **jdm das Leben** ~ **machen** to make sb's life a misery; **gib ihm Saures!** *(col)* let him have it! *(col)*.

**Sauer-:** ~**ampfer** *m* sorrel; ~**braten** *m* braised

beef (marinaded in vinegar), sauerbraten *(US)*.

**Sauerei** *f (col)* **(a)** *(Unflätigkeit)* ~**en erzählen** to tell filthy stories. **(b)** **so eine** ~! it's a bloody *(esp Brit col)* or downright disgrace. **(c)** *(Dreck)* mess.

**Sauer-:** ~**kirsche** *f* sour cherry; ~**kraut** *nt* sauerkraut, pickled cabbage.

**säuerlich** *adj (lit, fig)* sour; Wein *auch* sharp.

**Sauermilch** *f* sour milk.

**Sauerstoff** *m no pl* oxygen.

**Sauerstoff-** *in cpds* oxygen; ~**flasche** *f* oxygen cylinder; ~**gerät** *nt* breathing apparatus; *(Med)* *(für künstliche Beatmung)* respirator; *(für Erste Hilfe)* resuscitator; **s~haltig** *adj* containing oxygen; ~**mangel** *m* lack of oxygen; *(akut)* oxygen deficiency; ~**zufuhr** *f* oxygen supply.

**Sauer-:** ~**teig** *m* sour dough; **s~töpfisch** *adj (pej col)* sour; *Mensch auch* sour-faced.

**saufen** *pret* **soff**, *ptp* **gesoffen** *vti* **(a)** *(Tiere)* to drink. **(b)** *(col: Mensch)* to booze *(col)*, to drink. **das S~** boozing; **wie ein Loch** ~ to drink like a fish.

**Säufer(in** *f)* *m* - *(col)* boozer *(col)*, drunkard.

**Sauferei** *f (col)* **(a)** *(Trinkgelage)* booze-up *(col)*. **(b)** *no pl (Trunksucht)* boozing *(col)*.

**Säuferleber** *f (col)* gin-drinker's liver *(col)*.

**Sauf-:** ~**gelage** *nt (pej col)* drinking bout, booze-up *(col)*; ~**kumpan** *m (pej col)* drinking pal.

**saugen** *pret* **sog** *or* **saugte**, *ptp* **gesogen** *or* **gesaugt** *vti* to suck; *(col: mit Staubsauger)* to vacuum. **an etw** *(dat)* ~ to suck sth; **an Pfeife** to draw on sth.

**säugen** *vt* to suckle.

**Sauger** *m* - **(a)** *(auf Flasche)* teat *(Brit)*, nipple *(US)*. **(b)** *(col: Staub~)* vacuum (cleaner).

**Säugetier** *nt* mammal.

**Saug-:** **s~fähig** *adj* absorbent; ~**fähigkeit** *f* absorbency.

**Säugling** *m* baby, infant *(form)*.

**Säuglings-** *in cpds* baby, infant *(form)*; ~**alter** *nt* babyhood; **das Kind ist noch im** ~**alter** the child is still a baby; ~**heim** *nt* home for babies; ~**pflege** *f* babycare; ~**schwester** *f* infant nurse; ~**sterblichkeit** *f* infant mortality.

**Saug-:** ~**napf** *m* sucker; ~**rohr** *nt* pipette.

**Sau-:** ~**haufen** *m (col)* bunch of layabouts *(col)*; **s~kalt** *adj (col)* bloody *(esp Brit col)* or damn *(col)* cold; ~**klaue** *f (col)* scrawl *(col)*.

**Säule** *f* -**n** column; *(col: Pfeiler, fig: Stütze)* pillar.

**Säulengang** *m* colonnade.

**Saum** *m, pl* **Säume** hem; *(Naht)* seam.

**saumäßig** *(col)* **1** *adj* lousy *(col)*; *(zur Verstärkung)* hell of a *(col)*. **2** *adv siehe adj* lousily; like hell.

**säumen** *vt (Sew)* to hem; *(fig geh)* to line.

**säumig** *adj (geh)* Schuldner defaulting; Zahlung outstanding, overdue.

**saumselig** *adj (geh)* dilatory.

**Sauna** *f, pl* -**s** *or* **Saunen** sauna.

**saunieren** *vi* to have a sauna.

**Säure** *f* -**n** **(a)** *(Chem, Magen~)* acid. **(b)** *siehe* **sauer** **(a)** sourness; acidity.

**Säure-:** **s~arm** *adj* low in acid; **s~beständig**, **s~fest** *adj* acid-resistant; **s~frei** *adj* acid-free; ~**gehalt** *m* acid content.

**Sauregurkenzeit** *f (hum col)* bad time *or* period; *(in den Medien)* silly season.

**säurehaltig** *adj* acidic.

**Saurier** [-iɐ] *m* - dinosaur, saurian *(spec)*.

**Saus** *m*: **in** ~ **und Braus leben** to live like a lord.

**säuseln 1** *vi (Wind)* to murmur, to sigh; *(Blätter)* to rustle; *(Mensch)* to purr. **2** *vt* to murmur, to purr.

**sausen** *vi* **(a)** *(Ohren, Kopf)* to buzz; *(Wind)* to whistle; *(Sturm)* to roar. **(b)** *aux sein (Geschoß, Peitsche)* to whistle. (c) *aux sein (col: Mensch)* to tear *(col)*, to charge *(col)*; *(Fahrzeug)* to whizz *(col)*, to tear *(col)*. **in den Graben** ~ to shoot into the ditch; **durch eine Prüfung** ~ to fail *or* flunk *(col)* an exam.

**sausenlassen** *vt sep irreg (col)* **jdn/etw** ~ to drop sb/sth; **das Kino heute abend laß ich sausen** I'll not bother going to the cinema tonight.

**Sau-:** ~**stall** *m (col)* pigsty *(col)*; ~**wetter** *nt (col)* bloody *(Brit col) or* damn *(col)* awful weather; **s~wohl** *adj pred (col)* **ich fühle mich s~wohl** I feel bloody *(Brit col) or* really good.

**Savanne** [za'vanə] *f* **-n** savanna(h).

**Saxophon** [za'vanə] *nt* **-e** saxophone, sax *(col)*.

**Saxophonist(in** *f)* *m* saxophone player, saxophonist.

**SB-** [ɛs'be:-] *in cpds* self-service.

**S-Bahn** ['ɛs-] *f* = **Schnellbahn, Stadtbahn.**

**S-Bahnhof** ['ɛs-] *m* suburban line station.

**SBB** [ɛsbe:'be:] *f* = **Schweizerische Bundesbahn.**

**Scanner** ['skɛnɐ] *m* - *(Med, Comp)* scanner.

**Schabe** *f* **-n** cockroach.

**schaben** *vt* to scrape; *Fleisch* to chop finely; *Leder, Fell* to shave.

**Schaber** *m* - scraper.

**Schabernack** *m* **-e** prank, practical joke. **mit jdm einen** ~ **treiben** to play a prank on sb.

**schäbig** *adj* (a) *(abgetragen)* shabby. (b) *Kerl* mean; *Behandlung, Bezahlung* shabby.

**Schäbigkeit** *f siehe adj* (a) shabbiness. (b) meanness, shabbiness.

**Schablone** *f* **-n** (a) stencil; *(Muster)* template. (b) *(fig pej) (bei Arbeit, Arbeitsweise)* routine, pattern; *(beim Reden)* cliché. **in** ~**n denken** to think in a stereotyped way; **etw geht nach** ~ sth follows the set routine.

**schablonenhaft 1** *adj Denken etc* stereotyped; *Ausdrucksweise* cliché-ridden. **2** *adv* in stereotypes/ clichés.

**Schach** *nt no pl* chess; *(Stellung im Spiel)* check. ~ **(dem König)!** check; ~ **und matt** checkmate; **im** ~ **stehen** to be in check; **jdn in** ~ **halten** *(fig)* to hold sb in check; *(mit Pistole etc)* to keep sb covered.

**Schach-:** ~**brett** *nt* chessboard; **s~brettartig** *adj* chequered *(Brit)*, checkered *(US)*; ~**brettmuster** *nt* chequered *(Brit) or* checkered *(US)* pattern.

**schachern** *vi (pej)* **um etw** ~ to haggle over sth.

**Schach-:** ~**feld** *nt* square (on a chessboard); ~**figur** *f* chess piece; *(fig)* pawn; **s~matt** *adj (lit)* (check)mated; *(fig: erschöpft)* exhausted; **s~matt!** (check)mate; **jdn s~matt setzen** *(lit)* to (check)mate sb; *(fig)* to snooker sb *(col)*; ~**partie** *f* game of chess; ~**spiel** *nt (Spiel)* game of chess; *(Spielart)* chess *no art*; *(Brett und Figuren)* chess set; ~**spieler** *m* chess player.

**Schacht** *m* **-e** shaft; *(Brunnen~)* well.

**Schachtel** *f* **-n** (a) box; *(Zigaretten~)* packet, pack. **eine** ~ **Pralinen** a box of chocolates. (b) *(pej: Frau)* bag *(col)*.

**Schachtelsatz** *m* complicated *or* multi-clause sentence.

**Schach-:** ~**turnier** *nt* chess tournament; ~**zug** *m (fig)* move.

**schade** *adj pred* (**das ist aber**) ~! what a pity *or* shame; **es ist** ~ **um jdn/etw** it's a pity *or* shame about sb/sth; **um sie ist es nicht** ~ she's no great loss; **für etw zu** ~ **sein** to be too good for sth; **sich** *(dat)* **für etw zu** ~ **sein** to consider oneself too good for sth.

**Schädel** *m* - skull. **mir brummt der** ~ *(col)* my head is spinning; *(vor Kopfschmerzen)* my head is throbbing; **einen dicken** ~ **haben** *(fig col)* to be stubborn.

**Schädel-:** ~**bruch** *m* fractured skull; ~**decke** *f* top of the skull.

**schaden** *vi* +*dat* to damage, to harm; *einem Menschen* to harm, to hurt. **Rauchen schadet Ihnen** smoking is bad for you; **das schadet nichts** it does no harm; *(macht nichts)* that doesn't matter; **es kann nichts** ~, **wenn** ... it wouldn't do any harm if ...; **das schadet dir gar nichts** *(geschieht dir recht)* it serves you right.

**Schaden** *m* ≐ damage *no pl, no indef art (durch caused by)*; *(Personen~)* injury; *(Verlust)* loss; *(Unheil, Leid)* harm. **einen** ~ **verursachen** to cause damage; **ich habe einen** ~ **am Auto** my car has been damaged; ≈ **an der Lunge** lung damage; ≈ **aufweisen** to be defective; *(Organ)* to be damaged; **es soll sein** ~ **nicht sein** it will not be to his disadvantage; **den** ~ **von etw haben** to suffer for sth; **zu** ~ **kommen** to suffer; *(physisch)* to be injured; **an etw** *(dat)* ~ **nehmen** *(geh)* to damage sth; **jdm** ~ **zufügen** to harm sb; **durch** ~ **wird man klug** *(Prov)* you learn by your mistakes.

**Schadenersatz** *m* compensation, damages *pl*. ~ **leisten** to pay compensation.

**Schadenersatz-:** ~**anspruch** *m* claim for compensation; **s~pflichtig** *adj* liable for compensation.

**Schaden-:** ~**freiheitsrabatt** *m* no-claims bonus; ~**freude** *f* malicious glee, gloating; ... **sagte er mit** ~**freude** ... he gloated; **s~froh** *adj* gloating.

**Schadens-:** ~**begrenzung** *f* damage limitation; ~**ersatz** *m* = **Schadenersatz.**

**schadhaft** *adj no adv* faulty, defective; *(beschädigt)* damaged; *(abgenutzt) Kleidung* worn; *Zähne* decayed; *Gebäude* dilapidated.

**schädigen** *vt* to damage; *jdn* to hurt, to harm.

**Schädigung** *f siehe vt (gen* done to*)* damage; hurt, harm.

**schädlich** *adj* harmful; *Wirkung, Einflüsse* detrimental, damaging. ~ **für etw sein** to be damaging to sth.

**Schädlichkeit** *f* harmfulness.

**Schädling** *m* pest.

**Schädlings-:** ~**bekämpfung** *f* pest control *no art*; ~**bekämpfungsmittel** *nt* pesticide.

**schadlos** *adj* **sich an jdm/etw** ~ **halten** to take advantage of sb/sth.

**Schadstoff** *m* harmful substance, pollutant.

**Schadstoff-:** **s~arm** *adj* low-pollution *attr*; *Motor* low-emission; **s~arm sein** to contain a low level of pollutants; ~**begrenzung** *f (Aut)* emission control; ~**belastung** *f (von Umwelt)* pollution.

**Schaf** *nt* **-e** sheep; *(col: Dummkopf)* twit *(Brit col)*, dope *(col)*. **das schwarze** ~ **sein** to be the black sheep *(in +dat, gen of)*.

**Schafbock** *m* ram.

**Schäfchen** *nt* lamb, little sheep. ~ *pl (hum col: Anvertraute)* flock *sing*; **sein** ~ **ins trockene bringen** *(prov)* to see oneself all right *(col)*.

**Schäfchenwolken** *pl* cotton-wool clouds *pl*.

**Schäfer** *m* - shepherd.

**Schäferhund** *m* alsatian (dog) *(Brit)*, German shepherd (dog).

**Schäferin** *f* shepherdess.

**Schäferstündchen** *nt (euph hum)* lovers' meeting.

**Schaffell** *nt* sheepskin.

**Schaffen** *nt no pl* **die Freude am** ~ the joy of creation; **sein künstlerisches** ~ his works *pl* (of art).

**schaffen¹** *pret* **schuf**, *ptp* **geschaffen** *vt* to create; *(herstellen)* to make. **dafür ist er wie geschaffen** he's just made for it; **Platz** ~ to make room; **Ruhe** ~ to establish order.

**schaffen²** **1** *vt* (a) *(bewältigen)* to manage; *Prüfung* to pass. **schaffst du's noch?** *(col)* can you manage?; **so, das wäre geschafft!** there, that's done; **das ist nicht zu ~** that can't be done; **wir haben nicht viel geschafft** we haven't got much done. **(b)** *(col: erschöpfen)* **das hat mich geschafft** it took it out of me; *(nervlich)* it got on top of me; **geschafft sein** to be shattered *(col)* or pooped *(US col)*. **(c)** *(bringen)* **wie sollen wir das auf den Berg ~?** how will we manage to get that up the mountain?; **einen Koffer zum Bahnhof ~** to take *or* get a case to the station. **(d)** *(verursachen)* Ärger, Unruhe to cause, to create.

**2** *vi* **(a)** *(tun)* to do. **ich habe damit nichts zu ~** that has nothing to do with me; **was haben Sie dort zu ~?** what do you think you're doing (there)?; **sich** *(dat)* **an etw** *(dat)* **zu ~ machen** to busy oneself with sth; *(zum Schein)* to fiddle about with sth. **(b)** *(zusetzen)* **(jdm schwer) zu ~ machen** to cause sb (a lot of) trouble; *(bekümmern)* to worry sb (a lot). **(c)** *(S Ger: arbeiten)* to work.

**Schaffens-:** ~**drang** *m* energy; *(von Künstler)* creative urge; ~**kraft** *f* creativity.

**Schaffner(in** *f)* *m* - *(im Bus)* conductor/conductress; *(Rail)* guard *(Brit)*, conductor/conductress *(US)*.

**Schaffung** *f* creation.

**Schaf-:** ~**herde** *f* flock of sheep; ~**hirt** *m* shepherd.

**Schafott** *nt* -e scaffold.

**Schafschur** *f* sheep-shearing.

**Schafs-:** ~**käse** *m* sheep's milk cheese; ~**milch** *f* sheep's milk.

**Schafstall** *m* sheepfold.

**Schaft** *m* ≃e shaft *(auch Archit)*; *(von Gewehr)* stock; *(von Stiefel)* leg; *(von Schlüssel)* shank.

**Schaftstiefel** *pl* high boots *pl*; *(Mil)* jackboots *pl*.

**Schaf-:** ~**wolle** *f* sheep's wool; ~**zucht** *f* sheep breeding *no art*.

**Schah** *m* -s Shah.

**Schakal** *m* -e jackal.

**schäkern** *vi* *(col)* to flirt; *(necken)* to have a joke.

**Schal** *m* -s *or* -e scarf; *(Umschlagtuch)* shawl.

**schal** *adj* Getränk flat; *Wasser, Geschmack* stale; *(fig: geistlos)* Witz stale, weak.

**Schale** *f* -n **(a)** *(Schüssel)* bowl; *(flach)* dish; *(von Waage)* pan. **(b)** *(von Obst, Gemüse)* skin; *(abgeschält)* peel *no pl*; *(von Nüssen, Eiern, Muscheln)* shell; *(von Getreide)* husk. **sich in ~ werfen** *(col)* to dress up in one's glad rags *(col)*; **in seiner rauhen ~ steckt ein guter Kern** beneath that rough exterior (there) beats a heart of gold *(prov)*.

**schälen 1** *vti* to peel; *Tomate, Mandel* to skin; *Erbsen, Eier, Nüsse* to shell; *Getreide* to husk. **2** *vr* to peel. **sich aus den Kleidern ~** to peel off one's clothes.

**Schalk** *m* -e *or* ≃e *(dated)* joker. **ihm sitzt der ~ im Nacken** he's in a devilish mood.

**Schall** *m* -e *or* ≃e sound. **Name ist ~ und Rauch** names don't mean anything; **das ist alles ~ und Rauch** it's nothing but hollow words.

**Schall-:** s~**dämmen** *vt* to soundproof; s~**dämmend** *adj* sound-deadening; ~**dämpfer** *m* sound absorber; *(von Auto)* silencer *(Brit)*, muffler *(US)*; *(von Gewehr etc)* silencer; *(Mus)* mute; ~**dämpfung** *f* sound absorption; *(Abdichtung gegen Schall)* soundproofing; s~**dicht** *adj* soundproof.

**schallen** *vi* to sound; *(Stimme, Glocke, Beifall)* to ring (out); *(widerhallen)* to resound, to echo.

**schallend** *adj* Beifall, Ohrfeige resounding; *Gelächter* ringing. **~ lachen** to roar with laughter.

**Schall-:** ~**geschwindigkeit** *f* speed of sound; ~**grenze**, ~**mauer** *f* sound barrier.

**Schallplatte** *f* record.

**Schallplatten-** *in cpds* record; ~**hülle** *f* record sleeve.

**Schalotte** *f* -n shallot.

**schalt** *pret of* **schelten**.

**Schalt-:** ~**anlage** *f* switchgear; ~**bild** *nt* circuit diagram; ~**brett** *nt* switchboard.

**schalten 1** *vt* **(a)** to switch, to turn. **etw auf „2" ~** to switch sth to "2"; **in Reihe/parallel ~** *(Elec)* to connect in series/in parallel. **(b)** *Werbespot, Anzeige* to place. **2** *vi* **(a)** *(Gerät)* to switch *(auf +acc* to*)*; *(Aut)* to change gear. **in den 2. Gang ~** to change *or* shift *(US)* into 2nd gear. **(b)** **~ und walten** to bustle around; **frei ~ (und walten) können** to have a free hand. **(c)** *(col: begreifen)* to latch on *(col)*, to get it *(col)*; *(reagieren)* to react.

**Schalter** *m* - **(a)** *(Elec etc)* switch. **(b)** *(in Post, Bank, Amt)* counter; *(im Bahnhof)* ticket window.

**Schalter-:** ~**beamte(r)** *m* counter clerk; *(im Bahnhof)* ticket clerk; ~**halle** *f* *(in Post)* hall; *(in Bank)* (banking) hall; *(im Bahnhof)* booking hall; ~**stunden** *pl* hours of business *pl*.

**Schalt-:** ~**getriebe** *nt* manual transmission *or* gearbox *(Brit)*; ~**hebel** *m* switch lever; *(Aut)* gear lever *(Brit)*, gearshift *(US)*; **an den ~hebeln der Macht sitzen** to hold the reins of power; ~**jahr** *nt* leap year; ~**knüppel** *m* *(Aut)* gear lever *(Brit)*, gearshift *(US)*; *(Aviat)* joystick; ~**kreis** *m* *(Elec)* (switching) circuit; **integrierter ~kreis** integrated circuit; ~**plan** *m* circuit diagram; ~**pult** *nt* control desk; ~**stelle** *f* *(fig)* coordinating point; ~**tag** *m* leap day; ~**uhr** *f* time switch.

**Schaltung** *f* switching; *(Elec)* wiring; *(Aut)* gearchange, gearshift.

**Schaltzentrale** *f* *(lit)* control centre *(Brit)* or center *(US)*; *(fig)* nerve centre *(Brit)* or center *(US)*.

**Scham** *f* no *pl* **(a)** shame. **er wurde rot vor ~** he went red with shame; **er versteckte sich vor ~** he hid himself in shame; **nur keine falsche ~!** *(col)* no need to be embarrassed!; **ohne ~** unashamedly. **(b)** *(geh: Genitalien)* private parts *pl*; *(von Frau)* pudenda *pl*.

**Schambein** *nt* pubic bone.

**schämen** *vr* to be ashamed. **du solltest dich ~!** you ought to be ashamed of yourself!; **sich wegen jdm/etw ~** to be ashamed of sb/sth; **sich für jdn ~** to be ashamed for sb; **sich vor jdm ~** to feel ashamed in front of sb.

**Scham-:** ~**gefühl** *nt* sense of shame; ~**gegend** *f* pubic region; ~**haar** *nt* pubic hair; s~**haft** *adj* modest; *(verschämt)* bashful, coy; ~**lippen** *pl* labia *pl*, lips *pl* of the vulva; s~**los** *adj* shameless; *(unanständig auch)* Lüge brazen, barefaced; **sich s~los kleiden** to dress indecently; s~**losigkeit** *f* siehe *adj* shamelessness; indecency.

**Schampon** *nt* -s shampoo.

**schamponieren*** *vt* to shampoo.

**Scham-:** s~**rot** *adj* red (with shame); ~**röte** *f* blush of shame; **die ~röte stieg ihr ins Gesicht** her face flushed with shame; ~**teile** *pl* private parts *pl*, genitals *pl*.

**Schande** *f* no *pl* disgrace. **~ über jdn bringen** to disgrace sb; **jdm/einer Sache ~ machen** to be a disgrace to sb/sth; **zu meiner ~ muß ich gestehen, daß ...** to my shame I have to admit that ...

**schänden** *vt* to violate; *Ansehen, Namen* to dishonour *(Brit)*, to dishonor *(US)*, to discredit.

**Schandfleck** *m* blot *(in +dat* on*)*; *(Gebäude etc auch)* eyesore. **er war der ~ der Familie** he was the blot on the family name.

**schändlich** *adj* disgraceful, shameful.

**Schändlichkeit** *f* disgracefulness, shamefulness.

**Schand-**: ~**mal** nt brand, stigma; ~**tat** f disgraceful deed; (hum) escapade; **zu jeder** ~**tat bereit sein** (col) to be always ready for mischief (col).
**Schändung** f siehe vt violation; dishonouring (Brit), dishonoring (US).
**Schank-**: ~**betrieb** m bar service; ~**erlaubnis,** ~**konzession** f licence (of publican) (Brit), excise license (US); ~**tisch** m bar.
**Schanze** f -n (Mil) fieldwork, entrenchment; (Sport) (ski) jump, (jumping) hill.
**Schar** f -en crowd, throng (liter); (von Vögeln) flock; (von Insekten etc) swarm. **in** ~**en** in droves; **die Menschen kamen in (hellen)** ~**en nach Lourdes** people flocked to Lourdes.
**Scharade** f -n charade.
**scharen 1** vt **Menschen um sich** ~ to gather people around one. **2** vr **sich um jdn** ~ to gather around sb.
**scharenweise** adv (in bezug auf Menschen) in droves. **die Heuschrecken fielen** ~ **über die Saat her** swarms of locusts descended on the young crops.
**scharf** adj comp ⸚**er,** superl ⸚**ste(r, s)** or (adv) **am** ⸚**sten** (a) sharp; Verstand, Augen auch, Beobachter keen; Kälte, Wind biting; Ton piercing, shrill; Brille sharply focusing. **ein Messer** ~ **machen** to sharpen a knife; **etw** ~ **einstellen** Bild, Diaprojektor etc to bring sth into focus; Sender to tune sth in (properly); ~ **aufpassen/zuhören** to pay close attention/to listen closely; **jdn** ~ **ansehen** to give sb a scrutinizing look; (mißbilligend) to look sharply at sb; ~ **nachdenken** to have a good or long think, to think long and hard; ~ **kalkulieren** to calculate exactly; **mit** ~**em Blick** (fig) with penetrating insight; ~ **bremsen** to brake sharply or hard.
   (b) (hart, streng) Maßnahmen severe; (col) Prüfung strict, tough; Lehrer, Polizist tough; Bewachung close, tight; Hund fierce. **jdn** ~ **bewachen** to guard sb closely.
   (c) (schonungslos) Auseinandersetzung, Konkurrenz, Protest fierce; Worte, Kritik sharp, harsh. **eine** ~**e Zunge haben** to have a sharp tongue; **etw aufs** ⸚**ste verurteilen** to condemn sth in the strongest possible terms; **das war das** ⸚**ste!** (col) that put the lid on it! (col).
   (d) (stark gewürzt) hot; (mit Salz, Pfeffer) highly seasoned; Geruch, Geschmack pungent, acrid; Getränk (stark) strong; (brennend) fiery; Waschmittel, Lösung caustic. ~ **würzen** to season highly; **Fleisch** ~ **anbraten** to sear meat; ~**e Sachen** (col) hard stuff (col).
   (e) (echt) Munition etc live. **etw** ~ **machen** to arm sth; ~**e Schüsse abgeben** to fire live bullets; ~ **schießen** (lit) (mit ~er Munition) to shoot with live ammunition; (auf den Mann) to aim to hit.
   (f) (col) (geil) randy (Brit col), horny (col); (aufreizend) sexy (col); Film sexy (col), blue attr; (aufregend) Auto, Film cool (col), great (col). **jdn** ~ **machen** to turn sb on (col); **auf jdn/etw** ~ **sein** to be keen on sb/sth, to fancy sb/sth (col).
**Scharfblick** m (fig) perspicacity, keen insight.
**Schärfe** f -n siehe adj (a) sharpness; keenness; bite; shrillness; (an Kamera, Fernsehen) focus. (b) severity; toughness; closeness, tightness. (c) fierceness; sharpness, harshness. (d) hotness; pungency.
**Scharf|einstellung** f focusing.
**schärfen** vt (lit, fig) to sharpen.
**Scharf-**: **s**~**kantig** adj sharp-edged; **s**~**machen** vt sep (col) to stir up; ~**macher** m (col) agitator; ~**richter** m executioner; ~**schütze** m marksman; **s**~**sichtig** adj sharp-sighted; (fig) perspicacious; ~**sinn** m astuteness; **s**~**sinnig** adj astute.

**Scharlach** m (a) no pl scarlet. (b) (auch ~**fieber**) scarlet fever.
**scharlachrot** adj scarlet (red).
**Scharlatan** m -e charlatan; (Arzt auch) quack.
**Scharnier** -e, **Scharniergelenk** nt hinge.
**Schärpe** f -n sash.
**scharren** vti to scrape; (Pferd, Hund) to paw; (Huhn) to scratch.
**Scharte** f -n nick; (Schieß~) embrasure. **eine** ~ **auswetzen** (fig) to make amends.
**schartig** adj jagged, notched.
**Schaschlik** nt -s (shish-)kebab.
**schassen** vt (col) to boot out (col).
**Schatten** m - (lit, fig) shadow; (schattige Stelle) shade. **im** ~ **sitzen** to sit in the shade; **40 Grad im** ~ 40 degrees in the shade; **einen** ~ **auf etw** (acc) **werfen** (lit, fig) to cast a shadow on sth; **große Ereignisse werfen ihre** ~ **voraus** great events often cast their shadow before them; **in jds** ~ (dat) **stehen** (fig) to be in sb's shadow; **jdn/etw in den** ~ **stellen** (fig) to put sb/sth in the shade; **nur noch ein** ~ **(seiner selbst) sein** to be (only) a shadow of one's former self; ~ **unter den Augen** shadows under the eyes.
**Schatten-**: ~**dasein** nt shadowy existence; **s**~**haft** adj (lit, fig) shadowy; ~**kabinett** nt (Pol) shadow cabinet; **s**~**los** adj shadowless; ~**morelle** f morello cherry; ~**riß** m silhouette; ~**seite** f shady side; (fig: Nachteil) drawback; **die** ~**seite(n) des Lebens** the dark side of life; ~**spiel** nt shadow play; ~**wirtschaft** f black economy.
**schattieren*** vt to shade.
**Schattierung** f (lit, fig) shade; (Art) shading.
**schattig** adj shady.
**Schatulle** f -n casket; (Geld~) coffer.
**Schatz** m ⸚e (a) (lit, fig) treasure. ⸚**e** pl (Boden~) natural resources pl; (Reichtum) riches pl, wealth sing. (b) (Liebling) sweetheart.
**schätzbar** adj assessable. **schwer** ~ difficult to assess.
**Schätzchen** nt darling.
**schätzen 1** vt (a) (veranschlagen) to estimate (auf +acc at); Gemälde etc to value; (col: annehmen) to reckon. **die Besucherzahl wurde auf 500.000 geschätzt** the number of visitors was estimated at 500,000; **ich hätte sie älter geschätzt** I'd have said she was older. (b) (würdigen) to regard highly. **jdn** ~ to think highly of sb; **etw zu** ~ **wissen** to appreciate sth; **sich glücklich** ~ to consider oneself lucky. **2** vi (veranschlagen, raten) to guess. **schätz mal** have a guess.
**schätzenlernen** vt sep to come to appreciate.
**Schätzer** m - valuer; (Insur) assessor.
**Schatz-**: ~**gräber** m - treasure-hunter; ~**kammer** f treasure chamber or vault; ~**kanzler** m (Brit Pol) Chancellor of the Exchequer; ~**meister** m treasurer.
**Schätzung** f estimate; (das Schätzen) estimation; (von Wertgegenstand) valuation. **nach meiner** ~ ... I reckon that ...
**schätzungsweise** adv (so vermutet man) it is estimated; (ungefähr) roughly; (so schätze ich) I think. **wann wirst du** ~ **kommen?** when do you think you'll come?
**Schätzwert** m estimated value.
**Schau** f -en (a) (Vorführung) show; (Ausstellung auch) display, exhibition. **etw zur** ~ **stellen** (ausstellen) to put sth on show, to display sth; (fig) to make a show of sth; (protzen mit) to show off sth; **etw zur** ~ **tragen** to display sth. (b) (col) **eine** ~ **abziehen** to put on a show; **das ist nur** ~ it's only show; **jdm die** ~ **stehlen** to steal the show from sb.

**Schaubild** *nt* diagram; *(Kurve)* graph.
**Schauder** *m* - shudder; *(vor Angst, Kälte auch)* shiver.
**schauderhaft** *adj (fig col)* dreadful, awful.
**schaudern** *vi (vor Grauen, Abscheu)* to shudder; *(vor Kälte, Angst auch)* to shiver. **mich schauderte bei dem Gedanken** I shuddered *or* shivered at the thought (of it); **ihr schaudert vor ihm** he makes her shudder.
**schauen 1** *vi* to look. **traurig** *etc* ~ to look sad *etc*; **um sich** ~ to look around (one); **nach jdm/etw** ~ *(suchen)* to look for sb/sth; *(sich kümmern um)* to look after sb/sth; **da schau her!** *(S Ger)* well, well!; **schau, daß du ...** see (that) you ... **2** *vt (geh)* to see, to behold *(old, liter)*. **Gott** ~ to see God.
**Schauer** *m* - **(a)** *(Regen~)* shower. **(b)** *(Schauder)* shudder.
**Schauergeschichte** *f (col)* horror story.
**schauerlich** *adj* **(a)** horrific, horrible; *(gruselig)* eerie, creepy *(col)*. **(b)** *(col: fürchterlich)* dreadful, awful.
**Schauermärchen** *nt (col)* horror story.
**Schaufel** *f* **-n** shovel; *(kleiner: für Zucker etc)* scoop; *(Kehricht~)* dustpan; *(von Bagger)* scoop; *(von Schaufelrad)* paddle; *(von Turbine)* vane.
**schaufeln** *vti* to shovel; *Grab, Grube* to dig.
**Schaufenster** *nt* shop *(Brit)* or store *(US)* window.
**Schaufenster-:** ~**auslage** *f* window display; ~**bummel** *m* **einen** ~**bummel machen** to go window-shopping; ~**dekorateur** *m* window-dresser; ~**gestaltung** *f* window-dressing; ~**puppe** *f* display dummy.
**Schau-:** ~**geschäft** *nt* show business; ~**kampf** *m* exhibition bout; ~**kasten** *m* showcase, display cabinet.
**Schaukel** *f* **-n** swing.
**schaukeln 1** *vi* **(a)** *(mit Schaukel)* to swing; *(im Schaukelstuhl)* to rock. **(b)** *(Fahrzeug)* to bounce (up and down); *(Schiff)* to pitch and toss. **2** *vt* to rock. **wir werden das Kind** *or* **das schon** ~ *(col)* we'll manage it.
**Schaukel-:** ~**pferd** *nt* rocking horse; ~**stuhl** *m* rocking chair.
**Schau-:** **s**~**lustig** *adj* curious; ~**lustige** *pl decl as adj* (curious) onlookers *pl*, rubbernecks *pl (US col)*.
**Schaum** *m*, *pl* **Schäume** foam, froth; *(Seifen~)* lather; *(auf Getränken)* froth; *(von Bier)* head. ~ **vor dem Mund haben** *(lit, fig)* to froth *or* foam at the mouth; **etw zu** ~ **schlagen** *(Cook)* to beat sth until frothy; ~ **schlagen** *(fig col)* to talk a lot of hot air *(col)*.
**Schaumbad** *nt* bubble bath.
**schäumen** *vi* to foam, to froth; *(Shampoo, Waschmittel)* to lather (up). **vor Wut** ~ to be foaming with rage.
**Schaum-:** ~**festiger** *m* (styling) mousse; ~**gummi** *nt or m* foam rubber.
**schaumig** *adj siehe* **Schaum** frothy; lathery. **etw** ~ **schlagen** *(Cook)* to beat sth until frothy.
**Schaum-:** ~**krone** *f* white crest; ~**löffel** *m* skimmer; ~**schläger** *m (fig col)* windbag *(col)*; ~**schlägerei** *f (fig col)* hot air *(col)*; ~**stoff** *m* foam (material); ~**wein** *m* sparkling wine.
**Schau-:** ~**platz** *m* scene; **vom** ~**platz berichten** to give an on-the-spot report; ~**prozeß** *m* show trial.
**schaurig** *adj* gruesome; *(col: sehr schlecht)* abysmal *(col)*.
**schaurig-schön** *adj* gruesomely beautiful.
**Schauspiel** *nt (Theat)* drama, play; *(fig)* spectacle.
**Schauspieler** *m (also fig)* actor.
**Schauspielerei** *f* acting.

**Schauspielerin** *f (lit, fig)* actress.
**schauspielerisch 1** *adj* acting. **2** *adv* as regards acting.
**schauspielern** *vi insep* to act.
**Schauspiel-:** ~**haus** *nt* playhouse, theatre *(Brit)*, theater *(US)*; ~**schule** *f* drama school; ~**unterricht** *m* drama classes *pl*.
**Schau-:** ~**steller(in** *f)* *m* - (travelling *(Brit)* or traveling *(US)*) showman; ~**stück** *nt* showpiece; ~**tafel** *f* (notice) board; *(~bild)* diagram.
**Scheck** *m* **-s** cheque *(Brit)*, check *(US)*. **mit (einem)** or **per** ~ **bezahlen** to pay by cheque; **ein** ~ **über DM200** a cheque for 200 DM.
**Scheck-:** ~**betrug** *m* cheque *(Brit)* or check *(US)* fraud; ~**betrüger** *m* cheque *(Brit)* or check *(US)* fraud; ~**buch**, ~**heft** *nt* chequebook *(Brit)*, checkbook *(US)*.
**scheckig** *adj* spotted; *Pferd* dappled; *(verfärbt)* blotchy, patchy.
**Scheckkarte** *f* cheque card *(Brit)*, banker's card.
**scheel** *adj* **jdn** ~ **ansehen** to give sb a dirty look; *(abschätzig)* to look askance at sb.
**scheffeln** *vt Geld* to rake in *(col)*.
**Scheibe** *f* **-n** **(a)** disc, disk; *(Schieß~)* target; *(Eishockey)* puck; *(Wähl~)* dial; *(Tech: Dichtungs~)* washer; *(Töpfer~)* wheel; *(col: Schallplatte)* disc *(col)*. **(b)** *(abgeschnittene* ~*)* slice. **etw in** ~**n schneiden** to cut sth (up) into slices; **von ihm könntest du dir eine** ~ **abschneiden** *(fig col)* you could take a leaf out of his book *(col)*. **(c)** *(Glas~)* (window)pane.
**Scheiben-:** ~**bremse** *f* disc brake; ~**kleister** *interj (euph col)* sugar! *(euph col)*; ~**schießen** *nt* target shooting; ~**waschanlage** *f* windscreen *(Brit)* or windshield *(US)* washers *pl*; ~**wischer** *m* windscreen *(Brit)* or windshield *(US)* wiper.
**Scheich** *m* **-e** sheik(h).
**Scheide** *f* **-n** sheath; *(Vagina)* vagina.
**scheiden** *pret* **schied**, *ptp* **geschieden 1** *vt* **(a)** *(geh: trennen)* to separate. **(b)** *Ehe* to dissolve; *Eheleute* to divorce. **eine geschiedene Frau/ein geschiedener Mann** a divorcee; **sich** ~ **lassen** to get a divorce, to get divorced; **von dem Moment an waren wir (zwei) geschiedene Leute** *(col)* after that it was the parting of the ways for us *(col)*. **2** *vi aux sein (liter) (sich trennen)* to part; *(weggehen)* to depart. **aus dem Amt** ~ to retire from one's office; **aus dem Leben** ~ to depart this life. **3** *vr (Wege)* to divide; *(Meinungen)* to diverge.
**Scheideweg** *m (fig)* crossroads *sing.* **am** ~ **weg stehen** to be at a crossroads.
**Scheidung** *f* **(a)** *(das Scheiden)* separation. **(b)** *(Ehe~)* divorce. **in** ~ **leben** to be getting a divorce; **die** ~ **einreichen** to file a petition for divorce.
**Scheidungs-:** ~**grund** *m* grounds *pl* for divorce; *(hum: Mensch)* reason for the divorce; ~**klage** *f* petition for divorce; ~**prozeß** *m* divorce proceedings *pl*.
**Schein¹** *m no pl* **(a)** *(Licht)* light; *(matt)* glow. **(b)** *(An~)* appearances *pl*; *(Vortäuschung)* pretence *(Brit)*, pretense *(US)*, sham. ~ **und Sein** appearance and reality; **den** ~ **wahren** to keep up appearances; **etw nur zum** ~ **tun** only to pretend to do sth.
**Schein²** *m* **-e** *(Geld~)* note *(Brit)*, bill *(US)*; *(Bescheinigung)* certificate; *(Fahr~)* ticket.
**scheinbar** *adj* apparent; *(vorgegeben)* ostensible. **er hörte** ~ **interessiert zu** he listened with apparent interest.
**scheinen** *pret* **schien**, *ptp* **geschienen** *vi* **(a)** *(leuchten)* to shine. **(b)** *auch vi impers (den Anschein geben)* to seem, to appear. **mir scheint, (daß)** ... it seems to me that ...; **wie es scheint** apparently.

**Schein-**: **~gefecht** *nt* mock fight; **s~heilig** *adj* hypocritical; *(Arglosigkeit vortäuschend)* innocent; **tu nicht so s~heilig!** don't pretend to be so innocent; **~heilige(r)** *mf siehe adj* hypocrite; sham; **~heiligkeit** *f siehe adj* hypocrisy; feigned innocence; **~tod** *m* apparent death; **~werfer** *m (zum Beleuchten)* floodlight; *(im Theater)* spotlight; *(Such~)* searchlight; *(Aut)* (head)light, headlamp; **~werferlicht** *nt siehe* **~werfer** floodlight(ing); spotlight; searchlight (beam); beam of the headlights; *(fig)* limelight.

**Scheiß** *m no pl (col!)* shit *(col!)*, crap *(col!)*. **mach keinen ~!** don't be so damn *(col)* silly.

**Scheiß-** *in cpds (col!)* bloody *(Brit col)*, fucking *(col!!)*.

**Scheißdreck** *m (col!)* shit *(col!)*, crap *(col!)*; *(unangenehme Sache)* effing thing *(col!)*, bloody thing *(Brit col)*. **das geht dich einen ~ an** it's got buggerall to do with you *(col!)*; **einen ~ werd' ich tun!** like hell I will!

**Scheiße** *f no pl (col!)* shit *(col!)*, crap *(col!)*. **~ sein** to be bloody awful *(Brit col)* or goddamn *(col)* awful; **~!** bloody hell! *(Brit col)*, shit! *(col!)*, bugger *(col!)*; **in der ~ sitzen** to be in the shit *(col!)*.

**scheiß|egal** *adj (col)* **das ist mir doch ~!** I don't give a damn *(col)*.

**scheißen** *pret* **schiß**, *ptp* **geschissen** *vi (col!)* to shit *(col!)*, to crap *(col!)*. **auf etw (acc) ~** *(fig)* not to give a shit about sth *(col!)*.

**Scheißer** *m* - *(col!: Arschloch)* bugger *(col!)*.

**Scheiß-**: **s~freundlich** *adj (pej col)* as nice as pie *(iro col)*; **~haus** *nt (col!)* shithouse *(col!)*; **~kerl** *m (col!)* bastard *(col!)*, son-of-a-bitch *(US col!)*.

**Scheit** *m* -**e** log, piece of wood.

**Scheitel** *m* - **(a)** *(Haar~)* parting *(Brit)*, part *(US)*. **vom ~ bis zur Sohle** from top to toe. **(b)** *(höchster Punkt)* vertex.

**scheiteln** *vt* to part.

**Scheitelpunkt** *m* vertex.

**Scheiterhaufen** *m* (funeral) pyre; *(Hist: zur Hinrichtung)* stake.

**scheitern** *vi aux sein (an +dat because of)* *(Mensch, Plan)* to fail; *(Verhandlungen, Ehe)* to break down; *(Regierung)* to founder *(an +dat on)*.

**Scheitern** *nt no pl siehe vi* failure; breakdown; foundering. **das war zum ~ verurteilt** that was doomed to failure.

**Schelle** *f* -**n** **(a)** bell. **(b)** *(Tech)* clamp.

**schellen** *vi* to ring *(nach jdm* for sb*)*. **es hat geschellt** the bell has gone; *(an der Tür)* that was the doorbell.

**Schellfisch** *m* haddock.

**Schelm** *m* -**e** *(dated: Spaßvogel)* rogue.

**Schelmen-**: **~roman** *m* picaresque novel; **~streich** *m (dated)* roguish prank.

**schelmisch** *adj* mischievous.

**Schelte** *f* -**n** scolding; *(Kritik)* attack.

**schelten** *pret* **schalt**, *ptp* **gescholten** *(geh)* **1** *vt* to scold. **jdn einen Dummkopf ~** to call sb a blockhead. **2** *vi (schimpfen)* to curse.

**Schema** *nt, pl* **Schemen** *or* -**ta** scheme; *(Darstellung)* diagram; *(Muster)* pattern.

**Schemabrief** *m (Comm)* standard letter.

**schematisch** *adj* schematic; *(pej)* mechanical.

**Schemel** *m* - stool.

**schemenhaft** **1** *adj* shadowy. **2** *adv* **etw ~ sehen/zeichnen** to see the outlines of sth/to sketch sth in.

**Schenke** *f* -**n** tavern, inn.

**Schenkel** *m* - **(a)** *(Anat: Ober~)* thigh. **sich (dat) auf die ~ schlagen** to slap one's thighs. **(b)** *(Math: von Winkel)* side.

**schenken** **1** *vt* **(a)** **jdm etw ~** to give sb sth (as a present); **etw geschenkt bekommen** to get sth as a present; **etw zum Geburtstag geschenkt bekommen** to get sth for one's birthday; **ich möchte nichts geschenkt haben!** *(lit)* I don't want any presents!; *(fig: bevorzugt werden)* I don't want any special treatment!; **das ist geschenkt!** *(col: nicht der Rede wert)* that's no great shakes *(col)*; **das ist (fast) geschenkt!** *(col: billig)* that's dirt cheap *(col)*, that's just about giving it away; **einem Kind das Leben ~** *(geh)* to give birth to a child; **jdm seine Aufmerksamkeit ~** to give sb one's attention; **jdm Vertrauen ~** to put one's trust in sb; **einem geschenkten Gaul sieht man nicht ins Maul** *(Prov)* don't look a gift-horse in the mouth *(prov)*. **(b)** *(erlassen)* **jdm etw ~** to let sb off sth; **ihm ist nie etwas geschenkt worden** *(fig)* he never had it easy.

**2** *vr* **sich (dat) etw ~** to skip sth *(col)*; **deine Komplimente kannst du dir ~!** you can keep your compliments *(col)*; **er hat sich (dat) nichts geschenkt** he spared no pains.

**Schenkung** *f (Jur)* gift.

**Schenkungs|urkunde** *f* deed of gift.

**scheppern** *vi (col)* to clatter. **es hat gescheppert** *(Autounfall)* there was a bang.

**Scherbe** *f* -**n** fragment, (broken) piece; *(Glas~ etc)* broken piece of glass *etc*. **etw in ~n schlagen** to shatter sth; **in ~n gehen** to shatter; *(fig)* to fall to pieces; **~n bringen Glück** *(Prov)* broken crockery brings you luck.

**Schere** *f* -**n** **(a)** *(klein)* scissors *pl*; *(groß)* shears *pl*; *(fig: Kluft)* divide. **eine ~** a pair of scissors/shears. **(b)** *(Zool)* pincer; *(von Hummer, Krebs etc auch)* claw. **(c)** *(Turnen, Ringen)* scissors *sing*.

**scheren¹** *pret* **schor**, *ptp* **geschoren** *vt* to clip; *Schaf, (Tech)* to shear; *Haare* to crop; *Bart (rasieren)* to shave; *(stutzen)* to trim.

**scheren²** *vtr* **(a)** **sich nicht um jdn/etw ~** not to care about sb/sth. **(b)** *(col)* **scher dich (weg)!** beat it! *(col)*; **scher dich ins Bett!** get to bed!

**Scheren-**: **~schlag** *m* scissors kick; **~schnitt** *m* silhouette.

**Schererei** *f usu pl (col)* trouble *no pl*.

**Scherflein** *nt* **sein ~ (zu etw) beitragen** *(Geld)* to contribute one's mite (towards sth); *(fig)* to do one's bit (for sth).

**Scher-**: **~kopf** *m* shaving head; **~messer** *nt* shearing knife.

**Scherz** *m* -**e** joke. **zum/im ~** as a joke/in fun; **einen ~ machen** to make a joke; *(Streich)* to play a joke; **mach keine ~e!** *(col)* you're joking!; **(ganz) ohne ~!** *(col)* no kidding! *(col)*.

**Scherz|artikel** *m usu pl* joke (article).

**scherzen** *vi (geh)* to joke; *(albern)* to banter. **mit etw ist nicht zu ~** one can't trifle with sth.

**Scherz-**: **~frage** *f* riddle; **s~haft** *adj* jocular; *(spaßig)* Einfall playful; **etw s~haft sagen** to say sth as a joke *or* in fun; **~keks** *m (col)* joker *(col)*.

**scheu** *adj* shy. **mach doch die Pferde nicht ~** *(fig col)* keep your hair on *(col)*.

**Scheu** *f no pl* fear *(vor +dat* of*)*; *(Schüchternheit)* shyness; *(Hemmung)* inhibition; *(Ehrfurcht)* awe. **seine ~ verlieren** to lose one's inhibitions.

**scheuchen** *vt* to shoo (away). **jdn an die Arbeit ~** to make sb get down to work.

**scheuen** **1** *vt* *Kosten, Arbeit* to shy away from; *Menschen, Licht* to shun. **weder Mühe noch Kosten ~** to spare neither trouble nor expense. **2** *vr* **sich vor etw (dat) ~** *(Angst haben)* to be afraid of sth; *(zurückschrecken)* to shy away from sth. **3** *vi (Pferd etc)* to shy *(vor +dat* at*)*.

**Scheuer** f -n barn.
**Scheuer-**: ~**besen** m scrubbing broom; ~**bürste** f scrubbing brush; ~**lappen** m floorcloth.
**scheuern 1** vti **(a)** *(putzen)* to scour; *(mit Bürste)* to scrub. **(b)** *(reiben)* to chafe. **(c)** jdm eine ~ *(col)* to clout sb one *(col)*. **2** vt **sich (an etw** dat) ~ to rub (against sth); **sich** *(acc)* **(wund)** ~ to chafe oneself.
**Scheuer-**: ~**sand** m scouring powder; ~**tuch** nt floorcloth.
**Scheuklappe** f blinker. ~**n haben** *(lit, fig)* to be blinkered.
**Scheune** f -n barn.
**Scheunen-**: ~**drescher** m: **wie ein** ~**drescher fressen** *(col)* to eat like a horse *(col)*; ~**tor** nt barn door.
**Scheusal** nt, pl -e or *(col)* **Scheusäler** monster.
**scheußlich** adj dreadful; *(abstoßend häßlich)* hideous. **es hat** ~ **weh getan** *(col)* it was terribly painful.
**Scheußlichkeit** f *siehe* adj dreadfulness; hideousness.
**Schi** m -er or - = **Ski**.
**Schicht** f -en **(a)** *(Lage)* layer; *(dünne* ~) film; *(Farb~)* coat; *(der Gesellschaft)* level, stratum. **breite** ~**en der Bevölkerung** large sections of the population. **(b)** *(Ind)* shift. **er muß** ~ **arbeiten** he has to work shifts.
**Schicht-**: ~**arbeit** f shiftwork; ~**arbeiter** m shiftworker.
**schichten** vt to layer; *Holz, Bücher etc* to stack.
**Schicht-**: ~**stoff** m laminate; ~**torte** f layer cake.
**Schichtung** f layering; *(von Holz, Büchern etc)* stacking.
**Schicht-**: ~**wechsel** m change of shifts; **s~weise** adv in layers; *(Farbe, Lack)* in coats.
**Schick** m no pl style; *(von Frauenmode, Frau auch)* chic.
**schick** adj elegant, smart; *Frauenmode* chic; *Wohnung auch, Möbel* stylish; *Auto* smart.
**schicken 1** vti to send. **jdn einkaufen** ~ to send sb to do the shopping. **2** vr, vr impers *(sich ziemen)* to be fitting or proper. **3** vr *(dated: sich abfinden)* **sich in etw** *(acc)* ~ to resign or reconcile oneself to sth.
**Schickeria** f no pl *(iro)* smart set, in-people pl.
**Schicki, Schickimicki** m -s *(col)* trendy.
**schicklich** adj *Kleidung etc* proper, fitting; *Verhalten* seemly, becoming.
**Schicksal** nt -e fate, destiny; *(Pech)* fate. **das** ~ **wollte es, (daß)** ... as fate would have it, ...; **das sind (schwere)** ~**e** those are tragic cases; **er hat ein schweres** ~ **gehabt** fate has been unkind to him; **(das ist)** ~ *(col)* that's life; **jdn seinem** ~ **überlassen** to leave sb to his fate.
**schicksalhaft** adj fateful.
**Schicksals-**: ~**frage** f fateful question; ~**schlag** m great misfortune, stroke of fate.
**Schiebe-**: ~**dach** nt *(Aut)* sunroof; ~**fenster** nt sliding window.
**schieben** pret **schob**, ptp **geschoben 1** vt **(a)** to push, to shove; *(stecken)* to put. **etw von sich** *(dat)* ~ *(fig)* to put sth aside; *Schuld, Verantwortung* to reject sth; **etw vor sich** *(dat)* **her** ~ *(fig)* to put off sth; **etw auf jdn/etw** ~ to put the blame for sth onto sb/sth. **(b)** *(col: handeln mit)* to traffic in; *Drogen* to push *(col)*. **(c)** *(col)* **Wache** ~ to do guard duty. **2** vi **(a)** to push, to shove. **(b)** *(col)* **mit etw/ Drogen** ~ to traffic in sth/push *(col)* drugs. **(c)** *(col: betrügen)* to wangle *(col)*. **3** vr **(a)** *(mit Anstrengung)* to push, to shove. **(b)** *(sich bewegen)* to move.
**Schieber** m - **(a)** slide; *(am Ofen etc)* damper. **(b)** *(Schwarzhändler)* black marketeer; *(Waffen~)* gun-

runner; *(Drogen~)* pusher *(col)*.
**Schiebetür** f sliding door.
**Schiebung** f *(Betrug)* string-pulling; *(im Sport)* rigging; *(Schiebergeschäfte)* shady deals pl. **das war doch** ~ that was rigged or fixed *(col)*.
**schied** pret of **scheiden**.
**Schieds-**: ~**gericht** nt court of arbitration; ~**richter** m *(Sport)* referee; *(Hockey, Tennis)* umpire; *(Preisrichter)* judge; **s~richtern** vi insep *(col)* siehe ~**richter** to referee; to umpire; to judge; ~**spruch** m arbitration decision; ~**stelle** f arbitration service; ~**verfahren** nt arbitration proceedings pl.
**schief** adj crooked, not straight pred; *(nach einer Seite geneigt)* lopsided, tilted; *Winkel* oblique; *Blick* wry; *Absätze* worn(-down); *(fig: unzutreffend)* inappropriate; *Bild* distorted. ~**e Ebene** *(Phys)* inclined plane; **auf die** ~**e Bahn geraten** *(fig)* to leave the straight and narrow; **du siehst die Sache ganz** ~! *(fig)* you're looking at it all wrong!; **jdn** ~ **ansehen** *(fig)* to look askance at sb; **der S~e Turm von Pisa** the Leaning Tower of Pisa.
**Schiefer** m - *(Gesteinsart)* slate.
**Schiefer-**: ~**dach** nt slate roof; ~**tafel** f slate.
**schief-**: ~**gehen** vi sep irreg aux sein to go wrong; **es wird schon** ~**gehen!** *(hum)* it'll be OK *(col)*; ~**lachen** vr sep *(col)* to kill oneself (laughing) *(col)*; ~**laufen** vi sep irreg aux sein *(col)* to go wrong; ~**liegen** vi sep irreg *(col)* to be wrong.
**schielen** vi to squint, to be cross-eyed. **auf** or **mit einem Auge** ~ to have a squint in one eye; **auf etw** *(acc)* ~ *(col)* to steal a glance at sth; **nach etw** ~ to have an eye on sth.
**schien** pret of **scheinen**.
**Schienbein** nt shin; *(~knochen)* shinbone.
**Schienbeinschützer** m shin-pad.
**Schiene** f -n rail; *(Med)* splint. ~**n** *(Rail)* track sing, rails pl; **aus den** ~**n springen** to leave or jump the rails.
**schienen** vt *Arm, Bein* to splint.
**Schienen-**: ~**bus** m railcar; ~**fahrzeug** nt rail vehicle; ~**netz** nt *(Rail)* rail network; ~**strang** m (section of) track.
**schier 1** adj pure; *(fig)* sheer. **2** adv *(beinahe)* nearly, almost.
**Schieß-**: ~**befehl** m order to fire or shoot; ~**bude** f shooting gallery; ~**budenfigur** f *(fig col)* clown; ~**eisen** nt *(col)* shooter *(col)*, shooting iron *(US col)*.
**schießen** pret **schoß**, ptp **geschossen 1** vt to shoot; *Kugel, Rakete* to fire; *Tor auch* to score. **jdn in den Kopf** ~ to shoot sb in the head; **ein paar Bilder** ~ *(Phot col)* to take a few shots. **2** vi **(a)** to shoot. **auf jdn/etw** ~ to shoot at sb/sth; **aufs Tor** ~ to shoot at goal; **das ist zum S~** *(col)* that's a scream *(col)*. **(b)** aux sein to shoot; *(in die Höhe* ~) to shoot up. **aus dem Boden** ~ *(lit, fig)* to spring or sprout up; **er kam um die Ecke geschossen** he shot around the corner; **jdm durch den Kopf** ~ *(fig: Gedanke)* to flash through sb's mind; **das Blut schoß ihm ins Gesicht** blood rushed or shot to his face; **die Tränen schossen ihr in die Augen** tears flooded her eyes.
**Schießerei** f gun battle; *(das Schießen)* shooting.
**Schieß-**: ~**gewehr** nt *(hum)* gun; ~**hund** m: **wie ein** ~**hund aufpassen** *(col)* to watch like a hawk; ~**platz** m shooting or firing range; ~**pulver** nt gunpowder; ~**scharte** f embrasure; ~**scheibe** f target; ~**stand** m shooting range.
**Schiff** nt -e **(a)** ship. **(b)** *(Archit)* *(Mittel~)* nave; *(Seiten~)* aisle; *(Quer~)* transept.

**Schiffahrt** f shipping; *(~skunde)* navigation.
**Schiffahrts-:** **~gesellschaft** f shipping company; **~linie** f (a) *(Schiffsweg)* shipping route; (b) *(Unternehmen)* shipping line; **~straße** f, **~weg** m *(Kanal)* waterway; *(~linie)* shipping lane.
**Schiff-:** **s~bar** adj navigable; **~barkeit** f navigability; **~bau** m shipbuilding; **~bauer** m shipwright; **~bruch** m shipwreck; **~bruch erleiden** *(lit)* to be shipwrecked; *(fig)* to fail; *(Unternehmen)* to founder; **s~brüchig** adj shipwrecked; **~brüchige(r)** mf decl as adj shipwrecked person.
**Schiffchen** nt (a) *(zum Spielen)* little boat. (b) *(Mil, Fashion)* forage cap. (c) *(Tex, Sew)* shuttle.
**schiffen** *(col)* **1** vi *(urinieren)* to piss *(col!)*. **2** vi impers *(regnen)* to piss down *(col!)*.
**Schiffer** m - boatman, sailor; *(von Lastkahn)* bargee; *(Kapitän)* skipper.
**Schiffer-:** **~klavier** nt accordion; **~knoten** m sailor's knot; **~mütze** f yachting cap.
**Schiffschaukel** f swing boat.
**Schiffs-** in cpds ship's; **~eigner** m shipowner; **~junge** m ship's boy; **~karte** f chart; **~ladung** f shipload; **~mannschaft** f ship's crew; **~rumpf** m hull; **~schraube** f ship's propeller; **~taufe** f naming of a/the ship; **~verbindung** f (connecting) boat service; **~verkehr** m shipping; **~werft** f shipyard.
**Schiit(in** f**)** m **-en, en** Shiite.
**schiitisch** adj Shiite.
**Schikane** f **-n** (a) harassment. **das hat er aus reiner ~ gemacht** he did it out of sheer bloody-mindedness. (b) **mit allen ~n** *(col)* with all the trimmings. (c) *(Sport)* chicane.
**schikanieren*** vt to harass; *Ehepartner, Freundin etc* to mess around; *Mitschüler* to bully.
**schikanös** adj *Mensch* bloody-minded; *Maßnahme etc* harassing.
**Schild¹** m **-e** shield; *(von ~kröte)* shell. **etwas/nichts Gutes im ~e führen** *(fig)* to be up to something/to be up to no good.
**Schild²** nt **-er** *(Aushang, Verkehrs~)* sign; *(Wegweiser)* signpost; *(Namens~)* nameplate; *(Aut)* number plate *(Brit)*, license plate *(US)*; *(Preis~)* ticket; *(Etikett)* label; *(Plakat)* placard; *(an Monument, Haus, Grab)* plaque; *(von Mütze)* peak.
**Schildbürger(in** f**)** m *(hum)* fool.
**Schildbürgerstreich** m complete bungle.
**Schilddrüse** f thyroid gland.
**Schildermaler** m signwriter.
**schildern** vt to describe; *(skizzieren)* to outline; *Menschen, Landschaften* to portray. **~ Sie den Verlauf des Unfalls** give an account of how the accident happened.
**Schilderung** f *(Beschreibung)* description; *(Bericht)* account; *(literarische ~)* portrayal.
**Schild-:** **~kröte** f tortoise; *(Wasser~)* turtle; **~krötensuppe** f turtle soup; **~laus** f scale insect; **~patt** nt no pl tortoiseshell.
**Schilf** nt **-e** reed.
**Schilf-:** **~dach** nt thatched roof; **~gras** nt reed; **~rohr** nt reed.
**Schillerlocke** f (a) *(Gebäck)* cream horn. (b) *(Räucherfisch)* strip of smoked rock salmon.
**schillern** vi to shimmer.
**schillernd** adj shimmering; *(in Regenbogenfarben)* iridescent; *(fig) Charakter* enigmatic.
**Schilling** m **-** or *(bei Geldstücken)* **-e** shilling; *(Aus)* schilling.
**Schimmel¹** m **-** *(Pferd)* white horse, grey *(Brit)*, gray *(US)*.
**Schimmel²** m no pl mould *(Brit)*, mold *(US)*.

**schimm(e)lig** adj mouldy *(Brit)*, moldy *(US)*. **~ werden** to go mouldy.
**schimmeln** vi aux sein or haben *(Nahrungsmittel)* to go mouldy *(Brit)* or moldy *(US)*.
**Schimmelpilz** m mould *(Brit)*, mold *(US)*.
**Schimmer** m no pl glimmer, gleam; *(von Perlen, Seide)* shimmer; *(im Haar)* sheen. **beim ~ der Lampe** in the soft glow of the lamp; **keinen (blassen) ~ von etw haben** *(col)* not to have the slightest or faintest idea about sth.
**schimmern** vi to glimmer, to gleam; *(Perlen, Seide)* to shimmer.
**Schimpanse** m *(wk)* **-n, -n** chimpanzee, chimp *(col)*.
**Schimpf** m no pl **mit ~ und Schande** in disgrace.
**schimpfen 1** vi to get angry; *(sich beklagen)* to grumble; *(fluchen)* to swear, to curse. **mit jdm ~** to tell sb off; **auf** or **über jdn/etw ~** to bitch about sb/sth *(col)*, to curse (about or at) sb/sth. **2** vt *(pej: nennen)* to call. **3** vr **sich etw ~** *(col)* to call oneself sth.
**Schimpf-:** **~kanonade** f barrage of abuse; **~name** m nickname; **~wort** nt swearword.
**Schindel** f **-n** shingle.
**schinden** pret **schindete**, ptp **geschunden 1** vt (a) *Gefangene, Tiere* to maltreat. (b) *(col: herausschlagen)* Zeilen to pad (out); *Arbeitsstunden* to pile up. **Zeit ~** to play for time; **Mitleid ~** to angle for sympathy. **2** vr *(hart arbeiten)* to struggle. **sich mit etw ~** to slave away at sth.
**Schinderei** f *(Plackerei)* struggle; *(Arbeit)* slavery no indef art.
**Schindluder** nt *(col)* **mit jdm ~ treiben** to make sb suffer; **mit etw ~ treiben** to abuse sth.
**Schinken** m **-** (a) ham; *(gekocht und geräuchert auch)* gammon. (b) *(pej col)* hackneyed and clichéed play/book/film; *(großes Buch)* tome; *(großes Bild)* great daub *(pej col)*.
**Schinken-:** **~speck** m bacon; **~wurst** f ham sausage.
**Schippe** f **-n** shovel, spade. **jdn auf die ~ nehmen** *(fig col)* to pull sb's leg *(col)*.
**schippen** vt to shovel. **Schnee ~** to clear the snow.
**schippern** vi aux sein *(col)* to sail.
**Schiri** m **-s** *(Ftbl col)* ref *(col)*.
**Schirm** m **-e** *(Regen~)* umbrella; *(Sonnen~)* sunshade, parasol; *(Mützen~)* peak; *(Röntgen~, Wand~, Bild~)* screen; *(Lampen~)* shade.
**Schirm-:** **~bild** nt X-ray (picture); **~herr(in** f**)** m patron; *(Frau auch)* patroness; **~herrschaft** f patronage; **~mütze** f peaked cap; **~ständer** m umbrella stand.
**schiß** pret of **scheißen**.
**Schiß** m no pl *(col)* **(fürchterlichen) ~ haben** to be terrified *(vor +dat of)*.
**schizophren** adj (a) *(Med)* schizophrenic. (b) *(pej: widersinnig)* contradictory.
**Schizophrenie** f (a) *(Med)* schizophrenia. (b) *(pej: Widersinn)* contradictoriness.
**schlabberig** adj *(col)* Brei, Suppe watery; *Stoff* limp; *Hose etc* baggy.
**schlabbern** *(col)* **1** vi to slurp; *Kleidung* to hang loosely, to be baggy. **2** vt to slurp.
**Schlacht** f **-en** battle. **die ~ bei** or **um X** the battle of X; **jdm eine ~ liefern** to battle with sb.
**schlachten 1** vt to slaughter; *(hum)* Sparschwein to break into. **2** vi **heute wird geschlachtet** we're/they're etc slaughtering today.
**Schlachtenbummler** m *(col: Sport)* visiting or away supporter or fan.
**Schlachter(in** f**)** m **-** *(esp NGer)* butcher.

**Schlächter(in** *f)* *m* - *(dial, fig)* butcher.
**Schlächterei** *f (esp NGer)* butcher's (shop) *(Brit)*, butcher.
**Schlacht-:** ~**feld** *nt* battlefield; ~**fest** *nt esp country feast at which freshly slaughtered meat is served*; ~**hof** *m* slaughterhouse, abattoir; ~**messer** *nt* butcher's knife; ~**opfer** *nt* sacrifice; *(Mensch)* human sacrifice; ~**ordnung** *f* battle formation; ~**plan** *m* battle plan; *(für Feldzug)* campaign plan; *(fig auch)* plan of action; **s~reif** *adj (lit, fig)* ready for the slaughter; ~**ruf** *m* battle cry; ~**schiff** *nt* battleship.
**Schlachtung** *f* slaughter(ing).
**Schlachtvieh** *nt no pl* animals *pl* for slaughter.
**Schlacke** *f* **-n** clinker *no pl; (Aschenteile auch)* cinders *pl; (Metal, Geol)* slag *no pl; (Physiol)* waste products *pl.*
**schlackern** *vi (col)* to tremble, to shake; *(Kleidung)* to hang loosely, to be baggy. **mit den Ohren** ~ *(fig)* to be (left) speechless.
**Schlaf** *m no pl* sleep. **einen leichten/tiefen** ~ **haben** to be a light/deep sleeper; **keinen** ~ **finden** to be unable to sleep; **um seinen** ~ **kommen** to lose sleep; *(überhaupt nicht schlafen)* not to get any sleep; **jdn um seinen** ~ **bringen** to keep sb awake; ~ **haben** to be sleepy; **in tiefstem** ~ **liegen** to be sound or fast asleep; **das macht** or **kann er im** ~ *(fig col)* he can do that in his sleep.
**Schlaf|anzug** *m* pyjamas *pl (Brit)*, pajamas *pl (US).*
**Schläfchen** *nt* nap, snooze. **ein** ~ **machen** to have a nap or snooze.
**Schläfe** *f* **-n** temple. **graue** ~**n** greying *(Brit)* or graying *(US)* temples.
**schlafen** *pret* **schlief**, *ptp* **geschlafen** *vi* to sleep; *(col: nicht aufpassen) (bei bestimmter Gelegenheit)* to be asleep; *(immer)* not to pay attention. **er schläft immer noch** he's still asleep, he's still sleeping; ~ **gehen** to go to bed; **sich** ~ **legen** to lie down to sleep; **schläfst du schon?** are you asleep?; **lange** ~ to sleep for a long time; *(spät aufstehen)* to sleep late, to have a lie-in; **schlaf gut** sleep well; **bei jdm** ~ to stay overnight with sb; **mit jdm** ~ *(euph)* to sleep with sb; **das läßt ihn nicht** ~ *(fig)* it preys on his mind; **darüber muß ich erst mal** ~ *(fig: überdenken)* I'll have to sleep on it.
**Schlafengehen** *nt* going to bed. **vor dem** ~ before going to bed.
**Schlafenszeit** *f* bedtime.
**Schläfer(in** *f)* *m* - sleeper; *(fig)* dozy person *(col).*
**schlaff** *adj* limp; *(locker) Seil* slack; *Disziplin* lax; *Haut* loose; *Muskeln* flabby; *(erschöpft)* worn-out, exhausted; *(energielos)* listless.
**Schlaffheit** *f siehe adj* limpness; slackness; laxity; looseness; flabbiness; exhaustion; listlessness.
**Schlaf-:** ~**gast** *m* overnight guest; ~**gelegenheit** *f* place to sleep.
**Schlafittchen** *nt:* **jdn am** or **beim** ~ **nehmen** *(col)* to take sb by the scruff of the neck; *(zurechtweisen)* to give sb a dressing-down *(col).*
**Schlaf-:** ~**krankheit** *f* sleeping sickness; ~**lied** *nt* lullaby; **s~los** *adj (lit, fig)* sleepless; ~**losigkeit** *f* sleeplessness, insomnia *(Med);* ~**mittel** *nt* sleeping pill; *(fig iro)* soporific; ~**mütze** *f (col)* dope *(col);* **s~mützig** *adj (col)* dozy *(col)*, dopey *(col);* ~**raum** *m* dormitory *(Brit)*, dorm *(Brit col).*
**schläfrig** *adj* sleepy; *Mensch auch* drowsy.
**Schläfrigkeit** *f siehe adj* sleepiness; drowsiness.
**Schlaf-:** ~**rock** *m* dressing gown; **Äpfel im** ~**rock** baked apples in puff pastry; ~**saal** *m* dormitory; ~**sack** *m* sleeping bag; ~**stelle** *f* place to sleep; ~**störung** *f* sleeplessness, insomnia *(Med);* ~**ta-**

**blette** *f* sleeping pill; **s~trunken** *adv* drowsily, half-asleep; ~**wagen** *m* sleepingcar, sleeper *(Brit);* **s~wandeln** *vi insep aux sein or haben* to sleepwalk; ~**wandler(in** *f)* *m* - sleepwalker; **s~wandlerisch** *adj* **mit s~wandlerischer Sicherheit** intuitively, instinctively; ~**zimmer** *nt* bedroom.
**Schlag** *m* ⸚**e** (a) *(lit, fig)* blow; *(Faust~ auch)* punch; *(mit der Handfläche)* smack, slap; *(Handkanten~, Judo etc)* chop *(col); (Ohrfeige)* cuff, clout; *(Tritt)* kick; *(mit Rohrstock etc)* stroke; *(Peitschen~)* stroke, lash; *(Glocken~)* chime; *(~anfall, Ruder~, Schwimmen, Tennis)* stroke; *(Herz~, Wellen~)* beat; *(Blitz~)* bolt; *(Donner~)* clap; *(Strom~)* shock. **~e kriegen** to get a hiding or beating; **zum entscheidenden** ~ **ausholen** *(fig)* to launch the decisive blow; ~ **auf** ~ *(fig)* in quick succession; ~ **acht Uhr** *(col)* on the stroke of eight; **ein** ~ **ins Gesicht** *(lit, fig)* a slap in the face; **ein** ~ **ins Wasser** *(col)* a washout *(col);* **auf einen** ~ *(col)* all at once; **mit einem** ~ **berühmt werden** to become famous overnight; **sie haben keinen** ~ **getan** *(col)* they haven't done a stroke (of work); **einen** ~ **weghaben** *(col: blöd sein)* to have a screw loose *(col);* **ich dachte, mich trifft der** ~ *(col)* I was thunderstruck.
(**b**) *(col: Wesensart)* type (of person *etc).* **vom gleichen** ~ **sein** to be cast in the same mould *(Brit)* or mold *(US); (pej)* to be tarred with the same brush; **vom alten** ~ of the old school.
(**c**) *(col: Portion)* helping.
**Schlag-:** ~**abtausch** *m (Boxen)* exchange of blows; *(fig)* (verbal) exchange; **offener** ~**abtausch** public exchange (of views); ~**ader** *f* artery; ~**anfall** *m* stroke; **s~artig 1** *adj* sudden, abrupt; **2** *adv* suddenly; ~**ball** *m* rounders *sing; (Ball)* rounders ball; **s~bar** *adj* beatable; ~**baum** *m* barrier; ~**bohrer** *m*, ~**bohrmaschine** *f* hammer drill.
**schlagen** *pret* **schlug**, *ptp* **geschlagen 1** *vti* (a) to hit; *(hauen)* to beat; *(mit der flachen Hand)* to slap, to smack; *(mit der Faust)* to punch; *(treten)* to kick. **jdn bewußtlos** ~ to knock sb out or unconscious; *(mit vielen Schlägen)* to beat sb unconscious; **um sich** ~ to lash out; **mit der Faust auf den Tisch** ~ to thump on the table with one's fist; **jdm etw aus der Hand** ~ to knock sth out of sb's hand; **ihm schlug das Gewissen** his conscience pricked him; **einer Sache** *(dat)* **ins Gesicht** ~ *(fig)* to be a slap in the face for sth. (**b**) *Teig, Eier* to beat; *(mit Schneebesen)* to whisk; *Sahne* to whip. **ein Ei in die Pfanne** ~ to crack an egg into the pan. (**c**) *(läuten)* to chime; *Stunde* to strike. **die Uhr hat 12 geschlagen** the clock has struck 12; **eine geschlagene Stunde** a full hour. (**d**) *(flattern)* **mit den Flügeln** ~ to flap its wings.
**2** *vt* (a) *Gegner, Rekord* to beat. **jdn in etw** *(dat)* ~ to beat sb at sth; **na ja, ehe ich mich** ~ **lasse!** *(hum col)* I suppose you could twist my arm *(hum col);* **sich geschlagen geben** to admit defeat. (**b**) **das Schicksal schlug sie hart** fate dealt her a hard blow; **mit Blindheit geschlagen sein** to be blind. (**c**) *(fällen)* to fell. (**d**) *(Hunt: töten)* to kill. (**e**) *(spielen) Trommel* to beat; *(liter) Harfe, Laute* to pluck, to play. (**f**) *Kreis, Bogen* to describe; *Purzelbaum* to do; *Alarm* to raise; *Krach* to make. **Profit aus etw** ~ to make profit from sth; **eine Schlacht** ~ to fight a battle; **den Kragen nach oben** ~ to turn up one's collar. (**g**) *(wickeln)* to wrap.
**3** *vi* (a) *(Herz, Puls)* to beat; *(heftig)* to pound, to throb. (**b**) *(Regen)* to beat; *(Wellen auch)* to pound; *(Blitz)* to strike *(in etw (acc)* sth). (**c**) *(singen: Nachtigall, Fink)* to sing. (**d**) *(betreffen)* **in jds Fach** *(acc)* ~ to be in sb's field. (**e**) *aux sein or haben (Flammen)*

to shoot out *(aus of)*; *(Rauch)* to pour out *(aus of)*.
**(f)** *aux sein* **mit dem Kopf auf etw** *(acc)* ~ to hit one's head on sth; **auf die Nieren** *etc* ~ to affect the kidneys *etc*; **er schlägt sehr nach seinem Vater** he takes after his father a lot.

**4** *vr* **(a)** *(sich prügeln)* to fight; *(sich duellieren)* to duel. **als Schuljunge habe ich mich oft geschlagen** I often had fights when I was a schoolboy; **sich um etw** ~ *(lit, fig)* to fight over sth. **(b)** *(sich bewähren)* to do, to fare. **sich tapfer** *or* **gut** ~ to make a good showing. **(c)** *(sich begeben)* **sich nach links/Norden** ~ to strike out to the left/for the North; **sich auf jds Seite** *(acc)* ~ to side with sb; *(die Fronten wechseln)* to go over to sb.

**schlagend** *adj* **(a)** *Bemerkung, Vergleich* apt, appropriate; *Beweis* striking, convincing. **etw** ~ **beweisen/widerlegen** to prove/refute sth convincingly. **(b)** *Verbindung (Univ)* duelling.

**Schlager** *m* - **(a)** *(Mus)* pop song; *(erfolgreich)* hit song, hit. **(b)** *(col) (Erfolg)* hit; *(Verkaufs~)* bestseller.

**Schläger** *m* - **(a)** *(Tennis~, Federball~)* racket; *(Hockey~, Eishockey~)* stick; *(Golf~)* club; *(Kricket~, Baseball~, Tischtennis~)* bat; *(Polo~)* mallet. **(b)** *(Spieler) (Kricket)* batsman; *(Baseball)* batter. **(c)** *(Raufbold)* thug, ruffian.

**Schlägerei** *f* fight, brawl.

**Schlägerin** *f* = **Schläger (b), (c)**.

**Schlager-:** ~**musik** *f* pop music; ~**parade** *f* hit parade; ~**sänger** *m* pop singer.

**Schlägertyp** *m (col)* thug.

**Schlag-:** **s~fertig** *adj* quick-witted; ~**fertigkeit** *f* quick-wittedness; ~**instrument** *nt* percussion instrument; ~**kraft** *f (lit, fig)* power; *(Boxen)* punch(ing power); *(Mil)* strike power; **s~kräftig** *adj* powerful; *Beweise* clear-cut; ~**licht** *nt* **ein** ~**licht auf etw** *(acc)* **werfen** *(fig)* to highlight *or* spotlight sth; ~**loch** *nt* pothole; ~**mann** *m, pl* ~**männer** *(Rudern)* stroke; *(Kricket)* batsman; *(Baseball)* batter; ~**obers** *nt* -, - *(Aus)*, ~**rahm** *m (S Ger)*, ~**sahne** *f* (whipping) cream; *(geschlagen)* whipped cream; ~**seite** *f (Naut)* list; ~**seite haben** *(Naut)* to have a list; *(hum col)* to be half-seas over *(col)*; ~**stock** *m (form)* truncheon *(Brit)*, nightstick *(US)*; ~**wort** *nt* **(a)** *pl* ~**wörter** *(Stichwort)* headword; **(b)** *pl* ~**worte** *(Parole)* catchword, slogan; ~**zeile** *f* headline; ~**zeilen machen** *(col)* to hit the headlines; ~**zeug** *nt* drums *pl*; *(in Orchester)* percussion *no pl*; ~**zeuger(in)** *m* - drummer; *(in Orchester)* percussionist.

**schlaksig** *(col)* **1** *adj* gangling, gawky. **2** *adv* gawkily.

**Schlamassel** *m or nt* - *(col) (Durcheinander)* mix-up; *(mißliche Lage)* mess. **der** *or* **das (ganze)** ~ *(Zeug)* the whole caboodle *(col)*.

**Schlamm** *m* -**e** *or* -**e** mud; *(Schlick auch)* sludge.

**Schlammbad** *nt* mudbath.

**schlammig** *adj* muddy; *(schlickig auch)* sludgy.

**Schlampe** *f* -**n** *(pej col)* slut *(col)*.

**schlampen** *vi (col)* to be sloppy (in one's work).

**Schlamperei** *f (col)* sloppiness; *(schlechte Arbeit)* sloppy work; *(Unordentlichkeit)* untidiness. **das ist eine** ~**!** that's a disgrace.

**schlampig** *adj (col)* sloppy, careless; *(unordentlich)* untidy; *(liederlich)* slovenly.

**schlang** *pret of* **schlingen**.

**Schlange** *f* -**n** **(a)** snake, serpent *(liter)*; *(fig: Frau)* Jezebel. **eine falsche** ~ a snake in the grass. **(b)** *(Menschen~, Auto~)* queue *(Brit)*, line *(US)*. ~ **stehen** to queue (up) *(Brit)*, to stand in line *(US)*.

**schlängeln** *vr (Weg)* to wind (its way), to snake;

*(Fluß auch)* to meander; *(Schlange)* to wriggle. **eine geschlängelte Linie** a wavy line.

**Schlangen-:** ~**beschwörer** *m* - snake charmer; ~**biß** *m* snakebite; ~**gift** *nt* snake venom *or* poison; ~**haut** *f* snake's skin; *(Leder)* snakeskin; ~**linie** *f* wavy line; **(in)** ~**linien fahren** to swerve about; ~**mensch** *m* contortionist.

**Schlangestehen** *nt* queuing *(Brit)*, standing in line *(US)*.

**schlank** *adj* slim. **dieses Kleid macht sie** ~ this dress makes her look slim.

**Schlankheit** *f* slimness.

**Schlankheitskur** *f* diet. **eine** ~ **anfangen/machen** to go/be on a diet.

**schlankweg** *adv (col)* ablehnen, sagen point-blank, flatly.

**schlapp** *adj (col) (kraftlos)* shattered *(col)*; *(energielos)* listless; *(weichlich)* wimpish *(col)*; *(nach Krankheit etc)* run-down.

**Schlappe** *f* -**n** *(col)* setback; *(Sport)* thrashing *(col)*. **eine** ~ **einstecken (müssen)** to get one in the eye *(col)*; **jdm eine** ~ **beibringen** to give sb one in the eye *(col)*.

**Schlappen** *m* - *(col)* slipper.

**Schlapp-:** ~**hut** *m* floppy hat; **s~machen** *vi sep (col)* to wilt; *(zusammenbrechen)* to flop *(col)*, to flake out *(col)*; **die meisten Manager machen mit 40 s~** most managers are finished by the time they're 40; ~**schwanz** *m (pej col)* wimp *(col)*.

**Schlaraffenland** *nt* land of milk and honey.

**schlau** *adj* clever, smart; *(gerissen)* cunning; *Sprüche* clever. **ich werde nicht** ~ **aus ihm** I don't know what to make of him.

**Schlauberger** *m* - *(col)* clever dick *(col)*.

**Schlauch** *m, pl* **Schläuche (a)** *f* hose; *(für Fahrrad, Auto)* (inner) tube. **sein Zimmer war eine Art** ~ *(col)* his room was a sort of long, narrow corridor; **auf dem** ~ **stehen** *(col)* to be at a loose end. **(b)** *(col: Strapaze)* slog *(col)*, grind.

**Schlauchboot** *nt* rubber dinghy.

**schlauchen** *(col)* **1** *vt (Arbeit etc) jdn* to wear out. **2** *vi* **diese Arbeit schlaucht** this job takes it out of you.

**schlauchlos** *adj Reifen* tubeless.

**Schläue, Schlauheit** *f no pl* cunning.

**Schlaufe** *f* -**n** loop; *(Aufhänger)* hanger.

**Schlaukopf** *m*, **Schlaumeier** *m* - clever dick.

**Schlawiner** *m* - *(hum col)* crafty type, smooth operator.

**schlecht 1** *adj* **(a)** bad; *Geschmack, Leistung auch, Gesundheitszustand* poor. **das S~e in der Welt** the evil in the world; **nur S~es über jdn sagen** not to have a good word to say for sb; **jdm ist (es)** ~ **sb** feels ill *(bei Brechreiz)* sb feels sick; ~ **aussehen** *(Mensch)* to look ill, not to look well; *(Lage)* to look bad. **(b)** *pred (ungenießbar)* bad, off *(Brit)*. **die Milch ist** ~ the milk has gone off *or* is off.

**2** *adv* badly; *lernen, begreifen* with difficulty. **sich** ~ **vertragen** *(Menschen)* to get along badly; *(Dinge, Farben etc)* not to go well together; ~ **über jdn sprechen/von jdm denken** to speak/think ill of sb; **er kann** ~ **nein sagen** he finds it hard to say no; *(in diesem Fall)* he can hardly say no; **heute geht es** ~ today is not very convenient; **das läßt sich** ~ **machen** that's not really possible *or* on *(col)*; **er ist** ~ **zu verstehen** he is hard to understand; **ich kann sie** ~ **sehen** I can't see her very well; **auf jdn** ~ **zu sprechen sein** not to have a good word to say for sb; ~ **und recht, mehr** ~ **als recht** after a fashion; **er hat nicht** ~ **gestaunt** *(col)* he wasn't half surprised *(col)*.

**schlechtbezahlt** *adj attr* low-paid, badly paid.

**schlechterdings** *adv (völlig)* absolutely; *(nahezu)* virtually.

**schlecht-:** ~**gehen** *vi impers sep irreg aux sein* **es geht jdm** ~ sb is in a bad way; *(finanziell)* sb is doing badly; ~**gelaunt** *adj attr* bad-tempered; ~**hin** *adv (vollkommen)* quite, entirely; **er ist der romantische Komponist** ~**hin** he is the epitome of the Romantic composer; **Studenten** ~**hin** students as such *or* per se.

**Schlechtigkeit** *f* (a) *no pl* badness. (b) *(schlechte Tat)* misdeed.

**schlechtmachen** *vt sep* to denigrate, to run down.

**schlecken 1** *vti* to lick *(an etw (dat)* sth). **2** *vi (esp S Ger: Süßigkeiten essen)* to eat sweets *(Brit)* or candies *(US)*.

**Schleckermaul** *nt (hum col)* **sie ist ein richtiges** ~ she really has a sweet tooth.

**Schlegel** *m* - (a) stick. (b) *(Min)* miner's hammer. (c) *(S Ger, Aus: Cook)* leg.

**Schlehe** *f* -n sloe.

**schleichen** *pret* **schlich**, *ptp* **geschlichen 1** *vi aux sein* to creep; *(heimlich auch)* to sneak; *(Fahrzeug)* to crawl. **2** *vr* to creep, to sneak.

**schleichend** *adj attr* creeping; *Krankheit, Gift* insidious; *Fieber* lingering.

**Schleich-:** ~**handel** *m* illicit trading *(mit* in*)*; ~**weg** *m* secret path; **auf** ~**wegen** *(fig)* on the quiet; ~**werbung** *f* a plug.

**Schleier** *m* - *(lit, fig)* veil; *(von Wolken, Nebel auch)* haze. **einen** ~ **vor den Augen haben** to have a mist in front of one's eyes; **einen** ~ **über etw** *(acc)* **breiten** *(fig)* to draw a veil over sth.

**Schleier-:** ~**eule** *f* barn owl; **s**~**haft** *adj (col)* mysterious; **es ist mir völlig s**~**haft** it's a complete mystery to me; ~**kraut** *nt (Bot)* gypsophila.

**Schleife** *f* -n (a) loop *(auch Aviat, Comp)*; *(Straßen*~*)* twisty bend. (b) *(von Band)* bow; *(Schuh*~*)* bow(-knot); *(Fliege)* bow tie; *(Kranz*~*)* ribbon.

**schleifen¹ 1** *vt (lit, fig)* to drag; *(ziehen auch)* to haul; *(Mus)* Töne, Noten to slur. **2** *vi* (a) *aux sein or haben* to trail, to drag. (b) *(reiben)* to rub. **die Kupplung** ~ **lassen** *(Aut)* to slip the clutch; **die Zügel** ~ **lassen** *(lit, fig)* to slacken the reins.

**schleifen²** *pret* **schliff**, *ptp* **geschliffen** *vt Messer etc* to sharpen, to whet; *Parkett* to sand; *Edelstein, Glas* to cut; *siehe* **geschliffen.**

**Schleif-:** ~**lack** *m* (coloured *(Brit)* or colored *(US)*) lacquer *or* varnish; ~**maschine** *f* grinding machine; ~**papier** *nt* abrasive paper; ~**stein** *m* grindstone; **er sitzt da wie ein Affe auf dem** ~**stein** *(col)* he looks a proper Charlie sitting there *(col)*.

**Schleim** *m* -e (a) slime; *(Med)* mucus. (b) *(Cook)* gruel.

**Schleimer(in** *f)* *m* - *(col)* crawler *(col)*.

**Schleimhaut** *f* mucous membrane.

**schleimig** *adj* (a) slimy; *(Med)* mucous. (b) *(pej: unterwürfig)* slimy *(col)*.

**Schleim-:** **s**~**lösend** *adj* expectorant; ~**scheißer** *m (col!)* bootlicker *(col)*, arse-licker *(col!)*.

**schlemmen 1** *vi (üppig essen)* to feast. **2** *vt* to feast on.

**Schlemmer(in** *f)* *m* - gourmet, bon vivant.

**Schlemmerei** *f* feasting; *(Mahl)* feast.

**Schlemmerlokal** *nt* gourmet restaurant.

**schlendern** *vi aux sein* to stroll, to amble.

**Schlendrian** *m no pl (col)* casualness; *(Trott)* rut.

**Schlenker** *m* - swerve. **einen** ~ **machen** to swerve.

**schlenkern** *vti* to swing, to dangle.

**schlenzen** *vi (Sport)* to scoop.

**Schlepp** *m (Naut, fig)*: **jdn/etw in** ~ **nehmen** to take sb/sth in tow.

**Schleppe** *f* -n *(von Kleid)* train.

**schleppen 1** *vt (tragen) Lasten* to lug, to schlep *(US col)*; *(zerren)* to drag, to schlep *(US col)*; *Auto, Schiff* to tow; *(fig)* to drag. **2** *vr* to drag oneself; *(Verhandlungen etc)* to drag on.

**schleppend** *adj Gang* dragging, shuffling; *Abfertigung, Nachfrage* sluggish. **die Unterhaltung kam nur** ~ **in Gang** conversation was very slow to start.

**Schlepper** *m* - (a) *(Aut)* tractor. (b) *(Naut)* tug. (c) *(col: Kundenfänger)* tout.

**Schlepp-:** ~**kahn** *m* (canal) barge; ~**lift** *m* ski tow; ~**netz** *nt* trawl (net); ~**tau** *nt (Naut)* tow-rope; **jdn ins** ~**tau nehmen** *(col)* to take sb in tow.

**Schlesien** [-iən] *nt* Silesia.

**Schlesier(in** *f)* [-iɐ, -iɐrɪn] *m* - Silesian.

**schlesisch** *adj* Silesian.

**Schleswig-Holstein** *nt* Schleswig-Holstein.

**Schleuder** *f* -n (a) *(Waffe)* sling; *(Wurfmaschine)* catapult, slingshot *(US)*. (b) *(Zentrifuge)* centrifuge; *(Wäsche*~*)* spin-dryer *(Brit)*, dryer *(US)*.

**Schleuderhonig** *m* extracted honey.

**schleudern 1** *vti* (a) *(werfen)* to sling, to fling. (b) *(Tech)* to centrifuge, to spin; *Honig* to extract; *Wäsche* to spin-dry. **2** *vi aux sein or haben (Aut)* to skid. **ins S**~ **kommen** *or* **geraten** to go into a skid; *(fig col)* to run into trouble.

**Schleuder-:** ~**preis** *m* throwaway price; ~**sitz** *m (Aviat)* ejector seat; *(fig)* hot seat; ~**trauma** *nt (Med)* whiplash (injury); ~**ware** *f* cut-price goods *pl.*

**schleunigst** *adv* at once. **aber** ~! and be quick about it!

**Schleuse** *f* -n *(für Schiffe)* lock; *(zur Regulierung des Wasserlaufs)* sluice.

**schleusen** *vt Schiffe* to pass through a lock, to lock; *Wasser* to channel; *Menschen* to filter; *(fig: heimlich)* to smuggle.

**Schleusentor** *nt (für Schiffe)* lock gate.

**schlich** *pret of* **schleichen.**

**Schliche** *pl* **jdm auf die** ~ **kommen** to get wise to sb.

**schlicht** *adj* simple. **die** ~**e Wahrheit** the plain *or* simple truth; ~ **und einfach** plain and simple; **das ist** ~ **und einfach nicht wahr** that's just simply not true; **er sagte** ~ **und ergreifend nein** *(hum col)* he said quite simply no.

**schlichten** *vti Streit (vermitteln)* to mediate, to arbitrate *(esp Ind)*; *(beilegen)* to settle.

**Schlichter(in** *f)* *m* - mediator; *(Ind)* arbitrator.

**Schlichtheit** *f* simplicity.

**Schlichtung** *f siehe vti* arbitration; settlement.

**Schlick** *m* -e silt; *(Öl*~*)* slick.

**schlief** *pret of* **schlafen.**

**Schliefe** *f* -n fastening, fastener.

**schließen** *pret* **schloß**, *ptp* **geschlossen 1** *vt* (a) *(zumachen)* to close, to shut; *(verriegeln)* to bolt; *(Betrieb einstellen)* to close *or* shut down; *Stromkreis, (Fin) Position, (Comp) Datei* to close. **eine Lücke** ~ *(lit)* to close a gap; *(fig)* to fill a gap. (b) *(beenden) Versammlung* to close, to wind up; *Brief* to close. (c) *(eingehen) Vertrag, Bündnis* to conclude; *Frieden auch* to make; *Freundschaft* to form. **die Ehe** ~ to get married. (d) **etw in sich** *(dat)* ~ *(beinhalten: lit, fig)* to include sth; *(indirekt)* to imply sth; **jdn in die Arme** ~ to embrace sb; **jdn/etw in sein Herz** ~ to take sb/sth to one's heart; **daran schloß er eine Bemerkung** he added a remark (to this).

**2** *vr* to close, to shut. **sich um etw** ~ to close around sth.

**3** *vi* (a) to close, to shut; *(Betrieb einstellen)* to close *or* shut down. „**geschlossen**" "closed". (b) *(enden)* to close, to conclude; *(St Ex)* to close. (c) *(schlußfolgern)* to infer. **auf etw** *(acc)* ~ **lassen** to suggest sth; **von sich auf andere** ~ to judge others by one's own standards; *siehe* **geschlossen**.

**Schließfach** *nt* left-luggage *(Brit)* or baggage *(US)* locker; *(Bank~)* safe-deposit box.

**schließlich** *adv (endlich)* in the end; *(immerhin)* after all. **er kam** ~ **doch** he came after all.

**Schließung** *f* closing; *(von Vertrag)* conclusion; *(Betriebseinstellung)* closure.

**Schliff** *m* -e *(das Schleifen)* cutting; *(Ergebnis)* cut; *(fig: Umgangsformen)* refinement, polish. **einer Sache den letzten** ~ **geben** *(fig)* to put the finishing touch(es) to sth.

**schliff** *pret of* **schleifen**².

**schlimm** *adj* bad. **sich** ~ **verletzen** to hurt oneself badly; **das war** ~ that was terrible; **mit der neuen Frisur siehst du** ~ **aus** you look awful with that new hairdo; **das finde ich nicht** ~ I don't find that so bad; **das ist halb so** ~! that's not so bad!; **sie ist** ~ **dran** *(col)* she's in a bad way; **es steht** ~ **(um ihn)** things aren't looking too good (for him); **wenn es nichts S~eres ist!** if that's all it is!; **es gibt S~eres** it *or* things could be worse; **um so** ~**er** all the worse; **im** ~**sten Fall** if the worst comes to the worst.

**schlimmstenfalls** *adv* at (the) worst. ~ **müssen wir im Auto schlafen** if the worst comes to the worst we'll have to sleep in the car.

**Schlinge** *f* -**n** loop; *(an Galgen)* noose; *(Med: Armbinde)* sling; *(Falle)* snare. **den Kopf aus der** ~ **ziehen** *(fig)* to get out of a tight spot.

**Schlingel** *m* - rascal.

**schlingen** *pret* **schlang**, *ptp* **geschlungen 1** *vt (binden)* Knoten to tie; *(umbinden)* Schal to wrap. **2** *vr* **sich um etw** ~ to coil (itself) around sth. **3** *vi (hastig essen)* to bolt one's food.

**schlingern** *vi (Schiff)* to roll.

**Schlingpflanze** *f* creeper.

**Schlips** *m* -e *(col)* tie, necktie *(US)*. **mit** ~ **und Kragen** wearing a collar and tie; **jdm auf den** ~ **treten** to tread on sb's toes; **sich auf den** ~ **getreten fühlen** to feel offended.

**Schlitten** *m* - **(a)** sledge, sled; *(Pferde~)* sleigh; *(Rodel~)* toboggan. **mit jdm** ~ **fahren** *(col)* to give sb a rough time. **(b)** *(col: Auto)* motor *(col)*.

**Schlitten-:** ~**fahren** *nt* sledging; *(Rodeln)* tobogganing; ~**fahrt** *f* sledge ride; *(mit Rodel)* toboggan ride; ~**hund** *m* husky.

**schlittern** *vi aux sein* to slide; *(Wagen)* to skid.

**Schlittschuh** *m* (ice) skate. ~ **laufen** to (ice-)skate.

**Schlittschuh-:** ~**laufen** *nt* (ice-)skating; ~**läufer(in** *f)* *m* (ice-)skater.

**Schlitz** *m* -e slit; *(Einwurf~)* slot; *(Hosen~)* fly, flies *pl*.

**Schlitz-:** ~**auge** *nt* slant eye; *(pej: Chinese)* Chink *(pej)*; **s~äugig** *adj* slant-eyed.

**schlitzen** *vt* to slit.

**Schlitz-:** ~**ohr** *nt (fig)* crafty character, sly fox; **s~ohrig** *adj (fig)* crafty; ~**verschluß** *m (Phot)* focal-plane shutter.

**schlohweiß** *adj* Haare snow-white.

**schloß** *pret of* **schließen**.

**Schloß** *nt* ⁼**sser (a)** castle; *(Palast)* palace; *(großes Herrschaftshaus)* mansion. **(b)** *(Tür~ etc)* lock; *(Vorhänge~)* padlock; *(an Handtasche etc)* fastener. **ins** ~ **fallen** to lock (itself); **jdn hinter** ~ **und Riegel bringen** to put sb behind bars.

**Schlosser(in** *f)* *m* - fitter, metalworker; *(für Schlösser)* locksmith.

**Schlosserei** *f (~werkstatt)* metalworking shop.

**Schloß-:** ~**herr** *m* owner of a castle *etc*; *(Adliger)* lord of the castle; ~**hof** *m* courtyard; ~**hund** *m*

**heulen wie ein** ~**hund** *(col)* to howl one's head off *(col)*; ~**park** *m* castle *etc* grounds *pl*, estate.

**Schlot** *m* -e *(Schornstein)* chimney (stack), smokestack; *(von Vulkan)* chimney. **rauchen wie ein** ~ *(col)* to smoke like a chimney *(col)*.

**schlottern** *vi* **(a)** *(zittern)* to shiver; *(vor Angst)* to tremble. **er schlotterte mit den Knien** he was shaking at the knees. **(b)** *(Kleider)* to be baggy.

**Schlucht** *f* -**en** gorge, ravine.

**schluchzen** *vti (lit, fig)* to sob.

**Schluchzer** *m* - sob.

**Schluck** *m* -**e** drink; *(ein bißchen)* drop; *(das Schlucken)* swallow; *(großer)* gulp; *(kleiner)* sip. **etw** ~ **für** ~ **austrinken** to drink every drop; **einen kräftigen** ~ **nehmen** to take a long drink *or* a swig *(col)*.

**Schluck|auf** *m no pl* hiccups *pl.* **einen** ~ **haben** to have (the) hiccups.

**Schluckbeschwerden** *pl* difficulties *pl* in swallowing.

**Schlückchen** *nt dim of* **Schluck** sip.

**schlucken 1** *vt (lit, fig col)* to swallow; *(hastig)* to gulp down; *(col)* Alkohol to knock back *(col)*; *(col: verschlingen)* to swallow up; Benzin, Öl to guzzle. **2** *vi* to swallow; *(hastig)* to gulp.

**Schlucker** *m* - *(col)*: **armer** ~ poor devil.

**Schluck-:** ~**impfung** *f* oral vaccination; ~**specht** *m (col)* boozer *(col)*; **s~weise** *adv* in sips.

**schlud(e)rig** *adj (col)* Arbeit slipshod *no adv.* ~ **arbeiten** to work in a slipshod way.

**schludern** *vi (col)* to do sloppy work, to work sloppily.

**schlug** *pret of* **schlagen**.

**Schlummer** *m no pl (liter)* (light) slumber *(liter)*.

**Schlummerlied** *nt (geh)* lullaby.

**schlummern** *vi (liter)* to slumber *(liter)*.

**Schlummer-:** ~**rolle** *f* bolster; ~**taste** *f (an Radiowecker)* snooze button.

**Schlund** *m* ⁼**e** *(Anat)* pharynx, gullet; *(fig liter)* maw *(liter)*.

**schlüpfen** *vi aux sein* to slip; *(Küken)* to hatch (out).

**Schlüpfer** *m* - panties *pl*, knickers *pl*.

**Schlupfloch** *nt* gap; *(Versteck)* hideout; *(fig)* loophole.

**schlüpfrig** *adj* **(a)** slippery. **(b)** *(fig)* Bemerkung risqué, salacious.

**Schlupfwinkel** *m* hiding place; *(fig)* quiet corner.

**schlurfen** *vi aux sein* to shuffle.

**schlürfen** *vti* to slurp.

**Schluß** *m* ⁼**sse (a)** *no pl (Ende)* end. ~! that'll do!, stop!; ~ **für heute!** that'll do for today; ~ **damit!** stop it!; ... **und damit** ~! ... and that's that!; ~ **jetzt!** that's enough now!; **dann ist** ~ that'll be it; ~ **folgt** to be concluded; **zum** ~ **sangen wir** ... at the end we sang ...; **zum** ~ **möchte ich noch darauf hinweisen, daß** ... in conclusion I would like to point out that ...; ~ **machen** to call it a day; *(Selbstmord begehen)* to end it all; **mit der Arbeit** ~ **machen** to stop work; **mit jdm** ~ **machen** to break with sb. **(b)** *(Folgerung)* conclusion. **aus etw den** ~ **ziehen, daß** ... to draw the conclusion from sth that ...

**Schluß-** *in cpds* final; ~**akte** *f (Pol)* final agreement.

**Schlüssel** *m* - *(lit, fig)* key; *(Tech)* spanner *(Brit)*, wrench; *(Verteilungs~)* ratio (of distribution); *(Mus)* clef.

**Schlüssel-:** ~**anhänger** *m* keyring pendant; ~**bein** *nt* collarbone, clavicle *(form)*; ~**blume** *f* cowslip; ~**brett** *nt* keyboard; ~**bund** *m or nt* bunch of keys; ~**dienst** *m* key-cutting service; ~**erlebnis** *nt (Psych)* crucial experience; **s~fertig** *adj* Neubau ready for occupancy; ~**figur** *f* key figure; ~**industrie** *f* key industry; ~**kind** *nt (col)* latchkey child *(col)*; ~**loch** *nt* keyhole; ~**position** *f* key position; ~**ring** *m* key ring; ~**stellung** *f* key position; ~**wort** *nt* keyword; *(für Schloß)* combination.

**schlußfolgern** *vi insep* to conclude, to infer.

**Schluß-:** ~**folgerung** *f* conclusion, inference; ~**formel** *f (in Brief)* complimentary close; *(bei Vertrag)* final clause.

**schlüssig** *adj* conclusive. **sich** *(dat)* **(über etw** *acc)* ~ **sein** to have made up one's mind (about sth).

**Schluß-:** ~**kapitel** *nt* concluding *or* final chapter; ~**läufer** *m* last runner; *(in Staffel)* anchorman; ~**licht** *nt* rear light; *(col: bei Rennen etc)* back marker; ~**licht in der Klasse sein** to be bottom of the class; ~**pfiff** *m* final whistle; ~**phase** *f* final stages *pl*; ~**stand** *m* final result; *(von Spiel auch)* final score; ~**stein** *m (Archit, fig)* keystone; ~**strich** *m (fig)* final stroke; **einen** ~**strich unter etw** *(acc)* **ziehen** to consider sth finished; ~**verkauf** *m* (end-of-season) sale; ~**wort** *nt* closing words *pl*; *(~rede)* closing speech; *(Nachwort)* postscript.

**Schmach** *f no pl (geh)* ignominy *no indef art.*

**schmachten** *vi (geh: leiden)* to languish. **nach jdm/ etw** ~ to pine for sb/sth; **jdn** ~ **lassen** to torment sb.

**schmachtend** *adj* yearning, soulful; *Liebhaber* languishing.

**Schmachtfetzen** *m (hum)* tear-jerker *(col)*.

**schmächtig** *adj* frail, weedy *(pej)*.

**schmachvoll** *adj (geh) Niederlage* ignominious.

**schmackhaft** *adj (wohlschmeckend)* tasty. **jdm etw** ~ **machen** *(fig)* to make sth palatable to sb.

**schmähen** *vti (geh)* to abuse, to vituperate against *(liter)*.

**schmählich** *adj (geh)* ignominious; *(demütigend)* humiliating.

**Schmäh-:** ~**rede** *f (geh)* diatribe; ~**schrift** *f* defamatory piece of writing; *(Satire)* lampoon.

**Schmähung** *f (geh)* abuse, vituperation *(liter)*.

**schmal** *adj comp* **-er** *or* **≈er**, *superl* **-ste(r, s)** *or* **≈ste(r, s)** *or (adv)* **am -sten** *or* **≈sten (a)** narrow; *Hüfte auch, Mensch, Buch* slim; *Lippen* thin. **er ist sehr** ~ **geworden** he has got very thin. **(b)** *(fig: karg)* meagre *(Brit)*, meager *(US)*, slender.

**schmalbrüstig** *adj* narrow-chested; *(fig)* limited.

**schmälern** *vt* to diminish.

**Schmälerung** *f* diminishing.

**Schmal-:** ~**film** *m* cine film; ~**filmkamera** *f* cine-camera *(Brit)*, movie camera *(US)*; ~**seite** *f* narrow side; ~**spur** *f (Rail)* narrow gauge; ~**spur-** *in cpds (pej)* small-time; **s~spurig** *adj (Rail) Strecke* narrow-gauge.

**Schmalz**¹ *nt* **-e** fat; *(Schweine~)* lard; *(Braten~)* dripping.

**Schmalz**² *m no pl (pej col)* schmaltz *(col)*.

**schmalzen** *vti* to drool; *Lied* to croon.

**schmalzig** *adj (pej col)* schmaltzy *(col)*, slushy *(col)*.

**Schmankerl** *nt* **-n** *(S Ger, Aus) (Speise)* delicacy; *(fig)* gem.

**schmarotzen\*** *vi* to sponge, to freeload *(esp US) (bei* on, off*)*; *(Biol)* to be parasitic *(bei* on*)*.

**Schmarotzer(in** *f)* *m* - *(Biol)* parasite; *(fig auch)* sponger, freeloader *(esp US)*.

**Schmarr(e)n** *m* - **(a)** *(S Ger, Aus) (Cook) pancake cut up into small pieces*. **(b)** *(col: Quatsch)* rubbish *(col)*.

**Schmatz** *m* **-e** *(col: Kuß)* smacker *(col)*.

**schmatzen** *vi* to eat noisily. **schmatz nicht so!** don't make so much noise when you eat!

**Schmaus** *m, pl* **Schmäuse** *(dated)* feast.

**schmausen** *(geh)* **1** *vi* to feast. **2** *vt* to feast on.

**schmecken 1** *vi (Geschmack haben)* to taste *(nach* of*)*; *(gut* ~*)* to taste good. **ihm schmeckt es** *(gut*

*finden)* he likes it; *(Appetit haben)* he likes his food; **das schmeckt ihm nicht** *(lit, fig)* he doesn't like it; **nach etw** ~ *(fig)* to smack of sth; **das schmeckt nach mehr!** *(col)* it tastes moreish *(hum col)*; **schmeckt es (Ihnen)?** is it good?; are you enjoying your food *or* meal? *(esp form)*; **das hat geschmeckt** that was good; **das schmeckt nicht (gut)** it doesn't taste nice; **es sich** ~ **lassen** to tuck in. **2** *vt* to taste.

**Schmeichelei** *f* flattery.

**schmeichelhaft** *adj* flattering.

**schmeicheln** *vi* to flatter *(jdm* sb*)*. **es schmeichelt mir, daß ...** it flatters me that ...

**Schmeichler(in** *f)* *m* - flatterer; *(Kriecher)* sycophant.

**schmeichlerisch** *adj* flattering.

**schmeißen** *pret* **schmiß**, *ptp* **geschmissen** *(col)* **1** *vt* **(a)** *(werfen)* to sling *(col)*, to chuck *(col)*; *Tür* to slam. **sich jdm an den Hals** ~ *(fig)* to throw oneself at sb. **(b)** *(spendieren)* **eine Runde** *or* **Lage** ~ to stand a round. **(c)** *(managen)* **den Laden** ~ to run the (whole) show; **die Sache** ~ to handle it. **2** *vi (werfen)* to throw, to chuck *(col)*. **mit Steinen** ~ to throw stones; **mit etw um sich** ~ to chuck sth around *(col)*.

**Schmeißfliege** *f* bluebottle.

**Schmelz** *m* **-e** *(Glasur)* glaze; *(Zahn~)* enamel.

**schmelzen** *pret* **schmolz**, *ptp* **geschmolzen 1** *vi aux sein (lit, fig)* to melt; *(Reaktorkern)* to melt down. **2** *vt Metall, Fett* to melt; *Erz* to smelt.

**Schmelz-:** ~**hütte** *f* smelting plant *or* works *sing or pl*; ~**käse** *m* cheese spread; *(in Scheiben)* processed cheese; ~**ofen** *m* melting furnace; *(für Erze)* smelting furnace; ~**punkt** *m* melting point; ~**tiegel** *m (lit, fig)* melting pot; ~**wasser** *nt* melted snow and ice; *(Geog, Phys)* meltwater.

**Schmerbauch** *m (col)* paunch, potbelly.

**Schmerz** *m* **-en** pain; *(Kummer auch)* grief *no pl.* **ihre** ~**en** her pain; **er schrie vor** ~**en** he cried out in pain; ~**en haben** to be in pain; ~**en in den Ohren/ im Hals haben** to have earache/to have a sore throat; **jdm** ~**en bereiten** to cause sb pain; **jdn/etw mit** ~**en erwarten** to wait impatiently for sb/sth.

**schmerz|empfindlich** *adj Mensch* sensitive to pain; *Körperteil* tender.

**schmerzen** *(geh) vti* to hurt; *(Wunde etc)* to be sore; *(Kopf, Bauch auch)* to ache. **es schmerzt** *(lit, fig)* it hurts; **eine** ~**de Stelle** a painful spot *or* area.

**Schmerzens-:** ~**geld** *nt (Jur)* damages *pl*; ~**schrei** *m* scream of pain.

**Schmerz-:** **s~frei** *adj* free of pain; *Operation* painless; ~**grenze** *f* pain barrier; **s~haft** *adj (lit, fig)* painful; **s~lich** *adj (geh)* painful; *Lächeln* sad; **s~lindernd** *adj* pain-relieving; **s~los** *adj (lit, fig)* painless; ~**losigkeit** *f (lit, fig)* painlessness; ~**mittel** *nt* painkiller; ~**schwelle** *f* pain threshold; **s~stillend** *adj* painkilling, analgesic *(Med)*; **s~stillendes Mittel** painkilling drug, analgesic *(Med)*; ~**tablette** *f* painkiller, ≈ aspirin *(col)*; **s~verzerrt** *adj* agonized; **s~voll** *adj (fig)* painful.

**Schmetterling** *m (auch Schwimmart)* butterfly.

**Schmetterlings-:** ~**netz** *nt* butterfly net; ~**stil** *m* butterfly stroke.

**schmettern 1** *vt (schleudern)* to smash; *Tür* to slam; *(Sport) Ball* to smash. **2** *vi* **(a)** *(Sport)* to smash, to hit a smash. **(b)** *(Trompete etc)* to blare (out); *(Sänger)* to bellow; *(Vogel)* to sing, to warble.

**Schmied** *m* **-e** (black)smith.

**Schmiede** *f* **-n** smithy, forge.

**Schmiede-:** ~**arbeit** *f (das Schmieden)* forging; *(Gegenstand)* piece of wrought-iron work; ~**eisen**

*nt* wrought iron; **s~eisern** *adj* wrought-iron; **~hammer** *m* blacksmith's hammer.

**schmieden** *vt* to forge *(zu into)*; *(ersinnen) Plan* to hatch, to concoct; *(hum) Verse* to concoct. **geschmiedet sein** *(Gartentür etc)* to be made of wrought iron.

**Schmiedin** *f* = **Schmied**.

**schmiegen** *vr* **sich an jdn ~** to cuddle *or* snuggle up to sb; **sich an/in etw** *(acc)* **~** to nestle *or* snuggle into sth.

**schmiegsam** *adj* supple; *Stoff* soft; *(fig: anpassungsfähig)* adaptable, flexible.

**Schmiere** *f* **-n (a)** *(col)* grease; *(Salbe)* ointment. **(b)** *(pej) (schlechtes Theater)* fleapit. **(c) ~ stehen** *(col)* to be the lookout.

**schmieren 1** *vt* **(a)** *(streichen)* to smear; *Butter, Aufstrich* to spread; *Brot* to spread; *Salbe, Make-up* to rub in *(in +acc -to)*; *(einfetten, ölen)* to grease. **es läuft wie geschmiert** it's going like clockwork; **jdm eine ~** *(col)* to clout sb one *(col)*. **(b)** *(pej: schreiben)* to scrawl. **(c)** *(col: bestechen)* **jdn ~** to grease sb's palm *(col)*. **2** *vi* **(a)** *(pej) (schreiben)* to scrawl; *(malen)* to daub. **(b)** *(col: bestechen)* to give a bribe/bribes.

**Schmieren-: ~komödiant** *m (pej)* ham (actor); **~theater** *nt (pej: schlechtes Theater)* fleapit.

**Schmiererei** *f (pej col) (Geschriebenes)* scrawl, scribble; *(Parolen etc)* graffiti *pl*; *(Malerei)* daubing; *(Schriftstellerei)* scribbling; *(das Schmieren)* scrawling, scribbling.

**Schmier-: ~fett** *nt* (lubricating) grease; **~fink** *m (pej)* **(a)** *(Autor, Journalist)* hack, scribbler; **(b)** *(Schüler)* messy writer; **~geld** *nt (col)* bribe; **~heft** *nt* jotter.

**schmierig** *adj* greasy; *(fig: unanständig)* dirty, filthy.

**Schmier-: ~käse** *m* cheese spread; **~mittel** *nt* lubricant; **~öl** *nt* lubricating oil; **~papier** *nt* rough *or* scrap paper; **~seife** *f* soft soap.

**Schmierung** *f* lubrication.

**Schminke** *f* **-n** make-up.

**schminken 1** *vt* to make up. **sich** *(dat)* **die Lippen ~** to put on lipstick. **2** *vr* to put on make-up.

**Schmirgel** *m no pl* emery.

**schmirgeln 1** *vt* to sand, to rub down. **2** *vi* to sand.

**Schmirgelpapier** *nt* sandpaper.

**Schmiß** *m* **-sse (a)** *(Narbe)* duelling scar. **(b)** *(dated: Schwung)* dash, élan.

**schmiß** *pret of* **schmeißen**.

**schmissig** *adj (dated)* dashing; *Musik auch* spirited.

**Schmock** *m* **=e** *or* **-s** *(pej)* hack *(col)*.

**Schmöker** *m* **-** book *(usu of light literature)*; *(dick)* tome.

**schmökern** *(col)* **1** *vi* to bury oneself in a book; *(in Büchern blättern)* to browse. **2** *vt* to bury oneself in.

**schmollen** *vi* to pout; *(gekränkt sein)* to sulk.

**Schmoll-: ~mund** *m* pout; **~winkel** *m (col)* **im ~winkel sitzen** to have the sulks *(col)*.

**schmolz** *pret of* **schmelzen**.

**Schmorbraten** *m* pot-roast.

**schmoren 1** *vt* to braise. **2** *vi (Cook)* to braise; *(col: schwitzen)* to roast, to swelter. **jdn ~ lassen** to leave sb to stew.

**Schmorfleisch** *nt* stewing steak.

**Schmu** *m no pl (col)* cheating. **~ machen** to cheat.

**schmuck** *adj (dated) Haus etc* neat, tidy; *Bursche, Mädel* smart, spruce.

**Schmuck** *m* **(a)** *(~stücke)* jewellery *(Brit)* no pl, jewelry *(US)* no pl. **(b)** *(Verzierung)* decoration; *(fig)* embellishment.

**schmücken 1** *vt* to decorate, to adorn; *Rede* to em-

bellish. **~des Beiwerk** embellishment. **2** *vr (zum Fest etc) (Mensch)* to adorn oneself; *(Stadt)* to be decorated.

**Schmuck-: ~kästchen** *nt*, **~kasten** *m* jewellery *(Brit)* or jewelry *(US)* box; **s~los** *adj* plain; *(fig) Stil, Prosa etc* simple; **~losigkeit** *f siehe* **adj** plainness; simplicity; **~sachen** *pl* jewellery *(Brit)* sing, jewelry *(US)* sing; **~stück** *nt (Ring etc)* piece of jewellery *(Brit)* or jewelry *(US)*; *(fig: Prachtstück)* gem.

**schmudd(e)lig** *adj* messy; *(schmutzig auch)* dirty; *(schmierig, unsauber)* filthy.

**Schmuggel** *m no pl* smuggling.

**Schmuggelei** *f* smuggling *no pl*.

**schmuggeln** *vti (lit, fig)* to smuggle.

**Schmuggeln** *nt no pl* smuggling.

**Schmuggelware** *f* contraband *no pl*.

**Schmuggler(in** *f)* *m* **-** smuggler.

**schmunzeln** *vi* to smile (to oneself).

**Schmunzeln** *nt no pl (col)* (inward) smile.

**Schmus** *m no pl (col) (Unsinn)* nonsense; *(Schmeicheleien)* soft soap *(col)*.

**schmusen** *vi (col: zärtlich sein)* to cuddle. **mit jdm ~** to cuddle sb, to canoodle with sb *(col)*.

**Schmusepuppe** *f (col)* cuddly toy.

**Schmuser(in** *f)* *m* **-** *(col)* affectionate person. **er ist ein kleiner ~** he likes a cuddle.

**Schmusetier** *nt (col)* cuddly toy.

**Schmutz** *m no pl* dirt; *(fig auch)* filth, smut. **jdn/etw in den ~ ziehen** *(fig)* to drag sb/sth through the mud.

**schmutzen** *vi* to get dirty.

**Schmutz-: ~fink** *m (col) (unsauberer Mensch)* dirty slob *(col)*; *(Kind)* mucky pup *(col)*; *(fig: Mann)* dirty old man; **~fleck** *m* dirty mark.

**schmutzig** *adj* dirty. **sich ~ machen** to get oneself dirty; **~e Wäsche waschen** *(fig)* to wash one's dirty linen in public; **~ grinsen** to leer.

**Schmutzigkeit** *f* dirtiness.

**Schmutz-: ~kampagne** *f* smear campaign; **~titel** *m (Typ)* half-title; **~wäsche** *f* dirty washing; **~wasser** *nt* dirty water.

**Schnabel** *m* **=** **(a)** *(Vogel~)* beak, bill. **(b)** *(von Kanne)* spout. **(c)** *(col: Mund)* mouth. **halt den ~!** shut your mouth *(col)*; **reden, wie einem der ~ gewachsen ist** to say exactly what comes into one's head; *(unaffektiert)* to talk naturally.

**Schnabeltasse** *f* feeding cup.

**Schnack** *m* **-s** *(NGer col) (Unterhaltung)* chat; *(pej: Geschwätz)* silly talk.

**schnacken** *vi (NGer col)* to chat.

**Schnake** *f* **-n (a)** *(col: Stechmücke)* gnat, midge. **(b)** *(Weberknecht)* crane fly, daddy-longlegs.

**Schnalle** *f* **-n** *(Schuh~, Gürtel~)* buckle; *(an Handtasche, Buch)* clasp.

**schnallen** *vt* **(a)** to strap; *Gürtel* to buckle, to fasten. **(b)** *(col: begreifen)* to get *(col)*, to suss *(col)*. **hast du das immer noch nicht geschnallt?** have you still not got the message?

**Schnallenschuh** *m* buckled shoe.

**schnalzen** *vi* **mit den Fingern ~** to snap *or* click one's fingers; **mit der Zunge ~** to click one's tongue.

**Schnäppchen** *nt* bargain, snip *(col)*. **ein ~ machen** *(col)* to get a bargain.

**schnappen 1** *vi* **(a) nach jdm/etw ~** to snap at sb/ sth; *(greifen)* to snatch at sb/sth. **(b)** *aux sein* **die Tür schnappt ins Schloß** the door clicks shut. **2** *vt (col)* **(a)** *(ergreifen)* to snatch, to grab. **(b)** *(fangen)* to nab *(col)*.

**Schnapp-: ~messer** *nt* flick knife; **~schloß** *nt (an Tür)* springlock; *(an Schmuck)* spring clasp;

**~schuß** *m (Foto)* snap(shot); **~verschluß** *m* snap fastener.

**Schnaps** *m ⁼e (klarer ~)* schnaps; *(col: Branntwein)* spirits *pl*; *(col: Alkohol)* booze *(col)*, liquor *(esp US col)*.

**Schnäpschen** [ˈʃnɛpsçən] *nt (col)* little drink, wee dram *(esp Scot)*.

**Schnaps-:** **~flasche** *f* bottle of booze *(col) or* liquor *(esp US col)*; **~glas** *nt* small glass for spirits; **~idee** *f (col)* crackpot idea *(col)*; **~leiche** *f (col)* drunk.

**schnarchen** *vi* to snore.

**schnarren** *vi (Wecker etc)* to buzz; *(Maschine, Klingel)* to clatter. **mit ~der Stimme** in a rasping *or* grating voice.

**Schnatter-:** **~gans** *f (col)*, **~maul** *nt (col)* chatterbox.

**schnattern** *vi (Gans)* to gabble; *(Ente)* to quack; *(col: schwatzen)* to natter *(col)*.

**schnauben** *vi* to snort. **vor Wut ~** to snort with rage.

**schnaufen** *vi* **(a)** *(schwer atmen)* to wheeze; *(keuchen)* to puff, to pant. **(b)** *aux sein (sich keuchend bewegen: Auto)* to struggle.

**Schnaufer** *m - (col)* breath. **den letzten ~ tun** to breathe one's last.

**Schnauferl** *nt - (hum: Oldtimer)* veteran car.

**Schnauzbart** *m* walrus moustache *(Brit) or* mustache *(US)*.

**Schnauze** *f -n* **(a)** *(von Tier)* muzzle. **mit einer Maus in der ~** with a mouse in its mouth. **(b)** *(col) (von Fahrzeugen)* front; *(von Flugzeug, Schiff)* nose. **(c)** *(col!: Mund)* gob *(col)*, trap *(col)*. **~!** shut your trap *(col!)*; **auf die ~ fallen** to fall flat on one's face; *(fig)* to come a cropper *(col)*; **die ~ (gestrichen) voll haben** to be fed up to the back teeth *(col) (von etw* with sth*)*; **eine große ~ haben** to have a big mouth *(col)*; **die ~ halten** to hold one's tongue; **etw frei nach ~ machen** to do sth any old how *(col)*.

**schnauzen** *vi (col)* to shout; *(jdn anfahren)* to snap.

**Schnauzer** *m -* **(a)** *(Hund)* schnauzer. **(b)** *(col: Bart)* walrus moustache *(Brit) or* mustache *(US)*.

**Schnecke** *f -n* **(a)** *(Zool, fig)* snail; *(Nackt~)* slug; *(Cook auch)* escargot. **jdn zur ~ machen** *(col)* to give sb a real bawling-out *(col)*. **(b)** *(Cook: Gebäck)* ≈ Chelsea bun.

**Schnecken-:** **s~förmig** *adj* spiral; *(Archit)* ornament scroll-shaped; **~haus** *nt* snail-shell; **sich in sein ~haus zurückziehen** *(fig col)* to retreat into one's shell; **~tempo** *nt (col)* **im ~tempo** at a snail's pace.

**Schnee** *m no pl* **(a)** *(auch TV)* snow. **vom ~ eingeschlossen sein** to be snowbound; **das ist ~ von gestern** *(col)* that's old hat *(col)*. **(b)** *(Ei~)* whisked *(Brit) or* whipped *(US)* egg white. **Eiweiß zu ~ schlagen** to whisk *(Brit) or* whip *(US)* the egg white(s) till stiff.

**Schnee-:** **~ball** *m* snowball; **~ballschlacht** *f* snowball fight; **s~bedeckt** *adj* snow-covered; *Berg auch* snow-capped; **~besen** *m (Cook)* whisk; **s~blind** *adj* snowblind; **~decke** *f* blanket *or* covering of snow; **~fall** *m* snowfall, fall of snow; **~flocke** *f* snowflake; **s~frei** *adj* free of snow; **~gestöber** *nt (leicht)* snow flurry; *(stark)* snowstorm; **~glätte** *f* hard-packed snow *no pl*; **~glöckchen** *nt* snowdrop; **~grenze** *f* snowline; **~kette** *f (Aut)* snow chain; **~könig** *m:* **sich freuen wie ein ~könig** to be as pleased as Punch; **~mann** *m, pl* **~männer** snowman; **~matsch** *m* slush; **~mobil** *nt* snowmobile; **~pflug** *m (Tech, Ski)* snowplough *(Brit)*, snowplow *(US)*; **~regen** *m* sleet; **~schaufel** *f* snow

shovel, snowpusher *(US)*; **~schmelze** *f* thaw; **~schuh** *m* snowshoe; **s~sicher** *adj* **ein s~sicheres Gebiet** a region of guaranteed snowfall; **~sturm** *m* snowstorm; *(stärker)* blizzard; **~treiben** *nt* driving snow; **~verwehung, ~wehe** *f* snowdrift; **s~weiß** *adj* snow-white, as white as snow; *Haare* snowy-white; **~wittchen** *nt* Snow White.

**Schneid** *m no pl (col)* nerve, courage.

**Schneidbrenner** *m (Tech)* oxyacetylene cutter.

**Schneide** *f -n* (sharp *or* cutting) edge; *(von Messer, Schwert)* blade.

**schneiden** *pret* **schnitt**, *ptp* **geschnitten 1** *vi* to cut. **der Wind schneidet** the wind is biting.

  **2** *vt* **(a)** to cut; *(in Scheiben)* to slice; *(klein~) Gemüse etc* to chop; *(Sport) Ball* to slice; *(schnitzen) Namen, Figuren* to carve; *(Weg)* to cross. **sein schön/scharf geschnittenes Gesicht** his clean-cut/ sharp features; **die Luft ist zum S~** *(fig col)* there's an awful fug (in here) *(esp Brit)*; **die Atmosphäre ist zum S~** *(fig col)* you could cut the atmosphere with a knife; **jdn ~** *(beim Überholen)* to cut in on sb; *(ignorieren)* to cut sb dead; **weit/eng geschnitten sein** *(Sew)* to be cut wide/narrow, to be a generous/ tight fit. **(b)** *Film, Tonband* to edit. **(c)** *(col: operieren)* to operate on.

  **3** *vr* **(a)** *(Mensch)* to cut oneself. **sich in den Finger etc ~** to cut one's finger *etc.* **(b)** *(col: sich täuschen)* **da hat er sich aber geschnitten!** he's very much mistaken there. **(c)** *(Linien, Straßen etc)* to intersect.

**schneidend** *adj* biting; *Kälte auch* bitter; *Schmerz* sharp; *Stimme* piercing.

**Schneider** *m -* **(a)** *(Beruf)* tailor; *(Damen~)* dressmaker. **(b)** *(col)* **frieren wie ein ~** to be/get frozen to the marrow *(col)*; **aus dem ~ sein** *(fig)* to be out of the woods. **(c)** *(Gerät)* cutter; *(col: für Brot etc)* slicer. **(d)** *(Insekt)* daddy-longlegs.

**Schneiderei** *f* **(a)** *no pl (Handwerk)* tailoring; *(für Damen)* dressmaking. **(b)** *(Werkstatt)* tailor's/ dressmaker's workshop.

**Schneiderin** *f* tailor; *(Damen~)* dressmaker.

**Schneidermeister** *m* master tailor/dressmaker.

**schneidern 1** *vi (beruflich)* to be a tailor/ dressmaker; *(als Hobby)* to do dressmaking. **2** *vt* to make, to sew; *Herrenanzug* to tailor, to make.

**Schneider-:** **~puppe** *f* tailor's/dressmaker's dummy; **~sitz** *m* **im ~sitz sitzen** to sit cross-legged; **~werkstatt** *f* tailor's/dressmaker's workshop.

**Schneidezahn** *m* incisor.

**schneidig** *adj* dashing; *Tempo* fast.

**schneien 1** *vi impers* to snow. **es schneit** it is snowing. **2** *vt impers* **es schneite Konfetti** confetti rained down. **3** *vi aux sein (fig)* to rain down. **jdm ins Haus ~** *(col) (Besuch)* to drop in on sb; *(Rechnung, Brief)* to arrive through one's letterbox *or* in the mail.

**Schneise** *f -n* *(Wald~)* firebreak; *(Flug~)* flight path.

**schnell** *adj* quick; *Bedienung, Tempo auch, Auto, Zug, Strecke* fast; *Abreise, Hilfe* speedy. **~ gehen/ fahren** to walk/drive quickly *or* fast; **sie wird ~ böse** she loses her temper quickly; **diese dünnen Gläser gehen ~ kaputt** these thin glasses break easily; **er ist sehr ~ mit seinem Urteil** he's very quick to judge; **nicht so ~!** not so fast!; **ich muß mir nur noch ~ die Haare kämmen** I must just give my hair a quick comb; **sein Puls ging ~** his pulse was very fast; **das geht ~** *(grundsätzlich)* it doesn't take long; **das ging ~** that was quick; **wie heißt sie noch ~?** *(col)* what's her name again?; **das werden wir ~ erledigt haben** we'll soon have that finished; **~es Geld** *or* **eine ~e Mark (machen)** *(col)* (to make)

a fast buck *(col)*.
**Schnelläufer** *m (Sport)* sprinter.
**Schnell-:** ~**bahn** *f* high-speed railway *(Brit)* or railroad *(US)*; ~**boot** *nt* speedboat; ~**dienst** *m* express service.
**Schnelle** *f* -n **(a)** *no pl (Schnelligkeit)* quickness, speed. **(b)** *(Strom~)* rapids *pl*. **(c) etw auf die ~ machen** to do sth in a rush.
**schnellebig** *adj Zeit* fast-moving.
**schnellen** *vi aux sein (lit, fig)* to shoot. **in die Höhe ~** to shoot up.
**Schnell-:** ~**feuer** *nt (Mil)* rapid fire; ~**feuergewehr** *nt* automatic pistol; ~**gaststätte** *f* cafeteria, fast-food restaurant *(US)*; ~**gericht** *nt* **(a)** *(Jur)* summary court; **(b)** *(Cook)* convenience food, TV dinner *(US col)*; ~**hefter** *m* spring folder.
**Schnelligkeit** *f (von Auto, Verkehr)* speed; *(von Tempo auch)* quickness; *(von Schritten auch, von Puls)* rapidity; *(von Bote, Hilfe)* speediness.
**Schnell-:** ~**imbiß** *m* **(a)** *(Essen)* (quick) snack; **(b)** *(Raum)* snack bar; ~**kochtopf** *m (Dampfkochtopf)* pressure cooker; ~**kurs** *m* crash course; ~**paket** *nt* express parcel; ~**reinigung** *f* express cleaning service; ~**restaurant** *nt* fast-food restaurant.
**schnellstens** *adv* as quickly as possible.
**Schnell-:** ~**straße** *f* expressway; ~**zug** *m* fast train; *(Fern~zug)* express (train).
**Schnepfe** *f* -n *(Orn)* snipe.
**schnetzeln** *vt (S Ger, Sw) Fleisch* to shred.
**schneuzen** 1 *vr* to blow one's nose. 2 *vt einem Kind/sich die Nase ~* to blow a child's/one's nose.
**Schnickschnack** *m no pl (col: Unsinn)* twaddle *(col)* no indef art, poppycock *(col)* no indef art.
**schniefen** *vi (dial)* to sniffle.
**schniegeln** *vtr (col) siehe* **geschniegelt**.
**Schnippchen** *nt jdm ein ~ schlagen (col)* to play a trick on sb.
**schnippeln** *vti (col)* to snip *(an +dat at)*; *(mit Messer)* to hack *(an +dat at)*.
**schnippen** 1 *vi mit den Fingern ~* to snap one's fingers. 2 *vt etw von etw ~* to flick sth off or from sth.
**schnippisch** *adj* cocky, pert.
**Schnipsel** *m or nt* - *(col)* scrap; *(Papier~)* scrap of paper.
**schnitt** *pret of* **schneiden**.
**Schnitt** *m* -e **(a)** *(col)* cut; *(Haar~ auch)* haircut; *(von Gesicht, Augen)* shape; *(von Kleid etc auch)* styling; *(Sew: ~muster)* pattern. **(b)** *(Film)* editing *no pl*. ~: L. Schwarz editor - L. Schwarz. **(c)** *(Math) (~punkt)* (point of) intersection; *(Längs~, Quer~)* section; *(col: Durch~)* average. **im ~** on average.
**Schnitt-:** ~**blumen** *pl* cut flowers *pl*; ~**bohnen** *pl* French or green beans *pl*.
**Schnittchen** *nt* small open sandwich; *(Appetithappen)* canapé.
**Schnitte** *f* -n slice; *(belegt)* open sandwich; *(zusammengeklappt)* sandwich.
**Schnitt-:** s~**fest** *adj Tomaten* firm; ~**fläche** *f (Math)* section.
**schnittig** *adj* smart; *Auto, Formen auch* stylish; *Tempo auch* snappy *(col)*.
**Schnitt-:** ~**lauch** *m no pl* chives *pl*; ~**muster** *nt (Sew)* (paper) pattern; ~**punkt** *m* intersection; ~**stelle** *f (Comp)* interface; ~**wunde** *f* cut; *(tief)* gash.
**Schnitzarbeit** *f* (wood)carving.
**Schnitzel¹** *nt or m* - *(Papier~)* scrap of paper; *(Holz~)* shaving; *(Karotten~)* shred.
**Schnitzel²** *nt* - *(Cook)* veal/pork cutlet, schnitzel.
**Schnitzeljagd** *f* paper chase.

**schnitzeln** *vt* to shred.
**schnitzen** *vti* to carve.
**Schnitzelwerk** *nt (in Küchenmaschine)* shredder.
**Schnitzer** *m* - **(a)** woodcarver. **(b)** *(col) (in Benehmen)* boob *(Brit col)*, goof *(US col)*; *(Fehler)* howler *(col)*.
**Schnitzerei** *f* (wood-)carving.
**Schnitzerin** *f* = **Schnitzer (a)**.
**schnodd(e)rig** *adj (col)* offhand, brash.
**Schnodd(e)rigkeit** *f (col)* brashness.
**schnöd(e)** *adj (niederträchtig)* despicable; *Behandlung, Antwort* contemptuous. **schnöder Mammon/schnödes Geld** filthy lucre.
**Schnorchel** *m* - *(von U-Boot, Taucher)* snorkel.
**schnorcheln** *vi* to go snorkelling.
**Schnörkel** *m* - flourish; *(an Möbeln, Säulen)* scroll; *(fig: Unterschrift)* squiggle *(hum)*, signature.
**schnörkelig** *adj* ornate; *Rede auch* flowery.
**schnorren** *vti (col)* to cadge *(col) (bei from)*.
**Schnorrer(in** *f) m* - *(col)* cadger *(col)*.
**Schnösel** *m* - *(col)* snotty(-nosed) little upstart *(col)*.
**schnuckelig** *adj (col: gemütlich)* snug.
**Schnüffelei** *f (fig col: das Spionieren)* snooping *no pl (col)*.
**schnüffeln** 1 *vi* **(a)** *(schnuppern)* to sniff. **an etw** *(dat)* ~ to sniff (at) sth. **(b)** *(fig col: spionieren)* to snoop around *(col)*. **(c)** *(Dämpfe inhalieren)* to sniff (glue *etc*); *(regelmäßig)* to be a sniffer. 2 *vt Klebstoff etc* to sniff.
**Schnüffler(in** *f) m* - *(col) (fig)* snooper *(col)*, nosy parker *(col)*; *(Detektiv)* sleuth *(col)*; *(von Drogen)* sniffer; *(von Klebstoff)* glue-sniffer.
**Schnuller** *m* - *(col)* dummy *(Brit)*, pacifier *(US)*; *(auf Flasche)* teat *(Brit)*, nipple *(US)*.
**Schnulze** *f* -n *(col)* schmaltzy film/song *(col)*.
**schnupfen** *vti (Tabak)* ~ to take snuff.
**Schnupfen** *m* - cold, headcold. **(einen)** ~ **bekommen** to catch (a) cold; **(einen)** ~ **haben** to have a cold.
**Schnupftabak** *m* snuff.
**schnuppe** *adj pred (col)* **jdm** ~ **sein** to be all the same to sb; **das Wohl seiner Angestellten ist ihm völlig** ~ he couldn't care less about the welfare of his employees.
**schnuppern** *vti* to sniff. **an etw** *(dat)* ~ to sniff (at) sth.
**Schnur** *f* ¨e *(Bindfaden)* string; *(Kordel)* cord; *(Kabel)* flex, lead.
**Schnürchen** *nt* **es läuft** or **klappt alles wie am** ~ everything's going like clockwork.
**schnüren** 1 *vt Paket etc* to tie up; *Mieder* to lace (up). **Schuhe zum S~** lace-up shoes. 2 *vi (col: eng sein)* to be too tight.
**schnurgerade** *adj* (dead) straight.
**schnurlos** *adj Telefon* cordless.
**Schnurrbart** *m* moustache *(Brit)*, mustache *(US)*.
**schnurren** *vi (Katze)* to purr; *(Spinnrad etc)* to hum, to whirr.
**Schnurrhaare** *pl* whiskers *pl*.
**Schnür-:** ~**schuh** *m* laced shoe, lace-up; ~**senkel** *m* shoelace; *(für Stiefel)* bootlace; ~**stiefel** *m* lace-up boot.
**schnurstracks** *adv* straight, directly. ~ **auf jdn/etw zugehen** to make a bee-line for sb/sth *(col)*.
**schnurz** *adj (col)* = **schnuppe**.
**Schnute** *f* -n *(col, esp N Ger: Mund)* mouth, gob *(Brit col!)*. **eine** ~ **ziehen** to pout, to pull a face.
**schob** *pret of* **schieben**.
**Schober** *m* - *(Scheune)* barn.
**Schock** *m* -s shock. **unter** ~ **stehen** to be in (a state of) shock.
**Schockeinwirkung** *f* state of shock. **unter** ~ **ste-**

**hen** to be in (a state of) shock.

**schocken** *vt (col)* to shock.

**Schocker** *m - (col: Film, Roman)* sensational film/novel, shocker.

**schockieren\*** *vti* to shock; *(stärker)* to scandalize. **schockiert sein** to be shocked *(über +acc* at*)*.

**Schocktherapie** *f* shock therapy.

**Schöffe** *m (wk)* **-n, -n** ≃ lay judge.

**Schöffengericht** *nt* court *(with lay judges)*.

**Schöffin** *f* ≃ lay judge.

**Schokolade** *f* chocolate.

**Schokoladen-** *in cpds* chocolate; **s~braun** *adj* chocolate-coloured *(Brit)*, chocolate-colored *(US)*; **~riegel** *m* chocolate bar; **~seite** *f (fig)* attractive side.

**Scholle¹** *f* **-n** *(Fisch)* plaice.

**Scholle²** *f* **-n** *(Eis~)* (ice) floe; *(Erd~)* clod (of earth).

**Scholli** *m*: **mein lieber ~!** *(col) (drohend)* now look here!; *(erstaunt)* my oh my!

**schon** *adv* **(a)** *(bereits)* already; *(in Fragen: überhaupt ~)* ever. **er ist ~ da** he's there already, he's already there; **ist er ~ da?** is he there yet?; **warst du ~ dort?** have you been there yet?; *(je)* have you ever been there?; **mußt du ~ gehen?** must you go already, must you go so soon?; **er wollte ~ die Hoffnung aufgeben, als ...** he was just about to give up hope when ...; **ich warte nun ~ seit drei Wochen** I've already been waiting (for) three weeks; **~ am frühen Morgen** early in the morning; **~ damals** even then; **~ vor 100 Jahren** as far back as 100 years ago; **~ am nächsten Tag** the very next day; **der Briefträger kommt ~ um 6 Uhr** the postman comes as early as 6 o'clock; **ich habe das ~ mal gehört** I've heard that before; **das habe ich dir doch ~ hundertmal gesagt** I've told you that a hundred times (before); **das habe ich ~ oft gehört** I've heard that often; **ich bin ~ lange fertig** I've been ready for ages; **wartest du ~ lange?** have you been waiting (for) long?; **wie ~ so oft** as so often (before); **~ immer** always; **was, ~ wieder?** what — again?

**(b)** *(allein bloß)* just; *(ohnehin)* anyway. **allein ~ das Gefühl ...** just the very feeling ...; **~ die Tatsache, daß ...** the mere fact that ...; **wenn ich das ~ sehe/höre!** I can't bear to see/hear it; **~ weil** if only because.

**(c)** *(bestimmt)* all right. **du wirst ~ sehen** you'll see (all right); **das wirst du ~ noch lernen** you'll learn that one day.

**(d)** *(tatsächlich, allerdings)* really. **das ist ~ eine Frechheit!** that's a real cheek!; **da gehört ~ Mut** *etc* **dazu** that takes real courage *etc*; **das ist ~ möglich** that's quite possible; **das mußt du ~ machen!** you really ought to do that.

**(e)** *(einschränkend)* **ja ~, aber ...** *(col)* yes (well), but ...; **da haben Sie ~ recht, aber ...** yes, you're right (there), but ...

**(f) hör ~ auf damit!** will you stop that!; **so antworte ~!** come on, answer; **nun sag ~!** come on, tell me/us *etc*; **ich komme ja ~!** I'm just coming!; **das ist ~ möglich** that's quite possible; **was macht das ~, wenn ...** what does it matter if ...; **drei Seiten schreiben, was ist das ~?** write three pages? that's nothing; **und wenn ~!** *(col)* so what? *(col)*; **~ gut** *(col)* all right, okay *(col)*; **ich verstehe ~** I understand; **danke, es geht ~** thank you, I/we can manage.

**schön 1** *adj* **(a)** *(hübsch anzusehen)* beautiful, lovely; *Mann* handsome.

**(b)** *(nett, angenehm)* good; *Stimme, Musik, Wetter*

*auch* lovely; *Gelegenheit* great, splendid. **die ~en Künste** the fine arts; **die ~e Literatur** belletristic literature; **eines ~en Tages** one fine day; **das S~e beim Skilaufen ist ...** the nice *or* beautiful thing about skiing is ...; **~en Urlaub!** have a good *or* nice holiday; **~, daß du gekommen bist** (how) nice of you to come; **ein ~er frischer Wind** a nice cool wind.

**(c)** *(iro) Unordnung* fine, nice; *Überraschung* nice, lovely; *Unsinn* absolute. **da hast du etwas S~es angerichtet** you've made a fine *or* nice mess; **du bist mir ein ~er Freund/Held** *etc* a fine friend/hero *etc* you are; **das wäre ja noch ~er** *(col)* that's (just) too much!

**(d) das war nicht ~ von dir** *(col)* that wasn't very nice of you; **zu ~, um wahr zu sein** *(col)* too good to be true; **(also) ~, na ~** okay, all right; **~ und gut, aber ...** that's all very well but ...; **ein ~es Stück weiterkommen** to make good progress; **eine ganz ~e Menge** quite a lot.

**2** *adv* **(a)** *(bei Verben)* well; *scheinen* brightly; *schreiben* beautifully. **sich ~ anziehen** to get dressed up; **es ~ haben** to be well off; *(im Urlaub etc)* to have a good time (of it); **schlaf ~** sleep well; **erhole dich ~** have a good rest. **(b)** *(col: sehr, ziemlich)* really. **~ weich/warm** nice and soft/warm; **sich** *(dat)* **~ weh tun** to hurt oneself a lot; **sich ~ ärgern** to be very angry; **ganz ~ teuer/kalt** pretty expensive/cold; **ganz ~ lange** quite a while. **(c) iß mal ~ deinen Teller leer** eat it all up nicely (now); **sei ~ still/ordentlich** *etc (als Aufforderung)* be nice and quiet/tidy *etc*; **fahr ~ langsam** drive nice and slowly.

**schonen 1** *vt Gesundheit, Herz, Kleider* to look after, to take care of; *eigene Nerven, Bremsen* to go easy on; *jds Nerven* to spare; *Gegner, Kind* to be easy on; *Teppich, Füße* to save; *(schützen)* to protect. **ein Waschmittel, das die Wäsche schont** a detergent that is kind to your washing; **er muß den Arm noch ~** he still has to be careful with his arm. **2** *vr* to take things gently; *(auf sich aufpassen)* to look after *or* take care of oneself.

**schonend** *adj* gentle; *(rücksichtsvoll)* considerate. **jdm etw ~ beibringen** to break sth to sb gently; **etw ~ behandeln** to treat sth with care.

**Schoner¹** *m - (Naut)* schooner.

**Schoner²** *m -* cover; *(für Rückenlehnen)* antimacassar, chairback.

**Schön-: s~färben** *sep* **1** *vt (fig)* to gloss over; **2** *vi* to gloss things over; **~färberei** *f (fig)* glossing things over.

**Schon-: ~frist** *f* period of grace; **~gang** *m* **(a)** *(Aut)* overdrive; **(b)** *(bei Waschmaschine)* gentle action wash.

**schöngeistig** *adj* aesthetic *(Brit)*, esthetic *(US)*.

**Schönheit** *f* beauty.

**Schönheits-: ~chirurgie** *f* cosmetic surgery; **~fehler** *m* blemish; *(von Gegenstand)* flaw; **~ideal** *nt* ideal of beauty; **~königin** *f* beauty queen; **~operation** *f* cosmetic surgery *no pl, no art*; **~pflege** *f* beauty care; **~wettbewerb** *m* beauty contest.

**Schonkost** *f* light diet; *(Spezialdiät)* special diet.

**Schönling** *m (pej)* pretty boy *(col)*.

**Schön-: s~machen** *sep* **1** *vt Kind* to dress up; *Wohnung* to decorate; **2** *vr* to get dressed up; *(sich schminken)* to make (oneself) up; **~redner** *m* smooth talker, sweet talker *(US)*; **~schreibdrucker** *m* letter-quality printer; **~schrift** *f* **in ~schrift** in one's best (hand)writing; **s~tun** *vi sep irreg* **jdm s~tun** *(col: schmeicheln)* to flatter *or* soft-soap *(col)* sb; *(sich lieb Kind machen)* to play up to sb.

**Sch̲onung** *f* **(a)** *(Forest)* (protected) forest plantation area. **(b)** *(das Schonen) (von Gefühlen)* sparing; *(von Teppich, Kleidern)* saving; *(das Schützen)* protection. **der Patient braucht noch ein paar Wochen ~** the patient still needs to take things gently for a few weeks; **zur ~ meiner Gefühle** to spare my feelings; **zur ~ Ihrer Augen** to look after your eyes; **zur ~ des Getriebes** to give your gears an easier life. **(c)** *(Nachsicht, Milde)* mercy.

**Schonungs-:** **s~los** *adj* ruthless; *Wahrheit* blunt; *Kritik* savage; **~losigkeit** *f* ruthlessness; *(von Kritik)* savageness; **s~voll** *adj* gentle.

**Schönwetterperiode** *f* period of fine weather.

**Sch̲onzeit** *f* close season; *(fig)* honeymoon period.

**Sch̲opf** *m* ⸗e (shock of) hair. **eine Gelegenheit beim ~ ergreifen** *or* **fassen** to seize *or* grasp an opportunity with both hands.

**schöpfen** *vt* **(a)** *auch vi (aus* from*) Wasser* to scoop; *Suppe* to ladle. **(b)** *Atem* to draw, to take; *Mut, Kraft* to summon up; *Hoffnung* to find.

**Schöpfer** *m* - **(a)** creator; *(Gott)* Creator. **(b)** *(col: Schöpflöffel)* ladle.

**Schöpferin** *f* creator; *(Göttin)* Creator.

**schöpferisch** *adj* creative.

**Schöpferkraft** *f* creative power.

**Schöpf-:** **~kelle** *f,* **~löffel** *m* ladle.

**Schöpfung** *f* creation. **die ~** *(Rel)* the Creation; *(die Welt)* Creation.

**Schoppen** *m* - *(Glas Wein/Bier)* glass of wine/beer.

**sch̲or** *pret of* **scheren**[1].

**Sch̲orf** *m* -e crust, scaly skin; *(Wund~)* scab.

**Sch̲orle** *f* -n spritzer.

**Sch̲ornstein** *m* chimney; *(von Schiff)* funnel, (smoke)stack.

**Sch̲ornsteinfeger(in** *f)* *m* - chimney sweep.

**sch̲oß** *pret of* **schießen**.

**Sch̲oß** *m* ⸗e **(a)** lap. **die Hände in den ~ legen** *(fig)* to sit back (and take it easy); **das ist ihm nicht in den ~ gefallen** *(fig)* it didn't just fall into his lap. **(b)** *(liter: Mutterleib)* womb. **im ~e der Familie** in the bosom of one's family. **(c)** *(an Kleidungsstück)* tail.

**Sch̲oßhund** *m* lapdog.

**Sch̲ößling** *m* *(Bot)* shoot.

**Sch̲ote** *f* -n **(a)** *(Bot)* pod. **(b)** *(col)* yarn, tall story.

**Sch̲ott** *nt* -e(n) *(Naut)* bulkhead. **die ~en dichtmachen** *(fig col)* to shut up shop.

**Sch̲otte** *m (wk)* -n, -n Scot, Scotsman.

**Schotten-:** **~muster** *nt* tartan; **~rock** *m* kilt; *(für Frauen)* tartan skirt.

**Sch̲otter** *m* - gravel; *(im Straßenbau)* (road) metal; *(Rail)* ballast; *(col: Geld)* dough *(col)*.

**Schotter-:** **~decke** *f* gravel surface; **~straße** *f* gravel road.

**Sch̲ottin** *f* Scot, Scotswoman.

**sch̲ottisch** *adj* Scottish, Scots.

**Sch̲ottland** *nt* Scotland.

**schraffi̲eren*** *vt* to hatch.

**Schraffi̲erung** *f* hatching.

**schräg** **1** *adj* **(a)** *(geneigt)* sloping; *Augen* slanted, slanting; *Kante* bevelled *(Brit)*, beveled *(US)*. **(b)** *(nicht gerade, nicht parallel)* oblique. **(c)** *(col: verdächtig)* suspicious, fishy *(col)*. **ein ~er Vogel** a queer fish *(col)*. **(d)** *Musik, Vorstellungen, Leute* weird. **2** *adv* **(a)** *(geneigt)* at an angle; *halten* on the slant, slanting. **~ stehende Augen** slanting *or* slanted eyes. **(b)** *(nicht gerade, nicht parallel)* obliquely; *überqueren, gestreift* diagonally; *(Sew)* on the bias. **~ gegenüber/hinter** diagonally opposite/behind; **~ rechts/links** diagonally to the

right/left; **die Straße biegt ~ ab** the road forks off; **~ gedruckt** in italics.

**Schräge** *f* -n **(a)** *(schräge Fläche)* slope, sloping surface; *(schräge Kante)* bevel. **(b)** *(Schrägheit)* slant, angle; *(im Zimmer)* sloping ceiling.

**Schräg-:** **~heck** *nt* fastback; **~kante** *f* bevelled *(Brit)* or beveled *(US)* edge; **~lage** *f* angle, slant; *(von Flugzeug)* bank(ing); **~schrift** *f (Handschrift)* slanting hand(writing) *or* writing; *(Typ)* italics *pl*; **~streifen** *m* **(a)** *(Muster)* diagonal stripe; **(b)** *(Sew)* bias binding; **~strich** *m* oblique, slash.

**Schramme** *f* -n scratch.

**schrammen** *vt* to scratch.

**Schrank** *m* ⸗e cupboard, closet *(US)*; *(Kleider~)* wardrobe.

**Schränkchen** *nt* *dim of* **Schrank** small cupboard; *(Arznei~)* cabinet.

**Schranke** *f* -n barrier; *(fig) (Grenze)* limit; *(Hindernis)* barrier. **keine ~n kennen** to know no bounds; *(Mensch)* not to know when to stop; **einer Sache** *(dat)* **(enge) ~n setzen** to put a limit on sth; **jdn in seine ~n (ver)weisen** *(fig)* to put sb in his place.

**Schranken-:** **s~los** *adj (fig) Weiten* boundless, unlimited; *Forderungen* unrestrained; **~wärter** *m (Rail)* crossing keeper.

**Schrank-:** **~fach** *nt* shelf; **~koffer** *m* wardrobe trunk; **~wand** *f* wall unit.

**Schraubdeckel** *m* screw top.

**Schr̲aube** *f* -n **(a)** screw; *(ohne Spitze)* bolt. **bei ihr ist eine ~ locker** *(col)* she's got a screw loose *(col)*. **(b)** *(Naut, Aviat)* propeller, prop *(col)*. **(c)** *(Sport)* twist. **(d)** **alte ~** *(pej col)* old bag *(col)*.

**schr̲auben** *vti* to screw. **etw in die Höhe ~** *(fig) Preise, Rekorde* to push sth up; *Ansprüche* to raise; *siehe* **geschraubt.**

**Schrauben-:** **~dreher** *m* = **~zieher**; **~mutter** *f* nut; **~schlüssel** *m* spanner *(Brit)*, wrench; **~zieher** *m* - screwdriver.

**Schraub-:** **~stock** *m* vice; **~verschluß** *m* screw top *or* cap.

**Schr̲ebergarten** *m* allotment *(Brit)*.

**Schr̲eck** *m* -e fright, scare. **vor ~** in fright; *zittern* with fright; **zu meinem großen ~(en)** to my great horror *or* dismay; **einen ~(en) bekommen** to get a fright *or* scare; **auf den ~ (hin)** to get over the fright; **sich vom ersten ~ erholen** to recover from the initial shock; **mit dem ~(en) davonkommen** to get off with no more than a fright; **ach du ~** *(col)* (oh) crumbs! *(col)*; **o ~ laß nach** *(hum col)* for goodness sake! *(col)*.

**schr̲ecken** **1** *vt (ängstigen)* to frighten, to scare; *(stärker)* to terrify. **jdn aus dem Schlaf ~** to startle sb out of his sleep. **2** *vi aux sein* **aus dem Schlaf ~** to be startled out of one's sleep.

**Schr̲ecken** *m* - **(a)** = **Schreck.** **(b)** *(Furcht, Entsetzen)* terror, horror. **das Gleichgewicht des ~s** the balance of terror; **er war der ~ der ganzen Lehrerschaft** he was the terror of all the teachers.

**schr̲ecken\erregend** *adj* terrifying, horrifying.

**Schreckens-:** **s~bleich** *adj* as white as a sheet; **~herrschaft** *f* (reign of) terror; **~kammer** *f* chamber of horrors; **~nachricht** *f* terrible news *no pl or* piece of news.

**Schreck-:** **~gespenst** *nt* nightmare; **das ~gespenst der Inflation** the bogey of inflation; **s~haft** *adj* easily startled; **~haftigkeit** *f* jumpiness *(col)*.

**schr̲ecklich** *adj* terrible, dreadful; *(col: sehr, groß auch)* awful. **sich ~ freuen** *(col)* to be terribly *or* awfully pleased; **~ gerne!** *(col)* I'd absolutely love to.

**Schr̲ecklichkeit** *f* terribleness, dreadfulness.

**Schreck-:** **~schraube** *f (pej col)* (old) battle-axe

*(col)*; ~**schuß** *m* warning shot; ~**sekunde** *f* moment of shock.

**Schrei** *m* **-e** cry, shout; *(gellend)* scream; *(kreischend)* shriek; *(von Eule etc)* screech; *(von Hahn)* crow. **der ~ nach Freiheit/Rache** the call for freedom/revenge; **ein ~ der Entrüstung** an (indignant) outcry; **der letzte ~** *(col)* the latest thing, all the rage *(col)*.

**Schreib-:** ~**bedarf** *m* writing materials *pl,* stationery; ~**block** *m* (writing) pad.

**Schreibe** *f* **-n** *(col)* writing.

**schreiben** *pret* **schrieb**, *ptp* **geschrieben 1** *vt* **(a)** to write; *Scheck auch, Rechnung* to make out, to write out; *(mit Schreibmaschine)* to type (out); *Klassenarbeit, Übersetzung* to do; *(berichten: Zeitung etc)* to say. **jdm einen Brief ~** to write a letter to sb, to write sb a letter; **etw auf Diskette ~** *(Comp)* to write sth to disk; **wo steht das geschrieben?** where does it say that?; **es steht geschrieben** *(Rel)* it is written; **es steht Ihnen im Gesicht geschrieben** it's written all over your face. **(b)** *(orthographisch)* to spell. **ein Wort falsch ~** to misspell a word, to spell a word wrong(ly). **(c)** *(Datum)* **wir ~ heute den 10. Mai** today is May 10th; **man schrieb das Jahr 1939** the year was 1939, it was (in) 1939.

**2** *vi* to write; *(tippen)* to type; *(berichten)* to say. **jdm ~** to write to sb, to write sb *(US)*; **ich schrieb ihm, daß ...** I wrote and told him that ...; **an einem Roman ~** to be working on *or* writing a novel; **wieviel Silben schreibt sie pro Minute?** what is her (typing) speed?; **mit Bleistift ~** to write in pencil.

**3** *vr* **(a)** *(korrespondieren)* to write (to each other), to correspond. **(b)** *(geschrieben werden)* to be spelt. **wie schreibt sich das?** how is that spelt?

**Schreiben** *nt* - **(a)** *no pl* writing. **(b)** *(Mitteilung)* communication *(form)*; *(Comm: Brief)* letter.

**Schreiber(in** *f)* *m* - writer, author; *(Gerichts~)* clerk; *(pej: Schriftsteller)* scribbler.

**Schreiberei** *f* *(col)* writing *no indef art*; *(pej: von Schriftsteller)* scribbling.

**Schreiberling** *m* *(pej: Schriftsteller)* scribbler *(pej col)*.

**Schreib-:** **s~faul** *adj* lazy (about letter-writing); **er ist s~faul** he's a reluctant correspondent; ~**faulheit** *f* laziness (about letter-writing); ~**fehler** *m* (spelling) mistake; *(aus Flüchtigkeit)* slip of the pen; *(Tippfehler)* (typing) mistake *or* error; ~**heft** *nt* exercise book; ~**kraft** *f* typist; ~**maschine** *f* typewriter; **mit der ~maschine schreiben** to type; **mit der ~maschine geschrieben** typewritten, typed; ~**maschinenpapier** *nt* typing paper; ~**papier** *nt* writing paper; ~**schrift** *f* running (hand)writing; *(Typ)* script; ~**stube** *f* *(Mil)* orderly room; ~**tisch** *m* desk; ~**tischlampe** *f* desk lamp; ~**tischtäter** *m* mastermind behind the scenes (of a/the crime); ~**übung** *f* writing exercise; ~**ung** *f* spelling; ~**unterlage** *f* pad; *(auf ~tisch)* desk pad; ~**waren** *pl* stationery *sing,* writing materials *pl*; ~**warengeschäft** *nt* stationer's (shop); ~**warenhändler** *m* stationer; ~**weise** *f* *(Stil)* style; *(Rechtschreibung)* spelling; ~**zeug** *nt* writing things *pl*.

**schreien** *pret* **schrie**, *ptp* **geschrie(e)n 1** *vti* to shout, to cry out; *(gellend)* to scream; *(vor Angst, vor Schmerzen)* to cry out/to scream; *(kreischend)* to shriek; *(heulen: Kind)* to howl; *(jammern)* to moan; *(Eule etc)* to screech; *(Hahn)* to crow. **es war zum S~** *(col)* it was a scream *(col)* or a hoot *(col)*; **nach etw ~** *(fig)* to cry out for sth; **jdm etw ins Gesicht ~** to shout sth in sb's face. **2** *vr* **sich heiser ~** to shout oneself hoarse; *(Baby)* to cry itself hoarse.

**schreiend** *adj Farben* loud, garish; *Unrecht* glaring, flagrant.

**Schrei-:** ~**hals** *m* *(col)* *(Baby)* bawler *(col)*; *(Unruhestifter)* noisy troublemaker; ~**krampf** *m* screaming fit.

**Schrein** *m* **-e** *(geh)* shrine.

**Schreiner(in** *f)* *m* - carpenter; *(Möbel~)* cabinetmaker.

**schreinern 1** *vi* to do carpentry. **gut ~ können** to be good at carpentry. **2** *vt Schrank, Regale etc* to make.

**schreiten** *pret* **schritt**, *ptp* **geschritten** *vi aux sein* *(geh)* *(schnell gehen)* to stride; *(feierlich gehen)* to walk; *(stolzieren)* to strut. **zu etw ~** *(fig)* to proceed with sth; **zum Äußersten ~** to take extreme measures; **zur Abstimmung ~** to proceed to a/the vote.

**schrie** *pret of* **schreien**.

**schrieb** *pret of* **schreiben**.

**Schrieb** *m* **-e** *(col)* missive *(hum)*.

**Schrift** *f* **-en (a)** *(Schreibweise)* script; *(~system)* script; *(Typ)* type, typeface, font. **gotische ~** Gothic script; **er hat eine schlechte ~** he has bad handwriting. **(b)** *(~stück)* document; *(Broschüre)* leaflet; *(Buch)* work; *(kürzere Abhandlung)* paper. **seine früheren ~en** his early writings.

**Schrift-:** ~**art** *f* *(Hand~)* script; *(Typ)* type, typeface; ~**bild** *nt* script; ~**deutsch** *nt* written German; ~**form** *f* *(Jur)* **dieser Vertrag erfordert die ~form** this contract must be drawn up in writing; ~**führer** *m* secretary; ~**gelehrte(r)** *m* *(Bibl)* scribe.

**schriftlich 1** *adj* written. **in ~er Form** in writing; **die ~e Prüfung** the written exam. **2** *adv* in writing. **ich bin ~ eingeladen worden** I have had a written invitation; **das kann ich Ihnen ~ geben** *(fig col)* I can tell you that for free *(col)*.

**Schrift-:** ~**probe** *f* *(Hand~)* specimen of one's handwriting; ~**satz** *m* *(Jur)* legal document; ~**setzer** *m* typesetter, compositor; ~**sprache** *f* written language.

**Schriftsteller** *m* - author, writer.

**Schriftstellerin** *f* author(ess), writer.

**schriftstellerisch** *adj* literary. **sich ~ betätigen, ~ tätig sein** to write; **er ist ~ begabt** he has literary talent *or* talent as a writer.

**Schrift-:** ~**stück** *nt* paper; *(Jur)* document; ~**tum** *nt no pl* literature; ~**verkehr,** ~**wechsel** *m* correspondence; ~**zeichen** *nt* character; ~**zug** *m usu pl* stroke; *(Handschrift)* hand.

**schrill** *adj* shrill; *(fig) Mißklang* jarring; *Fest, Farbe* loud.

**schrillen** *vi* to shrill.

**schritt** *pret of* **schreiten**.

**Schritt** *m* **-e (a)** *(lit, fig)* step; *(hörbar)* footstep. **einen ~ zurücktreten** to take a step back; **ein paar ~e spazierengehen** to go for *or* take a short walk *or* stroll; **einen ~ machen** to take a step; **kurze/große ~e machen** to take small steps/long strides; **den ersten ~ tun** *(fig)* to make the first move; *(etw beginnen)* to take the first step; **~e gegen jdn/etw unternehmen** to take steps against sb/sth; **auf ~ und Tritt** *(lit, fig)* wherever *or* everywhere one goes; **~ für ~** step by step. **(b)** *(Gang)* walk, gait; *(Tempo)* pace. **~ halten** *(lit, fig)* to keep pace; **mit der Zeit ~ halten** to keep abreast of the times; **langsamen ~es** *(geh)* with slow steps. **(c)** *(~geschwindigkeit)* walking pace. **„~fahren"** "dead slow". **(d)** *(Maßangabe)* **mit zehn ~en Abstand** at a distance of ten paces. **(e)** *(Hosen~)* crotch.

**Schrittempo** *nt* walking speed.

**Schritt-:** ~**macher** *m* *(Sport, Med)* pacemaker; *(fig* *auch)* pacesetter; **s~weise 1** *adv* gradually, little by little; **2** *adj* gradual.

**schroff** *adj (rauh, barsch)* curt; *(kraß, abrupt)* abrupt; *(steil) Fels, Klippe* precipitous. **~e Gegensätze** stark *or* sharp contrasts.

**Schroffheit** *f siehe adj* curtness; abruptness; precipitousness; *(schroffes Wort)* curt remark.

**schröpfen** *vt jdn ~ (fig)* to fleece sb *(col).*

**Schrot** *m or nt* **-e (a)** whole-corn/-rye *etc* meal; *(Weizen)* wholemeal *(Brit)*, wholewheat *(US)*. **ein Schotte von echtem ~ und Korn** a true Scot; **vom alten ~ und Korn** *(fig)* of the old school. **(b)** *(Hunt)* shot.

**Schrotbüchse** *f* shotgun.

**schroten** *vt Getreide* to grind coarsely.

**Schrot-:** **~flinte** *f* shotgun; **~kugel** *f* pellet; **~ladung** *f* round of shot.

**Schrott** *m no pl* scrap metal. **ein Auto zu ~ fahren** to write off a car.

**Schrott-:** **~händler** *m* scrap dealer *or* merchant; **~haufen** *m (lit)* scrap heap; *(fig: Auto)* heap *(col)*; **~platz** *m* scrap yard; **s~reif** *adj* ready for the scrap heap; **~wert** *m* scrap value.

**schrubben** *vti* to scrub.

**Schrubber** *m* - (long-handled) scrubbing brush.

**Schrulle** *f* **-n (a)** *(Marotte)* quirk. **(b)** *(pej: alte Frau)* old crone.

**schrullig** *adj* odd, cranky.

**schrump(e)lig** *adj (col)* wrinkled.

**schrumpeln** *vi aux sein (col)* to go wrinkled.

**schrumpfen** *vi aux sein (lit, fig)* to shrink; *(Leber, Niere)* to atrophy; *(runzlig werden)* to get wrinkled; *(Exporte, Interesse)* to dwindle.

**Schrumpf-:** **~kopf** *m* shrunken head; **~leber** *f* cirrhosis of the liver.

**Schrumpfung** *f* shrinking; *(Raumverlust)* shrinkage; *(Med)* atrophy(ing); *(von Exporten)* dwindling.

**Schub** *m* **=e (a)** *(Stoß)* push, shove. **(b)** *(Phys)* thrust. **(c)** *(Gruppe, Anzahl)* batch.

**Schuber** *m* - slipcase.

**Schub-:** **~fach** *nt* drawer; **~karre** *f,* **~karren** *m* wheelbarrow; **~kasten** *m* drawer; **~kraft** *f (Phys)* thrust; **~lade** *f* **-n** drawer.

**Schubs** *m* **-e** *(col)* shove, push; *(Aufmerksamkeit erregend)* nudge.

**schubsen** *vti (col)* to shove, to push; *(Aufmerksamkeit erregend)* to nudge.

**schubweise** *adv* in batches.

**schüchtern** *adj* shy.

**Schüchternheit** *f* shyness.

**schuf** *pret of* **schaffen¹**.

**Schuft** *m* **-e** heel *(col)*, cad *(dated col).*

**schuften** *vi (col)* to graft (away) *(col)*, to slave away.

**Schufterei** *f (col)* graft *(col)*, hard work.

**schuftig** *adj* mean, shabby.

**Schuh** *m* **-e** shoe. **jdm etw in die ~e schieben** *(col)* to put the blame for sth on sb; **wissen, wo jdn der ~ drückt** to know what is troubling sb; **umgekehrt wird ein ~ draus!** *(col)* quite the reverse is true.

**Schuh-** *in cpds* shoe; **~anzieher** *m* shoehorn; **~creme** *f* shoe polish *or* cream; **~größe** *f* shoe size; **~löffel** *m* shoehorn; **~macher** *m* shoemaker; **~nummer** *f (col)* shoe size; **~plattler** *m* - *Bavarian folk dance*; **~putzer** *m* bootblack, shoeshine boy *(US)*; **ich bin doch nicht dein ~putzer!** I'm not your slave!; **~riemen** *m* strap of a/one's shoe); *(Schnürsenkel)* shoelace; **~sohle** *f* sole (of a/one's shoe); **~werk** *nt no pl* footwear; **~wichse** *f (col)* shoe polish.

**Schuko-** ®: **~steckdose** *f* safety socket *(Brit)* or out-

let *(US)*; **~stecker** *m* safety plug.

**Schul-:** **~abgänger(in** *f)* *m* - school-leaver; **~abschluß** *m* school-leaving qualification; **~anfang** *m* beginning of term; *(~eintritt)* first day at school; **~anfänger** *m* child just starting school; **~arbeit** *f usu pl* homework *no pl*; **~aufgaben** *pl* homework *sing*; **~bank** *f* school desk; **die ~bank drücken** *(col)* to go to school; **~beginn** *m (~jahrsbeginn)* beginning of the school year; *(nach Ferien)* beginning of term; **(der) ~beginn ist um neun** school starts at nine; **~behörde** *f* education authority; **~beispiel** *nt (fig)* classic example *(für of)*; **~besuch** *m* school attendance; **~bildung** *f* (school) education; **~buch** *nt* schoolbook, textbook; **~buchverlag** *m* educational publisher; **~bus** *m* school bus.

**schuld** *adj pred* **~ sein** *or* **haben** to be to blame *(an +dat* for); **er war** *or* **hatte ~ an dem Streit** the argument was his fault, he was to blame for the argument; **du hast** *or* **bist selbst ~** that's your own fault; **jdm/einer Sache ~ geben** to blame sb/sth.

**Schuld** *f* **-en (a)** *no pl (Ursache, Verantwortlichkeit)* **die ~ an etw** *(dat)* **haben** to be to blame for sth; **die ~ auf sich** *(acc)* **nehmen** to take the blame; **jdm die ~ geben** to blame sb; **jdm die ~ zuschieben, die ~ auf jdn schieben** to put the blame on sb; **die ~ bei anderen suchen** to try to blame somebody else; **das ist meine eigene ~** it's my own fault *or* all my fault; **durch meine/deine ~** because of me/you.

  **(b)** *no pl (~gefühl)* guilt; *(Unrecht)* wrong; *(Rel: Sünde)* sin. **ich bin mir keiner ~ bewußt** I'm not aware of having done anything wrong; **~ auf sich** *(acc)* **laden** to burden oneself with a deep sense of guilt; **für seine ~ büßen** to pay for one's sin/sins; **~ und Sühne** crime and punishment.

  **(c)** *(Zahlungsverpflichtung)* debt. **~en machen** to run up debts; **~en haben** to be in debt; **DM 10.000 ~en haben** to have debts of 10,000 DM; **ich stehe tief in seiner ~** *(fig)* I'm deeply indebted to him.

**Schuld-:** **~bekenntnis** *nt* confession; **s~beladen** *adj* burdened with guilt; **s~bewußt** *adj Mensch* feeling guilty; *Miene* guilty; **~bewußtsein** *nt* feelings of guilt *pl.*

**schulden** *vt* to owe. **das schulde ich ihm** I owe it to him; **jdm Dank ~** to owe sb a debt of gratitude.

**Schulden-:** **~eintreiber** *m (col)* debt collector; **s~frei** *adj* free of debt(s); *Grundstück etc* unmortgaged; **~last** *f* debts *pl.*

**Schuld-:** **~forderung** *f* claim; **~frage** *f* question of guilt; **s~frei** *adj* blameless; **~gefühl** *nt* feeling of guilt; **~gefühle haben** to feel guilty; **s~haft** *adj (Jur)* culpable.

**Schuldienst** *m* (school-)teaching *no art.* **im ~ sein** to be a teacher.

**schuldig** *adj* **(a)** *(schuldhaft, straffällig)* guilty; *(verantwortlich)* to blame *pred (an +dat* for); *(Rel)* sinful. **einer Sache** *(gen)* **~ sein, sich einer Sache** *(gen)* **~ machen** to be guilty of sth; **jdn ~ sprechen** to find sb guilty; **sich ~ bekennen** to admit one's guilt; *(Jur)* to plead guilty; **~ geschieden sein** to be the guilty party in a/the divorce. **(b)** *(geh: gebührend)* due. **jdm den ~en Respekt zollen** to give sb the respect due to him/her. **(c)** *(verpflichtet)* **jdm etw** *(acc)* **~ sein** *(lit, fig)* to owe sb sth; **was bin ich Ihnen ~?** how much do I owe you?; **jdm Dank ~ sein** to owe sb a debt of gratitude; **sie blieb mir die Antwort ~** she didn't have an answer.

**Schuldige(r)** *mf decl as adj* guilty person; *(zivilrechtlich)* guilty party.

**Schuldigkeit** *f no pl* duty. **seine ~ tun** to do one's duty.

**Schul-:** ~**direktor** *m* head teacher, headmaster *(esp Brit)*, principal; ~**direktorin** *f* head teacher, headmistress *(esp Brit)*, principal.

**Schuld-:** ~**komplex** *m* guilt complex; **s~los** *adj (an Verbrechen)* innocent *(an +dat* of*)*; *(an Fehler, Unglück etc)* blameless, free from blame; **s~los geschieden sein** to be the innocent party in a/the divorce; ~**losigkeit** *f siehe adj* innocence; blamelessness.

**Schuldner(in** *f) m* - debtor.

**Schuld-:** ~**prinzip** *nt (Jur)* principle of the guilty party; ~**schein** *m* IOU, promissory note; ~**spruch** *m* verdict of guilty.

**Schule** *f* -n school. **in die** ~ **kommen/gehen** to start school/go to school; **in der** ~ at school; **die** ~ **wechseln** to change schools; **von der** ~ **abgehen** to leave school; **durch eine harte** ~ **gegangen sein** *(fig)* to have learned in a hard school; ~ **machen** *(fig)* to become the accepted thing; **aus der** ~ **plaudern** to tell tales out of school *(col)*; **ein Kavalier der alten** ~ a gentleman of the old school.

**schulen** *vt* to train.

**Schüler(in** *f) m* - schoolboy/schoolgirl; *(älter)* school student; *(einer bestimmten Schule)* pupil; *(Jünger)* follower, disciple. **als** ~ **habe ich** ... when I was at school I ...; **alle** ~ **und** ~**innen dieser Stadt** the whole school population of this town.

**Schüler-:** ~**austausch** *m* school *or* student exchange; ~**ausweis** *m* (school) student card; ~**lotse** *m pupil acting as a road-crossing warden,* ≈ crossing guard *(US)*; ~**mitverwaltung** *f* school *or* student council; ~**schaft** *f* pupils *pl*; ~**zeitung** *f* school magazine *(written by pupils)*.

**Schul-:** ~**fach** *nt* school subject; ~**ferien** *pl* school holidays *pl (Brit) or* vacation; ~**fernsehen** *nt* schools' *or* educational television; ~**fest** *nt* school function; **s~frei** *adj* **s~freier Nachmittag** afternoon off (school), free afternoon; **s~frei haben** to have no school; ~**freund** *m* schoolfriend; ~**funk** *m* schools' broadcasting; ~**gebäude** *nt* school building; ~**gelände** *nt* school grounds *pl*; ~**geld** *nt* school fees *pl*; ~**heft** *nt* exercise book; ~**hof** *m* school playground *(Brit)*, schoolyard.

**schulisch** *adj Leistungen, Probleme* at school; *Angelegenheiten* school *attr.* **aus** ~**er Sicht** from the school angle.

**Schul-:** ~**jahr** *nt* school year; *(Klasse)* year; **ihre** ~**jahre** her schooldays; ~**junge** *m* schoolboy; ~**kamerad** *m* schoolmate, schoolfriend; ~**kenntnisse** *pl* knowledge *sing* acquired at school; ~**kind** *nt* schoolchild; ~**klasse** *f* (school) class; ~**leiter** *m* head teacher, headmaster *(esp Brit)*, principal; ~**leiterin** *f* head teacher, headmistress *(esp Brit)*, principal; ~**mädchen** *nt* schoolgirl; ~**medizin** *f* orthodox medicine; ~**meinung** *f* received opinion; ~**meister** *m (old, hum, pej)* schoolmaster; **s~meisterlich** *adj (pej)* schoolmasterish; **s~meistern** *insep* **1** *vt* to lecture (at *or* to); **2** *vi* to lecture; ~**ordnung** *f* school rules *pl*; ~**pflicht** *f* compulsory school attendance *no art*; **es besteht** ~**pflicht** school attendance is compulsory; **s~**ˈ**pflichtig** *adj Kind* required to attend school; ~**politik** *f* education policy; ~**rat** *m* school(s) inspector; ~**reife** *f* **die** ~**reife haben** to be ready to go to school; ~**schiff** *nt* training ship; ~**schluß** *m* end of school; ~**schluß ist um 13¹⁰** school finishes at 1.10; ~**sprecher(in** *f) m* head boy/girl *(Brit)*; ~**stunde** *f* (school) period *or* lesson; ~**tag** *m* schoolday; **der erste** ~**tag** the/one's first day at school; ~**tasche** *f* schoolbag.

**Schulter** *f* -n shoulder. **breite** ~**n haben** *(lit)* to be broad-shouldered, to have broad shoulders; *(fig)* to have a broad back; **er ließ die** ~**n hängen** he was slouching; *(niedergeschlagen)* he hung his head; **jdm auf die** ~ **klopfen** to give sb a slap on the back; *(lobend)* to pat sb on the back; **die** *or* **mit den** ~**n zucken** to shrug one's shoulders; **etw auf die leichte** ~ **nehmen** to take sth lightly.

**Schulter-:** ~**blatt** *nt* shoulder blade; **s~frei** *adj Kleid* off-the-shoulder; ~**höhe** *f* shoulder height; **in** ~**höhe** at shoulder level *or* height; ~**klappe** *f (Mil)* epaulette; **s~lang** *adj* shoulder-length.

**schultern** *vt* to shoulder.

**Schulter-:** ~**riemen** *m* shoulder strap; ~**stück** *nt* **(a)** *(Mil)* epaulette; **(b)** *(Cook)* piece of shoulder.

**Schultüte** *f large conical bag of sweets/candy given to children on their first day at school.*

**Schulung** *f (Ausbildung)* training; *(Kurs)* training course; *(Pol)* political instruction.

**Schul-:** ~**unterricht** *m* school lessons *pl*; ~**versager** *m* failure at school; ~**weg** *m* way to/ from school; *(Entfernung)* distance to/from school; ~**weisheit** *f (pej)* booklearning; ~**wesen** *nt* school system; ~**zeit** *f (~jahre)* schooldays *pl*; **nach 13jähriger** ~**zeit** after 13 years at school; ~**zeitung** *f* school magazine; ~**zeugnis** *nt* school report.

**schummeln** *vi (col)* to cheat *(bei etw* at sth*)*.

**schumm(e)rig** *adj Beleuchtung* dim; *Raum* dimly-lit. **bei** ~**em Licht** in the half-light.

**Schund** *m no pl (pej)* trash, rubbish.

**Schundroman** *m* trashy *or* pulp novel.

**schunkeln** *vi to link arms and sway from side to side in time to the music.*

**Schupo** *m* -s *(dated col)* = **Schutzpolizist** cop *(col)*.

**Schuppe** *f* -n **(a)** *(Bot, Zool)* scale. **es fiel mir wie** ~**n von den Augen** my eyes were opened, all was revealed. **(b)** *(Kopf~)* ~**n** *pl* dandruff *sing*.

**Schuppen** *m* - **(a)** shed. **(b)** *(col) (Haus etc)* hole *(pej col)*; *(übles Lokal)* dive *(col)*.

**schuppen 1** *vt Fische* to scale. **2** *vr* to flake.

**Schuppen-:** **s~artig** *adj* scale-like; ~**flechte** *f (Med)* psoriasis *(spec)*.

**schuppig** *adj* scaly; *(abblätternd auch)* flaking.

**Schur** *f* -en *(das Scheren)* shearing.

**Schür|eisen** *nt* poker.

**schüren** *vt* **(a)** *Feuer, Glut* to rake, to poke. **(b)** *(fig)* to stir up; *Zorn etc* to fan the flames of.

**schürfen 1** *vi (Min)* to prospect *(nach* for*)*. **tief** ~ *(fig)* to dig deep. **2** *vt Bodenschätze* to mine. **3** *vtr* to graze oneself. **sich am Knie** ~ to graze one's knee.

**Schürf-:** ~**recht** *nt* mining rights *pl*; ~**wunde** *f* graze, abrasion.

**Schürhaken** *m* poker.

**Schurke** *m (wk)* -n, -n *(dated)* villain, scoundrel.

**Schurwolle** *f* virgin wool. „**reine** ~" "pure new wool".

**Schurz** *m* -e apron; *(Lenden~)* loincloth.

**Schürze** *f* -n apron.

**Schürzen-:** ~**jäger** *m (col)* philanderer, one for the girls *(col)*; ~**zipfel** *m* apron string; **er hängt der Mutter noch am** ~**zipfel** he's still tied to his mother's apron strings.

**Schuß** *m* ⁼sse **(a)** shot; *(~ Munition)* round. **sechs** ~ *or* **Schüsse** six shots/rounds; **ein** ~ **ins Schwarze** *(lit, fig)* a bull's-eye; **weit vom** ~ **sein** *(fig col)* to be miles from where the action is *(col)*; *(abgelegen)* to be out in the sticks; **er ist keinen** ~ **Pulver wert** *(fig)* he is not worth tuppence *(Brit col) or* a red cent *(US col)*; **das war ein** ~ **vor den Bug** *(fig)* that was a warning shot across the bows; **ein** ~ **in den Ofen** *(col)* a complete waste of time. **(b)** *(Ftbl)* kick; *(zum Tor auch)* shot. **(c)** *(Ski)* schuss. **im** ~ **fahren** to schuss. **(d)** *(Spritzer)* *(von Wein, Essig etc)* dash; *(von Whisky)* shot; *(von Humor etc auch)* touch. **(e)** *(Tex)* weft. **(f)** *(col: mit Rauschgift)* shot. **einen ~ setzen** to shoot up *(col)*. **(g)** *(col)* **(gut) in ~ sein** to be in good shape *or* nick *(col)*; *(Mensch)* to be on form; **etw in ~ halten** to keep sth in good shape.

**Schuß-:** **~bereich** *m* (firing) range; **im ~bereich** within range; **s~bereit** *adj* ready to fire; *Gewehr auch* cocked.

**Schussel** *m* - *(col)* dolt *(col)*; *(zerstreut)* scatterbrain *(col)*.

**Schüssel** *f* **-n** bowl; *(Servier~ auch)* dish; *(Wasch~)* basin.

**schusselig** *adj (col)* daft; *(zerstreut)* scatterbrained *(col)*, muddle-headed *(col)*.

**Schuß-:** **~fahrt** *f (Ski)* schuss; *(das ~fahren)* schussing; **~feld** *nt* field of fire; *(Übungsplatz)* firing range; **s~fest** *adj* bulletproof; **~linie** *f* line of fire; *(fig auch)* firing line; **~verletzung** *f* bullet wound; **~waffe** *f* firearm; **~waffengebrauch** *m (form)* use of firearms; **~wechsel** *m* exchange of shots *or* fire; **~weite** *f* range (of fire); **in/außer ~weite** within/out of range; **~wunde** *f* bullet wound.

**Schuster** *m* - shoemaker; *(für Reparaturen)* shoe repairer. **auf ~s Rappen** *(hum)* by Shanks's pony; **~, bleib bei deinem Leisten!** *(Prov)* cobbler, stick to your last *(Prov)*.

**Schutt** *m no pl (Trümmer, Bau~)* rubble; *(Geol)* debris, detritus *(spec)*. **„~ abladen verboten"** "no tipping"; **in ~ und Asche liegen** to be in ruins.

**Schutt|abladeplatz** *m* tip, dump.

**Schüttel-:** **~frost** *m (Med)* shivering fit; **~frost haben** to have the shivers; **~lähmung** *f (Med)* Parkinson's disease.

**schütteln 1** *vt* to shake; *(rütteln)* to shake about, to jolt (about). **den** *or* **mit dem Kopf ~** to shake one's head; **von Fieber geschüttelt werden** to be racked with fever. **2** *vr* to shake oneself; *(vor Kälte)* to shiver *(vor with)*; *(vor Ekel)* to shudder *(vor with, in)*. **sich vor Lachen ~** to shake with laughter.

**schütten 1** *vt* to tip; *Flüssigkeiten* to pour; *(ver~)* to spill. **2** *vi impers (col)* **es schüttet** it's pouring (with rain), it's bucketing (down) *(col)*.

**schütter** *adj Haar* thin.

**Schutt-:** **~halde** *f* (rubble) tip; **~haufen** *m* pile *or* heap of rubble; **~platz** *m* (rubble) tip.

**Schutz** *m no pl* protection *(vor +dat, gegen* against, *from)*; *(Zuflucht auch)* shelter, refuge *(vor +dat, gegen* from); *(der Natur, Umwelt etc)* conservation; *(esp Mil: Deckung)* cover. **bei jdm ~ suchen** to look to sb for protection; to seek refuge with sb; **im ~ der Dunkelheit** under cover of darkness; **zum ~ der Augen** to protect the eyes; **jdn in ~ nehmen** *(fig)* to take sb's part.

**Schutz-:** **~anstrich** *m* protective coat; **~anzug** *m* protective clothing *no indef art, no pl*; **s~bedürftig** *adj* in need of protection; **~befohlene(r)** *mf decl as adj* = **Schützling**; **~behauptung** *f* lie to cover oneself; **~blech** *nt* mudguard; **~brief** *m (Insur)* (international) motoring cover; **~brille** *f* protective goggles *pl*; **~dach** *nt (vor Haustür)* porch; *(an Haltestelle)* shelter.

**Schütze** *m* *(wk)* **-n, -n** **(a)** marksman; *(Schießsportler)* rifleman; *(Bogen~)* archer; *(Ftbl: Tor~)* scorer. **(b)** *(Astrol)* Sagittarius *no art.* **sie ist ~** she's Sagittarius *or* a Sagittarian.

**schützen 1** *vt* to protect *(vor +dat, gegen* from, against*)*; *(esp Mil: Deckung geben)* to cover. **gesetzlich/urheberrechtlich geschützt** registered/ protected by copyright; **ein geschützter Platz** a sheltered spot *or* place; **vor Sonnenlicht ~!** keep

away from sunlight; **vor Nässe ~!** keep dry. **2** *vi* to give *or* offer protection *(vor +dat, gegen* against, from*)*; *(esp Mil: Deckung geben)* to give cover. **3** *vr* to protect oneself *(vor +dat, gegen* from, against*)*.

**schützend** *adj* protective. **ein ~es Dach** *(gegen Wetter)* a shelter.

**Schützenfest** *nt fair featuring shooting matches.*

**Schutz|engel** *m* guardian angel.

**Schützen-:** **~graben** *m* trench; **~hilfe** *f (fig)* support; **jdm ~hilfe geben** to back sb up; **~loch** *nt (Mil)* foxhole; **~panzer** *m* armoured *(Brit)* or armored *(US)* personnel carrier; **~verein** *m* rifle *or* shooting club.

**Schutz-:** **~farbe** *f (Biol)* protective *or* adaptive colouring *(Brit)* or coloring *(US)*; **~gebiet** *nt (Pol)* protectorate; **~gebühr** *f* (token) fee; **~geld** *nt* protection money; **~haft** *f (Jur)* protective custody; **~handschuh** *m* protective glove; **~haut** *f* protective covering; **~heilige(r)** *mf* patron saint; **~helm** *m* safety helmet; **~herrschaft** *f (Pol)* protection, protectorate; **~hülle** *f* protective cover; *(Buchumschlag)* dust cover *or* jacket; **s~impfen** *ptp* **s~geimpft** *vt* to vaccinate, to inoculate; **~impfung** *f* vaccination, inoculation; **~kleidung** *f* protective clothing.

**Schützling** *m* protégé; *(esp Kind)* charge.

**Schutz-:** **s~los** *adj (wehrlos)* defenceless *(Brit)*, defenseless *(US)*; *(gegen Kälte etc)* unprotected; **~macht** *f (Pol)* protecting power, protector; **~mann** *m, pl* **~leute** *(dated)* policeman, constable *(Brit)*; **~marke** *f* trademark; **~maßnahme** *f* precautionary measure; *(vorbeugend)* preventive measure; **~patron** *m* patron saint; **~schicht** *f* protective layer; *(Überzug)* protective coating; **~schild** *m* shield; *(von Polizist)* riot shield; *(an Geschützen)* gun shield; **~schirm** *m (Tech)* protective screen; **s~suchend** *adj* seeking protection; *(nach Obdach)* seeking refuge *or* shelter; **~umschlag** *m* dust cover *or* jacket; **~verband** *m (Med)* protective bandage *or* dressing; **~vorrichtung** *f* safety device; **~zoll** *m* protective duty *or* tariff.

**schwabbelig** *adj (col) Körperteil* flabby; *Gelee* wobbly.

**schwabbeln** *vi (col)* to wobble (about).

**Schwabe** *m (wk)* **-n, -n, Schwäbin** *f* Swabian.

**Schwaben** *nt* Swabia.

**Schwabenstreich** *m* piece of folly.

**schwäbisch** *adj* Swabian.

**schwach** *adj comp* **≃er,** *superl* **≃ste(r, s)** *or (adv)* **am ≃sten** weak *(auch Gram)*; *Gesundheit, Beteiligung, Gedächtnis* poor; *Ton, Anzeichen, Hoffnung* faint, slight; *Gehör* poor, dull; *Licht* poor, dim; *Wind* light; *(Comm) Nachfrage, Geschäft* slack, poor. **~e Augen** weak *or* poor (eye)sight; **das ist ein ~es Bild** *(col)* or **eine ~e Leistung** *(col)* that's a poor show *(col)*; **trotz des ~en Erfolges des Buchs** in spite of the book's lack of success; **jds ~e Seite** sb's weak point; **ein ~er Trost** cold *or* small comfort; **mach mich nicht ~!** *(col)* don't say that! *(col)*; **auf ~en Beinen** *or* **Füßen stehen** *(fig)* to be on shaky ground; *(Theorie)* to be shaky; **≃er werden** to grow weaker, to weaken; *(Augen)* to fail, to grow worse; *(Stimme)* to grow fainter; *(Licht)* to (grow) dim; *(Ton)* to fade; *(Nachfrage)* to fall off, to slacken; **~ besiedelt** *or* **bevölkert** sparsely populated; **~ besucht** poorly attended; **die S~en** the weak.

**Schwäche** *f* **-n** weakness; *(von Gesundheit)* poorness; *(von Licht)* dimness; *(von Nachfrage)* slackness. **er brach vor ~ zusammen** he was so weak he collapsed; **menschliche ~n** human failings *or* frailties; **eine ~ für etw haben** to have a weakness for sth.

**Schwäche|anfall** *m* sudden faint feeling.

**schwächen** *vt (lit, fig)* to weaken.

**Schwachheit** *f no pl (fig)* weakness, frailty.

**Schwachkopf** *m (col)* dimwit *(col)*, idiot.

**schwächlich** *adj* weakly; *(zart auch)* puny.

**Schwächling** *m* weakling.

**Schwach-:** ~**punkt** *m* weak point; **s~sichtig** *adj (Med)* poor- *or* weak-sighted; ~**sichtigkeit** *f (Med)* dimness of vision; ~**sinn** *m (Med)* mental deficiency; *(fig col) (unsinnige Tat)* idiocy *no indef art; (Quatsch)* rubbish *(col)*; **s~sinnig** *adj (Med)* mentally deficient; *(fig col)* daft *(col)*, idiotic; ~**sinnige(r)** *mf decl as adj* mental defective; *(fig col)* moron *(col)*, imbecile *(col)*; ~**stelle** *f* weak point; ~**strom** *m (Elec)* low-voltage current.

**Schwächung** *f* weakening.

**Schwaden** *m* - *usu pl* cloud.

**Schwadron** *f* -**en** *(Mil Hist)* squadron.

**schwadronieren\*** *vi* to bluster.

**Schwafelei** *f (pej col)* drivel *no pl (col)*, twaddle *no pl (col)*.

**schwafeln** *(pej col)* **1** *vi* to drivel (on) *(col)*; *(in einer Prüfung)* to waffle *(col)*. **2** *vt* **dummes Zeug** ~ to talk drivel *(col)*.

**Schwager** *m* ⸗ brother-in-law.

**Schwägerin** *f* sister-in-law.

**Schwalbe** *f* -**n** swallow. **eine** ~ **macht noch keinen Sommer** *(Prov)* one swallow doesn't make a summer *(Prov)*.

**Schwall** *m* -**e** flood, torrent.

**schwamm** *pret of* **schwimmen**.

**Schwamm** *m* ⸗**e** **(a)** sponge. **etw mit dem** ~ **abwischen** to sponge sth (down); ~ **drüber!** *(col)* (let's) forget it! **(b)** *(Haus~)* dry rot.

**schwammig** *adj* **(a)** *(lit)* spongy. **(b)** *(fig) Gesicht* puffy, bloated; *(vage) Begriff* woolly.

**Schwan** *m* ⸗**e** swan. **mein lieber** ~! *(col) (überrascht)* my goodness!; *(drohend)* now listen, my boy/girl.

**schwand** *pret of* **schwinden**.

**schwanen** *vi impers* **ihm schwante etwas** he sensed something might happen; **mir schwant nichts Gutes** I've a feeling something nasty is going to happen.

**Schwanen-:** ~**gesang** *m (fig)* swansong; ~**hals** *m* swan's neck; *(fig)* swanlike neck; *(Tech)* gooseneck, swan-neck.

**schwang** *pret of* **schwingen**.

**schwanger** *adj* pregnant. **im sechsten Monat** ~ five months pregnant.

**Schwangere** *f decl as adj* pregnant woman.

**schwängern** *vt* to make pregnant, to impregnate *(form)*. **mit etw geschwängert sein** *(fig)* to be impregnated with sth.

**Schwangerschaft** *f* pregnancy.

**Schwangerschafts-:** ~**abbruch** *m* termination of pregnancy, abortion; ~**gymnastik** *f* antenatal exercises *pl*; ~**test** *m* pregnancy test.

**Schwank** *m* ⸗**e** *(Liter)* merry *or* comical tale; *(Theat)* farce.

**schwanken** *vi* **(a)** *(wanken, sich wiegen)* to sway; *(Schiff) (auf und ab)* to pitch; *(seitwärts)* to roll; *(beben)* to rock. **(b)** *aux sein (gehen)* to stagger, to totter. **(c)** *(variieren)* to vary; *(Preise, Stimmung etc auch)* to fluctuate; *(Kompaßnadel etc)* to swing. **(d)** *(unschlüssig sein)* to waver; *(zögern)* to hesitate. **(e)** **ins S~ kommen** *(Baum, Gebäude etc)* to start to sway; *(Preise, Kurs etc)* to start to fluctuate *or* vary; *(Überzeugung etc)* to begin to waver.

**schwankend** *adj* **(a)** *siehe vi (a)* swaying; pitching; rolling; rocking. **(b)** *Mensch* staggering; *Gang* rolling; *Schritt* unsteady. **(c)** *siehe vi (c)* varying; fluc-

tuating *esp attr*; oscillating; *Kurs, Gesundheit auch* unstable. **(d)** *(unschlüssig)* uncertain, wavering *attr*; *(zögernd)* hesitant. ~ **werden** to waver.

**Schwankung** *f* **(a)** *(hin und her)* swaying *no pl*; *(auf und ab)* shaking *no pl*, rocking *no pl*. **um die** ~**en des Turms zu messen** to measure the extent to which the tower sways. **(b)** *siehe vi (c)* variation *(gen* in*)*; fluctuation.

**Schwanz** *m* ⸗**e** **(a)** *(lit, fig)* tail. **den** ~ **hängen lassen** *(lit)* to let its tail droop; *(fig col)* to be down in the dumps *(col)*; **kein** ~ *(col)* not a (blessed) soul *(col)*. **(b)** *(col!!: Penis)* prick *(col!!)*.

**schwänzen** *(col)* **1** *vt* **Stunde, Vorlesung** to skip *(col)*, to cut *(col)*; **Schule** to play truant *or* hooky *(esp US col)* from, to skive off *(Brit col)*. **2** *vi* to play truant, to play hooky *(esp US col)*, to skive *(Brit col)*.

**Schwanz-:** ~**feder** *f* tail feather; ~**flosse** *f (auch Aviat)* tail fin; **s~los** *adj* tailless.

**schwappen** *vi* **(a)** *(Wasser)* to slosh around. **(b)** *aux sein (über~)* to splash, to slosh.

**Schwarm** *m* ⸗**e** **(a)** swarm; *(Flugzeugformation)* flight. **(b)** *(col: Angebeteter)* idol. **der neue Englischlehrer ist ihr** ~ she's got a crush on the new English teacher *(col)*.

**schwärmen** *vi* **(a)** *aux sein* to swarm. **(b)** *(begeistert reden)* to enthuse *(von* about*)*, to go into raptures *(von* about*)*. **für jdn/etw** ~ to be raving about sb/sth *(col)*; **ins S~ kommen** *or* **geraten** to go into raptures.

**Schwärmer** *m* - *(Begeisterter)* enthusiast, zealot; *(Phantast)* dreamer, visionary; *(sentimentaler* ~*)* sentimentalist.

**Schwärmerei** *f (Begeisterung)* enthusiasm; *(in Worten ausgedrückt)* effusion *no pl*; *(Verzückung)* rapture.

**schwärmerisch** *adj (begeistert)* enthusiastic; *Worte, Übertreibung* effusive; *(verliebt)* infatuated; *(verzückt)* enraptured.

**Schwarte** *f* -**n** **(a)** *(Speck~)* rind. **(b)** *(col: Buch)* old book, tome *(hum)*.

**Schwartenmagen** *m (Cook)* brawn.

**Schwarz** *nt no pl* black. ~ **tragen, in** ~ **gehen** to wear black.

**schwarz** *adj comp* ⸗**er**, *superl* ⸗**este(r, s)** *or (adv)* **am** ⸗**esten** **(a)** *(lit, fig)* black. **das S~e Brett** the notice board *(Brit)*, the bulletin board *(US)*; ~**er Gürtel** *(Sport)* black belt; ~**er Humor** black humour *(Brit)* or humor *(US)*; ~**er Kaffee/Tee** black coffee/tea; **die S~e Kunst** *(Buchdruckerkunst)* (the art of) printing; *(Magie)* the Black Art; ~**e Liste** blacklist; **jdn auf die** ~**e Liste setzen** to blacklist sb, to put sb on the blacklist; ~**es Loch** black hole; **das S~e Meer** the Black Sea; **S~er Peter** *(Cards) children's card game*; **jdm den S~en Peter zuschieben** *(fig: die Verantwortung abschieben)* to pass the buck to sb *(col)*; **ein** ~**er Tag** a black day; **etw** ~ **auf weiß haben** to have sth in black and white; ~ **wie die Nacht/wie Ebenholz** jet-black; **in den** ~**en Zahlen** in the black; **sich** ~ **ärgern** to get extremely annoyed; **er wurde** ~ **vor Ärger** his face went black with fury; **mir wurde** ~ **vor den Augen** I blacked out; **da kannst du schreien, bis du** ~ **wirst** *(col)* you can shout until you're blue in the face *(col)*; **ins S~e treffen** *(lit, fig)* to score a bull's-eye.

**(b)** *(col: ungesetzlich)* illicit. **der** ~**e Markt** the black market; **sich** *(dat)* **etw** ~ **besorgen** to get sth illicitly/on the black market; ~ **über die Grenze gehen** to cross the border illegally.

**(c)** *(col: katholisch)* Catholic, Papist *(pej)*; *(Pol col: konservativ)* Christian Democrat; *(in Österreich)*

Austrian People's Party. **dort wählen alle** ~ they're all conservative voters there.

**Schwarz-:** ~**afrika** nt Black Africa; ~**arbeit** f illicit work; (nach Feierabend) moonlighting (col); **s**~**arbeiten** vi sep to do illicit work; to moonlight (col); ~**arbeiter** m person doing illicit work; moonlighter (col); **s**~**braun** adj dark brown; ~**brenner** m illicit distiller, moonshine distiller (col); ~**brennerei** f illicit still, moonshine still (col); ~**brot** nt (braun) brown rye bread; (Pumpernickel) black bread, pumpernickel; ~**drossel** f blackbird.

**Schwarze** f (wk) -n, -n (Negerin) black woman; (Schwarzhaarige) brunette.

**Schwärze** f no pl (Dunkelheit) blackness.

**schwärzen** vtr to blacken.

**Schwarze(r)** m decl as adj (Neger) black; (Schwarzhaariger) dark man/boy; (col: Katholik) Catholic, Papist (pej). **die** ~**n** (Pol col) the Christian Democrats; (in Österreich) the Austrian People's Party.

**Schwarz-:** **s**~**fahren** vi sep irreg aux sein (ohne zu zahlen) to travel without paying, to dodge paying the fare (col); ~**fahrer** m fare-dodger (col); ~**geld** nt illegal earnings; **s**~**haarig** adj black-haired; **eine** ~**haarige** a brunette; ~**handel** m no pl black market; (Tätigkeit) black-marketeering; **im** ~**handel** on the black market; ~**händler** m black marketeer; **s**~**hören** vi sep (Rad) to use a radio without having a licence (Brit) or license (US); ~**hörer** m (Rad) radio owner without a licence (Brit) or license (US); **s**~**malen** sep **1** vi to be pessimistic; **2** vt to be pessimistic about; ~**maler** m pessimist; ~**malerei** f pessimism; ~**markt** m black market; ~**marktpreis** m black-market price; **s**~**sehen** sep irreg **1** vt to be pessimistic about; **2** vi **(a)** to be pessimistic; **für jdn/etw s**~**sehen** to be pessimistic about sb/sth; **(b)** (TV) to watch TV without a licence (Brit) or license (US); ~**seher** m **(a)** pessimist; **(b)** (TV) (TV) licence-dodger (Brit) or license-dodger (US) (col); ~**seherei** f pessimism; ~**sender** m pirate (radio) station; ~**wald** m Black Forest; ~**wälder** adj attr Black Forest; ~**wälder Kirschtorte** Black Forest gateau.

**schwarzweiß** adj black and white.

**Schwarzweiß-:** ~**aufnahme** f black and white (shot); ~**fernseher** m black and white or monochrome television (set); ~**film** m black and white film; ~**foto** nt black and white (photo); **s**~**malen** vt sep (fig) to depict in black and white (terms).

**Schwarz-:** ~**wild** nt wild boars pl; ~**wurzel** f (Cook) salsify.

**Schwatz** m -e (col) chat, chinwag (col). **auf einen** ~ **kommen** to come for a chat.

**schwatzen, schwätzen** vti to talk; (pej) (unaufhörlich) to chatter; (über belanglose Dinge) to prattle; (Unsinn reden) to blather (col); (klatschen) to gossip. **dummes Zeug** ~ to talk a lot of rubbish (col).

**Schwätzer(in** f) m - (pej) chatterer; (Kind, Schüler) chatterbox; (Schwafler) windbag (col); (Klatschmaul) gossip.

**Schwätzerei** f (pej) (Gerede, im Unterricht) talk, chatter; (über Belanglosigkeiten, kindisch) prattle; (Unsinn) drivel (col); (Klatsch) gossip.

**schwatzhaft** adj talkative, garrulous; (klatschsüchtig) gossipy.

**Schwebe** f no pl **in der** ~ **sein** (fig) to be in the balance; (Jur, Comm) to be pending.

**Schwebe-:** ~**bahn** f suspension railway (Brit) or railroad (US); ~**balken** m (Sport) beam.

**schweben** vi **(a)** to hang; (in der Luft auch) to float; (Vogel etc) to hover. **ihr war, als ob sie schwebte** she felt as if she was floating on air; **etw schwebt jdm**

**vor Augen** (fig) sb has sth in mind; (Bild) sb sees sth in his/her mind's eye. **(b)** aux sein (durch die Luft gleiten) to float, to sail; (sich leichtfüßig bewegen) to glide, to float. **(c)** (schwanken) to hover, to waver; (Angelegenheit) to hang or be in the balance. ~**des Verfahren** (Jur) pending case.

**Schwebezustand** m (fig) state of suspense; (zwischen zwei Stadien) in-between state.

**Schwede** m (wk) -n, -n, **Schwedin** f Swede.

**Schweden** nt Sweden.

**schwedisch** adj Swedish. **hinter** ~**en Gardinen** (col) behind bars.

**Schwedisch(e)** nt Swedish; siehe **Deutsch(e)**.

**Schwefel** m no pl sulphur (Brit), sulfur (US).

**Schwefel-** in cpds sulphur (Brit), sulfur (US); **s**~**haltig** adj containing sulphur (Brit) or sulfur (US).

**schwef(e)lig** adj sulphurous (Brit), sulfurous (US).

**Schwefelsäure** f sulphuric (Brit) or sulfuric (US) acid.

**Schweif** m -e (auch Astron) tail.

**schweifen** vi aux sein (lit geh, fig) to roam. **warum in die Ferne** ~? why roam so far afield?

**Schweige-:** ~**geld** nt hush-money; ~**marsch** m silent march (of protest); ~**minute** f one minute('s) silence.

**schweigen** pret **schwieg**, ptp **geschwiegen** vi to be silent; (still sein auch) to keep quiet. ~ **Sie!** be silent or quiet!; **kannst du** ~? can you keep a secret?; **seit gestern** ~ **die Waffen** yesterday the guns fell silent; **plötzlich schwieg er** suddenly he fell or went silent; **zu etw** ~ to make no reply to sth; **ganz zu** ~ **von** ... to say nothing of ...

**Schweigen** nt no pl silence. **jdn zum** ~ **bringen** to silence sb (auch euph); **(es herrschte)** ~ **im Walde** (there was) dead silence.

**schweigend** adj silent. **die** ~**e Mehrheit** the silent majority; ~ **über etw** (acc) **hinweggehen** to pass over sth in silence.

**Schweigepflicht** f pledge of secrecy; (von Anwalt) requirement of confidentiality. **die ärztliche** ~ medical confidentiality or secrecy; **unter** ~ **stehen** to be bound to observe confidentiality.

**schweigsam** adj silent; (als Charaktereigenschaft) reticent; (verschwiegen) discreet.

**Schweigsamkeit** f siehe adj silence; reticence; discretion.

**Schwein** nt -e **(a)** pig, hog (US). **sich wie die** ~**e benehmen** (col) to behave like pigs (col). **(b)** (col: Mensch) pig (col); (gemein) swine (col), bastard (col!). **ein armes/faules** ~ a poor/lazy sod (col); **kein** ~ nobody, not one single person. **(c)** no pl (col: Glück) ~ **haben** to be lucky.

**Schweinchen** nt dim of **Schwein** little pig; (fig col: Schmutzfink) mucky pup (col).

**Schweine-:** ~**bauch** m (Cook) belly of pork; ~**braten** m (roh) joint of pork; (gebraten) roast pork; ~**filet** nt fillet of pork; ~**fleisch** nt pork; ~**geld** nt (col) **ein** ~**geld** a packet (col); ~**hund** m (pej col) bastard (col!), swine (col); **den inneren** ~**hund überwinden** (col) to conquer one's weaker self; ~**kotelett** nt pork chop; ~**lende** f loin of pork.

**Schweinerei** f (col) **(a)** no pl mess. **es ist eine** ~, **wenn** ... it's disgusting if ...; **so eine** ~! how disgusting! **(b)** (Gemeinheit) dirty or mean trick (col); (Zote) smutty or dirty joke; (unzüchtige Handlung) indecent act. ~**en machen** to do dirty or filthy things; **das Buch besteht nur aus** ~**en** the book is just a lot of dirt or filth.

**Schweine-:** ~**schmalz** nt dripping; (als Kochfett) lard; ~**schnitzel** nt pork cutlet; ~**stall** m (lit, fig)

pigsty, pig pen *(esp US)*.
**Schwein|igel** *m (col)* dirty pig *(col)*.
**schweinisch** *adj (col) Benehmen* piggish *(col)*, swinish *(col)*; *Witz* dirty.
**Schweinkram** *m (col)* dirt, filth.
**Schweins-**: ~**galopp** *m: im* ~**galopp davonlaufen** *(hum col)* to go galumphing off *(col)*; ~**haxe** *f (Cook)* knuckle of pork; ~**leder** *nt* pigskin; **s**~**ledern** *adj* pigskin; ~**ohr** *nt* pig's ear; *(Gebäck)* (kidney-shaped) pastry.
**Schweiß** *m no pl* sweat; *(von Mensch auch)* perspiration. **in** ~ **geraten** *or* **kommen** to break into a sweat; **der** ~ **brach ihm aus** he broke out in a sweat; **das hat viel** ~ **gekostet** it was a sweat *(col)*; **im** ~**e seines Angesichts** *(Bibl, liter)* in the sweat of his brow *(Bibl, liter)*.
**Schweiß-**: ~**ausbruch** *m* sweating *no indef art, no pl*; ~**band** *nt* sweatband; **s**~**bedeckt** *adj* covered in sweat; ~**brenner** *m (Tech)* welding torch; ~**drüse** *f (Anat)* sweat gland.
**schweißen** *vti (Tech)* to weld.
**Schweißer(in** *f)* *m - (Tech)* welder.
**Schweiß-**: ~**fuß** *m* sweaty foot; **s**~**gebadet** *adj* bathed in sweat; ~**naht** *f (Tech)* weld, welded joint; **s**~**naß** *adj* sweaty; ~**perle** *f* bead of perspiration *or* sweat; ~**stelle** *f* weld; **s**~**triefend** *adj* dripping with perspiration *or* sweat; ~**tropfen** *m* drop of sweat *or* perspiration; **s**~**überströmt** *adj* streaming with sweat.
**Schweiz** *f die* ~ Switzerland.
**Schweizer** *adj attr* Swiss. ~ **Käse** Swiss cheese.
**Schweizer(in** *f)* *m* - Swiss.
**Schweizer-**: ~**deutsch** *nt* Swiss German; ~**garde** *f* Swiss Guard.
**schweizerisch** *adj* Swiss.
**Schwelbrand** *m* smouldering *(Brit) or* smoldering *(US)* fire.
**schwelen** *vi* to smoulder *(Brit)*, to smolder *(US)*.
**schwelgen** *vi* to indulge oneself *(in +dat in)*. **wir schwelgten in Kaviar und Sekt** we feasted on caviar and champagne; **in Farben/Worten** ~ to revel in colour/in the sound of words; **in Gefühlen** ~ to revel in one's emotions; **in Erinnerungen** ~ to indulge in reminiscences.
**Schwelle** *f* -**n** *(Tür*~, *fig, Psych)* threshold. **an der** ~ **einer neuen Zeit** on the threshold of a new era; **an der** ~ **des Todes** at death's door.
**schwellen 1** *vi pret* **schwoll**, *ptp* **geschwollen** *aux sein* to swell. **der Wind schwoll zum Sturm** the wind grew into a storm; *siehe* **geschwollen**. **2** *vt (geh) Segel, Brust* to swell.
**Schwellen-**: ~**angst** *f (Psych)* fear of entering a place; *(fig)* fear of embarking on something new; ~**land** *nt* fast-developing nation.
**Schwellung** *f* swelling.
**Schwemme** *f* -**n** (a) *(für Tiere)* watering place. (b) *(Überfluß)* glut *(an +dat of)*.
**schwemmen** *vt (treiben) Sand etc* to wash.
**Schwengel** *m* - *(Glocken*~*)* clapper; *(Pumpen*~*)* handle.
**Schwenk** *m* -**s** *(Drehung)* wheel; *(Film)* pan, panning shot; *(fig)* about-turn. **einen** ~ **machen** *(Kolonne)* to swing *or* wheel around.
**Schwenk-**: ~**arm** *m* swivel arm; **s**~**bar** *adj* swivelling; *Geschütz* traversable.
**schwenken 1** *vt (schwingen)* to wave; *Lampe etc* to swivel; *Kran, Geschütz* to swing; *Kamera* to pan; *Kartoffeln* to toss; *Tanzpartnerin* to swing around, to spin (around). **2** *vi aux sein* to swing; *(Kolonne)* to wheel; *(Kamera)* to pan; *(fig)* to swing over, to switch. **links schwenkt!** *(Mil)* left wheel!

**Schwenker** *m* - *(Kognak*~*)* balloon glass.
**Schwenkung** *f* swing; *(Mil)* wheel; *(von Geschütz)* traverse; *(von Kamera)* pan(ning).
**schwer 1** *adj* **(a)** *(lit, fig)* heavy. **ein 10 kg** ~**er Sack** a sack weighing 10 kgs *or* 10kgs in weight; **wie** ~ **ist er?** how much does he weigh?; ~ **beladen/ bewaffnet sein** to be heavily laden/armed.
   **(b)** *(ernst) Sorge, Unrecht, Unfall, Verlust, Krankheit* serious, grave; *Fehler, Enttäuschung auch* big; *Strafe* severe. ~ **erkältet sein** to have a heavy cold; ~ **geprüft sein** to be sorely tried; ~ **verletzt/krank sein** to be seriously wounded/ill; ~ **verunglücken** to have a serious accident; ~ **betroffen sein** to be hard hit.
   **(c)** *(hart, anstrengend) Arbeit, Tag, Schicksal* hard; *Frage, Entscheidung auch* difficult, tough. **es** ~ **haben** to have a hard time (of it); ~ **schuften müssen** to have to work hard; **er lernt** ~ he's a slow learner; ~ **hören** to be hard of hearing; ~ **zu sehen/ sagen** hard *or* difficult to see/say; **sich** ~ **entschließen können** to find it hard *or* difficult to decide.
   **(d)** *(col)* ~**es Geld machen** to make a packet *(col)*; **ein** ~**er Junge** a (big-time) crook.
   **2** *adv (col: sehr)* really; *gekränkt, verletzt* deeply. **da mußte ich** ~ **aufpassen** I really had to watch out; ~ **betrunken** rolling drunk *(col)*; ~ **verdienen** to earn a packet *(col)*; ~ **im Irrtum sein** to be badly *or* seriously mistaken; **er ist** ~ **in Ordnung** he's a good sort *(col) or* regular guy *(US col)*.
**Schwer-**: ~**arbeit** *f* heavy labour *(Brit) or* labor *(US)*; ~**arbeiter** *m* labourer *(Brit)*, laborer *(US)*; ~**athlet** *m* weightlifter; boxer; wrestler; ~**athletik** *f* weightlifting sports, boxing, wrestling etc; **s**~**behindert** *adj* severely handicapped; ~**behinderte(r)** *mf* severely handicapped person; **s**~**beladen** *adj attr* heavily-laden; **s**~**bepackt** *adj attr* heavily-loaded *or* -laden; **s**~**beschädigt** *adj (dated)* = **s**~**behindert**; ~**beschädigte(r)** *mf (dated)* = **s**~**behinderte(r)**; **s**~**bewaffnet** *adj attr* heavily armed.
**Schwere** *f no pl siehe adj* **(a)** heaviness. **(b)** seriousness, gravity; severity. **(c)** hardness; difficulty.
**Schwere-**: **s**~**los** *adj* weightless; ~**losigkeit** *f* weightlessness.
**schwer|erziehbar** *adj attr* maladjusted.
**schwerfallen** *vi sep irreg aux sein* to be difficult *or* hard *(jdm* for sb*)*.
**schwerfällig** *adj Gang* clumsy, awkward; *Verstand* slow; *Stil* ponderous.
**Schwerfälligkeit** *f siehe adj* clumsiness, awkwardness; slowness; ponderousness.
**Schwer-**: ~**gewicht** *nt* **(a)** *(Sport, fig)* heavyweight; **(b)** *(Nachdruck)* emphasis; **das** ~**gewicht auf etw** *(acc)* **legen** to put the emphasis on sth; **s**~**-gewichtig** *adj* heavyweight; ~**gewichtler(in** *f)* *m* - *(Sport)* heavyweight; **s**~**hörig** *adj* hard of hearing; ~**hörigkeit** *f* hardness of hearing; ~**industrie** *f* heavy industry; ~**kraft** *f* gravity; **s**~**krank** *adj attr* seriously *or* critically ill; ~**kranke(r)** *mf* seriously *or* critically ill patient; **s**~**lich** *adv* hardly, scarcely; **s**~**machen** *vt sep* **es jdm/jdm das Leben s**~**machen** to make it/life difficult for sb; ~**metall** *nt* heavy metal; ~**mut** *f no pl* melancholy; **s**~**mütig** *adj* melancholy; **s**~**nehmen** *vt sep irreg* **etw s**~**nehmen** to take sth hard; ~**öl** *nt* heavy oil.
**Schwerpunkt** *m (Phys)* centre *(Brit) or* center *(US)* of gravity; *(fig) (Zentrum)* centre *(Brit)*, center *(US)*, main focus; *(Hauptgewicht)* main emphasis. **den** ~ **auf etw** *(acc)* **legen** to put the main emphasis *or* stress on sth.
**Schwerpunkt-**: ~**streik** *m* pinpoint strike;

~**verlagerung** f shift of emphasis.
**schwerreich** adj attr (col) stinking rich (col).
**Schwert** nt -er sword. **das ~ ziehen** to draw one's sword.
**Schwert-**: ~**fisch** m swordfish; ~**hieb** m sword stroke; ~**lilie** f (Bot) iris.
**schwertun** vr sep irreg (col) **sich** (dat) **mit jdm/etw ~** to find sb/sth heavy going.
**Schwertwal** m killer whale.
**Schwer-**: ~**verbrecher** m criminal, felon (esp Jur); **s~verdaulich** adj attr Speisen indigestible; (fig auch) difficult; **s~verdient** adj attr Geld hard-earned; **s~verletzt** adj attr seriously injured; ~**verletzte(r)** mf serious casualty; (bei Unfall etc auch) seriously injured person; **s~verständlich** adj attr difficult to understand, incomprehensible; **s~verwundet** adj attr seriously wounded; **s~wiegend** adj (fig) serious.
**Schwester** f -n sister; (Kranken~) nurse; (Stations~) sister; (Ordens~) nun, sister; (Gemeinde~) district nurse.
**Schwester-** in cpds sister; ~**firma** f sister or associate(d) company; ~**herz** nt (col) sis (col); **s~lich** adj sisterly.
**Schwestern-**: ~**heim** nt nurses' home; ~**helferin** f nursing auxiliary (Brit) or assistant (US); ~**schülerin** f student nurse.
**schwieg** pret of **schweigen**.
**Schwieger-**: ~**eltern** pl parents-in-law pl; ~**mutter** f mother-in-law; ~**sohn** m son-in-law; ~**tochter** f daughter-in-law; ~**vater** m father-in-law.
**Schwiele** f -n callus; (Vernarbung) welt.
**schwielig** adj Hände callused.
**schwierig** adj difficult; (schwer zu lernen etc auch) hard.
**Schwierigkeit** f difficulty. **in ~en geraten** to get into difficulties or trouble; **jdm ~en machen** to make difficulties or trouble for sb; **es macht mir überhaupt keine ~en** it won't be at all difficult for me; **mach keine ~en!** (col) don't be difficult, don't make any trouble; **ohne ~en** without any difficulty; ~**en haben, etw zu tun** to have difficulty in doing sth.
**Schwierigkeitsgrad** m degree of difficulty.
**Schwimm-**: ~**bad** nt swimming pool; (Hallenbad auch) swimming baths pl (Brit); ~**becken** nt (swimming) pool.
**schwimmen** pret **schwamm**, ptp **geschwommen** aux sein 1 vi (a) auch aux haben to swim. ~ **gehen** to go swimming or for a swim. (b) (auf dem Wasser treiben) to float. (c) (col: überschwemmt sein: Boden) to be swimming (col), to be awash. **in Fett** (dat) ~ to be swimming in fat; **in seinem Blut ~** to be soaked in blood; **im Geld ~** to be rolling in money (col). (d) (fig: unsicher sein) to be at sea, to flounder. **ins S~ geraten** (fig) to begin to flounder. (e) **es schwimmt mir vor den Augen** I feel dizzy. 2 vt auch aux haben (Sport) to swim.
**Schwimmer** m - (a) swimmer. (b) (Tech) float.
**Schwimmerbecken** nt swimmers' pool.
**Schwimmerin** f swimmer.
**Schwimm-**: ~**flosse** f (von Taucher) flipper; ~**fuß** m web foot; ~**halle** f swimming bath(s pl) (Brit), (indoor) swimming pool; ~**haut** f (Orn) web; ~**lehrer** m swimming instructor; ~**sport** m swimming no art; ~**stil** m stroke; (Technik) (swimming) style; ~**unterricht** m swimming lessons pl; ~**verein** m swimming club; ~**vogel** m waterfowl; ~**weste** f life jacket.
**Schwindel** m no pl (a) (Gleichgewichtsstörung) diz-

ziness. (b) (Lüge) lie; (Betrug) swindle, fraud, con (col). **das ist alles ~, was er da sagt** what he says is all a pack of lies or a big con (col).
**Schwindel|anfall** m dizzy turn, attack of dizziness.
**Schwindelei** f (col) (leichte Lüge) fib (col); (leichter Betrug) swindle.
**Schwindel-**: **s~erregend** adj (a) **in s~erregender Höhe** at a dizzy height; (b) Preise astronomical; ~**firma** f bogus firm or company; **s~frei** adj **s~frei sein** to have no fear of heights; **er ist nicht s~frei** he can't stand heights, he suffers from vertigo; ~**gefühl** nt feeling of dizziness.
**schwind(e)lig** adj dizzy. **mir ist ~** I feel dizzy.
**schwindeln** 1 vi (a) **mir schwindelt** I feel dizzy; **mir schwindelte der Kopf** my head was reeling; **in ~der Höhe** at a dizzy height. (b) (col: lügen) to fib (col), to tell fibs (col). 2 vt (col) **das ist alles geschwindelt** it's all lies. 3 vr **sich durch die Kontrollen ~** to con or wangle one's way through the checkpoints (col).
**schwinden** pret **schwand**, ptp **geschwunden** vi aux sein (abnehmen) to dwindle; (Schönheit) to fade, to wane; (Erinnerung, Angst, Zeit, Dunkelheit) to fade away; (Kräfte) to fade, to fail. **sein Mut schwand** his courage failed him; **ihm schwanden die Sinne** (liter) he grew faint.
**Schwindler(in** f) m - swindler; (Hochstapler) con-man (col); (Lügner) liar, fraud.
**schwindlig** adj = **schwind(e)lig**.
**Schwindsucht** f (dated) consumption.
**schwindsüchtig** adj (dated) consumptive.
**Schwinge** f -n (liter, Flügel) wing.
**schwingen** pret **schwang**, ptp **geschwungen** 1 vt to swing; (drohend) Schwert, Stock etc to brandish; Hut, Fahne to wave; siehe **geschwungen**. 2 vr **sich auf etw** (acc) ~ to leap or jump onto sth, to swing oneself onto sth; **sich in etw** (acc) ~ to vault into sth, to swing oneself into sth. 3 vi (a) to swing. (b) (vibrieren: Brücke, Saite) to vibrate.
**Schwinger** m - (Boxen) swing.
**Schwing-**: ~**flügel** m casement window; ~**schleifer** m (orbital) sander; ~**tor** nt up-and-over door; ~**tür** f swing door.
**Schwingung** f (Phys, fig) vibration; (von Wellen) oscillation. **etw in ~(en) versetzen** to start sth vibrating; to start sth oscillating.
**Schwips** m -e (col) **einen (kleinen) ~ haben** to be tiddly (Brit col) or (slightly) tipsy.
**schwirren** vi aux sein to whizz; (Bienen, Fliegen etc) to buzz. **Gerüchte ~ durch die Presse** the press is buzzing with rumours; **mir schwirrt der Kopf** my head is buzzing.
**Schwitzbad** nt Turkish bath; (Dampfbad) steam bath.
**Schwitze** f -n (Cook) roux.
**schwitzen** 1 vi (lit, fig) to sweat; (Fenster) to steam up. 2 vt (Cook) Mehl to brown in fat. 3 vr **sich naß ~** to get drenched in sweat.
**Schwitzkasten** m (Ringen) headlock. **jdn in den ~ nehmen** to put a headlock on sb.
**Schwof** m -e (col) hop (col), dance.
**schwofen** vi (col) to dance.
**schwoll** pret of **schwellen**.
**schwören** pret **schwor**, ptp **geschworen** vti to swear. **ich kann darauf ~, daß ...** I could swear to it that ...; **jdm/sich etw ~** to swear sth to sb/oneself; **auf jdn/etw ~** (fig) to swear by sb/sth.
**schwul** adj (col) gay, queer (col).
**schwül** adj (lit, fig) Tag, Stimmung sultry; Wetter auch close, muggy.
**Schwüle** f no pl siehe adj sultriness; closeness, mugginess.

**Schwulen-** *(col):* ~**bar** *f,* ~**lokal** *nt* gay bar.
**Schwule(r)** *mf decl as adj (col)* gay, queer *(pej col)*, fag *(US pej col)*.
**Schwulität** *f usu pl (col)* trouble *no indef art,* difficulty. **in** ~**en kommen** to get into a fix *(col)*; **jdn in** ~**en bringen** to get sb into trouble *or* hot water *(col)*.
**Schwulst** *m no pl (pej) (in der Sprache)* bombast, pompousness; *(in der Kunst)* ornateness.
**schwülstig** *adj (pej) Stil, Redeweise* bombastic, pompous.
**Schwund** *m no pl* **(a)** *(Abnahme)* decrease *(gen* in*)*, decline *(gen* in*)*, dwindling *(gen* of*)*. **(b)** *(von Material)* shrinkage. **(c)** *(Med)* atrophy.
**Schwung** *m ⁼e* **(a)** swing. **jdm/etw einen** ~ **geben** to give sb/sth a push. **(b)** *no pl (fig: Elan)* verve, zest; *(von Mensch auch)* go *(col)*; *(lit: Antrieb)* momentum. **in** ~ **kommen** *(lit: Schlitten etc)* to gather *or* gain momentum; *(fig auch)* to get going; **jdn/etw in** ~ **bringen** *(lit, fig)* to get sb/sth going; ~ **in die Sache bringen** *(col)* to liven things up; **in** ~ **sein** *(lit, fig)* to have got going; *(fig)* to be in full swing; **voller/ohne** ~ full of/lacking verve *or* zest. **(c)** *(Linienführung)* sweep. **der** ~ **ihrer Brauen** the arch of her eyebrows. **(d)** *no pl (col: Menge) (Sachen)* stack, pile *(col)*; *(Leute)* bunch *(col)*.
**Schwung-:** **s**~**haft** *adj Handel* flourishing, roaring; **sich s**~**haft entwickeln** to grow hand over fist; ~**kraft** *f* centrifugal force; **s**~**los** *adj* lacking in verve *or* zest; *Mensch auch* lacking go *(col)*; ~**rad** *nt* flywheel; **s**~**voll** *adj Linie, Bewegung* sweeping; *Rede, Aufführung* lively.
**Schwur** *m ⁼e (Eid)* oath; *(Gelübde)* vow.
**Schwurgericht** *nt court with a jury.* **vor das** ~ **kommen** to be tried by jury.
**SDR** [ɛsdeː'|ɛr] *m* = **Süddeutscher Rundfunk.**
**sechs** [zɛks] *num* six; *siehe* **vier.**
**Sechs-** ['zɛks-]: ~**eck** *nt* hexagon; **s**~**eckig** *adj* hexagonal.
**Sechserpackung** *f* six-pack.
**Sechs-** [zɛks-]: **s**~**fach 1** *adj* sixfold; **2** *adv* sixfold, six times; *siehe* **vierfach; s**~**hundert** *num* six hundred; **s**~**mal** *adv* six times; ~**tagerennen** *nt* six-day (bicycle) race; **s**~**tägig** *adj* six-day; **s**~**tausend** *num* six thousand.
**sechste(r, s)** ['zɛkstə] *adj* sixth. **einen** ~**n Sinn für etw haben** to have a sixth sense (for sth); *siehe* **vierte(r, s).**
**Sechstel** ['zɛkstl] *nt* - sixth.
**sechstens** ['zɛkstns] *adv* sixth(ly), in the sixth place.
**sechzehn** ['zɛçtseːn] *num* sixteen.
**Sechzehntel(note** *f) nt* - *(Mus)* semiquaver *(Brit)*, sixteenth note *(US)*.
**sechzig** ['zɛçtsɪç] *num* sixty; *siehe* **vierzig.**
**Sechziger(in** *f) m* - sixty-year-old.
**SED** [ɛs|eː'deː] *f (Hist)* = **Sozialistische Einheitspartei Deutschlands.**
**Sediment** *nt (Geol)* sediment.
**Sedimentgestein** *nt (Geol)* sedimentary rock.
**See¹** *f* -n ['zeːən] sea. **an der** ~ by the sea, at the seaside; **an die** ~ **fahren** to go to the sea(side); **auf hoher** ~ on the high seas; **auf** ~ at sea; **in** ~ **stechen** to put to sea.
**See²** *m* -n ['zeːən] lake; *(in Schottland)* loch.
**See-:** ~**aal** *m* **(a)** *(Zool)* conger (eel); **(b)** *(Comm)* dogfish; ~**bad** *nt (Kurort)* seaside resort; ~**bär** *m* **(a)** *(hum col)* seadog *(col)*; **(b)** *(Zool)* fur seal; ~**beben** *nt* seaquake; **s**~**fahrend** *adj attr Volk* seafaring; ~**fahrer** *m* seafarer; ~**fahrt** *f* **(a)** *(Fahrt)* (sea) voyage; *(Vergnügungs*~*)* cruise; **(b)** *(Schiffahrt)* seafaring *no art*; **s**~**fest** *adj* **s**~**fest sein**

to be a good sailor; ~**gang** *m* swell; **hoher** ~**gang** heavy seas *pl or* swell; **s**~**gestützt** *adj (Mil)* sea-based; ~**gras** *nt (Bot)* eelgrass, sea grass *or* hay; ~**hafen** *m* seaport; ~**handel** *m* maritime trade; ~**herrschaft** *f* naval *or* maritime supremacy; ~**höhe** *f* sea level; ~**hund** *m* seal; ~**hundfell** *nt* sealskin; ~**igel** *m* sea urchin; ~**jungfrau** *f (Myth)* mermaid; ~**kanal** *m* ship canal; ~**karte** *f* sea *or* nautical chart; ~**klima** *nt* maritime climate; **s**~**krank** *adj* seasick; **Paul wird leicht s**~**krank** Paul is a bad sailor; ~**krankheit** *f* seasickness; ~**lachs** *m (Cook)* pollack.
**Seele** *f* -n *(Rel, fig, Mensch)* soul; *(Herzstück, Mittelpunkt)* life and soul. **in tiefster** ~ *(geh)* in one's heart of hearts; **mit ganzer** ~ with all one's soul; **jdm aus der** ~ **sprechen** to express exactly what sb feels; **das liegt mir auf der** ~ it weighs heavily on my mind; **sich** *(dat)* **etw von der** ~ **reden** to get sth off one's chest; **sich** *(dat)* **die** ~ **aus dem Leib reden** *(col)* to talk until one is blue in the face *(col)*; **das tut mir in der** ~ **weh** I am deeply distressed; **zwei** ~**n und ein Gedanke** *(Prov)* two minds with but a single thought; **nun hat die liebe** *or* **arme** ~ **Ruh** now we should have some peace; **eine** ~ **von Mensch** an absolute dear.
**Seelen-:** ~**amt** *nt (Eccl)* requiem; ~**friede(n)** *m (geh)* peace of mind; ~**heil** *nt* salvation of one's soul; *(fig)* spiritual welfare; ~**leben** *nt* inner life; ~**ruhe** *f* calmness, coolness; **in aller** ~**ruhe** calmly; *(kaltblütig)* as cool as you please; **s**~**ruhig** *adv* calmly; *(kaltblütig)* as cool as you please, as cool as a cucumber *(col)*; ~**tröster** *m (hum: Schnaps)* pick-me-up *(col)*; **s**~**verwandt** *adj* congenial *(liter)*; **sie waren s**~**verwandt** they were kindred spirits; ~**verwandtschaft** *f* affinity; ~**wanderung** *f (Rel)* transmigration of souls, metempsychosis; ~**zustand** *m* psychological *or* mental state.
**See-:** ~**leute** *pl of* ~**mann;** ~**lilie** *f* sea lily.
**seelisch** *adj (Rel)* spiritual; *(geistig)* mental, psychological; *Belastung* emotional; *Grausamkeit* mental. ~ **bedingt sein** to have psychological causes.
**Seelöwe** *m* sea lion.
**Seelsorge** *f no pl* spiritual welfare.
**Seelsorger(in** *f) m* - pastor.
**See-:** ~**luft** *f* sea air; ~**macht** *f* sea *or* maritime power.
**Seemann** *m, pl* -**leute** sailor, seaman.
**seemännisch** *adj* nautical.
**Seemanns-:** ~**garn** *nt no pl (col)* sailor's yarn; ~**garn spinnen** to spin a yarn; ~**heim** *nt* sailors' home; ~**lied** *nt* sea shanty.
**Seemeile** *f* nautical *or* sea mile.
**Seengebiet** ['zeːən-] *nt* lakeland district.
**Seenot** *f no pl* distress. **in** ~ **geraten** to get into distress.
**Seenot-:** ~**(rettungs)dienst** *m* sea rescue service; ~**zeichen** *nt* nautical distress signal.
**See-:** ~**otter** *m* sea otter; ~**pferd(chen)** *nt* sea horse; ~**räuber** *m* pirate; ~**räuberei** *f* piracy; ~**recht** *nt* maritime law; ~**reise** *f* (sea) voyage; *(Kreuzfahrt)* cruise; ~**rose** *f* waterlily; ~**sack** *m* kitbag; ~**schaden** *m* damage at sea, average *(spec)*; ~**schiffahrt** *f* maritime *or* ocean shipping; ~**schlacht** *f* naval *or* sea battle; ~**stern** *m (Zool)* starfish; ~**streitkräfte** *pl* naval forces *pl*, navy; ~**tang** *m* seaweed; **s**~**tüchtig** *adj* seaworthy; ~**ufer** *nt* lakeside; ~**vogel** *m* sea bird; ~**volk** *nt (Nation)* seafaring nation *or* people; ~**weg** *m* sea route; **auf dem** ~**weg reisen** to go *or* travel by sea; ~**zeichen** *nt* navigational aid; ~**zunge** *f* sole.
**Segel** *nt* - sail. **mit vollen** ~**n** under full sail *or* can-

vas; *(fig)* with gusto; **die ~ streichen** *(Naut)* to strike sail; *(fig)* to give in.

**Segel-:** **~boot** *nt* sailing boat *(Brit)*, sailboat *(US)*; **s~fliegen** *vi infin only* to glide; **~fliegen** *nt* gliding; **~flieger** *m* glider pilot; **~flugzeug** *nt* glider; **~jacht** *f* (sailing) yacht, sailboat *(US)*; **~klub** *m* sailing club.

**segeln** *vti* **(a)** *aux haben or sein* to sail. **eine Strecke ~** to sail a course; **~ gehen** to go for a sail. **(b)** *aux sein (col)* **durch eine Prüfung ~** to flop in an exam *(col)*, to fail (in) an exam.

**Segeln** *nt no pl* sailing.

**Segel-:** **~ohren** *pl (hum)* floppy ears *pl (col)*; **~regatta** *f* sailing *or* yachting regatta; **~schiff** *nt* sailing ship *or* vessel; **~sport** *m* sailing *no art*; **~törn** *m* cruise *(on a yacht etc)*; **~tuch** *nt* canvas.

**Segen** *m* - **(a)** *(lit, fig)* blessing. **es ist ein ~, daß** ... it is a blessing that ...; **jdm den ~ erteilen** to give sb one's blessing *or* benediction; **meinen ~ hat er** *(col)* that's OK by me *(col)*, *(iro)* good luck to him. **(b)** *(col)* **der ganze ~** the whole lot.

**segensreich** *adj* beneficial; *Tätigkeit* beneficent.

**Segler** *m* - **(a)** *(Segelsportler)* yachtsman, sailor. **(b)** *(Schiff)* sailing vessel. **(c)** *(Orn)* swift.

**Seglerin** *f* yachtswoman.

**Segment** *nt* segment.

**segnen** *vt (Rel)* to bless; *siehe* **gesegnet**.

**Segnung** *f (Rel)* blessing, benediction.

**sehbehindert** *adj* partially sighted.

**sehen** *pret* **sah**, *ptp* **gesehen** **1** *vt* **(a)** to see; *(an~ auch)* to look at; *Fernsehsendung auch* to watch. **sieht man das?** does it show?; **das kann man ~** you can tell that (just by looking); **siehst du irgendwo mein Buch?** can you see my book anywhere?; **von ihm war nichts mehr zu ~** he was no longer to be seen; **darf ich das mal ~?** can I have a look at that?; **ich kann diesen Kerl nicht mehr ~** I can't stand the sight of that guy any more; **jdn kommen ~** to see sb coming; **jdn/etw zu ~ bekommen** to get to see sb/sth; **den möchte ich ~, der** ... I'd like to meet the man who ...; **da sieht man es mal wieder!** that's typical; **also, wir ~ uns morgen** right, I'll see you tomorrow; **das müssen wir erst mal ~** that remains to be seen; **das sehe ich noch nicht** *(col)* I still don't see that happening; **das wollen wir (doch) erst mal ~!** we'll see about that!

**(b)** *(beurteilen)* to see; *(deuten auch)* to look at. **wie siehst du das?** how do you see it?; **das darf man nicht so ~** that's not the way to look at it; **du siehst das nicht richtig** you've got it wrong; **das sehe ich anders** that's not how I see it; **rein menschlich gesehen** from a purely personal point of view; **so gesehen** looked at in this way; **du hast wohl keine Lust, oder wie sehe ich das?** *(col)* you don't feel like it, do you?

**(c)** **sich ~ lassen** to put in an appearance, to appear; **er läßt sich kaum noch bei uns ~** he hardly comes to see us any more; **er kann sich in der Nachbarschaft nicht mehr ~ lassen** he can't show his face in the neighbourhood any more; **kann ich mich in diesem Anzug ~ lassen?** do I look all right in this suit?; **das neue Rathaus kann sich ~ lassen** the new town hall is certainly worth a second glance.

**2** *vr* **sich betrogen/getäuscht ~** to see oneself cheated/deceived; **sich gezwungen ~, zu** ... to see *or* find oneself obliged to ...

**3** *vi* **(a)** to see. **siehe oben/unten** see above/below; **siehst du (wohl)!, siehste!** *(col)* you see!; **sieh doch!** look (here)!; **~ Sie mal!** look!; **er sieht gut/schlecht** he can/cannot see well; **laß mal ~** let me see *or* look *or* have a look, give us a look *(col)*; **na**

**siehst du** (there you are,) you see?; **wie ich sehe** ... I (can) see ...; **ich sehe schon, du willst nicht** I can see you don't want to; **da kann man mal ~** that just shows (you), that just goes to show; **mal ~, ob** ... *(col)* let's see if ...; **mal ~!** *(col)* we'll see; **sieh, daß du** ... see (that) you ... **(b)** *(herausragen)* **das Boot sah kaum aus dem Wasser** the boat hardly showed above the water. **(c)** *(zeigen, weisen)* **das Fenster sieht auf den Garten** the window looks onto the garden. **(d)** **nach jdm ~** *(jdn betreuen)* to look after sb; *(jdn besuchen)* to go/come to see sb; **nach etw ~** to look after sth. **(e)** **darauf ~, daß** ... to make sure (that) ...

**Sehen** *nt no pl* seeing; *(Sehkraft)* sight, vision. **ich kenne ihn nur vom ~** I only know him by sight.

**sehenswert** *adj* worth seeing.

**Sehenswürdigkeit** *f* sight. **die Kneipe ist wirklich eine ~!** that pub is really (a sight) worth seeing!

**Seher(in** *f*) ['ze:ɐ, -ərɪn] *m* - seer.

**seherisch** ['ze:ərɪʃ] *adj attr* prophetic.

**Seh-:** **~fehler** *m* visual *or* sight defect; **~kraft** *f* (eye)sight.

**Sehne** *f* -n **(a)** *(Anat)* tendon, sinew. **(b)** *(Bogen~)* string.

**sehnen** *vr* **sich nach jdm/etw ~** to long *or* yearn *(liter)* for sb/sth.

**Sehnen-:** **~scheidenentzündung** *f* tendovaginitis; **~zerrung** *f* pulled tendon.

**Sehnerv** *m* optic nerve.

**sehnig** *adj Mensch* sinewy, wiry; *Fleisch* stringy.

**sehnlich** *adj* ardent; *Erwartung* eager. **sein ~ster Wunsch** his fondest *or* most ardent *(liter)* wish.

**Sehnsucht** *f* ⁼e longing, yearning *(nach for)*. **~ haben** to have a longing *or* yearning; **~ nach jdm haben** to yearn for sb.

**sehnsüchtig** *adj* longing, yearning; *Wunsch etc* ardent; *Erwartung* eager.

**sehnsuchtsvoll** *adj* longing, yearning; *Blick, Brief, Schilderung* wistful.

**sehr** *adv* **(a)** *(mit adj, adv)* very. **er ist ~ dafür/dagegen** he is all for it/he is very much against it; **~ zu meiner Überraschung** very much to my surprise; **es geht ihm ~ viel besser** he is very much better; **wir haben ~ viel Zeit** we have plenty of time *or* lots of time; **wir haben nicht ~ viel Zeit** we don't have very much time.

**(b)** *(mit vb)* very much, a lot. **so ~** so much; **jdn so ~ schlagen, daß** ... to hit sb so hard that ...; **sich über etw** *(acc)* **so ~ ärgern/freuen, daß** ... to be so (very) annoyed/pleased about sth that ...; **wie ~** how much; **wie ~ er sich auch bemühte,** ... however much he tried ...; **sich** *(dat)* **etw ~ überlegen** to consider sth very carefully; **sich ~ anstrengen** to try very hard; **hat sie ~ geweint?** did she cry very much *or* a lot?; **freust du dich darauf? — ja, ~** are you looking forward to it? — yes, very much; **tut es weh? — ja, ~** does it hurt? — yes, a lot; **zu ~** too much.

**Seh-:** **~schwäche** *f* poor eyesight; **~test** *m* eye test; **~vermögen** *nt* powers of vision *pl*.

**sei** *imper sing, 1. and 3. pers sing subjunc of* **sein** *(imper)* be; *(subjunc)* am; is.

**seicht** *adj (lit, fig)* shallow.

**Seichtheit** *f (lit, fig)* shallowness.

**seid** *2. pers pl pres, imper pl of* **sein** are; *(imper)* be.

**Seide** *f* -n silk.

**Seidel** *nt* - *(Gefäß)* stein, beer mug.

**seiden** *adj attr (aus Seide)* silk, silken *(liter)*.

**Seiden-** *in cpds* silk; **~band** *nt* silk ribbon; **~gewebe** *nt* silk fabric; **~glanz** *m* silky *or* silken sheen; **~papier** *nt* tissue paper; **~raupe** *f* silkworm; ~**stoff** *m* silk cloth *or* fabric.

**seidig** *adj (wie Seide)* silky, silken.

**Seife** *f* **-n** soap.

**Seifen-**: ~**blase** *f* soap bubble; *(fig)* bubble; ~**blasen machen** to blow (soap) bubbles; ~**kistenrennen** *nt* soapbox derby; ~**lauge** *f* (soap)suds *pl*; ~**oper** *f (col)* soap (opera); ~**pulver** *nt* soap powder; ~**schale** *f* soap dish; ~**schaum** *m* lather; ~**spender** *m* soap dispenser; ~**wasser** *nt* soapy water.

**seifig** *adj* soapy.

**Seihe** *f* **-n** strainer, colander.

**seihen** *vt (Flüssigkeit abgießen von)* to strain.

**Seil** *nt* **-e** rope; *(Hoch~)* tightrope, highwire. **auf dem ~ tanzen** *(fig)* to be walking a tightrope.

**Seil-**: ~**bahn** *f* cable railway; *(Berg~ auch)* funicular; **s~hüpfen** *vi sep aux sein* to skip; ~**schaft** *f (Bergsteigen)* roped party; **s~springen** *vi sep irreg aux sein* to skip; ~**tanz** *m* tightrope *or* high-wire act; **s~tanzen** *vi sep* to walk the tightrope *or* high wire; ~**tänzer** *m* tightrope walker, high-wire performer; ~**winde** *f* winch.

**Sein** *nt no pl* being *no art*. **~ und Schein** appearance and reality; **~ oder Nichtsein** to be or not to be.

**sein¹** *pret* **war**, *ptp* **gewesen** *aux sein* **1** *vi* **(a)** to be. **wir waren** we were; **wir sind gewesen** we have been, we've been; **seien Sie nicht böse, aber ...** don't be angry but ...; **sei so nett und ...** be so kind as to ...; **das wäre gut** that would *or* that'd be a good thing; **es wäre schön gewesen** it would *or* it'd have been nice; **er ist Lehrer/ein Verwandter** he is a teacher/a relative; **was sind Sie (beruflich)?** what do you do?; **in der Küche sind noch viele** there's *or* there are still plenty in the kitchen; **wenn ich Sie wäre** if I were *or* was you; **er/sie war es nicht** it wasn't him/her; **das kann schon ~** that may well be; **das wär's!** that's all, that's it; **wie war das noch?** what was that again?; **bist du's/ist er's?** is that you/him?; **morgen bin ich in Rom** I'll *or* I will *or* I shall be in Rome tomorrow; **waren Sie mal in Rom?** have you ever been to Rome?; **wir waren essen** we went out for a meal; **wo warst du so lange?** what kept you?

**(b)** *(mit infin +zu)* **du bist nicht zu sehen** you cannot be seen; **das war ja vorauszusehen** that was to be expected; **wie ist das zu verstehen?** how is that to be understood?; **er ist nicht zu ersetzen** he cannot be replaced; **mit ihr ist ja nicht zu sprechen** you can't talk to her.

**(c) was ist?** what's the matter?, what is it?; **ist was?** what is it?; *(paßt dir was nicht)* is something the matter?; **das kann nicht ~** that can't be (true); **..., es sei denn, daß ... ...** unless ...; **wie dem auch sei** be that as it may; **wie wäre es mit ...?** how about ...?, what about ...?; **wie wäre es, wenn wir ihn besuchen würden?** what about *or* how about going to see him?; **wenn du nicht gewesen wärest ...** if it hadn't been for you ...; **er ist nicht mehr** *(euph)* he is no more *(euph liter)*; **mir ist kalt** I'm cold; **was ist Ihnen?** what's the matter with you?; **mir ist, als hätte ich ihn früher schon einmal gesehen** I have a feeling I've seen him before.

**2** *v aux* to have. **er war jahrelang krank gewesen** he had been *or* he'd been ill for years; **sie ist verschwunden** she has *or* she's disappeared; **sie ist gestern verschwunden** she disappeared yesterday; **sie sind geschlagen worden** they have been beaten.

**sein²** *poss pron (adjektivisch) (bei Männern)* his; *(bei Dingen)* its; *(bei Mädchen)* her; *(bei Tieren)* its, his/her; *(bei Ländern, Städten)* its, her; *(auf „man" bezüglich)* one's *(Brit)*, his *(US)*, your. **wenn man ~ Le-**

**ben betrachtet** when one looks at one's *or* his *(US)* life, when you look at your life; **jeder hat ~e Probleme** everybody has his *or* their *(col)* problems; **er ist gut ~e zwei Meter** *(col)* he's a good six feet six.

**seine(r, s)** *poss pron (substantivisch)* his. **der/die/das ~** *(geh)* his; **er hat das S~ getan** *(geh)* he did his bit; **jedem das S~** to each his own; **die S~n** *(geh)* his family, his people; *(auf „man" bezüglich)* one's *(Brit) or* his *(US)* family *or* people.

**seiner** *pers pron gen of* **er, es** *(geh)* **gedenke ~** remember him; **er war ~ nicht mächtig** he was not in control of himself.

**seiner-**: ~**seits** *adv (von ihm)* on his part; *(er selbst)* for his part; ~**zeit** *adv* at that time.

**seines** *poss pron siehe* **seine(r, s)**.

**seinesgleichen** *pron inv (gleichartig)* his kind *pl*; *(auf „man" bezüglich)* of one's own kind; *(pej)* the likes of him *pl*. **jdn wie ~ behandeln** to treat sb as an equal *or* on equal terms; **das sucht ~** it is unparalleled.

**seinet-**: ~**wegen** *adv* **(a)** *(wegen ihm)* because of him, on his account; *(um ihn)* about him; **(b)** *(von ihm aus)* as far as he is concerned; ~**willen** *adv:* **um ~willen** for his sake.

**seinige** *poss pron* **der/die/das ~** his.

**seinlassen** *vt sep irreg* **etw ~** *(aufhören)* to stop sth/doing sth; *(nicht tun)* to drop sth, to leave sth; **laß es sein!** stop that!

**seins** *poss pron* his.

**Seismograph** *m* seismograph.

**seit 1** *prep +dat (Zeitpunkt)* since; *(Zeitdauer)* for. **~ wann?** since when?; **~ Jahren** for years; **ich habe ihn schon ~ zwei Jahren nicht mehr gesehen** I haven't seen him for two years, I last saw him two years ago; **sie ist ~ Dienstag/~ etwa einer Woche hier** she has been here since Tuesday/for about a week. **2** *conj* since.

**seitdem 1** *adv* since then. **2** *conj* since.

**Seite** *f* **-n** side; *(Buch~, Zeitungs~)* page. **die hintere/vordere ~** the back/front; **auf beiden ~n des Hauses** on both sides of the house; **~ an ~ gehen** to walk at *or* by sb's side; **an jds ~** *(dat)* **gehen** to walk at *or* by sb's side; **jdn von der ~ ansehen** to give sb a sidelong glance; **zur ~ treten** to step aside; **die ~n wechseln** *(Sport)* to change ends *or* over; *(fig)* to change sides; **die Hände in die ~n gestemmt** with arms akimbo, with one's hands on one's hips; **jdm zur ~ stehen** *(fig)* to stand by sb's side; **das Recht ist auf ihrer ~** she has right on her side; **sich jdm an die ~ stellen** *(fig)* to put *or* set oneself beside sb; **jdn zur ~ nehmen** to take sb aside *or* on one side; **auf der einen ~ ..., auf der anderen (~) ...** on the one hand ..., on the other (hand) ...; **jds starke ~** sb's forte, sb's strong point; **jds schwache ~** sb's weakness, sb's weak spot; **sich von seiner besten ~ zeigen** to show oneself at one's best; **von dieser ~ kenne ich ihn gar nicht** I didn't know that side of him; **einer Sache** *(dat)* **die beste ~ abgewinnen** to make the best *or* most of sth; **von allen ~n** *(lit, fig)* from all sides; **nach allen ~n auseinandergehen** to scatter in all directions; **das habe ich von einer anderen ~ erfahren** *(fig)* I heard it from another source; **von meiner ~ aus** *(fig)* on my part.

**seiten** *prep +gen* **auf/von ~ of** on the part of.

**Seiten-** *in cpds* side; *(esp Tech, Sci etc)* lateral; ~**angabe** *f* page reference; ~**ansicht** *f* side view; *(Tech)* side elevation; ~**blick** *m* sidelong glance; **mit einem ~blick auf** *(+acc)* *(fig)* with one eye on; ~**einsteiger** *m (fig) non-specialist who has moved sideways into a responsible position*; ~**fläche** *f (Tech)* lateral face *or* surface; ~**hieb** *m (Fechten)* side cut; *(fig)* sideswipe; ~**lage** *f* side position; **in** ~**lage schlafen** to sleep on one's side; **s**~**lang** *adj* several pages long, going on for pages; ~**linie** *f (Tennis)* sideline; *(Ftbl etc)* touchline; ~**ruder** *nt (Aviat)* rudder.

**seitens** *prep +gen (form)* on the part of.

**Seiten-:** ~**scheitel** *m* side parting *(Brit)*, side part *(US)*; ~**schiff** *nt (Archit)* (side) aisle; ~**sprung** *m (fig)* infidelity; **einen** ~**sprung machen** to have an affair; ~**stechen** *nt* stitch; ~**stechen haben** to have a stitch; ~**stiche** *pl* = ~**stechen**; ~**straße** *f* side street, side road; ~**streifen** *m* verge, berm *(US)*; *(der Autobahn)* hard shoulder, emergency lane *(US)*; „~**streifen nicht befahrbar"** ''soft verges'' *(Brit)*, ''soft shoulder''; ~**tür** *f* side door; **s**~**verkehrt** *adj* the wrong way round; ~**wagen** *m* sidecar; ~**wechsel** *m (Sport)* changeover; ~**weg** *m* side road, byway; ~**wind** *m* crosswind; ~**zahl** *f* page number.

**seither** [zait'heːɐ] *adv* since then.

**seitlich 1** *adj* lateral *(esp Sci, Tech)*, side *attr.* **2** *adv* at the side; *(von der Seite)* from the side. ~ **von** at the side of; **die Kisten sind** ~ **grün bemalt** the sides of the boxes are painted green. **3** *prep +gen* to or at the side of.

**seitwärts** *adv* sideways.

**Sek., sek. = Sekunde** s, sec.

**Sekr. = Sekretär** sec.

**Sekret** *nt* **-e** *(Physiol)* secretion.

**Sekretär** *m* **(a)** secretary. **(b)** *(Schreibschrank)* bureau, secretaire.

**Sekretariat** *nt* office.

**Sekretärin** *f* secretary.

**Sekretion** *f (Physiol)* secretion.

**Sekt** *m* **-e** sparkling wine, ≃ champagne.

**Sekte** *f* **-n** sect.

**Sektierer(in** *f***)** *m* - sectarian.

**sektiererisch** *adj* sectarian.

**Sektion** *f* **(a)** section. **(b)** *(Obduktion)* post-mortem (examination), autopsy.

**Sektkelch** *m* champagne flute.

**Sektor** *m* sector *(auch Comp)*; *(Sachgebiet)* field.

**Sektschale** *f* champagne glass.

**Sekunda** *f, pl* **Sekunden** *(Sch dated) sixth and seventh year of German secondary school.*

**Sekundaner(in** *f***)** *m* - *(Sch dated) pupil in sixth and seventh year of German secondary school.*

**Sekundant** *m* second.

**sekundär** *adj* secondary.

**Sekundärliteratur** *f* secondary literature.

**Sekundarstufe** *f* secondary or high *(esp US)* school level.

**Sekunde** *f* **-n** *(auch Mus, Math)* second. **eine** ~, **bitte!** just a second, please; **auf die** ~ **genau** to the second.

**Sekunden-:** ~**bruchteil** *m* split second, fraction of a second; **s**~**lang 1** *adj* of a few seconds; **2** *adv* for a few seconds; ~**schnelle** *f* **in** ~**schnelle** in a matter of seconds; ~**zeiger** *m* second hand.

**sekundieren\*** *vi +dat* to second; *(unterstützen auch)* to back up.

**selber** *dem pron siehe* **selbst 1.**

**Selbermachen** *nt* do-it-yourself, DIY; *(von Kleidern etc)* making one's own. **Möbel zum** ~ do-it-yourself furniture.

**selbst 1** *dem pron* **(a) ich/er/das Haus** ~ I myself/he himself/the house itself; **du/Sie** ~ you yourself; **wir/sie/die Häuser** ~ we ourselves/they themselves/ the houses themselves; **sie ist die Tugend** ~ she's virtue itself; ~ **ist der Mann/die Frau!** self-reliance is the name of the game *(col)*; **er braut sein Bier** ~

he brews his own beer; **zu sich** ~ **kommen** to collect one's thoughts; **eine Sache um ihrer** ~ **willen tun** to do sth for its own sake; **wie geht's?** — **gut, und** ~? how are things? — fine, (and) yourself? **(b)** *(ohne Hilfe)* alone, on one's/his/your *etc* own. **das muß er** ~ **wissen** it's up to him; **das funktioniert von** ~ it works by itself *or* automatically; **er kam ganz von** ~ he came of his own accord. **2** *adv* even. ~ **Gott** even God (himself); ~ **wenn** even if.

**Selbst** *nt no pl* self.

**Selbst|achtung** *f* self-respect, self-esteem.

**selbständig** *adj* independent; *(steuerlich)* self-employed. ~ **denken** to think for oneself; ~**arbeiten/handeln** to work/act independently *or* on one's own; **sich** ~ **machen** *(beruflich)* to set up on one's own, to start one's own business; *(hum: verschwinden)* to grow legs *(hum)*.

**Selbständige(r)** *mf decl as adj* independent businessman/-woman; *(steuerlich)* self-employed person. **die** ~**n** the self-employed.

**Selbständigkeit** *f* independence; *(beruflich, steuerlich)* self-employment.

**Selbst-** *in cpds* self; ~**anzeige** *f* ~**anzeige erstatten** to come forward oneself; ~**auslöser** *m (Phot)* delayed-action shutter release, delay timer; ~**bedienung** *f* self-service; ~**bedienungsladen** *m* self-service shop *(Brit) or* store *(US)*; ~**befriedigung** *f* masturbation; *(fig)* self-gratification; ~**beherrschung** *f* self-control; *(Zurückhaltung)* self-restraint; **die** ~**beherrschung verlieren** to lose one's self-control *or* temper; ~**bekenntnis** *nt* confession; ~**bestätigung** *f* self-affirmation; **das empfand er als** ~**bestätigung** it boosted his ego; ~**bestimmung** *f* self-determination; ~**beteiligung** *f (Insur)* excess; ~**betrug** *m* self-deception.

**selbstbewußt** *adj (selbstsicher)* self-assured, self-confident.

**Selbstbewußtsein** *nt* self-assurance, self-confidence.

**Selbst-:** ~**bildnis** *nt* self-portrait; ~**darstellung** *f* self-portrayal; ~**disziplin** *f* self-discipline; ~**einschätzung** *f* self-assessment; ~**erfahrung** *f* self-awareness; ~**erfahrungsgruppe** *f* encounter group; ~**erhaltung** *f* self-preservation, survival; ~**erhaltungstrieb** *m* survival instinct; ~**erkenntnis** *f* self-knowledge; **s**~**ernannt** *adj* self-appointed; *(in bezug auf Titel)* self-styled; ~**fahrer** *m (Aut)* Autovermietung für ~**fahrer** self-drive car hire *(Brit) or* rental; **s**~**finanzierend** *adj* self-financing; **s**~**gebacken** *adj* home-baked, home-made; **s**~**gebaut** *adj* home-made, self-made; *Haus* self-built; ~**gedrehte** *f decl as adj* roll-up *(col)*; ~**gedrehte rauchen** to roll one's own; **s**~**gefällig** *adj* smug, complacent; ~**gefälligkeit** *f* smugness, complacency; **s**~**gemacht** *adj* home-made; *(Kleid etc)* self-made; **s**~**gerecht** *adj* self-righteous; ~**gerechtigkeit** *f* self-righteousness; ~**gespräch** *nt* ~**gespräche führen** to talk to oneself; **s**~**gestrickt** *adj* **(a)** *Pulli* hand-knitted; **ist das s**~**gestrickt?** did you knit it yourself?; **(b)** *(col) Methode* homespun, amateurish; **s**~**herrlich** *adj (pej)* **(a)** *(eigenwillig)* high-handed; **(b)** *(s~gerecht)* self-satisfied; ~**hilfe** *f* self-help; **zur** ~**hilfe greifen** to take matters into one's own hands; ~**hilfegruppe** *f* self-help group; ~**justiz** *f* arbitrary law; ~**justiz üben** to take the law into one's own hands; ~**klebeetikett** *nt* self-adhesive label; **s**~**klebend** *adj* self-adhesive.

**Selbstkosten** *pl (Comm)* prime costs *pl.*

**Selbstkosten-:** ~**beteiligung** *f (Insur)* excess; ~**preis** *m* cost price; **zum** ~**preis** at cost.

**Selbst-:** ~**kritik** *f* self-criticism; **s~kritisch** *adj* self-critical; ~**laut** *m* vowel; **s~los** *adj* selfless; ~**losigkeit** *f* selflessness.
**Selbstmord** *m (lit, fig)* suicide.
**Selbstmörder** *m* suicide.
**selbstmörderisch** *adj (lit, fig)* suicidal.
**Selbstmord-:** **s~gefährdet** *adj* suicidal; ~**versuch** *m* suicide attempt, attempted suicide.
**Selbst-:** **s~redend** *adv* of course, naturally; **s~reinigend** *adj* self-cleaning; **s~sicher** *adj* self-assured; ~**sicherheit** *f* self-assurance; ~**studium** *nt* private study; **etw im ~studium lernen** to learn sth by studying on one's own; ~**sucht** *f* egoism; **s~süchtig** *adj* egoistic; **s~tätig** *adj* **(a)** *(automatisch)* automatic, self-acting; **(b)** *(eigenständig)* independent; ~**test** *m* self-test; ~**tor** *nt (Sport, fig)* own goal; ~**tötung** *f* suicide; ~**überwindung** *f* willpower; **s~verdient** *adj* **s~verdientes Geld** money one has earned oneself; **s~vergessen** *adj* absent-minded; *Blick* faraway; ~**vergessenheit** *f* absent-mindedness; ~**verlag** *m* **im ~verlag erschienen** published privately (by the author); ~**verleugnung** *f* self-denial; ~**verschulden** *nt* one's own fault; **wenn ~verschulden vorliegt ...** if you yourself *etc* are at fault ...; **s~verschuldet** *adj* **wenn der Unfall s~verschuldet ist** if you are yourself to blame for the accident; ~**versorger** *m* ~**versorger sein** to be self-sufficient *or* self-reliant; **Urlaub für ~versorger** self-catering holiday.
**selbstverständlich 1** *adj Freundlichkeit* natural; *Wahrheit* self-evident. **das ist doch ~!** that goes without saying; **kann ich mitkommen? — ~** can I come too? — of course; **das ist keineswegs ~** it cannot be taken for granted; **etw für ~ halten, etw als ~ hinnehmen** to take sth for granted. **2** *adv* of course.
**Selbstverständlichkeit** *f* naturalness; *(Unbefangenheit)* casualness *no indef art*; *(von Wahrheit)* self-evidence; *(selbstverständliche Wahrheit etc)* self-evident truth *etc.* **etw für eine ~ halten** to take sth as a matter of course; **etw mit der größten ~ tun** to do sth as if it were the most natural thing in the world.
**Selbst-:** ~**verständnis** *nt* **nach seinem eigenen ~verständnis** as he sees himself; ~**versuch** *m* experiment on oneself; ~**verteidigung** *f* self-defence *(Brit)*, self-defense *(US)*; ~**vertrauen** *nt* self-confidence; ~**verwaltung** *f* self-administration; *(Regierung)* self-government; ~**wählferndienst** *m* *(Telec)* automatic dialling *(Brit)* or dial *(US)* service, subscriber trunk dialling *(Brit)*, STD *(Brit)*; ~**wertgefühl** *nt* feeling of one's own worth *or* value, self-esteem; **s~zufrieden** *adj* self-satisfied; ~**zufriedenheit** *f* self-satisfaction; ~**zweck** *m* end in itself; **als ~zweck** as an end in itself.
**selektiv** *adj* selective.
**Selen** *nt no pl* selenium.
**selig** *adj* **(a)** *(Rel)* blessed; *(old: verstorben)* late. **bis an mein ~es Ende** *(old, hum)* until the day I die. **(b)** *(überglücklich)* overjoyed; *Stunden* blissful.
**Seligkeit** *f* **(a)** *(Rel)* salvation. **(b)** *(Glück)* (supreme) happiness, bliss.
**Selig-:** **s~sprechen** *vt sep irreg (Eccl)* to beatify; ~**sprechung** *f (Eccl)* beatification.
**Sellerie** *m* -**(s)** celeriac; *(Stangen~)* celery.
**selten 1** *adj* rare. **2** *adv (nicht oft)* rarely, seldom; *(besonders)* exceptionally. **~ so gelacht!** *(col)* what a laugh! *(col)*.
**Seltenheit** *f* rarity. **das ist keine ~ bei ihr** it's nothing unusual with her.
**Seltenheitswert** *m* rarity value.

**Selters** *nt* -, - *(col)*, **Selter(s)wasser** *nt* soda (water).
**seltsam** *adj* strange; *(komisch auch)* odd.
**seltsamerweise** *adv* strangely enough.
**Seltsamkeit** *f* **(a)** *no pl* strangeness, oddness. **(b)** *(seltsame Sache)* oddity.
**Semantik** *f* semantics *sing*.
**semantisch** *adj* semantic.
**Semester** *nt* - *(Univ)* semester *(esp US)*, term *(of a half-year's duration)*. **im 7./8. ~ sein** to be in one's 4th year; **ein älteres ~** a senior student; *(hum)* **die älteren ~** the older generation.
**Semester-** *(Univ)*: ~**ferien** *pl* vacation *sing*; ~**schluß** *m* end of term, end of the semester *(US)*.
**Semi-** *in cpds* semi-; ~**finale** ['zeːmi-] *nt (Sport)* semifinal(s); ~**kolon** [zemi'koːlɔn] *nt, pl* -**s** *or* ~**kola** semicolon.
**Seminar** *nt* -**e** **(a)** *(Univ)* department; *(~übung)* seminar. **(b)** *(Priester~)* seminary. **(c)** *(Lehrer~, Studien~)* teacher training college, college of education.
**Semit(in** *f)* *m (wk)* -**en**, -**en** Semite.
**semitisch** *adj* Semitic.
**Semmel** *f* -**n** *(dial)* roll. **sie gehen weg wie warme ~n** *(col)* they're selling like hot cakes *(col)*.
**Semmel-:** ~**brösel(n)** *pl* breadcrumbs *pl*; ~**knödel** *(S Ger, Aus)* *m* bread dumpling.
**sen.** = **senior** sen.
**Senat** *m* -**e** *(Pol, Univ)* senate.
**Senator** *m*, **Senatorin** *f* senator.
**Sende-:** ~**bereich** *m* transmission range; ~**folge** *f* *(Serie)* series *sing*; *(einzelne Folge)* episode; *(Programmfolge)* programmes *pl*; ~**gebiet** *nt* area; ~**leiter** *m* producer.
**senden¹** *pret* **sandte**, *ptp* **gesandt 1** *vt* to send *(an +acc to)*. **jdm etw ~** to send sb sth, to send sth to sb. **2** *vi* **nach jdm ~** to send for sb.
**senden²** *vti (Rad, TV)* to broadcast; *Signal etc* to transmit.
**Sendepause** *f (Rad, TV)* interval.
**Sender** *m* - transmitter; *(~kanal) (Rad)* station; *(TV)* channel *(Brit)*, station *(esp US)*.
**Sende-:** ~**raum** *m* studio; ~**reihe** *f* (radio/ television) series; ~**schluß** *m (Rad, TV)* close-down; **bis zum ~schluß** until we close down; ~**turm** *m* radio tower; ~**zeichen** *nt* call sign; ~**zeit** *f* broadcasting time; **in der besten ~zeit** in prime time.
**Sendung** *f* **(a)** *no pl (das Senden)* sending. **(b)** *(Brief~)* letter; *(Päckchen)* packet; *(Paket)* parcel; *(Comm)* consignment. **(c)** *(Rad, TV)* programme *(Brit)*, program *(US)*; *(Rad auch)* broadcast; *(das Senden)* broadcasting. **auf ~ gehen/sein** to go/be on the air.
**Senegal** *nt* Senegal.
**Senegalese** *m (wk)* -**n**, -**n**, **Senegalesin** *f* Senegalese.
**senegalesisch, senegalisch** *adj* Senegalese.
**Senf** *m* -**e** mustard. **seinen ~ dazugeben** *(col)* to put one's oar in *(col)*.
**Senf-:** ~**früchte** *pl (Cook)* pickles *pl*; ~**gas** *nt (Chem)* mustard gas; ~**korn** *nt* mustard seed; ~**packung** *f (Med)* mustard poultice.
**sengen 1** *vt* to singe. **2** *vi* to scorch.
**senil** *adj (pej)* senile.
**Senilität** *f no pl (pej)* senility.
**senior** *adj* senior.
**Senior** *m* **(a)** *(auch ~chef)* boss; *(ältester Geschäftspartner)* senior partner. **kann ich mal den ~ sprechen?** can I speak to Mr X senior? **(b)** *(Sport)* senior player. **die ~en** the seniors. **(c)** ~**en** *pl* senior

citizens *pl*; *(hum)* old folk *pl*.
**Senioren-**: ~**heim** *nt* old people's home; ~**karte** *f* senior citizen's ticket; ~**mannschaft** *f* senior team; ~**paß** *m* senior citizen's travel pass.
**Senkblei** *nt* = **Senklot.**
**Senke** *f* -**n** valley.
**senken 1** *vt* to lower; *Lanze, Fahne* to dip; *Kopf* to bow; *(Tech) Schraube, Schacht* to sink. **2** *vr* to sink; *(Decke)* to sag; *(Stimme)* to drop.
**Senk-**: ~**fuß** *m (Med)* fallen arches *pl*; ~**grube** *f* cesspit; ~**lot** *nt* plumbline; *(Gewicht)* plummet.
**senkrecht** *adj* vertical; *(Math)* perpendicular.
**Senkrechte** *f decl as adj* vertical; *(Math)* perpendicular.
**Senkrechtstarter** *m (Aviat)* vertical take-off aircraft; *(fig col)* whizz kid *(col)*.
**Senkung** *f* **(a)** sinking; *(von Boden, Straße)* subsidence; *(von Wasserspiegel)* drop *(gen* in*)*; *(als Maßnahme)* lowering. **(b)** *(Vertiefung)* hollow, valley.
**Senner(in** *f) m* - (Alpine) dairyman/dairymaid.
**Sennerei** *f (Gebäude)* Alpine dairy.
**Sensation** *f* sensation.
**sensationell** [zɛnzatsio'nɛl] *adj* sensational.
**Sensations-**: ~**blatt** *nt* sensational paper; ~**lust** *f* desire for sensation; ~**nachricht** *f* scoop; ~**presse** *f* yellow press.
**Sense** *f* -**n** scythe. **dann ist** ~**!** *(col)* that's the end!
**sensibel** *adj* sensitive; *(heikel auch)* problematic, delicate.
**sensibilisieren*** *vt* to sensitize.
**Sensibilisierung** *f* sensitization.
**Sensibilität** *f* sensitivity.
**sensitiv** *adj (geh)* sensitive.
**Sensitivität** *f (geh)* sensitivity.
**Sensor** *m* sensor.
**Sensortaste** *f* touch-sensitive button.
**sentimental** *adj* sentimental.
**Sentimentalität** *f* sentimentality.
**Seoul** [se'u:l] *nt* Seoul.
**separat** *adj* separate; *Wohnung, Zimmer* self-contained.
**Separatismus** *m (Pol)* separatism.
**separatistisch** *adj (Pol)* separatist.
**Sepsis** *f, pl* **Sepsen** *(Med)* sepsis.
**Sept.** = **September** Sept.
**September** *m* - September; *siehe* **März.**
**Septime** *f* -**n** *(Mus)* seventh.
**septisch** *adj* septic.
**sequentiell** [zekven'tsiɛl] *adj (Comp)* sequential.
**Sequenz** *f* sequence.
**Serbe** *m (wk)* -**n, -n** Serbian.
**Serbien** ['zɛrbiən] *nt* Serbia.
**Serbin** *f* Serbian (woman/girl).
**serbisch** *adj* Serbian.
**Serbokroatisch(e)** *nt* Serbo-Croat; *siehe* **Deutsch(e).**
**Serenade** *f* serenade.
**Serie** ['ze:riə] *f* series *sing*. **in** ~ **gehen** to go into production; **in** ~ **hergestellt werden** to be produced in series.
**seriell** *adj Herstellung* series *attr*; *(Comp, Mus)* serial.
**Serien-** ['ze:riən-]: ~**anfertigung,** ~**herstellung** *f* series production; **s**~**mäßig 1** *adj Ausstattung* standard; *Herstellung* series *attr*; **2** *adv herstellen* in series; **das wird s**~**mäßig eingebaut** it's fitted as standard *or* a standard fitting; ~**modell** *nt (Auto)* standard *or* production model; ~**mörder** *m* serial killer; ~**nummer** *f* serial number; ~**produktion** *f* series production; **s**~**weise** *adv produzieren etc* in

series; *(col: in Mengen)* wholesale.
**seriös** *adj (anständig)* respectable; *Firma* reputable.
**Seriosität** *f siehe adj* respectability; reputableness.
**Sermon** *m* -**e** *(pej)* sermon, lecture.
**Serpentine** *f* winding road; *(Kurve)* double bend. **die Straße führt in** ~**n den Berg hinauf** the road winds *or* snakes its way up the mountain.
**Serum** *nt, pl* **Seren** serum.
**Service**[1] [zɛr'vi:s] *nt* - [zɛr'vi:sə] *(Geschirr)* dinner/coffee *etc* service; *(Gläser*~*)* set.
**Service**[2] ['sɔ:vɪs] *m or nt* -**s** *(Comm, Sport)* service.
**servieren*** [zɛr'vi:rən] *vti* to serve *(jdm etw* sb sth, sth to sb*)*.
**Serviererin** [zɛr'vi:rərɪn] *f* waitress.
**Servier-** [zɛr'vi:ɐ-]: ~**tisch** *m* serving table; ~**wagen** *m* trolley *(Brit)*, serving cart *(US)*.
**Serviette** [zɛr'viɛtə] *f* serviette.
**Servo-** ['zɛrvo-] *(Tech)*: ~**bremse** *f* servo brake; ~**lenkung** *f* power steering.
**Servus** ['zɛrvʊs] *interj (Aus, S Ger) (beim Treffen)* hello; *(beim Abschied)* goodbye, so long *(col)*.
**Sesam** *m* -**s** sesame; *(*~*samen)* sesame seeds *pl*. ~**, öffne dich!** open Sesame!
**Sessel** *m* - (easy) chair; *(Polstersessel)* armchair.
**Sessel-**: ~**lehne** *f* (chair) arm; ~**lift** *m* chairlift.
**seßhaft** *adj* settled; *(ansässig)* resident. ~ **werden** to settle down.
**Seßhaftigkeit** *f no pl* settled form of existence; *(von Lebensweise)* settledness.
**Set** *m or nt* -**s** **(a)** set. **(b)** *(Deckchen)* tablemat.
**Setter** *m* - setter.
**setzen 1** *vt* **(a)** to put, to place; *(bei Spielen) Stein, Figur* to move; *(bestimmen) Ziel, Grenze, Termin, Norm* to set. **etw auf die Rechnung** ~ to put sth on the bill; **etw an den Mund** ~ to put sth to one's mouth; **jdn an Land** ~ to put sb ashore; **jdn über den Fluß** ~ to take sb across the river; **Geld auf ein Pferd** ~ to put money on a horse; **auf seinen Kopf sind 100.000 Dollar gesetzt** there's 100,000 dollars on his head; **jdm ein Denkmal** ~ to build a monument to sb; **seinen Namen unter etw** *(acc)* ~ to put one's signature to sth; **seine Hoffnung in jdn/etw** ~ to put *or* place one's hopes in sb/sth; **dann setzt es was** *(col)* there'll be trouble; **jdm eine Spritze** ~ to give sb an injection. **(b)** *(Hort: pflanzen)* to plant.
    **2** *vr* **(a)** *(Platz nehmen)* to sit down; *(Vogel)* to alight. **sich auf einen Stuhl** ~ to sit down on a chair; **sich ins Auto** ~ to get into the car; **sich zu jdm** ~ to sit with sb. **(b)** *(Kaffee, Tee, Lösung)* to settle.
    **3** *vi* **(a)** *(bei Glücksspiel, Wetten)* to bet. **auf ein Pferd** ~ to bet on a horse; **auf jdn/etw** ~ *(lit, fig)* to back sb/sth. **(b)** *(Typ)* to set. **(c)** *(springen) (Pferd, Läufer)* to jump. **über einen Fluß** ~ to cross a river.
**Setzer(in** *f) m* - *(Typ)* typesetter.
**Setzerei** *f (Typ)* composing room; *(company)* typesetting firm.
**Setz-**: ~**kasten** *m* **(a)** *(Typ)* case; *(an Wand)* ornament shelf; **(b)** *(Hort)* seed box; ~**ling** *m (Hort)* seedling; ~**maschine** *f (Typ)* typesetting machine, typesetter.
**Seuche** *f* -**n** epidemic; *(fig pej)* scourge.
**Seuchen-**: **s**~**artig** *adj* epidemic; **sich s**~**artig ausbreiten** to reach epidemic proportions, to spread like the plague; ~**bekämpfung** *f* epidemic control; ~**gebiet** *nt* epidemic area; ~**gefahr** *f* danger of an epidemic.
**seufzen** *vti* to sigh.
**Seufzer** *m* - sigh.
**Sex** *m no pl* sex.
**Sex-**: ~**-Appeal** [-ə'pi:l] *m no pl* sex appeal;

~**bombe** *f (col)* sex bomb *(col)*; ~**film** *m* sex film; ~**foto** *nt* sexy photo.

**Sexismus** *m* sexism.

**sexistisch** *adj* sexist.

**Sexta** *f, pl* **Sexten** *(Sch dated)* first year in a German secondary school.

**Sextaner(in** *f)* *m* - *(Sch dated)* pupil in the first year of a German secondary school.

**Sextant** *m (Naut)* sextant.

**Sexte** *f* -**n** *(Mus)* sixth.

**Sextett** *nt* -**e** *(Mus)* sextet.

**Sexual|erziehung** *f* sex education.

**Sexualität** *f no pl* sexuality.

**Sexual-:** ~**kunde** *f (Sch)* sex education; ~**leben** *nt* sex life; ~**mörder** *m* sex murderer; ~**objekt** *nt* sex object; ~**täter** *m* sex offender; ~**trieb** *m* sex(ual) drive; ~**verbrechen** *nt* sex crime; ~**verbrecher** *m* sex offender; ~**wissenschaft** *f* sexology.

**sexuell** *adj* sexual.

**sexy** ['zɛksi] *adj pred (col)* sexy *(col)*.

**Seychellen** [zɛ'ʃɛlən] *pl (Geog)* Seychelles *pl.*

**sezieren\*** *vti (lit, fig)* to dissect.

**SFB** [ɛs|ɛf'beː] *m* = **Sender Freies Berlin.**

**Sfr, sFr** = **Schweizer Franken** sfr.

**Shampoo(n)** [ʃam'puː(n)] *nt* -**s** shampoo.

**Shorts** [ʃɔrts] *pl* (pair of) shorts.

**Show** [ʃoː] *f* -**s** show. **eine** ~ **abziehen** *(col)* to put on a show *(col).*

**Show-:** ~**geschäft** *nt* show business; ~**master** ['ʃoumaːstə] *m* - compère, emcee *(US).*

**Siam** [ziːam] *nt (old)* Siam.

**Siamese** *m (wk)* -**n**, -**n**, **Siamesin** *f* Siamese.

**siamesisch** *adj* ~**e Zwillinge** Siamese twins.

**Siamkatze** *f* Siamese (cat).

**Sibirien** [zi'biːriən] *nt* Siberia.

**Sibirier(in** *f)* *m* - Siberian.

**sibirisch** *adj* Siberian. ~**e Kälte** Siberian *or* Arctic conditions *pl.*

**sich** *refl pron* **(a)** *(acc)* *(+infin, bei „man")* oneself; *(3. pers sing)* himself; herself; itself; *(2. pers Höflichkeitsform)* yourself; yourselves; *(3. pers pl)* themselves. ~ **wiederholen** to repeat oneself/itself. **(b)** *(dat)* *(+infin, bei „man")* to oneself; *(3. pers sing)* to himself; to herself; to itself; *(2. pers Höflichkeitsform)* to yourself/yourselves; *(3. pers pl)* to themselves. ~ **die Haare waschen** to wash one's hair; **sie hat** ~ **einen Pullover gekauft** she bought herself a pullover. **(c)** *acc, dat (mit prep)* *(+infin, bei „man")* one; *(3. pers sing)* him; her; it; *(2. pers Höflichkeitsform)* you; *(3. pers pl)* them. **haben Sie Ihren Ausweis bei** ~**?** do you have your pass on you? **(d)** *(einander)* each other, one another. **(e)** *(impers)* **hier sitzt es** ~ **gut** it's good to sit here; **dieses Auto fährt** ~ **gut** this car is pleasant to drive.

**Sichel** *f* -**n** sickle; *(Mond~)* crescent.

**sicher 1** *adj* **(a)** *(gewiß)* certain, sure. **der** ~**e Tod** certain death; **(sich** *dat)* **einer Sache/jds** ~ **sein** to be sure of sth/sb; **soviel ist** ~ that much is certain. **(b)** *(geschützt)* safe; *(geborgen)* secure. **vor jdm/etw** ~ **sein** to be safe from sb/sth; ~ **leben** to lead a secure life; ~ **ist** ~ you can't be too sure. **(c)** *(zuverlässig)* reliable; *(fest)* Gefühl, Zusage definite; Hand, Job steady; Stellung secure. **(d)** *(selbstbewußt)* confident. ~ **wirken/auftreten** to give an impression of confidence. **2** *adv* **(a)** *fahren etc* safely. **(b)** *(natürlich)* of course. **du hast dich** ~ **verrechnet** you must have counted wrongly; **das weiß ich ganz** ~ I know that for certain; **aber er kommt** ~ **noch** I'm sure he'll come.

**sichergehen** *vi sep irreg aux sein* to be sure.

**Sicherheit** *f* **(a)** *no pl (Gewißheit)* certainty. **das ist mit** ~ **richtig** that is definitely right. **(b)** *no pl (Schutz, das Sichersein)* safety; *(als Aufgabe von Sicherheitsbeamten etc)* security. ~ **und Ordnung** law and order; **die öffentliche** ~ public security; **jdn/etw in** ~ **bringen** to get sb/sth to safety; ~ **im Straßenverkehr** road safety; **zu Ihrer eigenen** ~ for your own safety; **in** ~ **sein** to be safe. **(c)** *no pl (Zuverlässigkeit)* reliability; *(von Hand, Einkommen)* steadiness; *(von Stellung)* security. **(d)** *no pl (Selbstbewußtsein)* (self-)confidence. **(e)** *(Comm)* security; *(Pfand)* surety. ~ **leisten** *(Comm)* to offer security.

**Sicherheits-:** ~**abstand** *m* safe distance; ~**beamte(r)** *m* security officer; ~**bestimmungen** *pl* safety regulations *pl*; *(betrieblich, Pol etc)* security controls *pl*; ~**garantie** *f* safety guarantee; ~**glas** *nt* safety glass; ~**gurt** *m* seat belt; **s~halber** *adv* to be on the safe side; ~**kontrolle** *f* security check; ~**kräfte** *pl* security forces *pl*; ~**maßnahme** *f* safety precaution; *(betrieblich, Pol etc)* security measure; ~**nadel** *f* safety pin; ~**rat** *m* Security Council; ~**risiko** *nt* security risk; ~**schloß** *nt* safety lock; ~**truppen** *pl* security troops *pl*; ~**verschluß** *m* safety catch; ~**vorkehrung** *f* safety precaution; *(betrieblich, Pol etc)* security precaution; ~**vorschrift** *f* safety regulation.

**sicherlich** *adv (natürlich)* of course; *(bestimmt)* certainly.

**sichern 1** *vt* **(a)** *(gegen, vor +dat* against*)* to safeguard; *(absichern)* to protect; *(sicher machen)* Tür, Fahrrad etc to secure; Bergsteiger etc to belay; Waffe to put the safety catch on; *(Comp)* Daten to back up. **(b)** **jdm/sich etw** ~ to secure sth for sb/oneself. **2** *vr* to protect oneself *(vor +dat, gegen* against*).*

**sicherstellen** *vt sep* **(a)** Waffen, Heroin to take possession of. **(b)** *(garantieren)* to guarantee.

**Sicherung** *f* **(a)** *siehe vt (a)* safeguarding; protection; securing; belaying. **(b)** *(Schutz)* safeguard. **(c)** *(Elec)* fuse; *(von Waffe)* safety catch. **da ist (bei) ihm die** ~ **durchgebrannt** *(fig col)* he blew a fuse *(col).* **(d)** *(Comp)* back-up.

**Sicherungs-:** *(Comp)* ~**datei** *f* back-up file; ~**diskette** *f* back-up disk; ~**kopie** *f* back-up copy.

**Sicht** *f no pl* **(a)** *(Sehweite)* visibility. **die** ~ **betrug nur wenige Meter** visibility was only a few yards; **in** ~ **sein/kommen** to be in/come into sight; **auf lange/kurze** ~ *(fig)* in the long/short term; **planen for the long/short term. (b)** *(Ausblick, Gesichtspunkt)* view. **aus meiner/seiner** ~ from my/his point of view. **(c)** *(Comm)* **auf** *or* **bei** ~ at sight.

**sichtbar** *adj (lit, fig)* visible. ~ **werden** *(fig)* to become apparent.

**Sichtbeton** *m* exposed concrete.

**sichten** *vt* **(a)** *(durchsehen)* to look through; *(ordnen)* to sift through. **(b)** *(erblicken)* to sight.

**Sicht-:** ~**gerät** *(dat)* monitor; *(Comp auch)* VDU, visual display unit; ~**grenze** *f* visibility limit; ~**kontakt** *m* eye contact.

**sichtlich 1** *adj* obvious. **2** *adv* obviously, visibly.

**Sicht-:** ~**verhältnisse** *pl* visibility *sing*; ~**vermerk** *m* *(im Paß)* visa stamp; ~**weite** *f* visibility *no art*; **außer** ~**weite** out of sight.

**Sickergrube** *f* soakaway.

**sickern** *vi aux sein* to seep; *(in Tropfen)* to drip. **in die Presse** ~ *(fig)* to be leaked to the press.

**sie** *pers pron 3. pers* **(a)** *sing (von Frau, weiblichem Tier) (nom)* she; *(acc)* her; *(von Dingen)* it; *(acc)* them *pl.* ~ **ist es** it's her. **(b)** *pl (nom)* they; *(acc)* them. ~ **sind es** it's them.

**sinken**

**Sie** pers pron 2. pers sing or pl you. **jdn mit ~ anreden** to use the polite form of address to sb.
**Sieb** nt -e sieve; (Tee~) strainer; (Gemüse~) colander.
**Siebdruck** m (Verfahren) (silk-)screen printing; (Erzeugnis) (silk-)screen print.
**sieben[1] 1** vt to pass through a sieve; (Cook) to sift, to sieve. **2** vi (fig col) **bei der Prüfung wird stark gesiebt** the exam will weed a lot of people out.
**sieben[2]** num seven.
**Sieben** f - or -en seven; siehe **Vier**.
**Sieben-** in cpds siehe auch **Vier-**; **s~hundert** num seven hundred; **s~mal** adv seven times; **~meilenstiefel** pl (Liter) seven-league boots pl; **mit ~meilenstiefeln gehen** (col) to walk with giant strides; **~meter** m (Sport) penalty; **~sachen** pl (col) belongings pl; **~schläfer** m (Zool) dormouse; **s~tausend** num seven thousand.
**siebte(r, s)** adj seventh; siehe **vierte(r, s)**.
**Siebtel** nt - seventh.
**siebtens** adv seventh(ly), in the seventh place.
**siebzehn** num seventeen.
**siebzig** num seventy; siehe **vierzig**.
**siedeln** vi to settle.
**sieden 1** vi (Wasser, Zucker etc) to boil. **2** vt Seife, Leim to produce by boiling. **~d heiß** boiling hot.
**Siedepunkt** m (Phys, fig) boiling-point.
**Siedler(in** f) m - settler; (Bauer) smallholder.
**Siedlung** f **(a)** (Ansiedlung) settlement. **(b)** (Wohn~) housing estate (Brit), development.
**Sieg** m -e victory (über +acc over). **einen ~ erringen** to win a victory; **einer Sache** (dat) **zum ~ verhelfen** to help sth to triumph.
**Siegel** nt - seal.
**Siegellack** m sealing wax.
**siegeln** vt Urkunde to affix a/one's seal to; (ver~) Brief to seal.
**Siegelring** m signet ring.
**siegen** vi (Mil) to be victorious; (in Wettkampf) to win. **über jdn/etw ~** (fig) to triumph over sb/sth; (in Wettkampf) to beat sb/sth.
**Sieger(in** f) m - victor; (in Wettkampf) winner. **zweiter ~** runner-up; **~ werden** to win.
**Sieger-:** **~ehrung** f (Sport) presentation ceremony; **~macht** f usu pl (Pol) victorious power; **~pose** f victorious pose; **~urkunde** f (Sport) winner's certificate.
**Sieges-:** **s~bewußt** adj confident of victory; **~denkmal** nt victory monument; **~feier** f victory celebration; **~preis** m winner's prize; (Boxen) winner's purse; **s~sicher** adj certain of victory; **~zug** m triumphal march.
**siegreich** adj victorious, triumphant; (in Wettkampf) winning attr.
**siehe** imper sing of **sehen** see.
**Siel** nt or m -e (Schleuse) sluice; (Abwasserkanal) sewer.
**siezen** vt jdn/sich ~ to use the polite form of address to sb/each other.
**Signal** nt -e signal. **(ein) ~ geben** to give a signal.
**Signal|anlage** f signals pl, set of signals.
**signalisieren*** vt (lit, fig) to signal.
**Signal-:** **~lampe** f signal lamp; **~mast** m signal mast; **~wirkung** f **~wirkung haben** to act as a signal.
**Signatur** f **(a)** (Bibliotheks~) shelf mark. **(b)** (auf Landkarten) symbol.
**signieren*** vt to sign.
**Silbe** f -n syllable. **er hat es mit keiner ~ erwähnt** he didn't say a word about it.
**Silbentrennung** f hyphenation.

**Silber** nt no pl silver. **aus ~** made of silver.
**Silber-** in cpds silver; **~arbeit** f silverwork no pl; **~besteck** nt silver(ware); **~blick** m (col) squint; **s~farben** adj silver; **~fischchen** nt silverfish; **~folie** f silver foil; **~fuchs** m silver fox; **~geld** nt silver; **~hochzeit** f silver wedding (anniversary); **~löwe** m puma; **~medaille** f silver medal; **~möwe** f herring gull.
**silbern** adj silver. **~e Hochzeit** silver wedding (anniversary).
**Silber-:** **~papier** nt silver paper; **~pappel** f white poplar; **~schmied** m silversmith; **~stickerei** f (Kunst) silver embroidery; **~streif(en)** m (fig) **es zeichnete sich ein ~streif(en) am Horizont ab** there was light at the end of the tunnel; **~stück** nt silver coin; **~waren** pl silver(ware) sing; **s~weiß** adj silvery white.
**silbrig** adj silvery.
**Silhouette** [zi'luɛtə] f silhouette.
**Silikon** nt -e silicone.
**Silikose** f -n (Med) silicosis.
**Silizium** nt no pl silicon.
**Siliziumscheibe** f silicon chip.
**Silo** m -s silo.
**Silvester** [zɪl'vɛstɐ] m or nt - New Year's Eve.
**Simbabwe** nt Zimbabwe.
**Simbabwer(in** f) m Zimbabwean.
**simbabwisch** adj Zimbabwean.
**simpel** adj simple; (vereinfacht) simplistic.
**Simpel** m - (col) simpleton.
**Sims** m or nt -e (Fenster~) sill; (Gesims) ledge.
**Simulant(in** f) m malingerer.
**Simulator** m (Sci) simulator.
**simulieren*** vi **er simuliert nur** he's just putting it on. **2** vt **(a)** Krankheit to feign. **(b)** (Sci) to simulate.
**simultan** adj simultaneous.
**Simultandolmetscher** m simultaneous interpreter.
**sind** 1., 3. pers pl, bei Sie sing/pl pres of **sein** are.
**Sinfonie** f symphony.
**Sinfonie-:** **~konzert** nt symphony concert; **~orchester** nt symphony orchestra.
**sinfonisch** adj symphonic.
**Singapur** ['zɪŋgapuːɐ] nt Singapore.
**singen** pret **sang**, ptp **gesungen 1** vti **(a)** (lit, fig) to sing; (esp Eccl: eintönig, feierlich) to chant. **zur Gitarre ~** to sing to the guitar; **ein ~der Tonfall** a lilt; **jdn in den Schlaf ~** to sing sb to sleep. **(b)** (col: gestehen) to squeal (col). **2** vr **sich heiser ~** to sing oneself hoarse.
**Singhalese** [zɪŋga'leːzə] m (wk) -n, -n, **Singhalesin** f Sing(h)alese.
**singhalesisch** [zɪŋga'leːzɪʃ] adj Sing(h)alese.
**Singhalesisch(e)** nt decl as adj Sing(h)alese.
**Single[1]** ['sɪŋgl] f -s (CD, Schallplatte) single.
**Single[2]** ['sɪŋgl] m -s (Alleinlebender) single.
**Sing-:** **~sang** m -s (Gesang) monotonous singing; **~stimme** f vocal part.
**Singular** m -e singular. **im ~ stehen** to be (in the) singular.
**Sing-:** **~vogel** m songbird; **~weise** f way of singing.
**sinken** pret **sank**, ptp **gesunken** vi aux sein **(a)** to sink; (Ballon) to descend; (Nebel) to come down. **ins Bett ~** to fall into bed; **in jds Meinung/Achtung** (dat) **~** to go down in sb's estimation. **(b)** (Boden, Gebäude) to subside; (Fundament) to settle. **in Schutt und Asche ~** (geh) to fall in ruins. **(c)** (niedriger, geringer werden: Temperatur, Preise etc) to drop; (Ansehen) to diminish; (Hoffnung, Stimmung) to sink. **das Thermometer/Barometer sinkt** the temperature/

the barometer is falling; **den Mut/die Hoffnung** ~ **lassen** to lose courage/hope.

**Sinn** *m* **-e** (**a**) sense; *(Bedeutung)* meaning. **er war von** ~**en** he was out of his senses *or* mind; **im übertragenen** ~ in the figurative sense; **der Satz (er)gibt** *or* **macht keinen** ~ the sentence doesn't make sense.

(**b**) *(Gedanken, Denkweise)* mind. **sich** *(dat)* **jdn/ etw aus dem** ~ **schlagen** to put sb/sth out of one's mind; **es kam ihm gar nicht in den** ~, **ihr zu helfen** it did not occur to him to help her; **das will mir einfach nicht in den** ~ I just can't understand it; **das geht mir nicht aus dem** ~ I can't get it out of my mind; **etw im** ~ **haben** to have sth in mind.

(**c**) *(Verständnis)* feeling. ~ **für Humor haben** to have a sense of humour; **er hat keinen** ~ **für Kunst** he has no appreciation of art.

(**d**) *(Geist)* spirit. **im** ~**e des Gesetzes** according to the spirit of the law; **in jds** ~ *(dat)* **handeln** to act as sb would have wished; **das wäre nicht im** ~**e unserer Kunden** it would not be in the interests of our customers.

(**e**) *(Zweck)* point. **das ist nicht der** ~ **der Sache** that is not the point; **der** ~ **des Lebens** the meaning of life; **ohne** ~ **und Verstand sein** to make no sense at all; **das hat keinen** ~ there is no point in that.

**Sinn-:** ~**bild** *nt* symbol; **s**~**bildlich** *adj* symbolic(al).

**sinnen** *pret* **sann**, *ptp* **gesonnen** *vi (geh)* to ponder, to muse; *(grübeln)* to brood. **über etw** *(acc)* ~ to reflect on/brood over sth; **auf Verrat/Rache** *(acc)* ~ to plot treason/revenge.

**sinn-:** ~**entleert** *adj* empty of meaning; ~**entstellend** *adj* ~**entstellend sein** to distort the meaning.

**Sinnes-:** ~**eindruck** *m* sensory impression; ~**nerv** *m* sensory nerve; ~**organ** *nt* sense organ; ~**reiz** *m* sensory stimulus; ~**täuschung** *f* hallucination; ~**wandel** *m* change of mind.

**Sinngedicht** *nt* epigram.

**sinngemäß** *adj* (**a**) *(inhaltlich)* **etw** ~ **wiedergeben** to give the gist of sth. (**b**) *(esp Jur: analog)* corresponding, analogous. **etw** ~ **anwenden** to apply sth by analogy.

**sinnig** *adj* apt; *Vorrichtung* practical; *(iro: wenig sinnvoll)* clever.

**sinnlich** *adj* (**a**) *(vital, sinnenfroh)* sensuous; *(erotisch)* sensual. ~**e Liebe** sensual love. (**b**) ~ **wahrnehmbar** perceptible by the senses.

**Sinnlichkeit** *f (Vitalität)* sensuousness; *(Erotik)* sensuality.

**sinnlos** *adj* (**a**) *(unsinnig)* Redensarten, Geschwätz meaningless; *Verhalten, Töten* senseless. (**b**) *(zwecklos)* pointless; *Wut* blind. ~ **betrunken** blind drunk.

**Sinnlosigkeit** *f siehe adj* meaninglessness; senselessness; pointlessness.

**Sinn-:** ~**spruch** *m* aphorism; **s**~**verwandt** *adj* synonymous; **s**~**voll** *adj Satz* meaningful; *(fig)* sensible; *(nützlich)* useful.

**Sintflut** *f (Bibl)* Flood. **nach uns die** ~ it doesn't matter what happens after we've gone.

**sintflut|artig** *adj* ~**e Regenfälle** torrential rain.

**Sinus** *m* **-** (**a**) *(Math)* sine. (**b**) *(Anat)* sinus.

**Siphon** ['ziːfõ] *m* **-s** siphon.

**Sippe** *f* **-n** (extended) family; *(col: Verwandtschaft)* clan *(col)*.

**Sippschaft** *f (pej col)* tribe *(col)*.

**Sirene** *f* **-n** *(Tech, fig)* siren.

**sirren** *vi* = **surren**.

**Sirup** *m* **-e** syrup.

**Sisal(hanf)** *m no pl* sisal (hemp).

**Sit-in** [sɪt'|ɪn] *nt* **-s** sit-in. **ein** ~ **machen** to stage a sit-in.

**Sitte** *f* **-n** (**a**) *(Brauch)* custom; *(Mode)* practice. ~ **sein** to be the custom/the practice. (**b**) *usu pl (gutes Benehmen)* manners *pl*; *(Sittlichkeit)* morals *pl*. **gegen die (guten)** ~**n verstoßen** to offend common decency; **was sind denn das für** ~**n?** what sort of a way is that to behave!

**Sitten-:** ~**gesetz** *nt* moral law; ~**kodex** *m* moral code; ~**lehre** *f* ethics *sing*; **s**~**los** *adj* immoral; ~**losigkeit** *f* immorality; ~**polizei** *f* vice squad; ~**richter** *m* judge of public morals; **s**~**streng** *adj* puritanical; ~**strolch** *m* *(col)* sex offender; ~**verfall** *m* decline in moral standards; ~**wächter** *m (iro)* guardian of public morals; **s**~**widrig** *adj (form)* immoral.

**Sittich** *m* **-e** parakeet.

**sittlich** *adj* moral.

**Sittlichkeit** *f no pl* morality.

**Sittlichkeits-:** ~**delikt** *nt* sexual offence *(Brit)* or offense *(US)*; ~**verbrechen** *nt* sex crime; ~**verbrecher** *m* sex offender.

**sittsam** *adj* demure.

**Sittsamkeit** *f* demureness.

**Situation** *f* situation.

**situiert** *adj* **gut/schlecht** ~ **sein** to be well off/not well off.

**Sitz** *m* **-e** (**a**) *(~platz, Parl)* seat. (**b**) *(von Regierung, Universität, fig)* seat; *(Wohn~)* residence; *(von Firma, Verwaltung)* headquarters *pl*. (**c**) *no pl (Tech, von Kleidungsstück)* sit; *(von der Größe her)* fit. **einen guten/schlechten** ~ **haben** to sit/fit well/badly.

**Sitz-:** ~**bad** *nt* hip bath; ~**bank** *f* bench; ~**blockade** *f* sit-in; ~**ecke** *f* sitting area.

**sitzen** *vi pret* **saß**, *ptp* **gesessen** *aux haben or (Aus, S Ger, Sw)* **sein** (**a**) to sit; *(Vogel)* to perch. **er saß bei uns am Tisch** he was sitting at our table; **bleiben Sie bitte** ~**!** please don't get up; ~ **Sie bequem?** are you comfortable?; **etw im S**~ **tun** to do sth sitting down; **an einer Aufgabe** ~ to sit over a task; **einen** ~ **haben** *(col)* to have had one too many. (**b**) *(col: im Gefängnis* ~**)** to be inside *(col)*. (**c**) *(sein)* to be. **er sitzt im Kultusministerium** *(col)* he's in the ministry of culture. (**d**) *(angebracht sein)* to sit. **der Deckel sitzt fest** the lid is on tightly; **locker** ~ to be loose; **fest** ~ to be stuck tight(ly). (**e**) *(Kleid etc)* to fit. **deine Krawatte sitzt nicht richtig** your tie isn't straight. (**f**) *(col: treffen)* **das hat gesessen!** *(col)* that went home. (**g**) *(im Gedächtnis* ~**)** to have sunk in.

**sitzenbleiben** *vi sep irreg aux sein (col)* (**a**) *(Sch)* to stay down. (**b**) **auf einer Ware** ~ to be left with a product. (**c**) *(unverheiratete Frau)* to be left on the shelf *(col)*.

**sitzend** *adj attr Lebensweise etc* sedentary.

**sitzenlassen** *vt sep irreg ptp* ~ *or* **sitzengelassen** *(col)* (**a**) *(Sch: nicht versetzen)* to keep down (a year). (**b**) **eine Beleidigung auf sich** *(dat)* ~ to take an insult. (**c**) **jdn** ~ *(im Stich lassen)* to leave sb in the lurch; *Freund(in)* to stand sb up; *(nicht heiraten)* to jilt sb.

**Sitz-:** ~**fleisch** *nt (col)* ~**fleisch haben** to be able to sit still; ~**gelegenheit** *f* seat; ~**gruppe** *f* group of chairs; *(dreiteilig)* three-piece suite; ~**kissen** *nt* (floor) cushion; ~**ordnung** *f* seating plan; ~**platz** *m* seat; ~**reihe** *f* row of seats; ~**streik** *m* = **Sit-in**.

**Sitzung** *f* meeting; *(Jur)* session; *(Parlaments~)* sitting.

**Sitzungs-:** ~**periode** *f (Parl)* session; ~**saal** *m* conference hall.

**Sizilianer(in** *f)* *m* **-** Sicilian.

**sizilianisch** *adj* Sicilian.
**Sizilien** [zi'tsiːliən] *nt* Sicily.
**Skai** ® *nt no pl* imitation leather.
**Skala** *f, pl* **Skalen** scale; *(fig)* range.
**Skalp** *m* **-e** scalp.
**Skalpell** *nt* **-e** scalpel.
**skalpieren\*** *vt* to scalp.
**Skandal** *m* **-e** scandal; *(col: Krach)* fuss. **einen ~ machen** to cause a scandal; to make a fuss.
**Skandal-:** **~blatt** *nt (pej)* scandal sheet; **~geschichte** *f* (bit *or* piece of) scandal.
**skandalös** *adj* scandalous.
**Skandalpresse** *f (pej)* gutter press.
**skandieren\*** *vt* to chant; *Gedicht* to recite emphatically.
**Skandinavien** [skandi'naːviən] *nt* Scandinavia.
**Skandinavier(in** *f)* *m* - Scandinavian.
**skandinavisch** *adj* Scandinavian.
**Skat** *m* **-e** *(Cards)* skat.
**Skateboard** ['skeːtbɔːd] *nt* **-s** skateboard.
**Skateboard-:** **~bahn** *f* skateboard rink; **~fahren** *nt* skateboarding; **~fahrer** *m* skateboarder.
**Skelett** *nt* **-e** *(lit, fig)* skeleton.
**Skepsis** *f no pl* scepticism. **mit/voller ~** sceptically.
**Skeptiker(in** *f)* *m* - sceptic.
**skeptisch** *adj* sceptical.
**Sketch** [skɛtʃ] *m* **-e(s)** *(Art, Theat)* sketch.
**Ski** [ʃiː] *m* **-er** ['ʃiːɐ] ski. **~ laufen** *or* **fahren** to ski.
**Ski-** *in cpds* ski; **~anzug** *m* ski suit; **~brille** *f* skiing goggles *pl*; **~fahrer(in** *f)* *m* skier; **~gebiet** *nt* ski(ing) area; **~hütte** *f* ski hut *or* lodge *(US)*; **~kurs** *m* skiing course; **~lauf** *m,* **~laufen** *nt* skiing; **~läufer(in** *f)* *m* skier; **~lehrer** *m* ski instructor; **~lift** *m* ski lift; **~piste** *f* ski run; **~sport** *m* skiing; **~springen** *nt* ski jumping; **~stiefel** *m* ski boot; **~stock** *m* ski stick; **~urlaub** *m* skiing holiday; **~urlaubsort** *m* ski resort.
**Skizze** ['skɪtsə] *f* **-n** sketch; *(fig: Grundriß)* plan.
**Skizzen-** ['skɪtsn-]: **~block** *m* sketch pad; **~buch** *nt* sketchbook; **s~haft 1** *adj Zeichnung etc* roughly sketched; *Beschreibung etc* (given) in broad outline; **2** *adv* **etw s~haft zeichnen** to sketch sth. roughly.
**skizzieren\*** [skɪ'tsiːrən] *vt* to sketch; *(fig) Plan etc* to outline.
**Sklave** ['sklaːvə] *m (wk)* **-n, -n** slave. **~ einer Sache** *(gen)* **sein** *(fig)* to be a slave to sth.
**Sklaven-** ['sklaːvn-]: **~arbeit** *f* slavery; **~handel** *m* slave trade; **~treiber** *m* slave-driver.
**Sklaverei** [sklaːvə'rai] *f no pl (lit, fig)* slavery *no art.*
**Sklavin** ['sklaːvɪn] *f* slave.
**sklavisch** ['sklaːvɪʃ] *adj* slavish.
**Sklerose** *f* **-n** sclerosis.
**Skonto** *nt or m, pl* **-s** *or* **Skonti** cash discount.
**Skorbut** *m no pl* scurvy.
**Skorpion** *m* **-e** *(Zool)* scorpion; *(Astrol)* Scorpio.
**Skrupel** *m* - *usu pl* scruple. **er hatte keine ~, das zu tun** he had no scruples about doing it; **ohne ~** without scruples.
**Skrupel-:** **s~los** *adj* unscrupulous; **~losigkeit** *f* unscrupulousness.
**Skulptur** *f* sculpture.
**Skunk** *m* **-s** skunk.
**skurril** *adj (geh)* droll, comical.
**S-Kurve** ['ɛs-] *f* S-bend.
**Slalom** *m* **-s** slalom. **(im) ~ fahren** *(fig col)* to drive a zig-zag course.
**Slang** [slɛŋ] *m no pl* slang.
**Slawe** *m (wk)* **-n, -n, Slawin** *f* Slav.
**slawisch** *adj* Slavonic, Slavic *(esp US)*.
**Slip** *m* **-s** (pair of) briefs *pl*.

**Slipper** *m* - slip-on (shoe).
**Slogan** ['sloːgn] *m* **-s** slogan.
**Slowake** *m (wk)* **-n, -n Slowakin** *f* Slovak.
**Slowakei** *f die* ~ Slovakia.
**slowakisch** *adj* Slovak.
**Slowakisch(e)** *nt* Slovak; *siehe* **Deutsch(e)**.
**Slowene** *m (wk)* **-n, -n, Slowenin** *f* Slovene.
**Slowenien** [slo'veːniən] *nt* Slovenia.
**slowenisch** *adj* Slovenian.
**Slum** [slam] *m* **-s** slum.
**S.M.** = **Seine(r) Majestät** HM.
**Smaragd** *m* **-e** emerald.
**Smog** *m* **-s** smog.
**Smoking** ['smoːkɪŋ] *m* **-s** dinner jacket, tuxedo *(US)*.
**Snob** *m* **-s** snob.
**Snobismus** *m* snobbery, snobbishness.
**snobistisch** *adj* snobbish.
**SO** = **Südosten** SE.
**so 1** *adv* **(a)** *(mit adj, adv)* so; *(mit vb:* ~ *sehr)* so much. ~ **groß** *etc* so big *etc*; **eine ~ große Frau** such a big woman; ~ **groß wie** ... as big as ...; ~ **gut es geht** as best I/he *etc* can; **er ist nicht ~ dumm, das zu glauben** he's not so stupid as to believe that; **das hat ihn ~ geärgert, daß** ... that annoyed him so much that ...; ~ **ein Fehler** such a mistake; ~ **ein Idiot!** what an idiot!; **hast du ~ etwas schon einmal gesehen?** have you ever seen anything like it?; **na** ~ **was!** well I never!; ~ **etwas Schönes** such a beautiful thing; ~ **einer wie ich** somebody like me.
**(b)** *(auf diese Weise)* like this/that. **mach es nicht** ~ don't do it like that; **mach es ~, wie er es vorgeschlagen hat** do it the way he suggested; ~ **ist sie nun einmal** that's the way she is; **(ach)** ~ **ist das!** I see!; ~ **oder/und** ~ in one way or another; **und** ~ **weiter** and so on; **gut** ~**!** fine!; **das ist gut** ~ that's fine; **mir ist (es)** ~**, als ob** ... it seems to me as if ...; **das kam** ~: ... this is what happened ...; **es verhält sich** ~: ... the facts are as follows ...; **das habe ich nur** ~ **gesagt** I didn't really mean it.
**(c)** *(etwa)* about, or so. **ich komme** ~ **um 8 Uhr** I'll come at 8 or so.
**(d)** *(col: umsonst)* for nothing.
**(e)** *(als Füllwort) nicht übersetzt.* ~ **beeil dich doch!** do hurry up!; ~ **mancher** a number of people *pl*.
**2** *conj* **(a)** ~ **daß** so that. **(b)** ~ **wie es jetzt ist** as things are at the moment. **(c)** ~ **klein er auch sein mag** however small he may be.
**3** *interj* so; *(wirklich)* oh, really; *(abschließend)* well, right. **er ist schon da** — ~ **he's here already** — **is he?**; ~**, ~! well well.
**So.** = **Sonntag** Sun.
**s.o.** = **siehe oben.**
**sobald** *conj* as soon as.
**Söckchen** *nt* ankle sock.
**Socke** *f* **-n** sock. **sich auf die ~n machen** *(col)* to get going *(col)*; **von den ~n sein** *(col)* to be flabbergasted *(col)*.
**Sockel** *m* - base; *(von Denkmal, Statue auch)* pedestal.
**Soda** *nt no pl* soda.
**sodann** *adv* then.
**Sodawasser** *nt* soda water.
**Sodbrennen** *nt* heartburn.
**Sodomie** *f* buggery, bestiality.
**soeben** *adv* just (this moment).
**Sofa** *nt* **-s** sofa, settee *(esp Brit)*.
**Sofa-:** **~bett** *nt* sofa bed; **~kissen** *nt* sofa *or* scatter cushion.
**sofern** *conj* provided (that). ~ ... **nicht** if ... not.
**soff** *pret of* **saufen**.

**Sofia** ['zɔfia, 'zoːfia] *nt* Sofia.
**sofort** *adv* immediately. **komm hierher, und zwar ~!** come here this instant!; **(ich) komme ~!** (I'm) just coming!
**Sofort-:** ~**bildkamera** *f* Polaroid ® camera, instant camera; ~**hilfe** *f* emergency relief *or* aid.
**sofortig** *adj* immediate, instant.
**Sofortmaßnahme** *f* immediate measure.
**Soft|eis** ['sɔft-] *nt* soft ice-cream.
**Softi** *m* -**s** *(col)* caring type.
**Software** ['sɔftwɛːɐ] *f* -**s** *(Comp)* software.
**Softwarepaket** ['sɔftwɛːɐ-] *nt* software package.
**Sog** *m* -**e** *(saugende Kraft)* suction; *(von Strudel)* vortex; *(fig)* maelstrom.
**sog** *pret of* **saugen.**
**sog.** = **sogenannt.**
**sogar** *adv* even. **schön, ~ sehr schön** beautiful, in fact very beautiful.
**sogenannt** *adj attr* so-called.
**sogleich** *adv* = **sofort.**
**Sogwirkung** *f* suction; *(fig)* knock-on effect.
**Sohle** *f* -**n** **(a)** *(Fuß~ etc)* sole; *(Einlage)* insole. **auf leisen ~n** softly. **(b)** *(Boden)* bottom.
**Sohn** *m* ⁼**e** *(lit, fig)* son.
**Soja** *f,* **Sojen** soya.
**Soja-:** ~**bohne** *f* soya bean; ~**soße** *f* soya sauce.
**solang(e)** *conj* as long as, so long as.
**Solar-** *in cpds* solar.
**Solarium** *nt, pl* **Solarien** solarium.
**Solbad** *nt* saltwater bath; *(Schwimmbad)* saltwater pool.
**solch** *adj inv,* **solche(r, s)** *adj* such. **ein ~er Mensch** such a person; **wir haben ~en Durst** we're so thirsty; **~ ein langer Weg** such a long way; **~es** that kind of thing; **Rechtsanwälte gibt es ~e und ~e** there are lawyers and lawyers.
**solcherlei** *adj attr inv* such.
**Sold** *m no pl (Mil)* pay.
**Soldat** *m (wk)* -**en,** -**en** soldier. **~ spielen** to play soldiers.
**Soldaten-:** ~**friedhof** *m* military cemetery; ~**sprache** *f* military slang; ~**tum** *nt* soldiery *no art*; *(Tradition)* military tradition; ~**verband** *m* ex-servicemen's association.
**Soldatin** *f* (woman) soldier.
**soldatisch** *adj (militärisch)* military; *(soldaten-gemäß)* soldierly.
**Söldner(in** *f)* *m* - mercenary.
**Söldnertruppe** *f* mercenary force.
**Sole** *f* -**n** brine, salt water.
**Solei** ['zoːl|ai] *nt* pickled egg.
**solidarisch** *adj* **sich mit jdm ~ erklären** to declare one's solidarity with sb; **~ mit jdm handeln** to act in solidarity with sb.
**solidarisieren*** *vr* **sich ~ mit** to show (one's) solidarity with.
**Solidarität** *f* solidarity.
**Solidaritätsstreik** *m* sympathy strike.
**solid(e)** *adj* Haus, Möbel *etc* solid, sturdy; Arbeit, Wissen, Handwerker sound; Mensch, Lokal respectable; Firma sound, solid; Preise reasonable.
**Solist(in** *f)* *m (Mus)* soloist.
**Soll** *nt* -**(s)** **(a)** *(Schuld)* debit; *(Schuldseite)* debit side. **~ und Haben** debit and credit. **(b)** *(Comm)* quota. **sein ~ erfüllen** to meet one's target.
**sollen 1** *modal aux pret* **sollte,** *ptp* ~ **(a)** *(bei Befehl, Anordnung, Absicht)* to be (supposed) to. **was soll ich/er tun?** what shall *or* should I/should he do?; **er weiß nicht, was er tun soll** he doesn't know what to do; **sie sagte ihm, er solle draußen warten** she told him to wait outside; **was ich (nicht) alles tun/wissen**

**soll!** the things I'm supposed to do/know!; **es soll nicht wieder vorkommen** it won't happen again; **er soll reinkommen** tell him to come in; **niemand soll sagen, daß ...** let no one say that ...; **das Haus soll nächste Woche gestrichen werden** the house is to be painted next week; **was sollte ich/er deiner Meinung nach tun?** what do you think I/he should do *or* ought to do?; **das hättest du nicht tun ~** you shouldn't have done that.
**(b)** *(bei Gerücht, Vermutung)* to be supposed *or* meant to. **sie soll verheiratet sein** I've heard she's married; **Xanthippe soll zänkisch gewesen sein** Xanthippe is said to have been quarrelsome; **das soll gar nicht so einfach sein** they say it's not that easy; **was soll das heißen?** what's that supposed to mean?; **mir soll es gleich sein** it's all the same to me; **so etwas soll es geben** these things happen; **man sollte glauben, daß ...** you would think that ...; **sollte das möglich sein?** can that be possible?
**(c) sollte das passieren, ...** if that should happen ...; **er sollte sie nie wiedersehen** he was never to see her again; **es hat nicht ~ sein** *or* **sein ~** it wasn't to be.
**2** *vti pret* **sollte,** *ptp* **gesollt soll ich?** shall I?; **was soll das?** what's all this?; *(warum denn das)* what's that for?; **was soll's?** what the hell! *(col)*; **was soll ich dort?** what would I do there?; **das sollst du nicht** you shouldn't do that; **was man nicht alles soll!** *(col)* the things you're meant to do!
**Söller** *m* - balcony.
**Soll-:** ~**seite** *f (Fin)* debit side; ~**stärke** *f* required strength.
**solo** *adv (Mus)* solo; *(fig col)* on one's own, alone.
**Solo** *nt, pl* **Soli** solo.
**solvent** [zɔl'vɛnt] *adj (Fin)* solvent.
**Solvenz** [zɔl'vɛnts] *f (Fin)* solvency.
**Somali** *m* -**(s),** -**(s)** Somali.
**Somalia** *nt* Somalia.
**Somalier(in** *f)* [-iɐ, -iərɪn] *m* - Somali.
**somalisch** *adj* Somali.
**somit** *adv* consequently, therefore.
**Sommer** *m* - summer. **im ~** in (the) summer; **im nächsten ~** next summer; **~ wie Winter** all year round.
**Sommer-** *in cpds* summer; ~**abend** *m* summer('s) evening; ~**anfang** *m* beginning of summer; ~**ferien** *pl* summer holidays *pl (Brit) or* vacation *(US)*; *(Jur, Parl)* summer recess; ~**gast** *m* summer visitor; ~**haus** *nt* (summer) holiday home; ~**kleidung** *f* summer clothing.
**sommerlich** *adj* summer *attr*; *(sommerartig)* summery. **~ gekleidet sein** to be in summer clothes; **~ warm** warm and summery.
**Sommer-:** ~**loch** *nt (col)* silly season; ~**mantel** *m* summer coat; ~**monat** *m* summer month; ~**nacht** *f* summer('s) night; ~**pause** *f* summer break; *(Jur, Parl)* summer recess; ~**reifen** *m* standard tyre *(Brit) or* tire *(US) (not for winter use)*; ~**saison** *f* summer season; ~**schlußverkauf** *m* summer sale; ~**semester** *nt (Univ)* summer semester, ≈ summer term *(Brit)*; ~**sitz** *m* summer residence; ~**spiele** *pl* **die Olympischen ~spiele** the Summer Olympics; ~**sprosse** *f* freckle; **s~sprossig** *adj* freckled; ~**tag** *m* summer's day; ~**weizen** *m* spring wheat; ~**wetter** *nt* summer weather; ~**zeit** *f* summer time *no art.*
**Sonargerät** *nt* sonar (device).
**Sonate** *f* -**n** sonata.
**Sonde** *f* -**n** *(Space, Med)* probe.
**Sonder-** *in cpds* special; ~**anfertigung** *f* special model; ~**angebot** *nt* special offer; **im ~angebot**

**sein** to be on special offer; **~ausgabe** *f* **(a)** special edition; **(b)** **~ausgaben** *pl (Fin)* additional *or* extra expenses *pl*.

**sonderbar** *adj* strange, peculiar, odd.

**sonderbarerweise** *adv* strange to say.

**Sonder-**: **~beauftragte(r)** *mf (Pol)* special emissary; **~fahrt** *f* special excursion; **~fall** *m* special case; *(Ausnahme)* exception; **~genehmigung** *f* special permission; *(Schein)* special permit; **s~gleichen** *adv inv* **eine Frechheit s~gleichen** an incredible cheek; **~konto** *nt* special account.

**sonderlich 1** *adj attr* particular. **ohne ~e Begeisterung** without any particular enthusiasm. **2** *adv* particularly.

**Sonderling** *m* eccentric.

**Sonder-**: **~marke** *f* special issue (stamp); **~maschine** *f* special plane; *(Flug)* special flight; **~meldung** *f (Rad, TV)* special announcement; **~müll** *m* hazardous waste.

**sondern**[1] *conj* but. **nicht nur ..., ~ auch ...** not only ... but also ...

**sondern**[2] *vt (geh)* to separate; *siehe* **gesondert**.

**Sonder-**: **~nummer** *f* special issue; **~preis** *m* special (reduced) price; **~recht** *nt* (special) privilege; **~regelung** *f* special provision; **~schicht** *f* special shift; *(zusätzlich)* extra shift; **~schule** *f* special school; **~stellung** *f* special position; **~stempel** *m (bei der Post)* special postmark; **~wünsche** *pl* special requests *pl*; **~zug** *m* special train.

**sondieren*** *vti* to sound out. **das Terrain ~** to spy out the land; **die Lage ~** to find out how the land lies.

**Sondierungsgespräch** *nt* exploratory talk.

**Sonett** *nt* **-e** sonnet.

**Sonn|abend** *m (esp N Ger)* Saturday; *siehe* **Dienstag**.

**sonn|abends** *adv* on Saturdays, on a Saturday.

**Sonne** *f* **-n** sun. **an die ~ gehen** to go out in the sun; **geh mir aus der ~!** *(col)* get out of the way; *(aus dem Licht)* get out of the light.

**sonnen** *vr* to sun oneself. **sich in etw** *(dat)* **~** *(fig)* to bask in sth.

**Sonnen-**: **~anbeter** *m (lit, fig)* sun-worshipper; **~aufgang** *m* sunrise; **~bad** *nt* sunbathing *no pl*; **ein ~bad nehmen** to sunbathe; **s~baden** *vi sep infin, ptp only* to sunbathe; **~batterie** *f* solar battery; **~blende** *f (Aut)* sun visor; *(Phot)* lens hood.

**Sonnenblume** *f* sunflower.

**Sonnenblumen-**: **~kern** *m* sunflower seed; **~öl** *nt* sunflower oil.

**Sonnen-**: **~brand** *m* sunburn *no art*; **~bräune** *f* suntan; **~brille** *f* (pair of) sunglasses *pl*; **~deck** *nt (Naut)* sundeck; **~energie** *f* solar energy; **~finsternis** *f* solar eclipse; **~fleck** *m (Astron)* sunspot; **s~gebräunt** *adj* suntanned; **~gott** *m* sungod; **~hut** *m* sunhat; **~jahr** *nt (Astron)* solar year; **s~klar** *adj (col)* crystal clear; **~kollektor** *m* solar panel; **~kraftwerk** *nt* solar power station; **~kult** *m* sun cult; **~licht** *nt* sunlight; **~milch** *f* suntan lotion; **~öl** *nt* suntan oil; **~schein** *m* sunshine; **bei strahlendem ~schein** in brilliant sunshine; **~schirm** *m* sunshade; **~schutz** *m* protection against the sun; **~seite** *f (lit, fig)* sunny side; **~stand** *m* position of the sun; **~stich** *m* sunstroke *no art*; **du hast wohl einen ~stich!** *(col)* you must have been out in the sun too long!; **~strahl** *m* sunbeam; **~system** *nt* solar system; **~uhr** *f* sundial; **~untergang** *m* sunset; **~wende** *f* solstice.

**sonnig** *adj* sunny; *(fig)* cheerful; *(iron)* naive.

**Sonntag** *m* Sunday; *siehe* **Dienstag**.

**sonntäglich** *adj* Sunday *attr*. **~ gekleidet** dressed in one's Sunday best.

**sonntags** *adv* on Sundays, on a Sunday.

**Sonntags-** *in cpds* Sunday; **~arbeit** *f* Sunday working; **~ausflug** *m* Sunday trip; **~beilage** *f* Sunday supplement; **~dienst** *m (von Polizist etc)* Sunday duty; **~dienst haben** *(Apotheke)* to be open on Sundays; **~fahrer** *m (pej)* Sunday driver; **~kind** *nt (lit)* Sunday's child; **ein ~kind sein** *(fig)* to have been born under a lucky star; **~maler** *m* Sunday painter; **~staat** *m (hum)* Sunday best; **~zeitung** *f* Sunday paper.

**sonor** *adj* sonorous.

**sonst 1** *adv* **(a)** *(außerdem) (mit pron, adv)* else; *(mit n)* other. **~ noch Fragen?** any other questions?; **wer/wie** *etc* **(denn) ~?** who/how *etc* else?; **~ noch etwas?** is that all?, anything else?; **~ nichts** nothing else; **wo warst du ~ noch?** where else did you go?; **~ geht's dir gut?** *(iro col)* are you feeling okay? *(col)*. **(b)** *(andernfalls)* otherwise. **(c)** *(in anderer Hinsicht)* in other ways. **wenn ich Ihnen ~ noch behilflich sein kann** if I can help you in any other way. **(d)** *(gewöhnlich)* usually. **genau wie es ~ ist** just as it usually is; **genau wie/anders als ~** the same as/different from usual; **alles war wie ~** everything was as it always used to be. **2** *conj* otherwise, or (else).

**sonstig** *adj attr* other; *Fragen, Auskünfte etc* further. „**S~es**" "other".

**sonst-**: **~jemand** *indef pron (col)* = **~wer**; **~wann** *adv (col)* some other time; **~was** *indef pron (col)* **da kann ja ~was passieren** anything could happen; **ich habe ~was versucht** I've tried everything; **~wer** *indef pron (col)* somebody else; **er denkt, er ist ~wer** he thinks he's really somebody; **~wie** *adv (col)* **(in)** some other way; *(sehr)* like mad *(col)*; **~wo** *adv (col)* somewhere else; **~wohin** *adv (col)* somewhere else.

**so|oft** *conj* whenever.

**Sopran** *m* **-e** soprano; *(von Jungen)* treble.

**Sopranflöte** *f* descant recorder.

**Sopranistin** *f* soprano.

**Sorge** *f* **-n** **(a)** worry. **keine ~!** *(col)* don't worry!; **wir betrachten diese Entwicklung mit ~** we view this development with concern; **~n haben** to have problems; **ich habe solche ~** I'm so worried; **du hast ~n!** *(iro)* you think you've got troubles! *(col)*; **jdm ~n machen** *(Kummer bereiten)* to cause sb a lot of worry; **machen Sie sich** *(dat)* **deshalb keine ~n** don't worry about that; **lassen Sie das meine ~ sein** let me worry about that; **das ist nicht meine ~** that's not my problem; **dafür ~ tragen, daß ...** *(geh)* to see to it that ... **(b)** *(Für~, Jur)* care.

**sorgeberechtigt** *adj* **~ sein** to have custody.

**sorgen 1** *vi* **~ für** *(sich kümmern um)* to look after; *(vorsorgen für)* to provide for; *(herbeischaffen) Proviant, Musik* to provide; *(bewirken)* to ensure; **dafür ~, daß ...** to see to it that ...; **dafür ist gesorgt** that's taken care of. **2** *vr* to worry. **sich ~ um** to worry about.

**Sorgen-**: **~falte** *f* worry line; **s~frei** *adj* free of care; *(heiter)* carefree; **~kind** *nt (col)* problem child; **s~voll** *adj* worried; *Leben* full of worries.

**Sorgerecht** *nt (Jur)* custody.

**Sorgfalt** *f no pl* care. **ohne ~ arbeiten** to work carelessly; **viel ~ auf etw** *(acc)* **verwenden** to take a lot of care over sth.

**sorgfältig** *adj* careful.

**sorglos** *adj* carefree; *(leichtfertig)* careless.

**Sorglosigkeit** *f siehe adj* carefreeness; carelessness.

**sorgsam** *adj* careful.
**Sorte** *f* **-n** (a) type, kind; *(Qualität, Klasse)* grade; *(Marke)* brand. **beste** ~ top quality. (b) *(Fin) usu pl* foreign currency.
**sortieren*** *vt* to sort *(auch Comp)*. **etw in einen Schrank** ~ to tidy sth away into a cupboard.
**Sortierer(in** *f) m* - sorter.
**Sortiermaschine** *f* sorting machine.
**Sortiment** *nt* (a) assortment. (b) *(Buchhandel)* retail book trade.
**Sortimentsbuchhandlung** *f* retail bookshop *(Brit)* or bookstore *(US)*.
**SOS** [ɛs|oː'|ɛs] *nt* -, - SOS.
**sosehr** *conj* however much, no matter how much.
**soso** *interj* ~! I see!; *(erstaunt)* well well!; *(drohend)* well!
**Soße** *f* **-n** sauce; *(Braten~)* gravy; *(pej col: dickflüssige Brühe)* gunge *(col)*.
**Souffleur** [zu'fløːɐ] *m*, **Souffleuse** [zu'fløːzə] *f (Theat)* prompter.
**soufflieren*** [zu'fliːrən] *vti (Theat)* to prompt *(jdm sb)*.
**so|undso** *adv* ~ **lange** for such and such a time; ~ **viele** so and so many; **Paragraph** ~ article such-and-such; **er sagte, mach das** ~ he said, do it in such-and-such a way.
**so|undsovielte(r, s)** *adj* umpteenth. **am S~n** *(Datum)* on such and such a date.
**Souterrain** ['zuːtɛrɛ̃] *nt* **-s** basement.
**Souvenir** [zuvə'niːɐ] *nt* **-s** souvenir.
**souverän** [zuvə'rɛːn] *adj* sovereign *no adv*; *(fig)* supremely good; *(überlegen)* (most) superior *no adv*. **sein Gebiet** ~ **beherrschen** to have a commanding knowledge of one's field.
**Souveränität** [zuvərɛni'tɛːt] *f* sovereignty.
**soviel 1** *adv* so much. **halb** ~ half as much; ~ **wie** ... as much as ...; **noch einmal** ~ *(doppelt ~)* twice as much. **2** *conj* as far as. ~ **ich weiß(, nicht!)** (not) as far as I know.
**sovielmal** *adv* so many times.
**soweit 1** *adv* (a) on the whole; *(bis jetzt)* up to now; *(bis zu diesem Punkt)* thus far. ~ **wie möglich** as far as possible. (b) ~ **sein** to be finished *or (bereit)* ready; **es ist bald** ~ it's nearly time. **2** *conj* as far as; *(insofern)* in so far as.
**sowenig** *adv* no more, not any more *(wie than)*. ~ **wie möglich** as little as possible.
**sowie** *conj* (a) *(sobald)* as soon as. (b) *(und auch)* as well as.
**sowieso** *adv* anyway. **das** ~! obviously!
**sowjetisch** *adj (Hist)* Soviet.
**Sowjet-** *in cpds* Soviet; ~**republik** *f (Hist)* Soviet Republic; ~**russe** *m (Hist)* Soviet Russian; ~**union** *f (Hist)* Soviet Union.
**sowohl** *conj* ~ **X als** *or* **wie (auch) Y** both X and Y, X as well as Y.
**Sozi** *m* **-s** *(esp pej col)* Socialist.
**sozial** *adj* social; *(~ eingestellt)* public-spirited. ~**er Wohnungsbau** ≈ council housing *(Brit)*, state-subsidized housing; ~**er Friede** social harmony; ~ **denken** to be socially minded.
**Sozial-:** ~**abbau** *m* cuts *pl* in public spending; ~**abgaben** *pl* social security contributions *pl*; ~**amt** *nt* (social) welfare office; ~**arbeit** *f* social work; ~**arbeiter** *m* social worker; ~**ausgaben** *pl* public spending *sing*; ~**beruf** *m* caring profession; ~**demokrat** *m* social democrat; ~**demokratie** *f* social democracy; **s~demokratisch** *adj* social-democratic; ~**einrichtungen** *pl* social facilities *pl*; ~**fall** *m* hardship case; ~**gericht** *nt* (social) welfare tribunal; ~**hilfe** *f* supplementary benefit

*(Brit)*, welfare (aid) *(US)*.
**Sozialisation** *f (Psych, Sociol)* socialization.
**sozialisieren*** *vt (Psych, Sociol)* to socialize.
**Sozialismus** *m* socialism.
**Sozialist(in** *f) m* socialist.
**sozialistisch** *adj* socialist.
**Sozial-:** ~**kunde** *f* social studies *sing*; ~**leistungen** *pl* (state and employers') social security contributions; **s~liberal** *adj (BRD Pol)* Koalition liberal-social democrat; ~**pädagogik** *f* social education; ~**partner** *pl* unions and management; ~**plan** *m* redundancy payments scheme; ~**politik** *f* social policy; ~**staat** *m* welfare state; ~**station** *f* health and advice centre *(Brit)* or center *(US)*; ~**versicherung** *f* national insurance *(Brit)*, social security *(US)*; ~**wissenschaft** *f* social science; ~**wohnung** *f* ≈ council flat *(Brit)*, state-subsidized apartment.
**Sozio-:** ~**loge** *m (wk)*, ~**login** *f* sociologist; ~**logie** *f* sociology; **s~logisch** *adj* sociological.
**Sozius** *m* **-se** (a) *(Beifahrer)* pillion rider. (b) *(Partner)* partner.
**Soziussitz** *m* pillion (seat).
**sozusagen** *adv* so to speak, as it were.
**Spachtel** *m (Werkzeug)* spatula.
**Spachtelmasse** *f* filler.
**spachteln 1** *vt Mauerfugen, Ritzen* to fill (in). **2** *vi (col: essen)* to tuck in.
**Spagat** *m or nt* **-e** splits *pl*. ~ **machen** to do the splits.
**Spaghetti** [ʃpa'gɛti] *pl* spaghetti *sing*.
**spähen** *vi* to peer.
**Spähtrupp** *m (Mil)* reconnaissance party.
**Spalier** *nt* **-e** (a) *(für Pflanzen)* trellis. (b) *(von Menschen)* row, line; *(zur Ehrenbezeigung)* guard of honour *(Brit)* or honor *(US)*. ~ **stehen/ein** ~ **bilden** to form a guard of honour.
**Spalt** *m* **-e** (a) *(Öffnung)* gap, opening; *(Riß)* crack; *(Fels~)* crevice. **das Fenster einen** ~ **öffnen** to open the window slightly or a crack. (b) *(fig: Kluft)* split.
**spaltbar** *adj (Phys) Material* fissile.
**Spaltbreit** *m*: **etw einen** ~ **öffnen** to open sth slightly or a crack.
**Spalte** *f* **-n** (a) *(esp Geol)* fissure; *(in Wand)* crack. (b) *(Typ, Press)* column.
**spalten** *ptp auch* **gespalten** *vt (lit, fig)* to split; *Holz* to chop. **bei dieser Frage sind die Meinungen gespalten** opinions are divided on this question; *siehe* **gespalten.**
**Spaltung** *f (lit, fig)* splitting; *(in Partei etc)* split.
**Span** *m* **=e** *(Hobel~)* shaving; *(Metall~)* filing.
**Spanferkel** *nt* sucking pig.
**Spange** *f* **-n** clasp; *(Haar~)* hair slide *(Brit)*, barrette *(US)*; *(Schuh~)* strap; *(Arm~)* bangle; *(Zahn~)* brace.
**Spaniel** ['ʃpaːniɛl] *m* **-s** spaniel.
**Spanien** ['ʃpaːniən] *nt* Spain.
**Spanier(in** *f)* ['ʃpaːniɐ, -iərɪn] *m* - Spaniard. **die** ~ the Spanish, the Spaniards.
**spanisch** *adj* Spanish. ~**e Wand** (folding) screen; **das kommt mir** ~ **vor** *(col)* that seems odd to me; *siehe* **deutsch.**
**Spanisch(e)** *nt* Spanish; *siehe* **Deutsch(e).**
**Spankorb** *m* chip basket.
**Spann** *m* **-e** instep.
**spann** *pret of* **spinnen.**
**Spann-:** ~**beton** *m* prestressed concrete; ~**bettuch** *nt* fitted sheet.
**Spanne** *f* **-n** *(geh: Zeit~)* while; *(Gewinn~)* margin.
**spannen 1** *vt* (a) *Saite, Seil* to tighten; *Bogen* to draw; *Muskeln* to flex. (b) *(straff befestigen) Werk-*

*stück* to clamp; *Wäscheleine* to put up; *Netz, Plane* to stretch. **einen Bogen in die Schreibmaschine** ~ to insert a sheet of paper in the typewriter. **(c)** *(fig)* **seine Erwartungen zu hoch** ~ to pitch one's expectations too high. **2** *vr* **(a)** *(Haut, Muskeln)* to go *or* become taut. **(b) sich über etw** *(acc)* ~ *(Brücke)* to span sth. **3** *vi (Kleidungsstück)* to be (too) tight.

**spannend** *adj* exciting; *(stärker)* thrilling. **mach's nicht so** ~**!** *(col)* don't keep me/us in suspense.

**Spanner** *m* - **(a)** *(Hosen~)* hanger; *(Schuh~)* shoetree. **(b)** *(col: Voyeur)* peeping Tom.

**Spannkraft** *f (von Feder)* tension; *(von Muskel)* tone; *(fig)* vigour *(Brit)*, vigor *(US)*.

**Spannung** *f (lit, fig)* tension; *(Elec auch)* voltage; *(Mech)* stress. **mit großer/atemloser** ~ with great/ breathless excitement; **etw mit** ~ **erwarten** to await sth full of suspense.

**Spannungs-:** ~**feld** *nt (lit)* electric field; *(fig)* area of conflict; ~**gebiet** *nt (Pol)* flashpoint, area of tension; **s~geladen** *adj Atmosphäre* charged with tension; *Film, Erzählung etc* full of suspense; ~**prüfer** *m* voltage tester; ~**stoß** *m (Elec)* surge.

**Spannweite** *f (von Flügeln, Aviat)* (wing)span.

**Spanplatte** *f* chipboard.

**Spar-:** ~**brief** *m (Fin)* savings certificate; ~**buch** *nt* savings book; ~**büchse**, ~**dose** *f* moneybox; ~**einlage** *f* savings deposit.

**sparen 1** *vt* to save. **keine Kosten/Mühe** ~ to spare no expense/effort; **spar' dir deine guten Ratschläge!** *(col)* you can keep your advice!; **diese Mühe/diese Kosten hätten Sie sich** *(dat)* ~ **können** you could have saved *or* spared yourself the trouble/this expense. **2** *vi* to save; *(haushalten)* to economize. **an etw** *(dat)* ~ to be sparing with sth; *(mit etw haushalten)* to save *or* economize on sth; **er hatte nicht mit Lob gespart** he was lavish in his praise; **für** *or* **auf etw** *(acc)* ~ to save up for sth.

**Sparer(in** *f)* *m* - *(bei Bank etc)* saver.

**Sparflamme** *f* low flame. **auf** ~ *(fig col)* just ticking over *(col)*.

**Spargel** *m* - asparagus.

**Spar-:** ~**groschen** *m* nest egg; ~**guthaben** *nt* balance in a savings account; ~**kasse** *f* savings bank; ~**kassenbuch** *nt* savings book; ~**konto** *nt* savings account, deposit account *(Brit)*, thrift account *(US)*.

**spärlich** *adj* sparse; *Ausbeute, Reste, Kleidung, Kenntnisse* scanty; *Beleuchtung* poor. ~ **bevölkert** sparsely populated.

**Spar-:** ~**maßnahme** *f* economy (measure); ~**packung** *f* economy size; ~**politik** *f* cost-cutting policy; ~**prämie** *f* savings premium; ~**preis** *m* economy price.

**sparsam** *adj* thrifty; *(haushälterisch)* economical. ~ **leben** to live economically; ~ **im Verbrauch** economical; ~ **verwenden** to use sparingly.

**Sparsamkeit** *f* thrift; *(im Verbrauch)* economy; *(das Haushalten)* economizing.

**Sparschwein** *nt* piggy bank.

**spartanisch** *adj* Spartan. ~ **leben** to lead a Spartan life.

**Sparte** *f* -**n** **(a)** *(Comm)* *(Branche)* line of business; *(Teilgebiet)* area. **(b)** *(Rubrik)* column.

**Spar-:** ~**vertrag** *m* savings agreement; ~**zinsen** *pl* interest *no pl*; ~**zulage** *f* savings bonus.

**Spaß** *m* -**e** *(no pl: Vergnügen)* fun; *(Scherz)* joke; *(Streich)* prank. ~ **beiseite** joking apart; **viel** ~**!** have fun! *(auch iro)*; **an etw** *(dat)* ~ **haben** to enjoy sth; **es macht mir** ~**/keinen** ~ it's fun/no fun; **Hauptsache, es macht** ~ the main thing is to have fun; **(nur so,) zum** ~ for fun; **etw im** ~ **sagen** to say

sth in fun; **da hört der** ~ **auf** that's going beyond a joke; **ein teurer** ~ an expensive business; ~ **muß sein** there's no harm in a joke; **es war ein** ~**, ihm bei der Arbeit zuzusehen** it was a joy to see him at work; **sich** *(dat)* **einen** ~ **daraus machen, etw zu tun** to get enjoyment out of doing sth; **seinen** ~ **mit jdm treiben** to make fun of sb; **er versteht keinen** ~**!** he has no sense of humour *(Brit)* or humor *(US)*; **da verstehe ich keinen** ~**!** I won't stand for any nonsense.

**spaßen** *vi* **mit einer Blutvergiftung ist nicht zu** ~ blood poisoning is no joke; **mit ihm ist nicht zu** ~ he doesn't stand for any nonsense.

**spaßeshalber** *adv* for the fun of it, for fun.

**spaßig** *adj* funny, droll.

**Spaß-:** ~**macher** *m* joker; ~**verderber** *m* - spoilsport; ~**vogel** *m* joker.

**Spastiker(in** *f)* *m* - spastic.

**spastisch** *adj* spastic. ~ **gelähmt** suffering from spastic paralysis.

**spät** *adj* late; *Reue, Ruhm, Glück* belated. **am** ~**en Nachmittag** in the late afternoon; ~ **in der Nacht/ am Tage** late at night/in the day; **heute abend wird es** ~ it'll be a late night tonight; *(nach Hause kommen)* I/he *etc* will be late home this evening; **von früh bis** ~ from morning till night; **wie** ~ **ist es?** what's the time?; **zu** ~ too late; **er kommt morgens regelmäßig fünf Minuten zu** ~ he's always five minutes late in the mornings; **wir sind** ~ **dran** we're late.

**Spatel** *m* - *(Med)* spatula.

**Spaten** *m* - spade.

**Spatenstich** *m* **den ersten** ~ **tun** to turn the first sod.

**Spät|entwickler** *m* late developer.

**später** *comp of* **spät** *adj* later; *(zukünftig)* future. **was will sie denn** ~ **(einmal) werden?** what does she want to do when she grows up?; **an** ~ **denken** to think of the future; **bis** ~**!** see you later!

**spätestens** *adv* at the latest. ~ **morgen** tomorrow at the latest; ~ **um 8** by 8 at the latest; **bis** ~ **in einer Woche** in one week at the latest.

**Spät-:** ~**geburt** *f* late birth; ~**herbst** *m* late autumn *or* fall *(US)*; ~**lese** *f* late vintage; ~**nachmittag** *m* late afternoon; ~**schäden** *pl* long-term damage; ~**schicht** *f* late shift; ~**sommer** *m* late summer.

**Spatz** *m (wk)* -**en, -en (a)** sparrow. **wie ein** ~ **essen** to peck at one's food. **(b)** *(col: Kind)* tot *(col)*.

**Spätzle** *pl (Cook)* home-made pasta.

**Spätzünder** *m (hum col)* ~ **sein** *(schwer von Begriff)* to be slow on the uptake; *(spät im Leben mit etw anfangen)* to be a late starter.

**spazieren\*** *vi aux sein* to stroll. **wir waren** ~ we went for a walk *or* stroll.

**spazieren-:** ~**fahren** *sep irreg* **1** *vi aux sein* to go for a drive; **2** *vt* **jdn** ~**fahren** to take sb for a drive; **das Baby (im Kinderwagen)** ~**fahren** to take the baby for a walk (in the pram); ~**gehen** *vi sep irreg aux sein* to go for a walk.

**Spazier-:** ~**fahrt** *f* drive; **eine** ~**fahrt machen** to go for a run; ~**gang** *m* walk; **einen** ~**gang machen** to go for a walk; ~**gänger** *m* - stroller; ~**stock** *m* walking stick; ~**weg** *m* path, walk.

**SPD** [ɛspe:'de:] *f* - = **Sozialdemokratische Partei Deutschlands.**

**Specht** *m* -**e** woodpecker.

**Speck** *m* -**e** *(Schweine~)* bacon fat; *(Schinken~, durchwachsener ~)* bacon. ~ **ansetzen** *(col)* to get fat; **mit** ~ **fängt man Mäuse** *(Prov)* you need a sprat to catch a mackerel *(prov)*; **ran an den** ~ *(col)* let's get stuck in *(col)*.

**speckig** *adj* greasy.

**Speckschwarte** *f* bacon rind.

**Spediteur** [ʃpedi'tøːɐ] *m* haulage contractor; *(Umzugsfirma)* furniture remover *(Brit)* or mover.

**Spedition** *f (auch ~sfirma)* haulage contractor; *(Umzugsfirma)* removal firm *(Brit)*, furniture movers *pl (US)*.

**Speer** *m* **-e** spear; *(Sport)* javelin.

**Speer-:** **~spitze** *f (lit, fig)* spearhead; **~werfen** *nt (Sport)* das **~werfen** the javelin; **~werfer** *m (Sport)* javelin thrower.

**Speiche** *f* **-n** (a) spoke. (b) *(Anat)* radius.

**Speichel** *m no pl* saliva, spittle.

**Speichel-:** **~drüse** *f* salivary gland; **~lecker** *m* - *(pej col)* bootlicker *(col)*.

**Speicher** *m* - *(Lagerhaus)* storehouse; *(im Haus)* loft; *(Wasser~)* tank; *(Comp)* memory. **auf dem ~** in the loft.

**Speicherkapazität** *f* storage capacity; *(Comp)* memory capacity.

**speichern** **1** *vt* Vorräte, Energie, Daten to store; *(Comp: ab~)* to save. **2** *vr* to accumulate.

**Speicherung** *f* storing, storage.

**speien** *pret* **spie**, *ptp* **gespie(e)n** *vti* to spit; *Lava, Feuer* to spew (forth); *Wasser* to spout.

**Speise** *f* **-n** *(geh: Nahrung)* food; *(Gericht)* dish. **kalte und warme ~n** hot and cold meals.

**Speise-:** **~eis** *nt* ice cream; **~fett** *nt* cooking fat; **~gaststätte** *f* restaurant; **~kammer** *f* larder; **~karte** *f* menu.

**speisen** **1** *vti (geh)* to eat, to dine *(form)*. **2** *vt (liter, Tech)* to feed.

**Speise-:** **~öl** *nt* edible oil; *(zum Braten)* cooking oil; *(für Salat)* salad oil; **~reste** *pl* leftovers *pl*; **~röhre** *f (Anat)* gullet, oesophagus *(form)*; **~saal** *m* dining hall; *(in Hotel etc)* dining room; **~schrank** *m* larder; **~wagen** *m (Rail)* dining car; **~wärmer** *m* hotplate; **~zettel** *m* menu.

**Spektakel** *m* - *(col: Lärm)* row; *(Aufregung)* fuss.

**spektakulär** *adj* spectacular.

**Spektralfarbe** *f* colour *(Brit)* or color *(US)* of the spectrum.

**Spektrum** *nt, pl* **Spektren** spectrum.

**Spekulant(in** *f)* *m* speculator.

**Spekulation** *f (auch Fin)* speculation *(mit* in*)*. **~ mit Grundstücken** property speculation; **~en anstellen** to make speculations.

**Spekulatius** [ʃpeku'laːtsi̯ʊs] *m* **-**, **-** spiced biscuit *(Brit)* or cookie *(US)* *(eaten at Christmas)*.

**spekulativ** *adj* speculative.

**spekulieren*** *vi (auch Fin)* to speculate *(mit* in*)*. **auf etw** *(acc)* **~** *(col)* to have hopes of sth.

**Spelunke** *f* **-n** *(pej col)* dive *(col)*.

**Spelze** *f* **-n** *(Bot)* husk.

**spendabel** *adj (col)* generous, open-handed.

**Spende** *f* **-n** donation; *(Beitrag)* contribution.

**spenden** *vti* Lebensmittel, Geld, Organ to donate; *Blut* to give; *(beitragen)* Geld to contribute; *Trost* to give.

**Spenden-:** **~aktion** *f* fund-raising campaign; **~aufkommen** *nt* revenue from donations; **~aufruf** *m* appeal for donations; **~konto** *nt* donations account.

**Spender(in** *f)* *m* - donator; *(Beitragleistender)* contributor; *(Med)* donor.

**spendieren*** *vt* to buy, to get *(jdm etw* sb sth, sth for sb*)*. **spendierst du mir einen?** *(col)* are you going to buy me a drink?

**Spengler(in** *f)* *m* - *(dial: Klempner)* plumber.

**Sperber** *m* - sparrowhawk.

**Sperling** *m* sparrow.

**Sperma** *nt, pl* **Spermen** *or* **-ta** sperm.

**sperr|angelweit** *adv (col)* **~ offen** wide open.

**Sperrbezirk** *m* no-go area.

**Sperre** *f* **-n** (a) *(Schlagbaum, Bahnsteig~ etc)* barrier; *(Polizei~)* roadblock; *(Tech)* locking device. (b) *(Verbot, Sport)* ban; *(Comm)* embargo; *(Nachrichten~)* (news) blackout.

**sperren** **1** *vt* (a) *(schließen)* Grenze, Straße etc to close; *(Comm)* Konto to freeze; *Einfuhr, Ausfuhr, (Sport)* to ban; *(Tech)* to lock. **etw für jdn/etw ~** to close sth to sb/sth; **jdm das Gehalt ~** to stop sb's salary; **jdm den Strom/das Telefon ~** to cut off sb's electricity/telephone. (b) *(einschließen)* jdn in etw *(acc)* **~** to lock sb in sth. (c) *(Typ)* to space out. **2** *vr* **sich (gegen etw) ~** to ba(u)lk (at sth). **3** *vi (Sport)* to obstruct.

**Sperr-:** **~feuer** *nt (Mil, fig)* barrage; **~frist** *f* waiting period *(auch Jur)*; *(Sport)* (period of) suspension; **~gebiet** *nt* no-go area; **~gut** *nt* bulky freight; **~holz** *nt* plywood.

**sperrig** *adj* bulky; *(unhandlich)* unwieldy.

**Sperr-:** **~kette** *f* chain; *(an Haustür)* safety chain; **~konto** *nt* blocked account; **~müll** *m* bulky refuse; **~schrift** *f (Typ)* spaced type; **~sitz** *m (im Kino)* back seats *pl*; *(im Zirkus)* front seats *pl*; **~stunde** *f* closing time.

**Sperrung** *f* (a) *siehe vt (a)* closing; freezing; banning; locking. (b) *(Verbot, Sport)* ban.

**Spesen** *pl* expenses *pl*. **auf ~ reisen/essen** to travel/eat on expenses; **außer ~ nichts gewesen** *(col)* there was nothing doing *(col)*.

**Spesen-:** **s~frei** *adj* free of charge; **~konto** *nt* expense account.

**Spezi** *m* **-s** (a) *(S Ger col)* pal *(col)*, mate *(col)*. (b) *(Getränk)* Coca Cola ® *and lemonade.*

**Spezial-:** **~ausbildung** *f* specialized training; **~ausführung** *f* special model; **~fall** *m* special case; **~gebiet** *nt* special field; **~geschäft** *nt* specialist shop *(Brit)* or store *(US)*; **ein ~geschäft für Sportkleidung** a sportswear specialist.

**spezialisieren*** *vr* **sich (auf etw** *acc)* **~** to specialize (in sth).

**Spezialisierung** *f* specialization.

**Spezialist(in** *f)* *m* specialist *(für* in*)*.

**Spezialität** *f* speciality *(Brit)*, specialty *(US)*.

**speziell** **1** *adj* special. **2** *adv* (e)specially.

**spezifisch** *adj* specific.

**spezifizieren*** *vt* to specify.

**Sphäre** *f* **-n** *(lit, fig)* sphere.

**sphärisch** *adj* spherical; *Klänge, Musik* celestial.

**Sphinx** *f* **-e** sphinx.

**spicken** *vt* **1** *(Cook)* Braten to lard. **mit Fehlern gespickt** peppered with mistakes. **2** *vi (Sch col)* to crib *(col)* *(bei* off*)*.

**Spickzettel** *m (col)* crib.

**spie** *pret of* **speien**.

**Spiegel** *m* - (a) *(lit, fig)* mirror. **jdm den ~ vorhalten** *(fig)* to hold up a mirror to sb. (b) *(Wasser~, Alkohol~, Zucker~)* level.

**Spiegel-:** **~bild** *nt (lit, fig)* reflection; *(seitenverkehrtes Bild)* mirror image; **s~bildlich** *adj* Zeichnung etc mirror-image *attr*; **s~blank** *adj* shining.

**Spiegel|ei** *nt* fried egg.

**Spiegel-:** **~fechterei** *f (fig)* shadow-boxing; *(Vortäuschung)* bluff; **s~frei** *adj* Brille, Bildschirm etc non-reflecting; **~glas** *nt* mirror glass; **s~glatt** *adj* like glass *pred*.

**spiegeln** **1** *vi* to reflect; *(glitzern)* to gleam. **2** *vt* to reflect. **3** *vr* to be reflected *or* mirrored.

**Spiegel-:** **~reflexkamera** *f* reflex camera;

~**schrift** f mirror writing; **etw in ~schrift schreiben** to write sth backwards.
**Spiegelung** f reflection; *(Luft~)* mirage.
**spiegelverkehrt** *adj* in mirror image.
**Spiel** nt -e **(a)** game; *(Wettkampfs~ auch)* match; *(Theat: Stück)* play. **im ~ sein** *(fig)* to be at work; **das ~ verloren geben** *(fig)* to throw in the towel; **sein Geld beim ~ verlieren** to lose one's money gambling. **(b)** *(Bewegung, Zusammenspiel)* play. **das (freie) ~ der Kräfte** the (free) (inter)play of forces. **(c)** *(Spielzubehör)* game; *(Karten)* deck, pack; *(Satz)* set. **(d)** *(fig)* **das ist ein ~ mit dem Feuer** that's playing with fire; **leichtes ~ (mit or bei jdm) haben** to have an easy job of it (with sb); **das ~ ist aus** the game's up; **die Finger im ~ haben** to have a hand in affairs; **jdn/etw aus dem ~ lassen** to leave sb/sth out of it; **etw aufs ~ setzen** to put sth at stake; **auf dem ~(e) stehen** to be at stake; **sein ~ mit jdm treiben** to play games with sb.
**Spiel-: ~anzug** m playsuit; *(einteilig)* rompers pl *(Brit)*, creepers pl *(US)*; **~art** f variety; **~automat** m gambling machine; *(zum Geldgewinnen)* fruit machine *(Brit)*; **~ball** m *(fig)* plaything; **ein ~ball der Wellen sein** *(geh)* to be at the mercy of the waves; **~bank** f casino; **~dose** f musical box *(Brit)*, music box *(US)*.
**spielen 1** vt to play. **jdm einen Streich ~** to play a trick on sb; **Klavier ~** to play the piano; **was wird heute im Theater/Kino gespielt?** what's on at the theatre/cinema today?; **den Beleidigten ~** to act offended; **was wird hier gespielt?** *(col)* what's going on here? **2** vi to play; *(Theaterstück, Film)* to be on; *(beim Glücksspiel)* to gamble. **seine Beziehungen ~ lassen** to pull strings; **das Stück spielt im 18. Jahrhundert** the play is set in the 18th century; **mit dem Gedanken ~, etw zu tun** to toy with the idea of doing sth. **3** vr **sich warm ~** to warm up; **sich in den Vordergrund ~** to push oneself into the foreground.
**spielend 1** *adj* playing. **2** *adv* easily. **das ist ~ leicht** that's very easy.
**Spieler(in** f) m - player; *(Glücks~)* gambler.
**Spielerei** f no pl *(Kinderspiel)* child's play no art. **das ist nur ~** I am/he is etc just playing about.
**spielerisch 1** *adj (verspielt)* Geste, Katze etc playful. **(b)** *(Sport)* playing; *(Theat)* acting. **~es Können** playing/acting ability. **2** *adv* **(a)** *(verspielt)* playfully. **(b)** *(Sport)* in playing terms; *(Theat)* in acting terms.
**Spiel-: ~feld** nt field, pitch *(Brit)*; *(Tennis, Basketball)* court; **~figur** f piece; **~film** m feature film; **~folge** f *(Sport)* order of play; *(Theat)* programme *(Brit)*, program *(US)*; **~gefährte** m playmate; **~geld** nt *(Einsatz)* stake; **(b)** *(unechtes Geld)* toy money; **~halle** f amusement arcade; **~hölle** f gambling den; **~kamerad** m playmate; **~karte** f playing card; **~kasino** nt (gambling) casino; **~klasse** f division; **~leidenschaft** f gambling mania; **~macher** m key player; **~mannszug** m (brass) band; **~marke** f chip; **~minute** f minute (of play); **~plan** m *(Theat, Film)* programme *(Brit)*, program *(US)*; **ein Stück vom ~plan absetzen** to drop a play; **~platz** m *(für Kinder)* playground; **~raum** m room to move; *(fig)* scope; *(zeitlich)* time; *(bei Planung etc)* leeway; *(Tech)* clearance, (free) play; **~regel** f *(lit, fig)* rule of the game; **sich an die ~regeln halten** *(lit, fig)* to play the game; **gegen die ~regeln verstoßen** *(lit, fig)* not to play the game; **~sachen** pl toys pl; **~saison** f *(Theat, Sport)* season; **~schuld** f gambling debt; **~stand** m score; **bei einem ~stand von ...** with the score at ...; **~stein** m piece; **~straße** f play street;

~**sucht** f addiction to gambling; **~tag** m day (of play); **~tisch** m *(beim Glückspiel)* gaming table; **~trieb** m play instinct; **~uhr** f musical box *(Brit)*, music box *(US)*; **~verbot** nt *(Sport)* ban; **~verbot haben** to be banned; **~verderber(in** f) m - spoilsport; **~verlängerung** f extra time *(Brit)*, overtime *(US)*; **~verlauf** m action; **~waren** pl toys; **~warengeschäft** nt toy shop *(Brit)* or store *(US)*; **~weise** f way of playing; **~werk** nt musical box mechanism; **~wiese** f playing field; *(fig)* playground; **~zeit** f **(a)** *(Saison)* season; **(b)** *(~dauer)* playing time.
**Spielzeug** nt toy; toys pl; *(fig auch)* plaything.
**Spielzeug-** in cpds toy; **~eisenbahn** f toy train set.
**Spiel-: ~zimmer** nt playroom; **~zug** m move.
**Spieß** m -e **(a)** spear; *(Brat~)* spit; *(kleiner)* skewer. **am ~ gebraten** spitroast(ed); **wie am ~(e) schreien** *(col)* to squeal like a stuck pig; **den ~ umdrehen** *(fig)* to turn the tables. **(b)** *(Mil col)* sarge *(col)*.
**Spießbraten** m joint roasted on a spit.
**Spießbürger** m (petit) bourgeois.
**spießbürgerlich** *adj* (petit) bourgeois.
**spießen** vt **etw auf etw** *(acc)* **~** *(auf Pfahl)* to impale sth on sth; *(auf Gabel)* to skewer sth on sth.
**Spießer** m - *(col)* (petit) bourgeois.
**Spießgeselle** m *(hum: Komplize)* crony *(col)*.
**spießig** *adj (col)* (petit) bourgeois.
**Spießrute** f **~n laufen** *(fig)* to run the gauntlet.
**Spikes** [ʃpaiks, sp-] pl *(Sportschuhe)* spikes pl; *(Autoreifen)* studded tyres pl *(Brit)* or tires pl *(US)*; *(Stifte an Reifen)* studs pl.
**Spill** nt -(e)s, -e *(Naut)* capstan.
**Spinat** m no pl spinach.
**Spind** m or nt -e locker.
**Spindel** f -n spindle; *(Treppen~)* newel.
**spindeldürr** *adj (pej)* spindly, thin as a rake.
**Spinett** nt -e *(Mus)* spinet.
**Spinne** f -n spider; *(Wäsche~)* rotary clothes line.
**spinnefeind** *adj pred (col)* **sich** or **einander** *(dat)* **~ sein** to be deadly enemies.
**spinnen** pret **spann**, ptp **gesponnen 1** vti to spin; Lügen to concoct, to invent. **2** vi *(col) (leicht verrückt sein)* to be crazy; *(Unsinn reden)* to talk rubbish. **ich denk' ich spinne** I don't believe it; **du spinnst wohl!**, **spinnst du?** you must be crazy!
**Spinnen-: ~faden** m spider's thread; **~gewebe**, **~netz** nt cobweb.
**Spinner(in** f) m - **(a)** *(col)* nutcase *(col)*, screwball *(esp US col)*. **(b)** spinner.
**Spinnerei** f **(a)** *(Spinnwerkstatt)* spinning mill. **(b)** *(col)* crazy behaviour *(Brit)* or behavior *(US)* no pl; *(Idee)* crazy idea; *(Unsinn)* rubbish.
**spinnert** *adj (col)* crazy *(col)*.
**Spinn-: ~faser** f spinning fibre *(Brit)* or fiber *(US)*; **~gewebe** nt cobweb; **~rad** nt spinning-wheel; **~webe** f -n cobweb.
**Spion** m -e spy; *(col: Guckloch)* peephole.
**Spionage** [ʃpio'na:ʒə] f no pl espionage. **~ treiben** to spy.
**Spionage-: ~abwehr** f counter-intelligence; **~ring** m spy ring; **~satellit** m spy satellite.
**spionieren\*** vi to spy; *(col: nachforschen)* to snoop about *(col)*.
**Spionin** f (woman) spy.
**Spirale** f -n spiral; *(Med)* coil.
**Spiral-: ~feder** f coil spring; **s~förmig** *adj* spiral.
**Spiritismus** m spiritualism.
**Spiritist(in** f) m spiritualist.
**spiritistisch** *adj* spiritualist.
**spirituell** *adj* spiritual.
**Spirituosen** pl spirits pl.

**Spiritus** *m* -, *no pl (Alkohol)* spirit. **mit ~ kochen** to cook with a spirit stove; **etw in ~ legen** to put sth in alcohol.

**Spiritus-:** ~**kocher** *m* spirit stove; ~**lampe** *f* spirit lamp.

**spitz** *adj* (**a**) *(mit einer Spitze)* pointed; *Bleistift, Nadel etc* sharp; *(Math) Winkel* acute. ~**e Klammern** angle brackets; ~ **zulaufen** to taper; **etw mit ~en Fingern anfassen** *(col)* to pick sth up gingerly. (**b**) *(gehässig) Bemerkung* pointed, barbed; *Zunge* sharp.

**Spitz** *m* **-e** *(Hund)* spitz.

**Spitz-:** ~**bart** *m* goatee; **s~bekommen\*** *vt sep irreg (col)* **etw s~bekommen** to get wise to sth *(col)*; ~**bogen** *m* pointed arch; ~**bub(e)** *m* villain, rogue; *(col: Schlingel)* scamp *(col)*; **s~bübisch** *adj* mischievous.

**Spitze** *f* **-n** (**a**) point; *(Finger~, Nasen~, Bart~, Schuh~)* tip; *(Berg~, Fels~, Baum~, Turm~)* top. **auf der ~ stehen** to be upside down; **etw auf die ~ treiben** to carry sth too far; **einer Sache** *(dat)* **die ~ nehmen** *(fig)* to take the sting out of sth. (**b**) *(Führung)* head; *(vorderes Ende)* front; *(Tabellen~)* top; *(fig: Höchstwert)* peak. **an der ~ stehen** to be at the head; **an der ~ liegen** *(Sport, fig)* to be in the lead; **sich an die ~ setzen** *(in Wettbewerb etc, Sport)* to take the lead. (**c**) *(fig: Stichelei)* dig. **das ist eine ~ gegen Sie** that's a dig at you. (**d**) *(Gewebe)* lace. (**e**) *(col: prima)* great *(col)*.

**Spitzel** *m* - informer; *(Spion)* spy; *(Schnüffler)* snooper; *(Polizei~)* police informer.

**spitzen** *vt (spitz machen) Bleistift* to sharpen; *Lippen, Mund* to purse; *(zum Küssen)* to pucker; *Ohren (lit, fig)* to prick up.

**Spitzen-** *in cpds* top; *(aus Spitze)* lace; ~**belastung** *f* peak load; ~**bluse** *f* lace blouse; ~**erzeugnis** *nt* top-quality product; *(auf einem Gebiet)* leading product; ~**feld** *nt (Sport)* leading group; ~**funktionär** *m* top official; ~**gehalt** *nt* top salary; ~**geschwindigkeit** *f* top speed; ~**höschen** *nt* lace panties *pl*; ~**kandidat** *m* top candidate; ~**klasse** *f* top class; **Sekt der ~klasse** top-quality champagne; ~**kraft** *f* top professional; ~**leistung** *f* top performance; *(von Maschine, Auto)* peak performance; *(bei der Herstellung von Produkten, Energie)* peak output; ~**lohn** *m* top wage(s *pl*); **s~mäßig** *adj (col)* great *(col)*; ~**politiker** *m* leading politician; ~**position** *f* leading position; ~**qualität** *f* top quality; ~**reiter** *m (Sport)* leader; *(fig) (Kandidat)* front-runner; *(Ware)* top seller; *(Schlager)* number one; ~**sportler** *m* top(-class) sportsman; ~**stellung** *f* leading position; ~**technologie** *f* state-of-the-art technology; ~**verband** *m* leading organization; ~**verdiener** *m* top earner; ~**verkehrszeit** *f* peak period; ~**wein** *m* top-quality wine; ~**wert** *m* peak; ~**zeit** *f (Sport)* record time; *(Hauptverkehrszeit)* peak period, rush hour.

**Spitzer** *m* sharpener.

**Spitz-:** **s~findig** *adj* over-subtle; *(haarspalterisch)* hair-splitting; ~**findigkeit** *f* over-subtlety; *(Haarspalterei)* hair-splitting *no pl*; ~**hacke** *f* pickaxe *(Brit)*, pickax *(US)*; **s~kriegen** *vt sep (col)* = **s~bekommen;** ~**maus** *f* shrew; ~**name** *m* nickname; **mit dem ~namen ...** nicknamed ...; **s~züngig** *adj* sharp-tongued.

**Spleen** [ʃpliːn] *m* **-s** *(col) (Angewohnheit)* crazy habit; *(Idee)* crazy idea; *(Fimmel)* obsession. **du hast ja einen ~!** you're off your head *(col)*.

**spleenig** [ˈʃpliːnɪç] *adj (col)* crazy, nutty *(col)*.

**Splint** *m* **-e** cotter (pin), split pin.

**Splitt** *m* **-e** stone chippings *pl*; *(Streumittel)* grit.

**Splitter** *m* - splinter; *(Granat~)* fragment.

**Splitter-:** ~**bombe** *f (Mil)* fragmentation bomb; ~**gruppe** *f (Pol)* splinter group.

**splittern** *vi aux sein or haben (Holz, Glas)* to splinter.

**splitternackt** *adj* stark naked.

**Splitterpartei** *f (Pol)* splinter party.

**SPÖ** [ɛspeːˈløː] *f* = **Sozialistische Partei Österreichs** *Austrian Socialist Party.*

**Spoiler** [ˈʃpɔylɐ] *m* - *(Aut)* spoiler.

**sponsern** *vti* to sponsor.

**Sponsor** *m* **-en, Sponsorin** *f* sponsor.

**spontan** *adj* spontaneous.

**Spontaneität** [ʃpɔntaneiˈtɛːt] *f* spontaneity.

**sporadisch** *adj* sporadic.

**Spore** *f* **-n** *(Biol)* spore.

**Sporen** *pl (auch Zool, Bot)* spurs. **einem Pferd die ~ geben** to spur a horse; **sich** *(dat)* **die (ersten) ~ verdienen** *(fig)* to win one's spurs.

**Sport** *m no pl* sport. **treiben Sie ~?** do you go in for any sport?; **etw zum ~ betreiben** *(als Hobby)* to do sth as a hobby.

**Sport-** *in cpds* sports; *(US: esp Kleidung)* sport; ~**abzeichen** *nt* sports certificate; ~**angler** *m* angler; ~**anlage** *f* sports complex; ~**art** *f* (form of) sport; ~**artikel** *pl* sports *or* sport *(US)* equipment *with sing vb*; ~**arzt** *m* sports physician; **s~begeistert** *adj* keen on sport; ~**bericht** *m* sports report; ~**ereignis** *nt* sporting event; ~**fest** *nt* sports festival; *(Sch)* sports day *(Brit)*; ~**flieger** *m* amateur pilot; ~**flugzeug** *nt* sporting aircraft; ~**freund** *m* sport(s) fan; ~**geist** *m* sportsmanship; ~**geschäft** *nt* sports shop *(Brit)*, sport store *(US)*; ~**halle** *f* sports hall; ~**hemd** *nt* sports *or* sport *(US)* shirt; ~**hochschule** *f* college of physical education; ~**kleidung** *f* sportswear; ~**klub** *m* sports club; ~**lehrer(in** *f)* *m* sports instructor; *(Sch)* PE *or* physical education teacher.

**Sportler** *m* - sportsman, athlete.

**Sportlerin** *f* sportswoman, (woman) athlete.

**sportlich** *adj* (**a**) *Mensch, Auto* sporty; *Veranstaltung, Wettkampf* sporting; *(durchtrainiert)* athletic. (**b**) *(fair)* sportsmanlike *no adv*. (**c**) *Kleidung* (smart but) casual; *(wie Sportkleidung aussehend)* sporty.

**Sportlichkeit** *f* (**a**) *(von Menschen)* sportiness; *(Durchtrainiertheit)* athleticism. (**b**) *(Fairneß)* sportsmanship.

**Sport-:** ~**medizin** *f* sports medicine; ~**nachrichten** *pl* sports news *with sing vb or* reports *pl*; ~**platz** *m* playing *or* sports field; ~**rad** *nt* sports bike *(col)*; ~**reportage** *f* sports report; ~**schuh** *m* sports *or* sport *(US)* shoe; *(Freizeitschuh)* casual shoe.

**Sports-:** ~**freund** *m (fig col)* buddy *(col)*; ~**kanone** *f (col)* sporting ace *(col)*.

**Sport-:** ~**stadion** *nt* (sports) stadium; ~**unfall** *m* sporting accident; ~**veranstaltung** *f* sporting event; ~**verein** *m* sports club; ~**wagen** *m* sports car; *(für Kind)* pushchair *(Brit)*, (baby) stroller *(US)*; ~**zeitung** *f* sports paper; ~**zeug** *nt (col)* sport(s) things *pl*.

**Spot** [spɔt] *m* **-s** commercial, advertisement.

**Spott** *m no pl* mockery, ridicule. **seinen ~ mit jdm treiben** to make fun of sb.

**Spott-:** ~**bild** *nt (fig)* travesty; **s~billig** *adj* dirt-cheap *(col)*.

**spötteln** *vi* to mock *(über jdn/etw* sb/sth*)*.

**spotten** *vi* to mock. **über jdn/etw ~** to mock sb/sth; **das spottet jeder Beschreibung** that simply defies description.

**Spötter(in** *f)* *m* - mocker.

**Spott-:** ~**figur** *f* joke figure; **eine ~figur sein** to be an object of ridicule; ~**gedicht** *nt* satirical poem.

**spöttisch** *adj* mocking.
**Spott-:** ~**lied** *nt* satirical song; ~**name** *m* derisive nickname; ~**preis** *m* ridiculously low price; ~**rede** *f* satirical speech; ~**vers** *m* satirical verse.
**sprach** *pret of* **sprechen**.
**Sprach-:** ~**barriere** *f* language barrier; **s~begabt** *adj* good at languages; ~**begabung** *f* talent for languages.
**Sprache** *f* **-n** language; *(das Sprechen, Sprechweise)* speech; *(Fähigkeit zu sprechen)* faculty of speech. **eine ~ sprechen** to speak a language; **in französischer** *etc* ~ in French *etc*; **heraus mit der ~!** *(col)* come on, out with it!; **zur ~ kommen** to be mentioned; **etw zur ~ bringen** to bring sth up; **hast du die ~ verloren** have you lost your tongue?; **es verschlägt einem die ~** it takes your breath away.
**Sprachenschule** *f* language school.
**Sprach-:** ~**fehler** *m* speech defect; ~**forscher** *m* linguist; ~**forschung** *f* linguistic research; ~**führer** *m* phrasebook; ~**gebiet** *nt* language area; **ein französisches** *etc* ~**gebiet** a French-speaking *etc* area; ~**gebrauch** *m* usage; **moderner deutscher** ~**gebrauch** modern German usage; ~**gefühl** *nt* feeling for language; ~**gemeinschaft** *f* language community; ~**genie** *nt* linguistic genius; ~**geschichte** *f* linguistic history; **s~gewandt** *adj* articulate; ~**kenntnisse** *pl* linguistic proficiency *sing*; **mit englischen** ~**kenntnissen** with a knowledge of English; **haben Sie irgendwelche** ~**kenntnisse?** do you know any languages?; **s~kundig** *adj* **s~kundig sein** *(in einer bestimmten Sprache)* to know the language; ~**kurs(us)** *m* language course; ~**labor** *nt* language laboratory; ~**lehre** *f* grammar; ~**lehrer** *m* language teacher.
**sprachlich** *adj* linguistic; *Unterricht, Schwierigkeiten* language *attr*; *Fehler* grammatical. ~ **falsch/richtig** grammatically incorrect/correct.
**sprachlos** *adj* speechless.
**Sprachlosigkeit** *f* speechlessness.
**Sprach-:** ~**rohr** *nt* *(Megaphon)* megaphone; *(fig)* mouthpiece; ~**schöpfung** *f* linguistic innovation; ~**schule** *f* language school; ~**störung** *f* speech disorder; ~**studium** *nt* study of language; ~**übung** *f* language exercise; ~**unterricht** *m* language teaching; ~**urlaub** *m* language-learning holiday; ~**wissenschaft** *f* linguistics *sing*; ~**wissenschaftler** *m* linguist; **s~wissenschaftlich** *adj* linguistic.
**sprang** *pret of* **springen**.
**Spray** [ʃpreː, spreː] *m or nt* **-s** spray.
**Spraydose** ['ʃpreː-, 'spreː-] *f* aerosol (can), spray.
**sprayen** ['ʃpreːən, sp-] *vti* to spray.
**Sprech-:** ~**anlage** *f* intercom; ~**blase** *f* (speech) balloon; ~**chor** *m* chorus; *(fig)* chorus of voices; ~**einheit** *f* *(Telec)* unit.
**sprechen** *pret* **sprach**, *ptp* **gesprochen** **1** *vi* to speak *(über +acc, von* about, of*)*; *(reden, sich unterhalten auch)* to talk *(über +acc, von* about*)*. **viel ~** to talk a lot; **frei ~** to extemporize; **er spricht wenig** he doesn't say very much; **im Schlaf ~** to talk in one's sleep; **es spricht/es ~ ...** the speaker is/the speakers are ...; **nicht gut auf jdn zu ~ sein** to be on bad terms with sb; **wie sprichst du mit mir?** who do you think you're talking to?; **wir ~ nicht mehr miteinander** we are no longer on speaking terms; **mit wem spreche ich?** to whom am I speaking, please?; **darüber spricht man nicht** one doesn't talk about such things; ~ **wir von etwas anderem** let's change the subject; **es wird kaum noch von ihm gesprochen** he's hardly mentioned now; **es spricht für jdn/etw(, daß ...)** it says something for sb/sth (that ...); **das**

**spricht für ihn** that's a point in his favour *(Brit)* or favor *(US)*; **das spricht für sich (selbst)** that speaks for itself; **es spricht vieles dafür** there's a lot to be said for it; **es spricht vieles dafür, daß ...** there is every reason to believe that ...; **was spricht dafür/dagegen?** what is there to be said for/against it?; **er sprach vor den Studenten** he spoke to the students; **ganz allgemein gesprochen** generally speaking.
**2** *vt* **(a)** *(sagen)* to say, to speak; *eine Sprache* to speak; *Gebet, Gedicht* to say. ~ **Sie Japanisch?** do you speak Japanese?; **hier spricht man Spanisch** Spanish spoken. **(b)** *(mit jdm reden)* to speak to. **kann ich bitte Herrn Kurz ~?** may I speak to Mr Kurz, please?; **er ist nicht zu ~** he can't see anybody; **wir ~ uns noch!** you haven't heard the last of this! **(c)** *Urteil* to pronounce.
**Sprecher(in** *f)* *m* **-** speaker; *(Nachrichten~)* newsreader; *(für Dokumentarfilme etc)* narrator; *(Ansager)* announcer; *(Wortführer)* spokesperson; spokesman/-woman.
**Sprech-:** **s~faul** *adj* taciturn; ~**funk** *m* radiotelephone system; ~**funkgerät** *nt* radiotelephone; ~**gebühr** *f* *(Telec)* call charge; ~**muschel** *f* *(Telec)* mouthpiece; ~**organ** *nt* speech organ; ~**probe** *f* voice trial; ~**rolle** *f* speaking part; ~**schulung** *f* voice training; ~**stunde** *f* consultation (hour); *(von Arzt)* surgery *(Brit)*, doctor's office *(US)*; ~**stunden** consultation hours; *(von Arzt)* surgery *(Brit)*; ~**stundenhilfe** *f* doctor's receptionist; ~**übung** *f* speech exercise; ~**weise** *f* way of speaking; ~**werkzeuge** *pl* organs of speech; ~**zeit** *f* *(Telec)* call time; ~**zimmer** *nt* consulting room.
**Spreizdübel** *m* cavity plug.
**spreizen** **1** *vt* to spread. **2** *vr* *(sich sträuben)* to kick up *(col)*.
**Spreizfuß** *m* splayfoot.
**Spreng|arbeiten** *pl* blasting operations *pl*; „~" "blasting".
**sprengen** *vt* **(a)** to blow up; *Fels* to blast. **(b)** *Tür* to force (open); *Tresor* to break open; *Bande, Fesseln, (Spiel)bank* to break; *Versammlung* to break up. **(c)** *(besprizen)* to sprinkle.
**Spreng-:** ~**kapsel** *f* detonator; ~**kopf** *m* warhead; ~**körper** *m* explosive device; ~**kraft** *f* explosive force; ~**ladung** *f* explosive charge; ~**satz** *m* explosive device.
**Sprengstoff** *m* explosive.
**Sprengstoff|anschlag** *m* bomb attack. **auf ihn wurde ein ~ verübt** he was the subject of a bomb attack.
**Sprengung** *f* blowing-up; *(von Fels)* blasting; *(von Versammlung)* breaking-up.
**Sprenkel** *m* **-** *(Tupfen)* spot, speckle.
**sprenkeln** *vt* *Farbe* to sprinkle spots of; *siehe* **gesprenkelt**.
**Spreu** *f* *no pl* chaff. **die ~ vom Weizen trennen** *(fig)* to separate the wheat from the chaff.
**Sprichwort** *nt* **=er** proverb.
**sprichwörtlich** *adj* *(lit, fig)* proverbial.
**sprießen** *pret* **sproß** *or* **sprießte**, *ptp* **gesprossen** *vi aux* sein *(aus der Erde)* to spring up; *(Knospen)* to shoot.
**Springbrunnen** *m* fountain.
**springen** *pret* **sprang**, *ptp* **gesprungen** *vi aux sein* **(a)** *(lit, fig, Sport, bei Brettspielen)* to jump; *(mit Schwung auch)* to leap; *(beim Stabhochsprung)* to vault; *(Raubtier)* to pounce; *(sich springend fortbewegen)* to bound; *(hüpfen, seilhüpfen)* to skip; *(Ball etc)* to bounce; *(Wassersport)* to dive. **die Kinder kamen gesprungen** the children came running. **(b)** **etw ~ lassen** *(col)* to fork out for sth *(col)*; *Geld* to

fork out sth *(col)*; **für jdn etw ~ lassen** *(col)* to treat sb to sth. **(c)** *(Saite, Glas)* to break; *(Risse bekommen)* to crack.
**Springen** nt - *(Sport)* jumping; *(Stabhoch~)* vaulting.
**springend** adj der **~e Punkt** the crucial point.
**Springer(in** f) m - **(a)** jumper; *(Stabhoch~)* vaulter. **(b)** *(Chess)* knight. **(c)** *(Ind)* stand-in.
**Spring-:** **~flut** f spring tide; **~form** f *(Cook)* springform; **s~lebendig** adj lively, full of beans *(col)*; **~pferd** nt show-jumper; **~reiten** nt show-jumping; **~reiter** m show-jumper; **~rollo** nt roller blind; **~seil** nt skipping rope; **~turnier** nt show-jumping competition.
**Sprinkler** m - sprinkler.
**Sprint** m - sprint.
**sprinten** vti aux sein to sprint.
**Sprinter(in** f) m - sprinter.
**Sprit** m -e *(col)* **(a)** *(Benzin)* gas *(col)*, juice *(col)*. **(b)** *(Schnaps)* shorts pl.
**Spritz-:** **~beutel** m icing bag; **~düse** f nozzle.
**Spritze** f -n syringe; *(Feuer~, Garten~)* hose; *(Injektion)* injection. **eine ~ bekommen** to have an injection; **an der ~ hängen** *(col)* to be on heroin.
**spritzen 1** vti **(a)** to spray; *(verspritzen)* Wasser, Schmutz etc to splash; *(aus Wasserpistole etc)* to squirt. **jdn naß ~** to splash sb. **(b)** Wein to dilute with soda water/mineral water. **(c)** *(injizieren)* Serum etc to inject; Heroin etc auch to shoot *(col)*. **wir müssen (dem Kranken) Morphium ~** we have to give (the patient) a morphine injection. **2** vi aux haben or sein *(heißes Fett)* to spit; *(in einem Strahl)* to spurt; *(aus einer Tube etc)* to squirt.
**Spritzer** m - *(Farb~, Wasser~)* splash.
**spritzig** adj Wein tangy; Aufführung, Dialog etc sparkling; *(witzig)* witty.
**Spritz-:** **~lack** m spray paint; **~pistole** f spray-gun; **~tour** f *(col)* spin *(col)*; **~tülle** f nozzle.
**spröd(e)** adj Glas, Haar brittle; Haut rough; Stimme thin; *(abweisend)* aloof; Charme austere.
**sproß** pret of **sprießen**.
**Sproß** m -sse shoot.
**Sprosse** f -n *(lit, fig)* rung.
**Sprossenwand** f *(Sport)* wall bars pl.
**Sprößling** m shoot; *(fig hum)* offspring.
**Sprotte** f -n sprat.
**Spruch** m -e **(a)** saying; *(Wahl~)* motto; *(Bibel~)* quotation. **~e** *(col: Gerede)* patter no pl *(col)*; **~e klopfen** *(col)* to talk fancy *(col)*; **das sind doch nur ~e!** that's just talk. **(b)** *(Richter~)* judgement; *(Urteils~)* verdict; *(Schieds~)* ruling.
**Spruchband** nt banner.
**Sprüche-:** **~klopfer, ~macher** m *(col)* patter-merchant *(col)*.
**spruchreif** adj *(col)* **die Sache ist noch nicht ~** it's not definite yet.
**Sprudel** m - mineral water; *(Erfrischungsgetränk)* fizzy drink.
**sprudeln** vi **(a)** *(lit, fig)* to bubble; *(Sekt, Limonade)* to fizz. **(b)** aux sein *(hervor~)* *(Wasser etc)* to bubble; *(fig: Worte)* to pour out.
**sprudelnd** adj Getränk fizzy; *(fig)* effervescent.
**Sprudel-:** **~tablette** f effervescent tablet; **~wasser** nt sparkling mineral water.
**Sprühdose** f spray (can).
**sprühen 1** vi **(a)** aux haben or sein to spray; *(Funken)* to fly. **(b)** *(fig)* *(vor Witz etc)* to bubble over; *(Augen: vor Freude etc)* to sparkle. **2** vt to spray.
**sprühend** adj Laune, Temperament etc bubbling, effervescent; Witz sparkling, bubbling.
**Sprühregen** m drizzle.

**Sprung** m -e **(a)** jump; *(schwungvoll, fig: Gedanken~ auch)* leap; *(Hüpfer)* skip; *(von Raubtier)* pounce; *(Stabhoch~)* vault; *(Wassersport)* dive. **ein großer ~ nach vorn** *(fig)* a great leap forward; **damit kann man keine großen ~e machen** *(col)* you can't exactly live it up on that *(col)*; **immer auf dem ~ sein** *(col)* to be always on the go *(col)*; *(aufmerksam)* to be always on the ball *(col)*; **jdm auf die ~e helfen** *(wohlwollend)* to give sb a (helping) hand; *(drohend)* to show sb what's what. **(b)** *(col: kurze Strecke)* **auf einen ~ bei jdm vorbeikommen** to drop in to see sb *(col)*. **(c)** *(Riß)* crack. **einen ~ haben/bekommen** to be cracked/to crack.
**Sprung-:** **~brett** nt *(lit, fig)* springboard; **~feder** f spring; **s~haft 1** adj **(a)** Charakter volatile; Denken disjointed; **(b)** *(rapide)* rapid; **2** adv ansteigen, sich entwickeln by leaps and bounds; **~schanze** f *(Ski)* ski jump, jumping hill; **~seil** nt skipping rope; **~tuch** nt jumping sheet, life net *(US)*; **~turm** m diving platform.
**Spucke** f no pl *(col)* spittle, spit. **da bleibt einem die ~ weg!** *(col)* it's flabbergasting *(col)*; **mit Geduld und ~** *(col)* with a little application.
**spucken** vti to spit; *(fig col)* Lava, Flammen to spew (out). **in die Hände ~** *(fig)* to roll up one's sleeves.
**Spucknapf** m spittoon.
**Spuk** m -e *(Geistererscheinung)* apparition. **dem ~ ein Ende bereiten** *(fig)* to put an end to the nightmare.
**spuken** vi to haunt. **hier spukt es** this place is haunted; **es spukt auf dem Friedhof** the cemetery is haunted; **das spukt noch immer in den Köpfen** that still has a hold on people's minds.
**Spuk-:** **~geschichte** f ghost story; **s~haft** adj eerie.
**Spül-:** **~automat** m (automatic) dishwasher; **~becken** nt sink.
**Spule** f -n spool, reel; *(Nähmaschinen~, Ind)* bobbin; *(Elec)* coil.
**Spüle** f -n sink (unit); *(Spülbecken)* sink.
**spulen** vt to spool *(auch Comp)*, to reel.
**spülen** vti **(a)** *(aus~, ab~)* to rinse; *(Med)* to irrigate; *(abwaschen)* Geschirr to wash up *(Brit)*, to wash the dishes; *(auf der Toilette)* to flush. **Geschirr ~** to wash the dishes, to wash up *(Brit)*. **(b)** etw an Land ~ to wash sth ashore.
**Spül-:** **~maschine** f dishwasher; **s~maschinenfest** adj dishwasher-proof; **~mittel** nt washing-up liquid *(Brit)*, dish-washing liquid; **~schüssel** f washing-up bowl; **~tisch** m sink unit.
**Spülung** f rinsing; *(Wasser~)* flush; *(Med)* irrigation.
**Spülwasser** nt *(beim Abwaschen)* dishwater.
**Spund** m -e **(a)** bung, spigot. **(b)** pl -e **junger ~** *(dated col)* young pup *(dated col)*.
**Spundloch** nt bunghole.
**Spur** f -en **(a)** track *(auch Comp)*; *(Anzeichen, Beweisstück)* trace, sign. **von den Tätern fehlt jede ~** there is no trace of the criminals; **jds ~ aufnehmen** to take up sb's trail; **jdm auf der ~ sein** to be on sb's trail; **auf der richtigen ~ sein** *(lit, fig)* to be on the right track; **jdm auf die ~ kommen** to get onto sb; **(seine) ~en hinterlassen** *(fig)* to leave its mark. **(b)** *(fig: kleine Menge, Überrest)* trace; *(von Vernunft, Anstand etc)* scrap. **keine ~ von Anstand/Takt** *(col)* no decency/tact at all; **keine ~** *(col)* not at all/nothing at all; **eine ~ zu laut/grell** a shade too loud/garish. **(c)** *(Fahrbahn)* lane. **auf der linken ~ fahren** to drive in the left-hand lane; **in der ~ bleiben** to keep in lane.
**spürbar** adj noticeable, perceptible.

**spuren** vi (col) to obey; (sich fügen) to toe the line.

**spüren 1** vt to feel; (ahnen auch) to sense. **sie spürte, daß der Erdboden leicht bebte** she felt the earth trembling underfoot; **sie ließ mich ihr Mißfallen** ~ she let me know that she was displeased; **etw zu** ~ **bekommen** (lit) to feel sth; (fig) to get a taste of sth. **2** vti (Hunt) **(nach) etw** ~ to track sth.

**Spuren-**: ~**element** nt trace element; ~**sicherung** f securing of evidence.

**Spürhund** m tracker dog; (col: Mensch) sleuth.

**spurlos** adj without trace. ~ **an jdm vorübergehen** to have no effect on sb.

**Spür-**: ~**nase** f (Hunt) nose; ~**sinn** m (Hunt, fig) nose; (fig: Gefühl) feel.

**Spurt** m -s spurt.

**spurten** vi aux sein (Sport) to spurt; (col: rennen) to sprint.

**sputen** vr (dated col) to hurry.

**Squash** [skvɔʃ] nt no pl (Sport) squash.

**Sri Lanka** nt Sri Lanka.

**srilanker(in** f) m - Sri Lankan.

**srilankisch** adj Sri Lankan.

**SS** [ɛs'|ɛs] nt - (Univ) = **Sommersemester.**

**SSV** [ɛs|ɛs'fau] m = **Sommerschlußverkauf.**

**St.** = **(a) Stück. (b) Sankt** St.

**Staat** m -en **(a)** state; (Land) country. **beim** ~ **arbeiten** to be employed by the government. **(b)** (von Insekten) colony. **(c)** (fig) (Pracht) pomp; (Kleidung, Schmuck) finery. **damit ist kein** ~ **zu machen** that's nothing to write home about (col).

**Staaten-**: ~**bund** m confederation; **s~los** adj stateless.

**staatlich 1** adj state attr. **2** adv by the state. ~ **geprüft** state-certified.

**Staats-**: ~**affäre** f **(a)** (lit) affair of state; **(b)** (fig) major operation; ~**akt** m (lit) state occasion; ~**aktion** f major operation; ~**amt** nt public office; ~**angehörige(r)** mf decl as adj national; ~**angehörigkeit** f nationality; ~**anleihe** f government bond; ~**anwalt** m prosecuting attorney (US), public prosecutor; ~**apparat** m apparatus of state; ~**archiv** nt state archives pl; ~**ausgaben** pl public spending sing; ~**bank** f national bank; ~**bankrott** m national bankruptcy; ~**beamte(r)** m public servant; ~**begräbnis** nt state funeral; ~**besitz** m state or public property; **(in)** ~**besitz sein** to be state-owned; ~**besuch** m state visit; ~**betrieb** m state-owned enterprise; ~**bibliothek** f national library; ~**bürger** m citizen; ~**bürgerschaft** f nationality; ~**chef** m head of state; ~**dienst** m civil service; **s~eigen** adj state-owned, publicly owned; ~**eigentum** nt state or public property no art; ~**empfang** m state reception; ~**examen** nt ≈ university degree; ~**feiertag** m national holiday; ~**feind** m enemy of the state; ~**finanzen** pl public finances pl; ~**flagge** f national flag; ~**form** f type of state; ~**gebiet** nt national territory no art; ~**geheimnis** nt (lit, fig hum) state secret; ~**gelder** pl public funds pl; ~**gewalt** f authority of the state; ~**grenze** f state frontier; ~**haushalt** m national budget; ~**hoheit** f sovereignty; ~**interesse** nt interests pl of (the) state; ~**kasse** f treasury; ~**kirche** f state church; ~**kosten** pl public expenses pl; **auf** ~**kosten** at the public expense; ~**mann** m statesman; **s~männisch** adj statesmanlike; ~**oberhaupt** nt head of state; ~**präsident** m president; ~**recht** nt **(a)** national law; **(b)** (Verfassungsrecht) constitutional law; ~**regierung** f state government; ~**religion** f state religion; ~**rente** f state pension; ~**schuld** f (Fin) national debt; ~**sekretär** m (BRD:

*Beamter)* ≈ permanent secretary (Brit), senior official in government department; ~**sicherheit** f national security; ~**streich** m coup (d'état).

**Stab** m ⁼e **(a)** rod; (Gitter~) bar; (Bischofs~) crosier; (Hirten~) crook; (Dirigenten~, für Staffellauf) baton; (als Amtzeichen) mace; (für ~hochsprung) pole; (Meß~) (measuring) rod; (Zauber~) wand. **(b)** (Mitarbeiter~, Mil) staff; (von Experten) panel.

**Stäbchen** nt dim of **Stab** (Eß~) chopstick.

**Stab-**: ~**hochspringer** m pole-vaulter; ~**hochsprung** m pole vault.

**stabil** adj Möbel, Schuhe sturdy, robust; Währung, Beziehung, Charakter stable; Gesundheit sound.

**Stabilisator** [ʃtabili'zaːtoːɐ, st-] m stabilizer.

**stabilisieren*** vtr to stabilize.

**Stabilität** f stability.

**Stabreim** m alliteration.

**Stabs-**: ~**arzt** m (Mil) captain in the medical corps; ~**chef** m (Mil col) chief of staff; ~**offizier** m (Mil) staff officer; (Rang) field officer.

**stach** pret of **stechen.**

**Stachel** m -n (von Rosen etc) thorn; (von Kakteen, Igel) spine; (von ~schwein) quill, spine; (auf ~draht) barb; (zum Viehantrieb) goad; (Gift~: von Bienen etc) sting.

**Stachel-**: ~**beere** f gooseberry; ~**draht** m barbed wire.

**stach(e)lig** adj Rosen thorny; Kaktus, Igel spiny; (sich ~ anfühlend) prickly; Kinn, Bart bristly.

**Stachelschwein** nt porcupine.

**Stadion** nt, pl **Stadien** [-iən] stadium.

**Stadium** nt, pl **Stadien** [-iən] stage. **im vorgerückten/letzten** ~ (Med) at an advanced/a terminal stage.

**Stadt** f ⁼e **(a)** town; (Groß~) city. **die** ~ **Paris** the city of Paris; ~ **und Land** town and country; **in die** ~ **gehen** to go into town. **(b)** (~verwaltung) (town/city) council; (von Groß~) corporation. **bei der** ~ **arbeiten** or **angestellt sein** to be employed by the council.

**Stadt-**: **s~auswärts** adv out of town; ~**autobahn** f urban motorway (Brit) or freeway (US); ~**bad** nt municipal swimming pool; ~**bahn** f urban railway (Brit), city railroad (US); **s~bekannt** adj known all over town; ~**bewohner** m town-dweller; (von Groß~) city-dweller; ~**bezirk** m municipal district; ~**bibliothek**, ~**bücherei** f town/city library; ~**bummel** m stroll in the or through town.

**Städtebau** m urban development.

**stadt|einwärts** adv into town.

**Städte-**: ~**partnerschaft** f town twinning; ~**planung** f town planning.

**Städter(in** f) m - town-dweller; (Groß~) city-dweller.

**Stadt-**: ~**flucht** f exodus from the cities; ~**gebiet** nt municipal area; ~**gespräch** nt **(das)** ~**gespräch sein** to be the talk of the town; ~**grenze** f town/city boundary; ~**gue(r)rilla** f urban guerrilla; ~**halle** f municipal hall.

**städtisch** adj municipal, town/city attr; (nach Art einer Stadt) urban.

**Stadt-**: ~**kämmerer** m town/city treasurer; ~**kasse** f town/city treasury; ~**kern** m town/city centre (Brit) or center (US); ~**kreis** m town/city borough; ~**mauer** f city wall; ~**mitte** f town/city centre (Brit) or center (US); ~**park** m municipal park; ~**parlament** nt city council; ~**plan** m town plan, (street) map; ~**planung** f town planning; ~**rand** m outskirts pl (of a/the town/city); **am** ~**rand** on the outskirts (of the town/city); ~**rat** m (Behörde) (town/city) council; ~**reinigung** f

cleansing *(Brit) or* sanitation *(esp US)* department;
~**rundfahrt** *f* (sightseeing) tour of a/the town/city;
~**staat** *m* city state; ~**streicher(in** *f)* *m* - (town/
city) tramp; ~**teil** *m* district, part of town;
~**theater** *nt* municipal theatre *(Brit) or* theater
*(US)*; ~**tor** *nt* town/city gate; ~**verkehr** *m* urban
traffic; ~**verwaltung** *f (Behörde)* (town/city) council; ~**viertel** *nt* part of town; ~**zentrum** *nt* town/
city centre *(Brit) or* center *(US)*.

**Staffel** *f* -**n** **(a)** echelon; *(Aviat: Einheit)* squadron.
**(b)** *(Sport)* relay (race); *(Mannschaft)* relay team.
~ **laufen/schwimmen** to run/swim in a relay (race).

**Staffelei** *f* easel.

**Staffellauf** *m* relay (race).

**staffeln** *vt Gehälter, Fahrpreise* to grade; *Anfangs-
zeiten, Startplätze* to stagger.

**Staff(e)lung** *f siehe vt* grading; staggering.

**Stagnation** *f* stagnation.

**stagnieren*** *vi* to stagnate.

**stahl** *pret of* **stehlen.**

**Stahl** *m* -**e** *or* ≃**e** steel. **Nerven aus** *or* **wie** ~ nerves
of steel.

**Stahl-** *in cpds* steel; ~**bau** *m* steel-girder construction; ~**beton** *m* reinforced concrete; ~**blech** *nt*
sheet-steel.

**stählen** *vt* to harden, to toughen.

**stählern** *adj* steel; *(fig) Muskeln, Wille* of iron, iron
*attr; Nerven* of steel.

**Stahl-:** ~**feder** *f* steel nib; ~**gerüst** *nt* tubular steel
scaffolding; *(Gerippe)* steel-girder frame; **s~hart**
*adj* (as) hard as steel; ~**helm** *m (Mil)* steel helmet; ~**rohr** *nt* tubular steel; *(Stück)* steel tube;
~**roß** *nt (hum)* bike *(col)*; ~**träger** *m* steel girder;
~**werk** *nt* steelworks *sing or pl*; ~**wolle** *f* steel
wool.

**stak** *(geh) pret of* **stecken 1.**

**staksig** *adj (unbeholfen)* gawky. ~ **gehen** *(steif)* to
walk stiffly; *(unsicher)* to teeter.

**Stalinismus** *m* Stalinism.

**Stalin|orgel** *f (Hist)* multiple rocket launcher.

**Stall** *m* ≃**e** **(a)** *(Pferde~, Gestüt, Aut: Renn~)* stable;
*(Kuh~)* cowshed, (cow) barn *(US)*; *(Hühner~)* henhouse; *(Kaninchen~)* hutch; *(Schweine~)* (pig)sty,
(pig) pen *(esp US)*. **(b)** *(col: Hosenschlitz)* flies *pl*, fly
*(esp US)*.

**Stall-:** ~**bursche** *m* stable lad; ~**dung** *m* farmyard
manure; ~**meister** *m* head groom; ~**mist** *m* = ~-
**dung.**

**Stallung(en** *pl)* *f* stables *pl.*

**Stamm** *m* ≃**e** **(a)** *(Baum~)* trunk. **(b)** *(Ling)* stem. **(c)**
*(Volks~)* tribe; *(Abstammung)* line; *(Bakterien~)*
strain. **(d)** *(Personal, Kunden)* regulars *pl; (Arbeiter)*
regular workforce; *(Angestellte)* permanent staff *pl.*
**zum** ~ **gehören** to be one of the regulars *etc.*

**Stamm-:** ~**aktie** *f (St Ex)* ordinary *or* common *(US)*
share; ~**baum** *m* family tree; *(von Zuchttieren)*
pedigree; ~**buch** *nt book of family events with some
legal documents;* **jdm etw ins** ~**buch schreiben** *(fig)*
to put sb straight about sth; ~**datei** *f (Comp)* master file; ~**daten** *pl (Comp)* master data.

**stammeln** *vti* to stammer.

**stammen** *vi* to come *(von, aus* from*); (zeitlich)* to
date *(von, aus* from*).* **die Uhr stammt von seinem
Großvater** the watch was handed down from his
grandfather.

**Stamm-:** ~**form** *f* base form; ~**gast** *m* regular;
~**gericht** *nt* standard meal; ~**halter** *m* son and
heir.

**stämmig** *adj* stocky, thickset *no adv; (kräftig)* sturdy.

**Stamm-:** ~**kapital** *nt (Fin)* ordinary share *or* com-

mon stock *(US)* capital; ~**kneipe** *f (col)* local *(Brit
col)*; ~**kunde** *m* regular (customer); ~**lokal** *nt* favourite *(Brit) or* favorite *(US)* café/restaurant *etc;
(Kneipe)* local *(Brit)*, favorite bar *(US)*; ~**personal**
*nt* permanent staff *pl;* ~**platz** *m* usual seat; *(Stelle)*
usual place; ~**tisch** *m (Tisch in Gasthaus)* table reserved for the regulars; *(~tischrunde)* group of
regulars; ~**wähler** *m (Pol)* loyal voter.

**stampfen 1** *vi* **(a)** *(laut auftreten)* to stamp. **mit dem
Fuß** ~ to stamp one's foot. **(b)** *aux sein (gehen)* to
tramp; *(wütend)* to stamp; *(stapfen)* to trudge. **2** *vt*
**(a)** *(festtrampeln) Lehm, Sand* to stamp; *Trauben* to
press; *(mit den Füßen)* to tread. **(b)** *(mit Stampfer)*
to mash.

**Stampfer** *m* - *(Stampfgerät)* pounder; *(Cook)* mash-
er.

**Stampfkartoffeln** *pl (dial)* mashed potatoes *pl.*

**stand** *pret of* **stehen.**

**Stand** *m* ≃**e** **(a)** *(das Stehen)* standing position.
**aus dem** ~ from a standing position; **aus dem** ~
**(heraus)** *(col)* off the cuff; **bei jdm** *or* **gegen jdn ein-
en schweren** ~ **haben** *(fig)* to have a hard time of it
with sb. **(b)** *(Markt~ etc)* stall; *(Messe~)* stand;
*(Taxi~)* rank *(Brit)*, stand *(US)*. **(c)** *no pl (Lage)*
state; *(Niveau)* level; *(Zähler~ etc)* reading, level;
*(Konto~)* balance; *(Spiel~)* score. **beim jetzigen** ~
**der Dinge** the way things stand at the moment; **etw
auf den neuesten** ~ **bringen** to bring sth up to date;
**auf dem neuesten** ~ **der Technik sein** *(Gerät)* to be
state-of-the-art. **(d)** *(soziale Stellung)* station, status; *(Klasse)* rank, class; *(Beruf, Gewerbe)* profession.

**Standard-** *in cpds* standard.

**standardisieren*** *vt* to standardize.

**Standardisierung** *f* standardization.

**Standarte** *f* -**n** *(Mil, Pol)* standard.

**Standbild** *nt* statue; *(TV)* freeze frame.

**Ständchen** *nt* serenade. **jdm ein** ~ **bringen** to serenade sb.

**Ständer** *m* - stand; *(Pfeiler)* upright.

**Standes-:** ~**amt** *nt* registry office *(Brit)*;
**s~amtlich** *adj* **s~amtliche Trauung** civil *or (Brit)*
registry office wedding; **sich s~amtlich trauen lassen** to get married in a registry office *(Brit)*, to have
a civil marriage *(US)*; ~**beamte(r)** *m* registrar;
~**bewußtsein** *nt* status consciousness; ~**dünkel**
*m* snobbery; **s~gemäß 1** *adj* befitting one's rank;
**2** *adv* in a manner befitting one's rank;
~**organisation** *f* professional association;
~**unterschied** *m* class difference.

**Stand-:** **s~fest** *adj Tisch, Leiter* stable, steady; *(fig)*
steadfast; ~**festigkeit** *f* stability *(auch Sci); (fig
auch)* steadfastness; ~**foto** *nt* still (photograph);
~**gericht** *nt (Mil)* drumhead court martial; **vor ein
~gericht kommen** to be summarily court-
martialled *(Brit) or* court-martialled *(US)*; **s~haft**
*adj* steadfast; **er weigerte sich s~haft** he steadfastly
refused; ~**haftigkeit** *f* steadfastness; **s~halten** *vi
sep irreg (Mensch)* to stand firm; *(Gebäude, Brücke
etc)* to hold; *(+dat)* to stand up to; **Versuchungen**
*(dat)* **s~halten** to resist temptation; **einer Prüfung
s~halten** to stand up to close examination;
~**heizung** *f (Aut)* stationary heating.

**ständig** *adj* **(a)** *(dauernd)* permanent; *Mitglied* full.
~**er Ausschuß** standing committee. **(b)** *(unaufhörlich)* constant. **sie kommt** ~ **zu spät** she's always
late; **müssen Sie mich** ~ **unterbrechen?** do you have
to keep on interrupting me?

**Standlicht** *nt* sidelights *pl.* **mit** ~ **fahren** to drive on
sidelights.

**Stand|ort** *m* location; *(von Schütze, Schiff, fig)* position; *(Mil)* garrison; *(Bot)* habitat.

**Stand-:** **~pauke** *f (col)* lecture *(col)*; **jdm eine ~pauke halten** to give sb a lecture *(col)*; **~platz** *m* stand; **~punkt** *m (Meinung)* point of view; **auf dem ~punkt stehen, daß ...** to take the view that ...; **von seinem ~punkt aus** from his point of view; **s~rechtlich** *adj* summary; **jdn s~rechtlich erschießen** to put sb straight in front of a firing squad; **s~sicher** *adj* stable; *Mensch* steady (on one's feet/ skis *etc*); **~spur** *f (Aut)* hard shoulder *(Brit)*, emergency lane *(US)*; **~uhr** *f* grandfather clock.

**Stange** *f* **-n** **(a)** *(langer, Stab)* pole; *(Querstab)* bar; *(Ballett~)* barre; *(Kleider~, Teppich~)* rail; *(Gardinen~)* rod; *(Vogel~)* perch. **(b)** *(länglicher Gegenstand)* stick. **eine ~ Zigaretten** a carton of 200 cigarettes. **(c) ein Anzug von der ~** a suit off the peg; **bei der ~ bleiben** *(col)* to stick at it *(col)*; **jdm die ~ halten** *(col)* to stick up for sb *(col)*; **eine schöne ~ Geld** *(col)* a tidy sum *(col)*.

**Stangen-:** **~bohne** *f* runner *or (US)* pole bean; **~brot** *nt* French bread; *(Laib)* French loaf; **~spargel** *m* asparagus spears *pl*.

**stank** *pret of* **stinken**.

**stänkern** *vi (col)* to stir *(col)*.

**Stanniol** *nt* **-e** silver foil.

**Stanniolpapier** *nt* silver paper.

**Stanze** *f* **-n** die, stamp; *(Loch~)* punch.

**stanzen** *vt* to press; *(prägen)* to stamp; *Löcher* to punch.

**Stapel** *m* **-** **(a)** stack, pile. **(b)** *(Naut: Schiffs~)* stocks *pl*. **vom ~ laufen** to be launched.

**Stapellauf** *m (Naut)* launching.

**stapeln** 1 *vt* to stack; *(lagern)* to store. **2** *vr* to pile up.

**Stapelverarbeitung** *f (Comp)* batch processing.

**stapfen** *vi aux sein* to trudge, to plod.

**Star¹** *m* **-e** *(Orn)* starling.

**Star²** *m* **-e** *(Med)* **grauer/grüner ~** cataract/ glaucoma.

**Star³** [staːɐ, ʃtaːɐ] *m* **-s** *(Film etc)* star.

**starb** *pret of* **sterben**.

**Star-:** **~besetzung** *f* star cast; **~gast** *m* star guest.

**stark** *comp* **⁼er**, *superl* **⁼ste(r, s)** *or (adv)* **am ⁼sten** 1 *adj* **(a)** *(kräftig, konzentriert)* strong. **sich für etw ~ machen** *(col)* to stand up for sth; **das ist ein ~es Stück** *(col)* that's a bit much! **(b)** *(dick)* thick; *(euph: korpulent)* Dame, Herr large. **(c)** *(heftig)* Schmerzen, Kälte severe; *Regen, Verkehr, Raucher, Druck* heavy; *Sturm, Abneigung* violent; *Erkältung* bad, heavy; *Wind, Strömung, Eindruck* strong; *Beifall* hearty, loud; *Übertreibung* great. **(d)** *(leistungsfähig)* Motor powerful; *Sportler* able; *Mannschaft, Brille, Arznei* strong. **(e)** *(zahlreich)* Nachfrage great, big. **zehn Mann ~** ten strong; **das Buch ist 300 Seiten ~** the book is 300 pages long. **(f)** *(col: hervorragend)* Leistung, Werk great *(col)*. **2** *adv* *(mit vb)* a lot; *(mit adj, ptp)* very; *beschädigt etc* badly; *vergrößert, verkleinert* greatly. **~ wirken** to have a powerful effect; **~ gesalzen/gewürzt** very salty/highly spiced; **~ befahrene Straßen** bus roads; **er ist ~ erkältet** he has a bad cold.

**Starkbier** *nt* strong beer.

**Stärke¹** *f* **-n** **(a)** strength *(auch fig)*. **(b)** *(Dicke)* thickness; *(Macht)* power. **(c)** *(von Leid)* intensity; *(von Sturm, Abneigung)* violence. **(d)** *(Anzahl) (von Mannschaft)* size; *(von Nachfrage)* amount; *(Auflage)* size.

**Stärke²** *f* **-n** *(Chem, Wäsche~)* starch.

**Stärkemehl** *nt (Cook)* cornflour *(Brit)*, cornstarch *(US)*.

**stärken** 1 *vt* **(a)** *(lit, fig)* to strengthen; *Selbstbewußtsein* to boost; *Gesundheit* to improve. **(b)** *(erfrischen)* to fortify. **(c)** *Wäsche* to starch. **2** *vi* to be fortifying. **~des Mittel** tonic. **3** *vr* to fortify oneself.

**Starkstrom** *m (Elec)* heavy current; *(mit hoher Spannung)* high-voltage current.

**Starkstrom-** *in cpds* power; **~leitung** *f* power line.

**Stärkung** *f* **(a)** strengthening *(auch fig)*; *(des Selbstbewußtseins)* boosting. **(b)** *(Erfrischung)* refreshment. **eine ~ zu sich nehmen** to take some refreshment.

**Stärkungsmittel** *nt (Med)* tonic.

**starr** *adj* **(a)** stiff; *(unbeweglich)* rigid. **~ vor Frost** stiff with frost. **(b)** *(unbewegt)* Augen glassy; *Blick auch* fixed. **(c)** *(regungslos)* paralysed. **(d)** *(nicht flexibel)* Regelung, Prinzip inflexible, rigid.

**Starre** *f no pl* stiffness, rigidity.

**starren** *vi* **(a)** *(starr blicken)* to stare *(auf +acc* at*)*. **ins Leere ~** to stare into space; **vor sich *(acc)* hin ~** to stare straight ahead. **(b)** *(steif sein)* to be stiff *(von, vor +dat* with*)*. **vor Dreck ~** to be filthy.

**Starrheit** *f siehe adj (a)* stiffness; rigidity.

**Starr-:** **~kopf** *m (Mensch)* (stubborn) mule; **s~köpfig** *adj* stubborn; **~köpfigkeit** *f* stubbornness; **~krampf** *m (Med)* tetanus, lockjaw; **~sinn** *m* stubbornness; **s~sinnig** *adj* stubborn, mulish.

**Start** *m* **-s** **(a)** *(Sport)* start. **einen guten/schlechten ~ haben** *(lit, fig)* to get (off to) a good/bad start. **(b)** *(Aviat)* take-off; *(Raketen~)* launch.

**Start-:** **~automatik** *f (Aut)* automatic choke; **~bahn** *f (Aviat)* runway; **s~bereit** *adj (Sport, fig)* ready to go; *(Aviat)* ready for take-off; **~block** *m (Sport)* starting block.

**starten** 1 *vi aux sein* to start; *(Aviat)* to take off; *(zum Start antreten)* to take part. **2** *vt* Satelliten, Rakete to launch; *Motor* to start.

**Starter** *m* **-** *(Aut, Sport)* starter.

**Start-:** **~erlaubnis** *f (Sport)* permission to take part; *(Aviat)* clearance for take-off; **~hilfe** *f (Aviat)* rocket-assisted take-off; *(fig)* initial aid; **jdm ~hilfe geben** to help sb get off the ground; **~hilfekabel** *nt* jump leads *pl (Brit)*, jumper cables *pl (US)*; **s~klar** *adj (Aviat)* clear for take-off; *(Sport)* ready to start; **~kommando** *nt (Sport)* starting signal; **~linie** *f (Sport)* starting line; **~loch** *nt (Sport)* **in den ~löchern** on their marks; **~rampe** *f (Space)* launching pad; **~schuß** *m (Sport)* starting signal; *(fig)* signal *(zu* for*)*; **den ~schuß geben** to fire the pistol; *(fig: Erlaubnis geben)* to give the go-ahead; **~verbot** *nt (Aviat)* ban on take-off; *(Sport)* ban; **~verbot bekommen** to be banned; **~zeichen** *nt* starting signal

**Stasi** *m* **-**, **-s** = **Staatssicherheitsdienst** Stasi.

**Statik** ['ʃtaːtɪk, st-] *f* **(a)** *(Sci)* statics *sing*. **(b)** *(Build)* structural engineering.

**Statiker(in** *f)* *m* **-** *(Tech)* structural engineer.

**Station** *f* **(a)** station; *(Haltestelle)* stop; *(fig: Abschnitt: von Reise)* stage. **~ machen** to stop off. **(b)** *(Kranken~)* ward.

**stationär** [ʃtatsioˈnɛːɐ] *adj (Astron, Sociol)* stationary; *(Med)* in-patient *attr*. **~er Patient** in-patient; **~ behandeln** to treat in hospital.

**stationieren*** [ʃtatsioˈniːrən] *vt* Truppen to station; *Atomwaffen etc* to deploy.

**Stationierung** [ʃtatsioˈniːrʊŋ] *f siehe vt* stationing; deployment.

**Stations-:** **~arzt** *m* ward doctor; **~schwester** *f* ward sister; **~vorsteher** *m (Rail)* stationmaster.

**statisch** ['ʃtaːtɪʃ, st-] *adj (lit, fig)* static. ~ **einwand-frei** structurally sound.

**Statist** *m (Film)* extra; *(Theat)* supernumerary; *(fig)* cipher.

**Statistenrolle** *f (lit, fig)* minor role.

**Statistik** *f* (a) *(Wissenschaft)* statistics *sing*. (b) *(Aufstellung)* statistic. **die** ~**en** the statistics *pl*.

**Statistiker(in** *f)* *m* - statistician.

**statistisch** *adj* statistical.

**Stativ** *nt* tripod.

**statt** 1 *prep* +*gen* instead of. ~ **dessen** instead; ~ **meiner/seiner** in my/his place. 2 *conj* instead of. ~ **zu bleiben** instead of staying.

**Statt** *f no pl (form)* stead *(form)*, place. **an Kindes** ~ **annehmen** *(Jur)* to adopt.

**Stätte** *f* -**n** *(liter)* place.

**statt-:** **s**~**finden** *vi sep irreg* to take place; **s**~**haft** *adj pred* permitted; ~**halter** *m* governor.

**stattlich** *adj (hochgewachsen, groß) Tier* magnificent; *Bursche* strapping; *Erscheinung* imposing; *Gebäude, Park* splendid; *Sammlung* impressive; *Familie* large; *Summe* handsome.

**Statue** *f* -**n** statue.

**statuieren*** *vt* **ein Exempel (an jdm)** ~ to make an example (of sb); **ein Exempel mit etw** ~ to use sth as a warning.

**Statur** *f* build.

**Status** *m* - status. ~ **quo** status quo.

**Status-:** ~**symbol** *nt* status symbol; ~**zeile** *f (Comp)* status line.

**Statut** *nt* -**en** statute.

**Stau** *m* -**s** *(Wasserstauung)* build-up; *(Verkehrsstauung)* traffic jam. **ein** ~ **von 3 km** a 2 mile tailback *(Brit) or* line of traffic; **im** ~ **stehen** to sit in a (traffic) jam.

**Staub** *m, pl* -**e** *or* **Stäube** dust; *(Bot)* pollen. ~ **saugen** to vacuum; ~ **wischen** to dust; **sich vor jdm in den** ~ **werfen** to throw oneself at sb's feet; **sich aus dem** ~**e machen** *(col)* to clear off *(col)*.

**Stäubchen** *nt* speck of dust.

**Staubecken** *nt* reservoir.

**stauben** *vi* to be dusty; *(Staub machen)* to make a lot of dust.

**stäuben** *vt* **Mehl** *etc* **auf etw** *(acc)* ~ to sprinkle flour *etc* on sth.

**Staub-:** ~**fänger** *m (col)* dust collector; ~**flocke** *f* piece of fluff.

**staubig** *adj* dusty.

**Staub-:** ~**korn** *nt* speck of dust; ~**lappen** *m* duster; ~**lunge** *f (Med)* dust on the lung; *(von Kohlenstaub)* silicosis; **s**~**saugen** *vi insep, ptp* **s**~**gesaugt** to vacuum; ~**sauger** *m* vacuum cleaner; ~**sturm** *m* dust storm; ~**tuch** *nt* duster; ~**wedel** *m* feather duster; ~**wolke** *f* cloud of dust.

**stauchen** *vt* to compress *(auch Tech)*.

**Staudamm** *m* dam.

**Staude** *f* -**n** *(Hort)* herbaceous perennial; *(Busch)* shrub; *(Bananen*~*, Tabak*~*)* plant.

**stauen** 1 *vt* (a) *Wasser* to dam; *Blut* to stop the flow of. (b) *(Naut)* to stow. 2 *vr (sich anhäufen)* to pile up; *(ins Stocken geraten)* to get jammed; *(Wasser, Blut, fig)* to build up. **der Verkehr staute sich über eine Strecke von 4 km** there was a 2½ mile tailback *(Brit) or* line of traffic.

**Staumauer** *f* dam wall.

**staunen** *vi* to be astonished *(über +acc* at*)*. ~**d in** astonishment; **da kann man nur noch** ~ it's just amazing; **da staunst du, was?** *(col)* you didn't expect that, did you!

**Staunen** *nt no pl* astonishment, amazement *(über +acc* at*)*. **jdn in** ~ **versetzen** to amaze sb.

**Stau-:** ~**raum** *m* storage space; *(Naut)* stowage space; ~**see** *m* reservoir, artificial lake.

**Stauung** *f* (a) *(Stockung)* pile-up; *(von Verkehr)* tailback *(Brit)*, line of traffic. (b) *(von Wasser)* build-up (of water). (c) *(Blut*~*)* congestion *no pl*.

**Std.** = **Stunde** hr.

**stdl.** = **stündlich**.

**Steak** [steːk] *nt* -**s** steak.

**stechen** *pret* **stach**, *ptp* **gestochen** 1 *vti (Dorn, Stachel etc)* to prick; *(Insekt)* to sting; *(Mücken)* to bite; *(mit Messer etc)* to stab *(nach* at*)*. 2 *vi* (a) *(Sonne)* to beat down. (b) *(Cards)* to play a trump. **Karo sticht** diamonds are trumps. 3 *vt* (a) *(Cards)* to trump. (b) *Spargel, Torf* to cut. 4 *vr* to prick oneself *(an +dat* on, *mit* with*)*. **sich** *(acc or dat)* **in den Finger** ~ to prick one's finger. 5 *vti impers* **es sticht** it is prickly.

**Stechen** *nt* - (a) *(Sport)* play-off; *(beim Springreiten)* jump-off. (b) *(Schmerz)* sharp pain.

**stechend** *adj* piercing; *Schmerz* sharp; *(durchdringend) Augen auch* penetrating; *(beißend) Geruch* pungent.

**Stech-:** ~**karte** *f* clocking-in card; ~**mücke** *f* gnat; ~**schritt** *m (Mil)* goose step; ~**uhr** *f* time clock.

**Steck-:** ~**brief** *m* "wanted" poster; *(fig)* personal description; **s**~**brieflich** *adv* **s**~**brieflich gesucht werden** to be a wanted man/woman; ~**dose** *f (Elec)* socket *(Brit)*, outlet *(US)*.

**stecken** 1 *vi pret* **steckte** *or* **stak** *(geh)*, *ptp* **gesteckt** (a) *(festsitzen)* to be stuck; *(an- or eingesteckt sein)* to be; *(Nadel, Splitter etc)* to be (sticking); *(Brosche etc)* to be (pinned). **der Schlüssel steckt** the key is in the lock. (b) **wo steckt er?** where has he got to?; **darin steckt viel Mühe** a lot of work has gone into that; **da steckt etwas dahinter** *(col)* there's something behind it; **zeigen, was in einem steckt** to show what one is made of; **in einer Krise** ~ to be in the throes of a crisis.

2 *vt pret* **steckte**, *ptp* **gesteckt** (a) to put; *Haare* to put up; *Brosche* to pin *(an +acc* onto*)*. **die Hände in die Taschen** ~ to put one's hands in one's pockets; **das Hemd in die Hose** ~ to tuck one's shirt in (one's trousers); **jdn ins Gefängnis** ~ *(col)* to stick sb in prison *(col)*. (b) *(Sew)* to pin. (c) *(col: investieren) Geld, Mühe* to put *(in +acc* into*)*; *Zeit* to devote *(in +acc* to*)*. (d) *(pflanzen)* to set.

**Stecken-:** **s**~**bleiben** *vi sep irreg aux sein* to get stuck; *(in Rede)* to falter; **etw bleibt jdm im Halse s**~ *(lit, fig)* sth sticks in sb's throat; **s**~**lassen** *vt sep irreg* **den Schlüssel s**~**lassen** to leave the key in the lock; ~**pferd** *nt (lit, fig)* hobby-horse.

**Stecker** *m* - *(Elec)* plug.

**Steckling** *m (Hort)* cutting.

**Stecknadel** *f* pin. **man hätte eine** ~ **fallen hören können** you could have heard a pin drop; **eine** ~ **im Heuhaufen suchen** *(fig)* to look for a needle in a haystack.

**Steck-:** ~**nadelkissen** *nt* pincushion; ~**rübe** *f* swede, rutabaga *(US)*; ~**schloß** *nt* bicycle lock; ~**schlüssel** *m* socket spanner *(Brit) or* wrench *(US)*; ~**zwiebel** *f* bulb.

**Steg** *m* -**e** (a) *(Brücke)* footbridge; *(Landungs*~*)* landing stage *(Brit)*, jetty. (b) *(Mus, Brillen*~*)* bridge.

**Steghose** *f* stirrup pants *pl*.

**Stegreif** *m* **eine Rede aus dem** ~ **halten** to make an impromptu speech *or a* speech off the cuff.

**Stegreif-:** ~**rede** *f* impromptu speech; ~**spiel** *nt (Theat)* improvisation.

**Steh-** *in cpds* stand-up.

**Steh|aufmännchen** *nt (Spielzeug)* tumbler. **er ist ein richtiges** ~ *(fig)* he always bounces back.

**Steinobst**

**stehen** *pret* **stand**, *ptp* **gestanden** *aux haben or (S Ger, Aus, Sw)* **sein 1** *vi* **(a)** to stand; *(col: fertig sein)* to be finished; *(col: geregelt sein)* to be settled. **gebückt/krumm** ~ to slouch; **so wahr ich hier stehe** as sure as I'm standing here; **mit jdm/etw** ~ **und fallen** to depend on sb/sth; *(wesentlich sein für)* to stand or fall by sb/sth; **mit ihm steht und fällt die Firma** he's the linchpin of the company.

**(b)** *(sich befinden)* to be. **meine alte Schule steht noch** my old school is still there; **die Sonne steht abends im Westen** the sun in the evening is in the west; **unter Schock** ~ to be in a state of shock; **unter Drogeneinwirkung** ~ to be under the influence of drugs; **vor einer Entscheidung** ~ to be faced with a decision; **ich tue, was in meinen Kräften steht** I'll do everything I can.

**(c)** *(geschrieben, angezeigt sein)* to be. **wo steht das?** *(lit)* where does it say that?; **was steht da?** what does it say?; **das steht im Gesetz** the law says so; **es stand in der Zeitung** it was in the paper; **das steht in der Bibel** the Bible says so; **der Zeiger steht auf 4 Uhr** the clock says 4 (o'clock); **es steht 2:1 für München** the score is 2-1 to Munich; **wie steht das Pfund?** how does the pound stand?; **die Sache steht mir bis hier** *(col)* I'm sick and tired of it *(col)*.

**(d)** *(angehalten haben)* to have stopped. **meine Uhr steht** my watch has stopped; **der ganze Verkehr steht** all traffic is at a standstill.

**(e)** *(Gram) (bei Satzstellung)* to come; *(bei Zeit, Fall, Modus)* to be. **mit dem Dativ** ~ to take the dative.

**(f)** *(passen zu)* **jdm** ~ to suit sb.

**(g)** *(Belohnung, Strafe etc)* **auf Betrug steht eine Gefängnisstrafe** the penalty for fraud is imprisonment.

**(h)** *(Redewendungen)* **zu seinem Versprechen** ~ to stand by one's promise; **zu dem, was man gesagt hat,** ~ to stick to what one has said; **zu jdm** ~ to stand by sb; **wie** ~ **Sie dazu?** what are your views on that?; **für etw** ~ to stand for sth; **auf jdn/etw** ~ *(col)* to be mad about sb/sth *(col)*, to be into sb/sth *(col)*; **hinter jdm/etw** ~ to be behind sb/sth.

**2** *vr (col)* **sich gut/schlecht** ~ to be well-off/badly off; **sich gut/schlecht mit jdm** ~ *(sich verstehen)* to be on good/bad terms with sb.

**3** *vi impers* **es steht schlecht/gut um jdn** *(bei Aussichten)* things look bad/good for sb; *(gesundheitlich, finanziell)* sb is doing badly/well; **wie steht es damit?** how about it?

**4** *vt Posten, Wache* to stand. **sich** *(acc)* **müde** ~, **sich** *(dat)* **die Beine in den Bauch** *(col)* ~ to stand until one is ready to drop.

**Stehen** *nt no pl* standing; *(Halt)* stop, standstill. **zum** ~ **bringen** to stop; **zum** ~ **kommen** to stop.

**stehenbleiben** *vi sep irreg aux sein (anhalten)* to stop; *(nicht weitergehen) (Mensch, Tier)* to stay; *(Zeit)* to stand still; *(Auto, Zug)* to stand.

**stehend** *adj attr Fahrzeug* stationary; *Gewässer* stagnant; *(ständig) Heer* regular. ~**e Redensart** stock phrase.

**stehenlassen** *ptp* ~ *or* **stehengelassen** *vt sep irreg* to leave; *(Cook)* to let stand. **alles stehen- und liegenlassen** to drop everything; **jdn einfach** ~ to leave sb standing (there); **sich** *(dat)* **einen Bart** ~ to grow a beard.

**Steher** *m* - *(Pferderennen, fig)* stayer.

**Steh-:** ~**imbiß** *m* stand-up snack-bar; ~**kneipe** *f* stand-up bar; ~**kragen** *m* stand-up collar; ~**lampe** *f* standard lamp *(Brit)*, floor lamp *(US)*; ~**leiter** *f* stepladder.

**stehlen** *pret* **stahl**, *ptp* **gestohlen 1** *vti* to steal. **jdm**

**die Zeit** ~ to waste sb's time. **2** *vr* to steal. **sich aus dem Haus** ~ to steal out of the house.

**Steh-:** ~**platz** *m* **ich bekam nur noch einen** ~**platz** I had to stand; **ein** ~**platz kostet 10 Mark** a standing ticket costs 10 marks; ~**pult** *nt* high desk; ~**vermögen** *nt* staying power, stamina.

**Steiermark** *f* Steiermark.

**steif** *adj (lit, fig)* stiff; *Penis auch* erect; *Empfang* formal; *(gestärkt)* starched. ~ **und fest auf etw** *(dat)* **beharren** to insist stubbornly on sth.

**steifen** *vt* to stiffen; *Wäsche* to starch.

**Steifftier** ® *nt* soft toy (animal).

**Steig-:** ~**bügel** *m* stirrup; ~**eisen** *nt* climbing iron *usu pl*; *(Bergsteigen)* crampon.

**steigen** *pret* **stieg**, *ptp* **gestiegen** *aux sein* **1** *vi* **(a)** *(klettern)* to climb. **auf einen Berg** ~ to climb (up) a mountain; **aufs Fahrrad** ~ to get on(to) one's bicycle; **vom Fahrrad** ~ to get off one's bicycle; **aus dem Zug** ~ to get off the train. **(b)** *(sich aufwärts bewegen)* to rise; *(Flugzeug, Straße)* to climb; *(Nebel)* to lift; *(Fieber)* to go up. **Drachen** ~ **lassen** to fly kites; **das Blut stieg ihm in den Kopf** the blood rushed to his head; **in jds Achtung** *(dat)* ~ to rise in sb's estimation. **(c)** *(col: stattfinden)* to be on. **bei mir steigt morgen eine Party** I'm having a party tomorrow. **2** *vt Treppen, Stufen* to climb (up).

**Steiger** *m* - *(Min)* pit foreman.

**steigern 1** *vt* **(a)** to increase; *(verschlimmern) Übel, Zorn* to aggravate. **(b)** *(Gram)* to form the comparative and superlative of. **2** *vi* to bid *(um for)*. **3** *vr* **(a)** *(sich erhöhen)* to increase; *(Farben)* to be intensified; *(Zorn, Übel)* to be aggravated. **(b)** *(sich verbessern)* to improve.

**Steigerung** *f* **(a)** *siehe vt* **(a)** *(das Steigern)* increase *(gen in)*; aggravation. **(b)** *(Verbesserung)* improvement. **(c)** *(Gram)* comparison.

**Steigung** *f (Hang)* slope; *(von Hang, Straße, Math)* gradient.

**Steigungsgrad** *m* gradient.

**steil** *adj* **(a)** steep. **eine** ~**e Karriere** *(fig)* a rapid rise. **(b)** *(senkrecht)* upright. **sich** ~ **aufrichten** to sit/stand up straight. **(c)** *(Sport)* ~**er Paß** through ball.

**Steil-:** ~**hang** *m* steep slope; ~**küste** *f* steep coast; ~**paß** *m (Sport)* through ball.

**Stein** *m* -**e** **(a)** stone; *(Ziegel~)* brick; *(in Uhr)* jewel; *(Spiel~)* piece. **der** ~ **der Weisen** *(lit, fig)* the philosophers' stone; **es blieb kein** ~ **auf dem anderen** not a stone was left standing; **mir fällt ein** ~ **vom Herzen!** *(fig)* that's a load off my mind!; **bei jdm einen** ~ **im Brett haben** *(fig col)* to be well in with sb *(col)*; **den ersten** ~ **(auf jdn) werfen** to cast the first stone (at sb); **jdm** ~**e in den Weg legen** *(fig)* to make things difficult for sb; **es friert** ~ **und Bein** *(fig col)* it's freezing cold outside; ~ **und Bein schwören** *(fig col)* to swear blind *(col)*.

**Stein-:** ~**adler** *m* golden eagle; **s**~**alt** *adj* as old as the hills; ~**bock** *m* **(a)** *(Zool)* ibex; **(b)** *(Astrol)* Capricorn; ~**bohrer** *m* masonry drill; *(Gesteinsbohrer)* rock drill; ~**bruch** *m* quarry.

**steinern** *adj* stone; *(fig)* stony.

**Stein-:** ~**erweichen** *nt* **zum** ~**erweichen weinen** to cry heartbreakingly; ~**fußboden** *m* stone floor; ~**garten** *m* rockery; ~**gut** *nt* stoneware; **s**~**hart** *adj* rock-hard.

**steinig** *adj* stony.

**steinigen** *vt* to stone.

**Steinkohle** *f* hard coal.

**Steinkohlenbergbau** *m* coal mining.

**Stein-:** ~**krug** *m (Kanne)* stoneware jug; *(Becher)* stoneware mug; ~**meißel** *m* stone chisel; ~**metz** *m (wk)* -**en**, -**en** stonemason; ~**obst** *nt* stone fruit;

**~pilz** *m* cep; **~platte** *f* stone slab; *(zum Pflastern)* flagstone; **s~reich** *adj (col)* stinking rich *(col)*; **~salz** *nt* rock salt; **~schlag** *m* rockfall; „**Achtung ~schlag**" "danger falling stones"; **~tafel** *f* stone tablet; **~topf** *m* stoneware pot; **~wurf** *m (fig)* stone's throw; **~wüste** *f* stony desert; *(fig)* concrete jungle; **~zeit** *f* Stone Age.

**Steißbein** *nt (Anat)* coccyx.

**Stellage** [ʃtɛˈlaːʒə] *f* **-n** *(col: Gestell)* rack, frame.

**Stelldich|ein** *nt* **-(s)** *(dated)* rendezvous.

**Stelle** *f* **-n (a)** place; *(Fleck: rostend, naß, faul etc)* patch. **an dieser ~** in this place; **eine kahle ~ am Kopf** a bald patch on one's head; **eine empfindliche ~** *(lit)* a sensitive spot *or* place; *(fig)* a sensitive point; **eine schwache ~** a weak spot; **auf der ~ treten** *(lit)* to mark time; *(fig)* not to make any headway; **auf der ~** *(fig: sofort)* on the spot; *kommen, gehen* straight away; **nicht von der ~ kommen** not to make any progress; **sich nicht von der ~ rühren** to refuse to move; **zur ~ sein** to be on the spot; *(bereit, etw zu tun)* to be at hand.

**(b)** *(in Buch etc)* place; *(Abschnitt)* passage; *(Text~, esp beim Zitieren)* reference; *(Bibel~)* verse; *(Mus)* passage. **an dieser ~** here; **an anderer ~** elsewhere.

**(c) an erster ~** in the first place; **(bei jdm) an erster/letzter ~ kommen** to come first/last (for sb); **an führender ~ stehen** to be in a leading position; **an ~ von** *or (+gen)* in place of; **an jds ~** *(acc)/***an die ~ einer Sache** *(gen)* **treten** to take sb's place/the place of sth; **ich möchte jetzt nicht an seiner ~ sein** I wouldn't like to be in his position; **an deiner ~ würde ich ...** if I were you I would ...

**(d)** *(Math)* digit; *(hinter Komma)* place. **drei ~n hinter dem Komma** three decimal places.

**(e)** *(Posten)* job; *(Ausbildungs~)* place; *(Dienst~)* office; *(Behörde)* authority. **eine freie** *or* **offene ~** a vacancy; **ohne ~** without a job.

**stellen 1** *vt* **(a)** *(hin~)* to put. **jdm etw auf den Tisch ~** to put sth on the table for sb; **auf sich** *(acc)* **selbst gestellt sein** *(fig)* to have to fend for oneself. **(b)** *(arrangieren) Szene* to arrange; *Aufnahme* to pose. **eine gestellte Pose** a pose. **(c)** *(zur Verfügung ~)* to provide. **(d)** *(ein~)* to set *(auf +acc* at*)*; *Uhr etc* to set *(auf +acc* for*)*. **das Radio lauter/leiser ~** to turn the radio up/down. **(e)** *(finanziell)* **gut/besser gestellt** well-off/better off. **(f)** *Verbrecher* to catch; *(fig col)* to corner. **(g)** *Aufgabe, Bedingung* to set *(jdm* sb*)*; *Frage* to put *(jdm, an jdn* to sb*)*; *Antrag, Forderung* to make. **jdn vor ein Problem ~** to confront sb with a problem.

**2** *vr* **(a)** to (go and) stand *(an +acc* at, by*)*; *(sich auf~, sich einordnen)* to position oneself; *(sich aufrecht hin~)* to stand up. **sich gegen jdn/etw ~** *(fig)* to oppose sb/sth; **sich hinter jdn/etw ~** *(fig)* to support sb/sth.

**(b)** *(fig: sich verhalten)* **sich anders zu etw ~** to have a different attitude towards sth; **wie stellst du dich zu ...?** how do you regard ...?; **sich gut mit jdm ~** to get on good terms with sb.

**(c)** *(sich ein~: Gerät etc)* to set itself *(auf +acc* at*)*.

**(d)** *(sich ausliefern, antreten)* to give oneself up *(jdm* to sb*)*. **sich den Journalisten ~** to make oneself available to the reporters; **sich einer Herausforderung ~** to take up a challenge.

**(e)** *(sich ver~)* **sich krank/schlafend** *etc* **~** to pretend to be ill/asleep etc.

**Stellen-:** **~angebot** *nt* offer of employment; „**~angebote**" "situations vacant"; **~anzeige** *f* job advertisement *or* ad *(col)*; **~ausschreibung** *f* job advertisement; **~gesuch** *nt* advertisement seeking

employment; „**~gesuche**" "situations wanted"; **~markt** *m* job market; *(in Zeitung)* appointments section; **~suche** *f* = **Stellungssuche**; **~vermittlung** *f* employment bureau; **s~weise** *adv* in places; **s~weise Schauer** showers in places; **~wert** *m (fig)* status; **einen hohen ~wert haben** to play an important role.

**Stellplatz** *m (für Auto)* parking space.

**Stellung** *f (lit, fig, Mil)* position; *(Posten auch)* post. **in ~ bringen/gehen** to bring/get into position; **die ~ halten** *(Mil)* to hold one's position; *(hum)* to hold the fort; **~ beziehen** *(Mil)* to move into position; *(fig)* to make it clear where one stands; **zu etw ~ nehmen** to give one's opinion *or* to comment on sth; **für/gegen jdn/etw ~ nehmen** *or* **beziehen** to come out in favour *(Brit)* or favor *(US)* of/to come out against sb/sth; **in führender ~** in a leading position; **die rechtliche ~ des Mieters** the legal status of the tenant; **gesellschaftliche ~** social status *or* standing; **ohne ~ sein** *(arbeitslos)* to be unemployed.

**Stellungnahme** *f* **-n** statement *(zu* on*)*. **eine ~ zu etw abgeben** to make a statement on sth.

**Stellungs-:** **~krieg** *m* positional warfare *no indef art*; **s~los** *adj* unemployed; **~suche** *f* search for employment; **auf ~suche sein** to be looking for employment.

**Stell-:** **s~vertretend** *adj (von Amts wegen)* deputy *attr*; *(vorübergehend)* acting *attr*; **s~vertretend für jdn** acting for sb, on behalf of sb; **s~vertretend für jdn handeln** to act for sb; **~vertreter** *m* (acting) representative; *(von Amts wegen)* deputy; **~werk** *nt (Rail)* signal box *(Brit)* or tower *(US)*.

**Stelze** *f* **-n** stilt.

**stelzen** *vi aux sein (col)* to stalk.

**Stemm|eisen** *nt* crowbar.

**stemmen 1** *vt* **(a)** *(stützen)* to press; *Ellenbogen* to prop. **die Arme in die Seiten** *or* **Hüften gestemmt** with arms akimbo. **(b)** *(hoch~)* to lift (above one's head). **(c)** *(meißeln)* to chisel. **2** *vr* **sich gegen etw ~** to brace oneself against sth; *(fig)* to set oneself against sth.

**Stempel** *m* **-** **(a)** *(Gummi~)* (rubber) stamp. **(b)** *(Abdruck)* stamp; *(Post~)* postmark. **jdm/einer Sache einen/seinen ~ aufdrücken** *(fig)* to leave a/one's mark on sb/sth. **(c)** *(Tech) (Präge~)* die; *(stangenförmig, Loch~)* punch. **(d)** *(Bot)* pistil.

**Stempel-:** **~farbe** *f* stamping ink; **~geld** *nt (dated col)* dole (money) *(col)*; **~kissen** *nt* ink pad.

**stempeln 1** *vt* to stamp; *Brief* to postmark; *Briefmarke* to frank. **jdn zum Lügner ~** *(fig)* to brand sb as a liar. **2** *vi (col)* **(a)** **~ gehen** *(dated: arbeitslos sein/werden)* to be/go on the dole *(col)*. **(b)** *(Stempeluhr betätigen)* to clock in; *(beim Hinausgehen)* to clock out.

**Stempeluhr** *f* time clock.

**Stengel** *m* **-** stem, stalk. **vom ~ fallen** *(col: überrascht sein)* to be staggered *(col)*.

**Steno¹** *f no pl (col)* shorthand.

**Steno²** *nt* **-s** *(col)* = **Stenogramm**.

**Steno-:** **~block** *m* shorthand notebook *or* pad; **~gramm** *nt* text in shorthand; *(Diktat)* shorthand dictation; **~grammblock** *m* = **~block**; **~graph(in** *f***)** *m (im Büro)* shorthand secretary; *(esp in Gericht, bei Konferenz etc)* stenographer; **~graphie** *f* shorthand; **s~graphieren\* 1** *vt* to take down in shorthand; **2** *vi* to do shorthand; **s~graphisch** *adj* shorthand *attr*; **~typist(in** *f***)** *m* shorthand typist.

**Steppdecke** *f* quilt.

**Steppe** *f* **-n** steppe.

**steppen** *vti (Sew)* to quilt.

**Steppjacke** f quilted jacket.
**Step-**: ~**tanz** m tap dance; ~**tänzer** m tap dancer.
**Sterbe-**: ~**bett** nt deathbed; ~**fall** m death; ~**hilfe** f euthanasia; ~**kasse** f death benefit fund.
**sterben** pret **starb**, ptp **gestorben** vti aux sein to die. **einen schnellen Tod/eines natürlichen Todes** ~ to die quickly/to die a natural death; **an einer Krankheit/Verletzung** ~ to die of an illness/from an injury; **er stirbt vor Angst** (fig) he's frightened to death; **er ist für mich gestorben** (fig col) he might as well be dead as far as I'm concerned.
**Sterben** nt no pl death. **Angst vor dem** ~ fear of death; **im** ~ **liegen** to be dying.
**Sterbens-**: ~**angst** f (col) mortal fear; **s~elend** adj (col) wretched; **s~krank** adj mortally ill; **s~langweilig** adj (col) deadly boring; ~**wörtchen** nt (col) **er hat kein** ~**wörtchen gesagt** he didn't say a word.
**Sterbe-**: ~**rate** f death rate; ~**sakramente** pl last rites pl; ~**stunde** f dying hour; ~**urkunde** f death certificate; ~**ziffer** f death rate.
**sterblich** adj mortal.
**Sterbliche(r)** mf decl as adj mortal.
**Sterblichkeit** f mortality; (Zahl) death rate.
**Stereo** nt stereo.
**stereo** adj pred (in) stereo.
**Stereo-** in cpds stereo; (s~skopisch) stereoscopic; ~**anlage** f stereo system; ~**aufnahme** f stereo recording; ~**gerät** nt stereo unit; ~**kamera** f stereoscopic camera; **s~phon 1** adj stereophonic; **2** adv stereophonically; ~**skop** nt **-e** stereoscope; **s~skopisch** adj stereoscopic; ~**-Turm** m hi-fi stack; **s~typ** adj (fig) stereotyped.
**steril** adj (lit, fig) sterile.
**Sterilisation** f sterilization.
**sterilisieren*** vt to sterilize; Tier to neuter.
**Sterilisierung** f sterilization.
**Sterilität** f (lit, fig) sterility.
**Stern** m **-e** star. **das steht (noch) in den** ~**en** (fig) it's in the lap of the gods; **nach den** ~**en greifen** (fig) to reach for the stars; **sein** ~ **ist im Sinken** his star is on the decline; **mein guter** ~ my lucky star; **unter einem glücklichen** ~ **geboren sein** to be born under a lucky star; **unter einem guten** ~ **stehen** to be blessed with good fortune.
**Sternbild** nt (Astron) constellation; (Astrol) sign.
**Sternchen** nt dim of **Stern** (a) little star. (b) (Typ) asterisk.
**Sterndeuter** m astrologer.
**Sternen-**: ~**banner** nt Stars and Stripes sing; ~**himmel** m starry sky; **s~klar** adj starry attr.
**Stern-**: ~**fahrt** f (Mot, Pol) rally; **s~förmig** adj star-shaped; **s~hagelvoll** adj (col) legless (col); ~**kunde** f astronomy; ~**marsch** m (Pol) protest march; ~**schnuppe** f shooting star; ~**stunde** f great moment; ~**system** nt galaxy; ~**warte** f observatory; ~**zeichen** nt (Astrol) sign of the zodiac; **im** ~**zeichen der Jungfrau** under the sign of Virgo.
**stet** adj attr constant.
**Stethoskop** nt **-e** stethoscope.
**stetig** adj steady; (Math) Funktion continuous.
**stets** adv always.
**Steuer¹** nt **-** (Naut) helm, tiller; (Aut) (steering) wheel; (Aviat) controls pl. **am** ~ **stehen** (Naut) or **sein** (Naut, fig) to be at the helm; **am** ~ **sitzen** (col) (Aut) to be at the wheel; (Aviat) to be at the controls; **das** ~ **übernehmen** (lit, fig) to take over; **das** ~ **fest in der Hand haben** (fig) to be firmly in control; **das** ~ **herumreißen** (fig) to turn the tide of events.
**Steuer²** f **-n** (Abgabe) tax. ~**n** tax; (Arten von ~n)

taxes; ~**n zahlen** to pay tax.
**Steuer-**: ~**beamte(r)** m tax officer; **s~begünstigt** adj Investitionen, Hypothek tax-deductible; Waren taxed at a lower rate; ~**behörde** f tax authorities pl, inland (Brit) or internal (US) revenue authorities pl; ~**berater** m tax consultant; ~**bescheid** m tax assessment; ~**betrug** m tax evasion; ~**bord** nt no pl (Naut) starboard; **s~bord(s)** adv (Naut) to starboard; ~**einnahmen** pl revenue from taxation; ~**erhöhung** f tax increase; ~**erklärung** f tax return; ~**erlaß** m tax exemption; ~**erstattung** f tax rebate; ~**flucht** f tax evasion; ~**flüchtling** m tax exile; **s~frei** adj tax-free; ~**freibetrag** m tax allowance; ~**freiheit** f tax exemption; ~**gelder** pl taxpayers' money; ~**gerät** nt tuner-amplifier; (Elec, Comp) control unit; ~**hinterziehung** f tax evasion; ~**inspektor** m tax inspector; ~**jahr** nt tax year; ~**karte** f tax notice; ~**klasse** f tax bracket; ~**knüppel** m control column.
**steuerlich** adj tax attr. ~**e Belastung** tax burden.
**steuerlos** adj out of control; (fig) leaderless.
**Steuer-**: ~**mann** m, pl ~**männer** or ~**leute** helmsman; (als Rang) (first) mate; ~**marke** f revenue stamp; (für Hunde) dog licence disc (Brit), dog tag (US); ~**mittel** pl tax revenue; **etw aus** ~**mitteln finanzieren** to finance sth from the taxpayers' money; ~**moral** f taxpayers' honesty.
**steuern 1** vt to steer; Schiff auch to navigate; Flugzeug to pilot; (fig) Wirtschaft, Politik, (Comp) to control. **staatlich gesteuert** state-controlled; **einen Kurs** ~ (lit, fig) to steer a course. **2** vi (a) aux sein to head. (b) (am Steuer sein) (Naut) to be at the helm; (Aut) to be at the wheel; (Aviat) to be at the controls.
**Steuer-**: ~**oase** f, ~**paradies** nt tax haven; ~**pflicht** f liability to tax; **s~pflichtig** adj Einkommen taxable, liable to tax; ~**politik** f tax policy; ~**progression** f progressive taxation; ~**prüfer** m tax inspector; ~**prüfung** f tax inspector's investigation; ~**rad** nt (Aviat) control wheel; (Aut) (steering) wheel; ~**recht** nt tax law; ~**reform** f tax reform; ~**ruder** nt rudder; ~**satz** m rate of taxation; ~**schuld** f tax liability; ~**senkung** f tax cut.
**Steuerung** f (a) no pl (das Steuern) (Elec, Tech) control; (von Schiff) navigation; (von Flugzeug) piloting. (b) (Steuervorrichtung) (Aviat) controls pl; (Naut) steering apparatus. **automatische** ~ (Aviat) autopilot; (Naut) automatic steering (device).
**Steuer-**: ~**vergünstigung** f tax relief; ~**vorteil** m tax advantage; ~**zahler** m taxpayer.
**Steven** ['ʃteːvn] m **-** (Naut) (Vorder~) prow; (Achter~) stern.
**Steward** ['stjuːɐt] m **-s** (Naut, Aviat) steward.
**Stewardeß** ['stjuːɐdɛs] f **-ssen** stewardess.
**StGB** [ɛsteːgeːˈbeː] nt = **Strafgesetzbuch**.
**stibitzen*** vt (hum) to swipe (col), to pinch (col).
**Stich** m **-e** (a) (Insekten~) sting; (Mücken~) bite; (Nadel~) prick; (Messer~) stab. (b) (Schmerz) stabbing pain; (Seiten~) stitch; (fig) pang. (c) (Sew) stitch. (d) (Kupfer~, Stahl~) engraving. (e) (Schattierung) shade (in +acc of); (Tendenz) suggestion (in +acc of). **ein** ~ **ins Rote** a tinge of red. (f) (Cards) trick. **einen** ~ **machen** to get a trick. (g) **jdn im** ~ **lassen** to let sb down; (verlassen) to desert sb. (h) **einen** ~ **haben** (Eßwaren) to be bad or off (Brit); (Milch) to be sour; (col: Mensch: verrückt sein) to be nuts (col).
**Stichel** m **-** (Art) gouge.
**Stichelei** f (pej col: boshafte Bemerkung) dig. **deine ständigen** ~**en kannst du dir sparen** stop getting at me.

**sticheln** *vi (pej col)* to make snide remarks *(col)*.

**Stich-:** ~**flamme** *f* tongue of flame; **s~haltig** *adj* valid; *Beweis* conclusive; ~**haltigkeit** *f no pl* validity; conclusiveness.

**Stichling** *m (Zool)* stickleback.

**Stich-:** ~**probe** *f* spot check; ~**tag** *m* qualifying date; ~**waffe** *f* stabbing weapon; ~**wahl** *f (Pol)* final ballot, run-off *(US)*.

**Stichwort** *nt* (a) *pl* -**wörter** *(in Lexikon)* headword. (b) *pl* -**worte** *(Theat, fig)* cue. (c) *pl* -**worte** *usu pl* notes *pl*.

**Stichwort-:** **s~artig** *adj* abbreviated; **etw s~artig zusammenfassen** to summarize the main points of sth; ~**katalog** *m* classified catalogue; ~**verzeichnis** *nt* index.

**Stichwunde** *f* stab wound.

**Stick|arbeit** *f* embroidery.

**sticken** *vti* to embroider.

**Stickerei** *f* embroidery.

**stickig** *adj* Luft, Zimmer stuffy; *Klima* humid.

**Stickstoff** *m* nitrogen.

**stieben** *pret* **stob** *or* **stiebte**, *ptp* **gestoben** *or* **gestiebt** *vi (geh)* aux haben or sein *(sprühen)* (Funken, Staub, Schnee) to fly; *(Wasser)* to spray.

**Stiefbruder** *m* stepbrother.

**Stiefel** *m* - (a) boot. (b) *(Trinkgefäß)* large, boot-shaped beer glass.

**Stiefel-:** ~**absatz** *m* boot heel; ~**knecht** *m* bootjack.

**stiefeln** *vi aux sein (col)* to hoof it *(col)*; *siehe* **gestiefelt.**

**Stief-:** ~**eltern** *pl* stepparents *pl*; ~**kind** *nt* stepchild; *(fig)* poor cousin; ~**mutter** *f* stepmother; ~**mütterchen** *nt (Bot)* pansy; **s~mütterlich** *adj (fig)* **jdn/etw s~mütterlich behandeln** to treat sb as a poor relation/to pay little attention to sth; ~**schwester** *f* stepsister; ~**sohn** *m* stepson; ~**tochter** *f* stepdaughter; ~**vater** *m* stepfather.

**stieg** *pret of* **steigen.**

**Stiege** *f* -**n** *(Treppe)* (narrow) flight of stairs.

**Stieglitz** *m* -**e** goldfinch.

**Stiel** *m* -**e** (a) *(Griff)* handle; *(Pfeifen~, Glas~)* stem. (b) *(Stengel)* stalk.

**Stiel|augen** *pl (fig col)* **er machte** ~ his eyes (nearly) popped out of his head.

**stier** *adj (stumpfsinnig) Blick* vacant, blank.

**Stier** *m* -**e** (a) bull; *(junger ~)* bullock. **wütend wie ein** ~ beside oneself with rage. (b) *(Astrol)* Taurus.

**stieren** *vi* to stare *(auf +acc* at*)*.

**Stier-:** ~**kampf** *m* bullfight; ~**kampfarena** *f* bullring; ~**kämpfer** *m* bullfighter.

**stieß** *pret of* **stoßen.**

**Stift** *m* -**e** (a) *(Metall~)* pin; *(Nagel)* tack. (b) *(Blei~)* pencil. (c) *(col: Lehrling)* apprentice (boy).

**stiften** *vt* (a) *(spenden)* to donate; *(gründen) Kirche* to found. (b) *Verwirrung* to cause; *Unfrieden, Frieden* to bring about; *Ehe* to arrange.

**stiftengehen** *vi sep irreg aux sein (col)* to hop it *(col)*.

**Stifter(in** *f)* *m* - *(Gründer)* founder; *(Spender)* donator.

**Stiftung** *f* (a) *(Gründung)* foundation; *(Schenkung)* donation. (b) *(Organisation)* foundation.

**Stiftzahn** *m* post crown.

**Stigma** *nt* -**men** *or* -**ta** *(Bio, Rel, fig)* stigma.

**Stil** *m* -**e** style; *(Eigenart)* way, manner. **im großen** ~ on a grand scale, in a big way *(col)*; **schlechter** ~ bad style; **das ist schlechter** ~ *(fig)* that is bad form.

**Stil-:** ~**blüte** *f (hum)* stylistic howler; ~**bruch** *m* stylistic incongruity.

**Stilett** *nt* -**e** stiletto.

**Stil-:** ~**fehler** *m* stylistic lapse; ~**gefühl** *nt* feeling for style.

**stilisieren*** *vt* to stylize.

**Stilistik** *f (Liter)* stylistics *sing*.

**stilistisch** *adj* stylistic.

**still** *adj* (a) *(ruhig)* quiet, silent; *Seufzer, Plätzchen* quiet; *Gebet, Vorwurf, Beobachter* silent. ~ **werden** to go quiet; **im Saal wurde es** ~ the room fell silent; **um ihn ist es** ~ **geworden** you don't hear anything about him any more; ~ **weinen/leiden** to cry quietly/to suffer in silence; **in** ~**er Trauer** in silent grief; **im** ~**en** quietly; **ich dachte mir im** ~**en** I thought to myself; **die S~en im Lande** the quiet ones; **sei doch** ~! be quiet; ~**e Messe** silent mass. (b) *(unbewegt) Luft* still. **der S~e Ozean** the Pacific (Ocean); ~ **sitzen** to sit still; **die Füße** ~ **halten** to keep one's feet still; **er ist ein** ~**es Wasser** he's a deep one. (c) *(heimlich)* secret. **im** ~**en** in secret. (d) *(Comm) Teilhaber* sleeping *(Brit)*, silent *(US)*; *Reserven, Rücklagen* hidden. ~**e Beteiligung** sleeping partnership *(Brit)*, non-active interest.

**Stille** *f no pl* (a) *(Ruhe)* quiet(ness), peace(fulness); *(Schweigen)* silence. **die Beerdigung fand in aller** ~ **statt** it was a quiet funeral. (b) *(Unbewegtheit)* calm(ness); *(der Luft)* stillness. (c) *(Heimlichkeit)* secrecy. **in aller** ~ secretly.

**Stilleben** ['ʃtɪlleːbn] *nt* still life.

**stillegen** *vt sep* to close down.

**Stillegung** *f* closure.

**Stillehre** *f* stylistics *sing*.

**stillen** **1** *vt* (a) *(zum Stillstand bringen) Tränen* to stop; *Schmerzen* to ease. (b) *(befriedigen) Neugier, Hunger* to satisfy; *Durst auch* to quench. (c) *Säugling* to breast-feed. **2** *vi* to breast-feed. ~**de Mutter** nursing mother.

**stillgestanden** *interj (Mil)* halt!

**Stillhalte|abkommen** *nt (Fin, fig)* moratorium.

**stillhalten** *vi sep irreg* to keep still; *(fig)* to keep quiet.

**stilliegen** *vi sep irreg aux sein or haben* (a) *(außer Betrieb sein)* to be shut down. (b) *(lahmliegen)* to be at a standstill.

**Stillschweigen** *nt* silence. **über etw** *(acc)* ~ **bewahren** to keep quiet about sth; **etw mit** ~ **übergehen** to pass over sth in silence.

**stillschweigend** *adj* silent; *Einverständnis* tacit. **über etw** *(acc)* ~ **hinweggehen** to pass over sth in silence.

**stillsitzen** *vi sep irreg aux sein or haben* to sit still.

**Stillstand** *m* standstill; *(in Entwicklung)* halt. **zum** ~ **kommen** *(Verkehr)* to come to a standstill; **etw zum** ~ **bringen** to stop sth.

**stillstehen** *vi sep irreg aux sein or haben* (a) *(Produktion, Handel etc)* to be at a standstill; *(Herz)* to have stopped. (b) *(stehenbleiben)* to stop; *(Maschine)* to stop working.

**stillvergnügt** *adj* contented.

**Stil-:** ~**mittel** *nt* stylistic device; ~**möbel** *pl (Imitation)* reproduction furniture *sing*; *(antik)* period furniture *sing*; **s~voll** *adj* stylish; ~**wörterbuch** *nt* dictionary of correct usage.

**Stimm-:** ~**abgabe** *f* voting; ~**band** *nt usu pl* vocal cord; **s~berechtigt** *adj* entitled to vote; ~**berechtigte(r)** *mf decl as adj* person entitled to vote; ~**bezirk** *m* constituency; ~**bruch** *m* **er ist im** ~**bruch** his voice is breaking.

**Stimme** *f* -**n** (a) *(lit, fig)* voice; *(Mus: Part)* part; *(Orgel~)* register. **mit leiser/lauter** ~ in a soft/loud voice; **zweite** ~ *(in Chor)* second part; **bei einem Lied die erste/zweite** ~ **singen** to sing the top part of/descant to a song; **die ~n mehren sich, die ...** there is a growing body of opinion that ...; **der ~ des Gewissens folgen** to follow one's conscience. **(b)** *(Wahl/~)* vote. **eine/keine ~ haben** to have the vote/not to be entitled to vote; *(Mitspracherecht)* to have a/no say; **seine ~ abgeben** to vote; **jdm seine ~ geben** to vote for sb.

**stimmen 1** *vi* **(a)** *(richtig sein)* to be right. **stimmt es, daß ...?** is it true that ...?; **hier stimmt was nicht!** there's something wrong here; **stimmt so!** that's all right(, keep the change). **(b)** *(zusammenpassen)* to go (together). **(c)** *(wählen, sich entscheiden)* to vote. **für/gegen jdn/etw ~** to vote for/ against sb/sth. **2** *vt Instrument* to tune. **jdn froh/ traurig ~** to make sb (feel) cheerful/sad.

**Stimmen-:** **~gewirr** *nt* babble of voices; **~gleichheit** *f* tied vote; **bei ~gleichheit** in the event of a tie; **~mehrheit** *f* majority of votes.

**Stimm-:** **~enthaltung** *f* abstention; **~gabel** *f* tuning fork; **s~haft** *adj (Ling)* voiced; **s~haft ausgesprochen werden** to be voiced.

**stimmig** *adj* harmonious; *Argumente* coherent.

**stimmlich** *adj* vocal. **ihre ~en Qualitäten** the quality of her voice.

**Stimm-:** **s~los** *adj (Ling)* unvoiced; **s~los ausgesprochen werden** not to be voiced; **~recht** *nt* right to vote.

**Stimmung** *f* **(a)** *(auch St Ex)* mood; *(Moral)* morale. **in (guter)/gehobener ~** in a good mood/in high spirits; **in ~ kommen** to liven up; **ich bin nicht in der ~ dazu** I'm not in the mood for that. **(b)** *(Meinung)* opinion. **gegen/für jdn/etw ~ machen** to stir up (public) opinion against/in favour *(Brit)* or favor *(US)* of sb/sth.

**Stimmungs-:** **~kanone** *f (col)* life and soul of the party; **~lage** *f* atmosphere; **~mache** *f no pl (pej)* cheap propaganda; **~musik** *f* light music; **~umschwung** *m* change of atmosphere; *(Pol)* swing (in public opinion); **s~voll** *adj Bild* idyllic; *Atmosphäre* tremendous; *Gedicht* full of atmosphere.

**Stimm-:** **~vieh** *nt (pej)* gullible voters *pl*; **~volk** *nt* voters *pl*, electorate; **~zettel** *m* ballot paper.

**stimulieren*** *vt (Med, fig)* to stimulate.

**Stinkbombe** *f* stink bomb.

**stinken** *pret* **stank,** *ptp* **gestunken** *vi* to stink *(nach of)*. **er stinkt nach Kneipe** he smells of drink; **er stinkt vor Faulheit** he's bone-idle; **das stinkt zum Himmel** it's an absolute scandal; **die Sache stinkt mir** *(col)* I'm fed up to the back teeth (with it) *(col)*.

**Stink-:** **s~faul** *adj (col)* bone-lazy; **s~langweilig** *adj (col)* deadly boring; **s~normal** *adj (col)* dead normal *(col)*; **s~reich** *adj (col)* stinking rich *(col)*; **~tier** *nt* skunk; **~wut** *f (col)* raging temper; **eine ~wut (auf jdn) haben** to be livid (with sb).

**Stipendium** *nt* grant; *(als Auszeichnung etc erhalten)* scholarship.

**Stippvisite** *f (col)* flying visit.

**Stirn** *f* **-en** forehead. **es steht ihm auf der ~ geschrieben** *(geh)* it is written in his face; **die ~ haben, etw zu tun** to have the nerve to do sth; **jdm/einer Sache die ~ bieten** *(geh)* to stand up to sth.

**Stirn-:** **~band** *nt* headband; **~falte** *f* wrinkle (on one's forehead); **~glatze** *f* receding hairline; **~höhle** *f* (frontal) sinus; **~runzeln** *nt no pl* frown.

**stob** *pret of* **stieben.**

**stöbern** *vi* to rummage *(in +dat in, durch through)*.

**stochern** *vi* to poke *(in +dat at)*; *(im Essen)* to pick *(in +dat at)*. **sich** *(dat)* **in den Zähnen ~** to pick one's teeth.

**Stock** *m* ̈**-e** **(a)** stick; *(Rohr~)* cane; *(Takt~)* baton;

*(Zeige~)* pointer; *(Billard~)* cue. **am ~ gehen** *(lit)* to walk with a stick; *(fig col: verblüfft)* to be flabbergasted *(col)*. **(b)** *(Pflanze) (Reb~)* vine; *(Rosen~)* rose bush; *(Blumen~)* pot plant. **über ~ und Stein** up hill and down dale. **(c)** *pl* **-** *(~werk)* floor, storey *(Brit)*, story *(US)*. **im ersten ~** on the first floor *(Brit)*, on the second floor *(US)*.

**Stock-:** **s~betrunken** *(col)* *adj* blind drunk; **s~blind** *adj (col)* as blind as a bat; **s~dunkel** *adj (col)* pitch-dark.

**Stöckelschuh** *m* stiletto-heeled shoe.

**stocken** *vi* **(a)** *(Herz, Puls)* to miss a beat; *(nicht vorangehen) (Arbeit, Entwicklung)* to make no progress; *(Unterhaltung)* to flag; *(innehalten) (in der Rede)* to falter; *(im Satz)* to break off; *(Verkehr)* to be held up. **ihm stockte das Herz/der Puls** his heart/pulse missed a beat; **ihm stockte der Atem** he caught his breath; **ins S~ geraten** *(Gespräch)* to begin to flag. **(b)** *(stagnieren) (Verhandlungen)* to break off; *(Geschäfte, Handel)* to drop off. **(c)** *(gerinnen: Blut)* to thicken. **das Blut stockte ihm in den Adern** *(geh)* the blood froze in his veins.

**stockend** *adj* faltering, hesitant.

**Stock-:** **s~finster** *adj (col)* pitch-black; **~fisch** *m* dried cod; *(pej: Mensch)* dull old stick.

**Stockholm** *nt* Stockholm.

**Stock-:** **s~konservativ** *adj (col)* arch-conservative; **s~nüchtern** *adj (col)* stone-cold sober *(col)*; **s~sauer** *adj (col)* pissed off *(col!)*; **~schirm** *m* (walking-length) umbrella; **~schlag** *m* blow (with a stick); *(mit Rohr~)* stroke of the cane; **s~steif** *adj (col)* as stiff as a poker; **s~taub** *adj (col)* as deaf as a post.

**Stockung** *f* **(a)** hold-up *(gen, in +dat in)*; *(Verkehrs~)* traffic jam. **(b)** *(Pause) (im Gespräch)* lull; *(in der Rede)* hesitation.

**Stockwerk** *nt* floor, storey *(Brit)*, story *(US)*. **im 5. ~** on the 5th *(Brit)* or 6th *(US)* floor; **ein Haus mit vier ~en** a four-storey *(Brit)* or four-storied *(US)* building.

**Stoff** *m* **-e** **(a)** material, fabric; *(als Materialart)* cloth. **(b)** *(no pl: Materie)* matter. **(c)** *(Substanz, Chem)* substance; *(Papier~)* pulp. **(d)** *(Thema)* subject (matter); *(Unterhaltungs~, Diskussions~)* topic; *(Material)* material. **~ zum Lesen** reading matter. **(e)** *(col: Rauschgift)* dope *(col)*.

**Stoff-:** **~bahn** *f* length of material; **~ballen** *m* roll of cloth.

**Stoffel** *m* **-** *(pej col)* lout *(col)*, boor.

**stoff(e)lig** *adj (pej col)* uncouth, boorish.

**Stoffhandschuh** *m* fabric glove.

**stofflich** *adj (Philos)* material; *(den Inhalt betreffend)* as regards subject matter.

**Stoff-:** **~puppe** *f* rag doll; **~rest** *m* remnant; **~tier** *nt* soft toy.

**Stoffwechsel** *m* metabolism.

**Stoffwechselstörung** *f* metabolic disturbance.

**stöhnen** *vi* to groan. **~d** with a groan.

**stoisch** *adj* stoic(al); *(Philos)* Stoic.

**Stola** ['ʃtoːla, st-] *f, pl* **Stolen** stole.

**Stollen** *m* **-** **(a)** *(Min, Mil)* gallery, tunnel. **(b)** *(Cook)* *type of fruit loaf (eaten at Christmas)*, stollen *(US)*.

**stolpern** *vi aux sein* to stumble, to trip *(über +acc over)*; *(fig: zu Fall kommen)* to come a cropper *(col)*. **über jdn ~** *(fig)* to bump into sb; **über einen Hinweis ~** *(fig)* to stumble upon a clue.

**stolz** *adj* proud *(auf +acc of)*. **darauf kannst du ~ sein** that's something to be proud of. **(b)** *(imposant)* *Bauwerk* majestic; *(iro: stattlich)* Preis princely.

**Stolz** *m no pl* pride. **sein Garten ist sein ganzer ~** his garden is his pride and joy.

**stolzieren\*** *vi aux sein* to strut; *(hochmütig)* to stalk.

**stop** [ʃtɔp, stɔp] *interj* stop!

**stopfen 1** *vt* (a) *(füllen)* to stuff; *Pfeife, Loch* to fill. **jdm das Maul** *(col)* ~ to silence sb; **gierig stopfte er alles in sich hinein** he greedily stuffed down everything. (b) *(ausbessern, flicken) Loch, Strümpfe etc* to darn. **2** *vi* (a) *(Speisen) (ver~)* to cause constipation. (b) *(flicken)* to darn.

**Stopf-:** **~garn** *nt* darning thread; **~nadel** *f* darning needle.

**Stopp** *m* -s stop, halt; *(Lohn~)* freeze.

**Stoppball** *m* dropshot.

**Stoppel** *f* -n *(Getreide~, Bart~)* stubble.

**Stoppel-:** **~bart** *m* stubbly beard; **~feld** *nt* stubble field.

**stopp(e)lig** *adj Bart* stubbly; *Kinn auch* bristly.

**stoppen 1** *vt* to stop; *Zeit, Läufer* to time. **er hat die Zeit genau gestoppt** he timed exactly how long it took. **2** *vi* to stop.

**Stopper** *m* - *(Ftbl)* centre half.

**Stopp-:** **~licht** *nt* stoplight, brake light; **~schild** *nt* stop sign; **~straße** *f* road with stop signs; **~uhr** *f* stopwatch.

**Stöpsel** *m* - plug; *(Pfropfen)* stopper.

**stöpseln** *vti (Telec)* to connect.

**Stör** *m* -e *(Zool)* sturgeon.

**Stör-:** **~aktion** *f* disruptive action *no pl*; **s~anfällig** *adj* susceptible to interference.

**Storch** *m* ⸚e stork. **wie der ~ im Salat gehen** *(col)* to pick one's way carefully.

**Store** [ʃtoːɐ] *m* -s *usu pl* net curtain.

**stören 1** *vt* (a) *Schlaf, öffentliche Ordnung, Frieden etc* to disturb; *Verhältnis, Harmonie etc* to spoil; *Rundfunkempfang* to interfere with; *(absichtlich)* to jam. **jds Pläne** ~ to upset sb's plans. (b) *Prozeß, Vorlesung* to disrupt. (c) *(unangenehm berühren)* to disturb, to bother. **was mich an ihm/daran stört** what I don't like about him/it; **lassen Sie sich nicht ~!** don't let me disturb you; **stört es Sie, wenn ich rauche?** do you mind if I smoke?; **sie läßt sich durch nichts ~** she doesn't let anything bother her.

**2** *vr* **sich an etw** *(dat)* ~ to be bothered about sth; **ich störe mich an seiner Unpünktlichkeit** I take exception to his unpunctuality.

**3** *vi* (a) *(lästig, im Weg sein)* to get in the way; *(unterbrechen)* to interrupt; *(Belästigung darstellen: Musik, Lärm etc)* to be disturbing. **bitte nicht ~!** please do not disturb!; **ich möchte nicht ~** I don't want to be in the way; **etw als ~d empfinden** to find sth bothersome. (b) *(unangenehm auffallen)* to spoil the effect.

**Störenfried** *m* -e, **Störer** *m* - troublemaker.

**Stör-:** **~fall** *m* *(in Kraftwerk etc)* malfunction, accident; **~manöver** *nt* disruptive action.

**stornieren\*** *vti (Comm) Auftrag* to cancel; *Buchungsfehler* to reverse.

**Storno** *m or nt, pl* **Storni** *(Comm) (von Buchungsfehler)* reversal; *(von Auftrag)* cancellation.

**störrisch** *adj* stubborn, obstinate; *Kind* unmanageable; *Pferd* restive.

**Störsender** *m (Rad)* jamming transmitter.

**Störung** *f* (a) disturbance; *(von Ablauf, Verhandlungen etc)* disruption; *(Verkehrs~)* hold-up. (b) *(Tech)* fault. (c) *(Rad)* interference; *(absichtlich)* jamming. (d) *(Med)* disorder. **nervöse ~en** nervous trouble.

**Störungs-:** **s~frei** *adj* trouble-free; *(Rad)* free from interference; **~stelle** *f (Telec)* faults service.

**Stoß** *m* ⸚e (a) push, shove; *(leicht)* poke; *(mit Faust)* punch; *(mit Fuß)* kick; *(mit Ellbogen)* nudge; *(mit Kopf, Hörnern)* butt; *(Dolch~ etc)* stab; *(Fechten)*

thrust; *(Atem~)* gasp. **seinem Herzen einen ~ geben** to pluck up courage. (b) *(Anprall)* impact; *(Erd~)* tremor; *(eines Wagens)* jolt. (c) *(Stapel)* pile, stack. (d) *(Trompeten~ etc)* blast *(in +acc on)*.

**Stoßdämpfer** *m (Aut)* shock absorber.

**Stößel** *m* - pestle; *(Aut: Ventil~)* tappet.

**stoß\|empfindlich** *adj* susceptible to shock.

**stoßen** *pret* **stieß**, *ptp* **gestoßen 1** *vt* (a) to push, to shove; *(leicht)* to poke; *(mit Faust)* to punch; *(mit Fuß)* to kick; *(mit Ellbogen)* to nudge; *(mit Kopf, Hörnern)* to butt; *(stechen) Dolch* to plunge; *(Sport) Kugel* to put. **sich** *(dat)* **den Kopf** *etc* ~ to hit one's head *etc*; **jdn von sich** ~ to push sb away; *(fig)* to cast sb aside; **er stieß den Ball mit dem Kopf ins Tor** he headed the ball into the goal. (b) *(zerkleinern) Zimt, Pfeffer* to pound.

**2** *vr* to bump oneself. **sich an etw** *(dat)* ~ *(lit)* to bump oneself on sth; *(fig)* to take exception to sth.

**3** *vi* (a) *(mit den Hörnern)* to butt *(nach* at*)*. (b) *(Tech)* to butt *(an +acc* against*)*. (c) *(Gewichtheben)* to jerk. (d) *aux sein* **an etw** *(acc)* ~ to bump into sth; *(grenzen)* to border on sth; **gegen etw** ~ to run into sth; **zu jdm** ~ to meet up with sb; **auf jdn** ~ to bump into sb; **auf etw** *(acc)* ~ *(Schiff)* to hit sth; *(fig: entdecken)* to come across sth; **auf Erdöl** ~ to strike oil; **auf Widerstand** ~ to meet with resistance.

**Stoß-:** **s~fest** *adj* shockproof; **~gebet** *nt* quick prayer; **ein ~gebet zum Himmel schicken** to say a quick prayer; **~seufzer** *m* deep sigh; **s~sicher** *adj* shockproof; **~stange** *f (Aut)* bumper; **~trupp** *m (Mil)* raiding party; **~verkehr** *m* rush-hour traffic; **~waffe** *f* thrust weapon; **s~weise** *adv* (a) *(ruckartig)* by fits and starts; (b) *(stapelweise)* by the pile; **~zahn** *m* tusk; **~zeit** *f (im Verkehr)* rush hour; *(in Geschäft etc)* peak period.

**Stotterer** *m* -, **Stotterin** *f* stutterer.

**stottern** *vti* to stutter; *(Motor)* to splutter. **leicht/stark** ~ to stutter slightly/badly; **ins S~ kommen** to start stuttering.

**Stövchen** *nt* (teapot *etc*) warmer.

**Str.** = **Straße** St.

**Straf-:** **~anstalt** *f* penal institution, prison; **~antrag** *m* legal proceedings *pl*; **~antrag stellen** to institute legal proceedings; **~anzeige** *f* **~anzeige gegen jdn erstatten** to bring a charge against sb; **~arbeit** *f (Sch)* punishment; *(schriftlich)* lines *pl*; **~bank** *f (Sport)* penalty bench.

**strafbar** *adj Vergehen* punishable. **~e Handlung** punishable offence; **sich ~ machen** to commit an offence *(Brit)* or offense *(US)*.

**Strafe** *f* -n punishment; *(Jur, Sport)* penalty; *(Geld~)* fine; *(Gefängnis~)* sentence. **etw unter ~ stellen** to make sth a punishable offence *(Brit)* or offense *(US)*; **unter ~ stehen** to be a punishable offence *(Brit)* or offense *(US)*; **seine ~ absitzen** to serve one's sentence; **~ zahlen** to pay a fine; **100 Dollar ~ zahlen** to pay a 100 dollar fine; **zur ~** as a punishment; **~ muß sein!** discipline is necessary; **seine gerechte ~ bekommen** to get one's just deserts; **dieses Kind/diese Arbeit ist eine ~** *(col)* this child/job is a pain (in the neck) *(col)*.

**strafen** *vti* to punish. **mit etw gestraft sein** to be cursed with sth; **sie ist vom Schicksal gestraft** she is cursed by fate; **er ist gestraft genug** he has been punished enough.

**strafend** *adj attr* punitive; *Blick* reproachful.

**Straf-:** **~entlassene(r)** *mf decl as adj* discharged prisoner; **~erlaß** *m* remission (of sentence); **~expedition** *f* punitive expedition.

**straff** *adj Seil* tight, taut; *Haut* smooth; *(fig: streng)*

*Disziplin, Organisation* strict. ~ **sitzen** to fit tightly; **etw** ~ **spannen** to tighten sth; **das Haar** ~ **zurück-kämmen** to comb one's hair back severely.
**straffällig** *adj* ~ **werden** to commit a criminal offence *(Brit)* or offense *(US)*.
**Straffällige(r)** *mf decl as adj* offender.
**straffen 1** *vt* to tighten; *(raffen) Darstellung* to tighten up. **2** *vr* to tighten; *(Haut)* to become smooth.
**Straf-: s~frei** *adj* **s~frei ausgehen** to go unpunished; **~freiheit** *f* impunity; **~gebühr** *f* surcharge; **~gefangene(r)** *mf decl as adj* prisoner; **~gericht** *nt* criminal court; **ein ~gericht abhalten** to hold a trial; **das göttliche ~gericht** divine judgement; **~gesetz** *nt* penal law; **~gesetzbuch** *nt* Criminal Code; **~justiz** *f* criminal justice *no art*; **~kolonie** *f* penal colony; **~kompanie** *f (Mil)* punishment batallion.
**sträflich 1** *adj (lit, fig)* criminal. **2** *adv vernachlässigen etc* criminally.
**Sträfling** *m* prisoner.
**Sträflingskleidung** *f* prison clothing.
**Straf-: ~mandat** *nt* (parking *etc*) ticket; **~maß** *nt* sentence; **das höchste ~maß** the maximum penalty; **s~mildernd** *adj* mitigating; **~minute** *f (Sport)* minute's penalty; **vier ~minuten** four minutes' penalty; **~porto** *nt* excess postage; **~predigt** *f* dressing-down *(col)*; **jdm eine ~predigt halten** to give sb a dressing-down; **~prozeß** *m* criminal proceedings *pl*; **~prozeßordnung** *f* code of criminal procedure; **~punkt** *m (Sport)* penalty point; **~raum** *m (Sport)* penalty area; **~recht** *nt* criminal law; **s~rechtlich** *adj* criminal; **jdn/etw s~rechtlich verfolgen** to prosecute sb/sth; **~rechtsreform** *f* penal reform; **~register** *nt* criminal records *pl*; **~richter** *m* criminal judge; **~sache** *f* criminal matter; **~stoß** *m (Ftbl etc)* penalty (kick); *(Hockey etc)* penalty (shot); **~tat** *f* criminal offence *(Brit)* or offense *(US)*; **~täter** *m* offender; **~verfahren** *nt* criminal proceedings *pl*; **~verfolgung** *f* criminal prosecution; **s~versetzen*** *vt insep Beamte* to transfer for disciplinary reasons; **~verteidiger** *m* counsel for the defence *(Brit)* or defense *(US)*; **~vollzug** *m* penal system; **~vollzugsanstalt** *f (form)* penal institution; **s~würdig** *adj (form)* punishable; **~wurf** *m (Sport)* penalty throw; **~zettel** *m (col)* ticket.
**Strahl** *m* **-en** *(lit, fig)* ray; *(Radio~, Laser~ etc)* beam; *(Wasser~, Luft~)* jet.
**strahlen** *vi (Sonne, Licht etc)* to shine; *(Sender, fig: Gesicht)* to beam; *(radioaktiv)* to give off radioactivity. **er strahlte (übers ganze Gesicht)** he was beaming all over his face.
**Strahlen-: ~behandlung** *f* radiotherapy; **~belastung** *f* radiation.
**strahlend** *adj* radiant; *Wetter, Tag* bright; *(radioaktiv)* radioactive. **~es Lachen** beaming smile; **mit ~em Gesicht** with a beaming face; **~ weiß** gleaming white.
**Strahlen-: ~dosis** *f* dose of radiation; **s~förmig** *adj* radial; **s~geschädigt** *adj* suffering from radiation damage; **~krankheit** *f* radiation sickness; **~schäden** *pl* radiation injuries *pl*; **~schutz** *m* radiation protection; **~therapie** *f* radiotherapy; **s~verseucht** *adj* contaminated (with radiation).
**Strahler** *m* - *(Lampe)* spotlight.
**Strahltriebwerk** *nt* jet engine.
**Strahlung** *f* radiation.
**Strähne** *f* **-n** *(Haar~)* strand. **ich habe schon eine weiße** ~ I already have a white streak.
**strähnig** *adj Haar* straggly.
**stramm** *adj (straff) Seil, Hose* tight; *(schneidig) Hal-*

*tung, Soldat* erect; *(kräftig, drall) Mädchen, Junge* strapping; *Junge, Beine* sturdy; *Brust* firm; *(col) (tüchtig) Marsch, Arbeit* hard; *(überzeugt)* staunch. ~ **sitzen** *(Kleidung)* to be tight; **~e Haltung annehmen** to stand to attention; ~ **marschieren** *(col)* to march hard; **eine ~e Leistung** a solid achievement; ~ **konservativ** staunchly conservative.
**stramm-: ~stehen** *vi sep irreg (Mil col)* to stand to attention; **~ziehen** *vt sep irreg Seil, Hose* to pull tight; **jdm den Hosenboden ~ziehen** *(col)* to give sb a good hiding.
**Strampelhöschen** [-'hø:sçən] *nt* rompers *pl*.
**strampeln** *vi* **(a)** *Baby* to kick. **(b)** *aux sein (col: radfahren)* to pedal.
**Strand** *m* **≃e** *(Meeres~)* beach; *(Seeufer)* shore. **am** ~ on the beach.
**Strand-: ~anzug** *m* beach suit; **~bad** *nt* (seawater) swimming pool; *(Badeort)* bathing resort.
**stranden** *vi aux sein* to run aground; *(fig)* to fail.
**Strand-: ~gut** *nt (lit, fig)* flotsam and jetsam; **~hafer** *m* marram (grass); **~hotel** *nt* seaside hotel; **~kleidung** *f* beachwear; **~korb** *m wicker beach chair with a hood*; **~promenade** *f* promenade; **~räuber** *m* beachcomber.
**Strang** *m* **≃e** *(Nerven~, Muskel~)* cord; *(Rail: Schienen~)* track. **der Tod durch den** ~ death by hanging; **am gleichen** ~ **ziehen** *(fig)* to act in concert; **über die ~e schlagen** to run riot.
**strangulieren*** *vt* to strangle.
**Strapaze** *f* **-n** strain.
**strapazieren*** **1** *vt* to be a strain on; *Kleidung* to be hard on; *(fig col) Begriff* to flog *(col)*; *Nerven* to strain. **2** *vr* to tax oneself.
**strapazierfähig** *adj Schuhe, Kleidung* hardwearing; *(fig col) Nerven* tough.
**strapaziös** *adj (lit, fig)* wearing, exhausting.
**Straßburg** *nt* Strasbourg.
**Straße** *f* **-n** **(a)** road; *(in Stadt, Dorf)* street, road *(Brit)*; *(kleine Land~)* lane. **an der** ~ by the roadside; **auf der** ~ in the road/street; **auf die** ~ **gehen** *(lit)* to go out on the street; *(als Demonstrant)* to take to the streets; **auf der** ~ **liegen** *(fig col)* to be out of work; *(als Wohnungsloser)* to be on the streets; **jdn auf die** ~ **setzen** *Arbeiter* to sack sb *(col)*; *Mieter* to turn sb out (onto the streets); **über die** ~ **gehen** to cross (the road/street); **er wohnt drei ~n weiter** he lives three blocks further on; **dem Druck der** ~ **nachgeben** *(fig)* to give in to the demands of demonstrators. **(b)** *(Meerenge)* strait(s *pl)*. **(c)** *(Tech) (Fertigungs~)* (production) line.
**Straßen-: ~anzug** *m* lounge suit *(Brit)*, business suit *(US)*; **~arbeiten** *pl* roadworks *pl (Brit)*, roadwork *(US)*.
**Straßenbahn** *f (Wagen)* tram *(Brit)*, streetcar *(US)*.
**Straßenbahn-: ~fahrer** *m* tram *(Brit)* or streetcar *(US)* driver; **~haltestelle** *f* tram *(Brit)* or streetcar *(US)* stop; **~linie** *f* tramline *(Brit)*, streetcar line *(US)*; **~wagen** *m* tramcar *(Brit)*, streetcar *(US)*.
**Straßen-: ~bau** *m* road construction; **~bauarbeiten** *pl* roadworks *pl (Brit)*, roadwork *(US)*; **~beleuchtung** *f* street lighting; **~benutzungsgebühr** *f* (road) toll; **~decke** *f* road surface; **~ecke** *f* street corner; **~feger** *m* - road-sweeper; **~fest** *nt* street party; **~gabelung** *f* fork (in a/the road); **~glätte** *f* slippery road surface; **~graben** *m* ditch; **~händler** *m* street trader; **~junge** *m (pej)* street urchin; **~kampf** *m* street fighting *no pl*; **~karte** *f* road map; **~kehrer** *m* - roadsweeper; **~kind** *nt* child of the streets; **~kreuzer** *m* - *(col)* limousine; **~kreuzung** *f* crossroads *sing or pl*, intersection *(US)*; **~laterne** *f* street lamp; **~mädchen**

*nt* streetwalker; ~**netz** *nt* road network; ~**rand** *m* roadside; ~**raub** *m* mugging; ~**räuber** *m* mugger; ~**reinigung** *f* street cleaning; ~**rennen** *nt* road race; ~**sammlung** *f* street collection; ~**schild** *nt* street sign; ~**schlacht** *f* street battle; ~**schuh** *m* walking shoe; ~**seite** *f* side of a/the road; ~**sperre** *f* road block; ~**strich** *m* *(col)* streetwalking; **auf den** ~**strich gehen** to walk the streets; ~**theater** *nt* street theatre *(Brit)* or theater *(US)*; ~**überführung** *f* footbridge; ~**unterführung** *f* underpass; ~**verhältnisse** *pl* road conditions *pl*; ~**verkauf** *m* street-trading; take-away *(Brit)* or take-out *(US)* sales *pl*; ~**verkäufer** *m* street vendor; ~**verkehr** *m* road traffic; ~**verkehrsordnung** *f* *(Jur)* Road Traffic Act; ~**verzeichnis** *nt* index of street names; ~**wacht** *f* road patrol; ~**zustand** *m* road conditions *pl*; ~**zustandsbericht** *m* road report.

**Stratege** *m (wk)* -n, -n strategist.
**Strategie** *f* strategy.
**strategisch** *adj* strategic.
**Stratosphäre** *f no pl* stratosphere.
**sträuben 1** *vr* (a) *(Haare, Fell)* to stand on end; *(Gefieder)* to become ruffled. **da** ~ **sich einem die Haare** it's enough to make your hair stand on end. (b) *(fig)* to resist *(gegen etw sth)*. **es sträubt sich alles in mir, das zu tun** I am most reluctant to do it. **2** *vt* *Gefieder* to ruffle.
**Strauch** *m, pl* **Sträucher** bush, shrub.
**straucheln** *vi aux sein* (a) *(geh: stolpern)* to stumble. (b) *(fig)* to transgress; *(Mädchen)* to go astray.
**Strauchwerk** *nt no pl (Gebüsch)* bushes *pl*, shrubs *pl*; *(Gestrüpp)* undergrowth.
**Strauß¹** *m* -e *(Orn)* ostrich.
**Strauß²** *m, pl* **Sträuße** bunch; *(Blumen~)* bunch of flowers; *(als Geschenk)* bouquet, bunch of flowers.
**Strebe** *f* -n brace, strut; *(Decken~)* joist.
**Strebe-**: ~**balken** *m* diagonal brace; ~**bogen** *m* flying buttress.
**streben** *vi (geh)* (a) *(sich bemühen)* to strive *(nach* for*)*; *(Sch pej)* to swot *(col)*. **danach** ~, **etw zu tun** to strive to do sth. (b) *aux sein (sich bewegen)* **nach** or **zu etw** ~ to make one's way to sth.
**Streben** *nt no pl (Drängen)* striving *(nach* for*)*; *(nach Ruhm, Geld)* aspiration *(nach* to*)*; *(Bemühen)* efforts *pl*.
**Strebepfeiler** *m* buttress.
**Streber(in** *f)* *m* - *(pej col)* pushy person; *(Sch)* swot *(col)*.
**strebsam** *adj* assiduous, industrious.
**Strebsamkeit** *f no pl* assiduity, industriousness.
**Strecke** *f* -n (a) *(Entfernung)* distance; *(Math)* line. **eine** ~ **zurücklegen** to cover a distance. (b) *(Abschnitt)* *(von Straße, Fluß)* stretch; *(von Bahnlinie)* section. (c) *(Weg, Route)* route; *(Straße)* road; *(Bahnlinie, Sport: Bahn)* track; *(fig: Passage)* passage. **für die** ~ **London-Glasgow brauchen wir 5 Stunden** the journey from London to Glasgow will take us 5 hours; **auf der** ~ **Paris-Brüssel** on the way from Paris to Brussels; **auf der** ~ **bleiben** *(fig)* to fall by the wayside. (d) *(Hunt)* **zur** ~ **bringen** to bag.
**strecken 1** *vt* (a) *Arme, Beine* to stretch; *Hals* to crane. **die Zunge aus dem Mund** ~ to stick out one's tongue; **die Beine von sich** ~ to stretch out one's legs; **den Kopf aus dem Fenster** ~ to stick one's head out of the window. (b) *(Med)* *Bein, Arm* to straighten. (c) *(col: absichtlich verlängern)* *Vorräte, Geld* to eke out; *Arbeit* to drag out *(col)*; *Essen* to make go further. **2** *vr* (a) *(sich recken)* to stretch. **sich ins Gras** ~ to stretch out on the grass. (b) *(sich hinziehen)* to drag on.

**Strecken-**: ~**abschnitt** *m* *(Rail)* track section; ~**netz** *nt* rail network; ~**karte** *f* route map; ~**stillegung** *f* *(Rail)* line closure; **s~weise** *adv* in parts.
**Streich** *m* -e (a) *(Schabernack)* prank, trick. **jdm einen** ~ **spielen** *(lit)* to play a trick on sb; *(fig: Gedächtnis etc)* to play tricks on sb. (b) **auf einen** ~ at one blow; *(fig also)* in one go *(col)*.
**Streichel|einheiten** *pl (hum col)* a pat on the back.
**streicheln** *vti* to stroke. **jdm die Wange** ~ to stroke sb's cheek.
**streichen** *pret* **strich**, *ptp* **gestrichen 1** *vt* (a) to stroke. **etw glatt~** to smooth sth (out); **sich** *(dat)* **die Haare aus der Stirn** ~ to push one's hair back from one's forehead; *siehe* **gestrichen**. (b) *(auftragen)* *Butter, Leberwurst etc* to spread; *Salbe, Farbe etc* to apply, to put on. **sich** *(dat)* **ein Brot (mit Butter)** ~ to butter oneself a slice of bread; **ein Brot mit Marmelade** ~ to spread a slice of bread with jam. (c) *(an~: mit Farbe)* to paint. **frisch gestrichen!** wet paint. (d) *(tilgen)* *Zeile, Satz* to delete; *Auftrag, Zug etc* to cancel; *Schulden* to write off; *Zuschuß etc* to cut. **jdn/etw von der Liste** ~ to take sb/sth off the list.
    **2** *vi* (a) *(über etw hinfahren)* to stroke. **mit der Hand über etw** *(acc)* ~ to stroke sth; **sie strich ihm über das Haar** she stroked his hair. (b) *aux sein (streifen)* to brush past *(an etw (dat)* sth*)*. **um/durch etw** ~ *(herum~)* to prowl around/through sth; **die Katze strich mir um die Beine** the cat rubbed against my legs. (c) *(malen)* to paint.
**Streicher** *pl (Mus)* strings *pl*.
**Streich-**: **s~fähig** *adj* easy to spread; ~**holz** *nt* match; ~**holzschachtel** *f* matchbox; ~**instrument** *nt* string(ed) instrument; ~**käse** *m* cheese spread; ~**orchester** *nt* string orchestra.
**Streichung** *f* *(Tilgung)* *(von Zeile, Satz)* deletion; *(Kürzung)* cut; *(von Auftrag, Zug)* cancellation.
**Streifband** *nt* wrapper.
**Streifbandzeitung** *f newspaper sent at printed paper rate.*
**Streife** *f* -n *(Patrouille)* patrol. **auf** ~ **gehen/sein** to go/be on patrol; **ein Polizist auf** ~ a policeman on his beat.
**streifen 1** *vt* (a) to touch, to brush (against); *(Kugel)* to graze; *(Auto)* to scrape. **jdn mit einem Blick** ~ to glance fleetingly at sb. (b) *(flüchtig erwähnen)* to touch (up)on. (c) *(ab~, überziehen)* **die Schuhe von den Füßen** ~ to slip one's shoes off; **sich** *(dat)* **die Handschuhe über die Finger** ~ to pull on one's gloves. **2** *vi (geh)* (a) *aux sein (wandern)* to roam; *(Fuchs)* to prowl. (b) *aux sein (Blick etc)* **sie ließ ihren Blick über die Menge** ~ she scanned the crowd.
**Streifen** *m* - (a) *(Stück, Band)* strip; *(Loch~, Klebe~ etc)* tape. **ein** ~ **Land** a strip of land. (b) *(Strich)* stripe. **ein goldener** ~ **am Horizont** a streak of gold on the horizon. (c) *(Tresse)* braid; *(Mil)* stripe. (d) *(Film)* film *(Brit)*, movie *(esp US)*.
**Streifen-**: ~**dienst** *m* patrol duty; ~**wagen** *m* patrol car.
**Streif-**: ~**licht** *nt* *(fig)* highlight; **ein** ~**licht auf etw** *(acc)* **werfen** to highlight sth; ~**schuß** *m* graze; ~**zug** *m* *(Bummel)* expedition; *(fig: kurzer Überblick)* brief survey *(durch* of*)*.
**Streik** *m* -s strike. **zum** ~ **aufrufen** to call a strike; **in den** ~ **treten** to come out on strike, to strike.
**Streik-**: ~**aufruf** *m* strike call; ~**brecher(in** *f)* *m* - strikebreaker, scab *(pej)*.
**streiken** *vi* to be on strike; *(in den Streik treten)* to strike; *(hum col) (nicht funktionieren)* to pack up *(col)*; *(Gedächtnis)* to fail. **der Computer streikt** the

computer's packed up *(col)*, the computer's on the blink *(col)*; **da streike ich** *(col)* I refuse!
**Streikende(r)** *mf decl as adj* striker.
**Streik-**: ~**geld** *nt* strike pay; ~**kasse** *f* strike fund; ~**posten** *m* picket; ~**posten aufstellen** to put up pickets; ~**recht** *nt* right to strike; ~**welle** *f* wave of strikes.
**Streit** *m* -e argument *(über +acc about)*; *(leichter)* quarrel; *(Auseinandersetzung)* dispute. ~ **haben** to be arguing *or* quarrelling; **wegen etw mit jdm (einen)** ~ **haben** to argue with sb about sth; ~ **anfangen** to start an argument; **mit jdm in** ~ **liegen** to be at loggerheads with sb.
**Streit|axt** *f (Hist)* battleaxe *(Brit)*, battleax *(US)*.
**streiten** *pret* **stritt**, *ptp* **gestritten 1** *vi (über +acc* about, over*)* to argue; *(leichter)* to quarrel. **darüber läßt sich** ~ that's debatable; **die** ~**den Parteien** *(Jur)* the litigants. **2** *vr* to argue, to quarrel. **·wir wollen uns deswegen nicht** ~**!** don't let's fall out over that!
**Streit-**: ~**fall** *m* dispute, conflict; *(Jur)* case; **im** ~**fall** in case of dispute; **im** ~**fall Müller gegen Braun** in the case of Müller versus Braun; ~**frage** *f* point at issue; ~**gespräch** *nt* debate; ~**hahn** *m (col)* squabbler.
**streitig** *adj* **jdm etw** ~ **machen, jdm das Recht auf etw** *(acc)* ~ **machen** to dispute sb's right to sth.
**Streitigkeiten** *pl* quarrels *pl*, squabbles *pl*.
**Streit-**: ~**kräfte** *pl* armed forces *pl*; **s**~**lustig** *adj (aggressiv)* aggressive; ~**macht** *f* armed forces *pl*; ~**punkt** *m* contentious issue; ~**sache** *f* dispute; *(Jur)* case; ~**sucht** *f* quarrelsomeness; **s**~**süchtig** *adj* quarrelsome.
**streng** *adj* strict; *Blick, Bestrafung, Anforderung, Winter* severe; *Geruch, Geschmack* pungent. ~ **gegen jdn/etw vorgehen** to deal severely with sb/sth; ~ **aber gerecht** severe but just; **etw** ~ **befolgen** to keep strictly to sth; ~ **geheim** top secret; ~ **vertraulich** strictly confidential; ~ **nach Vorschrift** strictly according to regulations; ~ **verboten** strictly prohibited.
**Strenge** *f no pl siehe adj* strictness; severity; pungency.
**streng-**: ~**genommen** *adv* strictly speaking; *(eigentlich)* actually; ~**gläubig** *adj* strict.
**Streß** *m* -sse stress. **im** ~ **sein** to be under stress.
**stressen** *vt* to put under stress. **gestreßt sein** to be under stress.
**streßfrei** *adj* stress-free.
**streßsig** *adj* stressful.
**Streu** *f no pl* straw; *(aus Sägespänen)* sawdust.
**streuen 1** *vt Futter, Samen* to scatter; *Dünger, Sand* to spread; *Gewürze, Zucker etc* to sprinkle; *Straße* to grit; to salt. **2** *vi (mit Streumittel)* to grit; *(mit Salz)* to put down salt.
**Streuer** *m* - shaker; *(Salz*~*)* cellar; *(Pfeffer*~*)* pot.
**Streufahrzeug** *nt* gritter, sander.
**streunen** *vi* **(a)** to roam about; *(Hund, Katze)* to stray. ~**de Katzen** stray cats. **(b)** *aux sein* **durch etw** ~ to roam through sth.
**Streu-**: ~**salz** *nt* road salt; ~**sand** *m* sand; *(für Straße)* grit.
**Streusel** *nt* - *(Cook)* crumble (mixture).
**Streuselkuchen** *m thin sponge cake with crumble topping.*
**Streuung** *f (Statistik)* mean variation; *(Phys)* scattering.
**strich** *pret of* **streichen**.
**Strich** *m* -e **(a)** line; *(Quer*~*)* dash; *(Schräg*~*)* oblique, slash *(esp US)*; *(Feder*~, *Pinsel*~*)* stroke; *(von Land)* stretch. **jdm einen** ~ **durch die Rechnung machen** to thwart sb's plans; **einen** ~ **(unter etw**

*acc)* **machen** *(fig)* to forget sth; **unterm** ~ at the final count; **unterm** ~ **sein** *(col)* not to be up to scratch; **sie ist nur noch ein** ~ *(col)* she's as thin as a rake now; **ich habe heute keinen** ~ **gearbeitet** I haven't done a stroke of work today. **(b)** *(von Teppich)* pile; *(von Gewebe)* nap; *(von Fell, Haar)* direction of growth. **gegen den** ~ **bürsten** *(lit)* to brush the wrong way; **es geht (mir) gegen den** ~ *(col)* it goes against the grain; **nach** ~ **und Faden** *(col)* good and proper *(col)*. **(c)** *(Mus: Bogen*~*)* stroke, bow. **(d)** *(col) (Prostitution)* prostitution *no art*; *(Bordellgegend)* red-light district. **auf den** ~ **gehen** to be/go on the game *(col)*.
**Strichcode** *m* bar code *(Brit)*, universal product code *(US)*.
**stricheln** *vti (schraffieren)* to hatch. **eine gestrichelte Linie** a broken line.
**Strich-**: ~**junge** *m (col)* rent boy; ~**kode** *m* = ~**code**; ~**mädchen** *nt (col)* streetwalker *(col)*; ~**punkt** *m* semicolon; **s**~**weise** *adv (Met)* **s**~**weise Regen** rain in places.
**Strick** *m* -e rope. **jdm aus etw einen** ~ **drehen** to use sth against sb.
**stricken** *vti* to knit.
**Strickerei** *f* knitting *no indef art, no pl.*
**Strick-**: ~**jacke** *f* cardigan; ~**leiter** *f* rope ladder; ~**maschine** *f* knitting machine; ~**muster** *nt (lit)* knitting pattern; *(fig)* pattern; ~**nadel** *f* knitting needle; ~**waren** *pl* knitwear *sing*; ~**wolle** *f* knitting wool; ~**zeug** *nt* knitting.
**Striegel** *m* - currycomb.
**striegeln 1** *vt* to curry(comb); *(fig col: kämmen)* to comb. **2** *vr (col)* to spruce oneself up.
**Strieme** *f* -n weal.
**strikt** *adj* strict.
**Strippe** *f* -n *(col)* **(a)** *(Bindfaden)* string. **(b)** *(Telefonleitung)* phone. **an der** ~ **hängen** to be on the phone.
**strippen** *vi* to strip.
**Stripper(in** *f)* *m* - *(col)* stripper.
**Striptease** ['ʃtrɪptiːs] *m or nt no pl* striptease.
**stritt** *pret of* **streiten**.
**strittig** *adj* controversial. **noch** ~ still in dispute.
**Stroboskop** *nt* -e stroboscope.
**Stroh** *nt no pl* straw; *(Dach*~*)* thatch.
**Stroh-**: ~**ballen** *m* bale of straw; **s**~**blond** *adj Mensch* flaxen-haired; *Haare* flaxen; ~**blume** *f* everlasting flower; ~**dach** *nt* thatched roof; **s**~**dumm** *adj* thick *(col)*; ~**feuer** *nt*: **ein** ~**feuer sein** *(fig)* to be a passing fancy; ~**halm** *m* straw; **sich an einen** ~**halm klammern** to clutch at a straw; ~**hut** *m* straw hat; ~**kopf** *m (col)* blockhead *(col)*; ~**mann** *m, pl* ~**männer** *(fig)* front man; ~**sack** *m* **heiliger** ~**sack!** *(col)* good(ness) gracious (me)!; ~**witwe** *f* grass widow; ~**witwer** *m* grass widower.
**Strolch** *m* -e *(pej)* rogue, rascal.
**Strom** *m* =e **(a)** (large) river; *(Strömung)* current; *(von Besuchern)* stream. **ein reißender** ~ a raging torrent; **in** ~**en regnen** to be pouring with rain; **der Wein floß in** ~**en** the wine flowed like water; **mit dem/gegen den** ~ **schwimmen** *(lit, fig)* to swim with/against the current. **(b)** *(Elec)* current; *(Elektrizität)* electricity. ~ **führen** to be live; **unter** ~ **stehen** *(lit)* to be live; **der** ~ **ist ausgefallen** there has been a power failure *or* outage *(US)*.
**Strom-**: **s**~**ab(wärts)** *adv* downstream; ~**anschluß** *m* ~**anschluß haben** to be connected to the electricity mains; **s**~**auf(wärts)** *adv* upstream; ~**ausfall** *m* power failure *or* outage *(US)*.
**strömen** *vi aux sein* to stream; *(heraus*~*)* to pour *(aus from)*. **bei** ~**dem Regen** in (the) pouring rain.

**Strom-:** **s~führend** *adj attr (Elec)* live; **~kabel** *nt* electric cable; **~kreis** *m* (electrical) circuit; **~leitung** *f* electric cable; **~linienform** [-liːniən-] *f* streamlined design; **s~linienförmig** [-liːniən-] *adj* streamlined; **~netz** *nt* power supply system; **~quelle** *f* source of power; **~schnelle** *f* rapids *pl*; **~speicher** *m* (storage) battery; **~sperre** *f* power cut.

**Strömung** *f* current.

**Strom-:** **~verbrauch** *m* power consumption; **~versorgung** *f* power supply; **~zähler** *m* electricity meter.

**Strophe** *f* **-n** verse.

**strotzen** *vi* to abound *(von, vor +dat* with*); (von Kraft, Gesundheit)* to be bursting *(von* with*).* **von Schmutz ~** to be thick with dirt.

**strubb(e)lig** *adj (col)* Haar, Fell tousled.

**Strudel** *m* **-** **(a)** *(lit, fig)* whirlpool. **(b)** *(Cook)* strudel.

**strudeln** *vi* to whirl, to swirl.

**Struktur** *f* structure; *(von Stoff etc)* texture.

**Struktur-** *in cpds* structural; **~krise** *f (Econ)* structural crisis; **s~schwach** *adj* economically underdeveloped.

**strukturell** *adj* structural.

**strukturieren*** *vt* to structure.

**Strumpf** *m* ⁼e sock; *(Damen~)* stocking. **ein Paar ~e** a pair of socks/stockings; **auf ~en** in one's stockinged feet.

**Strumpf-:** **~band** *nt* garter; **~geschäft** *nt* hosiery shop *(Brit)* or store *(US)*; **~halter** *m* **-** suspender *(Brit)*, garter *(US)*; **~hose** *f* tights *pl (Brit)*, pantyhose; **eine ~hose** a pair of tights *(Brit)* or pantyhose; **~waren** *pl* hosiery *sing.*

**Strunk** *m* ⁼e stalk.

**struppig** *adj* unkempt; *Tier* shaggy.

**Stube** *f* **-n** room. **die gute ~** the parlour *(Brit)* or parlor *(US) (dated)*; **(immer) herein in die gute ~!** *(hum col)* come right in.

**Stuben-:** **~arrest** *m* confinement to one's room *or (Mil)* quarters; **~arrest haben** to be confined to one's room/quarters; **~fliege** *f* (common) housefly; **~hocker** *m* **-** *(pej col)* stay-at-home *(col)*; **s~rein** *adj* Katze, Hund house-trained; *(hum) Witz* clean.

**Stuck** *m no pl* stucco.

**Stück** *nt* **-e** *or (nach Zahlenangaben)* **-** **(a)** piece; *(von Vieh, Wild)* head; *(von Zucker)* lump; *(Seife)* bar; *(von Land)* plot. **ich nehme fünf ~** I'll take five; **20 ~ Vieh** 20 head of cattle; **sechs ~ von diesen Apfelsinen** six of these oranges; **50 Pfennig das ~** 50 pfennigs each; **am ~** in one piece; **aus einem ~** in one piece; **~ für ~** *(ein Exemplar nach dem andern)* one by one; **ein ~ Garten** a patch of garden; **das ist unser bestes ~** *(hum)* that is our pride and joy.
    **(b)** *(Teil, Abschnitt)* piece, bit; *(von Buch, Rede)* part. **~ für ~** *(einen Teil um den andern)* bit by bit; **in ~e gehen** to be broken to pieces; **etw in ~e schlagen** to smash sth to pieces; **ich komme ein ~ (des Weges) mit** I'll come part of the way with you; **ein ~ spazierengehen** to go for a walk; **das ist ein starkes ~!** *(col)* that's a bit much *(col)*; **große ~e auf jdn halten** to think highly of sb; **aus freien ~en** of one's own free will.
    **(c)** *(Bühnen~)* play; *(Musik~)* piece.

**Stückeschreiber** *m* dramatist, playwright.

**Stück-:** **~gut** *nt (Rail)* parcel service; **etw als ~gut schicken** to send sth as a parcel; **~kosten** *pl* unit cost; **~lohn** *m* piece(work) rate; **~preis** *m* unit price; **s~weise** *adv* bit by bit; **s~weise verkaufen** to sell individually; **~werk** *nt no pl* incomplete work; **~werk sein/bleiben** to be/remain incomplete;

**~zahl** *f* number of pieces.

**Student** *m* student.

**Studenten-:** **~ausweis** *m* student card; **~bewegung** *f* student movement; **~bude** *f (col)* student digs *pl*; **~futter** *nt* nuts and raisins; **~gemeinde** *f* student religious society; **~heim** *nt* = **~wohnheim**; **~schaft** *f* student body; **~verbindung** *f* students' society; **~werk** *nt* student administration; **~wohnheim** *nt* hall of residence.

**Studentin** *f* (female) student.

**studentisch** *adj attr* student *attr.*

**Studie** ['ʃtuːdiə] *f* study *(über +acc* of*).*

**Studien-** ['ʃtuːdiən-]: **~abschluß** *m* completion of a course of study; **~anfänger** *m* first-year student; **~aufenthalt** *m* study visit; **~beratung** *f* course guidance service; **~fach** *nt* subject; **~fahrt** *f* study trip; *(Sch)* educational trip; **~förderung** *f* study grant; *(an Universität)* university grant; **~gang** *m* course of studies; **~gebühren** *pl* tuition fees *pl*; **~jahr** *nt* academic year; **~jahre** *pl* university/college years *pl*; **~platz** *m* university place; **ein ~platz in Medizin** a place to study medicine; **~rat** *m*, **~rätin** *f teacher at a secondary school with tenure*; **~referendar** *m* student teacher; **~reform** *f* university/college reform; **~reise** *f* = **~fahrt**; **~seminar** *nt* teacher training course; **~zeit** *f* **(a)** student days *pl*; **(b)** *(Dauer)* duration of a/one's course of studies.

**studieren*** **1** *vi* to study; *(Student sein)* to be a student. **ich studiere an der Universität Bonn** I am (a student) at Bonn University; **wo haben Sie studiert?** what university/college did you go to?; **bei jdm ~** to study under sb. **2** *vt* to study; *(genau betrachten)* to scrutinize.

**Studierende(r)** *mf decl as adj* student.

**Studio** *nt* **-s** studio.

**Studiobühne** *f* studio theatre *(Brit)* or theater *(US)*.

**Studium** *nt* study; *(Hochschul~)* studies *pl.* **das ~ hat fünf Jahre gedauert** the course (of study) lasted five years; **während seines ~s** while he is/was *etc* a student.

**Stufe** *f* **-n** **(a)** step; *(Mus: Ton~)* degree; *(im Haar)* layer. **„Vorsicht ~"** "mind the step". **(b)** *(fig)* stage; *(Niveau)* level; *(Rang)* grade. **sich mit jdm/etw auf eine ~ stellen** to put oneself on a level with sb/sth.

**stufen** *vt* Schüler, Preise to grade.

**Stufen-:** **~barren** *m* asymmetric bars *pl*; **~heck** *nt (Aut)* notchback; **s~förmig** **1** *adj (lit)* stepped; Landschaft terraced; *(fig)* gradual; **2** *adv (lit)* in steps; angelegt in terraces; *(fig)* in stages; **~leiter** *f (fig)* ladder *(gen* to*);* **s~los** *adj* Übergang direct; *(fig: gleitend)* smooth; *(Tech)* infinitely variable; **~plan** *m* step-by-step plan *(zu* for*);* **~schnitt** *m (Frisur)* layered cut; **s~weise** **1** *adv* step by step; **2** *adj attr* gradual.

**stufig** *adj* stepped; Land etc terraced; Haar layered.

**Stufung** *f* gradation.

**Stuhl** *m* ⁼e **(a)** chair. **zwischen zwei ~en sitzen** *(fig)* to fall between two stools; **das haut einen vom ~** *(col)* it knocks you sideways *(col)*; **jdm den ~ vor die Tür setzen** *(fig)* to kick sb out *(col)*. **(b)** *(Königs~)* throne. **der Heilige ~** the Holy See. **(c)** *(~gang)* bowel movement; *(Kot)* stool.

**Stuhl-:** **~bein** *nt* chair leg; **~gang** *m no pl* bowel movement; **~lehne** *f* back of a chair.

**Stuka** *m* **-s =** **Sturzkampfflugzeug.**

**Stukkateur(in** *f***)** [ʃtʊkaˈtøːɐ, -ˈtøːrɪn] *m* plasterer.

**Stukkatur** *f* stucco, ornamental plasterwork.

**stülpen** *vt* den Kragen nach oben **~** to turn up one's collar; **etw auf/über etw** *(acc)* ~ to put sth on/over sth.

**stumm** *adj* **(a)** *(lit, fig)* dumb; *(schweigend)* mute. **die ~e Kreatur** *(geh)* the dumb creatures *pl*; ~ **vor Schmerz** in silent agony; **sie sah mich** ~ **an** she looked at me without speaking; ~ **bleiben** to stay silent. **(b)** *Rolle* non-speaking; *Film, Szene* silent.

**Stummel** *m* - *(Zigaretten~, Kerzen~)* stub; *(von Gliedmaßen, Zahn)* stump.

**Stummelschwanz** *m* stumpy tail; *(gestutzt)* dock.

**Stummfilm** *m* silent film *(Brit)* or movie *(esp US)*.

**Stumpen** *m* - cheroot.

**Stümper(in** *f)* *m* - *(pej)* amateur; *(Pfuscher)* bungler.

**Stümperei** *f* *(pej)* amateur work; *(Pfuscherei)* bungling; *(stümperhafte Arbeit)* botched job.

**stümperhaft** *adj (pej)* amateurish.

**stümpern** *vi (pfuschen)* to bungle. **bei einer Arbeit** ~ to botch a job.

**stumpf** *adj* **(a)** blunt; *Nase* snub, turned-up. **(b)** *(fig) Haar, Farbe, Mensch* dull. ~ **vor sich hin brüten** to sit brooding impassively. **(c)** *(Math) Winkel* obtuse.

**Stumpf** *m* ⁼e stump; *(Bleistift~)* stub. **etw mit** ~ **und Stiel ausrotten** to eradicate sth root and branch.

**Stumpf-:** ~**sinn** *m* mindlessness; *(Langweiligkeit)* tedium; **s~sinnig** *adj* mindless; *(langweilig)* tedious.

**Stunde** *f* -n **(a)** hour. **eine viertel/halbe/dreiviertel** ~ a quarter of an hour/half an hour/three-quarters of an hour; **eine halbe** ~ **Pause** a half-hour break; ~ **um** ~ hour after hour; **von** ~ **zu** ~ by the hour; **80 Kilometer in der** ~ 50 miles per hour. **(b)** *(Augenblick, Zeitpunkt)* time. **zu dieser** ~ at this/that time; **zu später** ~ at a late hour; **bis zur** ~ up to the present moment; **eine schwere** ~ a time of difficulty; **seine** ~ **hat geschlagen** *(fig)* his hour has come; **die** ~ **der Entscheidung** the moment of decision. **(c)** *(Unterricht, Sch)* lesson.

**stunden** *vt* **jdm etw** ~ to give sb time to pay sth.

**Stunden-:** ~**geschwindigkeit** *f* speed in kilometres *(Brit)* or kilometers *(US)* per hour; **eine ~geschwindigkeit von 80 km/h** a speed of 50 miles per hour; ~**glas** *nt* hour-glass; ~**kilometer** *pl* kilometres *(Brit)* or kilometers *(US)* per hour *pl*.

**stundenlang 1** *adj* lasting several hours. **nach ~em Warten** after hours of waiting. **2** *adv* for hours.

**Stunden-:** ~**lohn** *m* hourly wage; ~**lohn bekommen** to be paid by the hour; ~**plan** *m (Sch)* timetable; ~**satz** *m* hourly rate; **s~weise** *adv (pro Stunde)* by the hour; *(stündlich)* every hour; **Kellner s~weise gesucht** part-time waiters required; ~**zeiger** *m* hour hand.

**stündlich 1** *adj* hourly. **2** *adv* hourly, every hour.

**Stunk** *m no pl* ~ **machen** *(col)* to kick up a stink *(col)*.

**stupid(e)** *adj (geh)* mindless.

**Stups** *m* -e nudge.

**stupsen** *vt* to nudge.

**Stupsnase** *f* snub nose.

**stur** *adj* stolid; *Nein, Arbeiten* dogged; *(hartnäckig)* stubborn; *(querköpfig)* cussed. ~ **weitermachen** *etc* to carry on regardless; **er fuhr** ~ **geradeaus** he just carried straight on; **sich** ~ **stellen, auf** ~ **stellen** *(col)* to dig one's heels in; **ein ~er Bock** *(col)* a pigheaded fellow.

**Sturheit** *f siehe adj* stolidness; doggedness; stubbornness; cussedness.

**Sturm** *m* ⁼e **(a)** *(lit, fig)* storm; *(starker Wind auch)* gale. **die Zeichen stehen auf** ~ *(fig)* there's a storm brewing; **die Ruhe vor dem** ~ the calm before the

storm; **ein** ~ **im Wasserglas** *(fig)* a storm in a teacup; ~ **läuten** to keep one's finger on the doorbell; **ein** ~ **der Begeisterung** tempestuous enthusiasm. **(b)** *(Angriff)* all-out attack. **etw im** ~ **nehmen** *(Mil, fig)* to take sth by storm; **zum** ~ **blasen** *(Mil, fig)* to sound the attack; **gegen etw** ~ **laufen** *(fig)* to be up in arms against sth; **ein** ~ **auf die Banken** a run on the banks.

**Sturm-:** ~**angriff** *m (Mil)* all-out assault *(auf +acc* on*)*; ~**bö** *f* squall.

**stürmen 1** *vi* **(a)** *(Meer)* to rage; *(Sport, Mil)* to attack. **(b)** *aux sein (rennen)* to storm. **2** *vi impers* **es stürmt** it is blowing a gale. **3** *vt (Mil, fig)* to storm; *Bank etc* to make a run on.

**Stürmer** *m* - *(Sport)* forward; *(Ftbl auch)* striker.

**Sturm-:** ~**flut** *f* storm tide; **s~frei** *adj (Mil)* unassailable; **eine s~freie Bude** *(col)* a room free from disturbance.

**stürmisch** *adj* **(a)** *Meer* rough; *Wetter* blustery; *(mit Regen)* stormy. **(b)** *(fig)* tempestuous; *Entwicklung* rapid; *Liebhaber* passionate; *Beifall* tumultuous. **nicht so** ~ take it easy.

**Sturm-:** ~**schritt** *m (Mil, fig)* double-quick pace; **im ~schritt** at the double; ~**vogel** *m* petrel; ~**warnung** *f* gale warning; ~**wind** *m* gale.

**Sturz** *m* ⁼e fall; *(in Temperatur, Preis auch)* drop; *(Pol: durch Coup)* overthrow.

**Sturzbach** *m (lit)* fast-flowing stream.

**stürzen 1** *vi aux sein* **(a)** to fall *(auch Pol)*. **ins Wasser** ~ to plunge into the water; **vom Pferd** ~ to fall off a/one's horse; **er ist schwer gestürzt** he had a bad fall. **(b)** *(rennen)* to dash. **sie kam ins Zimmer gestürzt** she burst into the room. **2** *vt* **(a)** *(werfen)* to fling, to hurl; **jdn ins Unglück** ~ to bring disaster upon sb. **(b)** *(kippen)* to turn upside down. **„nicht ~!"** "this side up". **(c)** *(Pol) Regierung etc* to bring down; *(durch Coup)* to overthrow; *König* to depose. **3** *vr* **sich zu Tode** ~ to fall to one's death; *(absichtlich)* to jump to one's death; **sich aus dem Fenster** ~ to fling *or* hurl oneself out of the window; **sich auf jdn/etw** ~ to pounce on sb/sth; *auf Essen* to fall on sth; **sich in Schulden** ~ to plunge into debt; **sich ins Unglück** ~ to plunge headlong into disaster; **sich in Unkosten** ~ to go to great expense.

**Sturz-:** ~**flug** *m* (nose)dive; ~**helm** *m* crash helmet; ~**kampfflugzeug** *nt* dive bomber.

**Stuß** *m no pl (col)* nonsense, rubbish *(col)*.

**Stute** *f* -n mare.

**Stützbalken** *m* beam; *(in Decke)* joist.

**Stütze** *f* -n **(a)** support; *(Pfeiler)* pillar; *(Buch~)* rest. **(b)** *(Halt)* support; *(Fuß~)* footrest. **(c)** *(fig) (Hilfe)* help, aid *(für* to*)*; *(Beistand)* support; *(wichtiger Mensch)* mainstay. **die ~n der Gesellschaft** the pillars of society.

**stutzen¹** *vi* to stop short; *(zögern)* to hesitate.

**stutzen²** *vt* to trim; *Flügel, Hecke* to clip; *Schwanz* to dock.

**Stutzen** *m* - **(a)** *(Gewehr)* carbine. **(b)** *(Rohrstück)* connecting piece; *(Endstück)* nozzle.

**stützen 1** *vt (Halt geben)* to support; *Gebäude, Mauer* to shore up. **einen Verdacht auf etw** *(acc)* ~ to base a suspicion on sth; **die Ellbogen auf den Tisch** ~ to prop one's elbows on the table; **den Kopf in die Hände** ~ to rest one's head in one's hands. **2** *vr* **sich auf jdn/etw** ~ *(lit)* to lean on sb/sth; *(fig)* to count on sb/sth; *(Beweise, Theorie)* to be based on sb/sth.

**Stutzer** *m* - *(pej)* fop, dandy.

**stutzig** *adj pred* ~ **werden** *(argwöhnisch)* to become suspicious; **jdn** ~ **machen** to make sb suspicious.

**Stütz-:** ~**mauer** *f* retaining wall; ~**pfeiler** *m* sup-

porting pillar; ~**punkt** *m (Mil, fig)* base.
**Stützung** *f* support.
**Stützungskäufe** *pl (Fin)* support buying *sing.*
**StVO = Straßenverkehrsordnung.**
**stylen** ['stail-] *vt Wagen, Wohnung* to design; *Frisur* to style.
**Styling** ['stailiŋ] *nt* -**s**, *no pl* styling.
**Styropor** ® *nt* (expanded) polystyrene.
**s.u. = siehe unten.**
**sub|altern** *adj (pej) Stellung* subordinate.
**Subjekt** *nt* -**e** (**a**) subject. (**b**) *(pej: Mensch)* character *(col).*
**subjektiv** *adj* subjective.
**Subjektivität** [-vɪ'tɛːt] *f* subjectivity.
**Sub-:** ~**kontinent** *m* subcontinent; ~**kultur** *f* subculture.
**sublimieren\*** *vt (Psych, Chem)* to sublimate.
**Subsidiarität** *f* subsidiarity.
**Subskription** *f* subscription *(gen, auf +acc* to*).*
**substantiell** [zʊpstan'tsiɛl] *adj (fig geh: bedeutsam)* fundamental.
**Substantiv** ['zʊpstantiːf] *nt* -**e** noun.
**Substanz** [zʊp'stants] *f* (**a**) substance. (**b**) *(Fin)* capital assets *pl.* **von der** ~ **zehren** to live on one's capital.
**subtil** *adj (geh)* subtle; *Film etc* understated.
**subtrahieren\*** [zʊptra'hiːrən] *vti* to subtract.
**Subtraktion** *f* subtraction.
**subtropisch** ['zʊptroːpɪʃ] *adj* subtropical.
**Sub|unternehmer** *m* subcontractor.
**Subvention** [zʊpvɛn'tsioːn] *f* subsidy.
**subventionieren\*** [zʊpvɛntsio'niːrən] *vt* to subsidize.
**subversiv** [zʊpvɛr'ziːf] *adj* subversive. **sich** ~ **betätigen** to engage in subversive activities.
**Such-:** ~**aktion** *f* search operation; ~**anzeige** *f* missing person report; ~**dienst** *m* missing persons tracing service.
**Suche** *f no pl* search *(nach* for*).* **auf die** ~ **nach jdm/etw gehen** to go in search of sb/sth.
**suchen 1** *vt* (**a**) to look for; *(stärker, intensiv, Comp)* to search for. **Verkäufer(in) gesucht** sales person wanted; **gesucht** wanted *(wegen* for*)*; **was suchst du hier?** what are you doing here?; **du hast hier nichts zu** ~ you have no business (to be) here; **seinesgleichen** ~ to be unparalleled. (**b**) *(streben nach)* to seek. **ein Gespräch** ~ to try to have a talk. **2** *vi* to search, to hunt. **nach etw** ~ to look for sth; *(stärker)* to search for sth; **nach Worten** ~ to search for words; *(sprachlos sein)* to be at a loss for words; **such!** *(zu Hund)* seek!, find!
**Sucher** *m* - *(Phot)* viewfinder.
**Such-:** ~**lauf** *m (Comp, Rad)* search; ~**mannschaft** *f* search party; ~**meldung** *f* SOS message; ~**scheinwerfer** *m* searchlight.
**Sucht** *f* ⁼e addiction *(nach* to*)*; *(fig)* obsession *(nach* with*).* **eine krankhafte** ~ **haben, etw zu tun** *(fig)* to be completely obsessed with doing sth; **das kann zur** ~ **werden** one can get addicted to that; **an einer** ~ **leiden** to be an addict.
**Sucht-:** ~**droge** *f* addictive drug; **s**~**erzeugend** *adj* addictive.
**süchtig** *adj* addicted *(nach* to*).* ~ **machen** *(Droge)* to be addictive.
**Süchtige(r)** *mf decl as adj,* **Suchtkranke(r)** *mf* addict.
**Sud** *m* -**e** liquid; *(esp von Fleisch, für Suppe)* stock.
**Süd** *no art no pl (Naut, Met, liter)* south.
**Süd-** *in cpds* South; ~**afrika** *nt* South Africa; ~**amerika** *nt* South America.
**Sudan** [zu'daːn, 'zuːdan] *m* **der** ~ the Sudan.

**Sudanese** *m (wk)* -**n**, -**n**, **Sudanesin** *f* Sudanese.
**sudanesisch** *adj* Sudanese.
**Süd-:** **s**~**deutsch** *adj* South German; ~**deutschland** *nt* South(ern) Germany.
**Süden** *m no pl* south; *(von Land)* South. **aus dem** ~, **vom** ~ **her** from the south; **nach** ~ **hin** to the south; **weiter im** ~ further south.
**Süd-:** ~**europa** *nt* Southern Europe; ~**früchte** *pl* citrus and tropical fruit(s *pl*); ~**korea** *nt* South Korea; ~**küste** *f* south(ern) coast; ~**lage** *f* southern aspect; ~**länder(in** *f)* *m* - southerner; Mediterranean *or* Latin type; **s**~**ländisch** *adj* southern; *(italienisch, spanisch etc)* Latin.
**südlich 1** *adj* (**a**) southern; *Kurs, Richtung* southerly. (**b**) *(mediterran)* Mediterranean, Latin; *Temperament* Latin. **2** *adv* (to the) south. ~ **von Wien (gelegen)** (to the) south of Vienna; **es liegt weiter** ~ it is further (to the) south. **3** *prep +gen* (to the) south of.
**Süd|ost** *m (Met, Naut)* south-east.
**Süd|osten** *m* south-east; *(von Land)* South East. **aus** *or* **von** ~ from the south-east; **nach** ~ to the south-east.
**süd|östlich 1** *adj Gegend* south-eastern; *Wind* south-east(erly). **2** *adv* south-east. **3** *prep +gen* (to the) south-east of.
**Süd-:** ~**pol** *m* South Pole; ~**polarmeer** *nt* Antarctic Ocean; ~**see** *f* South Seas *pl*; ~**seite** *f* south side; *(von Berg)* south(ern) face; ~**staaten** *pl (US)* Southern States.
**südwärts** *adv* south(wards).
**Südwest** *m (Naut, Met)* south-west.
**Südwestafrika** *nt* South-West Africa.
**Südwesten** *m* south-west; *(von Land)* South West. **aus** *or* **von** ~ from the south-west; **nach** ~ to the south-west.
**südwestlich 1** *adj Gegend* south-western; *Wind* south-west(erly). **2** *adv* (to the) south-west. **3** *prep +gen* (to the) south-west of.
**Südwind** *m* south wind.
**Sueskanal** *m* Suez Canal.
**Suff** *m no pl (col)* **dem** ~ **ergeben sein** to be on the bottle *(col)*; **etw im** ~ **sagen** to say sth when under the influence *(col).*
**süffeln** *vi (col)* to tipple *(col).*
**süffig** *adj Wein etc* very drinkable. **ein** ~**er Wein** a wine that goes down very well.
**süffisant** *adj* smug, complacent.
**Suffix** *nt* -**e** suffix.
**suggerieren\*** *vt* to suggest. **jdm etw** ~ to influence sb by suggesting sth; **jdm** ~, **daß** ... to get sb to believe that ...
**Suggestion** *f* suggestion.
**Suggestivfrage** *f* leading question.
**suhlen** *vr (lit, fig)* to wallow.
**Sühne** *f* -**n** *(Rel, geh)* atonement; *(von Schuld)* expiation. ~ **leisten** to atone *(für* for*).*
**sühnen 1** *vt Unrecht, Verbrechen* to atone for; *Schuld* to expiate. **2** *vi* to atone.
**Sühnetermin** *m (Jur)* conciliatory hearing.
**Suite** ['sviːtə] *f* -**n** suite.
**sukzessiv(e)** *adj* gradual.
**Sulfat** *nt* sulphate *(Brit)*, sulfate *(US).*
**Sultan** *m* -**e** sultan.
**Sultanat** *nt* sultanate.
**Sultanine** *f (Rosine)* sultana.
**Sülze** *f* -**n** (**a**) brawn. (**b**) *(Aspik)* aspic.
**Sumatra** *nt* Sumatra.
**summarisch** *adj (auch Jur)* summary. **etw** ~ **zusammenfassen** to summarize sth.
**Sümmchen** *nt dim of* **Summe. ein schönes** ~

*(hum)* a tidy sum, a pretty penny *(col)*.
**Summe** f -n sum; *(fig)* sum total.
**summen 1** vt Melodie etc to hum. **2** vi to buzz; *(Mensch, Motor)* to hum.
**Summer** m - buzzer.
**summieren\* 1** vt to sum up. **2** vr to mount up. **das summiert sich** it (all) adds up.
**Summton** m buzz, buzzing sound.
**Sumpf** m ⁼e marsh; *(Morast)* mud; *(in tropischen Ländern)* swamp.
**Sumpf-:** ~**boden** m marshy ground; ~**fieber** nt malaria.
**sumpfig** adj marshy, swampy.
**Sumpf-:** ~**land** nt marshland; *(in tropischen Ländern)* swampland; ~**pflanze** f marsh plant; ~**vogel** m wader.
**Sund** m -e sound, straits pl.
**Sünde** f -n sin. **eine** ~ **begehen** to sin, to commit a sin.
**Sünden-:** ~**bekenntnis** nt confession of one's sins; *(Gebet)* confession (of sins); ~**bock** m *(col)* scapegoat; ~**fall** m *(Rel)* Fall; ~**register** nt *(fig)* list of sins; **jds** ~**register** the list of sb's sins.
**Sünder(in** f*)* m -s, - sinner. **armer** ~ *(fig)* poor wretch.
**sündhaft** adj *(lit)* sinful; *(fig col)* Preise wicked. ~ **teuer** *(col)* wickedly expensive.
**sündig** adj sinful.
**sündigen** vi to sin *(an +dat* against*)*; *(hum)* to indulge.
**Super** nt no pl *(Benzin)* four-star (petrol) *(Brit)*, premium gasoline *(US)*, super.
**super** *(col)* **1** adj inv super *(col)*. **2** adv *(mit vb)* incredibly well *(col)*.
**Super-** in cpds super-; *(sehr)* ultra-; ~**-8-Film** m super-8 film; ~**benzin** nt = Super; **s**~**klug** adj *(iro col)* brilliant; **du bist ein** ~**kluger** *(Besserwisser)* you are a (real) know-all *(col)*.
**Superlativ** m *(Gram, fig)* superlative.
**Super-:** ~**macht** f superpower; ~**mann** m, pl ~**männer** superman; ~**markt** m supermarket; **s**~**modern** adj *(col)* ultramodern; ~**star** m *(col)* superstar.
**Suppe** f -n soup; *(sämig mit Einlage)* broth; *(klare Brühe)* bouillon; *(fig col: Nebel)* pea-souper *(col)*. **du mußt die** ~ **auslöffeln, die du dir eingebrockt hast** *(col)* you've made your bed, now you must lie on it *(prov)*; **jdm die** ~ **versalzen** *(col)* to put a spoke in sb's wheel *(col)*.
**Suppen-** in cpds soup; ~**fleisch** nt meat for making soup; ~**gemüse** nt vegetables pl for making soup; ~**grün** nt herbs and vegetables pl for making soup; ~**huhn** nt boiling fowl; ~**kasper** m *(col)* poor eater; ~**kelle** f soup ladle; ~**löffel** m soup spoon; ~**schüssel** f tureen; ~**tasse** f soup bowl; ~**teller** m soup plate; ~**würfel** m stock cube; ~**würze** f soup seasoning.
**Surfbrett** ['zø:ɾɛf-] nt surfboard.
**surfen** ['zø:ɾɛfən] vi to surf.
**Surfer(in** f*)* ['zø:ɾɛfɐ, -əɾɪn] m - surfer.
**Surfing** ['zø:ɾɛfɪŋ] nt no pl *(Sport)* surfing.
**Surrealismus** m no pl surrealism.
**surrealistisch** adj surrealist(ic).
**surren** vi to hum; *(Insektenflügel)* to whirr.
**suspekt** [zʊs'pɛkt] adj suspicious. **jdm** ~ **sein** to seem suspicious to sb.
**suspendieren\*** [zʊspɛn'di:rən] vt to suspend *(von* from*)*.
**Suspendierung** f suspension.
**süß** adj *(lit, fig)* sweet. **gern** ~ **essen** to have a sweet tooth; **das** ~**e Leben** the good life; **(mein) S**~**er/**

**meine S**~**e** *(col)* my sweetheart.
**Süße** f no pl *(lit, fig)* sweetness.
**süßen 1** vt to sweeten; *(mit Zucker)* Tee, Kaffee to sugar. **2** vi **mit Honig** etc ~ to use honey etc as a sweetener.
**Süßholz** nt liquorice *(Brit)*, licorice *(US)*. ~ **raspeln** *(fig)* to turn on the blarney.
**Süßigkeit** f **(a)** no pl *(lit, fig)* sweetness. **(b)** ~**en** pl sweets pl *(Brit)*, candy *(US)*.
**Süßkirsche** f sweet cherry.
**süßlich** adj sweetish; *(unangenehm süß, fig)* Geschmack, Töne, Miene sickly sweet; *(kitschig)* mawkish.
**Süß-:** ~**most** m unfermented fruit juice; **s**~**sauer** adj sweet-and-sour; *Gurken etc* pickled; *(fig: gezwungen)* Lächeln forced; *Miene* artificially friendly; ~**speise** f sweet dish; ~**stoff** m sweetener; ~**waren** pl confectionery sing; ~**warengeschäft** nt sweetshop *(Brit)*, candy store *(US)*; ~**wasser** nt freshwater; ~**wasserfisch** m freshwater fish.
**SV** [ɛs'fau] m = **Sportverein**.
**SW** = **Südwesten** SW.
**Swahili** nt -, no pl *(Sprache)* Swahili; **siehe Deutsch(e)**.
**Swasiland** nt Swaziland.
**SWF** [ɛs've:|'ɛf] m = **Südwestfunk**.
**Swimming-pool** ['svɪmɪŋpu:l] m -s swimming pool.
**Sydney** ['zɪdnɪ] nt Sydney.
**Sylvester** nt - = **Silvester**.
**Symbiose** f -n symbiosis.
**Symbol** nt -e symbol.
**symbolhaft** adj symbolic.
**Symbolik** f symbolism.
**symbolisch** adj symbolic *(für of)*.
**symbolisieren\*** vt to symbolize.
**Symbolismus** m symbolism.
**Symmetrie** f symmetry.
**symmetrisch** adj symmetrical.
**Sympathie** [zvmpa'ti:] f *(Zuneigung)* liking; *(Mitgefühl, Solidaritätsgefühl)* sympathy. **für jdn/etw** ~ **haben** to have a liking for/a certain amount of sympathy with sb/sth; **durch seine Unverschämtheit hat er sich** *(dat)* **alle** ~**(n) verscherzt** he has turned everyone against him with his impertinence.
**Sympathie-:** ~**kundgebung** f demonstration of support; ~**streik** m sympathy strike.
**Sympathisant(in** f*)* m sympathizer.
**sympathisch** adj pleasant, nice. **er ist mir** ~ I like him.
**sympathisieren\*** vi to sympathize *(mit with)*.
**Symphonie** [zvmfo'ni:] f symphony.
**symphonisch** adj symphonic.
**Symposium** [zvm'po:zium] nt, pl **Symposien** [zvm'po:ziən] symposium.
**Symptom** nt -e symptom.
**symptomatisch** adj symptomatic *(für of)*.
**Synagoge** f -n synagogue.
**synchron** [zvn'kro:n] adj synchronous.
**Synchrongetriebe** [zvn'kro:n-] nt *(Aut)* synchromesh gearbox *(Brit)* or transmission *(US)*.
**Synchronisation** [zvnkroniza'tsio:n] f *(Film, TV)* dubbing; *(Tech)* synchronization.
**synchronisieren\*** [zvnkroni'zi:rən] vt Film to dub; *(Tech)* to synchronize.
**Synchronschwimmen** nt synchronized swimming.
**Syndikat** nt *(Kartell)* syndicate.
**Syndrom** nt -e syndrome.
**Synkope** [zvn'ko:pə] f -n *(Mus)* syncopation.

**synkopieren*** *vt* to syncopate.
**Synode** *f* **-n** *(Eccl)* synod.
**Synonym** [zyno'nyːm] *nt* **-e** synonym.
**synonym** [zyno'nyːm] *adj* synonymous.
**Synonymwörterbuch** *nt* dictionary of synonyms,
   ≃ thesaurus.
**syntaktisch** *adj* syntactic(al).
**Syntax** *f no pl* syntax.
**Synthese** *f* **-n** synthesis.
**Synthesizer** ['sɪntəsaizɐ] *m* **-** synthesizer.
**Synthetik** *f no pl (Kunstfaser)* synthetic fibre.
**synthetisch** *adj* synthetic.
**Syphilis** ['zyːfilɪs] *f no pl* syphilis.
**Syrer(in** *f)* *m* **-** Syrian.
**Syrien** ['zyːriən] *nt* Syria.
**syrisch** *adj* Syrian.
**System** [zʏs'teːm] *nt* **-e** system. **etw mit ~ machen**
   to do sth systematically; **hinter dieser Sache steckt**
   **~** there's method behind it; **~ in etw** *(acc)* **bringen**
   to get some system into sth; **ein ~ von Straßen/**
   **Kanälen** a road/canal system.

**System-:** **~analyse** *f (Comp)* systems analysis; **~-**
   **analytiker** *m (Comp)* systems analyst.
**Systematik** *f no pl* system.
**systematisch** *adj* systematic.
**systematisieren*** *vt* to systematize.
**System-:** **~diskette** *f (Comp)* systems disk;
   **~kritiker** *m* critic of the system; **s~kritisch** *adj*
   critical of the system; **~zwang** *m* obligation to
   conform (to the system).
**Szene** *f* **-n** *(Theat, fig, col: Drogen~ etc)* scene;
   *(Theat: Bühnenausstattung)* set; *(col: Milieu)* subculture. **hinter der ~** backstage; *(fig)* behind the
   scenes; **etw in ~ setzen** *(lit, fig)* to stage sth; **sich in**
   **~ setzen** to play to the gallery; **die ~ beherrschen**
   *(fig)* to dominate the scene *(gen* in*); (meistern)* to
   control things; **sich in der ~ auskennen** *(col)* to
   know the scene; **(jdm) eine ~ machen** to make a
   scene (in front of sb).
**Szenenwechsel** *m* scene change.
**Szenerie** *f (Theat, fig)* scenery.
**Szepter** ['stsɛptɐ] *nt* **-** sceptre *(Brit)*, scepter *(US)*.

# T

**T, t** [teː] nt -, - T, t. **T wie Theodor** ≃ T for Tommy.

**t** = Tonne.

**Tabak** ['taːbak, 'tabak] m -e tobacco; *(Schnupf~)* snuff.

**Tabak-** *in cpds* tobacco; **~händler** m tobacconist; **~laden** m tobacconist's *(Brit)*, tobacco store *(US)*.

**Tabaks-:** **~beutel** m tobacco pouch; **~dose** f tobacco tin; **~pfeife** f pipe.

**Tabak-:** **~steuer** f duty on tobacco; **~waren** pl tobacco goods.

**tabellarisch 1** *adj* tabular; *Lebenslauf* in tabular form. **2** *adv* in tables/a table.

**Tabelle** f table; *(Diagramm)* chart; *(Sport)* (league) table.

**Tabellen-:** **~form** f: **in ~form** in tabular form; *(als Diagramm)* as a chart; **~führer** m *(Sport)* league leaders pl; **~kalkulation** f *(Comp)* spreadsheet; **~platz** m *(Sport)* position in the league.

**Tablett** nt -s *or* -e tray. **jdm etw auf einem silbernen ~ servieren** *(fig: einfach machen)* to hand sb sth on a plate.

**Tablette** f tablet, pill.

**Tabu** nt -s taboo.

**tabu** *adj pred* taboo.

**tabuisieren*** *vt* to make taboo.

**Tabulator** m tabulator, tab *(col)*.

**tabulieren** *vt Spalten, Text* to tab *(col)*.

**Tach(e)les** *no art (col)* **(mit jdm) ~ reden** to have a frank talk with sb.

**Tacho** m -s *(col)* speedo *(Brit col)*, speedometer.

**Tachometer** m *or* nt - speedometer.

**Tadel** m - *(Verweis)* reprimand; *(Vorwurf)* reproach; *(Kritik)* criticism; *(geh: Makel)* blemish; *(Sch: Eintrag)* black mark. **ein Leben ohne jeden ~** *(geh)* a spotless life.

**tadellos 1** *adj* perfect; *(col)* splendid. **2** *adv* perfectly; *gekleidet* immaculately.

**tadeln** *vt jdn* to reprimand; *jds Benehmen* to criticize.

**tadelnd** *adj attr* reproachful.

**tadelnswert** *adj (geh)* reprehensible.

**Tadels|antrag** m *(Parl)* motion of censure.

**Tafel** f -n **(a)** *(Platte)* slab; *(Holz~)* panel; *(Wand~)* (black)board; *(Schreib~)* slate; *(Schokoladen~)* bar; *(Gedenk~)* plaque; *(Elec: Schalt~)* control panel, console; *(Anzeige~)* board. **(b)** *(Bildseite)* plate. **(c)** *(form: festlicher Speisetisch)* table; *(Festmahl)* meal; *(mittags)* luncheon *(form)*; *(abends)* dinner. **die ~ aufheben** to officially end the meal.

**Tafel-:** **~apfel** m eating apple; **~besteck** nt (best) silver; **t~fertig** *adj* ready to serve; **~freuden** pl culinary delights pl; **~geschirr** nt tableware; **~lappen** m (blackboard) duster.

**tafeln** *vi (geh)* to feast.

**täfeln** *vt* to panel.

**Tafel-:** **~obst** nt (dessert) fruit; **~öl** nt cooking/salad oil; **~salz** nt table salt; **~silber** nt silver.

**Täf(e)lung** f siehe **täfeln** (wooden) panelling *(Brit)*

*or* paneling *(US)*.

**Tafel-:** **~wasser** nt mineral water; **~wein** m table wine.

**Taft** m -e taffeta.

**Tag** m -e **(a)** day. **an dem/diesem ~** on that/this day; **am ~(e) des/der ...** (on) the day of ...; **am ~ during the day; alle ~e** *(col)*, **jeden ~** every day; **am vorigen ~(e)** the day before; **auf den ~ (genau)** to the day; **auf ein paar ~e** for a few days; **auf seine alten ~e** in his old age; **den ganzen ~ (lang), den lieben langen ~** *(lit, fig)* all day long; **eines ~es** one day; **sich** *(dat)* **einen schönen/faulen ~ machen** to have a nice/lazy day; **~ für ~** day by day; **von ~ zu ~** from day to day; **welcher ~ ist heute?** what day is it today?; **guten ~!** hello; *(esp bei Vorstellung)* how do you do; *(vormittags auch)* good morning; *(nachmittags auch)* good afternoon; **~!** *(col)* hello, hi *(col)*; **zweimal am ~(e)** *or* **pro ~** twice a day; **von einem ~ auf den anderen** overnight; **seinen guten/schlechten ~ haben** to have a good/bad day; **in den ~ hinein leben** to take each day as it comes; **~ und Nacht** night and day; **bei ~(e) ankommen** while it's light; *arbeiten, reisen* during the day; **es wird schon ~** it's getting light already; **an den ~ kommen** *(fig)* to come to light; **er legte großes Interesse an den ~** he showed great interest.

**(b)** *(col: Menstruation)* **ihre ~e** her period.

**(c)** *(Min)* **über/unter ~e arbeiten** to work above/below ground.

**tag|aus** *adv* **~, tagein** day in, day out.

**Tagdienst** m day duty.

**Tage-:** **~bau** m -e *(Min)* open-cast mining; **~blatt** nt daily (news)paper; **~buch** nt diary; *(über etw acc)* **~buch führen** to keep a diary (of sth); **~dieb** m *(dated)* idler; **~geld** nt daily allowance.

**tag|ein** *adv siehe* **tagaus.**

**Tage-:** **t~lang** *adj* lasting for days; **t~lange Regenfälle** several days' rain; **er war t~lang verschwunden** he disappeared for days; **~löhner(in** f) m - day labourer *(Brit)* or laborer *(US)*.

**tagen 1** *impers (geh)* **es tagt** day is breaking. **2** *vi (konferieren)* to meet; *Parlament* to sit.

**Tages-:** **~ablauf** m day, daily routine; **~anbruch** m daybreak, dawn; **~arbeit** f day's work; **~ausflug** m day trip; **~bedarf** m daily requirement; **~creme** f day cream; **~decke** f bedspread; **~fahrt** f day trip; **~fragen** pl issues of the day; **~geld** nt *(Fin)* overnight money; **~geschehen** nt events pl of the day; **~gespräch** nt talk of the town; **~karte** f **(a)** *(Speisekarte)* menu of the day; **(b)** *(Fahr-, Eintrittskarte)* day ticket; **~kasse** f **(a)** *(Theat)* box office; **(b)** *(Econ)* day's takings pl; **~klinik** f day clinic; **~kurs** m *(St Ex) (von Effekten)* current price; *(von Devisen)* current rate; **~lauf** m day; **~leistung** f daily workload; *(von Maschine, Schriftsteller etc)* daily output; **~licht** nt no pl daylight; **ans ~licht kommen** *(fig)* to come to light; **~lichtprojektor** m overhead projector; **~lohn** m day's wages; ~**marsch** *m* day's march; ~**menü** *nt* menu of the day; ~**mutter** *f* childminder; ~**nachrichten** *pl* (today's) news *sing*; ~**ordnung** *f* agenda; **etw auf die** ~**ordnung setzen** to put sth on the agenda; **auf der** ~**ordnung stehen** to be on the agenda; **zur** ~**ordnung übergehen** to proceed to the agenda; *(wie üblich weitermachen)* to carry on as usual; **an der** ~**ordnung sein** *(fig)* to be the order of the day; ~**ordnungspunkt** *m* item on the agenda; ~**presse** *f* daily newspapers *pl*; ~**ration** *f* daily rations *pl*; ~**reise** *f* (a) *(Entfernung)* day's journey; (b) *(Ausflug)* day trip; ~**satz** *m* daily rate; ~**stätte** *f (für Kinder)* day nursery *(Brit)*, daycare centre *(esp US)*; ~**tour** *f* = ~**fahrt**; ~**zeit** *f* time (of day); **zu jeder** ~**- und Nachtzeit** at all hours of the day and night; ~**zeitung** *f* daily (paper).

**Tage-:** **t~weise** *adv* on a daily basis; ~**werk** *nt (geh)* day's work.

**taghell** *adj* (as) bright as day. **es war schon** ~ it was already broad daylight.

**tägl.** = **täglich**.

**täglich** **1** *adj* daily; *(attr: gewöhnlich)* everyday. **das reicht gerade fürs** ~**e Leben** it's just about enough to get by on; **sein** ~**(es) Brot verdienen** to earn a living. **2** *adv* every day. **einmal** ~ once a day.

**tags** *adv* ~ **zuvor** the day before, the previous day; ~ **darauf** or **danach** the next or following day.

**Tagschicht** *f* day shift. ~ **haben** to be on day shift.

**tags|über** *adv* during the day.

**Tag-:** **t~täglich** **1** *adj* daily; **2** *adv* every (single) day; ~**traum** *m* daydream; ~**träumer** *m* daydreamer; ~ **-und Nachtdienst** *m* twenty-four hour service; ~**undnachtgleiche** *f* equinox.

**Tagung** *f* conference; *(von Ausschuß)* sitting, session.

**Tagungsort** *m* venue (of a/the conference).

**Tahiti** *nt* Tahiti.

**Taifun** *m* -e typhoon.

**Taille** ['taljə] *f* -n waist. **auf seine** ~ **achten** to watch one's waistline.

**Taillenweite** ['taljən-] *f* waist measurement.

**tailliert** [ta'jiːɐt] *adj* waisted, gathered at the waist.

**Taiwan** *nt* Taiwan.

**Taiwanese** *m wk* -n, -n, **Taiwanesin** *f* Taiwanese.

**taiwanesisch** *adj* Taiwan(ese).

**Takel** *nt* - *(Naut)* tackle.

**Takelage** [takə'laːʒə] *f* -n *(Naut)* rigging, tackle.

**takeln** *vt (Naut)* to rig.

**Takt** *m* -e (a) *(Mus)* bar; *(Phon, Poet)* foot. (b) *(Rhythmus)* time. **den** ~ **schlagen** to beat time; **gegen den** ~ out of time; **den** ~ **angeben** to give the beat, to beat time. (c) *(Aut)* stroke. (d) *(Ind)* phase. (e) *no pl (~gefühl)* tact.

**Taktgefühl** *nt* (a) (sense of) tact. (b) *(Mus)* sense of rhythm.

**taktieren*** *vi* to manoeuvre *(Brit)*, to maneuver *(US)*. **klug** ~ to use clever tactics; **so kann man nicht** ~ you can't use those tactics.

**Taktik** *f* tactics *pl*. **eine** ~ tactics *pl*.

**Taktiker(in** *f)* *m* - tactician.

**taktisch** *adj* tactical. ~ **klug vorgehen** to use clever tactics.

**Takt-:** **t~los** *adj* tactless; ~**losigkeit** *f* tactlessness; ~**stock** *m* baton; ~**strich** *m (Mus)* bar (line); **t~voll** *adj* tactful.

**Tal** *nt* ⁼er valley.

**tal|ab(wärts)** *adv* down into the valley.

**Talar** *m (Univ)* gown; *(Jur, Eccl)* robe(s).

**tal|aufwärts** *adv* up the valley.

**Tal-:** ~**brücke** *f* bridge over a valley; ~**enge** *f* gorge.

**Talent** *nt* -e (a) *(Begabung)* talent *(zu for)*. **ein großes** ~ **haben** to be very talented; **sie hat viel** ~ **zum Singen/zur Schauspielerin** she has a great talent for singing/acting. (b) *(Mensch)* talented person. **ein großes** ~ **sein** to be very talented; **junge** ~**e** young talent.

**talentiert** *adj* talented, gifted.

**Talfahrt** *f* descent; *(fig)* decline.

**Talg** *m* -e tallow; *(Cook)* suet; *(Haut~)* sebum.

**Talisman** *m* -e talisman, (lucky) charm; *(Maskottchen)* mascot.

**Talk** *m no pl* talc(um).

**Talkessel** *m* basin, hollow.

**Talkshow** ['tɔkʃoː] *f* -s *(TV)* talk show, chat show *(Brit)*.

**Tal-:** ~**senke** *f* hollow (of a/the valley); ~**sohle** *f* bottom of a/the valley; *(fig)* rock bottom; **in der** ~**sohle** *(fig)* at rock bottom; ~**sperre** *f* dam; **t~wärts** *adv* down to the valley.

**Tambour** ['tambuːɐ] *m* -e drummer.

**Tamburin** *nt* -e tambourine.

**Tampon** *m* -s tampon.

**tamponieren*** *vt (Med)* to plug, to tampon.

**Tamtam** *nt* -s (a) *(Mus)* tomtom. (b) *(col: Wirbel)* fuss, ballyhoo *(col)*; *(Lärm)* din *(col)*.

**Tand** *m no pl (liter)* knick-knacks *pl*; *(fig)* dross.

**tändeln** *vi (liter) (flirten)* to flirt; *(herumspielen)* to play around; *(trödeln)* to dilly-dally.

**Tandem** *nt* -s tandem.

**Tang** *m* -e seaweed.

**Tanga** *m* -s mini-bikini.

**Tangens** ['taŋgɛns] *m* - *(Math)* tan(gent).

**Tangente** [taŋ'gɛntə] *f* -n *(Math)* tangent; *(Straße)* bypass.

**Tanger** ['taŋɐ, 'tandʒɐ] *nt* Tangier(s).

**tangieren*** [taŋ'giːrən] *vt* Problem to touch on; *(betreffen)* to affect; *(col: kümmern)* to bother.

**Tango** ['taŋgo] *m* -s tango.

**Tank** *m* -s or -e tank.

**Tank-:** ~**anzeige** *f* fuel gauge; ~**deckel** *m* = ~**verschluß**.

**tanken** *vti* (a) *(bei Auto)* to fill up; *(bei Rennwagen, Flugzeug)* to refuel. **wo kann man hier** ~**?** where can I get petrol *(Brit)* or gas *(US)* around here?; **wir hielten an, um zu** ~ we stopped for petrol/gas; **ich tanke bleifrei** I use unleaded; **ich tanke nur 10 Liter/ für 10 Mark** I'll just put in 10 litres/10 marks' worth. (b) *(col)* frische Luft, neue Kräfte to get. **er hat ganz schön getankt** he's really tanked up *(col)*.

**Tanker** *m* - *(Naut)* tanker.

**Tank-:** ~**fahrzeug** *nt (Aut)* tanker; ~**lager** *nt* oil depot; *(für Benzin)* petrol *(Brit)* or gasoline *(US)* depot; ~**laster, ~lastzug** *m* tanker; ~**säule** *f* petrol pump *(Brit)*, gas(oline) pump *(US)*; ~**schiff** *nt* tanker; ~**stelle** *f* petrol *(Brit)* or gas(oline) *(US)* station; ~**uhr** *f* fuel gauge; ~**verschluß** *m* fuel cap; ~**wagen** *m* tanker; *(Rail)* tank wagon or car; ~**wart** *m* petrol pump *(Brit)* or gas station *(US)* attendant.

**Tanne** *f* -n fir, pine; *(Holz)* pine.

**Tannen-:** ~**baum** *m* fir tree, pine tree; *(Weihnachtsbaum)* Christmas tree; ~**nadel** *f* pine needle; ~**wald** *m* pine forest; ~**zapfen** *m* fir cone, pine cone.

**Tannin** *nt no pl* tannin.

**Tansania** *nt* Tanzania.

**Tansanier(in** *f)* ['tanˈzaːniɐ, -ərin] *m* - Tanzanian.

**tansanisch** *adj* Tanzanian.

**Tante** *f* -n (a) *(Verwandte)* aunt. (b) *(pej col: Frau)* old girl *(col)*. (c) *(baby-talk: Frau)* lady.

**Tante-Emma-Laden** *m (col)* corner shop.

**tantenhaft** adj (a) (col) old-maidish. (b) (pej: betu-lich) twee.
**Tantieme** [tā'tie:mə] f -n fee; (für Künstler) royalty.
**Tanz** m ⁼e dance. **dort ist heute abend** ~ there's a dance there this evening; **jdn zum** ~ **auffordern** to ask sb to dance.
**Tanz-**: ~**abend** m dance; ~**bar** f bar with dancing; ~**bär** m dancing bear; ~**bein** nt: **das** ~**bein schwingen** (hum) to shake a leg (hum); ~**boden** m (~**fläche**) dance floor; (Saal) dance hall; ~**café** nt café with dancing.
**tänzeln** vi aux haben or (bei Richtungsangabe) sein to mince; (Boxer) to skip; (Pferd) to step delicately.
**tanzen** vti aux haben or (bei Richtungsangabe) sein to dance; (auf dem Wasser) to bob; (Kreisel) to spin; (hüpfen) to hop. ~ **gehen** to go dancing; **Tango/Walzer** ~ to (dance the) tango/to waltz.
**Tänzer(in** f) m - dancer; (Partner) (dancing) partner.
**tänzerisch** adj dance-like. ~ **begabt** or **veranlagt sein** to have a talent for dancing; **sein** ~**es Können** his dancing ability.
**Tanz-**: ~**fläche** f dance floor; ~**gruppe** f dance group; ~**kapelle** f dance band; ~**kurs(us)** m dancing class or course; ~**lehrer** m dancing teacher; ~**lokal** nt café with dancing; ~**musik** f dance music; ~**saal** m dance hall; (in Hotel etc) ballroom; ~**schritt** m (dance) step; ~**schule** f dancing school; ~**sport** m competitive dancing; ~**stunde** f dancing lesson; ~**turnier** nt dancing competition.
**tapern** vi (col) to totter.
**Tapet** nt: **etw aufs** ~ **bringen** (col) to bring sth up; **aufs** ~ **kommen** (col) to be brought up.
**Tapete** f -n wallpaper no pl. **die** ~**n wechseln** (fig col) to have a change of surroundings.
**Tapeten-**: ~**bahn** f strip of wallpaper; ~**rolle** f roll of wallpaper; ~**wechsel** m (col) change of surroundings.
**tapezieren*** vt to (wall)paper. **neu** ~ to repaper.
**Tapezierer** m - paperhanger, decorator.
**tapfer** adj brave, courageous; (wacker) steadfast. **sich** ~ **schlagen** (col) to put on a brave show; **sich** ~ **halten** to be brave.
**Tapferkeit** f siehe adj bravery, courage; steadfastness.
**tappen** vi (a) aux sein (gehen) to go/come falteringly; (Bär) to lumber. **mit** ~**den Schritten gehen** to walk with a heavy tread; **in eine Falle** ~ (fig) to stumble into a trap. (b) (tasten) **nach etw** ~ to grope for sth; **im dunkeln** ~ (fig) to grope in the dark.
**täppisch** adj = tapsig.
**tapsen** vi aux sein (col) = tappen (a).
**tapsig** adj (col) awkward, clumsy.
**Tara** f, pl **Taren** (Comm) tare.
**Tarantel** f -n tarantula. **wie von der** ~ **gestochen** as if stung by a bee.
**Tarif** m -e rate; (Wasser~, Gas~ etc auch) tariff; (Gebühr auch) charge; (Verkehrs~) fares pl; (Lohn~) wage rate; (Gehalts~) salary scale. **die Gewerkschaft hat die** ~**e gekündigt** the union has put in a new wage claim; **nach/über/unter** ~ **bezahlen** to pay according to/above/below the (union) rate(s).
**Tarif-**: ~**abschluß** m wage settlement; ~**autonomie** f free collective bargaining; ~**gruppe** f grade; ~**kommission** f joint working party on pay.
**tariflich** adj agreed, union. **der** ~**e Mindestlohn** the agreed minimum wage.

**Tarif-**: ~**lohn** m standard wage; ~**ordnung** f pay scale; ~**partner** m **die** ~**partner** union and management; ~**runde** f pay round; ~**verhandlungen** pl pay negotiations pl; ~**vertrag** m pay agreement.
**tarnen** 1 vti to camouflage; (fig) Absichten, Identität etc to disguise. 2 vr (Tier) to camouflage itself; (Mensch) to disguise oneself.
**Tarnfarbe** f camouflage colour (Brit) or color (US)/paint.
**Tarnung** f camouflage; (von Agent etc) disguise.
**Tarock** m or nt -s tarot.
**Tasche** f -n (a) (Hand~) bag (Brit), purse (US); (Reise~, Schul~ etc) bag; (Akten~) (brief)case; (Backen~) pouch. (b) (bei Kleidungsstücken) pocket. **in die eigene** ~ **wirtschaften** to line one's own pockets; **etw in der** ~ **haben** (col) to have sth in the bag (col); **jdm das Geld aus der** ~ **ziehen** to get sb to part with his money; **etw aus der eigenen** ~ **bezahlen** to pay for sth out of one's own pocket; **jdm auf der** ~ **liegen** (col) to live off sb; **die Hände in die** ~**n stecken** (lit) to put one's hands in one's pockets; (fig) to stand idly by; **jdn in die** ~ **stecken** (col) to put sb in the shade (col).
**Taschen-**: ~**ausgabe** f pocket edition; ~**buch** nt paperback (book); ~**dieb** m pickpocket; ~**diebstahl** m pickpocketing; ~**format** nt pocket size; ~**geld** nt pocket money; ~**lampe** f torch (Brit), flashlight (US); ~**messer** nt pocket knife, penknife; ~**rechner** m pocket calculator; ~**schirm** m collapsible umbrella; ~**spieler** m conjurer; ~**spielertrick** m (fig) sleight of hand no indef art, no pl; ~**tuch** nt handkerchief; (aus Papier) tissue; ~**uhr** f pocket watch.
**Tasmanien** [-iən] nt Tasmania.
**Täßchen** nt dim of **Tasse** (little) cup. **ein** ~ **Kaffee** a quick cup of coffee.
**Tasse** f -n cup; (Suppen~) bowl. **eine** ~ **Kaffee** a cup of coffee; **er hat nicht alle** ~**n im Schrank** (col) he's not all there.
**Tastatur** f keyboard.
**Taste** f -n key; (Knopf an Gerät auch) button. **in die** ~**n greifen** to strike up a tune; **auf die** ~**n hauen** (col) to hammer away at the keyboard; „~ **drücken"** "push button".
**tasten** 1 vi to feel. **nach etw** ~ (lit, fig) to feel or grope for sth; ~**de Schritte** (lit, fig) tentative steps; ~**de Fragen** (fig) tentative questions. 2 vr to feel or grope one's way. 3 vti (drücken) to press; Telex, (Typ: setzen) to key.
**Tasten-**: ~**anschlag** m keystroke; ~**feld** nt (Comp) keypad; ~**instrument** nt (Mus) keyboard instrument; ~**telefon** nt push-button telephone.
**Tast-**: ~**organ** nt organ of touch; ~**sinn** m sense of touch.
**Tat** f -en (das Handeln) action; (Einzel~ auch) act; (Helden~, Un~) deed; (Leistung) feat; (Verbrechen) crime. **eine gute/böse** ~ a good/wicked deed; **etw in die** ~ **umsetzen** to put sth into action; **zur** ~ **schreiten** to act; **in der** ~ indeed; (wider Erwarten) actually.
**tat** pret of **tun**.
**Tatbestand** m (Jur) facts (of the case) pl.
**Taten-**: ~**drang** m energy; **t~los** adj idle; **t~los herumstehen** to stand idly by; **wir mußten t~los zusehen** we could only stand and watch.
**Täter(in** f) m - culprit; (Jur) perpetrator (form). **als** ~ **verdächtigt werden** to be a suspect; **wer war der** ~? who did it?
**Täterschaft** f guilt. **die** ~ **leugnen/zugeben** to deny/admit one's guilt.
**tätig** adj (a) attr active. ~**e Nächstenliebe** practical

charity; **in einer Sache ~ werden** *(form)* to take action on a matter. **(b)** *(arbeitend)* **~ sein** to work; **er ist im Bankwesen ~** he's in banking.

**tätigen** *vt (Comm)* to conclude; *(geh) Einkäufe* to carry out; *(geh) Anruf* to make.

**Tätigkeit** *f* activity; *(Beschäftigung)* occupation; *(Arbeit)* work; *(Beruf)* job. **in/außer ~ setzen** *Maschine* to start up/to stop.

**Tätigkeits-:** **~bereich** *m* field of activity; **~bericht** *m* progress report; **~beschreibung** *f* job description.

**Tat-:** **~kraft** *f no pl* energy, drive; **t~kräftig** *adj* energetic; *Hilfe* active.

**tätlich** *adj* violent. **gegen jdn ~ werden** to assault sb.

**Tätlichkeiten** *pl* violence *sing.* **es kam zu ~** there were violent scenes.

**Tat|ort** *m* scene of the crime.

**tätowieren\*** *vt* to tattoo.

**Tätowierung** *f* tattooing; *(Darstellung)* tattoo.

**Tatsache** *f* fact. **~?** *(col)* really?, no!; **das ist ~** *(col)* that's a fact; **jdn vor vollendete ~n stellen** to present sb with a fait accompli.

**Tatsachenbericht** *m* documentary (report).

**tatsächlich 1** *adj attr* real, actual. **2** *adv* actually, really, in fact. **willst du das ~ tun?** are you really *or* actually going to do it?; **da kommt er! — ~!** he's coming! — so he is!

**tätscheln** *vt* to pat.

**Tattergreis** *m (pej col)* old dodderer *(pej).*

**tatt(e)rig** *adj (col) Mensch* doddery; *Hände, Schriftzüge* shaky.

**Tat-:** **~verdacht** *m* suspicion *(of having committed a crime)*; **unter ~verdacht stehen** to be under suspicion; **t~verdächtig** *adj* suspected.

**Tatze** *f* **-n** *(lit, fig)* paw.

**Tau¹** *m no pl* dew.

**Tau²** *nt* **-e** *(Seil)* rope; *(Naut auch)* hawser.

**taub** *adj* deaf; *Glieder* numb; *Ähre* unfruitful; *Nuß* empty. **sich ~ stellen** to pretend not to hear; **gegen** *or* **für etw ~ sein** *(fig)* to be deaf to sth.

**Taube** *f* **-n** *(Zool)* pigeon; *(Turtel~, fig)* dove.

**Taubenschlag** *m* dovecot(e). **hier geht es zu wie im ~** *(fig)* like Waterloo Station here *(Brit col)*, it's like Grand Central Station here *(US col).*

**Taube(r)** *mf decl as adj* deaf person. **die ~n** the deaf.

**Taubheit** *f* deafness; *(von Körperteil)* numbness.

**Taub-:** **t~stumm** *adj* deaf and dumb, deaf-mute *attr*; **~stumme(r)** *mf* deaf-mute.

**tauchen 1** *vi* **(a)** *aux haben or sein* to dive *(nach for)*; *(als Sport auch)* to skin-dive; *(kurz ~)* to duck under; *(unter Wasser sein)* to stay under water; *(U-Boot auch)* to submerge. **(b)** *aux sein (fig: auf~)* to emerge *(aus out of, from).* **2** *vt (kurz ~)* to dip; *Menschen, Kopf* to duck; *(ein~)* to immerse.

**Taucher(in** *f) m* **-** diver.

**Taucher-:** **~anzug** *m* diving suit; **~brille** *f* diving goggles *pl*; **~glocke** *f* diving bell.

**Tauch-:** **~sieder** *m* **-** portable immersion heater; **~sport** *m* (skin-)diving; **~station** *f* **auf ~station gehen** *(U-Boot)* to dive; *(fig: sich zurückziehen)* to make oneself scarce; **auf ~station sein** *(U-Boot)* to be submerged.

**tauen** *vti (vi: aux haben or sein) (Schnee)* to melt, to thaw. **es taut** it is thawing.

**Taufbecken** *nt* font.

**Taufe** *f* **-n** baptism; *(Kindes~ auch)* christening; *(Schiffs~)* launching (ceremony).

**taufen** *vt* to baptize; *(nennen) Kind, Schiff etc* to christen. **sich ~ lassen** to be baptized; **jdn auf den**

**Namen Rufus ~** to christen sb Rufus.

**Täufer** *m* **-:** **Johannes der ~** John the Baptist.

**Täufling** *m* child/person to be baptized.

**Tauf-:** **~pate** *m* godfather; **~patin** *f* godmother; **~schein** *m* certificate of baptism; **~zeuge** *m* godparent.

**taugen** *vi* **(a)** *(geeignet sein)* to be suitable *(zu, für for).* **er taugt zu gar nichts** he is useless; **er taugt nicht zum Arzt** he wouldn't make a good doctor. **(b)** *(wert sein)* **etwas ~** to be all right; **nicht viel** *or* **wenig/nichts ~** to be not much good/to be no good.

**Taugenichts** *m* **-e** good-for-nothing.

**tauglich** *adj (zu for)* suitable; *(Mil)* fit.

**Tauglichkeit** *f* suitability; *(Mil)* fitness (for service).

**Taumel** *m no pl (geh: Schwindel)* (attack of) dizziness; *(liter: Rausch)* frenzy. **wie im ~** in a daze.

**taumeln** *vi aux sein* to stagger; *(zur Seite)* to sway.

**Tausch** *m* **-e** exchange, swap; *(~handel)* barter. **im ~ gegen etw** in exchange for sth; **einen guten/ schlechten ~ machen** to get a good/bad deal.

**tauschen 1** *vt (gegen for)* to exchange, to swap; *Güter* to barter; *(aus~) Briefmarken etc* to swap; *Geld* to change *(in +acc into).* **2** *vi* to swap; *(in Handel)* to barter. **ich möchte nicht mit ihm ~** I wouldn't like to be in his place.

**täuschen 1** *vt* to deceive; *Vertrauen* to betray. **wenn mich mein Gedächtnis nicht täuscht** if my memory serves me right; **wenn mich nicht alles täuscht** unless I'm completely wrong. **2** *vr* to be wrong *or* mistaken *(in +dat, über +acc about).* **3** *vi (irreführen: Aussehen etc)* to be deceptive.

**täuschend 1** *adj Nachahmung* remarkable; *Ähnlichkeit auch* striking. **2** *adv* **sich** *(dat)* **~ ähnlich sehen/ sein** to look/be remarkably alike *or* almost identical.

**Tausch-:** **~geschäft** *nt* exchange; *(Handel)* barter; **~handel** *m* barter.

**Täuschung** *f* **(a)** *(das Täuschen)* deception. **(b)** *(Irrtum)* mistake, error; *(falsche Wahrnehmung)* illusion; *(Selbst~)* delusion. **er gab sich einer ~** *(dat)* **hin** he was deluding himself.

**Täuschungsmanöver** *nt (Sport)* feint; *(col)* ploy.

**Tausend** *nt* **-e** thousand; *siehe* **Hundert.**

**tausend** *num* a *or* one thousand; *siehe* **hundert.**

**Tausender** *m* **-** **(a)** *(Zahl)* **ein ~** a figure in the thousands; **die ~** the thousands. **(b)** *(Geldschein)* thousand(-mark/dollar *etc* note).

**tausenderlei** *adj inv* a thousand kinds of.

**Tausend-:** **~füßler** *m* **-** centipede; **~jahrfeier** *f* millenary (celebrations); **t~jährig** *adj attr* thousand-year-old; *(t~ Jahre lang)* thousand-year (long); **t~mal** *adv* a thousand times; **~sas(s)a** *m* **-s** *(col)* hell of a guy *(col).*

**tausendste(r, s)** *adj* thousandth.

**Tau-:** **~tropfen** *m* dewdrop; **~werk** *nt no pl (Naut)* rigging; **~wetter** *nt* thaw; **es ist ~wetter** it is thawing; **~ziehen** *nt no pl (lit, fig)* tug of war.

**Taxi** *nt* **-s** taxi, cab. **~ fahren** to drive a taxi; *(als Fahrgast)* to go by taxi.

**taxieren\*** *vt Preis, Wert* to estimate *(auf +acc at)*; *Haus, Gemälde etc* to value *(auf +acc at).* **er hat mich richtiggehend taxiert** *(fig)* he looked me up and down.

**Taxi-:** **~fahrer** *m* taxi *or* cab driver, cabby *(col)*; **~fahrt** *f* taxi ride; **~stand** *m* taxi rank *(Brit) or* stand *(US).*

**Tb** [teː'beː] **-s** = **Tuberkulose** TB.

**Teak(holz)** ['tiːk-] *nt* teak. **ein Tisch aus ~** a teak table.

**Team** [tiːm] *nt* **-s** team.
**Team|arbeit** *f* teamwork.
**Technik** *f* (a) *(no pl: Technologie)* technology. **(b)** *(Arbeitsweise, Verfahren)* technique. **(c)** *(no pl: Funktionsweise)* workings *pl*, mechanics *pl*.
**Techniker(in** *f)* *m* - engineer; *(Beleuchtungs~, Labor~, fig: Fußballspieler, Künstler)* technician.
**Technikum** *nt, pl* **Technika** technical college.
**technisch** *adj* technical; *(technologisch)* technological. **er ist ~ begabt** he is technically minded; **~e Daten** (technical) specification; **T~e Fachschule/ Hochschule** technical college/university.
**Technokrat(in** *f)* *m (wk)* **-en, -en** technocrat.
**Technologie** *f* technology.
**Technologiepark** *m* science park.
**technologisch** *adj* technological.
**Techtelmechtel** *nt* - *(col)* affair, carry-on *(col)*.
**Teddy** ['tɛdi] *m* **-s** *(auch ~bär)* teddy (bear).
**TEE** [teːeːˈeː] *m* **-, -(s)** = **Trans-Europ(a)-Express** Trans-Europe Express.
**Tee** *m* **-s** tea. **einen im ~ haben** *(col)* to be tipsy *(col)*.
**Tee-:** **~beutel** *m* tea bag; **~gebäck** *nt no pl* sweet biscuits *pl*; **~glas** *nt* tea glass; **~kanne** *f* teapot; **~kessel** *m* kettle; **~licht** *nt* night-light; **~löffel** *m* teaspoon; *(Menge)* teaspoonful; **~mischung** *f* blend of tea.
**Teen** [tiːn] *m* **-s** *(col)*, **Teenager** ['tiːneːdʒɐ] *m* - teenager.
**Teenetz** *nt* tea filter.
**Teeny** ['tiːni:] *m* **-, Teenies** *(col)* teenybopper *(col)*.
**Teepause** *f* tea break.
**Teer** *m* **-e** tar.
**Teerdecke** *f* tarred (road) surface.
**teeren** *vt* to tar.
**Teer-:** **~gehalt** *m* tar content; **t~haltig** *adj* **eine wenig/stark t~haltige Zigarette** a low/high tar cigarette; **~pappe** *f* roofing felt.
**Tee-:** **~service** *nt* tea set; **~sieb** *nt* tea strainer; **~stube** *f* tearoom; **~tasse** *f* teacup.
**Teheran** *nt* Teheran.
**Teich** *m* **-e** pond.
**Teichhuhn** *nt* moorhen.
**Teig** *m* **-e** dough; *(Blätter~ etc)* pastry; *(Pfannkuchen~)* batter; *(in Rezepten auch)* mixture.
**teigig** *adj* doughy.
**Teigwaren** *pl (Nudeln)* pasta *sing*.
**Teil**[1] *m* **-e** (a) part. **zum ~** partly; **zum größten ~** for the most part, mostly; **er hat die Bücher darüber zum großen/größten ~ gelesen** he has read many/ most of the books about that. **(b)** *(auch nt: An~)* share. **zu gleichen ~en erben** to get an equal share of an inheritance; **er hat seinen ~ dazu beigetragen** he did his bit *or* share; **sich** *(dat)* **sein(en) ~ denken** *(col)* to draw one's own conclusions. **(c)** *(auch nt)* **ich für mein(en) ~ ...** I, for my part ...
**Teil**[2] *nt* **-e** (a) part; *(Bestand~ auch)* component; *(Ersatz~)* spare, (spare) part. **etw in seine ~e zerlegen** to take sth apart *or* to pieces. **(b)** = **Teil**[1] **(b, c)**.
**Teil-:** **t~bar** *adj* divisible; **~bereich** *m* part; **~betrag** *m* part (of an amount); *(auf Rechnung)* item; *(Rate)* instalment *(Brit)*, installment *(US)*; *(Zwischensumme)* subtotal.
**Teilchen** *nt* particle; *(dial: Gebäckstück)* small cake.
**teilen 1** *vt* (a) to divide *(durch* by). **geteilter Meinung sein** to have different opinions; **darüber sind die Meinungen geteilt** opinions differ *or* are divided on that. **(b)** *(auf~)* to share (out) *(unter +dat* amongst). **etw mit jdm ~** to share sth with sb. **(c)** *(an etw teilhaben)* to share. **sie haben Freud und Leid miteinander geteilt** they shared the rough and the

smooth; **sie teilten unser Schicksal** they shared our fate. **2** *vr* (a) *(in Gruppen)* to split up. **(b)** *(Straße, Fluß)* to fork, to divide; *(fig: Ansichten)* to differ. **(c)** **sich** *(dat)* **etw ~** to share sth; **teilt euch das!** share that between you. **3** *vi* to share. **er teilt nicht gern** he doesn't like sharing.
**Teil-:** **~erfolg** *m* partial success; **~gebiet** *nt (Bereich)* branch; *(räumlich)* area; **t~haben** *vi sep irreg (geh)* **an etw** *(dat)* **t~haben** to have a part in sth; **~haber(in** *f)* *m* - *(Comm)* partner.
**Teilkaskoversicherung** *f (Insur)* ≈ third party, fire and theft *(Brit)*.
**Teilnahme** *f no pl* (a) *(Anwesenheit)* attendance *(an +dat* at); *(Beteiligung)* participation *(an +dat* in). **(b)** *(Interesse)* interest *(an +dat* in); *(Mitgefühl)* sympathy. **jdm seine herzliche ~ aussprechen** to offer sb one's heartfelt condolences.
**teilnahmeberechtigt** *adj* eligible.
**teilnahms-:** **~los** *adj (gleichgültig)* indifferent, apathetic; *(stumm leidend)* listless; **~voll** *adj* compassionate, sympathetic.
**teilnehmen** *vi sep irreg* **an etw** *(dat)* **~** *(sich beteiligen)* to take part in sth; **an einem Ausflug ~** to go on an outing; **am Unterricht ~** to attend school.
**Teilnehmer(in** *f)* *m* - participant; *(bei Wettbewerb)* competitor, contestant; *(Kurs~)* student.
**teils** *adv* partly. **~ ..., ... partly ..., partly ...; bist du zufrieden? — ~, ~** are you happy? — sort of *(col)*.
**Teil-:** **~strecke** *f* stage; *(von Straße)* stretch; *(bei Bus etc)* fare stage; **~stück** *nt* part.
**Teilung** *f* division.
**teilweise 1** *adv* partly; *(manchmal)* sometimes. **~ sind sie interessiert** some of them are interested. **2** *adj attr* partial.
**Teilzahlung** *f* hire-purchase *(Brit)*, installment plan *(US)*; *(Rate)* instalment *(Brit)*, installment *(US)*. **auf ~** on hire-purchase/the installment plan.
**Teilzeit-:** **~arbeit** *f* part-time job/work; **t~beschäftigt** *adj* employed part-time; **~kraft** *f* part-time worker.
**Teint** [tɛ̃ː] *m* **-s** complexion.
**Tel.** = **Telefon(nummer)** tel.
**Tele-:** **~fax** *nt (Kopie, Gerät)* fax; **t~faxen** *vti insep* to fax; **~faxgerät** *nt* fax machine.
**Telefon** *nt* **-e** (tele)phone. **am ~** on the phone; **ans ~ gehen** to answer the phone.
**Telefon-** *in cpds* (tele)phone; **~anruf** *m* (tele)phone call; **~apparat** *m* telephone.
**Telefonat** *nt* (tele)phone call.
**Telefon-:** **~auskunft** *f* directory enquiries *pl*, information *(US)*; **~buch** *nt* telephone directory, phone book *(col)*; **~gebühr** *f* call charge; *(Grundgebühr)* telephone rental; **~gespräch** *nt* (tele)phone call; **~häuschen** *nt (col)* = **~zelle**.
**telefonieren*** *vi* to make a (tele)phone call. **er telefoniert gerade** he's on the phone; **bei jdm ~** to use sb's phone; **mit jdm ~** to speak to sb on the phone; **nach Hause ~** to phone *or* call *(esp US)* home; **ins Ausland ~** to make an international call; **nach Hamburg/Amerika ~** to call Hamburg/America.
**telefonisch** *adj* **~e Auskunft/Beratung** telephone information/advice service; **eine ~e Nachricht** a (tele)phone message; **jdm etw ~ mitteilen** to tell sb sth over the telephone; **etw ~ bestellen** to order sth on the phone *or* by phone; **ich bin ~ zu erreichen** I can be contacted by (tele)phone.
**Telefonist(in** *f)* *m* telephone operator; *(in Betrieb auch)* switchboard operator.
**Telefon-:** **~karte** *f* phonecard; **~leitung** *f* telephone line; **~netz** *nt* telephone network;

~**nummer** *f* (tele)phone number; ~**rechnung** *f* (tele)phone bill; ~**seelsorge** *f* die ~**seelsorge** ≃ the Samaritans *pl*; ~**verbindung** *f* telephone line; *(zwischen Orten)* telephone link; ~**zelle** *f* (tele)phone box *(Brit) or* booth; ~**zentrale** *f* (telephone) switchboard.

**Telegraf** *m (wk)* **-en, -en** telegraph.

**Telegrafie** *f* telegraphy.

**telegrafieren*** *vti* to telegram, to cable.

**telegrafisch** *adj* telegraphic. **jdm ~ Geld überweisen** to wire sb money.

**Telegramm** *nt* **-e** telegram.

**Tele-**: ~**heimarbeit** *f* telecommuting; ~**kolleg** *nt* ≃ Open University *(Brit)*; ~**kommunikation** *f* telecommunications *pl*; ~**kopie** *f* fax; ~**kopierer** *m* fax machine; ~**objektiv** *nt (Phot)* telephoto lens.

**Telepathie** *f* telepathy.

**telepathisch** *adj* telepathic.

**Teleskop** *nt* **-e** telescope.

**Telespiel** *nt* video game.

**Telex** *nt* **-e** telex.

**Teller** *m* - plate. **ein ~ Suppe** a plate of soup.

**Tellerwäscher** *m* dishwasher.

**Tempel** *m* - temple *(auch fig)*.

**Temperament** *nt* **(a)** *(Wesensart)* temperament. **ein hitziges ~ haben** to be hot-tempered. **(b)** *no pl (Lebhaftigkeit)* vitality, vivacity. **viel/kein ~ haben** to have plenty of spirit/to lack spirit; **sein ~ ist mit ihm durchgegangen** his feelings got the better of him.

**temperament-**: ~**los** *adj* lifeless; ~**voll** *adj* vivacious, lively; *Aufführung auch* spirited.

**Temperatur** *f* temperature. **erhöhte ~ haben** to have a temperature; **die ~en sind angestiegen/ gesunken** the temperature has risen/fallen.

**Temperatur-**: ~**anstieg** *m* rise in temperature; ~**regler** *m* thermostat; ~**rückgang** *m* fall in temperature; ~**schwankung** *f* variation in temperature; ~**sturz** *m* sudden drop in temperature.

**temperieren*** *vt* **etw ~** *(anwärmen)* to warm sth up; **der Raum ist angenehm temperiert** the room is at a pleasant temperature.

**Tempo** *nt* **-s (a)** *(Geschwindigkeit)* speed; *(Arbeits~, Schritt~ auch)* pace. **~!** *(col)* hurry up!; **nun mach mal ein bißchen ~!** *(col)* get a move on! *(col)*; ~ **100 fahren** to be doing 62 mph. **(b)** *(Mus) pl* **Tempi** tempo. **das ~ angeben** *(fig)* to set the pace.

**Tempo-**: ~**limit** *nt* speed limit; ~**(taschen)tuch** ® *nt* paper handkerchief, tissue; ~**überschreitung** *f* speeding.

**Tendenz** *f* trend; *(Neigung)* tendency; *(Absicht)* intention; *(no pl: Parteilichkeit)* bias, slant. **die ~ haben, zu ...** to have a tendency to ...; **er hat nationalistische ~en** he has nationalist leanings.

**tendenziell** *adj* **eine ~e Veränderung** a change in direction; **nur ~e Unterschiede** merely differences in emphasis.

**tendenziös** *adj* tendentious.

**tendieren*** *vi* **dazu ~, etw zu tun** to tend to do sth; **nach rechts ~** to have right-wing leanings *or* tendencies.

**Teneriffa** *nt* Tenerife.

**Tennis** *nt* **-,** *no pl* tennis.

**Tennis-** *in cpds* tennis; ~**platz** *m* tennis court; ~**schläger** *m* tennis racket.

**Tenor**[1] *m no pl* tenor; *(einer Rede etc)* thrust.

**Tenor**[2] *m* **⸚e** *(Mus)* tenor.

**Teppich** *m* **-e** carpet; *(Wand~)* tapestry. **etw unter den ~ kehren** *(lit, fig)* to sweep sth under the carpet.

**Teppich-**: ~**boden** *m* fitted carpet(s); ~**fliese** *f* carpet tile; ~**kehrmaschine** *f* carpet-sweeper;

~**klopfer** *m* carpet-beater.

**Termin** *m* **-e** date; *(für Fertigstellung)* deadline; *(Comm: Liefertag)* delivery date; *(bei Arzt, Besprechung etc)* appointment; *(Jur: Verhandlung)* hearing. **die ~e besprechen** to discuss the schedule; **der letzte ~** the deadline; *(bei Bewerbung etc)* the closing date; **sich *(dat)* einen ~ geben lassen** to make an appointment; **schon einen anderen ~ haben** to have a prior engagement; **auf ~ kaufen** *(Fin)* to buy forward.

**Terminal** ['tœrminəl] *nt or m* **-s** terminal.

**Termin-**: ~**börse** *f* futures market; **t~gemäß, t~gerecht** *adj, adv* on schedule; ~**geschäfte** *pl* futures.

**terminieren** *vt (befristen)* to limit; *(festsetzen)* to set a date for.

**Terminkalender** *m* (appointments *or* engagements) diary.

**terminlich** *adj* **etw ~ einrichten** to fit sth in (to one's schedule); ~**e Verpflichtungen** commitments.

**Terminologie** *f* terminology.

**Termin-**: ~**planer** *m* personal organizer; ~**planung** *f* time scheduling.

**Termite** *f* **-n** termite.

**Terpentin** *nt* **-e** turpentine; *(col:* ~**öl)** turps *(col)*.

**Terrain** [tɛˈrɛ̃ː] *nt* **-s** land, terrain; *(fig)* territory. **das ~ sondieren** *(Mil)* to reconnoitre *(Brit) or* reconnoiter *(US)* the terrain; *(fig)* to see how the land lies.

**Terrarium** *nt* terrarium.

**Terrasse** *f* **-n** terrace; *(Dach~)* roof garden.

**terrassenförmig 1** *adj* terraced. **2** *adv* in terraces.

**Terrier** ['tɛriɐ] *m* - terrier.

**Terrine** *f* tureen.

**territorial** *adj* territorial.

**Territorium** *nt* territory.

**Terror** *m no pl* terror; *(Terrorismus)* terrorism; *(~herrschaft)* reign of terror; *(Einschüchterung)* intimidation. **blutiger ~** terrorism and bloodshed; ~ **machen** *(col)* to raise hell *(col)*.

**Terror-**: ~**anschlag** *m* terrorist attack; ~**herrschaft** *f* reign of terror.

**terrorisieren*** *vt* to terrorize.

**Terrorismus** *m* terrorism.

**Terrorist(in** *f)* *m* terrorist.

**terroristisch** *adj* terrorist *attr*.

**Terror|organisation** *f* terrorist organization.

**Tertia** ['tɛrtsia] *f, pl* **Tertien** ['tɛrtsiən] *(Sch dated) (Unter-/Ober~)* fourth/fifth *year of German secondary school*.

**Tertianer(in** *f)* [tɛrtsiˈaːnɐ, -ərɪn] *m* - *(Sch dated) pupil in fourth/fifth year of German secondary school*.

**Terz** *f* **-en** *(Mus)* third; *(Fechten)* tierce.

**Terzett** *nt* **-(e)s, -e** *(Mus)* (vocal) trio.

**Tesafilm** ® *m* (type of) adhesive tape, ≃ Sellotape ® *(Brit)*, Scotch tape ® *(esp US)*.

**Test** *m* **-s** *or* **-e** test.

**Testament** *nt* **(a)** *(Jur)* will; *(fig)* legacy. **sein ~ machen** to make one's will. **(b)** *(Bibl)* **Altes/Neues ~** Old/New Testament.

**testamentarisch** *adj* testamentary. **etw ~ festlegen** to write sth in one's will.

**Testamentsvollstrecker** *m* executor.

**Testbild** *nt (TV)* testcard.

**testen** *vt* to test *(auf +acc* for*)*. **jdn auf seine Intelligenz ~** to test sb's intelligence.

**Test-**: ~**fahrer** *m* test driver; ~**fall** *m* test case; ~**person** *f* subject (of a test); ~**pilot** *m* test pilot; ~**stopp** *m* test ban.

**Tetanus** *m no pl* tetanus.

**teuer** *adj* expensive, dear *usu pred*; *(fig)* dear. **etw ~**

**kaufen/verkaufen** to buy/sell sth for a high price; **etw für teures Geld kaufen** to pay good money for sth; **teurer werden** *Milch, Porto etc* to go up (in price); **in Tokio lebt man ~** life is expensive in Tokyo; **das wird ihn ~ zu stehen kommen** *(fig)* that will cost him dear; **einen Sieg ~ erkaufen** to pay dearly for a victory.

**Teuerung** *f* rise in prices.

**Teuerungszulage** *f* cost of living supplement.

**Teufel** *m* - **(a)** *(lit, fig)* devil. **(b)** *(col)* **scher dich zum ~!** go to hell! *(col!)*; **jdn zum ~ jagen** to send sb packing *(col)*; **wer zum ~?** who the devil *(col)* or the hell *(col!)*?; **zum ~ mit dem Ding!** damn *(col)* or blast *(col)* the thing!; **den ~ an die Wand malen** *(schwarzmalen)* to imagine the worst; *(Unheil heraufbeschwören)* to tempt fate *or* providence; **wenn man vom ~ spricht** *(prov)* talk of the devil; **das müßte schon mit dem ~ zugehen** that really would be a stroke of bad luck; **der ~ steckt im Detail** it's the small things that cause problems; **in ~s Küche kommen** to get into a mess; **sich den ~ um etw kümmern** not to give a damn about sth *(col)*.

**Teufels-:** **~arbeit** *f* *(col)* hell of a job *(col)*; **~austreibung** *f* casting out of devils *no pl*, exorcism; **~kerl** *m* *(dated)* devil of a fellow *(dated)*; **~kreis** *m* vicious circle.

**teuflisch** *adj* fiendish, devilish, diabolical.

**Text** *m* **-e** text; *(einer Urkunde auch, eines Gesetzes)* wording; *(von Lied)* words *pl*; *(von Schlager)* lyrics *pl*; *(von Film, Rede etc)* script; *(Bild~)* caption; *(auf Plakat)* words *pl*.

**Text-:** **~aufgabe** *f* *(Math)* problem; **~buch** *nt* script; *(für Lieder)* songbook; **~dichter** *m* songwriter; *(bei Oper)* librettist; **~eingabe** *f* *(Comp)* text input.

**texten 1** *vt* to write. **2** *vi siehe* **Texter(in)** to write songs/copy.

**Texter(in** *f)* *m* - *(für Schlager)* songwriter; *(für Werbesprüche)* copywriter.

**Text|erfasser(in** *f)* *m* keyboarder.

**Textil-** *in cpds* textile; **~arbeiter** *m* textile worker; **~branche** *f* textile trade.

**Textilien** [-iən] *pl* textiles *pl*.

**Textilindustrie** *f* textile industry.

**Text-:** **~kritik** *f* textual criticism; **~stelle** *f* passage; **~system** *nt* word processor.

**Textverarbeitung** *f* word processing.

**Textverarbeitungs-:** **~programm** *nt* word-processing program; **~system** *nt* word processor, word-processing system.

**TH** [te:'ha:] *f* **-s** = **Technische Hochschule.**

**Thai** *nt* **-s** *(language)* Thai; *siehe* **Deutsch(e).**

**Thailand** *nt* Thailand.

**Thailänder(in** *f)* *m* - Thai.

**thailändisch** *adj* Thai.

**Theater** *nt* - **(a)** theatre *(Brit)*, theater *(US)*; *(~kunst auch)* drama; *(Schauspielbühne)* theatre *(Brit)* or theater *(US)* company. **beim/im ~ arbeiten** to be on the stage/work in the theatre; **zum ~ gehen** to go on the stage; **ins ~ gehen** to go to the theatre; **~ spielen** *(lit)* to act; *(fig)* to play-act. **(b)** *(fig)* carry-on *(col)*, fuss. **(ein) ~ machen** to make a (big) fuss *(mit jdm* of sb).

**Theater-** *in cpds* theatre *(Brit)*, theater *(US)*; **~aufführung** *f* stage production; *(Vorstellung, Darbietung)* stage performance; **~besucher** *m* theatre-goer *(Brit)*, theatergoer *(US)*; **~kritiker** *m* drama critic; **~stück** *nt* (stage) play.

**theatralisch** *adj* theatrical, histrionic.

**Theke** *f* **-n** *(Schanktisch)* bar; *(Ladentisch)* counter. **etw unter der ~ verkaufen** to sell sth under the

counter.

**Thema** *nt, pl* **Themen** *or* **-ta** subject, topic; *(Leitgedanke, Mus)* theme. **beim ~ bleiben/vom ~ abschweifen** to stick to/wander off the subject; **das ~ wechseln** to change the subject; **ein/kein ~ sein** to be/not to be an issue.

**Thematik** *f* topic.

**thematisch** *adj* thematic.

**Themenkreis** *m* topic.

**Themse** *f* Thames.

**Theologe** *m*, **Theologin** *f* theologian.

**Theologie** *f* theology.

**theologisch** *adj* theological.

**Theoretiker(in** *f)* *m* - theorist, theoretician.

**theoretisch** *adj* theoretical. **~ gesehen** in theory, theoretically.

**Theorie** *f* theory.

**Therapeut(in** *f)* *m (wk)* **-en, -en** therapist.

**therapeutisch** *adj* therapeutic(al).

**Therapie** *f* therapy.

**therapieren*** *vt* to give therapy to.

**Thermal-:** **~bad** *nt (Badeort)* spa; **~quelle** *f* thermal *or* hot spring.

**thermisch** *adj attr (Phys)* thermal.

**Thermo-** *in cpds* thermo-; **~drucker** *m* thermal printer.

**Thermometer** *nt* - thermometer.

**Thermosflasche** *f* thermos ® (flask).

**Thermostat** *m* **-e** thermostat.

**These** *f* **-n** hypothesis, thesis.

**Thrombose** *f* **-n** thrombosis.

**Thron** *m* **-e** throne. **von seinem ~ herabsteigen** *(fig)* to come down off one's high horse.

**thronen** *vi* to sit enthroned; *(fig: in exponierter Stellung sitzen)* to sit in state.

**Thron-:** **~erbe** *m*, **~erbin** *f* heir to the throne; **~folge** *f* line of succession; **~folger(in** *f)* *m* - heir to the throne, heir apparent.

**Thunfisch** *m* tuna (fish).

**Thymian** *m* **-e** thyme.

**Thüringen** *nt* Thuringia.

**Thüringer, thüringisch** *adj* Thuringian.

**Tibet** *nt* Tibet.

**Tibetaner(in** *f)* *m* **-**, **Tibeter(in** *f)* *m* - Tibetan.

**tibetanisch, tibetisch** *adj* Tibetan.

**tick** *interj* tick. **~ tack** tick-tock.

**Tick** *m* **-s** tic; *(col: Schrulle)* quirk. **Uhren sind sein ~** he has a thing about clocks *(col)*; **einen ~ haben** *(col)* to be crazy.

**ticken** *vi* to tick (away). **du tickst ja nicht richtig** you're off your rocker! *(col)*.

**tief 1** *adj* deep; *(niedrig) Ton, Ausschnitt* low; *(tiefgründig auch)* profound; *Schmerz* intense; *Not* dire; *Elend* utter. **~er Teller** soup plate; **die ~eren Ursachen** the underlying causes; **aus ~stem Herzen/ ~ster Seele** from the bottom of one's heart/the depths of one's soul; **im ~en Winter** in the depths of winter.

**2** *adv* **(a)** *(weit nach unten, innen etc)* deep; *untersuchen* in depth; *sich bücken* low. **~ in etw (acc) einsinken** to sink deep into sth; **3 Meter ~ fallen** to fall 10 feet; **~ sinken** *(fig)* to sink low; **(ganz) ~ unter uns** a long way below us, far below us; **~ verschneit** deep with snow; **bis ~ in die Nacht hinein** late into the night; **~ im Wald** deep in the forest; **~ in der Nacht** at dead of night; **~ in Gedanken (versunken)** deep in thought; **~ in Schulden stecken** to be deep in debt; **~ in die Tasche greifen müssen** *(col)* to have to dig deep in one's pocket. **(b)** *(schwer, stark)* deeply; *erschrecken* terribly. **~ atmen** to breathe deeply; **im Winter steht die Sonne**

~**er** the sun is lower (in the sky) in winter.

**Tief** *nt* **-e** *(Met)* depression; *(fig)* low. **ein moralisches** ~ *(fig)* a state of depression.

**Tief-:** ~**bau** *m* civil engineering *(excluding the construction of buildings)*; **t~betrübt** *adj attr* deeply distressed; ~**druck** *m* **(a)** *(Met)* low pressure, **(b)** *(Typ)* gravure; ~**druckgebiet** *nt (Met)* area of low pressure, depression.

**Tiefe** *f* **-n** *siehe* **tief** depth; lowness; profundity. **unten in der** ~ far below.

**Tief|ebene** *f* lowland plain.

**Tiefen-:** ~**psychologie** *f* depth psychology; ~**schärfe** *f (Phot)* depth of focus; ~**wirkung** *f* deep action.

**Tief-:** ~**flieger** *m* low-flying aircraft; ~**flug** *m* low-level *or* low-altitude flight; ~**gang** *m (Naut)* draught *(Brit)*, draft *(US)*; *(fig col)* depth; ~**garage** *f* underground car park *(Brit) or* parking lot *(US)*; **t~gefroren**, **t~gekühlt** *adj (gefroren)* frozen; **t~gestellt** *adj (Typ)* subscript; **t~greifend** *adj* far-reaching; **t~gründig** *adj* profound, deep; *(durchdacht)* well-grounded.

**Tiefkühl-:** ~**fach** *nt* freezer compartment; ~**kost** *f* frozen food; ~**truhe** *f* freezer, deep-freeze.

**Tief-:** ~**lader** *m* - low-loader; ~**land** *nt* lowlands *pl*; **t~liegend** *adj attr Gegend, Häuser* low-lying; *Augen* deep-set; *(nach Krankheit)* sunken; ~**parterre** *nt* basement; ~**punkt** *m* low; ~**schlag** *m (Boxen, fig)* hit below the belt; **t~schürfend** *adj* profound; *Ermittlung* in-depth; ~**see** *f* deep sea; ~**sinn** *m* profundity; **t~sinnig** *adj* profound; ~**stand** *m* low; **t~stapeln** *vi sep* to understate the case; *(in bezug auf eigene Leistung)* to be modest; ~**töner** *m* woofer.

**Tiegel** *m* - (sauce)pan; *(Chem)* crucible.

**Tier** *nt* **-e** animal; *(Haus~ auch)* pet; *(col: grausamer Mensch)* brute. **hohes** ~ *(col)* big shot *(col)*.

**Tier-** *in cpds* animal; *(Med)* veterinary; ~**arzt** *m* vet, veterinary surgeon *(form)*, veterinarian *(US)*; ~**freund** *m* animal lover; ~**futter** *nt* (animal) fodder; *(für Haustiere)* pet food; ~**garten** *m* zoo; ~**halter** *m (von Haustieren)* pet owner; *(von Nutztieren)* livestock owner; ~**handlung** *f* pet shop *(Brit) or* store *(US)*; ~**heim** *nt* animal home.

**tierisch** *adj* animal *attr*; *(fig) Roheit* bestial; *(fig col: unerträglich)* terrible. ~**er Ernst** *(col)* deadly seriousness.

**Tier-:** ~**kreis** *m* zodiac; ~**kreiszeichen** *nt* sign of the zodiac; ~**kunde** *f* zoology; **t~lieb** *adj* = **t~liebend**; ~**liebe** *f* love of animals; **t~liebend** *adj* fond of animals, animal-loving *attr*; ~**medizin** *f* veterinary medicine; ~**park** *m* zoo; ~**pfleger** *m* animal keeper; ~**quälerei** *f* cruelty to animals; ~**rechtler** *m* animal rights activist; ~**reich** *nt* animal kingdom; ~**schutz** *m* protection of animals; ~**schützer** *m* animal conservationist; ~**schutzverein** *m* society for the prevention of cruelty to animals; ~**versuch** *m* animal experiment; ~**welt** *f* animal kingdom.

**Tiger** *m* - tiger.

**Tigerin** *f* tigress.

**Tilde** *f* **-n** tilde.

**tilgen** *vt (geh) Schulden* to pay off.

**Tilgung** *f (von Schulden)* repayment.

**Tilgungsfonds** *m* sinking fund.

**tingeln** *vi (col)* to appear in small night-clubs/ theatres *(Brit) or* theaters *(US)* etc.

**Tinnef** *m no pl (col)* rubbish, trash *(col)*.

**Tinte** *f* **-n** ink. **in der** ~ **sitzen** *(col)* to be in the soup *(col)*.

**Tinten-:** ~**faß** *nt* inkpot; ~**fisch** *m* cuttlefish; *(Kal-*

*mar)* squid; *(achtarmig)* octopus; ~**fleck** *m* ink stain; ~**klecks** *m* ink blot; ~**strahldrucker** *m* inkjet printer.

**Tip** *m* **-s** *(Sport, St Ex)* tip; *(Andeutung)* hint; *(an Polizei)* tip-off. **kannst du mir einen** ~ **geben, wo ich ...?** can you give me an idea where I ...?

**Tippelbruder** *m (col)* tramp, gentleman of the road *(Brit hum)*, hobo *(US)*.

**tippeln** *vi aux sein (col) (gehen)* to foot it *(col)*; *(auf Zehenspitzen)* to tiptoe.

**tippen** *vti* **(a)** to tap *(an/auf/gegen etw (acc))* sth *l*; *(zeigen)* to touch *(auf or an etw (acc))* sth*)*. **jdm auf die Schulter** ~ to tap sb on the shoulder; **sich** *(dat)* **an die Stirn** ~ to tap one's forehead. **(b)** *(col: auf der Schreibmaschine)* to type *(an etw (dat))* sth*)*. **(c)** *(wetten)* to fill in one's coupon; *(im Toto auch)* to do the pools. **im Lotto** ~ to do the lottery. **(d)** *nur vi (col: raten)* to guess. **ich tippe auf Kohl** *(col)* I'll put my money on Kohl; **da hast du richtig getippt** you were on the right track there.

**Tippfehler** *m* typing error.

**Tippse** *f* **-n** *(pej)* typist.

**tipptopp** *(col)* **1** *adj* immaculate; *(prima)* first-class. **2** *adv* immaculately; *(prima)* really well.

**Tippzettel** *m (im Toto)* football pools coupon; *(im Lotto)* lottery coupon.

**Tirol** *nt* the Tyrol.

**Tiroler(in** *f)* *m* - Tyrolese, Tyrolean.

**tirolerisch** *adj* Tyrolese, Tyrolean.

**Tisch** *m* **-e** table; *(Schreib~)* desk. **bei** ~ at table; **bitte zu** ~**!** lunch/dinner is served!; **vor/nach** ~ before/after the meal; **unter den** ~ **fallen** *(col)* to go by the board; **jdn unter den** ~ **trinken** to drink sb under the table; **es wird gegessen, was auf den** ~ **kommt!** you'll eat what you're given; **zwei Parteien an einen** ~ **bringen** *(fig)* to get two parties round the conference table; **vom** ~ **sein** *(fig)* to be cleared out of the way.

**Tisch-** *in cpds* table; ~**dame** *f* dinner partner; ~**decke** *f* tablecloth; ~**gespräch** *nt* conversation at table; ~**herr** *m* dinner partner; ~**karte** *f* place card.

**Tischler** *m* - carpenter; *(Möbel~)* cabinet-maker.

**Tischlerei** *f (Werkstatt)* carpenter's/cabinet-maker's workshop.

**Tischlerhandwerk** *nt* carpentry; cabinet-making.

**Tischlerin** *f* = **Tischler**.

**tischlern** *(col)* **1** *vi* to do woodwork. **2** *vt Tisch, Regal etc* to make.

**Tisch-:** ~**nachbar** *m* neighbour *(Brit) or* neighbor *(US)* (at table); ~**ordnung** *f* seating plan; ~**rechner** *m* desk calculator; ~**rede** *f* after-dinner speech; ~**tennis** *nt* table tennis; ~**tuch** *nt* tablecloth; ~**wein** *m* table wine.

**Titel** *m* - title. **unter dem** ~ under the title.

**Titel-:** ~**anwärter** *m* (main) contender for the title; ~**bild** *nt* cover (picture); ~**blatt** *nt* title page.

**Titelei** *f (Typ)* prelims *pl*.

**Titel-:** ~**geschichte** *f* cover story; ~**kampf** *m (Sport)* finals *pl*; *(Boxen)* title fight; ~**melodie** *f (von Film)* theme tune; ~**rolle** *f* title role; ~**schutz** *m* copyright *(of a title)*; ~**seite** *f (von Zeitschrift)* cover; *(von Zeitung)* front page; ~**träger**, ~**verteidiger** *m* title holder.

**Titte** *f* **-n** *(col!)* tit *(col!)*.

**titulieren*** *vt jdn (bezeichnen)* to call *(mit etw* sth); *(anreden)* to address *(mit* as).

**tja** *interj* well.

**Toast** [to:st] *m* **-e** **(a)** *(Brot)* toast. **ein** ~ some toast. **(b)** *(Trinkspruch)* toast.

**toasten** ['to:stn] **1** *vi* to drink a toast *(auf +acc* to).

**2** vt Brot to toast.
**Toaster** ['toːstɐ] m - toaster.
**toben** vi (a) (wüten) to rage; (Mensch) to throw a fit; (vor Begeisterung etc) to go wild (vor with). **(b)** (ausgelassen spielen) to rollick (about).
**Tob-:** ~sucht f (bei Tieren) madness; (bei Menschen) maniacal rage; **er hat wieder mal die ~sucht** (col) he's in a mad fury again; **t~süchtig** adj Tier mad; Mensch in a mad fury; **~suchtsanfall** m (col) fit of rage.
**Tochter** f ⁼ daughter; (~firma) subsidiary.
**Tochtergesellschaft** f subsidiary (company).
**Tod** m -e death. ~ **durch Ersticken** death by suffocation; **eines natürlichen/gewaltsamen ~es sterben** to die of natural causes/to die a violent death; **sich zu ~e trinken** to drink oneself to death; **sich** (dat) **den ~ holen** to catch one's death (of cold); **sich zu ~(e) langweilen** to be bored to death; **zu ~e betrübt sein** to be in the depths of despair.
**tod|ernst** adj (col) deadly serious.
**Todes-:** ~angst f fear of death; **~ängste ausstehen** (col) to be scared to death (col); ~anzeige f obituary (notice); ~fall m death; (bei Unglück auch) fatality; (in der Familie auch) bereavement; ~jahr nt year of sb's death; ~kampf m death throes pl; **t~mutig** adj absolutely fearless; ~opfer nt death, casualty, fatality; **die Zahl der ~opfer** the death toll; ~qualen pl final agony sing; **~qualen ausstehen** (fig) to suffer agonies; ~stoß m death-blow; **jdm/einer Sache den ~stoß versetzen** (lit, fig) to deal sb/sth the death-blow; ~strafe f death penalty; ~stunde f hour of death; ~tag m day of sb's death; (Jahrestag) anniversary of sb's death; ~trieb m death wish; ~ursache f cause of death; ~urteil nt death sentence; ~verachtung f (col) **mit ~verachtung** with utter disgust.
**Tod-:** ~feind m deadly or mortal enemy; **t~krank** adj dangerously or critically ill.
**tödlich** adj fatal; Gefahr mortal; Gift deadly, lethal; (col) Langeweile deadly. ~ **verunglücken** to be killed in an accident.
**Tod-:** **t~müde** adj (col) dead tired (col); **t~schick** adj (col) dead smart (col); **t~sicher** (col) **1** adj dead certain (col); Methode, Tip sure-fire (col); **2** adv for sure; ~sünde f mortal or deadly sin; **t~unglücklich** adj (col) desperately unhappy.
**Toga** f, pl **Togen** toga.
**Toilette** [toa'lɛtə] f **(a)** (Abort) toilet. **öffentliche ~** public conveniences pl (Brit), comfort station (US); **auf die ~ gehen/auf der ~ sein** to go to/be in the toilet. **(b)** no pl (geh: Körperpflege) toilet.
**Toiletten-** [toa'lɛtn-] in cpds toilet; ~artikel pl toiletries pl; ~beutel m toilet bag; ~frau f, ~mann m toilet or lavatory (Brit) attendant; ~papier nt toilet paper; ~schrank m bathroom cabinet; ~wasser nt toilet water.
**toi, toi, toi** interj (col) good luck.
**Tokio** nt Tokyo.
**tolerant** adj tolerant (gegen of).
**Toleranz** f tolerance (gegen of).
**tolerieren*** vt to tolerate.
**toll** adj **(a)** (wild, ausgelassen) wild, mad. **(b)** (col: verrückt) mad, crazy. **(c)** (col: schlimm) terrible. **(d)** (col: großartig) fantastic (col), great (col) no adv.
**tollen** vi to romp about; (aux sein: laufen) to rush about.
**Toll-:** ~kirsche f deadly nightshade; **t~kühn** adj daredevil attr, daring; ~wut f rabies; **t~wütig** adj rabid.
**Tolpatsch** m -e (col) clumsy creature.
**Tölpel** m - (col) fool.

**Tomate** f -n tomato. **du treulose ~!** (col) you're a fine friend!
**Tomaten-** in cpds tomato; ~mark, ~püree nt tomato puree.
**Tombola** f, pl -s or **Tombolen** tombola.
**Ton¹** m -e (Erdart) clay.
**Ton²** m ⁼e **(a)** (Laut) sound; (von Zeitzeichen, im Telefon, Klangfarbe) tone; (Mus: Note) note. **den ~ angeben** (Mus) to give an A; (fig: Mensch) to set the tone; **keinen ~ herausbringen** not to be able to say a word; **keinen ~ sagen** not to utter a sound; **hast du ~e!** (col) did you ever! (col); **dicke or große ~e spucken** (col) to talk big. **(b)** (Betonung) stress; (Tonfall) intonation. **(c)** (Redeweise, Umgangs~) tone. **den richtigen ~ finden** to strike the right note; **ich verbitte mir diesen ~** I will not be spoken to like that; **einen anderen ~ anschlagen** to change one's tune; **der gute ~** good form. **(d)** (Farb~) tone; (Nuance) shade.
**Ton-:** ~abnehmer m pick-up; **t~angebend** adj who/which sets the tone; ~arm m pick-up arm; ~art f (Mus) key; (fig: Tonfall) tone.
**Tonband** nt tape; (col: Gerät) tape recorder.
**Tonband-:** ~aufnahme f tape recording; ~gerät nt (reel-to-reel) tape recorder.
**Tondichtung** f tone poem.
**tönen¹** vi (lit, fig: klingen) to sound; (schallen auch) to resound; (großspurig reden) to sound off.
**tönen²** vt to tint. **etw leicht rot** etc ~ to tinge sth (with) red etc.
**Toner** m - (für Kopierer etc) toner.
**Ton|erde** f aluminium (Brit) or aluminum (US) oxide.
**tönern** adj attr clay. **auf ~en Füßen stehen** (fig) to be shaky.
**Ton-:** ~fall m tone of voice; (Intonation) intonation; ~film m sound film, talkie (col); ~folge f sequence of notes/sounds; ~geschirr nt earthenware; ~höhe f pitch.
**Tonika** f, pl **Toniken** (Mus) tonic.
**Tonikum** nt, pl **Tonika** (Med) tonic.
**Ton-:** ~ingenieur m sound engineer; ~kopf m recording head; ~lage f pitch (level); (~umfang) register; ~leiter f scale; **t~los** adj toneless.
**Tonne** f -n **(a)** (Behälter) barrel; (aus Metall) drum; (Müll~) bin (Brit), trash can (US); (col: Mensch) fat-so (col). **grüne ~** container for recyclable waste. **(b)** (Gewicht) (1000 kg) tonne, metric ton; (Register~) (register) ton.
**Ton-:** ~spur f soundtrack; ~störung f sound interference; ~studio f recording studio; ~taube f clay pigeon.
**Tönung** f (das Tönen) tinting; (Farbton) tint, shade; (Haar~) hair colour.
**Tonwaren** pl earthenware sing.
**Top** nt (Fashion) top.
**Top-** in cpds top; ~angebot nt best offer.
**Topas** m -e topaz.
**Topf** m ⁼e pot; (Koch~ auch) (sauce)pan; (Nacht~) potty (col); (col: Toilette) loo (Brit col), john (US col). **alles in einen ~ werfen** (fig) to lump everything together.
**Topfblume** f (flowering) pot plant.
**Töpfer(in** f) m - potter.
**Töpferei** f pottery.
**töpfern 1** vi to do pottery. **2** vt to make (in clay).
**Töpfer-:** ~scheibe f potter's wheel; ~waren pl pottery sing; (irden) earthenware sing.
**Topfhandschuh** m ovenglove.
**topfit** ['tɔp'fɪt] adj pred (col) as fit as a fiddle (col).
**Topf-:** ~lappen m ovencloth; ~pflanze f potted

plant.
**Top-:** ~**lage** *f* prime location; ~**leistung** *f* outstanding achievement.
**Topographie** *f* topography.
**Tor** *nt* -e (a) *(lit, fig, Ski)* gate; *(Durchfahrt etc)* gateway; *(von Garage, Scheune)* door. (b) *(Sport)* goal. **im** ~ **stehen** to be in goal.
**Tor-:** ~**bogen** *m* arch, archway; ~**einfahrt** *f* entrance gate.
**Toresschluß** *m*: **(kurz) vor** ~ right at the last minute.
**Torf** *m no pl* peat.
**Torf-:** ~**boden** *m* peaty earth; ~**erde** *f* peat.
**torfig** *adj* peaty.
**Torf-:** ~**moor** *nt* peat bog *or (trocken)* moor; ~**stecher** *m* - peat-cutter.
**Torheit** *f* foolishness; *(Handlung)* foolish action.
**Torhüter** *m* goalkeeper.
**töricht** *adj* foolish; *Wunsch, Hoffnung* idle.
**torkeln** *vi aux sein* to stagger, to reel.
**Tor-:** ~**latte** *f* crossbar; ~**lauf** *m* slalom; ~**linie** *f* goal line; ~**mann** *m, pl* ~**männer** goalkeeper.
**Törn** *m (Naut)* (yacht) cruise.
**Tornister** *m* - *(Mil)* knapsack; *(dated: Schulranzen)* satchel.
**torpedieren\*** *vt (Naut, fig)* to torpedo.
**Torpedo** *m* -s torpedo.
**Tor-:** ~**pfosten** *m* gatepost; *(Sport)* goalpost; ~**schluß** *m (fig)* = ~**esschluß**; ~**schlußpanik** *f* *(col)* last minute panic; *(von Unverheirateten)* fear of being left on the shelf; ~**schütze** *m* (goal) scorer.
**Torte** *f* -n cake, gâteau; *(Obst~)* flan *(Brit)*, tart.
**Torten-:** ~**boden** *m* flan *(Brit)* or tart *(US)* base; ~**guß** *m* glaze; ~**heber** *m* - cake slice; ~**platte** *f* cake plate; ~**schaufel** *f* cake slice.
**Tortur** *f* torture; *(fig auch)* ordeal.
**Tor-:** ~**verhältnis** *nt* score; ~**wart** *m* goalkeeper.
**tosen** *vi* to roar, to thunder; *(Wind, Sturm)* to rage. ~**der Beifall** thunderous applause.
**Toskana** *f* **die** ~ Tuscany.
**tot** *adj (lit, fig)* dead; *Augen* sightless; *Haus, Stadt* deserted; *Gegend, Landschaft etc* bleak; *Wissen* useless; *Vulkan* extinct; *Farbe* lifeless; *(Rail) Gleis* disused. **mehr** ~ **als lebendig** *(fig col)* more dead than alive; ~ **geboren werden** to be stillborn; ~ **umfallen** to drop dead; **er war auf der Stelle** ~ he died instantly; **ein** ~**er Briefkasten** a dead-letter box; **der** ~**e Winkel** the blind spot; **ein** ~**er Punkt** *(Stillstand)* a standstill; *(in Verhandlungen)* deadlock; *(körperliche Ermüdung)* low point; **ein** ~**es Rennen** *(lit, fig)* a dead heat; **ein** ~**er Mann** *(fig col)* a goner *(col)*; **das T**~**e Meer** the Dead Sea.
**total 1** *adj* total. **2** *adv* totally.
**Totalausverkauf** *m* clearance sale.
**totalitär** *adj* totalitarian.
**Totalität** *f* totality, entirety.
**Total-:** ~**operation** *f* extirpation; *(col: von Gebärmutter)* hysterectomy; ~**schaden** *m* write-off.
**tot-:** ~**arbeiten** *vr sep (col)* to work oneself to death; ~**ärgern** *vr sep (col)* to be/become livid.
**töten** *vti (lit, fig)* to kill. **das kann einem den Nerv** ~ *(fig col)* that really gets on your *etc* nerves.
**Toten-:** ~**bett** *nt* deathbed; **t**~**blaß** *adj* deathly pale; ~**glocke** *f* death knell; ~**gräber** *m* gravedigger; ~**hemd** *nt* shroud; ~**klage** *f* lamentation of the dead; *(Liter)* dirge, lament; ~**kopf** *m* skull; *(als Zeichen)* death's-head; *(auf Piratenfahne, Arzneiflasche etc)* skull and crossbones; ~**messe** *f* requiem mass; ~**reich** *nt (Myth)* kingdom of the dead; ~**schein** *m* death certificate; **t**~**still** *adj*

deathly silent; ~**stille** *f* deathly hush; ~**starre** *f* rigor mortis; ~**wache** *f* wake.
**Tote(r)** *mf decl as adj* dead person, dead man/woman; *(bei Unfall etc)* fatality, casualty. **die** ~**n** the dead; **es gab drei** ~ three people were killed.
**Tot-:** **t**~**fahren** *vt sep irreg (col)* to knock down and kill; **t**~**geboren** *adj attr* stillborn; **ein** **t**~**geborenes Kind sein** *(fig)* to be doomed to failure; ~**geburt** *f* stillbirth; *(Kind)* stillborn baby; ~**gesagte(r)** *mf decl as adj* person *or* man/woman *etc* who has been declared dead; **t**~**kriegen** *vt sep (col)* **nicht t**~**zukriegen sein** to go on for ever; **t**~**lachen** *vr sep (col)* to die laughing *(col)*; **t**~**laufen** *vr sep irreg (col)* to peter out.
**Toto** *m* or *nt* -s (football) pools. **(im)** ~ **spielen** to do the pools.
**Toto-** *in cpds* pools; ~**schein**, ~**zettel** *m* pools coupon.
**Tot-:** **t**~**sagen** *vt sep* to declare dead; **t**~**schießen** *vt sep irreg (col)* to shoot dead; ~**schlag** *m (Jur)* manslaughter, homicide *(US)*; **t**~**schlagen** *vt sep irreg (lit, fig)* to kill; *(col) Menschen auch* to beat to death; ~**schläger** *m* cosh *(Brit)*, blackjack *(US)*; **t**~**schweigen** *vt sep irreg* to hush up *(col)*; **t**~**stellen** *vr sep* to pretend to be dead; **t**~**treten** *vt sep irreg* to trample to death.
**Tötung** *f* killing. **fahrlässige** ~ *(Jur)* manslaughter through culpable negligence.
**Toupet** [tu'pe:] *nt* -s toupee.
**toupieren\*** [tu'pi:rən] *vt* to backcomb.
**Tour** [tu:ɐ] *f* -en (a) *(Fahrt)* trip, outing; *(Ausflugs~)* tour; *(Spritz~)* *(mit Auto)* drive; *(mit Rad)* ride; *(Wanderung)* walk; *(Berg~)* climb. **eine** ~ **machen** to go on a trip *or* outing/tour; to go for a drive/ride/walk/climb. (b) *(Umdrehung)* revolution, rev *(col)*. **auf** ~**en kommen** *(Auto)* to get up speed; *(fig col)* to get into top gear; *(sich aufregen)* to get worked up *(col)*; **auf vollen** ~**en laufen** *(lit)* to run at full speed; *(fig)* to be in full swing; **in einer** ~ *(col)* the whole time. (c) *(col: Art und Weise)* ploy. **mit der** ~ **brauchst du mir gar nicht zu kommen** don't try that one on me; **auf die krumme** ~ by dishonest means.
**Touren-** ['tu:rən-]: ~**rad** *nt* tourer; ~**wagen** *m (Motorsport)* touring car; ~**zähler** *m* rev counter.
**Tourismus** [tu'rɪsmʊs] *m* tourism.
**Tourist(in f)** [tu'rɪst, -ɪn] *m* tourist.
**Touristik** [tu'rɪstɪk] *f* tourism, tourist industry.
**touristisch** [tu'rɪstɪʃ] *adj* tourist *attr*.
**Tournee** [tʊr'ne:] *f* -n [-e:ən] *or* -s tour.
**Trab** *m no pl* trot. **im** ~ at a trot; **(im)** ~ **reiten** to trot; **auf** ~ **sein** *(col)* to be on the go *(col)*; **jdn auf** ~ **bringen** *(col)* to make sb get a move on *(col)*.
**Trabant** *m (Astron, fig)* satellite.
**Trabantenstadt** *f* satellite town.
**traben** *vi* (a) *aux haben or sein* to trot. (b) *aux sein (col: laufen)* to trot.
**Trabrennen** *nt* trotting race.
**Tracht** *f* -en *(Kleidung)* dress; *(Volks~ etc)* costume; *(Schwestern~)* uniform. **eine** ~ **Prügel** a good thrashing.
**trachten** *vi (geh)* to strive *(nach* for, after*)*. **jdm nach dem Leben** ~ to be after sb's blood.
**trächtig** *adj Tier* pregnant.
**Tradition** [tradi'tsio:n] *f* tradition.
**traditionell** [traditsio'nɛl] *adj usu attr* traditional.
**traf** *pret of* **treffen**.
**Trafo** *m* -s *(col)* transformer.
**Tragbahre** *f* stretcher.
**tragbar** *adj* (a) *Apparat, Gerät* portable; *Kleid* wearable. (b) *(annehmbar)* acceptable *(für* to*)*; *(erträglich)* bearable; *(finanziell)* supportable.

**Trage** f -n *(Bahre)* stretcher.
**träge** adj (a) sluggish; *Mensch, Bewegung auch* lethargic. (b) *(Phys) Masse* inert.
**tragen** pret **trug**, ptp **getragen 1** vt (a) to carry; *(an einen Ort bringen)* to take. **etw mit sich** ~ to carry sth with one. (b) *Kleid, Brille etc* to wear; *(im Moment auch)* to have on; *Bart, Gebiß* to have; *Waffen* to carry. **getragene Kleider** second-hand clothes; *(abgelegt)* cast-offs. (c) *(stützen, halten, fig)* to support; *Schicksal, Leid etc* to bear, to endure. (d) *Zinsen* to yield; *Ernte auch* to produce; *(lit, fig) Früchte* to bear. (e) *(trächtig sein)* to be carrying. (f) *Verluste* to absorb; *Kosten* to bear, to carry; *Risiko, Folgen* to take; *(unterhalten) Verein* to support, to back. (g) *Titel, Aufschrift etc* to bear, to have; *Vermerk* to contain.
**2** vi (a) *(Baum, Acker etc)* to produce a crop. (b) *(reichen: Geschütz, Stimme)* to carry. (c) *(Eis)* to take weight. (d) **schwer an etw** *(dat)* ~ to have a job carrying sth; *(fig)* to find sth hard to bear. (e) **zum T~ kommen** to come to fruition; *(nützlich werden)* to come in useful.
**3** vr (a) **sich leicht** ~ to be easy to carry; **der Anzug trägt sich gut** this suit feels comfortable (on). (b) *(finanziell)* to be self-supporting.
**tragend** adj *Säule, Bauteil* load-bearing; *Idee, Motiv* fundamental.
**Träger** m - (a) *(an Kleidung)* strap; *(Hosen~)* braces pl *(Brit)*, suspenders pl *(US)*. (b) *(Holz~, Beton~)* (supporting) beam; *(Stahl~, Eisen~)* girder. (c) *(Tech: Stütze von Brücken etc)* support. (d) *(Mensch) (von Lasten)* bearer, porter; *(von Namen)* bearer; *(von Kleidung)* wearer. (e) *(fig) (der Kultur, Staatsgewalt etc)* representative; *(einer Veranstaltung)* sponsor.
**Trägerin** f = **Träger (d)**.
**Träger-:** ~**kleid** nt pinafore dress *(Brit)*, jumper *(US)*; ~**rakete** f booster, carrier rocket; ~**rock** m = ~**kleid**; *(für Kinder)* skirt with straps.
**Tragetasche** f carrier bag *(Brit)*, carry-all *(US)*.
**Trag-:** **t~fähig** adj *(Brücke, Balken)* able to take a load; *(Kompromiß, Beschluß)* acceptable; *(Mehrheit)* workable; ~**fläche** f wing; *(von Boot)* hydrofoil; ~**flächenboot**, ~**flügelboot** nt hydrofoil.
**Trägheit** f siehe adj sluggishness; lethargy; *(Faulheit)* laziness; *(Phys)* inertia.
**Tragik** f tragedy.
**Tragiker** m - tragedian.
**tragikomisch** adj tragicomical.
**Tragikomödie** f tragicomedy.
**tragisch** adj tragic. **etw** ~ **nehmen** *(col)* to take sth to heart; **das ist nicht so** ~ *(col)* it's not the end of the world.
**Trag-:** ~**korb** m pannier; ~**last** f load.
**Tragödie** [-iə] f *(Liter, fig)* tragedy.
**Trag-:** ~**pfeiler** m load-bearing pillar; *(von Brücke)* support; ~**riemen** m strap; ~**weite** f *(von Geschütz)* range; *(fig) (von Gesetz)* consequences pl; scope; **von großer** ~**weite sein** to have far-reaching consequences; ~**werk** nt *(Aviat)* wing assembly.
**Trainer(in** f) ['trɛːnɐ, 'trɛː-] m - coach, trainer; *(bei Fußball)* manager.
**trainieren*** [trɛ'niːrən, trɛː'n-] **1** vt to train; *Mannschaft, Sportler auch* to coach; *Sprung, Übung* to practise *(Brit)*, to practice *(US)*. **Fußball** ~ to do some football practice; **ein (gut) trainierter Sportler** an athlete who is in training; **jdn auf** or **für etw** *(acc)* ~ to train or coach sb for sth. **2** vi *(Sportler)* to train; *(Übungen machen)* to exercise; *(üben)* to practise *(Brit)*, to practice *(US)*. **auf** or **für etw** *(acc)* ~ to train/practise for sth. **3** vr to train *(auf +acc*

for*)*; *(üben)* to practise *(Brit)*, to practice *(US)*.
**Training** ['trɛːnɪŋ, 'trɛː-] nt -s training no pl; *(Fitneß~)* exercise no pl; *(Motorsport, fig: Übung)* practice.
**Trainings-:** ~**anzug** m tracksuit; ~**hose** f tracksuit trousers pl; ~**jacke** f tracksuit top; ~**runde** f practice lap; ~**schuh** m trainer; ~**zeit** f practice time.
**Trakt** m -e *(Gebäudeteil)* section; *(Flügel)* wing.
**Traktat** m or nt -e *(Abhandlung)* treatise; *(Flugschrift, religiöse Schrift)* tract.
**traktieren*** vt *(col) (schlecht behandeln)* to maltreat; *(quälen)* to torment.
**Traktor** m -en tractor; *(Comp)* tractor feed.
**trällern** vti to warble.
**Trampel** m or nt - clumsy clot *(col)*.
**trampeln 1** vi (a) to stamp. (b) *aux sein (schwerfällig gehen)* to stamp along. **über die Wiese** ~ to tramp across the meadow. **2** vt Weg to trample. **jdn zu Tode** ~ to trample sb to death.
**Trampel-:** ~**pfad** m track, path; ~**tier** nt *(Zool)* (Bactrian) camel; *(col)* clumsy oaf *(col)*.
**trampen** ['trɛmpn] vi aux sein to hitch-hike, to hitch *(col)*.
**Tramper(in** f) ['trɛmpɐ, -ərɪn] m - hitch-hiker.
**Trampolin** nt -e trampoline.
**Tran** m -e (a) *(von Fischen)* train oil. (b) *(col)* im ~ dop(e)y *(col)*; *(leicht betrunken)* merry *(col)*; **das habe ich im** ~ **ganz vergessen** I absent-mindedly forgot it altogether.
**tranchieren** [trã'fiːrən] vt to carve.
**Tranchiermesser** nt carving knife.
**Träne** f -n tear; *(einzelne* ~*)* tear(drop). **den** ~**n nahe sein** to be on the verge of tears; **zu** ~**n rühren** to move to tears; ~**n lachen** to laugh till one cries; **deswegen vergieße ich keine** ~**n** *(fig)* I'm not going to shed any tears over that; **bittere** ~**n weinen** to weep bitterly.
**tränen** vi to water.
**Tränen-:** ~**drüse** f lachrymal gland; **der Film drückt sehr auf die** ~**drüsen** the film is a real tearjerker; ~**gas** nt tear gas.
**Tranfunzel** f *(col)* slowcoach *(Brit col)*, slowpoke *(US col)*.
**tranig** adj *(col)* slow, sluggish.
**Trank** m ⁼e *(liter)* drink, draught *(liter)*.
**trank** pret of **trinken**.
**Tränke** f -n drinking trough.
**tränken** vt Tiere to water; *(durchnässen)* to soak.
**Trans|aktion** f transaction.
**trans|atlantisch** adj transatlantic.
**Transfer** m -s *(Econ, Sport, Aviat)* transfer; *(Psych)* transference.
**Transformation** f transformation.
**Transformator** m transformer.
**transformieren*** vt to transform.
**Transfusion** f transfusion
**Transistor** m transistor.
**Transistorradio** nt transistor (radio).
**Transit** m -e transit.
**transitiv** adj *(Gram)* transitive.
**Transit-:** ~**raum** m *(Aviat)* transit lounge; ~**schalter** m *(Aviat)* transit desk; ~**verkehr** m transit traffic.
**transparent** [transpa'rɛnt] adj transparent; *(fig geh) Argument* lucid, clear. **eine Entscheidung** ~ **machen** to make a decision-making process open.
**Transparent** [transpa'rɛnt] nt -e *(Reklameschild etc)* neon sign; *(Durchscheinbild)* transparency; *(Spruchband)* banner.
**Transparentpapier** nt waxed tissue paper; *(zum*

*Pausen)* tracing paper.

**Transparenz** [transpa'rɛnts] *f siehe adj* transparency; lucidity, clarity.

**transpirieren\*** [transpi'riːrən] *vi (geh)* to perspire.

**Transplantation** [transplanta'tsioːn] *f (Med)* transplant; *(von Haut)* graft; *(Bot)* grafting.

**transponieren\*** [transpo'niːrən] *vt (Mus)* to transpose.

**Transport** [trans'pɔrt] *m* -e (a) transport. ein ~ auf dem Landweg road transport; ein ~ des Kranken ist ausgeschlossen moving the patient is out of the question. (b) *(Fracht)* consignment, shipment; *(Menschen)* transport.

**transportabel** [transpor'taːbl] *adj* transportable.

**Transport|arbeiter** *m* transport worker.

**Transporter** [trans'pɔrtɐ] *m* - *(Schiff)* cargo ship; *(Flugzeug)* transport plane; *(Auto)* van.

**Transporteur** [transpor'tøːɐ] *m* removal man *(Brit)*, furniture mover.

**transportfähig** *adj* moveable.

**transportieren\*** [transpor'tiːrən] **1** *vt* to transport; *Patienten* to move; *Film* to wind on. **2** *vi (Förderband)* to move; *(Kamera)* to wind on.

**Transport-** [trans'pɔrt-]: ~**kosten** *pl* freight costs *pl*; ~**schiff** *nt* cargo ship; *(Mil)* transport ship; ~**unternehmen** *nt* haulier, haulage firm.

**Transsuse** *f* -n *(col)* slowcoach *(Brit col)*, slowpoke *(US col)*.

**Transvestit** [transvɛs'tiːt] *m (wk)* -en, -en transvestite.

**transzendental** *adj* transcendent(al).

**Trapez** *nt* -e *(von Artisten)* trapeze.

**trappeln** *vi aux sein* to clatter; *(Pony)* to clip-clop.

**Trara** *nt* -s *(fig col)* hullabaloo *(col) (um* about*)*. großes ~ um etw machen to make a great song and dance about sth.

**Trasse** *f* -n marked-out route *(for a road/railway)*.

**trat** *pret of* **treten**.

**Tratsch** *m no pl (col)* gossip, scandal.

**tratschen** *vi (col)* to gossip.

**Tratsch-**: ~**maul** *nt,* ~**tante** *f (pej col)* scandalmonger, gossip.

**Tratte** *f* -n *(Fin)* draft.

**Trau|altar** *m* altar.

**Traube** *f* -n *(Beere)* grape; *(ganze Frucht)* bunch of grapes; *(Menschen~)* bunch. ~**n** *(Fruchtart)* grapes.

**Trauben-**: ~**lese** *f* grape harvest; ~**saft** *m* grape juice; ~**zucker** *m* glucose, dextrose.

**trauen** **1** *vi +dat* to trust. **ich traute meinen Augen nicht** I couldn't believe my eyes. **2** *vr* to dare. **sich** *(acc)* ~, **etw zu tun** to dare (to) do sth; **ich trau' mich nicht** I daren't, I dare not; **sich auf die Straße** ~ to dare to go out (of doors). **3** *vt* to marry. **sich** ~ **lassen** to get married.

**Trauer** *f no pl (das Trauern, ~zeit, ~kleidung)* mourning; *(Schmerz, Leid)* sorrow, grief.

**Trauer-**: ~**anzeige** *f* obituary, death notice; ~**fall** *m* bereavement, death; ~**feier** *f* funeral service; ~**flor** *m* black ribbon; *(Armbinde)* black armband, mourning band; ~**gemeinde** *f* mourners *pl*; ~**kleidung** *f* mourning; ~**kloß** *m (col)* wet blanket *(col)*; ~**marsch** *m* funeral march; ~**miene** *f (col)* long face.

**trauern** *vi* to mourn *(um jdn/etw* sb/sth*)*.

**Trauer-**: ~**rand** *m* black edge *or* border; ~**ränder** *pl (col)* dirty fingernails; ~**schleier** *m* black veil; ~**spiel** *nt* tragedy; *(fig col)* fiasco; ~**weide** *f* weeping willow; ~**zug** *m* funeral procession.

**Traufe** *f* -n eaves *pl*.

**träufeln** *vt* to dribble.

**traulich** *adj* cosy *(Brit)*, cozy *(US)*.

**Traum** *m, pl* **Träume** *(lit, fig)* dream. **aus der** ~**!** it's all over; **das fällt mir nicht im** ~ **ein** I wouldn't dream of it.

**Trauma** *nt, pl* **Traumen** *or* -ta *(lit, fig)* trauma.

**traumatisch** *adj (lit, fig)* traumatic.

**Traum-**: ~**beruf** *m* dream job; ~**deutung** *f* interpretation of dreams.

**träumen** *vti (lit, fig)* to dream. **von jdm/etw** ~ to dream about sb/sth; **das hätte ich mir nicht** ~ **lassen** I'd never have thought it possible.

**Träumer(in** *f) m* - dreamer.

**Träumerei** *f* (a) *no pl (das Träumen)* (day)dreaming. (b) *(Vorstellung)* daydream.

**träumerisch** *adj* dreamy.

**traumhaft** *adj (phantastisch)* fantastic; *(wie im Traum)* dreamlike.

**Traum-**: **t~los** *adj* dreamless; ~**paar** *nt* perfect couple; ~**tänzer** *m* dreamer.

**traurig** *adj* sad; *Leben auch* unhappy; *Leistung, Rekord* pathetic, sorry; *Wetter* miserable.

**Traurigkeit** *f* sadness.

**Trau-**: ~**ring** *m* wedding ring; ~**schein** *m* marriage certificate.

**Trauung** *f* wedding.

**Trauzeuge** *m* witness *(at marriage ceremony)*.

**Treck** *m* -s trek, trail; *(Leute)* train.

**Treff** *m* -s *(col) (Treffen)* meeting, get-together *(col)*; *(~punkt)* haunt, rendezvous.

**treffen** *pret* **traf**, *ptp* **getroffen** **1** *vt* (a) *(durch Schlag etc)* to hit *(an/in +dat* on, *in +acc* in*)*; *(Blitz, Faust auch, Unglück)* to strike. **auf dem Photo bist du gut getroffen** *(col)* that's a good photo of you. (b) *(betreffen)* to hit, to affect; *(kränken)* to hurt. **er fühlte sich getroffen** he took it personally. (c) *(jdm begegnen)* to meet; *(an~)* to find. (d) *(finden)* to hit upon, to find; *(lit, fig) Ton* to hit. (e) **es (mit etw) gut/schlecht** ~ to be lucky/unlucky (with sth). (f) *Vereinbarung* to reach; *Entscheidung* to make, to take; *Maßnahmen* to take. **2** *vi* (a) *(Schlag, Schuß etc)* to hit. **nicht** ~ to miss. (b) *aux sein (stoßen)* **auf jdn/etw** ~ to meet sb/sth. (c) *(verletzen)* to hurt. **3** *vr (zusammen~)* to meet. **4** *vr impers* **es trifft sich, daß** ... it (just) happens that ...; **das trifft sich gut/schlecht, daß** ... it is convenient/inconvenient that ...

**Treffen** *nt* - meeting; *(Sport, Mil)* encounter.

**treffend** *adj* apt; *Ähnlichkeit* striking.

**Treffer** *m* - hit; *(Tor)* goal; *(fig: Erfolg)* hit; *(Gewinnlos)* winner.

**Treff-**: **t~lich** *adj (liter)* splendid; ~**punkt** *m* meeting place; **t~sicher** *adj* accurate; *Urteil* sound; ~**sicherheit** *f* accuracy; *(von Urteil)* soundness; *(beim Schießen)* marksmanship.

**Treib|eis** *nt* drift ice.

**treiben** *pret* **trieb**, *ptp* **getrieben** **1** *vt* (a) *(lit, fig)* to drive; *(auf Treibjagd) Wild* to beat; *Teig* to make rise; *(fig: drängen)* to rush; *(an~)* to push. **jdn zum Wahnsinn** ~ to drive sb mad; **jdn zur Eile/Arbeit** ~ to make sb hurry up/work; **die** ~**de Kraft** the driving force; **jdm den Schweiß/das Blut ins Gesicht** ~ to make sb sweat/blush. (b) *Geschäfte, Sport* to do; *Studien, Politik* to pursue; *Gewerbe* to carry on; *Unsinn* to be up to; *Aufwand* to create. **was treibst du?** what are you up to?; **Handel mit etw/jdm** ~ to trade in sth/with sb. (c) *(col)* **wenn du es weiter so treibst** ... if you carry on like that ...; **es toll** ~ to have a wild time; **es zu weit** ~ to go too far; **es mit jdm** ~ to have it off with sb. (d) *Blüten etc* to sprout; *(im Treibhaus)* to force. **2** *vi* (a) *aux sein (sich fortbewegen)* to drift. **sich** ~ **lassen** *(lit, fig)* to drift. (b) *(wachsen)* to sprout. (c) *(Hefe)* to make dough *etc* rise. ~**de Medikamente** diuretics.

**Treiben** *nt* - *(Getriebe)* hustle and bustle; *(von Schneeflocken)* swirling.
**Treiber** *m* - *(Hunt)* beater; *(Vieh~)* drover; *(Comp)* driver.
**Treib-:** ~**gas** *nt* propellant; ~**gut** *nt* flotsam and jetsam *pl.*
**Treibhaus** *nt* hothouse.
**Treibhaus-:** ~**effekt** *m* greenhouse effect; ~**gas** *nt* greenhouse gas.
**Treib-:** ~**holz** *nt* driftwood; ~**jagd** *f* shoot *(in which game is sent up by beaters)*; *(fig)* witchhunt; ~**mittel** *nt* *(in Sprühdosen)* propellant; *(Cook)* raising agent; ~**sand** *m* quicksand; ~**stoff** *m* fuel.
**Tremolo** *nt, pl* -s *or* **Tremoli** *(Mus)* tremolo.
**Trend** *m* -s trend. **voll im** ~ **liegen** *(col)* to be really trendy.
**Trendwende** *f* new trend.
**trennbar** *adj* separable.
**trennen 1** *vt* (a) to separate *(von* from*)*; *Kopf, Glied etc* to sever; *(abmachen)* to detach *(von* from*)*; *Aufgenähtes* to take off, to remove; *Saum, Naht* to undo; *Begriffe* to distinguish (between); *(nach Rasse, Geschlecht)* to segregate. **jetzt kann uns nichts mehr** ~ now nothing can ever come between us. (b) *(in Bestandteile zerlegen) Kleid* to take to pieces; *Wort* to split; *(Chem) Gemisch* to separate (out). **2** *vr (auseinandergehen)* to separate; *(Partner, Eheleute etc auch)* to split up; *(Abschied nehmen)* to part; *(Wege, Flüsse)* to divide. **sich von jdm/der Firma** ~ to leave sb/the firm; **die zwei Mannschaften trennten sich 2:2** the final score was 2:2; **sich von etw** ~ to part with sth; **hier** ~ **sich unsere Wege** *(fig)* now we must go our separate ways.
**Trennschärfe** *f* selectivity.
**Trennung** *f* separation; *(Abschied)* parting; *(in Teile)* division; *(von Wort)* division; *(Rassen~, Geschlechter~)* segregation.
**Trenn(ungs)-:** ~**linie** *f* *(lit, fig)* dividing line; ~**strich** *m* hyphen; ~**wand** *f* partition (wall); ~**zeichen** *nt* hyphen.
**trepp|auf** *adv* ~, **treppab** up and down stairs.
**Treppe** *f* -n stairs *pl*, staircase; *(im Freien)* steps *pl*. **eine** ~ a staircase, a flight of stairs/steps; **sie wohnt zwei** ~**n höher** she lives two flights up.
**Treppen-:** ~**absatz** *m* half-landing; ~**geländer** *nt* banister; ~**haus** *nt* stairwell; **im** ~**haus** on the stairs; ~**stufe** *f* step, stair.
**Tresen** *m* - *(Theke)* bar; *(Ladentisch)* counter.
**Tresor** *m* -e safe; *(Raum)* strongroom, vault.
**Tret-:** ~**auto** *nt* pedal car; ~**boot** *nt* pedal boat, pedalo; ~**eimer** *m* pedal bin.
**treten** *pret* **trat,** *ptp* **getreten 1** *vi* (a) **gegen etw** ~ to kick sth. (b) *aux sein* to step. **näher an etw** *(acc)* ~ to move *or* step closer to sth; **ans Fenster** ~ to go to the window; **jdm auf den Fuß** ~ to step *or* tread on sb's foot; **jdm auf die Füße** ~ *(fig)* to tread on sb's toes; **an jds Stelle** ~ to take sb's place; **aufs Gas(pedal)** ~ to press the accelerator; *(col: schnell fahren)* to step on it *(col)*. (c) **der Schweiß trat ihm auf die Stirn** sweat appeared on his forehead; **der Fluß trat über die Ufer** the river overflowed its banks. (d) *aux sein* **in den Streik** ~ to go on strike; **in den Stand der Ehe** ~ to enter into matrimony. **2** *vt* to kick; *(Sport) Ecke, Freistoß* to take. **jdn ans Bein** ~ to kick sb on the leg; **jdn mit dem Fuß** ~ to kick sb.
**Treter** *m* - *(col)* comfortable shoe.
**Tret-:** ~**mine** *f* *(Mil)* (anti-personnel) mine; ~**mühle** *f* *(lit, fig)* treadmill; **in der** ~**mühle sein** to be in a rut *(col)*; ~**roller** *m* scooter.
**treu 1** *adj Freund, Sohn, Kunde etc* loyal; *Hund, Gat-*

*te etc* faithful; *Abbild* true; *(~herzig)* trusting; *Miene* innocent. ~ **sein/bleiben** to be/remain faithful to sb; **seinen Grundsätzen** ~ **bleiben** to stay true to one's principles. **2** *adv* faithfully; *sorgen* devotedly; *(~herzig)* trustingly; *ansehen* innocently. ~ **und brav** dutifully.
**Treu-:** ~**bruch** *m* breach of faith; **t~brüchig** *adj* faithless, false; **t~doof** *adj* *(col)* naive.
**Treue** *f no pl siehe* **treu** loyalty; faithfulness; *(eheliche ~)* faithfulness, fidelity.
**Treu|eid** *m* oath of allegiance.
**Treueprämie** *f* long-service bonus.
**Treu-:** ~**hand** *f* *(col)*, ~**handanstalt** *f* trustee organization *(overseeing the transfer of GDR state-owned firms to private ownership)*; ~**händer(in** *f)* *m* trustee; ~**handgesellschaft** *f* trust company; ~**handvermögen** *nt* trust fund; **t~herzig** *adj* trusting; **t~los** *adj* disloyal, faithless; **t~los an jdm handeln** to fail sb; ~**losigkeit** *f* disloyalty, faithlessness.
**Triangel** *m or* *(Aus)* *nt* - triangle.
**Tribunal** *nt* -e tribunal.
**Tribüne** *f* -n *(Redner~)* platform; *(Zuschauer~, Zuschauer)* stand; *(Haupt~)* grandstand.
**Tribut** *m* -e *(lit, fig)* tribute; *(Opfer)* toll.
**Trichine** *f* trichina.
**Trichter** *m* - funnel; *(Bomben~)* crater; *(von Trompete etc)* bell; *(von Hörgerät)* trumpet; *(von Lautsprecher)* cone; *(Einfüll~)* hopper. **auf den** ~ **kommen** *(col)* to catch on *(col)*.
**Trick** *m* -s trick. **keine faulen** ~**s!** no funny business! *(col)*; **das ist der ganze** ~ that's all there is to it; **der** ~ **dabei ist, ...** the trick is to ...; **jdm einen** ~ **verraten** to give sb a tip.
**Trick-:** ~**betrug** *m* confidence trick; ~**film** *m* trick film; *(Zeichen~)* cartoon (film); **t~reich** *adj* *(col)* tricky; *(raffiniert)* clever.
**trieb** *pret of* **treiben.**
**Trieb** *m* -e (a) *(Psych, Natur~)* drive; *(Drang, Verlangen)* urge; *(Neigung, Hang)* inclination; *(Selbsterhaltungs~)* instinct. (b) *(Bot)* shoot.
**Trieb-:** ~**feder** *f* *(fig)* motivating force *(gen* behind*)*; **t~haft** *adj Handlungen* compulsive; **sie ist ein t~hafter Mensch** she is ruled by her physical desires; ~**kraft** *f* *(Mech)* motive power; *(fig)* driving force; ~**leben** *nt* *(Geschlechtsleben)* sex life; ~**rad** *nt* driving wheel; ~**täter** *m* sexual offender; ~**wagen** *m* *(Rail)* railcar; ~**werk** *nt* power plant; *(Düsentriebwerk)* jet engine.
**triefen** *vi* to be dripping wet; *(Nase)* to run; *(Auge)* to water. ~ **vor** to be dripping with; *(fig pej)* to gush with; ~**d (naß)** dripping wet.
**triefnaß** *adj* dripping wet.
**triezen** *vt* *(col)* jdn ~ to pester sb; *(schuften lassen)* to drive sb hard.
**triftig** *adj* cogent.
**Trigonometrie** *f* trigonometry.
**Trikolore** *f* -n tricolour *(Brit)*, tricolor *(US)*.
**Trikot** [tri'ko:, 'triko] *nt* -s *(Hemd)* shirt, jersey.
**Triller** *m* - *(Mus)* trill.
**trillern** *vti* to warble, to trill.
**Trillerpfeife** *f* (pea-)whistle.
**Trillion** *f* -en trillion *(Brit)*, quintillion *(US)*.
**Trilobal-Anzug** *m* shell suit.
**Trilogie** *f* trilogy.
**Trimester** *nt* - term.
**Trimm-:** ~**-Aktion** *f* keep-fit campaign; ~**-dich-Gerät** *nt* keep-fit apparatus; ~**-dich-Pfad** *m* keep-fit trail.
**trimmen 1** *vt Hund, Schiff, Flugzeug* to trim; *(col) Mensch, Tier* to teach, to train. **2** *vr* to do keep-fit

(exercises). **trimm dich durch Sport** keep fit with sport.
**Trinidad** *nt* Trinidad.
**trinkbar** *adj* drinkable.
**trinken** *pret* **trank,** *ptp* **getrunken** *vti* to drink; *ein Bier, Tasse Tee, Flasche Wein auch* to have. **er trinkt gern einen** *(col)* he likes his drink; **jdm zu ~ geben** to give sb something to drink; **auf jdn/etw ~** to drink to sb/to sth.
**Trinker(in** *f)* *m* - drinker; *(Alkoholiker)* alcoholic.
**Trinkerheil|anstalt** *f (old)* detoxification centre *(Brit)* or center *(US).*
**Trink-:** **t~fest** *adj* **ich bin nicht sehr t~fest** I can't hold my drink very well; **~geld** *nt* tip; **jdm ~geld geben** to tip sb, to give sb a tip; **~halle** *f (Kiosk)* refreshment kiosk; **~halm** *m* drinking straw; **~milch** *f* milk; **~schokolade** *f* drinking chocolate; **~spruch** *m* toast; **~wasser** *nt* drinking water.
**Trio** *nt* **-s** trio.
**Triole** *f* **-n** *(Mus)* triplet.
**Trip** *m* **-s** *(col: Ausflug, Drogenrausch)* trip.
**Tripolis** *nt* Tripoli.
**trippeln** *vi aux haben or (bei Richtungsangabe) sein* to trip; *(Kind, alte Dame)* to toddle.
**Tripper** *m* - gonorrhoea *no art (Brit)*, gonorrhea *no art (US).*
**trist** *adj* dreary, dismal; *Farbe* dull.
**Tritt** *m* **-e (a)** *(Schritt)* step. **im ~ marschieren/~ halten** to march/keep in step; **~ fassen** to find one's feet. **(b)** *(Fuß~)* kick. **jdm einen ~ geben** to give sb a kick, to kick sb; *(fig) (entlassen etc)* to kick sb out *(col)*; *(col: anstacheln)* to give sb a kick up the backside *(col)*. **(c)** *(bei ~leiter, Stufe)* step; *(Gestell)* steps *pl.*
**Tritt-:** **~brett** *nt* step; *(an Auto)* running board; **~brettfahrer** *m (fig col)* free-rider *(col)*; **er ist ein politischer ~brettfahrer** he has jumped on a political bandwagon; **~leiter** *f* stepladder.
**Triumph** *m* **-(e)s, -e** triumph. **~e feiern** to be a triumphant success.
**Triumphbogen** *m* triumphal arch.
**triumphieren\*** *vi (frohlocken)* to rejoice, to exult. **über jdn/etw ~** *(geh)* to triumph over sb/sth.
**triumphierend** *adj* triumphant.
**Triumphzug** *m* triumphal procession.
**trivial** [tri'viaːl] *adj* trivial.
**Trivialität** [triviali'tɛt] *f* triviality.
**Trivialliteratur** [tri'viaːl-] *f* light fiction.
**trocken** *adj (lit, fig)* dry. **da bleibt kein Auge ~** everyone is moved to tears; **~ aufbewahren/lagern** to keep/store in a dry place; **sich ~ rasieren** to use an electric razor; **auf dem ~en sitzen** *(col)* to be in a tight spot *(col).*
**Trocken-:** **~automat** *m* tumble dryer; **~blume** *f* dried flower; **~boden** *m* drying room *(in attic)*; **~dock** *nt* dry dock; **~futter** *nt* dried food; **~haube** *f* (salon) hairdryer.
**Trockenheit** *f (lit, fig)* dryness; *(Dürre)* drought.
**Trocken-:** **~kurs** *m (Ski)* ski training course using dry slopes; **t~legen** *vt sep* **(a)** *Baby* to change; **(b)** *Sumpf* to drain; **~milch** *f* dried milk; **~zeit** *f (Jahreszeit)* dry season.
**trocknen 1** *vt* to dry. **2** *vi aux sein* to dry.
**Troddel** *f* **-n** tassel.
**Trödel** *m no pl (col)* junk.
**Trödelmarkt** *m (col)* flea market.
**trödeln** *vi* to dawdle.
**Trödler(in** *f)* *m* - **(a)** *(Händler)* junk dealer. **(b)** *(col: langsamer Mensch)* dawdler.
**Trog** *m* ꞉e trough; *(Wasch~)* tub.

**trog** *pret of* **trügen.**
**trollen** *vr (col)* to push off *(col).*
**Trommel** *f* **-n** *(Mus, Tech)* drum. **die ~ rühren** *(fig col)* to drum up support.
**Trommel-:** **~bremse** *f* drum brake; **~fell** *nt* eardrum; **~feuer** *nt* drumfire, heavy barrage.
**trommeln 1** *vi* to drum; *(Regen)* to beat (down). **mit den Fingern ~** to drum one's fingers. **2** *vt Marsch, Lied* to play on the drum/drums.
**Trommel-:** **~schlag** *m* drum beat; *(das Trommeln)* drumming; **~stöcke** *pl* drumsticks *pl*; **~wirbel** *m* drumroll.
**Trommler(in** *f)* *m* - drummer.
**Trompete** *f* **-n** trumpet.
**trompeten\* 1** *vi* to trumpet. **2** *vt Marsch etc* to play on the trumpet.
**Trompeter(in** *f)* *m* - trumpeter.
**Tropen** *pl* tropics *pl.*
**Tropen-** *in cpds* tropical; **~helm** *m* pith-helmet, topee; **~wald** *m* tropical rainforest.
**Tropf** *m* ꞉e *(col)* **(a)** *einfältiger ~* twit *(Brit col)*, dummy *(col)*; *armer ~* poor devil. **(b)** *no pl (Infusion)* drip *(col).* **am ~ hängen** to be on a/the drip.
**tröpfeln 1** *vi (Leitung, aux sein: Flüssigkeit)* to drip; *(Nase)* to run. **2** *vi impers* **es tröpfelt** it's spitting *(col).* **3** *vt* to drip.
**tropfen** *vi* to drip; *(Nase)* to run.
**Tropfen** *m* - drop; *(Schweiß~ auch)* bead; *(fallender ~)* drip; *(col: kleine Menge)* drop. **~ pl (Medizin)** drops; **ein guter or edler ~** *(col)* a good wine; **bis auf den letzten ~** to the last drop; **ein ~ auf den heißen Stein** *(fig col)* a drop in the ocean.
**tropfenweise** *adv* drop by drop.
**Tropf-:** **t~naß** *adj* dripping wet; **~steinhöhle** *f* cave with stalactites/stalagmites.
**Trophäe** [tro'fɛːə] *f* **-n** trophy.
**tropisch** *adj* tropical.
**Trost** *m no pl* consolation, comfort. **jdm ~ zusprechen** to comfort sb; **das ist ein schwacher** *(iro)* **~** some comfort that is!; **du bist wohl nicht ganz bei ~!** *(col)* you must be out of your mind!
**trösten** *vt* to comfort. **sich/jdn über etw** *(acc)* **~** to get over sth/to help sb to get over sth; **es tröstet mich, daß ...** it is a comfort to me that ...
**tröstlich** *adj* comforting.
**trostlos** *adj* hopeless; *Jugend, Verhältnisse* miserable, wretched; *(öde, trist)* dreary.
**Trost-:** **~pflaster** *nt* consolation; **~preis** *m* consolation prize; **t~reich** *adj* comforting.
**Tröstung** *f* comfort; *(das Trösten)* comforting.
**Trott** *m no pl* (slow) trot; *(fig)* routine. **im ~** at a (slow) trot; **in den alten ~ zurückfallen** *(fig)* to slip back into the old routine.
**Trottel** *m* - *(col)* idiot, dope *(col).*
**trotten** *vi aux sein* to trot along.
**Trottoir** [trɔ'toaːɐ] *nt* **-s** *(dated, S Ger)* pavement.
**trotz** *prep +gen (geh) or +dat (col)* in spite of, despite. **~ allem** in spite of everything.
**Trotz** *m no pl* defiance; *(trotziges Verhalten)* contrariness. **jdm/einer Sache zum ~** in defiance of sb/sth.
**Trotz|alter** *nt* defiant age.
**trotzdem** *adv* nevertheless. **(und) ich mache es ~!** I'll do it all the same.
**trotzen** *vi* **(a)** *+dat* to defy; *der Kälte, dem Klima etc* to withstand; *der Gefahr* to brave. **(b)** *(trotzig sein)* to be awkward.
**trotzig** *adj* defiant; *Kind etc* difficult, awkward.
**Trotz-:** **~kopf** *m (col)* contrary so-and-so *(col)*; **~reaktion** *f* act of defiance.
**trüb(e)** *adj* **(a)** dull; *Flüssigkeit* cloudy; *Sonne, Licht*

dim. **im ~en fischen** *(col)* to fish in troubled waters. **(b)** *(fig: bedrückend, unerfreulich) Zeiten* bleak; *Erfahrung* grim. **~e Tasse** *(col)* drip *(col)*.

**Trubel** *m no pl* hurly-burly.

**trüben 1** *vt* **(a)** *Flüssigkeit* to make cloudy; *Glas, Metall* to dull; *Blick* to cloud. **sie sieht aus, als könnte sie kein Wässerlein ~** *(col)* she looks as if butter wouldn't melt in her mouth. **(b)** *(fig) Glück, Verhältnis* to spoil; *Bewußtsein, Verstand* to dull. **2** *vr (Flüssigkeit)* to go cloudy; *(Spiegel, Metall)* to become dull; *(geh) (Verstand)* to become dulled; *(Augen)* to dim; *(Himmel)* to cloud over; *(Glück, Freude)* to be marred.

**Trüb-:** **~sal** *f* gloom; **~sal blasen** *(col)* to mope; **t~selig** *adj* gloomy; *Behausung, Wetter* miserable; **~sinn** *m no pl* gloom, melancholy; **t~sinnig** *adj* gloomy, melancholy.

**trudeln** *vi aux sein or haben (Aviat)* to spin.

**Trüffel¹** *f* **-n** *(Pilz)* truffle.

**Trüffel²** *m* **-** truffle.

**Trug** *m no pl (liter)* deception; *(der Sinne)* illusion.

**trügen** *pret* **trog**, *ptp* **getrogen 1** *vt* to deceive. **wenn mich nicht alles trügt** unless I am very much mistaken. **2** *vi* to be deceptive.

**trügerisch** *adj (irreführend)* deceptive.

**Trugschluß** *m* fallacy.

**Truhe** *f* **-n** chest.

**Trümmer** *pl* rubble *sing*; *(Ruinen, fig: von Glück etc)* ruins *pl*; *(von Schiff, Flugzeug etc)* wreckage *sing*; *(Überreste)* remnants *pl*. **etw in ~ schlagen** to smash sth to pieces.

**Trümmer-:** **~feld** *nt* expanse of rubble/ruins; *(fig)* scene of devastation; **~haufen** *m* heap of rubble.

**Trumpf** *m* **⁼e** *(Cards)* (**~karte**, *auch fig*) trump card; *(Farbe)* trumps *pl*. **~ sein** to be trumps; *(fig col: modisch sein)* to be in *(col)*; **den ~ in der Hand haben/ aus der Hand geben** *(fig)* to hold the/throw away one's trump card.

**trumpfen 1** *vt* to trump. **2** *vi* to play a trump (card).

**Trumpf-:** **~farbe** *f* trumps *pl*; **~karte** *f (lit, fig)* trump (card).

**Trunk** *m* **⁼e** **(a)** *(old, liter)* draught *(old, liter)*. **(b)** **dem ~ verfallen sein** to be addicted to drink.

**Trunken-:** **~bold** *m* **-e** *(pej)* drunkard; **~heit** *f* drunkenness; **~heit am Steuer** drunken *or* drink driving.

**Trunksucht** *f* alcoholism.

**Trupp** *m* **-s** *(Einheit)* group; *(Mil)* squad.

**Truppe** *f* **-n** **(a)** *(Mil)* army, troops *pl*; *(Panzer~ etc)* corps *sing*. **~n** *pl* troops; **nicht von der schnellen ~ sein** *(col)* to be a slow worker. **(b)** *(Künstler~)* troupe, company.

**Truppen-:** **~abbau** *m* cutback in troop numbers; **~gattung** *f* corps *sing*; **~übung** *f* field exercise; **~übungsplatz** *m* military training area.

**Trut-:** **~hahn** *m* turkey(cock); **~henne** *f* turkey (hen); **~huhn** *nt usu pl* turkey.

**Tschad** *m* **-** **der ~** Chad.

**tschadisch** *adj* Chad *attr*.

**Tscheche** *m* **(wk)** **-n, -n, Tschechin** *f* Czech.

**Tschechien** [-iən] *nt* the Czech Republic.

**tschechisch** *adj* Czech. **T~e Republik** Czech Republic.

**Tschechoslowakei** *f (Hist)* **die ~** Czechoslovakia.

**tschüs** *interj (col)* cheerio *(Brit col)*, so long *(col)*.

**Tsetsefliege** *f* tsetse fly.

**TU** [te:'|u:] *f* **-** = **Technische Universität.**

**Tuba** *f*, *pl* **Tuben** *(Mus)* tuba.

**Tube** *f* **-n** tube. **auf die ~ drücken** *(col)* to get a move on *(col)*.

**Tuberkulose** *f* **-n** tuberculosis.

**tuberkulosekrank** *adj* tubercular.

**Tuch** *nt* **⁼er** **(a)** cloth; *(Hals~, Kopf~)* scarf. **das wirkt wie ein rotes ~ auf ihn** it's like a red rag to a bull. **(b)** *pl* **-e** *(old: Stoff)* cloth.

**Tuch-:** **~fabrik** *f* textile factory; **~fühlung** *f* physical contact; **auf ~fühlung mit jdm sein** to be close up against sb; **~händler** *m* cloth merchant.

**tüchtig 1** *adj* **(a)** *(fähig)* competent *(in +dat* at*)*; *(fleißig)* efficient. **etwas T~es lernen/werden** *(col)* to get a proper training/job; **~, ~!** not bad! **(b)** *(col: groß) Portion* big. **2** *adv* **(a)** *(fleißig, fest)* hard; *essen* heartily. **hilf ~ mit** go on, do your bit. **(b)** *(col: sehr)* good and proper *(col)*. **~ regnen** to pelt down *(col)*; **~ zulangen** to tuck in *(col)*.

**Tüchtigkeit** *f (Fähigkeit)* competence; *(von Arbeiter etc)* efficiency.

**Tücke** *f* **-n** **(a)** *(no pl: Bosheit)* malice, spite. **(b)** *(Gefahr)* danger, peril; *(von Krankheit)* perniciousness. **voller ~n stecken** to be difficult; *(gefährlich)* to be treacherous; **seine ~n haben** *(Maschine etc)* to be temperamental. **(c)** *(des Schicksals)* vagary *usu pl*.

**tückisch** *adj Mensch* malicious, spiteful; *Berge, Strom* treacherous; *Krankheit* pernicious.

**tüfteln** *vi (col)* to puzzle; *(basteln)* to fiddle about *(col)*. **an etw** *(dat)* **~** to fiddle about with sth; *(geistig)* to puzzle over sth.

**Tüftler(in** *f)* *m* **-** *(col) person who likes doing fiddly or finicky things.*

**Tugend** *f* **-en** virtue.

**Tugend-:** **~bold** *m* **-e** *(pej)* paragon of virtue; **t~haft** *adj* virtuous.

**Tukan** *m* **-e** toucan.

**Tüll** *m* **-e** tulle; *(für Gardinen)* net.

**Tülle** *f* **-n** spout.

**Tulpe** *f* **-n** *(Bot)* tulip; *(Glas)* tulip glass.

**tummeln** *vr* **(a)** to romp (about). **(b)** *(sich beeilen)* to hurry.

**Tummelplatz** *m* play area; *(fig)* hotbed.

**Tümmler** *m* **-** (bottle-nosed) dolphin.

**Tumor** *m* **-en** [tu'mo:rən] tumour *(Brit)*, tumor *(US)*.

**Tümpel** *m* **-** pond.

**Tumult** *m* **-e** commotion.

**tun** *pret* **tat**, *ptp* **getan 1** *vt* **(a)** to do; *Blick, Schritt* to take. **was ~?** what shall we do?; **du kannst ~ und lassen, was du willst** you can do as you please; **tu, was du nicht lassen kannst** well, if you must, you must; **damit ist es noch nicht getan** and that's not all; **etwas gegen etw ~** to do something about sth; **Sie müssen etwas für sich ~** *(sich etwas gönnen)* you should treat yourself; *(sich schonen)* you should take care of yourself; **so etwas tut man nicht!** that's just not done; **das hat nichts mit ihm zu ~** that is nothing to do with him; **ich habe mit mir (selbst) genug zu ~** I have enough problems of my own; **es mit jdm zu ~ bekommen** *(col)* to get into trouble with sb; **er hat es mit der Leber zu ~** *(col)* he has liver trouble; **was tut's?** what difference does it make?; **jdm etwas ~** to do something to sb; *(stärker)* to harm *or* hurt sb.

**(b)** *(col: an bestimmten Ort legen)* to put. **etw in die Tasche ~** to put sth in one's pocket.

**(c)** *(col: funktionieren)* **die Uhr tut es nicht mehr** this watch has had it *(col)*; **das Radio tut es wieder** the radio is going again.

**2** *vr (geschehen)* **es tut sich etwas** there is something happening; **hat sich in dieser Hinsicht schon etwas getan?** has anything been done about this?

**3** *vi* **(a) zu ~ haben** *(beschäftigt sein)* to be busy, to have work to do; **in der Stadt zu ~ haben** to have things to do in town; **mit jdm zu ~ haben** to deal with sb. **(b)** *(sich benehmen)* to act. **so ~, als ob ...** to pretend that ...; **tust du nur so dumm?** are you just acting stupid?; **sie tut nur so** she's only pretending. **(c) Sie täten gut daran, früh zu kommen** you would do well to come early.

**Tünche** *f* **-n** whitewash; *(fig)* veneer.

**tünchen** *vt* to whitewash.

**Tundra** *f, pl* **Tundren** tundra.

**Tunesien** [-iən] *nt* Tunisia.

**Tunesier(in** *f)* [-iɐ, -iərɪn] *m* - Tunisian.

**tunesisch** *adj* Tunisian.

**Tunichtgut** *m* **-e** good-for-nothing.

**Tunke** *f* **-n** sauce; *(Braten~)* gravy.

**tunken** *vt* to dip; *(stippen)* to dunk *(col)*; *jdn* to duck.

**tunlichst** *adv* if (at all) possible. **~ bald** as soon as possible.

**Tunnel** *m* - *or* **-s** tunnel.

**Tunte** *f* **-n** *(col)* fairy *(pej col)*, pansy *(pej col)*.

**Tüpfel** *m or nt* **-, Tüpfelchen** *nt* dot.

**tupfen** *vt* to dab. **getupft** spotted.

**Tupfen** *m* - spot; *(klein)* dot.

**Tupfer** *m* - swab.

**Tür** *f* **-en** door; *(Garten~)* gate. **in der ~** in the doorway; **an die ~ gehen** to answer the door; **Weihnachten steht vor der ~** Christmas is just around the corner; **jdn vor die ~ setzen** *(col)* to throw sb out; **jdm die ~ weisen** to show sb the door; **ein jeder kehre vor seiner ~** *(prov)* everyone should set his own house in order; **mit der ~ ins Haus fallen** *(col)* to blurt it/things out; **zwischen ~ und Angel** in passing.

**Tür|angel** *f* (door) hinge.

**Turban** *m* **-e** turban.

**Turbine** *f* turbine.

**Turbinenflugzeug** *nt* turbojet.

**Turbo** *m* **-s** *(Aut)* turbo.

**Turbo-**: **~lader** *m* turbocharger; **~motor** *m* turbocharged engine.

**turbulent** *adj* turbulent.

**Turbulenz** *f* turbulence *no pl.*

**Tür-**: **~drücker** *m* doorknob; *(col: Öffner)* buzzer; **~flügel** *m* door *(of a pair of doors)*; **~griff** *m* door handle.

**Türke** *m* *(wk)* **-n, -n, Türkin** *f* Turk.

**Türkei** *f* **die ~** Turkey.

**türken** *vt* *(col)* *Papiere, Zahlen* to fiddle. **getürkte Belege** falsified documents.

**Türkis** *m* **-e** *(Edelstein)* turquoise.

**türkis** *adj* turquoise.

**türkisch** *adj* Turkish.

**Türkisch(e)** *nt* Turkish; *siehe* **Deutsch(e)**.

**Tür-**: **~klinke** *f* door handle; **~klopfer** *m* doorknocker.

**Turm** *m* ⁼**e** **(a)** tower; *(spitzer Kirch~)* spire. **(b)** *(Chess)* castle, rook.

**türmen 1** *vt* to pile up. **2** *vr* to pile up; *(Wolken)* to build up; *(Wellen)* to tower up. **3** *vi aux sein (col: davonlaufen)* to run off.

**Turm-**: **~falke** *m* kestrel; **~schwalbe** *f* swift; **~uhr** *f* clock (on a/the tower); *(Kirch~uhr)* church clock.

**Turn|anzug** *m* leotard.

**turnen** *vi* **(a)** to do gymnastics; *(Sch)* to do gym. **am Reck ~** to do exercises on the horizontal bar. **(b)** *aux sein (herumklettern)* to climb about; *(Kind)* to romp.

**Turnen** *nt no pl* gymnastics *sing*; *(Sch)* gym, PE

*(col)*.

**Turner(in** *f)* *m* - gymnast.

**turnerisch** *adj* gymnastic.

**Turn-**: **~fest** *nt* gymnastics display; *(von Schule)* sports day; **~gerät** *nt* (piece of) gymnastic apparatus; **~halle** *f* gym(nasium); **~hemd** *nt* gym singlet; **~hose** *f* gym shorts *pl*.

**Turnier** *nt* **-e** tournament; *(Tanz~)* competition; *(Reit~)* show.

**Turnierpferd** *nt* show horse.

**Turn-**: **~lehrer** *m* gym teacher; **~schuh** *m* gym shoe; *(Trainingsschuh)* trainer, sneaker *(US)*; **~stunde** *f* gym lesson; **~übung** *f* gymnastic exercise.

**Turnus** *m* **-se** rota. **im (regelmäßigen) ~** in rotation.

**Turn-**: **~verein** *m* gymnastics club; **~zeug** *nt* gym kit.

**Tür-**: **~öffner** *m* buzzer (for opening the door); **~pfosten** *m* doorpost; **~rahmen** *m* doorframe; **~schild** *nt* doorplate; **~schloß** *nt* door lock; **~schwelle** *f* threshold; **~sprechanlage** *f* entryphone.

**turteln** *vi* to bill and coo.

**Turteltaube** *f (lit, fig col)* turtle-dove.

**Türvorleger** *m* doormat.

**Tusch** *m* **-e** *(Mus)* flourish.

**Tusche** *f* **-n** *(Auszieh~)* Indian ink; *(~farbe)* water colour *(Brit)* or color *(US)*.

**tuscheln** *vti* to whisper. **hinter seinem Rücken über jdn ~** to talk about sb behind his/her back.

**tuschen** *vt* to draw in Indian ink. **sich** *(dat)* **die Wimpern ~** to put one's mascara on.

**Tusch-**: **~farbe** *f* water colour *(Brit)* or color *(US)*; **~zeichnung** *f* pen-and-ink drawing.

**Tussi** *f* **-s** *(col)* female *(col)*.

**Tüte** *f* **-n** bag; *(Eis~)* cornet, cone; *(col: für Alkoholtest)* breathalyzer. **in die ~ blasen** *(col)* to be breathalyzed; **~n kleben** *(col)* to be in clink *(col)*; **das kommt nicht in die ~!** *(col)* no way! *(col)*.

**tuten** *vti* to toot; *(Schiff)* to sound its horn. **von T~ und Blasen keine Ahnung haben** *(col)* not to have a clue *(col)*.

**TÜV** [tyf] *m* **-s = Technischer Überwachungs-Verein** ≃ MOT *(Brit)*, vehicle inspection *(US)*. **das Auto ist durch den ~ gekommen** the car passed its MOT *or* vehicle inspection.

**TV** [teːˈfaʊ] *nt* **= Television** TV.

**Twen** *m* **-s** *person in his/her twenties*.

**Typ** *n* **-en** type; *(von Auto auch)* model; *(col: Mensch)* person, character; *(col: Mann, Freund)* guy *(col)*. **sie ist ein dunkler/blonder ~** she's dark/fair; **er ist nicht mein ~** *(col)* he's not my type *(col)*; **dein ~ wird verlangt** *(col)* you're wanted; **dein ~ ist nicht gefragt** *(col)* you're not wanted around here.

**Type** *f* **-n (a)** *(Druckbuchstabe)* character. **~n** *(Schrift)* type *sing*. **(b)** *(col: Mensch)* character.

**Typenrad** *nt* daisy wheel.

**Typenraddrucker** *m* daisy wheel printer.

**Typhus** *m no pl* typhoid (fever).

**Typhuskranke(r)** *mf* typhoid case.

**typisch** *adj* typical *(für of)*. **~ deutsch** typically German; **das ist ~ Mann/Frau** that's just typical of a man/woman.

**Typographie** *f* typography.

**Tyrann(in** *f)* *m (wk)* **-en, -en** tyrant.

**Tyrannei** *f* tyranny.

**tyrannisch** *adj* tyrannical.

**tyrannisieren\*** *vt* to tyrannize.

# U

**U, u** [uː] *nt* -, - U, u. **U wie Ulrich** ≃ U for Uncle.
**u.** = **und**.
**u.a.** = **und andere(s)**; **unter anderem/anderen**.
**u.ä.** = **und ähnliche(s)**.
**u.A.w.g.** = **um Antwort wird gebeten** RSVP.
**U-Bahn** ['uː-] *f* underground *(Brit)*, subway *(US)*; *(in London)* tube.
**U-Bahnhof** ['uː-] *m* underground *(Brit)* or subway *(US)* station.
**übel 1** *adj* bad; *Erkältung etc auch* nasty; *(moralisch auch)* wicked, evil. **er war übler Laune** he was in a bad mood; **das ist eine üble Sache!** it's a bad business; **in übler** *or* **~ster Weise** in a most unpleasant way; **mir wird ~** I feel sick. **2** *adv* badly. **etw ~ aufnehmen** to take sth badly; **das schmeckt gar nicht so ~** it doesn't taste so bad; **ich hätte nicht ~ Lust, jetzt nach Paris zu fahren** I wouldn't mind going to Paris now.
**Übel** *nt* - evil. **ein notwendiges/das kleinere ~** a necessary/the lesser evil; **das alte ~** the old trouble; **von ~ sein** to be a bad thing, to be bad; **zu allem ~** ... to make matters worse ...
**übelgelaunt** *adj attr* sullen, morose.
**Übelkeit** *f (lit, fig)* nausea.
**Übel-:** **ü~launig** *adj* ill-tempered; **ü~nehmen** *vt sep* **irreg etw ü~nehmen** to take sth amiss; **jdm etw ü~nehmen** to hold sth against sb; **ü~riechend** *adj* foul-smelling, evil-smelling; **~stand** *m* (social) evil *or* ill; **~täter** *m (geh)* wrongdoer.
**üben** *vtir* to practise *(Brit)*, to practice *(US)*; *(Mil)* to drill; *Gedächtnis, Muskeln etc* to exercise. **mit geübtem Auge** with a practised eye; **Kritik an etw** *(dat)* **~** to criticize sth; **sich in etw** *(dat)* **~** to practise sth.
**über 1** *prep* **(a)** +*acc (räumlich)* over; *(quer ~ auch)* across; *(weiter als)* beyond. **er lachte ~ das ganze Gesicht** he was beaming all over his face.
**(b)** +*dat (räumlich) (Lage, Standort)* over, above; *(jenseits)* over, across. **zwei Grad ~ Null** two degrees above zero; **~ jdm stehen** *(fig)* to be over *or* above sb.
**(c)** +*dat (zeitlich: bei, während)* over. **~ der Arbeit einschlafen** to fall asleep over one's work.
**(d)** +*acc* **Macht ~ jdn haben** to have power over sb; **sie liebt ihn ~ alles** she loves him more than anything; **das geht mir ~ den Verstand** that's beyond my understanding.
**(e)** +*acc (vermittels, auf dem Wege ~)* via. **die Nummer erfährt man ~ die Auskunft** you'll get the number from *or* through *or* via directory enquiries; **nach Köln ~ Aachen** to Cologne via Aachen.
**(f)** +*acc (zeitlich)* over. **~ Weihnachten** over Christmas; **den ganzen Sommer ~** all summer long; **~ Wochen** for weeks on end; **die ganze Zeit ~** all the time; **~ kurz oder lang** sooner or later.
**(g)** +*acc (bei Zahlenangaben)* **ein Scheck ~ DM200** a cheque for 200 DM; **Kinder ~ 14 Jahre** children over 14 years *or* of 14 and over.

**(h)** +*acc (betreffend)* about. **ein Buch ~ ...** a book about *or* on ...; **~ jdn/etw lachen** to laugh about *or* at sb/sth; **sich ~ etw freuen/ärgern** to be pleased/angry about *or* at sth.
**(i)** +*acc (steigernd)* **Fehler ~ Fehler** mistake upon *or* after mistake.
**2** *adv* **~ und ~** all over; **er wurde ~ und ~ rot** he went red all over.
**über|all** *adv* everywhere. **~ wo** wherever; **~ Bescheid wissen** *(wissensmäßig)* to have a wide-ranging knowledge; **es ist ~ dasselbe** it's the same wherever you go.
**über|all-:** **~her** *adv* from all over; **~hin** *adv* everywhere.
**Über-:** **ü~altert** *adj Gesellschaft* excessively geriatric; **~angebot** *nt* surplus *(an* +*dat* of*)*; **ü~ängstlich** *adj* overanxious; **ü~anstrengen\*** *insep* **1** *vt* to overstrain; *Kräfte* to overtax; *Augen* to strain; **2** *vr* to overstrain oneself; **~anstrengung** *f* overexertion; **eine ~anstrengung der Nerven/Augen** a strain on the nerves/eyes; **ü~antworten\*** *vt insep (geh)* **jdm etw ü~antworten** to entrust sth to sb; **ü~arbeiten\*** *insep* **1** *vt* to rework; **in einer ü~arbeiteten Fassung** published in a revised edition; **2** *vr* to overwork; **~arbeitung** *f no pl* **(a)** revision; **(b)** *(~anstrengung)* overwork; **ü~aus** *adv* extremely; **ü~backen\*** *vt insep irreg* to put in the oven/under the grill; **ü~backene Käseschnitten** cheese on toast.
**Überbau** *m* -e *(Build, Philos)* superstructure.
**überbauen\*** *vt insep* to build over; *(mit einem Dach)* to build a roof over.
**Über-:** **ü~beanspruchen\*** *vt insep* **(a)** *Menschen, Körper* to overtax; *Maschine* to overload; **(b)** *(arbeitsmäßig)* **ü~beansprucht sein** to be overworked; **(b)** *Einrichtungen, Dienste* to overburden; **ü~belegen\*** *vt insep usu ptp* to overcrowd; *Kursus, Fach etc* to oversubscribe; **ü~belichten\*** *vt insep (Phot)* to overexpose; **~beschäftigung** *f* overemployment; **ü~besetzt** *adj Abteilung* overstaffed; **~besetzung** *f* overmanning; **ü~betonen\*** *vt insep (fig)* to over-emphasize; **ü~betrieblich** *adj* industry-wide; **~bevölkerung** *f* overpopulation; **ü~bewerten\*** *vt insep (lit)* to overvalue; *(fig auch)* to overrate; *Schulleistung etc* to mark too high; *Äußerungen* to attach too much importance to; **~bezahlung** *f* overpayment; **ü~bieten\*** *insep irreg* **1** *vt (bei Auktion)* to outbid *(um* by*)*; *(fig)* to outdo; *Leistung, Rekord* to beat; **das ist kaum noch zu ü~bieten** *(Frechheit etc)* that's just about the limit!; **2** *vr* **sich in etw** *(dat)* **(gegenseitig) ü~bieten** to vie with each other in sth; **~bleibsel** *nt* - remnant; *(Speisereste)* left-overs *pl*; *(Brauch, Angewohnheit etc)* survival, hangover.
**Überblick** *m (über* +*acc* of*)* **(a)** *(freie Sicht)* view. **(b)** *(Einblick)* overview. **er hat keinen ~** he has no overall picture; **den ~ verlieren** to lose track (of things). **(c)** *(Abriß)* survey; *(Übersicht)* synopsis,

summary. **sich** *(dat)* **einen** ~ **verschaffen** to get a general idea.

**überblicken\*** *vt insep* **(a)** *(lit)* *Platz, Stadt* to overlook. **(b)** *(fig)* to see; *Lage etc auch* to grasp.

**überbringen\*** *vt insep irreg* **jdm etw** ~ to bring sb sth.

**Überbringer(in** *f)* *m* - bringer; *(von Scheck)* bearer.

**überbrücken\*** *vt insep Kluft, Zeitraum* to bridge; *Krisenzeiten* to get over; *Gegensätze* to reconcile.

**Überbrückung** *f* **hier sind 100 Mark zur** ~ here are 100 marks to tide you over.

**Überbrückungskredit** *m* bridging loan.

**Über-:** **ü~buchen\*** *vt insep* to overbook; **ü~dachen\*** *vt insep* to cover; **ü~dauern\*** *vt insep* to survive; **~decke** *f* bedspread; **ü~decken¹** *vt sep* to cover up *or* over; **jdm etw ü~decken** to cover sb with sth; **ü~decken²\*** *vt insep Riß, Geschmack* to cover up; **ü~dehnen\*** *vt insep Muskel etc* to strain; *Gummi, (fig) Begriff* to overstretch; **ü~denken\*** *vt insep irreg* to think over.

**überdies** *adv (geh) (außerdem)* moreover; *(ohnehin)* anyway.

**Über-:** **ü~dimensional** *adj* colossal, oversize; **~dosis** *f* overdose; *(zu große Zumessung)* excessive amount; **eine ~dosis nehmen** to (take an) overdose; **ü~drehen\*** *vt insep Uhr etc* to overwind; *Gewinde* to strip; **ü~dreht** *adj (col)* overexcited; **~druck** *m, pl* **~drücke** *(Tech)* excess pressure *no pl;* **ü~drucken** *vt insep* to overprint.

**Überdruß** *m no pl (Übersättigung)* surfeit *(an +dat of); (Widerwille)* aversion *(an +dat to).* **bis zum** ~ ad nauseam.

**überdrüssig** *adj* **jds/einer Sache** *(gen)* ~ **sein/werden** to be/grow weary of sb/sth.

**über-:** **~durchschnittlich 1** *adj* above-average; **2** *adv* exceptionally; **~eck** *adv* at right angles (to each other); **~eifrig** *adj* overzealous; **~eignen\*** *vt insep (geh)* **jdm etw ~eignen** to make sth over to sb; **~eilen\*** *vtr insep* to rush; **~eilen Sie nichts!** don't rush things!; **~eilt** *adj* (too) hasty.

**über|einander** *adv* **(a)** *(räumlich)* on top of each other; *hängen, wohnen* one above the other. **(b)** *reden etc* about each other.

**über|einander-:** **~legen** *vt sep* to put one on top of the other; **~liegen** *vi sep irreg* to lie on top of each other; **~schlagen** *vt sep irreg* **die Beine ~schlagen** to cross one's legs.

**über|einkommen** *vi sep irreg aux sein* to agree.

**Über|einkunft** *f* ⁼e agreement. **eine** ~ **treffen/erzielen** to make/reach an agreement.

**über|einstimmen** *vi sep* to agree; *(Angaben, Meßwerte etc)* to tally; *(Farben, Stile etc)* to match; *(mit Tatsachen)* to fit. **mit jdm in etw** *(dat)* ~ to agree with sb on sth.

**über|einstimmend 1** *adj* corresponding; *Meinungen* concurring; *Farben* matching. **nach ~en Meldungen** according to all reports. **2** *adv* **alle erklärten ~, daß** ... everybody agreed that ...

**Über|einstimmung** *f* correspondence, agreement; *(von Meinung)* agreement. **zwei Dinge in** ~ **bringen** to bring two things into line; **darin besteht bei allen Beteiligten** ~ all parties involved are agreed on that; **in** ~ **mit jdm/etw** in agreement with sb/in accordance with sth.

**über-:** **~empfindlich** *adj (gegen to)* oversensitive, hypersensitive *(auch Med);* **~erfüllen\*** *vt insep Norm, Soll* to exceed *(um by);* **~ernähren\*** *vt insep* to overfeed; **~essen** *pret* **~aß,** *ptp* **~gegessen** *vr insep* to overeat; **sich an Käse ~essen** to eat too much cheese.

**überfahren¹** *sep irreg* **1** *vt (mit Boot etc)* to take *or* ferry across. **2** *vi aux sein* to cross over.

**überfahren²\*** *vt insep irreg* **(a)** *jdn, Tier* to run over, to knock down. **(b)** *(hinwegfahren über)* to go *or* drive over. **(c)** *Ampel* to jump. **(d)** *(col: übertölpeln)* **jdn** ~ to stampede sb into it.

**Überfahrt** *f* crossing *(über +acc of).*

**Überfall** *m* attack *(auf +acc on); (auf offener Straße auch)* mugging *(auf +acc of); (auf Bank etc)* raid *(auf +acc on).*

**überfallen\*** *vt insep irreg* **(a)** to attack; *(auf offener Straße auch)* to mug; *Bank, Lager* to raid. **(b)** *(fig geh: Gefühle, Müdigkeit)* to come over.

**Über-:** **ü~fällig** *adj* overdue *usu pred;* **~fallkommando** *nt* flying squad; **ü~fliegen\*** *vt insep irreg* **(a)** to fly over, to overfly; **(b)** *(flüchtig ansehen) Buch etc* to take a quick look at; **~flieger** *m (fig)* high-flier; **ü~fließen** *vi sep irreg aux sein (Gefäß)* to overflow; *(fig: vor Dank etc auch)* to gush *(vor +dat with);* **ü~flügeln\*** *vt insep* to outdo.

**Überfluß** *m no pl* abundance *(an +dat of); (Luxus)* affluence. **Arbeit im** ~ plenty of work; **im** ~ **leben** to live in luxury; **zu allem** *or* **zum** ~ *(unnötigerweise)* superfluously; *(obendrein)* to crown it all *(col).*

**Überflußgesellschaft** *f* affluent society.

**überflüssig** *adj* superfluous; *(frei, entbehrlich)* spare; *(unnötig)* unnecessary; *(zwecklos)* useless.

**überflüssigerweise** *adv* superfluously.

**Über-:** **ü~fluten\*** *vt insep (lit, fig)* to flood; *(fig auch)* to inundate; **ü~fordern\*** *vt insep* to overtax; *jdn auch* to ask too much of; **ü~fragt** *adj pred* stumped; **da bin ich ü~fragt** there you've got me; **ü~fremden\*** *vt insep* to subject to too many foreign influences; **ü~fremdet** *adj (Land)* swamped by foreigners; **~fremdung** *f no pl* excessive foreign influence.

**überführen¹** *vt sep* to transfer; *Leiche* to transport; *Wagen* to drive.

**überführen²\*** *vt insep irreg* **(a)** *siehe* **überführen¹;** **(b)** *Täter* to convict *(gen of),* to find guilty *(gen of);* **(c)** **einen Fluß mit einer Brücke** ~ to build a bridge over a river.

**Überführung** *f* **(a)** transportation; **(b)** *no pl (Jur)* conviction; **(c)** *(Brücke über Straße etc)* bridge *(auch Rail),* overpass; *(Fußgänger~)* footbridge.

**über-:** **ü~füllt** *adj* overcrowded; *Kurs* oversubscribed; *(Comm) Lager* overstocked; **~füttern\*** *vt insep* to overfeed.

**Übergabe** *f no pl* handing over *no pl; (von Neubau)* opening; *(Mil)* surrender.

**Übergang** *m* **(a)** *(das Überqueren)* crossing. **(b)** *(Fußgänger~)* crossing, crosswalk *(US); (Brücke)* footbridge; *(Rail)* level *(Brit)* or grade *(US)* crossing. **(c)** *(fig: Wechsel)* transition.

**Übergangs-:** **~erscheinung** *f* temporary phenomenon; **ü~los** *adj* without a transition; **~lösung** *f* temporary solution; **~regierung** *f* caretaker government; **~stadium** *nt* transitional stage; **~zeit** *f* transitional period.

**übergeben\*** *insep irreg* **1** *vt* to hand over *(jdm to sb); (Mil auch)* to surrender. **eine Straße dem Verkehr** ~ to open a road to traffic. **2** *vr (sich erbrechen)* to vomit, to be sick *(Brit).*

**übergehen¹** *vi sep irreg aux sein* **(a)** **in etw** *(acc)* ~ to turn *or* change into sth; *(Farben)* to merge into sth; **in jds Besitz** *(acc)* ~ to become sb's property. **(b)** **auf jdn** ~ *(geerbt, übernommen werden)* to pass to sb. **(c)** **zu etw** ~ to change over to sth.

**übergehen²\*** *vt insep irreg* **jdn** to pass over; *Einwände etc auch* to ignore.

**Über-:** **ü~geordnet** *adj Behörde* higher; **~gepäck**

*nt* excess baggage; **ü~geschnappt** *adj (col)* crazy; **~gewicht** *nt* overweight; *(fig)* predominance; **~gewicht haben** to be overweight; **ü~gießen\*** *vt insep irreg* to pour over; *jdn* to douse; *Braten* to baste; **jdn/sich mit etw ü~gießen** to pour sth over sb/oneself; **ü~glücklich** *adj* overjoyed; **ü~greifen** *vi sep irreg (auf Rechte etc)* to encroach *(auf +acc* on*); (Feuer, Streik, Krankheit etc)* to spread *(auf +acc* to*);* **ineinander ü~greifen** to overlap; **ü~greifend** *adj (fig) Überlegungen* general; **~griff** *m (Einmischung)* encroachment *(auf +acc* on*); (Mil)* incursion *(auf +acc* into*);* **~größe** *f (bei Kleidung)* outsize; **ü~haben** *vt sep irreg (col)* **(a)** *(satt haben)* to be sick of *(col);* **(b)** *(übrig haben)* to have left (over); **für etw nichts ü~haben** not to like sth.

**überhandnehmen** *vi sep irreg* to get out of hand.

**Über-:** **~hang** *m* **(a)** *(Fels~)* overhang; **(b)** *(Comm: Überschuß)* surplus *(an +dat* of*);* **ü~hängen** *sep* **1** *vi irreg aux haben or sein* to overhang; **2** *vt* **sich** *(dat)* **einen Mantel ü~hängen** to put a coat over one's shoulders; **ü~hastet** *adj* overhasty; **ü~hastet sprechen** to speak too fast; **ü~häufen\*** *vt insep jdn* to overwhelm; **jdn mit Geschenken/ Vorwürfen ü~häufen** to heap presents/reproaches on sb.

**überhaupt** *adv* **(a)** *(in Fragen, Verneinungen)* at all. **~ nicht** not at all; **~ kein Grund** no reason at all *or* whatsoever; **hast du denn ~ keinen Anstand?** have you no decency at all?; **das habe ich ja ~ nicht gewußt** I had no idea at all. **(b)** *(sowieso, im allgemeinen)* in general; *(überdies, außerdem)* anyway, anyhow. **er ist ~ sehr schüchtern** he's altogether very shy; **er sagt ~ immer sehr wenig** he never says very much anyway *or* anyhow. **(c)** *(erst, eigentlich)* **waren Sie ~ schon in dem neuen Film?** have you actually been to the latest film?; **wenn ~** if at all; **wie ist das ~ möglich?** how is that (even) possible?; **wer sind Sie ~?** who are you anyway?

**über-:** **~heblich** *adj* arrogant; **Ü~heblichkeit** *f no pl* arrogance; **~hitzen\*** *vt insep* to overheat; **~hitzt** *adj (fig) Diskussion* very heated; **~höht** *adj Forderungen, Preise* exorbitant.

**überholen\*** *vti insep* **(a)** *Fahrzeug* to overtake *(Brit),* to pass; *(fig: übertreffen)* to overtake. **(b)** *Motor etc* to overhaul.

**Überhol-:** **~manöver** *nt* passing manoeuvre; **~spur** *f* fast lane.

**überholt** *adj* outdated.

**Überholverbot** *nt* ban on overtaking *(Brit) or* passing; *(als Schild etc)* no overtaking *(Brit),* no passing.

**überhören\*** *vt insep* not to hear; *(nicht hören wollen)* to ignore. **das möchte ich überhört haben!** (I'll pretend) I didn't hear that!

**Über-Ich** *nt* superego.

**über-:** **~irdisch** *adj* celestial, heavenly; **~kandidelt** *adj (col)* eccentric; **~kippen** *vi sep aux sein* to topple over; **~kleben\*** *vt insep* **die Kiste/Anschrift ~kleben** to stick something over the box/address; **~kochen** *vi sep aux sein (lit, fig)* to boil over; **~kommen\*** *vt insep irreg (geh: ergreifen)* to come over; **Furcht** *etc* **~kam ihn** he was overcome with fear *etc;* **~kriegen** *vt sep (col)* **(a)** *(~drüssig werden)* to get fed up with *(col);* **(b)** **eins ~kriegen** to get landed one *(col);* **~laden\* 1** *vt insep irreg* to overload; *(reichlich geben)* to shower; *(zu stark verzieren auch)* to clutter; **2** *adj Wagen* overloaded; *(fig) Stil* over-ornate; *Bild* cluttered; **~lagern\*** *insep* **1** *vt* **(a)** *Schichten* to overlie; *Sender* to blot out; **(b)** *Konflikt etc* to eclipse; **2** *vr (sich überschneiden)* to overlap; **~lang** *adj* too long; **~lappen\*** *vi r insep* to overlap.

**überlassen\*** *vt insep irreg* **jdm etw ~** *(haben lassen)* to let sb have sth; *(in Obhut geben)* to leave sth in sb's care; **es jdm ~, etw zu tun** to leave it up to sb to do sth; **das bleibt Ihnen ~** that's up to you; **jdn sich** *(dat)* **selbst ~** to leave sb to his/her own devices; **jdn seinem Schicksal ~** to leave *or* abandon sb to his/her fate.

**überlasten\*** *vt insep* to put too great a strain on; *jdn* to overtax; *(durch Gewicht, Elec)* to overload. **überlastet sein** to be under too great a strain; *(überfordert sein)* to be overtaxed; *(Elec etc)* to be overloaded.

**Überlauf** *m* overflow.

**überlaufen[1]\*** *vt insep irreg (Angst etc)* to seize. **es überlief ihn kalt** a cold shiver ran down his spine.

**überlaufen[2]** *vi sep irreg aux sein* **(a)** *(Wasser)* to overflow; *(überkochen)* to boil over. **(b)** *(Mil: überwechseln)* to desert *(zu to); (Pol)* to defect.

**überlaufen[3]** *adj* overcrowded; *Stadt (mit Touristen)* overrun.

**Überläufer** *m (Mil)* deserter; *(Pol)* defector.

**überleben\*** *insep* **1** *vti* **(a)** to survive; *Zeitraum auch* to last, to live through. **(b)** *(länger leben als)* to outlive. **2** *vr* **das hat sich überlebt** that's had its day.

**Überlebende(r)** *mf decl as adj* survivor.

**überlebensgroß** *adj* larger-than-life.

**Überlebenstraining** *nt* survival training; *(Kurs)* survival course.

**überlebt** *adj* outmoded, out-of-date.

**überlegen[1]** *insep* **1** *vi (nachdenken)* to think. **hin und her ~** to deliberate; **ohne zu ~** without thinking; *(ohne zu zögern)* without thinking twice. **2** *vt* to think over *or* about, to consider. **das werde ich mir ~** I'll think it over, I'll think about it; **ich habe es mir anders/noch mal überlegt** I've changed my mind; **wenn man es sich** *(dat)* **recht überlegt** when you think about it; **das hätten Sie sich** *(dat)* **vorher ~ müssen** you should have thought of that sooner.

**überlegen[2] 1** *adj* superior; *Sieg* convincing. **jdm ~ sein** to be superior to sb. **2** *adv* in a superior manner.

**Überlegenheit** *f no pl* superiority.

**überlegt 1** *adj* considered. **2** *adv* in a considered way.

**Überlegung** *f* consideration, thought; *(Bemerkung)* observation. **~en anstellen** to make observations *(zu* about *or* on*).*

**Über-:** **ü~leiten** *sep* **1** *vt Abschnitt etc* to link up *(in +acc* with*);* **2** *vi* **zu etw ü~leiten** to lead up to sth; **~leitung** *f* connection; *(zur nächsten Frage, Mus)* transition; **ü~lesen\*** *vt insep irreg* **(a)** *(flüchtig lesen)* to glance through; **(b)** *(übersehen)* to overlook, to miss; **ü~liefern\*** *vt insep Brauch* to hand down; **~lieferung** *f* tradition; **schriftliche ~lieferungen** (written) records; **ü~listen\*** *vt insep* to outwit.

**überm** = **über dem.**

**Über-:** **~macht** *f no pl* superior strength; **ü~mächtig** *adj Gewalt* superior; *Feind* powerful; *Wunsch* overpowering; **ü~malen\*** *vt insep* to paint over; **ü~mannen\*** *vt insep (geh)* to overcome; **~maß** *nt no pl* excess *(an +acc* of*);* **im ~maß** to excess; **er hat Zeit im ~maß** he has more than enough time; **ü~mäßig 1** *adj* excessive; *Schmerz, Sehnsucht* violent; *Freude* intense; **das war nicht ü~mäßig** that was not too brilliant; **2** *adv* excessively; *essen, trinken auch* to excess; **~mensch** *m* superman; **ü~menschlich** *adj* superhuman; **ü~mitteln\*** *vt insep* to convey *(jdm to sb); (telefonisch etc)* to transmit; **ü~morgen** *adv* the day after tomorrow; **ü~müden\*** *vt insep usu ptp* to overtire; ~**müdung** *f* overtiredness; ~**mut** *m* high spirits *pl*; **ü**~**mütig** *adj (ausgelassen)* high-spirited; *(zu mutig)* cocky *(col)*.

**übern** = **über den.**

**übernächste(r, s)** *adj attr* **das** ~ **Haus** the next house but one; **(die)** ~ **Woche** the week after next; **er kommt** ~**en Freitag** he's coming Friday week.

**Über-: ü**~**nachten*** *vi insep* to sleep; *(in Hotel)* to stay; *(eine Nacht)* to stay the night; **ü**~**nächtigt** *adj* bleary-eyed; ~**nachtung** *f* overnight stay; ~**nachtung mit Frühstück** bed and breakfast; ~**nahme** *f* -**n** takeover; *(von Ausdruck, Ansicht)* adoption; *(von Zitat, Wort)* borrowing; *(von Amt)* assumption; **durch** ~**nahme dieser Aufgabe** by taking on this task; ~**nahme|angebot** *nt* takeover bid; **ü**~**natürlich** *adj* supernatural; **ü**~**nehmen*** *insep irreg* **1** *vt* **(a)** *Aufgabe, Verantwortung, (Jur) Fall* to take on; *Amt* to assume; *Klasse* to take charge of; **lassen Sie mal, das ü**~**nehme ich!** let me take care of that; **den Befehl ü**~**nehmen** to take (over) command; **(b)** *(stellvertretend, ablösend)* to take over *(von* from*); Zitat, Wort* to take; **2** *vr* to take on too much; *(sich überanstrengen)* to overdo it; *(beim Essen)* to overeat; **ü**~**nimm dich nicht!** *(iro)* don't strain yourself! *(iro)*; **ü**~**ordnen** *vt sep* **jdn jdm ü**~**ordnen** to put sb over sb; **etw einer Sache** *(dat)* **ü**~**ordnen** to give sth precedence over sth; **ü**~**parteilich** *adj Zeitung* independent; *(Parl) Problem* all-party *attr; Amt, Präsident etc* above party politics; ~**produktion** *f* overproduction; **ü**~**prüfen*** *vt insep (auf +acc* for*)* to check; *Entscheidung, Lage, Frage* to examine; *Ergebnisse, Teilnehmer etc* to scrutinize; *(Pol)* **jdn** to screen.

**Überprüfung** *f* **(a)** *no pl siehe vt* checking; examination; scrutiny; *(Pol)* screening. **(b)** *(Kontrolle)* check.

**über-:** ~**quellen** *vi sep irreg aux sein* to overflow *(von, mit* with*); (Reis)* to boil over; ~**queren*** *vt insep* to cross; ~**ragen*** *vt insep* to tower above; *(fig: übertreffen)* to outshine *(an +dat, in +dat* in*);* ~**ragend** *adj* outstanding; *Bedeutung* paramount; ~**raschen*** *vt insep* to surprise; *(überrumpeln auch)* to take by surprise; **jdn bei etw** ~**raschen** to surprise *or* catch sb doing sth; ~**raschend** *adj* surprising; *Besuch* surprise *attr; Tod, Weggang* unexpected; ~**rascht** *adj* surprised *(über +acc* at*);* **jdn** ~**rascht ansehen** to look at sb in surprise.

**Überraschung** *f* surprise. **zu meiner** ~ to my surprise.

**Überraschungs-:** ~**angriff** *m* surprise attack; ~**effekt** *m* shock effect.

**überreden*** *vt insep* to persuade. **jdn** ~, **etw zu tun** to persuade sb to do sth, to talk sb into doing sth; **jdn zu etw** ~ to talk sb into sth.

**Überredung** *f* persuasion.

**Überredungskunst** *f* powers of persuasion *pl*.

**Über-: ü**~**regional** *adj* national; *Zeitung, Sender auch* nationwide; **ü**~**reich** *adj* lavish, abundant; *(zu reich)* overabundant; **ü**~**reich an etw** *(dat)* overflowing with sth; **jdn ü**~**reich beschenken** to lavish presents on sb; **ü**~**reichen*** *vt insep* **(jdm) etw ü**~**reichen** to hand sth over *(to* sb*);* **ü**~**reichlich** *adj* ample, abundant; *(zu reichlich)* overabundant; **in ü**~**reichlichem Maße** in abundance; **ü**~**reif** *adj* overripe; **ü**~**reizen*** *insep* **1** *vt Nerven, Augen* to overstrain; **2** *vtr (Cards)* to overbid; **ü**~**reizt** *adj Augen* overstrained; *(nervlich)* overwrought; *(zu erregt)* overexcited; **ü**~**rennen*** *vt insep irreg* to run down; *(Mil)* to overrun; ~**rest** *m* remnant, remains *pl*; ~**rollbügel** *m (Aut)* roll bar; **ü**~**rollen*** *vt insep* to run down; *(Mil, fig)* to overrun; **ü**~**rumpeln*** *vt*

*insep (col)* to take by surprise, to catch unawares; *(überwältigen)* to overpower; **ü**~**runden*** *vt insep (Sport)* to lap; *(fig)* to outstrip.

**übers** = **über das.**

**Über-: ü**~**säen*** *vt insep* to strew; **ü**~**sät** strewn; *(mit Abfall etc)* littered; *(mit Sternen) Himmel* studded; **ü**~**sättigen*** *vt insep* to satiate; *Markt* to oversaturate; ~**schall-** *in cpds* supersonic; **ü**~**schatten*** *vt insep (geh) (lit, fig)* to overshadow; *(fig: trüben)* to cast a shadow over; **ü**~**schätzen*** *vt insep* to overestimate; **ü**~**schaubar** *adj Plan* easily comprehensible, clear; *Zahl, Größe* manageable; *Gebiet, Abteilung etc* of a manageable size; **ü**~**schäumen** *vi sep aux sein* to froth over; *(fig)* to bubble over *(vor +dat* with*); (vor Wut)* to seethe; ~**schicht** *f (Ind)* extra shift; **ü**~**schlafen*** *vt insep irreg Problem* to sleep on.

**Überschlag** *m* **(a)** *(Berechnung)* (rough) estimate. **(b)** *(Drehung)* somersault.

**überschlagen¹*** *insep irreg* **1** *vt* **(a)** *(auslassen)* to skip (over). **(b)** *Kosten etc* to estimate (roughly). **2** *vr* **(a)** to somersault; *(Mensch: versehentlich)* to go head over heels; *(fig: Ereignisse)* to come thick and fast. **(b)** *(Stimme)* to crack.

**überschlagen²** *sep irreg* **1** *vt Beine* to cross; *Arme* to fold; *Decke* to fold back. **2** *vi aux sein* **(a)** *(Wellen)* to break. **(b)** *(Stimmung etc)* **in etw** *(acc)* ~ to turn into sth.

**Über-: ü**~**schnappen** *vi sep aux sein (Stimme)* to break; *(col: Mensch)* to crack up *(col);* **ü**~**schneiden*** *vr insep irreg (Flächen, fig: Ereignisse, Themen etc)* to overlap; *(unerwünscht)* to clash; *(Linien)* to intersect; **ü**~**schreiben*** *vt insep irreg* **(a)** *(betiteln)* to head; **(b)** **etw jdm** *or* **auf jdn ü**~**schreiben** to make sth over to sb; **(c)** *(Comp) Daten, Diskette* to overwrite; **ü**~**schreiten*** *vt insep irreg* to cross; *(fig)* to exceed; *Höhepunkt, Alter* to pass; ~**schrift** *f* heading; *(Schlagzeile)* headline; ~**schuh** *m* overshoe; **ü**~**schuldet** *adj* heavily in debt; *Grundstück* heavily mortgaged; ~**schuß** *m* surplus *(an +dat* of*);* **ü**~**schüssig** *adj* surplus; **ü**~**schütten*** *vt insep* **jdn/etw mit etw ü**~**schütten** to cover sb/sth with sth; *(mit Flüssigkeit)* to pour sth onto sb/sth; **jdn mit etw ü**~**schütten** *(fig: überhäufen)* to heap sth on sb; ~**schwang** *m no pl* exuberance; **ü**~**schwappen** *vi sep aux sein* to splash over; *(fig: sich ausbreiten)* to spill over; **ü**~**schwemmen*** *vt insep (lit, fig)* to flood; *(Touristen) Land etc auch* to overrun; *(mit Aufträgen)* to swamp, to inundate; ~**schwemmung** *f* flood; **ü**~**schwenglich** *adj* effusive, gushing *(pej);* ~**schwenglichkeit** *f* effusiveness.

**Übersee** *no art* **in/nach** ~ overseas; **aus/von** ~ from overseas.

**Übersee-:** ~**dampfer** *m* ocean liner; ~**hafen** *m* international port; ~**handel** *m* overseas trade.

**überseeisch** ['yːbeːzeːɪʃ] *adj* overseas.

**Überseeverkehr** *m* overseas traffic.

**übersehbar** *adj (fig) Folgen, Zusammenhänge etc* clear; *Kosten, Dauer etc* assessable.

**übersehen*** *vt insep irreg* **(a)** *Folgen, Zusammenhänge, Sachlage* to see clearly; *Fachgebiet* to have an overall view of; *(abschätzen) Schaden, Kosten, Dauer* to assess. **(b)** *(ignorieren, nicht erkennen)* to overlook; *(nicht bemerken)* to miss.

**übersein** *vi sep irreg aux sein (col)* **jdm ist etw über** sb is fed up with sth *(col)*.

**übersenden*** *vt insep irreg* to send.

**übersetzen¹*** *vti insep* **(a)** to translate. **aus dem** *or* **vom Englischen ins Deutsche** ~ to translate from English into German; **etw falsch** ~ to mistranslate

sth; **sich leicht/schwer ~ lassen** to be easy/hard to translate. **(b)** *(Tech: übertragen)* to transmit.
**übersetzen²** *sep* **1** *vi aux sein* to cross (over). **2** *vt (mit Fähre)* to take *or* ferry across.
**Übersetzer(in** *f) m* - translator.
**Übersetzung** *f* **(a)** translation. **(b)** *(Tech: Übertragung)* transmission.
**Übersetzungsbüro** *nt* translation bureau *or* agency.
**Übersicht** *f* **(a)** *no pl (Überblick)* overall view. **die ~ verlieren** to lose track. **(b)** *(Abriß, Resümee)* survey; *(Tabelle)* table.
**übersichtlich** *adj* Gelände *etc* open; Darstellung *etc* clear.
**Übersichtskarte** *f* general map.
**übersiedeln** *sep,* **übersiedeln\*** *insep vi aux sein* to move *(von* from, *nach, in +acc* to).
**Übersiedler(in** *f) m* migrant.
**über-:** **~sinnlich** *adv* supersensory; *(übernatürlich)* supernatural; **~spannen\*** *vt insep* **(a)** *(Brücke etc)* to span; **(b)** *(zu stark spannen)* to put too much strain on; **~spannt** *adj* Ideen, Forderungen wild, extravagant; *(exaltiert)* eccentric; *(hysterisch)* hysterical; *Nerven* overexcited; *Person* highly strung; **~spielen\*** *vt insep* **(a)** *(verbergen)* to cover (up); **(b)** *(übertragen)* Aufnahme to transfer *(auf +acc* to); **~spitzt 1** *adj (zu spitzfindig)* oversubtle; *(übertrieben)* exaggerated; **2** *adv* oversubtly; in an exaggerated fashion.
**überspringen¹\*** *vt insep irreg* **(a)** Hindernis, Höhe to jump, to clear. **(b)** *(auslassen)* to skip.
**überspringen²** *vi sep irreg aux sein (Begeisterung)* to spread quickly *(auf +acc* to).
**über-:** **~sprudeln** *vi sep aux sein (lit, fig)* to bubble over *(vor* with*)*; **~stehen\*** *vt insep irreg (durchstehen)* to come *or* get through; *(überleben)* to survive; *Gewitter* to weather, to ride out; *Krankheit* to get over; **~steigen\*** *vt insep irreg* **(a)** to climb over; **(b)** *(hinausgehen über)* to exceed, to go beyond; **~steigert** *adj* excessive; **~steuern\*** *vi insep (Aut)* to oversteer; **~stimmen\*** *vt insep* to outvote; *Antrag* to vote down; **~strapazieren\*** *insep* **1** *vt* to overtax; **2** *vr* to overtax oneself; **~streichen\*** *vt insep irreg* to paint/varnish over; **~streifen** *vt sep* **(sich** *dat)* **etw ~streifen** to slip sth on.
**überströmen¹\*** *vt insep (überfluten)* to flood. **von Blut überströmt sein** to be streaming with blood.
**überströmen²** *vi sep aux sein (lit, fig)* to overflow *(vor +dat* with*)*.
**überstülpen** *vt sep* **sich** *(dat)* **etw ~** to put on sth; **jdm/einer Sache etw ~** to put sth on sb/sth.
**Überstunde** *f* hour of overtime. **~n** overtime *sing;* **~n machen** to do overtime.
**über-:** **~stürzen\*** *insep* **1** *vt* to rush into; **2** *vr (Ereignisse etc)* to happen in a rush; *(Nachrichten)* to come fast and furious; **~stürzt** *adj* overhasty; **~tariflich** *adj, adv* above the agreed *or* union rate; **~tippen\*** *vt insep* to type over; **~tölpeln\*** *vt insep* to take in; **~tönen\*** *vt insep* to drown.
**Übertopf** *m* planter.
**Übertrag** *m* ᵉe amount carried forward.
**übertragbar** *adj* transferable *(auch Jur, Comp);* Methode, Maßstab applicable *(auf +acc* to*);* Krankheit infectious; *(durch Berührung)* contagious.
**übertragen¹\*** *v insep irreg* **1** *vt* **(a)** to transfer *(auch Jur, Psych, Comp);* Krankheit, *(Tech)* Bewegung to transmit; *Daten* to communicate. **(b)** *(übersetzen)* Text to render *(in +acc* into*)*. **(c)** *(anwenden)* Methode to apply *(auf +acc* to*)*. **(d)** Verantwortung *etc* to give *(jdm* sb*)*; *(auftragen)* Aufgabe to assign *(jdm* to sb*)*. **(e)** *(TV, Rad)* to broadcast; *(TV auch)* to

televise. **2** *vr (Eigenschaft, Krankheit etc, Tech)* to be transmitted *(auf +acc* to*)*; *(Heiterkeit etc)* to spread *(auf +acc* to*)*.
**übertragen²** *adj* Bedeutung *etc* figurative.
**Überträger** *m (Med)* carrier.
**Übertragung** *f siehe vt* **(a)** transference, transfer; transmission. **(b)** rendering. **(c)** application. **(d)** *(Aufgabe)* assignment. **(e)** *(TV, Rad)* transmission.
**Übertragungswagen** *m (TV, Rad)* outside broadcast vehicle.
**übertreffen\*** *insep irreg* **1** *vt* to surpass *(an +dat* in*)*; *(mehr leisten als auch)* to outdo; *(übersteigen auch)* to exceed. **2** *vr* **sich selbst ~** to surpass *or* excel oneself.
**übertreiben\*** *vti insep irreg* to exaggerate. **es mit der Sauberkeit ~** to carry cleanliness too far; **man kann es auch ~** you can overdo things.
**Übertreibung** *f* exaggeration.
**übertreten¹** *vi sep irreg aux sein* **(a)** *(Fluß)* to break its banks. **(b)** *(zu anderer Partei etc)* to go over *(zu* to*)*; *(zu anderem Glauben)* to convert *(zu* to*)*. **(c)** *(im Sport)* to overstep.
**übertreten²\*** *vt insep irreg* Gesetz to break.
**Übertretung** *f (von Gesetz etc)* violation; *(Jur: strafbare Handlung)* misdemeanour *(Brit),* misdemeanor *(US)*.
**Über-:** **ü~trieben** *adj* exaggerated; *(übermäßig)* Vorsicht, Training excessive; **~tritt** *m (über Grenze)* crossing *(über +acc* of*)*; *(zu anderem Glauben)* conversion; *(von Abtrünnigen, esp zu anderer Partei)* defection; **ü~trumpfen\*** *vt insep (Cards)* to overtrump; *(fig)* to outdo; **ü~tünchen\*** *vt insep* to whitewash; *(mit Farbton)* to distemper; *(fig)* to cover up; **ü~völkert** *adj* overpopulated; **~völkerung** *f* overpopulation; **ü~voll** *adj* overfull *(von* with*)*; **ü~vorteilen\*** *vt insep* to cheat; **ü~wachen\*** *vt insep (kontrollieren)* to supervise; *(beobachten)* to keep under observation; *Verdächtigen* to keep under surveillance; *(auf Monitor, mit Radar, fig)* to monitor; **~wachung** *f siehe vt* supervision; observation; surveillance; monitoring; **ü~wältigen\*** *vt insep (lit)* to overpower; *(zahlenmäßig)* to overwhelm; *(bezwingen, fig: Schlaf, Angst)* to overcome; **ü~wältigend** *adj* overwhelming; *Schönheit* stunning; *Gestank, Gefühl auch* overpowering; **ü~wechseln** *vi sep aux sein* to move *(in +acc* to*)*; *(zu Partei etc)* to go over *(zu* to*)*; *(Wild)* to cross over; **~weg** *m* **~weg für Fußgänger** pedestrian crossing; **ü~weisen\*** *vt insep irreg (an +acc* to*)* Geld to transfer; *Patienten* to refer.
**Überweisung** *f (Geld~)* (credit) transfer; *(von Patient)* referral.
**Überweisungs-:** **~auftrag** *m* (credit) transfer instruction; **~schein** *m (von Arzt)* letter of referral.
**Überweite** *f* extra-wide fitting, oversize.
**überwerfen¹\*** *vr insep irreg* **sich (mit jdm) ~** to fall out (with sb).
**überwerfen²** *vt sep irreg* to put over; *Kleidungsstück* to put on; *(sehr rasch)* to throw on.
**Über-:** **ü~wiegen\*** *insep irreg* **1** *vt* to outweigh; **2** *vi (das Übergewicht haben)* to predominate; **ü~wiegend 1** *adj* predominant; *Mehrheit* vast; **2** *adv* predominantly, mainly; **ü~winden\*** *insep irreg* **1** *vt* to overcome; **2** *vr* to overcome one's inclinations; **sich ü~winden, etw zu tun** to bring oneself to do sth; **~windung** *f* overcoming; *(Selbstüberwindung)* will power; **das hat mich viel ~windung gekostet** that was a real effort of will for me; **ü~wintern\*** *vi insep* to (spend the) winter; *(col: Winterschlaf halten)* to hibernate; **ü~wuchern\*** *vt insep* to overgrow; *(fig)* to obscure; **ü~wunden** *adj*

*Standpunkt, Haltung etc* of the past; *Angst* conquered; **~wurf** *m (Kleidungsstück)* wrap; **~zahl** *f no pl* **in der ~zahl sein** to be in the majority; *(Feind)* to be superior in number; **ü~zählig** *adj (überschüssig)* surplus; *(überflüssig)* superfluous; *(übrig)* spare.

**überzeugen*** *insep* **1** *vt* to convince; *(Jur)* to satisfy. **ich bin davon überzeugt, daß** ... I am convinced that ...; **er ist sehr von sich überzeugt** he is very sure of himself. **2** *vi* to be convincing. **3** *vr* **sich (selbst)** ~ to convince oneself *(von of)*; *(mit eigenen Augen)* to see for oneself.

**überzeugend** *adj* convincing.

**überzeugt** *adj attr* Marxist *etc* convinced; *Anhänger, Vegetarier etc* confirmed; *Christ, Moslem etc* committed.

**Überzeugung** *f* **(a)** *(das Überzeugen)* convincing. **(b)** *(Überzeugtsein)* conviction; *(Prinzipien)* convictions *pl.* **meiner ~ nach** ... I am convinced (that) ...; **zu der ~ gelangen, daß** ... to become convinced that ...

**Überzeugungskraft** *f* persuasiveness.

**überziehen¹*** *insep irreg* **1** *vt* **(a)** *(bedecken)* to cover; *(mit Schicht, Belag)* to coat; *(mit Metall)* to plate; *(mit Zuckerguß)* to ice, to frost *(esp US)*. **ein Bett frisch ~ lassen** to change the sheets; **Polstermöbel neu ~ lassen** to have furniture re-covered. **(b)** *Konto* to overdraw *(um +acc by)*. **(c)** *Redezeit, Sendezeit etc* to overrun. **(d)** *(übertreiben)* **sein Benehmen wirkte überzogen** his behaviour seemed exaggerated. **2** *vi (Fin)* to overdraw one's account; *(bei Rede, Sendung)* to overrun. **3** *vr (Himmel)* to cloud over.

**überziehen²** *vt sep irreg* **(a)** **(sich** *dat)* **etw ~** to put sth on. **(b)** **jdm eins ~** *(col)* to give sb a clout *(col)*.

**Überziehungskredit** *m* overdraft facility.

**Über-:** **ü~züchten*** *vt insep* to overbreed; **ü~zuckern*** *vt insep* to sugar; *(zu stark zuckern)* to put too much sugar in/on; **~zug** *m* **(a)** *(Beschichtung)* coat(ing); *(aus Metall)* plating; *(für Kuchen, esp aus Zuckerguß)* icing, frosting *(esp US)*; **(b)** *(von Bett, Sessel etc)* cover; *(von Kopfkissen auch)* (pillow) slip.

**üblich** *adj* usual; *(herkömmlich)* customary; *(typisch, normal)* normal. **wie ~** as usual; **das ist bei ihm so ~** that's usual for him; **allgemein ~ sein** to be common practice.

**üblicherweise** *adv* usually, normally.

**U-Boot** *nt* submarine, sub *(col)*.

**übrig** *adj* **(a)** *attr (verbleibend)* remaining; *(andere auch)* other. **meine ~en Sachen** the rest of my things. **(b)** *pred* left (over); *(zu entbehren)* spare. **etw ~ haben** to have sth left/to spare. **(c)** *(mögen)* **für jdn/etw nichts ~ haben** to have no time for sb/sth; **für jdn/etw etwas ~ haben** to like sb/sth. **(d)** *(substantivisch)* **das ~e** the rest, the remainder; **im ~en** moreover, also.

**übrig-:** **~behalten*** *vt sep irreg* to have left over; **~bleiben** *vi sep irreg* **aus sein** to be left over, to remain; **wieviel ist ~geblieben?** how much is left?; **was blieb mir anderes ~ als ...?** what choice did I have but ...?

**übrigens** *adv* incidentally, by the way.

**übriglassen** *vt sep irreg* to leave *(jdm* for sb*)*. **(einiges)/viel zu wünschen ~** *(col)* to leave something/a lot to be desired.

**Übung** *f* practice; *(Mil, Sport, Sch)* exercise; *(Feuerwehr~)* exercise, drill; *(Univ: Kursus)* seminar. **aus der ~ kommen/außer ~ sein** to get/be out of practice; **zur ~** as practice; **~ macht den Meister** *(Prov)* practice makes perfect *(Prov)*.

**Übungs-:** **~arbeit** *f (Sch)* mock test; **~aufgabe** *f (Sch)* exercise; **~buch** *nt (Sch)* book of exercises, workbook; **~heft** *nt (Sch)* exercise book; **~platz** *m* training ground; *(Mil)* drill ground.

**UdSSR** [uːdeːlɛslɛsˈlɛr] *f (Hist)* = **Union der Sozialistischen Sowjetrepubliken. die ~** the USSR.

**UEFA‡** **up** [uːˈleːfaːkap] *m (Ftbl)* UEFA Cup.

**Ufer** *nt* - *(Fluß~)* bank; *(See~)* shore. **direkt am ~ gelegen** right on the waterfront; **etw ans ~ spülen** to wash sth ashore; **das sichere ~ erreichen** to reach dry land.

**Ufer-:** **~befestigung** *f* bank reinforcement; **~böschung** *f* embankment; **u~los** *adj* endless; *(grenzenlos)* boundless; **ins u~lose gehen** to get out of hand; *(Debatte etc)* to go on forever; *(Kosten)* to go up and up; **~mauer** *f* sea wall; **~promenade** *f* lakeside/riverside walk; **~straße** *f* lakeside/riverside road.

**UFO, Ufo** [ˈuːfo] *nt* -(s), -s UFO, Ufo.

**Uganda** *nt* Uganda.

**Ugander(in** *f)* *m* - Ugandan.

**ugandisch** *adj* Ugandan.

**U-Haft** *f (col)* custody.

**Uhr** *f* -en clock; *(Armband~, Taschen~)* watch; *(Anzeiger)* gauge, dial. **auf die ~ sehen** to look at the clock/one's watch; **nach meiner ~** by my watch; **um drei (~)** at three (o'clock); **ein ~ dreißig** half past one, one-thirty; **wieviel ~ ist es?** what time is it?, what's the time?; **um wieviel ~?** at what time?; **rund um die ~** around the clock.

**Uhr(arm)band** *nt* watch strap, watch band *(US)*; *(aus Metall)* watch bracelet.

**Uhr-:** **~feder** *f* watch spring; **~kette** *f* watch chain; **~macher(in** *f)* *m* watchmaker; clockmaker; **~werk** *nt* clock/watch movement; **~zeiger** *m* (clock/watch) hand; **~zeigersinn** *m* im **~zeigersinn** clockwise; **entgegen dem ~zeigersinn** anticlockwise *(Brit)*, counterclockwise *(US)*; **~zeit** *f* time (of day).

**Uhu** [ˈuːhu] *m* -s eagle owl.

**Ukraine** *f* **die ~** the Ukraine.

**Ukrainer(in** *f)* *m* - Ukrainian.

**ukrainisch** *adj* Ukrainian.

**Ukrainisch(e)** *nt* Ukrainian; *siehe* **Deutsch(e).**

**UKW** [uːkaːˈveː] **Ultrakurzwelle** ≃ VHF, FM.

**Ulk** *m* -e *(col)* lark *(col)*; *(Streich)* practical joke; *(Spaß)* fun *no pl, no indef art.* **mit jdm seinen ~ treiben** *(Streiche spielen)* to play tricks on sb.

**ulkig** *adj (col)* funny.

**Ulknudel** *f (col)* joker *(col)*.

**Ulme** *f* -n elm.

**ultimativ** *adj* Forderung *etc* given as an ultimatum. **jdn ~ zu etw auffordern** to give sb an ultimatum to do sth.

**Ultimatum** *nt, pl* -s *or* **Ultimaten** ultimatum. **jdm ein ~ stellen** to give sb an ultimatum.

**Ultimo** *m* -s *(Comm)* last (day) of the mouth. **bis ~** *(fig)* till the last minute.

**Ultra** *m* -s *(pej)* extremist.

**Ultra-** *in cpds* ultra; **u~kurz** *adj (Phys)* ultra-short.

**Ultrakurzwelle** *f (Phys)* ultra-short wave; *(Rad)* ≃ very high frequency, ≃ frequency modulation.

**ultramodern** *adj* ultramodern.

**Ultraschall** *m (Phys)* ultrasound.

**Ultraschall-** *in cpds* ultrasound; **~gerät** *nt* ultrasound scanner; **~untersuchung** *f* scan *(Brit)*, ultrasound.

**ultraviolett** *adj* ultraviolet.

**um 1** *prep +acc* **(a)** **~ ...** **(herum)** around; **~ sich schauen** to look around (one) *or* about one; **~ Weihnachten/Ostern** around Christmas/Easter; **~**

**acht** at eight. **(b)** *(betreffend, über)* about. **es geht ~ das Prinzip** it's a question of principle; **der Kampf ~ den Titel** the battle for the title; **~ Geld spielen** to play for money; **die Sorge ~ die Zukunft** concern for *or* about the future. **(c)** *(bei Differenzangaben)* by. **~ 10% teurer** 10% more expensive; **~ einiges besser** quite a bit better; **etw ~ 4 cm verkürzen** to shorten sth by 4cm. **(d)** *(bei Verlust)* **jdn ~ etw bringen** to deprive sb of sth. **(e)** *(nach)* after, upon. **Stunde ~ Stunde** hour after *or* upon hour.

**2** *prep* +gen **~ ... willen** for the sake of ...; **~ Gottes willen!** for goodness *or (stärker)* God's sake!

**3** *conj* **(a)** **~ ... zu** (in order) to ...; **intelligent genug/zu intelligent, ~ ... zu** intelligent enough/too intelligent to ...; **er studierte jahrelang Jura, ~ dann Taxifahrer zu werden** he studied law for several years only to become a taxi-driver. **(b)** *(desto)* **~ so besser/schlimmer!** so much the better/worse!; **je mehr, ~ so besser** the more the better; **~ so mehr, als ...** all the more considering ...

**4** *adv* **(a)** *(ungefähr)* **~ (die) 30 Schüler** about *or* around 30 pupils. **(b)** *(vorbei)* **die zwei Stunden sind jetzt ~** the two hours are now up.

**um|adressieren\*** *vt sep* to readdress.

**um|ändern** *vt sep* to alter.

**um|arbeiten** *vt sep* to alter; *Buch etc* to rewrite; *Metall etc* to rework.

**um|armen\*** *vt insep* to embrace; *(fester)* to hug.

**Umbau** *m siehe vt* rebuilding, renovation; conversion; alterations *pl (+gen, von to)*; modification; reorganization; changing.

**umbauen¹** *sep* **1** *vt Gebäude (gründlich renovieren)* to rebuild, to renovate; *(zu etw anderem)* to convert *(zu into)*; *(umändern)* to alter; *Maschine etc* to modify; *(fig: Organisation)* to reorganize; *(Theat) Kulissen* to change. **2** *vi* to rebuild.

**umbauen²\*** *vt insep* to enclose. **umbauter Raum** enclosed area.

**umbenennen\*** *vt sep irreg* to rename *(in etw sth).*

**umbesetzen\*** *vt sep (Theat)* to recast; *Mannschaft* to change; *Posten, Stelle* to find someone else for.

**umbestellen\*** *vi sep* to change one's order.

**umbetten** *vt sep Kranken* to move (to another bed).

**umbiegen** *vt sep irreg* to bend.

**umbilden** *vt sep (fig)* to reorganize; *(Pol) Kabinett* to reshuffle *(Brit)*, to shake up *(US).*

**umbinden** *vt sep irreg* to put on; *(mit Knoten)* to tie on. **sich *(dat)* einen Schal ~** to put a scarf on.

**umblättern** *sep* **1** *vt* to turn (over). **2** *vi* to turn the page(s).

**umblicken** *vr sep* to look around *(nach at).*

**umbringen** *sep irreg* **1** *vt* to kill *(auch fig col)*, to murder. **2** *vr* to kill oneself.

**Umbruch** *m* **(a)** radical change. **(b)** *(Typ)* make-up (into page); *(umbrochener Satz)* page proofs.

**umbuchen** *sep* **1** *vi* to change one's reservation. **2** *vt* to change.

**umdenken** *vi sep irreg* to change one's ideas.

**umdirigieren\*** *vt sep* to redirect.

**umdisponieren\*** *vi sep* to change one's plans.

**umdrängen\*** *vt insep* to crowd around; *(stärker)* to mob.

**umdrehen** *sep* **1** *vt* to turn over; *(auf den Kopf)* to turn up (the other way); *(mit der Vorderseite nach hinten)* to turn around; *(von innen nach außen) Tasche etc* to turn inside out; *(um die Achse)* to turn around; *Schlüssel* to turn. **einem Vogel/jdm den Hals ~** to wring a bird's/sb's neck; **jdm den Arm ~** to twist sb's arm. **2** *vr* to turn around *(nach to look at)*; *(im Bett etc)* to turn over. **3** *vi* to turn around.

**Umdrehung** *f* turn; *(Phys, Mot)* revolution.

**um|einander** *adv* about each other; *(räumlich)* around each other. **sich ~ kümmern** to look after one another.

**um|erziehen\*** *vt sep irreg (Pol euph)* to re-educate *(zu to become).*

**umfahren¹** *vt sep irreg* to run over, to knock down.

**umfahren²\*** *vt insep irreg* to travel around; *(mit dem Auto)* to drive around; *(auf Umgehungsstraße)* to bypass; *(um etw zu vermeiden)* to make a detour around.

**umfallen** *vi sep irreg aux sein* to fall over *or* down; *(fig col: nachgeben)* to give in. **zum U~ müde sein** to be fit to drop.

**Umfang** *m, pl* **Umfänge (a)** *(von Kreis etc)* perimeter, circumference *(auch Geom)*; *(von Baum auch, Bauch~)* girth. **(b)** *(Fläche)* area; *(Rauminhalt)* capacity; *(Größe)* size; *(von Gepäck etc)* amount; *(von Buch)* length, extent. **das Buch hat einen ~ von 800 Seiten** the book is 800 pages long. **(c)** *(fig) (Ausmaß)* extent; *(Reichweite)* range; *(von Untersuchung etc)* scope; *(von Verkehr, Verkauf etc)* volume. **in großem ~** on a large scale; **in vollem ~** fully.

**umfangen\*** *vt insep irreg* **(a)** *(geh: umarmen)* to embrace. **(b)** *(fig: umgeben)* to envelop.

**umfangreich** *adj* extensive; *(geräumig)* spacious; *Buch* thick.

**umfassen\*** *vt insep* **(a)** to grasp, to clasp; *(umarmen)* to embrace. **(b)** *(einschließen) Zeitperiode* to cover; *(enthalten)* to contain.

**umfassend** *adj* extensive; *(vieles enthaltend)* comprehensive; *Vorbereitung* thorough; *Geständnis* full, complete.

**Umfeld** *nt* surroundings *pl*; *(fig)* sphere. **zum ~ von etw gehören** to be associated with sth.

**umfliegen\*** *vt insep irreg* to fly around.

**umformen** *vt sep* **(a)** to reshape *(in +acc into).* **(b)** *(Elec)* to convert.

**umformulieren\*** *vt* to reword.

**Umfrage** *f (Sociol)* survey; *(esp Pol)* (opinion) poll. **eine ~ halten** to carry out a survey/an opinion poll; **~ halten** to ask around.

**umfüllen** *vt sep* to transfer into another bottle/ container *etc.*

**umfunktionieren\*** *vt sep etw in (+acc) or zu etw ~* to change *or* turn sth into sth.

**Umgang** *m no pl* **(a)** contact; *(Bekanntenkreis)* acquaintances *pl*, friends *pl*. **schlechten ~ haben** to keep bad company; **keinen ~ mit jdm haben** to have nothing to do with sb; **er ist kein ~ für dich** he's not fit company for you. **(b)** **im ~ mit Jugendlichen** in dealing with young people; **an den ~ mit Kindern gewöhnt sein** to be used to children.

**umgänglich** *adj (entgegenkommend)* obliging; *(gesellig)* friendly.

**Umgangs-:** **~formen** *pl* manners *pl*; **~sprache** *f* colloquial language; **u~sprachlich** *adj* colloquial; **~ton** *m* tone, way of speaking; **hier herrscht ein höflicher ~ton** people talk politely here.

**umgeben\*** *vt insep irreg* to surround *(auch fig).* **mit einer Mauer/einem Zaun ~ sein** to be walled/ fenced in, to be surrounded by a wall/fence.

**Umgebung** *f (Umwelt)* surroundings *pl*; *(Nachbarschaft)* vicinity; *(gesellschaftlicher Hintergrund)* background; *(Freunde etc)* people *pl* about one. **in der näheren/weiteren ~ Münchens** in the immediate/general vicinity of Munich.

**umgehen¹** *vi sep irreg aux sein* **(a)** *(Gerücht, Grippe etc)* to go around *or* about; *(Gespenst)* to walk. **(b)** **mit jdm grob/behutsam ~** to treat sb roughly/ gently; **mit jdm/etw ~ können** to know how to handle sb/sth; **sorgsam/verschwenderisch mit etw ~** to be careful/lavish with sth.

**umgehen²\*** *vt insep irreg* to go around; *(vermeiden)* to avoid; *(Straße)* to bypass; *(Mil)* to outflank; *(fig)* to avoid; *Gesetz* to get around.

**umgehend 1** *adj* immediate. **2** *adv* immediately.

**Umgehungsstraße** *f* bypass.

**umgekehrt 1** *adj* reversed; *Reihenfolge* reverse; *(gegenteilig)* opposite; *(anders herum)* the other way around. **nein, ~!** no, the other way around; **genau ~!** just the opposite!; **in die ~e Richtung fahren** to go in the opposite direction; **im ~en Verhältnis zu etw stehen** *or* **sein** to be in inverse proportion to sth. **2** *adv (anders herum)* the other way around; *(dagegen)* conversely; *proportional* inversely. **... und ~ ...** and vice versa; **~ als** *or* **wie** *(col)* ... the other way around to what ...

**umgestalten\*** *vt sep* to alter; *(reorganisieren)* to reorganize; *(umbilden)* to remodel; *(umordnen)* to rearrange.

**umgewöhnen\*** *vr sep* to re-adapt.

**umgraben** *vt sep irreg* to dig over; *Erde* to turn.

**umgrenzen\*** *vt insep* to surround; *(umfassen auch)* to enclose; *(fig)* to delimit.

**umgruppieren\*** *vt sep Möbel etc* to rearrange; *Mitarbeiter* to regroup.

**umgucken** *vr sep (col)* = **umsehen.**

**umhaben** *vt sep irreg (col) Schal, Uhr* to have on.

**Umhang** *m, pl* **Umhänge** cape; *(länger)* cloak; *(Umhängetuch)* shawl, wrap.

**umhängen** *vt sep Rucksack etc* to put on; *Jacke, Schal etc* to drape around. **sich *(dat)* etw ~** to put sth on; to drape sth around one.

**Umhängetasche** *f* shoulder bag.

**umhauen** *vt sep irreg* **(a)** to cut down. **(b)** *(col: umwerfen)* to knock flying *(col)* or over. **(c)** *(col: erstaunen)* to bowl over *(col)*.

**umhegen\*** *vt insep (geh)* to care for lovingly.

**umher** *adv* around, about. **weit ~** all around.

**umher-** *pref siehe auch* **herum-** around, about; **~fahren** *vi sep irreg aux sein* to travel around; *(mit Auto)* to drive around; **~gehen** *vi sep irreg aux sein* to walk around; **~irren** *vi sep aux sein (in etw (dat) sth)* to wander around; *(Blick, Augen)* to roam about; **~laufen** *vi sep irreg aux sein* to walk around; *(rennen)* to run around; **im Garten ~laufen** to walk/run around the garden; **~schweifen** *vi sep aux sein* to roam about; **~wandern** *vi sep aux sein* to wander around *(in etw (dat) sth)*; **~ziehen** *vi sep irreg aux sein* to travel around *(in etw (dat) sth)*.

**umhinkönnen** *vi sep irreg* **er kann nicht umhin, das zu tun** he can't avoid doing it; *(einem Zwang folgend)* he can't help doing it.

**umhören** *vr sep* to ask around.

**umhüllen\*** *vt insep* to wrap (up) *(mit in)*.

**umkämpfen\*** *vt insep Entscheidung* to dispute; *Wahlkreis, Sieg* to contest. **die Stadt wurde wochenlang umkämpft** the battle for the city lasted weeks.

**Umkehr** *f no pl* **(a)** *(lit)* turning back. **jdn zur ~ zwingen** to force sb to turn back. **(b)** *(fig geh: Änderung)* change.

**umkehren** *sep* **1** *vi aux sein* to turn back; *(fig)* to change one's ways. **2** *vt Kleidungsstück* to turn inside out; *Reihenfolge* to reverse, to invert *(auch Gram, Mus)*. **das ganze Zimmer ~** *(col)* to turn the whole room upside down *(col)*. **3** *vr (Verhältnisse)* to become reversed.

**umkippen** *sep* **1** *vt* to tip over, to upset; *Auto, Boot* to overturn; *Leuchter, Vase* to knock over. **2** *vi aux sein* **(a)** to tip *or* fall over; *(Auto, Boot)* to overturn; *(volles Gefäß)* to tip over. **(b)** *(col: ohnmächtig wer-*

*den)* to keel over. **(c)** *(col: es sich anders überlegen)* to come around. **(d)** *(col: umschlagen)* to change abruptly *(in +acc into)*. **(e)** *(Fluß, See)* to reach the point of ecological breakdown.

**umklammern\*** *vt insep* to wrap one's arms/legs around; *(mit Händen)* to clasp; *(festhalten)* to cling to; *(Ringen)* to hold.

**umklappen** *sep* **1** *vt* to fold down. **2** *vi aux sein (col)* to pass out.

**Umkleidekabine** *f* changing cubicle *(Brit)*, dressing room *(US)*.

**umkleiden** *vr sep* to change (one's clothes).

**Umkleideraum** *m* changing room.

**umknicken** *sep* **1** *vt Ast* to snap; *Papier* to fold (over). **2** *vi aux sein (Ast)* to snap; *(Halm)* to get bent over. **mit dem Fuß ~** to twist one's ankle.

**umkommen** *vi sep irreg aux sein* to die, to be killed. **ich komme um vor Hitze** *(col)* I'm dying of heat *(col)*, the heat is killing me *(col)*.

**Umkreis** *m* **im ~ des Flughafens** in the airport area; **im näheren/weiteren ~** in the immediate/general vicinity; **im ~ von 20 km** within a radius of 12½ miles.

**umkreisen\*** *vt insep* to circle; *(Space)* to orbit.

**umkrempeln** *vt sep* **(a)** to turn up; *(mehrmals)* to roll up. **(b)** *(umwenden)* to turn inside out; *Betrieb* to shake up *(col)*. **jdn ~** *(fig col)* to change sb's ways.

**umladen** *vt sep irreg* to transfer; *(Naut)* to tranship.

**Umlage** *f* **eine ~ machen** to split the cost.

**umlagern¹\*** *vt insep* to besiege.

**umlagern²** *vt sep* to transfer *(in +acc into)*.

**Umland** *nt no pl* surrounding countryside.

**Umlauf** *m, pl* **Umläufe** **(a)** *(von Erde etc)* revolution; *(das Kursieren)* circulation *(auch fig)*. **im ~ sein** to be in circulation; **in ~ bringen** *or* **setzen** to circulate; *Geld* to put in circulation. **(b)** *(Rundschreiben)* circular.

**Umlaufbahn** *f* orbit.

**umlaufen** *vi sep irreg aux sein* to circulate.

**Umlaut** *m* umlaut.

**umlegen** *vt sep* **(a)** *(umhängen)* to put around; *Verband* to put on. **(b)** *Mauer, Baum* to bring down. **(c)** *(umklappen)* to tilt (over); *Kragen* to turn down. **(d)** *(verlegen) Kranke* to transfer; *Leitung* to re-lay. **(e)** *Termin* to change *(auf +acc to)*. **(f)** *(verteilen)* **die 20 Mark wurden auf uns fünf umgelegt** the five of us each had to pay a contribution towards the 20 marks. **(g)** *(col: ermorden)* to do in *(col)*.

**umleiten** *vt sep* to divert *(Brit)*, to detour *(US)*; *(Zug, Bus)* to reroute.

**Umleitung** *f* diversion *(Brit)*, detour *(US)*.

**umlernen** *vi sep* to retrain; *(fig)* to change one's ideas.

**umliegend** *adj* surrounding.

**ummelden** *vtr sep* **jdn/sich ~** to notify (the police of) a change in sb's/one's address.

**Umnachtung** *f* **geistige ~** mental derangement.

**um|ordnen** *vt sep* to rearrange.

**um|organisieren\*** *vt sep* to reorganize.

**um|orientieren\*** *vr sep (fig)* to reorientate oneself.

**umpflanzen** *vt sep* to transplant.

**umpflügen** *vt sep* to plough up.

**umquartieren\*** *vt sep* to move; *Truppen* to requarter.

**umrahmen\*** *vt insep* to frame.

**Umrahmung** *f* setting *(+gen, von for)*. **mit musikalischer ~** with music before and after.

**umranden\*** *vt insep* to edge, to border.

**umräumen** *sep* **1** *vt (anders anordnen)* to rearrange; *(an anderen Platz bringen)* to move. **2** *vi* to

rearrange the furniture.
**umrechnen** *vt sep* to convert *(in +acc into)*.
**Umrechnung** *f* conversion.
**Umrechnungskurs** *m* exchange rate.
**umreißen**[1] *vt sep irreg* to tear down; *(umwerfen)* to knock over.
**umreißen**[2]* *vt insep irreg* to outline.
**umrennen** *vt sep irreg* to (run into and) knock down.
**umringen*** *vt insep* to surround.
**Umriß** *m* outline; *(Kontur)* contour(s *pl*).
**umrühren** *vt sep* to stir.
**umrüsten** *vt sep* (a) *(Tech)* to adapt *(auf +acc to)*. (b) *(Mil)* to re-equip *(auf +acc with)*.
**ums** = **um das**.
**umsatteln** *sep* 1 *vt Pferd* to resaddle. 2 *vi (col: beruflich)* to change jobs.
**Umsatz** *m (Comm)* turnover. **500 Mark ~ machen** to turn over 500 marks.
**Umsatz-:** ~**beteiligung** *f* commission; ~**plus** *nt* increase in turnover; ~**steuer** *f* turnover *or* sales *(US)* tax.
**umsäumen*** *vt insep* to line; *(Sew)* to edge. **von Bäumen umsäumt** tree-lined.
**umschalten** *sep* 1 *vt (auf +acc to) Schalter* to flick; *Hebel* to throw; *Strom* to convert; *Gerät* to switch over. 2 *vi (mit Schalter)* to flick the/a switch; *(mit Hebel)* to move the/a lever; *(auf anderen Sender)* to change over *(auf +acc to)*; *(Aut)* to change *(Brit)*, to shift *(in +acc to)*. „**wir schalten jetzt um nach Hamburg**" "and now we go over to Hamburg".
**Umschalttaste** *f* shift key.
**Umschau** *f no pl (fig)* review. ~ **halten** to look around *(nach for)*.
**umschauen** *vr sep* = **umsehen**.
**umschichten** *vt sep* to restack.
**umschichtig** *adv* on a shift basis.
**umschiffen*** *vt insep* to sail around; *Erde auch* to circumnavigate.
**Umschlag** *m* (a) *(Veränderung)* (sudden) change *(+gen* in, *in +acc* into). (b) *(Hülle)* cover; *(Brief~)* envelope; *(als Verpackung)* wrapping; *(Buch~)* jacket. (c) *(Med)* compress; *(Packung)* poultice. (d) *(Ärmel~)* cuff; *(Hosen~)* turn-up *(Brit)*, cuff *(US)*. (e) *(umgeschlagene Gütermenge)* volume of goods handled.
**umschlagen** *sep irreg* 1 *vt* (a) *Seite etc* to turn over; *Ärmel, Hosenbein, Saum* to turn up; *Teppich, Decke* to turn back; *Kragen* to turn down. (b) *(um die Schultern) Schal* to put on. (c) *(absetzen) Güter* to handle. 2 *vi aux sein (sich ändern)* to change (suddenly); *(Wind auch)* to veer; *(Stimme)* to break. **in etw** *(acc)* ~ to change *or* turn into sth.
**Umschlag-:** ~**entwurf** *m* jacket design; ~**hafen** *m* port of transshipment; ~**klappe** *f* jacket flap; ~**platz** *m* trade centre *(Brit)* or center *(US)*.
**umschlingen*** *vt insep irreg (Pflanze)* to twine around; *jdn (mit den Armen)* ~ to embrace sb.
**umschmeißen** *vt sep irreg (col)* (a) *siehe* **umhauen** (b, c). (b) *(col) Pläne* to screw up *(col)*.
**umschreiben**[1] *vt sep irreg* (a) *Text etc* to rewrite; *(bearbeiten) Theaterstück etc* to adapt *(für for)*. (b) *Hypothek etc* to transfer *(auf +acc to)*.
**umschreiben**[2]* *vt insep irreg (mit anderen Worten)* to paraphrase; *(darlegen)* to outline; *(verhüllen) Sachverhalt* to refer to obliquely.
**Umschuldung** *f* rescheduling (of debts).
**umschulen** *vt sep* (a) to retrain; *(Pol euph)* to re-educate. (b) *(auf andere Schule)* to transfer (to another school).
**Umschulung** *f (beruflich)* retraining.

**umschütten** *vt sep (verschütten)* to spill, to upset.
**umschwärmen*** *vt insep* to swarm (a)round; *(verehren)* to idolize.
**Umschweife** *pl* **ohne** ~ straight out, plainly; **mach keine ~!** come (straight) to the point.
**umschwenken** *vi sep* (a) *aux sein or haben (Anhänger, Kran)* to swing out; *(fig)* to do an about-turn. (b) *(Wind)* to veer.
**Umschwung** *m* (a) *(Gymnastik)* circle. (b) *(fig) (Veränderung)* drastic change; *(ins Gegenteil)* about-turn.
**umsegeln*** *vt insep* to sail around; *Erde auch* to circumnavigate.
**umsehen** *vr sep irreg* to look around *(nach for)*; *(rückwärts)* to look back. **sich in der Stadt** ~ to have a look around the town; **sich in der Welt** ~ to see something of the world; **ich möchte mich nur mal** ~ *(in Geschäft)* I'm just looking; **du wirst dich noch ~!** *(col)* you're in for a shock!; **ohne mich wird er sich noch** ~ *(col)* he's not going to find it easy without me.
**umsein** *vi sep irreg aux sein (Zeit)* to be up.
**umseitig** *adj* overleaf *pred*.
**umsetzen** *sep* 1 *vt* (a) *Pflanzen* to transplant; *Schüler* to move. (b) *Waren* to turn over. (c) **etw in etw** *(acc)* ~ to convert sth into sth; **etw in die Tat** ~ to translate sth into action. 2 *vr (Schüler)* to change places.
**Umsicht** *f* circumspection.
**umsichtig** *adj* circumspect.
**umsiedeln** *vti sep (vi: aux sein)* to resettle. **von einem Ort an einen anderen** ~ to move from one place and settle in another.
**Umsiedler** *m* resettler.
**umso** *siehe* **um 3**.
**umsonst** *adv* (a) *(unentgeltlich)* free. (b) *(vergebens)* in vain, to no avail. (c) *(ohne Grund)* for nothing.
**umsorgen*** *vt insep* to care for.
**umspringen** *vi sep irreg aux sein* to change; *(Wind)* to veer around *(nach to)*. **so kannst du nicht mit ihr ~!** *(col)* you can't treat her like that!
**Umstand** *m, pl* **Umstände** (a) circumstance; *(Tatsache)* fact. **den Umständen entsprechend** much as one would expect (under the circumstances); **die näheren Umstände** further details; **in anderen Umständen sein** to be expecting; **unter diesen/keinen Umständen** under these/no circumstances; **unter Umständen** possibly. (b) **Umstände** *pl (Mühe, Schwierigkeiten)* bother *sing*; trouble *sing*; *(Förmlichkeit)* fuss *sing*; **jdm Umstände machen** to cause sb bother; **machen Sie bloß keine Umstände!** please don't go to any bother.
**umstandshalber** *adv* owing to circumstances. „**~ zu verkaufen**" "forced to sell".
**umständlich** *adj Arbeitsweise, Methode* (awkward and) involved; *(langsam und ungeschickt)* ponderous; *Vorbereitung* elaborate; *Erklärung, Übersetzung, Anleitung* long-winded; *Abfertigung* laborious; *Arbeit, Reise* awkward. **er ist fürchterlich** ~ he always makes such heavy weather of everything; **etw** ~ **machen** to make heavy weather *or* a meal *(col)* of doing sth; **etw** ~ **beschreiben** to describe sth in a roundabout way.
**Umstands-:** ~**kleid** *nt* maternity dress; ~**krämer** *m (col)* fusspot *(col)*, fussbudget *(US col)*; ~**wort** *nt* adverb.
**umstationieren*** *vt sep Truppen, Waffen* to redeploy.
**umstehend** *adj attr* (a) standing round about. **die U~en** the bystanders. (b) *(umseitig)* overleaf.
**umsteigen** *vi sep irreg aux sein* (a) to change *(nach*

for*)*. **(b)** *(fig col)* to change over, to switch (over) *(auf +acc* to*)*.

**umstellen**[1] *sep* **1** *vti* **(a)** *Möbel* to rearrange. **(b)** *Hebel* to move, adjust; *Fernsehgerät* to switch over; *Radio* to switch to another station; *Uhr* to reset, to put back/forward. **auf etw** *(acc)* ~ *(Betrieb)* to go *or* switch over to sth; *auf Erdgas etc* to convert to sth. **2** *vr* to move about; *(fig)* to get used to a different lifestyle. **sich auf etw** *(acc)* ~ to adjust to sth.

**umstellen**[2]* *vt insep* to surround.

**Umstellung** *f* **(a)** *(von Möbeln etc)* rearrangement. **(b)** *(von Hebel)* adjustment; *(von Uhr)* resetting. **(c)** *(fig: das Sichumstellen)* adjustment *(auf +acc* to*)*.

**umstimmen** *vt sep* **(a)** *Instrument* to retune. **(b)** *jdn* ~ to change sb's mind.

**umstoßen** *vt sep irreg Gegenstand* to knock over; *(fig) Plan etc* to change; *(Umstände)* to upset.

**umstritten** *adj (fraglich)* controversial; *(wird noch debattiert)* disputed.

**umstrukturieren*** *vt sep* to restructure.

**umstülpen** *vt sep* to turn upside down; *Tasche* to turn out.

**Umsturz** *m* coup (d'état).

**umstürzen** *sep* **1** *vt* to overturn; *(fig) Staat* to overthrow; *Demokratie* to destroy. **2** *vi aux sein* to fall; *(Möbelstück, Wagen etc)* to overturn.

**Umstürzler(in** *f)* *m* - subversive.

**umstürzlerisch** *adj* subversive.

**Umsturzversuch** *m* attempted coup.

**Umtausch** *m* exchange. **diese Waren sind vom ~ ausgeschlossen** these goods cannot be exchanged.

**umtauschen** *vt sep* to exchange; *Geld* to change *(in +acc* into*)*.

**umtopfen** *vt sep Blumen etc* to repot.

**umtreten** *vt sep irreg* to tread down.

**Umtriebe** *pl* machinations *pl.* **subversive ~** subversive activities.

**umtriebig** *adj (betriebsam)* go-getting.

**Umtrunk** *m* drink.

**umtun** *vr sep irreg (col)* to look around *(nach* for*)*.

**U-Musik** *f* = **Unterhaltungsmusik.**

**umverteilen*** *vt sep or insep* to redistribute.

**umwälzend** *adj (fig)* radical; *Veränderungen auch* sweeping; *Ereignisse* revolutionary.

**Umwälzung** *f (fig)* radical change.

**umwandeln** *vt sep* to transform *(in +acc* into*)*; *(Comm, Fin, Sci)* to convert *(in +acc* to*)*; *(Jur) Strafe* to commute *(in +acc* to*)*. **sie ist wie umgewandelt** she's a different person.

**Umwandlung** *f siehe vt* transformation; conversion; commutation.

**umwechseln** *vt sep Geld* to change *(in +acc* to, into*)*.

**Umweg** ['umveːk] *m* detour; *(fig)* roundabout way. **einen ~ machen/fahren** to go a long way around; *(absichtlich auch)* to make a detour; **auf ~en** *(fig)* in a roundabout way.

**Umwelt** *f no pl* environment.

**Umwelt-** *in cpds* environmental; **u~bedingt** *adj* caused by the environment; **~belastung** *f* ecological damage; **~bewußtsein** *nt* environmental awareness; **u~feindlich** *adj* damaging to the environment; **u~freundlich** *adj* environment-friendly; **~freundlich hergestellt** manufactured without harm to the environment; **u~gestört** *adj (Psych)* maladjusted; **~gift** *nt* environmental pollutant; **~katastrophe** *f* ecological disaster; **~kriminalität** *f* crimes against the environment; **~ministerium** *nt* Ministry of the Environment; **~politik** *f* ecological policy; **u~schädlich** *adj* harmful to the environment; **u~schonend** *adj*

environment-friendly; **~schutz** *m* environmental protection; **~schützer** *m* environmentalist; **~schutzpapier** *nt* recyled paper; **~steuer** *f* ecology tax; **~sünder** *m (col)* polluter of the environment; **~verschmutzung** *f* pollution (of the environment).

**umwenden** *sep irreg* **1** *vt* to turn over. **2** *vr* to turn (around) *(nach* to*)*.

**umwerben*** *vi insep irreg* to court.

**umwerfen** *vt sep irreg* **(a)** *Gegenstand* to knock over. **(b)** *(fig: ändern)* to upset. **(c)** *jdn (körperlich)* to knock down; *(Ringen)* to throw down; *(Drink)* to knock out; *(fig col)* to bowl over. **(d) sich** *(dat)* **etw** ~ to put sth around one's shoulders.

**umwerfend** *adj* fantastic; *(Erlebnis)* mind-blowing; *(Schönheit)* stunning. **von ~er Komik** hilarious.

**umwickeln*** *vt insep* to wrap around; *(mit Schnur)* to wind around.

**umzäunen*** *vt insep* to fence around.

**Umzäunung** *f* fencing.

**umziehen** *sep irreg* **1** *vi aux sein* to move *(nach* to*)*. **2** *vr* to change, to get changed.

**umzingeln*** *vt insep* to surround, to encircle.

**Umzug** ['umtsuːk] *m* **(a)** *(Wohnungs~)* move. **(b)** *(Festzug)* procession; *(Demonstration)* parade.

**Umzugs-:** **~karton** *m* packing case; **~kosten** *pl* removal expenses.

**UN** [uː'|ɛn] *pl* **die ~** the UN *sing.*

**un|ab|änderlich** *adj* **(a)** unalterable; *Entschluß, Urteil auch* irrevocable. **~ feststehen** to be absolutely certain. **(b)** *(ewig) Gesetze* immutable.

**un|abdingbar** *adj* indispensable; *Recht* inalienable.

**un|abhängig** *adj* independent *(von* of*)*. **~ davon, was Sie meinen** irrespective of what you think; **sich ~ machen** to go one's own way; **sich von jdm/etw ~ machen** to become independent of sb/sth.

**Un|abhängigkeit** *f* independence.

**un|abkömmlich** *adj (geh)* busy.

**un|abläsig** *adj* continual; *Versuche, Bemühungen* unremitting.

**un|absehbar** *adj* **(a)** *(fig) Folgen etc* unforeseeable; *Schaden* incalculable. **auf ~e Zeit** for an indefinite period. **(b)** *(lit)* interminable.

**un-:** **~absichtlich** *adj* unintentional; **~abweisbar** *adj* irrefutable; **~abwendbar** *adj* inevitable; **~achtsam** *adj (unaufmerksam)* inattentive; *(nicht sorgsam)* careless; *(unbedacht)* thoughtless; **~ähnlich** *adj* dissimilar; **jdm/einer Sache ~ähnlich sein** to be unlike sth/sb; **~anfechtbar** *adj Urteil* incontestable; *Argument etc* unassailable; *Beweis* irrefutable; **~angebracht** *adj Bemerkung* uncalled-for; *Sparsamkeit auch* misplaced; *(unzweckmäßig) Maßnahmen* inappropriate; **~angefochten** *adj* unchallenged *no adv*; *Testament, Wahlkandidat, Urteil* uncontested; **~angemeldet** *adj* unannounced *no adv*; *Besucher* unexpected; *Patient etc* without an appointment.

**un|angemessen** *adj (zu hoch)* unreasonable; *(unzulänglich)* inadequate. **einer Sache** *(dat)* **~ sein** to be inappropriate to sth.

**un|angenehm** *adj* unpleasant; *(peinlich) Zwischenfall, Begegnung* embarrassing. **~ werden** to get nasty; **~ auffallen** to make a bad impression; **~ berührt** embarrassed *(von* by*)*; **das ist mir immer so ~** I don't like that at all.

**un-:** **~angepaßt** *adj* non-conformist; **~angetastet** *adj* untouched; **~angetastet bleiben** *(Rechte)* not to be violated; **~angreifbar** *adj* unassailable; *Festung, Land* impregnable; **~annehmbar** *adj* unacceptable.

**Un|annehmlichkeit** *f usu pl* trouble *no pl.* **~en**

**haben/bekommen** to be in/to get into trouble.
**un|ansehnlich** adj unsightly; Frau etc plain; Tape-te, Möbel shabby.
**un|anständig** adj (a) (unerzogen) ill-mannered; (un-verschämt) rude. (b) (anstößig) improper; Wort, Witz dirty.
**Unanständigkeit** f siehe adj ill manners pl; rude-ness no pl; impropriety; dirtiness.
**un-:** ~antastbar adj inviolable, sacrosanct; ~appetitlich adj (lit, fig) unappetizing.
**Un|art** f bad habit.
**un|artig** adj naughty.
**Un-:** u~ästhetisch adj unsightly; Anblick unlovely; u~aufdringlich adj unobtrusive; Parfüm auch dis-creet; Mensch unassuming; u~auffällig 1 adj in-conspicuous; (unscheinbar, schlicht) unobtrusive; 2 adv unobtrusively, discreetly; u~auffindbar adj nowhere to be found; u~aufgefordert 1 adj unso-licited (esp Comm); 2 adv without being asked; u~aufgefordert zugesandte Manuskripte unsolicited manuscripts; u~aufhaltbar adj unstoppable; u~aufhaltsam adj (a) (unaufhaltbar) unstoppable; (b) (unerbittlich) inexorable; u~aufhörlich adj con-tinual, incessant; u~auflösbar adj Ehe indissol-uble; u~aufmerksam adj inattentive; ~aufmerk-samkeit f inattentiveness; u~aufrichtig adj insin-cere; ~aufrichtigkeit f insincerity; u~aufschieb-bar adj urgent; u~ausbleiblich adj inevitable, un-avoidable; u~ausgeglichen adj unbalanced; u~ausgegoren adj immature; Idee, Plan half-baked (col); u~ausgeschlafen adj tired; u~aus-gesetzt adj incessant, constant; u~ausge-sprochen adj unspoken; u~ausgewogen adj unbalanced; u~ausrottbar adj Unkraut inde-structible; (fig) Vorurteile etc ineradicable; u~aussprechlich adj (a) Wort, Name unpronounce-able; (b) Schönheit, Leid etc inexpressible; u~ausstehlich adj intolerable; u~ausweichlich adj inevitable; Folgen auch inescapable.
**unbändig** adj (a) Kind boisterous. sie freuten sich ~ they were jumping for joy. (b) (ungezügelt) unre-strained no adv; Haß, Zorn etc auch unbridled no adv; Hunger enormous.
**un-:** ~bar adj (Comm) etw ~bar bezahlen not to pay sth in cash; ~barmherzig adj merciless; ~beabsichtigt adj unintentional.
**unbe|achtet** adj unnoticed; Warnung, Vorschläge unheeded. wir wollen die weniger wichtigen Punkte zunächst ~ lassen let's leave aside the less impor-tant points for the time being.
**un-:** ~beanstandet adj etw ~beanstandet lassen to let sth pass or go; ~bebaut adj Land undeveloped; Feld uncultivated; ~bedacht adj rash; ~bedarft adj (col) (naiv) simple-minded; (unwissend) clueless (col); ~bedeckt adj bare; ~bedenklich 1 adj (un-gefährlich) completely harmless; 2 adv (ungefähr-lich) quite safely; (ohne zu zögern) without thinking twice (col); ~bedeutend adj insignificant; (gering-fügig) Änderung etc minor.
**unbedingt 1** adj attr absolute. **2** adv (auf jeden Fall) really; nötig, erforderlich absolutely. müßt ihr denn ~ in meinem Arbeitszimmer spielen? do you have to play in my study?; ~! absolutely!; nicht ~ not necessarily.
**Un-:** u~beeindruckt adj unimpressed; u~beeinflußt adj uninfluenced (von by); u~befahrbar adj Straße impassable; Gewässer un-navigable; u~befahren adj Straße, Seeweg un-used; u~befangen adj (a) (unparteiisch) impartial; (b) (natürlich) unselfconscious; (ungehemmt) unin-hibited; ~befangenheit f siehe adj impartiality;

naturalness; uninhibitedness; ~befestigt adj Straße unmetalled; u~befriedigend adj unsatisfactory; u~befriedigt adj (frustriert) unsatisfied; (unerfüllt auch) unfulfilled; (unzufrieden) dissatisfied; u~befristet adj permanent; u~befugt adj un-authorized; Eintritt für ~befugte verboten no admit-tance to unauthorized persons; u~begabt adj un-talented; u~beglichen adj unpaid, unsettled.
**unbegreiflich** adj incomprehensible. es wird mir im-mer ~ bleiben, wie/daß ... I shall never understand how/why ...
**unbegreiflicherweise** adv inexplicably.
**unbegrenzt** adj unlimited; Möglichkeiten, Energie etc auch limitless; Land, Meer etc boundless; Zeit-spanne, Frist indefinite. zeitlich ~ indefinite; ~, auf ~e Zeit indefinitely; „~ haltbar" "will keep indefi-nitely".
**unbegründet** adj unwarranted.
**unbehaart** adj hairless; (auf dem Kopf) bald.
**Unbehagen** nt uneasiness; (Unzufriedenheit) discon-tent (an +dat with); (körperlich) discomfort. jdm ~ bereiten to make sb feel uneasy.
**unbehaglich** adj uncomfortable; Gefühl uneasy.
**un-:** ~behelligt adj (unbelästigt) unmolested; (un-kontrolliert) unchecked; jdn ~behelligt lassen to leave sb alone; ~beherrscht adj uncontrolled; (Mensch) lacking self-control; (gierig) greedy; ~behindert adj unimpeded; ~beholfen adj clum-sy, awkward; (hilflos) helpless; ~beirrbar adj un-wavering; ~beirrt adj unswerving.
**unbekannt** adj unknown; Gesicht auch unfamiliar. das war mir ~ I was unaware of that; Angst ist ihm ~ he doesn't know what fear is; ~e Größe (Math, fig) unknown quantity; nach ~ verzogen moved — address unknown; ~e Täter person or persons un-known.
**Unbekannte** f (wk) -n, -n (Math) unknown.
**Unbekannte(r)** mf decl as adj stranger.
**unbekannterweise** adv grüße sie ~ von mir give her my regards although I don't know her.
**unbekleidet** adj bare. er war ~ he had nothing on.
**unbekümmert** adj (a) (unbesorgt) unconcerned. sei ganz ~ don't worry. (b) (sorgenfrei) carefree.
**unbelastet** adj (a) (ohne Last) unloaded, unladen. (b) (ohne Schulden) unencumbered. (c) (Pol: ohne Schuld) guiltless. (d) (ohne Sorgen) free from wor-ries.
**un-:** ~belebt adj Straße quiet; Natur inanimate; ~belehrbar adj fixed in one's views; Rassist etc dyed-in-the-wool attr; ~beleuchtet adj unlit; Fahr-zeug without lights; ~beliebt adj unpopular (bei with); U~beliebtheit f unpopularity (bei with); ~bemannt adj Raumflug unmanned; Fahrzeug driverless; ~bemerkbar adj imperceptible; ~bemerkt adj unnoticed; ~bemittelt adj without means; ~benommen adj pred (form) es bleibt or ist Ihnen ~benommen, zu ... you are at liberty to ...; ~benutzt adj unused; ~beobachtet adj unob-served, unnoticed; wenn er sich ~beobachtet fühlt ... when he thinks nobody is looking ...; ~bequem adj (ungemütlich) uncomfortable; (lästig) Situation awkward; Aufgabe unpleasant; (mühevoll) difficult; der Regierung ~bequem sein to be an embarrass-ment to the government; ~berechenbar adj un-predictable; u~berechtigt adj unwarranted; Sor-ge, Kritik etc unfounded; (unbefugt) unauthorized.
**unberücksichtigt** adj unconsidered. etw ~ lassen not to consider sth.
**unberührbar** adj untouchable.
**unberührt** adj (a) untouched; Bett unslept-in; Wald etc virgin; Natur unspoiled. ~ sein (Mädchen) to be

a virgin. **(b)** *(mitleidlos)* unmoved. **(c)** *(unbetroffen)* unaffected.

**unbeschadet** *prep +gen (form)* regardless of.

**unbeschädigt** *adj* undamaged; *Siegel* unbroken. ~ **bleiben** not to be damaged/broken; *(seelisch etc)* to come off unscathed

**unbeschäftigt** *adj (müßig)* idle; *(arbeitslos)* not working.

**unbescheiden** *adj* presumptuous.

**un-:** ~**bescholten** *adj (geh)* respectable; *Ruf* spotless; ~**beschrankt** *adj (Rail)* without gates.

**unbeschränkt** *adj* unlimited; *Macht* absolute.

**unbeschreiblich** *adj* indescribable.

**un-:** ~**beschrieben** *adj* blank; ~**beschwert** *adj* **(a)** *(sorgenfrei)* carefree; *Melodie* light; **(b)** *(ohne Gewicht)* unweighted.

**unbesehen** *adv* indiscriminately; *(ohne es anzusehen)* without looking at it/them. **das glaube ich dir** ~ I believe it if you say so.

**un-:** ~**besetzt** *adj* vacant; *Stuhl, Platz auch* unoccupied; *Bus, Zug* empty; *Schalter* closed; ~**besiegbar** *adj Armee etc* invincible; *(Sport auch)* unbeatable; ~**besiegt** *adj* undefeated; ~**besonnen** *adj* rash.

**unbesorgt 1** *adj* unconcerned. **Sie können ganz** ~ **sein** you can set your mind at rest. **2** *adv* without worrying.

**un-:** ~**bespielt** *adj Kassette, Band* blank; ~**beständig** *adj Wetter* unsettled, changeable; *Mensch* erratic; *(launisch)* moody; *Liebhaber* inconstant; ~**bestätigt** *adj* unconfirmed; ~**bestechlich** *adj* **(a)** *Mensch* incorruptible; **(b)** *Urteil, Blick* unerring; ~**bestimmbar** *adj* indeterminable; ~**bestimmt** *adj (ungewiß)* uncertain; *Gefühl, Erinnerung* vague; *(Gram)* indefinite; **auf** ~**bestimmte Zeit** indefinitely.

**unbestreitbar** *adj Tatsache* indisputable; *Verdienste, Fähigkeiten* unquestionable.

**unbestritten** *adj* undisputed, indisputable.

**unbeteiligt** *adj* **(a)** *(uninteressiert)* indifferent. **(b)** *(nicht teilnehmend)* uninvolved *no adv (an +dat, bei* in*)*; *(Jur, Comm)* disinterested.

**un-:** ~**betont** *adj* unstressed; ~**beugsam** *adj* uncompromising; *Wille* unshakable; ~**bewacht** *adj (lit, fig)* unguarded; *Parkplatz* unattended; ~**bewaffnet** *adj* unarmed; ~**bewältigt** *adj* unmastered; *Konflikt, Problem* unresolved; **Deutschlands** ~**bewältigte Vergangenheit** the past with which Germany has not yet come to terms; ~**beweglich** *adj* immovable; *(steif)* stiff; *(geistig)* rigid, inflexible; *(bewegungslos)* motionless; ~**bewegt** *adj* motionless; *(fig: unberührt)* unmoved; ~**bewiesen** *adj* unproven; ~**bewohnbar** *adj* uninhabitable; ~**bewohnt** *adj Gegend* uninhabited; *Haus* unoccupied; ~**bewußt** *adj* unconscious; *Reflex* involuntary; ~**bezahlbar** *adj* **(a)** *(zu teuer)* prohibitively expensive; **(b)** *(fig) (komisch)* priceless; *(nützlich)* invaluable; ~**bezahlt** *adj* unpaid; ~**bezähmbar** *adj Optimismus etc* irrepressible; *Verlangen* uncontrollable; ~**bezwinglich** *adj* unconquerable; *Gegner* invincible; *Festung* impregnable; *Drang* uncontrollable; ~**blutig 1** *adj* bloodless; **2** *adv* without bloodshed; ~**brauchbar** *adj (nutzlos)* useless; *(nicht zu verwenden)* unusable; ~**bürokratisch** *adj* without any red tape.

**und** *conj* and. ~**?** well?; ~ **dann?** then what?; **ich** ~ **ihm Geld leihen?** *(col)* what me, lend him money?; **er konnte** ~ **konnte nicht aufhören** he simply couldn't stop; **Unfälle, Staus,** ~ ~ ~ accidents, tailbacks etc etc etc; ... ~ **wenn ich selbst bezahlen muß** ... even if I have to pay myself.

**Undank** *m* ingratitude. ~ **ernten** to get no thanks; ~ **ist der Welt Lohn** *(Prov)* never expect thanks for anything.

**undankbar** *adj* ungrateful; *Arbeit* thankless.

**Undankbarkeit** *f* ingratitude.

**un-:** ~**definierbar** *adj* indefinable; ~**demokratisch** *adj* undemocratic; ~**denkbar** *adj* unthinkable, inconceivable; ~**denklich** *adj:* **seit** ~**denklichen Zeiten** *(geh)* since time immemorial.

**undeutlich** *adj* indistinct; *Erinnerung* vague; *Schrift* illegible; *Ausdrucksweise* unclear. ~ **sprechen** to speak indistinctly, to mumble.

**undicht** *adj Dose, Gefäß* not air-/water-tight. **das Rohr ist** ~ the pipe leaks; **das Fenster ist** ~ the window lets in a draught *(Brit)* or draft *(US)*; **eine** ~**e Stelle haben** *(Rohr etc)* to leak; *(Reifen)* to have a hole.

**undifferenziert** *adj* simplistic.

**Unding** *nt no pl* **es ist ein** ~**,** ... it is absurd ...

**Un-:** **u~diplomatisch** *adj* undiplomatic; **u~diszipliniert** *adj* undisciplined; **u~duldsam** *adj* intolerant *(gegen of)*; ~**duldsamkeit** *f no pl* intolerance *(gegen of)*; **u~durchdringlich** *adj Urwald* impenetrable; *Gesicht* inscrutable; **u~durchführbar** *adj* impracticable, unworkable; **u~durchlässig** *adj* impermeable *(gegen to)*; **u~durchschaubar** *adj* unfathomable; *Mensch* inscrutable; **u~durchsichtig** *adj Fenster* opaque; *Papier, Stoff* non-transparent; *(fig pej) Mensch, Methoden* devious; *Motive* obscure; ~**durchsichtigkeit** *f no pl siehe adj* opacity; non-transparency; deviousness; obscureness.

**un|eben** *adj* uneven; *Straße auch* bumpy.

**Un|ebenheit** *f siehe adj* unevenness; bumpiness. **kleine** ~**en** uneven patches.

**un-:** ~**echt** *adj* false; *Schmuck, Edelstein, Blumen etc* artifical, fake *(usu pej)*; ~**edel** *adj Metalle* base; ~**ehelich** *adj* illegitimate; ~**ehelich geboren sein** to be illegitimate; ~**ehrenhaft** *adj* dishonourable *(Brit)*, dishonorable *(US)*; ~**ehrlich** *adj* dishonest; ~**ehrlich spielen** to cheat; ~**eigennützig** *adj* unselfish, selfless.

**un|eingeschränkt** *adj* absolute, total; *Rechte, Handel* unrestricted; *Zustimmung* unqualified.

**Un-:** **u~einheitlich** *adj* non-uniform; *Preise* unsteady; **u~einheitlich sein** to vary; **u~einig** *adj* in disagreement; *Familie* divided; **(sich** *dat)* **über etw** *(acc)* **u~einig sein** to disagree about sth; ~**einigkeit** *f* disagreement *(gen between)*; **u~einnehmbar** *adj* impregnable.

**un|eins** *adj pred* divided. **(mit jdm)** ~ **sein/werden** to disagree with sb.

**un-:** ~**empfänglich** *adj (für* to*)* not susceptible; *(für Eindrücke, Atmosphäre)* insensitive; ~**empfindlich** *adj (gegen* to*)* insensitive; *Bazillen etc* immune; *Pflanzen* hardy; *Textilien* practical.

**un|endlich 1** *adj* infinite; *(zeitlich)* endless. **2** *adv* endlessly; *(fig: sehr)* terribly. ~ **lange diskutieren** to argue endlessly.

**Un|endlichkeit** *f* infinity; *(zeitlich)* endlessness.

**un-:** ~**entbehrlich** *adj* indispensable; ~**entgeltlich** *adj* free of charge.

**un|entschieden** *adj* undecided; *(entschlußlos)* indecisive; *(Sport)* drawn. ~ **enden** to end in a draw; ~ **spielen** to draw; **ein** ~**es Rennen** a dead heat.

**Un|entschieden** *nt - (Sport)* draw.

**un|entschlossen** *adj* undecided; *(entschlußlos) Mensch* indecisive.

**un|entschuldbar** *adj* inexcusable.

**un|entschuldigt 1** *adj* unexcused. ~**es Fernbleiben von der Arbeit/Schule** absenteeism/truancy. **2** *adv*

without an excuse.
**un|entwegt 1** *adj* constant, untiring. **einige U~e** a few stalwarts. **2** *adv* constantly, without tiring; *weiterarbeiten* unceasingly.
**un|erbittlich** *adj* relentless.
**Un-: u~erfahren** *adj* inexperienced; **u~erfindlich** *adj* incomprehensible; **u~erforschlich** *adj* impenetrable; *Wille* unfathomable; **u~erfreulich** *adj* unpleasant; **~erfreuliches** *(schlechte Nachrichten)* bad news *sing*; *(Übles)* bad things *pl*; **~erfüllbar** *adj* unrealizable; **u~erfüllt** *adj* unfulfilled; **u~ergiebig** *adj* Quelle, Thema unproductive; *Boden, Ernte, Nachschlagewerk* poor; **u~ergründlich** *adj* unfathomable; **u~erheblich** *adj* insignificant; **u~erhofft** *adj* unexpected.
**un|erhört[1] 1** *adj attr (ungeheuer)* enormous; *(empörend)* outrageous; *Frechheit* incredible. **2** *adv* incredibly. **~ viel** a tremendous amount (of).
**un|erhört[2]** *adj Bitte* unanswered.
**un-: ~erkannt** *adj* unrecognized; **~erklärlich** *adj* inexplicable; **~erklärt** *adj Phänomen* unexplained; *Krieg, Liebe* undeclared; **~erläßlich** *adj* imperative.
**un|erlaubt** *adj* forbidden; *Betreten, Parken* unauthorized; *(ungesetzlich)* illegal.
**un|erledigt** *adj* unfinished; *Post* unanswered; *Rechnung* outstanding; *(schwebend)* pending.
**un-: u~ermeßlich** *adj* immense, vast; **~ermüdlich** *adj* untiring; **u~erprobt** *adj* untested, untried; **u~erreichbar** *adj Ziel* unattainable; *Ort* inaccessible; *(telefonisch)* unobtainable; **~erreicht** *adj* unequalled; *Ziel* unattained; **~ersättlich** *adj* insatiable; **~erschlossen** *adj Land* undeveloped; *Boden* unexploited; *Vorkommen, Markt* untapped; **~erschöpflich** *adj* inexhaustible; **~erschrocken** *adj* intrepid, courageous; **~erschütterlich** *adj* unshakable; *Ruhe* imperturbable; **~erschwinglich** *adj* exorbitant, prohibitive; **für jdn ~erschwinglich sein** to be beyond sb's means; **~ersetzlich** *adj* irreplaceable; **~erträglich** *adj* unbearable; **~erwartet** *adj* unexpected; **~erwünscht** *adj Kind* unwanted; *Besuch, Effekt* unwelcome; **du bist hier ~erwünscht** you're not welcome here; **~erzogen** *adj* ill-mannered; *Kind auch* badly brought up.
**unfachmännisch** *adj* unprofessional.
**unfähig** *adj* **(a)** *attr* incompetent. **(b) ~ sein, etw zu tun** to be incapable of doing sth.
**Unfähigkeit** *f* **(a)** *(Untüchtigkeit)* incompetence. **(b)** *(Nichtkönnen)* inability.
**unfair** *adj* unfair *(gegenüber* to*)*.
**Unfall** *m, pl* **Unfälle** accident.
**Unfall-: ~arzt** *m* specialist for accidental injuries; **~flucht** *f* failure to stop after an accident; **~flucht begehen** to commit a hit-and-run offence *(Brit)* or offense *(US)*; **~folge** *f* result of an/the accident; **u~frei 1** *adj* accident-free; *Auto* with no accident damage; **2** *adv* without an accident; **~klinik** *f* accident hospital; **~opfer** *nt* casualty; **~ort** *m* scene of an/the accident; **~station** *f* casualty department; **~stelle** *f* scene of an/the accident; **u~trächtig** *adj* accident-prone; **~versicherung** *f* accident insurance; **~wagen** *m* car involved in an/the accident; *(col: Rettungswagen)* ambulance; **~zahl, ~ziffer** *f* number of accidents.
**unfaßbar, unfaßlich** *adj* incomprehensible.
**unfehlbar 1** *adj* infallible. **2** *adv* without fail.
**Unfehlbarkeit** *f* infallibility.
**un-: ~fein** *adj* unrefined; **das ist ~fein** that's bad manners; **~fertig** *adj* unfinished, incomplete; *Mensch* immature; **~flätig** *adj (geh)* offensive; **sich ~flätig ausdrücken** to use obscene language;

**~folgsam** *adj* disobedient; **~formatiert** *adj (Comp)* unformatted; **~förmig** *adj (formlos)* shapeless; *(groß)* cumbersome; *Füße, Gesicht* unshapely; **~frankiert** *adj* unstamped.
**unfrei** *adj* **(a)** not free. **(b)** *(befangen)* constrained, uneasy. **(c)** *Brief* unfranked.
**Unfreiheit** *f* lack of freedom.
**unfreiwillig** *adj* compulsory; *Witz, Fehler* unintentional. **ich war ~er Zeuge** I was an unwilling witness.
**unfreundlich** *adj* unfriendly *(zu, gegen* to*)*; *Landschaft, Zimmer, Farbe* cheerless; *Akt* hostile.
**Unfreundlichkeit** *f* unfriendliness; *(unfreundliche Bemerkung)* unpleasant remark.
**Unfriede(n)** *m* strife.
**un-: ~frisiert** *adj Haare* uncombed; *Mensch* with one's hair in a mess; **~fruchtbar** *adj* infertile; *(fig) Debatte etc* fruitless.
**Unfruchtbarkeit** *f siehe adj* infertility; fruitlessness.
**Unfug** ['ʊnfuːk] *m no pl* nonsense. **~ treiben** to get up to mischief; **wegen groben ~s** for causing a public nuisance.
**Ungar(in** *f)* ['ʊŋgar(ɪn)] *m (wk)* **-n, -n** Hungarian.
**ungarisch** ['ʊŋgarɪʃ] *adj* Hungarian.
**Ungarisch(e)** ['ʊŋgarɪʃ(ə)] *nt* Hungarian; *siehe* **Deutsch(e)**.
**Ungarn** ['ʊŋgarn] *nt* Hungary.
**ungastlich** *adj* inhospitable.
**unge|achtet** *prep +gen* in spite of, despite.
**un-: ~geahndet** *adj (Jur)* unpunished; **~geahnt** *adj* undreamt-of; **~gebärdig** *adj* unruly; **~gebeten** *adj* uninvited; **~gebildet** *adj* uncultured; *(ohne Bildung)* uneducated; **~geboren** *adj* unborn; **~gebräuchlich** *adj* uncommon; **~gebrochen** *adj* unbroken.
**ungebührlich** *adj* improper. **sich ~ aufregen** to get unduly excited.
**ungebunden** *adj* **(a)** *Buch* unbound; *Blumen* loose. **(b) in ~er Rede** in prose. **(c)** *Leben* (fancy-)free; *(unverheiratet)* unattached; *(Pol)* independent. **frei und ~** footloose and fancy-free.
**ungedeckt** *adj* **(a)** *(schutzlos)* unprotected; *(Sport) Tor* undefended; *Spieler* unmarked; *Scheck* uncovered. **(b)** *Tisch* unlaid *(Brit)*, not set *pred*.
**Ungeduld** *f* impatience. **vor ~** with impatience; **voller ~** impatiently.
**ungeduldig** *adj* impatient.
**unge|eignet** *adj* unsuitable.
**ungefähr 1** *adj attr* approximate, rough. **2** *adv* roughly, approximately. **(so) ~ dreißig** about *or* approximately thirty; **das kommt nicht von ~** it's no accident; **wo ~?** whereabouts?; **so ~!** more or less!; **damit ich ~ weiß, ...** so that I have a rough idea ...; **~ (so) wie** a bit like.
**un-: ~gefährdet** *adj* safe; **~gefährlich** *adj* safe; *Tier, Krankheit, Arzneimittel etc* harmless; **~gefällig** *adj Mensch* unobliging; **~gefärbt** *adj Haare, Stoff* undyed; *Lebensmittel* without colouring *(Brit)* or coloring *(US)*; **~gefedert** *adj* unsprung; *(ohne Feder)* without springs; **~gegliedert** *adj Körper* unjointed; *(fig)* disjointed; *Satz, Aufsatz etc* unstructured; **~gehalten** *adj* indignant *(über +acc* about*)*; **~geheizt** *adj* unheated.
**Ungeheuer** *nt* - monster.
**ungeheuer 1** *adj* **(a)** *(riesig)* enormous, immense. **(b)** = **ungeheuerlich**. **2** *adv (sehr)* enormously, tremendously; *(negativ)* terribly.
**ungeheuerlich** *adj* monstrous; *Verdacht, Dummheit* dreadful; *Leichtsinn* outrageous, appalling.
**un-: ~gehindert** *adj* unhindered; **~gehobelt** *adj*

*Benehmen, Mensch* boorish; ~**gehörig** *adj* impertinent.

**Ungehorsam** *m* disobedience; *(Mil)* insubordination. **ziviler** ~ civil disobedience.

**ungehorsam** *adj* disobedient.

**un-:** ~**gekämmt** *adj Haar* uncombed; ~**gekämmt aussehen** to look unkempt; ~**geklärt** *adj Abwasser* untreated; *Frage, Verbrechen* unsolved; *Ursache* unknown; ~**gekocht** *adj* raw; *Flüssigkeit* unboiled; *Obst etc* uncooked; ~**gekündigt** *adj*: **in** ~**gekündigter Stellung** not under notice (to leave); ~**gekünstelt** *adj* natural; ~**gekürzt** *adj* not shortened; *Buch* unabridged; *Film* uncut; *Ausgaben* not cut back; ~**geladen** *adj Kamera, Gewehr etc* unloaded; *Gäste* uninvited.

**ungelegen** *adj* inconvenient. **etw kommt jdm** ~ **sth** is inconvenient for sb; **komme ich (Ihnen)** ~**?** is this an inconvenient time for you?

**Ungelegenheiten** *pl* inconvenience *sing.* **jdm** ~ **bereiten** to inconvenience sb.

**un-:** ~**gelehrig** *adj* unteachable; ~**gelenkig** *adj* stiff; *(fig col: nicht flexibel)* inflexible; ~**gelernt** *adj attr* unskilled; ~**gelesen** *adj* unread; ~**geliebt** *adj* unloved; ~**gelogen** *adv* honestly; ~**gemacht** *adj Bett* unmade.

**ungemein** *adj* immense, tremendous.

**ungemustert** *adj* plain.

**un-:** ~**gemütlich** *adj* uncomfortable; *Mensch* awkward; *Land, Wetter, Wochenende* unpleasant; **mir wird es hier** ~**gemütlich** I'm getting a bit uncomfortable; **er kann** ~**gemütlich werden** he can get nasty; ~**genannt** *adj* anonymous; *Summe* undisclosed; ~**genau** *adj* inaccurate; *(vage)* vague; *(ungefähr)* approximate.

**Ungenauigkeit** *f siehe adj* inaccuracy; vagueness; approximateness.

**ungeniert** ['ʊnʒeniːɐt] **1** *adj* free and easy; *(bedenkenlos, taktlos)* uninhibited. **2** *adv* openly; *(bedenkenlos, taktlos)* without any inhibition.

**ungenießbar** *adj (nicht zu essen)* inedible; *(nicht zu trinken)* undrinkable; *(unschmackhaft)* unpalatable; *(col) Mensch* unbearable.

**ungenügend** *adj* inadequate, insufficient; *(Sch)* unsatisfactory.

**Un-:** **u**~**genutzt** *adj* unused; **eine Chance u**~**genutzt lassen** to miss an opportunity; **u**~**geordnet** *adj* disordered; **u**~**gepflegt** *adj Mensch* untidy; *Park, Hände etc* neglected; **sich u**~**gepflegt ausdrücken** to talk in a common way; **u**~**gerade** *adj* odd; **u**~**geraten** *adj Kind* ill-bred; **u**~**gerecht** *adj* unjust; **u**~**gerechtfertigt 1** *adj* unjustified; **2** *adv* unjustly; ~**gerechtigkeit** *f* injustice; **u**~**geregelt** *adj* irregular; **u**~**gereimt** *adj Verse* unrhymed; *(fig)* inconsistent; ~**gereimtheit** *f (fig)* inconsistency.

**ungern** *adv* reluctantly. **(höchst)** ~**!** if I/we really have to!

**un-:** ~**gerufen** *adj* without being called; ~**gerührt** *adj* unmoved; ~**gesagt** *adj* unsaid; **etw** ~**gesagt machen** to pretend sth has never been said; ~**gesäuert** *adj Brot* unleavened; ~**geschält** *adj* unpeeled; *Getreide, Reis* unhusked; ~**geschehen** *adj*: **etw** ~**geschehen machen** to undo sth.

**Ungeschicklichkeit** *f* clumsiness.

**ungeschickt** *adj* clumsy, awkward; *(unbedacht)* careless.

**un-:** ~**geschlechtlich** *adj* asexual; ~**geschliffen** *adj Edelstein* uncut; *Messer* blunt; *(fig) Benehmen* uncouth; ~**geschmälert** *adj* undiminished; ~**geschmeidig** *adj Stoff, Leder* rough; *Haar* coarse; ~**geschminkt** *adj* without make-up; *(fig) Wahrheit* unvarnished.

**ungeschoren** *adj* unshorn; *(fig)* spared. **jdn** ~ **lassen** *(col)* to spare sb; *(ungestraft)* to let sb off.

**un-:** ~**geschult** *adj* untrained; ~**geschützt** *adj* unprotected; *(Mil) Einheit* exposed; ~**gesehen** *adj* unseen; ~**gesetzlich** *adj* illegal; ~**gesichert** *adj* unsecured, not secured; *Schußwaffe* with the safety catch off; ~**gesittet** *adj* uncivilized; ~**gestört** *adj* undisturbed; *(Rad, TV etc)* without interference; ~**gestraft** *adv* with impunity.

**ungestüm** ['ʊnʒəʃtyːm] *adj* impetuous.

**un-:** ~**gesund** *adj* unhealthy; ~**getan** *adj* undone; ~**getragen** *adj Kleidung* unworn; ~**getrübt** *adj* clear; *Glück* perfect.

**Ungetüm** *nt* **-e** monster.

**un-:** ~**geübt** *adj* unpractised *(Brit)*, unpracticed *(US)*; *Mensch* out of practice; ~**gewandt** *adj* awkward.

**ungewiß** *adj* uncertain; *(vage)* vague. **jdn (über etw** *acc***) im ungewissen lassen** to leave sb in the dark (about sth).

**Ungewißheit** *f* uncertainty.

**ungewöhnlich 1** *adj* unusual. **2** *adv* unusually.

**ungewohnt** *adj* unusual; *(fremdartig)* strange, unfamiliar. **das ist mir** ~ I am not used to it.

**ungewollt** *adj* unwanted; *(unbeabsichtigt)* unintentional.

**Ungeziefer** *nt no pl* vermin.

**ungezogen** *adj* ill-mannered; *Kind* naughty.

**Ungezogenheit** *f siehe adj* bad manners *no indef art*; naughtiness.

**un-:** ~**gezügelt 1** *adj (unbeherrscht)* unbridled; *(ausschweifend)* dissipated; **2** *adv* without restraint; ~**gezwungen** *adj* casual, informal; **sich** ~**gezwungen bewegen** to feel quite free; **U**~**gezwungenheit** *f* casualness, informality; ~**giftig** *adj* non-poisonous.

**unglaubhaft** *adj* incredible, unbelievable.

**ungläubig 1** *adj* unbelieving; *(zweifelnd)* doubting. ~**er Thomas** doubting Thomas. **2** *adv* doubtingly, in disbelief.

**Ungläubige(r)** *mf* unbeliever.

**unglaublich** *adj* unbelievable, incredible.

**unglaubwürdig** *adj* implausible; *Dokument* dubious; *Mensch* unreliable. **sich** ~ **machen** to lose credibility.

**ungleich 1** *adj Charaktere* dissimilar; *Größe, Farbe* different; *(nicht gleichwertig, nicht vergleichbar) Mittel, Waffen* unequal; *(Math)* not equal. **2** *adv* much, incomparably.

**ungleichartig** *adj* dissimilar.

**Ungleich-:** ~**behandlung** *f no pl* discrimination; **u**~**mäßig** *adj* uneven; *Atemzüge, Gesichtszüge, Puls* irregular; ~**mäßigkeit** *f siehe adj* unevenness; irregularity.

**Unglück** *nt* **-e** *(Unfall, Vorfall)* accident; *(Schicksalsschlag)* disaster, tragedy; *(Unheil)* misfortune; *(Pech, im Aberglauben, bei Glücksspiel)* bad luck; *(Unglücklichsein)* unhappiness. **das ist auch kein** ~ that's not a disaster; **das** ~ **wollte es, daß ...** as (bad) luck would have it, ...; **zu allem** ~ to make matters worse; **ein** ~ **kommt selten allein** *(Prov)* it never rains but it pours *(Prov)*.

**unglücklich** *adj* **(a)** *(traurig)* unhappy; *Liebe* unrequited. **ich U**~**e(r)!** poor me! **(b)** *(bedauerlich)* sad, unfortunate. ~ **enden** to turn out badly.

**unglücklicherweise** *adv* unfortunately.

**unglückselig** *adj (liter)* unfortunate; *(armselig)* miserable; *(unglückbringend)* disastrous.

**Unglücks-:** ~**fall** *m* accident; ~**rabe** *m (col)* unlucky thing *(col)*; ~**zahl** *f* unlucky number.

**Ungnade** *f* **bei jdm in** ~ **fallen** to fall out of favour

*(Brit)* or favor *(US)* with sb.

**ungnädig** *adj* ungracious.

**ungültig** *adj* invalid; *(Sport)* Tor disallowed. ~ **wer-den** *(Paß)* to expire; **etw für** ~ **erklären** to declare sth null and void; **eine Ehe für** ~ **erklären** to annul a marriage.

**ungünstig** *adj* unfavourable *(Brit)*, unfavorable *(US)*, disadvantageous; *Termin* inconvenient; *Augenblick, Wetter* bad; *(nicht preiswert)* expensive.

**ungut** *adj* bad. **ein** ~**es Gefühl haben** to have an un-easy *or* bad feeling; **nichts für** ~! no offence *(Brit)* or offense *(US)*!

**un-:** ~**haltbar** *adj Zustand* intolerable; *Vorwurf, Behauptung etc* untenable; *Torschuß* unstoppable; ~**handlich** *adj* unwieldy.

**Unheil** *nt no pl* disaster. ~ **stiften** *or* **anrichten** to wreak havoc.

**unheilbar** *adj* incurable. ~ **krank sein** to be termi-nally ill.

**Unheil-:** **u**~**bringend** *adj* fateful, ominous; ~**stifter** *m* mischief-maker; **u**~**voll** *adj* disastrous.

**unheimlich 1** *adj* **(a)** *(angsterregend)* frightening, sinister. **das/er ist mir** ~ it/he gives me the creeps *(col)*. **(b)** *(col)* tremendous *(col)*. **2** *adv (col: sehr)* in-credibly *(col)*. ~ **viele Menschen** an incredible num-ber of people.

**un-:** ~**höflich** *adj* impolite; **U**~**höflichkeit** *f* impo-liteness; **U**~**hold** *m* **-e** monster; *(Press col)* fiend; ~**hörbar** *adj* inaudible; ~**hygienisch** *adj* unhygien-ic.

**Uni** *f* **-s** *(col)* university.

**uni** ['yni, y'niː] *adj pred* self-coloured *(Brit)*, self-colored *(US)*, plain.

**UNI EF** ['uːnitsɛf] *f* **(die)** ~ UNICEF.

**Uniform** *f* **-en** uniform.

**uniformieren**\* *vt (mit Uniform ausstatten)* to uni-form; *(einheitlich machen)* to make uniform.

**uniformiert** *adj* uniformed.

**Unikat** *nt* **-e** unique specimen.

**Unikum** *nt* **-s** *or* **Unika** *(col)* real character.

**un-:** ~**interessant** *adj* uninteresting; **sein Angebot ist für uns** ~**interessant** we're not interested in his offer; ~**interessiert** *adj (neutral)* disinterested; *(nicht interessiert)* uninterested.

**Union** *f* **-en** union. **die** ~ *(BRD Pol)* the CDU and CSU.

**Unionsparteien** *pl (BRD)* CDU and CSU parties *pl*.

**universal, universell** [univɛr-] *adj* universal.

**Universal-** [univɛr'zaːl-] *in cpds* universal; *Bildung etc* general; ~**genie** *nt* universal genius.

**Universität** [univɛrzi'tɛːt] *f* university. **die** ~ **Frei-burg, die Freiburger** ~ the University of Freiburg, Freiburg University; **auf die** ~ **gehen, die** ~ **besu-chen** to go to university.

**Universitäts-** *in cpds* university; ~**klinik** *f* univer-sity clinic *or* hospital; ~**studium** *nt (Ausbildung)* university education.

**Universum** [uni'vɛrzʊm] *nt no pl* universe.

**unken** *vi (col)* to prophesy gloom and doom.

**Unkenruf** *m (fig)* prophecy of doom.

**unkenntlich** *adj* unrecognizable; *Inschrift etc* indeci-pherable.

**Unkenntlichkeit** *f siehe adj* unrecognizableness; indecipherability. **bis zur** ~ beyond recognition.

**Unkenntnis** *f no pl* ignorance. **in** ~ **über etw** *(acc)* **sein** to be ignorant about sth.

**unklar** *adj* unclear; *Wetter* hazy. **ich bin mir darüber noch im** ~**en** I'm not quite clear about that yet; **jdn über etw** *(acc)* **im** ~**en lassen** to leave sb in the dark about sth; **nur** ~ **zu erkennen sein** not to be easily discernible.

**Unklarheit** *f* lack of clarity; *(über Tatsachen)* uncer-tainty. **darüber herrscht noch** ~ it is still unclear.

**un-:** ~**klug** *adj* unwise; ~**kollegial** *adj* uncoopera-tive; ~**kompliziert** *adj* straightforward, uncompli-cated; ~**kontrollierbar** *adj* uncontrollable; ~**kontrollierbar werden** *(Mißbrauch etc)* to get out of hand; ~**kontrolliert** *adj* unchecked; ~**konzentriert** *adj* lacking in concentration; **er ist so** ~**konzentriert** he can't concentrate; ~**korrekt** *adj* **(a)** improper; **(b)** *(unrichtig)* incorrect.

**Unkosten** *pl* costs *pl*; *(Ausgaben)* expenses *pl*. **sich in** ~ **stürzen** *(col)* to go to a lot of expense.

**Unkraut** *nt* weed. **von** ~ **übersät** overgrown with weeds; ~ **vergeht nicht** *(Prov)* it would take more than that to finish me/him *etc* off!

**Unkraut-:** ~**bekämpfung** *f* weed control; ~**vertilgungsmittel** *nt* weedkiller.

**unkündbar** *adj* permanent; *Vertrag* binding. **in** ~**er Stellung** in a permanent position.

**unkundig** *adj (geh)* ignorant *(+gen of)*. **des Lesens/ Schreibens** ~ **sein** to be illiterate.

**un-:** ~**längst** *adv (geh)* recently; ~**lauter** *adj* dis-honest; *Wettbewerb* unfair; ~**leserlich** *adj* unread-able; *Handschrift etc auch* illegible; ~**leugbar** *adj* undeniable; indisputable; ~**lieb** *adj*: **es ist mir nicht** ~**lieb, daß** ... I am quite glad that ...; ~**liebsam** *adj* unpleasant; ~**liniert** *adj Papier* unruled; ~**logisch** *adj* illogical; ~**lösbar** *adj Problem, (Chem)* insol-uble; *(untrennbar)* indissoluble; *Widerspruch* irre-concilable.

**Unlust** *f no pl* **(a)** *(Widerwille)* reluctance. **(b)** *(Lust-losigkeit)* listlessness.

**unlustig** *adj (gelangweilt)* bored; *(widerwillig)* reluc-tant.

**unmännlich** *adj* unmanly.

**Unmasse** *f (col)* load *(col)*. **eine** ~ **Leute** loads of people.

**unmaßgeblich** *adj* inconsequential. **nach meiner** ~**en Meinung** *(hum)* in my humble opinion *(hum)*.

**unmäßig** *adj* excessive, immoderate.

**Unmenge** *f* vast number; *(bei unzählbaren Begrif-fen)* vast amount. ~**n von Leuten** vast numbers of people.

**Unmensch** *m* monster.

**unmenschlich** *adj* inhuman.

**un-:** ~**merklich** *adj* imperceptible; ~**mißver-ständlich** *adj* unequivocal.

**unmittelbar 1** *adj* direct; *Nähe etc* immediate. **2** *adv* immediately; *(direkt)* directly. ~ **vor** *(+dat)* *(zeitlich)* immediately before; *(räumlich)* right *or* directly in front of; ~ **bevorstehen** to be imminent.

**un-:** ~**möbliert** *adj* unfurnished; ~**modern** *adj* old-fashioned.

**unmöglich 1** *adj* impossible. **das ist mir** ~ that is impossible for me; **U**~**es/das U**~**e** the impossible; ~ **aussehen** *(col)* to look ridiculous. **2** *adv (keines-falls)* not possibly; *(pej col: unpassend)* impossibly. **ich kann es** ~ **tun** I cannot possibly do it.

**Unmöglichkeit** *f* impossibility.

**Un-:** ~**moral** *f* immorality; **u**~**moralisch** *adj* im-moral; **u**~**motiviert 1** *adj* unmotivated; **2** *adv* without motivation; **u**~**mündig** *adj (minderjährig)* underage; **wir wollen nicht länger wie u**~**mündige behandelt werden** we don't want to go on being treated as though we are incapable of thinking for ourselves; **u**~**musikalisch** *adj* unmusical.

**Unmut** *m* ill-humour *(Brit)*, ill-humor *(US)*; *(Unzu-friedenheit)* displeasure *(über +acc at)*.

**un-:** ~**nachahmlich** *adj* inimitable; ~**nachgiebig** *adj* inflexible; *(fig) Mensch auch* intransigent; ~**nachsichtig 1** *adj* severe; *Strenge* unrelenting; **2**

*adv* mercilessly; *bestrafen* severely; ~**nahbar** *adj* unapproachable; ~**natürlich** *adj* unnatural; ~**normal** *adj* abnormal; ~**nötig** *adj* unnecessary; ~**nötigerweise** *adv* unnecessarily, needlessly.

**unnütz** *adj* useless; *Geschwätz* idle.

**UNO** ['uːno] *f no pl* **die** ~ the UN *sing*.

**un|ordentlich** *adj* untidy; *Lebenswandel* disorderly.

**Un|ordnung** *f* disorder *no indef art*; *(in Zimmer etc auch)* untidiness *no indef art*; *(Durcheinander)* mess. **mach nicht so eine** ~! don't make such a mess!

**un-**: ~**organisch** *adj* inorganic; ~**organisiert** *adj* disorganized; ~**orthodox** *adj* unorthodox; ~**pädagogisch** *adj* educationally unsound; *Lehrer etc* bad (as a teacher).

**unparteiisch** *adj* impartial.

**Unparteiische(r)** *mf decl as adj* neutral person. **der** ~ *(Sport)* the referee.

**Un-**: **u**~**passend** *adj* unsuitable; *Zeit auch* inconvenient; **u**~**päßlich** *adj (geh)* indisposed *(form)*; ~**person** *f* persona non grata; **u**~**persönlich** *adj* impersonal *(auch Ling)*; *Mensch* aloof; **u**~**politisch** *adj* unpolitical; **u**~**praktisch** *adj Mensch* unpractical; *Maschine, Lösung* impractical; **u**~*****problematisch** *adj* unproblematic; *(einfach)* uncomplicated; **u**~**produktiv** *adj* unproductive; **u**~**proportioniert** *adj* out of proportion; **u**~**pünktlich** *adj Mensch* unpunctual; *Zug* not on time; ~**pünktlich kommen/abfahren** to come/leave late; ~**pünktlichkeit** *f* unpunctuality; **u**~*****qualifiziert** *adj* unqualified; *Äußerung* incompetent; **u**~**rasiert** *adj* unshaven.

**Unrast** *f no pl (geh)* restlessness.

**Unrat** ['ʊnraːt] *m no pl (geh)* refuse; *(fig)* filth.

**un-**: ~**rationell** *adj* inefficient; ~**ratsam** *adj* inadvisable; ~**recht** *adj* wrong; **das ist mir gar nicht so** ~**recht** I don't really mind.

**Unrecht** *nt no pl* wrong, injustice. **zu** ~ *verdächtigt* wrongly, unjustly; **nicht zu** ~ not without good reason; **im** ~ **sein** to be wrong; **u**~ **haben** to be wrong; **jdm u**~ **tun** to do sb an injustice.

**unrechtmäßig** *adj* unlawful, illegal.

**un-**: ~**redlich** *adj* dishonest; ~**reell** *adj* unfair; *(unredlich)* dishonest; *Preis* unreasonable.

**unregelmäßig** *adj* irregular.

**Unregelmäßigkeit** *f* irregularity.

**Un-**: **u**~**reif** *adj* immature; *Obst* unripe; ~**reife** *f siehe adj* immaturity; unripeness.

**unrein** *adj* not clean; *Ton* impure; *Atem, Haut* bad; *Gedanken, Taten* impure. **etw ins** ~**e schreiben** to write sth out in rough.

**unrentabel** *adj* unprofitable.

**unrichtig** *adj* incorrect.

**Unruh** *f* -**en** *(von Uhr)* balance spring.

**Unruhe** *f* -**n** **(a)** *no pl* restlessness; *(Nervosität)* agitation; *(Besorgnis)* disquiet. **(b)** *no pl (Lärm)* noise, disturbance; *(Geschäftigkeit)* bustle. **(c)** *no pl (Unfrieden)* unrest *no pl*, trouble. ~ **stiften** to create unrest; *(in Familie, Schule)* to make trouble.

**Unruhe-**: ~**herd** *m* trouble spot; ~**stifter(in** *f)* *m* - troublemaker.

**unruhig** *adj* restless; *(nervös auch)* fidgety *no adv*; *(laut, belebt)* noisy; *Schlaf* fitful; *Zeit etc, Meer* troubled.

**unrühmlich** *adj* inglorious.

**uns 1** *pers pron acc, dat of* **wir** us; *(dat auch)* to/for us. **bei** ~ *(zu Hause, im Betrieb etc)* at our place; *(in unserer Beziehung)* between us; *(in unserem Land)* in our country; **ein Freund von** ~ a friend of ours. **2** *refl pron acc, dat* ourselves; *(einander)* each other, one another. ~ **selbst** ourselves; **unter** ~ **gesagt** between you and me; **mitten unter** ~ in our midst;

**hier sind wir unter** ~ we are alone here; **das bleibt unter** ~ it won't go any further.

**unsachgemäß** *adj* improper.

**unsachlich** *adj* unobjective; *(fehl am Platz)* uncalled-for. ~ **werden** to become personal.

**unsagbar, unsäglich** *adj (liter)* unspeakable.

**unsanft** *adj* rough; *(unhöflich)* rude. ~ **geweckt werden** to be rudely awakened.

**unsauber** *adj* **(a)** *(schmutzig)* dirty. **(b)** *Handschrift, Arbeit* untidy; *(nicht exakt) Schuß, Schnitt* inaccurate; *Klang* impure. **(c)** *(unmoralisch)* shady; *Spielweise* dirty.

**unschädlich** *adj* harmless; *Bombe auch* safe. **jdn** ~ **machen** *(col)* to take care of sb *(col)*.

**unscharf** *adj* blurred, fuzzy; *Foto auch* out of focus; *(Rad)* unclear.

**unschätzbar** *adj* incalculable; *Hilfe* invaluable. **von** ~**em Wert** invaluable; *Schmuck* priceless.

**unscheinbar** *adj* inconspicuous; *(unattraktiv) Mensch* unprepossessing.

**unschicklich** *adj* unseemly, improper.

**unschlagbar** *adj* unbeatable.

**unschlüssig** *adj* undecided. **er ist sich** *(dat)* **noch** ~ he's still undecided, he hasn't made up his mind yet.

**unschön** *adj (häßlich)* unsightly; *(stärker)* ugly; *Gesicht* plain; *(unangenehm)* unpleasant. ~**e Szenen** ugly scenes.

**Unschuld** *f no pl* innocence; *(Jungfräulichkeit)* virginity; *(fig: Mädchen)* innocent. **eine** ~ **vom Lande** a naïve country girl.

**unschuldig** *adj* innocent *(an +dat* of*)*. **schuldig oder** ~ guilty or not guilty; **er/sie ist noch** ~ he/she is still a virgin.

**Unschulds-**: ~**engel** *m*, ~**lamm** *nt (col)* little innocent; ~**miene** *f* innocent expression.

**unschwer** *adv* easily, without difficulty.

**unselbständig 1** *adj Denken, Handeln* lacking in independence; *Mensch auch* dependent, unable to stand on one's own two feet. **Einkünfte aus** ~**er Arbeit** income from (salaried) employment. **2** *adv (mit fremder Hilfe)* not independently.

**Unselbständige(r)** *mf decl as adj (Fin)* employed person.

**unselig** *adj* unfortunate; *(verhängnisvoll)* ill-fated.

**unser** *poss pron* our.

**unser|einer, unser|eins** *indef pron (col)* the likes of us *(col)*.

**uns(e)re(r, s)** *poss pron (substantivisch)* ours. **der/die/das** ~ *(geh)* ours; **wir tun das U**~ *(geh)* we are doing our bit; **die U**~**n** *(geh)* our family.

**unser(er)seits** *adv (auf unserer Seite)* for our part; *(von unserer Seite)* on our part.

**uns(e)resgleichen** *indef pron* people like us.

**uns(e)rige(r, s)** *poss pron (old, geh)* **der/die/das** ~ ours; *siehe* **uns(e)re(r, s)**.

**unseriös** *adj* **(a)** not serious. **(b)** *(unehrlich)* not straight, untrustworthy.

**unsert-**: ~**halben**, ~**wegen** *adv* on our behalf; ~**willen** *adv*: **um** ~**willen** for our sake.

**unsicher** *adj* **(a)** *(gefährlich)* dangerous, unsafe. **die Gegend** ~ **machen** *(fig col)* to knock about the district *(col)*. **(b)** *(nicht selbstbewußt)* insecure. **(c)** *(ungewiß, zweifelhaft)* unsure, uncertain; *Verhältnisse* unstable. **(d)** *(ungeübt, ungefestigt)* unsure; *Hand* unsteady; *Kenntnisse* shaky. ~ **auf den Beinen** unsteady on one's feet.

**Unsicherheit** *f siehe adj* **(a)** danger. **(b)** insecurity. **(c)** uncertainty; instability.

**unsichtbar** *adj (lit, fig)* invisible.

**Unsinn** *m no pl* nonsense *no indef art*, rubbish *no in-*

def art. ~ **machen** to do silly things; ~ **reden** to talk nonsense; **laß den ~!** stop fooling about!

**unsinnig** adj (sinnlos) nonsensical; (ungerechtfertigt) unreasonable.

**Unsitte** f (schlechte Gewohnheit) bad habit.

**unsittlich** adj immoral.

**unsolid(e)** adj Mensch free-living; (unredlich) Firma unreliable.

**un-:** ~**sozial** adj Verhalten antisocial; Politik unsocial; ~**spezifisch** adj non-specific; ~**sportlich** adj unathletic; (unfair) unsporting; ~**statthaft** adj (form) inadmissible; (~gesetzlich) illegal; (Sport) not allowed.

**unsterblich 1** adj immortal; Liebe undying. **jdn ~ machen** to immortalize sb. **2** adv (col) utterly.

**Unsterblichkeit** f immortality.

**unstet** ['ʊnʃteːt] adj Glück, Liebe fickle; Mensch restless; (wankelmütig) changeable; Entwicklung unsteady; Leben unsettled.

**Un-:** u~**stillbar** adj Durst unquenchable; Sehnsucht, Hunger insatiable; ~**stimmigkeit** f (Ungenauigkeit) inconsistency, discrepancy; (Streit) difference; u~**streitig** adv indisputably; ~**summe** f vast sum.

**unsympathisch** adj unpleasant, disagreeable. **das/ er ist mir ~** I don't like that/him.

**untad(e)lig** adj impeccable; Mensch beyond reproach.

**Untat** f atrocity.

**untätig** adj (müßig) idle; (nicht handelnd) passive; Vulkan inactive, dormant.

**un-:** ~**tauglich** adj (zu, für for) unsuitable; (für Wehrdienst) unfit; U~**tauglichkeit** f siehe adj unsuitability; unfitness; ~**teilbar** adj indivisible.

**unten** adv at the bottom; (tiefer, drunten) (down) below; (an der Unterseite) underneath; (in Gebäude) downstairs. ~ **am Berg/im Glas** at the bottom of the mountain/glass; **nach ~** down; **bis ~** to the bottom; **dort** or **da/hier ~** down there/here; **weiter ~** further down; ~ **bleiben** (fig) to stay down; **rechts/links ~** down on the right/left; **siehe ~** see below; **er ist bei mir ~ durch** (col) I'm through with him (col).

**unten-:** ~**an** adv (am unteren Ende) at the far end; (in Reihenfolge: lit, fig) at the bottom; **(bei jdm)** ~**an stehen** (fig) to be at the bottom of sb's list; ~**drunter** adv (col) underneath; ~**genannt** adj attr undermentioned; ~**stehend** adj following.

**unter** prep **(a)** +dat under; (drunter) underneath, below; (zwischen, innerhalb) among(st). ~ **18 Jahren** under 18 years (of age); **Temperaturen ~ 25 Grad** temperatures below 25 degrees; **sie waren ~ sich** (dat) they were by themselves; **jdn ~ sich haben** to have sb under one; ~ **anderem** among other things; ~ **uns (gesagt)** between you and me. **(b)** +acc under. **bis ~ das Dach voll mit ...** full to the rafters with...

**Unter-:** ~**abteilung** f subdivision; ~**arm** m forearm; ~**art** f (esp Biol) subspecies; ~**bau** m, pl -ten (von Gebäude) foundations pl; (bei Straßen) (road)bed; u~**belegt** adj Hotel etc not full; u~ undersubscribed; u~**belichten*** vti insep (Phot) to underexpose; ~**belichtung** f (Phot) underexposure; ~**beschäftigung** f (Econ) underemployment; u~**besetzt** adj understaffed; u~**bewerten*** vt insep to underrate; u~**bewußt** adj subconscious; ~**bewußtsein** nt subconscious; **im ~bewußtsein** subconsciously; u~**bezahlen*** vt insep to underpay; u~**bieten*** vt insep irreg Konkurrenten to undercut; (fig) to surpass; (Sport) Rekord, Zeit to beat; u~**binden*** vt insep irreg to stop, to prevent; u~**bleiben*** vi insep irreg aux sein **(a)** (aufhören) to stop; **in Zukunft muß das u~bleiben** that must not

happen again in the future; **(b)** (versäumt werden) to be omitted; ~**bodenschutz** m (Aut) underseal; u~**brechen*** vt insep irreg to interrupt; Reise, Eintönigkeit to break; (langfristig) to break off; Telefonverbindung to disconnect; Spiel to suspend, to stop; **wir sind u~brochen worden** (am Telefon) we've been cut off; ~**brecherkontakte** pl (Aut) contact breaker points pl; ~**brechung** f interruption; break (+gen in); (von Telefonverbindung) disconnection; (von Spiel) stoppage; **ohne ~brechung** without a break; u~**breiten*** vt insep Plan to present; **(jdm) einen Vorschlag u~breiten** to make a proposal (to sb).

**unterbringen** vt sep irreg **(a)** to put; Arbeitslose etc to fix up (bei with). **ich kann nicht alles im Schrank ~** I can't put or get everything in the cupboard; **ich kenne ihn, aber ich kann ihn nirgends ~** (col) I know him, but I just can't place him. **(b)** (Unterkunft geben) Menschen to accommodate; (in Haus, Hotel etc auch) to put up. **gut/schlecht untergebracht sein** to have good/bad accommodation (Brit) or accommodations (US); (versorgt werden) to be well/badly looked after.

**Unterbringung** f accommodation (Brit), accommodations pl (US).

**unterbuttern** vt sep (col) **(a)** (zuschießen) to throw in. **(b)** (unterdrücken) to sit on (col).

**unterderhand** adv secretly; verkaufen privately.

**unterdessen** adv (in the) meantime, meanwhile.

**Unterdruck** m (Phys) below atmospheric pressure.

**unterdrücken*** vt insep **(a)** Neugier, Lachen to suppress; Gähnen to stifle; Tränen, Bemerkung to hold back. **(b)** (beherrschen) Menschen to oppress; Freiheit, Revolution to suppress.

**Unterdrücker(in** f**)** m - oppressor.

**Unterdrückung** f siehe vt suppression; stifling; holding back; oppression.

**unterdurchschnittlich** adj below average.

**unter|einander** adv **(a)** (gegenseitig) each other; (miteinander) among ourselves/themselves etc. **(b)** (räumlich) one below the other.

**unter|einander-** pref **(a)** (durcheinander-) together. **(b)** (örtlich) one below the other.

**unter|entwickelt** adj underdeveloped.

**Unter|entwicklung** f underdevelopment.

**untere(r, s)** adj, superl **unterste(r, s)** lower.

**Unter-:** u~**ernährt** adj undernourished; ~**ernährung** f malnutrition.

**Unterfangen** nt - (geh) venture, undertaking.

**Unterführung** f underpass.

**Untergang** m **(a)** (von Schiff) sinking. **(b)** (von Gestirn) setting. **(c)** (das Zugrundegehen) (allmählich) decline; (völlig) destruction; (der Welt) end; (von Individuum) downfall, ruin. **dem ~ geweiht sein** to be doomed.

**untergeben** adj subordinate.

**Untergebene(r)** mf decl as adj subordinate.

**untergegangen** adj Volk etc extinct; Zivilisation, Kultur auch lost.

**untergehen** vi sep irreg aux sein **(a)** (versinken) to sink; (Schiff auch) to go down; (fig: im Lärm etc) to be drowned. **(b)** (Gestirn) to set. **(c)** (Kultur, Welt) to come to an end; (Individuum) to perish; (im Existenzkampf) to go under.

**Unter-:** u~**geordnet** adj Dienststelle subordinate; Bedeutung secondary; ~**geschoß** nt basement; ~**gewicht** nt **~gewicht haben** to be underweight; u~**gewichtig** adj underweight; u~**gliedern*** vt insep to subdivide; u~**graben**[1]**\*** vt insep irreg to undermine; u~**graben**[2] vt sep irreg Dung etc to dig in; ~**grenze** f lower limit.

**Untergrund** *m no pl* (a) *(Geol)* subsoil. (b) *(farblicher Hintergrund)* background. (c) *(Pol etc)* underground. **in den ~ gehen** to go underground.

**Untergrund-** *in cpds (Pol etc)* underground; **~bahn** *f* underground *(Brit)*, subway *(US)*.

**Unter-:** **~gruppe** *f* subgroup; **u~haken** *vr sep sich bei jdm u~haken* to link arms with sb.

**unterhalb 1** *prep +gen* below. **2** *adv* below. **~ von** below.

**Unterhalt** *m no pl* (a) *(Lebens~)* keep, maintenance *(esp Jur)*. **seinen ~ verdienen** to earn one's living; **seinen ~ haben** to earn enough. (b) *(Instandhaltung)* upkeep.

**unterhalten\*** *insep irreg* **1** *vt* (a) *(versorgen)* to support. (b) *Geschäft, Kfz* to run; *Konto* to have. (c) *(pflegen) Kontakte* to maintain. (d) *Gäste, Publikum* to entertain. **2** *vr* (a) *(sprechen)* to talk *(mit* to, with*)*. **sich mit jdm (über etw** *acc)* **~** to (have a) talk with sb (about sth). (b) *(sich vergnügen)* to enjoy oneself.

**Unterhalter(in** *f)* *m -* (a) entertainer. (b) *(Verdiener)* breadwinner.

**unterhaltsam** *adj* entertaining.

**Unterhalts-:** **~geld** *nt* maintenance; **~kosten** *pl* maintenance costs *pl*; **~pflicht** *f* obligation to pay maintenance.

**Unterhaltung** *f* (a) *(Gespräch)* talk, conversation. (b) *(Amüsement)* entertainment. (c) *no pl (Instandhaltung)* upkeep; *(von Gebäuden auch, von Kfz, Maschinen)* maintenance.

**Unterhaltungs-:** **~elektronik** *f* consumer electronics *sing*; **~literatur** *f* light fiction; **~musik** *f* light music; **~programm** *nt* light entertainment programme *(Brit)* or program *(US)*.

**Unterhändler** *m* negotiator.

**Unterhaus** *nt* House of Commons *(Brit)*, Lower House.

**Unterhemd** *nt* vest *(Brit)*, undershirt *(US)*.

**unterhöhlen\*** *vt insep* to hollow out; *(fig)* to undermine.

**Unterholz** *nt no pl* undergrowth.

**Unterhose** *f (Herren~)* (pair of) underpants *pl*; *(Damen~)* (pair of) pants *pl*. **lange ~n** long johns *pl*.

**unter|irdisch** *adj* underground.

**unterjochen\*** *vt insep* to subjugate.

**unterjubeln** *vt sep (col) jdm etw ~ (andrehen)* to palm sth off on sb *(col)*; *(anlasten)* to pin sth on sb *(col)*.

**unterkellern\*** *vt insep* to build with a cellar.

**Unter-:** **~kiefer** *m* lower jaw; **~klasse** *f* (a) subclass; (b) *(Sociol)* lower class; **~kleidung** *f* underwear, underclothes *pl*.

**unterkommen** *vi sep irreg aux sein* (a) *(Unterkunft finden)* to find accommodation *(Brit)* or accommodations *(US)*; *(col: Stelle finden)* to find a job *(als* as, *bei* with, at*)*. **bei jdm ~** to stay at sb's (place). (b) **so etwas ist mir noch nie untergekommen!** *(col)* I've never come across anything like it!

**Unterkommen** *nt -* *(Obdach)* accommodation *no pl (Brit)*, accommodations *(US)*. **bei jdm ein ~ finden** to be put up at sb's (place).

**Unter-:** **~körper** *m* lower part of the body; **u~kriegen** *vt sep (col)* **sich nicht u~kriegen lassen** not to let things get one down; **u~kühlen\*** *vt insep Körper* to expose to subnormal temperatures; **u~kühlt** *adj Körper* affected by hypothermia; *(fig) Atmosphäre, Mensch* cool; **~kühlung** *f (Med)* hypothermia.

**Unterkunft** *f, pl* **Unterkünfte** (a) accommodation *no pl (Brit)*, accommodations *pl (US)*. **~ und Verpflegung** board and lodging. (b) *(von Soldaten etc)* quarters *pl*; *(esp in Privathaus)* billet.

**Unterlage** *f* (a) base; *(für Teppich)* underlay; *(im Bett)* drawsheet. (b) *usu pl (Papiere)* document, paper.

**unterlassen\*** *vt insep irreg (nicht tun)* to refrain from; *(nicht durchführen)* not to carry out; *(auslassen)* to omit; *etwas Dummes etc* to refrain from doing. **er hat es ~, mich zu benachrichtigen** he failed *or* omitted to notify me.

**Unterlassung** *f (Versäumnis)* omission *(gen* of*)*, failure *(einer Handlung* to do sth*)*.

**Unterlauf** *m* lower reaches *(of a river)*.

**unterlaufen[1]\*** *insep irreg* **1** *vi +dat aux sein* **mir ist ein Fehler ~** I made a mistake. **2** *vt Bestimmungen* to get around; *(unterminieren)* to undermine.

**unterlaufen[2]** *adj* **mit Blut ~** bloodshot.

**unterlegen[1]** *vt sep* to put underneath.

**unterlegen[2]** *adj* inferior; *(besiegt)* defeated. **jdm ~ sein** to be inferior to sb; **zahlenmäßig ~ sein** to be outnumbered.

**Unterlegene(r)** *mf decl as adj* loser; *(Benachteiligter)* underdog.

**Unterleib** *m* abdomen.

**Unterleibs-** *in cpds* abdominal; **~krebs** *m* cancer of the abdomen; cancer of the womb.

**unterliegen\*** *vi insep irreg aux sein* (a) *(besiegt werden)* to be defeated *(+dat* by*)*. (b) *+dat (unterworfen sein)* to be subject to; *einer Gebühr, Steuer* to be liable to. **es unterliegt keinem Zweifel, daß ...** it's not open to any doubt that ...

**Unterlippe** *f* bottom *or* lower lip.

**unterm** = **unter dem**.

**untermalen\*** *vt insep (mit Musik)* to provide with background music.

**Untermalung** *f (musikalische)* **~** background music.

**untermauern\*** *vt insep (Build, fig)* to underpin.

**Untermensch** *m (pej)* subhuman creature.

**Untermiete** *f* subtenancy. **bei jdm zur ~ wohnen** to rent a room from sb.

**Untermieter(in** *f)* *m* lodger, subtenant *(Jur)*.

**unterminieren\*** *vt insep (lit, fig)* to undermine.

**untern** = **unter den**.

**unternehmen\*** *vt insep irreg* to do; *(durchführen auch)* to undertake; *Versuch, Vorstoß, Reise* to make. **etwas/nichts gegen jdn/etw ~** to do something/nothing about sb/sth.

**Unternehmen** *nt -* (a) *(Firma)* business, enterprise. (b) *(Aktion, Vorhaben)* undertaking, enterprise; *(Mil)* operation.

**unternehmend** *adj* enterprising.

**Unternehmens-:** **~berater** *m* management consultant; **~leitung** *f* management; **~planung** *f* business or corporate planning.

**Unternehmer(in** *f)* *m -* company owner; *(Arbeitgeber)* (business) employer; *(alten Stils)* entrepreneur; *(Industrieller auch)* industrialist. **die ~** the employers.

**unternehmerisch** *adj* entrepreneurial.

**Unternehmer-:** **~kreise** *pl* **in/aus ~kreisen** among/from industrialists; **~verband** *m* employers' association.

**Unternehmung** *f* (a) *siehe* **Unternehmen**. (b) *(Transaktion)* undertaking.

**Unternehmungs-:** **~geist** *m no pl* enterprise; **~lust** *f no pl* enterprise; **u~lustig** *adj* enterprising.

**Unter-:** **~offizier** *m* non-commissioned officer, NCO; **u~ordnen** *sep* **1** *vt* to subordinate *(+dat* to*)*; **2** *vr* to subordinate oneself *(+dat* to*)*; **~ordnung** *f* (a) *no pl* subordination; (b) *(Biol)* sub-order; **~organisation** *f* subsidiary organization;

**u~privilegiert** adj underprivileged; **~programm** nt (Comp) subroutine.

**unterreden*** vr insep **sich (mit jdm)** ~ to confer (with sb).

**Unterredung** f discussion; (Pol auch) talks pl.

**Unterricht** m no pl teaching; (Stunden) lessons pl, classes pl. ~ **in Mathematik/Englisch** maths/English lessons or classes; **seine Art des ~s** his way of teaching; **(jdm)** ~ **geben** to teach (sb) (in etw (dat) sth/; **am** ~ **teilnehmen** to attend classes; **zu spät zum** ~ **kommen** to be late for class.

**unterrichten*** insep **1** vt **(a)** Schüler, Fach to teach. **jdn in etw** (dat) ~ to teach sb sth. **(b)** (informieren) to inform (von, über +acc about). **gut unterrichtete Kreise** well-informed circles. **2** vi to teach. **3** vr **sich über etw** (acc) ~ to inform oneself about sth.

**Unterrichts-:** **~einheit** f teaching unit; **~fach** nt subject; **u~frei** adj Stunde, Tag free; **der Montag ist u~frei** there are no classes on Monday; **~gegenstand** m topic, subject; **~methode** f teaching method; **~mittel** nt teaching aid; **~stoff** m subject matter taught; **~stunde** f lesson; **~zwecke** pl **zu ~zwecken** for teaching purposes.

**Unterrock** m underskirt, slip.

**unterrühren** vt sep to stir or mix in.

**unters = unter das.**

**untersagen*** vt insep to forbid, to prohibit. **jdm etw** ~ to forbid sb sth.

**Untersatz** m mat; (für Blumentöpfe etc) base.

**unterschätzen*** vt insep to underestimate.

**unterscheiden*** insep irreg **1** vt to distinguish. **A nicht von B** ~ **können** to be unable to tell the difference between A and B, to be unable to tell A from B. **2** vi to differentiate, to distinguish. **3** vr **sich (von etw)** ~ to differ (from sth).

**Unterscheidung** f differentiation; (Unterschied) difference, distinction. **eine** ~ **treffen** to make a distinction.

**Unterschenkel** m lower leg.

**Unterschicht** f (Sociol) lower class.

**unterschieben¹*** vt insep irreg (col: unterstellen) **jdm etw** ~ to attribute sth to sb; **du unterschiebst mir immer, daß ich schwindle** you're always accusing me of cheating.

**unterschieben²** vt sep irreg **(a)** (lit) **etw unter etw** (acc) ~ to push sth under(neath) sth. **(b)** (fig) **jdm etw** ~ to foist sth on sb.

**Unterschied** m **-e** difference; (Unterscheidung auch) distinction. **einen** ~ **(zwischen zwei Dingen) machen** to make a distinction (between two things); **das macht keinen** ~ that makes no difference; **im** ~ **zu jdm/etw** in contrast to sb/sth; **alle ohne** ~ **halfen mit** everyone without exception lent a hand; **Männer und Frauen ohne** ~ **getötet** men and women were killed indiscriminately.

**unterschiedlich** adj different; (veränderlich) variable; (gemischt) varied, patchy. **das ist sehr** ~ it varies a lot; ~ **gut/lang** of varying quality/length.

**unterschiedslos 1** adj indiscriminate. **2** adv indiscriminately; (gleichmäßig) on an equal basis.

**unterschlagen*** vt insep irreg Geld to embezzle; Brief, Beweise to withhold; (col) Nachricht etc to keep quiet about.

**Unterschlagung** f (von Geld) embezzlement.

**Unterschlupf** m, pl **Unterschlüpfe** (Obdach) shelter; (Versteck) hiding place.

**unterschlüpfen** vi sep aux sein (col) to take cover or shelter; (Versteck finden) to hide out (col) (bei jdm at sb's).

**unterschreiben*** vti insep irreg to sign. **das kann ich ~!** (fig) I'll subscribe to that!

**unterschreiten*** vt insep irreg to fall short of; Temperatur, Zahlenwert to fall below.

**Unterschrift** f **(a)** signature. **seine** ~ **leisten** to give one's signature; **jdm etw zur** ~ **vorlegen** to give sb sth to sign. **(b)** (Bild~) caption.

**unterschrifts-:** **~berechtigt** adj authorized to sign; **~reif** adj Vertrag ready to be signed.

**unterschwellig** adj subliminal.

**Unterseeboot** nt submarine.

**unterseeisch** [-zeːɪʃ] adj undersea, submarine.

**Unter-:** **~seite** f underside; **~setzer** m - siehe **~satz**; **u~setzt** adj stocky; **u~spülen*** vt insep to undermine; **~stadt** f lower part of a/the town; **~stand** m shelter; (Mil) dugout.

**unterstehen*** insep irreg **1** vi +dat to be under; **jdm** to be subordinate to; (in Firma) to report to; **dem Gesetz** to be subject to. **2** vr to dare. **untersteh dich (ja nicht)!** (don't) you dare!

**unterstellen¹*** vt insep **(a)** (unterordnen) to subordinate (dat to/. **jdm/etw unterstellt sein** to be under sb/sth; (in Firma) to report to sb/sth; **jdm etw** ~ to put sb in charge of sth. **(b)** (annehmen) to assume, to suppose. **(c)** (pej: unterschieben) **jdm etw** ~ to insinuate that sb has done/said sth.

**unterstellen²** sep **1** vt (abstellen, unterbringen) to keep; Möbel auch to store; Auto to keep under cover. **2** vr to take shelter.

**Unterstellung** f (falsche Behauptung) misrepresentation; (Andeutung) insinuation. **das ist eine ~!** what are you insinuating!

**unterste(r, s)** adj superl of **untere(r, s)** lowest; (tiefste auch) bottom; (letzte) last. **das U~ zuoberst kehren** to turn everything upside down.

**untersteuern*** vi insep (Aut) to understeer.

**Unter-:** **u~streichen*** vt insep irreg (lit, fig) to underline; **~strömung** f (lit, fig) undercurrent; **~stufe** f (Sch) lower school, lower grade (US).

**unterstützen*** vt insep to support (auch fig, Comp).

**Unterstützung** f **(a)** no pl support (zu, für for). **(b)** (Zuschuß) assistance, aid; (col: Arbeitslosen~) unemployment benefit (Brit), welfare (US).

**unterstützungsbedürftig** adj needy.

**untersuchen*** vt insep **(a)** to examine (auf +acc for); (erforschen) to look into, to investigate; (chemisch, technisch etc) to test (auf +acc for). **sich ärztlich** ~ **lassen** to have a medical or a check-up; **etw gerichtlich** ~ to try sth (in court). **(b)** (nachprüfen) to check, to verify.

**Untersuchung** f siehe vt **(a)** examination; investigation (gen, über +acc into); test; (ärztlich) examination, check-up. **(b)** check, verification.

**Untersuchungs-:** **~ausschuß** m fact-finding committee; (nach Unfall etc) committee of inquiry; **~ergebnis** nt (Jur) findings pl; (Med) result of an/the examination; (Sci) test result; **~gefangene(r)** mf remand prisoner; **~gefängnis** nt remand prison; **~haft** f custody; **in ~haft sein** to be remanded in custody; **~richter** m examining magistrate.

**Untertage-** in cpds underground; **~arbeiter** m (coal)face worker; **~bau** m no pl underground mining.

**Untertan** m (wk) **-en**, **-en** (old: Staatsbürger) subject; (pej) underling (pej).

**untertan** adj pred subject (+dat to).

**untertänig** adj subservient, submissive. **jdn ~st bitten** to ask sb most humbly.

**Unter-:** **u~tariflich** adj Bezahlung below the agreed or union rate; **~tasse** f saucer; **~tauchen** sep **1** vi aux sein to dive (under); (fig) to disappear; **2** vt to immerse; jdn to duck; **~teil** nt or m bottom or lower part; **~teilen*** vt insep to subdivide (in +acc into); ~**teilung** f subdivision *(in +acc* into); ~**teller** m saucer; ~**titel** m subtitle; *(für Bild)* caption; ~**ton** m *(Mus, fig)* undertone; **u~treiben\*** *insep irreg* **1** vt to understate; **2** vi to play things down; ~**treibung** f understatement; **u~tunneln\*** vt *insep* to tunnel under; **u~vermieten\*** vti insep to sublet, to sublease; ~**versorgung** f inadequate provision; **u~wandern\*** vt *insep* to infiltrate; ~**wanderung** f infiltration.

**Unterwäsche** f *no pl* underwear *no pl*.

**Unterwasser-** *in cpds* underwater.

**unterwegs** adv on the way *(nach, zu* to); *(auf Reisen)* away. **bei ihnen ist wieder ein Kind ~** they've got another child on the way.

**unterweisen\*** vt insep irreg *(geh)* to instruct *(in +dat* in).

**Unterwelt** f *(lit, fig)* underworld.

**unterwerfen\*** insep irreg **1** vt **(a)** *Volk* to subjugate. **(b)** *(unterziehen)* to subject *(dat* to). **einer Sache** *(dat)* **unterworfen sein** to be subject to sth. **2** vr *(lit, fig)* **sich jdm/einer Sache ~** to submit to sb/sth.

**Unterwerfung** f *siehe vtr* subjugation; subjection; submission.

**unterworfen** adj **der Mode ~ sein** to be subject to fashion.

**unterwürfig** adj *(pej)* servile, obsequious.

**Unterwürfigkeit** f *(pej)* servility, obsequiousness.

**unterzeichnen\*** vt insep *(form)* to sign.

**Unterzeichner** m - signatory.

**Unterzeichnung** f signing.

**unterziehen[1]\*** insep irreg **1** vr **sich einer Sache** *(dat)* **~** to undergo sth; **sich einer Prüfung** *(dat)* **~** to take an examination. **2** vt to subject *(dat* to).

**unterziehen[2]** vt sep irreg *Kleidung* to put on underneath.

**Untiefe** f *(seichte Stelle)* shallow.

**Untier** nt monster.

**untragbar** adj intolerable, unbearable.

**untrennbar** adj inseparable. **mit etw ~ verbunden sein** *(fig)* to be inextricably linked with sth.

**untreu** adj *Liebhaber etc* unfaithful; *(einer Sache)* disloyal *(dat* to). **sich** *(dat)* **selbst ~ werden** to be untrue to oneself.

**Untreue** f *siehe adj* unfaithfulness; disloyalty.

**untröstlich** adj inconsolable *(über +acc* about).

**untrüglich** adj *Gedächtnis* infallible; *Zeichen* unmistakable

**Untugend** f vice; *(Angewohnheit)* bad habit.

**untypisch** adj uncharacteristic.

**un-:** ~**überbietbar** adj *Preis, Rekord etc* unbeatable; *Frechheit, Eifer* unparalleled; ~**überbrückbar** adj *(fig) Gegensätze etc* irreconcilable; *Kluft* unbridgeable; ~**überlegt** adj rash; ~**übersehbar** adj *Schaden etc* incalculable; *Menge* vast, immense; *(auffällig) Fehler etc* obvious; ~**übersichtlich** adj *Gelände* rugged; *Kurve* blind; *System, Plan* confused; ~**übertrefflich 1** adj matchless; *Rekord* unbeatable; **2** adv superbly, magnificently; ~**übertroffen** adj unsurpassed; ~**überwindlich** adj insurmountable; *Gegner, Heer* invincible; *Festung* impregnable; ~**üblich** adj not usual.

**un|umgänglich** adj essential; *(unvermeidlich)* inevitable.

**un|umschränkt** adj unlimited. **~ herrschen** to have absolute power.

**un|umstößlich** adj *Tatsache* incontrovertible; *Entschluß* irrevocable. **~ feststehen** to be absolutely definite.

**un-:** ~**umstritten** adj indisputable, undisputed; ~**umwunden** adv frankly; ~**unterbrochen** adj uninterrupted; *(unaufhörlich)* incessant;

~**veränderlich** adj unchanging; *(unwandelbar)* unchangeable; ~**verändert** adj unchanged; **du siehst ~verändert jung aus** you look just as young as ever; ~**verantwortlich** adj irresponsible; ~**verarbeitet** adj *(lit, fig)* raw; ~**veräußerlich** adj *Rechte* inalienable; ~**verbesserlich** adj incorrigible; ~**verbindlich** adj **(a)** *(nicht bindend)* not binding; *Besichtigung* free; **sich** *(dat)* **etw ~verbindlich schicken lassen** to have sth sent without obligation; ~**verbindlicher Richtpreis** recommended (retail) price; **(b)** *(vage, allgemein)* noncommittal; *(nicht entgegenkommend)* abrupt; ~**verbleit** adj *Benzin* unleaded; ~**verblümt** adj blunt; ~**verbraucht** adj *(fig)* unspent; ~**verbürgt** adj unconfirmed; ~**verdächtig** adj unsuspicious; *(nicht unter Verdacht stehend)* unsuspected, above suspicion; ~**verdaulich** adj *(lit, fig)* indigestible; ~**verdient** adj undeserved; ~**verdorben** adj *(lit, fig)* unspoilt, pure; ~**verdrossen** adj undeterred; *(unermüdlich)* untiring; ~**verdünnt** adj undiluted; ~**vereinbar** adj incompatible; ~**verfälscht** adj *(lit, fig)* unadulterated; *Dialekt* pure; *Natürlichkeit* unaffected; *Natur* unspoilt; ~**verfänglich** adj harmless.

**unverfroren** adj insolent.

**unvergänglich** adj *Werk* immortal; *Ruhm* undying; *Eindruck, Erinnerung* everlasting, abiding, *Melodien* evergreen.

**unvergessen** adj unforgotten.

**unvergeßlich** adj unforgettable. **das wird mir ~ bleiben** I'll never forget that.

**un-:** ~**vergleichlich** adj unique, incomparable; ~**verhältnismäßig** adv disproportionately; *(übermäßig)* excessively; ~**verheiratet** adj unmarried; ~**verhofft** adj unexpected; ~**verhohlen** adj open, unconcealed; ~**verhüllt** adj **(a)** *Tatsachen* undisguised; **(b)** *siehe* ~**verhohlen**; ~**verkäuflich** adj *(nicht absetzbar)* unsaleable; *(nicht zum Verkauf)* not for sale; ~**verkäufliches Muster** trade sample; ~**verkennbar** adj unmistakable; ~**verlangt** adj unsolicited; ~**verletzlich** adj *(fig) Rechte* inviolable; *(lit)* invulnerable; ~**vermeidlich** adj inevitable; *(nicht zu umgehen)* unavoidable; ~**vermindert** adj undiminished; ~**vermischt** adj unmixed; *(rein)* pure; ~**vermittelt** adj *(plötzlich)* sudden, unexpected.

**Unvermögen** nt *no pl* inability.

**unvermögend** adj *(arm)* without means.

**unvermutet** adj unexpected.

**Unvernunft** f *(Torheit)* stupidity; *(mangelnder Verstand)* irrationality; *(Uneinsichtigkeit)* unreasonableness.

**unvernünftig** adj *siehe n* stupid; irrational; unreasonable.

**unverrichtet** adj: ~**er Dinge zurückkehren** to return without having achieved anything.

**unverrückbar** adj *(fig)* unshakeable. **~ feststehen** to be absolutely definite.

**unverschämt** adj outrageous; *Mensch, Frage, Benehmen etc* impudent, impertinent; *Lüge auch* blatant, barefaced.

**Unverschämtheit** f **(a)** *no pl* outrageousness. **(b)** *(Bemerkung)* impertinence; *(Tat)* outrageous thing. **das ist eine ~!** it's outrageous!

**unverschuldet** adj occurring through no fault of one's own.

**unversehens** adv suddenly; *(überraschend)* unexpectedly.

**un-:** ~**versehrt** adj *Mensch (lit, fig)* unscathed; ~**versöhnlich** adj irreconcilable; ~**versorgt** adj *Familie, Kinder* unprovided for.

**Unverstand** m lack of judgement; *(Torheit)* folly.

**unverstanden** *adj* not understood; *(mißverstanden)* misunderstood.

**unverständlich** *adj* incomprehensible. **es ist mir ~** I cannot understand it.

**Unverständnis** *nt no pl* lack of understanding; *(für Kunst etc)* lack of appreciation.

**un-:** **~versucht** *adj:* **nichts ~versucht lassen** to leave no stone unturned, to try everything; **~verträglich** *adj* **(a)** *(streitsüchtig)* quarrelsome; **(b)** *(unverdaulich)* indigestible; *(Med: mit anderer Substanz etc)* incompatible; **~vertretbar** *adj* unjustifiable; **~verwandt** *adv* fixedly, steadfastly; **~verwechselbar** *adj* unmistakable, distinctive; **~verwundbar** *adj* *(lit, fig)* invulnerable; **~verwüstlich** *adj* indestructible; *Gesundheit* robust; *Mensch* irrepressible; **~verzagt** *adj* undaunted; **~verzeihlich** *adj* unforgivable; **~verzichtbar** *adj attr Recht* inalienable; *Anspruch* indisputable; *Bedingung* indispensable; **~verzinslich** *adj* interest-free; **~verzollt** *adj* duty-free; **~verzüglich 1** *adj* immediate; **2** *adv* immediately; **~vollendet** *adj* unfinished; **~vollkommen** *adj* *(unvollständig)* incomplete; *(fehlerhaft, mangelhaft)* imperfect.

**unvollständig** *adj* incomplete. **er hat das Formular ~ ausgefüllt** he didn't fill in all the details on the form.

**un-:** **~vorbereitet** *adj* unprepared *(auf +acc for)*; **eine ~vorbereitete Rede halten** to make an impromptu speech; **~voreingenommen** *adj* unbiased, unprejudiced; **~vorhergesehen** *adj* unforeseen; *Besuch* unexpected; **~vorhersehbar** *adj* unforeseeable; **~vorschriftsmäßig** *adj* not in keeping with the regulations; **~vorsichtig** *adj* careless; *(voreilig)* rash; **~vorstellbar** *adj* inconceivable; **~vorteilhaft** *adj* disadvantageous; *Kleid, Frisur etc* unbecoming; **~vorteilhaft aussehen** not to look one's best.

**Un-:** **u~wahr** *adj* untrue; **u~wahrhaftig** *adj* untruthful; *Gefühle* insincere; **~wahrheit** *f* untruth.

**unwahrscheinlich 1** *adj* improbable; *(col: groß)* incredible *(col)*. **2** *adv (col)* incredibly *(col)*.

**Unwahrscheinlichkeit** *f* improbability.

**unwandelbar** *adj (geh)* unalterable; *Treue* unwavering.

**unwegsam** *adj Gelände etc* rough.

**unweiblich** *adj* unfeminine.

**unweigerlich 1** *adj attr Folge* inevitable. **2** *adv* inevitably.

**unweit** *prep +gen, adv* not far from.

**Unwesen** *nt no pl (übler Zustand)* terrible state of affairs. **sein ~ treiben** *(Mörder etc)* to be up to his foul deeds.

**unwesentlich** *adj* irrelevant; *(unwichtig)* unimportant, insignificant.

**Unwetter** *nt* (thunder)storm. **ein ~ brach los** a storm broke.

**un-:** **~wichtig** *adj* unimportant; *(belanglos)* irrelevant; *(verzichtbar)* non-essential; **~widerlegbar** *adj* irrefutable; **~widerruflich** *adj* irrevocable; **es steht ~widerruflich fest, daß ...** it is absolutely definite that ...; **~widersprochen** *adj Behauptung* unchallenged; **~widerstehlich** *adj* irresistible; **~wiederbringlich** *adj (geh)* irretrievable.

**Unwille(n)** *m no pl* displeasure *(über +acc at)*; *(Ärger)* irritation. **jds ~n erregen** to incur sb's displeasure.

**unwillig** *adj (verärgert)* indignant *(über +acc about)*; *(widerwillig)* unwilling, reluctant.

**unwillkommen** *adj* unwelcome.

**unwillkürlich** *adj* spontaneous; instinctive.

**Un-:** **u~wirklich** *adj* unreal; **u~wirksam** *adj* ineffective; *Vertrag etc* void; **u~wirsch** *adj* surly, gruff; *Bewegung* brusque; **u~wirtlich** *adj* inhospitable; **u~wirtschaftlich** *adj* uneconomic; **~wissen** *nt* ignorance; **u~wissend** *adj* ignorant; *(unerfahren)* inexperienced; **~wissenheit** *f no pl siehe adj* ignorance; inexperience; **u~wissenschaftlich** *adj* unscientific; *Ausdrucksweise* unacademic; **u~wissentlich** *adv* unwittingly, unknowingly.

**unwohl** *adj (unpäßlich)* unwell; *(unbehaglich)* uneasy. **mir ist ~** I don't feel well.

**Unwohlsein** *nt* indisposition; *(unangenehmes Gefühl)* unease.

**un-:** **~wohnlich** *adj Zimmer etc* uncomfortable; **~würdig** *adj* unworthy *(+gen* of); *Verhalten* undignified; *Situation* degrading.

**Unzahl** *f* **eine ~ von** a host of.

**unzählbar** *adj* innumerable, countless; *(Gram)* uncountable.

**unzählig 1** *adj* innumerable, countless. **~e Male** countless times, time and again. **2** *adv* **~ viele** huge numbers.

**unzähmbar** *adj* untameable; *(fig auch)* indomitable.

**Unze** *f* **-n** ounce.

**Unzeit** *f* **zur ~** *(geh)* at an inopportune moment.

**un-:** **~zeitgemäß** *adj (altmodisch)* old-fashioned; **~zensiert** *adj* uncensored; *(Sch)* ungraded; **~zerbrechlich** *adj* unbreakable; **~zerstörbar** *adj* indestructible; **~zertrennlich** *adj* inseparable; **~zivilisiert** *adj* uncivilized.

**Unzucht** *f no pl (esp Jur)* sexual offence *(Brit)* or offense *(US)*. **~ mit jdm treiben** to fornicate with sb.

**unzüchtig** *adj (esp Jur)* indecent; *Reden* obscene.

**Un-:** **u~zufrieden** *adj* dissatisfied, discontent; **~zufriedenheit** *f no pl* dissatisfaction, discontent; **u~zugänglich** *adj Gegend* inaccessible; *Mensch* inapproachable; *(unaufgeschlossen gegen)* deaf *(+dat* to); **u~zulänglich** *adj* insufficient, inadequate; **~zulänglichkeit** *f* **(a)** insufficiency, inadequacy; **(b)** *usu pl* shortcomings *pl*; **u~zulässig** *adj (auch Jur)* inadmissible; *Gebrauch* improper; *Belastung, Geschwindigkeit* excessive; **u~zumutbar** *adj* unreasonable; **u~zurechnungsfähig** *adj* not responsible for one's actions; **jdn für u~zurechnungsfähig erklären lassen** *(Jur)* to have sb certified (insane); **u~zureichend** *adj* insufficient, inadequate; **u~zusammenhängend** *adj* incoherent; **u~zustellbar** *adj* undeliverable; **falls u~zustellbar, bitte an Absender zurück** if undelivered, please return to sender; **u~zuträglich** *adj* **jds Gesundheit u~zuträglich sein** to be bad for sb's health; **u~zutreffend** *adj* inapplicable; *(unwahr)* incorrect; **~zutreffendes bitte streichen** delete as applicable; **u~zuverlässig** *adj* unreliable; **~zuverlässigkeit** *f* unreliability; **u~zweckmäßig** *adj (nicht ratsam)* unadvisable; *(unpraktisch)* impractical; *(ungeeignet)* unsuitable; **u~zweideutig** *adj* unambiguous, unequivocal; *(fig: unanständig)* explicit; **u~zweifelhaft 1** *adj* indubitable, unquestionable; **2** *adv* without doubt.

**üppig** *adj Wachstum* luxuriant; *Vegetation auch* lush; *Haar* thick; *Mahl, Ausstattung* sumptuous; *Gehalt* lavish; *Figur, Frau* voluptuous; *Leben* luxurious; *Phantasie* rich. **~ leben** to live in style.

**Ur-** *in cpds (erste)* first; *(ursprünglich)* original; **~abstimmung** *f* (strike) ballot; **~ahn(e)** *m (Vorfahr)* forefather; *(~großvater)* great-grandfather; **~ahne** *f (Vorfahr)* forebear; *(~großmutter)* great-grandmother.

**Ural** *m* **der ~** the Urals *pl*, the Ural mountains *pl*.

**ur|alt** *adj* ancient.

**Uran** *nt no pl* uranium.
**ur|aufführen** *vt ptp* **uraufgeführt** to give the first performance of; *Film* to premiere.
**Ur|aufführung** *f* premiere; *(von Theaterstück etc auch)* first night; *(von Musikstück)* first performance.
**urbar** *adj* die Wüste/Land ~ **machen** to reclaim the desert/to cultivate land.
**Ur-**: ~**bevölkerung** *f* original inhabitants *pl*; ~**bild** *nt* archetype; ~**christentum** *nt* early Christianity; u~**eigen** *adj* very own; ~**einwohner** *m* original inhabitant; *(in Australien und Neuseeland)* Aborigine; ~**enkel** *m* great-grandchild, great-grandson; ~**enkelin** *f* great-granddaughter; ~**fassung** *f* original version; u~**gemütlich** *adj* really comfortable *or* cosy; ~**geschichte** *f* prehistory; ~**gewalt** *f* elemental force.
**Urgroß-**: ~**eltern** *pl* great-grandparents *pl*; ~**mutter** *f* great-grandmother; ~**vater** *m* great-grandfather.
**Urheber(in** *f)* *m* - originator; *(Jur: Verfasser)* author.
**Urheber-**: ~**recht** *nt* copyright *(an +dat* on*)*; u~**rechtlich** *adj* u~**rechtlich geschützt** copyright.
**urig** *adj (col) Mensch* ruggedly idiosyncratic; *Kneipe, Volksfest* ethnic.
**Urin** *m* -e urine.
**urinieren\*** *vi* to urinate.
**Ur-**: ~**knall** *m (Astron)* big bang; u~**komisch** *adj (col)* screamingly funny *(col)*.
**Urkunde** *f* -**n** document; *(Kauf~)* deed; *(Gründungs~ etc)* charter; *(Sieger~, Diplom, Bescheinigung etc)* certificate.
**urkundlich** *adj* documentary. ~ **verbürgt** authenticated; ~ **erwähnt** mentioned in a document, documented.
**Urlaub** *m* -e *(Ferien)* holiday(s) *(Brit)*, vacation *(US)*; *(esp Mil)* leave. ~ **haben** to have a holiday *or* vacation/to have leave; **in** ~ **fahren** to go on holiday *or* vacation/on leave; **(sich** *dat)* **einen Tag** ~ **nehmen** to take a day off.
**Urlauber(in** *f)* *m* - holiday-maker *(Brit)*, vacationist *(US)*.
**Urlaubs-**: ~**anspruch** *m* holiday *(Brit)* or vacation *(US)* entitlement; ~**gebiet** *nt* holiday *(Brit)* or vacation *(US)* area; ~**geld** *nt* holiday *(Brit)* or vacation *(US)* money; ~**ort** *m* holiday *(Brit)* or vacation *(US)* resort; u~**reif** *adj (col)* ready for a holiday *(Brit)* or vacation *(US)*; ~**reise** *f* holiday *(Brit)* or vacation *(US)* trip; ~**tag** *m* (one day of) holiday *(Brit)* or vacation *(US)*; **ich habe noch drei** ~**tage gut** I've still got three days' holiday *or* vacation to come; ~**vertretung** *f* temporary replacement; *(von Arzt, Anwalt)* locum; ~**zeit** *f* holiday *(Brit)* or vacation *(US)* period.
**Urmensch** *m* primeval man; *(col)* caveman *(col)*.
**Urne** *f* -**n** urn; *(Los~)* box; *(Wahl~)* ballot-box. **zur** ~ **gehen** to go to the polls.
**Urologe** *m*, **Urologin** *f* urologist.
**Ur-**: ~**oma** *f (col)* great-granny *(col)*; ~**opa** *m (col)* great-grandpa *(col)*; ~**pflanze** *f* primordial plant; u~**plötzlich** *adv (col)* all of a sudden.
**Ursache** *f* -**n** cause; *(Grund)* reason; *(Beweggrund)* motive. ~ **und Wirkung** cause and effect; **keine** ~**!** *(auf Dank)* don't mention it, you're welcome; *(auf Entschuldigung)* that's all right; **ohne (jede)** ~ **for** no reason (at all); **jdm** ~ **geben, etw zu tun** to give sb cause to do sth; **alle/keine** ~ **haben, etw zu tun** to have every/no reason to do sth.
**ursächlich** *adj (esp Philos)* causal. **in** ~**em Zusammenhang stehen** to be causally related.

**Ur-**: ~**schrei** *m (Psych)* primal scream; ~**schrift** *f* original (text).
**Ursprung** *m, pl* **Ursprünge** origin. **seinen** ~ **in etw** *(dat)* **haben** to originate in sth.
**ursprünglich 1** *adj* **(a)** *attr* original; *(anfänglich)* initial, first. **(b)** *(urwüchsig)* natural; *Natur* unspoilt. **2** *adv* originally; *(anfänglich)* initially.
**Ursprünglichkeit** *f* naturalness.
**Ursprungsland** *nt (Comm)* country of origin.
**Urteil** *nt* -e **(a)** judgement; *(Entscheidung)* decision; *(Meinung)* opinion. **nach meinem** ~ in my judgement/opinion; **ich kann darüber kein** ~ **abgeben** I am no judge of this; **sich** *(dat)* **ein** ~ **über etw** *(acc)* **erlauben/ein** ~ **über etw fällen** to pass judgement on sth; **sich** *(dat)* **kein** ~ **über etw** *(acc)* **erlauben können** to be in no position to judge sth; **zu dem** ~ **kommen, daß** ... to come to the conclusion that ...; **sich** *(dat)* **ein** ~ **über jdn/etw bilden** to form an opinion about sb/sth. **(b)** *(Jur: Gerichts~)* verdict; *(Richterspruch)* judgement; *(Strafmaß)* sentence; *(Schiedsspruch)* award; *(Scheidungsspruch)* decree. **das** ~ **über jdn sprechen** *(Jur)* to pass judgement on or upon sb.
**urteilen** *vi* to judge *(nach* by*)*. **über etw** *(acc)* ~ to judge sth; *(seine Meinung äußern)* to give one's opinion on sth.
**Urteils-**: ~**begründung** *f (Jur)* opinion; u~**fähig** *adj* competent to judge; *(umsichtig)* discriminating; ~**findung** *f (Jur)* reaching a verdict *no art*; ~**kraft** *f no pl* power of judgement; *(Umsichtigkeit)* discrimination; ~**spruch** *m (Jur)* judgement; *(von Geschworenen)* verdict; *(von Strafgericht)* sentence; *(von Schiedsgericht)* award; ~**verkündung** *f (Jur)* pronouncement of judgement; ~**vermögen** *nt* = ~**kraft**.
**Ur-**: ~**text** *m* original (text); ~**trieb** *m* basic drive; u~**tümlich** *adj* = u~**wüchsig**; ~**typ(us)** *m, pl* ~**typen** prototype.
**Uruguay** *nt* Uruguay.
**Uruguayer(in** *f)* *m* - Uruguayan.
**uruguayisch** *adj* Uruguayan.
**Ur|ur-** *in cpds* great-great-.
**Ur-**: ~**vater** *m* forefather; u~**verwandt** *adj Wörter* cognate; ~**viech**, ~**vieh** *nt (col)* real character; ~**wald** *m* primeval forest; *(in den Tropen)* jungle; ~**welt** *f* primeval world; u~**weltlich** *adj* primeval, primordial; u~**wüchsig** *adj* natural; *Natur* unspoilt; *(urweltlich) Flora* primeval; *(ursprünglich)* original; *(bodenständig)* rooted to the soil; *(unberührt) Land etc* untouched; *(urgewaltig) Kraft* elemental; *(derb, kräftig)* sturdy; *Mensch* rugged; *Humor, Sprache* earthy; ~**zeit** *f* primeval times *pl*; **seit** ~**zeiten** since primeval times; *(col)* for donkey's years *(col)*; u~**zeitlich** *adj* primeval; *Mensch* primitive; ~**zustand** *m* primordial state.
**USA** [uː|ɛsˈ|aː] *pl* die ~ the USA *sing*.
**Usambaraveilchen** *nt* African violet.
**usf.** = **und so fort**.
**Usurpator** *m (liter)* usurper.
**usurpieren\*** *vt (liter)* to usurp.
**usw.** = **und so weiter** etc.
**Utensil** *nt* -**ien** [-iən] utensil, implement.
**utilitaristisch** *adj* utilitarian.
**Utopie** *f* utopia.
**utopisch** *adj* utopian.
**u.U.** = **unter Umständen**.
**uV** [uːˈfau] = **ultraviolett** UV.
**UV-Strahlen** *pl* UV rays.
**Ü-Wagen** *m (Rad, TV)* outside broadcast vehicle.
**uzen** *vti (col)* to tease, to kid *(col)*.
**Uzname** *m (col)* nickname.

# V

**V, v** [faʊ] nt -, - V, v. **V wie Viktor** ≈ V for Victor.
**V** = (a) **Volt**. (b) **Volumen**.
**VAE** [faʊ|aː'|eː] pl = **Vereinigte Arabische Emirate** UAE.
**Vagabund** [vaga'bʊnt] m (wk) -en, -en vagabond.
**vag(e)** [vaːk,'vaːgə] adj vague.
**Vagheit** ['vaːkhait] f vagueness.
**Vagina** [va'giːna] f, pl **Vaginen** (Anat) vagina.
**Vakuum** ['vaːkuʊm] nt, pl **Vakuen** ['vaːkuən] (lit, fig) vacuum. **unter/im** ~ in a vacuum.
**Vakuum-** ['vaːkuʊm-] in cpds vacuum; ~**pumpe** f vacuum pump; **v~verpackt** adj vacuum-packed.
**Valentinstag** ['vaːlɛntiːns-] m (St) Valentine's Day.
**Valuta** [va'luːta] f, pl **Valuten** (Währung) foreign currency.
**Vamp** [vɛmp] m -s vamp.
**Vampir** [vam'piːɐ] m -e vampire.
**Vandalismus** [vanda'lɪsmʊs] m no pl vandalism.
**Vanille** [va'nɪljə, va'nɪlə] f no pl vanilla.
**Vanille-**: ~**eis** nt vanilla ice-cream; ~**geschmack** m vanilla flavour (Brit) or flavor (US); **mit** ~**geschmack** vanilla-flavoured (Brit) or -flavored (US); ~**soße** f vanilla sauce, ≈ custard; ~**zucker**, **Vanillinzucker** m vanilla sugar.
**variabel** [va'riaːbl] adj variable.
**Variable** [va'riaːblə] f (wk) -n, -n variable.
**Variante** [va'riantə] f -n variant (zu on).
**Variation** [varia'tsioːn] f variation. ~**en zu einem Thema** variations on a theme.
**Varieté** [varie'teː] nt -s (a) variety, vaudeville (US). (b) (Theater) variety theatre (Brit), music hall (Brit), vaudeville theater (US).
**Varieté-**: ~**nummer** f variety act; ~**theater** nt variety theatre (Brit), vaudeville theater (US).
**variieren*** [vari'iːrən] vti to vary.
**Vasall** [va'zal] m (wk) -en, -en (Hist, fig) vassal.
**Vase** ['vaːzə] f -n vase.
**Vater** m ⁼ (lit, fig) father. ~ **unser** (Rel) Our Father; **unsere** ⁓ pl (geh: Vorfahren) our (fore)fathers; **wie der** ~, **so der Sohn** (prov) like father, like son (prov); ~ **Staat** (hum) the State.
**Vater-**: ~**figur** f father figure; ~**freuden** pl joys of fatherhood pl; ~**haus** nt parental home.
**Vaterland** nt native country; (esp Deutschland auch) Fatherland. **unser** ~ our country.
**vaterländisch** adj national; (patriotisch) patriotic.
**Vaterlands-**: ~**liebe** f patriotism; **v~liebend** adj patriotic; ~**verräter** m traitor.
**väterlich** adj paternal, fatherly.
**väterlicherseits** adv on one's father's side. **meine Großeltern** ~ my paternal grandparents.
**Vater-**: ~**liebe** f fatherly love; **v~los** adj fatherless; ~**recht** nt patriarchy.
**Vaterschaft** f fatherhood no art; (esp Jur) paternity.
**Vaterschafts-**: ~**klage** f paternity suit; ~**urlaub** m paternity leave.
**Vater-**: ~**stadt** f home town; ~**stelle** f **bei jdm** ~**stelle vertreten** to take the place of sb's father;

~**tag** m Father's Day; ~**tier** nt sire; ~**unser** nt - **das** ~**unser** the Lord's Prayer.
**Vati** m -s (col) dad(dy) (col).
**Vatikan** [vati'kaːn] m Vatican.
**Vatikanstadt** [vati'kaːn-] f Vatican City.
**V-Ausschnitt** ['faʊ-] m V-neck.
**VB** = **Verhandlungsbasis** o.i.r.o.
**v. Chr.** = **vor Christus** BC.
**Veganer(in** f) [ve'gaːnɐ, -ərɪn] m - vegan.
**Vegetarier(in** f) [vege'taːriɐ, -iərɪn] m - vegetarian.
**vegetarisch** [vege'taːrɪʃ] adj vegetarian. ~ **leben** to be a vegetarian.
**Vegetarismus** [vegeta'rɪsmʊs] m no pl vegetarianism.
**Vegetation** [vegeta'tsioːn] f vegetation.
**vegetieren*** [vege'tiːrən] vi to vegetate; (kärglich leben) to eke out a bare existence.
**Vehikel** [ve'hiːkl] nt - (pej col) boneshaker (col).
**Veilchen** nt violet; (col: blaues Auge) shiner (col), black eye. **blau wie ein** ~ (col) roaring drunk (col).
**Vektor** ['vɛktɔr] m (Math, Phys) vector.
**Velo** ['veːlo] nt -s (Sw) bicycle, bike (col); (motorisiert) moped.
**Velours** [və'luːɐ, ve'luːɐ] m - (Tex) velour(s).
**Velours(leder)** [və'luːɐ-, ve'luːɐ-] nt - suede.
**Vene** ['veːnə] f -n vein.
**Venedig** [ve'neːdɪç] nt Venice.
**Venezianer(in** f) [vene'tsiaːnɐ, -ərɪn] m - Venetian.
**venezianisch** [vene'tsiaːnɪʃ] adj Venetian.
**Venezolaner(in** f) [venetso'laːnɐ, -ərɪn] m - Venezuelaner.
**venezolanisch** [venetso'laːnɪʃ] adj Venezuelan.
**Venezuela** [vene'tsueːla] nt Venezuela.
**Ventil** [vɛn'tiːl] nt -e valve; (fig) outlet.
**Ventilation** [vɛntila'tsioːn] f ventilation.
**Ventilator** [vɛnti'laːtɔr] m ventilator.
**Venus** ['veːnʊs] f no pl (Myth, Astron) Venus.
**ver|abreden*** **1** vt to arrange; Termin auch to agree. **es war eine verabredete Sache** it was arranged beforehand; **wir haben verabredet, daß wir uns um 5 Uhr treffen** we have arranged to meet at 5 o'clock; **schon verabredet sein** (für on) to have a prior engagement (esp form), to have something else on; **mit jdm verabredet sein** to have arranged to meet sb. **2** vr **sich mit jdm/miteinander** ~ to arrange to meet sb/to meet.
**Ver|abredung** f (Vereinbarung) arrangement, agreement; (Treffen) appointment; (esp mit Freund/Freundin) date. **ich habe eine** ~ I'm meeting somebody.
**ver|abreichen*** vt Tracht Prügel etc to give; Arznei auch to administer (form) (jdm to sb).
**ver|abscheuen*** vt to detest, to abhor, to loathe.
**ver|abscheuungswürdig** adj detestable.
**ver|abschieden*** **1** vt to say goodbye to; (entlassen) to discharge; (Pol) Haushaltsplan to adopt; Gesetz to pass. **2** vr **sich (von jdm)** ~ to say goodbye (to sb), to take one's leave (of sb).

Ver|abschiedung *f (von Beamten etc)* discharge; *(Pol) (von Gesetz)* passing; *(von Haushaltsplan)* adoption.

ver|achten* *vt* to despise; *(liter) Tod, Gefahr* to scorn. nicht zu ~ *(col)* not to be scoffed at.

ver|achtenswert *adj* despicable, contemptible.

ver|ächtlich *adj* contemptuous; *(verachtenswert)* despicable, contemptible.

Ver|achtung *f no pl* contempt *(von* for). jdn mit ~ strafen to treat sb with contempt.

ver|albern* *vt (col)* to make fun of.

ver|allgemeinern* *vti* to generalize.

Ver|allgemeinerung *f* generalization.

ver|alten* *vi aux sein* to become obsolete; *(Mode)* to go out of date.

ver|altet *adj* obsolete; *Mode* out-of-date.

Veranda [ve'randa] *f, pl* Veranden veranda, porch.

ver|änderlich *adj* variable; *Wetter, Mensch* changeable.

Ver|änderlichkeit *f siehe adj* variability; changeability.

ver|ändern* 1 *vt* to change. 2 *vr* to change; *(Stellung wechseln)* to change one's job; *(Wohnung wechseln)* to move. verändert aussehen to look different.

Ver|änderung *f* change. eine berufliche ~ a change of job.

ver|ängstigen* *vt (erschrecken)* to frighten; *(einschüchtern)* to intimidate.

ver|ankern* *vt (Naut, Tech)* to anchor; *(fig)* to embed *(in +dat* in).

Ver|ankerung *f (Naut, Tech)* anchoring; *(fig: von Rechten)* (firm) establishment.

ver|anlagen* *vt* to assess *(mit* at).

ver|anlagt *adj* melancholisch ~ sein to have a melancholy disposition; praktisch ~ sein to be practically minded; künstlerisch ~ sein to be artistic; zu *or* für etw ~ sein to be cut out for sth.

Ver|anlagung *f* (a) *(körperlich, esp Med)* predisposition; *(charakterlich, esp Hang)* nature, disposition; *(Hang)* tendency; *(allgemeine Fähigkeiten)* natural abilities *pl*; *(künstlerisches, praktisches etc Talent)* bent. (b) *(von Steuern)* assessment.

ver|anlassen* *vt* (a) etw ~ to arrange for sth; *(befehlen)* to order sth. (b) *auch vi (bewirken)* to give rise *(zu* to). jdn zu etw ~ to lead sb to sth; jdn (dazu) ~, etw zu tun to cause sb to do sth; was hat dich dazu veranlaßt? what made you do this?

Ver|anlassung *f* cause, reason. auf ~ von *or +gen* at the instigation of; keine ~ zu etw haben/keine ~ haben, etw zu tun to have no cause *or* reason for sth/to do sth.

ver|anschaulichen* *vt* to illustrate *(an +dat, mit* with). sich *(dat)* etw ~ to visualize sth.

Ver|anschaulichung *f* illustration. zur ~ as an illustration.

ver|anschlagen* *vt* to estimate *(auf +acc* at). etw zu hoch/niedrig ~ to overestimate/underestimate sth.

ver|anstalten* *vt* to organize, to arrange; *(kommerziell) Konzerte etc* to promote; *Party* to hold.

Ver|anstalter(in *f)* *m* - organizer; *(Comm: von Konzerten etc)* promoter.

Ver|anstaltung *f* (a) event *(von* organized by); *(feierlich, öffentlich)* function. (b) *no pl (das Veranstalten)* organization.

Ver|anstaltungs-: ~kalender *m* calendar of events, ≈ what's on; ~programm *nt* programme of events.

ver|antworten* 1 *vt* to accept responsibility for; *die Folgen auch, sein Tun* to answer for *(vor +dat*

to). wie könnte ich es denn ~, ...? it would be most irresponsible of me ...; eine nicht zu ~de Fahrlässigkeit inexcusable negligence. 2 *vr* sich für *or* wegen etw ~ to justify sth *(vor +dat* to).

ver|antwortlich *adj* responsible; *(haftbar)* liable. jdm (gegenüber) ~ sein to be responsible to sb; jdn für etw ~ machen to hold sb responsible for sth.

Ver|antwortung *f* responsibility *(für* for). auf eigene ~ on one's own responsibility; auf deine ~! on your head be it!; jdn zur ~ ziehen to call sb to account.

Ver|antwortungs-: v~bewußt *adj* responsible; ~bewußtsein *nt* sense of responsibility; ~gefühl *nt* sense of responsibility; v~los *adj* irresponsible; ~losigkeit *f no pl* irresponsibility; v~voll *adj* responsible.

ver|arbeiten* *vt* to use *(zu etw* to make sth); *(Tech, Biol, Comp)* to process; *Ton, Gold etc* to work; *(verbrauchen)* to consume; *Erlebnis etc* to assimilate, to digest. ~de Industrie processing industries *pl*; etw geistig ~ to assimilate *or* digest sth.

ver|arbeitet *adj* gut/schlecht ~ Rock etc well/badly finished *or* made.

Ver|arbeitung *f* (a) *(von Rohstoffen etc)* processing. (b) *(Ausführung)* finish.

ver|ärgern* *vt* to annoy.

ver|armen* *vi aux sein (lit, fig)* to become impoverished. verarmt impoverished.

ver|arschen* *vt (col!)* to take the piss out of *(col!)*; *(für dumm verkaufen)* to mess around *(col)*.

ver|arzten* *vt (col)* to fix up *(col)*.

ver|ästeln* *vr* to branch out; *(fig)* to ramify.

ver|ätzen* *vt Metall* to corrode; *Gesicht, Haut etc* to burn.

ver|ausgaben* *vr* to overexert oneself; *(finanziell)* to overspend. ich habe mich total verausgabt *(körperlich)* I'm completely worn out; *(finanziell)* I've spent every penny I've got.

ver|äußern* *vt (form: verkaufen)* to dispose of.

Verb [vɛrp] *nt* -en verb.

verbal [vɛr'baːl] *adj* verbal.

verballhornen* *vt* to parody; *(unabsichtlich)* to get wrong.

Verband *m* ⁼e (a) *(Med)* dressing; *(mit Binden)* bandage. (b) *(Bund)* association. (c) *(Mil)* unit.

Verband(s)-: ~kasten *m* first-aid box; ~päckchen *nt* gauze bandage; ~stoff *m* dressing; ~zeug *nt* first-aid materials.

verbannen* *vt* to banish *(auch fig)*, to exile *(aus* from, *auf* to).

Verbannte(r) *mf decl as adj* exile.

Verbannung *f* banishment, exile.

verbarrikadieren* 1 *vt* to barricade. 2 *vr* to barricade oneself in *(in etw (dat)* sth).

verbauen* *vt* (a) *(versperren)* to obstruct, to block. sich *(dat)* alle Chancen ~ to spoil one's chances. (b) *(verbrauchen) Holz, Geld* to use in building. (c) *(schlecht bauen)* to construct badly.

verbe|amten* *vt* to give the status of civil servant to.

verbeißen* *irreg* 1 *vt (fig col)* sich *(dat)* etw ~ *Schmerz* to hide sth; sich *(dat)* das Lachen ~ to keep a straight face. 2 *vr* sich in etw *(acc)* ~ *(fig)* to become obsessed with sth; *siehe* verbissen.

verbergen* *vtr irreg (lit, fig)* to hide *(vor +dat* from).

verbessern* 1 *vt* (a) to improve; *Leistung, Bestzeit* to improve on; *die Welt* to reform. eine neue, verbesserte Auflage a new revised edition. (b) *(korrigieren)* to correct. 2 *vr* to improve, to get better; *(beruflich, finanziell)* to better oneself; *(sich korrigieren)* to correct oneself.

**Verbęsserung** f **(a)** improvement *(von in)*; *(beruflich, finanziell)* betterment. **(b)** *(Berichtigung)* correction.

**verbeugen*** vr to bow *(vor +dat to)*.

**Verbeugung** f bow. **eine ~ vor jdm machen** to (make a) bow to sb.

**verbeulen*** vt to dent.

**verbiegen*** vtr irreg to bend; *(Holz)* to warp; *siehe* **verbogen**.

**verbiestert** adj *(col: mißmutig)* crotchety *(col)*.

**verbieten*** vt irreg to forbid; *(amtlich auch)* to prohibit; *Zeitung, Partei* to ban. **jdm ~, etw zu tun** to forbid sb to do sth; *(amtlich auch)* to prohibit sb from doing sth; *siehe* **verboten**.

**verbilden*** vt *(fig)* jdn to bring up badly; *Geschmack, Charakter* to spoil.

**verbilligen*** **1** vt to reduce the cost of; *Kosten, Preis* to reduce. **verbilligte Waren** reduced goods. **2** vr to become cheaper.

**verbinden*** irreg **1** vt **(a)** to connect; *Punkte* to join. **jdn (mit jdm) ~** *(Telec)* to put sb through (to sb); **falsch verbunden!** wrong number; **uns verbindet nichts** we have nothing in common; *siehe* **verbunden**. **(b)** *(verknüpfen)* to combine. **die damit verbundenen Kosten** the costs involved; **was ~ Sie mit diesem Begriff?** what do you associate with this concept? **(c)** *(Med)* to dress; *(mit Binden)* to bandage. **jdm die Augen ~** to blindfold sb. **2** vr **(a)** to combine *(zu to form)*. **(b)** *(assoziiert werden)* to be associated; *(hervorgerufen werden)* to be evoked *(mit by)*. **3** vi **(a) ich verbinde!** I'll put you through. **(b)** *(emotional)* to form a bond.

**verbindlich** adj **(a)** obliging. **(b)** *(verpflichtend)* obligatory, compulsory; *Regelung, Zusage* binding; *(verläßlich)* Auskunft reliable. **~ zusagen** to accept definitely.

**Verbindlichkeit** f *siehe* adj **(a)** obligingness. **~en** polite words pl. **(b)** no pl obligatory nature; binding nature; reliability. **(c) ~en** pl *(Comm, Jur)* obligations pl; *(finanziell auch)* liabilities pl.

**Verbindung** f **(a)** connection; *(einflußreiche Beziehung auch, Kontakt)* contact *(zu, mit with)*. **in ~ mit** *(zusammen mit)* in conjunction with; *(im Zusammenhang mit)* in connection with; **jdn/etw mit etw in ~ bringen** to connect sb/sth with sth; *(assoziieren)* to associate sb/sth with sth; **~ mit jdm aufnehmen** to contact sb; **(mit jdm) in ~ treten** to get in touch or contact (with sb), to contact sb; **mit jdm in ~ stehen** to be in touch or contact with sb. **(b)** *(Telec: Anschluß)* line. **telefonische ~** telephone link; **eine ~ (zu einem Ort) bekommen** to get through (to a place). **(c)** *(Kombination)* combination. **(d)** *(Vereinigung, Bündnis)* association; *(ehelich)* union; *(Univ: Burschenschaft)* fraternity. **(e)** *(Chem)* *(Prozeß)* combination; *(Ergebnis)* compound *(aus of)*.

**Verbindungs-** in cpds *(esp Tech, Archit)* connecting; **~mann** m, pl **~leute** or **~männer** intermediary; *(Agent)* contact; **~stelle** f join; *(von Gleisen)* junction; *(Amt)* liaison office.

**verbissen** adj grim; *Arbeiter, Gesicht* determined. **das darfst du nicht so ~ sehen** *(col)* you shouldn't be so rigid about it.

**verbitten*** vr irreg **das verbitte ich mir!** I won't have it!

**verbittern*** **1** vt to embitter, to make bitter. **2** vi aux sein to become embittered or bitter. **verbittert** embittered, bitter.

**Verbitterung** f bitterness.

**verblassen*** vi aux sein *(lit, fig)* to fade; *(Mond)* to pale.

**Verbleib** m no pl *(form)* whereabouts pl.

**verbleiben*** vi irreg aux sein to remain. ... **verbleibe ich Ihr ...** *(form)* ... I remain, Yours sincerely ...; **wir sind so verblieben, daß wir ...** we agreed to ...

**verbleit** adj Benzin leaded.

**verblichen** adj *(lit, fig)* faded.

**verblöden*** vi aux sein *(col)* to turn into a zombie *(col)*.

**verblüffen*** vt *(erstaunen)* to amaze; *(verwirren)* to baffle. **sich durch** or **von etw ~ lassen** to be taken in by sth.

**Verblüffung** f no pl *siehe* vt amazement; bafflement.

**verblühen*** vi aux sein *(lit, fig)* to fade.

**verbluten*** vi aux sein to bleed to death.

**verbogen** adj bent; *Rückgrat* curved.

**verbohren*** vr *(col)* **sich in etw** *(acc)* **~** to become obsessed with sth.

**verbohrt** adj Haltung stubborn, obstinate.

**verborgen[1]*** vt to lend out *(an +acc to)*.

**verborgen[2]** adj hidden. **etw/sich ~ halten** to keep sth hidden/to hide; **im V~en leben** to live hidden away; **im ~en liegen** to be not yet known; **~e Mängel** latent defects.

**Verbot** nt -e ban *(etw zu tun on doing sth)*. **er ging trotz meines ~s** he went even though I had forbidden him to do so.

**verboten** adj forbidden; *(amtlich auch)* prohibited; *(gesetzeswidrig)* Handel illegal; *Zeitung, Partei, Buch* etc banned. **Rauchen/Parken ~** no smoking/parking; **er sah ~ aus** *(col)* he looked a real sight *(col)*.

**Verbotsschild** nt sign (prohibiting something); *(im Verkehr)* prohibition sign.

**verbrämen*** vt *(geh)* Kleidungsstück to trim; *(fig)* Rede to pad; *Wahrheit* to gloss over; *Kritik* to veil *(mit in)*.

**verbrannt** adj burnt; *(fig)* Erde scorched.

**Verbrauch** m no pl consumption *(von, an +dat of)*; *(von Geld)* expenditure; *(von Kräften)* drain *(von, an +dat on)*.

**verbrauchen*** vt **(a)** to use; *Vorräte* to use up; *Nahrungsmittel etc auch* to consume. **der Wagen verbraucht 9 Liter Benzin auf 100 km** the car does 31 miles to the gallon. **(b)** *(abnützen)* Kräfte etc to exhaust; *Kleidung etc* to wear out. **sich ~** to wear oneself out; **verbrauchte Luft** stale air.

**Verbraucher(in** f**)** m - consumer.

**Verbraucher-** in cpds consumer; **~markt** m hypermarket; **~schutz** m consumer protection; **~verband** m consumer council.

**Verbrauchsgüter** pl consumer goods pl.

**Verbrechen** nt - *(lit, fig)* crime *(an +dat against)*.

**verbrechen*** vt irreg *(col: anstellen)* **was hast du wieder verbrochen?** what have you been up to this time?; **was habe ich denn verbrochen?** what am I supposed to have done?

**Verbrecher(in** f**)** m - criminal.

**Verbrecherbande** f gang of criminals.

**verbrecherisch** adj criminal.

**Verbrecherkartei** f file of offenders, ≃ rogues' gallery.

**verbreiten*** **1** vt to spread; *Zeitung* to circulate; *Wärme, Ruhe* to radiate; *Licht* to shed. **eine (weit) verbreitete Ansicht** a widely held opinion. **2** vr to spread. **sich über ein Thema ~** to expound on a subject.

**verbreitern*** vtr to widen.

**Verbreitung** f no pl *siehe* vt spreading; circulation; radiation; shedding.

**verbrennen*** irreg **1** vt to burn; *(einäschern)* Tote to cremate; *(versengen)* to scorch; *Haar* to singe; *(verbrühen)* to scald. **sich** *(dat)* **den Mund** ~ *(lit)* to burn one's mouth; *(fig)* to say too much. **2** *vr* to burn oneself; *(sich verbrühen)* to scald oneself. **3** *vi aux sein* to burn; *(Mensch, Tier)* to burn to death; *(Haus etc)* to burn down; *(durch Sonne, Hitze)* to be scorched. **alles verbrannte** everything was destroyed in the fire.

**Verbrennung** *f* **(a)** *no pl* burning; *(von Treibstoff)* combustion; *(von Leiche)* cremation. **(b)** *(Brandwunde)* burn; *(Verbrühung)* scald.

**Verbrennungs-:** ~**anlage** *f* incineration plant; ~**motor** *m* internal combustion engine.

**verbriefen\*** *vt* to document. **verbriefte Rechte** attested rights.

**verbringen** *vt irreg* to spend.

**verbrühen\*** **1** *vt* to scald. **2** *vr* to scald oneself.

**Verbrühung** *f* scalding; *(Wunde)* scald.

**verbuchen\*** *vt* to enter. **Erfolge (für sich)** ~ to notch up successes *(col)*.

**verbummeln\*** *(col)* **1** *vt (verlieren)* to lose; *Zeit* to waste, to fritter away; *Verabredung* to miss. **2** *vi aux sein (herunterkommen)* to go to seed.

**verbunden** *adj (form: dankbar)* **jdm (für etw)** ~ **sein** to be obliged to sb (for sth).

**verbünden\*** *vr* to form an alliance.

**Verbundenheit** *f no pl (von Völkern)* solidarity; *(mit Menschen, Natur)* closeness *(mit to)*; *(mit Land, Tradition)* attachment *(mit to)*.

**Verbündete(r)** *mf decl as adj* ally.

**Verbund-:** ~**glas** *nt* laminated glass; ~**system** *nt* integrated system.

**verbürgen\*** *vtr* to guarantee. **sich für jdn/etw** ~ to vouch for sb/sth; **verbürgte Nachricht** confirmed report; **ein verbürgtes Recht** an established right.

**verbüßen\*** *vt* to serve.

**verchromt\*** [fɛɛ'kroːmt] *adj* chromium-plated.

**Verchromung** [fɛɛ'kroːmʊŋ] *f* chromium-plating.

**Verdacht** *m no pl* suspicion. **jdn in** ~ **haben** to suspect sb; **im** ~ **stehen, etw getan zu haben** to be suspected of having done sth; **jdn wegen** ~**s einer Sache** *(gen)* **festnehmen** to arrest sb on suspicion of sth; **(gegen jdn)** ~ **schöpfen** to become suspicious (of sb); **es besteht** ~ **auf Krebs** *(acc)* cancer is suspected.

**verdächtig** *adj* suspicious. **sich** ~ **machen** to arouse suspicion; **einer Sache** *(gen)* ~ **sein** to be suspected of sth.

**verdächtigen\*** *vt* to suspect *(gen of)*.

**Verdächtige(r)** *mf decl as adj* suspect.

**Verdächtigung** *f* suspicion.

**verdammen\*** *vt* to damn; *(verurteilen)* to condemn.

**verdammt\*** *(col)* **1** *adj, adv* damned *(col)*. **das tut** ~ **weh** that hurts like hell *(col)*; **mir geht's** ~ **schlecht** I'm in a pretty bad way *(col)*. **2** *interj* ~! damn (it) *(col)*; ~ **noch mal!** *(col!)* bloody hell *(Brit col!)*, damn *(col)*.

**verdampfen\*** *vti (vi: aux sein)* to vaporize; *(Cook)* to boil away.

**verdanken\*** *vt* **jdm etw** ~ to owe sth to sb; **das haben wir ihm zu** ~ that's thanks to him.

**verdarb** *pret* of **verderben**.

**verdauen\*** *vti (lit, fig)* to digest.

**verdaulich** *adj* digestible. **leicht** ~ easy to digest.

**Verdauung** *f* digestion *no indef art*.

**Verdauungs-** *in cpds* digestive; ~**spaziergang** *m* constitutional; ~**störung** *f usu pl* indigestion *no pl*.

**Verdeck** *nt* **-e** *(von Kinderwagen)* hood *(Brit)*, canopy; *(von Auto)* hood *(Brit)*, soft top; *(von Schiff)* sundeck.

**verdecken\*** *vt* to hide, to conceal; *(zudecken)* to cover (up); *Sicht* to block. **verdeckt** concealed; *Widerspruch* hidden; **verdeckter Polizeieinsatz** undercover operation.

**verdenken\*** *vt irreg* **ich kann es ihm nicht** ~(, **daß er es getan hat)** I can't blame him (for doing it).

**verderben** *pret* **verdarb,** *ptp* **verdorben 1** *vt* to spoil; *(stärker)* to ruin; *Luft* to pollute; *(moralisch)* to corrupt; *(verwöhnen)* to spoil. **jdm etw** ~ to ruin sth for sb; **sich** *(dat)* **den Magen** ~ to give oneself an upset stomach; **sich** *(dat)* **die Augen** ~ to ruin one's eyes; **die Preise** ~ to force prices down; **jdm die Freude an etw** *(dat)* ~ to spoil sb's enjoyment of sth; **es (sich** *dat)* **mit jdm** ~ to fall out with sb; **sie will es (sich** *dat)* **nicht mit ihm** ~ she wants to keep on the right side of him. **2** *vi aux sein (Material)* to become spoiled/ruined; *(Nahrungsmittel)* to go bad; *(Ernte)* to be ruined; *(Mensch)* to become depraved.

**Verderben** *nt no pl* **(a)** ruin. **in sein** ~ **rennen** to be heading for disaster. **(b)** *(von Material)* spoiling, ruining; *(von Nahrungsmittel)* going off.

**verderblich** *adj* pernicious; *Lebensmittel* perishable.

**verdeutlichen\*** *vt (deutlicher machen)* to clarify; *(erklären)* to explain. **sich** *(dat)* **etw** ~ to think sth out for oneself.

**verdeutschen\*** *vt* to translate into German; *(eindeutschen)* to Germanize.

**verdichten\*** **1** *vt (Phys, fig)* to compress; *Gefühle* to intensify, to heighten. **2** *vr* to thicken; *(Gas)* to become compressed; *(fig: häufen)* to increase; *(Verdacht, Eindruck)* to deepen.

**Verdichter** *m* - compressor.

**verdicken\*** **1** *vt* to thicken. **2** *vr* to thicken; *(anschwellen)* to swell.

**verdienen\*** **1** *vt* **(a)** *(einnehmen)* to earn; *(Gewinn machen)* to make *(an +dat* on). **sich** *(dat)* **etw** ~ to earn the money for sth. **(b)** *(fig) Lob, Strafe* to deserve. **er verdient es nicht anders** he doesn't deserve anything else. **2** *vi* to earn; *(Gewinn machen)* to make (a profit) *(an +dat* on). **er verdient gut** he has a good income; **am Krieg** ~ to profit from war.

**Verdiener** *m* - earner.

**Verdienst¹** *m* **-e** income; *(Profit)* profit.

**Verdienst²** *nt* **-e (a)** *(Dank)* credit. **es ist sein** ~/**das** ~ **der Wissenschaftler(, daß...)** it is thanks to him/the scientists (that ...); **nach** ~ on merit. **(b)** *usu pl (um to) (Leistung)* contribution; *(um Wissenschaft, Staat)* service.

**Verdienst-:** ~**ausfall** *m* loss of earnings; ~**orden** *m* order of merit; **v~voll** *adj* commendable.

**verdient** *adj* **(a)** *Lohn, Strafe* rightful; *Ruhe, Lob* well-deserved. **(b)** *Wissenschaftler, Politiker, Sportler* of outstanding merit. **sich um etw** ~ **machen** to render outstanding services to sth.

**verdonnern\*** *vt (col: zu Haft etc)* to sentence *(zu* to). **jdn zu etw** ~, **jdn dazu** ~, **etw zu tun** to order sb to do sth as a punishment.

**verdoppeln\*** *vtr* to double.

**Verdoppelung** *f* doubling.

**verdorben 1** *ptp* of **verderben**. **2** *adj Lebensmittel* bad; *Magen* upset; *Stimmung, Urlaub, Freude* spoiled, ruined; *(moralisch)* corrupt; *(verzogen) Kind* spoiled.

**verdorren\*** *vi aux sein* to wither.

**verdrängen\*** *vt jdn* to drive out; *Gegner auch* to oust; *(ersetzen)* to replace; *(Phys) Wasser* to displace; *(Met)* to drive; *(fig) Sorgen* to dispel; *(Psych)* to repress, to suppress.

**Verdrängung** *f siehe vt* driving out; ousting; replacing; displacement; driving; dispelling; repression; suppression.

**verdrecken\*** *vti (vi: aux sein) (col)* to get filthy.

**verdrehen\*** vt (lit, fig) to twist; (verknacksen) to sprain; Hals to crick; Augen to roll. **das Recht** ~ to pervert the course of justice; **sich** (dat) **den Hals** ~ (fig col) to crane one's neck.

**verdreht** adj (col) crazy (col); Bericht confused.

**verdreifachen\*** vtr to treble, to triple.

**verdrießen** pret **verdroß**, ptp **verdrossen** vt jdn to annoy. **sich** (dat) **den Abend durch etw** ~ **lassen** to let sth spoil one's evening.

**verdrießlich** adj morose; Arbeit irksome.

**verdroß** pret of **verdrießen**.

**verdrossen 1** ptp of **verdrießen**. **2** adj (schlechtgelaunt) morose; (unlustig) Mensch, Gesicht unwilling, reluctant.

**Verdrossenheit** f (schlechte Laune) moroseness; (Lustlosigkeit) unwillingness, reluctance.

**verdrucken\*** vr (col) to make a misprint.

**verdrücken\* 1** vt Kleider to crumple; (col) Essen to put away (col). **2** vr (col) to beat it (col). **sich heimlich** ~ to slip away.

**Verdrückung** f (col: Bedrängnis) **in** ~ **geraten** to get into difficulties; **jdn in** ~ **bringen** to put sb under pressure.

**Verdruß** m -sse frustration. ~ **mit jdm haben** to get frustrated with sb; **zu jds** ~ to sb's annoyance.

**verduften** vi aux sein (col) to beat it (col).

**verdummen\* 1** vt jdn ~ (für dumm verkaufen) to make sb out to be stupid; (dumm machen) to dull sb's mind. **2** vi aux sein to become stultified.

**verdunkeln\* 1** vt to darken; Bühne auch, (im Krieg) to black out; (fig) Zusammenhänge etc to obscure. **die Sonne** ~ (Wolken) to obscure the sun. **2** vr to darken.

**Verdunk(e)lung** f (a) siehe vt darkening; blacking out; obscuring. **(b)** (Vorhang) curtain; (Jalousie) blind usu pl. **(c)** (Jur) suppression of evidence.

**verdünnen\* 1** vt to thin (down); (mit Wasser) to water down; Lösung to dilute. **den Teig mit Wasser** ~ to add water to the dough. **2** vr (Lösung) to become diluted; (schmaler werden) to become thinner.

**Verdünner** m - thinner; (esp für Farbe) thinners pl.

**verdünnisieren\*** vr (hum col) to beat a hasty retreat.

**verdunsten\*** vi aux sein to evaporate.

**Verdunster** m - humidifier.

**verdursten\*** vi aux sein to die of thirst.

**verdüstern\*** vtr to darken.

**verdutzt** adj, adv (col) taken aback; (verwirrt) baffled.

**ver|ebben\*** vi aux sein to subside.

**ver|edeln\*** vt Metalle, Erdöl to refine; Fasern to finish; Boden, Geschmack to improve.

**ver|ehren\*** vt to admire; (anbeten) to worship.

**Ver|ehrer(in** f) m - admirer.

**ver|ehrt** adj (sehr) ~e Anwesende/Gäste/~es Publikum Ladies and Gentlemen.

**Ver|ehrung** f admiration; (von Heiligen) worship; (Liebe) adoration.

**ver|eidigen\*** vt to swear in. **jdn auf etw** (acc) ~ to make sb swear on sth; **vereidigter Übersetzer** sworn translator.

**Ver|eidigung** f swearing in.

**Ver|ein** m -e organization, society; (Sport~) club; (col) crowd. **ein wohltätiger** ~ a charity; **im** ~ **mit** in conjunction with.

**ver|einbar** adj compatible; Aussagen consistent.

**ver|einbaren\*** vt (a) to agree; Zeit auch, Treffen to arrange. **(es)** ~, **daß** ... to agree/arrange that ... **(b)** **etw mit etw** ~ to reconcile sth with sth; **mit etw zu** ~ **sein** to be compatible with sth.

**Ver|einbarung** f siehe vt **(a)** (das Vereinbaren) agreeing; arranging; (Abmachung) agreement; arrangement. **laut** ~ as agreed; **nach** ~ by arrangement.

**ver|einen\* 1** vt to unite; Ideen, Prinzipien to reconcile. **vereint handeln** to act together; **Vereinte Nationen** United Nations sing. **2** vr to unite.

**ver|einfachen\*** vt to simplify.

**Ver|einfachung** f simplification.

**ver|einheitlichen\*** vt to standardize.

**ver|einigen\* 1** vt to unite; Kräfte, Eigenschaften to combine; Firmen to merge (zu into); Kapital to pool. **etw mit etw** ~ to combine sth with sth; (vereinbaren) to reconcile sth with sth; **in einer Hand vereinigt sein** to be held by the same person; **alle Stimmen auf sich** (acc) ~ to collect all the votes; **Vereinigtes Königreich** United Kingdom; **Vereinigte Staaten** United States sing; **Vereinigte Arabische Emirate** United Arab Emirates. **2** vr to unite; (sich verbünden auch) to join forces; (Firmen) to merge; (zusammenkommen) to combine; (Flüsse) to meet; (sich versammeln) to assemble.

**Ver|einigung** f **(a)** siehe vt uniting; combining; merging; pooling; (körperliche, eheliche ~) union. **(b)** (Organisation) organization.

**ver|einnahmen\*** vt (geh) to take. **jdn** ~ (fig) to make demands on sb; (Beruf) to occupy sb.

**ver|einsamen\*** vi aux sein to become isolated.

**Ver|einsamung** f isolation.

**Ver|einsmeier** m - (col) **er ist ein richtiger** ~ all he thinks about is his club.

**ver|einzelt 1** adj occasional; Regenfälle auch scattered. **2** adv occasionally.

**ver|eisen\*** vi aux sein to freeze; (Straße, Fensterscheibe) to ice over.

**ver|eist** adj Straßen, Fenster icy; Bäche frozen; Türschloß iced-up; Land covered in ice.

**ver|eiteln\*** vt to thwart, to foil.

**ver|eitern\*** vi aux sein to go septic. **vereitert sein** to be septic.

**Ver|eiterung** f sepsis.

**ver|elenden\*** vi aux sein to become impoverished.

**Ver|elendung** f impoverishment.

**ver|enden\*** vi aux sein to perish, to die.

**ver|engen\* 1** vr to narrow; (Gefäße, Pupille) to contract; (Kleid, Taille) to go in. **2** vt to make narrower; Kleid to take in.

**ver|erben\* 1** vt **(a)** Besitz to leave, to bequeath (dat, an +acc to). **(b)** Anlagen to pass on (dat, auf +acc to); Krankheit to transmit. **2** vr to be passed on/transmitted (auf +acc to).

**ver|erblich** adj Anlagen hereditary.

**Ver|erbung** f (von Besitz) leaving, bequeathing; (von Anlagen) passing on; (von Krankheit) transmission. **das ist** ~ (col) it's hereditary.

**ver|ewigen\* 1** vt to immortalize; Zustand, Verhältnisse to perpetuate. **2** vr (lit, fig) to immortalize oneself.

**Verf.** = **Verfasser.**

**verfahren[1]\*** vi irreg aux sein (vorgehen) to act, to proceed.

**verfahren[2]\*** irreg **1** vt Geld, Zeit to spend in travelling (Brit) or traveling (US); Benzin to use up. **2** vr to lose one's way; (fig) to get muddled.

**verfahren[3]** adj Angelegenheit muddled. **eine** ~**e Situation** a dead end.

**Verfahren** nt - (Vorgehen) actions pl; (~sweise) procedure; (Tech) process; (Methode) method; (Jur) proceedings pl. **ein** ~ **gegen jdn einleiten** to take legal proceedings against sb.

**Verfahrens-:** ~**regeln** pl code of practice; ~**weise**

*f* procedure.

**Verfall** *m no pl* **(a)** *(Zerfall)* decay; *(von Gebäude)* dilapidation; *(gesundheitlich, geistig, sittlich, von Kultur)* decline. **(b)** *(von Anspruch, Rechnung etc)* lapsing; *(von Scheck, Fahrkarte)* expiry.

**verfallen¹\*** *vi irreg aux sein* **(a)** *(zerfallen)* to decay; *(Bauwerk)* to fall into disrepair; *(Zellen)* to die; *(körperlich und geistig)* to deteriorate; *(Sitten, Reich)* to decline. **(b)** *(Geldscheine)* to become invalid; *(Scheck, Fahrkarte)* to expire; *(Termin, Anspruch)* to lapse. **(c)** *(abhängig werden)* **jdm/einer Sache ~/~ sein** to become/be a slave to sb/sth; **jdm völlig ~ sein** to be completely under sb's spell. **(d) auf etw** *(acc)* ~ to think of sth; *(aus Verzweiflung)* to resort to sth. **(e) in etw** *(acc)* ~ to sink into sth; **in einen tiefen Schlaf** ~ to fall into a deep sleep; **in einen Fehler** ~ to make a mistake.

**verfallen²** *adj Gebäude* dilapidated, ruined; *Mensch (körperlich)* emaciated; *(geistig)* senile; *(abgelaufen) Fahrkarte, Eintrittskarte* invalid; *Strafe* lapsed; *Scheck* expired.

**Verfalls-:** ~**datum** *nt* expiry date; *(der Haltbarkeit)* best-before date; ~**tag** *m* expiry date.

**verfälschen\*** *vt* to falsify; *Lebensmittel, Wein* to adulterate.

**verfangen\*** *irreg* **1** *vr* to get caught. **sich in Widersprüchen** ~ to contradict oneself. **2** *vi* to be accepted. **bei jdm nicht** ~ not to cut any ice with sb *(col)*.

**verfänglich** *adj Situation* awkward, embarrassing; *Aussage, Beweismaterial, Blicke* incriminating; *(gefährlich)* dangerous; *Angewohnheit* insidious; *Frage* tricky.

**verfärben\*** *vr* to change colour *(Brit)* or color *(US)*; *(Metall, Stoff)* to discolour *(Brit)*, to discolor *(US)*. **sich grün/rot** ~ to turn green/red.

**verfassen\*** *vt* to write; *Gesetz, Urkunde* to draw up.

**Verfasser(in** *f)* *m* - writer, author.

**Verfassung** *f* **(a)** *(Pol)* constitution. **(b)** *(Zustand)* state; *(körperlich)* state of health; *(seelisch)* state of mind. **sie ist in guter/schlechter** ~ she is in good/bad shape.

**Verfassungs-:** ~**änderung** *f* constitutional amendment; **v~feindlich** *adj* anticonstitutional; ~**gericht** *nt* constitutional court; **v~mäßig** *adj* constitutional; ~**schutz** *m* defence *(Brit)* or defense *(US)* of the constitution; *(Amt) office responsible for defending the constitution*; **v~treu** *adj* loyal to the constitution; **v~widrig** *adj* unconstitutional.

**verfaulen\*** *vi aux sein* to decay, to rot; *(fig)* to degenerate.

**verfault** *adj* decayed; *Fleisch, Obst etc* rotten; *Körper* decomposed.

**verfechten\*** *vt irreg* to defend; *Lehre* to advocate.

**Verfechter(in** *f)* *m* - advocate, champion.

**verfehlen\*** *vt (nicht treffen)* to miss. **den Zweck** ~ not to achieve its purpose; **das Thema** ~ to be completely off the subject.

**verfehlt** *adj* unsuccessful; *(unangebracht)* inappropriate. **etw für** ~ **halten** to regard sth as mistaken.

**Verfehlung** *f* **(a)** *(des Ziels)* missing. **(b)** *(Vergehen)* misdemeanour *(Brit)*, misdemeanor *(US)*; *(Sünde)* transgression.

**verfeinden\*** *vr* to quarrel. **sich mit jdm** ~ to make an enemy of sb; **verfeindet sein** to be enemies.

**verfeinern\*** **1** *vt* to improve; *Methode auch* to refine. **2** *vr* to improve; *(Methoden auch)* to become refined.

**verfeinert** *adj Methode, Geräte* sophisticated.

**Verfeinerung** *f siehe vb* improvement; refinement.

**verfestigen\*** **1** *vt* to harden; *Flüssigkeit* to solidify; *(verstärken)* to strengthen. **2** *vr* to harden; *(Flüssigkeit)* to solidify; *(Kenntnisse)* to be reinforced; *(Ideen, Gewohnheiten)* to become set.

**Verfettung** *f (von Organ, Muskeln)* fatty degeneration.

**verfeuern\*** *vt* to burn; *Munition* to fire; *(restlos)* to use up.

**verfilmen\*** *vt* to film, to make a film of.

**Verfilmung** *f* film (version).

**verfilzen\*** *vi aux sein (Wolle)* to become felted; *(Haare)* to become matted. **verfilzt** felted/matted.

**verfinstern\*** **1** *vt* to darken; *Sonne, Mond* to eclipse. **2** *vr (lit, fig)* to darken.

**verflachen\*** **1** *vi aux sein* to flatten out; *(fig: Diskussion)* to become superficial. **2** *vr (Gelände)* to flatten out.

**verflechten\*** *irreg* **1** *vt* to interweave; *Methoden* to combine; *Firmen* to interlink. **eng mit etw verflochten sein** *(fig)* to be closely linked with sth. **2** *vr* to interweave; *(sich verwirren)* to become entangled *(mit* in*)*; *(Methoden)* to combine.

**Verflechtung** *f (das Verflochtensein)* interconnection *(gen* between*)*; *(Pol, Econ)* integration.

**verfliegen\*** *irreg* **1** *vi aux sein (verfliegen; (Zeit)* to fly (past). **2** *vr* to stray; *(Pilot, Flugzeug)* to lose one's/its bearings.

**verfließen\*** *vi irreg aux sein (geh)* to go by, to pass.

**verflixt** *(col)* **1** *adj* darned *(col)*; *(kompliziert)* tricky. **2** *adv* darned *(col)*. **3** *interj* ~! blow! *(col)*.

**verflossen** *adj (col)* one-time *attr (col)*. **Ihr V~er** her former partner, her ex *(col)*.

**verfluchen\*** *vt* to curse.

**verflucht** *(col)* **1** *adj* damn *(col)*. ~ **(noch mal)!** damn (it) *(col)*. **2** *adv* damned *(col)*.

**verflüchtigen\*** **1** *vt* to evaporate. **2** *vr (Alkohol etc)* to evaporate; *(Duft)* to disappear; *(Gase)* to volatilize.

**verflüssigen\*** *vtr* to liquefy.

**verfolgen\*** *vt jdn, Ziel, Karriere etc* to pursue; *Idee, Gedanken* to follow up; *(politisch, religiös)* to persecute. **jdn politisch** ~ to persecute sb for political reasons; **jdn gerichtlich** ~ to prosecute sb; **jdn mit den Augen** ~ to follow sb with one's eyes.

**Verfolger(in** *f)* *m* - pursuer; *(politisch)* persecutor.

**Verfolgte(r)** *mf decl as adj (politisch)* victim of persecution.

**Verfolgung** *f* pursuit; *(politische)* persecution *no pl.* **die** ~ **aufnehmen** to take up the chase; **strafrechtliche** ~ prosecution.

**Verfolgungs-:** ~**jagd** *f* chase, pursuit; ~**rennen** *nt (Sport)* pursuit race; ~**wahn** *m* persecution mania.

**verformen\*** **1** *vt* to distort *(zu* into*)*; *(umformen)* to work. **verformt sein** to be out of shape; *(Mensch, Gliedmaßen)* to be deformed. **2** *vr* to go out of shape.

**verfrachten\*** *vt* to ship. **etw in eine Kiste** ~ *(col)* to dump sth in a crate.

**verfremden\*** *vt* to make unfamiliar.

**verfressen\*** *(col)* **1** *vt irreg Geld* to blow on food *(col)*. **2** *adj* greedy, piggish *(col)*.

**verfroren** *adj* sensitive to cold; *(durchgefroren)* frozen.

**verfrüht** *adj (zu früh)* premature; *(früh)* early.

**verfügbar** *adj* available.

**verfugen\*** *vt* to fit flush; *Fliesen* to grout.

**verfügen\*** **1** *vi* **über** *etw (acc)* ~ to have sth at one's disposal; *(besitzen)* to have sth; **über jdn/etw** ~ *(bestimmen über)* to be in charge of sb/sth; **du kannst doch nicht über mich** ~ you can't tell me what to do; **über etw** *(acc)* **frei** ~ **können** to be able to do as one wants with sth; ~ **Sie über mich** I am at your disposal. **2** *vt* to order; *(gesetzlich)* to decree.

**Verfügung** *f* **(a)** *no pl* **jdm etw zur ~ stellen** to put sth at sb's disposal; **jdm zur ~ stehen** to be at sb's disposal; **(jdm) zur ~ stehen** *(verfügbar sein)* to be available (to sb); **etw zur ~ haben** to have sth at one's disposal. **(b)** *(behördlich)* order; *(von Gesetzgeber)* decree; *(testamentarisch)* provision; *(Anweisung)* instruction.

**Verfügungsgewalt** *f (Jur)* right of disposal.

**verführen\*** *vt* to tempt; *(esp sexuell)* to seduce; **die Jugend, das Volk etc** to lead astray.

**Verführer** *m* - seducer.

**Verführerin** *f* seductress, temptress.

**verführerisch** *adj* seductive; *(verlockend)* tempting.

**Verführung** *f* seduction; *(von Jugend, Volk)* tempting; *(Verlockung)* enticement.

**verfüllen\*** *vt (mit Erde, Beton etc)* to fill in.

**verfüttern\*** *vt* **etw an die Vögel ~** to feed sth to the birds.

**Vergabe** *f* **-n** *(von Arbeiten)* allocation; *(von Stipendium, Auftrag etc)* award.

**vergällen\*** *vt (geh)* **jdm die Freude/das Leben ~** to spoil sb's fun/to sour sb's life.

**vergaloppieren\*** *vr (col: sich irren)* to be on the wrong track.

**vergammeln\*** *(col)* **1** *vi aux sein (Speisen)* to go bad; *(verlottern)* to go to the dogs *(col)*. **vergammelt aussehen** to look scruffy. **2** *vt Zeit* to waste.

**vergangen** *adj* **(a)** *(letzte)* last. **(b)** *Jahre* past; *Zeiten, Bräuche* bygone. **das V~e** the past.

**Vergangenheit** *f* past; *(Gram)* past (tense). **der ~ angehören** to be a thing of the past.

**Vergangenheitsbewältigung** *f* process of coming to terms with the past.

**vergänglich** *adj* transitory.

**Vergänglichkeit** *f no pl* transience, transitoriness.

**vergasen\*** *vt (töten)* to gas.

**Vergaser** *m* - *(Aut)* carburettor *(Brit)*, carburetor *(US)*.

**vergaß** *pret* of **vergessen**.

**vergeben\*** *irreg* **1** *vt* **(a)** *Auftrag, Preis* to award *(an +acc to)*; *Studienplätze, Stellen* to allocate; *(fig) Chance, Möglichkeit* to throw away. **ein Amt an jdn ~** to appoint sb to an office; **zu ~ sein** to be available; **~ sein** *(Wohnung, Plätze)* to have been taken; *(Stelle)* to have been filled; **er/sie ist schon ~** *(col)* he/she is already spoken for. **(b)** *(verzeihen)* to forgive. **jdm etw ~** to forgive sb (for) sth. **2** *vr* **sich** *(dat)* **etwas/nichts ~** to lose/not to lose face.

**vergebens** *adj pred, adv* in vain.

**vergeblich** **1** *adj* futile; *Bitten, Mühe auch* vain *attr*, in vain. **2** *adv* in vain.

**Vergebung** *f no pl* forgiveness.

**vergegenwärtigen\*** *vr* **sich** *(dat)* **etw ~** to imagine sth.

**Vergehen** *nt* - *(Verstoß)* offence *(Brit)*, offense *(US)*. **das ist doch kein ~, oder?** that's not a crime, is it?

**vergehen\*** *irreg* **1** *vi aux sein* **(a)** to pass; *(Liebe, Leidenschaft auch)* to die; *(Zeit, Jahre etc auch)* to go by; *(Schönheit, Glück)* to fade. **wie doch die Zeit vergeht** how time flies; **mir ist der Appetit vergangen** I have lost my appetite. **(b) vor etw** *(dat)* **~** to be dying of sth; **vor Angst ~** to be scared to death; **vor Sehnsucht ~** to pine away. **2** *vr* **sich an jdm ~** to do sb wrong; *(unsittlich)* to assault sb indecently; **sich gegen das Gesetz ~** to violate the law.

**vergeistigt** *adj* cerebral, spiritual.

**vergelten** *vt irreg* to repay. **jdm etw ~** to repay sb for sth.

**Vergeltung** *f (Rache)* retaliation. **~ üben** to take re-

venge *(an jdm on sb)*.

**Vergeltungs-:** **~maßnahme** *f* reprisal, retaliatory measure; **~schlag** *m* act of reprisal.

**vergesellschaften\*** *vt (Pol)* to nationalize.

**vergessen** *pret* **vergaß**, *ptp* **~** **1** *vti* to forget; *(liegenlassen auch)* to leave (behind). **... und nicht zu ~ seine Ehrlichkeit** ... and not forgetting his honesty; **das werde ich dir nie ~** I will never forget that; **das kannst du ~** *(col)* forget it. **2** *vr (Mensch)* to forget oneself.

**Vergessenheit** *f no pl* oblivion. **in ~ geraten** to fall into oblivion.

**vergeßlich** *adj* forgetful.

**Vergeßlichkeit** *f* forgetfulness.

**vergeuden\*** *vt* to waste, to squander.

**vergewaltigen\*** *vt* to rape; *(fig) Sprache etc* to mutilate.

**Vergewaltiger** *m* - rapist.

**Vergewaltigung** *f* rape.

**vergewissern\*** *vr* to make sure. **sich einer Sache** *(gen)* **or über etw** *(acc)* **~** to make sure of sth.

**vergießen\*** *vt irreg Kaffee, Wasser* to spill; *Blut auch, Tränen* to shed.

**vergiften\*** *vt (lit, fig)* to poison.

**Vergiftung** *f* poisoning *no pl*.

**vergilben\*** *vi aux sein* to go yellow. **vergilbt** yellowed.

**Vergißmeinnicht** *nt* -(e) forget-me-not.

**vergittert** *adj Fenster* barred.

**verglasen\*** *vt* to glaze.

**Vergleich** *m* -e **(a)** comparison. **~e ziehen** to make comparisons; **im ~ zu** *or* **mit** in comparison with; **in keinem ~ zu etw stehen** to be out of all proportion to sth; *(Leistungen)* not to compare with sth; **dem ~ mit jdm standhalten, den ~ mit jdm aushalten** to bear comparison with sb. **(b)** *(Jur)* settlement.

**vergleichbar** *adj* comparable.

**vergleichen\*** *irreg* **1** *vt* to compare. **etw mit etw ~** to compare sth to sth; *(prüfend)* to compare sth with sth; **vergleiche oben** compare above. **2** *vr* **(a) sich mit jdm ~** to compare oneself with sb. **(b)** *(Jur)* to reach a settlement, to settle.

**vergleichsweise** *adv* comparatively.

**verglimmen\*** *vi irreg aux sein (Zigarette)* to go out; *(Licht, Feuer auch)* to die away.

**verglühen\*** *vi aux sein (Feuer)* to die away; *(Draht)* to burn out; *(Raumkapsel, Meteor etc)* to burn up.

**vergnügen\*** *vr* to enjoy oneself. **sich mit jdm/etw ~** to amuse oneself with sb/sth; **sich mit Lesen ~** to amuse oneself by reading.

**Vergnügen** *nt* - *(Freude, Genuß)* pleasure; *(Spaß)* fun *no indef art*; *(Erheiterung)* amusement. **das macht** *or* **bereitet mir ~** I enjoy it, it gives me pleasure; **nur zum ~** just for pleasure *or* for the fun of it; **das war ein teures ~** *(iro)* that was an expensive business; **viel ~!** enjoy yourself/yourselves *(auch iro)*.

**vergnüglich** *adj* enjoyable; *(erheiternd)* amusing.

**vergnügt** *adj Stunden* enjoyable; *Mensch, Stimmung* cheerful.

**Vergnügung** *f* pleasure; *(Veranstaltung)* entertainment.

**Vergnügungs-:** **~industrie** *f* entertainment industry; **~park** *m* amusement park; **~reise** *f* pleasure trip; **~steuer** *f* entertainment tax; **~sucht** *f* craving for pleasure; **v~süchtig** *adj* pleasure-seeking; **~viertel** *nt* entertainments district.

**vergolden\*** *vt (mit Blattgold)* to gild; *(mit Gold)* to gold-plate; *(fig: verschönern)* to enhance.

**vergönnen\*** *vt (geh)* **es war ihr noch vergönnt, das**

**zu sehen** she was granted the privilege of seeing it.
**vergöttern\*** *vt* to idolize.
**vergraben\*** *irreg* **1** *vt* to bury. **2** *vr (lit, fig)* to bury oneself.
**vergrämt** *adj (kummervoll) Gesicht* troubled.
**vergreifen\*** *vr irreg* **(a)** to make a mistake. **sich im Ton/Ausdruck** ~ *(fig)* to adopt the wrong tone/use the wrong expression. **(b) sich an etw** *(dat)* ~ *(stehlen)* to misappropriate sth; **sich an jdm** ~ *(angreifen)* to lay hands on sb.
**vergreisen\*** *vi aux sein (Bevölkerung)* to age; *(Mensch)* to become senile.
**vergriffen** *adj* unavailable; *Buch* out of print.
**vergröbern\*** *vtr* to coarsen.
**vergrößern 1** *vt* to enlarge; *Gelände auch* to extend; *Firma, Absatzmarkt* to expand; *Anzahl, Probleme, Einfluß* to increase; *(Lupe, Brille)* to magnify. **2** *vr* to increase; *(räumlich)* to be extended; *(Firma, Absatzmarkt)* to expand; *(Organ)* to become enlarged.
**Vergrößerung** *f siehe vb* enlargement; extension; expansion; increase; magnification. **in 1.000facher** ~ magnified 1,000 times.
**Vergrößerungsglas** *nt* magnifying glass.
**vergucken\*** *vr (col)* **(a) da hab ich mich verguckt** I didn't see it properly. **(b) sich in jdn/etw** ~ to fall for sb/sth *(col)*.
**vergünstigt** *adj Lage* improved; *Preis* reduced.
**Vergünstigung** *f (Vorteil)* privilege; *(Preisermäßigung)* reduction.
**vergüten\*** *vt jdm etw* ~ *Unkosten* to reimburse sb for sth; *Arbeit, Leistung* to pay sb for sth.
**Vergütung** *f* reimbursement.
**verh.** = **verheiratet**.
**verhaften\*** *vt* to arrest. **Sie sind verhaftet!** you are under arrest!
**Verhaftete(r)** *mf decl as adj* person under arrest.
**Verhaftung** *f* arrest.
**verhallen\*** *vi aux sein (Geräusch etc)* to die away. **ungehört** ~ *(fig) Warnung* to go unheard *or* unheeded.
**verhalten¹\*** *vr irreg* **1 (a)** to behave; *(handeln)* to act. **sich ruhig** ~ to keep quiet; *(sich nicht bewegen)* to keep still. **(b)** *(Sache, Marktlage)* to be; *(Chem)* to react. **wie verhält sich die Sache?** how do things stand? **2** *vr impers* **wie verhält es sich damit?** *(wie ist die Lage?)* how do things stand?; *(wie wird das gehandhabt?)* how do you go about it?; **damit verhält es sich anders** the situation is different; **wenn sich das so verhält, ...** if that is the case ...
**verhalten²** **1** *adj* restrained; *Stimme* muted; *Atem* bated; *Wut* suppressed; *Tempo, Rhythmus* measured. **2** *adv* with restraint; *laufen* at a measured pace.
**Verhalten** *nt no pl (Benehmen)* behaviour *(Brit)*, behavior *(US)*; *(Vorgehen)* conduct; *(Chem)* reaction.
**Verhaltens-:** ~**forschung** *f* behavioural *(Brit) or* behavioral *(US)* science; **v~gestört** *adj* disturbed; ~**maßregel** *f* rule of conduct; ~**weise** *f* behaviour *(Brit)*, behavior *(US)*.
**Verhältnis** *nt* **(a)** *(Proportion)* proportion; *(Math, Mischungs~)* ratio. **im** ~ **zu** in relation *or* proportion to; **im** ~ **zu früher** in comparison with earlier times; **in keinem** ~ **zu etw stehen** to be out of all proportion to sth. **(b)** *(Beziehung)* relationship; *(zwischen Ländern, innerhalb einer Gruppe)* relations *pl (zu* with*)*; *(Einstellung)* attitude *(zu* to*)*. **(c)** *(Liebes~)* affair. **(d)** ~**se** *pl* conditions *pl; (finanzielle)* circumstances *pl;* **so wie die** ~**se liegen** as things stand; **aus welchen** ~**sen kommt er?** what sort of background does he come from?; **über seine** ~**se**

**leben** to live beyond one's means; **für klare** ~**se sorgen, klare** ~**se schaffen** to get things straight.
**Verhältnis-:** **v~mäßig** *adv* relatively; ~**mäßigkeit** *f* **die** ~**mäßigkeit der Mittel** the appropriateness of the means; ~**wahl(recht** *nt*) *f* proportional representation *no art*.
**verhandeln\*** **1** *vi* **(a)** to negotiate *(über +acc* about*); (col: diskutieren)* to argue. **über den Preis läßt sich** ~ *(col)* we can discuss the price. **(b)** *(Jur)* **gegen jdn/in einem Fall** ~ to hear sb's/a case. **2** *vt* **(a)** to negotiate. **(b)** *(Jur) Fall* to hear.
**Verhandlung** *f* **(a)** negotiations *pl; (das Verhandeln)* negotiation. ~**en führen** to negotiate. **(b)** *(Jur)* hearing; *(Straf~)* trial.
**Verhandlungs-:** ~**basis** *f* basis for negotiation(s); ~**basis DM 2.500** 2,500 DM or near offer; **v~bereit** *adj* ready to negotiate; **v~fähig** *adj (Jur)* able to stand trial; ~**partner** *m* negotiating party; **wer war Ihr** ~**partner?** who were you negotiating with?; ~**tisch** *m* negotiating table.
**verhangen** *adv* overcast.
**verhängen\*** *vt* **(a)** *Embargo, Strafe* to impose *(über +acc* on*); Ausnahmezustand* to declare *(über +acc* in*)*. **(b)** *(zuhängen)* to cover *(mit* with*)*.
**Verhängnis** *nt* fate. **jdm zum** ~ **werden** to be sb's undoing.
**verhängnisvoll** *adj* disastrous, fatal; *Tag* fateful.
**verharmlosen\*** *vt* to play down.
**verhärmt** *adj Mensch, Gesicht* careworn.
**verharren\*** *vi aux haben or sein* to pause; *(in einer bestimmten Stellung)* to remain. **auf einem Standpunkt** ~ to adhere to a viewpoint.
**verharschen\*** *vi aux sein (Schnee, Piste)* to crust.
**verhärten\*** *vtr* to harden.
**verhaspeln\*** *vr (col)* to get into a muddle.
**verhaßt** *adj* hated; *Arbeit, Pflicht* hateful. **sich** ~ **machen** to make oneself hated *(bei* by*)*.
**verhätscheln\*** *vt* to spoil, to pamper.
**Verhau** *m or nt* **-e** *(zur Absperrung)* barrier; *(Käfig)* coop.
**verhauen\*** *irreg (col)* **1** *vt* **(a)** *(verprügeln)* to beat up; *(zur Strafe)* to beat. **(b)** *Prüfung etc* to muff *(col)*. **2** *vr* **(a)** *(sich verprügeln)* to have a fight. **(b)** *(beim Schreiben etc)* to make a mistake. **(c)** *(sich irren)* to slip up *(col)*.
**verheben\*** *vr irreg* to hurt oneself lifting something.
**verheddern\*** *vr (col: lit, fig)* to get into a tangle.
**verheerend** *adj Sturm, Folgen* devastating, disastrous; *Anblick* ghastly.
**verhehlen\*** *vt* to conceal *(jdm* from sb*)*.
**verheilen\*** *vi aux sein (lit, fig)* to heal.
**verheimlichen\*** *vt* to keep secret, to conceal *(jdm* from sb*)*. **ich habe nichts zu** ~ I have nothing to hide.
**verheiraten\*** **1** *vt* to marry *(mit* to*)*. **2** *vr* to get married, to marry. **sich mit jdm** ~ to marry sb, to get married to sb.
**verheiratet** *adj* married.
**verheißen\*** *vt irreg (geh)* to promise.
**verheißungsvoll** *adj* promising; *Blicke* alluring.
**verheizen\*** *vt* to burn, to use as fuel. **Soldaten** ~ *(col)* to send soldiers to the slaughter.
**verhelfen\*** *vi irreg jdm zu etw* ~ to help sb to get sth.
**verherrlichen\*** *vt* to glorify.
**verheult** *adj Augen, Gesicht* puffy. **du siehst** ~ **aus** you look as though you've been crying.
**verhexen\*** *vt* to bewitch; *(col) Maschine etc* to put a jinx on *(col)*. **das ist doch wie verhext** *(col)* it's maddening *(col)*.

**verhindern\*** *vt* to prevent; *Versuch, Plan* to foil. **ich konnte es nicht ~, daß er die Wahrheit erfuhr** I couldn't prevent him from finding out the truth; **das läßt sich leider nicht ~** it can't be helped, unfortunately; **er war an diesem Abend (dienstlich) verhindert** he was unable to come that evening (for reasons of work); **ein verhinderter Politiker** *(col)* a frustrated politician.

**verhöhnen\*** *vt* to mock, to deride.

**verhökern\*** *vt (col)* to flog *(Brit col)*, to sell.

**Verhör** *nt* **-e** questioning, interrogation.

**verhören\*** **1** *vt* to question, to interrogate. **2** *vr* to mishear.

**verhüllen\*** **1** *vt* to veil; *Haupt, Körperteil* to cover. **2** *vr* to disguise oneself; *(Frau)* to veil oneself.

**verhüllend** *adj Ausdruck* euphemistic.

**verhungern\*** *vi aux sein (lit, fig)* to starve, to die of starvation.

**verhunzen\*** *vt (col)* to ruin.

**verhüten\*** *vt* to prevent.

**verhütten** *vt* to smelt.

**Verhütung** *f* prevention; *(Empfängnis~)* contraception.

**Verhütungsmittel** *nt* contraceptive.

**verhutzelt** *adj Gesicht, Männlein* wizened; *Haut* wrinkled; *Obst* shrivelled *(Brit)*, shriveled *(US)*.

**verifizieren\*** [verifi'tsiːrən] *vt* to verify.

**ver|innerlichen\*** *vt* to internalize.

**ver|irren\*** *vr* to get lost, to lose one's way; *(fig)* to go astray; *(Tier, Kugel)* to stray.

**Ver|irrung** *f* losing one's way *no art*; *(fig)* aberration.

**verjagen\*** *vt (lit, fig)* to chase away.

**verjähren\*** *vi aux sein (Jur)* to come under the statute of limitations; *(Anspruch)* to lapse.

**Verjährung** *f (Jur)* limitation; *(von Anspruch)* lapse.

**Verjährungsfrist** *f (Jur)* limitation period.

**verjubeln\*** *vt (col) Geld* to blow *(col)*.

**verjüngen\*** **1** *vt* to rejuvenate; *(jünger aussehen lassen)* to make look younger; *Baumbestand* to regenerate. **eine Mannschaft ~** to build up a younger team. **2** *vr* (**a**) to become younger; *(Haut, Erscheinung)* to become rejuvenated; *(jünger aussehen)* to look younger. (**b**) *(dünner werden)* to taper.

**verkabeln** *vt (TV)* to link up to the cable network.

**Verkabelung** *f (TV)* linking up to the cable network.

**verkalken\*** *vi aux sein (Arterien)* to become hardened; *(Gewebe)* to calcify; *(Wasserleitung etc)* to fur up; *(col: Mensch)* to become senile.

**verkalkt** *adj (col)* senile.

**verkalkulieren\*** *vr* to miscalculate.

**Verkalkung** *f siehe vi* hardening; calcification; furring; senility.

**verkannt** *adj* unrecognized.

**verkappt** *adj attr* hidden; *(Med)* undiagnosed.

**verkatert** *adj (col)* hung-over *(col)*.

**Verkauf** *m, pl* **Verkäufe** sale. **zum ~ stehen** to be up for sale.

**verkaufen\*** **1** *vti (lit, fig)* to sell *(für, um* for*)*. „**zu ~**" "for sale"; **jdm etw** *or* **etw an jdn ~** to sell sb sth, to sell sth to sb. **2** *vr (Ware)* to sell; *(Mensch)* to sell oneself.

**Verkäufer(in** *f)* *m -* seller; *(in Geschäft)* sales assistant *(Brit)*, sales clerk *(US)*; *(im Außendienst)* salesman/saleswoman, salesperson.

**verkäuflich** *adj* saleable, salable *(US)*, marketable; *(zu verkaufen)* for sale. **leicht/schwer ~** easy/hard to sell.

**Verkaufs-** *in cpds* sales; **~abteilung** *f* sales department; **~förderung** *f* sales promotion;

**~kampagne** *f* sales drive; **~leiter** *m* sales manager; **v~offen** *adj* open for business; **v~offener Samstag** *Saturday on which the shops are open all day*; **~personal** *nt* sales personnel; **~preis** *m* retail price; **~schlager** *m* big seller.

**Verkehr** *m no pl* (**a**) traffic; *(Beförderung, Verkehrsmittel)* transport, transportation *(US)*. **für den ~ freigeben** *Straße etc* to open to traffic; *Transportmittel* to bring into service; **aus dem ~ ziehen** to withdraw from service. (**b**) *(Verbindung)* contact, communication; *(Umgang)* company; *(Geschlechts~)* intercourse. (**c**) *(Umlauf)* circulation. **etw in (den) ~ bringen/aus dem ~ ziehen** to put sth into/withdraw sth from circulation.

**verkehren\*** **1** *vi* (**a**) *aux haben or sein (fahren)* to run; *(Flugzeug)* to fly. (**b**) *(Gast sein, Kontakt pflegen)* **bei jdm ~** to frequent sb's house; **mit jdm ~** to associate with sb; **in Künstlerkreisen ~** to move in artistic circles; **mit jdm brieflich/schriftlich ~** *(form)* to correspond with sb; **mit jdm (geschlechtlich) ~** to have (sexual) intercourse with sb. **2** *vtr* to turn *(in +acc* into*)*. **etw ins Gegenteil ~** to reverse sth.

**Verkehrs-** *in cpds* traffic; **~ader** *f* (traffic) artery; **~ampel** *f* traffic lights *pl (Brit)*, traffic light *(US)*; **~amt** *nt* = **~büro**; **v~arm** *adj Zeit, Straße* quiet; **ein v~armes Gebiet** an area with little traffic; **~aufkommen** *nt* volume of traffic; **~behinderung** *f (Jur)* obstruction (of traffic); **v~beruhigt** *adj* traffic-calmed; **~beruhigung** *f* traffic calming; **~betriebe** *pl* transport services *pl*; **~büro** *nt* tourist information office; **~delikt** *nt* traffic offence *(Brit)* or violation *(US)*; **~erziehung** *f* road safety training; **~flugzeug** *nt* commercial aircraft; **~funk** *m* radio traffic service; **~gefährdung** *f (durch Fahrer)* dangerous driving; **v~günstig** *adj* convenient; **~hindernis** *nt* (traffic) obstruction; **~hinweis** *m (Rad)* traffic announcement; **~insel** *f* traffic island; **~knotenpunkt** *m* traffic junction; **~kontrolle** *f* traffic check; **~minister** *m* minister of transport; **~mittel** *nt* means of transport *sing*; **öffentliche/private ~mittel** public/private transport; **~netz** *nt* traffic network; **~opfer** *nt* road casualty; **~polizei** *f* traffic police *pl*; **~regel** *f* traffic regulation; **v~reich** *adj Straße* busy; **v~reiche Zeit** peak (traffic) time; **~schild** *nt* road sign; **v~schwach** *adj Zeit* off-peak; **v~sicher** *adj Fahrzeug* roadworthy; *Brücke* safe (for traffic); **~sicherheit** *f* road safety; **~stau** *m* traffic jam; **~stockung** *f* traffic hold-up; **~sünder** *m (col)* traffic offender; **~teilnehmer** *m* road-user; **~tote(r)** *mf* road casualty; **v~tüchtig** *adj Fahrzeug* roadworthy; *Mensch* fit to drive; **~unfall** *m* road accident; **~unternehmen** *nt* transport company; **~unterricht** *m* road safety instruction; **~verbindung** *f* public transport facilities *pl*; *(Anschluß)* connection; **~verbund** *m* integrated transport system; **~verein** *m* local tourist organization; *(Büro)* tourist information office; **~verhältnisse** *pl* traffic situation *sing*; *(Straßenzustand)* road conditions *pl*; **~wesen** *nt* transport and communication *no art*; **v~widrig** *adj* contrary to road traffic regulations; **~zeichen** *nt* road sign.

**verkehrt** **1** *adj* wrong; *Welt* topsy-turvy. **2** *adv* wrongly. **etw ~ (herum) anhaben** to have sth on the wrong way around; **das V~este, was du tun könntest** the worst thing you could do.

**verkeilen\*** *vr* to become wedged together.

**verkennen\*** *vt irreg* to misjudge. **es ist nicht zu ~, daß ...** it is undeniable that ...; *siehe* **verkannt**.

**verketten\*** *vt Tür, Kiste* to put a chain on; *(fig)* to link.

**Verkettung** *f* eine ~ unglücklicher Umstände an unfortunate chain of events.
**verkitten*** *vt* to cement; *Fenster* to putty around.
**verklagen*** *vt* to sue *(wegen* for*)*. jdn auf etw *(acc)* ~ to take sb to court for sth.
**verklammern*** *vt* to staple together; *(fig)* to link.
**verklappen** *vt Abfallstoffe* to dump (at sea).
**verklärt** *adj* transfigured.
**verklausulieren*** *vt Vertrag* to hedge in with (restrictive) clauses.
**verkleben*** **1** *vt (zusammenkleben)* to stick together; *(zukleben)* to cover *(mit* with*)*. **2** *vi aux sein (Wunde)* to close; *(Augen)* to get gummed up; *(Briefmarken, Bonbons)* to stick together; *(Haare)* to become matted. mit etw ~ to stick to sth.
**verklebt** *adj* sticky; *Augen* gummed up; *Haare* matted.
**verkleckern*** *vr (col)* to spill.
**verkleiden*** **1** *vt* **(a)** to disguise; *(kostümieren)* to dress up. **(b)** *Schacht, Tunnel* to line; *(vertäfeln)* to panel; *Heizkörper* to cover in. **2** *vr* to disguise oneself; *(sich kostümieren)* to dress (oneself) up.
**Verkleidung** *f* **(a)** *(Kleidung)* disguise; *(Kostüm)* fancy dress. **(b)** *siehe vt (b)* lining; panelling *(Brit)*, paneling *(US)*; covering.
**verkleinern*** **1** *vt* to reduce; *Raum, Gebiet, Firma* to make smaller. **2** *vr* to be reduced; *(Raum, Gebiet, Firma)* to become smaller.
**Verkleinerung** *f* reduction.
**verklemmen*** *vr* to get stuck.
**verklemmt** *adj (col) Mensch* inhibited.
**verklingen*** *vi irreg aux sein* to die away.
**verklumpen*** *vi aux sein* to get lumpy.
**verknacksen*** *vt (col)* **(sich *dat*)** den Fuß ~ to twist one's ankle.
**verknallen*** *vr (col)* to fall head over heels *(in jdn* with sb*)* in love.
**verknappen*** *vt* to cut back.
**verkneifen*** *vr irreg (col)* sich *(dat)* ein Lächeln/eine Bemerkung ~ to suppress a smile/a remark; es sich *(dat)* ~, etw zu sagen/tun to stop oneself (from) saying/doing sth; ich konnte mir das Lachen nicht ~ I couldn't help laughing.
**verkniffen** *adj Gesicht (angestrengt)* strained; *(verbittert)* pinched. etw ~ sehen to take a narrow view of sth.
**verknöchert*** *adj (fig)* fossilized.
**verknoten*** **1** *vt* to tie, to knot; *(col) Paket* to tie up. **2** *vr* to become knotted.
**verknüpfen*** *vt* **(a)** to tie (together); *(Comp)* to integrate. **(b)** *(fig)* to combine; *(in Zusammenhang bringen)* to link, to connect; *Gedanken* to associate. ein Umzug ist immer mit großen Ausgaben verknüpft moving house always involves a lot of expense.
**verkochen*** *vti (vi: aux sein) (Flüssigkeit)* to boil away; *(Kartoffeln, Gemüse)* to overcook.
**verkohlen*** **1** *vi aux sein* to become charred. **2** *vt* **(a)** *Holz* to char. **(b)** *(col)* jdn ~ to have sb on *(col)*.
**verkommen¹*** *vi irreg aux sein* **(a)** *(Mensch)* to go to the dogs; *(moralisch)* to become dissolute; *(Kind)* to run wild. zu etw ~ to degenerate into sth. **(b)** *(Gebäude, Auto)* to fall to pieces; *(Stadt)* to become run-down; *(Gelände)* to run wild; *(Begabung)* to go to waste; *(Lebensmittel)* to go bad.
**verkommen²** *adj Mensch* depraved; *Auto, Gebäude* dilapidated; *Garten* wild.
**verkonsumieren*** *vt (col)* to get through; *(Essen auch)* to polish off.
**verkoppeln*** *vt* to connect, to couple; *(Space)* to link (up).

**verkorken*** *vt* to cork (up).
**verkorkst** *adj (col)* ruined; *Magen* upset. eine ~e Sache a mess.
**verkörpern*** *vt* to embody; *(Theat)* to play.
**Verkörperung** *f* embodiment.
**verköstigen*** *vt* to feed.
**verkrachen*** *vr (col)* sich (mit jdm) ~ to fall out (with sb).
**verkracht** *adj (col) Leben* ruined; *Typ* dead-beat *(col)*. sie sind ~ *(zerstritten)* they have fallen out with each other.
**verkraften*** *vt* to cope with; *(seelisch)* to come to terms with; *(finanziell, col: essen, trinken können)* to manage.
**verkrampfen*** *vr* to become cramped; *(Hände)* to clench up; *(Mensch)* to go tense. **verkrampft** *(fig)* tense.
**verkriechen*** *vr irreg* to creep away; *(fig)* to hide (oneself away). sich unter den *or* dem Tisch ~ to crawl *or* creep under the table.
**verkrümeln*** **1** *vr (col)* to disappear. **2** *vt* to crumble.
**verkrümmen*** *vtr* to bend; *(Rückgrat)* to become curved; *(Holz)* to warp; *(Baum)* to grow crooked.
**Verkrümmung** *f* bend *(gen* in*)*; *(von Fingern, Knochen, Bäumen)* crookedness *no pl.* ~ der Wirbelsäule curvature of the spine.
**verkrüppeln*** **1** *vt* to cripple. **2** *vi aux sein* to become crippled; *(Zehen, Füße)* to become deformed; *(Baum etc)* to grow stunted.
**verkrusten*** *vir (vi: aux sein)* to become encrusted.
**verkrustet** *adj Wunde* scabby; *(fig) Strukturen* rigid; *Ansichten* set.
**verkühlen*** *vr (col)* to get a chill.
**verkümmern*** *vi aux sein (Glied, Organ)* to atrophy; *(Pflanze)* to die; *(Talent)* to go to waste; *(Mensch)* to waste away. emotionell/geistig ~ to become emotionally/intellectually stunted.
**verkünden*** *vt* to announce; *Urteil* to pronounce; *Evangelium* to preach; *Gesetz* to promulgate.
**Verkünder(in** *f)* *m* - ein ~ des Evangeliums a preacher of the gospel.
**verkündigen*** *vt* to proclaim; *(iro)* to announce; *Evangelium auch* to preach.
**verkupfert** *adj* copper-plated.
**verkuppeln*** *vt (pej)* to pair off. jdn an jdn ~ *(Zuhälter)* to procure sb for sb.
**verkürzen*** **1** *vt* to shorten; *Strecke, Wege etc auch* to cut; *Aufenthalt* to cut short; *Haltbarkeit* to reduce; *(euph) Leiden* to end. sich *(dat)* die Zeit ~ to pass the time; verkürzte Arbeitszeit shorter working hours. **2** *vr* to be shortened; *(Strecke, Zeit auch)* to be cut; *(Haltbarkeit)* to be reduced; *(Leiden)* to be ended; *(Urlaub, Aufenthalt)* to be cut short.
**Verkürzung** *f siehe vb* shortening; cutting short; reduction; ending.
**Verl.** = **(a)** Verlag. **(b)** Verleger.
**verladen*** *vt irreg* to load.
**Verlag** *m* -e publisher, publishing house. in *or* bei welchem ~ ist das erschienen? who published it?
**verlagern*** *vtr (lit, fig)* to shift.
**Verlagerung** *f* shift.
**Verlags-:** ~anstalt *f* publishing firm; ~buchhandel *m* publishing trade; ~haus *nt* publishing house; ~programm *nt* list; ~wesen *nt* publishing *no art.*
**verlangen*** **1** *vt* **(a)** *(fordern)* to demand; *(wollen)* to want; *Preis* to ask; *Qualifikationen, Erfahrung* to require. **(b)** *(erwarten)* to ask *(von* of*)*. es wird von jdm verlangt, daß ... it is required *or* expected of sb that ...; das ist nicht zuviel verlangt it's not asking

too much. **(c)** *(fragen nach)* to ask for. **Sie werden am Telefon verlangt** you are wanted on the phone; **ich verlange den Geschäftsführer (zu sprechen)** I demand to see the manager. **2** *vi* ~ **nach** to ask for; *(sich sehnen nach)* to long for.

**Verlangen** *nt* - *(nach for)* desire; *(Sehnsucht)* yearning, longing; *(Begierde)* craving; *(Forderung)* request. **auf** ~ on demand; **auf** ~ **der Eltern** at the parents' request.

**verlängern\*** **1** *vt* to extend; *(zeitlich)* Wartezeit, Schmerzen *etc* to prolong; *(Hosenbein, Ärmel etc* to lengthen; *Paß, Abonnement etc* to renew. **ein verlängertes Wochenende** a long weekend. **2** *vr* to be extended; *(zeitlich auch, Leiden etc)* to be prolonged.

**Verlängerung** *f* **(a)** *siehe vt* extension; prolongation; lengthening; renewal. **(b)** *(von Spielzeit)* extra time *(Brit)*, overtime *(US)*.

**Verlängerungs-:** ~**kabel** *nt,* ~**schnur** *f (Elec)* extension lead.

**verlangsamen\*** *vtr* to slow down *or* up. **das Tempo** ~ to slow down.

**Verlaß** *m no pl* **darauf/auf ihn ist kein** ~ you can't rely on that/him.

**verlassen¹\*** *irreg* **1** *vt* to leave; *(fig: Mut etc)* to desert; *(im Stich lassen)* to desert, to abandon; *(Comp) Datei* to exit. **2** *vr* **sich auf jdn/etw** ~ to rely *or* depend on sb/sth; **darauf können Sie sich** ~ you can depend on that.

**verlassen²** *adj* deserted; *Auto* abandoned; *(öd)* desolate; *(einsam)* lonely. **einsam und** ~ all alone.

**verläßlich** *adj* reliable.

**Verlauf** *m, pl* **Verläufe** course; *(Ausgang)* end. **im** ~**(e) des Tages** *etc* during the course of the day *etc.* **einen guten/schlechten** ~ **nehmen** to go well/badly.

**verlaufen\*** *irreg* **1** *vi aux sein* **(a)** *(Tag, Prüfung)* to go; *(Kindheit)* to pass; *(Untersuchung)* to proceed. **(b)** *(sich erstrecken)* to run. **(c)** *(auseinanderfließen)* to run. **die Spur verlief im Sand** the track disappeared in the sand. **2** *vr* **(a)** *(sich verirren)* to get lost, to lose one's way. **(b)** *(Menschenmenge)* to disperse; *(Spur, Weg)* to disappear.

**Verlaufsform** *f (Gram)* continuous form.

**verlautbaren\*** *vti (form)* to announce.

**Verlautbarung** *f* announcement.

**verlauten\*** **1** *vi* **etwas** ~ **lassen** to give an indication. **2** *vi impers* **es verlautet, daß ...** it is reported that ...; **wie aus Bonn verlautet** according to reports from Bonn.

**verleben\*** *vt* to spend. **eine schöne Zeit** ~ to have a nice time.

**verlebt** *adj* worn out, dissipated.

**verlegen¹\*** **1** *vt* **(a)** *(an anderen Ort)* to transfer, to relocate. **(b)** *(verschieben)* to postpone *(auf +acc until)*; *(vorverlegen)* to bring forward *(auf +acc to)*. **(c)** *(an falschen Platz legen)* to mislay. **(d)** *Kabel, Fliesen etc* to lay. **(e)** *(drucken lassen)* to publish. **2** *vr* **sich auf etw** *(acc)* ~ to resort to sth; **sich aufs Unterrichten** ~ to take up teaching.

**verlegen²** *adj* embarrassed *no adv.* **um Worte** ~ **sein** to be at a loss for words.

**Verlegenheit** *f* **(a)** *no pl* embarrassment. **jdn in** ~ **bringen** to embarrass sb; **in** ~ **kommen** *or* **geraten** to get embarrassed. **(b)** *(unangenehme Lage)* embarrassing situation.

**Verleger(in** *f) m* - publisher.

**verleiden\*** *vt* **jdm etw** ~ to put sb off sth.

**Verleih** *m* **-e (a)** *(Unternehmen)* rental *or* hire *(Brit)* company; *(Auto~)* car rental *or* hire *(Brit)*; *(Film~)* distributor(s). **(b)** *(das Verleihen)* renting (out), hiring (out) *(Brit)*; *(Film~)* distribution. **der** ~ **von Büchern** the lending of books.

**verleihen\*** *vt irreg* **(a)** *(verborgen)* to lend *(an jdn to sb)*; *(gegen Gebühr)* to rent, to hire *(Brit)*. **(b)** *(zuerkennen)* to award *(jdm (to) sb)*; *Titel, Ehrenbürgerrechte* to confer *(jdm on sb)*. **(c)** *(geben, verschaffen)* to give.

**Verleiher** *m* - hire *(Brit)* or rental firm; *(von Filmen)* distributor; *(von Büchern)* lender.

**Verleihung** *f siehe vt (a, b)* **(a)** lending; renting, hiring *(Brit)*. **(b)** award(ing), conferment.

**verleimen\*** *vt* to glue.

**verleiten\*** *vt* **(a)** *(verlocken)* to tempt; *(verführen)* to lead astray. **jdn dazu** ~, **die Schule zu schwänzen** to encourage sb to play truant. **(b)** *(veranlassen)* **jdn zu etw** ~ to lead sb to sth.

**verlernen\*** *vt* to forget. **das Tanzen** ~ to forget how to dance.

**verlesen\*** *irreg* **1** *vt* **(a)** *(vorlesen)* to read (out). **(b)** *Gemüse, Linsen etc* to sort. **2** *vr* **ich habe mich wohl** ~ I must have misread it.

**verletzen\*** **1** *vt* **(a)** *(auch: fig)* to injure; *(in Kampf etc, mit Kugel, Messer)* to wound; *(fig)* jdn to hurt, to offend; *jds Schönheitssinn etc* to offend. **(b)** *Gesetz* to break; *Pflicht, Rechte, Intimsphäre* to violate. **2** *vr* to injure oneself.

**verletzend** *adj Bemerkung* hurtful.

**verletzlich** *adj* vulnerable.

**Verletzte(r)** *mf decl as adj* injured person; *(Unfall~ auch)* casualty; *(bei Kampf)* wounded person. **die** ~**n** the injured/the wounded.

**Verletzung** *f siehe vt* **(a)** injuring; wounding; *(fig)* hurting, offending. **(b)** breaking; violation. **(c)** *(Wunde)* injury.

**verleugnen\*** *vt* to deny; *Kind, Freunde* to disown. **er läßt sich immer** ~ he always pretends not to be there; **sich (selbst)** ~ to act against one's own convictions.

**verleumden\*** *vt* to slander; *(schriftlich)* to libel.

**verleumderisch** *adj siehe vt* slanderous; libellous *(Brit)*, libelous *(US)*.

**Verleumdung** *f (Bemerkung)* slander; *(Bericht)* libel.

**Verleumdungskampagne** *f* smear campaign.

**verlieben\*** *vr* to fall in love *(in +acc with)*.

**verliebt** *adj Benehmen, Blicke, Worte* amorous. **(in jdn)** ~ **sein** to be in love (with sb).

**Verliebtheit** *f* amorous state.

**verlieren** *pret* **verlor,** *ptp* **verloren** **1** *vti* to lose. **kein Wort über jdn/etw** ~ not to say a word about sb/sth; **das/er hat hier nichts verloren** *(col)* that/he has no business to be here; **sie hat an Schönheit verloren** she has lost some of her beauty; **sie/die Altstadt** *etc* **hat sehr verloren** she/the old town *etc* is not what she/it *etc* used to be; **durch etw** ~ to lose (something) by sth. **2** *vr (Menschen)* to lose each other; *(verschwinden)* to disappear; *(verhallen)* to fade away. **sich in etw** *(dat)* ~ to get lost in sth; *(fig)* to become absorbed in sth; *siehe* **verloren.**

**Verlierer(in** *f) m* - loser.

**Verlies** *nt* **-e** dungeon.

**verloben\*** *vr* to get engaged *(mit to)*. **verlobt sein** to be engaged.

**Verlobte(r)** *mf decl as adj* **mein** ~**r** my fiancé; **meine** ~ my fiancée; **die** ~**n** the engaged couple.

**Verlobung** *f* engagement; *(Feier)* engagement party.

**Verlobungs-** *in cpds* engagement.

**verlocken\*** *vti* to entice, to tempt.

**verlockend** *adj* enticing, tempting.

**Verlockung** *f* enticement, temptation.

**verlogen** *adj Mensch* lying; *Komplimente, Versprechungen* false; *Moral, Gesellschaft* hypocritical.

**Verlogenheit** *f siehe adj* mendacity *(form)*; falseness; hypocrisy.

**verlor** *pret of* **verlieren**.

**verloren 1** *ptp of* **verlieren**. **2** *adj* lost. **jdn/etw ~ geben** to give sb/sth up for lost; **auf ~em Posten kämpfen** *or* **stehen** to be fighting a losing battle; **der ~e Sohn** *(Bibl)* the prodigal son; **~e Eier** *(Cook)* poached eggs.

**verlorengehen** *vi sep irreg aux sein* to be lost. **an ihm ist ein Sänger verlorengegangen** he would have made a good singer.

**verlöschen\*** *vi aux sein* to go out; *(Inschrift, Farbe, Erinnerung)* to fade.

**verlosen\*** *vt* to raffle (off).

**Verlosung** *f (das Verlosen)* raffling; *(Lotterie)* raffle.

**verlöten\*** *vt* to solder.

**verlottern\*** *vi aux sein (col) (Stadt, Restaurant)* to become run down; *(Garten)* to run wild; *(Mensch)* to go to the dogs; *(moralisch)* to go to the bad.

**verlottert** *adj (col)* Stadt run-down; *Garten* wild; *Mensch, Aussehen* scruffy; *(moralisch)* dissolute.

**Verlust** *m* -e loss. **mit ~ verkaufen** to sell at a loss.

**Verlust-:** **~anzeige** *f* "lost" notice; **~betrieb** *m* loss-maker; **v~bringend** *adj* loss-making; **v~bringend arbeiten** to work at a loss; **~geschäft** *nt* **ein ~geschäft machen** to make a loss; **das war ein reines ~geschäft** that was a dead loss; **~liste** *f (Mil)* casualty list; **v~reich** *adj* with heavy losses.

**Verm.** = **Vermerk**.

**vermachen\*** *vt* **jdm etw ~** to leave *or* bequeath sth to sb.

**Vermächtnis** *nt* bequest, legacy; *(fig)* legacy.

**vermählen\*** *(form)* **1** *vt* to marry. **frisch vermählt sein** to be newly married. **2** *vr* **sich (mit jdm) ~** to marry (sb).

**Vermählte(r)** *mf decl as adj* **die beiden ~n** the newly-weds.

**Vermählung** *f (form)* marriage; *(Feier)* wedding ceremony.

**vermarkten\*** *vt* to market; *(fig)* to commercialize.

**vermasseln\*** *vt (col)* to mess up *(col)*.

**vermauern\*** *vt* to wall *or* brick up.

**vermehren\*** **1** *vt* to increase; *(fortpflanzen)* to breed. **diese Fälle treten vermehrt auf** these cases are happening increasingly often. **2** *vr* to increase; *(sich fortpflanzen)* to reproduce, to breed; *(Bakterien)* to multiply; *(Pflanzen)* to propagate.

**Vermehrung** *f siehe vb* increase; breeding; reproduction; multiplying; propagation.

**vermeidbar** *adj* avoidable.

**vermeiden\*** *vt irreg* to avoid. **~, daß etw passiert** to avoid letting sth happen; **es läßt sich nicht ~, daß ...** it is inevitable *or* unavoidable that ...

**vermeidlich** *adj* avoidable.

**vermeintlich** *adj attr* putative.

**vermengen\*** *vt* to mix; *(fig col: durcheinanderbringen)* to mix up.

**vermenschlichen\*** *vt* to humanize.

**Vermerk** *m* -e note, remark; *(im Kalender)* entry; *(in Paß)* observation; *(Stempel)* stamp.

**vermerken\*** *vt* to make a note of; *(in Paß, Karte)* to record. **sich (dat) etw ~** to make a note of sth; **jdm etw übel ~** to take sth amiss.

**vermessen¹\*** *vt irreg* to measure; *Land, Gelände* to survey.

**vermessen²** *adj (anmaßend)* presumptuous; *(kühn) Unterfangen* bold.

**Vermessenheit** *f no pl siehe adj* presumptuousness; boldness.

**Vermessung** *f* measurement; *(von Land, Gelände)* survey.

**Vermessungs-:** **~amt** *nt* land survey(ing) office; **~ingenieur** *m* land surveyor.

**vermiesen\*** *vt (col)* **jdm etw ~** to spoil sth for sb.

**vermietbar** *adj* rentable. **schlecht ~** difficult to rent.

**vermieten\*** *vti* to rent (out), to let (out) *(Brit)*; *Boot, Auto* to rent (out), to hire (out) *(Brit)*. **Zimmer zu ~** room to let *(Brit)* or for rent *(esp US)*.

**Vermieter** *m* - landlord.

**Vermieterin** *f* landlady.

**Vermietung** *f siehe vb* renting, letting *(Brit)*; rental, hiring.

**vermindern\*** **1** *vt* to reduce, to decrease; *Ärger* to lessen; *Schmerzen* to ease. **2** *vr siehe vt* to decrease; to lessen; to ease. **verminderte Zurechnungsfähigkeit** *(Jur)* diminished responsibility.

**Verminderung** *f siehe vb* reduction *(gen* of*)*, decrease *(gen* in*)*; lessening; easing.

**verminen\*** *vt* to mine.

**vermischen\*** **1** *vt* to mix; *Teesorten etc* to blend. **vermischte Schriften** miscellaneous writings. **2** *vr* to mix; *(Elemente, Klänge, Farben)* to blend.

**vermissen\*** *vt* to miss. **vermißt werden** to be missing; **vermißt sein, als vermißt gemeldet sein** to be reported missing; **etw an jdm ~** to find sb lacking in sth; **wir haben dich bei der Party vermißt** we didn't see you at the party; **etw ~ lassen** to be lacking in sth.

**Vermißten|anzeige** *f* missing persons report.

**Vermißte(r)** *mf decl as adj* missing person.

**vermittelbar** *adj* Idee, Gefühl communicable; *Arbeitsloser* placeable.

**vermitteln\*** **1** *vt* to arrange *(jdm* for sb*)*; *Stelle, Privatschüler* to find *(jdm* for sb*)*; *Aushilfskräfte, Arbeitslose etc* to place *(an eine Firma* with a firm*)*; *(Telec) Gespräch* to connect; *Lösung etc* to negotiate; *Gefühl, Bild, Idee* to convey, to give *(jdm* to sb*)*; *Wissen* to impart *(jdm* to sb*)*. **jdm etw ~** to get sth for sb. **2** *vi* to mediate. **~de Worte** conciliatory words.

**Vermittler(in** *f)* *m* - **(a)** mediator. **(b)** *(Comm)* agent; *(Fin, Heirats~)* broker; *(von Anleihe)* negotiator; *(Stellen~)* clerk in an employment agency.

**Vermittlung** *f* **(a)** *siehe vt* arranging; finding; placing; connection; negotiation; conveying; imparting. **durch seine freundliche ~** with his kind help. **(b)** *(Schlichtung)* mediation. **(c)** *(Stelle, Agentur)* agency; *(Heirats~)* marriage bureau; *(Wohnungs~)* letting agency; *(Arbeits~)* employment agency. **(d)** *(Telec)* exchange; *(in Firma etc)* switchboard.

**Vermittlungs-:** **~gebühr** *f* commission; **~stelle** *f* agency; *(Telec)* (telephone) exchange; *(in Firma etc)* switchboard.

**vermodern\*** *vi aux sein* to moulder, to decay.

**vermögen** *vt aux (geh)* **etw zu tun ~, (es) ~, etw zu tun** to be able to do sth; **Geduld vermag viel bei ihm** you can get a long way with him if you have patience.

**Vermögen** *nt* - **(a)** *(Reichtum, viel Geld)* fortune. **~ haben** to have money. **(b)** *(Besitz)* property. **mein ganzes ~ besteht aus ...** my entire assets consist of ... **(c)** *(Können)* ability, capacity.

**vermögend** *adj (reich)* wealthy, well-off.

**Vermögens-:** **~abgabe** *f* property levy; **~bildung** *f* creation of wealth; **~steuer** *f* wealth tax; **~verhältnisse** *pl* financial circumstances *pl*; **~verwaltung** *f* investment management; **~werte** *pl* assets *pl*; **v~wirksam** *adj* profitable; **sein Geld v~wirksam anlegen** to invest one's money profitably; **v~wirksame Leistungen** employers' contributions to a tax-deductible savings scheme.

**vermummen\*** *vr* **(a)** to wrap up (warm). **(b)** *(sich* *verkleiden)* to disguise. **vermummte Demonstranten** masked demonstrators.

**Vermummung** *f* disguise; *(von Demonstranten)* covering of the face.

**vermurksen\*** *vt (col)* **etw** ~ to make a mess of sth.

**vermuten\*** *vt* to suspect. **ich vermute es nur** that's only an assumption; **wir haben ihn dort nicht vermutet** we didn't expect to find him there; **es ist zu ~, daß …** it may be supposed that …

**vermutlich 1** *adj attr* presumable; *Täter* suspected. **2** *adv* presumably.

**Vermutung** *f (Annahme)* supposition, assumption; *(Verdacht)* suspicion. **die ~ liegt nahe, daß …** there are grounds for assuming that …; **meine ~en waren doch richtig** my guess was right.

**vernachlässigen\* 1** *vt* to neglect; *(Schicksal)* jdn to be unkind to. **das können wir ~** *(nicht berücksichtigen)* we can ignore that. **2** *vr* to neglect one's appearance.

**Vernachlässigung** *f* neglect.

**vernageln\*** *vt* to nail up. **etw mit Brettern ~** to board sth up.

**vernähen\*** *vt Wunde, Saum* to stitch (up).

**vernarben\*** *vi aux sein* to heal *or* close (up).

**vernarren\*** *vr (col)* **sich in jdn/etw ~** to fall for sb/ sth in a big way *(col)*; **in jdn/etw vernarrt sein** to be crazy about sb/sth *(col)*.

**vernaschen\*** *vt Süßigkeiten* to eat up; *Geld* to spend on sweets *(Brit)* or candy *(US)*; *(col) Mädchen, Mann* to make it with *(col)*.

**vernebeln\*** *vt (Mil)* to cover with a smoke screen; *(fig) Tatsachen* to obscure; *(col) Zimmer* to fug up.

**vernehmbar** *adj (hörbar)* audible.

**vernehmen\*** *vt irreg* **(a)** *(hören, erfahren)* to hear. **(b)** *(Jur) Zeugen, Angeklagte* to examine; *(Polizei)* to question.

**Vernehmen** *nt*: **dem ~ nach** from what I/we *etc* hear.

**vernehmlich** *adj* clear, audible.

**Vernehmung** *f (Jur: von Zeugen, Angeklagten)* examination; *(durch Polizei)* questioning.

**vernehmungsfähig** *adj* able to be examined/ questioned.

**verneigen\*** *vr* to bow. **sich vor jdm/etw ~** *(lit)* to bow to sb/sth; *(fig)* to bow down before sb/sth.

**verneinen\*** *vti Frage* to answer in the negative; *(leugnen) Tatsache, Existenz Gottes etc* to deny; *These* to dispute; *(Gram, Logik)* to negate. **die verneinte Form** the negative (form).

**verneinend** *adj (auch Gram)* negative.

**Verneinung** *f (Leugnung)* denial; *(von These etc)* disputing; *(Gram, Philos)* negation; *(verneinte Form)* negative.

**vernetzen\*** *vt* to link up; *(Comp)* to network.

**vernichten\*** *vt (lit, fig)* to destroy.

**vernichtend** *adj* devastating; *Niederlage* crushing. **jdn ~ schlagen** *(Mil, Sport)* to annihilate sb.

**Vernichtung** *f* destruction.

**Vernichtungs-**: **~krieg** *m* war of extermination; **~lager** *nt* extermination camp; **~schlag** *m* devastating blow; **~waffe** *f* doomsday weapon.

**verniedlichen\*** *vt* to trivialize.

**vernieten\*** *vt* to rivet.

**Vernissage** [vɛrnɪˈsaːʒə] *f* **-n** *(geh)* private view.

**Vernunft** *f no pl* reason. **zur ~ kommen** to come to one's senses; **~ annehmen** to see reason; **etw mit/ ohne ~ tun** to do sth sensibly/foolishly.

**Vernunft-**: **v~begabt** *adj* rational; **v~gemäß** *adv* rationally; **~glaube(n)** *m* rationalism; **~gründe** *pl* rational grounds *pl*; **~heirat** *f* marriage of convenience.

**vernünftig 1** *adj* sensible; *(logisch denkend)* rational; *(col: ordentlich, anständig)* decent; *Vorschlag* reasonable. **2** *adv siehe adj* sensibly; rationally; decently; reasonably; *(tüchtig)* properly *(col)*.

**Vernunft-**: **v~los** *adj* irrational; **~mensch** *m* rational person; **v~widrig** *adj* irrational.

**ver|öden\* 1** *vi aux sein* to become desolate; *(fig: geistig)* to become stultified. **2** *vt (Med) Krampfadern* to sclerose.

**ver|öffentlichen\*** *vti* to publish.

**Ver|öffentlichung** *f* publication.

**ver|ordnen\*** *vt* to prescribe *(jdm etw* sth for sb*)*.

**Ver|ordnung** *f* **(a)** *(Med)* prescription. **(b)** *(Verfügung)* decree.

**verpachten\*** *vt* to lease, to rent out *(an +acc* to*)*.

**Verpachtung** *f* lease.

**verpacken\*** *vt* to pack; *(verbrauchergerecht)* to package; *(einwickeln)* to wrap.

**Verpackung** *f siehe vt* packing; packaging; wrapping.

**Verpackungs-**: **~industrie** *f* packaging industry; **~müll** *m* superfluous packaging.

**verpassen\*** *vt* **(a)** *(versäumen)* to miss. **(b)** *(col: zuteilen)* **jdm etw ~** to give sb sth; *(aufzwingen)* to make sb have sth; **jdm eine Ohrfeige ~** to clout sb one *(col)*.

**verpatzen\*** *vt (col)* to spoil; *Examen* to make a mess of. **sich** *(dat)* **etw ~** to spoil sth/mess sth up *(col)*.

**verpennen\*** *(col)* **1** *vt (verpassen)* to miss by oversleeping; *(schlafend verbringen) Tag, Morgen etc* to sleep through. **2** *vir* to oversleep.

**verpesten\*** *vt* to pollute.

**verpetzen\*** *vt (col)* to tell on *(bei* to*)*.

**verpfänden\*** *vt* to pawn; *(Jur)* to mortgage.

**verpfeifen\*** *vt irreg (col)* to grass on *(bei* to*) (col)*.

**verpflanzen\*** *vt (lit, fig)* to transplant; *Haut* to graft.

**verpflegen\* 1** *vt* to feed. **2** *vr* **sich (selbst) ~** to feed oneself; *(selbst kochen)* to cook for oneself.

**Verpflegung** *f* **(a)** *(das Verpflegen)* catering; *(Mil)* rationing. **(b)** *(Essen)* food; *(Mil)* rations *pl*.

**verpflichten\* 1** *vt* **(a)** to oblige; *(durch Versprechen, Vertrag)* to commit. **verpflichtet sein, etw zu tun** to be obliged to do sth; **zu etw verpflichtet sein** to be committed to (doing) sth; **jdm verpflichtet sein** to be under an obligation to sb; **~d** *Zusage* binding. **(b)** *(einstellen)* to engage; *Sportler* to sign on. **2** *vi* to involve a commitment. **das verpflichtet zu nichts** there's no obligation involved. **3** *vr* to commit oneself. **sich zu etw ~** to commit oneself to (doing) sth.

**Verpflichtung** *f* **(a)** obligation *(zu etw* to do sth*)*; *(Pflicht auch, finanzielle ~)* commitment *(zu etw* to do sth*)*; *(Aufgabe)* duty. **(b)** *(Einstellung)* engaging; *(von Sportlern)* signing on.

**verpfuschen\*** *vt (col)* to make a mess of.

**verplanen\* 1** *vt Zeit* to book up; *Geld* to budget. **jdn ~** *(col)* to fill up all sb's spare time (for him/her). **2** *vr* to plan badly; *(falsch berechnen)* to miscalculate.

**verplappern\*** *vr (col)* to open one's big mouth *(col)*.

**verplempern\*** *vt (col)* to waste, to fritter away.

**verpönt** *adj* frowned upon *(bei* by*)*.

**verprassen\*** *vt* to blow *(col) (für* on*)*.

**verprellen\*** *vt* to put off, to intimidate.

**verprügeln\*** *vt* to thrash, to beat up.

**verpuffen\*** *vi aux sein* to (go) pop; *(fig)* to fall flat.

**verpulvern\*** *vt (col)* to squander.

**Verputz** *m no pl* plaster; *(Rauhputz)* roughcast.

**verputzen\*** *vt* **(a)** to plaster; *(mit Rauhputz)* to roughcast. **(b)** *(col: aufessen)* to polish off *(col)*.

**verqualmen\*** *vt Zimmer* to fill with smoke.

**verquer** *adj* skew-whiff *pred (col); (fig) Idee, Ansicht etc* oddball.

**verquicken\*** *vtr* to combine; *(vermischen)* to mix.

**verquirlen\*** *vt* to whisk.

**verquollen** *adj Augen* puffy, swollen.

**verrammeln\*** *vt* to barricade.

**verramschen\*** *vt (col)* to sell off cheap.

**Verrat** *m no pl* betrayal *(an +dat* of*); (Jur)* treason *(an +dat* against*).* ~ **an jdm üben** to betray sb.

**verraten\*** *irreg* **1** *vt* to betray; *(bekanntgeben, ausplaudern)* to tell; *(fig: erkennen lassen)* to show. **nichts** ~! don't say a word!; **er hat es** ~ he let it out. **2** *vr* to give oneself away.

**Verräter(in** *f***)** *m* - traitor *(+gen* to*).*

**verräterisch** *adj* treacherous; *(Jur)* treasonable; *Blick etc* telltale *attr.*

**verrauchen\*** **1** *vi aux sein (fig: Zorn)* to blow over. **2** *vt Zimmer* to fill with smoke; *Geld* to spend on smoking.

**verräuchern\*** *vt* to fill with smoke.

**verrechnen\*** **1** *vt (begleichen)* to settle; *Scheck* to clear; *Gutschein* to redeem. **etw mit etw** ~ *(gegeneinander aufrechnen)* to balance sth with sth. **2** *vr* to miscalculate; *(col: sich täuschen)* to be mistaken. **sich um eine Mark** ~ to be out by one mark.

**Verrechnungsscheck** *m* crossed *(Brit)* or non-negotiable cheque *(Brit)* or check *(US).*

**verrecken\*** *vi aux sein (col!)* to die; *(elend sterben)* to die a wretched death. **er ist elend verreckt** he died like a dog *(col).*

**verregnet** *adj* rainy, wet.

**verreiben\*** *vt irreg* to rub *(auf +dat* into*).*

**verreisen\*** *vi aux sein* to go away (on a trip). **er ist geschäftlich verreist** he's away on business.

**verreißen\*** *vt irreg (kritisieren)* to tear to pieces, to slate *(col).*

**verrenken\*** **1** *vt* to dislocate; *Hals* to crick. **2** *vr* to contort oneself.

**verrennen\*** *vr irreg* **sich in etw** *(acc)* ~ to get stuck on sth.

**verrichten\*** *vt Arbeit* to carry out.

**verriegeln\*** *vt* to bolt; *(Comp) Tastatur* to lock.

**verringern\*** **1** *vt* to reduce. **2** *vr* to decrease; *(Qualität, Leistungen)* to deteriorate.

**Verringerung** *f siehe vb* reduction; decrease; deterioration.

**verrinnen\*** *vi irreg aux sein (Wasser)* to trickle away *(in +dat* into*); (Zeit)* to elapse.

**Verriß** *m* **-sse** damning review. **einen** ~ **bekommen** to get a slating *(col).*

**verrohen\*** *vi aux sein* to become brutalized.

**Verrohung** *f* brutalization.

**verrosten\*** *vi aux sein* to rust. **verrostet** rusty.

**verrotten\*** *vi aux sein* to rot; *(organisch)* to decompose.

**verrucht** *adj* despicable; *(verrufen)* disreputable.

**verrücken\*** *vt* to move.

**verrückt** *adj* mad. ~ **auf** *(+acc)* or **nach** *(col)* crazy or mad about *(col);* **wie** ~ like mad or crazy *(col);* **die Leute kamen wie** ~ *(col)* loads of people came *(col);* **jdn** ~ **machen** *(col)* to drive sb crazy or mad; ~ **werden** *(col)* to go crazy; ~ **spielen** *(col)* to play up *(col).*

**Verrückte(r)** *mf decl as adj (col)* lunatic.

**Verruf** *m no pl* **in** ~ **kommen** to fall into disrepute.

**verrufen** *adj* disreputable.

**verrühren\*** *vt* to mix, to stir.

**verrußen\*** *vi aux sein* to get sooty.

**verrutschen\*** *vi aux sein* to slip.

**Vers** [fɛrs] *m* **-e** verse *(auch Bibl); (Zeile)* line.

**versachlichen\*** *vt* to objectify.

**versacken\*** *vi aux sein* **(a)** *(lit)* to sink. **(b)** *(fig col) (herunterkommen)* to go downhill; *(lange zechen)* to get involved in a booze-up *(col).*

**versagen\*** **1** *vt* **sich** *(dat)* **etw** ~ to deny oneself sth; **jdm etw** ~ to deny sb sth; *(verweigern)* to refuse sb sth; **etw bleibt jdm versagt** sth is denied sth. **2** *vi* to fail. **die Beine/Nerven** *etc* **versagten ihm** his legs/nerves *etc* gave way.

**Versagen** *nt no pl* failure; *(von Maschine)* breakdown. **menschliches** ~ human error.

**Versager** *m* - failure, flop *(col).*

**versalzen¹\*** *vt irreg* to put too much salt in/on; *(col: verderben)* to spoil.

**versalzen²** *adj Essen* too salty.

**versammeln\*** **1** *vt* to assemble. **2** *vr* to assemble; *(Parliament)* to sit; *(Ausschuß, Verein)* to meet.

**Versammlung** *f* meeting, assembly.

**Versammlungs-:** ~**freiheit** *f* freedom of assembly; ~**lokal** *nt* meeting place.

**Versand** *m no pl* dispatch; *(das Vertreiben)* distribution.

**Versand-:** ~**abteilung** *f* dispatch department; ~**anzeige** *f* dispatch note; ~**artikel** *m* article for dispatch; ~**bahnhof** *m* dispatch station; **v**~**bereit** *adj* ready for dispatch.

**versanden\*** *vi aux sein* to silt (up); *(fig)* to peter out.

**Versand-:** ~**gut** *nt* goods *pl* for dispatch; ~**handel** *m* mail order business; ~**haus** *nt* mail order firm; ~**kosten** *pl* transport(ation) costs *pl*; ~**tasche** *f* padded envelope, Jiffy bag ®; ~**weg** *m* **auf dem** ~**weg** by mail order.

**versauen\*** *vt (col)* to mess up *(col).*

**versauern\*** *vi aux sein (col)* to stagnate.

**versaufen\*** *irreg (col)* **1** *vt Geld* to spend on booze *(col).* **2** *vi aux sein (ertrinken)* to drown.

**versäumen\*** *vt* to miss; *Zeit* to lose; *Pflicht* to neglect. **(es)** ~**, etw zu tun** to fail to do sth; **das Versäumte** what one has missed; **die versäumte Zeit aufholen** to make up for lost time.

**Versäumnis** *nt (Fehler)* failing; *(Unterlassung)* omission.

**verschachern\*** *vt* to sell off.

**verschachtelt** *adj Satz* encapsulated, complex.

**verschaffen** **1** *vt* **jdm etw** ~ to provide sb with sth; *Erleichterung, Genugtuung* to give sb sth; *Respekt* to earn sb sth. **2** *vr* **sich** *(dat)* **etw** ~ to obtain sth; *Ansehen, Vorteil* to gain sth; *Ruhe, Respekt* to get sth; **sich mit Gewalt Zutritt** ~ to force an entry.

**verschalen\*** *vt Wand* to panel; *Heizung etc* to box in.

**verschämt** *adj* bashful, coy.

**verschandeln\*** *vt* to ruin.

**verschanzen\*** **1** *vt (Mil)* to fortify. **2** *vr (Mil, fig)* to entrench oneself *(hinter +dat* behind*); (sich verbarrikadieren)* to barricade oneself in *(in etw (dat)* sth*).*

**verschärfen\*** **1** *vt (erhöhen) Tempo* to increase; *Gegensätze* to intensify; *(verschlimmern) Lage* to aggravate; *(strenger machen) Kontrollen, Gesetze* to tighten up. **2** *vr siehe vt* to increase; to intensify; to become aggravated; to become tighter.

**verschärft** **1** *adj siehe vb* increased; intensified; aggravated; tightened. **2** *adv (intensiver)* more intensively; *(strenger)* more severely. ~ **aufpassen/kontrollieren** to keep a closer watch/a tighter control.

**Verschärfung** *f* intensification; *(der Lage)* aggravation; *(von Kontrollen etc)* tightening.

**verscharren\*** *vt* to bury.

**verschätzen\*** *vr* to miscalculate *(in etw (dat)* sth*).*

**verschneiden**

**verschenken*** vt (lit, fig) to give away.
**verscherzen*** vt sich (dat) etw ~ to forfeit sth; **es sich** (dat) **mit jdm** ~ to spoil things with sb.
**verscheuchen*** vt to scare off; (fig) Sorgen etc to drive away.
**verschicken*** vt (versenden) to send out; (zur Kur etc) to send away; (deportieren) to deport.
**verschieben*** irreg **1** vt (a) (verrücken) to move, to shift; (Rail) to shunt. (b) (auf später) to postpone (um for, auf +acc until). (c) (col) Waren, Devisen to traffic in. **2** vr to shift; (zeitlich) to be postponed.
**Verschiebung** f (zeitlich) postponement.
**verschieden 1** adj (a) (unterschiedlich) different. **die ~sten Farben** a great variety of colours; **das ist ganz** ~ (das kommt darauf an) that varies, that just depends. (b) attr (mehrere, einige) various, several. (c) (substantivisch) ~e pl various or several people; ~es several things; V~es (in Zeitung, Liste) miscellaneous. **2** adv differently. **die Häuser sind** ~ **hoch** the houses vary in height.
**verschieden|artig** adj different; (mannigfaltig) various, diverse. **die ~sten Dinge** all sorts of things.
**Verschiedenheit** f difference (gen of, in); (Unähnlichkeit) dissimilarity.
**verschiedentlich** adv (mehrmals) on several occasions.
**verschießen*** vt irreg Munition to use up.
**verschiffen*** vt to ship; Sträfling to transport.
**verschimmeln*** vi aux sein (Nahrungsmittel) to go mouldy (Brit) or moldy (US); (Leder, Papier etc) to get mildew (on it). **verschimmelt** mouldy (Brit), moldy (US); covered in mildew.
**verschlafen*** irreg **1** vir to oversleep. **2** vt Termin to miss by oversleeping; Tag to sleep through. **3** adj half-asleep; (trottelig) dozy (col); (fig) Städtchen etc sleepy.
**Verschlag** m ⁼e (Schuppen) shed; (für Kaninchen) hutch.
**verschlagen¹*** vt irreg (a) etw mit Brettern ~ to board sth up; **etw mit Nägeln** ~ to nail sth up. (b) Atem to take away. **das hat mir die Sprache** ~ it left me speechless. (c) (geraten lassen) to bring. **nach Australien** ~ **werden** to end up in Australia. (d) (Sport) Ball to mishit. (e) (verblättern) Seite, Stelle to lose.
**verschlagen²** adj Mensch, Blick etc sly.
**Verschlagenheit** f slyness.
**verschlammen*** vi aux sein to silt up.
**verschlampen*** (col) **1** vt (verlieren) to lose (col). **2** vi aux sein (Mensch) to go to seed (col).
**verschlechtern*** **1** vt to make worse. **2** vr to get worse, to deteriorate; (gehaltlich) to take a lower-paid job. **sich beruflich** ~ to take a worse job.
**Verschlechterung** f worsening, deterioration.
**verschleiern*** **1** vt to veil; (fig) to disguise; Blick to blur. **2** vr (Frau) to veil oneself; (Himmel) to become hazy; (Blick) to become blurred.
**Verschleierung** f veiling; (fig: von Tatsachen etc) cover-up.
**Verschleiß** m -e (lit, fig) wear and tear; (Verbrauch) consumption (an +dat of). **ein** ~ **deiner Kräfte** a drain on your strength; **er hat einen großen** ~ **an Freundinnen** (col) he gets through an enormous number of girlfriends.
**verschleißen** pret **verschliß**, ptp **verschlissen 1** vt to wear out; (verbrauchen) to use up. **2** vi aux sein to wear out. **3** vr to wear out; (Menschen) to wear oneself out.
**Verschleiß-:** ~erscheinung f sign of wear; ~teil nt part subject to wear.
**verschleppen*** vt (a) (entführen) jdn to abduct;

Kunstschätze etc to carry off. (b) (verbreiten) Seuche to spread. (c) (hinauszögern) to protract; (Pol) Gesetzesänderung etc to delay.
**verschleudern*** vt (Comm) to dump; (vergeuden) to squander.
**verschließbar** adj Tür, Zimmer etc lockable; Dose etc (re)sealable.
**verschließen*** irreg **1** vt (a) (abschließen) to lock up; (fig) to close, to shut; (versperren) to bar; (mit Riegel) to bolt. (b) (zumachen) to close; (mit Pfropfen) Flasche to cork. **die Augen (vor etw** dat) ~ to shut one's eyes (to sth). **2** vr (Reize, Sprache, Möglichkeit) to be closed (dat to); (Mensch: reserviert sein) to shut oneself off (dat from). **sich einer Sache** (dat) or **gegen etw** ~ to close one's mind to sth.
**verschlimmbessern** vt insep (hum) to try to improve and make worse, to miscorrect.
**verschlimmern*** **1** vt to make worse. **2** vr to get worse, to deteriorate.
**Verschlimmerung** f worsening, deterioration.
**verschlingen*** irreg **1** vt (a) (lit, fig) to devour; (Wellen etc, verbrauchen) to swallow up. (b) (verknoten) to entwine; Arme to fold. **ein verschlungener Pfad** a winding path. **2** vr to become entwined.
**verschliß** pret of **verschleißen**.
**verschlissen 1** ptp of **verschleißen**. **2** adj badly worn; (völlig) worn out.
**verschlossen** adj closed; (fig: unzugänglich) reserved. **etw bleibt jdm** ~ sth is a closed book to sb; **wir standen vor** ~**er Tür** we found the door locked.
**Verschlossenheit** f (von Mensch) reserve.
**verschlucken*** **1** vt to swallow; Geld to swallow up; Schall to deaden. **2** vr to swallow the wrong way; (fig) to splutter.
**Verschluß** m ⁼sse (a) (Schloß) lock; (luft-, wasserdicht, für Zoll) seal; (Deckel, Klappe) top, lid; (Pfropfen, Stöpsel) stopper; (an Kleidung) fastener. **etw unter** ~ **halten** to keep sth under lock and key. (b) (Phot) shutter.
**verschlüsseln*** vt to (put into) code, to encode.
**Verschluß-:** ~sache f item of classified information; ~zeit f (Phot) shutter speed.
**verschmachten*** vi aux sein to languish (vor +dat for). **(vor Durst/Hitze)** ~ (col) to be dying of thirst/heat (col).
**verschmähen*** vt to spurn.
**verschmälern*** vtr to narrow.
**verschmelzen*** irreg **1** vi aux sein to melt together; (Metalle) to fuse; (Farben) to blend; (fig) to blend (zu into). **2** vt Metalle to fuse; Farben to blend; (fig) to unify (zu into).
**verschmerzen*** vt to get over.
**verschmieren*** vt (a) Salbe, Schmiere to spread (in +dat over). (b) (verputzen) Löcher to fill (in). (c) (verwischen) Fenster, Gesicht to smear; Geschriebenes, Schminke to smudge. **2** vi to smudge.
**verschmiert** adj Hände smeary; Schminke smudged.
**verschmitzt** adj mischievous.
**verschmutzen*** **1** vt to dirty; Umwelt, Luft etc to pollute; Gewehr, Zündkerze to foul; Fahrbahn to make muddy; (Hund) Bürgersteig to foul. **2** vi aux sein to get dirty; (Umwelt, Luft etc) to become polluted.
**verschmutzt** adj dirty, soiled; Umwelt, Luft etc polluted.
**Verschmutzung** f dirtiness no pl; (von Umwelt, Luft etc) pollution.
**verschnaufen*** vir (col) to have a breather.
**verschneiden*** vt irreg (a) Rum etc to blend. (b) Flügel, Hecke to clip. (c) (falsch schneiden) to cut

wrongly. **(d)** *Tiere* to castrate.
**verschneit** *adj* snow-covered. **tief** ~ thick with snow.
**Verschnitt** *m* **(a)** *(von Rum etc)* blend. **(b)** *(Abfall)* clippings *pl.*
**verschnörkelt** *adj* ornate.
**verschnupft** *adj (col)* ~ **sein** to have a cold; *(beleidigt)* to be peeved *(col).*
**verschnüren*** *vt* to tie up.
**verschollen** *adj* missing; *Literaturwerk* forgotten.
**verschonen*** *vt* to spare *(jdn mit etw* sb sth*).* **von etw verschont bleiben** to escape sth.
**verschöne(r)n*** *vt* to improve (the appearance of); *Wohnung* to brighten up.
**Verschönerung** *f siehe vt* improvement; brightening up.
**verschränken*** *vt* to cross over; *Arme* to fold; *Beine* to cross; *Hände* to clasp.
**verschrauben*** *vt* to screw together.
**verschreckt** *adj* frightened, scared.
**verschreiben*** *irreg* **1** *vt* **(a)** *(verordnen)* to prescribe. **(b)** *Papier* to use up. **2** *vr* **(a)** *(falsch schreiben)* to make a slip (of the pen). **(b) sich einer Sache** *(dat)* ~ to devote oneself to sth.
**verschreibungspflichtig** *adj* only available on prescription.
**verschrie(e)n** *adj* notorious.
**verschroben** *adj* eccentric, odd.
**verschrotten*** *vt* to scrap.
**verschrumpeln*** *vi aux sein* to shrivel.
**verschüchtern*** *vt* to intimidate. **verschüchtert** timid.
**verschulden*** **1** *vt* to be to blame for. **2** *vi aux sein (in Schulden geraten)* to get into debt. **verschuldet sein** to be in debt.
**Verschulden** *nt no pl* fault. **ohne sein/mein** ~ through no fault of his/my own.
**Verschuldung** *f (Schulden)* indebtedness.
**verschütten*** *vt* **(a)** *Flüssigkeit* to spill. **(b)** *(zuschütten) Brunnen* to fill in. **(c) verschüttet werden** *(Mensch)* to be buried (alive); *(fig)* to be submerged.
**verschwägert** *adj* related (by marriage) *(mit to).*
**verschweigen*** *vt irreg Tatsachen, Wahrheit etc* to conceal *(jdm etw* sth from sb*).*
**verschweißen*** *vt* to weld together.
**verschwenden*** *vt* to waste *(auf or an +acc* on*).*
**Verschwender(in** *f) m* - spendthrift.
**verschwenderisch** *adj* wasteful; *Leben* extravagant; *(üppig)* lavish.
**Verschwendung** *f* waste.
**Verschwendungs-:** ~**sucht** *f no pl* extravagance; **v~süchtig** *adj* extravagant.
**verschwiegen** *adj Mensch* discreet; *Ort* secluded.
**Verschwiegenheit** *f no pl (von Mensch)* discretion. **zur** ~ **verpflichtet** bound to secrecy.
**verschwimmen*** *vi irreg aux sein* to become blurred. **ineinander** ~ to merge into one another; *siehe* **verschwommen**
**verschwinden*** *vi irreg aux sein* to disappear, to vanish. **verschwinde!** clear off! *(col)*; **neben jdm/etw** ~ *(in bezug auf Größe)* to look minute beside sb/sth.
**Verschwinden** *nt no pl* disappearance.
**verschwindend** *adj Anzahl, Menge* insignificant. ~ **wenig** very, very few; ~ **klein** minute.
**verschwistert** *adj (miteinander)* ~ **sein** to be brother and sister; *(Brüder)* to be brothers; *(Schwestern)* to be sisters; *(Städte)* to be twinned.
**verschwitzen*** *vt* **(a)** *Kleidung* to make sweaty. **(b)** *(fig col)* to forget.

**verschwitzt** *adj* sweat-stained; *Mensch* sweaty.
**verschwommen** *adj Foto, Umrisse* blurred; *Berge* hazy; *Begriffe, Erinnerung* vague.
**verschworen** *adj Gesellschaft* sworn.
**verschwören*** *vr irreg* **(a)** to conspire, to plot *(mit* with, *gegen* against*).* **sich zu etw** ~ to plot sth; **alles hat sich gegen mich verschworen** *(fig)* there's a conspiracy against me. **(b) sich einer Sache** *(dat)* ~ to give oneself over to sth.
**Verschwörer(in** *f) m* - conspirator, plotter.
**Verschwörung** *f* conspiracy, plot.
**verschwunden** *adj* missing.
**versehen*** *irreg* **1** *vt* **(a)** *Amt, Stelle* to hold; *Dienst* to perform; *(sich kümmern um)* to look after. **(b)** *(ausstatten)* **jdn mit etw** ~ to provide or supply sb with sth; **etw mit etw** ~ to put sth on/in sth; *(montieren)* to fit sth with sth; **mit etw** ~ **sein** to have sth; **jdn mit einer Vollmacht** ~ to invest sb with full powers. **2** *vr* **(a)** *(sich irren)* to make a mistake. **(b) sich mit etw** ~ *(sich versorgen)* to provide oneself with sth; *(sich ausstatten)* to equip oneself with sth. **(c) ehe man sich's versieht** before you know what's happening.
**Versehen** *nt* - mistake, error; *(Unachtsamkeit)* oversight. **aus** ~ by mistake, inadvertently.
**versehentlich** **1** *adj attr* inadvertent; *(irrtümlich)* erroneous. **2** *adv* inadvertently, by mistake.
**Versehrte(r)** *mf decl as adj* disabled person.
**verselbständigen*** *vr* to become independent.
**versenden*** *vt irreg or reg* to send.
**versengen*** *vt* **(a)** to scorch; *(Feuer)* to singe. **(b)** *(col: verprügeln)* to wallop *(col).*
**versenkbar** *adj Nähmaschine, Tischplatte* fold-away *attr*; *Scheinwerfer* retractable.
**versenken*** **1** *vt* **(a)** *Schiff etc* to sink; *Leiche, Sarg* to lower; *das eigene Schiff* to scuttle. **(b)** *Schraube* to countersink; *Tischplatte* to fold away. **2** *vr* **sich in etw** *(acc)* ~ to become immersed in sth.
**Versenkung** *f* **(a)** *siehe vt* **(a)** sinking; lowering; scuttling. **(b)** *(das Sichversenken)* immersion. **innere/mystische** ~ inner/mystic contemplation. **(c) in der** ~ **verschwinden** *(col)* to vanish; **aus der** ~ **auftauchen** to re-appear.
**versessen** *adj* **auf etw** *(acc)* ~ **sein** to be very keen on sth.
**versetzen*** **1** *vt* **(a)** to move, to shift; *(nicht geradlinig anordnen)* to stagger; *(beruflich)* to transfer, to move. **(b)** *(Sch: in höhere Klasse)* to move up. **(c)** *(col) (verkaufen)* to flog *(Brit col)*, to sell; *(verpfänden)* to pawn. **(d)** *(col: nicht erscheinen)* **jdn** ~ to stand sb up *(col).* **(e) etw in Bewegung** ~ to set sth in motion; **jdn in Wut/in fröhliche Stimmung** ~ to send sb into a rage/to put sb in a cheerful mood; **jdn in Angst** ~ to frighten sb; **jdn in die Lage** ~, **etw zu tun** to put sb in a position to do sth. **(f)** *Stoß, Schlag, Tritt etc* to give. **jdm einen Stich** ~ *(fig)* to cut sb to the quick, to wound sb (deeply).
**2** *vr (sich an andere Stelle setzen)* to move (to another place). **sich in jdn/in jds Lage** ~ to put oneself in sb's place; **sich in eine frühere Zeit** *etc* ~ to imagine oneself back in an earlier period.
**Versetzung** *f* **(a)** *(beruflich)* transfer. **(b)** *(Sch)* moving up. **seine** ~ **ist gefährdet** he's in danger of having to stay down. **(c)** *(nicht geradlinige Anordnung)* staggering. **(d)** *(Vermischung)* mixing.
**verseuchen*** *vt* to contaminate.
**Versfuß** *m (Poet)* (metrical) foot.
**Versicherer** *m* - insurer; *(bei Schiffen)* underwriter.
**versichern*** **1** *vt* **(a)** *(beteuern)* **jdm** ~, **daß** ... to assure sb that ...; **jdm etw** ~, **jdn einer Sache** *(gen)* ~ to assure sb of sth; **seien Sie versichert, daß** ... rest

assured that ... **(b)** *(gegen Diebstahl etc)* to insure. **2** *vr* **(a)** to insure oneself *(mit for)*. **(b)** *(sich vergewissern)* to make sure *or* certain.
**Versicherte(r)** *mf decl as adj* insured (party).
**Versicherung** *f siehe vt* **(a)** assurance. **(b)** insurance; *(~sgesellschaft)* insurance company.
**Versicherungs-:** ~**beitrag** *m* insurance premium; *(bei staatlicher Versicherung etc)* insurance contribution; ~**betrug** *m* insurance fraud; ~**dauer** *f* period of insurance; ~**fall** *m* im ~**fall** in the event of a claim; ~**gesellschaft** *f* insurance company; ~**kaufmann** *m* insurance broker; ~**nehmer** *m (form)* policy holder; ~**pflicht** *f* compulsory insurance; ~**police** *f* insurance policy; ~**prämie** *f* insurance premium; ~**schutz** *m* insurance cover; ~**summe** *f* sum insured; ~**träger** *m* = Versicherer; ~**vertreter** *m* insurance agent; ~**wert** *m* insurance value; ~**wesen** *nt* insurance (business).
**versickern*** *vi aux sein* to seep away; *(fig: Interesse etc)* to peter out.
**versiegeln*** *vt* to seal.
**versiegen*** *vi aux sein (lit, fig)* to dry up; *(Interesse)* to peter out; *(Humor, Kräfte)* to fail.
**versiert** [vɛr-] *adj* in etw *(dat)* ~ sein to be experienced *or (in bezug auf Wissen)* well versed in sth.
**versilbern*** *vt* to silver(-plate).
**versinken*** *vi irreg aux sein* to sink. **ich hätte im Boden/vor Scham** ~ **mögen** I wished the ground would swallow me up; **in etw** *(acc)* ~ *(fig)* in Trauer, Melancholie to sink into sth; in Anblick, Gedanken, Musik to lose oneself in sth.
**versinnbildlichen*** *vt* to symbolize.
**Version** [vɛr'zioːn] *f* version.
**versklaven*** [fɛɛ'sklaːvn] *vt (lit, fig)* to enslave.
**Vers-:** ~**lehre** *f* study of verse; ~**maß** *nt* metre *(Brit)*, meter *(US)*.
**versohlen*** *vt (col)* to belt *(col)*.
**versöhnen*** **1** *vt* to reconcile; *(besänftigen)* jdn, Götter to placate. ~**de Worte** conciliatory words. **2** *vr* to be(come) reconciled; *(Streitende)* to make it up. **sich mit etw** ~ to reconcile oneself to sth.
**versöhnlich** *adj* Mensch conciliatory; *(nichts nachtragend)* forgiving.
**Versöhnung** *f* reconciliation; *(Beschwichtigung)* appeasement.
**versonnen** *adj* Gesichtsausdruck pensive, thoughtful; *(träumerisch)* Blick dreamy.
**versorgen*** **1** *vt* **(a)** *(sich kümmern um)* to look after. **(b)** *(beliefern)* to supply. **(c)** *(unterhalten)* Familie to provide for, to support. **2** *vr* **sich mit etw** ~ to provide oneself with sth; **sich selbst** ~ to look after oneself.
**Versorger(in** *f)* *m* - **(a)** *(Ernährer)* provider, breadwinner. **(b)** *(Belieferer)* supplier.
**Versorgung** *f* **(a)** *(Pflege)* care. **(b)** *(Belieferung)* supply. **die** ~ **dieses Gebiets mit Bussen** the provision of bus services for this district. **(c)** *(Unterhalt)* **die** ~ **im Alter** providing for one's old age.
**Versorgungs-:** ~**ausgleich** *m (bei Scheidung)* maintenance; **v~berechtigt** *adj* entitled to maintenance; *(durch Staat)* entitled to benefit; ~**betrieb** *m* public utility; ~**güter** *pl* supplies *pl*; ~**netz** *nt (Wasser~, Gas~ etc)* (supply) grid; *(von Waren)* supply network.
**verspachteln*** *vt* Risse to fill (in).
**verspannen*** **1** *vt* to brace. **2** *vr (Muskeln)* to tense up. **verspannt** tense(d up).
**verspäten*** *vr (zu spät kommen)* to be late.
**verspätet** *adj* Zug, Flugzeug delayed, late *pred*; Ankunft, Frühling, Entwicklung late; Glückwunsch belated.

**Verspätung** *f (von Verkehrsmitteln)* delay; *(von Mensch)* late arrival; *(von Glückwunsch etc)* belatedness. **(10 Minuten)** ~ **haben** to be (10 minutes) late; **eine zweistündige** ~ a delay of two hours; **die** ~ **aufholen** to catch up lost time; **mit zwanzig Minuten** ~ twenty minutes late.
**verspeisen*** *vt (geh)* to consume.
**versperren*** *vt* to block.
**verspielen*** **1** *vt (lit, fig)* Geld, Chancen to gamble away; Vorteile to bargain away. **2** *vi (fig)* **jetzt hast du (bei ihr) verspielt** you've had it now (with her) *(col)*.
**verspielt** *adj* Kind, Katze playful; Frisur, Muster fanciful.
**versponnen** *adj* airy-fairy.
**verspotten*** *vt* to mock.
**versprechen*** *irreg* **1** *vt* to promise *(jdm etw sb sth)*. **nichts Gutes** ~ to be ominous. **2** *vr* **(a)** **sich** *(dat)* **viel/wenig von jdm/etw** ~ to have high hopes/ no great hopes of sb/sth. **(b)** *(etwas Nicht-Gemeintes sagen)* to make a slip of the tongue.
**Versprechen** *nt* - promise.
**Versprecher** *m* - *(col)* slip (of the tongue).
**Versprechung** *f* promise.
**verspritzen*** *vt* **(a)** to spray; *(versprengen)* to sprinkle. **(b)** *(verkleckern)* Farbe, Kleidung to sp(l)atter. **(c)** *(verbrauchen)* Wasser, Farbe etc to use.
**versprühen*** *vt* to spray; Funken to send out; *(verbrauchen)* to use. **Witz/Geist** ~ *(fig)* to scintillate.
**verspüren*** *vt* to feel, to be conscious of.
**verstaatlichen*** *vt* to nationalize.
**Verstaatlichung** *f* nationalization.
**verstädtern*** **1** *vt* to urbanize. **2** *vi aux sein* to become urbanized.
**Verstand** *m no pl (Fähigkeit zu denken)* reason; *(Intellekt)* mind, intellect; *(Vernunft)* (common) sense; *(Urteilskraft)* (powers *pl* of) judgement. **den** ~ **verlieren** to lose one's mind; **nicht recht** *or* **ganz bei** ~ **sein** not to be in one's right mind; **das geht über meinen** ~ it's beyond me; **etw ohne** ~ **tun** to do sth mindlessly.
**verstandesmäßig** *adj* rational.
**verständig** *adj (vernünftig)* sensible; *(einsichtig)* understanding.
**verständigen*** **1** *vt* to notify. **2** *vr* to communicate; *(sich einigen)* to come to an understanding.
**Verständigung** *f no pl* **(a)** *(Benachrichtigung)* notification. **(b)** *(das Sichverständigen)* communication *no indef art.* **(c)** *(Einigung)* understanding.
**verständlich** *adj (begreiflich)* understandable; *(intellektuell erfaßbar)* comprehensible; *(hörbar)* audible. **schwer** ~ hard to understand; **jdm etw** ~ **machen** to make sb understand sth; *(erklären)* to explain sth to sb; **sich** ~ **machen** to make oneself understood; *(sich klar ausdrücken)* to make oneself clear.
**verständlicherweise** *adv* understandably (enough).
**Verständlichkeit** *f no pl* comprehensibility; *(Hörbarkeit)* audibility.
**Verständnis** *nt no pl* understanding *(für of)*; *(Mitgefühl)* sympathy *(für for)*. **für etw kein** ~ **haben** to have no understanding of/sympathy for sth; **für Kunst** etc to have no appreciation of sth; **für Unordnung** etc to have no time for sth; **dafür hast du mein vollstes** ~ you have my fullest sympathy; **wir bitten um Ihr** ~ we apologize for any inconvenience.
**verständnis-:** ~**los** *adj* uncomprehending; *(ohne Mitgefühl)* unsympathetic *(für towards)*; *(für Kunst)* unappreciative *(für of)*; ~**voll** *adj* understanding; Blick knowing *no pred*.

**verstärken\*** **1** *vt* to strengthen, to reinforce; *Spannung, Zweifel* to increase; *(Elec, Mus)* to amplify; *(Mil)* to reinforce. **2** *vr (fig)* to intensify; *(sich vermehren)* to increase.

**Verstärker** *m* - *(Rad, Elec)* amplifier.

**verstärkt** **1** *adj* increased; *Wachsamkeit* greater; *(Mil)* reinforced. **2** *adv* to an increased extent.

**Verstärkung** *f siehe vt* strengthening; reinforcement; increase; amplification.

**verstauben\*** *vi aux sein* to get dusty; *(fig)* to gather dust. **verstaubt** dusty; *(fig) Ansichten* fuddy-duddy *(col)*.

**verstauchen\*** *vt* **sich** *(dat)* **die Hand/den Fuß** ~ to sprain one's hand/foot.

**Verstauchung** *f* sprain.

**verstauen\*** *vt Gepäck* to load *(in +dat* in).

**Versteck** *nt* **-e** hiding place; *(von Verbrechern)* hideout. ~ **spielen** to play hide-and-seek.

**verstecken\*** **1** *vt* to hide, to conceal *(vor* from). **2** *vr* to hide. **sich vor jdm** ~ to hide from sb; **sich vor jdm nicht zu ~ brauchen** *(fig)* not to need to fear comparison with sb.

**Versteckspiel** *nt (lit, fig)* hide-and-seek.

**versteckt** *adj* **(a)** hidden; *(nicht leicht sichtbar) Eingang, Tür* concealed; *(abgelegen auch) Ort* secret. **(b)** *(fig) Lächeln, Blick* furtive; *Andeutung* veiled; *Bedeutung* hidden.

**verstehen\*** *irreg* **1** *vti* **(a)** to understand. **etw unter etw** *(dat)* ~ to understand sth by sth; **wie soll ich das ~?** how am I supposed to take that?; **das ist nicht wörtlich zu ~** that isn't to be taken literally; **jdn/etw falsch ~** to misunderstand sb/sth; **jdm zu ~ geben, daß ...** to give sb to understand that ... **(b)** *(können, beherrschen)* to know. **es ~,** **es mit jdm/etw zu tun** to know how to do sth; **es mit Kindern ~** to be good with children; **etwas von etw ~** to know something about sth. **2** *vr* **(a)** to understand each other; *(auskommen)* to get on. **(b)** *(klar sein)* to go without saying. **das versteht sich von selbst** that goes without saying; **die Preise ~ sich einschließlich Lieferung** prices are inclusive of delivery. **(c)** *(auffassen)* **sich als etw** ~ to see oneself as sth. **(d)** **sich auf etw** *(acc)* ~ to be an expert at sth.

**versteifen\*** **1** *vt* to strengthen, to reinforce. **2** *vr* to stiffen up; *(fig: Haltung, Gegensätze)* to harden. **sich auf etw** *(acc)* ~ *(fig)* to become set on sth.

**versteigen\*** *vr irreg* **er hat sich zu der Behauptung verstiegen, daß ...** he presumed to claim that ...

**versteigern\*** *vt* to auction (off). **etw ~ lassen** to put sth up for auction.

**Versteigerung** *f* auction.

**versteinern\*** **1** *vi aux sein (Pflanzen, Tiere)* to fossilize; *(Holz)* to petrify. **2** *vr (fig) Miene* to harden.

**verstellbar** *adj* adjustable.

**verstellen\*** **1** *vt* **(a)** *(anders einstellen)* to adjust; *Möbel* to move; *(in Unordnung bringen)* to put in the wrong place; *(falsch einstellen)* to adjust wrongly; *Radio* to alter the tuning of; *Uhr* to set wrong. **(b)** *Stimme* to disguise. **(c)** *(versperren)* to block, to obstruct. **2** *vr* to move (out of position); *(fig)* to act a part. **sich vor jdm** ~ to pretend to sb.

**Verstellung** *f* **(a)** *(der Stimme)* disguise. **(b)** *(Unaufrichtigkeit)* pretence *(Brit)*, pretense *(US)*.

**versteuern\*** *vt* to pay tax on. **versteuert** taxed; **zu ~** taxable.

**verstiegen** *adj (fig: überspannt)* extravagant, fantastic.

**verstimmen\*** *vt* to put out of tune; *(fig)* to put out.

**verstimmt** *adj Klavier etc* out of tune; *(fig) Magen* upset; *(verärgert)* put out, disgruntled.

**Verstimmung** *f* disgruntlement; *(zwischen Parteien)* ill-feeling, ill-will.

**verstockt** *adj* obstinate, stubborn; *Sünder* unrepentant.

**verstohlen** *adj* furtive, surreptitious.

**verstopfen\*** *vt* to stop up; *Straße* to block, to jam.

**verstopft** *adj* blocked; *Straßen auch* jammed; *Mensch* constipated.

**Verstopfung** *f* blockage; *(Med)* constipation.

**verstorben** *adj* late, deceased.

**Verstorbene(r)** *mf decl as adj* deceased.

**verstört** *adj* disturbed; *(vor Angst)* distraught.

**Verstoß** *m* ⁼**e** violation *(gegen* of*)*.

**verstoßen\*** *irreg* **1** *vt jdn* to disown, to repudiate; *(ausschließen)* to expel *(aus* from*)*. **2** *vi* **gegen etw** ~ to offend against sth.

**Verstoßene(r)** *mf decl as adj* outcast.

**verstrahlen\*** *vt Tier, Menschen* to expose to radiation; *Gebäude, Gebiet auch* to make (highly) radioactive.

**verstrahlt** *adj* contaminated (by radiation).

**Verstrebung** *f (Strebebalken)* support(ing beam).

**verstreichen\*** *irreg* **1** *vt Salbe, Farbe* to put on; *Butter* to spread *(auf +dat* on*)*; *Riß* to fill (in); *(verbrauchen)* to use. **2** *vi aux sein (Zeit)* to pass (by); *(Frist)* to expire.

**verstreuen\*** *vt* to scatter; *(versehentlich)* to spill.

**verstricken\*** **1** *vt* **(a)** *Wolle* to use. **(b)** *(fig)* to involve. **2** *vr (fig)* to become entangled.

**Verstrickung** *f (fig)* entanglement.

**verstromen\*** *vt Kohle* to convert into electricity.

**verströmen\*** *vt (lit, fig)* to exude.

**verstümmeln\*** *vt* to mutilate, to maim; *(fig) Nachricht* to distort.

**verstummen\*** *vi aux sein (Mensch)* to go silent; *(Geräusch, Beifall)* to stop; *(langsam verklingen)* to die away; *(fig: sich legen)* to subside. **jdn/etw zum V~ bringen** to silence sb/sth.

**Versuch** *m* **-e** attempt *(zu tun* at doing, to do*)*; *(wissenschaftlich)* experiment, test. **einen ~ machen** to make an attempt; to do an experiment *or* a test; **das käme auf einen ~ an** we'd have to try it.

**versuchen\*** **1** *vt* **(a)** *(auch vi)* to try. **es mit jdm/etw** ~ to give sb/sth a try; **versuchter Mord** attempted murder; **das Unmögliche ~** to attempt the impossible. **(b)** *(in Versuchung führen)* to tempt. **2** *vr* **sich an** *or* **in etw** *(dat)* ~ to try one's hand at sth.

**Versucher(in** *f)* *m* - tempter/temptress.

**Versuchs-:** **~anstalt** *f* research institute; **~ballon** *m* sounding balloon; **einen ~ballon steigen lassen** *(fig)* to fly a kite; **~bohrung** *f* experimental drilling; **~kaninchen** *nt (fig)* guinea-pig; **~objekt** *nt* test object; *(fig: Mensch)* guinea-pig; **~person** *f* experimental subject; **~reihe** *f* series of experiments; **~stadium** *nt* experimental stage; **~strecke** *f* test track; **~tier** *nt* laboratory animal; **v~weise** *adv* as a trial, on a trial basis.

**Versuchung** *f* temptation. **jdn in ~ führen** to lead sb into temptation; **in ~ geraten** *or* **kommen** to be tempted.

**versumpfen\*** *vi aux sein* **(a)** *(Gebiet)* to become marshy. **(b)** *(fig col) (verwahrlosen)* to go to pot *(col)*; *(zechen)* to get involved in a booze-up *(col)*.

**versündigen\*** *vr (geh)* **sich an jdm/etw** ~ to sin against sb/sth.

**versunken** *adj* sunken, submerged; *Kultur* submerged; *(fig)* engrossed. **in Gedanken ~** lost in thought.

**Versunkenheit** *f no pl (fig)* absorption.

**versüßen\*** *vt (fig)* to sweeten *(jdm etw* sth for sb*)*.

**vertagen\*** **1** *vti* to adjourn; *(verschieben)* to postpone *(auf +acc* until*)*. **2** *vr* to adjourn.

**Vertagung** f *siehe vti* adjournment; postponement.
**vertauschbar** *adj* exchangeable *(gegen* for*)*; *(miteinander)* interchangeable.
**vertauschen\*** *vt* **(a)** to exchange *(gegen or mit* for*)*; *(miteinander)* to interchange. **vertauschte Rollen** reversed roles. **(b)** *(verwechseln) Mäntel etc* to mix up.
**Vertauschung** f *(Austausch)* exchange.
**verteidigen\*** **1** *vti* to defend. **2** *vr* to defend oneself; *(vor Gericht)* to conduct one's own defence *(Brit)* or defense *(US)*.
**Verteidiger(in** f) *m* - defender; *(Anwalt)* defence *(Brit)* or defense *(US)* lawyer. **der ~ des Angeklagten** the counsel for the defence.
**Verteidigung** f defence *(Brit)*, defense *(US)*. **zur ~ von** *or* **+gen** in defence of.
**Verteidigungs-** *in cpds* defence *(Brit)*, defense *(US)*; **~anlagen** *pl* defences *pl (Brit)*, defenses *pl (US)*; **~fähigkeit** f defensive capability; **~krieg** *m* defensive war; **~minister** *m* Minister of Defence *(Brit)*, Defense Secretary *(US)*; **~ministerium** *nt* Ministry of Defence *(Brit)*, Defense Department *(US)*; **~schlacht** f defensive battle; **~spieler** *m* defender; **~stellung** f defensive position; **~system** *nt* defence *(Brit)* or defense *(US)* system; **~waffe** f defensive weapon.
**verteilen\*** **1** *vt* *(an* +acc to, *unter* +acc among*)* to distribute; *Essen* to dish out; *(Theat) Rollen* to cast; *Investitionen, Lehrstoff* to spread *(über* +acc over*)*; *(Mil)* to deploy; *(verstreuen)* to spread out; *(streichen) Farbe etc* to spread; *(streuen) Sand* to sprinkle. **2** *vr* *(Menschen, Flüssigkeiten)* to spread out; *(Reichtum etc)* to be spread *or* distributed; *(zeitlich)* to be spread *(über* +acc over*)*.
**Verteiler** *m* - *(Comm, Aut)* distributor.
**Verteilung** f distribution.
**vertelefonieren\*** *vt (col) Zeit* to spend on the phone; *(Geld)* to spend on phone calls.
**verteuern\*** **1** *vt* to make more expensive. **2** *vr* to become more expensive.
**Verteuerung** f increase in price.
**verteufeln\*** *vt* to condemn.
**verteufelt** *(col)* **1** *adj Lage* devilish *(col)*, tricky. **2** *adv (mit adj)* damned *(col)*.
**vertiefen\*** **1** *vt (lit, fig)* to deepen; *(Sch) Lehrstoff* to consolidate. **2** *vr (lit, fig)* to deepen; *(fig: Lehrstoff)* to be consolidated. **sich in etw** *(acc)* **~** *(fig)* to become engrossed in sth.
**Vertiefung** f **(a)** *siehe vt* deepening; consolidation. **(b)** *(in Oberfläche)* depression. **(c)** *(in Arbeit etc)* absorption.
**vertikal** [vɛrti'kaːl] *adj* vertical.
**Vertikale** [vɛrti'kaːlə] f **-n** vertical line.
**vertilgen\*** *vt* **(a)** *Unkraut etc* to eradicate. **(b)** *(col: aufessen)* to demolish *(col)*.
**Vertilgungsmittel** *nt* weedkiller; *(Insekten~)* pesticide.
**vertippen\*** *vr (col)* to make a typing error.
**vertonen\*** *vt* to set to music; *Film etc* to add a soundtrack to.
**vertrackt** *adj (col)* complicated, tricky.
**Vertrag** *m* ⁼e contract; *(Abkommen)* agreement; *(Pol: Friedens~)* treaty. **unter ~ stehen** to be under contract.
**vertragen\*** *irreg* **1** *vt* to take; *(aushalten auch)* to stand. **Eier/Wolle vertrage ich nicht** eggs don't agree with me/I can't wear wool; **viel ~ können** *(col: Alkohol)* to have a considerable capacity (for drink). **2** *vr* **sich (mit jdm) ~** to get along (with sb); **sich wieder ~** to be friends again; **sich mit etw ~** *(Nahrungsmittel, Farbe)* to go with sth; *(Aussage, Verhal-*

*ten)* to be consistent with sth.
**vertraglich** **1** *adj* contractual. **2** *adv* by contract; *festgelegt* in the/a contract.
**verträglich** *adj (friedlich, umgänglich)* peaceable, easy-going; *Speise* digestible; *(bekömmlich)* wholesome; *Medikament* well tolerated *(für* by*)*. **gut ~** easily digestible.
**Verträglichkeit** f *no pl siehe adj* easy-going nature; digestibility; wholesomeness.
**Vertrags-:** **~bruch** *m* breach of contract; breaking of an/the agreement; breaking of a/the treaty; **v~brüchig** *adj* in breach of contract; **~entwurf** *m* draft contract/agreement/treaty; **v~gemäß** *adj, adv* as stipulated in the contract/agreement/treaty; **~händler** *m* concessionary; **v~schließend** *adj* contracting; **~werkstatt** f authorized repair shop; **v~widrig** **1** *adj* contrary to the contract/agreement/treaty; **2** *adv* in breach of contract/the agreement/the treaty.
**vertrauen\*** *vi* **jdm/einer Sache ~** to trust sb/sth; **auf jdn/etw ~** to trust in sb/sth.
**Vertrauen** *nt no pl* trust, confidence *(zu,* in +acc, *auf* +acc in*)*; *(Pol)* confidence. **im ~ (gesagt)** strictly in confidence; **im ~ darauf, daß** ... confident that ...; **~ zu jdm fassen** to gain confidence in sb; **jdn ins ~ ziehen** to take sb into one's confidence.
**vertrauen|erweckend** *adj Arzt, Mensch* who inspires confidence. **einen ~en Eindruck machen/~ aussehen** to inspire confidence.
**Vertrauens-:** **~arzt** *m doctor who examines patients signed off sick for a lengthy period*; **v~bildend** *adj Maßnahmen* designed to build up confidence; **~bruch** *m* breach of confidence; **~mann** *m, pl* **~leute** *or* **~männer** intermediary; **~person** f someone to confide in, confidant(e); **~sache** f *(vertrauliche Angelegenheit)* confidential matter; *(Frage des Vertrauens)* question of trust; **v~selig** *adj* trusting; **~stellung** f position of trust; **v~voll** *adj* trusting; **~votum** *nt (Parl)* vote of confidence; **v~würdig** *adj* trustworthy.
**vertraulich** **1** *adj* **(a)** *(geheim)* confidential. **(b)** *(freundschaftlich)* friendly; *(plump ~)* familiar. **~ werden** to get familiar; *(zudringlich)* to take liberties. **2** *adv* **(a)** confidentially. **(b)** in a friendly way.
**Vertraulichkeit** f confidentiality.
**verträumt** *adj* dreamy; *Städtchen etc* sleepy.
**vertraut** *adj* intimate; *(bekannt) Gesicht, Umgebung* familiar. **sich mit etw ~ machen** to familiarize oneself with sth; **sich mit dem Gedanken ~ machen, daß** ... to get used to the idea that ...; **mit jdm ~ werden** to become friendly with sb.
**Vertraute(r)** *mf decl as adj* close friend.
**Vertrautheit** f *no pl siehe adj* intimacy; familiarity.
**vertreiben\*** *vt irreg* **(a)** *Tiere, Menschen, Sorgen* to drive away; *(aus Haus, Land)* to drive out *(aus* of*)*; *(aus Amt, von Stellung)* to oust *(aus* from*)*; *Feind* to drive off. **jdm/sich die Zeit mit etw ~** to help sb pass the time/to pass the time with sth. **(b)** *(Comm) Waren* to market.
**Vertreibung** f *(aus* from*)* expulsion; *(aus Amt etc)* ousting; *(von Feind)* repelling.
**vertretbar** *adj* justifiable; *Theorie* tenable.
**vertreten\*** *vt irreg* **(a)** *(ersetzen)* to replace; *Kollegen, Lehrer* to cover for. **(b)** *jds Interessen, Firma, Wahlkreis* to represent; *Sache* to look after; *(Jur) Fall* to plead. **~ sein** to be represented. **(c)** *(Comm)* to be the agent for; *(Angestellter)* to represent. **(d)** *(verfechten) Standpunkt* to support; *Meinung* to hold; *Kunstrichtung* to represent; *(rechtfertigen)* to justify *(vor* to*)*. **(e)** **sich** *(dat)* **den Fuß ~** to twist one's ankle; **sich** *(dat)* **die Beine** *or* **Füße ~** *(col)* to

stretch one's legs.

**Vertreter(in** f) m - (a) representative; *(Comm)* *(Firma)* agent; *(Angestellter)* (sales) representative, rep *(col)*. (b) *(Ersatz)* replacement; *(im Amt)* deputy. (c) *(Verfechter) (von Doktrin)* supporter, advocate; *(von Meinung)* holder.

**Vertretung** f siehe vt *(a-d)* (a) replacement; *(Aushilfslehrer)* supply *(Brit)* or substitute *(US)* teacher. **die ~ (für jdn) übernehmen** to stand in (for sb); **in ~ +gen** on behalf of; *(in Briefen)* pp. (b) representation. **X übernimmt die ~ des Falles** *(Jur)* X is pleading the case. (c) *(Comm)* agency. (d) supporting; holding; representation.

**Vertretungs-:** ~**stunde** f *(Sch)* cover lesson; **v~weise** adv as a replacement; *(bei Amtsperson)* as a deputy.

**Vertrieb** m -e sales pl; *(von einem Produkt)* sale, marketing; *(im Großhandel)* distribution. **den ~ für eine Firma haben** to have the agency or dealership for a firm.

**Vertriebene(r)** mf decl as adj exile.

**Vertriebs-:** ~**abteilung** f sales department; ~**gesellschaft** f marketing company; ~**kosten** pl marketing costs pl; ~**rechte** pl distribution rights pl.

**vertrinken*** vt irreg to spend on drink.

**vertrocknen*** vi aux sein to dry out; *(Eßwaren)* to go dry; *(Pflanzen)* to shrivel; *(Quelle)* to dry up.

**vertrödeln*** vt *(col)* to fritter away.

**vertrösten*** vt to put off *(auf +acc until)*. **jdn auf ein andermal/auf später ~** to put sb off.

**vertun*** irreg **1** vt Zeit etc to waste. **2** vr *(col)* to make a mistake.

**vertuschen*** vt to hush up. **etw vor jdm ~** to keep sth from sb.

**Vertuschung** f cover-up.

**ver|übeln*** vt jdm etw ~ not to be at all pleased with sb for doing sth; **das kann ich dir nicht ~** I can't blame you for that.

**ver|üben*** vt to commit.

**ver|ulken*** vt *(col)* to make fun of.

**ver|unglimpfen*** vt jdn to disparage.

**ver|unglücken*** vi aux sein *(Mensch)* to have an accident; *(Fahrzeug)* to crash; *(fig col: mißlingen)* to go wrong. **mit dem Flugzeug ~** to be in a plane crash.

**ver|unglückt** adj *(fig)* Versuch etc unsuccessful.

**Ver|unglückte(r)** mf decl as adj casualty, victim.

**ver|unreinigen*** vt Fluß etc to pollute; *(beschmutzen)* to dirty; *(Hund etc)* to foul.

**Ver|unreinigung** f siehe vt pollution; dirtying; fouling.

**ver|unsichern*** vt to make unsure *(in +dat about)*. **sie versuchten, ihn zu ~** they tried to throw him; **verunsichert** unsure of oneself.

**ver|unstalten*** vt to disfigure.

**ver|untreuen*** vt to embezzle.

**Ver|untreuung** f embezzlement.

**ver|unzieren*** vt to spoil. **jdn** or **jds Gesicht ~** to spoil sb's looks.

**ver|ursachen*** vt to cause.

**Ver|ursacher(in** f) m - person/party responsible *(gen for)*, perpetrator *(gen of)*.

**ver|urteilen*** vt to condemn *(Jur)*; *(für schuldig befinden)* to convict *(für of)*; *(zu Strafe)* to sentence *(zu to)*. **jdn zu einer Geldstrafe von 1.000 DM ~** to fine sb DM 1,000.

**Ver|urteilte(r)** mf decl as adj convicted man/woman. **der zum Tode ~** the condemned man.

**Ver|urteilung** f condemnation; *(Jur)* conviction.

**vervielfachen*** vtr to multiply.

**vervielfältigen*** vt to duplicate.

**Vervielfältigung** f duplication; *(Abzug)* copy.

**vervierfachen*** vtr to quadruple.

**vervollkommnen*** **1** vt to perfect. **2** vr to make oneself perfect.

**vervollständigen*** **1** vt to complete. **2** vr to be completed.

**Vervollständigung** f completion.

**verwachsen¹*** vi irreg aux sein (a) *(zusammenwachsen)* to grow together; *(Narbe, Wunde)* to heal; *(Knochen)* to knit. (b) *(fig: Menschen)* to grow closer (together). **zu etw ~** to grow into sth; **mit etw ~** mit Aufgabe, Traditionen to become caught up in sth; **mit etw ~ sein** to have very close ties with sth.

**verwachsen²** adj (a) Mensch deformed; *(verkümmert)* stunted. (b) *(überwuchert)* overgrown.

**verwackelt** adj blurred.

**verwählen*** vr to dial the wrong number.

**verwahren*** **1** vt *(aufbewahren)* to keep safe. **2** vr **sich gegen etw ~** to protest against sth.

**verwahrlosen*** vi aux sein to go to pot *(col)*; *(Gebäude auch)* to fall into disrepair; *(Mensch)* to let oneself go; *(verwildern)* to run wild.

**verwahrlost** adj neglected. **sittlich ~** depraved.

**Verwahrung** f (a) no pl *(von Geld etc)* keeping; *(von Täter)* custody, detention. **jdm etw in ~ geben** to give sth to sb for safekeeping; **etw in ~ nehmen** to take sth into safekeeping; *(Behörde)* to take possession of sth; **jdn in ~ nehmen** to take sb into custody. (b) *(Einspruch)* protest.

**verwaist** adj orphaned; *(fig)* deserted.

**verwalten*** vt to manage; Amt to hold; *(Pol)* Provinz etc to govern; *(Beamte)* to administer; *(Rel)* to administer. **sich selbst ~** *(Pol)* to be self-governing.

**Verwalter(in** f) m - administrator.

**Verwaltung** f (a) siehe vt management; holding; government; administration. (b) *(Behörde, Abteilung)* administration; *(Haus~)* management. **städtische ~** municipal authorities pl.

**Verwaltungs-:** ~**angestellte(r)** mf administrative employee; ~**apparat** m administrative machinery; ~**beamte(r)** m government official; ~**bezirk** m administrative district; ~**gericht** nt Administrative Court; ~**weg** m **auf dem ~weg** through administrative channels.

**verwandeln*** **1** vt to change, to transform; *(umwandeln)* to convert. **jdn/etw in etw** *(acc)* **~** to turn sb/sth into sth; **ein Gebäude in einen Trümmerhaufen ~** to reduce a building to a pile of rubble; **er ist wie verwandelt** he's a changed man. **2** vi *(Sport sl)* **zum 1:0 ~** to make it 1-0. **3** vr to change. **sich in etw** *(acc)* **or zu etw ~** to change or turn into sth.

**Verwandlung** f change, transformation. **eine ~ durchmachen** to undergo a transformation.

**verwandt** adj *(lit, fig)* related *(mit to)*. **geistig ~ sein** *(fig)* to be kindred spirits.

**Verwandte(r)** mf decl as adj relation, relative.

**Verwandtschaft** f relationship; *(die Verwandten)* relations pl, relatives pl; *(fig)* affinity.

**verwandtschaftlich** adj family attr.

**verwarnen*** vt to caution, to warn; *(Ftbl)* to book.

**Verwarnung** f caution, warning; *(Ftbl)* booking.

**verwaschen** adj faded; *(verwässert)* Farbe watery.

**verwässern*** vt *(lit, fig)* to water down.

**verwechseln*** vt to confuse, to mix up. **jdn (mit jdm) ~** to confuse sb with sb; *(für jdn halten auch)* to mistake sb for sb; **sie sind sich zum V~ ähnlich** it's impossible to tell the difference between them.

**Verwechslung** f confusion; *(Irrtum)* mistake. **das muß eine ~ sein** there must be some mistake.

**verwegen** adj daring, bold; *(tollkühn)* foolhardy;

*(keck)* saucy.

**verwehen\* 1** *vt Rauch* to blow away; *Spur* to cover over. **2** *vi aux sein (Spur)* to be covered over.

**verwehren\*** *vt (geh)* **jdm etw** ~ to refuse *or* deny sb sth; **jdm** ~, **etw zu tun** to bar sb from doing sth.

**Verwehung** *f* drift.

**verweichlichen\* 1** *vt* **jdn** ~ to make sb soft; **ein verweichlichter Mensch** a weakling. **2** *vi aux sein* to get soft.

**Verweigerer** *m* refusenik; *(Kriegsdienst~)* conscientious objector.

**verweigern\*** *vt* to refuse; *Befehl* to refuse to obey; *Kriegsdienst* to refuse to do. **jdm etw** ~ to refuse *or* deny sb sth.

**Verweigerung** *f* refusal. ~ **des Kriegsdienstes** refusal to do (one's) military service; ~ **des Gehorsams** disobedience.

**verweilen\*** *vi (geh) (Mensch)* to stay; *(Blick, Gedanken)* to dwell. **bei einer Sache** ~ to dwell on sth.

**verweint** *adj Augen* tear-swollen; *Gesicht* tear-stained.

**Verweis** *m* **-e (a)** *(Rüge)* reprimand. **jdm einen** ~ **erteilen** to reprimand sb. **(b)** *(Hinweis)* reference *(auf +acc to)*.

**verweisen\*** *irreg* **1** *vt* **(a)** *(hinweisen)* **jdn auf etw** *(acc)*/**an jdn** ~ to refer sb to sth/sb. **(b)** *(von der Schule)* to expel. **jdn des Landes** ~ to deport sb; **jdm vom Platz** *or* **des Spielfeldes** ~ to send sb off; **jdn auf den zweiten Platz** ~ *(Sport)* to relegate sb to second place. **(c)** *(Jur)* to refer *(an +acc to)*. **2** *vi* **auf etw** *(acc)* ~ to refer to sth.

**verwelken\*** *vi aux sein (Blumen)* to wilt; *(fig)* to fade. **ein verwelktes Gesicht** a worn face.

**verweltlichen\*** *vt* to secularize.

**verwendbar** *adj* usable *(zu for)*. **das ist nur einmal** ~ it can be used once only.

**Verwendbarkeit** *f no pl* usability.

**verwenden 1** *vt* to use. **Mühe auf etw** *(acc)* ~ to put effort into sth; **Zeit auf etw** *(acc)* ~ to spend time on sth. **2** *vr* **sich (bei jdm) für jdn** ~ to approach sb on sb's behalf.

**Verwendung** *f* use; *(von Zeit, Geld)* expenditure *(auf +acc on)*.

**Verwendungs-:** ~**möglichkeit** *f* (possible) use; ~**weise** *f* manner of use; ~**zweck** *m* use, purpose.

**verwerfen\*** *irreg vt (ablehnen)* to reject; *(Jur) Klage, Antrag* to dismiss; *Urteil* to quash; *(kritisieren) Handlungsweise* to condemn.

**verwerflich** *adj* reprehensible.

**verwertbar** *adj* usable.

**verwerten\*** *vt (verwenden)* to utilize; *Erfindung, Material etc* to exploit.

**Verwertung** *f siehe vt* utilization; exploitation.

**verwesen\*** *vi aux sein* to decay; *(Leiche auch)* to decompose.

**Verweser** *m* **-** *(old, liter)* administrator.

**Verwesung** *f no pl siehe vi* decay; decomposition.

**verwickeln\* 1** *vt Fäden etc* to tangle (up). **jdn in etw** *(acc)* ~ to involve sb in sth. **2** *vr (Fäden etc)* to get tangled up. **sich in etw** *(acc)* ~ *(lit, fig)* to become entangled in sth.

**verwickelt** *adj (fig col: schwierig)* involved, complicated.

**Verwicklung** *f* involvement *(in +acc in)*; *(Komplikation)* complication; *(Verwirrung)* confusion.

**verwildern\*** *vi aux sein (Garten)* to become overgrown; *(Pflanzen)* to grow wild; *(Haustier)* to become wild.

**verwildert** *adj* wild; *Garten* overgrown; *Aussehen* unkempt.

**verwirken** *vt (geh)* to forfeit.

**verwirklichen\* 1** *vt* to realize; *Wunsch* to fulfil *(Brit)* or fulfill *(US)*; *Traum* to make come true. **2** *vr* to be realized; *(Mensch)* to fulfil *(Brit)* or fulfill *(US)* oneself.

**Verwirklichung** *f no pl* realization; *(von Wunsch, Selbst~)* fulfilment *(Brit)*, fulfillment *(US)*.

**verwirren\* 1** *vt* **(a)** *Haare* to tousle; *Fäden etc* to get tangled up. **(b)** *(durcheinanderbringen)* to confuse; *(konfus machen)* to bewilder. **2** *vr (Fäden etc)* to become tangled up; *(Haare)* to become tousled; *(fig)* to become confused.

**Verwirrspiel** *nt (fig)* confusion. **ein** ~ **mit jdm treiben** to try to confuse sb.

**Verwirrung** *f (Durcheinander)* confusion. **jdn in** ~ **bringen** to confuse sb.

**verwirtschaften\*** *vt* to squander away.

**verwischen\* 1** *vt (verschmieren)* to smudge; *(lit, fig) Spuren* to cover over; *(fig) Erinnerungen* to blur. **2** *vr (lit, fig)* to become blurred.

**verwittern\*** *vi aux sein* to weather.

**verwitwet** *adj* widowed.

**verwöhnen\* 1** *vt* to spoil; *(Schicksal)* to be good to. **2** *vr* to spoil oneself.

**verwöhnt** *adj* spoilt; *Kunde, Geschmack* discriminating.

**verworfen** *adj (geh)* depraved.

**verworren** *adj* confused, muddled; *(verwickelt)* intricate.

**verwundbar** *adj (lit, fig)* vulnerable.

**verwunden\*** *vt* to wound.

**verwunderlich** *adj* surprising; *(sonderbar)* strange, odd.

**verwundern\* 1** *vt* to astonish. **2** *vr* to be astonished *(über +acc at)*.

**Verwunderung** *f no pl* astonishment.

**Verwundete(r)** *mf decl as adj* casualty. **die** ~**n** *(Mil)* the wounded.

**Verwundung** *f* wound.

**verwünschen\*** *vt* **(a)** *(verfluchen)* to curse. **(b)** *(in Märchen: verzaubern)* to enchant; *(verhexen)* to bewitch.

**Verwünschung** *f (Fluch)* curse.

**verwurzelt** *adj* ~ **sein** *(Pflanze)* to be rooted; **(fest) in** *or* **mit etw** ~ *(fig)* deeply rooted in sth.

**verwüsten\*** *vt* to devastate, to ravage.

**Verwüstung** *f* devastation *no pl*, ravaging *no pl*.

**verzagen\*** *vi (geh)* to lose heart.

**verzagt** *adj* disheartened.

**verzählen\*** *vr* to miscount.

**verzahnen\*** *vt* to dovetail; *Zahnräder* to cut teeth in. **ineinander verzahnt sein** *(lit, fig)* to mesh.

**verzapfen\*** *vt (col) Unsinn* to come out with.

**verzärteln\*** *vt (pej)* to mollycoddle, to pamper.

**verzaubern\*** *vt* to cast a spell on; *(bezaubern)* to enchant; *(verhexen)* to bewitch. **jdn in etw** *(acc)* ~ to turn sb into sth.

**verzehnfachen\*** *vtr* to increase tenfold.

**Verzehr** *m no pl* consumption.

**verzehren\*** *vt (form: lit, fig)* to consume.

**verzeichnen\*** *vt* to record; *(in einer Liste auch)* to enter. **einen Erfolg zu** ~ **haben** to have scored a success.

**Verzeichnis** *nt* index; *(Tabelle)* table; *(Namens~, esp amtlich)* register; *(Aufstellung)* list; *(Comp)* directory.

**verzeihen\*** *pret* **verzieh,** *ptp* **verziehen** *vti (vergeben)* to forgive; *(entschuldigen)* to excuse, to pardon. **jdm (etw)** ~ to forgive sb (for sth); ~ **Sie!** excuse me!

**verzeihlich** *adj* forgivable; *(zu entschuldigen)* excusable.

**Verzeihung** *f no pl* forgiveness; *(Entschuldigung)* pardon. ~! excuse me!; **(jdn) um ~ bitten** *(sich entschuldigen)* to apologize (to sb).

**verzerren*** **1** *vti (lit, fig)* to distort; *Gesicht* to contort; *Sehne, Muskel* to strain, to pull. **etw verzerrt darstellen** *(fig)* to present a distorted picture of sth. **2** *vr* to become distorted; *(Gesicht etc)* to become contorted *(zu in)*.

**Verzerrung** *f (lit, fig)* distortion; *(von Gesicht)* contortion.

**verzetteln*** **1** *vt* to fritter away. **2** *vr* to dissipate one's energies *(an +dat* on*)*; *(bei Aufgabe)* to get bogged down.

**Verzicht** *m* **-e** renunciation *(auf +acc* of*)*; *(auf Anspruch)* abandonment *(auf ↑acc* of*)*; *(Opfer)* sacrifice; *(auf Thron)* abdication *(auf +acc* of*)*. **ein ~, der mir nicht schwerfällt** that's something I can easily do without.

**verzichten*** *vi* to do without; *(Opfer bringen)* to make sacrifices. **auf jdn/etw ~** *(ohne auskommen müssen)* to do without sb/sth; *(aufgeben)* to give up sb/sth; *auf Erbschaft* to renounce sth; *(von etw absehen) auf Kommentar, Anzeige etc* to abstain from sth; *auf Amt* to refuse sth; **auf den Thron ~** to abdicate; **sie verzichtete zugunsten ihrer Schwester auf das Auto** she let her sister have the car; **danke, ich verzichte** *(iro)* not for me, thanks.

**verzieh** *pret of* **verzeihen**.

**verziehen**[1]* *irreg* **1** *vt* **(a)** *Mund, Züge etc* to twist *(zu* into*)*. **das Gesicht ~** to pull a face; **den Mund ~** to turn up one's mouth; **keine Miene ~** not to turn a hair. **(b)** *Stoff* to pull out of shape; *Holz* to warp. **(c)** *(verwöhnen)* to spoil. **2** *vr* **(a)** *(Stoff)* to go out of shape; *(Holz)* to warp. **(b)** *(Mund, Gesicht etc)* to twist *(zu* into*)*. **(c)** *(verschwinden)* to disappear; *(Gewitter)* to pass; *(Nebel, Wolken)* to disperse. **3** *vi aux sein* to move *(nach* to*)*. **verzogen** *(Vermerk)* gone away.

**verziehen**[2] *ptp of* **verzeihen**.

**verzieren*** *vt* to decorate; *(verschönern)* to embellish.

**Verzierung** *f siehe vt* decoration; embellishment.

**verzinsen*** **1** *vt* to pay interest on. **das Geld wird mit 3% verzinst** 3% interest is paid on the money. **2** *vr* **sich (mit 6%) ~** to yield (6%) interest.

**verzinslich** *adj* interest-bearing *attr*. **~/fest ~ sein** to yield interest/a fixed rate of interest; **nicht ~** interest-free.

**verzogen** *adj Kind* spoilt.

**verzögern*** **1** *vt* to delay; *(verlangsamen)* to slow down. **2** *vr* to be delayed.

**Verzögerung** *f* **(a)** delay, hold-up. **(b)** *no pl (das Verzögern)* delaying; *(Verlangsamung)* slowing down.

**Verzögerungstaktik** *f* delaying tactics *pl*.

**verzollen*** *vt* to pay duty on. **haben Sie etwas zu ~?** have you anything to declare?; **verzollt** duty-paid.

**verzuckern*** **1** *vi aux sein (Honig etc)* to crystallize. **2** *vt* to put too much sugar on.

**verzückt** *adj* enraptured, ecstatic.

**Verzückung** *f no pl* rapture, ecstasy. **in ~ geraten** to go into ecstasies *(wegen* over*)*.

**Verzug** *m* delay; *(Fin)* arrears *pl*. **bei ~ (der Zahlungen)** on default of payment; **mit etw in ~ geraten** to fall behind with sth; *mit Zahlungen auch* to fall into arrears with sth; **in ~ bringen** to delay.

**verzweifeln*** *vi aux sein* to despair *(an +dat* of*)*. **es ist zum V~!** it drives you to despair!

**verzweifelt** *adj* desperate; *Blick, Stimme etc auch* despairing.

**Verzweiflung** *f (Gemütszustand)* despair; *(Ratlosig-*

*keit)* desperation. **jdn zur ~ treiben** to drive sb to despair.

**verzweigen*** *vr* to branch.

**verzweigt** *adj Baum, Firma* with a lot of branches; *Verkehrsnetz* complex.

**verzwickt** *adj (col)* tricky.

**Vesper** *f* **-n** *(Eccl)* vespers *pl*.

**Vesuv** [ve'zu:f] *m der ~* Vesuvius.

**Veteran** [vete'ra:n] *m (wk)* **-en, -en** *(Mil, fig)* veteran.

**Veto** ['ve:to] *nt* **-s** veto.

**Vetorecht** ['ve:to-] *nt* right of veto.

**Vetter** *m* **-n** cousin.

**Vetternwirtschaft** *f (col)* nepotism.

**vgl.** = **vergleiche** cf.

**v.H.** = **vom Hundert** per cent.

**VHS** [fauha:'|ɛs] *f* = **Volkshochschule**.

**via** ['vi:a] *adv* via.

**Viadukt** [via'dʊkt] *m* **-e** viaduct.

**Vibration** [vibra'tsio:n] *f* vibration.

**Vibrato** [vi'bra:to] *nt* vibrato.

**vibrieren*** [vi'bri:rən] *vi* to vibrate; *(Stimme)* to tremble.

**Video** ['vi:deo] *nt* **-s** video. **auf ~ aufnehmen** to video.

**Video-:** *in cpds* video; **~aufnahme, ~aufzeichnung** *f* video recording; **~band** *nt* videotape; **~gerät** *nt* video (recorder); **~kamera** *f* video camera; **~kassette** *f* video cassette; **~rekorder** *m* video recorder; **~technik** *f* video technology; **~spiel** *nt* video game; **~text** *m* teletext.

**Vieh** *nt no pl* **(a)** *(Nutztiere)* livestock; *(Rinder auch)* cattle *pl*. **(b)** *(col: Tier)* animal.

**Vieh-:** **~bestand** *m* livestock; **~futter** *nt* animal fodder; **~handel** *m* livestock/cattle trade.

**viehisch** *adj* brutish; *Schmerzen* beastly.

**Vieh-:** **~markt** *m* livestock/cattle market; **~seuche** *f* livestock disease; **~wagen** *m* cattle truck; **~zeug** *nt (col)* animals *pl*; **~zucht** *f* (live)stock/cattle breeding.

**viel** *indef pron, adj, comp* **mehr**, *superl* **meiste(r, s)** *or (adv)* **am meisten** **(a)** *sing (adjektivisch)* a lot of; *(fragend, verneint auch)* much; *(substantivisch)* a lot; *(fragend, verneint auch)* much. **~es** a lot of *or* many things; **sehr ~ Geld** a great deal of money, a very large sum of money; **in ~em** in many respects; **noch (ein)mal so ~ (Zeit etc)** as much (time *etc)* again; **gleich ~ (Gewinn etc)** the same amount (of profit *etc)*; **einer zu ~** one too many; **~ Neues/Schönes** *etc* a lot of *or* many new/beautiful *etc* things; **das ~e/sein ~es Geld** all that/all his money.

**(b)** **~e** *(adjektivisch)* many, a lot of; *(substantivisch)* many, a lot; **gleich ~e (Angestellte/Anteile** *etc)* the same number (of employees/shares *etc)*; **so/zu ~e (Menschen/Fehler** *etc)* so/too many (people/mistakes *etc)*; **aufgrund der ~en Fehler** because of all the mistakes; **~e hundert Menschen** many hundreds of people.

**(c)** *(adverbial: mit vb)* a lot, a great deal; *(fragend, verneint auch)* much. **er arbeitet ~/nicht ~** he works a lot/doesn't work much; **er arbeitet zu/so ~** he works too/so much *or* such a lot; **die Straße wird (sehr/nicht) ~ befahren** this street is (very/not very) busy; **sich ~ einbilden** to think a lot of oneself.

**(d)** *(adverbial: mit adj, adv)* much, a lot. **~ größer** much *or* a lot bigger; **~ zu ...** much too ...; **~ zu ~e** far too many.

**Viel-:** **v~beschäftigt** *adj attr* very busy; **v~deutig** *adj* ambiguous; **v~diskutiert** *adj attr* much dis-

cussed; ~**eck** *nt* polygon.
**vielerlei** *adj inv* (a) all sorts of. (b) *(substantivisch)* all sorts of things.
**vieler|orts** *adv* in many places.
**vielfach 1** *adj* multiple *attr.* **ein** ~**er Millionär** a multimillionaire; **auf** ~**e Weise** in many various ways; **auf** ~**en Wunsch** by popular request; **um ein** ~**es besser** many times better. **2** *adv* many times; *(in vielen Fällen)* in many cases; *(auf* ~*e Weise)* in many ways; *(col: häufig)* frequently. ~ **bewährt** tried and tested many times.
**Vielfache(s)** *nt decl as adj (Math)* multiple. **um ein** ~**s** many times over; **er verdient ein** ~**s von dem, was ich verdiene** his salary is many times larger than mine.
**Vielfalt** *f* (great) variety.
**vielfältig** *adj* varied, diverse.
**Viel-:** **v**~**farbig** *adj* multicoloured *(Brit)*, multicolored *(US)*; ~**fraß** *m* -e glutton; **v**~**gehaßt** *adj attr* much-hated; **v**~**geliebt** *adj attr* much-loved; **v**~**geprüft** *adj attr (hum)* sorely tried; **v**~**gereist** *adj attr* much-travelled *(Brit)*, much-traveled *(US)*; ~**götterei** *f* polytheism; **v**~**köpfig** *adj (col) Familie, Schar* large.
**vielleicht** *adv* (a) perhaps; *(in Bitten auch)* by any chance. **ja,** ~ yes, perhaps *or* maybe; ~ **sagst du mir mal, warum** you'd better tell me why; **hat er sich** ~ **verirrt/weh getan?** maybe he has got lost/hurt himself; **hast du ihm das** ~ **erzählt?** did you perhaps tell him that?; *(entsetzt: denn etwa)* you didn't tell him that, did you?; ~, **daß** ... it could be that ... (b) *(col: wirklich)* really. **soll ich** ~ **24 Stunden arbeiten?** am I really supposed to work 24 hours then?; **du bist** ~ **ein Idiot!** you really are an idiot!; **ich war** ~ **nervös!** I wasn't half nervous! *(Brit col)*, was I nervous!
**vielmalig** *adj attr* repeated.
**vielmals** *adv* **danke** ~! many thanks!; **ich bitte** ~ **um Entschuldigung!** I do apologize!; **er läßt** ~ **grüßen** he sends his best regards.
**vielmehr** *adv* rather; *(sondern, nur)* just.
**Viel-:** **v**~**sagend** *adj* meaningful, significant; **jdn v**~**sagend ansehen** to give sb a meaningful look; **v**~**schichtig** *adj (fig)* complex; ~**schreiber** *m* **er ist ein richtiger** ~**schreiber** *(pej)* he really churns out the stuff *(col)*; **v**~**seitig** *adj (lit)* many-sided; *Mensch, Gerät* versatile; *Interessen* varied; *Ausbildung* all-round *attr*; **auf v**~**seitigen Wunsch** by popular request; **v**~**seitig begabt/interessiert sein** to be versatile/to have varied interests; **v**~**sprachig** *adj* multilingual, polyglot; **v**~**stimmig** *adj* many-voiced; **v**~**versprechend** *adj* promising; ~**völkerstaat** *m* multiracial state; ~**weiberei** *f* polygamy; ~**zahl** *f* multitude.
**Vielzweck-** *in cpds* multipurpose.
**vier** *num* four. **sie ist** ~ **(Jahre)** she's four (years old); **mit** ~ **(Jahren)** at the age of four; **es ist** ~ **(Uhr)** it's four (o'clock); ~ **Uhr** ~ four minutes past four; **für** *or* **auf** ~ **Tage** for four days; **in** ~ **Tagen** in four days, in four days' time; **wir waren** ~ **there** were four of us; **jdn unter** ~ **Augen sprechen** to speak to sb in private; ~ **Augen sehen mehr als zwei** *(prov)* two heads are better than one *(prov)*; **alle** ~**e von sich strecken** *(col: ausgestreckt liegen)* to stretch out; **auf allen** ~**en** *(col)* on all fours.
**Vier** *f* -**en** four; *(Sch)* ≈ D. **die Herz** ~ the four of hearts.
**Vier-:** ~**beiner** *m* - *(hum)* four-legged friend *(hum)*; **v**~**beinig** *adj* four-legged; **v**~**blätt(e)rig** *adj* four-leaved; **v**~**blätt(e)riges Kleeblatt** four-leaf clover; ~**eck** *nt* four-sided figure; *(Rechteck)* rectangle;

*(Quadrat)* square; **v**~**eckig** *adj (rechteckig)* rectangular; *(quadratisch)* square; **v**~**einhalb** *num* four and a half.
**Vierer** *m* - *(Rudern, Sch)* four; *(Golf)* foursome.
**Vierer-:** ~**bande** *f* gang of four; ~**bob** *m* four-man bob; **v**~**lei** *adj inv* (a) *attr Brot, Käse, Wein* four kinds *or* sorts of; *Möglichkeiten, Größen* four different; (b) *(substantivisch)* four different things; *(vier Sorten)* four different kinds.
**vierfach 1** *adj* fourfold, quadruple. **die** ~**e Größe** four times the size; **in** ~**er Ausfertigung** in quadruplicate. **2** *adv* four times, fourfold. **das Papier** ~ **legen** to fold the paper in four.
**Vierfache(s)** *nt decl as adj* four times the amount, quadruple. **um das** ~ **zunehmen** to quadruple.
**Vier-:** ~**farbendruck** *m (Verfahren)* four-colour *(Brit)* or four-color *(US)* printing; *(Erzeugnis)* four-colour *(Brit)* or four-color *(US)* print; ~**farb(en)stift** *m* four-colour *(Brit)* or four-color *(US)* pen; **v**~**füßig** *adj* four-legged; ~**ganggetriebe** *nt* four-speed gearbox; **v**~**geschossig** *adj* four-storey *attr (Brit)*, four-story *attr (US)*; **v**~**händig** *adv* for four hands.
**vierhundert** *num* four hundred.
**vierhundertste(r, s)** *adj* four hundredth.
**Vier-:** **v**~**jährig** *adj Kind etc* four-year-old *attr*; *(vier Jahre dauernd)* four-year; **v**~**kant** *adj, adv (Naut)* square; ~**kant** *m or nt* -**e** *(Tech)* square; **v**~**kantig** *adj* square(-headed); **v**~**köpfig** *adj Ungeheuer* four-headed; **eine v**~**köpfige Familie** a family of four.
**Vierling** *m* quadruplet, quad.
**Viermächte|abkommen** *nt (Hist)* four-power agreement.
**Vier-:** **v**~**mal** *adj* four times; **v**~**malig** *adj* **nach v**~**maligem Versuch** after the fourth attempt; ~**master** *m* - *(Naut)* four-master; **v**~**motorig** *adj* four-engined; ~**radantrieb** *m (Aut)* four-wheel drive; **v**~**räd(e)rig** *adj* four-wheel *attr*, four-wheeled; **v**~**seitig** *adj* four-sided; *Abkommen, Verhandlungen* quadripartite; *Broschüre* four-page *attr*; ~**sitzer** *m* - four-seater; **v**~**sitzig** *adj* four-seater *attr*; **v**~**spurig** *adj* four-lane *attr*; **v**~**stellig** *adj* four-figure *attr*; **v**~**stimmig** *adj* four-part *attr*, for four voices; **v**~**stöckig** *adj* = **v**~**geschossig**.
**viert** *adj* **wir gingen zu** ~ four of us went.
**Vier-:** ~**tagewoche** *f* four-day week; **v**~**tägig** *adj attr (vier Tage dauernd)* four-day; ~**taktmotor** *m* four-stroke engine; **v**~**tausend** *num* four thousand; ~**tausender** *m* - *(Berg)* thirteen thousand-foot mountain.
**vierte** *adj siehe* **vierte(r, s)**.
**vierteilig** *adj* four-piece *attr*; *Roman* four-part *attr*.
**Viertel¹** ['fɪrtl] *nt* - quarter. **ein** ~ **Leberwurst/Wein** a quarter of (a pound of) liver sausage/a quarter-litre *(Brit)* or -liter *(US)* of wine; **(ein)** ~ **nach/vor sechs** (a) quarter past/to six; **(ein)** ~ **sechs** (a) quarter past five; **drei** ~ **sechs** (a) quarter to six.
**Viertel²** ['fɪrtl] *nt* - *(Stadtbezirk)* quarter, district.
**viertel** ['fɪrtl] *adj inv* quarter. **ein** ~ **Liter/Pfund** a quarter (of a) litre *(Brit)* or liter *(US)*/pound; **drei** ~ **Liter** three quarters of a litre *(Brit)* or liter *(US)*.
**Viertelfinale** *nt* quarter-finals *pl*.
**Vierteljahr** *nt* three months *pl*, quarter *(Comm, Fin)*.
**Vierteljahres-** *in cpds* quarterly; ~**schrift** *f* quarterly.
**Viertel-** [fɪrtl-]: ~**jahrhundert** *nt* quarter of a century; **v**~**jährig** *adj attr Kind etc* three-month-old; *Aufenthalt, Frist* three months; **v**~**jährlich 1** *adj* quarterly; *Kündigung* three months' *attr*; **2** *adv* quarterly, every three months.
**vierteln** ['fɪrtln] *vt (in vier Teile teilen)* to divide into

**four**; *Summe, Gewinn* to divide by four.

**Viertel-** ['fɪrtl-]: ~**note** *f* crotchet *(Brit)*, quarter note *(US)*; ~**pfund** *nt* ≈ quarter of a pound; ~**stunde** *f* quarter of an hour; **v~stündig** *adj attr* *Abstand* quarter-hour; **v~stündlich** *adv* every quarter of an hour; ~**ton** *m* quarter tone.

**viertens** *adv* fourth(ly), in the fourth place.

**Vierte(r)** *mf decl as adj* fourth. **Karl IV** *or* **der ~** Charles IV *or* the Fourth.

**vierte(r, s)** *adj* fourth. **der ~ Oktober** the fourth of October; **der ~ Stock** the fourth *(Brit)* *or* fifth *(US)* floor; **er war ~r im Rennen** he was *or* came fourth in the race; **du bist der ~, der mich das fragt** you're the fourth person to ask me that.

**vier-:** ~**türig** *adj* four-door *attr*; ~**undzwanzig** *num* twenty-four.

**Vierviertaltakt** [-'fɪrtl-] *m* four-four *or* common time.

**Vierwaldstätter See** *m* Lake Lucerne.

**vier-:** ~**wöchentlich** *adj, adv* every four weeks; ~**wöchig** *adj* four-week *attr*.

**vierzehn** ['fɪrtseːn] *num* fourteen. **~ Uhr** 2 p.m.; *(auf Fahrplan, Mil)* fourteen hundred hours, 14.00; **~ Tage** two weeks, a fortnight *sing (Brit)*.

**vierzehn-** ['fɪrtseːn-]: ~**tägig** *adj* two-week *attr*, lasting two weeks; ~**täglich** *adj, adv* fortnightly *(Brit)*, every two weeks.

**Vierzehntel** ['fɪrtseːntl] *nt* - fourteenth.

**vierzehnte(r, s)** ['fɪrtseːntə(r, s)] *adj* fourteenth.

**vierzig** ['fɪrtsɪç] *num* forty. **mit ~ (km/h) fahren** to drive at twenty-five (miles an hour); **Mitte (der) V~** in one's mid-forties.

**vierziger** ['fɪrtsɪgɐ] *adj attr inv* **die ~ Jahre** the forties.

**Vierziger(in** *f)* ['fɪrtsɪgɐ, -ərɪn] *m* - *(Mensch)* forty-year-old; *(Wein)* wine of vintage forty. **er ist Mitte der ~** he is in his mid-forties; **er ist in den ~n** he is in his forties.

**vierzigmal** *adv* forty times.

**Vierzigstel** ['fɪrtsɪçstl] *nt* - fortieth.

**vierzigstel** ['fɪrtsɪçstl] *adj inv* fortieth.

**vierzigste(r, s)** ['fɪrtsɪçstə(r, s)] *adj* fortieth.

**Vierzigstundenwoche** [fɪrtsɪç-] *f* forty-hour week.

**Vierzimmerwohnung** *f* four-room flat *(Brit)* *or* apartment.

**Vietnam** [viɛt'nam] *nt* Vietnam.

**Vietnamese** [viɛtna'meːzə] *m (wk)* **-n, -n, Vietnamesin** *f* Vietnamese.

**vietnamesisch** [viɛtna'meːzɪʃ] *adj* Vietnamese.

**Vignette** [vɪn'jɛtə] *f (Gebührenmarke)* motorway *(Brit)* *or* turnpike *(US)* toll sticker.

**Vikar** [vi'kaːɐ] *m* curate.

**Villa** ['vɪla] *f, pl* **Villen** villa.

**Villenviertel** ['vɪlən-] *nt* exclusive residential area.

**Violett** *nt* - violet.

**violett** [vio'lɛt] *adj* violet.

**Violine** [vio'liːnə] *f* violin.

**Violinist(in** *f)* [violi'nɪst(in)] *m* violinist.

**Violin-** [vio'liːn-]: ~**konzert** *nt* violin concerto; ~**schlüssel** *m* treble clef.

**Violoncello** [violɔn'tʃɛlo] *nt* cello.

**VIP** [vɪp] *(col)*, **V.I.P.** ['viː|ai'piː] *m* -, **-s** *(col)* VIP.

**Viper** ['viːpɐ] *f* **-n** viper, adder.

**Viren** ['viːrən] *pl of* **Virus.**

**virtuell** [vɪr'tuɛl] *adj* virtual. **~e Realität** virtual reality.

**virtuos** [vɪr'tuoːs] *adj* virtuoso *attr*. **~ spielen** to give a virtuoso performance.

**Virtuose** [vɪr'tuoːzə] *m (wk)* **-n, -n, Virtuosin** *f* virtuoso.

**virulent** [viru'lɛnt] *adj (Med, fig)* virulent.

**Virulenz** [viru'lɛnts] *f (Med, fig)* virulence.

**Virus** ['viːrʊs] *nt or m, pl* **Viren** *(auch Comp)* virus.

**Virus-** *in cpds* viral; ~**infektion** *f* virus infection.

**Visage** [vi'zaːʒə] *f* **-n** *(pej)* face, (ugly) mug *(col)*.

**Visagist(in** *f)* [viza'ʒɪst(in)] *m* make-up artist.

**vis-à-vis** [viza'viː] *(dated)* **1** *adv* opposite *(von* to*)*. **2** *prep +dat* opposite (to).

**Visier** [vi'ziːɐ] *nt* **-e (a)** *(am Helm)* visor. **(b)** *(an Gewehren)* sight.

**Vision** [vi'zioːn] *f* vision.

**Visite** [vi'ziːtə] *f* **-n** *(Med)* round. **um 9 Uhr ist ~** the doctors do their rounds at 9 o'clock.

**Visitenkarte** [vi'ziːtn-] *f (lit, fig)* visiting *or* calling *(US)* card.

**Viskose** [vɪs'koːzə] *f no pl* viscose.

**visuell** [vi'zuɛl] *adj* visual.

**Visum** ['viːzʊm] *nt, pl* **Visa** *or* **Visen** visa.

**Visumzwang** ['viːzʊm-] *m* obligation to hold a visa. **für X besteht ~** a visa is required for X.

**vital** [vi'taːl] *adj* energetic; *(lebenswichtig)* vital.

**Vitalität** [vitali'tɛːt] *f* vitality, vigour *(Brit)*, vigor *(US)*.

**Vitamin** [vita'miːn] *nt* **-e** vitamin.

**Vitamin-** [vita'miːn-]: **v~arm** *adj* low in vitamins; ~**bedarf** *m* vitamin requirement; **v~haltig** *adj* containing vitamins; **v~haltig sein** to contain vitamins; ~**mangel** *m* vitamin deficiency; **v~reich** *adj* rich in vitamins; ~**tablette** *f* vitamin pill.

**Vitrine** [vi'triːnə] *f (Schrank)* glass cabinet; *(Schaukasten)* showcase, display case.

**Vivisektion** [vivizɛk'tsioːn] *f* vivisection.

**Vize** ['fiːtsə] *m* - *(col)* number two *(col)*; *(~meister)* runner-up.

**Vize-** ['fiːtsə-] *in cpds* vice-; ~**kanzler** *m* vice-chancellor; ~**könig** *m* viceroy; ~**meister** *m* runner-up; ~**präsident** *m* vice-president.

**Vlies** [fliːs] *nt* **-e** fleece.

**V-Mann** ['fau-] *m* = **Verbindungsmann.**

**Vogel** *m* ⁼ *(lit, fig)* bird. **ein seltsamer** *or* **komischer ~** *(col)* an odd bird *(col)*; **ein lustiger ~** *(col)* a lively character *(col)*; **den ~ abschießen** *(col)* to surpass everyone *(iro)*; **einen ~ haben** *(col)* to have a screw loose *(col)*; **jdm den ~ zeigen** *(col)* ≈ to give sb the V sign *(Brit)* *or* the finger *(US)*.

**Vogel-:** ~**bauer** *nt* birdcage; ~**beere** *f (auch* ~**beerbaum)** rowan (tree), mountain ash; *(Frucht)* rowan (berry); ~**dreck** *m* bird droppings *pl*; ~**ei** *nt* bird's egg; **v~frei** *adj (Hist)* outlawed; ~**futter** *nt* bird food; *(Samen)* birdseed; ~**häuschen** *nt* nesting box, bird house *(US)*; ~**käfig** *m* bird cage; ~**kirsche** *f (wilde Süßkirsche)* wild cherry; ~**kunde** *f* ornithology. ~**nest** *nt* bird's nest; ~**perspektive** *f* bird's-eye view; ~**ruf** *m* bird call; ~**scheuche** *f (lit, fig col)* scarecrow; ~**schutz** *m* protection of birds; ~**schutzgebiet** *nt* bird sanctuary; ~**Strauß-Politik** *f* head-in-the-sand policy; ~**tränke** *f* bird bath; ~**warte** *f* ornithological station; ~**zug** *m* bird migration.

**Vogesen** [vo'geːzən] *pl* **die ~** the Vosges *pl*.

**Vokabel** [vo'kaːbl] *f* **-n** word. ~**n** *pl* vocabulary *sing*.

**Vokabular** [vokabu'laːɐ] *nt* **-e** vocabulary.

**Vokal** [vo'kaːl] *m* **-e** vowel.

**Vokalmusik** [vo'kaːl-] *f* vocal music.

**Volk** *nt* ⁼**er** people *pl*; *(~sstamm)* people *sing*; *(Zool)* colony; *(col: Gruppe)* crowd *pl*; *(pej: Pack)* rabble *pl*. **das ~ verlangt, daß ...** the people demand that ...; **viel ~** lots of people *pl*; **etw unters ~ bringen** *Nachricht* to spread sth; *Geld* to spend sth; **da verkehrt vielleicht ein ~!** there's a really strange crowd there!

**Völkchen** *nt (col: Gruppe)* lot *(col)*, crowd. **ein ~ für**

**sich sein** to be a race apart.
**Völker-**: ~**bund** m (Hist) League of Nations; ~**kunde** f ethnology; ~**mord** m genocide; ~**recht** nt international law; **v~rechtlich 1** adj Vertrag, Anerkennung under international law; Frage, Thema, Standpunkt of international law; **2** adv according to international law; ~**verständigung** f international understanding; ~**wanderung** f (Hist) migration of peoples; (hum) mass migration.
**volkreich** adj populous.
**Volks-** in cpds popular; (auf ein Land bezogen) national; (Pol, esp DDR) people's; ~**abstimmung** f plebiscite; ~**armee** f People's Army; ~**ausgabe** f popular edition; ~**befragung** f public opinion poll; ~**begehren** nt petition for a referendum; ~**belustigung** f public entertainment; ~**bibliothek** f public library; ~**bildung** f national education; (Erwachsenenbildung) adult education; ~**deutsche(r)** mf ethnic German; ~**dichter** m poet of the people; **v~eigen** adj (DDR) nationally-owned; (in Namen) People's Own; ~**einkommen** nt national income; ~**empfinden** nt public feeling; das gesunde ~**empfinden** popular sentiment; ~**entscheid** m referendum; ~**erhebung** f national uprising; ~**feind** m enemy of the people; **v~feindlich** adj hostile to the people; ~**fest** nt public festival; (Jahrmarkt) fair; ~**front** f (Pol) popular front; ~**gesundheit** f public health; ~**glaube(n)** m popular belief; ~**gruppe** f ethnic group; ~**held** m popular hero; (Held des Landes) national hero; ~**hochschule** f adult education centre (Brit) or center (US); ~**krankheit** f widespread disease; ~**kunde** f folklore; ~**lauf** m fun run; ~**lied** nt folk song; ~**märchen** nt folktale; ~**meinung** f public or popular opinion; ~**menge** f crowd, mob (pej); ~**mund** m vernacular; ~**musik** f folk music; ~**nähe** f popular appeal; ~**partei** f people's party; ~**polizei** f (DDR) People's Police; ~**republik** f people's republic; ~**sage** f folk legend; ~**schicht** f level of society; ~**schule** f (dated) ≈ elementary school; ~**seuche** f epidemic; ~**stamm** m tribe; ~**stimme** f voice of the people; ~**stück** nt dialect folk play; ~**tanz** m folk dance; ~**theater** nt folk theatre (Brit) or theater (US); ~**tracht** f traditional costume; ~**tum** nt national traditions pl, folklore; **v~tümlich** adj folk attr, folksy (col); (traditionell, überliefert) traditional; (beliebt) popular; ~**vermögen** nt national wealth; ~**versammlung** f people's assembly; (Kundgebung) public gathering; ~**vertreter** m representative of the people; ~**vertretung** f representative body (of the people); ~**wahl** f direct election(s pl); ~**wirt** m economist; ~**wirtschaft** f national economy; (Fach) economics sing, political economy; ~**wirtschaftler** m economist; ~**zählung** f (national) census; ~**zugehörigkeit** f ethnic origin.
**voll 1** adj full; Haar thick; Satz, Service, Erfolg complete; Wahrheit whole. ~ **von** or **mit etw** full of sth; (bedeckt mit) covered with sth; **mit ~em Mund** with one's mouth full; **aus dem ~en schöpfen** to draw on unlimited resources; **die Uhr schlägt nur alle ~en Stunden** the clock only strikes the full hour; **die Zahl ist** ~ the numbers are complete; **in ~er Fahrt** at full speed; **in ~er Größe** (Bild) life-size; (bei plötzlicher Erscheinung etc) large as life; **jdn nicht für ~ nehmen** not to take sb seriously; ~ **sein** (col) (satt) to be full (up); (betrunken) to be plastered (col). **2** adv fully. ~ **und ganz** completely, wholly; **eine Rechnung ~ bezahlen** to pay a bill in full.
**volladen** vt sep irreg to load up. **vollgeladen** fully-laden.

**voll|auf** adv fully, completely. **das genügt** ~ that's quite enough; ~ **zu tun haben** to have quite enough to do.
**vollaufen** vi sep irreg aux sein to fill up. **etw** ~ **lassen** to fill sth (up); **sich** ~ **lassen** (col) to get tanked up (col).
**Voll-**: **v~automatisch** adj fully automatic; ~**bad** nt (proper) bath; ~**bart** m (full) beard; **v~bekommen*** vt sep irreg to (manage to) fill; **v~berechtigt** adj attr with full rights; ~**beschäftigung** f full employment; ~**besitz** m: **im ~besitz +gen** in full possession of; ~**bild** nt (Med: von Krankheit) full-blown form.
**Vollblut** nt no pl thoroughbred.
**Vollblut-** in cpds (lit: Tier) thoroughbred; (fig) full-blooded.
**Voll-**: ~**blüter** m - thoroughbred; **v~blütig** adj thoroughbred; (fig) full-blooded; ~**bremsung** f emergency stop; **eine ~bremsung machen** to slam on the brakes (col); **v~bringen*** vt insep irreg (ausführen) to accomplish, to achieve; Wunder to perform; **v~busig** adj full-bosomed; ~**dampf** m (Naut) **mit ~dampf** at full steam; **v~elektronisch** adj fully electronic.
**voll|enden*** insep **1** vt to complete. **2** vr (zum Abschluß kommen) to come to an end; (vollkommen werden) to be completed.
**voll|endet** adj (vollkommen) completed; Tugend, Schönheit perfect; Mensch accomplished. **nach ~em 18. Lebensjahr** upon completion of one's 18th year.
**voll|ends** adv (a) (völlig) completely. (b) (besonders) especially.
**Voll|endung** f no pl completion; (Vollkommenheit) perfection.
**voller** adj full (gen of).
**Völlerei** f gluttony.
**voll|essen** vr sep irreg (col) to gorge oneself.
**Volleyball** ['vɔli-] m volleyball.
**vollfett** adj full fat.
**vollführen*** vt insep to execute, to perform.
**Voll-**: ~**gas** nt no pl full speed or throttle; ~**gas geben** to go flat out (col); **v~gefüllt** nt: **im ~gefühl +gen** fully aware of; ~**genuß** m: **im ~genuß +gen** in full enjoyment of; **v~gießen** vt sep irreg to fill (up); **v~gültig** adj attr Paß fully valid; Ersatz completely satisfactory; ~**gummi** nt or m solid rubber; ~**idiot** m (col) complete idiot.
**völlig 1** adj complete. **2** adv completely. **es genügt** ~ that's quite enough; **er hat** ~ **recht** he's absolutely right.
**Voll-**: **v~jährig** adj of age; **v~jährig werden/sein** to come/be of age; ~**jährige(r)** mf decl as adj major; ~**jährigkeit** f majority no art; **v~kaskoversichert** adj comprehensively insured; ~**kasko(versicherung** f) nt fully comprehensive insurance; **v~klimatisiert** adj fully air-conditioned.
**vollkommen 1** adj perfect; (völlig) complete, absolute. **sein Glück war** ~ his happiness was complete. **2** adv completely.
**Vollkommenheit** f no pl siehe adj perfection; completeness.
**Voll-**: ~**kornbrot** nt wholemeal (Brit) or wholewheat (US) bread; **v~machen** vt sep (a) Gefäß to fill (up); Zahl, Dutzend to make up; (b) (col) Hosen, Windeln to fill; ~**macht** f -en power, authority no pl, no indef art; (Urkunde) power of attorney; ~**matrose** m able-bodied seaman; ~**milch** f full-cream milk; ~**mitglied** nt full member; ~**mond** m full moon; **heute ist ~mond** there's a full moon tonight; **v~mundig** adj Wein full-bodied;

**~narkose** *f* general anaesthetic *(Brit) or* anesthetic *(US)*; **v~packen** *vt sep (lit, fig)* to pack full; *jdn* to load up; **~pension** *f* full board *(Brit)*, American plan *(US)*; **v~pumpen** *vt sep* to fill (up); **~rausch** *m* drunken stupor; **einen ~rausch haben** to be in a drunken stupor; **v~reif** *adj* fully ripe; **v~saugen** *vr sep irreg* to become saturated; **v~schlank** *adj* plump, stout; **v~schmieren** *sep* **1** *vt* to mess up; **2** *vr* to make oneself all messy; **v~schreiben** *vt sep irreg Heft, Seite* to fill; *Tafel* to cover (with writing).

**vollständig 1** *adj* complete; *Adresse* full *attr.* **etw ~ machen** to complete sth. **2** *adv* completely, entirely.

**Vollständigkeit** *f no pl* completeness.

**vollstopfen** *vt sep* to cram full.

**vollstrecken\*** *vt insep (Jur)* to execute.

**Vollstreckung** *f (Jur)* execution.

**Voll-: v~tanken** *vti sep* to fill up; **v~tönend** *adj* resonant, sonorous; **~treffer** *m (lit, fig)* bull's eye; **v~trunken** *adj* completely drunk; **~versammlung** *f* general assembly; **~waise** *f* orphan; **v~wertig** *adj* full *attr; Stellung* equal; *Ersatz* fully adequate; **~wertkost** *f* wholefoods *pl*; **v~zählig** *adj usu pred* complete; **sie waren v~zählig anwesend** they were all present.

**vollziehen\*** *insep irreg* **1** *vt* to carry out, to execute; *Trauung* to perform; *Ehe* to consummate; *Bruch* to make. **die ~de Gewalt** the executive (power). **2** *vr* to take place; *(jds Schicksal)* to be fulfilled.

**Vollziehung** *f siehe vt* carrying out, execution; performance; consummation; making.

**Vollzug** *m no pl* **(a)** *(Straf~)* penal system. **(b)** = **Vollziehung**.

**Vollzugs-: ~anstalt** *f (form)* penal institution; **~beamte(r)** *m (form)* warder.

**Volontär(in** *f)* [volon'tɛːɐ, -'tɛːərɪn] *m* trainee.

**volontieren\*** [volon'tiːrən] *vi* to be working as a trainee *(bei* with*)*.

**Volt** [vɔlt] *nt* - volt.

**Volt-** [vɔlt-]: **~meter** *nt* voltmeter; **~zahl** *f* voltage.

**Volumen** [vo'luːmən] *nt, pl* - *(lit, fig)* volume.

**vom** = **von dem. ~ 10. September an** from the 10th September.

**von** *prep +dat* **(a)** *(Ausgangspunkt)* from. **nördlich ~** to the north of; **~ ... an** from ...; **Waren ~ 5 Mark an** *or* **ab** goods from 5 marks (upwards); **~ heute an** *or* **ab** from today (on); **~ ... aus** from ...; **~ dort aus** from there; **etw ~ sich aus tun** to do sth of one's own accord; **~ ... bis** from ... to; **~ morgens bis abends** from morning till night; **~ ... zu** from ... to; **etw ~ etw nehmen/abreißen** to take/tear sth off sth; **~ einer Brücke springen** to jump off a bridge; **~ wo/wann ...?** where/when ... from?

**(b)** *(Ursache, Urheberschaft, im Passiv)* by. **das Gedicht ist ~ Schiller** the poem is by Schiller; **ein Kind ~ jdm kriegen** to have a child by sb; **~ etw müde** tired from sth.

**(c)** *(als Genitiv)* of. **jeweils zwei ~ zehn** two out of every ten; **ein Riese ~ einem Mann** *(col)* a giant of a man; **nett ~ dir** nice of you; **die Königin ~ England** the queen of England; **der Geburtstag ~ meinem Vater** my father's birthday; **ein „~ (und zu)" sein** to have a handle to one's name.

**(d)** *(über)* about. **er erzählte vom Urlaub** he talked about his holiday; **da weiß ich nichts ~** *(col)* I don't know anything about it.

**(e)** *(col)* **~ wegen** no way! *(col)*; **~ mir aus** OK by me.

**von|einander** *adv* from each other; *wissen* of each other.

**vonnöten** *adj:* **~ sein** to be necessary.

**vonstatten** *adv:* **~ gehen** *(stattfinden)* to take place; **alles ging gut ~** everything went well.

**vor 1** *prep +acc or dat* **(a)** *+dat (räumlich)* in front of; *(außerhalb von)* outside; *(~ Hintergrund)* against; *(in jds Achtung)* in the eyes of; *(bei Reihenfolge)* before. **~ der Kirche rechts abbiegen** turn right before the church; **~ allen Dingen, ~ allem** above all. **(b)** *+acc (Richtung)* in front of; *(außerhalb von)* outside. **(c)** *+dat (zeitlich)* before. **~ zwanzig (Minuten) ~ drei** twenty (minutes) to three; **das liegt noch ~ uns** this is still to come; **~ fünf Jahren** five years ago. **(d)** *+acc* **~ sich hin summen** to hum to oneself; **~ sich hin schreiben/arbeiten** to write/work away. **(e)** *+dat* **~ sich her** before one, in front of one. **(f)** *+dat (Ursache angebend)* with. **~ Kälte zittern** to shiver with cold; **~ Hunger sterben** to die of hunger; **~ lauter Arbeit** because of the amount of work. **(g) sich ~ jdm verstecken** to hide from sb. **2** *adv* **~ und zurück** backwards and forwards; **alle kleinen Kinder ~!** all small children to the front!; **da sei Gott ~** *(N Ger col)* God forbid.

**vor|ab** *adv* to begin with.

**Vor-: ~abdruck** *m* preprint; **~abend** *m* evening before; **am ~abend der Revolution** *(fig)* on the eve of revolution; **~ahnung** *f* premonition.

**voran** *adv* **(a)** *(vorn, an der Spitze)* first. **ihm/ihr ~** in front of him/her; **mit dem Kopf ~ fallen** to fall head first. **(b)** *(vorwärts)* forwards. **nur** *or* **immer ~** keep going.

**voran-** *pref siehe auch* **voraus-; ~bringen** *vt sep irreg* to make progress with; **~gehen** *vi sep irreg aux sein* **(a)** *(an der Spitze gehen)* to go first *or* in front; *(fig: Einleitung etc)* to precede *(dat* sth*)*; **jdm ~gehen** to go ahead of sb; **(b)** *(zeitlich vor jdm gehen)* to go on ahead; **einer Sache** *(dat)* **~gehen** to precede sth; **(c)** *auch vi impers (Fortschritte machen)* to make progress *or* headway; **~kommen** *vi sep irreg aux sein* to get on; **nur langsam ~kommen** to make slow progress.

**Vor-: ~anmeldung** *f* appointment; **~anschlag** *m* estimate.

**voran-: ~stellen** *vt sep* to put in front *(dat* of*)*; *(fig)* to give precedence *(dat* over*)*; **~treiben** *vt sep irreg* to drive forward.

**Vor-: ~ankündigung** *f* advance notice; **~arbeit** *f* preliminary work, groundwork; **v~arbeiten** *sep* **1** *vi* to work in advance; **2** *vr* to work one's way forward; **~arbeiter** *m* foreman; **~arbeiterin** *f* forewoman.

**voraus** *adv* **(a)** *(voran)* in front *(+dat* of*)*. **er ist den anderen/seiner Zeit ~** he is ahead of the others/his time. **(b)** *(vorher)* **im ~** in advance.

**Voraus-: v~blicken** *vi sep* to look ahead; **v~blickend 1** *adj* foresighted; **2** *adv* with regard to the future; **v~eilen** *vi sep aux sein (lit, fig)* to hurry on ahead; **v~fahren** *vi sep irreg aux sein (an der Spitze)* to drive/go in front *(dat* of*)*; *(früher)* to drive/go on ahead; **v~gehen** *vi sep irreg aux sein siehe* **vorangehen (a, b); v~gesetzt** *adj* **v~gesetzt, (daß) ...** provided (that) ...; **v~haben** *vt sep irreg* **jdm viel v~haben** to have a great advantage over sb; **v~planen** *vti sep* to plan ahead; **~sage** *f* prediction; *(Wetter~)* forecast; **v~sagen** *vt sep* to predict *(jdm* for sb*)*; *Wetter* to forecast; **jdm die Zukunft v~sagen** to foretell sb's future; **v~schauend** *adj, adv* = **v~blickend; v~schicken** *vt sep* to send on ahead *(dat* of*)*; *(fig: vorher sagen)* to say in advance *(dat* of*)*; **v~sehen** *vt sep irreg* to foresee.

**voraussetzen** *vt sep* to presuppose; *(als selbstver-*

*ständlich, sicher annehmen)* to take for granted; *(erfordern)* to require, to demand. **etw als bekannt ~** to assume that everyone knows sth.

**Voraussetzung** f prerequisite, (pre)condition; *(Qualifikation)* qualification; *(Erfordernis)* requirement; *(Annahme)* assumption. **unter der ~, daß ...** on condition that ...

**Voraus-:** ~**sicht** f foresight; *(Erwartung)* anticipation; **aller ~sicht nach** in all probability; **v~sichtlich 1** adj expected; **2** adv probably; **er wird v~sichtlich gewinnen** he is expected to win; ~**zahlung** f advance payment.

**Vorbau** m porch; *(Balkon)* balcony.

**vorbauen** sep **1** vt *(anbauen)* to build on (in front). **2** vi *(Vorkehrungen treffen)* to take precautions.

**Vorbedacht** m: **mit/ohne ~** *(Überlegung)* with/without due consideration; *(Absicht)* intentionally/unintentionally.

**Vorbedingung** f precondition.

**Vorbehalt** m **-e** reservation. **unter dem ~, daß ...** with the reservation that ...; **unter ~** with reservations.

**vorbehalten\*** vt sep irreg **sich** *(dat)* **etw ~** to reserve sth (for oneself); *Recht* to reserve sth; **diese Entscheidung bleibt ihm ~** this decision is left up to him; **alle Rechte ~** all rights reserved; **Änderungen (sind) ~** subject to alteration.

**vorbehaltlich** prep +gen *(form)* subject to.

**vorbehaltlos** adj unconditional, unreserved.

**vorbei** adv **(a)** *(räumlich)* past, by. **~ an** *(+dat)* past. **(b)** *(zeitlich)* **~ sein** *(Sorgen)* to be over; *(Schmerzen)* to be gone; **damit ist es nun ~** that's all over now; **aus und ~** over and done with.

**vorbei-** pref *(vorüber)* past; *(zu Besuch)* over; ~**bringen** vt sep irreg *(col)* to drop off; ~**dürfen** vi sep irreg *(col)* to be allowed past; **dürfte ich bitte ~?** could I get past or by, please?; ~**fahren** vi sep irreg aux sein to pass *(an jdm/etw* sb/sth*)*; **bei jdm ~fahren** vi sep irreg aux sein **(a)** *(lit, fig)* to go past, to pass *(an jdm/etw* sb/sth*)*; **an etw** *(dat)* ~**gehen** *(fig: nicht beachten)* to overlook sth; **bei jdm ~gehen** *(col)* to drop in on sb; **im V~gehen** *(lit, fig)* in passing; **(b)** *(vergehen)* to pass; **(c)** *(verfehlen)* to miss *(an etw* *(dat)* sth*)*; **Das Leben geht an ihm ~** life is passing him by; ~**kommen** vi sep irreg aux sein **(a)** to pass, to go past *(an jdm/etw* sb/sth*)*; *(an einem Hindernis)* to get past or by; **an einer Aufgabe nicht ~kommen** to be unable to avoid a task; **(b) bei jdm ~kommen** *(col)* to drop or call in on sb; ~**können** vi sep irreg to be able to get past or by *(an etw* *(dat)* sth*)*; ~**lassen** vt sep irreg to let past *(an jdm/etw* sb/sth*)*; ~**laufen** vi sep irreg aux sein *(an jdm/etw* sb/sth*)* to run past; *(col: ~gehen)* to go or walk past; ~**marschieren\*** vi sep aux sein to march past; ~**müssen** vi sep irreg to have to go past *(an jdm/etw* sb/sth*)*; **bei jdm ~müssen** *(col)* to have to call in at sb's; ~**reden** vi sep aux sein *(an etw* *(dat)* ~**reden** to talk around sth; **aneinander ~reden** to talk at cross purposes; ~**ziehen** vi sep irreg aux sein to file past *(an jdm/etw* sb/sth*)*.

**vorbelastet** adj handicapped; *(voreingenommen)* biased *(von* because of*)*.

**Vorbemerkung** f introductory remark.

**vorbereiten\*** vtr sep to prepare *(auf +acc* for*)*.

**vorbereitend** adj attr preparatory, preliminary.

**Vorbereitung** f preparation. ~**en (für** or **zu etw) treffen** to make preparations (for sth).

**Vorbereitungs-** in cpds preparatory.

**Vor-:** ~**besitzer** m previous owner; ~**besprechung** f preliminary meeting; **v~bestellen\*** vt sep to book (in advance), to reserve; ~**bestellung** f ad-

vance booking; **v~bestraft** adj previously convicted; **er ist schon einmal v~bestraft** he has a previous conviction; **v~beten** sep **1** vi to lead the prayer/prayers; **2** vt **jdm etw v~beten** *(fig col)* to keep spelling sth out for sb *(col)*.

**Vorbeugehaft** f preventive custody.

**vorbeugen** sep **1** vi to prevent *(einer Sache* *(dat)* sth*)*. **2** vtr to bend forward.

**vorbeugend** adj preventive.

**Vorbeugung** f prevention *(gegen, von* of*)*.

**Vorbeugungs-** in cpds preventive.

**Vorbild** nt model; *(Beispiel)* example *(für jdn* to sb*)*. **er/sein Verhalten kann uns zum ~ dienen** he/his behaviour is an example to us; **sich** *(dat)* **jdn zum ~ nehmen** to model oneself on sb.

**vorbildlich** adj exemplary; **sich benehmen** in an exemplary fashion.

**Vor-:** ~**bildung** f educational background; ~**bote** m *(fig)* herald.

**vorbringen** vt sep irreg *Plan* to propose; *Meinung, Wunsch, Forderung* to express, to state; *Einwand, Beschwerde* to make; *Entschuldigung* to offer.

**Vor-:** **v~christlich** adj pre-Christian; ~**dach** nt canopy; **v~datieren\*** vt sep to postdate; ~**denker** m prophet.

**Vorder-:** ~**achse** f front axle; ~**ansicht** f front view; ~**asien** nt Near East; ~**bein** nt foreleg.

**Vordere(r)** mf decl as adj person in front.

**vordere(r, s)** adj front.

**Vorder-:** ~**front** f frontage; ~**fuß** m forefoot; ~**grund** m foreground; *(fig)* fore(front); **sich in den ~grund drängen** to push oneself to the fore; **im ~grund stehen** *(fig)* to be to the fore; **v~gründig** adj *(oberflächlich)* superficial; ~**mann** m, pl ~**männer** person in front; **etw auf ~mann bringen** *(fig col)* to get sth into shape; ~**pfote** f front paw; ~**rad** nt front wheel; ~**radantrieb** m *(Aut)* front-wheel drive; ~**seite** f front; *(von Münze)* head; ~**sitz** m front seat.

**vorderste(r, s)** adj superl of **vordere(r, s)** front(most). **der/die V~ in der Schlange** the first person in the queue *(Brit)* or line *(US)*.

**Vorder-:** ~**teil** m or nt front; ~**tür** f front door; ~**zahn** m front tooth; ~**zimmer** nt front room.

**vordränge(l)n** vr sep to push to the front. **sich in der Schlange ~** to jump the queue *(Brit)*, to push to the front of the line *(US)*.

**vordringen** vi sep irreg aux sein to advance. **bis zu jdm/etw ~** to get as far as sb/sth.

**vordringlich** adj urgent, pressing.

**Vordruck** m form.

**vor|ehelich** adj attr premarital.

**vor|eilig** adj rash. ~**e Schlüsse ziehen** to jump to conclusions.

**vor|einander** adv *(räumlich)* in front of each other; *(einander gegenüber)* face to face.

**vor|eingenommen** adj prejudiced, biased.

**Vor|eingenommenheit** f no pl prejudice, bias.

**Vor|einstellung** f *(Comp)* default.

**vor|enthalten\*** vt sep irreg **jdm etw ~** to withhold sth from sb.

**Vor|entscheidung** f preliminary decision.

**vor|erst** adv for the time being.

**Vorfahr** m *(wk)* **-en, -en** forefather, ancestor.

**vorfahren** sep irreg **1** vi aux sein **(a)** to go or move forward. **(b)** *(ankommen)* to drive up. **(c)** *(früher fahren)* to go on ahead. **(d)** *(an der Spitze fahren)* to drive in front. **2** vt **(a)** *(weiter nach vorn fahren)* to move up or forward. **(b)** *(vor den Eingang fahren)* to drive up.

**Vorfahrt** f no pl right of way. „**~ (be)achten**" ''give way" *(Brit)*, "yield" *(US)*; **jdm die** ~ **nehmen** to ignore sb's right of way.

**Vorfahrts-:** **v~berechtigt** *adj* **v~berechtigt sein** to have the right of way; **~regel** *f* rule on the right of way; **~schild** *nt* give way *(Brit)* or yield *(US)* sign; **~straße** *f* major road.

**Vorfall** *m* incident, occurrence.

**vorfallen** *vi sep irreg aux sein* to occur, to happen.

**Vor-:** **~feld** *nt (fig)* run-up *(+gen* to*)*; **v~fertigen** *vt sep* to prefabricate; **~film** *m* short; **v~finden** *vt sep irreg* to find, to discover; **~freude** *f* anticipation; **~frühling** *m* early spring.

**vorfühlen** *vi sep (fig)* to put out feelers. **bei jdm** ~ to sound sb out.

**vorführen** *vt sep* **(a)** *(zeigen)* to present; *Film* to show; *Mode* to model; *Übung, (Vertreter) Gerät* to demonstrate *(dat* to*)*; *Theaterstück auch, Kunststücke* to perform *(dat* to, in front of*)*. **(b)** *Angeklagten* to bring forward.

**Vorführung** *f* presentation; *(von Filmen)* showing; *(von Mode)* modelling *(Brit)*, modeling *(US)*; *(von Geräten, Modellen, Übungen)* demonstration; *(von Theaterstück, Kunststücken)* performance.

**Vorführwagen** *m (Wagen)* demonstrator.

**Vorgabe** *f* handicap.

**Vorgang** *m* **(a)** *(Ereignis)* event, occurrence; *(Ablauf, Hergang)* series of events. **(b)** *(Sci)* process.

**Vorgänger(in** *f) m -* predecessor.

**Vorgarten** *m* front garden.

**vorgaukeln** *vt sep* **jdm etw** ~ to lead sb to believe in sth; **jdm** ~, **daß** ... to lead sb to believe that ...

**vorgeben** *vt sep irreg* **(a)** *(vortäuschen)* to pretend; *(fälschlich beteuern)* to profess. **(b)** *(Sport)* **50 Meter/5 Sekunden** ~ to give a start of 50 metres/5 seconds.

**Vorgebirge** *nt* foothills *pl.*

**vorgedruckt** *adj* pre-printed.

**vorgefaßt** *adj Meinung* preconceived.

**Vorgefühl** *nt* anticipation; *(böse Ahnung)* presentiment.

**vorgehen** *vi sep irreg aux sein* **(a)** *(handeln)* to act, to proceed. **gerichtlich gegen jdn** ~ to take legal action against sb. **(b)** *(geschehen, vor sich gehen)* to go on, to happen. **(c)** *(Uhr) (spätere Zeit anzeigen)* to be fast; *(zu schnell gehen)* to gain. **(d)** *(nach vorn gehen)* to go forward. **(e)** *(vorangehen)* to go first; *(früher gehen)* to go on ahead. **(f)** *(den Vorrang haben)* to come first, to have priority.

**Vorgehen** *nt no pl* action.

**Vor-:** **v~gerückt** *adj Stunde* late; *Alter* advanced; **~geschichte** *f* **(a)** *(eines Falles)* past history; **(b)** *(Urgeschichte)* prehistory, prehistoric times *pl*; **v~geschichtlich** *adj* prehistoric; **~geschmack** *m (fig)* foretaste; **v~geschritten** *adj* advanced; **im v~geschrittenen Alter** at an advanced age; **zu v~geschrittener Stunde** at a late hour.

**Vorgesetzte(r)** *mf decl as adj* superior.

**vorgestern** *adv* the day before yesterday. **von** ~ *(fig)* antiquated.

**vorgreifen** *vi sep irreg* to anticipate; *(verfrüht handeln)* to act prematurely. **jdm** ~ to forestall sb; **einer Sache** *(dat)* ~ to anticipate sth.

**Vorgriff** *m* anticipation *(auf +acc* of*)*.

**vorhaben** *vt sep irreg* to intend; *(planen)* to have planned. **was haben Sie heute vor?** what are your plans for today?, what do you have on today?

**Vorhaben** *nt plan; (Absicht)* intention.

**Vorhalle** *f (Diele)* entrance hall; *(von Parlament)* lobby.

**vorhalten** *sep irreg* **1** *vt* **(a)** **jdm etw** ~ *(vorwerfen)* to reproach sb for sth; *(als Beispiel)* to hold sth up

to sb. **(b)** *(vor den Körper halten)* to hold up; *(beim Niesen etc)* to put in front of one's mouth. **mit vorgehaltener Pistole** at gunpoint. **2** *vi (anhalten)* to last.

**Vorhaltung** *f usu pl* reproach.

**Vorhand** *f (Sport)* forehand.

**vorhanden** *adj (verfügbar)* available; *(existierend)* existing.

**Vorhang** *m, pl* **Vorhänge** curtain.

**Vorhängeschloß** *nt* padlock.

**Vorhaut** *f* foreskin.

**vorheizen** *vt* to preheat.

**vorher** *adv* before(hand); *(früher)* before. **am Tage** ~ the day before, the previous day.

**vorher-:** **~bestimmen\*** *vt sep* to determine in advance; *Schicksal* to predetermine; *(Gott)* to preordain; **es war ihm ~bestimmt** ... he was predestined ...; **~gehen** *vi sep irreg aux sein* to go before or in front; *(fig)* to precede; **~gehend** *adj Tag, Ereignisse* preceding.

**vorherig** [foːˈheːrɪç] *adj attr* prior, previous; *(ehemalig)* former.

**Vorherrschaft** *f* predominance, supremacy.

**vorherrschen** *vi sep* to predominate, to prevail.

**vorherrschend** *adj* predominant; *(weitverbreitet)* prevalent.

**Vorher-:** **~sage** *f* forecast; **v~sagen** *vt sep* = **voraussagen**; **v~sehbar** *adj* predictable; **v~sehen** *vt sep irreg* to foresee.

**vorhin** *adv* a little while ago.

**vorhinein** *adv:* **im** ~ in advance.

**Vor-:** **~hof** *m* forecourt; **~hut** *f* **-en** *(Mil)* advance guard.

**vorig** *adj attr* previous; *Jahr, Woche etc* last.

**Vor-:** **~jahr** *nt* previous year, year before; **v~jährig** *adj* of the previous year; **v~jammern** *vti sep* **jdm (etwas) v~jammern** to moan to sb *(von* about*)*; **~kämpfer(in** *f) m* pioneer *(für* of*)*; **v~kauen** *vt sep Nahrung* to chew; **jdm etw v~kauen** *(fig col)* to spoonfeed sth to sb *(col)*; **~kaufsrecht** *nt (Comm)* option *(an +dat* on, to buy*)*.

**Vorkehrung** *f* **~en treffen** to take precautions.

**Vorkenntnis** *f* previous knowledge *no pl.*

**vorknöpfen** *vt sep (fig col)* **sich** *(dat)* **jdn** ~ to take sb to task.

**vorkochen** *vt* to precook.

**vorkommen** *vi sep irreg aux sein* **(a)** *auch vi impers (sich ereignen)* to happen. **das soll nicht wieder** ~ it won't happen again; **so was soll** ~! that's life! **(b)** *(vorhanden sein, auftreten)* to occur; *(Pflanzen, Tiere)* to be found. **(c)** *(erscheinen)* to seem *(jdm* to sb*)*. **sich** *(dat)* **überflüssig** ~ to feel superfluous; **sich** *(dat)* **klug** ~ to think one is clever. **(d)** *(nach vorn kommen)* to come forward.

**Vorkommen** *nt -* *(no pl: das Auftreten)* occurrence; *(Min)* deposit.

**Vorkommnis** *nt* incident.

**Vorkoster** *m* taster; *(fig)* guinea pig.

**Vorkriegs-** *in cpds* pre-war; **~zeit** *f* pre-war period.

**vorladen** *vt sep irreg (bei Gericht)* to summons.

**Vorladung** *f* summons.

**Vorlage** *f* **-n** **(a)** *no pl (von Dokument, Scheck etc)* presentation; *(von Beweismaterial)* submission. **(b)** *(Muster) (zum Stricken, Nähen)* pattern; *(Liter)* model. **etw nach einer** ~ **machen** to model sth on sth. **(c)** *(Entwurf)* draft; *(Parl: Gesetzes~)* bill.

**vorlassen** *vt sep irreg* **(a)** *(col)* **jdn** ~ *(nach vorn gehen lassen)* to let sb go in front; *(überholen lassen)* to let sb past. **(b)** *(Empfang gewähren)* to allow in.

**Vorlauf** *m (Sport)* preliminary heat/round.

**vorlaufen** *vi sep irreg aux sein (col) (voraus)* to run on ahead; *(nach vorn)* to run to the front.

**Vorläufer** *m* forerunner *(auch Ski)*, precursor.

**vorläufig 1** *adj* temporary; *(provisorisch)* provisional. **2** *adv (einstweilig)* temporarily; *(fürs erste)* for the time being.

**vorlaut** *adj* cheeky, impertinent.

**Vorleben** *nt* past (life).

**Vorlege-:** ~**besteck** *nt* serving cutlery; *(Tranchierbesteck)* carvers *pl*; ~**löffel** *m* serving spoon.

**vorlegen** *vt sep* **(a)** to present; *Paß, Zeugnisse* to produce; *Beweismaterial* to submit; *(Pol) Entwurf* to table *(Brit)*, to introduce. **(b)** *Speisen* to serve; *(hinlegen) Futter* to put down *(dat* for*)*. **(c)** *Riegel* to put across.

**Vorleger** *m* - mat; *(Bett~ auch)* (bedside) rug.

**vorlehnen** *vr sep* to lean forward.

**Vorleistung** *f (Econ) (Vorausbezahlung)* advance (payment); *(Vorarbeit)* preliminary work; *(Pol)* prior concession.

**vorlesen** *vti sep irreg* to read aloud. **jdm (etw)** ~ to read (sth) to sb.

**Vorlesung** *f (Univ)* lecture; *(Vorlesungsreihe)* course (of lectures). **über etw** *(acc)* ~**en halten** to give (a course of) lectures on sth; ~**en hören** to go to lectures.

**Vorlesungsverzeichnis** *nt* lecture timetable.

**vorletzte(r, s)** *adj* last but one, penultimate. **im** ~**n Jahr** the year before last.

**Vorliebe** *f* predilection. **etw mit** ~ **tun** to particularly like doing sth.

**vorliebnehmen** *vi sep irreg* **mit jdm/etw** ~ to make do with sb/sth.

**vorliegen** *vi sep irreg (zur Verfügung stehen)* to be available; *(Urteil)* to be known; *(eingereicht, vorgelegt sein)* to have come in. **jdm** ~ *(Unterlagen, Akten etc)* to be with sb; **etw liegt gegen jdn vor** sb is charged with sth; **hier liegt ein Irrtum vor** there is an error here.

**vorliegend** *adj attr Gründe* existing; *Akten, Unterlagen* on hand; *Frage* at issue; *Ergebnisse* available.

**vorlügen** *vt sep irreg* **jdm etwas** ~ to lie to sb.

**vormachen** *vt sep* **(a)** **jdm etw** ~ *(zeigen)* to show sb how to do sth. **(b)** *(fig)* **jdm etwas** ~ *(täuschen)* to fool sb; **er läßt sich** *(dat)* **von niemandem etwas** ~ nobody can fool him; **mach mir doch nichts vor** don't try and fool me.

**Vormacht(stellung)** *f* supremacy *(gegenüber* over*)*.

**vormals** *adv* formerly.

**Vormarsch** *m (Mil)* advance. **im** ~ **sein** to be on the advance; *(fig)* to be gaining ground.

**vormerken** *vt sep* to make a note of; *(bei Bestellung auch)* to take an order for; *Plätze* to book. **sich für einen Kursus** ~ **lassen** to put oneself down for a course.

**Vormittag** *m* morning. **am** ~ in the morning.

**vormittag** *adv* **heute/gestern/morgen** ~ this/ yesterday/tomorrow morning.

**vormittags** *adv* in the morning; *(jeden Morgen)* in the morning(s).

**Vormonat** *m* previous month.

**Vormund** *m* -e guardian. **ich brauche keinen** ~ *(fig)* I don't need anyone to tell me what to do.

**Vormundschaft** *f* guardianship. **jdn unter** ~ **stellen** to place sb under the care of a guardian.

**vorn** *adv* **(a)** in front. *(am vorderen Ende, auf der Vorderseite)* at the front. **von** ~ from the front; **nach** ~ *(ganz nach* ~*)* to the front; *(weiter nach* ~*)* forwards; **von weit** ~ from the very front; ~ **im Buch/in der Schlange/auf der Liste** at the front of the book/queue *(Brit) or* line *(US)*/at the top of the list; **sich** ~ **anstellen** to join the front of the queue *(Brit) or* line *(US)*; ~ **im Bild** in the front of the picture; **von** ~ from the front; **jdn von** ~ **sehen** to see sb's face; ~ **im Auto/Bus** in the front of the car/ bus; **das Buch ist** ~ **schmutzig** the front of the book is dirty; **das Auto da** ~ the car ahead there; **sie waren ziemlich weit** ~ they were quite far ahead.

**(b)** *(am Anfang)* **von** ~ from the beginning; **von** ~ **anfangen** to start from the beginning; *(von neuem)* to start (all) over again; *(neues Leben)* to make a fresh start; **er betrügt sie von** ~ **bis hinten** he deceives her right, left and centre *(Brit) or* center *(US)*.

**Vorname** *m* Christian name, first name.

**vorne** *adv* = **vorn**.

**vornehm** *adj* **(a)** *(von hohem Rang) Familie, Kreise* distinguished; *(von adliger Herkunft)* aristocratic; *(fein) Herr, Dame* genteel; *Manieren, Art, Benehmen* refined; *(edel) Gesinnung, Charakter, Handeln* noble. **die** ~**e Gesellschaft** high society; **in** ~**en Kreisen** in polite society. **(b)** *(elegant, luxuriös)* smart, posh *(col)*; *Geschäft* exclusive, posh *(col)*; *Kleid, Äußeres* elegant, stylish.

**vornehmen** *vt sep irreg* **(a)** *(ausführen)* to carry out. **(b)** **sich** *(dat)* **etw** ~ *(in Angriff nehmen)* to get to work on sth; *(planen, vorhaben)* to intend to do sth; *(Vorsatz fassen)* to have resolved to do sth; **sich** *(dat)* **zuviel** ~ to take on too much. **(c)** **sich** *(dat)* **jdn** ~ *(col)* to have a word with sb.

**vornehmlich** *adv (hauptsächlich, vor allem)* principally; *(vorzugsweise)* first and foremost.

**vorneigen** *vtr sep* to lean forward.

**vorn(e)weg** *adv* in front; *(als erstes)* first.

**vorn-:** ~**herein** *adv:* **von** ~**herein** from the outset; ~**über** *adv* forwards.

**Vor|ort-** *m (Vorstadt)* suburb.

**Vor-Ort-** *in cpds* on-site; ~**-Kontrolle** *f* on-site supervision.

**Vor|ortzug** *m* suburban train; *(im Berufsverkehr)* commuter train.

**Vor-:** ~**platz** *m* forecourt; ~**posten** *m (Mil)* outpost; **v**~**preschen** *vi sep aux sein (lit, fig)* to press ahead; ~**programm** *nt (esp Film)* supporting programme *(Brit) or* program *(US)*; **v**~**programmieren*** *vt sep (lit, fig)* to preprogramme *(Brit)*, to preprogram *(US)*; **v**~**programmiert** *adj Erfolg, Antwort* automatic.

**Vorrang** *m no pl* ~ **haben** to have priority; *(vor +dat* over*)*; **jdm/einer Sache (den)** ~ **geben** *or* **einräumen** to give sb/a matter priority.

**vorrangig 1** *adj* of prime importance, priority *attr*. **2** *adv* as a matter of priority.

**Vorrangstellung** *f* pre-eminence *no indef art*.

**Vorrat** *m, pl* **Vorräte** *(an +dat of)* stock; *(von Waren) stocks pl*. **etw auf ~ kaufen** to stock up with sth; **Vorräte anlegen** to lay in a stock; **solange der** ~ **reicht** *(Comm)* while stocks last.

**vorrätig** *adj* in stock; *(verfügbar)* available. **etw nicht mehr** ~ **haben** to be out of sth.

**Vorrats-:** ~**kammer** *f* store cupboard; *(für Lebensmittel)* larder; ~**keller** *m* store room in the cellar; ~**raum** *m* store room; *(in Geschäft)* stock room.

**Vorraum** *m* anteroom; *(Büro)* outer office.

**vorrechnen** *vt sep* **jdm etw** ~ to calculate sth for sb; *(als Kritik)* to point sth out to sb.

**Vorrecht** *nt* prerogative; *(Vergünstigung)* privilege.

**Vorrede** *f* introductory speech; *(Theat)* prologue.

**vorreden** *vt sep (col)* **red mir doch nichts vor** don't give me that *(col)*.

**Vorredner** *m (vorheriger Redner)* previous speaker.

**Vorreiter** *m* forerunner. **den ~ für etw machen** to be the first to do sth.
**vorrennen** *vi sep irreg aux sein (col) (voraus)* to race ahead; *(nach vorn)* to run forward.
**Vorrichtung** *f* device, gadget.
**vorrücken** *sep* **1** *vt* to move forward. **2** *vi aux sein* to move forward; *(Mil)* to advance; *(Uhrzeiger)* to move on. **mit dem Stuhl ~** to move one's chair forward; *siehe* **vorgerückt**.
**Vorruhestand** *m* early retirement.
**Vorruheständler(in** *f)* *m* person taking early retirement.
**Vorrunde** *f (Sport)* preliminary round.
**vorsagen** *sep (Sch)* **1** *vt Lösung* to tell. **2** *vi jdm ~* to tell sb the answer.
**Vorsaison** *f* low season, early season.
**Vorsatz** *m* (firm) intention; *(Jur)* premeditation. **den ~ haben, etw zu tun** to intend to do sth; **den ~ fassen, etw zu tun** to resolve to do sth.
**vorsätzlich** *adj* deliberate; *(Jur)* wilful; *Mord* premeditated. **jdn ~ töten** to kill sb intentionally.
**Vorschau** *f* preview; *(Film)* trailer.
**Vorschein** *m* **zum ~ bringen** *(lit: zeigen)* to produce; *(fig: deutlich machen)* to bring to light; **zum ~ kommen** *(lit: sichtbar werden)* to appear; *(fig: entdeckt werden)* to come to light.
**vorschieben** *vt sep irreg* **(a)** *(davorschieben)* to push in front; *Riegel* to put across; *(nach vorn schieben)* to push forward. **(b)** *(Mil)* **vorgeschobener Posten** advance party. **(c)** *(fig: vorschützen)* to put forward as an excuse. **vorgeschobene Gründe** pretexts *pl*. **(d)** **jdn ~** to put sb forward as a front man.
**vorschießen** *sep irreg* **1** *vt jdm Geld ~* to advance sb money. **2** *vi aux sein* to shoot forward.
**Vorschiff** *nt (Naut)* forecastle.
**Vorschlag** *m* suggestion; *(Rat)* advice; *(Pol: von Kandidaten)* proposal. **auf ~ von** *or* **+gen** at or on the suggestion of.
**vorschlagen** *vt sep irreg* to suggest. **jdn für ein Amt ~** to propose sb for a post; **jdm ~, daß er etw tut** to suggest to sb that he do(es) sth.
**Vorschlaghammer** *m* sledgehammer.
**vorschnell** *adj = voreilig*.
**vorschreiben** *vt sep irreg (befehlen)* to stipulate; *(Menge, Dosis)* to prescribe. **ich lasse mir nichts ~** I won't be dictated to.
**vorschreiten** *vi sep irreg aux sein* to progress; *siehe* **vorgeschritten**.
**Vorschrift** *f* **-en** rule, regulation; *(Anweisung)* instruction. **nach ~ des Arztes** according to doctor's orders; **jdm ~en machen** to give sb orders; **Dienst nach ~** work to rule.
**vorschrifts-:** **~gemäß, ~mäßig** **1** *adj Signal, Verhalten* correct, proper *attr*; **2** *adv* according to (the) regulations; *(laut Anordnung)* as instructed; **~widrig** *adj, adv* contrary to regulations.
**Vorschub** *m*: **jdm/einer Sache ~ leisten** to encourage sb/sth.
**Vorschul-:** *in cpds* preschool.
**Vorschule** *f* nursery school.
**vorschulisch** *adj* preschool *attr*.
**Vorschuß** *m* advance.
**vorschützen** *vt sep* to put forward as a pretext; *Unwissenheit* to plead. **er schützte vor, daß ...** he pretended that ...
**vorschwärmen** *vti sep jdm von jdm/etw ~* to go into raptures over sb/sth.
**vorschweben** *vi sep jdm schwebt etw vor* sb has sth in mind.
**vorschwindeln** *vt sep jdm etwas ~* to lie to sb.
**vorsehen** *sep irreg* **1** *vt* to provide for; *(planen)* to

plan; *Zeit* to allow. **etw für etw ~** *(bestimmen)* to intend sth for sth; *Geld* to earmark sth for sth; **jdn für etw ~** *(bestimmen)* to designate sb for sth; **er ist für dieses Amt vorgesehen** we have him in mind for this post. **2** *vr (sich in acht nehmen)* to take care. **sich vor jdm/etw ~** to beware of sb/sth.
**Vorsehung** *f no pl* **die ~** Providence.
**vorsetzen** *vt sep* **(a)** to move forward; *Fuß* to put forward; *Schüler* to move (up) to the front. **(b)** *(davorsetzen)* to put in front *(vor +acc of)*. **(c)** **jdm etw ~** *(anbieten)* to serve sth up for sb.
**Vorsicht** *f no pl* care; *(bei Gefahr)* caution; *(Behutsamkeit)* wariness. **(jdn) zur ~ (er)mahnen** to advise sb to be careful/cautious/wary; **„~ Stufe"** ''mind the step''; **mit ~** carefully; cautiously; warily; **was er sagt, ist mit ~ zu genießen** *(hum col)* you have to take what he says with a pinch of salt *(col)*; **dieser Wein ist mit ~ zu genießen** *(col)* I should be a bit wary of this wine; **~ ist besser als Nachsicht** *(Prov)* better safe than sorry.
**vorsichtig** *adj* careful; *(besonnen)* cautious; *(mißtrauisch)* wary; *Schätzung* conservative.
**Vorsichts-:** **v~halber** *adv* as a precaution; **~maßnahme** *f* precaution; **~maßnahmen treffen** to take precautions.
**Vor-:** **~silbe** *f* prefix; **v~singen** *sep irreg* **1** *vti* **jdm (etw) v~singen** to sing (sth) to sb. **2** *vi (zur Prüfung)* to have a singing test; **v~sintflutlich** *adj (col)* antediluvian, antiquated.
**Vorsitz** *m* chairmanship; *(Amt eines Präsidenten)* presidency. **den ~ haben** *or* **führen (bei etw)** to be chairman *or* chairperson (of sth); *(bei Sitzung)* to chair sth.
**Vorsitzende(r)** *mf decl as adj* chairman/chairwoman, chairperson; *(von Verein)* president.
**Vorsorge** *f no pl (Vorsichtsmaßnahme)* precaution; *(vorherplanende Fürsorge)* provision(s *pl*) *no def art*; *(Med)* preventive care. **zur ~** as a precaution; **~ treffen** to take precautions; *(fürs Alter)* to make provisions.
**vorsorgen** *vi sep* to make provisions *(daß so that)*. **für etw ~** to make provisions for sth.
**Vorsorge|untersuchung** *f (Med)* regular check-up.
**vorsorglich** **1** *adj* precautionary; *Mensch* cautious. **2** *adv* as a precaution.
**Vorspann** *m* **-e** *(Film, TV)* opening credits *pl*.
**vorspannen** *vt sep Pferde* to harness.
**Vorspeise** *f* starter.
**vorspiegeln** *vt sep* to sham. **jdm ~(, daß ...)** to pretend to sb (that...).
**Vorspiegelung** *f* pretence *(Brit)*, pretense *(US)*. **das ist ~ falscher Tatsachen** that's false pretences.
**Vorspiel** *nt (Einleitung)* prelude; *(Theat)* prologue; *(Sport)* preliminary match; *(bei Geschlechtsverkehr)* foreplay.
**vorspielen** *sep* **1** *vt jdm etw ~ (Mus)* to play sth to sb; *(Theat)* to act sth to sb; *(fig)* to put on an act for sb. **2** *vi (vor Zuhörern)* to play; *(Mus, Theat) (zur Prüfung)* to do one's practical (exam). **jdm ~ *(Mus)*** to play for sb; *(Theat)* to act (a role) in front of sb.
**vorsprechen** *sep irreg* **1** *vt (vortragen)* to recite. **jdm etw ~** to pronounce sth for sb. **2** *vi* **(a)** *(form: jdn aufsuchen)* to call *(bei jdm* on sb). **(b)** *(Theat)* to audition. **jdn ~ lassen** to audition sb.
**vorspringen** *vi sep irreg aux sein* to leap out; *(vorwärts)* to jump forward; *(herausragen)* to jut out; *(Nase, Kinn)* to be prominent.
**vorspringend** *adj* projecting; *Nase, Kinn* prominent.
**Vorsprung** *m* **(a)** *(Archit)* projection; *(Fels~)* ledge.

**(b)** *(Sport, fig: Abstand)* lead *(vor +dat* over); *(Vorgabe)* start. **einen ~ vor jdm haben** to be ahead of sb.

**Vor-:** ~**stadt** f suburb; **v~städtisch** *adj* suburban.

**Vorstand** m *(leitendes Gremium)* board; *(von Verein)* committee; *(von Partei)* executive.

**Vorstands-:** ~**etage** f management suite; ~**mitglied** *nt siehe* **Vorstand** member of the board; committee member; member of the executive; ~**sitzung** f *(von Firma)* board meeting; ~**vorsitzende(r)** *mf decl as adj* chairman *or* chairperson of the board (of directors).

**vorstecken** *vt sep* to put forward; *Kopf* to stick out.

**vorstehen** *vi sep irreg aux haben or sein* **(a)** *(hervorragen)* to project; *(Zähne)* to protrude; *(Knochen, Kinn, Nase)* to be prominent. **(b)** *dem Haushalt* to preside over; *einer Firma, einer Partei* to be the chairman of; *einem Geschäft* to manage; *einer Abteilung* to head (up); *einem Amt* to hold.

**Vorsteher(in** f) m - *(von Abteilung)* head; *(von Gefängnis)* governor *(Brit)*, warden *(US)*; *(Bahnhofs~)* stationmaster.

**vorstellbar** *adj* conceivable. **das ist nicht ~** it's inconceivable.

**vorstellen** *sep* **1** *vt* **(a)** *Tisch, Stuhl, Auto* to move forward; *Bein* to put out; *Uhr* to put forward *(um* by). **(b)** *(col: davorstellen)* **etw ~** to put sth in front. **(c)** *(darstellen)* to represent; *(bedeuten)* to mean. **etwas ~** *(fig: Ansehen haben)* to count for something. **(d)** *(bekannt machen)* **jdn jdm ~** to introduce sb to sb. **(e)** *(bekanntmachen, vorführen)* to present. **jdm etw ~** to show sb sth.

**2** *vr* **(a)** **sich** *(dat)* **etw ~** to imagine sth; **sich** *(dat)* **etw unter etw** *(dat)* **~** *Begriff, Wort* to understand sth by sth; **darunter kann ich mir nichts ~** it doesn't mean anything to me; **stell dir das nicht so einfach vor** don't think it's so easy; **so stelle ich mir einen gelungenen Urlaub vor** that's my idea of a successful holiday. **(b)** *(sich nach vorn stellen)* to move forward. **(c)** *(sich bekannt machen)* to introduce oneself *(jdm* to sb); *(bei Bewerbung)* to go for an interview.

**Vorstellung** f **(a)** *(Gedanke)* idea; *(bildlich)* picture; *(Einbildung)* illusion; *(~skraft)* imagination. **sich** *(dat)* **eine ~ von etw machen** to form an idea *or* *(Bild)* picture of sth; **du machst dir keine ~, wie schwierig das ist** you have no idea how difficult that is. **(b)** *(Theat etc)* performance. **(c)** *(das Bekanntmachen)* *(zwischen Leuten)* introduction; *(Vorführung)* presentation; *(bei Bewerbung)* interview *(bei* with).

**Vorstellungs-:** ~**gespräch** *nt* interview; ~**kraft** f imagination; ~**vermögen** *nt* powers of imagination *pl*.

**Vorstoß** m *(Vordringen)* venture; *(Mil)* advance; *(fig: Versuch)* attempt.

**vorstoßen** *sep irreg* **1** *vt* to push forward. **2** *vi aux sein* to venture; *(Sport)* to attack; *(Mil)* to advance.

**Vorstrafe** f previous conviction.

**vorstrecken** *vt sep* to stretch forward; *Hände* to stretch out; *(fig) Geld* to advance *(jdm* sb).

**Vorstufe** f preliminary stage; *(von Entwicklung)* early stage.

**vorstürmen** *vi sep aux sein* to rush forward.

**Vortag** m previous day, day before.

**vortasten** *vr (lit, fig)* to feel one's way forward.

**vortäuschen** *vt sep Krankheit* to feign; *Schlag* to fake.

**Vortäuschung** f pretence *(Brit)*, pretense *(US)*, fake. **unter ~ falscher Tatsachen** under false pretences.

**Vorteil** m -e advantage *(auch Sport)*. **die Vor- und Nachteile** the pros and cons; **auf seinen ~ bedacht sein** to have an eye to one's own interests; **jdm gegenüber im ~ sein** to have an advantage over sb; **sich zu seinem ~ verändern** to change for the better; **von ~ sein** to be advantageous.

**vorteilhaft** *adj* advantageous; *Kleider* flattering; *Geschäft* lucrative. **~ aussehen** to look one's best; **etw ~ verkaufen** to sell sth for a profit.

**Vortrag** m, *pl* **Vorträge** **(a)** talk; *(formell)* lecture. **einen ~ halten** to give a talk/lecture. **(b)** *(Darbietung)* performance; *(von Gedicht)* reading.

**vortragen** *vt sep irreg (berichten)* to report; *(förmlich mitteilen)* *Fall, Forderung* to present; *Beschwerde* to lodge; *Meinung, Wunsch* to express; *(einen Vortrag halten über)* to give a talk/lecture on; *(vorsprechen) Gedicht* to recite; *(Mus)* to perform.

**Vortrags-:** ~**abend** m lecture evening; *(mit Gedichten)* poetry evening; *(mit Musik)* recital; ~**reihe** f series of talks/lectures.

**vortrefflich** *adj* splendid, superb.

**vortreten** *vi sep irreg aux sein* **(a)** *(lit)* to step forward. **(b)** *(hervorragen)* to project; *(Augen)* to protrude.

**Vortritt** m no pl priority. **jdm den ~ lassen** *(lit, fig)* to let sb go first.

**vorüber** *adv* **~ sein** *(räumlich, Jugend)* to be past; *(Gewitter etc)* to be over; *(Schmerz)* to have gone.

**vorüber-** *pref siehe auch* **vorbei-;** ~**gehen** *vi sep irreg aux sein* to pass *(an etw (dat)* sth); *(Gewitter)* to blow over; **im V~gehen** in passing; ~**gehend** *adj* *(flüchtig)* momentary; *Krankheit* short; *(zeitweilig)* temporary.

**Vor|urteil** *nt* prejudice *(gegenüber* against). **~e haben** to be prejudiced.

**vor|urteils-:** ~**frei,** ~**los** **1** *adj* unprejudiced; **2** *adv* without prejudice.

**Vor-:** ~**väter** *pl* forefathers *pl*; ~**verkauf** m advance booking; **sich** *(dat)* **Karten im ~verkauf besorgen** to buy tickets in advance; ~**verkaufsstelle** f advance booking office.

**vorverlegen\*** *vt sep* **(a)** *Termin* to bring forward. **(b)** *(Mil) Front, Gefechtslinie* to push forward.

**vorwagen** *vr sep* to venture forward.

**Vorwahl** f **(a)** preliminary election; *(US)* primary. **(b)** *(Telec)* = ~**nummer.**

**Vorwahlnummer** f area *or* dialling *or* dial *(US)* code.

**Vorwand** m, *pl* **Vorwände** pretext.

**vorwärmen** *vt sep* to pre-heat; *Teller* to heat.

**Vorwarnung** f *(advance)* warning.

**vorwärts** *adv* forwards, forward. **~!** *(col)* let's go *(col)*; *(Mil)* forward march!; **weiter ~** further on.

**Vorwärts-:** ~**bewegung** f forward movement; ~**gang** m forward gear; **v~gehen** *sep irreg aux sein (fig)* **1** *vi* to progress; **2** *vi impers* **mit etw geht es v~** sth is going well; **v~kommen** *vi sep irreg aux sein (fig)* to get on *(in, mit* with).

**Vorwäsche** f, **Vorwaschgang** m prewash.

**vorweg** *adv (an der Spitze)* at the front; *(vorher)* before(hand); *(von vornherein)* at the outset.

**Vorweg-:** ~**nahme** f -n anticipation; **v~nehmen** *vt sep irreg* to anticipate.

**Vorweihnachtszeit** f pre-Christmas period.

**vorweisen** *vt sep irreg* to show; *Zeugnisse* to produce. **etw ~ können** *(fig) Kenntnisse, Erfahrung* to possess sth.

**vorwerfen** *vt sep irreg* **(a)** *(fig)* **jdm etw/Unpünktlichkeit ~** to reproach sb sth/for being unpunctual; *(beschuldigen)* to accuse sb of sth/of being unpunctual; **das wirft er mir heute noch vor** he still holds it against me; **ich habe mir nichts vor-**

**zuwerfen** my conscience is clear. **(b)** *(lit)* **Tieren/ Gefangenen etw** ~ to throw sth down for the animals/prisoners.

**vorwiegend 1** *adj attr* predominant. **2** *adv* predominantly.

**Vorwissen** *nt* previous knowledge.

**vorwitzig** *adj (keck)* cheeky; *(vorlaut)* forward.

**Vorwort** *nt* -e foreword, preface.

**Vorwurf** *m, pl* **Vorwürfe** reproach; *(Beschuldigung)* accusation. **jdm/sich große Vorwürfe machen** to reproach sb/oneself; **ich habe mir keine Vorwürfe zu machen** my conscience is clear; **jdm etw zum ~ machen** to reproach sb with sth.

**vorwurfsvoll** *adj* reproachful.

**Vorzeichen** *nt (Omen)* omen; *(Med)* early symptom; *(Math)* sign. **positives/negatives ~** *(Math)* plus/minus (sign); **mit umgekehrtem ~** *(fig)* the other way around.

**vorzeichnen** *vt sep* Linien *etc* to sketch (out). **jdm etw ~** *(fig)* to map sth out for sb.

**Vorzeige-** *in cpds* Schüler, Sportler star; **~frau** *f* token woman.

**vorzeigen** *vt sep* to show, to produce.

**Vorzeit** *f* prehistoric times *pl*.

**vorzeitig** *adj* **1** early; Geburt, Altern *etc* premature. **2** *adv pensioniert* early; *gealtert* prematurely.

**vorzeitlich** *adj* prehistoric; *(fig)* archaic.

**vorziehen** *vt sep irreg* **(a)** *(hervorziehen)* to pull out; *(nach vorne ziehen)* Stuhl *etc* to pull up; *(zuziehen)* Vorhänge to draw. **etw hinter/unter etw** *(dat)* ~ to pull sth out from behind/under sth. **(b)** *(fig) (lieber mögen)* to prefer; *(bevorzugen)* jdn to favour *(Brit)*, to favor *(US)*. **etw einer anderen Sache** ~ to prefer sth to sth else; **es** ~, **etw zu tun** to prefer to do sth. **(c)** *(zuerst behandeln, abfertigen)* to give priority to. **(d)** *(Wahlen)* to bring forward. **vorgezogener Ruhestand** early retirement.

**Vorzimmer** *nt* anteroom; *(Büro)* outer office.

**Vorzimmerdame** *f* receptionist.

**Vorzug** *m, pl* **Vorzüge** preference; *(Vorteil)* advantage; *(gute Eigenschaft)* asset. **einer Sache** *(dat)* **den ~ geben** *(form)* to prefer sth.

**vorzüglich** *adj* excellent.

**Vorzugsaktien** *pl (St Ex)* preference shares *pl*.

**vorzugsweise** *adv* preferably; *(hauptsächlich)* chiefly. **etw ~ trinken** to prefer to drink sth.

**Votum** ['voːtʊm] *nt, pl* **Voten** vote.

**vulgär** [vʊlˈgɛːɐ] *adj* vulgar.

**Vulkan** [vʊlˈkaːn] *m* -e volcano. **ein Tanz auf dem ~** playing with fire.

**Vulkan\ausbruch** [vʊlˈkaːn-] *m* volcanic eruption.

**vulkanisch** [vʊlˈkaːnɪʃ] *adj* volcanic.

**vulkanisieren\*** [vʊlkaniˈziːrən] *vt* to vulcanize.

**v.u.Z.** = **vor unserer Zeitrechnung** BC.

# W

**W, w** [ve:] *nt* -, - W, w. **W wie Wilhelm** ≃ W for William.

**W = Westen** W.

**WAA** [ve:|a:'|a:] *f* = **Wiederaufbereitungsanlage.**

**Waage** *f* **-n** (a) *(Gerät)* scales *pl*; *(Feder~, Apotheker~)* balance. **eine ~** a pair of scales; **sich** *(dat)* **die ~ halten** *(fig)* to balance one another. **(b)** *(Astrol)* Libra.

**Waag(e)-: w~recht** *adj* horizontal; **~rechte** *f* horizontal.

**Waagschale** *f* (scale) pan. **(schwer) in die ~ fallen** *(fig)* to carry weight; **seine Autorität in die ~ werfen** *(fig)* to bring one's authority to bear.

**wabb(e)lig** *adj Pudding* wobbly; *Mensch* flabby.

**Wabe** *f* **-n** honeycomb.

**Wabenhonig** *m* comb honey.

**wach** *adj* awake *pred*; *(fig: aufgeweckt)* alert. **in ~em Zustand** in the waking state; **~ werden** to wake up.

**Wach-: ~ablösung** *f* changing of the guard; *(fig: Regierungswechsel)* change of government; *(Mensch)* relief guard; **~boot** *nt* patrol boat; **~dienst** *m* lookout; *(Mil)* guard (duty); *(Naut)* watch; *(Firma)* security firm; **~dienst haben/machen** to be on guard (duty); *(Naut)* to have the watch.

**Wache** *f* **-n** (a) *no pl (Wachdienst)* guard (duty). **(bei jdm) ~ halten** to keep watch (over sb); *(Kranken~)* to keep watch (at sb's bedside); **~ stehen** *or* **schieben** *(col)* to be on guard (duty); *(Dieb, Schüler etc)* to keep a lookout. **(b)** *(Mil) (Wachposten)* guard; *(Gebäude)* guardhouse. **(c)** *(Naut: Personen, Dauer)* watch. **~ haben** to be on watch. **(d)** *(Polizei~)* (police) station.

**wachen** *vi* (a) *(wach sein)* to be awake. **(b)** *(Wache halten)* to keep watch. **bei jdm ~** to sit up with sb; **über etw** *(acc)* **~** to (keep) watch over sth; *über Verkehr* to supervise sth.

**Wach-: w~habend** *adj attr* duty; **w~halten** *vt sep irreg (fig) Interesse etc* to keep alive; **~hund** *m* *(lit, fig)* watchdog; *(lit auch)* guard dog; **~macher** *m* *(col)* stimulant; **~mann** *m, pl* **-leute** watchman; **~mannschaft** *f* guards *pl*; *(Naut)* watch.

**Wacholder** *m* - *(Bot)* juniper (tree).

**Wacholder-: ~beere** *f* juniper berry; **~schnaps** *m spirit made from juniper berries,* ≃ gin.

**wach-: ~rufen** *vt sep irreg (fig) Erinnerung etc* to evoke; **~rütteln** *vt sep (fig)* to rouse.

**Wachs** [vaks] *nt* **-e** wax. **weich wie ~** as soft as butter.

**wachsam** *adj* vigilant; *(vorsichtig)* on one's guard.

**Wachsamkeit** *f no pl* vigilance; *(Vorsichtigkeit)* guardedness.

**wachsbleich** ['vax-] *adj* waxen.

**Wachschiff** *nt* patrol ship.

**wachsen¹** ['vaksn] *pret* **wuchs** [vu:ks], *ptp* **gewachsen** *vi aux sein* to grow. **in die Breite/Länge ~** to broaden (out)/to lengthen; **sich** *(dat)* **einen Bart ~ lassen** to grow a beard; **gut gewachsen** *Baum* well-grown; *Mensch* with a good figure.

**wachsen²** ['vaks] *vt* to wax.

**Wachs-:** ['vaks-]: **~farbe** *f* **(a)** *(Farbstift)* wax crayon; **(b)** *(Farbstoff)* wax dye; **~figur** *f* wax figure, waxwork; **~figurenkabinett** *nt* waxworks *pl* (exhibition); **~kerze** *f* wax candle; **~malkreide** *f*, **~malstift** *m* wax crayon; **~papier** *nt* waxed paper; **~stift** *m* wax crayon.

**Wachstube** ['vaxʃtu:bə] *f* guardroom; *(von Polizei)* duty room.

**Wachstuch** ['vaks-] *nt* oilcloth.

**Wachstum** ['vakstu:m] *nt no pl* growth. **im ~ zurückgeblieben** stunted.

**Wachstums-: ~branche** *f* growth industry; **w~fördernd** *adj* growth-promoting; **~grenze** *f* limits *pl* of growth; **w~hemmend** *adj* growth-inhibiting; **~rate** *f* growth rate; **~störung** *f* disturbance of growth.

**Wachtel** *f* **-n** quail.

**Wächter** *m* - guardian; *(Nacht~)* watchman.

**Wacht-: ~meister** *m* (police) constable *(Brit)*, patrolman *(US)*; **~posten** *m* sentry; *(Schüler, Dieb etc)* lookout.

**Wachtraum** *m* daydream.

**Wach(t)turm** *m* watchtower.

**Wach- und Schließgesellschaft** *f* security firm.

**wack(e)lig** *adj* wobbly; *(fig) Firma* shaky. **~ auf den Beinen sein** *(col: Patient)* to be wobbly on one's legs; **~ stehen** *(lit)* to be unsteady; *(fig: Unternehmen, Schüler)* to be shaky.

**Wackelkontakt** *m* loose connection.

**wackeln** *vi* (a) to wobble; *(zittern)* to shake; *(Zahn, Schraube)* to be loose; *(beim Fotografieren)* to move. **mit den Ohren/Hüften/dem Kopf/Schwanz ~** to waggle one's ears/wiggle one's hips/wag one's head/its tail. **(b)** *aux sein (langsam, unsicher gehen)* to totter; *(Kleinkind)* to toddle.

**wacker** *adj (tapfer)* brave, valiant. **sich ~ schlagen** *(col)* to put up a brave fight.

**Wade** *f* **-n** *(Anat)* calf.

**Waden-: ~bein** *nt* fibula; **~krampf** *m* cramp in one's calf; **~strumpf** *m* half stocking; **~wickel** *m (Med)* compress around the leg.

**Waffe** *f* **-n** *(lit, fig)* weapon; *(Schuß~)* gun; *(Mil: Waffengattung)* arm. **~n** *(Mil)* arms; **~n tragen** to carry arms; **die ~n strecken** *(lit, fig)* to surrender; **jdn mit seinen eigenen ~n schlagen** *(fig)* to beat sb at his own game.

**Waffel** *f* **-n** waffle; *(Keks, Eis~)* wafer; *(Eistüte)* cone.

**Waffeleisen** *nt* waffle iron.

**Waffen-** *in cpds* arms; **~arsenal** *nt* arsenal; *(von Staat)* stockpile; **~gattung** *f (Mil)* arm of the service; **~gewalt** *f* force of arms; **mit ~gewalt** by force of arms; **~handel** *m* arms trade; *(illegal auch)* gunrunning; **~händler** *m* arms dealer; *(illegal auch)* gunrunner; **~hilfe** *f* military assistance; **~lager** *nt (von Armee)* ordnance depot; *(von*

*Terroristen)* cache; **w~los** *adj* unarmed; **~ruhe** *f* ceasefire; **~schein** *m* firearms *or* gun licence *(Brit) or* license *(US)*; **~schmuggel** *m* gunrunning, arms smuggling; **~stillstand** *m* armistice.

**Wagemut** *m no pl (geh)* (heroic) daring *or* boldness.

**wagemutig** *adj* daring, bold.

**wagen 1** *vt* to venture; *(sich getrauen)* to dare. **es ~, etw zu tun** to venture to do sth; to dare (to) do sth; **wage nicht, mir zu widersprechen!** don't you dare (to) contradict me! **2** *vr* to dare. **sich an etw** *(acc)* **~** to venture to do sth; **sich auf ein Gebiet ~** to venture into an area.

**Wagen** *m* - *(Personen~)* car; *(Liefer~)* van; *(von Pferden gezogen)* wag(g)on, cart; *(Kutsche)* coach; *(Kinder~)* pram *(Brit)*, baby carriage *(US)*; *(Hand~)* (hand)cart; *(Kofferkuli, Einkaufs~)* trolley *(Brit)*, cart *(US)*; *(Schreibmaschinen~)* carriage; *(Eisenbahn~)* car, carriage *(Brit)*. **der Große ~** *(Astrol)* the Plough.

**wägen** *pret* **wog,** *ptp* **gewogen** *vt (old)* to weigh.

**Wagen-:** **~abteil** *nt (Rail)* compartment; **~führer** *m* driver; **~heber** *m* jack; **~ladung** *f (von Personenwagen)* carload; *(von Lastwagen)* lorryload *(Brit)*, truckload; *(von Eisenbahn)* wag(g)onload; **~park** *m* fleet of cars; **~rad** *nt* cartwheel; **~rücklauf** *m (an Schreibmaschine)* carriage return; **~wäsche** *f* carwash.

**Waggon** [vaˈgɔŋ] *m* **-s** (goods) wag(g)on *(Brit)*, freight car *(US)*; *(Ladung)* wag(g)onload/carload.

**Wag-:** **~hals** *m* daredevil; **w~halsig** *adj* foolhardy, daredevil *attr*.

**Wagnis** *nt* hazardous business; *(Risiko)* risk.

**Wahl** *f* **-en (a)** *(Auswahl)* choice. **die ~ fiel auf ihn** he was chosen; **aus freier ~** of one's own free choice; **wir hatten keine (andere) ~(, als)** we had no alternative *or* choice (but); **jdm die ~ lassen** to leave (it up to) sb to choose; **jdm etw zur ~ stellen** to give sb a choice of sth; **seine ~ treffen** to make one's selection; **wer die ~ hat, hat die Qual** *(Prov)* he is/you are *etc* spoilt for choice.

**(b)** *(Pol etc)* election; *(Abstimmung)* vote; *(geheim)* ballot. **seine ~ in den Vorstand/zum Präsidenten** his election to the board/as president; **zur ~ gehen** to go to the polls; **jdn zur ~ aufstellen** to put sb up as a candidate; **sich zur ~ stellen** to stand, to run (for parliament *etc)*; **die ~ annehmen** to accept the vote.

**(c)** *(Qualität)* **erste ~** top quality; *(Gemüse, Eier)* grade one; **Waren erster/zweiter ~** top-quality goods/seconds *pl*; **Gemüse zweiter ~** grade-two vegetables.

**Wählautomatik** *f (Telec)* automatic dialling *(Brit) or* dialing *(US)*.

**wählbar** *adj* eligible (for office).

**Wahl-:** **~benachrichtigung** *f* polling card; **w~berechtigt** *adj* entitled to vote; **~beteiligung** *f* turnout; **~bezirk** *m* ward.

**wählen 1** *vt* **(a)** to choose *(von* from, out of*)*; *siehe* **gewählt. (b)** *(Telec) Nummer* to dial. **(c)** *(Pol)* to elect; *(sich entscheiden für) Partei* to vote for. **jdn ins Parlament ~** to elect sb to Parliament; **jdn zum Präsidenten ~** to elect sb president. **2** *vi* **(a)** *(auswählen)* to choose. **(b)** *(Telec)* to dial. **(c)** *(Stimme abgeben)* to vote.

**Wähler(in** *f)* *m* - *(Pol)* elector, voter.

**Wahl|ergebnis** *nt* election result.

**wählerisch** *adj* particular; *Geschmack, Kunde* discriminating. **sei nicht so ~!** don't be so choosy *(col)*.

**Wählerschaft** *f no pl* electorate *sing or pl*.

**Wähler-:** **~stimme** *f* vote; **~verzeichnis** *nt* elec-

toral roll.

**Wahl-:** **~fach** *nt (Sch)* optional subject, elective *(US)*; **w~frei** *adj* optional; **w~freier Zugriff** *(Comp)* random access; **~gang** *m* ballot; **~geheimnis** *nt* secrecy of the ballot; **~geschenk** *nt* (pre-election) vote-catching gimmick; **~gesetz** *nt* electoral law; **~heimat** *f* adopted country; **~helfer** *m (im ~kampf)* election assistant; *(bei der Wahl)* polling officer; **~kabine** *f* polling booth; **~kampf** *m* election campaign; **~kreis** *m* constituency; **~lokal** *nt* polling station; **w~los 1** *adj* indiscriminate; **2** *adv* at random, haphazardly; *(nicht wählerisch)* indiscriminately; **~mann** *m, pl* **~männer** delegate; **~möglichkeit** *f* option; **~niederlage** *f* election defeat; **~ordnung** *f* election regulations *pl*; **~periode** *f* lifetime of a/the parliament; **~pflicht** *f* electoral duty; **~programm** *nt* election manifesto; **~recht** *nt* (right to) vote; **allgemeines ~recht** universal franchise; **das aktive ~recht** the right to vote; **das passive ~recht** eligibility (for political office); **~rede** *f* election speech; **~reform** *f* electoral reform.

**Wählscheibe** *f* dial.

**Wahl-:** **~schein** *m* polling card; **~sieg** *m* election victory; **~spruch** *m* motto; **~system** *nt* electoral *or* voting system; **~tag** *m* election day; **~urne** *f* ballot box; **~verfahren** *nt* electoral procedure; **~versammlung** *f* election meeting; **~versprechungen** *pl* election promises *pl*; **~vorschlag** *m* election proposal; **w~weise** *adv* alternatively; **w~weise Kartoffeln oder Reis** a choice of potatoes or rice.

**Wählzeichen** *nt (Telec)* dialling *(Brit) or* dial *(US)* tone.

**Wahn** *m no pl* illusion, delusion; *(Manie)* mania. **in dem ~ leben, daß ...** to labour *(Brit) or* labor *(US)* under the delusion that ...

**Wahnsinn** *m no pl* madness. **das ist doch (heller) ~, so ein ~!** that's sheer madness; **~!** *(col: toll)* fantastic!

**wahnsinnig 1** *adj (col) (verrückt)* mad, crazy; *(toll)* brilliant *(col)*, great *(col)*; *(attr: sehr groß, viel)* awful, dreadful. **eine ~e Arbeit** a terrific amount of work; **das macht mich ~** *(col)* it's driving me crazy; **~ werden** to go mad *(col)*; **ich werde ~!** it's mind-blowing! *(col)*. **2** *adv (col)* incredibly *(col)*. **~ verliebt** madly in love; **~ viele/viel** an incredible number/amount *(col)*.

**Wahnsinnige(r)** *mf decl as adj* lunatic.

**Wahnsinns-** *in cpds (col: verrückt)* crazy; *(col: prima)* incredible *(col)*.

**Wahn-:** **~vorstellung** *f* delusion; **w~witzig 1** *adj* crazy *attr*; **2** *adv* terribly.

**wahr** *adj Geschichte, Liebe, Glaube etc* true; *(echt) Kunst, Glück* real, genuine; *(attr: wirklich)* real, veritable. **im ~sten Sinne des Wortes** in the true sense of the word; **daran ist kein Wort ~ or kein ~es Wort** there's not a word of truth in it; **da ist etwas W~es daran** there's some truth in that; **da hast du ein ~es Wort gesprochen** *(col)* there's a lot of truth in that; **etw ~ machen** *Pläne* to make sth a reality; *Versprechung, Drohung* to carry sth out; **~ werden** to come true; **so ~ mir Gott helfe!** so help me God!; **das darf or kann doch nicht ~ sein!** *(col)* I don't believe it!; **das ist nicht das W~e** *(col)* it's no great shakes *(col)*.

**wahren** *vt Interessen, Rechte* to look after; *Autorität, Ruf, Würde* to preserve, to keep; *Geheimnis* to keep; *gute Manieren* to adhere to, to observe.

**währen** *vi (geh)* to last.

**während 1** *prep* +*gen or dat* during. **~ eines Zeit-**

**raums** over a period of time. **2** *conj* while.

**währenddessen** *adv* meanwhile.

**Wahr-: w~haben** *vt sep irreg* **etw nicht w~haben wollen** not to want to admit sth; **w~haft 1** *adj* real; **2** *adv* really, truly; **w~haftig** *adv* really; *(tatsächlich)* actually.

**Wahrheit** *f* truth. **in ~** in reality; **die ~ sagen** to tell the truth.

**wahrheits-: ~gemäß, ~getreu** *adj Bericht* truthful; *Darstellung* faithful; **~liebend** *adj* truth-loving; *(ehrlich)* truthful.

**Wahr-: w~nehmbar** *adj* perceptible; **mit bloßem Auge w~nehmbar** visible to the naked eye; **w~nehmen** *vt sep irreg* **(a)** *(sinnlich)* to perceive; *Veränderungen etc* to be aware of; **nichts mehr um sich herum w~nehmen** to be no longer aware of anything around one; **(b)** *Frist, Termin* to observe; *Gelegenheit* to take; *Interessen, Rechte* to look after; **~nehmung** *f siehe vt* **(a)** perception; awareness; **(b)** *(von Frist)* observing; *(von Interessen)* looking after; **w~sagen** *vi sep or insep* to tell fortunes; **aus den Karten w~sagen** to read cards; **~sager(in** *f)* *m* - fortune-teller; **~sagerei** *f no pl* fortune-telling; **~sagung** *f* prediction.

**wahrscheinlich 1** *adj* probable, likely; *(glaubhaft)* plausible. **2** *adv* probably.

**Wahrscheinlichkeit** *f* probability; *(Glaubhaftigkeit)* plausibility. **mit großer ~, aller ~ nach, in aller ~** in all probability.

**Währung** *f* currency.

**Währungs-** *in cpds* currency; **~einheit** *f* monetary unit; **~fonds** *m* Monetary Fund; **~krise** *f* monetary crisis; **~politik** *f* monetary policy; **~reform** *f* currency reform; **~system** *nt* monetary system; **~union** *f* monetary union.

**Wahrzeichen** *nt (von Stadt, Verein)* emblem; *(Gebäude, Turm etc)* symbol. **das ~ von Hamburg** Hamburg's most famous landmark.

**Waid-** *in cpds* = **Weid-**.

**Waise** *f* **-n** orphan. **~ sein** to be an orphan.

**Waisen-: ~haus** *nt* orphanage; **~kind** *nt* orphan; **~knabe** *m* **gegen dich ist er ein ~knabe** *(col)* he's no match for you; **~rente** *f* orphan's allowance.

**Wal** *m* **-e** whale.

**Wald** *m* ⸚**er** wood(s *pl)*; *(großer)* forest; *(no pl: ~land)* woodland(s *pl)*. **er sieht den ~ vor lauter Bäumen nicht** he can't see the wood for the trees.

**Wald-: ~ameise** *f* red ant; **~arbeiter** *m* forestry worker; **~blume** *f* woodland flower; **~brand** *m* forest fire.

**Wäldchen** *nt dim of* **Wald** copse.

**Wald-: ~erdbeere** *f* wild strawberry; **~horn** *nt (Mus)* French horn.

**waldig** *adj* wooded, woody.

**Wald-: ~land** *nt* woodland(s *pl)*; **~lauf** *m* cross-country running; *(einzelner Lauf)* cross-country run; **~lehrpfad** *m* woodland nature trail; **~meister** *m (Bot)* woodruff; **w~reich** *adj* densely wooded; **~sterben** *nt no pl* loss of trees due to pollution.

**Wald- und Wiesen-** *in cpds (col)* common-or-garden *(col)*.

**Wald-: ~weg** *m* woodland/forest path; **~wiese** *f* glade.

**Wal-: ~fang** *m* whaling; **~fänger** *m* whaler; **~fisch** *m (col)* whale.

**Waliser** *m* - Welshman.

**Waliserin** *f* Welshwoman.

**walisisch** *adj* Welsh.

**Walkman** ® ['vɔːkmən] *m* **-s** Walkman ®.

**Wall** *m* ⸚**e** embankment; *(Mil)* rampart; *(fig)* bul-

wark.

**Wallach** *m* **-e** gelding.

**wallen** *vi (Wasser, Soße, fig: Blut)* to boil; *(geh: fließen: Locken, Gewand)* to flow.

**wallfahren** *vi insep reg aux sein* to go on a pilgrimage.

**Wallfahrer(in** *f)* *m* - pilgrim.

**Wallfahrt** *f* pilgrimage.

**Wallone** *m (wk)* **-n, -n, Wallonin** *f* Walloon.

**Walnuß** *f* walnut.

**Walroß** *nt* **-sse** walrus.

**walten** *vi (geh)* to reign *(in +dat* over*)*; *(wirken: Mensch, Naturkräfte)* to be at work. **über jdm/etw ~** to rule (over) sb/sth; **Vernunft ~ lassen** to let reason prevail; **Vorsicht ~ lassen** to exercise caution.

**Walzblech** *nt* sheet metal.

**Walze** *f* **-n** roller.

**walzen** *vt* to roll.

**wälzen 1** *vt* **(a)** *(rollen)* to roll. **(b)** *(col) Akten, Bücher* to pore over; *Probleme, Gedanken, Pläne* to turn over in one's mind. **die Verantwortung auf jdn ~** to shift the responsibility onto sb. **2** *vr* to roll; *(schlaflos im Bett)* to toss and turn; *(fig: Menschenmenge, Wassermassen)* to surge.

**walzenförmig** *adj* cylindrical.

**Walzer** *m* - waltz.

**Wälzer** *m* - *(col)* heavy *or* weighty tome *(hum)*.

**Walz-: ~straße** *f* rolling train; **~werk** *nt* rolling mill.

**Wampe** *f* **-n** *(col)* paunch.

**wand** *pret of* **winden**.

**Wand** *f* ⸚**e** wall; *(nicht gemauerte Trenn~)* partition (wall); *(von Gefäß, Behälter, Schiff)* side; *(Fels~)* (rock) face; *(fig)* barrier, wall. **spanische ~** (folding) screen; **~ an ~** wall to wall; **in seinen (eigenen) vier ~en** *(fig)* within one's own four walls; **weiß wie die ~** as white as a sheet; **jdn an die ~ spielen** to put sb in the shade; *(Sport auch)* to outplay sb; **jdn an die ~ drücken** *(fig)* to push sb to the wall; **jdn an die ~ stellen** *(fig)* to put sb up against a wall (and shoot him/her); **er lachte, daß die ~e wackelten** *(col)* he made the whole room shake with his laughter; **das ist, um die ~e hochzugehen** *(col)* it's enough to drive you up the wall *(col)*.

**Wand-: ~behang** *m* wall hanging; **~bekleidung** *f* wall covering; *(aus Holz)* panelling *(Brit)*, paneling *(US)*; **~bord, ~brett** *nt* (wall) shelf.

**Wandel** *m no pl* change. **im ~ der Zeiten** throughout the ages.

**Wandel-: w~bar** *adj* changeable; **~halle** *f* foyer; *(im Parlament)* lobby.

**wandeln**[1] *vtr (ändern)* to change.

**wandeln**[2] *vi aux sein (geh: gehen)* to walk, to stroll. **ein ~des Wörterbuch** *(hum)* a walking encyclopedia.

**Wander-: ~ameise** *f* army ant; **~ausstellung** *f* touring exhibition; **~bühne** *f* touring company; **~düne** *f* shifting dune.

**Wanderer** *m* - hiker; *(esp in Verein)* rambler.

**Wander-: ~falke** *m* peregrine (falcon); **~ferien** *pl* walking holiday; **~freund(in** *f)* *m* hiker; **~karte** *f* map of walks; **~kleidung** *f* hiking outfit; **~leben** *nt* roving *or* wandering life; *(fig)* unsettled life; **~lied** *nt* hiking song; **~lust** *f* wanderlust.

**wandern** *vi aux sein* to hike; *(in Verein)* to ramble; *(umherschweifen)* to roam; *(Wanderbühne)* to travel; *(Tiere, Völker)* to migrate; *(Wolken)* to drift; *(weitergegeben werden)* to be passed on; *(col: in den Papierkorb)* to land.

**Wander-: ~niere** *f* floating kidney; **~pokal** *m* challenge cup; **~prediger** *m* itinerant preacher; **~preis** *m* challenge trophy; **~ratte** *f* brown rat.

**Wạnderschaft** *f no pl* travels *pl.* **auf (der)** ~ **sein** to be on one's travels; **auf** ~ **gehen** to go off on one's travels.

**Wạnder-:** ~**schauspieler** *m* travelling *(Brit)* or traveling *(US)* actor; ~**schuhe** *pl* walking shoes *pl*; ~**truppe** *f* touring company.

**Wạnderung** *f* (a) *(Ausflug)* walk. **eine** ~ **machen** to go on a ramble. (b) *(von Tieren, Völkern)* migration.

**Wạnder-:** ~**verein** *m* rambling club; ~**weg** *m* trail, (foot)path; ~**zirkus** *m* travelling *(Brit)* or traveling *(US)* circus.

**Wạnd-:** ~**gemälde** *nt* mural, wall painting; ~**kalender** *m* wall calendar; ~**karte** *f* wall map; ~**lampe** *f* wall lamp; ~**leuchter** *m* wall bracket.

**Wạndlung** *f (Wechsel, Wandel)* change; *(völlige Um~)* transformation. **eine** ~ **durchmachen** to undergo a change.

**Wand-:** ~**malerei** *f* mural painting; ~**schirm** *m* screen; ~**schrank** *m* wall cupboard; ~**tafel** *f* (black)board.

**wạndte** *pret of* **wenden**.

**Wạnd-:** ~**teller** *m* wall plate; ~**teppich** *m* tapestry, wall hanging; ~**uhr** *f* wall clock; ~**verkleidung** *f* wall covering; *(aus Holz)* panelling *(Brit)*, paneling *(US)*; ~**zeitung** *f* wall newspaper.

**Wạnge** *f* **-n** *(geh)* cheek.

**wạnkelmütig** *adj* fickle, inconstant.

**wạnken** *vi* (a) *(Mensch, Gebäude)* to sway; *(Knie)* to shake, to wobble; *(unsicher sein/werden)* to waver. **etw ins W~ bringen** *(fig) Thron, Regierung* to cause sth to totter; *Glauben, Mut* to shake sth. (b) *aux sein (gehen)* to stagger; *(alter Mensch)* to totter.

**wạnn** *interrog adv* when. ~ **(auch) immer** whenever; **seit** ~ **bist/hast du ...?** how long have you been/have you had ...?; *(entrüstet etc)* since when are you/do you have ...?

**Wạnne** *f* **-n** bath; *(Öl~)* sump *(Brit)*, oil pan *(US)*.

**Wạnze** *f* **-n** *(Zool, col: Abhörgerät)* bug.

**Wạppen** *nt* **-** coat of arms.

**Wạppen-:** ~**kunde** *f* heraldry; ~**tier** *nt* heraldic animal.

**wạppnen** *vr (fig)* **sich (gegen etw)** ~ to prepare (oneself) (for sth); **gewappnet sein** to be forearmed.

**war** *pret of* **sein¹** was.

**wạrb** *pret of* **werben**.

**Wạre** *f* **-n** product; *(einzelne ~)* article; *(als Sammelbegriff)* goods *pl.* ~**n** *pl* goods *pl.*

**Wạren-:** ~**angebot** *nt* range of goods for sale; ~**aufzug** *m* goods hoist; ~**haus** *nt* (department) store; ~**korb** *m (Econ)* basket of goods; ~**lager** *nt* warehouse; *(Bestand)* stocks *pl*; ~**muster** *nt*, ~**probe** *f* trade sample; ~**sendung** *f* trade sample *(sent by post)*; ~**test** *m* test of goods; ~**zeichen** *nt* trademark.

**wạrf** *pret of* **werfen**.

**wạrm** *adj comp* ⸗**er**, *superl* ⸗**ste(r, s)** *or (adv)* **am** ⸗**sten** *(lit, fig)* warm; *(col: homosexuell)* queer *(col)*. **mir ist** ~ I'm warm; **das Essen** ~ **machen** to heat up the food; **das Essen** ~ **stellen** to keep the food hot; **sich** ~ **anziehen** to dress up warmly; **sich** ~ **laufen** to warm up; **jdn/etw** ~**stens empfehlen** to recommend sb/sth warmly; **mit jdm** ~ **werden** *(col)* to get close to sb.

**Wạrm-:** ~**blüter** *m* **-** *(Zool)* warm-blooded animal; **w~blütig** *adj* warm-blooded.

**Wärme** *f no pl (lit, fig)* warmth; *(von Wetter etc, Phys)* heat. **10 Grad** ~ 10 degrees above zero; **ist das eine** ~**!** isn't it warm!

**Wärme-:** ~**austauscher** *m* heat exchanger; ~**dämmung** *f* (heat) insulation; ~**kraftwerk** *nt*

thermal power station; ~**leiter** *m* heat conductor.

**wärmen 1** *vt* to warm; *Essen* to heat up. **2** *vi (Kleidung, Sonne)* to be warm. **3** *vr* to warm up. **sich gegenseitig** ~ to keep each other warm.

**Wärme-:** ~**pumpe** *f* heat pump; ~**regler** *m* thermostat; ~**technik** *f* heat technology; ~**verlust** *m* heat loss.

**Wärmflasche** *f* hot-water bottle.

**Wạrm-:** ~**front** *f (Met)* warm front; **w~halten** *vt sep irreg* **sich (dat) jdn w~halten** *(fig col)* to keep in with sb *(col)*; **w~herzig** *adj* warm-hearted; **w~laufen** *vi sep irreg aux sein* to warm up; **den Motor w~laufen lassen** to warm up the engine; ~**luft** *f* warm air.

**Warmwạsser-:** ~**heizung** *f* hot-water central heating; ~**leitung** *f* hot-water pipe; ~**speicher** *m* hot-water tank.

**Wạrn-:** ~**anlage** *f* warning system; ~**blinkanlage** *f (Aut)* hazard warning lights *pl*; ~**dreieck** *nt* warning triangle.

**wạrnen** *vti* to warn *(vor +dat of)*. **jdn (davor)** ~**, etw zu tun** to warn sb not to do sth.

**Wạrn-:** ~**kreuz** *nt* warning cross; ~**schild** *nt* warning sign; ~**schuß** *m* warning shot; ~**streik** *m* token strike.

**Wạrnung** *f* warning *(vor +dat of)*.

**Wạrn-:** ~**vorrichtung** *f* warning system; ~**zeichen** *nt* warning sign; *(hörbar)* warning signal.

**Wạrschau** *nt* Warsaw.

**Wạrschauer** *adj attr* Warsaw. ~ **Pakt** *(Hist)* Warsaw Pact.

**Wạrte** *f* **-n** observation point; *(fig)* viewpoint. **von jds** ~ **(aus)** *(fig)* from sb's standpoint.

**Wạrte-:** ~**frist** *f* waiting period; *(für Lieferung)* delivery time; ~**halle** *f* waiting room; *(Aviat)* departure lounge; ~**liste** *f* waiting list.

**wạrten¹** *vi* to wait *(auf +acc for)*. **warte mal!** wait a minute; *(überlegend)* let me see; **na warte!** *(col)* just you wait!; **mit dem Essen auf jdn** ~ to wait for sb before eating; **lange auf sich** ~ **lassen** to be a long time (in) coming.

**wạrten²** *vt Auto, Maschine* to service.

**Wạrter(in** *f)* *m* **-** attendant; *(Tier~)* keeper; *(Gefängnis~)* warder/wardress *(Brit)*, guard.

**Wạrte-:** ~**raum**, ~**saal** *m* waiting room; ~**zeit** *f* waiting period; ~**zimmer** *nt* waiting room.

**Wạrtung** *f (von Auto, Maschine)* servicing; *(Instandhaltung)* maintenance. **das Auto muß zur** ~ the car has to go in for a service.

**warụm** *interrog adv* why. ~ **nicht gleich so!** why not do that in the first place.

**Wạrze** *f* **-n** wart; *(Brust~)* nipple.

**wạs 1** *interrog pron* (a) what. ~ **ist, kommst du mit?** well, are you coming?; ~ **denn?** what is it?; *(ungläubig)* what?; **wenn nicht das,** ~ **denn?** if not that, what then?; **wenn ein Unfall passiert,** ~ **dann?** what if there's an accident?; ~ **haben wir gelacht!** *(col)* how we laughed! (b) *(col: warum)* what ... for. (c) ~ **für ...** what sort *or* kind of ...; ~ **für ein schönes Haus!** what a lovely house! **2** *rel pron (auf Satz bezogen)* which. **das,** ~ **...** that which ..., what ...; **ich weiß,** ~ **ich/er tun soll** I know what to do/what he should do; ~ **auch (immer)** whatever; **alles,** ~ **...** everything *or* all (that) ...; **lauf,** ~ **du kannst!** *(col)* run as fast as you can! **3** *(col) indef pron abbr of* **etwas** something; *(fragend, verneint)* anything; *(Teil einer Menge)* some; any. **(na,) so** ~**!** well I never!; *siehe* **etwas**.

**Wạsch-:** ~**anlage** *f (für Autos)* carwash; ~**anleitung** *f* washing instructions *pl*; **w~bar** *adj* washable; ~**bär** *m* rac(c)oon; ~**becken** *nt* wash-

basin *(Brit)*, washbowl *(US)*; ~**beutel** *m* sponge bag; ~**brett** *nt* washboard.
**Wäsche** *f no pl* (**a**) washing; *(Schmutz~)* laundry. **große** ~ **haben** to have a large amount of washing (to do); **in der** ~ in the wash. (**b**) *(Bett~, Küchen~)* linen; *(Unter~)* underwear. **dumm aus der** ~ **gucken** *(col)* to look stupid.
**Wäschebeutel** *m* laundry bag.
**wasch|echt** *adj Farbe* fast; *(fig)* genuine.
**Wäsche-**: ~**klammer** *f* clothes peg *(Brit)*, clothespin *(US)*; ~**korb** *m* laundry basket; ~**leine** *f* (clothes)line.
**waschen** *pret* **wusch**, *ptp* **gewaschen 1** *vt* to wash; *Gold etc* to pan; *(fig col) Geld, Spenden* to launder. (**Wäsche**) ~ to do the washing; **etw** *(acc)* **warm/kalt** ~ to wash sth in hot/cold water; **sich** *(dat)* **die Hände** ~ to wash one's hands. **2** *vr* to wash (oneself/itself); *(Stoff)* to wash. **eine Geldbuße, die sich gewaschen hat** *(col)* a really heavy fine.
**Wäscherei** *f* laundry.
**Wäsche-**: ~**sack** *m* laundry bag; ~**schleuder** *f* spin-dryer *(Brit)*, dryer; ~**schrank** *m* linen cupboard; ~**spinne** *f* revolving clothes dryer; ~**ständer** *m* clothes horse; ~**stärke** *f* starch; ~**trockner** *m (Ständer)* clothes horse; *(Trockenautomat)* dryer.
**Wasch-**: ~**gang** *m* stage of the washing programme *(Brit)* or program *(US)*; ~**gelegenheit** *f* washing facilities *pl*; ~**haus** *nt* wash house, laundry; ~**kessel** *m* clothes boiler; ~**küche** *f* laundry room; ~**lappen** *m* flannel *(Brit)*, washcloth *(US)*; *(col: Feigling)* wimp *(col)*; ~**lauge** *f* suds *pl*; ~**maschine** *f* washing machine; **w~maschinenfest** *adj* machine-washable; ~**mittel** *nt* detergent; ~**pulver** *nt* washing powder *(Brit)*, soap powder; ~**salon** *m* launderette *(Brit)*, laundromat *(US)*; ~**schüssel** *f* washbasin *(Brit)*, washbowl *(US)*; ~**straße** *f (zur Autowäsche)* car wash; ~**wasser** *nt* washing water; ~**zettel** *m (Typ)* blurb; ~**zeug** *nt* toilet or washing things *pl*; ~**zuber** *m* washtub.
**Wasser** *nt* - (**a**) *no pl* water. **das ist** ~ **auf seine Mühle** *(fig)* this is all grist to his mill; **dort wird auch nur mit** ~ **gekocht** *(fig)* they're no different from anybody else (there); **ihr kann er nicht das** ~ **reichen** *(fig)* he can't hold a candle to her; **unter** ~ **stehen** to be flooded; **ins** ~ **fallen** *(fig)* to fall through; **sich über** ~ **halten** *(fig)* to keep one's head above water; **mit allen** ~**n gewaschen sein** *(col)* to be a shrewd customer; **ein Boot zu** ~ **lassen** to launch a boat; **nahe am** ~ **gebaut haben** *(col)* to be a crybaby *(col)*; ~ **lassen** *(Med)* to pass water. (**b**) *pl* ≈ *(Flüssigkeit) (Abwasch~ etc)* water; *(medizinisch)* lotion; *(Parfüm)* cologne; *(Mineral~)* mineral water. **das** ~ **läuft mir im Mund zusammen** my mouth is watering.
**Wasser-**: **w~abstoßend, w~abweisend** *adj* water-repellent; ~**anschluß** *m* mains water supply; **w~arm** *adj* arid; ~**ball** *m* (**a**) *(no pl: Spiel)* water polo; (**b**) *(Ball)* beach ball; *(fürs ~ballspiel)* water-polo ball; ~**bett** *nt* water bed.
**Wässerchen** *nt* **er sieht aus, als ob er kein** ~ **trüben könnte** he looks as if butter wouldn't melt in his mouth.
**Wasser-**: ~**dampf** *m* steam; **w~dicht** *adj (lit, fig)* watertight; *Uhr, Stoff etc* waterproof; ~**enthärter** *m* water softener; ~**fahrzeug** *nt* watercraft; ~**fall** *m* waterfall; ~**farbe** *f* watercolour *(Brit)*, watercolor *(US)*; **w~fest** *adj* waterproof; ~**floh** *m* water flea; ~**flugzeug** *nt* seaplane; **w~gekühlt** *adj* water-cooled; ~**glas** *nt (Trinkglas)* tumbler; ~**glätte** *f* aquaplaning conditions *pl*; ~**graben** *m*

*(Sport)* water jump; *(um Burg)* moat; ~**hahn** *m* tap, faucet *(US)*; ~**härte** *f* hardness of the water; ~**huhn** *nt* coot.
**wässerig** *adj (lit, fig)* watery. **jdm den Mund** ~ **machen** *(col)* to make sb's mouth water.
**Wasser-**: ~**kessel** *m* kettle; *(Tech)* boiler; ~**klosett** *nt* water closet; ~**kraft** *f* water power; ~**kraftwerk** *nt* hydroelectric power station; ~**kreislauf** *m (Met)* water cycle; ~**kühlung** *f* water-cooling; **mit** ~**kühlung** water-cooled; ~**lassen** *nt* passing water; ~**lauf** *m* watercourse; ~**leiche** *f* drowned corpse; ~**leitung** *f (Rohr)* water pipe; *(Anlagen)* plumbing *no pl*; ~**lilie** *f* water lily; **w~löslich** *adj* water-soluble; ~**mann** *m*, *pl* ~**männer** *(Astrol)* Aquarius *no art*; ~**melone** *f* water melon; ~**mühle** *f* water mill.
**wassern** *vi (Aviat)* to land on water.
**wässern** *vti* to water; *Erbsen etc* to soak. **mir** ~ **die Augen** my eyes are watering.
**Wasser-**: ~**pfeife** *f* hookah; ~**pflanze** *f* aquatic plant; ~**pistole** *f* water pistol; ~**rad** *nt* water wheel; ~**ratte** *f* water rat or vole; *(col: Schwimmer)* water baby; **w~reich** *adj Gebiet* abounding in water; *Fluß* containing a lot of water; ~**rohr** *nt* water pipe; ~**scheide** *f* watershed; **w~scheu** *adj* scared of water; ~**schildkröte** *f* turtle; ~**schutzpolizei** *f (auf Flüssen, ~wegen)* river police; *(im Hafen)* harbour *(Brit)* or harbor *(US)* police; *(auf der See)* coastguard service; ~**ski** *nt* water-skiing; ~**spiegel** *m (Oberfläche)* surface of the water; *(~stand)* water level; ~**sport** *m* **der** ~**sport** water sports *pl*; ~**spülung** *f* flush; ~**stand** *m* water level; **niedriger/hoher** ~**stand** low/high water; ~**stelle** *f* water(ing) hole.
**Wasserstoff** *m* hydrogen.
**Wasserstoff-**: **w~blond** *adj attr Haar* peroxide blonde; **eine** ~**blonde** a peroxide blonde *(col)*; ~**bombe** *f* H-bomb.
**Wasser-**: ~**strahl** *m* jet of water; ~**straße** *f* waterway; ~**sucht** *f* dropsy; ~**tank** *m* water tank; ~**tier** *nt* aquatic animal; ~**träger** *m* water carrier; ~**treten** *nt (Med)* paddling *(in cold water as therapy)*; ~**tropfen** *m* drop of water; ~**turm** *m* water tower; ~**uhr** *f* water meter; ~**verbrauch** *m* water consumption *no def art*; ~**versorgung** *f* water supply; ~**verunreinigung** *f* water pollution; ~**vogel** *m* waterfowl; ~**waage** *f* spirit level; ~**weg** *m* waterway; **auf dem** ~**weg** by water or *(Meer)* sea; ~**werfer** *m* water cannon; ~**werk** *nt* waterworks *sing or pl*; ~**wirtschaft** *f* water supply (and distribution); ~**zähler** *m* water meter; ~**zeichen** *nt* watermark.
**wäßrig** *adj* = **wässerig**.
**waten** *vi aux sein* to wade.
**watscheln** *vi aux sein* to waddle.
**Watt**[1] *nt* - *(Elec)* watt.
**Watt**[2] *nt* -**en** *(Geog)* mud flats *pl*.
**Watte** *f* -**n** cotton wool *(Brit)*, absorbent cotton *(US)*; *(zur Polsterung)* wadding.
**Wattebausch** *m* cotton ball.
**Wattenmeer** *nt* mud flats *pl*.
**Wattestäbchen** *nt* cotton bud.
**wattieren*** *vt* to pad; *(füttern)* to line with padding; *(und absteppen) Stoff* to quilt.
**Wattzahl** *f* wattage.
**WC** [ve:'tse:] *nt* -**s** WC.
**WDR** [ve:de:'er] *m* = **Westdeutscher Rundfunk**.
**weben** *pret* **webte** or *(liter, fig)* **wob**, *ptp* **gewebt** or *(liter, fig)* **gewoben** *vti (lit, fig)* to weave; *Spinnennetz* to spin.
**Weber(in** *f)* *m* - weaver.

**Weberei** f (a) *(Betrieb)* weaving mill. (b) *no pl (das Weben)* weaving.

**Web-:** ~**stuhl** m loom; ~**waren** pl woven goods pl.

**Wechsel** ['vɛksl] m - (a) change; *(abwechselnd)* alternation; *(Geld~)* exchange. **im** ~ *(abwechselnd)* in turn, alternately. (b) *(Staffel~)* change-over; *(Ftbl etc)* substitution. (c) *(Fin)* bill (of exchange).

**Wechsel-** ['vɛksl-]: ~**bad** nt alternating hot and cold baths pl; ~**bad der Gefühle** *(fig)* emotional roller-coaster; ~**beziehung** f correlation, interrelation; ~**fälle** pl vicissitudes pl; ~**geld** nt change; **w~haft** adj changeable; ~**jahre** pl menopause sing; **in die** ~**jahre kommen** to start the menopause; ~**kurs** m exchange rate.

**wechseln** ['vɛksln] **1** vt to change *(in +acc into)*; *(austauschen)* to exchange. **die Schule/das Hemd** ~ to change schools/one's shirt; **die Farbe** ~ to change colour *(Brit)* or color *(US)*; **Briefe** ~ to correspond *(mit with)*; **können Sie (mir) 10 Mark** ~? can you change 10 marks (for me)? **2** vi (a) to change; *(einander ablösen)* to alternate. **ich kann leider nicht** ~ I'm sorry, I don't have any change. (b) **über die Straße** ~ to cross the road.

**wechselnd** ['vɛkslnt] adj changing; *(einander ablösend)* alternating; *Stimmungen* changeable; *Winde, Bewölkung* variable. **mit** ~**em Erfolg** with varying (degrees of) success.

**Wechsel** ['vɛksl-]: ~**rahmen** m clip-on picture frame; **w~seitig** adj reciprocal; ~**spiel** nt interplay; ~**strom** m alternating current, A.C.; ~**stube** f bureau de change; **w~voll** adj varied; ~**wähler** m floating voter; **w~weise** adv in turn, alternately; ~**wirkung** f interaction.

**Wechsler** ['vɛkslɐ] m - *(Automat)* change dispenser.

**Weckdienst** m *(Telec)* alarm call service.

**wecken** vt to wake (up); *(fig)* to arouse; *Bedarf* to create; *Erinnerungen* to revive.

**Wecker** m - alarm clock. **jdm auf den** ~ **fallen** *(col)* to get on sb's nerves.

**Weck-:** ~**glas** ® nt preserving jar; ~**radio** nt radio-alarm clock; ~**ruf** m *(Telec)* alarm call.

**Wedel** m - *(Staub~)* feather duster.

**wedeln** vi **(mit dem Schwanz)** ~ to wag its tail; **mit etw** ~ *(winken)* to wave sth.

**weder** conj ~ ... **noch** ... neither ... nor ...

**weg** adv away. ~ **sein** to have or be gone; *(nicht hier, entfernt)* to be away; *(col: geistesabwesend)* to be not quite with it *(col)*; *(col: eingeschlafen)* to be out like a light *(col)*; *(col: begeistert)* to be taken *(von* with*)*; **über etw** *(acc)* ~ **sein** *(col: emotional)* to have got over sth; **über den Tisch** ~ across the table; **nichts wie** or **nur** ~ **von hier!** let's get out of here; ~ **da!** (get) out of the way!; ~ **damit!** *(mit Schere etc)* put it away!; **Hände** ~! hands off!; **in einem** ~ *(col)* non-stop.

**Weg** m -e (a) *(Pfad, fig)* path. **am** ~**e** by the wayside; **jdm den** ~ **versperren** to block sb's way; **jdm/einer Sache im** ~ **stehen** *(fig)* to stand in the way of sb/sth; **jdm Steine in den** ~ **legen** *(fig)* to put obstructions in sb's way; **jdm nicht über den** ~ **trauen** *(fig)* not to trust sb an inch; **etw aus dem** ~ **räumen** *(fig)* to get sth out of the way; **den** ~ **des geringsten Widerstandes gehen** to follow the line of least resistance.

(b) *(lit, fig: Route)* way; *(Entfernung)* distance; *(Reise)* journey; *(zu Fuß)* walk. **ich muß diesen** ~ **jeden Tag zweimal gehen** I have to walk this stretch twice a day; **den richtigen** ~ **einschlagen** *(lit)* to follow the right road; **jdm einen guten Rat mit auf den** ~ **geben** to give sb good advice to follow in life; **jdm/einer Sache aus dem** ~ **gehen** *(lit)* to get out of

sb's way/the way of sth; **jdm über den** ~ **laufen** *(fig)* to run into sb; **etw in die** ~**e leiten** to arrange sth; **auf dem besten** ~ **sein, etw zu tun** to be well on the way to doing sth.

(c) *(Mittel, Art und Weise)* way. **auf diesem** ~**e** this way; **auf diplomatischem** ~**e** through diplomatic channels; **auf legalem** ~**e** legally.

**wegbekommen*** vt sep irreg to get rid of *(von* from*)*; *Fleck* to get off; *(von bestimmtem Ort)* jdn to get away *(von* from*)*.

**Weg-:** ~**bereiter** m precursor, forerunner; ~**bereiter einer Sache** *(gen)* or **für etw sein** to pave the way for sth; ~**biegung** f turn, bend.

**weg-:** ~**blasen** vt sep irreg to blow away; **wie** ~**geblasen sein** *(fig)* to have vanished; ~**bleiben** vi sep irreg aux sein to stay away; **mir bleibt die Spucke** ~! *(col)* I'm absolutely flabbergasted!; ~**bringen** vt sep irreg to take away; *(zur Reparatur)* to take in; ~**denken** vt sep irreg: **das Auto ist aus unserem Leben nicht mehr** ~**zudenken** life today without the car is something that cannot be imagined; ~**dürfen** vi sep irreg to be allowed to leave; *(col: ausgehen dürfen)* to be allowed to go out.

**Wegelagerer** m - highwayman; *(zu Fuß)* footpad.

**wegen** prep +gen because of. **jdn** ~ **einer Sache bestrafen** to punish sb for sth; ~ **der Kinder** for the sake of the children; ~ **mir** *(col)* because of me; **von** ~! *(col)* you must be joking!

**Wegerich** m -e *(Bot)* plantain.

**wegfahren** vi sep irreg aux sein *(abfahren)* to leave; *(Auto, Fahrer)* to drive off; *(im Boot)* to sail away; *(zum Einkaufen, als Ausflug)* to go out; *(verreisen)* to go away.

**wegfallen** vi sep irreg aux sein to be discontinued; *(Bestimmung)* to cease to apply; *(unterbleiben)* to be lost; *(überflüssig werden)* to become unnecessary; *(ausgelassen werden)* to be omitted. ~ **lassen** to discontinue; *(auslassen)* to omit.

**weg-:** ~**fegen** vt sep *(lit, fig)* to sweep away; ~**fliegen** vi sep irreg aux sein to fly away; *(Hut)* to fly off; *(mit Flugzeug)* to leave; ~**führen** vt sep to lead away.

**Weggabelung** f fork (in the road).

**Weggang** m departure.

**weggeben** vt sep irreg *(verschenken)* to give away. **seine Wäsche (zum Waschen)** ~ to have one's washing done.

**weggehen** vi sep irreg aux sein to go, to leave; *(verreisen, umziehen etc)* to go away; *(ausgehen)* to go out; *(col: Fleck)* to come off; *(col: Ware)* to sell.

**weggucken** vi sep to look away.

**weghaben** vt sep irreg *(col) (erledigt haben)* to have got done; *(bekommen, verstanden haben)* to have got. **du hast deinen Denkzettel weg** you have had your punishment; **einen** ~ *(col: verrückt sein)* to have a screw loose *(col)*.

**weg-:** ~**helfen** vi sep irreg **jdm von irgendwo** ~**helfen** to help sb get away from a place; ~**holen** vt sep to take away; *(abholen)* to fetch; ~**hören** vi sep not to listen; ~**jagen** vt sep to chase away.

**wegkommen** vi sep irreg aux sein *(col)* (a) *(abhanden kommen)* to disappear; *(weggehen können)* to get away; *(aus dem Haus)* to get out. **mach, daß du wegkommst!** hop it! *(col)*; **gut/schlecht (bei etw)** ~ to come off well/badly (in sth). (b) = **hinwegkommen**.

**Weg-:** ~**kreuzung** f crossroads; ~**krümmung** f bend in the road.

**weg-:** ~**lassen** vt sep irreg *(auslassen)* to leave out; *(col: gehen lassen)* to let go; ~**laufen** vi sep irreg *aux sein* to run away *(vor +dat* from*);* **das läuft (dir) nicht ~!** *(fig hum)* that can wait; **~legen** *vt sep* to put away; *(zum späteren Verbrauch)* to put aside.

**wegmachen** *vt sep (col)* to get rid of.

**wegmüssen** *vi sep irreg* to have to go; *(entfernt werden)* to have to be removed. **ich muß eine Zeitlang aus New York weg** I must get out of New York for a while.

**wegnehmen** *vt sep irreg* to take; *(fortnehmen, entziehen)* to take away; *Platz* to take up. **Gas ~** *(Aut)* to take one's foot off the accelerator *or* gas *(US);* **jdm die Frau ~** to steal sb's wife.

**weg-:** **~packen** *vt sep* to pack away; **~putzen** *vt sep* to wipe away; *(col: essen)* to polish off.

**Wegrand** *m* wayside.

**weg-:** **~rationalisieren\*** *vt sep Arbeitsplätze* to rationalize away; **~räumen** *vt sep* to clear away; *(in Schrank)* to put away; **~reißen** *vt sep irreg* to tear away *(jdm* from sb*);* **~rennen** *vi sep irreg aux sein (col)* to run away; **~rücken** *vti sep (vi: aux sein)* to move away; **~rufen** *vt sep irreg* to call away; **~rutschen** *vi sep aux sein (aus der Hand etc)* to slip away; *(auf Eis etc)* to slide away; **~schaffen** *vt sep (beseitigen)* to get rid of; *(~räumen)* to clear away; *(~tragen)* to remove; **~schicken** *vt sep Brief, jdn* to send away; *(um etwas zu holen etc)* to send off; **~schleichen** *vir sep irreg (vi: aux sein)* to creep *or* steal away; **~schleppen** *vt sep* to drag away *or* off; *(tragen)* to carry off; **~schließen** *vt sep irreg* to lock away; **~schmeißen** *vt sep irreg (col)* to chuck away *(col);* **~schnappen** *vt sep (col)* **jdm etw ~schnappen** to snatch sth (away) from sb; **jdm die Freundin ~schnappen** to pinch sb's girlfriend *(col);* **~schütten** *vt sep* to tip away; **~schwemmen** *vt sep* to wash away; **~sehen** *vi sep irreg* to look away; **~setzen** *vt sep* to move (away); *(~stellen)* to put away; **~sollen** *vi sep irreg (col)* **das soll ~** that is to go; **ich soll von London ~** I am (supposed) to leave London; **~spülen** *vt sep* to wash away; **~stecken** *vt sep (lit)* to put away; *(col) Niederlage, Kritik* to take; *Enttäuschung* to get over; **~stehlen** *vr sep irreg* to steal away; **~stellen** *vt sep* to put away; **~sterben** *vi sep irreg aux sein (col)* to die off; **~stoßen** *vt sep irreg* to push away; *(mit Fuß)* to kick away; **~tragen** *vt sep irreg* to carry away; **~treiben** *sep irreg* **1** *vt Tier etc* to drive away; **2** *vi aux sein* to drift away; **~treten** *vi sep irreg aux sein (Mil)* to fall out; **~treten!** dismiss!; **geistig ~getreten sein** *(col: geistesabwesend)* to be not quite with it *(col);* **~tun** *vt sep irreg* to put away; **~wehen** *vti sep (vi: aux sein)* to blow away.

**Weg-:** **w~weisend** *adj* pioneering *attr*, revolutionary; **~weiser** *m* - sign; *(an einem Pfosten)* signpost; *(fig: Buch etc)* guide.

**Wegwerf-** *in cpds* disposable.

**weg-:** **~werfen** *vt sep irreg* to throw away; **das ist ~geworfenes Geld** that's money down the drain; **~werfend** *adj* disdainful; **W~werfgesellschaft** *f* throwaway society; **~wischen** *vt sep* to wipe off; **~wollen** *vi sep irreg (verreisen)* to want to go away; *(~gehen: von Party etc)* to want to leave; *(hinausgehen)* to want to go out; **~zaubern** *vt sep* to make disappear; **~ziehen** *sep irreg* **1** *vt* to pull away *(jdm* from sb*);* **2** *vi aux sein* to move away.

**weh** *adj (wund)* sore. **~ tun** *(lit, fig)* to hurt; **mir tut der Rücken ~** my back hurts; **sich/jdm ~ tun** *(lit, fig)* to hurt oneself/sb.

**wehe** *interj* **~ (dir), wenn du das tust** you'll regret it if you do that; **darf ich das anfassen? — ~ (dir)!** can I touch? — you dare!

**Wehe** *f* -n (a) *(Schnee~ etc)* drift. (b) *(Geburts~)* **~n** *pl* contractions; **in den ~n liegen** to be in labour *(Brit)* or labor *(US).*

**wehen** **1** *vi (Wind)* to blow; *(Fahne)* to flutter; *(Haare)* to blow about. **2** *vt* to blow *(von* off*);* *(sanft)* to waft.

**Weh-:** **~klage** *f (liter)* lament(ation); **w~leidig** *adj* oversensitive to pain; *(jammernd)* whining *attr;* *(voller Selbstmitleid)* self-pitying; **sei nicht so w~leidig!** stop feeling sorry for yourself; **~mut** *f no pl (geh)* melancholy; *(Sehnsucht)* wistfulness; **w~mütig** *adj siehe n* melancholy; wistful.

**Wehr¹** *f* -en (a) *(Feuer~)* fire brigade *(Brit)* or department *(US).* (b) **sich zur ~ setzen** to defend oneself.

**Wehr²** *nt* -e weir.

**Wehr-** *in cpds* defence *(Brit)*, defense *(US);* **~dienst** *m* military service; **seinen ~dienst (ab)leisten** to do one's military service; **jdn zum ~dienst einberufen** to call sb up, to draft sb *(US);* **~dienstverweigerer** *m* conscientious objector.

**wehren** **1** *vr* to defend oneself; *(aktiv kämpfen)* to (put up a) fight. **2** *vi +dat (geh)* **wehret den Anfängen!** these things must be nipped in the bud.

**Wehr-:** **~etat** *m* defence *(Brit)* or defense *(US)* budget; **w~fähig** *adj* fit for military service; **w~haft** *adj (geh)* able to put up a fight; *Stadt etc* well-fortified; **w~los** *adj* defenceless *(Brit)*, defenseless *(US);* *(fig: hilflos)* helpless; **jdm w~los ausgeliefert sein** to be at sb's mercy; **~pflicht** *f* **(allgemeine) ~pflicht** (universal) conscription; **w~pflichtig** *adj* liable for military service; **~pflichtige(r)** *mf decl as adj* person liable for military service; **~sold** *m* (military) pay; **~übung** *f* reserve duty training exercise.

**Wehwehchen** *nt (col)* (minor) complaint.

**Weib** *nt* -er woman, female *(pej)*, broad *(US col).*

**Weibchen** *nt* little woman; *(Zool)* female.

**Weiber-:** **~feind** *m* woman-hater, misogynist; **~geschichten** *pl* sexploits *pl (hum);* **~geschwätz** *nt (pej)* women's talk; **~held** *m (pej)* womanizer.

**weibisch** *adj* effeminate.

**weiblich** *adj* female; *(Gram, fraulich)* feminine.

**Weiblichkeit** *f* femininity; *(Frauen)* women.

**weich** *adj* soft *(auch fig, Ling, Phot, Typ);* *Ei* soft-boiled; *Fleisch, Gemüse* tender; *Währung, Wasser* soft. **~ werden** *(lit, fig)* to soften; **die Knie wurden mir ~** my knees turned to jelly; **~ machen** to soften.

**Weiche¹** *f* -n *(Seite)* side; *(von Tier auch)* flank.

**Weiche²** *f* -n *(Rail)* points *pl (Brit)*, switch *(US).* **die ~n stellen** *(lit)* to switch the points; *(fig)* to set the course.

**weichen¹** *vti (vi: aux haben or sein) (ein~)* to soak.

**weichen²** *pret* **wich,** *ptp* **gewichen** *vi aux sein* (a) to give way *(dat* to*);* *(zurück~)* to retreat *(dat, vor +dat* from*);* **(nicht) von jdm** *or* **jds Seite ~** (not) to leave sb's side. (b) *(Schmerz)* to go.

**Weich-:** **w~gekocht** *adj attr Ei* soft-boiled; *Fleisch, Gemüse* boiled until tender; **w~herzig** *adj* soft-hearted; **~holz** *nt* softwood; **~käse** *m* soft cheese.

**weichlich** *adj (lit, fig)* soft; *Charakter* weak.

**Weichling** *m (pej)* softy *(col).*

**Weich-:** **w~machen** *vt sep (fig)* to soften up; **~macher** *m (Chem)* softener; **w~spülen** *vt sep* to condition; *Wäsche* to use softener on; **~spüler** *m* conditioner; **~teile** *pl* soft parts *pl;* **~tier** *nt* mollusc.

**Weide¹** *f* -n *(Bot)* willow.

**Weide²** *f* -n *(Agr)* pasture; *(Wiese)* meadow. **auf der ~ sein** to be grazing.

**Weideland** nt *(Agr)* pasture, grazing (land).

**weiden 1** vi to graze. **2** vt to (put out to) graze. **3** vr **sich an etw** *(dat)* ~ *(fig)* to gloat over sth.

**Weiden-:** ~**baum** m willow tree; ~**busch** m willow bush; ~**kätzchen** nt willow catkin; ~**korb** m wicker basket; ~**rost** m cattle grid.

**Weideplatz** m pasture.

**weidlich** adv *(mit adj)* pretty. **etw** ~ **ausnutzen** to make full use of sth.

**Weid-:** ~**mann** m, pl ~**männer** *(liter)* huntsman, hunter; **w~männisch 1** adj huntsman's attr; **das ist nicht w~männisch** that's not done in hunting; **2** adv like a professional hunter.

**weigern** vr to refuse.

**Weigerung** f refusal.

**Weihe** f -n *(Eccl)* consecration; *(Priester~)* ordination.

**weihen** vt **(a)** *(Eccl)* to consecrate. **jdn zum Bischof/ Priester** ~ to consecrate sb bishop/ordain sb priest. **(b)** *(widmen)* **etw jdm/einer Sache** ~ to dedicate sth to sb/sth; **dem Untergang geweiht** *(liter)* doomed.

**Weiher** m - pond.

**Weihnachten** nt - Christmas. **fröhliche** ~! happy or merry Christmas!; **(an)** ~ at Christmas; ~ **nach Hause fahren** to go home for Christmas; **etw zu** ~ **bekommen/schenken** to get sth for Christmas/to give sth as a Christmas present; **weiße/grüne** ~ (a) white Christmas/(a) Christmas without snow.

**weihnachten** vi impers *(poet, iro)* **es weihnachtet sehr** Christmas is very much in evidence.

**weihnachtlich** adj Christmassy *(col)*.

**Weihnachts-** in cpds Christmas; ~**abend** m Christmas Eve; ~**baum** m Christmas tree; ~**einkauf** m Christmas shopping no pl; ~**feier** f Christmas celebration(s pl); ~**feiertag** m = ~**tag**; ~**fest** nt Christmas; ~**gans** f Christmas goose; **jdn ausnehmen wie eine** ~**gans** *(col)* to fleece sb *(col)*, to take sb to the cleaners *(col)*; ~**geld** nt Christmas bonus; ~**geschenk** nt Christmas present; ~**insel** f Christmas Island; ~**karte** f Christmas card; ~**lied** nt (Christmas) carol; ~**mann** m, pl ~**männer** Father Christmas, Santa Claus; *(pej col)* clown *(pej col)*; ~**markt** m Christmas fair; ~**tag** m **(erster)** ~**tag** Christmas Day; **zweiter** ~**tag** Boxing Day *(Brit)*; ~**zeit** f Christmas time.

**Weih-:** ~**rauch** m incense; ~**wasser** nt holy water.

**weil** conj because.

**Weilchen** nt **ein** ~ a while.

**Weile** f no pl while. **eine** ~ for a while.

**weilen** vi *(geh)* to be; *(bleiben)* to stay.

**Weiler** m - hamlet.

**Weimarer Republik** f Weimar Republic.

**Wein** m -e wine. **jdm reinen** ~ **einschenken** to tell sb the truth.

**Wein-** in cpds *(auf Getränk bezogen)* wine; *(auf Pflanze bezogen)* vine; ~**bau** m wine-growing; ~**bauer** m wine-grower; ~**beere** f grape; ~**berg** m vineyard; ~**bergschnecke** f snail; ~**brand** m brandy; ~**brennerei** f brandy distillery.

**weinen** vti to cry; *(aus Trauer auch)* to weep *(um for, über +acc)*. **sich** *(dat)* **die Augen rot** ~ to cry one's eyes out; **es ist zum W~!** it's enough to make you weep!

**weinerlich** adj whining, whiny *(col)*.

**Wein-:** ~**ernte** f grape harvest; ~**essig** m wine vinegar; ~**faß** nt wine cask; ~**flasche** f wine bottle; ~**garten** m vineyard; ~**gegend** f wine-growing area; ~**geist** m (ethyl) alcohol; ~**gut** nt wine-growing estate; ~**händler** m wine merchant; ~**handlung** f wine shop *(Brit)* or store; ~**karte** f wine list; ~**keller** m wine cellar; *(Lokal)* wine bar;

~**kelter** f wine press; ~**kenner** m wine connoisseur.

**Weinkrampf** m crying fit.

**Wein-:** ~**küfer** m cellarman; ~**land** nt winegrowing country; ~**laub** nt vine leaves pl; ~**lese** f grape harvest; ~**lokal** nt wine bar; ~**panscherei** f wine-adulterating; ~**probe** f wine tasting; ~**rebe** f vine; **w~rot** adj wine-red; ~**säure** f *(Chem)* tartaric acid; **w~selig** adj merry with wine; ~**stock** m vine; ~**stube** f wine bar; ~**traube** f grape.

**weise** adj wise.

**Weise** f -n **(a)** *(Verfahren etc)* manner. **auf diese** ~ in this way; **auf geheimnisvolle** etc ~ in a mysterious way; **in gewisser/keiner** ~ in a/no way; **in der** ~, **daß** ... in such a way that ... **(b)** *(liter: Melodie)* melody.

**weisen** pret **wies**, ptp **gewiesen** *(geh)* **1** vt **jdm etw** ~ *(lit, fig)* to show sb sth; **jdn aus dem Lande** ~ to expel sb; **jdn vom Platz** ~ *(Sport)* to order sb off (the field); **jdn von der Schule** ~ to expel sb (from school); **etw (weit) von sich** ~ *(fig)* to reject sth (emphatically). **2** vi to point *(nach* to(wards)*, auf +acc* at*)*.

**Weise(r)** m decl as adj wise man.

**Weisheit** f **(a)** no pl wisdom. **das ist auch nicht der** ~ **letzter Schluß** that's not exactly the ideal solution; **er hat die** ~ **nicht mit Löffeln gefressen** he's not so bright. **(b)** *(weiser Spruch)* wise saying; *(iro)* pearl of wisdom.

**Weisheitszahn** m wisdom tooth.

**weismachen** vt sep **jdm etw** ~ to make sb believe sth; **er wollte uns** ~, **daß** ... he would have us believe that ...; **das kannst du mir nicht** ~! you can't expect me to believe that.

**weiß** adj white. **ein** ~**es (Blatt) Papier** a blank sheet of paper; **ein** ~**er Fleck (auf der Landkarte)** a blank area (on the map); **das W~e Haus** the White House; **das W~e im Auge** the whites of one's eyes; **das W~e vom Ei** the white of an egg.

**Weiß** nt - white.

**weissagen** vt insep to foretell.

**Weissagung** f prophecy.

**Weiß-:** ~**bier** nt light, *fizzy beer made using top-fermented yeast*; ~**blech** nt tinplate; **w~blond** adj ash-blond(e); ~**brot** nt white bread; *(Laib)* white loaf; ~**buch** nt *(Pol)* white paper; ~**dorn** m *(Bot)* hawthorn.

**weißen** vt to whiten; *(tünchen)* to whitewash.

**Weiße(r)** mf decl as adj white, white man/woman.

**Weiß-:** ~**glut** f **jdn zur** ~**glut bringen** to make sb see red; **w~haarig** adj white-haired; ~**herbst** m ≈ rosé; ~**kohl** m white cabbage; **w~lich** adj whitish; ~**metall** nt white metal; ~**rußland** nt Byelorussia; ~**wal** m white whale; ~**waren** pl linen sing; ~**wein** m white wine; ~**wurst** f veal sausage.

**Weisung** f directive; *(Jur)* ruling. **auf** ~ on instructions.

**weit** siehe auch **weiter 1** adv **(a)** far. **es ist noch** ~ **bis Bremen** there's still a long way to go till Bremen; ~ **zurückliegen** to be far behind; *(zeitlich)* to be a long time ago; ~ **nach Mitternacht** well after midnight; ~ **und breit** for miles around; **ziemlich** ~ **am Ende** fairly near the end; **von** ~**em** from a long way off; ~ **entfernt** a long way away; ~**er entfernt** farther away; **ich bin** ~ **davon entfernt, das zu tun** I have no intention of doing that; ~ **gefehlt!** far from it; ~ **offen** wide open; ~ **herumkommen** to get around a lot; ~ **verbreitet** widespread.

**(b)** *(in Entwicklung)* ~ **fortgeschritten** well advanced; **wie** ~ **bist du?** how far have you got?; **er**

**hat es ~ gebracht** he has come a long way; **es so ~ bringen, daß ...** to bring it about that ...
**(c)** *(fig: erheblich) (mit comp adj, adv)* far; *(mit vb)* by far. **~ besser** far better; **bei ~em nicht so gut** *etc* **(wie...)** not nearly as good *etc* (as ...); **~ über 60** well over 60.
**(d) mit etw ist es nicht ~ her** *(col)* sth is not up to much *(col)*; **das würde zu ~ führen** that would be taking things too far; **zu ~ gehen** to go too far; **das geht zu ~** that's going too far; **etw zu ~ treiben** to carry sth too far.
**2** *adj* **(a)** wide; *(fig) Begriff, Horizont etc* broad; *Meer* open; *Herz* big. **im ~eren Sinne** in the broader *or* wider sense; **das ist ein ~es Feld** *(fig)* that is a big subject.
**(b)** *(lang) Reise, Wurf etc* long. **in ~en Abständen** at long intervals; **man hat hier einen ~en Blick** you can see a long way from here; **in ~er Ferne** in the far distance; **das liegt noch in ~er Ferne** it's still a long way away.
**Weit-:** **w~ab** *adv* **w~ab von** far (away) from; **w~aus** *adv* far; **w~aus besser** far better; **w~ausholend** *adj Geste etc* expansive; *(fig) Erzählung etc* long-drawn-out; **~blick** *m (fig)* far-sightedness; **w~blickend** *adj (fig)* far-sighted.
**Weite** *f -n (Ferne)* distance; *(Länge)* length; *(Größe)* expanse; *(Durchmesser)* width. **etw in der ~ ändern** to alter the width of sth.
**weiten** *vtr* to widen; *(Pupille)* to dilate.
**weiter 1** *adj* further; *(andere)* other. **2** *adv (noch hinzu)* further; *(außerdem)* furthermore; *(sonst)* otherwise; *(nachher)* afterwards. **nichts ~** *(darüber hinaus nichts)* nothing further; **~ nichts?** is that all?; **~ nichts als ...** nothing but ...; **ich brauche ~ nichts** that's all I need; **wenn es ~ nichts ist, ...** well, if that's all (it is), ...; **außer uns war ~ niemand da** there was nobody else there besides us; **das hat ~ nichts zu sagen** that doesn't really matter; **etw ~ tun** to continue to do sth; **immer ~ on** and on; *(Anweisung)* keep on (going); **was geschah (dann) ~?** what happened then?
**weiter-:** **~arbeiten** *vi sep* to work on; **an einer Sache** *(dat)* **~arbeiten** to do some more work on sth; **W~bestehen** *nt* continued existence; **~bewegen\*** *vtr sep* to move further; **~bilden** *vr sep* to continue one's education; **~bringen** *vt sep irreg* to take further; **das bringt uns auch nicht ~** that doesn't get us any further; **~denken** *vi sep irreg* to think things through; *(an Zukünftiges)* to think ahead; **~empfehlen\*** *vt sep irreg* to recommend (to one's friends *etc)*; **~entwickeln\*** *vtr sep* to develop *(zu* into); **~erzählen\*** *vt sep Geheimnis etc* to pass on.
**Weitere(s)** *nt decl as adj* further details *pl*. **das ~** the rest; **alles ~** all the rest; **bis auf w~s** for the time being.
**Weiter-:** **w~fahren** *vi sep irreg aux sein (Fahrt fortsetzen)* to travel on; **w~fliegen** *vi sep irreg aux sein* to fly on; **die Maschine fliegt in 10 Minuten w~** the plane will take off again in 10 minutes; **w~führen** *vti sep* to continue; **das führt nicht w~** *(fig)* that doesn't get us anywhere; **w~führend** *adj Schule* secondary *(Brit)*, high *(US)*; **w~geben** *vt sep irreg* to pass on; **w~gehen** *vi sep irreg aux sein* to go on; **so kann es nicht w~gehen** *(fig)* things can't go on like this; **wie soll es nun w~gehen?** what's going to happen now?; **w~helfen** *vi sep irreg* to help (along) *(jdm sb)*; **w~hin** *adv (außerdem)* furthermore; **etw w~hin tun** to carry on doing sth; **w~kommen** *vi sep irreg aux sein* to advance; **nicht w~kommen** *(fig)* to be stuck down;

**w~können** *vi sep irreg* to be able to carry on; **ich kann nicht w~** I can't go on; **w~laufen** *vi sep irreg aux sein* to run/walk on; *(Film, Produktion)* to go on; *(Gehalt)* to continue to be paid; **w~leben** *vi sep* to live on; **w~leiten** *vt sep* to pass on *(an +acc* to); *(senden)* to forward; **w~machen** *vti sep* to carry on *(etw* with sth); **w~reichen** *vt sep* to pass on; **~reise** *f* continuation of the/one's journey; **auf der ~reise nach ...** when I *etc* was travelling *(Brit)* or traveling *(US)* on to ...; **w~sagen** *vt sep* to pass on; **nicht w~sagen!** don't tell anyone!; **w~sehen** *vi irreg* to see; **w~senden** *vt sep irreg* to forward; **w~verarbeiten\*** *vt sep* to process; **w~verfolgen\*** *vt sep Idee* to follow up; **~verkauf** *m* resale; **w~verkaufen\*** *vti sep* to resell; **w~vermieten\*** *vt sep* to sublet; **w~wissen** *vi sep irreg* **nicht (mehr) w~wissen** *(verzweifelt sein)* to be at one's wits' end; **w~wollen** *vi sep irreg* to want to go on; **w~wursteln** *vi sep (col)* to muddle on; **w~ziehen** *vi irreg aux sein* to move on.
**Weit-:** **w~gehend 1** *adj Vollmachten etc* far-reaching, extensive; *Übereinstimmung etc* a large degree of; **2** *adv* to a large extent; **w~gereist** *adj attr* widely travelled *(Brit)* or traveled *(US)*; **w~her** *adv (auch* **von w~her)** from far away; **w~hergeholt** *adj attr* far-fetched; **w~herzig** *adj* generous; **w~hin** *adv* widely; *(weitgehend)* to a large extent; **w~hin unbekannt** largely unknown; **w~läufig** *adj* **(a)** *Park, Gebäude* spacious; *Dorf* sprawling *attr; (fig) Erzählung* long-drawn-out; **(b)** *Verwandte* distant; **w~maschig** *adj Netz* wide-meshed; **w~räumig** *adj* wide-ranging; **etw w~räumig umfahren** to keep well away from sth; **w~reichend** *adj (fig)* far-reaching; **w~schweifig** *adj* long-winded; **~sicht** *f (fig)* far-sightedness; **w~sichtig** *adj (lit, fig)* far-sighted; **~sichtigkeit** *f* far-sightedness; **~sprung** *m (Sport)* the long jump *or* broad jump *(US)*; **w~verbreitet** *adj attr* widespread; *Zeitung* with a wide circulation; **w~verzweigt** *adj attr Straßensystem* extensive; **~winkelobjektiv** *nt* wide-angle lens.
**Weizen** *m no pl* wheat.
**Weizen-:** **~bier** *nt* light, very fizzy beer made using wheat, malt and top-fermentation yeast; **~brot** *nt* wheat bread; **~keime** *pl (Cook)* wheatgerm *sing;* **~mehl** *nt* wheat flour; **~schrot** *m or nt* wheatmeal.
**welch** *interrog pron inv (geh)* **(a)** **~ friedliches Bild!** what a peaceful scene! **(b)** *(in indirekten Fragesätzen)* **~ ein(e)** what.
**welche(r, s) 1** *interrog pron* **(a)** *(adjektivisch)* what; *(bei Auswahl)* which. **~r Mensch könnte behaupten ...?** what person could claim ...?; **~s Kleid soll ich anziehen?** which dress shall I wear? **(b)** *(substantivisch)* which (one). **~r von den beiden?** which (one) of the two?; **~s sind die Symptome dieser Krankheit?** what are the symptoms of this illness? **(c)** *(in Ausrufen)* **~ Freude!** what joy! **2** *indef pron* some; *(in Fragen)* any. **ich habe keine Äpfel, haben Sie ~?** I don't have any apples, do you have any? **3** *rel pron (Mensch)* who; *(Sache)* which, that. **~(r, s) auch immer** whoever/whichever/whatever.
**welcher|art** *interrog adj inv (geh) (attributiv)* what kind of; *(substantivisch)* of what kind.
**welk** *adj Pflanze* wilted, faded; *Blatt* dead; *Gesicht* tired-looking.
**welken** *vi aux sein (lit, fig)* to fade, to wilt.
**Wellblech** *nt* corrugated iron.
**Welle** *f -n* **(a)** wave; *(Rad: Frequenz)* wavelength. **die weiche ~** *(col)* the soft line; **(hohe) ~n schlagen** *(fig)* to create (quite) a stir. **(b)** *(Tech)* shaft.

**wellen 1** *vt* to wave. **2** *vr* to be/become wavy. **gewelltes Haar** wavy hair.

**Wellen-:** ~**bad** *nt* wave pool; ~**bereich** *m (Phys, Telec)* frequency range; *(Rad)* waveband; ~**brecher** *m* breakwater; **w~förmig 1** *adj* wave-like; *Linie* wavy; **2** *adv* in the form of waves; ~**gang** *m no pl* waves *pl*, swell; **starker ~gang** heavy sea(s) *or* swell; ~**länge** *f (Phys, Telec)* wavelength; **die gleiche ~länge haben** *(col)* to be on the same wavelength *(col)*; ~**linie** *f* wavy line; ~**reiten** *nt (Sport)* surfing; ~**sittich** *m* budgerigar, budgie *(col)*.

**Wellfleisch** *nt* boiled pork.

**wellig** *adj Haar etc* wavy; *Oberfläche* uneven; *Hügelland* rolling.

**Wellpappe** *f* corrugated cardboard.

**Welpe** *m (wk)* **-n, -n** pup, whelp; *(von Wolf etc)* cub.

**Wels** *m* **-e** catfish.

**Welt** *f* **-en** *(lit, fig)* world. **die (große) weite ~** the big wide world; **der höchste Berg der ~** the highest mountain in the world; **die Alte/Neue/Freie/Dritte ~** the Old/New/Free/Third World; **die ~ der Oper** the world of opera; **eine ~ brach für ihn zusammen** his whole world collapsed about him; **das ist doch nicht die ~** it isn't as important as all that; **deswegen geht die ~ nicht unter** *(col)* it isn't the end of the world; **das kostet doch nicht die ~** it won't cost the earth; **zwischen ihnen liegen ~en** they are worlds apart; **auf der ~** in the world; **aus aller ~** from all over the world; **aus der ~ schaffen** to eliminate; **in aller ~** all over the world; **warum in aller ~ ...?** why on earth ...?; **um nichts in der ~** not for anything; **ein Kind in die ~ setzen** to bring a child into the world; **ein Mann/eine Dame von ~** a man/woman of the world; **vor aller ~** in front of everybody; **zur ~ bringen** to give birth to; **auf die ~ kommen** to be born.

**Welt-** *in cpds* world; ~**all** *nt no pl* universe; **w~anschaulich** *adj* ideological; ~**anschauung** *f (Philos, Pol)* world view; ~**atlas** *m* atlas of the world; ~**ausstellung** *f* world exhibition; ~**bank** *f* World Bank; **w~berühmt** *adj* world-famous; **w~beste(r, s)** *adj attr* world's best; **w~bewegend** *adj* world-shattering; ~**bild** *nt* conception of the world; *(jds Ansichten)* philosophy; ~**bürger** *m* citizen of the world.

**Weltenbummler** *m* globetrotter.

**Weltergewicht** *nt (Boxen)* welterweight.

**Welt-:** **w~fremd** *adj* unworldly; ~**frieden** *m* world peace; ~**geschichte** *f* world history; **w~geschichtlich** *adj* **von w~geschichtlicher Bedeutung** of great significance in world history; ~**gesundheitsorganisation** *f* World Health Organization; **w~gewandt** *adj* sophisticated; ~**handel** *m* world trade; ~**herrschaft** *f* world domination; ~**karte** *f* map of the world; ~**kirchenrat** *m* World Council of Churches; ~**klasse** *f* ~**klasse sein** to be world-class; ~**krieg** *m* world war; **der Erste/Zweite ~krieg** World War One/Two, the First/Second World War; ~**kugel** *f* globe; **w~läufig** *adj* cosmopolitan; **w~lich** *adj* worldly; *(säkular)* secular; ~**literatur** *f* world literature; ~**macht** *f* world power; **w~männisch** *adj* urbane; ~**markt** *m* world market; ~**meer** *nt* ocean; ~**meister** *m* world *or* world's *(US)* champion; ~**meisterschaft** *f* world *or* world's *(US)* championship; *(Ftbl)* World Cup; **w~offen** *adj* liberal-minded; ~**ordnung** *f* world order; ~**politik** *f* world politics *pl*; **w~politisch** *adj* **die w~politische Entwicklung** the development of world politics; **von w~politischer Bedeutung** of importance in world politics; ~**rang** *m* **von**

~**rang** world-famous; ~**rangliste** *f* world rankings *pl*.

**Weltraum** *m* (outer) space.

**Weltraum-** *in cpds* space; ~**behörde** *f* space agency; ~**fahrer** *m* space traveller *(Brit) or* traveler *(US)*; ~**forschung** *f* space research; ~**station** *f* space station; ~**waffen** *pl* space weapons *pl*.

**Welt-:** ~**reich** *nt* empire; ~**reise** *f* world tour; **eine ~reise machen** to go around the world; ~**rekord** *m* world record; ~**religion** *f* world religion; ~**revolution** *f* world revolution; ~**ruf** *m* world-wide reputation; ~**ruhm** *m* world fame; ~**sicherheitsrat** *m (Pol)* (United Nations) Security Council; ~**sprache** *f* world language; ~**stadt** *f* cosmopolitan city; **w~städtisch** *adj* cosmopolitan; ~**umsegelung** *f* circumnavigation of the globe; ~**untergang** *m (lit, fig)* end of the world; ~**untergangsstimmung** *f* black mood, gloom and doom *(col)*; ~**verbesserer** *m* starry-eyed idealist; **w~weit** *adj* world-wide; ~**wirtschaft** *f* world economy; ~**wirtschaftskrise** *f* world economic crisis; ~**wunder** *nt* **die sieben ~wunder** the Seven Wonders of the World; ~**zeituhr** *f* world clock.

**wem** *dat of* **wer 1** *interrog pron* who ... to, to whom. **mit ~ ...** who ... with, with whom; ~ **von euch soll ich den Schlüssel geben?** which (one) of you should I give the key to? **2** *rel pron (derjenige, dem)* the person (who ...) to; *(jeder, dem)* anyone to whom ... **~ ... auch (immer)** whoever ... to.

**wen** *acc of* **wer 1** *interrog pron* who, whom. **an ~ hast du geschrieben?** who did you write to?; ~ **von den Schülern kennst du?** which (one) of these pupils do you know? **2** *rel pron (derjenige, den)* the person (who *or* whom); *(jeder, den)* anyone (who *or* whom). ~**... auch immer** whoever ...

**Wende** *f* **-n** turn; *(Veränderung)* change; *(~punkt)* turning point. **die ~** *(Pol)* the reunification (of Germany).

**Wende-:** ~**hals** *m (fig col)* turncoat *(pej)*; ~**jacke** *f* reversible jacket; ~**kreis** *m* (a) tropic; (b) *(Aut)* turning circle.

**Wendeltreppe** *f* spiral staircase.

**wenden** *pret* **wendete** *or* **wandte,** *ptp* **gewendet** *or* **gewandt 1** *vt* to turn; *(auf die andere Seite)* to turn (over); *(Cook)* to toss. **bitte ~!** please turn over; **wie man es auch wendet** ... whichever way you look at it ... **2** *vr* to turn (around); *(Wetter, Glück)* to change. **sich nach links ~** to turn to the left; **sich zu jdm/etw ~** to turn towards sb/sth; **sich zum Besseren/Schlimmeren ~** to take a turn for the better/worse; **sich an jdn ~** *(um Auskunft)* to consult sb; *(um Hilfe)* to turn to sb; *(Buch etc)* to be directed at sb; **sich gegen jdn/etw ~** to come out against sb/sth. **3** *vi* to turn *(auch Sport)*; *(umkehren)* to turn around.

**Wende-:** ~**platz** *m* turning place; ~**punkt** *m* turning point.

**wendig** *adj (lit, fig)* agile; *Auto etc* manoeuvrable *(Brit)*, maneuverable *(US)*.

**Wendigkeit** *f siehe adj* agility; manoeuvrability *(Brit)*, maneuverability *(US)*.

**Wendung** *f* (a) turn; *(Veränderung)* change. **eine ~ zum Besseren nehmen** to take a turn for the better. (b) *(Rede~)* expression, phrase.

**wenig 1** *adj, indef pron* (a) *sing* (a) little. **ich habe ~** I have only a little; **hast du Zeit? — ~!** have you got time? — not much; **das ~e, was er übrig hatte** the little he had left; **es fehlte (nur) ~, und er wäre überfahren worden** he was very nearly run over; **er gibt sich mit ~ zufrieden** *(verlangt nicht viel)* he is satisfied with a little; *(ist selten zufrieden)* not much satisfies him; **sie hat zu ~ Geld** *etc* she doesn't have enough money *etc*; **ein Exemplar zu ~** one copy too few; **£20 zu ~** £20 too little. **(b)** **~e** *pl (ein paar)* a few; *(nicht viele)* few; **in ~en Tagen** in (just) a few days; **einige ~e Leute** a few people. **(c)** *(auch adv)* **ein ~ a little; ein ~ Salz** a little salt.

**2** *adv* little. **~ besser** little better; **~ bekannt** little-known *attr*, little known *pred*; **sie kommt (nur) ~ raus** she doesn't get out very often.

**weniger** *comp of* **wenig 1** *adj, indef pron* less; *pl* fewer. **~ werden** to get less and less. **2** *adv* less. **das finde ich ~ schön!** that's not so nice!; **je mehr ... desto ~ ...** the more ... the less ...; **sieben ~ drei ist vier** seven minus three is four.

**Wenigkeit** *f* **meine ~** *(hum col)* little me *(hum col)*.

**wenigstens** *adv* at least.

**wenigste(r, s)** *superl of* **wenig** *adj, indef pron,* **am ~n** *adv* least; *pl* fewest. **er hat von uns allen am ~n Geld/Sorgen** he has the least money/the fewest worries of any of us; **diese Farbe ist am ~n schön** this colour *(Brit)* or color *(US)* is the least attractive one; **die ~n glauben das** very few believe that.

**wenn** *conj* **(a)** *(konditional, bei Wünschen)* if. **selbst** or **und ~** even if; **~ ... auch ...** even though or if ...; **~ er auch noch so dumm sein mag, ...** however stupid he may be, ...; **~ schon!** so what? *(col)*; **~ es schon sein muß** well, if that's the way it's got to be; **~ wir erst die neue Wohnung haben** once we get the new flat; **~ ich doch ...** if only I ...; **außer ~** except if, unless. **(b)** *(zeitlich)* when. **immer ~** whenever; **außer ~** except when.

**Wenn** *nt*: **das ~ und Aber** (the) ifs and buts; **ohne ~ und Aber** without any ifs and buts.

**wenngleich** *conj (geh)* although.

**wennschon** *adv (col)* **(na,) ~!** so what? *(col)*; **~, dennschon!** in for a penny, in for a pound!

**wer 1** *interrog pron* who. **~ von ...** which (one) of ... **2** *rel pron (derjenige, der)* the person who; *(jeder, der)* anyone or anybody who. **~ ... auch (immer)** whoever ... **3** *indef pron (col: jemand)* somebody, someone. **ist da ~?** is anybody there?; **~ sein** to be somebody *(col)*.

**Werbe-** *in cpds* advertising; **~abteilung** *f* publicity department; **~agentur** *f* advertising agency; **~aktion** *f* advertising campaign; **~antwort** *f* business reply card; **~etat** *m* advertising budget; **~fernsehen** *nt* television commercials *pl*; **~film** *m* promotional film; *(Spot)* (filmed) commercial; **~funk** *m* radio commercials *pl*; **~gag** *m* publicity stunt or gimmick; **~geschenk** *nt* gift *(from a company)*, freebie *(col)*; *(zu Gekauftem)* free gift; **~grafiker** *m* commercial artist; **~kampagne** *f* publicity campaign; **~material** *nt* publicity material; **~muster** *nt* advertising sample.

**werben** *pret* **warb**, *ptp* **geworben 1** *vt Mitglieder, Soldaten* to recruit; *Kunden, Stimmen* to attract, to win. **2** *vi* to advertise. **für etw ~** to advertise sth; **für eine Partei ~** to try to get support for a party; **um Unterstützung ~** to try to enlist support; **um junge Wähler ~** to try to attract young voters; **um ein Mädchen ~** to court a girl.

**Werbe-:** **~schrift** *f* publicity leaflet; **~schriften** promotional literature *sing*; **~slogan** *m* publicity slogan; **~spot** *m* commercial; **~text** *m* advertising copy *no pl*; **~texter** *m* copywriter; **~träger** *m* advertising medium; **~trommel** *f*: **die ~trommel (für etw) rühren** *(col)* to beat the big drum (for sth) *(col)*; **w~wirksam** *adj* **w~wirksam sein** to be good publicity; **~wirksamkeit** *f* publicity value.

**Werbung** *f (esp Comm)* advertising; *(für Produkt auch)* publicity, promotion; *(Werbeabteilung)* pub-

licity department. **~ für etw machen** to advertise sth.

**Werbungskosten** *pl* (tax-deductible) professional or business expenses *pl*.

**Werdegang** *m no pl* development; *(beruflich)* career.

**werden** *pret* **wurde**, *ptp* **geworden** *aux sein* **1** *vi* to become; *(mit adj auch)* to get. **blind ~** to go blind; **krank ~** to fall ill; **rot ~** to turn red; **es wird kalt** it's getting cold; **mir wird warm** I'm getting warm; **mir wird schlecht** I feel sick; **anders ~** to change; **die Fotos sind gut geworden** the photos have come out well; **aus ihm ist ein großer Komponist geworden** he has become a great composer; **ich will Lehrer ~** I want to be a teacher; **Erster ~** to come or be first; **was soll das ~?** — **das wird ein Pullover** what's that going to be? — it's going to be a pullover; **daraus ist nichts geworden** it came to nothing; **es wird bald ein Jahr, daß ...** it's almost a year since ...; **es wird Zeit, daß er kommt** it's time (that) he came; **es wird Nacht/Tag** it's getting dark/light; **es wird Winter** winter is coming; **er wird am 8. Mai 36** he is 36 on the 8th of May; **er ist gerade 40 geworden** he has just turned 40; **was soll nun ~?** so what's going to happen now?; **es wird schon ~** *(col)* it'll come all right in the end; **er wird mal wie sein Vater** he's going to be like his father; **wie soll der Pullover ~?** what's the pullover going to be like?

**2** *aux* **(a)** *(bei Futur und Konjunktiv)* **er wird es tun** he will do it, he'll do it; **er wird das nicht tun** he will not or won't do that; **es wird gleich regnen** it's just about to rain; **wer wird denn gleich!** *(col)* come on, now!; **das würde ich gerne tun** I would or I'd gladly do that. **(b)** *(bei Vermutung)* **sie wird wohl in der Küche sein** she must be in the kitchen; **er wird (wohl) ausgegangen sein** he's probably gone out. **(c)** *(bei Passiv)* *ptp* **worden gebraucht ~** to be used; **er ist erschossen worden** he was shot/he has been shot; **hier wird nicht geraucht!** there's no smoking here; **mir wurde gesagt, daß ...** I was told ...

**werdend** *adj* **~e Mutter** expectant mother.

**werfen** *pret* **warf**, *ptp* **geworfen 1** *vt* to throw *(nach at)*; *Tor, Korb* to score. **Bomben ~** *(von Flugzeug)* to drop bombs; **eine Münze ~** to toss a coin; **„nicht ~"** "handle with care"; **Bilder an die Wand ~** to project pictures onto the wall; **etw auf jdn/etw ~** to throw sth at sb/sth; **etw auf den Boden ~** to throw sth to the ground; **billige Waren auf den Markt ~** to dump cheap goods on the market; **jdn aus der Firma ~** to throw sb out (of the firm); **jdn ins Gefängnis** *etc* **~** to throw sb into prison *etc*; **etw in den Briefkasten ~** to put sth in the letter box. **2** *vi* **(a)** to throw. **mit etw (auf jdn/etw) ~** to throw sth (at sb/sth); **mit Geld um sich ~** to throw one's money about; **mit Fremdwörtern um sich ~** to bandy foreign words about. **(b)** *(Tier)* to have its young. **3** *vr* to throw oneself *(auf +acc* (up)on, at*)*.

**Werfer(in** *f)* *m* - thrower; *(Cricket)* bowler; *(Baseball)* pitcher.

**Werft** *f* **-en** shipyard; *(für Flugzeuge)* hangar.

**Werft|arbeiter** *m* shipyard worker.

**Werg** *nt no pl* tow.

**Werk** *nt* **-e (a)** *(Arbeit)* work *no indef art*; *(geh: Tat)* deed, act; *(Kunst~, Buch)* work; *(Gesamt~)* works *pl*. **das ~ eines Augenblicks** the work of a moment; **das ist sein ~** this is his doing; **das ~ jahrelanger Arbeit** the product of many years of work; **gute ~e tun** to do good works; **ein ~ der Nächstenliebe** an act of charity; **ans ~ gehen** to set to work. **(b)** *(Betrieb, Fabrik)* works *sing* or *pl*, plant. **ab ~** *(Comm)* ex works. **(c)** *(Mechanismus)* works *pl*.

**Werk-** *in cpds* works, factory; *siehe auch* **Werk(s)-**; ~**bank** *f* workbench.
**werkeln** *vi (col)* to potter about.
**werken** *vi* to be busy. **W~** *(Sch)* handicrafts *pl*.
**Werk-:** ~**halle** *f* factory building; ~**meister** *m* foreman.
**Werk(s)-:** ~**angehörige(r)** *mf* factory employee; ~**arzt** *m* works *or* company doctor.
**Werkschutz** *m* works security service.
**Werks-:** **w~eigen** *adj* company *attr*; ~**fahrer** *m* works driver; ~**feuerwehr** *f* factory fire service; ~**gelände** *nt* factory premises *pl*; ~**kantine** *f* works canteen; ~**küche** *f* works kitchen; ~**leiter** *m* works director *or* manager; ~**leitung** *f* works *or* factory management; ~**spionage** *f* industrial espionage.
**Werk-:** ~**statt** *f* =**en** workshop *(auch fig)*; *(für Autoreparaturen)* garage; *(von Künstler)* studio; ~**stoff** *m* material; ~**stück** *nt* workpiece; ~**student** *m* working student.
**Werk(s)-:** ~**verkehr** *m* company transport; ~**wohnung** *f* company flat *(Brit)* or apartment.
**Werktag** *m* working day, workday.
**werktags** *adv* on working days.
**werktätig** *adj* working.
**Werktätige(r)** *mf decl as adj* working man/woman. **die ~n** the working people.
**Werk-:** ~**tisch** *m* worktable; ~**unterricht** *m* woodwork/metalwork *etc* instruction.
**Werkzeug** *nt (lit, fig)* tool.
**Werkzeug-:** ~**kasten** *m* toolbox; ~**macher** *m* toolmaker; ~**maschine** *f* machine tool.
**Wermut** *m no pl (~wein)* vermouth.
**Wermutstropfen** *m (fig geh)* **der einzige ~** the only cloud in the sky.
**wert** *adj* **(a)** **etw ~ sein** to be worth sth; **nichts ~ sein** to be worthless; **Berlin ist eine Reise ~** Berlin is worth a visit; **es ist der Mühe ~** it's worth the trouble; **es ist nicht der Rede ~** it's not worth mentioning; **er ist es nicht ~, daß man ihm vertraut** he doesn't deserve to be trusted. **(b)** *(nützlich)* useful. **ein Auto ist viel ~** a car is very useful; **das ist schon viel ~** that's really useful *or (erfreulich)* encouraging.
**Wert** *m* **-e** value; *(esp menschlicher)* worth; *(von Banknoten, Briefmarken)* denomination. **~e** *pl (Ergebnisse)* results *pl*; **im ~e von** to the value of; **an ~ verlieren** to decrease in value; **etw unter ~ verkaufen** to sell sth for less than its true value; **sie hat innere ~e** she has certain inner qualities; **~ auf etw** *(acc)* **legen** *(fig)* to attach importance to sth.
**Wert-:** ~**angabe** *f* declaration of value; ~**arbeit** *f* craftsmanship; **w~beständig** *adj* stable in value.
**werten** *vti (einstufen)* to rate *(als* as*)*; *Klassenarbeit etc* to grade; *(beurteilen)* to judge *(als* to be*)*; *(Sport) (als gültig ~)* to allow; *(Punkte geben)* to give a score. **ein Tor nicht ~** *(Ftbl etc)* to disallow a goal.
**Werte-:** ~**system** *nt* system of values; ~**wandel** *m* change in values.
**Wert-:** **w~frei** *adj* unbias(s)ed; *Wort* neutral; ~**gegenstand** *m* object of value; ~**gegenstände** *pl* valuables *pl*; **w~los** *adj* worthless; ~**losigkeit** *f* worthlessness; ~**marke** *f* stamp; *(Gutschein)* voucher; ~**maßstab** *m* standard; ~**minderung** *f* reduction in value; ~**papier** *nt* bond; ~**papiere** *pl* stocks and shares *pl*; ~**papierbörse** *f* stock market; ~**sache** *f* = ~**gegenstand**; ~**schätzung** *f (liter)* esteem; ~**steigerung** *f* increase in value.
**Wertung** *f* evaluation; *(von Jury etc)* judging; *(Punkte)* score.
**Wert-:** ~**urteil** *nt* value judgement; **w~voll** *adj*

valuable; ~**vorstellung** *f* moral concept.
**Wesen** *nt* **-** **(a)** *no pl* nature; *(Wesentliches)* essence. **es liegt im ~ der Sache, daß ...** it's in the nature of the thing that ... **(b)** *(Geschöpf)* being. **ein weibliches/männliches ~** a female/male.
**Wesens-:** ~**art** *f* nature; **w~gleich** *adj* essentially alike; **w~verwandt** *adj* related in character; ~**zug** *m* trait.
**wesentlich 1** *adj (hauptsächlich)* essential; *(grundlegend)* fundamental; *(wichtig)* important. **das W~e** the essential thing; *(von Text, Rede)* the gist; **im ~en** essentially; *(im großen)* in the main. **2** *adv* fundamentally; *(erheblich)* considerably. **es ist mir ~ lieber, wenn wir ...** I would much rather we ...
**weshalb 1** *interrog adv* why. **2** *rel adv* **der Grund, ~ ...** the reason why ...
**Wespe** *f* **-n** wasp.
**Wespen-:** ~**nest** *nt* wasps' nest; **in ein ~nest stechen** *(fig)* to stir up a hornets' nest; ~**stich** *m* wasp sting.
**wessen** *pron* **1** *gen of* **wer** *interrog* whose. **2** *gen of* **was** *(liter)* ~ **hat man dich angeklagt?** of what have you been accused?
**Wessi** *m* **-s** *(col)* West German.
**West** *m no pl (Naut, Met, liter)* west.
**West-** *in cpds (in Ländernamen) (politisch)* West; *(geographisch auch)* the West of ..., Western; ~**afrika** *nt* West Africa; **w~deutsch** *adj (Hist Pol)* West German; *(Geog)* Western German; ~**deutsche(r)** *mf (Hist Pol)* West German; *(Geog)* Western German; ~**deutschland** *nt (Hist Pol)* West Germany; *(Geog)* Western Germany.
**Weste** *f* **-n** waistcoat *(Brit)*, vest *(US)*. **eine reine ~ haben** *(fig)* to have a clean slate.
**Westen** *m no pl* west; *(von Land)* West. **der ~** *(Hist Pol)* the West; **im ~** in the West; **nach ~** to the West; **von ~, aus dem ~** from the West.
**Westentasche** *f* waistcoat *(Brit)* or vest *(US)* pocket. **etw wie seine ~ kennen** *(col)* to know sth like the back of one's hand *(col)*.
**Western** *m* **-** western.
**West-:** ~**europa** *nt* Western Europe; **w~europäisch** *adj* West(ern) European; **w~europäische Zeit** Greenwich Mean Time.
**Westfale** *m (wk)* **-n, -n, Westfälin** *f* Westphalian.
**Westfalen** *nt* Westphalia.
**westfälisch** *adj* Westphalian.
**West-:** ~**friesische Inseln** *pl* West Frisian Islands *pl*; ~**indien** *nt* the West Indies *pl*; **w~indisch** *adj* West Indian; **die ~indischen Inseln** the West Indies *pl*; ~**jordanland** *nt* West Bank; ~**küste** *f* west coast.
**westlich 1** *adj* western; *Wind, Richtung* westerly; *(Pol)* Western. **der ~ste Ort** the westernmost place. **2** *adv* (to the) west *(von* of*)*. **3** *prep +gen* (to the) west of.
**West-:** ~**mächte** *pl (Hist Pol)* **die ~mächte** the western powers *pl*; **w~östlich** *adj* west-to-east; **in w~östlicher Richtung** from west to east; **w~wärts** *adv* westward(s); ~**wind** *m* west wind.
**weswegen** *interrog adv* why.
**Wettbewerb** *m* competition. **mit jdm in ~ stehen/treten** to be in/enter into competition with sb.
**Wettbewerbs-:** ~**beschränkung** *f* restraint of trade; **w~fähig** *adj* competitive; ~**fähigkeit** *f* competitiveness; ~**teilnehmer** *m* competitor.
**Wettbüro** *nt* betting office.
**Wette** *f* **-n** bet *(auch Sport)*, wager. **eine ~ abschließen** to make a bet; **darauf gehe ich jede ~ ein** I'll bet you anything you like; **was gilt die ~?** what are you betting?; **die ~ gilt!** done!, you're on! *(col)*; **um**

die ~ **laufen** to run a race (with each other); **sie schreien um die** ~ they're having a screaming competition.

**Wętt|eifer** *m* competitive urge.

**wętt|eifern** *vi insep* **mit jdm um etw** ~ to compete with sb for sth.

**wętten** *vti* to bet. **(wollen wir)** ~? (do you) want to bet?; ~**, daß ich recht habe?** (I) bet you I'm right!; **so haben wir nicht gewettet!** that's not part of the bargain!; **auf etw** *(acc)* ~ to bet on sth; **mit jdm** ~ to bet with sb; **(mit jdm) um 5 Mark** ~ to bet *(sb)* 5 marks; **ich wette 100 gegen 1(, daß ...)** I'll bet 100 to 1 (that ...).

**Wętter¹** *m* - better.

**Wętter²** *nt* - **(a)** weather *no indef art.* **bei jedem** ~ in all weathers; **das ist vielleicht ein** ~! *(col)* what weather!; **was haben wir heute für** ~? what's the weather like today?; **wir haben herrliches** ~ the weather's marvellous. **(b)** *usu pl (Min)* air. **schlagende** ~ *pl* firedamp *sing.*

**Wętter-:** ~**amt** *nt* meteorological office; ~**aussichten** *pl* weather outlook; ~**beobachtung** *f* meteorological observation; ~**bericht** *m* weather report; *(Vorhersage)* weather forecast; ~**besserung** *f* improvement in the weather; **w~beständig** *adj* weatherproof; ~**dienst** *m* meteorological service; **w~empfindlich** *adj* sensitive to the weather; ~**fahne** *f* weather vane; **w~fest** *adj* weatherproof; **w~fühlig** *adj* sensitive to the weather; ~**hahn** *m* weathercock; ~**häuschen** *nt* weather house; ~**karte** *f* weather chart; ~**lage** *f* weather situation; ~**leuchten** *nt no pl* sheet lightning; ~**meldung** *f* meteorological report.

**węttern** *vi* to curse and swear. **gegen etw** ~ to rail against sth.

**Wętter-:** ~**regel** *f* weather saying; ~**satellit** *m* weather satellite; ~**schaden** *m* weather damage; ~**seite** *f* windward side; ~**station** *f* weather station; ~**störung** *f* meteorological disturbance; ~**umschlag** *m* sudden change in the weather; ~**verhältnisse** *pl* weather conditions *pl*; ~**vorhersage** *f* weather forecast; ~**warte** *f* weather station; **w~wendisch** *adj (fig)* moody; ~**wolke** *f* storm cloud.

**Wętt-:** ~**fahrt** *f* race; ~**kampf** *m* competition; ~**kämpfer** *m* competitor; ~**lauf** *m* race; **einen** ~**lauf machen** to run a race; **ein** ~**lauf mit der Zeit** a race against time; ~**läufer** *m* runner (in a/the race).

**węttmachen** *vt sep* to make up for; *Verlust etc* to make good.

**Wętt-:** ~**rennen** *nt (lit, fig)* race; ~**rüsten** *nt* arms race; ~**schein** *m* betting slip; ~**schuld** *f* betting debt; ~**streit** *m* competition.

**wętzen 1** *vt* to whet. **2** *vi aux sein (col)* to scoot *(col)*.

**Wętzstein** *m* whetstone.

**WEZ** [veːʔeːˈtsɛt] = **Westeuropäische Zeit** GMT.

**WG** [veːˈgeː] *f* -**s** = **Wohngemeinschaft.**

**Whisky** ['vɪski] *m* -**s** whisky, whiskey *(US)*.

**wich** *pret of* **weichen².**

**wichsen** ['vɪksn] **1** *vti Schuhe* to polish; *Boden etc* to wax. **2** *vi (col!: onanieren)* to jerk or toss off *(col!)*.

**Wicht** *m* -**e** *(Kobold)* goblin; *(kleiner Mensch)* titch *(col)*; *(fig: verachtenswerter Mensch)* scoundrel.

**Wichtel** *m* - **(a)** *(auch* ~**männchen)* gnome; *(Kobold)* goblin. **(b)** *(Pfadfinderin)* brownie.

**wichtig** *adj* important. **eine** ~**e Miene machen** (to try) to look important; **sich** ~ **tun** to throw one's weight about; **er will sich nur** ~ **machen** he just wants to get attention; **sich selbst/etw (zu)** ~ **nehmen** to take oneself/sth (too) seriously; **sich**

*(dat)* ~ **vorkommen** to be full of oneself; **alles W~e** everything of importance; **W~eres zu tun haben** to have more important things to do; **nichts W~eres zu tun haben** to have nothing better to do.

**Wịchtigkeit** *f* importance.

**Wịchtigtuer(in** *f)* *m* - *(pej)* pompous type *(col)*. **er ist so ein** ~ he is so full of his own importance.

**wichtigtuerisch** *adj* pompous, self-important.

**Wịcke** *f* -**n** *(Bot)* vetch; *(Garten~)* sweet pea.

**Wịckel** *m* - **(a)** *(Med)* compress. **(b)** *(Rolle)* reel; *(Locken~)* curler. **(c)** *(col)* **jdn am** ~ **kriegen/haben** to grab/have sb by the scruff of the neck; *(fig)* to give sb a good talking to *(col)*.

**Wịckel-:** ~**bluse** *f* wrap-around blouse; ~**kind** *nt* babe-in-arms; ~**kleid** *nt* wrap-around dress.

**wịckeln 1** *vt* **(a)** *(schlingen)* to wind *(um* around*)*; *Verband etc* to bind; *Haare* to put in curlers. **sich** *(dat)* **eine Decke um die Beine** ~ to wrap a blanket around one's legs; **da bist du schief gewickelt!** *(fig col)* you're very much mistaken. **(b)** *(einwickeln)* to wrap *(in +acc* in*)*; *(mit Verband)* to dress. **einen Säugling** ~ to put on *or (frisch* ~*)* to change a baby's nappy *(Brit)* or diaper *(US)*. **2** *vr* to wrap oneself *(in +acc* in*)*. **sich um etw** ~ to wrap itself around sth; *(Schlange, Pflanze)* to wind itself around sth.

**Wịckel-:** ~**raum** *m (in Kaufhaus etc)* mothers' (and babies') room; ~**rock** *m* wrap-around skirt; ~**tisch** *m* baby's changing table.

**Wịdder** *m* - ram; *(Astrol)* Aries.

**wịder** *prep +acc (geh)* against. ~ **Erwarten** contrary to expectations.

**widerfạhren\*** *vi, vi impers insep irreg aux sein +dat (geh)* to happen *(jdm* to sb*)*.

**Wịder-:** ~**haken** *m* barb; ~**hall** *m* echo; **(bei jdm) keinen** ~**hall finden** *(Interesse)* to meet with no response (from sb); **w~hallen** *vi sep* to echo *(von* with*)*.

**widerlẹgbar** *adj* refutable. **nicht** ~ irrefutable.

**widerlẹgen\*** *vt insep* to refute; *jdn* to prove wrong.

**Wịder-:** **w~lich** *adj* revolting; ~**ling** *m (pej col)* repulsive creep *(col)*; **w~natürlich** *adj* unnatural; **w~rechtlich** *adj* unlawful; **sich** *(dat)* **etw w~rechtlich aneignen** to misappropriate sth; ~**rede** *f* contradiction; **keine** ~**rede!** don't argue!

**Wịderruf** *m siehe vb* withdrawal; retraction; cancellation; withdrawal. **bis auf** ~ until revoked.

**widerrụfen\*** *insep irreg* **1** *vt Erlaubnis etc* to withdraw; *Aussage* to retract; *Befehl* to cancel. **2** *vi (bei Verleumdung etc)* to withdraw.

**Wịder-:** ~**sacher(in** *f)* *m* - adversary; **w~setzen** *vr insep* **sich jdm/einer Sache w~setzen** to oppose sb/sth; *der Polizei, Festnahme* to resist sb/sth; **einem Befehl** to refuse to comply with sth; **w~sinnig** *adj* absurd; **w~spenstig** *adj* unruly; *(störrisch)* stubborn; *Haar* unmanageable; ~**spenstigkeit** *f siehe adj* unruliness; stubbornness; **w~spiegeln** *sep* **1** *vt (lit, fig)* to reflect; **2** *vr (lit, fig)* to be reflected; ~**spieg(e)lung** *f* reflection.

**widersprẹchen\*** *insep irreg* **1** *vi* **jdm/einer Sache** ~ to contradict sb/sth; **das widerspricht meinen Grundsätzen** that goes against my principles. **2** *vr (einander)* to contradict one another. **sich (selbst)** ~ to contradict oneself.

**Wịderspruch** *m* **(a)** *(Gegensätzlichkeit)* contradiction. **ein** ~ **in sich** a contradiction in terms; **im** ~ **zu** contrary to; **in** ~ **zu etw geraten** to come into conflict with sth; **in** *or* **im** ~ **zu etw stehen** to conflict with sth. **(b)** *(Widerrede)* contradiction; *(Ablehnung)* opposition. **kein** ~! don't argue!; **er duldet keinen** ~ he won't have any argument; **es erhob sich** ~ there

was opposition *(gegen* to*)*; ~ **erheben** to protest.
**widersprüchlich** *adj* contradictory, inconsistent.
**widerspruchs-**: ~**frei** *adj Theorie* consistent; ~**los**
**1** *adj Zustimmung* unopposed; **2** *adv* without opposition; **etw** ~**los hinnehmen** to accept sth unquestioningly; ~**voll** *adj* full of inconsistencies.
**Widerstand** *m* ⁼e resistance; *(Ablehnung)* opposition. **jdm/einer Sache** ~ **leisten** to resist sb/sth; **auf**
~ **stoßen** to meet with resistance.
**Widerstands-**: ~**bewegung** *f* resistance movement; **w**~**fähig** *adj* robust; *Pflanze* hardy; *(Med,*
*Tech etc)* resistant *(gegen* to*)*; ~**fähigkeit** *f* siehe
*adj* robustness; hardiness; resistance *(gegen* to*)*;
~**kämpfer** *m* resistance fighter; ~**kraft** *f* (powers
of) resistance; **w**~**los** *adj, adv* without resistance;
~**nest** *nt (Mil)* pocket of resistance.
**widerstehen\*** *vi insep irreg* +*dat* **einer Sache** ~ to
resist sth; *einem Erdbeben etc* to withstand sth.
**widerstreben\*** *vi insep* +*dat* **jds sittlichem Empfin**
**den** ~ to go against sb's moral sense; **es wider**
**strebt mir, so etwas zu tun** I am reluctant to do
anything like that.
**Widerstreben** *nt no pl* reluctance.
**widerstrebend** *adj (gegensätzlich) Interessen* conflicting; *(widerwillig)* reluctant.
**widerwärtig** *adj* disgusting. **er ist mir** ~ he disgusts
me.
**Widerwille** *m (Abscheu, Ekel)* disgust *(gegen* for*)*,
revulsion; *(Abneigung)* distaste *(gegen* for*)*; *(Wider*
*streben)* reluctance.
**widerwillig** *adj* reluctant, unwilling.
**Widerworte** *pl* answering back *sing.* **er tat es ohne**
~ he did it without protest.
**widmen 1** *vt* **jdm etw** ~ to dedicate sth to sb. **2** *vr*
+*dat* to devote oneself to; *den Gästen, einer Aufga*
*be* to attend to.
**Widmung** *f (in Buch etc)* dedication *(an* +*acc* to*)*.
**widrig** *adj* adverse.
**wie 1** *interrog adv* how. ~ **anders …?** how else …?; ~
**wär's damit** *(col)* how about it? *(col)*; ~ **wär's mit**
**einem Whisky?** *(col)* how about a whisky?; **wie**
**wär's mit uns beiden?** *(col)* shall we?; ~ **ist er**
**(denn)?** what's he like?; **Sie wissen ja,** ~ **das so ist**
well, you know how it is; ~ **nennt man das?** what is
that called?; ~ **bitte?** pardon?; ~ **bitte?!** *(entrüstet)*
I beg your pardon!; **das macht dir Spaß,** ~**?** you
like that, don't you?; **und** ~**!, aber** ~**!** and how!
*(col)*; ~ **groß er ist!** isn't he big!
   **2** *adv* **(a)** *(relativ)* **die Art,** ~ **sie geht** the way she
walks. **(b)** *(in Verbindung mit auch)* ~ **stark du auch**
**sein magst** however strong you may be.
   **3** *conj* **(a)** *(vergleichend)* **so …** ~ as … as; **weiß** ~
**Schnee** (as) white as snow; **ein Mann** ~ **er** a man
like him; **in einer Lage** ~ **diese(r)** in a situation like
this; **ich fühlte mich** ~ **im Traum** I felt as if I was
dreaming; ~ **du weißt** as you know; ~ **noch nie** as
never before. **(b)** *(zum Beispiel)* ~ *(zum Beispiel)*
such as (for example). **(c)** *(und)* as well as. **Alte** ~
**Junge** old and young alike. **(d)** *(bei Verben der*
*Wahrnehmung)* **er sah,** ~ **es geschah** he saw it happen; **er hörte,** ~ **der Regen fiel** he heard the rain
falling. **(e)** *(zeitlich: als)* ~ **ich mich umdrehte, sah**
**ich …** as I turned round I saw …
**Wie** *nt no pl* **das** ~ **und Wann werden wir später be**
**sprechen** we'll talk about how and when later.
**Wiedehopf** *m* -e hoopoe.
**wieder** *adv* again. ~ **nüchtern** sober again; **immer** ~
again and again; ~ **ist ein Jahr vorbei** another year
has passed; **wie, schon** ~**?** what, again?; **das ist**
**auch** ~ **wahr** that's true; **da sieht man mal** ~**, …** it
just goes to show …; **das fällt mir schon** ~ **ein** I'll

remember it again.
**Wieder-** *pref* re-; *(bei Verben) (erneut)* again; *(zu*
*rück)* back; ~**aufbau** *m (lit, fig)* reconstruction;
**w**~**aufbauen** *vti* *sep* to reconstruct;
**w**~**aufbereiten\*** *vt sep* to recycle; *Atommüll* to
reprocess; ~**aufbereitungsanlage** *f* recycling
plant; *(für Atommüll)* reprocessing plant;
**w**~**aufforsten** *vti sep* to reforest; **w**~**aufführen**
*vt sep Theaterstück* to revive; *Film* to rerun;
**w**~**aufladbar** *adj* *Batterie* rechargeable;
**w**~**aufladen** *vt sep irreg* to recharge;
**w**~**aufleben** *vi sep aux sein* to revive; ~**aufleben**
*nt* revival; *(von Nationalismus etc auch)* resurgence; ~**aufnahme** *f* **(a)** *(von Tätigkeit etc)* resumption; **(b)** *(in Verein etc)* readmittance; *(von*
*Patienten)* readmission; **w**~**aufnehmen** *vt sep ir*
*reg* **(a)** to resume; *Gedanken, Hobby* to take up
again; *Thema* to revert to; *(Jur) Verfahren* to reopen; **(b)** *Menschen* to take back; *(in Verein, Klinik)*
to readmit; **w**~**aufrüsten** *vti sep* to rearm;
~**aufrüstung** *f* rearmament; **w**~**bekommen\*** *vt*
*sep irreg* to get back; **w**~**beleben\*** *vt sep* to revive; *(Med)* to resuscitate; ~**belebung** *f* revival;
*(Med)* resuscitation; **w**~**beschaffen\*** *vt sep* to recover; ~**beschaffung** *f* recovery; **w**~**bewaffnen\***
*vr sep* to rearm; ~**bewaffnung** *f* rearmament;
**w**~**bringen** *vt* *sep* *irreg* to bring back;
**w**~**einführen** *vt sep* to reintroduce; ~**einführung**
*f* reintroduction; ~**einnahme** *f (Mil)* recapture;
**w**~**einnehmen** *vt sep irreg (Mil)* to recapture;
**w**~**einsetzen** *sep* **1** *vt* to reinstate *(in* +*acc* in*)*; **2**
*vi (Regen)* to start up again; *(Med: Fieber, Schmer*
*zen)* to recur; ~**einsetzung** *f* reinstatement;
**w**~**einstellen** *vt sep* to re-engage; ~**einstellung** *f*
re-engagement; **w**~**entdecken\*** *vt sep (lit, fig)* to
rediscover; ~**entdeckung** *f* rediscovery;
**w**~**ergreifen\*** *vt* *sep* *irreg* to recapture;
~**ergreifung** *f* recapture; **w**~**erkennen\*** *vt sep ir*
*reg* to recognize; **er war nicht w**~**zuerkennen** he
was unrecognizable; **w**~**eröffnen\*** *vti sep* to reopen; **w**~**erscheinen\*** *vi sep irreg aux sein* to reappear; *(Buch etc)* to be republished;
**w**~**erstatten\*** *vt sep Unkosten etc* to refund *(jdm*
*etw* sb for sth*)*; ~**erstattung** *f* reimbursement;
**w**~**erwachen\*** *vi sep aux sein* to reawaken; **w**~
**finden** *sep irreg* **1** *vt* to find again; *(fig) Selbst*
*achtung etc* to regain; **2** *vr (nach Schock)* to recover; **sich irgendwo w**~**finden** to find oneself somewhere.
**Wiedergabe** *f* **(a)** *(von Rede, Ereignis)* account, report; *(Wiederholung)* repetition. **(b)** *(Darbietung:*
*von Stück)* performance. **(c)** *(von Tönen, Farben etc)*
reproduction.
**Wiedergabegerät** *nt* playback unit.
**wiedergeben** *vt sep irreg* **(a)** *Gegenstand, Geld* to
give back. **jdm ein Buch** ~ to give a book back to
sb. **(b)** *(erzählen)* to give an account of; *(wiederho*
*len)* to repeat. **(c)** *Gedicht* to recite; *Musikstück etc*
to perform. **(d)** *(reproduzieren) Töne, Farben etc* to
reproduce.
**Wieder-**: **w**~**geboren** *adj* reborn; ~**geburt** *f* rebirth; **w**~**gewinnen\*** *vt sep irreg (lit, fig)* to regain; *Land, Rohstoffe etc* to reclaim; *Geld, Selbst*
*vertrauen* to recover; **w**~**gutmachen** *vt sep* to
make good; *Schaden* to compensate for; *(Pol)* to
make reparations for; *(Jur)* to redress; ~**gut**
**machung** *f* compensation; *(Pol)* reparations *pl*;
*(Jur)* redress; **w**~**haben** *vt sep irreg (col)* to have
(got) back; **w**~**herstellen** *vt sep Gebäude, Frieden,*
*jds Gesundheit* to restore; *Beziehungen* to reestablish; *Patienten* to restore to health; ~**herstel-**

**lung** f restoration.
**wiederholbar** adj repeatable. **schwer** ~ hard to repeat.
**wiederholen**[1]* insep **1** vti to repeat; (mehrmals) Forderung etc to reiterate; Lernstoff to revise, to review (US); Spiel to replay; Rennen to rerun; Prüfung to resit, to retake. **eine Klasse** ~ (Sch) to repeat a year. **2** vr (Mensch) to repeat oneself; (Thema, Ereignis) to recur.
**wiederholen**[2] vt sep to get back.
**wiederholt** adj repeated. **zum** ~**en Male** once again.
**Wiederholung** f repetition; (von Aufführung) repeat performance; (von Sendung) repeat; (in Zeitlupe) replay; (von Lernstoff) revision, review (US); (von Spiel) replay.
**Wiederholungs-:** ~**kurs** m refresher course; ~**spiel** nt (Sport) replay; ~**täter** m (Jur) reoffender; (gewohnheitsmäßig) persistent offender; ~**zeichen** nt (Mus) repeat (mark).
**Wieder-:** ~**hören** nt (auf) ~**hören!** (am Telefon) goodbye!; **w~käuen** vti sep to ruminate; (fig col) to go over again and again; ~**käuer** m - ruminant.
**Wiederkehr** f no pl (geh) (Rückkehr) return; (wiederholtes Vorkommen) recurrence; (von Ereignis) anniversary.
**wiederkehren** vi sep aux sein to return; (sich wiederholen) to recur.
**wiederkehrend** adj recurrent.
**Wieder-:** **w~kennen** vt sep irreg (col) to recognize; **w~kommen** vi sep irreg aux sein to come back; **komm doch mal w~!** you must come again!; ~**kunft** f no pl (liter) return; **w~sehen** vt sep irreg to see again; ~**sehen** nt (another) meeting; (nach längerer Zeit) reunion; **sie hofften auf ein baldiges** ~**sehen** they hoped to meet again soon; **(auf)** ~**sehen!** goodbye!; **w~tun** vt sep irreg to do again.
**wiederum** adv **(a)** (andererseits) on the other hand; (allerdings) though. **(b)** (seinerseits etc) in turn. **er** ~ **wollte** ... he, for his part, wanted ...
**Wieder-:** **w~vereinigen*** sep **1** vt Menschen to reunite; Land to reunify; **2** vr to reunite; ~**vereinigung** f reunification; **w~verheiraten*** vr sep to remarry; ~**verheiratung** f remarriage; ~**verkauf** m resale; **w~verkaufen*** vt sep to re-sell; **w~verwendbar** adj reusable; **w~verwenden*** vt sep to reuse; ~**verwendung** f reuse; **w~verwertbar** adj recyclable; **w~verwerten*** vt sep to recycle; ~**verwertung** f recycling; ~**wahl** f re-election; **w~wählen** vt sep to re-elect.
**Wiege** f -n cradle. **es ist ihm auch nicht an der** ~ **gesungen worden, daß** ... no one could have foreseen that ...
**wiegen**[1] **1** vt to rock; Kopf to shake (slowly); Hüften to sway. **2** vr (Boot etc) to rock (gently); (Mensch) to sway. **sich in trügerischen Hoffnungen** ~ to nurture false hopes.
**wiegen**[2] pret **wog**, ptp **gewogen** vti to weigh. **schwer** ~ (fig) to carry a lot of weight; (Irrtum) to be serious; siehe **gewogen**.
**Wiegenlied** nt lullaby.
**wiehern** vi to neigh. **(vor Lachen)** ~ to bray with laughter.
**Wien** nt Vienna.
**Wiener** adj attr Viennese. ~ **Würstchen** frankfurter, wiener (sausage) (esp US); ~ **Schnitzel** Wiener schnitzel.
**Wiener(in** f) m - Viennese.
**wies** pret of **weisen**.
**Wiese** f -n meadow; (col: Rasen) lawn. **auf der grünen** ~ (fig) in the open countryside.

**Wiesel** nt - weasel. **schnell** or **flink wie ein** ~ quick as a flash.
**Wiesenblume** f meadow flower.
**wieso** interrog adv why. ~ **gehst du nicht?** how come you're not going? (col); ~ **weißt du das?** how do you come to know that?
**wieviel** interrog adv how much; (bei Mehrzahl) how many.
**wievielmal** interrog adv how many times.
**wievielte(r, s)** interrog adj **das** ~ **Kind ist das jetzt?** how many children is that now?; **den** ~**n Platz hat er im Wettkampf belegt?** where did he come in the competition?; **das** ~ **Mal bist du schon in England?** how often have you been to England?; **ich habe morgen Geburtstag!** – **der** ~ **ist es denn?** it's my birthday tomorrow! – how old will you be?; **den W~n haben wir heute?** what's the date today?
**wieweit** conj to what extent.
**Wikinger** m - Viking.
**wild** adj wild; Stamm savage; (ausgelassen) boisterous; (heftig) Kampf, (zornig) Blick fierce; (ungesetzlich) Parken etc illegal; Streik wildcat attr, unofficial. **den** ~**en Mann spielen** (col) to come the heavy (col); **der W~e Westen** the Wild West; **in** ~**er Ehe leben** (dated, hum) to live in sin; ~ **durcheinanderliegen** to be strewn all over the place; **dann ging alles** ~ **durcheinander** there was chaos then; **wie** ~ **rennen** to run like mad; ~ **drauflosreden** to talk nineteen to the dozen; **seid nicht so** ~**!** calm down a bit!; **einen Hund** ~ **machen** to drive a dog wild; ~ **werden** to go wild (auch col); **ich könnte** ~ **werden** (col) I could scream (col); **das ist nicht so** ~ (col) never mind; ~ **entschlossen** (col) dead set (col).
**Wild** nt no pl game; (Rot~) deer; (Fleisch von Rot~) venison.
**Wild-:** ~**bach** m torrent; ~**bahn** f **in freier** ~**bahn** in the wild; ~**bestand** m game population; ~**braten** m roast venison; ~**bret** nt no pl game; (von Rotwild) venison; ~**dieb** m poacher; ~**diebstahl** m poaching; ~**ente** f wild duck.
**Wilde(r)** mf decl as adj savage; (fig) maniac.
**Wilderer** m - poacher.
**wildern** vi (Mensch) to poach; (Hund etc) to kill game.
**Wild-:** ~**esel** m wild ass; ~**fang** m little rascal; **w~fremd** adj (col) **w~fremde Leute** complete strangers; ~**gans** f wild goose; ~**hüter** m gamekeeper; ~**katze** f wildcat; **w~lebend** adj attr living in the wild; ~**leder** nt suede.
**Wildnis** f (lit, fig) wilderness. **in der** ~ **leben** to live in the wild.
**Wild-:** ~**park** m game park; (für Rotwild) deer park; ~**reservat** nt game reserve; ~**schaden** m damage caused by game; ~**schutzgebiet** nt game preserve; ~**schwein** nt wild boar; **w~wachsend** adj attr wild(-growing); ~**wasser** nt white water; ~**wechsel** m „~**wechsel**" "wild animals"; ~**west** no art the Wild West; ~**westfilm** m western (film); ~**westroman** m western (novel); ~**wuchs** m (geh) rank growth; (fig) proliferation.
**Wilhelm** ['vɪlhɛlm] m ≃ William.
**Wille** m -ns, no pl will; (Absicht) intention. **nach jds** ~**n** as sb wanted/wants; **wenn es nach ihrem** ~**n ginge** if she had her way; **das geschah gegen meinen** ~**n** that was done against my will; **er mußte wider** ~**n lachen** he couldn't help laughing; **jds** ~**n tun** to do sb's will; **seinen** ~**n durchsetzen** to get one's (own) way; **jdm seinen** ~**n lassen** to let sb have his own way; **seinen eigenen** ~**n haben** to be self-willed; **beim besten** ~**n nicht** not with the best will in the world; **es war kein böser** ~ there was no

ill-will intended; **der gute ~** goodwill.
**willen** *prep siehe* **um 2**.
**willenlos** *adj* weak-willed. **völlig ~ sein** to have no will of one's own; **jds ~es Werkzeug sein** to be the mere tool of sb.
**willens** *adj (geh)* **~ sein** to be willing.
**Willens-:** **~äußerung** *f* expression of will; **~freiheit** *f* freedom of will; **~kraft** *f* willpower; **w~schwach** *adj* weak-willed; **~schwäche** *f* weakness of will; **w~stark** *adj* strong-willed; **~stärke** *f* willpower.
**willentlich** *adj* wilful *(Brit)*, willful *(US)*, deliberate.
**willig** *adj* willing.
**willkommen** *adj* welcome. **du bist (mir) immer ~** you are always welcome; **jdn ~ heißen** to welcome sb; **herzlich ~** welcome *(in +dat* to*)*; **es ist mir ganz ~, daß ...** I quite welcome the fact that ...
**Willkommen** *nt* - welcome.
**Willkommensgruß** *m* greeting, welcome.
**Willkür** *f no pl* capriciousness; *(politisch)* despotism; *(bei Handlungen)* arbitrariness. **das ist reinste ~** that is purely arbitrary.
**Willkür-:** **~akt** *m* despotic act; **~herrschaft** *f* tyranny.
**willkürlich** *adj* arbitrary; *Herrscher* autocratic.
**Wilna** *nt* Vilnius.
**wimmeln** *vi auch vi impers* **der See wimmelt von Fischen** the lake is teeming with fish; **hier wimmelt es von Mücken/Menschen** this place is swarming with midges/people.
**wimmern** *vi* to whimper.
**Wimpel** *m* - pennant.
**Wimper** *f* **-n** (eye)lash. **ohne mit der ~ zu zucken** *(fig)* without batting an eyelid.
**Wimperntusche** *f* mascara.
**Wind** *m* **-e (a)** wind. **bei ~ und Wetter** in all weathers; **der ~ dreht sich** the wind is changing direction; **merken, woher der ~ weht** *(fig)* to see which way the wind is blowing; **daher weht der ~!** *(fig)* so that's the way the wind is blowing; **seither weht ein anderer/frischer ~** *(fig)* things have changed since then; **viel ~ um etw machen** *(col)* to make a lot of fuss about sth; **das Mäntelchen** *or* **das Fähnchen nach dem ~ hängen** to trim one's sails to the wind; **jdm den ~ aus den Segeln nehmen** *(fig)* to take the wind out of sb's sails; **sich** *(dat)* **den ~ um die Ohren wehen lassen** to see a bit of the world; **etw in den ~ schlagen** to turn a deaf ear to sth; **in alle (vier) ~e** to the four winds; **von etw ~ bekommen** *(fig col)* to get wind of sth. **(b)** *(Med: Blähung)* wind.
**Wind-:** **~beutel** *m* **(a)** cream puff; **(b)** *(col: Mensch)* rake; **~bö(e)** *f* gust of wind.
**Winde¹** *f* **-n** *(Tech)* winch, windlass.
**Winde²** *f* **-n** *(Bot)* bindweed, convolvulus.
**Windel** *f* **-n** nappy *(Brit)*, diaper *(US)*.
**Windel-:** **~einlage** *f* nappy *(Brit)* or diaper *(US)* liner; **~höschen** *nt* plastic pants.
**windelweich** *adj* **jdn ~ schlagen** *(col)* to beat the living daylights out of sb *(col)*.
**winden** *pret* **wand**, *ptp* **gewunden 1** *vt* to wind; *Kranz* to bind. **2** *vr (Bach, Schlange, Pflanze)* to wind; *(Mensch) (durch Menge etc)* to wind (one's way); *(vor Schmerzen)* to writhe *(vor* with, in*)*; *(fig: ausweichen)* to try to wriggle out.
**Wind|energie** *f* wind energy.
**Windes|eile** *f* **etw in ~ tun** to do sth in no time (at all) *or (in großer Eile)* in a great rush; **sich in** *or* **mit ~ verbreiten** to spread like wildfire.
**Wind-:** **~fang** *m (Raum)* porch; **w~geschützt 1** *adj* sheltered (from the wind); **2** *adv* in a sheltered place; **~geschwindigkeit** *f* wind speed; **~hauch**

*m* breath of wind; **~hose** *f* vortex; **~hund** *m* **(a)** *(Hund)* greyhound; **(b)** *(fig pej)* rake.
**windig** *adj* windy; *Sache* dodgy *(col)*.
**Wind-:** **~jacke** *f* windcheater *(Brit)*, windbreaker ® *(US)*; **~jammer** *m* - *(Naut)* windjammer; **~kanal** *m* wind tunnel; **~kraftanlage** *f*, **~kraftwerk** *nt* wind power station; **~licht** *nt* storm lantern; **~mühle** *f* windmill; **gegen ~mühlen (an)kämpfen** *(fig)* to tilt at windmills; **~mühlenflügel** *m* windmill sail; **~park** *m* wind farm; **~pocken** *pl* chickenpox *sing*; **~rad** *nt (Tech)* wind turbine; **~richtung** *f* wind direction; **~rose** *f (Naut)* compass card; *(Met)* wind rose; **~sack** *m* windsock; **~schatten** *m* lee; *(von Autos)* slipstream; **w~schief** *adj* crooked; **~schirm** *m* windbreak; **~schutzscheibe** *f* windscreen *(Brit)*, windshield *(US)*; **~seite** *f* windward side; **~skala** *f* wind scale; **~stärke** *f (Met)* wind-force; **w~still** *adj* windless; *Ecke etc* sheltered; **wenn es völlig w~still ist** when there is no wind at all; **~stille** *f* calm; **~stoß** *m* gust of wind; **~surfbrett** *nt* windsurfing board; **~surfen** *nt* windsurfing; **w~surfen** *vi insep* to windsurf; **~surfer** *m* windsurfer.
**Windung** *f (von Weg, Fluß etc)* meander; *(von Schlange, Spule)* coil; *(von Schraube)* thread.
**Wink** *m* **-e** *(Zeichen)* sign; *(mit der Hand)* wave *(mit* of*)*; *(mit dem Kopf)* nod *(mit* of*)*; *(Hinweis, Tip)* hint, tip.
**Winkel** *m* - **(a)** angle. **(b)** *(fig: Ecke)* corner; *(Plätzchen)* place, spot. **jdn/etw in allen (Ecken und) ~n suchen** to look high and low for sb/sth.
**Winkel-:** **~advokat** *m (pej)* incompetent lawyer; **~eisen** *nt* angle iron.
**wink(e)lig** *adj Haus, Altstadt* full of nooks and crannies; *Gasse* twisty, windy.
**Winkel-:** **~messer** *m* - protractor; **~zug** *m (Trick)* dodge; *(Ausflucht)* evasion.
**winken** *ptp* **gewinkt** *or (col)* **gewunken 1** *vi* to wave *(jdm* to sb*)*. **sie winkte mit einem Fähnchen** she waved a flag; **einem Taxi ~** to hail a taxi; **dem Sieger winkt eine Reise nach Italien** the winner will receive (the attractive prize of) a trip to Italy. **2** *vt* to wave; *Abseits* to signal; *Taxi* to hail; *Kellner* to call. **jdn zu sich ~** to beckon sb over to one.
**winseln** *vti* to whimper; *(pej)* to grovel.
**Winter** *m* - winter. **es ist/wird ~** winter is here/is coming; **im/über den ~** in (the)/over the winter; **über den ~ kommen** to get through the winter.
**Winter-** *in cpds* winter; **~anfang** *m* beginning of winter; **~einbruch** *m* onset of winter; **~fell** *nt* winter coat; **w~fest** *adj* winterproof; *(Bot)* hardy; **~garten** *m* conservatory; **~getreide** *nt* winter crop; **~halbjahr** *nt* winter; **w~hart** *adj (Bot)* hardy; **~kleid** *nt* winter dress; *(Zool)* winter coat; **~kleidung** *f* winter clothing; **w~lich** *adj* wintry; *Kleidung* winter *attr*; **w~lich gekleidet** dressed for winter; **w~lich kalt** cold and wintry; **~mantel** *m* winter coat; **~obst** *nt* winter fruit; **~pause** *f* winter break; **~quartier** *nt* winter quarters *pl*; **~reifen** *m* winter tyre *(Brit)* or tire *(US)*; **~saat** *f* winter seed; **~sachen** *pl* winter clothes *pl*; **~schlaf** *m* hibernation; **~schlaf halten** to hibernate; **~schlußverkauf** *m* winter sale; **~semester** *nt* winter semester; **~spiele** *pl* **(Olympische) ~spiele** Winter Olympics *pl*; **~sport** *m* winter sports *pl*; *(Sportart)* winter sport; **~tag** *m* winter('s) day; **~zeit** *f* winter time; *(Jahreszeit)* winter.
**Winzer(in** *f) m* - wine-grower.
**winzig** *adj* tiny. **~ klein** minute, tiny little *attr*.
**Winzling** *m (col)* midget.

**Wipfel** m - treetop.
**Wippe** f -n seesaw.
**wippen** vi (auf und ab) to bob up and down; (hin und her) to teeter. ~**der Gang** bouncing gait.
**wir** pers pron we. ~ **alle/beide/drei** all/both/the three of us; ~ **Armen** we poor people; **wer ist da?** — ~ **(sind's)** who's there? — (it's) us; **trinken** ~ **erst mal einen** let's have a drink first.
**Wirbel** m - **(a)** (lit, fig) whirl; (in Fluß etc) whirlpool, eddy; (der Ereignisse) turmoil. **einen** ~ **um jdn/etw machen** to make a fuss about sb/sth. **(b)** (Haar~) crown. **(c)** (Anat) vertebra. **(d)** (Trommel~) (drum) roll.
**wirbellos** adj (Zool) invertebrate. **die W~en** the invertebrates.
**wirbeln** 1 vi **(a)** aux sein to whirl. **(b) mir wirbelt der Kopf** (col) my head is reeling. **(c)** (Trommeln etc) to roll. 2 vt to whirl.
**Wirbel-:** ~**säule** f (Anat) spinal column; ~**sturm** m whirlwind; ~**tier** nt vertebrate; ~**wind** m whirlwind.
**wirken¹** 1 vi **(a)** (Wirkung haben) to have an effect. **die Arznei hat nicht gewirkt** the medicine did not work; **schalldämpfend** ~ to have a soundproofing effect; **in diesem Rahmen wirkt das Bild viel besser** the picture looks much better in this frame; **etw auf sich** (acc) ~ **lassen** to take sth in. **(b)** (erscheinen) to seem, to appear. **nervös (auf jdn)** ~ to give (sb) the impression of being nervous; **sie wirkt abstoßend auf mich** I find her repulsive. **(c)** (geh: tätig sein) (Mensch) to work; (Einflüsse, Kräfte etc) to be at work. 2 vt (geh: tun) Gutes to do; Wunder to work.
**wirken²** vt Teppiche, Stoffe to weave.
**wirklich** 1 adj real. **im** ~**en Leben** in real life. 2 adv really. ~? really?
**Wirklichkeit** f reality. ~ **werden** to come true; **in** ~ in reality.
**wirklichkeits-:** ~**fremd** adj unrealistic; ~**getreu** adj realistic; **etw** ~**getreu abbilden** to paint a realistic picture of sth.
**wirksam** adj effective. **mit (dem)/am 1. Januar** ~ **werden** (form: Gesetz) to take effect on or from January 1st.
**Wirksamkeit** f effectiveness.
**Wirkstoff** m (esp Physiol) active substance.
**Wirkung** f effect (bei on); (von Tabletten etc) effects pl. **seine** ~ **tun** to have an effect; (Droge) to take effect; **ohne** ~ **bleiben** to have no effect; **seine** ~ **verfehlen** not to have the desired effect; **mit** ~ **vom 1. Januar** (form) with effect from January 1st.
**Wirkungs-:** ~**bereich** m field (of activity/interest etc); (Domäne) domain; ~**grad** m (degree of) effectiveness; **w~los** adj ineffective; ~**losigkeit** f ineffectiveness; **w~voll** adj effective; ~**weise** f (von Medikament) action; **die** ~**weise eines Kondensators** the way a condenser works.
**Wirkwaren** pl knitwear sing.
**wirr** adj confused; Blick crazed; (unordentlich) Haare tangled; Gedanken weird. **er ist** ~ **im Kopf** he is confused in his mind; **mach mich nicht** ~ don't confuse me; **alles lag** ~ **durcheinander** everything was in chaos.
**Wirren** pl confusion sing, turmoil sing.
**Wirrkopf** m (pej) muddle-head.
**Wirrwarr** m no pl confusion; (von Stimmen) hubbub; (von Fäden, Haaren etc) tangle.
**Wirsing** m no pl savoy cabbage.
**Wirt** m -e (Gastwirt, Vermieter) landlord.
**Wirtin** f landlady; (Gastgeberin) hostess.
**Wirtschaft** f **(a)** (Volks~) economy; (Geschäftsleben)

industry and commerce; (Finanzwelt) business world. **freie** ~ free market economy. **(b)** (Gast~) ≈ pub (Brit), saloon (US). **(c)** (col: Zustände) **eine schöne/saubere** ~ (iro) a fine state of affairs.
**wirtschaften** 1 vi **(a)** (sparsam sein) to economize. **gut** ~ **können** to be economical. **(b)** (col: sich betätigen) to busy oneself. 2 vt **jdn/etw zugrunde** ~ to ruin sb/sth financially.
**Wirtschafter(in** f) m - **(a)** (Verwalter) manager. **(b)** (im Haushalt, Heim etc) housekeeper.
**wirtschaftlich** adj economic; (sparsam) economical.
**Wirtschaftlichkeit** f economy; (eines Betriebes) economic viability.
**Wirtschafts-** in cpds economic; ~**asylant** m asylum-seeker (for financial reasons); ~**auskunftei** f credit investigation agency; ~**berater** m economic advisor; ~**beziehungen** pl business relations pl; ~**flüchtling** m financial refugee; ~**form** f economic system; ~**gebäude** nt working quarters pl; ~**gefüge** nt economic framework; ~**geld** nt housekeeping (money); ~**gemeinschaft** f economic community; ~**güter** pl economic goods pl; ~**hilfe** f economic aid; ~**krieg** m economic war/warfare; ~**kriminalität** f white-collar crime; ~**krise** f economic crisis; ~**lage** f economic situation; ~**minister** m minister of economic affairs; ~**ministerium** nt ministry of economic affairs; ~**ordnung** f economic order; ~**politik** f economic policy; ~**prüfer** m accountant; (zum Überprüfen der Bücher) auditor; ~**recht** nt commercial or business law; ~**spionage** f industrial espionage; ~**system** nt economic system; ~**union** f economic union; ~**verband** m business association; ~**wachstum** nt economic growth; ~**wissenschaft** f economics sing; ~**wissenschaftler** m economist; ~**wunder** nt economic miracle; ~**zeitung** f financial paper; ~**zweig** m branch of industry.
**Wirts-:** ~**haus** nt ≈ pub (Brit), saloon (US); (esp auf dem Land) inn; ~**leute** pl landlord and landlady; ~**stube** f lounge.
**Wisch** m -e (pej col) piece of paper; (mit Gedrucktem auch) piece of bumph (Brit col).
**wischen** 1 vti to wipe. **Staub** ~ to dust; **mit einem Tuch über den Tisch** ~ to wipe the table with a cloth; **sie wischte sich** (dat) **den Schweiß von der Stirn** she wiped the sweat from her brow; **Bedenken (einfach) vom Tisch** ~ (fig) to brush aside misgivings; **jdm eine** ~ (col) to clout sb one (col); **einen gewischt bekommen** (col: elektrischen Schlag) to get a shock. 2 vi aux sein (sich schnell bewegen) to whisk.
**Wischer** m - (Aut) wiper.
**Wischerblatt** nt (Aut) wiper blade.
**Wischiwaschi** nt no pl (pej col) drivel (col).
**Wischlappen** m cloth; (für Fußboden) floorcloth.
**Wisent** m -e bison.
**wispern** vti to whisper.
**Wißbegier(de)** f thirst for knowledge.
**wißbegierig** adj Kind eager to learn.
**wissen** pret **wußte**, ptp **gewußt** vti **(a)** to know (über +acc, von about). **ich weiß (es)** I know; **er weiß von nichts** he doesn't know anything about it; **weißt du schon das Neueste?** have you heard the latest?; **als ob ich das wüßte!** how should I know?; **von jdm/etw nichts** ~ **wollen** not to be interested in sb/sth; **er weiß es nicht anders/besser** he doesn't know any different/better; **das mußt du (selbst)** ~ that's for you to decide; **das hättest du ja** ~ **müssen!** you ought to have realized that; **man kann nie** ~ you never know; **weiß Gott** (col) God knows (col);

sie hält sich für wer weiß wie klug *(col)* she doesn't half think she's clever *(col)*; ... oder was weiß ich *(col)* ... or something; **er ist wieder wer weiß wo** *(col)* goodness knows where he's got to again *(col)*; **nicht, daß ich wüßte** not as far as I know; **gewußt wie/wo** *etc*! sheer brilliance!; **ich weiß sie in Sicherheit** I know that she is safe.

(b) *(sich erinnern)* to remember; *(sich vor Augen führen)* to realize. **ich weiß seine Adresse nicht mehr** I can't remember his address; **du mußt ~, daß ...** you must realize that ...

**Wissen** *nt no pl* knowledge. **meines ~s** to my knowledge; **etw gegen (sein) besseres ~ tun** to do sth against one's better judgement; **nach bestem ~ und Gewissen** to the best of one's knowledge and belief.

**Wissenschaft** *f* science.

**Wissenschaftler(in** *f)* *m* - scientist; *(Geistes~)* academic.

**wissenschaftlich** *adj* scientific; *(geistes~)* academic. **W~er Assistent** ≈ assistant lecturer; **~ arbeiten** to use a scientific approach.

**Wissens-:** **~durst** *m (geh)* thirst for knowledge; **~gebiet** *nt* field (of knowledge); **~stoff** *m* material; **w~wert** *adj* worth knowing.

**wissentlich** **1** *adv* knowingly, deliberately. **2** *adj* deliberate.

**wittern** **1** *vi (Wild)* to sniff the air. **2** *vt* to scent.

**Witterung** *f* (a) *(Wetter)* weather. **bei günstiger ~** if the weather is good. (b) *(Hunt) (Geruch)* scent *(von of)*; *(Geruchssinn)* sense of smell.

**Witterungs-** *in cpds* weather; **~einflüsse** *pl* effects *pl* of the weather; **~umschlag** *m* change in the weather.

**Witwe** *f* **-n** widow. **~ werden** to be widowed.

**Witwen-:** **~geld** *nt* widow's allowance; **~rente** *f* widow's pension; **~stand** *m* widowhood.

**Witwer** *m* - widower.

**Witz** *m* **-e** (a) *(Äußerung)* joke *(über +acc about)*. **einen ~ machen** to make a joke; **mach keine ~e!** don't be funny; **das ist doch wohl ein ~** he/you *etc* must be joking; **die Prüfung war ein ~** *(col)* the exam was a joke. (b) *(Geist)* wit. **der ~ an der Sache ist, daß ...** the great thing about it is that ...

**Witz-:** **~blattfigur** *f (fig col)* comic figure; **~bold** *m* **-e** joker; **du bist vielleicht ein ~bold!** *(iro)* you're a great one! *(iro)*.

**Witzelei** *f* teasing *no pl*.

**witzeln** *vi* to joke *(über +acc about)*.

**Witzfigur** *f (fig col)* figure of fun.

**witzig** *adj* funny.

**witzlos** *adj (col: unsinnig)* pointless, futile.

**WM** [ve:'|ɛm] *f* **-s** = **Weltmeisterschaft**.

**wo** **1** *interrog, rel adv* where; *(irgendwo)* somewhere. **überall, ~** wherever; **~ immer ...** wherever ...; **ach ~!** *(col)* nonsense! **2** *conj* **~ nicht/möglich** if not/possible; **~ er doch wußte, daß ich nicht kommen konnte** when he knew I couldn't come.

**wö. = wöchentlich** p.w.

**wo-:** **~anders** *adv* somewhere else; **~andersher** *adv* from somewhere else; **~andershin** *adv* somewhere else.

**wob** *pret of* **weben**.

**wobei** *adv* (a) *interrog* **~ ist das passiert?** when did that happen?; **~ hast du ihn erwischt?** what did you catch him at *or* doing? (b) *rel (während)* while. ... **sagte er, ~ er mich scharf ansah ...**, he said giving me a penetrating look; **..., ~ er das Buch aufschlug ...** opening the book; **~ mir gerade einfällt** which reminds me.

**Woche** *f* **-n** week. **zweimal in der ~** twice a week; **in**

dieser **~** this week.

**Wochenbett** *nt* **im ~ sterben** to die after childbirth; **während sie im ~ lag** during the period after the birth of her child.

**Wochen|end-** *in cpds* weekend.

**Wochen|ende** *nt* weekend. **schönes ~!** have a nice weekend; **verlängertes ~** long weekend.

**Wochen-:** **~karte** *f* weekly ticket; **w~lang** *adj, adv* for weeks; **~lohn** *m* weekly wage; **~markt** *m* weekly market; **~schau** *f* newsreel; **~tag** *m* weekday *(including Saturday)*; **was ist heute für ein ~tag?** what day is it today?; **w~tags** *adv* on weekdays *(including Saturday)*.

**wöchentlich** **1** *adj* weekly. **2** *adv* weekly; *(einmal pro Woche)* once a week. **sich ~ abwechseln** to take turns every week.

**Wochen-:** **w~weise** *adv* by the week; **~zeitschrift** *f* weekly (magazine); **~zeitung** *f* weekly (newspaper).

**Wöchnerin** *f woman who has recently given birth*.

**Wodka** *m* **-s** vodka.

**wodurch** *adv* (a) *interrog* how. (b) *rel* as a result of which.

**wofür** *adv* (a) *interrog* for what, what ... for. (b) *rel* for which, which ... for.

**wog** *pret of* **wiegen²**.

**Woge** *f* **-n** wave; *(fig auch)* surge.

**wogegen** *adv* (a) *interrog* against what, what ... against. (b) *rel* against which, which ... against.

**wogen** *vi (liter)* to surge *(auch fig)*.

**woher** *adv* (a) *interrog* where ... from. **~ weißt du das?** how do you (come to) know that?; **~ kommt es eigentlich, daß ...** how is it that ...? (b) *rel* from which, where ... from.

**wohin** *adv* (a) *interrog* where. (b) *rel* where. **~ man auch schaut** wherever you look.

**wohingegen** *conj* whereas, while.

**wohinter** *adv* (a) *interrog* what *or* where ... behind. (b) *rel* behind which.

**wohl** **1** *adv* (a) *(angenehm zumute)* happy; *(gesund)* well. **sich ~/~er fühlen** to feel happy/happier; *(gesundheitlich)* to feel well/better; **bei dem Gedanken ist mir nicht ~** I'm not very happy at the thought; **~ oder übel** whether one likes it *or* not; **~ dem, der ... happy the man who ...** (b) *(wahrscheinlich)* probably; *(iro: bestimmt)* surely. **er ist ~ schon zu Hause** he's probably at home by now; **das ist doch ~ nicht dein Ernst!** surely you're not serious! (c) *(vielleicht)* perhaps; *(etwa)* about. **das mag ~ sein** that may well be; **ob das ~ stimmt?** I wonder if that's true; **willst du das ~ lassen!** I wish you'd stop (doing) that. (d) *(durchaus)* well. **ich denke, ich verstehe dich sehr ~!** I think I understand you very well.

**2** *conj (zwar)* **er hat es ~ versprochen, aber ...** he may have promised, but ....

**Wohl** *nt no pl* welfare, well-being. **das öffentliche ~** the public good; **zu eurem ~** for your benefit *or* good; **zum ~!** cheers!; **auf dein ~!** your health!; **auf jds ~ trinken** to drink sb's health.

**Wohl-:** **w~auf** *adj pred* in good health; **~befinden** *nt* well-being; **w~begründet** *adj* well-founded; *Maßnahme, Strafe* well-justified; **~behagen** *nt* feeling of well-being; **w~behalten** *adj Mensch* safe and sound; *Gegenstand* intact; **w~bekannt** *adj* well-known; **w~beleibt** *adj (hum)* stout, portly; **w~durchdacht** *adj* well thought out; **~ergehen** *nt no pl* welfare; **w~erzogen** *adj (geh)* well-mannered.

**Wohlfahrt** *f no pl* welfare.

**Wohlfahrts-:** **~einrichtung** *f* social service; **~marke** *f* charity stamp; **~organisation** *f* charity; ~**pflege** f welfare work; **freie** ~**pflege** voluntary welfare work; ~**staat** m welfare state.

**Wohl-:** ~**gefallen** nt no pl pleasure; **sich in** ~**gefallen auflösen** (hum) (Gegenstände, Probleme) to vanish into thin air; (zerfallen) to fall apart; **w~gefällig** adj (gefallend) pleasing; **w~geformt** adj well-shaped; Körperteil shapely; Satz well-formed; ~**gefühl** nt sense of well-being; **w~gemeint** adj well-intentioned; **w~gemerkt** adv mind you; **w~genährt** adj well-fed; **w~geraten** adj (geh) Kind fine; Werk successful; ~**geruch** m (geh) pleasant smell; ~**geschmack** m (geh) pleasant taste; **w~gesinnt** adj (geh) well-disposed (dat towards); **w~habend** adj well-to-do.

**wohlig** adj pleasant; (gemütlich) cosy (Brit), cozy (US). ~ **warm** nice and warm.

**Wohl-:** ~**klang** m (geh) melodious sound; **w~klingend** adj melodious; ~**leben** nt (geh) life of luxury; **w~meinend** adj well-meaning; **w~proportioniert** adj well-proportioned; **w~riechend** adj fragrant; **w~schmeckend** adj (geh) tasty; ~**sein** nt **zum** ~**sein!** your very good health!

**Wohlstand** m no pl affluence, prosperity **im ~ leben** to be well off.

**Wohlstandsgesellschaft** f affluent society.

**Wohltat** f (a) (Genuß) relief. (b) (Gefallen) favour (Brit), favor (US); (gute Tat) good deed. **jdm eine ~ erweisen** to do sb a favour.

**Wohltäter(in** f) m benefactor; benefactress.

**wohltätig** adj charitable. **für ~e Zwecke** for charity.

**Wohltätigkeits-:** ~**basar** m charity bazaar; ~**verein** m charity.

**Wohl-:** **w~tuend** adj pleasant; **w~tun** vi sep irreg (angenehm sein) to do good (jdm sb); **das tut w~** that's good; **w~überlegt** adj etw **w~überlegt machen** to do sth after careful consideration; **w~verdient** adj well-deserved; ~**verhalten** nt good conduct; **w~weislich** adv very wisely; ~**wollen** nt no pl goodwill; **w~wollend** adj benevolent.

**Wohn-:** ~**anhänger** m caravan (Brit), trailer (US); ~**bau** m, pl **-ten** residential building; ~**block** m, pl **-s** block of flats (Brit), apartment house (US); ~**container** m Portakabin ®.

**wohnen** vi to live; (vorübergehend) to stay. **er wohnt (in der) Friedrichstraße 11** he lives at (number) 11 Friedrichstraße; **wir ~ da sehr schön** it's very nice where we live.

**Wohn-:** ~**fläche** f living space; ~**gebiet** nt, ~**gegend** f residential area; ~**geld** nt housing benefit; ~**gemeinschaft** f group of people sharing a/the flat (Brit) or apartment/house; **in einer** ~**gemeinschaft leben** to share a flat etc; **w~haft** adj (form) resident; ~**haus** nt residential building; ~**heim** nt (esp für Arbeiter) hostel; (für Studenten) hall (of residence), dormitory (US); (für Senioren) home; ~**komfort** m mit sämtlichem ~**komfort** with all mod cons; ~**komplex** m housing estate; ~**küche** f kitchen-cum-living room; ~**kultur** f style of home décor; ~**lage** f beste ~**lage** prime location; **unsere ~lage ist schön** where we live is very nice; **w~lich** adj cosy (Brit), cozy (US); **es sich** (dat) **w~lich machen** to make oneself comfortable; ~**mobil** nt camper; ~**ort** m place of residence; ~**qualität** f quality of housing; ~**raum** m living room; (no pl: ~fläche) living space; ~**siedlung** f housing estate (Brit) or development; ~**silo** m (pej) soulless tower block; ~**sitz** m domicile; **ohne festen** ~**sitz** of no fixed abode; ~**stadt** f residential town; ~**turm** m tower block.

**Wohnung** f flat (Brit), apartment. **1.000 neue ~en**

1,000 new homes.

**Wohnungs-:** ~**amt** nt housing office; ~**bau** m no pl house building no def art; ~**baugesellschaft** f housing association; ~**bauprogramm** nt housing programme (Brit) or program (US); ~**besetzer(in** f) m - squatter; ~**inhaber** m householder; (Eigentümer auch) owner-occupier; **w~los** adj homeless; ~**makler** m estate agent (Brit), realtor (US); ~**mangel** m housing shortage; ~**markt** m housing market; ~**not** f serious housing shortage; ~**suche** f flat-hunting (Brit); **auf ~suche sein** to be looking for a flat (Brit) or an apartment; ~**tür** f door (to the flat (Brit) or apartment); ~**wechsel** m change of address.

**Wohn-:** ~**viertel** nt residential area; ~**wagen** m caravan (Brit), trailer (US); ~**zimmer** nt living room.

**wölben** 1 vt to curve; Dach to vault. 2 vr to curve; (Tapete) to bulge out; (Decke, Brücke) to arch.

**Wölbung** f curvature; (kuppelförmig) dome; (bogenförmig) arch; (von Körperteil) curve.

**Wolf** m -̈e (a) wolf. **ein ~ im Schafspelz** a wolf in sheep's clothing; **mit den ~̈en heulen** (fig) to run with the pack. (b) (Tech) shredder; (Fleisch~) mincer (Brit), grinder (US).

**Wölfin** f she-wolf.

**Wolfram** nt no pl (Chem) tungsten.

**Wolfs-:** ~**hund** m Alsatian (Brit), German shepherd; **irischer ~hund** Irish wolfhound; ~**milch** f (Bot) spurge; ~**rachen** m (Med) cleft palate; ~**rudel** nt pack of wolves.

**Wolga** f Volga.

**Wolke** f -n (lit, fig) cloud. **aus allen ~n fallen** (fig) to be flabbergasted (col).

**Wolken-:** ~**bank** f cloudbank; ~**bruch** m cloudburst; **w~bruchartig** adj torrential; ~**decke** f cloud cover; ~**kratzer** m skyscraper; ~**kuckucksheim** nt cloud-cuckoo-land; **w~los** adj cloudless; **w~verhangen** adj overcast.

**wolkig** adj cloudy.

**Wolldecke** f (woollen (Brit) or woolen US) blanket.

**Wolle** f -n wool. **sich mit jdm in die ~ kriegen** (fig col) to start squabbling with sb; **sich mit jdm in der ~ haben** (fig col) to be at loggerheads with sb.

**wollen¹** adj attr woollen (Brit), woolen (US).

**wollen²** 1 modal aux ptp ~ to want to. **er will ein Haus kaufen** he wants to buy a house; **etw gerade tun ~** to be going to do sth; **wolltest du gerade weggehen?** were you just leaving?; **es sieht aus, als wollte es regnen** it looks as if it's going to rain; **es will einfach nicht klappen** it just won't work; **keiner will es gewesen sein** nobody will admit to it; **er will es gesehen haben** he claims to have seen it; **und so jemand** or **etwas** (col) **will Lehrer sein!** and he calls himself a teacher; **ich wollte, ich wäre ...** I wish I were ...; **darauf ~ wir mal anstoßen!** let's drink to that; **das will alles gut überlegt sein** that needs a lot of thought.

2 vti to want. **kommt er nun? – nein, er will nicht** is he coming? – no, he doesn't want to; **ich will nach Hause** I want to go home; **oh, das hab ich nicht gewollt** oh, I didn't mean to do that; **ich will, daß du genau zuhörst** I want you to listen carefully; **wer nicht will, der hat schon** if you don't like it, you can lump it (col); **ob du willst oder nicht** whether you like it or not; **er hat nichts zu ~** he has no say; **ich weiß nicht, was er will** (verstehe ihn nicht) I don't know what he's on about; siehe **gewollt**.

**Woll-:** ~**faser** f wool fibre (Brit) or fiber (US); ~**garn** nt woollen (Brit) or woolen (US) yarn.

**wollig** adj woolly.

**Woll-:** ~**jacke** *f* cardigan; ~**knäuel** *nt* ball of wool; ~**sachen** *pl* woollens *pl (Brit)*, woolens *pl (US)*; ~**stoff** *m* woollen *(Brit)* or woolen *(US)* material.

**Wollust** *f no pl (geh) (Sinnlichkeit)* sensuality; *(Lüsternheit)* lust.

**wollüstig** *adj (geh) (sinnlich)* sensual; *(lüstern)* lascivious.

**Wollwaren** *pl* woollens *pl (Brit)*, woolens *pl (US)*.

**womit** *adv* (a) *interrog* with what, what ... with. ~ **kann ich dienen?** what can I do for you? (b) *rel* with which; *(auf ganzen Satz bezüglich)* by which. **das ist es,** ~ **ich nicht einverstanden bin** that's what I don't agree with; ~ **ich nicht sagen will, daß** ... by which I don't mean that ...

**womöglich** *adv* possibly.

**wonach** *adv* (a) *interrog* after what, what ... after. ~ **sollen wir uns richten?** what should we go by? (b) *rel* **das war es,** ~ **ich mich erkundigen wollte** that was what I wanted to ask about.

**Wonne** *f* -**n** *(geh) (Glückseligkeit)* bliss *no pl*; *(Vergnügen)* joy, delight. **die** ~**n der Liebe** the joys of love; **es ist eine wahre** ~ it's a sheer delight.

**wonnevoll** *adj Gefühl* blissful; *Kind, Anblick* delightful. ~ **lächeln** to smile with delight.

**wonnig** *adj* delightful; *Gefühl* blissful.

**woran** *adv* (a) *interrog* ~ **liegt das?** what's the reason for it?; ~ **denkst du?** what are you thinking about?; ~ **ist er gestorben?** what did he die of? (b) *rel* by which. **das,** ~ **ich mich gerne erinnere** what I like to recall; ~ **ich merkte, daß** ... which made me realize that ...

**worauf** *adv* (a) *interrog (räumlich)* on what, what ... on. ~ **wartest du?** what are you waiting for? (b) *rel (zeitlich)* whereupon. ~ **er einen Wutanfall bekam** whereupon he flew into a rage; ~ **du dich verlassen kannst** of that you can be sure.

**woraus** *adv* (a) *interrog* out of what, what ... out of. ~ **schließt du das?** from what do you deduce that? (b) *rel* out of which, which ... out of. ~ **ich schließe, daß** ... from which I conclude that ...

**worden** *ptp of* **werden 2 (c).**

**worin** *adv siehe auch* **in** (a) *interrog* in what, what ... in. ~ **war das eingewickelt?** what was it wrapped in?; ~ **liegt der Unterschied/Vorteil?** where is the difference/advantage? (b) *rel* in which, which ... in. **das ist etwas,** ~ **wir nicht übereinstimmen** that's something we don't agree on.

**Wort** *nt* -**e** (a) *pl usu* -**er** *(Vokabel)* word. ~ **für** ~ word for word.

(b) *(Äußerung)* word. **genug der** ~**e!** enough talk!; ~**en Taten folgen lassen** to suit the action to the word; **mit einem** ~ in a word; **mit anderen** ~**en** in other words; **hast du (da noch)** ~**e!** it leaves you speechless; **mir fehlen die** ~**e** words fail me; **kein** ~ **von etw sagen** not to say one word about sth; **ich verstehe kein** ~! I don't understand a word (of it); *(hören)* I can't hear a word (that's being said); **ein** ~ **mit jdm sprechen** to have a word with sb; **ein ernstes** ~ **mit jdm reden** to have a serious talk with sb; **davon hat man mir kein** ~ **gesagt** they didn't say anything about that; **man kann sein eigenes** ~ **nicht (mehr) verstehen** you can't hear yourself speak; **um nicht viel(e)** ~**e zu machen** to make it brief; **jdm das** ~ **im Mund (her)umdrehen** to twist sb's words; **die passenden** ~**e für etw finden** to find the right words for sth; **jdm aufs** ~ **glauben** to believe sb implicitly; **jdm aufs** ~ **gehorchen** to obey sb's every word; **dabei habe ich auch (noch) ein** ~ **mitzureden** I (still) have something to say about that too.

(c) *no pl (Versprechen)* word. **jdn beim** ~ **nehmen** to take sb at his word; **ich gebe Ihnen mein** ~ darauf I give you my word on it; **sein** ~ **halten** to keep one's word.

(d) *no pl* **das große** ~ **führen** *(col)* to shoot one's mouth off *(col)*; **einer Sache** *(dat)* **das** ~ **reden** to put the case for sth; **das** ~ **an jdn richten** to address (oneself to) sb; **jdm ins** ~ **fallen** to interrupt sb; **zu** ~ **kommen** to get a chance to speak; **sich zu** ~ **melden** to ask to speak; **jdm das** ~ **erteilen** to allow sb to speak.

(e) *(Ausspruch)* saying; *(Zitat)* quotation; *(Rel)* Word. **ein** ~ **Goethes** a quotation from Goethe.

(f) *(Text)* words *pl.* **in** ~**en** in words; **in** ~ **und Bild** in words and pictures; **in** ~ **und Schrift** in speech and writing; **etw in** ~**e fassen** to put sth into words.

**Wort-:** ~**art** *f (Gram)* part of speech; ~**bruch** *m* **das wäre ein** ~**bruch** that would be breaking your/my *etc* word; **w**~**brüchig** *adj* false; **w**~**brüchig werden** to break one's word.

**Wörtchen** *nt dim of* **Wort da habe ich wohl ein** ~ **mitzureden** *(col)* I think I have some say in that.

**Wörter-:** ~**buch** *nt* dictionary; ~**verzeichnis** *nt* vocabulary; *(von Spezialbegriffen)* glossary.

**Wort-:** ~**fetzen** *pl* snatches of conversation; ~**führer(in** *f)* *m* spokesman/-woman; ~**gebühr** *f (Telec)* rate per word; ~**gefecht** *nt* battle of words; **w**~**getreu** *adj, adv* verbatim; **w**~**gewaltig** *adj* powerfully eloquent; **w**~**gewandt** *adj* eloquent; **w**~**karg** *adj* taciturn; ~**klauberei** *f* quibbling; ~**laut** *m* wording; **im** ~**laut** verbatim.

**wörtlich** *adj Bedeutung* literal; *Rede* direct. **etw** ~ **wiedergeben** to repeat sth word for word; **das hat er** ~ **gesagt** those were his very words.

**Wort-:** **w**~**los** *adj* silent; **2** *adv* without saying a word; ~**meldung** *f* **wenn es keine weiteren** ~**meldungen gibt** if nobody else wishes to speak; **w**~**reich** *adj Rede, Erklärung etc* wordy; *Sprache* rich in vocabulary; ~**schatz** *m* vocabulary; ~**spiel** *nt* pun; ~**stellung** *f (Gram)* word order; ~**wahl** *f* choice of words; ~**wechsel** *m* verbal exchange; **w**~**wörtlich 1** *adj* word-for-word; **2** *adv* quite literally.

**worüber** *adv* (a) *interrog* about what, what ... about; *(örtlich)* over what, what ... over. (b) *rel* about which, which ... about; *(örtlich)* over which, which ... over.

**worum** *adv* (a) *interrog* about what, what ... about. ~ **handelt es sich?** what's it about? (b) *rel* about which, which ... about.

**worunter** *adv* (a) *interrog* under what, what ... under. (b) *rel* under which, which ... under.

**wovon** *adv* (a) *interrog* from what, what ... from. (b) *rel* from which, which ... from. **das ist ein Gebiet,** ~ **er viel versteht** that is a subject he knows a lot about.

**wovor** *adv* (a) *interrog (örtlich)* before what, what ... before. ~ **fürchtest du dich?** what are you afraid of? (b) *rel* before which, which ... before.

**wozu** *adv* (a) *interrog* to what, what ... to; *(warum)* why. ~ **soll das gut sein?** what's the point of that? (b) *rel* to which, which ... to. **das,** ~ **ich am meisten neige** what I'm most inclined to do.

**Wrack** *nt* -**s** wreck.

**wringen** *pret* **wrang**, *ptp* **gewrungen** *vti* to wring.

**WS** [ve:'|ɛs] *nt (Univ)* = **Wintersemester.**

**WSV** [ve:|ɛs'fau] *m* = **Winterschlußverkauf.**

**Wucher** *m no pl* profiteering. ~ **treiben** to profiteer; **das ist der reinste** ~! that's daylight robbery! *(col)*.

**Wucherer** *m* - profiteer.

**Wuchergeschäft** *nt* profiteering *no pl.*

**wucherisch** *adj* profiteering; *Zinsen etc* extortionate.

**wuchern** vi (a) aux sein or haben (Pflanzen) to grow rampant. (b) (Kaufmann etc) to profiteer.

**wuchernd** adj Pflanzen rampant.

**Wucherpreis** m exorbitant price.

**Wucherung** f rank growth; (Med) growth.

**Wucherzins** m exorbitant interest no pl.

**wuchs** [vu:ks] pret of **wachsen**[1].

**Wuchs** [vu:ks] m no pl (Wachstum) growth; (von Mensch) stature.

**Wucht** f no pl force. **mit voller** ~ with full force; **er ist eine** ~! (col) he's smashing! (col).

**wuchten** vti to heave.

**Wuchtgeschoß** nt rubber bullet.

**wuchtig** adj massive; Schlag powerful.

**wühlen 1** vi (a) (nach for) to dig; (Maulwurf etc) to burrow; (Schwein, Vogel) to root. **in den Haaren** ~ to run one's fingers through one's hair. (b) (suchen) to rummage (nach etw for sth). **in den Schubladen** ~ to rummage through the drawers. (c) (Untergrundarbeit leisten) to stir things up. **2** vr **sich durch etw** ~ to burrow one's way through sth.

**Wühl-:** ~**maus** f vole; ~**tisch** m (col) bargain counter.

**Wulst** m or f ⸗e bulge.

**wulstig** adj bulging; Rand, Lippen thick.

**wund** adj sore. **sich** (dat) **die Füße** ~ **laufen** (lit) to get sore feet from walking; (fig) to walk one's legs off; **ein** ~**er Punkt** a sore point.

**Wundbrand** m gangrene.

**Wunde** f -n (lit, fig) wound. **alte** ~**n wieder aufreißen** (fig) to open up old sores; **an eine alte** ~ **rühren** (fig geh) to touch on a sore point; **Salz in eine/jds** ~ **streuen** (fig) to turn the knife in the wound.

**Wunder** nt - miracle (auch Rel), wonder. ~ **wirken** to work miracles; **das grenzt an ein** ~ it verges on the miraculous; **die** ~ **der Natur** the wonders of nature; **es ist ein/kein** ~, **daß** ... it's a wonder/no wonder or little wonder that ...; **es ist ein** ~, **daß er dick ist?** is it any wonder that he's fat?

**wunder** adv inv **meine Eltern denken, es ist** ~ **was passiert** my parents think goodness knows what has happened; **er glaubt, er ist** ~ **wer** he thinks he's so fantastic.

**wunderbar** adj (a) wonderful. (b) (übernatürlich) miraculous.

**wunderbarerweise** adv miraculously.

**Wunder-:** ~**droge** f wonder drug; **w**~**gläubig** adj **w**~**gläubig sein** to believe in miracles; ~**heiler** m faith-healer; ~**kerze** f sparkler; ~**kind** nt child prodigy; ~**land** nt wonderland; **w**~**lich** adj (a) (merkwürdig) strange, odd; (b) (w~sam) wondrous; ~**mittel** nt miracle cure.

**wundern 1** vr to be surprised (über +acc at). **du wirst dich** ~! you'll be amazed!; **ich wundere mich über gar nichts mehr** nothing surprises me any more; **dann darfst du dich nicht** ~, **wenn** ... then don't be surprised if ... **2** vt, vt impers to surprise. **es wundert mich, daß er noch nicht hier ist** I'm surprised that he isn't here yet; **das würde mich nicht** ~ I shouldn't be surprised.

**Wunder-:** **w**~**schön** adj beautiful; ~**täter** m miracle worker; **w**~**tätig** adj miraculous; Leben, Heilige miracle-working; ~**tüte** f surprise packet; **w**~**voll** adj marvellous (Brit), marvelous (US); ~**waffe** f wonder weapon; ~**werk** nt miracle.

**Wund-:** ~**fieber** nt traumatic fever; ~**infektion** f wound infection; **w**~**liegen** vr sep irreg to get bedsores; ~**pflaster** nt adhesive plaster; ~**salbe** f ointment; ~**starrkrampf** m tetanus.

**Wunsch** m ⸗e (a) wish; (sehnliches Verlangen) desire; (Bitte) request. **ein Pferd war schon immer mein** ~ I've always wanted a horse; **haben Sie (sonst) noch einen** ~? (beim Einkauf etc) is there anything else you'd like?; **alles geht nach** ~ everything is going smoothly; **auf** ~ on request; **auf jds (besonderen/ausdrücklichen)** ~ **hin** at sb's (special/ express) request. (b) usu pl (Glückwunsch) wish.

**Wunsch-:** ~**bild** nt ideal; ~**denken** nt wishful thinking.

**Wünschelrute** f divining rod.

**wünschen 1** vt (a) **sich** (dat) **etw** ~ to want sth; (den Wunsch äußern) to ask for sth; **ich wünsche mir das** I would like that; **ich wünsche mir, daß du ... I would like you to ...; **das habe ich mir von meinen Eltern zu Weihnachten gewünscht** I asked my parents to give me that for Christmas; **er wünscht sich** (dat) **diesen Mann als Lehrer** he wishes that this man was his teacher; **was wünschst du dir?** what would you like?; **du darfst dir etwas** ~ you may make a wish; **sie haben alles, was man sich** (dat) **nur** ~ **kann** they have everything you could possibly wish for.

(b) **jdm etw** ~ to wish sb sth; **jdm einen guten Morgen** ~ to wish sb good morning; **wir** ~ **dir gute Besserung/eine gute Reise** we hope you get well soon/have a pleasant journey; **ich wünschte, ich hätte dich nie gesehen** I wish I'd never seen you.

(c) (begehren, verlangen) to want. **was** ~ **Sie?** (in Geschäft) what can I do for you?; (in Restaurant) what would you like?; **wen** ~ **Sie zu sprechen?** to whom would you like to speak?

**2** vi to wish. **Sie** ~? what can I do for you?; **ganz wie Sie** ~ (just) as you wish; **zu** ~/**viel zu** ~ **übrig lassen** to leave something/a great deal to be desired.

**wünschenswert** adj desirable.

**Wunsch-:** **w**~**gemäß** adv as requested; ~**kind** nt wanted child; **sie war ein** ~**kind** she was planned; ~**konzert** nt (Rad) musical request programme (Brit) or program (US); **w**~**los** adj Mensch content(ed); **w**~**los glücklich** perfectly happy; ~**partner** m ideal partner; ~**sendung** f (Rad) request programme (Brit) or program (US); ~**traum** m dream; **das ist doch bloß ein** ~**traum** that's just a pipe-dream; ~**zettel** m list of things one would like.

**wurde** pret of **werden**.

**Würde** f -n (a) no pl dignity. **unter aller** ~ **sein** to be beneath contempt; **unter jds** ~ **sein** to be beneath sb or sb's dignity. (b) (Auszeichnung) honour (Brit), honor (US); (Titel) title; (Amt) rank.

**würdelos** adj undignified.

**Würdenträger(in** f) m - dignitary.

**würdevoll** adj = **würdig** (a).

**würdig** adj (a) dignified. **sich** ~ **verhalten** to behave with dignity. (b) (wert) worthy. **jds/einer Sache** (gen) ~/**nicht** ~ **sein** to be worthy/unworthy of sb/ sth.

**würdigen** vt (a) to appreciate; (lobend erwähnen) to acknowledge; (ehren) to pay tribute to. **etw zu** ~ **wissen** to appreciate sth. (b) (geh) **jdn einer Sache** (gen) ~ to deem sb worthy of sth; **jdn keines Blickes** ~ not to deign to look at sb.

**Würdigung** f (a) siehe vt appreciation; acknowledgement; (Ehrung) honour (Brit), honor (US). (b) (Rede, Artikel) appreciation.

**Wurf** m ⸗e (a) throw; (beim Kegeln etc) bowl. **mit dem Film ist ihm ein großer** ~ **gelungen** this film is a big hit for him (col). (b) no pl (das Werfen) throwing. (c) (Zool) litter.

**Würfel** m - (a) dice. ~ **spielen** to play at dice; **die** ~

**sind gefallen** the die is cast. **(b)** *(Math)* cube; *(Zucker~)* lump.

**Würfel-:** ~**becher** *m* shaker; **w~förmig** *adj* cube-shaped.

**würfeln** *vti* to throw; *(Würfel spielen)* to play at dice. **um etw** ~ to throw dice for sth.

**Würfel-:** ~**spiel** *nt* *(Partie)* game of dice; *(Spielart)* dice; ~**zucker** *m* cube sugar.

**Wurf-:** ~**geschoß** *nt* projectile; ~**messer** *nt* throwing knife; ~**pfeil** *m* dart; ~**ring** *m* quoit; ~**sendung** *f* circular; *(unerwünscht)* (item of) junk mail; ~**speer** *m* javelin; ~**waffe** *f* missile.

**Würgegriff** *m* *(lit, fig)* stranglehold.

**würgen 1** *vt* jdn to throttle; *(fig: Angst)* to choke. **2** *vi* **(a)** to choke. **an etw** *(dat)* ~ to choke on sth, to gag. **(b)** *(beim Erbrechen)* to retch. **mit Hängen und W~** by the skin of one's teeth.

**Wurm¹** *m* ⸗er worm; *(Made)* maggot. **da steckt der** ~ **drin** *(fig col)* there's something wrong somewhere; *(verdächtig)* there's something fishy about it *(col)*.

**Wurm²** *nt* ⸗er *(col: Kind)* (little) mite.

**wurmen** *vt, vt impers (col)* to rankle with.

**wurmig** *adj Obst* maggoty.

**Wurm-:** ~**kur** *f* worming treatment; ~**mittel** *nt* medicament against intestinal worms, vermifuge *(spec)*; **w~stichig** *adj Holz* full of worm-holes; *(madig auch) Obst* maggoty.

**Wurst** *f* ⸗e sausage; *(col: Kot)* turd *(col!)*. **jetzt geht es um die** ~ *(fig col)* the moment of truth has come; **das ist mir** ~ **or Wurscht** *(col)* I don't give a damn *(col)*.

**Wurst-:** ~**aufschnitt** *m* assortment of sliced sausage; ~**brot** *nt* open sausage sandwich; *(zusammengeklappt)* sausage sandwich.

**Würstchen** *nt* **(a)** *dim of* **Wurst** small sausage. **heiße** *or* **warme** ~ hot sausages. **(b)** *(pej: Mensch)* squirt *(col)*, nobody. **ein armes** ~ *(fig)* a poor soul.

**Würstchen-:** ~**bude** *f*, ~**stand** *m* sausage stand; hot-dog stand.

**wursteln** *vi (col)* to muddle along. **sich durchs Leben** ~ to muddle through life.

**Wurstfinger** *pl (pej col)* podgy fingers *pl*.

**wurstig** *adj (col)* couldn't-care-less *attr*.

**Wurstigkeit** *f (col)* couldn't-care-less attitude *(col)*.

**Wurst-:** ~**salat** *m* sausage salad; ~**waren** *pl* sausages *pl*; ~**zipfel** *m* sausage end.

**Würze** *f* -n *(Gewürz)* seasoning, spice; *(Aroma)* aroma; *(fig: Reiz)* spice.

**Wurzel** *f* -n **(a)** *(lit, fig)* root. **etw mit der** ~ **ausrotten** *(fig)* to eradicate sth; ~**n schlagen** *(lit)* to root; *(fig)* to put down roots. **(b)** *(Math)* root. ~**n ziehen** to find the roots; **(die)** ~ **aus 4 ist 2** the square root of 4 is 2.

**Wurzel-:** ~**gemüse** *nt* root vegetables *pl*; **w~los** *adj (lit, fig)* rootless.

**wurzeln** *vi (lit, fig)* to be rooted.

**Wurzel-:** ~**werk** *nt no pl* root system; ~**zeichen** *nt (Math)* radical sign.

**würzen** *vt (lit, fig)* to season.

**würzig** *adj Speise* tasty; *(scharf)* spicy; *Luft* tangy; *Wein, Bier* full-bodied.

**wusch** *pret of* **waschen.**

**Wuschelhaar** *nt (col)* mop of curly hair.

**wusch(e)lig** *adj (col) Tier* shaggy; *Haare* fuzzy.

**Wuschelkopf** *m (Mensch)* fuzzy-head *(col)*.

**wußte** *pret of* **wissen.**

**Wust** *m no pl (col) (Durcheinander)* jumble; *(Menge)* pile.

**wüst** *adj* **(a)** *(öde)* desert *attr*, desolate. **(b)** *(unordentlich)* wild. ~ **aussehen** to look a real mess. **(c)** *(ausschweifend)* wild. ~ **feiern** to have a wild party. **(d)** *(rüde) Beschimpfung* vile. **jdn** ~ **beschimpfen** to use foul language to sb.

**Wüste** *f* -n *(lit, fig)* desert; *(Ödland)* waste. **die** ~ **Gobi** the Gobi Desert; **jdn in die** ~ **schicken** *(fig)* to send sb packing *(col)*.

**Wüsten-:** ~**fuchs** *m* desert fox; ~**könig** *m (poet)* king of the desert *(poet)*; ~**schiff** *nt (poet)* ship of the desert *(poet)*.

**Wüstling** *m* lecher.

**Wut** *f no pl* **(a)** *(Zorn, Raserei)* rage. **(auf jdn/etw) eine** ~ **haben** to be furious (with sb/sth); **eine** ~ **im Bauch haben** *(col)* to be seething; **eine** ~ **haben** to be in a rage; **in** ~ **geraten** to fly into a rage; **jdn in** ~ **versetzen** to infuriate sb. **(b)** *(Verbissenheit)* frenzy. **mit einer wahren** ~ like crazy *(col)*.

**Wut-:** ~**anfall** *m* fit of rage; *(esp von Kind)* tantrum; ~**ausbruch** *m* outburst of fury.

**wüten** *vi (lit, fig) (toben)* to rage; *(zerstörerisch hausen)* to cause havoc.

**wütend** *adj* furious, enraged; *Menge* angry. **auf jdn/etw** *(acc)* ~ **sein** to be mad at sb/sth.

**wut|entbrannt** *adj* furious, enraged. ~ **hinauslaufen** to leave in a rage.

**Wüterich** *m* brute.

**wut-:** ~**schnaubend** *adj* snorting with rage; ~**verzerrt** *adj* distorted with rage.

**Wwe.** = **Witwe.**

**Wz** = **Warenzeichen** TM.

# X

**X, x** [ɪks] *nt* **-, -** X, x. **Herr X** Mr X; **jdm ein X für ein U vormachen** to put one over on sb *(col)*; **X wie Xanthippe** ≃ X for Xmas.

**Xanthippe** [ksan'tɪpə] *f* **-n** *(fig col)* shrew.

**X-Beine** ['ɪks-] *pl* knock-knees *pl*.

**x-beinig** ['ɪks-] *adj* knock-kneed.

**x-beliebig** [ɪks-] *adj* any old *(col)*. **wir können uns an einem ~en Ort treffen** we can meet anywhere you like *or* any old place you like *(col)*.

**xerographieren*** [kserogra'fiːrən] *vti insep* to Xerox ®.

**Xerokopie** [kseroko'piː] *f* Xerox ® (copy).

**xerokopieren*** [kseroko'piːrən] *vti insep* to Xerox.

**x-fach** ['ɪks-] *adj* **die ~e Menge** *(Math)* n times the amount.

**x-mal** ['ɪks-] *adv (col)* n (number of) times *(col)*.

**x-te** ['ɪkstə] *adj (Math, col)* nth. **zum ~n Male** for the nth *or* umpteenth time *(col)*.

**Xylophon** [ksylo'foːn] *nt* **-e** xylophone.

# Y

**Y, y** ['ʏpsilɔn] *nt* **-, -** Y, y. **Y wie Ypsilon** ≃ Y for yellow, Y for yoke *(US)*.

**Yankee** ['jɛŋki] *m* **-s** *(pej)* Yankee, yank.

**Yen** [jɛn] *m* **-(s)** yen.

**Yeti** ['jeːti] *m* **-s** yeti, abominable snowman.

**Yoga** ['joːgɑ] *m or nt no pl* yoga.

**Yogi** ['joːgi] *m* **-s** yogi.

**Ypsilon** ['ʏpsilɔn] *nt* **-s** y.

**Ytong** ® ['yːtɔn] *m* **-s** breeze block, cinder block *(US)*.

**Yucca** ['jʊka] *f* **-s** yucca.

**Yuppie** ['jʊpiː, 'japiː] *m* **-s** yuppie.

# Z

**Z, z** [tsɛt] *nt* **-, -** Z, z. **Z wie Zacharias** ≃ Z for Zebra.

**Zack** *m no pl (col)* **auf ~ sein** to be on the ball *(col)*.

**zack** *interj (col)* pow, zap *(col)*. **~ ~!** chop-chop! *(col)*; **bei uns muß alles ~, ~ gehen** we have to do everything chop-chop *(col)*.

**Zacke** *f* **-n**, **Zacken** *m* **-** point; *(von Gabel)* prong; *(von Kamm)* tooth; *(Berg~)* jagged peak.

**zacken** *vt* to serrate; *Saum, Papier* to pink.

**zackig** *adj* **(a)** *(gezackt)* jagged. **(b)** *(col) Soldat* smart; *Tempo, Musik* brisk. **... aber ein bißchen ~!** ... and make it snappy *(col)*!

**zaghaft** *adj* timid.

**Zaghaftigkeit** *f* timidity.

**Zagreb** *nt* Zagreb.

**zäh** *adj* tough; *(dickflüssig)* glutinous; *Verkehr etc* slow-moving; *(ausdauernd)* dogged. **ein ~es Leben haben** to have a tenacious hold on life; *(fig: Idee etc)* to die hard.

**zähflüssig** *adj* viscous; *Verkehr* slow-moving.

**Zähigkeit** *f* toughness; *(Ausdauer)* doggedness.

**Zahl** *f* **-en** number; *(in Statistik, als Größe auch)* figure. **~en nennen** to give figures; **eine fünfstellige ~** a five-figure number; **in großer ~** in great numbers.

**zahlbar** *adj* payable *(an +acc* to*)*.

**zählbar** *adj* countable.

**zählebig** *adj* hardy; *Vorurteil* persistent.

**zahlen** *vti* to pay. **Herr Ober, (bitte) ~!** waiter, the bill *or* check *(US)* please; **dort zahlt man gut/ schlecht** they pay well/badly; **wenn er nicht bald zahlt, dann ...** if he doesn't pay up soon, then ...; **laß mal, ich zahl's** no no, I'll pay; **ich zahle dir ein Bier**

I'll buy you a beer.
**zählen 1** *vi* **(a)** to count. **(b)** *(gehören)* **er zählt zu den besten Schriftstellern unserer Zeit** he ranks as one of the best authors of our time; **zählt Aids zu den unheilbaren Krankheiten?** is AIDS an incurable disease? **(c)** *(sich verlassen)* **auf jdn/etw ~** to count on sb/sth. **(d)** *(gelten)* to count. **2** *vt* to count. **seine Tage sind gezählt** his days are numbered; **der König zählt 5 Punkte** *(Cards)* the King counts as 5 points.
**Zahlen-:** **~angabe** *f* figure; **ich kann keine genauen ~angaben machen** I can't quote any precise figures; **~folge** *f* sequence of numbers; **~gedächtnis** *nt* memory for numbers; **~kombination** *f* combination (of figures); **z~mäßig** *adj* numerical; **z~mäßig überlegen** superior in numbers; **~material** *nt* figures *pl*; **~schloß** *nt* combination lock; **~verhältnis** *nt* (numerical) ratio; **~verriegelung** *f (Comp)* numbers lock.
**Zähler** *m* - **(a)** *(Math)* numerator. **(b)** *(Meßgerät)* meter.
**Zählerstand** *m* meter reading.
**Zahl-:** **~grenze** *f* fare stage; **~karte** *f* transfer form; **z~los** *adj* countless, innumerable; **~meister** *m (Naut)* purser; **z~reich** *adj* numerous; **~stelle** *f* payments office; **~tag** *m* payday.
**Zahlung** *f* payment. **in ~ geben/nehmen** to give/take in part-exchange; **gegen eine ~ von $500 erhalten Sie ...** on payment of $500 you will receive ...
**Zählung** *f* count.
**Zahlungs-:** **~anweisung** *f* transfer order; **~aufforderung** *f* request for payment; **~aufschub** *m* extension (of credit); **~bedingungen** *pl* terms (of payment) *pl*; **~befehl** *m* order to pay; **~bilanz** *f* balance of payments; **~empfänger** *m* payee; **z~fähig** *adj* able to pay; *Firma* solvent; **~fähigkeit** *f* ability to pay; solvency; **~frist** *f* period allowed for payment; **z~kräftig** *adj* wealthy; **~mittel** *nt* means *sing* of payment; *(Münzen, Banknoten)* currency; **gesetzliches ~mittel** legal tender; **z~pflichtig** *adj* obliged to pay; **~rückstände** *pl* arrears *pl*; **~schwierigkeiten** *pl* financial difficulties *pl*; **z~unfähig** *adj* unable to pay; *Firma* insolvent; **~unfähigkeit** *f* inability to pay; insolvency; **z~unwillig** *adj* unwilling to pay; **~verkehr** *m* transactions *pl*, payments *pl*; **~verpflichtung** *f* obligation to pay; **~verzug** *m* default; **~weise** *f* method of payment; **z~willig** *adj* willing to pay.
**Zählwerk** *nt* counter.
**Zahlwort** *nt* numeral.
**zahm** *adj* tame.
**zähmen** *vt* to tame; *(fig)* *Leidenschaft* to control.
**Zahn** *m* ⁼e tooth; *(von Briefmarke)* perforation; *(Rad~)* cog. **künstliche ~e** false teeth *pl*; **~e bekommen** to cut one's teeth; **die ersten/zweiten ~e** one's milk teeth/second set of teeth; **die dritten ~e** *(hum)* false teeth; **diese Portion reicht** *or* **ist für den hohlen ~** *(col)* that's hardly enough to satisfy a mouse *(col)*; **der ~ der Zeit** the ravages *pl* of time; **die ~e zeigen** to bare one's teeth; *(fig col)* to show one's teeth; **jdm einen ~ ziehen** *(lit)* to pull one of sb's teeth out; *(fig)* to put an idea out of sb's head; **jdm auf den ~ fühlen** *(aushorchen)* to sound sb out; *(streng befragen)* to give sb a grilling; **einen ~ draufhaben** *(col: Geschwindigkeit)* to be going like the clappers *(col)*; **einen ~ zulegen** *(col)* to get a move on *(col)*.
**Zahn-:** **~arzt** *m* dentist; **z~ärztlich** *adj* dental; **~arztpraxis** *f* dentist's surgery *(Brit)* or office *(US)*; **~belag** *m* plaque; **~bürste** *f* toothbrush; **~creme**

*f* toothpaste.
**zähne-:** **~fletschend** *adj attr, adv* snarling; **~klappernd** *adj attr, adv* with teeth chattering; **~knirschend** *adj attr, adv (fig)* gnashing one's teeth.
**zahnen** *vi* to teethe.
**Zahn-:** **~ersatz** *m* dentures *pl*; **~faule** *f* tooth decay; **~fleisch** *nt* gum(s *pl*); **auf dem ~fleisch gehen** *(col)* to be all in *(col)*, to be on one's last legs *(col)*; **~fleischbluten** *nt* bleeding of the gums; **~füllung** *f* filling; **~heilkunde** *f* dentistry; **~höhle** *f* pulp cavity; **~klammer** *f* brace; **~klinik** *f* dental hospital; **~krone** *f* crown; **z~los** *adj* toothless; **~lücke** *f* gap between one's teeth; **~medizin** *f* dentistry; **~pasta** *f* toothpaste; **~pflege** *f* dental hygiene; **~prothese** *f* (set of) dentures; **~pulver** *nt* tooth powder; **~putzbecher** *m* tooth mug; **~rad** *nt* cogwheel; **~radbahn** *f* rack-railway *(Brit)*, rack-railroad *(US)*; **~radgetriebe** *nt* gear mechanism; **~schmelz** *m* (tooth) enamel; **~schmerz** *m usu pl* toothache *no pl*; **~seide** *f* dental floss; **~spange** *f* brace; **~stein** *m* tartar; **~stocher** *m* - toothpick; **~techniker** *m* dental technician; **~weh** *nt* toothache; **~wurzel** *f* root (of a/the tooth).
**Zaire** [zaˈiːr] *nt* Zaire.
**Zander** *m* - *(Zool)* pike-perch.
**Zange** *f* -n *(Flach~, Rund~)* (pair of) pliers *pl*; *(Beiß~)* (pair of) pincers *pl*; *(Greif~, Zucker~)* (pair of) tongs *pl*; *(von Tier)* pincers *pl*. **jdn in die ~ nehmen** *(fig)* to put the screws on sb *(col)*.
**Zangengeburt** *f* forceps delivery.
**Zank** *m no pl* squabble. **~ und Streit** trouble and strife.
**Zank|apfel** *m (fig)* bone of contention.
**zanken** *vir* to squabble. **(sich) um etw ~** to quarrel over sth.
**zänkisch** *adj* quarrelsome; *Weib* nagging *attr*.
**Zäpfchen** *nt (Gaumen~)* uvula.
**Zapfen** *m* - *(Spund)* bung; *(Tannen~ etc)* cone; *(Holzverbindung)* tenon.
**zapfen** *vt* to tap, to draw.
**Zapfenstreich** *m (Mil)* tattoo.
**Zapf-:** **~hahn** *m* tap; **~säule** *f* petrol pump *(Brit)*, gas pump *(US)*.
**zapp(e)lig** *adj* wriggly; *(unruhig)* fidgety.
**zappeln** *vi* to wriggle; *(unruhig sein)* to fidget. **jdn ~ lassen** *(fig col)* to keep sb in suspense.
**Zar** *m (wk)* -en, -en tsar.
**Zarin** *f* tsarina.
**zaristisch** *adj* tsarist *no adv*.
**zart** *adj Haut, Töne* soft; *Braten, Gemüse* tender; *Gebäck, Teint, Kind, Gefühle* delicate; *Berührung* gentle. **im ~en Alter von ...** at the tender age of ...; **~ besaitet sein** to be very sensitive.
**Zart-:** **z~besaitet** *adj attr* highly sensitive; **z~bitter** *adj Schokolade* plain; **z~fühlend** *adj* sensitive; **~gefühl** *nt* delicacy of feeling, sensitivity.
**Zartheit** *f siehe adj* softness; tenderness; delicacy; gentleness.
**zärtlich** *adj* tender, affectionate.
**Zärtlichkeit** *f* **(a)** *no pl* affection, tenderness. **(b)** *(Liebkosung)* caress. **~en** *(Worte)* loving words.
**Zaster** *m no pl (col)* lolly *(col)*.
**Zäsur** *f* caesura; *(fig)* break.
**Zauber** *m* - *(lit, fig)* magic. **fauler ~** *(col)* humbug *no indef art*; **der ganze ~** *(col)* the whole caboodle *(col)*.
**Zauberei** *f no pl* magic.
**Zauberer** *m* - magician.
**Zauber-:** **~formel** *f* magic formula; **z~haft** *adj* enchanting; **~hand** *f*: **wie von** *or* **durch ~hand** as if by magic.

**Zauberin** f (female) magician.
**Zauber-**: ~**kunst** f magic; ~**künstler** m conjurer; ~**kunststück** nt conjuring trick; ~**mittel** nt magical cure; (Trank) magic potion.
**zaubern 1** vi to do magic; (Kunststücke vorführen) to do conjuring tricks. **ich kann doch nicht** ~**!** (col) I'm not a magician! **2** vt **etw aus etw** ~ to conjure sth out of sth.
**Zauber-**: ~**spruch** m spell; ~**stab** m wand; ~**trank** m magic potion; ~**trick** m conjuring trick; ~**wort** nt magic word.
**Zauderer** m - vacillator.
**zaudern** vi to vacillate. **etw ohne zu** ~ **tun** to do sth without hesitating.
**Zaum** m, pl **Zäume** bridle. **jdn/etw im** ~ **halten** (fig) to keep a tight rein on sb/sth; **seine Ungeduld im** ~**e halten** (fig) to control one's impatience.
**zäumen** vt to bridle.
**Zaumzeug** nt bridle.
**Zaun** m, pl **Zäune** fence. **einen Streit vom** ~ **brechen** to pick a quarrel.
**Zaun-**: ~**gast** m mere onlooker; ~**könig** m (Orn) wren; ~**pfahl** m (fencing) post; **jdm einen Wink mit dem** ~**pfahl geben** to drop sb a broad hint.
**zausen** vt to ruffle; Haare to tousle.
**z.B.** = **zum Beispiel** e.g.
**ZDF** [tsɛtde:ˈʔɛf] **Zweites Deutsches Fernsehen.**
**Zebra** nt -s zebra.
**Zebrastreifen** m zebra crossing (Brit), crosswalk (US).
**Zeche** f -n (a) (Rechnung) bill, check (US). **die (ganze)** ~ **(be)zahlen** (lit, fig) to foot the bill. (b) (Bergwerk) (coal) mine.
**zechen** vi to booze (col), to drink.
**Zecher(in** f) m - boozer (col), drinker.
**Zech-**: ~**kumpan** m (col) drinking mate; ~**preller** m - person who leaves a bar/restaurant without paying the bill; ~**prellerei** f leaving without paying the bill in a bar/restaurant; ~**tour** f pub crawl (esp Brit col), bar hop (US col).
**Zecke** f -n tick.
**Zeder** f -n cedar.
**Zeh** m -en, **Zehe** f -n toe; (Knoblauch~) clove. **jdm auf die** ~**en treten** (lit, fig) to tread on sb's toes.
**Zehen-**: ~**nagel** m toenail; ~**spitze** f tip of the toe; **auf (den)** ~**spitzen** on tiptoe; **auf (den)** ~**spitzen gehen** to tiptoe.
**zehn** num ten; siehe **vier.**
**Zehn** f -en ten; siehe **Vier.**
**Zehner** m - (a) (Math) ten. (b) (col) (Groschen) tenpfennig piece; (Schein) ten mark note (Brit) or bill (US), ≈ tenner (col).
**Zehner-**: ~**karte** f (für Bus etc) 10-journey ticket; (für Schwimmbad etc) 10-visit ticket; ~**packung** f packet of ten; ~**system** nt decimal system; ~**tastatur** f (Comp) numeric keypad.
**Zehn-**: ~**fingersystem** nt touch-typing method; ~**kampf** m (Sport) decathlon; ~**markschein** m ten mark note (Brit) or bill (US).
**zehntausend** num ten thousand. **Z~e von Menschen** tens of thousands of people.
**Zehntel** nt - tenth.
**zehnte(r, s)** adj tenth; siehe **vierte(r, s).**
**zehren** vi (a) **von etw** ~ (lit) to live off sth; (fig) to feed on sth. (b) **an jdm** or **jds Kräften** ~ to drain or sap sb's strength; **an jds Gesundheit** ~ to undermine sb's health.
**Zeichen** nt - sign; (Sci, auf Landkarte) symbol; (Schrift~, Comp) character; (Hinweis, Signal) signal; (Erkennungs~) identification; (Vermerk) mark. **es ist ein** ~ **unserer Zeit, daß ...** it is a sign of the

times that ...; **als** ~ **von etw** as a sign of sth; **als** ~ **der Verehrung** as a token of respect; **jdm ein** ~ **geben** to give sb a signal; **unser/Ihr** ~ (form) our/your reference; **er ist im** ~ or **unter dem** ~ **des Widders geboren** he was born under the sign of Aries; **unter dem** ~ **von etw stehen** (fig: Konferenz etc) to take place against a background of sth.
**Zeichen-**: ~**block** m sketch pad; ~**brett** nt drawing board; ~**code** m (Comp) character code; ~**erklärung** f (auf Fahrplänen etc) key (to the symbols); (auf Landkarte) legend; ~**kette** f (Comp) character string; ~**lehrer** m art teacher; ~**papier** nt drawing paper; ~**saal** m (Sch) art room; ~**satz** m (Comp) character set; ~**setzung** f punctuation; ~**sprache** f sign language; ~**stift** m drawing pencil; ~**stunde** f art lesson; ~**system** nt notation; ~**tisch** m drawing table; ~**trickfilm** m (animated) cartoon; ~**unterricht** m art teaching; (Unterrichtsstunde) art lesson.
**zeichnen 1** vt (a) to draw; (entwerfen) Plan to draft. (b) (kennzeichnen) to mark. **2** vi to draw. **gezeichnet: XY** signed, XY; **für etw verantwortlich** ~ (form) to be responsible for sth.
**Zeichner(in** f) m - draughtsman/-woman (Brit), draftsman/-woman (US); (Art auch) artist.
**zeichnerisch 1** adj Darstellung graphic. **sein** ~**es Können** his drawing ability. **2** adv ~ **begabt sein** to have a talent for drawing.
**Zeichnung** f (a) drawing. (b) (Muster) pattern; (von Gefieder, Fell) markings pl.
**zeichnungsberechtigt** adj authorized to sign.
**Zeigefinger** m index finger, forefinger.
**zeigen 1** vi to point (auf +acc to). **2** vt to show. **jdm etw** ~ to show sb sth or sth to sb; **dem werd' ich's (aber)** ~**!** (col) I'll show him!; **zeig mal, was du kannst!** let's see what you can do! **3** vr to appear; (Gefühle) to show. **in dem Kleid kann ich mich doch nicht** ~ I can't be seen in this dress; **er zeigte sich befriedigt** he gave every sign of being satisfied; **es zeigt sich, daß ...** it turns out that ...; **es wird sich** ~**, wer recht hat** we shall see who's right.
**Zeiger** m - pointer; (Uhr~) hand.
**Zeigestock** m pointer.
**Zeile** f -n line. **vielen Dank für Deine** ~**n** many thanks for your letter; **zwischen den** ~**n** between the lines.
**Zeilen-**: ~**abstand** m line spacing; ~**drucker** m line printer; ~**schalter** m line spacer; ~**umbruch** m (automatischer) ~**umbruch** (Comp) wordwrap; ~**vorschub** m line feed.
**Zeisig** m -e (Orn) siskin.
**Zeit** f -en (a) time; (Epoche) age. **die gute alte** ~ the good old days; **das waren noch** ~**en!** those were the days; **die** ~ **Goethes** the age of Goethe; **für alle** ~**en** for ever; **mit der** ~ **gehen** to move with the times; **die** ~ **wird knapp** time is running out; **die** ~ **wurde mir lang** time hung heavy on my hands; **eine Stunde** ~ **haben** to have an hour (to spare); **haben Sie vielleicht einen Augenblick** ~**?** do you have a moment?; **sich** (dat) **für jdn/etw** ~ **nehmen** to devote time to sb/sth; **damit hat es noch** ~ there's no hurry; **das hat** ~ **bis morgen** that can wait until tomorrow; **laß dir** ~ take your time; **auf unbestimmte** ~ for an indefinite period; **in letzter** ~ recently; **die ganze** ~ **über** the whole time; **mit der** ~ (allmählich) in time; **nach** ~ **bezahlt werden** to be paid by the hour; **auf** ~ **spielen** (Sport, fig) to play for time; **es wird** ~**, daß wir gehen** it's about time we left; **Soldat auf** ~ soldier serving for a set time; **seit dieser** ~ since then; **zur** ~ **Königin Viktorias** in Queen Victoria's times; **zu der** ~**, als ...** (at the time)

when ...; **von** ~ **zu** ~ from time to time; **zur** ~ at the moment. **(b)** *(Ling)* tense.

**zeit** *prep +gen* ~ **meines Lebens** in my lifetime.

**Zeit-**: ~**abschnitt** *m* period (of time); ~**alter** *nt* age; ~**angabe** *f* time; *(Datum)* date; ~**ansage** *f* *(Rad)* time check; *(Telec)* speaking clock; ~**arbeit** *f* temporary work/job; ~**aufnahme** *f (Phot)* time exposure; ~**aufwand** *m* time *(needed for a task)*; **mit großem** ~**aufwand verbunden sein** to be extremely time-consuming; ~**bombe** *f* time bomb; ~**druck** *m* pressure of time; **unter** ~**druck** under pressure; ~**fahren** *nt (Radsport)* time trial; ~**fehler** *m* time fault; ~**frage** *f* question of time; ~**gefühl** *nt* sense of time; ~**geist** *m* spirit of the times; **z**~**gemäß** *adj* up-to-date; **z**~**gemäß sein** to be in keeping with the times *or (in der Vergangenheit)* the period; ~**genosse** *m* contemporary; **z**~**genössisch** *adj* contemporary; ~**geschehen** *nt* events *pl* of the day; ~**geschichte** *f* contemporary history; ~**geschmack** *m* prevailing taste; **z**~**gleich 1** *adj Erscheinungen* simultaneous; *Läufer* with the same time; **2** *adv* at the same time.

**zeitig** *adj, adv* early.

**zeitigen** *vt (geh) Ergebnis* to bring about.

**Zeit-**: ~**karte** *f* season ticket; **z**~**kritisch** *adj Aufsatz* commenting on contemporary issues; ~**lang** *f* **eine** ~**lang** for a while *or* a time; **z**~**lebens** *adv* all one's life.

**zeitlich 1** *adj* temporal; *Reihenfolge* chronological. **in kurzem** ~**em Abstand** at short intervals (of time); **das Z**~**e segnen** *(euph)* to depart this life. **2** *adv* timewise *(col)*. **das kann sie** ~ **nicht einrichten** she can't find (the) time for that; **das ist** ~ **ungünstig** that's bad timing; ~ **unmöglich** not possible timewise; **ist das** ~ **begrenzt?** is there a time limit?

**Zeit-**: **z**~**los** *adj* timeless; ~**lupe** *f* slow motion *no art*; **Wiederholung in** ~**lupe** slow-motion replay; ~**lupentempo** *nt* **im** ~**lupentempo** *(fig)* at a snail's pace; ~**mangel** *m* **aus** ~**mangel** for lack of time; ~**nahme** *f* -**n** *(Sport)* timekeeping *no pl*; ~**not** *f* shortage of time; **in** ~**not sein** to be pressed for time; ~**plan** *m* schedule; ~**punkt** *m* time; **zu diesem** ~**punkt** at that time; ~**raffer** *m no pl* time-lapse photography; **z**~**raubend** *adj* time-consuming; ~**raum** *m* period of time; **in einem** ~**raum von** ... over a period of ...; ~**rechnung** *f* calendar; ~**schrift** *f* magazine; *(wissenschaftlich)* journal; ~**soldat** *m* regular soldier *(who has signed up for a fixed period of time)*; ~**spanne** *f* period of time; **z**~**sparend** *adj* timesaving; ~**tafel** *f* chronological table.

**Zeitung** *f* (news)paper.

**Zeitungs-** *in cpds* newspaper; ~**annonce,** ~**anzeige** *f* newspaper advertisement; *(Familienanzeige)* announcement in the paper; ~**artikel** *m* newspaper article; ~**ausschnitt** *m* newspaper *or* press cutting; ~**austräger** *m* paperboy/-girl; ~**beilage** *f* newspaper supplement; ~**händler** *m* newsagent *(Brit)*, news vendor *(US)*; ~**inserat** *nt* newspaper advertisement; ~**junge** *m* paperboy; ~**korrespondent** *m* newspaper correspondent; ~**leser** *m* newspaper reader; ~**papier** *nt* newsprint; *(als Altpapier)* newspaper; ~**redakteur** *m* newspaper editor; ~**ständer** *m* newspaper rack; ~**verleger** *m* newspaper publisher.

**Zeit-**: ~**unterschied** *m* time difference; ~**verlust** *m* loss of time; **ohne** ~**verlust** without losing any time; ~**verschwendung** *f* waste of time; ~**vertreib** *m* way of passing the time; *(Hobby)* pastime; **z**~**weilig** *adj* temporary; **z**~**weise** *adv* at times; ~**wort** *nt* verb; ~**zeichen** *nt* time signal;

~**zone** *f* time zone; ~**zünder** *m* time fuse.

**zelebrieren\*** *vt* to celebrate.

**Zelle** *f* -**n** cell *(auch Sci, Pol)*; *(Kabine)* cabin; *(Telefon~)* phone box *(Brit)* or booth.

**Zell-**: ~**gewebe** *nt* cell tissue; ~**kern** *m* nucleus (of a/the cell).

**Zellophan** *nt no pl* cellophane.

**Zell-**: ~**stoff** *m* cellulose; ~**teilung** *f* cell division.

**Zelluloid** [*auch* -'lɔyt] *nt no pl* celluloid.

**Zellulose** *f* -**n** cellulose.

**Zelt** *nt* -**e** tent; *(Zirkus~)* big top. **seine** ~**e aufschlagen/abbrechen** *(fig)* to settle down/to pack one's bags.

**Zelt-**: ~**bahn** *f* strip of canvas; ~**dach** *nt* tent roof.

**zelten** *vi* to camp.

**Zelt-**: ~**lager** *nt* camp; ~**mast** *m* tent pole; ~**pflock** *m* tent peg *(Brit)* or stake *(US)*; ~**plane** *f* tarpaulin; ~**platz** *m* camp site; ~**stange** *f* tent pole.

**Zement** *m* -**e** cement.

**zementieren\*** *vt* to cement; *(fig)* to reinforce.

**Zementmaschine** *f* cement mixer.

**Zenit** *m no pl (lit, fig)* zenith. **die Sonne steht im** ~ the sun is at its zenith.

**zensieren\*** *vt* **(a)** *auch vi (benoten)* to mark. **(b)** *(Bücher etc)* to censor.

**Zensor** *m* censor.

**Zensur** *f* **(a)** *(no pl)* censorship *no indef art*; *(Prüfstelle)* censors *pl.* **einer** ~ **unterliegen** to be censored. **(b)** *(Note)* mark.

**Zenti-**: ~**meter** *m or nt* centimetre *(Brit)*, centimeter *(US)*; ~**metermaß** *nt* (metric) tape measure.

**Zentner** *m* - (metric) hundredweight *(= 50 kilograms)*; *(Aus, Sw)* 100 kilograms.

**Zentner-**: ~**last** *f (fig)* great weight; **z**~**schwer** *adj (fig)* very heavy.

**zentral** *adj (lit, fig)* central.

**Zentral-** *in cpds* central; ~**afrikanische Republik** *f* Central African Republic; ~**bank** *f* central bank.

**Zentrale** *f* -**n** head office; *(für Taxis etc)* headquarters *sing or pl*; *(Telefon~)* exchange

**Zentral-**: ~**einheit** *f (Comp)* central processing unit, CPU; ~**heizung** *f* central heating.

**Zentralisation** *f* centralization.

**zentralisieren\*** *vt* to centralize.

**zentralistisch** *adj* centralist.

**Zentral-**: ~**komitee** *nt* central committee; ~**nervensystem** *nt* central nervous system; ~**verriegelung** *f (Aut)* central locking.

**zentrieren\*** *vti (Typ, Comp)* to centre *(Brit)*, to center *(US)*.

**zentrifugal** *adj* centrifugal.

**Zentrifugalkraft** *f* centrifugal force.

**Zentrifuge** *f* -**n** centrifuge.

**Zentrum** *nt, pl* **Zentren** *(lit, fig)* centre *(Brit)*, center *(US)*.

**Zeppelin** *m* -**e** zeppelin.

**Zepter** *nt* - sceptre *(Brit)*, scepter *(US)*. **das** ~ **führen** to wield the sceptre.

**zerbeißen\*** *vt irreg* to chew; *Bonbon, Keks etc* to crunch; *(beschädigen)* to chew to pieces.

**zerbersten\*** *vi irreg aux sein* to burst.

**zerbeulen\*** *vt* to dent. **zerbeult** battered.

**zerbomben\*** *vt* to flatten with bombs. **zerbombt** *Stadt* bombed.

**zerbrechen\*** *irreg* **1** *vt (lit)* to break into pieces; *Glas, Porzellan etc* to smash; *Ketten (lit, fig)* to break. **2** *vi aux sein* to break into pieces; *(Glas, Porzellan etc)* to smash; *(fig)* to be destroyed *(an +dat* by).

zerbrechlich adj fragile.
Zerbrechlichkeit f fragility.
zerbröckeln* vti to crumble.
zerdrücken* vt to squash; Gemüse to mash; (zerknittern) to crush.
Zeremonie f ceremony.
zeremoniell adj ceremonial.
Zeremonienmeister [-'mɔːniən-] m master of ceremonies.
zerfahren adj scatty; (unkonzentriert) distracted.
Zerfahrenheit f siehe adj scattiness; distraction.
Zerfall m no pl disintegration; (von Gebäude auch, von Atom) decay; (von Leiche, Holz etc) decomposition; (von Kultur, Gesundheit) decline.
zerfallen* 1 vi irreg aux sein (a) to disintegrate; (Atomkern) to decay; (Leiche, Holz etc) to decompose; (Reich, Moral, Gesundheit) to decline. (b) (sich gliedern) to fall (in +acc into). 2 adj Haus tumbledown.
zerfetzen* vt to tear to pieces.
zerfetzt adj Hose tattered; Arm lacerated.
zerfleddert adj (col) tattered.
zerfleischen* vt to tear to pieces.
zerfließen* vi irreg aux sein (Tinte, Makeup etc) to run.
zerfranst adj frayed.
zerfressen* vt irreg to eat away; (Motten, Mäuse etc) to eat. (von Motten/Würmern) ~ sein to be moth-/worm-eaten.
zerfurcht adj Stirn furrowed; Weg rutted.
zergehen* vi irreg aux sein to dissolve; (schmelzen) to melt. auf der Zunge ~ (Gebäck etc) to melt in the mouth.
zergliedern* vt (Biol) to dissect; (fig) to analyse.
zerhacken* vt to chop up.
zerhauen* vt irreg to chop in two; (in viele Stücke) to chop up.
zerkauen* vt to chew.
zerkleinern* vt to cut up; (zerhacken) to chop (up); (zerbrechen) to break up; (zermahlen) to crush.
zerklüftet adj Küste jagged. tief ~es Gestein deeply fissured rock.
zerknautschen* vt (col) to crease, to crumple.
zerknirscht adj overcome with remorse.
zerknittern* vt to crease, to crumple.
zerknüllen* vt to crumple up.
zerkochen* vti (vi: aux sein) to overcook.
zerkratzen* vt to scratch.
zerkrümeln* vt to crumble.
zerlassen* vt irreg Butter etc to melt.
zerlaufen* vi irreg aux sein to melt.
zerlegbar adj die Möbel waren leicht ~ the furniture could easily be taken apart.
zerlegen* vt to take apart; (zerschneiden) to cut up; (Fleisch) to carve up; (Biol) to dissect. etw in seine Einzelteile ~ to take sth to pieces.
zerlesen adj well-thumbed.
zerlumpt adj ragged.
zermahlen* vt to grind.
zermalmen* vt to crush.
zermartern* vr sich (dat) das Hirn ~ to rack one's brains.
zermürben* vt (fig) jdn ~ to wear sb down; ~d wearing.
zernagen* vt to gnaw to pieces.
zerpflücken* vt to pick to pieces.
zerplatzen* vi aux sein to burst.
zerquetschen* vt to crush; Kartoffeln to mash. 10 Mark und ein paar Zerquetschte (col) 10 marks something (or other), 10 marks odd.
Zerrbild nt (fig) caricature.

zerreden* vt to flog to death (col).
zerreiben* vt irreg (lit, fig) to crush.
zerreißen* irreg 1 vt to tear up; (aus Versehen) to tear; Faden, Seil etc to break; (zerfleischen) to tear apart. 2 vi aux sein (Stoff) to tear; (Band, Seil etc) to break.
Zerreißprobe f (lit) pull test; (fig) real test.
zerren 1 vt to drag; Sehne to pull. 2 vi an etw (dat) ~ to tug at sth.
zerrinnen* vi irreg aux sein (lit, fig) to melt away; (Geld) to disappear.
zerrissen adj (fig) Volk, Partei strife-torn; Mensch torn.
Zerrissenheit f (von Volk, Partei) disunity no pl; (innere ~) (inner) conflict.
Zerrspiegel m (lit) distorting mirror; (fig) travesty.
Zerrung f eine ~ a pulled ligament/muscle.
zerrütten* vt (lit, fig) to destroy; Nerven to shatter. eine zerrüttete Ehe a broken marriage.
Zerrüttung f destruction; (von Nerven) shattering; (von Ehe) breakdown.
Zerrüttungsprinzip nt (Jur) principle of irretrievable (marital) breakdown.
zersägen* vt to saw up.
zerschellen* vi aux sein (Schiff, Flugzeug) to be smashed to pieces.
zerschlagen* irreg 1 vt (a) (Mensch) to smash (to pieces). (b) (fig) Opposition to crush; Vereinigung to break up. 2 vr (Plan etc) to fall through; (Hoffnung) to be shattered. 3 adj pred washed out (col); (nach Anstrengung) shattered (col), worn out.
Zerschlagung f (fig) (von Bewegung, Opposition) crushing; (von Plänen etc) failure.
zerschlissen adj Kleider tattered.
zerschmelzen* vi irreg aux sein to melt.
zerschmettern* 1 vt to shatter; Feind to crush. 2 vi aux sein to shatter.
zerschneiden* vt irreg to cut; (in Stücke) to cut up.
zersetzen* 1 vt to decompose; (Säure) to corrode; (fig) to subvert. 2 vr to decompose; (durch Säure) to corrode.
zersetzend adj (fig) subversive.
Zersetzung f (Chem) decomposition; (durch Säure) corrosion; (fig: Untergrabung) subversion.
zerspalten* vt to split; Gemeinschaft to split up.
zersplittern* 1 vt to shatter; Holz to splinter; (fig) Kräfte, Zeit to dissipate. 2 vi aux sein to shatter; (Holz) to splinter; (fig) to split up. 3 vr (fig) to dissipate one's energies; (Gruppe, Partei) to become fragmented.
zerspringen* vi irreg aux sein to shatter; (einen Sprung bekommen) to crack.
zerstampfen* vt (zertreten) to stamp on; (zerkleinern) to crush.
zerstäuben* vt to spray.
Zerstäuber m - spray; (Parfüm~ auch) atomizer.
zerstechen* vt irreg (a) (Mücken) to bite (all over). (b) Material, Haut to puncture; Finger to prick.
zerstieben* vi irreg aux sein to scatter; (Wasser) to spray.
zerstören* vt to destroy; (Rowdys) to vandalize; Gesundheit to ruin.
Zerstörer m - (Naut) destroyer.
zerstörerisch adj destructive.
Zerstörung f no pl destruction no pl.
Zerstörungswut f destructive mania.
zerstoßen* vt irreg to crush.
zerstreiten* vr irreg to quarrel, to fall out.
zerstreuen* 1 vt (a) to scatter (in +dat over); (fig) to dispel. (b) jdn ~ to take sb's mind off things. 2 vr (a) (sich verteilen) to scatter; (fig) to be dispelled.

**(b)** *(sich ablenken)* to take one's mind off things.
**zerstreut** *adj (fig) Mensch* absent-minded.
**Zerstreutheit** *f no pl* absent-mindedness.
**Zerstreuung** *f* **(a)** *no pl siehe vt* scattering. **(b)** *(Ablenkung)* diversion. **zur** ~ as a diversion.
**zerstritten** *adj* estranged. **mit jdm** ~ **sein** to have fallen out with sb.
**zerstückeln*** *vt (lit)* to cut up; *Leiche* to dismember; *Land* to carve up.
**zerteilen*** *vt* to split up.
**Zertifikat** *nt* certificate.
**zertrampeln*** *vt* to trample on.
**zertrennen*** *vt* to sever; *(auftrennen) Nähte* to undo.
**zertreten*** *vt irreg* to crush (underfoot); *Rasen* to ruin.
**zertrümmern*** *vt* to smash; *Einrichtung* to smash up; *Ordnung* to wreck.
**Zervelatwurst** [tsɛrvəˈlaːt-] *f* German salami, cervelat.
**zerwühlen*** *vt* to ruffle up, to tousle; *Bett* to rumple (up); *(aufwühlen) Erdboden* to churn up.
**zerzaust** *adj* dishevelled *(Brit)*, disheveled *(US)*.
**Zeter** *nt:* ~ **und Mordio schreien** to scream blue murder.
**zetern** *vi (pej)* to clamour *(Brit)*, to clamor *(US)*; *(keifen)* to scold.
**Zettel** *m* - piece of paper; *(Notiz~)* note; *(Kartei~)* card; *(Kassen~)* receipt; *(Bekanntmachung)* notice; *(Formular)* form.
**Zettel-:** ~**kartei** *f* card index; ~**kasten** *m* file-card box; ~**wirtschaft** *f (pej)* **eine** ~**wirtschaft haben** to have bits of paper everywhere.
**Zeug** *nt no pl (col)* stuff *no indef art, no pl*; *(Unsinn)* nonsense, rubbish *(col)*; *(Kleidung)* things *pl (col)*. **altes** ~ junk, trash; **das** ~ **zu etw haben** to have (got) what it takes to be sth; **jdm etwas am** ~ **flicken** *(col)* to find fault with sb; **was das** ~ **hält** for all one is worth; *laufen* like mad; *fahren* flat out *(col)*; **sich ins** ~ **legen** to go flat out *(col)*; **dummes** ~ **reden** to talk a lot of nonsense.
**Zeuge** *m (wk)* -**n**, -**n** *(Jur, fig)* witness *(gen to)*. ~ **eines Unfalls sein** to be a witness to an accident.
**zeugen**[1] *vt Kind* to father.
**zeugen**[2] *vi* **(a) von etw** ~ to show sth. **(b)** *(aussagen)* to testify *(vor +dat to)*.
**Zeugen-:** ~**aussage** *f* testimony; ~**bank** *f*, ~**stand** *m* witness box *(Brit)*, witness stand *(US)*; ~**vernehmung** *f* examination of the witness(es).
**Zeugin** *f* witness.
**Zeugnis** *nt* **(a)** *(Bescheinigung)* certificate; *(Schul~)* report; *(von Arbeitgeber)* reference. **jdm ein** ~ **ausstellen** to give sb a reference. **(b)** *(esp liter: Zeugenaussage)* evidence. **für/gegen jdn** ~ **ablegen** to testify for/against sb.
**Zeugnis-:** ~**konferenz** *f (Sch) staff meeting to decide on marks etc*; ~**papiere** *pl* certificates *pl*; *(von Arbeitgeber)* references *pl*.
**Zeugung** *f* fathering.
**Zeugungs-:** **z**~**fähig** *adj* fertile; ~**fähigkeit** *f* fertility; **z**~**unfähig** *adj* sterile; ~**unfähigkeit** *f* sterility.
**z.H(d).** = **zu Händen** att, attn.
**Zi** = **Zimmer** rm.
**Zicke** *f* -**n** **(a)** nanny goat. **(b)** *(pej col: Frau)* old bag *(col)*.
**Zicken** *pl (col)* nonsense *no pl*. **mach bloß keine** ~**!** no nonsense now!; ~ **machen** to make trouble.
**zickig** *adj (albern)* silly; *(prüde)* prudish.
**Zickzack** *m* -**e** zigzag. **z**~ *or* **im** ~ **laufen** to zigzag.
**Zickzack-:** ~**kurs** *m* zigzag course; ~**linie** *f* zigzag;

~**schere** *f* pinking shears.
**Ziege** *f* -**n** **(a)** goat. **(b)** *(pej col: Frau)* cow *(col!)*.
**Ziegel** *m* - *(Backstein)* brick; *(Dach~)* tile. **ein Dach mit** ~**n decken** to tile a roof.
**Ziegel-:** ~**bau** *m, pl* -**ten** brick building; ~**brenner** *m* brickmaker; *(von Dachziegeln)* tilemaker; ~**dach** *nt* tiled roof.
**Ziegelei** *f* brickworks *sing or pl*; *(für Dachziegel)* tile-making works *sing or pl.*
**Ziegelstein** *m* brick.
**Ziegen-:** ~**bart** *m (hum: Bart)* goatee (beard); ~**bock** *m* billy goat; ~**fell** *nt* goatskin; ~**käse** *m* goat's milk cheese; ~**leder** *nt* kid (leather), kidskin; ~**milch** *f* goat's milk; ~**peter** *m* - mumps *sing.*
**Zieh-:** ~**brücke** *f* drawbridge; ~**brunnen** *m* well; ~**eltern** *pl* foster parents *pl.*
**ziehen** *pret* **zog**, *ptp* **gezogen** **1** *vt* **(a)** to pull; *(schleppen)* to drag; *Hut* to raise; *Handbremse* to put on; *(heraus~)* to pull out *(aus of)*; *Fäden* to take out. **den Ring vom Finger** ~ to pull one's ring off (one's finger); **die Mütze tiefer ins Gesicht** ~ to pull one's hat further down over one's face; **er zog noch einen Pullover übers Hemd** he put on a pullover over his shirt; **unangenehme Folgen nach sich** ~ to have unpleasant consequences. **(b)** *(zeichnen, anlegen) Kreis, Linie* to draw; *Graben, Furchen* to dig; *Mauer* to build; *Grenze* to set up. **(c)** *(herstellen) Draht, Kerzen, Kopien* to make; *(züchten) Blumen* to grow; *Tiere* to breed.
**2** *vi* **(a)** to pull. **an etw** *(dat)* ~ to pull (on *or* at) sth; **ein** ~**der Schmerz** an ache. **(b)** *aux sein (um~)* to move. **nach Bayern/in eine größere Wohnung** ~ to move to Bavaria/into a bigger flat; **zu jdm** ~ to move in with sb. **(c)** *aux sein (sich bewegen)* to move, to go; *(Soldaten)* to march; *(durchstreifen)* to roam. **in den Krieg** ~ to go to war. **(d)** *(mit Spielfigur)* to move. **mit dem Turm** ~ to move the rook; **wer zieht?** whose move is it? **(e)** *(Cook) (Tee, Kaffee)* to draw; *(in Kochwasser)* to simmer. **(f)** *(col: Eindruck machen)* **so was zieht bei mir nicht** I don't like that sort of thing; **so was zieht immer** that sort of thing always goes down well.
**3** *vi impers* **es zieht** there's a draught *(Brit)* or draft *(US)*; **wenn es dir zieht** if you're in a draught; *(von Schmerzen)* **mir zieht's im Rücken** my back hurts.
**4** *vt impers* **es zog ihn in die weite Welt** he felt drawn out into the big wide world.
**5** *vr* **(a)** *(sich erstrecken, verlaufen)* to stretch. **dieses Thema zieht sich durch das ganze Buch** this theme runs through the whole book. **(b)** *(sich dehnen)* to stretch; *(Holz)* to warp; *(Metall)* to bend.
**Ziehen** *nt no pl (Schmerz)* ache.
**Ziehharmonika** *f* concertina.
**Ziehung** *f* draw.
**Ziel** *nt* -**e** **(a)** *(Reise~)* destination; *(Absicht, Zweck)* goal, aim; *(von Wünschen, Spott)* object. **mit dem** ~ **zu gewinnen** with the aim of winning; **jdm/sich ein** ~ **stecken** to set sb/oneself a goal; **sich** *(dat)* **etw zum** ~ **setzen** to set sth as one's goal; **zum** ~ **kommen** *(fig)* to reach one's goal; **am** ~ **sein** to be at one's destination; *(fig)* to have reached one's goal. **(b)** *(Sport)* finish. **durchs** ~ **gehen** to cross the finishing line. **(c)** *(Mil etc)* target. **ins** ~ **treffen** to hit the target; **über das** ~ **hinausschießen** *(fig)* to overshoot the mark.
**Ziel-:** ~**band** *nt* finishing tape; **z**~**bewußt** *adj* purposeful.
**zielen** *vi* to aim *(auf +acc, nach at)*; *(fig)* to be aimed

*(auf +acc* at*).* **ich weiß, worauf deine Bemerkungen** ~ I know what you're driving at.

**Ziel-:** ~**fernrohr** *nt* telescopic sight; **z**~**genau** *adj* accurate; ~**gerade** *f* finishing straight *or* straight-away *(US)*; ~**gruppe** *f* target group; ~**hafen** *m* port of destination; ~**linie** *f (Sport)* finishing line; **z**~**los** *adj* aimless; ~**losigkeit** *f* lack of purpose; ~**ort** *m* destination; ~**scheibe** *f* target; ~**schießen** *nt* target practice; ~**setzung** *f* target, objective; **z**~**sicher** *adj* unerring; *Handeln* purposeful; ~**sprache** *f* target language; **z**~**strebig** **1** *adj* single-minded; **2** *adv* single-mindedly, full of determination; ~**strebigkeit** *f* single-mindedness; ~**vorstellung** *f* objective.

**ziemen** *vr, vr impers (geh)* **das/es ziemt sich nicht (für dich)** it is not proper (for you).

**ziemlich 1** *adv* **(a)** rather, quite, pretty *(col)*; *sicher, genau* reasonably. **wir haben uns** ~ **beeilt** we've hurried quite a bit; ~ **lange** quite a long time; ~ **viel** quite a lot. **(b)** *(col: beinahe)* almost, nearly. **so** ~ **more** or less; **so** ~ **alles** just about everything; **so** ~ **dasselbe** pretty much the same. **2** *adj attr Anzahl, Strecke* fair; *Vermögen* sizeable. **eine** ~**e Anstrengung** quite an effort.

**Zierat** *m* **-e** *(geh)* decoration.

**Zierde** *f* **-n** ornament, decoration; *(Schmuckstück)* adornment. **zur** ~ for decoration; **das alte Haus ist eine** ~ **der Stadt** the old house is one of the beauties of the town.

**zieren 1** *vt* to adorn; *(fig: auszeichnen)* to grace. **2** *vr (sich bitten lassen)* to need a lot of pressing; *(sich gekünstelt benehmen)* to be affected. **zier dich nicht!** don't be shy *or* silly *(col)*.

**Zier-:** ~**fisch** *m* ornamental fish; ~**garten** *m* ornamental garden; ~**leiste** *f* border; *(an Auto)* trim; *(an Wand, Möbeln)* moulding *(Brit)*, molding *(US)*.

**zierlich** *adj* dainty; *Frau auch* petite.

**Zierlichkeit** *f siehe adj* daintiness; petiteness.

**Zierpflanze** *f* ornamental plant.

**Ziffer** *f* **-n** **(a)** digit; *(Zahl)* figure, number. **römische/arabische** ~**n** roman/arabic numerals; **eine Zahl mit drei** ~**n** a three-figure number. **(b)** *(eines Paragraphen)* clause.

**Zifferblatt** *nt (an Uhr)* dial; *(hum: Gesicht)* face.

**zig** *adj inv (col)* umpteen *(col)*.

**Zigarette** *f* cigarette.

**Zigaretten-** *in cpds* cigarette; ~**automat** *m* cigarette machine; ~**dose** *f* cigarette box; ~**etui** *nt* cigarette case; ~**kippe** *f* cigarette end; ~**papier** *nt* cigarette paper; ~**pause** *f* break for a cigarette; ~**schachtel** *f* cigarette packet *or* pack; ~**spitze** *f* cigarette-holder; ~**stummel** *m* cigarette end.

**Zigarillo** *m or nt* **-s** cigarillo.

**Zigarre** *f* **-n** **(a)** cigar. **(b)** *(col: Verweis)* **jdm eine** ~ **verpassen** to give sb a dressing-down.

**Zigarren-** *in cpds* cigar; ~**kiste** *f* cigar box; ~**spitze** *f* cigar-holder; ~**stummel** *m* cigar butt.

**Zigeuner(in** *f) m* - gipsy.

**Zigeunerschnitzel** *nt (Cook) cutlet served in a spicy sauce with green and red peppers.*

**zigmal** *adv (col)* umpteen times *(col)*.

**Zikade** *f* cicada.

**Zimmer** *nt* - room. ~ **frei** vacancies.

**Zimmer-:** ~**antenne** *f* indoor aerial *(Brit)* or antenna *(US)*; ~**arbeit** *f* carpentry job; ~**brand** *m* fire in a/the room; ~**flucht** *f* suite of rooms; ~**handwerk** *nt* carpentry; ~**kellner** *m* room-waiter; ~**lautstärke** *f* **bitte auf** ~**lautstärke stellen** please keep volume down; ~**mädchen** *nt* chambermaid *(Brit)*, maid *(US)*; ~**mann** *m, pl*

~**leute** carpenter.

**zimmern 1** *vt* to make from wood. **2** *vi* to do wood-work.

**Zimmer-:** ~**nachweis** *m* accommodation service; ~**pflanze** *f* house plant; ~**suche** *f* room hunting; **auf** ~**suche sein** to be looking for rooms/a room; ~**temperatur** *f* room temperature; ~**vermittlung** *f* accommodation *(Brit)* or accommodations *(US)* agency.

**zimperlich** *adj* squeamish; *(prüde)* prissy; *(wehleidig)* soft. **da darf man nicht so** ~ **sein** you can't afford to be soft (in that case).

**Zimt** *m* **-e** *(Gewürz)* cinnamon.

**Zimt-:** ~**stange** *f* stick of cinnamon; ~**ziege** *f (col)* stupid cow *(col!)*.

**Zink** *nt no pl* zinc.

**Zinke** *f* **-n** *(von Gabel)* prong; *(von Kamm, Harke)* tooth.

**Zinken** *m* - **(a)** *(col: Nase)* hooter *(col)*. **(b)** = **Zinke.**

**zinken** *vt Karten* to mark.

**Zinn** *nt no pl* **(a)** tin. **(b)** *(Legierung)* pewter. **(c)** *(~produkte)* pewter, pewterware.

**Zinn-:** ~**becher** *m* pewter tankard; ~**bergwerk** *nt* tin mine.

**zinnoberrot** *adj* vermilion.

**Zinnsoldat** *m* tin soldier.

**Zins** *m* **-en** *usu pl (Geld~)* interest *no pl.* ~**en bringen** to earn interest; *(fig)* to pay dividends; **Darlehen zu 10%** ~**en** loan at 10% interest; **jdm etw mit** ~**en heimzahlen** *(fig)* to pay sb back for sth with interest.

**Zinseszins** *m* compound interest.

**Zins-:** **z**~**frei** *adj* interest-free; ~**fuß** *m* interest rate; **z**~**günstig** *adj* at a favourable rate of interest; **z**~**los** *adj* interest-free; ~**niveau** *nt* level of interest rates; ~**rechnung** *f* calculation of interest; ~**satz** *m* interest rate; ~**senkung** *f* reduction in the interest rate.

**Zionismus** *m* Zionism.

**Zionist(in** *f) m* Zionist.

**zionistisch** *adj* Zionist.

**Zipfel** *m* - *(von Tuch)* corner; *(von Mütze)* point; *(von Jacke)* tail; *(von Wurst)* end; *(von Land)* tip.

**Zipfelmütze** *f* pointed cap *or* hat.

**zirka** *adv* about.

**Zirkel** *m* - *(Gerät)* pair of compasses, compasses *pl*; *(Stech~)* pair of dividers, dividers *pl*.

**Zirkelschluß** *m* circular argument.

**zirkulieren\*** *vi* to circulate.

**Zirkus** *m* **-se** **(a)** circus. **(b)** *(col: Getue)* fuss, to-do *(col)*.

**Zirkus-** *in cpds* circus; ~**zelt** *nt* big top.

**zirpen** *vi* to chirp, to cheep.

**Zirrhose** [tsi'ro:zə] *f* **-n** cirrhosis.

**zischeln** *vi* to whisper.

**zischen 1** *vi* to hiss; *(Limonade)* to fizz; *(Fett)* to sizzle. **2** *vt* **(a)** *(~d sagen)* to hiss. **(b)** *(col: trinken)* **einen** ~ to have a quick one *(col)*. **(c)** *(col: ohrfeigen)* **jdm eine** ~ to belt *or* clout sb one *(col)*.

**Zischlaut** *m (Ling)* sibilant.

**ziselieren\*** *vt* to engrave.

**Zitadelle** *f* citadel.

**Zitat** *nt* **-e** quotation, quote. **ein falsches** ~ a misquotation; ~ **... Ende des** ~**s** quote ... unquote.

**Zither** *f* **-n** zither.

**zitieren\*** *vt* **(a)** to quote. **(b)** *(vorladen, rufen)* to summon *(vor +acc* before, *an +acc, zu* to*)*.

**Zitronat** *nt* candied lemon peel.

**Zitrone** *f* **-n** lemon; *(Getränk)* lemon drink. **jdn wie eine** ~ **auspressen** to squeeze sb dry.

**Zitronen-: z~gelb** *adj* lemon yellow; **~limonade** *f* lemonade; **~melisse** *f* (lemon) balm; **~presse** *f* lemon squeezer; **~saft** *m* lemon juice; **~säure** *f* citric acid; **~schale** *f* lemon peel.

**Zitrusfrucht** *f* citrus fruit.

**Zitter-:** **~aal** *m* electric eel; **~greis** *m (col)* old dodderer *(col)*.

**zitt(e)rig** *adj* shaky.

**zittern** *vi* to tremble *(vor +dat* with*)*. **am ganzen Körper ~** to shake all over; **mir ~ die Knie** my knees are trembling; **vor jdm ~** to be terrified of sb.

**Zittern** *nt no pl* shaking, trembling. **mit ~ und Zagen** in fear and trembling.

**Zitterpartie** *f (fig)* nail-biting business.

**Zitze** *f* -n teat.

**Zivi** *m* -s *(col)* = **Zivildienstleistende(r).**

**zivil** [tsi'viːl] *adj* (a) civilian; *Schaden* non-military. **~er Bevölkerungsschutz** civil defence *(Brit)* or defense *(US)*. (b) *(col: anständig)* civil; *Preise* reasonable.

**Zivil** [tsi'viːl] *nt no pl* **in ~** *Soldat* in civilian clothes, in civvies *(col)*; *Polizist* **in ~** plain-clothes policeman.

**Zivil-:** **~beruf** *m* civilian profession/trade; **~bevölkerung** *f* civilian population; **~courage** *f* courage *(to stand up for one's beliefs)*; **~dienst** *m* community service *(as alternative to military service)*; **~dienstleistende(r)** *m decl as adj* person doing community service or work *(instead of military service)*; **~ehe** *f* civil marriage; **~flughafen** *m* civil airport; **~gericht** *nt* civil court.

**Zivilisation** [tsiviliza'tsioːn] *f* civilization.

**Zivilisationskrankheit** [tsiviliza'tsioːns-] *f* illness caused by modern civilization.

**zivilisatorisch** [tsiviliza'toːrɪʃ] *adj* of civilization.

**zivilisieren\*** [tsivili'ziːrən] *vt* to civilize.

**zivilisiert** [tsivili'ziːɐt] *adj* civilized.

**Zivilist** [tsivi'lɪst] *m* civilian.

**Zivil-:** **~kleidung** *f* = **Zivil; ~leben** *nt* civilian life, civvy street *(col)*; **~luftfahrt** *f* civil aviation; **~person** *f* civilian; **~prozeß** *m* civil action; **~recht** *nt* civil law; **~richter** *m* civil court judge; **~sache** *f* matter for a civil court; **~schutz** *m* civil defence *(Brit)* or defense *(US)*.

**ZK** [tsɛt'kaː] *nt* -s = **Zentralkomitee.**

**Zobel** *m* - *(Zool, Pelz)* sable.

**zocken** *vi (col)* to gamble.

**Zofe** *f* -n lady's maid; *(von Königin)* lady-in-waiting.

**Zoff** *m no pl (col: Ärger)* trouble, ructions *pl*. **dann gibt's ~** then there'll be trouble.

**zog** *pret of* **ziehen.**

**zögerlich** *adj* hesitant.

**zögern** *vi* to hesitate. **er zögerte lange mit der Antwort** he hesitated a long time before replying.

**Zögern** *nt no pl* hesitation. **nach langem ~** after hesitating a long time.

**Zölibat** *nt or m no pl* celibacy. **im ~ leben** to lead a life of celibacy.

**Zoll¹** *m* - *(Measure)* inch.

**Zoll²** *m* ⁼e (a) *(Waren~)* customs duty; *(Brücken~, Straßen~)* toll. **darauf wird ~ erhoben** there is duty to pay on that. (b) *(Stelle)* **der ~** customs *pl*.

**Zoll|abfertigung** *f (Vorgang)* customs clearance.

**Zollager** *nt* bonded warehouse.

**Zoll-:** **~amt** *nt* customs house or office; **~beamte(r)** *m* customs officer; **~behörde** *f* customs authorities *pl*, customs *pl*; **~bestimmung** *f usu pl* customs regulation.

**zollen** *vt* **jdm Anerkennung/Achtung ~** to acknowledge/respect sb; **jdm Beifall ~** to applaud sb.

**Zoll-:** **~erklärung** *f* customs declaration; **~fahnder** *m* customs investigator; **~fahndung** *m* customs investigation department; **z~frei** *adj* duty-free; **etw z~frei einführen** to import sth free of duty; **~gebiet** *nt* customs area or territory; **~grenze** *f* customs border; **~kontrolle** *f* customs inspection or check; **~papiere** *pl* customs documents *pl*; **z~pflichtig** *adj* dutiable; **~schranke** *f* customs barrier; **~stock** *m* folding rule; **~tarif** *m* customs tariff; **~union** *f* customs union.

**Zombie** *m* -s *(lit, fig)* zombie.

**Zone** *f* -n zone; *(von Fahrkarte)* fare stage.

**Zonen-:** **~grenze** *f* zonal border; **die ~grenze** *(Hist col)* the border (with East Germany); **~randgebiet** *nt (Hist)* border area (with East Germany).

**Zoo** [tsoː] *m* -s zoo.

**Zoohandlung** [tsoː-] *f* pet shop.

**Zoologe** [tsoo'loːgə] *m (wk)* -n, -n, **Zoologin** *f* zoologist.

**Zoologie** [tsoolo'giː] *f* zoology.

**zoologisch** [tsoo'loːgɪʃ] *adj* zoological.

**Zoom** [zuːm] *nt* -s zoom shot; *(Objektiv)* zoom lens.

**Zoowärter** *m* zoo keeper.

**Zopf** *m* ⁼e pigtail; *(geflochten)* plait. **das Haar in ~e flechten** to plait one's hair; **ein alter ~ *(fig)*** an antiquated custom.

**Zopf-:** **~band** *nt* hair ribbon; **~spange** *f* clip.

**Zorn** *m no pl* anger. **der ~ Gottes** the wrath of God; **jds ~ heraufbeschwören** to incur sb's wrath; **in ~ geraten** to fly into a rage; **im ~** in a rage; **in gerechtem ~** in righteous indignation; **einen ~ auf jdn haben** to be furious with sb.

**Zorn(es)ausbruch** *m* fit of anger or rage.

**zornig** *adj* angry, furious. **(leicht) ~ werden** to lose one's temper (easily); **auf jdn ~ sein** to be angry with sb.

**Zote** *f* -n dirty joke.

**Zottelhaar** *nt (col)* shaggy hair.

**zottelig** *adj (col) Haar* shaggy.

**Zotteln** *pl (col: Haare)* shaggy locks.

**zotteln** *vi aux sein (col)* to amble.

**zottig** *adj Fell* shaggy.

**ZPO** [tsetpeː'ʔoː]⁼ **Zivilprozeßordnung.**

**z.T.** = **zum Teil.**

**Ztr.** = **Zentner.**

**zu 1** *prep +dat* **(a)** *(örtlich)* to. **~m Bahnhof** to the station; **~m Arzt gehen** to go to the doctor's *(Brit)* or doctor; **bis ~** as far as; **(bis) ~m Bahnhof sind es 8 km** it's 5 miles to the station; **~r Schule/Kirche gehen** to go to school/church; **~m Film/Ballett gehen** to go into films/to join the ballet; **~m Fenster herein/hinaus** in (at)/out of the window; **~r Decke sehen** to look (up) at the ceiling; **~ jdm/etw hinaufsehen** to look up at sb/sth; **sie sah ~ ihm hin** she looked towards him; **das Zimmer liegt ~r Straße hin** the room looks out onto the street; **ein Zimmer mit Blick ~m Meer** a room with a view of the sea; **die Tür ~m Keller** the door to the cellar; **~r Stadtmitte hin** towards the town/city centre *(Brit)* or center *(US)*; **~ meiner Linken** to or on my left; **~ Lande und ~ Wasser** on land and sea; **der Dom ~ Köln** Cologne Cathedral.

**(b)** *(zeitlich)* at. **~ später Stunde** at a late hour; **~ Mittag** *(am Mittag)* at noon; *(bis Mittag)* by midday; **~ Ostern** at Easter; **rechtzeitig ~m Essen kommen** to be in time for dinner; **bis ~m 15. April** until April 15th; *(nicht später als)* by April 15th; **der Wechsel ist ~m 15. April fällig** the bill is due on April 15th; **~m 31. Mai kündigen** to give in one's notice for

May 31st.

**(c)** *(Zusatz, Zusammengehörigkeit)* with. **Wein ~m Essen trinken** to drink wine with one's meal; **~r Gitarre singen** to sing to a/the guitar; **die Melodie ~ dem Lied** the tune of the song; **Vorwort/ Anmerkungen ~ etw** preface/notes to sth; **~ dem kommt noch, daß ich ...** on top of that I ...; **etw ~ etw legen** to put sth with sth; **sich ~ jdm setzen** to sit down beside sb; **setz dich doch ~ uns** (come and) sit with us; **Liebe ~ jdm** love for sb; **sein Verhältnis ~ ihr** his relationship with her.

**(d)** *(Zweck)* for. **Wasser ~m Waschen** water for washing; **Papier ~m Schreiben** paper to write on; **er sagte das nur ~ ihrer Beruhigung** he said that just to set her mind at rest; **etw ~m Geburtstag/~ Weihnachten bekommen** to get sth for one's birthday/for Christmas; **jdm ~ etw gratulieren** to congratulate sb on sth; **Ausstellung ~m Jahrestag der Revolution** exhibition to mark the anniversary of the revolution; **~ dieser Frage möchte ich folgendes sagen** I should like to comment as follows on this question.

**(e)** *(Folge, Umstand, Art und Weise)* **~ seinem Besten** for his own good; **~m Glück** luckily; **~ meiner Freude** *etc* to my joy *etc*; **~/~m Tode** to death; **es ist ~m Weinen** it's enough to make you (want to) weep; **~ Fuß/Pferd** on foot/horseback; **~ Schiff** by ship *or* sea.

**(f)** *(Veränderung)* into. **~ etw werden** to turn into sth; **Leder ~ Handtaschen verarbeiten** to make handbags out of leather; **jdn/etw ~ etw machen** to make sb/sth (into) sth; **~ Asche verbrennen** to burn to ashes; **jdn ~m König wählen** to choose sb as king; **jdn ~ etw ernennen** to nominate sb sth.

**(g)** *(bei Zahlen)* **drei ~ zwei** *(Sport)* three-two; **drei Sätze ~ zwei** *(Tennis)* three sets to two; **Äpfel ~ 30 Pfennig das Stück** apples at 30 pfennigs each; **~m halben Preis** at half price; **~m ersten Male** for the first time.

**2** *adv* **(a)** *(allzu)* too. **~ sehr** too much; **das war einfach ~ dumm!** *(col)* it was so stupid! **(b)** *(geschlossen)* shut, closed. **auf, ~** *(an Hähnen etc)* on, off; **Tür ~!** *(col)* shut the door; **die Geschäfte haben jetzt ~** the shops are closed now. **(c)** *(col: los, weiter)* **dann mal ~!** right, off we go!; **nur ~!** just keep on!; **mach ~!** hurry up! **(d)** *(örtlich)* toward(s). **auf den Wald ~** towards the forest.

**3** *conj* **(a)** *(mit Infinitiv)* to. **etw ~ essen** sth to eat; **der Fußboden ist noch ~ fegen** the floor still has to be swept; **er hat ~ gehorchen** he has to obey; **ohne es ~ wissen** without knowing it; **um besser sehen ~ können** in order to see better; **ich komme, um mich ~ verabschieden** I've come to say goodbye. **(b)** *(mit Partizip)* **noch ~ bezahlende Rechnungen** bills that are still to be paid; **nur winzige, leicht ~ übersehende Punkte** only very small points (that are) easily overlooked.

**4** *adj* *(col: geschlossen)* **eine ~e Tür** a closed door; *siehe* **zusein**.

**zu|aller-: ~erst** *adv* first of all; **~letzt** *adv* last of all.

**zu|arbeiten** *vi sep* **jdm ~** to do the groundwork for sb.

**zubauen** *vt sep* **Lücke** to fill in; **Platz, Gelände** to build up.

**Zubehör** *nt* **-e** equipment *no pl*; *(Zusatzgeräte, ~teile)* accessories *pl.* **Küche mit allem ~** fully equipped kitchen.

**Zubehörteil** *nt* accessory.

**zubeißen** *vi sep irreg* to bite.

**zubekommen\*** *vt sep irreg (col)* **Tür, Fenster** to get

shut *or* closed. **ich bekomme den Reißverschluß nicht zu** I can't get the zip done up.

**Zuber** *m* **-** (wash)tub.

**zubereiten\*** *vt sep* to prepare.

**Zubereitung** *f* preparation.

**zubilligen** *vt sep* **jdm etw ~** to allow sb sth.

**zubinden** *vt sep irreg* to tie up. **jdm die Augen ~** to blindfold sb.

**zublinzeln** *vi sep* **jdm ~** to wink at sb.

**zubringen** *vt sep irreg* **(a)** *(verbringen)* to spend. **(b)** *(herbeibringen)* to bring to, to take to.

**Zubringer** *m* **-** **(a)** *(Tech)* conveyor. **(b)** *(Straße)* feeder road. **(c)** *~(bus)* shuttle (bus); *(zum Flughafen)* airport bus.

**Zubrot** *nt (hum)* extra income. **ein kleines ~ verdienen** to earn a bit on the side *(col)*.

**Zucchini** [tsʊˈkiːni] *f* - courgette *(Brit)*, zucchini *(US)*.

**Zucht** *f* **(a)** *(Disziplin)* discipline. **~ und Ordnung** orderliness. **(b)** *(Aufzucht) (von Tieren)* breeding; *(von Pflanzen)* cultivation. **(c)** *(~generation)* stock.

**Zuchtbulle** *m* breeding bull.

**züchten** *vt* to breed; **Bienen** to keep; **Pflanzen** to grow; **Perlen, Bakterien** to cultivate.

**Züchter(in** *f)* *m* **-** *(von Tieren)* breeder; *(von Pflanzen)* grower; *(von Bienen)* keeper.

**Zuchthaus** *nt (Gebäude)* prison *(for capital offenders)*, penitentiary *(US)*.

**Zuchthäusler(in** *f)* *m* **-** *(col)* convict.

**Zuchthengst** *m* breeding stallion.

**züchtig** *adj (liter)* chaste; *(tugendhaft)* virtuous.

**züchtigen** *vt (geh)* to beat.

**Züchtigung** *f* beating. **körperliche ~** corporal punishment.

**Zucht-: ~perle** *f* cultured pearl; **~stute** *f* broodmare; **~tier** *nt* breeding animal.

**Züchtung** *f* **(a)** *siehe vt* breeding; keeping; growing; cultivation. **(b)** *(Zuchtart) (Pflanzen)* strain, variety; *(Tiere)* breed.

**Zuchtvieh** *nt* breeding cattle.

**zuckeln** *vi aux sein (col)* to trail, to traipse *(col)*.

**zucken 1** *vi* **(a)** *(nervös)* to twitch; *(vor Schreck)* to start; *(vor Schmerzen)* to flinch; *(verwundetes Tier)* to thrash about. **er zuckte ständig mit dem Mund** his mouth kept twitching; **mit den Schultern ~** to shrug (one's shoulders). **(b)** *(aufleuchten) (Blitz)* to flash; *(Flammen)* to flare up. **2** *vt* **die Schultern ~** to shrug (one's shoulders).

**zücken** *vt* **Schwert** to draw; *(col)* **Notizbuch, Brieftasche** to take out.

**Zucker** *m* *no pl* **(a)** sugar. **ein Stück ~** a lump of sugar. **(b)** *(Med)* *(~gehalt)* sugar; *(Krankheit)* diabetes *sing*. **~ haben** *(col)* to be a diabetic.

**Zucker-: ~dose** *f* sugar bowl; **~erbse** *f* mange-tout (pea); **~gehalt** *m* sugar content, **~guß** *m* icing, frosting *(esp US)*; **mit ~guß überziehen** to ice, to frost *(esp US)*; **~hut** *m* sugarloaf.

**zuck(e)rig** *adj* sugary.

**Zucker-: z~krank** *adj* diabetic; **~krankheit** *f* diabetes *sing*; **~lecken** *nt*: **das ist kein ~lecken** *(col)* it's no picnic *(col)*.

**zuckern** *vt* to sugar. **zu stark gezuckert** too sweet.

**Zucker-: ~raffinade** *f* refined sugar; **~rohr** *nt* sugar cane; **~rübe** *f* sugar beet; **~schlecken** *nt* = **~lecken**; **~spiegel** *m (Med)* (blood) sugar level; **~stange** *f* stick of rock *(Brit)* or candy *(US)*; **~streuer** *m* sugar sprinkler; **z~süß** *adj (lit, fig)* sugar-sweet, sugary; **~watte** *f* candy floss; **~zange** *f* sugar tongs *pl.*

**Zuckung** *f* twitch; *(krampfhaft)* convulsion.

**zudecken** *vt sep* to cover; *(im Bett)* to tuck up *or* in. **jdn/sich (mit etw) ~** to cover sb/oneself up (with sth); to tuck sb/oneself up (in sth).

**zud̲e̲m** *adv (geh)* moreover.

**zu̲drehen** *sep* **1** *vt Wasserhahn etc* to turn off; *(zu-wenden)* to turn *(dat* to*)*. **2** *vr* to turn *(dat* to*)*.

**zu̲dringlich** *adj Mensch* importunate; *(penetrant)* pushy *(col)*; *Nachbarn* prying. ~ **werden** *(zu einer Frau)* to make advances *(zu* to*)*.

**Zu̲dringlichkeit** *f siehe adj* importunity; pushiness *(col)*; prying; *(einer Frau gegenüber)* advances *pl*.

**zu̲drücken** *vt sep* to press shut. **jdm die Kehle** ~ to throttle sb.

**zu|e̲ilen** *vi sep aux sein* **auf jdn/etw** ~ to rush towards sb/sth.

**zu|eina̲nder** *adv (gegenseitig)* to each other; *Vertrauen* in each other; *(zusammen)* together. ~ **passen** to go together; *(Menschen)* to suit each other.

**zu|erke̲nnen*** *vt sep irreg Preis* to award *(jdm* to sb*)*; *Recht* to grant; *(vor Gericht) Entschädigung* to award *(jdm etw* sb sth*)*.

**zu|e̲rst** *adv* first; *(anfangs)* at first. ~ **an die Reihe kommen** to be first.

**zufa̲hren** *vi sep irreg aux sein* **(a) auf jdn/etw** ~ to drive/ride towards sb/sth. **(b) fahren Sie doch zu!** go on then!

**Zufa̲hrt** *f* approach (road); *(zu einem Haus)* drive-(way). „**keine** ~ **zum Krankenhaus**" ''no access to hospital''.

**Zufa̲hrtsstraße** *f* access road; *(zur Autobahn)* feeder road.

**Zufa̲ll** *m* chance; *(Zusammentreffen)* coincidence. **das ist** ~ it's pure chance; **durch** ~ (quite) by chance; **es ist kein** ~**, daß** ... it's no coincidence *or* accident that ...; **es war ein glücklicher** ~**, daß** ... it was lucky that ...; **welch ein** ~**!** what a coincidence!; **etw dem** ~ **überlassen** to leave sth to chance.

**zufa̲llen** *vi sep irreg aux sein* **(a)** *(sich schließen: Fenster etc)* to close. **die Tür fiel laut zu** the door slammed shut; **die Augen fielen ihm zu** *(er schlief ein)* he couldn't keep his eyes open. **(b) jdm** ~ *(Preis etc)* to go to sb; *(Aufgabe)* to fall to sb.

**zufällig** **1** *adj* chance *attr*; *Zusammentreffen auch* coincidental. **das war rein** ~ it was pure chance. **2** *adv* **(a)** by chance. **er ging** ~ **vorüber** he happened to be passing; **wenn Sie das** ~ **wissen sollten** if you (should) happen to know. **(b)** *(in Fragen)* by any chance.

**Zufa̲lls-** *in cpds* chance; ~**bekanntschaft** *f* chance acquaintance; ~**treffer** *m* fluke; **einen** ~**treffer machen** to have a lucky break.

**zufa̲ssen** *vi sep* **(a)** *(zugreifen)* to take hold of it/them; *(fig: schnell handeln)* to seize an/the opportunity. **(b)** *(helfen)* to lend a hand.

**zufl̲iegen** *vi sep irreg aux sein* **(a) auf etw** *(acc)* ~ to fly towards sth. **(b)** +*dat* to fly to. **der Vogel ist uns zugeflogen** the bird flew into our house/flat *etc*; **ihm fliegt alles nur so zu** *(fig)* everything comes so easily to him. **(c)** *(col: Fenster, Tür)* to slam shut.

**zufl̲ießen** *vi sep irreg aux sein* +*dat* to flow to(wards); *(fig: Geld)* to flow into.

**Zufl̲ucht** *f* refuge *(vor* +*dat* from*)*. **du bist meine letzte** ~ *(fig)* you are my last hope; **zu etw** ~ **nehmen** *(fig)* to resort to sth.

**Zufl̲uchts-**: ~**ort** *m*, ~**stätte** *f* place of refuge.

**Zuflu̲ß** *m* **(a)** *no pl* influx; *(Mech: Zufuhr)* supply. **(b)** *(Nebenfluß)* tributary; *(zu Binnensee)* inlet.

**zufl̲üstern** *vti sep* **jdm (etw)** ~ to whisper (sth) to sb.

**zuf̲o̲lge** *prep* +*dat (gemäß)* according to; *(auf Grund)* as a result of. **dem Bericht** ~ according to the report.

**zufr̲ieden** *adj* contented, content *pred*. **ein** ~**es Gesicht machen** to look pleased; ~ **lächeln** to smile contentedly; **mit jdm/etw** ~ **sein** to be satisfied *or* happy with sb/sth; **er ist mit nichts** ~ nothing pleases him.

**Zufr̲ieden-**: **z**~**geben** *vr sep irreg* **sich mit etw z**~**geben** to be satisfied with sth; ~**heit** *f* contentment, contentedness; *(Befriedigtsein)* satisfaction; **zur allgemeinen** ~**heit** to everyone's satisfaction; **z**~**lassen** *vt sep irreg* to leave alone; **laß mich damit z**~**!** *(col)* shut up about it! *(col)*; **z**~**stellen** *vt sep* to satisfy; **schwer z**~**zustellen sein** to be hard to please; **z**~**stellend** *adj* satisfactory.

**zufr̲ieren** *vi sep irreg aux sein* to freeze (over).

**zuf̲ügen** *vt sep* **(a)** *Leid* to cause. **jdm Schaden** ~ to harm sb; **jdm etw** ~ to cause sb sth. **(b)** *(col)* = **hinzufügen**.

**Zuf̲uhr** *f* -**en** *(Versorgung)* supply *(in* +*acc, nach* to*)*; *(Mil)* supplies *pl*; *(Met)* influx.

**zuf̲ühren** *sep* **1** *vt* +*dat* **(a)** *(versorgen mit)* to supply; *(Comp) Papier* to feed *(+dat* into*)*. **jdn etw** ~ to supply sb with sth. **(b)** *(bringen)* to bring. **jdn der gerechten Strafe** ~ to give sb the punishment he/she deserves. **2** *vi* **auf etw** *(acc)* ~ to lead to sth.

**Zug**[1] *m* ⸚e **(a)** *(Luft~)* draught *(Brit)*, draft *(US)*; *(Atem~)* breath; *(an eine Zigarette etc)* puff, drag; *(Schluck)* mouthful. **einen** ~ **machen** *(an Zigarette etc)* to take a drag; **das Glas in einem** ~ **leeren** to empty the glass with one gulp; **etw in vollen** ⸚**en genießen** to enjoy sth to the full; **in den letzten** ⸚**en liegen** *(col)* to be at one's last gasp; ~ **abbekommen** *or* **kriegen** *(col)* to get a stiff neck/shoulder *etc* from sitting in a draught.

**(b)** *no pl (von Vögeln, Menschen)* migration; *(der Wolken)* drifting. **im** ~**e** *(im Verlauf)* in the course *(gen* of*)*; **das liegt im** ~ **der Zeit** it's a sign of the times.

**(c)** *(beim Schwimmen)* stroke; *(beim Rudern)* pull *(mit* at*)*; *(bei Brettspiel)* move. **einen** ~ **machen** *(beim Schwimmen)* to do a stroke; ~ **um** ~ *(fig)* step by step; **zum** ~**e kommen** *(col)* to get a look-in *(col)*; **du bist am** ~ *(bei Brettspiel, fig)* it's your move; **etw in groben** ⸚**en darstellen/umreißen** to outline sth.

**(d)** *no pl (Ziehen)* pull, tug *(an* +*dat* on, at*)*.

**(e)** *(Gruppe) (von Menschen)* procession; *(Mil)* platoon; *(Abteilung)* section.

**Zug**[2] *m* ⸚e *(Eisenbahn~)* train; *(Last~)* truck and trailer. **mit dem** ~ **fahren** to go/travel by train.

**Zug**[3] *m* ⸚e *(Gesichts~, Charakter~)* feature; *(brutal etc)* streak; *(Anflug)* touch. **das war kein schöner** ~ **von dir** that wasn't nice of you.

**Zu̲gabe** *f* extra, bonus; *(Comm)* free gift; *(Theat)* encore. ~**!** encore!

**Zu̲g|abteil** *nt* railway *or* railroad *(US)* compartment.

**Zu̲gang** *m* **(a)** *(Eingang, Einfahrt)* entrance; *(Zutritt)* access *(zu* to*)*. **er hat keinen** ~ **zur Musik** music doesn't mean anything to him. **(b)** *(von Patienten)* admission; *(von Schülern)* intake; *(von Büchern)* acquisition.

**zuga̲nge** *adj pred*: **mit jdm/etw** ~ **sein** *(col)* to be busy with sb/sth; *(euph: sexuell)* to be carrying on with sb *(col)*.

**zugänglich** *adj (dat, für* to*)* *(erreichbar) Gelände, Ort* accessible; *öffentliche Einrichtungen* open; *(umgänglich) Mensch, Vorgesetzter* approachable. **etw der Allgemeinheit** ~ **machen** to open sth to the public; **für etw leicht/nicht** ~ **sein** to respond/not to respond to sth.

**Zugänglichkeit** *f (Erreichbarkeit)* accessibility; *(Ver-*

zukommen

*fügbarkeit)* availability; *(Umgänglichkeit)* approachability.

**Zug-:** ~**begleiter** m *(Rail)* guard *(Brit)*, conductor *(US)*; ~**brücke** f drawbridge.

**zugeben** vt sep irreg **(a)** *(zugestehen, einräumen)* to admit. **er gab zu, es getan zu haben** he admitted (to) having done it; **jdm gegenüber etw** ~ to admit or confess sth to sb; **zugegeben** granted. **(b)** *(hinzufügen)* to add. **(c)** *(zusätzlich geben)* to give as an extra. **jdm etw** ~ to give sb sth extra.

**zugegebenermaßen** adv admittedly.

**zugegen** adv *(geh)* ~ **sein** to be present.

**zugehen** sep irreg aux sein **1** vi **(a)** *(Tür, Deckel)* to shut. **der Koffer geht nicht zu** the case won't shut. **(b) auf jdn/etw** ~ to go towards sb/sth; **direkt auf jdn/etw** ~ to go straight up to sb/sth; **es geht auf den Winter zu** winter is drawing in; **er geht schon auf die Siebzig zu** he's getting on for seventy; **dem Ende** ~ to draw to a close. **(c)** +*dat (Nachricht etc)* to reach. **der Brief ist uns noch nicht zugegangen** the letter hasn't reached us yet. **2** vi impers **dort geht es ... zu** things are ... there; **hier geht es nicht mit rechten Dingen zu** there's something odd going on here.

**zugehörig** adj attr *(geh)* accompanying; *(verbunden)* affiliated *(dat to)*.

**Zugehörigkeit** f **(a)** *(zu Land, Glauben)* affiliation; *(Mitgliedschaft)* membership *(zu of)*. **(b)** *(Zugehörigkeitsgefühl)* sense of belonging.

**zugeknöpft** adj *(fig col) Mensch* reserved.

**Zügel** m - rein *(auch fig)*. **die** ~ **anziehen** *(lit)* to draw in the reins; *(fig)* to keep a tighter rein *(bei on)*; **die** ~ **fest in der Hand behalten** *(fig)* to keep things firmly in hand; **die** ~ **locker lassen** *(fig)* to give free rein *(bei to)*; **die** ~ **an sich** *(acc)* **reißen** *(fig)* to seize the reins.

**zugelassen** adj authorized; *Arzt* registered; *Auto* licensed. **amtlich/staatlich** ~ **sein** to be authorized/to be state-registered; **eine nicht** ~**e Partei** an illegal party; **als Kassenarzt** ~ **sein** ≃ to be registered as a National Health doctor *(Brit)* or panel doctor *(US)*.

**Zügel-:** **z**~**los** adj *(fig)* unbridled no adv, unrestrained; ~**losigkeit** f *(fig)* lack of restraint.

**zügeln 1** vt *Pferd* to rein in; *(fig)* to curb, to check. **2** vr to restrain oneself.

**zugesellen\*** vr sep **sich jdm** ~ *(Mensch)* to join sb.

**Zugeständnis** nt concession *(dat, an +acc to)*. ~**se machen** to make allowances.

**zugestehen\*** vt sep irreg *(einräumen) Recht* to concede, to grant; *(zugeben)* to admit. **jdm etw** ~ *(einräumen)* to grant sb sth.

**zugetan** adj **jdm/einer Sache** ~ **sein** to be fond of sb/sth.

**Zugewinn** m gain *(an +dat in)*.

**Zugewinngemeinschaft** f *(Jur)* joint ownership of property by a married couple.

**Zugezogene(r)** mf decl as adj newcomer.

**Zug-:** ~**folge** f *(Rail)* order of incoming trains; **z**~**frei** adj *Raum* draught-free *(Brit)*, draft-free *(US)*; ~**führer** m *(Rail)* chief guard *(Brit)* or conductor *(US)*.

**zugig** adj draughty *(Brit)*, drafty *(US)*.

**zügig** adj swift, speedy; *Handschrift* smooth.

**Zugkraft** f *(fig)* attraction, appeal.

**zugkräftig** adj *(fig) Werbetext, Titel* eye-catching; *Stück* crowd-pulling attr, popular.

**zugleich** adv *(auch ebenso)* at the same time.

**Zug-:** ~**luft** f draught *(Brit)*, draft *(US)*; ~**maschine** f towing vehicle; *(von Sattelschlepper)* traction engine; ~**personal** nt *(Rail)* train personnel; ~**pferd** nt draught *(Brit)* or draft *(US)* horse; *(fig)* crowd

puller.

**zugreifen** vi sep irreg **(a)** to grab it/them; *(fig)* to act fast or quickly; *(bei Tisch)* to help oneself. **(b)** *(Polizei)* to step in quickly. **(c)** *(Comp)* **auf etw** *(acc)* ~ to access sth.

**Zugrestaurant** nt dining car.

**Zugriff** m **(a) durch raschen** ~ by acting fast; **sich dem** ~ **der Polizei entziehen** to evade justice. **(b)** *(Comp)* access.

**Zugriffszeit** f *(Comp)* access time.

**zugrunde** adv **(a)** ~ **gehen** to perish; **jdn/etw** ~ **richten** to destroy sb/sth; *(finanziell)* to ruin sb/sth; **er wird daran nicht** ~ **gehen** he'll survive; *(finanziell)* it won't ruin him. **(b) einer Sache** *(dat)* ~ **liegen** to form the basis of sth; **etw einer Sache** *(dat)* ~ **legen** to base sth on sth.

**Zugtier** nt draught *(Brit)* or draft *(US)* animal.

**zugucken** vi sep = **zusehen**.

**Zug|unglück** nt train accident.

**zugunsten** prep ~ **von** or +gen in favour of *(Brit)*, in favor of *(US)*.

**zugute** adv **jdm etw** ~ **halten** to grant sb sth; *(Verständnis haben)* to make allowances for sth; **einer Sache/jdm** ~ **kommen** to come in useful for sth/to sb; *(Geld, Erlös)* to benefit sth/sb.

**Zug-:** ~**verbindung** f train connection; ~**verkehr** m *(Rail)* rail services pl; **starker** ~**verkehr** heavy rail traffic; ~**vieh** nt no pl draught *(Brit)* or draft *(US)* cattle; ~**vogel** m migratory bird; ~**zwang** m *(Chess)* zugzwang; **unter** ~**zwang stehen** *(fig)* to be under pressure (to take action).

**zuhaben** vi sep irreg *(col: Geschäft)* to be closed.

**zuhalten** sep irreg **1** vt to hold shut. **sich** *(dat)* **die Nase** ~ to hold one's nose; **sich** *(dat)* **die Augen/Ohren** ~ to put one's hands over one's eyes/ears. **2** vi **auf etw** *(acc)* ~ to head straight for sth.

**Zuhälter(in** f**)** m - pimp, procurer.

**zuhängen** vt sep to cover up or over.

**zuhauen** sep irreg **1** vt *Baumstamm* to hew; *Stein* to trim. **2** vi to strike out.

**zuhause** adv at home.

**Zuhause** nt no pl home.

**zuheilen** vi sep aux sein to heal up.

**Zuhilfenahme** f: **unter** ~ **von** or +gen with the aid of.

**zuhinterst** adv right at the back.

**zuhören** vi sep to listen *(dat to)*. **hör mal zu!** *(drohend)* now (just) listen (to me)!

**Zuhörer** m listener. **die** ~ *(das Publikum)* the audience sing.

**zujubeln** vi sep **jdm** ~ to cheer sb.

**zukehren** vt sep *(zuwenden)* to turn. **jdm das Gesicht** ~ to turn to face sb; **jdm den Rücken** ~ *(lit, fig)* to turn one's back on sb.

**zuklappen** sep **1** vt *Buch, Deckel* to close. **2** vi aux sein *(Tür etc)* to click shut.

**zukleben** vt sep *Briefumschlag* to stick down.

**zuknallen** vti sep *(vi: aux sein) (col)* to slam or bang (shut).

**zukneifen** vti sep irreg to pinch; *Augen* to screw up; *Mund* to shut tight(ly).

**zuknöpfen** vt sep to button (up); *siehe* **zugeknöpft**.

**zuknoten** vt sep to knot up.

**zukommen** vi sep irreg aux sein **(a) auf jdn/etw** ~ to come toward(s) or *(direkt)* up to sb/sth; **die Aufgabe, die nun auf uns zukommt** the task which now confronts us; **die Dinge auf sich** *(acc)* ~ **lassen** to take things as they come. **(b) jdm etw** ~ **lassen** *Brief etc* to send sb sth; *(schenken auch), Hilfe* to give sb sth. **(c)** +*dat (geziemen)* to befit, to become.

diesem Treffen kommt große Bedeutung zu this meeting is of the utmost importance.

**zukriegen** *vt sep (col)* = **zubekommen**.

**Zukunft** *f no pl (auch Gram)* future. **in ferner/naher** ~ in the distant/near future; **unsere gemeinsame** ~ our future together.

**zukünftig 1** *adj* future. **meine Z~e** *(col)*/**mein Z~er** *(col)* my future wife/husband. **2** *adv* in future.

**Zukunfts-:** ~**angst** *f* fear of the future; ~**aussichten** *pl* future prospects *pl*; ~**branche** *f* new *or* sunrise industry; ~**glaube** *m* belief in the future; **z~gläubig** *adj* believing in the future; ~**musik** *f (fig col)* pie in the sky *(col)*; ~**perspektive** *f* future prospects *pl*; ~**pläne** *pl* plans *pl* for the future; ~**roman** *m* novel set in the future; *(Science-fiction)* science fiction novel; **z~weisend** *adj* forward-looking.

**zulächeln** *vi sep* jdm ~ to smile at sb.

**Zulage** *f* **(a)** *(Geld~)* extra pay *no indef art*; *(Sonder~ auch)* bonus (payment). **eine** ~ **von 100 Mark** an extra 100 marks pay. **(b)** *(Gehaltserhöhung)* rise *(Brit)*, raise *(US)*.

**zulande** *adv* **bei uns** ~ in our country.

**zulangen** *vi sep (col: Dieb, beim Essen)* to help oneself.

**zulassen** *vt sep irreg* **(a)** *(Zugang gewähren)* to admit; *(amtlich)* to authorize; *Arzt* to register; *Kraftfahrzeug* to license; *Rechtsanwalt, Prüfling* to admit. **(b)** *(dulden, gestatten)* to allow, to permit. ~, **daß etw passiert** to allow sth to happen. **(c)** *(geschlossen lassen)* to leave closed.

**zulässig** *adj* permissible, permitted. ~**es Gesamtgewicht** *(Mot)* maximum laden weight; ~**e Höchstgeschwindigkeit** (upper) speed limit.

**Zulassung** *f* **(a)** *no pl (Erlaubnis, Gewährung von Zugang)* admission; *(amtlich)* authorization; *(von Auto)* licensing; *(als Arzt)* registration. **(b)** *(Dokument)* papers *pl*; *(Lizenz)* licence *(Brit)*, license *(US)*.

**Zulassungs-:** ~**anforderungen** *pl* entrance qualifications *pl*; ~**beschränkung** *f (esp Univ)* restriction on admissions; ~**stopp** *m (esp Univ)* block on admissions.

**Zulauf** *m no pl* **großen** ~ **haben** *(Geschäft)* to be very popular.

**zulaufen** *vi sep irreg aux sein* **(a) auf jdn/etw** ~ to run towards sb/sth. **(b)** *(auslaufen)* **spitz** ~ to taper. **(c)** *(Wasser etc)* **laß noch etwas kaltes Wasser** ~ run in some more cold water. **(d)** *(Tier)* **jdm** ~ to stray into sb's house/place; **eine zugelaufene Katze** a stray cat (which has adopted sb).

**zulegen** *sep* **1** *vt* **(a)** *(dazulegen)* to put on. **(b)** *Geld* to add; *(bei Verlustgeschäft)* to lose. **die fehlenden 20 Mark legte meine Mutter zu** my mother made up the remaining 20 marks. **(c) etwas Tempo** ~ *(col)* to get a move on *(col)*; **die Grünen konnten 5%** ~ the Greens managed to gain 5%. **2** *vi* **(a)** *(an Gewicht)* to put on (weight). **(b)** *(col) (sich mehr anstrengen)* to pull one's finger out *(col)*; *(sich steigern)* to do better; *(Sport)* to step up the pace *(col)*. **3** *vr* **sich** *(dat)* **etw/jdn** ~ *(col)* to get oneself sth/sb.

**zuleide** *adv* jdm etwas ~ **tun** to harm sb.

**zuleiten** *vt sep Wasser etc* to supply; *Post, Waren* to send on.

**Zuleitung** *f (Tech)* supply.

**zuletzt** *adv* **(a)** **im end.** ~ **kam sie doch** she came in the end; **wir blieben bis** ~ we stayed to the very end; **ganz** ~ at the very last moment. **(b)** *(als letzte(r, s), an letzter Stelle)* last. **ich kam** ~ I came last; **ganz** ~ last of all; **nicht** ~ **wegen** not least because of.

**zuliebe** *adv* etw jdm ~ **tun** to do sth for sb's sake.

**Zulieferbetrieb, Zulieferer** *m (Econ)* supplier.

**Zulu** ['tsuːlu] *mf* **-(s)** Zulu.

**zum** = **zu dem**.

**zumachen** *sep* **1** *vt (schließen)* to close; *(col: auflösen) Laden etc* to close (down). **2** *vi (col)* **(a)** *(den Laden* ~*)* to close (down); *(fig)* to call it a day. **(b)** *(sich beeilen)* to hurry up.

**zumal 1** *conj* ~ **(da)** especially as. **2** *adv (besonders)* especially.

**zumauern** *vt sep* to brick up, to wall up.

**zumeist** *adv* mostly.

**zumessen** *vt sep irreg Zeit* to allocate *(dat for)*; *Schuld* to attribute *(jdm to sb)*; *Bedeutung* to attach *(dat to)*.

**zumindest** *adv* at least.

**zumutbar** *adj* reasonable. **es ist mir nicht** ~, **das zu tun** I can't be expected to do that.

**zumute** *adv* **mir ist traurig** ~ I feel sad; **mir ist gar nicht danach** ~ I'm not in the mood (for it).

**zumuten** *vt sep* jdm etw ~ to expect sth of sb; **Sie wollen mir doch wohl nicht** ~, **diesen Unsinn zu lesen** you surely don't expect me to read this nonsense; **sich** *(dat)* **zuviel** ~ to take on too much.

**Zumutung** *f* unreasonable demand; *(Unverschämtheit)* nerve *(col)*. **das ist eine** ~! that's a bit much!

**zunächst** *adv* **(a)** *(zuerst)* first (of all). ~ **einmal** first of all. **(b)** *(vorläufig)* for the time being.

**zunageln** *vt sep Fenster etc* to nail up; *(mit Brettern, Pappe etc)* to board up; *Kiste etc* to nail down.

**zunähen** *vt sep* to sew up.

**Zunahme** *f* **-n** increase *(gen, an +dat* in*)*.

**Zuname** *m* surname, last name.

**zündeln** *vi* to play (about) with fire.

**zünden 1** *vi* to ignite; *(Streichholz)* to light; *(Motor)* to fire; *(Sprengkörper)* to go off; *(fig)* to kindle enthusiasm. **2** *vt* to ignite; *Rakete* to fire; *Sprengkörper* to detonate; *Feuerwerkskörper* to let off.

**zündend** *adj (fig)* stirring; *Idee* exciting.

**Zünder** *m* - tinder. ~ **kriegen/jdm** ~ **geben** *(col)* to get/to give sb a good hiding *(col)*.

**Zünder** *m* - igniter; *(für Sprengstoff, Bombe etc)* fuse; *(für Mine)* detonator.

**Zünd-:** ~**flamme** *f* pilot light; ~**holz** *nt* match; ~**hütchen** *nt* percussion cap; ~**kabel** *nt (Aut)* plug lead; ~**kapsel** *f* detonator; ~**kerze** *f (Aut)* spark plug, sparking plug *(Brit)*; ~**plättchen** *nt* cap; ~**schloß** *nt (Aut)* ignition lock; ~**schlüssel** *m (Aut)* ignition key; ~**schnur** *f* fuse; ~**spule** *f* ignition coil; ~**stoff** *m* inflammable matter; *(Sprengstoff)* explosives *pl*; *(fig)* inflammatory stuff.

**Zündung** *f* ignition; *(von Sprengkörper)* detonation. **die** ~ **einstellen** *(Aut)* to adjust the timing.

**zunehmen** *vi sep irreg* **1** *vi* to increase; *(an Weisheit etc)* to gain *(an +dat* in*)*; *(an Gewicht)* to put on weight; *(Mond)* to wax. **2** *vt (Mensch: an Gewicht)* to gain.

**zunehmend 1** *adj* increasing, growing. **bei** ~**em Alter** with advancing age; **wir haben** ~**en Mond** there is a crescent moon; **in** ~**em Maße** to an increasing degree. **2** *adv* increasingly.

**zuneigen** *sep +dat* **1** *vi* to be inclined towards. **jdm zugeneigt sein** *(geh)* to be well disposed towards sb. **2** *vr* to lean towards. **sich dem Ende** ~ *(geh)* to be drawing to a close; *(Vorräte etc)* to be running out.

**Zuneigung** *f* affection *(zu for)*.

**Zunft** *f* =**e** *(Hist)* guild; *(hum col)* brotherhood.

**zünftig** *adj Kleidung* professional; *(col: ordentlich)* proper. **eine** ~**e Ohrfeige** a hefty box on the ears.

**Zunge** *f* **-n** tongue; *(von Waage)* pointer. **das brennt auf der** ~ that burns the tongue; **jdm die** ~ **herausstrecken** to stick one's tongue out at sb; **eine**

**spitze/lose** ~ **haben** to have a sharp/loose tongue; **böse** ~**n behaupten, ...** malicious gossip has it ...; **mir liegt das Wort auf der** ~ the word is on the tip of my tongue; **mir hängt die** ~ **zum Hals heraus** *(col)* my tongue is hanging out; *(erschöpft)* I'm exhausted.

**züngeln** *vi (Schlange)* to dart its tongue in and out; *(Flammen)* to lick.

**Zungen-:** ~**brecher** *m* tongue-twister; **z~fertig** *adj (geh)* fluent; *(pej)* glib; ~**kuß** *m* French kiss; ~**spitze** *f* tip of the tongue; ~**wurst** *f* tongue sausage.

**Zünglein** *nt:* **das** ~ **an der Waage sein** *(fig)* to tip the scales.

**zunichte** *adv* ~ **machen/werden** *(geh)* to ruin/to be ruined.

**zunicken** *vi sep* **jdm** ~ to nod to sb; **jdm freundlich** ~ to give sb a friendly nod.

**zunutze** *adv* **sich** *(dat)* **etw** ~ **machen** *(verwenden)* to make use of sth; *(ausnutzen)* to take advantage of sth.

**zu|oberst** *adv* right at the top.

**zu|ordnen** *vt sep* +*dat* to assign to.

**zupacken** *vi sep (col)* **(a)** *(zugreifen)* to make a grab for it *etc.* **(b)** *(bei der Arbeit)* to get down to it. **(c)** *(helfen)* **mit** ~ to give me/them *etc* a hand.

**zupackend 1** *adj Film etc* hard-hitting; *(resolut)* determined. **2** *adv* purposefully.

**zupfen** *vti* to pick; *Saite, Augenbrauen* to pluck; *Unkraut, Fäden* to pull. **jdn am Ärmel** *etc* ~ to tug at sb's sleeve *etc*; **sich** *(dat or acc)* **am Bart** ~ to pull at one's beard.

**Zupf|instrument** *nt (Mus)* plucked string instrument.

**zuprosten** *vi sep* **jdm** ~ to drink sb's health.

**zur** = **zu der.**

**zuraten** *vi sep irreg* **jdm** ~**, etw zu tun** to advise sb to do sth.

**Zürcher(in** *f)* *m* - native of Zurich.

**Zürcher, zürcherisch** *adj* of Zurich.

**zurechnen** *vt sep* **(a)** *(col: dazurechnen)* to add to. **(b)** *(fig: zuordnen)* to class *(dat* with*)*; *Kunstwerk etc* to ascribe *(dat* to*)*.

**Zurechnungs-:** **z~fähig** *adj* of sound mind; *(esp Jur, fig col)* compos mentis *pred*; ~**fähigkeit** *f* soundness of mind; **verminderte** ~**fähigkeit** diminished responsibility.

**zurecht-:** ~**biegen** *vt sep irreg* to bend into shape; *(fig)* to twist; **er hat alles wieder** ~**gebogen** *(col)* he has straightened everything out again; ~**finden** *vr sep irreg* to find one's way *(in* +*dat* around*)*; **sich in der Welt nicht mehr** ~**finden** not to be able to cope with the world any longer; ~**kommen** *vi sep irreg aux sein* **(a)** *(fig)* to get on; *(schaffen)* to cope; *(genug haben)* to have enough; **(b)** *(rechtzeitig kommen)* to come in time; **(c)** *(finanziell)* to manage; ~**legen** *vt sep irreg* to lay out ready; **sich** *(dat)* **etw** ~**legen** to get sth out ready; *(fig)* to work sth out; ~**machen** *vt sep (col)* **(a)** *Zimmer, Essen etc* to prepare; *Bett* to make up; **(b)** *(anziehen)* to dress; *(schminken)* to make up; **sich** ~**machen** to get ready; to put on one's make-up; ~**rücken** *vt sep (lit, fig)* to put straight; *Brille, Hut etc* to adjust; ~**stutzen** *vt sep* to trim; *(fig)* to lick into shape; ~**weisen** *vt sep irreg (form)* to rebuke; *Schüler etc* to reprimand; **Z~weisung** *f siehe vt* rebuke; reprimand.

**zureden** *vi sep* **jdm** ~ to encourage sb; *(überreden)* to persuade sb; **wenn du ihm gut zuredest, hilft er dir** if you talk to him nicely, he'll help you.

**zureiten** *sep irreg* **1** *vt Pferd* to break in. **2** *vi aux*

*sein* **auf jdn/etw** ~ to ride toward(s) sb/sth.

**Zürich** *nt* Zurich.

**zurichten** *vt sep* **(a)** *Essen etc* to prepare. **(b)** *(verunstalten)* to make a mess of; *(verletzen)* to injure. **jdn übel** ~ to knock sb about.

**zürnen** *vi (geh)* **jdm** ~ to be angry with sb.

**zurück** *adv* back; *(mit Zahlungen)* behind; *(fig: zurückgeblieben: von Kind)* backward. **ein Schritt** ~ a step backwards; **in Mathematik (sehr)** ~ **sein** *(fig)* to be (really) behind in maths; ~**!** get back!; ~ **an Absender** return to sender; **einmal München und** ~ a return *(Brit)* or round-trip ticket *(US)* to Munich; **hinter jdm** ~ **sein** *(fig)* to lie behind sb; **es gibt kein Z~ (mehr)** there's no going back.

**zurück-:** ~**behalten*** *vt sep irreg* to keep (back); **er hat Schäden** ~**behalten** he suffered lasting damage; ~**bekommen*** *vt sep irreg* to get back; ~**berufen*** *vt sep irreg* to recall; ~**bewegen*** *vtr sep* to move back; ~**bilden** *vr sep (Geschwür)* to recede; *(Muskel)* to become wasted; *(Biol)* to regress.

**zurückbleiben** *vi sep irreg aux sein* **(a)** to stay behind. **(b)** *(übrigbleiben)* to be left, to remain. **ihm ist eine Narbe zurückgeblieben** he has been left with a scar. **(c)** *(nicht Schritt halten)* to fall behind; *(in Entwicklung)* to be retarded; *(Sport)* to be behind. **ihre Leistung blieb hinter meinen Erwartungen zurück** her performance did not come up to my expectations; *siehe* **zurückgeblieben.**

**zurück-:** ~**blicken** *vi sep* to look back *(auf* +*acc* at*)*; *(fig)* to look back *(auf* +*acc* on*)*; ~**bringen** *vt sep irreg* to bring back; *(wieder wegbringen)* to take back; ~**datieren*** *vt sep* to backdate; ~**denken** *vi sep irreg* to think back *(an* +*acc* to*)*; **so weit ich** ~**denken kann** as far as I can recall; ~**drängen** *vt sep* to force back; *(Mil)* to drive back; ~**drehen** *vt sep* to turn back; ~**dürfen** *vi sep irreg (col)* to be allowed back; ~**erhalten*** *vt sep irreg* to get back; ~**erinnern*** *vr sep* to remember; ~**erobern*** *vt sep (Mil)* to recapture; ~**erstatten*** *vt sep* to reimburse; ~**fahren** *sep irreg* **1** *vi aux sein* to return; **2** *vt* **(a)** to drive back; **(b)** *Produktion* to cut back; ~**fallen** *vi sep irreg aux sein* to fall back; *(Sport)* to drop back; *(in Leistungen)* to fall behind; *(fig) (an Besitzer)* to revert *(an* +*acc* to*)*; *(Schande, Vorwurf etc)* to reflect *(auf* +*acc* on*)*; ~**finden** *vi sep irreg* to find the way back; ~**fliegen** *vti sep irreg (vi aux sein)* to fly back; ~**fließen** *vi sep irreg aux sein (lit, fig)* to flow back; ~**fordern** *vt sep* **etw** ~**fordern** to ask for sth back; ~**fragen** *vi sep* to ask a question back; *(wegen Auskunft)* to check back *(bei* with*)*.

**zurückführen** *sep* **1** *vt* **(a)** *(zurückbringen)* to lead back. **(b)** *(ableiten aus)* to put down to. **2** *vi* to lead back. **es führt kein Weg zurück** *(fig)* there's no going back.

**zurückgeben** *vt sep irreg* to give back; *Ball, Beleidigung* to return.

**zurückgeblieben** *adj* **geistig/körperlich** ~ mentally/physically retarded.

**zurückgehen** *vi sep irreg aux sein* **(a)** to go back *(nach, in* +*acc* to, *fig: auf* +*acc* to*)*; *(zeitlich)* to date *(auf* +*acc* from*)*. **er ging zwei Schritte zurück** he took two steps back; **Waren/Essen** ~ **lassen** to send back goods/food. **(b)** *(zurückweichen)* to retreat, to fall back; *(fig: abnehmen)* to go down; *(Geschäft, Umsatz)* to fall off; *(Schmerz, Blutung)* to ease

**zurück-:** ~**gezogen** *adj Mensch* retiring; *Lebensweise* secluded; **er lebt sehr** ~**gezogen** he lives a very secluded life; ~**greifen** *vi sep irreg (fig)* to fall back *(auf* +*acc* on*)*; *(zeitlich)* to go back *(auf* +*acc* to*)*; ~**haben** *vt sep irreg (col)* to have back; **ich will**

**mein Geld ~haben** I want my money back.
**zurückhalten** *sep irreg* **1** *vt* to hold back; *(aufhalten) jdn* to hold up; *(nicht freigeben) Informationen* to withhold; *(unterdrücken) Tränen* to keep back. **jdn von etw** *(dat)* ~ to keep sb from sth. **2** *vr (sich beherrschen)* to restrain oneself; *(im Hintergrund bleiben)* to keep in the background; *(bei Verhandlung etc)* to keep a low profile. **Sie müssen sich beim Essen sehr** ~ you must cut down a lot on what you eat. **3** *vi* **mit etw** ~ *(verheimlichen)* to hold sth back.
**zurückhaltend** *adj* **(a)** *(restrained; (reserviert)* reserved; *Empfang, Nachfrage* low-key. **sich** ~ **über etw** *(acc)* **äußern** to be restrained in one's comments about sth. **(b)** *(nicht großzügig)* sparing.
**Zurück-:** ~**haltung** *f* restraint; *(Reserve)* reserve; **z~holen** *vt sep* to fetch back; **z~kaufen** *vt sep* to buy back; **z~kehren** *vi sep aux sein* to return *(von, aus* from; *nach, zu* to*)*; **z~kommen** *vi sep irreg aux sein* to come back *(fig: auf +acc* to*)*; **z~können** *vi sep irreg (col)* to be able to go back; **ich kann nicht mehr z~** *(fig)* there's no going back!; **z~kriegen** *vt sep (col)* to get back; **z~lassen** *vt sep irreg* **(a)** to leave; *(liegenlassen, fig: übertreffen)* to leave behind; **(b)** *(col: z~kehren lassen)* to allow back; **z~laufen** *vi sep irreg aux sein* to run back; *(z~gehen)* to walk back.
**zurücklegen** *sep* **1** *vt* **(a)** to put back. **(b)** *Kopf* to lay *or* lean back. **(c)** *(aufbewahren)* to put aside; *(sparen)* to lay aside. **jdm etw** ~ to keep sth for sb. **(d)** *Strecke* to cover, to do. **2** *vr* to lie back.
**Zurück-:** **z~lehnen** *vtr sep* to lean back; **z~liegen** *vi sep irreg* **(a)** *(im Rückstand liegen)* to be behind; **(b)** *(zeitlich)* **der Unfall liegt etwa eine Woche z~** the accident was about a week ago; **z~melden** *vtr sep* to report back; **z~müssen** *vi sep irreg (col)* to have to go back; ~**nahme** *f* -n *siehe* **z~nehmen** taking back; revoking; reversal; withdrawal; **z~nehmen** *vt sep irreg* to take back; *Verordnung* to revoke; *Entscheidung* to reverse; *Angebot* to withdraw; **sein Wort z~nehmen** to go back on one's word; **z~pfeifen** *vt sep irreg* **jdn z~pfeifen** *(fig col)* to bring sb back into line; **z~prallen** *vi sep aux sein* to bounce back; **z~reichen** *vi sep (Tradition etc)* to go back *(in +acc* to*)*; **z~reißen** *vt sep irreg* to pull back; **z~rollen** *vti sep (vi: aux sein)* to roll back; z~**rufen** *vti sep irreg* to call back; *Botschafter, fehlerhafte Autos* to recall; **jdn ins Leben z~rufen** to bring sb back to life; **jdm/sich etw ins Gedächtnis z~rufen** to remind sb of sth/to recall sth; **z~schalten** *vi sep* to change back; **z~schauen** *vi sep* to look back *(auf +acc lit* at, *(fig)* on*)*; **z~schicken** *vt sep* to send back; **z~schieben** *vt sep irreg* to push back.
**zurückschlagen** *sep irreg* **1** *vt* **(a)** *Ball* to return; *Angriff etc* to repulse. **(b)** *Decke* to fold back; *Kragen* to turn down. **2** *vi* to hit back.
**zurück-:** ~**schrauben** *vt sep Erwartungen* to lower; *Verbrauch etc* to cut back; **seine Ansprüche** ~**schrauben** to lower one's sights; ~**schrecken** *vi sep irreg aux sein or haben (fig)* to shy away *(vor +dat* from*)*; **vor nichts** ~**schrecken** to stop at nothing; ~**sehen** *vi sep irreg* to look back *(auf +acc lit* at, *(fig)* on*)*; ~**sehnen** *vr sep* to long to return *(nach* to*)*; **sich nach der guten alten Zeit** ~**sehnen** to long for the good old days; ~**senden** *vt sep irreg* to send back.
**zurücksetzen** *sep* **1** *vt (nach hinten)* to move back; *(an früherem Platz)* to put back; *(fig: benachteiligen)* to neglect. **2** *vr* to sit back. **3** *vi (mit Fahrzeug)* to reverse, to back.
**Zurück-:** ~**setzung** *f (fig: Benachteiligung)* neglect;

**z~sinken** *vi sep irreg aux sein* to sink back *(in +acc* into*)*; **z~spielen** *vti sep (Sport)* to play back; **z~stecken** *sep* **1** *vt* to put back; **2** *vi* **(a)** *(weniger Ansprüche stellen)* to lower one's expectations; **(b)** *(nachgeben)* to backtrack.
**zurückstehen** *vi sep irreg* **(a)** *(Haus etc)* to stand back. **(b)** *(verzichten)* to miss out. **(c)** *(hintangesetzt werden)* to take second place *(hinter +dat* to*)*.
**zurückstellen** *vt sep* **(a)** *(an seinen Platz, Uhr)* to put back; *(nach hinten)* to move back. **(b)** *Waren* to put aside *or* by. **(c)** *(fig) Schüler* to keep down. **jdn vom Wehrdienst** ~ to defer sb's military service. **(d)** *(fig: verschieben)* to defer; *Bedenken etc* to put aside. **persönliche Interessen hinter etw** *(dat)* ~ to put one's personal interests after sth.
**Zurück-:** ~**stellung** *f (Aufschub, Mil)* deferment; **z~stoßen** *vt sep irreg* to push back; *(fig)* to reject; **z~stufen** *vt sep* to downgrade; **z~tragen** *vt sep irreg* to carry back; **z~treiben** *vt sep irreg* to drive back.
**zurücktreten** *sep irreg* **1** *vi aux sein* **(a)** to step back; *(fig: Hochwasser)* to go down. **bitte ~!** stand back, please!; **einen Schritt** ~ to take a step back. **(b)** *(Regierung)* to resign; *(von einem Amt)* to step down. **(c)** *(von einem Vertrag etc)* to withdraw *(von* from*)*. **(d)** *(fig: geringer werden)* to decrease; *(Wald)* to recede. **hinter jdm/etw** ~ to come second to sb/sth. **2** *vti (mit Fuß)* to kick back.
**Zurück-:** **z~verfolgen*** *vt sep (fig)* to trace back; **z~verlangen*** *vt sep* to demand back; **z~verlegen*** *vt sep* **(a)** *(zeitlich)* to set back; **(b)** *Front etc, Wohnsitz* to move back; **z~versetzen*** *sep* **1** *vt* **(a)** *(in alten Zustand)* to restore *(in +acc* to*)*; *(in andere Zeit)* to take back *(in +acc* to*)*; **(b)** *Beamte etc* to transfer back; **2** *vr* to think oneself back *(in +acc* to*)*; **z~verweisen*** *vt sep irreg* to refer back; *(Parl) Gesetzentwurf* to recommit; **z~weichen** *vi sep irreg aux sein* to shrink back *(vor +dat* from*)*; **z~weisen** *vt sep irreg* to reject; *Bittsteller* to turn away; *(an der Grenze)* to turn back; ~**weisung** *f siehe vt* rejection; turning away; turning back; **z~werfen** *vt sep irreg Ball, Kopf* to throw back; *Feind auch* to repel; *Strahlen, Schall* to reflect; *(fig: wirtschaftlich)* to set back *(um by)*; **z~wollen** *vi sep (col)* to want to go back; **z~zahlen** *vt sep* to pay back; ~**zahlung** *f* repayment.
**zurückziehen** *sep irreg* **1** *vt* to pull back; *Antrag, Klage etc* to withdraw. **2** *vr* to withdraw *(von* from*)*; *(von Tätigkeit)* to retire; *siehe* **zurückgezogen. 3** *vi aux sein* to move back.
**Zuruf** *m* shout; *(aufmunternd)* cheer.
**zurufen** *vi sep irreg* **jdm etw** ~ to shout sth to sb.
**zus.** = **(a)** **zusammen. (b)** **zusätzlich.**
**Zusage** *f* -n **(a)** *(Verpflichtung)* commitment. **(b)** *(Annahme)* acceptance. **(c)** *(Versprechen)* promise.
**zusagen** *sep* **1** *vt (versprechen)* to promise; *(bestätigen)* to confirm. **2** *vi* **(a)** *(annehmen)* **(jdm)** ~ to accept (sb's invitation). **(b)** *(gefallen)* **jdm** ~ to appeal to sb.
**zusammen** *adv* together. **wir hatten** ~ **100 Mark zum Ausgeben** between us we had 100 marks to spend; **er verdient mehr als wir alle** ~ he earns more than the rest of us put together; **das macht** ~ **50 Mark** that makes 50 marks altogether.
**Zusammen-:** ~**arbeit** *f* co-operation; **z~arbeiten** *vi sep* to co-operate; ~**ballung** *f* accumulation; ~**bau** *m no pl* assembly; **z~bauen** *vt sep* to assemble; **etw wieder z~bauen** to reassemble sth; **z~beißen** *vt sep irreg* **die Zähne z~beißen** *(lit)* to clench one's teeth; *(fig)* to grit one's teeth;

z~**bekommen*** *vt sep irreg* to get together; *Wortlaut etc* to remember; z~**binden** *vt sep irreg* to tie together; z~**bleiben** *vi sep irreg aux sein* to stay together; z~**brauen** *sep* **1** *vt (col)* to concoct; **2** *vr (Gewitter, Unheil etc)* to be brewing.

**zusammenbrechen** *vi sep irreg aux sein* to collapse; *(Mensch auch, Verhandlungen, Telefonverbindungen)* to break down; *(Verkehr etc)* to come to a standstill, *(Computer, Börse)* to crash.

**zusammenbringen** *vt sep irreg* to collect; *Geld* to raise; *(ins Gedächtnis zurückrufen)* to remember; *(bekannt machen) Menschen* to bring together.

**Zusammenbruch** *m (von Beziehungen, Kommunikation, Nerven~)* breakdown; *(Comp, Fin)* crash; *(fig)* collapse.

**zusammen-**: ~**drängen** *vtr* to crowd together; ~**drücken** *vt sep* to press together; ~**fahren** *sep irreg* **1** *vi aux sein* (a) *(~stoßen)* to collide; (b) *(erschrecken)* to give a start; **2** *vt (col) Fahrzeug* to wreck; ~**fallen** *vi sep irreg aux sein* (a) *(einstürzen)* to collapse; (b) *(Ereignisse)* to coincide; ~**falten** *vt sep* to fold up.

**zusammenfassen** *sep* **1** *vt* to combine *(zu in)*. **2** *vti (das Fazit ziehen)* to summarize. ~**d kann man sagen, ...** to sum up, one can say ...

**Zusammen-**: ~**fassung** *f* (a) combination; (b) *(Überblick)* summary; z~**fegen** *vt sep* to sweep together; z~**finden** *vr sep irreg* to meet; *(sich versammeln)* to congregate; z~**flicken** *vt sep (col) Sache, Verletzten* to patch up; z~**fließen** *vi sep irreg aux sein* to meet; *(Farben)* to run together; ~**fluß** *m* confluence; z~**fügen** *sep* **1** *vt* to join together; *(Tech)* to fit together; **etw zu etw z~fügen** to join/fit sth together to make sth; **2** *vr* to fit together; z~**führen** *vt sep* to bring together; *Familie* to reunite; z~**gehen** *vi sep irreg aux sein (sich vereinen)* to unite; *(Linien etc)* to meet; z~**gehören*** *vi sep* to belong together; *(Gegenstände)* to go together, to match; z~**gehörig** *adj Kleidungsstücke etc* matching; ~**gehörigkeit** *f (Einheit)* unity; ~**gehörigkeitsgefühl** *nt* sense of belonging; *(in Familie)* sense of a common bond; z~**gesetzt** *adj* **aus etw z~gesetzt sein** to be composed of sth; z~**gesetztes Wort/Verb** compound (word)/verb; z~**gewürfelt** *adj* motley; z~**haben** *vt sep irreg (col)* **etw z~haben** to have got sth together; ~**halt** *m no pl* cohesion; *(Tech)* (cohesive) strength.

**zusammenhalten** *sep irreg* **1** *vt* to hold together; *(col) Geld etc* to hold on to. **2** *vi* to hold together; *(fig: Freunde, Gruppe etc)* to stick together.

**Zusammenhang** *m* connection *(von, zwischen +dat* between*)*; *(im Text)* context. **etw mit etw in ~ bringen** to connect sth with sth; **im** *or* **in ~ mit etw stehen** to be connected with sth; **etw aus dem ~ reißen** to take sth out of its context.

**zusammenhängen** *vi sep irreg* to be joined (together); *(fig)* to be connected. ~**d** *Erzählung* coherent.

**zusammenhang(s)los** **1** *adj* disjointed. **2** *adv* incoherently.

**Zusammen-**: z~**hauen** *vt sep irreg (col) (zerstören)* to smash to pieces; **jdn z~hauen** to beat sb up; z~**heften** *vt sep* to staple together; z~**heilen** *vi sep aux sein* to heal (up); *(Knochen)* to knit (together); z~**kehren** *vt sep* to sweep together; z~**klappbar** *adj* folding; z~**klappen** *sep* **1** *vt* to fold up; *Schirm* to shut; **2** *vi aux sein* (a) *(Stuhl etc)* to collapse; (b) *(fig col: vor Erschöpfung)* to flake out *(col)*; z~**kleben** *vti sep (vi: aux haben or sein)* to stick together; z~**kneifen** *vt sep irreg Lippen etc* to press together; *Augen* to screw up; z~**knüllen** *vt*

*sep* to crumple up; z~**kommen** *vi sep irreg aux sein* to meet; *(Umstände)* to combine; *(Geld)* to be collected; **er kommt viel mit Menschen zusammen** he meets a lot of people; z~**kratzen** *vt sep* to scrape together; z~**kriegen** *vt sep (col)* = z~**bekommen**; ~**kunft** *f, pl* ~**künfte** meeting; *(zwanglos)* get-together; z~**lassen** *vt sep irreg* to leave together.

**zusammenlaufen** *vi sep irreg aux sein* (a) *(an eine Stelle laufen)* to gather; *(Flüssigkeit)* to collect. (b) *(Farben)* to run together; *(Linien, Straßen)* to converge. (c) *(Stoff)* to shrink.

**zusammenleben** *vi sep* to live together.

**Zusammenleben** *nt* living together *no art.* **das menschliche ~** social existence.

**zusammen-**: ~**legen** *vt sep* (a) to fold (up); (b) *(stapeln)* to pile together; (c) *(vereinigen)* to put together, to combine; *Grundstücke* to join; *Termine* to combine; *Häftlinge, Patienten* to put together; **sie legten ihr Geld ~** they pooled their money; ~**nähen** *vt sep* to sew *or* stitch together.

**zusammennehmen** *sep irreg* **1** *vt* to gather up; *Mut* to summon up; *Gedanken* to collect. **alles zusammengenommen** all in all. **2** *vr* to pull oneself together.

**Zusammen-**: z~**packen** *vt sep* to pack up together; **pack (deine Sachen) z~!** get packed!; z~**passen** *vi sep* to be suited to each other; *(Farben, Stile)* to go together; z~**pferchen** *vt sep* to herd together; ~**prall** *m* collision; *(fig)* clash; z~**prallen** *vi sep aux sein* to collide; *(fig)* to clash; z~**pressen** *vt sep* to press together; z~**raffen** *sep* **1** *vt* (a) to bundle together; (b) *(fig) Mut* to summon up; (c) *(fig pej: anhäufen)* to amass, to pile up; **2** *vr* to pull oneself together; z~**rechnen** *vt sep* to add up; z~**reimen** *vt sep (col)* **das kann ich mir nicht z~reimen** I can't make head or tail of this; z~**reißen** *vr sep irreg* to pull oneself together; z~**rollen** *sep* **1** *vt* to roll up; **2** *vr* to curl up; *(Schlange)* to coil up; z~**rotten** *vr sep (pej)* to gang up *(gegen against)*; *(in aufrührerischer Absicht)* to form a mob; z~**rücken** *sep* **1** *vt Möbel etc* to move closer together; **2** *vi aux sein* to move up closer; z~**rufen** *vt sep irreg* to call together; z~**sacken** *vi sep aux sein* = z~**sinken**; z~**scharen** *vr sep* to gather; z~**schießen** *vt sep irreg* to shoot up; z~**schlagen** *sep irreg* **1** *vt* (a) *(aneinanderschlagen)* to knock together; *Hacken* to click; **die Hände überm Kopf z~schlagen** to throw up one's hands in horror; (b) *(verprügeln)* to beat up; *(zerschlagen)* to smash up; **2** *vi aux sein* **über jdm/etw z~schlagen** *(Wellen etc)* to close over sb/sth; z~**schließen** *vr sep irreg* to join together, to combine; *(Comm, Pol)* to merge; ~**schluß** *m siehe vr* combining; merger; z~**schmelzen** *vi sep irreg aux sein* (a) *(verschmelzen)* to fuse; (b) *(zerschmelzen)* to melt (away); *(Anzahl)* to dwindle; z~**schrecken** *vi sep irreg aux sein* to give a start; z~**schreiben** *vt sep irreg* (a) *Wörter* to write together; (b) *(pej: verfassen)* to dash off; **was der für einen Mist zusammenschreibt** what a load of rubbish he writes; z~**schrumpfen** *vi sep aux sein* to shrivel up; *(fig)* to dwindle *(auf +acc to)*.

**zusammensein** *vi sep irreg aux sein* **mit jdm ~** to be with sb; *(col: befreundet)* to be going out with sb; *(euph: mit jdm schlafen)* to sleep with sb.

**Zusammensein** *nt* (a) being together. (b) *(Zusammenkunft)* get-together.

**zusammensetzen** *sep* **1** *vt* to put together. **2** *vr* (a) to sit together; *(um etwas zu tun)* to get together. (b) **sich ~ aus** to consist of.

**Zusammen-:** ~**setzung** *f (Struktur)* composition; *(Mischung)* mixture; **das Team in dieser ~setzung** the team in this line-up; **z~sinken** *vi sep irreg aux sein* **(in sich) z~sinken** to slump; *(Gebäude)* to cave in; **z~sparen** *vt sep* to save up; ~**spiel** *nt* teamwork; *(von Kräften etc)* interaction; **z~stauchen** *vt sep (col)* to give a dressing-down *(col)*; **z~stecken** *sep* **1** *vt Einzelteile* to fit together; *(mit Nadeln etc)* to pin together; **die Köpfe z~stecken** *(col)* to go into a huddle; *(flüstern)* to whisper to each other; **2** *vi (col)* to be together; **z~stehen** *vi sep irreg* to stand together; *(Gegenstände)* to be together; *(fig)* to stand by each other.

**zusammenstellen** *vt sep* to put together; *(nach System)* to arrange; *Liste* to draw up.

**Zusammenstellung** *f* **(a)** *siehe vt* putting together; arranging; drawing up. **(b)** *(nach System)* arrangement; *(Liste)* list; *(Zusammensetzung)* composition; *(Übersicht)* survey.

**Zusammenstoß** *m* collision, crash; *(Mil, fig: Streit)* clash.

**zusammenstoßen** *sep irreg* **1** *vi aux sein (z~prallen)* to collide; *(Mil, fig: sich streiten)* to clash. **mit jdm ~** to collide with sb; *(fig)* to clash with sb; **sie stießen mit den Köpfen zusammen** they banged their heads together. **2** *vt* to knock together.

**Zusammen-:** **z~streichen** *vt sep irreg* to cut (down) *(auf +acc to)*; **z~strömen** *vi sep aux sein (Menschen)* to flock together; **z~stürzen** *vi sep aux sein (einstürzen)* to collapse; **z~suchen** *vt sep* to collect (together); **sich** *(dat)* **etw z~suchen** to find sth; **z~tragen** *vt sep irreg* to collect; **z~treffen** *vi sep irreg aux sein (Menschen)* to meet; *(Ereignisse)* to coincide; **mit jdm z~treffen** to meet sb; **z~treten** *vi sep irreg aux sein (Vorstand etc)* to meet; **z~trommeln** *vt sep (col)* to round up *(col)*; **z~tun** *sep* **1** *vt (col)* to put together; *(vermischen)* to mix; **2** *vr* to get together; **z~wachsen** *vi sep irreg aux sein* to grow together; *(Wunde)* to close; *(Knochen)* to knit; **z~wirken** *vi sep* to combine; **z~zählen** *vt sep* to add up.

**zusammenziehen** *sep irreg* **1** *vt* **(a)** to draw together; *(verengen)* to narrow; *Augenbrauen* to knit. **(b)** *(fig) Truppen, Polizei* to assemble. **(c)** *(kürzen) Wörter etc* to contract; *Zahlen* to add together. **2** *vr (esp Biol, Sci)* to contract; *(Gewitter)* to be brewing. **3** *vi aux sein* to move in together.

**zusammenzucken** *vi sep aux sein* to start.

**Zusatz** *m* addition; *(zu Gesetz)* amendment; *(Beimischung)* additive.

**Zusatz-** *in cpds* supplementary; ~**antrag** *m (Parl etc)* amendment; ~**bestimmung** *f* supplementary provision; ~**gerät** *nt* attachment; *(Comp)* peripheral (device).

**zusätzlich 1** *adj* additional. **2** *adv* in addition.

**Zusatz-:** ~**mittel** *nt*, ~**stoff** *m* additive.

**zuschanzen** *vt sep (col)* **jdm etw ~** to make sure sb gets sth.

**zuschauen** *vi sep* = **zusehen**.

**Zuschauer(in** *f)* *m* - spectator; *(TV)* viewer; *(Theat)* member of the audience; *(Beistehender)* onlooker. **die ~** *pl* the spectators *pl*; *(TV)* the viewers *pl*; *(Theat)* the audience *sing*.

**Zuschauer-:** ~**raum** *m* auditorium; ~**tribüne** *f (esp Sport)* stand.

**zuschaufeln** *vt sep* to fill up.

**zuschicken** *vt sep* **jdm etw ~** to send sth to sb *or* sb sth; **sich** *(dat)* **etw ~ lassen** to send for sth.

**zuschieben** *vt sep irreg* **(a)** **jdm etw ~** to push sth over to sb; **jdm die Schuld ~** to put the blame on

sb. **(b)** *(schließen)* to push shut.

**zuschießen** *sep irreg* **1** *vt* **(a)** **jdm den Ball ~** to kick the ball (over) to sb. **(b)** *Geld etc* to contribute. **Geld für etw ~** to put money towards sth. **2** *vi aux sein (col)* **auf jdn ~** to shoot up to sb.

**Zuschlag** *m* **(a)** *(Erhöhung)* surcharge *(esp Comm, Econ)*; *(auf Briefmarke)* supplement; *(Rail)* supplement *(für +acc* on*)*. **(b)** **er erhielt den ~** *(bei Auktion)* it was knocked down to him; *(bei Auftragsvergabe)* he won the order.

**zuschlagen** *sep irreg* **1** *vt* **(a)** *Tür, Fenster* to slam (shut). **(b)** *Gebiet* to annex *(dat* to*)*. **2** *vi* **(a)** *(kräftig schlagen)* to hit out *(auch fig)*. **schlag zu!** hit me/him/it *etc!* **(b)** *aux sein (Tür)* to slam (shut).

**Zuschlag(s)-** *(Rail)*: **z~frei** *adj Zug* not subject to a supplement; ~**karte** *f* supplementary ticket; **z~pflichtig** *adj Zug* subject to a supplement.

**zuschließen** *vt sep irreg* to lock; *Laden* to lock up.

**zuschmeißen** *vt sep irreg (col) Tür etc* to slam (shut).

**zuschmieren** *vt sep (col)* to smear over; *Löcher* to fill in.

**zuschnappen** *vi sep* **(a)** **der Hund schnappte zu** the dog snapped at me/him *etc*. **(b)** *aux sein (Schloß)* to snap shut.

**zuschneiden** *vt sep irreg* to cut to size; *(Sew)* to cut out. **auf etw** *(acc)* **zugeschnitten sein** *(fig)* to be geared to sth.

**Zuschneider** *m* cutter.

**zuschneien** *vi sep aux sein* to snow in.

**Zuschnitt** *m* **(a)** *no pl* cutting. **(b)** *(Form)* cut; *(fig)* calibre *(Brit)*, caliber *(US)*.

**zuschnüren** *vt sep* to tie up; *Schuhe, Mieder* to lace up. **die Angst schnürte ihm die Kehle zu** he was choked with fear.

**zuschrauben** *vt sep Hahn etc* to screw shut; *Deckel etc* to screw on.

**zuschreiben** *vt sep irreg (fig)* to ascribe *(dat* to*)*. **das hast du dir selbst zuzuschreiben** you've only got yourself to blame for that; **das ist nur seiner Dummheit zuzuschreiben** that can only be put down to his stupidity.

**Zuschrift** *f* letter; *(auf Anzeige)* reply.

**zuschulden** *adv:* **sich** *(dat)* **etwas ~ kommen lassen** to do something wrong.

**Zuschuß** *m* contribution; *(staatlich)* subsidy, grant.

**Zuschußbetrieb** *m* loss-making concern.

**zuschütten** *vt sep* to fill in; *(hin~)* to add.

**zusehen** *vi sep irreg* **(a)** to watch; *(unbeteiligter Zuschauer sein)* to look on; *(etw dulden)* to sit back (and watch). **jdm/(bei) einer Sache ~** to watch sb/sth; *(dulden)* to sit back and watch sb/sth; **jdm bei der Arbeit ~** to watch sb working; **ich kann doch nicht ~, wie er ...** *(dulden)* I can't sit back and watch him ... **(b)** *(dafür sorgen)* ~, **daß ...** to see to it that ..., to make sure (that) ...

**zusehends** *adv* visibly; *(rasch)* rapidly.

**zusein** *vi sep irreg aux sein (col)* to be shut.

**zusenden** *vt sep irreg* to send, to forward.

**zusetzen** *sep* **1** *vt (hinzufügen)* to add. **2** *vi* **jdm ~** *(unter Druck setzen)* to lean on sb *(col)*; *dem Gegner* to harass sb; *(schwer treffen)* to hit sb hard; *(Kälte, Krankheit etc)* to take a lot out of sb.

**zusichern** *vt sep* **jdm etw ~** to assure sb of sth; **mir wurde zugesichert, daß ...** I was assured that ...

**Zusicherung** *f* assurance.

**Zuspiel** *nt (Sport)* passing.

**zuspielen** *vt sep Ball* to pass *(dat* to*)*. **jdm etw ~** *(fig)* to pass sth on to sb; *(der Presse)* to leak sth to sb.

**zuspitzen** *sep* **1** *vt Stock etc* to sharpen. **2** *vr* to be pointed; *(fig: Lage)* to become acute.

**Zuspitzung** *f (fig: von Lage, Konflikt)* aggravation.

**zusprechen** *sep irreg* **1** *vt (Jur), Preis, Gewinn etc* to award; *Kind* to grant custody of. **jdm Mut/Trost ~** *(fig)* to encourage/comfort sb. **2** *vi* **dem Essen tüchtig ~** to tuck into the food.

**zuspringen** *vi sep irreg aux sein* **(a)** *(Schloß, Tür)* to snap shut. **(b) auf jdn ~** to leap towards sb.

**Zuspruch** *m no pl* **(a)** *(Worte)* words *pl*; *(Aufmunterung)* encouragement; *(tröstlich)* comfort. **(b) (großen) ~ finden** to be (very) popular.

**Zustand** *m* state; *(von Haus, Ware, Med)* condition; *(Lage)* state of affairs. **Zustände** *pl* conditions; **in gutem/schlechtem ~** in good/poor condition; *(Haus)* in good/bad repair; **in ungepflegtem/baufälligem ~** in a state of neglect/disrepair; **Zustände bekommen** *or* **kriegen** *(col)* to have a fit *(col)*; **das sind ja schöne Zustände!** *(iro)* that's a fine state of affairs! *(iro)*.

**zustande** *adv* **(a) ~ bringen** to manage; *Arbeit* to get done; *Ereignis, Frieden etc* to bring about. **(b) ~ kommen** *(erreicht werden)* to be achieved; *(geschehen)* to come about.

**zuständig** *adj* responsible; *Behörde etc* appropriate. **dafür ist er ~** that's his responsibility.

**Zuständigkeit** *f (Kompetenz)* competence; *(Verantwortlichkeit)* responsibility.

**Zuständigkeitsbereich** *m* area of responsibility.

**zustatten** *adj* **jdm ~ kommen** *(geh)* to come in useful for sb.

**zustecken** *vt sep* **(a)** *Kleid etc* to pin up. **(b) jdm etw ~** to slip sb sth.

**zustehen** *vi sep irreg* **ihm stehen 6 Wochen Urlaub zu** he is entitled to 6 weeks' holiday.

**zusteigen** *vi sep irreg aux sein* to get on, to board. **noch jemand zugestiegen?** *(in Zug)* tickets please!

**Zustellbezirk** *m* postal district.

**zustellen** *vt sep* **(a)** *Brief* to deliver. **(b)** *Tür etc* to block.

**Zusteller(in** *f)* *m* - deliverer; *(Briefträger)* postman *(Brit)*, mailman *(US)*.

**Zustellung** *f* delivery.

**zusteuern** *sep* **1** *vi aux sein* **auf etw** *(acc)* **~** *(geh)* to head for sth; *(beim Gespräch)* to steer toward(s) sth. **2** *vt (beitragen)* to contribute *(zu to)*.

**zustimmen** *vi sep* **(einer Sache** *dat)* **~** to agree (to sth); *(einwilligen)* to consent (to sth); **jdm (in einem Punkt) ~** to agree with sb (on a point).

**Zustimmung** *f (Einverständnis)* agreement, assent; *(Einwilligung)* consent; *(Beifall)* approval. **allgemeine ~ finden** to meet with general approval.

**zustopfen** *vt sep* to stop up, to plug.

**zustöpseln** *vt sep* *Flasche* to stopper; *(mit Korken)* to cork.

**zustoßen** *sep irreg* **1** *vt Tür etc* to push shut. **2** *vi* **(a)** to plunge a/the knife/sword *etc* in; *(Stier etc)* to strike. **(b)** *(passieren) aux sein* **jdm ~** to happen to sb.

**zustreben** *vi sep aux sein* **~ auf** *(+acc)* to make *or* head for; *(fig)* to strive for.

**Zustrom** *m no pl (fig: Menschenmenge)* stream (of visitors *etc)*; *(hineinströmend)* influx; *(Met)* inflow.

**zuströmen** *vi sep aux sein* **+dat** *(Fluß)* to flow toward(s); *(fig: Menschen)* to stream toward(s).

**zustürzen** *vi sep aux sein* **auf jdn/etw ~** to rush up to sb/sth.

**zutage** *adj* **etw ~ fördern** to unearth sth; **~ kommen** *or* **treten** to come to light.

**Zutaten** *pl (Cook)* ingredients *pl*; *(fig)* accessories *pl*.

**zuteil** *adv (geh)* **jdm wird etw ~** sb is granted sth, sth is granted to sb; **jdm etw ~ werden lassen** to give sb sth.

**zuteilen** *vt sep (jdm* to sb*)* to allocate; *Arbeitskraft* to assign.

**Zuteilung** *f siehe vt* allocation; assignment.

**zutiefst** *adv* deeply.

**zutragen** *sep irreg* **1** *vt (fig: weitersagen)* to report *(jdm* to sb*)*. **2** *vr (liter)* to take place.

**zuträglich** *adj* good *(dat* for*)*, beneficial *(dat* to*)*.

**zutrauen** *vt sep* **jdm etw ~** *(Aufgabe, Tat)* to believe sb (is) capable of (doing) sth; **sich** *(dat)* **~, etw zu tun** to think one can do sth; **sich** *(dat)* **zuviel ~** to overrate one's own abilities; **sich** *(dat)* **nichts ~** to have no confidence in oneself; **das hätte ich ihm nie zugetraut!** I would never have thought him capable of it!; **jdm viel/wenig ~** to think/not to think a lot of sb.

**Zutrauen** *nt no pl* confidence *(zu* in*)*. **zu jdm ~ fassen** to begin to trust sb.

**zutraulich** *adj Kind* trusting; *Tier* friendly.

**Zutraulichkeit** *f siehe adj* trusting nature, friendliness.

**zutreffen** *vi sep irreg (gelten)* to apply *(auf +acc, für* to*)*; *(stimmen)* to be correct, to be true. **das trifft zu** that is so.

**zutreffend** *adj* accurate. **Z~es bitte unterstreichen** underline where applicable.

**zutreten** *vi sep irreg* **(a)** to kick out. **(b)** *aux sein* **auf jdn/etw ~** to step up to sb/sth.

**zutrinken** *vi sep irreg* **jdm ~** to drink to sb; *(mit Trinkspruch)* to toast sb.

**Zutritt** *m no pl (Einlaß)* admittance; *(Zugang)* access. **kein ~, ~ verboten** no admittance; **sich ~ verschaffen** to gain admission; *(Dieb)* to gain access.

**zutun** *vt sep irreg* **(a) ich habe die ganze Nacht kein Auge zugetan** I didn't sleep a wink all night. **(b)** *(col: hinzufügen)* to add *(dat* to*)*.

**Zutun** *nt no pl* **es geschah ohne mein ~** I did not have a hand in the matter.

**zu|ungunsten** *prep +gen* to the disadvantage of.

**zu|unterst** *adv* right at the bottom.

**zuverlässig** *adj* reliable.

**Zuverlässigkeit** *f* reliability.

**Zuversicht** *f no pl* confidence.

**zuversichtlich** *adj* confident.

**Zuversichtlichkeit** *f* confidence.

**zuviel** *adj, adv* too much; *(col: zu viele)* too many. **viel ~** far too much; **da krieg' ich ~** *(col)* I blow my top *(col)*; **einer/zwei** *etc* **~** one/two *etc* too many; **was ~ ist, ist ~** that's just too much.

**zuvor** *adv* before. **im Jahr ~** the year before.

**zuvorderst** *adv* right at the front.

**zuvorkommen** *vi sep irreg aux sein +dat* to anticipate; *(verhindern) einer Gefahr etc* to forestall. **jemand ist uns zuvorgekommen** somebody beat us to it.

**zuvorkommend** *adj* obliging; *(hilfsbereit)* helpful; *(höflich)* courteous.

**Zuwachs** ['tsu:vaks] *m, pl* **Zuwächse** **(a)** *no pl (Wachstum)* growth *(an +dat* of*)*. **(b)** *(Ansteigen)* increase *(an +dat* in*)*. **~ bekommen** *(col: ein Baby)* to have an addition to the family.

**zuwachsen** ['tsu:vaksən] *vi sep irreg aux sein (Loch)* to grow over; *(Garten)* to become overgrown; *(Wunde)* to heal.

**Zuwachsrate** ['tsu:vaks-] *f* rate of increase.

**Zuwanderer** *m* immigrant.

**zuwandern** *vi sep aux sein* to immigrate.

**Zuwanderung** *f* immigration.

**zuwege** *adv* **etw ~ bringen** to manage sth; *(erreichen)* to achieve sth; **mit etw ~ kommen** to (be able to) cope with sth.

**zuweilen** *adv (geh)* (every) now and then.

**zuweisen** *vt sep irreg* to allocate *(jdm etw* sth to sb).

**zuwenden** *sep irreg* **1** *vt (lit, fig)* to turn *(dat* to, towards)*; **2** *vr* **sich jdm/einer Sache** ~ *(lit, fig)* to turn to sb/sth; *(sich widmen, liebevoll)* to devote oneself to sb/sth.

**Zuwendung** *f* (**a**) *(Liebe)* care. (**b**) *(Geldsumme)* sum (of money).

**zuwenig** *adj* too little; *(col: zu wenige)* too few. **du schläfst** ~ you don't get enough sleep; **zwei** ~ two too few.

**zuwerfen** *vt sep irreg* (**a**) *(hinwerfen)* **jdm etw** ~ to throw sth to sb; **jdm einen Blick** ~ to cast a glance at sb; **jdm einen bösen Blick** ~ to look daggers at sb. (**b**) *(schließen) Tür* to slam (shut).

**zuwider** *adj* **er/das ist mir** ~ I detest *or* loathe him/that.

**Zuwider-:** **z~handeln** *vi sep +dat (geh)* to go against; *einem Verbot, Befehl* to defy; *dem Gesetz* to contravene; **~handlung** *f (form)* contravention; **z~laufen** *vi sep irreg aux sein +dat* to run counter to.

**zuwinken** *vi sep* **jdm** ~ to wave to sb.

**zuzahlen** *sep* **1** *vt* **10 Mark** ~ to pay another 10 marks. **2** *vi* to pay extra.

**zuzählen** *vt sep (col)* to add; *(einbeziehen)* to include *(zu* in).

**zuziehen** *sep irreg* **1** *vt* (**a**) *Vorhang* to draw; *Tür* to pull shut; *Knoten* to tighten; *Arzt etc* to consult. (**b**) **sich** *(dat)* **jds Zorn** ~ to incur sb's anger; **sich** *(dat)* **eine Verletzung/Krankheit** ~ *(form)* to sustain an injury/to contract an illness. **2** *vr (Schlinge etc)* to tighten. **3** *vi aux sein* to move into the area.

**Zuzug** *m (Zustrom)* influx; *(von Familie etc)* move *(nach* to).

**zuzüglich** *prep +gen* plus.

**zuzwinkern** *vi sep* **jdm** ~ to wink at sb.

**ZVS** [tsɛtfau'|ɛs] *f* = **Zentralstelle für die Vergabe von Studienplätzen** ≃ UCCA *(Brit)*, SAT center *(US)*.

**zw.** = **zwischen**.

**zwang** *pret of* **zwingen**.

**Zwang** *m ⁼e* compulsion; *(Gewalt)* force; *(Verpflichtung)* obligation. **gesellschaftliche** ~̃e social constraints; **unter** ~ *(dat)* **stehen** to be under duress; **etw ohne** ~ **tun** to do sth without being forced to; **auf jdn** ~ **ausüben** to exert pressure on sb; **darf ich rauchen? — tu dir keinen** ~ an may I smoke? — feel free; **der** ~ **der Verhältnisse** the force of circumstances.

**zwängen** *vt* to force; *(hinein~)* to cram. **sich in/durch etw** *(acc)* ~ to squeeze into/through sth.

**Zwang-:** **z~haft** *adj (Psych)* compulsive; **z~los** *adj (ohne Förmlichkeit)* informal; *(locker)* casual; *(frei)* free; **da geht es recht z~los zu** things are very informal there; **~losigkeit** *f siehe adj* informality; casualness; freeness.

**Zwangs-:** **~abgabe** *f (Econ)* compulsory levy; **~arbeit** *f* hard labour *(Brit)* or labor *(US)*; **z~ernähren\*** *vt insep* to force-feed; **~ernährung** *f* force-feeding; **~jacke** *f (lit, fig)* straitjacket; **~lage** *f* predicament; **z~läufig** *adj* inevitable; **das mußte ja z~läufig so kommen** that had to happen; **~läufigkeit** *f* inevitability; **~maßnahme** *f* compulsory measure; *(Pol)* sanction; **~räumung** *f* eviction *(+gen* from)*; **~verkauf** *m* forced sale; **~versteigerung** *f* compulsory auction; **~vollstreckung** *f* execution; **~vorstellung** *f (Psych)* obsession; **z~weise** *adv* compulsorily.

**zwanzig** *num* twenty; *siehe* **vierzig**.

**Zwanziger(in** *f) m* - (**a**) man/woman in his/her twenties. (**b**) *(col: Geldschein)* twenty mark note *(Brit)* or bill *(US)*.

**Zwanzigmarkschein** *m* twenty mark note *(Brit)* or bill *(US)*.

**zwanzigste(r, s)** *adj* twentieth.

**zwar** *adv* (**a**) *(wohl)* **sie ist** ~ **sehr schön, aber** ... it's true she's very beautiful but ... (**b**) **und** ~ in fact, actually; **er ist tatsächlich gekommen, und** ~ **um 4 Uhr** he really did come, at 4 o'clock actually; **er hat mir das anders erklärt, und** ~ **so:** ... he explained it differently to me(, like this) ...; **mach deine Hausaufgaben, und** ~ **sofort** get on with your homework, now!

**Zweck** *m -e* (**a**) purpose. **einem** ~ **dienen** to serve a purpose; **Spenden für wohltätige** ~**e** donations to charity; **seinen** ~ **erfüllen** to serve its/one's purpose; **zu welchem** ~? for what purpose?; **einen** ~ **verfolgen** to have a specific aim. (**b**) *(Sinn)* point. **was soll das für einen** ~ **haben?** what's the point of that?; **es hat keinen** ~, **darüber zu reden** there is no point (in) talking about it.

**Zweck-:** **~bau** *m -ten* functional building; **z~dienlich** *adj* appropriate; *(nützlich)* useful; **z~dienliche Hinweise** (any) relevant information; **z~entfremden\*** *vt insep* to use for another purpose; **etw als etw z~entfremden** to use sth as sth else; **~entfremdung** *f* use for another purpose; **z~entsprechend** *adj* appropriate; **z~frei** *adj Forschung etc* pure; **z~gebunden** *adj* for a specific purpose; **~gemeinschaft** *f* partnership of convenience; **z~los** *adj* pointless; **es ist z~los, hier zu bleiben** it's pointless staying here; **~losigkeit** *f no pl* pointlessness; **z~mäßig** *adj (nützlich)* useful; *(wirksam)* effective; *(ratsam)* advisable; *(z~entsprechend) Arbeitskleider etc* suitable; **~mäßigkeit** *f (Nützlichkeit)* usefulness.

**zwecks** *prep +gen (form)* for (the purpose of).

**zwei** *num* two. **dazu gehören** ~ *(col)* it takes two; *siehe* **vier**.

**Zwei** *f -en* two; *(Sch)* ≃ B; *siehe* **Vier**.

**Zwei-:** **z~bändig** *adj* two-volume; **z~beinig** *adj* two-legged; **~bettzimmer** *nt* twin-bedded room; **z~deutig** *adj* ambiguous; *(schlüpfrig)* suggestive; **~deutigkeit** *f* (**a**) *siehe adj* ambiguity; suggestiveness; (**b**) *(Bemerkung)* ambiguous remark; *(Witz)* risqué joke; **z~dimensional** *adj* two-dimensional; **~drittelmehrheit** *f (Parl)* two-thirds majority; **z~eiig** *adj Zwillinge* non-identical.

**Zweier** *m* - two; *(Zweipfennigstück)* two pfennig piece; *siehe* **Vierer**.

**Zweier-:** **~beziehung** *f* relationship; **~bob** *m* two-man bob; **~kajak** *m or nt (Kanu)* double kayak; *(Disziplin)* kayak pairs.

**zweierlei** *adj inv attr Brot, Käse* two kinds *or* sorts of; *Möglichkeiten, Größen* two different. **auf** ~ **Art** in two different ways; ~ **Handschuhe/Strümpfe** *etc* odd gloves/socks *etc*.

**zweifach** *adj* double; *(zweimal)* twice; *siehe* **vierfach**.

**Zwei-:** **~familienhaus** *nt* two-family house; **z~farbig** *adj* two-colour *(Brit)*, two-color *(US)*.

**Zweifel** *m* - doubt. **außer** ~ beyond doubt; **im** ~ in doubt; **ohne** ~ without doubt; **über allen** ~ **erhaben** beyond all doubt; **es besteht kein** ~, **daß** ... there is no doubt that ...; **da habe ich meine** ~ I have my doubts; **etw in** ~ **ziehen** to call sth into question; **ich bin mir im** ~, **ob ich das tun soll** I'm in two minds whether I should do that.

**zweifelhaft** *adj* doubtful.

**zweifellos** *adv* undoubtedly.

**zweifeln** *vi* to doubt. **an etw/jdm** ~ to doubt sth/sb.

**Zweifels-:** ~**fall** *m* difficult *or* problem case. **im** ~**fall** in case of doubt; **z~frei 1** *adj* unequivocal; **2** *adv* beyond (all) doubt; **z~ohne** *adv* undoubtedly.
**Zweifler(in** *f*) *m* - sceptic.
**Zweifrontenkrieg** *m* war/warfare on two fronts.
**Zweig** *m* -**e (a)** *(Ast)* branch; *(dünner, kleiner)* twig. **(b)** *(fig)* branch; *(Abteilung)* department.
**Zweig-:** ~**betrieb** *m* branch; ~**gesellschaft** *f* subsidiary (company).
**zweigleisig** *adj* double-track *attr.* ~ **argumentieren** to argue along two different lines.
**Zweig-:** ~**linie** *f* branch line; ~**niederlassung** *f* subsidiary; ~**stelle** *f* branch (office); ~**werk** *nt* *(Fabrik)* branch.
**zwei-:** ~**händig** *adj* two-handed; *(Mus)* for two hands; ~**höck(e)rig** *adj Kamel* two-humped.
**zweihundert** *num* two hundred.
**zweijährig** *adj attr Kind etc* two-year-old *attr,* two years old; *(Dauer)* two-year *attr,* of two years.
**Zweikampf** *m* single combat; *(Duell)* duel.
**zweimal** *adv* twice. **sich** *(dat)* **etw** ~ **überlegen** to think twice about sth; **das lasse ich mir nicht** ~ **sagen** I don't have to be told twice.
**zweimalig** *adj attr* **nach** ~**er Aufforderung** after being told twice.
**Zwei-:** ~**markstück** *nt* two-mark piece; **z~motorig** *adj* twin-engined; ~**parteiensystem** *nt* two-party system; ~**pfennigstück** *nt* twopfennig piece; ~**rad** *nt* two-wheeler; **z~räd(e)rig** *adj* two-wheeled; ~**reiher** *m (Anzug)* double-breasted suit; **z~reihig 1** *adj* double-row *attr,* in two rows; *Anzug* double-breasted; **2** *adv* in two rows; ~**samkeit** *f (liter, hum)* togetherness; **z~schneidig** *adj (lit, fig)* double-edged; **das ist ein z~schneidiges Schwert** *(fig)* it cuts both ways; **z~seitig 1** *adj Vertrag etc* bilateral; *(Comp) Diskette* double-sided; **2** *adv* on two sides; ~**sitzer** *m* - *(Aut, Aviat)* two-seater; **z~sprachig** *adj* bilingual; ~**sprachigkeit** *f* bilingualism; **z~spurig** *adj* double-tracked, double-track *attr; Autobahn* two-lane *attr;* ~**spur(tonband)gerät** *nt* twin-track (tape) recorder; **z~stellig** *adj Zahl* two-digit *attr,* with two digits; **z~stimmig** *adj (Mus)* for two voices; **z~stimmig singen** to sing in two parts; **z~stöckig** *adj* two-storey *attr (Brit),* two-story *attr (US);* **z~stündig** *adj* two-hour *attr.*
**zweit** *adv:* **zu** ~ *(in Paaren)* in twos; **wir gingen zu** ~ **spazieren** the two of us went for a walk; **das Leben zu** ~ living with someone; *siehe* **vier.**
**Zwei-:** **z~tägig** *adj* two-day *attr,* of two days; ~**taktmotor** *m* two-stroke engine.
**Zweit-:** **z~älteste(r, s)** *adj* second eldest; ~**ausfertigung** *f (form)* copy; **z~beste(r, s)** *adj* second best.
**zwei-:** ~**teilen** *vt sep, infin, ptp only* to divide (into two); ~**teiler** *m (Fashion)* two-piece; ~**teilig** *adj Roman, Film* two-part *attr,* in two parts; *Kleidungsstück* two-piece.
**zweitens** *adv* secondly.
**zweite(r, s)** *adj* second. ~ **Klasse** *(Rail etc)* second class; **Bürger** ~**r Klasse** second-class citizen(s); **jeder** ~ *(lit, col: sehr viele)* every other; **zum** ~**n** secondly; **ein** ~**r Caruso** another Caruso; *siehe* **vierte(r, s).**
**Zweite(r)** *mf decl as adj* second; *(Sport etc)* runner-up. **wie kein z~r** like nobody else.
**Zweit-:** ~**frisur** *f* wig; ~**gerät** *nt (Rad, TV)* second set; **z~größte(r, s)** *adj* second biggest/largest; **z~klassig** *adj (fig)* second-class, second-rate *(pej);* **z~letzte(r, s)** *adj* last but one; **z~rangig** *adj* = **z~klassig;** ~**schlüssel** *m* duplicate key;

~**stimme** *f* second vote.
**zweitürig** *adj* two-door.
**Zweit-:** ~**wagen** *m* second car; ~**wohnung** *f* second home.
**Zwei-:** ~**vierteltakt** *m (Mus)* two-four time; **z~wöchig** *adj* two-week *attr,* of two weeks; ~**zeiler** *m (Liter)* couplet; **z~zeilig** *adj* two-lined; *(Typ) Abstand* double-spaced; **z~zeilig schreiben** to double-space; ~**zimmerwohnung** *f* two-room(ed) flat *(Brit) or* apartment; **z~zylindrig** *adj* two-cylinder *attr.*
**Zwerchfell** *nt (Anat)* diaphragm.
**Zwerg(in** *f*) *m* -**e** dwarf; *(fig: Knirps)* midget; *(pej: unbedeutender Mensch)* squirt *(col).*
**zwergenhaft** *adj* dwarfish; *(fig)* diminutive.
**Zwerg-:** ~**huhn** *nt* bantam; ~**pinscher** *m* pet terrier; ~**schule** *f (Sch col)* village school; ~**staat** *m* miniature state; ~**wuchs** *m* dwarfism; **z~wüchsig** *adj attr* dwarfish.
**Zwetsch(g)e** *f* -**n** plum.
**Zwetsch(g)enschnaps** *m* plum brandy.
**Zwickel** *m* - *(Sew)* gusset.
**zwicken 1** *vt* to pinch; *(leicht schmerzen)* to give a twinge. **2** *vt impers* **es zwickt mich in der Schulter** I've a twinge in my shoulder.
**Zwicker** *m* - pince-nez.
**Zwickmühle** *f* **in der** ~ **sitzen** *(fig)* to be in a dilemma.
**Zwieback** *m* -**e** *or* =**e** ≈ rusk.
**Zwiebel** *f* -**n** onion; *(Blumen~)* bulb; *(hum col: Uhr)* watch.
**Zwiebel-:** **z~förmig** *adj* onion-shaped; ~**kuchen** *m* onion tart; ~**ring** *m* onion ring; ~**suppe** *f* onion soup; ~**turm** *m* (tower with an) onion dome.
**Zwie-:** ~**gespräch** *nt* dialogue; ~**licht** *nt no pl* twilight; *(morgens)* half-light; **ins** ~**licht geraten sein** *(fig)* to appear in an unfavourable *(Brit) or* unfavorable *(US)* light; **z~lichtig** *adj (fig)* shady; ~**spalt** *m (der Gefühle etc)* conflict; *(zwischen Menschen)* rift, gulf; **z~spältig** *adj Gefühle* mixed, conflicting *attr;* **ein z~spältiger Mensch** a man/woman of contradictions; ~**sprache** *f (geh)* ~**sprache mit jdm halten** to commune with sb; ~**tracht** *f no pl* discord; ~**tracht säen** to sow discord.
**Zwilling** *m* -**e** twin; *(Gewehr)* double-barrelled *(Brit) or* double-barreled *(US)* gun. ~**e** *(Astrol)* Gemini.
**Zwillings-:** ~**bruder** *m* twin brother; ~**geburt** *f* twin birth; ~**paar** *nt* twins *pl;* ~**schwester** *f* twin sister.
**Zwinge** *f* -**n** *(Tech)* (screw) clamp; *(an Stock, Schirm)* tip; *(an Werkzeuggriff)* ferrule.
**zwingen** *pret* **zwang,** *ptp* **gezwungen 1** *vt* to force. **jdn** ~**, etw zu tun** to force sb to do sth; **jdn zu etw** ~ to force sb to do sth; **jdn zum Handeln** ~ to force sb to act; **die Regierung wurde zum Rücktritt gezwungen** the government was forced to resign; *siehe* **gezwungen. 2** *vr* to force oneself. **3** *vi* **zum Handeln/Umdenken** ~ to force *or* compel us/them *etc* to act/rethink.
**zwingend** *adj Notwendigkeit* urgent; *(logisch notwendig)* necessary; *Schluß, Beweis* conclusive; *Argument, Gründe* cogent.
**Zwinger** *m* - *(Käfig)* cage; *(Hunde~)* kennels *pl.*
**zwinkern** *vi* to blink; *(als Zeichen)* to wink; *(lustig)* to twinkle. **mit den Augen** ~ to blink (one's eyes).
**zwirbeln** *vt Bart* to twirl; *Schnur* to twist.
**Zwirn** *m* -**e** (strong) thread, yarn.
**Zwirnsfaden** *m* thread.
**zwischen** *prep* +*dat or (mit Bewegungsverben)* +*acc* between; *(bei mehreren auch)* among. **mitten** ~ right in the midst of.

**Zwischen-:** ~**akt** *m (Theat)* intermission; ~**aufenthalt** *m* stopover; ~**bemerkung** *f* interjection; **wenn Sie mir eine kurze ~bemerkung erlauben** if I may just interrupt; ~**bericht** *m* interim report; ~**bescheid** *m* provisional notification *no indef art*; ~**bilanz** *f (Comm)* interim balance; ~**deck** *nt (Naut)* 'tween deck; **im ~deck** 'tween decks; ~**ding** *nt* cross (between the two); **z~durch** *adv* **(a)** *(zeitlich)* in between times; *(inzwischen)* meantime; *(nebenbei)* on the side; **(b)** *(örtlich)* here and there; ~**ergebnis** *nt* interim result; *(Sport)* latest score; ~**fall** *m* incident; ~**finanzierung** *f* bridging finance; ~**frage** *f* (interposed) question; ~**gericht** *nt (Cook)* entrée; ~**größe** *f* in-between size; ~**handel** *m* wholesaling; ~**händler** *m* middleman; ~**lager** *nt* temporary store; **z~lagern** *vt insep inf and ptp only* to store (temporarily); ~**lagerung** *f* temporary storage; **z~landen** *vi sep aux sein (Aviat)* to stop over; ~**landung** *f (Aviat)* stopover; ~**lösung** *f* temporary solution; ~**mahlzeit** *f* snack (between meals); **z~menschlich** *adj attr* interpersonal; ~**musik** *f* interlude; ~**produkt** *nt* intermediate product; ~**prüfung** *f* intermediate examination; ~**raum** *m* gap, space; *(zeitlich)* interval; ~**ruf** *m* interruption; ~**rufe** heckling; ~**rufer(in** *f)* *m* - heckler; ~**runde** *f* intermediate round; ~**saison** *f* low season; **z~schalten** *vt sep (Elec)* to insert; *(fig)* to interpose; ~**schalter** *m (Elec)* circuit breaker; ~**speicher** *m (Comp)* cache (memory); ~**spiel** *nt (Mus)* intermezzo; *(Theat, fig)* interlude; ~**spurt** *m (Sport)* short burst (of speed); **z~staatlich** *adj attr* international; ~**stadium** *nt* intermediate stage; ~**station** *f* (intermediate) stop; **in London machten wir ~station** we stopped off in London; ~**stecker** *m (Elec)* adapter; ~**stück** *nt* connecting piece; ~**summe** *f* subtotal; ~**text** *m* inserted text; ~**ton** *m (Farbe)* shade; ~**töne** *(fig)* nuances; ~**wand** *f* dividing wall; *(Stellwand)* partition; ~**zeit** *f* **(a)** *(Zeitraum)* interval; **in der ~zeit** (in the) meantime; **(b)** *(Sport)* intermediate time; *(Ski)* split time; **z~zeitlich** *adv* in between; *(inzwischen)* (in the) meantime; ~**zeugnis** *nt (Sch)* mid-year report.

**Zwist** *m (rare)* **-e** *(geh)* discord; *(Fehde, Streit)* strife *no indef art.* **mit jdm in ~** *(acc)* **geraten** to become involved in a dispute with sb.

**Zwistigkeit** *f usu pl* dispute.

**zwitschern** *vti* to twitter. **einen ~** *(col)* to have a drink.

**Zwitter** *m* - hermaphrodite; *(fig)* cross *(aus* between*).*

**zwo** *num (Telec, col)* two.

**zwölf** *num* twelve. **~ Uhr mittags/nachts** (12 o'clock) midday/midnight; **fünf Minuten vor ~** *(fig)* at the eleventh hour; *siehe* **vier.**

**Zwölf-:** **z~fach** *adj* twelve-fold; *siehe* **vierfach;** ~**fingerdarm** *m* duodenum; ~**kampf** *m (Sport)* twelve-exercise event.

**zwölftens** *adv* twelfth(ly), in the twelfth place.

**zwölfte(r, s)** *adj* twelfth; *siehe* **vierte(r, s).**

**Zyankali** [tsya:n'ka:li] *nt no pl (Chem)* potassium cyanide.

**zyklisch 1** *adj* cyclic(al). **2** *adv* cyclically.

**Zyklon** *m* **-e** cyclone.

**Zyklus** ['tsy:klʊs] *m* **-, Zyklen** ['tsy:klən] cycle.

**Zylinder** *m* **- (a)** *(Math, Tech)* cylinder. **(b)** *(Hut)* top hat.

**zylindrisch** *adj* cylindrical.

**Zyniker(in** *f)* ['tsy:nikɐ, -ərɪn] *m* - cynic.

**zynisch** ['tsy:nɪʃ] *adj* cynical.

**Zynismus** *m* cynicism.

**Zypern** ['tsy:pɐn] *nt* Cyprus.

**Zypresse** *f (Bot)* cypress.

**Zypriot(in** *f)* *m (wk)* **-en, en** Cypriot.

**zypriotisch, zyprisch** ['tsy:prɪʃ] *adj* Cypriot.

**Zyste** ['tsʏstə] *f* **-n** cyst.

**z.Z(t).** = **zur Zeit.**

# A

**A, a** [eɪ] n A, a nt; (Sch: as a mark) sehr gut; (Mus) A, a nt. **A for Able** (Brit), **A for Andrew** (US) ≈ A wie Anton; **to get from A to B** von A nach B kommen; **A sharp/flat** (Mus) Ais, ais nt/As, as nt.

**a** [eɪ, ə] indef art, before vowel **an (a)** ein; (before feminine noun) eine. **so large ~ country** ein so großes Land; **an unusual feeling** ein merkwürdiges Gefühl. **(b)** (in negative constructions) **not ~** kein(e); **he didn't want ~ present** er wollte kein Geschenk. **(c)** (with profession, nationality etc) **he's ~ doctor/Frenchman** er ist Arzt/Franzose; **he's ~ famous doctor/Frenchman** er ist ein berühmter Arzt/Franzose. **(d)** (per) pro. **£4 ~ head** £4 pro Person; **50p ~ kilo** 50 Pence das or pro Kilo; **twice ~ month** zweimal im or pro Monat.

**AA** = **(a) Automobile Association** britischer Automobilklub ≈ ADAC m. **(b) Alcoholics Anonymous** Anonyme Alkoholiker, AA m.

**AAA** = **(a) Amateur Athletics Association** britischer Amateursportverband. **(b) American Automobile Club** amerikanischer Automobilklub ≈ ADAC m.

**aback** [əˈbæk] adv: **to be taken ~** erstaunt sein; (upset) betroffen sein.

**abandon** [əˈbændən] **1** vt **(a)** (leave, forsake) verlassen; wife, family also im Stich lassen; baby aussetzen; car (einfach) stehenlassen. **to ~ ship** das Schiff verlassen. **(b)** (give up) aufgeben. **to ~ play** das Spiel abbrechen. **(c)** (fig) **to ~ oneself to sth** sich einer Sache (dat) hingeben. **2** n **with ~** mit ganzer Seele.

**abandoned** [əˈbændənd] adj **(a)** (dissolute) verkommen. **(b)** (unrestrained) selbstvergessen.

**abashed** [əˈbæʃd] adj beschämt.

**abate** [əˈbeɪt] vi nachlassen.

**abatement** [əˈbeɪtmənt] Nachlassen nt. **noise ~** Bekämpfung f von Lärm.

**abattoir** [ˈæbətwɑːr] n Schlachthof m.

**abbey** [ˈæbɪ] n Abtei f; (church) Klosterkirche f.

**abbot** [ˈæbət] n Abt m.

**abbreviate** [əˈbriːvɪeɪt] vt abkürzen (to mit).

**abbreviation** [ə,briːvɪˈeɪʃən] n Abkürzung f.

**ABC¹** [ˈeɪbiːˈsiː] n (lit, fig) Abc nt. **it's as easy as ~** das ist doch kinderleicht.

**ABC²** = **American Broadcasting Company** amerikanische Rundfunkgesellschaft.

**abdicate** [ˈæbdɪkeɪt] **1** vt verzichten auf (+acc). **2** vi (monarch) abdanken.

**abdication** [,æbdɪˈkeɪʃən] n Abdankung f. **his ~ of the throne** sein Verzicht auf den Thron.

**abdomen** [ˈæbdəmen] n Unterleib m; (of insects) Hinterleib m.

**abdominal** [æbˈdɒmɪnl] adj Unterleibs-.

**abduct** [æbˈdʌkt] vt entführen.

**abduction** [æbˈdʌkʃən] n Entführung f.

**abductor** [æbˈdʌktər] n Entführer(in f) m.

**aberration** [,æbəˈreɪʃən] n Anomalie f; (in statistics) Abweichung f; (mistake) Irrtum m; (moral) Verirrung f. **in a moment of (mental) ~** in einem Augenblick geistiger Verwirrung.

**abet** [əˈbet] vt see **aid 2**.

**abeyance** [əˈbeɪəns] n no pl **to be in ~** (law, rule, issue) ruhen; (custom, office) nicht mehr ausgeübt werden.

**abhor** [əbˈhɔːr] vt verabscheuen.

**abhorrence** [əbˈhɒrəns] n Abscheu f (of vor +dat).

**abhorrent** [əbˈhɒrənt] adj abscheulich.

**abide** [əˈbaɪd] vt (usu neg, interrog) person ausstehen; (endure) aushalten. **I cannot ~ living here** ich kann es nicht ertragen, hier zu leben.

▶**abide by** vi +prep obj decision, law etc sich halten an (+acc). **I ~ ~ what I said** ich bleibe bei dem, was ich gesagt habe.

**ability** [əˈbɪlɪtɪ] n Fähigkeit f. **to the best of my ~** nach (besten) Kräften; (with mental activities) so gut ich kann; **his ~ in German** seine Fähigkeiten im Deutschen; **a man of many abilities** ein sehr vielseitiger Mensch.

**abject** [ˈæbdʒekt] adj state, liar, thief elend, erbärmlich; poverty bitter; apology demütig.

**ablaze** [əˈbleɪz] adv, adj pred in Flammen. **to be ~** in Flammen stehen; **to be ~ with light** hell erleuchtet sein.

**able** [eɪbl] adj **(a)** person fähig, kompetent; piece of work, exam paper, speech gekonnt. **(b) to be ~ to do sth** etw tun können; (be in a position to) in der Lage sein, etw zu tun.

**able-bodied** [,eɪblˈbɒdɪd] adj (gesund und) kräftig; (Mil) tauglich.

**able(-bodied) seaman** n Vollmatrose m.

**ablutions** [əˈbluːʃənz] npl (lavatory) sanitäre Einrichtungen pl.

**ably** [ˈeɪblɪ] adv gekonnt, fähig.

**abnormal** [æbˈnɔːməl] adj anormal; (deviant, Med) abnorm.

**abnormality** [,æbnɔːˈmælɪtɪ] n Anormale(s) nt; (deviancy, Med) Abnormität f.

**abnormally** [æbˈnɔːməlɪ] adv **(a)** see adj. **(b)** (exceptionally) außergewöhnlich.

**aboard** [əˈbɔːd] **1** adv (on plane, ship) an Bord. **all ~!** alle an Bord!; (on train, bus) alles einsteigen!; **to go ~** an Bord gehen. **2** prep **the ship** an Bord des Schiffes.

**abode** [əˈbəʊd] n (liter: dwelling) Aufenthalt m. **a humble ~** (iro) eine bescheidene Hütte (iro); **of no fixed ~** ohne festen Wohnsitz.

**abolish** [əˈbɒlɪʃ] vt abschaffen; law also aufheben.

**abolition** [,æbəʊˈlɪʃən] n Abschaffung f.

**abominable** [əˈbɒmɪnəbl] adj gräßlich, abscheulich. **A~ Snowman** Schneemensch m.

**abominably** [əˈbɒmɪnəblɪ] adv gräßlich, abscheulich. **~ rude** furchtbar unhöflich.

**abomination** [ə,bɒmɪ'neɪʃən] *n* **(a)** *no pl* Verabscheuung *f.* **to be held in ~ by sb** von jdm verabscheut werden. **(b)** *(thing)* Scheußlichkeit *f.*

**aborigine** [,æbə'rɪdʒɪnɪ] *n* Ureinwohner(in *f*) *m* (Australiens).

**abort** [ə'bɔːt] **1** *vi (Med: woman)* eine Fehlgeburt haben; *(Comp)* abbrechen. **2** *vt (Med) foetus* abtreiben; *(break off) mission, program etc* abbrechen.

**abortion** [ə'bɔːʃən] *n* Abtreibung *f.* **to have an ~** abtreiben lassen.

**abortive** [ə'bɔːtɪv] *adj (unsuccessful) attempt* gescheitert. **to be ~** scheitern, fehlschlagen.

**abound** [ə'baʊnd] *vi* im Überfluß vorhanden sein; *(persons)* sehr zahlreich sein. **to ~ in** reich sein an *(+dat).*

**about** [ə'baʊt] **1** *adv* **(a)** herum, umher; *(present)* in der Nähe. **to walk ~** herum- *or* umhergehen; **to leave things (lying) ~** Sachen herumliegen lassen; **to be (up and) ~ again** wieder auf den Beinen sein; **there's a lot of measles ~** die Masern gehen um; **there was nobody ~** es war keiner da; *(close at hand)* es war niemand in der Nähe; **is Paul ~?** ist Paul da?; **he's/it's ~ somewhere** er/es ist irgendwo in der Nähe; **it's the other way ~** es ist gerade umgekehrt.

  **(b) to be ~ to** im Begriff sein zu; *(esp US col: intending)* vorhaben, zu ...; **I was ~ to go out** ich wollte gerade ausgehen; **it's ~ to rain** es regnet gleich; **we are ~ to run out of petrol** uns geht gleich das Benzin aus; **are you ~ to tell me ...?** willst du mir etwa erzählen ...?

  **(c)** *(approximately)* ungefähr. **he's ~ 40** er ist ungefähr 40 *or* um die 40; **he is ~ the same, doctor** sein Zustand hat sich kaum geändert, Herr Doktor; **that's ~ it** das ist so ziemlich alles; **I've had ~ enough of this** jetzt reicht es mir aber allmählich *(col).*

  **2** *prep* **(a)** um (... herum); *(in)* in *(+dat)* (... herum). **the fields ~ the house** die Felder ums Haus; **scattered ~ the room** über das ganze Zimmer verstreut; **somewhere ~ here** hier irgendwo; **to do jobs ~ the house** sich im Haus nützlich machen; **he looked ~ him** er schaute sich um; **there's something ~ him** er hat so etwas an sich *(dat);* **while you're ~ it** wenn du schon dabei bist; **you've been a long time ~ it** du hast lange dazu gebraucht.

  **(b)** *(concerning)* über *(+acc).* **what's the film ~?** wovon handelt der Film?; **what's it all ~?** worum geht es eigentlich?; **he's promised to do something ~ it** er hat versprochen, (in der Sache) etwas zu unternehmen; **they fell out ~ money** sie haben sich wegen Geld zerstritten; **how *or* what ~ me?** und ich?, und was ist mit mir? *(col);* **how *or* what ~ going to the pictures?** wie wär's mit (dem) Kino?; **(yes,) what ~ it/him?** ja *or* na und(, was ist damit/ mit ihm)?

**about-face** [ə,baʊt'feɪs], **about-turn** [ə,baʊt'tɜːn] *n (Mil)* Kehrtwendung *f;* *(fig also)* Wendung *f* um hundertachtzig Grad. **to do an ~** kehrtmachen; *(fig)* sich um hundertachtzig Grad drehen.

**above** [ə'bʌv] **1** *adv* **(a)** *(in a higher position)* darüber. **from ~** von oben; **the flat ~** die Wohnung oben *or* (~ **that one**) darüber.

  **2** *prep* über *(+dat);* *(with motion)* über *(+acc);* *(upstream of)* oberhalb *(+gen).* **~ all** vor allem; **I couldn't hear ~ the din** ich konnte bei dem Lärm nichts hören; **to be ~ sb/sth** über jdm/etw stehen; **~ criticism/praise** über jede Kritik/jedes Lob erhaben; **he's ~ that sort of thing** er ist über so etwas erhaben; **he's not ~ a bit of blackmail** er ist sich *(dat)* nicht zu gut *or* zu schade für eine kleine Er-

pressung; **it's ~ my head** *or* **me** das ist mir zu hoch; **to be/get ~ oneself** *(col)* größenwahnsinnig werden.

  **3** *adj attr* **the ~ figures** die obengenannten Zahlen; **the ~ paragraph** der obige Abschnitt.

**above:** **~ board** *adj pred* korrekt; **~-mentioned** *adj* obenerwähnt.

**abrasion** [ə'breɪʒən] *n (Med)* (Haut)abschürfung *f.*

**abrasive** [ə'breɪsɪv] **1** *adj surface* rauh; *(fig) personality, person* aggressiv; *tongue, voice* scharf. **2** *n (cleanser)* Scheuermittel *nt;* *(~ substance)* Schleifmittel *nt.*

**abrasiveness** [ə'breɪsɪvnɪs] *n* Rauheit *f;* *(of personality)* Aggressivität *f.*

**abreast** [ə'brest] *adv* Seite an Seite. **to march four ~** im Viererglied *(Mil)* *or* zu viert nebeneinander marschieren; **to keep ~ of the news** mit den Nachrichten auf dem laufenden bleiben.

**abridged** [ə'brɪdʒd] *adj* gekürzt.

**abroad** [ə'brɔːd] *adv* **(a)** im Ausland. **to go ~** ins Ausland gehen; **from ~** aus dem Ausland. **(b) there is a rumour ~ that ...** es geht das Gerücht, daß ...

**abrupt** [ə'brʌpt] *adj* abrupt; *descent, drop* jäh; *manner, reply* schroff.

**abruptness** [ə'brʌptnɪs] *n* abrupte Art; *(of person)* schroffe Art; *(of descent, drop)* Steilheit *f;* *(of reply)* Schroffheit *f.*

**ABS = anti-lock braking system** ABS *nt.* **~ brakes** ABS-Bremsen *pl.*

**abscess** ['æbses] *n* Abszeß *m.*

**abscond** [əb'skɒnd] *vi* sich (heimlich) davonmachen; *(schoolboys also)* durchbrennen.

**absence** ['æbsəns] *n* **(a)** Abwesenheit *f;* *(from school, work etc also)* Fehlen *nt.* **in the ~ of the chairman** in Abwesenheit des Vorsitzenden; **in his ~** in seiner Abwesenheit. **(b)** *(lack)* Fehlen *nt.* **~ of enthusiasm** Mangel *m* an Begeisterung; **in the ~ of further evidence** in Ermangelung weiterer Beweise.

**absent** ['æbsənt] **1** *adj* **(a)** abwesend, nicht da. **to be ~ from school/work** in der Schule/am Arbeitsplatz fehlen. **(b)** *expression, look* (geistes)abwesend. **2** [æb'sent] *vr* **to ~ oneself (from)** *(not go, not appear)* fernbleiben *(+dat,* von); *(leave temporarily)* sich zurückziehen.

**absentee** [,æbsən'tiː] *n* Abwesende(r) *mf.* **there were a lot of ~s** es fehlten viele.

**absenteeism** [,æbsən'tiːɪzəm] *n* häufige Abwesenheit; *(of workers also)* Nichterscheinen *nt* am Arbeitsplatz; *(pej)* Krankfeiern *nt;* *(Sch)* Schwänzen *nt.*

**absently** ['æbsəntlɪ] *adv* (geistes)abwesend.

**absent-minded** [,æbsənt'maɪndɪd] *adj (lost in thought)* geistesabwesend; *(forgetful)* zerstreut; *look* abwesend.

**absent-mindedly** [,æbsənt'maɪndɪdlɪ] *adv* geistesabwesend. **he ~ forgot it** in seiner Zerstreutheit hat er es vergessen.

**absent-mindedness** [,æbsənt'maɪndɪdnɪs] *n see adj* Geistesabwesenheit *f;* Zerstreutheit *f;* Abwesenheit *f.*

**absolute** ['æbsəluːt] *adj* absolut; *idiot* ausgemacht.

**absolutely** ['æbsəluːtlɪ] *adv* absolut; *prove* eindeutig; *agree, trust also, true, correct* vollkommen, völlig; *deny, refuse* strikt; *forbidden* streng; *stupid also* völlig. **~!** genau!; **do you agree? — ~** sind Sie einverstanden? — vollkommen; **do you ~ insist?** muß das unbedingt sein? **~ amazing** wirklich erstaunlich; **you look ~ stunning** du siehst einfach umwerfend aus.

**absolution** [,æbsə'luːʃən] *n (Eccl)* Absolution *f.*

**absolve** [əb'zɒlv] *vt (from sins)* lossprechen *(from*

von); *(from blame)* freisprechen *(from* von).

**absorb** [əb'sɔːb] *vt* absorbieren; *liquid also* aufsaugen; *knowledge, news also* in sich *(acc)* aufnehmen; *shock* dämpfen; *costs etc* tragen. **to be/get ~ed in a book** in ein Buch vertieft sein/sich in ein Buch vertiefen; **she was completely ~ed in her family/job** sie ging völlig in ihrer Familie/Arbeit auf.

**absorbency** [əb'sɔːbənsɪ] *n* Saugfähigkeit *f.*

**absorbent** [əb'sɔːbənt] *adj* saugfähig, absorbierend.

**absorbent cotton** *n (US)* Watte *f.*

**absorbing** [əb'sɔːbɪŋ] *adj* fesselnd.

**absorption** [əb'sɔːpʃən] *n see vt* Absorption *f*; Aufsaugen *nt*; Aufnahme *f*; Dämpfung *f.*

**abstain** [əb'steɪn] *vi* (a) sich enthalten *(from gen)*. (b) *(in voting)* sich der Stimme enthalten.

**abstemious** [əb'stiːmɪəs] *adj person, life* enthaltsam; *meal, diet* bescheiden.

**abstention** [əb'stenʃən] *n* (a) *no pl* Enthaltung *f*; *(from alcohol also)* Abstinenz *f.* (b) *(in voting)* (Stimm)enthaltung *f.*

**abstinence** ['æbstɪnəns] *n* Abstinenz, Enthaltung *f (from* von).

**abstract¹** ['æbstrækt] **1** *adj* abstrakt. **in the ~** abstrakt; **~ noun** Abstraktum *nt.* **2** *n* (kurze) Zusammenfassung *f.*

**abstract²** [æb'strækt] *vt* abstrahieren; *information* entnehmen *(from* aus*)*; *metal etc* trennen.

**abstraction** [æb'strækʃən] *n* Abstraktion *f.*

**abstruse** [æb'struːs] *adj* abstrus.

**absurd** [əb'sɜːd] *adj* absurd. **don't be ~!** sei nicht albern; **you're just being ~** du bist ja nicht recht bei Trost!

**absurdity** [əb'sɜːdɪtɪ] *n* Absurde(s) *nt no pl (of* an +*dat)*; *(thing etc also)* Absurdität *f.*

**abundance** [ə'bʌndəns] *n* Fülle *f (of* von, gen*).* **in ~** in Hülle und Fülle; **an ~ of raw materials** großer Reichtum an Rohstoffen.

**abundant** [ə'bʌndənt] *adj* reich *(in* an +*dat)*; *time, proof* reichlich; *energy, self-confidence etc* ungeheuer.

**abundantly** [ə'bʌndəntlɪ] *adv* reichlich. **to make it ~ clear that ...** mehr als deutlich zu verstehen geben, daß ...

**abuse** [ə'bjuːs] **1** *n* (a) *no pl (insults)* Beschimpfungen *pl.* **a term of ~** ein Schimpfwort *nt.* (b) *(misuse)* Mißbrauch *m*; *(unjust practice)* Mißstand *m.* **the system is open to ~** das System kann leicht mißbraucht werden. **2** [ə'bjuːz] *vt* (a) *(revile)* beschimpfen. (b) *(misuse)* mißbrauchen; *one's health* Raubbau treiben mit.

**abusive** [əb'juːsɪv] *adj* beleidigend. **~ language** Beschimpfungen *pl*; **to be/become ~ (with sb)** (jdm gegenüber) beleidigend *or* ausfallend sein/werden.

**abut** [ə'bʌt] **1** *vi* stoßen *(on(to)* an +*acc)*; *(two things)* aneinanderstoßen. **2** *vt* anstoßen an +*acc.*

**abysmal** [ə'bɪzməl] *adj (fig)* entsetzlich; *performance, work etc* miserabel.

**abyss** [ə'bɪs] *n (lit, fig)* Abgrund *m.*

**Abyssinia** [æbɪ'sɪnɪə] *n* Abessinien *nt.*

**Abyssinian** [æbɪ'sɪnɪən] **1** *adj* abessinisch. **2** *n* Abessinier(in *f*) *m.*

**A/C** = **account** Kto.

**AC** = **alternating current.**

**academic** [ˌækə'demɪk] **1** *adj* (a) akademisch, wissenschaftlich; *person* intellektuell. **~ year** Studienjahr *nt.* (b) *(theoretical)* **out of ~ interest** aus rein akademischem Interesse; **it's purely ~ now** das ist jetzt nur noch eine rein theoretische Frage. **2** *n* Akademiker(in *f*) *m*; *(Univ)* Hochschullehrer *m.*

**academically** [ækə'demɪkəlɪ] *adv* wissenschaftlich. **~ gifted** intellektuell begabt; **to do well ~** in der

Schule gut sein; *(Univ)* mit dem Studium gut vorankommen.

**academy** [ə'kædəmɪ] *n* Akademie *f.*

**ACAS, Acas** ['eɪkæs] = **Advisory Conciliation and Arbitration Service** Schlichtungsstelle *f* für Arbeitskonflikte.

**accede** [æk'siːd] *vi* (a) **to ~ to the throne** den Thron besteigen. (b) *(agree)* zustimmen *(to dat).* (c) **to ~ to a treaty** einem Pakt beitreten.

**accelerate** [æk'seləreɪt] **1** *vt* beschleunigen. **2** *vi* beschleunigen; *(driver also)* Gas geben; *(speed, change, growth, inflation etc)* zunehmen.

**acceleration** [ækˌselə'reɪʃən] *n* Beschleunigung *f.*

**accelerator** [æk'seləreɪtəʳ] *n* (a) *(Aut)* Gaspedal *nt.* **to step on the ~** *(col)* aufs Gas treten *(col).* (b) *(Phys)* Beschleuniger *m.*

**accent** ['æksənt] *n* Akzent *m*; *(stress also)* Betonung *f.* **to speak without/with an ~** akzentfrei *or* ohne/mit Akzent sprechen; **to put the ~ on sth** *(fig)* den Akzent auf etw *(acc)* legen.

**accentuate** [æk'sentjʊeɪt] *vt* betonen; *(in speaking, Mus)* akzentuieren.

**accept** [ək'sept] **1** *vt* annehmen; *award, prize* entgegennehmen; *suggestion, work also, report, findings, person* akzeptieren; *responsibility* übernehmen; *(recognize)* need einsehen, anerkennen; *(allow, put up with)* behaviour, fate, conditions hinnehmen. **it is generally ~ed that ...** es ist allgemein anerkannt, daß ...; **we must ~ the fact that ...** wir müssen uns damit abfinden, daß ...; **it's the ~ed thing** es ist allgemein *or* so üblich. **2** *vi* annehmen; *(with offers also)* akzeptieren; *(with invitations)* zusagen.

**acceptability** [ək'septəbɪlətɪ] *n* Annehmbarkeit *f*; Zulässigkeit *f.*

**acceptable** [ək'septəbl] *adj* annehmbar *(to* für*)*, akzeptabel *(to* für*)*; *behaviour* zulässig; *(suitable)* gift passend.

**acceptance** [ək'septəns] *n see vt* Annahme *f*; Entgegennahme *f*; Akzeptierung *f*; Übernahme *f.* **to meet with general ~** allgemeine Anerkennung finden.

**access** ['ækses] **1** *n* (a) Zugang *m (to* zu*)*; *(to room, private grounds etc also)* Zutritt *m (to* zu*).* **this location offers easy ~ to shops and transport facilities** von hier sind Läden und Verkehrsmittel leicht zu erreichen; **the thieves gained ~ through the window** die Diebe gelangten durch das Fenster hinein; **~ road** Zufahrt(sstraße) *f.* (b) *(Comp)* Zugriff *m.* **~ time** Zugriffszeit *f.* **2** *vt (Comp)* file, data zugreifen auf (+*acc*).

**accessibility** [æksesɪ'bɪlɪtɪ] *n* Zugänglichkeit *f.*

**accessible** [æk'sesəbl] *adj information, person* zugänglich *(to dat)*; *place also* (leicht) zu erreichen *(to* für*).*

**accession** [æk'seʃən] *n* (a) *(to an office)* Antritt *m (to gen)*; *(also ~ to the throne)* Thronbesteigung *f.* (b) *(consent: to treaty, demand)* Zustimmung *(to* zu*)*, Annahme *(to gen) f.*

**accessory** [æk'sesərɪ] *n* (a) Extra *nt*; *(in fashion)* Accessoire *nt.* **accessories** *pl* Zubehör *nt.* (b) *(Jur)* Mitschuldige(r) *mf (to* an +*dat).*

**accident** ['æksɪdənt] *n (Mot, in home, at work)* Unfall *m*; *(Rail, Aviat, disaster)* Unglück *nt*; *(mishap)* Mißgeschick *nt*; *(chance occurrence)* Zufall *m.* **she has had an ~** sie hat einen Unfall gehabt *or (caused it)* gebaut *(col)*; *(by car, train etc also)* sie ist verunglückt; **by ~** *(by chance)* durch Zufall, zufällig; *(unintentionally)* aus Versehen.

**accidental** [ˌæksɪ'dentl] *adj (unplanned)* zufällig, Zufalls-; *(unintentional)* versehentlich. **~ death** Tod durch Unfall.

**accidentally** [ˌæksɪ'dentəlɪ] *adv (by chance)* zufällig;

*(unintentionally)* versehentlich.

**accident-prone** ['æksɪdənt,prəʊn] *adj* **to be ~** ständig Unfälle haben; *(be unlucky)* vom Pech verfolgt sein.

**acclaim** [ə'kleɪm] **1** *vt (applaud)* feiern *(as* als*)*. **to ~ sb the winner** jdn zum Sieger erklären. **2** *n* Beifall *m.*

**acclamation** [,æklə'meɪʃən] *n* Beifall *m no pl*; *(of critics also)* Anerkennung *f.*

**acclimatization** [ə,klaɪmətaɪ'zeɪʃən], *(US)* **acclimation** [,æklaɪ'meɪʃən] *n* Akklimatisierung *f (to* an +*acc)*.

**acclimatize** [ə'klaɪmətaɪz], *(US)* **acclimate** [ə'klaɪmət] *vt* gewöhnen *(to* an +*acc)*. **to become ~d** sich akklimatisieren.

**accolade** ['ækəleɪd] *n (award)* Auszeichnung *f*; *(praise)* Lob *nt.*

**accommodate** [ə'kɒmədeɪt] *vt* **(a)** *(provide lodging for)* unterbringen. **(b)** *(hold, have room for)* Platz haben für. **(c)** *theory, plan, forecasts* Rechnung tragen *(+dat)*. **(d)** *(form: oblige)* dienen *(+dat)*; *wishes* entgegenkommen *(+dat)*.

**accommodating** [ə'kɒmədeɪtɪŋ] *adj* entgegenkommend.

**accommodation** [ə,kɒmə'deɪʃən] *n (US* **~s** *pl)* Unterkunft *f*; *(room also)* Zimmer *nt*; *(flat also)* Wohnung *f.* **"~"** „Fremdenzimmer"; **they found ~ in a youth hostel** sie kamen in einer Jugendherberge unter; **seating ~** Sitzplätze *pl.*

**accommodation: ~ address** *n* Briefkastenadresse *f*; **~ bureau** *or* **service** *n* Wohnungsvermittlung *f*; *(for rooms)* Zimmervermittlung *f.*

**accompaniment** [ə'kʌmpənɪmənt] *n* Begleitung *f (also Mus).*

**accompanist** [ə'kʌmpənɪst] *n* Begleiter(in *f*) *m.*

**accompany** [ə'kʌmpənɪ] *vt* begleiten *(also Mus).*

**accomplice** [ə'kʌmplɪs] *n* Komplize *m,* Komplizin *f.*

**accomplish** [ə'kʌmplɪʃ] *vt* schaffen. **he ~ed a great deal in his short career** er hat in der kurzen Zeit seines Wirkens Großes geleistet; **that didn't ~ anything** damit war nichts erreicht.

**accomplished** [ə'kʌmplɪʃt] *adj (skilled) player* fähig; *performance* vollendet.

**accomplishment** [ə'kʌmplɪʃmənt] *n (skill)* Fertigkeit *f*; *(achievement)* Leistung *f.*

**accord** [ə'kɔːd] **1** *n* Übereinstimmung, Einigkeit *f.* **of one's/its own ~** von selbst; **with one ~** geschlossen; *sing, cheer, say etc* wie aus einem Mund(e); **to be in ~ with sth** mit etw in Einklang sein. **2** *vt* gewähren *(sb sth* jdm etw*).*

**accordance** [ə'kɔːdəns] *n* **in ~ with** entsprechend *(+dat)*, gemäß *(+dat)*; **to be in ~ with sth** einer Sache *(dat)* entsprechen.

**accordingly** [ə'kɔːdɪŋlɪ] *adv (correspondingly)* (dem)entsprechend; *(so, therefore also)* folglich.

**according to** [ə'kɔːdɪŋ'tuː] *prep* entsprechend *(+dat)*, nach. **~ this** danach; **~ the map** der Karte nach; **~ Peter** laut Peter, Peter zufolge; **~ what he says** seiner Aussage nach; **we did it ~ the rules** wir haben uns an die Regeln gehalten.

**accordion** [ə'kɔːdɪən] *n* Akkordeon *nt.*

**accost** [ə'kɒst] *vt* ansprechen, anpöbeln *(pej).*

**account** [ə'kaʊnt] *n* **(a)** *(description)* Darstellung *f*; *(report also)* Bericht *m.* **to keep an ~ of one's expenses** über seine Ausgaben Buch führen; **by all ~s** nach allem, was man hört; **to give an ~ of sth** über etw *(acc)* Bericht erstatten; **to give an ~ of oneself** Rede und Antwort stehen; **to give a good ~ of oneself** sich bewähren.

**(b)** *(consideration)* **to take ~ of sb/sth, to take sb/ sth into ~** jdn/etw in Betracht ziehen; **to take no ~**

**of sb/sth, to leave sb/sth out of ~** jdn/etw außer Betracht lassen; **on no ~, not on any ~** auf (gar) keinen Fall; **on this/that ~** deshalb; **on ~ of him/the weather** seinetwegen/wegen des Wetters; **on my/ his/their ~** meinet-/seinet-/ihretwegen; **on one's own ~** für sich (selbst).

**(c)** *(benefit)* **to turn sth to (good) ~** (guten) Gebrauch von etw machen, etw (gut) nützen.

**(d)** *(importance)* **of no ~** ohne Bedeutung.

**(e)** *(Fin, Comm) (at bank, shop)* Konto *nt (with* bei*)*; *(bill)* Rechnung *f.* **to buy sth on ~** etw auf (Kunden)kredit kaufen; **please charge it to my ~** stellen Sie es mir bitte in Rechnung; **£50 on ~** £50 als Anzahlung; **~ holder** Kontoinhaber(in *f*) *m*; **~ number** Kontonummer *f*; **~s department** Buchhaltung *f*; *(of shop)* Kreditbüro *nt.*

**(f)** **~s** *pl (of company, club)* (Geschäfts)bücher *pl.* **to keep the ~s** die Bücher führen.

►**account for** *vi +prep obj* **(a)** *(explain)* erklären; *(give account of) actions, expenditure* Rechenschaft ablegen über *(+acc)*. **all the children were ~ed ~** man wußte, wo alle Kinder waren; **there's no ~ing ~ taste** über Geschmack läßt sich (nicht) streiten. **(b)** **this area alone ~s ~ some 25% of the population** allein in diesem Gebiet leben etwa 25% der Bevölkerung. **(c)** *(be cause of death, downfall)* zur Strecke bringen; *(illness)* fertigmachen, den Rest geben *(+dat).*

**accountability** [ə,kaʊntə'bɪlətɪ] *n* Verantwortlichkeit *f (to sb* jdm gegenüber*).*

**accountable** [ə'kaʊntəbl] *adj* verantwortlich *(to sb* jdm*).* **to hold sb ~ (for sth)** jdn (für etw) verantwortlich machen.

**accountancy** [ə'kaʊntənsɪ] *n* Buchhaltung *f.*

**accountant** [ə'kaʊntənt] *n* Buchhalter(in *f*) *m*; *(external financial adviser)* Wirtschaftsprüfer(in *f*) *m*; *(tax ~)* Steuerberater(in *f*) *m.*

**accounting** [ə'kaʊntɪŋ] *n* Buchhaltung *f.*

**accounting: ~ method** *n* Buchhaltungsverfahren *nt*; **~ period** *n* Abrechnungszeitraum *m.*

**accredited** [ə'kredɪtɪd] *adj* (offiziell) zugelassen.

**accrue** [ə'kruː] *vi* **(a)** *(accumulate)* sich ansammeln; *(Fin: interest)* auflaufen. **~d charges/interest** aufgelaufene Kosten/Zinsen *pl.* **(b)** **to ~ to sb** *(honour, costs etc)* jdm erwachsen *(geh) (from* aus*).*

**accumulate** [ə'kjuːmjʊleɪt] **1** *vt* ansammeln, anhäufen; *evidence* sammeln. **2** *vi* sich ansammeln; *(possessions, wealth also)* sich anhäufen; *(evidence)* sich häufen.

**accumulation** [ə,kjuːmjʊ'leɪʃən] *n see vi* Ansammlung *f*; Anhäufung *f*; Häufung *f.*

**accumulator** [ə'kjuːmjʊleɪtə'] *n* Akkumulator *m.*

**accuracy** ['ækjʊrəsɪ] *n* Genauigkeit *f.*

**accurate** ['ækjʊrɪt] *adj* genau. **his aim was ~** er hat genau gezielt.

**accusation** [,ækjʊ'zeɪʃən] *n* Anschuldigung *f*; *(Jur)* Anklage *f*; *(reproach)* Vorwurf *m.*

**accusative** [ə'kjuːzətɪv] *n* Akkusativ *m.*

**accuse** [ə'kjuːz] *vt* **(a)** *(Jur)* anklagen *(of* wegen, gen*).* **(b)** **to ~ sb of doing sth** jdn beschuldigen *or* bezichtigen, etw getan zu haben; **are you accusing me of lying?** willst du (damit) vielleicht sagen, daß ich lüge?; **to ~ sb of being untidy** *or* **of untidiness** jdm vorwerfen, unordentlich zu sein.

**accused** [ə'kjuːzd] *n* **the ~** der/die Angeklagte; die Angeklagten *pl.*

**accusing** [ə'kjuːzɪŋ] *adj* anklagend.

**accustom** [ə'kʌstəm] *vt* **to be ~ed to sth/to doing sth** an etw *(acc)* gewöhnt sein/gewöhnt sein, etw zu tun; **to become ~ed to sth/to doing sth** sich an etw *(acc)* gewöhnen/sich daran gewöhnen, etw zu tun.

**accustomed** [əˈkʌstəmd] *adj* gewohnt.

**AC/DC** = **alternating current/direct current** Allstrom(-).

**ace** [eɪs] **1** *n (Cards, Tennis, col: expert)* As *nt*. **the ~ of clubs** das Kreuzas; **he came within an ~ of winning** er hätte um ein Haar gesiegt. **2** *adj swimmer, reporter etc* Star-; **an ~ party** *(col)* eine tolle Party.

**acerbity** [əˈsɜːbɪtɪ] *n* Schärfe *f*.

**ache** [eɪk] **1** *n* Schmerz *m*. **I have an ~ in my side** ich habe Schmerzen in der Seite; **just a few little ~s and pains** nur ein paar Wehwehchen *(col)*. **2** *vi* **(a)** weh tun, schmerzen. **my head/stomach ~s** mir tut der Kopf/Bauch weh; **it makes my heart ~ to see him** *(fig)* es tut mir in der Seele weh, wenn ich ihn sehe. **(b)** *(fig: yearn)* **to ~ to do sth** sich danach sehnen, etw zu tun.

**achieve** [əˈtʃiːv] *vt* erreichen, schaffen; *success* erzielen; *victory* erringen; *rank also, title* erlangen. **she ~d a great deal** *(did a lot of work)* sie hat eine Menge geleistet; *(was quite successful)* sie hat viel erreicht.

**achievement** [əˈtʃiːvmənt] *n* **(a)** *(act) see vt* Erreichen *nt*; Erzielen *nt*; Erringen *nt*; Erlangen *nt*. **(b)** *(thing achieved)* Leistung *f*; *(of civilization, technology)* Errungenschaft *f*. **that's quite an ~!** das ist wirklich eine Leistung! *(also iro)*.

**achiever** [əˈtʃiːvəʳ] *n* Leistungstyp *m (col)*.

**acid** [ˈæsɪd] **1** *adj (sour, Chem)* sauer; *(fig)* ätzend. **~ rain** saurer Regen; **~ test** *(fig)* Feuerprobe *f*. **2** *n* **(a)** *(Chem)* Säure *f*. **(b)** *(col: drug)* Acid *nt*.

**acidity** [əˈsɪdɪtɪ] *n* Säure *f*; *(Chem)* Säuregehalt *m*.

**acknowledge** [əkˈnɒlɪdʒ] *vt* anerkennen; *truth, fault, defeat etc* eingestehen, zugeben; *(note receipt of) letter etc* bestätigen; *(respond to) greetings, cheers etc* erwidern. **to ~ oneself beaten** sich geschlagen geben; **to ~ sb's presence** jds Anwesenheit zur Kenntnis nehmen.

**acknowledged** [əkˈnɒlɪdʒd] *adj attr* anerkannt.

**acknowledgement** [əkˈnɒlɪdʒmənt] *n see vt* Anerkennung *f*; Eingeständnis *nt*; Bestätigung *f*; Erwiderung *f*. **in ~ of** in Anerkennung *(+gen)*.

**acme** [ˈækmɪ] *n* Höhepunkt, Gipfel *m*; *(of elegance etc)* Inbegriff *m*.

**acne** [ˈæknɪ] *n* Akne *f*.

**acorn** [ˈeɪkɔːn] *n* Eichel *f*.

**acoustic** [əˈkuːstɪk] *adj* akustisch. **~ guitar** Akustikgitarre *f*; **~ screen** (schalldämpfende) Trennwand.

**acoustics** [əˈkuːstɪks] *n sing or pl* Akustik *f*.

**acquaint** [əˈkweɪnt] *vt* **(a)** *(make familiar)* bekannt machen. **to be ~ed/thoroughly ~ed with sth** mit etw bekannt/vertraut sein; **to become ~ed with sth** etw kennenlernen; **to ~ oneself with sth** sich mit etw vertraut machen. **(b)** *(with person)* **to be ~ed with sb** mit jdm bekannt sein; **to become** *or* **get ~ed** sich (näher) kennenlernen.

**acquaintance** [əˈkweɪntəns] *n* **(a)** *(person)* Bekannte(r) *mf*. **(b)** *(with person)* Bekanntschaft *f*; *(with subject etc)* Kenntnis *f (with gen)*. **to make sb's ~** jds Bekanntschaft machen; **it improves on ~** man kommt mit der Zeit auf den Geschmack.

**acquiesce** [ˌækwɪˈes] *vi* einwilligen *(in* in +*acc)*; *(submissively)* sich fügen *(in dat)*.

**acquiescence** [ˌækwɪˈesns] *n see vi* Einwilligung *f (in* in +*acc)*; Fügung *f (in* in +*acc)*.

**acquiescent** [ˌækwɪˈesnt] *adj* fügsam.

**acquire** [əˈkwaɪəʳ] *vt* erwerben; *habit* annehmen. **to ~ a taste for sth** Geschmack an etw *(dat)* finden; **it's an ~d taste** das ist (nur) etwas für Kenner.

**acquisition** [ˌækwɪˈzɪʃən] *n* **(a)** *(act)* Erwerb *m*. **(b)** *(thing acquired)* Anschaffung *f*.

**acquisitive** [əˈkwɪzɪtɪv] *adj* auf Erwerb aus, habgie-

rig *(pej)*.

**acquit** [əˈkwɪt] **1** *vt* freisprechen. **2** *vr* **he ~ted himself well** er hat seine Sache gut gemacht.

**acquittal** [əˈkwɪtl] *n* Freispruch *m*.

**acre** [ˈeɪkəʳ] *n* ≈ Morgen *m*.

**acrid** [ˈækrɪd] *adj taste* bitter; *(of wine)* sauer; *comment, smoke* beißend.

**acrimonious** [ˌækrɪˈməʊnɪəs] *adj discussion, argument* erbittert; *person, words* bissig.

**acrimony** [ˈækrɪmənɪ] *n see* **acrimonious** erbitterte Schärfe; Bissigkeit *f*.

**acrobat** [ˈækrəbæt] *n* Akrobat(in *f*) *m*.

**acrobatic** [ˌækrəʊˈbætɪk] *adj* akrobatisch.

**acrobatics** [ˌækrəʊˈbætɪks] *npl* Akrobatik *f*.

**acronym** [ˈækrənɪm] *n* Akronym *nt*.

**across** [əˈkrɒs] **1** *adv* **(a)** *(direction) (to the other side)* hinüber; *(from the other side)* herüber; *(crosswise)* (quer)durch. **to cut sth ~** etw (quer) durchschneiden; **he was already ~** er war schon drüben; **~ from your house** gegenüber von eurem Haus; **the stripes go ~ the material** der Stoff ist quer gestreift. **(b)** *(measurement)* breit; *(of round object)* im Durchmesser. **how far is it ~?** wie groß ist der Durchmesser? **(c)** *(in crosswords)* waagerecht.

**2** *prep* **(a)** *(direction)* über *(+acc)*; *(diagonally ~)* quer durch *(+acc)*. **to run ~ the road** über die Straße laufen; **a tree fell ~ the path** ein Baum fiel quer über den Weg. **(b)** *(position)* über *(+dat)*. **a tree lay ~ the path** ein Baum lag quer über dem Weg; **from ~ the sea** von jenseits des Meeres *(geh)*, von der anderen Seite des Meeres; **he lives ~ the street from us** er wohnt uns gegenüber; **from ~ the hall** von der anderen Seite des Saals.

**across-the-board** [əˈkrɒsðəˈbɔːd] *adj attr* generell.

**acrylic** [əˈkrɪlɪk] **1** *n* Acryl *nt*. **2** *adj* Acryl-.

**act** [ækt] **1** *n* **(a)** *(deed, thing done)* Tat *f*; *(official, ceremonial)* Akt *m*. **an ~ of mercy** ein Gnadenakt *m*; **an ~ of God** höhere Gewalt *no pl*; **an ~ of folly/madness** reine Dummheit/reiner Wahnsinn. **(b)** **to be in the ~ of doing sth** (gerade) dabei sein, etw zu tun; **to catch sb in the ~** jdn auf frischer Tat ertappen. **(c)** *(of Parliament)* Gesetz *nt*. **(d)** *(Theat) (of play, opera)* Akt *m*; *(turn)* Nummer *f*. **to get in on the ~** *(fig col)* mit von der Partie sein; **he's got his ~ together** *(col)* er hat die Sache im Griff. **(e)** *(fig: pretence)* **it's all an ~** das ist alles nur Theater *or* Schau *(col)*.

**2** *vt part* spielen; *play* aufführen. **to ~ the fool** herumalbern, den Clown spielen.

**3** *vi* **(a)** *(Theat) (perform)* spielen; *(to be an actor, fig)* schauspielern, Theater spielen. **he's only ~ing** er tut (doch) nur so; **to ~ stupid/innocent** den Dummen/Unschuldigen spielen *or* markieren *(col)*. **(b)** *(function) (brakes etc)* funktionieren; *(drug)* wirken. **to ~ as ...** wirken als ...; *(have function)* fungieren als ...; **it ~s as a deterrent** das wirkt abschreckend. **(c)** *(represent)* **to ~ for sb** jdn vertreten. **(d)** *(behave)* sich verhalten. **~ like a man!** sei ein Mann!; **she ~ed as though she was surprised** sie tat so, als ob sie überrascht wäre. **(e)** *(take action)* handeln. **he ~ed to stop it** er unternahm Schritte, um dem ein Ende zu machen.

►**act on** *or* **upon** *vi +prep obj* **(a)** *(affect)* wirken auf *(+acc)*. **(b)** *(take action on) warning, report* handeln auf *(+acc)* ... hin; *suggestion, advice* folgen *(+dat)*.

►**act out** *vt sep fantasies etc* durchspielen. **the affair was ~ed ~ at ...** die Affäre spielte sich in ... ab.

►**act up** *vi (col) (bad knee etc)* Ärger machen; *(person also)* Theater machen *(col)*; *(to attract attention)* sich aufspielen; *(machine also)* verrückt spie-

len _(col)._
**acting** ['æktɪŋ] **1** _adj_ **(a)** stellvertretend _attr._ **(b)** _attr_ _(Theat)_ schauspielerisch. **2** _n (Theat: profession)_ Schauspielerei _f._ **what was the/his** ~ **like?** wie waren die Schauspieler/wie hat er gespielt?; **I didn't like his** ~ ich mochte seine Art zu spielen nicht.

**action** ['ækʃən] _n_ **(a)** _no pl (activity)_ Handeln _nt_; _(of play, novel etc)_ Handlung _f._ **now is the time for** ~ die Zeit zum Handeln ist gekommen; **a man of** ~ ein Mann der Tat; **to take** ~ etwas _or_ Schritte unternehmen; **course of** ~ Vorgehen _nt._
  **(b)** _(deed)_ Tat _f._ **to suit the** ~ **to the word** dem Wort die Tat folgen lassen.
  **(c)** _(motion, operation)_ **in/out of** ~ _(machine)_ in/außer Betrieb; _(operational)_ einsatzfähig/nicht einsatzfähig; **to go into** ~ in Aktion treten; **to put a plan into** ~ einen Plan in die Tat umsetzen; **to put out of** ~ außer Gefecht setzen.
  **(d)** _(exciting events)_ Action _f (col)._ **a novel full of** ~ ein handlungsgeladener Roman; **to go where the** ~ **is** _(col)_ hingehen, wo was los ist _(col)._
  **(e)** _(Mil) (fighting)_ Aktionen _pl_; _(battle)_ Kampf _m_, Gefecht _nt._ **enemy** ~ feindliche Handlungen _or_ Aktionen _pl_; **killed in** ~ gefallen; **he saw** ~ **in the desert** er war in der Wüste im Einsatz; **they never went into** ~ sie kamen nie zum Einsatz.
  **(f)** _(way of operating) (of machine)_ Arbeitsweise _f_; _(of piano etc)_ Mechanik _f_; _(of watch, gun)_ Mechanismus _m_; _(way of moving: of athlete etc)_ Bewegung _f._ **to move with** _or_ **have an easy** ~ _(Sport)_ sich ganz leicht und locker bewegen.
  **(g)** _(esp Chem, Phys: effect)_ Wirkung _f (on_ auf _+acc)._
  **(h)** _(Jur)_ Klage _f._ **to bring an** ~ **(against sb)** eine Klage (gegen jdn) anstrengen.
**actionable** ['ækʃnəbl] _adj_ verfolgbar; _statement_ klagbar.
**action:** ~ **group** _n_ Initiative _f_; ~-**packed** _adj film, book_ aktions- _or_ handlungsgeladen; ~ **replay** _n_ Wiederholung _f._
**activate** ['æktɪveɪt] _vt_ betätigen; _(automatically) alarm etc_ auslösen; _(lever)_ in Gang setzen.
**active** ['æktɪv] _adj_ aktiv; _(also Gram)_; _mind, social life_ rege; _volcano also_ tätig; _dislike_ offen. **to be** ~ **in politics** politisch aktiv _or_ tätig sein; **to be under** ~ **consideration** ernsthaft erwogen werden; **on** ~ **service** _(Mil)_ im Einsatz; **he played an** ~ **part in it** er war aktiv daran beteiligt; ~ **partner** _(Comm)_ persönlich haftender Gesellschafter.
**actively** ['æktɪvlɪ] _adv_ aktiv.
**activist** ['æktɪvɪst] _n_ Aktivist(in _f_) _m._
**activity** [æk'tɪvɪtɪ] _n_ **(a)** _no pl_ Aktivität _f_; _(in classroom, station, on beach etc also)_ reges Leben; _(in market, town, office)_ Geschäftigkeit _f._ **sphere of** ~ Betätigungsfeld _nt._ **(b)** _(pastime)_ Betätigung _f._ **the church organizes many activities** die Kirche organisiert viele Veranstaltungen; **business/social activities** geschäftliche/gesellschaftliche Unternehmungen _pl._
**actor** ['æktər] _n (lit, fig)_ Schauspieler _m._
**actress** ['æktrɪs] _n (lit, fig)_ Schauspielerin _f._
**actual** ['æktjʊəl] _adj_ eigentlich; _reason, price also, result_ tatsächlich; _case, example_ konkret. **in** ~ **fact** eigentlich; **what were his** ~ **words?** was hat er genau gesagt?; **this is the** ~ **house** das ist hier das Haus.
**actuality** [,æktjʊ'ælɪtɪ] _n (reality)_ Wirklichkeit _f._
**actually** ['æktjʊəlɪ] _adv_ **(a)** _(to tell the truth, in actual fact)_ eigentlich; _(by the way)_ übrigens. **you don't know him, do you?** — ~ **I do** Sie kennen ihn (doch) nicht, oder? — doch, ich kenne ihn (tatsächlich); **I'm going soon, tomorrow** ~ ich gehe bald, genauer

gesagt morgen; **you're never home** — ~ **I was home last night** du bist nie zu Hause — doch, gestern abend war ich da. **(b)** _(truly, in reality, showing surprise)_ tatsächlich. **don't tell me you're** ~ **going now!** sag bloß, du gehst jetzt tatsächlich _or_ wirklich!; **oh, you're** ~ **in!** oh, du bist sogar da!; **I wasn't** ~ **there, but** ... ich war zwar selbst nicht dabei, aber ...; **as for** ~ **working** ... was die Arbeit selbst betrifft ...
**actuary** ['æktjʊərɪ] _n (Insur)_ Aktuar _m._
**actuate** ['æktjʊeɪt] _vt (lit)_ auslösen; _(fig)_ treiben.
**acuity** [ə'kju:ɪtɪ] _n_ Scharfsinn _m._
**acumen** ['ækjʊmen] _n_ Scharfsinn _m._ **business/political** ~ Geschäftssinn _m_/politische Klugheit.
**acupuncture** ['ækjʊ,pʌŋktʃər] _n_ Akupunktur _f._
**acute** [ə'kju:t] _adj_ **(a)** _(intense, serious, Med)_ akut; _pleasure_ intensiv. **(b)** _eyesight_ scharf; _hearing also, sense of smell_ fein. **(c)** _(shrewd)_ scharf; _person_ scharfsinnig; _child_ aufgeweckt. **(d)** _(Math) angle_ spitz.
**acutely** [ə'kju:tlɪ] _adv_ **(a)** _(intensely)_ akut; _feel_ intensiv; _embarrassed, uncomfortable_ äußerst. **(b)** _(shrewdly)_ scharfsinnig; _observe_ scharf.
**acuteness** [ə'kju:tnɪs] _n_ **(a)** _(of problem)_ Dringlichkeit _f._ **(b)** _see adj (b)_ Schärfe _f_; Feinheit _f._ **(c)** _see adj (c)_ Schärfe _f_; Scharfsinn _m_; Aufgewecktheit _f._
**AD** = **Anno Domini** A.D., a.D.
**ad** [æd] = **advertisement** Anzeige _f_, Inserat _nt._ **small** ~**s** Kleinanzeigen _pl._
**Adam** ['ædəm] _n_ Adam _m._ ~**'s apple** Adamsapfel _m_; **I don't know him from** ~ _(col)_ ich habe keine Ahnung, wer er ist _(col)._
**adamant** ['ædəmənt] _adj_ hart. **since you're** ~ da Sie darauf bestehen; **he was** ~ **about going** er bestand hartnäckig darauf zu gehen.
**adapt** [ə'dæpt] **1** _vt_ anpassen _(to_ dat_)_; _machine_ umstellen _(to, for_ auf _+acc)_; _vehicle, building_ umbauen _(to, for_ für_)_; _text, book etc_ adaptieren, bearbeiten _(for_ für_)._ **2** _vi_ sich anpassen _(to_ dat_)._
**adaptability** [ə,dæptə'bɪlɪtɪ] _n see adj_ Anpassungsfähigkeit _f_; Vielseitigkeit _f_; Flexibilität _f._
**adaptable** [ə'dæptəbl] _adj person_ anpassungsfähig; _vehicle_ vielseitig; _schedule_ flexibel.
**adaptation** [,ædæp'teɪʃən] _n (process)_ Adaptation _f (to_ an _+acc)_; _(of person, plant, animal)_ Anpassung _f (to_ an _+acc)_; _(of machine)_ Umstellung _f (to_ auf _+acc)_; _(of vehicle, building)_ Umbau _m_; _(of text)_ Bearbeitung _f._ ~ **for television** Fernsehbearbeitung _f._
**adapter, adaptor** [ə'dæptər] _n_ **(a)** _(of text)_ Bearbeiter(in _f_) _m._ **(b)** _(Elec)_ Adapter _m_; _(for two/three plugs)_ Doppel-/Dreifachstecker _m_; _(for several plugs)_ Mehrfachstecker _m._
**add** [æd] **1** _vt_ **(a)** _(Math)_ addieren; _(~ up)_ several numbers _also_ zusammenzählen. **(b)** hinzufügen _(to_ zu_)_; _ingredients, money also_ dazutun _(to_ zu_)_; _(say in addition also)_ dazusagen; _(build on)_ anbauen. ~**ed to which** ... hinzu kommt, daß ... **2** _vi (Math)_ addieren.
  ►**add to** _vi +prep obj (expand) collection_ erweitern; _(increase) problems_ vergrößern; _(improve) flavour_ steigern, verfeinern.
  ►**add up 1** _vt sep_ zusammenzählen. **2** _vi_ **(a)** _(figures etc)_ stimmen; _(fig: make sense)_ zusammenpassen. **it's beginning to** ~ jetzt wird so manches klar. **(b)** **to** ~ **to** _(column, figures, fig)_ ergeben; _(expenses also)_ sich belaufen auf _(+acc)_; **it doesn't** ~ ~ **to much** _(fig)_ das ist nicht berühmt _(col)._
**adder** ['ædər] _n_ Natter _f._
**addict** ['ædɪkt] _n (lit, fig)_ Süchtige(r) _mf._ **he's a TV/heroin** ~ er ist fernseh-/heroinsüchtig.

**addicted** [ə'dɪktɪd] *adj* süchtig. **to be/become ~ to heroin** heroinsüchtig sein/werden; **he's ~ to it** *(fig)* das ist bei ihm schon zur Sucht geworden.

**addiction** [ə'dɪkʃən] *n* Sucht *f (to* nach*); (no pl: state of dependence also)* Süchtigkeit *f.* ~ **to alcohol** Trunksucht *f.*

**addictive** [ə'dɪktɪv] *adj* suchterzeugend. ~ **drug** Suchtdroge *f.* **to be ~** *(lit)* süchtig machen; *(fig)* zu einer Sucht werden können.

**adding machine** ['ædɪŋməʃiːn] *n* Addiermaschine *f.*

**Addis Ababa** [ædɪs'æbəbə] *n* Addis Abeba *nt.*

**addition** [ə'dɪʃən] *n* **(a)** *(Math)* Addition *f.* **the ~ of one more country to the EC** die Erweiterung der EG um ein weiteres Land. **(b)** *(thing added)* Zusatz *m (to* zu*); (to list)* Ergänzung *f (to* zu*).* **they are expecting an ~ to their family** *(col)* sie erwarten (Familien)zuwachs. **(c) in ~** außerdem, obendrein; **in ~ to sth** zusätzlich zu etw.

**additional** [ə'dɪʃənl] *adj* zusätzlich. ~ **charge** Aufpreis *m;* **an ~ chapter** ein weiteres Kapitel.

**additive** ['ædɪtɪv] *n* Zusatz *m.*

**add-on** ['ædɒn] *n (Tech, Comp etc)* Zusatz *m.*

**address** [ə'dres] **1** *n* **(a)** *(also Comp)* Adresse *f.* **home ~** Privatadresse *f; (when travelling)* Heimatanschrift *f.* **(b)** *(speech)* Ansprache *f.* **(c) form of ~** (Form *f* der) Anrede *f.* **2** *vt* **(a)** *letter, parcel* adressieren *(to an +acc).* **(b)** *(direct) complaints, speech, remarks* richten *(to an +acc).* **(c)** *(speak to) meeting* sprechen zu; *jury* sich wenden an *(+acc); person* anreden. **3** *vr* **to ~ oneself to sb** *(speak to)* jdn ansprechen; **to ~ oneself to a task** *(form)* sich einer Aufgabe widmen.

**address book** *n* Adreßbuch *nt.*

**addressee** [ˌædre'siː] *n* Empfänger(in *f) m.*

**address label** *n* Adressenaufkleber *m.*

**Aden** ['eɪdn] *n* Aden *nt.* **Gulf of ~** Golf *m* von Aden.

**adenoids** ['ædɪnɔɪdz] *npl* Rachenmandeln *pl.*

**adept** ['ædept] *adj* geschickt *(in, at* in *+dat).* **she's quite ~ at that** sie hat ein Talent dafür.

**adequate** ['ædɪkwɪt] *adj* adäquat, angemessen; *(sufficient) supply, heating system* ausreichend; *time* genügend *inv.* **to be ~** *(sufficient)* (aus)reichen; *(good enough)* angemessen sein; **this is just not ~** das ist einfach unzureichend.

**adhere** [əd'hɪər] *vi* haften *(to an +dat).*
▶**adhere to** *vi +prep obj* festhalten an *(+dat).*

**adherence** [əd'hɪərəns] *n* Festhalten *nt (to an +dat).*

**adherent** [əd'hɪərənt] *n* Anhänger(in *f) m (of gen).*

**adhesive** [əd'hiːzɪv] **1** *n* Klebstoff *m.* **2** *adj* haftend; *(more firmly)* klebend. ~ **label** Klebeetikett *nt;* ~ **plaster** Heftpflaster *nt;* ~ **tape** Klebstreifen *m.*

**ad hoc** [ˌæd'hɒk] *adj, adv* ad hoc *inv.*

**adjacent** [ə'dʒeɪsənt] *adj* angrenzend; *room also, angles* Neben-. **to be ~ to sth** an etw *(acc)* angrenzen, neben etw *(dat)* liegen.

**adjective** ['ædʒektɪv] *n* Adjektiv, Eigenschaftswort *nt.*

**adjoin** [ə'dʒɔɪn] **1** *vt* grenzen an *(+acc).* **2** *vi* aneinander grenzen.

**adjoining** [ə'dʒɔɪnɪŋ] *adj room* Neben-, Nachbar-; *field* angrenzend; *(of two things)* nebeneinanderliegend. **in the ~ office** im Büro nebenan.

**adjourn** [ə'dʒɜːn] **1** *vt* **(a)** vertagen *(until* auf *+acc).* **he ~ed the meeting for three hours** er unterbrach die Konferenz für drei Stunden. **(b)** *(US: end)* beenden. **2** *vi* **(a)** sich vertagen *(until* auf *+acc).* **to ~ for lunch/one hour** für die Mittagspause/für eine Stunde unterbrechen. **(b) to ~ to the lounge** sich ins Wohnzimmer begeben.

**adjournment** [ə'dʒɜːnmənt] *n* Vertagung *f (until* auf *+acc); (within a day)* Unterbrechung *f.*

**adjudge** [ə'dʒʌdʒ] *vt* **to ~ sb (to be) guilty/the winner** jdn für schuldig/zum Sieger erklären.

**adjudicate** [ə'dʒuːdɪkeɪt] **1** *vt claim* entscheiden; *competition* Preisrichter sein bei. **2** *vi* entscheiden, urteilen *(on, in* bei*); (in dispute)* Schiedsrichter sein *(on* bei, in *+dat); (in competition, dog-show etc)* als Preisrichter fungieren.

**adjudicator** [ə'dʒuːdɪkeɪtər] *n (in competition)* Preisrichter(in *f) m; (in dispute)* Schiedsrichter(in *f) m.*

**adjust** [ə'dʒʌst] **1** *vt (set) machine, carburettor, brakes, knob etc* einstellen; *(alter) plan, terms* ändern; *height, speed* verstellen; *(correct, readjust)* nachstellen; *height, speed, flow* regulieren; *hat, tie* zurechtrücken. **to ~ sth to new requirements/conditions** etw neuen Erfordernissen/Bedingungen anpassen. **2** *vi (to new circumstances)* sich anpassen *(to dat); (to new requirements, demands)* sich einstellen *(to* auf *+acc).*

**adjustable** [ə'dʒʌstəbl] *adj tool, angle* verstellbar; *shape* veränderlich, variabel; *speed, temperature* regulierbar; *tax, rate of production* beweglich, flexibel; *person, animal, plant* anpassungsfähig. ~ **spanner** Engländer *m.*

**adjustment** [ə'dʒʌstmənt] *n* **(a)** *see vt* Einstellung *f;* Änderung *f;* Verstellen *nt;* Nachstellen *nt;* Regulierung *f.* **to make an ~ to sth** etw einstellen/verstellen/nachstellen *etc;* **to make ~s** Änderungen vornehmen. **(b)** *(socially etc)* Anpassung *f.*

**ad-lib** [æd'lɪb] **1** *adv* aus dem Stegreif. **2** *adj* improvisiert, Stegreif-. **3** *vti* improvisieren.

**Adm** = **Admiral** Adm.

**admin** ['ædmɪn] *(col)* = **administration. a lot of ~** viel Verwaltungsarbeit.

**administer** [əd'mɪnɪstər] *vt* **(a)** *institution, funds* verwalten; *business, affairs* führen; *(run) company, department* die Verwaltungsangelegenheiten regeln *(+gen).* **(b)** *(to sb* jdm*) medicine* verabreichen; *sacraments* spenden. **to ~ an oath to sb** jdm einen Eid abnehmen.

**administration** [ədˌmɪnɪs'treɪʃən] *n* **(a)** *no pl* Verwaltung *f; (of a project etc)* Organisation *f.* **(b) the Kohl ~** die Regierung Kohl. **(c)** *no pl (of remedy)* Verabreichung *f; (of sacrament)* Spenden *nt.* **the ~ of an oath** die Vereidigung; **the ~ of justice** die Rechtsprechung.

**administrative** [əd'mɪnɪstrətɪv] *adj* administrativ.

**administrator** [əd'mɪnɪstreɪtər] *n* Verwalter *m.*

**admirable** ['ædmərəbl] *adj* bewundernswert, erstaunlich; *(excellent)* ausgezeichnet.

**admiral** ['ædmərəl] *n* Admiral *m.*

**Admiralty** ['ædmərəltɪ] *n (Brit)* Marineministerium *nt.*

**admiration** [ˌædmə'reɪʃən] *n* Bewunderung *f.*

**admire** [əd'maɪər] *vt* bewundern.

**admirer** [əd'maɪərər] *n* Bewunderer(in *f) m; (dated, hum: of a woman)* Verehrer *m.*

**admissible** [əd'mɪsəbl] *adj* zulässig.

**admission** [əd'mɪʃən] *n* **(a)** *(entry)* Zutritt *m (to* zu*); (to club also, university)* Zulassung *f; (price)* Eintritt *m; (to hospital)* Einlieferung *f (to* in *+acc).* **(b)** *(confession)* Eingeständnis *nt.* **by his own ~** nach eigenem Eingeständnis; **that would be an ~ of failure** das hieße, sein Versagen einzugestehen.

**admission:** ~ **charge,** ~ **fee** *n* Eintrittsgeld *nt;* ~ **ticket** *n* Eintrittskarte *f.*

**admit** [əd'mɪt] *vt* **(a)** *(let in)* hinein-/hereinlassen; *(permit to join)* zulassen *(to* zu*),* aufnehmen *(to* in *+acc).* **to be ~ted to hospital** ins Krankenhaus eingeliefert werden; **children not ~ted** kein Zutritt für Kinder. **(b)** *(acknowledge)* zugeben. **he ~ted himself beaten** er gab sich geschlagen.

**admittance** [əd'mɪtəns] n (to building) Zutritt (to zu). "no ~" „Zutritt verboten".
**admittedly** [əd'mɪtɪdlɪ] adv zugegebenermaßen.
**admonish** [əd'mɒnɪʃ] vt ermahnen (for wegen).
**ad nauseam** [ˌæd'nɔːsɪæm] adv bis zum Überdruß, bis zum Gehtnichtmehr (col).
**ado** [ə'duː] n without further ~ ohne weiteres.
**adolescence** [ˌædəʊ'lesns] n Jugend f; (puberty) Pubertät f.
**adolescent** [ˌædəʊ'lesnt] 1 n Jugendliche(r) mf. 2 adj Jugend-; (in puberty) Pubertäts-; (immature) unreif. he is so ~ er steckt noch in der Pubertät.
**adopt** [ə'dɒpt] vt (a) child adoptieren; family, city, child in a different country die Patenschaft übernehmen für. your cat has ~ed me (col) deine Katze hat sich mir angeschlossen. (b) suggestion, method übernehmen; mannerisms annehmen. (c) (Pol) motion annehmen; candidate nominieren.
**adopted** [ə'dɒptɪd] adj son, daughter Adoptiv-, adoptiert. ~ country Wahlheimat f.
**adoption** [ə'dɒpʃən] n (a) (of child) Adoption f; (into the family) Aufnahme f. (b) (of method, idea) Übernahme f; (of mannerisms, law, candidate) Annahme f.
**adorable** [ə'dɔːrəbl] adj bezaubernd, hinreißend.
**adoration** [ˌædə'reɪʃən] n (grenzenlose) Liebe (of zu); (of God) Anbetung f.
**adore** [ə'dɔːʳ] vt über alles lieben.
**adorn** [ə'dɔːn] vt schmücken.
**adrenalin(e)** [ə'drenəlɪn] n Adrenalin nt. when the ~'s going ... wenn man richtig aufgedreht ist ...
**Adriatic (Sea)** [ˌeɪdrɪ'ætɪk('siː)] n Adria f.
**adrift** [ə'drɪft] adv, adj pred to be ~ (Naut) treiben; to come ~ (wire, hair etc) sich lösen; (plans) fehlschlagen; (theory) zusammenbrechen.
**adroit** [ə'drɔɪt] adj gewandt; mind scharf.
**adulation** [ˌædjʊ'leɪʃən] n Verherrlichung f.
**adult** ['ædʌlt] 1 n Erwachsene(r) mf. 2 adj person erwachsen; film für Erwachsene; (mature) decision reif. ~ education Erwachsenenbildung f.
**adulterate** [ə'dʌltəreɪt] vt drink panschen; food, (fig) text verhunzen (col).
**adulterer** [ə'dʌltərəʳ] n Ehebrecher m.
**adulteress** [ə'dʌltərɪs] n Ehebrecherin f.
**adultery** [ə'dʌltərɪ] n Ehebruch m. to commit ~ Ehebruch begehen.
**adulthood** ['ædʌlthʊd] n Erwachsenenalter nt.
**advance** [əd'vɑːns] 1 n (a) (progress) Fortschritt m. (b) (of science) Weiterentwicklung f; (of ideas, sea) Vordringen nt. recent ~s jüngste Entwicklungen; with the ~ of old age mit fortschreitendem Alter. (c) (Mil) Vorrücken nt. (d) (money) Vorschuß m (on auf +acc). (e) (amorous, fig) ~s pl Annäherungsversuche pl. (f) in ~ im voraus; (temporal also) vorher; to send sb on in ~ jdn vorausschicken; to arrive in ~ of the others vor den anderen ankommen.
2 vt (a) (move forward) date, time vorverlegen. (b) (further) work, project voranbringen; cause, interests fördern; growth vorantreiben. (c) suggestion, opinion vorbringen. (d) (pay beforehand) (sb jdm) (als) Vorschuß geben, vorschießen (col); (lend) als Kredit geben.
3 vi (a) (Mil) vorrücken. (b) (move forward) vorankommen. to ~ towards sb/sth auf jdn/etw zugehen/-kommen; to ~ upon sb drohend auf jdn zukommen. (c) (fig: progress) Fortschritte machen.
**advance booking** n Reservierung f; (Theat) Vorverkauf m.
**advanced** [əd'vɑːnst] adj student, level, age fortgeschritten; studies, mathematics etc höher; tech-

nology also, ideas fortschrittlich; version, model verbessert, neu(er); level of civilization hoch; position, observation post etc vorgeschoben. ~ in years in fortgeschrittenem Alter.
**advancement** [əd'vɑːnsmənt] n (furtherance) Förderung f.
**advance:** ~ notice or warning n Vorankündigung f; (of sth bad) Vorwarnung f; ~ party n (Mil, fig) Vorhut f; ~ payment n Vorauszahlung f.
**advantage** [əd'vɑːntɪdʒ] n Vorteil m (also Tennis). to have an ~ (over sb) (jdm gegenüber) im Vorteil sein; he had the ~ of greater experience er war durch seine größere Erfahrung im Vorteil; that gives you an ~ over me damit sind Sie mir gegenüber im Vorteil; to take ~ of sb/sth jdn/etw ausnutzen; he took ~ of her (euph) er hat sie mißbraucht; to turn sth to (good) ~ Nutzen aus etw ziehen; it would be to our ~ es wäre vorteilhaft für uns.
**advantageous** [ˌædvən'teɪdʒəs] adj vorteilhaft.
**advent** ['ædvənt] n (a) (of era) Beginn, Anbruch m; (of new invention etc) Aufkommen nt. (b) (Eccl) A~ Advent m.
**adventure** [əd'ventʃəʳ] n Abenteuer nt. an ~ into the unknown ein Vorstoß ins Unbekannte.
**adventurer** [əd'ventʃərəʳ] n Abenteurer(in f) m.
**adventurous** [əd'ventʃərəs] adj person abenteuerlustig; journey abenteuerlich; scheme gewagt.
**adverb** ['ædvɜːb] n Adverb, Umstandswort nt.
**adverbial** adj, ~ly adv [əd'vɜːbɪəl, -i] adverbial.
**adversary** ['ædvəsərɪ] n Widersacher(in f) m; (in contest) Gegner(in f) m.
**adverse** ['ædvɜːs] adj ungünstig; criticism, comment, reaction negativ; effect nachteilig.
**adversity** [əd'vɜːsɪtɪ] n no pl Not f. in ~ im Unglück, in der Not.
**advert** ['ædvɜːt] n (Brit) = advertisement.
**advertise** ['ædvətaɪz] vti (a) (publicize) Werbung or Reklame machen (für), werben (für). (b) (in paper etc) flat, table etc inserieren; job, post also ausschreiben. to ~ for sb/sth jdn/etw (per Anzeige) suchen.
**advertisement** [əd'vɜːtɪsmənt] n (a) (Comm) Werbung, Reklame f no pl; (in paper also) Anzeige f. he is not a good ~ for his school (fig) er ist nicht gerade ein Aushängeschild für seine Schule. (b) (announcement) Anzeige f; (in paper also) Inserat nt. to put an ~ in the paper (for sb/sth) eine Anzeige (für jdn/etw) in die Zeitung setzen.
**advertiser** ['ædvətaɪzəʳ] n (in paper) Inserent(in f) m.
**advertising** ['ædvətaɪzɪŋ] n Werbung, Reklame f. he is in ~ er ist in der Werbung (tätig).
**advertising** in cpds Werbe-; ~ agency n Werbeagentur f; ~ campaign n Werbekampagne f; ~ rates pl Anzeigenpreise pl.
**advice** [əd'vaɪs] n (a) no pl Rat m no pl. a piece of ~, some ~ ein Rat(schlag) m; to take sb's ~ jds Rat (be)folgen; take my ~ hör auf mich. (b) (Comm) Mitteilung f. ~ note (Brit) Benachrichtigung f.
**advisable** [əd'vaɪzəbl] adj ratsam.
**advise** [əd'vaɪz] vti (a) (give advice to) raten (+dat); (professionally) beraten. to ~ caution zur Vorsicht raten; I would ~ you to do it/not to do it ich würde dir zuraten/abraten; to ~ sb against sth/doing sth jdm von etw abraten/jdm abraten, etw zu tun. (b) (Comm: inform) verständigen. to ~ sb of sth jdn von etw in Kenntnis setzen.
**advisedly** [əd'vaɪzɪdlɪ] adv richtig. and I use the word ~ ich verwende bewußt dieses Wort.
**adviser** [əd'vaɪzəʳ] n Ratgeber(in f) m; (professional) Berater(in f) m.

**advisory** [əd'vaɪzərɪ] *adj* beratend. ~ **service** Beratungsdienst *m*; **to act in a purely ~ capacity** rein beratende Funktion haben.

**advocacy** ['ædvəkəsɪ] *n* Eintreten *nt (of für)*; *(of plan)* Befürwortung *f*.

**advocate** ['ædvəkɪt] **1** *n* **(a)** *(of cause etc)* Verfechter(in *f*), Befürworter(in *f*) *m*. **(b)** *(esp Scot: Jur)* (Rechts)anwalt *m*/-anwältin *f*. **2** ['ædvəkeɪt] *vt* eintreten für; *plan etc* befürworten.

**advt** = **advertisement**.

**Aegean** [iː'dʒiːən] *n* **the ~ (Sea)** das Ägäische Meer.

**aerate** ['ɛəreɪt] *vt liquid* mit Kohlensäure anreichern; *soil* auflockern.

**aerial** ['ɛərɪəl] **1** *n (esp Brit)* Antenne *f*. **2** *adj* Luft-.

**aerial:** ~ **photograph** *n* Luftbild *nt*, Luftaufnahme *f*; ~ **photography** *n* Luftaufnahmen *pl*.

**aero-** ['ɛərəʊ] *pref* aero- *(form)*, Luft-.

**aerobatics** ['ɛərəʊ'bætɪks] *npl* Kunstfliegen *nt*.

**aerobics** [ɛər'əʊbɪks] *n sing* Aerobic *nt*.

**aerodrome** ['ɛərədrəʊm] *n (Brit)* Flugplatz *m*.

**aerodynamic** ['ɛərəʊdaɪ'næmɪk] *adj* aerodynamisch.

**aerodynamics** ['ɛərəʊdaɪ'næmɪks] *n sing* Aerodynamik *f*.

**aerofoil** ['ɛərəʊfɔɪl] *n* Tragflügel *m*; *(on racing cars)* Spoiler *m*.

**aeronautic(al)** [ˌɛərə'nɔːtɪk(əl)] *adj* Luftfahrt-. ~ **engineering** Flugzeugbau *m*.

**aeronautics** [ˌɛərə'nɔːtɪks] *n sing* Luftfahrt *f*.

**aeroplane** ['ɛərəpleɪn] *n (Brit)* Flugzeug *nt*.

**aerosol** ['ɛərəsɒl] *n (can)* Spraydose *f*; *(mixture)* Aerosol *nt*.

**aerospace** *in cpds* Raumfahrt-.

**aesthete,** *(US)* **esthete** ['iːsθiːt] *n* Ästhet(in *f*) *m*.

**aesthetic,** *(US)* **esthetic** [iːs'θetɪk] *adj* ästhetisch.

**aesthetics,** *(US)* **esthetics** [iːs'θetɪks] *n sing* Ästhetik *f*.

**AEU** = **Amalgamated Engineering Union** *britische Ingenieurgewerkschaft*.

**afar** [ə'faːr] *adv (liter)* weit. **from ~** aus der Ferne.

**affable** ['æfəbl] *adj* umgänglich, freundlich.

**affair** [ə'fɛər] *n* **(a)** Sache, Angelegenheit *f*. **the Watergate ~** die Watergate-Affäre; **the state of ~s with the economy** die Lage der Wirtschaft; **in the present state of ~s** beim gegenwärtigen Stand der Dinge; **there's a fine state of ~s!** das sind ja schöne Zustände!; **private/business ~s** Privat-/Geschäftsangelegenheiten *pl*; **~s of state** Staatsangelegenheiten *pl*; **it's not your ~ what I do in the evenings** was ich abends tue, geht dich nichts an; **that's my/his ~!** das ist meine/seine Sache! **(b)** *(love ~)* Verhältnis *nt*, Affäre *f*.

**affect**[1] [ə'fekt] *vt* **(a)** *(have effect on)* sich auswirken auf *(+acc)*; *decision, sb's life also* beeinflussen; *health, person* schaden *(+dat)*. **(b)** *(concern)* betreffen. **(c)** *(emotionally)* berühren.

**affect**[2] *vt (feign)* vortäuschen, vorgeben.

**affectation** [ˌæfek'teɪʃən] *n (pretence)* Vortäuschung *f*; *(artificiality)* Affektiertheit *f no pl*.

**affected** [ə'fektɪd] *adj person, clothes* affektiert; *behaviour, style, accent also* gekünstelt.

**affection** [ə'fekʃən] *n (fondness)* Zuneigung *f no pl (for, towards zu)*. **I have a great ~ for her** ich mag sie sehr gerne; **you could show a little more ~ towards me** du könntest etwas liebevoller (zu mir) sein; **children who lacked ~** Kinder, denen die Liebe fehlte.

**affectionate** [ə'fekʃənɪt] *adj* liebevoll, zärtlich.

**affidavit** [ˌæfɪ'deɪvɪt] *n (Jur)* eidesstattliche Versicherung.

**affiliated** [ə'fɪlɪeɪtɪd] *adj* angeschlossen, Schwester-.

**affiliation** [əˌfɪlɪ'eɪʃən] *n* Angliederung *f (to, with* an

*+acc)*. **what are his political ~s?** was ist seine politische Zugehörigkeit?

**affinity** [ə'fɪnɪtɪ] *n* **(a)** *(liking)* Neigung *f (for, to* zu*)*; *(for person)* Verbundenheit *f (for, to* mit*)*. **(b)** *(resemblance, connection)* Verwandtschaft *f*.

**affirm** [ə'fɜːm] *vt* versichern; *(very forcefully)* beteuern.

**affirmation** [ˌæfə'meɪʃən] *n see vt* Versicherung *f*; Beteuerung *f*.

**affirmative** [ə'fɜːmətɪv] *adj* bejahend, positiv. **to answer in the ~** bejahend *or* mit „ja" antworten.

**affix** [ə'fɪks] *vt* anbringen *(to* auf *+dat)*.

**afflict** [ə'flɪkt] *vt* plagen, zusetzen *(+dat)*; *(emotionally, mentally also)* belasten; *(troubles, inflation, injuries)* heimsuchen. **the ~ed** die Leidenden *pl*.

**affliction** [ə'flɪkʃən] *n (distress)* Not *f*; *(pain)* Leiden *pl*; *(illness)* Beschwerde *f*.

**affluence** ['æflʊəns] *n* Reichtum, Wohlstand *m*.

**affluent** ['æflʊənt] *adj* reich, wohlhabend. **the ~ society** die Wohlstandsgesellschaft.

**afford** [ə'fɔːd] *vt* **(a)** *(also non-financially)* sich *(dat)* leisten. **I can't ~ to buy both of them** ich kann es mir nicht leisten, beide zu kaufen. **(b)** *(liter: provide) (sb sth* jdm etw*)* gewähren, bieten; *pleasure* bereiten.

**afforestation** [æˌfɒrɪs'teɪʃən] *n* Aufforstung *f*.

**affray** [ə'freɪ] *n (esp Jur)* Schlägerei *f*.

**affront** [ə'frʌnt] **1** *vt* beleidigen. **2** *n* Beleidigung *f (to sb* jds, *to sth* für etw*)*, Affront *m (to* gegen*)*.

**Afghan** ['æfgæn] **1** *n* **(a)** Afghane *m*, Afghanin *f*. **(b)** *(language)* Afghanisch *nt*. **(c)** *(dog)* Afghane *m*, afghanischer Windhund. **2** *adj* afghanisch.

**Afghanistan** [æf'gænɪstæn] *n* Afghanistan *nt*.

**afield** [ə'fiːld] *adv* **far ~** weit weg; **further ~** weiter entfernt.

**afloat** [ə'fləʊt] *adj pred, adv (Naut)* **to be ~** schwimmen; **the largest navy ~** die größte Flotte auf See; **to get a business ~** *(fig)* ein Geschäft auf die Beine stellen.

**afoot** [ə'fʊt] *adv* im Gange. **what's ~?** was geht hier vor?

**aforementioned** [əˌfɔː'menʃənd], **aforesaid** [əˌfɔː'sed] *adj attr (form)* obengenannt.

**afraid** [ə'freɪd] *adj pred and (frightened)* **to be ~ (of sb/sth)** (vor jdm/etw) Angst haben, sich (vor jdm/etw) fürchten; **don't be ~!** keine Angst!; **I am ~ of hurting him** *or* **that I might hurt him** ich fürchte, ihm weh zu tun *or* ich könnte ihm weh tun; **I was ~ of waking the children** ich wollte die Kinder nicht wecken; **he's not ~ to say what he thinks** er scheut sich nicht, zu sagen, was er denkt; **that's what I was ~ of, I was ~ that would happen** das habe ich befürchtet. **(b)** *(expressing polite regret)* **I'm ~ I can't do it** leider kann ich es nicht machen; **I'm ~ you'll have to wait** Sie müssen leider warten; **I'm ~ not/I'm ~ so** leider nicht/ja, leider.

**afresh** [ə'freʃ] *adv* noch einmal von vorn.

**Africa** ['æfrɪkə] *n* Afrika *nt*.

**African** ['æfrɪkən] **1** *n* **(a)** Afrikaner(in *f*) *m*. **(b)** *(US: black person)* Schwarze(r) *mf*. **2** *adj* afrikanisch. ~ **violet** Usambaraveilchen *nt*.

**Afrika(a)ner** [ˌæfrɪ'kɔːnər] *n* Afrika(a)nder(in *f*) *m*.

**Afrikaans** [ˌæfrɪ'kɔːns] *n* Afrikaans *nt*.

**Afro** ['æfrəʊ] **1** *pref* afro-, Afro-. **2** *n (hairstyle)* Afro-Look *m*.

**Afro-:** ~**-American 1** *adj* afro-amerikanisch. **2** *n* Afro-Amerikaner(in *f*) *m*; ~**-Asian 1** *adj* afro-asiatisch. **2** *n* Afro-Asiat(in *f*) *m*.

**aft** [ɑːft] *(Naut) adv* achtern. **to go ~** nach achtern gehen.

**after 1** *prep* nach *(+dat)*. **~ that** danach; **the week**

~ **next** übernächste Woche; **ten** ~ **eight** *(US)* zehn nach acht; **to run** ~ **sb** hinter jdm herlaufen; **he shut the door** ~ **her** er machte die Tür hinter ihr zu; ~ **what has happened** nach allem, was geschehen ist; **to do sth** ~ **all** etw schließlich doch tun; ~ **all our efforts!** und das, nachdem wir uns soviel Mühe gegeben haben!; **you tell me lie** ~ **lie** du erzählst mir eine Lüge nach der anderen; **day** ~ **day** Tag für Tag; **time** ~ **time** immer wieder; **mile** ~ **mile** Meile um Meile; ~ **El Greco** in der Art von El Greco; **to be** ~ **sb/sth** hinter jdm/etw hersein; **what are you** ~? was willst du?; *(looking for)* was suchst du?

**2** *adv (time, order)* danach. **the year/week** ~ das Jahr/die Woche danach or darauf.

**3** *conj* nachdem. ~ **finishing it I will/I went** ... wenn ich das fertig habe, werde ich .../als ich das fertig hatte, ging ich ...; ~ **arriving they went** ... nachdem sie angekommen waren, gingen sie ...

**4** *n* ~**s** *pl (Brit col)* Nachtisch *m*.

**after:** ~**birth** *n* Nachgeburt *f*; ~**burner** *n (Aviat)* Nachbrenner *m*; ~-**care** *n (of convalescent)* Nachbehandlung *f*; ~-**dinner** *adj speech, speaker* Tisch-; ~-**effect** *n* Nachwirkung *f*; ~-**life** *n* Leben *nt* nach dem Tode; ~**math** *n* Nachwirkungen *pl*; **in the** ~**math of sth** nach etw.

**afternoon** ['ɑːftə'nuːn] *n* Nachmittag *m*. **in the** ~ am Nachmittag, nachmittags; **at three o'clock in the** ~ (um) drei Uhr nachmittags; **on Sunday** ~ (am) Sonntag nachmittag; **this/tomorrow** ~ heute/morgen nachmittag; **good** ~! Guten Tag!

**after:** ~-**pains** *npl* Nachwehen *pl*; ~-**sales service** *n (Brit)* Kundendienst *m*; ~**shave, Rasierwasser** *nt*; ~**shave (lotion)** *n* Aftershave, Rasierwasser *nt*; ~**shock** *n (of earthquake)* Nachbeben *nt*; ~**thought** *n* nachträgliche Idee; *(hum: child)* Nachkömmling *m*.

**afterwards** ['ɑːftəwədz] *adv* nachher; *(after that, after an event etc)* danach, anschließend.

**again** [ə'gen] *adv* **(a)** wieder. ~ **and** ~ immer wieder; **to do sth** ~ etw noch (ein)mal tun; **not to do sth** ~ etw nicht wieder tun; **I'll ring** ~ **tomorrow** ich rufe morgen noch einmal an; **never** ~ nie wieder; **if that happens** ~ wenn das noch einmal passiert; **all over** ~ noch (ein)mal von vorn; **not** ~! schon wieder! **(b)** *(in quantity)* **as much** ~ doppelt soviel, noch (ein)mal soviel. **(c)** *(on the other hand)* wiederum; *(besides, moreover)* außerdem. **but then** ~, **it may not be true** vielleicht ist es auch gar nicht wahr.

**against** [ə'genst] *prep* gegen *(+acc)*. **he's** ~ **her going** er ist dagegen, daß sie geht; **to have something** ~ **sb/sth** etwas gegen jdn/etw haben; ~ **their wish** entgegen ihrem Wunsch; **the advantages of flying (as)** ~ **going by train** die Vorteile von Flugreisen gegenüber Bahnreisen.

**age** [eɪdʒ] **1** *n* **(a)** Alter *nt*. **what is her** ~, **what** ~ **is she?** wie alt ist sie?; **he is ten years of** ~ er ist zehn Jahre alt; **at the** ~ **of 15** im Alter von 15 Jahren, mit 15 Jahren; **when I was your** ~ als ich in deinem Alter war; **but he's twice your** ~ aber er ist doppelt so alt wie du; **over** ~ zu alt; **be** or **act your** ~! sei nicht kindisch! **(b)** *(length of life)* Lebensdauer *f*. **(c) to come of** ~ *(Jur)* volljährig or mündig werden, die Volljährigkeit erlangen; *(fig)* den Kinderschuhen entwachsen; **under** ~ minderjährig, unmündig. **(d)** *(period, epoch)* Zeit (alter *nt*) *f*. **the** ~ **of technology** das technologische Zeitalter; **down the** ~**s** durch alle Zeiten. **(e)** *(col: long time)* **I haven't seen him for** ~**s, it's been** ~**s since I saw him** ich habe ihn eine Ewigkeit or ewig nicht gesehen *(col)*; **it/he takes** ~**s** das dauert ewig/er braucht ewig *(col)*.

**2** *vi* alt werden, altern.

**3** *vt (worry, experience etc)* altern lassen; *(dress, hairstyle etc)* älter machen.

**aged** [eɪdʒd] **1** *adj* **(a)** im Alter von, ... Jahre alt, -jährig. **a boy** ~ **ten** ein zehnjähriger Junge. **(b)** ['eɪdʒɪd] *person* bejahrt, betagt. **2** ['eɪdʒɪd] *npl* **the** ~ die alten Menschen, die Alten *pl*.

**age:** ~ **difference** or **gap** *n* Altersunterschied *m*; ~-**group** *n* Altersgruppe *f*; ~**less** *adj* zeitlos; **one of those** ~**less people** eine(r) von denen, die nie alt werden; ~ **limit** *n* Altersgrenze *f*.

**agency** ['eɪdʒənsɪ] *n* **(a)** *(Comm)* Agentur *f*. **translation/tourist** ~ Übersetzungs-/Reisebüro *nt*; **they have the Citroën** ~ sie haben die Citroën-Vertretung. **(b) through the** ~ **of friends** durch die Vermittlung or mit Hilfe von Freunden.

**agenda** [ə'dʒendə] *n* Tagesordnung *f*. **on the** ~ auf dem Programm.

**agent** ['eɪdʒənt] *n* **(a)** *(Comm) (person)* Vertreter(in *f*) *m*; *(organization)* Vertretung *f*. **(b)** *(literary, press, secret ~ etc)* Agent(in *f*) *m*; *(Pol)* Wahlkampfleiter(in *f*) *m*. **you're a free** ~ du bist dein eigener Herr. **(c)** *(Chem, means)* Mittel *nt*.

**age-old** ['eɪdʒəʊld] *adj* uralt.

**aggravate** ['ægrəveɪt] *vt* **(a)** *(worsen)* verschlimmern. **(b)** *(annoy)* aufregen; *(deliberately)* reizen.

**aggravating** ['ægrəveɪtɪŋ] *adj* ärgerlich; *noise, child* lästig.

**aggravation** [ˌægrə'veɪʃən] *n* **(a)** Verschlimmerung *f*. **(b)** *(annoyance)* Ärger *m*. **her constant** ~ **made him** ... sie reizte ihn so, daß er ...

**aggregate** ['ægrɪgɪt] **1** *n* **(a)** Summe, Gesamtheit *f*. **they won on** ~ sie wurden Gesamtsieger. **(b)** *(Build)* Zuschlagstoffe *pl*. **2** *adj* gesamt, Gesamt-.

**aggression** [ə'greʃən] *n* Aggression *f*; *(of person: aggressiveness)* Aggressivität *f*. **an act of** ~ eine aggressive Handlung.

**aggressive** [ə'gresɪv] *adj* aggressiv; *salesman, businessman etc* dynamisch, aufdringlich *(pej)*.

**aggressiveness** [ə'gresɪvnɪs] *n see adj* Aggressivität *f*; Dynamik, Aufdringlichkeit *(pej) f*.

**aggressor** [ə'gresər] *n* Angreifer(in *f*) *m*.

**aggrieved** [ə'griːvd] *adj (offended)* verletzt *(at, by durch)*.

**aggro** ['ægrəʊ] *n (Brit col)* **(a)** *(bother)* Ärger *m*, Stunk *m (col)*. **all the** ~ **of moving house** das ganze Theater mit dem Umziehen. **(b)** *(fighting)* Schlägereien *pl*.

**aghast** [ə'gɑːst] *adj pred* entgeistert *(at über +acc)*.

**agile** ['ædʒaɪl] *adj person, thinker* beweglich; *body movements* geschmeidig; *animal* flink. **she has an** ~ **mind** sie ist geistig sehr rege.

**agility** [ə'dʒɪlɪtɪ] *n see adj* Beweglichkeit *f*; Geschmeidigkeit *f*; Flinkheit *f*.

**agitate** ['ædʒɪteɪt] **1** *vt* **(a)** *(excite, upset)* aufregen, aus der Fassung bringen. **(b)** *(lit: shake) liquid* schütteln. **2** *vi* agitieren. **to** ~ **for sth** sich für etw stark machen.

**agitated** ['ædʒɪteɪtɪd] *adj* aufgeregt, erregt. **to get** ~ sich aufregen.

**agitation** [ˌædʒɪ'teɪʃən] *n* **(a)** *(anxiety, worry)* Erregung *f*, Aufruhr *m*. **(b)** *(incitement)* Agitation *f*.

**agitator** ['ædʒɪteɪtər] *n (person)* Agitator(in *f*) *m*.

**AGM** = **annual general meeting** JHV *f*.

**agnostic** [æg'nɒstɪk] **1** *adj* agnostisch. **2** *n* Agnostiker(in *f*) *m*.

**agnosticism** [æg'nɒstɪsɪzəm] *n* Agnostizismus *m*.

**ago** [ə'gəʊ] *adv* vor. **years/a week/a little while** ~ vor Jahren/einer Woche/kurzem; **that was years/a week** ~ das ist schon Jahre/eine Woche her; **how long** ~ **is it since you last saw him?** wann haben Sie ihn das letzte Mal gesehen?; **how long** ~**?** wie lange ist das her?; **that was long** ~ das ist schon lange her; **as long** ~ **as 1950** schon 1950; **no longer** ~ **than yesterday** erst gestern (noch).

**agog** [ə'gɒg] adj pred gespannt. **to be** ~ **with curiosity** vor Neugierde platzen.

**agonize** ['ægənaɪz] vi sich (dat) den Kopf zermartern (over über +acc).

**agonizing** ['ægənaɪzɪŋ] adj qualvoll.

**agony** ['ægənɪ] n **(a)** Qual f; (mental also) Leid nt. **that's** ~ das ist eine Qual; **to be in** ~ schreckliche Schmerzen haben; **in an** ~ **of indecision** in qualvoller Unentschlossenheit; **put him out of his** ~ (lit) erlöse ihn von seiner Qual; (fig) nun spann ihn doch nicht länger auf die Folter.

**agony:** ~ **aunt** n (Brit col) Briefkastentante f (col); ~ **column** n (Brit col) Kummerkasten m.

**agrarian** [ə'grɛərɪən] adj Agrar-.

**agree** [ə'griː] pret, ptp ~**d 1** vt **(a)** price, date etc vereinbaren, abmachen. **we all** ~ **that** ... wir sind alle der Meinung, daß ...; **it was** ~**d that** ... man einigte sich darauf or es wurde beschlossen, daß ...; **to** ~ **to differ** sich (dat) verschiedene Meinungen zugestehen. **(b)** (consent) **to** ~ **to do sth** sich bereit erklären, etw zu tun. **(c)** (admit) zugeben. **I** ~ **(that) I was wrong** ich gebe zu, daß ich mich geirrt habe.

**2** vi **(a)** (hold same opinion) (two or more people) übereinstimmen; (one person) der gleichen Meinung sein. **to** ~ **with sb** jdm zustimmen; **I quite** ~ ganz meine Meinung!; **it's too late now, don't you** ~**?** meinen Sie nicht auch, daß es jetzt zu spät ist?; **to** ~ **with the figures** (accept) die Zahlen akzeptieren. **(b)** (come to an agreement) sich einigen, Einigkeit erzielen (about über +acc). **(c)** (people: get on together) miteinander auskommen. **(d)** (statements, figures, Gram) übereinstimmen. **(e)** **I don't** ~ **with children drinking wine** ich bin nicht damit einverstanden, daß Kinder Wein trinken. **(f)** (food, climate etc) **whisky doesn't** ~ **with me** Whisky bekommt mir nicht.

►**agree on** vi +prep obj sich einigen auf (+acc).
►**agree to** vi +prep obj zustimmen (+dat). **to** ~ ~ **the conditions** sich mit den Bedingungen einverstanden erklären.

**agreeable** [ə'griːəbl] adj **(a)** (pleasant) angenehm. **(b)** pred **are you** ~ **to that?** sind Sie damit einverstanden?

**agreed** [ə'griːd] adj **(a)** pred einig. **to be** ~ **on sth/on doing sthg** sich über etw einig sein/sich darüber einig sein, etw zu tun; **are we all** ~**?** sind wir uns da einig?; (on course of action) sind alle einverstanden? **(b)** (arranged) vereinbart; price also festgesetzt; time also verabredet. **it's all** ~ es ist alles abgesprochen; ~**?** einverstanden?

**agreement** [ə'griːmənt] n **(a)** (understanding, arrangement) Abmachung, Übereinkunft f; (treaty, contract) Abkommen nt, Vertrag m. **to reach an** ~ **(with sb)** (mit jdm) zu einer Einigung kommen. **(b)** (sharing of opinion) Einigkeit f. **by mutual** ~ in gegenseitigem Einvernehmen; **to be in** ~ **with sb** mit jdm einer Meinung sein; **to be in** ~ **with/about sth** mit etw übereinstimmen/über etw (acc) einig sein. **(c)** (consent) Zustimmung f (to zu). **(d)** (between figures, Gram etc) Übereinstimmung f.

**agricultural** [ˌægrɪ'kʌltʃərəl] adj produce, tool etc landwirtschaftlich; studies Landwirtschafts-. ~ **college** Landwirtschaftsschule f; ~ **show** Landwirtschaftsausstellung f; ~ **worker** Landarbeiter(in f) m; ~ **policy** Agrarpolitik f.

**agriculture** ['ægrɪkʌltʃər] n Landwirtschaft f.

**aground** [ə'graʊnd] adv **to go** or **run** ~ auflaufen, auf

Grund laufen.

**ah** [ɑː] interj ah; (pain) au; (pity) o, ach.

**aha** [ɑː'hɑː] interj aha.

**ahead** [ə'hed] adv **(a)** **there's some thick cloud** ~ da vorne ist eine große Wolke; **the German runner was/drew** ~ der deutsche Läufer lag vorn/zog nach vorne; **he is** ~ **by about two minutes** er hat etwa zwei Minuten Vorsprung; **we sent him on** ~ wir schickten ihn voraus; **in the months** ~ in den bevorstehenden Monaten; **I see problems** ~ ich sehe Probleme auf mich/uns etc zukommen. **(b)** ~ **of sb/sth** vor jdm/etw; **walk** ~ **of me** gehen Sie voran; **we arrived ten minutes** ~ **of time** wir kamen zehn Minuten vorher an; **to be** ~ **of one's time** (fig) seiner Zeit voraus sein.

**ahoy** [ə'hɔɪ] interj (Naut) ahoi. **ship** ~**!** Schiff ahoi!

**AI** = **artificial intelligence** KI f.

**aid** [eɪd] **1** n **(a)** no pl (help) Hilfe f. **(foreign)** ~ Entwicklungshilfe f; **with the** ~ **of** mit Hilfe (+gen); **to come to sb's** ~ jdm zu Hilfe kommen; **a sale in** ~ **of the blind** ein Verkauf zugunsten der Blinden; **what's all this wiring in** ~ **of?** (col) wozu sind all diese Drähte da or gut? **(b)** (useful person, thing) Hilfe f (to für); (piece of equipment) Hilfsmittel nt; (teaching ~) Lehrmittel nt. **2** vt unterstützen, helfen (+dat). **to** ~ **sb's recovery** zu jds Erholung beitragen; **to** ~ **and abet sb** (Jur) jdm Beihilfe leisten; (after crime) jdn begünstigen.

**aide** [eɪd] n Helfer(in f) m; (adviser) Berater(in f) m.

**AIDS** [eɪdz] n (Med) Aids nt. ~ **victim** Aids-Kranke(r) mf; ~ **virus** Aids-Erreger m.

**ailing** ['eɪlɪŋ] adj (lit) kränklich; (fig) industry, economy etc krankend, krank.

**ailment** ['eɪlmənt] n Gebrechen, Leiden nt. **minor** ~**s** leichte Beschwerden pl.

**aim** [eɪm] **1** n **(a)** Zielen nt. **to take** ~ zielen (at auf +acc); **his** ~ **was good** er zielte gut. **(b)** (purpose) Ziel nt, Absicht f. **what is your** ~ **in life?** was ist Ihr Lebensziel?; **what is your** ~ **in doing that?** was wollen Sie damit bezwecken?

**2** vt **(a)** guided missile, camera richten (at auf +acc); stone etc zielen mit (at auf +acc). **to** ~ **a pistol at sb/sth** eine Pistole auf jdn/etw richten, mit einer Pistole auf jdn/etw zielen. **(b)** (fig) remark, insult, criticism richten (at gegen). **this programme is** ~**ed at the general public** dieses Programm ist für die breite Öffentlichkeit gedacht; **to be** ~**ed at sth** (cuts, measure, new law etc) auf etw (acc) abzielen.

**3** vi **(a)** (with gun, punch etc) zielen (at, for auf +acc). **(b)** (try, strive for) **to** ~ **high** sich (dat) hohe Ziele setzen; **isn't that** ~**ing a bit high?** wollen Sie nicht etwas zu hoch hinaus?; **to** ~ **at** or **for sth** etw anstreben, auf etw (acc) abzielen; **he** ~**s at only spending £10 per week** er hat es sich zum Ziel gesetzt, mit £10 pro Woche auszukommen. **(c)** (col: intend) **to** ~ **to do sth** vorhaben, etw zu tun.

**aimless** ['eɪmlɪs] adj ziellos.

**aimlessness** ['eɪmlɪsnɪs] n Ziellosigkeit f.

**ain't** [eɪnt] (incorrect) = **am not**; **is not**; **are not**; **has not**; **have not**.

**air** [ɛər] **1** n **(a)** Luft f. **to go for a breath of (fresh)** ~ frische Luft schnappen (gehen); **by** ~ per or mit dem Flugzeug; (transport) auf dem Luftweg.

**(b)** (fig phrases) **there's something in the** ~ es liegt etwas in der Luft; **it's still all up in the** ~ (col) es ist noch alles offen; **to be up in the** ~ **about sth** (col) wegen etw aus dem Häuschen sein (col); **to clear the** ~ die Atmosphäre reinigen; **to be walking on** ~ wie auf Wolken gehen.

**(c)** (Rad, TV) **to be on the** ~ (programme) gesendet werden; (station) senden; **he's on the** ~ **every**

**day** er ist jeden Tag im Radio zu hören; **we come on the ~ at 6** unsere Sendezeit beginnt um 6; **to go off the ~** das Programm beenden.

**(d)** *(facial expression)* Miene *f*; *(appearance)* Aussehen *nt*; *(atmosphere)* Atmosphäre *f*. **there was an ~ of mystery about her** sie hatte etwas Geheimnisvolles an sich *(dat)*.

**(e)** **~s** *pl* Getue, Gehabe *nt*; **to give oneself ~s** vornehm tun; **~s and graces** Allüren *pl*.

**(f)** *(Mus)* Weise *f (old)*; *(tune also)* Melodie *f*.

**2** *vt* **(a)** *clothes, bed, room* (aus)lüften. **(b)** *anger, grievance* Luft machen *(+dat)*; *opinion* darlegen.

**3** *vi (clothes etc) (after washing)* nachtrocknen; *(after storage)* (aus)lüften.

**air** *in cpds* Luft-; **~ bag** *n (Aut)* Luftsack *m*, Airbag *m*; **~ base** *n* Luftwaffenstützpunkt *m*; **~bed** *n* Luftmatratze *f*; **~borne** *adj* **~borne troops** Luftlandetruppen *pl*; **to be ~borne** sich in der Luft befinden; **~ brake** *n (on truck)* Druckluftbremse *f*; **~ bubble** *n* Luftblase *f*; **~bus** *n* Airbus *m*; **~ cargo** *n* Luftfracht *f*; **~-conditioned** *adj* klimatisiert; **~-conditioning** *n (plant)* Klimaanlage *f*; **~-cooled** *adj* luftgekühlt; **~ cover** *n (Mil)* Luftunterstützung *f*; **~craft** *n, pl* **~craft** Flugzeug *nt*, Maschine *f*; **~craft carrier** *n* Flugzeugträger *m*; **~craft noise** *n* Fluglärm *m*; **~crew** *n* Flugpersonal *nt*; **~ display** *n* Flugschau *f*; **~drome** *n (US)* Flugplatz *m*; **~ fare** *n* Flugpreis *m*; **~field** *n* Flugplatz *m*; **~ force** *n* Luftwaffe *f*; **~freight 1** *n* Luftfracht *f*; **2** *vt* per Luftfracht senden; **~gun** *n* Luftgewehr *nt*; **~hole** *n* Luftloch *nt*; **~ hostess** *n* Stewardeß *f*.

**airily** [ˈɛərɪlɪ] *adv* leichthin, lässig.

**airiness** [ˈɛərɪnɪs] *n see adj (b)* Lässigkeit *f*; Vagheit *f*; Versponnenheit *f*.

**airing** [ˈɛərɪŋ] *n* **to give sth an ~** etw gut durch- *or* auslüften lassen; *(fig col) idea* etw darlegen.

**airing cupboard** *n (Brit)* (Wäsche)trockenschrank *m*.

**air:** **~ intake** *n* Lufteinlaß *m*; *(quantity)* Luftmenge *f*; **~lane** *n* Flugroute *f*; **~less** *adj (lit) space* luftleer; *(stuffy) room* stickig; *(with no wind) day* windstill; **~ letter** *n* Luftpostbrief *m*; **~lift** *n* Luftbrücke *f*; **~line** *n* **(a)** Fluggesellschaft, Fluglinie *f*. **(b)** *(for diver, at garage)* Luftschlauch *m*; **~liner** *n* Verkehrsflugzeug *nt*; **~lock** *n (in spacecraft etc)* Luftschleuse *f*; *(in pipe)* Luftsack *m*; **~mail** *n* Luftpost *f*; **to send sth (by) ~mail** etw per *or* mit Luftpost schicken; **~man** *n* Flieger *m*; **~ miss** *n (Aviat)* Beinahezusammenstoß *m*; **~ passenger** *n* Fluggast *m*; **~plane** *n (US)* Flugzeug *nt*; **~ pocket** *n* Luftloch *nt*; **~port** *n* Flughafen *m*; **~ raid** *n* Luftangriff *m*; **~-raid shelter** *n* Luftschutzkeller *m*; **~-raid warning** *n* Fliegeralarm *m*; **~ rifle** *n* Luftgewehr *nt*; **~-sea rescue service** *n* Seenotrettungsdienst *m*; **~ship** *n* Luftschiff *nt*; **~ show** *n* Luftfahrtausstellung *f*; **~sick** *adj* luftkrank; **~space** *n* Luftraum *m*; **~strip** *n* Start- und Lande-Bahn *f*; **~ speed** *n* Eigen- *or* Fluggeschwindigkeit *f*; **~ support** *n (Mil)* Luftunterstützung *f*; **~ terminal** *n* Terminal *m or nt*; **~tight** *adj* luftdicht; **~-to-~** *adj (Mil)* Luft-Luft-; **~-to-ground** *adj (Mil)* Luft-Boden-; **~-traffic control** *n* Flugleitung *f*; **~-traffic controller** *n* Fluglotse *m*; **~waves** *npl* Radiowellen *pl*; **~ waybill** *n* Luftfrachtbrief *m*; **~worthiness** *n* Flugtüchtigkeit *f*; **~worthy** *adj* flugtüchtig.

**airy** [ˈɛərɪ] *adj (+er)* **(a)** *room* luftig. **(b)** *(casual) manner, gesture* lässig, nonchalant; *(vague) promise* vage; *theory* versponnen.

**airy-fairy** [ˈɛərɪˈfɛərɪ] *adj (col)* versponnen; *excuse* windig; *talk also* larifari *inv (col)*.

**aisle** [aɪl] *n* Gang *m*; *(in church)* Seitenschiff *nt*; *(central ~)* Mittelgang *m*. **he had them rolling in the ~s** die Leute kugelten sich vor Lachen.

**aitch** [eɪtʃ] *n* h, H *nt*. **to drop one's ~es** den Buchstaben „h" nicht aussprechen.

**ajar** [əˈdʒɑːʳ] *adj, adv* angelehnt.

**AK** *(US Post)* = **Alaska**.

**aka** = **also known as** alias.

**akimbo** [əˈkɪmbəʊ] *adv:* **with arms ~** die Arme in die Hüften gestemmt.

**akin** [əˈkɪn] *adj pred* verwandt *(to mit)*.

**AL** *(US Post)* = **Alabama**.

**alabaster** [ˈæləbɑːstəʳ] *n* Alabaster *m*.

**à la carte** [ɑːlɑːˈkɑːt] *adj, adv* à la carte.

**alacrity** [əˈlækrɪtɪ] *n* Bereitwilligkeit *f*. **to accept with ~** ohne zu zögern annehmen.

**alarm** [əˈlɑːm] **1** *n* **(a)** *(warning)* Alarm *m*. **to give/sound the ~** Alarm geben *or (fig)* schlagen. **(b)** *(device)* Alarmanlage *f*. **(c) to cause a good deal of ~** große Unruhe auslösen. **2** *vt* **(a)** *(worry)* beunruhigen; *(frighten)* erschrecken. **don't be ~ed** erschrecken Sie nicht. **(b)** *(warn)* warnen; *fire brigade etc* alarmieren.

**alarm** *in cpds* Alarm-; **~ call** *n (Telec)* Weckruf *m*; **~ clock** *n* Wecker *m*.

**alarming** [əˈlɑːmɪŋ] *adj (worrying)* beunruhigend; *(frightening)* erschreckend; *news* alarmierend.

**alarmist** [əˈlɑːmɪst] *n* Unheilsprophet *m*.

**alas** [əˈlæs] *interj* leider.

**Alaska** [əˈlæskə] *n* Alaska *nt*.

**Albania** [ælˈbeɪnɪə] *n* Albanien *nt*.

**Albanian** [ælˈbeɪnɪən] **1** *adj* albanisch. **2** *n* **(a)** Albaner(in *f*) *m*. **(b)** *(language)* Albanisch *nt*.

**albatross** [ˈælbətrɒs] *n* Albatros *m*.

**albeit** [ɔːlˈbiːɪt] *conj (esp liter)* obgleich, wenn auch.

**albino** [ælˈbiːnəʊ] **1** *n* Albino *m*. **2** *adj* Albino-.

**album** [ˈælbəm] *n* Album *nt*.

**alchemy** [ˈælkɪmɪ] *n* Alchemie, Alchimie *f*.

**alcohol** [ˈælkəhɒl] *n* Alkohol *m*.

**alcoholic** [ˌælkəˈhɒlɪk] **1** *adj drink* alkoholisch. **2** *n* **to be an ~** Alkoholiker(in) sein.

**alcoholism** [ˈælkəhɒlɪzəm] *n* Alkoholismus *m*.

**alcove** [ˈælkəʊv] *n* Nische *f*.

**ale** [eɪl] *n (old)* Ale, Bier *nt*.

**alert** [əˈlɜːt] **1** *adj* aufmerksam; *(as character trait)* aufgeweckt; *mind* scharf, hell. **2** *vt* warnen *(to vor +dat)*. **3** *n* Alarm *m*. **to put troops on the ~** Truppen in Alarmbereitschaft versetzen; **to be on (the) ~** einsatzbereit sein; *(be on lookout)* auf der Hut sein *(for vor +dat)*.

**alertness** [əˈlɜːtnɪs] *n* Aufmerksamkeit *f*.

**Aleutian Islands** [əˈluːʃənˈaɪləndz], **Aleutians** [əˈluːʃənz] *npl* Aleuten *pl*.

**A level** [ˈeɪˌlevl] *n (Brit)* Abschluß *m* der Sekundarstufe 2; ≈ Abitur *nt no pl*.

**alfresco** [ælˈfreskəʊ] *adj, adv* im Freien.

**algae** [ˈælgɪ] *npl* Algen *pl*.

**algebra** [ˈældʒɪbrə] *n* Algebra *f*.

**Algeria** [ælˈdʒɪərɪə] *n* Algerien *nt*.

**Algerian** [ælˈdʒɪərɪən] **1** *n* Algerier(in *f*) *m*. **2** *adj* algerisch.

**Algiers** [ælˈdʒɪəz] *n* Algier *nt*.

**algorithm** [ˈælgəˌrɪðəm] *n* Algorithmus *m*.

**alias** [ˈeɪlɪæs] **1** *adv* alias. **2** *n* Deckname *m*.

**alibi** [ˈælɪbaɪ] *n* Alibi *nt*.

**alien** [ˈeɪlɪən] **1** *n (esp Pol)* Ausländer(in *f*) *m*; *(Sci-Fi)* außerirdisches Wesen. **2** *adj (foreign)* ausländisch; *(Sci-Fi)* außerirdisch; *(different, also Comp)* fremd. **to be ~ to sb's nature** jdm fremd sein.

**alienate** [ˈeɪlɪəneɪt] *vt people* befremden. **to be ~d**

from sb jdm entfremdet sein.

**alienation** [ˌeɪlɪə'neɪʃən] n Entfremdung f.

**alight¹** [ə'laɪt] vi (a) (form: person) aussteigen (from aus). (b) (bird) sich niederlassen (on auf +dat).

**alight²** adj pred to be ~ brennen; to keep the fire ~ das Feuer in Gang halten; to set sth ~ etw in Brand setzen or stecken.

**align** [ə'laɪn] vt (a) wheels of car, gun sights etc ausrichten; (bring into line also) in eine Linie bringen. (b) (Fin, Pol) currencies, policies aufeinander abstimmen. to ~ oneself with a party sich einer Partei anschließen.

**alignment** [ə'laɪnmənt] n Ausrichtung f; (of policies etc also) Orientierung f (with nach). to be out of ~ (wheels etc) nicht richtig ausgerichtet sein; (views, policies) nicht übereinstimmen; the new ~ of world powers die Neugruppierung der Weltmächte.

**alike** [ə'laɪk] adj pred, adv gleich; (similar) ähnlich. you men are all ~! ihr Männer seid doch alle gleich!; winter and summer ~ Sommer wie Winter.

**alimentary** [ˌælɪ'mentərɪ] adj (Anat) Verdauungs-. ~ canal Verdauungskanal m.

**alimony** ['ælɪmənɪ] n Unterhaltszahlung f. to pay ~ Unterhalt zahlen.

**alive** [ə'laɪv] adj (a) pred (living) lebendig, lebend attr. dead or ~ tot oder lebendig; to be ~ leben; the greatest violinist ~ der größte lebende Geiger; it's good to be ~ das Leben ist schön; to stay ~ am Leben bleiben; to keep sb/sth ~ (lit, fig) jdn/etw am Leben erhalten. (b) (lively) lebendig. (c) pred (aware) to be ~ to sth sich (dat) einer Sache (gen) bewußt sein. (d) to be ~ with tourists/fish/insects etc von Touristen/Fischen/Insekten etc wimmeln.

**alkali** ['ælkəlaɪ] n, pl -(e)s Alkali nt; (solution) Lauge f.

**alkaline** ['ælkəlaɪn] adj alkalisch. ~ solution Lauge f.

**all** [ɔːl] 1 adj (with pl n) alle no art; (with sing n) ganze(r, s), alle(r, s) no art. ~ the books/people alle Bücher/Leute, die ganzen Bücher/Leute; ~ the tobacco/milk/fruit der ganze Tabak/die ganze Milch/das ganze Obst; ~ my books/friends/strength all(e) meine Bücher/Freunde/meine ganze Kraft; ~ my life mein ganzes Leben (lang); ~ Spain ganz Spanien; we ~ sat down wir setzten uns alle; ~ day (long) den ganzen Tag (lang); I don't understand ~ that ich verstehe das alles nicht; in ~ respects in jeder Hinsicht; why me of ~ people? warum ausgerechnet ich?; of ~ the idiots! so ein Idiot!; with ~ possible speed so schnell wie möglich.

2 pron (a) (everything) alles; (everybody) alle pl. ~ of them/of it (sie) alle/alles; ~ of Paris/of the house ganz Paris/das ganze Haus; the score was two ~ es stand zwei zu zwei. (b) (phrases) at ~ überhaupt; nothing at ~ überhaupt or gar nichts; it's not bad at ~ das ist gar nicht schlecht; for ~ I know she could be ill was weiß ich, vielleicht ist sie krank; in ~ insgesamt; in ~ alles in allem; happiest of ~ am glücklichsten; the best car of ~ das allerbeste Auto.

3 adv (a) (quite, entirely) ganz. dressed ~ in white ganz in Weiß (gekleidet); an ~ wool carpet ein reinwollener Teppich; ~ along the road die ganze Straße entlang; I'll tell you ~ about it ich erzähl dir alles; that's ~ very well das ist alles ganz schön und gut; it's not as bad as ~ that so schlimm ist es nun auch wieder nicht; if at ~ possible wenn irgend möglich; to be ~ in (col) total erledigt sein (col); he's ~/not ~ there (col) er ist voll da/er ist nicht ganz da (col).

(b) ~ but fast; he ~ but died er wäre fast gestor-

ben.

(c) (with comp) ~ the happier noch glücklicher; ~ the sadder because ... um so trauriger, weil ...; ~ the more so since ... besonders weil ..., zumal ...

4 n one's ~ alles; to give one's ~ sein Letztes geben.

**all-American** adj team, player amerikanische(r, s) National-. an ~ boy ein richtiger amerikanischer Junge.

**allay** [ə'leɪ] vt verringern; doubt, fears, suspicion (weitgehend) zerstreuen.

**all:** ~-clear n Entwarnung f; ~-day adj ganztägig.

**allegation** [ˌælɪ'geɪʃən] n Behauptung f.

**allege** [ə'ledʒ] vt behaupten. he is ~d to have said that ... er soll angeblich gesagt haben, daß ...

**alleged** adj, ~ly adv [ə'ledʒd, ə'ledʒɪdlɪ] angeblich.

**allegiance** [ə'liːdʒəns] n Treue f (to dat).

**allegorical** adj, ~ly adv [ˌælɪ'gɒrɪkəl, -ɪ] allegorisch.

**allegory** ['ælɪgərɪ] n Allegorie f.

**all-embracing** [ˌɔːlɪm'breɪsɪŋ] adj (all)umfassend.

**Allen key** ® ['ælən,kiː] n Inbusschlüssel ® m.

**allergic** [ə'lɜːdʒɪk] adj (lit, fig) allergisch (to gegen).

**allergy** ['ælədʒɪ] n Allergie f (to gegen).

**alleviate** [ə'liːvɪeɪt] vt lindern.

**alleviation** [əˌliːvɪ'eɪʃən] n Linderung f.

**alley** ['ælɪ] n (between buildings) (enge) Gasse.

**alliance** [ə'laɪəns] n Verbindung f; (of institutions also, of states) Bündnis nt; (in historical contexts) Allianz f.

**Allied** ['ælaɪd] adj the ~ forces die Alliierten.

**alligator** ['ælɪgeɪtər] n Alligator m.

**all:** ~-important adj außerordentlich wichtig; the ~-important question die Frage, auf die es ankommt; ~-in adj (a) (inclusive) Inklusiv-; (b) (Sport) ~-in wrestling Freistilringen nt.

**alliteration** [əˌlɪtə'reɪʃən] n Alliteration f.

**all-night** [ˌɔːl'naɪt] adj attr café durchgehend geöffnet. to have an ~ party die ganze Nacht durchfeiern.

**allocate** ['æləʊkeɪt] vt (allot) zuteilen, zuweisen (to sb jdm); (apportion) verteilen (to auf +acc); tasks vergeben (to an +acc). to ~ money to or for a project Geld für ein Projekt bestimmen.

**allocation** [ˌæləʊ'keɪʃən] n (sum) Zuwendung f.

**allot** [ə'lɒt] vt zuteilen (to sb/sth jdm/etw); time vorsehen (to für); money bestimmen (to für).

**allotment** [ə'lɒtmənt] n (a) see vt Zuteilung f; Vorsehen nt; Bestimmung f. (b) (Brit: land) Schrebergarten m.

**all-out** [ˌɔːl'aʊt] 1 adj strike total; attack massiv; effort äußerste(r, s). to make an ~ attempt to do sth alles daransetzen, etw zu tun. 2 adv mit aller Kraft. to go ~ to do sth alles daransetzen, etw zu tun.

**allow** [ə'laʊ] 1 vt (a) (permit) sth erlauben, gestatten. to ~ sb sth/to do sth jdm etw erlauben/jdm erlauben, etw zu tun; to be ~ed to do sth etw tun dürfen; smoking is not ~ed Rauchen ist nicht gestattet; to ~ oneself sth sich (dat) etw erlauben; (treat oneself) sich (dat) etw gönnen; ~ me! gestatten Sie (form); to ~ sth to happen zulassen, daß etw geschieht; to ~ sb in/out jdn hinein-/hinauslassen; to be ~ed in/out/past hinein-/hinaus-/vorbeidürfen. (b) (recognize, accept) claim anerkennen; goal also geben. (c) (allocate, grant) discount geben; space lassen; time einplanen, einberechnen; (in tax, Jur) zugestehen. to ~ (yourself) an hour rechnen Sie mit einer Stunde; ~ 5 cms extra geben Sie 5 cm zu.

2 vi if time ~s falls es zeitlich möglich ist.

▶**allow for** vi +prep obj berücksichtigen.

**allowable** [ə'lauəbl] *adj* zulässig; *(in tax)* abzugsfähig.

**allowance** [ə'lauəns] *n* **(a)** finanzielle Unterstützung; *(paid by state)* Beihilfe *f*; *(father to child)* Unterhaltsgeld *nt*; *(for unsociable hours, overseas ~ etc)* Zulage *f*; *(on business trip)* Spesen *pl*; *(spending money)* Taschengeld *nt*. **clothing ~** Kleidungsgeld *nt*. **(b)** *(Fin: tax ~)* Freibetrag *m*. **(c)** *(Fin, Comm: discount)* (Preis)nachlaß *m* *(on* für*)*. **(d) to make ~(s) for sth** etw berücksichtigen; **you have to make ~s** Sie müssen (gewisse) Zugeständnisse machen.

**alloy** ['ælɔɪ] *n* Legierung *f*.

**all: ~-powerful** *adj* allmächtig; **~-purpose** *adj* Allzweck-.

**all right** ['ɔːl'raɪt] **1** *adj pred* in Ordnung, okay *(col)*. **it's ~** *(not too bad)* es geht; *(working properly)* es ist in Ordnung; **that's** *or* **it's ~** *(after thanks, apology)* schon gut; **to taste ~** ganz gut schmecken; **is it ~ for me to leave early?** kann ich früher gehen?; **it's ~ for you** du hast's gut; **are you ~?** *(healthy)* geht es Ihnen gut?; *(unharmed)* ist Ihnen etwas passiert?; **are you feeling ~?** fehlt Ihnen etwas?; *(iro)* sag mal, fehlt dir was?

**2** *adv* **(a)** *(satisfactory)* ganz gut, ganz ordentlich; *(safely)* gut. **did I do it ~?** habe ich es richtig gemacht?; **did you get home ~?** bist du gut nach Hause gekommen?; **did you get/find it ~?** haben Sie es denn bekommen/gefunden? **(b)** *(certainly)* schon. **he'll come ~** er wird schon kommen; **that's the boy ~** das ist der Junge; **he's a clever man ~** er ist schon intelligent; **oh yes, we heard you ~** o ja, und ob wir dich gehört haben.

**3** *interj* okay *(col)*; *(in agreement also)* in Ordnung. **~, ~!** **I'm coming** schon gut, schon gut, ich komme ja!

**all: ~-round** *adj* athlete Allround-; *improvement* in jeder Beziehung; **~-rounder** *n* Allroundmann *m*; *(Sport)* Allroundsportler(in *f*) *m*; **A~ Saints' Day** *n* Allerheiligen *nt*; **A~ Souls' Day** *n* Allerseelen *nt*; **~-terrain vehicle** *n* Geländefahrzeug *nt*; **~-time** *adj* record ungebrochen; **an ~-time high/low** der höchste/niedrigste Stand aller Zeiten.

**allude to** [ə'luːd] *vi* **+prep obj** anspielen auf *(+acc)*.

**allure** [ə'ljuər] *n* Reiz *m*.

**alluring** [ə'ljuərɪŋ] *adj* verführerisch.

**allusion** [ə'luːʒən] *n* Anspielung *f (to* auf *+acc)*.

**all-weather** ['ɔːl'weðər] *adj* Allwetter-.

**ally** ['ælaɪ] **1** *n* Verbündete(r) *mf*, Bundesgenosse *m*; *(Hist)* Alliierte(r) *m*. **2** [ə'laɪ] *vr* **to ~ o.s. with sb** sich mit jdm verbünden.

**almanac** ['ɔːlmənæk] *n* Almanach *m*.

**almighty** [ɔːl'maɪtɪ] **1** *adj* allmächtig; *(col)* Mords-, gewaltig. **2** *n* **the A~** der Allmächtige.

**almond** ['ɑːmənd] *n* Mandel *f*; *(tree)* Mandelbaum *m*. **~ paste** Marzipanmasse *f*.

**almost** ['ɔːlməust] *adv* beinahe, fast. **he ~ fell** er wäre fast gefallen.

**alms** [ɑːmz] *npl* Almosen *pl*.

**aloft** [ə'lɒft] *adv* *(into the air)* empor; *(in the air)* hoch droben.

**alone** [ə'ləun] **1** *adj pred* allein(e). **we're not ~ in thinking that** wir stehen mit dieser Meinung nicht allein. **2** *adv* allein(e). **to live on bread ~** von Brot allein leben; **the hotel ~ cost £35** das Hotel allein kostete (schon) £35, schon das Hotel kostete £35.

**along** [ə'lɒŋ] **1** *prep* *(direction)* entlang *(+acc)*, *(+acc) (col)*; *(position)* entlang *(+dat)*. **he walked ~ the river** er ging den Fluß entlang; **somewhere ~ here/there** irgendwo hier/dort (herum); *(in this/that direction)* irgendwo in dieser Richtung/der Richtung. **2** *adv* **to move ~** weitergehen; **he was just**

**strolling ~** er ist bloß so dahingeschlendert; **run ~** nun lauf!; **he'll be ~ soon** er muß gleich da sein; **I'll be ~ about eight** ich komme ungefähr um acht; **~ with** zusammen mit; **to come/sing ~ with sb** mit jdm mitkommen/mitsingen; **take an umbrella ~** nimm einen Schirm mit.

**alongside** [ə'lɒŋ'saɪd] **1** *prep* neben *(+dat)*. **we were moored ~ the pier** wir lagen am Pier vor Anker; **the houses ~ the river** die Häuser am Fluß; **he works ~ me** *(with)* er ist ein Kollege von mir; *(next to)* er arbeitet neben mir. **2** *adv* daneben; *(Naut)* längsseits. **a police car drew up ~** ein Polizeiauto hielt neben mir/ihm *etc* an; **they brought their dinghy ~** sie brachten ihr Dingi heran.

**aloof** [ə'luːf] **1** *adv* *(lit, fig)* abseits. **to remain ~** sich abseits halten. **2** *adj* unnahbar.

**aloofness** [ə'luːfnɪs] *n* Unnahbarkeit *f*.

**aloud** [ə'laud] *adv* laut.

**alpaca** [æl'pækə] *n* Alpaka *nt*.

**alphabet** ['ælfəbet] *n* Alphabet *nt*.

**alphabetic(al)** [ˌælfə'betɪk(əl)] *adj* alphabetisch. **in ~ order** in alphabetischer Reihenfolge.

**alphanumeric** [ˌælfənjuː'merɪk] *adj* alphanumerisch.

**alpine** ['ælpaɪn] *adj* alpin; *flowers, scenery* Alpen-, Gebirgs-.

**Alps** [ælps] *npl* Alpen *pl*.

**already** [ɔːl'redɪ] *adv* schon, bereits.

**alright** ['ɔːl,raɪt] *adj, adv* = **all right**.

**Alsace** ['ælsæs] *n* das Elsaß.

**Alsace-Lorraine** ['ælsæslə'reɪn] *n* Elsaß-Lothringen *nt*.

**alsatian** [æl'seɪʃən] *n (Brit: dog)* Schäferhund *m*.

**Alsatian** [æl'seɪʃən] **1** *adj* elsässisch. **2** *n (dialect)* Elsässisch *nt*.

**also** ['ɔːlsəu] *adv* **(a)** auch. **(b)** *(moreover)* ~, **I must explain that ...** außerdem muß ich erklären, daß ...

**also-ran** [ˌɔːlsəu'ræn] *n* **to be an ~** *(Sport, fig)* unter „ferner liefen" kommen.

**altar** ['ɒltər] *n* Altar *m*.

**alter** ['ɒltər] **1** *vt* ändern; *(modify also)* abändern. **to ~ sth completely** etw vollkommen verändern. **2** *vi* sich (ver)ändern.

**alteration** [ˌɒltə'reɪʃən] *n* Änderung *f*; *(modification also)* Abänderung *f*; *(of appearance)* Veränderung *f*; *(to building)* Umbau *m*. **to make ~s in** *or* **to sth** Änderungen an etw *(dat)* vornehmen.

**alternate** [ɒl'tɜːnɪt] **1** *adj* **(a)** **on ~ days** jeden zweiten Tag; **they put down ~ layers of brick and mortar** sie schichteten abwechselnd Ziegel und Mörtel aufeinander. **(b)** *(alternative)* Alternativ-. **2** ['ɒltəneɪt] *vi* (sich) abwechseln.

**alternately** [ɒl'tɜːnɪtlɪ] *adv* *(in turn)* wechselweise.

**alternating** ['ɒltɜːneɪtɪŋ] *adj* wechselnd. **~ current** Wechselstrom *m*.

**alternative** [ɒl'tɜːnətɪv] **1** *adj* Alternativ-. **~ route** Ausweichstrecke *f*. **2** *n* Alternative *f*.

**alternatively** [ɒl'tɜːnətɪvlɪ] *adv* **or ~** oder aber.

**alternator** ['ɒltɜːneɪtər] *n (Elec)* Wechselstromgenerator *m*; *(Aut)* Lichtmaschine *f*.

**although** [ɔːl'ðəu] *conj* obwohl, obgleich.

**altitude** ['æltɪtjuːd] *n* Höhe *f*. **at this ~** in dieser Höhe. **~ sickness** Höhenkrankheit *f*; **~ reading** Höhenanzeige *f*.

**alto** ['æltəu] *n* Alt *m*, Altstimme *f*; *(person)* Alt *m*; *(also ~ saxophone)* Altsaxophon *nt*.

**altogether** [ˌɔːltə'geðər] **1** *adv* **(a)** im ganzen, insgesamt. **taken ~,** *or* **~ it was very pleasant** alles in allem war es sehr nett. **(b)** *(wholly)* vollkommen, ganz und gar. **he wasn't ~ wrong/pleased** er hatte nicht ganz unrecht/war nicht besonders zufrieden. **2** *n* **in the ~** *(hum col)* hüllenlos, im Adamskostüm/

*(woman)* im Evaskostüm.

**altruism** ['æltru:ɪzəm] *n* Altruismus *m*.

**altruistic** [,æltru'ɪstɪk] *adj* altruistisch.

**aluminium** [,ælju'mɪnɪəm], *(US)* **aluminum** [ə'lu:mɪnəm] *n* Aluminium *nt*. ~ **foil** Alufolie *f*.

**always** ['ɔ:lweɪz] *adv* **(a)** immer. **(b) we could ~ go by train** wir könnten doch auch den Zug nehmen.

**Alzheimer's disease** ['ælts,haɪməz dɪ,zi:z] *n* Alzheimer-Krankheit *f*.

**am** [æm] *1st pers sing pres of* **be**.

**am, a.m.** = **ante meridiem** morgens. **10** ~ **10 Uhr** morgens *or* vormittags; **12** ~ **null Uhr, 12 Uhr** nachts.

**AM** = **amplitude modulation** AM.

**amalgam** [ə'mælgəm] *n* Amalgam *nt*; *(fig also)* Gemisch *nt*, Mischung *f*.

**amalgamate** [ə'mælgəmeɪt] **1** *vt companies* fusionieren; *departments* zusammenlegen. **2** *vi (companies)* fusionieren; *(metals)* amalgamieren.

**amass** [ə'mæs] *vt* anhäufen; *money also* scheffeln.

**amateur** ['æmətə'] **1** *n* Amateur *m*; *(pej)* Dilettant(in *f*) *m*. **2** *adj attr* Amateur-; *photographer also, painter* Hobby-. ~ **actor** Laiendarsteller *m*; ~ **dramatics** Laientheater *nt*.

**amateurish** ['æmətərɪʃ] *adj (pej)* dilettantisch; *performance, work also* laienhaft.

**amaze** [ə'meɪz] **1** *vt* erstaunen. **to be ~d at sth** über etw *(acc)* erstaunt sein; **you didn't know that? You ~ me!** das wußten Sie nicht? Das wundert mich aber. **2** *vi* **he/it never ceases to ~** er/es setzt einen immer wieder in Erstaunen.

**amazement** [ə'meɪzmənt] *n* Erstaunen *nt*. **much to my ~** zu meinem großen Erstaunen.

**amazing** [ə'meɪzɪŋ] *adj* erstaunlich; *(col)* holiday etc toll *(col)*.

**amazingly** [ə'meɪzɪŋlɪ] *adv* erstaunlich; *simple, obvious also* verblüffend. ~ **enough** erstaunlicherweise.

**Amazon** ['æməzən] *n* Amazonas *m*; *(Myth, fig)* Amazone *f*.

**ambassador** [æm'bæsədə'] *n* Botschafter(in *f*) *m*; *(fig)* Repräsentant(in *f*), Vertreter(in *f*) *m*.

**amber** ['æmbə'] **1** *n (substance)* Bernstein *m*; *(colour)* Bernsteingelb *nt*; *(Brit: in traffic lights)* Gelb *nt*. **2** *adj (~-coloured)* bernsteinfarben.

**ambidextrous** [,æmbɪ'dekstrəs] *adj* mit beiden Händen gleich geschickt, beidhändig.

**ambience** ['æmbɪəns] *n* Atmosphäre *f*, Ambiente *nt*.

**ambiguity** [,æmbɪ'gjʊɪtɪ] *n* Zweideutigkeit *f*.

**ambiguous** [æm'bɪgjʊəs] *adj* zweideutig.

**ambition** [æm'bɪʃən] *n* **(a)** *(desire)* Ambition *f*. **she has ~s in that direction/for her son** sie hat Ambitionen in dieser Richtung/ehrgeizige Pläne für ihren Sohn. **(b)** *(ambitious nature)* Ehrgeiz *m*.

**ambitious** [æm'bɪʃəs] *adj* ehrgeizig, ambitiös *(pej)*. **she is ~ for her husband** sie hat ehrgeizige Pläne für ihren Mann.

**ambivalent** [æm'bɪvələnt] *adj* ambivalent.

**amble** ['æmbl] *vi* schlendern.

**ambulance** ['æmbjʊləns] *n* Krankenwagen *m*.

**ambulance:** ~ **driver** *n* Krankenwagenfahrer *m*; **~man** *n* Sanitäter *m*; ~ **service** *n* Rettungsdienst *m*; ~ **worker** *n* Sanitäter(in *f*) *m*.

**ambush** ['æmbʊʃ] **1** *n* Überfall *m* (aus dem Hinterhalt). **to lie in ~ for sb** *(Mil, fig)* jdm im Hinterhalt auflauern. **2** *vt* (aus dem Hinterhalt) überfallen.

**ameba** *n (US)* = **amoeba**.

**amelioration** [ə,mi:lɪə'reɪʃən] *n (form)* Verbesserung *f*.

**amen** [,ɑ:'men] **1** *interj* amen. **2** *n* Amen *nt*.

**amenable** [ə'mi:nəbl] *adj* zugänglich *(to dat)*.

**amend** [ə'mend] *vt* ändern.

**amendment** [ə'mendmənt] *n* Änderung *f (to gen)*; *(Pol)* Zusatz(antrag) *m*. **the First/Second etc A~** *(US Pol)* das Erste/Zweite *etc* Amendement, Zusatz 1/2 *etc*.

**amends** [ə'mendz] *npl* **to make ~ (for sth)** etw wiedergutmachen.

**amenity** [ə'mi:nɪtɪ] *n* **(public)** ~ öffentliche Einrichtung; **the lack of amenities in many parts of the city** der Mangel an Einkaufs-, Unterhaltungs- und Transportmöglichkeiten in vielen Teilen der Stadt; **close to all amenities** in günstiger (Einkaufs- und Verkehrs)lage.

**America** [ə'merɪkə] *n* Amerika *nt*.

**American** [ə'merɪkən] **1** *adj* amerikanisch. ~ **football** Football *m*; ~ **Indian** Indianer(in *f*) *m*; ~ **plan** *(US)* Vollpension *f*. **2** *n* Amerikaner(in *f*) *m*.

**americanism** [ə'merɪkənɪzəm] *n (Ling)* Amerikanismus *m*.

**americanize** [ə'merɪkənaɪz] *vt* amerikanisieren.

**Amerindian** [æmə'rɪndɪən] *n* Indianer(in *f*) *m*.

**amethyst** ['æmɪθɪst] *n* Amethyst *m*; *(colour)* Amethystblau *nt*.

**Amex** ['æmeks] *n amerikanische Börse*.

**amiable** ['eɪmɪəbl] *adj* liebenswürdig.

**amicable** ['æmɪkəbl] *adj* freundlich; *relations* freundschaftlich; *(Jur) settlement* gütlich.

**amid(st)** [ə'mɪd(st)] *prep* inmitten *(+gen)*.

**amino acid** [ə'mi:nəʊ æsɪd] *n* Aminosäure *f*.

**amiss** [ə'mɪs] **1** *adj pred* **there's something ~** da stimmt irgend etwas nicht. **2** *adv* **to take sth ~** (jdm) etw übelnehmen; **a drink would not go ~** etwas zu trinken wäre gar nicht verkehrt.

**ammeter** ['æmɪtə'] *n* Amperemeter *nt*.

**ammo** ['æməʊ] *n (col)* Munition, Mun *(col) f*.

**ammonia** [ə'məʊnɪə] *n* Ammoniak *nt*.

**ammunition** [,æmjʊ'nɪʃən] *n (lit, fig)* Munition *f*. ~ **dump** *n* Munitionslager *nt*.

**amnesia** [æm'ni:zɪə] *n* Amnesie *f (form)*, Gedächtnisschwund *m*.

**amnesty** ['æmnɪstɪ] *n* Amnestie *f*.

**amoeba**, *(US)* **ameba** [ə'mi:bə] *n* Amöbe *f*.

**amok** [ə'mɒk] *adv* = **amuck**.

**among(st)** [ə'mʌŋ(st)] *prep* unter *(+acc or dat)*. ~ **other things** unter anderem; **this habit is widespread ~ the French** diese Sitte ist bei den Franzosen weitverbreitet; **there were ferns ~ the trees** zwischen den Bäumen wuchs Farnkraut.

**amoral** [æ'mɒrəl] *adj* amoralisch.

**amorous** ['æmərəs] *adj* amourös; *look also* verliebt. ~ **state** Verliebtheit *f*.

**amorphous** [ə'mɔ:fəs] *adj* amorph, formlos; *style, ideas, play, novel* strukturlos.

**amount** [ə'maʊnt] **1** *vi* **(a)** *(total)* sich belaufen *(to auf +acc)*. **(b)** *(be equivalent)* gleichkommen *(to +dat)*. **it ~s to the same thing** das läuft *or* kommt aufs gleiche hinaus; **he will never ~ to much** aus ihm wird nie etwas werden. **2** *n* **(a)** *(of money)* Betrag *m*. **total** ~ Gesamtsumme *f*, Endbetrag *m*; **a large/small ~ of money** eine große/geringe Summe. **(b)** *(quantity)* Menge *f*; *(of luck, intelligence, skill etc)* Maß *nt (of an +dat)*. **an enormous ~ of work** sehr viel Arbeit; **any ~ of food** jede Menge Essen; **no ~ of talking will convince him** du kannst reden, soviel du willst, aber du wirst ihn nicht überzeugen.

**amp(ère)** ['æmp(εə')] *n* Ampere *nt*.

**amphetamine** [æm'fetəmi:n] *n* Amphetamin *nt*.

**amphibian** [æm'fɪbɪən] *n* Amphibie *f*; *(vehicle)* Amphibienfahrzeug *nt*.

**amphibious** [æm'fɪbɪəs] *adj animal, (Mil)* amphibisch; *vehicle, aircraft* Amphibien-.

**amphitheatre,** *(US)* **amphitheater** ['æmfɪ,θɪətəʳ] *n* Amphitheater *nt*.

**ample** ['æmpl] *adj (+er)* **(a)** *(plentiful)* reichlich. **more than ~** überreichlich; **~ time** genügend Zeit. **(b)** *(large)* figure, proportions üppig; *boot of car etc* geräumig; *garden* weitläufig, ausgedehnt.

**amplifier** ['æmplɪfaɪəʳ] *n (Rad etc)* Verstärker *m*.

**amplify** ['æmplɪfaɪ] **(a)** *(Rad etc)* verstärken. **(b)** *(expand) statement, idea* näher *or* ausführlicher erläutern.

**amply** ['æmplɪ] *adv* reichlich.

**amputate** ['æmpjʊteɪt] *vti* amputieren.

**amputation** [,æmpjʊ'teɪʃən] *n* Amputation *f*.

**Amsterdam** [,æmstə'dæm] *n* Amsterdam *nt*.

**amuck** [ə'mʌk] *adv:* **to run ~** Amok laufen.

**amuse** [ə'mjuːz] **1** *vt* **(a)** *(cause mirth)* amüsieren, belustigen. **I was ~d to hear ...** es hat mich amüsiert *or* belustigt zu hören ...; **he was not ~d** er fand es überhaupt nicht komisch. **(b)** *(entertain)* unterhalten. **let the children do it if it ~s them** laß die Kinder doch, wenn es ihnen Spaß macht; **I have no problem keeping myself ~d** ich habe keinerlei Schwierigkeiten, mir die Zeit zu vertreiben. **2** *vr* **the children can ~ themselves for a while** die Kinder können sich eine Zeitlang selbst beschäftigen.

**amusement** [ə'mjuːzmənt] *n* **(a)** *(enjoyment, fun)* Vergnügen *nt*; *(pastime)* Zeitvertreib *m*. **the toys were a great source of ~** das Spielzeug bereitete großen Spaß; **I see no cause for ~** ich sehe keinen Grund zur Heiterkeit; **to my great ~/to everyone's ~** zu meiner großen/zur allgemeinen Belustigung. **(b)** *(entertainment: of guests)* Belustigung, Unterhaltung *f*. **(c)** **~s** *pl (place of entertainment)* Vergnügungsstätte *f usu pl*; *(at fair)* Attraktionen *pl*.

**amusement:** **~ arcade** *n* Spielhalle *f*; **~ park** *n* Vergnügungspark *m*.

**amusing** [ə'mjuːzɪŋ] *adj* amüsant. **I don't find that very ~** das finde ich gar nicht lustig.

**an** [æn, ən, n] *indef art see* **a.**

**anabolic steroid** [,ænə'bɒlɪk'stɪərɔɪd] *n* Anabolikum *nt*.

**anachronism** [ə'nækrənɪzəm] *n* Anachronismus *m*.

**anachronistic** [ə,nækrə'nɪstɪk] *adj* anachronistisch; *(not fitting modern times)* nicht zeitgemäß.

**anaemia,** *(US)* **anemia** [ə'niːmɪə] *n* Anämie, Blutarmut *f*.

**anaemic,** *(US)* **anemic** [ə'niːmɪk] *adj* **(a)** anämisch, blutarm. **(b)** *(fig)* saft- und kraftlos.

**anaesthetic,** *(US)* **anesthetic** [,ænɪs'θetɪk] *n* Narkose, Anästhesie *(spec)* *f*; *(substance)* Narkosemittel *nt*. **general ~** Vollnarkose *f*; **local ~** örtliche Betäubung, Lokalanästhesie *(spec)* *f*; **under the ~** in der Narkose.

**anaesthetist,** *(US)* **anesthetist** [æ'niːsθɪtɪst] *n* Anästhesist (in *f*) *m*.

**anagram** ['ænəgræm] *n* Anagramm *nt*.

**analgesic** [,ænəl'dʒiːzɪk] **1** *n* schmerzstillendes Mittel. **2** *adj* schmerzstillend.

**analog** ['ænəlɒg] *adj (Comp, Elec)* analog. **~ computer** Analogrechner *m*.

**analogous** [ə'næləgəs] *adj* analog *(to, with* zu*)*.

**analogue** ['ænəlɒg] **1** *n* Gegenstück *nt*, Parallele *f*. **2** *adj (Brit)* **= analog.**

**analogy** [ə'nælədʒɪ] *n* Analogie *f*. **to draw an ~** eine Analogie herstellen; **on the ~ of** analog zu.

**analyse,** *(US)* **analyze** ['ænəlaɪz] *vt* analysieren.

**analysis** [ə'næləsɪs] *n, pl* **analyses** [ə'næləsiːz] **(a)** Analyse *f*; **in the final ~** letzten Endes; **on (closer) ~** bei genauerer Untersuchung. **(b)** *(psycho~)* Psychoanalyse, Analyse *(col)* *f*.

**analyst** ['ænəlɪst] *n* Analytiker *m*.

**analytical** [,ænə'lɪtɪkəl] *adj* analytisch.

**analyze** ['ænəlaɪz] *vt (US)* **= analyse.**

**anarchic** [æ'nɑːkɪk] *adj* anarchisch.

**anarchist** ['ænəkɪst] *n* Anarchist (in *f*) *m*.

**anarchy** ['ænəkɪ] *n* Anarchie *f*.

**anathema** [ə'næθɪmə] *n no art (fig)* **it is ~ to me** das ist mir ein Greuel.

**Anatolia** [,ænə'təʊlɪə] *n* Anatolien *nt*.

**anatomical** [,ænə'tɒmɪkəl] *adj* anatomisch.

**anatomy** [ə'nætəmɪ] *n* Anatomie *f*.

**ANC = African National Congress** ANC *m*.

**ancestor** ['ænsestəʳ] *n* Vorfahr, Ahne *m*.

**ancestral** [æn'sestrəl] *adj* Ahnen-, seiner/ihrer Vorfahren. **~ home** Stammsitz *m*.

**ancestry** ['ænsɪstrɪ] *n (descent)* Abstammung, Herkunft *f*; *(ancestors)* Ahnenreihe, Familie *f*.

**anchor** ['æŋkəʳ] **1** *n (Naut)* Anker *m*. **to drop ~** vor Anker gehen; **to weigh ~** den Anker lichten; **to be** *or* **lie at ~** vor Anker liegen. **2** *vt (Naut, fig)* verankern. **3** *vi (Naut)* ankern.

**anchorage** ['æŋkərɪdʒ] *n (Naut)* Ankerplatz *m*.

**anchorman** ['æŋkəʳ,mæn] *n (TV etc)* Moderator (in *f*) *m*; *(in team)* Zentralfigur *f*; *(last runner in relay race)* Schlußläufer (in *f*) *m*.

**anchovy** ['æntʃəvɪ] *n* Sardelle, An(s)chovis *f*.

**ancient** ['eɪnʃənt] *adj* alt; *(col) person, clothes etc* uralt. **in ~ times** im Altertum; *(Greek, Roman also)* in der Antike; **~ Rome** das alte Rom; **~ monument** *(Brit)* historisches Denkmal, historische Stätte; **that's ~ history** *(fig)* das ist schon längst Geschichte.

**ancillary** [æn'sɪlərɪ] *adj (secondary)* Neben-; *(auxiliary) service, troops* Hilfs-.

**and** [ænd, ənd, nd, ən] *conj* und. **nice ~ early/warm** schön früh/warm; **try ~ come** versuch zu kommen; **~/or** und/oder; **~ so on** und so weiter; **better ~ better** immer besser; **for hours ~ hours** stundenlang, Stunde um Stunde; **for miles ~ miles** meilenweit; **I tried ~ tried** ich habe es immer wieder versucht; **three hundred ~ ten** dreihundert (und) zehn.

**Andes** ['ændiːz] *npl* **the ~** die Anden *pl*.

**Andorra** [æn'dɔːrə] *n* Andorra *nt*.

**Andorran** [æn'dɔːrən] **1** *n* Andorraner (in *f*) *m*. **2** *adj* andorranisch.

**anecdote** ['ænɪkdəʊt] *n* Anekdote *f*.

**anemia** *etc (US)* **= anaemia** *etc*.

**anemone** [ə'nemənɪ] *n (Bot)* Anemone *f*, Buschwindröschen *nt*; *(sea ~)* Seeanemone *f*.

**anesthetic** *etc (US)* **= anaesthetic** *etc*.

**anew** [ə'njuː] *adv* aufs neue. **to start ~** noch einmal *or* wieder von vorn anfangen.

**angel** ['eɪndʒəl] *n (lit, fig)* Engel *m*. **be an ~ and ...** sei so lieb und ...

**angel cake** *n* ≈ Biskuitkuchen *m*.

**angelic** [æn'dʒelɪk] *adj* **(a)** *(of angel)* Engels-; *hosts* himmlisch. **(b)** *(like an angel)* engelhaft.

**anger** ['æŋgəʳ] **1** *n* Ärger *m*; *(wrath: of gods etc)* Zorn *m*. **a fit of ~** ein Wutanfall *m*; **red with ~** rot vor Wut; **public ~** öffentliche Entrüstung. **2** *vt* verärgern.

**angina** [æn'dʒaɪnə] *n* Angina, Halsentzündung *f*. **~ pectoris** Angina pectoris *f*.

**angle**[1] ['æŋgl] *n* **(a)** Winkel *m*. **at an ~ of 40°** in einem Winkel von 40°; **at an ~** schräg; *(hat)* schief. **(b)** *(projecting corner)* Ecke *f*. **(c)** *(of problem etc: aspect)* Seite *f*. **(d)** *(point of view)* Standpunkt *m*, Position *f*. **to have an ~ on a story** *(journalist)* einen Bericht von einer gewissen Warte aus schreiben.

**angle**[2] *vi (Fishing)* angeln.

  ▶**angle for** *vi +prep obj (fig) compliments* fischen nach. **to ~ ~ sth** auf etw *(acc)* aus sein.

**angle brackets** npl spitze Klammern pl.

**angler** ['æŋglə'] n Angler(in f) m.

**Anglican** ['æŋglɪkən] 1 n Anglikaner(in f) m. 2 adj anglikanisch.

**anglicism** ['æŋglɪsɪzəm] n Anglizismus m.

**anglicize** ['æŋglɪsaɪz] vt anglisieren.

**angling** ['æŋglɪŋ] n Angeln nt.

**Anglo-** ['æŋgləʊ] pref Anglo-; (between two countries) Englisch-; ~-**German** adj deutsch-englisch.

**anglo:** ~**phile** ['æŋgləʊfaɪl] 1 n Anglophile(r) mf (form), Englandfreund m; 2 adj anglophil, englandfreundlich; **A**~-**Saxon** 1 n (a) (person, Hist) Angelsachse m, Angelsächsin f; (b) (language) Angelsächsisch nt; 2 adj angelsächsisch.

**Angola** [æŋ'gəʊlə] n Angola nt.

**Angolan** [æŋ'gəʊlən] 1 n Angolaner(in f) m. 2 adj angolanisch.

**angora** [æŋ'gɔːrə] n Angora(wolle f) nt.

**angrily** ['æŋgrɪlɪ] adv wütend.

**angry** ['æŋgrɪ] adj (+er) (a) böse; (wrathful) zornig; letter, look also, animal wütend. **to be** ~ **with** or **at sb** jdm or auf jdn böse sein; **to be/get** ~ **at** or **about sth** sich über etw (acc) ärgern; **don't get** ~! reg dich nicht auf!; **to make sb** ~ jdn verärgern; **it makes me so** ~ es ärgert mich furchtbar. (b) (fig) sea aufgewühlt; sky, clouds bedrohlich, finster; (inflamed) wound entzündet, böse.

**anguish** ['æŋgwɪʃ] n Qual f. **to cause sb great** ~ jdm großen Kummer bereiten.

**anguished** ['æŋgwɪʃt] adj qualvoll; look gequält.

**angular** ['æŋgjʊlə'] adj shape eckig; face, features kantig.

**animal** ['ænɪməl] 1 n Tier nt; (brutal person also) Bestie f. **man is a social** ~ der Mensch ist ein soziales Wesen. 2 adj attr story, picture Tier-; products, fat, lust tierisch. ~ **kingdom** Tierreich nt, Tierwelt f; ~ **lover** Tierfreund m; ~ **magnetism** körperliche Anziehungskraft; ~ **rights** der Tierschutz; ~ **rights activist** Tierrechtler(in f) m.

**animate** ['ænɪmeɪt] vt (enliven) beleben.

**animated** ['ænɪmeɪtɪd] adj lebhaft, rege; discussion also angeregt. ~ **cartoon** Zeichentrickfilm m.

**animation** [ˌænɪ'meɪʃən] n Lebhaftigkeit f; (Film) Animation f.

**animosity** [ˌænɪ'mɒsɪtɪ] n Animosität (geh), Feindseligkeit f (towards gegenüber, gegen).

**aniseed** ['ænɪsiːd] n Anis m.

**ankle** ['æŋkl] n Knöchel m.

**ankle:** ~-**deep** adj knöcheltief; ~ **sock** n Söckchen nt.

**annals** ['ænəlz] npl Annalen pl.

**annex** [ə'neks] 1 vt annektieren. 2 ['æneks] n (a) (to document etc) Anhang m. (b) (building) Nebengebäude nt; (extension) Anbau m.

**annexation** [ˌænek'seɪʃən] n Annexion f.

**annexe** ['æneks] n = **annex 2** (b).

**annihilate** [ə'naɪəleɪt] vt (lit, fig) vernichten; (col) person, team fertigmachen (col).

**annihilation** [ə,naɪə'leɪʃən] n (lit, fig) Vernichtung f. **our team's** ~ die vernichtende Niederlage unserer Mannschaft.

**anniversary** [ˌænɪ'vɜːsərɪ] n Jahrestag m; (wedding ~) Hochzeitstag m. **the** ~ **of his death** sein Todestag m.

**Anno Domini** ['ænəʊ'dɒmɪnaɪ] n (a) nach Christus, Anno Domini. (b) (col: age) Alter nt.

**annotate** ['ænəʊteɪt] vt mit Anmerkungen versehen. ~**d text** kommentierter Text.

**annotation** [ˌænəʊ'teɪʃən] n (notes, act) Kommentar m; (note) Anmerkung f.

**announce** [ə'naʊns] vt (lit, fig: person) bekanntgeben, verkünden; arrival, departure, radio programme ansagen; (over intercom) durchsagen; (formally) birth, marriage etc anzeigen; coming of spring etc ankündigen. **to** ~ **sb** jdn melden.

**announcement** [ə'naʊnsmənt] n (public declaration) Bekanntgabe, Bekanntmachung f; (of impending event, speaker) Ankündigung f; (over intercom etc) Durchsage f; (on radio etc) Ansage f; (written: of birth, marriage etc) Anzeige f.

**announcer** [ə'naʊnsə'] n (Rad, TV) Ansager(in f), Radio-/Fernsehsprecher(in f) m.

**annoy** [ə'nɔɪ] vt ärgern; (noise, questions etc) aufregen; (pester) belästigen. **to be** ~**ed that** ... ärgerlich or verärgert sein, weil ...; **to be** ~**ed with sb/about sth** sich über jdn/etw ärgern, (mit) jdm/über etw (acc) böse sein.

**annoyance** [ə'nɔɪəns] n (a) no pl (irritation) Ärger m. **to his** ~ zu seinem Ärger. (b) (nuisance) Plage, Belästigung f, Ärgernis nt.

**annoying** [ə'nɔɪɪŋ] adj ärgerlich; habit lästig.

**annual** ['ænjʊəl] 1 n (a) (Bot) einjährige Pflanze. (b) (book) Jahrbuch nt. 2 adj (happening once a year) jährlich; salary etc Jahres-. ~ **accounts** Jahresbilanz f; ~ **general meeting** (Brit) Jahreshauptversammlung f; ~ **report** Jahresbericht m.

**annually** ['ænjʊəlɪ] adv jährlich.

**annual:** ~ **ring** n (on tree) Jahresring m; ~ **subscription** n (to club etc) Jahresbeitrag m; (to publication) Jahresabonnement nt.

**annuity** [ə'njuːɪtɪ] n (Leib)rente f.

**annul** [ə'nʌl] vt annullieren; law, decree, judgement aufheben; contract, marriage also auflösen.

**annulment** [ə'nʌlmənt] n see vt Annullierung f; Aufhebung f; Auflösung f.

**Annunciation** [ə,nʌnsɪ'eɪʃən] n (Bibl) Mariä Verkündigung f.

**anode** ['ænəʊd] n Anode f.

**anoint** [ə'nɔɪnt] vt salben.

**anomalous** [ə'nɒmələs] adj (abnormal) anomal, ungewöhnlich; (improper) ungehörig.

**anomaly** [ə'nɒməlɪ] n Anomalie f; (impropriety) Ungehörigkeit f; (in law etc) Besonderheit f.

**anonymity** [ˌænə'nɪmɪtɪ] n Anonymität f.

**anonymous** [ə'nɒnɪməs] adj anonym.

**anorak** ['ænəræk] n (Brit) Anorak m.

**anorexia (nervosa)** [ænə'reksɪə(nɜː'vəʊsə)] n Magersucht f.

**another** [ə'nʌðə'] 1 adj (a) (additional) noch eine(r, s). ~ **one** noch eine(r, s); **take** ~ **ten** nehmen Sie noch (weitere) zehn; **I don't want** ~ **drink** ich möchte nichts mehr trinken; ~ **20 years and he** ... noch 20 Jahre, und er ...; **without** ~ **word** ohne ein weiteres Wort; **and (there's)** ~ **thing** und noch eins, und (da ist) noch etwas; ~ **Shakespeare** ein zweiter Shakespeare. (b) (different) ein anderer, eine andere, ein anderes. **that's quite** ~ **matter** das ist etwas ganz anderes. 2 pron ein anderer, eine andere, ein anderes. **have** ~! nehmen Sie (doch) noch einen/eins etc; **tell me** ~! (col) das glaubst du doch wohl selbst nicht!; **what with one thing and** ~ bei all dem Trubel; **is this** ~ **of your brilliant ideas?** ist das wieder so eine deiner Glanzideen?

**ANSI** = **American National Standards Institute** amerikanischer Normenausschuß.

**answer** ['ɑːnsə'] 1 n (a) Antwort f (to auf +acc). **there was no** ~ (to telephone, doorbell) es hat sich niemand gemeldet; **the** ~ **to our prayers** ein Geschenk des Himmels; **there's no** ~ **to that** (col) was soll man da groß machen/sagen! (col); **in** ~ **to your letter/my question** in Beantwortung Ihres Briefes (form)/auf meine Frage hin. (b) (solution) Lösung f *(to gen)*; *(remedy)* Heilmittel *nt (for* für), Mittel *nt (for* gegen). **his ~ to any difficulty is** ... seine Reaktion auf jede Schwierigkeit ist ...

**2** *vt* **(a)** antworten auf *(+acc)*, erwidern auf *(+acc) (geh)*; *person* antworten *(+dat)*; *exam questions* beantworten, antworten auf *(+acc)*; *objections, criticism also* beantworten. **will you ~ that?** *(phone/door)* gehst du ran/hin?; **to ~ the telephone/bell** *or* **door** das Telefon abnehmen, ans Telefon gehen/die Tür aufmachen. **(b)** *(fulfil)* description entsprechen *(+dat)*; *prayer (God)* erhören; *need* befriedigen. **(c)** *(Jur) charge* sich verantworten wegen *(+gen)*.

**3** *vi (also react)* antworten. **if the phone rings, don't ~** wenn das Telefon klingelt, geh nicht ran *or* nimm nicht ab.

▶**answer back** *vi* widersprechen; *(children also)* freche Antworten geben. **don't ~ ~!** keine Widerrede!

▶**answer for** *vi +prep obj* **(a)** *(be responsible for)* verantwortlich sein für; *(person also)* verantworten; *mistakes also* einstehen für. **he has a lot to ~ ~** er hat eine Menge auf dem Gewissen. **(b)** *(guarantee)* sich verbürgen für; *(speak for also)* sprechen für.

▶**answer to** *vi +prep obj* **(a)** *(be accountable to)* **to ~ ~ sb for sth** jdm für etw Rechenschaft schuldig sein. **(b) to ~ ~ a description** einer Beschreibung entsprechen. **(c) to ~ ~ the name of** ... auf den Namen ... hören. **(d) to ~ ~ the wheel/helm** auf das Steuer/Ruder ansprechen.

**answerable** [ˈɑːnsərəbl] *adj* **(a)** *(responsible)* **to be ~ to sb (for sth)** jdm gegenüber für etw verantwortlich sein. **(b)** *question* zu beantworten.

**answering machine** [ˈɑːnsərɪŋməˈʃiːn] *n*, **answerphone** [ˈɑːnsəfəʊn] *n* Anrufbeantworter *m*.

**ant** [ænt] *n* Ameise *f*.

**antagonism** [ænˈtægənɪzəm] *n* Antagonismus *m*; *(towards sb, ideas)* Feindseligkeit *f* *(to(wards)* gegenüber).

**antagonist** [ænˈtægənɪst] *n* Gegner, Antagonist *m*.

**antagonistic** [ænˌtægəˈnɪstɪk] *adj* feindselig. **to be ~ towards sb/sth** jdm/gegen etw feindselig gesinnt sein.

**antagonize** [ænˈtægənaɪz] *vt* gegen sich aufbringen.

**antarctic** [æntˈɑːktɪk] **1** *adj* antarktisch. **A~ Circle** südlicher Polarkreis; **A~ Ocean** Südpolarmeer *nt*. **2** *n* **the A~** die Antarktis.

**Antarctica** [æntˈɑːktɪkə] *n* die Antarktis.

**ante** [ˈæntɪ] *n (Cards)* Einsatz *m*. **to up the ~** *(fig col)* den Einsatz erhöhen.

**ante-** *pref* vor-.

**anteater** [ˈæntˌiːtər] *n* Ameisenbär *m*.

**antecedent** [ˌæntɪˈsiːdənt] *n* **~s** *(of person) (past history)* Vorleben *nt*; *(ancestry)* Abstammung *f*; *(of event)* Vorgeschichte *f*.

**ante-** **~date** *vt document, cheque* vordatieren *(to* auf *+acc)*; *event* vorausgehen *(+dat) (by* um); **~diluvian** *adj (lit, fig col)* vorsintflutlich.

**antelope** [ˈæntɪləʊp] *n* Antilope *f*.

**ante meridiem** [ˈæntɪməˈrɪdɪəm] *adv (abbr* **am)** morgens, vormittags.

**antenatal** [ˈæntɪˈneɪtl] *adj* vor der Geburt, pränatal *(form)*. **~ care/excercises** Schwangerschaftsfürsorge/-gymnastik *f*; **~ clinic** Sprechstunde *f* für werdende Mütter.

**antenna** [ænˈtenə] *n* **(a)** *pl* **-e** [ænˈteniː] *(Zool)* Fühler *m*. **(b)** *pl* **-e** *or* **-s** *(Rad, TV)* Antenne *f*.

**anteroom** [ˈæntɪruːm] *n* Vorzimmer *nt*.

**anthem** [ˈænθəm] *n* Hymne *f*; *(by choir)* Chorgesang *m*.

**anthill** [ˈæntˌhɪl] *n* Ameisenhaufen *m*.

**anthology** [ænˈθɒlədʒɪ] *n* Anthologie *f*.

**anthracite** [ˈænθrəsaɪt] *n* Anthrazit *m*.

**anthropoid** [ˈænθrəʊpɔɪd] *n* Anthropoid *m (spec)*; *(ape)* Menschenaffe *m*.

**anthropologist** [ˌænθrəˈpɒlədʒɪst] *n* Anthropologe *m*, Anthropologin *f*.

**anthropology** [ˌænθrəˈpɒlədʒɪ] *n* Anthropologie *f*.

**anti** [ˈæntɪ] *prep (col)* gegen *(+acc)*. **~ everything** grundsätzlich gegen alles.

**anti-** *in cpds* Anti-, anti-; **~-abortionist** *n* Abtreibungsgegner(in *f*) *m*; **~-aircraft** *adj* rocket Flugabwehr-; **~-aircraft gun** *n* Flakgeschütz *nt*; **~biotic** *n* Antibiotikum *nt*; **~body** *n* Abwehrstoff *m*.

**anticipate** [ænˈtɪsɪpeɪt] **1** *vt* **(a)** *(expect)* erwarten. **(b)** *(see in advance)* vorhersehen; *danger, action* vorausahnen; *(see in advance and cater for) objection, need etc* zuvorkommen *(+dat)*. **(c)** *(do before sb else)* zuvorkommen *(+dat)*. **2** *vi (chess-player etc)* vorauskalkulieren.

**anticipation** [ænˌtɪsɪˈpeɪʃən] *n* **(a)** *(expectation)* Erwartung *f*. **thanking you in ~** herzlichen Dank im voraus; **to wait in ~** gespannt warten. **(b)** **his uncanny ~ of every objection** die verblüffende Art, wie er jedem Einwand zuvorkam; **the driver showed good ~** der Fahrer zeigte gute Voraussicht. **(c)** *(of discovery, discoverer)* Vorwegnahme *f*; *(Mus: of theme)* Vorgriff *m (of* auf *+acc)*.

**anti-** **~climax** *n* Enttäuschung *f*; **~clockwise** *adv* nach links, gegen den Uhrzeigersinn.

**antics** [ˈæntɪks] *npl* Eskapaden *pl*; *(tricks)* Streiche, Mätzchen *(col) pl*.

**anti-** **~cyclone** *n* Hoch(druckgebiet) *nt*; **~dazzle** *adj* Blendschutz-; *mirror* Abblend-; *screen* blendfrei; **~depressant** *n* Mittel *nt* gegen Depressionen; **~dote** [ˈæntɪdəʊt] *n (Med, fig)* Gegenmittel *nt (for* gegen); **~freeze** *n* Frostschutz *m*; **~hero** *n* Antiheld *m*; **~histamine** *n* Antihistamin *nt*.

**Antilles** [ænˈtɪliːz] *npl* Antillen *pl*.

**anti-** **~lock braking system** *n* Antiblockiersystem, ABS *nt*; **~-marketeer** *n* EG-Gegner(in *f*) *m*; **~missile missile** *n* Raketenabwehrrakete *f*.

**antipathy** [ænˈtɪpəθɪ] *n* Antipathie, Abneigung *f (towards* gegen).

**antipodes** [ænˈtɪpədiːz] *npl* **the ~** die entgegengesetzten Teile der Erde. **A~** *(Brit)* Australien und Neuseeland.

**antiquarian** [ˌæntɪˈkwɛərɪən] *adj* antiquarisch. **~ bookshop** Antiquariat *nt*.

**antiquated** [ˈæntɪkweɪtɪd] *adj* antiquiert; *machines, ideas also* überholt; *institutions also* veraltet.

**antique** [ænˈtiːk] **1** *adj* antik. **2** *n* Antiquität *f*.

**antique dealer** *n* Antiquitätenhändler(in *f*) *m*.

**antiquity** [ænˈtɪkwɪtɪ] *n* das Altertum; *(Roman, Greek ~)* die Antike; *(great age)* großes Alter.

**anti-roll bar** *n (Brit Aut)* Stabilisator *m*.

**antirrhinum** [ˌæntɪˈraɪnəm] *n* Löwenmaul *nt*.

**anti-** **~rust** *adj* Rostschutz-; **~-Semitic** *adj* antisemitisch; **~-Semitism** *n* Antisemitismus *m*; **~septic 1** *n* Antiseptikum *nt*; **2** *adj* antiseptisch; **~social** *adj* unsozial; *(Psych)* asozial; **don't be ~social** *(don't be a spoilsport)* sei kein Spielverderber; *(don't be aloof etc)* mach doch mit; **~-theft system** *n* Diebstahlsicherung *f*.

**antithesis** [ænˈtɪθɪsɪs] *n*, *pl* **antitheses** [ænˈtɪθɪsiːz] *(direct opposite)* genaues Gegenteil *(to, of* gen); *(contrast)* Gegensatz *m*.

**anti-trust** *adj (US)* Antitrust-. **~ legislation** Kartellgesetzgebung *f*.

**antler** [ˈæntlər] *n* Geweihsprosse *f*. **(set** *or* **pair of) ~s**

Geweih *nt*.

**antonym** ['æntənɪm] *n* Antonym *nt*.

**Antwerp** ['æntwɜːp] *n* Antwerpen *nt*.

**anus** ['eɪnəs] *n* After *m*.

**anvil** ['ænvɪl] *n* Amboß *m*.

**anxiety** [æŋg'zaɪətɪ] *n* (a) Sorge *f*. **to suffer from ~** unter Angst leiden. (b) *(keen desire)* **in his ~ to get away** weil er unbedingt wegkommen wollte.

**anxious** ['æŋkʃəs] *adj* (a) *(worried)* besorgt; *person (as character trait)* ängstlich. **to be ~ about sb/sth** sich *(dat)* um jdn/etw Sorgen machen, um jdn/etw besorgt sein. (b) *(worrying)* **moment, minutes** der Angst, bang *(geh)*. **it's been an ~ time for us all** wir alle haben uns (in dieser Zeit) große Sorgen gemacht. (c) **to be ~ to do sth** etw unbedingt (tun) wollen; **they were ~ for news** sie warteten gespannt auf Nachricht; **we are ~ for a settlement** uns ist an einer Klärung sehr gelegen; **I am ~ for him to do it** mir liegt viel daran, daß er es tut.

**anxiously** ['æŋkʃəslɪ] *adv* (a) besorgt. (b) *(keenly)* gespannt.

**any** ['enɪ] 1 *adj* (a) *(in interrog, conditional, neg sentences) not translated*; *(emph: ~ at all) (with sing n) (with pl n)* irgendein(e); *(with pl n)* irgendwelche; *(with uncountable n)* etwas. **do you have ~ wine/cigarettes?** haben Sie Wein/Zigaretten?; **is there ~ hope (at all)?** besteht (überhaupt) noch Hoffnung?; **not ~** kein/keine; **not any ... at all** überhaupt kein/keine ...; **if I had any plan/ideas/money (at all)** wenn ich irgendeinen Plan/irgendwelche Ideen/(auch nur) etwas Geld hätte; **without ~ difficulty (at all)** ohne jede Schwierigkeit; **hardly ~ difference at all** kaum ein Unterschied.

(b) *(no matter which)* jede(r, s) (beliebige); *(with pl or uncountable n)* alle. **~ one will do** es ist jede(r, s) recht; **you can have ~ book/books you find** du kannst jedes Buch/alle Bücher haben, das/die du findest; **take ~ two points** wähle zwei beliebige Punkte; **~ one you like** was du willst; **~ one of us** jeder von uns.

2 *pron* (a) *(in interrog, conditional, neg sentences) (replacing sing n)* ein(e), welche(r, s); *(replacing pl n)* einige, welche; *(replacing uncountable n)* etwas, welche. **I need some butter/stamps, do you have ~?** ich brauche Butter/Briefmarken, haben Sie welche?; **have you seen ~ of my ties?** haben Sie eine von meinen Krawatten gesehen?; **haven't you ~ (at all)?** haben Sie (gar) keinen/keine/keines?; **the profits, if ~** die eventuellen Gewinne; **if ~ of you can sing** wenn (irgend) jemand *or* (irgend)einer/-eine von euch singen kann; **few, if ~, will come** wenn überhaupt, werden nur wenige kommen. (b) *(no matter which)* alle; *(very few)* die wenigen. **~ I have ...** alle/die wenigen, die ich habe ...

3 *adv* (a) **if it gets ~ colder** wenn es (noch) kälter wird; **not ~ colder/bigger** nicht kälter/größer; **it won't get ~ colder** es wird nicht mehr kälter; **we can't go ~ further** wir können nicht mehr weitergehen; **are you feeling ~ better?** geht es dir etwas besser?; **do you want ~ more soup?** willst du noch etwas Suppe?; **I don't want ~ more** ich möchte nichts mehr. (b) *(esp US col: at all)* **it didn't help them ~** es hat ihnen gar *or* überhaupt nichts genützt.

**anybody** ['enɪˌbɒdɪ] 1 *pron* (a) (irgend) jemand, (irgend)eine(r). **not ... ~** niemand, keine(r); **don't tell ~** erzähl das niemand(em) *or* keinem. (b) *(no matter who)* jede(r). **~ will tell you the same** jeder wird dir dasselbe sagen. 2 *n* **she'll never be ~** sie wird nie zu etwas bringen; **he's not just ~** er ist nicht einfach irgend jemand.

**anyhow** ['enɪhaʊ] *adv* (a) **~, that's what I think** das ist jedenfalls meine Meinung; **it's no trouble, I'm going there ~** es macht keine Mühe, ich gehe sowieso hin; **I told him not to, but he did it ~** ich habe es ihm verboten, aber er hat es trotzdem gemacht; **who cares, ~?** überhaupt, wen kümmert es denn schon? (b) *(carelessly)* irgendwie; *(at random also)* aufs Geratewohl.

**anyone** ['enɪwʌn] *pron, n* = **anybody**.

**anyplace** ['enɪpleɪs] *adv (US col)* = **anywhere**.

**anything** ['enɪθɪŋ] 1 *pron* (a) (irgend) etwas. **not ~** nichts; *(emph)* gar *or* überhaupt nichts. (b) *(no matter what)* alles. **~ you like** (alles,) was du willst; **they eat ~** sie essen alles; **not just ~** nicht bloß irgend etwas; **I wouldn't do it for ~** ich würde es um keinen Preis tun. 2 *adv (col)* **it isn't ~ like him** das sieht ihm überhaupt nicht ähnlich; **it didn't cost ~ like £100** es kostete bei weitem keine £100; **not ~ like as wet as ...** nicht annähernd so naß wie ...; **she's been working like ~ (col)** sie hat wie verrückt gearbeitet.

**anyway** ['enɪweɪ] *adv* = **anyhow (a)**.

**anywhere** ['enɪwɛər] *adv* (a) *be, stay, live* irgendwo; *go, travel* irgendwohin. **not ~** nirgends/ nirgendwohin; **I haven't found ~ to live yet** ich habe noch nichts gefunden, wo ich wohnen kann; **he'll never get ~** er wird es zu nichts bringen; **I wasn't getting ~** ich kam (einfach) nicht weiter. (b) *(no matter where) be, stay, live* überall; *go, travel* überallhin. **they could be ~** sie könnten überall sein; **~ you like** wo/wohin du willst.

**aorta** [eɪ'ɔːtə] *n* Aorta *f*.

**apart** [ə'pɑːt] *adv* (a) auseinander. **to sit with one's legs ~** mit gespreizten Beinen dasitzen; **I can't tell them ~** ich kann sie nicht auseinanderhalten; **to live ~** getrennt leben; **to come** *or* **fall ~** entzweigehen, auseinanderfallen. (b) *(to one side)* zur Seite, beiseite; *(on one side)* abseits *(from gen)*. **a class/thing ~** eine Klasse/Sache für sich. (c) *(excepted)* abgesehen von, bis auf *(+acc)*. **these problems ~** abgesehen von diesen Problemen; **~ from that** abgesehen davon.

**apartheid** [ə'pɑːteɪt] *n* Apartheid *f*.

**apartment** [ə'pɑːtmənt] *n* (a) *(Brit: room)* Raum *m*. (b) **~s** *pl (Brit: suite of rooms)* Appartement *nt*. (c) *(esp US: flat)* Wohnung *f*. **~ house** *or* *(US)* **block** *or* *(US)* **building** Wohnblock *m*.

**apathetic** [ˌæpə'θetɪk] *adj* apathisch, teilnahmslos.

**apathy** ['æpəθɪ] *n* Apathie, Teilnahmslosigkeit *f*.

**APB** *(US)* = **all points bulletin** ≈ allgemeine Fahndung.

**ape** [eɪp] 1 *n (lit, fig)* Affe *m*. 2 *vt* nachäffen *(pej)*, nachmachen.

**Apennines** ['æpəˌnaɪnz] *npl* Apenninen *pl*.

**aperitif** [əˌperɪ'tiːf] *n* Aperitif *m*.

**aperture** ['æpətjʊər] *n* Öffnung *f*; *(Phot)* Blende *f*. **at an ~ of f2.8** *(Phot)* bei *or* mit Blende 2,8.

**apex** ['eɪpeks] *n* Spitze *f*; *(fig)* Höhepunkt *m*.

**aphid** ['eɪfɪd] *n* Blattlaus *f*.

**aphorism** ['æfərɪzəm] *n* Aphorismus *m*.

**aphrodisiac** [ˌæfrəʊ'dɪzɪæk] *n* Aphrodisiakum *nt*.

**apiary** ['eɪpɪərɪ] *n* Bienenhaus *nt*.

**apiece** [ə'piːs] *adv* pro Stück; *(per person)* pro Person. **I gave them two ~** ich gab ihnen je zwei; **they had two ~** sie hatten jeder zwei.

**aplomb** [ə'plɒm] *n* Gelassenheit *f*.

**Apocalypse** [ə'pɒkəlɪps] *n* Apokalypse *f*.

**apocryphal** [ə'pɒkrɪfəl] *adj (untrue)* erfunden.

**apologetic** [əˌpɒlə'dʒetɪk] *adj gesture, look* entschuldigend *attr*. **he was most ~ (about it)** er entschuldigte sich vielmals (dafür).

**apologize** [ə'pɒlədʒaɪz] *vi* sich entschuldigen *(to* bei, *for* für*)*.

**apology** [ə'pɒlədʒɪ] *n* Entschuldigung *f*. **to make** *or* **offer sb an** ~ jdn um Verzeihung bitten; **I owe you an** ~ ich muß dich um Verzeihung bitten; **to make one's apologies** sich entschuldigen; **Mr Jones sends his apologies** Herr Jones läßt sich entschuldigen; **an** ~ **for a breakfast** ein erbärmliches Frühstück.

**apoplectic** [ˌæpə'plektɪk] *n (Med)* apoplektisch. **to be** ~ **with rage** *(fig col)* vor Wut fast platzen.

**apoplexy** ['æpəpleksɪ] *n* Schlaganfall *m*.

**apostle** [ə'pɒsl] *n (lit, fig)* Apostel *m*.

**apostrophe** [ə'pɒstrəfɪ] *n (Gram)* Apostroph *m*.

**appal,** *(US also)* **appall** [ə'pɔːl] *vt* entsetzen. **to be** ~**led (at** *or* **by sth)** *(über etw acc)* entsetzt sein.

**Appalachian Mountains** [ˌæpə'leɪtʃɪən'maʊntɪnz], **Appalachians** [ˌæpəleɪtʃɪənz] *npl* Appalachen *pl*.

**appalling** [ə'pɔːlɪŋ] *adj* entsetzlich.

**apparatus** [ˌæpə'reɪtəs] *n (lit, fig)* Apparat *m*; *(equipment also)* Ausrüstung *f*; *(in gym)* Geräte *pl*. **a piece of** ~ ein Gerät *nt*.

**apparent** [ə'pærənt] *adj* **(a)** *(obvious)* offensichtlich. **to be** ~ **to sb** jdm klar sein; **to become** ~ sich (deutlich) zeigen. **(b)** *(seeming)* scheinbar.

**apparently** [ə'pærəntlɪ] *adv* anscheinend.

**apparition** [ˌæpə'rɪʃən] *n* **(a)** *(ghost, hum: person)* Erscheinung *f*. **(b)** *(appearance)* Erscheinen *nt*.

**appeal** [ə'piːl] **1** *n* **(a)** *(request: for help, money etc)* Appell *m*, Bitte *f (for* um*)*; *(for mercy)* Gesuch *nt (for* um*)*. ~ **for funds** Spendenaufruf *m or* -aktion *f*; **to make an** ~ **to sb (to do sth)/to sb for sth** an jdn appellieren(, etw zu tun)/jdn um etw bitten. **(b)** *(against decision)* Einspruch *m*; *(Jur: against sentence)* Berufung *f*; *(actual trial)* Berufungsverhandlung *f*. **he lost his** ~ er verlor in der Berufung; **right of** ~ Einspruchsrecht *nt*; *(Jur)* Berufungsrecht *nt*; **Court of A**~ Berufungsgericht *nt*. **(c)** *(attraction)* Reiz *m (to* für*)*. **his music has a wide** ~ seine Musik findet großen Anklang.

  **2** *vi* **(a)** *(make request)* **to** ~ **to sb for sth** jdn um etw bitten; **to** ~ **to the public to do sth** die Öffentlichkeit (dazu) aufrufen, etw zu tun. **(b)** *(against decision: to authority etc)* Einspruch erheben *(to* bei*)*; *(Jur)* Berufung einlegen *(to* bei*)*. **(c)** *(apply: for support, decision)* appellieren *(to* an +*acc)*; *(Sport)* Einspruch erheben *(to* bei*)*. **to** ~ **to sb's better nature** an jds besseres Ich appellieren. **(d)** *(be attractive)* reizen *(to sb* jdn*)*, zusagen *(to sb* jdm*)*; *(plan, candidate, idea)* zusagen *(to sb* jdm*)*; *(book, magazine)* ansprechen *(to sb* jdn*)*. **how does that** ~**?** wie gefällt dir/Ihnen das?; **the story** ~**ed to his sense of humour** die Geschichte sprach seinen Sinn für Humor an.

**appealing** [ə'piːlɪŋ] *adj (attractive)* attraktiv, reizvoll; *character, smile* ansprechend, gewinnend.

**appear** [ə'pɪəʳ] *vi* **(a)** erscheinen; *(unexpectedly)* auftauchen; *(personality, ghost also)* sich zeigen; *(Theat)* auftreten. **to** ~ **in court** vor Gericht erscheinen; **to** ~ **for sb** jdn vertreten. **(b)** *(seem)* scheinen. **he** ~**ed (to be) tired** er schien müde zu sein; **it** ~**s that ...** anscheinend ...; **so it** ~**s, so it would** ~ so scheint es; **it** ~**s not** anscheinend nicht, es sieht nicht so aus; **it** ~**s from his statement that ...** aus seiner Bemerkung geht hervor, daß ...

**appearance** [ə'pɪərəns] *n* **(a)** Erscheinen *nt*; *(unexpected)* Auftauchen *nt or pl*; *(Theat)* Auftritt *m*. **many successful court** ~**s** viele erfolgreiche Auftritte vor Gericht; **to put in** *or* **make an** ~ sich sehen lassen. **(b)** *(look)* Aussehen *nt*; *(of person also)* Äußere(s) *nt*, äußere Erscheinung. ~**s** *(outward*

*signs)* der äußere (An)schein; **in** ~ dem Aussehen nach; **at first** ~ auf den ersten Blick; **for the sake of** ~**s** um den Schein zu wahren; *(as good manners)* der Form halber; **to keep up** ~**s** den (äußeren) Schein wahren; ~**s are often deceptive** der Schein trügt oft; **to all** ~**s** allem Anschein nach.

**appease** [ə'piːz] *vt person, anger* beschwichtigen, besänftigen; *hunger, curiosity* stillen.

**appeasement** [ə'piːzmənt] *n (esp Pol)* Beschwichtigung *f*.

**appellant** [ə'pelənt] *n (Jur)* Berufungskläger *m*.

**append** [ə'pend] *vt notes etc* anhängen *(to* an +*acc) (also Comp)*, hinzufügen; *signature* setzen *(to* under +*acc)*.

**appendage** [ə'pendɪdʒ] *n (fig)* Anhängsel *nt*.

**appendicitis** [əˌpendɪ'saɪtɪs] *n* Blinddarmentzündung *f*.

**appendix** [ə'pendɪks] *n, pl* **appendices** **(a)** *(Anat)* Blinddarm *m*. **to have one's** ~ **out** sich *(dat)* den Blinddarm herausnehmen lassen. **(b)** *(to book etc)* Anhang, Appendix *m*.

**appetite** ['æpɪtaɪt] *n (for* auf +*acc)* Appetit *m*; *(fig: desire)* Lust *f*. **to have an/no** ~ **for sth** Appetit/keinen Appetit auf etw *(acc)* haben; *(fig)* Verlangen/kein Verlangen nach etw haben; **to have a good** ~ einen guten *or* gesunden Appetit haben.

**appetizer** ['æpɪtaɪzəʳ] *n (food)* Appetitanreger *m*; *(drink)* appetitanregendes Getränk.

**appetizing** ['æpɪtaɪzɪŋ] *adj* appetitlich *(also fig)*; *smell* lecker.

**applaud** [ə'plɔːd] *vti (lit, fig)* applaudieren (+*dat)*; *(fig) efforts, courage* loben; *decision* begrüßen.

**applause** [ə'plɔːz] *n no pl (lit, fig)* Beifall *m*.

**apple** ['æpl] *n* Apfel *m*. **to be the** ~ **of sb's eye** jds Liebling sein.

**apple** *in cpds* Apfel-; ~-**pie** *n* = gedeckter Apfelkuchen; ~-**tree** *n* Apfelbaum *m*; ~ **turnover** *n* Apfeltasche *f*.

**appliance** [ə'plaɪəns] *n* Vorrichtung *f*; *(household* ~*)* Gerät *nt*.

**applicable** [ə'plɪkəbl] *adj* anwendbar *(to* auf +*acc)*; *(on forms)* zutreffend *(to* für*)*. **that isn't** ~ **to you** das trifft auf Sie nicht zu.

**applicant** ['æplɪkənt] *n (for job)* Bewerber(in *f*) *m (for* um, für*)*; *(for loan etc)* Antragsteller(in *f*) *m (for* für*)*.

**application** [ˌæplɪ'keɪʃən] *n* **(a)** *(for job etc)* Bewerbung *f (for* um, für*)*; *(for grant, loan etc)* Antrag *m (for* auf +*acc)*. ~ **form** Bewerbung(sformular *nt)* *f*; Antrag(sformular *nt)* *m*; *(for course, exhibition etc)* Anmeldeformular *nt*. **(b)** *(act of applying)* see **apply** **1** Anwendung *f*; Auftragen *nt*; Anlegen *nt*; Betätigung *f*; Verwertung *f*. **"for external** ~ **only"** *(Med)* „nur zur äußerlichen Anwendung"; ~ **program** *(Comp)* Anwenderprogramm *nt*; ~ **software** *(Comp)* Anwendersoftware *f*. **(c)** *(diligence, effort)* Fleiß, Eifer *m*.

**applied** [ə'plaɪd] *adj attr maths etc* angewandt.

**apply** [ə'plaɪ] **1** *vt* anwenden *(to* auf +*acc)*; *paint etc* auftragen *(to* auf +*acc)*; *dressing* anlegen; *brakes* betätigen; *results, findings* verwerten *(to* für*)*. **to** ~ **oneself** *or* **one's mind (to sth)** sich (bei etw) anstrengen. **2** *vi* **(a)** sich bewerben *(for* um, für*)*. **to** ~ **for a loan** einen Kredit beantragen. **(b)** *(be applicable)* gelten *(to* für*)*.

**appoint** [ə'pɔɪnt] *vt* **(a)** *(to a job)* einstellen; *(to a post)* ernennen. **to** ~ **sb sth** jdn zu etw ernennen. **(b)** *(designate, ordain)* bestimmen. **at the** ~**ed time** zur vereinbarten Zeit.

**-appointed** [-ə'pɔɪntɪd] *adj suf* well-~ gut ausgestattet.

**appointment** [əˈpɔɪntmənt] n (a) Verabredung f; (business ~, with doctor, lawyer etc) Termin m (with bei). **to make an ~ with sb** mit jdm eine Verabredung treffen; einen Termin mit jdm vereinbaren; **do you have an ~?** sind Sie angemeldet?; **by ~** auf Verabredung; (on business, to see doctor, lawyer etc) mit (Vor)anmeldung, nach Vereinbarung. **(b)** (act of appointing) see vt **(a)** Einstellung f; Ernennung f. "**by ~ (to Her Majesty)**" (on goods) „königlicher Hoflieferant". **(c)** (post) Stelle f. **~s (vacant)** Stellenangebote pl.

**apportion** [əˈpɔːʃən] vt aufteilen. **to ~ sth to sb** jdm etw zuteilen; **to ~ blame** Schuldige finden.

**apposite** [ˈæpəzɪt] adj treffend, passend.

**appraisal** [əˈpreɪzəl] n see vt Schätzung f; Beurteilung f.

**appraise** [əˈpreɪz] vt schätzen; character, ability beurteilen.

**appreciable** [əˈpriːʃəbl] adj beträchtlich, deutlich; difference, change also merklich.

**appreciate** [əˈpriːʃɪeɪt] **1** vt **(a)** (be aware of) sich (dat) bewußt sein (+gen); (understand) sb's wishes, reluctance etc also Verständnis haben für. **I ~ that you can't come** ich verstehe, daß Sie nicht kommen können. **(b)** (value, be grateful for) zu schätzen wissen. **thank you, I ~ it** vielen Dank, sehr nett von Ihnen; **I would really ~ that** das wäre mir wirklich sehr lieb. **(c)** (enjoy) art, music, poetry schätzen. **2** vi (Fin) im Wert steigen, an Wert gewinnen.

**appreciation** [əˌpriːʃɪˈeɪʃən] n **(a)** (awareness) Erkennen nt. **(b)** (esteem, respect) Anerkennung f; (of abilities, efforts also) Würdigung f; (of person also) Wertschätzung f; (gratitude) Dankbarkeit f. **in ~ of sth** in Anerkennung (+gen), zum Dank für etw. **(c)** (enjoyment, understanding) Verständnis nt; (of art) Sinn m (of für). **(d)** (Fin: increase) (Wert)steigerung f.

**appreciative** [əˈpriːʃɪətɪv] adj anerkennend; audience dankbar; (grateful) dankbar. **to be ~ of sth** etw zu schätzen wissen; of music, art etc Sinn für etw haben.

**apprehend** [ˌæprɪˈhend] vt (arrest) festnehmen.

**apprehension** [ˌæprɪˈhenʃən] n **(a)** (fear) Besorgnis, Befürchtung f. **a feeling of ~** eine dunkle Ahnung. **(b)** (arrest) Festnahme f.

**apprehensive** [ˌæprɪˈhensɪv] adj ängstlich. **to be ~ of sth/that** ... etw befürchten/fürchten, daß ...

**apprentice** [əˈprentɪs] n Lehrling m, Auszubildende(r) mf.

**apprenticeship** [əˈprentɪsʃɪp] n Lehre f.

**appro** [ˈæprəʊ] (esp Comm) = **approval**.

**approach** [əˈprəʊtʃ] **1** vi (physically) sich nähern, näherkommen; (date, summer etc) nahen.

**2** vt **(a)** (come near) sich nähern (+dat); (Aviat also) anfliegen; (in quality, stature) herankommen an (+acc). **to ~ thirty** auf die Dreißig zugehen. **(b)** person, committee herantreten an (+acc) (about wegen). **he is easy/difficult to ~** er ist leicht/nicht leicht ansprechbar. **(c)** (tackle) problem angehen.

**3** n **(a)** (drawing near) (Heran)nahen nt; (of troops, in time also) Heranrücken nt; (of night) Einbruch m; (Aviat) Anflug m (to auf +acc). **(b)** **to make ~es/an ~ to sb** (with request) an jdn herantreten; (make advances) Annäherungsversuche machen. **(c)** (way of tackling, attitude) Ansatz m (to zu). **an easy ~ to maths** ein einfacher Weg, Mathematik zu lernen; **his ~ to the problem** sein Problemansatz m; **you've got the wrong ~** du machst das verkehrt; **try a different ~** versuch's doch mal anders. **(d)** (access) Zugang, Weg m; (road also) Zufahrt(sstraße) f.

**approachable** [əˈprəʊtʃəbl] adj **(a)** person umgänglich, zugänglich. **(b)** place zugänglich.

**approach:** **~ path** n (Aviat) Einflugschneise f; **~ road** n (to city etc) Zufahrtsstraße f; (to motorway) Zubringer m.

**approbation** [ˌæprəˈbeɪʃən] n Billigung f; (from critics) Beifall m.

**appropriate¹** [əˈprəʊprɪɪt] adj **(a)** (suitable, fitting) passend, geeignet (for, to für); (to a particular occasion, situation) angemessen; name, remark also treffend. **(b)** (relevant) entsprechend; body, authority also zuständig. **where ~** wo es angebracht ist/war, an gegebener Stelle; **delete as ~** Nichtzutreffendes streichen.

**appropriate²** [əˈprəʊprɪeɪt] vt (authorities) beschlagnahmen; (take for oneself) sich (dat) aneignen, mit Beschlag belegen.

**appropriately** [əˈprəʊprɪɪtlɪ] adv treffend; dressed passend (for, to für); (to fit particular needs) designed, equipped zweckmäßig (for, to für).

**appropriateness** [əˈprəʊprɪɪtnɪs] n (suitability) Eignung f; (for a particular occasion, situation) Angemessenheit f.

**approval** [əˈpruːvəl] n Zustimmung (of zu), Billigung f. **to meet with sb's ~** jds Zustimmung or Beifall finden; **to show one's ~ of sth** zeigen, daß man einer Sache (dat) zustimmt or etw billigt; **on ~** (Comm) auf Probe; (to look at) zur Ansicht.

**approve** [əˈpruːv] **1** vt decision billigen, gutheißen; minutes, motion annehmen; project genehmigen. **an ~d campsite** ein empfohlener Campingplatz. **2** vi **I don't ~ of him/it** ich halte nichts von ihm/davon; **I don't ~ of children smoking** ich finde es nicht richtig, daß Kinder rauchen; **do you ~?** findest du das richtig or in Ordnung?

**approved school** [əˈpruːvdˈskuːl] n (Brit) Erziehungsheim nt.

**approx.** = **approximately** ca.

**approximate** [əˈprɒksmɪt] **1** adj ungefähr. **2** [əˈprɒksəmeɪt] vti **to ~ (to) sth** einer Sache (dat) in etwa entsprechen.

**approximately** [əˈprɒksmɪtlɪ] adv ungefähr.

**approximation** [əˌprɒksɪˈmeɪʃən] n Annäherung f (of, to an +acc); (figure, sum etc) (An)näherungswert m.

**APR** = **annual percentage rate** Jahreszinssatz m.

**apricot** [ˈeɪprɪkɒt] n Aprikose f.

**April** [ˈeɪprəl] n April m. **~ fool!** ≈ April, April!; **~ Fool's Day** der erste April; **to make an ~ fool of sb** jdn in den April schicken; see **September**.

**apron** [ˈeɪprən] n Schürze f; (Aviat) Vorfeld nt. **to be tied to one's mother's ~-strings** seiner Mutter (dat) am Schürzenzipfel hängen (col).

**apse** [æps] n Apsis f.

**APT** = **advanced passenger train** Hochgeschwindigkeitszug m.

**Apt.** = **apartment** Z., Zi.

**apt** [æpt] adj (+er) **(a)** (suitable, fitting) passend; comparison, remark also treffend. **(b)** (able, intelligent) begabt (at für). **(c)** (liable) **to be ~ to do sth** dazu neigen, etw zu tun.

**aptitude** [ˈæptɪtjuːd] n Begabung f. **~ test** Eignungsprüfung f.

**aptly** [ˈæptlɪ] adv passend.

**aqualung** [ˈækwəlʌŋ] n Tauchgerät nt.

**aquamarine** [ækwəməˈriːn] **1** n Aquamarin nt. **2** adj aquamarin(blau).

**aquaplaning** [ˈækwəpleɪnɪŋ] n Aquaplaning nt.

**aquarium** [əˈkwɛərɪəm] n Aquarium nt.

**Aquarius** [əˈkwɛərɪəs] n Wassermann m.

**aquatic** [əˈkwætɪk] adj Wasser-.

**aqueduct** ['ækwɪdʌkt] *n* Aquädukt *m or nt.*
**aquiline** ['ækwɪlaɪn] *adj nose* Adler-, gebogen.
**AR** *(US Post)* = **Arkansas**.
**Arab** ['ærəb] **1** *n* Araber *m (also horse),* Araberin *f.* **2** *adj attr* arabisch. ~ **customs/policies** die Bräuche/ Politik der Araber.
**arabesque** [,ærə'besk] *n* Arabeske *f.*
**Arabia** [ə'reɪbɪə] *n* Arabien *nt.*
**Arabian** [ə'reɪbɪən] *adj* arabisch. **the ~ Sea/desert** das Arabische Meer/die Arabische Wüste; **tales of the ~ Nights** Märchen aus Tausendundeiner Nacht.
**Arabic** ['ærəbɪk] **1** *n* Arabisch *nt.* **2** *adj* arabisch.
**arable** ['ærəbl] *adj land* bebaubar; *(being used)* Acker-.
**arbitrary** ['ɑːbɪtrərɪ] *adj* willkürlich.
**arbitrate** ['ɑːbɪtreɪt] **1** *vt dispute* schlichten. **2** *vi* vermitteln.
**arbitration** [,ɑːbɪ'treɪʃən] *n* Schlichtung *f.* ~ **(decision)** Schiedsspruch *m;* ~ **proceedings** Schiedsverfahren *nt;* **to go to ~** vor eine Schlichtungskommission gehen; *(dispute)* vor eine Schlichtungskommission gebracht werden.
**arbitrator** ['ɑːbɪtreɪtəʳ] *n* Vermittler *m; (esp Ind)* Schlichter *m.*
**arc** [ɑːk] *n* Bogen *m; (Elec)* Lichtbogen *m.*
**arcade** [ɑː'keɪd] *n (Archit)* Arkade *f; (shopping ~)* Passage *f.*
**arcane** [ɑː'keɪn] *adj* obskur.
**arch¹** [ɑːtʃ] **1** *n* **(a)** Bogen *m.* **(b)** *(Anat)* **fallen ~es** Senkfüße *pl.* **2** *vi* sich wölben; *(arrow etc)* einen Bogen beschreiben. **3** *vt back* krümmen. **the cat ~ed his back** die Katze machte einen Buckel.
**arch²** *adj attr* Erz-. ~ **traitor** Hochverräter *m.*
**archaeological, archeological** [,ɑːkɪə'lɒdʒɪkəl] *adj* archäologisch.
**archaeologist, archeologist** [,ɑːkɪ'ɒlədʒɪst] *n* Archäologe *m,* Archäologin *f.*
**archaeology, archeology** [,ɑːkɪ'ɒlədʒɪ] *n* Archäologie *f.*
**archaic** [ɑː'keɪɪk] *adj word etc* veraltet, archaisch *(spec); (col)* vorsintflutlich.
**arch: ~angel** ['ɑːk,eɪndʒəl] *n* Erzengel *m;* **~bishop** *n* Erzbischof *m;* **~duke** *n* Erzherzog *m.*
**arched** [ɑːtʃt] *adj* gewölbt; *window* (Rund)bogen-.
**arch-enemy** [,ɑːtʃ'enɪmɪ] *n* Erzfeind *m.*
**archeological** *etc* = **archaeological** *etc.*
**archer** ['ɑːtʃəʳ] *n* Bogenschütze *m.*
**archery** ['ɑːtʃərɪ] *n* Bogenschießen *nt.*
**archetypal** ['ɑːkɪtaɪpəl] *adj* archetypisch *(geh); (typical)* typisch.
**archetype** ['ɑːkɪtaɪp] *n* Urbild *nt,* Urtyp *m.*
**archipelago** [,ɑːkɪ'pelɪgəʊ] *n, pl* **-(e)s** Archipel *m.*
**architect** ['ɑːkɪtekt] *n (lit, fig)* Architekt(in *f) m.*
**architectural** [,ɑːkɪ'tektʃərəl] *adj* architektonisch.
**architecture** ['ɑːkɪtektʃəʳ] *n* Architektur *f (also Comp); (of building also)* Baustil *m.*
**archive** ['ɑːkaɪv] *n* Archiv *nt (also Comp).*
**archives** ['ɑːkaɪvz] *npl* Archiv *nt.*
**archway** ['ɑːtʃ,weɪ] *n* Torbogen *m.*
**arc lamp** ['ɑːk,læmp] *n* Bogenlampe *f.*
**arctic** ['ɑːktɪk] **1** *adj (lit, fig)* arktisch. **A~ Circle** nördlicher Polarkreis; **A~ Ocean** Nordpolarmeer *nt.* **2** *n* **the A~** die Arktis.
**arc welding** ['ɑːk,weldɪŋ] *n* (Licht)bogenschweißung *f.*
**ardent** ['ɑːdənt] *adj* leidenschaftlich; *supporter also* begeistert; *admirer also* glühend.
**ardour, (US) ardor** ['ɑːdəʳ] *n (of person)* Leidenschaft *f; (of feelings also)* Heftigkeit *f; (passion)* Leidenschaftlichkeit *f.*
**arduous** ['ɑːdjʊəs] *adj* beschwerlich, mühsam;

*course, work* anstrengend; *task* mühselig.
**are** [ɑːʳ] *2nd pers sing, 1st, 2nd, 3rd pers pl pres of* **be.**
**area** ['ɛərɪə] *n* **(a)** *(measure)* Fläche *f.*
  **(b)** *(region, district)* Gebiet *nt; (neighbourhood, vicinity)* Gegend *f; (separated off, piece of ground etc)* Gelände *nt; (on plan, diagram etc)* Bereich *m; (slum ~, residential ~, commercial ~ also)* Viertel *nt.* **in the ~** in der Nähe; **dining/sleeping ~** Eß-/ Schlafbereich *m;* **no smoking/reception ~** Nichtraucherzone *f/*Empfangsbereich *m;* **this ~ is for directors' cars** dieser Platz ist für die Direktorenwagen vorgesehen; **the infected ~s of the lungs** die befallenen Lungenpartien; **in the ~ of the station** in der Bahnhofsgegend; **the thief is still in the ~** der Dieb hält sich noch in der Umgebung auf; **in the London ~** im Raum London, im Londoner Raum; **~ code** *(Telec)* Vorwahl(nummer) *f;* **~ office** Bezirksbüro *nt.*
  **(c)** *(fig)* Bereich *m.* **his ~ of responsibility** sein Verantwortungsbereich *m;* **the ~s in which we agree** die Bereiche, in denen wir übereinstimmen; **~ of interest/study** Interessen-/Studiengebiet *nt;* **in the ~ of £100** um die hundert Pfund.
**arena** [ə'riːnə] *n (lit, fig)* Arena *f.*
**aren't** [ɑːnt] = **are not; am not;** *see* **be.**
**Argentine** ['ɑːdʒəntaɪn] **1** *n* **(a) the ~** Argentinien *nt.* **(b)** *(person)* Argentinier(in *f) m.* **2** *adj* argentinisch.
**Argentina** [,ɑːdʒən'tiːnə] *n* Argentinien *nt.*
**Argentinian** [,ɑːdʒən'tɪnɪən] **1** *n (person)* Argentinier(in *f) m.* **2** *adj* argentinisch.
**arguable** ['ɑːgjʊəbl] *adj* **(a)** *(capable of being maintained)* vertretbar. **it is ~ that** ... es läßt sich der Standpunkt vertreten, daß ... **(b)** *(doubtful)* **it is ~ whether** ... es ist (noch) die Frage, ob ...
**arguably** ['ɑːgjʊəblɪ] *adj* **this is ~ his best book** dies dürfte (wohl) sein bestes Buch sein.
**argue** ['ɑːgjuː] **1** *vi* **(a)** *(dispute)* streiten; *(quarrel)* sich streiten. **don't ~ (with me)!** keine Widerrede!; **there's no point in arguing** da erübrigt sich jede weitere Diskussion. **(b)** *(present reasons)* **he ~s that** ... er vertritt den Standpunkt, daß ..., er behauptet, daß ...; **to ~ for or in favour of sth** für etw sprechen; *(in book)* sich für etw aussprechen; **to ~ against sth** gegen etw sprechen; *(in book)* sich gegen etw aussprechen; **to ~ from a position of** ... von einem Standpunkt *(+gen)* aus argumentieren. **2** *vt (debate) issue* diskutieren, erörtern; *(Jur, present) case* vertreten. **a well ~d case** ein gut dargelegter Fall.
**argument** ['ɑːgjʊmənt] *n* **(a)** *(discussion)* Diskussion *f.* **for the sake of ~** rein theoretisch; **this is open to ~** darüber läßt sich streiten. **(b)** *(quarrel)* Auseinandersetzung *f.* **to have an ~** sich streiten. **(c)** *(reason)* Argument *nt; (line of reasoning)* Argumentation, Beweisführung *f; (statement of proof)* Beweis *m.* **(d)** *(theme: of play, book etc)* Aussage *f; (claim)* These *f.*
**argumentation** [,ɑːgjʊmen'teɪʃən] *n* Argumentation, Beweisführung *f.*
**argumentative** [,ɑːgjʊ'mentətɪv] *adj* streitsüchtig.
**argy-bargy** ['ɑːdʒɪ'bɑːdʒɪ] *n (col)* Hickhack *m or nt (col).*
**aria** ['ɑːrɪə] *n* Arie *f.*
**arid** ['ærɪd] *adj* dürr; *(fig) subject* trocken.
**aridity** [ə'rɪdɪtɪ] *n* Dürre *f; (fig)* Trockenheit *f.*
**Aries** ['ɛəriːz] *n (Astrol)* Widder *m.*
**arise** [ə'raɪz] *pret* **arose** [ə'rəʊz], *ptp* **arisen** [ə'rɪzn] *vi* **(a)** *(occur)* entstehen; *(misunderstanding, problem also)* aufkommen; *(protest, cry)* sich erheben; *(question)* sich stellen. **(b)** *(result)* **to ~ from sth**

sich aus etw ergeben. **(c)** *(old, liter: get up)* sich erheben *(liter)*.
**aristocracy** [ˌærɪsˈtɒkrəsɪ] *n* Aristokratie *f*.
**aristocrat** [ˈærɪstəkræt] *n* Aristokrat(in *f*) *m*, Adlige(r) *mf*.
**aristocratic** [ˌærɪstəˈkrætɪk] *adj (lit, fig)* aristokratisch, adlig; *(fig also)* vornehm.
**Aristotle** [ˈærɪstɒtl] *n* Aristoteles *m*.
**arithmetic** [əˈrɪθmətɪk] *n* Rechnen *nt*. **could you check my ~?** kannst du das mal nachrechnen?
**ark** [ɑːk] *n* Arche *f*. **Noah's ~** die Arche Noah.
**arm¹** [ɑːm] *n* **(a)** Arm *m*. **under one's ~** unter dem *or* unterm Arm; **to take sb in one's ~s** jdn in die Arme nehmen; **to put one's ~s around sb** jdn umarmen; **~ in ~** Arm in Arm; *(~s linked)* eingehakt, untergehakt; **to keep sb at ~'s length** *(fig)* jdn auf Distanz halten; **with open ~s** mit offenen Armen; **within ~'s reach** in Reichweite; **as long as your ~** *(fig)* ellenlang; **it cost him an ~ and a leg** *(col)* es kostete ihn ein Vermögen. **(b)** *(sleeve)* Arm, Ärmel *m*; *(of river)* (Fluß)arm *m*; *(of armchair)* (Arm)lehne *f*; *(of record player)* Tonarm *m*.
**arm²** **1** *vt person, nation etc* bewaffnen; *bomb* scharf machen. **to ~ sth with sth** etw mit etw ausrüsten; **to ~ oneself with sth** *(lit, fig)* sich mit etw bewaffnen; *(fig: non-aggressively)* sich mit etw wappnen; **he came ~ed with an excuse** er hatte eine Ausrede parat. **2** *vi* aufrüsten. **to ~ for war** zum Krieg rüsten.
**armada** [ɑːˈmɑːdə] *n* Armada *f*.
**armadillo** [ˌɑːməˈdɪləʊ] *n* Gürteltier *nt*.
**armament** [ˈɑːməmənt] *n* **(a)** **~s** *pl (weapons)* Ausrüstung *f*. **(b)** *(preparation)* Aufrüstung *f no pl*.
**armband** [ˈɑːmbænd] *n* Armbinde *f*.
**armchair** [ˌɑːmˈtʃɛəʳ] *n* Sessel, Lehnstuhl *m*. **~ detective** Amateurdetektiv *m*; **~ politician** Stammtischpolitiker *m*.
**armed** [ɑːmd] *adj* bewaffnet.
**armed: ~ forces** *pl* Streitkräfte *pl*; **~ robbery** *n* bewaffneter Raubüberfall.
**Armenia** [ɑːˈmiːnɪə] *n* Armenien *nt*.
**Armenian** [ɑːˈmiːnɪən] **1** *adj* armenisch. **2** *n* **(a)** *(person)* Armenier(in *f*) *m*. **(b)** *(language)* Armenisch *nt*.
**armful** [ˈɑːmfʊl] *n* Armvoll *m no pl*, Ladung *f (col)*.
**armistice** [ˈɑːmɪstɪs] *n* Waffenstillstand *m*.
**armour,** *(US)* **armor** [ˈɑːməʳ] *n* **(a)** Rüstung *f*; *(of animal)* Panzer *m*. **suit of ~** Rüstung *f*. **(b)** *(no pl: steel plates)* Panzerplatte(n *pl*) *f*. **(c)** *(vehicles)* Panzerfahrzeuge *pl*.
**armoured** [ˈɑːməd] *adj division, glass* Panzer-. **~ car** Panzerwagen *m*.
**armour: ~-piercing** *adj* panzerbrechend; **~-plated** *adj* gepanzert.
**armoury,** *(US)* **armory** [ˈɑːmərɪ] *n* Arsenal, Waffenlager *nt*; *(US: factory)* Munitionsfabrik *f*.
**arm: ~pit** *n* Achselhöhle *f*; **~rest** *n* Armlehne *f*.
**arms** [ɑːmz] *npl* **(a)** *(weapons)* Waffen *pl*. **to be up in ~ (about sth)** *(fig col)* (über etw *acc*) empört sein; **~ control** Rüstungskontrolle *f*; **~ freeze** Rüstungsstopp *m*; **~ race** Wettrüsten *nt*; **~ trade** Waffenhandel *m*; **~ dealer** Waffenhändler *m*. **(b)** *(Her)* Wappen *nt*.
**army** [ˈɑːmɪ] **1** *n* **(a)** Armee *f*, Heer *nt*. **to join the ~** zum Militär gehen. **(b)** *(fig)* Heer *nt*. **(c)** *(division)* Armee(korps *nt*) *f*. **2** *attr* Militär-; *discipline* militärisch; *life, slang* Soldaten-. **~ officer** Offizier *m* (in der Armee).
**aroma** [əˈrəʊmə] *n* Duft *m*, Aroma *nt*.
**aromatherapy** [əˌrəʊməˈθerəpɪ] *n* Aromatherapie *f*.
**aromatic** [ˌærəʊˈmætɪk] *adj* aromatisch.

**arose** [əˈrəʊz] *pret of* **arise**.
**around** [əˈraʊnd] **1** *adv* herum, rum *(col)*. **with gardens all ~** mit Gärten ringsherum; **I looked all ~** ich sah mich nach allen Seiten um; **books were lying all ~** überall lagen Bücher herum; **for miles ~** meilenweit im Umkreis; **is he ~?** ist er da?; **he's been ~!** der kennt sich aus!; **it's been ~ for ages** das ist schon uralt; **see you ~!** *(col)* bis bald! **2** *prep* **(a)** *(movement, position)* um *(+acc)*; *(in a circle)* um *(+acc)* ... herum. **(b)** *(in, through)* **to wander ~ the city** durch die Stadt spazieren; **to talk ~ a subject** um ein Thema herumreden. **(c)** *(approximately)* *(with date)* um *(+acc)*; *(with time of day)* gegen *(+acc)*; *(with weight, price)* etwa, um die *(col)*; *see also* **round**.
**arousal** [əˈraʊzəl] *n (sexual)* Erregung *f*.
**arouse** [əˈraʊz] *vt* **(a)** *(lit liter)* wecken. **(b)** *(excite)* erregen; *interest, suspicion etc also* (er)wecken.
**arr** *(Rail)* = **arrives** Ank.
**arrange** [əˈreɪndʒ] *vt* **(a)** *(order)* ordnen; *furniture, objects* aufstellen, hinstellen; *flowers* arrangieren; *room* einrichten. **(b)** *(fix)* vereinbaren, ausmachen; *details* regeln; *party* arrangieren, organisieren. **I have ~d for a car to pick you up** ich habe Ihnen einen Wagen bestellt, der Sie abholt; **if you could ~ to be there at five** wenn du es einrichten kannst, um fünf Uhr da zu sein; **that's easily ~d** das läßt sich leicht einrichten *or* arrangieren; **a meeting has been ~d for next month** nächsten Monat ist ein Treffen angesetzt; **good, that's ~d then** gut, das ist abgemacht!; **but you ~d to meet me!** aber du wolltest dich doch mit mir treffen! **(c)** *(Mus)* bearbeiten; *light music* arrangieren.
**arrangement** [əˈreɪndʒmənt] *n* **(a)** Anordnung *f*; *(of room)* Einrichtung *f*. **a floral ~** ein Blumenarrangement *nt*. **(b)** *(agreement)* Vereinbarung *f*; *(to meet)* Verabredung *f*; *(esp shifty)* Arrangement *nt*. **a special ~** eine Sonderregelung; **to have an ~ with sb** eine Regelung mit jdm getroffen haben; **to make an ~ with sb** eine Vereinbarung *or* Absprache mit jdm treffen; **to come to an ~ with sb** eine Regelung mit jdm treffen; *(settle dispute)* sich mit jdm einigen. **(c)** **~s** *pl (plans)* Pläne *pl*; *(preparations)* Vorbereitungen *pl*. **to make ~s for sth** für etw Vorbereitungen treffen; **to make ~s for sth to be done** veranlassen, daß etw getan wird. **(d)** *(Mus)* Bearbeitung *f*; *(light music)* Arrangement *nt*.
**arrant** [ˈærənt] *adj* **~ nonsense** barer Unsinn.
**array** [əˈreɪ] *n (collection)* Ansammlung *f*, Aufgebot *nt*. **in battle ~** in Kampfaufstellung.
**arrears** [əˈrɪəz] *npl* Rückstände *pl*; *(payments)* Zahlungsrückstände *pl*. **to be in ~ with sth** mit etw im Rückstand sein.
**arrest** [əˈrest] **1** *vt* **(a)** festnehmen, verhaften. **(b)** *(check)* hemmen; *sth unwanted* (Ein)halt gebieten *(+dat)*. **2** *n* Festnahme, Verhaftung *f*. **you are under ~** Sie sind festgenommen *or* verhaftet; **to put sb under ~** jdn festnehmen *or* verhaften.
**arresting** [əˈrestɪŋ] *adj (striking)* atemberaubend; *features* markant.
**arrival** [əˈraɪvəl] *n* **(a)** *(coming)* Ankunft *f no pl*; *(of person also)* Kommen, Eintreffen *nt no pl*; *(of train also, of goods, news)* Eintreffen *nt no pl*. **on ~** bei Ankunft; **~ lounge** Ankunftshalle *f*; **~ time** Ankunftszeit *f*; **~s board** *(Rail)* Ankunftstafel *f*; *(Aviat)* Ankunftsanzeige *f*. **(b)** *(person)* **new ~** Neuankömmling *m*; *(at school also)* Neue(r) *mf*.
**arrive** [əˈraɪv] *vi* ankommen, eintreffen *(geh)*. **to ~ home** nach Hause kommen; **the great day ~d** der große Tag kam.
▸**arrive at** *vi +prep obj decision* gelangen zu; *price*

sich einigen auf *(+acc)*.

**arrogance** ['ærəgəns] *n* Arroganz, Überheblichkeit *f*.

**arrogant** ['ærəgənt] *adj* arrogant, überheblich.

**arrow** ['ærəʊ] *n (weapon, sign)* Pfeil *m*.

**arrow:** ~**head** *n* Pfeilspitze *f*; ~ **key** *n (Comp)* Pfeiltaste *f*.

**arse** [ɑːs] *(col!)* Arsch *m (col!)*.

▶**arse about** *vi (col)* rumblödeln *(col)*.

**arsenal** ['ɑːsɪnl] *n (Mil) (store)* Arsenal *nt; (arms factory)* Waffenfabrik *f; (munitions factory)* Munitionsfabrik *f*.

**arsenic** ['ɑːsnɪk] *n* Arsen *nt*.

**arson** ['ɑːsn] *n* Brandstiftung *f*. ~ **attack** Brandanschlag *m*.

**arsonist** ['ɑːsənɪst] *n* Brandstifter(in *f*) *m*.

**art** [ɑːt] *n* **(a)** Kunst *f*. **there's an** ~ **to it** das ist eine Kunst; ~**s and crafts** Kunsthandwerk, Kunstgewerbe *nt;* **A~s Council** Kulturausschuß *m* der britischen Regierung; **a~s minister** *(Brit)* Kulturminister *m*. **(b)** ~**s** *(Univ)* Geisteswissenschaften *pl;* **Faculty of A~s** Philosophische Fakultät; ~**s subject** geisteswissenschaftliches Fach.

**art college** *n* Kunsthochschule *f*.

**art deco** ['ɑːt'dekəʊ] *n* Art deco *f*.

**artefact** *(Brit)*, **artifact** ['ɑːtɪfækt] *n* Artefakt *nt*.

**arterial** [ɑː'tɪərɪəl] *adj (Anat)* arteriell. ~ **road** Fernverkehrsstraße *f*.

**arteriosclerosis** [ɑː'tɪərɪəʊsklɪ'rəʊsɪs] *n (Med)* Arteriosklerose, Arterienverkalkung *f*.

**artery** ['ɑːtərɪ] *n* **(a)** *(Anat)* Arterie *f*, Schlagader *f*. **(b)** *(also* **traffic** ~*)* Verkehrsader *f*.

**art form** *n* Kunstgattung *f*. **to raise sth to an** ~ eine Kunst aus etw machen.

**artful** ['ɑːtfʊl] *adj person, trick* raffiniert, schlau.

**art gallery** *n* Kunstgalerie *f*.

**arthritic** [ɑː'θrɪtɪk] *adj* arthritisch. **she is** ~ sie hat Arthritis.

**arthritis** [ɑː'θraɪtɪs] *n* Arthritis, Gelenkentzündung *f*.

**Arthur** ['ɑːθər] *n* Art(h)ur *m*. **King**~ *(Hist, Myth)* König Artus.

**artichoke** ['ɑːtɪtʃəʊk] *n* Artischocke *f*.

**article** ['ɑːtɪkl] *n* **(a)** *(item)* Gegenstand *m; (in list)* Posten *m; (Comm)* Ware *f*, Artikel *m*. ~**s of clothing** Kleidungsstücke *pl;* **toilet** ~**s** Toilettenartikel *pl*. **(b)** *(in newspaper)* Artikel, Beitrag *m; (encyclopedia entry)* Eintrag *m*. **(c)** *(of constitution)* Artikel *m; (of treaty, contract)* Paragraph *m*. ~**s of association** Gesellschaftsvertrag *m*. **(d)** *(Gram)* Artikel *m*. **(e)** *(Brit Jur: of articled clerk)* **to be under** ~**s** Rechtsreferendar(in) sein.

**articled** ['ɑːtɪkld] *adj (Brit Jur)* ~ **clerk** Rechtsreferendar(in *f*) *m*.

**articulate** [ɑː'tɪkjʊlɪt] **1** *adj sentence, book* leicht verständlich. **to be** ~ sich gut *or* klar ausdrücken können; **clear and** ~ klar und deutlich. **2** [ɑː'tɪkjʊleɪt] *vt* **(a)** *(pronounce)* artikulieren. **(b)** *(state) reasons, views etc* darlegen. **(c)** ~**d lorry** *(Brit) or* **truck** Sattelschlepper *m*.

**articulation** [ɑːˌtɪkjʊ'leɪʃən] *n (of speech)* Artikulation *f*.

**artifact** *n* = **artefact**.

**artifice** ['ɑːtɪfɪs] *n (guile)* List *f no pl*.

**artificial** [ˌɑːtɪ'fɪʃəl] *adj (lit, fig)* künstlich; *(pej) smile* gekünstelt, unecht. ~ **insemination** künstliche Befruchtung; ~ **intelligence** künstliche Intelligenz; ~ **leather** Kunstleder *nt;* ~ **limb** Prothese *f;* ~ **respiration** künstliche Beatmung; ~ **silk** Kunstseide *f*.

**artificiality** [ˌɑːtɪfɪʃɪ'ælɪtɪ] *n* **(a)** Künstlichkeit *f*. **(b)** *(insincerity, unnaturalness)* Gekünsteltheit *f*.

**artificially** [ˌɑːtɪ'fɪʃəlɪ] *adv* künstlich; *(insincerely)* gekünstelt.

**artillery** [ɑː'tɪlərɪ] *n (weapons, troops)* Artillerie *f*.

**artisan** ['ɑːtɪzæn] *n* Handwerker *m*.

**artist** ['ɑːtɪst] *n* Künstler(in *f*) *m*.

**artiste** [ɑː'tiːst] *n* Künstler(in *f*) *m; (circus* ~*)* Artist(in *f*) *m*.

**artistic** [ɑː'tɪstɪk] *adj* künstlerisch; *(tasteful) arrangements* kunstvoll; *(appreciative of art)* kunstverständig. ~ **temperament** Künstlertemperament *nt;* **she's very** ~ sie ist künstlerisch veranlagt.

**artistry** ['ɑːtɪstrɪ] *n (lit, fig)* Kunst *f*.

**artless** ['ɑːtlɪs] *adj* unschuldig.

**Art Nouveau** ['ɑːnuː'vəʊ] *n* Jugendstil *m*.

**arts centre** *n* Kulturzentrum *nt*.

**art:** ~ **paper** *n* Kunstdruckpapier *nt;* ~ **school** *n* Kunsthochschule *f;* ~**work** *n (in book)* Bildmaterial *nt; (material for printing)* Druckvorlage *f*.

**arty** ['ɑːtɪ] *adj (+er) (col)* Künstler-; *type also, tie, clothes* verrückt *(col); person* künstlerisch angehaucht *(col); decoration, style* auf Kunst getrimmt *(col); film, novel* geschmäcklerisch.

**arty-farty** ['ɑːtɪ'fɑːtɪ] *adj (hum col) see* **arty**.

**as** [æz, əz] **1** *conj* **(a)** *(when, while)* als; *(two parallel actions)* während, als, indem. ~ **he got older** mit zunehmendem Alter; ~ **a child** als Kind. **(b)** *(since)* da. ~ **it's late** da es spät ist. **(c)** *(although)* **rich/big** ~ **he is** und wenn er noch so reich/groß ist; **much** ~ **I admire her, ...** so sehr ich sie auch bewundere, ...; **try** ~ **he might** so sehr er sich auch bemüht/bemühte. **(d)** *(manner)* wie. ~ **I said** wie gesagt; **do** ~ **you like** machen Sie, was Sie wollen; **leave it** ~ **it is** lassen Sie es so; **he drinks enough** ~ **it is** er trinkt sowieso schon genug; ~ **it were** sozusagen; **my husband** ~ **was** *(col)* mein verflossener *or (late)* verstorbener Mann. **(e)** *(phrases)* ~ **if** *or* **though** als ob; **he rose** ~ **if to go** er erhob sich, als wollte er gehen; **it isn't** ~ **if he didn't see me** schließlich hat er mich ja gesehen; ~ **for him/you** (und) was ihn/dich angeht; ~ **from** *or* **of the 5th/now** vom Fünften an/von jetzt an.

**2** *adv* ~ **...** ~ **so ... wie;** **not** ~ **...** ~ nicht so ... wie; **twice** ~ **old** doppelt so alt; **just** ~ **nice** genauso nett; **late** ~ **usual!** wie immer zu spät!; **is it** ~ **difficult** ~ **that?** ist das denn so schwierig?; ~ **many/much** ~ **I could** so viele/soviel ich (nur) konnte.

**3** *prep (in the capacity of)* als. **to be employed as a ...** als ... angestellt sein.

**asap** = **as soon as possible** baldmöglichst.

**asbestos** [æz'bestəs] *n* Asbest *m*.

**ascend** [ə'send] **1** *vi (rise)* aufsteigen. **in** ~**ing order** in aufsteigender Reihenfolge. **2** *vt stairs* hinaufsteigen; *mountain, throne* besteigen.

**ascendancy** [ə'sendənsɪ] *n* **to gain the** ~ **over sb** die Vorherrschaft über jdn gewinnen.

**ascendant** [ə'sendənt] *n* **to be in the** ~ *(Astrol)* im Aszendenten stehen; *(fig)* im Aufstieg begriffen sein.

**Ascension** [ə'senʃən] *n* **the** ~ (Christi) Himmelfahrt *f;* ~ **Day** Himmelfahrt(stag *m*) *nt*.

**ascent** [ə'sent] *n* Besteigung *f*, Aufstieg *m (of* auf *+acc)*.

**ascertain** [ˌæsə'teɪn] *vt* ermitteln, feststellen.

**ascetic** [ə'setɪk] **1** *adj* asketisch. **2** *n* Asket *m*.

**asceticism** [ə'setɪsɪzəm] *n* Askese *f*.

**ASCII** ['æski:] *(Comp)* = **American Standard Code for Information Interchange** ASCII(-Code *m*).

**ascribe** [ə'skraɪb] *vt* zuschreiben *(sth to sb* jdm etw*)*.

**aseptic** [eɪ'septɪk] *adj* aseptisch.

**ash**[1] [æʃ] *n (also* ~ **tree)** Esche *f*.

**ash**[2] *n* **(a)** Asche *f*. ~**es** Asche *f*; **to reduce sth to** ~**es** etw total *or* völlig niederbrennen; *(in war)* etw in Schutt und Asche legen. **(b)** *(Cricket)* **the A**~**es** Spielserie f zwischen Australien und England.

**ashamed** [ə'ʃeɪmd] adj beschämt. **to be** or **feel ~ (of sb/sth)** sich schämen (für jdn/für or wegen etw); **it's nothing to be ~ of** deswegen braucht man sich nicht zu schämen; ... **I'm ~ to say** ..., muß ich leider zugeben; **you ought to be ~ (of yourself)** du solltest dich (was) schämen!

**A shares** ['eɪʃɛəz] npl stimmrechtslose Aktien pl.

**ash: ~ blonde** adj aschblond; **~can** n (US) Mülltonne f.

**ashore** [ə'ʃɔːr] adv an Land. **to go ~** an Land gehen.

**ash: ~tray** n Aschenbecher m; **A~ Wednesday** n Aschermittwoch m.

**Asia** ['eɪʃə] n Asien nt.

**Asian** ['eɪʃn] **1** adj asiatisch. **2** n Asiat(in f) m.

**aside** [ə'saɪd] **1** adv (a) (with verb) zur Seite, beiseite. **to turn ~** sich zur Seite drehen, sich abwenden (esp fig). **(b)** (Theat etc) beiseite. **(c)** (esp US) **~ from** außer; **this criticism, ~ from being wrong, is** ... diese Kritik ist nicht nur falsch, sondern auch ... **2** n (Theat) **to say sth in an ~** etw beiseite sprechen.

**asinine** ['æsɪnaɪn] adj idiotisch.

**ask** [ɑːsk] **1** vt **(a)** (inquire) fragen; question stellen. **to ~ sb the way/the time/his opinion** jdn nach dem Weg/der Uhrzeit/seiner Meinung fragen; **to ~ if** ... (nach)fragen, ob ...; **he ~ed me where I'd been** er fragte mich, wo ich gewesen sei; **if you ~ me** wenn du mich fragst; **don't ~ me!** (col) was weiß ich! (col), da bin ich überfragt!; **I ~ you!** (col) ich muß schon sagen! **(b)** (invite) einladen; (in dancing) auffordern. **to ~ sb to lunch** jdn zum (Mittag)essen einladen; **to ~ sb in/up** jdn hereinbitten/heraufbitten; **to ~ sb back** jdn zu sich einladen. **(c)** (request) bitten (sb for sth jdn um etw); (require, demand) verlangen (sth of sb etw von jdm). **to ~ sb to do sth** jdn darum bitten, etw zu tun; **all I ~ is** ... ich will ja nur ...; **it's (not) ~ing too much** das ist (nicht) zuviel verlangt. **(d)** (Comm) price verlangen, fordern. **~ing price** Verkaufspreis m.

**2** vi **(a)** (inquire) fragen. **to ~ about sb/sth** sich nach jdm/etw erkundigen; **~ away!** frag nur!; **well may you ~** das fragt man sich mit Recht. **(b)** (request) bitten (for sth um etw). **I'm not ~ing for sympathy** ich will kein Mitleid; **it's yours for the ~ing** du kannst es haben(, du brauchst nur ein Wort zu sagen); **that's ~ing for trouble** das kann ja nicht gutgehen; **you ~ed for it** (col) du hast es herausgefordert; **to ~ for Mr X** Herrn X verlangen.

►**ask after** vi +prep obj sich erkundigen nach. **tell her I was ~ing ~ her** grüß sie schön von mir.

►**ask out** vt sep einladen.

**askance** [ə'skɑːns] adv **to look ~ at sb** jdn befremdet ansehen.

**askew** [ə'skjuː] adv schief.

**asleep** [ə'sliːp] adj pred **to be (fast) ~** (fest) schlafen; **to fall ~** einschlafen (also euph: die).

**asparagus** [əs'pærəgəs] n no pl Spargel m.

**aspect** ['æspekt] n **(a)** (of question etc) Aspekt m, Seite f. **(b)** (of building) **to have a southerly ~** Südlage haben.

**asperity** [æs'perɪtɪ] n Schroffheit f.

**aspersion** [ə'pɜːʃən] n: **to cast ~s upon sb/sth** abfällige Bemerkungen über jdn/etw machen.

**asphalt** ['æsfælt] n Asphalt m.

**asphyxia** [æs'fɪksɪə] n Erstickung f.

**asphyxiate** [æs'fɪksɪeɪt] vti ersticken. **to be ~d** ersticken.

**aspic** ['æspɪk] n (Cook) Aspik, Gelee m or nt.

**aspiration** [,æspə'reɪʃən] n Ziel, Bestreben nt.

**aspire** [ə'spaɪər] vi **to ~ to sth** nach etw streben; **to ~ to do sth** danach streben, etw zu tun.

**aspirin** ['æsprɪn] n Aspirin ® nt, ≈ Schmerztablette f.

**aspiring** [ə'spaɪərɪŋ] adj aufstrebend.

**ass¹** [æs] (lit, fig col) Esel m.

**ass²** n (US col!) = **arse**.

**assail** [ə'seɪl] vt (lit, fig) angreifen; (fig: with questions etc) überschütten, bombardieren.

**assailant** [ə'seɪlənt] n Angreifer(in f) m.

**assassin** [ə'sæsɪn] n Mörder(in f) m; (would-be ~) Attentäter(in f) m.

**assassinate** [ə'sæsɪneɪt] vt durch ein Attentat or einen Mordanschlag töten. **JFK was ~d in Dallas** JFK wurde in Dallas ermordet.

**assassination** [ə,sæsɪ'neɪʃən] n (geglücktes) Attentat, (geglückter) Mordanschlag (of auf +acc). **~ attempt** Attentat nt; **to plan an ~** ein Attentat planen.

**assault** [ə'sɔːlt] **1** n **(a)** (Mil) Sturm(angriff) m (on auf +acc); (fig) Angriff m (on gegen). **~ course** Hindernisstrecke f (esp für die Ausbildung von Truppen). **(b)** (Jur) Körperverletzung f. **~ and battery** Körperverletzung f; **indecent** or **sexual ~** Notzucht f. **2** vt angreifen; (Jur) tätlich werden gegen; (sexually) herfallen über (+acc); (rape) vergewaltigen.

**assemble** [ə'sembl] **1** vt zusammenbauen; car, machine etc also montieren. **2** vi sich versammeln.

**assembly** [ə'semblɪ] n **(a)** (gathering) Versammlung f. **(b)** (Sch) (tägliche) Versammlung f (mit Bekanntmachungen, einem Gebet und einem Kirchenlied). **(c)** (putting together) Zusammenbau m; (of machine, cars also) Montage f. **(d)** (thing assembled) Konstruktion f.

**assembly: ~ hall** n (Sch) Aula f; **~ language** n (Comp) Assemblersprache f; **~ line** n Montageband nt; **~ point** n Sammelplatz m.

**assent** [ə'sent] **1** n Zustimmung f. **2** vi **to ~ to sth** einer Sache (dat) zustimmen.

**assert** [ə'sɜːt] vt **(a)** (declare) behaupten; one's innocence beteuern. **(b)** **to ~ one's authority** seine Autorität geltend machen; **to ~ one's rights** sein Recht behaupten; **to ~ oneself** sich behaupten or durchsetzen (over gegenüber).

**assertion** [ə'sɜːʃən] n Behauptung f.

**assertive** [ə'sɜːtɪv] adj bestimmt.

**assess** [ə'ses] vt **(a)** einschätzen; proposal, advantages abwägen. **(b)** property schätzen; person (for tax purposes) veranlagen (at mit); tax festsetzen (at auf +acc); damages schätzen (at auf +acc).

**assessment** [ə'sesmənt] n see vt **(a)** Einschätzung f; Abwägen nt. **what's your ~ of the situation?** wie beurteilen Sie die Lage? **(b)** Schätzung f; Veranlagung f. **(c)** Festsetzung f; Schätzung f.

**assessor** [ə'sesər] n Schätzer m.

**asset** ['æset] n **(a)** usu pl Vermögenswert m; (on balance sheet) Aktivposten m. **~s** Vermögen nt; (on balance sheet) Aktiva pl; **~ stripping** Aufkauf von finanziell gefährdeten Firmen und anschließender Verkauf ihrer Vermögenswerte. **(b)** (fig) **to be an ~ to** vorteilhaft sein für; **the new man is an ~ to the company** der neue Mann ist ein Gewinn für die Firma.

**assiduous** [ə'sɪdjʊəs] adj gewissenhaft.

**assign** [ə'saɪn] vt (allot) zuweisen, zuteilen (to sb jdm); (Jur) übertragen (to sb jdm); room bestimmen (to für); meaning zuordnen (to dat); (attribute) novel, play, music zuschreiben (to dat). **she was ~ed to this school** sie wurde an diese Schule berufen.

**assignation** [,æsɪg'neɪʃən] n (lovers') Rendezvous nt.

**assignment** [ə'saɪnmənt] n **(a)** (task) Aufgabe f. **(b)** (to post etc) Berufung f. **(c)** (Jur) Übertragung f.

**assimilate** [ə'sımıleıt] *vt food, knowledge* aufnehmen; *(fig: into society etc also)* integrieren.

**assimilation** [ə,sımı'leıʃən] *n see vt* Aufnahme *f*; Integration *f.* **his powers of ~** seine geistige Aufnahmefähigkeit.

**assist** [ə'sıst] **1** *vt* helfen *(+dat)*; *(act as an assistant to)* assistieren *(+dat)*. **to ~ sb in doing *or* to do sth** jdm helfen, etw zu tun. **2** *vi* helfen. **to ~ with sth** bei etw helfen.

**assistance** [ə'sıstəns] *n* Hilfe *f.* **to come to sb's ~** jdm zu Hilfe kommen; **can I be of any ~?** kann ich irgendwie behilflich sein?

**assistant** [ə'sıstənt] **1** *n* Assistent(in *f*) *m*; *(Brit: shop ~)* Verkäufer(in *f*) *m.* **2** *adj attr manager etc* stellvertretend.

**associate** [ə'səuʃııt] **1** *n (colleague)* Kollege *m*, Kollegin *f*; *(Comm)* Partner(in *f*) *m*; *(accomplice)* Komplize *m*, Komplizin *f*; *(of a society)* außerordentliches Mitglied. **~ professor** *n (US)* außerordentlicher Professor. **2** [ə'səuʃıeıt] *vt* assoziieren *(also Psych).* **to ~ oneself with sb/sth** sich jdm/einer Sache anschließen; **to be ~d with sb/sth** mit jdm/einer Sache in Verbindung gebracht *or* assoziiert werden; **I don't ~ him with sport** bei ihm denke ich nicht an Sport. **3** [ə'səuʃıeıt] *vi* **to ~ with** verkehren mit.

**association** [ə,səusı'eıʃən] *n* **(a)** *no pl (with people)* Verkehr, Umgang *m*; *(co-operation)* Zusammenarbeit *f.* **he has had a long ~ with the party** er hat seit langem mit der Partei zu tun gehabt. **(b)** *(organization)* Verband *m.* **(c)** *(mental)* Assoziation *f (with an +acc) (also Psych).* **~ of ideas** Gedankenassoziation *f.*

**association football** *n (Brit)* Fußball *m*, Soccer *nt.*

**assorted** [ə'sɔ:tıd] *adj (mixed)* gemischt.

**assortment** [ə'sɔ:tmənt] *n* Mischung *f*; *(of goods)* Auswahl *f (of an +dat)*, Sortiment *nt (of von).*

**asst = assistant** Ass.

**assume** [ə'sju:m] *vt* **(a)** annehmen; *(presuppose)* voraussetzen. **let us ~ that you are right** nehmen wir an *or* gehen wir davon aus, Sie hätten recht; **assuming (that) ...** angenommen(, daß) ... **(b)** *power, control* übernehmen; *(forcefully)* ergreifen. **(c)** *(take on) title, guise, shape* annehmen. **under an ~d name** unter anderem Namen.

**assumption** [ə'sʌmpʃən] *n* **(a)** Annahme *f*; *(presupposition)* Voraussetzung *f.* **to go on the ~ that ...** von der Voraussetzung ausgehen, daß ...; **that's just an ~** das ist nur eine Vermutung. **(b)** *(of power, role etc)* Übernahme *f*; *(forcefully)* Ergreifen *nt.* **(c)** *(of guise, false name etc)* Annahme *f.* **(d)** *(Eccl)* **the A~** Mariä Himmelfahrt *f.*

**assurance** [ə'ʃuərəns] *n* **(a)** Versicherung *f*; *(promise also)* Zusicherung *f.* **he gave me his ~ that it would be done** er versicherte mir, daß es erledigt würde; **you have my ~ that ...** Sie können versichert sein, daß ... **(b)** *(self-confidence)* Sicherheit *f.* **(c)** *(confidence)* Zuversicht *f.* **(d)** *(esp Brit: life ~)* (Lebens)versicherung *f.*

**assure** [ə'ʃuər] *vt* **(a)** versichern *(+dat)*; *(promise)* zusichern *(+dat).* **to ~ sb of sth** *(of love, willingness etc)* jdn einer Sache *(gen)* versichern; *(of service, support, help)* jdm etw zusichern; **... I ~ you ...** das versichere ich Ihnen. **(b)** *(make certain of) success, happiness, future* sichern. **(c)** *(esp Brit: insure)* life versichern.

**assured** [ə'ʃuəd] *adj* sicher; *income, future also* gesichert. **to rest ~ that** sich sein, daß ...

**asterisk** ['æstərısk] *n* Sternchen *nt.*

**astern** [ə'stɜ:n] *(Naut) adv* achtern; *(towards the stern)* nach achtern; *(backwards)* achteraus.

**asteroid** ['æstərɔıd] *n* Asteroid *m.*

**asthma** ['æsmə] *n* Asthma *nt.*

**asthmatic** [æs'mætık] *n* Asthmatiker(in *f*) *m.*

**astigmatism** [æs'tıgmətızəm] *n* Astigmatismus *m.*

**astonish** [ə'stonıʃ] *vt* erstaunen, überraschen. **I was ~ed to learn that ...** ich war erstaunt, als ich hörte, daß ...

**astonishing** [ə'stonıʃıŋ] *adj* erstaunlich.

**astonishingly** [ə'stonıʃıŋlı] *adv* erstaunlich. **~ (enough)** erstaunlicherweise.

**astonishment** [ə'stonıʃmənt] *n* Erstaunen *nt (at über +acc).* **look of ~** erstaunter Blick; **she looked at me in ~** sie sah mich erstaunt an; **to my ~** zu meinem Erstaunen.

**astound** [ə'staund] *vt* in Erstaunen versetzen. **to be ~ed (at)** höchst erstaunt sein *(über +acc).*

**astounding** [ə'staundıŋ] *adj* erstaunlich.

**astray** [ə'streı] *adj* verloren. **to go ~** *(person) (lit)* vom Weg abkommen; *(fig: morally)* auf Abwege geraten; *(letter, object)* verlorengehen; **to lead sb ~** *(fig)* jdn vom rechten Weg abbringen; *(mislead)* jdn irreführen.

**astride** [ə'straıd] *prep* rittlings auf.

**astrologer** [əs'trolədʒər] *n* Astrologe *m*, Astrologin *f.*

**astrology** [əs'trolədʒı] *n* Astrologie *f.*

**astronaut** ['æstrənɔ:t] *n* Astronaut(in *f*) *m.*

**astronomer** [əs'tronəmər] *n* Astronom(in *f*) *m.*

**astronomical** [,æstrə'nomıkəl] *adj (fig also* **astronomic)** astronomisch.

**astronomy** [əs'tronəmı] *n* Astronomie *f.*

**astrophysics** [,æstrəu'fızıks] *n sing* Astrophysik *f.*

**astute** [ə'stju:t] *adj* schlau; *remark also* scharfsinnig; *mind* scharf.

**astuteness** [əs'tju:tnıs] *n see adj* Schlauheit *f*; Scharfsinnigkeit *f*; Schärfe *f.*

**asylum** [ə'saıləm] *n* **(a)** *(Pol)* Asyl *nt.* **~ seeker** Asylant(in *f*) *m*; **to ask for (political) ~** um (politisches) Asyl bitten. **(b)** *(lunatic ~)* (Irren)anstalt *f.*

**asymmetric(al)** [,eısı'metrık(əl)] *adj* asymmetrisch. **asymmetric bars** Stufenbarren *m.*

**at** [æt] *prep* **(a)** *(position)* an *(+dat)*, bei *(+dat)*; *(with place)* in *(+dat).* **~ the window/corner** am *or* beim Fenster/an der Ecke; **~ university/school/the hotel/the zoo** an *or* auf der Universität/in der Schule/im Hotel/im Zoo; **~ my brother's** bei meinem Bruder; **~ a party** auf *or* bei einer Party; **~ the station** am Bahnhof.

**(b)** *(direction)* **to aim/point etc ~ sb/sth** auf jdn/etw zielen/zeigen *etc*; **to look/growl etc ~ sb** jdn ansehen/anknurren *etc.*

**(c)** *(time, frequency, order)* **~ ten o'clock** um zehn Uhr; **~ night** bei Nacht; **~ Christmas/Easter** zu Weihnachten/Ostern; **~ your age/16** in deinem Alter/mit 16; **three ~ a time** drei auf einmal; **~ the start/end of sth** am Anfang/am Ende einer Sache.

**(d)** *(activity)* **~ play/work** beim Spiel/bei der Arbeit; **good/bad/an expert ~ sth** gut/schlecht/ein Experte in etw *(dat)*; **he's been ~ it all day** er ist schon den ganzen Tag dabei; **while we are ~ it** *(col)* wenn wir schon mal dabei sind.

**(e)** *(as a result of, upon)* auf *(+acc)* ... (hin). **~ his request** auf seine Bitte (hin); **~ her death** bei ihrem Tod; **~ that/this he left the room** daraufhin verließ er das Zimmer.

**(f)** *(with) delighted etc* über *(+acc).*

**(g)** *(rate, value, degree)* **~ 50 km/h** mit 50 km/h; **~ 50p a pound** für 50 Pence pro Pfund; **~ 5% interest** zu 5% Zinsen; **when the temperature is ~ 90** wenn die Temperatur 90° beträgt.

**ate** [et, eıt] *pret of* eat.

**atheism** ['eıθıızəm] *n* Atheismus *m.*

**atheist** ['eıθııst] *n* Atheist(in *f*) *m.*

**Athenian** [ə'θiːnɪən] **1** *n* Athener(in *f*) *m*. **2** *adj* athenisch; *(esp modern)* Athener.
**Athens** ['æθɪnz] *n* Athen *nt*.
**athlete** ['æθliːt] *n* Athlet(in *f*) *m*; *(in track and field events)* Leichtathlet(in *f*) *m*. **he is a natural** ~ er ist der geborene Sportler; ~**'s foot** Fußpilz *m*.
**athletic** *adj* [æθ'letɪk] sportlich; *build* athletisch.
**athletically** [æθ'letɪkəlɪ] *adv* athletisch.
**athletics** [æθ'letɪks] *n sing or pl* Leichtathletik *f*. ~ **meeting** Leichtathletikwettkampf *m*.
**Atlantic** [ət'læntɪk] **1** *n (also* ~ **Ocean)** Atlantik *m*, Atlantischer Ozean. **2** *adj* atlantisch. ~ **crossing** Atlantiküberquerung *f*.
**atlas** ['ætləs] *n* Atlas *m*.
**Atlas Mountains** *npl* Atlas *m*.
**atmosphere** ['ætməsfɪəʳ] *n (lit, fig)* Atmosphäre *f*; *(fig: of novel also)* Stimmung *f*.
**atmospheric** [,ætməs'ferɪk] *adj* atmosphärisch; *(full of atmosphere) description* stimmungsvoll. ~ **pollution** Luftbelastung *f*.
**atmospherics** [,ætməs'ferɪks] *npl (Rad)* atmosphärische Störungen *pl*.
**atom** ['ætəm] *n* Atom *nt*. ~ **bomb** Atombombe *f*.
**atomic** [ə'tɒmɪk] *adj* atomar.
**atomic** *in cpds* Atom-; ~ **age** *n* Atomzeitalter *nt*; ~ **bomb** *n* Atombombe *f*; ~ **energy** *n* Atom- or Kernenergie *f*; ~ **power** *n* Atomkraft *f*.
**atomizer** ['ætəmaɪzəʳ] *n* Zerstäuber *m*.
**atone** [ə'təʊn] *vi* **to** ~ **for sth** für etw sühnen *or* büßen.
**atonement** [ə'təʊnmənt] *n* Sühne, Buße *f*. **to make** ~ **for sth** für etw Sühne *or* Buße tun; **the A**~ *(Eccl)* das Sühneopfer (Christi).
**atrocious** [ə'trəʊʃəs] *adj* grauenhaft.
**atrocity** [ə'trɒsɪtɪ] *n* Grausamkeit *f*; *(act also)* Greueltat *f*.
**atrophy** ['ætrəfɪ] **1** *n* Atrophie *f*; *(Med)* Schwund *m*. **2** *vi* verkümmern, schwinden.
**attach** [ə'tætʃ] *vt* **(a)** *(join)* festmachen, befestigen *(to* an *+dat)*. **please find** ~**ed** ... beiliegend finden Sie ...; **is he/she** ~**ed?** ist er/sie schon vergeben? **(b) to be** ~**ed to sb/sth** *(be fond of)* an jdm/etw hängen. **(c)** *(attribute) value, importance* beimessen, zuschreiben *(to* dat).
**attaché** [ə'tæʃeɪ] *n* Attaché *m*. ~ **case** Aktenkoffer *m*.
**attachment** [ə'tætʃmənt] *n* **(a)** *(accessory)* Zusatzteil, Zubehörteil *nt*. **(b)** *(fig: affection)* Zuneigung *f* *(to* zu). **(c) he's (working) here on** ~ er ist (vorübergehend) hierher versetzt worden.
**attack** [ə'tæk] **1** *n* **(a)** *(Mil, Sport, fig)* Angriff *m (on* auf *+acc)*. **to be under** ~ angegriffen werden; *(fig also)* unter Beschuß stehen; **to leave oneself open to** ~ Angriffsflächen bieten. **(b)** *(Med etc)* Anfall *m*. **2** *vt* **(a)** *(Mil, Sport, fig)* angreifen; *(from ambush, in robbery etc)* überfallen. **(b)** *(tackle) task, problem* in Angriff nehmen.
**attacker** [ə'tækəʳ] *n* Angreifer *m*.
**attain** [ə'teɪn] *vt rank, age* erreichen; *knowledge* erlangen; *happiness, power* gelangen zu.
**attainment** [ə'teɪnmənt] *n* **(a)** *(act)* Erreichen *nt*; *(of knowledge, happiness, prosperity, power)* Erlangen *nt*. **(b)** *(usu pl: accomplishment)* Fertigkeit *f*.
**attempt** [ə'tempt] **1** *vt* versuchen; *task* sich versuchen an *(+dat)*. ~**ed murder** Mordversuch *m*. **2** *n* Versuch *m*. **an** ~ **on the record** ein Versuch, den Rekord zu brechen; **to make an** ~ **on sb's life** einen Anschlag auf jdn *or* jds Leben verüben; **he made no** ~ **to help us** er unternahm keinen Versuch, uns zu helfen; **at the first** ~ auf Anhieb, beim ersten Versuch; **in the** ~ dabei.

**attend** [ə'tend] **1** *vt* **(a)** *classes, church, meeting* besuchen; *wedding, funeral* anwesend sein bei *(+dat)*. **(b)** *(wait on) queen etc* bedienen. **2** *vi* **(a)** *(be present)* anwesend sein. **are you going to** ~**?** gehen Sie hin? **(b)** *(pay attention)* aufpassen.
▶**attend to** *vi +prep obj (see to)* sich kümmern um; *(pay attention to)* work *etc* Aufmerksamkeit schenken *(+dat)*; *customers* bedienen. **are you being** ~**ed** ~**?** werden Sie schon bedient?; **that's being** ~**ed** ~ das wird (bereits) erledigt.
**attendance** [ə'tendəns] *n* **(a)** Anwesenheit *f (at* bei*)*. **in** ~ anwesend; **regular** ~ **at school** regelmäßiger Schulbesuch. **(b)** *(number present)* Teilnehmerzahl *f*.
**attendant** [ə'tendənt] **1** *n (in art galleries, museums)* Aufseher(in *f*), Wärter(in *f*) *m*; *(in public toilets)* Toilettenwart *m*, Toilettenfrau *f*; *(in swimming baths)* Bademeister(in *f*) *m*. **2** *adj* damit verbunden. ~ **circumstances** Begleitumstände *pl*.
**attention** [ə'tenʃən] *n* **(a)** *no pl* Aufmerksamkeit *f*. **to call** *or* **draw sb's** ~ **to sth** jdn auf etw *(acc)* aufmerksam machen; **to attract sb's** ~ jdm auffallen; *(by waving etc)* jdn auf sich *(acc)* aufmerksam machen; **to turn one's** ~ **to sb/sth** jdm/einer Sache seine Aufmerksamkeit zuwenden; **to pay** ~**/no** ~ **to sb/sth** jdn/etw beachten/nicht beachten; **to pay** ~ **to the teacher** dem Lehrer zuhören; **to hold sb's** ~ jdn fesseln; **your** ~**, please** ich bitte um Aufmerksamkeit; *(over tannoy)* Achtung, Achtung!; **it has come to my** ~ **that** ... ich habe feststellen müssen, daß ...; **it has been brought to my** ~ **that** ... es ist mir zu Ohren gekommen, daß ...; **the bodywork needs a little** ~ an der Karosserie muß etwas getan werden. **(b)** ~**s** *pl (kindnesses)* Aufmerksamkeiten *pl*. **(c)** *(Mil)* **to stand at** ~ stillstehen; ~**!** stillgestanden! **(d)** *(Comm)* **for the** ~ **of** ... zu Händen von ...
**attentive** *adj*, ~**ly** *adv*, [ə'tentɪv, -lɪ] aufmerksam.
**attenuating** [ə'tenjʊeɪtɪŋ] *adj:* ~ **circumstances** mildernde Umstände.
**attest** [ə'test] *vt (certify)* bestätigen, bescheinigen; *signature also* beglaubigen.
▶**attest to** *vi +prep obj* bezeugen.
**attic** [ætɪk] *n* Dachboden, Speicher *m*; *(lived-in)* Mansarde *f*. **in the** ~ auf dem (Dach)boden.
**attire** [ə'taɪəʳ] *n no pl* Kleidung *f*. **ceremonial** ~ Festtracht *f*; *(of priest)* Ornat *nt*.
**attitude** [ætɪtjuːd] *n (way of thinking)* Einstellung *f (to, towards* zu*)*; *(way of acting, posture, manner)* Haltung *f (to, towards* gegenüber*)*. **well, if that's your** ~ ja, wenn du *so* denkst.
**attorney** [ə'tɜːnɪ] *n (US: lawyer)* (Rechts)anwalt *m*, (Rechts)anwältin *f*. ~ **general** *(US) (of state government)* ≃ Generalstaatsanwalt *m*; *(of federal government)* ≃ Generalbundesanwalt *m*; *(Brit)* ≃ Justizminister *m*.
**attract** [ə'trækt] *vt (also Phys)* anziehen; *sb's attention* auf sich *(acc)* ziehen *or* lenken; *(idea, music, place etc)* ansprechen. **she feels** ~**ed to him/to the idea** sie fühlt sich zu ihm hingezogen/die Idee reizt sie; **what** ~**s me about the place** was mich an dem Ort reizt.
**attraction** [ə'trækʃən] *n* **(a)** *(Phys, fig)* Anziehungskraft *f*. **to lose its** ~ seinen Reiz verlieren; **to have an** ~ **for sb** einen Reiz auf jdn ausüben, jdn reizen; **the** ~ **of the city** der Reiz der Großstadt. **(b)** *(attractive thing)* Attraktion *f*.
**attractive** [ə'træktɪv] *adj* attraktiv, reizvoll; *offer, price* verlockend.
**attractively** [ə'træktɪvlɪ] *adv* attraktiv; *furnish, paint* reizvoll.
**attractiveness** [ə'træktɪvnɪs] *n* Attraktivität *f*; *(of*

*house, furnishing, view etc)* Reiz *m*.
**attributable** [ə'trɪbjʊtəbl] *adj* **to be** ~ **to sb/sth** jdm/ einer Sache zuzuschreiben sein.
**attribute** [ə'trɪbjuːt] **1** *vt* **to** ~ **sth to sb** *play, remark etc* jdm etw zuschreiben; *intelligence, feelings etc* jdm etw zusprechen; **to** ~ **sth to sth** *success, accident etc* etw auf etw *(acc)* zurückführen. **2** ['ætrɪbjuːt] *n (quality)* Merkmal *nt*, Eigenschaft *f*.
**attributive** [ə'trɪbjʊtɪv] *(Gram) adj* attributiv.
**attrition** [ə'trɪʃən] *n* Zermürbung *f*. **war of** ~ *(Mil)* Zermürbungskrieg *m*.
**Atty Gen = Attorney General.**
**aubergine** ['əʊbəʒiːn] *n (Brit)* Aubergine *f*.
**auburn** ['ɔːbən] *adj hair* rotbraun, rostrot.
**auction** ['ɔːkʃən] **1** *n (also* ~ **sale)** Auktion, Versteigerung *f*. **2** *vt (also* ~ **off)** versteigern.
**auctioneer** [ˌɔːkʃə'nɪər] *n* Auktionator *m*.
**audacious** [ɔː'deɪʃəs] *adj* **(a)** *(impudent)* dreist, unverfroren. **(b)** *(bold)* kühn.
**audacity** [ɔː'dæsɪtɪ] *n* **(a)** *(impudence)* **to have the** ~ **to do sth** die Dreistigkeit *or* Unverfrorenheit besitzen, etw zu tun. **(b)** *(boldness)* Kühnheit *f*.
**audibility** [ˌɔːdɪ'bɪlɪtɪ] *n* Hörbarkeit *f*.
**audible** ['ɔːdɪbl] *adj* hörbar, (deutlich) vernehmbar. **she was hardly** ~ man konnte sie kaum hören.
**audibly** ['ɔːdɪblɪ] *adv* hörbar.
**audience** ['ɔːdɪəns] *n* **(a)** Publikum *nt no pl*; *(Theat, TV also)* Zuschauer *pl*; *(of speaker also)* Zuhörer *pl*; *(Rad, Mus also)* Zuhörerschaft *f*. **to have** ~ **appeal** publikumswirksam sein. **(b)** *(formal interview)* Audienz *f (with bei)*.
**audio** ['ɔːdɪəʊ] *in cpds* Ton-. ~ **cassette** *n* (Ton)kassette, Cassette *f*; ~ **engineer** *n* Toningenieur *m*; ~ **equipment** *n* HiFi-Geräte *pl*.
**audio:** ~ **typist** *n* Phonotypistin *f*; ~**-visual** *adj* audiovisuell.
**audit** ['ɔːdɪt] **1** *n* Buchprüfung *f*. **2** *vt* prüfen.
**audition** [ɔː'dɪʃən] **1** *n (Theat)* Vorsprechprobe *f*; *(Mus)* Probespiel *nt*; *(of singer)* Vorsingen *nt*. **2** *vt* vorsprechen/vorspielen/vorsingen lassen.
**auditor** ['ɔːdɪtər] *n* Wirtschaftsprüfer *m*.
**auditorium** [ˌɔːdɪ'tɔːrɪəm] *n* Auditorium *nt*; *(in theatre, cinema)* Zuschauerraum *m*.
**au fait** [ˌəʊ'feɪ] *adj* vertraut.
**Aug = August** Aug.
**augment** [ɔːg'ment] **1** *vt* vermehren; *income also* vergrößern. **2** *vi* zunehmen.
**augur** ['ɔːgər] *vi* **to** ~ **well/ill** etwas Gutes/nichts Gutes verheißen.
**august** [ɔː'gʌst] *adj* illuster; *occasion* erhaben.
**August** ['ɔːgəst] *n* August *m*; *see* **September.**
**aunt** [ɑːnt] *n* Tante *f*.
**auntie, aunty** ['ɑːntɪ] *n (col)* Tante *f*.
**au pair** ['əʊ'peə] *n, pl* - **-s** *(also* ~ **girl)** Au-pair(-Mädchen) *nt*.
**aura** ['ɔːrə] *n* Aura *f (geh)*, Ausstrahlung *f*. **she has an** ~ **of** ... sie strahlt ... aus.
**auspices** ['ɔːspɪsɪz] *npl* **under the** ~ **of** unter der Schirmherrschaft *(+gen)*.
**auspicious** [ɔː'spɪʃəs] *adj* günstig; *start* vielversprechend. **an** ~ **occasion** ein feierlicher Anlaß.
**Aussie** ['ɒzɪ] *(col)* Australier(in *f*) *m*.
**austere** [ɒs'tɪər] *adj* streng; *way of life also* asketisch; *room* schmucklos.
**austerity** [ɒs'terɪtɪ] *n* **(a)** *(severity)* Strenge *f*; *(simplicity)* strenge Einfachheit, Schmucklosigkeit *f*. **(b)** *(hardship)* **after the** ~ **of the war years** nach den Entbehrungen der Kriegsjahre; **a life of** ~ ein Leben der Entsagung; ~ **measures** Sparmaßnahmen *pl*.
**Australasia** [ˌɔːstrə'leɪsjə] *n* Australien und Ozea-

nien *nt*.
**Australia** [ɒs'treɪlɪə] *n* Australien *nt*.
**Australian** [ɒs'treɪlɪən] **1** *n* Australier(in *f*) *m*. **2** *adj* australisch.
**Austria** ['ɒstrɪə] *n* Österreich *nt*.
**Austrian** ['ɒstrɪən] **1** *n* Österreicher(in *f*) *m*; *(dialect)* Österreichisch *nt*. **2** *adj* österreichisch.
**Austro-** [ɒstrəʊ] *pref* Austro-. ~**-Hungarian** österreichisch-ungarisch.
**authentic** [ɔː'θentɪk] *adj* echt; *document etc* authentisch; *claim* berechtigt.
**authenticate** [ɔː'θentɪkeɪt] *vt* bestätigen; *signature, document* beglaubigen; *manuscript, work of art* für echt befinden.
**authenticity** [ˌɔːθen'tɪsɪtɪ] *n* Echtheit, Authentizität *(geh) f*; *(of claim to title)* Berechtigung *f*.
**author** ['ɔːθər] *n* Autor(in *f*), Schriftsteller(in *f*) *m*; *(of report, pamphlet)* Verfasser(in *f*) *m*; *(fig)* Urheber(in *f*) *m*.
**authoress** ['ɔːθərɪs] *n* Autorin *f*; Schriftstellerin *f*.
**authoritarian** [ˌɔːθɒrɪ'tɛərɪən] *adj* autoritär.
**authoritative** [ɔː'θɒrɪtətɪv] *adj* **(a)** *(commanding)* bestimmt, entschieden. **(b)** *(definitive)* maßgeblich, maßgebend. **from an** ~ **source** aus berufenem Munde.
**authority** [ɔː'θɒrɪtɪ] *n* **(a)** *(power)* Autorität *f*; *(right, entitlement)* Befugnis *f*; *(specifically delegated power)* Vollmacht *f*; *(permission)* Erlaubnis *f*. **people who are in** ~ Menschen, die Autorität haben; **the person in** ~ der Zuständige *or* Verantwortliche; **to be in** *or* **have** ~ **over sb** jdm übergeordnet sein; **on one's own** ~ auf eigene Verantwortung; **by what** ~ **do you claim the right to ...?** mit welcher Berechtigung verlangen Sie, daß ...?; **to have the** ~ **to do sth** berechtigt *or* befugt sein, etw zu tun; **to do sth on sb's** ~ etw in jds Auftrag *(dat)* tun; **to have** *or* **carry (great)** ~ viel gelten *(with bei)*; **to speak/write with** ~ mit Sachkenntnis sprechen/ schreiben.
**(b)** *(also pl: ruling body)* Behörde *f*; *(body of people)* Verwaltung *f*; **the authorities** die Behörden *pl*; **the university authorities** die Universitätsverwaltung; **the local** ~ die Gemeindeverwaltung; *(in town)* die Stadtverwaltung.
**(c)** *(expert)* Autorität *f*, Fachmann *m (on* auf dem Gebiet +gen); *(definitive book etc)* (anerkannte) Autorität; *(source)* Quelle *f*. **to have sth on good** ~ etw aus zuverlässiger Quelle wissen; **this book is the** ~ **on spelling** dieses Buch ist maßgebend für die Rechtschreibung.
**authorization** [ˌɔːθəraɪ'zeɪʃən] *n* Genehmigung *f*; *(delegated authority)* Vollmacht *f*; *(right)* Recht *nt*.
**authorize** ['ɔːθəraɪz] *vt* **(a)** *(empower)* berechtigen, ermächtigen. **to be** ~**d to do sth** *(have right)* das Recht haben, etw zu tun; **he was specially** ~**d to ...** er hatte eine Sondervollmacht, zu ...; ~**d representative** bevollmächtigter Vertreter. **(b)** *(permit)* genehmigen; *money, claim etc* bewilligen; *translation, biography etc* autorisieren. **the A**~**d Version** *englische Bibelfassung von 1611.*
**authorship** ['ɔːθəʃɪp] *n* Autorschaft *f*. **of unknown** ~ eines unbekannten Autors.
**autistic** [ɔː'tɪstɪk] *adj* autistisch.
**auto** ['ɔːtəʊ] *n (US)* Auto *nt*, Pkw *m*.
**auto-** ['ɔːtəʊ] *pref* auto-, Auto-.
**autobiographical** [ˌɔːtəʊbaɪəʊ'græfɪkəl] *adj* autobiographisch.
**autobiography** [ˌɔːtəʊbaɪ'ɒgrəfɪ] *n* Autobiographie *f*.
**autocratic** [ˌɔːtəʊ'krætɪk] *adj* autokratisch.
**autocue** ['ɔːtəʊkjuː] *n (Brit TV)* Teleprompter *m*.

**autofocus** ['ɔːtəufəukəs] *n (Phot)* Autofocus, Autofokus *m*.

**autograph** ['ɔːtəgrɑːf] **1** *n* Autogramm *nt*. **2** *vt* signieren.

**automat** ['ɔːtəmæt] *n (US)* Automatenrestaurant *nt*.

**automate** ['ɔːtəmeɪt] *vt* automatisieren.

**automatic** [ˌɔːtə'mætɪk] **1** *adj (lit, fig)* automatisch; ~ **choke** Startautomatik *f*; ~ **dialling** *(Brit) or* **dialing** *(US)* Wählautomatik *f*; ~ **exposure** Belichtungsautomatik *f*; ~ **transmission** Automatikgetriebe *nt*; **the** ~ **model** das Modell mit Automatik; ~ **pilot** Autopilot *m*. **2** *n (gun)* automatische Waffe; *(car)* Automatikwagen *m*.

**automatically** [ˌɔːtə'mætɪkəlɪ] *adv* automatisch.

**automation** [ˌɔːtə'meɪʃən] *n* Automatisierung *f*.

**automaton** [ɔː'tɒmətən] *n, pl* **-s** *or* **automata** [-etə] *(robot)* Roboter *m*; *(fig also)* Automat *m*.

**automobile** ['ɔːtəməbiːl] *n (esp US)* Auto(mobil), Kraftfahrzeug *nt*.

**autonomous** [ɔː'tɒnəməs] *adj* autonom.

**autonomy** [ɔː'tɒnəmɪ] *n* Autonomie *f*.

**autopilot** [ˌɔːtəu'paɪlət] *n* Autopilot *m*. **to be on** ~ *(col)* alles nur noch ganz automatisch machen.

**autopsy** ['ɔːtɒpsɪ] *n* Autopsie, Obduktion *f*.

**autumn** ['ɔːtəm] *(esp Brit)* **1** *n (lit, fig)* Herbst *m*. **in (the)** ~ im Herbst. **2** *adj attr* Herbst-, herbstlich.

**autumnal** [ɔː'tʌmnəl] *adj* herbstlich, Herbst-.

**auxiliary** [ɔːg'zɪlɪərɪ] **1** *adj* Hilfs-; *(emergency also)* Not-; *(additional) engine, generator etc* Zusatz-. ~ **nurse** *(female)* Schwesternhelferin *f*; *(male)* Hilfspfleger *m*. **2** *n* **(a)** *(Mil)* **auxiliaries** *pl* Hilfstruppe(n *pl)* *f*. **(b)** *(general: assistant)* Hilfskraft *f*, Helfer(in *f)* *m*. **(c)** *(~ verb)* Hilfsverb *nt*.

**AV** = **(a) audiovisual. (b) Authorized Version.**

**Av** = **Avenue.**

**avail** [ə'veɪl] **1** *vr* **to** ~ **oneself of sth** von etw Gebrauch machen. **2** *n* **of no** ~ erfolglos, ohne Erfolg; **to no** ~ vergebens, vergeblich.

**availability** [əˌveɪlə'bɪlɪtɪ] *n see adj* Erhältlichkeit *f*; Lieferbarkeit *f*; Verfügbarkeit *f*; *(presence: of secretarial staff, mineral ore etc)* Vorhandensein *nt*. **the market price is determined by** ~ der Marktpreis richtet sich nach dem vorhandenen Angebot; **the** ~ **of jobs** *etc* das Angebot an Stellen *etc*; **offer subject to** ~ (das Angebot gilt nur,) solange der Vorrat reicht.

**available** [ə'veɪləbl] *adj object* erhältlich; *(Comm) (from supplier also)* lieferbar; *(free) time, seats etc* frei; *(at one's disposal) means, resources etc* verfügbar. **to be** ~ *(at one's disposal)* zur Verfügung stehen; *(can be reached)* erreichbar sein; *(for discussion)* zu sprechen sein; **to make sth** ~ **to sb** jdm etw zur Verfügung stellen; *(accessible) knowledge etc* jdm etw zugänglich machen; **the best dictionary** ~**, the best** ~ **dictionary** das beste Wörterbuch, das es gibt; **to try every** ~ **means (to achieve sth)** nichts unversucht lassen(, um etw zu erreichen).

**avalanche** ['ævəlɑːnʃ] *n (lit, fig)* Lawine *f*.

**avant-garde** ['ævãŋ'gɑːd] **1** *n* Avantgarde *f*. **2** *adj* avantgardistisch.

**avarice** ['ævərɪs] *n* Habgier *f*.

**avaricious** [ˌævə'rɪʃəs] *adj* habgierig.

**Ave** = **Avenue.**

**avenge** [ə'vendʒ] *vt* rächen. **to** ~ **oneself on sb (for sth)** sich an jdm (für etw) rächen.

**avenue** ['ævənjuː] *n* **(a)** *(tree-lined)* Allee *f*; *(broad street)* Boulevard *m*. **(b)** *(fig)* ~**s of approach** Verfahrensweisen; **to explore every** ~ alle sich bietenden Wege prüfen.

**average** ['ævərɪdʒ] **1** *n* (Durch)schnitt *m*. **to do an** ~ **of 50 miles a day** durchschnittlich *or* im

(Durch)schnitt 80 Kilometer pro Tag fahren; **on** ~ durchschnittlich, im (Durch)schnitt; *(normally)* normalerweise; **above/below** ~ ~ überdurchschnittlich/unter dem Durchschnitt. **2** *adj* durchschnittlich; *(ordinary)* Durchschnitts-; *(not good or bad)* mittelmäßig. ~ **speed** Durchschnittsgeschwindigkeit *f*; **the** ~ **man, Mr A**~ der Durchschnittsbürger; **he's a man of** ~ **height** er ist mittelgroß. **3** *vt* **we** ~**d 50 mph** wir sind durchschnittlich 80 km/h gefahren; **the factory** ~**s 500 cars a week** die Fabrik produziert im (Durch)schnitt 500 Autos pro Woche.

▶**average out** *vi* durchschnittlich ausmachen *(at acc)*; *(balance out)* sich ausgleichen. **how does it** ~ ~ **on a weekly basis?** wieviel ist das durchschnittlich pro Woche?

**averse** [ə'vɜːs] *adj pred* **I am not** ~ **to a glass of wine** einem Glas Wein bin ich nicht abgeneigt.

**aversion** [ə'vɜːʃən] *n* Abneigung, Aversion *f (to gegen)*.

**avert** [ə'vɜːt] *vt* **(a)** *eyes* abwenden. **(b)** *(prevent)* verhindern; *suspicion* ablenken.

**aviary** ['eɪvɪərɪ] *n* Vogelhaus *nt*.

**aviation** [ˌeɪvɪ'eɪʃən] *n* Luftfahrt *f*. **the art of** ~ die Kunst des Fliegens.

**aviator** ['eɪvɪeɪtəʳ] *n* Flieger(in *f)* *m*.

**avid** ['ævɪd] *adj* **(a)** *(desirous)* gierig *(for nach)*. **(b)** *(keen)* begeistert, passioniert. **I am an** ~ **reader** ich lese leidenschaftlich gern.

**avidly** ['ævɪdlɪ] *adv* gierig; *(keenly)* eifrig; *read* leidenschaftlich gern.

**avionics** [ˌeɪvɪ'ɒnɪks] *n sing* Avionik *f*.

**avocado** [ˌævə'kɑːdəu] *n, pl* **-s** Avocado *f*.

**avoid** [ə'vɔɪd] *vt* vermeiden; *damage, accident also* verhüten; *person, danger* meiden, aus dem Weg gehen *(+dat)*; *obstacle* ausweichen *(+dat)*; *difficulty, duty, truth* umgehen. **in order to** ~ **being seen** um nicht gesehen zu werden; **I'm not going if I can possibly** ~ **it** wenn es sich irgendwie vermeiden läßt, gehe ich nicht hin.

**avoidable** [ə'vɔɪdəbl] *adj* vermeidbar. **if it's (at all)** ~ wenn es sich (irgend) vermeiden läßt.

**avoidance** [ə'vɔɪdəns] *n* Vermeidung *f*.

**avowed** [ə'vaud] *adj* erklärt.

**avuncular** [ə'vʌŋkjuləʳ] *adj* onkelhaft.

**AWACS, Awacs** ['eɪwæks] = **airborne warning and control system** AWACS, Frühwarnsystem *nt* der US-Luftwaffe.

**await** [ə'weɪt] *vt* erwarten; *future events, decision etc* entgegensehen *(+dat)*. **the long** ~**ed day** der langersehnte Tag.

**awake** [ə'weɪk] *pret* **awoke**, *ptp* **awoken** *or* **awaked** [ə'weɪkt] **1** *vi (lit, fig)* erwachen. **to** ~ **to sth** *(fig) (realize)* sich *(dat)* einer Sache *(gen)* bewußt werden. **2** *vt* wecken; *(fig) suspicion, interest etc also* erwecken. **3** *adj pred (lit, fig)* wach. **to be/stay** ~ wach sein/bleiben; **to keep sb** ~ jdn wachhalten; **wide** ~ *(lit)* hellwach; **to be** ~ **to sth** *(fig)* sich *(dat)* einer Sache *(gen)* bewußt sein.

**awaken** [ə'weɪkən] *vti* = **awake 1, 2.**

**awakening** [ə'weɪknɪŋ] *n (lit, fig)* Erwachen *nt*. **a rude** ~ *(lit, fig)* ein böses Erwachen.

**award** [ə'wɔːd] **1** *vt prize etc* zusprechen *(to sb jdm)*; *(present) prize, degree, medal etc* verleihen *(to sb jdm)*; *penalty, free kick* geben. **to be** ~**ed damages** Schadenersatz zugesprochen bekommen. **2** *n* **(a)** *(prize)* Preis *m*; *(for bravery)* Auszeichnung *f*. **(b)** *(Univ)* Stipendium *nt*.

**aware** [ə'weəʳ] *adj esp pred* bewußt. **to be/become** ~ **of sb/sth** sich *(dat)* jds/einer Sache bewußt sein/ werden; *(notice)* jdn bemerken/etw merken; **I was**

**not** ~ **(of the fact) that** ... es war mir nicht klar *or* bewußt, daß ...; **are you** ~ **that** ...? ist dir eigentlich klar, daß ...?; **not that I am** ~ **(of)** nicht daß ich wüßte; **as far as I am** ~ soviel ich weiß; **to make sb more** ~/~ **of sth** jds Bewußtsein wecken/jdm etw bewußt machen; **she's very** ~ **of language** sie ist sehr sprachbewußt.

**awareness** [ə'wɛənɪs] *n* Bewußtsein *nt*.

**awash** [ə'wɒʃ] *adj pred decks, rocks etc* überspült; *cellar, floor etc* unter Wasser.

**away** [ə'weɪ] *adv* **1 (a)** weg. **three miles** ~ **(from here)** drei Meilen (entfernt) von hier; **to look** ~ wegsehen; ~ **we go!** los (geht's)!; ~ **with it!** weg damit! **(b)** *(absent)* fort, weg. **he's** ~ **from work (with a cold)** er fehlt (wegen einer Erkältung); **he's** ~ **in London** er ist in London; **when I have to be** ~ wenn ich nicht da sein kann. **(c)** *(Sport)* **to play** ~ auswärts spielen; **to be** ~ **to** ... ein Auswärtsspiel bei ... haben. **(d) to put/give** ~ weglegen/ weggeben; **to gamble/die** ~ verspielen/verhallen; **to work/knit** *etc* ~ vor sich hin arbeiten/stricken *etc*; **ask** ~! frag nur! **(e)** *(col)* **he's** ~ **again** *(talking, giggling, drunk etc)* es geht wieder los; ~ **with you!** *(surprised)* ach wo! **2** *adj attr (Sport)* team auswärtig, Gast-; *match, win* Auswärts-.

**awe** [ɔː] **1** *n* Ehrfurcht *f.* **to be** *or* **stand in** ~ **of sb** Ehrfurcht vor jdm haben; *(feel fear)* große Furcht vor jdm haben. **2** *vt* ~**d by the beauty/silence** von der Schönheit/der Stille ergriffen.

**awe-inspiring** ['ɔːɪn,spaɪərɪŋ] *adj* ehrfurchtgebietend.

**awesome** ['ɔːsəm] *adj* ehrfurchtgebietend; *(col: fantastic)* überwältigend, toll *(col)*.

**awful** ['ɔːfəl] *adj (col)* schrecklich, furchtbar. **you are** ~! du bist wirklich schrecklich!; **it's not an** ~ **lot better** das ist nicht viel besser.

**awfully** ['ɔːflɪ] *adv (col)* furchtbar *(col)*, schrecklich *(col)*.

**awfulness** ['ɔːfəlnɪs] *n* Schrecklichkeit *f*, Furchtbar-

keit *f*.

**awkward** ['ɔːkwəd] *adj* **(a)** *(difficult)* schwierig; *time, moment, angle, shape* ungünstig. **(b)** *(embarrassing)* peinlich. **(c)** *(embarrassed)* verlegen; *silence* betreten. **the** ~ **age** das schwierige Alter; **to feel** ~ **in sb's company** sich in jds Gesellschaft *(dat)* nicht wohl fühlen. **(d)** *(clumsy)* unbeholfen.

**awkwardly** ['ɔːkwədlɪ] *adv see adj* **(a)** schwierig; ungünstig. **(b)** peinlich. **(c)** verlegen; betreten. **(d)** unbeholfen. **to fall** ~ unglücklich fallen.

**awkwardness** ['ɔːkwədnɪs] *n see adj* **(a)** Schwierigkeit *f*; Ungünstigkeit *f*. **(b)** Peinlichkeit *f*. **(c)** Verlegenheit *f*; Betretenheit *f*. **(d)** Unbeholfenheit *f*.

**awning** ['ɔːnɪŋ] *n (on window, of shop)* Markise *f*.

**awoke** [ə'wəʊk] *pret of* **awake.**

**awoken** [ə'wəʊkən] *ptp of* **awake.**

**AWOL** ['eɪwɒl] *(Mil)* = **absent without leave** unerlaubt von der Truppe entfernt.

**awry** [ə'raɪ] *adj pred, adv* schief. **to go** ~ *(plans etc)* schiefgehen.

**axe,** *(US)* **ax** [æks] **1** *n* Axt *f*, Beil *nt.* **to have an/no** ~ **to grind** *(fig)* ein/kein persönliches Interesse haben. **2** *vt plans, jobs* streichen; *person* entlassen.

**axiom** ['æksɪəm] *n* Axiom *nt*.

**axiomatic** [,æksɪəʊ'mætɪk] *adj* axiomatisch.

**axis** ['æksɪs] *n, pl* **axes** ['æksiːz] Achse *f.* **the A**~ **(powers)** *(Hist)* die Achsenmächte *pl*.

**axle** ['æksl] *n* Achse *f*.

**ayatollah** [,aɪə'tɒlə] *n* Ajatollah *m*.

**aye** [aɪ] **1** *interj (esp Scot, dial)* ja. ~, ~ **Sir** *(Naut)* jawohl, Herr Kapitän *etc*. **2** *n (esp Parl)* Jastimme *f*.

**AZ** *(US Post)* = **Arizona.**

**azalea** [ə'zeɪlɪə] *n* Azalee *f*.

**Azerbaijan** [,æzəbaɪ'dʒɑːn] *n* Aserbaidschan *nt*.

**Azerbaijani** [,æzəbaɪ'dʒɑːnɪ] **1** *adj* aserbaidschanisch. **2** *n* Aserbaidschane *m*, Aserbaidschanin *f*.

**Azores** [ə'zɔːz] *npl* Azoren *pl*.

**azure** ['æʒə<sup>r</sup>] **1** *n* Azur(blau *nt*) *m*. **2** *adj* azurblau.

# B

**B, b** [biː] *n* B, b *nt*; *(Sch: as a mark)* ≈ Zwei *f*, Gut *nt*; *(Mus)* H, h *nt*. **B for Benjamin** *(Brit)*, **B for Baker** *(US)* ≈ B wie Bertha; **B flat/sharp** *(Mus)* B, b *nt/* His, his *nt*.

**b** = **born** geb.

**BA** = **(a) Bachelor of Arts. (b) British Airways.**

**babble** ['bæbl] **1** *n* **(a)** Gemurmel *nt*; *(of baby, excited person etc)* Geplapper *nt*. ~ **(of voices)** Stimmengewirr *nt*. **(b)** *(of stream)* Murmeln *nt no pl* *(liter)*. **2** *vi* **(a)** *(person)* plappern. **(b)** *(stream)* murmeln *(liter)*.

**babe** [beɪb] *n* **(a)** *(esp liter)* Kindlein *nt (liter)*. ~ **in arms** Säugling *m*. **(b)** *(US col: as address)* Schätzchen *nt*.

**baboon** [bə'buːn] *n* Pavian *m*.

**baby** ['beɪbɪ] *n* **(a)** Kind, Baby *nt*; *(of animal)* Junge(s) *nt*. **to have a** ~ ein Kind *or* Baby bekommen; **I've known him since he was a** ~ ich kenne ihn von Kindesbeinen an; **the** ~ **of the family** das Nesthäkchen; **don't be such a** ~! stell dich nicht so an! *(col)*; **he's a big** ~ er ist ein großes Kind; **to be left holding the** ~ der Dumme sein *(col)*, die Sache ausbaden müssen *(col)*; **to throw out the** ~ **with the bathwater** das Kind mit dem Bade ausschütten. **(b)** *(col: girlfriend, boyfriend)* Schatz *m*. **(c)** *(esp US col: as address)* Schätzchen *nt (col)*; *(man to man)* Junge *m*. **(d)** *(col: responsibility)* **this is your** ~ das ist deine Sache *or (col)* dein Bier.

**baby** *in cpds* **(a)** *(for baby)* Baby-, Säuglings-. **(b)** *(little)* Klein-. **(c)** *(of animal)* ~ **crocodile** Krokodiljunge(s) *nt*.

**baby:** ~-**battering** *n* Kindesmißhandlung *f*; ~ **boom** *n* Baby-Boom *m*; ~ **boy** *n* Junge *m*; ~ **buggy** *n* (Klapp)sportwagen *m*; ~ **carriage** *n (US)* Kinderwagen *m*; ~ **clothes** *npl* Babykleidung *f*; ~ **face** *n* Kindergesicht *nt*; *(of adult male)* Milchgesicht *nt*; ~ **food** *n* Babynahrung *f*; ~ **girl** *nt* Mädchen *nt*; ~ **grand (piano)** *n* Stutzflügel *m*.

**babyhood** ['beɪbɪhʊd] *n* Säuglingsalter *nt*.

**babyish** ['beɪbɪʃ] *adj* kindisch.

**baby:** ~-**minder** *n* Tagesmutter *f*; ~-**sit** *pret, ptp* ~-**sat** *vi* babysitten; **she** ~-**sits for her** sie geht bei ihr babysitten; ~-**sitter** *n* Babysitter(in *f*) *m*; ~ **stroller** *n (US)* Sportwagen *m*; ~ **tooth** *n* Milchzahn *m*; ~-**walker** *n* Laufstuhl *m*.

**bachelor** ['bætʃələʳ] *n* **(a)** Junggeselle *m*. **(b)** *(Univ)* B~ **of Arts/Science** ≈ Magister *m* der Geisteswissenschaften/Naturwissenschaften.

**bachelor:** ~ **days** *npl* Junggesellenzeit *f*; ~ **flat** *n* Junggesellenwohnung *f*; ~ **girl** *n* Junggesellin *f*.

**bachelorhood** ['bætʃələhʊd] *n* Junggesellentum *nt*.

**bachelor pad** *n (col)* Junggesellenbude *f (col)*.

**bacillus** [bə'sɪləs] *n, pl* **bacilli** [bə'sɪlaɪ] Bazillus *m*.

**back** [bæk] **1** *n* **(a)** *(of person, animal, book)* Rücken *m*; *(of chair also)* (Rücken)lehne *f*. **with one's** ~ **to the engine** *(on train)* entgegen der Fahrtrichtung; **to break one's** ~ *(fig)* sich abrackern; **we've broken the** ~ **of the job** wir sind mit der Arbeit über den

Berg *(col)*; **behind sb's** ~ *(fig)* hinter jds Rücken *(dat)*; **to put one's** ~ **into sth** *(fig)* bei etw Einsatz zeigen; **to put** *or* **get sb's** ~ **up** jdn gegen sich aufbringen; **to turn one's** ~ **on sb** *(lit, fig)* sich von jdm abwenden; **he's at the** ~ **of all the trouble** er steckt hinter dem ganzen Ärger; **get off my** ~! *(col)* laß mich endlich in Ruhe!; **get these people off my** ~ *(col)* schaff mir diese Leute vom Hals! *(col)*; **to have one's** ~ **to the wall** *(fig)* in die Enge getrieben sein; **I was pleased to see the** ~ **of them** *(col)* ich war froh, sie endlich los zu sein *(col)*.

**(b)** *(as opposed to front)* Rück- *or* Hinterseite *f*; *(of hand, dress)* Rücken *m*; *(of house, page, cheque)* Rückseite *f*; *(of material)* linke Seite. **I know London like the** ~ **of my hand** ich kenne London wie meine Westentasche; **at the** ~ **of the book** hinten im Buch; **in** ~ **of** *(US)* hinter; **he drove into the** ~ **of me** er ist mir hinten reingefahren *(col)*; **in the** ~ **(of the car)** hinten (im Auto); **one consideration was at the** ~ **of my mind** ich hatte dabei eine Überlegung im Hinterkopf; **there's one other worry at the** ~ **of my mind** da ist noch etwas, das mich leise beunruhigt; **at the** ~ **of beyond** am Ende der Welt, j.w.d. *(hum)*.

**(c)** *(Ftbl)* Verteidiger *m*.

**2** *adj wheel, yard* Hinter-; *rent* ausstehend.

**3** *adv* zurück. ~ **and forth** hin und her; **to pay sth** ~ etw zurückzahlen; **to come/go** ~ zurückkommen/-gehen; **there and** ~ hin und zurück; **I'll never go** ~ da gehe ich nie wieder hin; **a week** ~ vor einer Woche; **as far** ~ **as the 18th century** *(dating back)* bis zurück ins 18. Jahrhundert.

**4** *prep (US)* ~ **of** hinter.

**5** *vt* **(a)** *(support)* unterstützen. **I will** ~ **you whatever you do** egal, was du tust, ich stehe hinter dir. **(b)** *(Betting)* setzen auf (+*acc*). **(c)** *(cause to move)* *car* zurücksetzen. **he** ~**ed his car into the tree/ garage** er fuhr rückwärts gegen den Baum/in die Garage.

**6** *vi (car, train)* zurücksetzen. **the car** ~**ed into the garage** das Auto fuhr rückwärts in die Garage; **she** ~**ed into me** sie fuhr rückwärts in mein Auto.

▶**back away** *vi* zurückweichen *(from* vor +*dat)*.

▶**back down** *vi (fig)* nachgeben, klein beigeben.

▶**back off** *vi* zurückweichen; *(stop harassing)* sich zurückhalten.

▶**back on to** *vi* +*prep obj* hinten angrenzen an (+*acc*).

▶**back out 1** *vi* **(a)** *(car etc)* rückwärts herausfahren. **(b)** *(fig: of contract, deal etc)* aussteigen *(of, from* aus) *(col)*. **2** *vt sep vehicle* rückwärts herausfahren *or* -setzen.

▶**back up 1** *vi* **(a)** *(car etc)* zurücksetzen. **to** ~ ~ **to sth** rückwärts an etw *(acc)* heranfahren. **(b)** *(US: drains)* **to have** ~**ed** ~ verstopft sein. **2** *vt sep* **(a)** *(support)* unterstützen; *(confirm)* story bestätigen; *(in discussion etc also)* den Rücken stärken (+*dat*); *claim, theory* untermauern. **he can** ~ **me** ~ **in this** er kann das bestätigen. **(b)** *car etc* zurückfahren. **(c)** *(Comp)* sichern.

**back**: ~**ache** *n* Rückenschmerzen *pl*; ~**bencher** *n* *(esp Brit)* einfache(r) Abgeordnete(r) *mf (der/die nicht zur Regierung gehört und auf den hinteren Reihen im britischen Parlament sitzt)*; ~**biting** *n* Lästern *nt*; ~**bone** *n (lit, fig)* Rückgrat *nt*; ~**breaking** *adj* äußerst anstrengend; ~ **burner** *n* to put sth on the ~ **burner** *(fig col)* etw zurückstellen; ~**chat** *n no pl* Widerrede *f*; ~**cloth** *n* Hintergrund *m*; ~**comb** *vt* hair toupieren; ~ **copy** *n* alte Ausgabe; ~**date** *vt* (zu)rückdatieren; ~**dated to May** rückwirkend ab Mai; ~ **door** *n (lit, fig)* Hintertür *f*; ~**drop** *n* = ~**cloth**.

**backer** ['bækəʳ] *n* **(a)** *(supporter)* his ~**s** (die,) die ihn unterstützen. **(b)** *(Comm)* Geldgeber *m*.

**back**: ~**fire 1** *n (Aut)* Fehlzündung *f*; **2** *vi* **(a)** *(Aut)* Fehlzündungen haben; **(b)** *(col: plan etc)* ins Auge gehen *(col)*; it ~**fired on us** der Schuß ging nach hinten los *(col)*; ~**gammon** *n* Backgammon *nt*; ~ **garden** *n* Garten *m* (hinter dem Haus).

**background** ['bækgraʊnd] **1** *n* **(a)** *(of painting etc, fig)* Hintergrund *m*. **to stay in the** ~ sich im Hintergrund halten. **(b)** *(educational etc)* Werdegang *m*; *(social)* Verhältnisse *pl*; *(family* ~*)* Herkunft *f no pl*; **he comes from a** ~ **of poverty** er kommt aus ärmlichen Verhältnissen. **(c)** *(of case, event, problem etc)* Zusammenhänge, Hintergründe *pl*. **the** ~ **to the crisis** die Hintergründe der Krise. **2** *cpds*: ~**information** Hintergrundinformationen *pl*; ~ **music** musikalische Untermalung; ~ **program** *(Comp)* Hintergrundprogramm *nt*; ~ **reading** Sekundärliteratur *f*.

**back**: ~**hand 1** *n (Sport)* Rückhand *f no pl*; ~**hand** **(stroke** *or* **shot)** Rückhandschlag *m*; **2** *adv* mit der Rückhand; ~**handed** *adj compliment* zweifelhaft; *shot* Rückhand-; ~**hander** *n (col: bribe)* Schmiergeld *nt*; **to give sb a** ~**hander** jdn schmieren *(col)*.

**backing** ['bækɪŋ] *n* **(a)** *(support)* Unterstützung *f*. **(b)** *(Mus) (also* ~ **group)** Begleitung *f*. **(c)** *(for picture frame, for strengthening)* Rücken(verstärkung *f*) *m*.

**back**: ~**lash** *n (Tech)* Gegenschlag *m*; *(play)* Spiel *nt*; *(fig)* Gegenreaktion *f*; ~**less** *adj dress* rückenfrei; ~**log** *n* Rückstände *pl*; **I have a** ~**log of work** ich bin mit der Arbeit im Rückstand; ~ **number** *(of paper)* alte Ausgabe *or* Nummer; ~**pack** *n* Rucksack *m*; ~**packer** *n* Rucksacktourist(in *f*) *m*; ~**packing** *n* Reisen *nt* mit dem Rucksack; ~ **pay** *n* Nachzahlung *f*; ~**pedal** *vi (lit)* rückwärts treten; *(fig col)* einen Rückzieher machen; ~**rest** *n* Rückenstütze *f*; ~ **room** *n* Hinterzimmer *nt*; ~ **seat** *n* Rücksitz *m*; **to take a** ~ **seat** *(col)* sich zurückhalten; ~**seat driver** *n* **she is a terrible** ~**seat driver** sie redet beim Fahren immer rein; ~**side** *n (col)* Hinterteil *nt (col)*; ~**slide** *vi* rückfällig werden; ~**space** *vi (Typing)* zurücksetzen; ~**stage** *adv, adj* hinter den Kulissen; *(in dressing-room area)* in der Garderobe; ~ **street** *n* Seitenstraßen *nt*; **he comes from the** ~ **streets of Liverpool** er kommt aus dem ärmeren Teil von Liverpool; ~**-street abortionist** *n* Engelmacher(in *f*) *m (col)*; ~**stroke** *n (Swimming)* Rückenschwimmen *nt*; ~ **to** ~ *adv* Rücken an Rücken *or* mit den Rückenseiten aneinander; ~ **to front** *adv* verkehrt herum; *read* von hinten nach vorne; ~**-up 1** *n* Unterstützung *f*; **2** *adj troops* Hilfs-. ~**-up copy/disk/file** *(Comp)* Sicherungskopie/-diskette/-datei *f*.

**backward** ['bækwəd] **1** *adj* **(a)** ~ **and forward movement** Vor- und Zurückbewegung *f*; **a** ~ **glance** ein Blick zurück. **(b)** *(fig)* **a** ~ **step/move** ein Schritt *m* zurück/eine (Zu)rückentwicklung. **(c)** *(retarded)* *child* zurückgeblieben; *region, country* rückständig.

**2** *adv* = **backwards**.

**backwardness** ['bækwədnɪs] *n (mental)* Zurückgebliebenheit *f*; *(of region)* Rückständigkeit *f*.

**backwards** ['bækwəd] *adv* rückwärts. **to fall** ~ nach hinten fallen; **to walk** ~ **and forwards** hin und her gehen; **to bend over** ~ **to do sth** *(col)* sich *(dat)* ein Bein ausreißen, um etw zu tun *(col)*; **I know it** ~ das kenne ich in- und auswendig.

**back**: ~**water** *n (lit)* Stauwasser *nt*; *(fig)* rückständiges Nest; **this town is a cultural** ~**water** kulturell gesehen ist diese Stadt tiefste Provinz; ~**yard** *n* **(a)** Hinterhof *m*; **(b)** *(US)* = ~ **garden**.

**bacon** ['beɪkən] *n* durchwachsener Speck. ~ **and eggs** Eier mit Speck; **to save sb's** ~ *(col)* jds Rettung sein.

**bacteria** [bæk'tɪərɪə] *npl* Bakterien *pl*.

**bacterial** [bæk'tɪərɪəl] *adj* Bakterien-, bakteriell.

**bacteriology** [bæk,tɪərɪ'ɒlədʒɪ] *n* Bakteriologie *f*.

**bad** [bæd] *adj, comp* **worse**, *superl* **worst** **(a)** schlecht; *risk* hoch; *word* unanständig; *(immoral, wicked also)* böse; *(naughty, misbehaved)* unartig, ungezogen; *dog* böse. **you** ~ **boy!** du Lümmel!; **I didn't mean that word in a** ~ **sense** ich habe das Wort nicht böse gemeint; **to go** ~ schlecht werden; **to be** ~ **for sb/sth** schlecht für jdn/etw sein; **he's** ~ **at tennis** er spielt schlecht Tennis; **it would not be a** ~ **thing** das wäre nicht schlecht; **(that's) too** ~**!** *(indignant)* (also) so was!; **(**~ **luck)** Pech!; **too** ~ **you couldn't make it** wirklich schade, daß Sie nicht kommen konnten; **to be in** ~ **with sb** *(US)* bei jdm schlecht angeschrieben sein.

**(b)** *(serious) wound, situation* schlimm. **he's got it** ~ *(col)* ihn hat's schwer erwischt *(col)*; **things are going from** ~ **to worse** es wird immer schlimmer.

**(c)** *(in poor health, sick) stomach* krank; *leg, knee, hand* schlimm. **he/the economy is in a** ~ **way** es geht ihm schlecht/es steht schlecht mit der Wirtschaft; **to feel** ~ sich nicht wohl fühlen; **I feel** ~ mir geht es nicht gut; **how is he?** — **he's not so** ~ wie geht es ihm? — nicht schlecht.

**(d)** *(regretful)* **I feel really** ~ **about not having told him** ich habe ein schlechtes Gewissen, daß ich ihm das nicht gesagt habe; **don't feel** ~ **about it** mach dir keine Gedanken (darüber).

**baddie** ['bædɪ] *n (col)* Schurke, Bösewicht *m*.

**bade** [beɪd] *pret of* **bid**.

**badge** [bædʒ] *n* Abzeichen *nt*; *(made of metal) (women's lib, joke* ~ *etc)* Button *m*; *(on car etc)* Plakette *f*. ~ **of office** Dienstmarke *f*.

**badger** ['bædʒəʳ] **1** *n* Dachs *m*. **2** *vt* zusetzen (+*dat*).

**badly** ['bædlɪ] *adv* **(a)** schlecht. **the party went** ~ die Party war ein Reinfall *(col)*. **(b)** *wounded, mistaken* schwer. ~ **beaten** *(Sport)* vernichtend geschlagen; *(as punishment)* schwer verprügelt. **(c)** *(very much)* äußerst, sehr; *in debt, overdrawn* hoch. **to want sth** ~ etw unbedingt wollen; **he** ~ **needs** *or* **wants a haircut** er muß dringend zum Friseur.

**bad-mannered** [,bæd'mænəd] *adj* unhöflich; *child also* ungezogen.

**badminton** ['bædmɪntən] *n* Federball *nt*; *(on court)* Badminton *nt*.

**bad-mouth** ['bædmaʊθ] *vt (US col)* herziehen über (+*acc*) *(col)*.

**bad-tempered** [,bæd'tempəd] *adj* schlechtgelaunt *attr*. **to be** ~ schlechte Laune haben; *(as characteristic)* ein reizbarer Mensch sein.

**baffle** ['bæfl] *vt (confound, amaze)* verblüffen; *(cause incomprehension)* vor ein Rätsel stellen. **a** ~**d look** ein verdutzter Blick; **it really** ~**s me how ...** es ist mir wirklich ein Rätsel, wie ...

**bafflement** ['bæflmənt] *n* Verblüffung *f*.

**ballistic**

**baffling** ['bæflɪŋ] *adj case* rätselhaft; *complexity* verwirrend; *mystery* unergründlich.

**bag** [bæg] *n* Tasche *f*; *(with drawstrings, pouch)* Beutel *m*; *(for school)* Schultasche *f*; *(made of paper, plastic)* Tüte *f*; *(sack)* Sack *m*; *(suitcase)* Reisetasche *f*. **~s** (Reise)gepäck *nt*; **to pack one's ~s** die Koffer packen; **to be a ~ of bones** *(fig col)* nur Haut und Knochen sein *(col)*; **it's in the ~** *(fig col)* das ist gelaufen *(col)*; **~s under the eyes** *(black)* Ringe *pl* unter den Augen; *(of skin)* Tränensäcke *pl*; **~s of** *(col: a lot)* jede Menge *(col)*; **(old) ~** *(pej col: woman)* (alte) Ziege *(pej col)*.

**bagel** ['beɪgəl] *n kleines ringförmiges Brötchen.*

**baggage** ['bægɪdʒ] *n (luggage)* (Reise)gepäck *nt.*

**baggage: ~ allowance** *n* Freigepäck *nt*; **~ car** *n (US)* Gepäckwagen *m*; **~ check** *n* (a) Gepäckkontrolle *f*; **(b)** *(US: ticket)* Gepäckschein *m*; **~ checkroom** *n (US)* Gepäckaufbewahrung *f*; **~ claim** *n* Gepäckausgabe *f*; **~ handler** *n* Gepäckträger *m.*

**baggy** ['bægɪ] *adj (+er) (ill-fitting)* (zu) weit; *skin* schlaff; *(out of shape) trousers, suit* ausgebeult; *jumper* ausgeleiert.

**Baghdad** [bæg'dæd] *n* Bagdad *nt.*

**bag lady** *n* Stadtstreicherin *f (, die ihre ganze Habe in Einkaufstaschen mit sich führt).*

**bagpiper** ['bægpaɪpəʳ] *n* Dudelsackpfeifer *m.*

**bagpipe(s** *pl*) ['bægpaɪp(s)] *n* Dudelsack *m.*

**bag-snatcher** ['bæg,snætʃəʳ] *n* Handtaschendieb *m.*

**Bahamas** [bə'hɑːməz] *npl* **the ~** die Bahamas.

**Bahrain** [bɑː'reɪn] *n* Bahrain *nt.*

**bail¹** [beɪl] *n (Jur)* Kaution *f.* **to stand ~ for sb** für jdn (die) Kaution stellen; **to grant ~** die Freilassung gegen Kaution bewilligen; **to let sb out on ~** jdn gegen Kaution freilassen.

▶**bail out** *vt sep* **(a)** *(Jur)* gegen Kaution freibekommen. **(b)** *(fig)* aus der Patsche helfen *(+dat) (col).*

**bail²** *vti* = **bale².**

**bailiff** ['beɪlɪf] *n (sheriff's ~)* Amtsdiener *m*; *(for property)* Gerichtsvollzieher *m*; *(in court)* Gerichtsdiener *m*; *(on estate)* (Guts)verwalter *m.*

**bait** [beɪt] **1** *n (lit, fig)* Köder *m.* **to swallow the** *or* **rise to the ~** *(lit, fig)* anbeißen. **2** *vt* **(a)** *hook, trap* mit einem Köder versehen. **(b)** *(torment) animal* (mit Hunden) hetzen; *person* quälen.

**baize** [beɪz] *n* Flausch *m.* **green ~** Billardtuch *nt.*

**bake** [beɪk] *vt* **(a)** *(Cook)* backen. **~d beans** *pl* gebackene Bohnen *pl*; **~d potatoes** *pl* in der Schale gebackene Kartoffeln *pl.* **(b)** *pottery, bricks* brennen; *(sun) earth* ausdörren.

**baker** ['beɪkəʳ] *n* Bäcker(in *f*) *m.* **~'s (shop)** *(Brit)* Bäckerei *f*; **~'s dozen** 13 (Stück).

**bakery** ['beɪkərɪ] *n* Bäckerei *f.*

**baking** ['beɪkɪŋ] *n (act) (Cook)* Backen *nt*; *(of earthenware)* Brennen *nt.*

**baking: ~ day** *n* Backtag *m*; **~ dish** *n* Backform *f*; **~ powder, ~ soda** *n* Backpulver *nt*; **~ tin** *n* Backform *f.*

**Balaclava** [,bælə'klɑːvə] *n* Kapuzenmütze *f.*

**balance** ['bæləns] **1** *n* **(a)** *(apparatus)* Waage *f.* **to be** *or* **hang in the ~** *(fig)* in der Schwebe sein. **(b)** *(counterpoise)* Gegengewicht *nt (to zu)*; *(fig also)* Ausgleich *m (to für).* **(c)** *(lit, fig: equilibrium)* Gleichgewicht *nt.* **to keep/lose one's ~** das Gleichgewicht halten/verlieren; **to throw sb off (his) ~** jdn aus dem Gleichgewicht bringen; **the ~ of power** das Gleichgewicht der Kräfte; **to strike the right ~** den goldenen Mittelweg finden; **on ~** *(fig)* alles in allem. **(d)** *(Comm, Fin: state of account)* Saldo *m*; *(with bank also)* Kontostand *m*; *(of company)* Bilanz *f.* **~ carried forward** Saldoübertrag *m*; **~ due** *(bank-*

*ing)* Soll *nt*; *(Comm)* Rechnungsbetrag *m*; **~ of payments/trade** Zahlungs-/Handelsbilanz *f.* **(e)** *(fig: remainder)* Rest *m.*

**2** *vt* **(a)** *(keep level, in equilibrium)* im Gleichgewicht halten; *(as trick) ball etc* balancieren; *(bring into equilibrium)* ins Gleichgewicht bringen. **(b)** *(weigh in the mind) two solutions* (gegeneinander) abwägen. **to ~ sth against sth** etw einer Sache *(dat)* gegenüberstellen. **(c)** *(equal, make up for)* ausgleichen. **(d)** *(Comm, Fin) account (add up)* abschließen; *(make equal)* ausgleichen. **to ~ the books** die Bilanz ziehen.

**3** *vi* **(a)** *(be in equilibrium)* Gleichgewicht halten; *(scales)* sich ausbalancieren. **he ~d on one foot** er balancierte auf einem Bein. **(b)** *(Comm, Fin: of accounts)* ausgeglichen sein. **the books don't ~** die Abrechnung stimmt nicht.

▶**balance out 1** *vt sep* ausgleichen. **they ~ each other ~** sie halten sich die Waage; *(personalities)* sie gleichen sich aus. **2** *vi* sich ausgleichen.

**balanced** ['bælənst] *adj* ausgewogen; *personality* ausgeglichen.

**balance sheet** *n (Fin)* Bilanz *f.*

**balancing** ['bælənsɪŋ]: **~ act** *n (lit, fig)* Balanceakt *m*; **~ trick** *n* Balancekunststück *nt.*

**balcony** ['bælkənɪ] *n* **(a)** Balkon *m.* **(b)** *(Theat)* oberster Rang.

**bald** [bɔːld] *adj (+er)* **(a)** *person* kahl, glatzköpfig; *tyre* abgefahren. **he is ~** er hat eine Glatze; **to go ~** eine Glatze bekommen; **~ patch** kahle Stelle. **(b)** *style, statement* knapp.

**baldly** ['bɔːldlɪ] *adv (fig: bluntly)* unverblümt.

**baldness** ['bɔːldnɪs] *n* **(a)** Kahlheit *f.* **(b)** *(of style, statement)* Knappheit *f.*

**bale¹** [beɪl] *n (of hay)* Ballen *m.*

**bale²** *vti (Naut)* schöpfen.

▶**bale out 1** *vi* **(a)** *(Aviat)* abspringen, aussteigen *(col) (of aus).* **(b)** *(Naut)* schöpfen. **2** *vt sep (Naut) water* schöpfen; *boat* ausschöpfen.

**Balearic** [,bælɪ'ærɪk] *adj* **the ~ Islands** die Balearen *pl.*

**baleful** ['beɪlfʊl] *adj (evil)* böse; *(sad)* traurig.

**balk, baulk** [bɔːk] *vi (person)* zurückschrecken *(at vor +dat)*; *(horse)* scheuen *(at bei).*

**Balkan** ['bɔːlkən] **1** *adj* Balkan-. **2** *n* **the ~s** der Balkan, die Balkanländer *pl.*

**ball¹** [bɔːl] *n* **(a)** Ball *m*; *(Billiards)* Kugel *f*; *(of wool, string)* Knäuel *m or nt*; *(US: baseball)* Baseball *nt.* **to keep the ~ rolling** die Sache in Gang halten; **to start** *or* **set the ~ rolling** *(fig)* den Stein ins Rollen bringen; **the ~ is with you** *or* **in your court** *(fig)* Sie sind am Ball *(col)*; **to play ~** *(fig)* mitmachen; **to be on the ~** *(fig col)* auf Zack *or* Draht sein *(col)*; **~ of the foot/thumb** Fuß-/Handballen *m.* **(b)** *(col!: testicle)* Ei *nt usu pl (col!)*; *pl also* Sack *m (col!).* **~s!** *(nonsense)* red keinen Scheiß! *(col!).*

**ball²** *n (dance)* Ball *m.* **to have a ~** *(col)* sich prima amüsieren *(col).*

**ballad** ['bæləd] *n (Mus, Liter)* Ballade *f.*

**ballast** ['bæləst] *n (Naut, Aviat, fig)* Ballast *m.*

**ball: ~-bearing** *n* Kugellager *nt*; **~ boy** *n (Tennis)* Balljunge *m*; **~-cock** *n* Schwimmerhahn *m.*

**ballerina** [,bælə'riːnə] *n* Ballerina *f.*

**ballet** ['bæleɪ] *n* Ballett *nt.*

**ballet: ~-dancer** *n* Ballettänzer(in *f*) *m*; **~shoe** *n* Ballettschuh *m.*

**ball: ~ game** *n* Ballspiel *nt*; *(US: baseball game)* Baseballspiel *nt*; **it's a whole new ~ game** *(fig col)* das ist 'ne ganz andere Sache *(col)*; **~ girl** *n (Tennis)* Ballmädchen *nt.*

**ballistic** [bə'lɪstɪk] *adj* ballistisch. **~ missile** Raketengeschoß *nt.*

**ballistics** [bə'lıstıks] *n sing* Ballistik *f.*

**balloon** [bə'luːn] **1** *n* Ballon *m; (toy also)* Luftballon *m; (in cartoon)* Sprechblase *f.* **the ~ went up** *(fig col)* da ist die Bombe geplatzt *(col).* **2** *vi* **(a) to go ~ing** auf Ballonfahrt gehen. **(b)** *(swell out)* sich blähen.

**balloonist** [bə'luːnıst] *n* Ballonfahrer(in *f*) *m.*

**ballot** ['bælət] **1** *n* (geheime) Abstimmung. **to decide sth by ~** über etw *(acc)* (geheim) abstimmen; **to take** *or* **hold a ~** (geheim) abstimmen. **2** *vt members* abstimmen lassen.

**ballot: ~-box** *n* Wahlurne *f;* **~-paper** *n* Stimmzettel *m.*

**ball: ~park** *n* **(a)** *(US)* Baseballstadion *nt;* **(b) ~park figure** Richtzahl *f;* **in that ~park** in dieser Größenordnung; **~-point (pen)** *n* Kugelschreiber *m;* **~room** *n* Ballsaal *m;* **~room dancing** *n* Gesellschaftstanz *m.*

**balls-up** ['bɔːlzʌp], *(esp US)* **ball up** ['bɔːlʌp] *n (col!)* Schlamassel *m (col);* Scheiß *m (col!).* **to make a ~ of sth** bei etw Mist *(col) or* Scheiße *(col!)* bauen.

**ballyhoo** [,bælı'huː] *n (col)* Trara *nt (col).*

**balm** [bɑːm] *n (lit, fig)* Balsam *m; (Bot)* Melisse *f.*

**balmy** ['bɑːmı] *adj (+er) (fragrant)* wohlriechend; *(mild)* sanft. **~ breezes** linde Lüfte *(geh).*

**balsa** ['bɔːlsə] *n (also ~ wood)* Balsa(holz) *nt.*

**balsam** ['bɔlsəm] *n* Balsam *m.*

**Balt** [bɔːlt] *n* Balte *m,* Baltin *f.*

**Baltic** ['bɔːltık] *adj* baltisch. **~ (Sea)** Ostsee *f;* **the ~ States** das Baltikum.

**balustrade** [,bælə'streıd] *n* Balustrade *f.*

**bamboo** [bæm'buː] *n* Bambus *m.*

**bamboozle** [bæm'buːzl] *vt (col) (baffle)* verblüffen; *(trick)* hereinlegen *(col).*

**ban** [bæn] **1** *n* Verbot *nt.* **to put a ~ on sth** etw verbieten; **a ~ on smoking** Rauchverbot *nt.* **2** *vt (prohibit)* verbieten; *footballer etc* sperren. **she was ~ned from driving** ihr wurde Fahrverbot erteilt.

**banal** [bə'nɑːl] *adj* banal.

**banality** [bə'nælıtı] *n* Banalität *f.*

**banana** [bə'nɑːnə] *n* Banane *f.* **~ republic** Bananenrepublik *f.*

**bananas** [bə'nɑːnəz] *adj pred (col: crazy)* bescheuert *(col).* **to go ~** durchdrehen *(col);* **this is driving me ~** dabei dreh' ich noch durch *(col).*

**banana skin** *n* Bananenschale *f.*

**band¹** [bænd] *n* **(a)** *(of cloth, iron)* Band *nt; (of leather)* Band *nt,* Riemen *m; (waist ~)* Bund *m; (on machine)* Riemen *m.* **(b)** *(stripe)* Streifen *m.*

**band²** *n* **(a)** Schar *f; (of robbers etc)* Bande *f; (of workers)* Trupp *m,* Kolonne *f.* **(b)** *(Mus)* Band *f; (dance ~)* Tanzkapelle *f; (brass ~, Mil etc)* (Musik)kapelle *f.*

▶**band together** *vi* sich zusammenschließen.

**bandage** ['bændıdʒ] **1** *n* Verband *m; (strip of cloth)* Binde *f.* **2** *vt (also ~ up) cut* verbinden; *broken limb* bandagieren.

**Band-Aid** ® ['bændeıd] *(US)* **1** *n* Heftpflaster *nt; (fig: temporary remedy)* behelfsmäßige Lösung, Behelf *m.* **2** *adj (also* **band-aid**) *(col: makeshift)* behelfsmäßig.

**B & B** [,biːənd'biː] *n* = **bed and breakfast.**

**bandit** ['bændıt] *n* Bandit, Räuber *m.*

**band: ~leader** *n* Bandleader *m;* **~saw** *n* Bandsäge *f.*

**bandsman** ['bændzmən] *n, pl* **-men** [-mən] Musiker *m.* **military ~** Mitglied *nt* eines Musikkorps.

**band: ~stand** *n* Musikpavillon *m;* **~wagon** *n:* **to jump** *or* **climb on the ~wagon** *(fig col)* auf den fahrenden Zug aufspringen; **~width** *n (Rad)* Band-

breite *f.*

**bandy** ['bændı] *adj* krumm. **~ legs** *(of people)* O-Beine.

▶**bandy about** *or* **around** *vt sep story* herumerzählen; *words, technical expressions* um sich werfen mit; *sb's name* immer wieder nennen.

**bandy-legged** [,bændı'legd] *adj* mit krummen Beinen; *person* O-beinig.

**bane** [beın] *n (cause of distress)* Fluch *m.* **he's the ~ of my life** mit ihm bin ich geschlagen.

**bang** [bæŋ] **1** *n (noise)* Knall *m; (of sth falling)* Plumps *m.* **there was a ~ outside** draußen hat es geknallt; **to go off with a ~** mit lautem Knall losgehen; *(col: be a success)* ein Bombenerfolg sein *(col).* **2** *adv* **(a) to go ~** knallen; *(gun also, balloon)* peng machen *(col); (balloon)* zerplatzen. **(b)** *(col)* **his answer was ~ on** seine Antwort war genau richtig; **she came ~ on time** sie war auf die Sekunde pünktlich. **3** *interj* peng. **~ went a £10 note** *(col)* und schon war ein 10-Pfund-Schein futsch *(col).* **4** *vt* **(a)** *(thump)* schlagen, knallen *(col).* **he ~ed his fist on the table** er schlug mit der Faust auf den Tisch. **(b)** *(shut noisily) door* zuknallen *(col).* **(c) to ~ one's head** *etc* **on sth** sich *(dat)* den Kopf *etc* an etw *(dat)* anschlagen. **5** *vi* **(a)** *(door: shut)* zuknallen *(col); (fireworks, gun)* knallen. **(b) to ~ on** *or* **at sth** gegen *or* an etw *(acc)* schlagen.

▶**bang down** *vt sep (hin)*knallen *(col).* **to ~ ~ the receiver** den Hörer aufknallen *(col).*

**banger** ['bæŋəʳ] *n* **(a)** *(col: sausage)* Wurst *f.* **(b)** *(col: old car)* Kiste *f (col).* **(c)** *(Brit: firework)* Knallkörper, Kracher *m.*

**Bangladesh** [,bæŋglə'deʃ] *n* Bangladesch *nt.*

**bangle** ['bæŋgl] *n* Armreif *m; (for ankle)* Fußreif *m.*

**bangs** [bæŋz] *npl (US: in hair)* Pony *m.*

**banish** ['bænıʃ] *vt person* verbannen; *cares, fear* vertreiben.

**banishment** ['bænıʃmənt] *n* Verbannung *f.*

**banisters** ['bænıstəz] *npl* Geländer *nt.*

**banjo** ['bændʒəu] *n, pl* **-es,** *(US)* **-s** Banjo *nt.*

**bank¹** [bæŋk] **1** *n* **(a)** *(of earth, sand)* Wall, Damm *m; (slope)* Böschung *f,* Abhang *m; (on racetrack)* Kurvenüberhöhung *f.* **(b)** *(of river, lake)* Ufer *nt.* **(c) ~ of clouds** Wolkenwand *or* -bank *f.* **2** *vi (Aviat)* eine Kurve fliegen.

**bank²** **1** *n (Fin, Med)* Bank *f.* **2** *vt money* einzahlen. **3** *vi* **where do you ~?** bei welcher Bank sind Sie?

▶**bank (up)on** *vi +prep obj* sich verlassen auf *(+acc).*

**bank: ~ account** *n* Bankkonto *nt;* **~ balance** *n* Kontostand *m;* **~book** *n* Sparbuch *nt;* **~ charges** *pl (Brit)* Bankgebühren *pl;* **~ clerk** *n* Bankangestellte(r) *mf.*

**banker** ['bæŋkəʳ] *n (Fin)* Bankier *m; (gambling)* Bankhalter *m.*

**banker's: ~ card** *n* Scheckkarte *f;* **~ order** *n* Bankauftrag *m.*

**bank holiday** *n (Brit)* öffentlicher Feiertag; *(US)* Bankfeiertag *m.*

**banking¹** ['bæŋkıŋ] *n (in road etc)* Überhöhung *f; (of aircraft)* Kurvenflug *m.*

**banking²** *n* Bankwesen *nt.* **he wants to go into ~** er will ins Bankfach gehen.

**banking hours** *npl* Schalterstunden *pl.*

**bank: ~loan** *n* Bankkredit *m;* **~ manager** *n* Filialleiter(in *f*) *m (einer Bank);* **~note** *n (Brit)* Banknote *f,* Geldschein *m;* **~ rate** *n* Diskontsatz *m.*

**bankrupt** ['bæŋkrʌpt] *adj (Jur)* bankrott. **to go ~** Bankrott machen; **to be ~** bankrott *or* pleite *(col)* sein.

**bankruptcy** ['bæŋkrəpsı] *n (lit, fig)* Bankrott *m.*

**bank:** ~ **statement** n Kontoauszug m; ~ **transfer** n Banküberweisung f.

**banner** ['bænər] n Banner nt (also fig); (in processions) Transparent nt. ~ **headlines** Schlagzeilen pl.

**bannisters** ['bænɪstəz] n = **banisters.**

**banns** [bæns] npl (Eccl) Aufgebot nt. **to read the ~** das Aufgebot verlesen.

**banquet** ['bæŋkwɪt] n (lavish feast) Festessen nt; (ceremonial dinner) Bankett nt.

**bantam** ['bæntəm] n Bantamhuhn nt.

**bantamweight** ['bæntəm,weɪt] n Bantamgewicht nt.

**banter** ['bæntər] n Geplänkel nt.

**Bantu** [,bæn'tu] **1** n (language) Bantu nt; (person) Bantu mf. **the ~** die Bantu pl. **2** adj Bantu-.

**BAOR** = **British Army of the Rhine** Britische Rheinarmee.

**baptism** ['bæptɪzəm] n Taufe f. ~ **of fire** (fig) Feuertaufe f.

**Baptist** ['bæptɪst] n Baptist(in f) m. **John the ~** Johannes der Täufer.

**baptize** [bæp'taɪz] vt taufen.

**bar¹** [bɑːr] **1** n (a) (of metal, wood) Stange f; (of toffee etc) Riegel m; (of electric fire) Element nt. ~ **of gold/silver** Gold-/Silberbarren m; **a ~ of chocolate, a chocolate ~** (slab) eine Tafel Schokolade; (smaller) ein Schokoladenriegel m; **a ~ of soap** ein Stück nt Seife. **(b)** (of window, cage) (Gitter)stab m; (of door) Stange f; (Sport) (of goal, high jump etc) Latte f; (horizontal ~) Reck nt. **behind ~s** hinter Gittern. **(c)** (fig: obstacle) Hindernis (to für) nt. **to be a ~ to sth** einer Sache (dat) im Wege stehen. **(d)** (for drinks) Bar f; (counter) Theke f, Tresen m. **(e)** (Jur) **the B~** die Anwaltschaft; **to be called or admitted** (US) **to the B~** als Anwalt zugelassen werden; "**prisoner at the ~**" „Angeklagter!". **(f)** (Mus) Takt m.

**2** vt **(a)** (obstruct) road versperren. **(b)** (fasten) door verriegeln. **(c)** (exclude, prohibit) person ausschließen; action, thing verbieten. **to ~ sb from a competition** jdn von (der Teilnahme an) einem Wettbewerb ausschließen.

**bar²**, **barring** prep **barring accidents** falls nichts passiert; **bar none** ohne Ausnahme.

**barb** [bɑːb] n (of fish-hook, arrow) Widerhaken m.

**Barbados** [bɑː'beɪdɒs] n Barbados nt.

**barbarian** [bɑː'bɛərɪən] **1** n (Hist, fig) Barbar(in f) m. **2** adj (Hist, fig) barbarisch.

**barbaric** [bɑː'bærɪk] adj barbarisch; guard etc grausam, roh; (fig col) conditions grauenhaft.

**barbarity** [bɑː'bærɪtɪ] n Barbarei f; (cruelty) Grausamkeit f.

**barbarous** ['bɑːbərəs] adj (Hist, fig) barbarisch; (cruel) grausam.

**barbecue** ['bɑːbɪkjuː] **1** n (Cook: grid) Grill m; (occasion) Grillparty f; (meat) Grillfleisch nt. **2** vt grillen; (on a spit) pig etc am Spieß braten.

**barbed wire** ['bɑːbd'waɪər] n Stacheldraht m.

**barber** ['bɑːbər] n (Herren)friseur m. **at/to the ~'s** (Brit) beim/zum Friseur.

**barbershop** [,bɑːbə'ʃɒp] n (US) Friseurgeschäft nt.

**Barbie doll** ® ['bɑːbɪ,dɒl] n Barbie-Puppe ® f.

**barbiturate** [bɑː'bɪtjʊrɪt] n Barbiturat nt.

**Barcelona** [,bɑːsɪ'ləʊnə] n Barcelona nt.

**bar:** ~ **chart** n Balkendiagramm nt; ~ **code** n Strichkode m.

**bard** [bɑːd] n (old) Barde m.

**bare** [bɛər] **1** adj (+er) **(a)** skin, floor nackt, bloß; countryside, room kahl. ~ **patch** kahle Stelle; **to lay ~ one's heart** sein Innerstes bloßlegen; **with his ~ hands** mit bloßen Händen; **a ~ statement of the**

**facts** eine reine Tatsachenfeststellung. **(b)** (scanty, mere) knapp. **a ~ majority** eine knappe Mehrheit; **with just the ~st hint of garlic** nur mit einer winzigen Spur Knoblauch. **2** vt parts of the body entblößen; (at doctor's) freimachen; end of a wire freilegen.

**bare:** ~**back** adv, adj ohne Sattel; ~**faced** adj liar unverfroren, schamlos; ~**foot** adv barfuß; ~**headed** adj ohne Kopfbedeckung; ~**legged** adj mit bloßen or nackten Beinen.

**barely** ['bɛəlɪ] adv (scarcely) kaum. **we ~ know him** wir kennen ihn kaum.

**bareness** ['bɛənɪs] n Nacktheit f; (of trees, countryside) Kahlheit f.

**bargain** ['bɑːgɪn] **1** n **(a)** (transaction) Handel m, Geschäft nt. **to make or strike a ~** sich einigen; **I'll make a ~ with you, if you ...** ich mache Ihnen ein Angebot, wenn Sie ...; **it's a ~!** abgemacht!; **you drive a hard ~** Sie stellen ja harte Forderungen!; **then it started raining into the ~** dann hat es (obendrein) auch noch angefangen zu regnen. **(b)** (cheap offer) Sonderangebot nt; (thing bought) Schnäppchen nt (col). **what a ~!** das ist aber günstig! **2** vi handeln (for um); (in negotiations) verhandeln.

▶**bargain for** vi +prep obj (col: expect) erwarten. **I hadn't ~ed ~ that** damit hatte ich nicht gerechnet; **I got more than I ~ed ~** ich habe vielleicht mein blaues Wunder erlebt! (col).

**bargain:** ~ **buy** n Preisschlager m; ~ **hunter** n auf Sonderangebote versessener Käufer.

**bargaining** ['bɑːgənɪŋ] n Handeln nt; (negotiating) Verhandeln nt.

**bargain:** ~ **offer** n Sonderangebot nt; ~ **price** n Sonderpreis m.

**barge** [bɑːdʒ] **1** n (for freight) Last- or Frachtkahn m; (unpowered) Schleppkahn m; (ceremonial) Barkasse f. **2** vt **he ~d me out of the way** er hat mich weggestoßen.

▶**barge in** vi (col) hinein-/hereinplatzen (col); (interrupt) dazwischenplatzen (col) (on bei).

▶**barge into** vi +prep obj **(a)** (knock against) person (hinein)rennen in (+acc) (col); (shove) (an)-rempeln; thing rennen gegen (col). **(b)** (col) room, party, conversation (hinein-/herein)platzen in (+acc) (col).

**barge pole** n: **I wouldn't touch it/him with a ~** (Brit col) von so etwas/so jemandem lasse ich die Finger (col); (because disgusting, unpleasant) das/den würde ich noch nicht mal mit der Kneifzange anfassen (col).

**baritone** ['bærɪtəʊn] n (voice, singer) Bariton m.

**barium** ['bɛərɪəm] n Barium nt. ~ **meal** Kontrastbrei m.

**bark¹** [bɑːk] n (of tree) Rinde, Borke f.

**bark²** **1** n (of dog) Bellen nt no pl. **his ~ is worse than his bite** (Prov) Hunde, die bellen, beißen nicht (Prov). **2** vi bellen. **to ~ at sb** jdn anbellen; (person) jdn anfahren; **to be ~ing up the wrong tree** (fig col) auf dem Holzweg sein (col).

▶**bark out** vt sep orders bellen.

**barkeep(er)** ['bɑːkiːp(ər)] n (US) Barkeeper m.

**barley** ['bɑːlɪ] n Gerste f. ~ **sugar** n Malzzucker m; (sweet) Malzbonbon m.

**bar line** n (Mus) Taktstrich m.

**bar:** ~**maid** n Bardame f; ~**man** n Barkeeper m.

**barmy** ['bɑːmɪ] adj (Brit col) bekloppt (col).

**barn** [bɑːn] n Scheune f.

**barnacle** ['bɑːnəkl] n Rankenfüßer m.

**barn:** ~ **dance** n Tanzveranstaltung f mit Volkstänzen; ~ **owl** n Schleiereule f; ~**yard** n (Bauern)hof m.

**barometer** [bə'rɒmɪtəʳ] *n (lit, fig)* Barometer *nt.*
**barometric pressure** [ˌbærəʊ'metrɪk'preʃəʳ] *n* Atmosphären- *or* Luftdruck *m.*
**baron** ['bærən] *n (lit, fig)* Baron *m.*
**baroness** ['bærənɪs] *n* Baronin *f.*
**baronet** ['bærənɪt] *n* Baronet *m.*
**baroque** [bə'rɒk] **1** *adj* barock, Barock-. **2** *n (style)* Barock *m or nt.*
**barracking** ['bærəkɪŋ] *n* Pfeifen *nt; (boos)* Buhrufe *pl.*
**barracks** ['bærəks] *npl (often with sing vb) (Mil)* Kaserne *f; (fig pej also)* Mietskaserne *f.*
**barrage** ['bærɑːʒ] *n* **(a)** *(across river)* Wehr *nt; (larger)* Staustufe *f.* **(b)** *(Mil)* Sperrfeuer *nt.* **a ~ of stones** ein Steinhagel *m.* **(c)** *(fig: of questions etc)* Hagel *m.*
**barrel** ['bærəl] *n* **(a)** Faß *nt; (for rainwater etc)* Tonne *f; (measure: of oil)* Barrel *nt.* **they've got us over a ~** *(col)* sie haben uns in der Zange *(col).* **(b)** *(of handgun)* Lauf *m; (of cannon etc)* Rohr *nt.*
**barrel organ** *n* Drehorgel *f,* Leierkasten *m.*
**barren** ['bærən] *adj (lit, fig)* unfruchtbar; *land also* karg; *landscape* kahl, öde.
**barrenness** ['bærənnɪs] *n see adj* Unfruchtbarkeit *f;* Kargheit *f;* Kahlheit *f,* Öde *f.*
**barricade** [ˌbærɪ'keɪd] **1** *n* Barrikade *f.* **2** *vt* verbarrikadieren.
**barrier** ['bærɪəʳ] *n (lit, fig)* Barriere *f; (railing etc)* Schranke *f; (crash ~)* Leitplanke *f.* **ticket ~** Sperre *f.*
**barrier cream** *n* (Haut)schutzcreme *f.*
**barring** ['bɑːrɪŋ] *prep =* **bar²**.
**barrister** ['bærɪstəʳ] *n (Brit)* Rechtsanwalt *m/* -anwältin *f (bei Gericht).*
**barrow** ['bærəʊ] *n* Karre(n *m) f.*
**bar stool** *n* Barhocker *m.*
**Bart.** = **baronet.**
**bartender** ['bɑːtendəʳ] *n (US)* Barkeeper *m.*
**barter** ['bɑːtəʳ] **1** *vt* tauschen *(for gegen).* **2** *vi* tauschen; *(as general practice also)* Tauschhandel treiben. **to ~ for sth** um etw handeln. **3** *n* (Tausch)handel *m.*
►**barter away** *vt sep one's rights* verspielen.
**base¹** [beɪs] **1** *n* **(a)** *(lowest part)* Basis *f; (support for statue etc)* Sockel *m; (of lamp, mountain)* Fuß *m.* **(b)** *(main ingredient)* Hauptbestandteil *m.* **(c)** *(Mil)* Stützpunkt *m; (for holidays)* Standort *m; (Baseball)* Base *nt,* Mal *nt.* **(d)** *(Chem)* Lauge, Base *f.* **2** *vt* **(a)** stellen. **to be ~d on** ruhen auf *(+dat); (statue)* stehen auf *(+dat);* **you need something to ~ it on** Sie brauchen dafür eine feste Unterlage. **(b)** *(fig) opinion, theory* basieren *(on* auf *+acc); hopes* setzen *(on* auf *+acc); relationship* bauen *(on* auf *+acc).* **to be ~d on sb/sth** auf jdm/etw basieren. **(c)** *(Mil)* stationieren. **the company/my job is ~d in London** die Firma hat ihren Sitz in London/ich arbeite hauptsächlich in London.
**base²** *adj (+er)* **(a)** *motive* niedrig; *person, action* gemein, niederträchtig. **(b)** *metal* unedel.
**baseball** ['beɪsbɔːl] *n* Baseball *m or nt.*
**base camp** *n* Basislager *nt.*
**-based** [beɪst] *adj suf* **London-~** mit Sitz in London.
**base line** *n (Tennis)* Grundlinie *f; (Baseball)* Verbindungslinie *f zwischen zwei Malen.*
**basement** ['beɪsmənt] *n (in building)* Untergeschoß *nt; (in house also)* Keller *m.* **~ flat** Kellerwohnung, Souterrainwohnung *f.*
**baseness** ['beɪsnɪs] *n see adj* **(a)** Niedrigkeit *f;* Gemeinheit, Niederträchtigkeit *f.*
**base rate** *n (Fin)* Leitzins *m.*
**bash** [bæʃ] *(col)* **1** *n* **(a)** Schlag *m.* **the bumper has had a ~** die Stoßstange hat eine Delle abgekriegt

*(col).* **(b)** *(fig)* **I'll have a ~ (at it)** ich probier's mal *(col).* **2** *vt person* (ver)hauen *(col); ball* knallen *(col); car, wing* eindellen *(col).* **to ~ one's head/shin (against** *or* **on sth)** sich *(dat)* den Kopf/das Schienbein (an etw *dat)* anschlagen; **to ~ sb on the head with sth** jdm etw auf den Kopf hauen *(col).*
►**bash in** *vt sep (col) door* einschlagen. **to ~ sb's head ~** jdm den Schädel einschlagen *(col).*
►**bash up** *vt sep (Brit col) person* vermöbeln *(col).*
**bashful** ['bæʃful] *adj* schüchtern; *smile, look* verschämt; *(embarrassed)* verlegen.
**-bashing** ['bæʃɪŋ] *suf (col)* **Paki/queer~** *(physical)* Überfälle *pl* auf Pakistaner/Schwule; *(verbal)* das Schlechtmachen von Pakistanern/Schwulen.
**Basic** ['beɪsɪk] *(Comp) =* **beginner's all-purpose symbolic instruction code** BASIC *nt.*
**basic** ['beɪsɪk] **1** *adj* **(a)** *(fundamental)* Grund-; *problem also, reason, issue* Haupt-; *points, issues* wesentlich. **there's no ~ difference** es besteht kein grundlegender Unterschied; **must you be so ~!** müssen Sie sich denn so direkt ausdrücken?; **~ rate** *(of wage)* Grundgehalt *nt; (of tax)* Eingangssteuersatz *m; ~* **salary** Grundgehalt *nt; ~* **English** englischer Grundwortschatz. **(b)** *(original)* zu Grunde liegend. **(c)** *(essential)* notwendig. **2** *npl* **the ~s** das Wesentliche.
**basically** ['beɪsɪkəlɪ] *adv* im Grunde; *(mainly)* im wesentlichen.
**basil** ['bæzl] *n (Bot)* Basilikum *nt.*
**basilica** [bə'zɪlɪkə] *n* Basilika *f.*
**basin** ['beɪsn] *n* **(a)** *(vessel)* Schüssel *f; (wash~)* (Wasch)becken *nt.* **(b)** *(Geog)* Becken *nt.*
**basis** ['beɪsɪs] *n (foundation)* Basis *f; (for assumption)* Grund *m.* **we're working on the ~ that** ... wir gehen von der Annahme aus, daß ...; **on the ~ of this evidence** aufgrund dieses Beweismaterials.
**bask** [bɑːsk] *vi (in sun)* sich aalen *(in* in *+dat).*
**basket** ['bɑːskɪt] *n* Korb *m; (for rolls, fruit etc)* Körbchen *nt.* **a ~ of currencies** ausgewählte Währungen.
**basket:** **~ball** *n* Basketball *m;* **~work** *n* Korbflechterei *f; (articles)* Korbarbeiten *pl;* **~work chair** *n* Korbstuhl *m.*
**Basle** [bɑːl] *n* Basel *nt.*
**Basque** [bæsk] **1** *n* **(a)** *(person)* Baske *m,* Baskin *f.* **(b)** *(language)* Baskisch *nt.* **2** *adj* baskisch.
**bass** [beɪs] *(Mus)* **1** *n* Baß *m.* **2** *adj* Baß-. **~ clef** Baßschlüssel *m; ~* **drum** große Trommel.
**bassoon** [bə'suːn] *n* Fagott *nt.*
**bastard** ['bɑːstəd] *n* **(a)** *(lit)* uneheliches Kind; *(fig: hybrid)* Kreuzung *f.* **(b)** *(col!: person)* Scheißkerl *m (col!).* **poor ~** armes Schwein *(col).*
**baste¹** [beɪst] *vt (Sew)* heften.
**baste²** *vt (Cook)* (mit Fett) begießen.
**bat¹** [bæt] *n (Zool)* Fledermaus *f.* **(as) blind as a ~** blind wie ein Maulwurf.
**bat²** *(Sport)* **1** *n (Baseball, Cricket)* Schlagholz *nt; (Table-tennis)* Schläger *m.* **off one's own ~** *(fig)* auf eigene Faust *(col).* **2** *vi (Baseball, Cricket)* Schlagmann sein. **3** *vt (US col)* **to ~ sth around** etw bekakeln *(col).*
**bat³** *vt* **without ~ting an eyelid** ohne mit der Wimper zu zucken; **he didn't ~ an eyelid** er blieb seelenruhig.
**batch** [bætʃ] *n (of loaves)* Schub *m; (of prisoners, recruits also)* Trupp *m; (of things dispatched)* Sendung *f; (of letters, work)* Stoß, Stapel *m.*
**batch:** *(Comp)* **~ file** *n* Batch-Datei *f;* **~ processing** *n* Stapelverarbeitung *f,* Batch-Betrieb *m.*
**bated** ['beɪtɪd] *adj:* **with ~ breath** mit angehaltenem Atem.
**bath** [bɑːθ] **1** *n* **(a)** Bad *nt.* **to have** *or* **take a ~**

baden; **a room with** ~ ein Zimmer mit Bad. **(b)** *(bathtub)* (Bade)wanne *f.* **(c) (swimming)** ~s *pl* (Schwimm)bad *nt*; **(public)** ~s *pl* Badeanstalt *f*; *(Hist)* Bäder *pl.* **2** *vt (Brit)* baden. **3** *vi (Brit)* (sich) baden.

**bath: B~ bun** *n Hefebrötchen nt mit Rosinen, Zitronat und Orangeat*; ~**chair** *n* Rollstuhl *m*; ~**cube** *n* Würfel *m* Badesalz.

**bathe** [beɪð] **1** *vt* baden; *(with cottonwool etc)* waschen. **to be** ~**d in light/sweat** in Licht/Schweiß gebadet sein. **2** *vi (US)* (sich) baden.

**bather** ['beɪðəʳ] *n* Badende(r) *mf.*

**bathing** ['beɪðɪŋ] *n* Baden *nt.*

**bathing:** ~**-cap** *n* Badekappe *f*; ~**-costume** *n (Brit)* Badeanzug *m*; ~**-trunks** *npl (Brit)* Badehose *f.*

**bath:** ~**mat** *n* Badematte *f*; ~**robe** *n* Bademantel *m*; ~**room** *n* Bad(ezimmer) *nt*; *(euph: lavatory)* Toilette *f*; ~**salts** *npl* Badesalz *nt*; ~ **sheet** *n* großes Badetuch *nt*; ~**towel** *n* Badetuch *nt*; ~**tub** *n* Badewanne *f.*

**baton** ['bætən] *n* **(a)** *(Mus)* Taktstock *m*; *(Mil)* (Kommando)stab *m*. **(b)** *(of policeman)* Schlagstock *m*; *(for directing traffic)* Stab *m*. **(c)** *(in relay race)* Staffelholz *nt*, Stab *m.*

**bats** [bæts] *adj pred (col)* beklopft *(col).*

**battalion** [bə'tælɪən] *n (Mil, fig)* Bataillon *nt.*

**batter¹** ['bætəʳ] *n (Cook)* Teig *m.*

**batter²** **1** *vt* **(a)** einschlagen auf *(+acc).* **the house was** ~**ed by the wind** der Wind rüttelte unentwegt am Haus. **(b)** *(damage)* übel zurichten; *car also, metal* zer- or verbeulen. **(c)** *(col)* opponent eins draufgeben *(+dat) (col).* **2** *vi* **to** ~ **at the door** an die Tür hämmern *(col).*

▶**batter down** *vt sep door* einschlagen.

**battered** ['bætəd] *adj* übel zugerichtet; *wife, baby* mißhandelt; *object* verbeult; *furniture* ramponiert *(col)*; *nerves* zerrüttet.

**battering** ['bætərɪŋ] *n (lit)* Schläge, Prügel *pl*; *(of baby, wife)* Mißhandlung *f.* **to take a real** ~ übel zugerichtet werden; **to give sb a** ~ jdm heftig zusetzen.

**battering ram** ['bætərɪŋ,ræm] *n* Rammbock *m.*

**battery** ['bætəri] *n* Batterie *f*; *(fig: of arguments etc)* Reihe *f.*

**battery:** ~**-charger** *n* Ladegerät *nt*; ~ **farming** *n* (Hühner- *etc*)batterien *pl*; ~ **hen** *n (Agr)* Batteriehuhn *nt*; ~**-powered** *adj* batteriebetrieben.

**battle** ['bætl] **1** *n (lit)* Schlacht *f*; *(fig)* Kampf *m.* **to give** ~ sich zum Kampf stellen; **to fight a** ~ eine Schlacht schlagen; **to fight one's own** ~s sich alleine durchsetzen; **killed in** ~ (im Kampf) gefallen; ~ **of words/wits** Wortgefecht *nt*/geistiger Wettstreit; ~ **of the sexes** Geschlechterkampf *m*; **that's half the** ~ damit ist schon viel gewonnen. **2** *vi* kämpfen *(for* um*).*

**battle:** ~**-axe**, ~**-ax** *(US) n (weapon)* Streitaxt *f*; *(col: woman)* Drachen *m (col)*; ~ **cry** *n* Schlachtruf *m*; ~**field**, ~**ground** *n* Schlachtfeld *nt.*

**battlements** ['bætlmənts] *npl* Zinnen *pl.*

**battle:** ~ **royal** *n (fig: quarrel)* heftige Auseinandersetzung *f*; ~**ship** *n* Schlachtschiff *nt.*

**batty** ['bæti] *adj (+er)* verrückt.

**bauble** ['bɔ:bl] *n* Flitter *m no pl.* ~**s** Flitterzeug *nt.*

**baud** [bɔ:d] *n (Comp)* Baud *nt.*

**baulk** [bɔ:k] *vi* = **balk.**

**bauxite** ['bɔ:ksaɪt] *n* Bauxit *m.*

**Bavaria** [bə'vɛərɪə] *n* Bayern *nt.*

**Bavarian** [bə'vɛərɪən] **1** *n* **(a)** *(person)* Bayer(in *f*) *m.* **(b)** *(dialect)* Bayrisch *nt.* **2** *adj* bay(e)risch.

**bawdy** ['bɔ:di] *adj (+er)* derb.

**bawl** [bɔ:l] *vi* **(a)** *(shout)* brüllen, schreien; *(sing)*

grölen *(col).* **(b)** *(col: weep)* heulen *(col).*

▶**bawl out** *vt sep* **(a)** *order* brüllen; *song* grölen *(pej col).* **(b)** *(col: scold)* ausschimpfen.

**bay¹** [beɪ] *n* Bucht *f.*

**bay²** *n* **(a)** *(Archit)* Erker *m.* **(b)** *(loading* ~*)* Ladeplatz *m.*

**bay³** **1** *n (of dogs)* Bellen *nt no pl*; *(Hunt)* Melden *nt no pl.* **to keep** *or* **hold sb/sth at** ~ jdn/etw in Schach halten. **2** *vi* bellen; *(Hunt also)* melden.

**bay⁴** *adj horse* (kastanien)braun.

**bayleaf** ['beɪli:f] *n* Lorbeerblatt *nt.*

**bayonet** ['beɪənɪt] **1** *n* Bajonett, Seitengewehr *nt.* ~ **fitting** *(Elec)* Bajonettfassung *f.* **2** *vt* mit dem Bajonett aufspießen.

**bay:** ~ **tree** *n* Lorbeerbaum *m*; ~ **window** *n* Erkerfenster *nt.*

**bazaar** [bə'zɑ:ʳ] *n* Basar *m.*

**BBC** = **British Broadcasting Corporation** BBC *f.*

**BC** = **(a)** **before Christ** v. Chr. **(b)** **British Columbia.**

**be** [bi:] *pres* **am, is, are,** *pret* **was, were,** *ptp* **been**
**1 (a)** *(with adj, n)* sein. **he is a soldier/a German** er ist Soldat/Deutscher; **who is that? — it's me/that's Mary** wer ist das? — ich bin's/das ist Mary; **if I were you** wenn ich Sie wäre; ~ **sensible!** sei vernünftig! **(b) how are you?** wie geht's?; **I'm better now** es geht mir jetzt besser; **to** ~ **hungry/thirsty** Hunger/Durst haben; **I am hot/cold** mir ist heiß/kalt. **(c)** *(age)* sein. **he'll** ~ **three** er wird drei (Jahre alt). **(d)** *(cost)* kosten. **how much is that?** wieviel *or* was kostet das?; *(altogether)* wieviel macht das? **(e)** *(Math)* sein. **two times two is** *or* **are four** zwei mal zwei ist vier. **(f)** *(with poss)* gehören *(+dat).* **that book is your brother's** das Buch gehört Ihrem Bruder. **(g)** *(in exclamations)* **was he pleased to hear it!** er war vielleicht froh, das zu hören!

**2** *aux* **(a)** *(+prp: continuous tenses)* **what are you doing?** was machst du da?; **she is always complaining** sie beklagt sich dauernd; **they're coming tomorrow** sie kommen morgen; **will you** ~ **seeing her tomorrow?** treffen Sie sie morgen?; **I'll** ~ **starting soon** ich fange gleich an; **I have been waiting for you for half an hour** ich warte schon seit einer halben Stunde auf Sie.

**(b)** *(+ptp: passive)* werden. **the box had been opened** die Schachtel war geöffnet worden; **the car is to** ~ **sold** das Auto soll verkauft werden.

**(c)** *(recommendation)* **he is to** ~ **pitied/not to** ~ **envied** er ist zu bedauern/nicht zu beneiden; **not to** ~ **confused with** nicht zu verwechseln mit.

**(d)** *(intention, obligation, command)* sollen. **I am to look after my mother** ich soll mich um meine Mutter kümmern; **he is not to open it** er soll es nicht öffnen.

**(e)** *(~ destined)* sollen. **she was never to return** sie sollte nie zurückkehren.

**(f)** *(suppositions, wishes)* **if it were** *or* **was to snow** falls *or* wenn es schneien sollte; **I would** ~ **surprised if ...** ich wäre überrascht, wenn ...

**(g)** *(in tag questions, short answers)* **he's always late, isn't he? — yes he is** er kommt doch immer zu spät, nicht? — ja, das stimmt; **he's never late, is he? — yes he is** er kommt nie zu spät, oder? — o, doch.

**3** *vi* **(a)** sein; *(remain)* bleiben. **to** ~ **or not to** ~ Sein oder Nichtsein; **will you** ~ **much longer?** dauert das noch lange?; **the powers that** ~ die zuständigen Stellen; **let me/him** ~ laß mich/ihn (in Ruhe); ~ **that as it may** wie dem auch sei. **(b)** *(be situated)* sein; *(town, country, carpet etc also)* liegen; *(car, bottle, chair also)* stehen. **(c)** *(visit, call)*

**I've been to Paris** ich war schon (ein)mal in Paris; **the postman has already been** der Briefträger war schon da. **(d) now you've been and done it** *(col)* jetzt hast du aber was angerichtet! *(col)*.
**4** *vb impers* **(a)** sein. **it is dark/morning** es ist dunkel/Morgen; **it's 5 km to the nearest town** es sind 5 km bis zur nächsten Stadt. **(b)** *(emphatic)* **it was us** *or* **we** *(form)* **who found it** *wir* haben das gefunden. **(c)** *(wishes etc)* **were it not for him, if it weren't** *or* **wasn't for him** wenn er nicht wäre.

**beach** [biːtʃ] *n* Strand *m*. **on the ~** am Strand.

**beach:** **~ball** *n* Wasserball *m*; **~ buggy** *n* Strandbuggy *m*; **~comber** *n* Strandgutsammler *m*; **~wear** *n* Badesachen *pl*; *(Fashion)* Strandkleidung *f*.

**beacon** ['biːkən] *n* *(fire, light)* Leuchtfeuer *nt*; *(radio ~)* Funkfeuer *nt*; *(one of a series of lights, radio ~s)* Bake *f*.

**bead** [biːd] *n* *(also sweat)* Perle *f*. **(string of) ~s** Perlenschnur *f*; *(necklace)* Perlenkette *f*.

**beady** ['biːdɪ] *adj* **I've got my ~ eye on you** *(col)* ich beobachte Sie genau!

**beak** [biːk] *n* Schnabel *m*.

**beaker** ['biːkər] *n* Becher *m*; *(Chem etc)* Becherglas *nt*.

**be-all and end-all** ['biːɔːlənd'endɔːl] *n* das A und O.

**beam** [biːm] **1** *n* **(a)** *(Build)* Balken *m*. **(b) to be broad in the ~** *(ship)* sehr breit sein; *(person)* breit gebaut sein. **(c)** *(of light etc)* Strahl *m*. **to drive on main** *or* **full** *or* *(US)* **high ~** mit Fernlicht fahren. **(d)** *(radio ~)* Leitstrahl *m*. **(e)** *(smile)* Strahlen *nt*. **2** *vi* strahlen. **to ~ down** *(sun)* niederstrahlen; **her face was ~ing with joy** sie strahlte übers ganze Gesicht; **to ~ at sb** jdn anstrahlen. **3** *vt* *(Rad, TV)* ausstrahlen.

**beam-ends** ['biːmendz] *npl* **to be on one's ~** auf *or* aus dem letzten Loch pfeifen.

**bean** [biːn] *n* Bohne *f*. **to be full of ~s** *(col)* putzmunter sein *(col)*.

**bean:** **~ bag** *n* mit *Bohnen gefülltes Säckchen zum Spielen*; *(seat)* Sitzsack *m*; **~pole** *n* *(lit, fig)* Bohnenstange *f*; **~sprout** *n* Sojabohnensprosse *f*.

**bear¹** [bɛər] *n* **(a)** Bär *m*. *(fig: person)* Brummbär *m (col)*. **(b)** *(Astron)* **the Great/Little B~** der Große/Kleine Bär.

**bear²** *pret* **bore**, *ptp* **borne 1** *vt* **(a)** *burden, weight, responsibility, fruit* tragen; *gift, message* bei sich tragen. **he was borne along by the crowd** die Menge trug ihn mit (sich). **(b)** *inscription, signature, name, title* tragen; *mark, traces also, likeness, relation* aufweisen. **(c)** *(have in heart or mind)* *love, hatred, grudge* empfinden. **(d)** *(endure, tolerate)* ertragen; *criticism, noise etc also* vertragen. **could you ~ to stay a little longer?** können Sie es noch ein bißchen länger hier aushalten?; **it doesn't ~ thinking about** man darf gar nicht daran denken. **(e)** *(give birth to)* gebären; *see* **born**.
**2** *vi* **(a)** *(move)* **to ~ right/left/north** sich rechts/links/nach Norden halten. **(b)** *(fruit-tree etc)* tragen. **(c) to bring one's mind to ~ on sth** sich auf etw konzentrieren; **to bring pressure to ~ on sb/sth** Druck auf jdn/etw ausüben.
**3** *vr* sich halten. **he bore himself with dignity** er hat Würde gezeigt.
▶**bear down** *vi* **to ~ ~ on sb/sth** *(driver etc)* auf jdn/etw zuhalten.
▶**bear out** *vt sep* bestätigen.
▶**bear up** *vi* sich halten. **he bore ~ well under the death of his father** er trug den Tod seines Vaters mit Fassung; **how are you? — ~ing ~!** wie geht's? — man lebt!

▶**bear with** *vi +prep obj* tolerieren. **if you would ~ ~ me for a couple of minutes** wenn Sie sich vielleicht noch zwei Minuten gedulden wollen.

**bearable** ['bɛərəbl] *adj* erträglich.

**beard** [bɪəd] **1** *n* Bart *m*; *(full-face)* Vollbart *m*. **2** *vt* **to ~ the lion in his den** *(fig)* sich in die Höhle des Löwen wagen.

**bearded** ['bɪədɪd] *adj* *man, animal* bärtig.

**bearer** ['bɛərər] *n* *(carrier)* Träger(in *f*) *m*; *(of news, banknote)* Überbringer *m*; *(of passport)* Inhaber(in *f*) *m*.

**bear hug** *n* ungestüme Umarmung.

**bearing** ['bɛərɪŋ] *n* **(a)** *(posture)* Haltung *f*; *(behaviour)* Verhalten *nt*. **(b)** *(relevance)* **to have some/no ~ on sth** von Belang/belanglos für etw sein; *(be/not be connected with)* einen gewissen/keinen Bezug zu etw haben. **(c)** *(direction)* **to take a compass ~** den Kompaßkurs feststellen; **to lose one's ~s** die Orientierung verlieren; **to get one's ~s** sich orientieren. **(d)** *(Tech)* Lager *nt*.

**bear:** **~ market** *n* *(St Ex)* Baisse(markt *m*) *f*; **~-skin** *n* *(Mil)* Bärenfellmütze *f*.

**beast** [biːst] *n* **(a)** Tier *nt*. **(b)** *(col: person)* Biest, Ekel *nt*. **it's a ~ (of a problem)** das (Problem) hat's in sich *(col)*.

**beastly** ['biːstlɪ] *adj* *(col)* scheußlich *(col)*; *person, conduct also* gemein.

**beat** [biːt] *(vb: pret ~, ptp ~en)* **1** *n* **(a)** *(of heart etc)* *(single ~)* Schlag *m*; *(repeated beating)* Schlagen *nt*. **(b)** *(of policeman, sentry)* Runde *f*, Rundgang *m*; *(district)* Revier *nt*. **to be on one's ~** seine Runde machen. **(c)** *(Mus, Poet)* Takt *m*; *(of metronome, baton)* Taktschlag *m*. **to have a strong ~** einen ausgeprägten Rhythmus haben.
**2** *vt* **(a)** *(hit)* schlagen; *person* (ver)prügeln; *carpet* klopfen. **~ it!** *(fig col)* hau ab! *(col)*, verschwinde! **(b)** *(hammer)* *metal* hämmern. **(c)** *(defeat)* schlagen; *record* brechen. **to ~ sb at chess/tennis** jdn im Schach/Tennis schlagen; **coffee ~s tea any day** Kaffee ist allemal besser als Tee; **that ~s everything** das schlägt dem Faß den Boden aus *(col)*; *(is very good)* darüber geht nichts; **that ~s me** *(col)* das ist mir ein Rätsel *(col)*. **(d)** *(be before)* *budget, crowds* zuvorkommen *(+dat)*. **to ~ sb to it** jdm zuvorkommen. **(e) the bird ~s its wings** der Vogel schlägt mit den Flügeln. **(f)** *(Mus)* **to ~ time** den Takt schlagen. **(g)** *cream, eggs* schlagen.
**3** *vi* **(a)** *(heart etc)* schlagen. **to ~ on the door (with one's fists)** (mit den Fäusten) gegen die Tür hämmern; **with ~ing heart** mit pochendem *or* klopfendem Herzen. **(b)** *(wind, waves)* schlagen; *(rain also)* trommeln; *(sun)* brennen.
**4** *adj* **(a)** *(col: exhausted)* **to be (dead) ~** total geschafft *or* erledigt sein *(col)*. **(b)** *(col: defeated)* **to be ~(en)** aufgeben müssen *(col)*, sich geschlagen geben müssen; **this problem's got me ~** mit dem Problem komme ich nicht klar *(col)*.
▶**beat back** *vt sep* *flames, enemy* zurückschlagen.
▶**beat down 1** *vi* *(rain)* herunterprasseln; *(sun)* herunterbrennen. **2** *vt sep* **(a)** *prices* herunterhandeln; *opposition* kleinkriegen *(col)*. **I managed to ~ him/her ~** ich konnte den Preis herunterhandeln. **(b)** *(flatten)* *door* einrennen.
▶**beat off** *vt sep* *attack, attacker* abwehren.
▶**beat out** *vt sep* *fire* ausschlagen; *dent* aushämmern; *rhythm* schlagen; *(on drum)* trommeln.
▶**beat up** *vt sep* **(a)** *person* zusammenschlagen. **(b)** *(Cook)* *eggs, cream* schlagen.

**beaten** ['biːtn] **1** *ptp of* **beat**. **2** *adj* **(a)** *metal* gehämmert. **(b) to be off the ~ track** abgelegen sein.

**beater** ['biːtər] *n* *(carpet ~)* Klopfer *m*; *(egg ~)*

Schneebesen m.

**beatify** [biːˈætɪfaɪ] vt (Eccl) seligsprechen.

**beating** [ˈbiːtɪŋ] n (a) (series of blows) Schläge, Prügel pl. **to give sb a ~** jdn verprügeln; **to get a ~** verprügelt werden; (as punishment also) Prügel bekommen. (b) (of drums, heart, wings) Schlagen nt. (c) (defeat) Niederlage f. **to take a ~** eine Schlappe einstecken (col). (d) **to take some ~** seines-/ihresgleichen suchen.

**beating-up** [ˌbiːtɪŋˈʌp] n **to get a ~** zusammengeschlagen werden; **to give sb a ~** jdn zusammenschlagen.

**beat-up** [ˈbiːtʌp] adj (col) ramponiert (col).

**beaut** [bjuːt] n (esp Austral col) Prachtexemplar nt. **it's a real ~** es ist einsame Klasse (col).

**beautician** [bjuːˈtɪʃən] n Kosmetiker(in f) m.

**beautiful** [ˈbjuːtɪfʊl] adj schön; (stronger) wunderschön; weather also, idea, meal herrlich; piece of work hervorragend.

**beautifully** [ˈbjuːtɪfəlɪ] adv schön; warm, simple herrlich; (well) sew, sing hervorragend.

**beautify** [ˈbjuːtɪfaɪ] vt verschönern.

**beauty** [ˈbjuːtɪ] n (a) Schönheit f. **~ is only skin-deep** (prov) der äußere Schein kann trügen; **~ is in the eye of the beholder** (Prov) schön ist, was gefällt; **the ~ of it is that ...** das Schöne daran ist, daß ... (b) (beautiful person) Schönheit f. (c) (good example) Prachtexemplar nt.

**beauty** in cpds Schönheits-; **~ contest** n Schönheitswettbewerb m; **~ queen** n Schönheitskönigin f; **~ spot** n (a) Schönheitsfleck m. (b) (place) schönes or hübsches Fleckchen (Erde); **~ treatment** n kosmetische Behandlung.

**beaver** [ˈbiːvəʳ] n Biber m. **to work like a ~** wie ein Wilder/eine Wilde arbeiten.

**becalm** [bɪˈkɑːm] vt (Naut) **to be/become ~ed** sich in einer Flaute befinden/in eine Flaute geraten.

**became** [bɪˈkeɪm] pret of **become.**

**because** [bɪˈkɒz] **1** conj weil. **that's ~ it's so far north** das liegt daran, daß es so weit nördlich liegt. **2** prep **~ of** wegen (+gen or (col) dat); **I only did it ~ of you** ich habe es nur deinetwegen getan.

**beck** [bek] n **to be at sb's ~ and call** nach jds Pfeife tanzen müssen.

**beckon** [ˈbekən] vti winken. **he ~ed me in/back/over** er winkte mich herein/zurück/herüber.

**become** [bɪˈkʌm] pret **became,** ptp **~ 1** vi werden. **to ~ old/fat/tired** alt/dick/müde werden; **to ~ accustomed to sb/sth** sich an jdn/etw gewöhnen; **to ~ interested in sb/sth** anfangen, sich für jdn/etw zu interessieren; **to ~ a problem/habit** zum Problem/zur Gewohnheit werden; **to ~ king/a doctor** König/Arzt werden; **what has ~ of him?** was ist aus ihm geworden? **2** vt (suit) stehen (+dat); (befit) sich schicken für.

**becoming** [bɪˈkʌmɪŋ] adj (fitting) schicklich; (flattering) vorteilhaft. **that dress/colour is very ~** das Kleid/die Farbe steht ihr/dir etc sehr gut.

**bed** [bed] **1** n (a) Bett nt. **to go to ~** zu or ins Bett gehen; **to go to ~ with sb** mit jdm ins Bett gehen; **to put sb to ~** jdn ins Bett bringen; **he must have got out of ~ on the wrong side** (col) er ist wohl mit dem linken Fuß zuerst aufgestanden; **to be in ~** im Bett sein; **his life is not exactly a ~ of roses** er ist nicht gerade auf Rosen gebettet; **can I have a ~ for the night?** kann ich hier/bei euch etc übernachten? (b) (sea ~) Grund, Boden m; (river ~) Bett nt. (c) (oyster ~, coral ~) Bank f. (d) (flower ~) Beet nt. **2** vt plant setzen, pflanzen.

▶**bed down** vi sein Lager aufschlagen.

**bed and breakfast** n Übernachtung f mit Früh-

stück. "**~**" „Fremdenzimmer".

**bed** in cpds Bett-; **~-bath** n (Kranken)wäsche f im Bett; **to give sb a ~-bath** jdn im Bett waschen; **~-bug** n Wanze f; **~-clothes** npl Bettzeug nt; **~cover** n Bettdecke f.

**bedding** [ˈbedɪŋ] n Bettzeug nt; (for horses) Streu f.

**bedding plant** n Setzling m (einer einjährigen Pflanze).

**bedevil** [bɪˈdevl] vt erschweren. **~led by misfortune/bad luck** vom Schicksal/Pech verfolgt.

**bedfellow** [ˈbedˌfeləʊ] n **to be** or **make strange ~s** (fig) ein merkwürdiges Gespann sein.

**bedlam** [ˈbedləm] n Chaos nt. **it was sheer ~ in the class** in der Klasse ging es zu wie im Irrenhaus.

**bed: ~-linen** n Bettwäsche f; **~-pan** n Bettpfanne f; **~post** n Bettpfosten m.

**bedraggled** [bɪˈdrægld] adj (wet) trief- or tropfnaß; (dirty) verdreckt; (untidy) person, appearance ungepflegt.

**bed-ridden** [ˈbedrɪdn] adj bettlägerig.

**bedroom** [ˈbedruːm] n Schlafzimmer nt.

**bedroom** in cpds Schlafzimmer-; **~ slipper** n Hausschuh m.

**Beds** = **Bedfordshire.**

**beds** = **bedrooms** Zi.

**bed-settee** [ˈbedseˈtiː] n Sofabett nt.

**bedside** [ˈbedsaɪd] n **to be/sit at sb's ~** an jds Bett (dat) sein/sitzen.

**bedside: ~ lamp** n Nachttischlampe f; **~ manner** n **he has a good/bad ~ manner** er kann gut/nicht gut mit den Kranken umgehen; **~ rug** n Bettvorleger m; **~ table** n Nachttisch m.

**bed: ~-sit(ter)** (col), **~-sitting room** n (Brit) möbliertes Zimmer; **~sore** n wundgelegene Stelle; **to get ~sores** sich wundliegen; **~spread** n Tagesdecke f; **~stead** [ˈbedsted] n Bettgestell nt; **~time** n **it's ~time** es ist Schlafenszeit; **his ~time is 10 o'clock** er geht um 10 Uhr schlafen; **it's past your ~time** du müßtest schon lange im Bett sein; **~time story** n Gutenachtgeschichte f; **~-wetting** n Bettnässen nt.

**bee** [biː] n Biene f. **he's got a ~ in his bonnet about cleanliness** er hat einen Sauberkeitstick (col).

**Beeb** [biːb] n **the ~** (Brit col) die BBC.

**beech** [biːtʃ] n (tree, wood) Buche f.

**beef** [biːf] **1** n (a) (meat) Rindfleisch nt. **roast ~** Roastbeef nt. (b) (col) (flesh) Speck m (col); (muscles) Muskeln pl. **2** vi (col: complain) meckern (col) (about über +acc). **what's he ~ing about?** was hat er zu meckern? (col).

**beef: ~burger** n Hamburger m; **~eater** n (a) Beefeater m; (b) (US col) Engländer(in f) m; **~ olive** n Rinderroulade f; **~steak** n Beefsteak nt.

**beefy** [ˈbiːfɪ] adj (+er) fleischig; (muscular) muskulös.

**bee: ~hive** n (a) Bienenstock m; (dome-shaped) Bienenkorb m; (b) (hairstyle) toupierte Hochfrisur; **~keeper** n Bienenzüchter(in f), Imker(in f) m; **~line** n **to make a ~line for sb/sth** schnurstracks auf jdn/etw zugehen.

**been** [biːn] ptp of **be.**

**beer** [bɪəʳ] n Bier nt. **two ~s, please** zwei Bier, bitte; **German ~s** deutsche Biere.

**beer** in cpds Bier-; **~ belly** n (col) Bierbauch m (col); **~-bottle** n Bierflasche f; **~ can** n Bierdose f; **~ cellar** n Bierkeller m; **~ glass** n Bierglas nt; **~mat** n Bierdeckel m.

**beeswax** [ˈbiːzwæks] n Bienenwachs nt.

**beet** [biːt] n Rübe f.

**beetle** [ˈbiːtl] n Käfer m.

**beetle-browed** [ˈbiːtlˌbraʊd] adj mit buschigen Augenbrauen.

**beetroot** ['biːt,ruːt] *n (Brit)* rote Bete *or* Rübe.

**befall** [bɪ'fɔːl] *pret* **befell** [bɪ'fel], *ptp* **befallen** [bɪ'fɔːlən] *vt* widerfahren *(+dat) (geh)*.

**befitting** [bɪ'fɪtɪŋ] *adj* geziemend *(dated)*. ~ **for a lady** für eine Dame schicklich.

**before** [bɪ'fɔːr] **1** *prep* **(a)** *(earlier than)* vor *(+dat)*. **the day** ~ **yesterday** vorgestern; ~ **Christ** *(abbr BC)* vor Christi Geburt *(abbr v. Chr.)*; ~ **now** früher; ~ **long** bald. **(b)** *(in place, rank, in the presence of)* vor *(+dat)*. ~ **my (very) eyes** vor meinen Augen; **the question** ~ **us** die uns vorliegende Frage; **ladies** ~ **gentlemen** Damen haben den Vortritt; **to appear** ~ **a court/judge** vor Gericht/einem Richter erscheinen. **(c)** *(rather than)* **he would die** ~ **betraying his country** er würde eher sterben als sein Land verraten.
  **2** *adv* **(a)** *(in time)* *(~ that)* davor; *(at an earlier time, ~ now)* vorher. **I have read** *etc* **this** ~ ich habe das schon einmal gelesen *etc*; **it has never happened** ~ das ist noch nie passiert; **two days** ~ zwei Tage davor *or* zuvor. **(b)** *(indicating order)* davor. **that chapter and the one** ~ dieses Kapitel und das davor.
  **3** *conj* **(a)** *(in time)* bevor. ~ **doing sth** bevor man etw tut; **it will be a long time** ~ **he comes back** es wird lange dauern, bis er zurückkommt. **(b)** *(rather than)* **he will die** ~ **he surrenders** eher will er sterben als sich geschlagen geben.

**beforehand** [bɪ'fɔːhænd] *adv* im voraus. **you must tell me** ~ Sie müssen mir vorher Bescheid sagen.

**befriend** [bɪ'frend] *vt* sich anfreunden mit; *(help)* sich annehmen *(+gen)*.

**befuddled** [bɪ'fʌdld] *adj (confused)* durcheinander *(pred)*.

**beg** [beg] **1** *vt* **(a)** *money, alms* betteln um. **(b)** *forgiveness, mercy* bitten um. **he** ~**ged to be allowed to** ... er bat darum, ... zu dürfen; **I** ~ **to differ** ich erlaube mir, anderer Meinung zu sein. **(c)** *(entreat) sb* anflehen. **(d) to** ~ **the question** um den eigentlichen Frage vorbeigehen. **2** *vi* **(a)** *(beggar)* betteln; *(dog)* Männchen machen. **(b)** *(for help, time etc)* bitten *(for* um*)*. **(c)** *(entreat)* **I** ~ **of you** ich bitte Sie. **(d) to go** ~**ging** *(col)* noch zu haben sein; *(to be unwanted)* keine Abnehmer finden.

**began** [bɪ'gæn] *pret of* **begin**.

**beggar** ['begər] *n* **(a)** Bettler(in *f*) *m*. ~**s can't be choosers** *(prov)* wer arm dran ist, kann nicht wählerisch sein. **(b)** *(col)* Kerl *m (col)*. **poor** ~**!** armer Kerl! *(col)*; **a lucky** ~ ein Glückspilz *m*.

**begging letter** ['begɪŋ ˌletər] *n* Bittbrief *m*.

**begin** [bɪ'gɪn] *pret* **began**, *ptp* **begun 1** *vt* **(a)** beginnen, anfangen; *song also* anstimmen; *bottle* anbrechen; *book* anfangen; *rehearsals, work* anfangen mit; *task* in Angriff nehmen. **to** ~ **to do sth** *or* **doing sth** anfangen *or* beginnen, etw zu tun; **that doesn't even** ~ **to compare with** ... das läßt sich nicht einmal annähernd mit ... vergleichen; **I can't** ~ **to thank you for what you've done** ich kann Ihnen gar nicht genug dafür danken, was Sie getan haben. **(b)** *(initiate)* anfangen; *fashion, custom, policy* einführen; *society, firm, movement* gründen; *(cause)* war auslösen.
  **2** *vi* anfangen, beginnen; *(new play etc)* anlaufen; *(custom)* entstehen; *(river)* entspringen. **to** ~ **by doing sth** etw zuerst (einmal) tun; **he began by saying that** ... er sagte einleitend, daß ...; ~**ning from Monday** ab Montag, von Montag an; **to** ~ **with there were only three** anfänglich waren es nur drei; **to** ~ **with, this is wrong, and** ... erstens einmal ist das falsch, dann ...; **to** ~ **on sth** mit etw anfangen

*or* beginnen; **since the world began** seit (An)beginn *or* Anfang der Welt.

**beginner** [bɪ'gɪnər] *n* Anfänger(in *f*) *m*. ~**'s luck** Anfängerglück *nt*.

**beginning** [bɪ'gɪnɪŋ] *n* Anfang *m. (temporal also)* Beginn *m; (of custom, movement)* Entstehen *nt no pl; (of river)* Ursprung *m*. **at the** ~ **of sth** am Anfang *or (temporal also)* zu Beginn einer Sache *(gen)*; **the** ~ **of time/the world** der Anbeginn der Welt; **in the** ~ *(Bibl)* am Anfang; **from the** ~ von Anfang an; **from** ~ **to end** von vorn bis hinten; *(temporal)* von Anfang bis Ende; **to begin at the** ~ ganz vorn anfangen; **Nazism had its** ~**s in Germany** der Nazismus hatte seine Anfänge in Deutschland.

**begonia** [bɪ'gəʊnɪə] *n* Begonie *f*.

**begrudge** [bɪ'grʌdʒ] *vt* **(a)** *(be reluctant)* **to** ~ **doing sth** etw widerwillig tun. **(b)** *(envy)* mißgönnen *(sb sth* jdm etw*)*. **no one** ~**s you your good fortune** wir gönnen dir ja dein Glück. **(c)** *(give unwillingly)* nicht gönnen *(sb sth* jdm etw*)*. **I shan't** ~ **you £5** du sollst die £5 haben.

**beguile** [bɪ'gaɪl] *vt* verführen; *(charm)* betören.

**beguiling** [bɪ'gaɪlɪŋ] *adj* betörend, verführerisch.

**begun** [bɪ'gʌn] *ptp of* **begin**.

**behalf** [bɪ'hɑːf] *n* **on** *or (US also)* **in** ~ **of** *(as spokesman)* im Namen von; *(as authorized representative)* im Auftrag von.

**behave** [bɪ'heɪv] **1** *vi* sich verhalten; *(people also)* sich benehmen. **to** ~ **well towards sb** jdn gut behandeln; ~**!** benimm dich!; **the car** ~**s well at high speeds** das Auto zeigt bei hoher Geschwindigkeit ein gutes Fahrverhalten. **2** *vr* **to** ~ **oneself** sich benehmen; ~ **yourself!** benimm dich!

**behaviour,** *(US)* **behavior** [bɪ'heɪvjər] *n* **(a)** *(manner, bearing)* Benehmen *nt; (esp of children also)* Betragen *nt*. **to be on one's best** ~ sich von seiner besten Seite zeigen. **(b)** *(towards others, of car)* Verhalten *nt (to(wards)* gegenüber*)*.

**behavioural,** *(US)* **behavioral** [bɪ'heɪvjərəl] *adj* Verhaltens-. ~ **science** Verhaltensforschung *f*.

**behaviourism,** *(US)* **behaviorism** [bɪ'heɪvjərɪzəm] *n* Behaviorismus *m*.

**behead** [bɪ'hed] *vt* enthaupten, köpfen.

**beheld** [bɪ'held] *pret, ptp of* **behold**.

**behest** [bɪ'hest] *n (liter)* Geheiß *nt (liter)*. **at his** ~ auf sein Geheiß *nt (liter)*.

**behind** [bɪ'haɪnd] **1** *prep* **(a)** *(stationary)* hinter *(+dat); (with motion)* hinter *(+acc)*. **come out from** ~ **the door** komm hinter der Tür (her)vor; **he came up** ~ **me** er trat von hinten an mich heran; **he has the workers** ~ **him** er hat die Arbeiter hinter sich *(dat)*; **to be** ~ **an idea** eine Idee unterstützen; **what is** ~ **this?** was steckt dahinter? **(b)** *(more backward than)* **to be** ~ **sb** hinter jdm zurücksein. **(c)** *(in time)* **to be** ~ **time** *(train etc)* Verspätung haben; *(with work etc)* im Rückstand sein; **to be** ~ **schedule** im Verzug sein; **to be (a bit)** ~ **the times** *(fig)* nicht (ganz) auf dem laufenden sein. **2** *adv* **(a)** *(in or at rear)* hinten; *(~ this, sb etc)* dahinter. **from** ~ von hinten; **to look** ~ zurückblicken. **(b)** *(late)* **I'm a bit** ~ **today** ich bin heute etwas spät dran; **to be** ~ **with one's studies/payments** mit seinen Studien/Zahlungen im Rückstand sein. **3** *n (col)* Hintern *m (col)*.

**behindhand** [bɪ'haɪndhænd] *adv* **to be** ~ **with sth** mit etw im Rückstand sein.

**behold** [bɪ'həʊld] *pret, ptp* **beheld** *vt (liter)* sehen, erblicken *(liter)*. ~**!** und siehe (da); *(Rel)* siehe.

**beige** [beɪʒ] **1** *adj* beige. **2** *n* Beige *nt*.

**being** ['biːɪŋ] *n* **(a)** *(existence)* Dasein, Leben *nt*. **to come into** ~ entstehen; *(club etc also)* ins Leben gerufen werden; **to bring into** ~ ins Leben rufen. **(b)** *(that which exists)* Geschöpf *nt.*

**Beirut** [beɪˈruːt] *n* Beirut *nt.*

**belabour,** *(US)* **belabor** [bɪˈleɪbəʳ] *vt* einschlagen auf *(+acc)*; *(with insults etc)* überhäufen.

**belated** [bɪˈleɪtɪd] *adj* verspätet.

**belch** [beltʃ] **1** *vi (person)* rülpsen, aufstoßen; *(volcano)* Lava ausstoßen; *(smoke, fire)* herausquellen. **2** *vt (also* ~ **forth** *or* **out)** *smoke, flames* ausstoßen. **3** *n* Rülpser *m (col).*

**beleaguered** [bɪˈliːɡəd] *adj (city)* belagert; *(army)* eingekesselt; *(fig)* umgeben.

**Belfast** [ˈbelfɑːst] *n* Belfast *nt.*

**belfry** [ˈbelfrɪ] *n* Glockenstube *f.*

**Belgian** [ˈbeldʒən] **1** *n* Belgier(in *f*) *m.* **2** *adj* belgisch.

**Belgium** [ˈbeldʒəm] *n* Belgien *nt.*

**Belgrade** [belˈɡreɪd] *n* Belgrad *nt.*

**belie** [bɪˈlaɪ] *vt* **(a)** *(prove false) words, proverb* Lügen strafen, widerlegen. **(b)** *(give false impression of)* hinwegtäuschen über *(+acc).*

**belief** [bɪˈliːf] *n* Glaube *m (in* an *+acc).* **it is beyond** ~ es ist nicht zu glauben; **in the** ~ **that ...** im Glauben, daß ...; **it is my** ~ **that ...** ich bin der Überzeugung, daß ...; **strong** ~**s** feste Überzeugungen; **to the best of my** ~ meines Wissens.

**believable** [bɪˈliːvəbl] *adj* glaubhaft, glaubwürdig.

**believe** [bɪˈliːv] **1** *vt* **(a)** *sth* glauben; *sb* glauben *(+dat).* **I don't** ~ **you** das glaube ich (Ihnen) nicht; **don't you** ~ **it** wer's glaubt, wird selig *(col);* **I would never have** ~**d it of him** das hätte ich nie von ihm geglaubt; **he could hardly** ~ **his eyes/ears** er traute seinen Augen/Ohren nicht. **(b)** *(think)* glauben. **I** ~ **so/not** ich glaube schon/nicht. **2** *vi (have a religious faith)* an Gott glauben.
► **believe in** *vi +prep obj* glauben an *(+acc).* **I** ~ ~ **giving people a second chance** ich gebe prinzipiell jedem noch einmal eine Chance; **he doesn't** ~ ~ **medicine/doctors** er hält nicht viel von Medikamenten/Ärzten.

**believer** [bɪˈliːvəʳ] *n* **(a)** *(Rel)* Gläubige(r) *mf.* **(b) to be a (firm** *or* **great )** ~ **in sth/in doing sth** (grundsätzlich) für etw sein/dafür sein, daß man etw tut.

**Belisha beacon** [bɪˈliːʃəˈbiːkən] *n (Brit) gelbes Blinklicht an Zebrastreifen.*

**belittle** [bɪˈlɪtl] *vt* herabsetzen.

**Belize** [beˈliːz] *n* Belize *nt.*

**bell** [bel] *n* **(a)** Glocke *f; (small: on toys etc)* Glöckchen *nt,* Schelle *f; (school* ~, *door*~, *of cycle)* Klingel *f; (Boxing)* Gong *m.* **(b)** *(sound of* ~*)* Läuten *nt; (of door*~, *telephone etc)* Klingeln *nt.* **was that the** ~? hat es gerade geklingelt *or* geläutet? **(c)** *(col: telephone call)* **to give sb a** ~ jdn anrufen.

**bell:** ~-**bottomed trousers,** ~-**bottoms** *npl* ausgestellte Hosen; ~-**boy** *n (US)* Page, Hoteljunge *m.*

**belle** [bel] *n* Schöne, Schönheit *f.* **the** ~ **of the ball** die Ballkönigin.

**bellhop** [ˈbel,hɒp] *n (US)* = **bell-boy.**

**bellicose** [ˈbelɪkəʊs] *adj nation, mood* kriegerisch.

**belligerence** [bɪˈlɪdʒərəns] *n see adj* **(a)** Kriegslust *f;* Streitlust *f;* Aggressivität *f.*

**belligerent** [bɪˈlɪdʒərənt] **1** *adj* **(a)** *nation* kriegerisch; *person, attitude* streitlustig; *speech* aggressiv. **(b)** *(waging war)* kriegführend. **2** *n (nation)* kriegführendes Land; *(person)* Streitende(r) *mf.*

**bell-jar** [ˈbeldʒɑːʳ] *n* (Glas)glocke *f.*

**bellow** [ˈbeləʊ] **1** *vi (animal, person)* brüllen; *(singing also)* grölen *(col).* **2** *vt (also* ~ **out)** brüllen; *song also* grölen *(col).* **3** *n* Brüllen *nt.*

**bellows** [ˈbeləʊz] *npl* Blasebalg *m.*

**bell:** ~**push** *n* Klingel *f;* ~-**ringer** *n* Glöckner *m;*

~-**ringing** *n* Glockenläuten *nt;* ~-**shaped** *adj* glockenförmig, kelchförmig; ~**tower** *n* Glockenturm *m.*

**belly** [ˈbelɪ] *n* Bauch *m.*

**belly:** ~-**ache 1** *n (col)* Bauchweh *nt (col),* Bauchschmerzen *pl;* **2** *vi (col: complain)* murren *(about* über *+acc);* ~ **button** *n (col)* Bauchnabel *m;* ~ **dance** *n* Bauchtanz *m;* ~ **dancer** *n* Bauchtänzerin *f.*

**bellyful** [ˈbelɪfʊl] *n* **to have had a** ~ **of sb/sth** *(col)* von jdm/etw die Nase voll haben *(col).*

**belly:** ~ **landing** *n* Bauchlandung *f;* ~ **laugh** *n* dröhnendes Lachen.

**belong** [bɪˈlɒŋ] *vi* **(a)** gehören *(to sb* jdm*).* **who does it** ~ **to?** wem gehört es?; **the lid** ~**s to this box** der Deckel gehört zu dieser Schachtel; **to** ~ **to a club** einem Club angehören. **(b)** *(be in right place)* gehören. **to feel that one doesn't** ~ das Gefühl haben, daß man nicht dazugehört; **where does this one** ~? wo gehört das hin?

**belongings** [bɪˈlɒŋɪŋz] *npl* Besitz *m,* Habe *f* (geh). **personal** ~ persönliches Eigentum, persönlicher Besitz; **all his** ~ sein ganzes Hab und Gut.

**beloved** [bɪˈlʌvɪd] **1** *adj* geliebt; *memory* lieb, teuer. **2** *n* Geliebte(r) *mf.*

**below** [bɪˈləʊ] **1** *prep* **(a)** *(under)* unterhalb *(+gen); (with line, level etc also)* unter *(+dat or with motion +acc).* **the sun disappeared** ~ **the horizon** die Sonne verschwand hinter dem Horizont; **to be** ~ **sb** *(in rank)* (rangmäßig) unter jdm stehen. **(b)** *(downstream from)* unterhalb *(+gen).* **2** *adv* unten. **they live one floor** ~ sie wohnen ein Stockwerk tiefer; **the flat** ~ die Wohnung darunter; *(below us)* die Wohnung unter uns; **see** ~ siehe unten; **15 degrees** ~ 15 Grad unter Null, 15 Grad minus.

**belt** [belt] **1** *n* **(a)** *(on clothes)* Gürtel *m; (for holding etc, seat*~*)* Gurt *m.* **that was below the** ~ das war ein Schlag unter die Gürtellinie; **to tighten one's** ~ *(fig)* (sich *dat*) den Gürtel *or* Riemen enger schnallen *(col).* **(b)** *(Tech)* (Treib)riemen *m; (conveyor* ~*)* Band *nt.* **(c)** *(tract of land)* Gürtel *m.* **industrial** ~ Industriegürtel *m.* **(d)** *(col: hit)* Schlag *m.* **2** *vt (col: hit)* verhauen *(col).* **she** ~**ed him one** sie knallte ihm eine *(col).* **3** *vi (col: rush)* rasen *(col).* **to** ~ **out** hinaus-/herausrasen *(col);* **we were really** ~**ing along** wir sind wirklich gerast *(col).*
► **belt out** *vt sep (col) tune* schmettern *(col).*
► **belt up 1** *vt sep jacket* den Gürtel *(+gen)* zumachen. **2** *vi* **(a)** *(col)* die Klappe *(col)* halten; *(stop making noise)* mit dem Krach aufhören *(col).* **(b)** *(hum: put seatbelt on)* sich anschnallen.

**beltway** [ˈbeltweɪ] *n (US)* Umgehungsstraße *f.*

**bemoan** [bɪˈməʊn] *vt* beklagen.

**bemused** [bɪˈmjuːzd] *adj (puzzled)* verwirrt.

**bench** [bentʃ] *n* **(a)** *(seat)* Bank *f.* **(b)** *(Jur: office of a judge)* Richteramt *nt; (judges generally)* Richter *pl; (court)* Gericht *nt.* **to be on the** ~ *(permanent office)* Richter sein; *(when in court)* der Richter sein. **(c)** *(work* ~*)* Werkbank *f; (in lab)* Experimentiertisch *m.*

**benchmark** [ˈbentʃmɑːk] *n (standard)* Maßstab *m.* ~ **price** Richtpreis *m;* ~ **figure** Eckwert *m.*

**bend** [bend] *(vb: pret, ptp* **bent)** **1** *n (in river, tube etc)* Krümmung, Biegung *f; (in road also)* Kurve *f.* **to drive sb round the** ~ *(col)* jdn verrückt *or* wahnsinnig machen *(col).* **2** *vt* **(a)** biegen; *arm, knee also* beugen; *(forwards)* back also, head beugen. **on** ~**ed knees** auf Knien; *(fig also)* kniefällig. **(b)** *(fig) rules* frei auslegen. **3** *vi* **(a)** sich biegen; *(pipe, rail also)* sich krümmen; *(forwards also) (tree, corn etc)* sich neigen; *(person)* sich beugen. **this metal** ~**s easily** *(a*

*bad thing)* dieses Metall verbiegt sich leicht; *(a good thing)* dieses Metall läßt sich leicht biegen. **(b)** *(river)* eine Biegung machen; *(road also)* eine Kurve machen. **(c)** *(fig: submit)* sich beugen, sich fügen *(to dat)*.
▶**bend down** *vi (person)* sich bücken.
▶**bend over 1** *vi (person)* sich bücken. **2** *vt sep* umbiegen.
**bender** ['bendə<sup>r</sup>] *n (col)* **to go on a ~** sich besaufen *(col)*; *(go on pubcrawl)* auf eine Sauftour gehen.
**bends** [bendz] *n* **the ~** die Taucherkrankheit *f*.
**beneath** [bɪ'niːθ] **1** *prep* **(a)** unter *(+dat or with motion +acc)*; *(with line, level etc also)* unterhalb *(+gen)*; *see* **below 1** (a). **(b)** *(unworthy of)* **it is ~ him** das ist unter seiner Würde. **2** *adv* unten; *see also* **below 2**.
**benediction** [ˌbenɪ'dɪkʃən] *n* Segen *m*; *(act of blessing)* Segnung *f*.
**benefactor** ['benɪfæktə<sup>r</sup>] *n* Wohltäter *m*; *(giver of money also)* Gönner *m*.
**beneficial** [ˌbenɪ'fɪʃəl] *adj* gut *(to für)*; *climate also* zuträglich *(geh) (to dat)*; *influence also* vorteilhaft; *advice* nützlich *(to für)*.
**beneficiary** [ˌbenɪ'fɪʃərɪ] *n* Nutznießer(in *f*) *m*; *(of will, insurance etc)* Begünstigte(r) *mf*.
**benefit** ['benɪfɪt] **1** *n* **(a)** *(advantage)* Vorteil *m*; *(profit)* Gewinn *m*. **for the ~ of your health** Ihrer Gesundheit zuliebe; **it is for his ~ that this was done** das ist seinetwegen geschehen; **to give sb the ~ of the doubt** im Zweifel zu jds Gunsten entscheiden. **(b)** *(allowance)* Unterstützung *f*; *(sickness ~)* Krankengeld *nt*; *(social security ~)* Sozialhilfe *f*. **(c)** *(special performance)* Benefizveranstaltung *f*. **~ (match)** Benefizspiel *nt*. **2** *vt* nützen *(+dat)*; *(healthwise)* guttun *(+dat)*. **3** *vi* profitieren *(from, by von)*; *(from experience also)* Nutzen ziehen *(from aus)*. **who will ~ from that?** wem wird das nützen?
**Benelux** ['benɪlʌks] *n* **the ~ (countries)** die Beneluxländer *pl*.
**benevolence** [bɪ'nevələns] *n see adj* Wohlwollen *nt*; Gutmütigkeit *f*; Güte *f*.
**benevolent** [bɪ'nevələnt] *adj* wohlwollend; *smile* gutmütig; *(as character trait)* gütig.
**Bengal** [beŋ'gɔːl] *n* Bengalen *nt*. **~ tiger** bengalischer Tiger.
**Bengali** [beŋ'gɔːlɪ] **1** *n (language)* Bengali *nt*; *(person)* Bengale *m*, Bengalin *f*. **2** *adj* bengalisch.
**benign** [bɪ'naɪn] *adj* **(a)** gütig; *influence* günstig; *climate* mild. **(b)** *(Med)* gutartig.
**bent** [bent] **1** *pret, ptp of* **bend**. **2** *adj* **(a)** *metal etc* gebogen; *(out of shape)* verbogen. **(b)** *(Brit col: dishonest) person* korrupt. **(c)** *(col: homosexual)* andersrum *pred (col)*. **(d)** **to be ~ on sth** etw unbedingt wollen/tun wollen. **3** *n (aptitude)* Neigung *f (for zu)*; *(type of mind, character)* Schlag *m*. **with or of a musical ~** mit einer musikalischen Veranlagung.
**bequeath** [bɪ'kwiːð] *vt* vermachen; *(fig also)* hinterlassen *(to sb jdm)*.
**bequest** [bɪ'kwest] *n (legacy)* Nachlaß *m*; *(to museum)* Stiftung *f*.
**berate** [bɪ'reɪt] *vt (liter)* schelten.
**bereaved** [bɪ'riːvd] *npl* **the ~** die Hinterbliebenen *pl*.
**bereavement** [bɪ'riːvmənt] *n (death in family)* Trauerfall *m*. **to feel a sense of ~ at sth** etw als schmerzlichen Verlust empfinden.
**bereft** [bɪ'reft] *adj* **to be ~ of sth** einer Sache *(gen)* bar sein *(geh)*; **~ of reason** ohne jede Vernunft.
**beret** ['bereɪ] *n* Baskenmütze *f*.
**Bering** ['beriŋ]: **~ Sea** *n* Beringmeer *nt*; **~ Straits** *npl* Beringstraße *f*.

**berk** [bɜːk] *n (Brit col!)* Dussel *m (col)*.
**Berks** [bɑːks] = **Berkshire**.
**Berlin** [bɜː'lɪn] *n* Berlin *nt*. **the ~ wall** die Mauer.
**Berliner** [bɜː'lɪnə<sup>r</sup>] *n* Berliner(in *f*) *m*.
**Bermuda** [bɜː'mjuːdə] *n* Bermuda *nt*. **~ shorts** Bermudashorts *pl*; **~ triangle** Bermuda-Dreieck *nt*.
**Berne** [bɜːn] *n* Bern *nt*.
**berry** ['berɪ] *n* Beere *f*. **as brown as a ~** ganz braungebrannt.
**berserk** [bə'sɜːk] *adj* wild. **to go ~** wild werden; *(audience)* zu toben anfangen; *(go mad)* überschnappen *(col)*.
**berth** [bɜːθ] **1** *n* **(a)** *(on ship)* Koje *f*; *(on train)* Bett *nt*. **(b)** *(Naut: place for ship)* Liegeplatz *m*. **to give sb/sth a wide ~** *(fig)* einen (weiten) Bogen um jdn/etw machen. **2** *vi* anlegen.
**beseech** [bɪ'siːtʃ] *pret, ptp* **~ed** *or (liter)* **besought** *vt person* anflehen, beschwören.
**beset** [bɪ'set] *pret, ptp* **~** *vt (difficulties, dangers)* (von allen Seiten) bedrängen; *(doubts)* befallen; *(temptations, trials)* heimsuchen. **to be ~ with danger** *(journey etc)* voller Gefahren sein.
**besetting** [bɪ'setɪŋ] *adj* **his ~ sin** eine ständige Untugend von ihm.
**beside** [bɪ'saɪd] *prep* **(a)** neben *(+dat or with motion +acc)*; *(at the edge of)* road, river an *(+dat or with motion +acc)*. **~ the road** am Straßenrand. **(b)** *(compared with)* neben *(+dat)*. **(c)** **to be ~ oneself (with anger/joy)** außer sich sein *(vor Wut/Freude)*.
**besides** [bɪ'saɪdz] **1** *adv* außerdem. **have you got any others ~?** haben Sie noch andere *or* noch welche? **2** *prep* außer *(+dat)*. **others ~ ourselves** außer uns noch andere; **~ which he was unwell** außerdem fühlte er sich nicht wohl.
**besiege** [bɪ'siːdʒ] *vt (Mil, fig)* belagern; *(with offers)* überhäufen; *(pester)* bestürmen.
**besotted** [bɪ'sɒtɪd] *adj* völlig vernarrt *(with in +acc)*.
**besought** [bɪ'sɔːt] *(liter) pret, ptp of* **beseech**.
**bespatter** [bɪ'spætə<sup>r</sup>] *vt* bespritzen.
**bespectacled** [bɪ'spektɪkld] *adj* bebrillt.
**bespoke** [bɪ'spəʊk] *adj garment* Maß-. **a ~ tailor** ein Maßschneider *m*.
**best** [best] **1** *adj, superl of* **good** beste(r,s) *attr*; *(most favourable)* route, price also günstigste(r, s) *attr*. **to be ~** am besten/günstigsten sein; **the ~ thing about her** das Beste an ihr; **may the ~ man win!** dem Besten der Sieg!; **the ~ part of the year** fast das ganze Jahr.
**2** *adv, superl of* **well** **(a)** am besten; *like* am liebsten; *enjoy* am meisten. **the ~ known title** der bekannteste Titel; **~ of all** am allerbesten/-liebsten/-meisten; **I helped him as ~ I could** ich half ihm, so gut ich konnte; **do as you think ~** tun Sie, was Sie für richtig halten; **you know ~** Sie müssen es (am besten) wissen. **(b)** **you had ~ go now** am besten gehen Sie jetzt.
**3** *n* **(a)** **the ~** der/die/das beste; **the ~ of the bunch** *(col)* der/die/das beste; **he can sing with the ~ of them** er kann sich im Singen mit den Besten messen; **to be in one's (Sunday) ~** im Sonntagsstaat sein. **(b)** **to do one's (level) ~** sein Bestes *or* möglichstes tun; **to make the ~ of it/a bad job** das Beste daraus machen; **the ~ of it is that ...** das Beste daran ist, daß ...; **I meant it for the ~** ich habe es doch nur gut gemeint; **to the ~ of my ability** so gut ich kann/konnte; **to the ~ of my knowledge** meines Wissens; **to look one's ~** so gut wie möglich aussehen; **he is at his ~ at about 8 in the evening** so gegen 8 Uhr abends ist seine beste Zeit; **at ~** bestenfalls; **all the ~!** alles Gute!
**best-before date** [ˌbestbɪ'fɔː,deɪt] *n* Haltbarkeits-

datum *nt.*
**bestial** ['bestɪəl] *adj acts, cruelty* bestialisch; *person, appearance* brutal; *(carnal)* tierisch.
**bestiality** [ˌbestɪ'ælɪtɪ] *n* Bestialität *f; (cruelty)* Brutalität *f.*
**best man** *n* Trauzeuge *m* (des Bräutigams).
**bestow** [bɪ'stəʊ] *vt (on or upon sb* jdm) *(grant, give)* schenken; *honour* erweisen; *title, medal* verleihen.
**best:** ~-**seller** *n* Verkaufs- *or* Kassenschlager *m; (book)* Bestseller *m;* ~-**selling** *adj article* meistverkauft; ~-**selling author** Erfolgsautor(in *f) m;* ~-**selling book** Bestseller *m.*
**bet** [bet] *(vb: pret, ptp* ~) **1** *n* Wette *f (on* auf +*acc); (money etc staked)* Wetteinsatz *m.* **to have a** ~ **with sb** mit jdm wetten; **it's a safe** ~ **that ...** *(fig)* höchstwahrscheinlich ... **2** *vt* (a) wetten, setzen *(against* gegen, *on* auf +*acc).* **I** ~ **him £5** ich habe mit ihm (um) £5 gewettet. **(b)** *(col)* wetten. **you can** ~ **your boots** *or* **your bottom dollar that ...** Sie können Gift darauf nehmen, daß ... *(col).* **3** *vi* wetten. **to** ~ **on a horse** auf ein Pferd setzen; **you** ~! *(col)* und ob! *(col).*
**bête noire** [bet'nwɑːʳ] *n* that's my/his ~ das ist mir/ihm besonders verhaßt.
**Bethlehem** ['beθlɪhem] *n* Bethlehem *nt.*
**betray** [bɪ'treɪ] *vt* verraten *(also Pol)* (to *dat or* (Pol) an +*acc); trust* enttäuschen; *sb's secrets also* preisgeben. **his accent** ~**ed him (as a foreigner)** sein Akzent verriet, daß er Ausländer war.
**betrayal** [bɪ'treɪəl] *n* Verrat *m (of gen); (instance)* Verrat *m (of* an +*dat); (of trust)* Enttäuschung *f; (of friends also)* Untreue *f (of* gegenüber); *(of plans also)* Preisgabe *f.*
**betrothal** [bɪ'trəʊðəl] *n (liter, hum)* Verlobung *f.*
**better** **1** *adj, comp of* **good** besser; *route, way also* günstiger. **he's much** ~ es geht ihm viel besser; **that's** ~! *(approval)* so ist es besser!; *(relief etc)* endlich!; **the** ~ **part of an hour** fast eine Stunde; **to go one** ~ einen Schritt weiter gehen; *(in offer)* höher gehen.
**2** *adv, comp of* **well** (a) besser; *like* lieber; *enjoy* mehr. **they are** ~ **off than we are** sie sind besser dran als wir; *(financially)* sie sind besser gestellt als wir; **all the** ~, **so much the** ~ um so besser; **to think** ~ **of it** es sich *(dat)* noch einmal überlegen. **(b) I had** ~ **go** ich gehe jetzt wohl besser; **you'd** ~ **do what he says** tun Sie lieber, was er sagt.
**3** *n* (a) **one's** ~**s** Leute, die über einem stehen; *(socially also)* Höhergestellte. **(b)** *(person, object)* **the** ~ der/die/das Bessere. **(c) it's a change for the** ~ es ist eine Wendung zum Guten; **it's done now, for** ~ **or worse** so oder so, es ist geschehen; **to get the** ~ **of sb** *(person)* jdn unterkriegen *(col); (illness)* jdn erwischen *(col); (problem etc)* jdm schwer zu schaffen machen.
**4** *vt (improve on)* verbessern; *(surpass)* übertreffen.
**5** *vr* **to** ~ **oneself** sich verbessern.
**betting:** ~ **man** *n* **I'm not a** ~ **man** ich wette eigentlich nicht; ~ **shop** *n* Wettannahme *f.*
**between** [bɪ'twiːn] **1** *prep* (a) zwischen (+*dat); (with movement)* zwischen (+*acc).* **sit down** ~ **those two boys** setz dich zwischen diese beiden Jungen; **in** ~ zwischen (+*dat/acc);* ~ **now and next week we must ...** bis nächste Woche müssen wir ...; **there's nothing** ~ **them** *(they're equal)* sie sind gleich gut; *(no relationship)* sie haben nichts miteinander. **(b)** *(amongst)* unter (+*dat/acc).* **we shared an apple** ~ **us** wir teilten uns *(dat)* einen Apfel; ~ **you and me he is not very clever** unter uns *(dat)* (gesagt), er ist nicht besonders gescheit; **that's just** ~ **ourselves**

das bleibt aber unter uns; **we have a car** ~ **the two/three of us** wir haben zu zweit/dritt ein Auto. **2** *adv (place)* dazwischen; *(time also)* zwischendurch. **in** ~ dazwischen; **the space/time** ~ der Zwischenraum/die Zwischenzeit, der Raum/die Zeit dazwischen.
**bevelled edge** *n* ['bevld'edʒ] *n* Schrägkante *f.*
**beverage** ['bevərɪdʒ] *n* Getränk *nt.*
**bevy** ['bevɪ] *n (of girls)* Schar *f.*
**bewail** [bɪ'weɪl] *vt (deplore)* beklagen; *(lament also)* bejammern; *sb's death also* betrauern.
**beware** [bɪ'weəʳ] *vti imper and infin only* **to** ~ **(of) sb/sth** sich vor jdm/etw hüten, sich vor jdm/etw in acht nehmen; ~ **of falling** passen Sie auf, daß Sie nicht fallen; "~ **of the dog**" „Vorsicht, bissiger Hund".
**bewilder** [bɪ'wɪldəʳ] *vt (confuse)* verwirren; *(baffle)* verblüffen.
**bewildered** [bɪ'wɪldəd] *adj (confused)* verwirrt; *(baffled)* verblüfft, perplex *(col).*
**bewildering** [bɪ'wɪldərɪŋ] *adj see vt* verwirrend; verblüffend.
**bewilderment** [bɪ'wɪldəmənt] *n see vt* Verwirrung *f;* Verblüffung *f.* **in** ~ verwundert.
**bewitch** [bɪ'wɪtʃ] *vt* verzaubern; *(fig)* bezaubern.
**bewitching** *adj,* ~**ly** *adv* [bɪ'wɪtʃɪŋ, -lɪ] bezaubernd, hinreißend.
**beyond** [bɪ'jɒnd] **1** *prep* (a) *(on the other side of)* hinter (+*dat),* jenseits (+*gen) (geh); (further than)* über (+*acc)* ... hinaus, weiter als. ~ **the Alps** jenseits der Alpen. **(b)** *(in time)* ~ **6 o'clock** nach 6 Uhr; ~ **the middle of June/the week** über Mitte Juni/der Woche hinaus. **(c) a task** ~ **her abilities** eine Aufgabe, die über ihre Fähigkeiten geht; **that's almost** ~ **belief** das ist fast unglaublich *or* nicht zu glauben; **that's** ~ **me** *(I don't understand)* das geht über meinen Verstand. **2** *adv (on the other side of)* jenseits davon *(geh).* **the world** ~ das Jenseits.
**BF** *(euph)* = **bloody fool.**
**bhp** = **brake horsepower** PS.
**bi-** [baɪ] *pref* bi, Bi-.
**biannual** [baɪ'ænjʊəl] *adj* halbjährlich.
**bias** ['baɪəs] *(vb: pret, ptp* ~**(s)ed)* **1** *n* (a) Voreingenommenheit *f; (of course, newspaper etc)* (einseitige) Ausrichtung *f (towards* auf +*acc); (of person)* Vorliebe *f (towards* für). **to have a** ~ **against sth** *(course, newspaper etc)* gegen etw eingestellt sein; *(person)* ein Vorurteil *nt* gegen etw haben; **to have a left-wing/right-wing** ~ nach links/rechts ausgerichtet sein. **(b)** *(Sew)* **on the** ~ schräg zum Fadenlauf. **2** *vt report, article etc* (einseitig) färben.
**bias(s)ed** ['baɪəst] *adj* voreingenommen; *report* einseitig.
**bib** [bɪb] *n* Latz *m; (for baby)* Lätzchen *nt.*
**Bible** ['baɪbl] *n* Bibel *f.*
**Bible** *in cpds* Bibel-; *story* biblisch; ~ **basher** *n (col)* Jesusjünger(in *f) m (col).*
**biblical** ['bɪblɪkəl] *adj* biblisch.
**bibliography** [ˌbɪblɪ'ɒgrəfɪ] *n* Bibliographie *f.*
**bibulous** ['bɪbjʊləs] *adj* trunksüchtig.
**bicarbonate of soda** [baɪˌkɑːbənɪtəv'səʊdə] *n (Cook)* Natron *nt; (Chem)* doppelt kohlensaures Natrium.
**bi-:** ~**centenary,** *(US)* ~**centennial** *n* Zweihundertjahrfeier *f (of gen).*
**biceps** ['baɪseps] *n* Bizeps *m.*
**bicker** ['bɪkəʳ] *vi* sich zanken. **they are always** ~**ing** sie liegen sich dauernd in den Haaren.
**bicycle** ['baɪsɪkl] *n* Fahrrad *nt.* **to ride a** ~ Fahrrad fahren, radfahren; ~ **kick** *(Football)* Fallrückzieher

*m; see* **cycle.**

**bid** [bɪd] **1** *vti* **(a)** *pret, ptp* ~ *(at auction)* bieten *(for* auf *+acc).* **(b)** *pret, ptp* ~ *(Cards)* reizen, bieten. **(c)** *pret* **bade,** *ptp* ~**den** *(say)* to ~ sb good-morning jdm einen guten Morgen wünschen; **to** ~ **farewell to sb** jdm Lebewohl sagen *(geh).* **2** *vi pret* **bad,** *ptp* ~**den everything** ~**s fair to be successful** es sieht alles recht erfolgversprechend aus. **3** *n* **(a)** *(at auction)* Gebot *nt (for* auf *+acc);* (Comm) Angebot *nt (for* für*).* **(b)** *(Cards)* Ansage *f.* **(c)** *(attempt)* Versuch *m.* **to make a** ~ **for power** nach der Macht greifen; **to make a** ~ **for freedom** versuchen, die Freiheit zu erlangen.

**bidden** ['bɪdn] *ptp of* **bid 1 (c).**

**bidder** ['bɪdə'] *n* Bietende(r) *mf.* **to sell to the highest** ~ an den Meistbietenden verkaufen.

**bidding** ['bɪdɪŋ] *n* **(a)** *(at auction)* Steigern, Bieten *nt.* **(b)** *(Cards)* Bieten, Reizen *nt.*

**bide** [baɪd] *vt* **to** ~ **one's time** den rechten Augenblick abwarten.

**bidet** ['biːdeɪ] *n* Bidet *nt.*

**biennial** [baɪ'enɪəl] **1** *adj (every two years)* zweijährlich. **2** *n (Bot)* zweijährige Pflanze.

**bier** [bɪə'] *n* Bahre *f.*

**biff** [bɪf] *n (col)* Stoß, Puff *(col) m.* **a** ~ **on the nose** eins auf die Nase *(col).*

**bifocal** [baɪ'fəukəl] **1** *adj* Bifokal-. **2** *n* ~**s** *pl* Bifokalbrille *f.*

**big** [bɪg] **1** *adj (+er)* groß. **a** ~ **man** ein großer, schwerer Mann; **my** ~ **brother** mein großer Bruder; **that's really** ~ **of you** *(iro)* wirklich nobel von dir *(iro);* **he is too** ~ **for his boots** *(col)* der ist ja größenwahnsinnig; **to have a** ~ **head** *(col)* eingebildet sein; **to earn** ~ **money** das große Geld verdienen *(col);* **to have** ~ **ideas** große Pläne haben; **what's the** ~ **idea?** *(col)* was soll denn das? *(col);* **to have a** ~ **mouth** *(col)* eine große Klappe haben *(col);* **to do things in a** ~ **way** alles im großen (Stil) tun; ~ **deal!** *(iro col)* na und? *(col); (that's not much etc)* ist ja toll! *(iro col).* **2** *adv* **to talk** ~ große Töne spucken *(col);* **to think** ~ im großen (Maßstab) planen.

**bigamist** ['bɪgəmɪst] *n* Bigamist *m.*

**bigamy** ['bɪgəmɪ] *n* Bigamie *f.*

**big: B**~ **Apple** *n* New York *nt;* ~ **bang** *n (Astron)* Urknall *m;* **B**~ **Brother** *n* der Große Bruder; ~ **business** *n (high finance)* Großkapital *nt;* ~ **dipper** *n (Brit: at fair)* Achterbahn *f;* ~ **end** *n (Tech)* Pleuelfuß *m;* ~ **game** *n (Hunt)* Großwild *nt;* ~**head** *n (col: person)* Angeber *m (col);* ~**headed** *adj (col)* angeberisch *(col);* ~ **name** *n (col: person)* Größe *f (in* in *+dat);* ~ **noise** *n (col)* hohes Tier *(col).*

**bigoted** ['bɪgətɪd] *adj* engstirnig.

**big:** ~ **shot** *n* hohes Tier *(col);* ~**-time** *n (col)* **to make** *or* **hit the** ~**-time** groß einsteigen *(col);* ~ **toe** *n* große Zehe; ~ **top** *n (circus)* Zirkus *m; (main tent)* Hauptzelt *nt;* ~ **wheel** *n* **(a)** *(US col)* = ~ **shot;** **(b)** *(Brit: at fair)* Riesenrad *nt;* ~**wig** *n (col)* hohes Tier *(col).*

**bike** [baɪk] *(col)* **1** *n* (Fahr)rad *nt; (motor* ~) Motorrad *nt.* **on your** ~! *(col: clear off)* verschwinde! **2** *vi* radeln *(col).*

**biker** ['baɪkə'] *n (col)* Motorradfahrer *m.*

**bikini** [bɪ'kiːnɪ] *n* Bikini *m.*

**bilateral** [baɪ'lætərəl] *adj* bilateral.

**bilberry** ['bɪlbərɪ] *n* Heidelbeere *f.*

**bile** [baɪl] *n (Med)* Galle *f.*

**bilge** [bɪldʒ] *n* **(a)** *(Naut)* Bilge *f.* **(b)** *(Brit col: nonsense)* Quatsch *m.*

**bilingual** [baɪ'lɪŋgwəl] *adj* zweisprachig. ~ **secretary** Fremdsprachenkorrespondentin, Fremdsprachensekretärin *f.*

**bilingualism** [baɪ'lɪŋgwəlɪzm] *n* Zweisprachigkeit *f.*

**bilious** ['bɪlɪəs] *adj (Med)* Gallen-. ~ **attack** Gallenkolik *f.*

**bill**[1] [bɪl] **1** *n (of bird, turtle)* Schnabel *m.* **2** *vi* **to** ~ **and coo** *(birds)* schnäbeln und gurren, turteln.

**bill**[2] **1** *n* **(a)** *(statement of charges)* Rechnung *f.* **could we have the** ~ **please** zahlen bitte!, wir möchten bitte zahlen. **(b)** *(US: banknote)* Banknote *f,* Schein *m.* **(c)** *(poster)* Plakat *nt; (on notice board)* Anschlag *m; (public announcement)* Aushang *m;* **"stick no** ~**s"** „Plakate ankleben verboten". **(d)** *(Theat)* Programm *nt.* **to top the** ~ Star *m* des Abends/der Saison sein; *(act)* die Hauptattraktion sein. **(e)** ~ **of fare** Speisekarte *f.* **(f)** *(Parl)* Gesetzentwurf *m.* **(g)** *(Comm)* ~ **of lading** Frachtbrief *m;* ~ **of exchange** Wechsel *m;* ~ **of sale** Verkaufsurkunde *f;* **to fit** *or* **fill the** ~ *(fig)* der/die/das richtige sein, passen.

**2** *vt* **(a)** *customers* eine Rechnung ausstellen *(+dat).* **we won't** ~ **you for that** *(make no charge)* wir werden Ihnen das nicht berechnen. **(b)** *play, actor* ankündigen. **he's** ~**ed at the Apollo** er tritt im Apollo auf.

**billboard** ['bɪlbɔːd] *n* Reklametafel *f.*

**billet** ['bɪlɪt] **1** *n (Mil)* Quartier *nt,* Unterkunft *f.* **2** *vt (Mil)* einquartieren *(on sb* bei jdm*).*

**billfold** ['bɪl,fəuld] *n (US)* Brieftasche *f.*

**billiard** ['bɪljəd] *adj attr* Billiard-. ~ **ball** Billardkugel *f;* ~ **cue** Queue *nt,* Billardstock *m.*

**billiards** ['bɪljədz] *n* Billard *nt.*

**billiard table** *n* Billardtisch *m.*

**billion** ['bɪljən] *n* **(a)** *(Brit)* Billion *f.* **(b)** *(US)* Milliarde *f.*

**billow** ['bɪləu] **1** *n (of smoke)* Schwaden *m.* **2** *vi (sail)* sich blähen; *(dress etc)* sich bauschen.

**billy(-goat)** ['bɪlɪ(gəut)] *n* Ziegenbock *m.*

**billy-ho** ['bɪlɪhəu] *n (col)* **like** ~ wie verrückt *(col).*

**bimbo** ['bɪmbəu] *n (pej col)* Puppe *f (col).*

**bin** [bɪn] *n (esp Brit) (for bread)* Brotkasten *m; (rubbish*~*)* Mülleimer *m; (dust*~*)* Mülltonne *f; (litter-*~*)* Abfallbehälter *m.*

**binary** ['baɪnərɪ] *adj* binär. ~ **form** *(Mus)* zweiteilige Form; ~ **system/number** *(Math)* Dualsystem *nt/* -zahl *f;* ~ **code** *(Comp)* Binärcode *m.*

**bind** [baɪnd] *pret, ptp* **bound 1** *vt* **(a)** *(make fast, tie together)* binden *(to* an *+acc); person* fesseln; *(fig)* verbinden *(to* mit*).* **bound hand and foot** an Händen und Füßen gefesselt. **(b)** *wound, arm etc* verbinden; *bandage* wickeln. **(c)** *(secure edge of)* einfassen. **(d)** *book* binden. **(e)** *(oblige)* **to** ~ **sb to sth/ to do sth** jdn zu etw verpflichten/jdn verpflichten, etw zu tun; *see* **bound**[3]. **2** *n (col: nuisance)* **to be (a bit of) a** ~ recht lästig sein.

▶**bind over** *vt sep (Jur)* **to** ~ **sb** ~ **(to keep the peace)** jdn verwarnen; **he was bound** ~ **for six months** er bekam eine sechsmonatige Bewährungsfrist.

▶**bind together** *vt sep (lit)* zusammenbinden; *(fig)* verbinden.

▶**bind up** *vt sep wound* verbinden; *hair* hochbinden. **to be bound** ~ **in** *(work etc)* verwachsen sein mit; **to be bound** ~ **with** *(person)* eng verbunden sein mit.

**binder** ['baɪndə'] *n* **(a)** *(machine)* Bindemaschine *f.* **(b)** *(for papers)* Hefter *m.*

**binding** ['baɪndɪŋ] **1** *n (of book)* Einband *m; (Sew)* Band *nt; (on skis)* Bindung *f.* **2** *adj agreement* bindend, verbindlich *(on* für*).*

**binge** [bɪndʒ] *n (col)* Gelage *nt.* **to go on a** ~ *(drinking)* auf Sauftour *(col)* gehen; *(eating)* eine Freßtour

**biting**

*(col)* machen.
**bingo** ['bɪŋgəʊ] *n* Bingo *nt.*
**bin liner** *n* Mülltüte *f.*
**binoculars** [bɪ'nɒkjʊləz] *npl* Fernglas *nt.*
**bio-** [baɪəʊ-]: ~**chemist** *n* Biochemiker(in *f*) *m*; ~**chemistry** *n* Biochemie *f*; ~**degradable** *adj* biologisch abbaubar; ~**diversity** *n* biologische Vielfalt.
**biographer** [baɪ'ɒgrəfə'] *n* Biograph(in *f*) *m.*
**biographic(al)** [ˌbaɪəʊ'græfɪk(əl)] *adj* biographisch.
**biography** [baɪ'ɒgrəfɪ] *n* Biographie *f.*
**biological** [ˌbaɪə'lɒdʒɪkəl] *adj* biologisch. ~ **washing powder** Bio-Waschmittel *nt.*
**biologist** [baɪ'ɒlədʒɪst] *n* Biologe *m*, Biologin *f.*
**biology** [baɪ'ɒlədʒɪ] *n* Biologie *f.*
**biophysics** [ˌbaɪəʊ'fɪzɪks] *n sing* Biophysik *f.*
**biopic** ['baɪəʊpɪk] *n* Filmbiographie *f.*
**bi:** ~**partite** *adj* zweiteilig; *(affecting two parties)* zweiseitig; ~**plane** *n* Doppeldecker *m.*
**birch** [bɜːtʃ] *n* Birke *f*; *(for whipping)* Rute *f.*
**bird** [bɜːd] *n* **(a)** Vogel *m.* **a little ~ told me** *(col)* das hat mir mein kleiner Mann im Ohr erzählt; **the early ~ catches the worm** ≈ Morgenstund hat Gold im Mund *(Prov)*; **a ~ in the hand is worth two in the bush** *(Prov)* der Spatz in der Hand ist besser als die Taube auf dem Dach *(Prov)*; **they are ~s of a feather** sie sind vom gleichen Schlag; ~**s of a feather flock together** gleich und gleich gesellt sich gern; **to tell sb about the ~s and the bees** jdm erzählen, wo die kleinen Kinder herkommen. **(b)** *(Brit col: girl)* Mieze *f* *(col)*. **(c) he's an odd ~** *(col)* er ist ein komischer Kauz.
**bird:** ~ **bath** *n* Vogeltränke *f*; ~-**cage** *n* Vogelkäfig *m*; ~ **call** *n* Vogelruf *m*; ~ **food** *n* Vogelfutter *nt*; ~ **sanctuary** *n* Vogelschutzgebiet *nt*; ~**seed** *n* Vogelfutter *nt.*
**bird's:** ~ **egg** *n* Vogelei *nt*; ~-**eye view** *n* Vogelperspektive *f*; ~ **nest** *n* Vogelnest *nt.*
**bird:** ~ **table** *n* Futterplatz *m* *(für Vögel)*; ~ **watcher** *n* Vogelbeobachter(in *f*) *m.*
**Biro** ® ['baɪərəʊ] *n* *(Brit)* Kugelschreiber, Kuli *(col)* *m.*
**birth** [bɜːθ] *n* **(a)** Geburt *f.* **to give ~ to** zur Welt bringen; **to give ~** entbinden; *(animal)* jungen. **(b)** *(parentage)* Abstammung, Herkunft *f.* **Scottish by ~** gebürtiger Schotte, gebürtige Schottin; **of good/low** *or* **humble ~** aus guter Familie/von niedriger Geburt. **(c)** *(fig)* Geburt *f*; *(of movement, fashion etc)* Aufkommen *nt*; *(of nation, party, company also)* Entstehen *nt*; *(of new era)* Anbruch *m*; *(of planet)* Entstehung *f.*
**birth:** ~ **certificate** *n* Geburtsurkunde *f*; ~ **control** *n* Geburtenkontrolle *f.*
**birthday** ['bɜːθdeɪ] *n* Geburtstag *m.* **what did you get for your ~?** was hast du zum Geburtstag bekommen?
**birthday:** ~ **cake** *n* Geburtstagskuchen *m* *or* -torte *f*; ~ **card** *n* Geburtstagskarte *f*; ~ **party** *n* Geburtstagsfeier *f*; *(with dancing etc)* Geburtstagsparty *f*; *(for child)* Kindergeburtstag *m*; ~ **present** *n* Geburtstagsgeschenk *nt*; ~ **suit** *n* *(col)* Adams-/Evaskostüm *nt* *(col)*.
**birth:** ~**mark** *n* Muttermal *nt*; ~**place** *n* Geburtsort *m*; ~**rate** *n* Geburtenrate *or* -ziffer *f*; ~**right** *n* *(fig: right)* angeborenes Recht.
**Biscay** ['bɪskeɪ] *n* **the Bay of** ~ der Golf von Biskaya *or* Biscaya.
**biscuit** ['bɪskɪt] **1** *n* **(a)** *(Brit)* Keks *m.* **that takes/you take the** ~! *(col)* das übertrifft alles; *(negatively)* das schlägt dem Faß den Boden aus! **(b)** *(US)* Brötchen *nt.* **2** *adj* *(colour)* beige.
**bisect** [baɪ'sekt] *vt* in zwei Teile teilen; *(Math)* halbieren.

**bisexual** [ˌbaɪ'seksjuəl] *adj* bisexuell; *(Biol)* zwittrig.
**bishop** ['bɪʃəp] *n* Bischof *m*; *(Chess)* Läufer *m.*
**bison** ['baɪsn] *n* *(American)* Bison *m*; *(European)* Wisent *m.*
**bit¹** [bɪt] *n* **(a)** *(for horse)* Gebiß(stange *f*) *nt.* **(b)** *(of drill)* Bohrer *m.*
**bit²** **1** *n* **(a)** *(piece)* Stück *nt*; *(smaller)* Stückchen; *(of glass also)* Scherbe *f*; *(share)* Teil *m*; *(passage in book etc)* Stelle *f.* **a ~** *(not much, small amount)* ein bißchen, etwas; **would you like a ~ of ice cream?** möchten Sie etwas Eis?; **there's a ~ of truth in what he says** daran ist schon etwas Wahres; **a ~ of advice/news** ein Rat *m*/eine Neuigkeit; **we had a ~ of trouble** wir hatten ein wenig Ärger; **it wasn't a ~ of help/use** das war überhaupt keine Hilfe/hat überhaupt nichts genützt; **there's quite a ~ of bread left** es ist noch eine ganze Menge Brot übrig; **in ~s and pieces** in Einzelteilen; **bring all your ~s and pieces** bring deine Siebensachen; **to come** *or* **fall to ~s** kaputtgehen.
**(b)** *(with time)* **a ~** ein Weilchen *nt.*
**(c)** *(with cost)* **a ~** eine ganze Menge.
**(d) to do one's ~** sein(en) Teil tun.
**(e) he's a ~ of a rogue/musician/an expert** er ist ein ziemlicher Schlingel/er ist gar kein schlechter Musiker/er versteht einiges davon.
**(f)** ~ **by** ~ Stück für Stück; *(gradually)* nach und nach; **he's every ~ a soldier** er ist durch und durch Soldat; **it/he is every ~ as good as ...** es/er ist genauso gut wie ...; **not a ~ of it** keine Spur *(col)*.
**(g) when it comes to the** ~ wenn es drauf ankommt.
**(h)** *(coin)* *(Brit)* Stück *nt*, Münze *f.* **2/4/6 ~s** *(US)* 25/50/75 Cent(s).
**(i)** *(Comp)* Bit *nt.*
**2** *adv* **a** ~ ein bißchen, etwas; **I'm not a ~ surprised** das wundert mich kein bißchen *(col)* *or* keineswegs; **he's improved quite a** ~ er hat sich ziemlich gebessert.
**bit³** *pret of* **bite.**
**bitch** [bɪtʃ] **1** *n* **(a)** *(of dog)* Hündin *f.* **terrier ~** weiblicher Terrier. **(b)** *(col: woman)* Miststück *nt* *(col)*; *(spiteful)* Hexe *f.* **2** *vi* *(col: complain)* bissige Bemerkungen machen *(about* über +*acc)*. **to ~ about sb** über jdn herziehen *(col)*.
**bitchiness** ['bɪtʃɪnɪs] *n see adj* Gehässigkeit, Gemeinheit *f*; Bissigkeit *f.*
**bitchy** ['bɪtʃɪ] *adj* *(+er)* *(col)* *woman* gehässig, gemein; *remark also* bissig.
**bite** [baɪt] *(vb: pret* **bit,** *ptp* **bitten)* **1** *n* **(a)** Biß *m.* **(b)** *(insect ~)* Stich *m*; *(flea ~)* Biß *m*; *(love ~)* (Knutsch)fleck *m* *(col)*. **(c)** *(Fishing)* **I think I've got a** ~ ich glaube, es hat einer angebissen. **(d)** *(of food)* Happen *m.* **there's not a** ~ **to eat** es ist überhaupt nichts zu essen da; **do you fancy a** ~ **(to eat)?** möchten Sie etwas essen? **2** *vt* *(person, dog)* beißen; *(insect)* stechen. **to ~ one's nails** an den Nägeln kauen; **to ~ the dust** *(col)* ins Gras beißen *(col)*; **once bitten twice shy** *(Prov)* (ein) gebranntes Kind scheut das Feuer *(Prov)*. **3** *vi* *(dog etc)* beißen; *(insects)* stechen; *(fish, fig col)* anbeißen.
▶**bite into** *vi +prep obj* *(person)* (hinein)beißen in (+*acc)*; *(teeth)* (tief) eindringen in (+*acc)*; *(acid, saw)* sich hineinfressen in (+*acc)*; *(screw, drill)* sich hineinbohren in (+*acc)*.
▶**bite off** *vt sep* abbeißen. **he won't** ~ **your head** ~ er wird dir schon nicht den Kopf abreißen; **to** ~ ~ **more than one can chew** sich *(dat)* zuviel zumuten.
▶**bite through** *vt insep* durchbeißen.
**biting** ['baɪtɪŋ] *adj* beißend; *cold, wind also* schneidend.

**bit part** *n* kleine Nebenrolle.
**bitten** ['bɪtn] *ptp of* **bite**.
**bitter** ['bɪtər] **1** *adj* (+er) bitter; *weather, wind* eisig; *enemy, struggle, opposition* erbittert. **it was a ~ pill to swallow** es war eine bittere Pille; **he's still ~ about it** er nimmt es mir/ihnen *etc* noch übel; **to the ~ end** bis zum bitteren Ende. **2** *n* (*Brit: beer*) ≃ Altbier *nt.*
**bitterly** ['bɪtəlɪ] *adv* (a) bitter; *complain also, weep* bitterlich; *oppose* erbittert; *criticize* scharf; *jealous* sehr. (b) *(showing embitteredness)* verbittert; *criticize* erbittert.
**bitterness** ['bɪtənɪs] *n see adj* Bitterkeit *f*; eisige Kälte; Erbittertheit *f.*
**bitter-sweet** ['bɪtə‚swiːt] *adj (lit, fig)* bittersüß.
**bitty** ['bɪtɪ] *adj* (+er) (*Brit col: scrappy*) zusammengestückelt *(col).*
**bitumen** ['bɪtjʊmɪn] *n* Bitumen *nt.*
**bivouac** ['bɪvʊæk] (*vb: pret, ptp ~ked*) **1** *n* Biwak *nt.* **2** *vi* biwakieren.
**bizarre** [bɪ'zaːr] *adj* bizarr.
**bk** = **book**.
**blab** [blæb] *vi* quatschen *(col); (talk fast, tell secret)* plappern; *(criminal)* singen *(col).*
**black** [blæk] **1** *adj* (+er) **(a)** schwarz. **~ man/woman** Schwarze(r) *mf*; **to beat sb ~ and blue** jdn grün und blau schlagen; **~ and white film** Schwarzweißfilm *m*; **the situation isn't as ~ and white as that** die Situation ist nicht so eindeutig schwarzweiß; **he's not so ~ as he's painted** er ist nicht so schlecht wie sein Ruf. **(b)** *future, prospects, mood* düster, finster. **things are looking ~** es sieht düster aus. **(c)** *(fig: angry) looks* böse. **he looked as ~ as thunder** er machte ein bitterböses Gesicht.
**2** *n* **(a)** *(colour)* Schwarz *nt.* **he is dressed in** *or* **wearing ~** er trägt Schwarz; **to wear ~ for sb** für jdn Trauer tragen; **it's written down in ~ and white** es steht schwarz auf weiß geschrieben; **in the ~** *(Fin)* in den schwarzen Zahlen. **(b)** *(negro)* Schwarze(r) *mf.*
**3** *vt* **(a)** schwärzen. **to ~ sb's eye** jdm ein blaues Auge schlagen. **(b)** *(Brit: trade union)* bestreiken; *goods* boykottieren.
▶**black out 1** *vi* das Bewußtsein verlieren, ohnmächtig werden. **2** *vt sep* **(a)** *building, stage* verdunkeln. **(b)** *(with ink, paint)* schwärzen.
**black:** **~ belt** *n (Sport)* Schwarzer Gürtel; **~berry** *n* Brombeere *f*; **~bird** *n* Amsel *f*; **~board** *n* Tafel *f*; **to write sth on the ~board** etw an die Tafel schreiben; **~ box** *n (Aviat)* Flugschreiber *m*; **~ bread** *n* Schwarzbrot *nt*; **~ cherry** *n* (Sauer)kirsche *f*; **~currant** *n* schwarze Johannisbeere; **B~ Death** *n (Hist)* Schwarzer Tod; **~ economy** *n* Schattenwirtschaft *f.*
**blacken** ['blækən] **1** *vt* schwarz machen; *one's face* schwarz anmalen; *(fig) character* verunglimpfen. **to ~ sb's name** jdn schlechtmachen. **2** *vi* schwarz werden.
**black:** **~ eye** *n* blaues Auge; **B~ Forest** *n* Schwarzwald *m*; **~head** *n* Mitesser *m*; **~ hole** *n (Astron)* schwarzes Loch; **~ humour** *(Brit) or* **humor** *(US) n* schwarzer Humor; **~ ice** *n* Glatteis *nt*; **~jack** *n (Cards)* Siebzehn und Vier; **~leg** *(Brit Ind) n* Streikbrecher(in *f*) *m*; **~ list** *n* schwarze Liste; **~list** *vt* auf die schwarze Liste setzen; **~ magic** *n* Schwarze Magie *f*; **~mail 1** *n* Erpressung *f*; **2** *vt* erpressen; **to ~mail sb into doing sth** jdn durch Erpressung dazu zwingen, etw zu tun; **B~ Maria** [‚blækmə'raɪə] *n* ≃ grüne Minna *(col);* **~ mark** *n* Tadel *m*; *(in school register)* Eintrag *m*; **~ market 1** *n* Schwarzmarkt *m*; **2** *adj attr* Schwarzmarkt-.

**blackness** ['blæknɪs] *n* Schwärze *f.*
**black:** **~out** *n* **(a)** *(Med)* Ohnmacht(sanfall *m*) *f no pl*; **(b)** *(light failure)* Stromausfall *m*; *(during war)* Verdunkelung *f*; *(TV)* Ausfall *m*; **(c)** *(news ~out)* (Nachrichten)sperre *f*; **~ pudding** *n* ≃ Blutwurst *f*; **B~ Sea** *n* Schwarzes Meer; **~ sheep** *n (fig)* schwarzes Schaf; **B~shirt** *n* Schwarzhemd *nt*; **~smith** *n* Schmied *m*; **~ spot** *n (also* **accident ~ spot)** Gefahrenstelle *f*; **~ tie** *n* schwarze Fliege; "**~ tie**" *(on invitation)* „Abendanzug".
**bladder** ['blædər] *n (Anat, Bot)* Blase *f.*
**blade** [bleɪd] *n (of knife, tool)* Klinge *f*, *(of oar, saw, propeller, windscreen wiper)* Blatt *nt*; *(of plough)* Schar *f*; *(of turbine, paddle wheel)* Schaufel *f*; *(of grass, corn)* Halm *m.*
**blame** [bleɪm] **1** *vt* **(a)** *(hold responsible)* die Schuld geben *(+dat).* **to ~ sb for sth/sth on sb** jdm die Schuld an etw *(dat)* geben; **you only have yourself to ~** das hast du dir selbst zuzuschreiben; **I'm to ~ for this** daran bin ich schuld. **(b)** *(reproach)* Vorwürfe machen *(sb for* jdm für *or* wegen). **nobody is blaming you** es macht Ihnen ja niemand einen Vorwurf. **(c)** **he decided to turn down the offer — well, I can't say I ~ him** er entschloß sich, das Angebot abzulehnen — das kann man ihm wahrhaftig nicht verdenken. **2** *n (responsibility)* Schuld *f.* **to put the ~ for sth on sb** jdm die Schuld an etw *(dat)* geben; **to take the ~** die Schuld auf sich *(acc)* nehmen; *(for sb's mistakes also)* den Kopf hinhalten; **the ~ lies with him** er hat *or* ist schuld (daran).
**blameless** ['bleɪmlɪs] *adj* schuldlos; *life* untadelig.
**blameworthy** ['bleɪmwɜːðɪ] *adj* schuldig.
**blanch** [blɑːntʃ] **1** *vt (Cook) vegetables* blanchieren. **2** *vi (with* vor *+dat) (person)* blaß werden.
**bland** [blænd] *adj* (+er) **(a)** *person* verbindlich; *face* ausdruckslos-höflich. **(b)** *food* mild, fade *(pej).* **(c)** *(mild, lacking distinction)* nichtssagend.
**blandishment** ['blændɪʃmənt] *n* Schmeichelei *f.*
**blank** [blæŋk] **1** *adj* (+er) **(a)** *piece of paper, page, wall* leer. **~ cheque** Blankoscheck *m*; *(fig)* Freibrief *m*; **there is a ~ space after each question** nach jeder Frage ist eine Lücke (gelassen). **(b)** *(expressionless) face, look* ausdruckslos; *(stupid)* verständnislos; *(puzzled)* verdutzt, verblüfft. **he just looked ~** er guckte mich nur groß an *(col)*; **my mind went ~** ich hatte Mattscheibe *(col).* **(c)** **~ verse** Blankvers *m.* **2** *n* **(a)** *(in document)* freier Raum, leere Stelle; *(~ document)* Formular *nt*; *(gap)* Lücke *f.* **(b)** **my mind was/went a complete ~** ich hatte totale Mattscheibe *(col)*; **to draw a ~** kein Glück haben. **(c)** *(also* **~ cartridge)** Platzpatrone *f.*
**blanket** ['blæŋkɪt] **1** *n (lit, fig)* Decke *f.* **a ~ of snow/ fog** eine Schnee-/Nebeldecke. **2** *adj attr statement* pauschal; *insurance etc* umfassend. **3** *vt (snow, smoke)* zudecken.
**blare** [blɛər] **1** *n (of car horn etc)* lautes Hupen; *(of trumpets etc)* Schmettern *nt.* **2** *vi see n* laut hupen; schmettern. **the music ~d through the hall** die Musik schallte durch den Saal.
▶**blare out 1** *vi (loud voice, music)* schallen; *(trumpets)* schmettern. **2** *vt sep (trumpets) tune* schmettern; *(radio) music* plärren; *(person) order, warning etc* brüllen.
**blasé** ['blɑːzeɪ] *adj* blasiert.
**blaspheme** [blæs'fiːm] *vi* Gott lästern.
**blasphemous** ['blæsfɪməs] *adj (lit, fig)* blasphemisch; *(lit also)* gotteslästerlich.
**blasphemy** ['blæsfɪmɪ] *n see adj* Blasphemie *f*; Gotteslästerung *f.*
**blast** [blɑːst] **1** *n* **(a)** Windstoß *m*; *(of hot air)* Schwall *m.* **(b)** *(sound: of trumpets)* Schmettern *nt*; *(of fog-*

*horn)* Tuten *nt.* **(c)** *(noise, explosion)* Explosion *f;* *(shock wave)* Druckwelle *f.* **to get the full ~ of sb's anger** jds Wut in voller Wucht abbekommen. **(d)** *(in quarrying etc)* Sprengung *f.* **(e) at full ~** *(lit, fig)* auf Hochtouren; **with the radio turned up (at) full ~** mit dem Radio voll aufgedreht. **2** *vt hole* sprengen; *rocket* schießen. **3** *interj (col)* **~ (it)!** verdammt! *(col).*

►**blast off** *vi (rocket, astronaut)* abheben, starten.
**blasted** ['blɑːstɪd] *adj (col)* verdammt *(col).*
**blast furnace** *n* Hochofen *m.*
**blasting** ['blɑːstɪŋ] *n (Tech)* Sprengen *nt.* **"danger ~ in progress"** „Achtung! Sprengarbeiten!"
**blast-off** ['blɑːstɒf] *n* Abschuß *m.*
**blatant** ['bleɪtənt] *adj (very obvious)* offensichtlich; *injustice also* eklatant; *error also* kraß; *liar* unverfroren; *disregard* offen.
**blaze**[1] [bleɪz] **1** *n (fire)* Feuer *nt;* *(of building etc also)* Brand *m;* *(of sun)* Glut *f.* **a ~ of lights/colour** ein Lichtermeer *nt*/Meer *nt* von Farben; **he went out in a ~ of glory** er trat mit Glanz und Gloria ab; **go to ~s** *(col)* scher dich zum Teufel! *(col);* **what/how the ~s ...?** *(col)* was/wie zum Teufel ...? *(col);* **like ~s** *(col)* wie verrückt *(col).* **2** *vi* **(a)** *(sun)* brennen; *(fire also)* lodern. **to ~ with anger** vor Zorn glühen. **(b)** *(guns)* feuern.
►**blaze away** *vi* **(a)** *(soldiers, guns)* drauflos feuern *(at auf +acc).* **(b)** *(fire etc)* lodern.
►**blaze up** *vi* auflodern.
**blaze**[2] **1** *n (of horse etc)* Blesse *f.* **2** *vt* **to ~ a trail** *(fig)* den Weg bahnen.
**blazer** ['bleɪzər] *n* Blazer *m.*
**blazing** ['bleɪzɪŋ] *adj building etc* brennend; *fire, torch* lodernd; *sun (hot)* brennend; *(fig) eyes* funkelnd *(with* vor *+dat);* *red* knall-, leuchtend.
**bldg** = **building.**
**bleach** [bliːtʃ] **1** *n* Bleichmittel *nt.* **2** *vt linen, bones, hair* bleichen.
**bleachers** ['bliːtʃəz] *npl (US)* unüberdachte Zuschauertribüne.
**bleak** [bliːk] *adj (+er)* **(a)** öde, trostlos. **(b)** *weather, wind* rauh, kalt. **(c)** *(fig) future etc* trostlos.
**bleakness** ['bliːknɪs] *n see adj* **(a)** Öde, Trostlosigkeit *f.* **(b)** Rauheit, Kälte *f.* **(c)** Trostlosigkeit *f.*
**bleary** ['blɪərɪ] *adj (+er) eyes* trübe; *(after sleep)* verschlafen.
**bleary-eyed** ['blɪərɪˌaɪd] *adj (after sleep)* verschlafen.
**bleat** [bliːt] *vi (sheep, calf)* blöken; *(goat, fig col)* meckern.
**bleed** [bliːd] *pret, ptp* **bled** [bled] **1** *vi* bluten. **to ~ to death** verbluten; **my heart ~s for you** *(iro)* ich fang gleich an zu weinen. **2** *vt* **(a)** *person* zur Ader lassen. **(b)** *(fig col)* schröpfen *(col) (for* um). **(c)** *(Aut) brakes* entlüften.
**bleeding** ['bliːdɪŋ] **1** *n* **(a)** *(loss of blood)* Blutung *f.* **(b)** *(taking blood)* Aderlaß *m.* **(c)** *(of brakes)* Entlüftung *f.* **2** *adj* **(a)** *wound* blutend; *(fig) heart* gebrochen. **(b)** *(Brit col!)* verdammt *(col).* **just a ~ minute** nun mal sachte *(col).*
**bleep** [bliːp] **1** *n (Rad, TV)* Piepton *m.* **2** *vi (transmitter)* piepen. **3** *vt person, esp doctor* rufen, anpiepen *(col).*
**bleeper** ['bliːpər] *n* Funkrufempfänger, Piepser *(col) m.*
**blemish** ['blemɪʃ] **1** *n (lit, fig)* Makel *m.* **2** *vt object* beschädigen; *work* beeinträchtigen; *reputation* beflecken.
**blend** [blend] **1** *n* Mischung *f.* **2** *vt* **(a)** *teas, colours etc* (ver)mischen. **(b)** *(Cook) (stir)* einrühren; *(in blender) liquids* mixen; *semi-solids* pürieren. **3** *vi*

**(a)** *(voices, colours)* verschmelzen. **(b)** *(also ~ in:* *go together, harmonize)* harmonieren *(with* mit*),* passen *(with* zu*).*
**blender** ['blendər] *n* Mixer *m,* Mixgerät *nt.*
**bless** [bles] *vt* segnen. **to be ~ed with** gesegnet sein mit; **~ you, you're an angel** *(col)* du bist wirklich ein Engel *(col);* **~ you!** *(to sneezer)* Gesundheit!; **~ my soul!** *(col)* du meine Güte! *(col).*
**blessed** ['blesɪd] **1** *adj* **(a)** *(Rel)* heilig. **B~ Virgin** Heilige Jungfrau (Maria). **(b)** *(euph col: cursed)* verflixt *(col).* **the whole ~ day** den lieben langen Tag *(col).* **2** *n* **the ~, the Blest** die Seligen *pl.*
**blessing** ['blesɪŋ] *n (Rel, fig)* Segen *m.* **he can count his ~s** da kann er von Glück sagen; **what a ~ that ...** welch ein Segen *or* Glück, daß ...; **it was a ~ in disguise** es war schließlich doch ein Segen.
**blew** [bluː] *pret* of **blow**[2].
**blight** [blaɪt] **1** *n (on plants)* Braunfäule *f.* **these slums are a ~ upon the city** *(fig)* diese Slums sind ein Schandfleck für die Stadt. **2** *vt plants* zerstören; *(fig) hopes* zunichte machen.
**blighter** ['blaɪtər] *n (Brit col)* Kerl *m (col).* **a poor ~** ein armer Hund *(col);* **what a lucky ~!** so ein Glückspilz!
**blind** [blaɪnd] **1** *adj (+er) person, obedience, fury* blind; *corner* unübersichtlich. **a ~ man/woman** ein Blinder/eine Blinde; **~ in one eye** auf einem Auge blind; **he was ~ to her faults** er sah ihre Fehler einfach nicht; **to be ~ to the possibilities** die Möglichkeiten nicht sehen; **to turn a ~ eye to sth** bei etw ein Auge zudrücken; **but he didn't take a ~ bit of notice** *(col)* aber er hat sich nicht die Spur darum gekümmert *(col).*
**2** *vt* blenden; *(love, hate etc)* blind machen *(to* für, gegen*).* **he was ~ed in the war** er ist kriegsblind; **to ~ sb with science** jdn mit Fachjargon beeindrucken (wollen).
**3** *n* **(a)** **the ~** die Blinden *pl;* **it's the ~ leading the ~** *(fig)* das hieße, einen Lahmen einen Blinden führen lassen. **(b)** *(window shade) (cloth)* Rollo *nt;* *(slats)* Jalousie *f;* *(outside)* Rolladen *m.*
**4** *adv* **(a)** *(Aviat) fly* blind. **(b)** **~ drunk** *(col)* sinnlos betrunken.
**blind: ~ alley** *n (lit, fig)* Sackgasse *f;* **~ date** *n* Rendezvous *nt* mit einem/einer Unbekannten.
**blinder** ['blaɪndər] *n (col: drinking spree)* Saufgelage *nt (col).*
**blind flying** *n (Aviat)* Blindflug *m.*
**blindfold** ['blaɪndfəʊld] **1** *vt* die Augen verbinden *(+dat).* **2** *n* Augenbinde *f.* **3** *adj* mit verbundenen Augen. **I could do it ~** *(col)* das mach' ich mit links *(col).*
**blinding** ['blaɪndɪŋ] *adj light* blendend; *truth* ins Auge stechend.
**blindingly** ['blaɪndɪŋlɪ] *adv* **it is ~ obvious** das sieht doch ein Blinder.
**blindly** ['blaɪndlɪ] *adv (lit, fig)* blind(lings).
**blind man's buff** *n* Blindekuh *no art.*
**blindness** ['blaɪndnɪs] *n (lit, fig)* Blindheit *f (to* gegenüber*).*
**blind spot** *n (Med)* blinder Fleck; *(Aut, Aviat)* toter Winkel; *(Rad)* tote Zone.
**blink** [blɪŋk] **1** *n* Blinzeln *nt.* **to be on the ~** *(col)* kaputt sein *(col).* **2** *vi* blinzeln; *(light)* blinken. **3** *vt* **to ~ one's eyes** mit den Augen zwinkern.
**blinkers** ['blɪŋkəz] *npl* Scheuklappen *pl.*
**blinkered** ['blɪŋkəd] *adj (fig)* engstirnig. **they are all so ~** sie laufen alle mit Scheuklappen herum.
**blip** [blɪp] *n* **(a)** *(sound)* Piepsen *nt.* **(b)** *(on radar screen)* leuchtender Punkt.
**bliss** [blɪs] *n* Glück *nt.* **this is ~!** das ist eine Wohl-

tat!; **a life of marital** ~ ein überaus glückliches Eheleben.

**blissful** ['blɪsfʊl] *adj time, ignorance* herrlich; *respite also* wohltuend; *happiness* höchste(s); *state, look, smile* (glück)selig; *moments* selig.

**blissfully** ['blɪsfəlɪ] *adv stretch* wohlig; *peaceful* herrlich; *smile* selig. ~ **happy** überglücklich; **to be ~ ignorant** herrlich ahnungslos sein.

**blister** ['blɪstər] **1** *n (on skin, paint)* Blase *f*. ~ **pack** Klarsichtpackung *f*. **2** *vi (skin)* Blasen bekommen; *(paintwork, metal)* Blasen werfen. **3** *vt* Blasen hervorrufen auf *(+dat)*.

**blithely** ['blaɪðlɪ] *adv ignore, carry on* munter. **he ~ ignored the problem** er setzte sich ungeniert über das Problem hinweg.

**blithering** ['blɪðərɪŋ] *adj (col)* ~ **idiot** Trottel *m (col)*.

**blitz** [blɪts] **1** *n* **(a)** Blitzkrieg *m*; *(aerial)* Luftangriff *m*. **the B~** *deutscher Luftangriff auf britische Städte 1940-41.* **(b)** *(fig col)* Blitzaktion *f*. **he had a ~ on his room** er machte gründlich in seinem Zimmer sauber. **2** *vt* heftig bombardieren.

**blizzard** ['blɪzəd] *n* Schneesturm, Blizzard *m*.

**bloated** ['bləʊtɪd] *adj* aufgedunsen. **I feel absolutely ~** *(col)* ich bin zum Platzen voll *(col)*.

**blob** [blɒb] *n (of water, honey, wax)* Tropfen *m*; *(of ink)* Klecks *m*; *(of paint)* Tupfer *m*; *(of ice-cream, mashed potatoes)* Klacks *m*.

**bloc** [blɒk] *n* **(a)** *(Pol)* Block *m*. **(b)** **en ~** en bloc.

**block** [blɒk] **1** *n* **(a)** Block, Klotz *m*. **(b)** *(building, of shares, seats, for writing, Comp)* Block *m*. ~ **of flats** *(Brit)* Wohnblock *m*; **to take a stroll around the ~** einen Spaziergang um den Block machen; **she lived in the next ~/three ~s from us** *(esp US)* sie wohnte im nächsten Block/drei Blocks *or* Straßen weiter. **(c)** *(obstruction: in pipe, Med)* Verstopfung *f*. **I've a mental ~ about it** dabei habe ich totale Mattscheibe *(col)*. **(d)** *(col: head)* Knüller *m*. **to knock sb's ~ off** jdm eins überziehen *(col)*. **2** *vt road* blockieren; *traffic also, progress* aufhalten; *pipe* verstopfen; *(Ftbl)* blocken; *ball* stoppen; *credit* sperren. **to ~ sb's way/view** jdm den Weg/die Sicht versperren.

▶**block off** *vt sep street* absperren; *fireplace* abdecken.

▶**block out** *vt sep* **(a)** *(obscure) light* nicht durchlassen; *sun also* verdecken. **(b)** *(obliterate) part of picture* wegretuschieren.

▶**block up** *vt sep* **(a)** *(obstruct) gangway* blockieren; *pipe* verstopfen. **my nose is all ~ed ~** meine Nase ist völlig verstopft. **(b)** *(close, fill in) window* zumauern; *hole* zustopfen.

**blockade** [blɒ'keɪd] **1** *n (Mil)* Blockade *f*. **2** *vt* blockieren, sperren.

**blockage** ['blɒkɪdʒ] *n* Verstopfung *f*.

**block:** ~ **and tackle** *n* Flaschenzug *m*; ~ **booking** *n* Gruppenbuchung *f*; *(Theat)* Gruppenbestellung *f*; ~**buster** *n (col)* Knüller *m (col)*; ~ **capitals** *npl* Blockschrift *f*; ~**head** *n (col)* Knallkopf *m (col)*; ~**letters** *npl* Blockschrift *f*; ~ **vote** *n* Stimmenblock *m*.

**bloke** [bləʊk] *n (Brit col)* Kerl *(col)*, Typ *(col) m*.

**blond** [blɒnd] *adj man, hair* blond.

**blonde** [blɒnd] **1** *adj woman* blond. **2** *n (woman)* Blondine *f*.

**blood** [blʌd] *n* Blut *nt*. **to give ~** Blut spenden; **it makes my ~ boil** das macht mich rasend; **she's after his ~** sie will ihm an den Kragen *(col)*; **his ~ ran cold** es lief ihn eiskalt über den Rücken; **it's like trying to get ~ out of a stone** das ist verlorene Liebesmüh; **there is bad ~ between them** sie sind einander feindlich gesinnt; **it's in his ~** das liegt ihm im Blut; ~ **is thicker than water** *(prov)* Blut ist

dicker als Wasser *(prov)*.

**blood** *in cpds* Blut-; ~ **bank** *n* Blutbank *f*; ~**bath** *n* Blutbad *nt*; ~ **brother** *n* Blutsbruder *m*; ~ **clot** *n* Blutgerinnsel *nt*; ~ **corpuscle** *n* Blutkörperchen *nt*; ~ **count** *n* Blutbild *nt*; ~**curdling** *adj* grauenerregend; ~ **donor** *n* Blutspender(in *f*) *m*; ~ **group** *n* Blutgruppe *f*; ~**hound** *n* **(a)** *(Zool)* Bluthund *m*; **(b)** *(fig: detective)* Schnüffler *m (col)*.

**bloodless** ['blʌdlɪs] *adj victory, coup* unblutig; *(pallid)* blutleer, bleich.

**blood:** ~**lust** *n* Blutrünstigkeit *f*; ~ **money** *n* Mordgeld *nt*; ~ **orange** *n* Blutorange *f*; ~**poisoning** *n* Blutvergiftung *f*; ~ **pressure** *n* Blutdruck *m*; **to have (high)** ~ **pressure** hohen Blutdruck haben; ~**red** *adj* blutrot; ~ **relation** *n* Blutsverwandte(r) *mf*; ~ **relationship** *n* Blutsverwandtschaft *f*; ~**shed** *n* Blutvergießen *nt*; ~**shot** *adj* blutunterlaufen; ~ **sports** *npl* Jagdsport, Hahnenkampf *etc*; ~**stain** *n* Blutfleck *m*; ~**stained** *adj* blutig, blutbefleckt; ~**stream** *n* Blut *nt*, Blutkreislauf *m*; ~ **test** *n* Blutprobe *f*; ~**thirsty** *adj* blutrünstig; ~ **transfusion** *n (Blut)* transfusion *f*; ~ **vessel** *n* Blutgefäß *nt*.

**bloody** ['blʌdɪ] **1** *adj (+er)* **(a)** *(lit)* blutig. **(b)** *(Brit col!: damned)* verdammt *(col)*, Scheiß- *(col!)*; *(in positive sense) genius, wonder* echt *(col)*, verdammt *(col)*. ~ **hell!** verdammt nochmal! *(col)*; **he is a ~ marvel** er ist verdammt gut *(col)*. **2** *adv (Brit col!)* verdammt *(col)*. ~ **cold/stupid** saukalt/saublöd *(col)*; *(in positive sense)* ~ **good** echt *or* verdammt gut *(col)*; ~ **brilliant** echt toll *(col)*.

**bloody-minded** ['blʌdɪ'maɪndɪd] *adj (Brit col)* stur *(col)*.

**bloom** [bluːm] **1** *n* **(a)** Blüte *f*. **to be in (full)** ~ in (voller) Blüte stehen; **in the ~ of youth** in der Blüte der Jugend. **(b)** *(on fruit)* satter Schimmer; *(on peaches)* Flaum *m*. **2** *vi (lit, fig)* blühen.

**bloomer** ['bluːmər] *n (col)* grober Fehler.

**blossom** ['blɒsəm] **1** *n* Blüte *f*. **in ~** in Blüte. **2** *vi (lit, fig)* blühen; *(person, trade etc also)* aufblühen. **to ~ into sth** zu etw aufblühen.

▶**blossom out** *vi (fig)* aufblühen *(into zu)*.

**blot** [blɒt] **1** *n* **(a)** *(of ink)* (Tinten)klecks *m*. **(b)** *(fig: on honour, reputation)* Fleck *m (on auf +dat)*. **a ~ on the landscape** ein Schandfleck in der Landschaft. **2** *vt* **(a)** *(make ink spots on)* beklecksen. **to ~ one's copybook** *(fig)* sich danebenbenehmen, es sich *(dat)* verderben *(with sb mit jdm)*. **(b)** *(dry) ink, page* löschen.

▶**blot out** *vt sep* **(a)** *(lit) words* verschmieren. **(b)** *(hide from view) landscape* verdecken; *(obliterate) memories* auslöschen.

**blotch** [blɒtʃ] *n (on skin)* Fleck *m*; *(of ink, colour also)* Klecks *m*.

**blotchy** ['blɒtʃɪ] *adj (+er) skin* fleckig; *drawing, paint* klecksig.

**blotter** ['blɒtər] *n* (Tinten)löscher *m*.

**blotting paper** ['blɒtɪŋ,peɪpər] *n* Löschpapier *nt*.

**blotto** ['blɒtəʊ] *adj pred (col: drunk)* sternhagelvoll *(col)*.

**blouse** [blaʊz] *n* **(a)** Bluse *f*. **(b)** *(US Mil)* (Feld)bluse *f*.

**blow¹** [bləʊ] *n (lit, fig)* Schlag *m (for, to* für*)*. **to come to ~s** handgreiflich werden; **at one ~** *(fig)* mit einem Schlag *(col)*.

**blow²** [bləʊ] *(vb: pret* **blew***, ptp* **~n)** **1** *vi* **(a)** *(wind)* wehen, blasen. **(b)** *(person)* blasen, pusten *(col) (on* auf *+acc)*. **(c)** *(move with the wind)* fliegen. **the door blew open/shut** die Tür flog auf/zu. **(d)** *(bugle)* blasen; *(whistle)* pfeifen. **(e)** *(fuse, light bulb, gasket)* durchbrennen.

**board**

**2** vt **(a)** (breeze) wehen; (strong wind, draught) blasen; (gale etc) treiben; (person) blasen, pusten (col). **the wind blew the ship off course** der Wind trieb das Schiff vom Kurs ab; **to ~ sb a kiss** jdm eine Kußhand zuwerfen; **to ~ one's nose** sich (dat) die Nase putzen. **(b)** glass, trumpet blasen; bubbles machen; (Hunt, Mil) horn blasen in (+acc). **the referee blew his whistle** der Schiedsrichter pfiff. **(c)** (burn out, ~ up) safe, bridge etc sprengen; transistor zerstören. **I've ~n a fuse/light bulb** mir ist eine Sicherung/Birne durchgebrannt; **to be ~n to pieces** (bridge, car) in die Luft gesprengt werden; (person) zerfetzt werden. **(d)** (col: spend extravagantly) money verpulvern (col). **(e)** (col: reveal) secret verraten. **(f)** (col: damn) ~! Mist! (col); ~ **the expense** das ist doch wurscht, was es kostet (col).

▶**blow away 1** vi (hat, paper etc) wegfliegen. **2** vt sep wegblasen; (breeze also) wegwehen.

▶**blow down 1** vi (tree etc) umgeweht werden. **2** vt sep (lit) umwehen.

▶**blow in 1** vi **(a)** (lit) (be blown down: window etc) eingedrückt werden; (be ~n inside: dust etc) hereingeweht werden; (wind) hereinwehen, hereinblasen. **(b)** (col: arrive unexpectedly) hereinschneien (col) (+prep obj, -to in +acc). **2** vt sep window, door etc eindrücken; dust etc hereinwehen (+prep obj, -to in +acc).

▶**blow off 1** vi wegfliegen. **2** vt sep (+prep obj) blasen von. **3** vt insep (fig) steam ablassen (col).

▶**blow out 1** vi (candle etc) ausgehen. **2** vt sep candle ausblasen; cheeks aufblasen. **to ~ one's brains** ~ sich (dat) eine Kugel durch den Kopf jagen. **3** vr (wind, storm) sich legen.

▶**blow over** vi (lit, fig: storm, dispute) sich legen.

▶**blow up 1** vi (be exploded) in die Luft fliegen; (bomb) explodieren; (gale, crisis, row) ausbrechen; (fig col: person) explodieren (col). **2** vt sep mine, bridge, person in die Luft jagen; tyre, balloon aufblasen; photo vergrößern; (exaggerate) event aufbauschen (into zu).

**blow:** ~-**by-**~ adj account detailliert; ~-**dry 1** n to have a ~-**dry** sich fönen lassen; **2** vt fönen; ~ **job** n (vulg) **to give sb a ~ job** jdm einen blasen (vulg); ~**lamp** n Lötlampe f.

**blown** [bləʊn] ptp of **blow²**.

**blow:** ~-**out** n **(a)** (col: meal) Schlemmerei f; **(b)** (burst tyre) **he had a ~-out** ihm ist ein Reifen geplatzt; **(c)** (Elec) **there's been a ~-out** die Sicherung ist durchgebrannt; ~ **pipe** n (weapon) Blasrohr nt; ~**torch** n Lötlampe f; ~-**up** n **(a)** (col: outburst) Wutausbruch m; (row) Krach m; **(b)** (Phot) Vergrößerung f.

**blowy** ['bləʊɪ] adj (+er) windig.

**blowzy** ['blaʊzɪ] adj (+er) (woman) schlampig (col).

**blubber** ['blʌbər] **1** n Walfischspeck m. **2** vi (col) flennen (col), heulen (col).

**blue** [bluː] **1** adj (+er) **(a)** blau. ~ **with cold** blau vor Kälte; **until you're ~ in the face** (col) bis zur Vergasung (col); **once in a ~ moon** alle Jubeljahre (einmal). **(b)** (col: miserable) melancholisch, trübsinnig. **to feel ~** niedergeschlagen sein. **(c)** (col: obscene) joke schlüpfrig; film Porno-, Sex-. **(d)** (Pol) konservativ. **2** n **(a)** Blau nt. **(b)** (liter: sky) Himmel m. **out of the ~** (fig col) aus heiterem Himmel (col). **(c)** (Pol) Konservative(r) mf. **(d)** (col) **to have (a fit of) the ~s** den Moralischen haben (col). **(e)** (Mus) **the ~s** pl der Blues.

**blue:** ~ **baby** n Baby nt mit angeborenem Herzfehler; ~**bell** n Sternhyazinthe f; (Scot) Glockenblume f; ~**berry** n Blau- or Heidelbeere f; ~ **blood** n blaues Blut; ~-**blooded** adj blaublütig; ~**bottle** n

Schmeißfliege f; ~ **cheese** n Blauschimmelkäse m; ~-**chip** adj company, shares führend; investment sicher; ~-**collar** adj ~-**collar worker/union/jobs** Arbeiter m/Arbeitergewerkschaft f/Stellen pl für Arbeiter; ~-**eyed** adj blauäugig; **sb's ~-eyed boy** (fig) jds Liebling m; ~-**pencil** vt (edit, revise) korrigieren; ~**print** n Blaupause f; (fig) Plan, Entwurf m; ~**stocking** n Blaustrumpf m; ~**tit** n Blaumeise f.

**bluff¹** [blʌf] **1** n (headland) Kliff nt; (inland) Felsvorsprung m. **2** adj rauh aber herzlich (col); honesty, answer aufrichtig.

**bluff²** **1** vti bluffen. **2** n Bluff m. **to call sb's ~** es darauf ankommen lassen; (make prove) jdn auf die Probe stellen.

▶**bluff out** vt sep **to ~ it ~** sich rausreden (col).

**bluish** ['bluːɪʃ] adj bläulich.

**blunder** ['blʌndər] **1** n Schnitzer m (col); (socially) Fauxpas m. **to make a ~** einen Bock schießen (col); (socially) einen Fauxpas begehen. **2** vi **(a)** einen Bock schießen (col); (socially) sich blamieren. **(b)** (move clumsily) tappen (into gegen).

**blunt** [blʌnt] **1** adj (+er) **(a)** stumpf. **with a ~ instrument** mit einem stumpfen Gegenstand. **(b)** (outspoken) person geradeheraus pred; speech unverblümt; facts nackt. **to be ~ about sth** sich unverblümt zu etw äußern. **2** vt knife etc stumpf machen; (fig) palate, senses abstumpfen.

**bluntly** ['blʌntlɪ] adv speak freiheraus.

**bluntness** ['blʌntnɪs] n **(a)** (of blade) Stumpfheit f. **(b)** (outspokenness) Unverblümtheit f

**blur** [blɜːr] **1** n verschwommener Fleck. **2** vt **(a)** inscription verwischen; writing also verschmieren; outline, photograph unscharf machen; sound verzerren. **to be/become ~red** undeutlich sein/werden; (image etc also) verschwommen sein/verschwimmen. **(b)** (fig) senses, mind trüben; meaning verwischen.

**blurb** [blɜːb] n Material nt, Informationen pl; (on book jacket) Klappentext m.

**blurt (out)** [blɜːt('aʊt)] vt sep herausplatzen mit (col).

**blush** [blʌʃ] **1** vi rot werden (with vor +dat). **2** n Erröten nt no pl. **with a ~** errötend.

**blusher** ['blʌʃər] n Rouge nt.

**bluster** ['blʌstər] vi (wind) toben; (person) ein großes Geschrei machen; (angrily also) toben.

**blustery** ['blʌstərɪ] adj wind, day stürmisch.

**Blvd.** = **Boulevard**.

**BM** = **British Museum**.

**BMA** = **British Medical Association** britischer Ärzteverband.

**B-Movie** ['biːmuːvɪ] n als Beiprogramm gezeigter Kinofilm.

**BO** [ˌbiːˈəʊ] (col) = **body odour** Körpergeruch m.

**boa** ['bəʊə] n Boa f. ~ **constrictor** Boa constrictor f.

**boar** [bɔːr] n (male pig) Eber m; (wild) Keiler m.

**board** [bɔːd] **1** n **(a)** Brett nt; (black~) Tafel f; (notice~) Schwarzes Brett; (sign~) Schild nt; (floor~) Diele(nbrett nt) f. **(b)** (provision of meals) Verpflegung f. ~ **and lodging** Kost und Logis; **full/half ~** (Brit) Voll-/Halbpension f. **(c)** (group of officials) Ausschuß m; (with advisory function, ~ of trustees) Beirat m; (permanent official institution: gas~, harbour ~ etc) Behörde f; (of company: also ~ of directors) Vorstand m; (including shareholders, advisers) Aufsichtsrat m. **to be on the ~** im Vorstand/Aufsichtsrat sein or sitzen; **B~ of Trade** (Brit) Handelsministerium nt. **(d)** (Naut, Aviat) **on ~** an Bord; **to go on ~** an Bord gehen. **(e)** (fig phrases) **across the ~** (fig) generell, pauschal; **to go by the ~**

*(dreams, hopes)* zunichte werden; *(principles)* über Bord geworfen werden.

  **2** *vt ship, plane* besteigen, an Bord *(+gen)* gehen/kommen; *train, bus* einsteigen in *(+acc)*; *(Naut: in attack)* entern.

  **3** *vi* **(a)** *(live)* in Pension sein *(with* bei*)*. **(b)** *(Sch)* Internatsschüler(in *f)* m sein. **(c)** *(Aviat)* die Maschine besteigen. "**flight ZA173 now ~ing through gate 13**" „Aufruf für Passagiere des Fluges ZA173, sich zum Flugsteig 13 zu begeben".

  ►**board up** *vt sep* mit Brettern vernageln.

**boarder** ['bɔːdə'] *n* **(a)** Pensionsgast *m.* **(b)** *(Sch)* Internatsschüler(in *f)* m.

**board game** *n* Brettspiel *nt.*

**boarding** ['bɔːdɪŋ-]: **~ card** *n* Bordkarte *f;* **~ house** *n* Pension *f;* **~ party** *n (Naut)* Enterkommando *nt;* **~ pass** *n* Bordkarte *f;* **~ school** *n* Internat *nt.*

**board:** **~ meeting** *n* Vorstandssitzung *f;* **~room** *n* Sitzungssaal *m;* **~walk** *n (US)* Holzsteg *m;* *(on beach)* hölzerne Uferpromenade.

**boast** [bəust] **1** *n* Prahlerei *f.* **it is their ~ that** ... sie rühmen sich, daß ... **2** *vi* angeben *(about, of* mit, *to sb* jdm gegenüber*).* **don't ~** gib nicht so an. **3** *vt (possess)* sich rühmen *(+gen) (geh).*

**boaster** ['bəustə'] *n* Prahler(in *f)* m.

**boastful** ['bəustfʊl] *adj* prahlerisch.

**boastfulness** ['bəustfʊlnɪs], **boasting** ['bəustɪŋ] *n* Prahlerei *f.*

**boat** [bəut] *n* Boot *nt;* *(sea-going, passenger ~)* Schiff *nt;* *(pleasure steamer etc)* Dampfer *m.* **by ~** mit dem Schiff; **to miss the ~** *(fig col)* den Anschluß verpassen; **we're all in the same ~** *(fig col)* wir sitzen alle im gleichen Boot.

**boat-building** *n* Bootsbau *m.*

**boater** ['bəutə'] *n* **(a)** *(hat)* steifer Strohhut. **(b)** *(person boating)* Bootsfahrer(in *f)* m.

**boat:** **~ hire** *n* Bootsverleih *m;* **~hook** *n* Bootshaken *m.*

**boating** ['bəutɪŋ] *n* Bootfahren *nt;* **~ holiday** Bootsferien *pl.*

**boat:** **~man** *n* Bootsführer *m;* *(hirer)* Bootsverleiher *m;* **~ people** *npl* Bootsflüchtlinge *pl;* **~ race** *n* Regatta *f.*

**boatswain, bosun, bo's'n** ['bəusn] *n* Bootsmann *m.*

**boat train** *n* Zug *m* mit Fährenanschluß.

**bob¹** [bɒb] *vi* sich auf und ab bewegen; *(rabbit)* hoppeln; *(bird's tail)* wippen; *(boxer)* tänzeln. **to ~ (up and down) in** *or* **on the water** auf dem Wasser schaukeln.

  ►**bob up** *vi (lit, fig)* auftauchen.

**bob²** *n, pl -* *(dated Brit col)* Shilling *m.* **that will cost a few ~** das wird einiges kosten.

**bob³** *n (haircut)* Bubikopf *m.*

**bob⁴** *n (sleigh)* Bob *m.*

**bobbin** ['bɒbɪn] *n* Spule *f;* *(cotton reel)* Rolle *f.*

**bobble** ['bɒbl] *n* Bommel *f,* Pompon *m.* **~ hat** Pudelmütze *f.*

**bobby** ['bɒbɪ] *n (dated Brit col)* Bobby *m.*

**bob:** **~cat** *n (US)* Luchs *m;* **~sleigh 1** *n* Bob *m;* **2** *vi* Bob fahren.

**bode** [bəud] *vi:* **to ~ well/ill** ein gutes/schlechtes Zeichen sein.

**bodge** [bɒdʒ] *n, vt see* **botch.**

**bodice** ['bɒdɪs] *n* **(a)** *(of dress)* Oberteil *nt.* **(b)** *(vest)* Unterhemd *nt.*

**bodily** ['bɒdɪlɪ] **1** *adj (physical)* körperlich. **~ needs** leibliche Bedürfnisse *pl;* **~ harm** Körperverletzung *f.* **2** *adv (forcibly)* gewaltsam.

**body** ['bɒdɪ] *n* **(a)** Körper *m;* *(of human also)* Leib *m*

*(geh).* **to keep ~ and soul together** Leib und Seele zusammenhalten. **(b)** *(corpse)* Leiche *f.* **(c)** *(of plane, ship)* Rumpf *m;* *(of speech, army)* Hauptteil *m.* **the main ~ of his readers/the students** das Gros seiner Leser/der Studenten. **(d)** *(of car)* Karosserie *f.* **(e)** *(group of people)* Gruppe *f.* **the student ~** die Studentenschaft. **(f)** *(organization)* Organ *nt;* *(committee)* Gremium *nt;* *(corporation)* Körperschaft *f.* **(g)** *(of wine)* Körper *m;* *(of hair)* Fülle *f;* *(of paper, cloth)* Festigkeit *f.*

**body:** **~building** *n* Bodybuilding *nt;* **~guard** *n (one person)* Leibwächter *m;* *(group)* Leibwache *f;* **~ language** *n* Körpersprache *f;* **~ search** *n* Leibesvisitation *f;* **~ shop** *n (Aut)* Karosseriewerkstatt *f;* **~ warmer** *n* Thermoweste *f;* **~work** *n (Aut)* Karosserie *f.*

**bog** [bɒg] *n* **(a)** Sumpf *m;* *(peat ~)* (Torf)moor *nt.* **(b)** *(Brit col: toilet)* Klo *nt (col).*

  ►**bog down** *vt sep* **to be** *or* **get ~ged ~** *(lit)* steckenbleiben; *(fig)* sich festgefahren haben; *(in details)* sich verzettelt haben.

**boggle** ['bɒgl] *vi (col)* **the mind ~s** *(faced with fact)* da bist du baff *(col) or* platt *(col);* *(faced with possibility)* das kann man sich *(dat)* kaum ausmalen.

**boggy** ['bɒgɪ] *adj (+er) ground* sumpfig.

**bogus** ['bəugəs] *adj doctor* falsch; *money* gefälscht; *company* Schwindel-; *claim* erfunden.

**Bohemia** [bəu'hiːmɪə] *n* Böhmen *nt.*

**Bohemian** [bəu'hiːmɪən] **1** *n* **(a)** Böhme *m,* Böhmin *f.* **(b)** *(fig)* b~ Bohemien *m.* **2** *adj* **(a)** böhmisch. **(b)** *(fig)* b~ *lifestyle* unkonventionell, unbürgerlich.

**boil¹** [bɔɪl] *n (Med)* Furunkel *m or nt.*

**boil²** *vi* **(a)** kochen; *(water also, Phys)* sieden. **the kettle is ~ing** das Wasser kocht. **(b)** *(fig col: be angry)* kochen, schäumen *(with* vor *+dat).* **2** *vt* kochen. **~ed/hard ~ed egg** weich-/hartgekochtes Ei; **~ed potatoes** Salzkartoffeln *pl.* **3** *n* **to bring to the ~** zum Kochen bringen; **he's gone off the ~** *(fig col)* er hat kein Interesse mehr.

  ►**boil away** *vi* **(a)** *(go on boiling)* weiterkochen. **(b)** *(evaporate)* verdampfen.

  ►**boil down 1** *vt sep* eindicken lassen. **2** *vi* **(a)** *(jam etc)* dickflüssig werden. **(b)** *(fig)* **what it ~s ~ to is that** ... das läuft darauf hinaus, daß ...

  ►**boil over** *vi* **(a)** *(lit)* überkochen. **(b)** *(fig) (situation, quarrel)* den Siedepunkt erreichen.

**boiler** ['bɔɪlə'] *n* **(a)** *(domestic)* Boiler, Warmwasserbereiter *m;* *(in ship, engine)* (Dampf)kessel *m.* **(b)** *(chicken)* Suppenhuhn *nt.*

**boiler:** **~maker** *n* Kesselschmied *m;* **~suit** *n* Overall, Blaumann *m (col) m.*

**boiling** ['bɔɪlɪŋ]: **~ hot** *adj* kochendheiß; **I'm ~ hot** mir ist schrecklich heiß; **~ point** *n (lit, fig)* Siedepunkt *m.*

**boisterous** ['bɔɪstərəs] *adj (exuberant) person* ausgelassen; *game etc also* wild.

**bold** [bəuld] *adj (+er)* **(a)** *(valiant)* kühn. **(b)** *(impudent)* dreist. **to be** *or* **make so ~ as to** ... sich erlauben, zu ... **(c)** *(striking) colours etc* kräftig; *handwriting, style* kraftvoll. **(d)** *(Typ)* fett. **~ type** Fettdruck *m.*

**boldness** ['bəuldnɪs] *n see adj (a), (b), (c)* Kühnheit *(geh) f;* Dreistigkeit *f;* Kräftigkeit *f.*

**Bolivia** [bə'lɪvɪə] *n* Bolivien *nt.*

**Bolivian** [bə'lɪvɪən] **1** *n* Bolivianer(in *f)* m. **2** *adj* bolivianisch.

**bollard** ['bɒlɑːd] *n (on road, quay)* Poller *m.*

**Bolshevik** ['bɒlʃəvɪk] **1** *n* Bolschewik *m.* **2** *adj* bolschewistisch.

**Bolshevism** ['bɒlʃəvɪzəm] *n* Bolschewismus *m.*

**bolshy** ['bɒlʃɪ] *(col) adj (+er) (uncooperative)* stur,

störrisch; *(aggressive)* pampig *(col)*.
**bolster** ['bəʊlstər] **1** *n (on bed)* Nackenrolle *f.* **2** *vt* *(also ~ up) (fig) person* Mut machen *(+dat)*; *status* aufbessern; *currency* stützen.
**bolt** [bəʊlt] **1** *n* **(a)** *(on door etc)* Riegel *m.* **(b)** *(Tech)* Bolzen *m.* **(c)** *(of lightning)* Blitzstrahl *m.* **it came/ was like a ~ from the blue** *(fig)* das war wie ein Blitz aus heiterem Himmel. **(d)** *(of crossbow)* Bolzen *m.* **(e)** *(of rifle)* Kammer *f.* **(f)** *(sudden dash)* Satz *m (col).* **he made a ~ for the door** er machte einen Satz zur Tür; **to make a ~ for it** abhauen *(col).* **2** *adv*: **~ upright** kerzengerade. **3** *vi* **(a)** *(horse)* durchgehen; *(person)* Reißaus nehmen *(col)*, abhauen *(col).* **(b)** *(move quickly)* sausen, rasen. **4** *vt* **(a)** *door, window* verriegeln. **(b)** *(Tech) machine parts* verschrauben *(to* mit*).* **to ~ together** verschrauben. **(c)** *(also ~ down)* one's food hinunterschlingen.
**bomb** [bɒm] **1** *n* Bombe *f.* **his party went like a ~** *(col)* seine Party war ein Bombenerfolg *(col)*; **the car goes like a ~** *(col)* der Wagen läuft verdammt gut *(col)*; **to cost a ~** *(col)* ein Wahnsinnsgeld kosten *(col)*; **to do a ~** *(US: fail)* durchfallen *(col).* **2** *vt* bombardieren; *(not from the air)* einen Bombenanschlag verüben auf *(+acc).*
▶**bomb along** *vi (col: drive fast)* dahinrasen *(col).*
**bombard** [bɒm'bɑːd] *vt (Mil, fig)* bombardieren *(with* mit*)*; *(Phys)* beschießen.
**bombardment** [bɒm'bɑːdmənt] *n (Mil)* Bombardierung *f (also fig)*, Bombardement *nt.*
**bombastic** [bɒm'bæstɪk] *adj* bombastisch.
**bomb:** **~ attack** *n* Bombenangriff *m*; **~ disposal expert** *n* Bombenräumexperte *m*; **~ disposal squad** *n* Bombenräumtrupp *m.*
**bomber** ['bɒmər] *n* **(a)** *(aircraft)* Bomber *m*, Bombenflieger *m.* **(b)** *(person) (Aviat)* Bombenschütze *m*; *(terrorist)* Bombenattentäter(in *f*) *m.*
**bomber jacket** *n* Fliegerjacke *f.*
**bombing** ['bɒmɪŋ] *n* Bombenangriff *m (of* auf *+acc).*
**bomb:** **~ scare** *n* Bombenalarm *m*; **~shell** *n* **this news was a ~shell** die Nachricht schlug wie eine Bombe ein; **~ site** *n* Trümmergrundstück *nt.*
**bona fide** ['bəʊnə'faɪdɪ] *adj (genuine)* echt. **it's a ~ offer** es ist ein Angebot auf Treu und Glauben.
**bonanza** [bə'nænzə] *n* **(a)** *(US Min)* reiche Erzader. **(b)** *(fig)* Goldgrube *f.* **the oil ~** der Ölboom.
**bond** [bɒnd] **1** *n* **(a)** *(agreement)* Übereinkommen *nt.* **to enter into a ~ with sb** ein Übereinkommen mit jdm treffen. **(b)** *(fig: link)* Band *nt (geh)*, Bindung *f.* **(c)** **~s** *pl (lit, fig: chains)* Bande *pl (geh).* **(d)** *(Comm, Fin)* Obligation *f*, Pfandbrief *m.* **government ~** Staatsanleihe *f.* **(e)** *(Comm: custody of goods)* Zollverschluß *m.* **goods in ~** Zollgut *nt.* **(f)** *(adhesion between surfaces)* Haftfestigkeit *f.* **2** *vt (Comm) goods* unter Zollverschluß nehmen. **3** *vi (glue)* binden.
**bondage** ['bɒndɪdʒ] *n* **(a)** *(lit)* Sklaverei *f*; *(in Middle Ages)* Leibeigenschaft *f.* **(b)** *(fig liter)* Versklavung *f.*
**bonded** ['bɒndɪd] *adj goods* unter Zollverschluß. **~ warehouse** Zollager *nt.*
**bone** [bəʊn] **1** *n* Knochen *m*; *(of fish)* Gräte *f.* **~s** *pl (of the dead)* Gebeine *pl*; **chilled to the ~** völlig durchgefroren; **to work one's fingers to the ~** sich *(dat)* die Finger abarbeiten; **~ of contention** Zankapfel *m*; **to have a ~ to pick with sb** *(col)* mit jdm ein Hühnchen zu rupfen haben *(col)*; **to make no ~s about saying what he thought** *(col)* er hat kein Blatt vor den Mund genommen; **I can feel it in my ~s** ich spüre es in den Knochen. **2** *vt* die Knochen lösen aus; *fish* entgräten.
**bone china** *n* feines Porzellan.
**bone:** **~-dry** *adj (col)* knochentrocken; **~-idle** *adj*

*(col)* stinkfaul *(col)*; **~ meal** *n* Knochenmehl *nt.*
**boner** ['bəʊnər] *n (US col)* Schnitzer *m.*
**bonfire** ['bɒnfaɪər] *n* Feuer *nt*; *(as beacon)* Leuchtfeuer *nt.* **~ night** 5. November *(Jahrestag m der Pulververschwörung).*
**bonk** [bɒŋk] *vti (col)* bumsen *(col).*
**bonkers** ['bɒŋkəz] *adj (Brit col)* meschugge *(col).*
**Bonn** [bɒn] **1** *n* Bonn *nt.* **2** *adj* Bonner.
**bonnet** ['bɒnɪt] *n* **(a)** *(woman's)* Haube *f*; *(baby's)* Häubchen *nt*; *(esp Scot: man's)* Mütze *f.* **(b)** *(Brit Aut)* Motor- *or* Kühlerhaube *f.*
**bonny** ['bɒnɪ] *adj (esp Scot)* schön; *baby* prächtig.
**bonus** ['bəʊnəs] *n* **(a)** Prämie *f*; *(on output, production also)* Zulage *f*; *(cost-of-living ~)* Zuschlag *m*; *(Christmas ~)* Gratifikation *f.* **(b)** *(Fin: on shares)* Extradividende *f.* **(c)** *(col: sth extra)* Zugabe *f.*
**bony** ['bəʊnɪ] *adj (+er) (of bone)* knöchern; *(like bone)* knochenartig; *person, knee, hips* knochig; *fish* mit viel Gräten; *meat* mit viel Knochen.
**boo** [buː] **1** *interj* buh. **he wouldn't say ~ to a goose** *(col)* er ist ein schüchternes Pflänzchen. **2** *vt actor, play, speaker* auspfeifen, ausbuhen. **to be ~ed off the stage** ausgepfiffen *or* ausgebuht werden. **3** *vi* buhen. **4** *n* Buhruf *m.*
**boob** [buːb] **1** *n* **(a)** *(Brit col: mistake)* Schnitzer *m.* **(b)** *(col: woman's breast)* Brust *f.* **2** *vi (Brit col)* einen Schnitzer machen; *(fail)* Mist bauen *(col).*
**booby:** **~ prize** *n* Trostpreis *m für den schlechtesten Teilnehmer*; **~ trap** **1** *n* **(a)** *(als Schabernack versteckt angebrachte)* Falle *f*; **(b)** *(Mil etc)* versteckte Bombe; **2** *vt* **the suitcase was ~-trapped** in dem Koffer war eine Bombe versteckt.
**book** [bʊk] **1** *n* **(a)** Buch *nt*; *(exercise ~)* Heft *nt.* **to bring sb to ~** jdn zur Rechenschaft ziehen; **he does everything by the ~** er hält sich bei allem strikt an die Vorschriften; **to be in sb's good/bad ~s** bei jdm gut/schlecht angeschrieben sein *(col)*; **to throw the ~ at sb** *(col)* jdn fertigmachen *(col)*; **in my ~** für mich; **he knows every trick in the ~** *(col)* er ist mit allen Wassern gewaschen *(col).* **(b)** *(of tickets)* Heft *nt*; *(thicker)* Block *m*; *(of matches)* Briefchen *nt.* **(c)** *(Comm, Fin)* **~s** *pl* Bücher *pl*; **to keep the ~s of a firm** die Bücher einer Firma führen. **2** *vt* **(a)** bestellen; *seat, room* buchen; *artiste* engagieren. **(b)** *driver* aufschreiben *(col)*; einen Strafzettel verpassen *(+dat) (col)*; *football player* verwarnen. **3** *vi see vt (a)* bestellen; buchen.
▶**book in** **1** *vi (in hotel etc)* sich eintragen. **we ~ed ~ at the Hilton** wir sind im Hilton abgestiegen. **2** *vt sep* **(a)** *(register)* eintragen. **(b)** *(make reservation for)* **to ~ sb ~to a hotel** jdm ein Hotelzimmer reservieren lassen.
▶**book up** **1** *vi* buchen. **2** *vt sep (usu pass)* reservieren lassen. **to be (fully) ~ed ~** (voll) ausgebucht sein.
**bookable** ['bʊkəbl] *adj seats* im Vorverkauf erhältlich.
**book:** **~binder** *n* Buchbinder *m*; **~binding** *n* Buchbinderei *f*; **~case** *n* Bücherregal *nt*; *(with doors)* Bücherschrank *m*; **~ club** *n* Buchgemeinschaft *f*; **~end** *n* Buchstütze *f*; **~ fair** *n* Buchmesse *f.*
**bookie** ['bʊkɪ] *n (col)* Buchmacher *m.*
**booking** ['bʊkɪŋ] *n* **(a)** *(Brit)* Buchung, Reservierung *f*; *(of artiste)* Engagement *nt.* **to make a ~** buchen. **(b)** *(Ftbl)* Verwarnung *f.*
**booking:** **~ clerk** *n* Fahrkartenverkäufer(in *f*) *m*; **~ office** *n (Brit) (Rail)* Fahrkartenschalter *m*; *(Theat)* Theaterkasse *f.*
**bookish** ['bʊkɪʃ] *adj* gelehrt *(pej, hum)*; *language, expression (pej)* trocken.
**book:** **~ jacket** *n* Schutzumschlag *m*; **~-keeper** *n*

Buchhalter(in *f*) *m*; **~-keeping** *n* Buchhaltung *or* -führung *f*.
**booklet** ['buklɪt] *n* Broschüre *f*.
**book:** ~**maker** *n* Buchmacher *m*; ~**mark** *n* Lesezeichen *nt*; ~ **review** *n* Buchbesprechung *f*; ~**seller** *n* Buchhändler(in *f*) *m*; ~**shelf** *n* Bücherbord *or* -regal *nt*; ~**shop** *(Brit)*, ~**store** *(US)* *n* Buchhandlung *f*; ~**stall** *n* Bücherstand *m*; ~**token** *n* Büchergutschein *m*; ~**worm** *n* Bücherwurm *m*.
**Boolean** ['buːlɪən] *adj algebra, logic* boolesch *attr*.
**boom**[1] [buːm] *n (across river etc)* Sperre *f*; *(at factory gate etc)* Schranke *f*; *(Naut)* Baum *m*; *(jib of crane)* Ausleger *m*; *(for microphone)* Galgen *m*.
**boom**[2] **1** *n (of sea, waves, wind)* Brausen *nt*; *(of thunder)* Grollen *nt*; *(of guns)* Donnern *nt*; *(of organ, voice)* Dröhnen *nt*. **2** *vi* (**a**) *(sea, wind)* brausen; *(thunder)* grollen. (**b**) *(also ~ out) (organ, person, voice)* dröhnen; *(guns)* donnern. **3** *interj* bum.
▶**boom out 1** *vi see* **boom**[2] **2** (**b**). **2** *vt sep (person) order* brüllen.
**boom**[3] **1** *vi (trade, sales)* einen Aufschwung nehmen. business is ~ing das Geschäft blüht *or* floriert. **2** *n (of business, fig)* Boom, Aufschwung *m*; *(period of economic growth)* Hochkonjunktur *f*.
**boomerang** ['buːməræŋ] **1** *n (lit, fig)* Bumerang *m*. **2** *vi (fig col: words, actions)* wie ein Bumerang zurückkommen *(on zu)*.
**boom town** *n schnell wachsende, florierende Stadt*.
**boon** [buːn] *n (blessing, advantage)* Segen *m*.
**boor** [buə<sup>r</sup>] *n* Rüpel, Flegel *m*.
**boorish** ['buərɪʃ] *adj* rüpelhaft, flegelhaft.
**boost** [buːst] **1** *n* Auftrieb *m no pl*; *(Elec, Aut)* Verstärkung *f*; *(for rocket)* Zusatzantrieb *m*. to give sb/sth a ~ jdm/einer Sache Auftrieb geben. **2** *vt production, economy* ankurbeln; *electric charge, heart etc* verstärken; *confidence, sb's ego* stärken; *morale* heben.
**booster** ['buːstə<sup>r</sup>] *n* (**a**) *(Elec)* Puffersatz *m*; *(Rad)* Zusatzverstärker *m*; *(TV)* Zusatzgleichrichter *m*; *(for heating)* Gebläse *nt*; *(~ rocket)* Booster *m*. (**b**) *(Med: also ~ shot)* Wiederholungsimpfung *f*.
**boot** [buːt] **1** *n* (**a**) Stiefel *m*. the ~ is on the other foot *(fig)* es ist genau umgekehrt; to give sb the ~ *(fig col)* jdn rausschmeißen *(col);* to get the ~ *(fig col)* rausgeschmissen werden *(col)*. (**b**) *(Brit: of car)* Kofferraum *m*. **2** *vt* (**a**) *(col: kick)* einen (Fuß)tritt geben *(+dat); ball* kicken. (**b**) *(Comp)* laden.
▶**boot out** *vt sep (col: lit, fig)* rausschmeißen *(col)*.
**booth** [buːð] *n* (**a**) *(at fair)* (Markt)bude *f*. (**b**) *(telephone ~)* Zelle *f*; *(polling ~, in language laboratory)* Kabine *f*.
**boot:** ~**lace** *n* Schnürsenkel *m*; ~**leg** *adj whisky etc* schwarz gebrannt; ~**legger** *n (US)* Bootlegger *m*; *(producer also)* Schwarzbrenner *m*; ~ **polish** *n* Schuhcreme *f*.
**booty** ['buːtɪ] *n (lit, fig)* Beute *f*.
**booze** [buːz] *(col)* **1** *n* Alkohol *m*. bring some ~ bring was zu trinken mit. **2** *vi* saufen *(col)*.
**boozer** ['buːzə<sup>r</sup>] *n* (**a**) *(pej col: drinker)* Säufer(in *f*) *(pej col)* *m*. (**b**) *(Brit col: pub)* Kneipe *f* *(col)*.
**booze-up** ['buːzʌp] *n (col)* Saufgelage *nt (col)*.
**border** ['bɔːdə<sup>r</sup>] **1** *n* (**a**) *(edge, side)* Rand *m*. (**b**) *(boundary, frontier)* Grenze *f*. north/south of the ~ *(Brit)* in/nach Schottland/England; ~ **crossing** Grenzübergang *m*; ~ **dispute** Grenzstreitigkeit *f*; ~ **incident** Grenzzwischenfall *m*. (**c**) *(in garden)* Rabatte *f*. (**d**) *(edging: on dress)* Bordüre *f*; *(of carpet)* Einfassung *f*; *(of picture)* Umrahmung *f*. **black** ~ *(on notepaper)* schwarzer Rand, Trauerrand *m*. **2** *vt* (**a**) *road* säumen; *garden etc* begrenzen; *(on all sides)*

umschließen. (**b**) *(land etc)* grenzen an *(+acc)*.
▶**border on** *vi +prep obj (lit, fig)* grenzen an *(+acc)*.
**border:** ~**line 1** *n (lit, fig)* Grenzlinie, Grenze *f*; to be on the ~**line** an der Grenze liegen; **2** *adj* ~**line case** Grenzfall *m*; ~ **town** *n* Grenzstadt *f*.
**bore**[1] [bɔː<sup>r</sup>] **1** *vt hole etc* bohren. **2** *vi* bohren *(for nach)*. **3** *n (hole)* Bohrloch *nt*; *(of tube, pipe)* Durchmesser *m*; *(of shotgun, cannon)* Kaliber *nt*.
**bore**[2] **1** *n* (**a**) *(person)* Langweiler *m*. the office ~ der Langweiler vom Dienst. (**b**) *(thing, profession, situation etc)* to be a ~ langweilig sein. (**c**) *(nuisance)* don't be a ~ nun hab dich doch nicht so!; oh what a ~! das ist aber auch zu dumm! **2** *vt* langweilen. to ~ sb stiff *or* to death *or* to tears jdn zu Tode langweilen; I'm ~d ich langweile mich.
**bore**[3] *pret of* **bear**[2].
**boredom** ['bɔːdəm] *n* Langeweile *f*.
**borehole** ['bɔːhəʊl] *n* Bohrloch *nt*.
**boring** ['bɔːrɪŋ] *adj* langweilig.
**born** [bɔːn] *adj* to be ~ geboren werden; *(fig)* entstehen; *(idea)* geboren werden; I was ~ in 1948 ich bin 1948 geboren; I wasn't ~ yesterday *(col)* ich bin nicht von gestern *(col)*; he is Chicago-~ er ist ein gebürtiger Chicagoer; high-/low-~ von vornehmer/niedriger Geburt; he is a ~ poet/teacher er ist der geborene Dichter/Lehrer; an Englishman ~ and bred ein echter *or* waschechter *(col)* Engländer.
**born-again** ['bɔːnəˌgen] *adj Christian etc* wiedergeboren.
**borne** [bɔːn] *ptp of* **bear**[2].
**borough** ['bʌrə] *n (also municipal ~)* Bezirk *m*.
**borrow** ['bɒrəʊ] *vt* sich *(dat)* leihen *(from von); library book* ausleihen; *word* entlehnen; *(fig) idea* übernehmen *(from von)*. to ~ money from the bank einen Kredit bei der Bank aufnehmen; he is living on ~ed time seine Uhr ist abgelaufen.
**borrower** ['bɒrəʊə<sup>r</sup>] *n (of books)* Entleiher(in *f*) *m*; *(of capital, loan etc)* Kreditnehmer(in *f*) *m*.
**borrowing** ['bɒrəʊɪŋ] *n see vt* Leihen *nt*; Ausleihen *nt*; Entlehnung *f*; Übernahme *f*. ~**s** *pl (Fin)* Anleihen *pl*; **government** ~ staatliche Kreditaufnahme.
**borstal** ['bɔːstl] *n (Brit obs)* Besserungsanstalt *f*.
**Bosnia** ['bɒznɪə] *n* Bosnien *nt*.
**Bosnian** ['bɒznɪən] **1** *adj* bosnisch. **2** *n* Bosnier(in *f*) *m*.
**bosom** ['buzəm] **1** *n (lit, fig: of person)* Busen *m*. in the ~ of the family im Schoß der Familie. **2** *adj attr friend etc* Busen-.
**boss** [bɒs] *n* Chef, Boß *(col)* *m*. industrial/union ~es Industrie-/Gewerkschaftsbosse *pl (col)*; OK, you're the ~ okay, du bestimmst.
▶**boss about** *or* **around** *vt sep (col)* rumkommandieren *(col)*.
**bossy** ['bɒsɪ] *adj (+er)* herrisch. don't you get ~ with me! kommandier mich nicht so rum! *(col)*.
**bosun** ['bəʊsn] *n* Bootsmann *m*.
**botanical** [bə'tænɪkəl] *adj* botanisch, Pflanzen-. ~ **gardens** botanischer Garten.
**botanist** ['bɒtənɪst] *n* Botaniker(in *f*) *m*.
**botany** ['bɒtənɪ] *n* Botanik, Pflanzenkunde *f*.
**botch** [bɒtʃ] *(col)* **1** *vt (also ~ up)* verpfuschen *(col)*. **2** *n* Murks *m (col)*.
**both** [bəʊθ] **1** *adj* beide. ~ (the) boys beide Jungen. **2** *pron* beide; *(two different things)* beides. ~ of them were there, they were ~ there sie waren (alle) beide da; come in ~ of you kommt beide herein. **3** *adv* ~ ... and ... sowohl ... als auch ...; ~ **you and I** wir beide; John and I ~ came John and ich sind beide gekommen; she was ~ laughing and crying sie lachte und weinte zugleich *or* gleichzeitig; is

it black or white? — ~ ist es schwarz oder weiß? — beides.

**bother** ['bɒðəʳ] **1** vt (a) stören; (pester) belästigen; (worry) Sorgen machen (+dat); (back, teeth etc) zu schaffen machen (+dat); (problem, question) beschäftigen. **I'm sorry to ~ you but ...** es tut mir leid, daß ich Sie damit belästigen muß, aber ...; **I shouldn't let it ~ you** machen Sie sich mal keine Sorgen; **don't ~ me!** laß mich in Frieden!; **could I ~ you for a light?** dürfte ich Sie vielleicht um Feuer bitten?; **what's ~ing you?** was haben Sie denn? **(b) I can't be ~ed with doing that** ich habe einfach keine Lust dazu; **do you want to stay or go? — I'm not ~ed** willst du bleiben oder gehen? — das ist mir egal.

**2** vti sich kümmern (about um). **don't ~!** nicht nötig!; (sarcastic) machen Sie sich (dat) keine Mühe!; **she didn't even ~ to ask/check** sie hat nicht einmal gefragt/nachgesehen; **you needn't ~ to come** Sie brauchen wirklich nicht (zu) kommen; **I didn't ~ about lunch** ich habe das Mittagessen ausgelassen.

**3** n (a) (nuisance) Plage f. **it's such a ~** das ist wirklich lästig; **I've forgotten it, what a ~** ich habe es vergessen, wie ärgerlich. **(b)** (trouble etc) Ärger m; (difficulties) Schwierigkeiten pl. **we had a spot** or **bit of ~ with the car** wir hatten Ärger mit dem Auto; **it wasn't any ~** (don't mention it) gern geschehen; (not difficult) das war ganz einfach; **the children were no ~ at all** wir hatten mit den Kindern überhaupt keine Probleme; **to go to a lot of ~ to do sth** sich (dat) mit etw viel Mühe geben.

**4** interj so was Dummes! (col).

**Bothnia** ['bɒθnɪə] n **Gulf of ~** Bottnischer Meerbusen.

**Botswana** [ˌbɒt'swɑːnə] n Botswana nt.

**bottle** ['bɒtl] **1** n Flasche f. **a ~ of wine** eine Flasche Wein; **to take to the ~** zur Flasche greifen. **2** vt in Flaschen abfüllen. **~d in ...** abgefüllt in ...

►**bottle up** vt sep emotion in sich (dat) aufstauen.

**bottled** ['bɒtld] adj wine in Flaschen (abgefüllt); beer Flaschen-; fruit eingemacht; gas in Flaschen.

**bottle:** **~ bank** n Altglascontainer m; **~-feed** vt mit der Flasche ernähren; **~ green** adj flaschengrün; **~neck** n (fig) Engpaß m; **~ opener** n Flaschenöffner m; **~ party** n Bottle-Party f; **~ rack** n Flaschengestell nt.

**bottom** ['bɒtəm] **1** n (a) (of receptacle) Boden m; (of mountain, pillar, spire) Fuß m; (of well, canyon) Grund m; (of page, screen, wall) (unteres) Ende; (of list, league) Ende nt. **at the ~** unten (an/in +dat); **to be (at the) ~ of the class** der/die Letzte in der Klasse sein; **~s up!** hoch die Tassen (col); **at ~** (fig) im Grunde; **the ~ fell out of his world** (col) für ihn brach eine Welt zusammen. **(b)** (underneath, underside) Unterseite f, untere Seite. **(c)** (of sea, lake, river) Grund, Boden m. **(d)** (of person) Hintern (col), Po (col) m; (of trousers etc) Hosenboden m. **(e)** (fig: cause) **to be at the ~ of sth** (person) hinter etw (dat) stecken; (thing) einer Sache zugrunde liegen; **to get to the ~ of sth** einer Sache (dat) auf den Grund kommen. **(f)** (Brit Aut: gear) **in ~** im ersten Gang.

**2** adj attr (lower) untere(r, s); (lowest) unterste(r, s); (Fin) Tiefst-; pupil schlechteste(r, s). **~ half** (of box etc) untere Hälfte; (of list, class) zweite Hälfte.

►**bottom out** vi (reach lowest point) die Talsohle erreichen (at bei).

**bottom:** **~ drawer** n (Brit) **to put sth away in one's ~ drawer** etw für die Aussteuer sparen; **~ gear** n (Brit Aut) erster Gang; **~less** adj (lit) bodenlos; a

**~less pit** (fig) ein Faß ohne Boden; **~ line** n (a) (of accounts etc) Saldo m; **(b)** (fig) Fazit nt; **that's the ~ line** darauf läuft es im Endeffekt hinaus; **~most** adj allerunterste(r, s).

**bough** [baʊ] n Ast m.

**bought** [bɔːt] pret, ptp of **buy**.

**boulder** ['bəʊldəʳ] n Felsblock, Felsbrocken m.

**bounce** [baʊns] **1** vi (a) (ball etc) springen; (Sport: ball) aufspringen. **the child ~d up and down on the bed** das Kind hüpfte auf dem Bett herum. **(b)** (col: cheque) platzen (col). **2** vt aufprallen lassen, prellen (Sport); **he ~d the baby on his knee** er ließ das Kind auf den Knien reiten. **3** n (a) (of ball: rebound) Aufprall m. **(b)** no pl (of ball) Sprungkraft f; (of rubber) Elastizität f; (col: of person) Schwung m (col).

►**bounce back** vi abprallen, zurückprallen; (fig col: person) sich nicht unterkriegen lassen (col).

►**bounce off** vt always separate **to ~ sth ~ sth** etw von etw abprallen lassen; **to ~ an idea ~ sb** eine Idee an jdm testen (col).

**bouncer** ['baʊnsəʳ] n (col) Rausschmeißer m (col).

**bouncing** ['baʊnsɪŋ] adj **~ baby** strammes Baby.

**bouncy** ['baʊnsɪ] adj (+er) (a) ball gut springend; mattress federnd; springs elastisch; ride holpernd. **(b)** (fig col: exuberant) übermütig.

**bound¹** [baʊnd] **1** n usu pl (lit, fig) Grenze f. **to keep within the ~s of propriety** im Rahmen bleiben; **within the ~s of probability** im Bereich des Wahrscheinlichen; **there are no ~s to his ambition** sein Ehrgeiz kennt keine Grenzen; **out of ~s** gesperrt.

**2** vt usu pass country begrenzen.

**bound²** **1** n Sprung, Satz m. **2** vi springen; (rabbit) hoppeln. **the dog came ~ing up** der Hund kam angesprungen.

**bound³** **1** pret, ptp of **bind**. **2** adj (a) (prisoner, book) gebunden. **~ hand and foot** an Händen und Füßen gebunden. **(b)** (sure) **he's ~ to do sth** er kommt bestimmt tun; **he's ~ to be late** er kommt garantiert zu spät; **it's ~ to happen** das muß so kommen. **(c)** (obliged) person verpflichtet; (by contract, word, promise) gebunden. **but I'm ~ to say ...** (col) aber ich muß schon sagen ...

**bound⁴** adj pred **to be ~ for London** (heading for) auf dem Weg nach London sein; **where are you ~ for?** wohin geht die Reise?, wohin wollen Sie?; **we were northward-/California-~** wir waren nach Norden/Kalifornien unterwegs.

**boundary** ['baʊndərɪ] n Grenze f. **~ stone** Grenzstein m.

**boundless** ['baʊndlɪs] adj (lit, fig) grenzenlos.

**bountiful** ['baʊntɪfʊl] adj großzügig; sovereign, god gütig; harvest, gifts (über)reich.

**bounty** ['baʊntɪ] n (a) (generosity) Freigebigkeit f; (of nature) reiche Fülle (geh). **(b)** (reward money) Kopfgeld nt. **~ hunter** Kopfgeldjäger m.

**bouquet** ['bʊkeɪ] n (a) Strauß m, Bukett nt (geh). **(b)** (of wine) Bukett nt, Blume f.

**bourbon** ['bɜːbən] n (also **~ whisky**) Bourbon m.

**bourgeois** ['bʊəʒwɑː] **1** n Bürger(in f) m; (pej) Spießbürger(in f) m. **2** adj bürgerlich; (pej) spießbürgerlich.

**bourgeoisie** [ˌbʊəʒwɑː'ziː] n Bürgertum nt, Bourgeoisie f.

**bout** [baʊt] n (a) (of flu etc) Anfall m; (of negotiations) Runde f. **a ~ of fever** ein Fieberanfall m; **a drinking ~** ein Trinkgelage f. **(b)** (Boxing, Wrestling, Fencing) Kampf m.

**boutique** [buː'tiːk] n Boutique f.

**bow¹** [bəʊ] n (a) (for arrows, Mus) Bogen m. **a ~ and arrow** Pfeil und Bogen pl. **(b)** (of ribbon etc) Schleife f.

**bow²** [baʊ] **1** *n (with head, body)* Verbeugung *f; (by young boy)* Diener *m.* **2** *vi* **(a)** sich verbeugen *(to sb* vor jdm*); (young boy)* einen Diener machen. **to ~ and scrape** katzbuckeln *(pej).* **(b)** *(bend: branches etc)* sich biegen. **(c)** *(fig: defer, submit)* sich beugen *(before* vor +*dat, under* unter +*dat, to* dat*).* **to ~ to the inevitable** sich in das Unvermeidliche fügen. **3** *vt* **to ~ one's head** den Kopf senken; *(in prayer)* sich verneigen.
▶**bow out** *vi (fig)* sich verabschieden.

**bow³** [baʊ] *n (also: ~s)* Bug *m.* **on the port ~** backbord voraus.

**Bow Bells** [ˌbaʊˈbelz] *npl* **he was born within the sound of ~** er ist ein waschechter Cockney *(Londoner).*

**bowel** [ˈbaʊəl] *n usu pl (Anat) (of person)* Eingeweide *nt usu pl; (of animal also)* Innereien *pl.* **a ~ movement** Stuhl(gang) *m;* **the ~s of the earth** das Erdinnere.

**bowl¹** [baʊl] *n* **(a)** Schüssel *f; (smaller, shallow also, finger~)* Schale *f; (for sugar etc)* Schälchen *nt; (for animals, prisoners also)* Napf *m.* **(b)** *(of pipe)* Kopf *m; (of lavatory)* Becken *nt.* **(c)** *(Geog)* Becken *nt.* **(d)** *(US: stadium)* Stadion *nt.*

**bowl²** **1** *n (Sport: ball)* Kugel *f.* **2** *vi (Cricket) (mit gestrecktem Arm)* werfen. **3** *vt* **(a)** *(roll) ball* rollen; *hoop also* treiben. **(b)** *(Cricket) ball* werfen; *batsman* ausschlagen.
▶**bowl over** *vt sep (lit, fig)* umwerfen. **he was ~ed ~ by the news** die Nachricht hat ihn überwältigt *or* umgehauen *(col).*

**bow-legged** [ˌbaʊˈlegɪd] *adj* O-beinig.

**bowler** [ˈbaʊləʳ] *n* **(a)** *(Cricket)* Werfer *m.* **(b)** *(Brit: also ~ hat)* Melone *f.*

**bowling** [ˈbaʊlɪŋ] *n* **(a)** *(Cricket)* Werfen *nt.* **(b)** *(tenpin ~)* Bowling *nt; (skittles)* Kegeln *nt.* **to go ~** bowlen/kegeln gehen.

**bowling:** **~ alley** *n* Kegelbahn *f;* **~ green** *n* Rasenfläche *f* für Bowling.

**bowls** [baʊlz] *n sing* Bowling *nt.*

**bow:** **~ tie** *n* Fliege *f;* **~ window** *n* ≃ Erkerfenster *nt.*

**box¹** [bɒks] **1** *vti (Sport)* boxen. **to ~ sb's ears** jdn ohrfeigen, jdm eine Ohrfeige geben. **2** *n* **a ~ on the ear** eine Ohrfeige.

**box²** *n* **(a)** Kiste *f; (cardboard ~)* Karton *m; (smaller)* Schachtel *f; (snuff~, cigarette ~ etc, biscuit tin)* Dose *f; (chocolates etc)* Schachtel *f; (jewellery ~)* Schatulle *f,* Kasten *m; (collection ~)* (Sammel)büchse *f; (in church)* Opferbüchse *f; (fixed to wall etc)* Opferstock *m.* **(b)** *(two-dimensional)* (umrandetes) Feld *f; (Baseball)* Box *f; (in road junction)* *gelb schraffierter Kreuzungsbereich.* **(c)** *(Theat)* Loge *f; (jury ~)* Geschworenenbank *f; (witness ~)* Zeugenstand *m; (press ~)* Pressekabine *f.* **(d)** *(Tech: housing)* Gehäuse *nt.* **gear ~** Getriebe *nt.* **(e)** *(sentry ~)* Schilderhaus *nt; (signal ~)* Häuschen *nt.* **(f)** *(horse ~)* Box *f.* **(g)** **PO B~** Postfach *nt.* **(h)** *(Brit: phone ~)* Zelle *f.* **(i)** *(Brit col: TV)* Glotze *f (col).*
▶**box in** *vt sep player* in die Zange nehmen; *parked car* einklemmen; *(fig)* einengen.

**boxer** [ˈbɒksəʳ] *n (Sport, dog)* Boxer *m.*

**boxer shorts** *npl (Brit)* Boxer-Shorts *pl.*

**box:** **~ file** *n* Flachordner *m;* **~ hedge** *n* Buchsbaumhecke *f.*

**boxing** [ˈbɒksɪŋ] *n* Boxen *nt.*

**boxing** *in cpds* Box-; **~ Day** *n (Brit)* zweiter Weihnachts(feier)tag; **~ match** *n* Boxkampf *m;* **~ ring** *n* Boxring *m.*

**box:** **~ junction** *n (Brit Mot)* gelb schraffierte Kreuzung *(, in die bei Stau nicht eingefahren werden darf);*

**~ kite** *n* Kastendrachen *m;* **~ number** *n (at post office)* Postfach *nt;* **~ office** *n* Kasse, Theater-/Kinokasse *f;* **~room** *n (Brit)* Abstellraum *m.*

**boy** [bɔɪ] *n* Junge *m; (lift~)* Boy *m.* **~s will be ~s** Jungen sind nun mal so; **a school for ~s** eine Jungenschule; **the old ~** *(boss)* der Alte *(col); (father)* mein *etc* Alter *(col);* **old ~** *(col)* alter Junge *(col);* **oh ~!** *(col)* Junge, Junge! *(col).*

**boycott** [ˈbɔɪkɒt] **1** *n* Boykott *m.* **2** *vt* boykottieren.

**boy:** **~friend** *n* Freund *m;* **~hood** *n* Kindheit *f; (as teenager)* Jugend(zeit) *f.*

**boyish** [ˈbɔɪɪʃ] *adj* jungenhaft; *(of woman) figure, appearance* knabenhaft.

**boy scout** *n* Pfadfinder *m.*

**BR** = **British Rail.**

**bra** [brɑː] *n* = **brassière** BH *m.*

**brace¹** [breɪs] *n, pl* - *(pair: of pheasants etc)* Paar *nt.*

**brace²** **1** *n* **(a)** *(Build)* Strebe *f.* **(b)** *(tool) (wheel ~)* Radschlüssel *m; (to hold bit)* Bohrwinde *f.* **~ and bit** Bohrer *m* (mit Einsatz). **(c)** *(on teeth)* Klammer, Spange *f; (Med)* Stützapparat *m.* **2** *vt* **(a)** (ab)stützen; *(horizontally)* verstreben; *(in vice etc)* verklammern. **3** *vr* **to ~ oneself for sth** sich auf etw *(acc)* gefaßt machen.

**bracelet** [ˈbreɪslɪt] *n* Armband *nt; (bangle)* Armreif *m.* **~s** *(col: handcuffs)* Handschellen *pl.*

**braces** [ˈbreɪsɪz] *npl (Brit)* Hosenträger *pl.*

**bracing** [ˈbreɪsɪŋ] *adj* anregend; *climate* Reiz-.

**bracken** [ˈbrækən] *n* Adlerfarn *m.*

**bracket** [ˈbrækɪt] **1** *n* **(a)** *(angle ~)* Winkelträger *m; (Archit)* Konsole *f.* **(b)** *(Typ)* Klammer *f.* **in ~s** in Klammern. **(c)** *(group)* Gruppe, Klasse *f.* **the lower income ~** die untere Einkommensgruppe. **2** *vt* **(a)** *(put in ~s)* einklammern. **(b)** *(also ~ together)* mit einer Klammer versehen; *(fig: group together)* zusammenfassen.

**brackish** [ˈbrækɪʃ] *adj water* brackig.

**brag** [bræg] *vti* prahlen, angeben *(about, of* mit*).*

**braggart** [ˈbrægət] *n* Prahler, Angeber *m.*

**braid** [breɪd] **1** *n* **(a)** *(of hair)* Zopf *m.* **(b)** *(trimming)* Borte *f; (self-coloured)* Litze *f.* **(c)** *(Mil)* Tressen *pl.* **gold ~** Goldtressen *pl.* **2** *vt (plait) hair, straw etc* flechten.

**braille** [breɪl] *n* Blinden- *or* Brailleschrift *f.*

**brain** [breɪn] **1** *n* **(a)** *(Anat, of machine)* Gehirn *nt.* **he's got cars on the ~** *(col)* er hat nur Autos im Kopf. **(b)** **~s** *pl (Anat)* Gehirn *nt; (Cook)* Hirn *nt.* **(c)** *(mind)* Verstand *m.* **~s** *pl (intelligence)* Intelligenz *f,* Grips *m (col),* Köpfchen *nt (col).* **he didn't have the ~s to warn us** er ist nicht einmal darauf gekommen, uns zu warnen; **he's the ~s of the family** er ist das Genie in der Familie. **2** *vt* **stop it or I'll ~ you!** *(col)* hör auf oder ich knall dir eine! *(col).*

**brain:** **~child** *n (invention)* Erfindung *f;* **~ damage** *n* **to have ~ damage** hirngeschädigt sein; **~-damaged** *adj* hirngeschädigt; **~ dead** *adj* hirntot; *(pej col)* hirnlos; **~ death** *n* Hirntod *m;* **~ drain** *n* Abwanderung *f* von Wissenschaftlern, Brain-Drain *m;* **~less** *adj plan, idea* hirnlos, dumm; *person also* unbedarft; **~storm** *n* **(a)** *(Brit)* to have a **~storm** geistig weggetreten sein *(col);* **(b)** *(US: ~wave)* Geistesblitz *m;* **~ storming** *n* gemeinsame Problembewältigung; **~ storming session** *n* Brainstorming *nt;* **~ teaser** *n* Denksportaufgabe *f;* **~ tumour** *(Brit) or* **tumor** *(US) n* Gehirntumor *m;* **~wash** *vt* einer Gehirnwäsche *(dat)* unterziehen; **to ~wash sb into believing that ...** jdm (ständig) einreden, daß ...; **~washing** *n* Gehirnwäsche *f;* **~wave** *n (fig)* Geistesblitz *m.*

**brainy** [ˈbreɪnɪ] *adj (+er) (col)* gescheit *(col),* intelligent.

**break**

**braise** [breɪz] vt (Cook) schmoren.
**brake** [breɪk] **1** n (Tech) Bremse f. **to put the ~s on**
(lit, fig) bremsen; **to put the ~s on sth** (fig) etw
bremsen. **2** vi bremsen.
**brake** in cpds Brems-; **~ drum** n Bremstrommel f;
**~ fluid** n Bremsflüssigkeit f; **~light** n Bremslicht
nt; **~ lining** n Bremsbelag m; **~ pad** n Brems-
klotz m; **~ pedal** n Bremspedal nt; **~ servo** n
Bremskraftverstärker m; **~ shoe** n Bremsbacke f.
**braking** ['breɪkɪŋ] n Bremsen nt. **~ distance** Bremsweg m.
**bramble** ['bræmbl] n **(a)** (thorny shoot) Dornenzweig
m. **(b)** (blackberry) Brombeere f; (bush) Brombeer-
strauch m.
**bran** [bræn] n Kleie f.
**branch** [brɑːntʃ] **1** n **(a)** (Bot) Zweig m; (growing
straight from trunk) Ast m. **(b)** (of river, pipe, duct)
Arm m; (of road) Abzweigung f; (of family, race,
language) Zweig m; (of railway) Nebenlinie f. **(c)**
(Comm) Filiale, Zweigstelle f; (of company, bank
also) Geschäftsstelle f. **2** vi (divide: river, road etc)
sich gabeln; (in more than two) sich verzweigen.
▶**branch off** vi (road) abzweigen; (driver) abbiegen.
▶**branch out** vi (company) sein Geschäft erweitern
or ausdehnen (into auf +acc). **to ~ ~ on one's own**
sich selbständig machen
**branch:** **~ line** n (Rail) Zweiglinie, Nebenlinie f; **~
manager** n Filialleiter(in f) m; **~ office** n Filiale,
Geschäftsstelle f.
**brand** [brænd] **1** n **(a)** (make) Marke f. **(b)** (mark) (on
cattle) Brandzeichen nt; (on criminal, prisoner, fig)
Brandmal nt. **2** vt **(a)** (Comm) goods mit seinem
Warenzeichen versehen. **~ed goods** Markenware f.
**(b)** cattle, property mit einem Brandzeichen kennzeichnen. **(c)** (stigmatize) person brandmarken.
**branding iron** ['brændɪŋˌaɪən] n Brandeisen nt.
**brandish** ['brændɪʃ] vt schwingen, fuchteln mit (col).
**brand:** **~ leader** n führende Marke; **~ loyalty** n
Markentreue f; **~ name** n Markenname m; **~-
new** adj nagelneu, brandneu (col).
**brandy** ['brændɪ] n Weinbrand m.
**brash** [bræʃ] adj (+er) frech, dreist; (tasteless) colour
grell; style etc aufdringlich.
**brass** [brɑːs] **1** n **(a)** Messing nt. **(b) the ~** (Mus) die
Blechbläser pl. **(c)** (col) **the top ~** die hohen Tiere
(col). **(d)** (col: money) Moos nt (col), Kies m (col). **2**
adj (made of ~) Messing-. **~ plate** Messingschild nt;
**~ section** (Mus) Blechbläser pl; **to get down to ~
tacks** (col) zur Sache kommen.
**brass band** n Blaskapelle f.
**brassière** ['bræsɪər] n (dated, form) Büstenhalter m.
**brat** [bræt] n (pej col) Balg m or nt (col), Gör nt (col).
**bravado** [brə'vɑːdəʊ] n (showy bravery) Wagemut
m; (hiding fear) gespielte Tapferkeit.
**brave** [breɪv] **1** adj (+er) mutig, unerschrocken; (suffering pain) smile tapfer. **be ~!** nur Mut!; (more seriously) sei tapfer! **2** n (Indian) Krieger m. **3** vt die
Stirn bieten (+dat); weather trotzen (+dat); death
tapfer ins Auge sehen (+dat).
▶**brave out** vt sep **you have to ~ it ~** das mußt du
durchstehen.
**bravely** ['breɪvlɪ] adv see adj mutig; tapfer.
**braveness** ['breɪvnɪs], **bravery** ['breɪvərɪ] n see adj
Mut m; Tapferkeit f.
**brawl** [brɔːl] **1** vi sich schlagen. **2** n Schlägerei f.
**brawn** [brɔːn] n **(a)** (Cook) Preßkopf m, Sülze f. **(b)**
Muskeln pl, Muskelkraft f.
**brawny** ['brɔːnɪ] adj (+er) muskulös, kräftig.
**bray** [breɪ] **1** n (of ass) (Esels)schrei m. **2** vi (ass)
schreien; (col: person) wiehern.

**brazen** ['breɪzn] adj (impudent) unverschämt, dreist;
lie schamlos.
▶**brazen out** vt sep **to ~ it ~** durchhalten; (by
lying) sich durchmogeln (col).
**brazier** ['breɪzɪər] n (Kohlen)feuer nt (im Freien);
(container) Kohlenbecken nt.
**brazil** [brə'zɪl] n (also ~ **nut**) Paranuß f.
**Brazil** [brə'zɪl] n Brasilien nt.
**Brazilian** [brə'zɪlɪən] **1** adj brasilianisch. **2** n Brasi-
lianer(in f) m.
**breach** [briːtʃ] **1** n **(a)** (of law) Übertretung f (of
gen), Verstoß m (of gegen). **a ~ of contract** ein Vertragsbruch m; **~ of the peace** (Jur) öffentliche Ruhestörung. **(b)** (in friendship etc) Bruch m. **(c)** (in
wall etc, in security) Lücke f. **to step into the ~** (fig)
in die Bresche springen. **2** vt wall eine Bresche
schlagen (in +acc); defences, security durchbrechen.
**bread** [bred] **1** n **(a)** Brot nt. **a piece of ~ and butter**
ein Butterbrot nt; **it's my ~ and butter** (fig) davon
lebe ich; **he knows which side his ~ is buttered (on)**
er weiß, wo was zu holen ist; **to earn one's daily ~**
(sich dat) sein Brot verdienen. **(b)** (col: money)
Moos nt (col), Kohle f (col). **2** vt panieren.
**bread:** **~bin** n Brotkasten m; **~board** n
Brot(schneide)brett nt; **~box** n (US) Brotkasten
m; **~crumb** n Brotkrume f or -krümel m;
**~crumbs** npl (Cook) Paniermehl nt; **in ~crumbs**
paniert; **~knife** n Brotmesser nt; **~line to be on
the ~line** (fig) nur das Allernotwendigste zum Leben haben; **~ slicer** n Brotmaschine f.
**breadth** [bretθ] n **(a)** Breite f; (of ideas, of theory)
(Band)breite f. **a hundred metres in ~** hundert Meter breit; **his ~ of outlook** (open-mindedness) seine
Aufgeschlossenheit; (variety of interests) seine Vielseitigkeit.
**breadwinner** ['bredwɪnər] n Ernährer m.
**break** [breɪk] (vb: pret **broke**, ptp **broken**) **1** n **(a)**
(in bone, pipe, end of relations etc) Bruch m; (gap)
(in wall, line) Lücke f; (in clouds) Spalt m. **~ in the
circuit** Stromkreisunterbrechung f. **(b)** (pause, rest,
Brit Sch) Pause f. **without a ~** ununterbrochen; **to
take or have a ~** (eine) Pause machen. **(c)** (change)
(in contest etc) Wende f; (holiday, change of activity
etc) Abwechslung f. **it makes a nice ~** das ist mal
etwas anderes; **~ in the weather** Wetterum-
schwung m. **(d)** **at ~ of day** bei Tagesanbruch. **(e)**
(col: escape) Ausbruch m. **they made a ~ for it** sie
versuchten zu entkommen. **(f)** (col: luck, opportunity) **to have a good/bad ~** Glück or Schwein (col)
nt/Pech nt haben; **we had a few lucky ~s** wir haben
ein paarmal Glück or Schwein (col) gehabt; **give
me a ~!** gib mir ein Chance! **(g)** (Snooker) Ballfol-
ge, Serie f.
  **2** vt **(a)** brechen; stick, glass zerbrechen; window
einschlagen; egg aufschlagen; surface, shell durchbrechen. **to ~ a leg** sich (dat) das Bein brechen; **to
~ surface** (submarine) auftauchen. **(b)** rule verletzen; appointment nicht einhalten. **(c)** journey, current, silence etc unterbrechen; monotony, routine
auflockern; holiday abbrechen. **(d)** sound barrier
durchbrechen; record brechen. **(e)** **he couldn't ~
the habit of smoking** er konnte sich das Rauchen
nicht abgewöhnen. **(f)** code entziffern; (Sport) serve
durchbrechen. **to ~ sb** (financially) jdn ruinieren;
(mentally) jdn mürbe machen; (with grief) jdn seelisch brechen; **to ~ the bank** die Bank sprengen.
**(g)** fall dämpfen, abfangen. **(h)** jail, one's bonds
ausbrechen aus. **(i)** news mitteilen. **how can I ~ it
to her?** wie soll ich es ihr bloß beibringen?
  **3** vi **(a)** brechen; (rope) zerreißen; (smash) ka-

puttgehen; *(cup, glass etc)* zerbrechen. **(b)** *(stop working etc: toy, watch)* kaputtgehen. **(c)** *(pause)* (eine) Pause machen. **(d)** *(wave)* sich brechen. **(e)** *(day, dawn)* anbrechen; *(suddenly: storm)* losbrechen. **(f)** *(change: weather, luck)* umschlagen. **(g)** *(disperse: clouds)* aufreißen. **(h)** *(stamina)* gebrochen werden; *(under interrogation etc)* zusammenbrechen. **after 6 months her health broke** nach 6 Monaten war ihre Gesundheit ruiniert. **(i)** *(voice: with emotion)* brechen. **his voice is beginning to ~** *(boy)* er kommt in den Stimmbruch; **his voice has broken** er hat den Stimmbruch schon hinter sich. **(j)** *(story, news, scandal)* bekannt werden. **(k) to ~ even** seine (Un)kosten decken. **(l)** **he's broken with her** er hat mit ihr Schluß gemacht.

▶**break away 1** *vi* **(a)** *(chair leg, handle etc)* abbrechen *(from* von*)*; *(railway coaches, boats)* sich losreißen *(from* von*)*. **(b)** *(dash away)* weglaufen *(from* von*)*; *(prisoner)* sich losreißen *(from* von*)*; *(Ftbl)* sich freispielen. **(c)** *(cut ties)* sich trennen *(from* von*)*. **2** *vt sep* abbrechen *(from* von*)*.

▶**break down 1** *vi* **(a)** *(vehicle)* eine Panne haben; *(machine)* ausfallen. **(b)** *(negotiations, plan)* scheitern; *(communications)* zum Erliegen kommen; *(law and order)* zusammenbrechen; *(marriage)* in die Brüche gehen. **(c)** *(argument, resistance, person: start crying)* zusammenbrechen. **(d)** *(be analysed)* *(expenditure)* sich aufschlüsseln *or* -gliedern; *(theory)* sich aufgliedern (lassen). **2** *vt sep* **(a)** *door* einrennen; *wall* niederreißen; *opposition* brechen; *reserve, shyness* überwinden; *suspicion* zerstreuen. **(b)** *expenditure* aufschlüsseln; *theory, argument* untergliedern; *substance* aufspalten.

▶**break in 1** *vi* **(a)** *(interrupt)* unterbrechen *(on sb/ sth* jdn/etw*)*. **(b)** *(enter illegally)* einbrechen. **2** *vt sep* **(a)** *door* aufbrechen. **(b)** *horse* zureiten; *shoes* einlaufen.

▶**break into** *vi +prep obj* **(a)** *house* einbrechen in *(+acc)*; *safe, car* aufbrechen. **(b)** *(use part of)* *savings, £5 note* anbrechen. **(c)** *(begin suddenly)* to **~ ~ song/a trot** zu singen/traben anfangen.

▶**break off 1** *vi* abbrechen; *(stop also)* aufhören. **we ~ ~ at 5 o'clock** wir hören um 5 Uhr auf. **2** *vt sep* abbrechen; *engagement* lösen. **she's broken it ~** sie hat die Verlobung gelöst.

▶**break out** *vi* **(a)** *(epidemic, fire, war)* ausbrechen. **(b) to ~ ~ in a rash/in(to) spots** einen Ausschlag/ Pickel bekommen; **he broke ~ in a cold sweat** ihm brach der Angstschweiß aus. **(c)** *(escape)* ausbrechen *(from, of* aus*)*.

▶**break through** *vi* durchbrechen.

▶**break up 1** *vi* **(a)** *(road)* aufbrechen; *(ice also)* bersten; *(ship in storm)* zerbersten. **(b)** *(clouds)* sich lichten; *(crowd, group)* auseinanderlaufen; *(meeting, partnership)* sich auflösen; *(marriage, relationship)* in die Brüche gehen; *(friends, partners)* sich trennen. **(c)** *(Brit Sch)* *(school)* aufhören. **when do you ~ ~?** wann fangen bei euch die Ferien an? **2** *vt sep* **(a)** *ground, road* aufbrechen; *ship (in breaker's yard)* abwracken. **(b)** *estate* aufteilen; *room also, paragraph, sentence* unterteilen; *empire, combine* auflösen; *lines, expanse of colour (make more interesting)* auflockern. **(c)** *marriage, home* zerstören; *meeting* auflösen; *crowd (police)* zerstreuen, auseinandertreiben. **~ it ~!** auseinander!

**breakable** ['breɪkəbl] **1** *adj* zerbrechlich. **2** *n* **~s** *pl* zerbrechliche Ware.

**breakage** ['breɪkɪdʒ] *n* Bruch *m*. **to pay for ~s** für zerbrochene Ware bezahlen.

**breakaway** ['breɪkə‚weɪ] **1** *n* **(a)** *(Pol)* Absplitterung *f*; *(of state also)* Loslösung *f*. **(b)** *(Sport)* Aus- or

Durchbruch *m*. **(c)** *(US Sport: false start)* Fehlstart *m*. **2** *adj* **~ group** Splittergruppe *f*.

**break: ~dance** *vi* Breakdance tanzen; **~dancing** *n* Breakdance *m*.

**breakdown** ['breɪkdaʊn] *n* **(a)** *(of machine)* Betriebsschaden *m*; *(of vehicle)* Panne *f*. **(b)** *(of communications, Med)* Zusammenbruch *m*. **(c)** *(of figures, expenditure etc)* Aufschlüsselung *f*; *(of thesis, theory etc)* Auf- *or* Untergliederung *f*. **(d)** *(Chem)* Aufspaltung *f*.

**breakdown: ~ service** *n* *(Brit)* Pannendienst *m*; **~ truck** *or* **van** *n* *(Brit)* Abschleppwagen *m*.

**breaker** ['breɪkər] *n* *(wave)* Brecher *m*.

**break-even (point)** [breɪk'iːvən, (‚pɔɪnt)] *n* Gewinnschwelle *f*.

**breakfast** ['brekfəst] **1** *n* Frühstück *nt*. **to have ~** frühstücken; **for ~** zum Frühstück. **2** *vi* frühstücken.

**breakfast** *in cpds* Frühstücks-; **~ cereal** *n* Getreideflocken *pl*; **~ television** *n* Frühstücksfernsehen *nt*.

**break-in** ['breɪkɪn] *n* Einbruch *m*.

**breaking** ['breɪkɪŋ] *n* **~ and entering** *(Jur)* Einbruch *m*.

**breaking point** *n* **(a)** *(Tech)* Festigkeitsgrenze *f*. **(b)** *(fig)* **she is at ~** sie ist nervlich am Ende.

**break: ~neck** *adj*: **at ~neck speed** mit halsbrecherischer Geschwindigkeit; **~-out** *n* Ausbruch *m*; **~point** *n* *(Tennis)* Breakpunkt *m*; **~through** *n* *(Mil, fig)* Durchbruch *m*; **~-up** *n* **(a)** *(lit) (of ship)* Zerbersten *nt*; *(of ice)* Bersten *nt*; **(b)** *(fig) (of friendship)* Bruch *m*; *(of marriage)* Zerrüttung *f*; *(of political party)* Zersplitterung *f*; *(of partnership, meeting)* Auflösung *f*; **~water** *n* Wellenbrecher *m*.

**breast** [brest] *n* *(lit, fig)* Brust *f*.

**breast: ~ cancer** *n* Brustkrebs *m*; **~fed** *adj* **to be ~fed** gestillt werden; **~feed** *vti* stillen; **~ screening** *n* Mammographie *f*; **~ stroke** *m* Brustschwimmen *nt*; **to do the ~ stroke** brustschwimmen.

**breath** [breθ] *n* **(a)** Atem *m*. **to take a deep ~** einmal tief Luft holen; **bad ~** Mundgeruch *m*; **with one's dying ~** mit dem letzten Atemzug; **out of ~** außer Atem, atemlos; **in the same ~** im selben Atemzug; **to take sb's ~ away** jdm den Atem verschlagen; **to say sth under one's ~** etw vor sich *(acc)* hin murmeln; **to go out for a ~ of (fresh) air** an die frische Luft gehen. **(b)** *(slight stirring)* **~ of wind** Lüftchen *nt*, Hauch *m*.

**breathalyze** ['breθəlaɪz] *vt* *(Brit)* (ins Röhrchen) blasen lassen.

**Breathalyzer** ® ['breθəlaɪzər] *n* *(Brit)* Promillemesser *m*. **to give sb a ~ (test)** jdn ins Röhrchen blasen lassen.

**breathe** [briːð] **1** *vi* atmen; *(col: rest)* verschnaufen, Luft holen. **now we can ~ again** jetzt können wir wieder aufatmen; *(have more space)* jetzt haben wir wieder Luft. **2** *vt air* einatmen. **to ~ one's last** seinen letzten Atemzug tun; **he ~d garlic all over me** ich mußte seinen Knoblauchatem über mich ergehen lassen; **he ~d new life into the firm** er brachte neues Leben in die Firma; **don't ~ a word** sag kein Sterbenswörtchen!

▶**breathe in** *vi*, *vt sep* einatmen.

▶**breathe out** *vi*, *vt sep* ausatmen.

**breather** ['briːðər] *n* *(short rest)* Atempause, Verschnaufpause *f*.

**breathing** ['briːðɪŋ] *n* *(respiration)* Atmung *f*. **~ space** *(fig)* Atempause, Ruhepause *f*.

**breathless** ['breθlɪs] *adj* atemlos; *(with exertion also)* außer Atem. **it left me ~** *(lit, fig)* es verschlug mir den Atem.

**bring**

**breath:** ~**taking** *adj* atemberaubend; ~ **test** *n* Atemalkoholtest *m*.

**bred** [bred] *pret, ptp of* **breed**.

**-bred** *suf* **well/ill-**~ gut/schlecht erzogen.

**breeches** ['brɪtʃɪz] *npl* Kniehose *f*; *(riding* ~*)* Reithose *f*.

**breed** [briːd] *(vb: pret, ptp* **bred***)* **1** *n (lit, fig) (species)* Art, Sorte *f*. **2** *vt* **(a)** *animals, flowers* züchten. **(b)** *(fig: give rise to)* erzeugen. **3** *vi (animals)* Junge haben; *(birds)* brüten.

**breeder** ['briːdəʳ] *n* **(a)** *(person)* Züchter *m*. **(b)** *(Tech: also* ~ **reactor***)* Brutreaktor, Brüter *m*.

**breeding** ['briːdɪŋ] *n* **(a)** *(reproduction)* Fortpflanzung und Aufzucht *f* der Jungen. **(b)** *(rearing)* Zucht *f*. **(c)** *(upbringing, good manners: also* **good** ~*)* gute Erziehung, Kinderstube *f*.

**breeding:** ~ **cattle** *n* Zuchtvieh *nt*; ~ **stallion** *n* Zuchthengst *m*.

**breeze** [briːz] **1** *n* Brise *f*. **2** *vi* **to** ~ **in/out** fröhlich angetrabt kommen/vergnügt abziehen *(of aus)*.

**breeze block** ['briːzblɒk] *n* Ytong ® *m*.

**breezy** ['briːzɪ] *adj (+er)* **(a)** *weather, day* windig; *corner also* luftig. **(b)** *manner* forsch-fröhlich.

**Breton** ['bretən] **1** *adj* bretonisch. **2** *n* **(a)** *(person)* Bretone *m*, Bretonin *f*. **(b)** *(language)* Bretonisch *nt*.

**brevity** ['brevɪtɪ] *n* Kürze *f*.

**brew** [bruː] **1** *n (beer)* Bräu *nt*; *(of tea)* Tee *m*, Gebräu *nt (iro)*; *(of herbs)* Aufguß *m*. **witch's** ~ Zaubertrank *m*. **2** *vt beer* brauen; *tea* aufgießen; *(fig) scheme, plot* ausbrüten. **3** *vi (beer)* gären; *(tea)* ziehen; *(make beer)* brauen. **there's something** ~**ing** da braut sich etwas zusammen.

**brewer** ['bruːəʳ] *n* Brauer *m*. ~**'s yeast** Bierhefe *f*.

**brewery** ['bruːərɪ] *n* Brauerei *f*.

**briar** ['braɪəʳ] *n* **(a)** *(wood)* Bruyère(holz) *nt*; ~ **(pipe)** Bruyère(pfeife) *f*. **(b)** *(rose)* wilde Rose; *(bramble runner)* Ranke *f*; *(thorn bush)* Dornbusch *m*.

**bribe** [braɪb] **1** *n* Bestechung *f*; *(money)* Bestechungsgeld *nt*. **to take a** ~ sich bestechen lassen. **2** *vt* bestechen. **to** ~ **sb to do sth** jdn bestechen, damit er/sie etw tut.

**bribery** ['braɪbərɪ] *n* Bestechung *f*.

**bric-à-brac** ['brɪkəbræk] *n* Nippes *m*.

**brick** [brɪk] *n* **(a)** Ziegel- *or* Backstein *m*. **he came down on me like a ton of** ~**s** *(col)* er hat mich völlig fertiggemacht *(col)*; **to drop a** ~ *(fig col)* ins Fettnäpfchen treten; **to drop sb/sth like a hot** ~ *(col)* jdn/etw wie eine heiße Kartoffel fallenlassen. **(b)** *(toy)* (Bau)klotz *m*. **box of (building)** ~**s** Baukasten *m*.

► **brick in** *or* **up** *vt sep door, window* zumauern.

**brick:** ~**layer** *n* Maurer *m*; ~ **red** *adj* ziegelrot; ~ **wall** *n (fig col)* **I might as well be talking to a** ~ **wall** ich könnte genausogut gegen eine Wand reden; ~**work** *n* Backsteinmauerwerk *nt*; ~**works** *n* Ziegelei *f*.

**bridal** ['braɪdl] *adj* Braut-; *procession, feast* Hochzeits-.

**bride** [braɪd] *n* Braut *f*. **the** ~ **and groom** Braut und Bräutigam, das Hochzeitspaar.

**bridegroom** ['braɪdgruːm] *n* Bräutigam *m*.

**bridesmaid** ['braɪdzmeɪd] *n* Brautjungfer *f*.

**bridge¹** [brɪdʒ] **1** *n* **(a)** *(lit, fig)* Brücke *f*. **(b)** *(Naut)* (Kommando)brücke *f*. **2** *vt river, railway* eine Brücke schlagen *or* bauen über *(+acc)*; *(fig)* überbrücken. **to** ~ **the gap** *(fig)* die Zeit überbrücken; *(between people)* die Kluft überbrücken.

**bridge²** *n (Cards)* Bridge *nt*.

**bridgehead** ['brɪdʒhed] *n* Brückenkopf *m*.

**bridging loan** ['brɪdʒɪŋ,ləʊn] *n (Brit)* Über-

brückungskredit *m*.

**bridle** ['braɪdl] **1** *n (of horse)* Zaum *m*. **2** *vt horse* aufzäumen; *(fig) emotions* im Zaum halten.

**bridlepath** ['braɪdl,pɑːθ] *n* Reitweg *m*.

**brief** [briːf] **1** *adj (+er)* kurz; *(curt also)* manner kurz angebunden. **in** ~ kurz (und gut). **2** *n* **(a)** *(Jur)* Auftrag *m (an einen Anwalt)*; *(document)* Unterlagen *pl* zu dem/einem Fall; *(instructions)* Instruktionen *pl*. **(b)** *(instructions)* Auftrag *m*. **3** *vt (employ) lawyer* beauftragen; *(give instructions to)* instruieren *(on über +acc)*; *(give information)* informieren *(on über +acc)*.

**briefcase** ['briːfkeɪs] *n* (Akten)tasche *f*.

**briefing** ['briːfɪŋ] *n (instructions)* Instruktionen *pl*, Anweisungen *pl*; *(also* ~ **session***)* Einsatzbesprechung *f*.

**briefly** ['briːflɪ] *adv* kurz.

**briefs** [briːfs] *npl* Slip *m*. **a pair of** ~ ein Slip.

**Brig.** = **Brigadier**.

**brigade** [brɪ'geɪd] *n (Mil)* Brigade *f*.

**brigadier (general)** [,brɪgə'dɪə('dʒenərəl)] *n* Brigadegeneral *m*.

**bright** [braɪt] *adj (+er)* **(a)** hell; *colour* leuchtend; *sunshine also, eyes* strahlend; *day, weather* heiter. ~ **red** knallrot; ~ **intervals** *or* **periods** *(Met)* Aufheiterungen *pl*; **the** ~ **lights** *(col)* der Glanz der Großstadt. **(b)** *(cheerful) person, smile* fröhlich, heiter. **I wasn't feeling too** ~ es ging mir nicht besonders gut; ~ **and early** in aller Frühe. **(c)** *(intelligent) person* intelligent; *child* aufgeweckt; *idea* glänzend; *(iro)* intelligent. **(d)** *future, prospects* glänzend. **things aren't looking too** ~ es sieht nicht gerade rosig aus; **we must look on the** ~ **side** wir müssen die Sache von der positiven Seite betrachten.

**brighten (up)** ['braɪtn(ʌp)] **1** *vt (sep)* **(a)** *(make cheerful) spirits, person* aufheitern; *room, atmosphere* aufhellen; *prospects, situation* verbessern. **(b)** *(make bright) colour, hair* aufhellen; *metal* aufpolieren. **2** *vi (weather, sky, face)* sich aufheitern; *(person)* fröhlicher werden; *(eyes)* aufleuchten; *(prospects)* besser werden; *(future)* freundlicher aussehen.

**brightly** ['braɪtlɪ] *adv shine* hell; *smile* fröhlich.

**brightness** ['braɪtnɪs] *n see adj* **(a)** Helligkeit *f*; Leuchten *nt*; Strahlen *nt*; Heiterkeit *f*. **(b)** Fröhlichkeit, Heiterkeit *f*. **(c)** Intelligenz *f*; Aufgewecktheit *f*.

**brill** [brɪl] *adj (Brit col)* toll *(col)*.

**brilliance** ['brɪljəns] *n* **(a)** *(of light)* heller Glanz, Strahlen *nt*. **(b)** *(of idea, achievement)* Großartigkeit *f*; *(of person)* Brillianz *f*. **a man of such** ~ ein Mann von so hervorragender Intelligenz.

**brilliant** ['brɪljənt] *adj* **(a)** *sunshine, light* strahlend; *colour* leuchtend. **(b)** *idea etc* großartig *(also iro)*; *scientist, achievement also* glänzend, brilliant. **she is a** ~ **woman** sie ist eine sehr intelligente Frau.

**brilliantly** ['brɪljəntlɪ] *adv* **(a)** *shine* hell; **(b)** *(very well)* großartig; *perform* brillant; *talented* glänzend; *witty* herrlich.

**brim** [brɪm] **1** *n (of cup)* Rand *m*; *(of hat also)* Krempe *f*. **2** *vi (with confidence, energy)* strotzen *(with vor +dat)*. **her eyes were** ~**ming with tears** ihre Augen standen voll Tränen.

► **brim over** *vi (lit, fig)* überfließen *(with vor +dat)*.

**brimful** ['brɪm'fʊl] *adj (lit)* randvoll; *(fig)* voll *(of, with von)*. **he is** ~ **of energy** er sprüht vor Energie.

**brine** [braɪn] *n* **(a)** *(salt water)* Sole *f*; *(for pickling)* Lake *f*. **(b)** *(sea water)* Salzwasser *nt*.

**bring** [brɪŋ] *pret, ptp* **brought** *vt* **(a)** bringen; *(also:* ~ **with one)** mitbringen. **did you** ~ **your guitar?** haben Sie Ihre Gitarre mitgebracht?; **to** ~ **tears to**

sb's eyes jdm die Tränen in die Augen treiben. **(b) I cannot ~ myself to speak to him** ich kann es nicht über mich bringen, mit ihm zu sprechen.

►**bring about** *vt sep* **(a)** *(cause)* herbeiführen, verursachen. **(b)** *(Naut)* wenden.

►**bring back** *vt sep* **(a)** *(lit)* *person, object, memories* zurückbringen. **(b)** *custom, death penalty* wieder einführen; *government* wiederwählen. **to ~ sb ~ to life** jdn wieder lebendig machen.

►**bring down** *vt sep* **(a)** *(out of air)* *(shoot down)* *bird, plane* herunterholen; *(land)* *plane, kite* herunterbringen. **(b)** *opponent, government* zu Fall bringen; *(by shooting)* *animal* zur Strecke bringen; *person* niederschießen. **(c)** *(reduce)* *temperature, prices* senken; *swelling* zurückgehen lassen.

►**bring forward** *vt sep* **(a)** *(lit)* *person, chair* nach vorne bringen. **(b)** *(fig: present)* *witness* vorführen; *evidence, argument* vorbringen. **(c)** *(advance time of)* *meeting* vorverlegen. **(d)** *(Comm)* *figure* übertragen.

►**bring in** *vt sep* **(a)** *(lit)* *person, object* hereinbringen *(prep obj, -to* in *+acc)*; *harvest* einbringen. **(b)** *(fig: introduce)* *fashion, custom* einführen. **(c)** *(involve, call in)* *police etc* einschalten *(on* bei). **(d)** *(Fin)* *income, money* (ein)bringen *(-to sb* jdm*)*; *(Comm)* *business* bringen. **(e)** *(Jur: jury)* *verdict* fällen.

►**bring off** *vt sep* **(a)** *people from wreck* retten, wegbringen *(prep obj* von*)*. **(b)** *(succeed with)* *plan* zustande *or* zuwege bringen. **he brought it ~!** er hat es geschafft! *(col)*.

►**bring on** *vt sep* **(a)** *(cause)* *illness, quarrel* herbeiführen, verursachen; *attack also* auslösen. **(b)** *(help develop)* *pupil* weiterbringen. **(c)** *(Theat)* *person* auftreten lassen; *thing* auf die Bühne bringen; *(Sport)* *player* einsetzen. **(d)** **you brought it ~ yourself** das hast du dir selbst zuzuschreiben.

►**bring out** *vt sep* *(lit, fig)* herausbringen; *(also ~* ~ **on strike***)* *workers* in den Streik treten lassen. **to ~ ~ the best/worst in sb** das Beste/Schlimmste in jdm zum Vorschein bringen.

►**bring round** *vt sep* **(a)** *(to one's house etc)* vorbeibringen. **(b)** *discussion* bringen *(to* auf *+acc)*. **(c)** *unconscious person* wieder zu Bewußtsein bringen. **(d)** *(convert)* herumkriegen *(col)*. **to ~ sb ~ to one's way of thinking** jdn von seiner Meinung überzeugen.

►**bring to** *vt always separate unconscious person* wieder zu Bewußtsein bringen.

►**bring up** *vt sep* **(a)** *(to a higher place)* heraufbringen. **(b)** *(raise, increase)* *amount* erhöhen *(to* auf *+acc)*; *level, standards* anheben. **to ~ sb ~ to a certain standard** jdn auf ein gewisses Niveau bringen. **(c)** *(rear)* *child, animal* groß- *or* aufziehen; *(educate)* erziehen. **a well brought-~ child** ein gut erzogenes Kind. **(d)** *(vomit up)* brechen. **(e)** *(mention)* *fact, problem* erwähnen.

**bring-and-buy sale** ['brɪŋnənd'baɪ,seɪl] *n (Brit)* Basar *m, wo mitgebrachte Sachen verkauft werden.*

**brink** [brɪŋk] *n (lit, fig)* Rand *m.* **on the ~ of sth/doing sth** *(lit, fig)* am Rande von etw/nahe daran, etw zu tun.

**brinkmanship** ['brɪŋkmənʃɪp] *n (col)* Spiel *nt* mit dem Feuer.

**briny** ['braɪnɪ] **1** *adj* salzhaltig, salzig. **2** *n (col)* See *f.*

**brisk** [brɪsk] *adj (+er)* **(a)** *person, way of speaking* forsch; *walk, pace* flott. **(b)** *(fig)* *trade, betting* lebhaft, rege. **(c)** *wind, weather* frisch.

**briskly** ['brɪsklɪ] *adv* flott.

**bristle** ['brɪsl] **1** *n (of brush, boar etc)* Borste *f; (of beard)* Stoppel *f.* **2** *vi* **(a)** *(animal's hair)* sich sträu-

ben. **(b)** *(fig: person)* zornig werden. **to ~ with anger** vor Wut schnauben. **(c)** *(fig)* **to be bristling with police** von Polizisten wimmeln; **bristling with difficulties** mit Schwierigkeiten gespickt.

**bristly** ['brɪslɪ] *adj (+er)* *animal, hair* borstig; *chin* Stoppel-, stoppelig.

**Brit** [brɪt] *n (col)* Brite *m,* Britin *f.*

**Britain** ['brɪtən] *n* Großbritannien *nt.*

**British** ['brɪtɪʃ] **1** *adj* britisch. **I'm ~** ich bin Brite/Britin; **the ~ Isles** die Britischen Inseln; **~ Rail** die britischen Eisenbahnen. **2** *n* **the ~** *pl* die Briten *pl.*

**Britisher** ['brɪtɪʃər] *n (US)* Brite *m,* Britin *f.*

**Briton** ['brɪtən] *n* Brite *m,* Britin *f.*

**Brittany** ['brɪtənɪ] *n* die Bretagne.

**brittle** ['brɪtl] *adj* spröde, zerbrechlich. **~ bones** schwache Knochen.

**broach** [brəʊtʃ] *vt* **(a)** *barrel* anstechen, anzapfen. **(b)** *subject, topic* anschneiden.

**broad** [brɔːd] *adj (+er)* **(a)** *(wide)* breit. **it's as ~ as it is long** *(fig)* es ist Jacke wie Hose *(col)*. **(b)** *(widely applicable)* *theory* umfassend; *(general)* allgemein. **(c)** *(not detailed)* *idea, outline* grob; *sense* weit. **as a very ~ rule** als Faustregel. **(d)** *(liberal)* *mind, attitude* großzügig, tolerant. **(e)** *hint* deutlich. **(f)** *(strongly marked)* *accent* stark.

**broad bean** *n* dicke Bohne, Saubohne *f.*

**broadcast** ['brɔːdkɑːst] *(vb: pret, ptp ~)* **1** *n (Rad, TV)* Sendung *f; (of match etc)* Übertragung *f.* **2** *vt* **(a)** *(Rad, TV)* senden, ausstrahlen; *football match, event* übertragen. **a ~ appeal** ein Aufruf im Rundfunk/Fernsehen. **(b)** *(fig)* *news, rumour etc* verbreiten. **3** *vi (Rad, TV: station)* senden.

**broadcaster** ['brɔːdkɑːstər] *n (Rad, TV)* *(announcer)* Rundfunk-/Fernsehsprecher(in *f)* *m; (personality)* Rundfunk-/Fernsehpersönlichkeit *f.*

**broadcasting** ['brɔːdkɑːstɪŋ] **1** *n (Rad, TV)* Sendung *f; (of event)* Übertragung *f.* **2** *attr (Rad)* Rundfunk-; *(TV)* Fernseh-. **~ station** *(Rad)* Rundfunkstation *f; (TV)* Fernsehstation *f.*

**broaden (out)** ['brɔːdn(aʊt)] **1** *vt (sep)* *road etc* verbreitern. **to ~ one's mind/one's horizons** *(fig)* seinen Horizont erweitern. **2** *vi* breiter werden, sich verbreitern.

**broad jump** *n (US Sport)* Weitsprung *m.*

**broadly** ['brɔːdlɪ] *adv* **(a)** *(in general terms)* allgemein, in großen Zügen. **~ speaking** ganz allgemein gesprochen. **(b)** *(greatly, widely)* *differ* beträchtlich. **(c)** *grin, smile, laugh* breit.

**broad: ~-minded** *adj* großzügig, tolerant; **~sheet** *n* Flugblatt *nt;* **~-shouldered** *adj* breitschult(e)rig; **~side** *(Naut)* Breitseite *f; (fig also)* Attacke *f;* **to fire a ~side** eine Breitseite abfeuern.

**brocade** [brəʊ'keɪd] *n* Brokat *m.*

**broccoli** ['brɒkəlɪ] *n* Brokkoli *pl.*

**brochure** ['brəʊʃjʊər] *n* Broschüre *f,* Prospekt *m.*

**brogue**[1] [brəʊg] *n (Irish accent)* irischer Akzent.

**brogue**[2] *n (shoe)* Budapester *m.*

**broil** [brɔɪl] *vti (Cook)* grillen.

**broiler** ['brɔɪlər] *n* Brathähnchen *nt.*

**broke** [brəʊk] **1** *pret of* **break. 2** *adj pred (col)* abgebrannt *(col)*, pleite *(col)*.

**broken** ['brəʊkən] **1** *ptp of* **break. 2** *adj* **(a)** kaputt *(col)*; *twig* geknickt; *bone* gebrochen; *rope also* gerissen; *(smashed)* *cup, glass etc also* zerbrochen. **(b)** *heart, spirit, man, promise* gebrochen; *health, marriage* zerrüttet. **from a ~ home** aus zerrütteten Familienverhältnissen. **(c)** *road, surface, ground* uneben; *coastline* zerklüftet. **(d)** *(interrupted)* *journey, line on road* unterbrochen; *line on paper* gestrichelt; *sleep* unruhig. **(e)** *English, German etc* gebrochen.

**broken:** ~**-down** *adj machine, car* kaputt *(col)*; ~**hearted** *adj* untröstlich.
**broker** ['brəʊkər] *n* Makler *m*.
**brokerage** ['brəʊkərɪdʒ] *n (fee)* Maklergebühr *f*; *(trade)* Maklergeschäft *nt*.
**brolly** ['brɒlɪ] *n (Brit col)* (Regen)schirm *m*.
**bromide** ['brəʊmaɪd] *n (Chem)* Bromid *nt*.
**bronchial** ['brɒŋkɪəl] *adj* bronchial. ~ **tubes** Bronchien *pl*.
**bronchitis** [brɒŋ'kaɪtɪs] *n* Bronchitis *f*.
**bronco** ['brɒŋkəʊ] *n (US) wildes oder halbwildes Pferd*.
**bronze** [brɒnz] **1** *n* Bronze *f*. **2** *vi (person)* braun werden. **3** *vt face, skin* bräunen. **4** *adj* Bronze-.
**Bronze Age** *n* Bronzezeit *f*.
**bronzed** [brɒnzd] *adj* (sonnen)gebräunt.
**brooch** [brəʊtʃ] *n* Brosche *f*.
**brood** [bruːd] **1** *n (lit, fig)* Brut *f*. **2** *vi* (a) *(bird)* brüten. (b) *(fig: person)* grübeln.
▶**brood over** or **(up)on** *vi +prep obj* nachgrübeln über *(+acc)*; *(despondently also)* brüten über *(+dat)*.
**broody** ['bruːdɪ] *adj* (a) *hen* brütig. **the hen is** ~ die Henne gluckt; **she is feeling** ~ *(hum col)* sie wünscht sich *(dat)* ein Kind. (b) *person* grüblerisch.
**brook¹** [brʊk] *n* Bach *m*.
**brook²** *vt (liter: tolerate)* dulden.
**broom** [bruːm] *n* Besen *m*. **a new** ~ **sweeps clean** *(Prov)* neue Besen kehren gut *(Prov)*.
**broom:** ~ **cupboard** *n* Besenschrank *m*; ~**stick** *n* Besenstiel *m*.
**Bros** *npl (Comm)* = **Brothers** Gebr.
**broth** [brɒθ] *n* Fleischbrühe *f*; *(thickened soup)* Suppe *f*.
**brothel** ['brɒθl] *n* Bordell *nt*, Puff *m (col)*.
**brother** ['brʌðər] *n* (a) Bruder *m*. **my/his** ~**s and sisters** meine/seine Geschwister; **oh** ~! *(esp US col)* Junge, Junge! *(col)*. (b) *(in trade unions)* Kollege *m*.
**brother:** ~**hood** *n* (a) Brüderlichkeit *f*; (b) *(organization)* Bruderschaft *f*; ~**hood of man** Gemeinschaft *f* der Menschen; ~**-in-law** *n, pl* ~**s-in-law** Schwager *m*.
**brotherly** ['brʌðəlɪ] *adj* brüderlich.
**brought** [brɔːt] *pret, ptp of* **bring**.
**brow** [braʊ] *n* (a) *(eyebrow)* Braue *f*. (b) *(forehead)* Stirn *f*. (c) *(of hill)* (Berg)kuppe *f*.
**browbeat** ['braʊbiːt] *pret* ~, *ptp* ~**en** *vt* unter Druck setzen.
**brown** [braʊn] **1** *adj (+er)* braun. **2** *n* Braun *nt*. **3** *vt (sun) skin, person* bräunen; *(Cook)* (an)bräunen; *meat also* anbraten. **4** *vi* braun werden.
**brown:** ~**ale** *n* Malzbier *nt*; ~ **bear** *n* Braunbär *m*; ~ **bread** *n* Grau- or Mischbrot *nt*; *(from wholemeal)* Vollkornbrot *nt*; *(darker)* Schwarzbrot *nt*.
**browned off** ['braʊnd'ɒf] *adj* **to be** ~ **with sb/sth** *(esp Brit col)* jdn/etw satt haben *(col)*.
**brownie** ['braʊnɪ] *n* (a) *(fairy)* Heinzelmännchen *nt*. (b) B~ Wichtel *f*; B~ **points** Pluspunkte *pl*. (c) *(cake) kleiner Schokoladenkuchen*.
**brownish** ['braʊnɪʃ] *adj* bräunlich.
**brown:** ~**owl** *n* (a) *(Orn)* Waldkauz *m*; (b) B~ **Owl** *(in Brownies)* die Weise Eule; ~ **paper** *n* Packpapier *nt*; ~ **rice** *n* ungeschälter Reis; ~ **sugar** *n* brauner Zucker.
**browse** [braʊz] **1** *vi* **to** ~ **among the books** in den Büchern schmökern; **to** ~ **(around)** sich umsehen. **2** *n* **to have a** ~ **(around)** sich umsehen.
**Bruges** [bruːʒ] *n* Brügge *nt*.
**bruise** [bruːz] **1** *n* blauer Fleck; *(on fruit)* Druckstelle *f*. **2** *vt person* einen blauen Fleck/blaue Flecke(n) schlagen *(+dat)*; *fruit* beschädigen; *(fig) feelings* verletzen. **3** *vi* **he** ~**s easily** er bekommt leicht

blaue Flecken.
**brunch** [brʌntʃ] *n* Brunch *m*.
**brunette** [bruː'net] **1** *n* Brünette *f*. **2** *adj* brünett.
**Brunswick** ['brʌnzwɪk] *n* Braunschweig *nt*.
**brunt** [brʌnt] *n* **to bear the** ~ **of the costs/attack** die Hauptlast der Kosten tragen/die volle Wucht des Angriffs mitbekommen.
**brush** [brʌʃ] **1** *n* (a) Bürste *f*; *(artist's* ~, *paint* ~, *shaving* ~*)* Pinsel *m*; *(with dustpan)* Handbesen *or* -feger *m*. (b) *(action)* **to give sth a** ~ etw bürsten; *jacket, shoes* etw abbürsten. (c) *(light touch)* leichte Berührung. (d) *(Mil: skirmish)* Zusammenstoß *m*. **to have a** ~ **with sb** mit jdm aneinandergeraten. **2** *vt* (a) bürsten; *(with hand)* wischen. **to** ~ **one's teeth/hair** sich *(dat)* die Zähne putzen/das Haar bürsten. (b) *(sweep) dirt* fegen, kehren; *(with hand, cloth)* wischen. (c) *(touch lightly)* streifen.
▶**brush against** *vi +prep obj* streifen.
▶**brush aside** *vt sep obstacle, person* (einfach) zur Seite schieben; *objections* (einfach) abtun.
▶**brush away** *vt sep* abbürsten; *(with hand, cloth)* wegwischen; *insects* verscheuchen.
▶**brush off** *vt sep* (a) *mud, snow* abbürsten; *insect* verscheuchen. (b) *(col: reject) person* abblitzen lassen *(col)*; *suggestion, criticism* zurückweisen.
▶**brush past** *vi* streifen *(prep obj acc)*.
▶**brush up** *vt sep* (a) *crumbs, dirt* auffegen, aufkehren. (b) *(fig: also* ~ ~ **on)** *subject, one's German etc* auffrischen.
**brush:** ~**-off** *n (col)* Abfuhr *f*; **to give sb the** ~**-off** jdn abblitzen lassen *(col)*, jdm einen Korb geben *(col)*; ~ **stroke** *n* Pinselstrich *m*; ~**work** *n (Art)* Pinselführung *f*.
**brusque** [bruːsk] *adj (+er)* brüsk, schroff.
**brusqueness** ['bruːsknɪs] *n* Schroffheit *f*.
**Brussels** ['brʌslz] **1** *n* Brüssel *nt*. **2** *attr* Brüsseler. ~ **sprouts** Rosenkohl *m*.
**brutal** ['bruːtl] *adj* brutal.
**brutality** [bruː'tælɪtɪ] *n* Brutalität *f*.
**brutally** ['bruːtəlɪ] *adv* brutal. ~ **frank** schonungslos offen.
**brute** [bruːt] **1** *n* (a) Tier, Vieh *(pej) nt*. (b) *(person)* brutaler Kerl; *(savage)* Bestie *f*. (c) *(col: thing)* **it's a** ~ **of a thing to lift** es ist verdammt schwer, das hochzuheben *(col)*. **2** *adj attr strength* roh; *passion* tierisch. **by** ~ **force** mit roher Gewalt.
**BSc** = **Bachelor of Science**.
**BSI** = **British Standards Institution** *britischer Normenausschuß*.
**BST** = **British Summer Time** *britische Sommerzeit*.
**Bt** = **baronet**.
**BT** = **British Telecom** *britisches Telekommunikationsunternehmen*.
**btu** = **British thermal unit** *britische Wärmeeinheit*.
**bubble** ['bʌbl] **1** *n* Blase *f*. **to blow** ~**s** Blasen machen. **2** *vi (liquid)* sprudeln; *(wine)* perlen; *(gas)* Blasen bilden.
▶**bubble over** *vi (lit)* überschäumen; *(fig)* übersprudeln *(with vor +dat)*.
**bubble:** ~ **bath** *n* Schaumbad *nt*; ~ **gum** *n* Kaugummi *m or nt*.
**bubbly** ['bʌblɪ] **1** *adj (+er) (lit)* sprudelnd; *(fig col) personality* temperamentvoll, lebendig. **2** *n (col: champagne)* Schampus *m (col)*.
**Bucharest** [,bjuːkə'rest] *n* Bukarest *nt*.
**buck** [bʌk] *n* (a) *(male) (of deer)* Bock *m*; *(of rabbit)* Rammler *m*. (b) *(US col: dollar)* Dollar *m*. **to make a fast** ~ *(also Brit)* schnell Kohle machen *(col)*. (c) **to pass the** ~ den Schwarzen Peter weitergeben; *(responsibility also)* die Verantwortung abschieben.
▶**buck up** *(col)* **1** *vi* (a) *(hurry up)* sich ranhalten

*(col)*, rasch *or* fix machen *(col)*. ~ ~! halt dich ran! *(col)*. **(b)** *(cheer up)* aufleben. ~ ~! Kopf hoch! **2** *vt sep* **(a)** *(make cheerful)* aufmuntern. **(b) to** ~ **one's ideas** ~ sich zusammenreißen *(col)*.

**bucket** ['bʌkɪt] **1** *n* Eimer *m; (of excavator)* Schaufel *f.* **a** ~ **of water** ein Eimer Wasser. **2** *vi (col)* **it's** ~**ing, the rain is** ~**ing (down)** es gießt wie aus Kübeln *(col)*.

**bucket:** ~ **seat** *n* Schalensitz *m;* ~ **shop** *n (travel agent)* Agentur *f* für Billigreisen.

**buckle** ['bʌkl] **1** *n* **(a)** *(on belt, shoe)* Schnalle, Spange *f.* **(b)** *(in metal etc)* Beule *f; (concave also)* Delle *f.* **2** *vt* **(a)** *belt, shoes* zuschnallen. **(b)** *wheel, girder etc* verbiegen; *(dent)* verbeulen. **3** *vi* **(a)** *(belt, shoe)* mit einer Schnalle *or* Spange geschlossen werden, geschnallt werden. **(b)** *(wheel, metal)* sich verbiegen.

▶**buckle down** *vi (col)* sich dranmachen *(to an* +dat*) (col)*.

**Bucks** [bʌks] *(Brit)* = **Buckinghamshire.**

**buck:** ~**skin** *n* Wildleder *nt;* ~**tooth** *m* vorstehender Zahn; ~**wheat** *n* Buchweizen *m.*

**bud** [bʌd] **1** *n* Knospe *f.* **to be in** ~ knospen, Knospen treiben. **2** *vi (plant, flower)* knospen, Knospen treiben; *(tree also)* ausschlagen.

**Budapest** [bjuːdə'pest] *n* Budapest *nt.*

**Buddha** ['budə] *n* Buddha *m.*

**Buddhism** ['budɪzəm] *n* Buddhismus *m.*

**Buddhist** ['budɪst] **1** *n* Buddhist(in *f*) *m.* **2** *adj* buddhistisch.

**budding** ['bʌdɪŋ] *adj* knospend; *(fig)* poet etc angehend.

**buddy** ['bʌdɪ] *n (US col)* Kumpel *m.*

**budge** [bʌdʒ] **1** *vi* **(a)** *(move)* sich rühren, sich bewegen. **(b)** *(fig: give way)* nachgeben, weichen. **I will not** ~ **an inch** ich werde keinen Fingerbreit nachgeben. **2** *vt (move)* (von der Stelle) bewegen. **we can't** ~ **him** *(fig)* er läßt sich durch nichts erweichen.

**budgerigar** ['bʌdʒərɪgɑːr] *n* Wellensittich *m.*

**budget** ['bʌdʒɪt] **1** *n* Etat *m,* Budget *nt; (Parl also)* Haushalt(splan) *m.* ~ **deficit** Haushaltsdefizit *nt;* ~ **speech** Etatrede *f.* **2** *vi* wirtschaften. **3** *vt money, time* verplanen.

▶**budget for** *vi* +prep obj (im Etat) einplanen.

**budgie** ['bʌdʒɪ] *n (col)* = **budgerigar.**

**Buenos Aires** ['bweɪnɒs'aɪrɪz] *n* Buenos Aires *nt.*

**buff** [bʌf] **1** *n* **(a)** *(colour)* Gelbbraun *nt.* **(b)** *(col: movie ~ etc)* Fan *m.* **2** *adj* gelbbraun.

**buffalo** ['bʌfələu] *n, pl* -es, *collective pl* - Büffel *m.*

**buffer** ['bʌfər] *n (lit, fig)* Puffer *m; (Rail: at terminus)* Prellbock *m; (Comp: memory)* Pufferspeicher *m.* **old** ~ *(col)* alter Heini *(col)*.

**buffer state** *n (Pol)* Pufferstaat *m.*

**buffet¹** ['bʌfɪt] **1** *n (blow)* Schlag *m.* **2** *vt* hin und her werfen. ~**ed by the wind** von Windböen geschüttelt.

**buffet²** ['bufeɪ] *n* Büffet *nt; (Brit Rail)* Speisewagen *m; (meal)* Büfettessen *nt; (cold ~)* kaltes Büfett.

**buffet:** ['bufeɪ-] ~ **car** *n (Brit Rail)* Speisewagen *m;* ~ **lunch/supper** *n* Büfettessen *nt.*

**bug** [bʌg] **1** *n* **(a)** *n* Wanze *f; (col: any insect)* Käfer *m.* ~**s** *pl* Ungeziefer *nt.* **(b)** *(bugging device)* Wanze *f.* **(c)** *(col: germ, virus)* Bazillus *f.* **he picked up a** ~ **while on holiday** er hat sich *(dat)* im Urlaub eine Krankheit geholt. **(d)** *(col: obsession)* **she's got the travel** ~ die Reiselust hat sie gepackt. **(e)** *(col: fault)* Fehler *m; (Comp)* Programmfehler *m.* **2** *vt* **(a)** *room, building* Wanzen *pl* einbauen in *(*+acc*) (col)*; *conversation, telephone lines* abhören. **(b)** *(col) (worry)* stören; *(annoy)* nerven *(col),* den Nerv töten *(*+dat*) (col)*. **don't let it** ~ **you** mach dir nichts draus *(col)*.

**bugbear** ['bʌgbɛər] *n* Problem *nt; (drawback)* Nachteil *m.*

**bugger** ['bʌgər] **1** *n (col!)* Scheißkerl *m (col!),* Arschloch *nt (col!); (when not contemptible)* Kerl *(col),* Typ *(col) m; (thing)* Scheißding *nt (col!).* **you lucky** ~! du hast vielleicht ein Schwein! *(col);* **to play silly** ~**s** *(col)* Scheiß machen *(col).* **2** *interj (col!)* Mist! *(col).* ~ **him** dieser Scheißkerl *(col!).*

▶**bugger off** *vi (Brit col!)* abhauen *(col).*

▶**bugger up** *vt sep (Brit col!)* versauen *(col!).*

**buggy** ['bʌgɪ] *n (also* **baby** ~) (Klapp)sportwagen *m.*

**bugle** ['bjuːgl] *n* Signalhorn *nt.*

**build** [bɪld] *(vb: pret, ptp* **built**) **1** *n* Körperbau *m.* **2** *vt* **(a)** bauen. **the house is being built** das Haus ist im Bau. **(b)** *(fig) new nation, relationship etc* aufbauen; *a better future* schaffen. **3** *vi* bauen.

▶**build on 1** *vt sep* anbauen. **2** *vi* **(a)** anbauen. **(b)** +*prep obj* bauen auf *(*+acc*).*

▶**build up 1** *vi* **(a)** entstehen; *(anticyclone, atmosphere also)* sich aufbauen; *(increase)* zunehmen; *(Tech: pressure)* sich erhöhen. **the music** ~**s** ~ **to a huge crescendo** die Musik steigert sich zu einem gewaltigen Crescendo. **(b)** *(traffic)* sich verdichten; *(queue, line of cars)* sich bilden. **2** *vt sep* **(a)** aufbauen *(into* zu*); finances* aufbessern. **to** ~ ~ **a reputation** sich *(dat)* einen Namen machen. **(b)** *(increase) ego, muscles* aufbauen; *production, pressure* steigern, erhöhen; *forces (mass)* zusammenziehen; *health* kräftigen; *sb's confidence* stärken. **to** ~ ~ **sb's hopes** jdm Hoffnung(en) machen. **(c)** *(with houses) area, land* (ganz) bebauen. **(d)** *(publicize) person* aufbauen.

**builder** ['bɪldər] *n (contractor)* Bauunternehmer *m.* ~**'s labourer** Bauarbeiter *m;* ~**'s merchant** Baustoffhändler *m.*

**building** ['bɪldɪŋ] *n* **(a)** Gebäude *nt; (usually big also)* Bau *m.* **(b)** *(act of constructing)* Bau *m,* Bauen *nt.*

**building:** ~ **block** *n (in toy set)* Bauklotz *m; (fig)* Baustein *m;* ~ **contractor** *n* Bauunternehmer *m;* ~ **industry** *n* Bauindustrie *f;* ~ **site** *n* Baustelle *f;* ~ **society** *n (Brit)* Bausparkasse *f;* ~ **trade** *n* Baugewerbe *nt.*

**build-up** ['bɪldʌp] *n* **(a)** *(publicity)* Werbung *f.* **they gave the play a good** ~ sie haben das Stück ganz groß herausgebracht *(col).* **(b)** *(of pressure)* Steigerung *f; (Tech also)* Verdichtung *f.* ~ **of troops** Truppenmassierungen *pl.*

**built** [bɪlt] *pret, ptp of* **build.**

**built:** ~-**in** *adj* **(a)** *cupboard etc* eingebaut, Einbau-; *(fig) safeguard* eingeplant; ~-**in obsolescence** geplanter Verschleiß; **(b)** *(inherent)* instinktiv; ~-**up area** *n* bebautes Gebiet; *(Mot)* geschlossene Ortschaft.

**bulb** [bʌlb] *n* **(a)** Zwiebel *f.* **(b)** *(Elec)* (Glüh)birne *f.* **(c)** *(of thermometer etc)* Kolben *m.*

**bulbous** ['bʌlbəs] *adj nose* Knollen-; *growth etc* knotig, Knoten-.

**Bulgaria** [bʌl'gɛərɪə] *n* Bulgarien *nt.*

**Bulgarian** [bʌl'gɛərɪən] **1** *adj* bulgarisch. **2** *n* **(a)** Bulgare *m,* Bulgarin *f.* **(b)** *(language)* Bulgarisch *nt.*

**bulge** [bʌldʒ] **1** *n (in surface)* Wölbung *f; (irregular)* Unebenheit *f,* Buckel *m (col); (in line)* Bogen *m; (in tyre)* Wulst *m; (in birth rate etc)* Zunahme *f (in* gen*).* **2** *vi* **(a)** *(also* ~ **out)** *(swell)* (an)schwellen; *(metal, sides of box)* sich wölben; *(stick out)* vorstehen. **(b)** *(pocket, sack)* prall gefüllt sein *(with* mit*).*

**bulimia** [bə'lɪmɪə] *n* Bulimie *f,* Kotz- und Freßsucht *f (col).*

**bulging** ['bʌldʒɪŋ] *adj stomach* vorstehend; *pocket, suitcase* prall gefüllt. ~ **eyes** Glotzaugen *pl.*

**bulk** [bʌlk] *n* **(a)** *(size)* Größe *f; (large shape)* (of *thing)* massige Form; *(of person, animal)* massige Gestalt. **(b)** *(main part) (also* **great** ~*)* größter Teil; *(of debt, loan also)* Hauptteil *m*; *(of work, mineral deposits also)* Großteil *m*; *(of people, votes also)* Gros *nt*; *(of property, legacy etc also)* Masse *f*. **(c)** *(Comm)* **in** ~ im großen, en gros; ~ **buying** Mengeneinkauf *m*.

**bulkhead** ['bʌlkhed] *n (Naut)* Schott *nt*; *(Aut)* Spritzwand *f*.

**bulky** ['bʌlkɪ] *adj (+er) object* sperrig; *book* dick; *sweater* unförmig; *person* massig, wuchtig.

**bull** [bʊl] *n* **(a)** Stier *m*; *(for breeding)* Bulle *m*. **to take the** ~ **by the horns** *(fig)* den Stier bei den Hörnern packen; **like a** ~ **in a china shop** *(col)* wie ein Elefant im Porzellanladen *(col)*. **(b)** *(male of elephant, whale etc)* Bulle *m*.

**bulldog** ['bʊldɒg] *n* Bulldogge *f*.

**bulldoze** ['bʊldəʊz] *vt (lit)* mit Bulldozern wegräumen. **to** ~ **sb into doing sth** jdn zwingen, etw zu tun; **she** ~**d her way through the crowd** sie boxte sich durch die Menge.

**bulldozer** ['bʊldəʊzə˚] *n* Planierraupe *f*, Bulldozer *m*.

**bullet** ['bʊlɪt] *n* Kugel *f*. ~**hole** Einschuß(loch *nt*) *m*.

**bulletin** ['bʊlɪtɪn] *n* Bulletin *nt*, amtliche Bekanntmachung; *(TV, Rad) (also* **news** ~*)* Nachrichtensendung *f*. ~ **board** *(US)* Schwarzes Brett.

**bullet:** ~**proof** *adj* kugelsicher; ~ **wound** *n* Schußwunde *or* -verletzung *f*.

**bull:** ~**fight** *n* Stierkampf *m*; ~**fighter** *n* Stierkämpfer *m*; ~**finch** *n* Dompfaff, Gimpel *m*; ~**frog** *n* Ochsenfrosch *m*.

**bullion** ['bʊljən] *n no pl* Gold-/Silberbarren *pl*.

**bull:** ~ **market** *n (St Ex)* Hausse(markt *m*) *f*; ~**necked** *adj* stiernackig.

**bullock** ['bʊlək] *n* Ochse *m*.

**bull:** ~**ring** *n* Stierkampfarena *f*; ~**'s eye** *n* **(a)** *(of target)* Scheibenmittelpunkt *m*, Scheibenzentrum *nt*; *(hit)* Schuß *m* ins Schwarze *or* Zentrum; **(b)** *(window pane)* Butzenscheibe *f*; ~**shit** *n (col!)* Scheiß *m (col)*.

**bully** ['bʊlɪ] **1** *n* Tyrann *m*; *(esp Sch)* Rabauke *m*. **you great big** ~ du Rüpel. **2** *vt* tyrannisieren, schikanieren; *(using violence)* drangsalieren, traktieren. **to** ~ **sb into doing sth** jdn so unter Druck setzen, daß er/sie etw tut.
▶**bully about** *or* **around** *vt sep* herumkommandieren, tyrannisieren.

**bulrush** ['bʊlrʌʃ] *n* Rohrkolben *m*.

**bulwark** ['bʊlwək] *n (lit, fig)* Bollwerk *nt*.

**bum¹** [bʌm] *n (esp Brit col)* Hintern *m (col)*.

**bum²** **1** *(col) n* **(a)** *(good-for-nothing)* Rumtreiber *m (col)*; *(young)* Gammler *m*; *(down-and-out)* Penner *m (col)*. **(b)** *(despicable person)* Saukerl *m (col)*. **2** *adj (bad)* beschissen *(col!)*. ~ **rap** *(US)* falsche Anklage.
▶**bum about** *or* **around** *vi (col)* rumgammeln *(col)*.

**bumble-bee** ['bʌmblbiː] *n* Hummel *f*.

**bumbling** ['bʌmblɪŋ] *adj* schusselig *(col)*.

**bumf** [bʌmf] *n (Brit col)* Papierkram *m (col)*.

**bump** [bʌmp] **1** *n* **(a)** *(blow, noise, jolt)* Bums *m (col)*; *(of sth falling also)* Plumps *m (col)*. **to get a** ~ **on the head** sich *(dat)* den Kopf anschlagen. **(b)** *(on any surface)* Unebenheit *f*; *(on head, knee etc)* Beule *f*; *(on car)* Delle *f*. **2** *vt* stoßen; *car wing etc, one's own car* eine Delle fahren in *(+acc)*; *another car* fahren in *(+acc)*. **to** ~ **one's head** sich *(dat)* den Kopf anstoßen *or* anschlagen *(on, against* an *+dat)*. **3** *vi (move joltingly)* holpern. **4** *adv* **to go** ~ bumsen *(col)*.

▶**bump into** *vi +prep obj* **(a)** stoßen gegen; *(driver, car)* fahren gegen; *another car* fahren in *(+acc)*. **(b)** *(col: meet)* zufällig treffen.
▶**bump off** *vt sep (col)* abmurksen *(col)*.

**bumper** ['bʌmpə˚] **1** *n (of car)* Stoßstange *f*. **2** *adj* ~ **crop** Rekordernte *f*.

**bumper car** *n* Autoskooter *m*.

**bumpkin** ['bʌmpkɪn] *n (also* **country** ~*)* (Bauern)tölpel *m*.

**bumptious** ['bʌmpʃəs] *adj* aufgeblasen.

**bumpy** ['bʌmpɪ] *adj (+er) surface* holp(e)rig; *flight* unruhig.

**bun** [bʌn] *n* **(a)** *(bread)* süßes Brötchen; *(iced* ~ *etc)* süßes Teilchen. **to have a** ~ **in the oven** *(col)* ein Kind kriegen *(col)*. **(b)** *(hair)* Knoten *m*.

**bunch** [bʌntʃ] *n* **(a)** *(of flowers)* Strauß *m*; *(of radishes)* Bund *nt*; *(of bananas)* Büschel *nt*. **a** ~ **of grapes** eine (ganze) Weintraube; ~ **of keys** Schlüsselbund *m*; **to wear one's hair in** ~**es** Rattenschwänze haben. **(b)** *(col: of people)* Grüppchen *nt*, Haufen *m (col)*. **(c)** *(col: a lot)* **thanks a** ~ *(esp iro)* schönen Dank.
▶**bunch together 1** *vt sep* ~**ed** ~ dicht zusammen. **2** *vi (people)* Grüppchen bilden.
▶**bunch up** *vi* **(a)** *(people)* Grüppchen bilden. **(b)** *(material)* sich bauschen.

**bundle** ['bʌndl] **1** *n* Bündel *nt*. **he is a** ~ **of nerves** er ist ein Nervenbündel; **that child is a** ~ **of mischief** das Kind hat nichts als Unfug im Kopf. **2** *vt* **(a)** bündeln. **(b)** *(put, send hastily) things* stopfen; *people* verfrachten, schaffen; *(into vehicle)* packen *(col)*.
▶**bundle off** *vt sep* **he was** ~**d** ~ **to Australia** er wurde nach Australien verfrachtet.
▶**bundle up** *vt sep (tie into bundles)* bündeln.

**bun fight** *n (col)* Festivitäten *pl*.

**bung** [bʌŋ] **1** *n (of cask)* Spund(zapfen) *m*. **2** *vt (Brit col: throw)* schmeißen *(col)*.
▶**bung up** *vt sep (col) pipe* verstopfen. **I'm all** ~**ed** ~ **meine Nase ist verstopft**.

**bungalow** ['bʌŋgələʊ] *n* Bungalow *m*.

**bungee jumping** ['bʌndʒɪ-] *n* Bungee-Springen *nt*.

**bungle** ['bʌŋgl] *vt* verpfuschen.

**bungler** ['bʌŋglə˚] *n* Stümper *m*.

**bungling** ['bʌŋglɪŋ] *adj person* ungeschickt, dusselig *(col)*; *attempt* stümperhaft.

**bunk¹** [bʌŋk] *n:* **to do a** ~ *(col)* türmen *(col)*.

**bunk²** *n (col: nonsense)* Quatsch *m (col)*.

**bunk³** *n (in ship)* Koje *f*; *(in train, dormitory)* Bett *nt*.

**bunk-beds** [bʌŋk'bedz] *npl* Etagenbett *nt*.

**bunker** ['bʌŋkə˚] *n (Naut, Golf, Mil)* Bunker *m*.

**bunkum** ['bʌŋkəm] *n (col)* Quatsch *m (col)*.

**bunny** ['bʌnɪ] *n (also* ~ **rabbit)** *(esp baby talk)* Hase *m*, Häschen *nt*.

**bunting** ['bʌntɪŋ] *n (flags)* bunte Fähnchen *pl*, Wimpel *pl*.

**buoy** [bɔɪ] *n* Boje *f*.
▶**buoy up** *vt sep (lit)* über Wasser halten; *(fig) person* Auftrieb geben *(+dat)*; *hopes* beleben.

**buoyancy** ['bɔɪənsɪ] *n* **(a)** *(of ship, object)* Schwimmfähigkeit *f*. **(b)** *(fig: cheerfulness)* Schwung, Elan *m*.

**buoyant** ['bɔɪənt] *adj* **(a)** *ship, object* schwimmend. **(b)** *(fig) person, mood* heiter; *(energetic) step* federnd. **(c)** *market* rege.

**BUPA** ['buːpə] *n* = **British United Provident Association** *private Krankenversicherung*.

**burble** ['bɜːbl] *vi (stream)* plätschern; *(person)* plappern; *(baby)* gurgeln.

**burden** ['bɜːdn] **1** *n* **(a)** *(lit)* Last *f*. **beast of** ~ Lasttier *nt*. **(b)** *(fig)* Belastung *f (on, to* für*)*. **I don't want to be a** ~ **to you** ich möchte Ihnen nicht zur

Last fallen; **the ~ of proof lies with him** er muß den Beweis dafür erbringen; *(Jur)* er trägt die Beweislast. **2** *vt* belasten.

**bureau** [bjʊə'rəʊ] *n* (a) *(Brit: desk)* Sekretär *m*. (b) *(US: chest of drawers)* Kommode *f*. (c) *(office)* Büro *nt*. (d) *(government department)* Amt *nt*.

**bureaucracy** [bjʊə'rɒkrəsɪ] *n* Bürokratie *f*.

**bureaucrat** ['bjʊərəʊkræt] *n* Bürokrat *m*.

**bureaucratic** [ˌbjʊərəʊ'krætɪk] *adj* bürokratisch.

**burger** ['bɜːgə'] *n (col)* Hamburger *m*.

**burglar** ['bɜːglə'] *n* Einbrecher(in *f*) *m*. **~ alarm** Alarmanlage *f*.

**burglarize** ['bɜːgləraɪz] *vt (US)* einbrechen in *(+acc)*. **he was ~d** bei ihm wurde eingebrochen.

**burglary** ['bɜːglərɪ] *n* Einbruch *m*.

**burgle** ['bɜːgl] *vt* einbrechen in *(+acc)*. **he was ~d** bei ihm wurde eingebrochen.

**Burgundy** ['bɜːgəndɪ] *n* Burgund *nt*; *(wine)* Burgunder *m*.

**burial** ['berɪəl] *n* Beerdigung *f*; *(~ ceremony also)* Begräbnis *nt*; *(in cemetery also)* Beisetzung *f (form)*. **~ ground** Begräbnisstätte *f*; **~ service** Trauerfeier *f*.

**burlesque** [bɜː'lesk] *n* (a) *(parody)* Parodie *f*; *(Theat)* Burleske *f*. (b) *(US Theat)* Varieté *nt*; *(show)* Varietévorstellung *f*.

**burly** ['bɜːlɪ] *adj (+er)* kräftig, stramm.

**Burma** ['bɜːmə] *n* Birma *nt*.

**Burmese** [bɜː'miːz] **1** *adj* birmanisch. **2** *n* Birmane *m*, Birmanin *f*; *(language)* Birmanisch *nt*.

**burn** *(vb: pret, ptp ~ed or ~t)* **1** *n (on skin)* Brandwunde *f*; *(on material)* verbrannte Stelle, Brandfleck *m*. **severe ~s** schwere Verbrennungen *pl*.

**2** *vt* (a) verbrennen; *village, building* niederbrennen. **to ~ oneself** sich verbrennen; **to be ~t to death** *(at stake)* verbrannt werden; *(in accident)* verbrennen; **to ~ a hole in sth** ein Loch in etw *(acc)* brennen; **to ~ one's boats or bridges** *(fig)* alle Brücken hinter sich *(dat)* abbrechen; **to ~ one's fingers** *(lit, fig)* sich *(dat)* die Finger verbrennen; **to ~ the midnight oil** *(fig)* bis tief in die Nacht arbeiten. (b) *meat, toast etc* verbrennen lassen; *(slightly)* anbrennen lassen. (c) *(acid)* ätzen. (d) *(use as fuel: ship etc)* befeuert werden mit; *(use up) petrol, electricity* verbrauchen.

**3** *vi* (a) brennen. (b) *(meat, pastry etc)* verbrennen; *(slightly)* anbrennen. **she ~s easily** sie bekommt leicht einen Sonnenbrand. (c) **to be ~ing to do sth** darauf brennen, etw zu tun; **he was ~ing with anger** er kochte vor Wut. (d) *(Space: rockets)* zünden.

►**burn down 1** *vi* (a) *(house etc)* ab- or niederbrennen. (b) *(fire, candle, wick)* herunterbrennen. **2** *vt sep* ab- or niederbrennen.

►**burn off** *vt sep paint etc* abbrennen.

►**burn out 1** *vi (fire, candle)* ausgehen; *(fuse)* durchbrennen; *(rocket)* den Treibstoff verbraucht haben. **2** *vr* (a) *(candle, lamp)* herunterbrennen; *(fire)* ab- or ausbrennen. (b) *(fig col)* **to ~ oneself ~** sich völlig verausgaben. **3** *vt sep usu pass* **~t ~ lorries/houses** ausgebrannte Lastwagen/Häuser.

►**burn up 1** *vi* (a) *(fire etc)* auflodern. (b) *(rocket etc)* verglühen. **2** *vt sep rubbish* verbrennen; *fuel, energy* verbrauchen; *excess fat also* abbauen.

**burner** ['bɜːnə'] *n (of cooker, lamp)* Brenner *m*.

**burning** ['bɜːnɪŋ] **1** *adj (lit, fig)* brennend. **2** *n* **I can smell ~** es riecht verbrannt.

**burnish** ['bɜːnɪʃ] *vt metal* polieren.

**burnt** [bɜːnt] *adj* verbrannt. **~ offering** *(Rel)* Brandopfer *nt*; *(hum: food)* angebranntes Essen.

**burp** [bɜːp] *(col)* **1** *vi* rülpsen *(col)*; *(baby)* aufstoßen.

**2** *vt baby* aufstoßen lassen. **3** *n* Rülpser *m (col)*.

**burrow** ['bʌrəʊ] **1** *n (of rabbit etc)* Bau *m*. **2** *vti (rabbits, dogs etc)* graben, buddeln *(col)*; *(person: in papers etc)* wühlen.

**bursar** ['bɜːsə'] *n* Schatzmeister *m*.

**bursary** ['bɜːsərɪ] *n* (a) *(grant)* Stipendium *nt*. (b) *(office)* Schatzamt *nt*.

**burst** [bɜːst] *(vb: pret, ptp ~)* **1** *n* (a) *(of shell etc)* Explosion *f*. (b) *(in pipe etc)* Bruch *m*. (c) *(of anger, enthusiasm, activity etc)* Ausbruch, Anfall *m*. **~ of laughter** Lachsalve *f*; **~ of applause** Beifallssturm *m*; **~ of speed** Spurt *m*; *(of cars etc)* Riesenbeschleunigung *f (col)*; **a ~ of automatic gunfire** eine Maschinengewehrsalve.

**2** *vi* (a) platzen. **to ~ open** *(box, door etc)* aufspringen; *(abscess, wound)* aufplatzen. (b) *(be very full)* platzen. **to fill sth to ~ing point** etw bis zum Platzen füllen; **to be ~ing with pride** vor Stolz platzen; **he was ~ing to tell us** *(col)* er brannte darauf, uns das zu sagen; **I'm ~ing** *(col)* ich platze gleich *(col)*. (c) **to ~ into tears/flames** in Tränen ausbrechen/in Flammen aufgehen; **he ~ into song** er fing plötzlich an zu singen; **the ~ into the room** er platzte ins Zimmer; **the sun ~ through the clouds** die Sonne brach durch die Wolken; **to ~ out laughing/crying** in Gelächter/Tränen ausbrechen.

**3** *vt balloon, bubble* zum Platzen bringen, platzen lassen; *boiler, pipe, dyke* sprengen. **the river has ~ its banks** der Fluß ist über die Ufer getreten; **to ~ one's sides with laughter** vor Lachen platzen.

**burton** ['bɜːtn] *n (Brit col)* **to have gone for a ~** im Eimer sein *(col)*; *(be lost)* futsch sein *(col)*.

**bury** ['berɪ] *vt* (a) *person, animal, differences* begraben; *(with ceremony also)* beerdigen; *(hide in earth) treasure, bones* vergraben; *(put in earth) end of post, roots* eingraben. **buried by an avalanche** von einer Lawine verschüttet *or* begraben; **to ~ one's head in the sand** *(fig)* den Kopf in den Sand stecken; **to ~ one's face in one's hands** das Gesicht in den Händen vergraben. (b) *(put, plunge) hands, fingers* vergraben *(in* in *+dat)*; *claws, teeth* schlagen *(in* in *+acc)*; *dagger* stoßen *(in* in *+acc)*. (c) **to ~ oneself in one's books** sich in seinen Büchern vergraben; **buried in thought** in Gedanken versunken.

**bus** [bʌs] **1** *n, pl* **-es** *or (US)* **-ses** (Omni)bus *m*. **by ~** mit dem Bus. **2** *vt (esp US)* mit dem Bus befördern.

**bus-:** **~ company** *n* Verkehrsbetrieb *m*; **~ conductor** *n* Busschaffner *m*; **~ depot** *n* Busdepot *nt*; **~ driver** *n* Busfahrer(in *f*) *m*; **~ fare** *n* Busfahrpreis *m*; **~ garage** *n* Busdepot *nt*.

**bush¹** [bʊʃ] *n* (a) *(shrub)* Busch, Strauch *m*; *(thicket: also ~es)* Gebüsch *nt*. **to beat about the ~** *(fig)* wie die Katze um den heißen Brei herumschleichen. (b) *(in Africa, Australia)* Busch *m*.

**bush²** *n (Tech)* Buchse *f*.

**bushy** ['bʊʃɪ] *adj (+er)* buschig.

**busily** ['bɪzɪlɪ] *adv* eifrig.

**business** ['bɪznɪs] *n* (a) Geschäft *nt*; *(enterprise also)* Betrieb *m*; *(line of ~)* Branche *f*. **to be in the plastics/insurance ~** in der Plastikbranche/im Versicherungsgewerbe sein; **to set up in ~** ein Geschäft gründen; **to go out of ~** zumachen; **to do ~ with sb** Geschäfte *pl* mit jdm machen; **~ is ~** Geschäft ist Geschäft; **he is here/away on ~** er ist geschäftlich hier/unterwegs; **to get down to ~** zur Sache kommen; **now we're in ~** *(fig col)* jetzt kann's losgehen *(col)*; **to mean ~** *(col)* es ernst meinen. (b) *(concern, col: affair)* Sache *f*; *(task, duty also)* Aufgabe *f*. **that's my ~** das ist meine Sache *or* Angelegenheit; **that's none of my/your ~** das geht mich/dich nichts an; **to make it one's ~ to do sth** es sich *(dat)* zur Aufgabe machen, etw zu tun; **you've no** ~ **doing that** du hast kein Recht, das zu tun. **(c) this will do the** ~ *(col: do the job)* das bringt's *(col)*.

**business:** ~ **address** *n* Geschäftsadresse *f*; ~ **card** *n* Visitenkarte *f*; ~ **expenses** *npl* Spesen *pl*; ~ **hours** *npl* Geschäftsstunden *pl*, Geschäftszeit *f*; ~ **letter** *n* Geschäftsbrief *m*.

**businesslike** ['bıznıslaık] *adj (good at doing business)* geschäftstüchtig; *person, manner* geschäftsmäßig; *prose* nüchtern.

**business:** ~ **lunch** *n* Geschäftsessen *nt*; ~**man** *n* Geschäftsmann *m*; ~ **park** *n* Industriegelände *nt*; ~ **school** *n* Wirtschaftshochschule *f*; *(part of university)* Wirtschaftsfakultät *f*; ~ **sense** *n* Geschäftssinn *m*; ~ **studies** *npl* Wirtschaftslehre *f*; ~ **trip** *n* Geschäftsreise *f*; ~**woman** *n* Geschäftsfrau *f*.

**busker** ['bʌskər] *n* Straßenmusikant *m*.

**bus:** ~ **lane** *n (Brit)* Busspur *f*; ~**man** *n*: **a** ~**man's holiday** *(fig)* Fortsetzung *f* der Arbeit im Urlaub; ~ **ride** *n* Busfahrt *f*; ~ **route** *n* Buslinie *f*; ~ **service** *n* Busverbindung *f*; *(network)* Busverbindungen *pl*; ~ **shelter** *n* Wartehäuschen *nt*; ~ **station** *n* Busbahnhof *m*; ~ **stop** *n* Bushaltestelle *f*.

**bust¹** [bʌst] *n* Büste *f*; *(Anat also)* Busen *m*. ~ **measurement** Brustumfang *m*, Oberweite *f*.

**bust²** *(vb: pret, ptp* ~*)* *(col)* **1** *adj* **(a)** *(broken)* kaputt *(col)*. **(b)** *(bankrupt)* pleite *(col)*. **2** *adv (bankrupt)* **to go** ~ pleite gehen *or* machen *(col)*. **3** *vt* kaputtmachen *(col)*; *drugs ring* auffliegen lassen *(col)*.

**bus ticket** *n* Busfahrschein *m*.

**bustle** ['bʌsl] **1** *n* Betrieb *m* *(of* in +*dat)*; *(of fair, streets also)* reges Treiben *(of auf or* in +*dat)*. **2** *vi* **to** ~ **about** geschäftig hin und her eilen.

**bustling** ['bʌslıŋ] *adj person* geschäftig; *place, scene* belebt, voller Leben.

**bust-up** ['bʌstʌp] *n (col)* Krach *m (col)*.

**busway** ['bʌsweı] *n (US)* Busspur *f*.

**busy** ['bızı] **1** *adj (+er)* **(a)** *(occupied) person* beschäftigt. **a very** ~ **man** ein vielbeschäftigter Mann; **are you** ~? haben Sie gerade Zeit?; **I was** ~ **studying when you called** ich war gerade beim Lernen, als Sie kamen; **let's get** ~ an die Arbeit! **(b)** *(active) life, time* bewegt; *place, street, town* belebt; *street (with traffic)* stark befahren. **it's been a** ~ **day/week** heute/diese Woche war viel los. **(c)** *(esp US) telephone line* besetzt. ~ **signal/tone** Besetztzeichen *nt*. **2** *vr* **to** ~ **oneself doing sth** sich damit beschäftigen, etw zu tun; **to** ~ **oneself with sth** sich mit etw beschäftigen.

**busybody** ['bızı'bɒdı] *n* Wichtigtuer *m*. **don't be such a** ~ misch dich nicht überall ein.

**but** [bʌt] **1** *conj* **(a)** aber. **(b) not X** ~ **Y** nicht X, sondern Y. **(c) never a week passes** ~ **she is ill** keine Woche vergeht, ohne daß sie krank ist.

**2** *adv nur.* **she's** ~ **a child** sie ist doch nur *or* doch noch ein Kind; **I cannot (help)** ~ **think that** ... ich kann nicht umhin, zu denken, daß ...; **you can** ~ **try** du kannst es immerhin versuchen.

**3** *prep* **no one** ~ **me could do it** niemand außer mir konnte es tun; **anything** ~ **that!** (alles,) nur das nicht!; **he/it was nothing** ~ **trouble** er/das hat nichts als *or* hat nur Schwierigkeiten gemacht; **the last house** ~ **one/two/three** das vorletzte/ vorvorletzte/drittletzte Haus; **the next street** ~ **one** die übernächste Straße; ~ **for you I would be dead** ohne Sie wäre ich tot, wenn Sie nicht gewesen wären, wäre ich tot.

**4** *n* **no** ~**s about it** kein Aber *nt*.

**butane** ['bju:teın] *n* Butan *nt*.

**butch** [bʊtʃ] *adj (col)* maskulin.

**butcher** ['bʊtʃər] **1** *n* **(a)** Fleischer, Metzger *m*. ~**'s (shop)** *(Brit)* Fleischerei, Metzgerei *f*; **at the** ~**'s** *(Brit)* beim Fleischer *or* Metzger. **(b)** *(fig: murderer)* Schlächter *m*. **2** *vt animals* schlachten; *people* abschlachten.

**butchery** ['bʊtʃərı] *n (slaughter)* Gemetzel *nt*.

**butler** ['bʌtlər] *n* Butler *m*.

**butt¹** [bʌt] *n (for wine)* großes Faß; *(for rainwater)* Tonne *f*.

**butt²** *n (also* ~ **end)** dickes Ende; *(of rifle)* (Gewehr)kolben *m*; *(of cigarette)* Stummel *m*.

**butt³** *n (US col: cigarette)* Kippe *f (col)*.

**butt⁴** *n* **(a)** *(target)* Schießscheibe *f*. **(b)** *usu pl (on shooting range)* Schießstand *m*. **(c)** *(fig: person)* **she's always the** ~ **of his jokes** sie ist immer (die) Zielscheibe seines Spottes.

**butt⁵** **1** *n* (Kopf)stoß *m*. **2** *vt* mit dem Kopf stoßen; *(goat also)* mit den Hörnern stoßen.

►**butt in** *vi* sich einmischen *(on* in +*acc)*.

**butter** ['bʌtər] **1** *n* Butter *f*. **she looks as if** ~ **wouldn't melt in her mouth** sie sieht aus, als ob sie kein Wässerchen trüben könnte. **2** *vt bread etc* mit Butter bestreichen, buttern.

►**butter up** *vt sep (col)* um den Bart gehen (+*dat)* *(col)*.

**butter:** ~ **bean** *n* Mondbohne *f*; ~**cup** *n* Butterblume *f*, Hahnenfuß *m*; ~**dish** *n* Butterdose *f*; ~**fingers** *n sing (col)* Tolpatsch *m (col)*.

**butterfly** ['bʌtəflaı] *n* **(a)** Schmetterling *m*. **I've got/I get butterflies (in my stomach)** mir ist/wird ganz flau im Magen *(col)*. **(b)** *(Swimming)* Schmetterlingsstil *m*.

**butterfly stroke** *n* Schmetterlingsstil *m*.

**butter:** ~ **knife** *n* Buttermesser *m*; ~**milk** *n* Buttermilch *f*.

**buttock** ['bʌtək] *n* (Hinter)backe, Gesäßhälfte *(form) f*. ~**s** *pl* Gesäß *nt*, Hintern *m (col)*.

**button** ['bʌtn] **1** *n* Knopf *m*. **2** *vt garment* zuknöpfen. **3** *vi (garment)* geknöpft werden.

►**button up** *vt sep* zuknöpfen.

**button:** ~**hole 1** *n* **(a)** *(in garment)* Knopfloch *nt*; **(b)** *(flower)* Blume *f* im Knopfloch; **2** *vt (fig)* zu fassen bekommen; *sth (dat)* schnappen *(col)*; ~ **mushroom** *n* junger Champignon.

**buttress** ['bʌtrıs] *n (Archit)* Strebepfeiler *m*; *(fig)* Pfeiler *m*.

**buxom** ['bʌksəm] *adj* drall.

**buy** [baı] *(vb: pret, ptp* **bought)** **1** *vt* **(a)** kaufen; *(Rail) ticket also* lösen. **(b)** *(fig) victory, fame* sich *(dat)* erkaufen; *time* gewinnen. **the victory was dearly bought** der Sieg war teuer erkauft. **(c) to** ~ **sth** *(col) (accept)* etw akzeptieren; *(believe)* jdm etw abnehmen *(col) or* abkaufen *(col)*; **I'll** ~ **that** das ist o.k. *(col)*; *(believe)* ja, das glaube ich. **2** *vi* kaufen. **3** *n (col)* Kauf *m*. **to be a good** ~ ein guter Kauf sein; *(clothes also, food)* preiswert sein.

►**buy back** *vt sep* zurückkaufen.

►**buy forward** *vi (Fin)* auf Termin kaufen.

►**buy in** *vt sep (acquire supply of) goods* einkaufen.

►**buy off** *vt sep (col: bribe)* kaufen *(col)*.

►**buy out** *vt sep shareholders etc* auszahlen; *firm* aufkaufen.

►**buy up** *vt sep* aufkaufen.

**buyer** ['baıər] *n* Käufer *m*; *(agent)* Einkäufer *m*. ~**'s market** Käufermarkt *m*.

**buy-out** ['baıaʊt] *n* Aufkauf *m*.

**buzz** [bʌz] **1** *vi* summen. **my head is** ~**ing** mir schwirrt der Kopf; *(from noise)* mir dröhnt der Kopf; **the town is** ~**ing** in der Stadt ist viel los. **2** *vt* **(a)** *(call) secretary* (mit dem Summer) rufen. **(b)** *(col: telephone)* anrufen. **(c)** *(plane)* plane, building dicht vorbeifliegen an *(+dat)*. **3** *n* **(a)** Summen *nt*. **(b)** *(of conversation)* Stimmengewirr *nt*. **(c)** *(col)* **to give sb a** ~ jdn anrufen; *secretary etc* jdn (mit dem Summer) rufen.

►**buzz off** *vi (Brit col)* abzischen *(col)*.
**buzzard** ['bʌzəd] *n* Bussard *m*.
**buzzer** ['bʌzəʳ] *n* Summer *m*.
**buzz word** *n* Modewort *nt*.
**by** [baɪ] **1** *prep* **(a)** *(close to)* bei, an *(+dat)*; *(with movement)* an *(+acc)*; *(next to)* neben *(+dat)*; *(with movement)* neben *(+acc)*. **a holiday** ~ **the sea** Ferien *pl* an der See; **come and sit** ~ **me** komm, setz dich neben mich.

**(b)** *(via)* über *(+acc)*.

**(c)** *(past)* **to go/rush** *etc* ~ **sb/sth** an jdm/etw vorbeigehen/-eilen *etc*.

**(d)** *(time: during)* ~ **day/night** bei Tag/Nacht.

**(e)** *(time: not later than)* bis. **can you do it** ~ **tomorrow?** kannst du es bis morgen machen?; ~ **tomorrow I'll be in France** morgen werde ich in Frankreich sein; ~ **the time I got there** ... bis ich dorthin kam ...; ~ **that time** *or* ~ **then it will be too late** bis dahin *or* dann ist es schon zu spät; ~ **now** inzwischen.

**(f)** *(indicating amount)* ~ **the metre/kilo/hour** meter-/kilo-/stundenweise; **one** ~ **one** einer nach dem anderen.

**(g)** *(indicating agent, cause)* von, durch. **killed** ~ **a bullet** durch eine *or* von einer Kugel getötet; **a painting** ~ **Picasso** ein Bild von Picasso; **surrounded** ~ umgeben von.

**(h)** *(indicating method, means, manner)* ~ **bus/car** mit dem *or* per Bus/Auto; ~ **land and (**~**) sea** zu Land und zu Wasser; **to pay** ~ **cheque** mit Scheck bezahlen; **made** ~ **hand/machine** handgearbeitet/ maschinell hergestellt; ~ **daylight/moonlight** bei Tag (eslicht)/im Mondschein; **to know sb** ~ **sight** jdn vom Sehen her kennen; **to be known** ~ **the name of** ... unter dem Namen ... bekannt sein; **to lead** ~ **the hand** an der Hand führen; **to grab sb** ~ **the collar** jdn am Kragen packen; **he had a daughter** ~ **his first wife** von seiner ersten Frau hatte er eine Tochter; ~ **myself/himself** *etc* allein; ~ **saving hard he managed to** ... durch eisernes Sparen ge-

lang es ihm, zu ...; ~ **saying that I didn't mean (that)** ... ich habe damit nicht gemeint (, daß) ...

**(i)** *(according to)* nach. **to judge** ~ **appearances** allem Anschein nach; **it's all right** ~ **me** von mir aus gern.

**(j)** *(measuring difference)* um. **broader** ~ **a metre** um einen Meter breiter; **it missed me** ~ **inches** es verfehlte mich um Zentimeter.

**(k)** *(Math, Measure)* **to divide/multiply** ~ dividieren durch/multiplizieren mit; **a room 20 metres** ~ **30** ein Zimmer 20 auf *or* mal 30 Meter.

**(l)** *(points of compass)* **South** ~ **South West** Süd-südwest.

**(m)** *(in oaths)* bei. **I swear** ~ **Almighty God** ich schwöre beim allmächtigen Gott.

**(n)** ~ **the way** übrigens.

**2** *adv* **(a)** *(past)* **to pass/wander/rush** *etc* ~ vorbei- *or* vorüberkommen/-wandern/-eilen *etc*. **(b)** *(in reserve)* **to put** *or* **lay** ~ beiseite legen. **(c)** *(phrases)* ~ **and** ~ irgendwann; *(with past tense)* nach einiger Zeit; ~ **and large** im großen und ganzen.

**bye** [baɪ] *interj (col)* tschüs. ~ **for now!** bis bald!
**bye-bye** ['baɪ'baɪ] **1** *interj (col)* Wiedersehen *(col)*. **2** *n* **to go** ~**s** *(baby-talk)* in die Heia gehen *(baby-talk)*.
**by(e)-election** [baɪɪ'lekʃən] *n* Nachwahl *f*.
**Byelorussia** [bjɛləu'rʌʃə] *n* Weißrußland *nt*.
**bygone** ['baɪgɒn] **1** *adj* längst vergangen. **2** *n* **to let** ~**s be** ~**s** die Vergangenheit ruhen lassen.
**by:** ~**law** *n* *(also* **bye-law)** Verordnung *f*; ~**-line** *n* *(Press)* Zeile mit dem Namen des Autors; ~**pass 1** *n* *(road)* Umgehungsstraße *f*; *(Tech: pipe etc, Med)* Bypass *m*; **2** *vt* town, village umgehen; *(Tech)* fluid, gas umleiten; *(fig)* person übergehen; *intermediate stage also* überspringen; *difficulties* umgehen; ~**pass operation** *n* Bypass-Operation *f*; ~**-product** *n* *(lit, fig)* Nebenprodukt *nt*; ~**-road** *n* Nebenstraße *f*; ~**stander** *n* Zuschauer *m*.
**byte** [baɪt] *n* *(Comp)* Byte *nt*.
**by:** ~**way** *n* Seitenweg *m*; ~**word** *n* Inbegriff *m*; **to be/become a** ~**word for sth** gleichbedeutend mit etw sein/werden.
**Byzantine** [baɪ'zæntaɪn] **1** *adj* byzantinisch. **2** *n* Byzantiner (in *f*) *m*.
**Byzantium** [baɪ'zæntɪəm] *n* Byzanz *nt*.

# C

**C, c** [si:] C, c nt *(also Mus)*; *(Sch: as a mark)* ≈ Drei f, Befriedigend nt; **C for Charlie** C wie Cäsar; **C sharp/flat** *(Mus)* Cis, cis nt/Ces, ces nt.

**C** = **(a) centigrade** C. **(b)** *(Pol)* **Conservative.**

**c** = **(a) cent** c, ct. **(b) circa** ca. **(c) century** Jh.

**CA** = **(a) chartered accountant. (b) Central America. (c)** *(US)* **California.**

**ca.** = **circa** ca.

**c/a** = **current account.**

**CAA** *(Brit)* = **Civil Aviation Authority** Zivilluft-fahrtbehörde f.

**cab** [kæb] n **(a)** *(taxi)* Taxi nt. ~ **driver** Taxifahrer(in f) m. **(b)** *(of lorry etc)* Führerhaus nt.

**cabaret** ['kæbəreɪ] n Varieté nt; *(satire)* Kabarett nt.

**cabbage** ['kæbɪdʒ] n **(a)** Kohl m. **(b)** *(col: person)* to become a ~ *(sick person)* dahinvegetieren.

**cabby** ['kæbɪ] n *(col: taxi driver)* Taxifahrer m.

**cabin** ['kæbɪn] n **(a)** *(hut)* Hütte f. **(b)** *(Naut)* Kabine f. **(c)** *(of lorries, buses etc)* Führerhaus nt. **(d)** *(Aviat)* Passagierraum m.

**cabin-:** ~**boy** n Schiffsjunge m; *(steward)* Kabinen-steward m; ~ **crew** n *(Aviat)* Flugpersonal nt; ~ **cruiser** n Kajütboot nt.

**cabinet** ['kæbɪnɪt] n **(a)** Schränkchen nt; *(for display)* Vitrine f; *(for TV, record-player)* Schrank m; *(loud-speaker ~)* Box f. **(b)** *(Pol)* Kabinett nt.

**cabinet:** ~**maker** n (Möbel)schreiner m; ~ **meet-ing** n Kabinettssitzung f; ~ **minister** n Mitglied nt des Kabinetts.

**cable** ['keɪbl] **1** n **(a)** Tau nt; *(of wire)* Drahtseil nt. **(b)** *(Elec)* Kabel nt. **(c)** *(~gram)* Telegramm nt. **2** vt information telegrafisch durchgeben. **to** ~ **sb** jdm telegrafieren. **3** vi telegrafieren, ein Telegramm schicken.

**cable:** ~**-car** n *(hanging)* Drahtseilbahn f; *(streetcar)* (gezogene) Straßenbahn f; ~ **laying** n Kabelver-legung f; ~ **railway** n (Stand)seilbahn f; ~ **televi-sion** n Kabelfernsehen nt.

**caboodle** [kə'buːdl] n: **the whole** ~ *(col)* der ganze Kram *(col)*.

**caboose** [kə'buːs] n *(US Rail)* Dienstwagen m.

**cache** [kæʃ] n **(a)** geheimes Lager. **(b)** *(Comp: also* ~ **memory)** Cache-Speicher m.

**cachet** ['kæʃeɪ] n Gütesiegel nt. **to have a certain** ~ ein gewisses Ansehen haben.

**cack-handed** ['kæk'hændəd] adj *(Brit col)* tolpatschig *(col)*.

**cackle** ['kækl] **1** n *(of hens)* Gackern nt; *(laughter)* meckerndes Gelächter. **2** vi *(hens)* gackern; *(laugh)* meckernd lachen.

**cacophony** [kæ'kɒfənɪ] n Mißklang m.

**cactus** ['kæktəs] n Kaktus m.

**CAD** = **computer-aided design** CAD nt.

**cad** [kæd] n *(dated)* Schurke m *(dated)*.

**cadaver** [kə'deɪvəʳ] n Kadaver m; *(of humans)* Lei-che f.

**cadaverous** [kə'dævərəs] adj *(corpse-like)* Kadaver-, Leichen-; *(gaunt)* ausgemergelt; *(pale)* leichenblaß.

**caddie** ['kædɪ] n *(golf* ~*)* Caddie, Golfjunge m.

**caddy** ['kædɪ] n **(a)** *(tea* ~*)* Behälter m, Dose f. **(b)** *(US: shopping trolley)* Einkaufswagen m.

**cadence** ['keɪdəns] n *(Mus)* Kadenz f; *(of voice)* Ton-fall m, Melodie f; *(rhythm)* Rhythmus m, Melodie f.

**cadenza** [kə'denzə] n *(Mus)* Kadenz f.

**cadet** [kə'det] n *(Mil etc)* Kadett m.

**cadge** [kædʒ] **1** vt (er)betteln, schnorren *(col) (from sb* bei *or* von jdm*)*. **could I** ~ **a lift?** könnten Sie mich vielleicht mitnehmen? **2** vi schnorren *(col)*.

**cadger** ['kædʒəʳ] n Schnorrer *(col)* m.

**Caesar** ['siːzəʳ] n Cäsar m; *(emperor)* Kaiser m.

**Caesarean, Caesarian** [siːˈzɛərɪən] n, adj ~ **(sec-tion)** *(Med)* Kaiserschnitt m.

**café** ['kæfeɪ] n Café nt.

**cafeteria** [ˌkæfɪˈtɪərɪə] n Cafeteria f.

**caffein(e)** ['kæfiːn] n Koffein nt.

**caftan** ['kæftæn] n Kaftan m.

**cage** [keɪdʒ] **1** n **(a)** Käfig m; *(small bird~)* Bauer nt or m. **(b)** *(of lift)* Aufzug m; *(Min)* Förderkorb m. **2** vt *(also* ~ **up)** in einen Käfig sperren.

**cagey** ['keɪdʒɪ] adj *(col)* vorsichtig; *(evasive)* auswei-chend. **what are you being so** ~ **about?** warum tust du so geheimnisvoll?

**cagily** ['keɪdʒɪlɪ] adv *see* **cagey.**

**caginess** ['keɪdʒɪnɪs] n *(col)* Vorsicht f; *(evasiveness)* ausweichende Art.

**cagoule** [kə'guːl] n Windjacke f.

**cahoots** [kə'huːts] n *(col)*: **to be in** ~ **with sb** mit jdm unter einer Decke stecken.

**cairn** [kɛən] n Steinhügel m.

**Cairo** ['kaɪərəʊ] n Kairo nt.

**cajole** [kə'dʒəʊl] vt gut zureden (+dat), beschwatzen *(col)*. **to** ~ **sb into doing sth** jdn dazu bringen, etw zu tun.

**cake** [keɪk] **1** n **(a)** Kuchen m; *(gateau)* Torte f. **a piece of** ~ *(fig col)* ein Kinderspiel nt, ein Klacks m *(col)*; **to sell like hot** ~**s** weggehen wie warme Sem-meln *(col)*; **you can't have your** ~ **and eat it** *(prov)* man kann nicht beides (gleichzeitig) haben. **(b)** *(of soap)* Stück nt; *(of chocolate)* Tafel f. **2** vt überkru-sten. **my shoes are** ~**d with mud** meine Schuhe sind dreckverkrustet. **3** vi eine Kruste bilden.

**cake:** ~ **mix** n Backmischung f; ~ **mixture** n Ku-chenteig m; ~ **shop** n Konditorei f; ~ **slice** n Tor-tenheber m; ~ **tin** n *(for baking)* Kuchenform f; *(for storage)* Kuchendose f.

**cal.** = **calorie(s)** cal.

**calamine** ['kæləmaɪn] n Galmei m. ~ **lotion** Galmei-lotion f.

**calamity** [kə'læmɪtɪ] n Katastrophe f.

**calcify** ['kælsɪfaɪ] **1** vt Kalk m ablagern auf/in (+dat). **2** vi verkalken.

**calcium** ['kælsɪəm] n Kalzium nt.

**calculate** ['kælkjʊleɪt] **1** vt **(a)** *costs* berechnen. **(b)** *(fig: estimate)* kalkulieren, schätzen. **(c) to be** ~**d to do sth** *(be intended)* auf etw *(acc)* abzielen. **this is** ~**d to drive you mad!** das macht dich doch ver-

rückt! (**d**) *(US col: suppose)* schätzen. **2** *vi (Math)*
rechnen.

▶**calculate on** *vi +prep obj* rechnen mit. **I had ~d
~ finishing by this week** ich hatte damit gerechnet,
noch in dieser Woche fertig zu werden.

**calculated** [ˈkælkjʊleɪtɪd] *adj (deliberate)* berechnet.
**to take a ~ risk** ein kalkuliertes Risiko eingehen.

**calculating** [ˈkælkjʊleɪtɪŋ] *adj* berechnend.

**calculation** [ˌkælkjʊˈleɪʃən] *n* Berechnung *f*; *(critical
estimation)* Schätzung *f*. **to do a quick ~** die Sache
schnell überschlagen.

**calculator** [ˈkælkjʊleɪtər] *n* Rechner *m*.

**calculus** [ˈkælkjʊləs] *n (Math)* Differential- und Inte-
gralrechnung *f*.

**Calcutta** [kælˈkʌtə] *n* Kalkutta *nt*.

**calendar** [ˈkæləndər] *n* (**a**) Kalender *m*. **~ month** Ka-
lendermonat *m*. (**b**) *(schedule)* Terminkalender *m*;
*(of events)* Veranstaltungskalender *m*. **Church ~**
Kirchenkalender *m*.

**calf¹** [kɑːf] *n, pl* **calves** (**a**) Kalb *nt*. **a cow in** *or* **with
~** eine trächtige Kuh. (**b**) *(young elephant, seal etc)*
Elefanten-/Robbenjunge(s) *etc nt*. (**c**) *(leather; also
~ skin)* Kalb(s)leder *nt*.

**calf²** *n, pl* **calves** *(Anat)* Wade *f*.

**caliber** *n (US)* = **calibre**.

**calibrate** [ˈkælɪbreɪt] *vt gun* kalibrieren; *meter, instrument* eichen.

**calibration** [ˌkælɪˈbreɪʃən] *n see vt* Kalibrieren *nt*;
Eichen *nt*; *(mark)* Kalibrierung *f*; Eichung *f*.

**calibre,** *(US)* **caliber** [ˈkælɪbər] *n (lit)* Kaliber *nt*; *(fig
also)* Format *nt*. **a man of his ~** ein Mann seines
Kalibers.

**calico** [ˈkælɪkəʊ] *n* Kattun *m*.

**California** [kælɪˈfɔːnɪə] *n* Kalifornien *nt*.

**Californian** [kælɪˈfɔːnɪən] **1** *adj* kalifornisch. **2** *n* Ka-
lifornier(in *f*) *m*.

**caliper** [ˈkælɪpə] *n* (**a**) *(US)* = **calliper**. (**b**)
*(Tech) (brake)* ~ Bremssattel *m*.

**call** [kɔːl] **1** *n* (**a**) *(shout, cry) (of person, bird etc)* Ruf
*m*; *(of bugle)* Signal *nt*. **to give sb a ~** jdn (herbei)rufen; *(wake sb)* jdn wecken; **within ~** in Rufweite *f*; **a ~ for help** *(lit, fig)* ein Hilferuf *m*.
   (**b**) *(telephone ~)* Anruf *m*. **I'll give you a ~** ich
rufe Sie an; **to take a ~** ein Gespräch entgegennehmen.
   (**c**) *(Aviat, fig: summons)* Aufruf *m*; *(of religion)*
Berufung *f*; *(fig: lure)* Verlockung *f*. **to be on ~** (Be-
reitschafts)dienst haben; **the ~ of duty** der Ruf der
Pflicht.
   (**d**) *(visit)* Besuch *m*. **to make** *or* **pay a ~ on sb** jdn
besuchen; **port of ~** Anlaufhafen *m*; *(fig)* Station *f*;
**to pay a ~** *(euph)* mal verschwinden *(col)*.
   (**e**) *(demand, claim)* Beanspruchung *f*; *(Comm)*
Nachfrage *f (for* nach*)*. **to have many ~s on one's
purse/time** finanziell/zeitlich sehr in Anspruch genommen sein.
   (**f**) **at** *or* **on ~** *(Fin)* auf Abruf.
   (**g**) *(need, occasion)* Grund *m*, Veranlassung *f*.
**there is no ~ for you to worry** es besteht kein
Grund zur Sorge; **there was no ~ for that!** das war
wirklich nicht nötig!
   (**h**) *(Cards)* Ansage *f*.
   **2** *vt* (**a**) *(shout out)* rufen. (**b**) *(name, consider)*
nennen. **to be ~ed** heißen; **what's he ~ed?** wie
heißt er?; **what's this ~ed in German?** wie heißt das
auf deutsch?; **~ it £5** sagen wir £5; **would you ~
German a difficult language?** würden Sie Deutsch
als schwierige Sprache bezeichnen? (**c**) *(summon)
person, doctor* rufen; *meeting* einberufen; *election*
ausschreiben; *strike* ausrufen; *(Jur) witness* aufrufen; *(subpoena)* vorladen; *(waken)* wecken. (**d**)

*(telephone)* anrufen. (**e**) *(Fin) bond* aufrufen; *loan*
abrufen.
   **3** *vi* (**a**) *(shout: person, animal)* rufen. **to ~ for
help** um Hilfe rufen; **to ~ to sb** jdm zurufen. (**b**)
*(visit)* vorbeigehen/-kommen. (**c**) *(Telec)* anrufen.
**who's ~ing, please?** wer spricht bitte?; **London
~ing!** *(Rad)* hier ist London; **thanks for ~ing** vielen
Dank für den Anruf.

▶**call aside** *vt sep person* beiseite rufen.

▶**call at** *vi +prep obj (person)* vorbeigehen bei;
*(Rail)* halten in *(+dat)*; *(Naut)* anlaufen.

▶**call away** *vt sep* weg- *or* abrufen. **I was ~ed ~ on
business** ich wurde geschäftlich abgerufen.

▶**call back 1** *vti sep* zurückrufen. **2** *vi (come back)*
**I'll ~ ~ later** ich komme später noch einmal wieder.

▶**call by** *vi* vorbeikommen.

▶**call for** *vi +prep obj* (**a**) *(send for) person* rufen;
*food, drink* kommen lassen; *(ask for)* verlangen
(nach). (**b**) *(need) courage, endurance* erfordern.
**that ~s ~ a drink/celebration!** darauf müssen wir
einen trinken!/das muß gefeiert werden! (**c**) *(collect) person, goods* abholen. **"to be ~ed ~"** *(goods
sent by rail)* „bahnlagernd"; *(by post)* „postlagernd"; *(in shop)* „wird abgeholt".

▶**call in 1** *vt sep* (**a**) *doctor* zu Rate ziehen. (**b**)
*(withdraw)* aus dem Verkehr ziehen. **2** *vi* vorbeischauen *(at, on* bei*)*.

▶**call off** *vt sep* (**a**) *(cancel)* absagen; *deal* rückgängig machen; *engagement* lösen. (**b**) *dog* zurückrufen.

▶**call on** *vi +prep obj* (**a**) *(visit)* besuchen. (**b**) =
**call upon.**

▶**call out 1** *vi* rufen. **2** *vt sep* (**a**) *names* aufrufen;
*(announce)* ansagen. (**b**) *doctor* rufen; *troops, fire
brigade* alarmieren. (**c**) *(order to strike)* zum Streik
aufrufen.

▶**call out for** *vi +prep obj food, drink* verlangen;
*help* rufen um.

▶**call round** *vi (col)* vorbeikommen.

▶**call up 1** *vt sep* (**a**) *(Mil) reservist* einberufen; *re-
inforcements* mobilisieren. (**b**) *(Telec)* anrufen. (**c**)
*(fig)* (herauf)beschwören; *memories* wachrufen.
**2** *vi (Telec)* anrufen.

▶**call upon** *vi +prep obj* (**a**) *(ask)* **to ~ ~ sb to do
sth** jdn bitten, etw zu tun. (**b**) *(invoke)* **to ~ ~ sb's
generosity** an jds Großzügigkeit *(acc)* appellieren;
**to ~ ~ God** Gott anrufen.

**Callanetics** [kæləˈnetɪks] *n* Callanetics *f*.

**callbox** [ˈkɔːlbɒks] *n (Brit)* Telefonzelle *f*.

**caller** [ˈkɔːlər] *n* (**a**) *(visitor)* Besuch(er) *m*. (**b**)
*(Telec)* Anrufer *m*.

**callgirl** [ˈkɔːlgɜːl] *n* Callgirl *nt*.

**calligraphy** [kəˈlɪgrəfɪ] *n* Kalligraphie, Schön-
schreibkunst *f*.

**call-in** [ˈkɔːlɪn] *n (US)* = **phone-in**.

**calling** [ˈkɔːlɪŋ] *n* Berufung *f*.

**calling card** *n (US)* Visitenkarte *f*.

**calliper,** *(US)* **caliper** [ˈkælɪpə] *n* (**a**) *esp pl* Tastzir-
kel *m*. (**b**) *(Med)* Beinschiene *f*.

**callous** [ˈkæləs] *adj (cruel)* gefühllos.

**callousness** [ˈkæləsnɪs] *n* Gefühllosigkeit *f*.

**callow** [ˈkæləʊ] *adj* unreif.

**call-up** [ˈkɔːlʌp] *n* Einberufung *f*.

**calm** [kɑːm] **1** *adj (+er)* ruhig; *weather* windstill.
**keep ~!** bleib ruhig! **2** *n* Ruhe *f*; *(at sea)* Flaute *f*;
*(of wind)* Windstille *f*. **the ~ before the storm** *(lit, fig)*
die Ruhe vor dem Sturm. **3** *vt* beruhigen.

▶**calm down 1** *vt sep* beruhigen. **2** *vi* sich beruhigen; *(wind)* abflauen.

**calmly** [ˈkɑːmlɪ] *adv speak, act* ruhig, gelassen.

**Calor gas** ® [ˈkæləˈgæs] *n* Butangas *nt*.

**calorie** ['kælərɪ] n Kalorie f.

**calorific** [,kælə'rɪfɪk] adj wärmeerzeugend. ~ **value** Heizwert m.

**calumny** ['kæləmnɪ] n Verunglimpfung f.

**calve** [kɑːv] vi kalben.

**calves** [kɑːvz] pl of **calf**[1], **calf**[2].

**CAM** = computer-aided manufacturing CAM f.

**cam** [kæm] n Nocken m.

**camber** ['kæmbə'] n Wölbung f.

**Cambodia** [kæm'bəʊdɪə] n Kambodscha nt.

**Cambodian** [kæm'bəʊdɪən] **1** adj kambodschanisch. **2** n (**a**) Kambodschaner(in f) m. (**b**) (language) Kambodschanisch nt.

**Cambs** = **Cambridgeshire**.

**camcorder** ['kæmkɔːdə'] n Camcorder m.

**came** [keɪm] pret of **come**.

**camel** ['kæməl] n Kamel nt.

**camel** in cpds (colour) kamelhaarfarben.

**camellia** [kə'miːlɪə] n Kamelie f.

**cameo** ['kæmɪəʊ] n (**a**) (jewellery) Kamee f. (**b**) ~ **part** Miniaturrolle f.

**camera**[1] ['kæmərə] n Kamera f; (for stills also) Fotoapparat m.

**camera**[2] n (Jur): **in** ~ unter Ausschluß der Öffentlichkeit; (fig) hinter verschlossenen Türen.

**camera:** ~**man** n, pl -**men** Kameramann m; ~-**ready (copy)** n Druckvorlage f.

**Cameroons** [,kæmə'ruːnz] npl the ~ Kamerun nt.

**camomile** ['kæməʊmaɪl] m Kamille f. ~ **tea** Kamillentee f.

**camouflage** ['kæməflɑːʒ] **1** n (Mil, fig) Tarnung f. **2** vt (Mil, fig) tarnen.

**camp**[1] [kæmp] **1** n (lit, fig) Lager nt. **to pitch** ~ ein Lager aufschlagen; **to strike** or **break** ~ das Lager abbrechen. **2** vi zelten, campen; (Mil) lagern. **to go** ~**ing** zelten or campen (gehen).
►**camp out** vi zelten.

**camp**[2] adj (theatrical, stagey) übertrieben; person's appearance aufgedonnert; (homosexual) schwul (col).

**campaign** [kæm'peɪn] **1** n (**a**) (Mil) Feldzug m. (**b**) (fig) Kampagne f. **2** vi (**a**) (Mil) einen Feldzug unternehmen. (**b**) (fig) (for für, against gegen) sich einsetzen; (politician, candidate) den Wahlkampf führen.

**campaigner** [kæm'peɪnə'] n (**a**) (Mil) Krieger m. **old** ~ Kriegsveteran m; (fig) alter Hase (col). (**b**) (fig) Befürworter(in f) m (for gen); Gegner(in f) m (against gen); (Pol) Wahlwerber(in f) m.

**camp bed** n (Brit) Campingliege f.

**camper** ['kæmpə'] n Camper(in f) m (col); (vehicle) Wohnmobil nt.

**camp:** ~**fire** n Lagerfeuer nt; ~ **follower** n Marketender(in f) m; ~ **followers** (fig) Mitläufer pl.

**camphor** ['kæmfə'] n Kampfer m.

**camping** ['kæmpɪŋ] n Zelten, Camping nt.

**camping** in cpds Camping-; ~ **ground** (US), ~ **site** n (also **camp site**) Campingplatz m.

**campus** ['kæmpəs] n Campus m, Universitätsgelände nt.

**camshaft** ['kæmʃɑːft] n Nockenwelle f.

**can**[1] [kæn] pret **could** modal aux können; (may also) dürfen. ~ **you speak German?** können or sprechen Sie Deutsch?; ~ **I come too?** kann ich mitkommen?; ~ **you hear me?** hören Sie mich?; **how** ~/**could you say such a thing!** wie können/konnten Sie nur so etwas sagen!; **he could be on the next train** er könnte mit dem nächsten Zug kommen; **you could have told me** das hättest du mir sagen können; **she was as happy as could be** sie war über alle Maßen glücklich; **he** ~'**t** or **couldn't have done that**

er kann das unmöglich getan haben; **as soon as it** ~ **be arranged** sobald es sich machen läßt.

**can**[2] **1** n (**a**) (container) Kanister m; (milk~) Kanne f; (esp US: garbage ~) (Müll)eimer m. **to carry the** ~ (fig col) die Sache ausbaden (col). (**b**) (tin) Dose f; (of food also) Büchse f. **a** ~ **of beer** eine Dose Bier. **2** vt foodstuffs in Dosen füllen.

**Canada** ['kænədə] n Kanada nt.

**Canadian** [kə'neɪdɪən] **1** adj kanadisch. **2** n Kanadier(in f) m.

**canal** [kə'næl] n (**a**) Kanal m. (**b**) (Anat) Gang m.

**canapé** ['kænəpeɪ] n Cocktailhappen m.

**Canaries** [kə'nɛərɪz] npl Kanarische Inseln pl.

**canary** [kə'nɛərɪ] n Kanarienvogel m.

**canary** in cpds (colour: also ~ **yellow**) kanariengelb.

**cancel** ['kænsəl] vt (**a**) (call off) absagen; (Comm) stornieren; plans aufgeben; train, bus streichen; invitation, deal rückgängig machen; subscription kündigen. **the last train has been** ~**led** der letzte Zug fällt aus. (**b**) cheque entwerten; (cross out) name etc (durch)streichen. (**c**) (Math) kürzen.
►**cancel out 1** vt sep (Math) aufheben; (fig) zunichte machen. **to** ~ **each other** ~ (Math) sich aufheben; (fig) sich die Waage halten. **2** vi (Math) sich aufheben.

**cancellation** [,kænsə'leɪʃən] n see vt (**a**) Absage f; Stornierung f; Aufgabe f; Streichung f; Kündigung f. (**b**) Entwertung f. (**c**) (Math) Kürzung f.

**cancer** ['kænsə'] n (Med) Krebs m; (fig) Krebsgeschwür nt. **C**~ (Astrol) Krebs m; ~ **patient** Krebskranke(r) mf; ~ **research** Krebsforschung f.

**cancerous** ['kænsərəs] adj krebsartig.

**candelabra** [,kændɪ'lɑːbrə] n Leuchter m.

**candid** ['kændɪd] adj offen, ehrlich.

**candidacy** ['kændɪdəsɪ] n Kandidatur f.

**candidate** ['kændɪdeɪt] n (Pol) Kandidat(in f) m.

**candidly** ['kændɪdlɪ] adv offen, ehrlich.

**candied** ['kændɪd] adj kandiert. ~ **orange/lemon peel** Orangeat/Zitronat nt.

**candle** ['kændl] n Kerze f. **he's burning the** ~ **at both ends** er arbeitet Tag und Nacht; **he can't hold a** ~ **to his brother** (col) er kann seinem Bruder nicht das Wasser reichen.

**candle** in cpds Kerzen-; ~**light** n Kerzenlicht nt; ~**stick** n Kerzenhalter m.

**candour, (US) candor** ['kændə'] n Offenheit, Ehrlichkeit f.

**candy** ['kændɪ] **1** n (US) (sweet) Bonbon m or nt; (sweets) Süßigkeiten pl; (bar of chocolate) (Tafel) Schokolade f; (individual chocolate) Praline f. **2** vt sugar kristallisieren lassen; fruit etc kandieren.

**candy:** ~**floss** n (Brit) Zuckerwatte f; ~ **store** n (US) Süßwarenhandlung f.

**cane** [keɪn] **1** n (**a**) (stem of bamboo, sugar etc) Rohr nt; (of raspberry) Zweig m; (for supporting plants) Stock m. **a chair made of** ~ ein Rohrstuhl m. (**b**) (walking stick) (Spazier)stock m; (instrument of punishment) (Rohr)stock m. **to get the** ~ Stockschläge bekommen. **2** vt mit dem Stock schlagen.

**cane sugar** n Rohrzucker m.

**canine** ['keɪnaɪn] **1** n (**a**) (animal) Hund m. (**b**) (also ~ **tooth**) Eckzahn m. **2** adj Hunde-.

**canister** ['kænɪstə'] n Behälter m.

**cannabis** ['kænəbɪs] n Cannabis m.

**canned** [kænd] (**a**) food Dosen-, in Dosen. ~ **music** (col) Musikberieselung f (col). (**b**) (col: drunk) voll (col).

**cannibal** ['kænɪbəl] **1** n (person) Kannibale, Menschenfresser m. **2** adj kannibalisch.

**cannibalism** ['kænɪbəlɪzəm] n Kannibalismus m.

**cannibalize** ['kænɪbəlaɪz] vt old car etc ausschlachten.

**cannon** ['kænən] *n (Mil)* Kanone *f.*
▶**cannon into** *vi +prep obj* prallen gegen.
**cannon:** ~**ball** *n* Kanonenkugel *f*; ~ **fodder** *n* Kanonenfutter *nt*.
**cannot** ['kænɒt] = **can not.**
**canoe** [kə'nu:] **1** *n* Kanu *nt.* **2** *vi* Kanu fahren.
**canoeing** [kə'nu:ɪŋ] *n* Kanusport *m*, Kanufahren *nt.*
**canoeist** [kə'nu:ɪst] *n* Kanufahrer(in *f*) *m*, Kanute *m.*
**canon**[1] ['kænən] *n (all senses)* Kanon *m.*
**canon**[2] *n (priest)* Kanoniker *m.*
**canonize** ['kænənaɪz] *vt (Eccl)* heiligsprechen.
**canoodle** [kə'nu:dl] *vi (col)* rumschmusen *(col).*
**can opener** *n* Dosen- *or* Büchsenöffner *m.*
**canopy** ['kænəpɪ] *n (awning)* Markise *f*; *(over entrance)* Vordach *nt*; *(of bed, throne)* Baldachin *m.*
**can't** [kɑ:nt] = **can not.**
**Cantab** ['kæntæb] = **Cantabrigiensis** von der Universität Cambridge.
**cantankerous** [kæn'tæŋkərəs] *adj* verdrießlich.
**cantata** [kæn'tɑ:tə] *n* Kantate *f.*
**canteen** [kæn'ti:n] *n* **(a)** *(restaurant)* Kantine *f*; *(in university)* Mensa *f.* **(b)** *(Mil) (flask)* Feldflasche *f*; *(mess tin)* Kochgeschirr *nt.* **(c)** *(of cutlery)* Besteckkasten *m.*
**canter** ['kæntə'] **1** *n* Kanter *m.* **2** *vi* langsam galoppieren.
**cantilever** ['kæntɪli:və'] *n* Ausleger *m.*
**cantilever** *in cpds* Ausleger-; ~ **bridge** *n* Auslegerbrücke *f.*
**canton** ['kæntɒn] *n* Kanton *m.*
**Cantonese** [ˌkæntə'ni:z] **1** *adj* kantonesisch. **2** *n* **(a)** Kantonese *m*, Kantonesin *f.* **(b)** *(language)* Kantonesisch *nt.*
**canvas** ['kænvəs] *n* Leinwand *f*; *(for sails)* Segeltuch *nt*; *(set of sails)* Segel *pl*; *(painting)* Gemälde *nt.* **under** ~ *(in a tent)* im Zelt; *(Naut)* mit gehißtem Segel.
**canvass** ['kænvəs] **1** *vt* **(a)** *(Pol) district* Wahlwerbung machen in *(+dat).* **to** ~ **voters** Wahlwerbung machen. **(b)** *customers, citizens etc* werben; *district* bereisen; *(sound out) opinions* erforschen. **2** *vi* **(a)** *(Pol)* um Stimmen werben *(for sb* für jdn*).* **(b)** *(Comm)* eine Werbekampagne durchführen.
**canvasser** ['kænvəsə'] *n* **(a)** *(Pol)* Wahlhelfer(in *f*) *m.* **(b)** *(Comm)* Vertreter(in *f*) *m.*
**canvassing** ['kænvəsɪŋ] *n* **(a)** *(Pol)* Wahlwerbung *f.* **(b)** *(Comm)* Von-Haus-zu-Haus-Gehen *nt.*
**canyon** ['kænjən] *n* Cañon *m.*
**CAP** = **Common Agricultural Policy** *gemeinsame Agrarpolitik (der EG)*, GAP *f.*
**cap** [kæp] **1** *n* **(a)** *(hat)* Mütze *f*; *(nurse's ~)* Haube *f*; *(for swimming)* Badekappe *f.* ~ **in hand** *(fig)* kleinlaut; **if the** ~ **fits(, wear it)** *(prov)* wem der Schuh paßt (, der soll ihn sich anziehen); **he's got his** ~ **for England, he's an English** ~ *(Sport)* er ist/war in der englischen Nationalmannschaft. **(b)** *(lid, cover: of bottle)* Deckel *m*; *(of fountain pen)* (Verschluß)kappe *f*; *(Mil: of shell, fuse)* Kapsel *f*; *(Aut: petrol ~, radiator ~)* Verschluß *m.* **(c)** *(contraceptive)* Pessar *nt.* **(d)** *(of tooth)* (Jacket)krone *f.*
   **2** *vt* **(a)** *(put ~ on) bottle etc* verschließen. **(b)** *(do or say better)* überbieten. **and then to** ~ **it all ...** und zur Krönung des Ganzen, ... **(c)** **he's been** ~**ped twice for England** er war zweimal in der englischen Nationalmannschaft.
**capability** [ˌkeɪpə'bɪlɪtɪ] *n (potential ability)* Fähigkeit *f*; *(no pl: capableness also)* Kompetenz *f.*
**capable** ['keɪpəbl] *adj* **(a)** *(skilful, competent)* fähig. **(b) to be** ~ **of doing sth** etw tun können; **it's** ~ **of speeds of up to ...** es erreicht Geschwindigkeiten

bis zu ...; **thank you but I'm quite** ~ **of doing that myself** danke, ich bin durchaus imstande, das allein zu machen.
**capacitor** [kə'pæsɪtə'] *n* Kondensator *m.*
**capacity** [kə'pæsɪtɪ] *n* **(a)** *(cubic content etc)* Fassungsvermögen *nt*; *(maximum output)* Kapazität *f*; *(maximum weight)* Höchstlast *f*; *(Aut: engine* ~*)* Hubraum *m.* **filled to** ~ randvoll; *(hall)* bis auf den letzten Platz besetzt; **to have a seating** ~ **of 400** 400 Sitzplätze haben; **working at full** ~ voll ausgelastet; **to play to a** ~ **audience** vor ausverkauftem Haus spielen. **(b)** *(ability)* Fähigkeit *f.* **this work is beyond his** ~ diese Arbeit übersteigt seine Fähigkeiten. **(c)** *(role, position)* Eigenschaft *f.* **in my** ~ **as a doctor** (in meiner Eigenschaft) als Arzt.
**cape**[1] [keɪp] *n* Cape *nt*, Umhang *m.*
**cape**[2] *n (Geog)* Kap *nt.* **the C**~ **of Good Hope** das Kap der guten Hoffnung; **C**~ **Horn** Kap Hoorn; **C**~ **Canaveral** Kap Canaveral.
**caper**[1] ['keɪpə'] **1** *vi* herumtollen. **2** *n (prank)* Kapriole *f.*
**caper**[2] *n (Bot, Cook)* Kaper *f.*
**Cape Town** *n* Kapstadt *nt.*
**capillary** [kə'pɪlərɪ] **1** *adj* kapillar, Kapillar-. ~ **action** Kapillarwirkung *f.* **2** *n* Kapillare *f.*
**capital** ['kæpɪtl] **1** *n* **(a)** *(also* ~ **city)** Hauptstadt *f.* **(b)** *(also* ~ **letter)** Großbuchstabe *m.* **please write in** ~**s** bitte in Blockschrift schreiben! **(c)** *no pl (Fin)* Kapital *nt.* **to make** ~ **out of sth** *(fig)* aus etw Kapital schlagen. **2** *adj* **(a)** ~ **letter** Großbuchstabe *m.* **(b)** *(dated: excellent)* prächtig.
**capital** *in cpds* Kapital-; ~ **assets** *npl* Kapitalvermögen *nt*; ~ **expenditure** *n* Kapitalaufwendungen *pl*; ~ **gains tax** *n* Kapitalertragssteuer *f*; ~ **goods** *npl* Investitionsgüter *pl*; ~**-intensive** *adj* kapitalintensiv; ~ **investment** *n* Kapitalanlage *f.*
**capitalism** ['kæpɪtəlɪzəm] *n* Kapitalismus *m.*
**capitalist** ['kæpɪtəlɪst] **1** *n* Kapitalist(in *f*) *m.* **2** *adj* kapitalistisch.
**capitalize** ['kæpɪtə,laɪz] *vt* **(a)** *(Fin)* kapitalisieren. **(b)** *(Typ) word* groß schreiben.
▶**capitalize on** *vi +prep obj (fig)* Kapital schlagen aus.
**capital:** ~ **offence** *(Brit) or* **offense** *(US) n* Kapitalverbrechen *nt*; ~ **punishment** *n* Todesstrafe *f.*
**capitulate** [kə'pɪtjuleɪt] *vi* kapitulieren *(also Mil) (to* vor *+dat)*, aufgeben *(to* gegenüber*).*
**caprice** [kə'pri:s] *n* Laune, Kaprice *(geh) f.*
**capricious** [kə'prɪʃəs] *adj* launisch, kapriziös *(geh).*
**Capricorn** ['kæprɪkɔ:n] *n* Steinbock *m.*
**caps** [kæps] *npl (col)* Großbuchstaben *pl.*
**capsize** [kæp'saɪz] **1** *vi* kentern. **2** *vt* zum Kentern bringen.
**capstan** ['kæpstən] *n (Naut)* Spill *nt.*
**capsule** ['kæpsju:l] *n* Kapsel *f.*
**captain** ['kæptɪn] *(abbr* **Capt)** **1** *n (Mil)* Hauptmann *m*; *(Naut, Aviat, Sport)* Kapitän *m*; *(US: in restaurant)* Oberkellner *m.* ~ **of industry** Industriekapitän *m.* **2** *vt (Sport) team* anführen; *(Naut) ship* befehligen. **he** ~**ed the team for years** er war jahrelang Kapitän der Mannschaft.
**captaincy** ['kæptənsɪ] *n* Befehl *m*; *(Sport)* Führung *f.*
**caption** ['kæpʃən] *n* Bildtext *m*; *(heading)* Überschrift *f*; *(Film: subtitle)* Untertitel *m.*
**captivate** ['kæptɪveɪt] *vt* bezaubern.
**captivating** ['kæptɪveɪtɪŋ] *adj* bezaubernd.
**captive** ['kæptɪv] **1** *n* Gefangene(r) *mf.* **to take sb** ~ jdn gefangennehmen. **2** *adj person* gefangen. **a** ~ **audience** ein geneigtes Publikum.
**captivity** [kæp'tɪvɪtɪ] *n* Gefangenschaft *f.*
**captor** ['kæptə'] *n* **his** ~**s were British** er wurde von

Briten gefangengehalten; **his ~s treated him kindly** er wurde während seiner Gefangenschaft gut behandelt.
**capture** ['kæptʃər] **1** *vt* **(a)** *town* einnehmen, erobern; *person* gefangennehmen; *animal* (ein)fangen. **(b)** *(fig: painter etc) atmosphere* einfangen; *attention, sb's interest* erregen. **(c)** *(Comp) data* erfassen. **2** *n* Eroberung *f*; *(of soldier, escapee)* Gefangennahme *f*; *(of animal)* Einfangen *nt*; *(Comp: of data)* Erfassung *f*.
**car** [kɑːʳ] *n* **(a)** Auto *nt*, Wagen *m*. **by** ~ mit dem Auto. **(b)** *(Rail, tram~)* Wagen *m*. **(c)** *(US: of elevator)* Fahrkorb *m*.
**carafe** [kə'ræf] *n* Karaffe *f*.
**caramel** ['kærəməl] *n* *(substance)* Karamel *m*; *(sweet)* Karamelbonbon *nt or m*.
**carat** ['kærət] *n* Karat *nt*. **nine ~ gold** neunkarätiges Gold.
**caravan** ['kærəvæn] *n* **(a)** *(Brit: trailer)* Wohnwagen, Caravan *m*. **(b)** *(gipsy ~)* Zigeunerwagen *m*. **(c)** *(desert ~)* Karawane *f*.
**caravanning** ['kærəvænɪŋ] *n* *(Brit)* Urlaub *m* im Wohnwagen.
**caravan site** *n* *(Brit)* Campingplatz *m* für Wohnwagen.
**caraway** ['kærəweɪ] *n* *(also ~ seeds)* Kümmel *m*.
**carbohydrate** ['kɑːbəʊ'haɪdreɪt] *n* Kohlehydrat *nt*.
**carbolic** [kɑː'bɒlɪk] *adj* ~ **acid** Karbolsäure *f*.
**car bomb** *n* Autobombe *f*.
**carbon** ['kɑːbən] *n* *(Chem)* Kohlenstoff *m*.
**carbon:** ~ **copy** *n* Durchschlag *m*; **to be a ~ copy of sth/sb** einer Sache/jdm aufs Haar gleichen *(col)*; ~ **dioxide** *n* Kohlendioxyd *nt*; ~ **fibre** *n* Kohlenstoffaser *f*.
**carbonize** ['kɑːbənaɪz] *vt* karbonisieren.
**carbon:** ~ **monoxide** *n* Kohlenmonoxyd *nt*; ~ **paper** *n* Kohlepapier *nt*.
**carbuncle** ['kɑː,bʌŋkl] *n* *(Med)* Karbunkel *m*.
**carburettor,** *(US)* **carburetor** [,kɑːbə'retəʳ] *n* Vergaser *m*.
**carcass** ['kɑːkəs] *n* **(a)** *(corpse)* Leiche *f*; *(of animal)* Kadaver *m*; *(at butcher's)* Rumpf *m*. **(b)** *(of ship)* Skelett *nt*.
**carcinogen** [kɑː'sɪnədʒən] *n* Krebserreger *m*.
**carcinogenic** [,kɑːsɪnə'dʒenɪk] *adj* krebserregend.
**carcinoma** [,kɑːsɪ'nəʊmə] *n* Karzinom *nt*.
**card** [kɑːd] *n* **(a)** *no pl (~board)* Pappe *f*. **(b)** *(greetings, visiting ~ etc)* Karte *f*. **(c)** *(playing ~)* (Spiel)karte *f*. **to play ~s** Karten spielen. **(d)** *(fig uses)* **to put one's ~s on the table** seine Karten auf den Tisch legen; **to play one's ~s right** taktisch geschickt vorgehen; **it's on the ~s** es ist zu erwarten.
**card:** ~**board** *n* Karton *m*, Pappe *f*; ~**board box** *n* (Papp)karton *m*; ~**-carrying member** *n* eingetragenes Mitglied; ~ **file** *n* Kartei *f*; ~ **game** *n* Kartenspiel *nt*.
**cardiac** ['kɑːdɪæk] *adj* Herz-. ~ **arrest** Herzstillstand *m*.
**cardigan** ['kɑːdɪgən] *n* Strickjacke *f*.
**cardinal** ['kɑːdɪnl] *n* *(Eccl)* Kardinal *m*.
**cardinal:** ~ **number** *n* Kardinalzahl *f*; ~ **sin** *n* Todsünde *f*.
**card index** *n* Kartei *f*; *(in library)* Katalog *m*.
**cardiogram** ['kɑːdɪəʊgræm] *n* Kardiogramm *nt*.
**cardiology** [,kɑːdɪ'ɒlədʒɪ] *n* Kardiologie *f*.
**card:** ~**phone** *n* Kartentelefon *nt*; ~**sharp(er)** *n* Falschspieler *m*; ~ **table** *n* Spieltisch *m*; ~ **trick** *n* Kartenkunststück *nt*.
**care** [kɛəʳ] **1** *n* **(a)** *(worry, anxiety)* Sorge *f* *(of* um*)*. **he hasn't a ~ in the world** er hat keinerlei Sorgen; **without a ~ in the world** völlig sorglos.

**(b)** *(carefulness, attentiveness)* Sorgfalt *f*. **to drive with(out) due ~ and attention** rücksichtslos fahren; **"fragile, with ~"**, **"handle with ~"** „Vorsicht, zerbrechlich"; **to take ~** aufpassen, achtgeben; **bye-bye, take ~** tschüs, mach's gut; **to take ~ to do sth** sich bemühen, etw zu tun; **take ~ not to drop it** paß auf, daß du es nicht fallenläßt; **you should take more ~ with** *or* **over the details** Sie sollten sich sorgfältiger mit den Einzelheiten befassen.
**(c)** *(of teeth, car etc)* Pflege *f*. **to take ~ of sth** auf etw *(acc)* aufpassen; *of one's appearance, hair, car* etw pflegen; *(not treat roughly) car, health* etw schonen.
**(d)** *(of old people, children)* Fürsorge *f*. **he needs medical ~** er muß ärztlich behandelt werden; **to take ~ of sb** sich um jdn kümmern; *of patients* jdn versorgen; *of one's family* für jdn sorgen; **he can take ~ of himself** er kommt schon alleine zurecht.
**(e)** ~ **of** *(abbr c/o)* bei; **to take/put a child into ~** ein Kind in Pflege nehmen/geben.
**(f) to take ~ of sb/sth** *(see to)* sich um jdn/etw kümmern; *of arrangements also* etw erledigen.
**(g)** *(caringness, concern)* Anteilnahme *f*.
**2** *vi* *(be concerned)* sich kümmern *(about* um*)*. **money is all he ~s about** er interessiert sich nur fürs Geld; **he ~s deeply about her** sie bedeutet ihm sehr viel; **I don't ~** das ist mir egal; **for all I ~** mei netwegen, von mir aus; **who ~s?** na und?
**3** *vt* **(a)** *(mind, be concerned)* **I don't ~ what people say** es ist mir egal, was die Leute sagen; **what do I ~?** was geht mich das an?; **I couldn't ~ less** das ist mir doch völlig egal. **(b)** *(like)* **would you ~ to take off your coat?** möchten Sie nicht (Ihren Mantel) ablegen?
►**care for** *vi* +*prep obj* **(a)** *(look after)* sich kümmern um; *invalid also* versorgen; *hands, furniture etc* pflegen. **(b)** *(like)* mögen. **I don't ~ ~ your tone of voice** wie reden Sie denn mit mir?; **would you ~ ~ a cup of tea?** hätten *or* möchten Sie gerne eine Tasse Tee?; **I never have much ~d ~ his films** ich habe mir noch nie viel aus seinen Filmen gemacht.
**career** [kə'rɪəʳ] **1** *n* Karriere *f*; *(profession)* Beruf *m*; *(working life)* Laufbahn *f*. ~**s adviser** *or* **officer** Berufsberater(in *f*) *m*; **to make a ~ for oneself** Karriere machen. **2** *attr* Karriere-; *soldier, diplomat* Berufs-. ~ **girl** *or* **woman** Karrierefrau *f*. **3** *vi* rasen. **to ~ along** dahinrasen.
**careerist** [kə'rɪərɪst] *n* Karrieremacher(in *f*) *m*.
**carefree** ['kɛəfriː] *adj* sorglos; *song* heiter.
**careful** ['kɛəfʊl] *adj* sorgfältig; *(cautious)* vorsichtig; *(with money etc)* sparsam. **~! Vorsicht!;** **to be ~** aufpassen *(of auf +acc)*; **be ~ what you do** nimm dich in acht; **be ~ (that) they don't hear you** gib acht, daß sie dich nicht hören; **be ~ with those glasses** geh vorsichtig mit den Gläsern um; **he is ~ with his money** er hält sein Geld gut zusammen.
**carefully** ['kɛəfəlɪ] *adv see adj*.
**careless** ['kɛəlɪs] *adj* *(negligent, heedless)* nachlässig; *driver* unvorsichtig; *driving* leichtsinnig; *remark* gedankenlos. ~ **mistake** Flüchtigkeitsfehler *m*.
**carelessly** ['kɛəlɪslɪ] *adv see adj*.
**carelessness** ['kɛəlɪsnɪs] *n see adj* Nachlässigkeit *f*; Unvorsicht(igkeit) *f*, Leichtsinn *m*; Gedankenlosigkeit *f*.
**carer** ['kɛərəʳ] *n* Betreuer(in *f*) *m*.
**caress** [kə'res] **1** *n* Liebkosung *f*, Streicheln *nt no pl*. **2** *vt* streicheln, liebkosen.
**care:** ~**taker** *n* Hausmeister *m*; ~**taker government** *n* Übergangsregierung *f*; ~**worn** *adj* von Sorgen gezeichnet, abgehärmt.
**car ferry** *n* Autofähre *f*.

**cargo** ['kɑːgəʊ] *n* (Schiffs)ladung *f.* ~ **boat** *or* **ship** Frachter *m*, Frachtschiff *nt*; ~ **plane** Transportflugzeug *nt.*

**car hire** *n* Autovermietung *f.*

**Caribbean** [ˌkærɪ'biːən, *(US)* kæ'rɪbiːən] **1** *adj* karibisch. ~ **Sea** Karibisches Meer. **2** *n* Karibik *f.*

**caricature** ['kærɪkətjʊəʳ] **1** *n* Karikatur *f.* **2** *vt* karikieren.

**caries** ['kɛəriːz] *n* Karies *f.*

**caring** ['kɛərɪŋ] *adj person* liebevoll; *government, society* sozial eingestellt.

**carload** ['kɑːləʊd] *n* Wagenladung *f.*

**carnage** ['kɑːnɪdʒ] *n* Gemetzel *nt.*

**carnal** ['kɑːnl] *adj* fleischlich, körperlich.

**carnation** [kɑː'neɪʃən] *n* Nelke *f.*

**carnival** ['kɑːnɪvəl] *n* **(a)** Karneval *m*; *(in SGer)* Fasching *m.* **(b)** *(US: funfair)* Kirmes *f.*

**carnivore** ['kɑːnɪvɔːʳ] *n* *(animal)* Fleischfresser *m*; *(plant)* fleischfressende Pflanze.

**carnivorous** [kɑː'nɪvərəs] *adj* fleischfressend.

**carol** ['kærəl] *n* Lied *nt.* **Christmas** ~ Weihnachtslied *nt*; ~ **singers** *npl* = Sternsinger *pl*; **to go** ~ **singing** Weihnachtslieder singen gehen.

**carouse** [kə'raʊz] *vi (old)* zechen.

**carousel** [ˌkæru'sel] *n* = **car(r)ousel.**

**carp¹** [kɑːp] *n (fish)* Karpfen *m.*

**carp²** *vi* etwas auszusetzen haben *(at* an *+dat).*

**car park** *n (Brit) (open air)* Parkplatz *m*; *(covered)* Parkhaus *nt.* **underground** ~ Tiefgarage *f*; ~ **ticket** Parkschein *m.*

**carpenter** ['kɑːpɪntəʳ] *n* Zimmermann *m*; *(for furniture)* Tischler *m.*

**carpentry** ['kɑːpɪntrɪ] *n* Zimmerhandwerk *nt*; *(as hobby)* Tischlern *nt.*

**carpet** ['kɑːpɪt] **1** *n (lit, fig)* Teppich *m*; *(fitted* ~*)* Teppichboden *m.* **2** *vt* **(a)** *floor* (mit Teppichen/Teppichboden) auslegen. **(b)** *(col: reprimand)* zur Minna machen *(col).*

**carpet bombing** *n* Flächenbombardierung *f.*

**carpeting** ['kɑːpətɪŋ] *n* Teppiche *pl*; *(wall-to-wall)* Teppichboden *m.*

**carpet:** ~ **slippers** *npl* Pantoffeln *pl*; ~ **sweeper** *n* Teppichkehrer *m*; ~ **tile** *n* Teppichfliese *f.*

**car:** ~ **phone** *n* Autotelefon *nt*; ~ **pool** *n (people)* Fahrgemeinschaft *f*; *(vehicles)* Fuhrpark *m*; ~**port** *n* Einstellplatz *m*; ~ **radio** *n* Autoradio *nt*; ~ **rental** *n (US)* Autovermietung *f.*

**carriage** ['kærɪdʒ] *n* **(a)** *(horse-drawn vehicle)* Kutsche *f*; *(esp US: baby* ~*)* Kinderwagen *m.* **(b)** *(Brit Rail)* Wagen *m.* **(c)** *(Comm: conveyance)* Beförderung *f.* ~ **free** frachtfrei; ~ **paid** frei Haus. **(d)** *(Typ)* Wagen *m.* ~ **return** Wagenrücklauf *m*; *(key)* Rücklauftaste *f*; *(Comp)* Return *nt.* **(e)** *(of person: bearing)* Haltung *f.*

**carriageway** ['kærɪdʒweɪ] *n (Brit)* Fahrbahn *f.*

**carrier** ['kærɪəʳ] *n* **(a)** *(goods haulier)* Spediteur *m.* **(b)** *(of disease)* Überträger *m.* **(c)** *(aircraft* ~*)* Flugzeugträger *m*; *(troop* ~*)* Transportflugzeug *nt/*-schiff *nt.* **(d)** *(Chem)* Träger(substanz *f*) *m.* **(e)** *(Brit also* ~ **bag)** Tragetüte *f.*

**carrier pigeon** *n* Brieftaube *f*; **by** ~ mit der Taubenpost.

**carrion** ['kærɪən] *n* Aas *nt.* ~ **crow** Rabenkrähe *f.*

**carrot** ['kærət] *n* Karotte, Möhre *f*; *(fig)* Köder *m.*

**car(r)ousel** [ˌkæru'sel] *n* **(a)** Karussell *nt.* **(b)** *(for slides)* Rundmagazin *nt.*

**carry** ['kærɪ] **1** *vt* **(a)** tragen; *message* (über)-bringen.
**(b)** *(vehicle: convey)* befördern. **the wind carried the sounds to him** der Wind trug die Laute zu ihm hin.

**(c)** *(have on person) documents, money* bei sich haben.

**(d)** *(fig)* **his voice carries conviction** seine Stimme klingt überzeugend; **the offence carries a penalty of £5** darauf steht eine Geldstrafe von £5; **it carries interest at 8%** es wirft 8% Zinsen ab; **you're** ~**ing things too far** *(fig)* du treibst es zu weit; **he carries himself well** er hat eine gute Haltung.

**(e)** *(bridge etc: support)* tragen. **he carries his drink well** er kann viel vertragen.

**(f)** *(Comm) goods, stock* führen, (auf Lager) haben; *(newspaper) story* bringen.

**(g)** *(Tech: pipe)* führen; *(wire)* (weiter)leiten.

**(h)** *(win)* einnehmen, erobern. **to** ~ **the day** den Sieg davontragen; **the motion was carried unanimously** der Antrag wurde einstimmig angenommen.

**2** *vi (voice, sound)* tragen. **the sound of the alphorn carried for miles** der Klang des Alphorns war meilenweit zu hören.

▶**carry away** *vt sep* **(a)** *(lit)* (hin)wegtragen; *(torrent, flood)* (hin)wegspülen. **(b)** *(fig)* **to get carried** ~ sich nicht mehr bremsen können; **don't get carried** ~! übertreib's nicht!

▶**carry back** *vt sep (fig) person* zurückversetzen *(to* in *+acc).*

▶**carry forward** *vt sep (Fin)* vortragen.

▶**carry off** *vt sep* **(a)** *(seize, carry away)* wegtragen. **(b)** *(win) prizes, medals* gewinnen. **(c) to** ~ **it** ~ es hinkriegen *(col).*

▶**carry on** **1** *vi* **(a)** *(continue)* weitermachen; *(life)* weitergehen. **(b)** *(col) (talk)* reden und reden; *(make a scene)* ein Theater machen *(col).* **to** ~ ~ **about sth** sich über etw *(acc)* auslassen. **(c)** *(have an affair)* etwas haben *(col) (with sb* mit jdm*).* **2** *vt sep* **(a)** *(continue) tradition* fortführen. **(b)** *(conduct) conversation, correspondence* führen; *profession, trade* ausüben.

▶**carry out** *vt sep* **(a)** *(lit)* heraustragen. **(b)** *order* ausführen; *plan, experiment* durchführen; *threats* wahrmachen.

▶**carry through** *vt sep (carry out)* zu Ende führen.

**carry:** ~**-all** *n* (Reise)tasche *f*; ~**cot** *n (Brit)* Babytragetasche *f*; ~**-on** *n (col)* Theater *nt (col).*

**carsick** ['kɑːsɪk] *adj* **I get** ~ mir wird beim Autofahren immer übel.

**cart** [kɑːt] **1** *n* Wagen, Karren *m*; *(US) (in supermarket)* Einkaufswagen *m*; *(for baggage)* Gepäckwagen *m.* **to put the** ~ **before the horse** *(fig)* das Pferd am Schwanz aufzäumen. **2** *vt (fig col)* schleppen; ~ **around** mit sich herumschleppen.

▶**cart away** *or* **off** *vt sep* abtransportieren.

**carte blanche** ['kɑːt'blɑ̃ʃ] *n no pl* **to give sb** ~ ~ jdm (eine) Blankovollmacht geben.

**cartel** [kɑː'tel] *n* Kartell *nt.*

**carthorse** ['kɑːthɔːs] *n* Zugpferd *nt.*

**cartilage** ['kɑːtɪlɪdʒ] *n* Knorpel *m.*

**cartography** [kɑː'tɒgrəfɪ] *n* Kartographie *f.*

**carton** ['kɑːtən] *n* Karton *m*; *(of cigarettes)* Stange *f*; *(of milk)* Tüte *f.*

**cartoon** [kɑː'tuːn] *n* **(a)** Cartoon *m or nt*; *(single picture)* Karikatur *f.* ~ **character** Comicfigur *f.* **(b)** *(Film, TV)* (Zeichen)trickfilm *m.*

**cartoonist** [ˌkɑː'tuːnɪst] *n* **(a)** *(in newspaper etc)* Karikaturist(in *f*) *m.* **(b)** *(Film, TV)* Trickzeichner(in *f*) *m.*

**cartridge** ['kɑːtrɪdʒ] *n (for rifle, pen)* Patrone *f*; *(Phot, for tape recorder)* Kassette *f*; *(for record player)* Tonabnehmer *m.*

**cartridge:** ~ **belt** *n* Patronengürtel *m*; ~ **case** *n* Patronenhülse *f*; ~ **paper** *n* Zeichenpapier *nt.*

**cartwheel** ['kɑːt,wiːl] n (lit) Wagenrad nt; (Sport) Rad nt. **to turn** or **do** ~s radschlagen.

**carve** [kɑːv] **1** vt (a) (Art: cut) wood schnitzen; stone etc (be)hauen. **to** ~ **sth on a stone** etw in einen Stein einmeißeln. (b) (Cook) tranchieren. **2** vi (Cook) tranchieren.
►**carve out** vt sep **to** ~ ~ **a career for oneself** sich (dat) eine Karriere aufbauen.
►**carve up** vt sep meat aufschneiden; body, (fig) country zerstückeln.

**carve-up** ['kɑːvʌp] n (col) Zerstückelung f; (of inheritance) Verteilung f.

**carving** ['kɑːvɪŋ] n (Art) (thing carved) Skulptur f; (in wood) Holzschnitt m. ~ **knife** Tranchiermesser nt.

**carwash** ['kɑːwɒʃ] n (place) Waschstraße f; (wash) Autowäsche f.

**cascade** [kæs'keɪd] **1** n Kaskade f. **2** vi (also ~ **down**) (onto auf +acc) (in Kaskaden) herabfallen; (hair) wallend herabfallen; (boxes etc) herunterpurzeln (col).

**case¹** [keɪs] n (a) (Med, Jur, instance) Fall m. **if that's the** ~ wenn das der Fall ist; **as the** ~ **may be** je nachdem; **it's a clear** ~ **of lying** das ist eindeutig gelogen; **in** ~ falls; **(just) in** ~ für alle Fälle; **in** ~ **of emergency** im Notfall m; **in any** ~ sowieso; **in this/ that** ~ in dem Fall; **the** ~ **for the defence/ prosecution** die Verteidigung/Anklage; **in the** ~ **Higgins v Schwarz** in der Sache Higgins gegen Schwarz; **the** ~ **for/against the abolition of capital punishment** die Argumente für/gegen die Abschaffung der Todesstrafe; **to put the** ~ **for sth** etw vertreten; **you've got a good** ~ was Sie sagen, ist durchaus gerechtfertigt; **there's a strong** ~ **for legalizing cannabis** es spricht viel für die Legalisierung von Marihuana. (b) (Gram) Fall, Kasus m. **in the genitive** ~ im Genitiv. (c) (col: person) Type f (col). **he's a** ~ das ist vielleicht 'ne Type (col); **a hard** ~ ein schwieriger Fall.

**case²** n (a) (suit~) Koffer m; (crate, packing ~) Kiste f; (display ~) Vitrine f. (b) (box) Schachtel f; (for spectacles) Etui nt; (pillow~) Bezug m; (for musical instrument) Kasten m.

**case:** ~**book** n (Med) (Kranken)fälle pl; (in social work, Jur) Fallsammlung f; ~**-hardened** adj verstählt; (fig) abgebrüht; ~ **history** n (Med) Krankengeschichte f; (Sociol, Psych) Vorgeschichte f.

**casement** ['keɪsmənt] n (frame) Fensterflügel m; (also ~ **window**) Flügelfenster nt.

**case:** ~ **study** n Fallstudie f; ~**work** n (Sociol) ≈ Sozialarbeit f.

**cash** [kæʃ] **1** n (a) Bargeld nt. ~ **in hand** Barbestand m; **to pay (in)** ~ bar bezahlen; **ready** ~ verfügbares Geld. (b) (immediate payment) Barzahlung f; (not credit) Sofortzahlung f. ~ **on delivery** per Nachnahme. (c) (money) Geld nt. **to be short of** ~ knapp bei Kasse sein (col). **2** vt cheque einlösen.
►**cash in 1** vt sep einlösen. **2** vi **to** ~ ~ **on sth** aus etw Kapital schlagen.

**cash:** ~**-and-carry 1** adj Cash-and-carry-; **2** n (for retailers) Cash and Carry m; (for public) Verbrauchermarkt m; ~ **book** n Kassenbuch nt; ~ **box** n Geldkassette f; ~ **card** n (Geld)automatenkarte f; ~ **desk** n Kasse f; ~ **dispenser** n Geldautomat m.

**cashew** [kæ'ʃuː] n (tree) Nierenbaum m; (nut) Cashewnuß f.

**cashflow** ['kæʃfləʊ] n Cash-flow m. ~ **problems** Liquiditätsprobleme.

**cashier** [kæ'ʃɪəʳ] n Kassierer(in f) m.

**cashless** ['kæʃləs] adj bargeldlos.

**cashmere** [kæʃ'mɪəʳ] n Kaschmir m.

**cash:** ~ **payment** n Barzahlung f; ~**point** n Geldautomat m; ~ **price** n Barzahlungspreis m; ~ **prize** n Geldpreis m; ~ **register** n Registrierkasse f; ~ **sale** n Barverkauf m.

**casing** ['keɪsɪŋ] n (Tech) Gehäuse nt.

**casino** [kə'siːnəʊ] n (Spiel)kasino nt.

**cask** [kɑːsk] n Faß nt.

**casket** ['kɑːskɪt] n Schatulle f; (US: coffin) Sarg m.

**Caspian Sea** ['kæspɪən'siː] n Kaspisches Meer.

**casserole** ['kæsərəʊl] **1** n (Cook) Kasserolle f. **2** vt (Brit) schmoren.

**cassette** [kæ'set] n Kassette f. ~ **deck** Kassettendeck nt; ~ **recorder** Kassettenrecorder m.

**cassock** ['kæsək] n Soutane f.

**cast** [kɑːst] (vb: pret, ptp ~) **1** n (a) (of dice, net, line) Wurf m. (b) (mould) (Guß)form f; (object moulded) Abdruck m; (in metal) (Ab)guß m. (c) (plaster ~) Gipsverband m. (d) (Theat) Besetzung f. ~ (in the order of appearance) Mitwirkende pl (in der Reihenfolge ihres Auftritts). (e) ~ **of mind** Gesinnung f. (f) (Med: squint) schielender Blick. **2** vt (a) werfen; anchor, net auswerfen; vote abgeben. **to** ~ **one's eyes over sth** einen Blick auf etw (acc) werfen. (b) (shed) **to** ~ **its skin** sich häuten. (c) (Tech, Art) gießen. ~ **iron** Gußeisen nt. (d) (Theat) parts, play besetzen. **he was** ~ **for the part of Hamlet** er sollte den Hamlet spielen. **3** vi (a) (Fishing) die Angel auswerfen. (b) (Theat) die Rollen verteilen.
►**cast about** or **around for** vi +prep obj suchen nach; for new job etc sich umsehen nach.
►**cast aside** vt sep cares, inhibitions ablegen; old clothes etc ausrangieren.
►**cast away** vt sep wegwerfen. **to be** ~ ~ (Naut) gestrandet sein.
►**cast down** vt sep eyes niederschlagen. **to be** ~ ~ (fig) niedergeschlagen sein.
►**cast off 1** vt sep (a) (get rid of clothes) abwerfen; friends fallenlassen. (b) stitches abketten. (c) (Naut) losmachen. **2** vi (a) (Naut) ablegen. (b) (in knitting) abketten.
►**cast on** vti sep (Knitting) anschlagen.
►**cast up** vt sep flotsam, sailors anspülen, an Land spülen.

**castanets** [,kæstə'nets] npl Kastagnetten pl.

**castaway** ['kɑːstəweɪ] n (lit, fig) Schiffbrüchige(r) mf.

**caste** [kɑːst] n Kaste f.

**caster** ['kɑːstəʳ] n = **castor**.

**castigate** ['kæstɪgeɪt] vt person (old: physically) züchtigen; (verbally) geißeln.

**Castile** [kæ'stiːl] n Kastilien nt.

**Castilian** [kæ'stɪljən] **1** adj kastilisch. **2** n (a) (language) Kastilisch nt. (b) (person) Kastilier(in f) m.

**casting** ['kɑːstɪŋ] n (a) (Tech, Art) Abguß m; (in metal) Guß m. (b) (Theat) Rollenverteilung f.

**casting vote** n ausschlaggebende Stimme.

**cast-iron** ['kɑːst,aɪən] adj (a) (lit) gußeisern. (b) (fig) will, constitution eisern; case, alibi hieb- und stichfest.

**castle** ['kɑːsl] **1** n (a) (fortress) Burg f; (mansion, great house) Schloß nt. **to build** ~s **in the air** Luftschlösser bauen. (b) (Chess) Turm m. **2** vi (Chess) rochieren.

**cast:** ~**-off 1** adj clothes abgelegt attr; **2** npl ~**-offs** (col) abgelegte Kleider.

**castor** ['kɑːstəʳ] n (a) (Brit: for sugar, salt etc) Streuer m. (b) (wheel) Rolle f, Rad nt.

**castor:** ~ **oil** n Rizinus(öl) nt; ~ **sugar** n (Brit) Kristallzucker m.

**castrate** [kæs'treɪt] vt kastrieren.

**casual** ['kæʒjʊəl] **1** adj (a) (not planned) zufällig; acquaintance, glance flüchtig. (b) (offhand, careless) lässig; *attitude* gleichgültig; *remark* beiläufig. **(c)** *(informal)* zwanglos; *clothes* leger. ~ **wear** Freizeitkleidung *f*. **(d)** *(irregular)* ~ **work/labour** Gelegenheitsarbeit *f*; ~ **worker/labourer** Gelegenheitsarbeiter(in *f*) *m*. **2** *n (*~ *worker)* Gelegenheitsarbeiter(in *f*) *m*. ~**s** Aushilfen *pl*.

**casually** ['kæʒjʊəlɪ] *adv (without planning)* zufällig; *(in an offhand manner)* beiläufig; *(informally)* zwanglos; *dressed* leger.

**casualty** ['kæʒjʊəltɪ] *n* **(a)** *(lit, fig)* Opfer *nt*; *(injured also)* Verletzte(r) *mf*; *(dead also)* Tote(r) *mf*. **(b)** *(also ~ ward)* Unfallstation *f*.

**cat** [kæt] *n* Katze *f*. **to let the ~ out of the bag** die Katze aus dem Sack lassen; **they fight like ~ and dog** sie vertragen sich wie Hund und Katze; **there isn't room to swing a ~ (in)** *(col)* man kann sich nicht rühren(, so eng ist es); **to be like a ~ on hot bricks** (wie) auf glühenden Kohlen sitzen; **that's put the ~ among the pigeons!** da hast du *etc* aber was (Schönes) angerichtet!; **he thinks he's the ~'s whiskers** *(col)* er hält sich für wer weiß was; **when the ~'s away the mice will play** *(prov)* wenn die Katze aus dem Haus ist, tanzen die Mäuse.

**cataclysm** ['kætəklɪzəm] *n* Verheerung *f*; *(fig)* Umwälzung *f*.

**catacombs** ['kætəkuːmz] *npl* Katakomben *pl*.

**catalogue**, *(US)* **catalog** ['kætəlɒg] **1** *n* Katalog *m*. **2** *vt* katalogisieren.

**catalyst** ['kætəlɪst] *n (lit, fig)* Katalysator *m*.

**catalytic converter** [‚kætə'lɪtɪk kən'vɜːtər] *n (Aut)* Katalysator *m*.

**catamaran** [‚kætəmə'ræn] *n* Katamaran *m*.

**catapult** ['kætəpʌlt] **1** *n (slingshot)* Schleuder *f*; *(Mil, Aviat)* Katapult *nt or m*. **2** *vt* schleudern; *(Aviat)* katapultieren.

**cataract** ['kætərækt] *n* **(a)** *(rapids)* Katarakt *m*. **(b)** *(Med)* grauer Star.

**catarrh** [kə'tɑːr] *n* Katarrh *m*.

**catastrophe** [kə'tæstrəfɪ] *n* Katastrophe *f*.

**catastrophic** [‚kætə'strɒfɪk] *adj* katastrophal.

**cat:** ~ **burglar** *n* Fassadenkletterer *m*; ~**call** *n (Theat)* ~**calls** Pfiffe und Buhrufe *pl*.

**catch** [kætʃ] *(vb: pret, ptp* **caught***)* **1** *n* **(a)** *(of ball etc)* **to make a (good)** ~ (gut) fangen. **(b)** *(Fishing, Hunt)* Fang *m*. **(c)** *(trick, snag)* Haken *m*. **there's a ~ in it somewhere** die Sache hat irgendwo einen Haken; a ~**-22 situation** *(col)* eine Zwickmühle; ~ **question** Fangfrage *f*. **(d)** *(device for fastening)* Verschluß(vorrichtung *f*) *m*; *(hook)* Haken *m*; *(latch)* Riegel *m*.

**2** *vt* **(a)** fangen; *thief* fassen, schnappen *(col)*; *(col: manage to see)* erwischen *(col)*. **to ~ sight/a glimpse of sb/sth** jdn/etw erblicken/flüchtig zu sehen bekommen; **he caught the waiter's eye** er machte den Ober auf sich aufmerksam; **this dress caught my eye** das Kleid ist mir ins Auge gefallen; **to ~ one's breath** *(after exercise etc)* Luft holen, verschnaufen *(col)*.

**(b)** *(take by surprise)* erwischen, ertappen. **to ~ sb at sth** jdn bei etw erwischen; **you won't ~ me doing that again!** *(col)* das mache ich bestimmt nicht wieder!; **caught in the act** auf frischer Tat ertappt.

**(c)** *train, bus* erreichen, kriegen *(col)*.

**(d)** *(get entangled)* coat hängenbleiben mit. **I caught my finger in the car door** ich habe mir den Finger in der Wagentür eingeklemmt.

**(e)** *(understand, hear)* mitkriegen *(col)*.

**(f)** **to** ~ **an illness** *(dat)* eine Krankheit holen *(col)*; **to** ~ **a cold** sich erkälten.

**(g)** *(hit)* treffen. **the blow/ball caught him on the**

**arm** der Schlag/Ball traf ihn am Arm; **you'll ~ it!** *(col)* du kannst was erleben!

**3** *vi* **(a)** *(with ball)* fangen. **(b)** *(fire)* in Gang kommen; *(wood etc)* Feuer fangen; *(Cook)* anbrennen. **(c)** *(get stuck)* sich verklemmen; *(get entangled)* hängenbleiben. **her dress caught in the door** sie blieb mit ihrem Kleid in der Tür hängen.

►**catch on** *vi (col)* **(a)** *(become popular)* (gut) ankommen. **(b)** *(understand)* kapieren *(col)*.

►**catch out** *vt sep (fig)* durchschauen; *(with trick question etc)* hereinlegen *(col)*. **I caught you ~ there!** du bist durchschaut; *(with trick question)* jetzt bist du aber reingefallen *(col)*.

►**catch up 1** *vi* aufholen. **to** ~ ~ **on sth** etw nachholen; **to** ~ ~ **on one's sleep** Schlaf nachholen; **to** ~ ~ **with sb** *(running, in work etc)* jdn einholen. **2** *vt sep* **(a) to** ~ **sb** ~ *(walking, working etc)* jdn einholen. **(b) to get caught** ~ **in sth** *(entangled)* sich in etw *(dat)* verfangen; *in traffic* in etw *(acc)* geraten; *in discussion* in etw *(acc)* verwickelt werden.

**catching** ['kætʃɪŋ] *adj (Med, fig)* ansteckend.

**catchment area** ['kætʃmənt-] *n* Einzugsgebiet *nt*.

**catch:** ~ **phrase** *n* Slogan *m*; ~ **word** *n* Schlagwort *nt*.

**catchy** ['kætʃɪ] *adj (+er) tune* eingängig. **to be** ~ leicht ins Ohr gehen.

**catechism** ['kætɪkɪzəm] *n* Katechismus *m*.

**categorical** [‚kætɪ'gɒrɪkəl] *adj* kategorisch.

**categorize** ['kætɪgəraɪz] *vt* kategorisieren.

**category** ['kætɪgərɪ] *n* Kategorie *f*.

**cater** ['keɪtər] *vi (provide food)* die Speisen und Getränke liefern.

►**cater for** *vi +prep obj* **(a)** *(serve)* mit Speisen und Getränken versorgen; *functions* ausrichten. **(b)** eingestellt sein auf *(+acc)*; *(also* **cater to***) needs, tastes* gerecht werden *(+dat)*. **we** ~ ~ **all sizes** wir führen alle Größen; **this magazine** ~**s** ~ **all ages** diese Zeitschrift hat jeder Altersgruppe etwas zu bieten.

**catering** ['keɪtərɪŋ] *n* Versorgung *f* mit Speisen und Getränken *(for gen)*; *(trade)* Gastronomie *f*. **who's doing the** ~? welche Firma liefert das Essen?; ~ **trade** Gastronomie *f*.

**caterpillar** ['kætəpɪlər] *n (Zool)* Raupe *f*; *(Tech)* Raupe(nkette) *f*; *(vehicle) (also* ~ **tractor***)* Raupenfahrzeug *nt*. ~**-track** Raupenkette *f*.

**caterwauling** ['kætəwɔːlɪŋ] *n* Gejaule *nt*.

**catgut** ['kætgʌt] *n* Katgut *nt*.

**cathedral** [kə'θiːdrəl] *n* Dom *m*, Kathedrale *f*.

**Catherine** ['kæθərɪn] *n* Katharina *f*. **c~ wheel** Feuerrad *nt*.

**catheter** ['kæθɪtər] *n* Katheter *m*.

**cathode** ['kæθəʊd] *n* Kathode *f*. ~**-ray tube** Kathodenstrahlröhre *f*.

**catholic** ['kæθəlɪk] *adj (varied, all-embracing)* vielseitig. **he's a man of very** ~ **tastes** er ist (ein) sehr vielseitig interessiert(er Mensch).

**Catholic 1** *adj (Eccl)* katholisch. **the** ~ **Church** die katholische Kirche. **2** *n* Katholik(in *f*) *m*.

**Catholicism** [kə'θɒlɪsɪzəm] *n* Katholizismus *m*.

**cat:** ~**kin** *n (Bot)* Kätzchen *nt*; ~ **litter** *n* Katzenstreu *f*; ~**nap** *n* **to have a** ~**nap** ein Nickerchen *nt* machen *(col)*; ~**'s eye** *n* Katzenauge *nt*.

**catsup** ['kætsəp] *n (US)* = **ketchup**.

**cattle** ['kætl] *npl* Rind(vieh) *nt*. ~ **breeding** Rinderzucht *f*; ~ **market** *(lit)* Viehmarkt *m*; *(fig col)* Fleischbeschau *f (col)*; ~ **truck** *(Rail)* Viehwagen *m*.

**catty** ['kætɪ] *adj (+er)* gehässig, boshaft.

**catwalk** ['kætwɔːk] *n* Steg *m*; *(for models)* Laufsteg *m*.

**Caucasian** [kɔː'keɪzɪən] **1** *adj* kaukasisch. **2** *n* Kaukasier(in *f*) *m*.

**Caucasus** ['kɔːkəsəs] *n* der Kaukasus.
**caucus** ['kɔːkəs] *n (committee)* Gremium *nt*; *(US: meeting)* Sitzung *f.*
**caught** [kɔːt] *pret, ptp of* catch.
**cauldron** ['kɔːldrən] *n* großer Kessel.
**cauliflower** ['kɒlɪflaʊəʳ] *n* Blumenkohl *m.*
**cause** [kɔːz] **1** *n* **(a)** Ursache *f (of* für*).* ~ **and effect** Ursache und Wirkung. **(b)** *(reason)* Grund *m.* there's no ~ for alarm es besteht kein Grund zur Aufregung. **(c)** *(purpose, ideal)* Sache *f.* in the ~ of justice im Namen der Gerechtigkeit; it's all in a good ~ es ist für eine gute Sache. **2** *vt* verursachen. to ~ grief to sb jdm Kummer machen; to ~ sb to do sth jdn veranlassen, etw zu tun.
**causeway** ['kɔːzweɪ] *n* Damm *m.*
**caustic** ['kɔːstɪk] *adj (Chem, fig)* ätzend; remark bissig. ~ soda Ätznatron *nt.*
**cauterize** ['kɔːtəraɪz] *vt (Med)* ausbrennen.
**caution** ['kɔːʃən] **1** *n* **(a)** Vorsicht *f.* "~!" „Vorsicht!"; to act with ~ umsichtig *or* vorsichtig vorgehen. **(b)** *(warning)* Warnung *f*; *(official)* Verwarnung *f.* **2** *vt (warn)* to ~ sb jdn warnen *(against* vor +dat*)*; *(officially)* jdn verwarnen.
**cautious** ['kɔːʃəs] *adj*, ~ly [-lɪ] *adv* vorsichtig *(of* in bezug auf +acc*).*
**cavalcade** [,kævəl'keɪd] *n* Kavalkade *f.*
**cavalier** [,kævə'lɪəʳ] **1** *n* Kavalier *m.* **2** *adj* person, nature unbekümmert.
**cavalry** ['kævəlrɪ] *n* Kavallerie *f.*
**cave** [keɪv] *n* Höhle *f.*
▶**cave in** *vi (ground, ceiling)* einstürzen.
**caveat** ['kævɪæt] *n* Vorbehalt *m.*
**cave:** ~man *n* Höhlenmensch *m*; *(fig)* Urmensch *m*; ~ painting *n* Höhlenmalerei *f.*
**cavern** ['kævən] *n* Höhle *f.*
**cavernous** ['kævənəs] *adj* pit tief; hole gähnend; eyes tiefliegend; cheeks eingefallen.
**caviar(e)** ['kævɪɑːʳ] *n* Kaviar *m.*
**cavil** ['kævɪl] *vi* kritteln. to ~ at sth an etw *(dat)* herumkritteln.
**cavity** ['kævɪtɪ] *n* Hohlraum *m*; *(in tooth)* Loch *nt.* nasal/chest ~ *(Anat)* Nasen-/Brusthöhle *f*; ~ wall Hohlwand *f*; ~ wall insulation Schaumisolierung *f* für Hohlwände.
**cavort** [kə'vɔːt] *vi* tollen, toben.
**caw** [kɔː] **1** *vi* krächzen. **2** *n* (heiserer) Schrei.
**cayenne pepper** ['keɪɛn'pepəʳ] *n* Cayennepfeffer *m.*
**CB** = **Citizens' Band** CB. ~ radio CB-Funk *m.*
**CBC** = **Canadian Broadcasting Corporation** kanadischer Rundfunk.
**CBE** = **Companion (of the Order) of the British Empire.**
**CBI** *(Brit)* = **Confederation of British Industry** ≈ BDI.
**CBS** = **Columbia Broadcasting System** CBS *f*; *amerikanischer Rundfunk.*
**cc** = **(a) cubic centimetre** ccm, cm³. **(b) carbon copy.**
**CCTV** = **closed circuit television.**
**CD** = **(a) compact disc** CD *f.* ~ player CD-Spieler *m.* **(b) corps diplomatique. (c) civil defence.**
**Cdr** = **Commander.**
**CD-ROM** ['siːdiː'rɒm] = **compact disc read-only memory** CD-ROM *f.*
**cease** [siːs] **1** *vi* aufhören. **2** *vt* beenden; fire, production einstellen. to ~ to exist aufhören zu bestehen; ~ fire! Feuer halt!
**ceasefire** [,siːs'faɪəʳ] *n* Feuerpause *f*; *(longer)* Waffenruhe *f.*
**ceaseless** ['siːslɪs] *adj* unaufhörlich; *(relentless)* vigi-

lance unablässig.
**cedar** ['siːdəʳ] *n* **(a)** *(tree)* Zeder *f.* **(b)** *(also ~ wood)* Zedernholz *nt.*
**cede** [siːd] *vt* territory abtreten *(to* an +acc*).* to ~ a point in einem Punkt nachgeben.
**cedilla** [sə'dɪlə] *n* Cedille *f.*
**Ceefax** ® ['siːfæks] *n* Videotext *m der BBC.*
**ceiling** ['siːlɪŋ] *n* **(a)** (Zimmer)decke *f.* **(b)** *(Aviat) (cloud* ~*)* Wolkengrenze *f*; *(aircraft's* ~*)* maximale Flughöhe. **(c)** *(fig: upper limit)* ober(st)e Grenze. to put a ~ on sth etw nach oben begrenzen.
**celebrate** ['selɪbreɪt] **1** *vt* **(a)** feiern. **(b)** mass, ritual zelebrieren. **2** *vi* feiern.
**celebrated** ['selɪbreɪtɪd] *adj* berühmt *(for* für*).*
**celebration** [,selɪ'breɪʃən] *n* **(a)** *(party, festival)* Feier *f.* **(b)** *(of mass)* Zelebration *f.*
**celebrity** [sɪ'lebrɪtɪ] *n* Berühmtheit *f*; *(person also)* berühmte Persönlichkeit.
**celeriac** [sə'lerɪæk] *n* (Knollen)sellerie *m.*
**celery** ['selərɪ] *n* Stangensellerie *m.*
**celestial** [sɪ'lestɪəl] *adj (heavenly)* himmlisch; *(Astron)* Himmels-.
**celibacy** ['selɪbəsɪ] *n* Zölibat *nt or m*; *(fig)* Enthaltsamkeit *f.*
**celibate** ['selɪbɪt] *adj (Rel)* ehelos; *(fig)* enthaltsam.
**cell** [sel] *n* Zelle *f.* ~ division Zellteilung *f.*
**cellar** ['selər] *n* Keller *m.*
**cellist** ['tʃelɪst] *n* Cellist(in *f*) *m.*
**cello, 'cello** ['tʃeləʊ] *n* Cello *nt.*
**cellophane** ® ['seləfeɪn] *n* Cellophan ® *nt.*
**cellular** ['seljʊləʳ] *adj* zellenförmig, Zell-. ~ phone Funktelefon *nt.*
**celluloid** ['seljʊlɔɪd] *n* Zelluloid *nt.*
**cellulose** ['seljʊləʊs] **1** *n* Zellulose *f.* **2** *adj* Zellulose-.
**Celsius** ['selsɪəs] *adj* Celsius.
**Celt** [kelt, selt] *n* Kelte *m*, Keltin *f.*
**Celtic** ['keltɪk, 'seltɪk] *adj* keltisch.
**cement** [sə'ment] **1** *n* **(a)** *(Build)* Zement *m.* ~ mixer Betonmischmaschine *f.* **(b)** *(glue)* Klebstoff *m*; *(for holes etc, fig)* Kitt *m.* **2** *vt (Build, fig)* zementieren; *(glue)* kleben; holes kitten.
**cemetery** ['semɪtrɪ] *n* Friedhof *m.*
**cenotaph** ['senətɑːf] *n* Kriegerdenkmal *nt.*
**censor** ['sensəʳ] **1** *n* Zensor *m.* **2** *vt* zensieren.
**censorship** ['sensəʃɪp] *n* Zensur *f.*
**censure** ['senʃəʳ] **1** *vt* tadeln. **2** *n* Tadel *m.* vote of ~ Tadelsantrag *m.*
**census** ['sensəs] *n* Volkszählung *f.* traffic ~ Verkehrszählung *f.*
**cent** [sent] *n* Cent *m.* I haven't a ~ *(US)* ich habe keinen Pfennig.
**centenarian** [,sentɪ'nɛərɪən] *n* Hundertjährige(r) *mf.*
**centenary** [sen'tiːnərɪ] *n (anniversary)* hundertster Jahrestag; *(birthday)* hundertster Geburtstag; *(100 years)* Jahrhundert *nt.*
**centennial** [sen'tenɪəl] **1** *adj* hundertjährig, hundertjährlich. **2** *n (esp US)* Hundertjahrfeier *f.*
**center** *n (US)* = **centre.**
**centigrade** ['sentɪgreɪd] *adj* Celsius-. one degree ~ ein Grad Celsius.
**centilitre, *(US)* centiliter** ['sentɪ,liːtəʳ] *n* Zentiliter *m or nt.*
**centimetre, *(US)* centimeter** ['sentɪ,miːtəʳ] *n* Zentimeter *m or nt.*
**centipede** ['sentɪpiːd] *n* Tausendfüßler *m.*
**central** ['sentrəl] **1** *adj* **(a)** zentral, Zentral-; *(main, chief)* Haupt-. **(b)** *(fig)* wesentlich; importance, figure zentral. **2** *n (US: exchange, operator)* (Telefon)zentrale *f.*
**central:** C~ African Republic *n* Zentralafrikanische Republik; C~ America *n* Mittelamerika *nt*;

**C~ Europe** *n* Mitteleuropa *nt*; **C~ European 1** *adj* mitteleuropäisch; **2** *n* Mitteleuropäer(in *f*) *m*; ~ **government** *n* Zentralregierung *f*; ~ **heating** *n* Zentralheizung *f*.

**centralize** ['sentrəlaɪz] *vt* zentralisieren.

**central locking** *n* (Aut) Zentralverriegelung *f*.

**centrally** ['sentrəlɪ] *adv* zentral. ~ **heated** zentralbeheizt.

**central:** ~ **nervous system** *n* Zentralnervensystem *nt*; ~ **processing unit** *n* (Comp) Zentraleinheit *f*; ~ **reservation** *n* (Brit) Mittelstreifen *m*; (with grass etc) Grünstreifen *m*; ~ **station** *n* Hauptbahnhof *m*.

**centre,** (US) **center** ['sentər] **1** *n* (a) Zentrum *nt*. (b) (middle) Mitte *f*; (of circle) Mittelpunkt *m*; (of place) Ortsmitte *f*; (town ~) Stadtmitte *f*. ~ **of gravity** Schwerpunkt *m*; ~ **of attraction** Hauptattraktion *f*; he always wants to be the ~ of attraction er will immer im Mittelpunkt stehen. **2** *vt* (a) (put in the middle, Typ, Comp) zentrieren; ball zur Mitte spielen or flanken. (b) (concentrate) konzentrieren.
►**centre (up)on** *vi* +prep obj (thoughts, talk etc) sich drehen um.

**centre:** ~-**fold** *n* doppelseitiges Bild in der Mitte einer Zeitschrift; ~-**forward** *n* (Sport) Mittelstürmer *m*; ~ **half** *n* (Sport) Stopper *m*; ~ **party** *n* Partei *f* der Mitte; ~-**piece** *n* (on table) Tafelaufsatz *m*; (main item) Kernstück *nt*.

**centrifugal** [,sentrɪ'fjuːgəl] *adj* zentrifugal. ~ **force** Zentrifugalkraft, Fliehkraft *f*.

**centrifuge** ['sentrɪfjuːʒ] *n* (Tech) Zentrifuge *f*.

**centurion** [sen'tjʊərɪən] *n* Zenturio *m*.

**century** ['sentjʊrɪ] *n* Jahrhundert *nt*. in the 20th ~ im 20. Jahrhundert.

**ceramic** [sɪ'ræmɪk] **1** *adj* keramisch, Keramik-. ~ **hob** (Glaskeramik-)Kochfeld *nt*. **2** *n* Keramik *f*.

**ceramics** [sɪ'ræmɪks] *n* (a) sing (art) Keramik *f*. (b) *pl* (articles) Keramiken *pl*.

**cereal** ['sɪərɪəl] *n* (a) (crop) Getreide *nt*. (b) (food) Getreideprodukt *nt*; (breakfast ~) Corn-flakes, Haferflocken etc, Cerealien *pl*.

**cerebral** ['serɪbrəl] *adj* (Physiol) zerebral; (intellectual) geistig. ~ **haemorrhage** Gehirnblutung *f*.

**ceremonial** [,serɪ'məʊnɪəl] **1** *adj* zeremoniell. **2** *n* Zeremoniell *nt*.

**ceremonious** [,serɪ'məʊnɪəs] *adj* förmlich.

**ceremony** ['serɪmənɪ] *n* (a) (event etc) Zeremonie *f*. (b) (formality) Förmlichkeit(en *pl*) *f*. to stand on ~ förmlich sein.

**cerise** [sə'riːz] **1** *adj* kirschrot. **2** *n* Kirschrot *nt*.

**cert** [sɜːt] *n* (col) a (dead) ~ eine todsichere Sache (col).

**certain** ['sɜːtən] *adj* (a) (positive, convinced) sicher; (inevitable, guaranteed) bestimmt. is he ~ weiß er das genau?; I don't know for ~, but ... ich bin mir nicht ganz sicher, aber ...; I can't say for ~ ich kann das nicht mit Sicherheit sagen; he is ~ to come er wird ganz bestimmt kommen; to make ~ of sth (check) etw nachprüfen; (ensure) für etw sorgen; be ~ to tell him vergessen Sie bitte nicht, ihm das zu sagen; that was ~ to happen das mußte ja so kommen. (b) (attr: not named or specified) gewiß; reason, conditions bestimmt. a ~ gentleman ein gewisser Herr; to a ~ extent in gewissem Maße.

**certainly** ['sɜːtənlɪ] *adv* (admittedly) sicher(lich); (positively, without doubt) bestimmt. ~ not! ganz bestimmt nicht!; ~! gewiß!

**certainty** ['sɜːtəntɪ] *n* (sure fact) Gewißheit *f*. to know for a ~ that ... mit Sicherheit wissen, daß ...; the ultimate ~ of death die letztliche Gewißheit des Todes.

**certifiable** [,sɜːtɪ'faɪəbl] *adj* (a) fact, claim nachweisbar. (b) (Psych) unzurechnungsfähig; (col: mad) nicht ganz bei Trost (col).

**certificate** [sə'tɪfɪkɪt] *n* Bescheinigung *f*; (of qualifications, health) Zeugnis *nt*.

**certify** ['sɜːtɪfaɪ] *vt* (a) bescheinigen; (Jur) beglaubigen. this is to ~ that ... hiermit wird bescheinigt or bestätigt, daß ...; certified public accountant (US) geprüfter Buchhalter; by certified mail (US) per Einschreiben. (b) (Psych) person für unzurechnungsfähig erklären.

**certitude** ['sɜːtɪtjuːd] *n* Gewißheit *f*.

**cervical** ['sɜːvɪkəl] *adj* zervikal (spec). ~ **cancer** Gebärmutterhalskrebs *m*; ~ **smear** (Gebärmutterhals)abstrich *m*.

**cervix** ['sɜːvɪks] *n* (of uterus) Gebärmutterhals *m*.

**Cesarean, Cesarian** [sɪ'zɛərɪən] (US) = **Caesarean**.

**cessation** [se'seɪʃən] *n* Ende *nt*; (of hostilities) Einstellung *f*.

**cesspit** ['sespɪt] *n* = **cesspool** (a).

**cesspool** ['sespuːl] *n* (a) Senkgrube *f*. (b) (fig) Sumpf *m*.

**CET** = **Central European Time** MEZ.

**Ceylon** [sɪ'lɒn] *n* (old) Ceylon *nt*.

**cf** = **confer** vgl.

**CFC** = **chlorofluorocarbon** FCKW *m*.

**ch** = (a) **chapter** Kap. (b) **central heating** ZH.

**Chad** [tʃæd] **1** *n* der Tschad. **2** *adj* tschadisch.

**chafe** [tʃeɪf] **1** *vt* (rub) (auf)scheuern. his shirt ~d his neck sein (Hemd)kragen scheuerte. **2** *vi* (a) (rub) sich aufscheuern; (cause soreness) scheuern. her skin ~s easily ihre Haut wird leicht wund. (b) (fig) sich ärgern, wütend werden (at, against über +acc).

**chaff** [tʃɑːf] *n* (a) (husks of grain) Spreu *f*. (b) (straw) Häcksel *m* or *nt*.

**chaffinch** ['tʃæfɪntʃ] *n* Buchfink *m*.

**chagrin** ['ʃægrɪn] **1** *n* Verdruß *m*. **2** *vt* verdrießen.

**chain** [tʃeɪn] **1** *n* (a) (lit, fig) Kette *f*. ~**s** (lit, fig: fetters) Ketten *pl*. (b) (of mountains) (Gebirgs)kette *f*. **2** *vt* (lit, fig) anketten. to ~ sb/sth to sth jdn/etw an etw (acc) ketten.

**chain:** ~ **reaction** *n* Kettenreaktion *f*; ~**saw** *n* Kettensäge *f*; ~-**smoke** *vi* eine nach der anderen rauchen (col); ~-**smoker** *n* Kettenraucher(in *f*) *m*; ~ **store** *n* Ladenkette *f*; (individual shop) Geschäft *nt* einer Ladenkette.

**chair** [tʃɛər] **1** *n* (a) (seat) Stuhl *m*; (arm~) Sessel *m*. (b) (in committees etc) Vorsitz *m*. to be in/take the ~ den Vorsitz führen. (c) (professorship) Lehrstuhl *m* (of für). (d) (US: electric ~) (elektrischer) Stuhl. **2** *vt* meeting den Vorsitz führen bei.

**chair:** ~**lift** *n* Sessellift *m*; ~**man** *n* Vorsitzende(r) *mf*; ~**manship** *n* Vorsitz *m*; ~**person** *n* Vorsitzende(r) *mf*; ~**woman** *n* Vorsitzende *f*.

**chalet** ['ʃæleɪ] *n* Chalet *nt*.

**chalice** ['tʃælɪs] *n* (poet, Eccl) Kelch *m*.

**chalk** [tʃɔːk] **1** *n* Kreide *f*. not by a long ~ (Brit col) bei weitem nicht; they're as different as ~ and cheese sie sind so verschieden wie Tag und Nacht. **2** *vt* message etc mit Kreide schreiben.
►**chalk up** *vt sep* (a) (lit) (mit Kreide) aufschreiben. (b) (fig) success, victory verbuchen. (c) (fig: mark up as credit) anschreiben (col).

**challenge** ['tʃælɪndʒ] **1** *n* (a) (to duel, match etc) Herausforderung *f* (to an +acc); (fig: demands) Anforderung(en *pl*) *f*. to issue a ~ to sb jdn herausfordern; the ~ of the unknown der Reiz des Unbekannten. (b) (bid: for leadership etc) Griff *m* (for nach). a direct ~ to his authority eine direkte Infragestellung seiner Autorität. **(c)** *(Mil: of sentry)* Anruf *m.* **(d)** *(Jur: of witness)* Ablehnung *f.* **2** *vt* **(a)** *person* herausfordern; *world record etc* überbieten wollen. **(b)** *(fig: make demands on)* fordern. **intellectually** ~**d** *(esp hum)* geistig minderbemittelt. **(c)** *(fig) remarks, sb's authority* in Frage stellen. **(d)** *(sentry)* anrufen. **(e)** *(Jur) witnesses* ablehnen; *evidence, verdict* anfechten.

**challenger** [ˈtʃælɪndʒəʳ] *n (to duel, match etc)* Herausforderer *m.*

**challenging** [ˈtʃælɪndʒɪŋ] *adj (provocative)* herausfordernd; *(thought-provoking)* reizvoll; *book* anregend; *(demanding)* anspruchsvoll. **I don't find this work** ~ **enough** diese Arbeit fordert mich nicht genügend.

**chamber** [ˈtʃeɪmbəʳ] *n* **(a)** *(old: room)* Kammer *f (old)*. **(b)** **C**~ **of Commerce** Handelskammer *f*; **the Upper/Lower C**~ *(Parl)* die Erste/Zweite Kammer. **(c)** *(Anat)* (Herz)kammer *f.*

**chamber**: ~**maid** *n (Brit)* Zimmermädchen *nt*; ~ **music** *n* Kammermusik *f*; ~ **orchestra** *n* Kammerorchester *nt*; ~ **pot** *n* Nachttopf *m.*

**chameleon** [kəˈmiːlɪən] *n (Zool, fig)* Chamäleon *nt.*

**chamois** [ˈʃæmwɑː] *n* **(a)** *also* [ˈʃæmɪ] *(leather)* Gamsleder *nt.* **a** ~ **(leather)** ein Ledertuch *nt*, ein Fensterleder *nt.* **(b)** *(Zool)* Gemse *f.*

**champagne** [ʃæmˈpeɪn] *n (unspecified)* Sekt *m*; *(French* ~*)* Champagner *m.*

**champion** [ˈtʃæmpjən] **1** *n* **(a)** *(Sport)* Meister(in *f) m.* ~**s** *(team)* Meister *m*; **world** ~ Weltmeister(in *f) m.* **(b)** *(of a cause)* Verfechter *m.* **2** *adj* **(a)** *(prize-winning)* siegreich; *show animal* preisgekrönt. ~ **boxer** Boxmeister. **(b)** *(N Engl col)* klasse *inv (col)*. **3** *vt person, action, cause* sich engagieren für.

**championship** [ˈtʃæmpjənʃɪp] *n* **(a)** *(Sport)* Meisterschaft *f.* **(b)** ~**s** *pl (event)* Meisterschaftskämpfe *pl.* **(c)** *(support)* Engagement *nt (of für).*

**chance** [tʃɑːns] **1** *n* **(a)** *(coincidence)* Zufall *m*; *(luck, fortune)* Glück *nt.* **by** ~ zufällig; **would you by any** ~ **be able to help?** könnten Sie mir vielleicht behilflich sein?

**(b)** *(possibility)* Chance(n *pl) f*; *(probability, likelihood)* Möglichkeit *f.* **the** ~**s are that** ... wahrscheinlich ...; **he has not much/a good** ~ **of winning** er hat wenig/gute Aussicht zu gewinnen; **to be in with a** ~ eine Chance haben; **he doesn't stand a** ~ er hat keine Chance(n); **no** ~! *(col)* (das) ist nicht drin *(col)*, nichts zu machen *(col)*; **the** ~ **of a lifetime** eine einmalige Chance; **you won't get another** ~ das ist eine einmalige Gelegenheit; **now's your** ~! das ist deine Chance!; **give me a** ~! nun mach aber mal langsam! *(col)*; **you never gave me a** ~ **to explain** du hast mir ja nie Gelegenheit gegeben, das zu erklären. **(c)** *(risk)* Risiko *nt.* **to take a** ~ ein Risiko eingehen.

**2** *attr* zufällig. ~ **meeting** zufällige Begegnung.

**3** *vt* **I'll** ~ **it!** *(col)* ich versuch's mal *(col)*; **to** ~ **one's luck** *(have a try)* sein Glück versuchen; *(risk)* das Glück herausfordern.

►**chance (up)on** *vi +prep obj person* zufällig treffen; *thing* zufällig stoßen auf *(+acc).*

**chancel** [ˈtʃɑːnsəl] *n* Chor, Altarraum *m.*

**chancellor** [ˈtʃɑːnsələʳ] *n (Jur, Pol, Univ)* Kanzler *m.* **C**~ **(of the Exchequer)** *(Brit)* Schatzkanzler *m.*

**chancy** [ˈtʃɑːnsɪ] *adj (col)* riskant.

**chandelier** [ˌʃændəˈlɪəʳ] *n* Kronleuchter *m.*

**change** [tʃeɪndʒ] **1** *n* **(a)** Veränderung *f*; *(modification)* Änderung *f (to gen).* **a** ~ **of air** eine Luftveränderung; **a** ~ **is as good as a rest** *(prov)* Abwechslung wirkt Wunder; **no** ~ unverändert; **a** ~ **for the**

**better/worse** eine Verbesserung/Verschlechterung; **the** ~ **of life** die Wechseljahre *pl*; **he needs a** ~ **of clothes** er braucht etwas zum Wechseln. **(b)** *(variety)* Abwechslung *f.* **(just) for a** ~ zur Abwechslung (mal); **that makes a** ~ das ist mal was anderes; *(iro)* das ist ja was ganz Neues! **(c)** *(of one thing for another)* Wechsel *m.* **a** ~ **of government** ein Regierungswechsel. **(d)** *no pl (money)* Wechselgeld *nt*; *(small* ~*)* Kleingeld *nt.* **can you give me** ~ **for a pound?** können Sie mir ein Pfund wechseln?; **keep the** ~ stimmt so!;_you won't get much ~ out of £5 von £5 wird nicht viel übrigbleiben.

**2** *vt* **(a)** *(replace)* wechseln; *address, name* ändern. **to** ~ **train/buses** *etc* umsteigen; **to** ~ **one's clothes** sich umziehen; **to** ~ **a wheel/the oil** ein Rad/das Öl wechseln; **to** ~ **hands** den Besitzer wechseln; **to** ~ **places with sb** mit jdm den Platz tauschen. **(b)** *(alter)* ändern; *(transform)* verwandeln. **to** ~ **sb/sth into sth** jdn/etw in etw *(acc)* verwandeln. **(c)** *(exchange: in shop etc)* umtauschen. **(d)** *money* wechseln; *(into other currency also)* (um)tauschen. **(e)** *(Aut)* **to** ~ **gear** schalten.

**3** *vi* **(a)** sich ändern; *(town, person also)* sich verändern. **you've** ~**d!** du hast dich aber verändert!; **to** ~ **into sth/sb** sich in etw *(acc)*/jdn verwandeln. **(b)** *(~ clothes)* sich umziehen. **she** ~**d into an old skirt** sie zog sich *(dat)* einen alten Rock an. **(c)** *(~ trains etc)* umsteigen. **all** ~! Endstation!, alles aussteigen! **(d)** *(~ gear)* schalten. **(e)** *(from one thing to another) (seasons)* wechseln. **to** ~ **to a different system** zu einem anderen System übergehen.

►**change down** *vi (Aut)* in einen niedrigeren Gang schalten.

►**change over** *vi* **(a)** *(change to sth different)* sich umstellen auf *(+acc).* **(b)** *(exchange places, activities etc)* wechseln. **do you mind if I** ~ ~? *(TV)* hast du was dagegen, wenn ich umschalte?

►**change up** *vi (Aut)* in einen höheren Gang schalten.

**changeability** [ˌtʃeɪndʒəˈbɪlɪtɪ] *n* Unbeständigkeit, Veränderlichkeit *f.*

**changeable** [ˈtʃeɪndʒəbl] *adj weather* unbeständig, veränderlich; *person* wankelmütig.

**change machine** *n* Geldwechsler *m.*

**changing** [ˈtʃeɪndʒɪŋ] **1** *adj* sich verändernd. **2** *n* **the** ~ **of the Guard** die Wachablösung.

**changing-room** [ˈtʃeɪndʒɪŋˈruːm] *n (Brit) (in store)* Ankleideraum *m*; *(Sport)* Umkleideraum *m.*

**channel** [ˈtʃænl] **1** *n* **(a)** *(watercourse)* (Fluß)bett *nt*; *(strait)* Kanal *m*; *(deepest part of river etc)* Fahrrinne *f.* **the (English) C**~ der Ärmelkanal; **C**~ **Islands** Kanalinseln *pl*; **C**~ **Tunnel** Kanaltunnel *m.* **(b)** *(fig, usu pl) (of bureaucracy etc)* Dienstweg *m*; *(of information etc)* Kanal *m*; *(of thought, interest etc)* Bahn *f.* **if you go through the right** ~**s** wenn Sie sich an die richtigen Stellen wenden. **(c)** *(groove)* Rinne *f.* **(d)** *(TV, Rad)* Kanal *m*, Programm *nt.* **2** *vt* **(a)** *(dig out, furrow)* way, course sich *(dat)* bahnen. **(b)** *(direct)* water, river (hindurch)leiten *(through* durch*).* **(c)** *(fig)* efforts, interest lenken *(into* auf *+acc).*

**chant** [tʃɑːnt] **1** *n (Eccl, Mus)* Gesang *m*; *(monotonous song)* Sprechgesang *m*; *(of football fans)* Sprechchor *m.* **2** *vt* im (Sprech)chor rufen; *(Eccl)* singen. **3** *vi* Sprechchöre anstimmen; *(Eccl)* singen.

**chaos** [ˈkeɪɒs] *n* Chaos, Durcheinander *nt.*

**chaotic** [keɪˈɒtɪk] *adj* chaotisch.

**chap**[1] [tʃæp] *n (Med: of skin)* **he's got** ~**s on his hands** seine Hände sind aufgesprungen.

**chap**[2] *n (Brit col: man)* Kerl *(col)*, Typ *(col) m.* **old** ~ alter Junge *(col)*. **the poor little** ~ der arme Kleine.

**chapel** [ˈtʃæpəl] *n* Kapelle *f.*

**chaperon(e)** ['ʃæpərəʊn] **1** *n* **(a)** *(for propriety)* Anstandsdame *f.* **(b)** *(escort)* Begleiter(in *f*) *m.* **2** *vt* **(a)** *(for propriety)* Anstandsdame spielen bei. **(b)** *(escort)* begleiten.

**chaplain** ['tʃæplɪn] *n* Kaplan *m.*

**chapter** ['tʃæptər] *n (of book)* Kapitel *nt; (fig: episode)* Abschnitt *m (in,* of in +*dat).* **to give ~ and verse (for sth)** *(fig)* etw genau belegen; **a ~ of accidents** eine Serie von Unfällen.

**char¹** [tʃɑːr] *vt (burn black)* verkohlen.

**char²** *(Brit col)* **1** *n (charwoman)* Putzfrau *f.* **2** *vi* putzen.

**character** ['kærɪktər] *n* **(a)** *(nature)* Charakter *m; (of people)* Wesen *nt no pl.* **it is out of ~ for him to behave like that** solches Benehmen ist untypisch für ihn; **to be of good/bad ~** ein guter/schlechter Mensch sein; **a man of ~** ein Mann von Charakter; **he's quite a ~** er ist ein richtiges Original. **(b)** *no pl (individuality) (of towns etc)* Charakter *m; (of person)* Persönlichkeit *f.* **(c)** *(in novel, Theat)* Figur *f.* **(d)** *(Typ, Comp)* Zeichen *nt.*

**character:** **~ actor** *n* Chargendarsteller *m;* **~ code** *n (Comp)* Zeichencode *m.*

**characteristic** [ˌkærɪktə'rɪstɪk] **1** *adj* charakteristisch, typisch *(of* für*).* **2** *n* (typisches) Merkmal.

**characteristically** [ˌkærɪktə'rɪstɪkəlɪ] *adv* typisch.

**characterization** [ˌkærɪktəraɪ'zeɪʃən] *n (in a novel etc)* Personenbeschreibung *f; (of one character)* Charakterisierung *f.*

**characterize** ['kærɪktəraɪz] *vt (be characteristic of)* kennzeichnen, charakterisieren; *(describe)* beschreiben.

**character:** **~less** *adj* nichtssagend; **~ part** *n* Charge *f;* **~ set** *n (Comp)* Zeichensatz *m;* **~ string** *n (Comp)* Zeichenkette *f.*

**charade** [ʃə'rɑːd] *n* Scharade *f; (fig)* Farce *f.*

**charcoal** ['tʃɑːkəʊl] *n* Holzkohle *f; (pencil)* Kohle(stift *m*) *f.*

**charcoal:** **~ drawing** *n* Kohlezeichnung *f;* **~ grey** *adj* anthrazitfarben.

**charge** [tʃɑːdʒ] **1** *n* **(a)** *(Jur: accusation)* Anklage *f (of* wegen*).* **to bring a ~ against sb** gegen jdn Anklage erheben; **he was arrested on a ~ of murder** er wurde wegen Mordverdacht festgenommen; **to be on a ~** *(soldier)* eine Disziplinarstrafe verbüßen.
**(b)** *(attack: of soldiers, bull etc)* Angriff *m.*
**(c)** *(fee)* Gebühr *f.* **what's the ~?** was kostet das?; **free of ~** kostenlos.
**(d)** *(explosive ~)* (Spreng)ladung *f; (in firearm, Elec, Phys)* Ladung *f.*
**(e)** *(position of responsibility)* Verantwortung *f (of* für*).* **to be in ~** verantwortlich sein; **who's in ~ here?** wer ist hier der Verantwortliche?; **the children were placed in their aunt's ~** die Kinder wurden ihrer Tante anvertraut; **to take ~ of sth** etw übernehmen; **he took ~ of the situation** er nahm die Sache in die Hand.
**2** *vt* **(a)** *(with gen) (Jur)* anklagen; *(fig)* beschuldigen. **(b)** *(attack)* stürmen; *troops* angreifen. **(c)** *(ask in payment)* berechnen. **I won't ~ you for that** dafür berechne ich Ihnen nichts. **(d)** *(record as debt)* in Rechnung stellen. **~ it to the company** stellen Sie das der Firma in Rechnung. **(e)** *firearm* laden; *(Phys, Elec), battery* (auf)laden.
**3** *vi* **(a)** *(attack)* stürmen; *(at people)* angreifen *(at sb* jdn*).* **~!** vorwärts! **(b)** *(col: rush)* rennen. **he ~d into the room/upstairs** er stürmte ins Zimmer/die Treppe hoch.

**charge:** **~ account** *n* Kunden(kredit)konto *nt;* **~ card** *n* Kundenkreditkarte *f.*

**chargé d'affaires** [ˌʃɑːʒeɪdæ'fɛər] *n* Chargé

d'affaires *m.*

**charge nurse** *n (Brit)* Stationsleiter(in *f*) *m (im Pflegedienst).*

**charger** ['tʃɑːdʒər] *n (battery ~)* Ladegerät *nt.*

**chariot** ['tʃærɪət] *n* Streitwagen *m.*

**charisma** [kæ'rɪzmə] *n* Charisma *nt.*

**charismatic** [ˌkærɪz'mætɪk] *adj* charismatisch.

**charitable** ['tʃærɪtəbl] *adj* gütig; *organization* Wohltätigkeits-; *(financially generous, tolerant)* großzügig; *thought, remark etc* freundlich.

**charity** ['tʃærɪtɪ] *n* **(a)** *(Christian virtue)* Nächstenliebe *f; (tolerance, kindness)* Güte *f.* **~ begins at home** *(Prov)* man sollte zuerst an seine eigene Familie/ sein eigenes Land *etc* denken; **to live on ~** von Almosen leben. **(b)** *(charitable society)* Wohltätigkeitsverein *m; (charitable purposes)* Wohlfahrt *f.* **a collection for ~** eine Sammlung für wohltätige Zwecke.

**charlady** ['tʃɑːˌleɪdɪ] *n (Brit dated)* Putzfrau *f.*

**charlatan** ['ʃɑːlətən] *n* Scharlatan *m.*

**Charlemagne** ['ʃɑːləmeɪn] *n (Hist)* Karl der Große.

**Charles** [tʃɑːlz] *n ≃* Karl *m.*

**charm** [tʃɑːm] **1** *n* **(a)** *(attractiveness)* Charme *m no pl; (of village, countryside)* Reiz *m.* **feminine ~s** weibliche Reize *pl;* **to turn on the ~** seinen (ganzen) Charme spielen lassen. **(b)** *(spell)* Bann *m.* **it worked like a ~** das hat hervorragend geklappt. **(c)** *(amulet)* Talisman *m; (trinket)* Anhänger *m.* **~ bracelet** Armband *nt* mit Anhängern. **2** *vt* **(a)** *(attract, please)* bezaubern. **(b) to lead a ~ed life** einen Schutzengel haben.

**charmer** ['tʃɑːmər] *n* **to be a real ~** wirklich charmant sein.

**charming** ['tʃɑːmɪŋ] *adj* reizend, charmant. **~!** *(iro)* wie reizend! *(iro).*

**chart** [tʃɑːt] **1** *n* **(a)** *(table)* Tabelle *f; (graph)* Schaubild *nt; (map, weather ~)* Karte *f.* **(b) ~s** *pl (top twenty)* Hitliste *f;* **~ topper** *(hit record)* Spitzenreiter *m.* **2** *vt (make a map of)* kartographisch erfassen; *(record progress of)* auswerten; *(keep a ~ of)* aufzeichnen; *(plan)* festlegen.

**charter** ['tʃɑːtər] **1** *n* **(a)** Charta *f; (of a society)* Satzung *f; (permission to become established)* Charter *f or m,* Freibrief *m.* **(b)** *(Naut, Aviat: hire)* **on ~** gechartert. **2** *vt plane, bus etc* chartern. **~ed accountant** *(Brit)* staatlich geprüfter Bilanzbuchhalter *m;* **~ flight** Charterflug *m.*

**charwoman** ['tʃɑːˌwʊmən] *n (Brit)* Putzfrau *f.*

**chary** ['tʃɛərɪ] *adj (+er) (cautious)* vorsichtig; *(sparing)* zurückhaltend *(of* mit*).* **he is ~ of giving praise** er spart mit Lob.

**chase** [tʃeɪs] **1** *n* Verfolgungsjagd *f; (Hunt)* Jagd *f.* **to give ~** die Verfolgung aufnehmen. **2** *vt* jagen; *(follow)* verfolgen. **he's been chasing that woman for months** er ist schon seit Monaten hinter der Frau her. **3** *vi* **to ~ after sb** hinter jdm herrennen *(col); (in vehicle)* hinter jdm herrasen *(col);* **to ~ around** herumrasen *(col).*
►**chase away** *or* **off 1** *vi* losrasen *(col).* **2** *vt sep* wegjagen; *(fig)* sorrow *etc* vertreiben.
►**chase up** *vt sep* person rankriegen *(col); information etc* ranschaffen *(col); (make hurry)* Dampf machen (+*dat*) *(col).*

**chasm** ['kæzəm] *n (Geol, fig)* Kluft *f.* **a yawning ~** ein gähnender Abgrund.

**chassis** ['ʃæsɪ] *n* Chassis *nt; (Aut)* Fahrgestell *nt.*

**chaste** [tʃeɪst] *adj (+er)* keusch.

**chastening** ['tʃeɪsnɪŋ] *adj experience* ernüchternd.

**chastise** [tʃæs'taɪz] *vt* züchtigen *(geh); (scold)* schelten.

**chastisement** ['tʃæstɪzmənt] *n see vt* Züchtigung *f*

**cherry**

*(geh)*; Schelte *f.*

**chastity** ['tʃæstɪtɪ] *n* Keuschheit *f.*

**chat** [tʃæt] *n* Unterhaltung *f.* **could we have a** ~ **about it?** können wir uns mal darüber unterhalten?; **she dropped in for a** ~ sie kam zu einem Schwätzchen rein *(col).*
▶**chat up** *vt sep (col) person* einreden auf *(+acc)*; *girl, boy* sich heranmachen an *(+acc)*, anmachen *(col).*

**chatline** *n Telefondienst m, der Anrufern die Teilnahme an einer Gesprächsrunde ermöglicht.*

**chat show** *n (Brit)* Talkshow *f.*

**chattels** ['tʃætlz] *npl* **all his (goods and)** ~ seine gesamte Habe.

**chatter** ['tʃætər] **1** *n (of person)* Geschwätz *nt; (of birds)* Gezwitscher *nt; (of teeth)* Klappern *nt.* **2** *vi see n* schwatzen; zwitschern; klappern.

**chatterbox** ['tʃætəbɒks] *n* Quasselstrippe *f (col).*

**chattering classes** ['tʃætərɪŋklɑːsɪz] *npl:* **the** ~ ~ *(often pej)* intellektuelle Schwätzer *pl (pej).*

**chatty** ['tʃætɪ] *adj (+er) person* geschwätzig.

**chauffeur** ['ʃəʊfər] *n* Chauffeur *m.*

**chauvinism** ['ʃəʊvɪnɪzəm] *n* Chauvinismus *m.*

**chauvinist** ['ʃəʊvɪnɪst] **1** *n (jingoist)* Chauvinist(in *f*) *m.* **male** ~ **pig** *(pej col)* Pascha *(col)*, Chauvi *(col) m.* **2** *adj* chauvinistisch.

**chauvinistic** [ˌʃəʊvɪ'nɪstɪk] *adj* chauvinistisch.

**cheap** [tʃiːp] *adj, adv (+er)* billig. **to buy sth on the** ~ *(col)* etw für einen Pappenstiel kaufen *(col)*; **it's** ~ **at the price** es ist sehr preiswert; **to feel** ~ sich *(dat)* schäbig vorkommen.

**cheapen** ['tʃiːpən] **1** *vt (lit, fig)* herabsetzen. **2** *vi* billiger werden.

**cheaply** ['tʃiːplɪ] *adv see adj.*

**cheapskate** ['tʃiːpskeɪt] *n (col)* Knicker *m (col).*

**cheat** [tʃiːt] **1** *vt* betrügen. **to** ~ **sb out of sth** jdn um etw betrügen. **2** *vi* betrügen; *(in exam, game etc)* mogeln *(col)*, schummeln *(Sch sl).* **3** *n* **(a)** *(person)* Betrüger(in *f*) *m; (in exam, game etc)* Mogler(in *f*) *(col)*, Schummler(in *f*) *(Sch sl) m.* **(b)** *(dishonest trick)* Betrug *m.*

**check** [tʃek] **1** *n* **(a)** *(examination)* Kontrolle *f.* **a random** ~ eine Stichprobe; **to keep a** ~ **on sb/sth** jdn/etw überwachen *or* kontrollieren. **(b)** *(restraint)* Hemmnis *nt.* **to keep one's temper in** ~ sich beherrschen; **to act as a** ~ **on sth** etw unter Kontrolle *(dat)* halten. **(c)** *(pattern)* Karomuster *nt; (square)* Karo *nt.* **(d)** *(Chess)* Schach *nt.* **to be in** ~ im Schach stehen; **to put sb in** ~ jdm Schach bieten. **(e)** *(US) (cheque)* Scheck *m; (bill)* Rechnung *f.* ~ **please** bitte (be)zahlen! **2** *vt* **(a)** *(examine)* überprüfen; *(in book)* nachschlagen; *tickets* kontrollieren. **(b)** *(act as control on)* kontrollieren; *anger* unterdrücken. **(c)** *(Chess)* Schach bieten *(+dat).* **(d)** *(US: tick)* abhaken. **3** *vi (make sure)* nachprüfen; *(ask also)* nachfragen *(with* bei*); (have a look)* nachsehen.
▶**check in 1** *vi (at airport)* einchecken; *(at hotel)* sich anmelden. **2** *vt sep (at airport) luggage* abfertigen lassen; *(at hotel) person* anmelden.
▶**check out 1** *vi* sich abmelden; *(leave hotel)* abreisen. **2** *vt sep figures, facts* überprüfen. ~ ~ **our new range** *(col)* sehen Sie sich *(dat)* unser neues Sortiment an.
▶**check up** *vi* überprüfen.
▶**check up on** *vi* +*prep obj* überprüfen; *(keep a check on) sb* kontrollieren.

**checkbook** ['tʃekbʊk] *n (US)* Scheckbuch *nt.*

**checked** [tʃekt] *adj* kariert.

**checkered** *adj (US)* = **chequered.**

**checkers** ['tʃekəz] *n (US)* Damespiel *nt.*

**check-in (desk)** ['tʃekɪn('desk)] *n* Abfertigung *f.*

**checking account** ['tʃekɪŋə'kaʊnt] *n (US)* Girokonto *nt.*

**check:** ~ **list** *n* Prüf- *or* Checkliste *f;* ~**mate** *n* Schachmatt *nt;* ~**out** *n (in supermarket)* Kasse *f;* ~**point** *n* Kontrollpunkt *m;* ~**room** *n (US) (Theat)* Garderobe *f; (Rail)* Gepäckaufbewahrung *f;* ~**-up** *n (Med)* Untersuchung *f;* **to have a** ~**-up** sich untersuchen lassen.

**cheddar** ['tʃedər] *n* Cheddar(käse) *m.*

**cheek** [tʃiːk] *n* **(a)** Backe, Wange *(geh) f.* **(b)** *(buttock)* Backe *f.* **(c)** *(impudence)* Frechheit *f.* **of all the** ~!, **the** ~ **of it!** so eine Frechheit *or* Unverschämtheit!

**cheekily** ['tʃiːkɪlɪ] *adv* frech.

**cheekiness** ['tʃiːkɪnɪs] *n* Frechheit *f.*

**cheeky** ['tʃiːkɪ] *adj (+er)* frech.

**cheep** [tʃiːp] **1** *n* Piepser *m.* **2** *vi* piepsen.

**cheer** [tʃɪər] **1** *n* Beifallsruf *m; (cheering)* Hurrageschrei *nt.* **three** ~**s for Mike!** ein dreifaches Hurra für Mike!; ~**s!** *(Brit col) (your health)* prost!; *(goodbye)* tschüs! *(col)*; *(thank you)* danke schön! **2** *vt* **(a)** *person* zujubeln. **(b)** *(gladden)* aufmuntern. **3** *vi* jubeln.
▶**cheer on** *vt sep* anfeuern.
▶**cheer up 1** *vt sep* aufmuntern; *room, place* freundlicher gestalten. **2** *vi* **he** ~**ed** ~ seine Stimmung hob sich; ~ ~! laß den Kopf nicht hängen!

**cheerful** ['tʃɪəfʊl] *adj* fröhlich, vergnügt; *colour etc* heiter; *room* freundlich; *prospect, news* erfreulich; *(iro)* heiter. **you're a** ~ **one!** *(iro)* du bist vielleicht ein Miesmacher! *(col).*

**cheerfully** ['tʃɪəfʊlɪ] *adv* fröhlich, vergnügt; *decorated* heiter.

**cheerfulness** ['tʃɪəfʊlnɪs] *n see adj* Fröhlichkeit, Vergnügtheit *f;* Heiterkeit *f;* Freundlichkeit *f;* Erfreulichkeit *f.*

**cheerily** ['tʃɪərɪlɪ] *adv* fröhlich, vergnügt.

**cheering** ['tʃɪərɪŋ] **1** *n* Jubel *m*, Jubeln *nt.* **2** *adj* **(a)** *news, prospect* beglückend. **(b)** *crowds* jubelnd.

**cheerio** ['tʃɪərɪ'əʊ] *interj (esp Brit col)* Wiedersehen *(col)*; *(to friends)* tschüs *(col)*; *(your health)* prost.

**cheerless** ['tʃɪəlɪs] *adj person* trübselig; *prospect* trübe; *scenery* grau.

**cheery** ['tʃɪərɪ] *adj (+er)* fröhlich.

**cheese** [tʃiːz] *n* Käse *m.*

**cheese** *in cpds* Käse-; ~**board** *n* Käsebrett *nt; (course)* Käseplatte *f;* ~**burger** *n* Cheeseburger *m;* ~**cake** *n (Cook)* Käsekuchen *m;* ~**cloth** *n (Tex)* Baumwollkrepp *m.*

**cheesed-off** [tʃiːzd'ɒf] *adj (Brit col)* angeödet *(col).*

**cheetah** ['tʃiːtə] *n* Gepard *m.*

**chef** [ʃef] *n* Küchenchef *m; (as profession)* Koch *m.*

**chemical** ['kemɪkəl] **1** *adj* chemisch. ~ **engineer** Chemotechniker(in *f*) *m.* **2** *n* Chemikalie *f.*

**chemist** ['kemɪst] *n* **(a)** *(scientist)* Chemiker(in *f*) *m.* **(b)** *(Brit: in shop)* Drogist(in *f*) *m; (dispensing)* Apotheker(in *f*) *m.* ~**'s shop** Drogerie *f;* Apotheke *f.*

**chemistry** ['kemɪstrɪ] *n* Chemie *f.* ~ **set** Chemiebaukasten *m.*

**chemotherapy** [ˌkeməʊ'θerəpɪ] *n* Chemotherapie *f.*

**cheque,** *(US)* **check** [tʃek] *n* Scheck *m.* **a** ~ **for £10** ein Scheck über £10; **to pay by** ~ mit (einem) Scheck bezahlen; ~**book** Scheckbuch *nt;* ~ **card** *(Brit)* Scheckkarte *f.*

**chequered,** *(US)* **checkered** ['tʃekəd] *adj (lit)* kariert; *(fig) career, history* bewegt.

**cherish** ['tʃerɪʃ] *vt* **(a)** *person* liebevoll sorgen für. **(b)** *feelings, hope* hegen.

**cheroot** [ʃə'ruːt] *n* Stumpen *m.*

**cherry** ['tʃerɪ] *n* Kirsche *f.* ~ **brandy** Cherry Brandy *m*; ~ **red** kirschrot; ~ **stone** Kirschkern *m*.

**cherub** ['tʃerəb] *n (fig: baby)* Engelchen *nt*.

**chess** [tʃes] *n* Schach(spiel) *nt*. ~ **board** Schachbrett *nt*; ~**man** Schachfigur *f*; ~ **player** Schachspieler(in *f*) *m*.

**chest¹** [tʃest] *n (for tea, tools etc)* Kiste *f*; *(piece of furniture)* Truhe *f*. ~ **of drawers** Kommode *f*.

**chest²** *n (Anat)* Brust *f*. **to get sth off one's** ~ *(fig col)* sich *(dat)* etw von der Seele reden; **to have a weak** ~ schwach auf der Brust sein *(col)*; ~ **measurement** Brustumfang *m*; ~ **specialist** Facharzt *m* für Lungenkrankheiten.

**chestnut** ['tʃesnʌt] **1** *n* **(a)** *(nut)* Kastanie *f*; *(tree)* Kastanie *f*, Kastanienbaum *m*. **(b)** *(colour)* Kastanienbraun *nt*. **(c)** *(horse)* Fuchs *m*. **(d)** **that's an old** ~ *(col: joke)* der Witz hat einen Bart *(col)*. **2** *adj (colour)* hair kastanienbraun.

**chew** [tʃuː] *vt* kauen.

►**chew over** *vi +prep obj (col)* facts, problem sich *(dat)* durch den Kopf gehen lassen.

►**chew up** *vt sep* pencil etc zerkauen; ground, road surface zerstören.

**chewing gum** ['tʃuːɪŋɡʌm] *n* Kaugummi *m or nt*.

**chewy** ['tʃuːwɪ] *adj* meat zäh.

**chic** [ʃiːk] *adj (+er)* schick, elegant.

**chicane** [ʃɪ'keɪn] *n (Sport)* Schikane *f*.

**chicanery** [ʃɪ'keɪnərɪ] *n* Machenschaften *pl*.

**chick** [tʃɪk] *n (of chicken)* Küken *nt*; *(young bird)* Junge(s) *nt*; *(col: girl)* Mädchen *nt*.

**chicken** ['tʃɪkɪn] **1** *n* **(a)** Huhn *nt*; *(for roasting, frying)* Hähnchen *nt*. **she's no** ~ *(col)* sie ist nicht mehr die Jüngste; **don't count your ~s (before they're hatched)** *(Prov)* man soll den Tag nicht vor dem Abend loben *(Prov)*; **it's a ~ and egg situation** *(col)* das ist eine Zwickmühle. **(b)** *(col: coward)* feiges Huhn *(col)*. **2** *adj (col)* feig.

►**chicken out** *vi (col)* kneifen *(col)*.

**chicken** *in cpds* Hühner-; ~**feed** *n* **(a)** *(lit)* Hühnerfutter *nt*; **(b)** *(col: insignificant sum)* ein Pappenstiel *(col)*; ~**pox** *n* Windpocken *pl*.

**chickpea** ['tʃɪk,piː] *n* Kichererbse *f*.

**chicory** ['tʃɪkərɪ] *n* Chicorée *f or m*; *(in coffee)* Zichorie *f*.

**chief** [tʃiːf] **1** *n, pl* **-s** *(of department or organization)* Leiter *m*; *(of tribe)* Häuptling *m*; *(of gang)* Anführer *m*; *(col: boss)* Chef *m*. ~ **of police** Polizeipräsident *m*; ~ **of staff** *(Mil)* Stabschef *m*. **2** *adj* **(a)** *(most important)* Haupt-, wichtigste(r, s). **the** ~ **thing** die Hauptsache. **(b)** *(most senior)* Haupt-. ~ **clerk** Bürochef *m*; ~ **constable** *(Brit)* Polizeipräsident *m*; ~ **engineer** *(Naut)* erster Maschinist; ~ **executive** *(officer)* Generaldirektor *m*; ~ **justice** *(Brit)* ≈ Oberrichter *m*; *(US)* Oberster Bundesrichter.

**chiefly** ['tʃiːflɪ] *adv* hauptsächlich, vor allem.

**chieftain** ['tʃiːftən] *n (of tribe)* Häuptling *m*.

**chiffon** ['ʃɪfɒn] **1** *n* Chiffon *m*. **2** *adj* Chiffon-.

**chilblain** ['tʃɪlbleɪn] *n* Frostbeule *f*.

**child** [tʃaɪld] *n, pl* **children** *(lit, fig)* Kind *nt*. **when I was a** ~ in meiner Kindheit.

**child:** ~ **abuse** *n* Kindesmißhandlung *f*; ~**bearing** *adj* **of** ~**-bearing age** im gebärfähigen Alter; ~ **benefit** *n* Kindergeld *nt*; ~**birth** *n* Geburt *f*; **to die in** ~**birth** bei der Geburt sterben; ~ **care** *n* Kinderpflege *f*; ~**hood** *n* Kindheit *f*; ~**hood memory** Kindheitserinnerung *f*.

**childish** ['tʃaɪldɪʃ] *adj (pej)* kindisch.

**childishness** ['tʃaɪldɪʃnɪs] *n (pej)* kindisches Gehabe.

**child:** ~ **labour** *(Brit) or* **labor** *(US) n* Kinderarbeit *f*; ~**less** *adj* kinderlos; ~**like** *adj* kindlich; ~**minder** *n* Tagesmutter *f*; ~ **prodigy** *n* Wunder-

kind *nt*; ~**proof** *adj* kindersicher.

**children** ['tʃɪldrən] *pl of* **child**.

**children's** *in cpds* Kinder-; ~ **books** *npl* Kinderbücher *pl*; ~ **choir** *n* Kinderchor *m*; ~ **game** *n* Kinderspiel *nt*; ~ **portion** *n* Kinderteller *m*.

**child:** ~'**s play** *n* ein Kinderspiel *nt*; ~ **welfare** *n* Jugendfürsorge *f*.

**Chile** ['tʃɪlɪ] *n* Chile *nt*.

**Chilean** ['tʃɪlɪən] **1** *adj* chilenisch. **2** *n* Chilene *m*, Chilenin *f*.

**chill** [tʃɪl] **1** *n* **(a)** Kälte *f*. **there's quite a** ~ **in the air** es ist ziemlich frisch draußen. **(b)** *(Med)* fieberhafte Erkältung; *(shiver)* Schauder *m*. **to catch a** ~ sich verkühlen. **2** *adj (lit, fig)* kühl. **3** *vt (a) (lit)* wine etc kalt stellen. **I was** ~**ed to the bone** etc die Kälte ging mir bis auf die Knochen. **(b)** *(fig)* blood gefrieren lassen.

►**chill out** *vi (col)* auftauen.

**chil(l)i** ['tʃɪlɪ] *n* Peperoni *pl*; *(spice, meal)* Chili *m*.

**chilly** ['tʃɪlɪ] *adj (+er) (lit, fig)* kühl. **I feel** ~ mir ist kühl.

**chime** [tʃaɪm] **1** *n* Geläut *nt*; *(of doorbell)* Läuten *nt* no *pl*. **2** *vt* schlagen. **3** *vi* läuten.

►**chime in** *vi (col)* sich einschalten.

**chiming clock** ['tʃaɪmɪŋ'klɒk] *n* Schlaguhr *f*.

**chimney** ['tʃɪmnɪ] *n* Schornstein *m*.

**chimney:** ~ **breast** *n* Kaminvorsprung *m*; ~**pot** *n* Schornsteinkopf *m*; ~ **sweep** *n* Schornsteinfeger *m*.

**chimp** [tʃɪmp] *(col)*, **chimpanzee** [,tʃɪmpæn'ziː] *n* Schimpanse *m*.

**chin** [tʃɪn] *n* Kinn *nt*. **keep your** ~ **up!** Kopf hoch!; **he took it on the** ~ *(fig col)* er hat es mit Fassung getragen.

**China** ['tʃaɪnə] *n* China *nt*. **the People's Republic of** ~ die Volksrepublik China.

**china** ['tʃaɪnə] **1** *n* Porzellan *nt*. **2** *adj* Porzellan-.

**china:** ~ **clay** *n* Kaolin *m*; **C**~**man** *n* Chinese *m*; **C**~ **Sea** *n* East/South **C**~ **Sea** Ost-/Südchinesisches Meer.

**Chinese** [tʃaɪ'niːz] **1** *n* **(a)** *(person)* Chinese *m*, Chinesin *f*. **(b)** *(language, fig: gibberish)* Chinesisch *nt*. **2** *adj* chinesisch. ~ **lantern** Lampion *m*; ~ **restaurant** Chinarestaurant *nt*.

**chink¹** [tʃɪŋk] *n* **(a)** Ritze *f*; *(in door)* Spalt *m*. ~ **of light** dünner Lichtstreifen; **the** ~ **in sb's armour** *(fig)* jds schwacher Punkt. **(b)** *(pej, hum: Chinaman)* **C**~ Schlitzauge *nt (col)*.

**chink²** **1** *n (sound)* Klimpern *nt*. **2** *vt* klimpern mit. **3** *vi* klimpern.

**chin:** ~**less** *adj* **to be** ~**less** ein fliehendes Kinn haben; ~ **strap** *n* Kinnriemen *m*.

**chintz** [tʃɪnts] **1** *n* Chintz *m*. **2** *attr* Chintz-.

**chinwag** ['tʃɪnwæg] *n (Brit col)* Schwatz *m (col)*.

**chip** [tʃɪp] **1** *n* **(a)** Splitter *m*; *(of wood)* Span *m*. **he's a** ~ **off the old block** er ist ganz der Vater; **to have a** ~ **on one's shoulder** einen Komplex haben *(about wegen)*. **(b)** *(Brit: potato* ~*)* ~**s** Pommes frites *pl*; *(US: crisps)* Chips *pl*. **(c)** *(in crockery, furniture etc)* abgeschlagene Stelle *f*. **(d)** *(in poker etc)* Chip *m*. **when the** ~**s are down** wenn es drauf ankommt. **(e)** *(Elec: micro*~*)* Chip *m*. **2** *vt* cup, stone anschlagen; varnish, paint abstoßen. **3** *vi (cup, china etc)* angeschlagen werden; *(paint, varnish)* abspringen.

►**chip in** *vi (col)* **(a)** *(interrupt)* sich einschalten. **(b)** *(contribute)* **he** ~**ped** ~ **with £3** er steuerte £3 bei.

►**chip off 1** *vt sep* paint etc wegschlagen; *piece of china* abschlagen. **2** *vi (paint etc)* absplittern.

**chipboard** ['tʃɪpbɔːd] *n* Spanholz *nt*.

**chipmunk** ['tʃɪpmʌŋk] *n* Backenhörnchen *nt*.

**chip pan** ['tʃɪp,pæn] *n (Brit)* Friteuse *f*.

chippings ['tʃɪpɪŋz] npl (road ~) Schotter m.
chippy ['tʃɪpɪ] n (Brit col) (a) (joiner) Schreiner m. (b) (also chip shop) Frittenbude f (col).
chiropodist [kɪ'rɒpədɪst] n Fußpfleger(in f) m.
chiropody [kɪ'rɒpədɪ] n Fußpflege f.
chirp [tʃɜːp] vi (birds) zwitschern; (crickets) zirpen.
chirpy ['tʃɜːpɪ] adj (+er) (col) munter.
chirrup ['tʃɪrəp] = chirp.
chisel ['tʃɪzl] 1 n Meißel m; (for wood) Beitel m. 2 vt meißeln; (in wood) stemmen. her finely ~led features ihr fein geschnittenes Gesicht.
chit [tʃɪt] n (also ~ of paper) Zettel m.
chitchat ['tʃɪt‚tʃæt] n (col) Geschwätz nt.
chivalrous ['ʃɪvəlrəs] adj ritterlich.
chivalry ['ʃɪvəlrɪ] n Ritterlichkeit f.
chives [tʃaɪvz] npl Schnittlauch m.
chivvy ['tʃɪvɪ] vt (Brit col) (also ~ along) antreiben.
chloride ['klɔːraɪd] n Chlorid nt.
chlorinate ['klɒrɪneɪt] vt water chloren.
chlorine ['klɔːriːn] n Chlor nt.
chloroform ['klɒrəfɔːm] n Chloroform nt.
chlorophyll ['klɒrəfɪl] n Chlorophyll nt.
choc-ice ['tʃɒkaɪs] n Eis nt mit Schokoladenüberzug.
chock [tʃɒk] n Bremskeil m.
chock-a-block ['tʃɒkəblɒk], chock-full ['tʃɒkful] adj (col) gerammelt voll (col).
chocolate ['tʃɒklɪt] 1 n Schokolade f. a ~ eine Praline; a box of ~s eine Schachtel Pralinen. 2 adj Schokoladen-; (also ~-coloured (Brit) or ~-colored US) schokoladenbraun.
chocolate in cpds Schokoladen-; ~ cake n Schokoladenkuchen m; ~ box 1 n Pralinenschachtel f; 2 adj Postkarten-.
choice [tʃɔɪs] 1 n (a) Wahl f. to make a ~ eine Wahl treffen; he had no ~ but to ... es blieb ihm nichts anderes übrig, als zu ...; take your ~ such dir etwas/eins aus; it was your ~ du wolltest es ja so. (b) (variety to choose from) Auswahl f (of an +dat, von). 2 adj goods, fruit, wine Qualitäts-. ~ fruit Obst erster Wahl.
choir ['kwaɪər] n Chor m. ~boy Sängerknabe m; ~master Chorleiter m; ~ stalls Chorgestühl nt.
choke [tʃəʊk] 1 vt (a) (stifle) ersticken; (throttle) (er)würgen, erdrosseln. (b) (fig) pipe etc verstopfen. 2 vi ersticken (on an +dat). 3 n (Aut) Choke m. ▶choke back vt sep tears, reply unterdrücken.
cholera ['kɒlərə] n Cholera f.
cholesterol [kɒ'lestərəl] n Cholesterin nt.
choose [tʃuːz] pret chose, ptp chosen 1 vt (aus)wählen. to ~ to do sth es vorziehen, etw zu tun. 2 vi to ~ (between or among/from) wählen (zwischen +dat/aus or unter +dat); there is nothing to ~ between them es ist kein Unterschied zwischen ihnen; I'll do it when I ~ ich mache es, wann es mir paßt (col).
choos(e)y ['tʃuːzɪ] adj (+er) wählerisch.
chop¹ [tʃɒp] 1 n (a) (blow) Schlag m. (b) (Cook) Kotelett nt. (c) (col) to get the ~ (be axed) gestrichen werden; (be fired) rausgeschmissen werden (col). 2 vt hacken; meat, vegetables etc kleinschneiden.
▶chop down vt sep tree fällen.
▶chop off vt sep abhacken.
▶chop up vt sep zerhacken.
chop² vi (fig) to ~ and change ständig seine Meinung ändern.
chopper ['tʃɒpər] n (a) (axe) Hackbeil nt. (b) (col: helicopter) Hubschrauber m.
chopping ['tʃɒpɪŋ]: ~ block n Hackklotz m; (for wood) Block m; ~ board n Hackbrett nt.
choppy ['tʃɒpɪ] adj (+er) sea kabbelig; wind böig.
chopstick ['tʃɒpstɪk] n Eßstäbchen nt.

choral ['kɔːrəl] adj Chor-. ~ society Gesangverein m.
chord [kɔːd] n (Mus) Akkord m. to strike the right/a sympathetic ~ (fig) den richtigen Ton treffen/auf Verständnis stoßen.
chore [tʃɔːr] n lästige Pflicht. ~s pl Hausarbeit f; to do the ~s den Haushalt machen.
choreographer [‚kɒrɪ'ɒgrəfər] n Choreograph(in f) m.
choreography [‚kɒrɪ'ɒgrəfɪ] n Choreographie f.
chorister ['kɒrɪstər] n (a) Chorsänger(in f) m; (boy) Chorknabe m. (b) (US: leader) Vorsänger m.
chortle ['tʃɔːtl] vi glucksen.
chorus ['kɔːrəs] 1 n (a) (refrain) Refrain m. (b) Chor m; (dancers) Tanzgruppe f. in ~ im Chor. 2 vi im Chor singen/sprechen/rufen.
chorus girl n (Revue)tänzerin f.
chose [tʃəʊz] pret of choose.
chosen ['tʃəʊzn] 1 ptp of choose. 2 adj the ~ people das auserwählte Volk.
choux pastry ['ʃuː‚peɪstrɪ] n Brandteig m.
chowder ['tʃaʊdər] n (US) sämige Fischsuppe.
Christ [kraɪst] n Christus m.
christen ['krɪsn] vt taufen. to be ~ed ... auf den Namen ... getauft werden.
christening ['krɪsnɪŋ] n Taufe f.
Christian ['krɪstɪən] 1 n Christ m. 2 adj (lit, fig) christlich.
Christianity [‚krɪstɪ'ænɪtɪ] n (faith, religion) Christentum nt; (body of Christians) Christenheit f.
Christian name n Vorname m.
Christmas ['krɪsməs] n Weihnachten nt. happy or merry ~! fröhliche Weihnachten!; at or for ~ zu Weihnachten.
Christmas: ~ cake n Früchtekuchen m mit Zuckerguß zu Weihnachten; ~ card n Weihnachtskarte f; ~ carol n Weihnachtslied nt; ~ Day n der erste Weihnachtstag; ~ Eve n Heiligabend m; ~ Island n Weihnachtsinsel f; ~ present n Weihnachtsgeschenk nt; ~ pudding n Plumpudding m; ~ tree n Weihnachtsbaum, Christbaum (esp S Ger) m.
chromatic [krə'mætɪk] adj (Art, Mus) chromatisch.
chrome [krəʊm], chromium ['krəʊmɪəm] n Chrom nt.
chromium: ~-plated adj verchromt; ~ plating n Verchromung f.
chromosome ['krəʊməsəʊm] n Chromosom nt.
chronic ['krɒnɪk] adj (a) (Med, fig) chronisch. (b) (col: terrible) miserabel (col).
chronicle ['krɒnɪkl] 1 n Chronik f. 2 vt aufzeichnen.
chronological [‚krɒnə'lɒdʒɪkəl] adj chronologisch.
chronology [krə'nɒlədʒɪ] n zeitliche Abfolge; (list of dates) Zeittafel f.
chrysalis ['krɪsəlɪs] n, pl -es (Biol) Puppe f.
chrysanthemum [krɪ'sænθəməm] n Chrysantheme f.
chubby ['tʃʌbɪ] adj (+er) pummelig, rundlich.
chuck [tʃʌk] 1 n (a) (col: throw) Wurf m. (b) (Tech: of drill) Spannfutter nt. 2 vt (col) (a) (throw) schmeißen (col). (b) (also: ~ away) wegschmeißen (col). (c) (also: ~ in) boyfriend etc Schluß machen mit (col); job hinschmeißen (col).
▶chuck out vt sep (col) rausschmeißen (col); old clothes etc wegschmeißen.
chuckle ['tʃʌkl] 1 n leises Lachen. 2 vi in sich (acc) hineinlachen.
chuffed [tʃʌft] adj (Brit col) vergnügt und zufrieden; (flattered) gebauchpinselt (col) (about wegen).
chug [tʃʌg] 1 n Tuckern nt. 2 vi tuckern.
▶chug along vi dahintuckern.
chum [tʃʌm] n (col) Kamerad, Kumpel (col) m.

**chump** [tʃʌmp] *n (col)* Trottel *m*.

**chunk** [tʃʌŋk] *n* großes Stück; *(of stone)* Brocken *m*.

**chunky** ['tʃʌŋkɪ] *adj (+er) (col) legs, arms* stämmig; *knitwear* dick; *meat* grob geschnitten; *book, format* kompakt; *glasses* schwer.

**church** [tʃɜːtʃ] *n* Kirche *f*. **to go to ~** in die Kirche gehen; **the C~ of England** die Anglikanische Kirche; **he has entered the C~** er ist Geistlicher geworden.

**church** *in cpds* Kirchen-; **~-goer** *n* Kirchgänger(in *f*) *m*; **~ hall** *n* Gemeindehalle *f*; **~ service** *n* Gottesdienst *m*; **~ spire** *n* Kirchturmspitze *f*; **~ steeple**, **~ tower** *n* Kirchturm *m*; **~ warden** *n* Gemeindevorsteher *m*; **~yard** *n* Kirchhof *m*.

**churlish** ['tʃɜːlɪʃ] *adj* ungehobelt.

**churn** [tʃɜːn] **1** *n (for butter)* Butterfaß *nt*; *(Brit: milk-~)* Milchkanne *f*. **2** *vt* **to ~ butter** buttern. **3** *vi (water)* wirbeln.

  ► **churn out** *vt sep* am laufenden Band produzieren.

  ► **churn up** *vt sep* aufwühlen.

**chute** [ʃuːt] *n* **(a)** Rutsche *f*; *(garbage ~)* Müllschlucker *m*. **(b)** *(in playground)* Rutschbahn *f*.

**chutney** ['tʃʌtnɪ] *n* Chutney *m*.

**CI = Channel Islands.**

**CIA = Central Intelligence Agency** CIA *m*.

**cicada** [sɪ'kɑːdə] *n* Zikade *f*.

**CID = Criminal Investigation Department.**

**cider** ['saɪdər] *n* ≈ Apfelwein, Cidre *m*.

**cider: ~ apple** *n* Mostapfel *m*; **~ press** *n* Apfelpresse *f*.

**cigar** [sɪ'ɡɑːr] *n* Zigarre *f*.

**cigarette** [ˌsɪɡə'ret] *n* Zigarette *f*.

**cigarette: ~ case** *n* Zigarettenetui *nt*; **~ end** *n* Zigarettenstummel *m*; **~ holder** *n* Zigarettenspitze *f*; **~ lighter** *n* Feuerzeug *nt*; *(in car)* Zigarettenanzünder *m*; **~ pack** *or* **~ packet** *n* Zigarettenschachtel *f*; **~ paper** *n* Zigarettenpapier *nt*.

**C-in-C = Commander-in-Chief.**

**cinch** [sɪntʃ] *n (col)* **it's a ~** *(easy)* das ist ein Klacks *(col)*; *(esp US: certain)* es ist todsicher *(col)*.

**cinder** ['sɪndər] *n* **~s** *pl* Asche *f*. **burnt to a ~** *(fig)* verkohlt.

**Cinderella** [ˌsɪndə'relə] *n* Aschenputtel *nt*.

**cinder track** *n* Aschenbahn *f*.

**cine-** ['sɪnɪ]: **~camera** *n (Brit)* (Schmal)filmkamera *f*; **~ film** *n* Schmalfilm *m*.

**cinema** ['sɪnəmə] *n (esp Brit)* Kino *nt*. **at/to the ~** im/ins Kino.

**cinemagoer** ['sɪnəməɡəʊər] *n (esp Brit)* Kinobesucher(in *f*) *m*.

**cine-projector** [ˌsɪnɪprə'dʒektər] *n (Brit)* Filmprojektor *m*.

**cinnamon** ['sɪnəmən] *n* Zimt *m*.

**cipher** ['saɪfər] *n* **(a)** Ziffer *f*; *(zero)* Null *f*. **(b)** *(code)* Chiffre *f*. **(c)** *(fig: nonentity)* Niemand *m no pl*.

**circa** ['sɜːkə] *prep* zirka.

**circle** ['sɜːkl] **1** *n* **(a)** Kreis *m*. **we're just going around in ~s** *(fig)* wir bewegen uns nur im Kreis; **to come full ~** *(fig)* zum Ausgangspunkt zurückkehren; **the family ~** der engere Familienkreis; **he's moving in different ~s now** er verkehrt jetzt in anderen Kreisen. **(b)** *(Brit: Theat)* Rang *m*. **2** *vt* **(a)** *(surround)* umgeben. **(b)** *(move around)* kreisen um. **(c)** *(draw a ~ round)* einen Kreis machen um. **3** *vi (fly in a ~)* kreisen.

**circuit** ['sɜːkɪt] *n* **(a)** *(journey around etc)* Rundgang *m*/-fahrt *f*/-reise *f* *(of* um*)*. **three ~s of the racetrack** drei Runden auf der Rennbahn. **(b)** *(Elec)* Stromkreis *m*; *(apparatus)* Schaltung *f*. **(c)** *(Sport: track)* Rennstrecke *f*.

**circuit: ~ board** *n (Elec)* Platine *f*; **~ breaker** *n* Stromkreisunterbrecher *m*; **~ diagram** *n* Schaltplan *m*.

**circuitous** [sɜː'kjuːɪtəs] *adj* umständlich.

**circuitry** ['sɜːkɪtrɪ] *n (Elec)* Schaltkreise *pl*.

**circular** ['sɜːkjʊlər] **1** *adj object* rund. **~ saw** Kreissäge *f*; **~ tour** Rundfahrt *f*/-reise *f*; **~ argument** Zirkelschluß *m*; **~ letter** Rundschreiben *nt*, Rundbrief *m*. **2** *n (in firm)* Rundschreiben *nt*; *(advertisement)* Wurfsendung *f*.

**circularize** ['sɜːkjʊləraɪz] *vt person* durch Rundschreiben informieren; *letter* zirkulieren lassen.

**circulate** ['sɜːkjʊleɪt] **1** *vi (blood, money)* zirkulieren; *(rumour)* kursieren; *(news)* sich verbreiten; *(person: at party)* die Runde machen. **2** *vt memo etc* zirkulieren lassen.

**circulation** [ˌsɜːkjʊ'leɪʃən] *n* **(a)** *(Med)* Kreislauf *m*; *(of traffic)* Fluß *m*; *(of money)* Umlauf *m*; *(of news, rumour)* Kursieren *nt*. **to have poor ~** Kreislaufstörungen haben; **to put notes into ~** Banknoten in Umlauf bringen; **new words which come into ~** neue Wörter, die in den Sprachgebrauch eingehen; **he's back in ~ now** *(col)* er mischt wieder mit *(col)*. **(b)** *(of newspaper etc)* Auflage(nziffer) *f*.

**circumcise** ['sɜːkəmsaɪz] *vt* beschneiden.

**circumcision** [ˌsɜːkəm'sɪʒən] *n* Beschneidung *f*.

**circumference** [sə'kʌmfərəns] *n* Umfang *m*.

**circumflex** ['sɜːkəmfleks] *n* Zirkumflex *m*.

**circumnavigate** [ˌsɜːkəm'nævɪɡeɪt] *vt* umfahren.

**circumscribe** ['sɜːkəmskraɪb] *vt* **(a)** *(Math)* einen Kreis beschreiben um. **(b)** *(restrict)* eingrenzen.

**circumspect** ['sɜːkəmspekt] *adj* umsichtig.

**circumstance** ['sɜːkəmstəns] *n* Umstand *m*. **in** *or* **under the ~s** unter diesen Umständen; **under no ~s** unter gar keinen Umständen; **in certain ~s** unter Umständen.

**circumstantial** [ˌsɜːkəm'stænʃəl] *adj* **(a)** *report* ausführlich. **(b)** *(Jur)* **~ evidence** Indizienbeweis *m*.

**circumvent** [ˌsɜːkəm'vent] *vt* umgehen.

**circus** ['sɜːkəs] *n* Zirkus *m*; *(in place names)* Platz *m*.

**cirrhosis** [sɪ'rəʊsɪs] *n* Zirrhose *f*.

**CIS = Commonwealth of Independent States** GUS *f*.

**cissy** ['sɪsɪ] *n* = **sissy**.

**cistern** ['sɪstən] *n* Zisterne *f*; *(of WC)* Spülkasten *m*.

**citadel** ['sɪtədl] *n* Zitadelle *f*.

**citation** [saɪ'teɪʃən] *n* **(a)** *(quote)* Zitat *nt*. **(b)** *(Mil)* Belobigung *f*.

**cite** [saɪt] *vt (quote)* zitieren.

**citizen** ['sɪtɪzn] *n* Bürger(in *f*) *m*. **C~s' Band** CB-Funk *m*.

**citizenship** ['sɪtɪznʃɪp] *n* Staatsbürgerschaft *f*.

**citric acid** ['sɪtrɪk 'æsɪd] *n* Zitronensäure *f*.

**citrus fruit** ['sɪtrəs fruːt] *n* Zitrusfrucht *f*.

**city** ['sɪtɪ] *n* **(a)** Großstadt *f*. **the ~ of Glasgow** die Stadt Glasgow. **(b)** *(in London)* **the C~** die City, das Banken- und Börsenviertel.

**city: ~ centre** *(Brit)* *or* **center** *(US)* *n* Stadtmitte *f*; **~ hall** *n* Rathaus *nt*; *(US: municipal government)* Stadtverwaltung *f*; **~ page** *n (Brit)* Wirtschaftsseite *f*; **~ slicker** *n (pej col)* feiner Pinkel aus der (Groß)stadt *(pej col)*; **C~ Technology College** *n* in einer Großstadt eingerichtetes Oberstufenkolleg *nt* mit technischem Schwerpunkt.

**civic** ['sɪvɪk] *adj rights* bürgerlich, Bürger-; *authorities* Stadt-, städtisch. **~ centre** *(Brit)* Verwaltungszentrum *nt* einer Stadt.

**civil** ['sɪvl] *adj* **(a)** *(of society)* bürgerlich; *duties* Bürger-. **(b)** *(polite)* höflich. **(c)** *(Jur)* zivilrechtlich.

**civil: ~ aviation** *n* Zivilluftfahrt *f*; **C~ Code** *n* Bürgerliches Gesetzbuch; **~ defence** *(Brit)* *or* **defense**

*(US) n* Zivilschutz *m*; ~ **disobedience** *n* ziviler Ungehorsam; ~ **engineer** *n* Bauingenieur *m*; ~ **engineering** *n* Hoch- und Tiefbau *m*.
**civilian** [sɪ'vɪlɪən] **1** *n* Zivilist *m*. **2** *adj* zivil, Zivil-. **in** ~ **clothes** in Zivil.
**civility** [sɪ'vɪlɪtɪ] *n* Höflichkeit *f*.
**civilization** [sɪvɪlaɪ'zeɪʃən] *n* **(a)** Zivilisation *f*. **(b)** *(of Greeks etc)* Kultur *f*.
**civilize** ['sɪvɪlaɪz] *vt* zivilisieren.
**civilized** ['sɪvɪlaɪzd] *adj* **(a)** zivilisiert. **(b)** *(cultured) lifestyle etc* kultiviert.
**civil law** *n* Bürgerliches Recht.
**civil liberties** *npl* Freiheitsrechte *pl*.
**civilly** ['sɪvɪlɪ] *adv* höflich.
**civil:** ~ **marriage** *n (esp US)* standesamtliche Trauung; ~ **rights** *npl* (staats)bürgerliche Rechte *pl*; ~ **rights demonstration/movement** Bürgerrechts-demonstration/-bewegung *f*; ~ **servant** *n* ≃ (Staats)beamte(r) *m*, (Staats)beamtin *f*; ~ **service** *n* ≃ Staatsdienst *m (ohne Richter und Lehrer)*; *(~ servants collectively)* Beamtenschaft *f*; ~ **war** *n* Bürgerkrieg *m*; ~ **wedding** *n* standesamtliche Trauung.
**civvies** ['sɪvɪz] *npl (Brit col)* Zivil *nt*.
**civvy street** ['sɪvɪ,striːt] *n (Brit col)* das Zivilleben.
**cl** = **centilitre(s)** cl.
**clad** [klæd] **1** *(old) pret, ptp of* **clothe**. **2** *adj (liter)* gekleidet.
**claim** [kleɪm] **1** *vt* **(a)** *(demand as one's own or due)* Anspruch erheben auf *(+acc)*; *benefits, sum of money (apply for)* beantragen; *lost property* abholen. **he** ~**ed diplomatic immunity** er berief sich auf seine diplomatische Immunität. **(b)** *(profess, assert)* behaupten. **the advantages** ~**ed for this technique** die Vorzüge, die man dieser Methode zuschreibt.
  **2** *vi* **(a)** *(Insur)* Ansprüche geltend machen; *(for damage done by people)* Schadenersatz verlangen. **(b)** *(for expenses etc)* **to** ~ **for sth** sich *(dat)* etw zurückzahlen lassen; **you can** ~ **for your travelling expenses** Sie können sich *(dat)* Ihre Reisekosten (zurück)erstatten lassen.
  **3** *n* **(a)** Anspruch *m*; *(pay~, Ind)* Forderung *f*. **to lay** ~ **to the title/property** *etc* Anspruch auf den Titel/das Grundstück *etc* erheben; **to put in a** ~ **(for sth)** etw beantragen; **he put in an expenses** ~ **for £100** er reichte Spesen in Höhe von £100 ein; **the** ~**s were all paid** *(Insur)* der Schaden wurde voll ersetzt. **(b)** *(assertion)* Behauptung *f*. **the book makes no** ~ **to be original** das Buch erhebt keinen Anspruch auf Originalität.
  ▶**claim back** *vt sep* zurückfordern. **to** ~ **sth** ~ **(as expenses)** sich *(dat)* etw zurückzahlen *or* -erstatten lassen.
**claimant** ['kleɪmənt] *n (for social security etc)* Antragsteller(in *f*) *m*; *(for inheritance etc)* Anspruchsteller(in *f*) *m (to auf +acc)*; *(Jur)* Kläger(in *f*) *m*.
**claim form** *n* Antragsformular *nt*.
**clairvoyant** [kleə'vɔɪənt] **1** *n* Hellseher(in *f*) *m*. **2** *adj* hellseherisch.
**clam** [klæm] *n* Venusmuschel *f*. **to shut up like a** ~ *(fig)* keinen Piep (mehr) sagen *(col)*.
**clamber** ['klæmbər] *vi* klettern. **to** ~ **up a hill** einen Berg hinaufklettern.
**clammy** ['klæmɪ] *adj (+er)* feucht, klamm.
**clamour, *(US)* clamor** ['klæmər] **1** *n* **(a)** *(noise)* Lärm *m*. **(b)** *(demand)* lautstark erhobene Forderung *(for nach)*. **2** *vi* **to** ~ **for sth** etw lautstark fordern.
**clamp** [klæmp] **1** *n* Schraubzwinge *f*; *(Med, Elec)* Klemme *f*. **2** *vt* (ein)spannen; *(for illegal parking) vehicle* krallen.

▶**clamp down 1** *vt sep (lit)* festmachen. **2** *vi (fig col: on expenses etc)* gewaltig bremsen *(col)*; *(police, government)* rigoros durchgreifen.
▶**clamp down on** *vi +prep obj (col) person* an die Kandare nehmen; *expenditure, activities* einen Riegel vorschieben *(+dat)*; *crime etc* zum Schlag ausholen gegen.
**clan** [klæn] *n (lit, fig)* Clan *m*.
**clandestine** [klæn'destɪn] *adj* geheim.
**clang** [klæŋ] **1** *n* Klappern *nt*; *(of hammer)* Dröhnen *nt*. **2** *vi* klappern; *(hammer)* dröhnen. **3** *vt* mit etw klappern.
**clanger** ['klæŋər] *n (Brit col)* Schnitzer *(col) m*. **to drop a** ~ ins Fettnäpfchen treten *(col)*.
**clank** [klæŋk] **1** *n* Klirren *nt*. **2** *vt* klirren mit. **3** *vi* klirren.
**clap** [klæp] **1** *n* Klatschen *nt no pl*; *(no pl: applause)* (Beifall)klatschen *nt*. **a** ~ **of thunder** ein Donnerschlag *m*. **2** *vt* **(a)** *(applaud)* Beifall klatschen *(sb jdm)*. **(b)** **to** ~ **one's hands** in die Hände klatschen. **(c)** **to** ~ **sb into prison** jdn ins Gefängnis stecken; **to** ~ **eyes on sb/sth** *(col)* jdn/etw zu Gesicht bekommen. **3** *vi* (Beifall) klatschen.
**clapped (out)** ['klæpt (aut)] *adj (col) thing* klapprig *(col)*; *person* fix und fertig *(col)*.
**clapping** ['klæpɪŋ] *n* Klatschen *nt*.
**claptrap** ['klæptræp] *n (col)* Geschwafel *nt (col)*.
**claret** ['klærət] *n (wine)* roter Bordeauxwein.
**clarification** [,klærɪfɪ'keɪʃən] *n* Klarstellung *f*.
**clarify** ['klærɪfaɪ] *vt* klären; *text* erklären.
**clarinet** [,klærɪ'net] *n* Klarinette *f*.
**clarinettist, *(US)* clarinetist** [klærɪ'netɪst] *n* Klarinettist(in *f*) *m*.
**clarity** ['klærɪtɪ] *n* Klarheit *f*.
**clash** [klæʃ] **1** *vi* **(a)** *(armies, demonstrators)* zusammenstoßen. **(b)** *(colours)* sich beißen; *(interests)* aufeinanderprallen; *(programmes, films)* sich überschneiden. **(c)** *(cymbals etc: also* ~ **together)** aneinanderschlagen; *(metal)* klirren. **2** *vt cymbals* schlagen. **3** *n* **(a)** *(of armies, demonstrators etc)* Zusammenstoß *m*. **(b)** *(of personalities)* grundsätzliche Verschiedenheit. **it's such a** ~ **of personalities** sie sind charakterlich grundverschieden. **(c)** *(of swords)* Aufeinanderprallen *nt*; *(between people)* Konflikt *m*. **there's a** ~ **of dates** die Termine überschneiden sich.
**clasp** [klɑːsp] **1** *n* **(a)** *(on brooch, purse etc)* (Schnapp)verschluß *m*. **(b)** *(with one's arms)* Umklammerung *f*; *(with hand)* Griff *m*. **2** *vt* **(a)** (er)greifen. **with his hands** ~**ed** mit gefalteten Händen; **to** ~ **sb in one's arms** jdn in die Arme schließen. **(b)** *(to fasten with a* ~*)* befestigen.
**class** [klɑːs] **1** *n* **(a)** *(group, division)* Klasse *f*. **in a** ~ **by himself/itself** weitaus der/das Beste. **(b)** *(social rank)* Schicht, Klasse *f*. **(c)** *(Sch, Univ)* Klasse *f*. **to give** *or* **take a Latin** ~ Latein unterrichten; **the French** ~ *(lesson)* die Französischstunde; *(people)* die Französischklasse; **an evening** ~ ein Abendkurs *m*. **(d)** *(col: quality, tone)* Stil *m*. **to have** ~ Stil haben; *(person)* Format haben. **2** *vt* einordnen, klassifizieren.
**class:** ~ **conscious** *adj* klassenbewußt, standesbewußt; ~ **consciousness** *n* Klassenbewußtsein *nt*; ~ **distinction** *n* Klassenunterschied *m*.
**classic** ['klæsɪk] **1** *adj (lit, fig)* klassisch. **2** *n* Klassiker *m*.
**classical** ['klæsɪkəl] *adj* klassisch; *education* humanistisch. ~ **scholar** Altphilologe *m*/-philologin *f*; ~ **studies** Altphilologie *f*.
**classicism** ['klæsɪsɪzəm] *n* Klassik *f*.
**classics** ['klæsɪks] *n sing (Univ)* Altphilologie *f*.

**classification** [ˌklæsɪfɪ'keɪʃən] *n* Klassifizierung *f.*

**classified** ['klæsɪfaɪd] *adj* in Klassen eingeteilt. ~ **ad(vertisement)** Kleinanzeige *f*; ~ **information** *(Mil)* Verschlußsache *f*; *(Pol)* Geheimsache *f.*

**classify** ['klæsɪfaɪ] *vt* klassifizieren.

**class:** ~**less** *adj* klassenlos; ~**mate** *n* Klassenkamerad(in *f*) *m*; ~**room** *n* Klassenzimmer *nt*; ~**war(fare)** *n* Klassenkrieg *m.*

**classy** ['klɑːsɪ] *adj (+er) (col)* nobel *(col).* ~ **woman** Klassefrau *f.*

**clatter** ['klætər] **1** *n* Klappern *nt.* **2** *vi* klappern. **the cart** ~**ed over the cobbles** der Wagen rumpelte über das Pflaster.

**clause** [klɔːz] *n* **(a)** *(Gram)* Satz *m.* **(b)** *(Jur etc)* Klausel *f.*

**claustrophobia** [ˌklɔːstrə'fəʊbɪə] *n* Platzangst *f.*

**claustrophobic** [ˌklɔːstrə'fəʊbɪk] *adj* klaustrophob(isch) *(Psych).* **I get this** ~ **feeling** ich kriege Platzangst *(col).*

**claw** [klɔː] **1** *n* Kralle *f*; *(of lions, birds of prey also)* Klaue *f*; *(of lobster etc)* Schere *f.* **to get one's** ~**s into sb** *(col)* jdn in die Krallen bekommen *(col).* **2** *vt* kratzen. **he** ~**ed back the sheets** er riß die Laken weg. **3** *vi* **to** ~ **at sth** sich an etw *(acc)* krallen.

**clay** [kleɪ] *n* Lehm *m.* **potter's** ~ Ton *m.*

**clay:** ~ **pigeon shooting** *n* Tontaubenschießen *nt*; ~ **pipe** *n* Tonpfeife *f.*

**clean** [kliːn] **1** *adj (+er)* sauber. **to wipe sth** ~ etw abreiben; ~ **licence** Führerschein *m* ohne Strafvermerk; **to make a** ~ **start** ganz von vorne anfangen; *(in life)* ein neues Leben anfangen; **to make a** ~ **breast of sth** sich *(dat)* etw von der Seele reden; **to give sb a** ~ **bill of health** *(doctor)* jdm gute Gesundheit bescheinigen; *(authorities)* jdn für unbedenklich erklären. **2** *adv* glatt. **I** ~ **forgot** das habe ich glatt(weg) vergessen *(col)*; **he got** ~ **away** er verschwand spurlos; **I'm** ~ **out of cigarettes** *(col)* ich habe keine Zigaretten mehr; **to cut** ~ **through** sth ganz durchschneiden/durchschlagen *etc*; **to come** ~ *(col)* auspacken *(col).* **3** *vt* saubermachen; *carpets, clothes, buildings* reinigen; *window, shoes* putzen; *fish, wound* säubern; *chicken* ausnehmen; *car* waschen. **to** ~ **one's teeth** sich *(dat)* die Zähne putzen.

►**clean off** *vt sep (wash)* abwaschen; *(wipe)* abwischen.

►**clean out** *vt sep* **(a)** *(lit)* gründlich saubermachen. **(b)** *(col: leave penniless) person* ausnehmen (wie eine Weihnachtsgans) *(col).* **the holiday has** ~**ed me** ~ nach dem Urlaub bin ich jetzt blank *(col).*

►**clean up 1** *vt sep* saubermachen; *old building, old painting* reinigen. **2** *vi (tidy up)* aufräumen; *(wash)* sich waschen; *(col: make money)* absahnen *(col).*

**clean-cut** ['kliːnkʌt] *adj features, lines* klar.

**cleaner** ['kliːnər] *n* **(a)** *(person)* Raumpfleger(in *f*) *m.* **a firm of office** ~**s** eine Büroreinigungsfirma. **(b)** *(shop)* ~'**s** Reinigung *f*; **to take sb to the** ~'**s** *(col)* jdn übers Ohr hauen *(col).* **(c)** *(substance)* Reinigungsmittel *nt.*

**cleaning lady** ['kliːnɪŋˌleɪdɪ] *n* Raumpflegerin, Putzfrau *(col) f.*

**cleanliness** ['klenlɪnɪs] *n* Reinlichkeit *f.*

**cleanly** ['kliːnlɪ] *adv* sauber.

**cleanness** ['kliːnnɪs] *n* Sauberkeit *f.*

**clean-out** ['kliːnaʊt] *n* **to have a** ~ gründlich saubermachen.

**cleanse** [klenz] *vt* reinigen; *(spiritually)* läutern *(of von).*

**cleanser** ['klenzər] *n* Reinigungsmittel *nt.*

**clean-shaven** ['kliːn'ʃeɪvn] *adj* glattrasiert.

**cleansing** ['klenzɪŋ] *adj agent, cream* Reinigungs-.

**clean-up** ['kliːnʌp] *n* Saubermachen *nt*; *(by police)* Säuberung *f.* **to give sth a** ~ etw saubermachen.

**clear** [klɪər] **1** *adj (+er)* **(a)** klar; *complexion, conscience* rein; *photograph* scharf. **on a** ~ **day** bei klarem Wetter.

**(b)** *(distinct, obvious)* klar. **it's still not** ~ **to me why** es ist mir immer noch nicht klar, warum; **to make it** ~ **to sb that** ... jdm klarmachen, daß ...; **let's get this** ~, **I'm the boss** eins wollen wir mal klarstellen: ich bin hier der Chef; **as** ~ **as day** sonnenklar; **as** ~ **as mud** *(col)* klar wie Kloßbrühe *(col).*

**(c) to be** ~ **on sth** über etw *(acc)* im klaren sein; **I'm not** ~ **on the implications** ich bin mir nicht sicher, was das bedeutet.

**(d)** *road, way* frei. *(on gate)* **"Keep** ~" „Ausfahrt freihalten"; **I want to keep the weekend** ~ ich möchte mir das Wochenende freihalten; **all** ~! (alles) frei!; **is it all** ~ **now?** ist alles in Ordnung?; **at last we were** ~ **of London** endlich hatten wir London hinter uns; **the shells landed well** ~ **of us** die Granaten schlugen ein ganzes Stück neben uns ein; **a** ~ **profit** ein Reingewinn *m*; **three** ~ **days** drei volle Tage; **a** ~ **majority** eine eindeutige Mehrheit; **to have a** ~ **lead** klar führen.

**2** *n* **to be in the** ~ nichts zu verbergen haben; *(clear of suspicion)* entlastet sein; **we're not in the** ~ **yet** *(not out of debt, difficulties)* wir sind noch nicht aus allem heraus; **this puts Harry in the** ~ damit ist Harry entlastet.

**3** *adv* **to keep** ~ **of sb/sth** jdm aus dem Wege gehen/etw meiden; **"keep** ~ **of the testing area"** „Versuchsgebiet nicht betreten"!; **stand** ~ **of the doors!** bitte von den Türen zurücktreten!

**4** *vt* **(a)** *(remove obstacles etc from) pipe* reinigen; *blockage* beseitigen; *road, snow* räumen; *(Comp) screen* löschen; *one's conscience* erleichtern. **to** ~ **the table** den Tisch abräumen; **to** ~ **a space for sth** für etw Platz schaffen; **to** ~ **the way for sb/sth** den Weg für jdn/etw freimachen; **to** ~ **the ground for further talks** den Boden für weitere Gespräche bereiten.

**(b)** *(free from guilt etc, Jur: find innocent) person* freisprechen; *one's/sb's name* reinwaschen.

**(c)** *(get past or over)* **he** ~**ed the bar easily** er übersprang die Latte mit Leichtigkeit.

**(d)** *debt* begleichen; *profit* machen.

**(e)** *stock etc* räumen.

**(f)** *(pass, OK)* abfertigen; *ship* klarieren; *expenses, appointment* bestätigen; *goods* zollamtlich abfertigen. **he's been** ~**ed by security** er ist von den Sicherheitsbehörden für unbedenklich erklärt worden; **you'll have to** ~ **that with the boss** das müssen Sie mit dem Chef abklären.

**(g)** *(Sport)* **to** ~ **the ball** klären.

**5** *vi (weather)* aufklaren; *(mist)* sich lichten.

►**clear away 1** *vt sep* wegräumen; *dishes also* abräumen. **2** *vi* **(a)** *(mist etc)* sich auflösen. **(b)** *(~ the table)* den Tisch abräumen.

►**clear off 1** *vt sep debts* begleichen; *stock* räumen. **2** *vi (col)* verschwinden *(col).*

►**clear out 1** *vt sep cupboard, room* ausräumen. **2** *vi (col)* verschwinden *(col).*

►**clear up 1** *vt sep* **(a)** *point, matter* klären; *mystery, crime* aufklären. **(b)** *(tidy)* aufräumen. **2** *vi* **(a)** *(weather)* sich aufklären; *(rain)* aufhören. **(b)** *(tidy up)* aufräumen.

**clearance** ['klɪərəns] *n* **(a)** *(act of clearing)* Beseitigung *f.* **slum** ~ Slumsanierung *f.* **(b)** *(free space)* Spielraum *m*; *(headroom)* lichte Höhe. **(c)** *(by cus-*

*toms)* Abfertigung *f*; *(by security)* Unbedenklichkeitserklärung *f*; *(authorization)* Genehmigung *f*. ~ **for take-off** Startfreigabe *f*. **(d)** *(Sport)* Abwehr *f*, Klärung *f*.
**clearance sale** *n (Comm)* Räumungsverkauf *m*.
**clear-cut** ['klɪə'kʌt] *adj* klar.
**clearing** ['klɪərɪŋ] *n (in forest)* Lichtung *f*.
**clearing:** ~ **bank** *n* Clearingbank *f*; ~ **house** *n* Clearingstelle *f*.
**clearly** ['klɪəlɪ] *adv* **(a)** *(distinctly)* klar. ~ **visible** gut zu sehen; **to stand out** ~ **from the rest** sich deutlich von den anderen abheben. **(b)** *(obviously)* eindeutig. ~ **we cannot allow ...** wir können keinesfalls zulassen, ...
**clearness** ['klɪənɪs] *n* Klarheit *f*; *(of photograph, outline)* Schärfe *f*.
**clear:** ~**-out** *n* Aufräumaktion *f*; **to have a** ~**-out** gründlich aufräumen; ~**way** *n (Brit)* Straße *f* mit Halteverbot.
**cleavage** ['kliːvɪdʒ] *n* **(a)** *(split)* Spalte *f*; *(fig)* Kluft *f*. **(b)** *(of woman's breasts)* Dekolleté *nt*.
**cleaver** ['kliːvə'] *n* Hackbeil *nt*.
**clef** [klef] *n* (Noten)schlüssel *m*.
**cleft** [kleft] **1** *adj* gespalten. ~ **palate** Gaumenspalte *f*; **to be in a** ~ **stick** in der Klemme sitzen *(col)*. **2** *n* Spalte *f*.
**clematis** ['klemətɪs] *n* Waldrebe, Klematis *f*.
**clemency** ['klemənsɪ] *n (of person)* Nachsicht *f (towards sb* jdm gegenüber*)*; *(of weather)* Milde *f*.
**clementine** ['kleməntaɪn] *n* Klementine *f*.
**clench** [klentʃ] *vt fist* ballen; *teeth* zusammenbeißen. **to** ~ **sth between one's teeth** etw zwischen die Zähne klemmen; **to** ~ **sth in one's hands** etw mit den Händen umklammern.
**clergy** ['klɜːdʒɪ] *npl* Klerus *m*, Geistlichkeit *f*.
**clergyman** ['klɜːdʒɪmən] *n, pl* **-men** [-mən] Geistlicher *m*.
**cleric** ['klerɪk] *n* Kleriker *m*.
**clerical** ['klerɪkəl] *adj* **(a)** *(Eccl)* geistlich. **(b)** ~ **staff** Büropersonal *nt*; ~ **error** Versehen *nt*.
**clerk** [klɑːk, *(US)* klɜːrk] *n* **(a)** (Büro)angestellte(r) *mf*. **(b)** **C~ of the Court** *(Jur)* Protokollführer(in *f*) *m*. **(c)** *(US: in shop)* Verkäufer(in *f*) *m*.
**clever** ['klevə'] *adj* **(a)** *(mentally bright)* klug; *machine also* clever. **to be** ~ **at French** gut in Französisch sein; **how** ~ **of you to remember my birthday!** wie aufmerksam von dir, daß du an meinen Geburtstag gedacht hast! **(b)** *(ingenious, skilful)* **be** ~ **at sth** Geschick zu etw haben, in etw *(dat)* geschickt sein; **to be** ~ **with one's hands** geschickte Hände haben. **(c)** *(cunning, smart)* schlau, clever *(col)*. ~ **Dick** Schlaumeier *m (col)*.
**cleverly** ['klevəlɪ] *adv* geschickt; *(wittily)* schlau.
**cleverness** ['klevənɪs] *n see adj* **(a)** Klugheit *f*. **(b)** Geschicktheit *f*. **(c)** Schläue, Cleverness *f*.
**clew** [kluː] *n (US)* = **clue.**
**cliché** ['kliːʃeɪ] *n* Klischee *nt*.
**click** [klɪk] **1** *n* Klicken *nt*; *(of latch, key in lock)* Schnappen *nt*; *(of tongue)* Schnalzen *nt*. **2** *vi* **(a)** *see n* klicken; schnappen; schnalzen. **(b)** *(col: be understood)* funken *(col)*. **suddenly it all** ~**ed (into place)** plötzlich hatte es gefunkt *(col)*. **(c)** *(col: get on well)* **they** ~**ed right from the moment they first met** zwischen ihnen hatte es vom ersten Augenblick an gefunkt *(col)*. **3** *vt heels* zusammenklappen; *fingers* schnippen mit; *tongue* schnalzen mit. **to** ~ **sth into place** etw einschnappen lassen.
**client** ['klaɪənt] *n* Kunde *m*, Kundin *f*; *(of lawyer)* Mandant *m*, Mandantin *f*.
**clientele** [ˌkliːɑːn'tel] *n* Kundschaft *f*. **the regular** ~ die Stammkundschaft.

**cliff** [klɪf] *n* Klippe *f*; *(inland also)* Felsen *m*. **the** ~**s of Dover** die Felsen von Dover.
**cliffhanger** ['klɪf,hæŋə] *n* Superthriller *m (col)*.
**climate** ['klaɪmɪt] *n (lit, fig)* Klima *nt*. **the two countries have very different** ~**s** die beiden Länder haben (ein) sehr unterschiedliches Klima; **to move to a warmer** ~ in eine wärmere Gegend ziehen; **the** ~ **of popular opinion** das öffentliche Klima.
**climatic** [klaɪ'mætɪk] *adj* klimatisch, Klima-.
**climax** ['klaɪmæks] *n (all senses)* Höhepunkt *m*.
**climb** [klaɪm] **1** *vt* **(a)** *(also* ~ **up)** klettern auf *(+acc)*; *wall also, hill* steigen auf *(+acc)*; *mountain* besteigen; *ladder, steps* hinaufsteigen; *pole, cliffs* hochklettern. **my car can't** ~ **that hill** mein Auto schafft den Berg nicht; **to** ~ **a rope** an einem Seil hochklettern. **(b)** *(also* ~ **over)** *wall etc* steigen or klettern über *(+acc)*. **2** *vi* klettern; *(as mountaineer)* bergsteigen; *(into train, car etc)* steigen; *(road)* ansteigen; *(aircraft)* (auf)steigen. **3** *n* **(a)** *(also fig)* Aufstieg *m*; *(of a mountain)* Besteigung *f*. **that was some** ~**!** das war eine Kletterei!; **we're going out for a** ~ wir machen eine Klettertour; *(as mountaineers)* wir gehen bergsteigen; **this face is a difficult** ~ diese Steilwand ist schwer zu besteigen. **(b)** *(of aircraft)* Steigflug *m*. **the plane went into a steep** ~ das Flugzeug zog steil nach oben.
  ▶**climb down** *vi* **(a)** *(lit)* *(person)* *(from tree, wall)* herunterklettern; *(from horse, mountain)* absteigen. **(b)** *(admit error)* klein beigeben.
  ▶**climb up 1** *vi* hinaufsteigen. **2** *vt see* **climb 1 (a)**.
**climbdown** ['klaɪmdaʊn] *n* Rückzieher *m (col)*.
**climber** ['klaɪmə'] *n* **(a)** *(mountaineer)* Bergsteiger(in *f*) *m*. **(b)** *(socially)* Aufsteiger *m*.
**climbing** ['klaɪmɪŋ] **1** *adj club* Berg(steiger)-. ~ **boot** Bergschuh *m*; ~ **frame** Klettergerüst *nt*; ~ **plant** Kletterpflanze *f*. **2** *n* Bergsteigen *nt*; *(rock* ~*)* Klettern *nt*. **we did a lot of** ~ wir sind viel geklettert.
**clinch** [klɪntʃ] **1** *vt argument* zum Abschluß bringen. **to** ~ **the deal** den Handel perfekt machen; **that** ~**es it** damit ist der Fall erledigt. **2** *n (Boxing)* Clinch *m*.
**cling** [klɪŋ] *pret, prep* **clung** *vi (hold on tightly)* sich festklammern *(to an* +*dat)*; *(to opinion also)* festhalten *(to an* +*dat)*; *(remain close)* sich halten *(to an* +*acc)*; *(clothes, fabric)* eng anliegen; *(smell)* haften *(to an* +*dat)*. **the boat clung to the shoreline** das Schiff hielt sich dicht an der Küste.
**clingfilm** ['klɪŋfɪlm] *n* Frischhaltefolie *f*.
**clinging** ['klɪŋɪŋ] *adj garment* enganliegend. **she's the** ~ **sort** sie ist wie eine Klette *(col)*.
**clinic** ['klɪnɪk] *n* Klinik *f*; *(surgery)* Sprechstunde *f*.
**clinical** ['klɪnɪkəl] *adj* **(a)** *(Med)* klinisch. **(b)** *(fig)* nüchtern.
**clink¹** [klɪŋk] **1** *vt* klirren lassen. **to** ~ **glasses with sb** mit jdm anstoßen. **2** *vi* klirren; *(jingle)* klimpern. **3** *n no pl* Klirren *nt*; Klimpern *nt*. **the** ~ **of glasses** das Klingen der Gläser.
**clink²** *n (col: prison)* Knast *m (col)*.
**clip¹** [klɪp] **1** *n* **(a)** *(for holding things)* Klammer *f*. **(b)** *(jewel)* Klips *m*. **2** *vt* **to** ~ **on** anklemmen; *papers* anheften.
**clip²** **1** *vt* scheren; *dog* trimmen; *hedge, fingernails* schneiden; *wings* stutzen; *(Brit)* *ticket* entwerten. **2** *n* **(a)** *see vt* Scheren *nt*; Trimmen *nt*; Schneiden *nt*; Stutzen *nt*. **(b)** *(from film)* Ausschnitt *m*. **(c)** **to give sb a** ~ **on the ear** jdm eine Ohrfeige geben.
**clip:** ~**board** *n* Klemmbrett *nt*; ~ **joint** *n (col)* Nepplokal *nt (col)*; ~**-on** *adj brooch* mit Klips; ~**-on earrings** Clips *pl*.
**clipped** [klɪpt] *adj accent* abgehackt.

**clipper** [ˈklɪpəʳ] *n (Naut)* Klipper *m.*

**clippers** [ˈklɪpəz] *npl (also* **pair of** *~s)* Schere *f; (for hair)* Haarschneidemaschine *f; (for fingernails)* Zwicker *m.*

**clipping** [ˈklɪpɪŋ] *n (newspaper ~)* Ausschnitt *m.*

**clique** [kliːk] *n* Clique *f.*

**cloak** [kləʊk] **1** *n (lit)* Umhang *m; (fig) (disguise)* Deckmantel *m; (veil: of secrecy etc)* Schleier *m.* **under the** *~* **of darkness** im Schutz der Dunkelheit. **2** *vt (fig)* hüllen.

**cloak:** *~*-**and-dagger** *adj* mysteriös; **a** *~*-**and-dagger operation** eine Nacht-und-Nebel-Aktion; *~***room** *n* **(a)** *(for coats)* Garderobe *f;* **(b)** *(Brit euph)* Waschraum *m (euph).*

**clobber** [ˈklɒbəʳ] *(col)* **1** *n (Brit)* Klamotten *pl (col).* **2** *vt (hit)* hauen *(col); (defeat)* haushoch schlagen.

**clock** [klɒk] **1** *n* **(a)** Uhr *f.* **around the** *~* rund um die Uhr; **to work against the** *~* gegen die Uhr arbeiten. **(b)** *(col) (speedometer, milometer)* Tacho *m (col); (of taxi)* Uhr *f.* **it's got 60,000 on the** *~* es hat einen Tachostand von 60 000 (Meilen). **2** *vt (Sport)* **he's** *~***ed the fastest time this year** er ist die schnellste Zeit dieses Jahres gelaufen/gefahren.

▶**clock in** *or* **on** *vi* (den Arbeitsbeginn) stempeln.

▶**clock off** *or* **out** *vi* (das Arbeitsende) stempeln.

▶**clock up** *vt sep* **(a)** *(athlete, competitor)* time laufen, schwimmen *etc.* **(b)** *speed, distance* zurücklegen. **(c)** *(col) success* verbuchen.

**clock** *in cpds* Uhr(en)-; *~* **face** *n* Zifferblatt *nt; ~*-**radio** *n* Radiouhr *f; ~***wise** *adj, adv* im Uhrzeigersinn; *~***work 1** *n (of clock)* Uhrwerk *nt; (of toy)* Aufziehmechanismus *m;* **like** *~***work** wie am Schnürchen; **2** *attr train, car* zum Aufziehen.

**clod** [klɒd] *n (of earth)* Klumpen *m.*

**clog** [klɒg] **1** *n (shoe)* Holzschuh *m. ~***s** *(modern)* Clogs *pl.* **2** *vt (also ~* **up)** *pipe, drain etc* verstopfen; *mechanism, wheels* blockieren. **3** *vi (also ~* **up)** *(pipe etc)* verstopfen; *(mechanism etc)* blockiert werden.

**cloister** [ˈklɔɪstəʳ] *n* **(a)** *(covered walk)* Kreuzgang *m.* **(b)** *(monastery)* Kloster *nt.*

**cloistered** [ˈklɔɪstəd] *adj (fig)* weltabgeschieden.

**clone** [kləʊn] **1** *n* Klon *m.* **2** *vt* klonen.

**close¹** [kləʊs] **1** *adj (+er)* **(a)** *(near)* in der Nähe *(to gen, von); (in time)* nahe (bevorstehend); *(fig) friend, co-operation, connection etc* eng; *relative* nahe; *resemblance* stark; *fight, result* knapp. **is Glasgow ~ to Edinburgh?** liegt Glasgow in der Nähe von Edinburgh?; **in** *~* **proximity** in unmittelbarer Nähe *(to gen);* **it's** *~***r to what we want** das kommt unseren Vorstellungen näher; **you're very** *~ (in guessing etc)* du bist dicht dran; *~* **combat** Nahkampf *m.*

**(b)** *(not spread out) handwriting, print* eng; *ranks* geschlossen.

**(c)** *examination, study* eingehend; *translation* originalgetreu. **to keep a** *~* **watch on sb** jdn scharf bewachen; **now pay** *~* **attention to me** jetzt hör mir gut zu!

**(d)** *(weather)* schwül; *(in room)* stickig.

**(e)** *~* **on** nahezu; *~* **on sixty/midnight** an die sechzig/kurz vor Mitternacht.

**2** *adv (+er)* nahe; *(spatially also)* dicht. *~* **by** in der Nähe; **stay** *~* **to me** bleib dicht bei mir; *~* **to the water/ground** nahe *or* dicht am Wasser/Boden; **to be** *~* **to tears** den Tränen nahe sein.

**close²** [kləʊz] **1** *vt* **(a)** schließen, zumachen; *(col) factory* stillegen. **to** *~* **one's eyes/ears to sth** sich einer Sache gegenüber blind/taub stellen. **(b)** *(bring to an end) meeting* schließen, beenden; *bank account etc* auflösen. **2** *vi (shut, come together)* sich schließen;

*(door, box, lid also)* zugehen; *(shop, factory)* schließen; *(come to an end)* schließen; *(tourist season)* zu Ende gehen. **3** *n* Ende *nt.* **to come to a** *~* zu Ende gehen; **to bring sth to a** *~* etw beenden.

▶**close down 1** *vi* **(a)** *(business, shop etc)* schließen, zumachen *(col); (factory: permanently)* stillgelegt werden. **(b)** *(Rad, TV)* das Programm beenden. **2** *vt sep shop etc* schließen; *factory (permanently)* stillegen.

▶**close in** *vi (night, darkness)* hereinbrechen; *(days)* kürzer werden; *(enemy etc)* bedrohlich nahekommen. **the police are closing** *~* **on him** die Polizei zieht das Netz um ihn zu.

▶**close off** *vt sep* (ab)sperren; *(separate off)* abteilen.

▶**close up 1** *vi* **(a)** *(line of people)* zusammenrücken. **(b)** *(lock up)* ab- *or* zuschließen. **2** *vt sep* **(a)** *shop* zumachen; *house* verschließen. **(b)** *(block up) hole* zumachen.

**closed-circuit television** [ˈkləʊzdˌsɜːkɪtˈtelɪˌvɪʒən] *n* interne Fernsehanlage; *(for supervision)* Fernsehüberwachungsanlage *f.*

**close-down** [ˈkləʊzdaʊn] *n* **(a)** *(of shop, business etc)* (Geschäfts)schließung *f; (of factory)* Stillegung *f.* **(b)** *(Rad, TV)* Sendeschluß *m.*

**closed shop** [ˈkləʊzdˈʃɒp] *n* Closed Shop *m.* **we have a** *~* wir haben Gewerkschaftszwang.

**close** [kləʊs]: *~*-**fitting** *adj* enganliegend; *~*-**knit** *adj* community und zusammengewachsen.

**closely** [ˈkləʊslɪ] *adv* eng, dicht; *work, connect* eng; *related* nah(e); *follow (in time)* dicht; *(attentively) watch, listen etc* genau; *guard* scharf, streng.

**closeness** [ˈkləʊsnɪs] *n (nearness, in time)* Nähe *f; (fig) (of friendship)* Innigkeit *f; (of examination, interrogation)* Genauigkeit *f; (of translation)* Texttreue *f; (of air, atmosphere)* Schwüle *f; (indoors)* stickige Luft; *(of race etc)* knapper Ausgang.

**close:** *~*-**run** *adj* race mit knappem Ausgang; **a** *~*-**run thing** eine knappe Sache; *~* **season** *n* Schonzeit *f; ~*-**shaven** *adj* glattrasiert.

**closet** [ˈklɒzɪt] *(vb: pret, ptp ~***ed** [ˈklɒzɪtɪd]*)* **1** *n* Wandschrank *m.* **2** *vt* **to be** *~***ed** hinter verschlossenen Türen sitzen *(with sb* mit jdm*).*

**close-up** [ˈkləʊsʌp] *n* Nahaufnahme *f.* **in** *~* in Nahaufnahme; *(of face)* in Großaufnahme.

**closing** [ˈkləʊzɪŋ] *adj remarks* abschließend. *~* **date** *(for competition etc)* Einsendeschluß *m; ~* **time** Ladenschluß *m; (Brit: in pub)* Polizeistunde *f; ~* **prices** *(St Ex)* Schlußnotierungen *pl.*

**closure** [ˈkləʊʒəʳ] *n* **(a)** Schließung *f; (of road)* Sperrung *f; (of factory, mine etc also)* Stillegung *f.* **(b)** *(object, stopper)* Verschluß *m.*

**clot** [klɒt] **1** *n* **(a)** *(of blood)* (Blut)gerinnsel *nt.* **(b)** *(col: person)* Trottel *m.* **2** *vi (blood, milk)* gerinnen.

**cloth** [klɒθ] *n* Tuch *nt; (for cleaning)* Lappen *m; (table~)* Tischdecke *f.* **a gentleman of the** *~* ein geistlicher Herr.

**clothe** [kləʊð] *pret, ptp* **clad** *(old) or ~***d** *vt (usu pass: dress)* kleiden.

**clothes** [kləʊðz] *npl (garments)* Kleider *pl; (clothing, outfit also)* Kleidung *f no pl.* **to put on/take off one's** *~* sich anziehen/ausziehen.

**clothes:** *~* **brush** *n* Kleiderbürste *f; ~* **drier** *n* Wäschetrockner *m; ~* **hanger** *n* Kleiderbügel *m; ~* **horse** *n* Wäscheständer *m; ~***line** *n* Wäscheleine *f; ~* **peg** *(Brit), ~* **pin** *(US)* *n* Wäscheklammer *f; ~* **shop** *n* Bekleidungsgeschäft *nt.*

**clothing** [ˈkləʊðɪŋ] *n* Kleidung *f.*

**clotted cream** [ˌklɒtɪdˈkriːm] *n Sahne f aus erhitzter Milch.*

**cloud** [klaʊd] **1** *n* Wolke *f.* **to have one's head in the**

**cobble**

~s in höheren Regionen schweben; **to be on ~ nine** *(col)* im siebten Himmel sein *(col)*; **every ~ has a silver lining** *(Prov)* kein Unglück ist so groß, es hat sein Glück im Schoß *(Prov)*; **~ of dust/smoke** Staub-/Rauchwolke *f*; **he's been under a ~ for weeks** *(under suspicion)* seit Wochen haftet ein Verdacht an ihm; *(in disgrace)* er steht schon seit Wochen in Ungnade. **2** *vt* **(a)** *(lit)* sky, view verhängen *(geh)*; mirror trüben. **a ~ed sky** ein bewölkter Himmel. **(b)** *(fig)* prospect, sb's enjoyment, mind, judgement etc trüben; friendship, sb's future überschatten. **to ~ the issue** *(complicate)* die Dinge unnötig kompliziert machen.
  ►**cloud over** *vi (sky)* sich bewölken; *(mirror etc)* beschlagen.
**cloud:** **~burst** *n* Wolkenbruch *m*; **~-cuckoo-land** *n* Wolkenkuckucksheim *nt*.
**cloudless** ['klaʊdlɪs] *adj* sky wolkenlos.
**cloudy** ['klaʊdɪ] *adj (+er)* sky bewölkt; liquid trüb.
**clout** [klaʊt] **1** *n* **(a)** *(col: blow)* Schlag *m*. **(b)** *influence* Schlagkraft *f*. **2** *vt (col)* hauen *(col)*. **to ~ sb one** jdm eine runterhauen *(col)*.
**clove** [kləʊv] *n* **(a)** Gewürznelke *f*. **(b)** **~ of garlic** Knoblauchzehe *f*.
**clover** ['kləʊvəʳ] *n* Klee *m*. **~ leaf** *(Bot, Mot)* Kleeblatt *nt*.
**clown** [klaʊn] **1** *n* Clown *m*; *(pej)* Trottel *m*. **to act the ~** den Hanswurst spielen. **2** *vi (also ~ about or around)* herumblödeln *(col)*.
**cloy** [klɔɪ] *vi (lit, fig)* zu süßlich sein/werden.
**cloying** ['klɔɪɪŋ] *adj* übermäßig süß.
**club** [klʌb] **1** *n* **(a)** *(weapon)* Knüppel *m*; *(golf~)* Golfschläger *m*. **(b)** *(Cards)* ~s *pl* Kreuz *nt*; *(Bridge)* Treff *nt*. **nine of ~s** die Kreuz-/Treff-Neun. **(c)** *(society)* Klub, Verein *m*. **to be in the ~** *(col)* ein Kind kriegen *(col)*; **join the ~!** *(col)* gratuliere! du auch!; **2** *vt* einknüppeln auf *(+acc)*.
  ►**club together** *vi* zusammenlegen.
**club:** **~ car** *n (US Rail)* Wagen *m* der Luxusklasse; **~ class** *n (Aviat)* Club-Klasse *f*; **~house** *n* Klubhaus *nt*.
**cluck** [klʌk] *vi (hen)* glucken.
**clue** [kluː] *n* Anhaltspunkt *m*; *(in crosswords)* Frage *f*. **I'll give you a ~** ich gebe dir einen Tip; **I haven't a ~!** (ich hab') keine Ahnung!
**clued-in** [ˌkluːd'ɪn] *(US)*, **clued-up** [ˌkluːd'ʌp] *adj (col)* im Bilde; *(about subject)* vertraut *(about* mit*)*.
**clueless** ['kluːlɪs] *adj (col)* unbedarft *(col)*.
**clump** [klʌmp] **1** *n (of trees, flowers etc)* Gruppe *f*; *(of earth)* Klumpen *m*. **2** *vi* **to ~ about** herumtrampeln.
**clumsily** ['klʌmzɪlɪ] *adv* ungeschickt; *(awkwardly)* unbeholfen.
**clumsiness** ['klʌmzɪnɪs] *n* Ungeschicklichkeit *f*; *(ungainliness)* Schwerfälligkeit *f*; *(awkwardness)* Unbeholfenheit *f*.
**clumsy** ['klʌmzɪ] *adj (+er)* **(a)** ungeschickt. **(b)** *(unwieldy)* plump; tool unhandlich; *(ungainly)* schwerfällig.
**clung** [klʌŋ] *pret, ptp of* **cling**.
**clunker** ['klʌŋkəʳ] *n (US col)* nutzloses Ding; *(car)* Klapperkiste *f (col)*.
**cluster** ['klʌstəʳ] *n (of trees, flowers, houses)* Gruppe *f*; *(of grapes)* Traube *f*.
  ►**cluster around** *vi +prep obj* sich scharen (um *+acc)*.
**clutch** [klʌtʃ] **1** *n* **(a)** *(Aut)* Kupplung *f*. **to let in/out the ~** ein-/auskuppeln. **(b)** *(fig)* **to fall into sb's ~es** jdm in die Hände fallen. **2** *vt* umklammern.
  ►**clutch at** *vi +prep obj (lit)* greifen nach *(+dat)*; *(fig)* sich klammern an *(+acc)*.

**clutter** ['klʌtəʳ] **1** *n (confusion)* Durcheinander *nt*; *(disorderly articles)* Kram *m (col)*. **2** *vt (also ~ up)* cupboard vollstopfen. **to be ~ed up with sth** mit etw vollgestopft sein; *(floor, desk etc)* mit etw übersät sein.
**cm** = **centimetre** cm.
**CNAA** *(Brit Univ)* = **Council for National Academic Awards** Kontrollausschuß *m* für neue Studiengänge.
**CND** = **Campaign for Nuclear Disarmament**.
**CO** = **(a) Commanding Officer**. **(b)** *(US)* Colorado.
**Co** = **(a) company** ≈ KG *f*. **& ~** und Co. **(b) county**.
**c/o** = **care of** bei, c/o.
**co-** [kəʊ-] *pref* Mit-, mit-.
**coach** [kəʊtʃ] **1** *n* **(a)** *(horsedrawn)* Kutsche *f*; *(state ~)* (Staats)karosse *f*; *(Rail)* (Eisenbahn)wagen *m*; *(motor ~)* (Reise)bus *m*. **(b)** *(tutor)* Nachhilfelehrer(in *f*) *m*; *(Sport)* Trainer(in *f*) *m*. **2** *vt* **(a)** *(Sport)* trainieren. **(b) to ~ sb for an exam** jdn auf eine Prüfung vorbereiten.
**coaching** ['kəʊtʃɪŋ] *n* Nachhilfe *f*; *(Sport)* Trainierstunden *pl*.
**coach** *(Brit):* **~ party** *n* Busreisegruppe *f*; **~ station** *n* Busbahnhof *m*; **~ trip** *n* Busfahrt *f*.
**coagulate** [kəʊ'ægjʊleɪt] **1** *vi* gerinnen. **2** *vt* gerinnen lassen.
**coal** [kəʊl] *n* Kohle *f*. **to haul sb over the ~s** jdm eine Standpauke halten; **to carry ~s to Newcastle** *(prov)* Eulen nach Athen tragen *(prov)*.
**coal** *in cpds* Kohlen-; **~ black** *adj* kohlrabenschwarz; **~-cellar** *n* Kohlenkeller *m*; **~-face** *n:* **to work at the ~-face** vor Ort arbeiten; **~field** *n* Kohlenrevier *nt*; **~ fire** *n* Kohlenfeuer *nt*; **~-fired** *adj* Kohle(n)-; **~-fired power station** Kohlekraftwerk *nt*.
**coalition** [ˌkəʊɪ'lɪʃən] *n* Koalition *f*.
**coal:** **~man** *n* Kohlenauslieferer *m*; **~ merchant** *n* Kohlenhändler *m*; **~-mine** *n* Grube, Zeche *f*; **~-miner** *n* Bergmann, Kumpel *(col)* *m*; **~-mining** *n* Kohle(n)bergbau *m*; **~ scuttle** *n* Kohleneimer *m*; **~shed** *n* Kohlenschuppen *m*.
**coarse** [kɔːs] *adj (+er)* **(a)** *(in texture)* grob. **(b)** *(uncouth)* gewöhnlich; person, manners ungehobelt; joke, language derb.
**coarsen** ['kɔːsn] **1** *vt* derb(er) machen; skin gerben. **2** *vi (person)* derb(er) werden.
**coast** [kəʊst] **1** *n* Küste *f*. **at/on the ~** an der Küste; **the ~ is clear** *(fig)* die Luft ist rein. **2** *vi (car, cyclist)* im Leerlauf fahren. **to ~ through an exam** eine Prüfung spielend schaffen.
**coastal** ['kəʊstəl] *adj* Küsten-.
**coaster** ['kəʊstəʳ] *n* **(a)** *(Naut)* Küstenmotorschiff *nt*. **(b)** *(drip mat)* Untersetzer *m*.
**coast:** **~guard** *n* Küstenwache *f*; **~line** *n* Küste *f*.
**coat** [kəʊt] **1** *n* **(a)** Mantel *m*; *(doctor's ~ etc also)* (Arzt)kittel *m*; *(jacket of suit etc)* Jacke *f*. **(b)** *(Her)* **~ of arms** Wappen *nt*. **(c)** *(of animal)* Fell *nt*. **(d)** *(of paint)* Anstrich *m*. **2** *vt (with paint etc)* streichen; *(with chocolate, icing etc)* überziehen. **~ed tongue** belegte Zunge.
**coat:** **~-hanger** *n* Kleiderbügel *m*; **~-hook** *n* Kleiderhaken *m*.
**coating** ['kəʊtɪŋ] *n* Überzug *m*; *(of paint)* Anstrich *m*.
**co-author** ['kəʊˌɔːθəʳ] *n* Mitverfasser *m*.
**coax** [kəʊks] *vt:* **to ~ sb into doing sth** jdn dazu bringen, etw zu tun; **to ~ sth out of sb** jdm etw entlocken.
**cobalt** ['kəʊbɒlt] *n* Kobalt *nt*.
**cobber** ['kɒbəʳ] *n (Austral col)* Kumpel *m (col)*.
**cobble** ['kɒbl] **1** *n (also ~stone)* Kopfstein *m*. **2** *vt* a

~**d street** eine Straße mit Kopfsteinpflaster.
►**cobble together** *vt sep (col) essay etc* zusammenschustern.
**cobbler** ['kɒblə'] *n* Schuster *m*.
**cobblestones** ['kɒblstəunz] *npl* Kopfsteinpflaster *nt*.
**COBOL** ['kəubɒl] *(Comp)* = **common business oriented language** COBOL *nt*.
**cobra** ['kəubrə] *n* Kobra *f*.
**cobweb** ['kɒbweb] *n* Spinn(en)webe *f*.
**cocaine** [kə'keɪn] *n* Kokain *nt*.
**cock** [kɒk] **1** *n* (a) *(rooster)* Hahn *m*. (b) *(male bird)* Männchen *nt*. (c) *(tap)* (Wasser)hahn *m*. **fuel** ~ Treibstoffhahn *m*. (d) *(col!: penis)* Schwanz *m (col!)*. **2** *vt ears* spitzen; *gun* entsichern. **the parrot** ~**ed its head on one side** der Papagei legte seinen Kopf schief.
►**cock up** *vt sep (Brit col)* vermasseln *(col)*.
**cock:** ~-**a-doodle-doo** *interj* kikeriki; ~-**a-hoop** *adj* ganz aus dem Häuschen; ~-**and-bull** *adj:* ~-**and-bull story** Lügengeschichte *f*.
**cockatoo** [ˌkɒkə'tuː] *n* Kakadu *m*.
**cockchafer** ['kɒkˌtʃeɪfə'] *n* Maikäfer *m*.
**cockerel** ['kɒkərəl] *n* junger Hahn.
**cock-eyed** [ˌkɒk'aɪd] *adj (col)* (a) *(crooked)* schief. (b) *(absurd)* verrückt.
**cockle** ['kɒkl] *n (shellfish)* Herzmuschel *f*.
**cockney** ['kɒknɪ] *n* Cockney *nt*; *(person)* Cockney *m*.
**cockpit** ['kɒkpɪt] *n (Aviat, Naut, of racing car)* Cockpit *nt*.
**cockroach** ['kɒkrəutʃ] *n* Küchenschabe *f*.
**cocksure** ['kɒk'ʃuə'] *adj (confident)* selbstsicher; *(convinced)* fest überzeugt. **to be** ~ **of oneself** von sich *(dat)* selber *or* selbst sehr überzeugt sein.
**cocktail** ['kɒkteɪl] *n* (a) Cocktail *m*. (b) *fruit* ~ Obstsalat *m*.
**cocktail** *in cpds* Cocktail-; ~ **bar** *n* Cocktail-Bar *f*; ~ **cabinet** *n* Hausbar *f*; ~ **dress** *n* Cocktailkleid *nt*; ~ **party** *nt* Cocktailparty *f*; ~ **shaker** *n* Mixbecher *m*.
**cock-up** ['kɒkʌp] *n (Brit col)* Stümperei *f (col)*. **to make a** ~ **of sth** etw vermasseln *(col)*.
**cocky** ['kɒkɪ] *adj (+er) (col)* großspurig.
**cocoa** ['kəukəu] *n* Kakao *m*.
**coconut** ['kəukənʌt] **1** *n* Kokosnuß *f*. **2** *attr* Kokos-. ~ **matting** Kokosläufer *m*; ~ **milk** Kokosmilch *f*; ~ **palm**, ~ **tree** Kokospalme *f*.
**cocoon** [kə'kuːn] **1** *n* Kokon *m*; *(fig: of scarves, blankets etc)* Hülle *f*. **2** *vt* einhüllen.
**COD** = **cash** *(Brit) or* **collect** *(US)* **on delivery** per Nachnahme.
**cod** [kɒd] *n* Kabeljau *m*.
**coddle** ['kɒdl] *vt child* verhätscheln.
**code** [kəud] *n* (a) *(cipher)* Kode, Code *m*. **in** ~ verschlüsselt; **to put into** ~ verschlüsseln; ~-**name** Deckname *m*; ~-**number** Kennziffer *f*; ~ **word** *(also Comp)* Kennwort *nt*. (b) *(rules)* ~ **of honour/ behaviour** Ehren-/Sittenkodex *m*; ~ **of practice** Verfahrensregeln *pl*. (c) *post (Brit) or* **zip** *(US)* ~ Postleitzahl *f*.
**co-defendant** [ˌkəudɪ'fendənt] *n* Mitangeklagte(r) *mf*.
**codeine** ['kəudiːn] *n* Kodein *nt*.
**codetermination** [ˌkəudɪtɜːmɪ'neɪʃən] *n* Mitbestimmung *f*.
**codger** ['kɒdʒə'] *n (col):* **old** ~ alter Kauz.
**cod-liver-oil** ['kɒdlɪvər'ɔɪl] *n* Lebertran *m*.
**co-driver** ['kəudraɪvə'] *n* Beifahrer *m*.
**co-ed, coed** ['kəu'ed] *n (col) (Brit: school)* gemischte Schule; *(US: girl student)* Studentin *f* an einer gemischten Universität.
**coeducation** ['kəuˌedjʊ'keɪʃən] *n* Koedukation *f*.

**coeducational** ['kəuˌedjʊ'keɪʃənl] *adj teaching* koedukativ; *school* gemischt.
**coerce** [kəu'ɜːs] *vt* zwingen. **to** ~ **sb into doing sth** jdn zwingen, etw zu tun.
**coercion** [kəu'ɜːʃən] *n* Zwang *m*; *(Jur)* Nötigung *f*.
**coexist** [ˌkəuɪg'zɪst] *vi* nebeneinander bestehen.
**coexistence** [ˌkəuɪg'zɪstəns] *n* Koexistenz *f*.
**C of E** = **Church of England**.
**coffee** ['kɒfɪ] *n* Kaffee *m*. **two** ~**s, please** zwei Kaffee, bitte.
**coffee** *in cpds* Kaffee-; ~ **bar** *n (Brit)* Café *nt*; ~ **bean** *n* Kaffeebohne *f*; ~ **break** *n* Kaffeepause *f*; ~ **cup** *n* Kaffeetasse *f*; ~ **filter** *n* Kaffeefilter *m*; ~ **grinder** *n* Kaffeemühle *f*; ~ **maker** *n* Kaffeemaschine *f*; ~ **pot** *n* Kaffeekanne *f*; ~ **table** *n* Couchtisch *m*.
**coffin** ['kɒfɪn] *n* Sarg *m*.
**co-founder** [ˌkəu'faundə'] *n* Mitbegründer(in *f*) *m*.
**cog** [kɒg] *n* Zahn *m*; *(~wheel)* Zahnrad *nt*. **he's only a** ~ **in the machine** *(fig)* er ist nur ein Rädchen im Getriebe.
**cogent** ['kəudʒənt] *adj argument, reason* zwingend; *reasoning* überzeugend.
**cogitate** ['kɒdʒɪteɪt] *vi* nachsinnen.
**cognac** ['kɒnjæk] *n* Kognak *m*; *(French)* Cognac *m*.
**cognate** ['kɒgneɪt] *adj* verwandt.
**cohabit** [kəu'hæbɪt] *vi* zusammenleben; *(esp Jur)* in nichtehelicher Lebensgemeinschaft leben.
**coherence** [kəu'hɪərəns] *n* (a) *(lit)* Kohärenz *f*. (b) *(of community)* Zusammenhalt *m*; *(of essay, symphony etc)* Geschlossenheit *f*. **his speech lacked** ~ seiner Rede *(dat)* fehlte der Zusammenhang.
**coherent** [kəu'hɪərənt] *adj* (a) *(comprehensible)* verständlich. (b) *(cohesive)* zusammenhängend; *logic, reasoning etc* schlüssig.
**cohesion** [kəu'hiːʒən] *n (fig)* Geschlossenheit *f*.
**cohesive** [kəu'hiːsɪv] *adj (fig)* geschlossen.
**coil** [kɔɪl] **1** *n* (a) *(of rope, wire etc)* Rolle *f*; *(on loop)* Windung *f*; *(of smoke)* Kringel *m*. ~ **spring** Spiralfeder *f*. (b) *(Elec)* Spule *f*. (c) *(contraceptive)* Spirale *f*. **2** *vt (also* ~ **up)** aufwickeln. **to** ~ **sth around sth** etw um etw wickeln; **the python** ~**ed itself up** die Pythonschlange rollte sich zusammen. **3** *vi* sich ringeln; *(river)* sich schlängeln.
**coin** [kɔɪn] **1** *n* Münze *f*. **the other side of the** ~ *(fig)* die Kehrseite der Medaille. **2** *vt money, phrase* prägen. ..., **to** ~ **a phrase** ..., um es mal so auszudrücken.
**coinage** ['kɔɪnɪdʒ] *n (of money, words)* Prägung *f*; *(coins)* Münzen *pl*.
**coin-box (telephone)** *n* Münzfernsprecher *m*.
**coincide** [ˌkəuɪn'saɪd] *vi (in time, place)* zusammenfallen; *(in area)* sich decken; *(agree)* übereinstimmen.
**coincidence** [kəu'ɪnsɪdəns] *n* Zufall *m*.
**coincidental** [kəuɪnsɪ'dentl] *adj* zufällig.
**coin-operated** *adj* Münz-; ~ **machine** Münzautomat *m*.
**coke** [kəuk] *n* Koks *m*.
**Coke** ® [kəuk] *n (col)* Cola *f*, Coke ® *nt*.
**Col** = **Colonel**.
**colander** ['kʌləndə'] *n* Durchschlag *m*, Sieb *nt*.
**cold** [kəuld] **1** *adj (+er)* kalt *(also fig)*; *reception, personality* kühl. **I am** ~ mir ist kalt, ich friere; **my hands are** ~/**are getting** ~ ich habe/bekomme kalte Hände; **to be** ~ **to sb** jdn kühl behandeln; **that leaves me** ~ das läßt mich kalt; **to be out** ~ bewußtlos sein; *(knocked out)* k.o. sein; **in** ~ **blood** kaltblütig; **to get** ~ **feet** *(fig col)* kalte Füße kriegen *(col)*; **to give sb the** ~ **shoulder** *(col)* jdm die kalte Schulter zeigen. **2** *n* (a) Kälte *f*. **to feel the** ~ käl-

teempfindlich sein; **to be left out in the** ~ *(fig)* ausgeschlossen werden. **(b)** *(Med)* Erkältung *f*; *(runny nose)* Schnupfen *m*. **to have a** ~ erkältet sein; **to get** *or* **catch a** ~ sich erkälten.

**cold:** ~**-blooded** *adj (Zool, fig)* kaltblütig; ~ **cream** *n* Cold Cream *f or nt*, Feuchtigkeitscreme *f*; ~ **cuts** *npl* Aufschnitt *m*; ~**-hearted** *adj* kaltherzig.

**coldly** ['kəʊldlɪ] *adv (lit, fig)* kalt; *answer, receive* betont kühl.

**cold:** ~**-shoulder** *vt (col)* links liegenlassen *(col)*; ~ **storage** *n* Kühllagerung *f*; **to put sth into** ~ **storage** *(lit) food* etw kühl lagern; *(fig) idea, plan* etw auf Eis legen; ~ **turkey** *n (also* ~ **turkey cure)** *(col)* sofortiger Totalentzug.

**coleslaw** ['kəʊlslɔː] *n* Krautsalat *m*.

**colic** ['kɒlɪk] *n* Kolik *f*.

**collaborate** [kə'læbəreɪt] *vi* **(a)** zusammenarbeiten. **(b)** *(with enemy)* kollaborieren.

**collaboration** [kə,læbə'reɪʃən] *n* **(a)** Zusammenarbeit *f*; *(of one party)* Mitarbeit *f*. **(b)** *(with enemy)* Kollaboration *f*.

**collaborator** [kə'læbəreɪtər] *n* **(a)** Mitarbeiter(in *f*) *m*. **(b)** *(with enemy)* Kollaborateur(in *f*) *m*.

**collage** [kɒ'lɑːʒ] *n* Collage *f*.

**collapse** [kə'læps] **1** *vi (lit, fig)* zusammenbrechen; *(building, wall, roof)* einstürzen; *(negotiations)* scheitern. **they all** ~**d with laughter** sie konnten sich alle vor Lachen nicht mehr halten; **his whole world** ~**d about him** für ihn brach eine Welt zusammen. **2** *n* Zusammenbruch *m*; *(heart attack)* Kollaps *m*; *(of building etc)* Einsturz *m*; *(of negotiations)* Scheitern *nt*.

**collapsible** [kə'læpsəbl] *adj bicycle, chair* zusammenklappbar, Klapp-.

**collar** ['kɒlər] **1** *n* Kragen *m*; *(for dogs)* Halsband *nt*; *(Mech: on pipe etc)* Bund *m*. ~**bone** Schlüsselbein *nt*. **2** *vt (capture)* fassen.

**collate** [kɒ'leɪt] *vt* vergleichen; *(assemble)* zusammentragen.

**collateral** [kɒ'lætərəl] *n (Fin)* (zusätzliche) Sicherheit.

**colleague** ['kɒliːg] *n* Kollege *m*, Kollegin *f*.

**collect** ['kɒlekt] **1** *vt* **(a)** *stamps etc, one's thoughts, money, facts* sammeln; *(accumulate)* ansammeln; *(furniture) dust etc* anziehen; *empty glasses, tickets etc* einsammeln; *litter* aufsammeln; *belongings* zusammenpacken; *taxes* einziehen; *debts* eintreiben; *rent, fares* kassieren. **(b)** *(pick up, fetch)* abholen *(from* bei*)*. **2** *vi (gather)* sich ansammeln; *(dust)* sich absetzen; *(~ money)* kassieren; *(for charity)* sammeln. **3** *adj (esp US)* ~ **call** R-Gespräch *nt*. **4** *adv (esp US)* **to call** ~ ein R-Gespräch führen.

**collected** [kə'lektɪd] *adj* **(a) the** ~ **works of Oscar Wilde** Oscar Wildes gesammelte Werke. **(b)** *(calm)* ruhig, gelassen.

**collection** [kə'lekʃən] *n* **(a)** *(group of people, objects)* Ansammlung *f*; *(of stamps, coins etc)* Sammlung *f*. **(b)** *(collecting) (of facts, information)* Zusammentragen *nt*; *(of goods)* Abholung *f*; *(from letterbox)* Leerung *f*; *(of stamps, coins)* Sammeln *nt*; *(of money, jumble for charity)* Sammlung *f*; *(in church)* Kollekte *f*; *(of debts)* Eintreibung *f*; *(of rent, fares)* Kassieren *nt*; *(of taxes)* Einzug *m*. **(c)** *(Fashion)* Kollektion *f*.

**collective** [kə'lektɪv] **1** *adj* kollektiv, Kollektiv-. ~ **bargaining** Tarifverhandlungen *pl*. **2** *n* Kollektiv *nt*.

**collector** [kə'lektər] *n* **(a)** *(of taxes)* Einnehmer(in *f*) *m*; *(of rent, cash)* Kassierer(in *f*) *m*; *(ticket ~)* Fahrkartenkontrolleur *m*. **(b)** *(of stamps, coins etc)* Sammler(in *f*) *m*. ~**'s item** Sammlerstück *nt*; ~**'s price** Liebhaberpreis *m*.

**college** ['kɒlɪdʒ] *n* **(a)** *(Univ)* College *nt*. **to go to** ~

*(university)* studieren. **(b)** *(of music, technology)* Fachhochschule *f*. ~ **of Art** Kunstakademie *f*.

**collide** [kə'laɪd] *vi* zusammenstoßen.

**collie** ['kɒlɪ] *n* Collie *m*.

**colliery** ['kɒlɪərɪ] *n* Grube, Zeche *f*.

**collision** [kə'lɪʒən] *n (lit)* Zusammenstoß *m*; *(fig)* Konflikt *m*, Kollision *f*. **on a** ~ **course** *(lit, fig)* auf Kollisionskurs.

**colloquial** [kə'ləʊkwɪəl] *adj* umgangssprachlich.

**collusion** [kə'luːʒən] *n* (geheime) Absprache.

**Cologne** [kə'ləʊn] **1** *n* Köln *nt*. **2** *adj* Kölner.

**cologne** [kə'ləʊn] *n* Kölnisch Wasser *nt*.

**Colombia** [kə'lɒmbɪə] *n* Kolumbien *nt*.

**Colombian** [kə'lɒmbɪən] **1** *adj* kolumbianisch. **2** *n* Kolumbianer(in *f*) *m*.

**colon¹** ['kəʊlən] *n (Anat)* Dickdarm *m*.

**colon²** *n (Gram)* Doppelpunkt *m*.

**colonel** ['kɜːnl] *n* Oberst *m*.

**colonial** [kə'ləʊnɪəl] **1** *adj* Kolonial-, kolonial. **2** *n* Bewohner(in *f*) *m* einer Kolonie/der Kolonien.

**colonialism** [kə'ləʊnɪəlɪzəm] *n* Kolonialismus *m*.

**colonist** ['kɒlənɪst] *n* Siedler(in *f*) *m*.

**colonize** ['kɒlənaɪz] *vt* kolonisieren.

**colonnade** [,kɒlə'neɪd] *n* Kolonnade *f*, Säulengang *m*.

**colony** ['kɒlənɪ] *n (also Zool)* Kolonie *f*; *(of ants, bees)* Staat *m*.

**color** *etc (US)* = **colour** *etc*.

**Colorado beetle** [,kɒlə'rɑːdəʊ'biːtl] *n* Kartoffelkäfer *m*.

**colossal** [kə'lɒsl] *adj* riesig; *prices, mistake* gewaltig.

**colour,** *(US)* **color** ['kʌlər] **1** *n* **(a)** *(lit, fig)* Farbe *f*. **what** ~ **is it?** welche Farbe hat es?; **let's see the** ~ **of your money first** *(col)* zeig erst mal dein Geld her *(col)*. **(b)** *(complexion)* (Gesichts)farbe *f*. **to get one's** ~ **back** wieder Farbe bekommen. **(c)** *(racial)* Hautfarbe *f*. **(d)** *(flag)* ~**s** Fahne *f*; **to nail one's** ~**s to the mast** *(fig)* Farbe bekennen; **to show one's true** ~**s** *(fig)* sein wahres Gesicht zeigen. **2** *vt* **(a)** *(lit)* anmalen. **(b)** *(fig)* beeinflussen; *(bias)* färben. **3** *vi* **(a)** *(leaves)* sich (ver)färben. **(b)** *(person: also* ~ **up)** rot werden.

▶**colour in** *vt sep* anmalen; *(Art)* kolorieren.

**colour** *in cpds* Farb-; *(racial)* Rassen-; *(Mil)* Fahnen-; ~**-bar** *n* Rassenschranke *f*; ~**-blind** *adj* farbenblind; ~**-code** *vt* farbig kennzeichnen; ~ **copier** *n* Farbkopierer *m*.

**coloured,** *(US)* **colored** ['kʌləd] **1** *adj* **(a)** bunt. **(b)** *(fig: biased)* gefärbt. **(c)** *person, race* farbig. ~ **man/woman** Farbige(r) *m*/Farbige *f*. **2** *n* Farbige(r) *mf*.

**-coloured,** *(US)* **-colored** *adj suf* **straw-/dark-**~ strohfarben/dunkel.

**colour:** ~**fast** *adj* farbecht; ~ **film** *n* Farbfilm *m*.

**colourful,** *(US)* **colorful** ['kʌləfʊl] *adj* **(a)** *(lit)* bunt. **(b)** *account etc* anschaulich; *life* bewegt; *personality* schillernd.

**colouring,** *(US)* **coloring** ['kʌlərɪŋ] *n (complexion)* Gesichtsfarbe *f*; *(substance)* Farbstoff *m*; *(colours)* Farben *pl*. ~ **book** Malbuch *nt*.

**colourless,** *(US)* **colorless** ['kʌləlɪs] *adj (lit, fig)* farblos.

**colour:** ~ **photograph** *n* Farbfoto *nt*; ~ **photography** *n* Farbfotografie *f*; ~ **scheme** *n* Farbzusammenstellung *f*; ~ **supplement** *n (Press)* Farbbeilage *f*; ~ **television** *n* Farbfernsehen *nt*; *(set)* Farbfernseher *m*.

**colt** [kəʊlt] *n* Fohlen *nt*.

**column** ['kɒləm] *n* **(a)** *(Archit, of smoke)* Säule *f*. **(b)** *(division of page)* Spalte *f*; *(article in newspaper)* Kolumne *f*.

**columnist** ['kɒləmnɪst] *n* Kolumnist(in *f*) *m*.

**coma** ['kəʊmə] *n* Koma *nt.* **to go into a** ~ ins Koma fallen; **to be in a** ~ im Koma liegen.

**comatose** ['kəʊmətəʊs] *adj* im Koma.

**comb** [kəʊm] **1** *n* Kamm *m.* **2** *vt* **(a)** kämmen. **to** ~ **one's hair** sich *(dat)* die Haare kämmen. **(b)** *(search)* durchkämmen.

►**comb out** *vt hair* durchkämmen.

**combat** ['kɒmbæt] **1** *n* Kampf *m.* **2** *vt (lit, fig)* bekämpfen.

**combatant** ['kɒmbətənt] *n (lit, fig)* Kämpfer *m.*

**combat:** ~ **jacket** *n* Feldjacke, Kampfjacke *f;* ~ **troops** *npl* Kampftruppen *pl.*

**combative** ['kɒmbətɪv] *adj* kämpferisch; *(fig)* konfliktfreudig.

**combination** [ˌkɒmbɪ'neɪʃən] *n* **(a)** Kombination *f;* *(combining: of organizations, people etc)* Zusammenschluß *m;* *(of events)* Verkettung *f.* **in** ~ zusammen. **(b)** *(for lock)* Kombination *f.* ~ **lock** Kombinationsschloß *nt.*

**combine** [kəm'baɪn] **1** *vt* verbinden, kombinieren. **2** *vi* sich zusammenschließen; *(Chem)* sich verbinden. **3** ['kɒmbaɪn] *n* **(a)** Konzern *m;* *(Hist: in socialist countries)* Kombinat *nt.* **(b)** *(also* ~ **harvester)** Mähdrescher *m.*

**combined** [kəm'baɪnd] *adj* gemeinsam; *talents, efforts* vereint. ~ **with** in Kombination mit; *(esp clothes, furniture)* kombiniert mit.

**combo** ['kɒmbəʊ] *n* Combo *f.*

**combustible** [kəm'bʌstɪbl] *adj* brennbar.

**combustion** [kəm'bʌstʃən] *n* Verbrennung *f.* ~ **chamber** Verbrennungsraum *m;* *(of jet engine)* Brennkammer *f.*

**come** [kʌm] *pret* **came**, *ptp* ~ **1** *vi* **(a)** kommen. ~ **and see me soon** besuchen Sie mich bald einmal; **he has** ~ **a long way** er kommt von weit her; *(fig)* er ist weit gekommen; **the project has** ~ **a long way** das Projekt ist schon ziemlich weit; **he came running/hurrying into the room** er kam ins Zimmer gerannt/er eilte ins Zimmer; **coming!** ich komme; ~ ~!, ~ **now!** *(fig)* komm, komm; **Christmas is coming** bald ist Weihnachten; **they came to a town/ castle** sie kamen in eine Stadt/an ein Schloß; **it came into my head that ...** es kam mir gedacht, daß ...; **May** ~**s before June** Mai kommt vor Juni; **it came as a shock to me** es war ein Schock für mich; ~ **what may** ganz gleich, was geschieht; **you could see it coming** das war ja zu erwarten; **she had it coming to her** *(col)* es geschah ihr recht; **people were coming and going all day** es war den ganzen Tag ein Kommen und Gehen; **to** ~ **for sb** *(collect)* jdn abholen; **we'll** ~ **after you** wir kommen nach; **he came third in the race** er wurde Dritter in dem Rennen; **it all came right in the end** schließlich ging alles doch noch gut; **how** ~? *(col)* wieso?

**(b)** *(be, become)* werden. **his dreams came true** seine Träume wurden wahr; **no good will** ~ **of it** das wird nicht gut ausgehen; **nothing came of it** es wurde nichts daraus; **that's what** ~**s of being careless** das kommt davon, wenn man unvorsichtig ist; **the handle has** ~ **loose** der Griff hat sich gelockert.

**(c)** *(Comm: be available)* erhältlich sein. **milk now** ~**s in plastic bottles** es gibt jetzt Milch in Plastikflaschen.

**(d) I have** ~ **to believe him** mittlerweile glaube ich ihm; **I'm sure you will** ~ **to agree with me** ich bin sicher, daß du mir schließlich zustimmst; *(now I)* ~ **to think of it** wenn ich es mir recht überlege; **the years/weeks to** ~ die kommenden Jahre/ Wochen; **the life to** ~ das ewige Leben.

**(e)** *(col uses)* ~ **next week** nächste Woche; **I've known him for three years** ~ **January** im Januar

kenne ich ihn drei Jahre; ~ **again?** wie bitte?; **she is as vain as they** ~ sie ist so eingebildet wie nur was *(col).*

**2** *vt* **don't** ~ **the innocent with me** *(col)* komm mir bloß nicht auf die unschuldige Tour *(col)*!

►**come about** *vi impers (happen)* passieren.

►**come across 1** *vi* **(a)** *(cross)* herüberkommen. **(b)** *(be understood)* verstanden werden; *(message, speech)* ankommen. **(c)** *(make an impression)* wirken. **2** *vi +prep obj (find)* finden. **if you** ~ ~ **my watch** wenn du zufällig meine Uhr siehst.

►**come along** *vi* **(a)** ~ ~! *(nun)* komm doch! **(b)** *(accompany)* mitkommen. **(c)** *(progress)* **to be coming** ~ **(nicely)** (gute) Fortschritte machen; **my play isn't coming** ~ **at all well** mein Stück macht überhaupt keine Fortschritte; **how's the thesis coming** ~? was macht die Doktorarbeit?

►**come apart** *vi* auseinandergehen; *(to be able to be taken apart)* zerlegbar sein.

►**come around** *vi* **(a)** *(call round)* vorbeikommen. **(b)** *(recur)* **Christmas has** ~ ~ **again** nun ist wieder Weihnachten. **(c)** *(change one's opinions)* es sich *(dat)* anders überlegen. **eventually he came** ~ **to our way of thinking** schließlich schloß er sich unserer Auffassung an. **(d)** *(regain consciousness)* wieder zu sich *(dat)* kommen.

►**come away** *vi* **(a)** *(leave)* (weg)gehen. ~ ~ **from there!** komm da weg! **(b)** *(become detached)* abgehen.

►**come back** *vi* **(a)** zurückkommen. **can I** ~ ~ **to you on that one?** kann ich später darauf zurückkommen? **(b)** *(return to one's memory)* **ah yes, it's all coming** ~ **(to me)** ach ja, jetzt fällt mir alles wieder ein; **your German will very quickly** ~ ~ **to you** du wirst ganz schnell wieder ins Deutsche reinkommen *(col).*

►**come by 1** *vi +prep obj (obtain)* kommen zu; *idea* kommen auf *(+acc).* **2** *vi (visit)* vorbeikommen.

►**come down** *vi* **(a)** *(from ladder, stairs)* herunterkommen. **(b)** *(be demolished: building etc)* abgerissen werden; *(fall down)* herunterfallen. **(c)** *(drop: prices)* sinken; *(seller)* heruntergehen *(to auf +acc).* **(d)** *(be a question of)* ankommen *(to auf +acc).* **it all** ~**s** ~ **to something very simple** das ist im Grunde ganz einfach. **(e)** *(lose social rank)* sinken. **you've** ~ ~ **in the world a bit** mit dir ist es aber abwärts gegangen. **(f)** *(US col: be planned)* **there's a robbery coming** ~ **tonight** für heute nacht ist ein Überfall geplant.

►**come down on** *vi +prep obj (rebuke)* zusammenstauchen *(col).*

►**come down with** *vi +prep obj illness* bekommen.

►**come forward** *vi* **(a)** sich melden. **(b) to** ~ ~ **with help/money** Hilfe/Geld anbieten.

►**come in** *vi* **(a)** hereinkommen. ~ ~! herein!; *(on radio)* ~ ~ ... melden ... **(b)** *(arrive)* ankommen; *(train)* einfahren; *(ship)* einlaufen. **(c)** *(be received as income)* **he has £10,000 coming** ~ **every year** er bekommt £10.000 im Jahr. **(d)** *(have a part to play)* **where do I** ~ ~? welche Rolle spiele ich dabei?; **that will** ~ ~ **useful** das kann man gut gebrauchen.

►**come in for** *vi +prep obj attention, admiration* erregen; *criticism etc* einstecken müssen.

►**come into** *vi +prep obj* **(a)** *(inherit) legacy etc* erben. **to** ~ ~ **one's own** zeigen, was in einem steckt. **(b)** *(be involved)* **I don't see where I** ~ ~ **all this** ich verstehe nicht, was ich mit der ganzen Sache zu tun habe; **money doesn't** ~ ~ **it** das hat nichts mit Geld zu tun.

►**come off 1** *vi* **(a)** *(off bicycle etc)* herunterfallen.

**(b)** *(button, handle, paint etc)* abgehen; *(stains, marks)* weggehen. **(c)** *(take place)* **her wedding didn't ~ ~ after all** aus ihrer Hochzeit ist nun doch nichts geworden. **(d)** *(col: succeed)* klappen *(col)*. **(e)** *(acquit oneself)* abschneiden. **2** *vi +prep obj* **(a)** *bicycle, horse etc* fallen von. **(b)** *(button, paint, stain)* abgehen von. **(c)** *(col)* **~ ~ it!** nun mach mal halblang! *(col)*.

►**come on 1** *vi* **(a)** *(follow)* nachkommen. **(b)** **~ ~!** komm!; **~ on!** komm schon! **(c)** *(continue to advance)* zukommen *(towards* auf *+acc).* **(d)** *(start) (night)* hereinbrechen; *(storm)* einsetzen. **I feel a cold coming ~** ich spüre die ersten Anzeichen einer Erkältung. **(e)** *(actor)* auftreten. **(f)** *(col)* **to ~ ~ strong** groß auftreten *(col)*. **(g)** **= ~ along (c)**.

►**come out** *vi* **(a)** herauskommen; *(book, magazine also)* erscheinen; *(new product)* auf den Markt kommen; *(film)* (in den Kinos) anlaufen; *(exam results, news also)* bekannt werden. **(b)** *(Ind)* **to ~ ~ (on strike)** in den Streik treten. **(c)** *(Phot: film, photograph)* **to ~ ~ well** gut werden; **let's hope the photos ~ ~** hoffentlich sind die Bilder etwas geworden. **(d)** *(stains, dye etc)* herausgehen. **(e) he came ~ in a rash** er bekam einen Ausschlag; **to ~ ~ against/in favour of sth** sich gegen/für etw aussprechen; **to ~ ~ of sth badly/well** bei etw schlecht/nicht schlecht wegkommen.

►**come out with** *vi +prep obj truth, facts* herausrücken mit; *(col) remarks, nonsense* von sich geben.

►**come over 1** *vi* herüberkommen. **he came ~ to England** er kam nach England; **he came ~ to our side** er trat auf unsere Seite über; **she came ~ giddy** *(col)* ihr wurde schwindelig; **it came ~ cloudy** es bewölkte sich. **2** *vi +prep obj (feelings)* überkommen. **what's ~ ~ you?** was ist denn in dich gefahren?

►**come round** *vi* **= come around.**

►**come through 1** *vi* **(a)** *(phone-call, order)* durchkommen. **your papers haven't ~ ~ yet** *(be cleared)* Ihre Papiere sind noch nicht fertig. **(b)** *(survive)* durchkommen. **2** *vi +prep obj (survive) illness, danger* überstehen.

►**come to 1** *vi (regain consciousness)* wieder zu sich *(dat)* kommen. **2** *vi +prep obj* **(a)** **he will never ~ ~ much** aus ihm wird nie etwas werden. **(b)** *(impers)* **if it ~s ~ that we're sunk** wenn es dazu kommt, sind wir verloren; **~ ~ that** *or* **if it ~s ~ that, he's just as good** was das betrifft, ist er genauso gut; **when it ~s ~ mathematics** wenn es um Mathematik geht; **it ~s ~ the same thing** das läuft auf dasselbe hinaus; **what are things** *or* **what is the world coming ~!** wohin soll das noch führen! **(c)** *(price, bill)* **it ~s ~ £20** es macht insgesamt £20; **how much does it ~ ~?** wieviel macht das? **(d)** *(touch on) point, subject etc* kommen auf *(+acc); (tackle) problem, job etc* herangehen an *(+acc).*

►**come together** *vi* zusammenkommen. **he and his wife have ~ ~ again** er ist wieder mit seiner Frau zusammen.

►**come under** *vi +prep obj* **(a)** **to ~ ~ sb's influence** unter jds Einfluß geraten; **this shop has ~ ~ new management** dieser Laden hat eine neue Geschäftsführung. **(b)** *category, heading* kommen unter *(+acc).*

►**come up** *vi* **(a)** *(lit)* hochkommen; *(diver, submarine)* nach oben kommen; *(sun, moon)* aufgehen. **you've ~ ~ in the world** du bist ja richtig vornehm geworden!; **he came ~ to me with a smile** er kam lächelnd auf mich zu. **(b)** *(Jur) (case)* verhandelt werden; *(accused)* vor Gericht stehen. **(c)** *(for discussion)* aufkommen; *(name)* erwähnt werden. **(d)**

*(number in lottery etc)* gewinnen. **to ~ ~ for sale/ auction** zum Verkauf/zur Auktion *etc* kommen. **(e)** *(post, job)* frei werden.

►**come up against** *vi +prep obj* stoßen auf *(+acc)*; *opposing team* treffen auf *(+acc).* **the new teacher keeps coming ~ ~ the headmaster** der neue Lehrer gerät ständig mit dem Direktor aneinander.

►**come (up)on** *vi +prep obj (find)* stoßen auf *(+acc).*

►**come up to** *vi +prep obj* **(a)** *(reach up to)* gehen *or* reichen bis zu *or* an *(+acc).* **(b)** *expectations* entsprechen *(+dat).* **(c)** *(col: approach)* **it's just coming ~ ~ 10** es ist gleich 10.

►**come up with** *vi +prep obj answer* haben; *plan* sich *(dat)* ausdenken; *suggestion* machen; *money (raise)* aufbringen; *(pay)* herausrücken *(col).*

**comeback** ['kʌmbæk] *n* **(a)** *(Theat etc, fig)* Comeback *nt.* **(b)** *(col: redress)* Anspruch *m* auf Schadenersatz; *(reaction)* Reaktion *f.* **we have no ~** wir können nichts machen.

**comedian** [kə'miːdɪən] *n* Komiker *m.*

**comedienne** [kə,miːdɪ'en] *n* Komikerin *f.*

**comedown** ['kʌmdaʊn] *n (col)* Abstieg *m.* **that's a bit of a ~ for you** das ist eine ziemliche Enttäuschung für dich.

**comedy** ['kɒmɪdɪ] *n* Komödie *f.*

**comer** ['kʌmər] *n* **"open to all ~s"** „Teilnahme für jedermann".

**comet** ['kɒmɪt] *n* Komet *m.*

**come-uppance** [,kʌm'ʌpəns] *n (col)*: **to get one's ~** die Quittung kriegen *(col).*

**comfort** ['kʌmfət] **1** *n* **(a)** Komfort *m no pl.* **to live in ~** komfortabel leben; **that car was a little too close for ~** dieses Auto ist mir zu nahe herangefahren. **(b)** *(consolation)* Trost *m.* **to take ~ from the fact that ...** sich damit trösten, daß ...; **your presence is a great ~ to me** es beruhigt mich sehr, daß Sie da sind; **small ~** schwacher Trost. **(c)** *(US)* **~ station** öffentliche Toilette. **2** *vt (console)* trösten.

**comfortable** ['kʌmfətəbl] *adj* **(a)** *armchair, shoes, life* bequem; *room, hotel etc* komfortabel; *temperature* angenehm. **to make sb/oneself ~** es jdm/sich bequem machen; *(make at home)* es jdm/sich gemütlich machen. **(b)** *(fig) income, pension* ausreichend; *life* angenehm; *majority, lead* sicher. **I don't feel too ~ about it** mir ist nicht ganz wohl bei dem Gedanken.

**comfortably** ['kʌmfətəblɪ] *adv* **(a)** *sit, dress etc* bequem; *furnished* komfortabel. **(b)** *(fig) win, lead* sicher; *live* angenehm; *afford* gut und gern; *claim, say* ruhig. **they are ~ off** es geht ihnen gut.

**comforter** ['kʌmfətər] *n (US) (on bed)* Deckbett *nt*; *(scarf)* Wollschal *m.*

**comforting** ['kʌmfətɪŋ] *adj* tröstlich.

**comfy** ['kʌmfɪ] *adj (+er) (col)* bequem; *room* gemütlich.

**comic** ['kɒmɪk] **1** *adj* komisch. **~ strip** Comic strip *m.* **2** *n* **(a)** *(person)* Komiker(in *f*) *m.* **(b)** *(magazine)* Comic-Heft(chen) *nt.* **(c)** *(US)* **~s** Comics *pl.*

**comical** ['kɒmɪkəl] *adj* komisch.

**coming** ['kʌmɪŋ] **1** *n* Kommen *nt.* **~ and going/~s and goings** Kommen und Gehen *nt.* **2** *adj (lit, fig)* kommend.

**comma** ['kɒmə] *n* Komma *nt.*

**command** [kə'mɑːnd] **1** *vt* **(a)** befehlen. **(b)** *army, ship* befehligen. **(c)** *resources, vocabulary* verfügen über *(+acc).* **to ~ sb's admiration/respect** jdm Bewunderung/Respekt abnötigen; **he ~s our admiration** wir bewundern ihn. **(d)** **to ~ a view of** eine Aussicht bieten über *+acc.* **2** *n* **(a)** *(order, also Comp)* Befehl *m.* **at/by the ~ of** auf Befehl *+gen*;

**on** ~ auf Befehl. **(b)** *(esp Mil: power, authority)* Kommando *nt.* **to be in** ~ das Kommando haben *(of* über *+acc)*; **to take** ~ das Kommando übernehmen *(of gen)*; ~ **economy** Kommandowirtschaft *f.* **(c)** *(fig: possession, mastery)* Beherrschung *f.* **he has a** ~ **of three foreign languages** er beherrscht drei Fremdsprachen; **to have sb/sth at one's** ~ über jdn/etw verfügen; **I am at your** ~ ich stehe zu Ihrer Verfügung.

**commandant** [ˌkɒmən'dænt] *n (Mil)* Kommandant *m.*

**commandeer** [ˌkɒmən'dɪər] *vt (Mil)* men einziehen; *(lit, fig)* stores, ship, car beschlagnahmen.

**commander** [kə'mɑːndər] *n* Führer *m*; *(Mil, Aviat)* Kommandant *m*; *(Naut)* Fregattenkapitän *m.* ~/ ~**s-in-chief** Oberbefehlshaber *m/pl.*

**commanding** [kə'mɑːndɪŋ] *adj* **(a)** ~ **officer** *(Mil)* befehlshabender Offizier. **(b)** *personality, voice, tone* gebieterisch.

**commandment** [kə'mɑːndmənt] *n (Bibl)* Gebot *nt.*

**command module** *n (Space)* Kommandokapsel *f.*

**commando** [kə'mɑːndəʊ] *n, pl* **-s** *(Mil: soldier)* Angehöriger *m* eines Kommando(trupp)s.

**command performance** *n (Theat)* königliche Galavorstellung.

**commemorate** [kə'meməreɪt] *vt* gedenken *(+gen).*

**commemoration** [kə,memə'reɪʃən] *n* Gedenken *nt.* **in** ~ **of** zum Gedenken an *(+acc).*

**commemorative** [kə'memərətɪv] *adj* Gedenk-. ~ **plaque** Gedenktafel *f.*

**commence** [kə'mens] *vti (form)* beginnen.

**commencement** [kə'mensmənt] *n (form)* Beginn *m.*

**commend** [kə'mend] **1** *vt (praise)* loben; *(recommend)* empfehlen. **2** *vr* **to** ~ **itself** sich empfehlen *(to dat).*

**commendable** [kə'mendəbl] *adj* lobenswert.

**commendation** [ˌkɒmen'deɪʃən] *n (praise)* Lob *nt*; *(award)* Auszeichnung *f.*

**commensurate** [kə'menʃərɪt] *adj* entsprechend *(with dat).* **to be** ~ **with sth** einer Sache *(dat)* entsprechen.

**comment** ['kɒment] **1** *n (remark)* Bemerkung *f (on, about* über *+acc,* zu*)*; *(esp official)* Kommentar *m (on* zu*).* **no** ~ kein Kommentar! **2** *vi* sich äußern *(on* über *+acc,* zu*).* **3** *vt* bemerken.

**commentary** ['kɒməntərɪ] *n* Kommentar *m (on* zu*).*

**commentate** ['kɒmenteɪt] *vi (Rad, TV)* Reporter(in) sein *(on* bei*).*

**commentator** ['kɒmenteɪtər] *n (Rad, TV)* Reporter(in *f) m.* **political** ~ politischer Kommentator.

**commerce** ['kɒmɜːs] *n* Handel *m.*

**commercial** [kə'mɜːʃəl] **1** *adj* Handels-; *ethics, training* kaufmännisch; *premises, vehicle* Geschäfts-; *production, radio, project, success, attitude etc* kommerziell. **the** ~ **world** die Geschäftswelt; **of no** ~ **value** ohne Verkaufswert. **2** *n (Rad, TV)* Werbespot *m.*

**commercial:** ~ **art** *n* Werbegrafik *f*; ~ **artist** *n* Werbegrafiker(in *f) m*; ~ **college** *n* Fachschule *f* für kaufmännische Berufe.

**commercialism** [kə'mɜːʃəlɪzəm] *n* Kommerzialisierung *f.*

**commercialize** [kə'mɜːʃəlaɪz] *vt* kommerzialisieren.

**commercial:** ~ **television** *n* durch Werbung finanziertes Fernsehen; ~ **traveller** *(Brit)* or **traveler** *(US) n* Handelsvertreter(in *f) m*; ~ **vehicle** *n* Nutzfahrzeug *nt.*

**commiserate** [kə'mɪzəreɪt] *vi* mitfühlen *(with* mit*).*

**commiseration** [kə,mɪzə'reɪʃən] *n* (An)teilnahme *f no pl.* **my** ~**s** herzliches Beileid *(on* zu*).*

**commission** [kə'mɪʃən] **1 (a)** *(for building, painting etc)* Auftrag *m.* **(b)** *(Comm: payment)* Provision *f.* **on** ~ auf Provision. **(c)** *(Mil)* Patent *nt.* **(d)** *(special committee)* Kommission *f.* **the (EC) C**~ die EG-Kommission. **(e)** *(use)* **in/out of** ~ in/außer Betrieb. **2** *vt* **(a)** *person* beauftragen; *book, painting* in Auftrag geben. **to** ~ **sb to do sth** jdn damit beauftragen, etw zu tun. **(b)** *(Mil) sb* zum Offizier ernennen. ~**ed officer** Offizier *m.* **(c)** *ship* in Dienst stellen; *power station etc* in Betrieb nehmen.

**commissionaire** [kə,mɪʃə'neər] *n* Portier *m.*

**commissioner** [kə'mɪʃənər] *n* **(a)** *(member of commission)* Ausschußmitglied *nt.* **(b)** *(of police)* Polizeipräsident *m.* **(c)** *(Jur)* ~ **for oaths** Notar(in *f) m.*

**commit** [kə'mɪt] **1** *vt* **(a)** *crime, suicide* begehen. **(b)** **to have sb** ~**ted (to an asylum)** jdn in eine Anstalt einweisen lassen; **to** ~ **sb for trial** jdn einem Gericht überstellen; **to** ~ **sth to writing** *or* **to paper** etw zu Papier bringen. **(c)** *(oblige)* festlegen *(to* auf *+acc)*; *manpower, resources* einsetzen. **that doesn't** ~ **you to buying the book** das verpflichtet Sie nicht zum Kauf des Buches. **2** *vr* sich festlegen *(to* auf *+acc).* **to** ~ **oneself on an issue** sich in einer Frage festlegen; **... without thereby** ~**ting myself to the whole contract** ... ohne damit an den ganzen Vertrag gebunden zu sein.

**commitment** [kə'mɪtmənt] *n (obligation)* Verpflichtung *f*; *(dedication)* Engagement *nt.*

**committed** [kə'mɪtɪd] *adj (dedicated)* engagiert.

**committee** [kə'mɪtɪ] *n* Ausschuß *m*, Komitee *nt.* ~ **meeting** Ausschußsitzung *f*; ~ **member** Ausschußmitglied *nt.*

**commodity** [kə'mɒdɪtɪ] *n* Ware *f*; *(agricultural)* Erzeugnis *nt.* ~ **market** Rohstoffmarkt *m.*

**common** ['kɒmən] **1** *adj (+er)* **(a)** *(shared by many)* gemeinsam. **it is** ~ **knowledge that** ... es ist allgemein bekannt, daß ... **(b)** *(frequently seen or heard etc)* häufig; *word* geläufig; *experience also* allgemein; *belief, custom, animal, bird* (weit)verbreitet; *(customary, usual)* normal. **(c)** *(ordinary)* gewöhnlich. **the** ~ **man** der Normalbürger; **the** ~ **people** die einfachen Leute; **the** ~ **cold** Schnupfen *m*; **it's only** ~ **decency** das gehört sich einfach. **(d)** *(vulgar, low-class)* gewöhnlich. **2** *n* **(a)** *(land)* Gemeindewiese *f.* **(b)** **to have sth in** ~ etw miteinander gemein haben.

**common denominator** *n (Math, fig)* gemeinsamer Nenner.

**commoner** ['kɒmənər] *n* Bürgerliche(r) *mf.*

**common-law** ['kɒmənlɔː] *adj* **she is his** ~**-law wife** sie lebt mit ihm in eheähnlicher Gemeinschaft.

**commonly** ['kɒmənlɪ] *adv* **(a)** *(often)* häufig; *(widely)* weithin. **a** ~ **held belief** eine weitverbreitete Ansicht. **(b)** *(vulgarly)* ordinär.

**common: C**~ **Market** *n* Gemeinsamer Markt; ~**-or-garden** *adj* Durchschnitts-, Feld-, Wald- und Wiesen- *(esp pej col)*; *topic, novel etc* ganz gewöhnlich; ~**place 1** *adj* alltäglich; *(banal)* remark banal; **2** *n* Gemeinplatz *m*; ~**room** *n* Aufenthaltsraum *m*; *(for teachers)* Lehrerzimmer *nt*; *(for lecturers)* Dozentenzimmer *nt.*

**Commons** ['kɒmənz] *npl* **the** ~ *(Parl)* das Unterhaus.

**common:** ~ **sense** *n* gesunder Menschenverstand; ~**sense** *adj* vernünftig; **C**~**wealth** *n* **the (British) C**~**wealth, the C**~**wealth of Nations** das Commonwealth.

**commotion** [kə'məʊʃən] *n* Aufruhr *m*; *(noise)* Lärm *m.* **to cause a** ~ Aufsehen erregen.

**communal** ['kɒmjuːnl] *adj* **(a)** *(of a community)* Gemeinde-. ~ **life** Gemeinschaftsleben *nt.* **(b)** *(owned, used in common)* gemeinsam.

**commune** ['kɒmjuːn] **1** *n* Kommune *f*. **2** [kə'mjuːn] *vi* to ~ **with nature** mit der Natur Zwiesprache halten.

**communicable** [kə'mjuːnɪkəbl] *adj disease* übertragbar; *idea* vermittelbar.

**communicant** [kə'mjuːnɪkənt] *n (Eccl)* Kommunikant(in *f*) *m*.

**communicate** [kə'mjuːnɪkeɪt] **1** *vt news etc* übermitteln; *ideas, feelings* vermitteln; *illness* übertragen *(to* auf *+acc)*. **2** *vi* **(a)** *(be in communication)* in Verbindung stehen. **(b)** *(convey or exchange thoughts)* sich verständigen. **he can't** ~ er hat keine Kommunikationsfähigkeiten. **(c)** *(rooms)* verbunden sein. **communicating rooms** Zimmer *pl* mit einer Verbindungstür.

**communication** [kə,mjuːnɪ'keɪʃən] *n* **(a)** Kommunikation *f*; *(of ideas, information)* Vermittlung *f*; *(of disease)* Übertragung *f*; *(between people)* Verständigung *f*; *(contact)* Verbindung *f*. **to be in** ~ **with sb** mit jdm in Verbindung stehen *(about* wegen*)*; **to get into** ~ **with sb about sth** sich mit jdm wegen etw in Verbindung setzen. **(b)** *(letter, message)* Mitteilung *f*. **(c)** ~**s** *(roads, railways, telegraph lines etc)* Kommunikationswege *pl*; *(Telec)* Nachrichtenwesen *nt*.

**communication:** ~ **cord** *n (Brit Rail)* ≃ Notbremse *f*; ~ **network** *n* Kommunikationsnetz *nt*; ~**s satellite** *n* Nachrichtensatellit *m*; ~ **studies** *npl* Kommunikationswissenschaften *pl*.

**communicative** [kə'mjuːnɪkətɪv] *adj* gesprächig. ~ **skills** Kommunikationsfähigkeit *f*.

**communion** [kə'mjuːnɪən] *n* **(a)** *(intercourse, exchange of feelings etc)* Zwiesprache *f*. **(b)** *(Eccl: also* C~*) (Protestant)* Abendmahl *nt*; *(Catholic)* Kommunion *f*. **to receive** *or* **take** ~ die Kommunion/das Abendmahl empfangen.

**communiqué** [kə'mjuːnɪkeɪ] *n* Kommuniqué *nt*, *(amtliche)* Verlautbarung.

**communism** ['kɒmjʊnɪzəm] *n* Kommunismus *m*.

**communist** ['kɒmjʊnɪst] **1** *n* Kommunist(in *f*) *m*. **2** *adj* kommunistisch.

**community** [kə'mjuːnɪtɪ] *n* **(a)** *(social etc group)* Gemeinde *f*. **(b)** *(the public)* Allgemeinheit *f*.

**community:** ~ **centre** *(Brit)* or **center** *(US)* *n* Gemeindezentrum *nt*; ~ **chest** *n (US)* Hilfsfonds *m*; ~ **relations** *npl* das Verhältnis zwischen den Bevölkerungsgruppen; ~ **service** *n (Jur)* sozialer Dienst *m*; ~ **spirit** *n* Gemeinschaftsgeist *m*.

**commutation ticket** [,kɒmjʊ'teɪʃən'tɪkɪt] *n (US)* Zeitkarte *f*.

**commute** [kə'mjuːt] **1** *vt* umwandeln. **2** *vi (be commuter)* pendeln.

**commuter** [kə'mjuːtəʳ] *n* Pendler(in *f*) *m*. ~ **train** Pendlerzug *m*; **the** ~ **belt** das Einzugsgebiet.

**compact**[1] [kəm'pækt] *adj (+er)* kompakt; *soil, snow* fest. ~ **disk** CD(-Platte) *f*.

**compact**[2] ['kɒmpækt] *n* **(a)** *(powder* ~*)* Puderdose *f*. **(b)** *(US: car)* Kompaktauto *nt*.

**compact**[3] ['kɒmpækt] *n (form: agreement)* Übereinkunft *f*.

**companion** [kəm'pænjən] *n* **(a)** Begleiter(in *f*) *m*. **travelling** ~ Reisegefährte *m*, Reisegefährtin *f*. **(b)** *(friend)* Freund(in *f*) *m*. **(c)** *(one of pair of objects)* Pendant *nt*. **(d)** *(lady's)* Hausdame *f*.

**companionable** [kəm'pænjənəbl] *adj* freundlich.

**companionship** [kəm'pænjənʃɪp] *n* Gesellschaft *f*.

**company** ['kʌmpənɪ] **1** *n* Gesellschaft *f*; *(guests)* Besuch *m*; *(Comm also)* Firma *f*; *(Theat)* (Schauspiel)truppe *f*. **ship's** ~ *(Naut)* Besatzung *f*; **to keep sb** ~ jdm Gesellschaft leisten; **she is not fit** ~ **for your sister** sie ist nicht der richtige Umgang für

deine Schwester; **to get into bad** ~ in schlechte Gesellschaft geraten; **we have** ~ **this evening** wir haben heute abend Besuch. **2** *attr* ~ **car** Firmenwagen *m*; ~ **law** Gesellschaftsrecht *nt*; ~ **policy** Geschäftspolitik *f*; ~ **report** Geschäftsbericht *m*; ~ **secretary** *(Brit)* ≃ Prokurist *m*.

**comparable** ['kɒmpərəbl] *adj* vergleichbar *(with, to* mit*)*.

**comparative** [kəm'pærətɪv] *adj* **(a)** *religion, philology etc* vergleichend. **the** ~ **form** *(Gram)* der Komparativ. **(b)** *(relative)* relativ. **to live in** ~ **luxury** relativ luxuriös leben.

**comparatively** [kəm'pærətɪvlɪ] *adv (relatively)* verhältnismäßig.

**compare** [kəm'pɛəʳ] **1** *vt* vergleichen *(with, to* mit*)*. ~**d with** verglichen mit; **they cannot be** ~**d** man kann sie nicht vergleichen; **to** ~ **notes** Eindrücke/Erfahrungen austauschen. **2** *vi* sich vergleichen lassen *(with* mit*)*. **it** ~**s badly/well** es schneidet vergleichsweise schlecht/gut ab. **3** *n:* **beyond** ~ unvergleichlich.

**comparison** [kəm'pærɪsn] *n* Vergleich *m (with, to* mit*)*. **in** ~ **with** im Vergleich zu.

**compartment** [kəm'pɑːtmənt] *n (in fridge, desk etc)* Fach *nt*; *(Rail)* Abteil *nt*.

**compass** ['kʌmpəs] *n* **(a)** Kompaß *m*. **(b)** ~**es** *pl*, **pair of** ~**es** Zirkel *m*. **(c)** *(fig: extent)* Rahmen *m*; *(of human mind, experience)* Bereich *m*.

**compassion** [kəm'pæʃən] *n* Mitgefühl *nt (for* mit*)*.

**compassionate** [kəm'pæʃənɪt] *adj* mitfühlend. **on** ~ **grounds** aus familiären Gründen; ~ **leave** Beurlaubung *f* wegen einer dringenden Familienangelegenheit.

**compatibility** [kəm,pætɪ'bɪlɪtɪ] *n* Vereinbarkeit *f*; *(Med)* Verträglichkeit *f*; *(Tech)* Kompatibilität *f*.

**compatible** [kəm'pætɪbl] *adj* vereinbar; *(Med)* verträglich; *people* zueinander passend; *colours, furniture* passend; *(Tech)* kompatibel.

**compatriot** [kəm'pætrɪət] *n* Landsmann *m*, Landsmännin *f*.

**compel** [kəm'pel] *vt* zwingen. **I feel** ~**led to tell you** ... ich sehe mich (dazu) gezwungen, Ihnen mitzuteilen, ...

**compelling** [kəm'pelɪŋ] *adj reason* zwingend; *performance* bezwingend.

**compendium** [kəm'pendɪəm] *n* Handbuch *nt*.

**compensate** ['kɒmpənseɪt] *vt (recompense)* entschädigen.

►**compensate for** *vi +prep obj (in money etc)* ersetzen; *(make up for, offset)* wieder ausgleichen.

**compensation** [,kɒmpən'seɪʃən] *n (damages)* Entschädigung *f*; *(fig)* Ausgleich *m*.

**compère** ['kɒmpɛəʳ] *(Brit)* **1** *n* Conférencier *m*. **2** *vt* **to** ~ **a show** bei einer Show der Conférencier sein.

**compete** [kəm'piːt] *vi* **(a)** konkurrieren. **to** ~ **with each other** sich (gegenseitig) Konkurrenz machen; **he can't** ~ **with her** er kann sich nicht mit ihr messen. **(b)** *(Sport)* teilnehmen.

**competence** ['kɒmpɪtəns], **competency** ['kɒmpɪtənsɪ] *n* Fähigkeit *f*; *(of doctor etc also)* Kompetenz *f*.

**competent** ['kɒmpɪtənt] *adj* fähig, befähigt *(in zu)*; *(in a particular field)* kompetent.

**competition** [,kɒmpɪ'tɪʃən] *n* **(a)** *no pl* Konkurrenz *f (for* um*)*. **(b)** *(contest)* Wettbewerb *m*; *(in newspapers etc)* Preisausschreiben *nt*. **beauty** ~ Schönheitswettbewerb *m*.

**competitive** [kəm'petɪtɪv] *adj* **(a)** *person, attitude* vom Konkurrenzdenken geprägt. ~ **sport** (Wett)kampfsport *m*; **a** ~ **examination** eine Auswahlprüfung. **(b)** *(Comm, Sport: able to compete)* *business, prices, salaries, car, athlete* konkurrenzfähig.

**competitiveness** [kəm'petɪtɪvnɪs] *n (Comm)* Konkurrenzfähigkeit *f*.

**competitor** [kəm'petɪtə*r*] *n* (a) Teilnehmer(in *f*) *m*. (b) *(Comm)* our ~s unsere Konkurrenz *f or* Konkurrenten *pl*.

**compilation** [ˌkɒmpɪ'leɪʃən] *n see vt* Zusammenstellung *f*; Zusammentragen *nt*; Verfassen *nt*.

**compile** [kəm'paɪl] *vt* zusammenstellen; *material* zusammentragen; *dictionary* verfassen.

**complacency** [kəm'pleɪsnsɪ] *n* Selbstgefälligkeit *f*.

**complacent** [kəm'pleɪsənt] *adj* selbstgefällig.

**complain** [kəm'pleɪn] *vi* sich beklagen *(about* über +*acc)*; *(to make a formal complaint)* sich beschweren *(about* über +*acc, to* bei*)*. (l) **can't** ~ *(col)* ich kann nicht klagen *(col)*.

**complaint** [kəm'pleɪnt] *n* (a) Klage *f*; *(formal* ~*)* Beschwerde *f*. (b) *(illness)* Beschwerden *pl*. **a very rare** ~ eine sehr seltene Krankheit.

**complement** ['kɒmplɪmənt] **1** *n* (a) *(also Gram)* Ergänzung *f (to gen)*. (b) *(full number)* volle Stärke; *(crew of ship)* Besatzung *f*. **our office has its full** ~ in unserem Büro sind alle Stellen besetzt. **2** ['kɒmplɪment] *vt* ergänzen. **to** ~ **each other** sich ergänzen.

**complementary** [ˌkɒmplɪ'mentərɪ] *adj* komplementär; *pair* zusammengehörig. **they have** ~ **interests** ihre Interessen ergänzen sich.

**complete** [kəm'pliːt] **1** *adj* (a) *(entire, whole)* ganz *attr*; *wardrobe, deck of cards* komplett; *(having the required numbers)* vollzählig; *edition* Gesamt-. ~ **with** komplett mit; **the** ~ **works of Shakespeare** die gesammelten Werke Shakespeares; **my happiness was** ~ mein Glück war vollkommen. (b) *attr (total, absolute)* völlig; *failure, disaster, victory* total; *satisfaction, approval* voll. **a** ~ **idiot** ein Vollidiot *m*; **we were** ~ **strangers** wir waren uns völlig fremd. (c) *(finished)* fertig. **2** *vt* (a) *(make whole) collection, set* vervollständigen. (b) *(fig) happiness* vollkommen machen. **and to** ~ **their misery** ... und zu allem Unglück ... (c) *(finish)* abschließen. (d) *form, questionnaire* ausfüllen.

**completely** [kəm'pliːtlɪ] *adv* völlig, vollkommen.

**completion** [kəm'pliːʃən] *n (finishing)* Fertigstellung *f*; *(of project, course, education)* Abschluß *m*. **on** ~ **of the contract/sale** bei Vertrags-/Kaufabschluß.

**complex** ['kɒmpleks] **1** *adj* komplex. **2** *n* (a) Komplex *m*. **industrial** ~ Industriekomplex. (b) *(Psych)* Komplex *m*. **he has a** ~ **about his big ears** er hat Komplexe wegen seiner großen Ohren.

**complexion** [kəm'plekʃən] *n* (a) Teint *m*; *(skin colour)* Gesichtsfarbe *f*. (b) *(fig: aspect)* Aspekt *m*. **to put a new/different/sinister** *etc* ~ **on sth** etw in einem neuen/anderen/düsteren *etc* Licht erscheinen lassen.

**complexity** [kəm'pleksɪtɪ] *n* Komplexität *f*.

**compliance** [kəm'plaɪəns] *n* Einverständnis *nt*; *(with rules etc)* Einhalten *nt (with gen)*. **in** ~ **with the law/our wishes** *etc* dem Gesetz/unseren Wünschen *etc* gemäß.

**complicate** ['kɒmplɪkeɪt] *vt* komplizieren.

**complicated** ['kɒmplɪkeɪtɪd] *adj* kompliziert.

**complication** [ˌkɒmplɪ'keɪʃən] *n* Komplikation *f*; *(condition)* Kompliziertheit *f*.

**complicity** [kəm'plɪsɪtɪ] *n* Mittäterschaft *f (in* bei*)*.

**compliment** ['kɒmplɪmənt] **1** *n* (a) Kompliment *nt (on* zu, wegen*)*. **to pay sb a** ~ jdm ein Kompliment machen. (b) *(form)* ~s *pl* Grüße *pl*; "**the** ~**s of the season**" „frohes Fest"; "**with the** ~**s of Mr X/the management**" „mit den besten Empfehlungen von

Herrn X/der Geschäftsleitung"; ~**s slip** *(Comm)* Empfehlungszettel *m*. **2** ['kɒmplɪment] *vt* ein Kompliment/Komplimente machen *(+dat) (on* wegen, zu*)*.

**complimentary** [ˌkɒmplɪ'mentərɪ] *adj* (a) *(praising)* schmeichelhaft. ~ **close** *(in letter)* Schlußformel *f*. (b) *(gratis) seat, ticket* Frei-.

**comply** [kəm'plaɪ] *vi (person)* einwilligen; *(object, system etc)* den Bedingungen entsprechen. **to** ~ **with a request/a wish/instructions** einer Bitte/einem Wunsch/den Anordnungen entsprechen *(form)*.

**component** [kəm'pəʊnənt] *n* Bestandteil *m*; *(Chem, Phys)* Komponente *f*.

**compose** [kəm'pəʊz] *vt* (a) *music* komponieren; *letter, poem* verfassen. (b) *(constitute, make up)* bilden. **to be** ~**d of** sich zusammensetzen aus. (c) **to** ~ **oneself** sich sammeln.

**composed** [kəm'pəʊzd] *adj* gefaßt.

**composer** [kəm'pəʊzə*r*] *n* (a) *(Mus)* Komponist(in *f*) *m*. (b) *(of letter, poem etc)* Verfasser(in *f*) *m*.

**composition** [ˌkɒmpə'zɪʃən] *n* (a) *(act) (of music)* Komponieren *nt*; *(of letter, poem etc)* Verfassen *nt*. (b) *(arrangement, Mus, Art)* Komposition *f*. (c) *(Sch: essay)* Aufsatz *m*. (d) *(constitution, make-up)* Zusammensetzung *f*. (e) ~ **soles** Kunststoffsohlen *pl*.

**compositor** [kəm'pɒzɪtə*r*] *n (Typ)* (Schrift)setzer(in *f*) *m*.

**compos mentis** ['kɒmpəs'mentɪs] *adj* voll zurechnungsfähig; *(clear-headed)* klar im Kopf *(col)*.

**compost** ['kɒmpɒst] *n* Kompost *m*. ~ **heap** Komposthaufen *m*.

**composure** [kəm'pəʊʒə*r*] *n* Fassung *f*.

**compote** ['kɒmpəʊt] *n* Kompott *nt*.

**compound** ['kɒmpaʊnd] **1** *n* (a) *(Chem)* Verbindung *f*; *(Gram) (also* ~ **noun)** Kompositum *nt*, zusammengesetztes Wort. (b) *(enclosed area)* Lager *nt*. **2** *adj* ~ **interest** Zinseszins *m*; ~ **fracture** komplizierter Bruch. **3** [kəm'paʊnd] *vt (make worse)* verschlimmern.

**comprehend** [ˌkɒmprɪ'hend] *vt* verstehen.

**comprehensibility** [ˌkɒmprɪˌhensɪ'bɪlɪtɪ] *n* Verständlichkeit *f*.

**comprehensible** *adj*, ~**bly** *adv* [ˌkɒmprɪ'hensəbl, -ɪ] verständlich.

**comprehension** [ˌkɒmprɪ'henʃən] *n (understanding)* Verständnis *nt*; *(school exercise)* Fragen *pl* zum Textverständnis.

**comprehensive** [ˌkɒmprɪ'hensɪv] *adj* umfassend, ausführlich; *measures, knowledge* umfassend. ~ **school** *(Brit)* Gesamtschule *f*; ~ **policy** *(Insur)* Vollkasko(versicherung *f*) *nt*.

**comprehensively** [ˌkɒmprɪ'hensɪvlɪ] *adv* umfassend. **to be** ~ **beaten** deutlich geschlagen werden.

**compress¹** [kəm'pres] **1** *vt* komprimieren *(into* auf +*acc)*; *materials* zusammenpressen *(into* zu*)*. **2** *vi* sich komprimieren lassen.

**compress²** ['kɒmpres] *n (Med)* Kompresse *f*.

**compressed air** [kəm'prest'ɛə*r*] *n* Preßluft *f*.

**compression** [kəm'preʃən] *n* Kompression *f*.

**compressor** [kəm'presə*r*] *n* Kompressor *m*.

**comprise** [kəm'praɪz] *vt* umfassen.

**compromise** ['kɒmprəmaɪz] **1** *n* Kompromiß *m*. **2** *adj attr* Kompromiß-. ~ **solution** Kompromißlösung *f*. **3** *vi* Kompromisse schließen *(about* in +*dat)*. **not prepared to** ~ nicht kompromißbereit. **4** *vt* kompromittieren.

**compulsion** [kəm'pʌlʃən] *n* Zwang *m*; *(Psych)* innerer Zwang. **under** ~ unter Druck; **you are under no** ~ niemand zwingt Sie.

**compulsive** [kəm'pʌlsɪv] *adj* Zwangs-; *behaviour* zwanghaft. **he is a** ~ **eater** er leidet an einem Eßzwang; **he is a** ~ **liar** er hat einen krankhaften Trieb zu lügen; **he's a** ~ **smoker** das Rauchen ist bei ihm zur Sucht geworden; **it makes** ~ **viewing** davon kann man sich nicht losreißen.

**compulsorily** [kəm'pʌlsərɪlɪ] *adv* zwangsweise.

**compulsory** [kəm'pʌlsərɪ] *adj* obligatorisch; *measures* Zwangs-; *subject* Pflicht-. **that is** ~ das ist Pflicht; **education is** ~ es besteht (allgemeine) Schulpflicht; ~ **purchase** Enteignung *f.*

**compunction** [kəm'pʌŋkʃən] *n (liter)* Schuldgefühle *pl.* **with no** ~ ohne sich schuldig zu fühlen.

**computation** [ˌkɒmpjʊ'teɪʃən] *n* Berechnung *f.*

**compute** [kəm'pjuːt] *vt* berechnen *(at* auf *+acc).*

**computer** [kəm'pjuːtər] *n* Computer, Rechner *m.* **to put sth on** ~ etw im Computer speichern.

**computer:** ~ **crime** *n* Computerkriminalität *f;* ~- **dating** *n* Partnervermittlung *f* per Computer; ~ **game** *n* Computerspiel *nt;* ~ **graphics** *npl* Computergrafik *f.*

**computerization** [kəmˌpjuːtəraɪ'zeɪʃən] *n (of information etc)* Computerisierung *f.* **the** ~ **of the factory** die Umstellung der Fabrik auf Computer.

**computerize** [kəm'pjuːtəraɪz] *vt information* computerisieren; *company, accounting methods* auf EDV umstellen.

**computer:** ~ **literate** *adj* **to be** ~ **literate** sich mit Computern auskennen; ~ **network** *n* Rechnerverbund *m;* ~-**operated** *adj* computergesteuert; ~ **program** *n* Programm *nt;* ~ **programmer** *n* Programmierer (in *f) m;* ~ **science** *n* Informatik *f;* ~ **typesetting** *n* Computersatz *m.*

**comrade** ['kɒmrɪd] *n* Kamerad *m; (Pol)* Genosse *m,* Genossin *f.*

**con**¹ [kɒn] *(col)* **1** *n* Schwindel *m.* ~ **man** Schwindler *m.* **2** *vt* hereinlegen *(col).* **he** ~**ned her out of all her money** er hat ihr ihr ganzes Geld abgeschwindelt.

**con**² *(col)* = **convict** Knastbruder *m (col).*

**concave** ['kɒn'keɪv] *adj* konkav; *mirror* Hohl-.

**conceal** [kən'siːl] *vt (hide)* verbergen; *(keep secret)* verheimlichen.

**concealed** [kən'siːld] *adj* verborgen; *lighting* indirekt; *entrance* verdeckt.

**concealment** [kən'siːlmənt] *n* Verheimlichung *f; (of evidence)* Unterschlagung *f.* **to stay in** ~ sich versteckt halten.

**concede** [kən'siːd] *vt* **(a)** *(yield) privilege* aufgeben; *lands* abtreten *(to* an *+acc); (Sport) corner, penalty* verursachen. **to** ~ **victory to sb** vor jdm kapitulieren; **to** ~ **a point to sb** *(in debate)* jdm in einem Punkt recht geben. **(b)** *(admit, grant)* einräumen. **to** ~ **defeat** sich geschlagen geben.

**conceit** [kən'siːt] *n (pride)* Einbildung *f.*

**conceited** [kən'siːtɪd] *adj* eingebildet.

**conceivable** [kən'siːvəbl] *adj* denkbar. **the worst** ~ **thing to say** das denkbar Schlechteste, was man sagen kann.

**conceivably** [kən'siːvəblɪ] *adv* **she may** ~ **be right** es ist durchaus denkbar, daß sie recht hat.

**conceive** [kən'siːv] **1** *vt* **(a)** *child* empfangen. **(b)** *(imagine)* sich *(dat)* vorstellen; *idea, plan* haben; *novel* die Idee haben zu. **I can't** ~ **why** ich verstehe nicht, warum. **2** *vi (woman)* empfangen.

**concentrate** ['kɒnsəntreɪt] **1** *vt* konzentrieren *(on* auf *+acc).* **to** ~ **one's mind on sth** seine Gedanken *or* sich auf etw *(acc)* konzentrieren. **2** *vi* **(a)** *(give one's attention)* sich konzentrieren. **(b)** *(people)* sich sammeln. **3** *n (Chem)* Konzentrat *nt.*

**concentration** [ˌkɒnsən'treɪʃən] *n* Konzentration *f.* **powers of** ~ Konzentrationsfähigkeit *f.*

**concentration camp** *n* Konzentrationslager, KZ *nt.*

**concentric** [kən'sentrɪk] *adj* konzentrisch.

**concept** ['kɒnsept] *n* Begriff *m; (conception)* Vorstellung *f.*

**conception** [kən'sepʃən] *n* **(a)** *(idea)* Vorstellung *f; (way sth is conceived)* Auffassung *f.* **the writer's powers of** ~ die Vorstellungskraft des Schriftstellers. **he has no** ~ **of how difficult it is** er macht sich *(dat)* keinen Begriff davon, wie schwer das ist. **(b)** *(of child)* die Empfängnis.

**concern** [kən'sɜːn] **1** *n* **(a)** *(connection)* **to have no** ~ **with sth** mit etw nichts zu tun haben. **(b)** *(business, affair)* Angelegenheit (en *pl) f; (matter of importance to a person)* Anliegen *nt.* **it's no** ~ **of his** das geht ihn nichts an; **what** ~ **is it of yours?** was geht Sie das an? **(c)** *(Comm)* Konzern *m.* **(d)** *(anxiety)* Sorge *f.* **a look of** ~ ein besorgter Blick; **there's some/no cause for** ~ es besteht Grund/kein Grund zur Sorge; **he showed great** ~ **for your safety** er zeigte sich sehr um Ihre Sicherheit besorgt.

**2** *vt* **(a)** *(be about)* handeln von.

**(b)** *(be the business of, involve)* angehen, betreffen. **that doesn't** ~ **you** das betrifft Sie nicht; *(as snub)* das geht Sie nichts an; **to whom it may** ~ *(on letter)* an den betreffenden Sachbearbeiter; *(on certificate)* „Bestätigung''; *(on reference)* „Zeugnis''; **as far as I'm** ~**ed** was mich betrifft; **as far as I'm** ~**ed you can do what you like** von mir aus kannst du tun und lassen, was du willst; **the persons** ~**ed** die Betroffenen.

**(c)** *(interest)* **he is only** ~**ed with facts** ihn interessieren nur die Fakten; *(is only dealing with)* ihm geht es nur um die Fakten.

**(d)** *(worry)* **there's no need for you to** ~ **yourself about that** darum brauchen Sie sich nicht zu kümmern; **to be** ~**ed about sth** sich *(dat)* um etw Sorgen machen, um etw besorgt sein; **don't** ~ **yourself** machen Sie sich keine Sorgen; **I was very** ~**ed about** *or* **for your safety** ich war sehr um Ihre Sicherheit besorgt.

**concerning** [kən'sɜːnɪŋ] *prep* bezüglich *(+gen),* hinsichtlich *(+gen).* ~ **your request** ... was Ihre Anfrage betrifft ...

**concert** ['kɒnsət] *n (Mus)* Konzert *nt.* **in** ~ *(fig)* gemeinsam.

**concerted** [kən'sɜːtɪd] *adj efforts* vereint; *action* gemeinsam.

**concert:** ~**goer** *n* Konzertbesucher (in *f) m;* ~ **grand** *n* Konzertflügel *m;* ~ **hall** *n* Konzertsaal *m.*

**concertina** [ˌkɒnsə'tiːnə] *n* Konzertina *f.*

**concertmaster** ['kɒnsətmæstər] *n (esp US)* Konzertmeister *m.*

**concerto** [kən'tʃɛːtəʊ] *n* Konzert *nt.*

**concert:** ~ **pianist** *n* Pianist (in *f) m;* ~ **pitch** *n* Kammerton *m;* ~ **tour** *n* Konzerttournee *f.*

**concession** [kən'seʃən] *n* Zugeständnis *nt (to* an *+acc); (Comm)* Konzession *f.*

**concessionary** [kən'seʃənərɪ] *adj (Comm)* Konzessions-; *rate, fare* ermäßigt.

**conciliate** [kən'sɪlɪeɪt] *vt (a) (placate)* besänftigen. **(b)** *(reconcile) opposing views* in Einklang bringen.

**conciliation** [kənsɪlɪ'eɪʃn] *n* Besänftigung *f; (in strikes)* Schlichtung *f.*

**conciliatory** [kən'sɪlɪətərɪ] *adj* versöhnlich; *(placatory)* beschwichtigend.

**concise** [kən'saɪs] *adj* prägnant; *(brief)* knapp. ~ **dictionary** Handwörterbuch *nt.*

**conclude** [kən'kluːd] **1** *vt* **(a)** *(end) meeting, letter, speech* schließen. **(b)** *(arrange) treaty, deal* abschließen. **(c)** *(decide)* **to** ~ **that** ... zu dem Schluß kommen, daß ...; **what do you** ~ **from this?** was schließen Sie daraus? **2** *vi (meetings, events)* enden; *(letter, speech)* schließen.

**concluding** [kən'kluːdɪŋ] adj abschließend; years, paragraph letzte(r, s).

**conclusion** [kən'kluːʒən] n (a) (end, settling) Abschluß m; (of essay, novel etc) Schluß m. in ~ zum (Ab)schluß. (b) (deduction) Schluß(folgerung f) m. **to come to the ~ that** ... zu dem Schluß kommen, daß ...

**conclusive** [kən'kluːsɪv] adj (convincing) überzeugend; (decisive, final) endgültig; (Jur) evidence einschlägig; proof schlüssig.

**conclusively** [kən'kluːsɪvlɪ] adv überzeugend; prove schlüssig.

**concoct** [kən'kɒkt] vt (a) (Cook etc) zusammenstellen. (b) (fig) sich (dat) zurechtlegen; new dress, hat zaubern; story, alibi sich (dat) ausdenken.

**concoction** [kən'kɒkʃən] n (food) Zusammenstellung f; (drink) Gebräu nt; (story) Lügengeschichte f; (fashion) Spielerei f.

**concord** ['kɒŋkɔːd] n (harmony) Eintracht f.

**concourse** ['kɒŋkɔːs] n (place) Eingangshalle f. **station** ~ Bahnhofshalle f.

**concrete**[1] ['kɒŋkriːt] adj object, example konkret.

**concrete**[2] n (Build) Beton m. ~ **mixer** Betonmischmaschine f; ~ **jungle** (fig) Betonwüste f. **2** adj Beton-. **3** vt wall, floor betonieren.

**concur** [kən'kɜːr] vi (a) (agree) übereinstimmen; (with a suggestion etc) beipflichten (with dat). **I ~ with that** ich pflichte dem bei. (b) (happen together) zusammentreffen.

**concurrent** [kən'kʌrənt] adj gleichzeitig.

**concuss** [kən'kʌs] vt (usu pass) **to be ~ed** eine Gehirnerschütterung haben.

**concussion** [kən'kʌʃən] n Gehirnerschütterung f.

**condemn** [kən'dem] vt (a) (censure, Jur, fig) verurteilen. **to ~ sb to death** jdn zum Tode verurteilen. (b) (declare unfit) building, slums für abbruchreif erklären; food für den Verzehr ungeeignet erklären.

**condemnation** [ˌkɒndem'neɪʃən] n Verurteilung f.

**condensation** [ˌkɒnden'seɪʃən] n (a) (of vapour) Kondensation f; (liquid formed) Kondensat nt. **the windows/walls are covered with** ~ die Fenster/Wände sind beschlagen. (b) (short form) Kurzfassung f.

**condense** [kən'dens] **1** vt (a) kondensieren. **~d milk** (gesüßte) Kondensmilch f. (b) (Phys) gas kondensieren; (compress) verdichten. (c) (shorten) zusammenfassen. **2** vi (gas) kondensieren.

**condenser** [kən'densər] n (Elec, Phys) Kondensator m.

**condescend** [ˌkɒndɪ'send] vi sich herablassen.

**condescending** [ˌkɒndɪ'sendɪŋ] adj (pej) herablassend.

**condescension** [ˌkɒndɪ'senʃən] n (pej) Herablassung f.

**condition** [kən'dɪʃən] **1** n (a) (determining factor) Bedingung f (also Jur, Comm); (prerequisite) Voraussetzung f. **on ~ that** ... unter der Voraussetzung, daß ...; **on no ~** auf keinen Fall; **to make ~s** Bedingungen stellen.

(b) **~s** pl (circumstances) Verhältnisse pl; **working ~s** Arbeitsbedingungen pl; **living ~s** Wohnverhältnisse pl.

(c) no pl (state) Zustand m. **he is in good/bad ~** er ist in guter/schlechter Verfassung; **it is in good/bad ~** es ist in gutem/schlechtem Zustand; **you're in no ~ to drive** du bist nicht fahrtüchtig; **to be in/out of ~** eine gute/keine Kondition haben; **to keep in/get into ~** in Form bleiben/kommen.

(d) (Med) Beschwerden pl. **he has a heart ~** er ist herzkrank.

**2** vt (a) (esp pass: determine) bedingen. **to be ~ed**

**by** bedingt sein durch. (b) (Psych etc: train) konditionieren; (accustom) gewöhnen. **~ed reflex** bedingter Reflex.

**conditional** [kən'dɪʃənl] adj (a) mit Vorbehalt, bedingt. **to be ~ (up)on sth** von etw abhängen. (b) (Gram) konditional, Bedingungs-. ~ **clause** Bedingungssatz m; **the ~ mood/tense** das Konditional.

**conditionally** [kən'dɪʃnəlɪ] adv unter or mit Vorbehalt.

**conditioner** [kən'dɪʃənər] n (for hair) Pflegespülung f; (for fabrics) Weichspüler m.

**condo** ['kɒndəʊ] n (US col) = **condominium**.

**condolence** [kən'dəʊləns] n Beileid nt no pl. **letter of** ~ Kondolenzbrief m.

**condom** ['kɒndəm] n Kondom nt or m.

**condominium** [ˌkɒndə'mɪnɪəm] n (US) Eigentumswohnung f; (block) Eigentumsblock m.

**condone** [kən'dəʊn] vt (overlook) hinwegsehen über (+acc); (tacitly approve) (stillschweigend) dulden.

**conducive** [kən'djuːsɪv] adj dienlich (to dat).

**conduct 1** ['kɒndʌkt] n (a) (behaviour) Verhalten, Benehmen nt (towards gegenüber). (b) (management) Führung f. **2** [kən'dʌkt] vt (a) (guide) führen. **~ed tour (of)** (Brit) (of country) Gesellschaftsreise f (durch); (of building) Führung f (durch). (b) (direct, manage) führen; meeting leiten; investigation durchführen. (c) (Mus) dirigieren. (d) (Phys, Physiol) leiten; lightning ableiten. **3** [kən'dʌkt] vr **to ~ oneself** sich benehmen.

**conduction** [kən'dʌkʃən] n (Phys) Leitung f.

**conductivity** [ˌkɒndʌk'tɪvɪtɪ] n (Phys) Leitfähigkeit f.

**conductor** [kən'dʌktər] n (a) (Mus) Dirigent(in f) m. (b) (bus, tram ~) Schaffner m; (US Rail: guard) Zugführer m. (c) (Phys) Leiter m; (lightning ~) Blitzableiter m.

**conductress** [kən'dʌktrɪs] n (on bus etc) Schaffnerin f.

**conduit** ['kɒndɪt] n Leitungsrohr nt.

**cone** [kəʊn] n (a) Kegel m. (b) (Bot) Zapfen m. (c) (ice-cream ~) (Eis)tüte f.

**cone-shaped** ['kəʊn'ʃeɪpt] adj kegelförmig.

**confab** ['kɒnfæb] n (col) kleine Besprechung.

**confection** [kən'fekʃən] n (sweets) Konfekt nt; (creation) Kreation f.

**confectioner's** [kən'fekʃənəz] n (Brit) Süßwarenladen m.

**confectionery** [kən'fekʃənərɪ] n Süßwaren pl; (chocolates) Konfekt nt.

**confederate** [kən'fedərɪt] **1** adj system konföderiert; nations verbündet. **2** n (Pol: ally) Verbündete(r) m; (pej: accomplice) Komplize m (pej).

**confederation** [kən,fedə'reɪʃən] n (a) (Pol) (alliance) Bündnis nt; (system of government) Staatenbund m. **the Swiss C~** die Schweizer Eidgenossenschaft. (b) (association) Bund m. **C~ of British Industry** Verband m der britischen Industrie.

**confer** [kən'fɜːr] **1** vt title, degree verleihen (on, upon sb jdm). **2** vi sich beraten.

**conference** ['kɒnfərəns] n Konferenz f; (more informal) Besprechung f. **to be in ~** in or bei einer Konferenz/Besprechung sein.

**conference:** ~ **call** n (Telec) Konferenzschaltung f; ~ **centre** n Kongreßzentrum nt; ~ **room** n Konferenzzimmer nt; (smaller) Besprechungszimmer nt; ~ **table** n Konferenztisch m.

**confess** [kən'fes] **1** vt (a) (acknowledge) gestehen. (b) (Eccl) sins bekennen; (to priest) beichten; (priest) penitent die Beichte abnehmen (+dat). **2** vi (a) gestehen (to acc). **to ~ to sth** etw gestehen. (b) (Eccl) beichten.

**confession** [kən'feʃən] n (a) Eingeständnis nt; (of

*guilt, crime etc)* Geständnis *nt.* **I have a ~ to make** ich muß dir etwas gestehen. **(b)** *(Eccl: of sins)* Beichte *f.* **~ of faith** Glaubensbekenntnis *nt*; **to make one's ~** seine Sünden bekennen.

**confessional** [kən'feʃənl] *n* Beichtstuhl *m*.

**confessor** [kən'fesər] *n (Eccl)* Beichtvater *m*.

**confetti** [kən'fetiː] *n no pl* Konfetti *nt*.

**confidant** [ˌkɒnfɪ'dænt] *n* Vertraute(r) *m*.

**confidante** [ˌkɒnfɪ'dænt] *n* Vertraute *f*.

**confide** [kən'faɪd] **1** *vt* anvertrauen *(to sb* jdm*).* **2** *vi* **to ~ in sb** jdn ins Vertrauen ziehen.

**confidence** ['kɒnfɪdəns] *n* **(a)** *(trust)* Vertrauen *nt*; *(confident expectation)* Zuversicht *f.* **to have (every/ no) ~ in sb/sth** (volles/kein) Vertrauen zu jdm/etw haben; **I have every ~ that ...** ich bin ganz zuversichtlich, daß ...; **to give/ask for a vote of ~** *(Parl)* das Vertrauen aussprechen/die Vertrauensfrage stellen; **motion/vote of no ~** Mißtrauensantrag *m*/ -votum *nt*. **(b)** *(self-~)* (Selbst)vertrauen *nt.* **(c)** *(confidential relationship)* Vertrauen *nt.* **in (strict) ~** (streng) vertraulich; **to take sb into one's ~** jdn ins Vertrauen ziehen. **(d)** *(information confided)* vertrauliche Mitteilung.

**confidence: ~ trick** *n* = **con trick; ~trickster** *n* = **con-man.**

**confident** ['kɒnfɪdənt] *adj* **(a)** *(sure)* überzeugt; *look etc* zuversichtlich. **(b)** *(self-assured)* (selbst)sicher.

**confidential** [ˌkɒnfɪ'denʃəl] *adj information* vertraulich. **~ secretary** Privatsekretär(in *f) m*.

**confidentiality** [ˌkɒnfɪˌdenʃɪ'ælɪtɪ] *n* Vertraulichkeit *f.*

**confidentially** [ˌkɒnfɪ'denʃəlɪ] *adv* im Vertrauen.

**confidently** ['kɒnfɪdəntlɪ] *adv* zuversichtlich; *(self-~)* selbstsicher.

**configuration** [kənˌfɪgjʊ'reɪʃən] *n (also Comp)* Konfiguration *f.*

**confine** [kən'faɪn] *vt* **(a)** *(keep in)* (ein)sperren. **~d to bed/the house** ans Bett/ans Haus gefesselt; **to be ~d to barracks** Kasernenarrest haben. **(b)** *(limit)* beschränken *(to* auf *+acc).* **to ~ oneself to doing sth** sich darauf beschränken, etw zu tun.

**confined** [kən'faɪnd] *adj space* beschränkt; *atmosphere* beengend.

**confinement** [kən'faɪnmənt] *n* **(a)** *(imprisonment)* *(act)* Einsperren *nt*; *(in jail)* Haft *f.* **(b)** *(dated: childbirth)* Niederkunft *(dated) f.*

**confines** ['kɒnfaɪnz] *npl* Grenzen *pl.*

**confirm** [kən'fɜːm] *vt* **(a)** *(verify)* bestätigen. **(b)** *(strengthen)* bestärken; *one's resolve* bekräftigen. **(c)** *(Eccl)* konfirmieren; *Roman Catholic* firmen.

**confirmation** [ˌkɒnfə'meɪʃən] *n* **(a)** Bestätigung *f.* **(b)** *(Eccl)* Konfirmation *f*; *(of Roman Catholics)* Firmung *f.* **~ candidate** Konfirmand(in *f) m*.

**confirmed** [kən'fɜːmd] *adj* erklärt; *bachelor* eingefleischt.

**confiscate** ['kɒnfɪskeɪt] *vt* beschlagnahmen.

**confiscation** [ˌkɒnfɪs'keɪʃn] *n* Beschlagnahme *f.*

**conflict 1** ['kɒnflɪkt] *n* Konflikt *m*; *(between two accounts etc)* Widerspruch *m*; *(fighting)* Zusammenstoß *m.* **to come into ~ with sb/sth** mit jdm/etw in Konflikt geraten; **~ of interests/opinions** Interessen-/Meinungskonflikt *m.* **2** [kən'flɪkt] *vi* im Widerspruch stehen *(with* zu*).*

**conflicting** [kən'flɪktɪŋ] *adj* widersprüchlich.

**conform** [kən'fɔːm] *vi (things: comply with)* entsprechen *(to dat)*; *(people: socially)* sich anpassen *(to* an *+acc)*; *(things, people: to rules etc)* sich richten *(to* nach*).*

**conformist** [kən'fɔːmɪst] *n* Konformist(in *f) m*.

**conformity** [kən'fɔːmɪtɪ] *n* **(a)** *(uniformity)* Konformismus *m*. **(b)** *(compliance)* Übereinstimmung *f*;

*(socially)* Anpassung *f (with* an *+acc).* **to be in ~ with sth** einer Sache *(dat)* entsprechen; **in ~ with** entsprechend *(+dat).*

**confound** [kən'faʊnd] *vt (amaze)* verblüffen; *(throw into confusion)* verwirren. **~ it!** *(col)* verflixt noch mal! *(col).*

**confounded** [kən'faʊndɪd] *adj (col)* verflixt *(col)*; **~ noise** Heidenlärm *m (col).*

**confront** [kən'frʌnt] *vt* **(a)** *(face)* gegenübertreten *(+dat)*; *(problems, decisions)* sich stellen *(+dat).* **(b)** *(bring face to face with)* konfrontieren. **to ~ sb with sb/sth** jdn mit jdm/etw konfrontieren.

**confrontation** [ˌkɒnfrən'teɪʃən] *n* Konfrontation *f (also Pol)*; *(with witnesses, evidence etc)* Gegenüberstellung *f.*

**confuse** [kən'fjuːz] *vt* **(a)** *(bewilder, perplex)* verwirren, durcheinanderbringen. **(b)** *(mix up)* verwechseln.

**confused** [kən'fjuːzd] *adj (muddled)* konfus; *person also* verwirrt; *idea, report, situation* verworren.

**confusing** [kən'fjuːzɪŋ] *adj* verwirrend.

**confusion** [kən'fjuːʒən] *n* **(a)** *(disorder)* Durcheinander *nt*; *(jumble)* Wirrwarr *m.* **(b)** *(perplexity)* Verwirrung *f*; *(mental ~: after drugs, blow on head etc)* Verwirrtheit *f.* **in the ~ of the moment** im Eifer des Gefechts. **(c)** *(mixing up)* Verwechslung *f.*

**congeal** [kən'dʒiːl] *vi* erstarren; *(glue, mud)* hart werden; *(blood)* gerinnen.

**congenial** [kən'dʒiːnɪəl] *adj (pleasant)* angenehm.

**congenital** [kən'dʒenɪtl] *adj deficiency, disease* angeboren. **~ defect** Geburtsfehler *m*; **~ idiot** *(col)* Vollidiot *m (col).*

**conger** ['kɒŋgər] *n (also ~ eel)* Seeaal *m.*

**congest** [kən'dʒest] *vt* verstopfen.

**congested** [kən'dʒestɪd] *adj* überfüllt; *roads, nose* verstopft.

**congestion** [kən'dʒestʃən] *n (traffic ~)* Stau *m*; *(of town etc)* Verstopfung *f*; *(overpopulation)* Übervölkerung *f*; *(Med)* Blutstau *m*; *(nasal ~)* verstopfte Nase.

**conglomerate** [kən'glɒmərɪt] *n (also Geol, fig)* Konglomerat *nt*; *(Comm: combine)* Mischkonzern *m.*

**conglomeration** [kənˌglɒmə'reɪʃən] *n* Ansammlung *f.*

**Congo** ['kɒŋgəʊ] *n* Kongo *m.*

**Congolese** [ˌkɒŋgəʊ'liːz] **1** *adj* kongolesisch. **2** *n* Kongolese *m*, Kongolesin *f.*

**congratulate** [kən'grætjʊleɪt] *vt* gratulieren *(+dat) (on* zu*).*

**congratulations** [kənˌgrætjʊ'leɪʃənz] **1** *npl* Glückwünsche *pl.* **2** *interj* (ich) gratuliere!; **~ (on your success)!** herzlichen Glückwunsch (zu deinem Erfolg)!

**congregate** ['kɒŋgrɪgeɪt] *vi* sich sammeln; *(on a particular occasion)* sich versammeln.

**congregation** [ˌkɒŋgrɪ'geɪʃən] *n* **(a)** Versammlung *f.* **(b)** *(Eccl)* Gemeinde *f.*

**congress** ['kɒŋgres] *n* **(a)** *(meeting)* Kongreß *m*; *(of political party)* Parteitag *m.* **(b)** **C~** *(US etc Pol)* der Kongreß.

**congressional** [kən'greʃənl] *adj (US Pol)* Kongreß-.

**Congressman** ['kɒŋgresmən] *n, pl* **-men** [-mən] Kongreßabgeordnete(r) *m*.

**Congresswoman** ['kɒŋgresˌwʊmən] *n, pl* **-women** [-ˌwɪmɪn] Kongreßabgeordnete *f.*

**conic** ['kɒnɪk] *adj (Math)* konisch. **~ section** Kegelschnitt *m.* **(b)** *(also ~al)* kegelförmig.

**conifer** ['kɒnɪfər] *n* Nadelbaum *m.* **~s** Nadelhölzer *pl.*

**coniferous** [kə'nɪfərəs] *adj tree, forest* Nadel-.

**conjecture** [kən'dʒektʃər] **1** *vt* mutmaßen *(geh).*

**2** *vi* Mutmaßungen anstellen. **3** *n* Mutmaßung *f.*
**conjugal** [ˈkɒndʒʊɡəl] *adj bliss, duties* ehelich.
**conjugate** [ˈkɒndʒʊɡeɪt] *vt (Gram)* konjugieren.
**conjugation** [ˌkɒndʒʊˈɡeɪʃən] *n (Gram)* Konjugation *f.*
**conjunction** [kənˈdʒʌŋkʃən] **(a)** *(Gram)* Konjunktion *f.* **(b)** *(association)* Verbindung *f.* **in ~** zusammen.
**conjunctivitis** [kənˌdʒʌŋktɪˈvaɪtɪs] *n (Med)* Bindehautentzündung *f.*
**conjure** [ˈkʌndʒəʳ] *vti* zaubern.
   ►**conjure up** *vt sep ghost, spirits* beschwören; *(fig)* *memories etc* heraufbeschwören.
**conjurer, conjuror** [ˈkʌndʒərəʳ] *n* Zauberkünstler (in *f*) *m.*
**conjuring** [ˈkʌndʒərɪŋ] *n* Zaubern *nt;* **~ set** Zauberkasten *m;* **~ trick** Zauberkunststück *nt.*
   ►**conk out** [kɒŋkˈaʊt] *vi (col)* den Geist aufgeben; *(person)* umkippen *(col).*
**conker** [ˈkɒŋkəʳ] *n (Brit col)* (Roß)kastanie *f.*
**con-man** [ˈkɒnmæn] *n, pl* **-men** [-men] *(col)* Schwindler *m;* *(pretending to have social status)* Hochstapler *m.*
**Conn** *(US)* = **Connecticut.**
**connect** [kəˈnekt] **1** *vt* **(a)** *(join)* verbinden *(to, with* mit*);* *(Elec etc: also ~* **up***)* *appliances, subscribers* anschließen *(to* an *+acc).* **I'll ~ you** *(Telec)* ich verbinde (Sie); **to be ~ed** *(two things)* miteinander verbunden sein. **(b)** *(fig: associate)* in Verbindung bringen *(with* mit*).* **(c)** *(esp pass: link) ideas, theories etc* verbinden. **to be ~ed with** eine Beziehung haben zu; *(be related to)* verwandt sein mit. **2** *vi (rooms)* eine Verbindung haben *(to, with* zu*);* *(train, plane)* Anschluß haben *(with* an *+acc).* **his punch didn't ~** sein Schlag hat nicht getroffen.
**connecting** [kəˈnektɪŋ]: **~ door** *n* Verbindungstür *f;* **~ flight** *n* Anschlußflug *m;* **~ rod** *n (Tech)* Pleuelstange *f;* **~ thread** *n* Leitfaden *m.*
**connection, connexion** [kəˈnekʃən] *n* **(a)** Verbindung *f (to, with* zu, mit*);* *(wire)* Leitung *f;* *(to mains)* Anschluß *m (to* an *+acc);* *(connecting part)* Verbindung (sstück *nt*) *f.* **parallel/series ~** Parallel-/Reihenschaltung *f.* **(b)** *(fig: link)* Zusammenhang *m.* **the two events are not ~ed** zwischen den beiden Ereignissen besteht kein Zusammenhang; **in this ~** in diesem Zusammenhang; **in ~ with** im Zusammenhang mit. **(c)** *(relationship, business ~)* Beziehung *f (with* zu*);* *(family ~)* familiäre Beziehung. **to have ~s** Beziehungen haben; **there is some distant family ~ between them** sie sind weitläufig miteinander verwandt. **(d)** *(Rail etc)* Anschluß *m.*
**conning tower** [ˈkɒnɪŋtaʊəʳ] *n* Kommandoturm *m.*
**connivance** [kəˈnaɪvəns] *n (tacit consent)* stillschweigendes Einverständnis.
**connive** [kəˈnaɪv] *vi* **(a)** *(conspire)* sich verschwören. **(b)** *(deliberately overlook)* **to ~ at sth** etw stillschweigend dulden.
**connoisseur** [ˌkɒnəˈsɜːʳ] *n* Kenner *m.*
**connotation** [ˌkɒnəʊˈteɪʃən] *n* Assoziation *f.*
**conquer** [ˈkɒŋkəʳ] *vt* **(a)** *(lit) country, the world* erobern; *enemy, nation* besiegen. **(b)** *(fig) mountain* bezwingen; *people, sb's heart* erobern.
**conquering** [ˈkɒŋkərɪŋ] *adj hero* siegreich.
**conqueror** [ˈkɒŋkərəʳ] *n (of country, heart)* Eroberer *m;* *(fig)* Sieger *m (of* über *+acc);* *(of mountain)* Bezwinger *m (of* gen*).*
**conquest** [ˈkɒŋkwest] *n* Eroberung *f;* *(of enemy etc, disease)* Sieg *m (of* über *+acc);* *(col: person)* Eroberung *f;* *(of mountain)* Bezwingung *f.*
**conscience** [ˈkɒnʃəns] *n* Gewissen *nt.* **to have a clear/easy/bad ~** ein reines/gutes/schlechtes Gewissen haben *(about* wegen*);* **to have sth on one's ~** etw auf dem Gewissen haben; **with an easy ~** mit

ruhigem Gewissen; **in (all) ~** allen Ernstes.
**conscience-stricken** [ˈkɒnʃəns,strɪkən] *adj* schuldbewußt.
**conscientious** [ˌkɒnʃɪˈenʃəs] *adj,* **~ly** [-lɪ] *adv (diligent)* gewissenhaft; *(conscious of one's duty)* pflichtbewußt. **~ objector** Wehrdienst- *or* Kriegsdienstverweigerer *m (aus Gewissensgründen).*
**conscientiousness** [ˌkɒnʃɪˈenʃəsnɪs] *n* Gewissenhaftigkeit *f;* *(sense of duty)* Pflichtbewußtsein *nt.*
**conscious** [ˈkɒnʃəs] *adj* **(a)** *(Med)* bei Bewußtsein. **(b)** *(aware, also Psych.)* **to be/become ~ of sth** sich *(dat)* einer Sache *(gen)* bewußt sein/werden. **(c)** *(deliberate)* bewußt.
**consciousness** [ˈkɒnʃəsnɪs] *n* **(a)** *(Med)* Bewußtsein *nt.* **to lose/regain ~** das Bewußtsein verlieren/wiedererlangen. **(b)** *(awareness)* Wissen *nt (of* um*).*
**conscript** [kənˈskrɪpt] **1** *vt* einziehen; *army* ausheben. **2** [ˈkɒnskrɪpt] *n* Wehrpflichtige(r) *m.*
**conscription** [kənˈskrɪpʃən] *n* Wehrpflicht *f;* *(act of conscripting)* Einberufung *f;* *(of army)* Aushebung *f.*
**consecrate** [ˈkɒnsɪkreɪt] *vt (lit, fig)* weihen.
**consecration** [ˌkɒnsɪˈkreɪʃən] *n* Weihe *f;* *(in mass)* Wandlung *f.*
**consecutive** [kənˈsekjʊtɪv] *adj* aufeinanderfolgend; *numbers* fortlaufend. **on four ~ days** vier Tage hintereinander.
**consecutively** [kənˈsekjʊtɪvlɪ] *adv* nacheinander, hintereinander.
**consensus** [kənˈsensəs] *n* Übereinstimmung *f.* **the ~ is that ...** man ist allgemein der Meinung, daß ...; **that's the ~ of opinion** das ist die allgemeine Meinung.
**consent** [kənˈsent] **1** *vi* zustimmen *(to* dat*).* **to ~ to do sth** sich bereit erklären, etw zu tun. **2** *n* Zustimmung *f (to* zu*).* **it is by common ~ ...** man hält es allgemein für ...; **by mutual ~** in gegenseitigem Einverständnis; **the age of ~** das Ehemündigkeitsalter; **she's below the age of ~** sie ist noch minderjährig.
**consequence** [ˈkɒnsɪkwəns] *n* **(a)** *(result, effect)* Folge *f.* **in ~** folglich; **in ~ of** infolge *(+gen);* **in ~ of which** infolgedessen; **to take the ~s** die Konsequenzen tragen. **(b)** *(importance)* Bedeutung *f.* **it's of no ~** das spielt keine Rolle.
**consequent** [ˈkɒnsɪkwənt] *adj attr* daraus folgend; *(temporal)* darauffolgend.
**consequently** [ˈkɒnsɪkwəntlɪ] *adv* folglich.
**conservation** [ˌkɒnsəˈveɪʃən] *n (also Phys)* Erhaltung *f.* **~ area** *(in the country)* Naturschutzgebiet *nt;* *(in town)* unter Denkmalschutz stehendes Gebiet.
**conservationist** [ˌkɒnsəˈveɪʃənɪst] *n* Umweltschützer (in *f*) *m;* *(as regards old buildings etc)* Denkmalpfleger (in *f*) *m.*
**conservative** [kənˈsɜːvətɪv] **1** *adj (also Pol)* konservativ. **at a ~ estimate** bei vorsichtiger Schätzung; **the C~ Party** *(Brit)* die Konservative Partei. **2** *n (Pol:* C~*)* Konservative(r) *mf.*
**conservatoire** [kənˈsɜːvətwɑːʳ] *n* Konservatorium *nt.*
**conservatory** [kənˈsɜːvətrɪ] *n* **(a)** *(sunroom)* Wintergarten *m.* **(b)** *(esp US: Mus etc)* Konservatorium *nt.*
**conserve** [kənˈsɜːv] *vt* erhalten; *one's strength* schonen; *energy* sparen.
**consider** [kənˈsɪdəʳ] *vt* **(a)** *(reflect upon) plan, idea, offer* nachdenken über *(+acc).* **I'll ~ the matter** ich werde mir die Sache durch den Kopf gehen lassen; **have you ~ed the possibility of ...?** haben Sie an die Möglichkeit gedacht, zu...?; **I wouldn't even ~ it!** ich denke nicht daran! **(b)** *(bear in mind)* in Erwägung ziehen; *(take into account)* denken an *(+acc),* berücksichtigen; *person, feelings also* Rücksicht nehmen auf *(+acc).* **~ how much you owe him**

**construction**

bedenken Sie, wieviel Sie ihm schulden; **all things** ~**ed** alles in allem. **(c)** *(regard as)* betrachten als; *person* halten für. **to ~ oneself lucky** sich glücklich schätzen.

**considerable** [kən'sɪdərəbl] *adj* beträchtlich.

**considerably** [kən'sɪdərəblɪ] *adv* beträchtlich.

**considerate** [kən'sɪdərɪt] *adj* rücksichtsvoll *(to(wards)* gegenüber*)*; *(kind)* aufmerksam.

**consideration** [kən,sɪdə'reɪʃən] *n* **(a)** *no pl (careful thought)* Überlegung *f.* **I'll give it my ~** ich werde es mir überlegen. **(b)** *no pl (regard, account)* **to take sth into ~** etw berücksichtigen; **to leave sth out of ~** etw außer acht lassen; **he's under ~ for the job** er wird für die Stelle in Erwägung gezogen; **it's under ~** es wird zur Zeit geprüft. **(c)** *no pl (thoughtfulness)* Rücksicht *f (for* auf +*acc).* **to have ~ for sb's feelings** Rücksicht auf jds Gefühle nehmen; **his lack of ~ (for others)** seine Rücksichtslosigkeit (anderen gegenüber). **(d)** *(sth taken into account)* Faktor *m.* **money is no ~** Geld spielt keine Rolle; **his first ~ is his family** seine Familie spielt für ihn die größte Rolle. **(e)** *(payment)* **for a ~** gegen Entgelt.

**considered** [kən'sɪdəd] *adj attr opinion* ernsthaft.

**considering** [kən'sɪdərɪŋ] **1** *prep* ~ **my age** für mein Alter, wenn man mein Alter bedenkt. **2** *conj* ~ **(that) he's been ill ...** wenn man bedenkt, daß er krank war ...

**consign** [kən'saɪn] *vt* **(a)** *(Comm: send)* versenden. **to ~ sth to the w.p.b./rubbish heap** *(hum)* etwas in den Papierkorb/auf den Abfallhaufen werfen. **(b)** *(entrust)* anvertrauen *(to* +*dat).*

**consignee** [,kɒnsaɪ'niː] *n* Empfänger *m.*

**consignment** [kən'saɪnmənt] *n (Comm) (goods)* Sendung *f; (bigger)* Ladung *f.* ~ **note** Frachtbrief *m.*

**consist** [kən'sɪst] *vi* **to ~ of** bestehen aus; **to ~ in sth** in etw *(dat)* bestehen.

**consistency** [kən'sɪstənsɪ] *n* **(a)** *see adj* **(a)** Konsequenz *f;* Übereinstimmung *f;* Folgerichtigkeit *f;* Beständigkeit *f.* **his statements lack ~** seine Aussagen widersprechen sich. **(b)** *(of substance)* Konsistenz *f.*

**consistent** [kən'sɪstənt] *adj* **(a)** konsequent; *statements* übereinstimmend; *argument* folgerichtig; *quality* beständig. **(b)** *(in agreement)* **to be ~ with sth** einer Sache *(dat)* entsprechen.

**consistently** [kən'sɪstəntlɪ] *adv* **(a)** *argue* konsequent. **(b)** *(uniformly)* durchweg. **(c)** *(in agreement)* entsprechend *(with dat).*

**consolation** [,kɒnsə'leɪʃən] *n* Trost *m no pl.* **words of ~** tröstende Worte; ~ **prize** Trostpreis *m.*

**console¹** [kən'səʊl] *vt* trösten.

**console²** ['kɒnsəʊl] *n* **(a)** *(control panel)* (Kontroll)pult *nt; (of organ)* Spieltisch *m.* **(b)** *(cabinet)* Schrank *m.* **(c)** *(ornamental bracket)* Konsole *f.*

**consolidate** [kən'sɒlɪdeɪt] *vt* **(a)** *(confirm)* festigen. **(b)** *(combine)* zusammenlegen; *companies* zusammenschließen; *funds, debts* konsolidieren.

**consolidation** [kən,sɒlɪ'deɪʃən] *n see vt* **(a)** Festigung *f.* **(b)** Zusammenlegung *f;* Zusammenschluß *m;* Konsolidierung *f.*

**consommé** [kɒn'sɒmeɪ] *n* Kraftbrühe *f.*

**consonant** ['kɒnsənənt] *n (Phon)* Konsonant *m.* ~ **shift** Lautverschiebung *f.*

**consort 1** ['kɒnsɔːt] *n (form: spouse)* Gemahl(in *f)* *m (form).* **2** [kən'sɔːt] *vi (form)* verkehren *(with* mit*).*

**consortium** [kən'sɔːtɪəm] *n* Konsortium *nt.*

**conspicuous** [kən'spɪkjʊəs] *adj* auffällig; *road signs* deutlich sichtbar; *lack of sth* offensichtlich; *bravery* bemerkenswert. **to be/make oneself ~** auffallen; **to be/not to be ~ for sth** sich/sich nicht gerade durch etw auszeichnen; **he was ~ by his absence** er glänz-

te durch Abwesenheit.

**conspicuously** [kən'spɪkjʊəslɪ] *adv* auffällig; *(obviously)* offensichtlich; *(outstandingly)* bemerkenswert.

**conspiracy** [kən'spɪrəsɪ] *n* Verschwörung *f.* **a ~ of silence** ein verabredetes Schweigen.

**conspirator** [kən'spɪrətər] *n* Verschwörer *m.*

**conspiratorial** [kən,spɪrə'tɔːrɪəl] *adj* verschwörerisch.

**conspire** [kən'spaɪər] *vi* sich verschwören *(against* gegen*); (events)* zusammenkommen.

**constable** ['kʌnstəbl] *n (Brit: police* ~*)* Polizist(in *f) m.*

**constabulary** [kən'stæbjʊlərɪ] *n (Brit)* Polizei *f no pl.*

**constancy** ['kɒnstənsɪ] *n* Beständigkeit *f; (of feelings)* Unveränderlichkeit *f; (of friend, lover)* Treue *f;* ~ **of purpose** Ausdauer *f.*

**constant** ['kɒnstənt] **1** *adj* **(a)** *(continuous)* ständig. **(b)** *(unchanging)* gleichbleibend, konstant. **(c)** *(steadfast)* beständig. **2** *n (Math, Phys, fig)* Konstante *f.*

**constantly** ['kɒnstəntlɪ] *adv* ständig.

**constellation** [,kɒnstə'leɪʃən] *n* Sternbild *nt.*

**consternation** ['kɒnstə'neɪʃən] *n (dismay)* Bestürzung *f; (worry)* Sorge *f; (confusion)* Aufruhr *m.* **to my great ~** zu meiner großen Bestürzung; **with a look of ~ on his face** mit bestürzter Miene; **the news filled me with ~** ich war bestürzt, als ich das hörte.

**constipated** ['kɒnstɪpeɪtɪd] *adj* verstopft. **he is ~** er hat Verstopfung.

**constipation** [,kɒnstɪ'peɪʃən] *n no pl* Verstopfung *f.*

**constituency** [kən'stɪtjʊənsɪ] *n (Pol)* Wahlkreis *m.* ~ **party** Parteiorganisation *f in einem Wahlkreis.*

**constituent** [kən'stɪtjʊənt] **1** *n* **(a)** *(Pol)* Wähler(in *f) m.* **(b)** *(part, element)* Bestandteil *m.* **2** *adj* **(a)** *(Pol) assembly* konstituierend. **(b)** *attr part, element* einzeln.

**constitute** ['kɒnstɪtjuːt] *vt* **(a)** *(make up)* bilden. **(b)** *(amount to)* darstellen. **(c)** *(set up)* gründen.

**constitution** [,kɒnstɪ'tjuːʃən] *n* **(a)** *(Pol)* Verfassung *f; (of club etc)* Satzung *f.* **(b)** *(of person)* Konstitution *f.* **(c)** *(way sth is made)* Aufbau *m; (what sth is made of)* Zusammensetzung *f.* **(d)** *(setting up)* Gründung *f.*

**constitutional** [,kɒnstɪ'tjuːʃənl] **1** *adj* **(a)** *(Pol) reform, crisis, court* Verfassungs-; *monarchy* konstitutionell; *government, action* verfassungsmäßig. ~ **law** Verfassungsrecht *nt;* **it's not ~** das ist verfassungswidrig. **(b)** *(Med)* konstitutionell. **2** *n (hum col)* Spaziergang *m.*

**constrain** [kən'streɪn] *vt* zwingen; *one's temper* zügeln. **to find oneself/feel** ~**ed to ...** sich gezwungen sehen/fühlen, zu ...

**constraint** [kən'streɪnt] *n* **(a)** *(compulsion)* Zwang *m.* **(b)** *(restriction)* Beschränkung *f.* **to place** ~**s on sth** einer Sache *(dat)* Zwänge auferlegen. **(c)** *(in manner etc)* Gezwungenheit *f; (embarrassment)* Befangenheit *f.*

**constrict** [kən'strɪkt] *vt* **(a)** einengen; *muscle* zusammenziehen; *vein* verengen. **(b)** *movements* einschränken *(also fig).*

**constriction** [kən'strɪkʃən] *n* **(a)** *(of muscles)* Zusammenziehen *nt.* **(b)** *(of movements etc)* Einschränkung *f.*

**construct** [kən'strʌkt] *vt* bauen; *geometrical figure* konstruieren; *sentence* bilden; *theory* entwickeln.

**construction** [kən'strʌkʃən] *n* **(a)** *see vt* Bau *m;* Konstruktion *f;* Entwicklung *f.* **under ~** in *or* im Bau. **(b)** *(way sth is constructed)* Struktur *f; (of building)* Bauweise *f; (of machine, bridge)* Konstruktion *f.* **(c)** *(sth constructed)* Bau *m*; *(bridge, machine)* Konstruktion *f.* **(d)** *(interpretation)* Deutung *f.* **to put a wrong ~ on sth** etw falsch auffassen. **(e)** *(Gram)* Konstruktion *f.* **sentence ~** Satzbau *m*.

**construction industry** *n* Bauindustrie *f.*

**constructive** [kən'strʌktɪv] *adj* konstruktiv.

**construe** [kən'struː] *vt (interpret)* auffassen.

**consul** ['kɒnsəl] *n* Konsul *m*.

**consular** ['kɒnsjʊlə<sup>r</sup>] *adj* konsularisch.

**consulate** ['kɒnsjʊlɪt] *n* Konsulat *nt*.

**consult** [kən'sʌlt] **1** *vt* sich besprechen mit; *lawyer, doctor etc* konsultieren; *dictionary* nachschlagen in *(+dat)*; *map* nachsehen auf *(+dat)*; *oracle* befragen; *horoscope* nachlesen. **he did it without ~ing anyone** er hat das getan, ohne jemanden zu fragen. **2** *vi (confer)* sich beraten *(with mit)*.

**consultancy** [kən'sʌltənsɪ] *n (act)* Beratung *f*; *(business)* Beratungsbüro *nt*.

**consultant** [kən'sʌltənt] **1** *n* **(a)** *(Brit Med)* Facharzt *m*, Fachärztin *f.* **~ gynaecologist** Facharzt/-ärztin für Frauenkrankheiten. **(b)** *(other professions)* Berater(in *f*) *m*. **2** *adj attr* beratend.

**consultation** [ˌkɒnsəl'teɪʃən] *n* Besprechung *f*; *(of doctor, lawyer)* Konsultation *f (of gen)*. **in ~ with** in gemeinsamer Beratung mit.

**consulting** [kən'sʌltɪŋ] *adj* **~ hours/room** *(Brit)* Sprechstunde *f*/-zimmer *nt*.

**consumables** [kən'sjuːməblz] *npl* Konsumgüter *pl*; *(Comp)* Verbrauchsmaterial *nt*.

**consume** [kən'sjuːm] *vt* **(a)** *food, drink* zu sich nehmen; *(Econ)* konsumieren. **(b)** *(destroy)* vernichten; *(use up)* verbrauchen. **he was ~d with jealousy** er wurde von Eifersucht verzehrt *(geh)*.

**consumer** [kən'sjuːmə<sup>r</sup>] *n* Verbraucher(in *f*) *m*.

**consumer** *in cpds* Verbraucher-; **~ durables** *npl* Gebrauchsgüter *pl*; **~ goods** *npl* Konsumgüter *pl*.

**consumerism** [kən'sjuːmərɪzəm] *n* Konsumdenken *nt*.

**consumer:** **~ protection** *n* Verbraucherschutz *m*; **~s' advice centre** *(Brit) or* **center** *(US)* *n* Verbraucherzentrale *f*; **~ society** *n* Konsumgesellschaft *f*.

**consummate 1** [kən'sʌmɪt] *adj* vollendet. **with ~ ease** mit spielender Leichtigkeit. **2** ['kɒnsəmeɪt] *vt marriage* vollziehen.

**consummation** [ˌkɒnsə'meɪʃən] *n (of marriage)* Vollzug *m*; *(fig: peak)* Höhepunkt *m*.

**consumption** [kən'sʌmpʃən] *n* **(a)** Konsum *m*; *(of non-edible products)* Verbrauch *m*. **this letter is for private ~ only** *(col)* der Brief ist nur für den privaten Gebrauch; **not fit for human ~** zum Verzehr ungeeignet. **(b)** *(Med old)* Schwindsucht *f*.

**cont** = **(a) containing, contents** Inh. **(b) continued** Forts.

**contact** ['kɒntækt] **1** *n* **(a)** Kontakt *m*; *(communication also)* Verbindung *f.* **to be in ~ with sb/sth** *(be touching)* jdn/etw berühren; *(in communication)* mit jdm/etw in Kontakt stehen; **to come into ~ with sb/sth** *(lit, fig)* mit jdm/etw in Berührung kommen; **he has no ~ with his family** er hat keinen Kontakt zu seiner Familie; **to make ~ with sb/sth** *(get in touch with)* sich mit jdm/etw in Verbindung setzen; **I finally made ~ with him at his office** ich habe ihn schließlich im Büro erreicht; **to lose ~ (with sb/ sth)** den Kontakt (zu jdm/etw) verlieren; **point of ~** *(Math, fig)* Berührungspunkt *m*.

**(b)** *(Elec) (act)* Kontakt *m*; *(equipment)* Kontaktstück *nt*. **to make/break ~** den Kontakt herstellen/ unterbrechen.

**(c)** *(person)* Kontaktperson *f (also Med)*; *(in espionage)* Verbindungsmann, V-Mann *m*. **~s** *pl* Kontakte *pl*; **to make ~s** Kontakte herstellen.

**2** *vt person, agent* sich in Verbindung setzen mit.

**I've been trying to ~ you for hours** ich versuche schon seit Stunden, Sie zu erreichen.

**contact:** **~ adhesive** *n* Kontaktklebstoff *m*; **~-breaker** *n* Unterbrecher *m*; **~ lens** *n* Kontaktlinse *f*.

**contagion** [kən'teɪdʒən] *n (contact)* Ansteckung *f*; *(disease)* Ansteckungskrankheit *f*; *(epidemic)* Seuche *f (also fig)*; *(fig: spreading influence)* schädlicher Einfluß.

**contagious** [kən'teɪdʒəs] *adj (Med, fig)* ansteckend.

**contain** [kən'teɪn] *vt* **(a)** *(hold within itself)* enthalten. **(b)** *(have capacity for)* fassen. **(c)** *emotions, oneself* beherrschen; *disease, inflation* in Grenzen halten; *epidemic, flood* unter Kontrolle bringen.

**container** [kən'teɪnə<sup>r</sup>] **1** *n* **(a)** Behälter *m*. **(b)** *(Comm)* Container *m*. **2** *adj attr* Container-. **~ ship** Containerschiff *nt*; **by ~ transport** per Container.

**containerize** [kən'teɪnəraɪz] *vt freight* in Container verpacken; *port* auf Container umstellen.

**contaminate** [kən'tæmɪneɪt] *vt* verunreinigen; *(poison)* vergiften; *(radioactivity)* verseuchen; *(fig) mind* verderben.

**contd** = **continued** Forts., Fortsetzung *f*.

**contemplate** ['kɒntəmpleɪt] *vt* **(a)** *(look at)* betrachten. **(b)** *(reflect upon)* nachdenken über *(+acc)*; *(consider)* a purchase, action in Erwägung ziehen; a holiday denken an *(+acc)*.

**contemplation** [ˌkɒntəm'pleɪʃən] *n* **(a)** *(looking)* Betrachtung *f*. **(b)** *(thinking)* Nachdenken *nt (of* über *+acc)*; *(deep thought)* Betrachtung *f*, Kontemplation *(esp Rel)* *f*.

**contemplative** [kən'templətɪv] *adj look* nachdenklich; *life* beschaulich, kontemplativ *(esp Rel)*.

**contemporary** [kən'tempərərɪ] **1** *adj* **(a)** *(of the same time)* events gleichzeitig; *literature* zeitgenössisch; *(of the same age)* gleich alt. **(b)** *(of the present time)* life heutig; *art* zeitgenössisch, modern. **~ history** Zeitgeschichte *f*. **2** *n* Altersgenosse *m*/ -genossin *f*; *(in history)* Zeitgenosse *m*/-genossin *f*.

**contempt** [kən'tempt] *n* **(a)** Verachtung *f*; *(disregard also)* Geringschätzung *f (for* von*)*. **to hold in ~** verachten; **beneath ~** unter aller Kritik. **(b)** *(Jur: also ~ of court)* Mißachtung *f* des Gerichts.

**contemptible** [kən'temptəbl] *adj* verachtenswert.

**contemptuous** [kən'temptjʊəs] *adj manner, look* verächtlich. **to be ~ of sb/sth** jdn/etw verachten.

**contend** [kən'tend] **1** *vi* **(a)** kämpfen. **to ~ for sth** um etw kämpfen; **you'll have me to ~ with** dann bekommst du es mit mir zu tun. **(b)** *(cope)* **to ~ with sb/sth** mit jdm/etw fertig werden. **2** *vt* behaupten.

**contender** [kən'tendə<sup>r</sup>] *n* Anwärter(in *f*) *m (for* auf *+acc)*; *(Sport)* Wettkämpfer(in *f*) *m (for* um*)*. **the (main) ~s for the title** die Titelanwärter.

**content¹** [kən'tent] **1** *adj* zufrieden *(with* mit*)*. **2** *n* Zufriedenheit *f*; *see* **heart** **(a)**. **3** *vt person* zufriedenstellen. **to ~ oneself with** sich zufriedengeben mit.

**content²** ['kɒntent] *n* **(a)** **~s** *pl* Inhalt *m*; **(table of) ~s** Inhaltsverzeichnis *nt*. **(b)** *no pl (substance)* Gehalt *m*.

**contented** *adj*, **~ly** *adv* [kən'tentɪd, -lɪ] zufrieden.

**contention** [kən'tenʃən] *n* **(a)** *(dispute)* Streit *m*. **the matter in ~** die strittige Angelegenheit. **(b)** *(assertion)* Behauptung *f*.

**contentment** [kən'tentmənt] *n* Zufriedenheit *f*.

**contest** ['kɒntest] **1** *n* Kampf *m (for* um*)*; *(beauty ~ etc)* Wettbewerb *m*. **boxing ~** Boxkampf *m*; **election ~** Wahlkampf *m*. **2** [kən'test] *vt* **(a)** *(fight over)* kämpfen um; *(Pol: candidate)* seat sich bewerben um; *(oppose)* kämpfen gegen. **(b)** *statement* bestreiten; *(Jur)* will anfechten.

**contestant** [kən'testənt] *n* (Wettbewerbs)teilnehmer(in *f*) *m*; *(Parl, in quiz)* Kandidat(in *f*) *m*; *(Sport)* (Wettkampf)teilnehmer(in *f*) *m*. **the ~s in the election** die Wahlkandidaten.

**context** ['kɒntekst] *n* Zusammenhang *m*. **out of ~** aus dem Zusammenhang gerissen.

**continent** ['kɒntɪnənt] *n* Kontinent, Erdteil *m*; *(mainland)* Festland *nt*. **the C~** *(Brit)* Kontinentaleuropa *nt*; **on the C~** auf dem europäischen Festland.

**continental** [,kɒntɪ'nentl] **1** *adj* **(a)** *(Geog)* kontinental. **(b)** *(Brit: European)* europäisch. **~ breakfast** kleines Frühstück *(Kaffee und Brötchen)*. **2** *n* (Festlands)europäer(in *f*) *m*.

**contingency** [kən'tɪndʒənsɪ] *n* möglicher Fall. **in this ~** in diesem Fall; **~ fund** Eventualfonds *m*; **a ~ plan** ein Ausweichplan *m*.

**contingent** [kən'tɪndʒənt] **1** *adj* **~ upon** *(form)* abhängig von; **to be ~ upon** abhängen von. **2** *n* Kontingent *nt*; *(Mil)* Trupp *m*.

**continual** [kən'tɪnjʊəl] *adj (frequent)* dauernd; *(unceasing)* ununterbrochen.

**continually** [kən'tɪnjʊəlɪ] *adv see adj* dauernd; ununterbrochen.

**continuance** [kən'tɪnjʊəns] *n* **(a)** *(duration)* Dauer *f*. **(b)** *(continuation)* Fortsetzung *f*.

**continuation** [kən,tɪnjʊ'eɪʃən] *n* Fortsetzung *f*.

**continue** [kən'tɪnjuː] **1** *vt* fortsetzen. **to ~ to read, to ~ reading** weiterlesen; **to be ~d** Fortsetzung folgt; **~d existence** Weiterbestehen *nt*. **2** *vi (go on) (person)* weitermachen; *(crisis, speech)* (an)dauern; *(weather)* anhalten; *(road etc)* sich fortsetzen; *(concert etc)* weitergehen. **he ~s (to be) optimistic** er ist nach wie vor optimistisch.

**continuity** [,kɒntɪ'njuːɪtɪ] *n* **(a)** Kontinuität *f*. **the story lacks ~** der Geschichte fehlt der rote Faden. **(b)** *(Film)* **~ girl** Scriptgirl *nt*.

**continuous** [kən'tɪnjʊəs] *adj* dauernd, ständig; *line* ununterbrochen; **~ paper** or **stationery** *(Comp)* Endlospapier *nt*; *(pre-printed)* Endlosformular *nt*; **~ performance** *(Film)* durchgehende Vorstellung; **present/past ~** *(Gram)* Verlaufsform *f* Präsens/Imperfekt.

**continuously** [kən'tɪnjʊəslɪ] *adv see adj* dauernd, ständig; ununterbrochen.

**contort** [kən'tɔːt] *vt features* verziehen *(into* zu*)*; *limbs* verrenken. **a face ~ed by pain** ein schmerzverzerrtes Gesicht.

**contortion** [kən'tɔːʃən] *n (esp of acrobat)* Verrenkung *f*; *(of features)* Verzerrung *f*.

**contortionist** [kən'tɔːʃənɪst] *n* Schlangenmensch *m*.

**contour** ['kɒntʊəʳ] *n* Kontur *f*.

**contour:** **~ line** *n (Geog)* Höhenlinie *f*; **~ map** *n* Höhenlinienkarte *f*.

**contraband** ['kɒntrəbænd] **1** *n no pl (goods)* Schmuggelware *f*; *(form: smuggling)* Schleichhandel *m*. **2** *adj* Schmuggel-.

**contraception** [,kɒntrə'sepʃən] *n* Empfängnisverhütung *f*.

**contraceptive** [,kɒntrə'septɪv] **1** *n* empfängnisverhütendes Mittel. **2** *adj* empfängnisverhütend; *pill* Antibaby-.

**contract¹** ['kɒntrækt] **1** *n* **(a)** Vertrag *m*; *(Comm: order)* Auftrag *m*. **to enter into a ~ (with sb)** (mit jdm) einen Vertrag schließen; **to put work out to ~** Arbeiten außer Haus machen lassen. **(b)** *(Bridge)* Kontrakt *m*. **~ bridge** Kontrakt-Bridge *nt*. **2** *adj price, date* vertraglich festgelegt. **~ work** Auftragsarbeit *f*. **3** [kən'trækt] *vt* **(a)** *debts* machen; *illness* erkranken an *(+dat)*. **(b)** *(enter into) marriage, alliance* eingehen. **4** [kən'trækt] *vi (Comm)* **to ~ to do**

**sth** sich vertraglich verpflichten, etw zu tun.
▶**contract in** *vi* sich anschließen *(-to* dat*)*; *(into insurance scheme)* beitreten *(-to* dat*)*.
▶**contract out 1** *vi (withdraw)* austreten *(of* aus*)*; *(not join)* sich nicht anschließen *(of* dat*)*; *(of insurance scheme)* nicht beitreten *(of* dat*)*. **2** *vt sep (Comm) work* vergeben *(to* an *+acc)*.

**contract²** [kən'trækt] **1** *vt* zusammenziehen. **2** *vi (muscle, metal etc)* sich zusammenziehen.

**contraction** [kən'trækʃən] *n* **(a)** *(shrinking)* Zusammenziehung *f*. **(b)** *(in childbirth)* Wehe *f*.

**contractor** [kən'træktəʳ] *n (individual)* Auftragnehmer *m*; *(building ~)* Bauunternehmer *m*.

**contractual** [kən'træktʃʊəl] *adj* vertraglich.

**contradict** [,kɒntrə'dɪkt] *vt* widersprechen *(+dat)*.

**contradiction** [,kɒntrə'dɪkʃən] *n* Widerspruch *m (of* zu*)*. **full of ~s** voller Widersprüchlichkeiten.

**contradictory** [,kɒntrə'dɪktərɪ] *adj* widersprüchlich.

**contra-flow** ['kɒntrə,fləʊ] *n (Mot)* Gegenverkehr *m (auf einem Fahrstreifen)*.

**contraindication** [,kɒntrə,ɪndɪ'keɪʃən] *n (Med)* Kontraindikation *f*.

**contralto** [kən'træltəʊ] **1** *n (voice)* Alt *m*. **2** *adj voice* Alt-. **the ~ part** die Altstimme.

**contraption** [kən'træpʃən] *n (col)* Apparat *m (col)*; *(vehicle)* Vehikel *nt (col)*.

**contrary¹** ['kɒntrərɪ] **1** *adj (opposite)* entgegengesetzt; *development, tendency* gegenläufig. **2** *n* Gegenteil *nt*. **on the ~** im Gegenteil; **do you have information to the ~?** liegen Ihnen gegenteilige Informationen vor?; **unless you hear to the ~** sofern Sie nichts Gegenteiliges hören. **3** *adv* **~ to expectations** wider Erwarten; **~ to what he said** im Gegensatz zu dem, was er gesagt hat.

**contrary²** [kən'trɛərɪ] *adj (awkward)* widerspenstig.

**contrast** ['kɒntrɑːst] **1** *n* **(a)** Gegensatz *m (with, to* zu*)*; *(visual)* Kontrast *m (with, to* zu*)*. **by** or **in ~** im Gegensatz dazu. **(b)** *(Art, Phot, TV)* Kontrast *m*. **2** [kən'trɑːst] *vt* gegenüberstellen *(with* dat*)*. **3** [kən'trɑːst] *vi* im Gegensatz stehen *(with* zu*)*; *(colours)* sich abheben *(with* von*)*.

**contrasting** [kən'trɑːstɪŋ] *adj* gegensätzlich.

**contravene** [,kɒntrə'viːn] *vt* verstoßen gegen.

**contravention** [,kɒntrə'venʃən] *n* Verstoß *m (of* gegen*)*. **to act in ~ of sth** einer Sache *(dat)* zuwiderhandeln.

**contretemps** ['kɒntrə,tɒŋ] *n no pl* Zwischenfall *m*.

**contribute** [kən'trɪbjuːt] **1** *vt* beitragen *(to* zu*)*; *money, supplies* beisteuern *(to* zu*)*; *(to charity)* spenden *(to* für*)*. **to ~ one's share** sein(en) Teil (dazu) beitragen. **2** *vi* beitragen *(to* zu*)*; *(to pension fund etc)* einen Beitrag leisten *(to* zu*)*; *(to newspaper)* schreiben *(to* für*)*; *(to present)* beisteuern *(to* zu*)*; *(to charity)* spenden *(to* für*)*.

**contribution** [,kɒntrɪ'bjuːʃən] *n* Beitrag *m (to* zu*)*; *(to charity)* Spende *f*. **the beer is my ~** das Bier stelle ich.

**contributor** [kən'trɪbjʊtəʳ] *n (to magazine etc)* Mitarbeiter(in *f*) *m (to* an *+dat)*; *(of goods, money)* Spender(in *f*) *m*.

**contributory** [kən'trɪbjʊtərɪ] *adj* **(a)** **that's a ~ factor** dieser Faktor spielt eine Rolle; **~ negligence** *(Jur)* Mitverschulden *nt*. **(b)** *pension scheme* beitragspflichtig.

**con trick** *n (col)* Schwindel *m*.

**contrite** ['kɒntraɪt] *adj* reuig.

**contrition** [kən'trɪʃən] *n* Reue *f*. **act of ~** *(Eccl)* Buße *f*.

**contrivance** [kən'traɪvəns] *n (device)* Vorrichtung *f*; *(mechanical)* Gerät *nt*.

**contrive** [kən'traɪv] *vt* **(a)** *plan* ersinnen. **to ~ a**

**means of doing sth** einen Weg finden, etw zu tun. **(b)** *(manage, arrange)* bewerkstelligen. **to ~ to do sth** *(also iro)* es fertigbringen, etw zu tun; **he always ~s to get his own way** er versteht (es) immer, seinen Kopf durchzusetzen.

**contrived** [kən'traɪvd] *adj* gestellt; *style* gekünstelt.

**control** [kən'trəʊl] **1** *n* **(a)** *no pl (supervision)* Aufsicht *f (of* über +*acc)*; *(of situation, emotion)* Beherrschung *f (of gen)*; *(authority, power)* Gewalt *f (over* über +*acc)*; *(of prices)* Kontrolle *f (of gen)*; *(of traffic)* Regelung *f (of gen)* etc. **to be in ~ of sth** *business, office* etw leiten; *group of children* etw beaufsichtigen; **to have sth under ~** etw in der Hand haben; **to be in ~ of one's emotions** Herr seiner Gefühle sein; **to have no ~ over sb** keinen Einfluß auf jdn haben; **to lose ~ (of sth)** die Gewalt (über etw *acc)* verlieren; **to lose ~ of the situation** nicht mehr Herr der Lage sein; **to be/get out of ~** *(child, class)* außer Rand und Band sein/geraten; *(situation)* außer Kontrolle sein/geraten; **the car went out of ~** das Auto geriet außer Kontrolle; **under state ~** unter staatlicher Aufsicht; **to be under ~** unter Kontrolle sein; **he was beyond parental ~** er war seinen Eltern über den Kopf gewachsen; **circumstances beyond our ~** nicht in unserer Hand liegende Umstände; **his ~ of the ball** seine Ballführung.

**(b)** *(check)* Kontrolle *f (on gen,* über +*acc)*. **wages/price ~s** Lohn-/Preiskontrolle *f*.

**(c)** *(~ room)* die Zentrale; *(Aviat)* der Kontrollturm.

**(d)** *(knob, switch)* Regler *m*; *(of vehicle, machine)* Schalter *m*. **to be at the ~s** *(of spaceship, airliner)* am Kontrollpult sitzen; *(of small plane, car)* am Steuer sitzen; **to take over the ~s** das Steuer übernehmen.

**(e)** *(Sci: group)* Kontrollgruppe *f*.

**(f)** *(Comp)* **~-F1** Control-F1.

**2** *vt* **(a)** *(direct, manage)* kontrollieren; *business* führen; *organization* in der Hand haben; *child, class* fertigwerden mit; *car* steuern, lenken; *traffic* regeln; *emotions* beherrschen; *hair* bändigen. **to ~ oneself/one's temper** sich beherrschen; **~ yourself!** nimm dich zusammen! **(b)** *(regulate) temperature, speed* regulieren; *prices etc* kontrollieren; *disease* unter Kontrolle bringen; *population* eindämmen.

**control: ~ centre** *n* Kontrollzentrum *nt*; **~ column** *n* Steuerknüppel *m*; **~ experiment** *n* Kontrollversuch *m*; **~ key** *n (Comp)* Control-Taste *f*; **~ knob** *n (TV, Rad etc)* Regler, Kontrollknopf *m*.

**controlled** [kən'trəʊld] *adj emotion* beherrscht; *conditions* kontrolliert; *prices* gebunden; *temperature* geregelt.

**controller** [kən'trəʊlə\*] *n* **(a)** *(Rad)* Intendant *m*; *(Aviat)* (Flug)lotse *m*. **(b)** *(Tech)* Regler *m*.

**controlling** [kən'trəʊlɪŋ] *adj attr factor* beherrschend; *body* Aufsichts-. **~ interest** Mehrheitsanteil *m*.

**control: ~ panel** *n* Schalttafel *f*; *(on aircraft, TV)* Bedienungsfeld *nt*; *(on car)* Armaturenbrett *nt*; **~ point** *n* Kontrollpunkt *m*; **~ room** *n* Kontrollraum *m*; *(Mil)* (Operations)zentrale *f*; *(of police)* Zentrale *f*; **~ tower** *n (Aviat)* Kontrollturm *m*; **~ unit** *n (Comp, Elec)* Steuereinheit *f*.

**controversial** [ˌkɒntrə'vɜːʃəl] *adj* umstritten.

**controversy** ['kɒntrəvɜːsɪ, kən'trɒvəsɪ] *n* Kontroversen *pl*. **to give rise to ~** Anlaß zu Kontroversen geben.

**contusion** [kən'tjuːʒən] *n* Quetschung *f*.

**conundrum** [kə'nʌndrəm] *n (lit, fig)* Rätsel *nt*.

**conurbation** [ˌkɒnɜː'beɪʃən] *n* Ballungsgebiet *nt*.

**convalesce** [ˌkɒnvə'les] *vi* genesen *(from, after* von*)*.

**convalescence** [ˌkɒnvə'lesəns] *n* Genesung *f*; *(period)* Genesungszeit *f*.

**convalescent** [ˌkɒnvə'lesənt] **1** *n* Genesende(r) *mf*. **2** *adj* genesend. **to be ~** auf dem Wege der Besserung sein; **~ home** Genesungsheim *nt*.

**convection** [kən'vekʃən] *n* Konvektion *f*.

**convector** [kən'vektə\*] *n (also ~ heater)* Heizlüfter *m*.

**convene** [kən'viːn] **1** *vt meeting* einberufen. **2** *vi* sich versammeln.

**convener** [kən'viːnə\*] *n Person, die Versammlungen einberuft.*

**convenience** [kən'viːnɪəns] *n* **(a)** *no pl (usefulness)* Annehmlichkeit *f*; *(expediency)* Zweckmäßigkeit *f*. **~ foods** Fertiggerichte *pl*; **flag of ~** *(Naut)* Billigflagge *f*. **(b)** *no pl* **these chairs are for the ~ of customers** diese Stühle sind für unsere Kunden gedacht; **at your own ~** wann es Ihnen paßt; **at your earliest ~** *(Comm)* möglichst bald. **(c)** *(convenient thing, amenity)* Annehmlichkeit *f*. **a house with every ~** ein Haus mit allem Komfort. **(d)** *(Brit form: public ~)* (öffentliche) Toilette.

**convenient** [kən'viːnɪənt] *adj (useful)* praktisch; *area, house (for shops etc)* günstig gelegen; *time* günstig. **if it is ~ for you** wenn es Ihnen (so) paßt; **is tomorrow ~ (for you)?** paßt (es) Ihnen morgen?; **the trams are very ~** *(nearby)* die Straßenbahnhaltestellen liegen sehr günstig; *(useful)* die Straßenbahn ist sehr praktisch.

**conveniently** [kən'viːnɪəntlɪ] *adv* günstigerweise; *situated* günstig; *(usefully) designed* praktisch.

**convent** ['kɒnvənt] *n* (Frauen)kloster *nt*. **~ school** Klosterschule *f*.

**convention** [kən'venʃən] *n* **(a)** *(social rule)* Sitte *f*; Konvention *f*. **it's a ~ that ...** es ist so üblich *or* Sitte, daß ... **(b)** *(conference)* Tagung *f*; *(Pol)* Versammlung *f*.

**conventional** [kən'venʃənl] *adj dress* konventionell; *beliefs* herkömmlich; *style* traditionell.

**conventionally** [kən'venʃnəlɪ] *adv see adj* konventionell; herkömmlicherweise; traditionell.

**converge** [kən'vɜːdʒ] *vi (road, lines)* zusammenlaufen *(at in* +*dat)*; *(fig: views etc)* sich aneinander annähern. **to ~ on sb/sth/New York** von überallher zu jdm/etw/nach New York strömen.

**convergence** [kən'vɜːdʒəns] *n see vi* Zusammenlaufen *nt*; Annäherung *f*. **point of ~** Schnittpunkt *m*; *(of rays)* Brennpunkt *m*.

**conversant** [kən'vɜːsənt] *adj* vertraut *(with* mit*)*.

**conversation** [ˌkɒnvə'seɪʃən] *n* Gespräch *nt*; *(Sch)* Konversation *f*. **to make ~** sich unterhalten; **to get into/be in ~ with sb** mit jdm ins Gespräch kommen/im Gespräch sein; **deep in ~** ins Gespräch vertieft; **his ~ is very amusing** er ist ein sehr unterhaltsamer Gesprächspartner; **a subject of ~** ein Gesprächsthema *nt*; **that was a ~ stopper** *(col)* das hat uns die Sprache verschlagen *(col)*; **the art of ~** die Kunst des (guten) Gesprächs.

**conversational** [ˌkɒnvə'seɪʃənl] *adj tone, style* Unterhaltungs-. **~ German** gesprochenes Deutsch.

**conversationalist** [ˌkɒnvə'seɪʃnəlɪst] *n* guter Gesprächspartner, gute Gesprächspartnerin.

**conversation: ~ mode** *n (Comp)* Dialogbetrieb *m*; **~ piece** *n (item provoking talk)* Gesprächsgegenstand *m*; *(Theat: play)* Konversationsstück *nt*.

**converse¹** [kən'vɜːs] *vi (form)* sich unterhalten.

**converse²** ['kɒnvɜːs] **1** *adj* umgekehrt; *opinions etc* gegenteilig. **2** *n (opposite)* Gegenteil *nt*.

**conversely** [kɒn'vɜːslɪ] *adv* umgekehrt.

**conversion** [kən'vɜːʃən] *n* **(a)** Konversion *f (into* in +*acc)*; *(Rugby, US Ftbl)* Verwandlung *f*; *(of meas-*

*ures)* Umrechnung *f (into* in *+acc)*; *(of building)* Umbau *m (into* zu). ~ **table** Umrechnungstabelle *f.* **(b)** *(Rel, fig)* Bekehrung *f (to* zu).

**convert** ['kɒnvɜːt] **1** *n (lit, fig)* Bekehrte(r) *mf*; *(to another denomination)* Konvertit(in *f) m.* **2** [kən'vɜːt] *vt* **(a)** konvertieren *(into* in *+acc)*; *(Rugby, US Ftbl)* verwandeln; *measures* umrechnen *(into* in *+acc)*; *attic* ausbauen *(into* zu); *building* umbauen *(into* zu). **(b)** *(Rel, fig)* bekehren *(to* zu); *(to another denomination)* konvertieren. **3** [kən'vɜːt] *vi* sich verwandeln lassen *(into* in *+acc).*

**converter** [kən'vɜːtə˞] *n (Elec)* Konverter *m*; *(for AC/DC)* Stromgleichrichter *m.*

**convertible** [kən'vɜːtəbl] **1** *adj* verwandelbar; *currency* konvertibel. ~ **sofa** Bettcouch *f.* **2** *n (car)* Kabriolett *nt.*

**convex** [kɒn'veks] *adj lens, mirror* konvex.

**convey** [kən'veɪ] *vt* **(a)** befördern; *goods* spedieren; *water* leiten. **(b)** *idea* vermitteln; *meaning* klarmachen; *best wishes* übermitteln. **words cannot** ~ **what I feel** was ich empfinde, läßt sich nicht mit Worten ausdrücken; **the name** ~**s nothing to me** der Name sagt mir nichts. **(c)** *(Jur) property* übertragen *(to* auf *+acc).*

**conveyance** [kən'veɪəns] *n (transport)* Beförderung *f.* ~ **of goods** Güterverkehr *m*; **means of** ~ Beförderungsmittel *nt.*

**conveyancing** [kən'veɪənsɪŋ] *n (Jur)* (Eigentums)übertragung *f.*

**conveyor** [kən'veɪə˞] *n (of message etc)* Überbringer(in *f) m*; *(Tech)* Förderer *m.* ~ **belt** Fließband *nt*; *(for transport, supply)* Förderband *nt.*

**convict 1** ['kɒnvɪkt] *n* Strafgefangene(r) *mf.* **2** [kən'vɪkt] *vt (Jur) person* verurteilen *(of* wegen). **a** ~**ed criminal** ein überführter Verbrecher.

**conviction** [kən'vɪkʃən] *n* **(a)** *(Jur)* Verurteilung *f.* **(b)** *(belief, act of convincing)* Überzeugung *f.* **to carry** ~ überzeugend klingen; *see* **courage.**

**convince** [kən'vɪns] *vt* überzeugen.

**convincing** *adj,* ~**ly** *adv* [kən'vɪnsɪŋ, -lɪ] überzeugend.

**convivial** [kən'vɪvɪəl] *adj* heiter und unbeschwert; *(sociable)* gesellig.

**convoluted** ['kɒnvəluːtɪd] *adj (involved)* verwickelt; *style* gewunden.

**convoy** ['kɒnvɔɪ] *n* **(a)** *(escort)* Geleit *nt.* **under** ~ mit Geleitschutz; **to be on** ~ **duty** als Geleitschutz abgeordnet sein. **(b)** *(vehicles under escort, fig)* Konvoi *m.* **in** ~ im Konvoi.

**convulse** [kən'vʌls] *vt land* erschüttern; *muscles* krampfhaft zusammenziehen. **to be** ~**d with laughter/pain** sich vor Lachen schütteln/vor Schmerzen krümmen.

**convulsion** [kən'vʌlʃən] *n* **(a)** *(Med)* Schüttelkrampf *m no pl.* **(b)** *(caused by social upheaval etc)* Erschütterung *f.* **(c)** *(col: of laughter)* **to go into/be in** ~**s** sich vor Lachen biegen.

**convulsive** [kən'vʌlsɪv] *adj* Krampf-. ~ **laughter** Lachkrämpfe *pl.*

**coo** [kuː] **1** *vi (pigeon, fig)* gurren. **2** *n* Gurren *nt.* **3** *interj (Brit col)* ui.

**cook** [kʊk] **1** *n* Koch *m,* Köchin *f.* **too many** ~**s spoil the broth** *(Prov)* viele Köche verderben den Brei *(Prov).* **2** *vt* **(a)** *food, meal* zubereiten; *(in water, milk etc)* kochen; *(fry, roast)* braten; *pie, pancake* backen. **to** ~ **sb's goose** *(fig)* jdm die Suppe versalzen. **(b)** *(col: falsify) accounts* frisieren *(col).* **3** *vi (person, food)* kochen; *(fry, roast)* braten; *(pie)* backen. **what's** ~**ing?** *(fig col)* was ist los?

▶**cook up** *vt sep (fig col) story, excuse* zurechtbasteln *(col).* ~**ed** ~ **story** Lügenmärchen *nt.*

**cookbook** ['kʊkbʊk] *n* Kochbuch *nt.*

**cooker** ['kʊkə˞] *n (Brit)* **(a)** *(stove)* Herd *m.* ~ **hood** Abzugshaube *f.* **(b)** *(apple)* Kochapfel *m.*

**cookery** ['kʊkərɪ] *n* Kochen *nt (also Sch).* ~ **book** Kochbuch *nt.*

**cookhouse** ['kʊkhaʊs] *n (Naut)* Kombüse *f*; *(Mil)* Feldküche *f.*

**cookie, cooky** ['kʊkɪ] *n* **(a)** *(US: biscuit)* Keks *m.* **that's the way the** ~ **crumbles** *(col, also Brit)* so ist das nun mal (im Leben). **(b)** *(col: smart person)* Typ *m.* **he's a pretty sharp** ~ er ist ein richtiger Schlauberger.

**cooking** ['kʊkɪŋ] *n* Kochen *nt*; **plain** ~ Hausmannskost *f*; **French** ~ die französische Küche.

**cooking** *in cpds* Koch-; ~ **apple** *n* Kochapfel *m*; ~ **chocolate** *n* Blockschokolade *f*; ~ **foil** *n* Alufolie *f.*

**cookout** ['kʊkaʊt] *n (US)* Kochen *nt* am Lagerfeuer; *(on charcoal brazier)* Grillparty *f.*

**cool** [kuːl] **1** *adj (+er)* **(a)** *weather, drink* kühl; *clothes* luftig. **"keep in a** ~ **place"** „kühl aufbewahren". **(b)** *person* besonnen. **keep** ~! reg dich nicht auf!; **to be** ~ **to(wards)** sb sich jdm gegenüber kühl verhalten; **play it** ~! immer mit der Ruhe! **(c)** *(audacious)* unverfroren. **a** ~ **customer** *(col)* ein lässiger Typ *(col)*; **that was very** ~ **of him** da hat er sich ein starkes Stück geleistet. **(d)** *(col: of money)* glatt *(col).* **he earns a** ~ **forty thousand a year** er verdient glatte vierzigtausend im Jahr *(col).* **(e)** *disco, dress etc* cool, stark *(col).* ~ **jazz** Cool Jazz *m.*

**2** *n* **(a)** *(lit, fig)* Kühle *f.* **the** ~ **of the evening** die Abendkühle. **(b)** *(col)* **keep your** ~! reg dich nicht auf!; **to lose one's** ~ durchdrehen *(col).*

**3** *vt* **(a)** kühlen; *(~ down)* abkühlen; *wine* kalt stellen. **(b)** ~ **it!** *(relax)* reg dich ab; *(don't cause trouble)* mach keinen Ärger! *(col).*

**4** *vi (lit, fig)* abkühlen; *(anger)* sich legen; *(interest)* nachlassen.

▶**cool down 1** *vi* **(a)** *(lit)* abkühlen. **(b)** *(feelings, fig: person)* sich abkühlen; *(critical situation)* sich beruhigen. **to let things** ~ ~ die Sache etwas ruhen lassen. **2** *vt sep food, drink* abkühlen; *(let* ~ ~*)* abkühlen lassen.

▶**cool off** *vi* **(a)** *(liquid, food)* abkühlen; *(person)* sich abkühlen. **(b)** *(fig)* (sich) abkühlen; *(enthusiasm, interest)* nachlassen; *(become less angry)* sich abreagieren; *(become less friendly)* kühler werden *(towards sb* jdm gegenüber*).*

**coolant** ['kuːlənt] *n* Kühlmittel *nt.*

**cool:** ~ **bag** *n* Kühltasche *f*; ~ **box** *n* Kühlbox *f.*

**cooler** ['kuːlə˞] *n* **(a)** *(for wine)* Kühler *m.* **(b)** *(col: solitary)* Bau *m (col).*

**cooling** ['kuːlɪŋ] *adj drink, shower* kühlend. ~ **fan** Ventilator *m.*

**cooling-off** ['kuːlɪŋˈɒf] **1** *n (in relationship etc)* Abkühlung *f.* **2** *adj* ~ **period** Zeitraum *für Schlichtungsverhandlungen (bei Arbeitskämpfen).*

**cooling tower** *n* Kühlturm *m.*

**coolly** ['kuːlɪ] *adv* **(a)** *(calmly)* ruhig, gefaßt. **(b)** *(unenthusiastically, in an unfriendly way)* kühl. **(c)** *(audaciously)* unverfroren.

**coolness** ['kuːlnɪs] *n see adj* **(a)** Kühle *f*; Luftigkeit *f.* **(b)** Besonnenheit *f.* **(c)** Unverfrorenheit *f.*

**coop** [kuːp] *n (also hen ~)* Hühnerstall *m.*

▶**coop up** *vt sep person* einsperren; *several people* zusammenpferchen.

**co-op** ['kəʊˈɒp] *n* Genossenschaft *f*; *(shop)* Coop *m.*

**cooperate** [kəʊˈɒpəreɪt] *vi* zusammenarbeiten; *(not be awkward)* mitmachen.

**cooperation** [kəʊˌɒpəˈreɪʃən] *n* Kooperation, Zusammenarbeit *f*; *(help)* Mitarbeit *f.*

**cooperative** [kəʊˈɒpərətɪv] **1** *adj* **(a)** *(willing to com-*

*ply)* kooperativ; *(willing to help)* hilfsbereit. **(b)** ~ **society** Genossenschaft *f*; ~ **farm** Bauernhof *m* auf Genossenschaftsbasis. **2** *n* Genossenschaft *f*; *(also* ~ **farm)** Bauernhof *m* auf Genossenschaftsbasis.

**coopt** [kəʊ'ɒpt] *vt* (hinzu)wählen. **he was ~ed onto the committee** er wurde vom Komitee dazugewählt.

**coordinate** [kəʊ'ɔːdnɪt] **1** *n (Math etc)* Koordinate *f*. **~s** *(clothes)* Kleidung *f* zum Kombinieren. **2** [kəʊ'ɔːdɪneɪt] *vt* koordinieren.

**coordination** [kəʊ,ɔːdɪ'neɪʃən] *n* Koordination *f*.

**coordinator** [kəʊ'ɔːdɪneɪtə'] *n* Koordinator *m*.

**coot** [kuːt] *n* Wasserhuhn *nt*.

**co-owner** [kəʊ'əʊnə'] *n* Mitbesitzer(in *f*) *m*.

**cop** [kɒp] **1** *n* **(a)** *(col: policeman)* Polizist(in *f*), Bulle *(pej col) m*. **(b)** *(Brit col)* **it's not much** ~ das ist nichts Besonderes. **2** *vt (col: catch) sb* schnappen *(col)*. **you'll** ~ **it when your dad gets home** du kannst was erleben, wenn dein Vater nach Haus kommt!; **he's ~ped it** *(died)* er mußte dran glauben *(col)*; **hey,** ~ **a load of this!** he, hör/sieh dir das mal an! *(col)*.

▶**cop out** *vi (col)* sich drücken *(of* vor*)*.

**cope** [kəʊp] *vi* zurechtkommen; *(with work)* es schaffen. **to** ~ **with** fertigwerden mit; **she can't** ~ **with the stairs any more** sie schafft die Treppe nicht mehr.

**Copenhagen** [,kəʊpn'heɪgən] *n* Kopenhagen *nt*.

**copier** ['kɒpɪə'] *n (copyist)* Kopist(in *f*) *m*; *(machine)* Kopierer *m*, Kopiergerät *nt*.

**co-pilot** ['kəʊ'paɪlət] *n* Kopilot *m*.

**copious** ['kəʊpɪəs] *adj supply* reichlich; *information, illustrations* zahlreich.

**cop-out** ['kɒpaʊt] *n (col)* Rückzieher *m (col)*.

**copper** ['kɒpə'] *n* **(a)** *(metal)* Kupfer *nt*. **(b)** *(colour)* Kupferrot *nt*. **(c)** *(coin)* Pfennig *m*. **~s** Kleingeld *nt*. **(d)** *(col: policeman)* Polizist(in *f*), Bulle *(pej col) m*.

**copper:** ~ **beech** *n* Rotbuche *f*; **~-coloured** *(Brit)* or **~-colored** *(US) adj* kupferfarben; **~plate 1** *vt* verkupfern; **2** *adj* **~plate engraving** Kupferstich *m*; **~plate handwriting** lateinische (Ausgangs)schrift; *(best writing)* Schönschrift *f*.

**copse** [kɒps] *n* Wäldchen *nt*.

**copulate** ['kɒpjʊleɪt] *vi* kopulieren.

**copulation** [,kɒpjʊ'leɪʃən] *n* Kopulation *f*.

**copy** ['kɒpɪ] **1** *n* **(a)** Kopie *f*; *(carbon)* Durchschlag *m*; *(Phot)* Abzug *m*. **to write out a fair** ~ **of sth** etw ins reine schreiben. **(b)** *(of book etc)* Exemplar *nt*. **(c)** *(Press etc) (material)* Stoff *m*; *(text)* Text *m*. **that's always good** ~ das zieht immer. **(d)** *(in advertising)* Werbetext *m*. **2** *vi* **(a)** *(imitate)* nachahmen. **(b)** *(Sch etc)* abschreiben. **3** *vt* **(a)** *(make a ~ of)* see *n* kopieren; einen Durchschlag machen von; abziehen; *(write out again)* abschreiben. **(b)** *(imitate)* nachmachen; *accent etc* nachahmen. **(c)** *(Sch etc) sb else's work* abschreiben. **(d)** *(send)* **to** ~ **sth to sb** einen Durchschlag von etw an jdn senden.

**copy:** **~book 1** *n* Schönschreibheft *nt*; **2** *adj attr* mustergültig; **~cat** *n (col)* **she's a terrible ~cat** sie macht immer alles nach.

**copyright** ['kɒpɪraɪt] **1** *n* Urheberrecht, Copyright *nt*. **2** *adj* urheberrechtlich geschützt.

**copy:** ~ **typist** *n* Schreibkraft *f*; **~writer** *n* Werbetexter(in *f*) *m*.

**coral** ['kɒrəl] *n* **(a)** Koralle *f*. **(b)** *(colour: also* ~ **pink)** Korallenrot *nt*.

**coral** *in cpds* Korallen-; ~ **necklace** *n* Korallenkette *f*; ~ **reef** *n* Korallenriff *nt*; **C~ Sea** *n* Korallenmeer *nt*.

**cord** [kɔːd] *n* **(a)** Schnur *f*; *(for clothes)* Kordel *f*. **(b)** *(Tex)* = **corduroy**. **~s** *pl (also* **a pair of ~s)** Kordho-

sen *pl*.

**cordial** ['kɔːdɪəl] **1** *adj*, **~ly** ['kɔːdɪəlɪ] *adv* herzlich. **2** *n (soft drink)* Fruchtsaftkonzentrat *nt*; *(alcoholic)* Fruchtlikör *m*.

**cordless** ['kɔːdlɪs] *adj (Telec)* schnurlos.

**cordon** ['kɔːdn] *n* Postenkette *f*. **to put a** ~ **around sth** etw (hermetisch) abriegeln.

▶**cordon off** *vt sep area, building* abriegeln.

**corduroy** ['kɔːdərɔɪ] *n* Kordsamt *m*. **~s** Kordhosen *pl*.

**CORE** [kɔː'] *(US)* = **Congress of Racial Equality** *Verband m zur Bekämpfung von Rassendiskriminierung.*

**core** [kɔː'] **1** *n (lit, fig)* Kern *m*; *(of apple, pear)* Kerngehäuse *nt*; *(of rock)* Innere(s) *nt*. ~ **subject** *(Sch)* Hauptfach, Pflichtfach *nt*; ~ **time** Kernarbeitszeit *f*; **rotten/English to the** ~ *(fig)* durch und durch schlecht/englisch; **to get to the** ~ **of the matter** *(fig)* zum Kern der Sache kommen. **2** *vt fruit* entkernen; *apple, pear* das Kerngehäuse *(+gen)* ausschneiden.

**co-respondent** ['kəʊrɪs'pɒndənt] *n (Jur)* Mitbeklagte(r) *mf (im Scheidungsprozeß)*.

**Corfu** [kɔː'fuː] *n* Korfu *nt*.

**corgi** ['kɔːgɪ] *n* Corgi *m*.

**coriander** [,kɒrɪ'ændə'] *n* Koriander *m*.

**cork** [kɔːk] **1** *n* **(a)** *no pl (substance)* Kork *m*. **(b)** *(stopper)* Korken *m*. **(c)** *(Fishing: also* ~ **float)** Schwimmer *m*. **2** *vt (also* ~ **up)** *bottle, wine* verkorken. **3** *adj* Kork-.

**corkage** ['kɔːkɪdʒ] *n* Korkengeld *nt*.

**corked** [kɔːkt] *adj* **the wine is** ~ der Wein schmeckt nach Kork.

**cork:** **~screw** *n* Korkenzieher *m*; **~screw curls** *npl* Korkenzieherlocken *pl*; ~ **tile** *n* Korkfliese *f*; **~-tipped** *adj cigarette* mit Korkfilter; ~ **tree** *n* Korkbaum *m*.

**cormorant** ['kɔːmərənt] *n* Kormoran *m*.

**corn**[1] [kɔːn] *n* **(a)** *no pl (Brit: cereal)* Getreide *nt*. **(b)** *(seed of* ~*)* Korn *nt*. **(c)** *no pl (esp US: sweet* ~*)* Mais *m*; ~ **on the cob** Maiskolben *m*.

**corn**[2] *n* Hühnerauge *nt*. ~ **plaster** Hühneraugenpflaster *nt*.

**cornea** ['kɔːnɪə] *n* Hornhaut *f*.

**corned beef** ['kɔːnd'biːf] *n* Corned beef *nt*.

**corner** ['kɔːnə'] **1** *n* **(a)** Ecke *f*; *(of sheet)* Zipfel *m*; *(of mouth, eye)* Winkel *m*; *(in road)* Kurve *f*. **at** *or* **on the** ~ an der Ecke; **it's just around the** ~ es ist gleich um die Ecke; **to turn the** ~ *(lit)* um die Ecke biegen; **we've turned the** ~ **now** *(fig)* wir sind jetzt über den Berg; **out of the** ~ **of one's eye** aus dem Augenwinkel (heraus); **to cut** **~s** *(lit)* Kurven schneiden; *(fig)* das Verfahren abkürzen; **to drive sb into a** ~ *(fig)* jdn in die Enge treiben; **all four ~s of the world** die ganze Welt. **(b)** *(out-of-the-way place)* Winkel *m*. **(c)** *(Ftbl)* Eckball *m*, Ecke *f*. **to take a** ~ eine Ecke ausführen.

**2** *vt* **(a)** *(lit, fig: trap)* in die Enge treiben. **(b)** *(Comm) the market* monopolisieren.

**3** *vi (take a* ~*) (person)* Kurven/die Kurve nehmen. **this car ~s well** dieses Auto hat eine gute Kurvenlage.

**corner** *in cpds* Eck-; ~ **cupboard** *n* Eckschrank *m*; ~ **flag** *n (Sport)* Eckfahne *f*.

**cornering** ['kɔːnərɪŋ] *n (of car)* Kurvenlage *f*; *(of driver)* Kurventechnik *f*.

**corner:** ~ **kick** *n (Ftbl)* Eckstoß *m*; ~ **seat** *n (Rail)* Eckplatz *m*; ~ **shop** *n* Laden *m* an der Ecke; **~stone** *n (lit, fig)* Eckstein *m*.

**cornet** ['kɔːnɪt] *n* **(a)** *(Mus)* Kornett *nt*. **(b)** *(ice-cream* ~*)* (Eis)tüte *f*.

**corn:** **~field** *n (Brit)* Weizenfeld *nt*; *(US)* Maisfeld nt; ~**flakes** npl Corn-flakes ® pl; ~**flour** n (Brit) Stärkemehl nt; ~**flower** n Kornblume f.

**cornice** ['kɔ:nɪs] n (Archit: of wall, column) (Ge)sims nt; (fig: of snow) Wächte f.

**Cornish** ['kɔ:nɪʃ] 1 adj aus Cornwall. 2 n (dialect) Kornisch nt.

**corn:** ~**meal** n (US) Maismehl nt; ~ **oil** n (Mais)keimöl nt; ~ **pone** n (US) Maisbrot nt; ~**starch** n (US) Stärkemehl nt.

**cornucopia** [kɔ:njʊ'kəʊpɪə] n Füllhorn nt; (fig: abundance) Fülle f.

**Cornwall** ['kɔ:nwɔ:l] n Cornwall nt.

**corn whiskey** n (US) Maiswhiskey m.

**corny** ['kɔ:nɪ] adj (+er) (col) joke blöd (col); (sentimental) kitschig. **what a** ~ **old joke!** der Witz hat (so) einen Bart (col).

**corollary** [kə'rɒlərɪ] n (logische) Folge, Korollar nt (also Math).

**coronary** ['kɒrənərɪ] 1 adj (Med) Koronar- (spec). ~ **thrombosis** Herzinfarkt m. 2 n Herzinfarkt m.

**coronation** [,kɒrə'neɪʃən] n Krönung f.

**coroner** ['kɒrənər] n Beamter, der Todesfälle untersucht, die nicht eindeutig eine natürliche Ursache haben.

**coronet** ['kɒrənɪt] n Krone f; (jewellery) Krönchen nt.

**Corp** = **Corporation** ≃ GmbH f.

**corporal**[1] ['kɔ:pərəl] n (abbr **corp**) (Mil) Stabsunteroffizier m.

**corporal**[2] adj körperlich. ~ **punishment** Prügelstrafe f.

**corporate** ['kɔ:pərɪt] adj (a) (of a group) gemeinsam. (b) (of a corporation) korporativ; (of a company) Firmen-. ~ **body** Körperschaft f; ~ **image** or **identity** Firmenimage nt; ~ **planning** Unternehmensplanung f.

**corporation** [,kɔ:pə'reɪʃən] n (a) (municipal ~) Gemeinde f. (b) (Brit Comm: incorporated company) Handelsgesellschaft f; (US Comm: limited liability company) Gesellschaft f mit beschränkter Haftung. (c) (Brit hum: large belly) Schmerbauch m (col).

**corps** [kɔ:r] n, pl - (Mil) Korps nt. ~ **de ballet** Corps de ballet nt.

**corpse** [kɔ:ps] n Leiche f.

**corpulence** ['kɔ:pjʊləns] n Korpulenz f.

**corpulent** ['kɔ:pjʊlənt] adj korpulent.

**Corpus Christi** ['kɔ:pəs'krɪstɪ] n (Eccl) Fronleichnam m.

**corpuscle** ['kɔ:pʌsl] n Korpuskel nt (spec). **blood** ~ Blutkörperchen nt.

**corral** [kə'rɑ:l] n (esp US) Korral m.

**correct** [kə'rekt] 1 adj (right) richtig; (proper) korrekt. **am I** ~ **in thinking** ...? gehe ich recht in der Annahme, daß ...?; **you are** ~ Sie haben recht; **it's the** ~ **thing to do** das gehört sich so. 2 vt korrigieren; bad habit sich/jdm abgewöhnen. ~ **me if I'm wrong** Sie können mich gern berichtigen; **I stand** ~**ed** ich nehme alles zurück.

**correction** [kə'rekʃən] n see vt Korrektur f; Abgewöhnung f. ~ **key** Korrekturtaste f; ~ **tape** (on typewriter) Korrekturband nt.

**correctly** [kə'rektlɪ] adv richtig; behave korrekt.

**correctness** [kə'rektnɪs] n Korrektheit f.

**correlate** ['kɒrɪleɪt] 1 vt two things zueinander in Beziehung setzen. **to** ~ **sth with sth** etw mit etw in Beziehung setzen. 2 vi (two things) sich entsprechen. **to** ~ **with sth** mit etw in Beziehung stehen.

**correlation** [,kɒrɪ'leɪʃən] n (interdependence) Wechselbeziehung f; (Math, Statistics) Korrelation f.

**correspond** [,kɒrɪs'pɒnd] vi (a) (be equivalent) entsprechen (to, with dat); (to one another) sich entsprechen. (b) (exchange letters) korrespondieren

(with mit).

**correspondence** [,kɒrɪs'pɒndəns] n (a) (agreement, equivalence) Übereinstimmung f (between zwischen, with mit). (b) (letter-writing, letters) Korrespondenz f. **to be in** ~ **with sb** mit jdm in Briefwechsel stehen.

**correspondence:** ~ **college** n Institut nt für Fernunterricht; ~ **column** n (Press) Leserbriefspalte f; ~ **course** n Fernkurs m.

**correspondent** [,kɒrɪs'pɒndənt] n (a) (letter-writer) Briefschreiber(in f) m. **to be a bad** ~ schreibfaul sein. (b) (Press) Korrespondent(in f) m.

**corresponding** adj, ~**ly** adv [,kɒrɪs'pɒndɪŋ, -lɪ] entsprechend.

**corridor** ['kɒrɪdɔ:r] n Korridor m; (in train, bus) Gang m.

**corroborate** [kə'rɒbəreɪt] vt bestätigen.

**corroboration** [kə,rɒbə'reɪʃən] n Bestätigung f.

**corrode** [kə'rəʊd] 1 vt metal zerfressen; (fig) zerstören. 2 vi (metal) korrodieren.

**corrosion** [kə'rəʊʒən] n Korrosion f; (fig) Zerstörung f.

**corrosive** [kə'rəʊzɪv] 1 adj korrosiv; (fig) zerstörerisch. 2 n Korrosion verursachendes Mittel.

**corrugated** ['kɒrəgeɪtɪd] adj gewellt. ~ **cardboard** Wellpappe f; ~ **iron** Wellblech nt.

**corrupt** [kə'rʌpt] 1 adj verdorben; (open to bribery) korrupt. 2 vt (morally) verderben; (ethically, also Comp) korrumpieren; (form: bribe) bestechen.

**corruption** [kə'rʌpʃən] n (a) (act: of person) Korruption f; (Comp: of data) Korrumpierung f. (b) (corrupt nature) Verdorbenheit f; (by bribery) Bestechlichkeit f; (of morals) Verfall m.

**corset** ['kɔ:sɪt] n (also ~**s**) Korsett nt. **surgical** ~ Stützkorsett nt.

**Corsica** ['kɔ:sɪkə] n Korsika nt.

**Corsican** ['kɔ:sɪkən] 1 adj korsisch. 2 n Korse m, Korsin f.

**cortège** [kɔ:'teɪʒ] n (retinue) Gefolge nt; (procession) Prozession f; (funeral ~) Leichenzug m.

**cortisone** ['kɔ:tɪzəʊn] n Kortison nt.

**corvette** [kɔ:'vet] n (Naut) Korvette f.

**cos**[1] [kɒs] n (also ~ **lettuce**) römischer Salat.

**cos**[2] = **cosine** cos.

**cos**[3] [kɒz] (col) = **because**.

**cosh** [kɒʃ] (Brit col) 1 vt eins über den Schädel ziehen (+dat) (col). 2 n (instrument) Totschläger m.

**cosily** ['kəʊzɪlɪ] adv behaglich.

**cosine** ['kəʊsaɪn] n Kosinus m.

**cosiness** ['kəʊzɪnɪs] n Behaglichkeit f; (warmth) mollige Wärme.

**cosmetic** [kɒz'metɪk] 1 adj kosmetisch. **she's had** ~ **surgery** sie hat eine Schönheitsoperation gehabt. 2 n Kosmetikum nt.

**cosmic** ['kɒzmɪk] adj kosmisch.

**cosmonaut** ['kɒzmənɔ:t] n Kosmonaut(in f) m.

**cosmopolitan** [,kɒzmə'pɒlɪtən] 1 adj kosmopolitisch. 2 n Kosmopolit m.

**cosmos** ['kɒzmɒs] n Kosmos m.

**Cossack** ['kɒsæk] 1 n Kosak(in f) m. 2 adj Kosaken-.

**cosset** ['kɒsɪt] vt verwöhnen.

**cost** [kɒst] (vb: pret, ptp ~) 1 vt (a) (lit, fig) kosten. **how much does it** ~? wieviel kostet es?; **how much will it** ~ **to have it repaired?** wieviel kostet die Reparatur?; **it** ~ **(him) a lot of money** das hat (ihn) viel Geld gekostet; **it** ~ **him a great effort** es kostete ihn viel Mühe; ~ **what it may** koste es, was es wolle; **politeness doesn't** ~ **(you) anything** es kostet (dich) nichts, höflich zu sein. (b) pret, ptp ~**ed** (work out ~ of) project etc veranschlagen (at mit); (Comm: put a price on); articles for sale auszeichnen

*(at* mit*)*.
**2** *n* **(a)** Kosten *pl (of* für*)*. **to bear the ~ of sth** die
Kosten für etw tragen; **to buy sth at ~** etw zum
Selbstkostenpreis kaufen. **(b)** *(fig)* Preis *m.* **at all ~s**
um jeden Preis; **whatever the ~** koste es, was es
wolle; **at the ~ of one's health/job/marriage** *etc* auf
Kosten seiner Gesundheit/Stelle/Ehe *etc*; **he found
out to his ~ that ...** er machte die bittere Erfahrung, daß ... **(c)** *(Jur)* ~s *pl* Kosten *pl*; **to be ordered
to pay ~s** zur Übernahme der Kosten verurteilt
werden.
**cost accountant** *n* Kostenbuchhalter(in *f) m.*
**co-star** ['kəustɑːʳ] **1** *n (Film, Theat)* einer der Haupt-
darsteller. **2** *vi* **she was ~ring with Robert Redford**
sie spielte neben Robert Redford in einer der
Hauptrollen.
**Costa Rica** ['kɒstə'riːkə] *n* Costa Rica *nt.*
**cost:** **~ centre** *n* Kostenstelle *f*; **~-conscious** *adj*
kostenbewußt; **~-cutting** *n* Sparmaßnahmen *pl*;
**~-cutting policy** Sparpolitik *f*; **~-effective** *adj* rentabel.
**costing** ['kɒstɪŋ] *n* Kalkulation *f.*
**costly** ['kɒstlɪ] *adj* kostspielig.
**cost:** **~ of living** *n* Lebenshaltungskosten *pl*; **~-of-
living index** *n* Lebenshaltungskostenindex *m*; **~
price** *n (Brit)* Selbstkostenpreis *m.*
**costume** ['kɒstjuːm] *n* Kostüm *nt*; *(bathing ~)* Badeanzug *m.* **national ~** Nationaltracht *f.*
**costume:** **~ ball** *n* Kostümfest *nt*; **~ jewellery**
*(Brit)* or **jewelry** *(US) n* Modeschmuck *m.*
**cosy,** *(US)* **cozy** ['kəuzɪ] **1** *adj (+er) room, atmosphere* behaglich; *(warm)* mollig warm. **warm and ~**
mollig warm. **2** *n (tea ~)* Wärmer *m.*
**cot** [kɒt] *n* **(a)** *(esp Brit: child's bed)* Kinderbett *nt.*
**(b)** *(US: camp bed)* Feldbett *nt*; **~ death** Krippentod *m.*
**cottage** ['kɒtɪdʒ] *n* Cottage, Häuschen *nt*; *(US: in institution)* Wohneinheit *f.*
**cottage:** **~ cheese** *n* Hüttenkäse *m*; **~ hospital** *n*
*(Brit) kleines Krankenhaus für leichtere Fälle*; **~ industry** *n* Heimindustrie *f*; **~ pie** *n Hackfleisch nt
mit Kartoffelbrei überbacken.*
**cotter-pin** ['kɒtəpɪn] *n* Splint *m.*
**cotton** ['kɒtn] **1** *n* Baumwolle *f*; *(plant)* Baumwoll-
strauch *m*; *(sewing thread)* (Baumwoll)garn *nt.* **absorbent ~** *(US)* Watte *f.* **2** *adj* Baumwoll-.
▶**cotton on** *vi (col)* es kapieren *(col)*. **~ ~ to sth**
etw kapieren *(col)*.
**cotton** *in cpds* Baumwoll-; **~ batting** *n (US)* Gaze
*f*; **~ bud** *n* Wattestäbchen *nt*; **~ candy** *n (US)*
Zuckerwatte *f*; **~ mill** *n* Baumwollspinnerei *f*; **~-
picking** *adj (US col)* verdammt *(col)*; **~ print** *n (fabric)* bedruckter Baumwollstoff; **~ reel** *n* Garnrolle *f*;
**~tail** *n (US)* Kaninchen *nt*; **~wool** *n (Brit)* Watte *f*; **to
wrap sb in ~wool** *(fig)* jdn in Watte packen.
**couch** [kautʃ] **1** *n* Couch *f.* **~ potato** *(esp US col)*
Dauerglotzer(in *f) m (col)*. **2** *vt (put in words)* formulieren.
**couchette** [kuːʃet] *n (Rail)* Liegewagenplatz *m.*
**cough** [kɒf] **1** *n* Husten *m.* **2** *vti* husten.
▶**cough up** *vt sep (lit)* aushusten. **2** *vt insep (fig
col) money* rausrücken *(col)*. **3** *vi (fig col)* blechen
*(col)*.
**cough:** **~ drop** *n* Hustenpastille *f*; **~ mixture** *n*
Hustensaft *m*; **~ sweet** *n* Hustenbonbon *m.*
**could** [kud] *pret of* **can**[1].
**couldn't** ['kudnt] = **could not.**
**council** ['kaunsl] **1** *n* Rat *m.* **city/town ~** Stadtrat *m*;
**C~ of Europe** Europarat *m*; **C~ of Ministers** Ministerrat *m.* **2** *attr estate (Brit)* ≈ des sozialen Woh-
nungsbaus. **~ flat/house** *(Brit)* ≈ Sozialwohnung *f*;

**~ housing** *(Brit)* ≈ sozialer Wohnungsbau; **~ chamber** Sitzungssaal *m* des Rats; **~man** *(US)* = **councillor;** **~ meeting** Ratssitzung *f*; **~ tax** *(Brit)* Ge-
meindesteuer *f.*
**councillor,** *(US)* **councilor** ['kaunsələʳ] *n* Ratsmit-
glied *nt*; *(town ~)* Stadtrat *m*/-rätin *f.*
**counsel** ['kaunsl] **1** *n* **(a)** *(form: advice)* Rat(schlag)
*m.* **(b)** *(Jur)* Rechtsanwalt *m.* **~ for the defence/
prosecution** Verteidiger(in *f) m*/Vertreter(in *f) m*
der Anklage, ≈ Staatsanwalt *m*/-anwältin *f.* **2** *vt
(form) person* beraten; *course of action* raten zu.
**counselling,** *(US)* **counseling** ['kaunsəlɪŋ] *n* Beratung *f*; *(Psych)* psychologische Beratung.
**counsellor,** *(US)* **counselor** ['kaunsələʳ] *n* **(a)** *(adviser)* Berater(in *f) m*; *(Psych)* psychologische(r)
Berater(in *f) m.* **(b)** *(US, Ir: lawyer)* Rechtsanwalt
*m*/-anwältin *f.*
**count**[1] [kaunt] **1** *n* **(a)** Zählung *f*; *(of votes)* (Stimmen)auszählung *f.* **she lost ~ when she was interrupted** sie kam mit dem Zählen durcheinander, als
sie unterbrochen wurde; **I've lost all ~** ich habe
völlig die Übersicht verloren; **he was out for the ~**
*(Sport)* er wurde ausgezählt; *(fig)* er war k.o. **(b)**
*(Jur: charge)* Anklagepunkt *m.* **on that ~** *(fig)* in
dem Punkt; **on all ~s** in jeder Hinsicht.
**2** *vt* **(a)** (ab)zählen; *(~ again)* nachzählen; *votes*
(aus)zählen. **to ~ the cost** *(lit)* auf die Kosten achten. **(b)** *(consider)* betrachten; *(include)* mitzählen.
**to ~ sb among one's friends** jdn zu seinen Freunden
zählen; **~ yourself lucky that ...** Sie können von
Glück sagen, daß ...; **ten people ~ing the children**
zehn Leute, die Kinder mitgerechnet.
**3** *vi* **(a)** zählen. **~ing from today** von heute an (gerechnet). **(b)** *(be considered)* betrachtet werden;
*(be included)* mitgezählt werden; *(be important)*
wichtig sein. **that doesn't ~** das zählt nicht; **to ~
against sb** gegen jdn sprechen.
▶**count in** *vt sep* mitzählen. **you can ~ me ~!** da
bin ich dabei.
▶**count on** *vi +prep obj (depend on)* rechnen mit.
**you can ~ ~ him to help you** du kannst auf seine
Hilfe zählen.
▶**count out** *vt sep* **(a)** *(Sport)* auszählen. **(b)**
*money, books etc* abzählen. **(c)** *(col: exclude)* **(you
can) ~ me ~ (of that)!** ohne mich!, da mache ich
nicht mit!
▶**count up** *vt sep* zusammenzählen.
▶**count upon** *vi +prep obj* = **count on.**
**count**[2] *n* Graf *m.*
**countable** ['kauntəbl] *adj* zählbar *(also Gram).*
**countdown** ['kauntdaun] *n* Countdown *m.* **to start
the ~** mit dem Countdown beginnen.
**countenance** ['kauntɪnəns] **1** *n (old, form: face)* Antlitz *nt (old)*. **to keep one's ~** *(fig)* die Haltung bewahren. **2** *vt behaviour* gutheißen.
**counter** ['kauntəʳ] **1** *n* **(a)** *(in shop)* Ladentisch *m*;
*(in cafe)* Theke *f*; *(in bank, post office)* Schalter *m.* **~
clerk** Schalterbeamte(r) *m*/-beamtin *f*; **under-the-~
dealings** *(fig)* undurchsichtige Geschäfte. **(b)** *(for
games)* Spielmarke *f.* **(c)** *(Tech)* Zähler *m.* **2** *vt (retaliate against)* antworten auf *(+acc)*. **3** *vi* kontern
*(also Sport).* **4** *adv* **~ to** gegen *(+acc)*; **to run ~ to
sb's wishes** jds Wünschen *(dat)* zuwiderlaufen.
**counter:** **~act** *vt (make ineffective)* neutralisieren;
*(act in opposition to)* entgegenwirken *(+dat)*; *disease* bekämpfen; **~action** *n see vt* Neutralisierung
*f*; Gegenwirkung *f*; Bekämpfung *f*; **~attack 1** *n*
Gegenangriff *m*; **2** *vi* einen Gegenangriff starten;
**~balance 1** *n* Gegengewicht *nt*; **2** *vt* ausgleichen;
**~clockwise** *adj, adv (US)* = **anti-clockwise;**
**~espionage** *n* Gegenspionage *f.*

**counterfeit** ['kaʊntəfiːt] **1** adj gefälscht; (fig) falsch. ~ **money** Falschgeld nt. **2** n Fälschung f. **3** vt fälschen.
**counterfoil** ['kaʊntəfɔɪl] n (Brit) Kontrollabschnitt m.
**counterintelligence** [ˌkaʊntərɪn'telɪdʒəns] n Gegenspionage f.
**countermand** ['kaʊntəmɑːnd] vt order aufheben; attack, plan rückgängig machen.
**counter:** ~**measure** n Gegenmaßnahme f; ~**offensive** n (Mil) Gegenoffensive f; ~-**offer** n Gegenangebot nt; ~**pane** n Tagesdecke f; ~**part** n (equivalent) Gegenüber nt; (complement) Gegenstück nt; ~ **point** n (Mus) Kontrapunkt m; ~-**productive** adj widersinnig; measures destruktiv; that'd be ~-**productive** das würde den Zweck verfehlen; that runs the risk of being ~-**productive** es besteht die Gefahr, daß dadurch das Gegenteil bewirkt wird; ~-**proposal** n Gegenvorschlag m; ~**sign** vt cheque etc gegenzeichnen; ~**sink** vt hole senken; screw versenken; ~**weight** n Gegengewicht nt.
**countess** ['kaʊntɪs] n Gräfin f.
**countless** ['kaʊntlɪs] adj unzählig attr, zahllos attr.
**countrified** ['kʌntrɪfaɪd] adj ländlich.
**country** ['kʌntrɪ] n **(a)** (state) Land nt. his own ~ seine Heimat; to die for one's ~ für sein Land sterben; to go to the ~ (Pol) Wahlen ausschreiben. **(b)** no pl (as opposed to town) Land nt. in/to the ~ auf dem/aufs Land; the surrounding ~ die Umgebung; there's some lovely ~ up north die Landschaft im Norden ist herrlich.
**country** in cpds Land-; ~-**and-western** n Country-und-Western-Musik f; ~ **bumpkin** n (pej) Bauerntölpel (col) m; (girl) Bauerntrampel m (col); ~ **cousin** n Vetter m/Cousine f vom Lande; ~ **dancing** n Volkstanz m; ~ **dweller** n Landbewohner(in f) m; ~ **house** n Landhaus nt; ~**man** n **(a)** Landsmann m; his fellow ~**men** seine Landsleute; **(b)** (country-dweller) Landbewohner m; ~ **people** npl Leute pl vom Land(e); ~**side** n (scenery) Landschaft f; (rural area) Land nt; it's beautiful ~**side** das ist eine herrliche Landschaft; ~ **town** n Kleinstadt f (auf dem Land); ~-**wide** adj landesweit; ~**woman** n **(a)** Landsmännin f; **(b)** (country dweller) Landbewohnerin f.
**county** ['kaʊntɪ] n (Brit) Grafschaft f; (US) (Verwaltungs)bezirk m.
**county:** ~ **council** n (Brit) Grafschaftsrat m; ~ **seat** n (US) Hauptstadt f eines Verwaltungsbezirks; ~ **town** n (Brit) Hauptstadt f einer Grafschaft.
**coup** [kuː] n **(a)** (successful action) Coup m. **(b)** (~ d'état) Staatsstreich m.
**coupé** ['kuːpeɪ] n (car) Coupé nt.
**couple** ['kʌpl] **1** n **(a)** (pair) Paar nt; (married ~) Ehepaar nt. **(b)** (col) a ~ (two) zwei; (several) ein paar; a ~ of friends ein paar Freunde; a ~ of times ein paarmal. **2** vt ideas etc verbinden; carriages etc koppeln.
**coupling** ['kʌplɪŋ] n **(a)** (linking) Verbindung f; (of carriages etc) Kopplung f. **(b)** (device) Kupplung f.
**coupon** ['kuːpɒn] n **(a)** (voucher) Gutschein m. **(b)** (Ftbl) Wettschein m.
**courage** ['kʌrɪdʒ] n Mut m. I haven't the ~ to refuse ich habe einfach nicht den Mut, nein zu sagen; to have the ~ of one's convictions Zivilcourage haben; to take one's ~ in both hands sein Herz in beide Hände nehmen.
**courageous** adj, ~**ly** adv [kə'reɪdʒəs, -lɪ] mutig.
**courgette** ['kʊəʒet] n (Brit) Zucchini f.
**courier** ['kʊrɪər] n (messenger) Kurier m; (tourist guide) Reiseleiter(in f) m. ~ **service** Kurierdienst

m.
**course**¹ [kɔːs] n **(a)** (direction) Kurs m; (of river, history) Lauf m; (fig: of illness) Verlauf m. to set ~ for a place Kurs auf einen Ort nehmen; to change ~ den Kurs ändern; to be on/off ~ auf Kurs sein/vom Kurs abgekommen sein; to let sth take its ~ einer Sache (dat) ihren Lauf lassen; which ~ of action did you take? wie sind Sie vorgegangen?; the best ~ would be ... das beste wäre ...; we have no other ~ (of action) but to ... es bleibt uns nichts anderes übrig als zu ...
**(b)** in the ~ of his life/the next few weeks/the meeting etc während seines Lebens/der nächsten paar Wochen/der Versammlung etc; in the ~ of time/the conversation im Laufe der Zeit/Unterhaltung; in the ordinary ~ of things unter normalen Umständen; to be in the ~ of construction sich im Bau befinden.
**(c)** of ~ (admittedly) natürlich; (obviously) selbstverständlich; of ~ I will! aber natürlich; of ~ I'm coming natürlich komme ich.
**(d)** (Sch, Univ) Studium nt; (shorter, summer ~ etc) Kurs(us) m; (at work) Lehrgang m; (Med: of treatment) Kur f. to go to/on a French ~ einen Französischkurs(us) besuchen; a ~ of lectures eine Vorlesungsreihe; a ~ of treatment eine Behandlung.
**(e)** (Sports) (race ~) Kurs m; (golf ~) Platz m.
**(f)** (Cook) Gang m. a three-~ meal ein Essen mit drei Gängen.
**course**² vi (blood, tears) strömen.
**court** [kɔːt] **1** n **(a)** (Jur) Gericht nt; (room) Gerichtssaal m. to appear in ~ vor Gericht erscheinen; his suggestion was ruled out of ~ (fig) sein Vorschlag wurde verworfen; to take sb to ~ jdn vor Gericht bringen. **(b)** (royal) Hof m. **(c)** (Sport) Platz m. **2** vt **(a)** (dated) woman den Hof machen (+dat). **(b)** (fig) danger herausfordern. that's ~**ing disaster** das könnte katastrophale Folgen haben. **3** vi (dated) she's ~**ing** sie hat einen Freund; ~**ing couple** Liebespaar nt.
**court card** n (Brit) Bildkarte f.
**courteous** ['kɜːtɪəs] adj höflich.
**courtesy** ['kɜːtɪsɪ] n Höflichkeit f. by ~ of ... freundlicherweise zur Verfügung gestellt von ...; you might have had the ~ to ... sie hätten doch so freundlich sein können und ...
**courtesy:** ~ **coach** n gebührenfreier Bus; ~ **light** n (Aut) Innenleuchte f; ~ **visit** n Höflichkeitsbesuch m.
**courthouse** ['kɔːthaʊs] n (Jur) Gerichtsgebäude nt.
**courtier** ['kɔːtɪər] n Höfling m.
**court:** ~-**martial** ['kɔːt'mɑːʃəl] **1** n (Mil) Militärgericht nt. **2** vt jdn vor das Militärgericht stellen; ~**room** n Gerichtssaal m.
**courtship** ['kɔːtʃɪp] n (dated) (Braut)werbung f (dated) (of um).
**court:** ~ **shoe** n Pumps m; ~**yard** n Hof m.
**cousin** ['kʌzn] n (male) Vetter, Cousin m; (female) Cousine f.
**cove**¹ [kəʊv] n (Geog) (kleine) Bucht f.
**cove**² n (dated Brit col: fellow) Kerl m (col).
**covenant** ['kʌvɪnənt] **1** n Schwur m; (Bibl) Bund m; (Jur) Verpflichtung f zu regelmäßigen Spenden. **2** vt to ~ to do sth durch ein Abkommen versprechen, etw zu tun.
**Coventry** ['kɒvəntrɪ] n: to send sb to ~ (Brit col) jdn schneiden (col).
**cover** ['kʌvər] **1** n **(a)** (lid) Deckel m; (of lens) (Schutz)kappe f; (on chair etc) Bezug m; (for typewriter etc) Hülle f; (on lorries, tennis court) Plane f; (over merchandise) Decke f; (quilt) (Bett)decke f.

**(b)** *(of book)* Einband *m*; *(of magazine)* Umschlag *m*. **to read a book from** ~ **to** ~ ein Buch von der ersten bis zur letzten Seite lesen.

**(c)** *(Comm: envelope)* Umschlag *m*. **under separate** ~ mit getrennter Post.

**(d)** *no pl (shelter, protection)* Schutz *m (from* vor +*dat*, gegen*)*; *(Mil)* Deckung *f (from* vor +*dat*, gegen*)*. **to take** ~ *(from rain)* sich unterstellen; *(Mil)* in Deckung gehen *(from* vor +*dat)*; **under the** ~ **of the trees** im Schutz der Bäume; **under** ~ **of darkness** im Schutz(e) der Dunkelheit; **to give sb** ~ *(Mil)* jdm Deckung geben.

**(e)** *(Hunt)* Deckung *f*. **to break** ~ aus der Deckung hervorbrechen.

**(f)** *(place at meal)* Gedeck *nt*.

**(g)** *(Comm, Fin)* Deckung *f*; *(insurance* ~*)* Versicherung *f*. **to take out** ~ **against fire** eine Feuerversicherung abschließen; **do you have adequate** ~**?** sind Sie ausreichend versichert?

**(h)** *(assumed identity)* Tarnung *f*. **to operate under** ~ als Agent tätig sein; **under** ~ **as** getarnt als.

**2** *vt* **(a)** bedecken; *(cover over)* zudecken; *(with loose cover)* chair etc beziehen. **to** ~ **oneself in** or **with glory** Ruhm ernten; *(iro)* sich mit Ruhm bekleckern *(iro col)*; ~**ed in** or **with shame** zutiefst beschämt.

**(b)** *(hide)* verbergen.

**(c)** *(Mil, Sport, Chess: protect)* decken. **he only said that to** ~ **himself** er hat das nur gesagt, um sich zu decken; **I'll keep you** ~**ed** ich gebe dir Deckung.

**(d)** *(point weapon at)* door etc sichern; *sb* in Schach halten; *(be on guard near)* sichern. **to keep sb** ~**ed** jdn in Schach halten; **I've got you** ~**ed!** *(with gun etc)* ich hab' auf dich angelegt; *(fig: Chess etc)* ich hab' dich.

**(e)** *(Fin)* loan decken; *(Insur)* versichern *(for* gegen*)*. **will £3** ~ **the petrol?** reichen £3 für das Benzin?; **we've** ~**ed most eventualities** wir haben die meisten Eventualitäten abgedeckt.

**(f)** *(Press: report on)* berichten über *(+acc)*.

**(g)** *(travel)* miles, distance zurücklegen; *(deal with)* topics behandeln. **we've** ~**ed a lot today** wir haben heute viel geschafft.

**(h)** *(salesman etc)* territory zuständig sein für.

►**cover for** *vi* + *prep obj* vertreten.

►**cover over** *vt sep* zudecken.

►**cover up 1** *vi* **(a)** *(wrap up)* sich einmummen. **(b)** *(conceal a fact)* alles vertuschen. **to** ~ ~ **for sb** jdn decken. **2** *vt sep* **(a)** *child* zudecken. **(b)** *(hide)* truth, facts vertuschen.

**coverage** ['kʌvərɪdʒ] *n no pl* **(a)** *(in media)* Berichterstattung *f (of* über +*acc)*. **to give full** ~ **to an event** ausführlich über ein Ereignis berichten. **(b)** *(Insur)* Versicherung *f*.

**cover:** ~**all** *n usu pl (US)* Overall *m*; ~ **charge** *n* Kosten *pl* für ein Gedeck; ~ **girl** *n* Titelmädchen *nt*.

**covering** ['kʌvərɪŋ] *n* Decke *f*; *(floor* ~*)* Belag *m*. **a** ~ **of dust/snow** eine Staub-/Schneedecke.

**covering letter,** *(US)* **cover letter** *n* Begleitbrief *m*.

**cover:** ~ **lesson** *n* Vertretungsstunde *f*; ~ **note** *n* Deckungszusage *f*; ~ **price** *n* Einzel-(exemplar)preis *m*; ~ **story** *n (of paper)* Titelgeschichte *f*.

**covert** ['kʌvət] *adj* threat, attack versteckt; *glance* verstohlen.

**cover-up** ['kʌvərʌp] *n* Vertuschung *f*.

**covet** ['kʌvɪt] *vt* begehren.

**covetous** ['kʌvɪtəs] *adj* begehrlich.

**cow¹** [kaʊ] *n* **(a)** Kuh *f*. ~ **elephant** Elefantenkuh *f*; **you'll be waiting till the** ~**s come home** *(fig col)* da kannst du warten, bis du schwarz wirst *(col)*. **(b)** *(pej col: woman) (stupid)* Kuh *f (col)*; *(nasty)* gemeine Ziege *(col)*.

**cow²** *vt* person, animal einschüchtern. **she had a** ~**ed look about her** sie machte einen eingeschüchterten Eindruck.

**coward** ['kaʊəd] *n* Feigling *m*.

**cowardice** ['kaʊədɪs], **cowardliness** ['kaʊədlɪnɪs] *n* Feigheit *f*.

**cowardly** ['kaʊədlɪ] *adj* feig(e).

**cow:** ~**boy** *n* **(a)** Cowboy *m*; **(b)** *(fig col) (incompetent)* Pfuscher *m*; *(dishonest)* Gauner *m*; ~**catcher** *n (Rail)* Schienenräumer *m*.

**cower** ['kaʊər] *vi* sich ducken; *(squatting)* kauern.

**cowhide** ['kaʊhaɪd] *n* **(a)** *(untanned)* Kuhhaut *f*; *(no pl: leather)* Rindsleder *nt*. **(b)** *(US: whip)* Lederpeitsche *f*.

**cowl** [kaʊl] *n* **(a)** *(monk's hood)* Kapuze *f*. **(b)** *(chimney* ~*)* (Schornstein)kappe *f*.

**cowman** ['kaʊmən] *n, pl* -**men** [-mən] *(farm labourer)* Stallbursche *m*; *(US: cattle rancher)* Viehzüchter *m*.

**co-worker** ['kəʊ'wɜːkər] *n* Kollege *m*, Kollegin *f*.

**cow:** ~**shed** *n* Kuhstall *m*; ~**slip** *n (Brit: primrose)* Schlüsselblume *f*; *(US: kingcup)* Sumpfdotterblume *f*.

**cox** [kɒks] **1** *n* Steuermann *m*. **2** *vt crew* Steuermann sein für. **3** *vi* steuern.

**coy** [kɔɪ] *adj* (+*er*) *(affectedly shy)* verschämt; *(coquettish)* kokett.

**cozy** *adj (US)* = **cosy.**

**cp** = **compare** vgl.

**CPA** *(US)* = **certified public accountant.**

**Cpl** = **Corporal.**

**c.p.s.** = **(a)** *(Phys)* **cycles per second. (b)** *(Comp)* **characters per second.**

**CPU** *(Comp)* = **central processing unit.**

**crab** [kræb] *n* Krabbe *f*.

**crab apple** *n* Holzapfel *m*.

**crack** [kræk] **1** *n* **(a)** Riß *m*; *(between floorboards etc)* Ritze *f*; *(wider hole etc)* Spalte *f*; *(in pottery etc)* Sprung *m*. **at the** ~ **of dawn** in aller Frühe. **(b)** *(sharp noise) (of wood etc breaking)* Knacks *m*; *(of gun, whip)* Knall(en *nt no pl*) *m*; *(of thunder)* Schlag *m*. **(c)** *(sharp blow)* Schlag *m*. **to give sb/oneself a** ~ **on the head** jdm eins auf den Kopf geben/sich *(dat)* den Kopf anschlagen. **(d)** *(col) (gibe)* Stichelei *f*; *(joke)* Witz *m*. **(e)** *(col: attempt)* **to have a** ~ **at sth** etw mal probieren *(col)*. **(f)** *(Drugs)* Crack *nt*.

**2** *adj attr* erstklassig; *(Mil)* Elite-. ~ **shot** Meisterschütze *m*.

**3** *vt* nuts, *(col)* safe, *(fig)* code knacken; *problem, case* lösen; *joke* reißen; *whip* knallen mit. **I think I've** ~**ed it** ich glaube, ich hab's.

**4** *vi* **(a)** *(get a* ~*)* *(pottery)* springen; *(ice, road)* einen Riß/Risse bekommen; *(lips, skin)* spröde werden; *(bones)* einen Knacks bekommen *(col)*; *(break)* brechen. **(b)** *(twigs, joints)* knacken; *(whip, gun)* knallen. **(c)** *(col)* **to get** ~**ing** loslegen *(col)*.

►**crack down** *vi (clamp down)* hart durchgreifen *(on* bei*)*.

►**crack up 1** *vi* **(a)** *(break into pieces)* zerbrechen. **(b)** *(fig col: person)* zusammenbrechen. **2** *vt sep (col)* **he's/it's not all he's/it's** ~**ed** ~ **to be** so toll ist er/es dann auch wieder nicht.

**cracked** [krækt] *adj* **(a)** *plate* gesprungen; *rib* angebrochen; *walls* rissig. **(b)** *(col: mad)* übergeschnappt *(col)*.

**cracker** ['krækər] *n* **(a)** *(biscuit)* Kräcker *m*. **(b)**

*(fire~)* Knallkörper *m*; *(Christmas ~)* Knallbonbon *nt*.

**crackers** ['krækəz] *adj pred (Brit col)* übergeschnappt *(col)*.

**crackle** ['krækl] **1** *vi (dry leaves, paper)* rascheln; *(fire)* knistern; *(twigs, telephone line)* knacken. **2** *n (crackling noise) see vi* Rascheln *nt*; Knistern *nt*; Knacken *nt*.

**crackling** ['kræklɪŋ] *n no pl* **(a)** = **crackle 2. (b)** *(Cook)* Kruste *f (des Schweinebratens)*.

**crackpot** ['krækpɒt] *adj (col)* verrückt, irre.

**cradle** ['kreɪdl] **1** *n* Wiege *f*; *(of phone)* Gabel *f*. **from the ~ to the grave** von der Wiege bis zur Bahre. **2** *vt (hold)* (in den Armen) halten. **he was cradling his injured arm** er hielt sich *(dat)* (behutsam) seinen verletzten Arm.

**cradle-song** ['kreɪdlsɒŋ] *n* Wiegenlied *nt*.

**craft** [krɑːft] *n* **(a)** *(handicraft)* Kunst *f*; *(trade)* Handwerk *nt*; *(weaving, pottery etc)* Kunstgewerbe *nt*. **(b)** *no pl (skill)* Geschick(lichkeit *f*) *nt*, Kunstfertigkeit *f*. **(c)** *no pl (cunning)* List *f*. **(d)** *pl - (boat)* Boot *nt*.

**craftsman** ['krɑːftsmən] *n, pl* **-men** [-mən] Handwerker *m*.

**craftsmanship** ['krɑːftsmənʃɪp] *n* Handwerkskunst *f*; *(of person)* handwerkliches Können.

**crafty** ['krɑːftɪ] *adj (+er) (shrewd)* schlau; *(sly)* durchtrieben.

**crag** [kræg] *n* Fels *m*.

**craggy** ['krægɪ] *adj (+er) (rocky)* felsig; *(jagged)* zerklüftet; *face* kantig.

**cram** [kræm] **1** *vt* **(a)** *(fill)* vollstopfen; *(stuff in)* hineinstopfen *(in(to)* in *+acc)*; *people* hineinzwängen *(in(to)* in *+acc)*. **the room was ~med** der Raum war gestopft voll; **he ~med his hat (down) over his eyes** er zog sich *(dat)* den Hut tief ins Gesicht. **(b)** *(Sch) subject* pauken *(col)*, büffeln *(col)*; *pupil* pauken mit *(col)*. **2** *vi (swot)* pauken *(col)*, büffeln *(col)*.

**cramp** [kræmp] **1** *n (Med)* Krampf *m*. **2** *vt (also ~ up) persons* zusammenpferchen. **to ~ sb's style** jdm im Weg sein.

**cramped** [kræmpt] *adj* **(a)** *space* beschränkt. **we are very ~ (for space)** wir sind räumlich sehr beschränkt. **(b)** *position* verkrampft.

**crampon** ['kræmpən] *n* Steigeisen *nt*.

**cranberry** ['krænbərɪ] *n* Preiselbeere *f*.

**crane** [kreɪn] **1** *n* **(a)** Kran *m*. **~ driver** *n* Kranführer *m*. **(b)** *(Orn)* Kranich *m*. **2** *vt*: **to ~ one's neck** den Hals recken. **3** *vi (also ~ forward)* den Hals *or* den Kopf recken.

**cranefly** *n* Weberknecht *m*.

**cranium** ['kreɪnɪəm] *n, pl* **crania** *(Anat)* Schädel *m*.

**crank¹** [kræŋk] *n (eccentric)* Spinner(in *f*) *m (col)*; *(US: cross person)* Griesgram *m*.

**crank²** **1** *n (Mech)* Kurbel *f*. **2** *vt (also: ~ up)* ankurbeln.

**crankshaft** ['kræŋkʃɑːft] *n (Mech)* Kurbelwelle *f*.

**cranky** ['kræŋkɪ] *adj (+er)* **(a)** *(eccentric)* verrückt. **(b)** *(US: bad-tempered)* griesgrämig.

**crap** [kræp] *n (lit, fig: col!)* Scheiße *f (col!)*. **to go for a ~** aufs Scheißhaus gehen *(col!)*; **don't talk ~** red' kein Blech *(col)*.

**crap game** *n (US)* Würfelspiel *nt (mit zwei Würfeln)*.

**crappy** ['kræpɪ] *adj (col!)* beschissen *(col!)*.

**crash** [kræʃ] **1** *n* **(a)** *(noise)* Krach(en *nt*) *m no pl*; *(of thunder etc)* Schlag *m*. **(b)** *(accident)* Unfall *m*; *(collision also)* Zusammenstoß *m*; *(with several cars)* Karambolage *f*; *(plane ~)* (Flugzeug)unglück *nt*. **to have a ~** einen (Auto)unfall haben. **(c)** *(Fin, Comp)* Zusammenbruch *m*. **2** *vt car* einen Unfall haben mit; *plane* abstürzen mit. **to ~ one's car into sth** mit dem Auto gegen etw krachen. **3** *vi* **(a)** *(have an accident)* verunglücken; *(plane)* abstürzen. **to ~ into sth** gegen etw krachen. **(b)** *(move with a ~)* krachen. **to ~ to the ground/through sth** zu Boden/durch etw krachen; **his whole world ~ed about him** eine Welt brach für ihn zusammen. **(c)** *(stock market, computer)* zusammenbrechen.
►**crash out** *vi (col: fall asleep)* sich hinhauen *(col)*; *(without meaning to)* wegtreten *(col)*.

**crash:** **~ barrier** *n (Brit)* Leitplanke *f*; **~ course** *n* Intensivkurs *m*; **~ diet** *n* radikale Diät *f*; **~ dive** *n* Schnelltauchmanöver *nt*; **2** *vti* schnelltauchen; **~ helmet** *n* Sturzhelm *m*; **~-land** *vi* eine Bruchlandung machen; **~-landing** *n* Bruchlandung *f*.

**crass** [kræs] *adj (+er) (unsubtle)* kraß.

**crate** [kreɪt] *n (also col: car, plane)* Kiste *f*; *(of bottles)* Kasten *m*.

**crater** ['kreɪtər] *n* Krater *m*.

**cravat(te)** [krə'væt] *n* Halstuch *nt*.

**crave** [kreɪv] *vt (liter: beg)* erbitten; *attention, drink etc* sich sehnen nach.

**craving** ['kreɪvɪŋ] *n* Verlangen *nt*. **to have a ~ for sth** Verlangen nach etw haben.

**crawfish** ['krɔːfɪʃ] *n* Languste *f*.

**crawl** [krɔːl] **1** *n* **(a)** *(on hands and knees)* Kriechen *nt*; *(slow speed)* Kriechtempo *nt*. **to go at/be reduced to a ~** im Schneckentempo vorankommen/fahren müssen. **(b)** *(swimming stroke)* Kraulstil *m*. **to do the ~** kraulen. **2** *vi* **(a)** kriechen; *(baby, insects)* krabbeln. **(b)** *(be infested)* wimmeln *(with* von*)*. **the place is ~ing!** hier wimmelt es von Ungeziefer! **(c)** *(col: suck up)* kriechen *(to* vor *+dat)*.

**crawler lane** ['krɔːlələɪn] *n (Brit Aut)* Kriechspur *f*.

**crayfish** ['kreɪfɪʃ] *n* **(a)** *(freshwater)* Flußkrebs *m*. **(b)** *(saltwater: also* **crawfish***)* Languste *f*.

**crayon** ['kreɪən] *n (pencil)* Buntstift *m*; *(wax ~)* Wachs(mal)stift *m*; *(chalk ~)* Pastellstift *m*.

**craze** [kreɪz] **1** *n (of person)* Fimmel *m (col)*. **it's the latest ~** es ist jetzt in *(col)*. **2** *vt* **(a)** *(make insane)* **to be half ~d with grief** vor Schmerz halb wahnsinnig sein; **he had a ~d look** er sah wie wahnsinnig aus. **(b)** *glazing* rissig machen.

**crazy** ['kreɪzɪ] *adj (+er)* **(a)** verrückt *(with* vor *+dat)*. **to drive sb ~** jdn verrückt machen; **to go ~** verrückt werden. **(b)** *(col: enthusiastic)* verrückt *(col)*. **to be ~ about sb/sth** ganz verrückt auf jdn/etw sein *(col)*. **(c)** *angle, tilt* unwahrscheinlich.

**crazy paving** *n* Mosaikpflaster *nt*.

**CRC** = **(a)** **camera-ready copy.** **(b)** *(US)* **Civil Rights Commission.**

**creak** [kriːk] **1** *n* Knarren *nt no pl*; *(of hinges, bed)* Quietschen *nt no pl*; *(of knees etc)* Knacken *nt no pl*. **2** *vi* knarren; *(hinges, bed)* quietschen; *(knees etc)* knacken.

**cream** [kriːm] **1** *n* **(a)** Sahne *f*; *(~ pudding, artificial ~)* Creme *f*. **~ of tomato/chicken soup** Tomaten-/Hühnercremesuppe *f*. **(b)** *(lotion)* Creme *f*. **(c)** *(colour)* Creme *f*. **(d)** *(fig: best)* **the ~** die Besten; *(of society)* die Elite *f*. **2** *adj (colour)* cremefarben. **3** *vt* **(a)** *(put ~ on)* face etc eincremen. **(b)** *butter etc* cremig rühren; *potatoes* pürieren. **~ed potatoes** Kartoffelpüree *nt*. **(c)** *milk* entrahmen.
►**cream off** *vt sep (lit)* abschöpfen; *(fig)* absahnen.

**cream:** **~ cake** *n* Sahnetorte *f*; **~ cheese** *n* (Doppelrahm)frischkäse *m*.

**creamery** ['kriːmərɪ] *n* Molkerei *f*.

**cream tea** *n (Brit)* Nachmittagstee *m mit kleinen Kuchen, Marmelade und Sahne*.

**creamy** ['kriːmɪ] *adj (+er) (tasting of cream)* sahnig; *(smooth)* cremig.

**crease** [kriːs] **1** *n* Falte *f*. **to put a ~ in a pair of trou-**

**sers** eine Falte in eine Hose bügeln. **2** *vt (deliberately) clothes* Falten/eine Falte machen in *(+acc)*; *paper* falzen; *(unintentionally)* zerknittern. **3** *vi* knittern.

**crease-resistant** ['kriːsrɪzɪstənt] *adj* knitterfrei.

**create** [kriː'eɪt] **1** *vt* **(a)** schaffen; *fashion* kreieren; *the world, man* erschaffen; *fuss* verursachen; *difficulties, impression* machen; *(Comp) file* anlegen. **to ~ a sensation** eine Sensation sein; **to ~ a fuss** Theater machen *(col)*. **(b)** *peer* ernennen. **2** *vi (Brit col)* Theater machen *(col)*.

**creation** [kriː'eɪʃən] *n* **(a)** *no pl see vt* Schaffung *f*; Kreation *f*; Erschaffung *f*; Verursachung *f*; Ernennung *f*. **(b)** *no pl* **the C~** die Schöpfung. **(c)** *(Art)* Werk *nt*; *(Fashion)* Kreation *f*.

**creative** [krɪ'eɪtɪv] *adj* kreativ.

**creativity** [ˌkriːeɪ'tɪvɪtɪ] *n* Kreativität *f*.

**creator** [krɪ'eɪtər] *n* Schöpfer(in *f*) *m*.

**creature** ['kriːtʃər] *n* Geschöpf *nt*. **she's a poor/funny ~** sie ist ein armes/komisches Geschöpf; **~ of habit** Gewohnheitstier *nt*.

**creature comforts** *npl* leibliches Wohl.

**crèche** [kreɪʃ] *n (Brit)* (Kinder)krippe *f*.

**credence** ['kriːdəns] *n no pl* Glaube *m*. **to lend ~ to sth** etw glaubwürdig erscheinen lassen.

**credentials** [krɪ'denʃəlz] *npl (references)* Referenzen *pl*; *(papers of identity)* (Ausweis)papiere *pl*.

**credibility** [ˌkredə'bɪlɪtɪ] *n* Glaubwürdigkeit *f*. **there's a ~ gap** es besteht ein Mangel an Glaubwürdigkeit.

**credible** *adj*, **~bly** *adv* ['kredɪbl, -ɪ] glaubwürdig.

**credit** ['kredɪt] **1** *n* **(a)** *no pl (Fin)* Kredit *m*. **the bank will let me have £5,000 ~** die Bank räumt mir einen Kredit von £5.000 ein; **his ~ is good** er ist kreditwürdig; **to give sb ~** jdm Kredit geben; **to be in ~** Geld auf dem Konto haben. **(b)** *no pl (honour)* Ehre *f*; *(recognition)* Anerkennung *f*; *(Sch, Univ: distinction)* Auszeichnung *f*. **he's a ~ to his family** er macht seiner Familie Ehre; **that's to his ~** das muß man ihm hoch anrechnen; **to take the ~ for sth** das Verdienst für etw in Anspruch nehmen; **I gave you ~ for more sense** ich habe Sie für vernünftiger gehalten. **(c)** *(esp US Univ)* Schein *m*. **(d)** **~s** *pl (Film etc) (opening ~s)* Vorspann *m*; *(closing ~s)* Nachspann *m*.

**2** *vt* **(a)** *(believe)* glauben. **would you ~ it!** ist das denn die Möglichkeit! **(b)** *(attribute)* zuschreiben *(+dat)*. **I ~ed him with more sense** ich habe ihn für vernünftiger gehalten; **it's ~ed with (having) magic powers** ihm werden Zauberkräfte zugeschrieben. **(c)** *(Fin)* gutschreiben. **to ~ a sum to sb's account** jds Konto *(dat)* einen Betrag gutschreiben.

**creditable** ['kredɪtəbl] *adj (praiseworthy)* lobenswert.

**credit:** **~ account** *n* Kreditkonto *nt*; **~ card** *n* Kreditkarte *f*; **~ control** *n* Kreditüberwachung *f*; **~ facilities** *npl* Kreditmöglichkeiten *pl*; **~ limit** Kreditgrenze *f*; **~ note** *n (Brit)* Gutschrift *f*.

**creditor** ['kredɪtər] *n* Gläubiger *m*.

**credit:** **~ side** *n (lit, fig)* Habenseite *f*; **on the ~ side** he's young für ihn spricht, daß er jung ist; **~ squeeze** *n* Kreditbeschränkung *f*; **~ terms** *npl* Kreditbedingungen *pl*; **~-worthy** *adj* kreditwürdig.

**credulity** [krɪ'djuːlɪtɪ] *n no pl* Leichtgläubigkeit *f*.

**credulous** ['kredjuləs] *adj* leichtgläubig.

**creed** [kriːd] *n (Eccl)* Glaubensbekenntnis *nt*.

**creek** [kriːk] *n (esp Brit: inlet)* (kleine) Bucht; *(US: brook)* Bach *m*. **to be up the ~** *(col: be in trouble)* in der Tinte sitzen *(col)*.

**creep** [kriːp] *(vb: pret, ptp* **crept***)* **1** *vi* **(a)** schleichen; *(crawl)* kriechen. **ivy is a ~ing plant** Efeu ist eine Kletterpflanze; **time's ~ing on** die Zeit verrinnt. **(b)** **the story made my flesh ~** bei der Geschichte über-

lief es mich kalt. **2** *n* **(a)** *(col: unpleasant person)* fieser Typ *(col)*. **(b)** **this old house gives me the ~s** *(col)* in dem alten Haus kriege ich das kalte Grausen *(col)*.

▶**creep in** *vi (mistakes, new tone etc)* sich einschleichen *(-to* in *+acc)*.

▶**creep over** *vi +prep obj (pleasant feeling)* überkommen.

▶**creep up** *vi* **(a)** *(person)* sich heranschleichen *(on* an *+acc)*; *(prices)* (in die Höhe) klettern. **(b)** **to ~ ~ on sb** *(time, exam)* langsam auf jdn zukommen; **old age is ~ing ~ on him** er wird langsam alt.

**creeper** ['kriːpər] *n* **(a)** *(plant) (along ground)* Kriechpflanze *f*; *(upwards)* Kletterpflanze *f*. **(b)** **~s** *pl (col: shoes)* Leisetreter *pl (col)*; *(US: baby's suit)* einteiliger Spielanzug.

**creepy** ['kriːpɪ] *adj (+er) (frightening)* unheimlich.

**creepy-crawly** ['kriːpɪ'krɔːlɪ] *(col) n* Krabbeltier *nt (col)*.

**cremate** [krɪ'meɪt] *vt* einäschern.

**cremation** [krɪ'meɪʃən] *n* Einäscherung *f*.

**crematorium** [ˌkremə'tɔːrɪəm], *(esp US)* **crematory** ['kremə,tɔːrɪ] *n* Krematorium *nt*.

**creosote** ['krɪəsəʊt] **1** *n* Kreosot *nt (ein Holzschutzmittel)*. **2** *vt* mit Kreosot streichen.

**crêpe** [kreɪp] *n*: **~ bandage** *n* elastischer Verband; **~ paper** *n* Kreppapier *nt*; **~ rubber 1** *n* Kreppgummi *m*; **2** *adj* Kreppgummi-; **~-soled** [kreɪp'səʊld] *adj* mit Kreppsohle(n).

**crept** [krept] *pret, ptp of* **creep**.

**crescendo** [krɪ'ʃendəʊ] *n (Mus)* Crescendo *nt*; *(fig)* Zunahme *f*.

**crescent** ['kresnt] **1** *n* Halbmond *m*; *(street)* (halbkreisförmige) Straße. **2** *adj* **~-shaped** halbmondförmig; **the ~ moon** die Mondsichel.

**cress** [kres] *n* (Garten)kresse *f*; *(water~)* Brunnenkresse *f*.

**crest** [krest] *n* **(a)** *(of bird)* Haube *f*; *(of cock)* Kamm *m*; *(on hat etc)* Federbusch *m*. **(b)** *(Her)* Helmzierde *f*; *(coat of arms)* Wappen *nt*. **(c)** *(of wave, hill, Anat: of horse etc)* Kamm *m*; *(fig: of excitement, popularity)* Höhepunkt *m*; *(Phys: of oscillation)* Scheitel(punkt) *m*. **he's riding on the ~ of a wave** *(fig)* er schwimmt ganz oben.

**crestfallen** ['krest,fɔːlən] *adj* niedergeschlagen.

**Cretan** ['kriːtən] **1** *adj* kretisch. **2** *n* Kreter(in *f*) *m*.

**Crete** [kriːt] *n* Kreta *nt*.

**cretin** ['kretɪn] *n (Med)* Kretin *m*; *(col)* Schwachkopf *m (col)*.

**crevasse** [krɪ'væs] *n* (Gletscher)spalte *f*.

**crevice** ['krevɪs] *n* Spalte *f*.

**crew**[1] [kruː] **1** *n* **(a)** Mannschaft *(also Sport) f*; *(including officers: of ship also, of plane, tank)* Besatzung *f*. **50 passengers and 20 ~** 50 Passagiere und 20 Mann Besatzung; **the ground ~** *(Aviat)* das Bodenpersonal. **(b)** *(col: gang)* Bande *f*. **they were a motley ~** sie waren ein bunt zusammengewürfelter Haufen *(col)*. **2** *vt yacht* die Mannschaft sein von. **3** *vi* **to ~ for sb** *(Sailing)* bei jdm den Vorschotmann machen.

**crew**[2] *(old) pret of* **crow**.

**crew:** **~-cut** ['kruːkʌt] *n* Bürstenschnitt *m*; **~ neck** *n* runder Halsausschnitt; *(also ~ neck pullover or sweater)* Pullover *m* mit rundem Halsausschnitt.

**crib** [krɪb] **1** *n* **(a)** *(manger, nativity scene)* Krippe *f*; *(US: cot)* Kinderbett *nt*. **~ death** *(US)* Krippentod *m*. **(b)** *(Sch: cheating aid)* Spickzettel *m (col)*. **2** *vti (esp Sch col)* spicken *(col)*.

**crick** [krɪk] **1** *n* **a ~ in one's neck** ein steifer Hals, ein steifes Genick *(col)*. **2** *vt* **to ~ one's neck** einen steifen Hals bekommen.

**cricket¹** ['krɪkɪt] *n (insect)* Grille *f.*
**cricket²** *n (Sport)* Kricket *nt.* **that's not** ~ *(fig col)* das ist nicht fair.
**cricket** *in cpds* Kricket-; ~ **bat** *n* (Kricket)-schlagholz *nt.*
**crime** [kraɪm] *n* Straftat *f; (robbery etc also, fig)* Verbrechen *nt.* **it's a** ~ **to throw away all that good food** es ist eine Sünde, all das gute Essen wegzuwerfen.
**Crimea** [kraɪ'mɪə] *n* **the** ~ die Krim.
**crime:** ~ **prevention** *n* Verbrechensverhütung *f;* ~ **rate** *n* Verbrechensrate *f;* ~ **wave** *n* Welle *f* von Straftaten.
**criminal** ['krɪmɪnl] **1** *n* Straftäter(in *f*) *m; (guilty of capital crimes also, fig)* Verbrecher(in *f*) *m.* **2** *adj* **(a)** kriminell, verbrecherisch. **C~ Investigation Department** Kriminalpolizei *f;* ~ **code** Strafgesetzbuch *nt;* ~ **law** Strafrecht *nt;* ~ **lawyer** Anwalt *m* für Strafsachen; *(specializing in defence)* Strafverteidiger *m;* **to have a** ~ **record** vorbestraft sein. **(b)** *(fig)* kriminell.
**criminology** [ˌkrɪmɪ'nɒlədʒɪ] *n* Kriminologie *f.*
**crimp** [krɪmp] *vt hair* mit der Brennschere wellen.
**crimson** ['krɪmzn] **1** *adj* purpurrot; *sky* blutrot. **to turn** ~ *(person, face)* knallrot *(col)* or dunkelrot anlaufen. **2** *n* Purpurrot *nt.*
**cringe** [krɪndʒ] *vi* **(a)** *(shrink back)* zurückschrecken *(at* vor *+dat); (fig)* schaudern. **to** ~ **before sb** vor jdm zurückschrecken; **he** ~**d at the thought** er *or* ihn schauderte bei dem Gedanken; **his jokes make me** ~ bei seinen Witzen kriege ich zuviel. **(b)** *(fawn)* kriechen *(to* vor *+dat).* **cringing behaviour** kriecherisches Benehmen.
**crinkle** ['krɪŋkl] **1** *n* (Knitter)falte *f.* **2** *vt paper, dress etc* (zer)knittern. **3** *vi (paper, foil, dress etc)* knittern; *(face, skin)* (Lach)fältchen bekommen; *(edges of paper)* sich wellen; *(curl: hair)* sich krausen.
**crinkly** ['krɪŋklɪ] *adj (+er) (col) paper etc* zerknittert; *hair* kraus.
**cripple** ['krɪpl] **1** *n* Krüppel *m.* **2** *vt person* zum Krüppel machen; *legs etc* verkrüppeln; *ship, plane* aktionsunfähig machen; *(fig) industry* lahmlegen. **the ship was** ~**d** das Schiff war nicht mehr aktionsfähig; ~**d with rheumatism** von Rheuma praktisch gelähmt.
**crippling** ['krɪplɪŋ] *adj taxes* erdrückend.
**crisis** ['kraɪsɪs] *n, pl* **crises** ['kraɪsiːz] Krise *f.*
**crisp** [krɪsp] **1** *adj (+er) apple, lettuce* knackig; *bread, biscuits, bacon* knusprig; *snow* verharscht; *leaves* trocken; *appearance* adrett; *style* knapp; *air* frisch. **2** *n (Brit: potato* ~*)* Chip *m usu pl.*
**crispbread** ['krɪspbred] *n* Knäckebrot *nt.*
**criss-cross** ['krɪskrɒs] **1** *adv* kreuz und quer. **2** *adj pattern* Kreuz-. **3** *vi (lines)* sich kreuzen.
**crit** [krɪt] *n (col)* Kritik *f.*
**criterion** [kraɪ'tɪərɪən] *n, pl* **criteria** [kraɪ'tɪərɪə] Kriterium *nt.*
**critic** ['krɪtɪk] *n* Kritiker(in *f*) *m.*
**critical** ['krɪtɪkəl] *adj* kritisch. **to be** ~ **of sb/sth** *(criticize)* jdn/etw kritisieren; *(have* ~ *attitude)* jdm/einer Sache kritisch gegenüberstehen; **that's** ~ *(crucial)* das ist entscheidend.
**critically** ['krɪtɪkəlɪ] *adv* **(a)** kritisch. **(b)** ~ **ill** schwer krank.
**criticism** ['krɪtɪsɪzəm] *n* Kritik *f.*
**criticize** ['krɪtɪsaɪz] *vti* kritisieren.
**critique** [krɪ'tiːk] *n* Kritik *f.*
**croak** [krəʊk] **1** *n (of frog)* Quaken *nt no pl; (of raven, person)* Krächzen *nt no pl.* **2** *vti (frog)* quaken; *(raven, person)* krächzen.
**croaky** ['krəʊkɪ] *adj (+er) (col) voice* heiser.

**Croat** ['krəʊæt] *n (person)* Kroate *m*, Kroatin *f; (language)* Kroatisch *nt.*
**Croatia** [krəʊ'eɪʃɪə] *n* Kroatien *nt.*
**Croatian** [krəʊ'eɪʃɪən] *adj* kroatisch.
**crochet** ['krəʊʃeɪ] **1** *n* Häkelei *f.* ~ **hook** Häkelnadel *f.* **2** *vti* häkeln.
**crock** [krɒk] *n old* ~ *(car)* alte Kiste.
**crockery** ['krɒkərɪ] *n (Brit)* Geschirr *nt.*
**crocodile** ['krɒkədaɪl] *n* **(a)** Krokodil *nt.* ~ **tears** Krokodilstränen. **(b)** *(Brit Sch)* **to walk in a** ~ zwei und zwei hintereinandergehen.
**crocus** ['krəʊkəs] *n* Krokus *m.*
**croft** [krɒft] *n (esp Scot)* kleines Pachtgrundstück; *(house)* Kate *f.*
**crofter** ['krɒftər] *n (esp Scot)* Kleinpächter(in *f*) *m.*
**croissant** ['krwɑːsɒŋ] *n* Hörnchen *nt.*
**crony** ['krəʊnɪ] *n* Freund(in *f*), Spießgeselle *(hum) m.*
**crook** [krʊk] **1** *n* **(a)** *(dishonest person)* Gauner(in *f*) *m (col).* **(b)** *(of shepherd)* Hirtenstab *m; (of bishop)* Bischofsstab *m.* **(c)** *(bend: in road, river)* Biegung *f; (in arm)* Beuge *f.* **2** *vt finger* krümmen; *arm* beugen.
**crooked** ['krʊkɪd] *adj (lit) (bent)* krumm; *smile* schief; *(fig col: dishonest) method* krumm; *person* unehrlich.
**croon** [kruːn] *vti (sing softly)* leise singen; *(sentimentally)* schmalzig singen *(pej col).*
**crooner** ['kruːnər] *n* Schnulzensänger *m (pej col).*
**crop** [krɒp] **1** *n* **(a)** *(produce)* Ernte *f; (species grown)* (Feld)frucht *f; (fig: large number)* Schwung *m.* **a good** ~ **of potatoes** eine gute Kartoffelernte. **(b)** *(of bird)* Kropf *m.* **(c)** *(of whip)* Stock *m; (hunting* ~*)* Reitpeitsche *f.* **(d)** *(hairstyle)* Kurzhaarschnitt *m.* **2** *vt hair* stutzen.
▶**crop up** *vi* aufkommen. **something's** ~**ped** ~ es ist etwas dazwischengekommen.
**cropper** ['krɒpər] *n (col)* **to come a** ~ *(lit: fall)* hinfliegen *(col); (fig: fail)* auf die Nase fallen.
**crop spraying** *n* Schädlingsbekämpfung *f (durch Besprühen).*
**croquet** ['krəʊkeɪ] *n* Krocket(spiel) *nt.*
**croquette** [krəʊ'ket] *n* Krokette *f.*
**cross¹** [krɒs] **1** *n* **(a)** Kreuz *nt.* **we all have our** ~ **to bear** wir haben alle unser Kreuz zu tragen. **(b)** *(bias)* **on the** ~ schräg. **(c)** *(hybrid)* Kreuzung *f; (fig)* Mittelding *nt.*
**2** *attr (transverse) street etc* Quer-.
**3** *vt* **(a)** *road, river, Channel* überqueren; *(on foot)* überschreiten; *country, desert* durchqueren. **to** ~ **the road** über die Straße gehen; **to** ~ **sb's path** *(fig)* jdm über den Weg laufen; **it** ~**ed my mind that ...** es fiel mir ein, daß ...; **we'll** ~ **that bridge when we come to it** lassen wir das Problem erst mal auf uns zukommen. **(b)** *(intersect)* kreuzen. **to** ~ **one's legs** die Beine übereinanderschlagen; **the lines are** ~**ed** *(Telec)* die Leitungen überschneiden sich; **I'm keeping my fingers** ~**ed for you** *(col)* ich drücke dir die Daumen *(col).* **(c)** **to** ~ **oneself** sich bekreuzigen; **my/your heart** *(col)* Ehrenwort. **(d)** *(mark with a* ~*)* ankreuzen. ~**ed cheque** Verrechnungsscheck *m.* **(e)** *(go against) plans* durchkreuzen. **to** ~ **sb** jdn verärgern. **(f)** *animal, fruit* kreuzen.
**4** *vi* **(a)** *(across road)* hinübergehen; *(across Channel etc)* überfahren. **(b)** *(lines, letters)* sich kreuzen. **our paths have** ~**ed several times** *(fig)* unsere Wege haben sich öfters gekreuzt.
▶**cross off** *vt sep* streichen *(prep obj* aus, von*).*
▶**cross out** *vt sep* ausstreichen.
▶**cross over 1** *vi* die Straße überqueren. **2** *vi + prep obj road, street* überqueren.
**cross²** *adj (+er)* böse. **to be** ~ **with sb** mit jdm *or* auf jdn böse sein.

**cross:** ~**bar** *n (of bicycle)* Stange *f*; *(Sport)* Querlatte *f*; ~**-bencher** ['krɒsbentʃəʳ] *n (Parl) Abgeordnete(r)*, *der/die weder der Regierungs- noch der Oppositionspartei angehört*; ~**bow** *n* Armbrust *f*; ~**breed** *(Zool, Biol)* **1** *n* Kreuzung *f*; **2** *vt* kreuzen; ~**-Channel ferry** *n* Kanalfähre *f*; ~**-check 1** *n* Gegenprobe *f*; **2** *vt facts, figures* überprüfen; ~**-country 1** *adj* Querfeldein-; *vehicle* gelandegängig; **2** *adv* querfeldein; **3** *n (also* ~**-country race)** Querfeldeinrennen *nt*; ~**-country skiing** Langlauf *m*; ~**-examination** *n* Kreuzverhör *nt (of* über +*acc)*; ~**-examine** *vt* ins Kreuzverhör nehmen; ~**-eyed** *adj* schielend; ~**-fertilization** *n, no pl (Bot)* Fremdbestäubung *f*; *(fig)* gegenseitige Befruchtung; ~**fire** *n* Kreuzfeuer *nt*; **to be caught in the** ~**fire** *(lit, fig)* ins Kreuzfeuer geraten.

**crossing** ['krɒsɪŋ] *n* **(a)** *(act)* Überquerung *f*; *(sea* ~*)* Überfahrt *f*. **(b)** *(*~ *place)* Übergang *m*; *(crossroads)* Kreuzung *f*. ~ **guard** *(US)* ≃ Schülerlotse *m*.

**cross-legged** [ˌkrɒs'legɪd] *adj, adv* mit gekreuzten Beinen; *(on ground)* im Schneidersitz.

**crossly** ['krɒslɪ] *adv* böse, verärgert.

**cross:** ~**patch** *n (col)* Brummbär *m (col)*; ~**purposes** *npl* **to be at** ~**-purposes** aneinander vorbeireden; ~**-reference** *n* Querverweis *m (to auf* +*acc)*; ~**roads** *n sing or pl (lit)* Kreuzung *f*; *(fig)* Scheideweg *m*; ~ **section** *n* Querschnitt *m (of durch)*; ~**walk** *n (US)* Fußgängerüberweg *m*; ~**wind** *n* Seitenwind *m*; ~**word (puzzle)** *n* Kreuzworträtsel *nt*.

**crotch** [krɒtʃ] *n* **(a)** *(in tree etc)* Gabelung *f*. **(b)** *(of trousers)* Schritt *m*; *(Anat)* Damm(gegend *f) m*.

**crotchet** ['krɒtʃɪt] *n (Mus)* Viertelnote *f*.

**crotchety** ['krɒtʃətɪ] *adj (col)* miesepetrig *(col)*.

**crouch** [kraʊtʃ] *vi* sich zusammenkauern. **to** ~ **down** sich niederkauern.

**croupier** ['kruːpɪeɪ] *n* Croupier *m*.

**crouton** ['kruːtɒn] *n* Crouton *m*.

**crow**[1] [krəʊ] *n (Orn)* Krähe *f*. **as the** ~ **flies** (in der) Luftlinie.

**crow**[2] **1** *n (of cock, baby)* Krähen *nt*. **2** *vi* **(a)** *pret* ~**ed** *or (old)* **crew,** *ptp* ~**ed** *(cock)* krähen. **(b)** *pret, ptp* ~**ed** *(baby)* krähen; *(boast)* sich brüsten *(about mit)*.

**crowbar** ['krəʊbaːʳ] *n* Brecheisen *nt*.

**crowd** [kraʊd] **1** *n* **(a)** Menschenmenge *f*; *(Sport, Theat)* Zuschauermenge *f*. ~**s of people** Menschenmassen *pl*; ~ **scene** *(Theat)* Massenszene *f*. **(b)** *(set)* Clique *f*. **the university** ~ die Leute von der Uni; **they're a nice** ~ sie sind alle sehr nett. **(c)** *no pl (the masses)* **the** ~ die (breite) Masse; **to go with** *or* **follow the** ~ mit der Herde laufen. **2** *vi* (sich) drängen. **to** ~ **together/in** sich zusammendrängen/(sich) hereindrängen; **to** ~ **around sb/sth** (sich) um jdn/etw scharen. **3** *vt* **to** ~ **the streets** die Straßen bevölkern.

►**crowd out** *vt sep (not let in)* wegdrängen. **the pub was** ~**ed** ~ das Lokal war gerammelt voll *(col)*.

**crowded** ['kraʊdɪd] *adj train etc* überfüllt.

**crowd puller** ['kraʊd,pʊləʳ] *n* Publikumsmagnet *m*.

**crown** [kraʊn] **1** *n* **(a)** Krone *f*. **the C**~ die Krone. **(b)** *(of head)* Wirbel *m*; *(of hat)* Kopf *m*; *(of road)* Wölbung *f*; *(of tooth)* Krone *f*. **2** *vt* **(a)** *(lit, fig)* krönen. **he was** ~**ed king** er ist zum König gekrönt worden; ~**ed head** gekröntes Haupt; **to be** ~**ed with success** von Erfolg gekrönt sein; **to** ~ **it all it began to snow** *(col)* zur Krönung des Ganzen begann es zu schneien. **(b)** *(in draughts etc)* eine Dame bekommen mit. **(c)** *tooth* überkronen. **(d)** *(col: hit)* **I'll** ~ **you!** ich hau dir gleich eine runter! *(col)*.

**crown:** ~ **cap** *n* Kronkorken *m*; ~ **court** *n (Brit) Bezirksgericht nt für Strafsachen.*

**crowning** ['kraʊnɪŋ] **1** *n* Krönung *f*. **2** *adj achievement* krönend.

**crown:** ~ **jewels** *npl* Kronjuwelen *pl*; ~ **prince** *n* Kronprinz *m*; ~ **princess** *n* Kronprinzessin *f*; ~ **witness** *n (Brit)* Zeuge *m*/Zeugin *f* der Anklage.

**crow's nest** *n (Naut)* Mastkorb *m*; *(on foremast)* Krähennest *nt*.

**crucial** ['kruːʃəl] *adj* **(a)** *(decisive)* entscheidend *(to für)*. **(b)** *(col: very important)* sehr wichtig.

**crucible** ['kruːsɪbl] *n* (Schmelz)tiegel *m*.

**crucifix** ['kruːsɪfɪks] *n* Kruzifix *nt*.

**crucifixion** [ˌkruːsɪ'fɪkʃən] *n* Kreuzigung *f*.

**crucify** ['kruːsɪfaɪ] *vt* **(a)** kreuzigen. **(b)** *(fig) play, author* verreißen; *person* in der Luft zerreißen *(col)*. **(c)** *(mortify) the flesh* abtöten.

**crude** [kruːd] *adj (+er)* **(a)** *(unprocessed)* Roh-. ~ **oil** Rohöl *nt*. **(b)** *expression etc* ordinär. **(c)** *implement* primitiv; *manners* ungehobelt, grob.

**crudely** ['kruːdlɪ] *adv* primitiv; *draw* grob; *behave* ungehobelt.

**crudeness** ['kruːdnɪs], **crudity** ['kruːdɪtɪ] *n* **(a)** *(vulgarity)* Derbheit *f*. **(b)** *see adj (c)* Primitivität *f*; Ungehobeltheit(s) *nt (of gen, in* +*dat)*.

**cruel** ['krʊəl] *adj* grausam *(to zu)*. **that is** ~ **to animals** das ist Tierquälerei.

**cruelly** ['krʊəlɪ] *adv (+vb)* grausam; *(+adj)* auf grausame Art.

**cruelty** ['krʊəltɪ] *n* Grausamkeit *f (to gegenüber)*. ~ **to children** Kindesmißhandlung *f*; ~ **to animals** Tierquälerei *f*; **physical/mental** ~ Grausamkeit *f*/ seelische Grausamkeit.

**cruet** ['kruːɪt] *n (set)* Gewürzständer *m*; *(for oil)* Krug *m*.

**cruise** [kruːz] **1** *vi* eine Kreuzfahrt/Kreuzfahrten machen; *(ship)* kreuzen; *(car)* Dauergeschwindigkeit fahren. **cruising speed** *(Aut)* Reisegeschwindigkeit *f*. **2** *n* Kreuzfahrt *f*. **to go on/for a** ~ eine Kreuzfahrt machen.

**cruise missile** *n* Cruise-Missile *nt*, Marschflugkörper *m*.

**cruiser** ['kruːzəʳ] *n (Naut)* Kreuzer *m*; *(pleasure* ~*)* Vergnügungsjacht *f*.

**crumb** [krʌm] **1** *n* **(a)** *(of bread etc)* Krümel *m*; *(inside of loaf)* Krume *f*. **a few** ~**s of information** ein paar Informationsbrocken; **that's one** ~ **of comfort** das ist (wenigstens) ein winziger Trost. **(b)** *(col: fool)* Depp *m (col)*. **2** *interj* ~**s!** *(col)* Mensch! *(col)*.

**crumble** ['krʌmbl] **1** *vt* zerkrümeln. **2** *vi (brick)* bröckeln; *(bread etc)* krümeln; *(also* ~ **away)** *(earth, building)* zerbröckeln; *(opposition)* sich auflösen. **3** *n (Cook)* Obst *nt* mit Streusel; *(topping)* Streusel *pl*.

**crumbly** ['krʌmblɪ] *adj (+er) stone* bröckelig; *cake, bread* krümelig, bröselig.

**crummy** ['krʌmɪ] *adj (+er) (col)* mies *(col)*.

**crumpet** ['krʌmpɪt] *n* **(a)** *(Cook) kleiner dicker Pfannkuchen.* **(b)** *(esp Brit col: women)* Miezen *pl (col)*.

**crumple** ['krʌmpl] **1** *vt (also* ~ **up)** *paper, dress* zerknittern; *(screw up)* zusammenknüllen; *metal* eindrücken. **2** *vi (lit, fig: collapse)* zusammenbrechen.

**crumple zone** *n (Aut)* Knautschzone *f*.

**crunch** [krʌntʃ] **1** *vt apple, biscuit etc* mampfen *(col)*. **2** *vi (gravel, snow etc)* knirschen; *(gears)* krachen. **3** *n (sound)* Krachen *nt*; *(of footsteps, gravel etc)* Knirschen *nt*. **when it comes to the** ~ wenn es darauf ankommt.

**crunchy** ['krʌntʃɪ] *adj (+er) apple* knackig; *biscuit* knusprig; *snow* verharscht.

**crusade** [kruː'seɪd] *n (Hist, fig)* Kreuzzug *m*.

**crusader** [kruːˈseɪdəʳ] n (Hist) Kreuzritter m.

**crush** [krʌʃ] 1 n (a) (crowd) Gedränge nt. ~ **barrier** Absperrung f. (b) (col) **to have a ~ on sb** für jdn schwärmen. 2 vt (a) (squeeze) quetschen; fruit etc zerdrücken; (kill) zu Tode quetschen; spices, garlic (zer)stoßen; stone zerkleinern; scrap metal zusammenpressen; (crease) zerknittern; (screw up) zerknüllen. (b) (fig) hopes, sb vernichten; people unterdrücken. 3 vi (clothes) knittern.

**crushing** [ˈkrʌʃɪŋ] adj defeat, reply vernichtend.

**crust** [krʌst] n (all senses) Kruste f. **the earth's** ~ die Erdkruste.

**crustacean** [krʌsˈteɪʃən] n Schalentier nt.

**crusty** [ˈkrʌstɪ] adj (+er) knusprig; (fig: irritable) barsch.

**crutch** [krʌtʃ] (a) n (for walking) Krücke f. (b) = **crotch** (b).

**crux** [krʌks] n (of problem) Kern m. **the ~ of the matter** der springende Punkt.

**cry** [kraɪ] 1 n (a) Schrei m; (call) Ruf m. **to utter a ~** einen Schrei ausstoßen; **a ~ of pain** ein Schmerzensschrei m; **a ~ for help** ein Hilferuf m. (b) (slogan) Parole f. (c) (weep) **a ~ will do you good** weine ruhig, das wird dir guttun. 2 vi (a) (weep) weinen; (baby) schreien. **she was ~ing for her mother** sie weinte nach ihrer Mutter. (b) (call) rufen; (louder, animal, bird) schreien. **to ~ for help** um Hilfe rufen/schreien. 3 vt (a) (shout out) rufen; (louder) schreien. (b) bitter tears etc weinen. **to ~ one's heart out** herzzerreißend weinen. **to ~ oneself to sleep** sich in den Schlaf weinen.

►**cry off** vi einen Rückzieher machen.

►**cry out** vi (a) aufschreien. **to ~ ~ to sb** jdm etwas zuschreien. (b) (fig) **this door is ~ing ~ for a coat of paint** diese Tür schreit danach, gestrichen zu werden.

**crying** [ˈkraɪɪŋ] 1 adj (fig) injustice schreiend; need dringend. **it is a ~ shame** es ist ein Jammer. 2 n (weeping) Weinen nt.

**crypt** [krɪpt] n Krypta f; (burial ~) Gruft f.

**cryptic** [ˈkrɪptɪk] adj remark hintergründig; riddle verschlüsselt.

**crystal** [ˈkrɪstl] 1 n (a) (Chem, Rad) Kristall m. (b) (on watch) (Uhr)glas nt. (c) (also ~ glass) Kristall nt. 2 adj (a) (crystalline) kristallin; (~-glass) Kristall-; (quartz) Quarzkristall-. (b) (fig) waters, lake kristallklar.

**crystal:** ~ **ball** n Glaskugel f; ~-**clear** adj (lit, fig) glasklar; ~-**gazing** n Hellseherei f.

**crystallization** [ˌkrɪstəlaɪˈzeɪʃən] n Kristallisierung f.

**crystallize** [ˈkrɪstəlaɪz] 1 vt (lit) zum Kristallisieren bringen; (fig) feste Form geben (+dat). 2 vi (lit) kristallisieren; (fig) feste Form annehmen.

**crystallized** [ˈkrɪstəlaɪzd] adj fruit kandiert.

**c/s** = **cycles per second** Hz.

**CSE** (Brit old) = **Certificate of Secondary Education** ≃ Hauptschulabschluß m.

**CS gas** n (Brit) ≃ Tränengas nt.

**CST** (US) = **Central Standard Time** mittelamerikanische Zeit.

**ct** = (a) **cent** ct. (b) **carat** Kt.

**CT** (US) = **Connecticut.**

**cub** [kʌb] n (a) (of animal) Junge(s) nt. (b) (also ~ scout) Wölfling m.

**Cuba** [ˈkjuːbə] n Kuba nt.

**Cuban** [ˈkjuːbən] 1 adj kubanisch. 2 n Kubaner(in f) m.

**cubby-hole** [ˈkʌbɪhəʊl] n (a) (compartment) Fach nt. (b) (room) Kabäuschen nt (col).

**cube** [kjuːb] n (a) (shape, object) Würfel m. ~ **sugar** Würfelzucker m. (b) (Math) dritte Potenz. ~ **root** Kubikwurzel f.

**cubic** [ˈkjuːbɪk] adj (a) (of volume) Kubik-. ~ **capacity** Fassungsvermögen nt; (of engine) Hubraum m. (b) (Math) kubisch. ~ **equation** Gleichung f dritten Grades.

**cubicle** [ˈkjuːbɪkəl] n Kabine f.

**cubism** [ˈkjuːbɪzəm] n Kubismus m.

**cuckoo** [ˈkʊkuː] 1 n Kuckuck m. 2 adj pred (col) meschugge (col). ~ **clock** Kuckucksuhr f.

**cucumber** [ˈkjuːkʌmbəʳ] n (Salat)gurke f. **as cool as a ~** seelenruhig.

**cud** [kʌd] n **to chew the ~** (lit) wiederkäuen; (fig) vor sich hingrübeln.

**cuddle** [ˈkʌdl] 1 n Liebkosung f. **to give sb a ~** jdn in den Arm nehmen; **to have a ~** schmusen. 2 vt in den Arm nehmen.

►**cuddle down** vi sich kuscheln.

►**cuddle up** vi sich kuscheln (to, against an +acc).

**cuddly** [ˈkʌdlɪ] adj (+er) (wanting a cuddle) anschmiegsam; (good to cuddle) doll zum Liebhaben, knuddelig (col). ~ **toy** Schmusetier nt (col).

**cudgel** [ˈkʌdʒəl] 1 n Knüppel m. **to take up the ~s for sb/sth** (fig) für jdn/etw eine Lanze brechen. 2 vt prügeln. **to ~ one's brains** (fig) sich (dat) das (Ge)hirn zermartern.

**cue** [kjuː] n (a) (Theat, fig) Stichwort nt; (action) (Einsatz)zeichen nt; (Mus) Einsatz m. **to take one's ~ from sb** sich nach jdm richten; **right on ~** (Theat) genau aufs Stichwort; (fig) wie gerufen. (b) (Billiards) Queue nt.

►**cue in** vt sep den Einsatz geben (+dat); (TV, Film) scene abfahren lassen; tape etc (rechtzeitig) einspielen.

**cuff¹** [kʌf] n (a) Manschette f. **off the ~** (fig) aus dem Stegreif; remark aus dem Handgelenk. (b) (US: of trousers) (Hosen)aufschlag m.

**cuff²** vt (strike) einen Klaps geben (+dat).

**cuff-link** [ˈkʌflɪŋk] n Manschettenknopf m.

**cuisine** [kwɪˈziːn] n Küche f.

**cul-de-sac** [ˈkʌldəsæk] n (esp Brit) Sackgasse f.

**culinary** [ˈkʌlɪnərɪ] adj kulinarisch; skill etc Koch-.

**cull** [kʌl] 1 n (a) (selection) Auswahl f. (b) (killing of surplus) ~ **of seals** Robbenschlag m. 2 vt (a) (pick) flowers pflücken. (b) (collect) entnehmen (from dat). (c) (kill as surplus) **to ~ seals** Robbenschlag m betreiben.

**culminate** [ˈkʌlmɪneɪt] vi gipfeln (in in +dat).

**culmination** [ˌkʌlmɪˈneɪʃən] n Höhepunkt m; (end) Ende nt.

**culottes** [kjuːˈlɒts] npl Hosenrock m. **a pair of ~** ein Hosenrock.

**culpable** [ˈkʌlpəbl] adj (form) schuldig. ~ **homicide** (Jur) fahrlässige Tötung; ~ **negligence** grobe Fahrlässigkeit.

**culprit** [ˈkʌlprɪt] n Schuldige(r) mf; (Jur) Täter(in f) m.

**cult** [kʌlt] n (Rel, fig) Kult m. **to make a ~ of sth** (einen) Kult mit etw treiben.

**cultivate** [ˈkʌltɪveɪt] vt (a) soil bebauen; crop anbauen. (b) (fig) friendship, links etc pflegen; skill, taste entwickeln.

**cultivation** [ˌkʌltɪˈveɪʃən] n see vt (a) Bebauung f; Anbau m. (b) Pflege f (of von); Entwicklung f.

**cultural** [ˈkʌltʃərəl] adj Kultur-; differences, events kulturell. ~ **centre** Kulturzentrum nt.

**culture** [ˈkʌltʃəʳ] n (a) Kultur f. ~ **shock** Kulturschock m. (b) (Agr, Biol, Med) Kultur f; (of animals) Zucht f.

**cultured** [ˈkʌltʃəd] adj kultiviert; (Agr) Kultur-; (Biol, Med) gezüchtet. ~ **pearl** Zuchtperle f.

**cumbersome** [ˈkʌmbəsəm] adj clothing hinderlich;

*vehicle* schwer zu manövrieren; *suitcases, parcels* sperrig; *procedure* beschwerlich.

**cumin** ['kʌmɪn] *n* Kreuzkümmel *m.*

**cumulative** ['kjuːmjʊlətɪv] *adj* kumulativ. ~ **effect** Gesamtwirkung *f;* **the** ~ **debts of ten years** die Schulden, die sich im Laufe von zehn Jahren angehäuft haben/hatten.

**cunning** ['kʌnɪŋ] **1** *n (cleverness)* Schlauheit *f.* **2** *adj* schlau; *person also* gerissen; *expression* verschmitzt; *gadget* raffiniert.

**cup** [kʌp] **1** *n* **(a)** Tasse *f; (goblet)* Pokal *m; (mug)* Becher *m.* **a** ~ **of tea** eine Tasse Tee; **that's just/ that's not my** ~ **of tea** *(fig col)* das ist genau/ist nicht mein Fall *(col).* **(b)** *(prize, football* ~ *etc)* Pokal *m.* **(c)** *(of bra)* Körbchen *nt.* **2** *vt hands* hohl machen. ~**ped hand** hohle Hand; **he** ~**ped his chin in his hand** er stützte das Kinn in die Hand; **to** ~ **one's hands around sth** etw mit der hohlen Hand umfassen.

**cupboard** ['kʌbəd] *n* Schrank *m.* ~ **love** fauler Schmus *(col).*

**cup: C**~ **Final** *n* Pokalendspiel *nt;* ~**ful** *n, pl* ~**sful** *or* ~**fuls** Tasse *f;* ~ **size** *n (of bra)* Körbchengröße *f;* ~ **tie** *n* Pokalspiel *nt;* **C**~**-Winners** *npl* Pokalsieger *m.*

**cupola** ['kjuːpələ] *n* Kuppel *f.*

**curable** ['kjʊərəbl] *adj* heilbar.

**curate** ['kjʊərɪt] *n (Catholic)* Kaplan *m; (Protestant)* Vikar *m.*

**curator** [kjʊə'reɪtəʳ] *n (of museum etc)* Kustos *m.*

**curb** [kɜːb] **1** *n* **(a)** *(of harness) (bit)* Kandare *f; (chain)* Kinnkette *f.* **(b)** *(fig)* Behinderung *f; (deliberate)* Beschränkung *f.* **(c)** *(esp US)* = **kerb. 2** *vt horse, (fig)* zügeln; *immigration etc* beschränken.

**curd** [kɜːd] *n (often pl)* Quark *m.* ~ **cheese** Quark *m.*

**curdle** ['kɜːdl] **1** *vt (lit, fig)* gerinnen lassen. **2** *vi* gerinnen. **his blood** ~**d** das Blut gerann ihm in den Adern.

**cure** [kjʊəʳ] **1** *vt* **(a)** *(Med) illness, person* heilen. **to be/get** ~**d (of sth)** *(von etw)* geheilt sein/werden; **to** ~ **sb (of sth)** jdn *(von etw)* heilen. **(b)** *(fig) inflation, ill etc* abhelfen *(+dat).* **to** ~ **sb of sth** jdn von etw kurieren. **(c)** *food* haltbar machen; *(salt)* pökeln; *(smoke)* räuchern; *skins, tobacco* trocknen. **2** *n (Med) (remedy)* (Heil)mittel *nt (for gegen); (treatment)* Heilverfahren *nt (for sb* für jdn, *for sth* gegen etw); *(recovery)* Heilung *f; (health* ~*)* Kur *f; (fig: remedy)* Mittel *nt (for gegen).* **to take** *or* **follow a** ~ zur *or* in Kur gehen.

**cure-all** ['kjʊərɔːl] *n (lit, fig)* Allheilmittel *nt.*

**curettage** ['kjʊəretɪdʒ] *n (Med)* Ausschabung *f.*

**curfew** ['kɜːfjuː] *n* Ausgangssperre *f.*

**curio** ['kjʊərɪəʊ] *n* Kuriosität *f.*

**curiosity** [,kjʊərɪ'ɒsɪtɪ] *n* **(a)** *no pl (inquisitiveness)* Neugier *f.* ~ **killed the cat** *(Prov)* sei nicht so neugierig. **(b)** *(object, person)* Kuriosität *f.*

**curious** ['kjʊərɪəs] *adj* **(a)** *(inquisitive)* neugierig. **I'm** ~ **to know what he'll do** ich bin mal gespannt, was er macht; **I'd be** ~ **to know ...** ich wüßte gern, ... **(b)** *(odd)* sonderbar.

**curiously** ['kjʊərɪəslɪ] *adv* **(a)** neugierig. **(b)** *behave, speak etc* eigenartig. ~ **enough** merkwürdigerweise.

**curl** [kɜːl] **1** *n (of hair)* Locke *f.* **a** ~ **of smoke** ein Rauchkringel *m.* **2** *vt hair* locken; *(with curlers)* in Locken legen; *lips* kräuseln. **3** *vi (hair)* sich locken; *(tightly)* sich kräuseln; *(naturally)* lockig sein. **his lips** ~**ed** er kräuselte die Lippen.

▶**curl up** *vi (animal)* sich zusammenrollen; *(person)* sich zusammenkuscheln; *(leaf)* sich einrollen. **to** ~ ~ **in an armchair** sich in einen Sessel kuscheln; **to** ~

~ **with a good book** es sich *(dat)* mit einem guten Buch gemütlich machen.

**curler** ['kɜːləʳ] *n (hair* ~*)* Lockenwickler *m.* **to put one's** ~**s in** sich *(dat)* die Haare eindrehen.

**curlew** ['kɜːljuː] *n* Brachvogel *m.*

**curling** ['kɜːlɪŋ] *n (Sport)* Curling, Eisschießen *nt.*

**curling-irons** ['kɜːlɪŋ,aɪənz] *or* **curling-tongs** ['kɜːlɪŋ,tɒŋz] *npl* Lockenschere *f; (electric)* Lockenstab *m.*

**curly** ['kɜːlɪ] *adj (+er) hair* lockig; *(tighter)* kraus. ~ **tail** Ringelschwanz *m.*

**currant** ['kʌrənt] *n* **(a)** *(dried fruit)* Korinthe *f.* ~ **bun** Rosinenbrötchen *nt.* **(b)** *(Bot)* Johannisbeere *f.*

**currency** ['kʌrənsɪ] *n* **(a)** *(Fin)* Währung *f.* **foreign** ~ Devisen *pl.* **(b)** *(of ideas etc)* Verbreitung *f; (of expression)* Gebräuchlichkeit *f.* **to be in** ~ in Umlauf sein.

**currency:** ~ **market** *n* Devisenmarkt *m;* ~ **speculator** *n* Währungsspekulant(in *f*) *m.*

**current** ['kʌrənt] **1** *adj (present)* gegenwärtig; *edition* letzte(r, s); *opinion* verbreitet. **to be no longer** ~ nicht mehr aktuell sein; *(coins)* nicht mehr in Umlauf sein; **in** ~ **use** allgemein gebräuchlich. **2** *n* **(a)** *(Elec)* Strom *m; (of water also)* Strömung *f; (of air)* Luftströmung *f.* **(b)** *(fig: of events, opinions etc)* Tendenz *f.* **to go against the** ~ **of popular opinion** gegen den Strom der öffentlichen Meinung anschwimmen.

**current:** ~ **account** *n (Brit)* Girokonto *nt;* ~ **affairs** aktuelle Fragen *pl;* ~ **assets** *npl* Umlaufvermögen *nt.*

**currently** ['kʌrəntlɪ] *adv* zur Zeit.

**curriculum** [kə'rɪkjʊləm] *n, pl* **curricula** Lehrplan *m.* ~ **vitae** Lebenslauf *m.*

**curry**[1] ['kʌrɪ] *(Cook) n* Curry *m or nt.* ~**-powder** Currypulver *nt.*

**curry**[2] *vt horse* striegeln. **to** ~ **favour** *(Brit) or* **favor** *(US)* **(with sb)** sich (bei jdm) einschmeicheln.

**curse** [kɜːs] **1** *n (lit, fig)* Fluch *m.* **to put sb under a** ~ jdn mit einem Fluch belegen; ~**s!** *(col)* verflucht! *(col);* **it's the** ~ **of my life** damit bin ich gestraft; **the** ~ *(col: menstruation)* die Tage *pl (col);* **she has the** ~ sie hat ihre Tage *(col).* **2** *vt* **(a)** *(to put a curse on)* verfluchen. ~ **you/it!** *(col)* verflucht! *(col);* ~ **these trains!** *(col)* diese verfluchten Züge! *(col).* **(b)** *(swear at or about)* fluchen über *(+acc).* **(c)** *(fig: to afflict)* **to be** ~**d with sb/sth** mit jdm/etw gestraft sein. **3** *vi* fluchen.

**cursor** ['kɜːsəʳ] *n (Comp)* Cursor *m.*

**cursory** ['kɜːsərɪ] *adj glance* flüchtig.

**curt** [kɜːt] *adj (+er) person* kurz angebunden; *nod, refusal* kurz.

**curtail** [kɜː'teɪl] *vt* kürzen.

**curtain** ['kɜːtn] *n* Vorhang *m (also Theat).* **to draw the** ~**s** *(open)* den Vorhang/die Vorhänge aufziehen; *(close)* den Vorhang/die Vorhänge zuziehen; **the** ~ **rises/falls** der Vorhang hebt sich/fällt; **if you get caught up** ~**s for you** *(col)* wenn sie dich erwischen, bist du weg vom Fenster *(col).*

▶**curtain off** *vt sep* durch einen Vorhang abtrennen.

**curtain:** ~**-call** *n (Theat)* Vorhang *m;* **to get/take a** ~**-call** einen Vorhang bekommen/vor den Vorhang treten; ~ **hook** *n* Gardinengleithaken *m;* ~ **rail** *n* Vorhangschiene *f;* ~**-raiser** *n (Theat)* kurzes Vorspiel; ~ **ring** *n* Gardinenring *m;* ~ **rod** *n* Gardinenstange *f.*

**curts(e)y** ['kɜːtsɪ] *n* Knicks *m; (to royalty)* Hofknicks *m.* **to drop a** ~ einen Knicks machen.

**curvaceous** [kɜː'veɪʃəs] *adj figure, woman* kurvenreich.

**curvature** ['kɜːvətʃəʳ] n Krümmung f; (misshapen) Verkrümmung f. ~ **of the spine** (normal) Rückgratkrümmung f; (abnormal) Rückgratverkrümmung f.

**curve** [kɜːv] **1** n Kurve f; (of body, vase etc) Rundung f; (of river) Biegung f; (of archway) Bogen m. **there's a ~ in the road** die Straße macht einen Bogen. **2** vt biegen; arch, roof wölben. **3** vi **(a)** (road) einen Bogen machen; (river) eine Biegung machen. **the road ~s around the city** die Straße macht einen Bogen um die Stadt. **(b)** (be curved) (arch) sich wölben; (hips, breasts) sich runden; (metal strip etc) sich biegen.

**curved** [kɜːvd] adj line gebogen; arch gewölbt; hips rund.

**cushion** ['kʊʃən] **1** n Kissen nt; (pad, fig: buffer) Polster nt; (Billiards) Bande f. **2** vt fall, blow auffangen. **to ~ sb against sth** jdn gegen etw abschirmen.

**cushy** ['kʊʃɪ] adj (+er) (col) bequem. **to be onto/have a ~ number** eine ruhige Kugel schieben (col).

**cuss** [kʌs] n **(a)** (person) Kauz m (col). **(b)** (oath) Fluch m.

**cussed** ['kʌsɪd] adj (col) stur.

**cussedness** ['kʌsɪdnɪs] n (col) Sturheit f.

**custard** ['kʌstəd] n (pouring ~) ≃ Vanillesoße f; (set) ≃ Vanillepudding m.

**custard:** ~ **cream (biscuit)** n Doppelkeks m (mit Vanillecremefüllung); ~ **powder** n ≃ Vanillepuddingpulver nt; **~-tart** n ≃ Puddingteilchen nt.

**custodian** [kʌs'təʊdɪən] n (of park, museum) Aufseher m; (of treasure) Hüter m.

**custody** ['kʌstədɪ] n **(a)** (keeping, guardianship) Obhut f; (Jur: of children) Vormundschaft f (of für, über +acc). **to place sth in sb's ~** etw jdm zur Aufbewahrung anvertrauen; **the money is in safe ~** das Geld ist gut aufgehoben; **the mother was awarded ~ of the children** die Kinder wurden der Mutter zugesprochen. **(b)** (police) Haft f. **to take sb into ~** jdn verhaften.

**custom** ['kʌstəm] n **(a)** (convention) Sitte f, Brauch m; (habit) (An)gewohnheit f. **as was his ~** wie er es gewohnt war. **(b)** no pl (Comm) Kundschaft f. **to get sb's ~** jdn als Kunden gewinnen. **(c)** ~s pl Zoll m; **(the) C~s** der Zoll; **C~s and Excise** (Brit) die Zollbehörde; **to go through ~s** durch den Zoll gehen.

**customary** ['kʌstəmərɪ] adj (conventional) üblich; (habitual) gewohnt. **it's ~ to wear a tie** man trägt gewöhnlich eine Krawatte.

**custom-built** ['kʌstəmbɪlt] adj spezialgefertigt.

**customer** ['kʌstəməʳ] n **(a)** (Comm: patron) Kunde m, Kundin f. **our ~s** unsere Kundschaft; ~ **service** Kundendienst m. **(b)** (col: person) Kunde m (col).

**customize** ['kʌstəmaɪz] vt individuell aufmachen.

**custom-made** ['kʌstəmmeɪd] adj maßgefertigt; clothes maßgeschneidert; furniture, car spezialgefertigt.

**customs:** ~ **barrier** n Zollschranke f; ~ **clearance** n Zollabfertigung f; ~ **declaration** n Zollerklärung f; ~ **documents** npl Zollpapiere pl; ~ **duty** n Zoll(abgabe f) m; ~ **inspection** n Zollkontrolle f; ~ **officer** n Zollbeamte(r) m.

**cut** [kʌt] (vb: pret, ptp ~) **1** n **(a)** Schnitt m. **to make a ~ in sth** einen Einschnitt in etw (acc) machen; **the ~ and thrust of politics** das Spannungsfeld der Politik; **the ~ and thrust of the debate** die Hitze der Debatte. **(b)** (reduction) (in gen) (in prices) Senkung f; (in wages etc) Kürzung f; (in production, output) Einschränkung f. **he had to take a ~ in (his) salary** er mußte eine Gehaltskürzung hinnehmen. **(c)** (of meat) Stück nt. **(d)** (col: share) Anteil m. **(e)** (short route) Abkürzung f. **(f)** (Elec) Unterbrechung f (in gen). **power ~** Stromausfall m. **(g)** (Cards) **it's your**

~ **du hebst ab. (h) he's a ~ above the rest of them** er ist den anderen um einiges überlegen.

**2** adj usu attr flowers Schnitt-; bread geschnitten; grass gemäht; prices herabgesetzt.

**3** vt **(a)** schneiden; grass mähen; cake anschneiden; (~ out) fabric, suit zuschneiden; (~ off) abschneiden. **to ~ one's finger** (with knife etc) sich (dat) in den Finger schneiden; **to ~ one's nails** sich (dat) die Nägel schneiden; **to ~ sth in half/three** etw halbieren/dritteln; **to ~ to pieces** zerstückeln; **to get one's hair ~** sich (dat) die Haare schneiden lassen; **to ~ sb free/loose** jdn losschneiden.

**(b)** (shape) steps schlagen; channel, trench ausheben; figure (in wood) schnitzen (in aus); (in stone) hauen (in aus); diamond schleifen; key anfertigen. **to ~ one's coat according to** or **to suit one's cloth** (fig) sich nach der Decke strecken.

**(c)** (fig: break off) electricity abstellen; ties, links abbrechen. **to ~ a long story short,** ... der langen Rede kurzer Sinn ist ....

**(d)** person schneiden. **to ~ sb dead** jdn wie Luft behandeln.

**(e)** class schwänzen (col).

**(f)** (intersect) schneiden.

**(g)** (reduce) prices senken; expenses, salary kürzen; production, output einschränken.

**(h)** part of text streichen; part of film herausschneiden.

**(i)** (cause pain to) **it ~ me to the quick** es schnitt mir ins Herz.

**(j) to ~ a tooth** einen Zahn bekommen.

**(k)** (Cards) **to ~ the cards/the pack** abheben.

**(l) aren't you ~ting it a bit fine?** ist das nicht ein bißchen knapp?

**4** vi **(a)** (knife, scissors) schneiden. **to ~ both ways** (fig) auch umgekehrt zutreffen; (have disadvantages too) ein zweischneidiges Schwert sein. **(b)** (intersect: lines, roads) sich schneiden. **(c)** (Cards) abheben. **to ~ and run** abhauen (col).

▶**cut away** vt sep wegschneiden.

▶**cut back 1** vi **(a)** (go back) zurückgehen/-fahren. **(b)** (reduce expenditure etc) sich einschränken. **to ~ ~ on smoking** weniger rauchen. **2** vt sep **(a)** plants, shrubs zurückschneiden. **(b)** production zurückschrauben.

▶**cut down 1** vt sep **(a)** tree fällen. **(b)** number, expenses einschränken. **to ~ sb ~ to size** jdn auf seinen Platz verweisen. **2** vi (reduce intake, expenditure etc) sich einschränken. **to ~ ~ on sth** etw einschränken.

▶**cut in** vi **(a)** (interrupt) sich einschalten. **(b)** (Aut) **to ~ ~ in front of sb** jdn schneiden.

▶**cut into** vi +prep obj savings ein Loch reißen in (+acc).

▶**cut off** vt sep **(a)** (lit, fig) abschneiden; allowance sperren. **to ~ ~ the enemy's retreat** dem Feind den Rückzug abschneiden; **we're very ~ ~ out here** wir leben hier draußen sehr abgeschieden. **(b)** (disinherit) enterben. **to ~ sb ~ without a penny** jdn völlig enterben. **(c)** (disconnect) telephone etc abstellen. **operator, I've been ~ ~** wir sind unterbrochen worden.

▶**cut out 1** vi (engine) aussetzen. **2** vt sep **(a)** (remove by cutting) ausschneiden; malignant growth etc herausschneiden. **(b)** dress zuschneiden. **(c)** (delete) (heraus)streichen; (not bother with) verzichten auf (+acc); smoking, swearing etc aufhören mit. ~ **it ~!** (col) laß das (sein)! (col). **(d)** (fig) **to be ~ ~ for sth** zu etw gemacht sein. **(e) to have one's work ~ ~** alle Hände voll zu tun haben.

▶**cut up 1** vi **to ~ ~ rough** Krach schlagen (col).

**2** *vt sep* **(a)** *meat* aufschneiden; *wood* spalten. **(b)** *pass (col: upset)* **he was very ~ ~ about it** das hat ihn schwer getroffen. **(c)** *(Aut col)* schneiden.

**cut-and-dried** [ˌkʌtən'draɪd] *adj* **it's ~** *(fixed beforehand)* das ist eine abgemachte Sache; *(unchangeable)* das ist festgelegt.

**cut-back** ['kʌtbæk] *n* **(a)** Kürzung *f.* **(b)** *(Film)* Rückblende *f.*

**cute** [kjuːt] *adj (+er)* **(a)** *(col: sweet)* süß. **(b)** *(esp US col: clever) idea, gadget* dufte *(col)*; *(shrewd) person, move* clever *(col)*.

**cut glass** *n* geschliffenes Glas.

**cuticle** ['kjuːtɪkl] *n (of nail)* Nagelhaut *f.* **~ remover** Nagelhautentferner *m.*

**cutie** ['kjuːtɪ] *n (esp US col: attractive woman)* dufte Biene *(col)*; *(child)* süßer Fratz *(col)*.

**cutlery** ['kʌtlərɪ] *n no pl (esp Brit)* Besteck *nt.*

**cutlet** ['kʌtlɪt] *n (boneless chop)* Schnitzel *nt; (of chopped meat)* (paniertes) Hacksteak.

**cut: ~-off** *n* **(a)** *(Tech: device)* Ausschaltmechanismus *m*; **(b)** *(also* **~-off point)** Trennlinie *f;* **~-out** *n* **(a)** *(model)* Ausschneidemodell *nt;* **(b)** *(of engine)* Aussetzen *nt;* **it has an automatic ~-out** es setzt automatisch aus; **~-price** *adj (Brit)*, **~-rate** *adj (US)* zu herabgesetzten Preisen.

**cut-throat** ['kʌtθrəʊt] **1** *n (murderous type)* Verbrechertyp *(col) m.* **2** *adj* **(a)** *competition* mörderisch. **(b)** **~ razor** (offenes) Rasiermesser.

**cutting** ['kʌtɪŋ] **1** *n* **(a)** Schneiden *nt; (~ off)* Abschneiden *nt; (of prices)* Senkung *f; (of expenses, salary)* Kürzung *f; (of production)* Drosselung *f; (of part of text)* Streichung *f; (of film)* Schnitt *m.* **~ room** *(Film)* Schneideraum *m.* **(b)** *(from newspaper)* Ausschnitt *m.* **(c)** *(Hort)* Ableger *m.* **to take a ~** einen Ableger nehmen. **2** *adj* **(a)** *edge* scharf. **(b)** *(fig) wind, cold* schneidend; *remark, tongue* spitz.

**cuttlefish** ['kʌtlfɪʃ] *n* Tintenfisch *m.*

**CV = curriculum vitae.**

**CWO, cwo = cash with order** Barzahlung *f* bei Auftragserteilung.

**cwt = hundredweight.**

**cyanide** ['saɪənaɪd] *n* Zyanid *nt.* **~ poisoning** Blausäurevergiftung *f.*

**cybernetics** [ˌsaɪbə'netɪks] *n sing* Kybernetik *f.*

**cyclamen** ['sɪkləmən] *n* Alpenveilchen *nt.*

**cycle** ['saɪkl] **1** *n* **(a)** Zyklus *m; (of events)* Gang *m.* **(b)** *(bicycle)* (Fahr)rad *nt; (col: motorbike)* Maschine *f (col).* **~ clip** Hosenklammer *f;* **~ race** Radrennen *nt;* **~ track** *(path)* Radweg *m; (for racing)* Radrennbahn *f.* **2** *vi* mit dem (Fahr)rad fahren.

**cycling** ['saɪklɪŋ] *n* Radfahren *nt.* **I enjoy ~** ich fahre gern Rad.

**cycling: ~ holiday** *n* Urlaub *m* mit dem Fahrrad; **~ shorts** *npl* Radlerhose *f;* **~ tour** *n* Radtour *f.*

**cyclist** ['saɪklɪst] *n* (Fahr)radfahrer(in *f) m.*

**cyclone** ['saɪkləʊn] *n* Zyklon *m.*

**cygnet** ['sɪgnɪt] *n* Schwanjunge(s) *nt.*

**cylinder** ['sɪlɪndə'] *n (Math, Aut)* Zylinder *m.* **a four-~ car** ein Vierzylinder *m.*

**cylinder: ~ block** *n (Aut)* Zylinderblock *m;* **~ head** *n (Aut)* Zylinderkopf *m;* **~ head gasket** *n* Zylinderkopfdichtung *f.*

**cylindrical** [sɪ'lɪndrɪkəl] *adj* zylindrisch.

**cymbal** ['sɪmbəl] *n* Beckenteller *m.* **~s** Becken *nt.*

**cynic** ['sɪnɪk] *n* Zyniker(in *f) m.*

**cynical** ['sɪnɪkəl] *adj* zynisch.

**cynicism** ['sɪnɪsɪzəm] *n* **(a)** *no pl* Zynismus *m.* **(b)** *(cynical remark)* zynische Bemerkung.

**cypress** ['saɪprɪs] *n* Zypresse *f.*

**Cypriot** ['sɪprɪət] **1** *adj* zypriotisch. **2** *n* Zypriot(in *f) m.*

**Cyprus** ['saɪprəs] *n* Zypern *nt.*

**cyst** [sɪst] *n* Zyste *f.*

**cystitis** [sɪs'taɪtɪs] *n* Blasenentzündung *f.*

**CZ** *(US)* **= Canal Zone.**

**czar** [zɑː'] *n* Zar *m.*

**czarina** [zɑː'riːnə] *n* Zarin *f.*

**Czech** [tʃek] **1** *adj* tschechisch. **the ~ Republic** die Tschechische Republik, Tschechien *nt.* **2** *n* **(a)** Tscheche *m*, Tschechin *f.* **(b)** *(language)* Tschechisch *nt.*

**Czechoslovakia** ['tʃekəʊsləˈvækɪə] *n (Hist)* die Tschechoslowakei.

**Czechoslovak(ian)** ['tʃekəʊsləˈvæk(ɪən)] *(Hist)* **1** *adj* tschechoslowakisch. **2** *n* Tschechoslowake *m*, Tschechoslowakin *f.*

# D

**D, d** [di:] *n* D, d *nt*; *(Sch: as a mark)* ≃ Vier *f.* **D for David** *(Brit)*, **D for dog** *(US)* ≃ D wie Dora; **D sharp/flat** Dis *(Mus)*, dis *nt*/Des, des *nt.*
**D** *(US Pol)* = **Democratic** dem.
**d** = **(a)** *(Brit old)* **pence. (b) died** gest.
**'d** = **had**; **would.**
**DA** *(US)* = **District Attorney.**
**D/A** = **deposit account.**
**dab¹** [dæb] **1** *n* Klecks *m*; *(of powder, cream etc)* Tupfer *m*; *(of liquid, perfume, glue etc)* Tropfen *m*; *(of butter)* Klacks *m*. a ~ of ointment ein bißchen Salbe; to give sth a ~ of paint etw kurz überstreichen. **2** *vt (with powder etc)* betupfen; *(with towel etc)* tupfen. to ~ one's eyes sich *(dat)* die Augen tupfen.
▶**dab at** *vi +prep obj* betupfen.
▶**dab on** *vt sep* tupfend auftragen *(prep obj auf +acc).*
**dab²** *adj (col)* to be a ~ hand at sth/doing sth ein As in etw *(dat)* sein/sich darauf verstehen, etw zu tun.
**dabble** ['dæbl] *vi* to ~ in sth sich nebenbei mit etw beschäftigen.
**dachshund** ['dækshʊnd] *n* Dackel *m.*
**dad** [dæd], **daddy** ['dædɪ] *n (col)* Vater, Papa *(col)*, Vati *m (col).*
**daddy-longlegs** [ˌdædɪ'lɒŋlegz] *n, pl* - *(Brit)* Schnake *f*; *(US)* Weberknecht *m.*
**daffodil** ['dæfədɪl] *n* Osterglocke, Narzisse *f.*
**daft** [dɑːft] *adj (+er)* doof *(col)*, blöd *(col)*. he's ~ about her *(col)* er ist verrückt nach ihr *(col).*
**dagger** ['dægəʳ] *n* Dolch *m.* to be at ~s drawn with sb *(fig)* mit jdm auf Kriegsfuß stehen; to look ~s at sb jdn mit Blicken durchbohren.
**dago** ['deɪɡəʊ] *n (pej)* Südländer, Kanake *(pej col!) m.*
**dahlia** ['deɪlɪə] *n* Dahlie *f.*
**daily** ['deɪlɪ] **1** *adj* täglich; *wage, newspaper, requirement, ration* Tages-. ~ grind täglicher Trott; on a ~ basis tageweise. **2** *adv* täglich. **3** *n* **(a)** *(newspaper)* Tageszeitung *f.* **(b)** *(also ~ help)* Putzfrau *f.*
**dainty** ['deɪntɪ] *adj (+er)* zierlich; *manners* geziert; *lace, handkerchief, movements* fein; *food* appetitlich. ~ morsel Leckerbissen *m.*
**dairy** ['dɛərɪ] *n* Molkerei *f*; *(on farm)* Milchkammer *f*; *(shop)* Milchgeschäft *nt.*
**dairy:** ~ butter *n* Markenbutter *f*; ~ cow *n* Milchkuh *f*; ~ farm *n* Milchbetrieb *m*; ~ farmer *n* Milchbauer *m*; ~ farming *n* Milchviehhaltung *f*; ~ ice cream *n* Milchspeiseeis *nt*; ~ produce *n* Milch- or Molkereiprodukte *pl.*
**dais** ['deɪɪs] *n* Podium *nt.*
**daisy** ['deɪzɪ] *n* Gänseblümchen *nt.* as fresh as a ~ taufrisch; to be pushing up the daisies *(col)* sich *(dat)* die Radieschen von unten besehen *(col)*; ~ wheel Typenrad *nt*; ~ wheel printer Typenraddrucker *m.*
**dale** [deɪl] *n (N Engl, liter)* Tal *nt.*
**dally** ['dælɪ] *vi (waste time)* (herum)trödeln.

**Dalmatia** [dæl'meɪʃə] *n* Dalmatien *nt.*
**Dalmatian** [dæl'meɪʃən] *n (dog)* Dalmatiner *m.*
**dam** [dæm] **1** *n (lit, fig)* Damm *m*; *(reservoir)* Stausee *m.* **2** *vt (also ~ up) river, lake* stauen.
**damage** ['dæmɪdʒ] **1** *n* **(a)** Schaden *m (to an +dat).* to do a lot of ~ großen Schaden anrichten; to do sb/sth a lot of ~ jdm/einer Sache *(dat)* großen Schaden zufügen; that did a lot of ~ to his reputation das hat seinem Ruf sehr geschadet; ~ limitation Schadensbegrenzung *f.* **(b)** *(Jur)* ~s Schaden(s)ersatz *m.* **(c)** *(col: cost)* what's the ~? was kostet der Spaß? *(col).* **2** *vt* beschädigen; *health, reputation, relations* schaden *(+dat)*, schädigen. to ~ one's eyesight sich *(dat)* die Augen verderben; smoking can ~ your health Rauchen schadet Ihrer Gesundheit.
**damaging** ['dæmɪdʒɪŋ] *adj* schädlich *(to für).*
**Damascus** [də'mɑːskəs] *n* Damaskus *nt.*
**damask** ['dæməsk] *n* Damast *m.*
**dame** [deɪm] *n* **(a)** D~ *britischer Titel.* **(b)** *(Theat: in pantomime)* (komische) Alte. **(c)** *(US col)* Weib *nt (col).*
**dammit** ['dæmɪt] *interj (col)* verdammt *(col).* as near as ~ beinahe; *(approximately)* ungefähr.
**damn** [dæm] **1** *interj (col)* verdammt *(col).*
**2** *n (col)* he doesn't care *or* give a ~ er schert sich einen Dreck (darum) *(col)*; I don't give a ~ das ist mir scheißegal *(col!).*
**3** *adj attr (col)* verdammt. I couldn't see a ~ thing so ein Mist *(col)*, ich konnte überhaupt nichts sehen.
**4** *adv (col)* verdammt. I should ~ well hope so das will ich aber auch stark hoffen; ~-all nicht die Bohne *(col)*; I've done ~-all today ich hab heute rein gar nichts gemacht *(col).*
**5** *vt* **(a)** *(Rel)* verdammen. **(b)** *(judge and condemn)* verurteilen; *book etc also* verreißen. **(c)** *(col)* ~ him/you! der kann/du kannst mich mal! *(col!)*; ~ it! verdammt (noch mal)! *(col)*; well, I'll be ~ed! Donnerwetter! *(col)*; I'll be ~ed if I'll go there ich denke nicht daran, da hinzugehen; I'll be ~ed if I know weiß der Teufel *(col).*
**damnation** [dæm'neɪʃən] **1** *n (Eccl)* Verdammnis *f.* **2** *interj (col)* verdammt *(col).*
**damned** [dæmd] *adj* **(a)** *soul* verdammt. **(b)** *(col)* = damn 3. **2** *adv* = damn 4.
**damnedest** ['dæmdɪst] *n* to do *or* try one's ~ *(col)* sein möglichstes tun.
**damning** ['dæmɪŋ] *adj* vernichtend; *evidence* belastend.
**damp** [dæmp] **1** *adj (~er)* feucht. a ~ squib *(fig)* ein Reinfall *m.* **2** *n* Feuchtigkeit *f.* **3** *vt* **(a)** befeuchten. **(b)** *(fig) enthusiasm etc* dämpfen. to ~ sb's spirits jdm einen Dämpfer aufsetzen. **(c)** *sounds, vibrations* dämpfen; *(also ~ down) fire* ersticken.
**damp course** *n* Dämmschicht, Isolierschicht *f.*
**dampen** ['dæmpən] *vt* = **damp** 3 (a, b).
**damper** ['dæmpəʳ] *n* **(a)** *(of chimney)* (Luft)klappe *f*;

*(of piano)* Dämpfer *m.* **(b) to put a ~ on sth** einer Sache *(dat)* einen Dämpfer aufsetzen.

**damp-proof** ['dæmpruːf] *adj* feuchtigkeitsbeständig. **~ course = damp course.**

**damson** ['dæmzən] *n (fruit)* Damaszenerpflaume *f.*

**dance** [dɑːns] **1** *n* Tanz *m*; *(occasion also)* Tanzabend *m*; *(school etc)* Ball *m*. **she's led him a fine ~** sie hat ihn ganz schön an der Nase herumgeführt. **2** *vti* tanzen. **to ~ for joy** einen Freudentanz aufführen.

**dance** *in cpds* Tanz-; **~ band** *n* Tanzkapelle *f*; **~ floor** *n* Tanzboden *m*; *(in restaurant)* Tanzfläche *f*; **~ hall** *n* Tanzsaal *m*; **~ music** *n* Tanzmusik *f.*

**dancer** ['dɑːnsər] *n* Tänzer(in *f*) *m.*

**dancing** ['dɑːnsɪŋ] **1** *n* Tanzen *nt.* **2** *attr* Tanz-. **~ girl** Tänzerin *f.*

**dandelion** ['dændɪlaɪən] *n* Löwenzahn *m.*

**dandruff** ['dændrəf] *n* Schuppen *pl.*

**dandy** ['dændɪ] **1** *n* Dandy, Geck *m.* **2** *adj (esp US col)* prima *(col).*

**Dane** [deɪn] *n* Däne *m*, Dänin *f.*

**danger** ['deɪndʒər] *n* **(a)** Gefahr *f.* **to put sb/sth in ~** jdn/etw in Gefahr bringen; **to be in ~ of doing sth** Gefahr laufen, etw zu tun; **out of ~** außer Gefahr; **there is no ~ of that** die Gefahr besteht nicht; **to be a ~ to sb/sth** für jdn/etw eine Gefahr bedeuten. **(b)** "**~**" „Achtung, Lebensgefahr!"; "**~, ice**" „Glatteisgefahr".

**danger: ~ area** *n* Gefahrenzone *f or* -bereich *m*; **~ list: on/off the ~ list** in/außer Lebensgefahr; **~ money** *n* Gefahrenzulage *f.*

**dangerous** ['deɪndʒrəs] *adj* gefährlich.

**dangerously** ['deɪndʒrəslɪ] *adv* gefährlich. **the deadline is getting ~ close** der Termin rückt bedenklich nahe; **to be ~ ill** schwerkrank sein.

**danger: ~ signal** *n (lit, fig)* Warnsignal *nt*; **~ zone** *n* Gefahrenzone *f.*

**dangle** ['dæŋgl] **1** *vt* baumeln lassen. **to ~ sth before sb** *(fig)* jdm etw in Aussicht stellen. **2** *vi* baumeln.

**Danish** ['deɪnɪʃ] **1** *adj* dänisch. **~ blue (cheese)** dänischer Edelpilzkäse *m*; **~ pastry** Plundergebäck *nt.* **2** *n (language)* Dänisch *nt.*

**dank** [dæŋk] *adj (unangenehm)* feucht.

**Danube** ['dænjuːb] *n* Donau *f.*

**dapper** ['dæpər] *adj* gepflegt, gediegen.

**dappled** ['dæpld] *adj* gefleckt; *(with small flecks)* gesprenkelt; *horse* scheckig.

**dare** [dɛər] **1** *vi (be bold enough)* es wagen; *(have the confidence)* sich trauen. **he wouldn't ~!** er wird sich schwer hüten; **you ~!** untersteh dich!; **how ~ you!** was fällt dir ein! **2** *vt* **(a) to ~ (to) do sth** (es) wagen, etw zu tun, sich trauen, etw zu tun; **he ~ not** *or* **doesn't ~** *or* **~n't do it** das wagt er nicht; **don't (you) ~ say that to me** untersteh dich, das zu mir zu sagen. **(b) I ~ say it gets quite cold here in winter** ich nehme an, daß es hier im Winter ziemlich kalt wird; **I ~ say he'll be there** es kann (gut) sein, daß er dort ist; **he was very sorry — I ~ say** es tat ihm sehr leid — das glaube ich gerne. **(c)** *(challenge)* **I ~ you to jump off** wetten, daß du dich nicht zu springen traust! **3** *n* **to do sth for a ~** etw als Mutprobe tun.

**daredevil** ['dɛəˌdevl] **1** *n* Draufgänger *m.* **2** *adj* waghalsig.

**daring** ['dɛərɪŋ] **1** *adj* kühn; *(in physical matters)* waghalsig; *opinion, dress* gewagt. **2** *n* Kühnheit *f*; *(in physical matters)* Waghalsigkeit *f.*

**dark** [dɑːk] **1** *adj (+er) (lit, fig)* dunkel; *thoughts, threats* finster. **it's getting ~** es wird dunkel; **~ blue** dunkelblau; **to keep sth ~** etw geheimhalten. **2** *n* **(a)** Dunkelheit *f.* **after ~** nach Einbruch der Dunkelheit; **until ~** bis zum Einbruch der Dunkelheit. **(b)** *(fig)* **to be in the ~** keine Ahnung haben *(about* von*)*; **he has kept me in the ~** er hat mich im dunkeln gelassen; **it was a shot in the ~** das war nur auf gut Glück gesagt/geraten *etc.*

**dark: D~ Ages** *npl* finsteres Mittelalter; **~ chocolate** *n* Zartbitterschokolade *f.*

**darken** ['dɑːkən] **1** *vt* dunkel machen; *sky also* verdunkeln; *(before storm)* verfinstern; **never ~ my door again!** lassen Sie sich hier nicht mehr blicken! **2** *vi see* **vt** dunkel werden; sich verdunkeln; sich verfinstern.

**dark: ~-eyed** ['dɑːkaɪd] *adj* dunkeläugig; **~ glasses** *npl* Sonnenbrille *f*; **~-haired** *adj* dunkelhaarig; **~ horse** *n (fig)* stilles Wasser; *(unexpected winner)* Außenseiter *m.*

**darkly** ['dɑːklɪ] *adj (lit, fig)* dunkel.

**darkness** ['dɑːknɪs] *n* Dunkelheit *f.* **the house was in ~** das Haus lag im Dunkeln.

**dark: ~room** *n (Phot)* Dunkelkammer *f*; **~-skinned** ['dɑːkskɪnd] *adj* dunkelhäutig.

**darling** ['dɑːlɪŋ] **1** *n* Liebling, Schatz *m.* **be a ~ and ... sei so lieb und ... 2** *adj wife etc* lieb.

**darn¹** [dɑːn] *(Sew)* **1** *n* gestopfte Stelle. **2** *vt* stopfen.

**darn²** *(col)* **1** *adj, adv, interj* verflixt *(col).* **2** *vt see* **damn 5 (c).**

**darned** [dɑːnd] *adj, adv (col)* verflixt *(col).*

**darning** ['dɑːnɪŋ] *n* Stopfen *nt*; *(things to be darned)* Stopfsachen *pl.* **I've a lot of ~ to do** ich habe viel zu stopfen; **~ needle** Stopfnadel *f.*

**dart** [dɑːt] **1** *n* **(a)** *(movement)* **to make a sudden ~ at sb/sth** einen plötzlichen Satz auf jdn/etw zu machen. **(b)** *(weapon)* Pfeil *m*; *(Sport)* (Wurf)pfeil *m.* **(c)** *(Sew)* Abnäher *m.* **2** *vi* flitzen; *(fish)* schnellen. **to ~ out** *(person)* heraus-/hinausflitzen; *(fish, tongue)* hervorschnellen; **he ~ed behind a bush** er hechtete hinter einen Busch. **3** *vt* **to ~ a glance at sb** jdm einen Blick zuwerfen.

**dart board** *n* Dartscheibe *f.*

**darts** [dɑːts] *n sing* Darts, Pfeilwurfspiel *nt.*

**dash** [dæʃ] **1** *n* **(a)** *(sudden rush)* **he made a ~ for the door** er stürzte auf die Tür zu; **she made a ~ for it** sie rannte, so schnell sie konnte. **(b)** *(style, vigour)* Schwung, Elan *m.* **to cut a ~** eine schneidige Figur machen. **(c)** *(small amount)* etwas, ein bißchen; *(of wine, vinegar, spirits also)* Schuß *m*; *(of seasoning etc also)* Prise *f.* **(d)** *(Typ)* Gedankenstrich *m.* **(e) = dashboard. 2** *vt* **(a)** *(throw violently)* schleudern. **to ~ sth to pieces** etw in tausend Stücke zerschlagen; **to ~ one's head against sth** mit dem Kopf gegen etw schlagen. **(b)** *sb's hopes* zunichte machen. **3** *vi* **(a) to ~ into a room** in ein Zimmer stürzen; **to ~ away/back/up** davon-/zurück-/hinaufstürmen. **(b)** *(knock, be hurled)* schlagen; *(waves also)* peitschen. **4** *interj* **~ (it)!** *(col)* verflixt! *(col).*

▶**dash off 1** *vt sep letter* hinwerfen. **2** *vi* losstürzen.

**dashboard** ['dæʃbɔːd] *n* Armaturenbrett *nt.*

**dashing** ['dæʃɪŋ] *adj* flott, schneidig.

**dastardly** ['dæstədlɪ] *adj* niederträchtig.

**DAT** *n abbr* (= **digital audio tape**) DAT *nt, Band mit digitaler Tonaufzeichnung.*

**data** ['deɪtə] *pl of* **datum** *usu with sing vb* Daten *pl.* **a piece of ~** eine Angabe.

**data: ~ bank** *n* Datenbank *f*; **~base** *n* Datenbank *f*; **~ capture** *n* Datenerfassung *f*; **~ processing** *n* Datenverarbeitung *f*; **~ protection** *n* Datenschutz *m*; **~ retrieval** *n* Datenabruf *m*; **~ transmission** *n* Datenübertragung *f.*

**date¹** [deɪt] *n (fruit)* Dattel *f*; *(tree)* Dattelpalme *f.*

**date²** **1** *n* **(a)** Datum *nt*; *(historical* ~) Jahreszahl *f*; *(for appointment)* Termin *m*. ~ **of birth** Geburtsdatum *nt*; **what's the** ~ **today?** der wievielte ist heute?, welches Datum haben wir heute?; **what** ~ **is he coming on?** an welchem Tag kommt er?; **to** ~ bis heute. **(b)** *(appointment)* Verabredung *f*; **who's his** ~? mit wem geht er aus?; **to make a** ~ **with sb** sich mit jdm verabreden; **she's out on a** ~ sie hat eine Verabredung.

   **2** *vt* **(a)** mit dem Datum versehen; *letter etc also* datieren. **a coin** ~**d 1390** eine Münze von 1390. **(b)** *(establish age of) work of art etc* datieren. **that really** ~**s you** daran merkt man, wie alt Sie sind. **(c)** *(take out) girlfriend etc* ausgehen mit; *(regularly also)* gehen mit *(col)*.

   **3** *vi* **(a)** **to** ~ **back to** zurückdatieren auf (+*acc*); **to** ~ **from** zurückgehen auf *(+acc)*. **(b)** *(become old-fashioned)* veralten.

**dated** ['deɪtɪd] *adj* altmodisch.

**date:** ~ **line** *n (Geog)* Datumsgrenze *f*; ~ **palm** *n* Dattelpalme *f*; ~ **stamp** *n* Datumsstempel *m*.

**dative** ['deɪtɪv] *n* Dativ *m*. **in the** ~ **(case)** im Dativ.

**daub** [dɔːb] *vt walls, canvas, face* beschmieren; *paint, slogans, make-up* schmieren.

**daughter** ['dɔːtə*r*] *n* Tochter *f*. ~-**in-law** Schwiegertochter *f*.

**daunt** [dɔːnt] *vt* entmutigen. **nothing** ~**ed** unverzagt.

**daunting** ['dɔːntɪŋ] *adj* entmutigend.

**dauntless** ['dɔːntlɪs] *adj* unerschrocken, beherzt.

**davenport** ['dævnpɔːt] *n* **(a)** *(esp US: sofa)* Sofa *nt*. **(b)** *(Brit: desk)* Sekretär *m*.

**dawdle** ['dɔːdl] *vi (be too slow)* trödeln; *(stroll)* bummeln.

**dawdler** ['dɔːdlə*r*] *n* Trödler (in *f*) *m*.

**dawn** [dɔːn] **1** *n* (Morgen)dämmerung *f*; *(time of day)* Tagesanbruch *m*; *(fig)* Anbruch *m*. **at** ~ bei Tagesanbruch; **it's almost** ~ es dämmert schon bald; **from** ~ **to dusk** von morgens bis abends. **2** *vi* **(a)** **day was already** ~**ing** es dämmerte schon; **the day will** ~ **when** ... *(fig)* der Tag wird kommen, wo ... **(b)** *(fig: new age etc)* dämmern, anbrechen. **(c)** **it suddenly** ~**ed on him that** ... es dämmerte ihm, daß ...

**dawn chorus** *n* Morgenkonzert *nt* der Vögel.

**day** [deɪ] *n* **(a)** Tag *m*. **it will arrive any** ~ **now** es muß jeden Tag kommen; **what** ~ **is it today?** welcher Tag ist heute?; **what** ~ **of the month is it?** der wievielte ist heute?; **the** ~ **before yesterday** vorgestern; **(on) the** ~ **after/before** am Tag danach/zuvor; **two years ago to the** ~ auf den Tag genau vor zwei Jahren; **one** ~ eines Tages; **one of these** ~**s** irgendwann (einmal), eines Tages; ~ **in,** ~ **out** tagein, tagaus; **they went to London for the** ~ sie machten einen Tagesausflug nach London; **for** ~**s on end** tagelang; ~ **after** ~ Tag für Tag; ~ **by** ~ jeden Tag, täglich; **the other** ~ neulich; **at the end of the** ~ *(fig)* letzten Endes; **to live from** ~ **to** ~ von einem Tag auf den andern leben; **I remember it to this** ~ daran erinnere ich mich noch heute; **for** ~**s on end** tagelang; **he's fifty if he's a** ~ er ist mindestens fünfzig; **to travel during the** *or* **by** ~ tagsüber *or* am Tag reisen; **good** ~! guten Tag!; *(good-bye)* auf Wiedersehen; **to be paid by the** ~ tageweise bezahlt werden; **let's call it a** ~ machen wir Schluß; **to have a nice/lazy** ~ einen schönen Tag verbringen/einen Tag faulenzen; **have a nice** ~! *(esp US)* schönen Tag noch!; **did you have a nice** ~? na, wie war's?; **to have a good/bad** ~ einen guten/schlechten Tag haben; **that'll be the** ~ das möcht' ich sehen *or* erleben.

   **(b)** *(period of time: often pl)* **these** ~**s** heute, heut-

zutage; **what are you doing these** ~**s?** was machst du denn so?; **in this** ~ **and age** heutzutage; **in** ~**s to come** in künftigen Zeiten; **in his younger** ~**s** als er noch jünger war; **in Queen Victoria's** ~, **in the** ~**s of Queen Victoria** zu Königin Viktorias Zeiten; **the happiest** ~**s of my life** die glücklichste Zeit meines Lebens; **those were the** ~**s** das waren noch Zeiten; **in the old** ~**s** früher; **in the good old** ~**s** in der guten alten Zeit; **it's early** ~**s yet** es ist noch zu früh; **he/this machine has seen better** ~**s** er/diese Maschine hat (auch) schon bessere Tage gesehen; **to end one's** ~**s in misery** im Elend sterben.

   **(c)** *(with poss adj: lifetime, best time)* **famous in her** ~ in ihrer Zeit berühmt; **it has had its** ~ es hat seine Glanzzeit überschritten; **his** ~ **will come** sein Tag wird kommen.

   **(d)** *no pl (contest, battle)* **to win** *or* **carry the** ~ siegen; **to lose the** ~ (den Kampf) verlieren; **that saved the** ~ das war die Rettung.

**day:** ~ **boy** *n (Sch)* Externe(r) *m*; ~ **break** *n* Tagesanbruch *m*; **at** ~**break** bei Tagesanbruch; ~ **care** *n* **to be in** ~ **care** in einer Tagesstätte untergebracht sein; ~ **care centre** *n (esp US)* Kindertagesstätte *f*; ~**dream** **1** *n* Tagtraum *m*; **2** *vi* mit offenen Augen träumen; ~ **dreamer** *n* Tagträumer *m*; ~ **girl** *n (Sch)* Externe *f*.

**daylight** ['deɪlaɪt] *n* Tageslicht *nt*. **at** ~ bei Tage; **it is still** ~ es ist noch hell; **it was broad** ~ es war hellichter Tag; **in broad** ~ am hellichten Tage; **I began to see** ~ *(fig) (to understand)* mir ging ein Licht auf; *(to see the end appear)* so langsam habe ich Land gesehen *(col)*; **to beat the living** ~**s out of sb** *(col)* jdn windelweich schlagen *(col)*; **to scare the living** ~**s out of sb** *(col)* jdm einen fürchterlichen Schreck einjagen *(col)*.

**daylight:** ~ **robbery** *n (col)* Halsabschneiderei *f (col)*; ~ **saving time** *n* Sommerzeit *f*.

**day:** ~ **nursery** *n* Kindertagesstätte *f*; ~ **release course** *n* Fortbildungskurs *m (für den man einen Tag pro Woche freigestellt wird)*; ~ **return (ticket)** *n (Brit Rail)* Tagesrückfahrkarte *f*; ~ **school** *n* Tagesschule *f*; ~ **shift** *n* Tagschicht *f*; **to be on** ~ **shift** Tagschicht arbeiten.

**daytime** ['deɪtaɪm] **1** *n* Tag *m*. **in the** ~ bei Tage, tagsüber. **2** *attr* am Tage.

**day:** ~-**to-day** *adj occurrence* alltäglich; **on a** ~-**to-day basis** tageweise; ~ **trip** *n* Tagesausflug *m*; ~**tripper** *n* Tagesausflügler (in *f*) *m*.

**daze** [deɪz] **1** *n* Benommenheit *f*. **in a** ~ ganz benommen. **2** *vt* benommen machen.

**dazzle** ['dæzl] *vt (lit, fig)* blenden.

**dazzling** ['dæzlɪŋ] *adj (lit)* blendend.

**dB** = **decibel** dB.

**DC** = **(a)** **direct current**. **(b)** *(US Post)* **District of Columbia**.

**D/D** = **direct debit**.

**D-day** ['diːdeɪ] *n (Hist)* Tag der Invasion durch die Alliierten (6.6.44); *(fig)* der Tag X.

**DDT** [diːdiː'tiː] *n* DDT *nt*.

**DE** *(US Post)* = **Delaware**.

**deacon** ['diːkən] *n* Diakon *m*.

**deaconess** ['diːkənes] *n* Diakonisse *f*.

**dead** [ded] **1** *adj* **(a)** *(lit, fig)* tot; *plant also* abgestorben. **to drop (down)** ~ tot umfallen; **over my** ~ **body** *(col)* nur über meine Leiche *(col)*. **(b)** *(not sensitive) limbs* abgestorben, taub. **my fingers are** ~ meine Finger sind wie abgestorben; **to be** ~ **from the neck up** *(col)* nur Stroh im Kopf haben *(col)*, gehirnamputiert sein *(col)*; **to be** ~ **to the world** vollkommen weggetreten sein *(col)*. **(c)** *(Elec) cable* stromlos; *(Telec)* tot. **to go** ~ ausfallen; **the line**

went ~ die Leitung war plötzlich tot. (**d**) *(burnt out)* fire aus *pred*; *match* abgebrannt. (**e**) *(absolute, exact)* total, völlig. ~ **silence** Totenstille *f*; ~ **calm** *(Naut)* totale Windstille; **to come to a ~ stop** völlig zum Stillstand kommen; **to hit sth ~ centre** etw genau in der Mitte treffen. (**f**) *(col: exhausted)* völlig kaputt *(col)*.

  **2** *adv* (**a**) *(exactly)* genau. ~ **straight** schnurgerade; **to be ~ on time** auf die Minute pünktlich kommen; ~ **on course** voll *or* genau auf Kurs. (**b**) *(col: very)* total *(col)*, völlig. ~ **drunk/tired** total betrunken/todmüde; **you're ~ right** Sie haben völlig recht; ~ **slow** ganz langsam; *(on sign)* „Schritt fahren"; **to be ~ certain about sth** bei etw todsicher sein. (**c**) **to stop ~** abrupt stehenbleiben *or (talking)* innehalten.

  **3** *n* (**a**) **the ~** *pl* die Toten *pl*. (**b**) **at ~ of night** mitten in der Nacht; **in the ~ of winter** mitten im Winter.

**dead-beat** ['ded'biːt] *adj (col)* völlig kaputt *(col)*.

**deaden** ['dedn] *vt sound, noise* dämpfen; *pain* mildern; *force, blow* abschwächen; *nerve* abtöten.

**dead:** ~**end** *n* Sackgasse *f*; **a ~-end job** ein Job *m* ohne Aufstiegsmöglichkeiten; ~ **heat** *n* totes Rennen; ~**line** *n* (letzter) Termin; *(for application etc)* Abgabetermin *m*; **to set a ~line** eine Frist setzen; **to work to a ~line** auf einen Termin hinarbeiten; ~**lock** *n* **to reach (a)** ~**lock** sich festfahren; **to break the ~lock** aus der Sackgasse herauskommen; ~ **loss** *n (col)* böser Reinfall *(col)*; *(person)* hoffnungsloser Fall *(col)*.

**deadly** ['dedlɪ] **1** *adj (+er)* (**a**) tödlich; *sin, enemy* Tod-; *wit, sarcasm* vernichtend. **he's in ~ earnest** er meint es todernst, es ist sein völler Ernst. (**b**) *(col: boring)* todlangweilig. **2** *adv boring* tod-. ~ **pale** totenbleich.

**deadly nightshade** ['dedlɪ'naɪtʃeɪd] *n (Bot)* Tollkirsche *f*.

**dead:** ~**pan** *adj face* unbewegt; *style, humour* trocken; **D~ Sea** *n* Totes Meer; ~ **season** *n* tote Saison; ~ **weight** *n (Tech)* Eigengewicht *nt*; **to be a ~ weight** furchtbar schwer sein.

**deaf** [def] *adj (+er)* taub. **as ~ as a (door)post** stocktaub; **to turn a ~ ear to sb/sth** sich jdm/einer Sache *(dat)* gegenüber taub stellen.

**deaf:** ~**-aid** *n* Hörgerät *nt*; ~**-and-dumb** *adj* taubstumm; *language* Taubstummen-.

**deafen** ['defn] *vt (lit)* taub machen; *(fig)* betäuben.

**deafening** ['defnɪŋ] *adj noise* ohrenbetäubend; *row* lautstark. **a ~ silence** ein eisiges Schweigen.

**deaf-mute** ['def'mjuːt] *n* Taubstumme(r) *mf*.

**deafness** ['defnɪs] *n (lit, fig)* Taubheit *f (to* gegenüber*)*.

**deal¹** [diːl] **1** *n* **a good** *or* **great ~** eine Menge, (ziemlich) viel; **not a great ~** nicht (besonders) viel; **there's a great** *or* **good ~ of truth in what he says** es ist schon ziemlich viel Wahres an dem, was er sagt; **and that's saying a good ~** und damit ist schon viel gesagt; **to mean a great ~ to sb** jdm viel bedeuten. **2** *adv* **a good** *or* **great ~** viel; **not a great ~** nicht viel.

**deal²** *(vb: pret, ptp* **dealt) 1** *n* (**a**) *(Comm: also* **business ~)** Geschäft *nt*; *(arrangement)* Abmachung *f*; *(official)* Abkommen *nt*. **to do a ~ with sb** mit jdm ein Geschäft *or* einen Deal *(col)* machen; **it's a ~** abgemacht!; **I'll make a ~ with you** ich schlage Ihnen ein Geschäft vor; **to give sb a fair ~** jdn anständig behandeln; **a better ~ for the lower paid** bessere Bedingungen für die schlechter bezahlten Arbeiter; **it's the usual ~** es gibt das Übliche. (**b**) *(Cards)* **it's your ~** Sie geben. **2** *vti (Cards)* geben,

austeilen.

▶**deal in** *vi +prep obj (Comm)* handeln mit.

▶**deal out** *vt sep gifts, money* verteilen *(to* an *+acc)*; *cards* geben *(to* dat*)*. **to ~ ~ justice** Recht sprechen.

▶**deal with** *vi +prep obj* (**a**) *(do business with)* verhandeln mit. (**b**) *(manage, handle)* sich kümmern um; *(with job)* sich befassen mit; *(successfully)* fertigwerden mit; *(Comm)* orders erledigen; *(be responsible for)* zuständig sein für. **to know how to ~ sb** wissen, wie man mit jdm umgeht; **I'll ~ ~ you later!** dich knöpf ich mir später vor *(col)*. (**c**) *(be concerned with)* *(book, film etc)* handeln von; *(author)* sich befassen mit.

**deal³** *n (wood)* Kiefern- *or* Tannenholz *nt*.

**dealer** ['diːlə<sup>r</sup>] *n (Comm)* Händler *m*. **a ~ in furs** ein Pelzhändler.

**dealership** ['diːləʃɪp] *n* Vertrieb *m*.

**dealing** ['diːlɪŋ] *n* (**a**) *(trading)* Handel *m*. **there's some crooked ~ involved here** da ist irgend etwas gemauschelt worden *(col)*. (**b**) ~**s** *pl (Comm)* Geschäfte *pl*; *(generally)* Umgang *m*; **to have ~s with sb** mit jdm zu tun haben.

**dealt** [delt] *pret, ptp of* **deal²**.

**dean** [diːn] *n (Eccl, Univ)* Dekan *m*.

**dear** [dɪə<sup>r</sup>] **1** *adj (+er)* (**a**) **I hold him/it ~** er/es ist mir lieb und teuer; **that is my ~est wish** das ist mein sehnlichster Wunsch; **my ~ chap** mein lieber Freund. (**b**) *(in letter-writing)* **D~ Daddy/John** lieber Vati/John!; ~ **Sir** sehr geehrter Herr X; *(to firm etc)* sehr geehrte (Damen und) Herren; ~ **Madam** sehr geehrte Frau X; ~ **Sirs** sehr geehrte Damen und Herren; ~ **Mr Kemp** sehr geehrter Herr Kemp; *(less formal)* lieber Herr Kemp!; **D~ John letter** *(US col)* Abschiedsbrief *m*. (**c**) *(expensive)* teuer. **2** *interj* ~ ~!, ~ **me!** (du) meine Güte!; **oh** ~! oje! **3** *n* **hello/thank you** ~ hallo/vielen Dank; **yes,** ~ ja, Liebling; **be a** ~ *(col)* sei so lieb *or* gut; **poor** ~ der/die Arme. **4** *adv (lit, fig) buy, pay, sell* teuer.

**dearly** ['dɪəlɪ] *adv* (**a**) *love* von ganzem Herzen. **I should ~ like to live here** ich würde für mein Leben gern hier wohnen. (**b**) *(lit, fig) pay etc* teuer.

**dearth** [dɜːθ] *n* Mangel *m (of* an *+dat)*. ~ **of ideas** Ideenarmut *f*.

**death** [deθ] *n* Tod *m*; *(of plans, hopes etc)* Ende *nt*. **the number of ~s** die Todesfälle; **to be afraid of ~** sich vor dem Tod fürchten; **a fight to the ~** ein Kampf auf Leben und Tod; **to put sb to ~** jdn hinrichten; **to drink oneself to ~** sich zu Tode trinken; **to be at ~'s door** an der Schwelle des Todes stehen; **it will be the ~ of you** *(col)* das wird dein Tod sein; **he will be the ~ of me** *(col) (he's so funny)* ich lach' mich noch einmal tot über ihn *(col)*; *(he's annoying)* er bringt mich noch ins Grab; **to catch one's ~ (of cold)** *(col)* sich *(dat)* den Tod holen; **I am sick to ~ of all this** *(col)* das alles hängt mir gründlich zum Halse raus.

**death:** ~**bed** *n* Sterbebett *nt*; ~**-blow** *n (lit, fig)* Todesstoß *m*; ~ **certificate** *n* Totenschein *m*; ~ **duties** *npl (Brit)* Erbschaftssteuer *f*.

**deathly** ['deθlɪ] **1** *adj (+er)* ~ **hush** Totenstille *f*; ~ **silence** eisiges Schweigen; ~ **pallor** Totenblässe *f*. **2** *adv* ~ **pale** totenblaß.

**death:** ~**-mask** *n* Totenmaske *f*; ~ **penalty** *n* Todesstrafe *f*; ~ **rate** *n* Sterbeziffer *f*; ~ **sentence** *n* Todesurteil *nt*; ~ **throes** *npl* Todeskampf *m*; ~ **toll** *n* Zahl *f* der Todesopfer; ~**-trap** *n* Todesfalle *f*; ~**-watch beetle** *n* Klopfkäfer *m*; ~**-wish** *n* Todestrieb *m*.

**deb** [deb] *n (col)* Debütantin *f*.

**debacle** [deˈbɑːkl] *n* Debakel *nt*.

**debar** [dɪ'bɑːʳ] vt ausschließen (from von).

**debase** [dɪ'beɪs] vt person erniedrigen; qualities mindern, herabsetzen; coinage den Wert mindern von; language entstellen.

**debatable** [dɪ'beɪtəbl] adj fraglich.

**debate** [dɪ'beɪt] **1** vti debattieren, diskutieren (with mit, about über +acc). he was debating with himself whether to go or not er überlegte hin und her, ob er gehen sollte; debating society Debattierklub m. **2** n Debatte f. after much ~ nach langer Debatte or Diskussion.

**debauched** [dɪ'bɔːtʃt] adj verkommen; life ausschweifend.

**debauchery** [dɪ'bɔːtʃərɪ] n Ausschweifung f. a life of ~ ein ausschweifendes Leben.

**debenture** [dɪ'bentʃəʳ] n (Fin) Schuldschein m.

**debilitate** [dɪ'bɪlɪteɪt] vt schwächen.

**debility** [dɪ'bɪlɪtɪ] n Schwäche f.

**debit** ['debɪt] **1** n Debetposten m, Soll nt. ~s Debet, Soll nt; ~ balance Debetsaldo m; ~ note Lastschrift f; ~ side Sollseite f; on the ~ side there's the weather (fig) als Minuspunkt ist das Wetter zu erwähnen. **2** vt to ~ sb/sb's account with a sum jdn/jds Konto mit einem Betrag belasten.

**debonair** [ˌdebə'nɛəʳ] adj flott.

**debrief** [ˌdiː'briːf] vt befragen. to be ~ed Bericht erstatten.

**debris** ['debriː] n Trümmer pl, Schutt m.

**debt** [det] n Schuld f. ~ of honour Ehrenschuld f; National D~ Staatsschulden pl; to be in ~ verschuldet sein (to gegenüber); to be £5 in ~ £5 Schulden haben (to bei); to get into ~ Schulden machen; to be out of ~ schuldenfrei sein; to repay a ~ (lit, fig) eine Schuld begleichen; I shall always be in your ~ ich werde ewig in Ihrer Schuld stehen.

**debt collector** n Inkassobeauftragte(r) mf, Schuldeneintreiber (col) m.

**debtor** ['detəʳ] n Schuldner(in f) m.

**debug** [ˌdiː'bʌg] vt (also Comp) entwanzen.

**debunk** [ˌdiː'bʌŋk] vt claim entlarven; politician vom Sockel stoßen.

**début** ['deɪbjuː] n (lit, fig) Debüt nt. to make one's ~ sein Debüt geben.

**débutante** ['debjuːtɑːnt] n Debütantin f.

**Dec** = **December** Dez.

**decade** ['dekeɪd] n Jahrzehnt nt.

**decadence** ['dekədəns] n Dekadenz f.

**decadent** ['dekədənt] adj dekadent.

**decaffeinated** [ˌdiː'kæfɪneɪtɪd] adj koffeinfrei, entkoffeiniert.

**decal** [dɪ'kæl] n (US) Aufkleber m.

**decamp** [dɪ'kæmp] vi (col) sich aus dem Staube machen.

**decant** [dɪ'kænt] vt umfüllen.

**decanter** [dɪ'kæntəʳ] n Karaffe f.

**decapitate** [dɪ'kæpɪteɪt] vt enthaupten, köpfen.

**decarbonize** [ˌdiː'kɑːbənaɪz] vt dekarbonisieren, entkohlen.

**decathlete** [dɪ'kæθliːt] n Zehnkämpfer m.

**decathlon** [dɪ'kæθlɒn] n Zehnkampf m.

**decay** [dɪ'keɪ] **1** vi verfallen; (rot) verwesen, verfaulen; (food) schlecht werden, verderben; (beauty) verblühen, vergehen; (civilization, race) untergehen; (one's faculties) verkümmern. **2** n see vi Verfall m; Verwesung f; Verderben nt; (of civilization) Untergang m; (of one's faculties) Verkümmern nt. to fall into ~ in Verfall geraten.

**decease** [dɪ'siːs] n (Jur, form) Ableben nt (form).

**deceased** [dɪ'siːst] (Jur, form) **1** adj verstorben. **2** n: the ~ der/die Tote or Verstorbene; die Toten or Verstorbenen pl.

**deceit** [dɪ'siːt] n Betrug m no pl, Täuschung f.

**deceitful** [dɪ'siːtful] adj falsch, betrügerisch.

**deceitfulness** [dɪ'siːtfulnɪs] n Falschheit f; (deceitful acts) Betrügereien pl.

**deceive** [dɪ'siːv] vt täuschen, irreführen; one's wife, husband betrügen. to ~ sb into thinking sth jdm etw einreden; are my eyes deceiving me? täuschen mich meine Augen?; to ~ oneself sich (dat) selbst etwas vormachen.

**decelerate** [diː'seləreɪt] vi (car, train) langsamer werden; (driver) die Geschwindigkeit herabsetzen.

**deceleration** [diːˌselə'reɪʃən] n see vi Langsamerwerden nt; Herabsetzung f der Geschwindigkeit.

**December** [dɪ'sembəʳ] n Dezember m; see September.

**decency** ['diːsənsɪ] n Anstand m. it's only common ~ to ... es gehört sich einfach, zu ...; have you no sense of ~? haben Sie denn kein Anstandsgefühl!; they didn't even have the ~ ... sie haben es nicht einmal für nötig gehalten, ...

**decent** ['diːsənt] adj anständig. are you ~? (col) bist du schon angezogen?

**decentralization** ['diːˌsentrəlaɪ'zeɪʃən] n Dezentralisierung f.

**decentralize** [diː'sentrəlaɪz] vti dezentralisieren.

**deception** [dɪ'sepʃən] n Betrug m no pl (of an +dat); (of public etc) Täuschung f.

**deceptive** [dɪ'septɪv] adj irreführend; similarity täuschend; simplicity trügerisch. to be ~ täuschen, trügen (geh); appearances can be ~ der Schein trügt.

**deceptively** [dɪ'septɪvlɪ] adv täuschend.

**decibel** ['desɪbel] n Dezibel nt.

**decide** [dɪ'saɪd] **1** vt (a) (come to a decision) (sich) entscheiden; (take it into one's head) beschließen. did you ~ anything? habt ihr irgendwelche Entscheidungen getroffen?; I have ~d we are making a big mistake ich bin zu der Überzeugung gekommen, daß wir einen großen Fehler machen; I'll ~ what we do! ich bestimme, was wir tun! (b) (settle) question, war entscheiden. that ~s it damit ist die Sache entschieden; that eventually ~d me das hat schließlich für mich den Ausschlag gegeben. **2** vi (sich) entscheiden. I don't know, you ~ ich weiß nicht, entscheiden or bestimmen Sie!; to ~ for/against sth (sich) für/gegen etw entscheiden.

▶**decide on** vi +prep obj sich entscheiden für.

**decided** [dɪ'saɪdɪd] adj (a) (clear, definite) entschieden; difference deutlich. (b) (determined) manner entschlossen, bestimmt.

**decidedly** [dɪ'saɪdɪdlɪ] adv (definitely) entschieden.

**deciding** [dɪ'saɪdɪŋ] adj entscheidend.

**deciduous** [dɪ'sɪdjuəs] adj ~ tree Laubbaum m.

**decimal** ['desɪməl] **1** adj Dezimal-. ~ currency Dezimalwährung f; to three ~ places auf drei Dezimalstellen; ~ point Komma nt; ~ system Dezimalsystem nt. **2** n Dezimalzahl f.

**decimalization** [ˌdesɪməlaɪ'zeɪʃən] n Umstellung f auf das Dezimalsystem.

**decimate** ['desɪmeɪt] vt dezimieren.

**decipher** [dɪ'saɪfəʳ] vt (lit, fig) entziffern.

**decision** [dɪ'sɪʒən] n (a) Entscheidung f (on über +acc), Entschluß m; (esp of committee etc) Beschluß m. to make a ~ eine Entscheidung treffen or fällen, einen Entschluß/Beschluß fassen; it's your ~ das mußt du entscheiden; to come to a ~ zu einer Entscheidung kommen. (b) no pl (of character) Entschlossenheit f.

**decision:** ~**-maker** n Entscheidungsträger m; ~**-making** n Entscheidungsfindung f; ~**-making**

**skills** *npl* Entschlußfähigkeit *f.*
**decisive** [dɪ'saɪsɪv] *adj* **(a)** entscheidend; *factor also* ausschlaggebend. **(b)** *manner, answer* entschlossen; *person* entschlußfreudig.
**deck** [dek] **1** *n* **(a)** *(Naut)* Deck *nt.* **on** ~ auf Deck; **to go up on** ~ an Deck gehen; **to go (down) below** ~**(s)** unter Deck gehen. **(b)** *(of bus)* **top** *or* **upper** ~ Oberdeck *nt.* **(c)** *(of cards)* Spiel *nt.* **(d)** *(hi-fi unit)* Laufwerk *nt.* **cassette** ~ Kassettendeck *nt*; **record** ~ Plattenspieler *m.* **2** *vt (also* ~ **out)** schmücken.
**deckchair** ['dektʃɛəʳ] *n* Liegestuhl *m.*
**declaim** [dɪ'kleɪm] *vi* deklamieren.
**declaration** [deklə'reɪʃən] *n* Erklärung *f.*
**declare** [dɪ'klɛəʳ] *vt* erklären; *results* bekanntgeben; *goods* angeben. **have you anything to** ~? haben Sie etwas zu verzollen?; **to** ~ **one's income** sein Einkommen angeben; **to** ~ **war (on sb)** (jdm) den Krieg erklären; **to** ~ **sb the winner** jdn zum Sieger erklären; **he** ~**d that** ... er behauptete, daß ...
**declared** [dɪ'klɛəd] *adj* erklärt.
**declassify** [diː'klæsɪfaɪ] *vt information* freigeben.
**declension** [dɪ'klenʃən] *n (Gram)* Deklination *f.*
**decline** [dɪ'klaɪn] **1** *n* **(a)** Rückgang *m*; *(of empire, a party's supremacy)* Untergang, Niedergang *m.* **to be on the** ~ *see vi.* **(b)** *(Med)* Verfall *m.* **2** *vt* **(a)** *invitation, honour* ablehnen. **he** ~**d to come** er hat es abgelehnt, zu kommen. **(b)** *(Gram)* deklinieren. **3** *vi* **(a)** *(prices, value)* sinken; *(popularity, enthusiasm, interest)* abnehmen; *(population, influence, business)* zurückgehen; *(empire)* verfallen; *(fame)* verblassen; *(health)* sich verschlechtern. **in his declining years** gegen Ende seines Lebens. **(b)** *(refuse, say no)* ablehnen. **(c)** *(Gram)* dekliniert werden.
**declutch** [‚diː'klʌtʃ] *vi* auskuppeln.
**decode** [‚diː'kəʊd] *vt* entschlüsseln; *(Comp, TV)* dekodieren, decodieren.
**decoder** [‚diː'kəʊdəʳ] *n (Comp, TV etc)* Decoder *m.*
**decommission** [‚diːkə'mɪʃən] *vt power station* stillegen; *warship* außer Dienst nehmen.
**decompose** [‚diːkəm'pəʊz] *vi (Chem, Phys)* zerlegt werden; *(rot)* sich zersetzen; *(body)* verwesen.
**decomposition** [‚diːkɒmpə'zɪʃən] *n (Chem, Phys)* Zerlegung *f*; *(rotting)* Zersetzung *f*; *(of body)* Verwesung *f.*
**decompression** [‚diːkəm'preʃən] *n* Dekompression, Druckverminderung *f.* ~ **chamber** *n* Dekompressionskammer *f.*
**decongestant** [‚diːkən'dʒestənt] *n (Med)* (die Nasenschleimhaut) abschwellendes Mittel *nt.*
**decontaminate** [‚diːkən'tæmɪneɪt] *vt* entgiften; *(from radioactivity)* entseuchen.
**decontamination** [‚diːkəntæmɪ'neɪʃən] *n see vt* Entgiftung *f*; Entseuchung *f.*
**decontrol** [‚diːkən'trəʊl] *vt prices* freigeben.
**décor** ['deɪkɔːʳ] *n (in room)* Ausstattung *f*; *(Theat)* Bühnenbild *nt.*
**decorate** ['dekəreɪt] *vt* **(a)** *cake, hat* verzieren; *street, Christmas tree* schmücken; *room (paint)* streichen; *(paint and wallpaper)* streichen und tapezieren. **(b)** *soldier* dekorieren, auszeichnen.
**decoration** [‚dekə'reɪʃən] *n* **(a)** *(act: of room etc)* Tapezieren *nt*; *(An)*streichen *nt.* *(on cake, hat etc)* Verzierung *f*; *(on Christmas tree, in street)* Schmuck *m no pl.* **Christmas** ~**s** Weihnachtsdekorationen *pl or* -schmuck *m*; **interior** ~ Innenausstattung *f.* **(c)** *(Mil)* Auszeichnung *f.*
**decorative** ['dekərətɪv] *adj* dekorativ.
**decorator** ['dekəreɪtəʳ] *n (Brit)* Maler und Tapezierer *m.*
**decorous** ['dekərəs] *adj* schicklich.
**decorum** [dɪ'kɔːrəm] *n* Anstand *m.*

**decoy** ['diːkɔɪ] *n (lit, fig)* Köder *m*; *(person)* Lockvogel *m.*
**decrease** [diː'kriːs] **1** *vi* abnehmen; *(figures, output, birthrate, production)* zurückgehen; *(strength, enthusiasm, intensity)* nachlassen. **it** ~**s in value** es verliert an Wert. **2** *vt* verringern, reduzieren. **3** ['diːkriːs] *n see vi* Abnahme *f*; Rückgang *m*; Nachlassen *nt.* **to be on the** ~ *see vi.*
**decreasing** [diː'kriːsɪŋ] *adj see vi* abnehmend; zurückgehend; nachlassend.
**decreasingly** [diː'kriːsɪŋlɪ] *adv* immer weniger.
**decree** [dɪ'kriː] **1** *n (Pol, of king etc)* Erlaß *m*; *(of tribunal, court)* Entscheid *m*, Urteil *nt.* ~ **nisi/absolute** vorläufiges/endgültiges Scheidungsurteil. **2** *vt* verordnen, verfügen.
**decrepit** [dɪ'krepɪt] *adj* altersschwach; *building also* baufällig.
**decry** [dɪ'kraɪ] *vt* schlechtmachen.
**dedicate** ['dedɪkeɪt] *vt* **(a)** *church* weihen. **(b)** *book, music* widmen *(to sb* jdm*).* **to** ~ **oneself** *or* **one's life to sth** sich *or* sein Leben einer Sache widmen.
**dedicated** ['dedɪkeɪtɪd] *adj* **(a)** *attitude* hingebungsvoll; *service* treu; *teacher etc* engagiert. **she's a** ~ **nurse** sie ist Krankenschwester mit Leib und Seele. **(b)** *(Comp)* dediziert.
**dedication** [‚dedɪ'keɪʃən] *n* **(a)** *(quality)* Hingabe *f (to an* +*acc); (to work)* Engagement *nt.* **(b)** *(of church)* Weihe *f.* **(c)** *(in book)* Widmung *f.*
**deduce** [dɪ'djuːs] *vt* folgern, schließen *(from* aus*).*
**deduct** [dɪ'dʌkt] *vt* abziehen *(from* von*); (from wages also)* einbehalten. **to** ~ **sth from the price** etw vom Preis nachlassen.
**deductible** [dɪ'dʌktəbl] *adj* abziehbar; *(tax* ~*)* absetzbar.
**deduction** [dɪ'dʌkʃən] *n* **(a)** *(act of deducting)* Abzug *m*; *(sth deducted) (from price)* Nachlaß *m*; *(from wage)* Abzug *m.* **(b)** *(sth deduced)* (Schluß)-folgerung *f.*
**deed** [diːd] *n* **(a)** Tat *f.* **good** ~ gute Tat; **in word and** ~ in Wort und Tat. **(b)** *(Jur)* Urkunde *f.* ~ **of covenant** Vertragsurkunde *f.*
**deem** [diːm] *vt* **to** ~ **sb/sth (to be) sth** jdn/etw für etw erachten *(geh)* or halten.
**deep** [diːp] **1** *adj* (+*er*) tief; *(profound)* *thinker, book, remark* tiefsinnig; *concern, interest* groß; *sorrow* tief (empfunden). **two metres** ~ **in snow/water** mit zwei Meter Schnee bedeckt/zwei Meter tief unter Wasser; **to go off (at) the** ~ **end** *(col)* an die Decke gehen *(col)*; **to plunge in at the** ~ **end** *(col)* sich kopfüber in die Sache stürzen; **to be thrown in at the** ~ **end** *(col)* gleich zu Anfang richtig ranmüssen *(col)*; ~ **in thought/a book** in Gedanken/in ein Buch vertieft; **he's a** ~ **one** *(col)* er ist ein stilles Wasser. **2** *adv* (+*er*) tief. ~ **into the night** bis tief in die Nacht hinein; **they stood ten** ~ sie standen in zehn Reihen hintereinander. **3** *n (liter)* **the** ~ das Meer, die See.
**deepen** ['diːpən] **1** *vt (lit, fig)* vertiefen. **2** *vi (lit, fig)* tiefer werden; *(concern, interest)* zunehmen; *(mystery)* größer werden.
**deep:** ~**-freeze 1** *n* Tiefkühltruhe *f*; *(upright)* Gefrierschrank *m*; **2** *vt* einfrieren; ~**-fry** *vt* fritieren, in schwimmendem Fett ausbacken.
**deeply** ['diːplɪ] *adv* **(a)** *dig, cut, breathe* tief; *think, consider also* gründlich. **(b)** *grateful, concerned* zutiefst; *offended also, indebted* tief; *love* innig; *interested* höchst; *aware* voll(kommen).
**deep:** ~**-rooted** *adj (fig)* tiefverwurzelt; ~**-sea** *adj plant, current, animal* Meeres-; ~**-sea diver** *n* Tiefseetaucher *m*; ~**-sea fishing** *n* Hochseefischerei *f*; ~**-seated** *adj* tiefsitzend; ~**-set** *adj* tiefliegend; **D**~

defy

**South** n Tiefer Süden.
**deer** [dɪər] n, pl - Hirsch m; (roe ~) Reh nt. **are there any ~ here?** gibt es hier Wild?
**deer:** ~ **park** n Wildpark m; **~skin** n Hirsch-/Rehleder nt; **~stalker** n (hat) ≃ Sherlock-Holmes-Mütze f; **~stalking** n Pirschen nt, Pirsch f.
**deface** [dɪ'feɪs] vt verunstalten.
**de facto** [deɪ'fæktəʊ] adj, adv de facto.
**defamation** [ˌdefə'meɪʃən] n Diffamierung, Verleumdung f. ~ **of character** Rufmord m.
**defamatory** [dɪ'fæmətərɪ] adj diffamierend.
**default** [dɪ'fɔːlt] **1** n (a) (failure to appear) (Jur) Nichterscheinen nt vor Gericht; (Sport) Nichtantreten nt; (failure to perform duty) Versäumnis nt. **to win by ~** (Sport) kampflos gewinnen. (b) ['diːfɔːlt] (Comp) Default m, Voreinstellung f. **2** vi (not appear) (Jur) nicht erscheinen; (Sport) nicht antreten; (not perform duty, not pay) säumig sein. **to ~ in one's payments** seinen Zahlungsverpflichtungen nicht nachkommen. **3** ['diːfɔːlt] attr (Comp) voreingestellt. ~ **drive** Standardlaufwerk nt.
**defeat** [dɪ'fiːt] **1** n (defeating) Sieg m (of über +acc); (of motion, bill) Ablehnung f; (being defeated) Niederlage f. **to admit ~** sich geschlagen geben. **2** vt army, team besiegen, schlagen; government also eine Niederlage beibringen (+dat); motion, bill ablehnen; **that would be ~ing the purpose** das würde den Zweck verfehlen.
**defeatism** [dɪ'fiːtɪzəm] n Defätismus m.
**defeatist** [dɪ'fiːtɪst] **1** n Defätist m. **2** adj defätistisch.
**defecate** ['defəkeɪt] vi den Darm entleeren.
**defect**[1] ['diːfekt] n Fehler, Schaden m; (in mechanism also) Defekt m. **physical ~** Mißbildung f; (less serious) Schönheitsfehler m; **a character ~** ein Charakterfehler m.
**defect**[2] [dɪ'fekt] vi sich absetzen; (fig) abtrünnig werden. **to ~ to the enemy** zum Feind übergehen or überlaufen.
**defection** [dɪ'fekʃən] n (Pol) Überlaufen nt, (fig) Abtrünnigkeit f, Abfall m.
**defective** [dɪ'fektɪv] adj fehlerhaft; machine also defekt; hearing, sight mangelhaft, gestört.
**defector** [dɪ'fektər] n Überlaufer(in f) m; (fig) Abtrünnige(r) mf.
**defence,** (US) **defense** [dɪ'fens] n Verteidigung f; (Sport also) Abwehr f. **in his ~** zu seiner Verteidigung; **to come to sb's ~** jdn verteidigen; **to put up a stubborn ~** sich hartnäckig verteidigen; **his only ~ was ...** seine einzige Rechtfertigung war ...; **counsel for the ~** Verteidiger(in f) m; **as a ~ against** als Schutz gegen; **~s** (Mil) Verteidigungsanlagen pl; **Ministry of D~** Verteidigungsministerium nt.
**defence:** ~ **expenditure** n Verteidigungsausgaben pl; **~less** adj schutzlos; ~ **mechanism** n Abwehrmechanismus m.
**defend** [dɪ'fend] vt verteidigen (also Jur) (against gegen). **to ~ oneself** sich verteidigen.
**defendant** [dɪ'fendənt] n Angeklagte(r) mf; (in civil cases) Beklagte(r) mf.
**defender** [dɪ'fendər] n Verteidiger m.
**defending** [dɪ'fendɪŋ] adj: ~ **counsel** Verteidiger(in f) m.
**defense** etc [dɪ'fens] (US) = **defence** etc.
**defensive** [dɪ'fensɪv] **1** adj defensiv (also fig), Verteidigungs-. ~ **capability** Verteidigungsfähigkeit f. **2** n (Mil) Abwehraktion f. **to be on the ~** (Mil, fig) in der Defensive sein.
**defer**[1] [dɪ'fɜːr] vt (delay) verschieben; event also verlegen. **~red terms** Ratenkauf m.
**defer**[2] vi (submit) **to ~ to sb/sb's wishes** sich jdm

beugen or fügen/sich jds Wünschen (dat) fügen.
**deference** ['defərəns] n Achtung f, Respekt m. **out of ~ to** aus Achtung or Respekt vor (+dat).
**deferential** [ˌdefə'renʃəl] adj ehrerbietig, respektvoll.
**deferment** [dɪ'fɜːmənt] n see **defer**[1] Verschiebung f; Verlegung f.
**defiance** [dɪ'faɪəns] n Trotz m. **in ~ of sb/sb's orders** jdm/jds Anordnungen zum Trotz.
**defiant** [dɪ'faɪənt] adj aufsässig; esp child also, answer trotzig; (challenging) attitude herausfordernd.
**deficiency** [dɪ'fɪʃənsɪ] n Mangel m; (in character, system) Schwäche f. ~ **disease** Mangelkrankheit f.
**deficient** [dɪ'fɪʃənt] adj unzulänglich. **sb/sth is ~ in sth** jdm/einer Sache fehlt es an etw (dat).
**deficit** ['defɪsɪt] n Defizit nt.
**defile**[1] ['diːfaɪl] n Hohlweg m.
**defile**[2] [dɪ'faɪl] vt (pollute) verschmutzen; (desecrate) schänden, entweihen.
**define** [dɪ'faɪn] vt (a) festlegen, bestimmen; word definieren. **to ~ one's position** seinen Standpunkt klarmachen. (b) **to be clearly ~d against the sky** sich klar gegen den Himmel abzeichnen.
**definite** ['defɪnɪt] adj answer, decision klar, eindeutig; date, agreement, plan fest, definitiv; improvement, lisp deutlich; manner, tone bestimmt. **is that ~?** ist das sicher?; **the date is not ~ yet** der Termin steht noch nicht fest; **she was very ~ about it** sie war sich (dat) sehr sicher; (insistent) sie bestand darauf; **can't you be more ~?** können Sie sich etwas genauer festlegen?; ~ **article** (Gram) bestimmter Artikel.
**definitely** ['defɪnɪtlɪ] adv bestimmt; decide, arrange fest, definitiv. **he ~ wanted to come** er wollte auf jeden Fall kommen; **that's ~ an improvement** das ist eindeutig eine Verbesserung.
**definition** [ˌdefɪ'nɪʃən] n (a) (of word, concept) Definition f. (b) (of powers, duties, boundaries) Festlegung, Bestimmung f. (c) (Phot, TV) Bildschärfe f; (Opt: of lens) Schärfe f.
**definitive** [dɪ'fɪnɪtɪv] adj victory, answer entscheiden; (authoritative) book maßgeblich (on für).
**deflate** [ˌdiː'fleɪt] vt tyre etwas Luft/die Luft ablassen aus. **to ~ the currency** eine Deflation herbeiführen; **he was a bit ~d** es war ein ziemlicher Dämpfer für ihn.
**deflation** [ˌdiː'fleɪʃən] n (Fin) Deflation f.
**deflationary** [ˌdiː'fleɪʃənərɪ] adj (Fin) deflationär.
**deflect** [dɪ'flekt] vt ablenken; (Phys) light beugen.
**deflower** [ˌdiː'flaʊər] vt entjungfern, deflorieren.
**defog** [diː'fɒg] vt (US) = **demist**.
**defogger** [diː'fɒgər] n (US) = **demister**.
**deforestation** [diːˌfɒrɪ'steɪʃən] n Entwaldung f.
**deform** [dɪ'fɔːm] vt deformieren, verunstalten.
**deformed** [dɪ'fɔːmd] adj limb, body mißgebildet.
**deformity** [dɪ'fɔːmɪtɪ] n Mißbildung f.
**defraud** [dɪ'frɔːd] vt **to ~ sb of sth** jdn um etw betrügen.
**defray** [dɪ'freɪ] vt tragen, übernehmen.
**defrock** [ˌdiː'frɒk] vt aus dem Priesteramt verstoßen.
**defrost** [ˌdiː'frɒst] vt entfrosten; fridge abtauen; food auftauen.
**defroster** [ˌdiː'frɒstər] n (US) Defroster m; (blower) Gebläse nt.
**deft** [deft] adj (+er) flink, geschickt.
**defunct** [dɪ'fʌŋkt] adj institution etc eingegangen; law außer Kraft.
**defuse** [ˌdiː'fjuːz] vt (lit, fig) entschärfen.
**defy** [dɪ'faɪ] vt (a) (disobey) person sich widersetzen (+dat); orders, law, death, danger trotzen (+dat).

**(b)** *(fig) efforts* widerstehen *(+dat)*. **to ~ definition** sich nicht erklären *or* definieren lassen; **to ~ description** jeder Beschreibung spotten. **(c)** *(challenge)* **I ~ you to do better** machen Sie es doch besser, wenn Sie können.

**degeneracy** [dɪ'dʒenərəsɪ] *n* Degeneriertheit *f.*

**degenerate** [dɪ'dʒenərɪt] **1** *adj* degeneriert; *race, morals also* entartet. **2** *n* degenerierter Mensch. **3** [dɪ'dʒenəreɪt] *vi* degenerieren; *(people, morals also)* entarten.

**degradation** [ˌdegrə'deɪʃən] *n* Erniedrigung *f.*

**degrade** [dɪ'greɪd] *vt* erniedrigen.

**degrading** [dɪ'greɪdɪŋ] *adj* erniedrigend.

**degree** [dɪ'griː] *n* **(a)** Grad *m no pl.* **it was 35 ~s in the shade** es waren 35 Grad im Schatten. **(b)** *(extent)* **to some ~, to a (certain) ~** zu einem gewissen Grad, in gewissem Maße; **to a high ~** in hohem Maße; **to such a ~ that** ... so sehr, daß ...; **to what ~ was he involved?** inwieweit war er verwickelt?; **by ~s** nach und nach; **first/second ~ murder** *(Jur)* Mord *m*/Totschlag *m.* **(c)** *(Univ)* akademischer Grad. **when did you do your ~?** wann haben Sie das Examen gemacht?; **he has a ~ in English** er hat ein abgeschlossenes Anglistikstudium; **she has a ~** sie hat einen Universitätsabschluß.

**dehydrate** [ˌdiːhaɪ'dreɪt] *vt* Wasser entziehen *(+dat).*

**dehydrated** [ˌdiːhaɪ'dreɪtɪd] *adj vegetables, milk* Trocken-; *person, skin* ausgetrocknet.

**dehydration** [ˌdiːhaɪ'dreɪʃən] *n* Austrocknung *f.*

**de-ice** [ˌdiː'aɪs] *vt* enteisen.

**de-icer** [ˌdiː'aɪsər] *n* Enteiser *m*; *(spray for cars)* Defroster *m.*

**deign** [deɪn] *vt* **to ~ to do sth** sich herablassen, etw zu tun.

**deity** ['diːɪtɪ] *n* Gottheit *f.* **the D~** Gott *m.*

**déjà vu** ['deɪʒɑː'vjuː] *n* Déjà-vu-Erlebnis *nt.* **a feeling of ~** das Gefühl, das schon einmal gesehen *or* erlebt zu haben.

**dejected** [dɪ'dʒektɪd] *adj* niedergeschlagen, deprimiert.

**dejection** [dɪ'dʒekʃən] *n* Niedergeschlagenheit *f.*

**de jure** [ˌdiː'dʒʊərɪ] *adj, adv* de jure.

**delay** [dɪ'leɪ] **1** *vt* **(a)** *(postpone)* verschieben, aufschieben. **he ~ed writing the letter** er schob den Brief auf. **(b)** *(hold up) person, train* aufhalten. **the flight was ~ed** das Flugzeug hatte Verspätung; *(leaving)* der Abflug verzögerte sich; **we'll be ~ed** wir werden uns verspäten; **~ing tactics** Verzögerungstaktik *f.* **2** *vi* **to ~ in doing sth** es aufschieben, etw zu tun; **don't ~!** verlieren Sie keine Zeit! **3** *n (hold-up)* Verzögerung *f*; *(to train, plane)* Verspätung *f*; **there are ~s to all trains** alle Züge haben Verspätung; **without ~** unverzüglich; **without further ~** gleich.

**delayed-action** [dɪ'leɪdˌækʃən] *adj attr bomb, mine* mit Zeitzünder. **~ shutter release** *(Phot)* Selbstauslöser *m.*

**delectable** [dɪ'lektəbl] *adj* köstlich; *(fig)* reizend.

**delegate** ['delɪgeɪt] **1** *vt* delegieren. **to ~ sb to do sth** jdn damit beauftragen, etw zu tun. **2** *vi* delegieren. **3** ['delɪgət] *n* Delegierte(r) *mf.*

**delegation** [ˌdelɪ'geɪʃən] *n* Delegation *f (to an +acc).*

**delete** [dɪ'liːt] *vt* streichen *(from von)*; *tape recording, (Comp)* löschen.

**deletion** [dɪ'liːʃən] *n see vt* Streichung *f*; Löschung *f.*

**Delhi** ['delɪ] *n* Delhi *nt.*

**deli** ['delɪ] *n (esp US col)* = **delicatessen.**

**deliberate** [dɪ'lɪbərɪt] **1** *adj* **(a)** *(intentional)* absichtlich; *action, insult, lie also* bewußt. **(b)** *(cautious, thoughtful)* besonnen; *action* (wohl)überlegt; *(slow)*

*movement, step* bedächtig. **2** [dɪ'lɪbəreɪt] *vi (ponder)* nachdenken *(on über +acc)*; *(discuss)* sich beraten *(on über +acc, wegen).* **3** [dɪ'lɪbəreɪt] *vt (ponder)* bedenken, überlegen; *(discuss)* beraten.

**deliberately** [dɪ'lɪbərɪtlɪ] *adv* **(a)** absichtlich, bewußt. **(b)** *(purposefully, slowly)* bedächtig.

**deliberation** [dɪˌlɪbə'reɪʃən] *n* **(a)** *(consideration)* Überlegung *f.* **(b)** *(discussion)* Beratungen *pl (of, on* in *+dat,* über *+acc).*

**delicacy** ['delɪkəsɪ] *n see adj* **(a)** Feinheit *f*; Zerbrechlichkeit *f*; Zartheit *f*; Empfindlichkeit *f.* **the ~ of his health** seine schwächliche Konstitution. **(b)** Feinfühligkeit *f*; Empfindlichkeit *f*; Empfindsamkeit *f.* **(c)** Heikle *nt (of an +dat).* **(d)** *(food)* Delikatesse *f.*

**delicate** ['delɪkɪt] *adj* **(a)** *fabric etc* fein, zart; *(fragile)* zerbrechlich; *person* zart; *stomach* empfindlich. **to have very ~ health** sehr anfällig sein. **(b)** *(sensitive) person* feinfühlig; *instrument* empfindlich; *playing* empfindsam. **(c)** *operation, situation* heikel, delikat.

**delicately** ['delɪkɪtlɪ] *adv* fein; *(tactfully)* taktvoll.

**delicateness** ['delɪkɪtnɪs] *n see* **delicacy (a), (b), (c).**

**delicatessen** [ˌdelɪkə'tesn] *n* Feinkostgeschäft *nt.*

**delicious** [dɪ'lɪʃəs] *adj* köstlich, lecker *(col).*

**delight** [dɪ'laɪt] **1** *n* Freude *f.* **to my ~** zu meiner Freude; **he takes great ~ in doing that** es bereitet ihm große Freude, das zu tun; **he's a ~ to watch** es ist eine Freude, ihm zuzusehen. **2** *vt* erfreuen. **3** *vi* sich erfreuen *(in an +dat).*

**delighted** [dɪ'laɪtɪd] *adj* **to be ~** sich sehr freuen *(at* über *+acc, that* daß*);* **I'd be ~ to help you** ich würde Ihnen sehr gern helfen.

**delightful** [dɪ'laɪtfʊl] *adj* reizend; *weather, party, meal* wunderbar.

**delightfully** [dɪ'laɪtfəlɪ] *adv* wunderbar.

**delimit** [diː'lɪmɪt] *vt* abstecken, abgrenzen.

**delineate** [dɪ'lɪnɪeɪt] *vt (draw)* skizzieren; *(describe)* beschreiben.

**delinquency** [dɪ'lɪŋkwənsɪ] *n* Kriminalität *f.*

**delinquent** [dɪ'lɪŋkwənt] **1** *adj* **(a)** straffällig. **(b)** *(US) bill* überfällig; *account* rückständig. **2** *n* Delinquent *m.*

**delirious** [dɪ'lɪrɪəs] *adj (Med)* im Delirium; *(fig)* im Taumel. **~ with joy** im Freudentaumel.

**deliriously** [dɪ'lɪrɪəslɪ] *adv* **~ happy** überglücklich.

**delirium** [dɪ'lɪrɪəm] *n (Med)* Delirium *nt.*

**deliver** [dɪ'lɪvər] **1** *vt* **(a)** *goods* liefern; *note, message* überbringen; *(on regular basis) letters, papers etc* zustellen. **to ~ sth to sb** jdm etw liefern/zustellen; **to ~ sth to the door** etw ins Haus liefern; **he ~ed me right to the door** er brachte mich bis zur Tür; **to ~ the goods** *(fig col)* es bringen *(col)*, es schaffen. **(b)** *(liter: rescue)* befreien. **(c)** *(pronounce) speech* halten; *ultimatum* stellen; *verdict* verkünden. **(d)** *baby* zur Welt bringen. **(e)** *(aim) blow* versetzen. **2** *vi* **(a)** liefern. **(b)** **they didn't ~** *(fig col)* sie brachten's nicht *(col).*

**deliverance** [dɪ'lɪvərəns] *n (liter)* Erlösung *(from* von*) f.*

**delivery** [dɪ'lɪvərɪ] *n* **(a)** *(of goods)* Lieferung *f*; *(of parcels, letters)* Zustellung *f.* **to take ~ of sth** etw in Empfang nehmen; **to pay on ~** bei Empfang zahlen. **(b)** *(Med)* Entbindung *f.* **(c)** *(of speaker)* Vortragsweise *f.*

**delivery:** **~ boy** *n* Bote *m*; *(for newspapers)* Austräger *m*; **~ date** *n* Liefertermin *m*; **~ note** *n* Lieferschein *m*; **~ van** *n (Brit)* Lieferwagen *m.*

**delouse** [ˌdiː'laʊs] *vt* entlausen.

**delphinium** [del'fɪnɪəm] *n* Rittersporn *m.*

**deny**

**delta** ['deltə] *n* Delta *nt.* ~ **wing** Deltaflügel *m.*
**delude** [dɪ'luːd] *vt* täuschen, irreführen *(with* mit*).*
**to** ~ **sb into thinking sth** jdm etw weismachen; **to**
~ **oneself** sich *(dat)* Illusionen machen, sich *(dat)* etwas vormachen.
**deluge** ['deljuːdʒ] **1** *n* Überschwemmung *f; (of rain)*
Wolkenbruch *m; (fig: of letters etc)* Flut *f.* **2** *vt (lit,*
*fig)* überschwemmen, überfluten.
**delusion** [dɪ'luːʒən] *n* Illusion *f,* Irrglaube *m no pl.*
**de luxe** [dɪ'lʌks] *adj* Luxus-.
**delve** [delv] *vi (into book)* sich vertiefen *(into* in
+*acc).* **to** ~ **into one's pocket** tief in die Tasche
greifen.
**Dem** *(US Pol)* = **Democrat** dem.
**demagogue** ['deməgɒg] *n* Demagoge *m,* Demago-
gin *f.*
**demand** [dɪ'mɑːnd] **1** *vt* verlangen, fordern *(of, from*
von*); (situation, task etc)* erfordern; **he** ~**ed to see**
**my passport** er verlangte meinen Paß. **2** *n* **(a)** Forderung *f (for* nach*).* **by popular** ~ auf allgemeinen
Wunsch; **to make** ~**s on sb** Forderungen an jdn
stellen; **I have many** ~**s on my time** ich habe sehr
viele Verpflichtungen. **(b)** *no pl (Comm)* Nachfrage
*f,* Bedarf *m (for* nach*).* **to be in great** ~ *(article, per-*
*son)* sehr gefragt sein.
**demanding** [dɪ'mɑːndɪŋ] *adj child* anstrengend; *task*
*also, teacher, boss* anspruchsvoll. **physically** ~ körperlich anstrengend.
**demarcate** ['diːmɑːkeɪt] *vt* abgrenzen, demarkieren.
**demarcation** [ˌdiːmɑː'keɪʃən] *n* Abgrenzung, De-
markation *f.* ~**-line** Demarkationslinie *f;* ~ **dispute**
Streit *m* um den Zuständigkeitsbereich.
**demeaning** [dɪ'miːnɪŋ] *adj* erniedrigend.
**demeanour,** *(US)* **demeanor** [dɪ'miːnəʳ] *n (behav-*
*iour)* Benehmen, Auftreten *nt.*
**demented** [dɪ'mentɪd] *adj* verrückt, wahnsinnig.
**demerara (sugar)** [ˌdeməˈrɛərə('ʃʊgəʳ)] *n* brauner
Rohrzucker.
**demi** ['demɪ-] *pref* Halb-, halb-. ~**god** Halbgott *m.*
**demilitarize** [ˌdiːˈmɪlɪtəraɪz] *vt* demilitarisieren.
**demise** [dɪ'maɪz] *n (form)* Ableben *nt (geh); (fig: of*
*institution, newspaper etc)* Ende *nt.*
**demist** [ˌdiː'mɪst] *vt windscreen* freimachen.
**demister** [ˌdiː'mɪstəʳ] *n (Brit)* Defroster *m; (blower)*
Gebläse *nt.*
**demitasse** ['demɪtæs] *n (US) (cup)* Mokkatasse *f;*
*(coffee)* Kaffee *m.*
**demo** ['deməʊ] *n (col)* = **demonstration** Demo *f*
*(col).*
**demob** [diː'mɒb] *(col),* **demobilize** [diː'məʊbɪlaɪz]
*vt* aus dem Kriegsdienst entlassen.
**democracy** [dɪ'mɒkrəsɪ] *n* Demokratie *f.*
**democrat** ['deməkræt] *n* Demokrat(in *f) m.*
**democratic** *adj,* ~**ally** *adv* [ˌdemə'krætɪk, -əlɪ] demokratisch. *(US Pol)* **D**~ **Party** Demokratische Partei.
**demography** [dɪ'mɒgrəfɪ] *n* Demographie *f.*
**demolish** [dɪ'mɒlɪʃ] *vt building* ab- or einreißen; *(fig)*
*opponent, theory* zunichte machen, vernichten;
*(hum) cake etc* vertilgen.
**demolition** [ˌdemə'lɪʃən] *n* Abbruch *m.*
**demon** ['diːmən] *n* Dämon *m; (col: child)* Teufel *m.*
**to be a** ~ **for work** ein Arbeitstier sein.
**demonstrable** ['demənstrəbl] *adj* offensichtlich, beweisbar.
**demonstrably** ['demənstrəblɪ] *adv* beweisbar. ~
**false** nachweislich falsch.
**demonstrate** ['demənstreɪt] **1** *vt* **(a)** zeigen, beweisen. **(b)** *appliance etc* vorführen. **2** *vi (Pol)* demonstrieren.
**demonstration** [ˌdemən'streɪʃən] *n* **(a)** Beweis *m;*

*(of appliance)* Vorführung *f.* **(b)** *(Pol)* Demonstration *f.*
**demonstrative** [dɪ'mɒnstrətɪv] *adj* demonstrativ.
**he's not very** ~ er zeigt seine Gefühle nicht.
**demonstrator** ['demənstreɪtəʳ] *n* **(a)** *(Comm)* Vor-
führer(in *f) m; (car)* Vorführwagen *m.* **(b)** *(Pol)* De-
monstrant(in *f) m.*
**demoralize** [dɪ'mɒrəlaɪz] *vt* entmutigen; *troops etc*
demoralisieren.
**demote** [dɪ'məʊt] *vt (Mil)* degradieren *(to* zu*); (in*
*business etc)* zurückstufen.
**demotion** [dɪ'məʊʃən] *n (Mil)* Degradierung *f; (in*
*business etc)* Zurückstufung *f.*
**demur** [dɪ'mɜːʳ] *(form)* **1** *vi* Einwände erheben *(at*
gegen*).* **2** *n without* ~ widerspruchslos.
**demure** [dɪ'mjʊəʳ] *adj (+er) (coy)* spröde; *(sedate)*
ernst, gesetzt.
**den** [den] *n* **(a)** *(of lion etc)* Höhle *f; (of fox)* Bau *m.* ~
**of iniquity** Lasterhöhle *f;* ~ **of thieves** Spelunke,
Räuberhöhle *(hum) f.* **(b)** *(room)* Bude *f (col).*
**denationalization** ['diːˌnæʃnəlaɪ'zeɪʃən] *n* Entstaat-
lichung *f.*
**denationalize** [ˌdiː'næʃnəlaɪz] *vt* entstaatlichen.
**denial** [dɪ'naɪəl] *n* **(a)** *(of accusation, guilt)* Leugnen
*nt.* **an official** ~ ein offizielles Dementi. **(b)** *(of re-*
*quest etc)* Ablehnung *f; (official)* abschlägiger Bescheid; *(of rights)* Verweigerung *f.*
**denier** ['denɪəʳ] *n (of stockings)* Denier *nt.*
**denigrate** ['denɪgreɪt] *vt* verunglimpfen.
**denim** ['denɪm] *n* **(a)** Jeansstoff *m.* **(b)** *attr* Jeans-. ~
**jacket** Jeansjacke *f.* **(c)** ~**s** *pl* (Blue) Jeans *pl.*
**Denmark** ['denmɑːk] *n* Dänemark *nt.*
**denomination** [dɪˌnɒmɪ'neɪʃən] *n* **(a)** *(Eccl)* Konfession *f.* **(b)** *(of money)* Nennwert *m.*
**denominational** [dɪˌnɒmɪ'neɪʃənəl] *adj* konfessionell.
**denominator** [dɪ'nɒmɪneɪtəʳ] *n (Math)* Nenner *m.*
**denote** [dɪ'nəʊt] *vt* bedeuten.
**dénouement** [dɪ'nuːmɒŋ] *n* Ausgang *m.*
**denounce** [dɪ'naʊns] *vt* **(a)** *(accuse)* anprangern; *(in-*
*form against)* anzeigen, denunzieren *(sb to sb* jdn
bei jdm*).* **(b)** *(condemn) alcohol, habit etc* verurteilen.
**dense** [dens] *adj (+er)* **(a)** dicht. **(b)** *(col: stupid)*
beschränkt.
**densely** ['denslɪ] *adv* ~ **populated** dicht bevölkert.
**density** ['densɪtɪ] *n* Dichte *f.* **population** ~ Bevölke-
rungsdichte *f.*
**dent** [dent] **1** *n (in metal)* Beule, Delle *(col) f.* **that**
**made a** ~ **in his savings** *(col)* das hat ein Loch in
seine Ersparnisse gerissen. **2** *vt car* eindellen, verbeulen; *(col) pride* anknacksen *(col).*
**dental** ['dentl] *adj* Zahn-; *treatment* zahnärztlich. ~
**care** Zahnpflege *f;* ~ **floss** Zahnseide *f;* ~ **surgeon**
Zahnarzt *m*/-ärztin *f.*
**dentifrice** ['dentɪfrɪs] *n* Zahnpasta *f.*
**dentist** ['dentɪst] *n* Zahnarzt *m,* Zahnärztin *f.* **at the**
~**'s** beim Zahnarzt; ~**'s surgery** *(Brit)* or **office** *(US)*
Zahnarztpraxis *f.*
**dentistry** ['dentɪstrɪ] *n* Zahnmedizin *f.*
**dentures** ['dentʃəz] *npl (partial* ~*)* Zahnprothese *f;*
*(full* ~*)* Gebiß *nt.*
**denude** [dɪ'njuːd] *vt* entblößen *(of gen).*
**denunciation** [dɪˌnʌnsɪ'eɪʃən] *n see* **denounce** Anprangerung *f;* Denunziation *f;* Verurteilung *f.*
**deny** [dɪ'naɪ] *vt* **(a)** *charge, accusation etc* bestreiten,
leugnen; *(officially)* dementieren. **do you** ~ **having**
**said that?** leugnen or bestreiten Sie, das gesagt zu
haben?; **I don't** ~ **it** das streite ich gar nicht ab. **(b)**
*(refuse)* **to** ~ **sb a request/his rights** jdm eine Bitte
abschlagen/seine Rechte vorenthalten; **I can't** ~ **her**

**anything** ich kann ihr nichts abschlagen; **to ~ one-self sth** auf etw *(acc)* verzichten. **(c)** *religion, principles* verleugnen.

**deodorant** [diːˈəʊdərənt] **1** *n* Deodorant *nt*. **2** *adj* desodorierend.

**dep** = **departure** Abf.

**depart** [dɪˈpɑːt] *vi* **(a)** *(go away)* weggehen; *(on journey)* abreisen; *(by bus, car etc)* wegfahren; *(train, bus etc)* abfahren. **(b)** *(deviate: from opinion etc)* abweichen, abgehen.

**departed** [dɪˈpɑːtɪd] *n* **the (dear) ~** der/die (liebe) Verstorbene; **die (lieben) Verstorbenen** *pl*.

**department** [dɪˈpɑːtmənt] *n* **(a)** Abteilung *f*; *(in civil service)* Ressort *nt*. **D~ of Employment** *(Brit)* Arbeitsministerium *nt*; **D~ of State** *(US)* Außenministerium *nt*; **that's not my ~** *(fig)* dafür bin ich nicht zuständig. **(b)** *(Univ)* Seminar *nt*.

**departmental** [ˌdiːpɑːtˈmentl] *adj* **(a)** Abteilungs-. **(b)** *(Univ)* Seminar-.

**department store** *n* Kaufhaus, Warenhaus *nt*.

**departure** [dɪˈpɑːtʃər] *n* **(a)** *(of person)* Weggang *m*; *(on journey)* Abreise *f (from* aus*)*; *(of vehicle)* Abfahrt *f*; *(of plane)* Abflug *m*. **~ board** *(Aviat)* Abfluganzeige *f*; *(Rail)* Abfahrtstafel *f*; **~ lounge** Abflughalle *f*; **~ time** *(Aviat)* Abflugzeit *f*; *(Rail, bus)* Abfahrtszeit *f*; **point of ~** *(fig)* Ausgangspunkt *m*. **(b)** *(fig: from custom, truth)* Abweichen *nt (from* von*)*. **a new ~** eine neue Richtung.

**depend** [dɪˈpend] *vi* **(a)** abhängen *(on sb/sth* von jdm/etw*)*. **it all ~s** das hängt ganz davon ab(, ob ...); **that ~s** das kommt darauf an; **~ing on his mood/how late we arrive** je nach seiner Laune/je nachdem, wie spät wir ankommen. **(b)** *(rely)* sich verlassen *(on, upon* auf +*acc)*. **you can ~ (up)on it!** darauf können Sie sich verlassen! **(c)** *(person: be dependent on)* **to ~ on** angewiesen sein auf *(+acc)*.

**dependable** *adj* zuverlässig, verläßlich.

**dependant, dependent** [dɪˈpendənt] *n* Abhängige(r) *mf*. **do you have ~s?** haben Sie (abhängige) Angehörige?

**dependence** [dɪˈpendəns] *n* Abhängigkeit *f (on* von*)*.

**dependency** [dɪˈpendənsɪ] *n* *(country)* Abhängigkeitsgebiet *nt*.

**dependent** [dɪˈpendənt] **1** *adj* abhängig *(on, upon* von*)*. **to be ~ on sb's good will** auf jds Wohlwollen *(acc)* angewiesen sein. **2** *n* = **dependant**.

**depict** [dɪˈpɪkt] *vt* schildern.

**depilatory** [dɪˈpɪlətərɪ] *n* Enthaarungsmittel *nt*. **~ cream** Enthaarungscreme *f*.

**deplete** [dɪˈpliːt] *vt* verringern.

**depletion** [dɪˈpliːʃən] *n* Verringerung *f*.

**deplorable** [dɪˈplɔːrəbl] *adj* beklagenswert, bedauerlich.

**deplore** [dɪˈplɔːr] *vt* *(regret)* bedauern, beklagen; *(disapprove of)* mißbilligen.

**deploy** [dɪˈplɔɪ] *vt* *(Mil, fig)* einsetzen. **the troops ~ed in Germany** die in Deutschland stationierten Truppen.

**deployment** [dɪˈplɔɪmənt] *n* Einsatz *m*.

**depopulate** [ˌdiːˈpɒpjʊleɪt] *vt* entvölkern.

**depopulation** [ˈdiːˌpɒpjʊˈleɪʃən] *n* Entvölkerung *f*.

**deport** [dɪˈpɔːt] *vt* *prisoner* deportieren; *alien* abschieben.

**deportation** [ˌdiːpɔːˈteɪʃən] *n see vt* Deportation *f*; Abschiebung *f*.

**deportment** [dɪˈpɔːtmənt] *n* Haltung *f*; *(behaviour)* Verhalten, Benehmen *nt*.

**depose** [dɪˈpəʊz] *vt* absetzen.

**deposit** [dɪˈpɒzɪt] **1** *vt* **(a)** *(put down)* hinlegen; *(upright)* hinstellen. **(b)** *money, valuables* deponie-

ren *(with* bei*)*. **2** *n* **(a)** *(Fin: in bank)* Einlage *f*, Guthaben *nt*. **(b)** *(Comm)* *(part payment)* Anzahlung *f*; *(returnable security)* Kaution *f*; *(for bottle)* Pfand *nt*. **to lose one's ~** *(Pol)* seine Kaution verlieren. **(c)** *(Chem: in wine, Geol)* Ablagerung *f*; *(of ore, coal, oil)* (Lager)stätte *f*.

**deposit account** *n* *(Brit)* Sparkonto *nt*.

**depositor** [dɪˈpɒzɪtər] *n* Einzahler(in *f*) *m*.

**depository** [dɪˈpɒzɪtərɪ] *n* Lagerhaus *nt*.

**depot** [ˈdepəʊ] *n* *(bus garage etc)* Depot *nt*; *(store also)* Lager(haus) *nt*.

**deprave** [dɪˈpreɪv] *vt* verderben.

**depraved** [dɪˈpreɪvd] *adj* verkommen.

**depravity** [dɪˈprævɪtɪ] *n* Verkommenheit *f*.

**deprecate** [ˈdeprɪkeɪt] *vt* *(form)* mißbilligen.

**deprecating** [ˈdeprɪkeɪtɪŋ], **deprecatory** [ˈdeprɪkətərɪ] *adj* mißbilligend; *smile, gesture* abwehrend.

**depreciate** [dɪˈpriːʃɪeɪt] *vi* an Wert verlieren; *(currency)* an Kaufkraft verlieren.

**depreciation** [dɪˌpriːʃɪˈeɪʃən] *n* Wertminderung *f*; *(for tax)* Abschreibung *f*; *(of currency)* Kaufkraftverlust *m*.

**depress** [dɪˈpres] *vt* **(a)** *person* deprimieren; *(discourage)* entmutigen. **(b)** *(form)* *lever* niederdrücken.

**depressant** [dɪˈpresnt] *n* Beruhigungsmittel *nt*.

**depressed** [dɪˈprest] *adj* **(a)** *person* deprimiert. **don't get ~** sei nicht deprimiert. **(b)** *industry* notleidend. **~ area** Notstandsgebiet *nt*.

**depressing** [dɪˈpresɪŋ] *adj* deprimierend.

**depression** [dɪˈpreʃən] *n* **(a)** Depressionen *pl*. **(b)** *(in ground)* Vertiefung, Senke *f*. **(c)** *(Met)* Tief(druckgebiet) *nt*. **(d)** *(Econ)* Depression *f*. **the D~** *(Hist)* die Weltwirtschaftskrise.

**deprivation** [ˌdeprɪˈveɪʃən] *n* **(a)** *(depriving)* Entzug *m*; *(Psych)* Deprivation *f*; *(of rights)* Beraubung *f*. **(b)** *(state)* Entbehrung *f*.

**deprive** [dɪˈpraɪv] *vt* **to ~ sb of sth** jdm etw nehmen; **they had been ~d of ...** *(had lacked)* ihnen fehlte ...; **to ~ oneself of sth** auf etw *(acc)* verzichten.

**deprived** [dɪˈpraɪvd] *adj* benachteiligt; *area* strukturschwach.

**dept** = **department** Abt.

**depth** [depθ] *n* *(lit, fig)* Tiefe *f*. **the ~s of the ocean** die Tiefen des Ozeans; **at a ~ of 3 metres** in einer Tiefe von 3 Metern, in 3 Meter Tiefe; **to get out of one's ~** *(lit, fig)* den Boden unter den Füßen verlieren; **sorry, I'm out of my ~ there** es tut mir leid, aber da muß ich passen; **with great ~ of feeling** sehr gefühlvoll; **in ~** eingehend, intensiv; **in the ~s of despair** in tiefster Verzweiflung; **in the ~s of winter/the forest** im tiefsten Winter/Wald; **~ charge** Wasserbombe *f*; **~ of field** *(Phot)* Tiefenschärfe *f*.

**deputation** [ˌdepjʊˈteɪʃən] *n* Abordnung *f*.

**deputize** [ˈdepjʊtaɪz] *vi* vertreten *(for sb* jdn*)*.

**deputy** [ˈdepjʊtɪ] **1** *n* Stellvertreter(in *f*) *m*. **2** *adj attr* stellvertretend.

**derail** [dɪˈreɪl] *vt* zum Entgleisen bringen, entgleisen lassen. **to be ~ed** entgleisen.

**derailment** [dɪˈreɪlmənt] *n* Entgleisung *f*.

**deranged** [dɪˈreɪndʒd] *adj* *mind* gestört. **to be (mentally) ~** geistesgestört sein.

**Derby** [ˈdɑːbɪ, *(US)* ˈdɜːbɪ] *n* **(a)** *(US: also ~ hat)* Melone *f*. **(b)** *(Sport)* *(race)* Derby *nt*. **local d~** *(match)* Lokalderby *nt*.

**deregulate** [diːˈregjʊleɪt] *vt* deregulieren; *buses etc* dem freien Wettbewerb überlassen.

**deregulation** [ˌdiːregjʊˈleɪʃən] *n see vt* Deregulierung *f*; Wettbewerbsfreiheit *f (of* für*)*.

**derelict** [ˈderɪlɪkt] *adj* *(abandoned)* verlassen;

*(ruined)* verfallen, heruntergekommen.

**dereliction** [ˌderɪˈlɪkʃən] *n* ~ **of duty** Pflichtversäumnis *nt*.

**deride** [dɪˈraɪd] *vt* verhöhnen.

**derision** [dɪˈrɪʒən] *n* Hohn, Spott *m*. **object of** ~ Zielscheibe *f* des Spotts.

**derisive** [dɪˈraɪsɪv] *adj* spöttisch, höhnisch.

**derisory** [dɪˈraɪsərɪ] *adj* (a) *amount, offer* lächerlich. (b) = **derisive**.

**derivation** [ˌderɪˈveɪʃən] *n* Ableitung *f*.

**derivative** [dɪˈrɪvətɪv] **1** *adj* abgeleitet; *literary work etc* nachgeahmt, imitiert. **2** *n* Ableitung *f*.

**derive** [dɪˈraɪv] **1** *vt ideas, names* her- *or* ableiten *(from* von*)*; *profit* ziehen *(from* aus*)*; *satisfaction, comfort* beziehen *(from* aus*)*. **this word is** ~**d from the Greek** dieses Wort stammt aus dem Griechischen; **to** ~ **pleasure from sth** Freude an etw *(dat)* haben. **2** *vi* **to** ~ **from** sich her- *or* ableiten von; *(power, fortune)* beruhen auf *(+dat)*; *(ideas)* stammen von.

**dermatitis** [ˌdɜːməˈtaɪtɪs] *n* Hautentzündung, Dermatitis *f*.

**dermatology** [ˌdɜːməˈtɒlədʒɪ] *n* Dermatologie *f*.

**derogatory** [dɪˈrɒgətərɪ] *adj* abfällig, abschätzig.

**derrick** [ˈderɪk] *n* Ladebaum *m*; *(above oil well)* Bohrturm *m*.

**derust** [diːˈrʌst] *vt* entrosten.

**derv** [dɜːv] *n (Brit)* Diesel(kraftstoff) *m*.

**DES** *(Brit)* = **Department of Education and Science** Bildungs- *und* Wissenschaftsministerium.

**desalinate** [diːˈsælɪneɪt] *vt* entsalzen.

**descant** [ˈdeskænt] *n (Mus)* Diskant *m*. ~ **recorder** Sopranflöte *f*.

**descend** [dɪˈsend] **1** *vi* (a) *(go down)* herunter-/hinuntergehen; *(lift, vehicle)* herunter-/hinunterfahren; *(land)* abfallen. (b) *(attack, visit)* **to** ~ **(up)on sb** jdn überfallen. (c) *(lower oneself)* **to** ~ **to sth** sich zu etw herablassen; **he even** ~**ed to bribery** er scheute selbst vor Bestechung nicht zurück. **2** *vt* (a) *stairs* hinunter-/heruntergehen. (b) **to be** ~**ed from** abstammen von.

**descendant** [dɪˈsendənt] *n* (a) Nachkomme *m*. (b) *(Astron, Astrol)* **in the** ~ im Deszendenten.

**descent** [dɪˈsent] *n* (a) Abstieg *m*. (b) *(ancestry)* Abstammung, Herkunft *f*. (c) *(fig: into crime etc)* Absinken *nt (into* in *+acc)*.

**describe** [dɪˈskraɪb] *vt* (a) beschreiben. (b) *(+as)* bezeichnen. **he** ~**s himself as a doctor** er bezeichnet sich als Arzt.

**description** [dɪˈskrɪpʃən] *n* (a) Beschreibung *f*. **beyond** ~ unbeschreiblich. (b) *(+as)* Bezeichnung *f*. (c) *(sort)* **vehicles of every** ~ Fahrzeuge aller Art.

**descriptive** [dɪˈskrɪptɪv] *adj* (a) beschreibend; *account, adjective, passage* anschaulich. (b) *linguistics, science etc* deskriptiv.

**desecrate** [ˈdesɪkreɪt] *vt* entweihen, schänden.

**desegregate** [ˌdiːˈsegrɪgeɪt] *vt school* die Rassentrennung aufheben an *+dat*.

**desegregation** [ˈdiːˌsegrɪˈgeɪʃən] *n* Aufhebung *f* der Rassentrennung *(of* in *+dat)*.

**desert¹** [ˈdezət] **1** *n (lit, fig)* Wüste *f*. **2** *adj attr* Wüsten-. ~ **island** einsame *or* verlassene Insel.

**desert²** [dɪˈzɜːt] **1** *vt (leave)* verlassen; *cause, party* im Stich lassen. **the place was** ~**ed** es war dort wie ausgestorben. **2** *vi (Mil)* desertieren. **to** ~ **to the rebels** zu den Rebellen überlaufen.

**deserter** [dɪˈzɜːtər] *n (Mil, fig)* Deserteur *m*.

**desertion** [dɪˈzɜːʃən] *n* (a) *(act)* Verlassen *nt*; *(Mil)* Fahnenflucht *f*. (b) *(state)* Verlassenheit *f*.

**deserts** [dɪˈzɜːts] *npl* **to get one's just** ~ bekommen, was man verdient hat.

**deserve** [dɪˈzɜːv] *vt* verdienen. **he** ~**s to win** er verdient den Sieg; **he** ~**s to be punished** er verdient es, bestraft zu werden.

**deservedly** [dɪˈzɜːvɪdlɪ] *adv* verdientermaßen.

**deserving** [dɪˈzɜːvɪŋ] *adj person, cause* verdienstvoll. **to be** ~ **of sth** etw verdienen.

**desiccated** [ˈdesɪkeɪtɪd] *adj* getrocknet; *(fig)* vertrocknet. ~ **coconut** Kokosflocken *pl*.

**design** [dɪˈzaɪn] **1** *n* (a) Design *nt*, Ausführung *f*; *(of vehicle, machine)* Konstruktion *f*; *(plan: of building etc)* Entwurf *m*. **a new** ~ *(Aut)* ein neues Modell. (b) *(pattern)* Muster *nt*. (c) *(intention)* Plan *m*, Absicht *f*. **by** ~ absichtlich; **to have** ~**s on sb/sth** es auf jdn/etw abgesehen haben. **2** *vt* (a) entwerfen; *machine* konstruieren. (b) *(intend)* **to be** ~**ed for sb/sth** für jdn/etw vorgesehen *or* bestimmt sein.

**designate** [ˈdezɪgneɪt] **1** *vt* bezeichnen; *(appoint)* ernennen. **to** ~ **sb as sth** jdn zu etw ernennen. **2** [ˈdezɪgnɪt] *adj* **the Prime Minister** ~ der designierte Premierminister.

**designation** [ˌdezɪgˈneɪʃən] *n see vt* Bezeichnung; Ernennung *f*.

**designer** [dɪˈzaɪnər] **1** *n* Designer(in *f*) *m*; *(fashion* ~*)* Mode-Designer(in *f*) *m*; *(of machines etc)* Konstrukteur(in *f*) *m*; *(Theat)* Bühnenbildner(in *f*) *m*. **2** *adj attr* Designer-. ~ **stubble** *(hum)* Dreitagebart *m (col)*.

**desirable** [dɪˈzaɪərəbl] *adj* wünschenswert, erwünscht; *position, offer, house, area* reizvoll, attraktiv; *woman* begehrenswert.

**desire** [dɪˈzaɪər] **1** *n (for nach)* Wunsch *m*; *(longing)* Sehnsucht *f*; *(sexual)* Verlangen, Begehren *nt*. **I have no** ~ **to see him** ich habe kein Verlangen, ihn zu sehen; **I have no** ~ **to cause you any trouble** ich möchte Ihnen keine Unannehmlichkeiten bereiten. **2** *vt* wünschen; *woman* begehren; *peace* wollen. **it leaves much to be** ~**d** das läßt viel zu wünschen übrig.

**desirous** [dɪˈzaɪərəs] *adj* **to be** ~ **of sth** *(form)* nach etw verlangen.

**desist** [dɪˈzɪst] *vi (form)* Abstand nehmen, absehen *(from doing sth* davon, etw zu tun*)*.

**desk** [desk] *n* Schreibtisch *m*; *(for pupils, teacher)* Pult *nt*; *(Brit: in shop, restaurant)* Kasse *f*; *(in hotel)* Empfang *m*. ~ **information** *(computing)* Information(sschalter *m) f*; ~ **copy** Arbeitsexemplar *nt*; ~ **job** Bürojob *m*; ~ **lamp** Schreibtischlampe *f*.

**desktop** [ˈdesktɒp]: ~ **computer** *n* Desktop-Computer *m*; ~ **publishing** *n* Desktop Publishing *nt*.

**desolate** [ˈdesəlɪt] **1** *adj* (a) *place (devastated)* verwüstet; *(barren)* trostlos; *(fig)* outlook trostlos. (b) *(grief-stricken)* tieftraurig, zu Tode betrübt. **2** [ˈdesəleɪt] *vt country* verwüsten.

**desolation** [ˌdesəˈleɪʃən] *n* (a) *(by war)* Verwüstung *f*. (b) *(of landscape, grief)* Trostlosigkeit *f*.

**despair** [dɪˈspeər] **1** *n* Verzweiflung *f (about, at* über *+acc)*. **in** ~ aus Verzweiflung. **2** *vi* verzweifeln, alle Hoffnung aufgeben. **to** ~ **of doing sth** alle Hoffnung aufgeben, etw zu tun.

**despairing** [dɪsˈpeərɪŋ] *adj* verzweifelt.

**despatch** [dɪˈspætʃ] *vt, n* = **dispatch**.

**desperate** [ˈdespərɪt] *adj* verzweifelt; *criminal* zum Äußersten entschlossen; *(urgent) need etc* dringend; *measures* extrem. **to get** ~ verzweifeln, in Verzweiflung geraten; **to be** ~ **for sth** etw dringend brauchen; **I'm/it's not that** ~! so dringend ist es nicht!; **I was** ~ **to get the job** ich wollte die Stelle unbedingt haben; **things are getting** ~ die Lage wird allmählich verzweifelt.

**desperately** [ˈdespərɪtlɪ] *adv* verzweifelt; *(urgently)* *need* dringend. ~ **in love** verliebt bis über beide Ohren; ~ **ill** schwer krank; **do you want ...? — not** ~ möchten Sie ...? — nicht unbedingt.

**desperation** [ˌdespəˈreɪʃən] *n* Verzweiflung *f*. **an act of** ~ eine Verzweiflungstat; **in (sheer)** ~ aus (reiner) Verzweiflung; **to drive sb to** ~ jdn zur Verzweiflung bringen.

**despicable** [dɪˈspɪkəbl] *adj* abscheulich.

**despise** [dɪˈspaɪz] *vt* verachten.

**despite** [dɪˈspaɪt] *prep* trotz *(+gen)*. ~ **what she says** trotz allem, was sie sagt.

**despondency** [dɪˈspɒndənsɪ] *n* Niedergeschlagenheit *f*.

**despondent** [dɪˈspɒndənt] *adj* niedergeschlagen *(about* wegen*)*.

**despot** [ˈdespɒt] *n (lit, fig)* Despot *m*.

**despotic** [desˈpɒtɪk] *adj (lit, fig)* despotisch.

**despotism** [ˈdespətɪzəm] *n* Despotie *f*.

**des res** [ˈdezˈrez] *n (Brit hum col)* attraktiver Wohnsitz.

**dessert** [dɪˈzɜːt] *n* Nachtisch *m*, Dessert *nt*. **~spoon** Dessertlöffel *m*.

**destabilize** [diːˈsteɪbɪlaɪz] *vt* destabilisieren.

**destination** [ˌdestɪˈneɪʃən] *n* Reiseziel *nt*; *(of goods)* Bestimmungsort *m*.

**destined** [ˈdestɪnd] *adj* **to be** ~ **to do sth** dazu bestimmt *or* ausersehen sein, etw zu tun; **we were** ~ **to meet** das Schicksal wollte es, daß wir uns begegnen; **I was** ~ **never to see them again** ich sollte sie nie (mehr) wiedersehen; ~ **for** *(ship, consignment)* unterwegs nach.

**destiny** [ˈdestɪnɪ] *n* Schicksal *nt*.

**destitute** [ˈdestɪtjuːt] *adj (poverty-stricken)* mittellos. **to be utterly** ~ bettelarm sein.

**destroy** [dɪˈstrɔɪ] *vt* zerstören; *documents, manuscripts etc also* vernichten; *(fire also)* verwüsten; *(kill)* vernichten; *animal* töten; *influence, hopes, chances* zunichte machen; *reputation* ruinieren.

**destroyer** [dɪˈstrɔɪəʳ] *n (Naut)* Zerstörer *m*.

**destruction** [dɪˈstrʌkʃən] *n* Zerstörung *f*; *(of enemy, people, documents)* Vernichtung *f*.

**destructive** [dɪˈstrʌktɪv] *adj wind, fire, war* zerstörerisch; *tendencies, criticism* destruktiv.

**desultory** [ˈdesəltərɪ] *adj reading* flüchtig; *manner, attempt* halbherzig; *conversation* zwanglos.

**detach** [dɪˈtætʃ] *vt (separate, unfasten)* lösen *(from* von*)*; *section of form* abtrennen *(from* von*)*; *part of machine, hood* abnehmen *(from* von*)*. **to become ~ed from sth** sich von etw lösen.

**detachable** [dɪˈtætʃəbl] *adj* abnehmbar.

**detached** [dɪˈtætʃt] *adj* **(a)** *(unbiased)* objektiv; *(unemotional)* kühl, distanziert. **(b)** *building* freistehend. ~ **house** Einzelhaus *nt*.

**detachment** [dɪˈtætʃmənt] *n* **(a)** *(emotionlessness)* Distanz *f*; *(objectivity)* Abstand *m*. **(b)** *(Mil)* Sonderkommando *nt*, Abordnung *f*.

**detail** [ˈdiːteɪl] **1** *n* **(a)** Detail *nt*; *(particular)* Einzelheit *f*; *(part of painting, photo etc)* Ausschnitt *m*; *(insignificant circumstance)* unwichtige Einzelheit. **in** ~ im Detail, in Einzelheiten; **in great** ~ in allen Einzelheiten, ausführlich; **there's one little** ~ **you've forgotten** eine Kleinigkeit haben Sie vergessen; **further ~s** nähere *or* weitere Einzelheiten; **to go into ~s** ins Detail gehen; **his attention to** ~ seine Sorgfalt. **(b)** *(Mil)* Sondertrupp *m*. **2** *vt* **(a)** ausführlich *or* detailliert beschreiben. **(b)** *(Mil)* troops abkommandieren.

**detailed** [ˈdiːteɪld] *adj* ausführlich, detailliert.

**detain** [dɪˈteɪn] *vt* aufhalten; *(police)* in Haft nehmen.

**detainee** [ˌdiːteɪˈniː] *n* Häftling *m*.

**detect** [dɪˈtekt] *vt* entdecken; *(see, make out)* ausfindig machen; *crime* aufdecken; *a tone of sadness, movement* wahrnehmen; *gas* aufspüren.

**detection** [dɪˈtekʃən] *n* Entdeckung *f*; *(of gases)* Aufspüren *nt*. **to escape** ~ nicht entdeckt werden.

**detective** [dɪˈtektɪv] *n* Kriminalbeamte(r) *mf*; *(private* ~*)* Detektiv *m*.

**detective:** ~ **inspector** *n* Kriminalinspektor *m*; ~ **sergeant** *n* Kriminalmeister *m*; ~ **story** *n* Kriminalgeschichte *f*, Krimi *(col) m*; ~ **work** *n* kriminalistische Arbeit.

**detector** [dɪˈtektəʳ] *n (Rad, Tech)* Detektor *m*. ~ **van** Funkmeßwagen *m*.

**détente** [deɪˈtɑːnt] *n* Entspannung *f*.

**detention** [dɪˈtenʃən] *n (captivity)* Haft *f*, Gewahrsam *m*; *(act)* Festnahme *f*; *(Sch)* Nachsitzen *nt*. **he's in** ~ *(Sch)* er muß nachsitzen.

**deter** [dɪˈtɜːʳ] *vt* **to** ~ **sb from doing sth** jdn davon abhalten, etw zu tun.

**detergent** [dɪˈtɜːdʒənt] *n* Reinigungsmittel *nt*; *(for clothes)* Waschmittel *nt*.

**deteriorate** [dɪˈtɪərɪəreɪt] *vi* sich verschlechtern; *(materials)* verschleißen; *(building)* verfallen.

**deterioration** [dɪˌtɪərɪəˈreɪʃən] *n see vi* Verschlechterung *f*; Verschleiß *m*; Verfall *m*.

**determination** [dɪˌtɜːmɪˈneɪʃən] *n* **(a)** *(firmness)* Entschlossenheit *f*. **(b)** *(establishing)* Determinierung *f*; *(of character, future also)* Bestimmung *f*; *(of cause, nature, position)* Ermittlung, Bestimmung *f*; *(of frontiers)* Festsetzung *f*.

**determine** [dɪˈtɜːmɪn] *vt* **(a)** *sb's character, future* bestimmen. **(b)** *(settle, fix) conditions, price* festsetzen. **(c)** *(ascertain)* ermitteln, bestimmen. **(d)** *(resolve) issue* entscheiden.

**determined** [dɪˈtɜːmɪnd] *adj* entschlossen. **he's** ~ **to make me lose my temper** *(col)* er legt es darauf an, mich wütend zu machen.

**deterrent** [dɪˈterənt] **1** *n* Abschreckungsmittel *nt*. **2** *adj attr* Abschreckungs-.

**detest** [dɪˈtest] *vt* verabscheuen, hassen.

**detestable** [dɪˈtestəbl] *adj* widerwärtig, abscheulich.

**detestation** [ˌdiːtesˈteɪʃən] *n* Abscheu *m (of* vor *+dat)*.

**dethrone** [diːˈθrəʊn] *vt* entthronen.

**detonate** [ˈdetəneɪt] *vt* zur Explosion bringen.

**detonation** [ˌdetəˈneɪʃən] *n* Zündung *f*.

**detonator** [ˈdetəneɪtəʳ] *n* Zünd- *or* Sprengkapsel *f*.

**detour** [ˈdiːˌtʊəʳ] **1** *n* Umweg *m*; *(for traffic)* Umleitung *f*. **2** *vt (esp US) traffic* umleiten.

**detoxification** [ˌdiːtɒksɪfɪˈkeɪʃən] *n* Entgiftung *f*.

**detract** [dɪˈtrækt] *vi* **to** ~ **from sth** etw beeinträchtigen; *pleasure, merit also* etw schmälern.

**detractor** [dɪˈtræktəʳ] *n* Kritiker (in *f) m*.

**detriment** [ˈdetrɪmənt] *n* Schaden, Nachteil *m*. **to the** ~ **of** zum Schaden *(+gen)*; **without** ~ **to** ohne Schaden für.

**detrimental** [ˌdetrɪˈmentl] *adj (to health, reputation)* schädlich *(to* dat*)*; *effect also* nachteilig *(to* für*)*; *(to case, cause)* abträglich *(to* dat*)*.

**deuce** [djuːs] *n* **(a)** *(Cards)* Zwei *f*. **(b)** *(Tennis)* Einstand *m*. **(c) why the** ~ **...?** *(col)* warum zum Teufel ...? *(col)*.

**Deutschmark, deutschmark** [ˈdɔɪtʃmɑːk] *n* Deutsche Mark, D-Mark *f*.

**devaluation** [ˌdiːvæljuˈeɪʃən] *n* Abwertung *f*.

**devalue** [diːˈvæljuː] *vt* abwerten.

**devastate** [ˈdevəsteɪt] *vt (lit)* town, land verwüsten; *(fig) opposition* vernichten. **I was ~d** *(col)* das hat mich umgehauen *(col)*.

**devastating** [ˈdevəsteɪtɪŋ] *adj (lit, fig)* verheerend, vernichtend; *news* niederschmetternd; *wit, humour* umwerfend; *grief* überwältigend.

**devastatingly** ['devəsteɪtɪŋlɪ] *adv beautiful, funny* umwerfend.

**devastation** [ˌdevə'steɪʃən] *n* Verwüstung *f.*

**develop** [dɪ'veləp] **1** *vt* **(a)** *(also Phot)* entwickeln. **to ~ a taste for sth** Geschmack an etw *dat* finden. **(b)** *idea, thesis* (weiter)entwickeln; *(unfold)* plot of novel entfalten; *(Mus)* theme durchführen. **(c)** *natural resources, region* erschließen; *old part of town* sanieren; *business (expand)* ausbauen; *(from scratch)* aufziehen. **2** *vi* sich entwickeln. **to ~ into sth** sich zu etw entwickeln; **it later ~ed that ...** später stellte sich heraus, daß ...

**developer** [dɪ'veləpəʳ] *n* **(a)** = **property ~**. **(b)** *(Phot)* Entwickler *m.* **(c)** **late ~** Spätentwickler *m.*

**developing** [dɪ'veləpɪŋ] **1** *adj crisis, storm* aufkommend; *industry* neu entstehend; *interest* wachsend. **~ country** Entwicklungsland *nt.* **2** *n* *(Phot)* Entwickeln *nt.*

**development** [dɪ'veləpmənt] *n* **(a)** Entwicklung *f.* **to await ~s** die Entwicklung abwarten. **(b)** *(of subject, plot etc)* Ausführung *f;* *(of interests also)* Entfaltung *f;* *(of argument etc)* (Weiter)entwicklung *f;* *(Mus)* Durchführung *f.* **(c)** *(of site, new town)* Erschließung *f;* *(of old part of town)* Sanierung *f;* *(of industry)* *(from scratch)* Entwicklung *f;* *(expansion)* Ausbau *m.* **we live in a new ~** wir leben in einer neuen Siedlung; **~ area** Entwicklungsgebiet *nt;* **~ costs** Erschließungskosten *pl.*

**deviant** ['diːvɪənt] *adj behaviour* abweichend.

**deviate** ['diːvɪeɪt] *vi* abweichen *(from* von*).*

**deviation** [ˌdiːvɪ'eɪʃən] *n* Abweichung *f.*

**device** [dɪ'vaɪs] *n* **(a)** *(gadget etc)* Gerät *nt;* *(extra fitment)* Vorrichtung *f;* *(explosive ~)* Sprengkörper *m.* **(b)** **to leave sb to his own ~s** jdn sich *(dat)* selbst überlassen.

**devil** ['devl] *n* **(a)** *(lit, fig col)* Teufel *m.* **be a ~!** riskier mal was!; **he's a ~ for changing his mind** er ändert ständig seine Meinung.
**(b)** *(col: as intensifier)* **I had the ~ of a job getting here** es war verdammt schwierig, hierher zu kommen; **how/what/why/who the ~ ...?** wie/was/warum/wer zum Teufel ...?; **to work like the ~** wie ein Pferd schuften *(col);* **the ~ of a noise** ein Höllenlärm; **there will be the ~ to pay** das dicke Ende kommt nach.
**(c)** *(in expressions)* **(to be) between the D~ and the deep blue sea** (sich) in einer Zwickmühle (befinden); **go to the ~!** *(col)* scher dich zum Teufel! *(col);* **talk of the ~!** wenn man vom Teufel spricht!; **give the ~ his due** das muß der Neid ihm lassen; **to have the ~'s own luck** *(col)* ein Schweineglück *(col) or* unverschämtes Glück haben; **better the ~ you know (than the ~ you don't)** *(prov)* von zwei Übeln wählt man besser das, was man schon kennt; **(the) ~ take the hindmost** den Letzten beißen die Hunde *(Prov).*

**devilish** ['devlɪʃ] *adj* **(a)** teuflisch. **(b)** *(col: terrible)* schrecklich.

**devil-may-care** [ˌdevlmeɪ'kɛəʳ] *adj* leichtsinnig.

**devilment** ['devlmənt] *n* **out of sheer ~** aus lauter Übermut.

**devil's advocate** *n* Advocatus Diaboli *m.*

**devious** ['diːvɪəs] *adj* **(a)** *path, argumentation* gewunden. **by a ~ route** auf einem Umweg. **(b)** *(dishonest)* *method* krumm *(col),* fragwürdig; *person* verschlagen, hinterhältig.

**devise** [dɪ'vaɪz] *vt* sich *(dat)* ausdenken.

**devoid** [dɪ'vɔɪd] *adj:* **~ of** bar *(+gen),* ohne.

**devolution** [ˌdiːvə'luːʃən] *n* *(of power)* Übertragung *f (from ... to* von ... auf *+acc);* *(Pol)* Dezentralisie-

rung *f.*

**devolve** [dɪ'vɒlv] *(on, upon* auf *+acc)* **1** *vi* übergehen. **2** *vt* übertragen.

**devote** [dɪ'vəʊt] *vt* widmen *(to dat);* *resources* bestimmen *(to* für*).*

**devoted** [dɪ'vəʊtɪd] *adj* ergeben; *followers, service* treu; *admirer* eifrig. **she's ~ to him/her family** sie liebt ihn/ihre Familie über alles.

**devotee** [ˌdevəʊ'tiː] *n* Anhänger(in *f*) *m;* *(of a writer)* Verehrer(in *f*) *m;* *(of music also, poetry)* Liebhaber(in *f*) *m.*

**devotion** [dɪ'vəʊʃən] *n* *(to friend, wife etc)* Ergebenheit *f (to* gegenüber*);* *(to work)* Hingabe *f (to* an *+acc).* **~ to duty** Pflichteifer *m.*

**devour** [dɪ'vaʊəʳ] *vt (lit, fig)* verschlingen.

**devout** [dɪ'vaʊt] *adj (+er) person* fromm; *hope* sehnlich(st).

**dew** [djuː] *n* Tau *m.* **~drop** Tautropfen *m.*

**dewy-eyed** ['djuːaɪd] *adj (innocent, naive)* naiv; *(trusting)* vertrauensselig. **to go all ~** feuchte Augen bekommen.

**dexterity** [deks'terɪtɪ] *n* Geschick *nt.*

**dext(e)rous** ['dekstrəs] *adj (skilful)* geschickt.

**DHSS** *(Brit old)* = **Department of Health and Social Security** Ministerium *nt* für Gesundheit und Soziales.

**diabetes** [ˌdaɪə'biːtiːz] *n* Diabetes *m,* Zucker *no art (col).*

**diabetic** [ˌdaɪə'betɪk] **1** *adj* **(a)** zuckerkrank. **(b)** *beer, chocolate* Diabetiker-. **2** *n* Zuckerkranke(r) *mf,* Diabetiker(in *f*) *m.*

**diabolic(al)** [ˌdaɪə'bɒlɪk(əl)] *adj* **(a)** diabolisch, teuflisch. **(b)** *(col) weather, heat* saumäßig *(col).*

**diadem** ['daɪədem] *n* Diadem *nt.*

**diagnose** ['daɪəgnəʊz] *vt (Med, fig)* diagnostizieren.

**diagnosis** [ˌdaɪəg'nəʊsɪs] *n, pl* **diagnoses** [ˌdaɪəg'nəʊsiːz] Diagnose *f.*

**diagnostic** [ˌdaɪəg'nɒstɪk] *adj* diagnostisch.

**diagonal** [daɪ'ægənl] **1** *adj* diagonal. **2** *n* Diagonale *f.*

**diagonally** [daɪ'ægənəlɪ] *adv cut, fold* diagonal. **~ across sth** schräg über etw *(acc);* **~ opposite sth** einer Sache *(dat)* schräg gegenüber.

**diagram** ['daɪəgræm] *n* Schaubild *nt,* graphische Darstellung; *(Math)* Diagramm *nt.*

**dial** ['daɪəl] **1** *n* *(of clock)* Zifferblatt *nt;* *(of speedometer, pressure gauge)* Skala *f;* *(Telec)* Wählscheibe *f.* **~ code** *(US)* Vorwahl *f;* **~ tone** *(US)* Amtszeichen *nt.* **2** *vti (Telec)* wählen. **you can ~ London direct** man kann nach London durchwählen; **to ~ 999** den Notruf wählen.

**dialect** ['daɪəlekt] *n* Dialekt *m;* *(local, rural also)* Mundart *f.*

**dialling** ['daɪəlɪŋ]: **~ code** *n* Vorwahl *f;* **~ tone** *n* *(Brit Telec)* Amtszeichen *nt.*

**dialogue** ['daɪəlɒg] *n* Dialog *m.*

**dialysis** [daɪ'æləsɪs] *n* Dialyse *f.*

**diameter** [daɪ'æmɪtəʳ] *n* Durchmesser *m.* **it is one metre in ~** es hat einen Durchmesser von einem Meter.

**diametrically** [ˌdaɪə'metrɪkəlɪ] *adv* **~ opposed (to)** diametral entgegengesetzt *(+dat).*

**diamond** ['daɪəmənd] *n* **(a)** Diamant *m.* **~ jubilee** 60-jähriges Jubiläum; **~ wedding** *n* diamantene Hochzeit. **(b)** **~s** *(Cards)* Karo *nt;* **the King of ~s** der Karokönig.

**diaper** ['daɪəpəʳ] *n (US)* Windel *f.* **~ liner** Windeleinlage *f.*

**diaphanous** [daɪ'æfənəs] *adj* durchscheinend.

**diaphragm** ['daɪəfræm] *n (Anat, Phys, Med)* Diaphragma *nt;* *(abdominal also)* Zwerchfell *nt;* *(contraceptive also)* Pessar *nt.*

**diarrhoea,** *(US)* **diarrhea** [ˌdaɪə'riːə] *n* Durchfall *m*. **to have verbal** ~ die Laberkrankheit haben *(col)*.

**diary** ['daɪərɪ] *n (of personal experience)* Tagebuch *nt*; *(for noting dates)* (Termin)kalender *m*. **to keep a** ~ Tagebuch führen.

**diatribe** ['daɪətraɪb] *n* Schmährede *f*.

**dice** [daɪs] **1** *n, pl* - Würfel *m*. **to throw (the)** ~, **to play** ~ würfeln. **2** *vi* **to** ~ **with death** sein Leben riskieren. **3** *vt (Cook)* in Würfel schneiden.

**dicey** ['daɪsɪ] *adj (Brit col)* riskant.

**dichotomy** [dɪ'kɒtəmɪ] *n* Trennung, Dichotomie *f*.

**dick** [dɪk] *n* **(a)** *(col: detective)* Schnüffler *m (col)*. **(b)** *(col!: penis)* Schwanz *m (col!)*.

**dickhead** ['dɪkhɛd] *n (Brit col!)* Knallkopf *m (col)*.

**dicky** ['dɪkɪ] *adj (col) heart* angeknackst *(col)*.

**dickybird** ['dɪkɪbɜːd] *n (baby-talk)* Piepmatz *m (baby-talk)*.

**dictate** [dɪk'teɪt] **1** *vti* diktieren. **2** ['dɪkteɪt] *n usu pl* Diktat *nt*; *(of reason)* Gebote *pl*.
►**dictate to** *vi* +*prep obj person* diktieren *(+dat)*, Vorschriften machen *(+dat)*. **I won't be** ~**d** ~ ich lasse mir keine Vorschriften machen.

**dictating machine** [dɪk'teɪtɪŋ mə'ʃiːn] *n* Diktiergerät *nt*.

**dictation** [dɪk'teɪʃən] *n (also Sch)* Diktat *nt*.

**dictator** [dɪk'teɪtər] *n (Pol, fig)* Diktator *m*.

**dictatorial** [ˌdɪktə'tɔːrɪəl] *adj (Pol, fig)* diktatorisch.

**dictatorship** [dɪk'teɪtəʃɪp] *n (Pol, fig)* Diktatur *f*.

**diction** ['dɪkʃən] *n (way of speaking)* Diktion *f*.

**dictionary** ['dɪkʃənrɪ] *n* Wörterbuch *nt*.

**did** [dɪd] *pret of* **do**.

**didactic** [dɪ'dæktɪk] *adj* didaktisch.

**diddle** ['dɪdl] *vt (col)* übers Ohr hauen *(col)*.

**didn't** ['dɪdənt] = **did not**; *see* **do**.

**die**[1] [daɪ] **1** *vi* **(a)** sterben *(of sth* an etw *dat)*; *(love)* vergehen; *(memory)* (ent)schwinden; *(custom)* aussterben. **the secret** ~**d with him** er nahm das Geheimnis mit ins Grab; **old habits** ~ **hard** der Mensch ist ein Gewohnheitstier; **to** ~ **of hunger** verhungern; **to be dying** im Sterben liegen; **never say** ~! nur nicht aufgeben!; **to** ~ **laughing** *(col)* sich totlachen *(col)*. **(b) to be dying to do sth** *(fig)* darauf brennen, etw zu tun; **I'm dying to know what happened** ich will unbedingt wissen, was passiert ist. **2** *vt* **to** ~ **a hero's/a violent death** den Heldentod/eines gewaltsamen Todes sterben.
►**die away** *vi (sound, voice)* leiser werden; *(wind, anger)* sich legen.
►**die down** *vi* nachlassen; *(fire)* herunterbrennen; *(storm, wind also)* sich legen.
►**die off** *vi* wegsterben.
►**die out** *vi* aussterben.

**die**[2] *n, pl* **dice**: **the** ~ **is cast** *(fig)* die Würfel sind gefallen.

**die-hard** ['daɪhɑːd] *adj* zäh; *(pej)* reaktionär; *conservative* Erz-.

**diesel** ['diːzəl] *n* **(a)** *(also* ~ **fuel)** Diesel(kraftstoff) *m*. **(b)** *(car)* Diesel *m*; *(train)* Dieseltriebwagen *m*; *(locomotive)* Diesellok *f*.

**diesel:** ~ **engine** *n* Dieselmotor *m*; ~ **oil** *n* Dieselöl *nt*; ~ **train** *n* Dieseltriebwagen *m*.

**diet** ['daɪət] **1** *n* Ernährung *f*; *(special* ~*)* Diät *f*; *(slimming* ~*)* Abmagerungs- *or* Schlankheitskur *f*. **to be/go on a** ~ eine Schlankheitskur machen; **to live on a** ~ **of ...** sich von ... ernähren. **2** *vi* eine Schlankheitskur machen.

**dietetics** [daɪə'tetɪks] *n sing* Ernährungswissenschaft *f*.

**dietician** [ˌdaɪə'tɪʃən] *n* Ernährungswissenschaftler(in *f*) *m*; *(in hospital)* Diätassistent(in *f*) *m*.

**differ** ['dɪfər] *vi* **(a)** *(be different)* sich unterscheiden *(from* von*)*. **tastes** ~ die Geschmäcker sind verschieden *(hum col)*. **(b)** *(disagree)* **to** ~ **with sb over sth** über etw *(acc)* anderer Meinung sein als jd.

**difference** ['dɪfrəns] *n* **(a)** Unterschied *m (in, between* zwischen +*dat)*. **that makes a big** ~ **to me** das ist für mich ein großer Unterschied; **that makes a big** ~ das ändert die Sache völlig; **what** ~ **does it make if ...?** was macht es schon, wenn ...?; **what** ~ **is that to you?** was macht dir das aus?; **it makes no** ~ **to me** das ist mir egal; **cooperation makes all the** ~ gute Zusammenarbeit ist alles; **a car with a** ~ *(col)* das besondere Auto. **(b)** *(between numbers, amounts)* Differenz *f*. **(c)** *(quarrel)* **a** ~ **of opinion** eine Meinungsverschiedenheit; **to settle one's** ~**s** die Meinungsverschiedenheiten beilegen.

**different** ['dɪfrənt] *adj* andere(r, s), anders *pred (from, to* als*); two people, things* verschieden, unterschiedlich. **completely** ~ völlig verschieden; *(changed)* völlig verändert; **that's** ~! das ist was anderes!; **in what way are they** ~? worin unterscheiden sie sich?

**differential** [ˌdɪfə'renʃəl] *n* **(a)** *(difference)* Unterschied *m*. **wage** ~ Gehaltsunterschiede *pl*. **(b)** *(Aut)* Differential(getriebe) *nt*.

**differentiate** [ˌdɪfə'renʃɪeɪt] *vti* unterscheiden *(between people)* einen Unterschied machen.

**differently** ['dɪfrəntlɪ] *adv* anders *(from* als*); (from one another)* verschieden, unterschiedlich.

**difficult** ['dɪfɪkəlt] *adj* schwierig, schwer; *writer* kompliziert, schwierig; *neighbour, child* schwierig. **I find it** ~ **to believe that** es fällt mir schwer, das zu glauben; **he's just trying to be** ~ er will nur Schwierigkeiten machen; **she is** ~ **to get on with** es ist schwer, mit ihr auszukommen.

**difficulty** ['dɪfɪkəltɪ] *n* Schwierigkeit *f*. **with/without** ~ mit/ohne Schwierigkeiten *pl*; **a slight** ~ **in breathing** leichte Atembeschwerden *pl*; **there was some** ~ **in finding him** es war schwierig, ihn zu finden; **to get into difficulties** in Schwierigkeiten geraten.

**diffidence** ['dɪfɪdəns] *n* Bescheidenheit *f*.

**diffident** ['dɪfɪdənt] *adj* bescheiden; *smile* zaghaft.

**diffuse** [dɪ'fjuːz] **1** *vt* ausstrahlen; *light* streuen; *knowledge, news* verbreiten. **2** [dɪ'fjuːs] *adj (verbose) style, writer* langatmig, weitschweifig.

**diffusion** [dɪ'fjuːʒən] *n* Ausbreitung *f*; *(of light)* Streuung *f*; *(of knowledge, news)* Verbreitung *f*.

**dig** [dɪg] *(vb: pret, ptp* **dug***)* **1** *vt* **(a)** *ground* graben. **(b)** *(poke, thrust)* bohren *(sth into* etw in etw *acc)*. **(c)** *(col) (enjoy)* stehen auf *(+acc)*; *(understand)* kapieren *(col)*. **2** *vi* graben; *(dog, pig also)* wühlen; *(Tech)* schürfen; *(Archeol)* Ausgrabungen machen. **to** ~ **for minerals** Erz schürfen; **to** ~ **in one's pockets** *(fig)* tief in seinen Taschen nach etw suchen *or* wühlen. **3** *n* **(a)** **to give sb a** ~ **in the ribs** jdm einen Rippenstoß geben. **(b)** *(sarcastic remark)* Seitenhieb *m*, Spitze *f*. **to have a** ~ **at sb/sth** eine Spitze gegen jdn loslassen *(col)*. **(c)** *(Archeol)* (Aus)grabung *f*; *(site)* Ausgrabungsstätte *f*.
►**dig in** *vi* **(a)** *(also* ~ **oneself** ~*) (Mil, fig)* sich eingraben. **(b)** *(col: eat)* reinhauen *(col)*. **2** *vt sep compost* untergraben. **to** ~ **one's heels** ~ *(fig)* sich stur stellen.
►**dig out** *vt sep (lit, fig)* ausgraben *(of* aus*)*.
►**dig up** *vt sep (lit, fig)* ausgraben; *earth* aufwühlen; *lawn, garden* umgraben; *weeds* jäten. **where did you** ~ **him** ~? *(col)* wo hast du den denn aufgegabelt? *(col)*

**digest** [daɪ'dʒest] **1** *vt (lig, fig)* verdauen. **2** ['daɪdʒest] *n (of book, facts)* Zusammenfassung *f*.

**digestible** [dɪ'dʒestəbl] *adj* verdaulich.

**digestion** [dɪ'dʒestʃən] *n* Verdauung *f*.

**digestive** [dɪ'dʒestɪv] *adj* Verdauungs-. ~ **(biscuit)** *(Brit) Keks m aus Vollkornschrot.*

**digger** ['dɪgəʳ] *n (excavator)* Bagger *m.*

**digit** ['dɪdʒɪt] *n (Math)* Ziffer *f.*

**digital** ['dɪdʒɪtəl] *adj* Digital-, digital. ~ **computer** Digitalrechner *m*; ~ **recording** Digitalaufnahme *f.*

**digitize** ['dɪdʒɪtaɪz] *vt (Comp)* digitalisieren.

**dignified** ['dɪgnɪfaɪd] *adj person* würdig; *behaviour, manner* würdevoll.

**dignify** ['dɪgnɪfaɪ] *vt* ehren, auszeichnen.

**dignitary** ['dɪgnɪtərɪ] *n* Würdenträger(in *f*) *m.* **the local dignitaries** die Honoratioren am Ort.

**dignity** ['dɪgnɪtɪ] *n* Würde *f.* **that would be beneath my** ~ das wäre unter meiner Würde.

**digress** [daɪ'gres] *vi* abschweifen.

**digression** [daɪ'greʃən] *n* Abschweifung *f*, Exkurs *(geh) m.*

**digs** [dɪgz] *npl (Brit)* Bude *f (col).* **to be in** ~ ein möbliertes Zimmer *or* eine Bude *(col)* haben.

**dike** [daɪk] *n, vt =* **dyke.**

**dilapidated** [dɪ'læpɪdeɪtɪd] *adj house* verfallen, baufällig; *car* ramponiert; *appearance* schäbig.

**dilapidation** [dɪ,læpɪ'deɪʃən] *n* Baufälligkeit *f*, Verfall *m.*

**dilate** [daɪ'leɪt] **1** *vt* weiten. **2** *vi (pupils)* sich erweitern.

**dilation** [daɪ'leɪʃən] *n (of pupils)* Erweiterung *f.*

**dilatory** ['dɪlətərɪ] *adj* **(a)** *person* langsam; *reply* verspätet. **to be** ~ sich *(dat)* Zeit lassen. **(b)** *action, policy* Verzögerungs-, Hinhalte-.

**dilemma** [daɪ'lemə] *n* Dilemma *nt.* **to be in a** ~ sich in einem Dilemma befinden, in der Klemme sitzen *(col).*

**dilettante** [,dɪlɪ'tæntɪ] *n, pl* **dilettanti** [,dɪlɪ'tæntɪ] Amateur(in *f*), Dilettant(in *f*) *m.*

**diligence** ['dɪlɪdʒəns] *n* Eifer *m*; *(in work also)* Fleiß *m.*

**diligent** *adj*, **~ly** *adv* ['dɪlɪdʒənt, -lɪ] *person* eifrig; *(in work also)* fleißig; *search, work* sorgfältig, genau.

**dill** [dɪl] *n* Dill *m.*

**dilly-dally** [,dɪlɪ'dælɪ] *vi* trödeln.

**dilute** [daɪ'luːt] *vt orange juice etc* verdünnen; *(fig)* mildern, (ab)schwächen.

**dim** [dɪm] **1** *adj (+er)* **(a)** *light, eyesight, sound* schwach; *colour* matt; *memory, outline, shape* verschwommen. **the room grew** ~ im Zimmer wurde es dunkel. **(b)** *(col: stupid)* schwer von Begriff. **(c)** *(col)* **to take a** ~ **view of sb/sth** nicht viel von jdm/ etw halten. **2** *vt light* abdunkeln. **to** ~ **one's headlights** *(esp US)* abblenden. **3** *vi (lamps)* schwächer werden; *(memory)* nachlassen.

**dime** [daɪm] *n (US)* Zehncentstück *nt.*

**dimension** [daɪ'menʃən] *n* Dimension *f*; *(measurement)* Abmessung(en *pl*) *f*, Maß *nt.*

**-dimensional** [-daɪ'menʃənl] *adj suf* -dimensional.

**diminish** [dɪ'mɪnɪʃ] **1** *vt* verringern, herabsetzen; *value* mindern. **~ed responsibility** *(Jur)* verminderte Zurechnungsfähigkeit; **~ed** *(Mus)* vermindert. **2** *vi* sich verringern; *(authority, strength also)* abnehmen; *(value also)* sich vermindern.

**diminutive** [dɪ'mɪnjʊtɪv] **1** *adj* winzig, winzig klein. **2** *n (Gram)* Verkleinerungsform *f*, Diminutiv(um) *nt.*

**dimly** ['dɪmlɪ] *adv shine* schwach; *hear, remember also* undeutlich; *see* verschwommen.

**dimmer** ['dɪməʳ] *n (Elec)* Dimmer *m*; *(US Aut; also* ~ **switch)** Abblendschalter *m.*

**dimness** ['dɪmnɪs] *n see adj* **(a)** Schwäche *f*; Mattheit *f*; Verschwommenheit *f.*

**dimple** ['dɪmpl] *n (on cheek, chin)* Grübchen *nt.*

**dim:** **~-wit** *n (col)* Blödmann *m (col)*; **~-witted** *adj (col)* blöd *(col)*, dämlich *(col).*

**din** [dɪn] **1** *n* Lärm *m*, Getöse *nt.* **2** *vt* **to** ~ **sth into sb** jdm etw einbleuen.

**dine** [daɪn] **1** *vi* speisen, dinieren *(geh) (on etw).* **2** *vt* bewirten, beköstigen.

**diner** ['daɪnəʳ] *n* **(a)** *(person)* Speisende(r) *mf*; *(in restaurant)* Gast *m.* **(b)** *(US)* Eßlokal *nt.* **(c)** *(Rail)* Speisewagen *m.*

**ding-dong** ['dɪŋ'dɒŋ] *n* **(a)** Bimbam *nt.* **(b)** *(fight)* harter Kampf.

**dinghy** ['dɪŋɪ] *n* Ding(h)i *nt*; *(inflatable)* Schlauchboot *nt.*

**dingo** ['dɪŋgəʊ] *n* Dingo *m*, australischer Wildhund.

**dingy** ['dɪndʒɪ] *adj place, furniture* schmuddelig.

**dining** ['daɪnɪŋ]: ~ **area** *n* Eßbereich *m*; ~ **car** *n* Speisewagen *m*; ~ **hall** *n* Speisesaal *m*; ~ **room** *n* Eßzimmer *nt*; *(in hotel)* Speisesaal *m*; ~ **table** *n* Eßtisch *m.*

**dinky¹** ['dɪŋkɪ] *adj (Brit col)* schnuckelig *(col).*

**dinky²** *n (col)* = **double income no kids yet.** ~**s** noch kinderlose Doppelverdiener *pl.*

**dinner** ['dɪnəʳ] *n* (Haupt)mahlzeit *f*, Abendessen *nt*; *(formal)* (Abend)essen *nt*; *(lunch)* Mittagessen *nt.* **to be at** ~ beim Essen sein.

**dinner:** ~ **dance** *n* Abendessen *nt* mit Tanz; ~ **jacket** *n (Brit Sch)* Smokingjacke *f*; ~ **lady** *n (Brit Sch)* Serviererin *f* beim Mittagessen; ~ **party** *n* Abendgesellschaft *f* (mit Essen); **to have a small** ~ **party** ein kleines Essen geben; ~ **service** *n* Tafelservice *nt*; ~ **table** *n* Eßtisch *m*; ~ **time** *n* Essenszeit *f.*

**dinosaur** ['daɪnəsɔːʳ] *n* Dinosaurier *m.*

**dint** [dɪnt] *n* **by** ~ **of** durch.

**diocese** ['daɪəsɪs] *n* Diözese *f*, Bistum *nt.*

**diode** ['daɪəʊd] *n* Diode *f.*

**dioptre,** *(US)* **diopter** [daɪ'ɒptəʳ] *n* Dioptrie *f.*

**dioxide** [daɪ'ɒksaɪd] *n* Dioxyd *nt.*

**dip** [dɪp] **1** *vt* **(a)** *(in(to)* in +*acc) (into liquid)* tauchen; *pen, hand* eintauchen; *bread* (ein)tunken, stippen *(col).* **(b)** *(into bag, basket)* hand stecken. **(c)** *(Brit Aut)* headlights abblenden. **2** *vi (ground)* sich senken; *(temperature, pointer on scale)* fallen. **the sun** ~**ped behind the mountains** die Sonne verschwand hinter den Bergen. **3** *n* **(a)** *(swim)* **to go for a** ~ kurz schwimmen gehen. **(b)** *(for cleaning animals)* Desinfektionslösung *f.* **(c)** *(in ground)* Mulde *f.* **(d)** *(Cook)* Dip *m.*

▶**dip into** *vi* +*prep obj* **(a)** *(lit)* **she** ~**ped** ~ **her handbag** sie griff in ihre Handtasche. **(b)** **to** ~ ~ **one's savings** an seine Ersparnisse gehen. **(c)** *book* einen kurzen Blick werfen in (+*acc*).

**Dip** = **Diploma** Dipl.

**diphtheria** [dɪf'θɪərɪə] *n* Diphtherie *f.*

**diphthong** ['dɪfθɒŋ] *n* Diphthong *m.*

**diploma** [dɪ'pləʊmə] *n* Diplom *nt.*

**diplomacy** [dɪ'pləʊməsɪ] *n (Pol, fig)* Diplomatie *f.*

**diplomat** ['dɪpləmæt] *n (Pol, fig)* Diplomat *m.*

**diplomatic** *adj*, **~ally** *adv* [,dɪplə'mætɪk, -əlɪ] *(lit, fig)* diplomatisch.

**diplomatic:** ~ **bag** *n* Diplomatenpost *f*; ~ **corps** *n* diplomatisches Korps; ~ **immunity** *n* Immunität *f*; ~ **service** *n* diplomatischer Dienst.

**dipsomania** [,dɪpsəʊ'meɪnɪə] *n* Trunksucht *f.*

**dipsomaniac** [,dɪpsəʊ'meɪnɪæk] *n* Trunksüchtige(r) *mf.*

**dip:** ~**stick** *n (for oil)* Ölmeßstab *m*; ~**switch** *n (Aut)* Abblendschalter *m.*

**DIP switch** ['dɪpswɪtʃ] *n (Comp)* DIP-Schalter *m.*

**dire** ['daɪəʳ] *adj* schrecklich, furchtbar; *poverty* äußerste(r, s). ~ **necessity** dringende Notwendigkeit; **to be in** ~ **need of sth** etw dringend brauchen.

**direct** [daɪ'rekt] **1** *adj* direkt; *train* durchgehend; *opposite* genau. **~ access** *(Comp)* Direktzugriff *m*; **~ current** Gleichstrom *m*; **~ debit** *(Brit) (transaction)* automatische Abbuchung; *(order)* Einzugsauftrag *m*; **~ hit** Volltreffer *m*; **~ mail(ing)** Postwurfsendungen *pl*; **~ object** direktes Objekt, Akkusativobjekt *nt*; **~ speech** direkte Rede. **2** *vt* **(a)** *(address, aim) remark, letter* richten *(to* an *+acc)*; *efforts* richten *(towards* auf *+acc).* **can you ~ me to the town hall?** können Sie mir sagen, wie ich zum Rathaus komme? **(b)** *person's work, business* leiten, lenken; *traffic* regeln. **(c)** *(order)* anweisen *(sb to do sth* jdn, etw zu tun*)*, befehlen *(sb to do sth* jdm, etw zu tun*)*; *(Jur) jury* Rechtsbelehrung erteilen *(+dat).* **(d)** *film, play* Regie führen bei; *radio/TV programme* leiten. **3** *adv* direkt.
**direction** [dɪ'rekʃən] *n* **(a)** *(lit, fig: way)* Richtung *f.* **~ indicator** *(Aut)* Winker *m*; *(flashing)* Blinker *m*; **in the wrong/right ~** *(lit, fig)* in die falsche/richtige Richtung; **in the ~ of Hamburg** in Richtung Hamburg; **a sense of ~** *(lit)* Orientierungssinn *m*; *(fig)* ein Ziel *nt* (im Leben). **(b)** *(management: of company etc)* Leitung *f.* **(c)** *(of film, actors)* Regie *f*; *(of radio/TV programme)* Leitung *f.* **(d)** **~s** *pl (instructions)* Anweisungen *pl*; *(to a place)* Wegbeschreibung *f*; *(for use)* (Gebrauchs)anweisung *f.*
**directive** [dɪ'rektɪv] *n* Direktive, Weisung *f.*
**directly** [dɪ'rektlɪ] **1** *adv* direkt, unmittelbar; *(in a short time)* sofort, gleich. **2** *conj* sobald. **he'll come ~ he's ready** er kommt, sobald er fertig ist.
**directness** [daɪ'rektnɪs] *n* Direktheit *f.*
**director** [dɪ'rektəʳ] *n* **(a)** *(of company, institution)* Direktor(in *f*), Leiter(in *f*) *m*; *(Univ)* Rektor(in *f*) *m*. **D~ of Public Prosecutions** *(Brit)* ≃ Oberstaatsanwalt *m*; **(b)** *(Rad, TV)* Direktor(in *f*) *m*; *(Film, Theat)* Regisseur(in *f*) *m*.
**directorship** [dɪ'rektəʃɪp] *n* Direktorstelle *f.*
**directory** [dɪ'rektərɪ] *n* Adreßbuch *nt*; *(telephone ~)* Telefonbuch *nt*; *(trade ~)* Branchenverzeichnis *nt*; *(Comp)* Verzeichnis *nt.* **~ enquiries** *or (US)* **assistance** *(Telec)* (Fernsprech)auskunft *f.*
**dirge** [dɜːdʒ] *n* Klagegesang *m.*
**dirt** [dɜːt] *n (lit, fig)* Schmutz, Dreck *m*; *(soil)* Erde *f.* **to treat sb like ~** jdn wie (den letzten) Dreck behandeln *(col).*
**dirt: ~ cheap** *adj, adv (col)* spottbillig; **~ farmer** *n (US)* Kleinbauer *m.*
**dirtiness** ['dɜːtɪnɪs] *n* Schmutzigkeit *f.*
**dirt road** *n (US)* unbefestigte Straße.
**dirty** ['dɜːtɪ] **1** *adj (+er)* **(a)** schmutzig; *wound* verschmutzt. **~ weather** Sauwetter *nt (col)*; **to give sb a ~ look** *(fig)* jdm einen bösen Blick zuwerfen; **~ work** Dreckarbeit *f.* **(b)** *(fig: obscene)* schmutzig, unanständig; *story, joke also* zotig. **to have a ~ mind** eine schmutzige Phantasie haben; **~ old man** geiler Bock *(col!)*; **they're having a ~ weekend** *(col)* sie sind zusammen übers Wochenende weggefahren. **2** *vt* beschmutzen. **3** *n* **to do the ~ on sb** *(Brit col)* jdn reinlegen *(col).*
**disability** [ˌdɪsə'bɪlɪtɪ] *n* Behinderung *f.* **~ allowance** Behindertenfreibetrag *m*; **~ pension** Invalidenrente *f.*
**disable** [dɪs'eɪbl] *vt tank, gun* unbrauchbar machen; *ship* kampfunfähig machen.
**disabled** [dɪs'eɪbld] **1** *adj* **(a)** *person* behindert. **(b)** *tank, gun* unbrauchbar; *ship* nicht seetüchtig. **2** *npl* **the ~** die Behinderten *pl.*
**disadvantage** [ˌdɪsəd'vɑːntɪdʒ] *n* Nachteil *m.* **to his ~** zu seinem Nachteil. **to be at a ~** sich im Nachteil befinden, benachteiligt sein.
**disadvantaged** [ˌdɪsəd'vɑːntɪdʒd] *adj* benachteiligt.

**disadvantageous** *adj* [ˌdɪsædvɑːn'teɪdʒəs] nachteilig.
**disaffected** [ˌdɪsə'fektɪd] *adj* entfremdet.
**disagree** [ˌdɪsə'griː] *vi* **(a)** *(with person, views, figures)* nicht übereinstimmen; *(with plan, suggestion etc)* nicht einverstanden sein; *(two people)* sich nicht einig sein. **(b)** *(quarrel)* eine Meinungsverschiedenheit haben. **(c)** *(climate, food)* **to ~ with sb** jdm nicht bekommen.
**disagreeable** [ˌdɪsə'griːəbl] *adj* unangenehm; *person* unsympathisch.
**disagreement** [ˌdɪsə'griːmənt] *n* **(a)** *(with opinion, between opinions)* Uneinigkeit *f.* **(b)** *(quarrel)* Meinungsverschiedenheit *f.* **(c)** *(between reports)* Diskrepanz *f.*
**disallow** [ˌdɪsə'lau] *vt evidence, goal* nicht anerkennen; *claim also* zurückweisen.
**disappear** [ˌdɪsə'pɪəʳ] *vi* verschwinden.
**disappearance** [ˌdɪsə'pɪərəns] *n* Verschwinden *nt.*
**disappoint** [ˌdɪsə'pɔɪnt] *vt* enttäuschen.
**disappointed** [ˌdɪsə'pɔɪntɪd] *adj* enttäuscht.
**disappointing** [ˌdɪsə'pɔɪntɪŋ] *adj* enttäuschend.
**disappointment** [ˌdɪsə'pɔɪntmənt] *n* Enttäuschung *f.*
**disapproval** [ˌdɪsə'pruːvl] *n* Mißbilligung *f.*
**disapprove** [ˌdɪsə'pruːv] **1** *vt* mißbilligen. **2** *vi* dagegen sein. **he ~s of children smoking** er mißbilligt es, wenn Kinder rauchen.
**disapproving** [ˌdɪsə'pruːvɪŋ] *adj* mißbilligend.
**disarm** [dɪs'ɑːm] **1** *vt (lit, fig)* entwaffnen. **2** *vi (Mil)* abrüsten.
**disarmament** [dɪs'ɑːməmənt] *n* Abrüstung *f.* **~ talks** Abrüstungsgespräche *pl.*
**disarming** *adj*, **~ly** *adv* [dɪs'ɑːmɪŋ, -lɪ] entwaffnend.
**disarray** [ˌdɪsə'reɪ] *n* Unordnung *f.*
**disaster** [dɪ'zɑːstəʳ] *n* Katastrophe *f*; *(Aviat, Min, Rail also)* Unglück *nt.* **~ area** Katastrophengebiet *nt*; **~ movie** Katastrophenfilm *m.*
**disastrous** [dɪ'zɑːstrəs] *adj* katastrophal.
**disband** [dɪs'bænd] **1** *vt* auflösen. **2** *vi (soldiers, club members)* auseinandergehen.
**disbelief** ['dɪsbə'liːf] *n* **in ~** ungläubig.
**disbelieve** ['dɪsbə'liːv] *vt* nicht glauben.
**disc, (***esp US***) disk** [dɪsk] *n* **(a)** Scheibe *f*; *(Anat)* Bandscheibe *f.* **(b)** *(record)* Platte *f.* **(c)** *(Comp)* Diskette *f.*
**discard** [dɪ'skɑːd] *vt unwanted article* ausrangieren; *person* abschieben; *idea, plan* verwerfen; *cards* abwerfen.
**disc: ~ brake** *n* Scheibenbremse *f*; **~ drive** *n (Comp)* Diskettenlaufwerk *nt.*
**discern** [dɪ'sɜːn] *vt* erkennen.
**discernible** [dɪ'sɜːnəbl] *adj* erkennbar.
**discerning** [dɪ'sɜːnɪŋ] *adj clientele, reader* anspruchsvoll, kritisch. **to the ~ eye** für den Kenner.
**discernment** [dɪ'sɜːnmənt] *n (ability to discern)* feines Gespür. **a man of ~** ein Mann mit Geschmack.
**discharge** [dɪs'tʃɑːdʒ] **1** *vt* **(a)** *prisoner, patient, soldier* entlassen; *accused* freisprechen. **~d prisoner** Strafentlassene(r) *mf.* **(b)** *(emit) (Elec)* entladen; *liquid, gas (pipe etc)* ausstoßen; *(Med)* absondern. **(c)** *(unload) ship, cargo* löschen. **(d)** *(gun)* abfeuern. **(e)** *debt* begleichen; *obligation, duty* nachkommen *(+dat)*; *function* erfüllen. **2** *vi (wound, sore)* eitern. **3** ['dɪstʃɑːdʒ] *n* **(a)** *(dismissal) see vt (a)* Entlassung *f*; Freispruch *m*; *(of soldier)* Abschied *m.* **(b)** *(Elec)* Entladung *f*; *(of gas)* Ausströmen *nt*; *(of liquid, Med: vaginal ~)* Ausfluß *m*; *(of pus)* Absonderung *f.* **(c)** *(of debt)* Begleichung *f*; *(of obligation, duty, function)* Erfüllung *f.*
**disciple** [dɪ'saɪpl] *n (lit, fig)* Jünger *m.*

**disciplinarian** [,dısıplı'nɛərıən] *n* Zuchtmeister (in *f*) *m*.

**disciplinary** ['dısıplınərı] *adj* Disziplinar-, disziplinarisch. **to take ~ action against sb** ein Disziplinarverfahren gegen jdn einleiten.

**discipline** ['dısıplın] **1** *n* Disziplin *f*. **2** *vt* **(a)** *(train, make obedient)* disziplinieren. **(b)** *(punish)* bestrafen; *(physically)* züchtigen.

**disc jockey** *n* Diskjockey *m*.

**disclaim** [dıs'kleım] *vt* abstreiten.

**disclaimer** [dıs'kleımər] *n* Dementi *nt*.

**disclose** [dıs'kləʊz] *vt secret* enthüllen; *intentions, news* bekanntgeben.

**disclosure** [dıs'kləʊʒər] *n* **(a)** *see vt* Enthüllung *f*; Bekanntgabe *f*. **(b)** *(fact revealed)* Mitteilung *f*.

**disco** ['dıskəʊ] *n* Disko *f*.

**discoloration** [dıs,kʌlə'reıʃən] *n (mark)* Verfärbung *f*.

**discolour,** *(US)* **discolor** [dıs'kʌlər] **1** *vt* verfärben. **2** *vi* sich verfärben.

**discomfiture** [dıs'kʌmfıtʃər] *n* Unbehagen *nt*.

**discomfort** [dıs'kʌmfət] *n (lit)* Beschwerden *pl*; *(fig: uneasiness, embarrassment)* Unbehagen *nt*.

**disconcert** [,dıskən'sɜːt] *vt* aus der Fassung bringen.

**disconnect** ['dıskə'nekt] *vt pipe etc* trennen; *(cut off supply of) gas, electricity* abstellen. **I've been ~ed** *(for non-payment)* man hat mir das Telefon/den Strom/das Gas *etc* abgestellt. **to ~ an appliance** den Stecker eines Geräts herausziehen.

**disconsolate** [dıs'kɒnsəlıt] *adj* niedergeschlagen.

**discontent(ment)** ['dıskən'tent(mənt)] *n* Unzufriedenheit *f*.

**discontent(ed)** ['dıskən'tent(ıd)] *adj* unzufrieden *(with, about* mit*)*.

**discontinue** ['dıskən'tınjuː] *vt* aufgeben; *class, project, conversation* abbrechen; *(Comm) line* auslaufen lassen.

**discord** ['dıskɔːd] *n* **(a)** Uneinigkeit *f*. **(b)** *(Mus)* Dissonanz *f*.

**discordant** [dıs'kɔːdənt] *adj meeting, atmosphere* unharmonisch; *(Mus)* dissonant.

**discotheque** ['dıskəʊtek] *n* Diskothek *f*.

**discount** ['dıskaʊnt] **1** *n* Rabatt *m*; *(for cash)* Skonto *nt or m*. **to give a ~ on sth** Rabatt auf etw *(acc)* geben. **2** *vt* **(a)** *(Comm)* nachlassen. **(b)** [dıs'kaʊnt] *(dismiss)* abtun; *person's opinion* unberücksichtigt lassen.

**discount:** **~ rate** *n* Diskontsatz *m*; **~ shop, ~ store** *n* Discountgeschäft *nt*.

**discourage** [dıs'kʌrıdʒ] *vt* **(a)** *(dishearten)* entmutigen. **(b)** *(dissuade)* **to ~ sb from sth** jdm von etw abraten; *(successfully)* jdn von etw abbringen.

**discouragement** [dıs'kʌrıdʒmənt] *n* **(a)** *(depression)* Mutlosigkeit *f*. **(b)** **to be a ~** entmutigend sein.

**discouraging** [dıs'kʌrıdʒıŋ] *adj* entmutigend.

**discourteous** [dıs'kɜːtıəs] *adj* unhöflich.

**discourtesy** [dıs'kɜːtısı] *n* Unhöflichkeit *f*.

**discover** [dıs'kʌvər] *vt* entdecken; *(notice) mistake, loss also* feststellen, bemerken.

**discovery** [dıs'kʌvərı] *n* Entdeckung *f*.

**discredit** [dıs'kredıt] **1** *vt* **(a)** *report, theory* in Mißkredit bringen. **(b)** *(disbelieve)* keinen Glauben schenken *(+dat)*. **2** *n* **(a)** *no pl* **to bring ~ on sb** jdn in Mißkredit bringen. **(b)** **to be a ~ to sb** jdm keine Ehre machen.

**discreet** *adj*, **~ly** *adv* [dı'skriːt, -lı] diskret; *(in quiet taste also)* dezent.

**discrepancy** [dı'skrepənsı] *n* Diskrepanz *f (between* zwischen *+dat)*.

**discretion** [dı'skreʃən] *n* **(a)** Diskretion *f*. **(b)** to

**leave sth to sb's ~** etw jdm anheimstellen; **use your own ~** es steht in Ihrem Ermessen.

**discretionary** [dı'skreʃənərı] *adj* **~ powers** Ermessensspielraum *m*.

**discriminate** [dı'skrımıneıt] *vi* **(a)** *(distinguish)* unterscheiden *(between* zwischen *+dat)*. **(b)** **to ~ against/in favour of sb** jdn diskriminieren/bevorzugen.

**discriminating** [dı'skrımıneıtıŋ] *adj person, judgement, mind* kritisch.

**discrimination** [dı,skrımı'neıʃən] *n* **(a)** Diskriminierung *f*. **racial ~** Rassendiskriminierung *f*; **sexual ~** Diskriminierung auf Grund des Geschlechts. **(b)** *(discernment)* kritisches Urteilsvermögen.

**discus** ['dıskəs] *n* Diskus *m*.

**discuss** [dı'skʌs] *vt* besprechen; *politics, theory* erörtern, diskutieren.

**discussion** [dı'skʌʃən] *n* Diskussion *f*; *(meeting)* Besprechung *f*.

**disdain** [dıs'deın] **1** *vt* verachten. **he ~ed to notice them** er hielt es für unter seiner Würde, ihnen Beachtung zu schenken. **2** *n* Verachtung *f*.

**disdainful** *adj*, **~ly** *adv* [dıs'deınfʊl, -fəlı] verächtlich.

**disease** [dı'ziːz] *n (lit, fig)* Krankheit *f*.

**diseased** [dı'ziːzd] *adj (lit, fig)* krank.

**disembark** [,dısım'bɑːk] **1** *vt* ausschiffen. **2** *vi* von Bord gehen.

**disembarkation** [,dısembɑː'keıʃən] *n* Landung *f*.

**disembodied** [,dısım'bɒdıd] *adj* körperlos; *voice* geisterhaft.

**disenchanted** [,dısın'tʃɑːntıd] *adj* **to be ~ with sb/sth** von jdm/etw enttäuscht sein; **I've become ~ with it** ich halte nicht mehr viel davon.

**disenfranchise** [,dısın'fræntʃaız] *vt person* die bürgerlichen Ehrenrechte aberkennen *(+dat)*.

**disengage** [,dısın'geıdʒ] *vt* **to ~ the clutch** *(Aut)* auskuppeln.

**disentangle** [,dısın'tæŋgl] *vt (lit, fig)* entwirren.

**disfavour,** *(US)* **disfavor** [dıs'feıvər] *n (displeasure)* Ungnade *f*; *(dislike)* Mißfallen *nt*. **to fall into/be in ~** in Ungnade fallen/sein *(with* bei*)*.

**disfigure** [dıs'fıgər] *vt* verunstalten; *person also* entstellen.

**disfigurement** [dıs'fıgəmənt] *n see vt* Verunstaltung *f*; Entstellung *f*.

**disgorge** [dıs'gɔːdʒ] *vt* ausspeien.

**disgrace** [dıs'greıs] **1** *n* Schande *f*; *(person)* Schandfleck *m (to gen)*. **to be in/fall into ~** in Ungnade *(gefallen)* sein/fallen *(with* bei*)*. **2** *vt* Schande machen *(+dat)*; *country, family also* Schande bringen über *(+acc)*. **to ~ oneself** sich blamieren.

**disgraceful** [dıs'greısfʊl] *adj* erbärmlich (schlecht); *behaviour* skandalös. **it's ~ or a ~ business** es ist eine Schande.

**disgracefully** [dıs'greısfəlı] *adv (+adj)* erbärmlich; *(+vb)* erbärmlich schlecht; *behave* skandalös.

**disgruntled** [dıs'grʌntld] *adj* verstimmt.

**disguise** [dıs'gaız] **1** *vt* verkleiden; *voice* verstellen; *interest, feelings* verbergen. **there's no disguising the fact that ...** es läßt sich nicht verhehlen, daß ... **2** *n (lit)* Verkleidung *f*; *(of voice)* Verstellung *f*; *(fig)* Deckmantel *m*. **in ~** verkleidet.

**disgust** [dıs'gʌst] **1** *n* Ekel *m*; *(at sb's behaviour)* Entrüstung, Empörung *f*. **2** *vt (person, sight)* anekeln, anwidern; *(actions)* empören.

**disgusted** [dıs'gʌstıd] *adj* angeekelt; *(at sb's behaviour)* empört. **I am ~ with you** ich bin empört über dich.

**disgusting** [dıs'gʌstıŋ] *adj* widerlich; *(physically nauseating also)* ekelhaft. **that's ~** das ist eine

Schweinerei *(col)*.

**dish** [dɪʃ] *n* **(a)** Schale *f*; *(for serving also)* Schüssel *f*. **(b)** ~es *pl (crockery)* Geschirr *nt*; **to do the** ~es abwaschen. **(c)** *(food)* Gericht *nt*. **(d)** *(also* ~ **aerial** *(Brit)* or **antenna** *(US))* Parabolantenne, Schüssel *(col) f*.
▶**dish out** *vt sep (col)* austeilen.
▶**dish up** *vt sep (lit, fig)* auftischen.

**disharmony** [ˌdɪs'hɑːmənɪ] *n (lit, fig)* Disharmonie *f*.

**dishcloth** ['dɪʃklɒθ] *n* Geschirrtuch *nt*; *(for washing)* Spültuch *nt*.

**dishearten** [dɪs'hɑːtn] *vt* entmutigen. **don't be** ~**ed** nur Mut.

**disheartening** [dɪs'hɑːtnɪŋ] *adj* entmutigend.

**dished** [dɪʃt] *adj (Tech)* konkav (gewölbt); *wheels* gestürzt.

**dishevelled,** *(US)* **disheveled** [dɪ'ʃevəld] *adj* ramponiert *(col)*, unordentlich; *hair* zerzaust.

**dishonest** *adj,* ~**ly** *adv* [dɪs'ɒnɪst, -lɪ] unehrlich.

**dishonesty** [dɪs'ɒnɪstɪ] *n* Unehrlichkeit *f*.

**dishonour,** *(US)* **dishonor** [dɪs'ɒnəʳ] *n* Schande *f*. **to bring** ~ **upon sb** Schande über jdn bringen.

**dishonourable,** *(US)* **dishonorable** [dɪs'ɒnərəbl] *adj* unehrenhaft.

**dish:** ~ **rack** *n* Geschirrständer *m*; *(in* ~*washer)* Einsatzkorb *m*; ~ **towel** *n (US, Scot)* Geschirrtuch *nt*; ~**washer** *n (person)* Tellerwäscher(in *f*) *m*; *(machine)* Geschirrspülmaschine *f*; ~**washing liquid** *n (US)* Geschirrspülmittel *nt*; ~**water** *n* Abwasch- or Spülwasser *nt*; **this coffee is like** ~**water** der Kaffee schmeckt wie Spülwasser.

**dishy** ['dɪʃɪ] *adj (+er) (Brit col)* dufte *(col)*.

**disillusion** [ˌdɪsɪ'luːʒən] *vt* desillusionieren. **to become** ~**ed** seine Illusionen verlieren; **I'm completely** ~**ed** ich habe alle meine Illusionen verloren.

**disillusionment** [ˌdɪsɪ'luːʒənmənt] *n* Desillusionierung *f*.

**disincentive** [ˌdɪsɪn'sentɪv] *n* Entmutigung *f*. **it acts as a** ~ es wirkt abschreckend.

**disinclination** [ˌdɪsɪnklɪ'neɪʃən] *n* Abneigung, Unlust *f*.

**disinclined** [ˌdɪsɪn'klaɪnd] *adj* abgeneigt.

**disinfect** [ˌdɪsɪn'fekt] *vt* desinfizieren.

**disinfectant** [ˌdɪsɪn'fektənt] *n* Desinfektionsmittel *nt*.

**disinfection** [ˌdɪsɪn'fekʃən] *n* Desinfektion *f*.

**disinformation** [ˌdɪsɪnfɔː'meɪʃən] *n* Desinformation *f*.

**disinherit** [ˌdɪsɪn'herɪt] *vt* enterben.

**disintegrate** [dɪs'ɪntɪgreɪt] *vi* zerfallen; *(rock, cement)* auseinanderbröckeln; *(vehicle)* sich in seine Bestandteile auflösen; *(group also, institution)* sich auflösen.

**disintegration** [dɪsˌɪntɪ'greɪʃən] *n see vi* Zerfall *m*; Auseinanderbröckeln *nt*; Auflösung *f*.

**disinterested** [dɪs'ɪntrɪstɪd] *adj (unbiased)* unvoreingenommen.

**disjointed** *adj* [dɪs'dʒɔɪntɪd] zusammenhanglos.

**disk** [dɪsk] *n (Comp)* Diskette *f*; *(video etc)* Platte *f*. ~ **drive** Diskettenlaufwerk *nt*; **hard** ~ Festplatte *f*.

**diskette** [dɪs'ket] *n* Diskette *f*.

**dislike** [dɪs'laɪk] **1** *vt* nicht mögen, nicht gern haben. **to** ~ **doing sth** etw ungern tun. **I don't** ~ **him** ich habe nichts gegen ihn. **2** *n* Abneigung *f (of gegen)*. **to take a** ~ **to sb/sth** eine Abneigung gegen jdn/etw entwickeln.

**dislocate** ['dɪsləʊkeɪt] *vt (Med)* verrenken; *(fig) plans* durcheinanderbringen. **to** ~ **one's shoulder** sich *(dat)* den Arm auskugeln.

**dislodge** [dɪs'lɒdʒ] *vt obstruction, stone* entfernen; *(accidentally)* verschieben; *enemy* verdrängen.

**disloyal** [dɪs'lɔɪəl] *adj* treulos; *(esp Pol)* illoyal *(to* gegenüber*)*.

**disloyalty** [dɪs'lɔɪəltɪ] *n* Treulosigkeit *f*; *(esp Pol)* Illoyalität *f (to* gegenüber*)*.

**dismal** ['dɪzməl] *adj* trübe, trist; *person* trübsinnig; *failure, result* kläglich.

**dismantle** [dɪs'mæntl] *vt* auseinandernehmen; *scaffolding* abbauen; *(fig) system* demontieren.

**dismay** [dɪs'meɪ] **1** *n* Bestürzung *f*. **in** ~ bestürzt. **2** *vt* bestürzen.

**dismiss** [dɪs'mɪs] *vt* **(a)** *(from job)* entlassen. **(b)** *(allow to go)* entlassen; *assembly* auflösen. **(c)** *objection* abtun. **(d)** *(Jur) accused* entlassen; *appeal* abweisen. **to** ~ **a case** eine Klage abweisen.

**dismissal** [dɪs'mɪsəl] *n* Entlassung *f*; *(of assembly)* Auflösung *f*; *(of objection)* Zurückweisung *f*; *(of appeal)* Abweisung *f*.

**dismissive** [dɪs'mɪsɪv] *adj remark* wegwerfend; *gesture* abweisend.

**dismount** [dɪs'maʊnt] *vi* absteigen.

**disobedience** [ˌdɪsə'biːdɪəns] *n* Ungehorsam *m (to* gegenüber*)*.

**disobedient** [ˌdɪsə'biːdɪənt] *adj* ungehorsam.

**disobey** [ˌdɪsə'beɪ] *vt* nicht gehorchen *(+dat)*; *rule* übertreten.

**disobliging** [ˌdɪsə'blaɪdʒɪŋ] *adj* ungefällig.

**disorder** [dɪs'ɔːdəʳ] *n* **(a)** Durcheinander *nt*; *(in room etc also)* Unordnung *f*. **in** ~ durcheinander; in Unordnung. **(b)** *(rioting)* Unruhen *pl*. **(c)** *(Med)* Störung *f*.

**disordered** [dɪs'ɔːdəd] *adj room* unordentlich; *plans* wirr; *existence, thoughts* ungeordnet.

**disorderly** [dɪs'ɔːdəlɪ] *adj desk, room* unordentlich; *life* unsolide; *mind* wirr; *(unruly) crowd* aufrührerisch. ~ **conduct** *(Jur)* ungebührliches Benehmen.

**disorganized** [dɪs'ɔːgənaɪzd] *adj* durcheinander *pred*, desorganisiert; *life, person* chaotisch.

**disorientated** [dɪs'ɔːrɪənteɪtɪd] *adj* desorientiert.

**disown** [dɪs'əʊn] *vt* verleugnen; *child* verstoßen. **I'll** ~ **you if you go out in that hat** wenn du mit dem Hut ausgehst, tue ich so, als ob ich nicht zu dir gehöre.

**disparage** [dɪ'spærɪdʒ] *vt* herabsetzen.

**disparagement** [dɪ'spærɪdʒmənt] *n* Herabsetzung *f*.

**disparaging** [dɪ'spærɪdʒɪŋ] *adj* abschätzig.

**disparate** ['dɪspərɪt] *adj* ungleich.

**disparity** [dɪ'spærɪtɪ] *n* Ungleichheit *f*.

**dispassionate** [dɪs'pæʃənɪt] *adj* objektiv.

**dispatch** [dɪ'spætʃ] **1** *vt* **(a)** senden, schicken; *person, troops etc also* entsenden. **(b)** *(deal with) job etc* (prompt) erledigen. **(c)** *(kill)* töten. **2** *n* **(a)** *see vt* Senden, Schicken *nt*; Entsendung *f*; prompte Erledigung; *(kill)* Tötung *f*. ~ **department** Versandabteilung *f*; ~ **note** *(in advance)* Versandanzeige *f*; *(with goods)* Begleitschein *m*; **date of** ~ Absendedatum *nt*; **with** ~ prompt. **(b)** *(message)* Depesche *f*; *(Press)* Bericht *m*. **to be mentioned in** ~**es** *(Mil)* in den Kriegsberichten erwähnt werden; ~ **rider** *(Mil)* Melder *m*.

**dispel** [dɪ'spel] *vt clouds, fog* auflösen, vertreiben; *doubts, fears* zerstreuen; *sorrows* vertreiben.

**dispensable** [dɪ'spensəbl] *adj* entbehrlich.

**dispensary** [dɪ'pensərɪ] *n (in hospital)* (Krankenhaus)apotheke *f*; *(in chemist's)* Apothekenabteilung *f*.

**dispensation** [ˌdɪspen'seɪʃən] *n (handing out)* Verteilung *f*. ~ **of justice** Rechtsprechung *f*; **by a special** ~ durch besondere Verfügung.

**dispense** [dɪ'spens] *vt* **(a)** verteilen, austeilen *(to* an *+acc)*. **(b)** *medicine* abgeben; *prescription* zubereiten.

▶**dispense with** vi +prep obj verzichten auf (+acc).

**dispenser** [dɪ'spensəʳ] n (container) Spender m; (slot-machine) Automat m.

**dispensing** [dɪ'spensɪŋ]: ~ **chemist** n (Brit) Apotheker(in f) m; ~ **chemist's** n (Brit) Apotheke f.

**dispersal** [dɪ'spɜːsəl] n see vb Verstreuen nt; Verteilung f; Verbreitung f; Auflösung f.

**disperse** [dɪ'spɜːs] 1 vt (scatter widely) verstreuen; (Bot) seed verteilen; (fig) knowledge etc verbreiten. 2 vi sich auflösen.

**dispirited** [dɪ'spɪrɪtɪd] adj entmutigt.

**dispiriting** adj, ~**ly** adv [dɪ'spɪrɪtɪŋ, -lɪ] entmutigend.

**displace** [dɪs'pleɪs] vt (move) verschieben; (replace) ablösen, ersetzen; water, air verdrängen. ~**d person** Verschleppte(r) mf.

**displacement** [dɪs'pleɪsmənt] n see vt Verschiebung f; Ablösung f; Verdrängung f.

**display** [dɪ'spleɪ] 1 vt (a) zeigen; (ostentatiously) new clothes etc also vorführen; exam results, notice aushängen. (b) (Comm) goods ausstellen. 2 n (a) **to make a great ~ of sth** etw groß zur Schau stellen; **a ~ of temper** ein Wutanfall m. (b) (of paintings etc) Ausstellung f; (dancing ~ etc) Vorführung f; (military, air ~) Schau f. (c) (Comm) Auslage f. **the goods on ~** die ausgestellte Ware. (d) (visual ~: on calculator etc) Anzeige f.

**display:** ~ **advertisement** n Display-Anzeige f; ~ **cabinet** n Schaukasten m; ~ **case** n Vitrine f; ~ **unit** n (Comp) (Daten)sichtgerät nt.

**displease** [dɪs'pliːz] vt mißfallen (+dat), nicht gefallen (+dat).

**displeasure** [dɪs'pleʒəʳ] n Mißfallen nt (at über +acc).

**disposable** [dɪ'spəʊzəbl] adj (a) (to be thrown away) Wegwerf-; handkerchief, nappy also Papier-; bottle, syringe Einweg-. ~ **towel** Einmalhandtuch nt. (b) (available) verfügbar.

**disposal** [dɪ'spəʊzəl] n (a) see **dispose of** (a) Loswerden nt; Beseitigung f; Erledigung f. (waste) ~ **unit** Müllschlucker m. (b) **to be at sb's** ~ jdm zur Verfügung stehen; **to put sth at sb's** ~ jdm etw zur Verfügung stellen.

**dispose** [dɪ'spəʊz] vt (form: arrange) anorden; troops aufstellen. **to be well/ill** ~**d towards sb** jdm wohlwollen/übelwollen.

▶**dispose of** vi +prep obj (a) (get rid of) loswerden; rubbish beseitigen; opponent, difficulties aus dem Weg räumen; matter erledigen. (b) (have at disposal) fortune, time verfügen über (+acc).

**disposition** [ˌdɪspə'zɪʃən] n (temperament) Veranlagung f. **her cheerful/friendly** ~ ihre fröhliche/freundliche Art.

**dispossess** ['dɪspə'zes] vt enteignen.

**disproportionate** [ˌdɪsprə'pɔːʃnɪt] adj **a** ~ **amount of money** ein unverhältnismäßig hoher/niedriger Geldbetrag.

**disproportionately** [ˌdɪsprə'pɔːʃnɪtlɪ] adv unverhaltnismäßig.

**disprove** [dɪs'pruːv] vt widerlegen.

**disputable** [dɪ'spjuːtəbl] adj sehr zweifelhaft.

**dispute** [dɪ'spjuːt] 1 vt (a) statement bestreiten; claim to sth, will anfechten. (b) **the issue was hotly** ~**d** das Thema wurde heftig diskutiert. (c) (contest) championship jdm streitig machen. 2 vi (argue) streiten. 3 n also ['dɪspjuːt] (a) no pl (arguing, controversy) Disput m, Kontroverse f. **to be beyond** ~ außer Frage stehen; **without** ~ zweifellos; **to be open to** ~ umstritten sein. (b) (argument) Streit m; (debate) Kontroverse f. **industrial** ~ Arbeitskampf

m; **to be in** ~ (on strike) im Ausstand sein.

**disqualification** [dɪsˌkwɒlɪfɪ'keɪʃən] n (a) Ausschluß m; (Sport also) Disqualifikation f. ~ (**from driving**) Führerscheinentzug m. (b) (disqualifying factor) Grund m zur Disqualifikation.

**disqualify** [dɪs'kwɒlɪfaɪ] vt ungeeignet machen (from für); (Sport etc) disqualifizieren. **to** ~ **sb from driving** jdm den Führerschein entziehen.

**disquiet** [dɪs'kwaɪət] n Unruhe f.

**disquieting** [dɪs'kwaɪətɪŋ] adj beunruhigend.

**disregard** [ˌdɪsrɪ'gɑːd] 1 vt ignorieren; remark, feelings also nicht beachten (+acc); danger, advice, authority also mißachten. 2 n Mißachtung f (for gen); (for money) Geringschätzung f (for gen).

**disrepair** [ˌdɪsrɪ'pɛəʳ] n Baufälligkeit f. **in a state of** ~ baufällig; **to fall into** ~ verfallen.

**disreputable** [dɪs'repjʊtəbl] adj verrufen, berüchtigt.

**disrepute** [ˌdɪsrɪ'pjuːt] n schlechter Ruf. **to bring sth into** ~ etw in Verruf bringen; **to fall into** ~ in Verruf kommen or geraten.

**disrespect** [ˌdɪsrɪs'pekt] n Respektlosigkeit f (for gegenüber).

**disrespectful** adj [ˌdɪsrɪs'pektfʊl] respektlos (to gegenüber).

**disrupt** [dɪs'rʌpt] vt stören; train service, communications unterbrechen.

**disruption** [dɪs'rʌpʃən] n see vt Störung f; Unterbrechung f.

**disruptive** [dɪs'rʌptɪv] adj störend. ~ **action** Störmanöver nt.

**dissatisfaction** [ˌdɪssætɪs'fækʃən] n Unzufriedenheit f.

**dissatisfied** [dɪs'sætɪs'faɪd] adj unzufrieden.

**dissect** [dɪ'sekt] vt plant präparieren; animal also sezieren.

**dissection** [dɪ'sekʃən] n see vt Präparieren nt; Sezieren nt.

**disseminate** [dɪ'semɪneɪt] vt verbreiten.

**dissension** [dɪ'senʃən] n Meinungsverschiedenheit, Differenz f.

**dissent** [dɪ'sent] 1 vi anderer Meinung sein, differieren (geh). 2 n Meinungsverschiedenheit f. **to voice/express one's** ~ (**with sth**) erklären, daß man (mit etw) nicht übereinstimmt.

**dissenter** [dɪ'sentəʳ] n Abweichler(in f) m.

**dissertation** [ˌdɪsə'teɪʃən] n wissenschaftliche Arbeit; (PhD) Dissertation f.

**disservice** [dɪs'sɜːvɪs] n **to do sb a** ~ jdm einen schlechten Dienst erweisen.

**dissident** ['dɪsɪdənt] 1 n Dissident(in f), Regimekritiker(in f) m. 2 adj regimekritisch.

**dissimilar** [dɪ'sɪmɪləʳ] adj verschieden (to von).

**dissimilarity** [ˌdɪsɪmɪ'lærɪtɪ] n Verschiedenheit f.

**dissipate** ['dɪsɪpeɪt] vt (a) doubts, fears zerstreuen. (b) energy, fortune verschwenden.

**dissipated** ['dɪsɪpeɪtɪd] adj behaviour, society zügellos; person also leichtlebig; (in appearance) verlebt; life ausschweifend.

**dissipation** [ˌdɪsɪ'peɪʃən] n see vt (a) Zerstreuung f. (b) Verschwendung f. (c) (debauchery) Ausschweifung f.

**dissociate** [dɪ'səʊʃɪeɪt] vt trennen. **to** ~ **oneself from sb/sth** sich von jdm/etw distanzieren.

**dissolute** ['dɪsəluːt] adj person zügellos; way of life also ausschweifend; appearance verlebt.

**dissolution** [ˌdɪsə'luːʃən] n Auflösung f.

**dissolve** [dɪ'zɒlv] 1 vt auflösen. 2 vi sich (auf)lösen; (fig) sich in nichts auflösen. **it** ~**s in water** es ist wasserlöslich; **to** ~ **into tears** in Tränen zerfließen.

**dissuade** [dɪ'sweɪd] vt **to** ~ **sb from doing sth** jdn davon abbringen, etw zu tun.

**distaff** ['dıstɑːf] *n* **on the ~ side** mütterlicherseits.

**distance** ['dıstəns] *n* Entfernung *f*; *(gap, interval)* Abstand *m*; *(distance covered)* Strecke *f*, Weg *m*. **at a ~ of two metres** in zwei Meter(n) Entfernung; **what's the ~ from London to Glasgow?** wie weit ist es von London nach Glasgow?; **in the (far) ~** (ganz) in der Ferne, (ganz) weit weg; **he admired her at a ~** *(fig)* er bewunderte sie aus der Ferne; **it's within walking ~** es ist zu Fuß erreichbar; **it's no ~** es ist überhaupt nicht weit; **seen from a ~ it looks different** von weitem sieht das ganz anders aus; **quite a ~ (away)** ziemlich weit (entfernt); **the fight went the ~** der Kampf ging über alle Runden; **to go the ~** durchhalten; **to keep one's ~** *(lit, fig)* auf Distanz bleiben; **at this ~ in time** nach einem so langen Zeitraum; **to keep sb at a ~** jdn auf Distanz halten.

**distance:** **~ event** *n* Langstreckenlauf *m*; **~ runner** *n* Langstreckenläufer(in *f*) *m*.

**distant** ['dıstənt] *adj* **(a)** *country* weit entfernt, fern. **we had a ~ view of the church** wir sahen in der Ferne die Kirche. **(b)** *(with time)* age fern, weit zurückliegend; *recollection* entfernt. **that was in the ~ past** das liegt weit zurück; **in the not too ~ future** in nicht allzu ferner Zukunft. **(c)** *relationship, likeness, cousin* entfernt. **(d)** *(fig: aloof)* person, manner distanziert, reserviert.

**distaste** [dıs'teıst] *n* Widerwille *m* *(for gegen)*. **to have a ~ for sth** eine Abneigung gegen etw haben.

**distasteful** [dıs'teıstfʊl] *adj* *task* unangenehm; *photo, magazine* geschmacklos. **to be ~ to sb** jdm zuwider *or* unangenehm sein.

**distemper**[1] [dıs'tempəʳ] *n* *(paint)* Temperafarbe *f*.

**distemper**[2] *n* *(Vet)* Staupe *f*.

**distend** [dı'stend] **1** *vt* *sails, stomach* (auf)blähen. **2** *vi* sich blähen.

**distil, *(US)* distill** [dı'stıl] *vt* *(Chem)* destillieren; *whisky etc also* brennen.

**distiller** [dı'stıləʳ] *n* Destillateur, (Branntwein)brenner *m*.

**distillery** [dı'stılərı] *n* (Branntwein)brennerei *f*.

**distinct** [dı'stıŋkt] *adj* **(a)** deutlich, klar; *landmark, shape also* klar erkennbar; *accent, likeness also* ausgeprägt. **I had the ~ feeling that ...** ich hatte das bestimmte Gefühl, daß ... **(b)** *(different)* verschieden; *(separate)* getrennt. **as ~ from** im Unterschied zu; **to keep A ~ from B** A und B auseinanderhalten.

**distinction** [dı'stıŋkʃən] *n* **(a)** *(difference)* Unterschied *m*; *(act of distinguishing)* Unterscheidung *f*. **to make a ~ (between two things)** (zwischen zwei Dingen) einen Unterschied machen. **(b)** *no pl (pre-eminence)* Rang *m*. **with ~** sich hervortun *or* auszeichnen; **a pianist of ~** ein Pianist von Rang. **(c)** *(Sch, Univ: grade)* **he got a ~ in French** er hat das Französischexamen mit Auszeichnung bestanden.

**distinctive** [dı'stıŋktıv] *adj* *colour, plumage* auffällig; *(unmistakable)* unverkennbar; *characteristic, feature* besondere(s).

**distinctly** [dı'stıŋktlı] *adv* deutlich; *rude* ausgesprochen; *better* entschieden.

**distinguish** [dı'stıŋgwıʃ] **1** *vt* **(a)** unterscheiden. **(b)** *(make out)* landmark, shape erkennen. **2** *vi* **to ~ between** unterscheiden zwischen *(+dat)*. **3** *vr* **to ~ oneself** sich auszeichnen.

**distinguishable** [dı'stıŋgwıʃəbl] *adj* unterscheidbar; *(discernible)* erkennbar. **they are barely ~** sie sind kaum auseinanderzuhalten.

**distinguished** [dı'stıŋgwıʃt] *adj* **(a)** *(eminent)* pianist, scholar von hohem Rang; *career* hervorragend. **(b)** *(refined, elegant)* person, manner distinguiert *(geh)*, vornehm.

**distinguishing** [dı'stıŋgwıʃıŋ] *adj* kennzeichnend, charakteristisch. **the ~ feature of his work is ...** was seine Arbeit kennzeichnet, ist ...

**distort** [dı'stɔːt] *vt* verzerren; *truth, words* verdrehen.

**distortion** [dı'stɔːʃən] *n see vt* Verzerrung *f*; Verdrehung *f*.

**distract** [dı'strækt] *vt* ablenken.

**distracted** [dı'stræktıd] *adj* *(worried)* besorgt, beunruhigt; *(distraught)* außer sich *(with vor +dat)*.

**distraction** [dı'strækʃən] *n* **(a)** *(from work etc)* Ablenkung *f*. **(b)** *(entertainment)* Zerstreuung *f*. **(c)** *(anxiety)* Ruhelosigkeit, Unruhe *f*; *(distraughtness)* Verstörtheit *f*. **to drive sb to ~** jdn wahnsinnig machen.

**distraught** [dı'strɔːt] *adj* verzweifelt.

**distress** [dı'stres] **1** *n* **(a)** *(physical)* Leiden *nt*; *(mental)* Kummer *m*, Sorge *f*. **to be in great ~** sehr leiden. **(b)** *(danger)* **a ship/plane in ~** ein Schiff in Seenot/ein Flugzeug in Not; **~ signal** Notsignal *nt*. **2** *vt* Sorge bereiten *(+dat)*. **please don't ~ yourself** machen Sie sich *(dat)* bitte keine Sorgen!

**distressed** [dı'strest] *adj* **(a)** *(upset)* bekümmert; *(grief-stricken)* verzweifelt *(about über +acc)*. **(b)** *(poverty-stricken)* verarmt; *circumstances* erbärmlich.

**distressing** [dı'stresıŋ] *adj* *(upsetting)* besorgniserregend; *(stronger)* erschütternd.

**distribute** [dı'strıbjuːt] *vt* verteilen; *(Comm)* goods vertreiben; *films* verleihen.

**distribution** [ˌdıstrı'bjuːʃən] *n see vt* Verteilung *f*; *(Comm)* Vertrieb *m*; Verleih *m*. **~ network** Vertriebsnetz *nt*; **~ rights** Vertriebsrechte *pl*.

**distributor** [dı'strıbjʊtəʳ] *n* Verteiler *m* *(also Aut)*; *(Comm)* *(wholesaler)* Großhändler *m*; *(retailer)* Händler *m*; *(of films)* Verleih(er) *m*.

**district** ['dıstrıkt] *n* Gegend *f*; *(of town also)* Viertel *nt*; *(administrative)* (Verwaltungs)bezirk *m*.

**district:** **~ attorney** *n* *(US)* Bezirksstaatsanwalt *m*; **~ council** *n* *(Brit)* Bezirksrat *m*; **~ manager** *n* Bezirksleiter *m*; **~ nurse** *n* Gemeindeschwester *f*.

**distrust** [dıs'trʌst] **1** *vt* mißtrauen *(+dat)*. **2** *n* Mißtrauen *nt* *(of gegenüber)*.

**distrustful** [dıs'trʌstfʊl] *adj* mißtrauisch *(of gegenüber)*.

**disturb** [dı'stɜːb] **1** *vt* **(a)** stören. **(b)** *(alarm)* person beunruhigen. **(c)** *waters* bewegen; *sediment* aufwirbeln; *papers* durcheinanderbringen. **2** *vi* **"please do not ~"** „bitte nicht stören".

**disturbance** [dı'stɜːbəns] *n* **(a)** *(political)* Unruhe *f*; *(in pub, street)* (Ruhe)störung *f*. **to cause a ~** eine Ruhestörung verursachen. **(b)** *(in work, routine)* Störung *f*.

**disturbed** [dı'stɜːbd] *adj* **(a)** *(mentally)* geistig gestört; *(socially)* verhaltensgestört. **(b)** *(worried)* beunruhigt *(at, by über +acc, von)*. **to have a ~ night** eine unruhige Nacht verbringen.

**disturbing** [dı'stɜːbıŋ] *adj* *(alarming)* beunruhigend; *(distracting)* störend. **some viewers may find these scenes ~** einige Zuschauer könnten an diesen Szenen Anstoß nehmen.

**disuse** [dıs'juːs] *n* **to fall into ~** nicht mehr benutzt werden.

**disused** [dıs'juːzd] *adj* *building* leerstehend; *mine, railway line* stillgelegt.

**ditch** [dıtʃ] **1** *n* Graben *m*. **2** *vt* *(col: get rid of)* person loswerden; *boyfriend* abservieren *(col)*; *project* fallenlassen.

**dither** ['dıðəʳ] **1** *n* **to be all of a ~** ganz aufgeregt sein. **2** *vi* zaudern, schwanken.

**ditto** ['dıtəʊ] *n* ebenfalls. **I'd like coffee — ~ (for me)**

*(col)* ich möchte Kaffee — ich auch.

**ditty** ['dɪtɪ] *n* Liedchen *nt*.

**divan** [dɪ'væn] *n* Diwan *m*. ~ **bed** Liege *f*.

**dive** [daɪv] *(vb: pret* ~**d** *or (US)* **dove,** *ptp* ~**d)* **1** *n* **(a)** *(by swimmer)* Sprung *m*; *(by diver)* Tauchgang *m*; *(by submarine)* Tauchmanöver *nt*; *(by plane)* Sturzflug *m*; *(Ftbl)* Hechtsprung *m*. **the deepest ~ yet made** die bisher größte Tauchtiefe; **to make a ~ for sth** *(fig col)* sich auf etw *(acc)* stürzen; **the dollar took a ~** *(col)* der Dollar sackte ab *(col)*. **(b)** *(pej col: club etc)* Spelunke *f (col)*. **2** *vi* **(a)** *(person)* springen; *(under water)* tauchen; *(submarine)* untertauchen; *(plane)* einen Sturzflug machen; *(goalkeeper etc)* hechten. **to ~ for pearls** nach Perlen tauchen. **(b)** *(col)* **he ~d into the crowd/under the table** er verschwand blitzschnell in der Menge/unter dem Tisch; **to ~ for cover** blitzschnell in Deckung gehen; **he ~d under the sheets** er versteckte sich schnell unter der Bettdecke.

**dive:** ~**-bomb** *vt* im Sturzflug bombardieren; ~**-bomber** *n* Sturzkampfbomber, Stuka *m*.

**diver** ['daɪvə'] *n (also bird)* Taucher *m*; *(off high board)* Turmspringer(in *f)* *m*; *(off springboard)* Kunstspringer(in *f)* *m*.

**diverge** [daɪ'vɜ:dʒ] *vi* abweichen *(from* von*)*; *(two things)* auseinandergehen.

**divergence** [daɪ'vɜ:dʒəns] *n* Abweichung *f*.

**divergent** [daɪ'vɜ:dʒənt] *adj opinions etc* auseinandergehend.

**diverse** [daɪ'vɜ:s] *adj* verschieden(artig).

**diversification** [daɪ,vɜ:sɪfɪ'keɪʃən] *n (Comm)* Diversifikation *f*.

**diversify** [daɪ'vɜ:sɪfaɪ] **1** *vt* abwechslungsreich(er) gestalten; *business etc* diversifizieren *(Comm)*. **2** *vi (Comm)* diversifizieren.

**diversion** [daɪ'vɜ:ʃən] *n* **(a)** *(of stream, esp Brit: of traffic)* Umleitung *f*. **(b)** *(relaxation)* Unterhaltung *f*. **(c)** *(Mil, fig)* Ablenkung *f*. **to create a ~** ablenken.

**diversity** [daɪ'vɜ:sɪtɪ] *n* Vielfalt *f*.

**divert** [daɪ'vɜ:t] *vt* **(a)** *traffic, stream* umleiten; *attention* ablenken; *conversation* in eine andere Richtung lenken; *blow* abwenden. **(b)** *(amuse)* unterhalten.

**divest** [daɪ'vest] *vt* berauben *(sb of sth* jdn einer Sache *gen)*. **to ~ oneself of one's coat** *(hum)* sich seines Mantels entledigen.

**divide** [dɪ'vaɪd] **1** *vt* **(a)** *(separate)* trennen. **(b)** *(split into parts: also* ~ **up)** *money, work* teilen *(into* in +*acc)*; *(in order to distribute)* aufteilen. **(c)** *(Math)* dividieren, teilen *(by* durch*)*. **what is 12** ~**d by 3?** wieviel ist 12 (geteilt) durch 3? **2** *vi* **(a)** *(river, road, cells)* sich teilen. **to ~ (up) into groups** sich in Gruppen aufteilen. **(b)** *(Brit Parl)* **the House** ~**d** das Parlament stimmte durch Hammelsprung ab.

►**divide off** *vt sep* (ab)trennen.

►**divide out** *vt sep* aufteilen *(among* unter +*acc or* dat*)*.

►**divide up 1** *vi see* **divide 2 (a)**. **2** *vt sep see* **divide 1 (b)**.

**divided** [dɪ'vaɪdɪd] *adj* geteilt. ~ **highway** *(US)* zweispurige (Schnell)straße *f*; ~ **skirt** Hosenrock *m*; **a people** ~ **against itself** ein gespaltenes Volk.

**dividend** ['dɪvɪdend] *n (Fin)* Dividende *f*. **to pay** ~**s** *(fig)* sich bezahlt machen.

**dividers** [dɪ'vaɪdəz] *npl* Stechzirkel *m*.

**dividing** [dɪ'vaɪdɪŋ] *adj* ~ **wall** Trennwand *f*; ~ **line** *(lit, fig)* Trennungslinie *f*.

**divine** [dɪ'vaɪn] **1** *adj (Rel)* göttlich; *(fig col)* bezaubernd. **2** *vt* **(a)** *the future* weissagen, prophezeien; *sb's intentions* erahnen. **(b)** *water, metal* aufspüren.

**diving** ['daɪvɪŋ] *n (under water)* Tauchen *nt*; *(into wa-*

*ter)* Springen *nt*; *(Sport)* Kunstspringen *nt*.

**diving:** ~**-bell** *n* Taucherglocke *f*; ~**-board** *n* Sprungbrett *nt*; ~**-suit** *n* Taucheranzug *m*.

**divinity** [dɪ'vɪnɪtɪ] *n* **(a)** *(divine being)* Gottheit *f*. **(b)** *(Sch)* Religion *f*.

**divisible** [dɪ'vɪzəbl] *adj* teilbar *(by* durch*)*.

**division** [dɪ'vɪʒən] *n* **(a)** *(dividing)* Teilung *f*; *(Math)* Teilen *nt*, Division *f*. ~ **sign** Teilungszeichen *nt*; ~ **of labour** Arbeitsteilung *f*. **(b)** *(Mil)* Division *f*. **(c)** *(in administration)* Abteilung *f*. **(d)** *(in room)* Trennwand *f*; *(fig: between social classes etc)* Schranke *f*; *(dividing line: lit, fig)* Trennungslinie *f*. **(e)** *(fig: discord)* Uneinigkeit *f*. **(f)** *(Brit Parl)* Abstimmung *f* durch Hammelsprung. **(g)** *(Sport)* Liga *f*.

**divisive** [dɪ'vaɪsɪv] *adj* **to be** ~ Uneinigkeit schaffen.

**divorce** [dɪ'vɔ:s] **1** *n* Scheidung *f (from* von*)*; *(fig)* Trennung *f*. **he wants a** ~ er will sich scheiden lassen; **to get a** ~ **(from sb)** sich (von jdm) scheiden lassen. **2** *vt* **(a)** sich scheiden lassen von. **to get** ~**d** sich scheiden lassen. **(b)** *(fig)* trennen.

**divorced** [dɪ'vɔ:st] *adj* geschieden *(from* von*)*.

**divorcee** [dɪ,vɔ:'si:] *n* geschiedener Mann, geschiedene Frau. **he is a** ~ er ist geschieden.

**divulge** [daɪ'vʌldʒ] *vt* preisgeben *(sth to sb* jdm etw*)*.

**Dixie** ['dɪksɪ] *n (also* ~**land)** Dixie(land) *m*.

**DIY** = **do-it-yourself**.

**dizziness** ['dɪzɪnɪs] *n* Schwindelgefühl *nt*.

**dizzy** ['dɪzɪ] *adj (+er)* **(a)** *(lit, fig)* *person* schwind(e)lig; *height* schwindelerregend. ~ **spell** Schwindelanfall *m*; **I feel** ~ mir ist schwindlig. **(b)** *(col: foolish)* verrückt.

**DJ** = **(a) dinner jacket. (b) disc jockey**.

**Djakarta** [dʒə'kɑ:tə] *n* Jakarta *nt*.

**dl** = **decilitre(s)** dl.

**dm** = **decimetre(s)** dm.

**DNA** = **de(s)oxyribonucleic acid** DNS *f*.

**do** [du:] *(vb: pret* **did,** *ptp* **done)* 1** *aux* **(a)** ~ **you understand?** verstehen Sie?; **I** ~ **not** *or* **don't understand** ich verstehe nicht; **didn't you know?, did you not know?** haben Sie das nicht gewußt?

**(b)** *(for emphasis: with stress on do)* ~ **come!** kommen Sie doch (bitte)!; ~ **shut up!** (nun) sei doch (endlich) ruhig!; ~ **I remember him!** und ob ich mich an ihn erinnere!; **but I** ~ **like it** aber es gefällt mir wirklich; **so you** ~ **know them!** Sie kennen sie also tatsächlich!; *(and were lying etc)* Sie kennen sie also doch!

**(c)** *(used to avoid repeating vb)* **you speak better than I** ~ Sie sprechen besser als ich; **he likes cheese and so** ~ **I** er ißt gern Käse und ich auch; **neither** ~ **I** ich auch nicht.

**(d)** *(in question tags)* oder. **you know him, don't you?** Sie kennen ihn doch, oder?; **he didn't go, did he?** er ist (doch) nicht gegangen, oder?

**(e)** *(in answers: replacing vb)* **do you see them often?** — **yes, I** ~/**no, I don't** sehen Sie sie oft? — ja/nein; **they speak French** — **oh,** ~ **they?** sie sprechen Französisch — ja?, wirklich?; **may I come in?** — ~! darf ich hereinkommen? — ja, bitte; **shall I open the window?** — **no, don't!** soll ich das Fenster öffnen? — nein, bitte nicht!

**2** *vt* **(a)** tun, machen; *puzzle, housework, military service, translation, film* machen. **what are you** ~**ing on Saturday?** was machen Sie am Samstag?; **I've got nothing to** ~ ich habe nichts zu tun; **are you** ~**ing anything this evening?** haben Sie heute abend schon etwas vor?; **what shall we** ~ **for money?** wo kriegen wir jetzt (das) Geld her?; **we'll have to** ~ **something about this** wir müssen da etwas unternehmen; **how do you** ~ **it?** wie macht man das?; *(in amazement)* wie machen Sie das bloß?; **what's**

**to be done?** was ist da zu tun?; **what can you ~?** was kann man da machen?; **sorry, it can't be done** tut mir leid, es läßt sich nicht machen; **what can I ~ for you?** was kann ich für Sie tun?; *(by shop assistant also)* was darf's sein?; **can you ~ it by yourself?** schaffst du das allein?; **what do you want me to ~ (about it)?** und was soll ich da tun *or* machen?; **Brecht doesn't ~ anything for me** Brecht sagt mir nichts; **that's done it** *(col)* da haben wir's, da haben wir die Bescherung; **that does it!** jetzt reicht's mir!; **now what have you done!** was hast du jetzt wieder angestellt?; **we don't ~ lunches** wir haben keinen Mittagstisch.

**(b)** *(arrange, fix etc)* **to ~ the flowers** die Blumen arrangieren; **to ~ one's hair** sich *(dat)* die Haare machen *(col)*; **who does your hair?** zu welchem Friseur gehen Sie?; **to ~ one's nails** sich *(dat)* die Nägel schneiden *or (varnish)* lackieren; **you ~ the painting and I'll ~ the papering** du streichst und ich tapeziere; **I'll ~ the talking** ich übernehme das Reden.

**(c)** *(Sch etc: study)* **we've done Milton** wir haben Milton durchgenommen; **I've never done any German** ich habe nie Deutsch gelernt.

**(d)** *(in pret, ptp only: complete, accomplish)* **the work's done now** die Arbeit ist gemacht *or* getan *or* fertig; **what's done cannot be undone** was geschehen ist, kann man nicht ungeschehen machen; **done!** abgemacht!

**(e)** *(visit)* city, museum besuchen; *(take in also)* mitnehmen *(col)*.

**(f)** *(Aut etc)* schaffen, machen *(col)*. **this car does 125** das Auto schafft *or* macht *(col)* 200; **we did London to Edinburgh in 8 hours** wir haben es in 8 Stunden von London bis Edinburgh geschafft.

**(g)** *(be suitable)* passen *(sb jdm)*; *(be sufficient for)* reichen *(sb jdm)*. **that will ~ me nicely** *(enough)* das reicht dicke *(col)*; *(just right)* das paßt mir gut.

**(h)** *(take off, mimic)* nachmachen.

**(i)** *(col: cheat)* übers Ohr hauen *(col)*.

**(j)** *(Cook)* machen *(col)*. **to ~ the cooking** kochen; **how do you like your steak done?** wie möchten Sie Ihr Steak?; *see also* **done 2(a)**.

**(k)** *(col: in prison)* 6 years (ab)sitzen.

**3** *vi* **(a)** *(act)* **~ as I ~** mach es wie ich; **he did well to take advice** er tat gut daran, sich beraten zu lassen. **(b)** *(get on, fare)* **how are you ~ing?** wie geht's (Ihnen)?; **the patient is ~ing very well** dem Patienten geht es recht ordentlich; **he's ~ing well at school** er macht sich in der Schule; **his business is ~ing well** sein Geschäft geht gut; *see also* **well²**. **(c)** *(finish)* **have you done?** sind Sie endlich fertig? **(d)** *(suit, be convenient)* gehen. **that will never ~!** das geht nicht!; **this room will ~** das Zimmer ist in Ordnung; **will she/it ~?** geht sie/das?; **this coat will ~ as a cover** dieser Mantel muß als Decke herhalten; **you'll have to make ~ with £10** Sie werden mit £10 auskommen müssen. **(e)** *(be sufficient)* reichen. **will £1 ~?** reicht £1?; **yes, that'll ~** ja, das reicht; **that'll ~!** jetzt reicht's aber! **(f)** *(col: char)* putzen *(for bei)*.

**4** *n (col)* **(a)** Veranstaltung *f*; *(party)* Fete *f (col)*. **(b)** *(in phrases)* **it's a poor ~!** *(col)* das ist ja ein schwaches Bild! *(col)*; **the ~s and don'ts** was man wissen sollte; *(for behaviour)* die Verhaltensregeln *pl*; **fair ~s all round** *(col)* gleiches Recht für alle.

▶**do away with** *vi +prep obj* **(a)** *custom, law* abschaffen; *building* abreißen. **(b)** *(kill)* umbringen.

▶**do by** *vi +prep obj* **to ~ well/badly ~ sb** jdn gut/schlecht behandeln.

▶**do for** *vi +prep obj (col: finish off)* person fertigmachen *(col)*; *project* zunichte machen. **to be done ~** *(person)* erledigt *or* fertig *(col)* sein; *(project)* gestorben sein *(col)*.

▶**do in** *vt sep (col)* **(a)** *(kill)* um die Ecke bringen *(col)*. **(b)** **to be done ~** *(exhausted)* fertig sein *(col)*.

▶**do out** *vt sep* **(a)** *room* auskehren. **(b)** **to ~ sb ~ of a job/£100** jdn um eine Stelle/£ 100 bringen.

▶**do up 1** *vi (dress etc)* zugemacht werden. **2** *vt sep* **(a)** *(fasten)* zumachen. **(b)** *(parcel together)* goods zusammenpacken. **to ~ sth ~ in a parcel etw** einpacken. **(c)** *house, room* renovieren. **to ~ oneself ~** sich zurechtmachen.

▶**do with** *vi +prep obj* **(a)** *(with can or could: need)* brauchen. **it could ~ ~ a clean** es müßte mal saubergemacht werden. **(b)** **what has that got to ~ ~ it?** was hat das damit zu tun?; **that has nothing to ~ ~ you!** das geht Sie gar nichts an!; **it's to ~ ~ this letter you sent** es geht um den Brief, den Sie geschickt haben; **money has a lot to ~ ~ it** Geld spielt eine große Rolle dabei. **(c)** **what have you done ~ my gloves/your face?** was haben Sie mit meinen Handschuhen/Ihrem Gesicht gemacht? **(d)** **he doesn't know what to ~ ~ himself** er weiß nicht, was er mit sich anfangen soll. **(e)** **to be done ~ sb/sth** *(finished)* mit jdm/etw fertig sein.

▶**do without** *vi +prep obj* auskommen ohne. **I can ~ ~ your advice** Sie können sich Ihre Ratschläge sparen; **I could have done ~ that!** das hätte mir (wirklich) erspart bleiben können; **you'll have to ~ ~** Sie müssen so zurechtkommen.

**DOA** = **dead on arrival**.

**d.o.b.** = **date of birth**.

**docile** ['dəʊsaɪl] *adj* sanftmütig; *horse* fromm.

**dock¹** [dɒk] **1** *n* Dock *nt*; *(for berthing)* Pier, Kai *m*. **~s** *pl* Hafen *m*. **2** *vt* docken; *(Space also)* ankoppeln. **3** *vi (Naut)* anlegen; *(Space)* ankoppeln.

**dock²** *n (Jur)* Anklagebank *f*.

**dock³** *vt* **(a)** *dog's tail* kupieren; *horse's tail* stutzen. **(b)** *wages* kürzen *(by um)*.

**docker** ['dɒkər] *n (Brit)* Hafenarbeiter, Docker *m*.

**docket** ['dɒkɪt] *n (on parcel etc)* Warenbegleitschein *m*.

**docking** ['dɒkɪŋ] *n (Space)* Ankoppelung *f*.

**dockyard** ['dɒkjɑːd] *n* Werft *f*.

**doctor** ['dɒktər] **1** *n* **(a)** *(Med)* Arzt *m*, Ärztin *f*. **D~ Smith** Dr. Schmidt; **it's just what the ~ ordered** *(fig col)* das ist genau das richtige. **(b)** *(Univ etc)* Doktor *m*. **Dear Dr Smith** Sehr geehrter Herr Dr./Sehr geehrte Frau Dr. Smith. **2** *vt* **(a)** *(col: castrate)* kastrieren. **(b)** *(tamper with)* accounts frisieren; *text, document* verfälschen. **the wine's been ~ed** dem Wein ist etwas beigemischt worden.

**doctorate** ['dɒktərɪt] *n* Doktortitel *m*; *see* **PhD**.

**doctrinaire** [ˌdɒktrɪ'neər] *adj* doktrinär.

**doctrine** ['dɒktrɪn] *n* Doktrin, Lehre *f*.

**docudrama** [dɒkju'drɑːmə] *n* Dokumentarspiel *nt*.

**document** ['dɒkjʊmənt] **1** *n* Papier *nt*; *(certificate)* Dokument *nt*, Urkunde *f*. **2** *vt* belegen.

**documentary** [ˌdɒkjʊ'mentərɪ] **1** *n* Dokumentarfilm *m*. **2** *adj* dokumentarisch.

**documentation** [ˌdɒkjʊmen'teɪʃən] *n* Dokumentation *f*.

**DOD** *(US)* = **Department of Defense** Verteidigungsministerium *nt*.

**dodderer** ['dɒdərər] *n (col)* Tattergreis *(col)* m.

**doddering** ['dɒdərɪŋ], **doddery** ['dɒdərɪ] *adj* tatterig *(col)*. **the ~ old fool** *(col)* der vertrottelte alte Opa *(col)*.

**doddle** ['dɒdl] *n (Brit col)* Kinderspiel *nt*.

**dodge** [dɒdʒ] **1** *n (trick)* Trick, Kniff *m*. **to be up to all the ~s** mit allen Wassern gewaschen sein; **a tax**

~ ein Steuertrick. **2** *vt blow, question* ausweichen *(+dat)*; *tax* umgehen; *(shirk) work, military service* sich drücken vor *(+dat)*. **to ~ the issue** dem Problem ausweichen. **3** *vi* **to ~ out of the way** zur Seite springen; *(to escape notice)* blitzschnell verschwinden; **to ~ through the traffic** sich durch den Verkehr schlängeln.

**dodgem** ['dɒdʒəm] *n (Brit)* (Auto)skooter *m*.

**dodgy** ['dɒdʒɪ] *adj (+er) (Brit col: tricky) situation* vertrackt *(col)*; *(risky)* gewagt; *(dubious)* zweifelhaft; *engine, part* defekt; *translation, spelling* fehlerhaft.

**dodo** ['dəʊdəʊ] *n* **as dead as the** *or* **a ~** völlig überholt.

**DOE** = **(a)** *(Brit)* **Department of the Environment** Umweltministerium *nt*. **(b)** *(US)* **Department of Energy** Energieministerium *nt*.

**doe** [dəʊ] *n (roe deer)* Ricke *f*; *(red deer)* Hirschkuh *f*; *(rabbit)* Weibchen *nt*.

**does** [dʌz] *3rd pers sing of* **do**.

**doesn't** ['dʌznt] = **does not**.

**doff** [dɒf] *vt hat* ziehen, lüften.

**dog** [dɒg] **1** *n* **(a)** Hund *m*. **(b)** *(fig phrases)* **it's a ~'s life** es ist ein Hundeleben; **to go to the ~s** vor die Hunde gehen *(col)*; **~ in the manger** Spielverderber(in *f*) *m*; **~-in-the-manger attitude** mißgünstige Einstellung; **every ~ has his day** jeder hat einmal Glück; **it's a case of ~ eat ~** es ist ein Kampf aller gegen alle; **you can't teach an old ~ new tricks** der Mensch ist ein Gewohnheitstier; **~'s dinner** *(fig col)* Schlamassel *m (col)*. **(c)** *(male fox, wolf)* Rüde *m*. **(d)** *(col: man)* **lucky ~** Glückspilz *m*; **dirty ~** gemeiner Hund; **sly ~** gerissener Hund *(col)*. **(e)** *(US col) (failure)* Pleite *f (col)*; *(ugly woman)* Schreckschraube *f (col)*. **2** *vt* **to ~ sb's footsteps** jdm hart auf den Fersen sein/bleiben; **~ged by misfortune** vom Pech verfolgt.

**dog:** **~ biscuit** *n* Hundekuchen *m*; **~-collar** *n (lit)* Hundehalsband *nt*; *(vicar's)* steifer Halskragen *(von Geistlichen)*; **~-eared** ['dɒgɪəd] *adj* mit Eselsohren; **~-eat-dog society** *n* Ellenbogengesellschaft *f*; **~fight** *n (Aviat)* Luftkampf *m*; **~fish** *n* Hundshai *m*; **~ food** *n* Hundefutter *nt*.

**dogged** ['dɒgɪd] *adj* beharrlich, zäh.

**doggerel** ['dɒgərəl] *n* Knittelvers *m*.

**doggie bag** ['dɒgɪˌbæg] *n* Tüte *f für Essensreste, die nach Hause mitgenommen werden*.

**doggo** ['dɒgəʊ] *adv (col)*: **to lie ~** sich nicht mucksen *(col)*.

**dog:** **~house** *n* **he's in the ~house** *(col)* er ist in Ungnade; *(with wife)* bei ihm hängt der Haussegen schief; **~ leg** *n* Knick *m*; **~ licence** *n* Hundemarke *f*.

**dogma** ['dɒgmə] *n* Dogma *nt*.

**dogmatic** [dɒg'mætɪk] *adj* dogmatisch *(about* in *+dat)*.

**do-gooder** ['duːˈgʊdər] *n (pej)* Weltverbesserer *m*.

**dogsbody** ['dɒgzbɒdɪ] *n* **she's/he's the general ~** sie/er ist Mädchen für alles.

**dog:** **~ tag** *n (US Mil col)* Hundemarke *(col) f*; **~-tired** *adj* hundemüde.

**doing** ['duːɪŋ] *n* **this is your ~** das ist dein Werk; **that takes some ~** da gehört (schon) etwas dazu; **~s** *pl* Taten *pl*.

**doings** ['duːɪŋz] *n sing (Brit col)* Dingsbums *nt (col)*.

**do-it-yourself** ['duːɪtjəˈself] **1** *adj manual* für Heimwerker. **~ shop** Heimwerkermarkt *m*. **2** *n* Heimwerken, Do-it-yourself *nt*.

**doldrums** ['dɒldrəmz] *npl* **to be in the ~** Trübsal blasen; *(business etc)* in einer Flaute stecken.

**dole** [dəʊl] *n (Brit col)* Arbeitslosenunterstützung *f*. **to go/be on the ~** stempeln (gehen).

**►dole out** *vt sep* austeilen, verteilen.

**doleful** ['dəʊlfʊl] *adj* trübselig.

**doll** [dɒl] *n* **(a)** Puppe *f*. **~'s house** Puppenhaus *nt*. **(b)** *(esp US col: girl)* Mädchen *nt*; *(pretty girl)* Puppe *f (col)*.

**►doll up** *vt sep (col)* **to ~ oneself ~, to get ~ed ~** sich herausputzen *or* aufdonnern *(col)*.

**dollar** ['dɒlər] *n* Dollar *m*. **~ bill** Dollarnote *f*.

**dollop** ['dɒlə] *n (col)* Schlag, Klacks *m (col)*.

**dolly-bird** ['dɒlɪbɜːd] *n (col)* Puppe *f (col)*.

**Dolomites** ['dɒləmaɪts] *npl* Dolomiten *pl*.

**dolphin** ['dɒlfɪn] *n* Delphin *m*.

**dolt** [dəʊlt] *n* Tölpel *m*.

**domain** [dəʊ'meɪn] *n* **(a)** *(estate)* Gut *nt*; *(belonging to state, Crown)* Domäne *f*. **(b)** *(fig)* Domäne *f*.

**dome** [dəʊm] *n (Archit)* Kuppel *f*; *(of heaven, skull)* Gewölbe *nt*.

**domed** [dəʊmd] *adj forehead* gewölbt.

**domestic** [də'mestɪk] *adj* **(a)** *bliss, life* häuslich. **~ servants** Hausangestellte *pl*; **~ waste** Hausmüll *m*. **(b)** *produce* einheimisch. **~ policy** Innenpolitik *f*; **~ news** Nachrichten *pl* aus dem Inland; **~ trade** Binnenhandel *m*; **~ flight** Inlandsflug *m*. **(c)** **~ animal** Haustier *nt*.

**domesticate** [də'mestɪkeɪt] *vt* zähmen; *(house-train)* stubenrein machen.

**domesticated** [də'mestɪkeɪtɪd] *adj* zahm; *cat, dog* stubenrein. **she's very ~** sie ist sehr häuslich.

**domesticity** [ˌdəʊmes'tɪsɪtɪ] *n* häusliches Leben.

**domestic science** *n* Hauswirtschaftslehre *f*.

**domicile** ['dɒmɪsaɪl] *n (Admin)* Wohnsitz *m*.

**dominance** ['dɒmɪnəns] *n* Vorherrschaft, Dominanz *f (also Biol) (over über +acc)*.

**dominant** ['dɒmɪnənt] **1** *adj* beherrschend, dominierend; *feature also* hervorstechend; *gene, (Mus)* dominant. **~ male** *(lit, fig)* Platzhirsch *m*. **2** *n (Mus)* Dominante *f*.

**dominate** ['dɒmɪneɪt] **1** *vi* dominieren. **2** *vt* beherrschen; *(species, gene)* dominieren.

**domination** [ˌdɒmɪ'neɪʃən] *n* (Vor)herrschaft *f*.

**domineer** [ˌdɒmɪ'nɪər] *vi* tyrannisieren *(over sb* jdn*)*.

**domineering** [ˌdɒmɪ'nɪərɪŋ] *adj* herrisch; *mother-in-law, husband etc also* herrschsüchtig.

**Dominican** [də'mɪnɪkən] *(Eccl, Geog)* **1** *adj* dominikanisch. **~ Republic** Dominikanische Republik. **2** *n* Dominikaner(in *f*) *m*.

**dominion** [də'mɪnɪən] *n* **(a)** *no pl* Herrschaft *f (over über +acc)*. **(b)** *(territory)* Herrschaftsgebiet *nt*; *(Brit Pol)* Dominion *nt*.

**domino** ['dɒmɪnəʊ] *n, pl* **-es** Domino(stein) *m*. **(game of) ~es** Dominospiel *nt*.

**don¹** [dɒn] *n (Brit Univ)* Universitätsdozent *m*.

**don²** *vt garment* anziehen.

**donate** [dəʊ'neɪt] *vt* spenden.

**donation** [dəʊ'neɪʃən] *n* Spende *f*; *(large scale)* Stiftung *f*.

**done** [dʌn] **1** *ptp of* **do**. **2** *adj* **(a)** *(finished) work* erledigt; *(cooked) vegetables* gar; *meat* durch. **to get sth ~** *(finished)* etw fertigkriegen; **well/lightly ~** *meat* durch(gebraten)/nur angebraten. **(b)** **it's not the ~ thing** das tut man nicht.

**donkey** ['dɒŋkɪ] *n* Esel *m*. **~'s years** *(col)* eine Ewigkeit.

**donkey:** **~ jacket** *n* dicke (gefütterte) Jacke; **~work** *n* Routinearbeit, Dreckarbeit *(pej) f*.

**donor** ['dəʊnər] *n (also Med)* Spender(in *f*) *m*.

**don't** [dəʊnt] = **do not**.

**donut** ['dəʊnʌt] *n (esp US)* = **doughnut**.

**doodle** ['duːdl] **1** *vti* kritzeln. **2** *n* Gekritzel *nt*.

**doom** [duːm] **1** *n (fate)* Schicksal *nt*; *(ruin)* Verhängnis *nt*. **2** *vt* verurteilen, verdammen. **to be ~ed ver-**

loren sein; **the project was ~ed from the start** das Vorhaben war von Anfang an zum Scheitern verurteilt.

**doomsday** ['du:mzdeɪ] *n* der Jüngste Tag. **otherwise we'll be here till ~** *(col)* sonst sind wir in zwanzig Jahren noch hier.

**door** [dɔ:ʳ] *n* (**a**) Tür *f; (entrance: to cinema etc)* Eingang *m.* **was that the ~?** hat es geklingelt/geklopft?; **to pay at the ~** *(Theat etc)* an der Kasse zahlen; **he lives three ~s away** er wohnt drei Häuser weiter. (**b**) *(phrases)* **to lay sth at sb's ~** jdm etw anlasten; **to leave the ~ open for further negotiations** die Tür für weitere Verhandlungen offen lassen; **to open the ~ to sth** einer Sache *(dat)* Tür und Tor öffnen; **to show sb the ~** jdm die Tür weisen; **out of ~s** im Freien.

**door** *in cpds* Tür-; **~bell** *n* Türklingel *f;* **~ handle** *n* Türklinke *f;* **~keeper** *n* Portier *m;* **~ knob** *n* Türknauf *m;* **~knocker** *n* Türklopfer *m;* **~man** *n* Portier *m;* **~mat** *n* Fußmatte *f; (fig)* Fußabtreter *m;* **~nail** *n*: **as dead as a ~nail** mausetot; **~post** *n* **deaf as a ~post** stocktaub; **~step** *n* (Tür)schwelle *f;* **on my ~step** *(fig)* direkt vor meiner Tür; **~stop** *n* Türanschlag *m;* **~-to-~** *adj* (**a**) **~-to-~ salesman** Vertreter *m;* (**b**) *delivery* ins Haus; **~way** *n (of room)* Tür *f; (of building, shop)* Eingang *m.*

**dope** [dəʊp] **1** *n* (**a**) *no pl (col: drugs)* Stoff *m (col),* Dope *nt (col); (Sport)* Aufputschmittel *nt.* (**b**) *no pl (col: information)* Information(en *pl*) *f.* (**c**) *(col: stupid person)* Esel *m (col).* **2** *vt* dopen.

**dopey, dopy** ['dəʊpɪ] *adj (+er) (col) (stupid)* bekloppt *(col); (sleepy, half-drugged)* benebelt *(col).*

**dormant** ['dɔ:mənt] *adj (Zool, Bot)* ruhend; *volcano* untätig; *energy* verborgen. **to lie ~** *(evil etc)* schlummern.

**dormer (window)** ['dɔ:mə('wɪndəʊ)] *n* Mansardenfenster *nt.*

**dormitory** ['dɔ:mɪtrɪ] *n* Schlafsaal *m; (US: building)* Wohnheim *nt.* **~ town** Schlafstadt *f.*

**dormouse** ['dɔ:maʊs] *n, pl* **dormice** ['dɔ:maɪs] Haselmaus *f.*

**dorsal** ['dɔ:sl] *adj* **~ fin** Rückenflosse *f.*

**dosage** ['dəʊsɪdʒ] *n* Dosis *f.*

**dose** [dəʊs] **1** *n (Med)* Dosis *f.* **a ~ of flu** eine Grippe; **he's all right in small ~s** er ist nur (für) kurze Zeit zu ertragen. **2** *vt person* Arznei geben *(+dat).* **she's always dosing herself** sie nimmt *or* schluckt ständig Medikamente.

**doss** [dɒs] *vi (Brit col: also ~ down)* pennen *(col),* sich hinhauen *(col).*

**dosshouse** ['dɒshaʊs] *n (Brit col)* Penne *f (col).*

**dossier** ['dɒsɪeɪ] *n* Dossier *m or nt.*

**DOT** *(US)* = **Department of Transportation** Verkehrsministerium *nt.*

**dot** [dɒt] **1** *n* Punkt *m.* **to arrive on the ~** auf die Minute pünktlich (an)kommen. **2** *vt* **to ~ one's i's and cross one's t's** genau sein; **~ted line** punktierte Linie; **to sign on the ~ted line** *(fig)* seine Zustimmung geben; **a field ~ted with flowers** ein mit Blumen übersätes Feld; **~ted about the country** über das ganze Land verstreut.

**dotage** ['dəʊtɪdʒ] *n* **to be in one's ~** senil sein.

**►dote on** ['dəʊtɒn] *vi +prep obj* abgöttisch lieben.

**doting** ['dəʊtɪŋ] *adj* **her ~ parents** ihre Eltern, die sie abgöttisch lieb(t)en.

**dot matrix printer** *n* Matrixdrucker *m.*

**dotty** ['dɒtɪ] *adj (+er) (Brit col)* kauzig, schrullig. **to be ~ about sb/sth** nach jdm/etw verrückt sein *(col).*

**double** ['dʌbl] **1** *adj (twice as much)* doppelt; *(having two similar parts, for two)* Doppel-. **a ~ whisky** ein doppelter Whisky; **her salary is ~ what it was ten**

years ago ihr Gehalt hat sich in den letzten zehn Jahren verdoppelt; **~ bottom** doppelter Boden; **~ "p"** Doppel-p; **~ seven five four/~ seven five** *(Telec)* siebenundsiebzig vierundfünfzig/sieben sieben fünf; **~ room** Doppelzimmer *nt;* **it has a ~ meaning** es ist zwei- *or* doppeldeutig; **~ standards** Doppelmoral *f;* **to lead a ~ life** ein Doppelleben führen.

**2** *adv* (**a**) *(twice)* doppelt. **I have ~ what you have** ich habe doppelt soviel wie du; **to see ~** doppelt sehen. (**b**) **to be bent ~ with pain** sich vor Schmerzen krümmen; **fold the paper ~** falte das Papier (einmal).

**3** *n* (**a**) *(twice)* das Doppelte, das Zweifache. (**b**) *(person)* Ebenbild *nt,* Doppelgänger(in *f*) *m; (Film, Theat: stand-in)* Double *nt.* (**c**) **at the ~** *(also Mil)* im Laufschritt; *(fig)* auf der Stelle.

**4** *vt (increase twofold)* verdoppeln.

**5** *vi* (**a**) sich verdoppeln. (**b**) *(Film, Theat)* **to ~ for sb** jds Double sein, jdn doubeln; **he ~s as the butler and the duke** er hat eine Doppelrolle als Butler und Herzog.

**►double back 1** *vi* kehrtmachen; *(road, river)* sich zurückschlängeln. **2** *vt sep blanket* umschlagen.

**►double up** *vi* (**a**) *(with pain)* sich krümmen; *(with laughter)* sich biegen. **he ~d ~ when the bullet hit him** er brach zusammen, als die Kugel ihn traf. (**b**) *(share room)* das Zimmer/Büro *etc* teilen; *(share bed)* in einem Bett schlafen.

**double:** **~ agent** *n* Doppelagent *m;* **~ bar** *n (Mus)* Doppelstrich *m;* **~-barrelled,** *(US)* **~-barreled** [ˌdʌbl'bærəld] *adj gun* doppelläufig; **~-barrel(l)ed name** *(hum)* Doppelname *m;* **~ bass** *n* Kontrabaß *m;* **~ bed** *n* Doppelbett *nt;* **~ bend** *n* S-Kurve *f;* **~ bill** *n (Theat)* Vorstellung *f* mit zwei Stücken; **~-book** *vt seat, room* zweimal reservieren; **to ~-book sb** einen schon vergebenen Platz/ein schon vergebenes Zimmer für jdn reservieren; **~-breasted** *adj* zweireihig; **~-breasted jacket/suit** Zweireiher *m;* **~-check** *vti* noch einmal (über)prüfen; **~ chin** *n* Doppelkinn *nt;* **~ cream** *n* Sahne *f* mit hohem Fettgehalt; **~-cross** *vt (col)* ein falsches Spiel treiben mit; **~-dealing** *n* Betrügerei(en *pl*) *f;* **~-decker** *n* Doppeldecker *m;* **~-declutch** *vi (Aut)* mit Zwischengas schalten; **~ density** *adj (Comp) disk* mit doppelter Dichte; **~ dutch** *n (Brit)* Kauderwelsch *nt;* **it's ~ dutch to me** das sind böhmische Dörfer für mich; **~-edged** *adj (lit, fig)* zweischneidig; **~ entendre** ['du:blɑ:n'tɑ:ndr] *n* Zweideutigkeit *f;* **~ fault** *n (Tennis)* Doppelfehler *m;* **~-glazed** *adj* mit Doppelverglasung; **~ glazing** *n* Doppelverglasung *f;* **~-jointed** *adj* sehr gelenkig; **~-page spread** *n* Doppelseite *f;* **~ park** *vi* in zweiter Reihe parken; **~-quick** *adj (col)* **in ~-quick time** in Null Komma nichts *(col).*

**doubles** ['dʌblz] *n sing or pl (Sport)* Doppel *nt.*

**double:** **~-sided** *adj (Comp) disk* zweiseitig; **~-sided adhesive tape** Doppelklebeband *nt;* **~ spacing** *n* doppelter Zeilenabstand; **~ take** *n* he did a **~ take** er mußte zweimal hinsehen; **~talk** *n (ambiguous)* doppeldeutiges Gerede; *(deceitful)* doppelzüngiges Gerede; **~ time** *n* doppelter Lohn; **~ vision** *n* **to have ~ vision** doppelt sehen; **~ whammy** *n (col)* Doppelschlag *m.*

**doubling** ['dʌblɪŋ] *n* Verdoppelung *f.*

**doubly** ['dʌblɪ] *adv* doppelt.

**doubt** [daʊt] **1** *n* Zweifel *m.* **his honesty is in ~** seine Ehrlichkeit wird angezweifelt; **I am in no ~ as to what he means** ich bin mir völlig im klaren darüber, was er meint; **I have my ~s whether he will come** ich bezweifle, daß er kommt; **there's no ~ about it** daran gibt es keinen Zweifel; **I have no ~s**

**dozen**

about taking the job ich habe keine Bedenken, die Stelle anzunehmen; **no** ~ **he will come tomorrow** höchstwahrscheinlich kommt er morgen; **without (a)** ~ ohne Zweifel; **yes, no** ~ ja, zweifellos; **it's beyond** ~ **that** … es steht außer Zweifel, daß …; **when in** ~ im Zweifelsfall. **2** vt bezweifeln; sb's honesty, truth of statement anzweifeln, Zweifel haben an (+dat). **I** ~ **it (very much)** das bezweifle ich (sehr).

**doubter** ['daʊtər] n Skeptiker, Zweifler m.

**doubtful** ['daʊtfʊl] adj **(a)** (uncertain) unsicher, zweifelhaft; outcome, result, future ungewiß. **to be** ~ **about sb/sth** wegen jdm/etw Bedenken haben; **I'm a bit** ~ ich habe so meine Bedenken; **to look** ~ (person) skeptisch dreinblicken; **the weather looked a bit** ~ es sah nach schlechtem Wetter aus. **(b)** (of questionable character) zweifelhaft; person, affair also zwielichtig.

**doubtfully** ['daʊtfəlɪ] adv skeptisch.

**doubtfulness** ['daʊtfʊlnɪs] n see adj **(a)** Unsicherheit f; Ungewißheit f. **(b)** Zweifelhaftigkeit f; Zwielichtigkeit f.

**doubtless** ['daʊtlɪs] adj zweifelsohne.

**douche** [duːʃ] n Spülung f.

**dough** [dəʊ] n Teig m; (col: money) Kohle f (col).

**doughnut** ['dəʊnʌt] n Berliner m.

**dour** ['dʊər] adj mürrisch, verdrießlich; struggle hart, hartnäckig.

**douse** [daʊs] vt **(a)** Wasser schütten über (+acc); plants reichlich wässern. **(b)** light ausmachen.

**dove¹** [dʌv] n (lit, fig) Taube f.

**dove²** [dəʊv] (US) pret of **dive**.

**dovecot(e)** ['dʌvkɒt] n Taubenschlag m.

**dovetail** ['dʌvteɪl] **1** n ~ **joint** Schwalbenschwanzverbindung f. **2** vt plans koordinieren. **3** vi (plans) übereinstimmen.

**dowager** ['daʊədʒər] n (adelige) Witwe.

**dowdy** ['daʊdɪ] adj (+er) ohne jeden Schick; (down-at-heel) schäbig.

**Dow Jones** [daʊ'dʒəʊnz] n (US) (also ~ **industrial average**) Dow-Jones-Index m.

**down¹** [daʊn] **1** adv **(a)** (towards speaker) herunter, herab; (away from speaker) hinunter, hinab; (downstairs also) nach unten. ~**!** (to dog) Platz!; **to jump** ~ hinunter-/herunterspringen; ~ **with the traitors!** nieder mit den Verrätern!; **on his way** ~ **from the hilltop** beim Abstieg; **all the way** ~ **to the bottom** bis ganz nach unten.

**(b)** (position) unten. ~ **there** da unten; ~ **here** hier unten; **don't kick** or **hit a man when he's** ~ (fig) man soll jemanden nicht fertigmachen, wenn es ihm schon schlecht geht; **the sun is** ~ die Sonne ist untergegangen; **I'll be** ~ **in a minute** ich komme sofort runter; **I've been** ~ **with flu** ich habe mit Grippe im Bett gelegen; **he was (feeling) a bit** ~ er fühlte sich ein wenig niedergeschlagen or down (col); **they'll be** ~ **on you** (police etc) du bekommst Ärger mit ihnen; **it's** ~ **to you to decide** die Entscheidung liegt bei Ihnen.

**(c)** **he came** ~ **from London yesterday** er kam gestern aus London; ~ **South** im Süden/in den Süden; ~ **here in Italy** hier unten in Italien; **he's** ~ **at his brother's** er ist bei seinem Bruder; **from 1700** ~ **to the present** von 1700 bis zur Gegenwart.

**(d)** (in volume, degree, activity, status) **the tyres are** ~ die Reifen sind platt; **his temperature has gone** ~ sein Fieber ist zurückgegangen; **the price is** ~ **on last week** der Preis ist gegenüber der letzten Woche gefallen; **I'm £2** ~ **on what I expected** ich habe £2 weniger, als ich dachte; **they're still three goals** ~ sie liegen immer noch mit drei Toren zurück.

**(e)** (in writing, planning) **I've got it** ~ **in my diary** ich habe es in meinem Kalender notiert; **to be** ~ **for the next race** für das nächste Rennen gemeldet sein; **it's** ~ **for next month** es steht für nächsten Monat auf dem Programm.

**(f)** (as deposit) **to pay £2** ~ £2 anzahlen; **how much do they want** ~**?** was verlangen sie als Anzahlung?

**2** prep **(a)** (indicating movement to) **to go/come** ~ **the hill/street** den Berg/die Straße hinuntergehen/herunterkommen; **she let her hair fall** ~ **her back** sie ließ ihr Haar über die Schultern fallen; **he ran his finger** ~ **the list** er ging mit dem Finger die Liste durch. **(b)** (at a lower part of) **the other skiers were further** ~ **the slope** die anderen Skifahrer waren weiter unten; **she lives** ~ **the street** sie wohnt hier in der Straße. **(c)** ~ **the ages/centuries** Jahrhunderte (hindurch). **(d)** (along) **he was walking/coming** ~ **the street** er ging/kam die Straße entlang. **(e)** (Brit col: to, in, at) **he's gone** ~ **the pub** er ist in die Kneipe gegangen; **she's** ~ **the shops** sie ist einkaufen gegangen.

**3** n **to have a** ~ **on sb** (col) jdn auf dem Kieker haben (col).

**4** vt opponent niederschlagen; beer runterkippen (col). **to** ~ **tools** die Arbeit niederlegen.

**down²** n (feathers) Daunen, Flaumfedern pl; (youth's beard) Flaum m.

**down³** n usu pl on the ~**s** im Hügelland.

**down-:** ~-**and-out 1** n (tramp) Penner m (col); **2** adj heruntergekommen; ~-**at-heel** adj schäbig; ~**beat** n (Mus) erster Taktteil; ~**cast** adj niedergeschlagen; ~**fall** n Sturz, Fall m; (of empire also) Untergang m; (cause of ruin: drink etc) Ruin m; ~**grade** vt hotel, job herunterstufen; person also degradieren; ~-**hearted** adj niedergeschlagen; ~**hill** adv **to go** ~**hill** (road) bergab führen or gehen; (fig) (person) auf dem absteigenden Ast sein; (work, health) sich verschlechtern; ~**load** vt (Comp) laden; ~**market** adj product für den Massenmarkt; area, shop etc weniger vornehm; ~ **payment** n Anzahlung f; ~**pour** n Wolkenbruch m; ~**right 1** adj refusal, lie glatt; rudeness, scoundrel, liar ausgesprochen; **2** adv rude ausgesprochen; ~**size** vt gesundschrumpfen; ~**stairs 1** adv go, come nach unten; be unten; **2** adj **the** ~**stairs rooms** die unteren Zimmer; **our** ~**stairs neighbours** die Nachbarn unter uns; ~**stream** adv flußabwärts (from von); ~-**to-earth** adj nüchtern; advice praktisch; ~**town 1** adj im Zentrum; ~**town district** Zentrum nt, Innenstadt f; (US) Geschäftsviertel nt; **in** ~**town Houston** im Zentrum von Houston; **2** adv **to go** ~**town** in die Stadt or ins Zentrum gehen; ~ **train** n Zug, der von der Stadt aufs Land fährt oder von der Hauptstadt abgeht; ~-**trodden** adj people unterdrückt; ~ **under** (Brit col) **1** n Australien nt. **2** adv in/nach Australien.

**downward** ['daʊnwəd] **1** adj movement, pull nach unten. ~ **trend** Abwärtstrend m. **2** adv (also **downwards**) go, look nach unten. **to slope gently** ~ sanft abfallen; **from the President** ~ beim Präsidenten angefangen.

**downwind** ['daʊnwɪnd] adv in Windrichtung (of, from +gen).

**dowry** ['daʊrɪ] n Mitgift f.

**doz** = **dozen**.

**doze** [dəʊz] **1** n Nickerchen nt. **2** vi (vor sich hin) dösen.

▶**doze off** vi einschlafen, einnicken.

**dozen** ['dʌzn] n Dutzend nt. **half a** ~ ein halbes Dutzend; ~**s** (fig col) eine ganze Menge; ~**s of times**

*(col)* x-mal *(col)*.

**dozy** ['dəʊzɪ] *adj (+er) (sleepy)* verschlafen.

**DP** = **data processing** DV *f.*

**DPP** = **Director of Public Prosecutions.**

**dpt** = **department** Abt.

**Dr** = **doctor** Dr.

**Dr.** = **Drive** Str.

**drab** [dræb] *adj (+er)* trist; *colour also* düster.

**draft** [drɑːft] **1** *n* **(a)** *(rough outline)* Entwurf *m.* ~ **contract** Vertragsentwurf *m.* **(b)** *(Fin, Comm)* Wechsel *m.* **(c)** *(US Mil: conscription)* Einberufung *f* (zum Wehrdienst). **(d)** *(US)* = **draught. 2** *vt* **(a)** *letter, contract* entwerfen. **(b)** *(US Mil) conscript* einberufen.

**draftsman** *(US)* = **draughtsman.**

**drafty** *(US)* = **draughty.**

**drag** [dræg] **1** *n* **(a)** *(aerodynamic)* Luftwiderstand *m.* **(b)** *(col: hindrance)* **to be a** ~ **on sb** für jdn ein Klotz am Bein sein. **(c)** *(col)* **what a** ~! *(boring)* Mann, ist der/die/das langweilig! *(col)*; *(nuisance)* so'n Mist *(col)*; **(d)** *(col: pull on cigarette)* Zug *m (on, at an +dat)*. **(e)** *(women's clothing)* **in** or **wearing** ~ in Frauenkleidung. **2** *vt* **(a)** *person, object* schleppen, schleifen. **to** ~ **one's feet** *(fig)* alles/die Sache schleifen lassen; **to** ~ **the truth out of sb** die Wahrheit mühsam aus jdm herausholen. **(b)** *river* absuchen. **3** *vi (time, work)* sich hinziehen; *(play, book, conversation)* sich in die Länge ziehen.

▶**drag along** *vt sep person* mitschleppen.

▶**drag away** *vt sep (lit, fig)* wegschleppen. **you'll have to** ~ **him** ~ **from the television** den muß man mit Gewalt vom Fernseher wegziehen.

▶**drag down** *vt sep (lit)* herunterziehen; *(fig)* mit sich ziehen. **to** ~ **sb** ~ **to one's level** *(fig)* jdn auf sein eigenes Niveau herunterziehen.

▶**drag in** *vt sep (fig) subject* aufs Tapet bringen; *remark* anbringen.

▶**drag on** *vi* sich in die Länge ziehen; *(meeting, lecture also)* sich hinziehen. **it** ~**ged** ~ **for 3 hours** es zog sich über 3 Stunden hin.

**dragnet** ['drægnet] *n* Schleppnetz *nt.*

**dragon** ['drægən] *n (lit, fig col)* Drache *m.*

**dragonfly** ['drægənˌflaɪ] *n* Libelle *f.*

**dragoon** [drə'guːn] **1** *n (Mil Hist)* Dragoner *m.* **2** *vt* **to** ~ **sb into doing sth** jdn mit Gewalt dazu bringen, etw zu tun.

**drain** [dreɪn] **1** *n* **(a)** *(pipe)* Rohr *nt*; *(under sink etc)* Abfluß(rohr *nt*) *m*; *(under the ground)* Kanalisationsrohr *nt.* ~**s** *(system)* Kanalisation *f*; **open** ~ (Abfluß)rinne *f*; **to throw one's money down the** ~ *(fig col)* das Geld zum Fenster hinauswerfen; **this country's going down the** ~ *(col)* dieses Land geht vor die Hunde *(col)*. **(b)** *(on resources etc)* Belastung *f (on gen)*. **it has been a great** ~ **on her strength** das hat sehr an ihren Kräften gezehrt. **2** *vt* **(a)** *land, marshes* entwässern; *vegetables* abgießen; *reservoir* trockenlegen; *boiler, radiator* das Wasser ablassen aus; *engine oil* ablassen. **(b)** *(fig)* **to feel** ~**ed (of energy)** sich ausgelaugt fühlen; **to** ~ **a country of resources** ein Land ausbeuten; **to** ~ **sb dry** jdn ausnehmen *(col)*. **(c)** *glass* austrinken, leeren. **3** *vi (vegetables, dishes)* abtropfen.

▶**drain away** *vi (liquid)* ablaufen; *(strength)* dahinschwinden.

▶**drain off** *vt sep* abgießen.

**drainage** ['dreɪnɪdʒ] *n* **(a)** *(draining)* Dränage *f*; *(of land also)* Entwässerung *f.* **(b)** *(system)* Entwässerungssystem *nt*; *(in house, town)* Kanalisation *f.* **(c)** *(sewage)* Abwasser *nt.*

**drain:** ~ **cover** *n* Kanaldeckel *m*; ~**ing board,** *(US)*

~ **board** *n* Ablauf *m*; ~ **pipe** *n* Abflußrohr *nt.*

**drake** [dreɪk] *n* Erpel, Enterich *m.*

**drama** ['drɑːmə] *n* Drama *nt.* **the** ~ **of the situation** die Dramatik der Situation.

**drama:** ~ **critic** *n* Theaterkritiker(in *f*) *m*; ~ **student** *n* Schauspielschüler(in *f*) *m.*

**dramatic** [drə'mætɪk] *adj* dramatisch.

**dramatist** ['dræmətɪst] *n* Dramatiker(in *f*) *m.*

**dramatize** ['dræmətaɪz] **1** *vt* **(a)** *novel* für die Bühne/das Fernsehen bearbeiten. **(b)** *(make vivid)* dramatisieren. **2** *vi (exaggerate)* übertreiben.

**drank** [dræŋk] *pret of* **drink.**

**drape** [dreɪp] **1** *vt* drapieren; *person* hüllen. **2** *n* ~**s** *pl (US)* Vorhänge *pl.*

**draper** ['dreɪpər] *n (Brit)* Stoffhändler *m.*

**drapery** ['dreɪpərɪ] *n (Brit) (cloth etc)* Stoff *m*; *(business: also* ~ **shop)** Stoffgeschäft *nt.*

**drastic** ['dræstɪk] *adj* drastisch; *need* dringend; *change* radikal. **things are getting** ~ die Sache wird kritisch.

**drastically** ['dræstɪkəlɪ] *adv* drastisch; *need* dringend; *alter* radikal.

**drat** [dræt] *interj (col)* ~ **(it)**! verflixt! *(col)*.

**draught, *(US)* draft** [drɑːft] *n* **(a)** *(Luft)*zug *m.* **there's a terrible** ~ **in here** hier zieht es fürchterlich; **are you in a** ~? zieht es Ihnen?; **a nice cool** ~ etwas frische Luft. **(b)** *(swallow, drink)* Zug *m.* **(c)** *(~ beer)* Faß- or Schankbier *nt.* **on** ~ vom Faß. **(d)** *(Naut)* Tiefgang *m.* **(e)** *(Brit: game)* ~**s** *(+sing vb)* Damespiel *nt*; *(+pl vb: pieces)* Damesteine *pl.*

**draught:** ~ **beer** *n* Faßbier *nt*; ~**board** *n* Damebrett *nt*; ~**proof 1** *adj window, door* dicht; **2** *vt* (gegen Zugluft) abdichten.

**draughtsman, *(US)* draftsman** ['drɑːftsmən] *n, pl* -**men** [-mən] *(Tech)* Zeichner *m.*

**draughtsmanship, *(US)* draftsmanship** ['drɑːftsmənʃɪp] *n* zeichnerisches Können.

**draughty, *(US)* drafty** ['drɑːftɪ] *adj (+er)* zugig. **it's** ~ **in here** hier zieht es.

**draw¹** [drɔː] *pret* **drew,** *ptp* **drawn 1** *vt (lit, fig)* zeichnen; *line* ziehen. **we must** ~ **the line somewhere** *(fig)* irgendwo muß Schluß sein. **2** *vi* zeichnen.

**draw²** *(vb: pret* **drew,** *ptp* **drawn) 1** *vt* **(a)** *(pull)* ziehen; *bolt* zurückschieben; *bow* spannen; *curtains (open)* aufziehen; *(shut)* zuziehen; *(Med) abscess* schneiden; *cork* herausziehen. **he drew his hat over his eyes** er zog sich *(dat)* den Hut ins Gesicht.

**(b)** *(obtain from source)* holen; *salary* beziehen. **to** ~ **a bath** das Badewasser einlassen; **to** ~ **money from the bank** Geld (vom Konto) abheben; **to** ~ **comfort from sth** sich mit etw trösten; **to** ~ **a smile from sb** jdm ein Lächeln entlocken; **to** ~ **a (deep) breath** (tief) Luft holen.

**(c)** *(attract) interest* erregen; *customer, crowd* anlocken. **to feel** ~**n towards sb** sich zu jdm hingezogen fühlen.

**(d) he refuses to be** ~**n** *(will not speak)* aus ihm ist nichts herauszubringen; *(will not be provoked)* er läßt sich auf nichts ein; **I won't be** ~**n on that one** dazu möchte ich mich nicht äußern.

**(e)** *conclusion, comparison* ziehen; *distinction* treffen.

**(f)** *(Sport)* **to** ~ **a match** unentschieden spielen.

**(g) France has been** ~**n against Scotland** Frankreich ist für die Begegnung mit Schottland ausgelost worden.

**(h)** *(Cook) fowl* ausnehmen.

**2** *vi* **(a)** *(move, come)* kommen. **he drew towards the door** er bewegte sich zur Tür; **he drew to one side** er ging/fuhr zur Seite; **he drew over to the kerb**

er fuhr an den Straßenrand; **to ~ to an end** zu Ende gehen; **he drew ahead of** or **away from the other runners** er zog den anderen Läufern davon. (**b**) *(allow airflow: of chimney, pipe)* ziehen. (**c**) *(Sport)* unentschieden spielen. **they drew 2-2** sie trennten sich 2:2 unentschieden. (**d**) *(infuse: tea)* ziehen.
 **3** n (**a**) *(lottery)* Ziehung, Ausspielung f; *(for sports competitions)* Auslosung f. (**b**) *(Sport)* Unentschieden nt. **the match ended in a ~** das Spiel endete unentschieden. (**c**) *(attraction: play, film etc)* (Kassen)schlager, Knüller *(col)* m; *(person)* Attraktion f. (**d**) **to be quick on the ~** *(lit)* schnell mit der Pistole sein; *(fig)* schlagfertig sein.
 ▶**draw back 1** vi zurückweichen. **2** vt sep zurückziehen; *curtains* also aufziehen.
 ▶**draw in 1** vi (**a**) *(train)* einfahren; **to ~ ~ at the kerb** am Bordstein (an)halten. (**b**) *(get shorter: days)* kürzer werden. **2** vt sep (**a**) *breath, air* einziehen. (**b**) *(attract, gain) crowds* anziehen. (**c**) **to ~ ~ one's claws** *(lit, fig)* die Krallen einziehen.
 ▶**draw on 1** vi **as the night drew ~** mit fortschreitender Nacht; **winter ~s ~** der Winter naht; **time is ~ing ~** es wird spät. **2** vi **+prep obj** *(use as source: also ~ upon)* sich stützen auf (+acc). **3** vt sep *stockings, gloves* anziehen.
 ▶**draw out 1** vi (**a**) *(train)* ausfahren; *(car)* herausfahren *(of* aus*)*. (**b**) *(days)* länger werden. **2** vt sep (**a**) *(take out)* herausziehen. (**b**) *(prolong)* in die Länge ziehen, hinausziehen. (**c**) **to ~ sb ~** *(of his shell)* jdn aus der Reserve locken.
 ▶**draw together** vt sep *threads* miteinander verknüpfen.
 ▶**draw up 1** vi *(stop: car)* (an)halten. **2** vt sep (**a**) *(formulate)* entwerfen; *contract, agreement* also, *will* aufsetzen; *list* aufstellen. (**b**) *chair* heranziehen; **to ~ oneself ~** *(to one's full height)* sich (zu seiner vollen Größe) aufrichten. (**c**) *(set in line) troops* aufstellen.
 **draw:** **~back** n Nachteil m; **~bridge** n Zugbrücke f.
 **drawer** n (**a**) [drɔːr] *(in desk etc)* Schublade f. (**b**) ['drɔːər] *(person: of pictures)* Zeichner m. (**c**) ['drɔːər] *(of cheque etc)* Aussteller m.
 **drawing** ['drɔːɪŋ] n Zeichnung f. **I'm no good at ~** ich kann nicht gut zeichnen.
 **drawing:** **~-board** n Reißbrett nt; **well, it's back to the ~-board** *(fig)* das muß noch einmal ganz neu überdacht werden; **~-pin** n *(Brit)* Reiß- or Heftzwecke f; **~ room** n Wohnzimmer nt; *(in mansion)* Salon m.
 **drawl** [drɔːl] **1** vi schleppend sprechen. **2** vt schleppend aussprechen. **3** n schleppende Sprache.
 **drawn** [drɔːn] **1** ptp of **draw¹, draw².** **2** adj (**a**) *(from tiredness)* abgespannt; *(from worry)* abgehärmt, verhärmt; *(with pain)* schmerzverzerrt. (**b**) *game, match* unentschieden.
 **drawstring** ['drɔːstrɪŋ] n Kordel f zum Zuziehen.
 **dread** [dred] **1** vt sich fürchten vor (+dat), große Angst haben vor (+dat). **I ~ to think what may happen** ich wage nicht daran zu denken, was passieren könnte. **2** n Furcht f.
 **dreadful** ['dredfʊl] adj schrecklich, furchtbar. **I feel ~** *(ill)* ich fühle mich schrecklich or scheußlich; *(mortified)* es ist mir schrecklich peinlich.
 **dreadfully** ['dredfəlɪ] adv schrecklich.
 **dreadlocks** ['dredlɒks] npl Haartracht f der Rastafaris, Dreadlocks pl.
 **dream** [driːm] *(vb: pret, ptp* **dreamt** or **~ed)** **1** n Traum m. **to have a bad ~** schlecht träumen; **sweet ~s!** träum was Schönes!; **to have a ~ about**

sb/sth von jdm/etw träumen; **in a ~** *(fig)* wie im Traum; **the house of his ~s** das Haus seiner Träume, sein Traumhaus; **happy beyond her wildest ~s** glücklicher als in ihren kühnsten Träumen; **to have ~s of becoming rich** davon träumen, reich zu werden; **it worked like a ~** *(col)* es hat hervorragend geklappt; **you're a ~!** du bist ein Schatz; **a ~ of a hat** ein traumhaft schöner Hut.
 **2** vi *(lit, fig)* träumen *(about, of* von*)*. **I'm sorry, I was ~ing** Verzeihung, ich habe gerade geträumt.
 **3** vt *(lit, fig)* träumen; *dream* haben. **I wouldn't ~ of it** das würde mir nicht im Traum einfallen; **I never ~t (that) he would come** ich hätte mir nie träumen lassen, daß er kommen würde.
 **4** adj attr *car, holiday, world* Traum-.
 ▶**dream up** vt sep *(col) idea* sich *(dat)* ausdenken.
 **dreamer** ['driːmər] n Träumer(in f) m.
 **dreamless** ['driːmlɪs] adj *sleep* traumlos.
 **dreamt** [dremt] pret, ptp of **dream.**
 **dreamy** [driːmɪ] adj (+er) verträumt.
 **dreary** ['drɪərɪ] adj (+er) eintönig; *weather* trüb; *person, speech* langweilig.
 **dredge** [dredʒ] vt *river, canal* ausbaggern.
 ▶**dredge up** vt sep *(lit)* ausbaggern; *(fig) unpleasant facts* ausgraben.
 **dredger** ['dredʒər] n Bagger m.
 **dregs** [dregz] npl (**a**) (Boden)satz m. (**b**) *(fig)* Abschaum m.
 **drench** [drentʃ] vt durchnässen. **absolutely ~ed** durch und durch naß, völlig durchnäßt.
 **Dresden** ['drezdən] n Dresden nt; **~ china** ≈ Meißner Porzellan nt.
 **dress** [dres] **1** n (**a**) *(for woman)* Kleid nt. (**b**) *no pl (clothing)* Kleidung f. **in eastern ~** orientalisch gekleidet. **2** vt (**a**) *(clothe)* anziehen. **to get ~ed** sich anziehen; **to ~ sb in sth** jdm etw anziehen; **~ed in black** schwarz gekleidet. (**b**) *(Naut) ship* beflaggen. (**c**) *(Cook) salad* anmachen; *chicken* bratfertig machen. (**d**) *skins* gerben; *material* appretieren; *timber* hobeln; *stone* schleifen. (**e**) *wound* verbinden. **3** vi sich anziehen, sich kleiden. **to ~ in black** sich schwarz kleiden.
 ▶**dress up 1** vi *(smartly)* sich feinmachen; *(in fancy dress)* sich verkleiden. **~ed ~ as Father Christmas** als Weihnachtsmann (verkleidet). **2** vt sep *(disguise)* verkleiden.
 **dressage** ['dresɑːʒ] n Dressur f.
 **dress:** **~ circle** n erster Rang; **~ designer** n Modezeichner(in f) m.
 **dresser¹** ['dresər] n (**a**) *(Theat)* Garderobier m, Garderobiere f. (**b**) **she's a stylish ~** sie ist immer sehr elegant (gekleidet).
 **dresser²** n (**a**) Anrichte f. (**b**) *(US: dressing-table)* Frisierkommode f.
 **dressing** ['dresɪŋ] n (**a**) *(Med: bandage, ointment)* Verband m. (**b**) *(Cook)* Soße f.
 **dressing:** **~ down** n **to give sb a ~ down** jdn herunterputzen *(col)*; **~-gown** n Morgenrock m; **~-room** n *(Theat)* (Künstler)garderobe f; *(Sport)* Umkleidekabine f; **~-table** n Frisierkommode f.
 **dress:** **~maker** n (Damen)schneider(in f) m; **~making** n Schneidern nt; **~ rehearsal** n *(lit, fig)* Generalprobe f; **~ shirt** n Frackhemd nt; **~ uniform** n Galauniform f.
 **dressy** ['dresɪ] adj (+er) *(col) person* fein angezogen; *clothes* elegant.
 **drew** [druː] pret of **draw¹, draw².**
 **dribble** ['drɪbl] **1** vi (**a**) *(liquids)* tropfen; *(baby, person)* sabbern; *(animal)* geifern. (**b**) *(Sport)* dribbeln. (**c**) *(people)* **to ~ back/in** nach und nach zurückkommen/hereinkommen. **2** vt (**a**) *(Sport)* to

~ **the ball** mit dem Ball dribbeln. **(b)** *(baby etc)* kleckern.

**dribs and drabs** ['drɪbzən'dræbz] *npl*: **in** ~ kleckerweise *(col)*.

**dried** [draɪd] *adj* getrocknet; *fruit also* Dörr-. ~ **milk** Trockenmilch *f*, Milchpulver *nt*; ~ **flower** Trockenblume *f*.

**drier** *n* = **dryer**.

**drift** [drɪft] **1** *vi* **(a)** *(Naut)* treiben; *(sand)* wehen. **to** ~ **off course** abtreiben; **as the smoke** ~**ed away** als der Rauch abzog. **(b)** *(fig: person)* sich treiben lassen. **to let things** ~ die Dinge treiben lassen; **he** ~**ed into marriage** er ist in die Ehe hineingeschlittert *(col)*; **the nation was** ~**ing towards a crisis** das Land trieb auf eine Krise zu; **young people are** ~**ing away from the villages** junge Leute wandern aus den Dörfern ab; **to** ~ **apart** *(people)* sich auseinanderleben. **2** *n* **(a)** *(of air, water)* Strömung *f*; *(of events)* Lauf *m*. **(b)** *(of sand, snow)* Verwehung *f*. **(c)** *(of ship, aircraft)* (Ab)drift, Abweichung *f*. **(d)** *continental* ~ Kontinentalverschiebung *f*. **(e)** *(of questions)* Richtung, Tendenz *f*. **if I get your** ~ wenn ich Sie recht verstehe.

**drifter** ['drɪftər] *n (person)* Gammler *m*. **he's a bit of a** ~ er hält es nirgends lange aus.

**driftwood** ['drɪftwʊd] *n* Treibholz *nt*.

**drill**[1] [drɪl] **1** *n* Bohrer *m*. **2** *vti* bohren *(for nach)*.

**drill**[2] **1** *n no pl (esp Mil, fig)* Drill *m*; *(marching etc)* Exerzieren *nt*. **2** *vt* **(a)** *soldiers* drillen; *(in marching etc)* exerzieren lassen. **(b)** **to** ~ **pupils in grammar** mit den Schülern Grammatik pauken; **I** ~**ed it into him** ich habe es ihm eingebleut *(col)*. **3** *vi (Mil)* gedrillt werden; *(marching etc)* exerzieren.

**drill**[3] *n (Tex)* Drillich *m*.

**drill**: ~ **bit** *n* Bohrer *m*; ~ **ground** *n* Exerzierplatz *m*.

**drilling** ['drɪlɪŋ] *n (for oil)* Bohrung *f*. ~ **rig** Bohrturm *m*; *(at sea)* Bohrinsel *f*.

**drily** ['draɪlɪ] *adv* trocken.

**drink** [drɪŋk] *(vb: pret* **drank**, *ptp* **drunk***)* **1** *n* **(a)** Getränk *nt*. **food and** ~ Essen und Getränke; **may I have a** ~? kann ich etwas zu trinken haben?; **would you like a** ~ **of water?** möchten Sie etwas Wasser?; **to give sb a** ~ jdm etwas zu trinken geben. **(b)** *(alcoholic)* Drink *m*. **let's have a** ~ trinken wir was; **I need a** ~! ich brauche was zu trinken!; **he likes a** ~ er trinkt gern (einen); **to ask friends in for** ~**s** Freunde zu einem Drink einladen; **he's got a few** ~**s in him** *(col)* er hat einige Gläser intus *(col)*. **(c)** *no pl (alcoholic liquor)* Alkohol *m*. **he has a** ~ **problem** er trinkt; **his worries/she drove him to** ~ vor Kummer/wegen ihr fing er an zu trinken; **to smell of** ~ eine Fahne haben.

**2** *vt* trinken. **would you like something to** ~? möchten Sie etwas zu trinken (haben)?; **this coffee isn't fit to** ~ diesen Kaffee kann man nicht trinken.

**3** *vi* trinken. **he doesn't** ~ er trinkt nicht; **his father drank** sein Vater war Trinker; **one shouldn't** ~ **and drive** nach dem Trinken soll man nicht fahren; **to** ~ **to sb/sth** auf jdn/etw trinken.

▶**drink in** *vt sep air* tief einatmen; *(fig) a sight, his words etc (begierig)* in sich *(acc)* aufnehmen.

▶**drink up** *vti* austrinken.

**drinkable** ['drɪŋkəbl] *adj* trinkbar.

**drink-driving** ['drɪŋk'draɪvɪŋ] *n* Trunkenheit *f* am Steuer.

**drinker** ['drɪŋkər] *n* Trinker(in *f*) *m*.

**drinking** ['drɪŋkɪŋ] *n* Trinken *nt*. ~ **and driving** Trunkenheit *f* am Steuer.

**drinking**: ~ **chocolate** *n* Trinkschokolade *f*; ~ **fountain** *n* Trinkwasserbrunnen *m*; ~**-up time** *n*

*(Brit)* die letzten zehn Minuten vor der Polizeistunde; ~**-water** *n* Trinkwasser *nt*.

**drinks**: ~ **can** *n* Getränkedose *f*; ~ **machine** *n* Getränkeautomat *m*.

**drip** [drɪp] **1** *vi* tropfen. **to be** ~**ping with sweat/ blood** schweißgebadet/blutüberströmt sein. **2** *vt liquid* träufeln, tropfen. **you're** ~**ping paint over my coat** du tropfst mir Farbe auf den Mantel. **3** *n* **(a)** *(sound)* Tropfen *nt*. **(b)** *(drop)* Tropfen *m*. **(c)** *(Med)* Tropf *(col)* *m*. **to be on a** ~ eine Infusion bekommen, am Tropf hängen *(col)*. **(d)** *(col: silly person)* Flasche *f (col)*.

**drip-dry** ['drɪp'draɪ] *adj shirt etc* bügelfrei.

**dripping** ['drɪpɪŋ] **1** *n (Cook)* Bratenfett *nt*. **2** *adj* **(a)** *tap* tropfend; *washing* tropfnaß. **(b)** *(col: also* ~ **wet)** *person, coat, clothes* triefend, klatschnaß *(col)*.

**drive** [draɪv] *(vb: pret* **drove**, *ptp* **driven***)* **1** *n* **(a)** *(Aut: journey)* Fahrt *f*. **to go for a** ~ (ein bißchen) spazierenfahren; **to go for a** ~ **to the coast** ans Meer fahren; **one hour's** ~ **from London** eine Autostunde von London (entfernt). **(b)** *(to house: also* ~**way)** Einfahrt *f*; *(longer)* Auffahrt, Zufahrt *f*. **(c)** *(Golf, Tennis)* Treibschlag *m*. **(d)** *(Psych etc)* Trieb *m*; *(energy)* Schwung, Elan *m*. **sex** ~ Sexualtrieb *m*. **(e)** *(Comm, Pol etc)* Aktion *f*; *(Mil)* Offensive *f*. **sales** ~ Verkaufskampagne *f*. **(f)** *(Mech: power transmission)* Antrieb *m*; *(Comp)* Laufwerk *nt*. **(g)** *(Aut: steering)* Steuerung *f*. **left-hand** ~ Linkssteuerung *f*.

**2** *vt* **(a)** *animals, dust, clouds etc* treiben. **to** ~ **a nail into sth** einen Nagel in etw *(acc)* einschlagen; **the gale drove the ship off course** der Sturm trieb das Schiff vom Kurs ab. **(b)** *car, train* fahren. **he** ~**s a taxi** er fährt Taxi; **I'll** ~ **you home** ich fahre Sie nach Hause. **(c)** *(provide power for) (belt, shaft)* antreiben; *(electricity, fuel)* betreiben. **(d)** *(cause to become)* treiben. **to** ~ **sb mad** jdn verrückt machen; **to** ~ **sb to desperation** jdn zur Verzweiflung treiben; **I was** ~**n to it** ich wurde dazu getrieben. **(e)** *(force to work hard)* **you're driving him too hard** Sie nehmen ihn zu hart ran *(col)*; **he** ~**s himself very hard** er fordert viel von sich.

**3** *vi* **(a)** fahren; *(go by car)* mit dem Auto fahren. **he's learning to** ~ er lernt Auto fahren. **(b)** **the rain was driving in our faces** der Regen peitschte uns *(dat)* ins Gesicht.

▶**drive along 1** *vi (vehicle, person)* dahinfahren. **2** *vt sep (wind, current) person, boat* (voran)treiben.

▶**drive at** *vi +prep obj* hinauswollen auf *(+acc)*. **what are you driving** ~? worauf wollen Sie hinaus?

▶**drive away 1** *vi (car, person)* wegfahren. **2** *vt sep (lig, fig) person, cares* vertreiben.

▶**drive back 1** *vti (in vehicle)* zurückfahren. **2** *vt sep person, enemy* zurücktreiben.

▶**drive home** *vt sep nail, argument* einhämmern. **how can I** ~ **it** ~ **to him that ...?** wie kann ich (es) ihm nur klarmachen, daß ...?

▶**drive off 1** *vi (person, car)* weg- or abfahren. **2** *vt sep person, enemy* vertreiben.

▶**drive on 1** *vi (person, car)* weiterfahren. **2** *vt sep (encourage)* antreiben; *(to sth bad)* anstiften.

▶**drive out** *vt sep person* hinaustreiben *or* -jagen; *evil thoughts* austreiben.

▶**drive up** *vi (car, person)* vorfahren.

**drive-in** ['draɪv,ɪn] *adj* ~ **bank** Autoschalter *m*; ~ **cinema** Autokino *nt*.

**drivel** ['drɪvl] *n (pej)* Blödsinn *m*.

**driven** ['drɪvn] *ptp of* **drive**.

**drive-on** ['draɪv,ɒn] *adj* ~ **car ferry** Roll-on-roll-off-Autofähre *f*.

**driver** ['draɪvər] *n* Fahrer(in *f*) *m*; *(Brit: of locomotive)* Führer *m*.

**driver's**: ~ **license** n (US) Führerschein m; ~ **seat** n Fahrersitz m.

**drive**: ~ **shaft** n Antriebswelle f; (Aut) Kardanwelle f; ~**way** n Auffahrt f; (longer) Zufahrtsstraße f.

**driving** ['draɪvɪŋ] **1** n Fahren nt. his ~ is awful er fährt kriminell; **dangerous** ~ (Jur) verkehrsgefährdendes (Fahr)verhalten. **2** adj **the** ~ **force** die treibende Kraft; ~ **rain** peitschender Regen.

**driving**: ~ **instructor** n Fahrlehrer(in f) m; ~ **lesson** n Fahrstunde f; ~ **licence** n (Brit) Führerschein m; ~ **mirror** n Rückspiegel m; ~ **school** n Fahrschule f; ~ **seat** n Fahrersitz m; **to be in the** ~ **seat** (fig) die Zügel in der Hand haben; ~ **test** n Fahrprüfung f.

**drizzle** ['drɪzl] **1** n Nieselregen m. **2** vi nieseln.

**droll** [drəʊl] adj drollig, ulkig.

**dromedary** ['drɒmɪdərɪ] n Dromedar nt.

**drone** [drəʊn] **1** n (a) (bee, fig) Drohne f. (b) (sound) (of bees) Summen nt; (of engine) Brummen nt; (way of speaking) monotone Stimme. **2** vi (bee) summen; (engine) brummen; (speak: also ~ away or on) eintönig sprechen; (in reciting) leiern. **he** ~**d on for hours** er redete stundenlang in seinem monotonen Tonfall.

**drool** [druːl] vi sabbern.

►**drool over** vi +prep obj child vernarrt sein in (+acc); beautiful object in Ekstase geraten über (+acc); porno magazine sich aufgeilen an (+dat) (col!).

**droop** [druːp] vi (a) (lit) (person) vornüber gebeugt stehen; (shoulders) herabhängen; (head) herunterfallen; (eyelids) herunterhängen; (with sleepiness) zufallen; (flowers) die Köpfe hängen lassen; (one's hand, breasts) schlaff herunterhängen. (b) (fig: interest, energy) erlahmen; (audience etc) abschlaffen. **don't let your spirits** ~ laß den Mut nicht sinken.

**drop** [drɒp] **1** n (a) (of liquid, also fig) Tropfen m. **a** ~ **of blood** ein Blutstropfen m; **it's a** ~ **in the ocean** (fig) das ist ein Tropfen auf den heißen Stein; **a** ~ **of wine?** ein Schlückchen Wein?; **he's had a** ~ **too much** er hat einen über den Durst getrunken. (b) (sweet) Drops m. (c) (fall: in temperature, prices) Rückgang m; (sudden) Sturz m. **a** ~ **in prices** ein Preissturz m/-rückgang m; **a** ~ **in salary** eine Gehaltseinbuße. (d) (difference in level) Höhenunterschied m; (fall) Sturz, Fall m; (parachute jump) (Ab)sprung m. **there's a** ~ **of ten metres down to the ledge** bis zu dem Felsvorsprung geht es zehn Meter hinunter; **it's a long** ~ es geht tief hinunter. (e) (of supplies, arms) Abwurf m. (f) **to have the** ~ **on sb** (fig) jdn ausstechen können.

**2** vt (a) (allow to fall) fallen lassen; bomb, supplies, burden abwerfen; parachutist absetzen; voice senken; (Knitting) stitch fallen lassen; (lower) hemline herunterlassen. **I** ~**ped my watch** meine Uhr ist (mir) runtergefallen; **he** ~**ped me in it** (col) er hat mir das eingebrockt.

(b) (set down) (from car) person absetzen; thing abliefern; (from boat) cargo löschen.

(c) (utter casually) remark, name fallenlassen; clue geben; hint machen. **he let** ~ **that ...** (deliberately) er erwähnte so nebenbei, daß ...

(d) (send) postcard schreiben. ~ **me a line** schreib mir ein paar Zeilen.

(e) (omit) word, reference auslassen; (deliberately also) weglassen (from in +dat); programme absetzen. **to** ~ **sb from a team** jdn aus einer Mannschaft nehmen.

(f) candidate, minister, friend fallenlassen; girlfriend Schluß machen mit.

(g) (give up) aufgeben; idea, plan also fallenlassen; (Jur) case niederschlagen. **you'll find it hard to** ~ **the habit** es wird Ihnen schwerfallen, sich (dat) das abzugewöhnen; **let's** ~ **the subject** lassen wir das Thema; **you'd better** ~ **the idea** schlagen Sie sich (dat) das aus dem Kopf; ~ **it!** (col) hör auf (damit)!; ~ **everything!** (col) laß alles stehen und liegen!

(h) (lose) money, game, point verlieren.

**3** vi (a) (fall: object) (herunter)fallen. **don't let it** ~ laß es nicht fallen; **to** ~ **to one's knees** auf die Knie fallen or sinken; **I'm ready to** ~ (with fatigue) ich bin zum Umfallen müde; **to work till one** ~s arbeiten bis zum Gehtnichtmehr (col); **she** ~**ped into an armchair** sie ließ sich in einen Sessel fallen; **to** ~ (**down**) **dead** tot umfallen. (b) (rate, temperature etc) sinken; (wind) sich legen; (voice) sich senken. (c) **you can't just let the matter** ~ Sie können die Sache nicht einfach auf sich beruhen lassen; **shall we let it** ~? sollen wir es darauf beruhen lassen?

►**drop back** or **behind** vi zurückfallen.

►**drop by** vi (col) vorbeikommen, hereinschauen.

►**drop down** vi (fall) herunterfallen.

►**drop in** vi (col: visit casually) **to** ~ ~ **on sb** bei jdm vorbeischauen; **to** ~ ~ **at the grocer's** beim Lebensmittelgeschäft vorbeigehen.

►**drop off 1** vi (a) (fall off) abfallen; (come off) abgehen. (b) (fall asleep) einschlafen; (for brief while) einnicken. (c) (sales) zurückgehen; (speed, interest, popularity) nachlassen. **2** vt sep (from car etc) person absetzen; thing abliefern.

►**drop out** vi (a) (of box etc) herausfallen (of aus). (b) (from competition etc) ausscheiden (of aus); (of society) aussteigen. **to** ~ ~ **of university** sein Studium abbrechen.

**drop**: ~ **handlebars** npl Rennlenker m; ~ **kick** n (Rugby) Dropkick m; ~-**leaf table** n Tisch m mit herunterklappbaren Seitenteilen.

**droplet** ['drɒplɪt] n Tröpfchen nt.

**dropout** ['drɒpaʊt] n Aussteiger m (col).

**dropper** ['drɒpəʳ] n (Med) Pipette f; (on bottle) Tropfer m.

**droppings** ['drɒpɪŋz] npl (of rabbits, sheep etc) Köttel pl (col). **horse** ~ Pferdeäpfel pl.

**drop shot** n (Tennis) Stoppball m.

**dross** [drɒs] n no pl (fig) Schund m. **everything else is** ~ alles andere ist eitel und nichtig.

**drought** [draʊt] n Dürre f.

**drove** [drəʊv] **1** pret of **drive**. **2** n (of animals) Herde f; (of people) Schar f.

**drown** [draʊn] **1** vi ertrinken. **a** ~**ing man will clutch at a straw** (prov) dem Verzweifelten ist jedes Mittel recht. **2** vt (a) animal, sorrows ertränken. **to be** ~**ed** ertrinken. (b) (also ~ **out**) noise, voice übertönen; speaker niederschreien.

**drowse** [draʊz] vi (vor sich (acc) hin) dösen.

**drowsiness** ['draʊzɪnɪs] n Schläfrigkeit f.

**drowsy** ['draʊzɪ] adj (+er) schläfrig; (after sleep) verschlafen; afternoon träge.

**drudge** [drʌdʒ] n (person) Arbeitstier nt (col).

**drudgery** ['drʌdʒərɪ] n stumpfsinnige Plackerei. **it's sheer** ~ es ist eine einzige Plackerei.

**drug** [drʌg] **1** n (Med) Medikament, Arzneimittel nt; (Sport) Dopingmittel nt; (addictive) Droge f. **to be on** ~s drogenabhängig sein; (Med) Medikamente nehmen; (Sport) sich dopen. **2** vt person betäuben; food, drink ein Betäubungsmittel mischen in (+acc). **to be in a** ~**ged sleep** in tiefer Betäubung liegen.

**drug**: ~ **addict** n Drogenabhängige(r) mf; ~ **addiction** n Drogenabhängigkeit, Drogensucht f.

**druggist** ['drʌgɪst] n (US) Drogist(in f) m.

**drug**: ~ **peddler**, ~ **pusher** *n* Dealer *m (col)*; ~-**store** *n (US)* Drugstore *m*; ~ **taking** *n* Einnehmen *nt* von Drogen; *(Sport)* Doping *nt*.

**drum** [drʌm] **1** *n* **(a)** *(Mus)* Trommel *f*. **the** ~**s** *(in pop, jazz)* das Schlagzeug. **(b)** *(for oil, petrol)* Tonne *f*; *(cylinder, machine part)* Trommel *f*. **(c)** *(ear* ~*)* Trommelfell *nt*. **2** *vi (Mus, with fingers, rain)* trommeln. **the noise is still** ~**ming in my ears** das Geräusch dröhnt mir noch in den Ohren. **3** *vt* **to** ~ **one's fingers on the table** mit den Fingern auf den Tisch trommeln.

►**drum into** *vt always separate* **to** ~ **sth** ~ **sb** jdm etw einbleuen *(col)*.

►**drum up** *vt sep enthusiasm* erwecken; *support* auftreiben. **to** ~ ~ **business** Aufträge anbahnen.

**drummer** ['drʌməʳ] *n* Trommler *m*; *(in band, pop-group)* Schlagzeuger *m*.

**drum**: ~ **roll** *n* Trommelwirbel *m*; ~**stick** *n* **(a)** *(Mus)* Trommelschlegel *or* -stock *m*; **(b)** *(on chicken etc)* Keule *f*.

**drunk** [drʌŋk] **1** *ptp of* **drink**. **2** *adj* betrunken. **to get** ~ **(on)** betrunken werden (von); *(on purpose)* sich betrinken (mit); **to arrest sb for being** ~ **and disorderly** *(Jur)* jdn wegen Trunkenheit und ruhestörenden Lärms verhaften; ~ **with success** vom Erfolg berauscht. **3** *n* Betrunkene(r) *mf*; *(habitually)* Trinker(in *f*), Säufer(in *f*) *(col) m*.

**drunkard** ['drʌŋkəd] *n* Säufer(in *f*) *m (col)*.

**drunken** ['drʌŋkən] *adj* betrunken. ~ **orgy** Sauforgie *f*; ~ **brawl** Schlägerei *f* mit/von Betrunkenen; ~ **driving** *(Jur)* Trunkenheit *f* am Steuer.

**drunkenness** ['drʌŋkənnɪs] *n (state)* Betrunkenheit *f*; *(habit, problem)* Trunksucht *f*.

**dry** [draɪ] **1** *n* **come into the** ~ komm ins Trockene; **to give sth a** ~ etw trocknen. **2** *adj (+er)* trocken. **the river ran** ~ der Fluß trocknete aus; **to be on** ~ **land** festen Boden unter den Füßen haben; **as** ~ **as a bone** *land, clothes* knochentrocken *(col)*; *mouth, ditches* völlig ausgetrocknet; **to feel/to be** ~ *(thirsty)* eine trockene Kehle haben *(col)*. **3** *vt* trocknen; *skin* austrocknen; *fruit also* dörren; *dishes, one's hands* abtrocknen. **to** ~ **one's eyes** sich *(dat)* die Tränen abwischen; **to** ~ **oneself** sich abtrocknen. **4** *vi* trocken werden.

►**dry off** *vi* trocknen.

►**dry out 1** *vi (clothes)* trocknen; *(ground, skin etc)* austrocknen; *(col: alcoholic)* eine Entziehungskur machen. **2** *vt sep clothes* trocknen; *ground, skin* austrocknen.

►**dry up 1** *vi* **(a)** *(stream, well)* austrocknen, versiegen; *(moisture)* trocknen; *(inspiration, source of income)* versiegen. **(b)** *(dishes)* abtrocknen. **(c)** *(actor)* steckenbleiben *(col)*. **(d)** *(col: be quiet)* ~ ~! halt den Mund! *(col)*. **2** *vt sep mess* aufwischen; *dishes* abtrocknen.

**dry**: ~-**clean** *vt* chemisch reinigen; ~-**cleaners** *npl* chemische Reinigung; ~-**cleaning** *n* chemische Reinigung; ~ **dock** *n (Naut)* Trockendock *nt*.

**dryer, drier** ['draɪəʳ] *n (for clothes)* Wäschetrockner *m*; *(spin* ~*)* Wäscheschleuder *f*; *(for hair)* Fön, Haartrockner *m*; *(hood)* Trockenhaube *f*.

**dry**: ~ **goods** *npl (Comm)* Kurzwaren *pl*; ~ **ice** *n* Trockeneis *nt*.

**drying-up** ['draɪɪŋ'ʌp] *n* Abtrocknen *nt*. **to do the** ~ abtrocknen.

**dry land** *n* fester Boden.

**dryly** ['draɪlɪ] *adv* trocken.

**dryness** ['draɪnɪs] *n* Trockenheit *f*.

**dry**: ~ **rot** *n* (Haus- *or* Holz)schwamm *m*; ~ **run** *n* Probelauf *m*; ~ **ski slope** *n* Trockenskipiste *f*.

**DSS** = **Department of Social Security** ≃ Sozial-

ministerium *nt*.

**DST** *(US)* = **Daylight Saving Time**.

**DTI** *(Brit)* = **Department of Trade and Industry** ≃ Wirtschaftsministerium *nt*.

**DTP** = **desktop publishing** DTP *nt*.

**DTs** ['di:'ti:z] *npl* **to have the** ~ das Zittern haben.

**dual** ['djʊəl] *adj (double)* doppelt, Doppel-. ~ **carriageway** *(Brit)* zweispurige Straße, Schnellstraße *f*; ~ **control** *(Aut)* Doppelsteuerung *f*; ~ **nationality** doppelte Staatsangehörigkeit; ~ **role** *(Theat, fig)* Doppelrolle *f*.

**duality** [dju:'ælɪtɪ] *n* Dualität *f*.

**dual-purpose** ['djʊəl'pɜ:pəs] *adj* zweifach verwendbar.

**dub** [dʌb] *vt* **(a)** *(nickname)* taufen. **(b)** *film* synchronisieren.

**dubious** ['dju:bɪəs] *adj* zweifelhaft; *matter also* dubios; *look* zweifelnd. **I'm very** ~ **about it** ich habe da (doch) starke Zweifel.

**dubiously** ['dju:bɪəslɪ] *adv look* zweifelnd; *behave* zweifelhaft, fragwürdig.

**Dublin** ['dʌblɪn] *n* Dublin *nt*.

**duchess** ['dʌtʃɪs] *n* Herzogin *f*.

**duchy** ['dʌtʃɪ] *n* Herzogtum *nt*.

**duck** [dʌk] **1** *n* **(a)** *(bird)* Ente *f*. **he took to it like a** ~ **to water** da war er sofort in seinem Element; **it's like water off a** ~**'s back** das prallt alles an ihm/ihr *etc* ab. **(b)** *(Cricket)* **to be out for a** ~ ohne Punktgewinn aus sein. **2** *vi* **(a)** *(also* ~ **down)** sich ducken. **he** ~**ed under the water** er tauchte (im Wasser) unter. **(b)** **he** ~**ed out of the room** er verschwand aus dem Zimmer. **3** *vt* **(a)** *(push under water)* untertauchen. **(b)** **to** ~ **one's head** den Kopf einziehen. **(c)** *(avoid) difficult question etc* ausweichen *(+dat)*.

**duckboards** ['dʌkbɔ:dz] *npl* Lattenrost *m*.

**ducking** ['dʌkɪŋ] *n* Untertauchen *nt*. **to give sb a** ~ jdn untertauchen.

**duckling** ['dʌklɪŋ] *n* Entenküken, Entlein *nt*.

**duck**: ~ **pond** *n* Ententeich *m*; ~ **weed** *n* Entenflott *nt*.

**duct** [dʌkt] *n* **(a)** *(Anat)* Röhre *f*. **tear** ~ Tränenkanal *m*. **(b)** *(for liquid, gas)* Leitung *f*.

**dud** [dʌd] *(col)* **1** *adj* **(a)** ~ **shell/bomb** Blindgänger *m*. **(b)** *actor, teacher* mies *(col)*, schlecht; *coin* falsch; *cheque* ungedeckt; *(forged)* gefälscht. ~ **note** Blüte *f (col)*. **2** *n* **(a)** *(shell, bomb)* Blindgänger *m*. **(b)** *(cheque)* ungedeckter *or (forged)* gefälschter Scheck; *(banknote)* Blüte *f (col)*. **(c)** *(person)* Blindgänger *(col)*, Versager *m*.

**dude** [dju:d] *n (US)* Städter *m*, feiner Stadtpinkel *(pej col)*. ~ **ranch** Touristenranch *f*.

**dudgeon** ['dʌdʒən] *n*: **in high** ~ sehr empört.

**due** [dju:] **1** *adj* **(a)** *(to be paid, owing)* fällig. ~ **date** Fälligkeitsdatum *nt*; **the sum which is** ~ **to him** die Summe, die ihm zusteht; **the amount** ~ **as compensation** der Betrag, der als Schadenersatz gezahlt werden soll; **to fall** ~ fällig werden *or* sein; **I am** ~ **six days off/(for) a rise** mir stehen sechs Tage Urlaub zu/mir steht eine Gehaltserhöhung zu.

**(b)** *(expected, scheduled)* **to be** ~ **to do sth** etw tun sollen; **the train is** ~ **at midday** der Zug soll laut Fahrplan um zwölf Uhr ankommen; **I'm** ~ **in London tomorrow** ich soll morgen in London sein; **he's** ~ **back tomorrow** er müßte morgen zurück sein; **when is the baby/she** ~? wann soll das Baby kommen/bekommt sie ihr Baby?

**(c)** *(proper, suitable)* gebührend. **with all** ~ **respect** bei allem Respekt; **we'll let you know in** ~ **course** wir werden Sie zu gegebener Zeit benachrichtigen; **he was, in** ~ **course, to become** ... im Laufe der Zeit sollte er ... werden; **after** ~ **consideration** nach reif-

licher Überlegung.
   **(d)** ~ **to** aufgrund *(+gen)*, wegen *(+gen or dat)*;
**what's it ~ to?** worauf ist dies zurückzuführen?; **it
is ~ to you that ...** wir haben es Ihnen zu verdanken, daß ...
   **2** *adv* ~ **west** direkt nach Westen; ~ **east of the
village** genau im Osten des Dorfes.
   **3** *n* **(a)** ~**s** *pl (fees)* Gebühr *f*, Gebühren *pl.* **(b)** *no
pl* **(to) give him his** ~, **he did try hard** das muß man
ihm lassen, er hat sich wirklich angestrengt.
**duel** ['djʊəl] **1** *n (lit, fig)* Duell *nt.* **2** *vi* sich duellieren.
**duet** [djuː'et] *n* Duo *nt; (for voices)* Duett *nt.*
**duffel** ['dʌfl]: ~ **bag** *n* Matchbeutel *or* -sack *m*; ~-
**coat** *n* Dufflecoat *m.*
**dug** *pret, ptp of* **dig**.
**dugout** ['dʌgaʊt] *n* **(a)** *(Mil)* Schützengraben *m.* **(b)**
*(also* ~ *canoe)* Einbaum *m.*
**duke** [djuːk] *n* Herzog *m.*
**dull** [dʌl] **1** *adj (+er)* **(a)** *colour, light* trüb, matt;
*weather* trüb; *sound* dumpf. **(b)** *(boring)* langweilig; *person, evening also* lahm; *(lacking spirit) person, mood* lustlos. **as ~ as ditchwater** stinklangwei-
lig *(col).* **(c)** *(also* ~-**witted)** *person* schwerfällig. **(d)**
*blade* stumpf; *pain* dumpf. **(e)** *market* flau; *trade,
business* schleppend. **2** *vt* **(a)** *sense, powers of
memory* schwächen; *mind* abstumpfen. **(b)** *pain,
grief* betäuben; *pleasure* dämpfen. **(c)** *sound* dämpfen. **(d)** *edge, blade* stumpf machen.
**duly** ['djuːlɪ] *adv* entsprechend; *(properly)* gebührend, wie es sich gehört; *(according to regulations
etc)* vorschriftsmäßig. **and the parcel ~ arrived the
next morning** und das Paket kam dann auch am
nächsten Morgen.
**dumb** [dʌm] *adj (+er)* **(a)** stumm. **the ~** die Stum-
men *pl*; ~ **animals** die Tiere *pl*; **he was struck ~** es
verschlug ihm die Sprache; ~ **waiter** Speiseaufzug
*m; (trolley)* Serviertisch *m*, stummer Diener. **(b)**
*(esp US col: stupid)* doof *(col)*, dumm.
**dumbbell** ['dʌmbel] *n (Sport)* Hantel *f.*
**dumbfound** ['dʌmfaʊnd] *vt* verblüffen. **I'm ~ed!** ich
bin sprachlos!
**dumbness** ['dʌmnɪs] *n* **(a)** Stummheit *f.* **(b)** *(esp US
col: stupidity)* Doofheit *(col)*, Dummheit *f.*
**dumbo** ['dʌmbəʊ] *n (col)* Doofi *m (col).*
**dummy** ['dʌmɪ] **1** *n* **(a)** *(sham object)* Attrappe *f;
(for clothes)* (Kleider)puppe *f.* **(b)** *(Brit: baby's teat)*
Schnuller *m.* **(c)** *(Ftbl etc)* Finte *f.* **2** *adj attr* unecht.
**a ~ rifle** eine Gewehrattrappe; ~ **run** Probelauf *m.*
**dump** [dʌmp] **1** *n* **(a)** *(pile of rubbish)* Abfallhaufen
*m; (place)* Müllkippe *f.* **(b)** *(Mil)* Depot *nt.* **(c)** *(pej
col: town)* Kaff *nt (col); (house, building)* Loch *nt
(pej col).* **(d)** *(col)* **to be (down) in the ~s** deprimiert
sein. **2** *vt* **(a)** *rubbish* abladen; *(at sea)* verklappen;
*(col) person, girlfriend* abschieben; *car* abstellen,
loswerden. **(b)** *(put down) load* abladen; *bags etc
(drop)* fallen lassen; *(leave)* lassen. **(c)** *(Comm)
goods* zu Dumpingpreisen verkaufen.
**dumpling** ['dʌmplɪŋ] *n* **(a)** *(Cook)* Kloß, Knödel *m.*
**(b)** *(col: person)* Dickerchen *nt (col).*
**dump truck** *n* Kipper *m.*
**dumpy** ['dʌmpɪ] *adj person* pummelig.
**dun** [dʌn] *adj* graubraun.
**dunce** [dʌns] *n (Sch)* langsamer Schüler; *(stupid person)* Dummkopf *m.*
**dune** [djuːn] *n* Düne *f.*
**dung** [dʌŋ] **1** *n* Dung *m.* **2** *vt field* düngen.
**dungarees** [ˌdʌŋgə'riːz] *npl* Latzhose *f.*
**dungeon** ['dʌndʒən] *n* Verlies *nt*, Kerker *m.*
**dunghill** ['dʌŋhɪl] *n* Misthaufen *m.*
**dunk** [dʌŋk] *vt* (ein)tunken.
**dunno** ['dʌnəʊ] = **(I) don't know.**

**duo** ['djuːəʊ] *n* Duo *nt.*
**duodenal** [ˌdjuːəʊ'diːnl] *adj* ~ **ulcer** Zwölffinger-
darmgeschwür *nt.*
**duodenum** [ˌdjuːəʊ'diːnəm] *n* Zwölffingerdarm *m.*
**dupe** [djuːp] **1** *vt* betrügen. **he was ~d into believing
it** er fiel darauf herein. **2** *n* Betrogene(r) *mf.*
**duplex** ['djuːpleks] *n (esp US: also:* ~ **apartment)**
zweistöckige Wohnung.
**duplicate** ['djuːplɪkeɪt] **1** *vt document* ein Duplikat
*nt* anfertigen von; *(on machine)* vervielfältigen; *(repeat) action* wiederholen; *(wastefully)* doppelt *or*
zweimal machen. **2** ['djuːplɪkɪt] *n (of document)* Duplikat *nt; (of work of art)* Kopie *f; (of key)* Zweit-
schlüssel *m.* **3** ['djuːplɪkɪt] *adj* doppelt, zweifach.
**duplicating** ['djuːplɪkeɪtɪŋ] *n (of documents)* Vervielfältigung *f.* ~ **machine** Vervielfältigungsapparat *m.*
**duplication** [ˌdjuːplɪ'keɪʃən] *n (of efforts, work)* Wiederholung *f.*
**duplicator** ['djuːplɪkeɪtə'] *n* Vervielfältigungsapparat *m.*
**duplicity** [djuː'plɪsɪtɪ] *n* Doppelspiel *nt.*
**durability** [ˌdjʊərə'bɪlɪtɪ] *n (of material)* Haltbarkeit
*f; (of metal)* Widerstandsfähigkeit *f.*
**durable** ['djʊərəbl] *adj friendship* dauerhaft; *material*
haltbar; *metal* widerstandsfähig.
**duration** [djʊə'reɪʃən] *n (of play, war etc)* Länge,
Dauer *f.* **for the ~** bis zum Ende.
**duress** [djʊə'res] *n* **under ~** unter Zwang.
**durex** ® ['djʊəreks] *n* Gummi *(col) m.*
**during** ['djʊərɪŋ] *prep* während *(+gen).*
**dusk** [dʌsk] *n (twilight)* (Abend)dämmerung *f;
(gloom)* Finsternis *f.* **at ~** bei Einbruch der Dunkelheit.
**dusky** ['dʌskɪ] *adj (+er) maiden* dunkelhäutig.
**dust** [dʌst] **1** *n no pl* **(a)** Staub *m.* **when the ~ had
settled** *(fig)* als sich die Wogen wieder etwas ge-
glättet hatten. **(b)** **to give sth a ~** etw abstauben. **2**
*vt* **(a)** *furniture* abstauben; *room* Staub wischen in
*(+dat).* **(b)** *(Cook)* bestäuben.
**dust:** ~**bin** *n (Brit)* Mülltonne *f*; ~**bin liner** *n* Müllsack *m*; ~ **bowl** *n* Trockengebiet *nt*; ~**cart** *n (Brit)*
Müllwagen *m*; ~**cover** *n (on furniture)* Schonbezug
*m.*
**duster** ['dʌstə'] *n* Staubtuch *nt.*
**dusting** ['dʌstɪŋ] *n* Staubwischen *nt; (Cook)* Bestäuben *nt.* **to give sth a ~** etw abstauben.
**dust:** ~ **jacket** *n* (Schutz)umschlag *m*; ~**man** *n
(Brit)* Müllmann *m (col)*; **the ~men come on Fridays**
freitags ist Müllabfuhr; ~**pan** *n* Kehrschaufel *f*; ~
**sheet** *n* Staubdecke *f*; ~ **storm** *n* Staubsturm *m*;
~-**up** *n (col)* Schlägerei *f.*
**dusty** ['dʌstɪ] *adj (+er) table, path* staubig.
**Dutch** [dʌtʃ] **1** *adj* holländisch, niederländisch *(esp
form).* ~ **auction** *Versteigerung f mit stufenweise er-
niedrigtem Ausbietungspreis;* **I need a little ~ courage**
*(col)* ich muß mir ein bißchen Mut antrinken; ~
**elm disease** Ulmenkrankheit *f;* **to talk to sb like a ~
uncle** *(col)* jdm eine Standpauke halten. **2** *adv* **to go
~** *(col)* getrennte Kasse machen. **3** *n* **(a)** **the ~**
die Holländer *or* Niederländer *pl.* **(b)** *(language)* Holländisch, Niederländisch *(esp form) nt.*
**Dutchman** ['dʌtʃmən] *n, pl* **-men** [-mən] Holländer,
Niederländer *(esp form) m.* **he did say that or I'm a
~** *(col)* ich fresse einen Besen, wenn er das nicht
gesagt hat *(col).*
**Dutchwoman** ['dʌtʃˌwʊmən] *n, pl* **-women**
[-ˌwɪmɪn] Holländerin, Niederländerin *(esp form) f.*
**dutiable** ['djuːtɪəbl] *adj* zollpflichtig.
**dutiful** ['djuːtɪfʊl] *adj child* gehorsam; *husband, employee* pflichtbewußt.
**dutifully** ['djuːtɪfəlɪ] *adv* pflichtbewußt; *(esp iro)* treu

und brav.

**duty** ['djuːtɪ] *n* **(a)** Pflicht *f.* **to do one's ~ by sb** seine Pflicht gegenüber jdm tun *or* erfüllen; **I feel ~ bound to say that ...** ich fühle mich verpflichtet zu sagen, daß ...; **to make it one's ~ to do sth** es sich *(dat)* zur Pflicht machen, etw zu tun. **(b)** *(often pl: responsibility)* Aufgabe, Pflicht *f.* **to take up one's duties** seine Pflichten aufnehmen; **to be on ~** *(doctor etc)* im Dienst sein; *(Sch etc)* Aufsicht haben; **who's on ~ tomorrow?** wer hat morgen Dienst/ Aufsicht?; **to be off ~** nicht im Dienst sein. **(c)** *(Fin: tax)* Zoll *m.*

**duty:** **~-free 1** *adj* zollfrei; **~-free shop** Duty-free-Shop *m;* **2** *n* zollfreie Ware; **~ officer** *n* Offizier *m* vom Dienst.

**duvet** ['djuːveɪ] *n (Brit)* Steppdecke *f.*

**DVLA, DVLC** *(Brit)* = **Driver and Vehicle Licensing Agency/Centre** Zulassungsstelle *f* für Kraftfahrzeuge.

**dwarf** [dwɔːf] **1** *n, pl* **dwarves** [dwɔːvz] Zwerg *m.* **2** *adj* **tree, star** Zwerg-. **3** *vt* überragen; *(through achievements, ability etc)* in den Schatten stellen.

**dwell** [dwel] *pret, ptp* **dwelt** *vi (liter: live)* leben, wohnen.

►**dwell (up)on** *vi +prep obj* **(a)** verweilen bei; *(stress unnecessarily etc)* herumreiten auf *(+dat).* **(b)** *(Mus)* **note** halten.

**dwelling** ['dwelɪŋ] *n (form: also ~ place)* Wohnsitz *m (form),* Wohnung *f.*

**dwelt** [dwelt] *pret, ptp of* **dwell.**

**dwindle** ['dwɪndl] *vi (strength, interest)* schwinden; *(numbers, audiences)* zurückgehen; *(supplies)* zur Neige gehen.

**dwindling** ['dwɪndlɪŋ] *adj* schwindend; *resources* versiegend.

**dye** [daɪ] **1** *n* Farbstoff *m.* **hair ~** Haarfärbemittel *nt;* **the ~ will come out in the wash** die Farbe geht beim Waschen heraus. **2** *vt* färben.

**dyed-in-the-wool** ['daɪdɪnðə‚wʊl] *adj* durch und durch *pred; attitude* eingefleischt. **~ conservative** Erzkonservative(r) *mf.*

**dying** ['daɪɪŋ] *adj person* sterbend; *tradition, race, civilization* aussterbend; *embers* verglühend. **to my ~ day** bis an mein Lebensende; **~ wish** letzter Wunsch; **~ words** letzte Worte.

**dyke, dike** [daɪk] *n* **(a)** *(channel)* (Entwässerungs)graben, Kanal *m.* **(b)** *(barrier)* Deich, Damm *m.* **(c)** *(col: lesbian)* Lesbe *f (col).*

**dynamic** [daɪ'næmɪk] *adj* dynamisch.

**dynamism** ['daɪnəmɪzəm] *n* Dynamismus *m;* *(of person)* Dynamik *f.*

**dynamite** ['daɪnəmaɪt] **1** *n (lit)* Dynamit *nt; (fig)* Sprengstoff *m.* **she's ~** sie ist eine Wucht *(col);* **this story's ~** diese Geschichte wird wie eine Bombe einschlagen. **2** *vt bridge* sprengen.

**dynamo** ['daɪnəməʊ] *n* Dynamo *m.*

**dynasty** ['dɪnəstɪ] *n* Dynastie *f.*

**dysentery** ['dɪsɪntrɪ] *n* Dysenterie, Ruhr *f.*

**dyslexia** [dɪs'leksɪə] *n* Legasthenie *f.*

**dyslexic** [dɪs'leksɪk] **1** *adj* legasthenisch. **2** *n* Legastheniker(in *f*) *m.*

**dyspepsia** [dɪs'pepsɪə] *n* Verdauungsstörung *f.*

**dystrophy** ['dɪstrəfɪ] *n* Dystrophie *f.*

# E

**E, e** [i:] *n* E, e *nt*; *(Mus)* E, e *nt*. **E for Edward** *(Brit)*, **E for Easy** *(US)* ≃ E wie Emil; **E flat/sharp** Es, es *nt/* Eis, eis *nt*.

**E** = (a) **east** O. (b) **eastern**.

**ea.** = **each**.

**each** [i:tʃ] **1** *adj* jede(r, s). ~ **(and every) one of us** jeder (einzelne) von uns. **2** *pron* (a) jede(r, s). **a little of** ~ **please** von jedem etwas, bitte; **we** ~ **had our own ideas about it** jeder von uns hatte seine eigene Vorstellung davon. (b) ~ **other** einander; **they get on** ~ **other's nerves** sie gehen sich *(dat) or* einander auf die Nerven; **we visit** ~ **other** wir besuchen uns (gegenseitig); **on top of** ~ **other/next to** ~ **other** aufeinander/nebeneinander. **3** *adv* je. **two classes of 20 pupils** ~ zwei Klassen mit je 20 Schülern; **the books are £1** ~ die Bücher kosten je £1; **carnations at one mark** ~ Nelken zu einer Mark das Stück; **it cost them £10** ~ das hat sie pro Person £10 gekostet.

**eager** ['i:gər] *adj* eifrig. **to be** ~ **to do sth** etw unbedingt tun wollen; ~ **to learn** lernbegierig; **to be** ~ **for sth** auf etw *(acc)* erpicht sein; ~ **beaver** *(col)* Arbeitstier *nt (col)*.

**eagerly** ['i:gəlɪ] *adv* eifrig; *look, wait* gespannt.

**eagerness** ['i:gənɪs] *n* Eifer *m*.

**eagle** ['i:gl] *n* Adler *m*.

**eagle-eyed** ['i:gl'aɪd] *adj* **the** ~ **detective** der Detektiv mit seinen Adleraugen.

**E & O E** *(Comm)* = **errors and omissions excepted** Irrtum vorbehalten.

**ear¹** [ɪər] *n (Anat, fig)* Ohr *nt*. **to keep one's** ~**s open** die Ohren offenhalten; **to keep an** ~ **to the ground** die Ohren aufsperren; **to be all** ~**s** ganz Ohr sein; **your** ~**s must have been burning** Ihnen müssen die Ohren geklungen haben; **it goes in one** ~ **and out the other** das geht zum einen Ohr hinein und zum anderen wieder heraus; **to be up to the** ~**s in debt** bis über beide Ohren verschuldet sein; **he'll be out on his** ~ *(col)* dann fliegt er raus *(col)*; **to have a good** ~ **for music** musikalisch sein; **to play by** ~ *(lit)* nach Gehör spielen; **to play it by** ~ *(fig)* improvisieren.

**ear²** *n (of grain)* Ähre *f*.

**ear:** ~**ache** *n* Ohrenschmerzen *pl*; ~**-drum** *n* Trommelfell *nt*.

**earl** [ɜːl] *n* Graf *m*.

**early** ['ɜːlɪ] **1** *adj* (+*er*) früh; *(sooner than expected)* zu früh; *fruit, vegetable* Früh-. **it was** ~ **in the morning** es war früh am Morgen; **to be an** ~ **riser** Frühaufsteher sein; **in the** ~ **hours** in den frühen Morgenstunden; **in the** ~ **morning/afternoon** am frühen Morgen/Nachmittag; **in** ~ **spring/summer** zu Beginn des Frühjahrs/im Frühsommer; **in his** ~ **youth** in seiner frühen Jugend; **at an** ~ **age** von frühester Jugend an; **she's in her** ~ **forties** sie ist Anfang Vierzig; **to take** ~ **retirement** sich vorzeitig pensionieren lassen; **at the earliest possible moment** so bald wie (irgend) möglich.

**2** *adv* früh. **you're** ~ **today** Sie sind heute ja früh dran; **sorry, am I** ~? bin ich zu früh?; **earlier (on) this evening** früher am Abend; **I saw him** ~ **in the week** ich habe ihn Anfang der Woche gesehen; **earlier on that year Jim had ...** Jim hatte früher in dem Jahr ...; **the earliest he can come is Friday** er kann frühestens (am) Freitag kommen; **as** ~ **as 1935** schon 1935; **she left ten minutes** ~ sie ist zehn Minuten früher gegangen.

**early:** ~ **bird** *n (in morning)* Frühaufsteher(in *f*) *m*; *(arriving etc)* Frühankömmling *m*; **the** ~ **bird catches the worm** *(Prov)* Morgenstund(e) hat Gold im Mund(e) *(Prov)*; *(first come, first served)* wer zuerst kommt, mahlt zuerst *(Prov)*; ~ **closing** *n* **it's** ~ **closing today** die Geschäfte haben heute nachmittag geschlossen; ~ **diagnosis** *n (Med)* Früherkennung *f*; ~ **retirement** *n* vorgezogener Ruhestand; **to take** ~ **retirement** vorzeitig in den Ruhestand gehen; ~**-warning system** *n* Frühwarnsystem *nt*.

**ear:** ~**mark** *vt (fig)* vorsehen; ~**-muffs** *npl* Ohrenschützer *pl*.

**earn** [ɜːn] *vt* verdienen; *(Fin) interest* bringen. ~**ed income** Arbeitseinkommen *nt*.

**earner** ['ɜːnər] *n (person)* Verdiener(in *f*) *m*; *(Brit col: income source)* Einnahmequelle *f*.

**earnest** ['ɜːnɪst] **1** *adj* ernsthaft; *hope* aufrichtig. **2** *n* **in** ~ *(with determination)* ernsthaft; *(without joking)* im Ernst; **this time I'm in** ~ diesmal meine ich es ernst; **it is snowing in** ~ **now** jetzt schneit es richtig.

**earnestness** ['ɜːnɪstnɪs] *n* Ernsthaftigkeit *f*; *(of voice)* Ernst *m*.

**earnings** ['ɜːnɪŋz] *npl* Verdienst *m*.

**ear:** ~, **nose and throat** *adj attr (Med)* Hals-Nasen-Ohren-; ~**-phones** *npl* Kopfhörer *pl*; ~**-plug** *n* Ohropax ® *nt*; ~**-ring** *n* Ohrring *m*; ~**-shot** *n:* **out of/within** ~**shot** außer/in Hörweite; ~**-splitting** *adj* ohrenbetäubend.

**earth** [ɜːθ] **1** *n* (a) *(also Brit Elec)* Erde *f*. **the** ~**'s atmosphere** die Erdatmosphäre; **on** ~ auf der Erde; **to the ends of the** ~ bis ans Ende der Welt; **where/who** *etc* **on** ~? *(col)* wo/wer *etc* ... bloß?; **nothing on** ~ **will stop me now** keine Macht der Welt hält mich jetzt noch auf; **you look like nothing on** ~ *(col)* du siehst unmöglich aus *(col)*; **it cost the** ~ *(col)* das hat ein Vermögen gekostet *(col)*; **to bring sb down to** ~ **(with a bump)** *(fig)* jdn (unsanft) wieder auf den Boden der Tatsachen zurückholen. (b) *(of fox)* Bau *m*. **to go to** ~ im Bau untertauchen; *(criminal)* untertauchen; **to run sb to** ~ *(fig)* jdn ausfindig machen. **2** *vt (Brit Elec)* erden.

**earthenware** ['ɜːθənwɛər] **1** *n (material)* Ton *m*; *(products)* Tonwaren *pl*; *(dishes etc)* Tongeschirr *nt*. **2** *adj* aus Ton, Ton-.

**earthly** ['ɜːθlɪ] **1** *adj* (a) irdisch. ~ **paradise** Paradies *nt* auf Erden. (b) *(col)* **there is no** ~ **reason to think ...** es besteht nicht der geringste Grund für die Annahme ... **2** *n (col)* **she hasn't an** ~ sie hat nicht die geringste Chance.

**earth:** ~**-moving equipment** *n* Erdräummaschinen *pl*; ~**quake** *n* Erdbeben *nt*; ~**works** *npl* Erdarbeiten *pl*; ~**worm** *n* Regenwurm *m*.

**earthy** ['ɜːθɪ] *adj (+er)* **(a)** *taste, smell* erdig. **(b)** *person, humour* derb.

**earwig** ['ɪəwɪg] *n* Ohrwurm *m*.

**ease** [iːz] **1** *n* **(a)** Behagen *nt*. **I am never at** ~ **in his company** in seiner Gegenwart bin ich immer etwas befangen; **to put** *or* **set sb at his** ~ jdm die Befangenheit nehmen; **to put** *or* **set sb's mind at** ~ jdn beruhigen; **to feel at** ~ **with sb** sich bei jdm wohlfühlen; **(stand) at** ~! *(Mil)* rührt euch! **(b) with** ~ mit Leichtigkeit; **a life of** ~ ein Leben der Muße. **2** *vt* **(a)** *pain* lindern; *mind* erleichtern. **(b)** *rope, strap* lockern; *pressure, tension* verringern. **(c) to** ~ **in the clutch** *(Aut)* die Kupplung langsam kommen lassen; **he** ~**d the lid off** er löste behutsam den Deckel. **3** *vi* nachlassen; *(situation)* sich entspannen.
►**ease off** *or* **up** *vi (slow down, relax)* langsamer werden; *(driver)* verlangsamen; *(situation)* sich entspannen; *(pain, rain)* nachlassen. **the doctor told him to** ~ ~ der Arzt riet ihm, etwas kürzer zu treten.

**easel** ['iːzl] *n* Staffelei *f*.

**easily** ['iːzɪlɪ] *adv* leicht. **he is** ~ **the best** er ist mit Abstand der beste; **it's** ~ **25 miles** es sind gut und gerne 25 Meilen.

**easiness** ['iːzɪnɪs] *n* Leichtigkeit *f*.

**east** [iːst] **1** *n* **(a)** Osten *m*. **in/to the** ~ im Osten/nach Osten; **from the** ~ von Osten; **to the** ~ **of** östlich von. **(b)** *(Geog, Pol)* **the E**~ der Osten; **from the E**~ aus dem Osten. **2** *adv* nach Osten, ostwärts. **it faces** ~ es geht nach Osten; ~ **of** östlich von. **3** *adj* östlich, Ost-. ~ **wind** Ostwind *m*; **E**~ **Africa** Ostafrika *nt*; **the E**~ **End** der (Londoner) Osten; **E**~ **Berlin** Ostberlin *nt*.

**eastbound** ['iːstbaʊnd] *adj traffic etc* in Richtung Osten.

**Easter** ['iːstər] **1** *n* Ostern *nt*. **at** ~ an *or* zu Ostern. **2** *adj attr week, egg, holidays etc* Oster-. ~ **Monday** Ostermontag *m*; ~ **Sunday,** ~ **Day** Ostersonntag *m*; ~ **Island** Osterinsel *f*.

**easterly** ['iːstəlɪ] *adj* östlich, Ost-.

**eastern** ['iːstən] *adj* Ost-, östlich; *attitude* orientalisch. **the** ~ **bloc** *(Hist)* der Ostblock; **E**~ **Europe** Osteuropa *nt*.

**east: E**~ **German** *adj* ostdeutsch; *(Hist: GDR)* DDR-; **E**~ **Germany** *n (Hist)* die DDR; ~**ward(s)** *adv* ostwärts, nach Osten.

**easy** ['iːzɪ] **1** *adj (+er)* **(a)** leicht. **it's** ~ **for you to talk** du hast gut reden; **he was an** ~ **winner** er hat mühelos gewonnen; **he is** ~ **to get on with** mit ihm kann man gut auskommen; ~ **money** leicht verdientes Geld. **(b)** *(free from discomfort etc)* bequem, leicht; *manners, movement* ungezwungen; *style* flüssig. **in** ~ **stages** in bequemen Etappen; **on** ~ **terms** *(Comm)* zu günstigen Bedingungen; **I'm** ~ *(col)* mir ist alles recht. **2** *adv* **(that's) easier said than done** (das) ist leichter gesagt als getan; ~**!**, **it** ~ **does it!** immer sachte!; **to take things** *or* **it** ~ *(healthwise)* sich schonen; **take it** ~**!** *(don't worry)* nimm's nicht so schwer; *(don't get carried away, don't rush)* immer mit der Ruhe!; **to go** ~ **on sth** sparsam mit etw umgehen; **to go** ~ **on sb** nicht zu hart mit jdm sein; **take it** ~**!** *(Mil)* rührt euch!

**easy:** ~ **chair** *n* Sessel *m*; ~ **come** ~ **go 1** *interj* wie gewonnen, so zerronnen *(Prov)*; **2** *adj* ~**-come**~**-go** unbekümmert; ~**-going** *adj (not anxious)* gelassen; *(lax)* lässig.

**eat** [iːt] *(vb: pret* **ate***, ptp* **eaten***) vti (person)* essen; *(animal)* fressen. **to** ~ **one's breakfast** frühstücken; **he's** ~**ing us out of house and home** *(col)* er frißt uns noch die Haare vom Kopf *(col)*; **to** ~ **one's words** alles zurücknehmen; **he won't** ~ **you** *(col)* er wird dich schon nicht fressen *(col)*; **what's** ~**ing you?** *(col)* was hast du denn?
►**eat away** *vt sep (sea)* auswaschen; *(acid)* zerfressen.
►**eat into** *vi +prep obj metal* anfressen; *capital* angreifen.
►**eat out 1** *vi* essen gehen. **2** *vt sep* **to** ~ **one's heart** ~ Trübsal blasen.
►**eat up 1** *vt sep* **(a)** aufessen; *(animal)* auffressen. **(b)** *(fig: use up)* verbrauchen. **this car** ~**s** ~ **the miles** der Wagen gibt ganz schön was her *(col)*. **2** *vi* aufessen.

**eatable** ['iːtəbl] *adj* eßbar, genießbar.

**eaten** ['iːtn] *ptp of* **eat**.

**eater** ['iːtər] *n* Esser(in *f*) *m*.

**eating:** ~ **apple** *n* Eßapfel *m*; ~ **place** *n* Eßlokal *nt*.

**eau de Cologne** ['əʊdəkə'ləʊn] *n* Kölnisch Wasser *nt*.

**eaves** [iːvz] *npl* Dachvorsprung *m*.

**eavesdrop** ['iːvzdrɒp] *vi (heimlich)* lauschen. **to** ~ **on a conversation** ein Gespräch belauschen.

**ebb** [eb] **1** *n (also* ~**tide)* Ebbe *f*. ~ **and flow** Ebbe und Flut *f*; *(fig)* Auf und Ab *nt*; **at a low** ~ *(fig)* in einem Tief. **2** *vi* **(a)** *(tide)* zurückgehen. **to** ~ **and flow** *(lit, fig)* kommen und gehen. **(b)** *(fig: also* ~ **away)** *(enthusiasm etc)* verebben.

**ebony** ['ebənɪ] *n* Ebenholz *nt*.

**ebullient** [ɪ'bʌlɪənt] *adj* überschwenglich; *mood* übersprudelnd.

**EC** = **European Community** EG *f*. ~ **country** EG-Staat *m*.

**eccentric** [ɪk'sentrɪk] **1** *adj* exzentrisch. **2** *n* Exzentriker(in *f*) *m*.

**eccentricity** [ˌeksən'trɪsɪtɪ] *n* Exzentrizität *f*.

**ecclesiastical** [ɪˌkliːzɪ'æstɪkəl] *adj* kirchlich.

**ECG** = **electrocardiogram** EKG *nt*.

**echo** ['ekəʊ] **1** *n* Echo *nt*. **2** *vt sound* zurückwerfen; *(fig)* wiedergeben. **3** *vi* widerhallen *(with* von*)*; *(room)* hallen. **it** ~**es in here** hier ist ein Echo.

**éclair** [eɪ'kleər] *n* Eclair *nt*, Liebesknochen *m*.

**eclipse** [ɪ'klɪps] **1** *n (Astron)* ~ **of the sun/moon** Sonnen-/Mondfinsternis *f*. **2** *vt (Astron)* verfinstern; *(fig)* in den Schatten stellen.

**ECM** *(US)* = **European Common Market**.

**ecological** [ˌiːkəʊ'lɒdʒɪkəl] *adj* ökologisch. ~ **damage** Umweltbelastung *f*; ~ **disaster** Umweltkatastrophe *f*.

**ecologically** [ˌiːkəʊ'lɒdʒɪkəlɪ] *adv* ökologisch. ~ **harmful** umweltschädlich.

**ecologist** [ɪ'kɒlədʒɪst] *n* Ökologe *m*, Ökologin *f*.

**ecology** [ɪ'kɒlədʒɪ] *n* Ökologie *f*.

**economic** [ˌiːkə'nɒmɪk] *adj* wirtschaftlich, ökonomisch; *aid, crisis, policy, development, system, miracle* Wirtschafts-. ~ **upturn/downturn** Konjunkturaufschwung *m*/Konjunkturabschwung *m*.

**economical** [ˌiːkə'nɒmɪkəl] *adj* wirtschaftlich, ökonomisch; *person* sparsam. **to be** ~ **with sth** *(also fig)* mit etw sparsam umgehen; **to be** ~ **(to run)** *(car)* wirtschaftlich sein.

**economically** [ˌiːkə'nɒmɪkəlɪ] *adv* wirtschaftlich; *(thriftily)* sparsam.

**economics** [ˌiːkə'nɒmɪks] *n* **(a)** *with sing or pl vb* Volkswirtschaft *f*; *(management studies)* Betriebswirtschaft *f*. **(b)** *pl (economic aspect)* Wirtschaftlichkeit *f*. **the** ~ **of the situation** die wirtschaftliche

**efficient**

Seite der Situation.

**economist** [ɪ'kɒnəmɪst] n see **economics** Volkswirt(in f); Betriebswirt(in f) m.

**economize** [ɪ'kɒnəmaɪz] vi sparen.
►**economize on** vi +prep obj sparen.

**economy** [ɪ'kɒnəmɪ] n **(a)** (system) Wirtschaft f no pl; (from a monetary aspect) Konjunktur f. **(b)** (in time, money) Einsparung f; (measure) Sparmaßnahme f. **a false ~** falsche Sparsamkeit; **economies of scale** (Comm) Einsparungen pl durch erhöhte Produktion. **(c)** (thrift) Sparsamkeit f. **~ of effort** geringer Kräfteaufwand.

**economy: ~ class** n Economyklasse f; **~ drive** n Sparmaßnahmen pl; **~ size** n Sparpackung f.

**ecosystem** ['iːkəʊsɪstəm] n Ökosystem nt.

**ecstasy** ['ekstəsɪ] n Ekstase f. **to go into ecstasies over sth** über etw (acc) in Verzückung geraten.

**ecstatic** [eks'tætɪk] adj ekstatisch, verzückt.

**ECU, ecu** ['eɪkjuː] = **European Currency Unit** Ecu m.

**Ecuador** ['ekwədɔːr] n Ecuador, Ekuador nt.

**ecumenical** [ˌiːkjʊ'menɪkəl] adj ökumenisch.

**eczema** ['eksɪmə] n (Haut)ausschlag m.

**ed** = **(a) edition** Ausg. **(b) edited** herausg.

**Ed** = **editor** Herausg.

**eddy** ['edɪ] **1** n Wirbel m. **2** vi wirbeln.

**edge** [edʒ] **1** n **(a)** (of knife) Schneide f. **to take the ~ off sth** (fig) sensation etw (dat) die Wirkung nehmen; **that took the ~ off my appetite** das nahm mir erst einmal den Hunger; **the noise sets my teeth on ~** das Geräusch geht mir durch und durch; **to be on ~** nervös sein; **to have the ~ on sb/sth** jdm/etw (gerade noch) überlegen sein. **(b)** (outer limit) Rand m; (of cloth, table, of brick) Kante f; (of lake, river also) Ufer nt.
**2** vt **(a)** (put a border on) besetzen, einfassen. **(b) to ~ one's way towards sth** (slowly) sich allmählich auf etw (acc) zubewegen; (carefully) sich vorsichtig auf etw (acc) zubewegen; **she ~d her way through the crowd** sie schlängelte sich durch die Menge.
**3** vi sich schieben. **to ~ away from sb/sth** sich allmählich immer weiter von jdm/etw entfernen; **to ~ up to sb** sich an jdn heranmachen; **he ~d past me** er schob sich an mir vorbei.

**edgeways** ['edʒweɪz] adv mit der Schmalseite voran. **I couldn't get a word in ~** ich bin überhaupt nicht zu Wort gekommen.

**edginess** ['edʒɪnɪs] n Nervosität f.

**edging** ['edʒɪŋ] n Borte, Einfassung f.

**edgy** ['edʒɪ] adj (+er) person nervös.

**edible** ['edɪbl] adj eßbar, genießbar.

**edict** ['iːdɪkt] n Erlaß m.

**edifice** ['edɪfɪs] n Gebäude nt.

**edify** ['edɪfaɪ] vt erbauen.

**edifying** ['edɪfaɪɪŋ] adj erbaulich.

**Edinburgh** ['edɪnbərə] n Edinburg(h) nt.

**edit** ['edɪt] vt series, newspaper, magazine herausgeben; book, text redigieren; film, tape schneiden.

**edition** [ɪ'dɪʃən] n Ausgabe f; (printing) Auflage f.

**editor** [edɪtər] n Herausgeber(in f) m; (publisher's) (Verlags)lektor(in f) m; (of newspaper) Chefredakteur(in f) m; (Film) Cutter(in f) m. **political/sports ~** politischer Redakteur/Sportredakteur m.

**editorial** [edɪ'tɔːrɪəl] **1** adj redaktionell, Redaktions-. **~ assistant** Redaktionsassistent(in f) m; **~ office** Redaktion f; (Publishing also) (Verlags)lektorat nt; **~ staff** Redaktion(sangestellte pl) f. **2** n Leitartikel m.

**EDP** = **electronic data processing** EDV f.

**EDT** (US) = **Eastern Daylight Time** Sommerzeit im Osten der USA und Kanadas.

**educate** ['edjʊkeɪt] vt erziehen; the mind schulen; one's tastes (aus)bilden. **he was ~d at Eton** er ist in Eton zur Schule gegangen.

**educated** ['edjʊkeɪtɪd] adj gebildet. **~ guess** wohlbegründete Vermutung.

**education** [ˌedjʊ'keɪʃən] n Erziehung f; (studies, training) Ausbildung f; (knowledge, culture) Bildung f. **College of E~** Pädagogische Hochschule; (for graduates) Studienseminar nt; **~ authority** Schulbehörde f; **(school) ~ is free** die Schulausbildung ist kostenlos.

**educational** [edjʊ'keɪʃənl] adj pädagogisch; films, games also Lehr-; experience lehrreich. **~ method** Erziehungsmethode f; **~ publisher** Schulbuchverlag m; **~ system** Erziehungswesen nt.

**educationalist** [ˌedjʊ'keɪʃnəlɪst] n Pädagoge m, Pädagogin f.

**educator** ['edjʊkeɪtər] n Pädagoge, Erzieher m.

**Edwardian** [ed'wɔːdɪən] adj aus der Zeit Eduards VII.

**EEC** = **European Economic Community** EWG f.

**EEG** = **electroencephalogram** EEG nt.

**eel** [iːl] n Aal m.

**EENT** (US) = **eye, ear, nose and throat** Augen und HNO.

**eerie** ['ɪərɪ] adj (+er) unheimlich.

**EET** = **Eastern European Time** OEZ f.

**efface** [ɪ'feɪs] vt auslöschen.

**effect** [ɪ'fekt] **1** n **(a)** (result) Wirkung f, Effekt m; (repercussion) Auswirkung f. **the ~ of this is that ...** das hat zur Folge, daß ...; **to feel the ~s of an accident/of drink** die Folgen eines Unfalls/des Trinkens spüren; **to no ~** ohne Erfolg; **to have an ~ on sb/sth** eine Wirkung auf jdn/etw haben; **to take ~** (drug) wirken. **(b)** (impression) Wirkung f, Effekt m. **to create an ~** eine Wirkung or einen Effekt erzielen; **it's all done solely for ~** das wird alles bloß des Effekts wegen getan. **(c)** (meaning) **an announcement to the ~ that ...** eine Erklärung des Inhalts, daß ...; **... or words to that ~** ... oder etwas in diesem Sinne. **(d) ~s** pl (property) Effekten pl; **personal ~s** persönliches Eigentum. **(e) in ~** effektiv. **(f)** (of laws) **to be in ~** gültig or in Kraft sein; **to come into ~** in Kraft treten; **to put sth into ~** etw in Kraft setzen.
**2** vt bewirken, herbeiführen; (form) sale tätigen.

**effective** [ɪ'fektɪv] adj **(a)** wirksam, effektiv. **to become ~** (law) in Kraft treten; (drug) wirken. **(b)** (creating impression) wirkungsvoll, effektvoll. **(c)** (real) contribution tatsächlich; profit also effektiv.

**effectively** [ɪ'fektɪvlɪ] adv see adj **(a)** wirksam, effektiv. **(b)** wirkungsvoll. **(c)** (in effect) effektiv.

**effectiveness** [ɪ'fektɪvnɪs] n see adj **(a)** Wirksamkeit f. **(b)** Wirkung f, Effekt m.

**effectual** [ɪ'fektjʊəl] adj wirksam.

**effeminate** [ɪ'femɪnɪt] adj weibisch.

**effervesce** [efə'ves] vi sprudeln.

**effervescence** [efə'vesns] n (lit) Sprudeln nt; (fig) überschäumendes Temperament.

**effervescent** [ˌefə'vesnt] adj sprudelnd; (fig) überschäumend.

**effete** [ɪ'fiːt] adj schwach; person saft- und kraftlos.

**efficacious** [efɪ'keɪʃəs] adj wirksam.

**efficacy** ['efɪkəsɪ] n Wirksamkeit f.

**efficiency** [ɪ'fɪʃənsɪ] n (of person) Tüchtigkeit f; (of machine, factory) Leistungsfähigkeit f; (of method, organization) Rationalität, Effizienz (geh) f.

**efficient** [ɪ'fɪʃənt] adj person fähig; worker, secretary etc also tüchtig; machine, factory, company leistungsfähig; method, organization rationell. **to be ~ at sth/at doing sth** etw gut verstehen/es gut verstehen, etw zu tun; **the ~ working of a machine** das gute Funktionieren einer Maschine.

**efficiently** [ɪ'fɪʃəntlɪ] *adj* gut. **they handled the sale ~** sie haben den Verkauf gekonnt abgewickelt.

**effigy** ['efɪdʒɪ] *n* Bildnis *nt*.

**effluent** ['efluənt] *n (sewage)* Abwasser *nt*.

**effort** ['efət] *n* **(a)** *(attempt)* Bemühung *f; (strain, hard work)* Anstrengung, Mühe *f*. **their ~s to reach an agreement** ihre Bemühungen um eine Einigung; **to make an ~ to do sth** sich bemühen *or* anstrengen, etw zu tun; **to make every possible ~** to do sth sich *(dat)* die größte Mühe geben, etw zu tun; **he made no ~ to be polite** er gab sich *(dat)* keine Mühe, höflich zu sein; **it's an ~** es kostet einige Mühe; **if it's not too much of an ~ for you** *(iro)* wenn es dir nicht zu viel Mühe macht; **come on, make an ~** komm, streng dich ein bißchen an. **(b)** *(col)* **it was a poor ~** das war eine schwache Leistung; **his first ~ at making a film** sein erster Versuch, einen Film zu drehen.

**effortless** ['efətlɪs] *adj* mühelos; *style* flüssig.

**effortlessly** ['efətlɪslɪ] *adv* mühelos.

**effortlessness** ['efətlɪsnɪs] *n* Mühelosigkeit *f; (of style)* Flüssigkeit *f*.

**effrontery** [ɪ'frʌntərɪ] *n* Unverschämtheit *f*.

**effusive** *adj*, **~ly** *adv* [ɪ'fjuːsɪv, -lɪ] überschwenglich.

**effusiveness** [ɪ'fjuːsɪvnɪs] *n* Überschwenglichkeit *f*.

**EFL** = **English as a foreign language** Englisch als Fremdsprache.

**e.g., eg** = **for example** z.B.

**egalitarian** [ɪˌgælɪ'tɛərɪən] *adj* egalitär *(geh)*; *principle also* Gleichheits-.

**egg** [eg] *n* Ei *nt*. **to put all one's ~s in one basket** *(fig)* alles auf eine Karte setzen; **to have ~ all over one's face** *(fig col)* dumm dastehen *(col)*.

▶**egg on** *vt sep* anstacheln.

**egg: ~-cup** *n* Eierbecher *m; ~head n (pej col)* Intellektuelle(r) *mf*, Eierkopf *m (col); ~-plant n* Aubergine *f; ~shell n* Eierschale *f; ~-spoon n* Eierlöffel *m; ~ timer n* Eieruhr *f; ~ whisk n* Schneebesen *m; ~-white n* Eiweiß *nt; ~ yolk n* Eidotter *m*, Eigelb *nt*. ·

**ego** ['iːgəʊ] *n (Psych)* Ego, Ich *nt; (col)* Selbstbewußtsein *nt; (conceit)* Einbildung *f*. **this will boost his ~** das wird ihm Auftrieb geben.

**egocentric(al)** [egəʊ'sentrɪk(əl)] *adj* egozentrisch.

**egoism** ['egəʊɪzəm] *n* Egoismus *m*, Selbstsucht *f*.

**egotism** ['egəʊtɪzəm] *n* Egotismus *m*.

**egotist** ['egəʊtɪst] *n* Egotist *m*.

**egotistic(al)** [ˌegəʊ'tɪstɪk(əl)] *adj* ichbezogen.

**ego-trip** ['iːgəʊtrɪp] *n (col)* Egotrip *m (col)*. **he's on one of his ~s** er gibt wieder so an.

**Egypt** ['iːdʒɪpt] *n* Ägypten *nt*.

**Egyptian** [ɪ'dʒɪpʃən] **1** *adj* ägyptisch. **2** *n* **(a)** Ägypter(in *f*) *m*. **(b)** *(language)* Ägyptisch *nt*.

**eiderdown** ['aɪdədaʊn] *n (quilt)* Daunendecke *f*.

**eight** [eɪt] **1** *adj* acht. **2** *n* Acht *f; see* **six**.

**eighteen** ['eɪ'tiːn] *adj* achtzehn.

**eighteenth** ['eɪ'tiːnθ] *adj* achtzehnte(r, s); *see* **sixteenth**.

**eighth** [eɪtθ] **1** *adj* achte(r, s). **~ note** *(US Mus)* Achtelnote *f*. **2** *n (fraction)* Achtel *nt; (of series)* Achte(r,s); *see* **sixth**.

**eightieth** ['eɪtɪɪθ] *adj* achtzigste(r, s); *see* **sixtieth**.

**eighty** ['eɪtɪ] *adj* achtzig; *see* **sixty**.

**Eire** ['ɛərə] *n* Irland *nt*.

**either** ['aɪðər] **1** *adj, pron* **(a)** *(one or other)* eine(r, s) (von beiden). **there are two boxes, take ~** hier sind zwei Schachteln, nimm eine davon. **(b)** *(each, both)* jede(r, s), beide *pl*. **~ day would suit me** beide Tage passen mir; **which bus will you take?** — **~**

**(will do)** welchen Bus wollen Sie nehmen? — das ist egal; **on ~ side of the street** auf beiden Seiten der Straße; **it wasn't in ~ (box)** es war in keiner der beiden (Kisten); **~ way we lose out** wir machen auf jeden Fall einen Verlust.

**2** *adv, conj* **(a)** *(after neg statement)* auch nicht. **he can't act ~** schauspielern kann er auch nicht; **I haven't ~** ich auch nicht. **(b)** **~ ... or** entweder ... oder; *(after a negative)* weder ... noch; **~ be quiet or go out!** entweder bist du ruhig oder du gehst!; **I have never been to Paris, nor to Rome ~** ich bin bisher weder in Paris noch in Rom gewesen.

**ejaculate** [ɪ'dʒækjʊleɪt] *vi* aufschreien; *(Physiol)* ejakulieren.

**ejaculation** [ɪˌdʒækjʊ'leɪʃən] *n (cry)* Ausruf *m; (Physiol)* Ejakulation *f*, Samenerguß *m*.

**eject** [ɪ'dʒekt] **1** *vt* heckler, tenant hinauswerfen; *cartridge, cassette* auswerfen. **2** *vi (pilot)* den Schleudersitz betätigen.

**ejection** [ɪ'dʒekʃən] *n* Hinauswurf *m; (of cartridge, cassette)* Auswerfen *nt*.

**ejector seat** [ɪ'dʒektəˌsiːt] *n (Aviat)* Schleudersitz *m*.

▶**eke out** ['iːkaʊt] *vt sep* strecken. **to ~ ~ a living** sich recht und schlecht durchschlagen.

**EKG** *(US)* = **electrocardiogram** EKG.

**el** [el] *(US col)* = **elevated railroad**.

**elaborate** [ɪ'læbərɪt] **1** *adj design, hairstyle, pattern, drawing* kunstvoll; *style (of writing) also* ausführlich, detailliert; *plan* ausgeklügelt; *preparations* kompliziert. **an ~ meal** ein großes Menü. **2** [ɪ'læbəreɪt] *vt (work out)* ausarbeiten; *(describe)* ausführen. **3** [ɪ'læbəreɪt] *vi* **could you ~ (on that)?** könnten Sie das etwas näher ausführen?

**elaborately** [ɪ'læbərɪtlɪ] *adv* kunstvoll; *detailed* ausführlich.

**elaboration** [ɪˌlæbə'reɪʃən] *n* Ausarbeitung *f*.

**elapse** [ɪ'læps] *vi* vergehen, verstreichen.

**elastic** [ɪ'læstɪk] **1** *adj (lit, fig)* elastisch. **~ band** *(Brit)* Gummiband *nt*. **2** *n* Gummi(band) *nt* *m*.

**elasticated** [ɪ'læstɪkeɪtɪd] *adj* Elastik-.

**elasticity** [ˌiːlæs'tɪsɪtɪ] *n* Elastizität *f*.

**elated** [ɪ'leɪtɪd] *adj* begeistert.

**elation** [ɪ'leɪʃən] *n* Begeisterung *f (at über +acc)*.

**elbow** ['elbəʊ] **1** *n* Ellbogen *m*. **out at the ~s** an den Ellbogen durchgewetzt. **2** *vt* **he ~ed his way through the crowd** er boxte sich durch die Menge; **to ~ sb aside** jdn beiseite stoßen.

**elbow: ~-grease** *n (col)* Muskelkraft *f; ~-room n (col: lit, fig)* Ellbogenfreiheit *f (col)*.

**elder¹** ['eldər] **1** *adj attr comp of* **old** *brother, sister* ältere(r, s). **~ statesman** erfahrener Staatsmann. **2** *n* **(a) respect your ~s and betters** du mußt Respekt vor Älteren haben. **(b)** *(of tribe, Church)* Älteste(r) *m*.

**elder²** ['eldər] *n (Bot)* Holunder *m*.

**elderberry** ['eldəˌberɪ] *n* Holunderbeere *f*.

**elderly** ['eldəlɪ] *adj* ältlich, ältere(r, s) *attr*.

**eldest** ['eldɪst] *adj attr superl of* **old** älteste(r, s).

**elect** [ɪ'lekt] **1** *vt* **(a)** wählen. **he was ~ed chairman** er wurde zum Vorsitzenden gewählt. **(b)** *(choose)* **to ~ to do sth** sich dafür entscheiden, etw zu tun. **2** *adj* **the president ~** der designierte Präsident.

**election** [ɪ'lekʃən] *n* Wahl *f*. **~ campaign** Wahlkampf *m; ~ manifesto** Wahlprogramm *nt*.

**electioneering** [ɪˌlekʃə'nɪərɪŋ] *n* Wahlkampf *m; (propaganda)* Wahlpropaganda *f*.

**elective** [ɪ'lektɪv] **1** *adj* Wahl-; *(US: optional)* wahlfrei. **2** *n (US Sch)* Wahlfach *nt*.

**elector** [ɪ'lektər] *n* Wähler(in *f*) *m*.

**electoral** [ɪ'lektərəl] *adj* Wahl-. **~ college** Wahlmännergremium *nt; ~ roll** Wählerverzeichnis *nt*.

**electorate** [ɪ'lektərɪt] *n* Wähler *pl*, Wählerschaft *f.*

**electric** [ɪ'lektrɪk] *adj* elektrisch; *car, vehicle etc* Elektro-. **the atmosphere was** ~ es herrschte Hochspannung; **the effect was** ~ *(col)* das hatte eine elektrisierende Wirkung.

**electrical** [ɪ'lektrɪkəl] *adj* Elektro-, elektrisch. ~ **engineer** Elektrotechniker *m;* ~ **engineering** Elektrotechnik *f.*

**electrically** [ɪ'lektrɪkəlɪ] *adv* elektrisch.

**electric:** ~ **blanket** *n* Heizdecke *f;* ~ **chair** *n* elektrischer Stuhl; ~ **cooker** *n* Elektroherd *m;* ~ **current** *n* elektrischer Strom; ~ **fire** *n* elektrisches Heizgerät.

**electrician** [ɪlek'trɪʃən] *n* Elektriker *m.*

**electricity** [ɪlek'trɪsɪtɪ] *n* Elektrizität *f;* *(electric power for use)* Strom *m.* **to turn off the** ~ den Strom abschalten.

**electricity:** ~ **bill** *n* Stromrechnung *f;* ~ **board** *n* *(Brit)* Elektrizitätswerk *nt;* ~ **meter** *n* Stromzähler *m.*

**electric:** ~ **light** *n* elektrisches Licht; ~ **locomotive** *n* Elektrolok *f;* ~ **motor** *n* Elektromotor *m.*

**electrics** [ɪ'lektrɪks] *npl* Elektrik *f.*

**electric:** ~ **shock** *n* elektrischer Schlag; ~ **shock treatment** (Elektro)schocktherapie *f.*

**electrification** [ɪ,lektrɪfɪ'keɪʃən] *n* Elektrifizierung *f.*

**electrify** [ɪ'lektrɪfaɪ] *vt* **(a)** *(Rail)* elektrifizieren. **(b)** *(charge with electricity)* unter Strom setzen. **(c)** *(fig)* elektrisieren.

**electrifying** [ɪ'lektrɪfaɪɪŋ] *adj* *(fig)* elektrisierend.

**electrocardiogram** [ɪ,lektrəʊ'kɑːdɪəʊ,græm] *n* Elektrokardiogramm *nt.*

**electrocute** [ɪ'lektrəkjuːt] *vt* durch einen (Strom)schlag töten; *(execute)* auf dem elektrischen Stuhl hinrichten.

**electrocution** [ɪ,lektrə'kjuːʃən] *n* Tötung *f* durch Stromschlag; *(execution)* Hinrichtung *f* auf dem elektrischen Stuhl.

**electrode** [ɪ'lektrəʊd] *n* Elektrode *f.*

**electrolysis** [ɪlek'trɒlɪsɪs] *n* Elektrolyse *f.*

**electromagnetic** [ɪ'lektrəʊmæg'netɪk] *adj* elektromagnetisch.

**electron** [ɪ'lektrɒn] *n* Elektron *nt.* ~ **microscope** Elektronenmikroskop *nt.*

**electronic** [ɪlek'trɒnɪk] *adj* elektronisch. ~ **banking** elektronischer Geldverkehr; ~ **data processing** elektronische Datenverarbeitung; ~ **flash (unit)** *(Phot)* Elektronenblitz(gerät *nt*) *m;* ~ **mail** elektronische Post; ~ **mailbox** elektronischer Briefkasten.

**electronics** [ɪlek'trɒnɪks] *n* Elektronik *f.*

**electroplated** [ɪ'lektrəʊpleɪtɪd] *adj* (galvanisch) versilbert/verchromt *etc.*

**elegance** [ˈelɪgəns] *n* Eleganz *f.*

**elegant** *adj,* ~**ly** *adv* [ˈelɪgənt, -lɪ] elegant.

**elegiac** [ˌelɪ'dʒaɪək] *adj* elegisch.

**elegy** [ˈelɪdʒɪ] *n* Elegie *f.*

**element** [ˈelɪmənt] *n* *(also Elec)* Element *nt;* *(usu pl: of a subject also)* Grundbegriff *m.* **the** ~ **of chance** das Zufallselement; **there's an** ~ **of danger** es besteht eine gewisse Gefahr dabei; **to be in one's** ~ in seinem Element sein; **to be out of one's** ~ *(with people)* sich fehl am Platz fühlen; *(with subject)* sich nicht auskennen.

**elementary** [ˌelɪ'mentərɪ] *adj* **(a)** *(simple)* einfach, elementar. **(b)** *(basic)* elementar, Grund-. ~ **course** Grundkurs *m.*

**elephant** [ˈelɪfənt] *n* Elefant *m.*

**elevate** [ˈelɪveɪt] *vt* **(a)** heben. **(b)** **elevating reading** erbauliche Lektüre.

**elevated** [ˈelɪveɪtɪd] *adj* **(a)** *position* hoch(liegend), höher; *platform* erhöht. ~ **railway** *or* *(US)* **railroad**

Hochbahn *f.* **(b)** *(fig) position, style* gehoben; *thoughts* erhaben.

**elevation** [ˌelɪ'veɪʃən] *n* **(a)** *(lit)* Hebung *f.* **(b)** *(of thought)* Erhabenheit *f;* *(of position, style)* Gehobenheit *f.* **(c)** *(above sea level)* Höhe *f* über dem Meeresspiegel; *(hill)* Anhöhe *f.* **(d)** *(Archit: drawing)* Aufriß *m.* **front** ~ Frontansicht *f.*

**elevator** [ˈelɪveɪtər] *n* *(US)* Fahrstuhl, Aufzug *m.*

**eleven** [ɪ'levn] **1** *n* **(a)** *(number)* Elf *f.* **(b)** *(Sport)* Elf *f.* **the second** ~ die zweite Mannschaft. **2** *adj* elf; *see* **six.**

**elevenses** [ɪ'levnzɪz] *n sing or pl (Brit)* zweites Frühstück.

**eleventh** [ɪ'levnθ] *adj* elfte(r, s). **at the** ~ **hour** *(fig)* in letzter Minute; *see* **sixth.**

**elf** [elf] *n, pl* **elves** Elf *m,* Elfe *f; (mischievous)* Kobold *m.*

**elicit** [ɪ'lɪsɪt] *vt* entlocken *(from sb jdm).*

**eligibility** [ˌelɪdʒə'bɪlɪtɪ] *n* Berechtigung *f.* **graded in order of** ~ nach Eignung geordnet.

**eligible** [ˈelɪdʒəbl] *adj* in Frage kommend; *(for competition etc also)* teilnahmeberechtigt; *(for grants etc also)* berechtigt; *(for membership)* aufnahmeberechtigt. **an** ~ **bachelor** ein begehrter Junggeselle.

**eliminate** [ɪ'lɪmɪneɪt] *vt* **(a)** ausschließen; *competitor* ausschalten. **our team was** ~**d in the second round** unsere Mannschaft schied in der zweiten Runde aus. **(b)** *(kill)* ausschalten, eliminieren.

**elimination** [ɪ,lɪmɪ'neɪʃən] *n see vt* **(a)** Ausschluß *m;* Ausschaltung *f.* **by (a) process of** ~ durch negative Auslese. **(b)** Ausschaltung, Eliminierung *f.*

**élite** [eɪ'liːt] *n* Elite *f.*

**élitism** [eɪ'liːtɪzəm] *n* Elitedenken *nt.*

**élitist** [eɪ'liːtɪst] *adj* elitär.

**elixir** [ɪ'lɪksər] *n* Elixier *nt,* Auszug *m.*

**Elizabethan** [ɪ,lɪzə'biːθən] *adj* elisabethanisch.

**elk** [elk] *n* Elch *m.*

**ellipse** [ɪ'lɪps] *n* Ellipse *f.*

**elliptic(al)** [ɪ'lɪptɪk(əl)] *adj* elliptisch.

**elm** [elm] *n* Ulme *f.*

**elocution** [ˌelə'kjuːʃən] *n* Sprechtechnik *f.* ~ **classes** Sprecherziehung *f.*

**elongate** [ˈiːlɒŋgeɪt] *vt* verlängern.

**elope** [ɪ'ləʊp] *vi* durchbrennen *(col).*

**elopement** [ɪ'ləʊpmənt] *n* Durchbrennen *nt (col).*

**eloquence** [ˈeləkwəns] *n see adj* Wortgewandtheit *f;* Wohlgesetztheit *f;* Beredtheit *f.*

**eloquent** [ˈeləkwənt] *adj* wortgewandt; *speech* wohlgesetzt; *(fig) gesture* beredt, vielsagend.

**else** [els] *adv* **(a)** *(after pron)* andere(r, s). **anybody** ~? *(in addition)* sonst (noch) jemand?; **anybody** ~ **would have done it** jeder andere hätte es gemacht; **somebody** ~ *(in addition)* sonst jemand; *(somebody different)* jemand anders; **I don't know anybody** ~ ich kenne sonst niemanden; **have you anything** ~? haben Sie sonst noch etwas?; **something** ~ sonst etwas; etwas anderes; **anywhere** ~ sonstwo; **but they haven't got anywhere** ~ to go aber sie können sonst nirgendwo hingehen; **somewhere** ~ woanders, anderswo; *(with motion)* woandershin, anderswohin.

**(b)** *(after pron, neg)* **nobody** ~, **no one** ~ sonst niemand, niemand anders; **nobody** ~ **understood** niemand anders hat es verstanden; **nothing** ~ sonst nichts, nichts anderes; **nothing** ~, **thank you** danke, nichts weiter; **nowhere** ~ sonst nirgends, nirgendwo anders; **there's nothing** ~ **for it but to go** da hilft nichts, ich muß gehen.

**(c)** *(after interrog)* **where** ~? wo sonst?; **who** ~? wer sonst?; **what** ~? was sonst?; **what** ~ **could I do?** was konnte ich sonst tun?

**(d)** *(adv of quantity)* **and much** ~ und vieles ande-

re; **there is little ~ to be done** da bleibt nicht viel zu tun übrig.
**(e)** *(otherwise, if not)* sonst, andernfalls. **do it now (or) ~ you'll be punished** tu es jetzt oder es setzt Strafe; **you better had, or ~ ...!** mach das bloß, sonst ...!

**elsewhere** [,els'wɛəʳ] *adv* woanders, anderswo; *(to another place)* woandershin, anderswohin. **in Wales and ~** unter anderem in Wales.

**ELT** = **English Language Teaching** englischer Sprachunterricht.

**elucidate** [ɪ'luːsɪdeɪt] *vt text* erklären; *mystery* aufklären.

**elucidation** [ɪ,luːsɪ'deɪʃən] *n see vt* Erklärung *f*; Aufklärung *f*.

**elude** [ɪ'luːd] *vt observation, justice* sich entziehen *(+dat)*; *question* ausweichen *(+dat)*; *police, enemy* entkommen *(+dat)*. **success has ~d him** der Erfolg wollte sich nicht einstellen.

**elusive** [ɪ'luːsɪv] *adj* schwer faßbar; *concept, meaning also* schwer definierbar; *thoughts, memory* flüchtig; *happiness* unerreichbar; *answer* ausweichend; *person* schwer zu erreichen; *animal, criminal* schwer zu fangen.

**elves** [elvz] *pl of* **elf**.

**emaciated** [ɪ'meɪsɪeɪtɪd] *adj* ausgezehrt.

**emanate** ['eməneɪt] *vi* ausgehen *(from* von*)*; *(light also)* ausstrahlen *(from* von*)*; *(documents, instructions etc)* stammen *(from* aus*)*.

**emancipate** [ɪ'mænsɪpeɪt] *vt (lit, fig)* emanzipieren.

**emancipated** [ɪ'mænsɪpeɪtɪd] *adj (lit, fig)* emanzipiert.

**emancipation** [ɪ,mænsɪ'peɪʃən] *n (lit, fig)* Emanzipation *f*.

**embalm** [ɪm'bɑːm] *vt corpse* einbalsamieren.

**embankment** [ɪm'bæŋkmənt] *n* Böschung *f*; *(for railway)* Bahndamm *m*; *(holding back water)* Deich *m*; *(road beside a river)* Uferstraße *f*.

**embargo** [ɪm'bɑːgəʊ] *n, pl* **-es** Embargo *nt*. **to put an ~ on sth** ein Embargo über etw *(acc)* verhängen.

**embark** [ɪm'bɑːk] **1** *vt* einschiffen. **2** *vi* **(a)** *(Naut)* sich einschiffen; *(troops)* eingeschifft werden. **(b)** *(fig)* **to ~ up(on) sth** mit etw anfangen.

**embarkation** [,embɑː'keɪʃən] *n* Einschiffung *f*. **~ papers** Bordpapiere *pl*.

**embarrass** [ɪm'bærəs] *vt* in Verlegenheit bringen; *(generosity etc also)* beschämen. **I feel so ~ed about it** das ist mir so peinlich; **she was ~ed by the question** die Frage war ihr peinlich.

**embarrassed** [ɪm'bærəst] *adj* verlegen.

**embarrassing** [ɪm'bærəsɪŋ] *adj* peinlich.

**embarrassment** [ɪm'bærəsmənt] *n* Verlegenheit *f*. **to cause ~ to sb** jdn in Verlegenheit bringen; **much to my ~ she ... sie ...**, was mir sehr peinlich war; **financial ~** finanzielle Verlegenheit.

**embassy** ['embəsɪ] *n* Botschaft *f*.

**embedded** [ɪm'bedɪd] *adj (also Comp)* eingebettet. **~ in concrete** einbetoniert; **the screws were so firmly ~ that ...** die Schrauben steckten so fest, daß ...; **to be ~ in sth** *(fig)* fest in etw *(dat)* verwurzelt sein.

**embellish** [ɪm'belɪʃ] *vt (adorn)* schmücken; *(fig) tale, account* ausschmücken; *truth* beschönigen.

**embellishment** [ɪm'belɪʃmənt] *n* Schmuck *m*; *(act)* Verschönerung *f*.

**embers** ['embəz] *npl* Glut *f*.

**embezzle** [ɪm'bezl] *vt* unterschlagen.

**embezzlement** [ɪm'bezlmənt] *n* Unterschlagung *f*.

**embittered** [ɪm'bɪtəd] *adj person* verbittert; *relations* vergiftet.

**emblem** ['embləm] *n* Emblem *nt*.

**embodiment** [ɪm'bɒdɪmənt] *n* Verkörperung *f*. **to be the ~ of virtue** die Tugend in Person sein.

**embody** [ɪm'bɒdɪ] *vt* **(a)** *ideal etc* verkörpern. **(b)** *(include)* enthalten.

**embolism** ['embəlɪzəm] *n (Med)* Embolie *f*.

**emboss** [ɪm'bɒs] *vt metal, leather* prägen. **~ed wallpaper** Prägetapete *f*; **an ~ed silver tray** ein Silbertablett mit Relief.

**embrace** [ɪm'breɪs] **1** *vt* **(a)** *(hug)* umarmen, in die Arme schließen. **(b)** *religion* annehmen; *cause* sich annehmen *(+gen)*. **(c)** *(include)* umfassen, erfassen. **2** *vi* sich umarmen. **3** *n* Umarmung *f*.

**embroider** [ɪm'brɔɪdəʳ] *vt* **(a)** besticken; *pattern* sticken. **(b)** *(fig) facts, truth* ausschmücken.

**embroidery** [ɪm'brɔɪdərɪ] *n* **(a)** Stickerei *f*. **(b)** *(fig)* Ausschmückungen *pl*.

**embroil** [ɪm'brɔɪl] *vt* **to become ~ed in a dispute** in einen Streit verwickelt werden.

**embryo** ['embrɪəʊ] *n (lit, fig)* Embryo *m*; *(fig)* Keim *m*. **in ~** *(lit, fig)* im Keim.

**embryonic** [,embrɪ'ɒnɪk] *adj* embryonisch; *(fig)* keimhaft.

**emend** [ɪ'mend] *vt text* verbessern, korrigieren.

**emerald** ['emərəld] **1** *n (stone)* Smaragd *m*; *(colour)* Smaragdgrün *nt*. **2** *adj* Smaragd-. **the E~ Isle** die Grüne Insel.

**emerge** [ɪ'mɜːdʒ] *vi* **(a)** auftauchen. **he ~d the winner** er ging als Sieger hervor; **we ~d into the bright daylight** wir kamen heraus in das helle Tageslicht; **one arm ~d from beneath the blanket** ein Arm kam unter der Decke hervor. **(b)** *(come into being: life, new nation)* entstehen. **(c)** *(truth, nature of problem etc)* sich herausstellen. **it now ~s that ...** es stellt sich jetzt heraus, daß ...

**emergence** [ɪ'mɜːdʒəns] *n* Auftauchen *nt*; *(of new nation etc)* Entstehung *f*; *(of school of thought)* Aufkommen *nt*.

**emergency** [ɪ'mɜːdʒənsɪ] *n* Notfall *m*; *(state of ~)* Notlage *f*. **in case of ~** im Notfall; **to declare a state of ~** den Notstand ausrufen.

**emergency** *in cpds* Not-; **~ brake** *n* Notbremse *f*; **~ exit** *n* Notausgang *m*; **~ landing** *n* Notlandung *f*; **~ lane** *n (US)* Seitenstreifen *m*; **~ rations** *npl* Notverpflegung *f*; **~ room** *n (US)* Unfallstation *f*; **~ service** *n* Notdienst *m*; **~ session** *n* Krisensitzung *f*; **~ stop** *n (Aut)* Vollbremsung *f*; **~ ward** *n* Unfallstation *f*.

**emergent** [ɪ'mɜːdʒənt] *adj nations* aufstrebend.

**emery** ['emərɪ]: **~ board** *n* Papiernagelfeile *f*; **~ paper** *n* Schmirgelpapier *nt*.

**emetic** [ɪ'metɪk] *n* Brechmittel *nt*.

**emigrant** ['emɪgrənt] *n* Auswanderer *m*; *(esp for political reasons)* Emigrant(in *f*) *m*.

**emigrate** ['emɪgreɪt] *vi* auswandern; *(esp for political reasons)* emigrieren.

**emigration** [,emɪ'greɪʃən] *n* Auswanderung *f*; *(esp for political reasons)* Emigration *f*.

**émigré** ['emɪgreɪ] *n* Emigrant(in *f*) *m*.

**eminence** ['emɪnəns] *n* **(a)** *(distinction)* hohes Ansehen. **(b)** *(form: of ground)* Erhebung *f*. **(c)** *(Eccl)* **His/Your E~** Seine/Eure Eminenz.

**eminent** ['emɪnənt] *adj person* (hoch)angesehen; *suitability, fairness* ausgesprochen, eminent.

**eminently** ['emɪnəntlɪ] *adv* ausgesprochen.

**emissary** ['emɪsərɪ] *n* Abgesandte(r) *mf*.

**emission** [ɪ'mɪʃən] *n (of heat also, of sound, smoke)* Abgabe *f*; *(of liquid)* Ausströmen *nt*; *(of lava)* Ausstoßen *nt*. **~ control** *(Aut)* Schadstoffbegrenzung *f*.

**emit** [ɪ'mɪt] *vt light* ausstrahlen; *radiation also* emittieren; *heat also, sound, smoke* abgeben; *lava, cry* ausstoßen.

**emotion** [ɪˈməʊʃən] *n* (a) Gefühl *nt*, Emotion *f*. (b) *no pl (state of being moved)* Bewegtheit *f*. **to show no ~** unbewegt bleiben; **in a voice full of ~** mit bewegter Stimme.

**emotional** [ɪˈməʊʃənl] *adj* (a) emotional, emotionell; *story, film, speech also* gefühlsbetont; *moment, writing also* gefühlvoll; *decision also* gefühlsmäßig; *day, experience* erregend; *letter* erregt. **~ state** Zustand *m* der Erregung; **it has an ~ appeal** es appelliert an das Gefühl. (b) *person* (leicht) erregbar, emotional. **don't get so ~ about it** reg dich nicht so darüber auf.

**emotionalism** [ɪˈməʊʃnəlɪzəm] *n* Gefühlsbetontheit *f*. **the article was sheer ~** der Artikel war reine Gefühlsduselei.

**emotionally** [ɪˈməʊʃnəlɪ] *adv behave, react* gefühlsmäßig, emotional; *(with feeling) speak* gefühlvoll; *(showing one is upset)* erregt. **an ~ deprived child** ein Kind *nt* ohne Nestwärme; **to be ~ disturbed** seelisch gestört sein; **I don't want to get ~ involved (with her)** ich will mich (bei ihr) nicht ernsthaft engagieren.

**emotive** [ɪˈməʊtɪv] *adj* gefühlsbetont; *word also* emotional gefärbt; *force of a word* emotional.

**empathy** [ˈempəθɪ] *n* Einfühlungsvermögen *nt*.

**emperor** [ˈempərər] *n* Kaiser *m*.

**emphasis** [ˈemfəsɪs] *n* Betonung *f*. **to say sth with ~** etw mit Nachdruck betonen; **to lay ~ or put the ~ on sth** etw betonen; **this year the ~ is on ...** dieses Jahr liegt der Akzent auf ...; **there is too much ~ on ... ...** wird zu sehr betont; **a change of ~** eine Akzentverschiebung.

**emphasize** [ˈemfəsaɪz] *vt* betonen.

**emphatic** [ɪmˈfætɪk] *adj tone, manner* nachdrücklich, entschieden; *denial also* energisch.

**emphatically** [ɪmˈfætɪkəlɪ] *adv state* mit Nachdruck, ausdrücklich; *deny, refuse* strikt, energisch. **most ~ not** auf gar keinen Fall.

**empire** [ˈempaɪər] *n* Reich *nt*; *(fig: esp Comm)* Imperium *nt*.

**empirical** [emˈpɪrɪkəl] *adj* empirisch.

**employ** [ɪmˈplɔɪ] *vt* (a) beschäftigen; *(take on)* anstellen; *private detective* beauftragen. **he's ~ed in a bank** er ist bei einer Bank angestellt. (b) *(use) method* anwenden; *time* verbringen.

**employee** [ˌɪmplɔɪˈiː] *n* Angestellte(r) *mf*. **~s and employers** Arbeitnehmer und Arbeitgeber; **the ~s (of one firm)** die Belegschaft.

**employer** [ɪmˈplɔɪər] *n* Arbeitgeber(in *f*) *m*.

**employment** [ɪmˈplɔɪmənt] *n* (a) *(work)* Stellung, Arbeit *f*. **to take up ~ with sb** eine Stelle bei jdm annehmen; **to seek ~ with sb** sich bei jdm bewerben; **to be in ~** angestellt sein; **place of ~** Arbeitsplatz *m*. (b) *(act of employing)* Beschäftigung *f*; *(taking on)* Einstellen *nt*. (c) *(use: of method)* Anwendung *f*; *(of word)* Verwendung *f*.

**employment:** **~ agency** *n* Stellenvermittlung *f*; **~ exchange** *(dated)*, **~ office** *n* Arbeitsamt *nt*.

**empower** [ɪmˈpaʊər] *vt* **to ~ sb to do sth** jdn ermächtigen, etw zu tun.

**empress** [ˈemprɪs] *n* Kaiserin *f*.

**empties** [ˈemptɪz] *npl (bottles)* leere Flaschen; *(any containers)* Leergut *nt*.

**emptiness** [ˈemptɪnɪs] *n* Leere *f*.

**empty** [ˈemptɪ] 1 *adj (+er)* leer; *(not occupied) house* leerstehend *attr*; *head* hohl. 2 *vt* leeren; *box, room also* ausräumen; *house* räumen; *glass, bottle also (by drinking)* austrinken. **he emptied it into another container** er goß es in ein anderes Gefäß um. 3 *vi (water)* abfließen; *(rivers)* münden *(into* in +*acc)*;

*(theatre, streets)* sich leeren.

**empty:** **~-handed** *adj* **to return ~-handed** mit leeren Händen zurückkehren; **~-headed** *adj* strohdumm.

**EMS** = **European Monetary System** EWS *nt*.

**emu** [ˈiːmjuː] *n* Emu *m*.

**EMU** = **European Monetary Union** EWU *f*.

**emulate** [ˈemjʊleɪt] *vt* nacheifern *(+dat)*.

**emulation** [ˌemjʊˈleɪʃən] *n* Nacheiferung *f*; *(Comp)* Emulation *f*.

**emulsion** [ɪˈmʌlʃən] *n* (a) Emulsion *f*. (b) *(also ~ paint)* Dispersionsfarbe *f*.

**enable** [ɪˈneɪbl] *vt* **to ~ sb to do sth** es jdm ermöglichen, etw zu tun.

**enact** [ɪˈnækt] *vt* (a) *(Pol) law* erlassen. (b) *(perform) play* aufführen. **the drama which was ~ed yesterday** *(fig)* das Drama, das sich gestern abgespielt hat.

**enamel** [ɪˈnæməl] 1 *n* Emaille *f*; *(~ paint)* Emaillelack *m*; *(of teeth)* Zahnschmelz *m*. 2 *vt* emaillieren.

**encampment** [ɪnˈkæmpmənt] *n* Lager *nt*.

**encase** [ɪnˈkeɪs] *vt* verkleiden *(in* mit)*; *wires, pipes* umgeben *(in* mit).

**encash** [ɪnˈkæʃ] *vt cheque etc* einlösen.

**enchant** [ɪnˈtʃɑːnt] *vt* (a) *(delight)* bezaubern, entzücken. (b) *(put under spell)* verzaubern.

**enchanting** [ɪnˈtʃɑːntɪŋ] *adj* bezaubernd.

**enchantment** [ɪnˈtʃɑːntmənt] *n* (a) *(delight)* Entzücken *nt*. (b) *(charm)* Zauber *m*.

**enchantress** [ɪnˈtʃɑːntrɪs] *n* Zauberin *f*.

**encircle** [ɪnˈsɜːkl] *vt* umgeben, umfassen; *(troops)* einkreisen; *building* umstellen.

**enc(l)** = **enclosure(s)** Anl.

**enclave** [ˈenkleɪv] *n* Enklave *f*.

**enclose** [ɪnˈkləʊz] *vt* (a) *(shut in)* einschließen; *(surround)* umgeben; *(with fence etc)* einzäunen. **the garden is completely ~d** der Garten ist völlig abgeschlossen. (b) *(in envelope)* beilegen, beifügen. **please find ~d ...** in der Anlage übersenden wir Ihnen ...; **to ~ sth in a letter** einem Brief etw beilegen; **the ~d cheque** der beiliegende Scheck.

**enclosure** [ɪnˈkləʊʒər] *n* (a) *(for animals)* Gehege *nt*; *(on racecourse)* Zuschauerbereich *m*. (b) *(act)* Einzäunung *f*. (c) *(with letter)* Anlage *f*. (d) *(for loudspeaker)* Box *f*.

**encode** [ɪnˈkəʊd] *vt (also Comp)* kodieren.

**encoder** [ɪnˈkəʊdər] *n (also Comp)* Kodierer *m*, Kodiergerät *nt*.

**encompass** [ɪnˈkʌmpəs] *vt (include)* umfassen.

**encore** [ˈɒŋkɔːr] 1 *interj* da capo, Zugabe. 2 *n* Zugabe *f*. **to give an ~** eine Zugabe spielen/singen.

**encounter** [ɪnˈkaʊntər] 1 *vt* stoßen auf *(+acc)*; *(liter) person* begegnen *(+dat)*, treffen. 2 *n* Begegnung *f*, Treffen *nt*; *(in battle)* Zusammenstoß *m*.

**encourage** [ɪnˈkʌrɪdʒ] *vt person* ermutigen, ermuntern *(to* zu)*; *(motivate)* anregen; *arts, industry* fördern; *team* anfeuern; *sb's bad habits* unterstützen. **you'll only ~ him to think there's still hope** er wird dann nur noch eher glauben, daß noch Hoffnung besteht; **this ~s me to think that ...** das läßt mich vermuten, daß ...

**encouragement** [ɪnˈkʌrɪdʒmənt] *n* Ermutigung *f*, Ermunterung *f*; *(motivation)* Anregung *f*; *(support)* Unterstützung, Förderung *f*. **to give sb ~** jdn ermuntern.

**encouraging** [ɪnˈkʌrɪdʒɪŋ] *adj* ermutigend. **you are not very ~** du machst mir/uns *etc* nicht gerade Mut.

**encroach** [ɪnˈkrəʊtʃ] *vi* **to ~ (up)on** *land* vordringen in *(+acc)*; *sphere, rights* eingreifen in *(+acc)*; *time* in Anspruch nehmen.

**encrusted** [ɪnˈkrʌstɪd] verkrustet; *(with pearls etc)*

besetzt.

**encumber** [ɪnˈkʌmbəʳ] *vt* **to be** ~**ed with sth** *(person)* mit etw beladen sein; *with debts* mit etw belastet sein; *(room)* mit etw überladen sein.

**encumbrance** [ɪnˈkʌmbrəns] *n (also Jur)* Belastung *f.*

**encyclop(a)edia** [ɪn‚saɪkləʊˈpiːdɪə] *n* Lexikon *nt,* Enzyklopädie *f.*

**encyclop(a)edic** [ɪn‚saɪkləʊˈpiːdɪk] *adj* enzyklopädisch.

**end** [end] **1** *n* **(a)** Ende *nt; (of finger)* Spitze *f.* **at the** ~ **of the procession** am Schluß der Prozession; **the fourth from the** ~ *(from the back)* der/die/das vierte von hinten; *(from the side)* der/die/das vierte von links/rechts; **from** ~ **to** ~ von einem Ende zum anderen; **to stand on** ~ *(box etc)* hochkant stehen; *(hair)* zu Berge stehen; **for hours on** ~ stundenlang ununterbrochen; ~ **to** ~ mit den Enden aneinander; **to change** ~**s** *(Sport)* die Seiten wechseln; **to make** ~**s meet** *(fig)* zurechtkommen, sich über Wasser halten; **we've got some problems at this** ~ wir haben hier *or* bei uns einige Probleme.
  **(b)** *(remnant) (of rope)* Ende *nt; (of candle, cigarette)* Stummel *m.*
  **(c)** *(conclusion)* Ende *nt.* **the** ~ **of the month** das Monatsende; **at/towards the** ~ **of December** Ende/ gegen Ende Dezember; **is there no** ~ **to this?** hört das denn nie auf?; **we shall never hear the** ~ **of it** das werden wir noch lange zu hören kriegen; **to be at an** ~ zu Ende sein; **to be at the** ~ **of one's patience** mit seiner Geduld am Ende sein; **to see a film/read a book to the** ~ einen Film/ein Buch bis zu Ende sehen/lesen; **that's the** ~ **of him** er ist erledigt; **that's the** ~ **of that** das ist damit erledigt; **to come to an** ~ zu Ende gehen; **in the** ~ schließlich, zum Schluß; **to put an** ~ **to sth** einer Sache *(dat)* ein Ende setzen; **to come to a bad** ~ ein böses Ende nehmen; **to meet one's** ~ den Tod finden.
  **(d)** *(col phrases)* **no** ~ **of famous people** unheimlich viele berühmte Leute *(col);* **it's done him no** ~ **of harm** es hat ihm irrsinnig geschadet *(col);* **to think no** ~ **of sb** große Stücke auf jdn halten; **you're the** ~ du bist wirklich das Letzte.
  **(e)** *(purpose)* Ziel *nt,* Zweck *m.* **with this** ~ **in view** mit diesem Ziel vor Augen; **an** ~ **in itself** Selbstzweck *no art;* **the** ~ **justifies the means** *(prov)* der Zweck heiligt die Mittel *(prov).*
  **2** *adj attr* letzte(r, s); *house also* End-.
  **3** *vt* beenden; *speech, broadcast, series also, one's days* beschließen. **the novel to** ~ **all novels** der größte Roman aller Zeiten.
  **4** *vi* enden. **we'll have to** ~ **soon** wir müssen bald Schluß machen; **to be** ~**ing** zu Ende gehen; **where's it all going to** ~? wo soll das nur enden?
  ►**end up** *vi* enden, landen *(col).* **to** ~ ~ **doing sth** schließlich etw tun; **to** ~ ~ **as a lawyer/an alcoholic** schließlich Rechtsanwalt werden/als Alkoholiker enden.

**endanger** [ɪnˈdeɪndʒəʳ] *vt* gefährden. ~**ed species** vom Aussterben bedrohte Art.

**endear** [ɪnˈdɪəʳ] *vt* beliebt machen *(to bei).*

**endearing** [ɪnˈdɪərɪŋ] *adj smile, personality* gewinnend; *characteristic also* liebenswert.

**endearment** [ɪnˈdɪəmənt] *n* **term of** ~ Kosename *m.*

**endeavour,** *(US)* **endeavor** [ɪnˈdevəʳ] **1** *n* Anstrengung, Bemühung *f.* **to make every** ~ **to do sth** sich nach Kräften bemühen, etw zu tun. **2** *vt* sich bemühen.

**endemic** [enˈdemɪk] *adj (lit, fig)* endemisch.

**ending** [ˈendɪŋ] *n (of book, events)* Ausgang *m; (last part)* Ende *nt,* Schluß *m; (of word)* Endung *f.* **happy**

~ **Happy-End** *nt.*

**endive** [ˈendaɪv] *n* Endiviensalat *m.*

**endless** [ˈendlɪs] *adj* endlos; *possibilities* unendlich. **this job is** ~ diese Arbeit nimmt kein Ende.

**endlessly** [ˈendlɪslɪ] *adv* endlos; *(ceaselessly)* unaufhörlich.

**endorse** [ɪnˈdɔːs] *vt* **(a)** *cheque* auf der Rückseite unterzeichnen. **(b)** *(Brit) driving licence* einen Strafvermerk machen auf *(+dat).* **(c)** *(approve)* billigen. **I** ~ **that** dem stimme ich zu.

**endorsement** [ɪnˈdɔːsmənt] *n* **(a)** *(on cheque)* Indossament *nt.* **(b)** *(Brit: on driving licence)* Strafvermerk *m* auf dem Führerschein. **(c)** *(of opinion)* Billigung *f.*

**endow** [ɪnˈdaʊ] *vt institution* eine Stiftung machen an *(acc); prize* stiften. ~**ed with sth** *(fig: with characteristic)* mit etw ausgestattet.

**endowment** [ɪnˈdaʊmənt] *n* **(a)** Stiftung *f.* **(b)** *(talent)* Begabung *f; (physical)* Merkmal *nt.* ~ **assurance** Erlebensversicherung *f.*

**end:** ~**product** *n* Endprodukt *nt; (fig)* Produkt *nt;* ~ **result** *n* Endergebnis *nt.*

**endurable** [ɪnˈdjʊərəbl] *adj* erträglich.

**endurance** [ɪnˈdjʊərəns] *n (powers of* ~*)* Durchhaltevermögen *nt.* **tried beyond** ~ über die Maßen gereizt; ~ **test** Belastungsprobe *f.*

**endure** [ɪnˈdjʊəʳ] **1** *vt* **(a)** *(undergo) pain, insults* (er)leiden. **(b)** *(put up with)* ertragen. **she can't** ~ **being laughed at** sie kann es nicht vertragen, wenn man über sie lacht. **2** *vi* Bestand haben.

**enduring** [ɪnˈdjʊərɪŋ] *adj value, fame* bleibend; *friendship, peace* dauerhaft; *hardship* anhaltend.

**end user** *n (esp Comp)* Endbenutzer *m.*

**enemy** [ˈenəmɪ] **1** *n (lit, fig)* Feind *m.* **to make enemies** sich *(dat)* Feinde machen; **he is his own worst** ~ er schadet sich *(dat)* selbst am meisten. **2** *adj attr* feindlich; *position, advance, morale* des Feindes. ~ **action** Feindeinwirkung *f.*

**energetic** [‚enəˈdʒetɪk] *adj* voller Energie, energiegeladen; *(active)* aktiv; *manager, government* tatkräftig; *dancing, music, prose* schwungvoll; *protest, denial* energisch. **she is a very** ~ **person** sie steckt voller Energie.

**energetically** [‚enəˈdʒetɪkəlɪ] *adv* voller Energie; *dance, perform* schwungvoll; *protest, say* energisch.

**energize** [ˈenədʒaɪz] *vt* Antrieb geben *(+dat); (Elec)* unter Strom setzen.

**energy** [ˈenədʒɪ] *n* Energie *f;* ~ **crisis** *n* Energiekrise *f;* ~ **industry** *n* Energiewirtschaft *f;* ~**-saving** *adj* energiesparend; ~ **source** *n* Energiequelle *f.*

**enervate** [ˈenɜːveɪt] *vt* entkräften.

**enervating** [ˈenɜːveɪtɪŋ] *adj* strapaziös.

**enfeeble** [ɪnˈfiːbl] *vt* schwächen.

**enforce** [ɪnˈfɔːs] *vt* durchführen; *one's claims, rights* geltend machen; *silence, discipline* sorgen für, schaffen; *obedience* sich *(dat)* verschaffen. **the police** ~ **the law** die Polizei sorgt für die Einhaltung der Gesetze.

**enforcement** [ɪnˈfɔːsmənt] *n* Durchführung *f.*

**enfranchise** [ɪnˈfræntʃaɪz] *vt (Pol)* das Wahlrecht erteilen *(+dat).*

**engage** [ɪnˈgeɪdʒ] **1** *vt* **(a)** *workers* einstellen; *actor* engagieren; *lawyer* sich *(dat)* nehmen. **(b)** *the attention* in Anspruch nehmen. **to** ~ **sb in conversation** jdn in ein Gespräch verwickeln. **(c)** *the enemy* angreifen. **(d)** *(Tech) gears* ineinandergreifen lassen. **to** ~ **a gear** einen Gang einlegen; **to** ~ **the clutch** (ein)kuppeln. **2** *vi* **(a)** **to** ~ **in sth** sich an etw *(dat)* beteiligen; **to** ~ **in politics** sich politisch betätigen. **(b)** *(gears)* ineinandergreifen; *(clutch)* fassen.

**engaged** [ɪnˈgeɪdʒd] adj (a) verlobt. **to get ~** sich verloben (to mit); **the ~ couple** die Verlobten pl. (b) (occupied) beschäftigt. (c) **the parties ~ in this dispute** die streitenden Parteien. (d) (Brit) toilet, phone besetzt. **~ tone** Besetztzeichen nt.

**engagement** [ɪnˈgeɪdʒmənt] n (a) (appointment) Verabredung f; (of actor etc) Engagement nt. **I have a previous ~** ich bin schon anderweitig verpflichtet; **public ~s** öffentliche Verpflichtungen pl. (b) (to marry) Verlobung f. **~ ring** Verlobungsring m. (c) (form: undertaking) Verpflichtung f. (d) (Mil) Gefecht nt.

**engaging** [ɪnˈgeɪdʒɪŋ] adj personality einnehmend; smile, look, tone gewinnend.

**engender** [ɪnˈdʒendər] vt (fig) erzeugen.

**engine** [ˈendʒɪn] n (a) Maschine f; (of car, plane etc) Motor m; (jet ~) Triebwerk nt. (b) (Rail) Lokomotive, Lok f.

**engine driver** n (Brit) Lok(omotiv)führer(in f) m.

**engineer** [ˌendʒɪˈnɪər] 1 n (a) Techniker(in f) m; (with university degree etc) Ingenieur(in f) m. **the E~s** (Mil) die Pioniere pl. (b) (Naut: on merchant ships) Maschinist m; (in Navy) Schiffsingenieur m. (c) (US Rail) Lokführer(in f) m. 2 vt (a) konstruieren. (b) (fig) election, campaign organisieren; downfall einfädeln.

**engineering** [ˌendʒɪˈnɪərɪŋ] n (a) Technik f; (mechanical ~) Maschinenbau m; (engineering profession) Ingenieurwesen nt. (b) (design) Konstruktion f.

**engine:** **~ failure** n Maschinenschaden m; (Aut) Motorschaden m; **~ room** n (Naut) Maschinenraum m; **~ trouble** n Defekt m am Motor.

**England** [ˈɪŋglənd] n England nt.

**English** [ˈɪŋglɪʃ] 1 adj englisch. **he is ~** er ist Engländer. 2 n (a) **the ~** pl die Engländer pl. (b) Englisch nt; (as university subject) Anglistik f. **can you speak ~?** können Sie Englisch?; **he doesn't speak ~** er spricht kein Englisch; **they were speaking ~** sie sprachen englisch; **in ~** auf englisch; **to translate sth into/from (the) ~** etw ins Englische/aus dem Englischen übersetzen.

**English:** **~ Channel** n Ärmelkanal m; **~man** n Engländer m; **~-speaker** n Englischsprachige(r) mf; **~-speaking** adj englischsprachig; **~woman** n Engländerin f.

**engrave** [ɪnˈgreɪv] vt eingravieren. **it is ~d on my memory** (fig) es hat sich mir (unauslöschlich) eingeprägt.

**engraving** [ɪnˈgreɪvɪŋ] n (picture) Stich m.

**engrossed** [ɪnˈgrəʊst] adj **to be ~ in sth** in etw (acc) vertieft sein.

**engrossing** [ɪnˈgrəʊsɪŋ] adj fesselnd.

**engulf** [ɪnˈgʌlf] vt verschlingen.

**enhance** [ɪnˈhɑːns] vt verbessern; chances also, price, value, attraction erhöhen.

**enigma** [ɪˈnɪgmə] n Rätsel nt.

**enigmatic** [ˌenɪgˈmætɪk] adj rätselhaft.

**enjoy** [ɪnˈdʒɔɪ] 1 vt (a) genießen. **he ~s swimming/reading** er schwimmt/liest gern; **I ~ed the book/film** das Buch/der Film hat mir gefallen; **he ~ed the meal** das Essen hat ihm gut geschmeckt; **I've ~ed talking to you** es war mir eine Freude, mich mit Ihnen zu unterhalten; **I didn't ~ it at all** es hat mir überhaupt keinen Spaß gemacht. (b) good health sich erfreuen (+gen) (geh); rights, advantages genießen. 2 vr **to ~ oneself** sich amüsieren; **~ yourself!** viel Spaß!

**enjoyable** [ɪnˈdʒɔɪəbl] adj nett; film, book also unterhaltsam; evening also, meal angenehm.

**enjoyment** [ɪnˈdʒɔɪmənt] n Vergnügen nt, Spaß m

(of an +dat). **he got a lot of ~ from this book** das Buch machte ihm großen Spaß.

**enlarge** [ɪnˈlɑːdʒ] 1 vt vergrößern; hole, field of knowledge erweitern. **~d edition** erweitert; (Med: organ) vergrößert. 2 vi **to ~ (up)on sth** sich über etw (acc) genauer äußern.

**enlargement** [ɪnˈlɑːdʒmənt] n Vergrößerung f.

**enlighten** [ɪnˈlaɪtn] vt aufklären (on, as to, about über +acc).

**enlightened** [ɪnˈlaɪtnd] adj aufgeklärt.

**enlightening** [ɪnˈlaɪtnɪŋ] adj aufschlußreich.

**enlightenment** [ɪnˈlaɪtnmənt] n Aufklärung f. **the age of E~** das Zeitalter der Aufklärung.

**enlist** [ɪnˈlɪst] 1 vi (Mil etc) sich melden (in zu). 2 vt soldiers einziehen; supporters, sympathy, support gewinnen. **~ed man** (US) gemeiner Soldat.

**enlistment** [ɪnˈlɪstmənt] n see vt Einziehung f; Gewinnung f.

**enliven** [ɪnˈlaɪvn] vt beleben.

**en masse** [ɑ̃ˈmæs] adv en masse.

**enmity** [ˈenmɪtɪ] n Feindschaft f.

**ennoble** [ɪˈnəʊbl] vt (lit) adeln.

**enormity** [ɪˈnɔːmɪtɪ] n no pl (of offence) ungeheures Ausmaß.

**enormous** [ɪˈnɔːməs] adj gewaltig, enorm; person riesig; patience enorm. **an ~ number of people** ungeheuer viele Menschen; **an ~ amount of money/time** eine Unmenge Geld/Zeit.

**enormously** [ɪˈnɔːməslɪ] adv enorm, ungeheuer.

**enough** [ɪˈnʌf] 1 adj, n genug, genügend attr. **to be ~** genügen, reichen; **is there ~ milk?** ist genug Milch da?; **will that be ~?** reicht das?; **I've had ~, I'm going home** mir reicht's, ich gehe nach Hause; **I've had ~ of your impudence** jetzt habe ich aber genug von deiner Frechheit; **now children, that's ~!** Kinder, jetzt reicht es aber!; **this noise is ~ to drive me mad** dieser Lärm macht mich noch ganz verrückt; **~ is ~** was zuviel ist, ist zuviel. 2 adv (+adj) genug; (+vb also) genügend. **not big ~** nicht groß genug; **he knows well ~ what I said** er weiß ganz genau, was ich gesagt habe; **she's pleasant ~** sie ist so weit ganz nett; **he was kind ~ to lend me the money** er war so gut und hat mir das Geld geliehen; **he sings well ~** er singt ganz ordentlich; **funnily ~** komischerweise; **and sure ~, he didn't come** und er kam auch prompt nicht.

**enquire** [ɪnˈkwaɪər] 1 vt **he ~d what/whether/when** etc ... er erkundigte sich, was/ob/wann etc ... 2 vi sich erkundigen (about nach).

►**enquire into** vi +prep obj untersuchen.

**enquiring** [ɪnˈkwaɪərɪŋ] adj fragend. **he has an ~ mind** er ist eine Forschernatur.

**enquiry** [ɪnˈkwaɪərɪ, (US) ˈɪnkwɪrɪ] n (a) (question) Anfrage f (about über +acc); (for tourist information, direction etc) Erkundigung f (about über +acc, nach). **to make enquiries** Erkundigungen einziehen; (police etc) Nachforschungen anstellen (about sb über jdn, about sth nach etw). (b) (investigation) Untersuchung f.

**enrage** [ɪnˈreɪdʒ] vt wütend machen.

**enrich** [ɪnˈrɪtʃ] vt bereichern; soil, food anreichern.

**enrichment** [ɪnˈrɪtʃmənt] n Bereicherung f; (of soil) Anreicherung f.

**enrol, (US) enroll** [ɪnˈrəʊl] 1 vt einschreiben; members also aufnehmen; (Univ) immatrikulieren. 2 vi sich einschreiben; (in the army) sich melden (in zu); (for course also, at school) sich anmelden; (Univ also) sich immatrikulieren.

**enrolment** [ɪnˈrəʊlmənt] n see vt Einschreibung f; Aufnahme f; Immatrikulation f.

**en route** [ɒnˈruːt] adv unterwegs. **~ to Paris** auf

dem Weg nach Paris.

**ensconce** [ɪn'skɒns] *vr* sich (häuslich) niederlassen *(in* in +*dat)*.

**ensemble** [ãːn'sãːmbl] *n* Ensemble *nt*.

**ensign** ['ensaɪn] *n* (a) *(flag)* Nationalflagge *f*. (b) *(US Naut)* Fähnrich *m* zur See.

**enslave** [ɪn'sleɪv] *vt* zum Sklaven machen.

**ensnare** [ɪn'snɛəʳ] *vt (lit)* fangen; *(fig) (woman)* umgarnen; *(charms)* berücken, bestricken.

**ensue** [ɪn'sjuː] *vi* folgen *(from* aus*)*.

**ensuing** [ɪn'sjuːɪŋ] *adj* folgend.

**en suite** [ɒn'swiːt] *adj, n* ~ **(bathroom)** eigenes Bad.

**ensure** [ɪn'ʃʊəʳ] *vt* sicherstellen; *(secure)* sichern. **to ~ that** ... *(guarantee)* gewährleisten, daß ....

**ENT** *(Med)* = **ear, nose and throat** HNO.

**entail** [ɪn'teɪl] *vt* expense, suffering mit sich bringen; risk, difficulty also verbunden sein mit.

**entangle** [ɪn'tæŋgl] *vt* **to become ~d in sth** sich in etw *(dat)* verfangen; *(fig)* sich in etw *(acc)* verstricken.

**entanglement** [ɪn'tæŋglmənt] *n* (a) *(barbed wire)* Verhau *m*. (b) *(fig: in affair etc)* Verwicklung *f*.

**enter** ['entəʳ] **1** *vt* (a) *(towards speaker)* hereinkommen in *(+acc)*; *(away from speaker)* hineingehen in *(+acc)*; *(walk into)* building etc also betreten; *(drive into)* car park einfahren in *(+acc)*; *(turn into)* road etc einbiegen in *(+acc)*; *(river etc)* münden in *(+acc)*; *(penetrate: bullet etc)* eindringen in *(+acc)*; *(climb into)* bus einsteigen in *(+acc)*; *(cross border of)* country einreisen in *(+acc)*. **the thought never ~ed my mind** so etwas wäre mir nie eingefallen. (b) **to ~ the Army/Navy** zum Heer/zur Marine gehen; **to ~ the Church** Geistlicher werden; **to ~ a university** auf die Universität gehen. (c) *(write down, record)* eintragen *(in* in +*acc)*; *(Comp)* data eingeben. **~ key** *(Comp)* Enter-Taste *f*. (d) *(enrol)* pupil anmelden; horse melden. (e) race, contest sich beteiligen an *(+dat)*. (f) *(submit)* appeal, plea einlegen.

**2** *vi* (a) *(towards speaker)* hereinkommen; *(away from speaker)* hineingehen; *(walk in)* eintreten. (b) *(Theat)* auftreten. (c) *(for race, exam etc)* sich melden *(for* zu*)*.

▶**enter into** *vi* +*prep obj* (a) negotiations aufnehmen; contract, alliance schließen, eingehen; conversation anknüpfen. (b) *(figure in)* eine Rolle spielen bei. **that doesn't ~ ~ it** das spielt dabei keine Rolle.

▶**enter (up)on** *vi* +*prep obj (begin)* antreten; new era eintreten in *(+acc)*.

**enteritis** [ˌentə'raɪtɪs] *n* Dünndarmentzündung *f*.

**enterprise** ['entəpraɪz] *n* Unternehmen *nt*; *(initiative)* Initiative *f*; *(adventurousness)* Unternehmungsgeist *m*. **free/private** ~ freies/privates Unternehmertum; ~ **zone** wirtschaftliches Fördergebiet.

**enterprising** ['entəpraɪzɪŋ] *adj* unternehmungslustig; idea, venture kühn.

**entertain** [ˌentə'teɪn] **1** *vt* (a) *(offer hospitality to)* einladen; *(to meal)* bewirten. **to ~ sb to dinner** jdn zum Essen einladen. (b) *(amuse)* unterhalten. (c) thought sich tragen mit; suspicion, doubt hegen; hope nähren; proposal, offer, idea in Erwägung ziehen. **2** *vi (have visitors)* Gäste haben.

**entertainer** [ˌentə'teɪnəʳ] *n* Entertainer (in *f*) *m*.

**entertaining** [ˌentə'teɪnɪŋ] **1** *adj* unterhaltsam. **2** *n* **she does a lot of** ~ sie hat sehr oft Gäste.

**entertainment** [ˌentə'teɪnmənt] *n* (a) Unterhaltung *f*. **for my own** ~ nur so zum Vergnügen. (b) *(performance)* Darbietung *f*. (c) *(of guests)* Bewirtung *f*. ~ **allowance** Aufwandspauschale *f*.

**enthral(l)** [ɪn'θrɔːl] *vt* begeistern; *(exciting story etc also)* fesseln.

**enthralling** [ɪn'θrɔːlɪŋ] *adj* spannend.

**enthuse** [ɪn'θjuːz] *vi* schwärmen *(over* von*)*.

**enthusiasm** [ɪn'θjuːzɪæzəm] *n* Begeisterung *f*, Enthusiasmus *m (for* für*)*.

**enthusiast** [ɪn'θjuːzɪæst] *n* Enthusiast *m*. **sports/jazz** ~ begeisterter Sport-/Jazzfan *m*.

**enthusiastic** [ɪnˌθjuːzɪ'æstɪk] *adj* begeistert, enthusiastisch. **to be/get** ~ **about sth** von etw begeistert sein/sich für etw begeistern.

**entice** [ɪn'taɪs] *vt* locken; *(lead astray)* verführen, verleiten. **to ~ sb into doing sth** jdn dazu verleiten, etw zu tun; **to ~ sb away** jdn weglocken.

**enticement** [ɪn'taɪsmənt] *n (lure)* Verlockung *f*.

**enticing** [ɪn'taɪsɪŋ] *adj* verlockend.

**entire** [ɪn'taɪəʳ] *adj* ganz; set, waste of time vollständig.

**entirely** [ɪn'taɪəlɪ] *adv* ganz. **I'm not** ~ **surprised** das kommt für mich nicht ganz überraschend.

**entirety** [ɪn'taɪərətɪ] *n* **in its** ~ in seiner Gesamtheit.

**entitle** [ɪn'taɪtl] *vt* (a) **it is** ~**d** ... es hat den Titel ... (b) *(give the right)* **to** ~ **sb to sth/to do sth** jdn zu etw berechtigen/jdn dazu berechtigen, etw zu tun; *(to compensation, legal aid)* jdm den Anspruch auf etw *(acc)* geben; **to be** ~**d to sth/to do sth** das Recht auf etw *(acc)* haben/das Recht haben, etw zu tun; *to compensation, legal aid, holiday* Anspruch *m* auf etw *(acc)* haben.

**entitlement** [ɪn'taɪtlmənt] *n* Berechtigung *f (to* zu*)*; *(to compensation, holiday etc)* Anspruch *m (to* auf +*acc)*.

**entity** ['entɪtɪ] *n (separate)* ~ eigenständiges Gebilde; *(person)* eigenständiges Wesen; **as a complete** ~ als Ganzes.

**entomology** [ˌentə'mɒlədʒɪ] *n* Insektenkunde *f*.

**entourage** [ˌɒntu'rɑːʒ] *n* Gefolge *nt*.

**entrails** ['entreɪlz] *npl* Eingeweide *pl*.

**entrance¹** [ɪn'trɑːns] *vt* in Entzücken versetzen.

**entrance²** ['entrəns] *n* (a) *(way in)* Eingang *m*; *(for vehicles)* Einfahrt *f*; *(hall)* Eingangshalle *f*. (b) *(entering)* Eintritt *m*; *(Theat)* Auftritt *m*. **to make one's** ~ *(Theat)* auftreten; *(fig also)* erscheinen. (c) *(admission)* Eintritt *m (to* in +*acc)*; *(to club etc)* Zutritt *m (to* zu*)*.

**entrance:** ~ **examination** *n* Aufnahmeprüfung *f*; ~ **fee** *n* Eintrittsgeld *nt*; *(for club)* Aufnahmegebühr *f*; ~ **qualifications** *npl* Zulassungsanforderungen *pl*; ~ **ramp** *n (US)* Auffahrt *f*; ~ **visa** *n* Einreisevisum *nt*.

**entrancing** [ɪn'trɑːnsɪŋ] *adj* bezaubernd.

**entrant** ['entrənt] *n (in contest)* Teilnehmer (in *f*) *m*; *(in exam)* Prüfling *m*.

**entreat** [ɪn'triːt] *vt* anflehen *(for* um*)*.

**entreaty** [ɪn'triːtɪ] *n* dringende Bitte.

**entrée** ['ɒntreɪ] *n* Hauptgericht *nt*.

**entrenched** [ɪn'trentʃt] *adj* idea, belief etc (fest) verwurzelt; position festgefahren.

**entrepreneur** [ˌɒntrəprə'nɜːʳ] *n* Unternehmer *m*.

**entrepreneurial** [ˌɒntrəprə'nɜːrɪəl] *adj* unternehmerisch.

**entrust** [ɪn'trʌst] *vt* anvertrauen *(to sb* jdm*)*. **to** ~ **sb with a task** jdn mit einer Aufgabe betrauen.

**entry** ['entrɪ] *n* (a) *(into* +*acc)* Eintritt *m*; *(by car etc)* Einfahrt *f*; *(into country)* Einreise *f*; *(Theat)* Auftritt *m*. **"no ~"** *(on door etc)* „Zutritt verboten"; *(on one-way street)* „keine Einfahrt". (b) *(way in, doorway)* Eingang *m*; *(for vehicles)* Einfahrt *f*. (c) *(in diary, account book etc)* Eintrag *m*. *(for race etc)* Meldung *f*. **there is a large** ~ **for the race** für das Rennen sind viele Meldungen eingegangen.

**entry:** ~ **fee** *n (for competition)* Teilnahmegebühr *f*; *(to club)* Aufnahmegebühr *f*; ~ **form** *n* Anmeldefor-

**erect**

mular *nt*; ~ **permit** *n* Passierschein *m*; *(into country)* Einreiseerlaubnis *f*; ~ **phone** *n* Türsprechanlage *f*; ~ **visa** *n* Einreisevisum *nt*.
**entwine** [ɪn'twaɪn] *vt* ineinanderschlingen.
**enumerate** [ɪ'njuːməreɪt] *vt* aufzählen.
**enumeration** [ɪ,njuːmə'reɪʃən] *n* Aufzählung *f*.
**enunciate** [ɪ'nʌnsɪeɪt] *vti* artikulieren.
**enunciation** [ɪ,nʌnsɪ'eɪʃən] *n* Artikulation *f*.
**envelop** [ɪn'veləp] *vt* einhüllen.
**envelope** ['envələʊp] *n* Umschlag *m*.
**enviable** ['envɪəbl] *adj* beneidenswert.
**envious** *adj*, ~**ly** *adv* ['envɪəs, -lɪ] neidisch *(of* auf +*acc)*.
**environment** [ɪn'vaɪərənmənt] *n* Umwelt *f*; *(of town etc, physical surroundings)* Umgebung *f*; *(social, cultural also)* Milieu *nt*. **Department of the E~** *(Brit)* ≈ Umweltministerium *nt*.
**environmental** [ɪn,vaɪərən'mentl] *adj* Umwelt-. ~ **pollution** Umweltverschmutzung *f*; ~ **protection** Umweltschutz *m*; ~ **studies** *(Sch)* Umweltkunde *f*.
**environmentalist** [ɪn,vaɪərən'mentəlɪst] *n* Umweltschützer(in *f*) *m*.
**environment-friendly** *adj* umweltfreundlich.
**envisage** [ɪn'vɪzɪdʒ] *vt* sich *(dat)* vorstellen; *(expect)* erwarten.
**envoy** ['envɔɪ] *n* Bote *m*; *(diplomat)* Gesandte(r) *mf*.
**envy** ['envɪ] **1** *n* Neid *m*. **his house was the** ~ **of his friends** seine Freunde beneideten ihn um sein Haus. **2** *vt person* beneiden. **to** ~ **sb sth** jdn um etw beneiden.
**enzyme** ['enzaɪm] *n* Enzym, Ferment *nt*.
**EPA** *(US)* = **Environmental Protection Agency** US-Umweltbehörde *f*.
**ephemeral** [ɪ'femərəl] *adj* flüchtig.
**epic** ['epɪk] **1** *adj poetry* episch; *film, novel* Monumental-; *performance, match* gewaltig; *journey* lang und abenteuerlich. **2** *n (poem, film)* Epos *nt*; *(match)* gewaltiges Spiel.
**epicentre, *(US)* epicenter** ['epɪsentər] *n* Epizentrum *nt*.
**epidemic** [epɪ'demɪk] **1** *n* Epidemie *(also fig)*, Seuche *f*. **2** *adj* epidemisch.
**epigram** ['epɪgræm] *n* Epigramm, Sinngedicht *nt*.
**epilepsy** ['epɪlepsɪ] *n* Epilepsie *f*.
**epileptic** [,epɪ'leptɪk] **1** *adj* ~ **fit** epileptischer Anfall. **2** *n* Epileptiker(in *f*) *m*.
**epilogue** ['epɪlɒg] *n* Epilog *m*, Nachwort *nt*.
**Epiphany** [ɪ'pɪfənɪ] *n* das Dreikönigsfest.
**episcopal** [ɪ'pɪskəpəl] *adj* bischöflich, Bischofs-.
**episode** ['epɪsəʊd] *n* Episode *f*; *(of story, TV, Rad)* Fortsetzung *f*; *(incident also)* Begebenheit *f*.
**epistle** [ɪ'pɪsl] *n (Bibl)* Brief *m* *(to* an +*acc)*.
**epitaph** ['epɪtɑːf] *n* Epitaph *nt*; *(on grave)* Grabinschrift *f*.
**epithet** ['epɪθet] *n* Beiname *m*.
**epitome** [ɪ'pɪtəmɪ] *n* Inbegriff *m* *(of gen,* an +*dat)*.
**epitomize** [ɪ'pɪtəmaɪz] *vt* verkörpern.
**epoch** ['iːpɒk] *n* Zeitalter *nt (also Geol)*, Epoche *f*.
**epoch-making** ['iːpɒk,meɪkɪŋ] *adj* epochemachend, epochal.
**EPOS** *abbr* = **electronic point of sale** elektronisches Kassenterminal.
**equable** ['ekwəbl] *adj person, temperament* ausgeglichen; *climate* gleichmäßig.
**equal** ['iːkwəl] **1** *adj* (a) gleich *(to* +*dat)*. **they are about** ~ **in value** sie haben ungefähr den gleichen Wert; **to be on** ~ **terms** auf der gleichen Stufe stehen *(with* mit*)*; ~ **opportunities** Chancengleichheit *f*; **E~ Opportunities Commission** *(Brit)* Kommission *f* für Gleichberechtigung am Arbeitsplatz; **(all) other things being** ~ unter sonst gleichen Umständen;

**now we're** ~ jetzt sind wir quitt. **(b) to be** ~ **to the situation/task** der Situation/Aufgabe gewachsen sein; **to feel** ~ **to sth** sich zu etw imstande *or* in der Lage fühlen.
**2** *n (in rank)* Gleichgestellte(r) *mf*. **she is his** ~ sie ist ihm ebenbürtig; **he has no** ~ er hat nicht seinesgleichen; **our** ~**s** unseresgleichen; **to treat sb as an** ~ jdn als ebenbürtig behandeln.
**3** *vt (be same as, Math)* gleichen; *(match, measure up to)* gleichkommen *(+dat)*; *record* erreichen. **three times three** ~**s nine** drei mal drei (ist) gleich neun; **not to be** ~**led** unvergleichlich.
**equality** [ɪ'kwɒlɪtɪ] *n* Gleichheit *f*.
**equalize** ['iːkwəlaɪz] *vti* ausgleichen.
**equalizer** ['iːkwəlaɪzər] *n* (a) *(Sport)* Ausgleich *m*; *(Ftbl etc also)* Ausgleichstreffer *m*. (b) *(US col: gun)* Kanone *f (col)*.
**equally** ['iːkwəlɪ] *adv* (a) *divide, distribute* gleichmäßig. ~ **gifted** gleich begabt *pred,* gleichbegabt *attr*. (b) *(just as)* genauso. (c) **but then,** ~, **one must concede** ... aber dann muß man ebenso zugestehen, daß ...
**equals sign** ['iːkwəlz'saɪn] *n* Gleichheitszeichen *nt*.
**equanimity** [,ekwə'nɪmɪtɪ] *n* Gleichmut *m*.
**equate** [ɪ'kweɪt] *vt (identify)* gleichsetzen; *(treat as the same)* auf die gleiche Stufe stellen.
**equation** [ɪ'kweɪʒən] *n (Math, fig)* Gleichung *f*.
**equator** [ɪ'kweɪtər] *n* Äquator *m*.
**equatorial** [,ekwə'tɔːrɪəl] *adj* äquatorial, Äquatorial-.
**equestrian** [ɪ'kwestrɪən] *adj* Reit-.
**equidistant** [iːkwɪ'dɪstənt] *adj* gleich weit entfernt.
**equilateral** [iːkwɪ'lætərəl] *adj* gleichseitig.
**equilibrium** [,iːkwɪ'lɪbrɪəm] *n* Gleichgewicht *nt*.
**equine** ['ekwaɪn] *adj* Pferde-.
**equinox** ['iːkwɪnɒks] *n* Tagundnachtgleiche *f*.
**equip** [ɪ'kwɪp] *vt* ausrüsten; *kitchen* ausstatten; *office, laboratory* einrichten. **he's well** ~**ped for the job** *(fig)* er hat das nötige Rüstzeug für die Stelle.
**equipment** [ɪ'kwɪpmənt] *n no pl* Ausrüstung *f*. **office** ~ Büroeinrichtung *f*; **electrical/kitchen** ~ Elektro-/Küchengeräte *pl*.
**equitable** ['ekwɪtəbl] *adj* fair, gerecht.
**equity** ['ekwɪtɪ] *n* (a) Fairneß *f*. (b) *(Brit Fin)* ~ **capital** Eigenkapital *nt*; **equities** *pl* Stammaktien *pl*; **equities market** Aktienmarkt *m*.
**equivalence** [ɪ'kwɪvələns] *n* Entsprechung *f*.
**equivalent** [ɪ'kwɪvələnt] **1** *adj* (a) *(equal)* gleichwertig. **that's** ~ **to saying** ... das ist gleichbedeutend damit, zu sagen ... (b) *(corresponding)* entsprechend, äquivalent. **it is** ~ **to £30** das entspricht £30; **that's** ~ **to lying** das ist soviel wie gelogen. **2** *n* Äquivalent *nt*; *(counterpart)* Pendant *nt*. **what is the** ~ **in German marks?** was ist der Gegenwert in DM?; **the German** ~ **of the English word** die deutsche Entsprechung des englischen Wortes.
**equivocal** [ɪ'kwɪvəkəl] *adj* zweideutig; *outcome* nicht eindeutig.
**equivocate** [ɪ'kwɪvəkeɪt] *vi* ausweichen.
**equivocation** [ɪ,kwɪvə'keɪʃən] *n* Ausflüchte *pl*.
**ER** *(Brit)* = **Elizabeth Regina.**
**ERA** *(US)* = **Equal Rights Amendment** *Verfassungsartikel m zur Gleichberechtigung.*
**era** ['ɪərə] *n* Ära *f*; *(Geol)* Erdzeitalter *nt*.
**eradicate** [ɪ'rædɪkeɪt] *vt* ausrotten.
**erase** [ɪ'reɪz] *vt* ausradieren; *(from tape, computer)* löschen; *(from the mind)* streichen *(from* aus*)*.
**eraser** [ɪ'reɪzər] *n* Radiergummi *nt or m*.
**erect** [ɪ'rekt] **1** *adj* aufrecht, gerade. **2** *vt monument* errichten *(to sb* jdm*)*; *flats, factory* bauen; *collapsible furniture, scaffolding* aufstellen; *tent* aufschla-

gen; *mast* aufrichten.
**erection** [ɪˈrekʃən] *n* **(a)** *see vt* Errichten *nt*; Bau *m*;
Aufstellen *nt*; Aufschlagen *nt*; Aufrichten *nt*. **(b)**
*(building, structure)* Gebäude *nt*, Bau *m*. **(c)** *(Physiol)*
Erektion *f*.
**ergonomic** [ˌɜːgəʊˈnɒmɪk] *adj* ergonomisch.
**ergonomics** [ˌɜːgəʊˈnɒmɪks] *n sing* Ergonomie *f*.
**ermine** [ˈɜːmɪn] *n* Hermelin *nt*; *(fur)* Hermelin *m*.
**erode** [ɪˈrəʊd] *vt (sea)* auswaschen; *(rust)* zerfressen;
*(fig) confidence* untergraben.
**erogenous** [ɪˈrɒdʒənəs] *adj* erogen.
**erosion** [ɪˈrəʊʒən] *n (by water)* Erosion *f*; *(fig: of love
etc)* Schwinden *nt*.
**erotic** [ɪˈrɒtɪk] *adj* aufreizend; *book, film* erotisch.
**eroticism** [ɪˈrɒtɪsɪzəm] *n* Erotik *f*.
**err** [ɜːr] *vi* **(a)** sich irren. **it is better to ~ on the side
of caution** man sollte im Zweifelsfall lieber zu vorsichtig sein; **to ~ is human** *(Prov)* Irren ist menschlich *(Prov)*. **(b)** *(sin)* sündigen.
**errand** [ˈerənd] *n (shopping etc)* Besorgung *f*; *(to
give a message etc)* Botengang *m*. **to run ~s (for sb)**
(für jdn) Besorgungen/Botengänge machen; **~ of
mercy** Rettungsaktion *f*; **~ boy** Laufjunge *m*.
**erratic** [ɪˈrætɪk] *adj* unberechenbar; *results* stark
schwankend; *work* ungleichmäßig.
**erroneous** [ɪˈrəʊnɪəs] *adj* falsch; *belief* irrig.
**error** [ˈerər] *n* Fehler *m*. **to be in ~** sich im Irrtum
befinden; **in ~** aus Versehen, irrtümlicherweise; **to
see the ~ of one's ways** seine Fehler einsehen; **~
message** *(Comp)* Fehlermeldung *f*.
**erstwhile** [ˈɜːstwaɪl] *adj (old, liter)* ehemalig.
**erudite** [ˈerʊdaɪt] *adj* gelehrt; *person also* gebildet.
**erudition** [ˌerʊˈdɪʃən] *n* Gelehrsamkeit *f*.
**erupt** [ɪˈrʌpt] *vi (volcano, war)* ausbrechen; *skin* aufbrechen; *(fig: person)* explodieren.
**eruption** [ɪˈrʌpʃən] *n (of volcano, anger, violence)*
Ausbruch *m*; *(rash etc)* Hautausschlag *m*.
**escalate** [ˈeskəleɪt] **1** *vt war* ausweiten; *costs*
sprunghaft erhöhen. **2** *vi* sich ausweiten, eskalieren; *(costs)* sprunghaft ansteigen.
**escalation** [ˌeskəˈleɪʃən] *n* Eskalation *f*.
**escalator** [ˈeskəleɪtər] *n* Rolltreppe *f*.
**escapade** [ˌeskəˈpeɪd] *n* Eskapade *f*.
**escape** [ɪˈskeɪp] **1** *vi* **(a)** *(from pursuers)* entkommen
*(from dat)*; *(from prison, cage)* ausbrechen *(from
aus)*; *(water)* auslaufen *(from aus)*; *(gas)* ausströmen *(from aus)*. **he was shot while trying to ~** er
wurde bei einem Fluchtversuch erschossen; **an ~d
prisoner/tiger** ein entsprungener Häftling/
ausgebrochener Tiger; **he ~d from the fire** er ist
dem Feuer entkommen; **a room which I can ~ to**
ein Zimmer, in das ich mich zurückziehen kann.
**(b)** *(get off, be spared)* **to ~ with a warning/a few
cuts** mit einer Verwarnung/ein paar Schnittwunden
davonkommen; **the others were killed, but he ~d**
die anderen kamen um, aber er kam mit dem Leben davon.
　**2** *vt* **(a)** *pursuers* entkommen *(+dat)*. **(b)** *(avoid)*
*consequences, punishment, disaster* entgehen *(+dat)*.
**he narrowly ~d being run over** er wäre um ein Haar
überfahren worden; **but you can't ~ the fact that ...**
aber du kannst nicht abstreiten, daß ... **(c)** *his
name ~s me* sein Name ist mir entfallen; **nothing
~s him** ihm entgeht nichts; **to ~ sb's notice** jdm
entgehen.
　**3** *n* **(a)** Flucht *f*; *(from prison etc)* Ausbruch *m*.
**to make an ~** ausbrechen; **there's been an ~** jemand ist ausgebrochen; **to have a miraculous ~**
*(from accident, illness)* auf wunderbare Weise davonkommen; **fishing is his ~** Angeln ist seine Zuflucht; **there's no ~** *(fig)* es gibt keinen Ausweg. **(b)**

*(of water)* Ausfließen *nt*; *(of gas)* Ausströmen *nt*; *(of
steam, gas, in a machine)* Entweichen *nt*.
**escape: ~ artist** *n* Entfesselungskünstler(in *f*) *m*;
**~ bid** *n* Fluchtversuch *m*; **~ clause** *n (Jur)* Be-
freiungsklausel *f*; **~ hatch** *n (Naut)* Notluke *f*; **~
key** *n (Comp)* Escape-Taste *f*; **~ route** *n* Flucht-
weg *m*; **~ velocity** *n (Space)* Fluchtgeschwindig-
keit *f*.
**escapism** [ɪˈskeɪpɪzəm] *n* Wirklichkeitsflucht *f*.
**escapist** [ɪˈskeɪpɪst] *adj literature* der Wirklichkeitsflucht.
**escapologist** [ˌeskəˈpɒlədʒɪst] *n* Entfesselungskünst-
ler(in *f*) *m*.
**escarpment** [ɪˈskɑːpmənt] *n* Steilhang *m*; *(as fortification)* Böschung *f*.
**escort** [ˈeskɔːt] **1** *n* **(a)** Geleitschutz *m*; *(vehicles,
ships etc)* Eskorte *f*. **under ~** unter Bewachung. **(b)**
*(companion)* Begleiter(in *f*) *m*; *(hired female)* ≃ Hostess *f*. **2** [ɪˈskɔːt] *vt* begleiten; *(Mil, Naut)* Ge-
leit(schutz) geben *(+dat)*.
**escort: ~ agency** *n* ≃ Hostessenagentur *f*; **~ duty**
*n* Geleitdienst *m*; **to be on ~ duty** Geleitschutz geben müssen; **~ vessel** *n (Naut)* Geleitschiff *nt*.
**Eskimo** [ˈeskɪməʊ] **1** *adj* Eskimo-. **2** *n* **(a)** Eskimo *m*,
Eskimofrau *f*. **(b)** *(language)* Eskimosprache *f*.
**esophagus** *n (esp US)* = **oesophagus**.
**esoteric** [ˌesəʊˈterɪk] *adj* esoterisch.
**esp** = **especially** bes.
**ESP** = **(a) extra-sensory perception** außersinnliche Wahrnehmung, ASW. **(b) English for Special
Purposes** *Englischunterricht m für Studenten mit
meist technischen Hauptfächern.*
**especial** [ɪˈspeʃəl] *adj* besondere(r, s).
**especially** [ɪˈspeʃəli] *adv* besonders. **you ~ ought to
know that** gerade du solltest das wissen; **I came ~
to see you** ich bin eigens gekommen, um dich zu
besuchen; **~ as I am his godmother** zumal ich seine
Patin bin.
**espionage** [ˈespɪəˌnɑːʒ] *n* Spionage *f*.
**esplanade** [ˌespləˈneɪd] *n (Strand)* promenade *f*.
**espouse** [ɪˈspaʊz] *vt cause* eintreten für.
**espresso** [eˈspresəʊ] *n* Espresso *m*.
**esquire** [ɪˈskwaɪər] *n (Brit: on envelope, abbr* **Esq***)*
**James Jones, Esq** Herrn James Jones.
**essay** [ˈeseɪ] *n* Essay *m or nt*; *(esp Sch)* Aufsatz *m*.
**essence** [ˈesəns] *n* **(a)** Wesen *nt*. **in ~** im wesentlichen; **speed is of the ~** Geschwindigkeit ist von
entscheidender Bedeutung. **(b)** *(Chem, Cook)* Essenz *f*. **meat ~** Fleischextrakt *m*.
**essential** [ɪˈsenʃəl] **1** *adj* **(a)** *(necessary, vital)* (unbedingt) erforderlich. **it is ~ that you understand this**
du mußt das unbedingt verstehen; **the ~ thing is to
...** wichtig ist vor allem, zu ... **(b)** *(of the essence,
basic)* wesentlich; *question* entscheidend. **2** *n* **the
~s** das Wesentliche; *(most important points)* die
wichtigen Punkte, die Essentials *pl*. **with only the
bare ~s** nur mit dem Allernotwendigsten ausgestattet.
**essentially** [ɪˈsenʃəli] *adv (basically)* im Grunde genommen; *(in essence)* im wesentlichen.
**EST** *(US)* = **Eastern Standard Time** *ostamerika-
nische Zeit.*
**establish** [ɪˈstæblɪʃ] **1** *vt* **(a)** *(found, set up)* gründen;
*government* bilden; *custom, new procedure* einfüh-
ren; *relations* aufnehmen; *post* einrichten; *power,
authority, reputation* sich *(dat)* verschaffen; *peace*
stiften; *order* (wieder)herstellen; *precedent* setzen;
*committee* einsetzen. **(b)** *(prove)* *fact, innocence* beweisen; *claim* unter Beweis stellen. **(c)** *(determine)*
*identity, facts* ermitteln. **(d)** *(gain acceptance for)*
*product, ideas* Anerkennung finden für. **2** *vr (in busi-*

**evasive**

*ness)* **to ~ oneself** sich niederlassen.
**established** [ɪ'stæblɪʃt] *adj* **(a)** *reputation* gefestigt.
**well-~ business** gut eingeführte Firma. **(b)** *(accepted) fact* feststehend; *procedure, author* anerkannt; *belief* herrschend; *laws, order* bestehend.
**establishment** [ɪ'stæblɪʃmənt] *n* **(a)** *see vt (a)* Gründung *f*; Bildung *f*; Einführung *f*; Aufnahme *f*; Einrichtung *f*; *(of power, authority)* Festigung *f*; Stiftung *f*; (Wieder)herstellung *f*; Setzen *nt*; Einsetzen *nt*. **(b)** *(proving)* Beweis *m*. **(c)** *(determining)* Ermittlung *f*. **(d)** *(institution etc)* Institution *f*; *(hospital, school etc also)* Anstalt *f*. **commercial ~** kommerzielles Unternehmen. **(e)** *(Mil, Naut etc: personnel)* Truppenstärke *f*. **(f)** *(Brit)* **the E~** das Establishment.
**estate** [ɪ'steɪt] *n* **(a)** *(land)* Gut *nt*. **(b)** *(Jur)* Besitz(tümer *pl) m*, Eigentum *nt*; *(of deceased)* Nachlaß *m*, Erbmasse *f*. **(c)** *(esp Brit) (housing ~)* Siedlung *f*; *(trading ~)* Industriegelände *nt*.
**estate: ~ agent** *n (Brit)* Immobilienmakler(in *f) m*; **~ car** *n (Brit)* Kombi(wagen) *m*.
**esteem** [ɪ'stiːm] **1** *vt (form: consider)* betrachten. **2** *n* Wertschätzung *f*. **to hold sb/sth in (high) ~** von jdm/etw eine hohe Meinung haben.
**esthete** *etc (US)* = **aesthete** *etc*.
**estimate** ['estɪmɪt] **1** *n* **(a)** Schätzung *f*. **it's just an ~** das ist nur geschätzt; **at a rough ~** grob geschätzt. **(b)** *(Comm: of cost)* (Kosten)voranschlag *m*. **2** ['estɪmeɪt] *vt* schätzen. **his wealth is ~d at ...** sein Vermögen wird auf ... geschätzt.
**estimation** [,estɪ'meɪʃən] *n* **(a) in my ~** meiner Einschätzung nach. **(b)** *(esteem)* Achtung *f*. **he went up/down in my ~** er ist in meiner Achtung gestiegen/gesunken.
**estimator** ['estɪmeɪtə'] *n (Insur)* Schätzer *m*.
**Estonia** [e'stəunɪə] *n* Estland *nt*.
**Estonian** [e'stəunɪən] **1** *adj* estnisch. **2** *n* **(a)** *(person)* Este *m*, Estin *f*. **(b)** *(language)* Estnisch *nt*.
**estrange** [ɪ'streɪndʒ] *vt person* entfremden *(from +dat)*. **to be/become ~d from sb** sich jdm entfremdet haben/entfremden; **his ~d wife** seine von ihm getrennt lebende Frau.
**estrangement** [ɪ'streɪndʒmənt] *n* Entfremdung *f (from* von*)*.
**estrogen** ['iːstrəudʒən] *n (US)* Östrogen *nt*.
**estuary** ['estjuərɪ] *n* Mündung *f*.
**ETA** = **estimated time of arrival** voraussichtliche Ankunft.
**et al** [et'æl] *adv* et al.
**etc** = **etcetera** usw, etc.
**etcetera** [ɪt'setərə] *adv* und so weiter.
**etch** [etʃ] *vti* ätzen; *(in copper)* stechen; *(in other metals)* radieren.
**etching** ['etʃɪŋ] *n see vb* **(a)** Ätzen *nt*; Stechen *nt*; Radieren *nt*. **(b)** *(picture)* Ätzung *f*; Stich *m*; Radierung *f*.
**ETD** = **estimated time of departure** voraussichtliche Abfahrt.
**eternal** [ɪ'tɜːnl] *adj (lit, fig)* ewig. **the ~ triangle** *(fig)* das Dreiecksverhältnis.
**eternity** [ɪ'tɜːnɪtɪ] *n (lit, fig)* Ewigkeit *f*. **from here to ~** bis in alle Ewigkeit.
**ether** ['iːθə'] *n (Chem, poet)* Äther *m*.
**ethereal** [ɪ'θɪərɪəl] *adj* ätherisch; *regions* himmlisch.
**ethic** ['eθɪk] *n* Ethik *f*, Ethos *nt*.
**ethical** ['eθɪkəl] *adj* ethisch *attr*. **it is not ~ to ...** es ist unmoralisch, zu ...
**ethics** ['eθɪks] *n* **(a)** *sing* Ethik *f*. **(b)** *pl (morality)* Moral *f*. **the ~ of abortion** die moralischen Aspekte der Abtreibung.
**Ethiopia** [,iːθɪ'əupɪə] *n* Äthiopien *nt*.

**Ethiopian** [,iːθɪ'əupɪən] **1** *adj* äthiopisch. **2** *n* Äthiopier(in *f) m*.
**ethnic** ['eθnɪk] *adj* ethnisch, Volks-; *clothes* folkloristisch; *atmosphere, pub* urtümlich, urwüchsig. **~ groups/minority** ethnische Gruppen *pl*/Minderheit *f*; **~ cleansing** *(Pol)* ethnische Säuberung; **~ violence** Rassenkrawalle *pl*.
**ethos** ['iːθɒs] *n* Gesinnung *f*, Ethos *nt*.
**etiquette** ['etɪket] *n* Etikette *f*.
**ETV** *(US)* = **Educational Television** Schulfernsehen *nt*.
**etymological** *adj*, **~ly** *adv* [,etɪmə'lɒdʒɪkəl, -ɪ] etymologisch.
**etymology** [,etɪ'mɒlədʒɪ] *n* Etymologie *f*.
**EU** *abbr* = **European Union** EU *f*.
**eucalyptus** [,juːkə'lɪptəs] *n* Eukalyptus *m*.
**Eucharist** ['juːkərɪst] *n (Eccl)* **the ~** *(Protestant)* das (heilige) Abendmahl; *(Catholic)* die Eucharistie.
**eulogy** ['juːlədʒɪ] *n* Lobrede *f*.
**eunuch** ['juːnək] *n* Eunuch *m*.
**euphemism** ['juːfəmɪzəm] *n* beschönigender Ausdruck, Euphemismus *m*.
**euphemistic** [,juːfə'mɪstɪk] *adj* euphemistisch.
**euphoria** [juː'fɔːrɪə] *n* Euphorie *f*.
**euphoric** [juː'fɒrɪk] *adj* euphorisch.
**Eurasia** [juə'reɪʃə] *n* Eurasien *nt*.
**Eurasian** [juə'reɪʃn] **1** *adj* eurasisch. **2** *n* Eurasier(in *f) m*.
**Euratom** [juə'rætəm] = **European Atomic Energy Community** Euratom *f*.
**eureka** [juə'riːkə] *interj* heureka, ich hab's!
**Eurocheque** ['juərəu,tʃek] *n* Euroscheck *m*.
**Eurocrat** ['juərəukræt] *n* Eurokrat(in *f) m*.
**Eurodollar** ['juərəudɒlə'] *n* Eurodollar *m*.
**Europe** ['juərəp] *n* Europa *nt*.
**European** [,juərə'piːən] **1** *adj* europäisch. **~ Community** Europäische Gemeinschaft; **~ Economic Community** Europäische Wirtschaftsgemeinschaft; **~ Monetary System** Europäisches Währungssystem; **~ Parliament** Europäisches Parlament; **~ Union** Europäische Union; **~ elections** Europawahlen *pl*. **2** *n* Europäer(in *f) m*.
**eurosceptic** ['juərəuskeptɪk] *n* Euroskeptiker *m*.
**euthanasia** [,juːθə'neɪzɪə] *n* Euthanasie *f*.
**evacuate** [ɪ'vækjueɪt] *vt* räumen; *people* evakuieren.
**evacuation** [ɪ,vækju'eɪʃən] *n see vt* Räumung *f*; Evakuierung *f*.
**evacuee** [ɪ,vækju'iː] *n* Evakuierte(r) *mf*.
**evade** [ɪ'veɪd] *vt blow, question, sb's eyes* ausweichen *(+dat)*; *pursuit, pursuers, justice* sich entziehen *(+dat)*.
**evaluate** [ɪ'væljueɪt] *vt house, worth etc* schätzen *(at* auf *+acc)*; *chances, usefulness* einschätzen; *evidence, results* auswerten; *pros and cons* (gegeneinander) abwägen; *achievement* bewerten.
**evaluation** [ɪ,vælju'eɪʃən] *n see vt* Schätzung *f*; Einschätzung *f*; Auswertung *f*; Abwägung *f*; Bewertung *f*.
**evangelic(al)** [,iːvæn'dʒelɪk(əl)] *adj* evangelisch.
**evangelist** [ɪ'vændʒəlɪst] *n (Bibl)* Evangelist(in *f) m*; *(preacher)* Prediger(in *f) m*.
**evaporate** [ɪ'væpəreɪt] **1** *vi* **(a)** *(liquid)* verdunsten. **(b)** *(fig: disappear)* sich in Luft auflösen. **2** *vt* **~d milk** Kondensmilch *f*.
**evaporation** [ɪ,væpə'reɪʃən] *n* Verdampfen *nt*; *(fig)* Schwinden *nt*.
**evasion** [ɪ'veɪʒən] *n* Ausweichen *nt (of* vor *+dat)*.
**evasive** [ɪ'veɪzɪv] *adj answer* ausweichend; *meaning, truth* schwer zu fassen. **he was very ~ about it** er wollte (dazu) nicht mit der Sprache herausrücken; **to take ~ action** *(Mil, fig)* ein Ausweichmanöver ma-

chen.

**eve** [iːv] *n* Vorabend *m.* **on the ~ of** am Tage vor *(+dat)*; am Vorabend *(+gen).*

**even** ['iːvən] **1** *adj* **(a)** *surface, ground* eben. **to be ~ with sth** mit etw abschließen. **(b)** *(regular) layer etc* gleichmäßig; *progress* stetig; *temper* ausgeglichen. **(c)** *quantities, distances, values* gleich. **the score is ~** es steht unentschieden; **I will get ~ with you for that** das werde ich dir heimzahlen; **that makes us ~** *(in game)* damit steht es unentschieden; *(fig)* damit sind wir quitt. **(d)** *number* gerade.

    **2** *adv* **(a)** sogar, selbst. **they ~ denied its existence** sie leugneten sogar seine Existenz; **~ better/ more beautiful** sogar (noch) besser/schöner. **(b)** **not ~** nicht einmal; **with not ~ a smile** ohne auch nur zu lächeln. **(c)** **~ if/though** selbst wenn; **~ as I spoke** ... noch während ich redete ...; **~ so** (aber) trotzdem.

    ▶**even out 1** *vi* **(a)** *(prices)* sich einpendeln. **(b)** *(ground)* eben werden. **2** *vt sep* **(a)** *prices* ausgleichen. **that should ~ things ~ a bit** dadurch müßte ein gewisser Ausgleich erzielt werden. **(b)** *ground, cement* ebnen.

**even-handed** [ˌiːvən'hændɪd] *adj* gerecht.

**evening** ['iːvnɪŋ] *n* Abend *m.* **in the ~** abends, am Abend; **this/tomorrow ~** heute/morgen abend; **one ~** eines Abends; **every Monday ~** jeden Montagabend.

**evening** *in cpds* Abend-; **~ class** *n* Abendkurs *m*; **~ dress** *n (men's)* Abendanzug *m*; *(women's)* Abendkleid *nt*; **~ paper** *n* Abendzeitung *f.*

**evenly** ['iːvənlɪ] *adv* gleichmäßig. **they were ~ matched** sie waren einander ebenbürtig.

**evensong** ['iːvənsɒŋ] *n* Abendgottesdienst *m.*

**event** [ɪ'vent] *n* **(a)** *(happening)* Ereignis *nt.* **in the normal course of ~s** normalerweise. **(b)** *(function)* Veranstaltung *f.* **what is your best ~?** *(Sport)* in welcher Disziplin sind Sie am besten? **(c)** **in the ~ of war/fire** im Kriegsfalle/im Falle eines Brandes; **in any ~** ohnehin, sowieso; **in the ~** im Endeffekt; **at all ~s** auf jeden Fall.

**even-tempered** [ˌivən'tempəd] *adj* ausgeglichen.

**eventer** [ɪ'ventər] *n (Sport)* Militaryreiter(in *f*) *m.*

**eventful** [ɪ'ventfʊl] *adj* ereignisreich.

**eventing** [ɪ'ventɪŋ] *n (Sport)* Military *f.*

**eventual** [ɪ'ventʃʊəl] *adj* **the decline and ~ collapse of ...** der Niedergang und schließliche vollkommene Zerfall des ...

**eventuality** [ɪˌventʃʊ'ælɪtɪ] *n* möglicher Fall. **be ready for any ~** sei auf alle Eventualitäten gefaßt.

**eventually** [ɪ'ventʃʊəlɪ] *adv* schließlich, endlich.

**ever** ['evər] *adv* **(a)** je(mals). **not ~** nie; **nothing ~ happens** es passiert nie etwas; **it hardly ~ snows here** hier schneit es kaum (jemals); **if I ~ catch you doing that again** wenn ich dich noch einmal dabei erwische; **seldom, if ~** selten, wenn überhaupt; **he's a rascal if ~ there was one** er ist ein richtiggehender kleiner Halunke; **as if I ~ would** als ob ich das jemals täte; **don't you ~ say that again!** sag das ja nie mehr!; **have you ~ been to Glasgow?** bist du schon einmal in Glasgow gewesen?; **more beautiful than ~** schöner denn je; **the first ~** der/ die/das allererste; **the coldest night ~** die kälteste Nacht aller Zeiten.

    **(b)** **~ since then** seit der Zeit, seitdem; **for ~** für immer; **it seemed to go on for ~ (and ~)** es schien ewig zu dauern; **~ increasing powers** ständig wachsende Macht.

    **(c)** *(intensive)* **no government be it ~ so powerful** keine noch so mächtige Regierung; **the best grandmother ~** die beste Großmutter, die es je gegeben

hat; **did you ~!** *(col)* also so was!; **why ~ not?** warum denn bloß nicht?

    **(d)** *(col)* **~ so/such** unheimlich; **~ so slightly drunk** ein ganz klein wenig betrunken; **I am ~ so sorry** es tut mir schrecklich leid; **thank you ~ so much** ganz herzlichen Dank.

**Everest** ['evərest] *n* **(Mount)** ~ der Mount Everest.

**evergreen** ['evəgriːn] **1** *adj* immergrün; *(fig) topic* immer aktuell. **2** *n* immergrüner Baum/Busch; *(fig: song)* Evergreen *m.*

**everlasting** [ˌevə'lɑːstɪŋ] *adj (lit, fig)* ewig. **~ flower** Strohblume *f.*

**evermore** [ˌevə'mɔːr] *adv* immer. **for ~** in alle Ewigkeit.

**every** ['evrɪ] *adj* jede(r, s). **he is ~ bit as clever as his brother** er ist ganz genauso schlau wie sein Bruder; **I have ~ reason to believe that ...** ich habe allen Grund anzunehmen, daß ...; **I have ~ confidence in him** ich habe vollstes Vertrauen zu ihm; **we wish you ~ success/happiness** wir wünschen Ihnen viel Erfolg/Glück; **his ~ word** jedes Wort, das er sagte; **~ fifth day, ~ five days** jeden fünften Tag, alle fünf Tage; **~ other day** jeden zweiten Tag, alle zwei Tage; **~ so often, ~ now and then** *or* **again** hin und wieder, ab und zu.

**everybody** ['evrɪbɒdɪ] *pron* jeder(mann), alle *pl.* **~ knows ~ else here** hier kennt jeder jeden.

**everyday** ['evrɪdeɪ] *adj* alltäglich; *language* Umgangs-.

**everyone** ['evrɪwʌn] *pron* = **everybody.**

**everything** ['evrɪθɪŋ] *n* alles. **~ possible** alles Mögliche; **~ you have** alles, was du hast.

**everywhere** ['evrɪweər] *adv* überall; *(with direction)* überallhin. **from ~** überallher, von überall; **~ you look** wo man auch hinsieht.

**evict** [ɪ'vɪkt] *vt tenants* zur Räumung zwingen *(from gen).*

**eviction** [ɪ'vɪkʃən] *n* Zwangsräumung *f (from aus).* **~ notice** *or* **order** Räumungsbefehl *m.*

**evidence** ['evɪdəns] **1** *n* **(a)** Beweis(e *pl*) *m*; *(Jur) (object)* Beweisstück *nt*; *(testimony)* Aussage *f.* **there wasn't enough ~** die Beweise reichten nicht aus; **all the ~ was against his claim** alles sprach gegen seine Behauptung; **to give ~ (for/against sb)** (für/gegen jdn) aussagen; **the ~ for the defence** die Beweisführung für die Verteidigung. **(b)** **to be in ~** sichtbar sein; **ideas which have been very much in ~ recently** Ideen, die in letzter Zeit deutlich in Erscheinung getreten sind. **2** *vt* zeugen von.

**evident** *adj,* **~ly** *adv* ['evɪdənt, -lɪ] offensichtlich.

**evil** ['iːvl] **1** *adj* böse; *person also, reputation, influence* schlecht; *(col) smell* übel. **2** *n* Böse(s) *nt.* **an ~ ein Übel** *nt*; **the lesser of two ~s** das kleinere von zwei Übeln; **social ~s** soziale Mißstände.

**evil: ~-doer** *n* Übeltäter(in *f*) *m*; **~-minded** *adj* bösartig.

**evince** [ɪ'vɪns] *vt* an den Tag legen.

**evocation** [ˌevə'keɪʃən] *n* Heraufbeschwören *nt.*

**evocative** [ɪ'vɒkətɪv] *adj* evokativ *(geh).* **to be ~ of sth** etw heraufbeschwören.

**evoke** [ɪ'vəʊk] *vt* heraufbeschwören; *memory also* wachrufen; *admiration* hervorrufen.

**evolution** [ˌiːvə'luːʃən] *n* Entwicklung *f*; *(Biol etc)* Evolution *f.* **theory of ~** Abstammungslehre *f.*

**evolutionary** [ˌiːvə'luːʃnərɪ] *adj* evolutionär.

**evolve** [ɪ'vɒlv] **1** *vt* entwickeln. **2** *vi* sich entwickeln, sich herausbilden.

**ewe** [juː] *n* Mutterschaf *nt.*

**ex-** [eks-] *pref* **(a)** ehemalig, Ex-. **~-wife** frühere Frau, Exfrau *f.* **(b)** *(Comm)* **~-works** ab Werk.

**exacerbate** [ek'sæsəbeɪt] *vt pain, disease* verschlim-

mern; *situation* verschärfen.
**exact** [ɪg'zækt] **1** *adj* genau; *figures, analysis etc also*
exakt. **it's the ~ opposite** es ist genau umgekehrt;
**please tender the ~ fare** bitte das abgezählte Fahrgeld bereithalten. **2** *vt money, ransom* fordern
*(from* von*)*.
**exacting** [ɪg'zæktɪŋ] *adj* anspruchsvoll. **to be too/
very ~ with sb** zu viel/sehr viel von jdm verlangen.
**exactitude** [ɪg'zæktɪtjuːd] *n* Genauigkeit *f*.
**exactly** [ɪg'zæktlɪ] *adj* genau. **I'm not ~ sure who he
is** ich bin mir nicht ganz sicher, wer er ist; **it's not
~ a detective story** es ist eigentlich keine Kriminalgeschichte; **he wasn't ~ pleased** er war nicht gerade erfreut.
**exactness** [ɪg'zæktnɪs] *n* Genauigkeit *f*.
**exaggerate** [ɪg'zædʒəreɪt] *vti* übertreiben; *(intensify)
effect* verstärken.
**exaggerated** [ɪg'zædʒəreɪtɪd] *adj* übertrieben. **to
have an ~ opinion of oneself** eine übertrieben hohe
Meinung von sich haben.
**exaggeration** [ɪg,zædʒə'reɪʃən] *n* Übertreibung *f*.
**exalted** [ɪg'zɔːltɪd] *adj position, style* hoch.
**exam** [ɪg'zæm] *n* Prüfung *f*.
**examination** [ɪg,zæmɪ'neɪʃən] *n* **(a)** *(Sch etc)* Prüfung *f*; *(Univ also)* Examen *nt*. **~ candidate** Prüfling,
Prüfungskandidat *m*; **~ paper** Prüfungsbogen *m*;
*(questions)* Prüfungsaufgaben *pl*. **(b)** *(study, inspection)* Prüfung, Untersuchung *f*; *(of machine,
passports)* Kontrolle *f*; *(of question)* Untersuchung
*f*; *(of accounts)* Prüfung *f*. **the matter is still under ~**
die Angelegenheit wird noch geprüft *or* untersucht.
**(c)** *(of accused, witness)* Vernehmung *f*; *(of case)*
Untersuchung *f*.
**examine** [ɪg'zæmɪn] *vt* **(a)** *(for* auf *+acc)* untersuchen; *document, accounts* prüfen; *machine, passports, luggage* kontrollieren. **(b)** *pupil, candidate*
prüfen *(in* in *+dat, on* über *+acc)*. **(c)** *accused, witness* verhören.
**examiner** [ɪg'zæmɪnəʳ] *n* *(Sch, Univ)* Prüfer (in *f*) *m*.
**example** [ɪg'zɑːmpl] *n* Beispiel *nt*. **for ~** zum Beispiel; **to set a good/bad ~** ein gutes/schlechtes Beispiel geben; **to make an ~ of sb** an jdm ein Exempel statuieren.
**exasperate** [ɪg'zɑːspəreɪt] *vt* zur Verzweiflung bringen. **to get ~d** verzweifeln *(with* an *+dat)*; **~d at** *or*
**by** verärgert über *(+acc)*.
**exasperating** [ɪg'zɑːspəreɪtɪŋ] *adj* ärgerlich; *delay,
difficulty, job* leidig *attr*. **it's so ~!** es ist wirklich
zum Verzweifeln!
**exasperation** [ɪg,zɑːspə'reɪʃən] *n* Verzweiflung *f*
*(with* über *+acc)*.
**excavate** ['ekskəveɪt] **1** *vt ground* ausschachten;
*(machine)* ausbaggern; *(Archeol) remains* ausgraben. **2** *vi (Archeol)* Ausgrabungen machen.
**excavation** [,ekskə'veɪʃən] *n* *(Archeol)* (Aus)-
grabung *f*; *(of tunnel etc)* Graben *nt*. **~(s)** *(site)* Ausgrabungsstätte *f*.
**excavator** ['ekskəveɪtəʳ] *n* *(machine)* Bagger *m*.
**exceed** [ɪk'siːd] *vt (in value, amount, length of time)*
übersteigen *(by* um*)*; *(go beyond)* hinausgehen über
*(+acc)*; *expectations, desires* übertreffen; *limits,
powers, speed limit* überschreiten. **amounts ~ing/
not ~ing £50** Beträge über/bis zu £50.
**exceedingly** [ɪk'siːdɪŋlɪ] *adv* äußerst.
**excel** [ɪk'sel] **1** *vi* sich auszeichnen, sich hervortun
*(in* in *+dat, at* bei*)*. **2** *vr* **to ~ oneself** *(oft iro)* sich
selbst übertreffen.
**excellence** ['eksələns] *n* Vorzüglichkeit *f*.
**Excellency** ['eksələnsɪ] *n* **Your ~** Eure Exzellenz.
**excellent** ['eksələnt] *adj* ausgezeichnet.
**except** [ɪk'sept] **1** *prep* außer *(+dat)*. **what can they**

**do ~ wait?** was können sie anderes tun als warten?; **~ for** abgesehen von, bis auf *(+acc)*; **~ that ...**
außer daß ...; **~ for the fact that** abgesehen davon,
daß ...; **~ if** außer wenn; **~ when** außer wenn. **2**
*conj* **I'd refuse ~ I need the money** ich würde ablehnen, doch ich brauche das Geld. **3** *vt* ausnehmen.
**~ing** außer *(+dat)*; **not ~ing X** X nicht ausgenommen.
**exception** [ɪk'sepʃən] *n* **(a)** Ausnahme *f*. **to make an
~** eine Ausnahme machen; **with the ~ of** mit Ausnahme von; **as an ~** ausnahmsweise; **the ~ proves
the rule** *(prov)* Ausnahmen bestätigen die Regel
*(prov)*. **(b)** **to take ~ to sth** Anstoß *m* an etw *(dat)*
nehmen.
**exceptional** [ɪk'sepʃnl] *adj* außergewöhnlich. **apart
from ~ cases** abgesehen von Ausnahmefällen.
**exceptionally** [ɪk'sepʃnəlɪ] *adv (outstandingly)*
außergewöhnlich; *(as an exception)* ausnahmsweise.
**excerpt** ['eksɜːpt] *n* Auszug *m*.
**excess** [ɪk'ses] *n* **(a)** Übermaß *nt (of* an *+dat)*. **to
drink to ~** übermäßig trinken; **to carry sth to ~** etw
übertreiben. **(b)** **~es** *pl* Exzesse *pl*; *(brutalities also)*
Ausschreitungen *pl*. **(c)** *(amount left over)* Überschuß *m*. **(d)** **in ~ of** über *+dat*; **to be in ~ of** überschreiten.
**excess** *in cpds weight, production* Über-; **~ baggage** *n* Übergepäck *nt*; **~ fare** *n* Nachlösegebühr
*f*; **I had to pay ~ fare** ich mußte nachlösen.
**excessive** [ɪk'sesɪv] *adj* übermäßig; *praise also* übertrieben. **I think you're being ~** ich finde, Sie übertreiben.
**excessively** [ɪk'sesɪvlɪ] *adv* **(a)** *(to excess) (+vb)* eat,
drink* übermäßig; *(+adj) optimistic, severe* allzu. **(b)**
*(extremely)* äußerst.
**exchange** [ɪks'tʃeɪndʒ] **1** *vt books, glances, seats* tauschen; *foreign currency* umtauschen *(for* in *+acc)*;
*ideas, experiences etc* austauschen. **to ~ words/
letters/blows** einen Wortwechsel haben/einen Briefwechsel führen/sich schlagen; **to ~ one thing for
another** eine Sache gegen eine andere austauschen
*or (in shop)* umtauschen.
**2** *n* **(a)** *(of goods, stamps)* Tausch *m*; *(of prisoners, views)* Austausch *m*; *(of one bought item for another)* Umtausch *m*. **in ~** dafür; **in ~ for money**
gegen Geld; **in ~ for lending me your car** dafür, daß
Sie mir Ihr Auto geliehen haben. **(b)** *(Fin: place)*
Wechselstube *f*. **~ control** Devisenkontrolle *f*; **~
rate** Wechselkurs *m*. **(c)** *(telephone)* **~** Fernamt *nt*;
*(in office etc)* (Telefon)zentrale *f*.
**3** *adj attr student, teacher, engine etc* Austausch-.
**exchequer** [ɪks'tʃekəʳ] *n* Finanzministerium *nt*; *(esp
in GB)* Schatzamt *nt*.
**excise** ['eksaɪz] *n* Verbrauchssteuer *f*.
**excitable** [ɪk'saɪtəbl] *adj* (leicht) erregbar.
**excite** [ɪk'saɪt] *vt* aufregen, aufgeregt machen;
*(rouse enthusiasm in)* begeistern; *sentiments, (sexually)* erregen; *imagination* anregen.
**excited** [ɪk'saɪtɪd] *adj* aufgeregt; *(worked up, not
calm also, sexually)* erregt; *(enthusiastic)* begeistert.
**don't get ~!** *(angry etc)* reg dich nicht auf!; **don't
get too ~** *(iro)* freu dich nicht zu früh!; **aren't you
~ about the holidays?** freust du dich nicht schon
auf die Ferien?
**excitement** [ɪk'saɪtmənt] *n* Aufregung *f*; *(not being
calm etc also, sexual)* Erregung *f*. **a mood of ~** eine
spannungsgeladene Stimmung; **what's all the ~
about?** wozu die ganze Aufregung?; **his novel has
caused great ~** sein Roman hat große Begeisterung
ausgelöst.
**exciting** [ɪk'saɪtɪŋ] *adj* aufregend; *story, film, event,*

*adventure also* spannend; *new author* sensationell. **isn't that** ~**!** ist das nicht prima?; **how** ~ **for you** wie schön für dich!, wie aufregend *(also iro)*.

**excl** = **excluding** exkl.

**exclaim** [ɪk'skleɪm] *vt* ausrufen.

**exclamation** [,ekskləˈmeɪʃən] *n* Ausruf *m (also Gram)*. ~ **mark** *or (US)* **point** Ausrufezeichen *nt*.

**exclude** [ɪk'sklu:d] *vt* ausschließen. **to** ~ **sb from the team** jdn aus der Mannschaft ausschließen.

**excluding** [ɪk'sklu:dɪŋ] *prep* außer *(+dat)*, exklusive *(+gen)*. ~ **VAT** ohne MWSt.

**exclusion** [ɪk'sklu:ʒən] *n* Ausschluß *m (from* von*)*. **you can't just think about your job to the** ~ **of everything else** du kannst nicht ausschließlich an deine Arbeit denken; ~ **clause** *(Insur)* Haftungsausschlußklausel *f*.

**exclusive** [ɪk'sklu:sɪv] *adj* **(a)** *group, club etc* exklusiv; *report, interview also* Exklusiv-. ~ **right** ausschließliches Recht, Alleinrecht *nt*; **they are mutually** ~ sie schließen einander aus. **(b)** *(sole)* ausschließlich, einzig. **(c)** *from* **15th to 20th June** ~ vom 15. bis zum 20. Juni ausschließlich; ~ **of** ausschließlich *(+gen)*, exklusive *(+gen)*; ~ **of service** ohne Bedienung.

**exclusively** [ɪk'sklu:sɪvlɪ] *adv* ausschließlich.

**excommunicate** [,ekskəˈmju:nɪkeɪt] *vt* exkommunizieren.

**excommunication** [,ekskəmju:nɪ'keɪʃən] *n* Exkommunikation *f*.

**excrement** ['ekskrɪmənt] *n* Kot *m*, Exkremente *pl*.

**excruciating** [ɪk'skru:ʃɪeɪtɪŋ] *adj* *pain, noise* gräßlich, entsetzlich.

**excruciatingly** [ɪk'skru:ʃɪeɪtɪŋlɪ] *adv* **it was** ~ **painful** es hat scheußlich weh getan *(col)*; ~ **funny** urkomisch.

**excursion** [ɪk'skɜ:ʃən] *n* Ausflug *m*. **to go on an** ~ einen Ausflug machen; ~ **ticket** verbilligte Fahrkarte.

**excuse** [ɪk'skju:z] **1** *vt* **(a)** entschuldigen. **he** ~**d himself for being late** er entschuldigte sich, daß er zu spät kam; **to** ~ **sb for having done sth** jdm verzeihen, daß er etwas getan hat; **I think I can be** ~**d for believing him** man kann es mir wohl nicht übelnehmen, daß ich ihm geglaubt habe; **if you will** ~ **the expression** wenn Sie mir den Ausdruck gestatten; ~ **me!** *(to get attention, sorry)* Entschuldigung!, entschuldigen Sie!; *(indignant)* erlauben Sie mal! **(b)** *(from obligation)* **to** ~ **sb from (doing) sth** jdn von einer Sache befreien, jdm etw erlassen; **you are** ~**d** ihr könnt gehen; **can I be** ~**d?** darf ich mal verschwinden *(col)*?

**2** [ɪks'kju:s] *n* Entschuldigung *f*. **there's no** ~ **for it** dafür gibt es keine Entschuldigung; **to make** ~**s for sb** jdn entschuldigen; **he's only making** ~**s** er sucht nur nach einer Ausrede; **a good** ~ **for a party** ein guter Grund, eine Party zu feiern.

**ex-directory** [,eksdaɪ'rektərɪ] *adj (Brit)* **to be** ~ *(person)* nicht im Telefonbuch stehen; *(number)* eine Geheimnummer sein.

**execrable** ['eksɪkrəbl] *adj* abscheulich.

**execute** ['eksɪkju:t] *vt* **(a)** *plan, order, (Comp) command* ausführen; *duties* erfüllen. **beautifully** ~**d** *(music)* wunderbar gespielt. **(b)** *criminal* hinrichten. **(c)** *(Jur)* *will* vollstrecken.

**execution** [,eksɪ'kju:ʃən] *n* **(a)** *see vt* **(a)** Ausführung *f*; Erfüllung *f*. **in the** ~ **of his duties** bei der Ausübung seines Amtes. **(b)** *(Mus)* Vortrag *m*; *(musician's skill)* Ausführung *f*. **(c)** *(as punishment)* Hinrichtung *f*. **(d)** *(Jur: of will)* Vollstreckung *f*.

**executioner** [,eksɪ'kju:ʃnər] *n* Henker *m*.

**executive** [ɪg'zekjʊtɪv] **1** *adj* *powers, committee etc*

Exekutiv-; *(Comm)* geschäftsführend. ~ **director** Vorstandsmitglied *nt*; ~ **position** leitende Stellung *or* Position. **2** *n* **(a)** leitender Angestellter, leitende Angestellte, Manager *m*. ~ **(brief)case** Diplomatenkofferchen *nt*. **(b)** *(of government)* Exekutive *f*; *(of association)* Vorstand *m*.

**executor** [ɪg'zekjʊtər] *n (of will)* Testamentsvollstrecker *m*.

**exemplary** [ɪg'zemplərɪ] *adj* vorbildlich, beispielhaft. ~ **punishment** exemplarische Strafe.

**exemplify** [ɪg'zemplɪfaɪ] *vt* (anhand von Beispielen) erläutern.

**exempt** [ɪg'zempt] **1** *adj* befreit *(from* von*)*. **2** *vt person* befreien.

**exemption** [ɪg'zempʃən] *n* Befreiung *f*.

**exercise** ['eksəsaɪz] **1** *n* **(a)** *no pl (of right)* Wahrnehmung *f*; *(of physical, mental power)* Ausübung *f*. **(b)** *(bodily or mental, drill, Mus etc)* Übung *f*. **to do one's** ~**s in the morning** Morgengymnastik machen. **(c)** *no pl (physical)* Bewegung *f*. **physical** ~ (körperliche) Bewegung; **you should take more** ~ Sie sollten mehr Bewegung haben; **what do you do for** ~**?** wie halten Sie sich fit? **(d)** *(Mil: usu pl)* Übung *f*. **2** *vt* **(a)** *body, mind* trainieren; *(Mil)* *troops* exerzieren; *dog* spazierenführen. **(b)** *(use)* *control, power* ausüben; *a right also* geltend machen; *tact, discretion* üben. **3** *vi* **if you** ~ **regularly** wenn Sie sich viel bewegen.

**exercise:** ~ **bike** *n* Heimtrainer *m*, Trimmrad *nt*; ~ **book** *n* Heft *nt*.

**exert** [ɪg'zɜ:t] **1** *vt pressure, influence* ausüben *(on* auf *+acc)*; *authority* geltend machen *(on* bei*)*. **2** *vr* **to** ~ **oneself** sich anstrengen.

**exertion** [ɪg'zɜ:ʃən] *n* **(a)** *(effort)* Anstrengung *f*. **after the day's** ~**s** nach des Tages Mühen. **(b)** *(of pressure, influence)* Ausübung *f (on* auf *+acc)*.

**exeunt** ['eksɪʌnt] *(in stage directions)* ab.

**ex gratia** [eks'greɪʃə] *adj payment* Sonder-.

**exhale** [eks'heɪl] *vti* ausatmen.

**exhaust** [ɪg'zɔ:st] **1** *vt (use up, tire)* erschöpfen. **2** *n (Aut etc)* Auspuff *m*; *(~ gases)* Auspuffgase *pl*.

**exhausted** [ɪg'zɔ:stɪd] *adj* erschöpft.

**exhaust fumes** *npl* Abgase *pl*.

**exhausting** [ɪg'zɔ:stɪŋ] *adj* anstrengend.

**exhaustion** [ɪg'zɔ:stʃən] *n* Erschöpfung *f*.

**exhaustive** [ɪg'zɔ:stɪv] *adj* erschöpfend.

**exhaust:** ~ **pipe** *n* Auspuffrohr *nt*; ~ **system** *n* Auspuff *m*.

**exhibit** [ɪg'zɪbɪt] **1** *vt* **(a)** ausstellen; *merchandise also* auslegen. **(b)** *skill, ingenuity* zeigen, an den Tag legen. **2** *vi* ausstellen. **3** *n (in an exhibition)* Ausstellungsstück *nt*; *(Jur)* Beweisstück *nt*.

**exhibition** [,eksɪ'bɪʃən] *n* **(a)** Ausstellung *f*; *(of articles for sale)* Auslage *f*. **(b)** **to make an** ~ **of oneself** sich danebenbenehmen *(col)*.

**exhibition bout** *n* Schaukampf *m*.

**exhibitionist** [,eksɪ'bɪʃənɪst] *n* Exhibitionist(in *f*) *m*.

**exhibitor** [ɪg'zɪbɪtər] *n* Aussteller *m*.

**exhilarate** [ɪg'zɪləreɪt] *vt* in Hochstimmung versetzen; *(sea air etc)* beleben, erfrischen.

**exhilarated** [ɪg'zɪləreɪtɪd] *adj* erregt. **to feel** ~ in Hochstimmung sein.

**exhilarating** [ɪg'zɪləreɪtɪŋ] *adj sensation, speed* erregend; *music* anregend; *air etc* belebend.

**exhilaration** [ɪg,zɪlə'reɪʃən] *n* Hochgefühl *nt*.

**exhort** [ɪg'zɔ:t] *vt* ermahnen.

**exhumation** [,ekshju:'meɪʃən] *n* Exhumierung *f*.

**exhume** [eks'hju:m] *vt* exhumieren.

**exile** ['eksaɪl] **1** *n (person)* Verbannte(r) *mf*; *(banishment)* Exil *nt*, Verbannung *f*. **in** ~ im Exil. **2** *vt* verbannen *(from* aus*)*.

**exist** [ɪg'zɪst] vi (a) existieren, bestehen. **it doesn't ~ das gibt es nicht; to continue to ~** fortbestehen; **there ~s a tradition that** ... es gibt den Brauch, daß ...; **she ~s on very little** sie kommt mit sehr wenig aus; **we manage to ~** wir kommen gerade aus. (b) (be found: plants, minerals etc) vorkommen.

**existence** [ɪg'zɪstəns] n (a) Existenz f; (of custom, tradition, institution also) Bestehen nt. **to be in ~** existieren, bestehen; **to come into ~** entstehen; (person) auf die Welt kommen; **to go out of ~** zu existieren aufhören; **the only one in ~** der einzige, den es gibt. (b) (life) Dasein nt, Existenz f.

**existential** [ˌegzɪs'tenʃəl] adj existentiell.

**existentialism** [ˌegzɪs'tenʃəlɪzəm] n Existentialismus m.

**existing** [ɪg'zɪstɪŋ] adj law bestehend; director gegenwärtig.

**exit** ['eksɪt] **1** n Ausgang m; (for vehicles) Ausfahrt f. **he made a very dramatic ~** sein Abgang war sehr dramatisch; **~ poll** bei Wahlen unmittelbar nach Verlassen der Wahllokale durchgeführte Umfrage; **~ ramp** (US) Ausfahrt f; **~ visa** Ausreisevisum nt. **2** vi (from stage) abgehen; (Comp) das Programm/die Datei verlassen.

**exodus** ['eksədəs] n Auszug m; (Bibl, fig) Exodus m. **general ~** allgemeiner Aufbruch.

**ex officio** [ˌeksəˈfɪʃɪəʊ] **1** adj leader, member von Amts wegen. **2** adv **to act ~** kraft seines Amtes handeln.

**exonerate** [ɪg'zɒnəreɪt] vt entlasten (from von).

**exorbitant** [ɪg'zɔːbɪtənt] adj price astronomisch; demands maßlos, übertrieben. **that's ~!** das ist Wucher!

**exorcism** ['eksɔːsɪzəm] n Exorzismus m.

**exorcize** ['eksɔːsaɪz] vt exorzieren; evil spirit also austreiben.

**exotic** [ɪg'zɒtɪk] adj exotisch.

**expand** [ɪk'spænd] **1** vt ausdehnen, erweitern; ideas entwickeln. **~ed polystyrene** Styropor ® nt. **2** vi (gases, universe) sich ausdehnen; (business) expandieren, sich ausweiten; (knowledge, influence, market) wachsen. **could you ~ on that?** könnten Sie das näher ausführen?

**expandable** [ɪk'spændəbl] adj erweiterbar; (Comp) ausbaufähig.

**expanse** [ɪk'spæns] n Fläche f; (of sea) Weite f no pl.

**expansion** [ɪk'spænʃən] n (of gas, metal, property) Ausdehnung f; (of business, production, knowledge) Erweiterung f; (territorial, economic) Expansion f; (of subject, idea) Entwicklung f; (of experience, influence) Vergrößerung f.

**expansionism** [ɪk'spænʃənɪzəm] n Expansionspolitik f.

**expansionist** [ɪk'spænʃənɪst] adj expansionistisch.

**expansive** [ɪk'spænsɪv] adj person mitteilsam.

**expat** [ˌeks'pæt] (col) see **expatriate 2**.

**expatriate** [eks'pætrɪət] **1** adj im Ausland lebend. **2** n im Ausland Lebende(r) mf. **the ~s in Abu Dhabi** die Ausländer in Abu Dhabi.

**expect** [ɪk'spekt] **1** vt (a) (anticipate) erwarten; esp sth bad also rechnen mit. **that was to be ~ed** das war zu erwarten; **I know what to ~** ich weiß, was mich erwartet; **I ~ed as much** das habe ich erwartet; **I was ~ing him to come** ich habe eigentlich erwartet, daß er kommt.

(b) (suppose) annehmen. **will they be on time?** — **yes, I ~ so** kommen sie pünktlich? — ja, ich glaube schon; **I ~ it will rain** es wird wohl regnen; **I ~ he turned it down** ich nehme an, er hat abgelehnt; **well, I ~ he's right** er wird schon recht haben.

(c) (demand) **to ~ sth of** or **from sb** etw von jdm

erwarten; **to ~ sb to do sth** erwarten, daß jd etw tut; **are we ~ed to tip the waiter?** müssen wir dem Kellner Trinkgeld geben?; **what do you ~ me to do about it?** was soll ich da machen?

(d) (await) erwarten; baby also bekommen. **we'll ~ you when we see you** (col) wenn ihr kommt, dann kommt ihr (col).

**2** vi **she's ~ing** sie ist in anderen Umständen.

**expectancy** [ɪk'spektənsɪ] n Erwartung f.

**expectant** [ɪk'spektənt] adj erwartungsvoll; mother werdend.

**expectantly** [ɪk'spektəntlɪ] adv erwartungsvoll; wait gespannt.

**expectation** [ˌekspek'teɪʃən] n (a) Erwartung f. **in ~ of** in Erwartung (+gen); **contrary to all ~(s)** wider Erwarten; **beyond all ~(s)** über Erwarten; **to come up to sb's ~s** jds Erwartungen (dat) entsprechen. (b) (prospect) Aussicht f.

**expedience** [ɪk'spiːdɪəns], **expediency** [ɪk'spiːdɪənsɪ] n (a) (self-interest) Zweckdenken nt, Berechnung f. (b) (of measure etc) Zweckdienlichkeit f; (advisability) Ratsamkeit f.

**expedient** [ɪk'spiːdɪənt] adj (politic) zweckdienlich; (advisable) angebracht, ratsam.

**expedite** ['ekspɪdaɪt] vt beschleunigen.

**expedition** [ˌekspɪ'dɪʃən] n Expedition f; (Mil) Feldzug m.

**expeditionary** [ˌekspɪ'dɪʃənrɪ] adj **~ force** Expeditionskorps nt.

**expel** [ɪk'spel] vt vertreiben; (from country) ausweisen (from aus); (from school) verweisen (from von, gen); (from party) ausschließen (from aus).

**expend** [ɪk'spend] vt time, energy aufwenden (on für); (use up) resources verbrauchen.

**expendable** [ɪk'spendəbl] adj entbehrlich; people überflüssig.

**expenditure** [ɪk'spendɪtʃəʳ] n (money spent) Ausgaben pl; (of time, energy) Aufwand m (of an +dat).

**expense** [ɪk'spens] n (a) Kosten pl. **at great ~** unter großem Kostenaufwand; **it's a big ~** es ist eine große Ausgabe; **to go to great ~ to repair the house** es sich (dat) etwas kosten lassen, das Haus instand zu setzen; **don't go to any ~ over our visit** stürz dich nicht in Unkosten wegen unseres Besuchs; **at sb's ~/at the ~ of sth** (lit, fig) auf jds Kosten (acc)/auf Kosten einer Sache (gen); **at my own ~** auf eigene Kosten. (b) (Comm: usu pl) Spesen pl. **to incur ~s** Unkosten haben; **it's on ~s** das geht auf Spesen; **~ account** Spesenkonto nt.

**expensive** [ɪk'spensɪv] adj teuer.

**experience** [ɪk'spɪərɪəns] **1** n (a) Erfahrung f. **~ shows that** ... die Erfahrung lehrt, daß ...; **from my own personal ~** aus eigener Erfahrung; **he has no ~ of living in the country** er kennt das Landleben nicht; **to have a lot of teaching ~** große Erfahrung als Lehrer haben. (b) (event experienced) Erlebnis nt. **I had a nasty ~** mir ist etwas Unangenehmes passiert; **to go through** or **have a painful ~** Schreckliches erleben; **to have an ~** eine Erfahrung machen; **what an ~!** das war vielleicht was!; **it was a new ~ for me** es war völlig neu für mich.

**2** vt (a) erleben; pain, hunger also erfahren; difficult times durchmachen. **to ~ difficulties** Schwierigkeiten haben. (b) (feel) empfinden.

**experienced** [ɪk'spɪərɪənst] adj erfahren (in in +dat); eye, ear geschult.

**experiment** [ɪk'sperɪmənt] **1** n Versuch m, Experiment nt. **to do an ~** einen Versuch or ein Experiment machen. **2** vi experimentieren (on mit).

**experimental** [ɪk,sperɪ'mentl] adj experimentell; also method, science Experimental-; farm, engine,

*period* Versuchs-; *theatre, cinema* Experimentier-. **at the ~ stage** im Versuchsstadium.
**experimentally** [ɪk,sperɪ'mentəlɪ] *adv* versuchsweise.
**experimentation** [ɪk,sperɪmen'teɪʃən] *n* Experimentieren *nt.*
**expert** ['ekspɜːt] **1** *n* Fachmann, Experte *m,* Expertin *f; (Jur)* Sachverständige(r) *mf.* **~'s eye** Kennerblick *m.* **2** *adj work, repair* fachmännisch, geschickt; *driver etc* geschickt, ausgezeichnet; *approach, advice* fachmännisch. **~ opinion** Gutachten *nt;* **~ witness** sachverständiger Zeuge, Gutachter *m;* **the ~ touch** die Meisterhand; **~ system** *(Comp)* Expertensystem *nt.*
**expertise** [,ekspɜː'tiːz] *n* Sachkenntnis *f (in* auf dem Gebiet *+gen); (manual)* Geschick *nt (in* bei*).*
**expertly** ['ekspɜːtlɪ] *adv* fachmännisch; *drive etc* geschickt, ausgezeichnet.
**expire** [ɪk'spaɪər] *vi* **(a)** *(passport, time limit)* ablaufen. **(b)** *(liter: die)* seinen Geist aufgeben *(liter).*
**expiry** [ɪk'spaɪərɪ] *n* Ablauf *m.* **~ date** Ablauftermin *m; (of voucher)* Verfallsdatum *nt.*
**explain** [ɪk'spleɪn] *vt* erklären *(to sb* jdm*); situation also* erläutern; *mystery* aufklären. **he'd better ~ himself** will hoffe, er kann das erklären.
▶**explain away** *vt sep* eine Erklärung finden für.
**explanation** [,eksplə'neɪʃən] *n see vt* Erklärung *f;* Erläuterung *f;* Aufklärung *f.* **what can you say in ~ of this?** wie erklären Sie das?
**explanatory** [ɪk'splænətərɪ] *adj* erklärend. **a few ~ remarks** ein paar Worte zur Erklärung.
**expletive** [ɪk'spliːtɪv] *n* Kraftausdruck *m.*
**explicit** [ɪk'splɪsɪt] *adj* ausdrücklich, explizit *(geh); text, meaning* klar; *sex scene* deutlich, unverhüllt.
**explicitly** [ɪk'splɪsɪtlɪ] *adv* ausdrücklich.
**explode** [ɪk'spləʊd] **1** *vi (lit, fig)* explodieren. **to ~ with laughter** in schallendes Gelächter ausbrechen. **2** *vt* **(a)** *bomb, mine* sprengen; *dynamite, gas* zur Explosion bringen. **(b)** *(fig) theory, argument* zu Fall bringen.
**exploit** ['eksplɔɪt] **1** *n (heroic)* Heldentat *f.* **~s** *(adventures)* Abenteuer *pl.* **2** [ɪks'plɔɪt] *vt coal seam, (pej) workers* ausbeuten; *situation, (pej) friend, good nature* ausnutzen; *product* nutzen.
**exploitation** [,eksplɔɪ'teɪʃən] *n see vt* Ausbeutung *f;* Ausnutzung *f;* Nutzung *f.*
**exploration** [,eksplɔː'reɪʃən] *n* Erforschung, Erkundung *f; (of topic, Med)* Untersuchung *f.* **a voyage of ~** *(lit, fig)* eine Entdeckungsreise.
**exploratory** [ɪk'splɒrətərɪ] *adj drilling* Probe-. **~ operation** *(Med)* Explorationsoperation *f;* **~ talks** Sondierungsgespräche *pl.*
**explore** [ɪk'splɔːr] **1** *vt (lit, fig)* erforschen; *(Med)* untersuchen. **2** *vi* **to go exploring** auf Entdeckungsreise gehen.
**explorer** [ɪk'splɔːrər] *n* Forscher(in *f*) *m.*
**explosion** [ɪk'spləʊʒən] *n (lit, fig)* Explosion *f; (fig: of anger)* Wutausbruch *m.*
**explosive** [ɪk'spləʊzɪv] **1** *adj (lit, fig)* explosiv. **~ device** Sprengkörper *m.* **2** *n* Sprengstoff *m.*
**exponent** [ɪk'spəʊnənt] *n (of theory)* Vertreter(in *f*) *m.*
**export** [ɪk'spɔːt] **1** *vti* exportieren *(also Comp).* **2** ['ekspɔːt] *n* Export *m.* **~ drive** Exportkampagne *f.*
**exporter** [ɪk'spɔːtər] *n* Exporteur *m (of* von*); (country also)* Exportland *nt (of* für*).*
**export: ~ licence** *n* Ausfuhrgenehmigung *f;* **~ manager** *n* Exportleiter(in *f*) *m;* **~ trade** *n* Exporthandel *m.*
**expose** [ɪk'spəʊz] *vt* **(a)** *rocks, remains* freilegen; *electric wire, nerve also* bloßlegen. **to be ~d to view**

sichtbar sein. **(b)** *(to danger, sunlight, radiation, criticism)* aussetzen *(to dat).* **"not to be ~d to heat"** „vor Hitze schützen". **(c)** *(display)* one's ignorance offenbaren; *(indecently)* oneself entblößen. **(d)** *abuse, treachery* aufdecken; *imposter, thief* entlarven. **to ~ sb/sth to the press** jdn/etw der Presse ausliefern. **(e)** *(Phot)* belichten.
**exposé** [ek'spəʊzeɪ] *n* Exposé *nt.*
**exposed** [ɪk'spəʊzd] *adj* **(a)** *(to weather) place* ungeschützt. **~ to the wind** dem Wind ausgesetzt. **(b)** *(insecure)* **to feel ~** sich allen Blicken ausgesetzt fühlen. **(c)** *(visible)* sichtbar. **the ~ parts of an engine** die freiliegenden Teile eines Motors.
**exposition** [ekspə'zɪʃən] *n (of theory)* Darlegung *f; (Mus)* Exposition *f.*
**expostulate** [ɪk'spɒstjʊleɪt] *vi* protestieren.
**expostulation** [ɪk,spɒstjʊ'leɪʃən] *n* Protest *m.*
**exposure** [ɪk'spəʊʒər] *n* **(a)** *(to sunlight, air, danger)* Aussetzung *f (to dat).* **to be suffering from ~** an Unterkühlung leiden; **to die of ~** erfrieren. **(b)** *(displaying)* Entblößung *f.* **indecent ~** Exhibitionismus *m.* **(c)** *(unmasking)* Bloßstellung *f; (of thief, murderer)* Entlarvung *f; (of abuses, vices, scandals, crime)* Aufdeckung *f.* **(d)** *(Phot)* Belichtung(szeit) *f.* **~ meter** Belichtungsmesser *m.* **(e)** *(Media)* Publicity *f.*
**expound** [ɪk'spaʊnd] *vt* darlegen, erläutern.
**express** [ɪk'spres] **1** *vt* ausdrücken. **to ~ oneself** sich ausdrücken. **2** *adj instructions* ausdrücklich; *intention* bestimmt. **3** *adv* **to send sth ~** etw per Expreß schicken. **4** *n (train)* Schnellzug *m.*
**express: ~ delivery** *n* Eilsendung *f;* **~ freight** *n* Eilgut *nt.*
**expression** [ɪk'spreʃən] *n* Ausdruck *m.* **as an ~ of our gratitude** zum Ausdruck unserer Dankbarkeit; **you could tell by his ~ that ...** man konnte an seinem Gesichtsausdruck erkennen, daß ...
**expressionism** [ɪk'spreʃənɪzəm] *n* Expressionismus *m.*
**expressionist** [ɪk'spreʃənɪst] **1** *n* Expressionist(in *f*) *m.* **2** *adj* expressionistisch.
**expressive** *adj,* **~ly** *adv* [ɪk'spresɪv, -lɪ] ausdrucksvoll.
**expressly** [ɪk'spreslɪ] *adv deny etc* ausdrücklich.
**express: ~ train** *n* Schnellzug *m;* **~way** *n* Schnellstraße *f.*
**expulsion** [ɪk'spʌlʃən] *n (from country)* Ausweisung *f (from* aus*); (from school)* Verweisung *f* (von der Schule); *(from party)* Ausschluß *m (from* aus*).*
**expurgate** ['ekspɜːgeɪt] *vt* zensieren. **~d edition** bereinigte Fassung.
**exquisite** [ɪk'skwɪzɪt] *adj workmanship* ausgezeichnet; *dress, painting* exquisit; *taste* gepflegt; *view* herrlich; *food, wine, sense of humour, pleasure* köstlich.
**exquisitely** [ɪk'skwɪzɪtlɪ] *adv* ausgezeichnet; *perfumed, dressed* exquisit.
**ex-serviceman** [eks'sɜːvɪsmən] *n, pl* **-men** [-mən] altgedienter Soldat, Veteran *m.*
**ext** = **extension** App.
**extant** [ek'stænt] *adj* noch vorhanden.
**extempore** [ɪks'tempərɪ] *adj* **to give an ~ speech** eine Rede aus dem Stegreif halten.
**extemporize** [ɪk'stempəraɪz] *vti* aus dem Stegreif sprechen; *(make do, also Mus)* improvisieren.
**extend** [ɪk'stend] **1** *vt* **(a)** *(stretch out) arms* ausstrecken. **(b)** *line, visit, passport, holidays* verlängern. **(c)** *(enlarge) research, powers, limits, knowledge* erweitern; *house* anbauen an *(+acc); frontiers of a country* ausdehnen. **(d)** *(offer) (to sb* jdm*) help* gewähren; *hospitality, friendship* erweisen; *condolences* aussprechen. **to ~ a welcome to sb** jdn will-

kommen heißen. **2** *vi (wall, garden)* sich erstrecken *(to, as far as* bis*)*; *(over period of time)* sich hinziehen.

**extension** [ɪk'stenʃən] *n* **(a)** *(of property)* Vergrößerung *f*; *(of business, knowledge also)* Erweiterung *f*; *(of powers, franchise, research, frontiers)* Ausdehnung *f*; *(of road, line, period of time)* Verlängerung *f*; *(of house)* Anbau *m*. **(b)** *(Telec)* (Neben)anschluß *m*. ~ **3714** Apparat 3714; ~ **cable** Verlängerungskabel *nt*; ~ **lead** Verlängerungsschnur *f*; ~ **ladder** Ausziehleiter *f*.

**extensive** [ɪk'stensɪv] *adj land, forest* ausgedehnt; *knowledge, press coverage, research, enquiries, operations, alterations* umfangreich; *damage* beträchtlich; *use* häufig; *plans, reforms, influence* weitreichend.

**extensively** [ɪk'stensɪvlɪ] *adv* weit; *study, investigate, cover* ausführlich; *altered, reformed, damaged* beträchtlich; *used* häufig, viel; *travel* viel.

**extent** [ɪk'stent] *n (length)* Länge *f*; *(size)* Ausdehnung *f*; *(range, scope)* Umfang *m*; *(of damage, commitments also)* Ausmaß *nt*. **to some** ~ bis zu einem gewissen Grade; **to what** ~ inwieweit; **to a certain** ~ in gewissem Maße; **to a large** ~ in hohem Maße; **to such an** ~ **that** ... dermaßen, daß ...; **debts to the** ~ **of £5,000** Schulden in Höhe von £5000.

**extenuating** [ɪk'stenjʊeɪtɪŋ] *adj* ~ **circumstances** mildernde Umstände *pl*.

**exterior** [ɪk'stɪərɪər] **1** *adj surface* äußere(r, s), Außen-. **2** *n (of house etc)* Außenseite *f*; *(of person)* Äußere(s) *nt*. **on the** ~ außen.

**exterminate** [ɪk'stɜːmɪneɪt] *vt* ausrotten.

**extermination** [ɪk,stɜːmɪ'neɪʃən] *n* Ausrottung *f*.

**external** [ɪk'stɜːnl] **1** *adj wall* äußere(r, s), Außen-; *factors, help* extern. **for** ~ **use only** *(Med)* nur äußerlich (anzuwenden); ~ **trade** Außenhandel *m*. **2** *n (fig)* ~**s** *pl* Äußerlichkeiten *pl*.

**externally** [ek'stɜːnəlɪ] *adv* äußerlich.

**extinct** [ɪk'stɪŋkt] *adj volcano, love* erloschen; *species* ausgestorben.

**extinction** [ɪk'stɪŋkʃən] *n (of race)* Aussterben *nt*; *(annihilation)* Vernichtung *f*.

**extinguish** [ɪk'stɪŋgwɪʃ] *vt fire* löschen; *hopes, passion* zerstören.

**extinguisher** [ɪk'stɪŋgwɪʃər] *n* Feuerlöscher *m*.

**extol** [ɪk'stəʊl] *vt* preisen, rühmen.

**extort** [ɪk'stɔːt] *vt* erpressen *(from* von*)*.

**extortion** [ɪk'stɔːʃən] *n* Erpressung *f*. **this is sheer** ~! *(col)* das ist ja Wucher!

**extortionate** [ɪk'stɔːʃənɪt] *adj prices* Wucher-; *tax, demand* ungeheuer.

**extra** ['ekstrə] **1** *adj* zusätzlich. **we need an** ~ **chair** wir brauchen noch einen Stuhl; **to make an** ~ **effort** sich besonders anstrengen; ~ **charge** Zuschlag *m*; **there will be no** ~ **charge** das wird nicht extra berechnet; ~ **time** *(Brit Ftbl)* Verlängerung *f*; ~ **pay** eine Zulage; **for** ~ **safety** zur größeren Sicherheit; **we need an** ~ **10 minutes** wir brauchen 10 Minuten mehr; **I have brought an** ~ **pair of shoes** ich habe noch ein Paar Schuhe mitgebracht. **2** *adv* **(a)** *(especially)* extra, besonders. **(b)** *(in addition)* extra. **3** *n* **(a)** *(perk)* Zusatzleistung *f*; *(for car)* Extra *nt*. **they regard it as an** ~ sie betrachten es als Luxus. **(b)** ~**s** *pl (*~ *expenses)* zusätzliche Kosten *pl*; *(in restaurant)* Zusätzliches *nt*. **(c)** *(Film, Theat)* Statist(in *f*) *m*. **(d)** *(remainder)* Rest *m*.

**extract** [ɪk'strækt] **1** *vt* **(a)** herausziehen *(from* aus*)*; *juice, minerals, oil* gewinnen *(from* aus*)*; *tooth* ziehen. **(b)** *(fig) information, confession, money* herausholen *(from* aus*)*. **(c)** *quotation, passage* herausziehen. **2** ['ekstrækt] *n (from book etc)* Auszug *m*. **beef**

~ Fleischextrakt *m*.

**extraction** [ɪk'strækʃən] *n* **(a)** *see vt* Herausziehen *nt*; Gewinnung *f*; Ziehen *nt*; Herausholen *nt*. **he had to have three** ~**s** ihm mußten drei Zähne gezogen werden. **(b)** **of Spanish** ~ spanischer Abstammung.

**extractor** [ɪk'stræktər]: ~ **fan** *n* Sauglüfter *m*; ~ **hood** *n* Abzugshaube *f*.

**extracurricular** [,ekstrəkə'rɪkjʊlər] *adj* außerhalb des Stundenplans.

**extradite** ['ekstrədaɪt] *vt* ausliefern.

**extradition** [,ekstrə'dɪʃən] *n* Auslieferung *f*. ~ **treaty** Auslieferungsvertrag *m*.

**extramarital** [,ekstrə'mærɪtl] *adj* außerehelich.

**extramural** [,ekstrə'mjʊərəl] *adj courses* Volkshochschul-.

**extraneous** [ɪk'streɪnɪəs] *adj influence* extern. ~ **to** *(unrelated)* irrelevant für.

**extraordinarily** [ɪk'strɔːdnrɪlɪ] *adv* außerordentlich.

**extraordinary** [ɪk'strɔːdnrɪ] *adj* **(a)** *(beyond what is common)* außerordentlich; *(not usual)* ungewöhnlich. **(b)** *(odd, peculiar)* sonderbar, seltsam; *(amazing)* erstaunlich. **(c)** *(special)* ~ **meeting** Sondersitzung *f*; ~ **general meeting** außerordentliche Hauptversammlung.

**extrapolate** [ek'stræpəleɪt] *vti* extrapolieren *(from* aus*)*.

**extrapolation** [ek,stræpə'leɪʃən] *n* Extrapolation *f*.

**extrasensory** [,ekstrə'sensərɪ] *adj* ~ **perception** außersinnliche Wahrnehmung.

**extra-special** [,ekstrə'speʃəl] *adj* ganz besondere(r, s).

**extraterrestrial** [,ekstrətɪ'restrɪəl] *adj* außerirdisch.

**extravagance** [ɪk'strævəgəns] *n* **(a)** Luxus *m no pl*. **her** ~ ihre Verschwendungssucht. **(b)** *(wastefulness)* Verschwendung *f*. **(c)** *(of ideas, theories)* Ausgefallenheit *f*; *(of claim, demand)* Übertriebenheit *f*. **(d)** *(extravagant action)* Extravaganz *f*.

**extravagant** [ɪk'strævəgənt] *adj* **(a)** *(lavish)* taste, habit teuer, kostspielig; *wedding, lifestyle* aufwendig; *price* überhöht. **she is** ~ sie gibt das Geld mit vollen Händen aus; **go on, be** ~ gönn dir doch den Luxus. **(b)** *(wasteful)* verschwenderisch. **(c)** *behaviour* extravagant; *ideas also* ausgefallen; *claim, demand* übertrieben.

**extravagantly** [ɪk'strævəgəntlɪ] *adv see adj* **(a)** luxuriös; *spend* mit vollen Händen. **(b)** verschwenderisch. **(c)** *furnish, dress, behave* extravagant; *praise, act* überschwenglich.

**extreme** [ɪk'striːm] **1** *adj* äußerste(r, s); *(exaggerated, drastic, Pol)* extrem; *praise, flattery* übertrieben; *exaggeration, demands* maßlos; *penalty* höchste(r, s). **the** ~ **right** ganz rechts; ~ **old age** ein äußerst hohes Alter; **an** ~ **case** ein Extremfall *m*. **2** *n* Extrem *nt*. ~**s of temperature** extreme Temperaturen *pl*; **in the** ~ im höchsten Grade; **to go from one** ~ **to the other** von einem Extrem ins andere fallen; **to go to** ~**s** es übertreiben; **to drive sb to** ~**s** jdn zum Äußersten treiben.

**extremely** [ɪk'striːmlɪ] *adv* äußerst, höchst. **was it difficult?** — ~ war es schwierig? — sehr!

**extremist** [ɪk'striːmɪst] **1** *adj* extremistisch. **2** *n* Extremist(in *f*) *m*.

**extremity** [ɪk'stremɪtɪ] *n* **(a)** *(furthest point)* äußerstes Ende. **(b)** *(state of distress)* Not *f*. **(c)** **to resort to extremities** zu extremen Mitteln greifen. **(d)** **extremities** *pl (hands and feet)* Extremitäten *pl*.

**extricate** ['ekstrɪkeɪt] *vt* befreien *(from* aus*)*.

**extrovert** ['ekstrəʊvɜːt] **1** *adj* extrovertiert. **2** *n* extrovertierter Mensch.

**extrusion** [ɪk'struːʒən] *n (Tech) (of metal)* Fließpressen *nt*; *(of plastic)* Extrudieren *nt*.

**exuberance** [ɪgˈzuːbərəns] *n (of person)* Überschwenglichkeit *f*; *(of joy, youth, feelings)* Überschwang *m*; *(joy)* überschwengliche Freude *(at* über +*acc)*; *(of prose, style)* Vitalität *f*.

**exuberant** [ɪgˈzuːbərənt] *adj* überschwenglich; *style* übersprudelnd, vital; *music* mitreißend.

**exude** [ɪgˈzjuːd] *vt (liquid)* ausscheiden; *confidence* ausstrahlen; *(pej) charm* triefen vor *(+dat)*.

**exult** [ɪgˈzʌlt] *vi* frohlocken.

**exultant** [ɪgˈzʌltənt] *adj* jubelnd; *shout also* Jubel-. **to be ~** jubeln.

**exultation** [ˌegzʌlˈteɪʃən] *n* Jubel *m*.

**eye** [aɪ] **1** *n* Auge *nt*; *(of needle)* Öhr *nt*. **with one's ~s closed/open** mit geschlossenen/offenen Augen; *(fig)* blind/mit offenen Augen; **an ~ for an ~(, a tooth for a tooth)** *(prov)* Auge um Auge(, Zahn um Zahn) *(prov)*; **to be all ~s** große Augen machen; **that's one in the ~ for him** *(col)* da hat er eins aufs Dach gekriegt *(col)*; **to cast** *or* **run one's ~s over sth** etw überfliegen; **to look sb (straight) in the ~** jdm in die Augen sehen; **to set** *or* **clap** *(col)* **~s on sb/sth** jdn/etw zu Gesicht bekommen; **(why don't you) use your ~s!** hast du keine Augen im Kopf?; **with one's own ~s** mit eigenen Augen; **before my very ~s** (direkt) vor meinen Augen; **under the watchful ~ of the guard** unter der Aufsicht des Wächters; **to keep an ~ on sb/sth** *(look after)* auf jdn/etw aufpassen; **to keep one's ~ on the ball/main objective** sich auf den Ball/die Hauptsache konzentrieren; **you can't take your ~s off them for a moment** man kann sie keinen Moment aus den Augen lassen; **he couldn't take his ~s off her/the cake** er konnte einfach den Blick nicht von ihr/dem Kuchen wenden; **to keep one's ~s open** die Augen offenhalten; **to keep an ~ out for a hotel** nach einem Hotel Ausschau halten; **to keep an ~ on expenditure** auf seine Ausgaben achten; **to open sb's ~s to sb/sth** jdm die Augen über jdn/etw öffnen; **to close one's ~s to sth** die Augen vor etw *(dat)* verschließen; **to see ~ to ~ with sb** mit jdm einer Meinung sein; **to make ~s at sb** jdm schöne Augen machen; **to catch sb's ~** jds Aufmerksamkeit erregen; **that colour caught my ~**

die Farbe fiel mir ins Auge; **in the ~s of the law** in den Augen des Gesetzes; **in my ~s** in meinen Augen; **with an ~ to the future** im Hinblick auf die Zukunft; **with an ~ to buying sth** in der Absicht, etw zu kaufen; **I've got my ~ on you** ich beobachte dich genau; **to have one's ~ on sth** *(want)* auf etw *(acc)* ein Auge geworfen haben; **to have an ~ on sb for a job** jdn für eine Stelle im Auge haben; **he has a good ~ for colour** er hat ein Auge für Farben; **you need an ~ for detail** man muß einen Blick fürs Detail haben; **to be up to the ~s in work** *(col)* in Arbeit ersticken *(col)*.

**2** *vt* mustern. **to ~ sb up and down** jdn von oben bis unten mustern.

►**eye up** *vt sep girls, boys* mustern, begutachten.

**eye** *in cpds* Augen-; **~ball** *n* Augapfel *m*; **~brow** *n* Augenbraue *f*; **to raise one's ~brows** *(fig)* die Stirn runzeln; **he never raised an ~brow** *(fig)* er hat sich nicht einmal gewundert; **~brow pencil** *n* Augenbrauenstift *m*; **~-catching** *adj* auffallend; *publicity, poster also* auffällig; **~ contact** *n* Blickkontakt *m*; **~ drops** Augentropfen *pl*.

**eyeful** [ˈaɪfʊl] *n (col)* **to get an ~** *(get sth in eye)* etw ins Auge bekommen; **get an ~ of this** guck dir das mal an *(col)*; **she's quite an ~** *(col)* sie hat allerhand zu bieten.

**eye:** **~glasses** *npl (US)* Brille *f*; **~lash** *n* Augenwimper *f*; **~let** [ˈaɪlɪt] *n* Öse *f*; **~-level** *adj attr grill* in Augenhöhe; **~lid** *n* Augenlid *nt*; **~ liner** *n* Eyeliner *m*; **~-opener** *n* **that was a real ~-opener to me** das hat mir die Augen geöffnet; **~shade** *n* Augenblende *f*; **~shadow** *n* Lidschatten *m*; **~sight** *n* Sehkraft *f*; **to have good/poor ~sight** gute/schlechte Augen haben; **to lose one's ~sight** das Augenlicht verlieren *(geh)*, erblinden; **~sore** *n* Schandfleck *m*; **this carpet is a real ~sore** dieser Teppich sieht fürchterlich aus; **~strain** *n* Überanstrengung *f* der Augen; **~ tooth** *n* Eckzahn *m*; **I'd give my ~ teeth for that** darum würde ich alles geben; **~wash** *n (fig col)* Gewäsch *nt (col)*; *(deception)* Augenwischerei *f*; **~witness** *n* Augenzeuge *m*; **~witness account** *or* **report** Augenzeugenbericht *m*.

**eyrie** [ˈɪərɪ] *n* Horst *m*.

# F

**F, f** [ef] *n* F, f *nt.* **F for Frederick** *(Brit),* **F for Fox** *(US)* ≃ F wie Friedrich; ~ **sharp** Fis, fis *nt.*

**F** = **(a) Fahrenheit** F. **(b)** *(US)* **freeway.** **(c) franc** F.

**f** = **(a) feminine** f. **(b)** *(Mus)* **forte** f. **(c)** *(Phot)* **f8/f11** *etc* Blende 8/11 *etc.* **(d) and following (page)** f.

**FA** *(Brit)* = **Football Association** *englischer Fußballbund.*

**fable** ['feɪbl] *n* Fabel *f;* *(fig: lie)* Märchen *nt.*

**fabric** ['fæbrɪk] *n* **(a)** *(Tex)* Stoff *m.* **(b)** *(of building)* Bausubstanz *f;* *(of society)* Struktur *f.*

**fabricate** ['fæbrɪkeɪt] *vt* **(a)** *story* erfinden. **(b)** *(manufacture)* herstellen.

**fabrication** [ˌfæbrɪ'keɪʃən] *n* **(a)** *(lie etc)* Erfindung *f.* **(b)** *(manufacture)* Herstellung *f.*

**fabulous** ['fæbjʊləs] *adj* sagenhaft; *(col: wonderful)* toll *(col).*

**façade** [fə'sɑːd] *n* *(lit, fig)* Fassade *f.*

**face** [feɪs] **1** *n* Gesicht *nt;* *(of clock)* Zifferblatt *nt;* *(rock* ~*)* (Steil)wand *f;* *(coal*~*)* Streb *m;* *(of playing card)* Bildseite *f;* *(of coin)* Vorderseite *f.* **I don't want to see your ~ here again** ich möchte Sie hier nie wieder sehen; **we were standing ~ to ~** wir standen einander gegenüber; **to bring two people ~ to ~** zwei Leute einander gegenüberstellen; **to come ~ to ~ with sb/death** jdn treffen/dem Tod ins Auge sehen; **he told him so to his ~** er sagte ihm das (offen) ins Gesicht; **he shut the door in my ~** er schlug mir die Tür vor der Nase zu; **he laughed in my ~** er lachte mir ins Gesicht; **to look/be able to look sb in the ~** jdn ansehen/jdm in die Augen sehen können; **in the ~ of great difficulties** trotz größter Schwierigkeiten; **courage in the ~ of the enemy** Tapferkeit vor dem Feind; **to make** *or* **pull a ~** das Gesicht verziehen; **to make** *or* **pull ~s** Grimassen schneiden *(at sb* jdm*);* **to put a good ~ on it** gute Miene zum bösen Spiel machen; **to put a brave ~ on it** sich *(dat)* nichts anmerken lassen; *(do sth one dislikes)* (wohl oder übel) in den sauren Apfel beißen; **to save/lose ~** das Gesicht wahren/verlieren; **to be ~ up/down** *(person)* mit dem Gesicht nach oben/unten liegen; *(thing)* mit der Vorderseite nach oben/unten liegen; **to work at the (coal)~** vor Ort arbeiten; **the ~ of the town** das Stadtbild; **he vanished off the ~ of the earth** *(col)* er war wie vom Erdboden verschwunden; **on the ~ of it** so, wie es aussieht; **to have the ~ to do sth** *(col)* die Stirn haben, etw zu tun.

**2** *vt* **(a)** *(be opposite)* gegenübersein/-stehen/-liegen *etc (+dat);* *(window, door) north, south* gehen nach; *street, garden etc* liegen zu; *(building, room) north, south* liegen nach. **~ this way!** bitte sehen Sie hierher!; **he was facing me at dinner** er saß mir beim Essen gegenüber; **the picture facing page 16** die Abbildung gegenüber Seite 16; **to sit facing the engine** *(on train)* in Fahrtrichtung sitzen.

**(b)** *(fig)* *possibility, prospect* rechnen müssen mit.

**to be ~d with sth** sich einer Sache *(dat)* gegenübersehen; **he is facing a charge of murder** er steht unter Mordanklage.

**(c)** *situation, danger, criticism* sich stellen *(+dat);* *person, enemy* gegenübertreten *(+dat).* **to ~ (the) facts** den Tatsachen ins Auge sehen; **let's ~ it** machen wir uns doch nichts vor; **I can't ~ it** ich bringe es einfach nicht über mich; **I couldn't ~ another drink** ich könnte jetzt nichts Alkoholisches mehr verkraften.

**(d)** *building, wall* verkleiden.

**3** *vi (house, room)* liegen *(towards park* dem Park zu, *onto road* zur Straße, *away from road* nicht zur Straße*);* *(window)* gehen *(onto, towards* auf *+acc,* zu, *away from* nicht auf *+acc).* **in which direction was he facing?** in welche Richtung stand er?

►**face up to** *vi +prep obj fact, truth* ins Gesicht sehen *(+dat);* *possibility* sich abfinden mit; *responsibility* auf sich *(acc)* nehmen. **he won't ~ ~ ~ the fact that ...** er will es nicht wahrhaben, daß ...

**face** *in cpds* Gesichts-; **~cloth** *n (Brit)* Waschlappen *m;* **~ cream** *n* Gesichtscreme *f;* **~ flannel** *n (Brit)* = **~cloth;** **~less** *adj (fig)* anonym; **~lift** *n (lit)* Gesichts(haut)straffung *f;* *(fig: for car, building etc)* Verschönerung *f;* **to have a ~lift** sich *(dat)* das Gesicht liften lassen; *(fig)* ein neues Aussehen bekommen; **~ pack** *n* Gesichtspackung *f;* **~ powder** *n* Gesichtspuder *m;* **~-saving** *adj* **a ~-saving excuse** eine Entschuldigung, um das Gesicht zu wahren.

**facet** ['fæsɪt] *n (lit)* Facette *f;* *(fig)* Aspekt *m.*

**facetious** [fə'siːʃəs] *adj* witzelnd. **to be ~ (about sth)** (über etw *acc)* Witze machen.

**face: ~-to-~** *adj* persönlich; *confrontation* direkt; **~ value** *n (Fin)* Nennwert *m;* **to take sth at (its) ~ value** *(fig)* etw für bare Münze nehmen; **to take sb at ~ value** jdm unbesehen glauben.

**facial** ['feɪʃəl] **1** *adj* Gesichts-. **2** *n (col)* kosmetische Gesichtsbehandlung.

**facile** ['fæsaɪl] *adj* **(a)** *(glib, superficial)* oberflächlich. **(b)** *(easy) victory* leicht.

**facilitate** [fə'sɪlɪteɪt] *vt* erleichtern; *(make possible)* ermöglichen.

**facility** [fə'sɪlɪtɪ] *n* **(a)** Einrichtung *f;* *(possibility)* Möglichkeit *f;* *(esp US: installation)* Anlage *f.* **facilities for the disabled** Einrichtungen *pl* für Behinderte; **sports facilities** Sportanlagen *pl;* **cooking facilities** Kochgelegenheit *f.* **(b)** *no pl (ease)* Leichtigkeit *f;* *(dexterity)* Gewandtheit *f.*

**facing** ['feɪsɪŋ] **1** *n (on wall)* Verkleidung *f;* *(Sew)* Besatz *m.* **2** *adj* **~ page** gegenüberliegende Seite.

**facsimile** [fæk'sɪmɪlɪ] *n* **(a)** Faksimile *nt.* **(b)** *(Telec)* Telebrief *m.*

**fact** [fækt] *n* Tatsache *f.* **to know for a ~ that ...** (es) ganz sicher wissen, daß ...; **the ~ is that ...** die Sache ist die, daß ...; **to stick to the ~s** bei den Tatsachen bleiben; **is that a ~?** tatsächlich?; **the ~ that ...** (die Tatsache,) daß ...; **~ and fiction** Dichtung und Wahrheit; **founded on ~** auf Tatsachen beruhend; **to tell sb the ~s of life** jdn aufklären; **the ~s of the case** der Sachverhalt; **in ~, as a matter of ~** eigentlich; *(to intensify previous statement)* sogar; **I bet you haven't done that! − as a matter of ~ I have!** du hast das bestimmt nicht gemacht! − oh doch!; **do you know Sir Charles? − as a matter of ~ he's my uncle** kennen Sie Sir Charles? − ja, er ist nämlich mein Onkel.

**fact-finding** ['fæktfaɪndɪŋ] *adj commission* Untersuchungs-; *mission* Erkundungs-. **~ tour** Informationsreise *f.*

**faction** ['fækʃən] *n (group)* Gruppe *f;* *(Pol)* Fraktion *f;* *(splinter group)* Splittergruppe *f.*

**factor** ['fæktər] *n* Faktor *m.*

**factory** ['fæktərɪ] *n* Fabrik *f.*

**factory: ~ farming** *n industriell betriebene Viehzucht;* **~ inspector** *n* Gewerbeaufsichtsbeamte(r) *m;* **~ worker** *n* Fabrikarbeiter(in *f*) *m.*

**factsheet** ['fæktʃiːt] *n* Informationsblatt *nt.*

**factual** ['fæktjʊəl] *adj* sachlich, Tatsachen-. **~ error** Sachfehler *m.*

**faculty** ['fækəltɪ] *n* **(a)** Fähigkeit *f.* **~ of reason** Vernunft *f;* **~ of speech/sight** Sprech-/Sehvermögen *nt;* **to be in (full) possession of one's faculties** im Vollbesitz seiner Kräfte sein. **(b)** *(Univ)* Fakultät *f.* **the F~** *(staff)* der Lehrkörper.

**fad** [fæd] *n* Tick *m (col);* *(fashion)* Masche *f (col).*

**fade** [feɪd] *vi* verblassen; *(flower, beauty)* verblühen. **he ~d from sight** er verschwand; *see* **fade away.**

►**fade away** *vi (memory)* verblassen; *(hopes)* zerrinnen; *(interest, strength, inspiration)* nachlassen; *(sound)* verklingen; *(voice)* immer schwächer werden.

►**fade in** *vt sep (TV, Film)* allmählich einblenden.

►**fade out 1** *vi* **(a)** *(TV, Film)* abblenden. **(b) to ~ ~ of sb's life** aus jds Leben verschwinden. **2** *vt sep (TV, Film)* abblenden.

**faded** ['feɪdɪd] *adj* verblaßt; *flowers, beauty* verblüht.

**fade** *(Rad, TV, Film):* **~-in** *n* Einblendung *f;* **~-out** *n* Abblende *f.*

**faeces,** *(US)* **feces** ['fiːsiːz] *n pl* Kot *m.*

**Faeroe Islands** ['fɛərəʊˌaɪləndz], **Faeroes** ['fɛərəʊz] *npl* Färöer *pl.*

**fag** [fæg] *(col)* **1** *n* **(a)** *(Brit: cigarette)* Zigarette *f,* Glimmstengel *m (col).* **(b)** *(Brit Sch) junger Internatsschüler, der einem älteren bestimmte Dienste zu leisten hat.* **(c)** *(esp US col: homosexual)* Schwule(r) *m (col).* **2** *vt* **to be ~ged (out)** kaputt or geschafft sein *(col).*

**fag end** *n*̩ **(a)** *(Brit col: cigarette end)* Kippe *f (col).* **(b)** *(col: last part)* letztes Ende.

**faggot,** *(US)* **fagot** ['fægət] *n* **(a)** *(Brit col: cigarette end)* Reisigbündel *nt.* **(b)** *(Cook)* Frikadelle *f (meist mit Schweineleber).* **(c)** *(esp US col: homosexual)* Schwule(r) *m (col).*

**Fahrenheit** ['færənhaɪt] *n* Fahrenheit *nt.*

**fail** [feɪl] **1** *vi* **(a)** keinen Erfolg haben; *(in mission, life etc)* versagen; *(plan, experiment, marriage)* scheitern; *(undertaking, attempt)* fehlschlagen; *(applicant, application)* nicht angenommen werden; *(election candidate, in exam, play)* durchfallen; *(business)* eingehen. **they ~ed (in doing sth)** es gelang ihnen nicht(, etw zu tun); **to ~ in one's duty** seine Pflicht nicht tun; **to ~ by 5 votes** *(person)* um 5 Stimmen geschlagen werden; **if all else ~s** wenn alle Stricke reißen. **(c)** a **~ed teacher** als Lehrer hat er versagt. **(b)** *(health)* sich verschlechtern; *(hearing, eyesight)* nachlassen. **he is ~ing fast** sein Zustand verschlechtert sich zusehends. **(c)** *(generator, battery)* ausfallen; *(brakes, heart)* versagen; *(supply)* ausbleiben. **the crops ~ed** es gab eine

Mißernte.

**2** *vt* **(a)** *candidate* durchfallen lassen. **to ~ an exam** eine Prüfung nicht bestehen. **(b)** *(let down: person, memory)* im Stich lassen; *(not live up to sb's expectations)* enttäuschen. **words ~ me** mir fehlen die Worte. **(c) to ~ to do sth** etw nicht tun; *(neglect)* (es) versäumen, etw zu tun; **I ~ to see why** es ist mir völlig unklar, warum; *(indignantly)* ich sehe gar nicht ein, warum.

**3** *n without* **~** ganz bestimmt; *(inevitably)* garantiert.

**failing** ['feɪlɪŋ] **1** *n* Schwäche *f.* **2** *prep* **~ an answer** mangels (einer) Antwort *(geh);* **~ him see if Harry knows** und wenn er es nicht weiß, versuch es bei Harry; **~ this/that** (oder) sonst, und wenn das nicht möglich ist.

**failsafe** ['feɪlseɪf] *adj device* (ab)gesichert.

**failure** ['feɪljər] *n* **(a)** Mißerfolg *m;* *(of plan, experiment, marriage)* Scheitern *nt;* *(of undertaking, attempt)* Fehlschlag *m;* *(in exam, Theat: of play also)* Durchfall *m;* *(of business)* Eingehen *nt.* **it ended in ~** es schlug fehl; **~ rate** *(in exams)* Durchfallquote *f;* *(of machine)* Fehlerquote *f.* **(b)** *(person)* Versager *m,* Niete *f (col) (at in +dat).* **(c)** *(omission, neglect)* **because of his ~ to reply** weil er es versäumt hat zu antworten; **~ to observe a law** Nichtbeachtung *f* eines Gesetzes; **that was a ~ on my part** das war mein Fehler. **(d)** *(of generator, engine)* Ausfall *m;* *(of brakes, heart)* Versagen *nt;* *(of supply)* Ausbleiben *nt.* **~ of crops** Mißernte *f.*

**faint** [feɪnt] **1** *adj (+er)* **(a)** schwach; *voice (feeble)* matt; *(distant, not loud)* leise. **I haven't the ~est (idea)** ich habe keinen blassen Schimmer *(col).* **(b) I feel a bit ~** mir ist ganz schwach; **she felt ~** ihr wurde schwach; **~ with hunger** schwach vor Hunger. **2** *n* Ohnmacht *f.* **3** *vi* ohnmächtig werden *(with, from* vor *+dat).*

**faint-hearted** [ˌfeɪnt'hɑːtɪd] *adj* zaghaft.

**faint-heartedness** [ˌfeɪnt'hɑːtɪdnɪs] *n* Zaghaftigkeit *f,* Kleinmut *m.*

**faintly** ['feɪntlɪ] *adv* schwach; *hope, sound* leise; *smell, smile, interested* leicht; *similar, resemble* entfernt.

**faintness** ['feɪntnɪs] *n (dizziness)* Schwächegefühl *nt.*

**fair¹** [fɛər] **1** *adj (+er)* **(a)** *(just)* fair *(to/on sb* jdm gegenüber, gegen jdn).* **that's a ~ comment** das stimmt; **it's only ~ to ask him** man sollte ihn fairerweise fragen; **it's only ~ to expect ...** man kann doch wohl zu Recht erwarten ...; **~ enough!** na gut; **that's ~ enough** das ist nur recht und billig; **~'s ~!** wir wollen doch fair bleiben; **to give sb a ~ crack of the whip** jdm eine faire Chance geben; **by ~ means or foul** mit allen Mitteln; **that's a ~ sample of ...** das ist ziemlich typisch für ...

**(b)** *(reasonable)* ganz ordentlich. **only ~** nur mäßig; **he's a ~ judge of character** er hat eine gute Menschenkenntnis; **to have a ~ idea of sth** eine ungefähre Vorstellung von etw haben; **a ~ chance of success** ganz gute Erfolgsaussichten *pl.*

**(c)** *(reasonably large, fast, strong) sum, number* ansehnlich; *wind* frisch. **a ~ amount** ziemlich viel; **at a ~ speed** ziemlich schnell.

**(d)** *(fine) weather* heiter. **the ~ sex** das schöne Geschlecht.

**(e)** *person (light-haired)* blond; *(light-skinned)* hell.

**2** *adv* **to play ~** *(Sport)* fair spielen; *(fig)* fair sein; **~ and square** *(honestly)* offen und ehrlich; *(accurately, directly)* direkt; **it ~ took my breath away** *(col)* das hat mir glatt den Atem verschlagen.

**fair²** *n* (Jahr)markt *m;* *(Brit: fun ~)* Volksfest *nt,* Rummel *m (col);* *(Comm: trade ~)* Messe *f.*

**fair:** ~ **copy** n Reinschrift f; **to write out a** ~ **copy of sth** etw ins reine schreiben; ~ **game** n (lit) jagdbares Wild; (fig) Freiwild nt; ~**ground** n see **fair²** Markt(platz) m; Rummelplatz m; ~**-haired** adj blond; ~**-haired boy** n (US) Liebling m.

**fairly** ['fɛəlɪ] adv (a) (justly) gerecht. ~ **and squarely beaten** nach allen Regeln der Kunst geschlagen. (b) (rather) ziemlich. **it's** ~ **freezing** (col) es ist ganz schön kalt (col).

**fair-minded** ['fɛəmaɪndɪd] adj gerecht.

**fairness** ['fɛənɪs] n (a) Fairneß f. **in all** ~ gerechterweise; **in (all)** ~ **to him, he didn't have the same chance** gerechterweise muß man sagen, daß er nicht die gleichen Chancen hatte. (b) (of hair) Blondheit f; (of skin) Hellhäutigkeit f.

**fair:** ~ **play** n (Sport, fig) faires Verhalten, Fair play nt; ~**-sized** adj recht groß; ~**way** n (Golf) Fairway nt; ~**-weather** adj friends nur in guten Zeiten.

**fairy** ['fɛərɪ] n (a) Fee f. (b) (pej col: homosexual) Schwule(r) m (col), Tunte f (col).

**fairy:** ~ **godmother** n (lit, fig) gute Fee; ~**land** n Märchenland nt; ~ **lights** npl bunte Lichter pl; ~ **queen** n Elfenkönigin f; ~ **story,** ~ **tale** n (lit, fig) Märchen nt.

**fait accompli** [ˌfeɪtə'kɒmpliː] n **to present sb with a** ~ jdn vor vollendete Tatsachen stellen.

**faith** [feɪθ] n (a) (trust) Vertrauen nt (in zu); (in human nature, science etc, religious ~) Glaube m (in an +acc). **to have** ~ **in sb** jdm (ver)trauen; **to have** ~ **in sth** Vertrauen in etw (acc) haben; **act of** ~ Vertrauensbeweis m; **to keep/break** ~ **with sb** jdm treu bleiben/untreu werden; **to act in good/bad** ~ in gutem Glauben/böser Absicht handeln. (b) (religion) Glaube m no pl.

**faithful** ['feɪθfʊl] **1** adj (a) treu (to +dat). (b) account genau; translation wortgetreu. **2** npl **the** ~ (Rel) die Gläubigen pl.

**faithfully** ['feɪθfəlɪ] adv (a) treu; promise fest. **yours** ~ (Brit form) mit freundlichen Grüßen, hochachtungsvoll (form). (b) report etc genau; translate wortgetreu.

**faithfulness** ['feɪθfʊlnɪs] n (loyalty) Treue f (to zu).

**faith:** ~ **healer** n Gesundbeter(in f) m; ~ **healing** n Gesundbeten nt; ~**less** adj treulos.

**fake** [feɪk] **1** n (object) Fälschung f; (jewellery) Imitation f; (person: trickster) Schwindler(in f) m. **2** adj unecht; passport, banknote gefälscht. **3** vt vortäuschen; picture, document, results etc fälschen; bill, burglary, crash fingieren.

**falcon** ['fɔːlkən] n Falke m.

**Falkland Islands** ['fɔːklənd,aɪləndz], **Falklands** ['fɔːkləndz] npl Falkland-Inseln pl.

**fall** [fɔːl] (vb: pret **fell**, ptp **fallen**) **1** n (a) Sturz, Fall m; (of empire etc) Untergang m. **the F~ (of Man)** (Eccl) der Sündenfall; **to have a** ~ (hin)fallen, stürzen; **it's a long** ~ **from up here** von hier oben geht es tief hinunter. (b) (of town, fortress etc) Einnahme f; (of country) Zusammenbruch m; (of government) Sturz m. (c) ~ **of rain/snow** Regen-/Schneefall m; ~ **of rock** Steinschlag m. (d) (in gen) (lowering) Sinken nt; (sudden) Sturz m; (in population, membership) Abnahme f; (of prices, currency) (gradual) Sinken nt; (sudden) Sturz m. (e) (of roof, ground) Gefälle nt; (steeper) Abfall m. (f) (water~: also ~s) Wasserfall m. **the Niagara F~s** die Niagarafälle. (g) (Wrestling) Schultersieg m. (h) (US: autumn) Herbst m. **in the** ~ im Herbst.

**2** vi (a) fallen; (Sport, from a height, badly) stürzen; (object: to the ground) herunter-/hinunterfallen.

(b) (temperature, price) fallen; (population, mem-

bership etc) abnehmen; (wind) sich legen; (land) abfallen. **his face fell** er machte ein langes Gesicht; **to** ~ **in sb's estimation** or **eyes** in jds Achtung (dat) sinken.

(c) (country) eingenommen werden; (government, ruler) gestürzt werden. **three seats fell to the Liberals** drei Sitze gingen an die Liberalen.

(d) (night) hereinbrechen.

(e) (birthday, Easter etc) fallen (on auf +acc). **that** ~**s outside the scope** ... das fällt nicht in den Bereich ...; **to** ~ **into three sections** sich in drei Teile gliedern.

(f) (phrases) **her eyes fell on a strange object** ihr Blick fiel auf einen merkwürdigen Gegenstand; **the responsibility** ~**s on you** Sie tragen die Verantwortung; **it** ~**s to** or **on me to** ... es fällt mir zu, zu ...; **the blame for that** ~**s on him** ihn trifft die Schuld daran; **to** ~ **asleep** einschlafen; **to** ~ **ill** krank werden, erkranken (geh); **to** ~ **silent** still werden; **to** ~ **in love with sb** sich in jdn verlieben; **it's all** ~**ing into place now** (becoming clear) jetzt wird mir das Ganze klar; **to** ~ **into a deep sleep** in tiefen Schlaf fallen; **to** ~ **into bad ways** auf die schiefe Bahn geraten; **to** ~ **to doing sth** anfangen, etw zu tun.

**3** vt **to** ~ **a victim to sb/sth** jdm/einer Sache zum Opfer fallen.

▶**fall about** vi **to** ~ ~ **laughing** sich krank lachen (col).

▶**fall apart** vi auseinanderfallen; (fig: marriage etc) auseinandergehen.

▶**fall away** vi (a) (ground) abfallen. (b) (crumble: plaster, river bank) abbröckeln (from von).

▶**fall back** vi zurückweichen (also Mil).

▶**fall back on** vi +prep obj zurückgreifen auf (+acc).

▶**fall behind** vi (in race, school etc) zurückbleiben (prep obj hinter +dat); (with rent, work etc) in Rückstand geraten.

▶**fall down** vi (person) hinfallen; (statue, vase) herunterfallen; (house, scaffolding) einstürzen. **where he/the plan** ~**s is** ... (fig) woran es ihm/dem Plan fehlt, ist ...; **that was where we fell** ~ (fig) daran sind wir gescheitert; **he's been** ~**ing** ~ **on the job** (fig) er hat schlechte Arbeit geleistet.

▶**fall for** vi +prep obj (a) (fall in love with) sich verknallen in (+acc) (col). **I really fell** ~ **him/it** er/das hatte es mir angetan. (b) (be taken in by) hereinfallen auf (+acc).

▶**fall in** vi (a) (into water etc) hineinfallen. (b) (collapse) einstürzen. (c) (Mil) (in Reih und Glied) antreten; (one soldier) ins Glied treten.

▶**fall in with** vi +prep obj (a) (meet) sich anschließen (+dat); bad company geraten in (+acc). (b) (agree to) mitmachen bei; request unterstützen.

▶**fall off** vi (a) (lit) herunterfallen (prep obj von). (b) (decrease) zurückgehen; (supporters) abfallen; (support, enthusiasm) nachlassen.

▶**fall out** vi (a) (of bed, boat, window) herausfallen. **to** ~ ~ **of sth** aus etw fallen. (b) (quarrel) sich (zer)streiten. (c) (Mil) wegtreten. (d) (happen) just **wait and see how things** ~ ~ warte erst mal ab, wie sich die Dinge entwickeln; **if everything** ~**s** ~ **all right** wenn alles wunschgemäß verläuft.

▶**fall over** vi (a) (person) hinfallen; (collapse) umfallen. (b) +prep obj (trip over) stone, sb's legs fallen über (+acc). **to** ~ ~ **oneself to do sth** sich (dat) die größte Mühe geben, etw zu tun.

▶**fall through** vi (plan) ins Wasser fallen.

▶**fall to** vi (col) (start eating) sich dranmachen (col); (start fighting, working) loslegen (col).

**fallacious** [fə'leɪʃəs] adj irrig; argument trugschlüssig.

**fallacy** ['fæləsɪ] *n* Irrtum *m*; *(in logic)* Trugschluß *m*.

**fallen** ['fɔːlən] **1** *ptp of* **fall**. **2** *adj* women, angel gefallen; *leaf* abgefallen. **3** *npl* **the F~** *(Mil)* die Gefallenen *pl*.

**fall guy** ['fɔːlgaɪ] *n (esp US col) (scapegoat)* Sündenbock *m*.

**fallible** ['fæləbl] *adj* fehlbar.

**falling** ['fɔːlɪŋ]: **~-off** *n* = **fall-off**; **~ star** *n* Sternschnuppe *f*.

**fall-off** ['fɔːlɒf] *n (in gen)* Rückgang *m*; *(in numbers, attendances)* Abfall *m*; *(in support)* Nachlassen *nt*.

**Fallopian tube** [fə'ləupɪən'tjuːb] *n* Eileiter *m*.

**fallout** ['fɔːlaut] *n* radioaktiver Niederschlag, Fallout *m*. **~ shelter** Atombunker *m*.

**fallow** ['fæləu] *adj land* brach. **to lie ~** brachliegen.

**false** [fɔːls] *adj* falsch; *lover* treulos; *ceiling, floor* Zwischen-. **under ~ pretences** *(Brit)* or **pretenses** *(US)* unter Vorspiegelung falscher Tatsachen; **a box with a ~ bottom** ein Kiste mit doppeltem Boden.

**false alarm** *n* blinder Alarm.

**falsehood** ['fɔːlshud] *n (lie)* Unwahrheit *f*.

**falsely** ['fɔːlslɪ] *adv* falsch; *believe, claim, declare* fälschlicherweise; *accuse* zu Unrecht.

**falseness** ['fɔːlsnɪs] *n* Falschheit *f*; *(of lover etc)* Untreue *f*.

**false: ~ start** *n* Fehlstart *m*; **~ teeth** *npl (Brit)* (künstliches) Gebiß.

**falsetto** [fɔːl'setəu] **1** *n (voice)* Fistelstimme *f*; *(Mus)* Falsett *nt*. **2** *adv sing* im Falsett.

**falsies** ['fɔːlsɪz] *npl (col)* Gummibusen *m (col)*.

**falsify** ['fɔːlsɪfaɪ] *vt records, evidence* fälschen; *report, story* entstellen.

**falter** ['fɔːltər] *vi (speaking)* stocken; *(steps, horse)* zögern. **he never ~ed (in his resolve)** er war unbeirrbar (in seiner Entschlossenheit).

**fame** [feɪm] *n* Ruhm *m*. **to win ~** sich *(dat)* einen Namen machen.

**familiar** [fə'mɪljər] *adj* **(a)** *surroundings, sight, scene* vertraut; *street, person, feeling, phrase, song* bekannt; *complaint, event* häufig. **his face is ~** das Gesicht ist mir bekannt; **it looks very ~** es kommt mir sehr bekannt vor; **that sounds ~** das habe ich schon mal gehört; **to be on ~ ground with sth** in etw *(dat)* zu Hause sein; **to be ~ with sb/sth** mit jdm/etw vertraut sein; **to make oneself ~ with sth** sich mit etw vertraut machen. **(b)** *(friendly) language, gesture* familiär; *(overfriendly)* plumpvertraulich. **the ~ term of address** die Anrede mit „du"; **to be on ~ terms with sb** mit jdm auf freundschaftlichem Fuß stehen; **~ language/expressions** Umgangssprache *f*/umgangssprachliche Ausdrücke *pl*.

**familiarity** [fə,mɪlɪ'ærɪtɪ] *n* **(a)** *no pl (knowledge)* Vertrautheit *f*. **(b)** *(between people)* vertrauliches Verhältnis; *(of language etc)* Familiarität *f*; *(pej)* plumpe Vertraulichkeit. **~ breeds contempt** *(Prov)* allzu große Vertraulichkeit erzeugt Verachtung.

**familiarize** [fə'mɪlɪəraɪz] *vt* **to ~ sb/oneself with sth** jdn/sich mit etw vertraut machen.

**family** ['fæmɪlɪ] *n* Familie *f*; *(including cousins, aunts etc)* Verwandtschaft *f*. **to start a ~** eine Familie gründen; **has he any ~?** hat er Familie?; **it runs in the ~** das liegt in der Familie; **he's one of the ~** er gehört zur Familie.

**family: ~ allowance** *n* Kindergeld *nt*; **~ business** *n* Familienbetrieb *m*; **~ doctor** *n* Hausarzt *m*/-ärztin *f*; **~ life** *n* Familienleben *nt*; **~ man** *n (home-loving)* häuslich veranlagter Mann; *(with a ~)* Familienvater *m*; **~ planning** *n* Familienpla-

nung *f*; **~ planning clinic** *n* Familienberatungsstelle *f*; **~ resemblance** *n* Familienähnlichkeit *f*; **~-size** *adj* in Haushaltsgröße; *car, packets* Familien-; **~ tree** *n* Stammbaum *m*.

**famine** ['fæmɪn] *n* Hungersnot *f*.

**famished** ['fæmɪʃt] *adj (col)* ausgehungert. **I'm absolutely ~** ich sterbe vor Hunger *(col)*.

**famous** ['feɪməs] *adj* berühmt *(for durch, für)*.

**famously** ['feɪməslɪ] *adv (dated col)* famos *(dated)*, prima *(col)*.

**fan**[1] [fæn] **1** *n (hand-held)* Fächer *m*; *(mechanical, extractor ~, Aut)* Ventilator *m*. **2** *vt (wind)* umwehen; *(person)* fächeln *(+dat)*. **to ~ sb/oneself** jdm/sich (Luft) zufächeln; **to ~ the flames** *(fig)* Öl ins Feuer gießen.

▶**fan out** *vi (troops, searchers)* ausschwärmen.

**fan**[2] *n (supporter)* Fan *m*. **I'm a great ~ of his/hers** ich halte viel von ihm/ihr.

**fanatic** [fə'nætɪk] *n* Fanatiker(in *f*) *m*.

**fanatic(al)** [fə'nætɪk(əl)] *adj* fanatisch.

**fanaticism** [fə'nætɪsɪzəm] *n* Fanatismus *m*.

**fan belt** *n (Aut)* Keilriemen *m*.

**fancied** ['fænsɪd] *adj* **(a)** *(imaginary)* eingebildet. **(b)** *(Sport)* **~ horse** *or* **runner** Favorit *m*.

**fancier** ['fænsɪər] *n* Liebhaber(in *f*) *m*.

**fanciful** ['fænsɪful] *adj story, idea* phantastisch; *explanation* weit hergeholt; *pattern* phantasievoll.

**fan club** *n* Fanclub *m*.

**fancy** ['fænsɪ] **1** *n* **a passing ~** nur so eine Laune; **he's taken a ~ to her** sie hat es ihm angetan; **to take** *or* **catch sb's ~** jdm gefallen; **to tickle sb's ~** jdn reizen; **just as the ~ takes me/you** ganz nach Lust und Laune.

**2** *vt* **(a)** **~ that!** so was!; **~ seeing you here!** so was, Sie hier zu sehen!; **~ him winning!** wer hätte gedacht, daß er gewinnt!; **I rather ~ he has gone out** ich glaube, er ist weggegangen.

**(b)** *(like)* **he fancies the idea/her** die Idee/sie gefällt ihm; **he fancies a house on Crete** *(would like to have)* er hätte gern ein Haus auf Kreta; **he fancies a walk/steak** er hat Lust zu einem Spaziergang/auf ein Steak; **I don't ~ the idea** ich habe keine Lust dazu; **I didn't ~ that job** die Stelle hat mich nicht gereizt; **he fancies his chances** er meint, er hätte Chancen; **I don't ~ my chances of getting that job** ich rechne mir keine großen Chancen aus, die Stelle zu bekommen; **he really fancies himself** er ist sehr von sich eingenommen; **he fancies himself as an actor** er hält sich für einen guten Schauspieler.

**3** *adj (+er) (elaborate) hairdo, footwork* kunstvoll; *(unusual) food, pattern, cigarettes, furnishings* ausgefallen; *baking, cakes, bread* fein; *(col) gadget, car etc* schick *(col)*; *idea* überspannt; *cure* seltsam; *price* gepfeffert *(col)*. **nothing ~** etwas ganz Einfaches.

**fancy: ~ dress** *n* (Masken)kostüm *nt*; **in ~ dress** verkleidet, kostümiert; **~-dress ball/party** *n* Maskenball *m*/Kostümfest *nt*; **~ goods** *npl* Geschenkartikel *pl*; **~ man** *n (col: lover)* Liebhaber *m*; **~ woman** *n (col)* Geliebte *f*.

**fanfare** ['fænfɛər] *n* Fanfare *f*.

**fanfold paper** ['fænfəuld 'peɪpər] *n (Comp)* Endlospapier *nt*.

**fang** [fæŋ] *n* Fang *m*; *(of snake)* Giftzahn *m*.

**fan: ~ heater** *n* Heizlüfter *m*; **~ light** *n* Oberlicht *nt*; **~ mail** *n* Verehrerpost *f*; **~ oven** *n* Heißluftherd *m*.

**fantasia** [fæn'teɪzjə] *n* Fantasie *f*.

**fantasize** ['fæntəsaɪz] *vi* phantasieren.

**fantastic** [fæn'tæstɪk] *adj* phantastisch.

**fantasy** ['fæntəzɪ] *n* Phantasie *f*.

**fasten**

**fanzine** ['fænziːn] n Fan-Magazin nt.
**far** [fɑːr] see also comp **further, farther,** superl
**furthest, farthest 1** adv weit. **not ~ (away) from
here** nicht weit von hier; **I'll go with you as ~ as the
gate** ich komme/gehe bis zum Tor mit; **~ and wide**
weit und breit; **from ~ and wide** von nah und fern;
**~ above** hoch über (+dat); **~ away** weit weg; **~
away in the distance** weit in der Ferne; **~ into the
jungle** weit in den Dschungel hinein; **I won't be ~
away** ich bin ganz in der Nähe; **~ out** weit draußen; **have you come ~?** kommen Sie von weit her?;
**as ~ back as I can remember** so weit ich mich erinnern kann; **as ~ back as 1945** schon (im Jahre)
1945; **~ into the night** bis spät in die Nacht; **~
longer/better** weit länger/besser; **it's ~ beyond
what I can afford** das übersteigt meine Mittel bei
weitem; **as** or **so ~ as I'm concerned** was mich betrifft; **it's all right as ~ as it goes** das ist soweit
ganz gut; **in so ~ as** insofern als; **~ and away the
best, by ~ the best** bei weitem der/die/das Beste; **~
from satisfactory** alles andere als befriedigend; **~
from liking him I find him quite unpleasant** nicht
nur, daß ich ihn nicht leiden kann, ich finde ihn sogar ausgesprochen unsympathisch; **~ from it!** ganz
und gar nicht; **~ be it from me to ...** es sei mir
fern, zu ...; **so ~** (up to now) bis jetzt; (up to this
point) soweit; **so ~ so good** so weit, so gut; **so ~
and no further** bis hierher und nicht weiter; **to go ~**
(money, supplies etc) weit reichen; (person: succeed) es weit bringen; **I would go so ~ as to say ...**
ich würde so weit gehen zu sagen ...; **that's going
too ~** das geht zu weit; **to carry a joke too ~** einen
Spaß zu weit treiben; **you're not ~ out** (in guess) da
liegst du nicht schlecht; **that was not ~ off** (aim)
das war knapp daneben; (guess) das war schon
nicht schlecht; **~ gone** (col: drunk) schon ziemlich
hinüber (col).
   **2** adj country weit entfernt. **the ~ end of the room**
das andere Ende des Zimmers; **the ~ window/wall**
das Fenster/die Wand am anderen Ende des Zimmers; **the ~ one** das da drüben; **in the ~ distance**
in weiter Ferne; **the ~ left/right** (Pol) die äußerste
Linke/Rechte; **it's a ~ cry from ...** (fig) das ist etwas
ganz anderes als ...; **it's a ~ cry from what she
promised at first** ursprünglich hat sie etwas ganz
anderes versprochen.
**faraway** ['fɑːrəweɪ] adj attr place abgelegen; (fig:
dreamy) verträumt.
**farce** [fɑːs] n (Theat, fig) Farce f.
**farcical** ['fɑːsɪkəl] adj (fig: absurd) absurd.
**fare** [fɛər] **1** n **(a)** (charge) Fahrpreis m; (on plane)
Flugpreis m; (on boat) Preis m für die Überfahrt;
(money) Fahrgeld nt. **what is the ~?** was kostet die
Fahrt/der Flug/die Überfahrt? **(b)** (old, form: food)
Kost f. **2** vi **he ~d well** es erging ihm gut; **how did
you ~** wie erging es dir?
**Far: ~ East** n **the ~** der Ferne Osten; **~ Eastern**
adj fernöstlich; **~ Eastern travel** Fernostreisen pl.
**fare stage** n Teilstrecke f; (point) Zahlgrenze f.
**farewell** [fɛəˈwel] **1** n Abschied m. **to bid sb ~** jdm
auf Wiedersehen sagen. **2** interj (old) leb(e) wohl
(dated).
**farewell** in cpds Abschieds-.
**far: ~-fetched** adj weithergeholt attr, weit hergeholt
pred; **~-flung** adj (distant) abgelegen.
**farm** [fɑːm] **1** n Bauernhof m; (bigger) Gut(shof m)
nt; (in US, Australia) Farm f. **2** attr produce, buildings Landwirtschafts-; labourer Land-. **~ animals**
Tiere auf dem Bauernhof. **3** vt land bebauen. **4** vi
Landwirtschaft betreiben.
▶**farm out** vt sep work vergeben (on, to an +acc);

children in Pflege geben (to dat, bei).
**farmer** ['fɑːmər] n Bauer m, Bäuerin f, Landwirt(in
f) m; (in US, Australia) Farmer m; (gentleman ~)
Gutsherr m; (tenant ~) Pächter m. **~'s wife** Bäuerin f.
**farm: ~hand** n Landarbeiter m; (living on small
farm) Knecht m; **~house** n Bauernhaus nt.
**farming** ['fɑːmɪŋ] n Landwirtschaft f; (animals also)
Viehzucht f.
**farm: ~ land** n Ackerland nt; **~stead** n Bauernhof
m, Gehöft nt; **~ worker** n Landarbeiter m; **~yard**
n Hof m; **~yard manure** n Stalldung m.
**Far North** n **the ~** der Hohe Norden.
**far: ~-off** adj (weit)entfernt; **~-out** adj (col: excellent) toll (col). **~-reaching** adj weitreichend; **~-
seeing** adj weitblickend; **~-sighted** adj (lit) weitsichtig; (fig) person weitblickend; (taking precautionary measures) umsichtig; measures auf weite
Sicht geplant.
**fart** [fɑːt] (col) **1** n Furz m (col!). **2** vi furzen (col!).
**farther** ['fɑːðər] comp of **far 1** adv see **further 1** (a).
**2** adj **at the ~ end** am anderen Ende.
**farthest** ['fɑːðɪst] adj, adv superl of **far** see **furthest
1, 2.**
**farthing** ['fɑːðɪŋ] n (old Brit) Viertelpenny m.
**fascia** ['feɪʃə] n (Brit Aut) Armaturentafel f.
**fascinate** ['fæsɪneɪt] vt faszinieren. **it ~s me how ...**
ich finde es erstaunlich, wie ...
**fascinating** ['fæsɪneɪtɪŋ] adj faszinierend.
**fascination** [ˌfæsɪˈneɪʃən] n Faszination f. **to have a
~ for sb** auf jdn einen besonderen Reiz ausüben;
**his ~ with the cinema** die Faszination, die das Kino
auf ihn ausübt.
**fascism** ['fæʃɪzəm] n Faschismus m.
**fascist** ['fæʃɪst] **1** n Faschist(in f) m. **2** adj faschistisch.
**fashion** ['fæʃən] **1** n **(a)** no pl (manner) Art (und
Weise) f. **in the Indian ~** nach Art der Indianer; **in
the usual ~** wie üblich; **well, after a ~** na ja, so
einigermaßen; **to do sth after** or **in a ~** etw schlecht
und recht machen. **(b)** (in clothing, latest style)
Mode f. **in ~** modern; **it's the/all the ~** es ist Mode/
große Mode; **to come into/go out of ~** in Mode/aus
der Mode kommen; **this year's ~s** die Mode in diesem Jahr. **(c)** (custom) **it was the ~ in those days**
das war damals Sitte. **2** vt gestalten.
**fashionable** ['fæʃnəbl] adj clothes, person modisch;
illness, colour Mode-; area, address vornehm; pub,
artist, author in Mode. **it's (very) ~** es ist (große)
Mode.
**fashion** in cpds Mode-; **~-conscious** adj modebe-
wußt; **~ designer** n Modezeichner(in f) m; **~
model** n Mannequin nt; (man) Dressman m; **~
parade** n, **~ show** n Mode(n)schau f.
**fast¹** [fɑːst] **1** adj (+er) **(a)** schnell; film hoch-
empfindlich. **he's a ~ worker** (lit) er arbeitet
schnell; (fig) er geht mächtig ran (col); **to pull a ~
one (on sb)** (col) jdn übers Ohr hauen (col); **~ train**
D-Zug m. **(b) to be ~** (clock, watch) vorgehen. **(c)**
(fig: immoral) locker. **~ woman** leichtlebige Frau.
**(d)** (firm) fest; friend gut. **(e)** colour, dye farbecht.
**2** adv **(a)** schnell. **(b)** (firmly) fest. **to stick ~** festsitzen; (with glue) festkleben; **to hold ~ to sth** an etw
(dat) festhalten; **to play ~ and loose with sb** mit
jdm ein falsches Spiel treiben; **to be ~ asleep** tief
schlafen.
**fast²** **1** vi (not eat) fasten. **2** n Fasten nt; (period of
fasting) Fastenzeit f.
**fast: ~back** n (Aut) Fließheck nt; **~ breeder reactor** n schneller Brüter.
**fasten** ['fɑːsn] **1** vt (attach) befestigen (to, onto an

+*dat)*; *buttons, dress etc* zumachen; *(lock) door* (ab)schließen. **to ~ two things together** zwei Dinge aneinander befestigen; **to ~ the blame on sb** die Schuld auf jdn schieben. **2** *vi (door etc)* sich schließen lassen. **the dress ~s at the back** das Kleid wird hinten zugemacht; **this piece ~s in here** dieses Teil wird hier befestigt.

►**fasten down** *vt sep* festmachen.

►**fasten on 1** *vt sep* befestigen (+*prep obj, -to* an +*dat)*. **2** *vi +prep obj (fig)* **the teacher always ~s ~ Smith** der Lehrer hackt immer auf Smith herum *(col)*.

►**fasten onto** *vi +prep obj (fig)* **to ~ ~ sb** sich an jdn hängen; **to ~ ~ an idea** eine Idee aufgreifen.

►**fasten up** *vt sep dress etc* zumachen.

**fastener** ['fɑːsnə'], **fastening** ['fɑːsnɪŋ] *n* Verschluß *m*.

**fast: ~ food** *n* Fast-Food *nt*; **~ food restaurant** *n* Schnellrestaurant *nt*; **~ forward** *n (on tape deck)* Vorlauf *m*.

**fastidious** [fæs'tɪdɪəs] *adj* wählerisch *(about* in bezug auf +*acc)*.

**fast lane** *n* Überholspur *f*. **life in the ~** *(fig)* Leben *nt* mit Tempo.

**fat** [fæt] **1** *n (Anat, Cook)* Fett *nt*. **to live off the ~ of the land** *(fig)* wie die Made im Speck leben *(col)*; **to put on ~** Speck ansetzen; **to run to ~** in die Breite gehen *(col)*. **2** *adj* (+*er)* **(a)** dick, fett *(pej)*. **to get ~** dick werden. **(b)** *meat* fett. **(c)** *(fig) volume, wallet, cigar* dick; *salary, cheque, profit* üppig, fett *(col)*; *part in play* umfangreich. **(d)** *(iro col)* **a ~ lot of good you are!** Sie sind ja 'ne schöne Hilfe! *(iro col)*; **a ~ lot he knows!** er hat doch überhaupt keine Ahnung!; **a ~ chance he's got** da hat er ja Mordschancen *(iro col)*.

**fatal** ['feɪtl] *adj (lit)* tödlich *(to* für); *(fig)* verheerend; *day, decision* schicksalsschwer. **that would be ~** das wäre das Ende *(to gen)*; **to deal sb/sth a ~ blow** *(fig)* jdm/einer Sache einen vernichtenden Schlag versetzen; **it's ~ to say that** das ist fatal, so etwas zu sagen.

**fatalism** ['feɪtəlɪzəm] *n* Fatalismus *m*.

**fatalist** ['feɪtəlɪst] *n* Fatalist(in *f) m*.

**fatalistic** [ˌfeɪtə'lɪstɪk] *adj* fatalistisch.

**fatality** [fə'tælɪtɪ] *n* Todesfall *m*; *(in accident, war etc)* (Todes)opfer *nt*.

**fatally** ['feɪtəlɪ] *adv wounded* tödlich. **to be ~ attracted to sb** jdm hoffnungslos verfallen sein.

**fate** [feɪt] *n* Schicksal *nt*. **to leave sb to his ~** jdn seinem Schicksal überlassen; **to meet one's ~** *(die)* vom Schicksal ereilt werden.

**fated** ['feɪtɪd] *adj* unglückselig; *project, plan* zum Scheitern verurteilt. **to be ~** unter einem ungünstigen Stern stehen; **they were ~ never to meet again** es war ihnen bestimmt, sich nie wiederzusehen.

**fateful** ['feɪtfʊl] *adj (disastrous)* verhängnisvoll; *(momentous)* schicksalsschwer.

**fathead** ['fæthed] *n (col)* Blödian *m (col)*.

**father** ['fɑːðə'] **1** *n* **(a)** *(lit, fig)* Vater *m*. **to be a ~ to sb** jdm ein Vater sein; **from ~ to son** vom Vater auf den Sohn; **like ~ like son** der Apfel fällt nicht weit vom Stamm *(prov)*; **F~'s Day** Vatertag *m*. **(b)** *(priest)* Pfarrer *m*. **yes, ~** ja, Herr Pfarrer. **2** *vt child* zeugen.

**father: F~ Christmas** *n* der Weihnachtsmann; **~-figure** *n* Vaterfigur *f*; **~hood** *n* Vaterschaft *f*; **~-in-law** *n, pl* ~**s-in-law** Schwiegervater *m*; **~land** *n* Vaterland *nt*; **~less** *adj* vaterlos.

**fatherly** ['fɑːðəlɪ] *adj* väterlich.

**fathom** ['fæðəm] **1** *n* Faden *m*. **2** *vt (also ~ out)* verstehen. **I just can't ~ him (out)** er ist mir ein Rätsel.

**fatigue** [fə'tiːg] **1** *n* **(a)** Erschöpfung *f*; *(metal ~)* Ermüdung *f*. **(b)** *(Mil: ~ duty)* **to be on ~** Arbeitsdienst haben. **2** *vt (tire)* ermüden; *(exhaust)* erschöpfen.

**fatigue: ~ dress** *n* Arbeitsanzug *m*; **~ party** *n* Arbeitskommando *nt*.

**fatness** ['fætnɪs] *n* Dicke *f*.

**fatso** ['fætsəʊ] *n (col)* Dicke(r) *mf (col)*.

**fatten** ['fætn] *vt (also ~ up)* *animals* mästen; *people* herausfüttern *(col)*.

**fattening** ['fætnɪŋ] *adj* **chocolate is ~** Schokolade macht dick.

**fatty** ['fætɪ] **1** *adj* fett; *(greasy)* fettig; *acid, tissue* Fett-. **~ degeneration** *(Med)* Verfettung *f*. **2** *n (col)* Dickerchen *nt (col)*.

**fatuous** ['fætjʊəs] *adj statement* albern.

**faucet** ['fɔːsɪt] *n (US)* Hahn *m*.

**fault** [fɔːlt] **1** *n* **(a)** Fehler *m*; *(Tech)* Defekt *m*; *(Geol)* Verwerfung *f*; *(Tennis)* Fehler *m*. **generous to a ~** übermäßig großzügig; **to find ~ with sb/sth** etwas an jdm/etw auszusetzen haben; **he/my memory was at ~** er war im Unrecht/mein Gedächtnis hat mich getrogen. **(b)** *no pl* **it's my ~** es ist meine Schuld; **whose ~ is it?** wer ist schuld?; **it's all your own ~** Sie sind selbst schuld. **2** *vt* etwas auszusetzen haben an *(+dat)*. **I can't ~ it** ich habe nichts daran auszusetzen; *(can't disprove it)* ich kann es nicht widerlegen.

**fault: ~-finder** *n* Krittler(in *f) m*; **~-finding** *n* Krittelei *f*.

**faultless** ['fɔːltlɪs] *adj appearance* tadellos; *(without mistakes)* fehlerlos; *English* fehlerfrei.

**faulty** ['fɔːltɪ] *adj* (+*er)* fehlerhaft; *(Tech)* defekt. **~ design** Fehlkonstruktion *f*.

**fauna** ['fɔːnə] *n* Fauna *f*.

**faux pas** [fəʊ'pɑː] *n* Fauxpas *m*.

**favour, (US) favor** ['feɪvə'] **1** *n* **(a)** *no pl (goodwill)* Gunst *f*. **to find ~ with sb** bei jdm Anklang finden; **to be in ~ with sb** bei jdm gut angeschrieben sein; *(fashion, pop star, writer etc)* bei jdm beliebt sein; **to be/fall out of ~** in Ungnade (gefallen) sein/fallen; *(fashion, pop star, writer etc)* nicht mehr beliebt sein *(with* bei)/nicht mehr ankommen *(with* bei*)*.

**(b) to be in ~ of sth** für etw sein; **in his ~** zu seinen Gunsten; **all those in ~ (raise their hands)** alle, die dafür sind(, Hand hoch!); **I'm in ~ of staying** ich bin dafür zu bleiben.

**(c)** *(partiality)* Vergünstigung *f*. **to show ~ to sb** jdn bevorzugen.

**(d)** *(kindness)* Gefallen *m*. **to ask a ~ of sb** jdn um einen Gefallen bitten; **to do sb a ~** jdm einen Gefallen tun; **do me a ~!** *(col)* sei so gut!; **do me the ~ of shutting up!** *(col)* tu mir den Gefallen und halt den Mund!; **as a ~** aus Gefälligkeit; **as a ~ to him** ihm zuliebe.

**2** *vt* **(a)** *plan, idea (be in ~ of)* für gut halten; *(prefer)* bevorzugen. **(b)** *(oblige, honour)* beehren *(form)*. **(c)** *(US: resemble)* ähneln (+*dat)*.

**favourable, (US) favorable** ['feɪvərəbl] *adj* günstig *(for, to* für); *(expressing approval)* positiv.

**favourably, (US) favorably** ['feɪvərəblɪ] *adv see adj* vorteilhaft; positiv. **to be ~ impressed** einen positiven Eindruck haben; **to be ~ disposed to sb/sth** jdm wohlgesinnt sein/einer Sache *dat* positiv gegenüberstehen.

**favoured, (US) favored** ['feɪvəd] *adj* **the/a ~ few** die wenigen Auserwählten/einige (wenige) Auserwählte.

**favourite, (US) favorite** ['feɪvərɪt] **1** *n (person)* Liebling *m*; *(Sport)* Favorit(in *f) m*. **this one is my**

~ das habe ich am liebsten; **we sang all the old** ~s wir haben all die alten Lieder gesungen. **2** adj attr Lieblings-.

**favouritism,** *(US)* **favoritism** ['feɪvərɪtɪzəm] n Günstlingswirtschaft f; *(in school)* Lieblingswirtschaft f.

**fawn¹** [fɔːn] **1** n **(a)** Hirschkalb nt; *(of roe deer)* Rehkitz nt. **(b)** *(colour)* Beige nt. **2** adj beige.

**fawn²** vi *(dog)* (mit dem Schwanz) wedeln; *(fig: person)* katzbuckeln *(on* vor +dat).

**fax** [fæks] **1** n *(document, machine)* (Tele)fax nt. **2** vt (tele)faxen.

**faze** [feɪz] vt *(esp US col)* aus der Fassung bringen.

**FBI** *(US)* = **Federal Bureau of Investigation** FBI nt.

**FC** = **Football Club** FC m.

**FCO** *(Brit)* = **Foreign and Commonwealth Office.**

**fear** [fɪər] **1** n **(a)** Angst f *(of* vor +dat). **in** ~ **and trembling** mit schlotternden Knien; **to go in** ~ **of one's life** ständig um sein Leben bangen; **for** ~ **that** ... aus Angst, daß ...; **she talked quietly for** ~ **of waking the child** sie sprach leise, um das Kind nicht aufzuwecken; **without** ~ **or favour** *(Brit)* **or favor** *(US)* ganz gerecht; **to put the** ~ **of God into sb** *(col)* jdm gewaltig Angst einjagen *(col)*. **(b) no** ~! *(col)* nie im Leben! *(col)*; **there's no** ~ **of that happening again** keine Angst, das passiert so leicht nicht wieder; **there's not much** ~ **of his coming** es ist kaum zu befürchten, daß er kommt.

**2** vt (be)fürchten; *God* Ehrfurcht haben vor *(+dat).* **I** ~ **the worst** ich befürchte das Schlimmste; **he's a man to be** ~ed er ist ein Mann, vor dem man Angst haben muß.

**3** vi **to** ~ **for** fürchten um; **never** ~! keine Angst.

**fearful** ['fɪəfʊl] adj **(a)** *(terrible)* furchtbar. **(b)** *(apprehensive)* ängstlich. **to be** ~ **for one's/sb's life** um sein/jds Leben fürchten.

**fearfully** ['fɪəfəlɪ] adv *see adj* **(a)** furchtbar. **(b)** ängstlich.

**fearless** ['fɪəlɪs] adj furchtlos. **to be** ~ **of sth** keine Angst vor etw *(dat)* haben.

**fearlessly** ['fɪəlɪslɪ] adv furchtlos.

**fearlessness** ['fɪəlɪsnɪs] n Furchtlosigkeit f.

**fearsome** ['fɪəsəm] adj furchterregend.

**feasibility** [,fiːzə'bɪlɪtɪ] n **(a)** *(of plan etc)* Machbarkeit f. ~ **study** Machbarkeitsstudie f; **the** ~ **of doing sth** die Möglichkeit, etw zu tun. **(b)** *(plausibility: of story etc)* Wahrscheinlichkeit f.

**feasible** ['fiːzəbl] adj **(a)** machbar; *plan* realisierbar. **(b)** *(likely)* excuse plausibel.

**feast** [fiːst] **1** n **(a)** Festessen nt; *(Hist)* Festgelage nt. **a** ~ **for the eyes** eine Augenweide. **(b)** *(Eccl)* Fest nt. ~ **day** n Feiertag m. **2** vi *(lit)* ein Festgelage halten. **to** ~ **on sth** sich an etw *(dat)* gütlich tun. **3** vt **to** ~ **one's eyes on sth** seine Augen an etw *(dat)* weiden.

**feat** [fiːt] n Leistung f; *(heroic, courageous etc)* Heldentat f; *(skilful)* Meisterleistung f.

**feather** ['feðər] **1** n Feder f. ~s *(plumage)* Gefieder nt; **as light as a** ~ federleicht; **that's a** ~ **in his cap** das ist ein Ruhmesblatt nt für ihn; **you could have knocked me down with a** ~ *(col)* ich war wie vom Donner gerührt; **birds of a** ~ **flock together** *(Prov)* gleich und gleich gesellt sich gern *(Prov).* **2** vt **to** ~ **one's nest** *(fig)* sein Schäfchen ins trockene bringen.

**feather:** ~-**bed** n mit Federn gefüllte Matratze; ~**brained** adj dümmlich; ~ **duster** n Staubwedel m; ~**weight** *(Boxing)* **1** n Federgewicht nt; *(fig)* Leichtgewicht nt; **2** adj Federgewicht-.

**feature** ['fiːtʃər] **1** n **(a)** *(facial)* (Gesichts)zug m. **(b)** *(characteristic)* Merkmal, Kennzeichen nt. **a** ~ **of his**

style is ... sein Stil ist durch ... gekennzeichnet; **a** ~ **of this book is** ... das Buch zeichnet sich durch ... aus; **special** ~ Besonderheit f; **new** ~ Neuheit f. **(c)** *(focal point: of room etc)* besonderes *or* herausragendes Merkmal. **to make a** ~ **of sth** etw besonders betonen. **(d)** *(Press)* (Sonder)beitrag m; *(Rad, TV)* (Dokumentar)bericht m. **(e)** *(~ film)* Spielfilm m. **2** vt *(Press)* story, picture bringen. **this film** ~s ... in diesem Film spielt ... mit. **3** vi vorkommen; *(Film)* (mit)spielen. **it** ~s **prominently in** ... es spielt in *(+dat)* ... eine bedeutende Rolle.

**feature:** ~ **film** n Spielfilm m; ~-**length** adj film mit Spielfilmlänge; ~**less** adj ohne besondere Merkmale; ~ **story** n Sonderbericht m, Feature nt; ~ **writer** n Journalist, der Features schreibt.

**Feb** = **February** Febr.

**February** ['febrʊərɪ] n Februar m; *see* **September.**

**feces** ['fiːsiːz] npl *(US)* = **faeces.**

**feckless** ['feklɪs] adj nutzlos.

**fed¹** [fed] pret, ptp of **feed.**

**fed²** n *(US col)* FBI-Mann m.

**Fed** n *(US col)* = **Federal Reserve System.**

**federal** ['fedərəl] **1** adj Bundes-; *system etc* föderalistisch. ~ **state** *(in US)* (Einzel)staat m; **the F**~ **Republic of Germany** die Bundesrepublik Deutschland; **F**~ **Reserve System** *(US)* Zentralbanksystem nt. **2** n *(US col)* FBI-Mann m.

**federalism** ['fedərəlɪzəm] n Föderalismus m.

**federation** [,fedə'reɪʃən] n *(act)* Zusammenschluß m; *(league)* Föderation f, Bund m.

**fed up** ['fed'ʌp] adj *(col)* **I'm** ~ ich habe die Nase voll *(col)*; **I'm** ~ **with him/it** er/es hängt mir zum Hals heraus *(col)*; **I'm** ~ **waiting for him** ich habe es satt, auf ihn zu warten.

**fee** [fiː] n Gebühr f; *(of doctor, lawyer, artist, tutor)* Honorar nt; *(of stage performer)* Gage f. **(school)** ~s Schulgeld nt.

**feeble** ['fiːbl] adj *(+er)* schwach; *joke* lahm; *attempt* kläglich.

**feeble-minded** [,fiːbl'maɪndɪd] adj dümmlich.

**feed** [fiːd] *(vb: pret, ptp* **fed)** **1** n *(of animals)* Futter nt; *(col: of person)* Essen nt. **when is the baby's next** ~? wann wird das Baby wieder gefüttert?; **to have a good** ~ *(col)* tüchtig futtern *(col).* **2** vt **(a)** *(provide food for)* verpflegen; *family* ernähren. **(b)** *(give food to)* füttern. **to** ~ **oneself** *(child)* allein essen (können); **to** ~ **sth to sb/an animal** jdm/einem Tier etw zu essen/fressen geben. **(c)** *machine* versorgen; *furnace* beschicken; *meter* Geld einwerfen in *(+acc)*; *(fig)* hope, imagination nähren. **to** ~ **sth into a machine** etw in eine Maschine geben; **to** ~ **sb with information** jdn mit Informationen versorgen; **the data is fed into the computer** die Daten werden in den Computer eingegeben. **(d)** *(Tech: insert)* führen. **3** vi *(animal)* fressen; *(baby)* gefüttert werden.

▶**feed back** vt sep information zurückleiten *(to an +acc).*

▶**feed in** vt sep data etc eingeben.

▶**feed on 1** vi +prep obj sich (er)nähren von. **2** vt sep +prep obj animal, baby füttern mit; person ernähren mit.

**feedback** ['fiːdbæk] n *(Elec)* Rückkopplung f; *(fig)* Reaktion f, Feedback nt. ~ **of information** Rückinformation f; **to provide more** ~ **about sth** ausführlicher über etw *(acc)* berichten.

**feeder** ['fiːdər] n **(a)** *(bottle)* Flasche f. **(b)** *(source)* *(road)* Zubringer m; *(Elec)* Speiseleitung f.

**feeding** ['fiːdɪŋ] n: ~ **bottle** *(Brit)* Flasche f; ~ **time** n *(for animal)* Fütterungszeit f; *(for baby)* Zeit f für die Mahlzeit.

**feel** [fiːl] n *(vb: pret, ptp* **felt)** **1** vt **(a)** *(touch)* fühlen;

*(examining)* befühlen. **to ~ one's way** sich vortasten; **to ~ one's way into sth** sich in etw *(acc)* einfühlen. **(b)** *(be aware of)* fühlen, spüren; *pain, emotions, loss* empfinden; *(be affected by) heat, cold, insult* leiden unter *(+dat)*. **I can't ~ anything in my left leg** ich habe kein Gefühl im linken Bein; **I felt it move** ich spürte, wie es sich bewegte; **I could ~ him getting angry** ich merkte, daß er wütend wurde; **I bet she felt that!** das hat bestimmt weh getan. **(c)** *(think)* glauben. **what do you ~ about him/it?** was halten Sie von ihm/davon?; **it was felt that ...** man war der Meinung, daß ...; **he felt it necessary** er hielt es für notwendig; **don't ~ you have to ...** glauben Sie nicht, Sie müßten ...

**2** *vi* **(a)** *(physically or mentally)* sich fühlen. **to ~ well/ill** sich wohl/elend fühlen; **to ~ convinced/certain** überzeugt/sicher sein; **to ~ hungry/thirsty/sleepy** hungrig/durstig/müde sein; **I ~ hot/cold** mir ist heiß/kalt; **he doesn't ~ quite himself today** er ist heute nicht ganz auf der Höhe; **I felt sad/strange** mir war traurig/komisch zumute; **I felt as though I'd never been away** mir war, als ob ich nie weggewesen wäre; **I felt as if I was going to be sick** ich dachte, ich müßte mich übergeben; **how do you ~ about him?** *(emotionally)* was empfinden Sie für ihn?; **you can imagine how I felt** Sie können sich *(dat)* vorstellen, wie mir zumute war; **what does it ~ like** *or* **how does it ~ to be all alone?** wie fühlt man sich *or* wie ist das so ganz allein?; **it ~s like flying** es ist wie Fliegen.

**(b)** *(to the touch)* sich anfühlen. **to ~ hard** sich hart anfühlen; **the room/air ~s warm** das Zimmer/die Luft kommt einem warm vor.

**(c)** *(think, have opinions)* meinen. **how do you ~ about these developments?** was meinen Sie zu dieser Entwicklung?; **that's just how I ~** das meine ich auch.

**(d) to ~ like** *(have desire for)* Lust haben auf *(+acc)*; *(for food)* Appetit haben auf *(+acc)*; **I ~ like eating something/going for a walk** ich könnte jetzt etwas essen/ich habe Lust spazierenzugehen; **I felt like screaming/giving up** ich hätte am liebsten geschrie(e)n/aufgegeben; **if you ~ like it** wenn Sie Lust haben.

**3** *n* **let me have a ~ (of it)!** laß (mich) mal fühlen!; **it has a velvety ~** es fühlt sich samtig an; **he recognizes things by their ~** er erkennt Dinge daran, wie sie sich anfühlen; **to get/have a ~ for sth** *(fig)* Gefühl für etw bekommen/haben.

▶**feel about** *or* **around** *vi* umhertasten; *(in drawer, bag etc)* herumtasten.

▶**feel for** *vi +prep obj* **(a)** *(sympathize with)* Mitgefühl haben mit. **I ~ ~ you** Sie tun mir leid. **(b)** *(search for)* tasten nach.

▶**feel up to** *vi +prep obj* sich gewachsen fühlen *(+dat)*. **I don't ~ ~ ~ it** ich fühle mich nicht dazu in der Lage.

**feeler** ['fiːlə<sup>r</sup>] *n (Zool, fig)* Fühler *m*. **to put out ~s** seine Fühler ausstrecken; **~ gauge** Fühl(er)lehre *f*.

**feeling** ['fiːlɪŋ] *n* **(a)** Gefühl *nt*. **I've lost all ~ in my right arm** ich habe kein Gefühl mehr im rechten Arm; **I've a funny ~ she won't come** ich hab so das Gefühl, daß sie nicht kommt. **(b)** *(opinion: also ~s)* Meinung, Ansicht *f (on zu)*. **there was a general ~ that ...** man war allgemein der Ansicht, daß ...; **bad/good ~** Verstimmung *f*/Wohlwollen *nt*; **there's been a lot of bad ~ about this decision** wegen dieser Entscheidung hat es viel böses Blut gegeben. **(c)** **~s** Gefühle *pl*; **you've hurt his ~s** Sie haben ihn verletzt; **no hard ~s** nichts für ungut.

**fee-paying** ['fiːˌpeɪɪŋ] *adj school* Privat-; **~ pupils** Schüler, deren Eltern Schulgeld zahlen.

**feet** [fiːt] *pl of* **foot.**

**feign** [feɪn] *vt* vortäuschen.

**feint** [feɪnt] *n (Sport)* Finte *f*.

**feline** ['fiːlaɪn] *adj (lit)* Katzen-; *(fig)* katzenhaft.

**fell¹** [fel] *pret of* **fall.**

**fell²** *n (skin)* Fell *nt*.

**fell³** *adj* **with one ~ blow** mit einem einzigen gewaltigen Hieb; **at one ~ swoop** mit einem Schlag.

**fell⁴** *vt tree* fällen; *person* niederstrecken; *animal* zur Strecke bringen.

**fell⁵** *n (Brit)* Berg *m*; *(moorland)* Hochmoor *nt*.

**fellow** ['feləʊ] *n* **(a)** Mann, Typ *(col) m*. **(b)** *(comrade)* Kamerad *m*; *(colleague)* Kollege *m*, Kollegin *f*. **(c)** *(of a society)* Mitglied *nt*; *(Univ)* Fellow *m*.

**fellow:** **~ citizen** *n* Mitbürger(in *f*) *m*; **~ countryman** *n* Landsmann *m*/-männin *f*; **~ countrymen** *npl* Landsleute *pl*; **~ feeling** *n* Mitgefühl *nt*; *(togetherness)* Zusammengehörigkeitsgefühl *nt*; **~ men** *npl* Mitmenschen *pl*; **~ passenger** *n* Mitreisende(r) *mf*.

**fellowship** ['feləʊʃɪp] *n* **(a)** *no pl* Kameradschaft *f*; *(company)* Gesellschaft *f*. **(b)** *(society, club etc)* Gesellschaft *f*. **(c)** *(Univ: scholarship)* Forschungsstipendium *nt*; *(job)* Position *f eines Fellow*.

**fellow:** **~ student** *n* Kommilitone *m*, Kommilitonin *f*; **~ sufferer** *n* Leidensgenosse *m*/-genossin *f*; **~ traveller** *(Brit)* or **traveler** *(US) n* **(a)** *(lit)* Mitreisende(r) *mf*; **(b)** *(Pol)* Sympathisant(in *f*) *m*; **~ worker** *n* Kollege *m*, Kollegin *f*, Mitarbeiter(in *f*) *m*.

**felon** ['felən] *n (Schwer)* verbrecher *m*.

**felony** ['felənɪ] *n (schweres)* Verbrechen *nt*.

**felt¹** [felt] *pret, ptp of* **feel.**

**felt²** *n* Filz *m*.

**felt-tip (pen)** ['felttɪp('pen)] *n* Filzstift *m*.

**female** ['fiːmeɪl] **1** *adj* weiblich; *labour, rights* Frauen-. **a ~ doctor/student/slave/dog** eine Ärztin/Studentin/Sklavin/Hündin; **~ impersonator** Frauenimitator *m*; **that's a typical ~ attitude** (das ist) typisch Frau. **2** *n* **(a)** *(animal)* Weibchen *nt*. **(b)** *(col: woman)* Frau *f*; *(pej)* Weib *nt (pej)*.

**feminine** ['femɪnɪn] **1** *adj (also Gram)* weiblich, feminin. **2** *n (Gram)* Femininum *nt*. **in the ~** in der weiblichen *or* femininen Form.

**femininity** [ˌfemɪˈnɪnɪtɪ] *n* Weiblichkeit *f*.

**feminism** ['femɪnɪzəm] *n* Feminismus *m*.

**feminist** ['femɪnɪst] **1** *n* Feminist(in *f*) *m*. **2** *adj* feministisch.

**femur** ['fiːmə<sup>r</sup>] *n* Oberschenkelknochen *m*.

**fen** [fen] *n* Moorland, Sumpfland *nt*. **the F~s** *die Niederungen in East Anglia*.

**fence** [fens] **1** *n* **(a)** Zaun *m*; *(Sport)* Hindernis *nt*. **to sit on the ~** *(fig)* nicht Partei ergreifen; **don't sit on the ~** entscheiden Sie sich. **(b)** *(col: receiver of stolen goods)* Hehler *m*. **2** *vt (also ~ in)* land einzäunen, umzäunen. **3** *vi (Sport)* fechten.

▶**fence in** *vt sep* einzäunen, umzäunen. **to ~ sb ~** *(fig)* jds Freiheit beschneiden.

▶**fence off** *vt sep piece of land* abzäunen.

**fencer** ['fensə<sup>r</sup>] *n* Fechter(in *f*) *m*.

**fencing** ['fensɪŋ] *n* **(a)** *(Sport)* Fechten *nt*. **(b)** *(fences)* Zaun *m*, Einzäunung *f*.

**fend** [fend] *vi* **to ~ for oneself** *(provide)* für sich (selbst) sorgen; **could she ~ for herself in the big city?** könnte sie sich in der großen Stadt allein durchschlagen?

▶**fend off** *vt sep* abwehren.

**fender** ['fendə<sup>r</sup>] *n* **(a)** *(in front of fire)* Kamingitter *nt*. **(b)** *(US Aut)* Kotflügel *m*; *(of bicycle etc)* Schutzblech *nt*. **~-bender** *(col)* kleiner Blechschaden.

**fennel** ['fenl] *n (Bot)* Fenchel *m*.

**ferment** ['fɜ:ment] **1** n (fig) Unruhe f. **the city/he was in a state of** ~ es gärte in der Stadt/in ihm. **2** [fə'ment] vi (lit, fig) gären. **3** [fə'ment] vt (lit) fermentieren; (fig) unrest anwachsen lassen.
**fermentation** [,fɜ:men'teɪʃən] n Gärung f.
**fern** [fɜ:n] n Farn(kraut nt) m.
**ferocious** [fə'rəʊʃəs] adj appearance, animal wild; glance, look grimmig; criticism, competition scharf; fight, temper, attack heftig.
**ferociously** [fə'rəʊʃəslɪ] adv grimmig; growl wild; fight, resist heftig.
**ferocity** [fə'rɒsɪtɪ] n see adj Wildheit f; Grimmigkeit f; Schärfe f; Heftigkeit f.
**ferret** ['ferɪt] **1** n Frettchen nt. **2** vi (also ~ **about** or **around**) herumstöbern, herumschnüffeln (pej).
▶**ferret out** vt sep aufstöbern.
**fer(r)ule** ['feru:l] n Zwinge f.
**ferry** ['ferɪ] **1** n Fähre f. **2** vt (by boat: also ~ **across** or **over**) übersetzen; (by plane, car etc) transportieren. **to** ~ **sb across a river** jdn über einen Fluß setzen; **to** ~ **sb/sth back and forth** jdn/etw hin- und herbringen.
**ferry:** ~**boat** n Fährboot nt; ~**man** n Fährmann m.
**fertile** ['fɜ:taɪl] adj (lit, fig) fruchtbar.
**fertility** [fə'tɪlɪtɪ] **1** n (lit, fig) Fruchtbarkeit f. **2** attr cult, symbol Fruchtbarkeits-. ~ **drug** Fruchtbarkeitspille f.
**fertilization** [,fɜ:tɪlaɪ'zeɪʃən] n Befruchtung f.
**fertilize** ['fɜ:tɪlaɪz] vt befruchten; land düngen.
**fertilizer** ['fɜ:tɪlaɪzər] n Dünger m. **artificial** ~ Kunstdünger m.
**fervent** ['fɜ:vənt], **fervid** ['fɜ:vɪd] adj leidenschaftlich; tone of voice, expression, prayer inbrünstig.
**fervour,** (US) **fervor** ['fɜ:vər] n Leidenschaft f.
**fester** ['festər] vi (wound) eitern.
**festival** ['festɪvəl] n (a) (Eccl etc) Fest nt. (b) (cultural) Festspiele pl; (esp pop ~) Festival nt.
**festive** ['festɪv] adj festlich. **the** ~ **season** die Festzeit.
**festiveness** ['festɪvnɪs] n Festlichkeit f.
**festivity** [fe'stɪvɪtɪ] n (a) (gaiety) Feststimmung f. (b) (celebration) Feier f. **festivities** pl Feierlichkeiten pl.
**festoon** [fe'stu:n] vt **to** ~ **sb/sth with sth** jdn mit etw behängen/etw mit etw schmücken.
**FET** = (Elec) **field effect transistor** FET m.
**fetal** adj (esp US) = **foetal**.
**fetch** [fetʃ] vt (a) (bring) holen; (collect) person, thing abholen. (b) sigh, groan ausstoßen. (c) (bring in) money (ein)bringen. (d) (col) **to** ~ **sb a blow/one** jdm eine langen (col).
▶**fetch back** vt sep zurückholen.
▶**fetch in** vt sep hereinbringen.
▶**fetch up 1** vi (col) landen (col). **2** vt sep (Brit: vomit) erbrechen.
**fetching** ['fetʃɪŋ] adj reizend; smile gewinnend.
**fête** [feɪt] **1** n Fest nt. **2** vt (make much of) sb, sb's success feiern.
**fetid** ['fetɪd] adj übelriechend.
**fetish** ['fetɪʃ] n Fetisch m. **to have a** ~ **about cleanliness** einen Sauberkeitstick haben (col).
**fetishist** ['fetɪʃɪst] n Fetischist m.
**fetter** ['fetər] **1** vt prisoner fesseln; goat anpflocken; (fig) in Fesseln legen. **2** n ~**s** pl (Fuß)fesseln pl; (fig) Fesseln pl.
**fettle** ['fetl] n **to be in fine** ~ in bester Form sein.
**fetus** n (US) = **foetus**.
**feud** [fju:d] **1** n (lit, fig) Fehde f. **2** vi (lit, fig) sich befehden.
**feudal** ['fju:dl] adj Feudal-, feudal. ~ **system** Feudal-

system nt.
**feudalism** ['fju:dəlɪzəm] n Feudalismus m.
**fever** ['fi:vər] n (lit, fig) Fieber nt no pl. **to have a** ~ eine Fieberkrankheit haben; (high temperature) Fieber haben; **in a** ~ **of excitement** in fieberhafter Erregung; **to reach** ~ **pitch** auf dem Siedepunkt angelangt sein; **to be working at** ~ **pitch** auf Hochtouren arbeiten.
**feverish** ['fi:vərɪʃ] adj (Med) fiebernd attr; (fig) activity fieberhaft. **he's still** ~ er hat noch Fieber.
**feverishly** ['fi:vərɪʃlɪ] adv fieberhaft.
**few** [fju:] adj (+er), pron **(a)** (not many) wenige. **we are very** ~ wir sind nur sehr wenige; ~ **and far between** dünn gesät; **he has as** ~ **books as you** er hat genauso wenig(e) Bücher wie du; **as** ~ **as six objections** bloß sechs Einwände; **there were three too** ~ es waren drei zuwenig da; **he is one of the** ~ **people who** ... er ist einer der wenigen, die ...; **its days are** ~ es hat nur ein kurzes Leben; **the lucky** ~ die wenigen Glücklichen; **as** ~ **as you** genauso wenige wie du; **however** ~ **there may be** wie wenige auch immer da sind; **I've got too** ~ **as it is** ich habe sowieso schon zu wenig(e); **there are too** ~ **of you** ihr seid zu wenige; **the** ~ **who knew him** die wenigen, die ihn kannten.
**(b) a** ~ ein paar; **a** ~ **more days** noch ein paar Tage; **a** ~ **times** ein paar Male; **he's had a good** ~ **drinks** er hat ziemlich viel getrunken; **quite a** ~ **books** ziemlich viele Bücher; **in the next** ~ **days** in den nächsten paar Tagen; **every** ~ **days** alle paar Tage.
**fewer** ['fju:ər] adj, pron comp of **few** weniger. **no** ~ **than** nicht weniger als.
**fewest** ['fju:ɪst] adj, pron superl of **few** die wenigsten.
**ff.** = **and following (pages)** ff.
**FH** (Brit) = **fire hydrant.**
**fiancé** [fɪ'ā:ŋseɪ] n Verlobte(r) m.
**fiancée** [fɪ'ā:ŋseɪ] n Verlobte f.
**fiasco** [fɪ'æskəʊ] n Fiasko nt.
**fib** [fɪb] (col) **1** n (that's a) ~! das ist geflunkert! (col); **don't tell** ~**s** flunker nicht! (col). **2** vi flunkern (col).
**fibber** ['fɪbər] n (col) Flunkerer m (col).
**fibre,** (US) **fiber** ['faɪbər] n Faser f; (roughage) Ballaststoffe pl. **moral** ~ Charakterstärke f.
**fibre,** (US) **fiber:** ~**board** n Faserplatte f; ~**glass** (US: ®) **1** n Fiberglas nt; **2** adj Fiberglas-; ~ **optics** n sing Faseroptik f.
**fibrositis** [,faɪbrə'saɪtɪs] n Bindegewebsentzündung f.
**fibrous** ['faɪbrəs] adj faserig.
**fiche** [fi:ʃ] n = **microfiche.**
**fickle** ['fɪkl] adj unbeständig, launenhaft.
**fickleness** ['fɪklnɪs] n Unbeständigkeit f.
**fiction** ['fɪkʃən] n no pl (Liter) Prosaliteratur f; (category) Belletristik f. **work of** ~ Erzählung f; (longer) Roman m; **light** ~ (leichte) Unterhaltungsliteratur; **that's pure** ~ (fig) das ist frei erfunden.
**fictional** ['fɪkʃənl] adj erfunden. **a** ~ **character** eine Gestalt aus der Literatur.
**fictionalize** ['fɪkʃənəlaɪz] vt fiktionalisieren.
**fiction-writer** n Belletrist(in f) m.
**fictitious** [fɪk'tɪʃəs] adj (a) (imaginary) frei erfunden. (b) (false) falsch.
**fiddle** ['fɪdl] **1** n (a) (Mus col) Geige f. **to play second** ~ **to sb** (fig) in jds Schatten (dat) stehen; **he refuses to play second** ~ (fig) er will immer die erste Geige spielen; **as fit as a** ~ kerngesund. (b) (Brit col: cheat) Schiebung f; (with money) faule Geschäfte pl (col). **it's a** ~ das ist Schiebung!; **there are so many** ~**s going on** es wird so viel getrickst (col); **to be on**

the ~ krumme Dinger machen *(col)*; **tax** ~ Steuermanipulation *f.* **2** *vi (fidget, play around)* herumspielen. **to** ~ **with sth** an etw *(dat)* herumspielen *or* herumdoktern *(col)*. **3** *vt (col) accounts, results* frisieren *(col)*; *election* manipulieren. **he** ~**d it so that ...** er hat es so getrickst, daß ... *(col)*. **4** *interj* ach du liebe Zeit.

**fiddler** ['fɪdləʳ] *n* **(a)** *(Mus col)* Geiger(in *f*) *m.* **(b)** *(col: cheat)* Schwindler(in *f*) *m.*

**fiddlesticks** ['fɪdlstɪks] *interj (nonsense)* Unsinn, Quatsch *(col)*; *(bother)* du liebe Zeit.

**fiddling** ['fɪdlɪŋ] *adj (trivial)* läppisch.

**fiddly** ['fɪdlɪ] *adj (+er) (col: intricate)* knifflig *(col)*.

**fidelity** [fɪ'delɪtɪ] *n* **(a)** Treue *f (to* zu*).* **(b)** *(Rad etc)* Klangtreue *f.*

**fidget** ['fɪdʒɪt] **1** *vi* zappeln. **to** ~ **with sth** mit etw herumfummeln; **don't** ~ zappel nicht so rum! **2** *n (person)* Zappelphilipp *m (col).*

**fidgety** ['fɪdʒɪtɪ] *adj* zappelig; *audience etc* unruhig.

**field** [fi:ld] **1** *n* **(a)** *(lit, fig)* Feld *nt*; *(for root vegetables)* Acker *m*; *(area of grass)* Wiese *f*; *(for cows, horses etc)* Weide *f.* **he's working in the** ~**s** er arbeitet auf dem Feld *or* Acker; ~ **of battle** Schlachtfeld *nt*; ~ **of vision** Blickfeld *nt*; **magnetic** ~ Magnetfeld *nt.* **(b)** *(Sport: ground)* Platz *m*; *(competitors)* Feld *nt.* **there's a very strong** ~ das Feld der Teilnehmer ist sehr stark; **the rest of the** ~ *(runners)* die übrigen Läufer; **to lead the** ~ *(fig)* führend sein; **to take the** ~ auf den Platz kommen. **(c)** *(of study, work etc)* Gebiet *nt.* **to be first in the** ~ **with sth** *(Comm)* etw als Erster auf den Markt bringen; **studies in the** ~ **of medicine** Studien auf dem Gebiet der Medizin; **this is, of course, a very broad** ~ das ist natürlich ein weites Feld; **what** ~ **are you in?** auf welchem Gebiet arbeiten Sie?; **to test sth in the** ~ etw in der Praxis ausprobieren.

**2** *vt (Cricket, Baseball etc) ball* auffangen und zurückwerfen; *(fig) question etc* abblocken, abwehren; *team, side* aufs Feld *or* auf den Platz schicken.

**field day** *n* **I had a** ~ an dem Tag bin ich wirklich auf meine Kosten gekommen.

**fielder** ['fi:ldəʳ] *n (Cricket, Baseball etc)* Fänger *m.*

**field:** ~ **events** *npl (Athletics)* Sprung- und Wurfdisziplinen *pl*; ~ **glasses** *npl* Feldstecher *m*; ~ **goal** *n (US Ftbl)* Feldtor *nt*; ~ **gun** *n (Mil)* Feldgeschütz *nt*; ~ **hockey** *n (US)* Hockey *nt*; ~ **hospital** *n (Mil)* (Feld)lazarett *nt*; ~ **marshal** *n (Mil)* Feldmarschall *m*; ~**mouse** *n* Feldmaus *f*; ~ **sports** *npl* Sport *m* im Freien *(Jagen und Fischen)*; ~ **study** *n* Feldforschung *f*; **a** ~ **study** eine Feldstudie; ~ **test**, ~ **trial** *n* Feldversuch *m*; ~**work** *n (of geologist etc)* Arbeit *f* im Gelände; *(of sociologist etc)* Feldarbeit *f.*

**fiend** [fi:nd] *n* Teufel *m.* **tennis** ~ *(col)* Tennisnarr *m*; **a fresh-air** ~ *(col)* ein Frischluftfanatiker *m.*

**fiendish** ['fi:ndɪʃ] *adj* teuflisch; *(col) pace, heat* höllisch *(col)*; *problem* vertrackt *(col).*

**fiendishly** ['fi:ndɪʃlɪ] *adv* teuflisch; *difficult, complicated* verteufelt *(col).*

**fierce** [fɪəs] *adj (+er) appearance* wild; *glance, look* böse, grimmig; *dog* bissig; *criticism, competition* scharf; *fight, resistance, temper, attack (lit, fig)* heftig; *heat, sun* glühend.

**fiercely** ['fɪəslɪ] *adv see adj.*

**fierceness** ['fɪəsnɪs] *n see adj* Wildheit *f*; Grimmigkeit *f*; Bissigkeit *f*; Schärfe *f*; Heftigkeit *f*; Glut *f.*

**fieriness** ['faɪərɪnɪs] *n* Feuer *nt*; *(of temper)* Hitzigkeit *f.*

**fiery** ['faɪərɪ] *adj (+er) (lit, fig)* feurig; *sunset* rotglühend. **to have a** ~ **temper** ein Hitzkopf *m* sein.

**FIFA** ['fi:fə] = **Federation of International Football Associations** FIFA *f.*

**fife** [faɪf] *n (Mus)* Querpfeife *f.*

**fifteen** ['fɪf'ti:n] **1** *adj* fünfzehn. **2** *n* Fünfzehn *f.*

**fifteenth** ['fɪf'ti:nθ] *adj* fünfzehnte(r, s); *see* **sixteenth.**

**fifth** [fɪfθ] **1** *adj* fünfte(r, s). **2** *n* Fünfte(r, s); *(part, fraction)* Fünftel *nt*; *(Mus)* Quinte *f*; *see* **sixth.**

**fiftieth** ['fɪftɪɪθ] *adj* fünfzigste(r, s); *see* **sixtieth.**

**fifty** ['fɪftɪ] **1** *adj* fünfzig. **2** *n* Fünfzig *f*; *see* **sixty.**

**fifty-fifty** ['fɪftɪ'fɪftɪ] **1** *adj* halbe-halbe, fifty-fifty. **we have a** ~ **chance of success** unsere Chancen stehen fifty-fifty. **2** *adv* **to go** ~ **(with sb)** (mit jdm) halbe-halbe machen.

**fig**[1] [fɪg] *n* Feige *f.* ~ **tree** Feigenbaum *m*; **I don't care** *or* **give a** ~ *(col)* ich kümmere mich einen Dreck darum *(col).*

**fig**[2] = **figure** Abb.

**fight** [faɪt] *(vb: pret, ptp* **fought***)* **1** *n (lit, fig)* Kampf *m*; *(fist ~, scrap)* Schlägerei *f*; *(argument, row)* Streit *m.* **to have a** ~ **with sb** sich mit jdm schlagen; *(argue)* sich mit jdm streiten; **to put up a good** ~ *(lit, fig)* sich tapfer schlagen; **he won't give in without a** ~ er ergibt sich nicht kampflos; **there was no** ~ **left in him** sein Kampfgeist war erloschen.

**2** *vi* kämpfen; *(have punch-up etc)* sich schlagen; *(argue)* sich streiten. **to** ~ **over sth** um etw kämpfen; *(quarrel)* sich über etw *(acc)* streiten; *(to gain sth, also for sth)* sich um etw streiten; **to** ~ **for one's life** um sein Leben kämpfen.

**3** *vt person* kämpfen mit; *(have punch-up with)* sich schlagen mit; *fire, disease, cuts, policy* bekämpfen; *decision* ankämpfen gegen. **I'm prepared to** ~ **the government on this** ich bin bereit, das mit der Regierung durchzukämpfen; **you can't** ~ **the whole company** du kannst es nicht mit der ganzen Firma aufnehmen; **to** ~ **an action at law** einen Prozeß vor Gericht durchfechten; **to** ~ **one's way out of the crowd** sich aus der Menge freikämpfen.

▶**fight back 1** *vi (in fight)* zurückschlagen; *(Mil)* sich verteidigen; *(in argument)* sich wehren; *(after illness)* zu Kräften kommen; *(Sport)* einen Gegenangriff unternehmen; *(pull back)* aufholen. **2** *vt sep tears etc* unterdrücken.

▶**fight down** *vt sep anxiety* unterdrücken.

▶**fight off** *vt sep (Mil, fig) attack, disease* abwehren; *sleep* ankämpfen gegen; *a cold* ankämpfen gegen.

▶**fight on** *vi* weiterkämpfen.

▶**fight out** *vt sep* **to** ~ **it** ~ es untereinander ausfechten.

**fighter** ['faɪtəʳ] *n* **(a)** Kämpfer *m*; *(Boxing)* Fighter *m.* **he's a** ~ *(fig)* er ist eine Kämpfernatur. **(b)** *(Aviat: plane)* Jagdflugzeug *nt.*

**fighter:** ~**-aircraft** *n* Kampfflugzeug *nt*; ~**-bomber** *n* Jagdbomber *m*; ~**-interceptor** *n* Abfangjäger *m*; ~**-pilot** *n* Jagdflieger *m.*

**fighting** ['faɪtɪŋ] *n (Mil)* Kampf *m*; *(punch-ups etc)* Schlägereien *pl*; *(verbal)* Streit *m.* ~ **broke out** Kämpfe brachen aus.

**fighting:** ~ **chance** *n* gute Chancen *pl*; **he's in with** *or* **he has a** ~ **chance** er hat eine Chance, wenn er sich anstrengt; ~ **fit** *adj* topfit *(col)*; ~ **forces** *npl* Kampftruppen *pl*; ~ **spirit** *n* Kampfgeist *m*; ~ **strength** *n (Mil)* Kampfstärke *f.*

**fig leaf** *n* Feigenblatt *nt.*

**figment** ['fɪgmənt] *n* **a** ~ **of the imagination** pure Einbildung.

**figurative** ['fɪgjʊrətɪv] *adj use, sense* übertragen.

**figure** ['fɪgəʳ] **1** *n* **(a)** *(number)* Zahl *f*; *(digit also)* Ziffer *f*; *(sum)* Summe *f.* **he's good at** ~**s** er ist ein guter Rechner; **three-~ number** dreistellige Zahl; **the costs run into six ~s** die Kosten belaufen sich auf über 100.000 Pfund/Dollar etc. **(b)** *(in geometry, dancing, drawing)* Figur f. **~ of eight** Acht f. **(c)** *(human form)* Gestalt f. **(d)** *(shapeliness)* Figur f. **she has a good ~** sie hat eine gute Figur; **he's a fine ~ of a man** er ist ein Bild von einem Mann. **(e)** *(personality)* Persönlichkeit f; *(character in novel etc)* Gestalt f. **(f) ~ of speech** Redensart f. **(g)** *(illustration)* Abbildung f.

2 vt *(imagine)* sich *(dat)* vorstellen; *(US col: think, reckon)* schätzen *(col)*.

3 vi **(a)** *(appear)* erscheinen. **he ~d prominently in the talks** er spielte eine bedeutende Rolle bei den Gesprächen. **(b)** *(col: make sense)* hinkommen *(col)*. **that ~s** das hätte ich mir denken können.

▶**figure on** vi +prep obj *(esp US)* rechnen mit.

▶**figure out** vt sep **(a)** *(understand)* schlau werden aus. **(b)** *(work out)* ausrechnen; *answer, how to do sth* herausbekommen; *solution* finden.

**figure:** **~-conscious** adj figurbewußt; **~head** n *(Naut, fig)* Galionsfigur f; **~-hugging** adj figurbetont; **~-skater** n Eiskunstläufer(in f) m; **~-skating** n Eiskunstlaufen nt.

**Fiji** ['fi:dʒi:] n Fidschiinseln pl.

**filament** ['fɪləmənt] n *(Elec)* (Glüh)faden m.

**filch** [fɪltʃ] vt mausen *(col)*.

**file¹** [faɪl] 1 n *(tool)* Feile f. 2 vt feilen. **to ~ one's fingernails** sich *(dat)* die Fingernägel feilen; **to ~ sth away** or **down** etw abfeilen.

**file²** 1 n **(a)** *(holder)* Aktenordner m; *(for card index)* Karteikasten m. **it's in the ~s somewhere** das muß irgendwo bei den Akten sein. **(b)** *(documents, information)* Akte f *(on sb* über jdn, *on sth* zu etw). **on ~** aktenkundig; **to keep a ~ on sb/sth** eine Akte über jdn/etw führen. **(c)** *(Comp)* Datei f. **data on ~** gespeicherte Daten. 2 vt **(a)** *letters* ablegen. **(b)** *(Jur)* petition einreichen.

▶**file away** vt sep *papers* zu den Akten legen.

**file³** 1 n *(row)* Reihe f. **in single ~** im Gänsemarsch; *(Mil)* in Reihe. 2 vi **to ~ in** hereinmarschieren; **they ~d out of the classroom** sie gingen/kamen nacheinander aus dem Klassenzimmer; **the troops ~d past the general** die Truppen marschierten am General vorbei.

**file:** **~ card** n Karteikarte f; **~ clerk** n *(US)* Angestellte(r) mf in der Registratur; **~ management** n *(Comp)* Dateiverwaltung f; **~ name** n *(Comp)* Dateiname m.

**filial** ['fɪlɪəl] adj Kindes-. **with due ~ respect** mit dem Respekt, den eine Tochter/ein Sohn schuldig ist.

**filibuster** ['fɪlɪbʌstər] vi *(esp US)* Obstruktion betreiben.

**filigree** ['fɪlɪgri:] n Filigran(arbeit f) nt.

**filing:** **~ cabinet** n Aktenschrank m; **~ clerk** n *(Brit)* Angestellte(r) mf in der Registratur.

**filings** ['faɪlɪŋz] npl Späne pl.

**filing tray** n Ablagekorb m.

**Filipino** [fɪlɪ'pi:nəʊ] 1 n Filipino m. 2 adj philippinisch.

**fill** [fɪl] 1 vt füllen; *pipe* stopfen; *teeth* plombieren; *(wind)* sails blähen; *post, position (employer)* besetzen; *(employee)* einnehmen; *need* entsprechen *(+dat)*. **~ed with anger/admiration** voller Zorn/ Bewunderung; **the thought ~ed him with horror** der Gedanke erfüllte ihn mit Entsetzen. 2 vi sich füllen. 3 n **to drink one's ~** seinen Durst löschen; **to eat one's ~** sich satt essen; **I've had my ~ of him/it** *(col)* ich habe von ihm/davon die Nase voll *(col)*.

▶**fill in** 1 vi **to ~ ~ for sb** für jdn einspringen. 2 vt sep **(a)** *hole* auffüllen; *door, fireplace* zumauern;

*(fig)* gaps stopfen. **(b)** *form* ausfüllen; *name, details, missing word* eintragen. **(c) to ~ sb ~ (on sth)** jdn (über etw *acc*) aufklären or ins Bild setzen.

▶**fill out** 1 vi **(a)** *(sails etc)* sich blähen. **(b)** *(person: become fatter)* fülliger werden; *(cheeks, face)* voller werden. 2 vt sep *form* ausfüllen; *essay, article etc* strecken.

▶**fill up** 1 vi *(Aut)* (auf)tanken; *(hall, barrel etc)* sich füllen. 2 vt sep *tank, cup* vollfüllen; *(driver)* volltanken; *hole* stopfen; *(Brit)* form ausfüllen. **~ her ~!** *(Aut col)* volltanken bitte!

**filler** ['fɪlər] n **(a)** *(for cracks)* Spachtelmasse f. **(b)** *(Ling)* **~ (word)** Füllwort nt.

**filler cap** n Tankdeckel m.

**fillet** ['fɪlɪt] 1 n *(Brit)* Filet nt. **~ steak** Filetsteak nt; **~ of pork** Schweinefilet nt. 2 vt filetieren.

**filling** ['fɪlɪŋ] 1 n **(a)** *(in tooth)* Füllung, Plombe f. **I had to have three ~s** ich mußte mir drei Zähne plombieren lassen. **(b)** *(in pie, tart)* Füllung f; *(for sandwich)* Belag m. 2 adj *food* sättigend.

**filling station** n Tankstelle f.

**fillip** ['fɪlɪp] n *(fig)* Ansporn m.

**filly** ['fɪlɪ] n Stutfohlen nt; *(dated col)* Mädel nt *(dated)*.

**film** [fɪlm] 1 n **(a)** Film m; *(of dust, of ice)* Schicht f; *(of mist, on the eye)* Schleier m; *(thin membrane)* Häutchen nt; *(on teeth)* Belag m. **(b)** *(Phot)* Film m. **to make a ~** einen Film drehen; **to go to the ~s** ins Kino gehen. 2 vt *play* verfilmen; *scene* filmen; *people* einen Film machen von. 3 vi filmen.

**film:** **~ camera** n Filmkamera f; **~ clip** n Filmausschnitt m; **~ crew** n Kamerateam nt; **~ director** n Filmregisseur(in f) m; **~ fan** n Filmfan m; **~ festival** n Filmfestspiele pl; **~ guide** n Kinoprogramm nt; **~-maker** n Filmemacher(in f) m; **~ projector** n Projektor m; **~ rights** npl Filmrechte pl; **~ script** n Drehbuch nt; **~set** n Filmkulisse f; **~ show** n Filmvorführung f; **~star** n Filmstar m; **~strip** n Filmstreifen m; **~ studio** n Filmstudio nt; **~ version** n Verfilmung f.

**Filofax** ® ['faɪləʊfæks] n Filofax ® m, Terminplaner m.

**filter** ['fɪltər] 1 n Filter m; *(Brit: for traffic)* Abbiegespur f. 2 vt *liquids, air* filtern. 3 vi *(light)* durchscheinen. **to ~ to the left** *(Brit Aut)* sich links einordnen.

▶**filter back** vi *(people)* allmählich zurückkommen.

▶**filter in** vi *(people)* allmählich hereinkommen; *(news)* durchsickern.

▶**filter out** vt sep *(lit)* herausfiltern.

▶**filter through** vi *(liquid, sound, news)* durchsickern; *(light)* durchscheinen.

**filter:** **~ coffee** n Filterkaffee m; **~ lane** n *(Brit)* Abbiegespur f; **~ paper** n Filterpapier nt; **~ tip** n Filter m; **~-tipped** adj *cigarette* Filter-.

**filth** [fɪlθ] n *(lit)* Schmutz, Dreck m; *(fig)* Schweinerei f.

**filthy** ['fɪlθɪ] adj *(+er)* schmutzig, dreckig; *(col)* weather Sau- *(col)*; day Mist-; temper übel; *(obscene)* unanständig. **don't be ~** du Ferkel!; **a ~ habit** eine widerliche Angewohnheit; **~ lucre** *(hum)* schnöder Mammon *(esp hum)*; **~ rich** *(col)* stinkreich *(col)*.

**fin** [fɪn] n *(of fish)* Flosse f; *(Aviat)* Seitenflosse f; *(of bomb, rocket, ship)* Stabilisierungsfläche f.

**final** ['faɪnl] 1 adj *(last)* letzte(r, s); *examination, act, chapter, chord* Schluß-; *(definite)* decision, version endgültig. **~ score** Schlußstand m; **~ round/lap** Endrunde f; **~ stage** Endstadium nt; **that's not ~ yet** das steht noch nicht endgültig fest; **you're not going and that's ~** du gehst nicht, und damit Schluß! 2 n **(a) ~s** pl *(Univ)* Abschlußprüfung f. **(b)**

*(Sport)* Finale *nt*; *(in quiz etc)* Endrunde *f*. **the ~s** das Finale; die Endrunde.

**finale** [fɪ'nɑːlɪ] *n (Mus, fig)* Finale *nt*.

**finalist** ['faɪnəlɪst] *n (Sport)* Endrundenteilnehmer(in *f*), Finalist(in *f*) *m*.

**finality** [faɪ'nælɪtɪ] *n (of decision etc)* Endgültigkeit *f*; *(of tone of voice)* Entschiedenheit *f*.

**finalize** ['faɪnəlaɪz] *vt* fertigmachen; *plans, arrangements* endgültig festlegen; *deal* zum Abschluß bringen; *draft* die endgültige Form geben *(+dat)*. **to ~ a decision** eine endgültige Entscheidung treffen.

**finally** ['faɪnəlɪ] *adv* schließlich; *(expressing relief etc)* endlich.

**finance** [faɪ'næns] **1** *n* Finanzen *pl*. **~ company** Finanzierungsgesellschaft *f*; **high ~** Hochfinanz *f*; **it's a question of ~** das ist eine Geldfrage. **2** *vt* finanzieren.

**financial** [faɪ'nænʃəl] *adj* finanziell; *crisis, policy* Finanz-; *news, page* Wirtschafts-. **~ director** Leiter *m* der Finanzabteilung; **~ statement** Jahresabschluß *m*; *(balance sheet)* Bilanz *f*; **the ~ year** das Geschäftsjahr.

**financially** [faɪ'nænʃəlɪ] *adv* finanziell. **the company is ~ sound** die Finanzlage der Firma ist gesund.

**financier** [faɪ'nænsɪəʳ] *n* Finanzier *m*.

**finch** [fɪntʃ] *n* Fink *m*.

**find** [faɪnd] *(vb: pret, ptp* **found**) **1** *vt* (a) finden. **this flower is found all over England** diese Blume findet man in ganz England; **do you know where there is a chemist's to be found?** wissen Sie, wo hier eine Apotheke ist?; **there wasn't one to be found** es war keine(r) zu finden; **we left everything as we found it** wir haben alles so gelassen, wie wir es vorgefunden haben; **he was found dead in bed** er wurde tot im Bett aufgefunden; **where am I going to ~ the money/time?** wo nehme ich nur das Geld/die Zeit her?; **I ~ myself in an impossible situation** ich befinde mich in einer unmöglichen Situation; **he awoke to ~ himself in prison/hospital** er erwachte und fand sich im Gefängnis/Krankenhaus wieder; **I found myself unable/forced to ...** ich sah mich außerstande/gezwungen, zu ...

(b) *(supply)* besorgen *(sb sth* jdm etw*)*. **go and ~ me a needle** hol mir doch mal eine Nadel!

(c) *(discover, ascertain)* feststellen. **we found the car wouldn't start** es stellte sich heraus, daß das Auto nicht anspringen wollte; **if you still ~ you can't do it** wenn Sie feststellen, daß Sie es immer noch nicht können.

(d) *(consider to be)* finden. **I ~ Spain too hot** ich finde Spanien zu heiß; **I don't ~ it easy to tell you this** es fällt mir nicht leicht, Ihnen das zu sagen; **did you ~ her a good worker?** fanden Sie, daß sie gut arbeitet?; **I ~ it impossible to understand him** ich kann ihn einfach nicht verstehen.

(e) **£100 per week all found** £100 pro Woche, (und freie) Kost und Logis.

(f) *(Jur)* **to ~ sb guilty** jdn für schuldig befinden; **how do you ~ the accused?** wie lautet Ihr Urteil?

(g) *(Comp)* suchen.

**2** *vi (Jur)* **to ~ for/against the accused** den Angeklagten freisprechen/schuldig sprechen.

**3** *n* Fund *m*.

▶**find out 1** *vt sep answer, sb's secret* herausfinden. **don't get found ~** laß dich nicht erwischen; **you've been found ~** du bist ertappt. **2** *vi* es herausfinden. **to ~ ~ about sb/sth** *(learn facts)* etwas über jdn/etw erfahren; **if his wife ~s ~ about it/her** wenn seine Frau davon/von ihr erfährt.

**finder** ['faɪndəʳ] *n* Finder(in *f*) *m*. **~s keepers** *(col)* wer's findet, dem gehört's.

**findings** ['faɪndɪŋz] *n pl* Ergebnis(se *pl*) *nt*; *(medical)* Befund *m*.

**fine¹** [faɪn] **1** *n (Jur)* Geldstrafe *f*. **2** *vt* zu einer Geldstrafe verurteilen. **he was ~d £10** er mußte £10 Strafe bezahlen; **he was ~d for speeding** er mußte Strafe für zu schnelles Fahren zahlen.

**fine²** *adj (+er)* (a) *weather* schön. **one ~ day** eines schönen Tages. (b) *(good)* gut; *person* fein; *specimen, chap, woman* prächtig; *pianist, novel, painting, shot* großartig; *holiday, meal, view* herrlich; *(elegant)* *clothes, manners etc* fein. **this is a ~ time to ...** *(iro)* das ist genau der richtige Augenblick, zu ...; **a ~ friend you are** *(iro)* du bist mir ja ein schöner Freund!; **that's a ~ thing to say** *(iro)* das ist ja wirklich nett, so was zu sagen!; **this is a ~ state of affairs** *(iro)* das sind ja schöne Zustände!; **that's ~ by me** ich habe nichts dagegen; **(that's) ~** gut, in Ordnung; **I'm/he is ~ now** es geht mir/ihm wieder gut; **how are you? — ~** wie geht's? — gut. (c) *(delicate, thin)* *workmanship, dust, distinction* fein. **~ tuning** Feinabstimmung *f*; **to appeal to sb's ~r feelings** an jds besseres Ich appellieren; **there's a very ~ line between ...** es besteht ein feiner Unterschied zwischen ...

**fine art** *n* (a) *usu pl* **the ~s** die schönen Künste *pl*. (b) **he's got it down to a ~** er hat den Bogen heraus *(col)*.

**finely** ['faɪnlɪ] *adv* fein; *worked* schön.

**fineness** ['faɪnnɪs] *n* Feinheit *f*; *(of weather)* Schönheit *f*; *(of quality)* Güte *f*.

**finery** ['faɪnərɪ] *n (of dress)* Staat *m*.

**finesse** [fɪ'nes] *n (skill)* Gewandtheit *f*; *(cunning)* Finesse *f*.

**fine-tooth comb** ['faɪn'tuːθkəʊm] *n*: **to go through sth with a ~** etw genau unter die Lupe nehmen.

**fine-tune** ['faɪntjuːn] *vt (lit, fig)* feinabstimmen.

**finger** ['fɪŋgəʳ] **1** *n* Finger *m*. **she can twist him around her little ~** sie kann ihn um den (kleinen) Finger wickeln; **to have a ~ in every pie** überall die Finger im Spiel haben; **I didn't lay a ~ on her** ich habe sie nicht angerührt; **he didn't lift a ~ to help me** er hat keinen Finger gerührt, um mir zu helfen; **he didn't lift a ~** er hat keinen Finger krumm gemacht; **I can't put my ~ on it, but ...** ich kann es nicht genau ausmachen, aber ...; **you've put your ~ on it there** da haben Sie den kritischen Punkt berührt; **to get or pull one's ~ out** *(col) (do properly)* Nägel mit Köpfen machen; *(speed up)* Dampf dahinter machen *(col)*. **2** *vt* anfassen; *(toy, meddle with)* herumfingern an *(+dat)*.

**finger: ~ board** *n* Griffbrett *nt*; **~bowl** *n* Fingerschale *f*.

**fingering** ['fɪŋgərɪŋ] *n (Mus) (in the notation)* Fingersatz *m*; *(of keys, strings)* (Finger)technik *f*.

**finger: ~mark** *n* Fingerabdruck *m*; **~nail** *n* Fingernagel *m*; **~ print 1** *n* Fingerabdruck *m*; **2** *vt* **to ~print sb/sth** jdm Fingerabdrücke *pl* abnehmen/von etw Fingerabdrücke *pl* abnehmen; **~tip** *n* Fingerspitze *f*; **to have sth at one's ~tips** *(fig) (know very well)* etw aus dem Effeff kennen *(col)*; *(have at one's disposal)* etw parat haben; **~tip control** *n (of steering wheel etc)* mühelose Steuerung.

**finicky** ['fɪnɪkɪ] *adj person* schwer zufriedenzustellen, pingelig *(col)*; *work, job* kniff(e)lig *(col)*; *detail* winzig.

**finish** ['fɪnɪʃ] **1** *n* (a) *(end)* Schluß *m*, Ende *nt*; *(of race)* Finish *nt*; *(~ing line)* Ziel *nt*. **he's got a good ~** er hat einen starken Endspurt; **to be in at the ~** *(fig)* den Schluß miterleben; **to fight to the ~** bis zum letzten Augenblick kämpfen. (b) *(of products)* Finish *nt*; *(of material)* Appretur *f*. **paint with a**

**gloss/matt** ~ Farbe mit Hochglanzeffekt/mattem Glanz; **this one has a better** ~ das ist besser verarbeitet. **2** vt **(a)** beenden; *course, work, business also* abschließen. **to** ~/**have** ~**ed doing sth** mit etw fertig werden/sein; **to** ~ **writing/reading sth** etw zu Ende schreiben/lesen; **to have** ~**ed sth** etw fertig haben; *task, course* mit etw fertig sein; **when do you** ~ **work?** wann machen Sie Feierabend?; **give me time to** ~ **my drink** laß mich austrinken; ~ **what you're doing** mach das erst fertig; **that last kilometre nearly** ~**ed me** *(col)* dieser letzte Kilometer hat mich beinahe geschafft *(col)*. **(b)** *(give* ~ *to)* den letzten Schliff geben *(+dat)*; *piece of handiwork* verarbeiten; *industrial product* ein schönes Finish geben *(+dat)*. **the paintwork isn't very well** ~**ed** der Lack hat keine besonders schöne Oberfläche. **3** vi **(a)** zu Ende sein; *(person: with task etc)* fertig sein; *(come to an end,* ~ *work)* aufhören; *(piece of music, story etc)* enden. **when does the film** ~? wann ist der Film aus?; **we'll** ~ **by singing a song** wir wollen mit einem Lied schließen, zum Schluß singen wir ein Lied; **I've** ~**ed** ich bin fertig. **(b)** *(Sport)* das Ziel erreichen. **to** ~ **second** als zweiter durchs Ziel gehen.

►**finish off 1** vi aufhören, Schluß machen. **2** vt sep **(a)** *piece of work* fertigmachen. **to have a liqueur to** ~ ~ **the meal** zum Abschluß des Essens noch einen Likör trinken. **(b)** *food* aufessen; *drink* austrinken. **(c)** *(kill)* den Gnadenstoß geben *(+dat)*; *(by shooting)* den Gnadenschuß geben *(+dat)*. **(d)** *(do for)* person den Rest geben *(+dat)*.

►**finish up 1** vi *(end up in a place)* landen *(col)*. **he** ~**ed** ~ **a nervous wreck** er war zum Schluß ein Nervenbündel; **I'll just** ~ ~ **by doing it all again** zum Schluß muß ich doch alles noch mal machen. **2** vt sep = **finish off 2 (b)**.

►**finish with** vi +prep obj **have you** ~**ed** ~ **the paper?** haben Sie die Zeitung fertiggelesen?; **I've** ~**ed** ~ **him** ich will nichts mehr mit ihm zu tun haben; *(with boyfriend)* ich habe mit ihm Schluß gemacht.

**finished** ['fɪnɪʃt] adj **(a)** *item, product* fertig; *(polished)* poliert; *performance* ausgereift; *appearance* vollendet. ~ **goods** Fertigprodukte pl; **a beautifully** ~ **car** ein wunderschön lackierter Wagen. **(b) to be** ~ *(person, task etc)* fertig sein; *(exhausted, done for etc)* erledigt sein; **the wine is** ~ es ist kein Wein mehr da; **I'm** ~ **with politics** mit der Politik ist es für mich vorbei; **it's all** ~ **(between us)** es ist alles aus (zwischen uns).

**finishing** ['fɪnɪʃɪŋ]: ~ **line** n Ziellinie f; ~ **post** n Zielpfosten m; ~ **school** n (Mädchen)pensionat nt; ~ **straight** or *(US)* **straightaway** n Zielgerade f; ~ **touches** npl **to put the** ~ **touches to sth** einer Sache *(dat)* den letzten Schliff geben.

**finite** ['faɪnaɪt] adj *(limited)* begrenzt; *number* endlich.

**Finland** ['fɪnlənd] n Finnland nt.

**Finn** [fɪn] n Finne m, Finnin f.

**Finnish** ['fɪnɪʃ] **1** adj finnisch. **2** n Finnisch nt.

**fiord** [fjɔːd] n Fjord m.

**fir** [fɜː'] n Tanne f; *(*~ *wood)* Tanne(nholz nt) f. ~ **cone** Tannenzapfen m.

**fire** [faɪə'] **1** n *(lit, fig, Mil)* Feuer nt; *(electric, gas)* Ofen m; *(destructive: forest* ~, *house* ~*)* Brand m. **the house was on** ~ das Haus brannte; **to set** ~ **to sth, to set sth on** ~ etw anzünden; *(so as to destroy)* etw in Brand stecken; **to catch** ~ Feuer fangen; **you're playing with** ~ *(fig)* du spielst mit dem Feuer; **there was a** ~ **next door** nebenan hat es gebrannt; **to come under** ~ *(lit, fig)* unter Beschuß geraten.

**2** vt **(a)** *gun* abschießen; *shot* abfeuern; *rocket* zünden. **to** ~ **a gun at sb** auf jdn schießen; **to** ~ **questions at sb** Fragen auf jdn abfeuern. **(b)** *pottery* brennen. **(c)** *(fig)* imagination beflügeln. **(d)** *(col: dismiss)* feuern *(col)*.

**3** vi **(a)** *(shoot)* schießen *(at auf +acc)*. ~! Feuer! **(b)** *(engine)* zünden. **the engine is only firing on three cylinders** der Motor läuft nur auf drei Zylindern.

►**fire away** vi *(col: begin)* losschießen *(col)*.

**fire:** ~ **alarm** n Feueralarm m; *(apparatus)* Feuermelder m; ~**arm** n Schußwaffe f; ~**ball** n *(in explosion)* Feuerball m; *(fig col: person)* Energiebündel nt; ~ **brigade** n *(Brit)* Feuerwehr f; ~**cracker** n Knallkörper m; ~ **department** n *(US)* Feuerwehr f; ~ **drill** n *(for firemen)* Feuerwehrübung f; *(for passengers etc)* Probealarm m; ~**eater** n Feuerschlucker m; ~**engine** n Feuerwehrauto nt; ~ **escape** n *(staircase)* Feuertreppe f; *(ladder)* Feuerleiter f; ~ **extinguisher** n Feuerlöscher m; ~**fighting** n Feuerbekämpfung f; ~**fly** m Leuchtkäfer m; ~**guard** n (Schutz)gitter nt *(vor dem Kamin)*; ~ **hazard** n **to be a** ~ **hazard** feuergefährlich sein; ~ **hose** n Feuerspritze f; ~ **hydrant** n Hydrant m; ~ **insurance** n Feuer- or Brandversicherung f; ~**light** n Schein m des Feuers; ~ **lighter** n Feueranzünder m; ~**man** n Feuerwehrmann m; ~**place** n Kamin m; ~**plug** n *(US)* Hydrant m; ~**power** n *(of guns, aircraft, army)* Feuerkraft f; ~ **practice** n = ~ **drill**; ~**proof** adj feuerfest; ~ **regulations** npl Brandschutzbestimmungen pl; ~**resistant** adj feuerbeständig; ~ **risk** n Feuergefahr f; ~ **screen** n Ofenschirm m; F~ **Service** n Feuerwehr f; ~**side** n **to sit by the** ~**side** am Kamin sitzen; ~ **station** n Feuerwehrzentrale f; ~**woman** n Feuerwehrfrau f; ~**wood** n Brennholz nt; ~**work** n Feuerwerkskörper m; ~**works** *(display)* Feuerwerk nt; **there'll be** ~**works if he finds out** *(col)* wenn er das erfährt, dann kracht's.

**firing** ['faɪrɪŋ] n **(a)** *(of pottery)* Brennen nt. **(b)** *(Mil)* Feuer nt; *(of gun, shot, rocket)* Abfeuern nt. **(c)** *(Aut: of engine)* Zündung f.

**firing:** ~ **line** n *(lit, fig)* Schußlinie f; ~ **squad** n Erschießungskommando nt.

**firm¹** [fɜːm] n Firma f.

**firm²** **1** adj *(+er)* fest. **to be** ~ **with sb** jdm gegenüber bestimmt auftreten; **to be a** ~ **believer in sth** fest von etw überzeugt sein. **2** adv **to stand** ~ **on sth** *(fig)* fest bei etw bleiben.

**firmly** ['fɜːmlɪ] adv fest; *say* bestimmt. ~ **built** stabil gebaut.

**firmness** ['fɜːmnɪs] n Festigkeit f.

**first** [fɜːst] **1** adj erste(r, s). **who's** ~? wer ist der erste?; **I'm** ~, **I've been waiting longer than you** ich bin zuerst an der Reihe, ich warte schon länger als Sie; ~ **things** ~ eins nach dem anderen; **you have to put** ~ **things** ~ du mußt wissen, was dir am wichtigsten ist; **he doesn't know the** ~ **thing about it/cars** davon/von Autos hat er keinen blassen Schimmer *(col)*; **in the** ~ **place** zunächst einmal; **why didn't you say so in the** ~ **place?** warum hast du denn das nicht gleich gesagt?

**2** adv **(a)** zuerst; *arrive, leave* als erste(r, s); *(in listing)* erstens. ~ **come** ~ **served** *(prov)* wer zuerst kommt, mahlt zuerst *(Prov)*; **ladies** ~! Ladies first!; **you** ~ du zuerst; **he says** ~ **one thing then another** er sagt mal so, mal so; **my health comes** ~ meine Gesundheit ist mir am wichtigsten; **he always puts his job** ~ seine Arbeit kommt bei ihm immer vor allem anderen; ~ **and foremost** zunächst; **I must finish this** ~ ich muß das erst fertigmachen; **think** ~ überlegen Sie es sich. **(b)** *(for the ~ time)* zum ersten Mal. **when did you** ~ **meet him?** wann haben Sie ihn das erste Mal getroffen?; **when it** ~ **became known that** ... als zuerst bekannt wurde, daß ... **(c)** *(in preference)* eher, lieber. **I'd die** ~! eher würde ich sterben!

**3** *n* **(a) the** ~ der/die/das Erste; **they were the** ~ **to come** sie kamen als erste; **this is the** ~ **I've heard of it** das ist mir ja ganz neu; **at** ~ zuerst; **from the** ~ von Anfang an; **from** ~ **to last** von Anfang bis Ende. **(b)** *(Brit Univ)* **he got a** ~ ≈ er bestand (sein Examen) mit „sehr gut". **(c)** *(Aut)* ~ **(gear)** der erste (Gang); **in** ~ im ersten (Gang); *see* **sixth**.

**first:** ~ **aid** *n* Erste Hilfe; ~ **aid box,** ~ **aid kit** *n* Verbandskasten *m;* ~ **aid dressing** *n* Notverband *m;* ~ **aid post,** ~ **aid station** *n* Sanitätswache *f;* ~**-born 1** *adj* erstgeboren; **2** *n* Erstgeborene(r) *mf;* ~**-class 1** *adj* erstklassig; ~**-class compartment** Abteil *nt* erster Klasse; ~**-class mail** *bevorzugt beförderte Post;* **he's** ~**-class at tennis** er ist ein erstklassiger Tennisspieler; **that's absolutely** ~**-class** das ist einfach Spitze *(col);* ~**-class degree** *(Brit)* ≈ sehr gutes Examen; **2** *adv* **travel** erster Klasse; ~ **cousin** *n* Vetter *m* ersten Grades; ~ **edition** *n* Erstausgabe *f;* ~ **form** *n (Brit Sch)* erste Klasse; ~**-generation** *adj* **citizen, computer** der ersten Generation; ~**-hand** *adj, adv* aus erster Hand; ~ **hand experience** eigene Erfahrung; **F~ Lady** *n (US)* First Lady *f.*

**firstly** ['fɜːstlɪ] *adv* erstens, zunächst (einmal).

**first:** ~ **name** *n* Vorname *m;* ~ **night** *n (Theat)* Premiere *f;* ~ **offender** *n* Ersttäter(in *f*) *m;* **he is a** ~ **offender** er ist nicht vorbestraft; ~ **officer** *n (Naut)* Erster Offizier; ~**-past-the-post system** *n (Pol)* Mehrheitswahlrecht *nt;* ~ **performance** *n (Theat)* Premiere *f; (first ever)* Uraufführung *f;* ~ **rate** *adj* erstklassig; ~ **strike** *n* Erstschlag, Ersteinsatz *m* (von Atomwaffen); ~ **work** *n* Erstlingswerk *nt,* ~**-year student** *n* Studienanfänger(in *f*) *m.*

**firth** [fɜːθ] *n (Scot)* Meeresarm *m.*

**fir tree** *n* Tannenbaum *m.*

**fiscal** ['fɪskəl] *adj* Finanz-. ~ **year** Steuerjahr *nt.*

**fish** [fɪʃ] **1** *n, pl* - *or (esp for different types)* **-es** Fisch *m.* ~ **and chips** Fisch und Pommes frites; **to drink like a** ~ *(col)* wie ein Loch saufen *(col);* **like a** ~ **out of water** wie ein Fisch auf dem Trockenen; **a queer** ~ *(col)* ein komischer Kauz. **2** *vi* fischen; *(with rod)* angeln. **to go** ~**ing** fischen/angeln gehen; **to go salmon** ~**ing** auf Lachsfang gehen. **3** *vt* fischen; *(with rod)* angeln; *river* fischen/angeln in *(+dat).*

►**fish for** *vi +prep obj* fischen/angeln; *(fig) compliments* fischen nach. **they were** ~**ing** ~ **information** sie waren auf Informationen aus.

►**fish out** *vt sep* herausfischen *(of or from sth* aus etw*).*

►**fish up** *vt sep (from water)* herausziehen.

**fish:** ~**bone** *n* (Fisch)gräte *f;* ~**cake** *n* Fischfrikadelle *f.*

**fisherman** ['fɪʃəmən] *n, pl* **-men** [mən] Fischer *m; (amateur)* Angler *m.*

**fishery** ['fɪʃərɪ] *n (area)* Fischereizone *f; (industry)* Fischerei *f.*

**fish:** ~**-eye lens** *n (Phot)* Fischauge *nt;* ~ **farm** *n* Fischzucht *f;* ~ **finger** *n (Brit)* Fischstäbchen *nt;* ~**hook** *n* Angelhaken *m.*

**fishing** ['fɪʃɪŋ] *n* Fischen *nt; (with rod)* Angeln *nt; (as industry)* Fischerei *f.*

**fishing:** ~ **boat** *n* Fischerboot *nt;* ~ **grounds** *npl*

Fischgründe *pl;* ~ **industry** *n* Fischindustrie *f;* ~-**line** *n* Angelschnur *f;* ~-**net** *n* Fischnetz *nt;* ~-**port** *n* Fischereihafen *m;* ~-**rod** *n* Angelrute *f;* ~ **tackle** *n (for sport)* Angelgeräte *pl; (for industry)* Fischereigeräte *pl;* ~ **village** *n* Fischerdorf *nt.*

**fish:** ~ **knife** *n* Fischmesser *nt;* ~ **market** *n* Fischmarkt *m;* ~ **meal** *n* Fischmehl *nt;* ~**monger** *n (Brit)* Fischhändler(in *f*) *m;* ~-**net stockings** *npl* Netzstrümpfe *pl;* ~ **shop** *n* Fischgeschäft *nt;* ~ **slice** *n* (Braten)wender *m;* ~ **stick** *n (US)* Fischstäbchen *nt;* ~ **tank** *n (in house)* Aquarium *nt; (on fish farm)* Fischteich *m.*

**fishy** ['fɪʃɪ] *adj (+er)* **(a)** *smell* Fisch-. **(b)** *(col)* verdächtig; *excuse, story* faul *(col).*

**fission** ['fɪʃən] *n (Phys)* Spaltung *f.*

**fissure** ['fɪʃəʳ] *n* Spalt(e *f*) *m; (deep)* Kluft *f.*

**fist** [fɪst] *n* Faust *f.*

**fist:** ~**fight** *n* Faustkampf *m;* ~**ful** *n* Handvoll *f.*

**fit**[1] [fɪt] **1** *adj (+er)* **(a)** *(suitable)* geeignet. ~ **to eat** eßbar; **is this meat still** ~ **to eat?** kann man dieses Fleisch noch essen?; ~ **for habitation** bewohnbar; **to be** ~ **to be seen** sich sehen lassen können; **you're not** ~ **to be spoken to** du verdienst es nicht, daß man sich mit dir unterhält; **I'll do as I think** ~ ich handle, wie ich es für richtig halte; **to see** ~ **to do sth** es für angebracht halten, etw zu tun; **he did not see** ~ **to apologize** er hat es nicht für nötig gehalten, sich zu entschuldigen; **to be** ~ **to drop (with tiredness)** zum Umfallen müde sein. **(b)** *(in health)* gesund; *sportsman etc* fit, in Form. **she is not yet** ~ **to travel** sie ist noch nicht reisefähig.

**2** *n (of clothes)* **it is a very good** ~ es sitzt *or* paßt sehr gut; **it's a tight** ~ *(suitcase, parking)* es paßt gerade (noch); *(clothing)* es sitzt sehr eng; **in order to ensure a smooth** ~ *(of parts)* damit es genau paßt.

**3** *vt* **(a)** *(cover, sheet, nut etc)* passen auf *(+acc); (key etc)* passen in *(+acc); (clothes etc)* passen *(+dat).* **this coat** ~**s you better** dieser Mantel paßt Ihnen besser. **(b)** *(be suitable for) sb's plans, a theory etc* passen in *(+acc).* **(c) to** ~ **a dress on sb** jdm ein Kleid anpassen. **(d)** *(put on, attach)* anbringen *(to an +dat); tyre* montieren; *(put in)* einbauen *(in +acc); (furnish, provide)* ausstatten. **to** ~ **a key in the lock** einen Schlüssel ins Schloß stecken. **(e)** *(match) description, facts* entsprechen *(+dat); (person)* passen auf *(+acc).*

**4** *vi (clothes, parts)* passen. **the facts don't** ~ die Fakten sind widersprüchlich; **it all** ~**s** es paßt alles zusammen.

►**fit in 1** *vt sep* **(a)** *(find space for)* unterbringen. **(b)** *(find time for) person* einen Termin geben *(+dat); meeting* unterbringen. **I'll** ~ **you** ~ **somehow** ich werde Sie schon irgendwie einschieben. **(c)** *(make harmonize)* **to** ~ **sth** ~ **with sth** etw mit etw in Einklang bringen. **(d)** *(fit, put in)* einbauen.

**2** *vi* **(a)** *(go into place)* hineinpassen. **(b)** *(plans, ideas, word)* passen; *(facts etc)* übereinstimmen; *(match)* dazupassen. **how does this** ~ ~? wie paßt das ins Ganze?; **I see, it all** ~**s** ~ **now** jetzt paßt alles zusammen; **does that** ~ ~ **with your plans?** läßt sich das mit Ihren Plänen vereinbaren?; **he wants everybody to** ~ ~ **with him** er will, daß sich jedermann nach ihm richtet; **he doesn't** ~ ~ **here/with the others** er paßt hier nicht her/nicht zu den anderen; **the new director didn't** ~ ~ **in** der neue Direktor hat nicht in die Firma gepaßt; **try to** ~ ~ **in (with the others)** versuche, dich den anderen anzupassen.

►**fit out** *vt sep (for expedition)* ausrüsten; *person, ship* ausstatten.

**fit**[2] *n (Med, fig)* Anfall *m.* ~ **of coughing/anger**

Husten-/Wutanfall *m*; **in a ~ of anger** in einem Anfall von Wut; **in ~s and starts** sporadisch; **to be in ~s of laughter** sich vor Lachen biegen; **he'd have a ~** *(fig col)* er würde (ja) einen Anfall kriegen *(col)*.

**fitful** ['fɪtfʊl] *adj sleep* unruhig; *enthusiasm* sporadisch.

**fitfully** ['fɪtfəlɪ] *adv progress* stoßweise; *blow* sporadisch; *sleep* unruhig.

**fitment** ['fɪtmənt] *n (furniture)* Einrichtungsgegenstand *m*; *(of machine, car)* Zubehörteil *nt*.

**fitness** ['fɪtnɪs] *n* (**a**) *(health)* Gesundheit *f*; *(condition)* Fitness, Fitneß *f*. **~ training** *or (US)* **activity** Fitneß- *or* Konditionstraining *nt*. (**b**) *(suitability)* Eignung *f*; *(of remark etc)* Angemessenheit *f*.

**fitted** ['fɪtɪd] *adj garment* tailliert. **~ carpet** Teppichboden *m*; **~ kitchen/cupboards** Einbauküche *f*/Einbauschränke *pl*; **~ sheet** Spannbettuch *nt*.

**fitter** ['fɪtəʳ] *n (Tech)* Monteur *m*; *(for machines)* (Maschinen)schlosser *m*.

**fitting** ['fɪtɪŋ] **1** *adj (suitable)* passend. **it is not ~ for a lady** ... es schickt sich nicht für eine Dame ... **2** *n* (**a**) *(of suit etc)* Anprobe *f*. **~ room** Anproberaum *m*. (**b**) *(part)* Zubehörteil *nt*. **~s** Ausstattung *f*; *(furniture)* Einrichtung *f*; **bathroom ~s** Armaturen *pl*; **electrical ~s** Elektroinstallationen *pl*.

**five** [faɪv] **1** *adj* fünf. **2** *n* Fünf *f*; *see* **six**.

**five:** **~-and-ten** *n (US)* billiges Kaufhaus; **~-day week** *n* Fünftagewoche *f*; **~-o'clock shadow** *n* nachmittäglicher Anflug von Bartstoppeln.

**fiver** ['faɪvəʳ] *n (col) (£5 note)* Fünfpfundschein *m*; *($5 bill)* Fünfdollarschein *m*.

**fix** [fɪks] **1** *vt* (**a**) *(make firm)* befestigen *(sth to sth* etw an/auf etw *+dat)*; *(install)* new aerial, new dynamo etc anbringen; *(fig)* ideas, images festsetzen; *attention* richten *(on* auf *+acc)*. **to ~ a stake in the ground** einen Pfahl im Boden verankern; **to ~ sth in one's mind** sich *(dat)* etw fest einprägen; **to ~ one's eyes on sb/sth** jdn/etw fixieren. (**b**) *(arrange)* arrangieren; *date, price, limit* festsetzen; *(agree on)* ausmachen; *tickets, taxi etc* besorgen. (**c**) *(straighten out)* regeln. **I'll ~ him** *(col)* den nehme ich mir vor *(col)*. (**d**) *(repair)* in Ordnung bringen; *(put in good order, adjust)* machen *(col)*. (**e**) *drink, meal* machen. **to ~ one's hair** sich frisieren. (**f**) *(col)* race, fight manipulieren. **the whole thing was ~ed** das war eine abgekartete Sache *(col)*.

**2** *n* (**a**) *(col)* **to be in a ~** in der Klemme sitzen *(col)*; **to get oneself into a ~** sich *(dat)* eine schöne Suppe einbrocken *(col)*. (**b**) *(Naut)* **to take a ~ on sth** etw orten. (**c**) *(col: of drugs)* Fix *m (col)*. **to give oneself a ~** fixen *(col)*. (**d**) *(col)* **the fight was a ~** der Kampf war eine abgekartete Sache *(col)*.

▶**fix on 1** *vt sep* festmachen *(prep obj* auf *+dat)*; *(fit on)* anbringen. **2** *vi +prep obj (decide on)* sich entscheiden für; *(US col: intend)* vorhaben.

▶**fix up** *vt sep* (**a**) *shelves* anbringen. (**b**) *(arrange)* arrangieren; *holidays etc* festmachen. **have you got anything ~ed ~ for this evening?** haben Sie (für) heute abend schon etwas vor? (**c**) **to ~ sb ~ with sth** jdm etw besorgen; **when you get yourself ~ed ~ (with a room)** wenn du ein Zimmer gefunden hast.

**fixation** [fɪk'seɪʃən] *n (Psych)* Fixierung *f*. **a ~ about cleanliness** ein Sauberkeitsfimmel *m (col)*.

**fixative** ['fɪksətɪv] *n* Fixativ *nt*.

**fixed** [fɪkst] *adj* (**a**) fest; *idea* fix; *smile* starr. **~ assets** feste Anlagen *pl*; **~ capital** Anlagekapital *nt*; **~ costs** Fixkosten *pl*; **~ price** Festpreis *m*; **~-wing aircraft** Starrflügler *m*. (**b**) *(col)* **how are you ~ for money** etc? wie steht's (denn) bei dir mit Geld etc? *(col)*; **how are you ~ for tonight?** was hast du heute abend vor?

**fixedly** ['fɪksɪdlɪ] *adv stare, look* starr.

**fixings** ['fɪksɪŋz] *npl (US Cook)* Beilagen *pl*.

**fixture** ['fɪkstʃəʳ] *n* (**a**) *(of a building etc)* **~s** Ausstattung *f*; **~s and fittings** Anschlüsse und unbewegliches Inventar *(form)*. (**b**) *(Brit Sport)* Veranstaltung *f*; *(match)* Spiel *nt*.

**fizz** [fɪz] *vi (champagne etc)* perlen, sprudeln.

▶**fizzle out** *vi (firework, enthusiasm)* verpuffen; *(plan)* im Sande verlaufen.

**fizzy** ['fɪzɪ] *adj (+er)* sprudelnd. **to be ~** sprudeln; **a ~ drink** eine Brause.

**fjord** [fjɔːd] *n* Fjord *m*.

**FL** *(US)* = **Florida**.

**flab** [flæb] *n (col)* Speck *m*.

**flabbergasted** ['flæbəɡɑːstɪd] *adj (col)* platt *(col)*.

**flabby** ['flæbɪ] *adj (+er)* schlaff; *(fat)* stomach wabbelig.

**flag¹** [flæɡ] *n* Fahne *f*; *(small, on map, chart, for charity)* Fähnchen *nt*; *(national also, Naut)* Flagge *f*. **~ of convenience** *(Naut)* Billigflagge *f*; **to keep the ~ flying** die Fahne hochhalten.

▶**flag down** *vt sep taxi etc* anhalten.

**flag²** *vi (grow weaker etc)* nachlassen; *(person)* ermüden.

**flag³** *n (also* **~stone**) Steinplatte *f*.

**flag:** **~ day** *n (Brit)* Tag *m*, an dem für einen wohltätigen Zweck gesammelt wird; **F~ Day** *(US)* 14. Juni, Gedenktag der Einführung der amerikanischen Nationalflagge; **~pole** *n* Fahnenstange *f*.

**flagrant** ['fleɪɡrənt] *adj* eklatant, kraß; *injustice* himmelschreiend; *disregard* unverhohlen.

**flag:** **~ship** *n* Flaggschiff *nt*; **~stone** *n* Steinplatte *f*; **~ stop** *n (US)* Bedarfshaltestelle *f*.

**flail** [fleɪl] *vt* **he ~ed his arms about** er schlug (mit den Armen) wild um sich.

**flair** [fleəʳ] *n (talent)* Talent *nt*; *(stylishness)* Flair *nt*.

**flak** [flæk] *n* Flakfeuer *nt*. **~ jacket** kugelsichere Weste; **to get a lot of ~ for sth** *(fig col)* wegen etw unter Beschuß geraten.

**flake** [fleɪk] **1** *n (of snow, soap)* Flocke *f*; *(of paint, rust)* Splitter *m*; *(of skin)* Schuppe *f*. **2** *vi (also* **~ off**) *(plaster)* abbröckeln; *(paint)* abblättern.

▶**flake out** *vi (col) (pass out, fall over)* aus den Latschen kippen *(col)*; *(fall asleep)* einpennen *(col)*.

**flaky** ['fleɪkɪ] *adj (+er) (paint)* abblätternd; *(skin)* schuppig. **~ pastry** Blätterteig *m*.

**flamboyance** [flæm'bɔɪəns] *n* Extravaganz *f*; *(of colour)* Pracht *f*.

**flamboyant** [flæm'bɔɪənt] *adj* extravagant; *colours* prächtig.

**flame** [fleɪm] *n (also fig col: sweetheart)* Flamme *f*. **the house was in ~s** das Haus stand in Flammen.

**flamethrower** ['fleɪmˌθrəʊəʳ] *n* Flammenwerfer *m*.

**flaming** ['fleɪmɪŋ] *adj* (**a**) *(lit)* lodernd; *(fig)* passion glühend; *row* heftig. **he was in a ~ temper** *(col)* er kochte vor Wut *(col)*. (**b**) *(Brit col!: bloody)* verdammt *(col)*.

**flamingo** [flə'mɪŋɡəʊ] *n, pl* **-(e)s** Flamingo *m*.

**flammable** ['flæməbl] *adj* feuergefährlich.

**flan** [flæn] *n (Brit)* Kuchen *m*. **fruit ~** Obstkuchen *m*.

**Flanders** ['flɑːndəz] *n* Flandern *nt*.

**flange** [flændʒ] *n* Flansch *m*.

**flank** [flæŋk] **1** *n (of animal, Mil)* Flanke *f*. **2** *vt* flankieren.

**flannel** ['flænl] **1** *n* (**a**) Flanell *m*. **~s** *pl (trousers)* Flanellhose *f*. (**b**) *(Brit: face-~)* Waschlappen *m*. (**c**) *(Brit col: waffle)* Geschwafel *nt (col)*. **2** *adj trousers etc* Flanell-.

**flannelette** [ˌflænə'let] *n* Baumwollflanell *m*. **~ sheet** Biberbettuch *nt*.

**flap** [flæp] **1** *n* **(a)** *(of pocket, Aviat)* Klappe *f; (of table)* ausziehbarer Teil. **a ~ of skin** *(Med)* ein Hautlappen *m.* **(b)** *(sound) (of sails etc)* Flattern *nt; (of wings)* Schlagen *nt.* **(c) to give sth a ~** *(shake out)* etw ausschütteln. **(d)** *(col)* **to be in a ~** rotieren *(col);* **to get in(to) a ~** in Panik geraten; **there's a big ~ on** es herrscht große Panik. **2** *vi* **(a)** *(wings)* schlagen; *(sails, tarpaulin etc)* flattern. **his ears were ~ping** *(col)* er spitzte die Ohren. **(b)** *(col)* in Panik sein. **to start to ~** in Panik geraten; **don't ~** reg dich nicht auf! **3** *vt* **to ~ its wings** mit den Flügeln schlagen.

**flapjack** ['flæpdʒæk] *n* Gebäck *nt aus Haferflocken, Sirup etc; (US: pancake)* Pfannkuchen *m.*

**flare** [flɛəʳ] **1** *n* **(a)** Auflodern *nt.* **(b)** *(signal)* Leuchtsignal *nt; (from pistol)* Leuchtrakete *f; (landing ~)* Leuchtfeuer *nt.* **(c)** *(Fashion)* ausgestellter Schnitt. **(d)** *(solar ~)* Sonneneruption *f.* **2** *vi* **(a)** *(match, torch)* aufleuchten. **(b)** *(nostrils)* sich blähen. ▸**flare up** *vi* auflodern; *(fig) (person)* aufbrausen; *(fighting, epidemic)* ausbrechen.

**flared** [flɛəd] *adj trousers, skirt* ausgestellt.

**flare: ~ path** *n (Aviat)* Leuchtpfad *m; ~* **pistol** *n* Leuchtpistole *f; (sudden dispute)* (plötzlicher) Krach; *(fighting)* (plötzlicher) Ausbruch von Kämpfen.

**flash** [flæʃ] **1** *n* **(a)** Aufblinken *nt no pl; (very bright)* Aufblitzen *nt no pl; (of metal, jewels etc)* Blinken *nt no pl; (Mot)* Lichthupe *f no pl.* **to give sb a ~** *(Mot)* jdn (mit der Lichthupe) anblinken; **~ of lightning** Blitz *m.* **(b)** *(fig: news ~)* Kurzmeldung *f. ~* **of wit/ inspiration** Geistesblitz *m;* **in a ~** im Nu; **as quick as a ~** blitzschnell; **a ~ in the pan** *(col)* ein Strohfeuer *nt.* **(c)** *(Phot)* Blitz(licht *nt) m.* **to use a ~** Blitzlicht benutzen. **(d)** *(US col: torch)* Taschenlampe *f.*

**2** *vi* **(a)** aufblinken; *(very brightly)* aufblitzen; *(repeatedly: indicators etc)* blinken; *(metal, jewels, eyes)* blitzen. **(b)** *(move quickly) (vehicle)* sausen. **to ~ past** *or* **by** vorbeisausen; *(holidays etc)* vorbeifliegen; **the thought ~ed through my mind that ...** es schoß mir durch den Kopf, daß ...

**3** *vt* **(a)** *light* aufblitzen lassen; *SOS, message* blinken. **to ~ one's headlights** die Lichthupe betätigen; **to ~ one's headlights at sb, to ~ sb** jdn mit der Lichthupe anblinken; **she ~ed him a look of contempt** sie blitzte ihn verächtlich an. **(b)** *(col: show off: also ~* **around)** protzen mit; *diamond ring* blitzen lassen. **don't ~ all that money around** wedel nicht so mit dem vielen Geld herum! *(col).*

**flash: ~back** *n (Film)* Rückblende *f; ~***bulb** *n (Phot)* Blitzbirne *f; ~***cube** *n (Phot)* Blitz(licht)würfel *m.*

**flasher** ['flæʃəʳ] *n (Brit col)* Exhibitionist *m.*

**flash: ~ gun** *n* Elektronenblitzgerät *nt; ~* **Harry** *n (col)* Lackaffe *m (pej col); ~***light** *n* **(a)** *(Phot)* Blitzlicht *nt;* **(b)** *(esp US: torch)* Taschenlampe *f; ~* **photography** *n* Blitz(licht)fotografie *f; ~* **point** *n (Chem)* Flammpunkt *m; (fig)* Siedepunkt *m.*

**flashy** ['flæʃɪ] *adj (+er)* auffällig.

**flask** [flɑːsk] *n* Flakon *m; (Chem)* Glaskolben *m; (vacuum ~)* Thermosflasche *f.*

**flat¹** [flæt] **1** *adj (+er)* **(a)** flach; *tyre, nose, feet* platt; *surface* eben; *battery* leer. **as ~ as a pancake** *(col) (tyre)* total platt; *(countryside)* total flach; *(girl)* flach wie ein Brett; **to fall ~ on one's face** auf die Nase fallen. **(b)** *(fig: dull)* fad(e); *painting, photo* kontrastarm; *colour* matt; *joke* abgedroschen; *business, market* flau; *beer, wine* schal, abgestanden. **she felt a bit ~** sie hatte zu nichts Lust; **to fall ~** *(joke)* nicht ankommen; *(play etc)* durchfallen. **(c)** *refusal, denial* glatt. **and that's ~** und damit basta.

**(d)** *(Mus)* instrument zu tief (gestimmt); *voice* zu tief. **A ~** As *nt.* **(e)** *(Comm)* Pauschal-. **~ rate of pay** Pauschallohn *m; ~* **rate** Pauschale *f; ~* **fare** Einheitstarif *m.*

**2** *adv (+er)* **(a)** *refuse* rundweg; *tell* klipp und klar. **in ten seconds ~** in sage und schreibe (nur) zehn Sekunden; **~ broke** *(Brit col)* total pleite *(col).* **(b)** *(Mus)* **to sing/play ~** zu tief singen/spielen. **(c) ~ out** *(col: asleep, drunk)* hinüber *(col);* **to go ~ out** voll aufdrehen *(col); (in car also)* Spitze fahren *(col);* **to work ~ out** auf Hochtouren arbeiten; **to be lying ~ out** platt am Boden liegen.

**3** *n* **(a)** *(of hand)* Fläche *f.* **(b)** *(Mus)* Erniedrigungszeichen, b *nt.* **(c)** *(Aut)* Platte(r) *m (col),* (Reifen)panne *f.*

**flat²** *n (Brit: apartment)* Wohnung *f.*

**flat: ~-chested** *adj* flachbrüstig; **~ feet** *npl* Plattfüße *pl; ~***fish** *n* Plattfisch *m; ~***-footed** *adj* plattfüßig; **~let** *n (Brit)* kleine Wohnung.

**flatly** ['flætlɪ] *adv deny, refuse* rundweg; *say* klipp und klar.

**flatmate** ['flætmeɪt] *n (Brit)* Mitbewohner(in *f) m.*

**flatness** ['flætnɪs] *n (of land etc)* Flachheit *f.*

**flat: ~ race** *n* Flachrennen *nt; ~* **season** *n* Flachrennsaison *f.*

**flatten** ['flætn] **1** *vt path, road, field* ebnen; *(storm etc) crops* zu Boden drücken; *trees* umwerfen; *town* dem Erdboden gleichmachen. **that'll ~ him** *(fig col)* das wird bei ihm die Luft rauslassen *(col).* **2** *vr* **to ~ oneself against sth** sich platt gegen etw drücken. ▸**flatten out 1** *vi* eben(er) werden. **2** *vt sep path* ebnen; *metal* glatt hämmern; *map, paper, fabric* glätten.

**flatter** ['flætəʳ] *vt* schmeicheln *(+dat).* **it ~s your figure** das ist sehr vorteilhaft; **you can ~ yourself on being ...** Sie können sich *(dat)* etwas darauf einbilden, daß Sie ...

**flatterer** ['flætərəʳ] *n* Schmeichler(in *f) m.*

**flattering** ['flætərɪŋ] *adj* schmeichelhaft; *clothes* vorteilhaft.

**flattery** ['flætərɪ] *n* Schmeicheleien *pl.*

**flat top** *n (US col: aircraft carrier)* Flugzeugträger *m.*

**flatulence** ['flætjʊləns] *n* Blähungen *pl.*

**flatware** ['flætwɛəʳ] *n (US) (cutlery)* Besteck *nt; (plates etc)* Geschirr *nt.*

**flaunt** [flɔːnt] *vt* zur Schau stellen.

**flautist** ['flɔːtɪst] *n* Flötist(in *f) m.*

**flavour, *(US)* flavor** ['fleɪvəʳ] **1** *n (taste)* Geschmack *m; (flavouring)* Aroma *nt; (fig: atmosphere)* Atmosphäre *f.* **20 ~s** 20 Geschmackssorten. **2** *vt* Geschmack geben *(+dat).* **pineapple-~ed** mit Ananasgeschmack.

**flavouring, *(US)* flavoring** ['fleɪvərɪŋ] *n (Cook)* Aroma *nt.* **vanilla ~** Vanillearoma *nt.*

**flaw** [flɔː] *n* Fehler *m; (in diamond)* Unreinheit *f.*

**flawless** ['flɔːlɪs] *adj* fehlerlos; *complexion* makellos; *diamond* lupenrein.

**flax** [flæks] *n (Bot)* Flachs *m.*

**flaxen** ['flæksən] *adj* flachsfarben. **~-haired** flachsblond.

**flay** [fleɪ] *vt (skin)* animal abziehen; *(whip)* auspeitschen; *(fig: criticize)* kein gutes Haar lassen an *(+dat).*

**flea** [fliː] *n* Floh *m.* **to send sb off with a ~ in his/her ear** *(col)* jdn wie einen begossenen Pudel abziehen lassen.

**flea: ~-bite** *n* Flohbiß *m; ~* **collar** *n* Flohhalsband *nt; ~***pit** *n (Brit col)* Flohkino *nt (col).*

**fleck** [flɛk] **1** *n (of red etc)* Tupfen *m;* Fleck(en) *m.* **a ~ of dust** ein Stäubchen *nt.* **2** *vt* sprenkeln; *(with mud etc)* bespritzen. **blue ~ed with**

white blau mit weißen Tupfen.

**fled** [fled] pret, ptp of **flee**.

**fledg(e)ling** ['fledʒlɪŋ] n (bird) Jungvogel m.

**flee** [fliː] pret, ptp **fled** 1 vi fliehen, flüchten (from vor +dat). 2 vt town, country flüchten aus; danger entfliehen (+dat).

**fleece** [fliːs] 1 n Vlies nt; (fabric) (natural) Schaffell nt; (artificial) Webpelz m. 2 vt (fig col: rob) schröpfen.

**fleecy** ['fliːsɪ] adj (+er) blanket flauschig. ~ clouds Schäfchenwolken pl; ~ lining Wattierung f.

**fleet** [fliːt] n (a) (Naut) Geschwader nt; (entire naval force) Flotte f. (b) (of buses etc) (Fuhr)park m.

**fleeting** adj, ~ly adv ['fliːtɪŋ, -lɪ] flüchtig.

**Flemish** ['flemɪʃ] 1 adj flämisch. 2 n (a) the ~ pl die Flamen pl. (b) (language) Flämisch nt.

**flesh** [fleʃ] n Fleisch nt; (of fruit) (Frucht)fleisch nt. one's own ~ and blood sein eigen(es) Fleisch und Blut; it was more than a ~ and blood could bear das war einfach nicht zu ertragen; to go the way of all ~ den Weg allen Fleisches gehen; in the ~ in Person; ~pots pl Fleischtöpfe pl; ~ wound Fleischwunde f.
►**flesh out** vt sep idea ausgestalten.

**fleshy** ['fleʃɪ] adj (+er) fleischig.

**flew** [fluː] pret of **fly²**, **fly³**.

**flex** [fleks] 1 n (Brit) Schnur f; (heavy duty) Kabel nt. 2 vt body, knees beugen; muscles (lit, fig) spielen lassen.

**flexibility** [ˌfleksɪ'bɪlɪtɪ] n see adj Biegsamkeit f; Flexibilität f.

**flexible** ['fleksəbl] adj wire biegsam; (fig) flexibel. ~ working hours gleitende Arbeitszeit.

**flex(i)time** ['fleks(ɪ)taɪm] n Gleitzeit f.

**flick** [flɪk] 1 n (of tail) kurzer Schlag. **hot water at the** ~ **of a switch** auf Knopfdruck heißes Wasser; **she gave the room a quick** ~ **with the duster** sie ging kurz mit dem Staublappen durch das Zimmer. 2 vt whip schnalzen mit; switch anknipsen; dust, ash wegschnipsen; (with cloth) wegwedeln. **she** ~ed **her hair out of her eyes** sie strich sich (dat) die Haare aus den Augen. 3 vi **the snake's tongue** ~ed **in and out** die Schlange züngelte.
►**flick off** vt sep wegschnipsen.
►**flick through** vi +prep obj (schnell) durchblättern.

**flicker** ['flɪkər] 1 vi (flame, candle) flackern; (TV) flimmern; (needle on dial) zittern; (eyelid) zucken. 2 n see vi Flackern nt; Flimmern nt; Zittern nt; Zucken nt. **a** ~ **of hope** ein Hoffnungsschimmer m.

**flick knife** n Klappmesser nt.

**flicks** [flɪks] npl (Brit col) Kintopp m or nt (col).

**flier** ['flaɪər] n (a) (pilot) Flieger(in f) m. (b) (US: train) Schnellzug m. (c) (Sport: quick start) **to get off to a** ~ einen ausgezeichneten Start machen. (d) (leaflet) Flugblatt nt.

**flies** [flaɪz] npl of **fly**.

**flight¹** [flaɪt] n (a) Flug m. **in** ~ (birds) im Flug; (Aviat) in der Luft; ~**s of fancy** geistige Höhenflüge pl. (b) ~ (of stairs) Treppe f; **he lives six** ~**s up** er wohnt sechs Treppen hoch.

**flight²** n Flucht f. **to put the enemy to** ~ den Feind in die Flucht schlagen; **to take (to)** ~ die Flucht ergreifen.

**flight:** ~ **attendant** n Flugbegleiter(in f) m; ~ **crew** n Flugbesatzung f; ~ **deck** n (Naut) Flugdeck nt; (Aviat) Cockpit nt; ~ **engineer** n Bordingenieur m; ~**less** adj nicht flugfähig; ~ **path** n Flugbahn f; (of individual plane) Flugroute f; **incoming/outgoing** ~ **path** Einflug-/Ausflugschneise f; ~ **recorder** n Flugschreiber m.

**flighty** ['flaɪtɪ] adj (+er) (fickle) flatterhaft.

**flimsy** ['flɪmzɪ] adj (+er) material dünn; clothing dürftig; house, aircraft leicht gebaut; excuse fadenscheinig.

**flinch** [flɪntʃ] vi zurückzucken. **without** ~**ing** ohne mit der Wimper zu zucken; **to** ~ **from a task** vor einer Aufgabe zurückschrecken.

**fling** [flɪŋ] (vb: pret, ptp **flung**) 1 n (fig col) **to have a** ~ **at sth, to give sth a** ~ etw (aus)probieren; **to have a** ~ **at doing sth** einen Anlauf machen, etw zu tun (col); **to have a** or **one's** ~ sich austoben. 2 vt (lit, fig) schleudern. **to** ~ **the window open/shut** das Fenster aufstoßen/zuwerfen; **the door was flung open** die Tür flog auf; **to** ~ **one's arms around sb's neck** jdm die Arme um den Hals werfen; **to** ~ **one's coat** sich (dat) den Mantel überwerfen; **to** ~ **oneself into a job** sich auf eine Aufgabe stürzen; **to** ~ **oneself out of the window/into a chair** sich aus dem Fenster stürzen/in einen Sessel werfen.
►**fling away** vt sep wegwerfen; (fig) money verschwenden.
►**fling back** vt sep one's head zurückwerfen.
►**fling down** vt sep (lit) herunterwerfen.
►**fling out** vt sep object wegwerfen; person hinauswerfen.

**flint** [flɪnt] n Feuerstein m.

**flip** [flɪp] 1 vt schnippen, schnipsen. **to** ~ **a book open** ein Buch aufschlagen; **to** ~ **one's lid** (col) durchdrehen (col). 2 vi (col) durchdrehen (col). 3 interj (Brit col) verflixt (col).
►**flip off** vt sep wegschnipsen; ash from cigarette abschnippen.
►**flip over** 1 vt sep umdrehen; pages of book wenden. 2 vi sich (um)drehen.
►**flip through** vi +prep obj book durchblättern.

**flip:** ~**chart** n Flip-Chart f; ~ **pack** n Klappschachtel f.

**flippancy** ['flɪpənsɪ] n Leichtfertigkeit f.

**flippant** ['flɪpənt] adj leichtfertig.

**flipper** ['flɪpər] n Flosse f.

**flipping** ['flɪpɪŋ] adj, adv (Brit col) verflixt (col).

**flip:** ~**side** n (of record) B-Seite f; ~ **top** n Klappdeckel m.

**flirt** [flɜːt] 1 vi flirten; (with idea) liebäugeln. **to** ~ **with death** den Tod herausfordern. 2 n **he/she is just a** ~ er/sie will nur flirten.

**flirtation** [flɜː'teɪʃən] n Flirt m.

**flit** [flɪt] 1 vi (a) (bats, butterflies etc) flattern; (person, image) huschen. **to** ~ **in and out** (person) reinund rausflitzen (col). (b) (Brit: move house secretly) sich bei Nacht und Nebel davonmachen. 2 n (Brit) **to do a** (moonlight) ~ bei Nacht und Nebel ausziehen.

**float** [fləʊt] 1 n (a) (on fishing-line, Tech) Schwimmer m; (on trawl net) Korken m. (b) (vehicle) (in procession) Festwagen m; (electric ~ for deliveries) Elektrolieferwagen m. (c) (ready cash: in till) Wechselgeld nt no indef art; (loan to start business) Startkapital nt. 2 vi (a) (on water) schwimmen; (move gently) treiben; (in air) schweben. (b) (Comm: currency) floaten. 3 vt (a) boat zu Wasser bringen. (b) (Comm, Fin) company gründen; shares auf den Markt bringen; bond issue ausgeben; currency freigeben, floaten lassen.
►**float away** vi (on water) wegtreiben; (in air) davonschweben; (fig: person) hinwegschweben.
►**float off** 1 vi see **float away**. 2 vt ship flottmachen.

**floating** ['fləʊtɪŋ] adj raft, logs treibend; population wandernd; kidney Wander-; decimal point Gleit-. ~ **voter** Wechselwähler m.

**flock** [flɒk] **1** *n (of sheep, geese, Eccl)* Herde *f*; *(of birds, people)* Schar *f*. **2** *vi* in Scharen kommen. **to ~ in** hinein-/hereinströmen; **to ~ around sb** sich um jdn scharen.

**floe** [fləʊ] *n* Eisscholle *f*.

**flog** [flɒg] *vt* **(a)** prügeln; *thief, mutineer* auspeitschen. **you're ~ging a dead horse** *(col)* Sie verschwenden Ihre Zeit; **to ~ sth to death** *(fig)* etw zu Tode reiten. **(b)** *(Brit col: sell)* verkloppen *(col)*.

**flogging** ['flɒgɪŋ] *n* Tracht *f* Prügel; *(Jur)* Prügelstrafe *f*; *(of thief, mutineer)* Auspeitschen *nt*.

**flood** [flʌd] **1** *n (of water, fig)* Flut *f*. **~s** Hochwasser *nt*; **the F~** die Sintflut; **the river is in ~** der Fluß führt Hochwasser; **she had a ~ in the kitchen** ihre Küche stand unter Wasser; **she was in ~s of tears** sie war in Tränen gebadet; **bathed in a ~ of light** lichtüberflutet. **2** *vt (lit, fig, Comm)* überschwemmen. **to ~ the carburettor** den Motor absaufen lassen *(col)*; **~ed with light** lichtdurchflutet. **3** *vi* **(a)** *(river)* über die Ufer treten; *(bath etc)* überlaufen. **(b)** *(people)* strömen.

▶**flood in** *vi (lit, fig)* hinein-/hereinströmen. **the letters just ~ed ~** eine Flut von Briefen ging ein.

▶**flood out** *vt sep house* überfluten. **the villagers were ~ed ~** die Dorfbewohner wurden durch das Hochwasser obdachlos.

**floodgate** ['flʌdgeɪt] *n* Schleusentor *nt*. **to open the ~s** *(fig)* Tür und Tor öffnen *(to dat)*.

**flooding** ['flʌdɪŋ] *n* Überschwemmung *f*.

**flood:** **~light** *(vb: pret, ptp ~lit)* **1** *vt buildings* anstrahlen; *football pitch* mit Flutlicht beleuchten; **2** *n* **under ~lights** unter *or* bei Flutlicht; **~lit 1** *pret, ptp of* **~light**; **2** *adj* **~lit football** Fußball *m* bei Flutlicht; **~-tide** *n* Flut *f*; **~water** *n* Hochwasser *nt*.

**floor** [flɔːʳ] **1** *n* **(a)** Boden *m*; *(of room)* (Fuß)boden *m*; *(dance-~)* Tanzboden *m*. **to take the ~** *(dance)* aufs Parkett gehen; *(speak)* das Wort ergreifen; **to have the ~** *(speaker)* das Wort haben; **a question from the ~** eine Frage aus der Zuhörerschaft; *(Parl)* eine Frage aus dem Haus. **(b)** *(storey)* Stock(werk *nt)* *m.* **first ~** *(Brit)* erster Stock; *(US)* Erdgeschoß *nt*; **on the second ~** *(Brit)* im zweiten Stock; *(US)* im ersten Stock. **2** *vt* **(a)** *room etc* mit einem (Fuß)boden versehen. **(b)** *(knock down)* opponent zu Boden schlagen. **(c)** *(Aut)* **to ~ the accelerator** das Gaspedal durchtreten. **(d)** *(silence)* die Sprache verschlagen *(+dat)*; *(puzzle)* verblüffen; *(defeat: question, problem etc)* schaffen *(col)*.

**floor:** **~board** *n* Diele *f*; **~cloth** *n* Putzlappen *m*.

**flooring** ['flɔːrɪŋ] *n* Fußbodenbelag *m*.

**floor:** **~ lamp** *n (US)* Stehlampe *f*; **~ polish** *n* Bohnerwachs *nt*; **~ show** *n* Show *f (im Nachtklub oder Kabarett)*; **~-walker** *n (Comm)* Ladenaufsicht *f*.

**floozie, floozy** ['fluːzɪ] *n (col)* Flittchen *nt (col)*.

**flop** [flɒp] **1** *vi* **(a)** *(col: person: into chair etc)* sich hinplumpsen lassen. **(b)** *(col: fail)* durchfallen. **2** *n (col: failure)* Reinfall *m*; *(person)* Niete *f*.

**flophouse** ['flɒphaʊs] *n (US col)* billige Absteige.

**floppy** ['flɒpɪ] *adj (+er)* schlaff; *hat, ears* Schlapp-; *clothes* weit. **~ disk** Floppy-Disk, Diskette *f*.

**flora** ['flɔːrə] *n* Flora *f*.

**floral** ['flɔːrəl] *adj arrangement* Blumen-; *fabric, dress* geblümt.

**Florence** ['florəns] *n* Florenz *nt*.

**Florentine** ['florəntaɪn] **1** *adj* florentinisch. **2** *n* Florentiner(in *f*) *m.*

**florid** ['florɪd] *adj* **(a)** *complexion* kräftig. **(b)** *style, writing* blumig.

**florist** ['florɪst] *n* Florist(in *f*) *m.* **~'s (shop)** Blumengeschäft *nt*.

**flotation** [fləʊ'teɪʃən] *n (of firm)* Gründung *f*.

**flotilla** [fləʊ'tɪlə] *n* Flotille *f*.

**flotsam** ['flotsəm] *n (lit, fig)* **~ and jetsam** Strandgut *nt*.

**flounce¹** [flaʊns] *vi* **to ~ in/out** herein-/herausstolzieren.

**flounce²** *n (frill)* Volant *m*, Rüsche *f*.

**flounder¹** ['flaʊndəʳ] *n (fish)* Flunder *f*.

**flounder²** *vi* **to ~ through the mud/snow** sich durch den Schlamm/Schnee schleppen; **to start to ~** *(speaker etc)* ins Schwimmen kommen.

**flour** ['flaʊəʳ] *n* Mehl *nt*.

**flourish** ['flʌrɪʃ] **1** *vi (plants, person)* (prächtig) gedeihen; *(business)* blühen, florieren; *(type of literature, painting)* seine Blütezeit haben. **2** *vt (wave about)* schwenken. **3** *n* **(a)** *(curve, decoration etc)* Schnörkel *m.* **(b)** *(movement)* schwungvolle Bewegung. **(c)** *(Mus) (fanfare)* Fanfare *f*; *(decorative passage)* Verzierung *f*.

**flourishing** ['flʌrɪʃɪŋ] *adj plant, person* blühend *attr*; *business* florierend *attr*.

**flout** [flaʊt] *vt* mißachten.

**flow** [fləʊ] **1** *vi* **(a)** *(lit, fig)* fließen; *(prose)* flüssig sein. **where the river ~s into the sea** wo der Fluß ins Meer mündet; **to keep the conversation ~ing** das Gespräch in Gang halten; **to keep the traffic ~ing** den Verkehr nicht ins Stocken kommen lassen; **to ~ in** *(water, people, money)* hinein-/hereinströmen. **(b)** *(tide)* steigen. **2** *n* Fluß *m.* **the ~ of traffic/information** der Verkehrs-/Informationsfluß; **the tide is on the ~** die Flut kommt; **the ~ of his style** sein flüssiger Stil; **~chart** Flußdiagramm *nt*.

**flower** ['flaʊəʳ] **1** *n* Blume *f*; *(blossom, fig)* Blüte *f*. **in ~** in Blüte; **to be in the ~ of youth** in der Blüte seiner Jugend stehen. **2** *vi (lit, fig)* blühen.

**flower:** **~ arrangement** *n* Blumengesteck *nt*; **~bed** *n* Blumenbeet *nt*; **~ garden** *n* Blumengarten *m*; **~pot** *n* Blumentopf *m*; **~ power** *n* Flower-power *f*; **~-seller** *n* Blumenverkäufer(in *f*) *m*; **~ shop** *n* Blumengeschäft *nt*; **~ tub** *n* Blumenkübel *m*; **~ show** *n* Blumenschau *f*.

**flowery** ['flaʊərɪ] *adj perfume, (fig) language* blumig; *dress, material* geblümt.

**flowing** ['fləʊɪŋ] *adj* fließend; *dress, hair also* wallend; *style* flüssig.

**flown** [fləʊn] *ptp of* **fly²**, **fly³**.

**flu, 'flu** [fluː] *n* Grippe *f*. **to have (the) ~** (die *or* eine) Grippe haben.

**fluctuate** ['flʌktjʊeɪt] *vi* schwanken.

**fluctuation** [ˌflʌktjʊ'eɪʃən] *n* Schwankung *f*; *(fig: of opinions)* Schwanken *nt no pl*.

**flue** [fluː] *n* Rauchabzug *m*.

**fluency** ['fluːənsɪ] *n* Flüssigkeit *f*; *(of speaker)* Gewandtheit *f*. **because of his ~ in English** ... da er fließend Englisch spricht/sprach ...

**fluent** ['fluːənt] *adj style* flüssig; *speaker, writer* gewandt; *Italian, Russian etc* fließend. **to be ~ in Italian, to speak ~ Italian** fließend Italienisch sprechen.

**fluently** ['fluːəntlɪ] *adv speak a language* fließend; *express oneself* gewandt.

**fluff** [flʌf] **1** *n no pl (on young animals)* Flaum *m*; *(from material)* Fusseln *pl*; *(dust)* Staubflocken *pl*. **a bit of ~** eine Staubflocke/Fussel; *(hum col: girl)* eine Mieze *(col)*. **2** *vt* **(a)** *(also ~ out)* feathers aufplustern; *(also ~ up)* pillows aufschütteln. **(b)** *(col: make mistake in)* vermasseln *(col)*.

**fluffy** ['flʌfɪ] *adj (+er) bird* flaumig; *material, toy* kuschelig, weich; *hair* duftig.

**fluid** ['fluːɪd] **1** *adj substance, style* flüssig; *(fig) situation* ungewiß. **the situation is still ~** die Dinge sind

noch im Fluß. **2** *n* Flüssigkeit *f*.
**fluke** [fluːk] *n (col)* Dusel *m (col)*. **it was a (pure)** ~ das war (einfach) Dusel *(col)*.
**fluky** ['fluːkɪ] *n (col) wind* wechselnd. ~ **shot** Zufallstreffer *m*.
**flummox** ['flʌmǝks] *vt (col)* durcheinanderbringen.
**flung** [flʌŋ] *pret, ptp of* **fling**.
**flunk** [flʌŋk] *vt (col)* **to** ~ **German/an exam** in Deutsch/bei einer Prüfung durchsausen *(col)*.
**flunk(e)y** ['flʌŋkɪ] *n* Lakai *m*.
**fluorescent** [fluǝ'resǝnt] *adj* Leucht-; *lighting, tube* Leuchtstoff-.
**fluoride** ['fluǝraɪd] *n* Fluorid *nt*. ~ **toothpaste** Fluorzahnpasta *f*.
**flurry** ['flʌrɪ] *n* **(a)** *(of snow)* Gestöber *nt*; *(of wind)* Stoß *m*. **(b)** *(fig)* **all in a** ~ in großer Aufregung; **a** ~ **of activity** eine Hektik.
**flush¹** [flʌʃ] **1** *n* **(a)** *(lavatory ~)* (Wasser)spülung *f*. **(b)** *(blush)* Röte *f*. **hot ~es** *(Med)* fliegende Hitze. **(c)** *(of beauty, youth)* Blüte *f*; *(of excitement)* Welle *f*. **in the (first)** ~ **of victory** im (ersten) Siegestaumel; **in the first** ~ **of youth** in der ersten Jugendblüte. **2** *vi* **(a)** *(person, face)* rot werden *(with* vor *+dat)*. **(b)** *(lavatory)* spülen. **3** *vt* spülen. **to** ~ **the lavatory** spülen; **to** ~ **sth down the lavatory** etw die Toilette hinunterspülen.
▸**flush away** *vt sep* wegspülen.
▸**flush out** *vt sep bottle* ausspülen; *dirt* wegspülen; *birds, spies* aufstöbern.
**flush²** *adj pred* **(a)** bündig. ~ **against the wall** direkt an die/der Wand. **(b)** *(col: with money)* **to be** ~ gut bei Kasse sein *(col)*.
**flush³** *n (Cards)* Flöte, Sequenz *f*; *(Poker)* Flush *m*.
**flushed** [flʌʃt] *adj person* rot *(with* vor*)*.
**fluster** ['flʌstǝr] **1** *vt* nervös machen; *(confuse)* durcheinanderbringen. **she got ~ed** sie wurde nervös; sie kam durcheinander. **2** *n* **in a (real)** ~ (ganz) nervös; *(confused)* (völlig) durcheinander.
**flute** [fluːt] *n* Querflöte *f*.
**fluted** ['fluːtɪd] *adj column* kanneliert.
**flutter** ['flʌtǝr] **1** *vi (flag, wings, heart)* flattern. **to** ~ **away** davonflattern. **2** *vt (birds) wings* flattern mit. **to** ~ **one's eyelashes at sb** mit den Wimpern klimpern. **3** *n* Flattern *nt (also Med)*. **(all)** **in** *or* **of a** ~ *(fig)* in heller Aufregung; **to have a** ~ *(Brit col: gamble)* sein Glück (beim Wetten) versuchen.
**flux** [flʌks] *n* **in a state of** ~ im Fluß.
**fly¹** [flaɪ] *n* Fliege *f*. **he wouldn't hurt a** ~ er könnte keiner Fliege etwas zuleide tun; **the** ~ **in the ointment** der Haken bei der Sache; **there are no flies on him** *(col)* ihn legt man nicht so leicht rein *(col)*.
**fly²** *(vb: pret* **flew***, ptp* **flown***)* **1** *vi* **(a)** fliegen. **(b)** *(move quickly) (time)* (ver)fliegen; *(people)* sausen *(col)*; *(sparks)* stieben, fliegen. **how time flies!** wie die Zeit vergeht!; **to** ~ **past** *(car, person)* vorbeisausen *(col)*; **I must** ~ ich muß jetzt wirklich schnell los; **the door flew open** die Tür flog auf; **to** ~ **into a rage** einen Wutanfall bekommen; **to (let)** ~ **at sb** *(col)* auf jdn losgehen; **he really let** ~ er legte kräftig los; **to knock sb/sth** ~**ing** jdn/etw umwerfen. **(c)** *(flag)* wehen. **2** *vt aircraft, route* fliegen; *kite* steigen lassen; *Atlantic* überfliegen; *flag* führen.
▸**fly away** *vi (person, plane, bird)* wegfliegen; *(fig: cares)* schwinden.
▸**fly in** *vti sep* einfliegen. **she flew** ~ **from New York** sie ist mit dem Flugzeug aus New York angekommen.
▸**fly off** *vi* **(a)** *(plane, person)* abfliegen; *(bird)* wegfliegen. **(b)** *(come off: hat, lid etc)* wegfliegen; *(button)* abspringen.
▸**fly out 1** *vi* ausfliegen. **I'll** ~ ~ **and come back by**

**ship** ich werde hin fliegen und mit dem Schiff zurückkommen. **2** *vt sep (to an area)* hinfliegen; *(out of an area)* ausfliegen.
**fly³** *pret* **flew***, ptp* **flown** **1** *vi (flee)* fliehen. **to** ~ **for one's life** um sein Leben laufen/fahren *etc*. **2** *vt* **to** ~ **the country** aus dem Land flüchten.
**fly⁴** *n (on trousers: also flies)* (Hosen)schlitz *m*.
**fly⁵** *adj (col: crafty)* clever, gerissen.
**fly:** ~**-away** *adj hair* fliegend; ~**-by-night** *adj firm, operation* zweifelhaft, windig *(col)*.
**flyer** ['flaɪǝr] *n =* **flier**.
**flying** ['flaɪɪŋ] **1** *n* Fliegen *nt*. **he likes** ~ er fliegt gerne. **2** *adj* fliegend; *boat* Flug-.
**flying:** ~**-bomb** *n* V-Rakete *f*; ~ **buttress** *n* Strebebogen *m*; ~ **colours** *(Brit) or* **colors** *(US) npl* **to come through/pass** *etc* **with** ~ **colours** glänzend abschneiden; ~ **fish** *n* fliegender Fisch; ~ **jump** *n* **to take a** ~ **jump** einen großen Satz machen; ~ **picket** *n* mobiler Streikposten; ~ **saucer** *n* fliegende Untertasse; ~ **start** *n (Sport)* fliegender Start; **to get off to a** ~ **start** *(Sport)* hervorragend wegkommen; *(fig)* einen glänzenden Start haben; ~**-time** *n* Flugzeit *f*; ~ **visit** *n* Blitzbesuch *m*.
**fly:** ~**leaf** *n* Vorsatzblatt *nt*; ~**over** *n* Überführung *f*; ~**paper** *n* Fliegenfänger *m*; ~**past** *n* Luftparade *f*; ~**sheet** *n (entrance)* Überdach *nt*; *(outer tent)* Überzelt *nt*; ~**-spray** *n* Insektenspray *m or nt*; ~**swat(ter)** *n* Fliegenklatsche *f*; ~**weight** *n (Boxing)* Fliegengewicht *nt*; ~**wheel** *n* Schwungrad *nt*.
**FM = frequency modulation** FM.
**FO = Foreign Office.**
**foal** [fǝul] *n* Fohlen, Füllen *nt*.
**foam** [fǝum] **1** *n* Schaum *m*. **2** *vi* schäumen. **to** ~ **at the mouth** *(lit)* Schaum vor dem Mund/Maul haben; *(fig: person)* vor Wut schäumen.
**foam rubber** *n* Schaumgummi *m*.
**fob¹** ['efǝubiː] *= ***free on board.**
**fob²** [fɔb] *vt sep* **to** ~ **sb off (with promises)** jdn (mit leeren Versprechungen) abspeisen; **to** ~ **sb off with sth** jdm etw andrehen.
**foc** *(Brit Comm) = ***free of charge.**
**focal** ['fǝukǝl] *adj* ~ **length** Brennweite *f*; ~ **point** *(lit, fig)* Brennpunkt *m*.
**fo'c'sle** ['fǝuksl] *n = ***forecastle** Vorschiff *nt*.
**focus** ['fǝukǝs] **1** *n, pl* **foci** ['fǝukɪ] *(Phys, Math, fig)* Brennpunkt *m*; *(of earthquake, Med)* Herd *m*. **in** ~ *camera* (scharf) eingestellt; *photo* scharf; **out of** ~ *(lit) camera* unscharf eingestellt; *photo* unscharf; **he was the** ~ **of attention** er stand im Mittelpunkt. **2** *vt instrument* einstellen *(on* auf *+acc)*; *(fig) one's efforts* konzentrieren *(on* auf *+acc)*; **to** ~ **one's attention on sth** sich auf etw *(acc)* konzentrieren. **3** *vi* **to** ~ **on sth** sich auf etw *(acc)* konzentrieren; **his eyes** ~**ed on the book** sein Blick richtete sich auf das Buch; **I can't** ~ **properly** ich kann nicht mehr klar sehen.
**fodder** ['fɔdǝr] *n (lit, fig)* Futter *nt*.
**foe** [fǝu] *n (liter)* Feind, Widersacher *(geh) m*.
**foetal,** *(esp US)* **fetal** ['fiːtl] *adj* fötal.
**foetus,** *(esp US)* **fetus** ['fiːtǝs] *n* Fötus *m*.
**fog** [fɔg] *n* Nebel *m*.
**fogbound** ['fɔgbaund] *adj ship, plane* durch Nebel festgehalten; *airport* wegen Nebel(s) geschlossen.
**fogey** ['fǝugɪ] *n (col)* **old** ~ alter Kauz *(col)*.
**foggy** ['fɔgɪ] *adj (+er)* neb(e)lig. **I haven't the foggiest (idea)** *(col)* ich habe keinen blassen Schimmer *(col)*.
**fog:** ~**horn** *n (Naut)* Nebelhorn *nt*; ~ **light** *n (Aut)* Nebelscheinwerfer *m*; *(rear* ~ *light)* Nebelschlußleuchte *f*.
**foible** ['fɔɪbl] *n* Eigenheit *f*.

**foil¹** [fɔɪl] *n (metal)* Folie *f.* **to act as a ~ to sb** *(fig)* jdm als Hintergrund dienen.

**foil²** *n (Fencing)* Florett *nt.*

**foil³** *vt plans* durchkreuzen; *attempts* vereiteln; *person* einen Strich durch die Rechnung machen *(+dat).*

**foist** [fɔɪst] *vt* **to ~ sth (off) on sb** *goods* jdm etw andrehen; **to ~ oneself on(to) sb** sich jdm aufdrängen.

**fold¹** [fəʊld] **1** *n* Falte *f.* **2** *vt paper* (zusammen)-falten; *blanket* zusammenlegen. **to ~ sth in two/four** etw (einmal) falten/zweimal falten; **to ~ one's arms** die Arme verschränken; **he ~ed the book in some paper** er schlug das Buch in Papier ein. **3** *vi* **(a)** *(chair, table)* sich zusammenklappen lassen. **(b)** = **fold up.**
▶**fold away 1** *vi (table, bed)* zusammenklappbar sein. **2** *vt sep table, bed* zusammenklappen; *clothes* zusammenlegen.
▶**fold up 1** *vi (business)* eingehen *(col)*; *(play)* abgesetzt werden. **2** *vt sep paper* zusammenfalten.

**fold²** *n (pen)* Pferch *m.*

**foldaway** ['fəʊldəweɪ] *adj attr* zusammenklappbar.

**folder** ['fəʊldər] *n* **(a)** *(for papers)* Aktenmappe *f.* **(b)** *(brochure)* Informationsblatt *nt.*

**folding** ['fəʊldɪŋ] *adj attr* **~ bed** Klappbett *nt*; **~ chair** Klappstuhl *m*; **~ doors** Falttür *f.*

**foliage** ['fəʊlɪɪdʒ] *n* Blätter *pl*; *(of tree)* Laub *nt.*

**folio** ['fəʊlɪəʊ] *n* **(a)** *(sheet)* Folio *nt.* **(b)** *(volume)* Foliant *m.*

**folk** [fəʊk] *npl* Leute *pl.* **the young/old ~** die Jungen/Alten; **my ~s** *(col)* meine Leute *(col).*

**folk: ~ dance** *n* Volkstanz *m*; **~lore** *n* Folklore *f*; **~ music** *n* Volksmusik *f*; *(English, Irish etc)* Folk *m*; **~ singer** *n* Sänger(in *f*) *m* von Volksliedern/Folksongs; **~ song** *n* Volkslied *nt*; *(English, Irish etc)* Folksong *m*; **~ tale** *n* Volksmärchen *nt.*

**follow** ['fɒləʊ] **1** *vt (also understand)* folgen *(+dat)*; *(pursue also)* verfolgen; *advice, instructions also* befolgen; *profession* ausüben; *career, serial, speech, news* verfolgen; *athletics etc* sich interessieren für. **he ~ed me about** er folgte mir überall hin; **he ~ed me out** er folgte mir nach draußen; **we're being ~ed** wir werden verfolgt; **to have sb ~ed** jdn verfolgen lassen; **the reaction that ~ed this** die darauf folgende Reaktion; **do you ~ me?** können Sie mir folgen?; **which team do you ~?** für welchen Verein sind Sie? **2** *vi* **(a)** folgen *(on sth* auf etw *acc).* **as ~s** wie folgt; **what is there to ~?** was gibt es anschließend?; **what ~s** das Folgende. **(b)** *(results, deduction)* folgen *(from* aus*).* **it doesn't ~ that ...** daraus folgt nicht, daß ...; **that doesn't ~** nicht unbedingt! **(c)** *(understand)* folgen. **I don't ~** das verstehe ich nicht.
▶**follow on** *vi (come after)* später kommen.
▶**follow through 1** *vt sep argument* durchdenken; *idea, plan* (zu Ende) verfolgen. **2** *vi (Sport)* durchschwingen.
▶**follow up** *vt sep* **(a)** *(take further action on)* request nachgehen *(+dat)*; *offer, suggestion* aufgreifen. **(b)** *(investigate further)* sich näher befassen mit; *matter* weiterverfolgen; *rumour* nachgehen *(+dat).* **(c)** *(reinforce)* success, victory fortsetzen; *advantage* ausnutzen. **you should ~ ~ the letter with a phonecall** zusätzlich zu dem Brief sollten Sie noch anrufen.

**follower** ['fɒləʊər] *n (fan etc)* Anhänger(in *f*) *m.*

**following** ['fɒləʊɪŋ] **1** *adj* **(a)** folgend. **the ~ day** der (darauf)folgende Tag. **(b)** **a ~ wind** Rückenwind *m.* **2** *n* **(a)** *(followers)* Anhängerschaft *f.* **(b)** **he said the**

~ er sagte folgendes.

**follow-up** ['fɒləʊˌʌp] *n* Weiterverfolgen *nt*; *(event, programme etc coming after)* Fortsetzung *f (to* gen*).* **what was the ~ to this?** was folgte darauf?

**follow-up: ~ advertising** *n* Nachfaßwerbung *f*; **~ care** *n (Med)* Nachbehandlung *f*; **~ interview** *n* zweites Vorstellungsgespräch; **~ letter** *n* Nachfaßschreiben *nt.*

**folly** ['fɒlɪ] *n* Torheit *f.*

**fond** [fɒnd] *adj (+er)* **(a)** **to be ~ of sb** jdn gern mögen; **to be ~ of sth** etw gern mögen; **to be ~ of doing sth** etw gern tun. **(b)** *(loving)* liebevoll; *hope* sehnsüchtig. **(c)** *(vain)* illusion verloren; *hope* kühn.

**fondant** ['fɒndənt] *n* Fondant *m.*

**fondle** ['fɒndl] *vt* (zärtlich) spielen mit; *(stroke)* streicheln; *person* schmusen mit.

**fondly** ['fɒndlɪ] *adv look etc* liebevoll. **he ~ believed/imagined that ...** er hoffte vergebens, daß ...

**fondness** ['fɒndnɪs] *n* Begeisterung *f*; *(for people)* Zuneigung *f (for* zu*)*; *(for food, place)* Vorliebe *f (for* für*).*

**fondue** ['fɒnduː] *n* Fondue *nt.*

**font** [fɒnt] *n* **(a)** *(Eccl)* Taufstein *m.* **(b)** *(Typ)* Schrift *f.*

**food** [fuːd] *n* Essen *nt*; *(for animals)* Futter *nt*; *(nourishment)* Nahrung *f*; *(~stuff)* Nahrungsmittel *nt*; *(groceries)* Lebensmittel *pl.* **canned ~s** Konserven *pl*; **I haven't any ~ in the house** ich habe nichts zu essen im Haus; **to be off one's ~** keinen Appetit haben; **~ for thought** *(fig)* Stoff *m* zum Nachdenken.

**food: ~ chain** *n* Nahrungskette *f*; **~ poisoning** *n* Lebensmittelvergiftung *f*; **~ processor** *n* Küchenmaschine *f*; **~ shop** *(Brit)* or **store** *n* Lebensmittelgeschäft *nt*; **~stuff** *n* Nahrungsmittel *nt.*

**fool** [fuːl] **1** *n* Dummkopf, Narr *(also jester) m.* **don't be a ~!** sei nicht (so) dumm!; **some ~ of a civil servant** irgend so ein blöder Beamter; **I was a ~ not to realize** wie konnte ich nur so dumm sein und das nicht merken; **to play** *or* **act the ~** herumalbern; **to make a ~ of sb** jdn lächerlich machen; **he made a ~ of himself in the discussion** er hat sich in der Diskussion blamiert; **to live in a ~'s paradise** in einem Traumland leben. **2** *vi* herumalbern. **I was only ~ing** das war doch nur Spaß. **3** *vt (trick)* hereinlegen *(col)*; *(disguise, phoney accent etc)* täuschen. **you had me ~ed** ich habe das tatsächlich geglaubt; **they ~ed him into believing that ...** sie haben ihm weisgemacht, daß ...; **you could have ~ed me!** *(iro)* was du nicht sagst!
▶**fool about** *or* **around** *vi* **(a)** *(waste time)* herumtrödeln. **(b)** *(play the fool)* herumalbern. **(c)** **to ~ ~ with sth** mit etw Blödsinn machen.

**foolhardy** ['fuːlˌhɑːdɪ] *adj* tollkühn.

**foolish** ['fuːlɪʃ] *adj* dumm. **he's afraid of looking ~** er will sich nicht blamieren.

**foolishly** ['fuːlɪʃlɪ] *adv* **~, I assumed ...** törichterweise habe ich angenommen, ...

**foolishness** ['fuːlɪʃnɪs] *n* Dummheit *f.*

**foolproof** ['fuːlpruːf] *adj* narrensicher.

**foolscap** ['fuːlskæp] *n* ≈ Kanzleipapier *nt.*

**foot** [fʊt] **1** *n, pl* **feet** **(a)** *(also bottom, measure)* Fuß *m.* **to be on one's feet** *(lit, fig)* auf den Beinen sein; **to put sb (back) on his feet (again)** *(lit,fig)* jdm (wieder) auf die Beine helfen; **on ~** zu Fuß; **the first time he set ~ in the office** als er das erste Mal das Büro betrat; **to rise/jump to one's feet** aufstehen/aufspringen; **to put one's feet up** *(lit)* die Füße hochlegen; *(fig)* es sich *(dat)* bequem machen. **(b)** *(fig phrases)* **he never puts a ~ wrong** er macht nie einen Fehler; **to catch sb on the wrong ~** jdn überrumpeln; **to put one's ~ down** *(act with decision)* ein Machtwort sprechen; *(forbid, refuse)* es strikt verbieten; *(Aut)* Gas geben; **to put one's ~ in it** ins Fettnäpfchen treten *(col)*; **to put one's best ~ forward** *(hurry)* die Beine unter den Arm nehmen; *(do one's best)* sich anstrengen; **to find one's feet** sich eingewöhnen; **to fall on one's feet** auf die Füße fallen; **to have one ~ in the grave** mit einem Bein im Grab stehen; **to get/be under sb's feet** jdm in Weg sein; **to get off on the right/wrong ~** einen guten/ schlechten Start haben; **to stand on one's own feet** auf eigenen Füßen stehen.

**2** *vt bill* bezahlen.

**footage** ['futɪdʒ] *n* Filmmaterial *nt*.

**foot-and-mouth (disease)** [ˌfutən'mauθ(dɪˌziːz)] *n* Maul- und Klauenseuche *f*.

**football** ['futbɔːl] *n (also ball)* Fußball *m*; *(American ~)* Football *m*. **~ boot** Fußballschuh *m*; **~ pitch** Fußballplatz *m*; **~ player** Fußball(spiel)er *m*; *(US)* Football-Spieler *m*; **~ pools** Fußballtoto *nt*.

**footballer** ['futbɔːlər] *n* Fußball(spiel)er *m*.

**foot:** **~ brake** *n* Fußbremse *f*; **~bridge** *n* Fußgängerbrücke *f*; **~ fault** *n (Tennis)* Fußfehler *m*; **~hills** *npl* (Gebirgs)ausläufer *pl*; **~hold** *n* Halt *m*; *(fig)* sichere (Ausgangs)position.

**footing** ['futɪŋ] *n* **(a)** *(lit)* Halt *m*. **to lose one's ~** den Halt verlieren; **to miss one's ~** danebentreten. **(b)** *(fig)* Basis *f*; *(relationship)* Beziehung *f*. **on an equal ~ (with each other)** auf gleicher Basis.

**footlights** ['futlaɪts] *npl (Theat)* Rampenlicht *nt*.

**footling** ['fuːtlɪŋ] *adj* albern, läppisch.

**foot:** **~loose** *adj* **~loose and fancy-free** frei und ungebunden; **~man** *n* Lakai *m*; **~mark** *n* Fußabdruck *m*; **~note** *n* Fußnote *f*; **~path** *n* Fußweg *m*; *(Brit: pavement)* Bürgersteig *m*; **~print** *n* Fußabdruck *m*; **~prints** *npl* Fußspuren *pl*; **~rest** *n* Fußstütze *f*; **~sore** *adj* **to be ~sore** wunde Füße haben; **~step** *n* Schritt *m*; **to follow in sb's ~steps** *(fig)* in jds Fußstapfen treten; **~stool** *n* Schemel *m*; **~wear** *n* Schuhwerk *nt*; **~work** *n no pl (Boxing)* Beinarbeit *f*.

**for¹** [fɔːr] **1** *prep* **(a)** für. **what ~?** wofür?, wozu?; **what is this knife ~?** wozu dient dieses Messer?; **he does it ~ pleasure** er macht es zum Vergnügen; **what did you do that ~?** warum haben Sie das getan?; **a room ~ working in** ein Zimmer zum Arbeiten; **this will do ~ a hammer** das kann man als Hammer nehmen; **the train ~ Stuttgart** der Zug nach Stuttgart; **to leave ~ Germany** nach Deutschland abreisen; **he swam ~ the shore** er schwamm in Richtung Küste; **to make ~ home** sich auf den Heimweg machen; **to do sth ~ oneself** etw alleine tun; **you're ~ it!** *(col)* jetzt bist du dran! *(col)*; **oh ~ a cup of tea!** jetzt eine Tasse Tee, das wäre schön!

**(b)** *(indicating suitability)* **it's not ~ you to blame him** Sie haben kein Recht, ihm die Schuld zu geben; **it's not ~ me to say** es steht mir nicht zu, mich dazu zu äußern.

**(c)** *(representing, instead of)* **I'll see him ~ you if you like** wenn Sie wollen, gehe ich an Ihrer Stelle zu ihm; **to act ~ sb** für jdn handeln; **D ~ David** *(Telec)* D wie Dora.

**(d)** *(in defence, in favour of)* für. **are you ~ or against it?** sind Sie dafür oder dagegen?; **I'm all ~ it** ich bin ganz dafür.

**(e)** *(with regard to)* **anxious ~ sb** um jdn besorgt; **~ my part** was mich betrifft; **as ~ him/that** was ihn/das betrifft; **young ~ a president** jung für einen Präsidenten; **it's all right** *or* **all very well ~ you (to talk)** Sie haben gut reden.

**(f)** *(because of)* **~ this reason** aus diesem Grund; **he did it ~ fear of being left** er tat es aus Angst, zu-

rückgelassen zu werden; **he is famous ~ his big nose** er ist wegen seiner großen Nase berühmt; **to shout ~ joy** vor Freude jauchzen; **to go to prison ~ theft** wegen Diebstahl(s) ins Gefängnis wandern; **to choose sb ~ his ability** jdn wegen seiner Fähigkeiten wählen; **if it were not ~ him** wenn er nicht wäre; **do it ~ me** tu es für mich.

**(g)** *(in spite of)* trotz *(+gen or (col) +dat)*. **~ all his wealth** trotz all seines Reichtums; **~ all that** trotz allem.

**(h)** *(in contrast)* **~ one man who would do it there are ten who wouldn't** auf einen, der es tun würde, kommen zehn, die es nicht tun würden.

**(i)** *(in time)* seit; *(with future tense)* für. **I have not seen her ~ two years** ich habe sie seit zwei Jahren nicht gesehen; **he's been here ~ ten days** er ist seit zehn Tagen hier; **then I did not see her ~ two years** dann habe ich sie zwei Jahre lang nicht gesehen; **he walked ~ two hours** er ist zwei Stunden lang gewandert; **I am going away ~ a few days** ich werde (für) ein paar Tage wegfahren; **he won't be back ~ a week** er wird erst in einer Woche zurück sein; **can you get it done ~ Monday/this time next week?** können Sie es bis Montag/bis in einer Woche fertig haben?; **~ a while/time** (für) eine Weile/einige Zeit.

**(j)** *(distance)* **the road is lined with trees ~ two miles** die Straße ist auf zwei Meilen mit Bäumen gesäumt; **we walked ~ two miles** wir sind zwei Meilen weit gelaufen.

**(k)** *(with infin clauses)* **~ this to be possible** damit dies möglich wird/wurde; **I brought it ~ you to see** ich habe es mitgebracht, damit Sie es sich *(dat)* ansehen können; **the best would be ~ you to go** das beste wäre, wenn Sie weggingen; **their one hope is ~ him to return** ihre einzige Hoffnung ist, daß er zurückkommt.

**2** *conj* denn. **~ it was he who ...** denn er war es, der ...

**for²** ['efəʊɑːr] = **free on rail** frei Bahn.

**forage** ['fɒrɪdʒ] **1** *n* Futter *nt*. **2** *vi* nach Futter suchen; *(fig: rummage)* herumwühlen *(for* nach). **~-cap** Schiffchen *nt*.

**foray** ['fɒreɪ] *n* (Raub)überfall *m*; *(fig)* Exkurs *m (into* in *+acc)*.

**forbad** [fɔː'bæd], **forbade** [fɔː'beɪd] *pret of* **forbid**.

**forbearance** [fɔː'bɛərəns] *n* Nachsicht *f*.

**forbid** [fə'bɪd] *pret* **forbad(e)**, *ptp* **forbidden** [fə'bɪdn] *vt* verbieten. **to ~ sb to do sth** jdm verbieten, etw zu tun; **smoking ~den** Rauchen verboten; **it is ~den to ...** es ist verboten, zu ...

**forbidding** [fə'bɪdɪŋ] *adj rocks, cliffs* bedrohlich; *sky* düster; *prospect* grauenhaft; *look, person* streng.

**force** [fɔːs] **1** *n* **(a)** *no pl (physical strength, power)* Kraft *f*; *(of blow, of impact)* Wucht *f*; *(physical coercion)* Gewalt *f*. **to resort to ~** Gewalt anwenden; **by ~** gewaltsam; **a ~ 5 wind** Windstärke 5; **they came in ~** sie kamen in großer Zahl; **~s of Nature** Naturgewalten *pl*; **there are various ~s at work here** hier sind verschiedene Kräfte am Werk; **to come into/ be in ~** *(law etc)* in Kraft treten/sein. **(b)** *no pl (of argument)* Überzeugungskraft *f*; *(of music, phrase)* Eindringlichkeit *f*; *(of character)* Stärke *f*; *(of words, habit)* Macht *f*. **(c)** *(body of men)* **the ~s** *(Mil)* die Streitkräfte *pl*; **work ~** Arbeitskräfte *pl*; **sales ~** Verkaufspersonal *nt*; **the (police) ~** die Polizei; **to join** *or* **combine ~s** sich zusammentun.

**2** *vt* **(a)** *(compel)* zwingen. **to ~ sb/oneself to do sth** jdn/sich zwingen, etw zu tun; **he was ~d to resign** er wurde gezwungen zurückzutreten; *(felt obliged to)* er sah sich gezwungen zurückzutreten;

to ~ sth (up)on sb *present, one's company* jdm etw aufdrängen; *conditions* jdm etw auferlegen; *decision, war* jdm etw aufzwingen; **I don't want to ~ myself on you** ich möchte mich Ihnen nicht aufdrängen.

**(b)** *(break open) lock* aufbrechen. **to ~ an entry** sich *(dat)* gewaltsam Zutritt verschaffen.

**(c)** *(push, squeeze)* **to ~ books into a box** Bücher in eine Kiste zwängen; **if it won't go in, don't ~ it** versuche es nicht mit Gewalt, wenn es nicht hineinpaßt; **to ~ one's way through** sich gewaltsam einen Weg bahnen; **to ~ a car off the road** ein Auto von der Fahrbahn drängen.

**(d)** *surrender* erzwingen. **to ~ a smile** gezwungen lächeln; **to ~ a confession out of sb** ein Geständnis von jdm erzwingen.

▶**force back** *vt sep* zurückdrängen; *tear* unterdrücken.

▶**force down** *vt sep food* hinunterquälen; *aeroplane* zur Landung zwingen.

**forced** [fɔːst] *adj smile, translation* gezwungen. ~ **landing** Notlandung *f*; ~ **march** Gewaltmarsch *m*.

**force-feed** ['fɔːsfiːd] *vt* zwangsernähren.

**forceful** ['fɔːsfʊl] *adj person* energisch; *character* stark; *language, style* eindringlich; *argument* wirkungsvoll.

**forcefully** ['fɔːsfəlɪ] *adv* eindringlich.

**forcemeat** ['fɔːsmiːt] *n (Cook)* Fleischfüllung, Farce *f*.

**forceps** ['fɔːseps] *npl (also* **pair of** ~*)* Zange *f*. ~ **delivery** Zangengeburt *f*.

**forcible** ['fɔːsəbl] *adj* **(a)** *entry* gewaltsam. **(b)** *language, style* eindringlich; *argument, reason* zwingend.

**forcibly** ['fɔːsɪblɪ] *adv (by force)* mit Gewalt; *(vigorously)* eindringlich.

**ford** [fɔːd] **1** *n* Furt *f*. **2** *vt* durchqueren.

**fore** [fɔːr] **1** *n* **to the ~** im Vordergrund; **to come to the ~** ins Blickfeld geraten. **2** *adv (Naut)* ~ **and aft** längsschiffs.

**fore:** ~**arm** *n* Unterarm *m*; ~**bear** *n* Vorfahr(in *f*), Ahn(e *f*) *m*; ~**boding** [fɔː'bəudɪŋ] *n (presentiment)* (Vor)ahnung *f*; ~**cast 1** *vt* vorhersagen; **2** *n* Vorhersage *f*; ~**castle** ['fəuksl] *n (Naut)* Vorschiff *nt*; ~**close** *vi (on loan, mortgage)* ein Darlehen/eine Hypothek kündigen; **to ~close on sth** etw kündigen; ~**court** *n* Vorhof *m*; *(of garage)* Vorplatz *m*; ~**father** *n* Ahn, Vorfahr *m*; ~**finger** *n* Zeigefinger *m*; ~**front** *n* **in the ~ of** an der Spitze *(+gen)*; ~**go** *pret* ~**went**, *ptp* ~**gone** verzichten auf *(+acc)*; ~**going** *adj* vorhergehend; ~**gone 1** *ptp of* ~**go**; **2** *adj:* **it was a** ~**gone conclusion** es stand von vornherein fest; ~**ground** *n* Vordergrund *m*; **in the** ~**ground** im Vordergrund; ~**hand** *n (Sport)* Vorhand *f*; ~**head** ['fɔːhed, 'fɒrɪd] *n* Stirn *f*.

**foreign** ['fɒrən] *adj* ausländisch; *customs, appearance* fremdartig; *policy, trade* Außen-; *business* Auslands-. **is he ~?** ist er Ausländer?; ~ **countries** das Ausland; **lying is ~ to him** Lügen ist ihm fremd.

**foreign:** ~ **affairs** *npl* Außenpolitik *f*; **F~ and Commonwealth Office** *n (Brit)* Außenministerium *nt*; ~ **correspondent** *n* Auslandskorrespondent(in *f*) *m*; ~ **currency** *n* Devisen *pl*.

**foreigner** ['fɒrənər] *n* Ausländer(in *f*) *m*.

**foreign:** ~ **exchange** *n* Devisen *pl*; ~ **exchange market** *n* Devisenmarkt *m*; ~ **investment** *n* Auslandsinvestition *f*; ~ **language** *n* Fremdsprache *f*; ~ **legion** *n* Fremdenlegion *f*; **F~ Minister** *n* Außenminister *m*; **F~ Office** *n (Brit)* Außenministerium *nt*; **F~ Secretary** *n (Brit)* Außenminister *m*;

**F~ Service** *n (Brit)* diplomatischer Dienst.

**fore:** ~ **leg** *n* Vorderbein *nt*; ~**man** [-mən] *n, pl* ~**men** [-mən] *(in factory)* Vorarbeiter *m*; *(on building site)* Polier *m*; *(Jur: of jury)* Obmann *m*; ~**most** *adj (lit)* erste(r, s), vorderste(r, s); *(fig) writer, politician etc* führend; ~**name** *n* Vorname *m*.

**forensic** [fə'rensɪk] *adj* forensisch. ~ **science** Kriminaltechnik *f*; ~ **medicine** Gerichtsmedizin *f*; ~ **expert** Spurensicherungsexperte *m*.

**fore:** ~**play** *n* Vorspiel *nt*; ~**runner** *n* Vorläufer *m*; ~**see** *pret* ~**saw**, *ptp* ~**seen** *vt* vorhersehen; ~**seeable** *adj* voraussehbar; **in the** ~**seeable future** in absehbarer Zeit; ~**shadow** *vt* ahnen lassen, andeuten; ~ **shore** *n* Küstenvorland *nt*; *(beach)* Strand *m*; ~**shorten** *vt* perspektivisch verkürzen; **this has a** ~**shortening effect** das läßt es kürzer erscheinen; ~**sight** *n* Weitblick *m*; ~**skin** *n* Vorhaut *f*.

**forest** ['fɒrɪst] *n* Wald *m*. ~ **ranger** *(US)* Förster *m*.

**forestall** [fɔː'stɔːl] *vt sb, rival* zuvorkommen *(+dat)*; *objection* vorwegnehmen.

**forester** ['fɒrɪstər] *n* Förster *m*.

**forestry** ['fɒrɪstrɪ] *n* Forstwirtschaft *f*.

**fore:** ~**taste** *n* Vorgeschmack *m*; ~**tell** *pret, ptp* ~**told** *vt* vorhersagen; ~**thought** *n* Vorbedacht *m*.

**forever** [fər'evər] *adv* **(a)** *(constantly)* ständig, ewig *(col)*. **(b)** *(eternally)* ewig.

**fore:** ~**warn** *vt* vorher warnen; ~**warned is forearmed** *(Prov)* Gefahr erkannt, Gefahr gebannt *(prov)*; ~**went** *pret of* ~**go**; ~**woman** *n, pl* ~**women** Vorarbeiterin *f*; ~**word** *n* Vorwort *nt*.

**forfeit** ['fɔːfɪt] **1** *vt (esp Jur)* verwirken; *(fig) health, sb's respect* einbüßen. **2** *n (in game)* Pfand *nt*.

**forgave** [fə'geɪv] *pret of* **forgive**.

**forge** [fɔːdʒ] **1** *n (workshop)* Schmiede *f*; *(furnace)* Esse *f*. **2** *vt* **(a)** *metal, (fig) friendship* schmieden. **(b)** *signature, banknote* fälschen. **3** *vi* **to ~ ahead** vorwärtskommen; *(in one's career)* seinen Weg machen; *(Sport)* vorstoßen.

**forger** ['fɔːdʒər] *n* Fälscher(in *f*) *m*.

**forgery** ['fɔːdʒərɪ] *n (act, thing)* Fälschung *f*.

**forget** [fə'get] *pret* **forgot**, *ptp* **forgotten 1** *vt* vergessen; *ability, language* verlernen. **never to be forgotten** unvergeßlich; **and don't you ~ it!** und daß du das ja nicht vergißt!; **I ~ his name** sein Name ist mir entfallen; **I ~ what I wanted to say** ich weiß nicht mehr, was ich sagen wollte; **to ~ past quarrels** vergangene Streitigkeiten ruhen lassen; ~ **it!** schon gut!; **you might as well ~ it** *(col)* das kannst du vergessen *(col)*. **2** *vi* es vergessen. **don't ~!** vergiß es nicht!

▶**forget about** *vi +prep obj* vergessen.

**forgetful** [fə'getfʊl] *adj (absent-minded)* vergeßlich; *(of one's duties etc)* nachlässig *(of gegenüber)*.

**forgetfulness** [fə'getfʊlnɪs] *n* Vergeßlichkeit *f*.

**forget-me-not** [fə'getmɪnɒt] *n* Vergißmeinnicht *nt*.

**forgettable** [fə'getəbl] *adj* **that's really ~** das kann man getrost vergessen.

**forgivable** [fə'gɪvəbl] *adj* verzeihlich.

**forgive** [fə'gɪv] *pret* **forgave**, *ptp* **forgiven** [fə'gɪvn] *vti* vergeben, verzeihen *(esp Eccl)*. **to ~ sb for sth** jdm etw verzeihen *or* vergeben; **to ~ sb for doing sth** jdm verzeihen *or* vergeben, daß er/sie etw getan hat; ~ **me, but ...** Entschuldigung, aber ...

**forgiveness** [fə'gɪvnɪs] *n, no pl (willingness to forgive)* Versöhnlichkeit *f*. **to ask/beg (sb's)** ~ (jdn) um Verzeihung *or* Vergebung *(esp Eccl)* bitten.

**forgiving** [fə'gɪvɪŋ] *adj* versöhnlich.

**forgot** [fə'gɒt] *pret of* **forget**.

**forgotten** [fə'gɒtn] *ptp of* **forget**.

**fork** [fɔːk] **1** n (implement) Gabel f; (in road) Gabelung f. **2** vi (roads, branches) sich gabeln. **to ~ right** (road) nach rechts abzweigen; (driver) nach rechts abbiegen.
►**fork out** vti sep (col: pay) blechen (col).

**forked** [fɔːkt] adj branch, road, tail gegabelt; lightning zickzackförmig; tongue gespalten.

**fork-lift truck** [,fɔːklɪft'trʌk] n Gabelstapler m.

**forlorn** [fə'lɔːn] adj (deserted) verlassen; person einsam und verlassen; attempt verzweifelt; hope schwach.

**form** [fɔːm] **1** n (a) Form f. **~ of government** Regierungsform f; **a human ~** eine menschliche Gestalt; **in the ~ of** in Form von or +gen; (with reference to people) in Gestalt von or +gen; **to be in fine/good ~** gut in Form sein, in guter Form sein; **to be on/off ~** in/nicht in Form sein; **he was in great ~ that evening** er war an dem Abend in Hochform; **on past ~** auf dem Papier. **(b)** no pl (etiquette) **he did it for ~'s sake** er tat es der Form halber; **it's bad ~** so etwas tut man einfach nicht; **what's the ~?** (col) was ist üblich? **(c)** (questionnaire, document) Formular nt. **application ~** Bewerbungsbogen m. **(d)** (esp Brit: bench) Bank f. **(e)** (Brit Sch) Klasse f.
**2** vt **(a)** (shape, mould) object, character formen (into zu). **(b)** (develop) liking entwickeln; friendship schließen; opinion sich (dat) bilden; impression gewinnen; plan entwerfen. **(c)** (constitute, make up) part, basis, government, circle, queue, (Gram) bilden; company gründen.
**3** vi (take shape) Gestalt annehmen.

**formal** ['fɔːməl] adj **(a)** formell; reception, welcome feierlich; education, training offiziell. **~ dance/dress** Gesellschaftstanz m/-kleidung f. **(b)** (in form) distinction etc formal.

**formality** [fɔː'mælɪtɪ] n **(a)** no pl (of person, dress etc) Förmlichkeit f. **(b)** (matter of form) Formalität f. **it's a mere ~** es ist (eine) reine Formsache.

**formalize** ['fɔːməlaɪz] vt rules, grammar formalisieren; agreement, relationship formell machen.

**formally** ['fɔːməlɪ] adv **(a)** formell; welcome feierlich; educate, train offiziell. **to be ~ dressed** Gesellschaftskleidung tragen. **(b)** (in form) different, alike formal.

**format** ['fɔːmæt] **1** n (as regards size) Format nt; (as regards content) Aufmachung f; (Rad, TV: of programme) Struktur f. **2** vt (Comp) text formatieren.

**formation** [fɔː'meɪʃən] n **(a)** (act of forming, of character) Formung f; (of government, committee; Gram) Bildung f; (of company, society) Gründung f. **(b)** (of aircraft, dances) Formation f.

**formative** ['fɔːmətɪv] adj formend. **it had a ~ influence on him** es hat ihn entscheidend geprägt; **~ years** Entwicklungsjahre pl.

**former** ['fɔːmə'] **1** adj **(a)** früher, ehemalig. **in a ~ life** in einem früheren Leben; **in ~ times/days** früher. **(b)** (first-mentioned) erstere(r, s). **2** n **the ~** der/die/das erstere.

**formerly** ['fɔːməlɪ] adv früher.

**form feed** n (Comp) Papiervorschub m.

**formica** ® [fɔː'maɪkə] n ≈ Resopal ® nt.

**formidable** ['fɔːmɪdəbl] adj person, rock-face furchterregend; opponent gefährlich; obstacles, debts, problems, task gewaltig, enorm; piece of work beeindruckend.

**formula** ['fɔːmjʊlə] n, pl **-s** or **-e** ['fɔːmjuliː] Formel f; (for lotion, medicine, soap powder) Rezeptur f. **F~ One** (Sport) Formel Eins; **all his books use the same ~** alle seine Bücher sind nach demselben Rezept geschrieben.

**formulate** ['fɔːmjʊleɪt] vt formulieren.

**fornicate** ['fɔːnɪkeɪt] vi Unzucht treiben.

**forsake** [fə'seɪk] pret **forsook** [fə'sʊk], ptp **forsaken** [fə'seɪkn] vt verlassen; bad habits aufgeben.

**fort** [fɔːt] n (Mil) Fort nt. **to hold the ~** (fig) die Stellung halten.

**forte** ['fɔːtɪ] n (strong point) Stärke f.

**forth** [fɔːθ] adv **to set ~** (liter) ausziehen (liter); **from this day ~** (liter) von diesem Tag an; **and so ~** und so weiter.

**forthcoming** [,fɔːθ'kʌmɪŋ] adj **(a)** event bevorstehend; book in Kürze erscheinend; film, play in Kürze anlaufend. **(b) to be ~** (money) kommen; (help) erfolgen. **(c)** (esp Brit: informative) mitteilsam (about ... was ... betrifft).

**forthright** ['fɔːθraɪt] adj offen.

**forthwith** [,fɔːθ'wɪθ] adv (form) umgehend.

**fortieth** ['fɔːtɪɪθ] adj vierzigste(r, s); see **sixtieth**.

**fortification** [,fɔːtɪfɪ'keɪʃən] n **(a)** (act) (Mil) Befestigung f; (of food, drink) Stärkung f. **(b)** (often pl: Mil) Festungsanlagen pl.

**fortify** ['fɔːtɪfaɪ] vt (Mil) town befestigen; (food, drink) stärken. **fortified wine** süßer, starker Wein.

**fortitude** ['fɔːtɪtjuːd] n (innere) Stärke f.

**fortnight** ['fɔːtnaɪt] n (Brit) vierzehn Tage.

**fortnightly** ['fɔːtnaɪtlɪ] (Brit) **1** adj vierzehntägig. **2** adv alle vierzehn Tage.

**FORTRAN** ['fɔːtræn] (Comp) = **formula translator** FORTRAN nt.

**fortress** ['fɔːtrɪs] n Festung f.

**fortuitous** [fɔː'tjuːɪtəs] adj zufällig.

**fortunate** ['fɔːtʃənɪt] adj glücklich. **to be ~** (person) Glück haben; **it was ~ that** ... es war ein Glück, daß ...

**fortunately** ['fɔːtʃənɪtlɪ] adv zum Glück, glücklicherweise.

**fortune** ['fɔːtʃuːn] n **(a)** (fate) Geschick nt; (chance) Zufall m. **he had the good ~ to have rich parents** er hatte das Glück, reiche Eltern zu haben; **by good ~** glücklicherweise. **(b)** (money) Vermögen nt. **to make a ~** ein Vermögen erwerben; **it costs a ~** es kostet ein Vermögen.

**fortune: ~ hunter** n Mitgiftjäger m; **~-teller** n Wahrsager(in f) m; **~-telling** n Wahrsagerei f.

**forty** ['fɔːtɪ] **1** adj vierzig. **to have ~ winks** (col) ein Nickerchen machen (col). **2** n Vierzig f; see **sixty**.

**forum** ['fɔːrəm] n Forum nt.

**forward** ['fɔːwəd] **1** adv (also **~s**) (ahead) vorwärts; (to the front) nach vorn. **please step ~** bitte vortreten; **backward(s) and ~(s)** hin und her; **from this time ~** (from then) seitdem; (from now) von jetzt an. **2** adj **(a)** (in place) vordere(r, s); (in direction) Vorwärts-. **this seat is too far ~** dieser Sitz ist zu weit vorn. **(b)** (planning) Voraus-; (Comm) buying, selling Termin-. **good ~ thinking!** gut vorausgedacht! **(c)** (presumptuous, pert) dreist; (precocious) frühreif. **3** n (Sport) Stürmer m. **4** vt **(a)** (advance) plans vorantreiben. **(b)** (dispatch) goods senden; (send on) letter nachsenden; (to another office etc) weiterleiten. **please ~** bitte nachsenden.

**forwarding** ['fɔːwədɪŋ]: **~ address** n Nachsendeadresse f; **~ agent** n Spediteur m.

**forward-looking** ['fɔːwədlʊkɪŋ] adj person fortschrittlich, progressiv; plan vorausblickend.

**forwards** ['fɔːwədz] adv = **forward 1**.

**fossil** ['fɒsl] n Fossil nt. **~ fuels** fossile Brennstoffe pl.

**fossilized** ['fɒsɪlaɪzd] adj versteinert; (fig) customs verkrustet.

**foster** ['fɒstə'] **1** vt **(a)** child (parents) in Pflege nehmen; (authorities: ~ out) in Pflege geben (with bei). **(b)** (encourage, promote) fördern. **2** adj attr Pflege-.

~ **mother/father/parents/child** Pflegemutter *f*/Pflegevater *m*/Pflegeeltern *pl*/Pflegekind *nt*.

**fought** [fɔːt] *pret, ptp of* **fight**.

**foul** [faʊl] **1** *adj* (+*er*) *smell* übel; *water* faulig; *air* schlecht; *food* verdorben; *(horrible) day, weather, mood* ekelhaft; *person, behaviour* gemein, fies *(col)*; *language* unflätig. **a lot of ~ play** *(Sport)* eine Menge Fouls; **the police suspect ~ play** es besteht Verdacht auf einen unnatürlichen Tod; **to fall ~ of sb/the law** mit jdm/dem Gesetz in Konflikt geraten. **2** *n (Sport)* Foul *nt*. **3** *vt* **(a)** *(pollute) air* verpesten; *(dog) pavement* verunreinigen. **(b)** *(get in the way) mechanism* blockieren; *(entangle) fishing line* verheddern; *(seaweed etc) propeller* sich verheddern in (+*dat*). **(c)** *also vi (Sport)* foulen.

**foul-: ~-mouthed** *adj* unflätig; **~-smelling** *adj* übelriechend; **~-tempered** *adj* äußerst übellaunig.

**found¹** [faʊnd] *pret, ptp of* **find**.

**found²** *vt* **(a)** *(set up)* gründen. **(b) to ~ sth on sth** *opinion, belief* etw auf etw (*dat*) gründen; **to be ~ed on sth** auf etw (*dat*) basieren.

**foundation** [faʊnˈdeɪʃən] *n* **(a)** *(of business, colony)* Gründung *f*. **(b)** *(institution)* Stiftung *f*. **(c) ~s** *pl (of house etc)* Fundament *nt*; *(of road)* Unterbau *m*; *(fig: basis)* Grundlage *f*. **it has no ~ in fact** es beruht nicht auf Tatsachen.

**foundation: ~ cream** *n* Grundierungscreme *f*; **~ garment** *n* Mieder *nt*; **~ stone** *n* Grundstein *m*.

**founder¹** [ˈfaʊndər] *n (of school etc)* Gründer(in *f*) *m*; *(of charity, museum)* Stifter(in *f*) *m*.

**founder²** *vi (ship)* sinken; *(fig: project)* scheitern.

**founding** [ˈfaʊndɪŋ]: **F~ Fathers** *npl (US)* Väter *pl*; **~ member** *n* Mitbegründer(in *f*) *m*.

**foundry** [ˈfaʊndrɪ] *n* Gießerei *f*.

**fount** [faʊnt] *n* **(a)** *(lit liter, fig)* Quelle *f*. **(b)** *(Typ)* Schrift *f*.

**fountain** [ˈfaʊntɪn] *n* Brunnen *m*; *(with upward jets)* Springbrunnen *m*; *(fig: source)* Quelle *f*.

**fountain-pen** [ˈfaʊntɪnˌpen] *n* Füllfederhalter, Füller *m*.

**four** [fɔːr] **1** *adj* vier. **2** *n* Vier *f*. **on all ~s** auf allen vieren; *see* **six**.

**four: ~-door** *attr* viertürig; **~-footed** *adj* vierfüßig; **~-leaf clover** *n* vierblättriges Kleeblatt; **~-letter word** *n* Vulgärausdruck *m*; **~-poster (bed)** *n* Himmelbett *nt*; **~some** *n* Quartett *nt*; *(Sport)* Viererspiel *nt*; **to go out in a ~some** zu viert ausgehen; **~-star (petrol)** *n (Brit)* Super(benzin) *nt*; **~-stroke** *adj engine* Viertakt-.

**fourteen** [ˈfɔːˈtiːn] **1** *adj* vierzehn. **2** *n* Vierzehn *f*.

**fourteenth** [ˈfɔːˈtiːnθ] *adj* vierzehnte(r, s); *see* **sixteenth**.

**fourth** [fɔːθ] **1** *adj* vierte(r, s). **2** *n (fraction)* Viertel *nt*; *(in series)* Vierte(r, s). **to drive in ~** im vierten Gang fahren; *see* **sixth**.

**four-wheel drive** [ˈfɔːwiːlˈdraɪv] *n* Allradantrieb *m*.

**fowl** [faʊl] *n (poultry)* Geflügel *nt*; *(one bird)* Huhn *nt*; Gans *f etc*.

**fox** [fɒks] **1** *n (lit, fig)* Fuchs *m*. **2** *vt (deceive)* täuschen; *(bewilder)* verblüffen.

**fox: ~ cub** *n* Fuchsjunge(s) *nt*, Fuchswelpe *m*; **~glove** *n (Bot)* Fingerhut *m*; **~-hunting** *n* Fuchsjagd *f*; **~ terrier** *n* Foxterrier *m*; **~trot** *n* Foxtrott *m*.

**foxy** [ˈfɒksɪ] *adj* (+*er*) listig, pfiffig. **~ lady** *(US col)* scharfe Frau *(col)*.

**foyer** [ˈfɔɪeɪ] *n (in theatre)* Foyer *nt*; *(in hotel, esp US: in apartment house)* Eingangshalle *f*.

**fr** = **franc** fr.

**Fr** = **(a) Father. (b) Friar.**

**fracas** [ˈfrækɑː] *n* Aufruhr, Tumult *m*.

**fraction** [ˈfrækʃən] *n (Math)* Bruch *m*; *(fig)* Bruchteil *m*. **a ~ better/shorter** (um) eine Spur besser/kürzer; **for a ~ of a second** einen Augenblick lang; **it missed me by a ~ of an inch** es verfehlte mich um Haaresbreite.

**fractional** *adj*, **~ly** *adv* [ˈfrækʃnl, -əlɪ] *(fig)* geringfügig.

**fractious** [ˈfrækʃəs] *adj* verdrießlich.

**fracture** [ˈfræktʃər] **1** *n* Bruch *m*. **2** *vti* brechen. **he ~d his shoulder** er hat sich (*dat*) die Schulter gebrochen; **~d skull** Schädelbruch *m*.

**fragile** [ˈfrædʒaɪl] *adj china, glass, relationship* zerbrechlich; *material, plant* zart; *(with age)* brüchig; *(fig) person (in health)* gebrechlich; *health* anfällig; *ego* labil. **he's feeling a bit ~ this morning** *(col)* er fühlt sich heute morgen ein bißchen angeschlagen.

**fragment** [ˈfrægmənt] **1** *n* **(a)** Bruchstück *nt*; *(of china, glass)* Scherbe *f*; *(of paper, letter)* Schnipsel *m*; *(of programme etc)* kleiner Teil. **~s of conversation** Gesprächsfetzen *pl*. **(b)** *(esp Liter, Mus: unfinished work)* Fragment *nt*. **2** [frægˈment] *vi (rock, glass)* (zer)brechen.

**fragmentary** [ˈfrægməntərɪ] *adj (lit, fig)* fragmentarisch.

**fragmented** [frægˈmentɪd] *adj* bruchstückhaft; *(broken up)* unzusammenhängend.

**fragrance** [ˈfreɪgrəns] *n* Duft *m*.

**fragrant** [ˈfreɪgrənt] *adj* duftend. **~ smell** Duft *m*.

**frail** [freɪl] *adj* (+*er*) zart; *(infirm)* gebrechlich; *health* anfällig; *(fig) hope* schwach.

**frailty** [ˈfreɪltɪ] *n see adj* Zartheit *f*; Gebrechlichkeit *f*; Anfälligkeit *f*; Schwäche *f*.

**frame** [freɪm] **1** *n (basic structure, of picture, window, door, bicycle)* Rahmen *m*; *(of building, of ship)* Gerippe *nt*; *(of spectacles: also ~s)* Gestell *nt*; *(of human, animal)* Gestalt *f*; *(Film, Phot)* (Einzel)bild *nt*. **his massive ~** sein massiver Körper; **~ of mind** *(mental state)* Verfassung *f*; *(mood)* Stimmung *f*; **~ of reference** Bezugssystem *nt*. **2** *vt* **(a)** *picture* rahmen; *(fig) face etc* umrahmen. **(b)** *law, plan* entwerfen; *idea* entwickeln; *(express) answer, excuse* formulieren; *sentence* bilden. **(c) he's been ~ed** *(col)* die Sache wurde ihm angehängt *(col)*.

**frame: ~house** *n* Holzhaus *nt*; **~-up** *n (col)* Komplott *nt*; **~work** *n (lit)* Grundgerüst *nt*; *(fig) (of novel etc also)* Gerippe *nt*; *(of society, state etc)* Gefüge *nt*; **within the ~work of ...** im Rahmen (+*gen*) ...; **outside the ~work of ...** außerhalb des Rahmens (+ *gen*) ...

**franc** [fræŋk] *n (French)* Franc *m*; *(Swiss)* Franken *m*.

**France** [frɑːns] *n* Frankreich *nt*.

**franchise** [ˈfræntʃaɪz] *n* **(a)** *(Pol)* Wahlrecht *nt*. **(b)** *(Comm)* Lizenz *f*. **~ system** Franchise-System *nt*.

**Francis** [ˈfrɑːnsɪs] *n* Franz *m*. **St ~ (of Assisi)** der heilige Franziskus (von Assisi).

**Franco-** [ˈfræŋkəʊ-] *in cpds* französisch-. **the ~-Prussian War** der Deutsch-Französische Krieg.

**Franconia** [fræŋˈkəʊnɪə] *n* Franken *nt*.

**frank¹** [fræŋk] *adj* (+*er*) offen *(with* zu*)*. **to be (perfectly) ~** ehrlich gesagt.

**frank²** *vt letter* frankieren; *(postmark, cancel) stamp, letter* stempeln.

**frankfurter** [ˈfræŋkˌfɜːtər] *n* Frankfurter (Würstchen *nt*) *f*.

**frankincense** [ˈfræŋkɪnsens] *n* Weihrauch *m*.

**franking machine** [ˈfræŋkɪŋməˈʃiːn] *n* Frankiermaschine *f*.

**frankly** [ˈfræŋklɪ] *adv* offen; *(to tell the truth)* ehrlich gesagt.

**frankness** [ˈfræŋknɪs] *n* Offenheit *f*.

**frantic** ['fræntɪk] *adj effort, cry, scream* verzweifelt; *activity* fiebrig; *desire* übersteigert; *person* außer sich *(with* vor *+dat)*. **to drive sb ~** jdn zur Verzweiflung treiben.

**frantically** ['fræntɪkəlɪ] *adv try, scream* verzweifelt; *gesticulate, rush around* (wie) wild; *(col: terribly)* furchtbar. **~ in love** rasend verliebt *(col)*.

**fraternal** [frə'tɜ:nl] *adj* brüderlich.

**fraternity** [frə'tɜ:nɪtɪ] *n* **(a)** *no pl* Brüderlichkeit *f*. **(b)** *(community)* Vereinigung *f*; *(US Univ)* Verbindung *f*. **the legal/medical ~** die Juristen *pl*/Mediziner *pl*.

**fraternization** [‚frætənaɪ'zeɪʃən] *n* (freundschaftlicher) Umgang, *(Mil also)* Fraternisieren *nt*.

**fraternize** ['frætənaɪz] *vi* freundschaftlichen Umgang haben, *(Mil also)* fraternisieren.

**fraud** [frɔ:d] *n* Betrug *m*; *(person)* Betrüger(in *f*) *m*; *(thing)* (reiner) Schwindel. **~ squad** Betrugsdezernat *nt*.

**fraudulent** ['frɔ:djʊlənt] *adj* betrügerisch.

**fraught** [frɔ:t] *adj* geladen *(with* mit*)*; *(col: atmosphere)* gespannt. **~ with danger** gefahrvoll.

**fray¹** [freɪ] *n* Schlägerei *f*; *(Mil)* Kampf *m*. **ready for the ~** *(lit, fig)* kampfbereit.

**fray²** **1** *vt cloth* ausfransen; *cuff, rope* durchscheuern. **my nerves are ~ed** ich bin mit den Nerven herunter *(col)*; **tempers were ~ed** die Gemüter waren erhitzt. **2** *vi (cloth)* (aus)fransen; *(cuff, trouser turn-up, rope)* sich durchscheuern.

**FRCM** *(Brit)* = **Fellow of the Royal College of Music.**

**FRCS** *(Brit)* = **Fellow of the Royal College of Surgeons.**

**freak** [fri:k] **1** *n (plant)* Mißbildung *f*; *(person, animal also)* Mißgeburt *f*; *(event)* außergewöhnlicher Zufall; *(snowstorm etc)* Anomalie *f*; *(col: weird person)* komischer Vogel *(col)*; *(col: freaked-out person)* Ausgeflippte(r) *mf (col)*. **~ of nature** Laune *f* der Natur; **movie ~** *(col)* Kinofan *m*; **health ~** *(col)* Gesundheitsapostel *m* *(col)*. **2** *adj weather, conditions* anormal; *(Statistics) values* extrem; *victory* Überraschungs-.
▶**freak out** *vi (col)* ausflippen *(col)*; *(of society)* aussteigen.

**freakish** ['fri:kɪʃ] *adj* **(a)** *see* **freak 2. (b)** *(changeable) weather* launisch; *person* ausgeflippt *(col)*; *hairstyle, idea* verrückt *(col)*.

**freaky** ['fri:kɪ] *adj (+er) (col)* verrückt *(col)*; *(freaked out)* ausgeflippt *(col)*.

**freckle** ['frekl] *n* Sommersprosse *f*.

**freckled** ['frekld] *adj* sommersprossig.

**Frederick** ['fredrɪk] *n* Friederich *m*.

**free** [fri:] **1** *adj (+er)* **(a)** frei. **to set sb/an animal ~** jdn/ein Tier freilassen; **he is ~ to go** es steht ihm frei zu gehen; **you're ~ to choose** die Wahl steht Ihnen frei; **you're ~ to refuse** Sie können auch ablehnen; **I'm not ~ to do it** es steht mir nicht frei, es zu tun; **feel ~!** *(col)* bitte, gerne!; **feel ~ to go when you like** Sie dürfen gehen, wann Sie wollen; **to give sb a ~ hand** jdm freie Hand lassen; **are you ~ tonight?** hast du heute abend Zeit?; **am I ~ to speak here?** kann ich hier unbesorgt reden?; **he left one end of the string ~** er ließ ein Ende des Bindfadens lose; **~ from pain/worry** schmerzfrei/sorgenfrei; **~ from blame/responsibility** frei von Schuld/Verantwortung; **~ of sth** frei von etw.
**(b)** *(costing nothing)* kostenlos, *(Comm)* gratis. **it's ~** das kostet nichts; **admission ~** Eintritt frei; **to get sth ~** etw umsonst bekommen; **we got in ~ or for ~** *(col)* wir kamen umsonst rein; **~ sample** Gratisprobe *f*; **~ on board** *(Comm)* frei Schiff.

**(c)** *(lavish)* großzügig; *language, behaviour* ungezwungen; *(over-familiar)* plump-vertraulich.
**2** *vt prisoner (release)* freilassen; *(help escape)* befreien; *nation* befreien; *(untie) person* losbinden; *pipe* freimachen. **to ~ oneself from sth** sich von etw frei machen.

**freebie** ['fri:bi:] *n (col)* Werbegeschenk *nt*.

**free collective bargaining** *n* Tarifautonomie *f*.

**freedom** ['fri:dəm] *n* Freiheit *f*. **~ of speech** Redefreiheit *f*; **~ of the press** Pressefreiheit *f*; **the ~ of the city** die (Ehren)bürgerrechte *pl*; **to give sb the ~ of one's house** jdm sein Haus zur freien Verfügung stellen.

**freedom fighter** *n* Freiheitskämpfer(in *f*) *m*.

**free:** **~ enterprise** *n* freies Unternehmertum; **~ fall** *n* freier fall; **F~fone** ® *n* call **F~fone 0800** rufen Sie gebührenfrei 0800 an; **~-for-all** *n* Gerangel *nt (col)*; *(fight)* Schlägerei *f*; **~ gift** *n (Comm)* Werbegeschenk *nt*; **~hold** *n* **to own sth ~hold** etw besitzen; **~hold property** *n* (freier) Grundbesitz; **~ house** *n (Brit)* Wirtshaus *nt, das nicht an eine bestimmte Brauerei gebunden ist*; **~ kick** *n (Sport)* Freistoß *m*; **~lance 1** *n* Freiberufler(in *f*) *m*; *(with particular firm)* freier Mitarbeiter, freie Mitarbeiterin; **2** *adj* frei(schaffend); **3** *adv* freiberuflich; **4** *vi* freiberuflich tätig sein; *(with particular firm)* als freier Mitarbeiter/freie Mitarbeiterin tätig sein; **~load** *vi (esp US col)* schmarotzen *(col) (on* bei*)*. **~loader** *n (col)* Schmarotzer(in *f*) *m (col)*.

**freely** ['fri:lɪ] *adv* frei; *give* großzügig. **I ~ admit ...** ich gebe offen zu ...

**free:** **~mason** *n* Freimaurer *m*; **F~post** ® *n (Brit Post)* ≃ „Gebühr zahlt Empfänger"; **~-range** *adj (Brit) chicken* Farmhof-; *hen* freilaufend; *eggs* von freilaufenden Hühnern.

**freesia** ['fri:zɪə] *n (Bot)* Freesie *f*.

**free:** **~ sample** *n* Gratisprobe *f*; **~ speech** *n* Redefreiheit *f*; **~style** *n* Kür *f*; *(Swimming)* Freistil *m*; **~-trade** *n* Freihandel *m*; **~way** *n (US)* Autobahn *f*; **~wheel** *vi* im Freilauf fahren; **~wheeling** *adj discussion* offen; **~ will** *n (Philos)* freier Wille; **he did it of his own ~ will** er hat es aus freien Stücken getan.

**freeze** [fri:z] *(vb: pret* **froze,** *ptp* **frozen)* **1** *vi* **(a)** *(Met)* frieren; *(water)* gefrieren; *(rivers)* zufrieren; *(pipes)* einfrieren. **I'm/my hands are freezing** mir ist/meine Hände sind eiskalt; **to ~ to death** *(lit)* erfrieren; *(fig)* sich zu Tode frieren. **(b)** *(blood)* gefrieren; *(smile)* erstarren. **(c)** *(keep still)* **he froze in his tracks** er blieb wie angewurzelt stehen; **~!** keine Bewegung! **2** *vt water* gefrieren; *food, wages* einfrieren; *assets* festlegen; *(stop) film* anhalten. **3** *n (Met)* Frost *m*. **a wages ~** ein Lohnstopp *m*.
▶**freeze out** *vt sep (col)* rausekeln *(col)*.
▶**freeze over** *vi (lake)* überfrieren; *(windows)* vereisen.
▶**freeze up** *vi* zufrieren; *(lock also, pipes)* einfrieren; *(windows)* vereisen.

**freeze:** **~-dried** *adj* gefriergetrocknet; **~ frame** *n (TV)* Standbild *nt*.

**freezer** ['fri:zər] *n* Tiefkühltruhe *f*; *(upright)* Gefrierschrank *m*. **~ compartment** Gefrierfach *nt*.

**freezing** ['fri:zɪŋ] **1** *adj* eiskalt. **2** *n* **below ~** unter dem Gefrierpunkt; **~ point** Gefrierpunkt *m*.

**freight** [freɪt] **1** *n* Fracht *f*. **2** *vt (transport)* verfrachten.

**freight:** **~car** *n (US Rail)* Güterwagen *m*; **~ depot** *n (Rail)* Güterbahnhof *m*.

**freighter** ['freɪtər] *n (Naut)* Frachter *m*; *(Aviat)* Frachtflugzeug *nt*.

**freight:** **~ plane** *n* Frachtflugzeug *nt*; **~ train** *n*

Güterzug *m.*

**French** [frentʃ] **1** *adj* französisch. **2** *n* **(a)** **the** ~ *pl* die Franzosen *pl.* **(b)** *(language)* Französisch *nt*; *see* **English.**

**French:** ~ **bean** *n* grüne Bohne; ~ **bread** *n* Stangenbrot *nt*; ~-**Canadian 1** *adj* frankokanadisch; **2** *n* Frankokanadier(in *f*) *m*; ~ **dressing** *n* Vinaigrette *f*; ~ **fries** *npl (esp US)* Pommes frites *pl*; ~ **Guiana** *n* Französisch-Guayana *nt*; ~ **horn** *n (Mus)* (Wald)horn *nt*; ~ **letter** *n (Brit col)* Pariser *m (col)*; ~**man** *n* Franzose *m*; ~ **polish 1** *n* Möbelpolitur *f* mit Schellack; **2** *vt* lackieren; ~ **window(s** *pl***)** *n* Verandatür *f*; ~**woman** *n* Französin *f.*

**frenetic** [frəˈnetɪk] *adj* frenetisch, rasend.

**frenzied** [ˈfrenzɪd] *adj* wahnsinnig; *applause, activity* rasend.

**frenzy** [ˈfrenzɪ] *n* Raserei *f.* **in a** ~ in heller Aufregung.

**frequency** [ˈfriːkwənsɪ] *n* Häufigkeit *f*; *(Phys)* Frequenz *f.* **high/low** ~ Hoch-/Niederfrequenz *f*; ~ **band** Frequenzband *nt.*

**frequent** [ˈfriːkwənt] **1** *adj* häufig. **he's a** ~ **visitor to our house** er kommt uns oft besuchen. **2** [friˈkwent] *vt* oft besuchen.

**frequently** [ˈfriːkwəntlɪ] *adv* oft, häufig.

**fresco** [ˈfreskəʊ] *n* Fresko(gemälde) *nt.*

**fresh** [freʃ] **1** *adj* (+er) **(a)** *food, breeze* frisch. **it's still** ~ **in my memory** es ist mir noch frisch in Erinnerung; ~ **water** *(not salt)* Süßwasser *nt*; **in the** ~ **air** an der frischen Luft. **(b)** *(new) supplies, sheet of paper, ideas, approach, courage* neu. **to make a** ~ **start** einen neuen Anfang machen. **(c)** *(esp US: cheeky)* **don't get** ~ **(with me)!** werd nicht frech! **2** *adv* (+er) *baked, picked* frisch. ~ **from the oven** frisch aus dem Ofen; ~ **out of college** frisch von der Schule; **to come** ~ **to sth** neu zu etw kommen.

**freshen** [ˈfreʃn] *vi (wind)* auffrischen.

▶**freshen up** *vir (person)* sich frischmachen.

**fresher** [ˈfreʃəʳ] *n (Brit Univ col)* Erstsemester *nt.*

**freshly** [ˈfreʃlɪ] *adv* frisch.

**freshman** [ˈfreʃmən] *n, pl* -**men** [-mən] *(US)* = **fresher.**

**freshness** [ˈfreʃnɪs] *n see adj* **(a)** Frische *f.* **(b)** Neuheit *f.* **(c)** Frechheit *f.*

**freshwater** [ˈfreʃwɔːtəʳ] *adj attr* Süßwasser-.

**fret¹** [fret] *vi* sich *(dat)* Sorgen machen. **don't** ~ beruhige dich; **the child is** ~**ting for his mother** das Kind jammert nach seiner Mutter.

**fret²** *n (on guitar etc)* Bund *m.*

**fretful** [ˈfretfʊl] *adj child* quengelig.

**fret:** ~**saw** *n* Laubsäge *f*; ~**work** *n (in wood)* Laubsägearbeit *f.*

**Freudian** [ˈfrɔɪdɪən] *adj (Psych, fig)* Freudsch *attr.* ~ **slip** Freudscher Versprecher.

**FRG** = **Federal Republic of Germany** BRD *f.*

**Fri** = **Friday** Fr.

**friar** [ˈfraɪəʳ] *n* Mönch *m.*

**fricassee** [ˈfrɪkəseɪ] *n* Frikassee *nt.*

**friction** [ˈfrɪkʃən] **(a)** Reibung *f.* ~ **tape** *(US)* Isolierband *nt.* **(b)** *(fig)* Reibereien *pl.*

**Friday** [ˈfraɪdɪ] *n* Freitag *m*; *see* **Tuesday.**

**fridge** [frɪdʒ] *n (Brit)* Kühlschrank *m.*

**fridge-freezer** [ˈfrɪdʒˈfriːzəʳ] *n* Kühl- und Gefrierkombination *f.*

**fried** [fraɪd] *adj* gebraten; *potatoes, chicken* Brat-. ~ **egg** Spiegelei *nt.*

**friend** [frend] *n* Freund(in *f*) *m*; *(less intimate)* Bekannte(r) *mf.* **to make** ~**s with sb** sich mit jdm anfreunden; **to be** ~**s with sb** mit jdm befreundet sein; **we're just (good)** ~**s** wir sind nur gut befreun-

det; **Society of F**~**s** Quäker *pl.*

**friendliness** [ˈfrendlɪnɪs] *n see adj* Freundlichkeit *f*; Freundschaftlichkeit *f.*

**friendly** [ˈfrendlɪ] **1** *adj* (+er) *person, smile, welcome* freundlich; *advice, feelings* freundschaftlich; *game, match* Freundschafts-. **to be** ~ **to sb** zu jdm freundlich sein; **to be** ~ **with sb** mit jdm befreundet sein; **friendly fire** *(Mil)* Beschuß *m* durch die eigene Seite. **2** *n (Sport)* Freundschaftsspiel *nt.*

**friendship** [ˈfrendʃɪp] *n* Freundschaft *f.*

**Friesian** [ˈfriːʒən] **1** *adj* friesisch; *cattle* holsteinfriesisch. **2** *n (person)* Friese *m*, Friesin *f*; *(bull/ cow)* Holstein-Friese *m*/-Friesin *f.*

**frieze** [friːz] *n (picture)* Fries *m*; *(thin band)* Zierstreifen *m.*

**frigate** [ˈfrɪgɪt] *n (Naut)* Fregatte *f.*

**fright** [fraɪt] *n* Schreck(en) *m.* **to get a** ~ einen Schreck bekommen; **to give sb a** ~ jdm einen Schreck(en) einjagen; **to take** ~ es mit der Angst zu tun bekommen; **she looks a** ~ *(col)* sie sieht verboten aus *(col).*

**frighten** [ˈfraɪtn] *vt* Angst machen (+dat); *(give a sudden fright)* erschrecken.

▶**frighten away** *or* **off** *vt sep* abschrecken; *(deliberately)* verscheuchen.

**frightened** [ˈfraɪtnd] *adj* verängstigt; *voice* angsterfüllt. **to be** ~ **of sth** vor etw *(dat)* Angst haben; **to be** ~ **of doing sth** Angst davor haben, etw zu tun; **I was** ~ **out of my wits/to death** ich war zu Tode erschrocken.

**frightening** [ˈfraɪtnɪŋ] *adj* furchterregend.

**frightful** *adj*, ~**ly** *adv* [ˈfraɪtfʊl, -fəlɪ] furchtbar.

**frigid** [ˈfrɪdʒɪd] *adj manner, welcome* kühl; *(Physiol, Psych)* frigid(e).

**frigidity** [frɪˈdʒɪdɪtɪ] *n* Kühle *f*; *(Physiol, Psych)* Frigidität *f.*

**frill** [frɪl] *n (on dress, shirt etc)* Rüsche *f.* **with all the** ~**s** mit allem Drum und Dran *(col).*

**frilly** [ˈfrɪlɪ] *adj* (+er) mit Rüschen, Rüschen-.

**fringe** [frɪndʒ] *n (on shawl)* Fransen *pl*; *(Brit: hair)* Pony *m*; *(fig: periphery)* Rand *m.* **on the** ~**(s) of society** am Rande der Gesellschaft.

**fringe:** ~ **benefits** *npl* zusätzliche Leistungen *pl*; ~ **group** *n* Randgruppe *f*; ~ **theatre** avantgardistisches Theater.

**frisk** [frɪsk] **1** *vi (leap about)* umhertollen. **2** *vt suspect etc* durchsuchen.

**frisky** [ˈfrɪskɪ] *adj* (+er) verspielt.

**fritter¹** [ˈfrɪtəʳ] *vt (also* ~ **away)** *money, time* verzetteln, verplempern *(col).*

**fritter²** *n (Cook)* Schmalzgebackene(s) *nt no pl* mit Füllung.

**frivolity** [frɪˈvɒlɪtɪ] *n* Frivolität *f.*

**frivolous** [ˈfrɪvələs] *adj* frivol; *person, life, remark* leichtfertig.

**frizz(l)y** [ˈfrɪz(l)ɪ] *adj* (+er) *hair* kraus.

**fro** [frəʊ] *adv see* **to 4, to-ing and fro-ing.**

**frock** [frɒk] *n* Kleid *nt*; *(of monk)* Kutte *f.*

**frog** [frɒg] *n* **(a)** Frosch *m.* **to have a** ~ **in one's throat** einen Frosch im Hals haben. **(b)** **F**~ *(Brit pej col: French person)* Franzose *m*, Französin *f.*

**frog:** ~**man** *n* Froschmann *m*; ~**march** *vt (Brit)* (weg)schleifen; *(carry)* zu viert wegtragen; **they** ~**marched him in** sie schleppten ihn herein *(col)*; ~ **spawn** *n* Froschlaich *m.*

**frolic** [ˈfrɒlɪk] *vi (vb: pret, ptp* ~**ked** *(also* ~ **about** *or* **around)** umhertoben.

**from** [frɒm] *prep* **(a)** *(indicating starting place)* von (+dat); *(indicating place of origin)* aus (+dat). **where has he come** ~ **today?** von wo ist er heute gekommen?; **where is he** ~? woher kommt er?; **he comes**

~ **York** er kommt aus York; ~ **London to Edinburgh** von London nach Edinburgh; ~ **house to house** von Haus zu Haus.

**(b)** *(indicating time) (in past)* seit *(+dat)*; *(in future)* ab *(+dat)*, von *(+dat)* ... an. ~ **now on** von jetzt an; **as** ~ **May 6th** vom 6. Mai an.

**(c)** *(indicating distance)* von *(+dat)* *(... weg)*; *(from town etc also)* von *(+dat)* ... entfernt. **the house is 10 km** ~ **the coast** das Haus ist 10 km von der Küste entfernt; **to go away** ~ **home** von zu Haus weggehen.

**(d)** *(indicating origin)* von *(+dat)*; *(out of)* aus *(+dat)*. **tell him** ~ **me** ... richten Sie ihm von mir aus, ...; **an invitation** ~ **the Smiths** eine Einladung von den Smiths; **"~ ..."** *(on envelope, parcel)* „Absender ...", „Abs. ..."; **where did you get that** ~? wo hast du das her?; **I got it** ~ **the library/Gloria** ich habe es aus der Bibliothek/von Gloria; **to drink** ~ **a stream/glass** aus einem Bach/Glas trinken; **a quotation** ~ **Shakespeare** ein Zitat nach Shakespeare; **translated** ~ **the English** aus dem Englischen übersetzt; **painted** ~ **life** nach dem Leben gemalt.

**(e)** *(indicating lowest amount)* ab *(+dat)*. ~ **£2 (upwards)** ab £2; **dresses (ranging)** ~ **£20 to £30** Kleider zwischen £20 und £30; **there were** ~ **10 to 15 people there** es waren zwischen 10 und 15 Personen da.

**(f)** *(indicating change)* **things went** ~ **bad to worse** es wurde immer schlimmer; **he went** ~ **office boy to director** er stieg vom Laufjungen zum Direktor auf; **a price increase** ~ **1 mark to 1 mark 50** eine Preiserhöhung von 1 DM auf 1,50 DM.

**(g)** *(indicating difference)* **he is quite different** ~ **the others** er ist ganz anders als die anderen; **to tell black** ~ **white** Schwarz und Weiß auseinanderhalten.

**(h)** *(because of, due to)* **to act** ~ **conviction** aus Überzeugung handeln; **to die** ~ **fatigue** an Erschöpfung sterben; **weak** ~ **hunger** schwach vor Hunger; ~ **experience** aus Erfahrung; ~ **what I heard** nach dem, was ich gehört habe; ~ **what I can see** ... nach dem, was ich sehen kann, ...; ~ **the look of things** ... (so) wie die Sache aussieht, ...

**(i)** *(+prep)* ~ **above** *or* **over sth** über etw *(acc)* hinweg; ~ **beneath** *or* **underneath sth** unter etw *(dat)* hervor; ~ **out of sth** aus etw heraus; ~ **among the trees** zwischen den Bäumen hervor; ~ **inside/outside the house** von drinnen/draußen.

**front** [frʌnt] **1** *n* **(a)** Vorderseite *f*; *(forward part)* Vorderteil *nt*. **in** ~ vorne; *(in line, race etc also)* an der Spitze; **in** ~ **of sb/sth** vor jdm/etw; **at the** ~ **of** *(inside)* vorne in *(+dat)*; *(outside)* vor *(+dat)*; *(at the head of)* an der Spitze *(+gen)*; **to be in** ~ vorne sein; *(Sport)* vorn(e) liegen; **in** *or* **at the** ~ **of the class** vorne im Klassenzimmer. **(b)** *(Mil, Pol, Met)* Front *f*. **they were attacked on all** ~s *(Mil)* sie wurden an allen Fronten angegriffen; *(fig)* sie wurden von allen Seiten angegriffen; **cold** ~ *(Met)* Kalt(luft)front *f*; **we must present a united** ~ wir müssen eine geschlossene Front bilden. **(c)** *(Brit: at sea)* Strandpromenade *f*. **(d)** *(outward appearance)* Fassade *f*. **to put on a bold** ~ eine tapfere Miene zur Schau stellen; **it's just a** ~ das ist nur Fassade; **the fruit shop was just a** ~ das Obstgeschäft diente nur zur Tarnung.

**2** *vi* **the house/windows** ~ **onto the street** die Häuser liegen/die Fenster gehen auf die Straße hinaus.

**3** *adj* vorderste(r, s); *row, page also* erste(r, s); *tooth, wheel, view* Vorder-. ~ **seat** Platz *m* in der ersten Reihe; *(Aut)* Vordersitz *m*.

**frontage** ['frʌntɪdʒ] *n (of building)* Front *f*.

**frontal** ['frʌntl] *adj (Mil)* Frontal-. ~ **view** Vorderansicht *f*.

**front:** ~ **bench** *n (Parl)* vorderste *or* erste Reihe *(wo die führenden Politiker sitzen)*; ~ **desk** *n (US)* Rezeption *f*; ~ **door** *n* Haustür *f*; ~ **garden** *n* Vorgarten *m*.

**frontier** ['frʌntɪəʳ] *n (lit, fig)* Grenze *f*.

**frontispiece** ['frʌntɪspiːs] *n* Titelseite *f*; *(illustration)* Bildseite *f*.

**front:** ~ **line** *n* Front(linie) *f*; ~-**line** *adj troops* Front-; *(fig) management etc* in vorderster Front; ~ **man** *n* Mann *m* an der Spitze; *(pej)* Strohmann *m*; ~ **page** *n* Titelseite *f*; ~-**page** *adj news* auf der ersten Seite; ~ **room** *n* Vorderzimmer *nt*; *(Brit: sitting room)* Wohnzimmer *nt*; ~-**runner** *n (fig)* Spitzenreiter, Favorit *m*; ~-**wheel drive** *n (Aut)* Vorderradantrieb *m*.

**frost** [frɒst] **1** *n* Frost *m*; *(on leaves etc)* Rauhreif *m*. **ten degrees of** ~ zehn Grad Kälte. **2** *vt (esp US) cake* glasieren.

**frost:** ~**bite** *n* Frostbeulen *pl*; *(more serious)* Erfrierungen *pl*; ~**bitten** *adj hands, feet* erfroren; ~ **damage** *n* Frostschaden *m*.

**frosted** ['frɒstɪd] *adj* **(a)** ~ **glass** Mattglas *nt*; *(textured)* geriffeltes Glas. **(b)** *(esp US) cake* mit Zuckerguß überzogen, glasiert.

**frosting** ['frɒstɪŋ] *n (esp US: icing)* Zuckerguß *m*.

**frosty** ['frɒstɪ] *adj (+er) (lit, fig)* frostig.

**froth** [frɒθ] **1** *n (on liquids, Med)* Schaum *m*. **2** *vi* schäumen. **the dog was** ~**ing at the mouth** der Hund hatte Schaum vor dem Maul.

**frothy** ['frɒθɪ] *adj* schäumend; *cream* schaumig.

**frown** [fraʊn] **1** *n* Stirnrunzeln *nt no pl*. **to give a** ~ die Stirn(e) runzeln; **angry** ~ finsterer Blick; **worried/puzzled** ~ sorgenvoller/verdutzter Gesichtsausdruck. **2** *vi (lit, fig)* die Stirn(e) runzeln *(at über +acc)*. **to** ~ **at sb** jdn finster ansehen.

►**frown (up)on** *vi +prep obj (fig) suggestion, idea* mißbilligen.

**froze** [frəʊz] *pret of* **freeze**.

**frozen** ['frəʊzn] **1** *ptp of* **freeze**. **2** *adj river* zugefroren. **I'm absolutely** ~ **stiff** ich bin völlig erfroren; ~ **foods** Tiefkühlkost *f*; ~ **peas** gefrorene Erbsen *pl*.

**FRS** = **(a)** *(Brit)* **Fellow of the Royal Society. (b)** *(US)* **Federal Reserve System.**

**frugal** ['fruːgəl] *adj person* sparsam; *meal* einfach.

**fruit** [fruːt] *n (as collective)* Obst *nt*; *(Bot)* Frucht *f*. **what is your favourite** ~? welches Obst magst du am liebsten?; **to bear** ~ *(lit, fig)* Früchte tragen; **the** ~**(s) of my labour** die Früchte *pl* meiner Arbeit.

**fruiterer** ['fruːtərəʳ] *n (esp Brit)* Obsthändler(in *f*) *m*.

**fruitful** ['fruːtfʊl] *adj (lit, fig)* fruchtbar.

**fruition** [fruːˈɪʃən] *n* **to come to** ~ sich verwirklichen.

**fruit:** ~ **juice** *n* Fruchtsaft *m*; ~ **knife** *n* Obstmesser *nt*.

**fruitless** ['fruːtlɪs] *adj (fig)* fruchtlos.

**fruit:** ~ **machine** *n (Brit)* Spielautomat *m*; ~ **salad** *n* Obstsalat *m*; ~ **tree** *n* Obstbaum *m*.

**fruity** ['fruːtɪ] *adj (+er) (like fruit)* fruchtartig; *taste, wine* fruchtig; *voice* rauchig; *(col: salacious) remark, story* saftig *(col)*.

**frump** [frʌmp] *n (pej)* Vogelscheuche *f (col)*.

**frustrate** [frʌˈstreɪt] *vt hopes* zunichte machen; *plans, plot* durchkreuzen; *person* frustrieren.

**frustrated** [frʌˈstreɪtɪd] *adj person* frustriert.

**frustrating** [frʌˈstreɪtɪŋ] *adj* frustrierend.

**frustration** [frʌˈstreɪʃən] *n* Frustration *f no pl*; *(of hopes, plans, plot)* Zerschlagung *f*.

**fry**[1] [fraɪ] *npl* **small** ~ *(unimportant people)* kleine Fische *pl (col)*.

**fry²** *vt* (in der Pfanne) braten; *see* **fried**.

**frying pan** ['fraɪɪŋ,pæn] *n* Bratpfanne *f*. **(to jump) out of the ~ into the fire** *(prov)* vom Regen in die Traufe (kommen) *(prov)*.

**fry:** **~pan** *n (US)* = **frying pan**; **~-up** *n* Pfannengericht *nt*.

**ft** = **foot** ft; **feet** ft.

**FT** *(Brit)* = **Financial Times** *Wirtschaftstageszeitung f*.

**fuchsia** ['fjuːʃə] *n* Fuchsie *f*.

**fuck** [fʌk] *(col!!)* **1** *vt* **(a)** *(lit)* ficken *(col!!)*. **(b)** **~ you!** leck mich am Arsch *(col!!)*. **2** *interj* (verdammte) Scheiße *(col!)*.
   ►**fuck off** *vi (col!!)* ~ ~! verpiß dich! *(col!!)*.

**fucking** ['fʌkɪŋ] *adj (col!!)* Scheiß- *(col!)*.

**fuddled** ['fʌdld] *adj (muddled)* verwirrt; *(tipsy)* beschwipst.

**fuddy-duddy** ['fʌdɪ,dʌdɪ] *n (col)* alter Kauz *(col)*, Fossil *nt*.

**fudge** [fʌdʒ] **1** *n (Cook)* ≃ Karamel *m*. **2** *vt (fake) story etc* (frei) erfinden; *(dodge) issue* ausweichen *(+dat)*.

**fuel** [fjuəl] **1** *n* Brennstoff *m*; *(for vehicle)* Kraftstoff *m*; *(petrol)* Benzin *nt*; *(Aviat, Space)* Treibstoff *m*. **to add ~ to the flames** *(fig)* Öl ins Feuer gießen. **2** *vt stove, furnace etc (fill)* mit Brennstoff versorgen; *(drive, propel)* antreiben.

**fuel:** **~ cell** *n* Brennstoffzelle *f*; **~ consumption** *n* Kraftstoffverbrauch *m*; **~ gauge** *n* Tankuhr *f*; **~ injection** *n* (Benzin)einspritzung *f*; **engine with ~ injection** Einspritzmotor *m*; **~ oil** *n* Gasöl *nt*; **~ pump** *n* Benzinpumpe *f*; **~ rod** *n* Brennstab *m*; **~ tank** *n* Tank *m*; *(for oil)* Öltank *m*.

**fug** [fʌg] *n (esp Brit col)* Mief *m (col)*.

**fugitive** ['fjuːdʒɪtɪv] **1** *n* Flüchtling *m*. **he is a ~ from the law** er ist auf der Flucht vor dem Gesetz. **2** *adj* flüchtig.

**fugue** [fjuːg] *n (Mus)* Fuge *f*.

**fulfil,** *(US)* **fulfill** [fʊl'fɪl] *vt* erfüllen; *promise* halten. **to be ~led** *(wish etc)* sich erfüllen; **to feel ~led** sich ausgefüllt fühlen; *(in job etc)* Erfüllung finden.

**fulfilment,** *(US)* **fulfillment** [fʊl'fɪlmənt] *n* Erfüllung *f*.

**full** [fʊl] **1** *adj (+er)* voll; *description, report* vollständig; *understanding, sympathy* vollste(r, s); *figure* füllig; *skirt* weit. **~ of ...** voller *(+gen)* ...; **he's ~ of good ideas** er steckt voll(er) guter Ideen; **a look ~ of hate** ein haßerfüllter Blick; **I am ~ (up)** *(col)* ich bin voll bis obenhin *(col)*; **we are ~ up for July** wir sind für Juli völlig ausgebucht; **for the ~er figure** für vollschlanke Damen; **at ~ speed** in voller Fahrt; **to fall ~ length** der Länge nach hinfallen; **roses in ~ bloom** Rosen in voller Blüte; **I waited two ~ hours** ich habe zwei ganze Stunden gewartet; **the ~ particulars** die genauen Einzelheiten; **~ employment** Vollbeschäftigung *f*; **~ house** *(Theat)* ausverkauftes Haus; **~ marks** *(Sch)* die beste Note, ≃ eine Eins; **~ member** Vollmitglied *nt*; **~ name** Vor- und Zuname *m*; **to be ~ of oneself** von sich (selbst) eingenommen sein; **she was ~ of it** sie hat gar nicht mehr aufgehört, davon zu reden; **the papers were ~ of it for weeks** die Zeitungen waren wochenlang voll davon.

   **2** *adv* **it is a ~ five miles from here** es sind volle fünf Meilen von hier; **I know ~ well that ...** ich weiß sehr wohl, daß ...; **to hit sb ~ in the face** jdn voll ins Gesicht schlagen.

   **3** *n* **in ~** vollständig; **to write one's name in ~** seinen Namen ausschreiben; **to pay in ~** den vollen Betrag bezahlen; **to the ~** vollständig.

**full:** **~-back** *n (Sport)* Verteidiger *m*; **~ beam** *n*

*(Aut)* Fernlicht *nt*; **~-blooded** [,fʊl'blʌdɪd] *adj (vigorous)* kräftig; **~-blown** *adj (fig) doctor, theory* richtiggehend; **~-bodied** *adj wine* vollmundig; **~-cream milk** *n* Vollmilch *f*; **~-face helmet** *n* Integralhelm *m*; **~-fledged** *adj (US)* = **fully-fledged**; **~-grown** *adj* ausgewachsen; **~-length** *adj portrait* lebensgroß; *film* abendfüllend; **~ moon** *n* Vollmond *m*.

**fullness** ['fʊlnɪs] *n (of detail)* Vollständigkeit *f*; *(of skirt)* Weite *f*; *(of sound)* Fülle *f*. **in the ~ of time** *(eventually)* zu gegebener Zeit; *(at predestined time)* als die Zeit gekommen war.

**full:** **~-page** *adj* ganzseitig; **~-scale** *adj drawing* in Originalgröße; *operation, search* großangelegt; *revision* umfassend; *attack* General-; **~ stop** *n* Punkt *m*; **to come to a ~ stop** zum völligen Stillstand kommen; **~-time 1** *adv work* ganztags; **2** *adj employment* Ganztags-.

**fully** [fʊlɪ] *adv* völlig; *equipped* vollständig; *dressed* fertig. **it's ~ two years ago** es ist gut zwei Jahre her; **I ~ expected that ...** ich habe fest damit gerechnet, daß ...

**fully:** **~-fledged** *adj bird* flügge; *(fig: qualified)* richtiggehend; **~-qualified** *adj* vollqualifiziert *attr*.

**fulsome** ['fʊlsəm] *adj praise* übertrieben.

**fumble** ['fʌmbl] **1** *vi (also ~ about)* umhertasten. **to ~ in the dark** im Dunkeln herumtasten; **to ~ in one's pockets** in seinen Taschen wühlen; **to ~ with sth** an etw *(dat)* herumfummeln. **2** *vt* verpfuschen *(col)*. **to ~ the ball** den Ball nicht sicher fangen.

**fume** [fjuːm] **1** *vi (liquids)* dampfen; *(fig col: person)* kochen *(col)*. **2** *npl* **~s** Dämpfe *pl*; *(of car)* Abgase *pl*.

**fumigate** ['fjuːmɪgeɪt] *vt* ausräuchern.

**fun** [fʌn] **1** *n* Spaß *m*. **for** *or* **in ~ *(as a joke)*** als Scherz; **it's ~** es macht Spaß; **it's no ~** es macht keinen Spaß; **we just did it for ~ *or* for the ~ of it** wir haben das nur zum Spaß gemacht; **to spoil the ~** den Spaß verderben; **he's good ~** er ist ganz lustig; **have ~!** viel Spaß!; **that should be ~ and games** das kann ja (noch) heiter werden *(col)*; **there'll be the usual ~ and games** *(iro: trouble/fuss)* es wird die üblichen Scherereien *(col)*/das übliche Theater *(col)* geben; **to make ~ of** *or* **poke ~ at sb/sth** sich über jdn/etw lustig machen. **2** *adj attr (col)* lustig. **~ run** Volkslauf *m*.

**function** ['fʌŋkʃən] **1** *n* **(a)** *(purpose, Math)* Funktion *f*. **~ key** *(Comp)* Funktionstaste *f*; **in his ~ as judge** in seiner Eigenschaft als Richter. **(b)** *(reception)* Empfang *m*; *(official ceremony)* Feier *f*. **2** *vi* funktionieren. **to ~ as** fungieren als; *(thing also)* dienen als.

**functional** ['fʌŋkʃənəl] *adj* funktionell; *(able to operate)* funktionsfähig.

**fund** [fʌnd] **1** *n* **(a)** *(Fin)* Fonds *m*. **~s** *pl* Mittel *pl*; **I'm short of ~s,** **my ~s are low** ich bin knapp bei Kasse *(col)*. **(b)** *(of wisdom, humour etc)* Schatz *(of* von*)*, Vorrat *(of an +dat)* *m*. **2** *vt scheme, project* finanzieren.

**fundamental** [,fʌndə'mentl] **1** *adj (basic)* grundlegend; *indifference, problem* grundsätzlich. **to be ~ to sth** für etw von grundlegender Bedeutung sein; **our ~ needs/beliefs** unsere Grundbedürfnisse *pl*/Grundüberzeugungen *pl*. **2** *n usu pl* Grundlage *f*.

**fundamentalist** [,fʌndə'mentəlɪst] *n* Fundamentalist(in *f*) *m*.

**fundamentally** [,fʌndə'mentəlɪ] *adv* grundlegend; *(in essence)* im Grunde; *(in principle)* grundsätzlich.

**fund:** **~-raiser** *n* Spendenbeschaffer(in *f*) *m*; **~-raising** *n* Geldbeschaffung *f*.

**funeral** ['fjuːnərəl] *n* Beerdigung *f*. **well that's your ~**

*(col)* na ja, das ist dein Problem *(col)*.

**funeral:** ~ **director** *n* Beerdigungsunternehmer *m*; ~ **parlour** *n* Leichenhalle *f*; ~ **procession** *n* Leichenzug *m*; ~ **service** *n* Trauergottesdienst *m*, Trauerfeier *f*.

**funereal** [fjuː'nɪərɪəl] *adj voice, expression* trübselig, Trauer-. ~ **pace** Kriechtempo *nt*.

**funfair** ['fʌnfɛəʳ] *n (Brit)* Kirmes *f*.

**fungus** ['fʌŋgəs] *n, pl* **fungi** ['fʌŋgaɪ] Pilz *m*.

**funicular (railway)** [fjuː'nɪkjʊlə('reɪlweɪ)] *n* Seilbahn *f*.

**funk** [fʌŋk] **1** *n* **to be in a (blue)** ~ *(col)* ganz schön Bammel haben *(col)*. **2** *vt* kneifen vor *(+dat) (col)*.

**funnel** ['fʌnl] *n (for pouring)* Trichter *m*; *(Naut, Rail)* Schornstein *m*.

**funnily** ['fʌnɪlɪ] *adv* komisch. ~ **enough** komischerweise.

**funny** ['fʌnɪ] *adj (+er)* **(a)** *(comic)* komisch. **are you being** ~**?** das soll wohl ein Witz sein?; **it's not** ~ das ist *or* das finde ich überhaupt nicht komisch. **(b)** *(strange)* seltsam, komisch. **it's a** ~ **thing, only last week** ... (das ist doch) komisch, erst letzte Woche ...; **to get** ~ **with sb** *(col)* jdm dumm kommen *(col)*; ~ **business** *(col)* faule Sache *(col)*; **no** ~ **business** *or* **tricks!** *(col)* keine faulen Tricks! *(col)*; ~ **money** *(col)* ein Wahnsinnsgeld *nt (col)*; **I felt all** ~ *(col)* mir war ganz komisch; ~ **bone** *n* Musikantenknochen *m*.

**fur** [fɜːʳ] **1** *n (on animal)* Fell *nt*; *(for clothing)* Pelz *m*; *(in kettle)* Kesselstein *m*. **2** *attr coat, stole* Pelz-. ~ **hat** Pelzmütze *f*.

**furious** ['fjʊərɪəs] *adj person* wütend; *struggle* wild; *speed* rasend. **to be** ~ **with sb** auf jdn wütend sein.

**furiously** ['fjʊərɪəslɪ] *adv* wütend; *fight* wild; *work, drive, pedal* wie wild *(col)*.

**furl** [fɜːl] *vt sail, flag* einrollen.

**furlong** ['fɜːlɒŋ] *n* Achtelmeile *f*.

**furnace** ['fɜːnɪs] *n* Hochofen *m*; *(Metal)* Schmelzofen *m*.

**furnish** ['fɜːnɪʃ] *vt* **(a)** *house* einrichten. ~**ed room** möbliertes Zimmer; ~**ing fabrics** Dekorationsstoffe *pl*. **(b)** *information, reason, excuse* liefern. **to** ~ **sb with sth** jdm mit etw versorgen.

**furnishings** ['fɜːnɪʃɪŋz] *npl* Mobiliar *nt*; *(with carpets etc)* Einrichtung *f*.

**furniture** ['fɜːnɪtʃəʳ] *n* Möbel *pl*. **a piece of** ~ ein Möbelstück *nt*; **he's part of the** ~ *(fig col)* er gehört zum Inventar.

**furniture:** ~ **polish** *n* Möbelpolitur *f*; ~ **van** *n* Möbelwagen *m*.

**furore** [fjʊə'rɔːrɪ], *(US)* **furor** ['fjʊrɔːʳ] *n* Protest(e *pl) m*. **to cause a** ~ einen Skandal verursachen.

**furrier** ['fʌrɪəʳ] *n* Kürschner(in *f) m*.

**furrow** ['fʌrəʊ] **1** *n (Agr)* Furche *f*; *(on brow)* Runzel *f*. **2** *vt brow* runzeln. ~**ed brow** zerfurchte Stirn.

**furry** ['fɜːrɪ] *adj (+er) animal* Pelz-; *toy* Plüsch-; *tongue* belegt.

**further** ['fɜːðəʳ] **1** *adv, comp of* **far (a)** *(in place, time, fig)* weiter. ~ **on** weiter entfernt; ~ **back** *(in place, time)* weiter zurück; *(in time)* früher; **nothing is** ~ **from my thoughts** nichts liegt mir ferner. **(b)** *(more)* **he didn't question me** ~ er hat mich nichts weiter gefragt; **until you hear** ~ bis auf weiteres; **and** ~ ... und darüber hinaus ...; ~ **to your letter of** ... *(Comm)* in bezug auf Ihren Brief vom ... *(form)*. **2** *adj* **(a)** see **farther. (b)** *(additional)* weiter. **until** ~ **notice** bis auf weiteres; ~ **particulars** nähere Einzelheiten *pl*; ~ **education** Fortbildung *f*; *(at university)*

Hochschulausbildung *f*. **3** *vt one's interests, a cause* fördern.

**furtherance** ['fɜːðərəns] *n* Förderung *f*.

**furthermore** ['fɜːðəmɔːʳ] *adv* außerdem.

**furthermost** ['fɜːðəməʊst] *adj* äußerste(r, s).

**furthest** ['fɜːðɪst] **1** *adv* **the** ~ **north you can go** soweit nach Norden wie möglich. **2** *adj* am weitesten entfernt. **5 km at the** ~ höchstens 5km.

**furtive** ['fɜːtɪv] *adj action* heimlich; *behaviour, person* heimlichtuerisch; *look* verstohlen.

**furtively** ['fɜːtɪvlɪ] *adv* verstohlen; *behave* verdächtig.

**fury** ['fjʊərɪ] *n (of person)* Wut *f*; *(of storm)* Ungestüm *nt*. **she flew into a** ~ sie kam in Rage; **like** ~ *(col)* wie verrückt *(col)*.

**fuse,** *(US)* **fuze** [fjuːz] **1** *vt* **(a)** *metals* verschmelzen. **(b)** *(Brit Elec)* **to** ~ **the lights** die Sicherung für die Lampen durchbrennen lassen. **2** *vi* **(a)** *(metals)* sich verbinden; *(fig)* verschmelzen. **(b)** *(Brit Elec)* durchbrennen. **the lights** ~**d** die Sicherung für die Lampen war durchgebrannt. **3** *n (Elec)* Sicherung *f*; *(Brit Elec: act of fusing)* Kurzschluß *m*; *(in bombs)* Zündschnur *f*. **she's got** *or* **she's on a short** ~ *(fig col)* ihr brennt leicht die Sicherung durch *(col)*.

**fuse box** *n* Sicherungskasten *m*.

**fused** [fjuːzd] *adj plug etc* gesichert.

**fuselage** ['fjuːzəlɑːʒ] *n* (Flugzeug)rumpf *m*.

**fuse wire** *n* Schmelzdraht *m*.

**fusillade** [ˌfjuːzɪ'leɪd] *n* Salve *f*.

**fusion** ['fjuːʒən] *n (of metal, fig)* Verschmelzung *f*; *(Phys: also* **nuclear** ~*)* (Kern)fusion *f*.

**fuss** [fʌs] **1** *n* Theater *nt (col)*; *(bother)* Umstände *pl (col)*, Aufheben(s) *nt*. **don't go to a lot of** ~ mach dir keine Umstände; **to make a** ~, **to kick up a** ~ Krach schlagen *(col)*; **to make a** ~ **about** *or* **over sth** viel Aufhebens um etw machen; **to make a** ~ **of sb** *(spoil)* VIP, *guest* viel Wirbel um jdn machen *(col)*; *children* jdn verwöhnen; **a lot of** ~ **about nothing** viel Lärm um nichts. **2** *vi (do unnötig)* aufregen; *(get into a* ~*)* sich *(dat)* Umstände *pl* machen. **3** *vt person* nervös machen; *(pester)* keine Ruhe lassen *(+dat)*.

▶**fuss about** *vi* herumfuhrwerken *(col)*.

▶**fuss over** *vi +prep obj* sich *(dat)* große Umstände machen mit.

**fussy** ['fʌsɪ] *adj (+er) (fastidious)* heikel, pingelig *(col)*; *(choosy)* wählerisch; *(elaborate) dress, pattern* verspielt. **what do you want to do? — I'm not** ~ was willst du machen? — ist mir egal.

**futile** ['fjuːtaɪl] *adj* sinnlos.

**futility** [fjuː'tɪlɪtɪ] *n* Sinnlosigkeit *f*.

**futon** ['fuːtɒn] *n* Futon *m*.

**future** ['fjuːtʃəʳ] **1** *n* **(a)** Zukunft *f*. **in the near** ~ bald; **there's no** ~ **in it** das hat keine Zukunft. **(b)** *(St Ex)* ~**s** Termingeschäfte *pl*. **2** *adj* (zu)künftig. **at some** ~ **date** zu einem späteren Zeitpunkt; **the** ~ **tense** *(Gram)* das Futur, die Zukunft.

**futuristic** [ˌfjuːtʃə'rɪstɪk] *adj* futuristisch.

**fuze** *n (US)* = **fuse**.

**fuzz** [fʌz] *n* **(a)** *(fluff)* Flaum *m*. **(b) the** ~ *(col)* die Polypen *pl (col)*.

**fuzzy** ['fʌzɪ] *adj (+er)* **(a)** *hair* kraus. **(b)** *(col) picture, sound, memory* verschwommen.

**FWD** *(Aut)* = **front-wheel drive.**

**fwd** = **forward.**

**f.w.d.** *(Aut)* = **front-wheel drive.**

**fwy** *(US)* = **freeway.**

**f-word** *n:* **the** ~ das Wort „fuck".

# G

**G, g** [dʒiː] *n* G, g *nt*. **G for George** ≃ G wie Gustav; **G** *(US col)* tausend Dollar *pl.* ~ **sharp/flat** Gis, gis *nt*/Ges, ges *nt*.

**G** *(US)* = **general** *film* jugendfrei.

**g** = (a) **gram(s), gramme(s)** g. (b) **gravity** g.

**GA** *(US Post)* = **Georgia.**

**gab** [gæb] *(col)* **1** *n* **to have the gift of the** ~ nicht auf den Mund gefallen sein. **2** *vi* quatschen *(col)*.

**gabardine** [ˌgæbəˈdiːn] *n* Gabardine *m*.

**gabble** [ˈgæbl] **1** *vi (geese, person)* schnattern. **don't** ~ **red' nicht so schnell. 2** *vt* herunterrasseln *(col)*.
▶**gabble away** *vi* drauflosschnattern *(col)*.

**gable** [ˈgeɪbl] *n* Giebel *m*. ~ **end** Giebelwand *f*.

**gabled** [ˈgeɪbld] *adj* ~ **roof** Giebeldach *nt*.

**Gabon** [gəˈbɒn] *n* Gabun *nt*.

**gad** [gæd]: **gad about** *vi (col)*: **to** ~ **about** herumziehen; **to** ~ **about the country** im Land herumziehen.

**gadget** [ˈgædʒɪt] *n* Gerät *nt*. **with a lot of** ~s mit allen Schikanen *(col)*.

**gadgetry** [ˈgædʒɪtrɪ] *n* Vorrichtungen *pl*; *(superfluous equipment)* technische Spielereien *pl*.

**Gaelic** [ˈgeɪlɪk] **1** *adj* gälisch. **2** *n (language)* Gälisch *nt*.

**gaff** [gæf] *n*: **to blow the** ~ *(col)* nicht dichthalten *(col)*.

**gaffe** [gæf] *n* Fauxpas *m*; *(verbal)* taktlose Bemerkung. **to make a** ~ einen Fauxpas begehen.

**gaffer** [ˈgæfəʳ] *n (col) (boss)* Boß *m (col)*; *(old man)* Opa *m (col)*.

**gag** [gæg] **1** *n* (a) Knebel *m*. (b) *(col: joke)* Gag *m*. **2** *vt* knebeln *(auch fig)*.

**gaga** [ˈgɑːgɑː] *adj (col)* old person verkalkt *(col)*. **to go** ~ verkalken *(col)*.

**gage** [geɪdʒ] *n, vt (US)* = **gauge.**

**gaggle** [ˈgægl] *n (of geese)* Schar *f*.

**gaiety** [ˈgeɪtɪ] *n* Fröhlichkeit *f*.

**gaily** [ˈgeɪlɪ] *adv* fröhlich. ~ **coloured** farbenfroh.

**gain** [geɪn] **1** *n no pl (advantage)* Vorteil *m*; *(profit)* Gewinn *m*; *(increase)* Zunahme *f (in gen)*. **it will be to your** ~ es wird zu Ihrem Vorteil sein; **to do sth for** ~ etw des Geldes wegen tun; **his loss is our** ~ wir profitieren von seinem Verlust; **the Liberals made several** ~s die Liberalen gewannen einige Sitze.
**2** *vt* (a) *(obtain, win)* gewinnen; *knowledge, wealth* erwerben; *advantage, respect, entry* sich *(dat)* verschaffen. **what does he hope to** ~ **by it?** was erhofft er sich *(dat)* davon?; **to** ~ **experience** Erfahrung sammeln; **we have nothing to** ~ **by staying** wir haben nichts davon, wenn wir noch bleiben. (b) *(reach) shore, summit* erreichen. (c) *(increase)* **to** ~ **height** (an) Höhe gewinnen; **to** ~ **speed** schneller werden; **she has** ~**ed weight** sie hat zugenommen; **as he** ~**ed confidence** als seine Selbstsicherheit zunahm; **my watch** ~s **five minutes each day** meine Uhr geht fünf Minuten pro Tag vor.
**3** *vi* (a) *(watch)* vorgehen. (b) *(profit: person)* profitieren *(by* von*)*. **society/you would** ~ **from that** das wäre für die Gesellschaft/für Sie von Vorteil. (c) **to** ~ **in prestige** an Ansehen gewinnen.
▶**gain on** *vi +prep obj (close gap)* einholen.

**gainful** [ˈgeɪnfʊl] *adj occupation etc* einträglich. **to be in** ~ **employment** erwerbstätig sein.

**gait** [geɪt] *n* Gang *m*; *(of horse)* Gangart *f*.

**gal** = **gallon(s).**

**gala** [ˈgɑːlə] *n (festive occasion)* großes Fest; *(Theat, Film, ball)* Galaveranstaltung *f*. ~ **performance** Galavorstellung *f*.

**Galapagos Islands** [gəˈlæpəgəsˈaɪləndz] *npl* Galapagosinseln *pl*.

**galaxy** [ˈgæləksɪ] *n (Astron)* Sternsystem *nt*. **the G**~ die Milchstraße.

**gale** [geɪl] *n* Sturm *m*. **it was blowing a** ~ ein Sturm wütete; ~ **force** Sturmstärke *f*; ~ **force 8** Windstärke 8.

**Galicia** [gəˈlɪsɪə] *n (in E Europe)* Galizien *nt*; *(in Spain)* Galicien *nt*.

**gall** [gɔːl] **1** *n* (a) *(Physiol, Bot)* Galle *f*. (b) *(col)* **of all the** ~! so eine Frechheit! **2** *vt (fig: anger)* maßlos ärgern.

**gallant** [ˈgælənt] *adj (brave)* tapfer; *(chivalrous, noble)* edel, ritterlich; *(to women)* galant.

**gallantly** [ˈgæləntlɪ] *adv (bravely)* tapfer; *(nobly)* edelmütig; *(chivalrously)* galant.

**gallantry** [ˈgæləntrɪ] *n (bravery)* Tapferkeit *f*; *(chivalry)* Edelmut *m*; *(to women)* Galanterie *f*.

**gall bladder** *n* Gallenblase *f*.

**galleon** [ˈgælɪən] *n* Galeone *f*.

**gallery** [ˈgælərɪ] *n (balcony, Art)* Galerie *f*; *(Theat)* oberster Rang. **to play to the** ~ *(fig)* sich in Szene setzen.

**galley** [ˈgælɪ] *n* (a) *(Naut) (ship)* Galeere *f*; *(kitchen)* Kombüse *f*. ~ **slave** Galeerensklave *m*. (b) *(Typ) (also* ~ **proof)** Fahne (nabzug *m*) *f*.

**Gallic** [ˈgælɪk] *adj* gallisch.

**gallicism** [ˈgælɪsɪzəm] *n* Gallizismus *m*.

**galling** [ˈgɔːlɪŋ] *adj* äußerst ärgerlich.

**gallivant** [ˌgælɪˈvænt] *vi* **to** ~ **about** *(col)* sich herumtreiben.

**gallon** [ˈgælən] *n* Gallone *f*.

**gallop** [ˈgæləp] **1** *n* Galopp *m*. **at full** ~ im gestreckten Galopp. **2** *vi* galoppieren. **to** ~ **through a book/one's work** ein Buch im Eiltempo lesen *(col)*/seine Arbeit im Eiltempo erledigen *(col)*.

**galloping** [ˈgæləpɪŋ] *adj (lit, fig)* galoppierend.

**gallows** [ˈgæləʊz] *n* Galgen *m*.

**gallstone** [ˈgɔːlstəʊn] *n* Gallenstein *m*.

**Gallup poll** ® [ˈgæləpˌpəʊl] *n* Meinungsumfrage *f*.

**galore** [gəˈlɔːʳ] *adv* in Hülle und Fülle.

**galvanize** [ˈgælvənaɪz] *vt* (a) *(Elec)* galvanisieren. (b) *(fig)* elektrisieren. **to** ~ **sb into action** jdn plötzlich aktiv werden lassen.

**Gambia** [ˈgæmbɪə] *n* Gambia *nt*.

**Gambian** [ˈgæmbɪən] **1** *adj* gambisch. **2** *n* Gambier(in *f*) *m*.

**gambit** [ˈgæmbɪt] *n* (a) *(Chess)* Gambit *nt*. (b) *(fig)*

(Schach)zug m. **his favourite conversational ~ is** ... er fängt eine Unterhaltung am liebsten mit ... an.

**gamble** ['gæmbl] **1** n (fig) Risiko nt. **it's a ~** es ist riskant; **I'll take a ~ on it** ich riskiere es. **2** vi **(a)** (lit) (um Geld) spielen (with mit); (on horses etc) wetten. **to ~ on the stock exchange** an der Börse spekulieren. **(b)** (fig) **she was gambling on him being late** sie hat sich darauf verlassen, daß er sich verspäten würde; **to ~ with sth** etw aufs Spiel setzen.
▶**gamble away** vt sep verspielen.

**gambler** ['gæmblə<sup>r</sup>] n (lit, fig) Spieler(in f) m.

**gambling** ['gæmblɪŋ] n Spielen nt (um Geld); (on horses etc) Wetten nt. **to disapprove of ~** gegen das Glücksspiel/Wetten sein; **~ debts** Spielschulden pl.

**gambol** ['gæmbəl] vi herumspringen.

**game¹** [geɪm] n **(a)** Spiel nt; (of table tennis) Satz m; (of billiards, board-games etc, informal tennis match) Partie f. **~s** (Sch) Sport m; **to have** or **play a ~ of** football/tennis/chess etc Fußball/Tennis/Schach etc spielen; **he plays a good ~** er spielt gut; **to have a ~ with sb, to give sb a ~** mit jdm spielen; **to be off one's ~** nicht in Form sein; **~ of chance** Glücksspiel nt; **~ set and match to X** Satz und Spiel (geht an) X.
**(b)** (fig) Spiel nt. **to play the ~** sich an die Spielregeln halten; **to play ~s with sb** mit jdm spielen; **the ~ is up** das Spiel ist aus; **to play sb's ~** jdm in die Hände spielen; **two can play at that ~** wie du mir, so ich dir (col); **to beat sb at his own ~** jdn mit seinen/ihren eigenen Waffen schlagen; **to give the ~ away** alles verraten; **to spoil sb's little ~** jdm die Suppe versalzen (col); **I wonder what his little ~ is?** ich frage mich, was er im Schilde führt.
**(c)** (col: business, profession) Branche f. **how long have you been in this ~?** wie lange machen Sie das schon?; **to be/go on the ~** auf den Strich gehen (col).
**(d)** (Hunt) Wild nt; (Cook also) Wildbret nt.

**game²** adj (brave) mutig. **to be ~ for sth** (bei) etw mitmachen; **to be ~ for anything** für alles zu haben sein (col).

**game:** **~ bird** n Federwild nt no pl; **~keeper** n Wildhüter m; **~ park** n Wildpark m; **~ plan** n (Sport) Spielplan m; (fig) Strategie f.

**games:** **~manship** n gerissene Spieltaktik f; **~ master** n Sportlehrer m; **~ mistress** n Sportlehrerin f.

**gaming machine** ['geɪmɪŋməˈʃiːn] n Spielautomat m.

**gamma ray** ['gæməˈreɪ] n Gammastrahl m.

**gammon** ['gæmən] n Schinken m.

**gamut** ['gæmət] n (fig) Skala f. **to run the (whole) ~ of emotion(s)** die ganze Skala der Gefühle durchlaufen.

**gander** ['gændə<sup>r</sup>] n Gänserich m.

**gang** [gæŋ] n Schar f; (of workers, prisoners) Kolonne f; (of criminals, youths, terrorists) Bande f; (of friends etc, clique) Clique f (col).
▶**gang up** vi sich zusammentun. **to ~ ~ on sb** sich gegen jdn verschwören.

**Ganges** ['gændʒiːz] n Ganges m.

**gangling** ['gæŋglɪŋ] adj schlaksig.

**gangplank** ['gæŋplæŋk] n Laufplanke f.

**gangrene** ['gæŋgriːn] n Brand m.

**gangrenous** ['gæŋgrɪnəs] adj brandig.

**gangster** ['gæŋstə<sup>r</sup>] n Gangster m.

**gangway** ['gæŋweɪ] **1** n **(a)** (Naut) (gangplank) Landungsbrücke f; (ladder) Fallreep nt. **(b)** (aisle) Gang m. **2** interj Platz da.

**gantry** ['gæntrɪ] n (for crane) Portal nt; (on motorway) Schilderbrücke f; (Rail) Signalbrücke f; (for rocket) Abschußrampe f.

**gaol** [dʒeɪl] n, vt = **jail**.

**gap** [gæp] n (lit, fig) Lücke f; (chink) Spalt m; (in surface) Ritze f; (Tech: spark ~) Abstand m; (fig) (in conversation, narrative, time) Pause f; (gulf) Kluft f.

**gape** [geɪp] vi **(a)** (person) den Mund aufreißen; (chasm etc) gähnen; (seam, wound) klaffen. **(b)** (stare: person) starren. **to ~ at sb/sth** jdn/etw (mit offenem Mund) anstarren.

**gaping** ['geɪpɪŋ] adj **(a)** klaffend; chasm gähnend. **(b)** (staring) gaffend; (astonished) staunend.

**garage** ['gærɑːʒ, (US) gəˈrɑːʒ] **1** n (for parking) Garage f; (for petrol) Tankstelle f; (for repairs etc) (Reparatur)werkstatt f. **~ sale** meist in einer Garage durchgeführter Verkauf von Haushaltsgegenständen. **2** vt in einer Garage abstellen.

**garb** [gɑːb] n Gewand nt; (col) Kluft f (col).

**garbage** ['gɑːbɪdʒ] n (lit: esp US) Abfall, Müll m; (fig) (useless things) Schund m (col); (nonsense) Quatsch m (col).

**garbage:** **~ can** n (US) Mülleimer m; (outside) Mülltonne f; **~ disposal unit** n Müllschlucker m.

**garbled** ['gɑːbld] adj entstellt. **the message got ~ on its way** die Nachricht kam völlig entstellt an; **the facts got a little ~** die Tatsachen sind etwas durcheinandergeraten.

**garda** ['gɑːdə] n (Ir) (police) Polizei f; (policeman) Polizist m.

**garden** ['gɑːdn] n Garten m; (often pl: park) Gartenanlagen pl. **everything in the ~ is lovely** (col) Friede, Freude, Eierkuchen (col).

**garden:** **~ centre** n Gartencenter nt; **~ city** n Gartenstadt f.

**gardener** ['gɑːdnə<sup>r</sup>] n Gärtner(in f) m.

**gardening** ['gɑːdnɪŋ] n Gartenarbeit f.

**garden** in cpds Garten-; **~ party** n Gartenfest nt; **~ path** n: **to lead sb up the ~ path** (col) jdn an der Nase herumführen; **~ shears** npl Heckenschere f; **~ shed** n ≈ Geräteschuppen m.

**gargle** ['gɑːgl] **1** vi gurgeln. **2** n (liquid) Gurgelwasser nt. **to have a ~** gurgeln.

**gargoyle** ['gɑːgɔɪl] n Wasserspeier m.

**garish** ['gɛərɪʃ] adj lights etc grell; colour etc also knallig (col); clothes knallbunt.

**garishly** ['gɛərɪʃlɪ] adv in grellen Farben; lit grell.

**garland** ['gɑːlənd] n Kranz m; (festoon) Girlande f.

**garlic** ['gɑːlɪk] n Knoblauch m. **~ bread** Knoblauchbrot nt; **~ press** Knoblauchpresse f.

**garment** ['gɑːmənt] n Kleidungsstück nt. **~ industry** (US) Bekleidungsindustrie f.

**garnet** ['gɑːnɪt] n Granat m.

**garnish** ['gɑːnɪʃ] vt garnieren.

**garret** ['gærət] n Dachboden m; (room) Dachkammer f.

**garrison** ['gærɪsən] **1** n Garnison f. **2** vt troops in Garnison legen; town mit einer Garnison belegen.

**garrulous** ['gærʊləs] adj geschwätzig.

**garter** ['gɑːtə<sup>r</sup>] n Strumpfband nt; (US: suspender) Strumpfhalter m. **~ belt** (US) Hüftgürtel m.

**gas** [gæs] **1** n **(a)** Gas nt. **(b)** (US: petrol) Benzin nt. **(c)** (anaesthetic) Lachgas nt. **to have ~** Lachgas bekommen. **2** vt vergasen. **to ~ oneself** sich mit Gas vergiften. **3** vi (col: talk) schwafeln (col).

**gas** in cpds Gas-; **~bag** n (col) Schwätzer(in f) m (col); **~ can** n (US) Benzinkanister m; **~ chamber** n Gaskammer f; **~ cooker** n Gasherd m; **~ cylinder** n Gasflasche f; **~ fire** n Gasofen m; **~-fired** adj power station, boiler Gas-.

**gaseous** ['gæsɪəs] adj gasförmig.

**gash** [gæʃ] **1** *n (wound)* klaffende Wunde; *(in earth, tree)* (klaffende) Spalte; *(in upholstery)* tiefer Schlitz. **2** *vt* aufschlitzen; *furniture, wood* tief einkerben. **he ~ed his knee** er hat sich *(dat)* das Knie aufgeschlagen.

**gasket** ['gæskɪt] *n (Tech)* Dichtung *f*.

**gas:** **~ lighter** *n* Gasanzünder *m*; *(cigarette lighter)* Gasfeuerzeug *nt*; **~ main** *n* Gasleitung *f*; **~man** *n* Gasmann *m (col)*; **~ mask** *n* Gasmaske *f*; **~ meter** *n* Gaszähler *m*.

**gasoline** ['gæsəʊliːn] *n (US)* Benzin *nt*.

**gasometer** [gæ'sɒmɪtəʳ] *n* Gasometer *m*.

**gas oven** *n* Gasherd *nt*.

**gasp** [gɑːsp] **1** *n (for breath)* tiefer Atemzug. **to give a ~ of surprise** vor Überraschung die Luft anhalten; **to be at one's last ~** in den letzten Zügen liegen. **2** *vi (continually)* keuchen; *(once)* tief einatmen; *(with surprise etc)* nach Luft schnappen *(col)*. **to make sb ~** jdm den Atem nehmen; **to ~ for breath** nach Atem ringen.

**gas:** **~ pipe** *n* Gasleitung *f*; **~ pump** *n (US)* Zapfsäule *f*; **~ ring** *n* Gasbrenner *m*; **~ station** *n (US)* Tankstelle *f*; **~ stove** *n* Gasherd *m*.

**gassy** ['gæsɪ] *adj drink* kohlensäurehaltig.

**gas:** **~ tank** *n* **(a)** *(US)* Benzintank *m*; **(b)** *(Brit: for butane etc)* Gastank *m*; **~ tap** *n* Gashahn *m*.

**gastric:** **~ acid** *n* Magensäure *f*; **~ flu** *n* Darmgrippe *f*; **~ ulcer** *n* Magengeschwür *nt*.

**gastritis** [gæs'traɪtɪs] *n* Gastritis *f*.

**gastroenteritis** ['gæstrəʊˌentə'raɪtɪs] *n* Magen-Darm-Entzündung *f*.

**gastronomic** [ˌgæstrə'nɒmɪk] *adj* gastronomisch.

**gastronomy** [gæs'trɒnəmɪ] *n* Gastronomie *f*.

**gasworks** ['gæswɜːks] *n sing or pl* Gaswerk *nt*.

**gate** [geɪt] *n* **(a)** Tor *nt*; *(small, garden ~)* Pforte *f*; *(five-barred ~)* Gatter *nt*; *(in airport)* Flugsteig *m*; *(of level-crossing)* Schranke *f*; *(sports ground entrance)* Einlaß *m*. **(b)** *(Sport) (attendance)* Zuschauerzahl *f*; *(entrance money)* Einnahmen *pl*.

**gateau** ['gætəʊ] *n* Torte *f*.

**gate:** **~-crash 1** *vt* **to ~-crash a party** in eine Party hineinplatzen; **2** *vi* ohne Einladung hingehen; **~-crasher** *n* ungeladener Gast; **~ money** *n* Eintrittsgelder *pl*; **~post** *n* Torpfosten *m*; **between you, me and the ~post** *(col)* unter uns gesagt; **~way** *n (lit, fig)* Tor *nt (to* zu*)*; *(archway)* Torbogen *m*.

**gather** ['gæðəʳ] **1** *vt* **(a)** *(collect, bring together)* sammeln; *people* versammeln; *flowers, fruit* pflücken; *potatoes, corn etc* ernten; *harvest* einbringen; *taxes* einziehen; *(collect up) broken glass, pins etc* aufsammeln; *one's belongings* (zusammen)packen. **to ~ one's strength/thoughts** Kräfte sammeln/seine Gedanken ordnen; **to ~ dust** verstauben.

**(b)** *(increase)* **to ~ speed** schneller werden; **to ~ strength** stärker werden.

**(c)** *(infer)* schließen *(from* aus*)*. **I ~ed that** das dachte ich mir; **I ~ from the papers that he has ...** wie ich aus den Zeitungen ersehe, hat er ...; **as far as I could ~** nach dem, was ich in Erfahrung bringen konnte; **I ~ she won't be coming** ich nehme an, daß sie nicht kommt; **as you will have/might have ~ed** wie Sie bestimmt/vielleicht bemerkt haben.

**(d)** **she ~ed her mink around her** sie hüllte sich in ihren Nerz.

**(e)** *(Sew)* raffen.

**2** *vi* **(a)** *(people)* sich versammeln; *(objects, dust etc)* sich (an)sammeln; *(clouds)* sich zusammenziehen; *(storm)* sich zusammenbrauen. **(b)** *(increase: darkness etc)* zunehmen *(in* an +*dat)*.

▶**gather around** *vi* **come on, children, ~ ~!** kommt

alle her, Kinder!; **they ~ed ~ the fire** sie scharten sich um das Feuer.

▶**gather up** *vt sep* aufsammeln; *one's belongings* zusammenpacken; *hair* hochstecken; *(fig) pieces* auflesen.

**gathering** ['gæðərɪŋ] *n* Versammlung *f*; *(meeting)* Treffen *nt*.

**GATT** [gæt] = **General Agreement on Tariffs and Trade** GATT.

**gauche** [gəʊʃ] *adj* ungeschickt.

**gaudy** ['gɔːdɪ] *adj (+er)* knallig *(col)*.

**gauge** [geɪdʒ] **1** *n* **(a)** *(instrument)* Meßgerät *nt*; *(to measure diameter, width etc)* (Meß)lehre *f*; *(dial)* Anzeiger *m*. **pressure/wind ~** Druck-/Windmesser *m*; **oil ~** Ölstandsanzeiger *m*. **(b)** *(of wire, sheet metal etc)* Stärke *f*; *(of tube)* Durchmesser *m*; *(Rail)* Spurweite *f*. **(c)** *(fig)* Maßstab *m (of* für*)*. **2** *vt* **(a)** *(measure)* messen. **(b)** *(fig: appraise) character* beurteilen; *reaction* abschätzen.

**gaunt** [gɔːnt] *adj (+er)* hager; *(from suffering)* abgezehrt.

**gauntlet** ['gɔːntlɪt] *n* (Stulpen)handschuh *m*; *(of armour)* Panzerhandschuh *m*. **to throw down the ~** *(fig)* den Fehdehandschuh hinwerfen; **to run the ~** *(fig)* Spießruten laufen; **to (have to) run the ~ of sth** einer Sache *(dat)* ausgesetzt sein.

**gauze** [gɔːz] *n* Gaze *f*; *(Med also)* Mull *m*.

**gave** [geɪv] *pret of* **give**.

**gawk** [gɔːk] *vi (col) see* **gawp**.

**gawky** ['gɔːkɪ] *adj (+er) person, movement* schlaksig, staksig *(col)*; *animal* staksig *(col)*.

**gawp** [gɔːp] *vi (col)* glotzen *(col)*. **to ~ at sb/sth** jdn/etw anglotzen *(col)*.

**gay** [geɪ] **1** *adj (+er)* **(a)** *(happy)* fröhlich; *colours also* bunt; *company, occasion* lustig; *life* flott. **~ dog** *(col)* lockerer Vogel *(col)*. **(b)** *(homosexual)* schwul *(col)*. **2** *n* Schwule(r) *m*.

**gaze** [geɪz] **1** *n* Blick *m*. **2** *vi* starren. **to ~ at sb/sth** jdn/etw anstarren.

**gazelle** [gə'zel] *n* Gazelle *f*.

**gazette** [gə'zet] *n* Zeitung *f*; *(government publication)* Amtsblatt *nt*.

**gazetteer** [ˌgæzɪ'tɪəʳ] *n* alphabetisches Ortsverzeichnis *(mit Ortsbeschreibung)*.

**gazump** [gə'zʌmp] *vt (Brit)* entgegen vorheriger Zusage ein Haus an einen Höherbietenden verkaufen.

**GB** = **Great Britain** GB, Großbritannien *nt*.

**GBH, gbh** = **grievous bodily harm** schwere Körperverletzung.

**GC** *(Brit)* = **George Cross** Tapferkeitsmedaille *f*.

**GCE** *(Brit)* = **General Certificate of Education.**

**GCSE** *(Brit)* = **General Certificate of Secondary Education.**

**Gdns** = **Gardens.**

**GDP** = **gross domestic product.**

**GDR** *(Hist)* = **German Democratic Republic** DDR *f*.

**gear** [gɪəʳ] **1** *n* **(a)** *(~ wheel)* Zahnrad *nt*; *(Aut etc: ratio)* Gang *m*. **~s** *pl (mechanism)* Getriebe *nt*; *(on bicycle)* Gangschaltung *f*; **to put the car into ~** einen Gang einlegen; **to leave the car in ~/out of ~** den Gang eingelegt lassen/das Auto im Leerlauf lassen; **to change ~** schalten; **to change into third ~** in den dritten Gang schalten. **(b)** *(equipment)* Ausrüstung *f*; *(tools)* Gerät *nt*; *(belongings, clothes)* Sachen *pl*. **2** *vt (fig)* **to be ~ed to sth** auf etw *(acc)* ausgerichtet sein; *(have facilities for)* auf etw *(acc)* eingerichtet sein.

**gear:** **~box** *n* Getriebe *nt*; **~lever** *n (Brit)* Schaltknüppel *m*; *(column-mounted)* Schalthebel *m*; **~ shift** *n (esp US)* = **~ lever**; **~ wheel** *n* Zahnrad *nt*.

**gee** [dʒiː] *interj* **(a)** *(esp US col)* Mann! *(col)*. ~ **whiz!** Mensch Meier! *(col)*. **(b)** ~ **up!** hü!

**geek** [giːk] *n (col)* Knallkopf *m (col)*.

**geese** [giːs] *pl of* **goose.**

**Geiger counter** [ˈgaɪgəˌkaʊntəʳ] *n* Geigerzähler *m*.

**gel** [dʒel] **1** *n* Gel *nt*. **2** *vi* gelieren; *(fig: plan, idea)* Gestalt annehmen.

**gelatin(e)** [ˈdʒelətiːn] *n* Gelatine *f*.

**gelding** [ˈgeldɪŋ] *n (horse)* Wallach *m*.

**gelignite** [ˈdʒelɪgnaɪt] *n* Gelatinedynamit *nt*.

**gem** [dʒem] *n* Edelstein *m*; *(cut also)* Juwel *nt*; *(fig) (person)* Juwel *nt*; *(of collection etc)* Prachtstück *nt*. **it's a real** ~ *(fig)* es ist einmalig gut.

**Gemini** [ˈdʒemɪniː] *n* Zwillinge *pl*. **he's a** ~ er ist Zwilling.

**gen** [dʒen] *n (Brit col)* Informationen *pl*.

**Gen** = **General** Gen.

**gender** [ˈdʒendəʳ] *n* Geschlecht *nt*.

**gene** [dʒiːn] *n* Gen *nt*, Erbfaktor *m*.

**genealogy** [ˌdʒiːnɪˈælədʒɪ] *n* Stammbaumforschung *f*; *(ancestry)* Stammbaum *m*.

**general** [ˈdʒenərəl] **1** *adj* **(a)** allgemein; *view, enquiry also* General-; *agency* General-; *user, reader* Durchschnitts-; *(vague)* unbestimmt. **as a** ~ **rule** im allgemeinen; **in** ~ **use** allgemein in Gebrauch; **for** ~ **use** für den allgemeinen Gebrauch; *(for use by everybody)* für die Allgemeinheit; ~ **headquarters** *(Mil)* Generalhauptquartier *nt*; **to explain sth in** ~ **terms** etw allgemein erklären; **the** ~ **idea is that ...** wir hatten uns das so gedacht, daß ...; **that was the** ~ **idea** so war das (auch) gedacht; **the** ~ **idea is to wait and see** wir wollen einfach mal abwarten; **to give sb a** ~ **idea of sth** jdm eine ungefähre Vorstellung von etw geben; **OK, I've got the** ~ **idea** OK, ich hab' verstanden, um was es geht *(col)*.

**(b)** *(after official title)* Ober-. **Consul** ~ Generalkonsul *m*.

**2** *n* **(a) in** ~ im allgemeinen. **(b)** *(Mil)* General *m*; *(Caesar, Napoleon etc)* Feldherr *m*.

**general:** ~ **anaesthetic** *(Brit)*, ~ **anesthetic** *(US) n* Vollnarkose *f*; **G**~ **Certificate of Education** *n (Brit)* (old: O Level) *früherer Abschluß der Sekundarstufe*, ≃ Mittlere Reife; *(A level) Abschluß m der Oberstufe*, ≃ Abitur *nt*; **G**~ **Certificate of Secondary Education** *n (Brit) Abschluß m der Sekundarstufe*, ≃ Mittlere Reife; ~ **delivery** *adv (US)* postlagernd; ~ **election** *n* Parlamentswahlen *pl*.

**generality** [ˌdʒenəˈrælɪtɪ] *n* **to talk in generalities** ganz allgemein sprechen.

**generalization** [ˌdʒenərəlaɪˈzeɪʃən] *n* Verallgemeinerung *f*.

**generalize** [ˈdʒenərəlaɪz] *vti* verallgemeinern. **to** ~ **about sth** etw verallgemeinern.

**general knowledge** *n* Allgemeinbildung *f*.

**generally** [ˈdʒenərəlɪ] *adv (usually)* im allgemeinen; *(for the most part also)* im großen und ganzen; *(widely, not in detail)* allgemein. ~ **speaking** im großen und ganzen.

**general:** ~ **manager** *n* Hauptgeschäftsführer(in *f*) *m*; ~ **practitioner** *n* praktischer Arzt, praktische Ärztin; ~ **public** *n* breite Öffentlichkeit *f*; ~**purpose** *adj* Mehrzweck-; ~ **staff** *n (Mil)* Generalstab *m*; ~ **store** *n* Gemischtwarenhandlung *f*; ~ **strike** *n* Generalstreik *m*.

**generate** [ˈdʒenəreɪt] *vt (lit, fig)* erzeugen. **generating station** Kraftwerk *nt*.

**generation** [ˌdʒenəˈreɪʃən] *n* **(a)** *(lit, fig)* Generation *f*. ~ **gap** Generationsunterschied *m*. **(b)** *(act of generating)* Erzeugung *f*.

**generator** [ˈdʒenəreɪtəʳ] *n* Generator *m*.

**generic** [dʒɪˈnerɪk] *adj (Biol)* Gattungs-. ~ **name** *or*

**term** Oberbegriff *m*.

**generosity** [ˌdʒenəˈrɒsɪtɪ] *n* Großzügigkeit *f*.

**generous** [ˈdʒenərəs] *adj* **(a)** großzügig. **(b)** *(large, plentiful)* reichlich; *figure* üppig.

**generously** [ˈdʒenərəslɪ] *adv* großzügig; *(plentifully)* reichlich.

**genesis** [ˈdʒenɪsɪs] *n* Entstehung *f*. **(the Book of) G**~ die Schöpfungsgeschichte.

**genetic** [dʒɪˈnetɪk] *adj* genetisch. ~ **engineering** Gentechnologie, experimentelle Genetik; ~ **fingerprinting** genetischer Fingerabdruck; ~ **make-up** Erbgut *nt*.

**genetics** [dʒɪˈnetɪks] *n sing* Genetik *f*.

**Geneva** [dʒɪˈniːvə] *n* Genf *nt*. **Lake** ~ der Genfer See; ~ **Convention** Genfer Konvention *f*.

**genial** [ˈdʒiːnɪəl] *adj (lit, fig)* freundlich; *jovial* leutselig; *company* angenehm.

**geniality** [ˌdʒiːnɪˈælɪtɪ] *n* Freundlichkeit *f*.

**genitals** [ˈdʒenɪtlz] *npl* Geschlechtsorgane *pl*.

**genitive** [ˈdʒenɪtɪv] *n (Gram)* Genitiv *m*. **in the** ~ im Genitiv.

**genius** [ˈdʒiːnɪəs] *n*, *pl* **-es** *or* **genii** Genie *nt*; *(mental or creative capacity also)* schöpferische Kraft. **a man of** ~ ein genialer Mensch; **to have a** ~ **for sth** eine besondere Gabe für etw haben; **he has a** ~ **for saying the wrong thing** er hat ein Talent dafür, immer das Falsche zu sagen.

**Genoa** [ˈdʒenəʊə] *n* Genua *nt*.

**genocide** [ˈdʒenəʊsaɪd] *n* Völkermord *m*.

**genre** [ˈʒɑ̃ːŋrə] *n* Gattung *f*.

**gent** [dʒent] *n (col)* = **gentleman.** ~**s' shoes** *(Comm)* Herrenschuhe *pl*; **"G**~**s"** *(Brit)* „Herren"; **where is the** ~**s?** wo ist die Herrentoilette?

**genteel** [dʒenˈtiːl] *adj* vornehm, fein.

**gentile** [ˈdʒentaɪl] **1** *n* Nichtjude *m*. **2** *adj* nichtjüdisch.

**gentle** [ˈdʒentl] *adj (+er)* sanft; *smack, breeze also, exercise* leicht; *knock, sound* leise; *rebuke also, heat* mild; *person, disposition* sanftmütig; *animal* zahm. **the** ~ **sex** das zarte Geschlecht; **to be** ~ **with sb** mit jdm sanft umgehen; **to be** ~ **with sth** mit etw behutsam umgehen.

**gentleman** [ˈdʒentlmən] *n*, *pl* **-men** [-mən] *(man)* Herr *m*; *(well-mannered, well-born)* Gentleman *m*.

**gentlemen's agreement** Gentlemen's Agreement *nt*; **gentlemen!** meine Herren!

**gentlemanly** [ˈdʒentlmənlɪ] *adj* zuvorkommend.

**gentleness** [ˈdʒentlnɪs] *n see adj* Sanftheit *f*; Leichtheit *f*; Milde *f*; Sanftmut *m*; Zahmheit *f*.

**gently** [ˈdʒentlɪ] *adv see adj* **to handle sb/sth** ~ mit jdm/etw behutsam umgehen; ~ **does it!** sachte, sachte!

**gentry** [ˈdʒentrɪ] *npl* (niederer) Adel *m*.

**genuine** [ˈdʒenjʊɪn] *adj* echt; *manuscript* Original-; *offer* ernstgemeint; *(sincere)* aufrichtig.

**genuinely** [ˈdʒenjʊɪnlɪ] *adv* wirklich; *(sincerely also)* aufrichtig.

**genuineness** [ˈdʒenjʊɪnnɪs] *n* Echtheit *f*; *(sincerity)* Aufrichtigkeit *f*.

**genus** [ˈdʒenəs] *n*, *pl* **genera** *(Biol)* Gattung *f*.

**geographer** [dʒɪˈɒgrəfəʳ] *n* Geograph(in *f*) *m*.

**geographical** [dʒɪəˈgræfɪkəl] *adj* geographisch.

**geography** [dʒɪˈɒgrəfɪ] *n* Geographie *f*; *(Sch also)* Erdkunde *f*.

**geological** [dʒɪəʊˈlɒdʒɪkəl] *adj* geologisch.

**geologist** [dʒɪˈɒlədʒɪst] *n* Geologe *m*, Geologin *f*.

**geology** [dʒɪˈɒlədʒɪ] *n* Geologie *f*.

**geometric(al)** [dʒɪəʊˈmetrɪk(əl)] *adj* geometrisch.

**geometry** [dʒɪˈɒmɪtrɪ] *n* Geometrie *f*.

**geophysics** [ˌdʒɪːəʊˈfɪzɪks] *n sing* Geophysik *f*.

**George** [dʒɔːdʒ] *n* Georg *m*.

**Georgia** ['dʒɔːdʒə] *n (in former USSR)* Georgien *nt.*
**Georgian** ['dʒɔːdʒɪən] **1** *adj* georgisch. **2** *n* Georgier(in *f*) *m*; *(language)* Georgisch *nt.* **3** *adj (Brit Hist)* georgianisch.
**geranium** [dʒɪ'reɪnɪəm] *n* Geranie *f.*
**geriatric** [ˌdʒerɪ'ætrɪk] **1** *adj* geriatrisch; *nurse, nursing* Alten-; *home* Alters-; *patient* der Geriatrie. ~ **medicine** Altersheilkunde *f.* **2** *n* alter Mensch.
**geriatrics** [ˌdʒerɪ'ætrɪks] *n sing* Geriatrie *f.*
**germ** [dʒɜːm] *n (lit, fig)* Keim *m*; *(of particular illness)* Krankheitserreger *m*; *(esp of cold)* Bazillus *m.* **don't spread your ~s around** behalte deine Bazillen für dich.
**German** ['dʒɜːmən] **1** *adj* deutsch. **2** *n* **(a)** Deutsche(r) *mf.* **(b)** *(language)* Deutsch *nt; see* **English.**
**German Democratic Republic** *n (Hist)* Deutsche Demokratische Republik.
**Germanic** [dʒɜː'mænɪk] *adj* germanisch.
**Germanize** ['dʒɜːmənaɪz] *vt* germanisieren; *word* eindeutschen.
**German:** ~ **measles** *n sing* Röteln *pl*; ~ **shepherd** *n* deutscher Schäferhund; ~**-speaking** *adj* deutschsprachig; ~**-speaking Switzerland** die Deutschschweiz.
**Germany** ['dʒɜːmənɪ] *n* Deutschland *nt.*
**germinate** ['dʒɜːmɪneɪt] *vi (lit, fig)* keimen.
**germination** [ˌdʒɜːmɪ'neɪʃən] *n* Keimung *f.*
**germ warfare** *n* bakteriologische Kriegführung.
**gerund** ['dʒerənd] *n* Gerundium *nt.*
**gestation** [dʒe'steɪʃən] *n (of animals)* Trächtigkeit *f*; *(of humans)* Schwangerschaft *f*; *(fig)* Reifwerden *nt.*
**gesticulate** [dʒe'stɪkjʊleɪt] *vi* gestikulieren.
**gesture** ['dʒestʃəᵊ] **1** *n (lit, fig)* Geste *f.* **as a ~ of support** als Zeichen der Unterstützung. **2** *vi* gestikulieren. **to ~ to sb to do sth** jdm durch Gesten zu verstehen geben, etw zu tun.
**get** [get] *pret* **got,** *ptp* **got** *or (US)* **gotten 1** *vt* **(a)** *(receive)* bekommen, kriegen *(col)*; *wealth, glory* kommen zu; *time, personal characteristics, idea* haben *(from* von*).* **where did you ~ it (from)?** woher hast du das?; **this country ~s very little rain** in diesem Land regnet es sehr wenig; **where do you ~ that idea (from)?** wie kommst du denn auf die Idee?; **I got quite a surprise/shock** ich war ziemlich überrascht/ich habe einen ziemlichen Schock bekommen *or* gekriegt *(col)*; **I don't ~ much from his lectures** seine Vorlesungen geben mir nicht viel; **he's only in it for what he can ~** er will nur dabei profitieren; **you'll ~ it!** *(col: be in trouble)* du wirst was erleben! *(col).*
**(b)** *(obtain by one's own efforts) object* sich *(dat)* besorgen; *visa, money also* sich *(dat)* beschaffen; *(find) staff, partner, job* finden; *(buy)* kaufen; *(buy and keep) large item, car, pet* sich *(dat)* anschaffen. **not to be able to ~ sth** etw nicht bekommen *or* kriegen *(col)*; **to ~ sb/oneself sth, to ~ sth for sb/oneself** jdm/sich etw besorgen; **to need to ~ sth** etw brauchen; **I've still three to ~** ich brauche noch drei; **you'll have to ~ a job/flat** Sie müssen zusehen, daß Sie eine Stelle/Wohnung bekommen *or* finden; **why don't you ~ a flat of your own?** warum schaffen Sie sich *(dat)* nicht eine eigene Wohnung an?; *(rent)* warum nehmen Sie sich *(dat)* nicht eine eigene Wohnung?; **what are you ~ting her for Christmas?** was schenkst du ihr zu Weihnachten?; **I got her a doll for Christmas** ich habe für sie eine Puppe zu Weihnachten besorgt; **we could ~ a taxi** wir könnten (uns *dat*) ein Taxi nehmen; **could you ~ me a taxi?** könnten Sie mir ein Taxi besorgen?; **could you ~ that?** *(telephone)* gehst du ran? *(col)*; *(door)* gehst du?

**(c)** *(fetch) person, doctor, object* holen. **to ~ sb from the station** jdn vom Bahnhof abholen; **I got him a drink** ich habe ihm etwas zu trinken geholt; **can I ~ you a drink?** möchten Sie etwas zu trinken?
**(d)** *(catch)* bekommen, kriegen *(col)*; *cold, illness also* sich *(dat)* holen; *(hit)* treffen, erwischen *(col).* **to ~ sb by the arm/leg** jdn am Arm/Bein packen; **it** *or* **the pain ~s me here** *(col)* es tut hier weh; ~ **him/it!** *(to dog)* faß!; **the bullet got him in the neck** die Kugel traf ihn in den Hals; **(I've) got him/it!** *(col)* ich hab' ihn/ich hab's *(col)*; **got you!** *(col)* hab' dich (erwischt)! *(col)*; **he's out to ~ you** *(col)* er hat's auf dich abgesehen *(col)*; **we'll ~ them yet!** *(col)* die werden wir schon noch kriegen! *(col)*; **I'll ~ you for that!** *(col)* das wirst du mir büßen!; **you've got me there!** *(col)* da bin ich überfragt.
**(e)** *(Telec) (contact)* erreichen; *number* bekommen; *(put through to, get for sb)* geben. ~ **me Mr Johnston please** verbinden Sie mich bitte mit Herrn Johnston.
**(f)** *(prepare) meal* machen. **I'll ~ you some breakfast** ich mache dir etwas zum Frühstück.
**(g)** *(send, take)* bringen. **to ~ sb to hospital** jdn ins Krankenhaus bringen; **to ~ sth to sb** jdm etw zukommen lassen; *(take it oneself)* jdm etw bringen; **where does that ~ us?** *(col)* was bringt uns *(dat)* das? *(col)*; **this discussion isn't ~ting us anywhere** diese Diskussion führt zu nichts; **we'll ~ you there somehow** irgendwie kriegen wir dich schon dahin *(col)*; **how am I going to ~ myself home?** wie komme ich nach Hause?
**(h)** *(manage to move)* bekommen, kriegen *(col).* **we'll never ~ this piano upstairs** das Klavier kriegen wir nie nach oben *(col).*
**(i)** *(understand)* kapieren *(col)*; *(hear)* mitbekommen, mitkriegen *(col).* **I don't ~ it/you** *(col)* da komme ich nicht mit *(col)*/ich verstehe nicht, was du meinst; ~ **it?** kapiert? *(col).*
**(j)** *(col) (annoy)* ärgern, aufregen; *(upset)* an die Nieren gehen (+ *dat*) *(col).*
**(k)** **to ~ sb to do sth** *(have sth done by sb)* etw von jdm machen lassen; *(persuade sb)* jdn dazu bringen, etw zu tun; **I'll ~ him to phone you back** ich sage ihm, er soll Sie zurückrufen; **you'll never ~ him to understand** du wirst es nie schaffen, daß er das versteht.
**(l)** **to ~ sth done** *(do)* etw machen; *(cause to be done)* etw machen lassen; **to ~ one's hair cut** sich *(dat)* die Haare schneiden lassen; **I'll soon ~ the grass cut** den Rasen habe ich schnell gemäht; *(by sb else)* ich lasse bald den Rasen mähen; **I'm not going to ~ much done** ich werde nicht viel schaffen; **to ~ things done** etwas fertigkriegen *(col)*; **you'll ~ me thrown out** du bringst es noch so weit, daß ich hinausgeworfen werde.
**(m)** *(cause to be)* **I can't ~ the car to start/door to open** ich kriege das Auto nicht an *(col)*/die Tür nicht auf *(col)*; **once I've got this machine to work** wenn ich die Maschine erst einmal zum Laufen gebracht habe; **to ~ sb talking** jdn zum Sprechen bringen; **to ~ sth clean/shut** etw sauber-/zukriegen *(col)*; **that'll ~ it clean/shut** damit wird es sauber/geht es zu; **to ~ sb drunk** jdn betrunken machen; **to ~ the children to bed** die Kinder ins Bett bringen; **to ~ one's arm broken** sich *(dat)* den Arm brechen; **to ~ one's hands dirty** sich *(dat)* die Hände schmutzig machen; **to ~ one's things packed** seine Sachen packen.
**(n) to have got sth** *(have)* etw haben.
**(o)** *(col: forming passive)* werden. **I got paid** ich wurde bezahlt.

**2** *vi* (**a**) *(go)* gehen; *(arrive)* kommen. **to ~ home/here** nach Hause kommen/hier ankommen; **I've got as far as page 16** ich bin bis Seite 16 gekommen; **~ (lost)!** verschwinde!; **to ~ there** *(succeed)* es schaffen *(col)*; *(understand)* dahinterkommen *(col)*; **now we're ~ting there** *(to the truth)* jetzt kommt's raus! *(col)*; **to ~ somewhere/nowhere** *(in job, career etc)* es zu etwas/nichts bringen; *(with work, in discussion etc)* weiterkommen/nicht weiterkommen; **to ~ somewhere/nowhere (with sb)** (bei jdm) etwas/nichts erreichen.

(**b**) *(become, be)* werden. **to ~ old/tired** *etc* alt/müde *etc* werden; **I'm/the weather is ~ting cold/warm** mir wird es/es wird kalt/warm; **to ~ dressed/shaved/washed** *etc* sich anziehen/rasieren/waschen *etc*; **you could ~ killed** du riskierst dein Leben; **how do people ~ that way?** *(col)* wie wird man nur so? *(col)*.

(**c**) *(start)* **I got to like him** er ist mir sympathisch geworden; **to ~ to like sth** an etw *(dat)* Gefallen finden; **to ~ to be ...** (mit der Zeit) ... werden; **to ~ working/scrubbing** *etc* anfangen zu arbeiten/schrubben *etc*; **I got talking to him** ich kam mit ihm ins Gespräch; **let's ~ started** fangen wir an!; **we got to talking about that** wir kamen darauf zu sprechen; **I got to thinking ...** ich habe mir überlegt, ...

(**d**) *(~ chance to)* **to ~ to do sth** die Möglichkeit haben, etw zu tun; **to ~ to see sb** jdn zu sehen bekommen.

(**e**) *(be obliged to)* **to have got to do sth** etw tun müssen; **I've got to** ich muß.

▶**get about** *vi (after illness)* auf den Beinen sein; *(socially)* herumkommen; *(news, rumour)* sich verbreiten *(prep obj* in +*dat)*.

▶**get across 1** *vi* (**a**) *(cross)* hinüber-/herüberkommen; *(+prep obj)* road, river kommen über *(+acc)*. (**b**) *(play, comedian etc)* ankommen *(to* bei*)*; *(teacher etc)* sich verständlich machen *(to dat)*; *(idea, meaning)* klarwerden *(to dat)*. **2** *vt always separate* (**a**) *(transport)* hinüber-/herüberbringen. **to ~ sth ~ sth** etw über etw *(acc)* (hinüber-/herüber)bringen. (**b**) *(communicate)* klarmachen *(to sb* jdm*)*.

▶**get along** *vi* (**a**) gehen. **I must be ~ting ~** ich muß jetzt gehen; **~ ~ with you!** *(col)* jetzt hör aber auf! *(col)*. (**b**) *(manage)* zurechtkommen. (**c**) *(progress)* vorankommen; *(work, patient, wound etc)* sich machen. (**d**) *(be on good terms)* auskommen *(with* mit*)*. **they ~ ~ quite well** sie kommen ganz gut miteinander aus.

▶**get around 1** *vi +prep obj* problem etc herumkommen um; *law, regulations* umgehen. **to ~ ~ the conference table** sich an einen Tisch setzen. **2** *vt always separate* (**a**) *(make agree)* herumbringen *or* -kriegen *(col)*. **I'm sure I can ~ her ~ to my way of thinking** ich bin sicher, daß ich sie überzeugen kann. (**b**) *+prep obj* zusammenbringen. **to ~ people (together) ~ the conference table** Leute an einem Tisch zusammenbringen.

▶**get around to** *vi +prep obj (col)* **to ~ ~ ~ sth/doing sth** zu etw kommen/dazu kommen, etw zu tun.

▶**get at** *vi +prep obj* (**a**) *(gain access to, reach)* herankommen an *(+acc)*; *town, house* erreichen; *(take, eat etc)* food, money gehen an *(+acc)*. **put it where the dog/child won't ~ ~ it** stellen Sie es irgendwohin, wo der Hund/das Kind nicht drankommt *(col)*; **let me ~ ~ him!** *(col)* na, wenn ich den erwische! *(col)*; **the mice have been ~ting ~ the cheese again** die Mäuse waren wieder am Käse. (**b**) *(ascertain)* truth herausfinden; facts kommen an *(+acc)*. (**c**)

*(col: mean)* **what are you ~ting ~?** worauf wollen Sie hinaus? (**d**) **to ~ ~ ~ sb** *(col) (criticize)* an jdm etwas auszusetzen haben *(col)*; *(nag)* an jdm herumnörgeln *(col)*.

▶**get away** *vi (leave)* wegkommen; *(prisoner, thief)* entkommen *(from sb* jdm*)*. **there's no ~ting ~ from the fact that ...** man kommt nicht um die Tatsache herum, daß ...; **to ~ ~ from it all** sich von allem frei machen; **~ ~ (with you)!** *(col)* ach, hör auf! *(col)*.

▶**get away with** *vi +prep obj* (**a**) *(steal)* entkommen mit. (**b**) *(col: escape punishment)* **you'll never ~ ~ ~ that** damit wirst du nicht durchkommen; das wird nicht gutgehen; **he got ~ ~ it** er ist ungeschoren davongekommen *(col)*; **the things he ~s ~ ~!** was er sich *(dat)* alles erlauben kann!

▶**get back 1** *vi* zurückkommen; zurückgehen. **I must be ~ting ~ (home)** ich muß langsam wieder nach Hause; **~ ~!** zurück(treten)! **2** *vt sep* (**a**) *possessions* zurückbekommen. **now that I've got you/it ~** jetzt, wo ich dich/es wiederhabe. (**b**) *(bring back)* zurückbringen.

▶**get back at** *vi +prep obj (col)* sich rächen an *(+dat)*. **to ~ ~ ~ sb for sth** jdm etw heimzahlen *(col)*.

▶**get back to** *vi +prep obj (esp Comm)* sich wieder in Verbindung setzen mit. **I'll ~ ~ ~ you on that** ich werde darauf zurückkommen.

▶**get behind** *vi (with work, payments)* in Rückstand geraten.

▶**get by** *vi* (**a**) *(move past)* vorbeikommen *(prep obj* an +*dat)*. (**b**) *(manage)* **she ~s ~ on very little money** sie kommt mit sehr wenig Geld aus; **I can just about ~ ~ in German** ich komme mit meinem Deutsch gerade so durch.

▶**get down 1** *vi* (**a**) *(descend)* hinunter-/heruntersteigen *(prep obj, from* von*)*; *(from horse, bicycle)* absteigen *(from* von*)*. **~ ~!** runter! *(col)*. (**b**) *(leave table)* aufstehen. **2** *vt sep* (**a**) *(take down)* herunternehmen. (**b**) *(reduce)* inflation etc herunterbekommen *(to* auf +*acc)*. (**c**) *(swallow)* food hinunterbringen. **~ this ~ (you)!** *(col)* trink/iß das! (**d**) *(make a note of)* aufschreiben. (**e**) *(col: depress)* fertigmachen *(col)*. **don't let it ~ you** laß dich davon nicht unterkriegen *(col)*.

▶**get down to** *vi +prep obj* sich machen an *(+acc)*; *(find time to do)* kommen zu.

▶**get in 1** *vi* (**a**) *(enter)* hinein-/hereinkommen *(prep obj, -to* in +*acc)*; *(into car, train etc)* einsteigen *(prep obj, -to* in +*acc)*. **to ~ ~(to) the bath** in die Badewanne steigen; **he can't ~ ~** er kommt nicht herein/hinein. (**b**) *(arrive: train, bus)* ankommen. (**c**) *(be admitted)* angenommen werden; *(be elected)* gewählt werden. (**d**) *(get home)* nach Hause kommen. **2** *vt* (**a**) *sep (bring in)* hinein-/hereinbringen *(prep obj, -to* in +*acc)*; *(fetch)* herein-/hineinholen *(-to* in +*acc)*; *(col)* groceries, drink, supplies sich eindecken mit. (**b**) *sep (submit)* forms einreichen. (**c**) *sep (insert into, find room for)* hineinbringen; *(fig)* punch, request, words anbringen. (**d**) *sep (send for)* doctor etc holen. (**e**) *always separate* **to ~ one's eye/hand ~** in Übung kommen.

▶**get in on** *vi +prep obj (col)* mitmachen bei. **to ~ ~ ~ the act** mitmischen *(col)*.

▶**get into 1** *vi +prep obj* (**a**) *rage, debt, company* geraten in *(+acc)*. **what's got ~ him?** *(col)* was ist bloß in ihn gefahren? *(col)*. (**b**) *bad habits* sich *(dat)* angewöhnen. (**c**) *(get involved in)* book sich einlesen bei; *work* sich einarbeiten in *(+acc)*. (**d**) *(put on)* clothes anziehen. **2** *vt +prep obj always separate* **you'll ~ me ~ trouble** wegen dir komme ich noch in

Schwierigkeiten; **to ~ sb ~ bad habits** jdm schlechte Angewohnheiten beibringen.
►**get in with** *vi +prep obj bad company* geraten in *(+acc); (ingratiate)* sich gut stellen mit.
►**get off 1** *vi* **(a)** *(from bus, train etc)* aussteigen *(prep obj aus); (from bicycle, horse)* absteigen *(prep obj von)*. **~ ~ the grass!** gehen Sie vom Rasen runter!; **to tell sb where to ~ ~** *(col)* jdm gründlich die Meinung sagen *(col)*; **he knows where he can ~ ~!** *(col)* der kann mich mal! *(col!)*. **(b)** *(leave)* wegkommen. **it's time you got ~ to school** es ist Zeit, daß ihr in die Schule geht; **to ~ ~ to a good/bad start** einen guten/schlechten Anfang machen. **(c)** *(escape, be let off)* davonkommen *(col)*. **to ~ ~ with a fine** mit einer Geldstrafe davonkommen; **I got ~ having to do the work** ich bin um die Arbeit herumgekommen. **(d)** *(fall asleep)* **to ~ ~ (to sleep)** einschlafen. **(e)** *(from work etc)* gehen können. **what time do you ~ ~ work?** wann hören Sie mit der Arbeit auf?
**2** *vt* **(a)** *sep (remove)* wegbekommen, wegkriegen *(col) (prep obj* von*); clothes, shoes* ausziehen; *lid, wrapping* abmachen *(prep obj* von*); (manage to ~ ~)* abbekommen *(prep obj* von*); stains* herausmachen *(prep obj* aus*); (manage to ~ ~)* herausbekommen *or -kriegen (col) (prep obj* aus*).* **~ your dirty hands ~ that** nimm deine schmutzigen Hände da weg! **(b)** *always separate (send off) mail, children* losschicken. **to ~ sb/sth ~ to a good start** jdm/einer Sache zu einem guten Start verhelfen; **when she'd got the children ~ to school** als sie die Kinder versorgt und in die Schule geschickt hatte; **to ~ sb ~ (to sleep)** jdn zum Schlafen bringen. **(c)** *sep (lawyer) accused* freibekommen. **(d)** *always separate (from work etc) day, afternoon* freibekommen. **I've got the day ~** ich habe heute frei.
►**get off with** *vi +prep obj (col: start a relationship with)* aufreißen *(col)*.
►**get on 1** *vi* **(a)** *(climb on)* hinauf-/heraufsteigen *(prep obj* auf *+acc)*; *(on bus, train etc)* einsteigen *(prep obj, -to in +acc)*; *(on bicycle, horse etc)* aufsteigen *(prep obj, -to* auf *+acc)*. **to ~ ~ sth** auf etw *(acc)* aufsteigen *etc.*
**(b)** *(continue: with work etc)* weitermachen. **~ ~ with it!** nun mach schon! *(col)*; **this will do to be ~ting ~ with** das tut's wohl für den Anfang *(col)*.
**(c)** *(get late, old)* **time is ~ting ~** es wird langsam spät; **he is ~ting ~ (in years)** er wird langsam alt; **he's ~ting ~ for 40** er geht auf die 40 zu; **there were ~ting ~ for 60** es waren fast 60.
**(d) = get along (a).**
**(e)** *(progress)* vorankommen; *(work also, patient, pupil)* Fortschritte machen. **to ~ ~ in the world** es zu etwas bringen; **how did you ~ ~ in the exam?** wie ging's (dir) in der Prüfung?; **how are you ~ting ~?** wie geht's?; **to ~ ~ without sb/sth** ohne jdn/etw zurechtkommen.
**(f)** *(have a good relationship)* sich verstehen, auskommen *(with* mit*)*. **they don't ~ ~ (with each other)** sie kommen nicht miteinander aus.
**2** *vt sep (prep obj* auf *+acc) clothes, shoes* anziehen; *hat, kettle* aufsetzen; *lid, cover* drauftun.
►**get on to** *vi +prep obj (col)* **(a)** *new subject* übergehen zu. **(b)** *(contact)* sich in Verbindung setzen mit. **I'll ~ ~ ~ him about it** ich werde ihn daraufhin ansprechen.
►**get out 1** *vi* **(a)** heraus-/hinauskommen *(of aus); (climb out)* hinaus-/heraussteigen *(of aus); (of bus, train, car)* aussteigen *(of aus); (of business, contract)* aussteigen *(col) (of aus)*. **he has to ~ ~ of the country** er muß das Land verlassen; **let's ~ ~ (of here)!** bloß weg hier! *(col)*; **~ ~ (of my room)!** raus (aus

meinem Zimmer)! *(col)*; **to ~ ~ of bed** aufstehen; **I don't ~ ~ ~ much these days** ich komme in letzter Zeit nicht viel raus *(col)*. **(b)** *(lit, fig: escape, leak out) (of aus)* herauskommen; *(animal, prisoner also)* entkommen; *(news)* an die Öffentlichkeit dringen.
**2** *vt sep* **(a)** *(remove) (of aus) cork, splinter, stain etc* herausmachen; *people* hinaus-/herausbringen; *(send out)* hinausschicken. **~ him ~ of my house** schaff mir ihn aus dem Haus! **(b)** *(take out) car, wallet* herausholen *(of aus)*. **(c)** *(withdraw) money* abheben *(of von)*. **(d)** *(borrow from library)* ausleihen *(of aus)*. **(e) you only ~ ~ what you put in** Sie bekommen nur das zurück, was Sie hineinstecken.
►**get out of 1** *vi +prep obj see also* **get out 1** *duty, obligation* herumkommen um; *difficulty* herauskommen aus. **you can't ~ ~ ~ it now** jetzt kannst du nicht mehr zurück. **2** *vt +prep obj always separate see also* **get out 2 (a-c)** *words, confession, truth* herausbekommen *or -kriegen (col)* aus; *profit* machen bei; *benefit, little, nothing* haben von; *pleasure* haben an *(+dat)*. **to ~ the best/most ~ ~ sth** etw voll ausnutzen; **and what do I ~ ~ ~ it?** und was habe ich davon?
►**get over 1** *vi* **(a)** *(cross)* hinüber-/herübergehen *(prep obj* über *+acc); (climb over)* hinüber-/herübersteigen; *(+prep obj)* steigen über *(+acc)*. **they got ~ to the other side** sie gelangten auf die andere Seite. **(b)** *+prep obj (lit, fig: recover from) disappointment, loss, fact, experience* (hin)wegkommen über *(+acc); shock, illness* sich erholen von. **I can't ~ ~ the fact that ...** ich komme gar nicht darüber hinweg, daß ...; **I can't ~ ~ it** *(col)* da komm ich nicht drüber weg *(col)*. **(c)** *+prep obj (overcome) problem, nervousness* überwinden.
**2** *vt* **(a)** *always separate (transport across)* hinüber-/herüberbringen *(prep obj* über *+acc); (fetch)* holen; *(help sb to cross, climb)* hinüber-/herüberhelfen *(sb* jdm*) (prep obj* über *+acc)*. **(b)** *sep information, ideas etc* verständlich machen *(to dat); (impress upon)* klarmachen *(to dat)*. **she ~s her songs ~ well** sie kommt mit ihren Liedern gut an.
►**get over with** *vt always separate* hinter sich *(acc)* bringen. **let's ~ it ~ (~)** bringen wir's hinter uns.
►**get round (to) = get around (to).**
►**get through 1** *vi* **(a)** *(person, thing)* durchkommen *(prep obj* durch*); (news)* durchdringen; *(Telec)* durchkommen *(col) (to sb* zu jdm*, to* London nach London*)*. **to ~ ~ to the second round/final** in die zweite Runde/Endrunde kommen. **(b)** *(communicate, be understood) (person)* durchdringen zu; *(idea etc)* klarwerden *(to dat)*. **(c)** *+prep obj (finish) work* fertigmachen, erledigen; *(manage to ~ ~)* schaffen *(col); book* fertiglesen, auslesen. **when I've got ~ this** wenn ich damit fertig bin. **(d)** *+prep obj (survive) days, time* herumbekommen, herumkriegen *(col)*. **(e)** *+prep obj (consume, use up)* verbrauchen; *clothes, shoes* abnutzen; *food* aufessen; *fortune* durchbringen *(col)*.
**2** *vt always separate* **(a)** *person, object, proposal* durchbekommen, durchbringen *(prep obj* durch*); message* durchgeben *(to dat); supplies* durchbringen. **it was his English that got him ~** er hat das nur aufgrund seines Englisch geschafft; **he got the team ~ to the finals** er hat die Mannschaft in die Endrunde gebracht. **(b)** *(make understand)* **to ~ sth ~ (to sb)** jdm etw klarmachen.
►**get through with** *vi +prep obj (col: finish)* hinter sich bringen; *job also, formalities, subject* erledigen.
►**get to** *vi +prep obj* **(a)** *(arrive at)* kommen zu; *hotel, town also* ankommen in *(+dat)*. **where have you

got ~ **with that book?** wie weit seid ihr mit dem Buch? **(b)** *(col: annoy, upset)* aufregen.
▶**get together 1** *vi* zusammenkommen; *(estranged couple)* sich versöhnen; *(combine forces)* sich zusammenschließen. **to ~ ~ about sth** zusammenkommen und etw beraten; **why don't we ~ ~ later and have a drink?** warum treffen wir uns nicht später und trinken einen? **2** *vt sep people, parts, collection* zusammenbringen; *documents* zusammensuchen; *thoughts, ideas* sammeln. **to ~ one's things ~** seine Sachen zusammenpacken; **to ~ it ~** *(col)* es bringen *(col)*.
▶**get up 1** *vi* **(a)** *(stand up, get out of bed)* aufstehen. **(b)** *(climb up)* hinauf-/heraufsteigen *(prep obj* auf *+acc)*. **(c)** *(wind)* aufkommen; *(sea)* stürmisch werden. **2** *vt* **(a)** *always separate (get out of bed)* aus dem Bett holen; *(help stand up)* aufhelfen *(+dat)*. **(b)** *sep steam* aufbauen. **to ~ ~ speed** sich beschleunigen. **(c)** *sep (organize)* organisieren; *play also* auf die Beine stellen *(col)*. **(d)** *always separate (dress up)* zurechtmachen. **to ~ oneself ~ as sb/sth** sich als jd/etw verkleiden; **to ~ sth ~ to look like sth** etw als etw aufmachen.
▶**get up to** *vi +prep obj* **(a)** *(lit, fig: reach)* erreichen; *standard* herankommen an *(+acc)*; *page* kommen bis. **(b)** *(be involved in)* anstellen *(col)*. **to ~ ~ ~ mischief** etwas anstellen; **what have you been ~ting ~ ~?** was hast du getrieben? *(col)*.
**get:** ~-**at-able** [ˌgetˈætəbl] *adj (col)* leicht erreichbar; ~**away 1** *n* Flucht *f*; **to make one's ~away** sich davonmachen *(col)*; **2** *adj attr* Flucht-; ~**away vehicle** Fluchtfahrzeug *nt*; *(party)* Party *f*; ~-**up** *n (col)* Aufmachung *f (col)*; ~-**up-and-go** *n (col)* Elan *m*; ~-**well card** *n* Karte *f* mit Genesungswünschen.
**geyser** [ˈgiːzəʳ] *n* **(a)** *(Geol)* Geiser, Geysir *m*. **(b)** *(domestic ~)* Durchlauferhitzer *m*.
**Ghana** [ˈgɑːnə] *n* Ghana *nt*.
**Ghanaian** [gɑːˈneɪən] **1** *adj* ghanaisch. **2** *n (person)* Ghanaer(in *f*) *m*.
**ghastly** [ˈgɑːstlɪ] *adj* **(a)** *crime etc* entsetzlich; *mistake* schrecklich. **(b)** *(col: awful)* gräßlich *(col)*, scheußlich *(col)*.
**Ghent** [gent] *n* Gent *nt*.
**gherkin** [ˈgɜːkɪn] *n* Gewürzgurke *f*.
**ghetto** [ˈgetəʊ] *n* G(h)etto *nt*.
**ghettoblaster** [ˈgetəʊblɑːstəʳ] *n (col)* großer Radiorecorder.
**ghost** [gəʊst] **1** *n (apparition)* Gespenst *nt*; *(of sb)* Geist *m*. **I haven't the ~ of a chance** ich habe nicht die geringste Chance; **to give up the ~** *(col)* den Geist aufgeben *(col)*. **2** *vt* **to ~ sb's speeches** für jdn Reden (als Ghostwriter) schreiben.
**ghostly** [ˈgəʊstlɪ] *adj (+er)* gespenstisch.
**ghost** *in cpds* Geister-; ~ **story** *n* Gespenstergeschichte *f*; ~ **town** *n* Geisterstadt *f*; ~**writer** *n* Ghostwriter *m*.
**ghoulish** [ˈguːlɪʃ] *adj* makaber; *laughter, interest* schaurig.
**G.I.** *n* GI, US-Soldat *m*.
**giant** [ˈdʒaɪənt] **1** *n* Riese *m*; *(fig)* Größe *f*; *(company)* Gigant *m*. **2** *adj* riesig, Riesen-. ~**(-size) packet** Riesenpackung *f*; ~ **panda** Großer Panda *m*.
**gibber** [ˈdʒɪbəʳ] *vi (ape)* schnattern; *(idiot)* brabbeln. ~**ing idiot** *(col)* Blödmann *m (col)*.
**gibberish** [ˈdʒɪbərɪʃ] *n* Kauderwelsch *nt*.
**gibbet** [ˈdʒɪbɪt] *n* Galgen *m*.
**gibbon** [ˈgɪbən] *n* Gibbon *m*.
**gibe** [dʒaɪb] **1** *n* Stichelei *f*. **2** *vi* sticheln. **to ~ at sb/sth** höhnische Bemerkungen über jdn/etw machen.

**giblets** [ˈdʒɪblɪts] *npl* Geflügelinnereien *pl*.
**Gibraltar** [dʒɪˈbrɔːltəʳ] *n* Gibraltar *nt*.
**giddiness** [ˈgɪdɪnɪs] *n* Schwindelgefühl *nt*.
**giddy** [ˈgɪdɪ] *adj (+er)* schwind(e)lig; *feeling* Schwindel-. **I feel ~** mir ist schwind(e)lig.
**gift** [gɪft] *n* **(a)** Geschenk *nt*. **a free ~** ein (Werbe)geschenk *nt*; **it was a ~** *(col: easy)* das war ja geschenkt *(col)*. **(b)** *(talent)* Begabung *f*. **to have a ~ for sth** ein Talent für etw haben.
**gifted** [ˈgɪftɪd] *adj* begabt *(in für)*.
**gift:** ~ **horse** *n*: **don't look a ~ horse in the mouth** *(prov)* einem geschenkten Gaul schaut man nicht ins Maul *(prov)*; ~ **pack** *n* Geschenkpackung *f*; ~ **token** *n* Geschenkgutschein *m*; ~-**wrap 1** *vt* als Geschenk verpacken; **2** *n* Geschenkpapier *nt*.
**gig** [gɪg] *n (col: concert)* Gig *m (col)*.
**giga-** [ˈgɪgə-] *pref* Giga-.
**gigantic** [dʒaɪˈgæntɪk] *adj* riesig, riesengroß.
**giggle** [ˈgɪgl] **1** *n* Gekicher *nt no pl*. **it was a bit of a ~** *(col)* es war ganz lustig; **to get the ~s** anfangen herumzukichern *(col)*; **she's got the ~s** sie kann nicht aufhören zu kichern. **2** *vi* kichern.
**gigolo** [ˈʒɪgələʊ] *n* Gigolo *m*.
**gild** [gɪld] *vt* vergolden. **to ~ the lily** des Guten zuviel tun.
**gill**[1] [gɪl] *n (of fish)* Kieme *f*.
**gill**[2] [dʒɪl] *n (Measure)* Gill *nt*.
**gilt** [gɪlt] *n (material)* Vergoldung *f*.
**gilt-edged** [ˌgɪltˈedʒd] *adj (Fin)* mündelsicher; *(fig)* solide.
**gimlet** [ˈgɪmlɪt] *n* Vorbohrer *m*.
**gimmick** [ˈgɪmɪk] *n* Gag *m (col)*; *(gadget)* Spielerei *f*. **sales ~** Verkaufstrick *m*.
**gimmickry** [ˈgɪmɪkrɪ] *n* Effekthascherei *f*; *(advertising, sales)* Gags *pl*; *(gadgetry)* Spielereien *pl*.
**gimmicky** [ˈgɪmɪkɪ] *adj* effekthascherisch.
**gin** [dʒɪn] *n (drink)* Gin *m*. ~ **and tonic** Gin Tonic *m*.
**ginger** [ˈdʒɪndʒəʳ] **1** *n* Ingwer *m*. **2** *adj biscuit etc* Ingwer-; *hair* rotblond; *cat* rötlichgelb.
▶**ginger up** *vt sep (col)* in Schwung bringen *(col)*.
**ginger:** ~-**ale** *n* Ginger Ale *nt*; ~ **beer** *n (Brit)* Ingwerlimonade *f*; ~**bread** *n* Lebkuchen *m* mit *Ingwergeschmack*; ~-**haired** *adj* rotblond.
**gingerly** [ˈdʒɪndʒəlɪ] *adv* behutsam; *(because sth is cold, hot etc)* zaghaft.
**gingham** [ˈgɪŋəm] *n* Gingan *m*.
**ginormous** [dʒaɪˈnɔːməs] *adj (col)* riesig *(col)*.
**ginseng** [ˈdʒɪnseŋ] *n* Ginseng *m*.
**gipsy** [ˈdʒɪpsɪ] *n* Zigeuner(in *f*) *m*.
**giraffe** [dʒɪˈrɑːf] *n* Giraffe *f*.
**girder** [ˈgɜːdəʳ] *n* Träger *m*.
**girdle** [ˈgɜːdl] *n (corset)* Hüfthalter *m*.
**girl** [gɜːl] *n* Mädchen *nt*; *(daughter also)* Tochter *f*; *(hum: woman)* Frau *f*. **an English ~** eine Engländerin; **factory ~** Fabrikarbeiterin *f*; **shop ~** Verkäuferin *f*; **the ~s** *(colleagues)* meine/ihre etc Kolleginnen; *(friends)* meine/ihre etc Freundinnen; **the old ~** die Alte *(col)*; *(col: wife, mother)* meine/seine etc Alte *(col)*.
**girl:** ~ **Friday** *n* Allround-Sekretärin *f*; ~**friend** *n* Freundin *f*; ~**guide** *n (Brit)* Pfadfinderin *f*.
**girlish** [ˈgɜːlɪʃ] *adj* mädchenhaft.
**girl scout** *n (US)* Pfadfinderin *f*.
**girl's** [gɜːlz]: ~ **name** *n* Mädchenname *m*; ~ **school** *n* Mädchenschule *f*.
**giro** [ˈdʒaɪrəʊ] *n (Brit) (bank ~)* Giro(verkehr *m*) *nt*; *(post-office ~)* Postscheckdienst *m*.
**girth** [gɜːθ] *n* **(a)** *(circumference, of waist)* Umfang *m*. **(b)** *(harness)* (Sattel)gurt *m*.
**gismo** *n (US col)* = **gizmo**.
**gist** [dʒɪst] *n no pl* Wesentliche(s) *nt*. **that was the ~**

of what he said das war im wesentlichen, was er gesagt hat.

**git** [gɪt] *n (Brit col)* Idiot *m*.

**give** [gɪv] *(vb: pret* **gave**, *ptp* **given***)* **1** *vt* **(a)** geben *(sb sth, sth to sb* jdm etw*)*; *(as present)* schenken *(sb sth, sth to sb* jdm etw*)*; *one's name, particulars* angeben; *(let sb know by phone, letter etc) decision, results* mitteilen; *(produce) results* bringen; *pleasure, joy, pain* bereiten; *trouble* machen; *one's love, attention* schenken; *punishment* erteilen. **they gave us roast beef for lunch** sie servierten uns Roastbeef zum (Mittag)essen; **what will you ~ me for it?** was gibst du mir dafür?; **what did you ~ for it?** was hast du dafür bezahlt?; **11 o'clock, ~ or take a few minutes** so gegen 11 Uhr; **six foot, ~ or take a few inches** ungefähr sechs Fuß; **to ~ as good as one gets** sich kräftig wehren; **he gave everything he'd got** *(fig)* er holte das Letzte aus sich heraus; **to ~ sb one's cold** *(col)* jdn mit seiner Erkältung anstecken; **I'd ~ a lot/the world/anything to know ...** ich würde viel/alles darum geben, wenn ich wüßte, ...; **what gave you that idea?** wie kommst du denn auf die Idee?; **to ~ sb five years** jdn zu fünf Jahren verurteilen; **~ me Spain (every time)!** *(col)* es geht doch nichts über Spanien; **~ yourself more time/half an hour** lassen Sie sich mehr Zeit/rechnen Sie mit einer halben Stunde; **how long do you ~ that marriage?** wie lange gibst du dieser Ehe? *(col)*; **I'll ~ you that** zugegeben; **he's a good worker, I'll ~ him that** eines muß man ihm lassen, er arbeitet gut; **he wouldn't ~ me his decision/opinion** er wollte mir seine Entscheidung/Meinung nicht sagen.

**(b)** *(hold, perform) party, dinner, play* geben; *speech* halten; *song* singen; *toast* ausbringen *(to sb* auf jdn*)*. **~ us a song** sing uns was vor; **I ~ you Mary** *(as toast)* auf Mary!; *(as speaker)* ich gebe Mary das Wort.

**(c)** *(devote)* widmen *(to sb* jdm*)*. **he has ~n himself entirely to medicine** er hat sich ganz der Medizin verschrieben.

**(d) to ~ a cry/groan/laugh/sigh** schreien/stöhnen/lachen/seufzen; **to ~ sb a look/smile** jdn ansehen/anlächeln; **to ~ sb a push/kick** jdm einen Stoß/Tritt geben; **to ~ one's hair a brush/wash** sich *(dat)* die Haare bürsten/waschen.

**2** *vi* **(a)** *(~ money etc)* spenden. **you have to be prepared to ~ and take** man muß zu Kompromissen bereit sein. **(b)** *(also ~ way) (lit, fig: collapse, yield)* nachgeben; *(health, nerve, voice)* versagen; *(break: rope, cable)* reißen. **something's got to ~** *(col)* etwas muß sich einfach ändern. **(c)** *(lit, fig: bend, be flexible)* nachgeben; *(bed)* federn; *(shoe)* sich weiten.

**3** *n* Nachgiebigkeit *f*; *(of floor, bed, chair)* Federung *f*.

▶**give away** *vt sep* **(a)** weggeben; *(as present)* verschenken. **at £5 I'm practically giving it ~** ich will £5 dafür, das ist fast geschenkt. **(b)** *bride (als Brautvater etc)* zum Altar führen. **(c)** *(fig: betray)* verraten *(to sb* an jdn*)*. **to ~ the game ~** *(col)* alles verraten.

▶**give back** *vt sep* zurückgeben.

▶**give in** **1** *vi (surrender)* sich ergeben *(to sb* jdm*)*; *(in guessing game etc)* aufgeben; *(accede, back down)* nachgeben *(to dat)*. **to ~ ~ to blackmail** auf Erpressung eingehen. **2** *vt sep document, essay* einreichen; *parcel* abgeben.

▶**give off** *vt sep heat, gas* abgeben; *smell* verbreiten; *rays* ausstrahlen.

▶**give on to** *vi +prep obj (window)* hinausgehen auf *(+acc)*; *(door) garden* hinausführen in *(+acc)*.

▶**give out** **1** *vi (supplies, strength)* zu Ende gehen or *(in past tense)* sein; *(engine, machine)* versagen.

**2** *vt sep* **(a)** *(distribute)* verteilen. **(b)** *(announce)* bekanntgeben. **to ~ oneself ~ as sth** sich als etw ausgeben. **3** *vt insep* = **give off**.

▶**give over** **1** *vt sep* **(a)** *(hand over)* übergeben *(to dat)*. **(b)** *(set aside, use for)* to be ~ **~ to sth** für etw beansprucht werden. **2** *vi (col: stop)* **~ ~!** hör auf!

▶**give up** **1** *vi* aufgeben. **I ~ ~** ich gebe auf, ich geb's auf *(col)*. **2** *vt sep* **(a)** aufgeben; *claim also* verzichten auf *(+acc)*. **I'm trying to ~ ~ smoking** ich versuche, das Rauchen aufzugeben; **to ~ sb ~ as dead** jdn für tot halten; **I'd ~n you ~** *(expected visitor etc)* ich hatte nicht mehr damit gerechnet, daß du kommst. **(b)** *land, territory* abgeben *(to dat)*; *seat, place* freimachen *(to für)*; *ticket* abgeben *(to* bei*)*. **(c)** *(to authorities)* übergeben *(to dat)*. **to ~ oneself ~** sich stellen; *(after siege)* sich ergeben. **(d)** *(devote)* widmen. **to ~ ~ one's life to music** sein Leben ganz der Musik widmen. **(e)** *(disclose) secret, treasure* enthüllen *(geh)*.

▶**give way** *vi* **(a)** *(lit)* = **give 2 (b)**. **(b)** *(fig: yield)* nachgeben *(to dat)*. **to ~ ~ to intimidation** sich einschüchtern lassen; **don't ~ ~ to despair** überlaß dich nicht der Verzweiflung. **(c)** *(be superseded)* **to ~ ~ to sth** von etw abgelöst werden. **(d)** *(Brit Mot)* **who has to ~ ~ here?** wer hat hier Vorfahrt?; **"~ ~"** „Vorfahrt beachten".

**give: ~ and take** *n* Kompromißbereitschaft *f*; *(in personal relationships)* (gegenseitiges) Geben und Nehmen *nt*; **~-away** *n (col)* **the expression on her face was a ~-away** ihr Gesichtsausdruck verriet alles; **that exam question was a ~-away** diese Prüfungsfrage war geschenkt *(col)*; **~-away price** *n (col)* Schleuderpreis *m*.

**given** ['gɪvn] **1** *ptp of* **give**. **2** *adj* **(a)** *(with indef art)* bestimmt; *(with def art)* angegeben. **(b)** **~ name** *(esp US)* Vorname *m*. **(c) to be ~ to sth** zu etw neigen; **to be ~ to doing sth** gewohnt sein, etw zu tun. **3** *conj* **~ sth** *(provided with)* vorausgesetzt, man/er *etc* hat etw; *(in view of)* angesichts einer Sache *(gen)*; **~ that he ...** *(in view of the fact)* angesichts der Tatsache, daß er ...; *(assuming)* vorausgesetzt, (daß) er ...; **~ these circumstances/conditions** unter diesen Umständen/Voraussetzungen.

**giver** ['gɪvər] *n* Spender(in *f*) *m*.

**gizmo** ['gɪzməʊ] *n (col)* Ding *nt (col)*.

**glacé** ['glæseɪ] *adj* glasiert; *fruit* kandiert.

**glacier** ['glæsɪər] *n* Gletscher *m*.

**glad** [glæd] *adj (+er)* froh. **to be ~ at** or **about sth** sich über etw *(acc)* freuen; **I'm so ~!** das freut mich; **you'll be ~ to hear that ...** es wird Sie freuen, daß ...; **we would be ~ of your help** wir wären froh, wenn Sie helfen könnten; **I'd be ~ to** aber gern!; **to give sb the ~ eye** *(col)* jdm schöne Augen machen *(col)*; **to put on one's ~ rags** *(col)* sich in Schale werfen *(col)*.

**gladden** ['glædn] *vt person, heart* erfreuen.

**glade** [gleɪd] *n* Lichtung *f*.

**gladiator** ['glædɪeɪtər] *n* Gladiator *m*.

**gladiolus** [‚glædɪ'əʊləs] *n, pl* **gladioli** [‚glædɪ'əʊlaɪ] Gladiole *f*.

**gladly** ['glædlɪ] *adv (willingly)* gern.

**glam** [glæm] *adj (col)* todschick *(col)*.

**glamorize** ['glæməraɪz] *vt author, war* glorifizieren; **the mundane** idealisiert darstellen.

**glamorous** ['glæmərəs] *adj* bezaubernd; *film star, life* glamourös; *job* Traum-.

**glamorously** ['glæmərəslɪ] *adv* glamourös.

**glamour, (US) glamor** ['glæmər] *n* Glamour *m*; *(of occasion, situation)* Glanz *m*.

**glance** [glɑːns] **1** *n* Blick *m*. **at a ~** auf einen Blick;

**glottal stop**

**at first** ~ auf den ersten Blick; **to take a (quick)** ~ **at sth** einen kurzen Blick auf etw (acc) werfen. **2** vi **to** ~ **at sb/sth** einen kurzen Blick auf jdn/etw (acc) werfen; **to** ~ **at/through the newspaper** einen kurzen Blick in die Zeitung werfen/die Zeitung durchblättern; **he** ~**d around the room** er sah sich kurz im Zimmer um.
▶**glance off** vi (bullet etc) abprallen (prep obj von).

**glancing** ['glɑːnsɪŋ] adj **to strike sth a** ~ **blow** etw nur streifen.

**gland** [glænd] n Drüse f.

**glandular** ['glændjʊləʳ] adj Drüsen-. ~ **fever** Drüsenfieber nt.

**glare** [glɛəʳ] **1** n **(a)** greller Schein; (from sun, bulb, lamp also) grelles Licht. **the** ~ **of the sun** das grelle Sonnenlicht; **to avoid the** ~ **of publicity** das grelle Licht der Öffentlichkeit scheuen. **(b)** (stare) stechender Blick. **2** vi **(a)** (light, sun) grell scheinen; (headlights) grell leuchten. **(b)** (stare) **to** ~ **at sb/sth** jdn/etw zornig anstarren.

**glaring** ['glɛərɪŋ] adj sun, colour grell; (fig) omission eklatant; mistake grob; contrast kraß; injustice (himmel)schreiend.

**glasnost** ['glæznɒst] n Glasnost f.

**glass** [glɑːs] n Glas nt; (dated: mirror) Spiegel m; (barometer) Barometer nt. **a** ~ **of wine** ein Glas Wein; **wine by the** ~ offener Wein; ~**es** pl (spectacles) Brille f; (binoculars) Fernglas nt.

**glass** in cpds Glas-; ~**-blower** n Glasbläser (in f) m; ~**-blowing** n Glasbläserei f; ~ **fibre** (Brit) or **fiber** (US) n Glasfaser f; ~**-ful** n Glas nt (**of wine** etc Wein etc); ~**house** n (Brit Hort) Gewächshaus nt; (Mil sl) Bau m (col); ~**ware** n Glaswaren pl; ~ **wool** n Glaswolle f; ~**works** n sing or pl Glasfabrik f.

**glassy** ['glɑːsɪ] adj (+er) surface, sea etc spiegelglatt; eye, look glasig.

**Glaswegian** [glæz'wiːdʒən] **1** n Glasgower (in f) m. **2** adj Glasgower.

**glaucoma** [glɔː'kəʊmə] n grüner Star, Glaukom nt (form).

**glaze** [gleɪz] **1** n (on pottery, tiles, Cook) Glasur f; (on paper, fabric) Appretur f; (on painting) Lasur f. **2** vt **(a)** door, window verglasen. **(b)** pottery, tiles glasieren; fabric, paper appretieren; painting lasieren. ~**d tile** Kachel f. **(c)** (Cook) glasieren. **3** vi (eyes: also ~ over) glasig werden.

**glazier** ['gleɪzɪəʳ] n Glaser m.

**gleam** [gliːm] **1** n **(a)** Schimmer m; (of metal, water) Schimmern nt. **(b)** (fig) **a** ~ **of humour/intelligence** ein Anflug m von Humor/Intelligenz; **he had a** ~ **in his eye** seine Augen funkelten. **2** vi schimmern; (hair also) glänzen; (eyes) funkeln. **to make sth** ~ (by polishing) etw auf Hochglanz bringen; ~**ing** (shiny) glänzend.

**glean** [gliːn] vt (lit) corn nachlesen; (fig) facts, news ausfindig machen. **to** ~ **sth from sb/sth** etw von jdm in Erfahrung bringen/etw einer Sache (dat) entnehmen.

**glee** [gliː] n Freude f; (malicious) Schadenfreude f. ~ **club** (esp US) Männergesangverein m.

**gleeful** ['gliːfʊl] adj fröhlich; (malicious) schadenfroh.

**glen** [glen] n (esp Scot) Tal nt.

**glib** [glɪb] adj (pej) zungenfertig; reply, remark leichtfertig; talker, speech, style glatt. **don't be so** ~ sei nicht so oberflächlich.

**glibly** ['glɪblɪ] adv (pej) speak gewandt; reply, remark etc leichthin.

**glide** [glaɪd] vi **(a)** gleiten; (through the air also) schweben. **(b)** (plane) im Gleitflug fliegen; (glider)

gleiten.

**glider** ['glaɪdəʳ] n (Aviat) Segelflugzeug nt.

**gliding** ['glaɪdɪŋ] n (Aviat) Segelfliegen nt.

**glimmer** ['glɪməʳ] **1** n (of light, candle etc) Schimmer m; (of fire) Glimmen nt. **a** ~ **of hope** ein Hoffnungsschimmer m. **2** vi (light, water) schimmern; (fire) glimmen.

**glimpse** [glɪmps] **1** n Blick m. **to catch a** ~ **of sb/sth** einen flüchtigen Blick von jdm/etw erhaschen. **2** vt flüchtig sehen.

**glint** [glɪnt] **1** n (of light, metal) Glitzern nt no pl; (of eyes) Funkeln nt no pl. **he has a wicked/merry** ~ **in his eyes** seine Augen funkeln böse/lustig. **2** vi glitzern; (eyes) funkeln.

**glisten** ['glɪsn] vi glitzern.

**glitter** ['glɪtəʳ] **1** n Glitzern nt; (of eyes, diamonds) Funkeln nt; (fig) Glanz, Prunk m. **2** vi glitzern; (eyes, diamonds) funkeln. **all that** ~**s is not gold** (Prov) es ist nicht alles Gold, was glänzt (Prov).

**glitterati** [ˌglɪtə'rɑːtɪ] npl (col) Hautevolee f.

**glitzy** ['glɪtsɪ] adj (col) glanzvoll; dress todschick (col).

**gloat** [gləʊt] vi sich großtun (over mit/); (over sb's misfortune) sich hämisch freuen (over über +acc). **to** ~ **over one's possessions** sich an seinen Reichtümern weiden; **there's no need to** ~! das ist kein Grund zur Schadenfreude!

**global** ['gləʊbl] adj global; peace, war Welt-. ~ **warming** globaler Temperaturanstieg.

**globe** [gləʊb] n (sphere) Kugel f; (map) Globus m. **all over the** ~ auf der ganzen Erde or Welt; ~**-trotter** Globetrotter m.

**globule** ['glɒbjuːl] n Kügelchen nt; (of oil, water) Tröpfchen nt.

**gloom** [gluːm] n **(a)** (darkness) Düsterkeit f. **(b)** (sadness) düstere or gedrückte Stimmung. **a life of** ~ ein trauriges Leben.

**gloomily** ['gluːmɪlɪ] adv (fig) düster.

**gloomy** ['gluːmɪ] adj (+er) room etc düster; atmosphere also gedrückt; thoughts also, character trübsinnig; news also bedrückend; outlook on life pessimistisch. **to take a** ~ **view of things** schwarzsehen; **to feel** ~ bedrückt sein.

**glorification** [ˌglɔːrɪfɪ'keɪʃən] n Verherrlichung f.

**glorified** ['glɔːrɪfaɪd] adj **just a** ~ **snack-bar** nur eine bessere Imbißstube.

**glorify** ['glɔːrɪfaɪ] vt verherrlichen.

**glorious** ['glɔːrɪəs] adj weather, sky, day, feeling etc herrlich; deed, victory ruhmreich.

**glory** ['glɔːrɪ] **1** n **(a)** (honour, fame) Ruhm m. **covered in** ~ ruhmbedeckt. **(b)** (beauty, magnificence) Herrlichkeit f. **the rose in all its** ~ die Rose in ihrer ganzen Pracht; **the glories of Nature** die Schönheiten der Natur; **Rome at the height of its** ~ Rom in seiner Blütezeit. **2** vi **to** ~ **in sth** etw genießen; **to** ~ **in one's strength** mit seiner Kraft protzen; **to** ~ **in one's/sb's success** sich in seinem/jds Erfolg sonnen; **to** ~ **in the name of** ... den stolzen Namen ... führen.

**glory-hole** ['glɔːrɪˌhəʊl] n (col) Rumpelecke f.

**Glos** (Brit) = **Gloucestershire**.

**gloss¹** [glɒs] n Glanz m; (fig: of respectability etc) Schein m.
▶**gloss over** vt sep (try to conceal) vertuschen; (make light of) beschönigen.

**gloss²** n (note) Anmerkung f.

**glossary** ['glɒsərɪ] n Glossar nt.

**gloss (paint)** n Glanzlack (farbe f) m.

**glossy** ['glɒsɪ] adj (+er) glänzend; paper, paint, print Glanz-. ~ **(magazine)** Illustrierte f.

**glottal stop** [ˌglɒtl'stɒp] n (Phon) Knacklaut m.

**glove** [glʌv] *n* Handschuh *m*. **to fit (sb) like a ~** (jdm) wie angegossen passen; **~ box** *or* **compartment** Handschuhfach *nt*; **~ puppet** Handpuppe *f*.

**glow** [gləʊ] **1** *vi* glühen; *(colour, hands of clock)* leuchten; *(lamp also, candle)* scheinen. **she/her cheeks ~ed with health** sie hatte ein blühendes Aussehen. **2** *n* Glühen *nt*; *(of colour, clock hands)* Leuchten *nt*; *(of lamp, candle)* Schein *m*; *(of fire, sunset, passion)* Glut *f*. **to feel a warm ~** *(of happiness)* ein warmes Glücksgefühl verspüren.

**glower** ['glaʊəʳ] *vi* ein finsteres Gesicht machen. **to ~ at sb** jdn finster ansehen.

**glowing** ['gləʊɪŋ] *adj* **(a)** glühend; *candle, colour,* eyes leuchtend; *cheeks, complexion* blühend. **(b)** *(fig)* account, description begeistert; *praise, report* überschwenglich. **to paint sth in ~ colours** *(fig)* etw in den leuchtendsten Farben schildern.

**glow-worm** ['gləʊˌwɜːm] *n* Glühwürmchen *nt*.

**glucose** ['gluːkəʊs] *n* Traubenzucker *m*.

**glue** [gluː] **1** *n* Klebstoff *m*. **2** *vt* kleben. **to ~ sth together** etw zusammenkleben; **to ~ sth down/on** etw fest-/ankleben; **to ~ sth to sth** etw an etw *(acc)* kleben; **to keep one's eyes ~d on** *or* **to sb/sth** jdn/etw nicht aus den Augen lassen; **his eyes were ~d to the screen** seine Augen hingen an der Leinwand; **he's ~d to the TV all evening** er hängt den ganzen Abend vorm Fernseher *(col)*; **he stood there as if ~d to the spot** er stand wie angewurzelt da.

**glue:** **~-sniffer** *n* (Klebstoff-)Schnüffler(in *f*) *m* *(col)*; **~-sniffing** *n* (Klebstoff-)Schnüffeln *nt* *(col)*.

**glum** [glʌm] *adj (+er)* niedergeschlagen, bedrückt. **to feel ~** bedrückt sein.

**glut** [glʌt] **1** *vt (Comm)* market überschwemmen. **2** *n* Schwemme *f*; *(of manufactured goods also)* Überangebot *nt (of* an *+dat)*. **a ~ of apples** eine Apfelschwemme.

**glutinous** ['gluːtɪnəs] *adj* klebrig.

**glutton** ['glʌtn] *n* Vielfraß *m*. **a ~ for work/punishment** ein Arbeitstier *nt (col)*/Masochist *m*.

**gluttonous** ['glʌtənəs] *adj* gierig; *person* gefräßig.

**gluttony** ['glʌtənɪ] *n* Völlerei *f*.

**glycerin(e)** ['glɪsəriːn] *n* Glyzerin *nt*.

**GM** = **(a)** *(Brit)* **George Medal** *Tapferkeitsmedaille f*. **(b)** = **General Motors**.

**gm** = **gram(s)** g.

**GMT** = **Greenwich Mean Time** WEZ.

**gnarled** [nɑːld] *adj* tree knorrig; *hand* knotig.

**gnash** [næʃ] *vt* **to ~ one's teeth** mit den Zähnen knirschen.

**gnat** [næt] *n* (Stech)mücke *f*.

**gnaw** [nɔː] **1** *vi* nagen. **to ~ at sb/sth** an etw *(dat)* nagen; *(fig)* jdn/etw quälen. **2** *vt* nagen an *(+dat)*; *hole* nagen.

**gnawing** ['nɔːɪŋ] *adj (fig)* quälend; *doubt, hunger* nagend.

**gnome** [nəʊm] *n* Gnom *m*.

**GNP** = **gross national product**.

**gnu** [nuː] *n* Gnu *nt*.

**go** [gəʊ] *(vb: pret* went, *ptp* gone*)* **1** *vi* **(a)** gehen; *(vehicle, by vehicle)* fahren; *(plane)* fliegen; *(road)* führen. **to ~ to France** nach Frankreich fahren; **I have to ~ to the doctor/London** ich muß zum Arzt (gehen)/nach London; **to ~ for a swim** schwimmen gehen; **to ~ fishing/shopping** angeln/einkaufen gehen; **where do we ~ from here?** *(fig)* und was (wird) jetzt?; **you're ~ing too fast for me** *(lit, fig)* du bist mir zu schnell; **just look at him ~!** schau mal, wie schnell er ist!; **the favourite is ~ing well** der Favorit liegt gut im Rennen; **to ~ looking for sb/sth** nach jdm/etw suchen; **to ~ for a doctor/newspaper** einen Arzt/eine Zeitung holen (gehen);

there he ~es! da ist er ja!; **who ~es there?** *(guard)* wer da?; **you ~ first** geh du zuerst!; **you ~ next** du bist der nächste; **there you ~ again!** *(col)* du fängst ja schon wieder an!; **here we ~ again!** *(col)* jetzt geht das schon wieder los! *(col)*; **~ and shut the door** mach mal die Tür zu; **he's gone and lost his new watch** *(col)* er hat seine neue Uhr verloren; **don't ~ telling him** geh jetzt nicht hin und erzähl ihm das *(col)*; **there you ~** *(col) (giving sth)* bitte.

**(b)** *(depart)* gehen; *(vehicle, by vehicle also)* (ab)fahren; *(plane, by plane also)* (ab)fliegen. **has he gone yet?** ist er schon weg?; **I must ~** *or* **get ~ing now** ich muß jetzt gehen *or* weg; **when I'm gone** *(left)* wenn ich weg bin; *(dead)* wenn ich nicht mehr (da) bin; **~!** *(Sport)* los!; **here ~es!** jetzt geht's los! *(col)*.

**(c)** *(disappear, vanish)* verschwinden; *(pain, spot, mark etc also)* weggehen; *(be used up)* aufgebraucht werden; *(time)* vergehen. **it has gone** *(disappeared)* es ist weg; *(used up, eaten etc)* es ist alle *(col)*; **where has it gone?** wo ist es hin *or* geblieben?; **gone are the days when ...** die Zeiten sind vorbei, wo ...; **I don't know where the money ~es** ich weiß nicht, wo all das Geld bleibt; **all his money ~es on CDs** sein ganzes Geld geht für CDs drauf *(col)*; **£50 a week ~es in** *or* **on rent** £50 die Woche sind für die Miete (weg); **how is the time ~ing?** wie steht's mit der Zeit?; **it's just gone three** es ist gerade drei vorbei; **two days to ~ till ...** noch zwei Tage bis ...; **only two more patients to ~** nur noch zwei Patienten; **he'll have to ~** er wird gehen müssen; **that settee will have to ~** das Sofa muß weg.

**(d)** *(be sold)* **the hats aren't ~ing very well** die Hüte gehen nicht sehr gut; **to be ~ing cheap** billig sein; **it went for £5** es ging für £5 weg; **they are ~ing at 20p each** sie werden zu 20 Pence das Stück verkauft; **~ing, ~ing, gone!** zum ersten, zum zweiten, und zum dritten!

**(e)** *(prize, 1st place etc)* gehen *(to* an *+acc)*; *(inheritance)* zufallen *(to sb* jdm*)*.

**(f)** *(extend)* gehen. **the garden ~es down to the river** der Garten geht bis zum Fluß hinunter; **£5 won't ~ far** mit £5 kommt man nicht weit.

**(g)** *(run, function)* gehen; *(car, machine also)* laufen; *(workers)* arbeiten. **to get ~ing** in Schwung kommen; **to get sth ~ing, to make sth ~** etw in Gang bringen; *party* etw in Fahrt bringen; *business* etw auf Vordermann bringen; **to get sb ~ing** jdn in Fahrt bringen; **to get ~ing with sth** etw in Angriff nehmen; **to keep ~ing** *(person)* weitermachen; *(machine, engine, business)* weiterlaufen; *(car)* weiterfahren; **keep ~ing!** weiter!; **this medicine/prospect kept her ~ing** dieses Medikament/diese Aussicht hat sie durchhalten lassen; **here's £50/some work to keep you ~ing** hier hast du erst mal £50/etwas Arbeit, damit du beschäftigt bist.

**(h)** *(happen, turn out)* *(project, things)* gehen; *(event, evening)* verlaufen. **I've forgotten how the words ~** ich habe den Text vergessen; **how does the story/tune ~?** wie war die Geschichte doch noch mal/wie geht die Melodie?; **the decision went in his favour/against him** die Entscheidung fiel zu seinen Gunsten/Ungunsten aus; **how's it ~ing?, how ~es it?** *(col)* wie geht's (denn so)?; **how did it ~?** wie war's?; **how did the exam/your holiday ~?** wie ging's in der Prüfung/wie war der Urlaub?; **how's the essay ~ing?** was macht der Aufsatz?; **everything is ~ing well** alles läuft gut; **if everything ~es well** wenn alles gutgeht; **we'll see how things ~** *(col)* wir werden sehen, wie es läuft *(col)*; **she has**

**a lot** ~**ing for her** sie ist gut dran.

**(i)** *(fail, break, wear out)* kaputtgehen; *(health, strength, eyesight etc)* nachlassen; *(fail: brakes, steering)* versagen. **the jumper has gone at the elbows** der Pullover ist an den Ärmeln durch *(col)*; **his mind is** ~**ing** er läßt geistig sehr nach; **there** ~**es another bulb/button!** schon wieder eine Birne kaputt/ein Knopf ab!

**(j)** *(be permitted, accepted)* gehen *(col)*. **anything** ~**es!** alles ist erlaubt; **what I say** ~**es!** was ich sage, wird gemacht!; **that** ~**es for me too** *(that applies to me)* das gilt auch für mich; *(I agree with that)* das meine ich auch.

**(k)** *(be available)* **there are no jobs** ~**ing** es sind keine Stellen zu haben; **is there any tea** ~**ing?** gibt es Tee?; **I'll have whatever is** ~**ing** ich nehme, was es gibt.

**(l)** *(be, become)* werden. **to** ~ **deaf/mad/grey** taub/verrückt/grau werden; **I went cold** mir wurde kalt.

**(m)** *(fit)* passen; *(belong, be placed)* hingehören; *(in drawer, cupboard etc)* (hin)kommen. **the books** ~ **in that cupboard** die Bücher kommen in den Schrank dort; **4 into 3 won't** ~ 3 durch 4 geht nicht.

**(n)** *(match)* dazu passen. **to** ~ **with sth** zu etw passen.

**(o)** *(contribute)* **the money** ~**es to help the poor** das Geld soll den Armen helfen; **the money will** ~ **towards the holiday** das ist Geld für den Urlaub; **the qualities that** ~ **to make a great man** die Eigenschaften, die einen großen Mann ausmachen.

**(p)** *(make a sound or movement)* machen. **to** ~ **bang/ticktock** peng/ticktack machen; **there** ~**es the bell** es klingelt; **as the bell went** als es klingelte.

**(q)** *(US)* **food to** ~ Essen zum Mitnehmen.

**(r) he's not bad as boys** ~ verglichen mit anderen Jungen ist er nicht übel.

**2** *aux vb* **I'm** ~**ing to do it** ich werde es tun; **I was** ~**ing to do it** ich wollte es tun; **I had been** ~**ing to do it** ich hatte es tun wollen; **I wasn't** ~**ing to do it (anyway)** ich hätte es (sowieso) nicht gemacht.

**3** *vt (col)* **to** ~ **it** *(~ fast)* ein tolles Tempo draufhaben *(col)*; *(work hard)* sich hineinknien *(col)*; **to** ~ **it alone** einen Alleingang machen; *(in business)* sich selbständig machen; **I could** ~ **a beer** ich könnte ein Bier vertragen *(col)*.

**4** *n, pl* **-es (a)** *(col: energy)* Schwung *m*. **(b) to be on the** ~ auf Trab sein *(col)*; **to keep sb on the** ~ jdn auf Trab halten; **he's got two books on the** ~ er schreibt an zwei Büchern gleichzeitig; **it's all** ~ es ist wirklich was los *(col)*. **(c)** *(attempt)* Versuch *m*. **it's your** ~ du bist dran *(col)*; **you've had your** ~ du warst schon dran *(col)*; **to have a** ~ es probieren; **to have a** ~ **at sb** *(criticize)* jdn runterputzen *(col)*; *(fight)* es mit jdm aufnehmen; **to have a** ~ **at doing sth** versuchen, etw zu tun; **at** *or* **in one** ~ auf einen Schlag *(col)*; **drink** in einem Zug *(col)*; **can I have a** ~? darf ich mal? **(d)** *(success)* **to make a** ~ **of sth** in etw *(dat)* Erfolg haben; **(it's) no** ~ *(col)* das ist nicht drin *(col)*. **(e) from the word** ~ von Anfang an; **all systems (are)** ~ (es ist) alles klar.

▶**go about 1** *vi* herumgehen; *(by vehicle)* herumfahren; *(rumour, flu etc)* umgehen; *(ship)* wenden. **2** *vi +prep obj* task, problem anpacken. **we must** ~ ~ **it carefully** wir müssen vorsichtig vorgehen; **how does one** ~ ~ **getting seats?** wie bekommt man Plätze?; **to** ~ ~ **one's business** seinen Geschäften nachgehen.

▶**go after** *vi +prep obj* nachgehen *(+dat)*, nachlaufen *(+dat)*; *(in vehicle)* nachfahren *(+dat)*; *criminal*

jagen; *job, girl* sich bemühen um; *(Sport) record* einstellen wollen.

▶**go against** *vi +prep obj* **(a)** *(luck)* sein gegen; *(events)* ungünstig verlaufen für; *(evidence, appearance)* sprechen gegen. **the verdict went** ~ **her** das Urteil fiel zu ihren Ungunsten aus. **(b)** *(be contrary to)* im Widerspruch stehen zu; *principles, conscience* gehen gegen.

▶**go ahead** *vi* **(a)** *(go in front)* vorangehen; *(go earlier)* vorausgehen; *(in race)* sich an die Spitze setzen. **(b)** *(work, project)* vorangehen. **he just went** ~ **and did it** er hat es einfach gemacht; ~ ~! nur zu!; **to** ~ ~ **with sth** etw durchführen.

▶**go along** *vi* **(a)** *(walk along)* entlanggehen. **as one** ~**es** ~ *(while walking)* unterwegs; *(bit by bit)* nach und nach; *(at the same time)* nebenbei. **(b) to** ~ ~ **with** *(accompany)* mitgehen mit; *(agree)* zustimmen *+dat*.

▶**go around** *vi* **(a)** *(turn, spin)* sich drehen. **(b)** *(make a detour)* **we went** ~ **by Winchester** wir machten einen Umweg über Winchester. **(c)** *(visit)* vorbeigehen *(to bei)*. **(d)** *(tour: round museum etc)* herumgehen *(prep obj in +dat)*. **(e)** *(be sufficient)* (aus)reichen. **there's enough food to** ~ ~ es ist genügend zu essen da. **(f)** = **go about 1**.

▶**go at** *vi +prep obj (col: attack) person* losgehen auf *(+acc) (col)*; *task* sich machen an *(+acc)*. **he really went** ~ **it** er hat richtig losgelegt *(col)*.

▶**go away** *vi* (weg)gehen; *(for a holiday)* wegfahren. "**gone** ~" *(on letter)* „verzogen"; **the smell won't** ~ ~ der Geruch geht nicht mehr weg.

▶**go back** *vi* zurückgehen; *(to a subject)* zurückkommen *(to auf +acc)*; *(revert: to habits, methods etc)* zurückkehren *(to zu)*; *(clock: be put back)* zurückgestellt werden. **to** ~ ~ **to the beginning** wieder von vorn anfangen; **there's no** ~**ing** ~ **now** jetzt gibt es kein Zurück mehr; **we** ~ ~ **a long way** wir kennen uns schon seit langem.

▶**go back on** *vi +prep obj* zurücknehmen; *decision* rückgängig machen.

▶**go by** *vi (person, opportunity)* vorbeigehen *(prep obj an +dat)*; *(vehicle)* vorbeifahren *(prep obj an +dat)*; **as time went** ~ mit der Zeit. **2** *vi +prep obj* **(a)** *(base judgement on)* gehen nach; *compass, watch etc* sich richten nach; *(stick to) rules* sich halten an *(+acc)*. **if that's anything to** ~ ~ wenn man danach gehen kann; ~**ing** ~ **what he said** nach dem, was er sagte; **that's not much to** ~ ~ das will nicht viel heißen. **(b) to** ~ ~ **the name of X** X heißen.

▶**go down** *vi* **(a)** hinuntergehen *(prep obj acc)*; *(by vehicle, lift)* hinunterfahren *(prep obj acc)*; *(sun, moon)* untergehen; *(Theat: curtain)* fallen; *(fall: boxer etc)* zu Boden gehen.

**(b)** *(ship, person: sink)* untergehen; *(be defeated)* geschlagen werden *(to von)*.

**(c)** *(Brit Univ)* die Universität verlassen; *(for vacation)* in die Semesterferien gehen.

**(d)** *(be accepted, approved)* ankommen *(with bei)*. **that won't** ~ ~ **well with him** das wird er nicht gut finden; **he went** ~ **big in the States** *(col)* in den Staaten kam er ganz groß heraus *(col)*.

**(e)** *(floods, temperature etc)* zurückgehen; *(taxes, value)* weniger werden; *(prices)* sinken; *(balloon, tyre)* Luft verlieren; *(deteriorate: neighbourhood)* herunterkommen. **he has gone** ~ **in my estimation** er ist in meiner Achtung gesunken.

**(f)** *(be noted)* vermerkt werden. **to** ~ ~ **to posterity/in history** der Nachwelt überliefert werden/in die Geschichte eingehen.

**(g) to** ~ ~ **with a cold** eine Erkältung bekommen.

▶**go for** *vi +prep obj* (a) *(col: attack)* losgehen auf *(+acc)* *(col)*; *(verbally)* herziehen über *(+acc)*. (b) *(col: admire, like)* gut finden. (c) *(aim at)* zielen auf *(+acc)*; *(fig)* aussein auf *(+acc)* *(col)*.

▶**go in** *vi (enter, fit in)* hineingehen; *(sun)* verschwinden.

▶**go in for** *vi +prep obj* (a) *(enter for)* teilnehmen an *(+dat)*. (b) *(be interested in)* stehen auf *(+acc)* *(col)*; *(as career)* gewählt haben. **to ~ ~ ~ sports/ tennis** *(play oneself)* Sport treiben/Tennis spielen; *(be interested in)* sich für Sport/Tennis interessieren; **to ~ ~ ~ growing vegetables** sich auf den Gemüseanbau verlegen.

▶**go into** *vi +prep obj* (a) *house, hospital, politics* gehen in *(+acc)*; *the army, navy etc* gehen zu. **to ~ ~ teaching** Lehrer werden. (b) *(crash into)* car (hinein)fahren in *(+acc)*; *wall* fahren gegen. (c) *explanation, description etc* geben. (d) *trance, coma* fallen in *(+acc)*. (e) *(look into)* sich befassen mit; *(treat, explain at length)* abhandeln. **I don't want to ~ ~ that now** darauf möchte ich jetzt nicht (näher) eingehen.

▶**go off 1** *vi* (a) *(leave)* weggehen; *(by vehicle)* wegfahren. **he went ~ to the States** er fuhr in die Staaten; **to ~ ~ with sth** *(steal)* mit etw auf und davon gehen *(col)*. (b) *(light)* ausgehen; *(electricity)* ausfallen. **the water/gas went off** wir hatten plötzlich kein Wasser/Gas mehr. (c) *(gun, bomb, alarm, alarm clock)* losgehen. (d) *(food)* schlecht werden; *(person, work)* nachlassen. (e) *(go to sleep)* einschlafen. (f) *(take place)* verlaufen. **to ~ ~ well/ badly** gut/schlecht gehen. **2** *vi +prep obj (lose liking for)* nicht mehr mögen. **I've gone ~ him/it** ich mache mir nichts mehr aus ihm/daraus.

▶**go on 1** *vi* (a) *(walk on etc)* weitergehen; *(by vehicle)* weiterfahren; *(ahead of others)* vorausgehen.
(b) *(light, power)* angehen.
(c) *(carry on, continue)* weitergehen; *(person)* weitermachen. **to ~ ~ with sth** mit etw weitermachen; **to ~ ~ working** weiterarbeiten; **I want to ~ ~ being a teacher** ich möchte weiterhin Lehrer bleiben; **~ ~, tell me/try!** na, sag schon/na, versuch's doch!; **to have enough to be ~ing ~ with** fürs erste genug haben; **he went ~ to say that** ... dann sagte er, daß ...; **I can't ~ ~** ich kann nicht mehr; **as time ~es ~** im Laufe der Zeit; **don't ~ ~ (about it)** nun hör aber (damit) auf; **you do ~ ~ a bit** du weißt manchmal nicht, wann du aufhören solltest; **to ~ ~ about sb/sth** *(talk a lot)* stundenlang von jdm/etw erzählen; *(complain)* dauernd über jdn/etw schimpfen; **to ~ ~ at sb** an jdm herumnörgeln.
(d) *(happen)* vor sich gehen; *(party, argument etc)* im Gange sein. **this has been ~ing ~ for a long time** das geht schon lange so; **what's ~ing ~ here?** was geht hier vor?
**2** *vi +prep obj (be guided by)* gehen nach. **we haven't got much to ~ ~** wir haben nicht viel, worauf wir uns stützen können.

▶**go on for** *vi +prep obj fifty, one o'clock* zugehen auf *(+acc)*. **there were ~ing ~ ~ twenty people there** es waren fast zwanzig Leute da.

▶**go out** *vi* (a) *(leave)* hinausgehen. **to ~ ~ of a room** aus einem Zimmer gehen. (b) *(shopping etc)* weggehen; *(socially, to theatre etc, with girl-/boy-friend)* ausgehen. **to ~ ~ for a meal** essen gehen. (c) *(fire, light)* ausgehen. **to ~ ~ like a light** *(col)* sofort wegsein *(col)*. (d) *(tide)* zurückgehen. (e) **my heart went ~ to him** ich fühlte mit ihm mit. (f) *(Sport: be defeated)* ausscheiden. (g) *(circular)* (hinaus)gehen; *(Rad, TV: programme)* ausgestrahlt werden.

▶**go over 1** *vi* (a) *(cross)* hinübergehen; *(by vehi-*

*cle)* hinüberfahren. (b) *(change sides etc)* übergehen *(to* zu*)*; *(to another party)* überwechseln *(to* zu*)*. (c) *(TV, Rad: to news desk etc)* umschalten. (d) *(be received: play, remarks etc)* ankommen. **2** *vi +prep obj* (a) *(examine)* accounts durchgehen; *house, luggage* durchsuchen; *(medically)* person untersuchen; *(see over)* house etc sich *(dat)* ansehen. (b) *lesson, facts* durchgehen. **to ~ ~ sth in one's mind** etw überdenken.

▶**go past** *vi (prep obj* an *+dat)* vorbeigehen; *(vehicle)* vorbeifahren; *(time)* vergehen.

▶**go round** *vi =* **go around.**

▶**go through 1** *vi (lit, fig)* durchgehen; *(business deal)* abgeschlossen werden. **2** *vi +prep obj* (a) *hole, door, customs etc* gehen durch. (b) *illness, formalities etc* durchmachen. (c) *(examine, discuss)* durchgehen. (d) *(search)* pocket, suitcase durchsuchen. (e) *(use up)* aufbrauchen; *money* ausgeben; *shoes* durchlaufen *(col)*. **he has gone ~ the seat of his trousers** er hat seine Hose durchgesessen.

▶**go through with** *vi +prep obj* plan durchziehen *(col)*. **she couldn't ~ ~ ~ it** sie brachte es nicht fertig.

▶**go together** *vi (harmonize)* zusammenpassen; *(events, conditions)* zusammen auftreten.

▶**go under 1** *vi (sink)* untergehen; *(businessman)* scheitern; *(company)* eingehen *(col)*. **2** *vi +prep obj* **to ~ ~ the name of X** als X bekannt sein.

▶**go up** *vi* (a) *(price, temperature etc)* steigen. (b) *(climb)* hinaufsteigen *(prep obj* acc*)*. (c) *(lift)* hochfahren; *(balloon)* aufsteigen; *(Theat: curtain)* hochgehen; *(be built: new flats etc)* gebaut werden. (d) *(explode)* in die Luft gehen. **to ~ ~ in flames** in Flammen aufgehen.

▶**go without 1** *vi +prep obj* **to ~ ~ sth** auf etw *(acc)* verzichten. **2** *vi* darauf verzichten.

**goad** [gəʊd] *vt (taunt)* aufreizen. **to ~ sb into sth** jdn zu etw anstacheln.

▶**goad on** *vt sep* anstacheln.

**go-ahead** ['gəʊəhed] **1** *adj* fortschrittlich. **2** *n* **to give sb/sth the ~** jdm/für etw grünes Licht geben.

**goal** [gəʊl] *n* (a) *(Sport)* Tor *nt*. (b) *(aim, objective)* Ziel *nt*.

**goalie** ['gəʊlɪ] *n (col)* Tormann *m*.

**goal: ~keeper** *n* Torwart *m*; **~-kick** *n* Abstoß *m* (vom Tor); **~-post** *n* Torpfosten *m*; **to move the ~-posts** *(fig col)* die Spielregeln ändern; **~-scorer** *n* Torschütze *m*.

**goat** [gəʊt] *n* Ziege *f*. **to get sb's ~** *(col)* jdn auf die Palme bringen *(col)*.

**gob** [gɒb] *n (Brit col!: mouth)* Schnauze *f (col!)*.

**gobble** ['gɒbl] *vt* verschlingen.

▶**gobble down** *vt sep* hinunterschlingen.

▶**gobble up** *vt sep (lit, fig)* verschlingen.

**gobbledygook** ['gɒbldɪˌguːk] *n (col)* Kauderwelsch *nt*.

**go-between** ['gəʊbɪˌtwiːn] *n* Vermittler(in *f*) *m*.

**Gobi Desert** ['gəʊbɪˈdezət] *n* Wüste *f* Gobi.

**goblin** ['gɒblɪn] *n* Kobold *m*.

**gobsmacked** ['gɒbsmækt] *adj (col)* platt *(col)*.

**god** [gɒd] *n* Gott *m*. **G~ forbid** *(col)* Gott behüte; **G~ (only) knows** *(col)* wer weiß; **(my) G~!** *(col)*, **good G~!** *(col)* O Gott! *(col)*, großer Gott! *(col)*; **for G~'s sake!** *(col)* um Gottes willen! *(col)*; **the ~s** *(Brit Theat col)* die Galerie, der Olymp *(col)*.

**god: ~child** *n* Patenkind *nt*; **~dam** *adj (esp US col)* Scheiß- *(col!)*, gottverdammt *(col)*; **~daughter** *n* Patentochter *f*.

**goddess** ['gɒdɪs] *n* Göttin *f*.

**god: ~father** *n* Pate *m*; **~fearing** *adj* gottesfürchtig; **~forsaken** *adj (col)* gottverlassen; **~less** *adj* gottlos.

**godly** ['gɒdlɪ] *adj (+er)* fromm, gottesfürchtig.

**god:** ~**mother** *n* Patin *f*; ~**parent** *n* Pate *m,* Patin *f*; ~**send** *n* Geschenk *nt* des Himmels; ~**son** *n* Patensohn *m*.

**go-getter** ['gəʊ'getər] *n (col)* Tatmensch *m*.

**goggle** ['gɒgl] *vi* **to** ~ **at sb/sth** jdn/etw anglotzen *(col)*.

**goggle:** ~**-box** *n (Brit col)* Glotze *f (col)*; ~**-eyed** *adj* glotzäugig.

**goggles** ['gɒglz] *npl* Schutzbrille *f*.

**going** ['gəʊɪŋ] **1** *n* **it's slow** ~ es geht nur langsam; **that's good** ~ das ist ein flottes Tempo; **the** ~ **is good/hard** *(in racing)* die Bahn ist gut/hart; **the road was heavy/rough** ~ man kam auf der Straße nur schwer/mit Mühe voran; **it's heavy** ~ **talking to him** es ist sehr mühsam, sich mit ihm zu unterhalten; **while the** ~ **is good** solange es noch geht. **2** *adj attr* business gutgehend; *price* aktuell.

**going-over** [ˌgəʊɪŋ'əʊvər] *n (examination)* Untersuchung *f*; *(col: beating-up)* Abreibung *f*. **to give sth a good** ~ etw gründlich untersuchen; **to give sb a good** ~ *(col)* jdm eine tüchtige Abreibung verpassen *(col)*.

**goings-on** [ˌgəʊɪŋ'zɒn] *npl (col)* Dinge *pl*. **there have been strange** ~ da sind seltsame Dinge passiert.

**goitre,** *(US)* **goiter** ['gɔɪtər] *n* Kropf *m*.

**go-kart** ['gəʊˌkɑːt] *n* Go-Kart *m*.

**gold** [gəʊld] **1** *n* **(a)** Gold *nt*. **(b)** *(colour)* Goldton *m*. **2** *adj* golden; *(made of* ~ *also)* Gold-.

**gold card** *n* Goldcard *f*.

**golden** ['gəʊldən] *adj (lit, fig)* golden; *opportunity* einmalig. ~ **brown** goldbraun; ~ **eagle** Steinadler *m*; ~ **handshake** *(col)* großzügige Abfindung; ~ **hello** *(col)* Einstellungsprämie *f*; ~ **jubilee** goldenes Jubiläum; ~ **labrador** Goldener Labrador; ~ **rule** goldene Regel; ~ **wedding (anniversary)** goldene Hochzeit.

**gold:** ~**finch** *n* Stieglitz, Distelfink *m*; ~**fish** *n* Goldfisch *m*; ~ **leaf** *n* Blattgold *nt*; ~ **medal** *n* Goldmedaille *f*; ~ **medallist** *n* Goldmedaillengewinner(in *f*) *m*; ~ **mine** *n (lit, fig)* Goldgrube *f*; ~ **plate** *n (plating)* Vergoldung *f*; *(articles)* vergoldetes Gerät; ~**smith** *n* Goldschmied *m*.

**golf** [gɒlf] *n* Golf *nt*.

**golf:** ~**ball** *n* Golfball *m*; *(on typewriter)* Kugelkopf *m*; ~ **club** *n* Golfschläger *m*; *(association)* Golfklub *m*; ~ **course** *n* Golfplatz *m*.

**golfer** ['gɒlfər] *n* Golfer(in *f*), Golfspieler(in *f*) *m*.

**gondola** ['gɒndələ] *n* Gondel *f*.

**gondolier** [ˌgɒndə'lɪər] *n* Gondoliere *m*.

**gone** [gɒn] **1** *ptp of* **go. 2** *adj pred* **to be** ~ **on sb/sth** von jdm/etw ganz weg sein *(col)*; **she's six months** ~ *(pregnant)* sie ist im siebten Monat. **3** *prep* **it's just** ~ **three** es ist gerade drei Uhr vorbei.

**goner** ['gɒnər] *n (col)* **to be a** ~ *(car etc)* kaputt sein *(col)*; *(patient)* es nicht mehr lange machen; *(professionally: person, company)* weg vom Fenster sein *(col)*.

**gong** [gɒŋ] *n* Gong *m*; *(Brit col: medal)* Blech *nt (col)*.

**gonorrhoea** [ˌgɒnə'rɪə] *n* Gonorrhö *f*, Tripper *m*.

**goo** [guː] *n (col)* Papp *m (col)*.

**good** [gʊd] **1** *adj, comp* **better,** *superl* **best (a)** gut. **that's a** ~ **one!** *(joke)* der ist gut!, das ist ein guter Witz *(also iro)*; *(excuse)* wer's glaubt, wird selig! *(col)*; **it's no** ~ **doing it like that** es hat keinen Sinn, das so zu machen; **that's no** ~ das ist nichts; **to be** ~ **at sport/languages** gut im Sport/in Sprachen sein; **to be** ~ **at sewing/typing** gut nähen/maschineschreiben können; **I'm not very** ~ **at that** das kann ich nicht besonders gut; **to be** ~ **for sb**

jdm guttun; *(be healthy also)* gesund sein; **to be** ~ **for toothache/one's health** gut gegen Zahnschmerzen/für die Gesundheit sein; **to drink more than is** ~ **for one** mehr trinken, als einem guttut; **to be** ~ **with people** mit Menschen umgehen können; **it's too** ~ **to be true** es ist zu schön, um wahr zu sein; **to feel** ~ sich wohl fühlen; **I don't feel too** ~ ich fühle mich nicht wohl; **that's (not)** ~ **enough** das reicht (nicht); **if he gives his word, that's** ~ **enough for me** wenn er sein Wort gibt, reicht mir das; **it's just not** ~ **enough!** so geht das nicht!; **his attitude/behaviour is just not** ~ **enough** er hat einfach nicht die richtige Einstellung/sein Benehmen ist nicht akzeptabel; ~ **morning/afternoon** guten Morgen/Tag; **that's** ~! gut!, prima!; **(it's)** ~ **to see you/to be here** (es ist) schön, dich zu sehen/hier zu sein; ~**, I think that'll be all** gut, ich glaube das reicht; **very** ~**, sir** jawohl; ~ **for you/him!** das hast du/hat er gut gemacht!, *(iro also)* das ist ja toll!

**(b)** *(favourable)* moment, chance, opportunity günstig, gut. **a** ~ **day for a picnic** ein guter Tag für ein Picknick; **it's a** ~ **thing** *or* **job I was there** (nur) gut, daß ich dort war.

**(c)** *(enjoyable)* holiday, evening schön. **the** ~ **life** das süße Leben; **to have a** ~ **time** sich gut amüsieren; **have a** ~ **time!** viel Spaß *or* Vergnügen!; **did you have a** ~ **day?** wie ging's (dir) heute?; **have a** ~ **day!** schönen Tag noch!

**(d)** *(kind)* gut, lieb. **to be** ~ **to sb** gut zu jdm sein; **that's very** ~ **of you** das ist sehr lieb *or* nett von Ihnen; **(it was)** ~ **of you to come** nett, daß Sie gekommen sind; **would you be** ~ **enough to tell me ...** wären Sie so nett, mir zu sagen ... *(also iro)*; **she was** ~ **enough to help us** sie war so gut und hat uns geholfen; **with every** ~ **wish** mit den besten Wünschen.

**(e)** *(well-behaved, obedient)* artig, brav *(col)*. **(as)** ~ **as gold** sehr artig *or* brav *(col)*; **be a** ~ **girl/boy** sei artig *or* brav *(col)*; **be a** ~ **girl/boy and ...** sei so lieb und ...; **my** ~ **man** *(dated)* mein guter Mann *(dated)*; ~ **girl/boy!** das ist lieb!; *(well done)* gut!; ~ **old Charles!** der gute alte Charles!

**(f)** **is his credit** ~? ist er kreditfähig?; **what** *or* **how much is he** ~ **for?** *(will he give us)* mit wieviel kann man bei ihm rechnen?; *(does he have)* wieviel hat er?; **he/the car is** ~ **for another few years** mit ihm kann man noch ein paar Jahre rechnen/das Auto hält *or* tut's *(col)* noch ein paar Jahre.

**(g)** *(thorough)* gut, gründlich. **to give sth a** ~ **clean** etw gründlich reinigen; **to have a** ~ **laugh** ordentlich lachen; **to take a** ~ **look at sth** sich *(dat)* etw gut ansehen.

**(h)** *(considerable, not less than)* hour, while gut; amount, distance, way also schön. **it's a** ~ **8 km** es sind gute 8 km; **a** ~ **deal of effort/money** beträchtliche Mühe/ziemlich viel Geld; **a** ~ **many/few people** ziemlich viele/nicht gerade wenig Leute.

**(i)** **as** ~ **as** so gut wie; **as** ~ **as new/settled** so gut wie neu/abgemacht; **he was as** ~ **as his word** er hat sein Wort gehalten; **he as** ~ **as called me a liar** er nannte mich praktisch einen Lügner.

**2** *adv* schön. **a** ~ **strong stick/old age** ein schön(er) starker Stock/ein schön(es) hohes Alter; ~ **and strong** *(col)* schön stark *(col)*.

**3** *n* **(a)** *(what is morally right)* Gute(s) *nt*. **to do** ~ Gutes tun; **to be up to no** ~ *(col)* nichts Gutes im Schilde führen *(col)*.

**(b)** *(advantage, benefit)* Wohl *nt*. **the common** ~ das Gemeinwohl; **for the** ~ **of the nation** zum Wohl(e) der Nation; **I did it for your own** ~ es war nur zu deinem Besten; **for the** ~ **of one's health** *etc* seiner Gesundheit *etc* zuliebe; **that's all to the ~** das kann nur von Vorteil sein; **he'll come to no ~** mit ihm wird es noch ein böses Ende nehmen; **what's the ~ of hurrying?** wozu eigentlich die Eile?; **he's no ~ to us** er nützt uns *(dat)* nichts; **it's no ~ complaining to me** es ist sinnlos, sich bei mir zu beklagen; **if that is any ~ to you** wenn es dir hilft; **the applicant was no ~** der Bewerber war nicht gut; **he wasn't any ~ for the job** er eignete sich nicht für die Arbeit; **is this one any ~?** was ist mit dieser/diesem?; **it's no ~,** it won't start es hat keinen Zweck, es springt nicht an; **what ~ will that do you?** was hast du davon?; **that won't do you much/any ~** das hilft dir auch nicht viel/nichts; *(will be unhealthy etc)* das ist nicht gut für dich; **a (fat) lot of ~ that will do!** *(iro col)* als ob das etwas helfen würde! *(iro)*.

(c) *(for ever)* **for ~ (and all)** für immer (und ewig).

**good:** **~bye,** *(US)* **~by 1** *n* Abschied *m*; **to say ~bye (to sb)** sich (von jdm) verabschieden; **to say ~bye to sth** einer Sache *(dat)* Lebewohl sagen; **2** *interj* auf Wiedersehen; **~-for-nothing 1** *n* Nichtsnutz *m*; **2** *adj* nichtsnutzig; **G~ Friday** *n* Karfreitag *m*; **~-humoured,** *(US)* **~-humored** *adj* gut gelaunt; *(~-natured)* gutmütig.

**goodies** ['gʊdɪz] *pl of* **goody.**

**good:** **~-looking** *adj* gutaussehend; **~-natured** *adj* gutmütig.

**goodness** ['gʊdnɪs] *n* Güte *f*. **~ knows** *(col)* weiß der Himmel *(col)*; **for ~' sake** *(col)* um Himmels willen *(col)*; **I wish to ~ I had gone** *(col)* wenn ich doch bloß gegangen wäre!; **(my) ~!,** ~ **gracious!** *(col)* ach du meine Güte! *(col)*.

**goods** [gʊdz] *npl* Güter *pl (also Comm)*; *(merchandise also)* Waren *pl*; *(possessions also)* Habe *f (geh)*. **~ train/yard** *(Brit)* Güterzug *m*/-bahnhof *m*; **one's ~ and chattels** sein Hab und Gut *(also Jur)*; **to deliver or produce the ~** *(col)* es (wirklich) bringen *(col)*.

**good:** **~-sized** *adj* ziemlich groß; **~-tempered** *adj* **person** verträglich; *animal* gutartig; **~will** *n* Wohlwollen *nt*; *(between nations, Comm)* Goodwill *m*; **a gesture of ~will** ein Zeichen seines/ihres *etc* guten Willens; **to gain sb's ~will** jds Gunst gewinnen; **~will mission/tour** Goodwillreise *f*.

**goody** ['gʊdɪ] **1** *(col) interj* toll, prima. **2** *n* **(a)** *(person)* Gute(r) *mf*. **(b)** *pl (delicacies)* gute Sachen *pl*; *(accessories)* Zubehör *nt*. **computer/hifi goodies** Computerzeug *nt (col)*/Hifigeräte *pl*.

**goody-goody** ['gʊdɪ,gʊdɪ] *n (col)* Tugendlamm *nt (col)*.

**gooey** ['guːɪ] *adj (+er) (col) (sticky)* klebrig; *toffees, centres of chocolates* weich und klebrig.

**goof** [guːf] *vi (col: blunder)* Mist bauen *(col)*.

**goose** [guːs] *n, pl* **geese** *(lit, fig col)* Gans *f*.

**gooseberry** ['gʊzbərɪ] *n* Stachelbeere *f*. **to play ~** *(Brit col)* das fünfte Rad am Wagen sein *(col)*.

**goose:** **~flesh** *n,* **~pimples** *npl* Gänsehaut *f*; **~step 1** *n* Stechschritt *m*; **2** *vi* im Stechschritt marschieren.

**GOP** *(US Pol)* = **Grand Old Party** republikanische Partei.

**gore¹** [gɔːʳ] *n (liter: blood)* Blut *nt*.

**gore²** *vt* aufspießen.

**gorge** [gɔːdʒ] **1** *n (Geog)* Schlucht *f*. **2** *vr* sich vollessen; *(animal)* gierig fressen. **to ~ oneself on sth** etw verschlingen.

**gorgeous** ['gɔːdʒəs] *adj* großartig, sagenhaft *(col)*.

**gorilla** [gə'rɪlə] *n* Gorilla *m*.

**gormless** ['gɔːmlɪs] *adj (Brit col)* doof *(col)*.

**gorse** [gɔːs] *n* Stechginster *m*.

**gory** ['gɔːrɪ] *adj (+er)* battle *etc* blutig. **the ~ details** *(fig)* die peinlichen Einzelheiten.

**gosh** [gɒʃ] *interj* Mensch! *(col)*, Mann! *(col)*.

**gosling** ['gɒzlɪŋ] *n* junge Gans, Gänschen *nt*.

**go-slow** ['gəu'sləu] *n (Brit)* Bummelstreik *m*.

**gospel** ['gɒspəl] *n (Bibl)* Evangelium *nt*. **to take sth as ~** etw für bare Münze nehmen *(col)*; **the ~ truth** *(col)* die reine Wahrheit.

**gossamer** ['gɒsəməʳ] **1** *n* **(a)** Spinnfäden *pl*. **(b)** *(Tex)* hauchdünne Gaze. **2** *adj* hauchdünn.

**gossip** ['gɒsɪp] **1** *n* **(a)** Klatsch *(col) m*; *(chat)* Schwatz *m*. **to have a ~ with sb** mit jdm schwatzen. **(b)** *(person)* Klatschbase *f*. **2** *vi* schwatzen *(col)*; *(maliciously)* klatschen.

**gossip:** **~ column** *n* Klatschspalte *f*; **~ columnist** *n* Klatschkolumnist (in *f*) *m*.

**got** [gɒt] *pret, ptp of* **get.**

**Goth** [gɒθ] *n* Gote *m*.

**Gothic** ['gɒθɪk] **1** *adj* gotisch. **~ novel** Schauerroman *m*. **2** *n (Art)* Gotik *f*.

**gotten** ['gɒtn] *(esp US) ptp of* **get.**

**gouge** [gaudʒ] **1** *n (tool)* Hohlmeißel *m*; *(groove)* Furche *f*. **2** *vt* bohren. **the river ~d a channel in the mountainside** der Fluß grub sich *(dat)* sein Bett in den Berg.

►**gouge out** *vt sep* herausbohren. **to ~ sb's eyes ~** jdm die Augen ausstechen.

**goulash** ['guːlæʃ] *n* Gulasch *nt*.

**gourd** [guəd] *n* Flaschenkürbis *m*.

**gourmand** ['guəmənd] *n* Schlemmer *m*.

**gourmet** ['guəmeɪ] *n* Feinschmecker, Gourmet *m*.

**gout** [gaut] *n (Med)* Gicht *f*.

**govern** ['gʌvən] *vt* **(a)** *(rule)* country regieren; *province, colony, school etc* verwalten. **(b)** *(control)* bestimmen; *(legislation)* regeln. **(c)** *(Mech)* regulieren. **(d)** *(Gram)* case regieren.

**governess** ['gʌvənɪs] *n* Gouvernante *f*.

**governing** ['gʌvənɪŋ] *adj* **(a)** *(ruling)* regierend. **the ~ party** die Regierungspartei; **~ body** Vorstand *m*. **(b)** *(guiding, controlling)* entscheidend. **~ principle** Leitgedanke *m*.

**government** ['gʌvənmənt] *n* Regierung *f*.

**government** *in cpds* Regierungs-, der Regierung.

**government:** **~ backing** *n* staatliche Unterstützung; **~ department** *n* Ministerium *nt*; **~ grant** *n* (staatliche) Subvention; **~ intervention** *n* staatlicher Eingriff; **~ securities** *npl (Fin)* Staatsanleihen *pl*.

**governor** ['gʌvənəʳ] *n* **(a)** *(of colony, state etc)* Gouverneur *m*. **(b)** *(esp Brit: of bank, prison)* Direktor *m*; *(of school)* ≃ Mitglied *nt* des Schulbeirats. **the (board of) ~s** der Vorstand; *(of bank also)* das Direktorium; *(of school)* ≃ der Schulbeirat. **(c)** *(Brit col) (boss)* Chef *m (col)*. **(d)** *(Mech)* Regler *m*.

**govt** = **government** Reg.

**gown** [gaun] *n* **(a)** Kleid *nt*; *(evening ~)* Abendkleid *nt*. **(b)** *(academic)* Robe *f*; *(of clergyman, judge)* Talar *m*.

**GP** = **(a)** *(Sport)* **Grand Prix. (b)** *(Brit)* **general practitioner.**

**GPO** = **(a)** *(Brit old)* **General Post Office. (b)** *(US)* **Government Printing Office** Staatsdruckerei *f*.

**grab** [græb] **1** *n* **(a)** Griff *m*. **to make a ~ at sth** nach etw greifen. **(b)** *(Mech)* Greifer *m*. **(c)** *(col)* **to be up for ~s** zu haben sein *(col)*. **2** *vt* *(seize)* packen; *(greedily also)* sich *(dat)* schnappen *(col)*; *(take)* wegschnappen *(col)*; *(col: catch) person* schnappen *(col)*; *chance* beim Schopf ergreifen *(col)*. **he ~bed my sleeve** er packte mich am Ärmel; **to ~ sth away from sb** jdm etw wegreißen; **how does that ~ you?** *(col)* was hältst du davon?; **it didn't ~ me** *(col)* es hat mich nicht angemacht *(col)*. **3** *vi* **to** ~ **at** greifen nach, packen *(+acc)*.

**grace** [greɪs] **1** *n* Anmut *f.* **to do sth with (a) good/ bad** ~ etw bereitwillig/widerwillig tun; **he took it with good/bad** ~ er machte gute Miene zum bösen Spiel/er war sehr ungehalten darüber; **he had the** ~ **to apologize** er war so anständig, sich zu entschuldigen; **he didn't even have the** ~ **to apologize** er brachte es nicht einmal fertig, sich zu entschuldigen; **social** ~**s** (gesellschaftliche) Umgangsformen *pl*; **to give sb a few days'** ~ jdm ein paar Tage Zeit lassen; *(Comm)* jdm ein paar Tage Aufschub gewähren; **to say** ~ das Tischgebet sprechen; **by the** ~ **of God** durch die Gnade Gottes; **to fall from** ~ in Ungnade fallen; ~ **note** *(Mus)* Verzierung *f.* **2** *vt* **(a)** *(adorn)* zieren *(geh)*. **(b)** *(honour)* beehren *(with* mit*) (geh)*. **to** ~ **the occasion with one's presence** sich *(dat)* die Ehre geben.

**graceful** ['greɪsfʊl] *adj* anmutig; *outline, appearance also, behaviour* gefällig.

**gracefully** ['greɪsfəlɪ] *adv move* anmutig. **he gave in** ~ er gab gelassen nach.

**gracefulness** ['greɪsfʊlnɪs] *n* Anmut *f.*

**gracious** ['greɪʃəs] **1** *adj* liebenswürdig; *(lenient)* gnädig *(also iro)*. ~ **living** feudaler Lebensstil. **2** *interj* **(good)** ~**!** *(col)* du meine Güte!

**graciously** ['greɪʃəslɪ] *adv* gnädig.

**gradation** [grə'deɪʃən] *n* Abstufung *f.*

**grade** [greɪd] **1** *n* **(a)** *(standard)* Niveau *nt*; *(of goods)* (Güte)klasse *f.* **high-/low-**~ **goods** hoch-/minderwertige Ware; **to make the** ~ *(fig)* es schaffen *(col)*. **(b)** *(job* ~*)* Position, Stellung *f*; *(Mil)* Rang, (Dienst)grad *m*; *(salary* ~*)* Klasse, Stufe *f.* **(c)** *(Sch) (mark)* Note *f*; *(esp US: class)* Klasse *f.* **(d)** *(US)* = **gradient. 2** *vt* **(a)** klassifizieren; *eggs, goods also* sortieren; *students* einstufen. **(b)** *(Sch: mark)* benoten.

**grade:** ~ **crossing** *n (US)* Bahnübergang *m*; ~ **school** *n (US)* = Grundschule *f.*

**gradient** ['greɪdɪənt] *n* Neigung *f*; *(upward also)* Steigung *f*; *(downward also)* Gefälle *nt*. **a** ~ **of 1 in 10** eine Steigung/ein Gefälle von 10%.

**gradual** ['grædjʊəl] *adj* allmählich; *slope* sanft.

**gradually** ['grædjʊəlɪ] *adv* nach und nach, allmählich; *slope* sanft.

**graduate¹** ['grædjʊɪt] *n (Univ)* (Hochschul)absolvent(in *f*) *m*; *(US Sch)* Schulabgänger(in *f*) *m.* **high-school** ~ = Abiturient(in *f*) *m.*

**graduate²** ['grædjʊeɪt] **1** *vi (Univ)* graduieren; *(US Sch)* die Abschlußprüfung bestehen *(from* an *+dat)*. **2** *vt (mark)* einteilen.

**graduation** [ˌgrædjʊ'eɪʃən] *n* **(a)** *(Univ, US Sch: ceremony)* (Ab)schlußfeier *f (mit feierlicher Überreichung der Zeugnisse)*. **(b)** *(mark)* (Maß)einteilung *f.*

**graffiti** [grə'fiːtɪ] *npl* Graffiti *pl.*

**graft** [grɑːft] **1** *n* **(a)** *(Bot)* (Pfropf)reis *nt*; *(Med)* Transplantat *nt.* **(b)** *(col: corruption)* Schiebung *f.* **(c)** *(col: hard work)* Schufterei *f (col)*. **2** *vt (Bot)* (auf)pfropfen *(on* auf *+acc)*; *(Med)* übertragen *(on* auf *+acc)*, einpflanzen *(in* in *+acc)*; *(fig: incorporate)* einbauen *(onto* in *+acc)*. **3** *vi (col: work hard)* schuften *(col) (at* an *+dat)*.

**grain** [greɪn] *n* **(a)** *no pl* Getreide, Korn *nt.* **(b)** *(of corn, sand etc)* Korn *nt*; *(fig)* Spur *f*; *(of truth also)* Körnchen *nt.* **(c)** *(of leather)* Narben *m*; *(of cloth)* Strich *m*; *(of wood, marble)* Maserung *f*; *(Phot)* Korn *nt.* **it goes against the** ~ **(with sb)** *(fig)* es geht (jdm) gegen den Strich.

**grainy** ['greɪnɪ] *adj (+er) texture* körnig.

**gram(me)** [græm] *n* Gramm *nt.*

**grammar** ['græmər] *n* Grammatik *f.* **that's bad** ~ das ist grammat(ikal)isch falsch.

**grammar school** *n (Brit)* = Gymnasium *nt.*

**grammatical** [grə'mætɪkəl] *adj* grammat(ikal)isch; *rules, mistakes also* Grammatik-; *(correct)* grammat(ikal)isch richtig. **this is not** ~ das ist grammat(ikal)isch falsch.

**gramophone** ['græməfəʊn] *n (Brit)* Grammophon ® *nt.* ~ **record** Schallplatte *f.*

**gran** [græn] *n (col)* Oma *(col) f.*

**granary** ['grænərɪ] *n* Getreidespeicher *m.*

**grand** [grænd] **1** *adj (+er)* großartig; *building, display* prachtvoll; *(lofty) idea* hochfliegend; *(dignified) air, person* würdevoll; *(posh) dinner party, person* vornehm. **to have a** ~ **time** sich glänzend amüsieren. **2** *n (col)* = Riese *m (col) (1000 Dollar/Pfund)*. **50** ~ **50** Riesen *(col)*.

**grand:** ~**child** *n* Enkel(kind *nt*) *m*; ~**(d)ad** *n (col)* Opa *(col)*, Opi *(col) m*; ~**daughter** *n* Enkelin *f.*

**grandeur** ['grændjər] *n (of scenery, music)* Erhabenheit *f*; *(of manner also)* Würde *f*; *(of position, event also)* Glanz *m.*

**grand:** ~**father** *n* Großvater *m*; ~**father clock** *n* Standuhr *f*; ~ **finale** *n* großes Finale.

**grandiose** ['grændɪəʊs] *adj house, idea, speech* grandios *(also pej)*, großartig; *(pej: pompous) style* schwülstig, bombastisch.

**grand jury** *n (US Jur)* Großes Geschworenengericht.

**grandly** ['grændlɪ] *adv see adj* großartig; prachtvoll; würdevoll; vornehm.

**grand:** ~**ma** *n (col)* Oma *f (col)*; ~**mother** *n* Großmutter *f*; **G**~ **National** *n* Grand National *nt (bedeutendes Hindernisrennen in GB)*.

**grand:** ~ **opera** *n* große Oper; ~**pa** *n (col)* Opa *m (col)*; ~**parent** *n* Großvater *m*/-mutter *f*; ~**parents** *npl* Großeltern *pl*; ~ **piano** *n* Flügel *m*; **G**~ **Prix** *n* Grand Prix *m*; ~ **slam** *(Bridge)* Großschlemm *m*; **to win the** ~ **slam** *(Sport)* alle Wettbewerbe der Spielserie gewinnen; ~**son** *n* Enkel(sohn) *m*; ~**stand** *n* Haupttribüne *f*; **to have a** ~**stand view of sth** direkten Blick auf etw *(acc)* haben; ~ **total** *n* Gesamtsumme *f.*

**granite** ['grænɪt] *n* Granit *m.*

**granny, grannie** ['grænɪ] *n* **(a)** *(col)* Oma *(col) f.* **(b)** *(also* ~ **knot)** Altweiberknoten *m.*

**grant** [grɑːnt] **1** *vt* **(a)** gewähren *(sb* jdm*)*; *privilege also* zugestehen *(sb* jdm*)*; *prayer* erhören; *honour* erweisen *(sb* jdm*)*; *permission* erteilen *(sb* jdm*)*; *(fulfil) wish* erfüllen. **(b)** *(admit, agree)* zugeben, zugestehen. ~**ing** *or* ~**ed that this is true** ... angenommen, das ist wahr ...; **I** ~ **you** that da gebe ich dir recht; **to take sb/sth for** ~**ed** jdn/etw als selbstverständlich hinnehmen; **to take it for** ~**ed that** ... es als selbstverständlich betrachten, daß ...; **you take too much for** ~**ed** für dich ist zu vieles (einfach) selbstverständlich. **2** *n (of money)* Subvention *f*; *(for studying etc)* Ausbildungsbeihilfe *f*; *(scholarship)* Stipendium *nt.*

**granular** ['grænjʊlər] *adj* körnig.

**granulated sugar** ['grænjʊleɪtɪd'ʃʊgər] *n* Zuckerraffinade *f.*

**granule** ['grænjuːl] *n* Körnchen *nt.*

**grape** [greɪp] *n* (Wein)traube *f.*

**grape:** ~**fruit** *n* Grapefruit *f*; ~ **juice** *n* Traubensaft *m*; ~**vine** *n* Weinstock *m*; *(col)* Nachrichtendienst *m (col)*; **I heard it on the** ~**vine** es ist mir zu Ohren gekommen.

**graph** [grɑːf] *n* Diagramm, Schaubild *nt.* ~ **paper** Diagrammpapier, Millimeterpapier *nt.*

**graphic** ['græfɪk] *adj* **(a)** grafisch, graphisch. ~ **arts**

Grafik, Graphik *f*; ~ **artist** *or* **designer** Grafiker(in f) *m*, Graphiker(in *f*) *m*; **in** ~ **detail** in aller Deutlichkeit. (**b**) *(vivid) description* anschaulich.

**graphics** ['græfɪks] *n* (**a**) *pl (drawings)* grafische *or* graphische Darstellungen *pl*. (**b**) *(Comp)* Grafik *f*.

**graphite** ['græfaɪt] *n* Graphit *m*.

**graphologist** [græ'fɒlədʒɪst] *n* Graphologe *m*, Graphologin *f*.

**graphology** [græ'fɒlədʒɪ] *n* Graphologie *f*.

**grapple** ['græpl] *vi (lit)* ringen, kämpfen. **to** ~ **with a problem** sich mit einem Problem auseinandersetzen.

**grappling iron** ['græplɪŋ‚aɪən] *n* Haken *m*; *(Naut)* Enterhaken *m*.

**grasp** [grɑːsp] **1** *n* (**a**) *(hold)* Griff *m*. **to be within sb's** ~ (für jdn) in greifbare Nähe gerückt sein. (**b**) *(fig: understanding)* Verständnis *nt*. **to have a good** ~ **of sth** etw gut beherrschen; **it is beyond/within his** ~ das geht über seinen Verstand/das kann er begreifen. **2** *vt* (**a**) *(catch hold of)* ergreifen, greifen nach; *(hold tightly)* festhalten. (**b**) *(fig: understand)* begreifen, erfassen.

**grasping** ['grɑːspɪŋ] *adj (fig)* habgierig.

**grass** [grɑːs] **1** *n* (**a**) Gras *nt*; *(lawn)* Rasen *m*; *(pasture)* Weide(land *nt*) *f*. **to let the** ~ **grow under one's feet** *(fig)* lange zögern; **to put out to** ~ auf die Weide führen *or* treiben; *(fig: sb)* aufs Abstellgleis schieben. (**b**) *(col: marijuana)* Gras *nt (col)*. (**c**) *(Brit col: informer)* Spitzel *m (col)*. **2** *vi (Brit col)* singen *(col)* (**to** bei*)*; **to** ~ **on sb** jdn verpfeifen *(col)*.

**grass:** ~**hopper** *n* Heuschrecke *f*, Grashüpfer *m (col)*; ~**land** *n* Grasland *nt*; ~-**roots 1** *npl* Volk *nt*; *(of a party)* Basis *f*; **2** *adj attr* an der Basis; **at** ~-**roots level** an der Basis; **a** ~-**roots initiative** eine Bürgerinitiative; ~ **skirt** *n* Bastrock *m*; ~ **snake** *n* Ringelnatter *f*; ~ **widow** *n* Strohwitwe *f*; ~ **widower** *n* Strohwitwer *m*.

**grassy** ['grɑːsɪ] *adj (+er)* mit Gras bewachsen.

**grate**[1] [greɪt] *n* Gitter *nt*; *(in fire)* (Feuer)rost *m*; *(fireplace)* Kamin *m*.

**grate**[2] **1** *vt* (**a**) *(Cook)* reiben; *vegetables also* raspeln. (**b**) *(scrape)* streifen; *(make a grating noise with)* kratzen mit; *one's teeth* knirschen mit. **2** *vi (make a noise)* kratzen; *(chalk also, rusty door)* quietschen. **to** ~ **on sb's nerves** jdm auf die Nerven gehen; **it** ~**s on the ears** es tut in den Ohren weh.

**grateful** ['greɪtfʊl] *adj* dankbar *(to sb* jdm*)*.

**gratefully** ['greɪtfəlɪ] *adv* dankbar.

**grater** ['greɪtə*r*] *n* Reibe *f*; *(for vegetables also)* Raspel *f*.

**gratification** [‚grætɪfɪ'keɪʃən] *n (pleasure)* Genugtuung *f*; *(of desires)* Befriedigung *f*.

**gratify** ['grætɪfaɪ] *vt (give pleasure)* erfreuen; *(satisfy)* befriedigen, zufriedenstellen.

**gratifying** ['grætɪfaɪɪŋ] *adj* (sehr) erfreulich.

**grating**[1] ['greɪtɪŋ] *n* Gitter *nt*.

**grating**[2] *adj* kratzend; *sound (squeaking)* quietschend; *(rasping)* knirschend; *voice* schrill.

**gratis** ['grætɪs] *adj, adv* gratis.

**gratitude** ['grætɪtjuːd] *n* Dankbarkeit *f (to* gegenüber*)*.

**gratuitous** [grə'tjuːɪtəs] *adj* überflüssig, unnötig.

**gratuity** [grə'tjuːɪtɪ] *n* Gratifikation, (Sonder)zuwendung *f*; *(form: tip)* Trinkgeld *nt*.

**grave**[1] [greɪv] *n (lit, fig)* Grab *nt*. **he's digging his own** ~ *(fig)* er schaufelt sich selbst sein Grab; **to turn in one's** ~ sich im Grabe herumdrehen.

**grave**[2] *adj (+er)* ernst; *danger, risk* groß; *error* schwer, gravierend; *news* schlimm.

**grave-digger** ['greɪv‚dɪgə*r*] *n* Totengräber *m*.

**gravel** ['grævəl] **1** *n* Kies *m*; *(large chippings)* Schot-

ter *m*. ~ **path** Kiesweg *m*.

**gravelly** ['grævəlɪ] *adj (fig) voice* rauh.

**gravely** ['greɪvlɪ] *adv* ernst. ~ **ill** schwer krank; **you are** ~ **mistaken** Sie irren sich schwer.

**grave:** ~**stone** *n* Grabstein *m*; ~**yard** *n* Friedhof *m*.

**gravitate** ['grævɪteɪt] *vi* **to** ~ **towards sth** von etw angezogen werden.

**gravitation** [‚grævɪ'teɪʃən] *n (Phys)* Gravitation, Schwerkraft *f*; *(fig)* Tendenz *f (towards* zu*)*.

**gravitational** [‚grævɪ'teɪʃənl] *adj* Gravitations-. ~ **field** Gravitations- *or* Schwerefeld *nt*; ~ **force** Schwerkraft *f*; ~ **pull** Erdanziehung *f*.

**gravity** ['grævɪtɪ] *n* (**a**) *(Phys)* Schwere, Schwerkraft *f*. **centre of** ~ Schwerpunkt *m*; **force of** ~ Schwerkraft *f*; **specific** ~ spezifisches Gewicht. (**b**) *(seriousness)* Ernst *m*; *(of danger)* Größe *f*; *(of error)* Schwere *f*. **such was the** ~ **of the news that** ... die Nachricht war so schlimm, daß ...

**gravy** ['greɪvɪ] *n (juice)* Fleischsaft, Bratensaft *m*; *(sauce)* Soße *f*. ~ **boat** Sauciere, Soßenschüssel *f*; **to get on the** ~ **train** *(col)* auch ein Stück vom Kuchen abbekommen *(col)*.

**gray** [greɪ] *(esp US)* = **grey**.

**graze**[1] [greɪz] *vi (cattle etc)* grasen, weiden.

**graze**[2] **1** *vt (touch lightly)* streifen; *(scrape skin off)* aufschürfen. **to** ~ **one's knees** sich *(dat)* die Knie aufschürfen. **2** *n* Schürfwunde *f*.

**grazing** ['greɪzɪŋ] *n (also* ~ **land)** Weideland *nt*.

**grease** [griːs] **1** *n* Fett *nt*; *(lubricant)* Schmierfett *nt*. **2** *vt* fetten; *(Aut, Tech)* schmieren. **like** ~**d lightning** *(col)* wie ein geölter Blitz.

**grease:** ~**gun** *n* Fettpresse *f*; ~**paint** *n (Theat)* (Fett)schminke *f*; ~**proof paper** *n (Brit)* Butterbrotpapier *nt*.

**greasy** ['griːsɪ] *adj (+er)* (**a**) fettig; *food* fett; *machinery, axle* ölig; *hands, clothes* schmierig; *(slippery) road* rutschig. (**b**) *(fig pej) person* schmierig.

**great** [greɪt] **1** *adj (+er)* (**a**) groß. ~ **big** *(col)* riesig, Mords- *(col)*; **a** ~ **friend of ours** ein besonders guter Freund von uns; **of no** ~ **importance** ziemlich unwichtig; **a** ~ **number of, a** ~ **many** eine große Anzahl, sehr viele; **he lived to a** ~ **age** er erreichte ein hohes Alter; **to take a** ~ **interest in** sich sehr interessieren für; **Frederick the G**~ Friedrich der Große; **the** ~ **thing is** ... das Wichtigste ist ...; ~ **minds think alike** *(col)* große Geister denken gleich. (**b**) *(col: excellent)* Klasse *(col)*, Spitze *(col)*. **to be** ~ **at football/singing** ein großer Fußballspieler/Sänger sein; **he's a** ~ **one for criticizing others** im Kritisieren anderer ist er (ganz) groß. **2** *n usu pl* (~ **person)** Größe *f*.

**great:** ~-**aunt** *n* Großtante *f*; **G**~ **Barrier Reef** *n* Großes Barriereriff; **G**~ **Britain** *n* Großbritannien *nt*; **G**~ **Dane** *n* Deutsche Dogge.

**greater** ['greɪtə*r*] *adj, comp of* **great** größer. **to pay** ~ **attention** besser aufpassen; **G**~ **London** Groß-London *nt*.

**greatest** ['greɪtɪst] *adj, superl of* **great** größte(r, s). **he's the** ~ *(col)* er ist der Größte.

**great:** ~-**grandchild** *n* Urenkel *m*; ~-**grandparents** *npl* Urgroßeltern *pl*; **the G**~ **Lakes** *npl* die Großen Seen *pl*.

**greatly** ['greɪtlɪ] *adv* außerordentlich, sehr; *improved* bedeutend; *superior* bei weitem.

**greatness** ['greɪtnɪs] *n* Größe *f*.

**great:** ~-**uncle** *n* Großonkel *m*; **the G**~ **War** *n* der Erste Weltkrieg.

**Grecian** ['griːʃən] *adj* griechisch.

**Greece** [griːs] *n* Griechenland *nt*.

**greed** [griːd] *n* Gier *f (for* nach +*dat)*; *(for material* *wealth also)* Habsucht, Habgier *f; (gluttony)* Gefräßigkeit *f.* ~ **for power** Machtgier *f.*

**greedily** ['gri:dɪlɪ] *adv* gierig.

**greediness** ['gri:dɪnɪs] *n* Gier *f; (gluttony)* Gefräßigkeit *f.*

**greedy** ['gri:dɪ] *adj (+er)* gierig *(for* auf *+acc,* nach*); (for material wealth also)* habgierig; *(gluttonous)* gefräßig. ~ **for power** machtgierig.

**greedyguts** ['gri:dɪgʌts] *n (col)* Freßsack *m (col).*

**Greek** [gri:k] **1** *adj* griechisch. ~ **Orthodox** griechisch-orthodox. **2** *n* **(a)** Grieche *m,* Griechin *f.* **(b)** *(language)* Griechisch *nt.* **it's all** ~ **to me** *(col)* das sind für mich böhmische Dörfer *(col).*

**green** [gri:n] **1** *adj (+er) (lit, fig, Pol)* grün; *(gullible)* naiv. **to turn** ~ *(lit)* grün werden; *(fig: person)* (ganz) grün im Gesicht werden; *(with envy)* blaß *or* grün vor Neid werden. **2** *n* **(a)** *(colour)* Grün *nt.* **(b)** *(piece of land)* Rasen *m,* Grünfläche *f; (Golf)* Grün *nt; (village* ~*)* (Dorf)wiese *f.* **(c)** ~**s** *pl (Cook)* Grüngemüse *nt.* **(d)** *(Pol)* **G**~ Grüne(r) *mf;* **the G**~**s** die Grünen.

**green:** ~**back** *n (US col)* Lappen *(col),* Geldschein *m;* ~ **belt** *n* Grüngürtel *m;* ~ **card** *n (Mot Insur)* grüne Karte; *(US)* (unbefristete) Aufenthaltsgenehmigung.

**greenery** ['gri:nərɪ] *n* Grün *nt; (foliage)* grünes Laub.

**green:** ~ **field site** *n* unerschlossenes Bauland; ~ **fingers** *npl* **to have** ~ **fingers** eine Hand für Pflanzen haben; ~**fly** *n* Blattlaus *f;* ~**gage** *n* Reneklode *f;* ~**grocer** *n (esp Brit)* (Obst- und) Gemüsehändler *m;* ~**house** *n* Gewächshaus *nt;* ~ **house effect** *n* Treibhauseffekt *m.*

**Greenland** ['gri:nlənd] *n* Grönland *nt.*

**Greenlander** ['gri:nləndə'] *n* Grönländer(in *f) m.*

**green:** ~ **light** *n* **to give sb the** ~ **light** jdm grünes Licht geben; **the G**~ **Party** *n (Pol)* die Grünen *pl;* ~ **pepper** *n* (grüne) Paprikaschote; ~ **salad** *n* Blattsalat *m.*

**Greenwich (Mean) Time** ['grenɪdʒ('mi:n),taɪm] *n* westeuropäische Zeit.

**greet** [gri:t] *vt (welcome)* begrüßen; *(receive, meet)* empfangen; *(say hallo to)* grüßen; *news, decision* aufnehmen. **a terrible sight** ~**ed his eyes/him** ihm bot sich ein fürchterlicher Anblick.

**greeting** ['gri:tɪŋ] *n* Gruß *m; (welcoming)* Begrüßung *f; (receiving, meeting)* Empfang *m.* ~**s card/ telegram** Grußkarte *f/*-telegramm *nt.*

**gregarious** [grɪ'gɛərɪəs] *adj animal* Herden-; *person* gesellig.

**Gregorian** [grɪ'gɔ:rɪən] *adj chant, calendar* Gregorianisch.

**gremlin** ['gremlɪn] *n (hum)* Maschinenteufel *m (hum).*

**Grenada** [grə'neɪdə] *nt* Grenada *nt.*

**grenade** [grɪ'neɪd] *n* Granate *f.*

**Grenadian** [grə'neɪdɪən] **1** *adj* grenadisch. **2** *n* Grenader(in *f) m.*

**grew** [gru:] *pret of* **grow.**

**grey,** *(esp US)* **gray** [greɪ] **1** *adj (+er) (lit, fig)* grau. **to go** *or* **turn** ~ grau werden; **little** ~ **cells** *(col)* kleine graue Zellen *pl (col);* ~ **matter** *(col)* graue Zellen *pl;* **a** ~ **area** *(fig)* eine Grauzone. **2** *n (colour)* Grau *nt.* **3** *vi* grau werden. **his** ~**ing hair** sein graumeliertes Haar.

**grey:** ~**-haired** *adj* grauhaarig; ~**hound** *n* Windhund *m;* ~**hound racing** *n* Hunderennen *nt.*

**grid** [grɪd] *n (grating)* Gitter *nt; (on barbecue)* Rost *m; (on map)* Gitter, Netz *nt; (electricity, gas network)* Verteilernetz *nt; (Motor-racing: starting* ~*)* Start(platz) *m; (US Ftbl)* Spielfeld *nt.* **the (national)**

~ *(Elec)* das Überland(leitungs)netz; ~ **square** Planquadrat *nt.*

**gridiron** ['grɪd,aɪən] *n* **(a)** *(Cook)* (Brat)rost *m.* **(b)** *(US Ftbl)* Spielfeld *nt.*

**gridlock** ['grɪdlɒk] *n (US Mot)* totaler Stau *(esp in der Innenstadt).*

**grief** [gri:f] *n* Leid *nt,* Kummer *m; (because of loss)* große Trauer, Schmerz *m.* **to come to** ~ *(be hurt, damaged)* zu Schaden kommen; *(car)* auf der Strecke bleiben; *(fail)* scheitern.

**grievance** ['gri:vəns] *n* Beschwerde *f; (resentment)* Groll *m.* ~ **procedure** Beschwerdeweg *m;* **to air one's** ~**s** seine Beschwerden vorbringen.

**grieve** [gri:v] **1** *vt* Kummer bereiten *(+dat),* betrüben. **it** ~**s me to see that ...** es stimmt mich traurig, daß ... **2** *vi* trauern *(at, about* über *+acc).* **to** ~ **for sb/sth** um jdn/etw trauern.

**grievous** ['gri:vəs] *adj* ~ **bodily harm** *(Jur)* schwere Körperverletzung.

**grill** [grɪl] **1** *n* **(a)** *(on cooker)* Grill *m; (food)* Grillgericht *nt,* Grillteller *m.* **(b)** = **grille. 2** *vt* **(a)** *(Cook)* grillen. **(b)** *(col: interrogate)* in die Zange nehmen *(col).*

**grille** [grɪl] *n* Gitter *nt; (on window)* Fenstergitter *nt; (to speak through)* Sprechgitter *nt; (Aut)* Kühlergrill *m.*

**grilling** ['grɪlɪŋ] *n* strenges Verhör. **to give sb a** ~ jdn in die Zange nehmen *(col).*

**grim** [grɪm] *adj (+er) struggle* verbissen, unerbittlich; *(stern) face, smile* grimmig; *(fig) landscape, prospects, weather* trostlos; *news, tale, task* grauenhaft; *winter, times* hart; *determination* eisern; *necessity, truth* bitter. **to look** ~ *(person)* ein grimmiges Gesicht machen; *(things, prospects)* trostlos aussehen; **to hold on (to sth) like** ~ **death** sich verbissen (an etw *dat)* festhalten.

**grimace** ['grɪməs] **1** *n* Grimasse *f.* **to make a** ~ eine Grimasse schneiden. **2** *vi* Grimassen schneiden.

**grime** [graɪm] *n* (festsitzender) Schmutz; *(on buildings)* Ruß *m.*

**grimly** ['grɪmlɪ] *adv fight, hold on etc* verbissen; *smile* grimmig.

**grimness** ['grɪmnɪs] *n see adj* Verbissenheit, Unerbittlichkeit *f;* Grimmigkeit *f;* Trostlosigkeit *f;* Grauenhaftigkeit *f.*

**grimy** ['graɪmɪ] *adj (+er)* verschmutzt.

**grin** [grɪn] **1** *n see vi* Lächeln *nt;* Grinsen *nt.* **2** *vi (with pleasure)* lächeln; *(in scorn, cheekily)* grinsen. **to** ~ **and bear it** gute Miene zum bösen Spiel machen; **to** ~ **at sb** jdn anlächeln/angrinsen.

**grind** [graɪnd] *(vb: pret, ptp* **ground) 1** *vt* **(a)** *corn, coffee* mahlen. **to** ~ **one's teeth** mit den Zähnen knirschen. **(b)** *gem, lens, knife* schleifen. **(c) ground down by poverty** von Armut niedergedrückt. **2** *vi (brakes, teeth, gears)* knirschen. **to** ~ **to a halt** *(lit)* quietschend zum Stehen kommen; *(fig)* stocken; *(production etc)* zum Erliegen kommen; *(negotiations)* sich festfahren. **3** *n (col)* **the daily** ~ der tägliche Trott; **it's a bit of a** ~ das ist ganz schön mühsam *(col).*

**grinder** ['graɪndə'] *n (meat*~*)* Fleischwolf *m; (coffee*~*)* Kaffeemühle *f; (for sharpening)* Schleifmaschine *f.*

**grinding** ['graɪndɪŋ] *adj* ~ **poverty** drückende Armut.

**grindstone** ['graɪndstəun] *n* Schleifstein *m.* **to keep one's/sb's nose to the** ~ hart arbeiten/jdn hart arbeiten lassen.

**grip** [grɪp] **1** *n* **(a)** Griff *m; (on rope also, on road)* Halt *m.* **to get a** ~ **on oneself** *(col)* sich zusammenreißen *(col);* **to have a good** ~ **of a subject** ein Thema im Griff haben; **to release one's** ~ loslassen *(on* *sth* etw*)*; **to lose one's** ~ *(lit)* den Halt verlieren; *(fig)* nachlassen; **I must be losing my** ~ mit mir geht's bergab; **the country is in the** ~ **of winter** der Winter herrscht im Land; **to get** *or* **come to** ~**s with sth** etw in den Griff bekommen; **to get** *or* **come to** ~**s with sb** gegen jdn handgreiflich werden. (**b**) *(handle)* Griff *m*. (**c**) *(travelling-bag)* Reisetasche *f*.

2 *vt* packen; *hand also, (fig: fear etc also)* ergreifen; *(film, story etc also)* fesseln. **the car/tyre** ~**s the road well** der Wagen liegt gut auf der Straße/der Reifen greift gut.

**gripe** [graɪp] **1** *vi (col: grumble)* meckern *(col).* **to** ~ **at sb** jdn anmotzen *(col).* **2** *n* (**a**) **the** ~**s** *pl* Darmkrämpfe *pl.* (**b**) *(col: complaint)* Meckerei *f (col).*

**gripping** ['grɪpɪŋ] *adj* story spannend, fesselnd.

**grisly** ['grɪzlɪ] *adj (+er)* grausig, gräßlich.

**grist** [grɪst] *n* **it's all** ~ **to his mill** das kann er alles verwerten.

**gristle** ['grɪsl] *n* Knorpel *m.*

**grit** [grɪt] **1** *n* (**a**) *(dust, in eye)* Staub *m*; *(gravel)* Splitt *m*; *(for roads)* Streusand *m.* (**b**) *(courage)* Mut *m.* (**c**) *(US)* ~**s** *pl* Grütze *f.* **2** *vt* (**a**) *road* streuen. (**b**) **to** ~ **one's teeth** die Zähne zusammenbeißen.

**gritty** ['grɪtɪ] *adj* (**a**) *(like grit)* sandig. (**b**) *(col: brave)* tapfer.

**grizzle** ['grɪzl] *vi (Brit col)* quengeln.

**grizzly** ['grɪzlɪ] *n (also* ~ *bear)* Grisly(bär) *m.*

**groan** [grəʊn] **1** *n* Stöhnen *nt no pl*; *(of pain also, of planks etc)* Ächzen *nt no pl.* **to let out** *or* **give a** ~ (auf)stöhnen. **2** *vi* stöhnen *(with* vor +*dat)*; *(with pain also, beneath weight)* ächzen *(with* vor +*dat).*

**grocer** ['grəʊsəʳ] *n (dated)* Lebensmittelhändler, Kaufmann *(dated) m.*

**grocery** ['grəʊsərɪ] *n* (**a**) Lebensmittelgeschäft *nt.* (**b**) **groceries** *pl (goods)* Lebensmittel *pl.*

**grog** [grɒg] *n* Grog *m.*

**groggy** ['grɒgɪ] *adj (+er) (col)* groggy *inv (col).*

**groin** [grɔɪn] *n (Anat)* Leiste *f.*

**groom** [gruːm] **1** *n* (**a**) *(in stables)* Reitknecht *m.* (**b**) *(bride~)* Bräutigam *m.* **2** *vt* (**a**) *horse* striegeln. **well** ~**ed** *(person)* gepflegt. (**b**) **to** ~ **sb for an office** jdn auf *or* für ein Amt vorbereiten.

**groove** [gruːv] *n* Rille *f*; *(in face)* Furche *f.* **to be stuck in a** ~ *(fig)* aus dem Trott nicht mehr herauskommen.

**grope** [grəʊp] **1** *vi (also* ~ **around** *or* **about)** *(her-um)*tasten *(for* nach*)*; *(for words)* suchen *(for* nach*).* **2** *vt (col) girl* befummeln *(col).* **to** ~ **one's way in/out** sich hinein-/hinaustasten.

**gross¹** [grəʊs] *n no pl* Gros *nt.*

**gross²** [grəʊs] **1** *adj (+er)* (**a**) *(fat)* fett, feist. (**b**) *(coarse, vulgar)* derb. (**c**) *(extreme, flagrant)* grob; *impertinence* ungeheuerlich. (**d**) *(total)* brutto; *income, profit, weight* Brutto-. **he earns £250** ~ er verdient £250 brutto; ~ **national product** Bruttosozialprodukt *nt.* **2** *vt* brutto verdienen.

**grossly** ['grəʊslɪ] *adv* (**a**) *(coarsely)* derb. (**b**) *(extremely)* ungeheuer; *exaggerated* grob.

**grotesque** [grəʊ'tesk] *adj* grotesk.

**grotto** ['grɒtəʊ] *n, pl* -**(e)s** Grotte *f.*

**grotty** ['grɒtɪ] *adj (+er) (col)* mies *(col).*

**grouch** [graʊtʃ] *(col)* **1** *n* (**a**) *(complaint)* Beschwerde *f.* **she's always got a** ~ sie hat immer was zu meckern *(col).* (**b**) *(person)* Meckerer *m (col).* **2** *vi* meckern *(col).*

**grouchy** ['graʊtʃɪ] *adj (+er)* griesgrämig.

**ground¹** [graʊnd] **1** *n* (**a**) *(soil, terrain, fig)* Boden *m.* **snow on high** ~ Schnee in höheren Lagen; **hilly** ~ hügeliges Gelände; **there is common** ~ **between us** uns verbindet einiges; **to be on dangerous** ~ *(fig)*

sich auf gefährlichem Boden bewegen; **to meet sb on his own** ~ zu jdm kommen; **to cut the** ~ **from under sb's feet** jdm den Boden unter den Füßen wegziehen; **to gain/lose** ~ Boden gewinnen/verlieren; *(disease, rumour)* um sich greifen/im Schwinden begriffen sein; **to break new** ~ *(fig)* etwas völlig Neuartiges darstellen; *(person)* Neuland betreten; **to go over the** ~ *(fig)* alles durchgehen; **to cover a lot of** ~ *(lit)* eine weite Strecke zurücklegen; *(fig)* eine Menge Dinge behandeln; **to hold** *or* **stand one's** ~ *(lit)* nicht von der Stelle weichen; *(fig)* seinen Mann stehen, sich nicht unterkriegen lassen; **to shift one's** ~ *(fig)* seine Haltung ändern; **above/below** ~ über/unter der Erde; *(Min)* über/unter Tage; **to fall to the** ~ zu Boden fallen; **to burn sth to the** ~ etw niederbrennen; **it suits me down to the** ~ das paßt mir ausgezeichnet; **to get off the** ~ *(plane etc)* abheben; *(plans, project etc)* ins Rollen kommen; **to get sth off the** ~ etw ins Rollen bringen; **to go to** ~ *(fox)* im Bau verschwinden; *(person)* untertauchen *(col)*; **to run sb/sth to** ~ jdn/etw ausfindig machen; **to run sb/oneself into the** ~ *(col)* jdn/sich kaputtmachen *(col)*; **to run a car into the** ~ ein Auto schrottreif fahren.

(**b**) *(pitch)* Feld *nt*, Platz *m*; *(parade* ~, *drill*~*)* Platz *m.*

(**c**) ~**s** *pl (premises, land)* Gelände *nt*; *(gardens)* Anlagen *pl.*

(**d**) ~**s** *pl (sediment)* Satz *m.*

(**e**) *(esp US Elec)* Erde *f.*

(**f**) *(reason)* Grund *m.* **to have** ~**s for sth** Grund zu etw haben; **to be** ~**(s) for sth** Grund für *or* zu etw sein; ~**s for divorce** Scheidungsgrund *m*; **on the** ~**(s) of** aufgrund *(+gen)*, auf Grund von; **on the** ~**s that** auf Grund der Tatsache, daß; **on health** ~**s** aus gesundheitlichen Gründen.

**2** *vt* (**a**) *ship* auf Grund setzen. **to be** ~**ed** aufgelaufen sein. (**b**) *plane (for mechanical reasons)* aus dem Verkehr ziehen; *pilot* sperren. **to be** ~**ed by bad weather** wegen schlechten Wetters nicht starten können. (**c**) *(esp US Elec)* erden. (**d**) *(base)* **to be** ~**ed on sth** sich auf etw *(acc)* gründen.

**ground²** *pret, ptp of* **grind.** **2** *adj coffee* gemahlen. ~ **beef** *(US)* Hackfleisch *m*; ~ **glass** geschliffenes Glas; *(particles)* Glaspulver *nt*; ~ **rice** Reismehl *nt.*

**ground:** ~ **cloth** *n (US)* Zeltboden(plane *f*) *m*; ~ **control** *n (Aviat)* Bodenkontrolle *f*; ~ **crew** *n* Bodenpersonal *nt*; ~ **floor** *n* Erdgeschoß *nt*; ~ **frost** *n* Bodenfrost *m.*

**grounding** ['graʊndɪŋ] *n* (**a**) *(basic knowledge)* Grundwissen *nt.* **to give sb a** ~ **in English** jdm die Grundlagen *pl* des Englischen beibringen. (**b**) *(Aviat) (of plane)* Startverbot *nt*; *(of pilot)* Sperren *nt.*

**ground:** ~**less** *adj* grundlos, unbegründet; ~ **level** *n* Boden *m*; **below** ~ **level** unter dem Boden; **at** ~ **level** *live* im Erdgeschoß; ~ **mist** *n* Bodennebel *m*; ~**nut** *n* Erdnuß *f*; ~ **plan** *n* Grundriß *m*; ~ **rules** *npl* Grundregeln *pl*; ~**sheet** *n* Zeltboden(plane *f*) *m.*

**groundskeeper** ['graʊndzkiːpəʳ] *n (US)*, **groundsman** ['graʊndzmən] *n, pl* -**men** *(esp Brit)* Platzwart *m.*

**ground:** ~ **staff** *n* Bodenpersonal *nt*; ~ **swell** *n* Dünung *f*; ~**-to-air missile** *n* Boden-Luft-Rakete *f*; ~**work** *n* Vorarbeit *f.*

**group** [gruːp] **1** *n* Gruppe *f*; *(Comm also)* Konzern *m*; *(theatre* ~ *also)* Ensemble *nt.* **2** *attr* Gruppen-; *discussion, activities* in der Gruppe. **3** *vt* gruppieren. **to** ~ **together** *(in one* ~*)* zusammentun; *(in several* ~*s)* in Gruppen einteilen; **the books were** ~**ed ac-**

**cording to subject** die Bücher standen nach Sach-
gruppen geordnet.
**group:** ~ **booking** *n* Gruppenbuchung *f*; ~ **captain**
*n (Aviat)* Oberst *m*; ~ **practice** *n* Gemeinschafts-
praxis *f*; ~ **therapy** *n* Gruppentherapie *f.*
**grouse¹** [graʊs] *n, pl* - Rauhfußhuhn *nt*; *(red ~)*
Schottisches Moorhuhn.
**grouse²** *(col)* **1** *n (complaint)* Beschwerde *f.* **to have
a good** ~ herummeckern *(col)*. **2** *vi* meckern *(col)*
*(about über +acc)*.
**grouting** ['graʊtɪŋ] *n* Fugenkitt *m.*
**grove** [grəʊv] *n (liter)* Hain *m (poet)*.
**grovel** ['grɒvl] *vi* kriechen *(to sb vor jdm)*.
**grow** [grəʊ] *pret* **grew**, *ptp* **grown 1** *vt* (a) *plants*
ziehen; *(commercially) potatoes, coffee etc* anbauen;
*(cultivate) flowers* züchten. **(b) to** ~ **one's beard/hair**
sich *(dat)* einen Bart/die Haare wachsen lassen. **2**
*vi* (a) wachsen; *(hair also)* länger werden; *(in numbers)* zunehmen; *(in size also)* sich vergrößern; *(fig:
become more mature)* sich weiterentwickeln. **to** ~
**in stature/wisdom** an Ansehen/Weisheit zunehmen;
**to** ~ **in popularity** immer beliebter werden; **it'll** ~
**on you** du wirst schon noch Geschmack daran
finden. **(b)** *(become)* werden. **to** ~ **old** alt werden;
**to** ~ **to hate/love sb** jdn hassen/lieben lernen; **to** ~
**to enjoy sth** langsam Gefallen an etw *(dat)* finden.
►**grow apart** *vi (fig)* sich auseinanderentwickeln.
►**grow away** *vi (fig)* **to** ~ ~ **from sb** sich jdm entfremden.
►**grow into** *vi +prep obj* **(a)** *clothes, job* hinein-
wachsen in *(+acc)*. **(b)** *(become)* sich entwickeln zu,
werden zu. **to** ~ ~ **a man/woman** zum Mann/zur
Frau heranwachsen.
►**grow out of** *vi +prep obj* **(a)** *clothes* herauswachsen aus; *habit* ablegen. **(b)** *(arise from)* entstehen aus.
►**grow up** *vi (spend childhood)* aufwachsen; *(become adult)* erwachsen werden; *(fig) (custom,
hatred)* aufkommen; *(city)* entstehen. **what are you
going to do when you** ~ ~? was willst du mal werden, wenn du groß bist?; ~ ~! sei nicht kindisch!,
werde endlich erwachsen!; **to** ~ ~ **into a beauty**
sich zu einer Schönheit entwickeln.
**grower** ['grəʊə<sup>r</sup>] *n (of fruit, vegetables)* Anbauer *m*;
*(of flowers)* Züchter *m*; *(of tobacco, coffee)* Pflanzer
*m.*
**growing** ['grəʊɪŋ] *adj (lit, fig)* wachsend; *child* heran-
wachsend. ~ **pains** *(Med)* Wachstumsschmerzen *pl*;
*(fig)* Kinderkrankheiten *pl.*
**growl** [graʊl] **1** *n* Knurren *nt no pl*; *(of bear)* Brummen *nt no pl.* **2** *vi* knurren; *(bear)* böse brummen.
**to** ~ **at sb** jdn anknurren/anbrummen.
**grown** [grəʊn] **1** *ptp of* **grow**. **2** *adj* erwachsen. **fully**
~ ausgewachsen.
**grown-up** [ˌgrəʊn'ʌp] **1** *adj* erwachsen; *clothes,
shoes* Erwachsenen-. **2** *n* Erwachsene(r) *mf.*
**growth** [grəʊθ] *n* (a) Wachstum *nt*; *(of person also)*
Entwicklung *f*; *(increase in quantity, fig: of love, interest etc)* Anwachsen *nt*; *(increase in size also)* Vergrößerung *f*; *(of capital etc)* Zuwachs *m.* ~ **industry**
Wachstumsindustrie *f*; ~ **rate** Wachstumsrate *f.* **(b)**
**with a two days'** ~ **on his face** mit zwei Tage alten
Bartstoppeln. **(c)** *(Med)* Wucherung *f.*
**grub** [grʌb] **1** *n* **(a)** *(larva)* Larve *f.* **(b)** *(col: food)*
Fressalien *pl (hum, col)*. ~**('s) up!** antreten zum Es-
senfassen! *(col)*. **2** *vi (also* ~ **about** *or* **around)** wühlen *(in* in *+dat)*.
**grubby** ['grʌbɪ] *adj (+er)* schmuddelig *(col)*; *hands*
dreckig *(col)*.
**grudge** [grʌdʒ] **1** *n* Groll *m (against* gegen*).* **to bear
sb a** ~**/have a** ~ **against sb** einen Groll gegen jdn

hegen/auf jdn haben; **I bear him no** ~ ich nehme
ihm das nicht übel; **to bear** ~**s** nachtragend sein. **2**
*vt* **to** ~ **sb sth** jdm etw nicht gönnen; **I don't** ~ **you
your success/these pleasures** ich gönne Ihnen Ihren
Erfolg/das Vergnügen; **to** ~ **doing sth** etw mit Widerwillen tun.
**grudging** ['grʌdʒɪŋ] *adj person, attitude* unwirsch;
*contribution, gift* widerwillig gegeben; *admiration,
praise, support* widerwillig.
**grudgingly** ['grʌdʒɪŋlɪ] *adv* widerwillig.
**gruel** [grʊəl] *n* Schleimsuppe *f.*
**gruelling, *(US)* grueling** ['grʊəlɪŋ] *adj task, day etc*
aufreibend; *climb, race* äußerst strapaziös. ~ **pace**
mörderisches Tempo.
**gruesome** ['gruːsəm] *adj* grausig, schaurig.
**gruff** [grʌf] *adj (+er)* barsch, schroff.
**grumble** ['grʌmbl] **1** *n (complaint)* Murren *nt no pl.*
**2** *vi* murren *(about, over* über *+acc)*; *(thunder, gunfire)* grollen. **grumbling appendix** Blinddarmreizung
*f.*
**grumbler** ['grʌmblə<sup>r</sup>] *n* Nörgler(in *f*) *m.*
**grumpy** *adj*, ~**ily** *adv* ['grʌmpɪ, -lɪ] *(+er)* brummig,
grantig.
**grunge** [grʌndʒ] *n* Grunge *nt.*
**grunt** [grʌnt] **1** *n* Grunzen *nt no pl*; *(of pain, in exertion)* Ächzen *nt no pl.* **2** *vi* grunzen; *(with pain, exertion)* ächzen. **3** *vt reply* brummen, knurren.
**G-string** ['dʒiːstrɪŋ] *n (clothing)* Minislip *m.*
**GT** *(Aut)* = **gran turismo** GT.
**GU** *(US Post)* = **Guam.**
**guarantee** [ˌgærən'tiː] **1** *n* Garantie *f (of* für*)*; *(certificate)* Garantieschein *m.* **to have a 6-month** ~ 6
Monate Garantie haben; **while it is under** ~ solange
noch Garantie darauf ist; **that's no** ~ **that ... das**
heißt noch lange nicht, daß ...; **I give you my** ~ das
garantiere ich Ihnen. **2** *vt* garantieren. **to be** ~**d for
three years** drei Jahre Garantie haben; **I** ~ **to come
tomorrow** ich komme garantiert morgen; **that's a**
~**d success** das wird garantiert ein Erfolg; ~**d price**
Garantiepreis *m.*
**guarantor** [ˌgærən'tɔː<sup>r</sup>] *n* Garant *m*; *(Jur)* Bürge *m.*
**guard** [gɑːd] **1** *n* **(a)** *(Mil)* Wache *f*; *(single soldier
also)* Wachtposten *m*; *(no pl: squad also)* Wachmannschaft *f*; *(security~)* Sicherheitsbeamte(r) *m*,
Sicherheitsbeamtin *f*; *(at factory gates, in park etc)*
Wächter(in *f*) *m*; *(esp US: prison ~)* Gefängniswär-
ter(in *f*) *m*; *(Brit Rail)* Schaffner(in *f*) *m.* **the G**~**s**
*(Brit)* das Garderegiment; ~ **of honour** *(Brit)* or **hon-
or** *(US)* Ehrenwache *f*; **to change** ~ Wachablösung
machen; **under** ~ unter Bewachung; **to be under** ~
bewacht werden; **to keep sb/sth under** ~ jdn/etw
bewachen; **to be on** ~, **to stand** *or* **keep** ~ Wache
halten; **to put a** ~ **on sb/sth** jdn/etw bewachen lassen.
  **(b)** *(Boxing, Fencing)* Deckung *f.* **to take** ~ in Ver-
teidigungsstellung gehen; **to drop** *or* **lower one's** ~
*(col)* seine Deckung vernachlässigen; *(fig)* seine Reserve aufgeben; **to catch sb off (his/her)** ~ jdn überrumpeln; **to be on one's** ~ **(against sth)** *(fig)* (vor
etw *dat)* auf der Hut sein; **to put sb on his/her** ~
**(against sth)** jdn (vor etw *dat)* warnen.
  **(c)** *(safety device, for protection)* Schutz *m (against*
gegen*)*; *(on machinery also)* Schutzvorrichtung *f*;
*(fire ~)* Schutzgitter *nt.*
  **2** *vt prisoner, place, valuables* bewachen; *treasure
also, secret* hüten; *luggage* aufpassen auf *(+acc)*;
*(protect) person, place* schützen *(from, against* vor
*+dat)*.
►**guard against** *vi +prep obj (take care to avoid)*
*suspicion* sich in acht nehmen vor *(+dat)*; *hasty reaction, bad habit* sich hüten vor *(+dat)*; *illness, mis-*

**guard dog**

*understandings* vorbeugen *(+dat)*; *accidents* verhüten. **you must ~ ~ catching cold** Sie müssen aufpassen, daß Sie sich nicht erkälten; **in order to ~ ~ this** um dem vorzubeugen.

**guard:** ~ **dog** *n* Wachhund *m*; ~ **duty** *n* Wachdienst *m*; **to be on** ~ **duty** Wache haben.

**guarded** ['gɑːdɪd] *adj reply* zurückhaltend.

**guardhouse** ['gɑːdhaʊs] *n (Mil)* Wachstube *f*; *(for prisoners)* Bunker *m*.

**guardian** ['gɑːdɪən] *n* Hüter, Wächter *m*; *(Jur)* Vormund *m*.

**guard:** ~**-rail** *n* Schutzgeländer *nt*; ~**room** *n* Wachstube *f*.

**guardsman** ['gɑːdzmən] *n, pl* **-men** [-mən] Wachtposten *m*; *(member of guards regiment)* Gardist *m*; *(US: in National Guard)* Nationalgardist *m*.

**guard's van** ['gɑːdzvæn] *n (Brit Rail)* Schaffnerabteil *nt*, Dienstwagen *m*.

**Guatemala** [ˌgwɑːtɪˈmɑːlə] *n* Guatemala *nt*.

**Guatemalan** [ˌgwɑːtɪˈmɑːlən] **1** *adj* guatemaltekisch. **2** *n* Guatemalteke *m*, Guatemaltekin *f*.

**guer(r)illa** [gəˈrɪlə] **1** *n* Guerillakämpfer(in *f*) *m*. **2** *attr* Guerilla-. ~ **warfare** Guerillakrieg *m*.

**guess** [ges] **1** *n* Vermutung, Annahme *f*; *(estimate)* Schätzung *f*. **to have a** ~ **(at sth)** (etw) raten; *(estimate)* (etw) schätzen; **it was just a** ~ ich habe nur geraten; **it was just a lucky** ~ das war ein Zufallstreffer *m*; **I'll give you three** ~**es** dreimal darfst du raten; **at a rough** ~ grob geschätzt; **my** ~ **is that ...** ich schätze *or* vermute, daß ...; **your** ~ **is as good as mine!** *(col)* da kann ich auch nur raten!; **it's anybody's** ~ *(col)* das wissen die Götter *(col)*.

**2** *vi (a)* raten. **to keep sb** ~**ing** jdn im ungewissen lassen; **he's only** ~**ing** das ist eine reine Vermutung von ihm; **you'll never** ~**!** das wirst du nie erraten; **to** ~ **at sth** etw raten. **(b)** *(esp US)* schätzen, glauben. **I** ~ **not** wohl nicht; **he's right, I** ~ er hat wohl recht; **is he coming?** — **I** ~ **so** kommt er? — ich glaube schon.

**3** *vt* raten; *(correctly)* erraten; *(estimate) weight* schätzen. **I** ~**ed as much** das habe ich mir schon gedacht; ~ **what!** *(col)* stell dir vor! *(col)*.

**guessing game** ['gesɪŋgeɪm] *n (lit, fig)* Ratespiel *nt*.

**guesstimate** ['gestɪmɪt] *n* grobe Schätzung.

**guesswork** ['geswɜːk] *n* Raten *nt*. **(pure)** ~ (reine) Vermutung.

**guest** [gest] *n* Gast *m*. ~ **of honour** *(Brit)* or **honor** *(US)* Ehrengast *m*; **be my** ~ *(col)* nur zu! *(col)*.

**guest** *in cpds* Gast-; ~ **appearance** *n* Gastauftritt *m*; ~**-house** *n* Pension *f*; ~ **list** *n* Gästeliste *f*; ~**room** *n* Gästezimmer *nt*.

**guffaw** [gʌˈfɔː] **1** *n* schallendes Lachen *no pl*. **2** *vi* schallend (los)lachen.

**guidance** ['gaɪdəns] *n (direction)* Führung, Leitung *f*; *(counselling)* Beratung *f (on* über *+acc)*; *(from superior, parents, teacher etc)* Anleitung *f*. **for your** ~ zu Ihrer Orientierung; ~ **system** *(on rocket)* Steuerungssystem *nt*.

**guide** [gaɪd] **1** *n* **(a)** *(person)* Führer(in *f*) *m*; *(fig: indication, pointer)* Anhaltspunkt *m (to* für); *(model)* Leitbild *nt*. **(b)** *(Tech)* Leitvorrichtung *f*. **(c)** *(Brit: girl* ~) Pfadfinderin *f*. **(d)** *(instructions)* Anleitung *f*; *(manual)* Handbuch *nt (to* gen); *(travel* ~) (Reise)führer *m*. **2** *vt people, blind man etc* führen; *discussion also* leiten; *missile, sb's behaviour* lenken. **to** ~ **a plane in** ein Flugzeug einweisen; **to be** ~**d by sb/sth** *(person)* sich von jdm/etw leiten lassen.

**guide-book** ['gaɪdbʊk] *n* Reiseführer *m*.

**guided missile** [ˌgaɪdɪdˈmɪsaɪl] *n* ferngelenktes Geschoß.

**guide-dog** ['gaɪddɒg] *n* Blindenhund *m*.

**guided tour** [ˌgaɪdɪdˈtʊər] *n* Führung *f (of* durch).

**guidelines** ['gaɪdlaɪnz] *npl* Richtlinien *pl*.

**guiding** ['gaɪdɪŋ]: ~ **hand** *n* leitende Hand; ~ **principle** *n* Leitmotiv *nt*.

**guild** [gɪld] *n (Hist)* Zunft, Gilde *f*; *(association)* Verein *m*.

**guildhall** ['gɪldhɔːl] *n (town hall)* Rathaus *nt*.

**guile** [gaɪl] *n* Tücke, (Arg)list *f*.

**guillotine** [ˌgɪləˈtiːn] *n* Guillotine *f*; *(for paper)* (Papier)schneidemaschine *f*.

**guilt** [gɪlt] *n* Schuld *f (for, of* an *+dat)*. **to feel** ~ **about sth** sich wegen etw schuldig fühlen; ~ **complex** Schuldkomplex *m*.

**guiltily** ['gɪltɪlɪ] *adv* schuldbewußt; *act* verdächtig.

**guiltless** ['gɪltlɪs] *adj* schuldlos *(of* an *+dat)*.

**guilty** ['gɪltɪ] *adj (+er)* schuldig *(of* gen); *look, voice* schuldbewußt; *conscience, thought* schlecht. **the** ~ **person/party** der/die Schuldige/die schuldige Partei; **verdict of** ~ Schuldspruch *m*; **to find sb** ~**/not** ~ **(of a crime)** jdn (eines Verbrechens) für schuldig/nicht schuldig befinden; **we're all** ~ **of neglecting the problem** uns alle trifft Schuld, daß das Problem vernachlässigt wurde; **I've been** ~ **of that myself** den Fehler habe ich auch schon begangen; **I feel very** ~ **(about ...)** ich habe ein sehr schlechtes Gewissen (wegen ...).

**Guinea** ['gɪnɪ] *n* Guinea *nt*.

**guinea** ['gɪnɪ] *n (Brit old)* Guinee *f (21 Shillings, heute £1.05)*.

**guinea:** ~**-fowl** *n* Perlhuhn *nt*; ~**-pig** *n* Meerschweinchen *nt*; *(fig)* Versuchskaninchen *nt*.

**guise** [gaɪz] *n* **in the** ~ **of a clown/swan** als Clown verkleidet/in Gestalt eines Schwans.

**guitar** [gɪˈtɑːr] *n* Gitarre *f*.

**guitarist** [gɪˈtɑːrɪst] *n* Gitarrist(in *f*) *m*.

**gulch** [gʌltʃ] *n (US)* Schlucht *f*.

**gulf** [gʌlf] *n (bay)* Golf, Meerbusen *m*; *(lit, fig: chasm)* tiefe Kluft. **G~ Stream** Golfstrom *m*; **the (Persian) G~** der Persische Golf; **the G~ War** der Golfkrieg; **the G~ States** die Golfstaaten *pl*.

**gull** [gʌl] *n (sea~)* Möwe *f*.

**gullet** ['gʌlɪt] *n* Speiseröhre, Kehle *f*.

**gullible** ['gʌlɪbl] *adj* leichtgläubig.

**gully** ['gʌlɪ] *n (ravine)* Schlucht *f*; *(narrow channel)* Rinne *f*.

**gulp** [gʌlp] **1** *n* Schluck *m*. **at a/one** ~ auf einen Schluck. **2** *vt (also* ~ **down)** *drink* herunterstürzen; *food* herunterschlingen; *medicine* hinunterschlucken. **what?, he** ~**ed** was?, preßte er hervor.

**gum**[1] [gʌm] *n (Anat)* Zahnfleisch *nt no pl*.

**gum**[2] **1** *n (Bot)* Gummi *nt*; *(glue)* Klebstoff *m*; *(chewing* ~) Kaugummi *m*; *(sweet)* Weingummi *m*. **2** *vt (stick together)* kleben; *(spread* ~ *on)* gummieren.

▶**gum up** *vt sep* verkleben. **to** ~ ~ **the works** *(fig col)* die Sache vermasseln *(col)*.

**gum:** ~**boil** *n* Zahnfleischabszeß *m*; ~**boot** *n* Gummistiefel *m*.

**gumption** ['gʌmpʃən] *n (col)* Grips *m (col)*. **to have the** ~ **to do sth** geistesgegenwärtig genug sein, etw zu tun.

**gum:** ~**-shield** *n* Zahnschutz *m*; ~**-tree** *n* **to be up a** ~**-tree** *(Brit col)* aufgeschmissen sein *(col)*.

**gun** [gʌn] **1** *n* **(a)** *(cannon etc)* Kanone *f*, Geschütz *nt*; *(rifle)* Gewehr *nt*; *(pistol etc)* Pistole *f*. **to carry a** ~ (mit einer Schußwaffe) bewaffnet sein; **to draw a** ~ **on sb** jdn mit einer Schußwaffe bedrohen; **big** ~ *(fig col)* hohes Tier *(col) (in* in *+dat)*; **to stick to one's** ~**s** nicht nachgeben; **to jump the** ~ *(Sport)* Frühstart machen; *(fig)* voreilig sein *or* handeln. **(b)** *(spray~)* Pistole *f*. **2** *vi (col)* **to be** ~**ning for sb**

*(fig)* jdn auf dem Kieker haben *(col)*; *for opponent* jdn auf die Abschußliste gesetzt haben.
▶**gun down** *vt sep* niederschießen.
**gun:** ~ **battle** *n* Schießerei *f*; ~**boat** *n* Kanonenboot *nt*; ~ **carriage** *n* Lafette *f*; ~ **crew** *n* Geschützbedienung *f*; ~ **dog** *n* Jagdhund *m*; ~**-fight** *n* Schießerei *f*; *(Mil)* Feuergefecht *nt*; ~**fire** *n* Schießerei *f*, Schüsse *pl*; *(Mil)* Geschützfeuer *nt*.
**gunge** [gʌndʒ] *n (Brit col)* klebriges Zeug *(col)*.
**gungho** ['gʌŋ'həʊ] *adj* übereifrig.
**gunman** ['gʌnmən] *n, pl* **-men** Bewaffnete(r) *m*. **they saw the** ~ sie haben den Schützen gesehen.
**gunner** ['gʌnəʳ] *n (Mil)* Artillerist *m*; *(title)* Kanonier *m*; *(Naut)* Geschützführer *m*; *(in plane)* Bordschütze *m*.
**gun:** ~**point** *n* **to hold sb at** ~**point** jdn mit einer Pistole/einem Gewehr bedrohen; **to force sb to do sth at** ~**point** jdn mit Waffengewalt zwingen, etw zu tun; **to surrender at** ~**point** sich unter Waffengewalt ergeben; ~**powder** *n* Schießpulver *nt*; ~**runner** *n* Waffenschmuggler *m*; ~**running** *n* Waffenschmuggel *m*; ~**shot** *n* Schuß *m*; *(range)* Schußweite *f*; ~**shot wound** Schußwunde *f*; ~**smith** *n* Büchsenmacher *m*; ~**wale** ['gʌnl] *n (Naut)* Dollbord *nt*.
**gurgle** ['gɜːgl] **1** *n (of liquid)* Gluckern *nt no pl*. **2** *vi (liquid)* gluckern; *(person)* glucksen *(with* vor *+dat)*.
**guru** ['gʊruː] *n* Guru *m*.
**gush** [gʌʃ] **1** *n (of liquid)* Strahl, Schwall *m*; *(of words)* Schwall *m*; *(of emotion)* Ausbruch *m*. **2** *vi* **(a)** *(also* ~**out**) *(water)* herausprudeln; *(smoke, blood)* hervorquellen; *(flames)* herausschlagen. **(b)** *(col: talk)* schwärmen *(col) (about,* over von*)*.
**gushing** ['gʌʃɪŋ] *adj (fig)* überschwenglich.
**gusset** ['gʌsɪt] *n (in garment)* Keil, Zwickel *m*.
**gust** [gʌst] *n (of wind, rain)* Böe *f*.
**gusto** ['gʌstəʊ] *n* Begeisterung *f*. **to do sth with** ~ etw mit Schwung tun.
**gusty** ['gʌstɪ] *adj (+er) wind, day* böig, stürmisch.
**gut** [gʌt] **1** *n* **(a)** *(Anat)* Darm *m*; *(stomach, paunch)* Bauch *m*; *(for racket, violin) (also* ~ *strings)* Darmsaiten *pl*. **(b)** *pl (col: stomach)* Eingeweide *pl*; *(fig col: internal parts)* Innereien *pl (hum)*. **to hate sb's**

~**s** *(col)* jdn auf den Tod nicht ausstehen können *(col)*; **I'll have his** ~**s for garters** *(col)* den mache ich zur Minna *(col)*; ~ **reaction** rein gefühlsmäßige Reaktion. **(c)** *(col: courage)* ~**s** *pl* Mut, Mumm *m (col)*. **2** *vt* **(a)** *animal* ausnehmen. **(b)** **it was completely** ~**ted by the fire** es war völlig ausgebrannt.
**gutsy** ['gʌtsɪ] *adj (+ er) (col: brave)* tapfer.
**gutter** ['gʌtəʳ] **1** *n (on roof)* Dachrinne *f*; *(in street, fig)* Gosse *f*. **2** *vi (candle, flame)* flackern.
**gutter:** ~**-press** *n* Boulevardpresse *f*; ~**snipe** *n* Gassenkind *nt*.
**guttural** ['gʌtərəl] *adj* guttural, kehlig.
**guy**[1] [gaɪ] *n (col: man)* Typ *(col)*, Kerl *(col) m*. **hey you** ~**s** he Leute *(col)*.
**guy**[2] *n (also* ~**-rope**) *(for tent)* Zeltschnur *f*.
**Guyana** [gaɪ'ænə] *n* Guyana *nt*.
**guzzle** ['gʌzl] *vti (eat)* futtern *(col)*; *(drink)* herunterstürzen, saufen *(col)*; *petrol* schlucken *(col)*.
**gym** [dʒɪm] *n (gymnasium)* Turnhalle *f*; *(gymnastics)* Turnen *nt*.
**gymkhana** [dʒɪm'kɑːnə] *n* Reiterfest *nt*.
**gymnasium** [dʒɪm'neɪzɪəm] *n* Turnhalle *f*.
**gymnast** ['dʒɪmnæst] *n* Turner(in *f*) *m*.
**gymnastic** [dʒɪm'næstɪk] *adj* turnerisch; *exercise* Turn-. ~ **display** Turnfest *nt*.
**gymnastics** [dʒɪm'næstɪks] *n* **(a)** *sing (discipline)* Gymnastik *f no pl*; *(with apparatus)* Turnen *nt no pl*. **(b)** *pl (exercises)* Übungen *pl*.
**gym** *in cpds* Turn-; ~ **shoe** *n (Brit)* Turnschuh *m*; ~**slip** *n (Brit)* Schultragerrock *m*.
**gynaecological,** *(US)* **gynecological** [ˌgaɪnɪkə-'lɒdʒɪkəl] *adj* gynäkologisch. ~ **illness** Frauenleiden *nt*.
**gynaecologist,** *(US)* **gynecologist** [ˌgaɪnɪ'kɒlə-dʒɪst] *n* Gynäkologe *m*, Gynäkologin *f*, Frauenarzt *m*/-ärztin *f*.
**gynaecology,** *(US)* **gynecology** [ˌgaɪnɪ'kɒlədʒɪ] *n* Gynäkologie, Frauenheilkunde *f*.
**gypsy** ['dʒɪpsɪ] *n* Zigeuner(in *f*) *m*.
**gyrate** [ˌdʒaɪə'reɪt] *vi (rotate)* sich drehen; *(dancer)* sich drehen und winden.
**gyrocompass** ['dʒaɪərəʊ'kʌmpəs] *n* Kreisel-Magnetkompaß *m*.
**gyroscope** ['dʒaɪərəˌskəʊp] *n* Gyroskop *nt*.

# H

**H, h** [eɪtʃ] *n* H, h *nt.* **H for Harry** *(Brit),* **H for How** *(US)*
≃ H wie Heinrich.

**h** = **hour(s)** h.

**habeas corpus** ['heɪbɪəs'kɔːpəs] *n (Jur)* **to issue a
writ of** ~ einen Vorführungsbefehl erteilen.

**haberdashery** [ˌhæbə'dæʃərɪ] *n (Brit)* Kurzwaren *pl;
(US: men's clothing)* Herrenartikel *pl.*

**habit** ['hæbɪt] *n* **(a)** Gewohnheit *f.* **to be in the** ~ **of
doing sth** die Angewohnheit haben, etw zu tun; **it
became a** ~ es wurde zur Gewohnheit; **out of sheer
** ~ aus reiner Gewohnheit; **I don't make a** ~ **of asking strangers in** (für) gewöhnlich bitte ich Fremde
nicht herein; **don't make a** ~ **of it** lassen Sie (sich
*dat*) das nicht zur Gewohnheit werden; **to get into/
to get sb into the** ~ **of doing sth** sich/jdm angewöhnen, etw zu tun; **to get into bad** ~**s** schlechte Gewohnheiten annehmen; **to get out of/to get sb out
of the** ~ **of doing sth** sich/jdm abgewöhnen, etw zu
tun. **(b)** *(costume)* Gewand *nt; (monk's also)* Habit
*nt or m.* **(riding)** ~ Reitkleid *nt.*

**habitable** ['hæbɪtəbl] *adj* bewohnbar.

**habitat** ['hæbɪtæt] *n* Heimat *f; (of animals also)* Le-
bensraum *m; (of plants also)* Standort *m.*

**habitation** [ˌhæbɪ'teɪʃən] *n* **unfit for human** ~ für
Wohnzwecke nicht geeignet.

**habit-forming** ['hæbɪtˌfɔːmɪŋ] *adj (Droge)* süchtig
machend. **is this** ~**?** wird man davon abhängig?

**habitual** [hə'bɪtjʊəl] *adj* gewohnt; *drinker, gambler,
liar* gewohnheitsmäßig.

**habitually** [hə'bɪtjʊəlɪ] *adv* gewohnheitsmäßig; *(constantly)* ständig.

**habitué** [hə'bɪtjʊeɪ] *n* regelmäßiger Besucher, regelmäßige Besucherin.

**hack¹** [hæk] **1** *n (cut)* Kerbe *f; (action)* Hieb *m; (kick)*
Tritt *m.* **2** *vt* hacken. **to hack sb/sth to pieces** jdn
zerstückeln/etw (in Stücke) hacken; **to** ~ **one's way
through (sth)** sich *(dat)* einen Weg (durch etw)
schlagen. **3** *vi (chop, also Comp)* hacken *(into* in
+*acc).*
▶**hack down** *vt sep bushes etc* umhauen; *people
also* niedermetzeln.

**hack²** *n* **(a)** *(hired horse)* Mietpferd *nt; (worn-out
horse)* Klepper *m.* **(b)** *(pej: writer)* Schreiberling *m;
(journalist also)* Schmierfink *m.*

**hacker** ['hækər] *n (Comp)* Hacker *m.*

**hacking** ['hækɪŋ] **1** *adj* **(a)** ~ **cough** trockener Husten. **(b)** ~ **jacket** Sportsakko *m or nt; (for riding)*
Reitjacke *f.* **2** *n (also Comp)* Hacken *nt.*

**hackle** ['hækl] *n* **to get sb's** ~**s up** jdn auf die Palme
bringen *(col);* **to have one's** ~**s up** auf (hundert)achtzig sein *(col).*

**hackney cab** ['hæknɪˌkæb], **hackney carriage**
['hæknɪˌkærɪdʒ] *n (also form: taxi)* Droschke *f.*

**hackneyed** ['hæknɪd] *adj* abgedroschen.

**hacksaw** ['hæksɔː] *n* Metallsäge *f.*

**had** [hæd] *pret, ptp of* **have.**

**haddock** ['hædək] *n* Schellfisch *m.*

**hadn't** ['hædnt] = **had not.**

**haematology,** *(US)* **hematology** [ˌhiːmə'tɒlədʒɪ] *n*
Hämatologie *f.*

**haematoma,** *(US)* **hematoma** [ˌhiːmə'təʊmə] *n*
Bluterguß *m.*

**haemoglobin,** *(US)* **hemoglobin** [ˌhiːməʊ'gləʊbɪn]
*n* Hämoglobin *nt,* roter Blutfarbstoff.

**haemophilia,** *(US)* **hemophilia** [ˌhiːməʊ'fɪlɪə] *n*
Bluterkrankheit *f.*

**haemophiliac,** *(US)* **hemophiliac** [ˌhiːməʊ'fɪlɪæk]
*n* Bluter *m.*

**haemorrhage,** *(US)* **hemorrhage** ['hemərɪdʒ] **1** *n*
Blutung *f.* **2** *vi* bluten.

**haemorrhoids,** *(US)* **hemorrhoids** ['hemərɔɪdz]
*npl* Hämorrhoiden *pl.*

**hag** [hæg] *n* Hexe *f.*

**haggard** ['hægəd] *adj* ausgezehrt; *(from tiredness)*
abgespannt; *(from worry)* abgehärmt.

**haggis** ['hægɪs] *n mit gehackten Schafsinnereien und
Haferschrot gefüllter Schafsmagen.*

**haggle** ['hægl] *vi (bargain)* feilschen *(about or over
um); (argue also)* sich streiten *(over wegen).*

**haggling** ['hæglɪŋ] *n* Feilschen *nt.*

**Hague** [heɪg] *n* **the** ~ Den Haag *m.*

**hail¹** [heɪl] **1** *n (lit, fig)* Hagel *m.* **2** *vi* hageln.
▶**hail down** *vi (stones etc)* niederhageln *(on sb/sth*
auf jdn/etw*).*

**hail²** **1** *vt* **(a)** **to** ~ **sb/sth as sth** jdn/etw als etw
feiern. **(b)** *(call)* zurufen *(+dat); ship* anrufen; *taxi*
herbeiwinken. **within** ~**ing distance** in Rufweite. **2**
*vi* **a ship** ~**ing from London** ein Schiff *nt* mit (dem)
Heimathafen London; **he** ~**s from Ireland** er
stammt aus Irland. **3** *interj* ~ **Caesar!** heil dir, Cäsar; **the H**~ **Mary** das Ave Maria.

**hail-fellow-well-met** ['heɪlfeləʊˌwel'met] *adj*
plump-vertraulich.

**hail:** ~**stone** *n* Hagelkorn *nt;* ~**storm** *n* Ha-
gel(schlag) *m.*

**hair** [heər] **1** *n* Haar *nt; (collective: on head)* Haare
*pl,* Haar *nt.* **a fine head of** ~ schönes volles Haar;
**body** ~ Körperbehaarung *f;* **to do one's** ~ sich frisieren, sich *(dat)* die Haare (zurecht)machen *(col);*
**to have one's** ~ **cut/done** sich *(dat)* die Haare
schneiden/frisieren lassen; **her** ~ **is always perfect**
sie ist immer sehr gut frisiert; **to let one's** ~ **down**
*(fig)* aus sich *(dat)* herausgehen; **keep your** ~ **on!**
*(col)* ruhig Blut!; **that film really made my** ~ **stand
on end** bei dem Film lief es mir eiskalt den Rücken
herunter; **not a** ~ **of his head was harmed** ihm wurde kein Haar gekrümmt; **not a** ~ **out of place** *(fig)*
wie aus dem Ei gepellt; **the best cure for a hangover is a** ~ **of the dog (that bit you)** einen Kater kuriert man am besten, wenn man mit dem anfängt,
womit man aufgehört hat.
**2** *attr mattress, sofa* Roßhaar-.

**hair:** ~**brush** *n* Haarbürste *f;* ~ **clip** *n* Clip *m; (for
ponytail etc)* Haarspange *f;* ~ **colour** *n* Haarfarbe
*f;* ~ **conditioner** *n* Pflegespülung *f;* ~ **cream** *n*
Haarpomade *f;* ~**cut** *n* Haarschnitt *m; (hairdo)*

Frisur f; **to have** or **get a ~cut** sich (dat) die Haare schneiden lassen; **I need a ~cut** ich muß mir die Haare schneiden lassen; **~do** n (col) Frisur f; **~dresser** n Friseur m, Friseuse f; **~dresser's**, **~dressing salon** n Friseursalon m; **~ dryer** n Haartrockner m; (hand-held also) Fön ® m; (over head also) Trockenhaube f; **~-grip** n (Brit) Haarklemme f; **~ lacquer** n Haarspray m or nt; **~-line** n (a) Haaransatz m; (b) (thin line) haarfeine Linie; (in telescope, on sight) Faden m; **~-line crack**, **~-line fracture** n Haarriß m; **~net** n Haarnetz nt; **~ oil** n Haaröl nt; **~-piece** n Haarteil nt; (for men) Toupet nt; **~pin** n Haarnadel f; **~pin (bend)** n Haarnadelkurve f; **~-raising** adj haarsträubend; **~ remover** n Enthaarungsmittel nt; **~'s breadth** n **by a ~'s breadth** um Haaresbreite; **~-splitting 1** n Haarspalterei f; **2** adj haarspalterisch; **~spray** n Haarspray m or nt; **~style** n Frisur f.

**hairy** ['hɛərɪ] adj (+er) (a) stark behaart. (b) (col) situation haarig (col); film etc gruselig (col); driving kriminell (col).

**Haiti** ['heɪtɪ] n Haiti nt.

**Haitian** ['heɪʃɪən] **1** adj haitianisch, haitisch. **2** n Haitianer(in f) m.

**hake** [heɪk] n Seehecht m.

**halcyon** ['hælsɪən] adj: **~ days** glückliche Tage pl.

**hale** [heɪl] adj kräftig. **~ and hearty** gesund und munter.

**half** [hɑːf] **1** n, pl **halves** (a) Hälfte f. **to cut in ~** halbieren; **to break/tear sth in ~** etw entzweibrechen/-reißen; **~ of it/them** die Hälfte davon/ von ihnen; **~ the book/money** die Hälfte des Buches/Geldes; **he's not ~ the man he used to be** er ist längst nicht mehr das, was er einmal war; **~ a cup/an hour** eine halbe Tasse/Stunde; **~ a second!** (einen) Augenblick mal!; **to go halves** halbe-halbe machen (col); **he is too clever by ~** (col) er ist ein richtiger Schlaumeier; **not ~ enough** längst nicht genug; **one and a ~** eineinhalb, anderthalb; **an hour and a ~** eineinhalb or anderthalb Stunden; **not to do things by halves** keine halben Sachen machen; **~ and ~** halb und halb; **that's not the ~ of it** (col) und das ist längs noch nicht alles (col).

(b) (Sport) (of match) Halbzeit f; (player) Läufer(in f) m.

(c) (of ticket) Abschnitt m der Fahrkarte; (travel, admission fee) halbe Karte (col).

(d) (beer) kleines Bier.

**2** adj halb. **a ~ cup** eine halbe Tasse.

**3** adv (a) halb. **I ~ thought ...** ich hätte fast gedacht ...; **I was ~ afraid that ...** ich habe fast befürchtet, daß ...; **the work is only ~ done** die Arbeit ist erst zur Hälfte erledigt; **that's ~ right** das ist zur Hälfte richtig. (b) (Brit col) **he's not ~ stupid/rich** er ist unheimlich dumm/reich (col); **not ~ bad** gar nicht schlecht; **not ~!** und wie!, und ob! (c) **it's ~ past three** or **~ three** (col) es ist halb vier. (d) **~ as big as** halb so groß wie; **~ as big again** anderthalbmal so groß.

**half**: **~ back** n (Sport) Läufer(in f) m; **~-baked** adj (fig col) person, plan blöd; **~-breed** n (person) Mischling m; (animal) Rassenmischung f; (horse) Halbblut nt; **~ brother** n Halbbruder m; **~-caste** n Mischling m; **~-cock** n: **to go off at ~-cock** (col) ein Reinfall m sein (col); **~-crown** n (in old Brit system) Zweieinhalbschillingstück nt; **~-cut** adj (Brit col: drunk) besoffen (col!); **~-day** (holiday) n halber freier Tag; **we've got a ~-day (holiday)** wir haben einen halben Tag frei; **~-empty** adj halbleer attr, halb leer pred; **~-fare 1** n halber Fahrpreis; **2** adv zum halben Preis; **~-full** adj halbvoll

attr, halb voll pred; **~-hearted** adj halbherzig; manner lustlos; **~-heartedly** adv agree mit halbem Herzen; **to do sth ~-heartedly** etw ohne rechte Lust tun; **~-holiday** n (Brit) halber Urlaubstag/ Feiertag; **we've got a ~-holiday tomorrow afternoon** wir haben morgen nachmittag frei; **~-hour** n halbe Stunde; **~-hourly 1** adj halbstündlich; **2** adv jede halbe Stunde; **~-light** n Dämmerlicht, Halbdunkel nt; **~-mast** n: **at ~-mast** (also hum) (auf) halbmast; **~-measures** npl **we don't believe in ~-measures** wir machen keine halben Sachen; **~-moon** n Halbmond m; **~-note** n (US Mus) halbe Note; **~ pay** n halber Lohn; (salary) halbes Gehalt; **~penny** ['heɪpnɪ] n (old) halber Penny; **~-pint** n (a) ≈ Viertelliter m or nt; (of beer also) kleines Bier; (b) (col: person) halbe Portion (col); **~-price** n **at ~-price** zum halben Preis; **~-sister** n Halbschwester f; **~-term** n (Brit) Ferien pl in der Mitte des Trimesters; **~-timbered** adj Fachwerk-; **~-time** n (a) (Sport) Halbzeit f; (b) (Ind) **to be on ~-time** kurzarbeiten; **~-title** n (Typ) Schmutztitel m; **~-tone** n (Art, Phot, US Mus) Halbton m; **~-truth** n Halbwahrheit f.

**halfway** ['hɑːf,weɪ] **1** adj attr **when we reached the ~ stage** or **point on our journey** als wir die Hälfte der Reise hinter uns (dat) hatten; **the project is at the ~ stage** das Projekt ist zur Hälfte abgeschlossen. **2** adv **~way to** auf halbem Weg nach; **we drove ~ to London** wir fuhren die Hälfte der Strecke nach London; **~ between two points** (in der Mitte or genau) zwischen zwei Punkten; **~ up the hill** auf halber Höhe des Berges; **we went ~ up the hill** wir gingen den Berg halb hinauf; **~ through a book** halb durch ein Buch (durch); **this money will go ~ towards paying ...** diese Summe wird die Hälfte der Kosten für ... decken; **to meet sb ~** (lit, fig) jdm (auf halbem Weg) entgegenkommen. **3** attr **~ house** n (fig) Zwischending nt; (compromise) Kompromiß m.

**half**: **~-wit** n (fig) Schwachkopf m; **~-witted** ['hɑːf,wɪtɪd] adj schwachsinnig; **~-yearly** adj, adv halbjährlich.

**halibut** ['hælɪbət] n Heilbutt m.

**halitosis** [,hælɪ'təʊsɪs] n Mundgeruch m.

**hall** [hɔːl] n (a) (of house) Flur m; (large) Diele f. (b) (large building) Halle f; (large room) Saal m; (village ~) Gemeindehalle f; (school assembly ~) Aula f. (c) (mansion) Herrenhaus nt; (students'; also **~ of residence**) Studenten(wohn)heim nt.

**hallelujah** [,hælɪ'luːjə] interj halleluja(h).

**hallmark** ['hɔːlmɑːk] n (a) (Feingehalts)stempel m. (b) (fig) Kennzeichen nt (of gen, für).

**hallo** [hə'ləʊ] interj, n = **hello**.

**hallowed** ['hæləʊd] adj (lit, fig) geheiligt.

**Hallowe'en** [,hæləʊ'iːn] n Tag m vor Allerheiligen.

**hall**: **~ porter** n Portier m; **~-stand** n (Flur)garderobe f; (treelike) Garderobenständer m.

**hallucinate** [hə'luːsɪneɪt] vi halluzinieren.

**hallucination** [hə,luːsɪ'neɪʃən] n Halluzination f.

**hallway** ['hɔːlweɪ] n Korridor m.

**halo** ['heɪləʊ] n, pl **-(e)s** (of saint) Heiligenschein m; (Astron) Hof m.

**halogen** ['hælə,dʒən] n Halogen nt.

**halt** [hɔlt] **1** n (a) (stop) Pause f; (Mil) Halt m; (in production) Stopp m. **to come to a ~** zum Stillstand kommen; **to call a ~** to sth einer Sache (dat) ein Ende bereiten; **shall we call a ~?** wollen wir jetzt Schluß machen?; **~ sign** Stoppschild nt. (b) (small station) Haltepunkt m. **2** vi zum Stillstand kommen; (person) stehenbleiben; (Mil) halten. **to ~ briefly** kurz haltmachen. **3** vt anhalten; production, *traffic also* zum Stillstand bringen. **4** *interj* halt; *(Mil)* stillgestanden; *(traffic sign)* stop.

**halter** [ˈhɒltəʳ] *n (horse's)* Halfter *nt*.

**halterneck** [ˈhɒltənek] *n (dress)* rückenfreies Kleid; *(top)* Top *nt* mit Nackenband.

**halting** [ˈhɒltɪŋ] *adj walk* unsicher; *speech* stockend; *admission etc* zögernd; *verse* holp(e)rig. **in a ~ voice** zögernd, stockend.

**halve** [hɑːv] *vt* **(a)** halbieren. **(b)** *(reduce by one half)* auf die Hälfte reduzieren.

**halves** [hɑːvz] *pl of* **half**.

**ham** [hæm] **1** *n* **(a)** *(Cook)* Schinken *m*. **(b)** *(Theat) (also ~* **actor)** Schmierenkomödiant(in *f*) *m*. **(c)** *(Rad col)* Funkamateur *m*. **2** *adj attr acting* übertrieben. **3** *vi (Theat)* chargieren, übertrieben spielen.
  ►**ham up** *vt sep (col)* **to ~ it ~** zu dick auftragen.

**hamburger** [ˈhæm,bɜːgəʳ] *n* (flache) Frikadelle *f*; *(with bread)* Hamburger *m*.

**ham-fisted** [ˌhæmˈfɪstɪd] *adj* ungeschickt.

**hamlet** [ˈhæmlɪt] *n* Weiler *m*, kleines Dorf.

**hammer** [ˈhæməʳ] **1** *n* Hammer *m*. **to go at it ~ and tongs** *(col)* sich ins Zeug legen *(col)*; *(quarrel)* sich in die Haare kriegen *(col)*; **to come under the ~** *(auction)* unter den Hammer kommen; **in the ~** **(throwing)** *(Sport)* im Hammerwurf. **2** *vt* **(a)** *nail, metal* hämmern. **to ~ a nail into a wall** einen Nagel in die Wand schlagen; **to ~ sth into shape** *metal* etw zurechthämmern; *(fig) plan, agreement* etw ausarbeiten; **to ~ sth into sb's head, to ~ it home to sb** jdm etw einbleuen *(col)*. **(b)** *(col: defeat badly)* eine Schlappe beibringen *(+dat) (col)*. **3** *vi* hämmern. **to ~ (away) at the door** an die Tür hämmern.
  ►**hammer out** *vt sep (fig) plan, solution* ausarbeiten; *tune* hämmern.

**hammer drill** *n* Schlagbohrmaschine *f*.

**hammering** [ˈhæmərɪŋ] *n* **our team took a ~** *(col)* unsere Mannschaft mußte eine Schlappe einstecken *(col)*.

**hammock** [ˈhæmək] *n* Hängematte *f*.

**hamper¹** [ˈhæmpəʳ] *n* Korb *m*; *(as present)* Geschenkkorb *m*.

**hamper²** *vt* behindern. **to be ~ed** gehandikapt sein.

**hamster** [ˈhæmstəʳ] *n* Hamster *m*.

**hamstring** [ˈhæmstrɪŋ] *(vb: pret, ptp* **hamstrung** [ˈhæmstrʌŋ]) **1** *n (Anat)* Kniesehne *f*. **2** *vt (fig)* **to be hamstrung** außer Gefecht gesetzt sein; *(project)* lahmliegen.

**hand** [hænd] **1** *n* **(a)** Hand *f*; *(of clock)* Zeiger *m*. **on ~s and knees** auf allen vieren; **to take sb by the ~** jdn bei der Hand nehmen; **~s up!** Hände hoch!; *(Sch)* meldet euch!; **~s off** *(col)* Hände weg!; **keep your ~s off it** laß die Finger davon!; **made by ~** handgearbeitet; **to raise an animal by ~** ein Tier mit der Flasche aufziehen; **to live from ~ to mouth** von der Hand in den Mund leben; **with a heavy/firm ~** *(fig)* mit harter/starker Hand.
  **(b)** *(side, direction, position)* Seite *f*. **on the right ~** auf der rechten Seite, rechts; **on my right ~** rechts von mir; **on all ~s** auf allen Seiten; **on the one ~ ... on the other ~ ...** einerseits ..., andererseits ...
  **(c)** *(agency, possession etc)* **it's the ~ of God** das ist die Hand Gottes; **it's in your own ~s what you do now** Sie haben es selbst in der Hand, was Sie jetzt tun; **to put sth into sb's ~s** jdm etw in die Hand geben; **to leave sb/sth in sb's ~s** jdn in jds Obhut lassen/jdm etw überlassen; **I'm in your ~s** ich verlasse mich ganz auf Sie; **to fall into the ~s of sb** jdm in die Hände fallen; **to be in good ~s** in guten Händen sein; **he has too much time on his ~s** er hat zuviel Zeit zur Verfügung; **I've got enough**

**on my ~s already** ich habe schon genug am Hals *(col)*; **to get sb/sth off one's ~s** jdn/etw loswerden; **to take sb/sth off sb's ~s** jdm jdn/etw abnehmen.
  **(d)** *(applause)* **they gave him a big ~** er bekam großen Applaus.
  **(e)** *(worker)* Arbeitskraft *f*; *(Naut)* Besatzungsmitglied *nt*. **to take on ~s** Leute einstellen; *(Naut)* Leute anheuern; **~s** Belegschaft *f*; **all ~s on deck!** alle Mann an Deck!; **to be an old ~ (at sth)** ein alter Hase (in etw *dat*) sein.
  **(f)** *(Measure: of horse)* ≈ 10cm.
  **(g)** *(handwriting)* Handschrift *f*.
  **(h)** *(Cards)* Blatt *nt*; *(person)* Mann *m*; *(game)* Runde *f*. **a good/bad ~** gute/schlechte Karten; **3 ~s** *(people)* 3 Mann; **to show one's ~** *(fig)* sich *(dat)* in die Karten sehen lassen.
  **(i)** **Christmas is (close) at ~** Weihnachten steht vor der Tür; **at first/second ~** aus erster/zweiter Hand; **according to the information on ~** den vorliegenden Informationen zufolge; **to keep sth at ~** etw in Reichweite haben; **it's quite close at ~** es ist ganz in der Nähe; **he had the situation well in ~** er hatte die Situation im Griff; **to take sb in ~** *(discipline)* jdn zur Räson bringen; *(look after)* nach jdm sehen; **stock in ~** *(Comm)* Warenlager *nt*; **he still had £600/a couple of hours in ~** er hatte £600 übrig/noch zwei Stunden Zeit; **the matter in ~** die zur Debatte stehende Angelegenheit; **work in ~** Arbeit, die zur Zeit erledigt wird; **a matter/project etc is in ~** eine Sache/ein Projekt *nt etc* wird bearbeitet; **to put sth in ~** dafür sorgen, daß etw erledigt wird; **the children got out of ~** die Kinder waren nicht mehr zu bändigen; **matters got out of ~** die Dinge sind außer Kontrolle geraten; **I don't have the letter to ~** ich habe den Brief gerade nicht zur Hand.
  **(j)** *(phrases)* **to keep one's ~ in** in Übung bleiben; **to eat out of sb's ~** *(lit, fig)* jdm aus der Hand fressen; **to force sb's ~** auf jdn Druck ausüben; **to wait on sb ~ and foot** jdn von vorne und hinten bedienen; **he never does a ~'s turn** er rührt keinen Finger; **to have a ~ in sth** *(in decision)* an etw *(dat)* beteiligt sein; *(in crime)* die Hand bei etw im Spiel haben; **to lend** *or* **give sb a ~** jdm zur Hand gehen; **give me a ~!** hilf mir mal!; **to be ~ in glove with sb** mit jdm unter einer Decke stecken; **to have one's ~s full with sth** mit etw alle Hände voll zu tun haben; **to win ~s down** spielend gewinnen; **he is making money ~ over fist** er scheffelt das Geld nur so; **we're losing money/staff ~ over fist** wir verlieren haufenweise Geld/Personal; **to have the upper ~** die Oberhand behalten; **to gain the upper ~** die Oberhand gewinnen; **to ask for a lady's ~ (in marriage)** um die Hand einer Dame anhalten.
  **2** *vt (give)* reichen, geben *(sth to sb, sb sth* jdm etw*)*. **you've got to ~ it to him** *(fig)* das muß man ihm lassen *(col)*.
  ►**hand back** *vt sep* zurückgeben.
  ►**hand down** *vt sep* **(a)** *(lit)* herunter-/hinunterreichen *or* -geben *(to sb* jdm*)*. **(b)** *(fig)* weitergeben; *tradition, story also* überliefern *(to an +acc)*; *heirloom etc* vererben *(to dat)*.
  ►**hand in** *vt sep* abgeben; *forms, resignation* einreichen.
  ►**hand on** *vt sep* weitergeben *(to an +acc)*.
  ►**hand out** *vt sep* austeilen *(to sb* an jdn*)*; *advice* erteilen *(to sb* jdm*)*.
  ►**hand over 1** *vt sep (pass over)* (herüber-/hinüber)reichen *(to dat)*; *(give up)* (her)geben *(to dat)*; *(to third party)* (ab)geben *(to dat)*; *criminal, prisoner* übergeben *(to dat)*; *(from one state to another)* ausliefern; *leadership* abtreten *(to an +acc)*; *the*

*controls, business* übergeben *(to dat,* an *+acc).* **2** *vi* **when the Conservatives** ~**ed** ~ **to Labour** als die Konservativen die Regierung an Labour abgaben; **when the chairman** ~**ed** ~ **to his successor** als der Vorsitzende das Amt an seinen Nachfolger abgab. ►**hand round** *vt sep* herumreichen; *(distribute) papers* austeilen.

**hand:** ~**bag** *n* Handtasche *f;* ~ **baggage** *n* Handgepäck *nt;* ~**ball** *n* **(a)** Handball *m;* **(b)** *(Ftbl: foul)* Handspiel *nt;* ~**bill** *n* Handzettel *m;* ~**book** *n* Handbuch *nt; (tourist's)* Reiseführer *m;* ~**brake** *n (Brit)* Handbremse *f.*

**h & c** = **hot and cold (water)** k.u.w.

**hand:** ~**cart** *n* Handwagen *m;* ~ **controls** *npl (Aut)* Handbedienung *f;* ~**cuff** *vt* Handschellen anlegen *(+dat);* ~**cuffs** *npl* Handschellen *pl;* ~ **dryer** *n* Händetrockner *m.*

**handful** ['hændfʊl] *n* **(a)** Handvoll *f; (of hair, fur)* Büschel *nt.* **by the** ~, **in** ~**s** büschelweise. **(b)** *(small number)* Handvoll *f.* **(c)** *(fig)* **those children are a** ~ die Kinder können einen ganz schön in Trab halten.

**hand-grenade** ['hændgrɪneɪd] *n* Handgranate *f.*

**handicap** ['hændɪkæp] **1** *n* Handikap *nt; (in horse racing, golf also)* Vorgabe *f; (physical, mental also)* Behinderung *f.* **to be under a great** ~ stark gehandikapt sein. **2** *vt* ein Handikap *nt* darstellen für. **to be (physically/mentally)** ~**ped** (körperlich/geistig) behindert sein; ~**ped children** behinderte Kinder *pl.*

**handicraft** ['hændɪkrɑːft] *n* **(a)** *(work)* Kunsthandwerk *nt; (needlework etc)* Handarbeit *f; (woodwork, modelling etc)* Werken *nt.* **(b)** *(skill)* Geschick *nt,* Handfertigkeit *f.*

**handily** ['hændɪlɪ] *adv* **(a)** *situated* günstig. **(b)** *(US: easily)* mit Leichtigkeit.

**handiness** ['hændɪnɪs] *n (of shops etc)* günstige Lage.

**handiwork** ['hændɪwɜːk] *n no pl* **(a)** *(lit)* Arbeit *f; (Sch: subject)* Werken *nt; (needlework etc)* Handarbeit *f.* **(b)** *(fig)* Werk *nt; (pej)* Machwerk *nt.*

**handkerchief** ['hæŋkətʃɪf] *n* Taschentuch *nt.*

**handle** ['hændl] **1** *n* Griff *m; (of door also)* Klinke *f; (of broom, comb)* Stiel *m; (of basket, bucket, cup etc)* Henkel *m.* **to fly off the** ~ *(col)* an die Decke gehen *(col).*

**2** *vt* **(a)** *(touch, use hands on)* anfassen; *(Ftbl) ball* mit der Hand berühren. **be careful how you** ~ **that** gehen Sie vorsichtig damit um; **"**~ **with care"** „Vorsicht Glas/Blumen/lebende Tiere *etc".*

**(b)** *(deal with) person, animal, tool, weapon, machine etc* umgehen mit; *tool also* handhaben; *legal or financial matters* erledigen; *legal case, order, contract* bearbeiten; *applicant, matter, problem* sich befassen mit; *material for essay etc* bearbeiten; *(tackle) problem, interview etc* anpacken; *(cope with) child, drunk, situation, problem* fertigwerden mit; *vehicle, plane, ship* steuern. **how would you** ~ **the situation?** wie würden Sie sich in der Situation verhalten?; **you keep quiet, I'll** ~ **this** sei mal still und laß mich nur machen *(col);* **who's handling the publicity for this?** wer macht die Öffentlichkeitsarbeit dafür?

**3** *vi (ship, plane)* sich steuern lassen; *(car, motorbike)* sich fahren.

**4** *vr* **he** ~**s himself well in a fight** er kann sich in einer Schlägerei behaupten.

**handle:** ~**bar moustache** *n* Schnauzbart *m;* ~**bar(s)** *n(pl)* Lenkstange *f.*

**handler** ['hændlər] *n (dog-* ~) Hundeführer *m.*

**handling** ['hændlɪŋ] *n* **(a)** *(touching)* Berühren *nt.* **(b)** *(of plant, problem)* Behandlung *f; (of person, patient etc also)* Umgang *m (of mit);* *(of tool, weapon,*

*machine)* Handhabung *f; (of legal or financial matters)* Erledigung *f; (of order, contract, legal case)* Bearbeitung *f.* **his** ~ **of the situation** die Art, wie er die Situation angepackt hat; **he/it needs careful** ~ man muß vorsichtig mit ihm/damit umgehen; ~ **charge** *(Admin)* Bearbeitungsgebühr *f.* **(c)** *(of vehicle)* Fahrverhalten *nt.* **what's its** ~ **like?** wie fährt es sich?

**hand:** ~**luggage** *n* Handgepäck *nt;* ~~**made** *adj* handgearbeitet; **this is** ~~**made** das ist Handarbeit; ~~**me-down** *n (col)* abgelegtes Kleidungsstück; ~**out** *n (col: money)* (Geld)zuwendung *f; (leaflet)* Flugblatt *nt; (publicity* ~*)* Reklamezettel *m;* ~~**painted** *adj* handbemalt; ~~**picked** *adj (specially selected)* handverlesen; ~**rail** *n (of stairs etc)* Geländer *nt; (of ship)* Reling *f;* ~**set** *n (Telec)* Hörer *m;* ~**shake** *n* Händedruck *m.*

**hands-off** ['hændz'ɒf] *adj* passiv. ~ **manager** Geschäftsführer, der die Zügel gern locker läßt.

**handsome** ['hænsəm] *adj* gutaussehend; *furniture, building* schön; *(noble, generous)* großzügig, nobel *(col); profit, inheritance etc* stattlich, beträchtlich. **he is** ~**/he has a** ~ **face** er sieht gut aus.

**handsomely** ['hænsəmlɪ] *adv* **(a)** *(elegantly)* elegant. **(b)** *(generously)* großzügig.

**hands-on** ['hændz'ɒn] *adj* aktiv. ~ **manager** Geschäftsführer, der die Zügel gern fest in der Hand hält.

**hand:** ~~**stand** *n* Handstand *m;* ~~**to-**~ *adj* ~~**to-**~ **fighting** Nahkampf *m;* ~~**to-mouth** *adj* ~ **existence** kümmerlich, armselig; **to lead a** ~~**to-mouth** **existence** von der Hand in den Mund leben; ~ **towel** *n* (Hände)handtuch *nt;* ~**writing** *n* Handschrift *f;* ~**written** *adj* handgeschrieben.

**handy** ['hændɪ] *adj (+er)* **(a)** *person* geschickt. **to be** ~ **at doing sth** ein Geschick *nt* für etw haben. **(b)** *pred (close at hand)* in der Nähe *(for +gen).* **to keep sth** ~ etw griffbereit haben. **(c)** *(convenient, useful)* praktisch. **it'll come in** ~ das kann ich gut gebrauchen; **he's a very** ~ **person to have around** man kann ihn gut (ge)brauchen *(col);* **he's very** ~ **about the house** er kann im Haus vieles selbst erledigen.

**handyman** ['hændɪmæn] *n, pl* -**men** [-mən] *(odd-job man)* Handwerker *m; (do-it-yourselfer)* Bastler *m.*

**hang** [hæŋ] *(vb: pret, ptp* **hung**) **1** *vt* **(a)** hängen; *painting* aufhängen; *door, gate* einhängen; *wallpaper* kleben. **to** ~ **wallpaper** tapezieren; **to** ~ **sth from sth** etw an etw *(dat)* aufhängen; **the walls were hung with tapestries** die Wände waren mit Gobelins behängt; **to** ~ **one's head** den Kopf hängen lassen. **(b)** *pret, ptp* **hanged** *criminal* hängen. **to** ~ **oneself** sich erhängen; ~ **him** *(col)* zum Kuckuck mit ihm! *(col);* **I'm** ~**ed if I know** *(col)* weiß der Kuckuck *(col);* ~ **it!** *(col)* so ein Mist! *(col).*

**2** *vi* **(a)** hängen *(on an (+dat), from* von*); (drapery, clothes, hair)* fallen. **time** ~**s heavy on my hands** die Zeit wird mir sehr lang. **(b)** *(criminal)* gehängt werden. **(c) it/he can go** ~! *(col)* es/er kann mir gestohlen bleiben *(col).*

**3** *n* **(a)** *(of drapery)* Fall *m; (of suit)* Sitz *m.* **(b)** **you'll soon get the** ~ **of it** *(col)* du wirst bald den richtigen Dreh finden *(col).*

►**hang about** *or* **around 1** *vi (col) (wait)* warten; *(loiter)* sich herumtreiben *(col).* **to keep sb** ~**ing** ~ jdn warten lassen; ~ **about, I didn't say that** Moment mal, das habe ich nicht gesagt *(col);* **he doesn't** ~ ~ *(is fast)* er ist einer von der schnellen Truppe. **2** *vi +prep obj* **to** ~ ~ **a place** sich an einem Ort herumtreiben *(col).*

►**hang back** *vi (lit)* sich zurückhalten; *(hesitate)* zögern.

▶**hang in** *vi (col)* just ~ ~ **there!** bleib am Ball! *(col)*.

▶**hang on 1** *vi* (**a**) *(hold)* sich festhalten *(to sth an etw dat)*. (**b**) *(hold out)* durchhalten; *(Telec)* am Apparat bleiben; *(col: wait)* warten. ~ ~ (**a minute)** warte mal, einen Augenblick (mal). **2** *vi +prep obj* (**a**) **to** ~ ~ **sb's arm** an jds Arm *(dat)* hängen; **he** ~**s** ~ **her every word** er hängt an ihren Lippen. (**b**) *(depend on)* **it all** ~**s** ~ **his decision** alles hängt von seiner Entscheidung ab.

▶**hang on to** *vi +prep obj (keep)* behalten.

▶**hang out 1** *vi* (**a**) *(tongue, shirt tails etc)* heraushängen *(of aus +dat)*. (**b**) *(col: live)* sich aufhalten; *(be usually found also)* herumhängen *(col)*. (**c**) **they hung** ~ **for more pay** sie hielten an ihrer Lohnforderung fest. (**d**) *(col)* **to let it all** ~ ~ die Sau rauslassen *(col)*. **2** *vt sep* hinaushängen.

▶**hang together** *vi (people)* zusammenhalten; *(argument, report)* zusammenhängend sein; *(alibi etc)* keine Widersprüche aufweisen.

▶**hang up 1** *vi (Telec)* auflegen. **he hung** ~ **on me** er legte einfach auf. **2** *vt sep* aufhängen.

**hangar** [ˈhæŋəʳ] *n* Flugzeughalle *f.*

**hangdog** [ˈhændɒg] *adj look* niedergeschlagen; *(ashamed)* zerknirscht.

**hanger** [ˈhæŋəʳ] *n (for clothes)* (Kleider)bügel *m; (loop on garment)* Aufhänger *m.*

**hanger-on** [ˌhæŋərˈɒn] *n, pl* **-s-on** *(sponger)* Schmarotzer *m.* **he came with all his hangers-on** er kam mit seinem ganzen Gefolge.

**hang:** ~**-glider** *n (device)* Drachen *m; (person)* Drachenflieger(in *f*) *m;* ~**-gliding** *n* Drachenfliegen *nt.*

**hanging** [ˈhæŋɪŋ] **1** *n* (**a**) *(col)* Todesstrafe *f; (of criminal)* Erhängen *nt; (event)* Hinrichtung *f* (durch den Strang). (**b**) *(curtains etc)* ~**s** *pl* Vorhänge *pl; (tapestry)* Wandbehang *m.* **2** *attr* hängend; *bridge* Hänge-.

**hang:** ~**man** *n* Henker *m;* ~**-out** *n (col) (place where one lives)* Bude *f (col); (pub, café etc)* Stammlokal *nt; (of group)* Treff *m (col);* ~**over** *n* (**a**) Kater *m (col);* (**b**) *(sth left over)* Überbleibsel *nt;* ~**up** *n (col)* Komplex *m (about wegen); (obsession)* Fimmel *m (col) (about mit).*

**hank** [hæŋk] *n (of wool etc)* Strang *m; (of hair, fur)* Büschel *nt.*

**hanker** [ˈhæŋkəʳ] *vi* Verlangen haben *(for or after sth* nach etw*).*

**hankering** [ˈhæŋkərɪŋ] *n* Verlangen *nt.* **to have a** ~ **for sth** Verlangen nach etw haben.

**hanky** [ˈhæŋkɪ] *n (col)* Taschentuch *nt.*

**hanky-panky** [ˈhæŋkɪˈpæŋkɪ] *n (col)* (**a**) *(dishonest dealings)* Mauscheleien *pl (col).* **there's some** ~ **going on** hier ist was faul *(col).* (**b**) *(love affair)* Techtelmechtel *nt (col).* (**c**) *(sexy behaviour)* Gefummel *nt (col).*

**Hanover** [ˈhænəʊvəʳ] *n* Hannover *nt.*

**Hansard** [ˈhænsɑːd] *n* der Hansard, die britischen Parlamentsberichte.

**Hanseatic** [ˌhænzɪˈætɪk] *adj towns* Hanse-. ~ **League** Hansebund *m.*

**Hants** [hænts] *(Brit)* = **Hampshire.**

**haphazard** *adj,* ~**ly** *adv* [ˌhæpˈhæzəd, -lɪ] willkürlich.

**happen** [ˈhæpən] *vi* (**a**) geschehen; *(special or important event also)* sich ereignen; *(esp unexpected, unintentional or unpleasant event also)* passieren; *(process also)* vor sich gehen. **it all** ~**ed like this** ... das Ganze war so ...; **it's all** ~**ing here today** *(col)* heute ist hier ganz schön was los *(col);* **what's** ~**ing?** was ist los?; **you can't just let things** ~ du kannst die Dinge nicht einfach laufen lassen; **don't let it** ~

**again** daß das nicht noch mal passiert!; **these things** ~ so was kommt (schon mal) vor; **what has** ~**ed to him?** was ist mit ihm?; *(in accident etc)* was ist ihm passiert?; **what's** ~**ed to your leg?** was ist mit deinem Bein passiert?; **if anything should** ~ **to me** wenn mir etwas passieren sollte; **it all** ~**ed so quickly** es ging alles so schnell.

(**b**) *(chance)* **how does it** ~ **that ...?** wie kommt es, daß ...?; **it might** ~ **that ...** es könnte sein, daß ...; **how do you** ~ **to know?** wie kommt es, daß du das weißt?; **to** ~ **to do sth** zufälligerweise etw tun; **do you** ~ **to know whether ...?** wissen Sie zufällig, ob ...?; **I just** ~**ed to come along when ...** ich kam zufällig (gerade) vorbei, als ...; **as it** ~**s I'm going there today** zufällig(erweise) gehe ich heute (dort)hin; **he** ~**s to be the boss** er ist nun einmal der Chef.

▶**happen (up)on** *vi +prep obj* zufällig stoßen auf *(+acc); person* zufällig treffen.

**happening** [ˈhæpnɪŋ] *n* Ereignis *nt; (not planned)* Vorfall *m; (Theat)* Happening *nt.*

**happily** [ˈhæpɪlɪ] *adv* (**a**) glücklich; *(cheerfully also)* fröhlich; *(contentedly also)* zufrieden. **they lived** ~ **ever after** *(in fairy tales)* und wenn sie nicht gestorben sind, dann leben sie noch heute. (**b**) *(fortunately)* glücklicherweise. (**c**) *(worded)* treffend.

**happiness** [ˈhæpɪnɪs] *n* Glück *nt; (disposition)* Fröhlichkeit *f.*

**happy** [ˈhæpɪ] *adj (+er)* (**a**) *(about* über *+acc)* glücklich; *(cheerful also)* fröhlich. **a** ~ **event** ein freudiges Ereignis; **that's all right, (I'm/I'll be)** ~ **to help** schon gut, ich helfe (doch) gern; **yes, I'd be** ~ **to** ja, sehr gern(e); **to be** ~ **to do sth** sich freuen, etw tun zu können; **I'm very** ~ **for you** ich freue mich für dich; **the** ~ **few** die wenigen Auserwählten. (**b**) *phrase, solution* glücklich. (**c**) *(content)* zufrieden. **we're not** ~ **with it** wir sind damit nicht zufrieden. (**d**) ~ **anniversary/birthday** herzlichen Glückwunsch zum Hochzeitstag/Geburtstag; ~ **Easter** frohe Ostern; ~ **New Year** ein gutes neues Jahr.

**happy:** ~**-go-lucky** *adj* unbekümmert; ~ **hour** *n* Zeit, in der Bars, Pubs etc Getränke zu ermäßigten Preisen anbieten.

**harangue** [həˈræŋ] **1** *n (scolding)* (Straf)predigt *f; (encouraging)* Appell *m.* **2** *vt see n* eine (Straf)predigt halten *(+dat);* einen Appell richten an *(+acc).*

**harass** [ˈhærəs] *vt* belästigen; *(mess around)* schikanieren; *(Mil)* immer wieder überfallen. **don't** ~ **me** dräng mich doch nicht so!; **they eventually** ~**ed him into resigning** sie setzten ihm so lange zu, bis er schließlich zurücktrat.

**harassed** [ˈhærəst] *adj* mitgenommen; *(worried)* von Sorgen gequält.

**harassment** [ˈhærəsmənt] *n (act)* Belästigung *f; (messing around)* Schikanierung *f; (state)* Bedrängnis *f; (Mil)* Kleinkrieg *m.* **police** ~ Schikane *f* von seiten der Polizei.

**harbour,** *(US)* **harbor** [ˈhɑːbəʳ] **1** *n* Hafen *m.* ~ **dues** Hafengebühren *pl.* ~ **master** *n* Hafenmeister *m.* **2** *vt* (**a**) *criminal etc* Unterschlupf gewähren *(+dat).* (**b**) *suspicions, feelings, grudge* hegen.

**hard** [hɑːd] **1** *adj (+er)* (**a**) hart; *voice, tone also* schroff. **a** ~ **man** ein harter Mann; *(ruthless)* ein knallharter Typ *(col);* **don't be** ~ **on the boy** sei nicht zu streng zu dem Jungen; **no** ~ **feelings** nichts für ungut. (**b**) *(difficult)* schwer; *(complicated also)* schwierig; *(~ to endure)* hart. ~ **of hearing** schwerhörig; **I find it** ~ **to believe that ...** ich kann es kaum glauben, daß ...; **he is** ~ **to get on with** es ist schwierig, mit ihm auszukommen; **it's** ~ **going**

es ist mühsam; ~ **luck!**, ~ **lines!** (so ein) Pech!

**2** adv (+er) **(a)** mit aller Kraft; (violently) heftig; run schnell; breathe, work schwer. **to listen** ~ genau hinhören; **think** ~ denk mal scharf nach; **think** ~**er** denk mal ein bißchen besser nach; **he has obviously thought** ~ **about this** er hat es sich (dat) offensichtlich gut überlegt; **if you try** ~ wenn du dich richtig bemühst; **try** ~**er** gib dir doch ein bißchen mehr Mühe; **you're not trying** ~ **enough** du strengst dich nicht genügend an; **you're trying too** ~ du bemühst dich zu sehr; **he tried as** ~ **as he could** er hat sich nach Kräften bemüht; **to look** ~ **at sb/sth** sich jdn/etw genau ansehen; **to be** ~ **at it** (col) schwer am Werk sein (col).

**(b)** (in, with difficulty) **to be** ~ **put to it to do sth** es sehr schwer finden, etw zu tun; **to be** ~ **up** (col) knapp bei Kasse sein (col); **he's** ~ **up for ...** (col) es fehlt ihm an ... (+dat); **to be** ~ **done by** übel dran sein; **he took it pretty** ~ es traf ihn ziemlich schwer; **old traditions die** ~ alte Traditionen lassen sich nicht so leicht abschaffen.

**(c)** rain, snow stark. **it was freezing** ~ es herrschte strenger Frost.

**hard:** ~ **and fast** adj fest; rules also bindend; ~**back 1** adj book gebunden; **2** n gebundene Ausgabe; ~**bitten** adj person abgebrüht; manager knallhart (col); ~**board** n Hartfaserplatte f; ~**boiled** adj **(a)** egg hartgekocht; **(b)** (fig: shrewd) ausgekocht (col); (unsentimental) abgebrüht (col); ~ **cash** n Bargeld nt; ~ **copy** n Ausdruck m; ~ **core** n **(a)** (for building, road) Packlage f; **(b)** (fig) harter Kern; (pornography) harter Porno (col); ~**core** adj resistance vom harten Kern; pornography hart; ~ **court** n Hartplatz m; ~ **disk** n (Comp) Festplatte f; ~ **drinker** n starker Trinker; ~ **drug** n harte Droge; ~**earned** adj wages sauer verdient; victory hart erkämpft.

**harden** ['hɑːdn] **1** vt steel härten; body, muscles kräftigen. **this** ~**ed his attitude** dadurch hat sich seine Haltung verhärtet; **to** ~ **oneself to sth** (physically) sich gegen etw abhärten; (emotionally) gegen etw unempfindlich werden. **2** vi (substance) hart werden; (attitude) sich verhärten.

**hardened** ['hɑːdnd] adj steel gehärtet; person abgehärtet; criminal Gewohnheits-; sinner verstockt. **to be** ~ **to** or **against the cold/sb's insensitivity** gegen die Kälte abgehärtet sein/an jds Gefühllosigkeit (acc) gewöhnt sein; **he's** ~ **to it** (he doesn't mind) macht ihm nichts aus.

**hardening** ['hɑːdnɪŋ] n ~ **of the arteries** Arterienverkalkung f.

**hard:** ~**fought** adj battle erbittert; game hart; ~ **hat** n Schutzhelm m; (worker) Bauarbeiter m; ~**headed** adj nüchtern; ~**hearted** adj hartherzig (towards sb jdm gegenüber); ~**hitting** adj (lit) schlagkräftig; (fig: criticism, speech etc) gnadenlos; ~ **labour** (Brit) or **labor** (US) n Zwangsarbeit f; ~ **line** n harte Linie; **to take a** ~ **line** eine harte Linie verfolgen; ~**liner** n Vertreter(in f) m der harten Linie; ~ **liquor** n Schnaps m; ~**luck story** n Leidensgeschichte f.

**hardly** ['hɑːdlɪ] adv kaum. **I need** ~ **tell you that ...** ich muß Ihnen wohl kaum sagen, daß ...; ~ **ever** fast nie; **he had** ~ **gone** or ~ **had he gone when ...** er war kaum gegangen, als ...; **he would** ~ **have said that** das hat er wohl kaum gesagt; ~! (wohl) kaum; ~ **ideal conditions** wohl kaum ideale Bedingungen.

**hardness** ['hɑːdnɪs] n **(a)** Härte f. **(b)** see adj **(b)** Schwere f; Schwierigkeit f; Härte f. ~ **of hearing** Schwerhörigkeit f.

**hard:** ~**-nosed** adj abgebrüht; ~**-pressed** adj hart bedrängt; (with work) stark belastet; ~ **sell** n aggressive Verkaufstaktik, Hard selling nt.

**hardship** ['hɑːdʃɪp] n (condition) Not f; (instance) Härte f; (deprivation) Entbehrung f. **a temporary** ~ eine vorübergehende Notlage; **to suffer great** ~**s** große Not leiden; **if it's not too much (of a)** ~ **for you** wenn es dir nicht zuviel Mühe macht.

**hard:** ~ **shoulder** n (Brit) Seitenstreifen m; ~**top** n Hardtop nt or m; ~**ware** n **(a)** Eisenwaren pl; (household goods) Haushaltswaren pl; **(b)** (Comp) Hardware f; **(c)** (Mil) (Wehr)material nt; ~**ware store** n Eisenwarenhandlung f; (including household goods) Haushalts- und Eisenwarengeschäft nt; ~**-wearing** adj widerstandsfähig; cloth, clothes strapazierfähig; ~**-won** adj schwer erkämpft; ~**wood** n Hartholz nt; ~**-working** adj person fleißig; engine schwer belastet.

**hardy** ['hɑːdɪ] adj (+er) **(a)** (tough) zäh; person also abgehärtet; plant (frost)unempfindlich. ~ **annual** winterharte einjährige Pflanze. **(b)** (bold) person unerschrocken.

**hare** [hɛəʳ] **1** n (Feld)hase m. **2** vi (col) flitzen (col).

**hare:** ~**-brained** adj behämmert (col); ~**lip** n Hasenscharte f.

**harem** ['hɑːriːm] n Harem m.

**haricot** ['hærɪkəʊ] n ~ **bean** (Brit) Gartenbohne f.

**hark** [hɑːk] vi ~! (liter) horch(t)!; ~ **at him!** (col) hör ihn dir/hört ihn euch nur an! (col).

►**hark back** vi zurückkommen (to auf +acc). **he's always** ~**ing** ~ **to the good old days** er fängt immer wieder von der guten alten Zeit an.

**harm** [hɑːm] **1** n (bodily) Verletzung f; (material, to relations, psychological) Schaden m. **to do** ~ **to sb** jdm eine Verletzung zufügen/jdm Schaden zufügen; **to do** ~ **to sth** einer Sache (dat) schaden; **you will come to no** ~ es wird Ihnen nichts geschehen; **it will do more** ~ **than good** es wird mehr schaden als nützen; **it won't do you any** ~ es wird dir nicht schaden; **I see no** ~ **in the odd cigarette** ich finde nichts dabei, wenn man ab und zu eine Zigarette raucht; **to mean no** ~ es nicht böse meinen; **I don't mean him any** ~ ich meine es nicht böse mit ihm; **there's no** ~ **in asking/trying** es kann nicht schaden, zu fragen/es zu versuchen; **where's** or **what's the** ~ **in that?** was kann denn das schaden?; **out of** ~**'s way** in Sicherheit; **to stay out of** ~**'s way** der Gefahr (dat) aus dem Weg gehen.

**2** vt schaden (+dat); person verletzen.

**harmful** ['hɑːmfʊl] adj schädlich (to für); remarks verletzend.

**harmless** adj, ~**ly** adv ['hɑːmlɪs, -lɪ] harmlos.

**harmlessness** ['hɑːmlɪsnɪs] n Harmlosigkeit f.

**harmonica** [hɑː'mɒnɪkə] n Harmonika f.

**harmonious** adj, ~**ly** adv [hɑː'məʊnɪəs, -lɪ] harmonisch.

**harmonium** [hɑː'məʊnɪəm] n Harmonium nt.

**harmonize** ['hɑːmənaɪz] **1** vt (Mus) harmonisieren; plans, colours aufeinander abstimmen. **2** vi (notes, colours, people etc) harmonieren; (sing) mehrstimmig singen.

**harmony** ['hɑːmənɪ] n Harmonie f; (fig: harmonious relations) Eintracht f. **to be in/out of** ~ **with** (lit) harmonieren/nicht harmonieren mit; (fig also) in Einklang/nicht in Einklang sein mit; **to sing in** ~ mehrstimmig singen.

**harness** ['hɑːnɪs] **1** n Geschirr nt; (of parachute) Gurtwerk nt; (for baby) Laufgurt m. **to die in** ~ (fig, often hum) in den Sielen sterben. **2** vt **(a)** horse anschirren. **to** ~ **a horse to a carriage** ein Pferd vor einen Wagen spannen. **(b)** (utilize) river etc nutzbar

machen; *resources* (aus)nutzen.
**harp** [hɑːp] *n* Harfe *f.*
►**harp on 1** *vi (col)* don't ~ ~ so reite nicht so darauf herum! **2** *vt to* ~ ~ *sth* auf etw *dat* herumreiten; **to keep** ~**ing** ~ *sth* immer wieder mit etw kommen *(col).*
**harpist** [ˈhɑːpɪst] *n* Harfenspieler(in *f*) *m*, Harfenist(in *f*) *m.*
**harpoon** [hɑːˈpuːn] **1** *n* Harpune *f.* **2** *vt* harpunieren.
**harpsichord** [ˈhɑːpsɪkɔːd] *n* Cembalo *nt.*
**harrow** [ˈhærəʊ] **1** *n* Egge *f.* **2** *vt* eggen.
**harrowed** [ˈhærəʊd] *adj look* gequält.
**harrowing** [ˈhærəʊɪŋ] *adj* grauenhaft.
**harry** [ˈhærɪ] *vt* zusetzen *(+dat).*
**harsh** [hɑːʃ] *adj (+er)* rauh. **(a)** *(severe)* hart; *words, tone of voice also* barsch; *(too strict)* streng. **don't be too** ~ **with him** sei nicht zu streng mit ihm. **(b)** *colour, light, sound* grell; *taste* herb.
**harshly** [ˈhɑːʃlɪ] *adv (severely)* hart, streng; *speak* barsch.
**harshness** [ˈhɑːʃnɪs] *n see adj* Rauheit *f*; Härte *f*; Strenge *f*; Grelle *f*; Herbheit *f.*
**harvest** [ˈhɑːvɪst] **1** *n* Ernte *f*; *(of wines, berries also)* Lese *f.* **2** *vt (also fig)* ernten; *vines also* lesen; *(bring in)* einbringen. **3** *vi* ernten.
**harvester** [ˈhɑːvɪstəʳ] *n (person)* Erntearbeiter(in *f*) *m*; *(machine)* Mähmaschine *f*; *(combine* ~*)* Mähdrescher *m.*
**harvest:** ~ **festival** *n* Erntedankfest *nt*; ~ **time** *n* Erntezeit *f.*
**has** [hæz] *3rd pers sing pres of* **have.**
**has-been** [ˈhæzbiːn] *n (pej)* vergessene Größe.
**hash** [hæʃ] *n* **(a)** *(Cook)* Haschee *nt.* **(b)** *(col: mess)* **to make a** ~ **of sth** etw verpfuschen *(col).* **(c)** *(col: hashish)* Hasch *nt (col).*
**hashish** [ˈhæʃɪʃ] *n* Haschisch *nt.*
**hasn't** [ˈhæznt] = **has not.**
**hassle** [ˈhæsl] *(col)* **1** *n* Ärger *m*; *(bother, fuss)* Theater *nt (col).* **getting there is such a** ~ es ist so umständlich, dorthin zu kommen; **we had a bit of** ~ **with the police** wir hatten ein bißchen Ärger mit der Polizei; **this job is constant** ~ bei diesem Job ist man ständig im Streß *(col).* **2** *vt (mess around)* schikanieren; *(keep on at)* bedrängen.
**hassock** [ˈhæsək] *n* Kniekissen *nt.*
**haste** [heɪst] *n* Eile *f.* **to make** ~ sich beeilen; **more** ~ **less speed** *(Prov)* eile mit Weile *(Prov).*
**hasten** [ˈheɪsn] **1** *vi* sich beeilen. **I** ~ **to add that ...** ich muß allerdings hinzufügen, daß .... **2** *vt* beschleunigen. **the strain of office** ~**ed his death** die Belastung durch sein Amt trug zu seinem vorzeitigen Tod bei; **to** ~ **sb's departure** jdn zum Aufbruch drängen.
**hastily** [ˈheɪstɪlɪ] *adv* **(a)** *(hurriedly)* hastig. **(b)** *(rashly)* vorschnell.
**hastiness** [ˈheɪstɪnɪs] *n* **(a)** Eile *f.* **(b)** *(rashness)* Voreiligkeit *f.*
**hasty** [ˈheɪstɪ] *adj (+er)* **(a)** *(hurried)* eilig. **they made a** ~ **exit** sie gingen eilig hinaus; **don't be so** ~ nicht so hastig! **(b)** *(rash)* vorschnell.
**hat** [hæt] *n* **(a)** Hut *m.* **(b)** *(fig phrases)* **I'll eat my** ~ **if ...** ich fresse einen Besen, wenn ... *(col)*; **I take my** ~ **off to him** Hut ab vor ihm!; **to talk through one's** ~ *(col)* dummes Zeug reden; **to keep sth under one's** ~ *(col)* etw für sich behalten; **at the drop of a** ~ auf der Stelle; **that's old** ~ *(col)* das ist Schnee von gestern *(col)*; **to pass around the** ~ **for sb** für jdn den Hut rumgehen lassen *(col).*
**hatbox** [ˈhætbɒks] *n* Hutschachtel *f.*
**hatch¹** [hætʃ] *(also* ~ **out) 1** *vt* ausbrüten; *(fig)* plot *also* aushecken. **2** *vi (bird)* ausschlüpfen. **when will**

**the eggs** ~**?** wann schlüpfen die Jungen aus?
**hatch²** *n (Naut)* Luke *f.* **(service)** ~ *(Brit)* Durchreiche *f*; **down the** ~! *(col)* hoch die Tassen! *(col).*
**hatchback** [ˈhætʃbæk] *n (car)* Schrägheck *nt* (mit Heckklappe); *(door)* Heckklappe *f.*
**hatchet** [ˈhætʃɪt] *n* Beil *nt.* **to bury the** ~ das Kriegsbeil begraben; ~ **man** *(killer)* gedungener Mörder; *(fig)* Vollstreckungsbeamte(r) *m.*
**hatching** [ˈhætʃɪŋ] *n (Art)* Schraffur *f.*
**hate** [heɪt] **1** *vt* hassen; *(detest also)* verabscheuen; *(dislike also)* nicht leiden können. **to** ~ **the sound of sth** etw nicht hören können; **to** ~ **to do sth** *or* **doing sth** es hassen, etw zu tun; *(weaker)* etw äußerst ungern tun; **I** ~ **seeing her in pain** ich kann es nicht ertragen, sie leiden zu sehen; **I** ~ **the idea of leaving** der Gedanke, wegzumüssen, ist mir äußerst zuwider; **I** ~ **to bother you** es ist mir sehr unangenehm, daß ich Sie belästigen muß; **I** ~ **having to say it but ...** es fällt mir sehr schwer, das sagen zu müssen, aber ...; **I should** ~ **to keep you waiting** ich möchte Sie auf keinen Fall warten lassen. **2** *n* Haß *m (for, of* auf *+acc).* ~ **mail** beleidigende Briefe *pl*; **it's one of his pet** ~**s** das kann er auf den Tod nicht ausstehen.
**hateful** [ˈheɪtfʊl] *adj* abscheulich.
**hatpin** [ˈhætpɪn] *n* Hutnadel *f.*
**hatred** [ˈheɪtrɪd] *n* Haß *m (for* auf *+acc).*
**hatstand** [ˈhætstænd] *n* Garderobenständer *m*; *(for hats only)* Hutständer *m.*
**hatter** [ˈhætəʳ] *n* Hutmacher(in *f*) *m*; *(seller)* Hutverkäufer(in *f*) *m.*
**hat:** ~**-tree** *n (US)*=**hatstand**; ~**-trick** *n* Hattrick *m.*
**haughtily** [ˈhɔːtɪlɪ] *adv see adj* hochmütig; überheblich.
**haughty** [ˈhɔːtɪ] *adj (+er)* hochmütig; *(towards people)* überheblich.
**haul** [hɔːl] **1** *n* **(a)** *(journey)* Strecke *f.* **it's a long** ~ es ist ein weiter Weg; **short/long** ~ **aircraft** Kurz-/Langstreckenflugzeug *nt.* **(b)** *(Fishing)* (Fisch)fang *m*; *(from robbery)* Beute *f*; *(col: of presents)* Ausbeute *f (col).* **2** *vt* ziehen; *heavy objects also* schleppen.
►**haul down** *vt sep flag, sail* einholen.
**haulage** [ˈhɔːlɪdʒ] *n* **(a)** Transport *m.* ~ **contractor** *(firm)* Spedition(sfirma) *f*; *(person)* Spediteur *m.* **(b)** *(charges)* Transportkosten *pl.*
**haulier** [ˈhɔːlɪəʳ] *n* Spediteur *m*; *(company)* Spedition *f.*
**haunch** [hɔːntʃ] *n (of person)* Hüfte *f*; *(of animal)* *(hindquarters)* Hinterbacke *f*; *(top of leg)* Keule *f*; *(Cook)* Lendenstück *nt.* ~**es** Gesäß *nt*; *(of animal)* Hinterbacken *pl*; **he was sitting on his** ~**es** er saß in der Hocke; ~ **of venison** *(Cook)* Rehkeule *f.*
**haunt** [hɔːnt] **1** *vt* **(a)** *(ghost)* house spuken in *(+dat)*, umgehen in *(+dat).* **(b)** *(fig: memory etc)* verfolgen. **the nightmares which** ~**ed him** die Alpträume, die ihn heimsuchten. **(c)** *(frequent)* häufig besuchen. **2** *n* **this is one of his favourite** ~**s** hier hält er sich sehr gerne auf.
**haunted** [ˈhɔːntɪd] *adj* **(a)** Spuk-. **a** ~ **house** ein Haus *nt*, in dem es spukt; **this place is** ~ hier spukt es. **(b)** *look* gehetzt; *person* ruhelos.
**haunting** [ˈhɔːntɪŋ] *adj doubt* quälend; *tune, visions, poetry* eindringlich. **these** ~ **final chords** diese Schlußakkorde, die einen nicht loslassen.
**Havana** [həˈvænə] *n* Havanna *nt.*
**have** [hæv] *pret, ptp* **had,** *3rd pers sing pres* **has 1** *vt* **(a)** *(possess)* haben. **she has** **(got** *esp Brit)* **blue eyes** sie hat blaue Augen; ~ **you** **(got** *esp Brit)* *or* **do you** ~ **a suitcase?** hast du einen Koffer?; **I** ~**n't** **(got** *esp Brit)* *or* **I don't** ~ **a pen** ich habe keinen Kugel-

schreiber.

(b) to ~ **breakfast/lunch/dinner** frühstücken/zu Mittag essen/zu Abend essen; **what will you ~?** — **I'll ~ the steak** was möchten Sie gern(e)? — ich möchte gern das Steak; **he had a cigarette/a drink/a steak** er rauchte eine Zigarette/trank etwas/aß ein Steak; **will you ~ some more?** möchten Sie gern (noch etwas) mehr?; ~ **another one** nimm noch eine/einen/eines; *(drink)* trink noch einen; *(smoke)* rauch noch eine.

(c) *(receive, obtain, get)* haben. **I ~ it on good authority/from her that ...** ich habe aus zuverlässiger Quelle/von ihr erfahren, daß ...; **to let sb ~ sth** jdm etw geben; **it's nowhere to be had** es ist nirgends zu haben *or* kriegen *(col)*; **she's having a baby** sie bekommt ein Kind.

(d) *(maintain, insist)* **he will ~ it that Paul is guilty** er besteht darauf, daß Paul schuldig ist; **he won't ~ it that Paul is guilty** er will nichts davon hören, daß Paul schuldig ist; **as Professor James would ~ it** *(according to)* laut Professor James; *(as he would put it)* um es mit Professor James zu sagen.

(e) *(neg: refuse to allow)* **I won't ~ this nonsense** dieser Unsinn kommt (mir) nicht in Frage!; **I won't ~ it!** das lasse ich mir nicht bieten!

(f) *(hold)* (gepackt) haben. **the dog had (got) him by the ankle** der Hund hatte ihn am Knöchel gepackt; **I ~ (got) him where I want him** ich habe ihn endlich soweit; **I'll ~ you** *(col)* dich krieg ich (beim Kragen); **you ~ me there** da bin ich überfragt.

(g) *(causative)* **to ~ sth done** etw tun lassen; **to ~ one's hair cut/a suit made** sich *(dat)* die Haare schneiden lassen/einen Anzug machen lassen; **to ~ sb do sth** jdn etw tun lassen; **they had him shot** sie ließen ihn erschießen; **I'd ~ you understand ...** Sie müssen nämlich wissen ...; **what would you ~ me say?** was soll ich dazu sagen?; **they soon had the carpet down** sie waren schnell mit dem Teppichverlegen fertig; **when she had the lid off** als sie den Deckel herunterhatte.

(h) *(experience, suffer)* **he had his car stolen** man hat ihm sein Auto gestohlen; **I've had three windows broken** (bei) mir sind drei Fenster eingeworfen worden; **I had my friends turn against me** ich mußte es erleben, wie *or* daß sich meine Freunde gegen mich wandten.

(i) **to ~ a walk** spazierengehen; **to ~ a dream** träumen.

(j) *party* geben, machen; *meeting* abhalten. **are you having a reception?** gibt es einen Empfang?

(k) *(phrases)* **let him ~ it!** gib's ihm! *(col)*; **he/that coat has had it** *(col)* der ist weg von Fenster *(col)*/ der Mantel hat ausgedient; **if I miss the last bus, I've had it** *(col)* wenn ich den letzten Bus verpasse, bin ich geliefert *(col)*; **to ~ a pleasant evening** einen netten Abend verbringen; ~ **a good time!** viel Spaß!; **you've been had!** *(col)* da hat man dich übers Ohr gehauen *(col)*; **thanks for having me** vielen Dank für Ihre Gastfreundschaft.

**2** *aux* (a) haben; *(esp with vbs of motion)* sein. **to ~ been** gewesen sein; **to ~ seen/heard** gesehen/ gehört haben; **to ~ gone/run** gegangen/gelaufen sein; **I ~ /had been** ich bin/war gewesen; **I ~ /had seen** ich habe/hatte gesehen; **had I seen him** hätte ich ihn gesehen; **having seen him** *(since)* da ich ihn gesehen habe/hatte; *(after)* als ich ihn gesehen hatte; **I ~ lived** *or* ~ **been living here for 10 years/since January** ich wohne schon 10 Jahre/seit Januar hier; **you *have* grown** du bist aber gewachsen.

(b) *(in tag questions etc)* **you've seen her, ~n't you?** du hast sie gesehen, oder nicht?; **you ~n't seen her, ~ you?** du hast sie nicht (etwa) gesehen, oder?; **you ~n't seen her — yes, I ~** du hast sie nicht gesehen — doch; **you've made a mistake — no I ~n't** du hast einen Fehler gemacht — nein(, hab' ich nicht *col*); **you've dropped your book — so I ~** du hast dein Buch fallen lassen — tatsächlich!; **I ~ seen a ghost — ~ you?** ich habe ein Gespenst gesehen — tatsächlich?; **I've lost it — you ~n't** *(disbelieving)* ich habe es verloren — das darf doch nicht wahr sein!

**3** *modal aux (+infin)* **I ~ to do it, I ~ got to do it** *(Brit)* ich muß es tun; **I don't ~ to do it, I ~n't got to do it** *(Brit)* ich muß es nicht tun, ich brauche es nicht zu tun; **do you ~ to go now?, ~ you got to go now?** *(Brit)* müssen Sie jetzt unbedingt gehen?; **you didn't ~ to tell her** das mußten Sie ihr nicht unbedingt sagen; **it has to be a mistake!** das muß wohl ein Irrtum sein!

►**have around** *vt always separate* (a) *(bei sich)* zu Besuch haben; *(invite)* einladen. (b) **he's useful to ~** es ist ganz praktisch, ihn zur Hand zu haben.

►**have in** *vt always separate* (a) *decorators etc* im Haus haben; *doctor* holen. (b) **to ~ it ~ for sb** *(col)* jdn auf dem Kieker haben *(col)*.

►**have off** *vt always separate* **to ~ it ~ with sb** *(col)* es mit jdm treiben *(col)*.

►**have on 1** *vt sep clothes, radio* anhaben. **2** *vt always separate* (a) *(have sth arranged)* vorhaben; *(be busy with)* zu tun haben. ~ **you got anything ~ for tonight?** hast du heute abend etwas vor? (b) *(col: deceive)* übers Ohr hauen *(col)*; *(tease)* auf den Arm nehmen *(col)*. (c) **to ~ nothing ~ sb** gegen jdn nichts in der Hand haben; **they've got nothing ~ me!** mir kann keiner was! *(col)*.

►**have out** *vt always separate* (a) **he was having his tonsils ~** ihm wurden die Mandeln herausgenommen. (b) *(discuss)* **to ~ it ~ with sb** etw mit jdm ausdiskutieren; **I'll ~ it ~ with him** ich werde mit ihm reden.

►**have up** *vt always separate (col: in court)* **to be had ~ for sth** wegen etw vors Gericht kommen.

**haven** ['heɪvn] *n (fig)* Zufluchtsstätte *f*.

**haversack** ['hævəsæk] *n* Rucksack *m*.

**haves** [hævz] *npl (col)* **the ~ and the have-nots** die Betuchten und die Habenichtse *(col)*.

**havoc** ['hævək] *n* verheerender Schaden; *(devastation also)* Verwüstung *f*; *(chaos)* Chaos *nt*. **to wreak ~ in** *or* **with sth, to play ~ with sth** bei etw verheerenden Schaden anrichten.

**Hawaii** [həˈwaɪiː] *n* Hawaii *nt*.

**Hawaiian** [həˈwaɪjən] **1** *adj* hawaiisch. **2** *n* (a) *(person)* Hawaiianer(in *f*) *m*. (b) *(language)* Hawaiisch *nt*.

**hawk¹** [hɔːk] *n (Orn)* Habicht *m*; *(sparrow ~)* Sperber *m*; *(falcon)* Falke *m*. **to have eyes like a ~** Augen wie ein Luchs haben; **the ~s and the doves** *(fig)* die Falken und die Tauben.

**hawk²** *vt* hausieren (gehen) mit; *(in street)* verkaufen.

**hawker** ['hɔːkə$^r$] *n (pedlar) (door-to-door)* Hausierer(in *f*) *m*; *(in street)* Straßenhändler(in *f*) *m*.

**hawk-eyed** ['hɔːkaɪd] *adj* scharfsichtig. **to be ~** Adleraugen haben.

**hawser** ['hɔːzə$^r$] *n (Naut)* Trosse *f*.

**hawthorn** ['hɔːθɔːn] *n* Weiß- *or* Rotdorn *m*.

**hay** [heɪ] *n* Heu *nt*. **to make ~** Heu machen; **to hit the ~** *(col)* sich in die Falle hauen *(col)*; **to make ~ while the sun shines** *(Prov)* das Eisen schmieden, solange es heiß ist *(Prov)*.

**hay:** ~ **fever** *n* Heuschnupfen *m*; ~**making** *n* Heuernte *f*; ~**stack** *n* Heuhaufen *m*.

**haywire** ['heɪwaɪə$^r$] *adj pred (col)* **to be (all) ~**

(vollständig) durcheinander sein; **to go** ~ *(plans)* über den Haufen geworfen werden *(col)*; *(machinery)* verrückt spielen *(col)*.

**hazard** [ˈhæzəd] **1** *n* **(a)** *(danger)* Gefahr *f*; *(risk)* Risiko *nt*. **it's a fire** ~ es stellt eine Feuergefahr dar; ~ **warning lights** *(Aut)* Warnblinkanlage *f*. **(b)** *(chance)* **game of** ~ Glücksspiel *nt*. **2** *vt life, reputation* riskieren, aufs Spiel setzen. **if I might** ~ **a suggestion** wenn ich mir einen Vorschlag erlauben darf; **to** ~ **a guess** (es) wagen, eine Vermutung anzustellen.

**hazardous** [ˈhæzədəs] *adj* gefährlich, risikoreich. ~ **pay** *(US)* Gefahrenzulage *f*; ~ **waste** Sondermüll *m*.

**haze** [heɪz] *n* Dunst *m*.

**hazel** [ˈheɪzl] **1** *n (Bot)* Hasel(nuß)strauch *m*. **2** *adj (colour)* haselnußbraun.

**hazelnut** [ˈheɪzlnʌt] *n* Haselnuß *f*.

**hazy** [ˈheɪzɪ] *adj (+er)* **(a)** dunstig, diesig; *mountains* im Dunst (liegend). **(b)** *(unclear)* verschwommen. **I'm** ~ **about what happened** ich kann mich nur verschwommen daran erinnern, was geschah.

**HB** = **hard black** *(on pencils)* HB.

**H-bomb** [ˈeɪtʃbɒm] *n* H-Bombe *f*.

**HE** = **His Excellency** S.E.

**he** [hiː] **1** *pers pron* er. **so** ~**'s the one** der *(col)* or er ist es also!; **Harry Rigg? who's** ~? Harry Rigg? wer ist das denn?; ~ **who** *(liter)* derjenige, der. **2** *n* **it's a** ~ *(col: baby)* es ist ein er.

**head** [hed] **1** *n* **(a)** Kopf *m*. **from** ~ **to foot** von Kopf bis Fuß; ~ **downwards** mit dem Kopf nach unten; **to stand on one's** ~ auf dem Kopf stehen; **you could do it standing on your** ~ *(col)* das kann man ja im Schlaf machen; **to fall** ~ **over heels in love with sb** sich bis über beide Ohren in jdn verlieben; **to keep one's** ~ **above water** *(fig)* sich über Wasser halten; **to talk one's** ~ **off** *(col)* reden wie ein Wasserfall *(col)*; **to shout one's** ~ **off** *(col)* sich *(dat)* die Lunge aus dem Leib schreien *(col)*; **to have a good/bad** ~ **for heights** schwindelfrei/nicht schwindelfrei sein; **I've got some** ~ **this morning** *(col)* ich habe heute morgen einen ziemlichen Brummschädel *(col)*; **to give sb his** ~ jdn machen lassen; **on your (own)** ~ **be it** auf Ihre eigene Verantwortung; **he gave orders over my** ~ er hat über meinen Kopf (hin)weg Anordnungen gegeben; **to go to one's** ~ einem zu Kopf steigen; **I can't make** ~ **nor tail of it** daraus werde ich nicht schlau.

**(b)** *(mind, intellect)* Kopf, Verstand *m*. **use your** ~ streng deinen Kopf an; **to get sth into one's** ~ *(understand)* etw begreifen; **he won't get it into his** ~ **that** ... es will ihm nicht in den Kopf, daß ...; **to take it into one's** ~ **to do sth** sich *(dat)* in den Kopf setzen, etw zu tun; **it never entered his** ~ **that** ... es kam ihm nie in den Sinn, daß ...; **what put that idea into his** ~? wie kommt er denn darauf?; **to get sth out of one's** ~ sich *(dat)* etw aus dem Kopf schlagen; **he has a good business** ~ er hat einen ausgeprägten Geschäftssinn; **he has a good** ~ **on his shoulders** er ist ein kluger Kopf; **he has an old** ~ **on young shoulders** er ist sehr reif für sein Alter; **two** ~**s are better than one** *(prov)* besser zwei als einer allein; **we put our** ~**s together** wir haben unsere Köpfe zusammengesteckt; **to be above** *or* **over sb's** ~ über jds Horizont *(acc)* gehen; **to keep one's** ~ den Kopf nicht verlieren; **to lose one's** ~ den Kopf verlieren; **he is off his** ~ *(col)* er ist (ja) nicht (ganz) bei Trost *(col)*; **to be soft in the** ~ *(col)* einen (kleinen) Dachschaden haben *(col)*.

**(c) twenty** ~ **of cattle** zwanzig Stück Vieh; **to pay 10 marks a** ~ 10 Mark pro Kopf bezahlen.

**(d)** *(of flower, lettuce, nail, page)* Kopf *m*; *(of arrow, spear)* Spitze *f*; *(of bed)* Kopf(ende *nt*) *m*; *(on* *beer)* Blume *f*; *(of corn)* Ähre *f*; *(of stream) (upper area)* Oberlauf *m*; *(source)* Ursprung *m*; *(of tape-recorder)* Tonkopf *m*. ~ **of steam** Dampfdruck *m*; **at the** ~ **of the list/stairs** oben auf der Liste/an der Treppe; **at the** ~ **of the table** am Kopf(ende) des Tisches; **at the** ~ **of the queue/procession** an der Spitze der Schlange/des Zuges; **if things come to a** ~ wenn sich die Sache zuspitzt.

**(e)** *(of family)* Oberhaupt *nt*; *(of business, organization)* Chef(in *f*) *m*; *(Sch col)* Schulleiter(in *f*) *m*. ~ **of department** Abteilungsleiter(in *f*) *m*; *(Sch, Univ)* Fachbereichsleiter(in *f*) *m*; ~ **of state** Staatsoberhaupt *nt*.

**(f)** *(~ing, in essay etc)* Rubrik *f*.

**(g)** *(of coin)* ~**s or tails?** Kopf oder Zahl?; ~**s I win** bei Kopf gewinne ich.

**2** *vt* **(a)** *(lead)* anführen; *(be in charge of also)* führen; *list also* an der Spitze stehen von. **(b)** *(direct)* steuern *(towards, for* in Richtung*)*. **(c) in the chapter** ~**ed** ... in dem Kapitel mit der Überschrift ...; ~**ed writing paper** Schreibpapier mit Briefkopf. **(d)** *(Ftbl)* köpfen.

**3** *vi* gehen; *(in vehicle)* fahren. **where are you** ~**ing** *or* ~**ed?** wohin gehen/fahren Sie?

►**head back** *vi* zurückgehen/-fahren. **to be** ~**ing** ~ auf dem Rückweg sein.

►**head for** *vi* +*prep obj place, person* zugehen/zufahren auf *(+acc)*, zusteuern auf *(+acc)*; *town, country* gehen/fahren in Richtung *(+gen)*; *(ship also)* Kurs halten auf *(+acc)*. **where are you** ~**ing** *or* ~**ed** ~? wohin gehen/fahren Sie?; **you're** ~**ing** ~ **trouble** du bist auf dem besten Weg, Ärger zu bekommen.

►**head off** *vt sep* abfangen; *war, strike* abwenden.

►**head up** *vt sep delegation etc* leiten.

**head** *in cpds (top, senior)* Ober-; ~**ache** *n* Kopfschmerzen *pl*; *(col: problem)* Problem *nt*; **to have a** ~**ache** Kopfschmerzen haben; **this is a bit of a** ~**ache** das macht mir/uns ziemliches Kopfzerbrechen; ~**band** *n* Stirnband *nt*; ~**board** *n* Kopfteil *nt*; ~ **cold** *n* Schnupfen *m*; ~**dress** *n* Kopfschmuck *m*.

**header** [ˈhedəʳ] *n* **(a)** *(dive)* Kopfsprung *m*. **(b)** *(Ftbl)* Kopfball *m*.

**head:** ~**first** *adv (lit, fig)* kopfüber; ~**gear** *n* Kopfbedeckung *f*; ~**-hunt** *vt* abwerben; ~**-hunter** *n (lit, fig)* Kopfjäger *m*.

**heading** [ˈhedɪŋ] *n* Überschrift *f*; *(on letter, document)* Kopf *m*; *(in encyclopedia)* Stichwort *nt*.

**head:** ~**lamp**, ~**light** *n* Scheinwerfer *m*; ~**land** *n* Landspitze *f*; ~**line** *n (Press)* Schlagzeile *f*; **to hit the** ~**lines** Schlagzeilen machen; **the news** ~**lines** *(TV, Rad)* das Wichtigste in Kürze; ~**long** *adj, adv fall* der Länge nach; *rush* Hals über Kopf; ~**master** *n* Schulleiter *m*; ~**mistress** *n* Schulleiterin *f*; ~ **office** *n* Zentrale *f*; ~**-on** *1 adj* ~**on collision** Frontalzusammenstoß *m*; **2** *adj* frontal; **to meet** *or* **tackle sth** ~**-on** etw geradewegs angehen; ~**phones** *npl* Kopfhörer *pl*; ~**quarters** *n sing or pl (Mil)* Hauptquartier *nt*; *(Comm)* Zentrale *f*; *(of political party)* Parteizentrale *f*; **police** ~**quarters** Polizeipräsidium *nt*; ~**rest**, *(Aut)* ~ **restraint** *n* Kopfstütze *f*; ~**room** *n* lichte Höhe; *(in car)* Kopfraum *m*; ~**scarf** *n* Kopftuch *nt*; ~**set** *n* Kopfhörer *pl*; ~ **start** *n* **he's got a** ~ **start on us** er ist uns weit voraus; ~**stone** *n (on grave)* Grabstein *m*; ~**strong** *adj* dickköpfig; ~ **teacher** *n (Brit)* = ~**master**, ~**mistress**; ~ **waiter** *n* Oberkellner *m*; ~**way** *n* **to make** ~**way** *(lit, fig)* vorankommen; ~**wind** *n* Gegenwind *m*; ~**word** *n* Stichwort *nt*.

**heady** [ˈhedɪ] *adj (+er) (lit, fig)* berauschend.

**heat up**

**heal** [hiːl] **1** *vi (Med, fig)* heilen. **2** *vt (Med)* heilen; *(fig) differences etc* beilegen.
▶**heal up 1** *vi* zuheilen. **2** *vt sep* zuheilen lassen.
**health** [helθ] *n* Gesundheit *f*. **in good/poor** ~ bei guter/schlechter Gesundheit; **how is his** ~? wie geht es ihm gesundheitlich?; **to be good/bad for one's** ~ gesund/ungesund sein; ~ **and safety regulations** Arbeitsschutzvorschriften *pl*; **Ministry of H**~ Gesundheitsministerium *nt*; **to drink (to) sb's** ~ auf jds Wohl *(acc)* trinken; **your** ~! zum Wohl!
**health:** ~ **centre** *n* **(a)** Ärztezentrum *nt*; **(b)** = ~ **club**; ~ **certificate** *n* Gesundheitsattest *nt*; ~ **club** *n* Fitness-Center *nt*; ~ **farm** *n* Gesundheitsfarm *f*; ~ **food** *n* Reformkost *f*, Biokost *f (col)*; ~ **food shop** *(Brit) or* **store** *(esp US) n* Reformhaus *nt*, Bioladen *m (col)*; ~ **hazard** *n* Gefahr *f* für die Gesundheit; ~ **insurance** *n* Krankenversicherung *f*; ~ **resort** *n* Kurort *m*; **H**~ **Service** *n (Brit)* Gesundheitswesen *nt*; **H**~ **Service doctor** Kassenarzt *m/* -ärztin *f*; ~ **visitor** *n* Sozialarbeiter(in *f*) *m (in der Gesundheitsfürsorge)*.
**healthy** ['helθɪ] *adj (+er) (lit, fig)* gesund.
**heap** [hiːp] **1** *n* **(a)** Haufen *m*; *(col: old car)* Klapperkiste *f (col)*. **he fell in a** ~ **on the floor** er sackte zu Boden. **(b)** ~**s of** *(col)* eine Menge *(col)*; **we've got** ~**s of time** wir haben jede Menge Zeit *(col)*. **2** *vt* häufen. **to** ~ **praises on sb** jdn mit Lob überschütten; ~**ed spoonful** gehäufter Löffel.
▶**heap up 1** *vt sep* aufhäufen. **2** *vi* sich häufen.
**hear** [hɪəʳ] *pret, ptp* **heard 1** *vt (also learn)* hören. **to make oneself** ~**d** sich *(dat)* Gehör verschaffen; **you're not going, do you** ~ **me!** du gehst nicht, hörst du (mich)!; **to** ~ **him speak you'd think ...** wenn man ihn so reden hört, könnte man meinen, ...; **I've often** ~**d say** *or* **it said that ...** ich habe oft sagen hören, daß ...; **I** ~ **you're going away** ich höre, Sie gehen weg; **I must be** ~**ing things** ich glaube, ich höre nicht richtig; **to** ~ **a case** *(Jur)* einen Fall verhandeln.
**2** *vi* **(a)** hören. ~, ~! (sehr) richtig!; *(Parl)* hört!, hört! **(b)** *(get news)* hören. **yes, so I** ~ ja, ich habe es gehört; **you'll be** ~**ing from me!** *(threatening)* Sie werden noch von mir hören!; **to** ~ **about sth** von etw hören *or* erfahren; **have you** ~**d about John?** **he's getting married** haben Sie schon gehört? John heiratet; **never** ~**d of him/it** nie (von ihm/davon) gehört; **I've** ~**d of him** ich habe schon von ihm gehört; **he was never** ~**d of again** man hat nie wieder etwas von ihm gehört; **I've never** ~**d of such a thing!** das ist ja unerhört!; **I won't** ~ **of it** *(allow)* ich will davon nichts hören.
▶**hear out** *vt sep person* ausreden lassen.
**heard** [hɜːd] *pret, ptp of* **hear**.
**hearing** ['hɪərɪŋ] *n* **(a)** *(sense)* Gehör *nt*; *(ability)* Hörvermögen *nt*. **(b)** **within/out of** ~ in/außer Hörweite. *(Pol)* Hearing *nt*, Anhörung *f*; *(Jur)* Verhandlung *f*. **to give sb a** ~ jdn anhören; **he didn't get a fair** ~ man hörte ihn nicht richtig an; *(Jur)* er bekam keinen fairen Prozeß.
**hearing aid** *n* Hörgerät *nt*.
**hearsay** ['hɪəseɪ] *n* Gerüchte *pl*. **to have sth on** ~ etw vom Hörensagen wissen.
**hearse** [hɜːs] *n* Leichenwagen *m*.
**heart** [hɑːt] *n* **(a)** *(lit, fig)* Herz *nt*. **to break sb's** ~ jdm das Herz brechen; **to break one's** ~ **over sth** sich über etw *(acc)* zu Tode grämen; **you're breaking my** ~ *(iro)* ich fang' gleich an zu weinen *(iro)*; **after my own** ~ ganz nach meinem Herzen; **to have a change of** ~ sich anders besinnen; **to learn/know sth by** ~ etw auswendig lernen/wissen; **in my** ~ **of** ~**s** im Grunde meines Herzens; **with all my** ~ von

ganzem Herzen; **from the bottom of one's** ~ aus tiefstem Herzen; **to take sth to** ~ sich *(dat)* etw zu Herzen nehmen; **we have your interests at** ~ Ihre Interessen liegen uns am Herzen; **to set one's** ~ **on sth** sein Herz an etw *(acc)* hängen *(geh)*; **to one's** ~**'s content** nach Herzenslust; **most men are boys at** ~ die meisten Männer sind im Grunde (ihres Herzens) noch richtige Kinder; **his** ~ **isn't in it** er ist nicht mit dem Herzen dabei; **to lose** ~ den Mut verlieren; **to take** ~ Mut fassen; **to put new** ~ **into sb** jdn mit neuem Mut erfüllen; **his** ~ **is in the right place** *(col)* er hat das Herz auf dem rechten Fleck *(col)*; **to have a** ~ **of stone** ein Herz aus Stein haben; **to wear one's** ~ **on one's sleeve** aus seinem Herzen keine Mördergrube machen *(col)*; **my** ~ **was in my mouth** *(col)* mir schlug das Herz bis zum Hals; **have a** ~! *(col)* gib deinem Herzen einen Stoß! *(col)*; **not to have the** ~ **to do sth** es nicht übers Herz bringen, etw zu tun; **she has a** ~ **of gold** sie hat ein goldenes Herz; **my** ~ **sank** *(apprehension)* mir rutschte das Herz in die Hose *(col)*; *(sadness)* das Herz wurde mir schwer; *(discouraged)* mein Mut sank; **the** ~ **of the matter** der Kern der Sache; **in the** ~ **of the forest** mitten im Wald.
**(b)** *(Cards)* ~**s** *pl* Herz *nt*; *(Bridge)* Coeur *nt*; **queen of** ~**s** Herzdame *f*.
**heart:** ~**ache** *n* Kummer *m*; ~ **attack** *n* Herzinfarkt *m*; **I nearly had a** ~ **attack** *(fig col: shock)* ich habe fast einen Herzschlag gekriegt *(col)*; ~**beat** *n* Herzschlag *m*; ~**break** *n* großer Kummer; ~**breaking** *adj* herzzerreißend; **it's** ~**breaking** es bricht einem das Herz; ~**broken** *adj* todunglücklich; ~**burn** *n* Sodbrennen *nt*; ~ **condition** *n* Herzleiden *nt*.
**hearten** ['hɑːtn] *vt* ermutigen.
**heartening** ['hɑːtnɪŋ] *adj news* ermutigend.
**heart:** ~ **failure** *n* Herzversagen *nt*; ~**felt** *adj* tief empfunden; *sympathy* herzlichst.
**hearth** [hɑːθ] *n* Feuerstelle *f*; *(whole fireplace)* Kamin *m*. ~**rug** Kaminvorleger *m*.
**heartily** ['hɑːtɪlɪ] *adv* herzlich; *sing* kräftig; *eat* herzhaft. **I** ~ **agree** ich stimme voll und ganz zu.
**heart:** ~**land** *n* a Tory ~**land** eine Hochburg der Konservativen; ~**less** *adj* herzlos; *(cruel also)* grausam; ~**rending** *adj* herzzerreißend; ~**searching** *n* Gewissenserforschung *f*; ~**strings** *npl* **to pull** *or* **tug at the/sb's** ~**strings** auf die/bei jdm auf die Tränendrüsen drücken *(col)*; ~**throb** *n (col)* Schwarm *m (col)*; ~**to-**~ *adj, n* **to have a** ~**to-**~ **(talk) with sb** sich mit jdm ganz offen aussprechen; ~ **transplant** *n* Herztransplantation *f*; ~**trouble** *n* Herzbeschwerden *pl*; ~**warming** *adj* herzerfreuend.
**hearty** ['hɑːtɪ] *adj (+er)* herzlich; *slap also, meal, appetite* herzhaft, kräftig; *dislike* tief; *person (robust)* kernig; *(cheerful)* laut und herzlich.
**heat** [hiːt] **1** *n* **(a)** *(lit, fig)* Hitze *f*; *(pleasant, Phys)* Wärme *f*; *(of curry etc)* Schärfe *f*; *(*~*ing)* Heizung *f*. **in the** ~ **of the day** wenn es heiß ist; **in the** ~ **of the moment** in der Hitze des Gefechts; *(when upset)* in der Erregung; **to take the** ~ **out of the situation** die Situation entschärfen; **to put the** ~ **on** *(col)* Druck machen *(col)*; **to put the** ~ **on sb** *(col)* jdn unter Druck setzen; **the** ~ **is off** *(col)* der Druck ist weg *(col)*; *(danger is past)* die Gefahr ist vorbei. **(b)** *(Sport)* Vorlauf *m*; *(Boxing etc)* Vorkampf *m*. **final** ~ Ausscheidungskampf *m*. **(c)** *(Zool)* Brunst *f*; *(of dogs, cats)* Läufigkeit *f*. **on** ~ brünstig; läufig. **2** *vt* erhitzen; *room* heizen; *pool, house* beheizen.
▶**heat up 1** *vi* warm werden; *(get very hot)* sich erhitzen; *(discussion)* hitzig werden. **2** *vt sep* er-

wärmen; *food* heiß machen.
**heated** ['hiːtɪd] *adj (lit)* geheizt; *pool* beheizt; *(fig) words, discussion* hitzig, erregt. **things got rather** ~ die Gemüter erhitzten sich sehr.
**heatedly** ['hiːtɪdlɪ] *adv* hitzig.
**heater** ['hiːtəʳ] *n* Ofen *m; (electrical also)* Heizgerät *nt; (in car)* Heizung *f.*
**heat:** ~ **exchanger** *n* Wärmeaustauscher *m;* ~ **exhaustion** *n* Hitzeerschöpfung *f.*
**heath** [hiːθ] *n* Heide *f.*
**heathen** ['hiːðən] **1** *adj* heidnisch, Heiden-; *(fig)* unkultiviert. **2** *n* Heide *m,* Heidin *f; (fig)* unkultivierter Mensch.
**heather** ['heðəʳ] *n* Heidekraut *nt,* Erika *f.*
**Heath Robinson** [ˌhiːθˈrɒbɪnsən] *adj (col) gadget* wunderlich.
**heating** ['hiːtɪŋ] *n (in house etc)* Heizung *f.* ~ **costs** Heizkosten *pl;* ~ **oil** Heizöl *nt.*
**heat:** ~**-resistant** *adj* hitzebeständig; ~ **shield** *n* Hitzeschild *m;* ~**stroke** *n* Hitzschlag *m;* ~ **treatment** *n (Med)* Wärmebehandlung *f;* ~**wave** *n* Hitzewelle *f.*
**heave** [hiːv] **1** *vt (lift)* (hoch)hieven *(onto* auf +*acc); (drag)* schleppen; *(throw)* werfen; *sigh, sob* ausstoßen. **to** ~ **anchor** den Anker lichten; **to** ~ **a sigh of relief** erleichtert aufseufzen. **2** *vi* **(a)** *(pull)* ziehen. **(b)** *(bosom, sea)* sich heben und senken; *(stomach)* sich umdrehen. **(c)** *pret, ptp* **hove** *(Naut)* **to** ~ **in(to) sight** in Sicht kommen.
▶**heave to** *vi (Naut)* beidrehen.
**heave ho** *interj* hau ruck.
**heaven** ['hevn] *n* **(a)** *(lit, fig col)* Himmel *m.* **in** ~ im Himmel; **to go to** ~ in den Himmel kommen; **he is in (his seventh)** ~ er ist im siebten Himmel; **to move** ~ **and earth** Himmel und Hölle in Bewegung setzen; **it was** ~ es war einfach himmlisch; **the** ~**s opened** der Himmel öffnete seine Schleusen. **(b)** *(col) (good)* ~**s!** (du) lieber Himmel! *(col);* **would you like to?** — **(good)** ~**s no!** möchten Sie? — um Himmels willen, bloß nicht!; ~ **knows what** ... weiß der Himmel, was ... *(col);* **for** ~**'s sake!** um Himmels willen!
**heavenly** ['hevnlɪ] *adj (lit, fig col)* himmlisch. ~ **body** Himmelskörper *m.*
**heavily** ['hevɪlɪ] *adv* schwer; *move, walk* schwerfällig; *rain, smoke, drink, rely, populated, influenced, in debt* stark; *lose, tax* hoch; *sleep* tief. ~ **built** kräftig gebaut; **time hung** ~ **on his hands** die Zeit verging ihm nur langsam; ~ **committed** stark engagiert; **to be** ~ **subscribed** viele Abonnenten haben.
**heaviness** ['hevɪnɪs] *n* Schwere *f.*
**heavy** ['hevɪ] **1** *adj (+er)* **(a)** schwer; *features* grob; *rain, cold also, traffic, drinker, smoker* stark; *expenses, taxes* hoch; *line* dick; *sleep* tief; *crop* reich; *(~-handed) manner, style* schwerfällig; *silence* bedrückend; *weather, air* drückend, schwül; *sky* bedeckt; *(tiring) day* anstrengend. **with a** ~ **heart** schweren Herzens, mit schwerem Herzen; ~ **artillery** schwere Artillerie; ~ **goods vehicle** Lastkraftwagen *m;* ~ **industry** Schwerindustrie *f;* **to be** ~ **on petrol** viel Benzin brauchen; **the going was** ~ wir kamen nur schwer voran; **the conversation was** ~ **going** die Unterhaltung war mühsam; **this book is very** ~ **going** das Buch liest sich schwer. **(b)** *(col: strict)* streng *(on* mit*).* **2** *n (col: thug)* Schlägertyp *m.*
**heavy:** ~**-duty** *adj tyres etc* strapazierfähig; *boots* Arbeits-; *machine* Hochleistungs-; ~**-handed** *adj* ungeschickt; ~ **metal** *n (Mus)* Heavy Metal *m;* ~**set** *adj (US)* kräftig gebaut; ~**weight** *n (Boxing)* Schwergewicht *nt; (fig col)* großes Tier *(col).*

**Hebrew** ['hiːbruː] **1** *adj* hebräisch. **2** *n* **(a)** Hebräer(in *f*) *m.* **(b)** *(language)* Hebräisch *nt.*
**Hebrides** ['hebrɪdiːz] *npl* Hebriden *pl.*
**heck** [hek] *interj (col)* oh ~! zum Kuckuck! *(col);* **I've a** ~ **of a lot to do** ich habe irrsinnig viel zu tun *(col).*
**heckle** ['hekl] **1** *vt speaker* (durch Zwischenrufe) stören. **2** *vi* Zwischenrufe machen.
**heckler** ['hekləʳ] *n* Zwischenrufer *m.*
**heckling** ['heklɪŋ] *n* Zwischenrufe *pl.*
**hectare** ['hektɑːʳ] *n* Hektar *m or nt.*
**hectic** ['hektɪk] *adj* hektisch.
**he'd** [hiːd] = **he would; he had.**
**hedge** [hedʒ] **1** *n* Hecke *f; (fig: protection)* Schutz *m (against* gegen*).* **2** *vi* Fragen ausweichen, kneifen *(col) (at* bei*).* **3** *vt investment* absichern. **to** ~ **one's bets** *(lit, fig)* sich absichern.
**hedgehog** ['hedʒhɒg] *n* Igel *m.*
**hedge:** ~**hop** *vi* tief fliegen; ~**row** *n* Hecke *f;* ~**trimmer** *n* (elektrische) Heckenschere.
**hedonism** ['hiːdənɪzəm] *n* Hedonismus *m.*
**hedonist** ['hiːdənɪst] *n* Hedonist(in *f*) *m.*
**hedonistic** [hiːdəˈnɪstɪk] *adj* hedonistisch.
**heebie-jeebies** ['hiːbɪˈdʒiːbɪz] *npl* **he gives me the** ~ *(col)* wenn ich ihn sehe, bekomm' ich eine Gänsehaut *(col).*
**heed** [hiːd] **1** *n* **to take** ~ achtgeben; **to take** *or* **pay** ~**/no** ~ **of sb/sth** jdn/etw beachten/nicht beachten. **2** *vt* beachten; *advice* hören auf (+*acc*).
**heedful** ['hiːdfʊl] *adj* **to be** ~ **of sth** auf etw *(acc)* hören.
**heedless** ['hiːdlɪs] *adj* rücksichtslos. **to be** ~ **of sth** auf etw *(acc)* nicht achten.
**heel** [hiːl] **1** *n* **(a)** Ferse *f; (of shoe)* Absatz *m.* **to be right on sb's** ~**s** jdm auf den Fersen folgen; *(fig: chase)* jdm auf den Fersen sein; **to follow hard upon sb's** ~**s** jdm dicht auf den Fersen sein; **to be down at** ~ *(person)* schäbig aussehen; *(shoes)* abgelaufen sein; **to take to one's** ~**s** sich aus dem Staub(e) machen; ~! *(to dog)* (bei) Fuß!; **to bring sb to** ~ jdn an die Kandare nehmen *(col);* **to turn on one's** ~ auf dem Absatz kehrtmachen; **to cool** *or* **kick one's** ~**s** *(col) (wait)* warten; *(do nothing)* Däumchen drehen; ~ **bar** Absatz(schnell)dienst *m.* **(b)** *(pej col: person)* Scheißkerl *m (col!).* **2** *vt* **to** ~ **shoes** auf Schuhe neue Absätze machen; **to be well** ~**ed** *(col)* betucht sein *(col).*
**hefty** ['heftɪ] *adj (+er) (col)* kräftig; *book* dick; *object, workload* schwer; *sum of money, amount* ganz schön *(col).*
**heifer** ['hefəʳ] *n* Färse *f.*
**height** [haɪt] *n* **(a)** Höhe *f; (of person)* Größe *f.* **what** ~ **are you?** wie groß sind Sie? **(b)** *(high place)* ~**s** *pl* Höhen *pl;* **to scale the** ~**s of Everest** den Mount Everest besteigen; **fear of** ~**s** Höhenangst *f;* **to be afraid of** ~**s** nicht schwindelfrei sein. **(c)** *(fig)* Höhe *f; (of success, stupidity also)* Gipfel *m.* **at the** ~ **of his power** auf der Höhe seiner Macht; **at the** ~ **of the season** in der Hauptsaison; **at the** ~ **of the storm** als das Gewitter am heftigsten war; **dressed in the** ~ **of fashion** nach der neuesten Mode gekleidet; **at the** ~ **of summer** im Hochsommer.
**heighten** ['haɪtn] *vt (raise)* höher stellen; *(emphasize) colour etc* hervorheben; *(increase) anger, effect etc* verstärken; *intensity* steigern.
**heinous** ['heɪnəs, 'hiːnəs] *adj* abscheulich.
**heir** [ɛəʳ] *n* Erbe *m (to* gen*).* ~ **apparent** gesetzlicher Erbe; ~ **to the throne** Thronfolger *m.*
**heiress** ['ɛəres] *n* Erbin *f.*
**heirloom** ['ɛəluːm] *n* Erbstück *nt.*
**heist** [haɪst] *n (esp US col)* Raubüberfall *m.*

**held** [held] *pret, ptp of* **hold.**
**helical** ['helɪkəl] *adj gear* schrägverzahnt. ~ **spring** Schraubenfeder *f.*
**helicopter** ['helɪkɒptər] *n* Hubschrauber *m.*
**Heligoland** ['helɪgəʊlænd] *n* Helgoland *nt.*
**heliport** ['helɪpɔːt] *n* Hubschrauberflugplatz, Heliport *m.*
**helium** ['hiːlɪəm] *n* Helium *nt.*
**hell** [hel] *n* (a) Hölle *f.* **to go to ~** *(lit)* in die Hölle kommen.
(b) *(fig uses)* **all ~ was let loose** die Hölle war los; **it's ~ working there** es ist die reinste Hölle, dort zu arbeiten; **life became ~** das Leben wurde zur Hölle; **she made his life ~** sie machte ihm das Leben zur Hölle; **to give sb ~** *(col)* jdm die Hölle heiß machen; *(make life unpleasant)* jdm das Leben zur Hölle machen; **there'll be ~ when he finds out** *(col)* wenn er das erfährt, ist der Teufel los *(col)*; **to play ~ with sth** *(col)* etw total durcheinanderbringen *(col)*; **for the ~ of it** *(col)* nur zum Spaß *or* aus Jux.
(c) *(col: intensifier)* **a ~ of a noise** ein Höllenlärm *m* *(col)*; **to work like ~** wie wild arbeiten *(col)*; **to run like ~** laufen, was die Beine hergeben; **we had a ~ of a time** *(bad, difficult)* es war grauenhaft; *(good)* wir haben uns prima amüsiert *(col)*; **a ~ of a lot** verdammt viel *(col)*; **that's one** *or* **a ~ of a problem/difference/bruise** das ist ein verdammt schwieriges Problem/ein wahnsinniger Unterschied/Bluterguß *(col)*; **to ~ with him** hol ihn der Teufel *(col)*, der kann mich mal *(col)*; **to ~ with it!**, **~!** verdammt noch mal *(col!)*; **go to ~!** scher dich zum Teufel! *(col)*; **what the ~ do you want?** was willst du denn, verdammt noch mal? *(col!)*; **oh, what the ~!** ach, was soll's! *(col)*.
**he'll** [hiːl] = **he shall, he will.**
**hell-bent** *adj* versessen *(on* auf *+acc).*
**hellish** ['helɪʃ] *adj (col)* höllisch *(col)*; **exams** verteufelt schwer *(col)*.
**hello** [hə'ləʊ] *interj* hallo. **say ~ to your parents (from me)** grüß deine Eltern (von mir).
**helm** [helm] *n* Ruder *nt.* **to be at the ~** *(lit, fig)* am Ruder sein.
**helmet** ['helmɪt] *n* Helm *m*; *(Fencing)* Maske *f.*
**helmsman** ['helmzmən] *n, pl* **-men** [-mən] Steuermann *m.*
**help** [help] **1** *n* Hilfe *f.* **with the ~ of** mit Hilfe *(+gen)*; **he is beyond ~** ihm ist nicht mehr zu helfen; **to go/come to sb's ~** jdm zu Hilfe eilen/kommen; **to be of ~ to sb** jdm behilflich sein; *(thing also)* jdm nützen; **you're a great ~!** *(iro)* du bist mir eine schöne Hilfe!; **we are short of ~ in the shop** wir haben nicht genügend (Hilfs)kräfte im Geschäft; **there's no ~ for it** da ist nichts zu machen.
**2** *vti* (a) helfen *(+dat)*. **to ~ sb (to) do sth** jdm (dabei) helfen, etw zu tun; **~!** Hilfe!; **can I ~ you?** kann ich (Ihnen) behilflich sein?; **that won't ~ you** das wird Ihnen nichts nützen; **this will ~ the pain** das wird gegen die Schmerzen helfen; **it will ~ the corn to grow** es wird das Wachstum des Getreides fördern; **every little** *or* **it all ~s** Kleinvieh macht auch Mist *(col)*.
(b) **to ~ sb down** jdm hinunter-/herunterhelfen; **to ~ sb off with his coat** jdm aus dem Mantel helfen; **to ~ sb over the street** jdm über die Straße helfen; **to ~ sb through a difficult time** jdm in einer schwierigen Zeit beistehen; **to ~ sb up** *(from floor, chair etc)* jdm aufhelfen *or* *(up stairs etc)* hinaufhelfen.
(c) **to ~ oneself to sth** sich mit etw bedienen; **she ~ed him to potatoes** sie gab ihm Kartoffeln; **~**

**yourself!** bedienen Sie sich doch!
(d) **he can't ~ it, he was born with it** er kann nichts dafür, das ist angeboren; **he can't ~ it!** *(col: he's stupid)* er ist nun mal so (dumm); **don't say more than you can ~** sagen Sie nicht mehr als unbedingt nötig; **not if I can ~ it** nicht, wenn ich es irgendwie vermeiden kann; **I couldn't ~ laughing** ich mußte (einfach) lachen; **I had to do it, I couldn't ~ myself** ich mußte es einfach tun; **one cannot ~ wondering whether ...** man muß sich wirklich fragen, ob ...; **it can't be ~ed** es läßt sich nicht ändern.
►**help out 1** *vi* aushelfen *(with* bei*).* **2** *vt sep* helfen *(+dat)* *(with* mit*).*
**helper** ['helpər] *n* Helfer(in *f*) *m*; *(assistant)* Gehilfe *m*, Gehilfin *f.*
**helpful** ['helpfʊl] *adj person* hilfsbereit; *(useful)* **gadget, advice** nützlich. **you have been very ~** Sie haben mir sehr geholfen.
**helpfully** ['helpfəlɪ] *adv* hilfreich.
**helpfulness** ['helpfʊlnɪs] *n* Hilfsbereitschaft *f.*
**helping** ['helpɪŋ] **1** *n (at table)* Portion *f.* **to take a second ~ of sth** sich *(dat)* noch einmal von etw nehmen. **2** *adj attr* **to lend sb a ~ hand** jdm behilflich sein.
**helpless** ['helplɪs] *adj* hilflos. **she was ~ with laughter** sie konnte sich vor Lachen kaum halten.
**helplessly** ['helplɪslɪ] *adv* hilflos.
**helplessness** ['helplɪsnɪs] *n* Hilflosigkeit *f.*
**helpline** ['helplaɪn] *n (for emergencies)* Notruf *m*; *(for information)* Informationsdienst *m.*
**Helsinki** ['helsɪŋkɪ] *n* Helsinki *nt.*
**helter-skelter** ['heltə'skeltər] **1** *adv* Hals über Kopf *(col)*. **2** *n (Brit: on fairground)* Rutschbahn *f.*
**hem** [hem] **1** *n* Saum *m.* **2** *vt* säumen.
►**hem in** *vt sep* **troops** einschließen; *(fig)* einengen.
**he-man** ['hiːmæn] *n, pl* **-men** [-men] *(col)* sehr männlicher Typ; *(muscle-man)* Muskelprotz *m (col)*.
**hematology** *n (US)* = **haematology.**
**hemisphere** ['hemɪsfɪər] *n* Hemisphäre *f.*
**hemline** ['hemlaɪn] *n* Saum *m.* **~s are lower again** die Röcke sind wieder länger geworden.
**hemlock** ['hemlɒk] *n (poison)* Schierling(saft) *m.*
**hemo-** ['hiːmo-] *pref (US) see* **haemo-.**
**hemp** [hemp] *n* Hanf *m.*
**hemstitch** ['hemstɪtʃ] *n* Hohlsaum *m.*
**hen** [hen] *n* Huhn *nt*, Henne *f*; *(female bird)* Weibchen *nt.* **~ battery** Legebatterie *f.*
**hence** [hens] *adv* (a) *(for this reason)* also. **~ the name** daher der Name. (b) *(from now)* **two years ~** in zwei Jahren.
**henceforth** [,hens'fɔːθ] *adv (from then on)* von da an; *(from now on)* von nun an.
**henchman** ['hentʃmən] *n, pl* **-men** [-mən] *(pej)* Handlanger *m.*
**henna** ['henə] **1** *n* Henna *f or nt.* **2** *vt* mit Henna färben.
**hen:** **~ night** *n* Damenabend *m (esp für eine Braut)*; **~-party** *n (col)* Damengesellschaft *f*; *(before wedding)* für die Braut arrangierte Damengesellschaft; **~peck** *vt* a **~pecked husband** ein Pantoffelheld *m (col)*; **he is ~pecked** er steht unterm Pantoffel *(col)*.
**hepatitis** [,hepə'taɪtɪs] *n* Hepatitis *f.*
**her** [hɜːr] **1** *pers pron* (a) *(dir obj, with prep +acc)* sie; *(indir obj, with prep +dat)* ihr. **with her books all around ~** mit ihren Büchern um sich. (b) **it's ~** sie ist's; **who, ~?** wer, sie? **2** *poss adj* ihr; *see* **my.**
**herald** ['herəld] **1** *n (Hist)* Herold *m*; *(fig)* (Vor)bote *m (geh)*. **2** *vt* ankündigen.
**heraldic** [he'rældɪk] *adj* heraldisch, Wappen-.
**heraldry** ['herəldrɪ] *n (science)* Wappenkunde *f.*

**herb** [hɜːb] *n* Kraut *nt.* ~ **garden** Kräutergarten *m.*
**herbaceous** [hɜːˈbeɪʃəs] *adj* ~ **border** Staudenrabatte *f*; ~ **plant** Staude *f.*
**herbal** [ˈhɜːbəl] *adj* Kräuter-.
**herd** [hɜːd] **1** *n* Herde *f*; *(of deer)* Rudel *nt.* **the common** ~ die breite Masse. **2** *vt (drive) cattle, prisoners* treiben; *(tend) cattle* hüten.
  ►**herd together 1** *vi* sich zusammendrängen. **2** *vt sep* zusammentreiben.
**herd instinct** *n* Herdentrieb *m.*
**here** [hɪəʳ] *adv* **(a)** hier; *(with motion)* hierher; ~ **I am** hier bin ich; **spring is** ~ der Frühling ist da; ~ **and now** auf der Stelle; **this one** ~ der/die/das hier; **I won't be** ~ **for lunch** ich bin zum Mittagessen nicht da; ~ **and there** hier und da; ~, **there and everywhere** überall; **around/about** ~ ungefähr hier; **up/down to** ~ bis hierher; **it's in/over** ~ es ist hier (drin)/hier drüben; **put it in/over** ~ stellen Sie es hier herein/hierher; **from** ~ **on in** *(esp US)* von nun an.
  **(b)** *(phrases)* ~ **you are** *(giving sb sth)* hier (bitte); *(on finding sb)* da bist du ja!; *(on finding sth)* da ist es ja; ~ **we are, home again** so, da wären wir wieder zu Hause; ~ **he comes** da kommt er ja; **look out,** ~ **he comes** Vorsicht, er kommt!; ~ **goes!** *(before attempting sth)* dann mal los; ~, **let me do that** komm, laß mich das mal machen; ~**'s to you!** *(in toasts)* auf Ihr Wohl!; **it's neither** ~ **nor there** es spielt keine Rolle.
**here:** ~**abouts** [ˈhɪərəbaʊts] *adv* hier herum; ~**after 1** *adv (in books, contracts)* im folgenden. **2** *n* **the** ~**after** das Jenseits; ~**by** *adv (form)* hiermit.
**hereditary** [hɪˈredɪtərɪ] *adj* erblich, Erb-.
**heredity** [hɪˈredɪtɪ] *n* Vererbung *f.*
**heresy** [ˈherəsɪ] *n* Ketzerei *f.*
**heretic** [ˈherətɪk] *n* Ketzer(in *f*) *m.*
**heretical** [hɪˈretɪkəl] *adj* ketzerisch.
**here:** ~**upon** *adv* daraufhin; ~**with** *adv (form)* hiermit.
**heritage** [ˈherɪtɪdʒ] *n (lit, fig)* Erbe *nt.*
**hermaphrodite** [hɜːˈmæfrədaɪt] *n* Zwitter *m.*
**hermetic** [hɜːˈmetɪk] *adj* hermetisch.
**hermetically** [hɜːˈmetɪkəlɪ] *adv* ~ **sealed** hermetisch verschlossen *or (fig)* abgeriegelt.
**hermit** [ˈhɜːmɪt] *n* Einsiedler(in *f*) *m (also fig).*
**hernia** [ˈhɜːnɪə] *n* (Eingeweide)bruch *m.*
**hero** [ˈhɪərəʊ] *n, pl* -**es** Held *m*; *(fig: object of hero-worship also)* Idol *nt.*
**heroic** [hɪˈrəʊɪk] **1** *adj* heldenhaft; *behaviour, action also, words* heroisch; *effort* gewaltig. **2** *n* ~**s** *pl (acts)* Heldentaten *pl*; *(words)* hochtrabende Worte *pl*; *(of actor)* übertriebenes Pathos.
**heroin** [ˈherəʊɪn] *n* Heroin *nt.* ~ **addict** Heroinsüchtige(r) *mf.*
**heroine** [ˈherəʊɪn] *n* Heldin *f.*
**heroism** [ˈherəʊɪzəm] *n* (Helden)mut *m.*
**heron** [ˈherən] *n* Reiher *m.*
**hero-worship** [ˈhiːrəʊˌwɜːʃɪp] **1** *n* Verehrung *f*; *(of popstar etc)* Schwärmerei *f.* **2** *vt* verehren; *popstar etc* schwärmen für.
**herring** [ˈherɪŋ] *n* Hering *m.*
**herringbone pattern** [ˈherɪŋbəʊnˈpætən] *n* Fischgrät(en)muster *nt.*
**hers** [hɜːz] *poss pron* ihre(r, s); *see* **mine¹.**
**herself** [hɜːˈself] *pers pron* **(a)** *(dir and indir obj, with prep)* sich; *see* **myself. (b)** *(emph)* (sie) selbst.
**Herts** [hɑːts] = **Hertfordshire.**
**Herzegovina** [ˌhɜːtsəgəʊˈviːnə] *n* Herzegowina *nt.*
**he's** [hiːz] = **he is; he has.**
**hesitant** [ˈhezɪtənt] *adj answer, smile* zögernd; *person also* unentschlossen. **I was rather** ~ **about doing**

**it** ich hatte Bedenken, ob ich es tun sollte.
**hesitate** [ˈhezɪteɪt] *vi* zögern. **he who** ~**s is lost** *(Prov)* wer lange zögert, hat das Nachsehen; **even he would** ~ **at murder** selbst er hätte bei einem Mord Bedenken; **he** ~**s at nothing** er schreckt vor nichts zurück; **I am still hesitating about what to do** ich bin mir immer noch nicht schlüssig, was ich tun soll; **I wouldn't** ~ **to say so** ich hätte keine Hemmungen, es zu sagen; **don't** ~ **to ask me** fragen Sie ruhig; **please don't** ~ **to get in touch if ...** wenden Sie sich bitte an mich/uns, falls ....
**hesitation** [ˌhezɪˈteɪʃən] *n* Zögern *nt.* **without the slightest** ~ ohne auch nur einen Augenblick zu zögern; **I have no** ~ **in saying that ...** ich kann ohne weiteres sagen, daß ....
**hessian** [ˈhesɪən] *n* Sackleinen *nt.*
**heterogeneous** [ˌhetərəʊˈdʒiːnɪəs] *adj* heterogen.
**heterosexual** [ˌhetərəʊˈseksjʊəl] **1** *adj* heterosexuell. **2** *n* Heterosexuelle(r) *mf.*
**het up** [ˈhetˌʌp] *adj (col)* aufgeregt.
**hew** [hjuː] *pret* ~**ed,** *ptp* **hewn** *or* ~**ed** *vt* hauen; *(shape)* behauen.
**hex** [heks] *n* **to put a** ~ **on sth** etw verhexen.
**hexagon** [ˈheksəgən] *n* Sechseck *nt.*
**hexagonal** [hekˈsægənəl] *adj* sechseckig.
**hey** [heɪ] *interj* he. ~ **presto!** Hokuspokus (Fidibus).
**heyday** [ˈheɪdeɪ] *n* Glanzzeit, Blütezeit *f.* **in his** ~ in seiner Glanzzeit.
**HF** = **high frequency** HF.
**HGV** *(Brit)* = **heavy goods vehicle** LKW *m.*
**HI** *(US Post)* = **Hawaii.**
**hi** [haɪ] *interj* hallo.
**hiatus** [haɪˈeɪtəs] *n (gap)* Lücke *f.*
**hibernate** [ˈhaɪbəneɪt] *vi* Winterschlaf halten.
**hibernation** [ˌhaɪbəˈneɪʃən] *n* Winterschlaf *m.*
**hiccough, hiccup** [ˈhɪkʌp] *n* Schluckauf *m*; *(col: in plans etc)* kleines Problem; *(interruption)* Unterbrechung *f.* **to have the** ~**s** (den) Schluckauf haben.
**hick** [hɪk] *n (US col)* Hinterwäldler *m (col).*
**hide¹** [haɪd] *(vb: pret* **hid** [hɪd], *ptp* **hidden** [ˈhɪdn] *or* **hid)** **1** *vt (from* vor +*dat)* verstecken; *truth, tears, feelings, face* verbergen; *(from view) moon, rust* verdecken. **2** *vi* sich verstecken *(from sb* vor jdm). **he was hiding in the cupboard** er hielt sich im Schrank versteckt. **3** *n* Versteck *nt.*
  ►**hide away 1** *vi* sich verstecken. **2** *vt sep* verstecken.
  ►**hide out** *vi* sich verstecken.
**hide²** *n (of animal)* Haut *f*; *(of furry animal)* Fell *nt*; *(processed)* Leder *nt.* **I haven't seen** ~ **nor hair of him for weeks** *(col)* ich habe ihn in den letzten Wochen nicht mal von weitem gesehen.
**hide:** ~**-and-seek** *n* Versteckspiel *nt*; ~**away** *n* Versteck *nt*; ~**bound** *adj person, views* engstirnig.
**hideous** *adj*, ~**ly** *adv* [ˈhɪdɪəs, -lɪ] grauenhaft, scheußlich.
**hideout** [ˈhaɪdaʊt] *n* Versteck *nt.*
**hiding¹** [ˈhaɪdɪŋ] *n* **to be in** ~ sich versteckt halten; **to go into** ~ untertauchen; ~ **place** Versteck *nt.*
**hiding²** *n* **(a)** *(beating)* **to give sb a good** ~ jdm eine Tracht Prügel geben; **to be on a** ~ **to nothing** keine Aussicht auf Erfolg haben. **(b)** *(defeat)* Schlappe *f (col).*
**hierarchy** [ˈhaɪərɑːkɪ] *n* Hierarchie *f.*
**hieroglyphic** [ˌhaɪərəˈglɪfɪk] **1** *adj* hieroglyphisch. **2** *n* ~**s** *pl* Hieroglyphen(schrift *f*) *pl.*
**hi-fi** [ˈhaɪfaɪ] *n* Hi-Fi *nt*; *(system)* Hi-Fi-Anlage *f.*
**higgledy-piggledy** [ˈhɪgldɪˈpɪgldɪ] *adv* wie Kraut und Rüben (durcheinander) *(col).*
**high** [haɪ] **1** *adj (+er)* **(a)** hoch *pred*, hohe(r, s) *attr*; *altitude* groß; *wind* stark; *complexion, colour*

(hoch)rot. **a building 80 metres** ~ ein 80 Meter hohes Gebäude; **on one of the ~er floors** in einem der oberen Stockwerke; **the river is quite** ~ der Fluß führt ziemlich viel Wasser; **he left her ~ and dry** er hat sie sitzenlassen; **to be left ~ and dry** auf dem Trockenen sitzen *(col)*; **on the ~est authority** von höchster Stelle; **to act ~ and mighty** erhaben tun; **to be on one's ~ horse** *(fig)* auf dem hohen Roß sitzen; **to pay a ~ price for sth** *(lit, fig)* etw teuer bezahlen; **in ~ spirits** in Hochstimmung; **to have a ~ old time** *(col)* mächtig Spaß haben *(col)*; **it's ~ time you went home** es wird höchste Zeit, daß du nach Hause gehst.

(**b**) *(col)* *(on drugs)* high *(col)*. **to get ~ on sth** sich mit etw anturnen *(col)*.

(**c**) *meat* angegangen.

**2** *adv (+er)* hoch. ~ **up** *(position)* hoch oben; *(motion)* hoch hinauf; **one floor ~er** ein Stockwerk höher; **to go as ~ as £200** bis zu £200 (hoch)gehen; **feelings ran ~** die Gemüter erhitzten sich; **to search ~ and low** überall suchen.

**3** *n* (**a**) **the orders come from on ~** *(hum col)* der Befehl kommt von oben. (**b**) **unemployment has reached a new ~** die Arbeitslosenziffern haben einen neuen Höchststand erreicht. (**c**) *(Met)* Hoch *nt.* (**d**) *(US Aut: top gear)* **in ~** im höchsten Gang. (**e**) *(US col: high school)* Penne *f (col).*

**high:** ~ **altar** *n* Hochaltar *m*; ~**ball** *n (US)* Highball *m*; ~ **boy** *n (US)* hohe Kommode; ~**brow 1** *n* Intellektuelle(r) *mf*; **2** *adj interests* intellektuell; *tastes, music* anspruchsvoll; ~**chair** *n* Hochstuhl *m*; **H~ Church** *adj* der Hochkirche; *people* hochkirchlich eingestellt; ~**class** *adj* hochwertig; ~ **commissioner** *n* Hochkommissar *m*; ~ **court** *n* oberstes Gericht; ~ **diving** *n* Turmspringen *nt.*

**higher** ['haɪə<sup>r</sup>] **1** *adj mathematics, education, lifeforms* höher. **H~ National Certificate** *(Brit)* ≃ Berufsschulabschluß *m*; **H~ National Diploma** *(Brit) Qualifikationsnachweis m in technischen Fächern.* **2** *n* **H~s** *(Scot Sch)* ≃ Abschluß *m* der Sekundarstufe 2.

**high:** ~ **explosive** *n* hochexplosiver Sprengstoff; ~ **finance** *n* Hochfinanz *f*; ~ **flier** *n (col)* Hochbegabte(r) *mf*, Überflieger *m*; ~**-flown** *adj style, speech* hochgestochen; ~ **frequency** *adj* Hochfrequenz-; **H~ German** *n* Hochdeutsch *nt*; ~**-grade** *adj* hochwertig; *ore* gediegen; ~**-handed** *adj* eigenmächtig; *character* überheblich; ~**-heeled** *adj* hochhackig; ~ **heels** *npl* hohe Absätze *pl*; ~ **jinks** *npl* *(col)* **there were ~ jinks** es ging hoch her *(col)*; ~ **jump** *n (Sport)* Hochsprung *m*; **to be for the ~ jump** *(fig col)* dran sein *(col)*; **h~lands** *npl* Berg- or Hochland *nt*; **the (Scottish) H~lands** das schottische Hochland; ~**-level** *adj talks* auf höchster Ebene; *(Comp) language* höher; ~ **life** *n* Leben *nt* in großem Stil; ~**light 1** *n (Art, Phot)* Glanzlicht *nt*; *(in hair)* Strähne *f*; *(fig)* Höhepunkt *m*; ~**lights** *(in hair)* Strähnchen *pl*; **2** *vt need, problem* hervorheben; ~**lighter** *n (pen)* Leuchtstift *m*; *(for hair)* Aufheller *m.*

**highly** ['haɪlɪ] *adv* hoch-. **to be ~ paid** hoch bezahlt werden; **to think ~ of sb** eine hohe Meinung von jdm haben; **to speak ~ of sb** sich sehr positiv über jdn äußern; ~**-strung** nervös.

**high:** **H~ Mass** *n* Hochamt *nt*; ~**-minded** *adj* hochgesinnt; *ideals* hoch.

**highness** ['haɪnɪs] *n* Her **H~** Ihre Hoheit.

**high:** ~**-performance** *adj* Hochleistungs-; ~**pitched** *adj sound* hoch; ~ **point** *n* Höhepunkt *m*; ~**-powered** *adj* (**a**) *car, engine* stark, Hochleistungs-; (**b**) *(fig) businessman, politician, academic* Spitzen-; *conversation* sehr anspruchsvoll; ~

**pressure** *adj* (**a**) ~**-pressure area** Hochdruckgebiet *nt*; (**b**) *(fig) salesman* aufdringlich; *sales technique* aggressiv; ~ **priest** *n (lit, fig)* Hohepriester *m*; ~**ranking** *adj* von hohem Rang; ~**-resolution** *adj (Comp)* hochauflösend; ~**-rise building** *n* Hochhaus *nt*; ~**-rise flats** *npl* Wohnhochhaus *nt*; ~**-risk** *adj* risikoreich; ~ **school** *n (US)* Oberschule *f*; **the ~ seas** *npl* die Meere *pl*; **on the ~ seas** auf hoher See; ~ **season** *n (Brit)* Hochsaison *f*; ~**-security** *adj prison, wing* Hochsicherheits-; ~ **society** *n* High-Society *f*; ~**-speed** *adj* Schnell-; *train* Hochgeschwindigkeits-; *drill* mit hoher Umdrehungszahl; ~**-speed film** hoch(licht)empfindlicher Film; ~**-spirited** *adj* in Hochstimmung; ~ **spot** *n* Höhepunkt *m*; ~ **street** *n (Brit)* Hauptstraße *f*; ~**strung** *adj (US)* nervös; ~ **summer** *n* Hochsommer *m*; ~ **tea** *n* (frühes) Abendessen; ~**-tech** ['haɪˌtek] *adj see* hitech; ~**-tension,** ~**-voltage** *adj (Elec)* Hochspannungs-; ~ **tide** *n* Flut *f*; ~ **treason** *n* Hochverrat *m*; ~**way** *n* Landstraße *f*; **public** ~**way** öffentliche Straße; **H~way Code** *n* Straßenverkehrsordnung *f*; ~**wayman** *n* Wegelagerer *m.*

**hijack** ['haɪdʒæk] **1** *vt* entführen; *lorry* überfallen. **2** *n see* Entführung *f*; Überfall *m (of* auf +*acc).*

**hijacker** ['haɪdʒækə<sup>r</sup>] *n* Entführer *m.*

**hike** [haɪk] **1** *vi* wandern. **2** *n* Wanderung *f.*

**hiker** ['haɪkə<sup>r</sup>] *n* Wanderer *m*, Wanderin *f.*

**hiking** ['haɪkɪŋ] *n* Wandern *nt.*

**hilarious** [hɪ'lɛərɪəs] *adj* sehr komisch.

**hilariously** [hɪ'lɛərɪəslɪ] *adv* ~ **funny** zum Schreien.

**hilarity** [hɪ'lærɪtɪ] *n* **his statement caused some ~** seine Behauptung löste Heiterkeit aus.

**hill** [hɪl] *n* Hügel *m*; *(higher)* Berg *m*; *(incline)* Hang *m*. **built on a ~** am Hang *or* am Berg gebaut; **up ~ and down dale** bergauf und bergab; **that joke's as old as the ~s** der Witz hat so einen Bart; **to be over the ~** *(fig col)* die besten Jahre hinter sich *(dat)* haben.

**hillbilly** ['hɪlbɪlɪ] *(US col)* *n* Hinterwäldler *m (pej).*

**hillock** ['hɪlək] *n* Anhöhe *f.*

**hill:** ~**side** *n* Hang *m*; ~ **top** *n* Gipfel *m.*

**hilly** ['hɪlɪ] *adj (+er)* hüg(e)lig; *(higher)* bergig.

**hilt** [hɪlt] *n* Heft *nt.* **up to the ~** *(fig)* voll und ganz; *(involved, in debt also)* bis über beide Ohren *(col).*

**him** [hɪm] *pers pron* (**a**) *(dir obj, with prep* +*acc)* ihn; *(indir obj, with prep* +*dat)* ihm. **with his things all around ~** mit seinen Sachen um sich. (**b**) *(emph)* er. **it's ~** er ist's; **who, ~?** wer, er?

**Himalayas** [ˌhɪmə'leɪəz] *npl* Himalaya *m.*

**himself** [hɪm'self] *pers pron* (**a**) *(dir and indir obj, with prep)* sich; *see* myself. (**b**) *(emph)* (er) selbst.

**hind¹** [haɪnd] *n (Zool)* Hirschkuh *f.*

**hind²** *adj, superl* **hindmost** hintere(r, s). ~ **legs** Hinterbeine *pl*; **she could talk the ~ legs off a donkey** *(col)* sie redet wie ein Buch *(col).*

**hinder** ['hɪndə<sup>r</sup>] *vt (obstruct)* behindern; *(delay) person* aufhalten. **to ~ sb from doing sth** jdn daran hindern, etw zu tun.

**hind:** ~**most** *adj* hinterste(r, s); ~**quarters** *npl* Hinterteil *nt*; *(of horse)* Hinterhand *f.*

**hindrance** ['hɪndrəns] *n* Behinderung *f.* **to be a ~** hinderlich sein.

**hindsight** ['haɪndsaɪt] *n:* **with ~** im nachhinein.

**Hindu** ['hɪnduː] **1** *adj* hinduistisch, Hindu-. ~ **people** Hindu(s) *pl.* **2** *n* Hindu *m.*

**Hinduism** ['hɪnduːɪzəm] *n* Hinduismus *m.*

**hinge** [hɪndʒ] **1** *n (of door)* Angel *f*; *(of box etc)* Scharnier *nt.* **2** *vi (fig)* abhängen *(on* von).

**hint** [hɪnt] **1** *n* (**a**) *(suggestion)* Andeutung *f*, Wink *m.* **to give a/no ~ of sth** etw andeuten/nicht andeuten; **give me a ~** gib mir einen Anhaltspunkt; **to drop a**

~ eine Andeutung machen; **OK, I can take a** ~ schon recht, ich habe den Wink verstanden. **(b)** *(trace)* Spur *f.* **a** ~ **of garlic** eine Spur Knoblauch; **not a** ~ **of tiredness** keine Spur von Müdigkeit; **with the** ~ **of a smile** mit dem Anflug eines Lächelns. **(c)** *(tip, piece of advice)* Tip *m.* ~**s for travellers** Reisetips *pl.* **2** *vt* andeuten *(to gegenüber).* **what are you** ~**ing (at)?** was wollen Sie damit andeuten?

**hip** [hɪp] *n* Hüfte *f.*

**hip** *in cpds* Hüft-; ~ **bath** *n* Sitzbad *nt;* ~**-bone** *n* Hüftknochen *m;* ~**-flask** *n* Flachmann *(col) m;* ~ **joint** *n (Anat)* Hüftgelenk *nt;* ~ **pocket** *n* Gesäßtasche *f.*

**hippopotamus** [ˌhɪpəˈpɒtəməs] *n, pl* **-es** *or* **hippopotami** [ˌhɪpəˈpɒtəmaɪ] Nilpferd *nt.*

**hippy, hippie** [ˈhɪpɪ] *n* Hippie *m.*

**hire** [haɪəʳ] **1** *n* Mieten *nt; (of car also, suit)* Leihen *nt.* **for** ~ *(taxi)* frei; **it's on** ~ es ist geliehen/gemietet. **2** *vt* mieten; *cars also, suits* leihen; *staff* einstellen. ~**d assassin** gedungener Mörder; ~**d car** *(Brit)* Mietwagen *m;* ~**d hand** Lohnarbeiter *m.*
▶**hire out** *vt sep* vermieten, verleihen.

**hire:** ~ **car** *n* Mietwagen *m;* ~ **purchase** *n (Brit)* Ratenkauf *m;* **on** ~ **purchase** auf Raten *or* Teilzahlung.

**his** [hɪz] **1** *poss adj* sein; *see* **my.** **2** *poss pron* seine(r, s); *see* **mine**[1].

**Hispanic** [hɪsˈpænɪk] **1** *adj* hispanisch; *community* spanisch. **2** *n* Hispano-Amerikaner(in *f*) *m.*

**hiss** [hɪs] **1** *vi* zischen; *(cat)* fauchen. **2** *vt actor* auszischen.

**historian** [hɪsˈtɔːrɪən] *n* Historiker(in *f*) *m.*

**historic** [hɪsˈtɒrɪk] *adj* historisch.

**historical** [hɪsˈtɒrɪkəl] *adj* historisch; *studies, investigation also* geschichtlich, Geschichts-. ~ **monument** Baudenkmal *nt.*

**history** [ˈhɪstərɪ] *n* Geschichte *f.* **to make** ~ Geschichte machen; **he has a** ~ **of violence** er hat eine Vorgeschichte als Gewalttäter; **the family has a** ~ **of heart disease** in der Familie hat es schon immer Fälle von Herzleiden gegeben; **that's all** ~ **now** *(fig)* das gehört jetzt alles der Vergangenheit an.

**history** *in cpds* Geschichts-.

**histrionics** [ˌhɪstrɪˈɒnɪks] *npl* theatralisches Getue.

**hit** [hɪt] *(vb: pret, ptp* ~*)* **1** *n* **(a)** *(blow)* Schlag *m; (on target, Fencing)* Treffer *m.* **(b)** *(success, also Theat)* Erfolg, Knüller *(col) m; (song)* Schlager, Hit *m.* **to be** *or* **make a** ~ **with sb** bei jdm gut ankommen.

**2** *vt* **(a)** *(strike)* schlagen; *(missile, bullet etc)* treffen. **to** ~ **sb a blow** jdm einen Schlag versetzen; **to** ~ **one's head against sth** sich *(dat)* den Kopf an etw *(dat)* stoßen; **the car** ~ **a tree** das Auto fuhr gegen einen Baum; **he was** ~ **by a stone** er wurde von einem Stein getroffen; **he was** ~ **in the leg** er wurde ins Bein getroffen; **the commandos** ~ **the town at dawn** die Kommandos griffen die Stadt im Morgengrauen an; **it** ~**s you (in the eye)** *(fig)* das springt einem ins Auge; **that** ~ **home** *(fig)* das saß *(col);* **then it** ~ **me** dann wurde es mir plötzlich klar; **you won't know what's** ~ **you** *(col)* du wirst dein blaues Wunder erleben *(col).*

**(b)** *(affect adversely)* treffen. **to be hard** ~ **by sth** von etw schwer getroffen werden; **this tax will** ~ **the poor** diese Steuer wird die Armen treffen.

**(c)** *(achieve, reach) likeness, top C* treffen; *speed, level etc* erreichen. **to** ~ **the papers** in die Zeitungen kommen; **to** ~ **town** *(col)* die Stadt erreichen; **we're going to** ~ **the rush hour** wir geraten direkt in den Stoßverkehr; **the driver** ~ **a patch of ice** der Fahrer geriet auf eine vereiste Stelle; **to** ~ **a problem** auf ein Problem stoßen.

**(d)** *(fig col phrases)* **to** ~ **the bottle** zur Flasche greifen; **to** ~ **the ceiling** *or* **roof** an die Decke *or* in die Luft gehen *(col);* **to** ~ **the road** sich auf den Weg *or* die Socken *(col)* machen.

**3** *vi* **(a)** *(strike)* schlagen. **he** ~**s hard** er schlägt hart zu. **(b)** *(collide)* zusammenstoßen.
▶**hit back 1** *vi (lit, fig)* zurückschlagen. **he** ~ ~ **at his critics** er gab seinen Kritikern Kontra. **2** *vt sep* zurückschlagen.
▶**hit off** *vt sep* **(a)** *(portray)* **he** ~ **him** ~ **beautifully** er hat ihn ausgezeichnet getroffen. **(b) to** ~ **it** ~ **with sb** *(col)* prima mit jdm auskommen *(col).*
▶**hit out** *vi (lit)* losschlagen *(at sb* auf jdn*); (fig)* scharf angreifen *(at or against sb* jdn*).*
▶**hit (up)on** *vi +prep obj* stoßen auf *(+acc).*

**hit-and-run** [ˈhɪtənˈrʌn] *n* **there was a** ~ **here last night** hier hat heute nacht jemand (einen Unfall gebaut und) Fahrerflucht begangen.

**hitch** [hɪtʃ] **1** *n* Schwierigkeit *f.* **(technical)** ~ (technische) Störung; **without a** ~ reibungslos; **but there's one** ~ aber die Sache hat einen Haken. **2** *vt* **(a)** *(fasten)* anbinden *(to an +dat).* **(b)** *(col)* **to get** ~**ed** heiraten. **(c) to** ~ **a lift** trampen, per Anhalter fahren. **3** *vi (~-hike)* trampen, per Anhalter fahren.
▶**hitch up** *vt sep* **(a)** *horses* anschirren. **(b)** *trousers* hochziehen.

**hitch:** ~**-hike** *vi* per Anhalter fahren, trampen; ~**-hiker** *n* Anhalter(in *f*), Tramper(in *f*) *m;* ~**-hiking** *n* Trampen *nt.*

**hitech** [ˈhaɪˌtek] *adj* High-Tech-. **this is too** ~ **for me** die Technik ist mir zu raffiniert.

**hither** [ˈhɪðəʳ] *adv (obs)* hierher. ~ **and thither** *(liter)* hierhin und dorthin.

**hitherto** [ˌhɪðəˈtuː] *adv* bisher, bis jetzt.

**hit:** ~ **list** *n (lit, fig)* Abschußliste *f (col);* ~**man** *n (col)* Killer *m (col);* ~**-or-miss** *adj* auf gut Glück *pred; methods, planning* schlampig; ~ **parade** *n (dated)* Hitparade *f;* ~ **record** *n* Schlagerplatte *f;* ~ **song** *n* Schlager *m;* ~ **tune** *n* Schlagermelodie *f.*

**HIV** = **human immunodeficiency virus** HIV.

**hive** [haɪv] *n (bee* ~*)* Bienenstock *m.* **the office was a** ~ **of activity** in dem Büro ging es zu wie in einem Bienenstock.
▶**hive off 1** *vt sep department* ausgliedern. **2** *vi* **(a)** *(branch out)* sich absetzen. **(b)** *(col: slip away)* abschwirren *(col).*

**hl** = **hectolitre(s)** hl.

**HM** = **His/Her Majesty** S.M./I.M.

**HMI** *(Brit)* **His/Her Majesty's Inspector** Schulrat *m.*

**HMS** *(Brit)* **His/Her Majesty's Ship** Schiff *nt* der königlichen Flotte.

**HMSO** *(Brit)* **His/Her Majesty's Stationery Office** Staatsdruckerei *f.*

**HNC** *(Brit)* = **Higher National Certificate.**

**HND** *(Brit)* = **Higher National Diploma.**

**hoard** [hɔːd] **1** *n* Vorrat *m; (treasure)* Hort *m.* **a** ~ **of weapons** ein Waffenlager *nt.* **2** *vt (also* ~ **up)** *food etc* hamstern; *money* horten.

**hoarding** *n (Brit) (fence)* Bretterzaun *m.* **(advertisement)** ~ Plakatwand *f.*

**hoarfrost** [ˈhɔːˌfrɒst] *n* (Rauh)reif *m.*

**hoarse** [hɔːs] *adj (+er)* heiser.

**hoax** [həʊks] **1** *n (joke)* Streich *m; (false alarm)* blinder Alarm. **2** *vt* anführen. **he** ~**ed him into paying money** er hat ihm Geld abgeschwindelt.

**hoaxer** [ˈhəʊksəʳ] *n (in bomb scares etc)* jd, *der einen blinden Alarm auslöst.*

**hob** [hɒb] *n (on modern cooker)* Kochmulde *f.*

**hobble** [ˈhɒbl] *vi* humpeln.

**hobby** ['hɒbɪ] n Hobby nt.
**hobby-horse** ['hɒbɪ,hɔːs] n (lit, fig) Steckenpferd nt.
**hobnailed** ['hɒbneɪld] adj ~ **boots** genagelte Schuhe pl.
**hobnob** ['hɒbnɒb] vi to ~ **with sb** mit jdm verkehren; **the people he ~s** mit seine Kumpel (col).
**hobo** ['həʊbəʊ] n (US: tramp) Penner m (col).
**hock¹** [hɒk] n (Brit: wine) weißer Rheinwein.
**hock²** n (col) **in** ~ (pawned) versetzt.
**hockey** ['hɒkɪ] n Hockey nt; (US) Eishockey nt. ~ **stick** Hockeyschläger m.
**hocus-pocus** ['həʊkəs'pəʊkəs] n Hokuspokus m.
**hodge-podge** ['hɒdʒpɒdʒ] n see **hotchpotch**.
**hoe** [həʊ] n Hacke f.
**hog** [hɒg] **1** n (Mast)schwein nt; (US: pig) Schwein nt; (pej col: person) Schwein nt (col); (greedy) Vielfraß m (col). **2** vt (col) in Beschlag nehmen.
**Hogmanay** [,hɒgmə'neɪ] n (Scot) Silvester nt.
**hoi polloi** [,hɔɪpə'lɔɪ] n (pej) Pöbel m.
**hoist** [hɔɪst] **1** vt hochheben; (pull up) hochziehen; flag, sails hissen. **to be ~ with one's own petard** (prov) in die eigene Falle gehen. **2** n Hebevorrichtung f; (lift) (Lasten)aufzug m.
**hoity-toity** [,hɔɪtɪ'tɔɪtɪ] (col) adj hochnäsig.
**hold** [həʊld] (vb: pret, ptp **held**) **1** n (a) Griff m (also Wrestling); (Mountaineering) Halt m; (fig) Einfluß m (over auf +acc). **to seize** or **grab** ~ **of sb/sth** (lit) jdn/etw fassen or packen; **to get (a)** ~ **of sth** sich an etw (dat) festhalten; **to have/catch** ~ **of sth** (lit) etw festhalten/etw fassen or packen; **to get** ~ **of sb** (fig) jdn finden; (on phone etc) jdn erreichen; **to get** or **lay** ~ **of sth** (fig) etw auftreiben (col); **where did you get** ~ **of that idea?** wie kommst du denn auf die Idee?; **to have a** ~ **over** or **on sb** (fig) (großen) Einfluß auf jdn ausüben; **to get (a)** ~ **of oneself** (fig) sich in den Griff bekommen; **get (a)** ~ **of yourself!** reiß dich zusammen! (b) (Naut, Aviat) Laderaum m. (c) (Telec) **to put sb on** ~ jdn auf Warteposition schalten; (fig) **to put sth on** ~ etw auf Eis legen.
  **2** vt (a) (grasp) halten. **to** ~ **hands** sich an der Hand halten; (lovers, children etc) Händchen halten; **this car** ~**s the road well** dieses Auto hat eine gute Straßenlage; **to** ~ **oneself upright** sich aufrecht halten.
  (b) (contain) enthalten; (have capacity of: tank etc) fassen; (bus, hall etc) Platz haben für. **this room** ~**s twenty people** in diesem Raum haben zwanzig Personen Platz; **the box will** ~ **all my books** in der Kiste ist Platz für alle meine Bücher; **what does the future** ~? was bringt die Zukunft?
  (c) (believe) meinen; (maintain also) behaupten. **to** ~ **sth to be true/immoral** etw für wahr/unmoralisch etc halten; **to** ~ **the belief that ...** glauben, daß ...; **to** ~ **the view that ...** die Meinung vertreten, daß ...; **she held her grandchild dear** ihr Enkelkind bedeutete ihr sehr viel.
  (d) (keep back) train aufhalten; one's breath anhalten; suspect, hostages etc festhalten; confiscated goods etc zurückhalten; (discontinue) fire einstellen. **to** ~ **sb (prisoner)** jdn gefangenhalten; **there's no** ~**ing him** er ist nicht zu bremsen (col); ~ **it!** (col) Moment mal (col); (taking photograph) so ist gut; ~ **everything!** (col) stop!
  (e) (possess, occupy) post, position innehaben; passport haben; shares besitzen; (Sport) record halten; (Mil) position halten.
  (f) (keep, not let go) **to** ~ **its value** seinen Wert behalten; **to** ~ **one's ground** or **own** sich behaupten (können); **I'll** ~ **you to that!** ich werde Sie beim Wort nehmen.
  (g) **he can't** ~ **his whisky/liquor** er verträgt kei-

nen Whisky/nichts; **she can** ~ **her drink** sie kann etwas vertragen.
  (h) meeting abhalten.
  **3** vi (a) (rope, nail etc) halten. ~ **still!** halt still!; ~ **tight!** festhalten!; **will the good weather** ~? wird sich das gute Wetter wohl halten?; **if his luck** ~**s** wenn ihm das Glück treu bleibt. (b) (be valid) gelten.
  ►**hold against** vt always separate **to** ~ **sth** ~ **sb** jdm etw übelnehmen.
  ►**hold back 1** vi sich zurückhalten; (fail to act) zögern. **to** ~ ~ **from doing sth** es unterlassen, etw zu tun. **2** vt sep zurückhalten; floods (auf)stauen; tears also unterdrücken; emotions verbergen, unterdrücken; information geheimhalten. **to** ~ **sb** ~ **from doing sth** jdn daran hindern, etw zu tun; **nothing can** ~ **him** ~ **now** jetzt ist er nicht mehr aufzuhalten or zu bremsen; **he was** ~**ing something** ~ **from me** er verheimlichte mir etwas.
  ►**hold down** vt sep (keep on ground) unten halten; (keep in place) (fest)halten; (keep low) prices niedrig halten. **he can't** ~ **any job** ~ **for long** er kann sich in keiner Stellung lange halten.
  ►**hold forth** vi sich auslassen (on über +acc).
  ►**hold in** vt sep stomach einziehen.
  ►**hold off 1** vi (keep away) sich fernhalten (from von); (not act) warten; (enemy) nicht angreifen; (rain, storm) ausbleiben. **I hope the rain** ~**s** ~ ich hoffe, daß es nicht regnet. **2** vt sep enemy, attack abwehren; visitor etc hinhalten.
  ►**hold on 1** vi (maintain grip) sich festhalten; (endure, resist) durchhalten; (wait) warten. ~ ~ **Moment** (mal)!; (Telec) einen Moment bitte. **2** vt sep **to be held** ~ **by sth** mit etw befestigt sein.
  ►**hold on to** vi +prep obj (a) **to** ~ ~ ~ **sth** an etw (dat) festhalten. (b) hope nicht aufgeben; idea festhalten an (+dat). (c) (keep) behalten. **to** ~ ~ ~ **the lead** in Führung bleiben.
  ►**hold out 1** vi (a) (supplies etc) reichen. (b) (endure, resist) durchhalten. **to** ~ ~ **against sb** sich gegen jdn behaupten; **to** ~ ~ **for sth** auf etw (dat) bestehen. **2** vt sep (a) ausstrecken. **to** ~ ~ **sth to sb** jdm etw hinhalten; ~ **your hand** halt die Hand auf; **she held** ~ **her arms** sie breitete die Arme aus. (b) (fig) prospects bieten. **I don't** ~ ~ **much hope** ich habe nicht mehr viel Hoffnung.
  ►**hold out on** vi +prep obj (col) **you've been** ~**ing** ~ ~ **me** du verheimlichst mir doch was (col).
  ►**hold over** vt sep question, matter vertagen; decision verschieben (until auf +acc).
  ►**hold up 1** vi (a) (tent, wall etc) stehen bleiben. (b) (belief) standhalten; (theory) sich halten lassen; (evidence) sich als stichhaltig erweisen. **2** vt sep (a) hochhalten; face nach oben wenden. ~ ~ **your hand** hebt die Hand; **to** ~ **sth** ~ **to the light** etw gegen das Licht halten. (b) (support) halten; (from the side) stützen; (from beneath) tragen. (c) **to** ~ **sb** ~ **as sth** jdn als etw hinstellen. (d) (stop) anhalten; (delay) people aufhalten; talks, delivery verzögern. (e) (rob) überfallen.
  ►**hold with** vi +prep obj (col) **I don't** ~ ~ **that** ich bin gegen so was (col).
**holdall** ['həʊldɔːl] n (Brit) Reisetasche f.
**holder** ['həʊldər] n (of title, office, record, passport) Inhaber(in f) m; (object) Halter m.
**holding** ['həʊldɪŋ] n (land) Land nt; (with buildings) Gut nt. ~**s** pl (property) (Grund)besitz m; (Fin) Anteile pl; (stocks) Aktienbesitz m; ~ **company** Dachgesellschaft f.
**hold-up** ['həʊldʌp] n (a) (delay) Verzögerung f; (Brit: of traffic) Stockung f. **what's the** ~? warum dauert

das so lange?; **there's been a ~ in our plans** unsere Pläne haben sich verzögert. **(b)** *(robbery)* bewaffneter Raubüberfall.

**hole** [həʊl] **1** *n* Loch *nt*; *(rabbit's, fox's)* Bau *m*, Höhle *f*; *(pej col)* Loch *nt (col)*; *(town)* Kaff *(col) nt*. **~ in the heart** Loch *nt* in der Herzscheidewand; **to make a ~ in sb's savings** ein Loch in jds Ersparnisse reißen; **I need that like (I need) a ~ in the head** *(col)* das ist das letzte, was ich gebrauchen kann. **2** *vt* ein Loch machen in *(+acc)*. **to be ~d** ein Loch bekommen; **the ship was ~d by an iceberg** der Eisberg schlug das Schiff leck.

► **hole up** *vi (esp US col: hide)* sich verkriechen.

**holiday** ['hɒlədɪ] *n* **(a)** *(day off)* freier Tag; *(public ~)* Feiertag *m*. **to take a ~** einen Tag frei nehmen. **(b)** *(esp Brit: period) often pl* Urlaub *m*, Ferien *pl (esp Sch)*. **on ~** in den Ferien; im Urlaub; **to go on ~** Urlaub machen; **where are you going for your ~?** wohin fahren Sie in den Ferien *or* im Urlaub?; **to take a ~** Urlaub nehmen; **I need a ~** ich bin urlaubsreif.

**holiday: ~ camp** *n* Feriendorf *nt*; **~ home** *n* Ferienhaus *nt*; *(flat)* Ferienwohnung *f*; **~maker** *n (esp Brit)* Urlauber(in *f*) *m*; **~ pay** *n* Urlaubsgeld *nt*; **~ resort** *n* Ferienort *m*; **~ season** *n* Urlaubszeit, Ferienzeit *f*.

**holiness** ['həʊlɪnɪs] *n* **His H~** Seine Heiligkeit.

**Holland** ['hɒlənd] *n* Holland *nt*.

**hollow** ['hɒləʊ] **1** *adj (+er) (lit, fig)* hohl; *person* innerlich hohl; *life* inhaltslos; *sympathy, praise* unaufrichtig; *promise* leer; *victory* wertlos; *eyes* tiefliegend. **2** *adv sound* hohl. **they beat us ~** *(col)* sie haben uns haushoch geschlagen. **3** *n (in ground)* Mulde *f*. **the ~ of one's hand** die hohle Hand.

► **hollow out** *vt sep* aushöhlen.

**holly** ['hɒlɪ] *n* Stechpalme *f*.

**hollyhock** ['hɒlɪhɒk] *n* Malve *f*.

**holocaust** ['hɒləkɔːst] *n* Inferno *nt*. **nuclear ~** atomare Katastrophe; **the H~** *(Hist)* der Holocaust.

**hologram** ['hɒləgræm] *n* Hologramm *nt*.

**holster** ['həʊlstər] *n* (Pistolen)halfter *nt or f*.

**holy** ['həʊlɪ] *adj (+er)* heilig; *bread, ground* geweiht. **~ water** Weihwasser *nt*; **the H~ Bible** die Bibel; **H~ Communion** *(Catholic)* Heilige Kommunion; *(Protestant)* Heiliges Abendmahl; **H~ Ghost** *or* **Spirit** Heiliger Geist; **the H~ Land** das Heilige Land; **H~ Week** Karwoche *f*; **~ smoke** *(col)* heiliger Strohsack! *(col)*.

**homage** ['hɒmɪdʒ] *n* Huldigung *f*; *(for elders)* Ehrerbietung *f*. **to pay ~ to sb** jdm huldigen; **in silent ~** in stummer Ehrerbietung.

**home** [həʊm] **1** *n* **(a)** *(house)* Heim *nt*; *(country, area etc)* Heimat *f*. **gadgets for the ~** praktische Haushaltsgeräte; **his ~ is in Brussels** er ist in Brüssel zu Hause; **Bournemouth is his second ~** Bournemouth ist seine zweite Heimat (geworden); **haven't you got a ~ to go to?** hast du kein Zuhause?; **he invited us around to his ~** er hat uns zu sich (nach Hause) eingeladen; **away from ~** von zu Hause weg; **a long way from ~** weit von zu Hause weg; **to live away from ~** nicht zu Hause wohnen; **hasn't this hammer got a ~?** gehört der Hammer nicht irgendwohin?; **to find a ~ for sth** etw irgendwo unterbringen; **it's a ~ from ~** es ist wie zu Hause; **at ~** zu Hause; *(Sport)* auf eigenem Platz; **he doesn't feel at ~ in English** er fühlt sich im Englischen nicht sicher; **to make oneself at ~** es sich *(dat)* bequem machen; **to make sb feel at ~** es jdm gemütlich machen; **~ sweet ~** *(Prov)* trautes Heim, Glück allein *(Prov)*.

**(b)** *(institution)* Heim *nt*.

**(c)** *(Zool, Bot)* Heimat *f*.

**2** *adv* **(a)** *(position)* zu Hause, daheim; *(with verb of motion)* nach Hause, heim. **to go ~** nach Hause gehen/fahren; *(to country)* heimfahren; **on the way ~** auf dem Heimweg *or* Nachhauseweg; **to return ~ from abroad** aus dem Ausland zurückkommen. **(b)** **to drive a nail ~** einen Nagel einschlagen; **to bring** *or* **get sth ~ to sb** jdm etw klarmachen; **his words went ~** seine Worte hatten ihre Wirkung.

► **home in on** *vi +prep obj target* sich ausrichten auf *(+acc)*; *essential point* herausgreifen.

**home: ~ address** *n* Heimatadresse *or* -anschrift *f*; *(as opposed to business address)* Privatanschrift *f*; **~ birth** *n* Hausgeburt *f*; **~-brew** *n* selbstgebrautes Bier; **~ comforts** *npl* häuslicher Komfort; **~-coming** *n* Heimkehr *f*; **~ computer** *n* Heimcomputer *m*; **H~ Counties** *npl Grafschaften, die an London angrenzen*; **~ economics** *n sing* Hauswirtschaft (slehre) *f*; **~ front** *n* **on the ~ front** *(Mil, Pol)* im eigenen Land; *(in personal, family contexts)* zu Hause; **~ game** *n (Sport)* Heimspiel *nt*; **~ ground** *n (Sport)* eigener Platz; **to be on ~ ground** *(fig)* sich auf vertrautem Terrain bewegen; **~-grown** *adj vegetables* selbstgezogen; *(not imported)* einheimisch; **~ help** *n* (Haushalts)hilfe *f*; **~ improvement** *n* Modernisierung *f*; *(extension)* Anbau *m*; **~ key** *n (Comp)* Home-Taste *f*; **~land** *n* Heimat(land *nt*) *f*; *(in S Africa)* Homeland *nt*; **~less** *adj* heimatlos; *tramp* obdachlos; **~ life** *n (family life)* Familienleben *nt*; *(private life)* Privatleben *nt*; **~ loan** *n* Hypothek *f*.

**homely** ['həʊmlɪ] *adj (+er)* **(a)** *(home-loving)* häuslich; *atmosphere* heimelig; *style* anspruchslos; *advice* einfach. **(b)** *(US: plain) person* unscheinbar; *face* reizlos.

**home: ~-made** *adj* selbstgemacht; **~maker** *n (US) (housewife)* Hausfrau *f*; *(social worker)* Familienfürsorger(in *f*) *m*; **~ market** *n* Inlandsmarkt *m*; **~ news** *n* Meldungen *pl* aus dem Inland; **H~ Office** *n (Brit)* Innenministerium *nt*; *(with relation to aliens)* Einwanderungsbehörde *f*.

**homeopath** *etc (US) see* **homoeopath** *etc*.

**home: ~-owner** *n* Hauseigentümer(in *f*) *m*; *(of flat/apartment)* Wohnungseigentümer(in *f*) *m*; **~ port** *n* Heimathafen *m*; **~ rule** *n* Selbstverwaltung *f*; **~ sales** *npl* Inlandsumsatz *m*; **H~ Secretary** *n (Brit)* Innenminister *m*; **~sick** *adj* **to be ~sick** Heimweh haben *(for nach)*; **~spun** *adj (fig: simple)* einfach; *(pej)* hausbacken; **~stead** *n* **(a)** Heimstätte *f*; **(b)** *(US)* Heimstätte *f* für Siedler; **~ straight, ~ stretch** *n (Sport)* Zielgerade *f*; **~ team** *n (Sport)* Gastgeber *pl*; **~ town** *n* Heimatort *m*; **~ truth** *n* ungeschminkte Wahrheit; **to tell sb some ~ truths** jdm deutlich die Meinung sagen.

**homeward** ['həʊmwəd] *adj journey, flight* Heim-. **we are ~-bound** es geht Richtung Heimat; **~(-bound) traffic** Rückreiseverkehr *m*.

**homeward(s)** ['həʊmwəd(z)] *adv* nach Hause; *(to country also)* in Richtung Heimat.

**homework** ['həʊmwɜːk] *n (Sch)* Hausaufgaben *pl*; **to give sb sth for ~** jdm etw aufgeben; **what have you got for ~?** was hast du auf?; **he hadn't done his ~** *(fig col)* er hatte sich mit der Materie nicht vertraut gemacht.

**homey** ['həʊmɪ] *adj (+er) (US col)* gemütlich.

**homicidal** [ˌhɒmɪ'saɪdl] *adj* gemeingefährlich.

**homicide** ['hɒmɪsaɪd] *n* Totschlag *m*. **culpable ~** Mord *m*; **~ (squad)** Mordkommission *f*.

**homily** ['hɒmɪlɪ] *n* Predigt *f*.

**homing** ['həʊmɪŋ] *adj (Mil)* zielsuchend. **~ pigeon** Brieftaube *f*; **~ instinct** Heimfindevermögen *nt*.

**homoeopath,** *(US)* **homeopath** ['həʊmɪəʊpæθ] *n*

Homöopath (in *f*) *m*.

**homoeopathic,** *(US)* **homeopathic** [ˌhəʊmɪəʊ-ˈpæθɪk] *adj* homöopathisch.

**homoeopathy,** *(US)* **homeopathy** [ˌhəʊmɪˈɒpəθɪ] *n* Homöopathie *f*.

**homogeneous** [ˌhɒməˈdʒiːnɪəs] *adj* homogen.

**homogenize** [həˈmɒdʒənaɪz] *vt* homogenisieren.

**homosexual** [ˌhɒməʊˈseksjʊəl] **1** *adj* homosexuell. **2** *n* Homosexuelle (r) *mf*.

**homosexuality** [ˌhɒməʊseksjʊˈælɪtɪ] *n* Homosexualität *f*.

**Hon.** = (a) **honorary**. (b) **Honourable**.

**Honduras** [hɒnˈdjʊərəs] *n* Honduras *nt*.

**hone** [həʊn] **1** *n* Schleifstein *m*. **2** *vt* (fein) schleifen. **to ~ sth to perfection** *(fig)* einer Sache den letzten Schliff geben.

**honest** [ˈɒnɪst] *adj* ehrlich; *business, action also* anständig; *truth* rein. **he made an ~ woman of her** *(col)* er machte sie zu seiner Frau.

**honestly** [ˈɒnɪstlɪ] *adv* ehrlich. **~!** *(in exasperation)* also ehrlich!

**honesty** [ˈɒnɪstɪ] *n* Ehrlichkeit *f*. **in all ~** ganz ehrlich; **~ is the best policy** *(Prov)* ehrlich währt am längsten *(Prov)*.

**honey** [ˈhʌnɪ] *n* Honig *m*; *(col)* Schätzchen *nt*.

**honey:** **~ bee** *n* Honigbiene *f*; **~comb 1** *n* (Bienen) wabe *f*; **2** *vt usu pass* durchlöchern.

**honeymoon** [ˈhʌnɪmuːn] *n* Flitterwochen *pl*; *(trip)* Hochzeitsreise *f*. **to be on one's ~** in den Flitterwochen/auf Hochzeitsreise sein; **the ~ is over** *(fig)* die Schonzeit ist vorbei.

**honeysuckle** [ˈhʌnɪˌsʌkl] *n* Geißblatt *nt*.

**Hong Kong** [ˈhɒŋˈkɒŋ] *n* Hongkong *nt*.

**honk** [hɒŋk] **1** *vi (car)* hupen; *(geese)* schreien. **2** *vt* horn drücken auf *(+acc)*.

**honky** [ˈhɒŋkɪ] *n (negro pej sl)* Weiße (r) *mf*.

**honorary** [ˈɒnərərɪ] *adj secretary* ehrenamtlich; *member, president* Ehren-. **~ degree** *ehrenhalber verliehener akademischer Grad*.

**honour,** *(US)* **honor** [ˈɒnə<sup>r</sup>] **1** *n* (a) Ehre *f*. **he made it a point of ~** er betrachtete es als Ehrensache; **to put sb on his ~** jdn auf sein Ehrenwort verpflichten; **man of ~** Ehrenmann *m*; **word of ~** Ehrenwort *nt*; **to be an ~ to sth** einer Sache *(dat)* Ehre machen; **in ~ of sb/sth** zu Ehren von jdm/etw; *(of dead person, past thing)* in ehrendem Andenken an jdn/etw; **he is (in) ~ bound to do it** es ist Ehrensache für ihn, das zu tun; **to do the ~s** *(col)* die Honneurs machen. **(b)** *(title)* **Your H~** Hohes Gericht; **His H~** das Gericht. **(c)** *(distinction, award)* **~s** Auszeichnung (en *pl*) *f*; *(Univ: also* **~s degree)** *akademischer Grad mit Prüfung im Spezialfach*.

**2** *vt* (a) *person* ehren. **to ~ sb with a title** jdm einen Titel verleihen; **I should be ~ed if you ...** es wäre mir eine Ehre, wenn Sie ...; **he ~ed us with his presence** *(also iro)* er beehrte uns mit seiner Gegenwart. **(b)** *cheque* annehmen; *obligation* nachkommen *(+dat)*; *commitment* stehen zu.

**honourable,** *(US)* **honorable** [ˈɒnərəbl] *adj* ehrenhaft; *peace, discharge* ehrenvoll. **to receive ~ mention** erwähnt werden; **the H~ member for X** *(Parl)* der Herr/die Frau Abgeordnete für X.

**Hons** *(Univ)* = **honours**.

**hood** [hʊd] *n* (a) Kapuze *f*; *(Aut: roof)* Verdeck *nt*; *(US Aut)* (Motor) haube *f*; *(on cooker)* Abzugshaube *f*. **(b)** *(esp US col)* Gangster *m (col)*.

**hoodlum** [ˈhuːdləm] *n* Rowdy *m*; *(member of gang)* Gangster *m (col)*.

**hoodwink** [ˈhʊdwɪŋk] *vt (col)* (he) reinlegen *(col)*.

**hoof** [huːf] *n*, *pl* **-s** *or* **hooves** Huf *m*.

**hook** [hʊk] **1** *n* Haken *m (also Boxing)*. **to put the door on the ~** die Tür festhaken; **he swallowed the story ~, line and sinker** er hat die Geschichte tatsächlich ganz geschluckt *(col)*; **by ~ or by crook** auf Biegen und Brechen; **to get sb off the ~** *(col)* jdn herausreißen *(col)*; **that lets me off the ~** *(col)* damit bin ich aus dem Schneider *(col)*; **to leave the phone off the ~** nicht auflegen. **2** *vt* (a) *door, gate* festhaken *(to* an *+acc)*. **to ~ a trailer to a car** einen Anhänger an ein Auto hängen. **(b)** *fish* an die Angel bekommen; *husband* sich *(dat)* angeln. **to be/get ~ed (on sth)** *(on drugs)* (von etw) abhängig sein/werden; *(on food, place)* auf etw *(acc)* stehen *(col)*; **he's ~ed on the idea** er ist von der Idee besessen.

▶**hook on 1** *vi* (an) gehakt werden *(to* an *+acc)*; *(with towbar)* angekoppelt werden *(to* an *+acc)*. **2** *vt sep* **to ~ sth ~ to sth** *(with towbar)* etw an etw *(acc)* (an) koppeln.

▶**hook up 1** *vi (col)* **to ~ ~ with sb** sich jdm anschließen. **2** *vt sep dress etc* zuhaken; *(Rad, TV)* anschließen *(with* an *+acc)*; *trailer* anhängen.

**hook and eye** *n* Haken und Öse *no art, pl vb*.

**hooked nose** [ˈhʊktˈnəʊz] *n* Hakennase *f*.

**hooker** [ˈhʊkə<sup>r</sup>] *n (esp US col)* Nutte *f (col!)*.

**hook:** **~-nosed** *adj* hakennasig; **~-up** *n (Rad, TV)* gemeinsame Ausstrahlung.

**hooligan** [ˈhuːlɪɡən] *n* Rowdy *m*.

**hooliganism** [ˈhuːlɪɡənɪzəm] *n* Rowdytum *nt*.

**hoop** [huːp] *n* Reifen *m*; *(on animal)* Ring *m*. **to put sb through the ~** *(fig col)* jdn durch die Mangel drehen *(col)*.

**hooray** [həˈreɪ] *interj* hurra. **H~ Henry/Henrietta** *(col) junge (r) Angehörige (r) der Oberschicht mit auffälligem Gehabe*, ≈ Schickimicki *m*.

**hoot** [huːt] **1** *n* (a) *(of owl)* Ruf *m*. **~s of laughter** johlendes Gelächter; **I don't care two ~s** *(col)* das ist mir völlig schnuppe *(col)*; **to be a ~** *(col) (person, event etc)* zum Schießen sein *(col)*. **(b)** *(Aut)* Hupen *nt no pl*; *(of train, hooter)* Pfeifen *nt no pl*. **2** *vi* (a) *(owl)* schreien. **(b)** *(Aut)* hupen; *(train, factory hooter)* pfeifen.

**hooter** [ˈhuːtə<sup>r</sup>] *n* (a) *(Brit Aut)* Hupe *f*; *(at factory)* Sirene *f*. **(b)** *(Brit col: nose)* Zinken *m (col)*.

**hoover** ® [ˈhuːvə<sup>r</sup>] *(Brit)* **1** *n* Staubsauger *m*. **2** *vti* (staub) saugen.

**hooves** [huːvz] *pl of* **hoof**.

**hop¹** [hɒp] **1** *n* (a) (kleiner) Sprung; *(of person, bird also)* Hüpfer *m*; *(of rabbit also)* Satz *m*. **to catch sb on the ~** *(fig col)* jdn überraschen; **to keep sb on the ~** *(fig col)* jdn in Trab halten. **(b)** *(col: dance)* Tanz *m*. **(c)** *(Aviat col)* Sprung *m*. **a short ~** ein Katzensprung *m (col)*. **2** *vi (animal)* hüpfen. **~ in, said the driver** steigen Sie ein, sagte der Fahrer; **~ it!** *(col)* zieh Leine *(col)*.

**hop²** *n (Bot)* Hopfen *m*.

**hope** [həʊp] **1** *n* Hoffnung *f*. **past** *or* **beyond all ~** hoffnungslos; **the patient is beyond all ~** für den Patienten besteht keine Hoffnung mehr; **to have ~s of doing sth** hoffen, etw zu tun; **well, we live in ~** nun, wir hoffen eben (weiter); **there's no ~ of that** da braucht man sich gar keine Hoffnungen zu machen; **to lose ~ of doing sth** die Hoffnung aufgeben, etw zu tun; **what a ~!** *(col)*, **some ~ (s)!** *(col)* schön wär's! *(col)*.

**2** *vi* hoffen *(for* auf *+acc)*. **to ~ for the best** das Beste hoffen; **I ~ so/not** hoffentlich/hoffentlich nicht; **to ~ against hope that ...** trotz allem die Hoffnung nicht aufgeben, daß ...

**3** *vt* hoffen. **I ~ to see you** hoffentlich sehe ich Sie; **hoping to hear from you** ich hoffe, von Ihnen zu hören.

**hopeful** [ˈhəʊpfʊl] **1** *adj* hoffnungsvoll; *situation,* *sign* vielversprechend. **they weren't very** ~ sie hatten keine große Hoffnung; **to be** ~ **that** ... hoffen, daß ...; **you're** ~! du bist vielleicht ein Optimist! *(col).* **2** *n (col)* **a young** ~ *(hoping to succeed)* ein hoffnungsvoller junger Mensch.

**hopefully** ['həʊpfəlɪ] *adv* (**a**) hoffnungsvoll. (**b**) ~ **it won't rain** hoffentlich regnet es nicht.

**hopeless** ['həʊplɪs] *adj situation, outlook* hoffnungslos; *liar, drunkard etc* unverbesserlich; *weather, food* unmöglich *(col).* **it's** ~ **even to try** es hat gar keinen Wert, es überhaupt zu versuchen; **you're** ~ du bist ein hoffnungsloser Fall; **he's** ~ **at maths** in Mathematik ist er eine Niete *(col).*

**hopelessly** ['həʊplɪslɪ] *adv* hoffnungslos. **we were** ~ **lost** wir hatten uns ganz und gar verirrt.

**hopper** ['hɒpər] *n (Tech)* Einfülltrichter *m.*

**hopping mad** ['hɒpɪŋ'mæd] *adj (col)* fuchsteufelswild *(col).*

**hop:** ~**scotch** *n* Himmel-und-Hölle(-Spiel) *nt;* ~, **step and jump** *n* Dreisprung *m.*

**horde** [hɔːd] *n (of animals, children)* Horde *f.*

**horizon** [hə'raɪzn] *n (lit, fig)* Horizont *m.* **on the** ~ am Horizont.

**horizontal** [ˌhɒrɪ'zɒntl] *adj* horizontal.

**hormone** ['hɔːməʊn] *n* Hormon *nt.* **hormone replacement therapy** Hormonersatztherapie *f.*

**horn** [hɔːn] *n (of cattle, Mus)* Horn *nt;* *(Aut)* Hupe *f;* *(Naut)* (Signal)horn *nt;* *(of snail, insect)* Fühler *m.* ~**s** *pl (of deer)* Geweih *nt;* **to sound the** ~ *(Aut)* hupen; *(Naut)* das Horn ertönen lassen; **to draw in one's** ~**s** *(fig: spend less)* den Gürtel enger schnallen; **the H**~ *(Geog)* Kap Hoorn.

**horned** [hɔːnd] *adj* gehörnt.

**hornet** ['hɔːnɪt] *n* Hornisse *f.*

**horn:** ~**pipe** *n englischer Seemannstanz;* ~-**rimmed spectacles** *npl* Hornbrille *f.*

**horny** ['hɔːnɪ] *adj (+er) hands etc* schwielig; *(col: randy)* geil *(col).*

**horoscope** ['hɒrəskəʊp] *n* Horoskop *nt.*

**horrendous** [hɒ'rendəs] *adj crime* abscheulich; *prices* horrend.

**horrible** ['hɒrɪbl] *adj* schrecklich. **don't be** ~ sei nicht so gemein *(col).*

**horribly** ['hɒrɪblɪ] *adv* schrecklich.

**horrid** ['hɒrɪd] *adj* entsetzlich, schrecklich. **he was** ~ **to her** er war gemein zu ihr.

**horrific** [hɒ'rɪfɪk] *adj* entsetzlich; *story, film* erschreckend.

**horrify** ['hɒrɪfaɪ] *vt* entsetzen.

**horrifying** *adj,* ~**ly** *adv* ['hɒrɪfaɪɪŋ, -lɪ] schrecklich, entsetzlich.

**horror** ['hɒrər] **1** *n* Entsetzen *nt;* *(strong dislike)* Horror *m (of* vor +*dat);* *(of war etc)* Greuel *m.* **she shrank back in** ~ sie fuhr entsetzt zurück; **to be a real** ~ *(col)* furchtbar sein *(col);* **you little** ~! *(col)* du kleines Ungeheuer! *(col).* **2** *attr story, films* Horror-.

**horror-stricken** ['hɒrərstrɪkn], **horror-struck** ['hɒrərstrʌk] *adj* von Entsetzen gepackt.

**hors d'oeuvre** [ɔː'dɜːv] *n* Vorspeise *f.*

**horse** [hɔːs] *n* Pferd *(also Gymnastics),* Roß *(liter, pej) nt.* **wild** ~**s would not drag me there** keine zehn Pferde würden mich dahin bringen; **I could eat a** ~ ich könnte ein ganzes Pferd essen; **information straight from the** ~'**s mouth** Informationen aus erster Hand.

**horse:** ~**back: on** ~**back** *adv* zu Pferd; ~-**box** *n* Pferdetransporter *m;* ~ **chestnut** *n* Roßkastanie *f;* ~-**drawn** *adj* von Pferden gezogen, pferdebespannt; ~-**drawn cart** Pferdewagen *m;* ~**fly** *n* Bremse *f;* ~**hair** *n* Roßhaar *nt;* ~**man** *n* Reiter *m;*

~**manship** *n* Reitkunst *f;* ~**play** *n* Balgerei *f;* ~**power** *n* Pferdestärke *f;* *(with figure)* PS *nt;* ~**racing** *n (races)* Pferderennen *pl;* ~**radish** *n* Meerrettich *m;* ~**shoe** *n* Hufeisen *nt;* ~ **show** *n* Pferdeschau *f;* ~-**trading** *n (fig)* Kuhhandel *m;* ~**whip 1** *n* Reitpeitsche *f;* **2** *vt* auspeitschen; ~**woman** *n* Reiterin *f.*

**hors(e)y** ['hɔːsɪ] *adj (+er) (col) (fond of horses)* pferdenärrisch; *appearance* pferdeähnlich.

**horticultural** [ˌhɔːtɪ'kʌltʃərəl] *adj* Garten(bau)-.

**horticulture** ['hɔːtɪkʌltʃər] *n* Gartenbau *m.*

**hose**[1] [həʊz] **1** *n (also* ~**pipe)** Schlauch *m.* **2** *vt (also* ~ **down)** abspritzen.

**hose**[2] *n no pl (Comm: stockings)* Strumpfwaren *pl.*

**hosiery** ['həʊzɪərɪ] *n* Strumpfwaren *pl.*

**hospice** ['hɒspɪs] *n* Hospiz *nt.*

**hospitable** [hɒs'pɪtəbl] *adj* gastfreundlich.

**hospital** ['hɒspɪtl] *n* Krankenhaus *nt,* Klinik *f.* **in** or *(US)* **in the** ~ im Krankenhaus; **he's got to go to** or *(US)* **to the** ~ er muß ins Krankenhaus (gehen); ~ **bed** Krankenhausbett *nt;* ~ **porter** Pfleger(in *f) m;* ~ **ship** Lazarettschiff *nt.*

**hospitality** [ˌhɒspɪ'tælɪtɪ] *n* Gastfreundschaft *f.*

**hospitalize** ['hɒspɪtəlaɪz] *vt* ins Krankenhaus einweisen.

**host**[1] [həʊst] **1** *n* Gastgeber *m;* *(in own home also)* Hausherr *m.* **2** *vt TV programme, games* Gastgeber sein bei.

**host**[2] *n* Menge *f.* **for a whole** ~ **of reasons** aus einer ganzen Reihe von Gründen.

**hostage** ['hɒstɪdʒ] *n* Geisel *f.* **to take sb** ~ jdn als Geisel nehmen; ~ **crisis** Geiseldrama *nt;* ~-**taker** Geiselnehmer *m;* ~-**taking** Geiselnahme *f.*

**hostel** ['hɒstəl] *n* (Wohn)heim *nt.*

**hostess** ['həʊstes] *n* Gastgeberin *f;* *(in own home also)* Hausherrin *f;* *(in night-club)* Hosteß *f;* *(air-*~*)* Stewardeß *f.*

**hostile** ['hɒstaɪl] *adj* feindlich; *person also* feindlich gesinnt; *reception, looks* feindselig. **to be** ~ **to sb** sich jdm gegenüber feindselig verhalten; **don't be so** ~ seien Sie nicht so aggressiv!

**hostility** [hɒs'tɪlɪtɪ] *n* Feindlichkeit *f (to, towards* gegenüber*);* *(between people)* Feindschaft *f.* **hostilities** *pl (warfare)* Feindseligkeiten *pl.*

**hot** [hɒt] *adj (+er)* (**a**) heiß; *meal, tap* warm; *curry* scharf. **I am** or **feel** ~ mir ist (es) heiß. (**b**) *(col: good, competent)* stark *(col);* *person also* fähig. **he's** ~ **at German** er ist gut in Deutsch; **he/it isn't (all) that** ~ so umwerfend ist er/das auch wieder nicht *(col);* **I'm not feeling too** ~ mir geht's nicht besonders *(col).* (**c**) *(Aut col: tuned)* frisiert *(col).* (**d**) *(fig)* ~ **favourite** der große Favorit; ~ **news** das Neueste vom Neuen; **the pace was so** ~ das Tempo war so scharf; **to get into** ~ **water** in Teufels Küche kommen *(col);* **to be all** ~ **and bothered** *(col)* ganz aufgeregt sein *(about wegen);* **to be in** ~ **pursuit of sb** jdm nacheilen; **it's getting too** ~ **for him here** hier wird ihm der Boden unter den Füßen zu heiß. (**e**) *(col: stolen)* heiß *(col).*

►**hot up** *vi (col) (pace)* schneller werden; *(situation)* sich zuspitzen; *(party)* in Schwung kommen.

**hot:** ~ **air** *n (fig)* leeres Gerede; ~-**air balloon** *n* Heißluftballon *m;* ~-**bed** *n (fig)* Nährboden *m (of* für*);* ~-**blooded** *adj* heißblütig.

**hotchpotch** ['hɒtʃpɒtʃ] *n* Mischmasch *m.*

**hot:** ~ **cross bun** *n Rosinenbrötchen mit einem Kreuz darauf, in der Karwoche gegessen;* ~ **dog** *n* Hot dog *m.*

**hotel** [həʊ'tel] *n* Hotel *nt.*

**hotelier** [həʊ'telɪər] *n* Hotelier *m.*

**hotel:** ~ **industry,** ~ **trade** *n* Hotelgewerbe *nt;* ~

**room** *n* Hotelzimmer *nt.*
**hot:** ~**foot 1** *adv* schleunigst; **2** *vt (col)* **to** ~**foot it home** schleunigst nach Hause gehen; ~**head** *n* Hitzkopf *m;* ~**headed** *adj* hitzköpfig; ~**house** *n (lit, fig)* Treibhaus *nt;* ~ **line** *n (Pol)* heißer Draht.
**hotly** ['hɒtlɪ] *adv contested* heiß. **he was** ~ **pursued by the police** die Polizei war ihm dicht auf den Fersen.
**hot:** ~**plate** *n* Kochplatte *f; (plate-warmer)* Warmhalteplatte *f;* ~**pot** *n (esp Brit)* Fleischeintopf *m* mit Kartoffeleinlage; ~ **potato** *n (fig col)* heißes Eisen; ~**rod** *n (Aut)* hochfrisiertes (altes) Auto; ~ **seat** *n* **to be in the** ~ **seat** auf dem Schleudersitz sein; ~ **shoe** *n (Phot)* Steckschuh *m;* ~ **spot** *n (Pol)* Krisenherd *m;* ~ **spring** *n* heiße Quelle, Thermalquelle *f;* ~ **stuff** *n (col)* **it's/he's** ~ **stuff** das/er ist große Klasse *(col);* ~**-tempered** *adj* jähzornig; ~**-water bottle** *n* Wärmflasche *f.*
**hound** [haʊnd] **1** *n (Hunt)* (Jagd)hund *m; (any dog)* Hund *m.* **the** ~**s** die Meute. **2** *vt* hetzen.
▶**hound down** *vt sep* Jagd machen auf *(+acc); (criminal also)* zur Strecke bringen.
▶**hound out** *vt sep* vertreiben *(of* aus).
**hour** ['aʊəʳ] *n* Stunde *f.* ~ **after** ~ Stunde um Stunde; ~ **by** ~ mit jeder Stunde; **on the** ~ zur vollen Stunde; **every** ~ **on the** ~ jede volle Stunde; **at an early/a late** ~ früh/spät; **at all** ~**s (of the day and night)** zu jeder (Tages- und Nacht)zeit; **to drive at 50 miles an** ~ 80 Stundenkilometer fahren; **to be paid by the** ~ stundenweise bezahlt werden; **for** ~**s** stundenlang; **he took** ~**s to do it** er brauchte stundenlang dazu; **it's three** ~**s (from here) by car** es ist drei Autostunden entfernt; ~**s** *pl (of banks, shops etc)* Geschäftszeit(en *pl) f;* **after** ~**s** *(in pubs)* nach der Polizeistunde; *(in office etc)* nach Dienstschluß; **to work long** ~**s** eine lange Arbeitszeit haben; **the man of the** ~ der Mann der Stunde.
**hour:** ~ **glass** *n* Sanduhr *f;* ~ **hand** *n* Stundenzeiger *m,* kleiner Zeiger.
**hourly** ['aʊəlɪ] *adj, adv* stündlich. ~ **rate/wage** Stundensatz/-lohn *m.*
**house 1** [haʊs] *n, pl* **houses** ['haʊzɪz] **(a)** Haus *nt.* **at my** ~ bei mir (zu Hause); **to my** ~ zu mir (nach Hause); **to set up** ~ einen eigenen Hausstand gründen; *(in particular area)* sich niederlassen; **to put one's** ~ **in order** *(fig)* seine Angelegenheiten in Ordnung bringen; **he's getting on like a** ~ **on fire** *(col)* er kommt prima voran *(col);* **they get on like a** ~ **on fire** *(col)* sie kommen ausgezeichnet miteinander aus; **as safe as** ~**s** *(Brit)* bombensicher *(col);* **on the** ~ auf Kosten des Hauses; *(on the company)* auf Kosten der Firma; **he brought the** ~ **down** *(col)* er riß alle von den Sitzen *(col);* **full** ~ *(Cards)* Full House *nt.*
  **(b)** *(Pol)* **the upper/lower** ~ das Ober-/Unterhaus; **H**~ **of Commons/Lords** *(Brit)* (britisches) Unter-/Oberhaus; **H**~ **of Representatives** *(US)* Repräsentantenhaus *nt;* **the H**~**s of Parliament** das Parlament(sgebäude).
  **2** [haʊz] *vt people, goods* unterbringen.
**house** *in cpds* Haus-; ~ **arrest** *n* Hausarrest *m;* ~**boat** *n* Hausboot *nt;* ~**bound** *adj* ans Haus gefesselt; ~**breaker** *n* Einbrecher *m;* ~**breaking** *n* Einbruch *m;* ~**-broken** *adj (US)* = ~**-trained**; ~**coat** *n* Morgenmantel *m;* ~**guest** *n* (Haus)gast *m.*
**household** ['haʊshəʊld] *n* Haushalt *m.* ~ **goods** Haushaltswaren *pl;* **to be a** ~ **name** *or* **word** ein Begriff sein.
**householder** ['haʊs,həʊldəʳ] *n* Haus-/Wohnungsinhaber(in *f) m.*
**house:** ~**-hunting** *n* Haussuche *f;* ~**husband** *n*

Hausmann *m;* ~**keeper** *n* Haushälterin *f;* ~**keeping** *n* Haushalten *nt; (also* ~**keeping money)** Haushaltsgeld *nt;* ~**man** *n (Brit)* Assistenzarzt *m;* ~ **plant** *n* Zimmerpflanze *f;* ~**-proud** *adj* **she is** ~**-proud** sie ist eine penible Hausfrau; ~**room** *n* **I wouldn't give it** ~**room** *(col)* so etwas kommt mir nicht in die Wohnung/ins Haus; ~**-to**~ *adj collection* Haus-; **a** ~**-to**~ **search** eine Suche von Haus zu Haus; ~**-trained** *adj* stubenrein; ~ **warming (party)** *n* Einzugsparty *f;* ~**wife** *n* Hausfrau *f;* ~**wifely** *adj* hausfraulich; ~**work** *n* Hausarbeit *f.*
**housing** ['haʊzɪŋ] *n* **(a)** *(act)* Unterbringung *f.* **(b)** *(houses)* Wohnungen *pl; (temporary)* Unterkunft *f.* **(c)** *(building of houses)* Wohnungsbau *m.* **(d)** *(Tech)* Gehäuse *nt.*
**housing** *in cpds* Wohnungs-; ~ **association** *n* Wohnungsbaugesellschaft *f;* ~ **conditions** *npl* Wohnbedingungen *pl;* ~ **development** *or (Brit also)* **estate** *n* Wohnsiedlung *f;* ~ **programme** *n* Wohnungsbauprogramm *nt.*
**hove** [həʊv] *pret, ptp of* **heave** *(Naut).*
**hovel** ['hɒvəl] *n* armselige Hütte; *(fig pej)* Bruchbude *f (col).*
**hover** ['hɒvəʳ] *vi* schweben; *(stand around)* sich herumdrücken *(col).* **a smile** ~**ed on her lips** ein Lächeln lag auf ihren Lippen; **he** ~**ed between two alternatives** er schwankte zwischen zwei Möglichkeiten.
▶**hover about** *or* **around** *vi (persons)* herumlungern; *(helicopter etc)* (in der Luft) kreisen.
**hover:** ~**craft** *n* Luftkissenboot, Hovercraft *nt;* ~**port** *n* Anlegestelle *f* für Hovercrafts.
**how** [haʊ] *adv* **(a)** wie. ~**'s that?,** ~ **come?** *(col)* wie kommt (denn) das?; ~ **is it that ...?** wie kommt es, daß ...?; ~ **do you know that?** woher wissen Sie das?; ~ **much** wieviel; **I know** ~ **much he loves her** ich weiß, wie sehr er sie liebt; ~ **many** wie viele; ~ **do you do?** Guten Tag/Abend!, angenehm! *(form);* ~ **are you?** wie geht es Ihnen?; ~**'s work?** was macht die Arbeit? *(col);* ~ **are things at school?** wie geht's in der Schule? ~ **about ...** wie wäre es mit ...; ~ **about it?** wie wäre es damit? **(b) and** ~! und ob!; ~ **he's grown!** er ist aber groß geworden; ~ **strange!** seltsam!; ~ **kind of him!** wie nett von ihm! **(c)** *(that)* daß. **she told me** ~ **she had seen him there** sie sagte mir, daß sie ihn dort gesehen hat.
**however** [haʊ'evəʳ] **1** *conj* jedoch, aber. **2** *adv* ~ **strong he is** wie stark er auch ist; ~ **you do it** wie du es auch machst; **do it** ~ **you like** mach's, wie du willst; ~ **much you cry** und wenn du noch so weinst; ~ **did you manage it?** wie hast du das bloß geschafft?
**howitzer** ['haʊɪtsəʳ] *n* Haubitze *f.*
**howl** [haʊl] **1** *n* Schrei *m; (of animal, wind)* Heulen *nt no pl.* ~**s of protest** Protestgeschrei *nt.* **2** *vi* brüllen; *(animal)* jaulen; *(wind)* heulen. **to** ~ **with laughter** in brüllendes Gelächter ausbrechen.
▶**howl down** *vt sep* niederbrüllen.
**howler** ['haʊləʳ] *n (col)* Hammer *m (col).*
**HP, hp** = **(a)** *(Brit)* **hire purchase. (b) horse power** PS.
**HQ** = **headquarters.**
**HR** *(US)* = **House of Representatives.**
**HRH** = **His/Her Royal Highness** S.M./I.M.
**hr(s)** = **hour(s)** h.
**HRT** *n abbr* = **hormone replacement therapy.**
**HS** *(US)* = **High School.**
**ht** = **height.**
**hub** [hʌb] *n* (Rad)nabe *f; (fig)* Zentrum *nt.*
**hubbub** ['hʌbʌb] *n* Tumult *m.*
**hubcap** ['hʌbkæp] *n* Radkappe *f.*

**huddle** ['hʌdl] **1** *n (of people)* Gruppe *f.* **in a** ~ dicht zusammengedrängt; **to go into a** ~ *(col)* die Köpfe zusammenstecken. **2** *vi* (sich) kauern.
▶**huddle together** *vi* sich aneinanderkauern. **to be** ~**d** ~ aneinanderkauern.
▶**huddle up** *vi* sich zusammenkauern. **to be** ~**d** ~ zusammenkauern.
**hue¹** [hjuː] *n* Farbe *f; (shade, fig)* Schattierung *f.*
**hue²** *n:* ~ **and cry** Zeter und Mordio *nt.*
**huff** [hʌf] *n* **to be in a** ~ eingeschnappt sein *(col)*; **to go into a** ~ einschnappen *(col).*
**hug** [hʌg] **1** *n* Umarmung *f.* **2** *vt* umarmen; *coast etc* sich dicht halten an *(+acc).* **It** ~**s the figure** es liegt eng an.
**huge** [hjuːdʒ] *adj (+er)* riesig.
**hulk** [hʌlk] *n (col: person)* Klotz *m (col).*
**hulking** ['hʌlkɪŋ] *adj:* ~ **great** massig; **a** ~ **great wardrobe** ein Ungetüm *nt* von einem Kleiderschrank.
**hull** [hʌl] *n (Naut)* Schiffskörper *m.*
**hullabaloo** [ˌhʌləbə'luː] *n (col: noise)* Radau *m.*
**hullo** [hʌ'ləʊ] *interj* = **hello.**
**hum** [hʌm] **1** *n see vi* **(a)** Summen *nt;* Surren *nt; (of voices)* Gemurmel *nt.* **2** *vi* **(a)** *(insect, person)* summen; *(small machine, camera etc)* surren. **HQ was** ~**ming with activity** im Hauptquartier ging es zu wie in einem Bienenstock; **to** ~ **and haw** *(col)* herumdrucksen *(col) (over, about* um*).* **(b)** *(col: smell)* stinken *(col).* **3** *vt tune* summen.
**human** ['hjuːmən] **1** *adj* menschlich. **I'm only** ~ ich bin auch nur ein Mensch; ~ **chain** Menschenkette *f;* ~ **form** Menschengestalt *f;* ~ **nature** die menschliche Natur; ~ **rights** Menschenrechte *pl.* **2** *n (also* ~ **being)** Mensch *m.*
**humane** [hjuː'meɪn] *adj* human, menschlich. ~ **killer** Mittel *nt* zum schmerzlosen Töten.
**humanism** ['hjuːmənɪzəm] *n* Humanismus *m.*
**humanist** ['hjuːmənɪst] **1** *n* Humanist *m.* **2** *adj* humanistisch.
**humanitarian** [hjuːˌmænɪ'tɛərɪən] *adj* humanitär.
**humanity** [hjuː'mænɪtɪ] *n* **(a)** *(mankind)* die Menschheit. **(b)** *(humaneness)* Menschlichkeit *f.* **(c) (the) humanities** *pl* (die) Geisteswissenschaften *pl; (Latin and Greek)* Altphilologie *f.*
**humanly** ['hjuːmənlɪ] *adv* menschlich. **to do all that is** ~ **possible** alles menschenmögliche tun.
**humble** ['hʌmbl] **1** *adj (+er) (unassuming)* bescheiden; *(meek, Rel)* demütig. **in my** ~ **opinion** meiner bescheidenen Meinung nach; **to eat** ~ **pie** klein beigeben. **2** *vt* demütigen.
**humbly** ['hʌmblɪ] *adv* bescheiden, demütig *(esp Rel); apologize* zerknirscht.
**humbug** ['hʌmbʌg] *n* **(a)** *(col)* Humbug *m.* **(b)** *(Brit: sweet)* Pfefferminzbonbon *nt.*
**humdinger** ['hʌmdɪŋəʳ] *n (col: person, thing)* **to be a** ~ Spitze sein *(col).*
**humdrum** ['hʌmdrʌm] *adj* stumpfsinnig.
**humid** ['hjuːmɪd] *adj* feucht.
**humidifier** [hjuː'mɪdɪfaɪəʳ] *n* Luftbefeuchter *m.*
**humidity** [hjuː'mɪdɪtɪ] *n* (Luft)feuchtigkeit *f.*
**humiliate** [hjuː'mɪlɪeɪt] *vt see n* demütigen; beschämen.
**humiliation** [hjuːˌmɪlɪ'eɪʃən] *n* Demütigung *f; (because of one's own actions)* Beschämung *f no pl.*
**humility** [hjuː'mɪlɪtɪ] *n* Demut *f; (unassumingness)* Bescheidenheit *f.*
**hummingbird** ['hʌmɪŋbɜːd] *n* Kolibri *m.*
**humorist** ['hjuːmərɪst] *n* Humorist(in *f*) *m.*
**humorous** ['hjuːmərəs] *adj person* humorvoll; *story etc also, situation* lustig; *idea* witzig.
**humour,** *(US)* **humor** ['hjuːməʳ] **1** *n* **(a)** Humor *m.*

**a sense of** ~ (Sinn *m* für) Humor *m;* **a story full of** ~ eine humorvolle Geschichte. **(b)** *(mood)* Stimmung, Laune *f.* **to be in a good** ~ in guter Stimmung sein; **he took it with good** ~ er nahm es gelassen auf. **2** *vt whims* nachgeben *(+dat).* **to** ~ **sb** jdm seinen Willen lassen.
**humourless,** *(US)* **humorless** ['hjuːməlɪs] *adj* humorlos, ohne jeden Humor.
**hump** [hʌmp] **1** *n* **(a)** *(Anat)* Buckel *m; (of camel)* Höcker *m.* **(b)** *(hillock)* Hügel, Buckel *(esp S Ger) m.* **(c)** *(Brit col)* **he's got the** ~ er ist sauer *(col).* **2** *vt (col: carry)* schleppen.
**humpbacked** ['hʌmpˌbækt] *adj person* buck(e)lig; *(Brit) bridge* gewölbt.
**humus** ['hjuːməs] *n* Humus *m.*
**hunch** [hʌntʃ] **1** *n (feeling)* Gefühl *nt,* Ahnung *f.* **to have a** ~ **that ...** das (leise) Gefühl haben, daß ... **2** *vt (also* ~ **up)** *back* krümmen; *shoulders* hochziehen. **he was** ~**ed (up) over his desk** er saß über seinen Schreibtisch gebeugt.
**hunch:** ~**back** *n (person)* Buck(e)lige(r) *mf; (back)* Buckel *m;* ~**-backed** *adj* buck(e)lig.
**hundred** ['hʌndrɪd] **1** *adj* hundert. **a** *or* **one** ~ **years** (ein)hundert Jahre; **two** ~ **years** zweihundert Jahre; **a** *or* **one** ~ **and one** (ein)hundert(und)eins; **a** ~ **per cent fit** hundertprozentig fit. **2** *n* hundert *num; (written figure)* Hundert *f.* ~**s** *(lit, fig)* Hunderte *pl;* **one in a** ~ einer unter hundert; ~**s of times** *(fig)* hundertmal; **they came in their** ~**s** sie kamen zu Hunderten.
**hundredth** ['hʌndrɪdθ] **1** *adj (in series)* hundertste(r, s). **2** *n (fraction)* Hundertstel *nt.*
**hundredweight** ['hʌndrɪdweɪt] *n* Zentner *m; (Brit)* 50,8 kg; *(US)* 45,4 kg.
**hung** [hʌŋ] *pret, ptp of* **hang.**
**Hungarian** [hʌŋ'gɛərɪən] **1** *adj* ungarisch. **2** *n* **(a)** Ungar(in *f*) *m.* **(b)** *(language)* Ungarisch *nt.*
**Hungary** ['hʌŋgərɪ] *n* Ungarn *nt.*
**hunger** ['hʌŋgəʳ] *n (lit, fig)* Hunger *m (for* nach*).* **to die of** ~ verhungern; **to go on (a)** ~ **strike** in (den) Hungerstreik treten.
**hung:** ~ **over** *adj (col)* verkatert *(col);* ~ **parliament** *n* Parlament *nt* ohne klare Mehrheitsverhältnisse.
**hungrily** ['hʌŋgrɪlɪ] *adv (lit, fig)* hungrig.
**hungry** ['hʌŋgrɪ] *adj (+er) (lit, fig)* hungrig. **to be/get** ~ Hunger haben/bekommen; **to go** ~ hungern; ~ **for power** machthungrig.
**hunk** [hʌŋk] *n* Stück *nt.* **a gorgeous** ~ **(of a man)** *(col)* ein *Mann*! *(col).*
**hunky-dory** [ˌhʌŋkɪ'dɔːrɪ] *adj (col)* **that's** ~ das ist prima *(col).*
**hunt** [hʌnt] **1** *n* Jagd *f; (fig: search)* Suche *f.* **to have a** ~ **for sth** nach etw fahnden *(col).* **2** *vt* jagen; *criminal also* fahnden nach; *missing article, person* suchen. **3** *vi* **(a)** jagen. **to go** ~**ing** jagen, auf die Jagd gehen. **(b)** *(search)* suchen *(for* nach*).*
▶**hunt down** *vt sep* (unerbittlich) Jagd machen auf *(+acc); (capture)* zur Strecke bringen.
▶**hunt out** *vt sep sth* hervorkramen *(col).*
▶**hunt up** *vt sep history, origins* forschen nach.
**hunter** ['hʌntəʳ] *n* Jäger *m; (horse)* Jagdpferd *nt.*
**hunting** ['hʌntɪŋ] *n* die Jagd. **to go** ~ auf die Jagd gehen; ~ **horn** Jagdhorn *nt.*
**huntsman** ['hʌntsmən] *n, pl* **-men** [-mən] Jagdreiter *m.*
**hurdle** ['hɜːdl] *(Sport, fig)* Hürde *f.* ~**s** *sing (race)* Hürdenlauf *m.*
**hurdler** ['hɜːdləʳ] *n (Sport)* Hürdenläufer(in *f*) *m.*
**hurl** [hɜːl] *vt* schleudern. **to** ~ **oneself at sb** sich auf jdn stürzen; **to** ~ **abuse at sb** jdn wüst beschimpfen

*(col).*

**hurly-burly** ['hɜːlɪ'bɜːlɪ] *n* Rummel *m (col).*

**hurrah** [hʊ'rɑː], **hurray** [hʊ'reɪ] *interj* hurra.

**hurricane** ['hʌrɪkən] *n* Orkan *m; (tropical)* Hurrikan *m.* ~ **lamp** Sturmlaterne *f.*

**hurried** ['hʌrɪd] *adj* eilig; *letter, essay* hastig geschrieben; *work* in Eile gemacht.

**hurriedly** ['hʌrɪdlɪ] *adv* eilig.

**hurry** ['hʌrɪ] **1** *n* Eile *f.* **in my** ~ **to get it finished** ... vor lauter Eile, damit fertig zu werden ...; **to do sth in a** ~ etw hastig tun; **I need it in a** ~ ich brauche es dringend; **to be in a** ~ es eilig haben; **I won't do that again in a** ~! *(col)* das mache ich so schnell nicht wieder!; **what's the** ~? warum so eilig?; **is there any** ~ **for it?** eilt das?; **there's no** ~ es eilt nicht.

**2** *vi* sich beeilen; *(run/go quickly)* laufen; *(in car etc)* schnell fahren. **there's no need to** ~ (es besteht) kein Grund zur Eile; **can't you make her** ~? kannst du sie nicht zur Eile antreiben?; **don't** ~! immer mit der Ruhe!; **I must** ~ **back** ich muß schnell zurück.

**3** *vt work etc* schneller machen; *(do too quickly)* überstürzen. **troops were hurried to the spot** es wurden schleunigst Truppen dorthin gebracht; **don't** ~ **me** hetz mich nicht so!; **don't** ~ **your meal** lassen Sie sich Zeit beim Essen!

▶**hurry along 1** *vi* sich beeilen. **to** ~ ~ **the road** die Straße schnell entlangfahren. **2** *vt sep person* weiterdrängen; *(with work etc)* zur Eile antreiben; *things, work etc* vorantreiben.

▶**hurry away** *or* **off 1** *vi* schnell weggehen. **2** *vt sep* schnell wegbringen.

▶**hurry on** *vi* weiterlaufen.

▶**hurry up 1** *vi* sich beeilen. ~ ~! beeil dich! **2** *vt sep* zur Eile antreiben; *work* vorantreiben.

**hurt** [hɜːt] *(vb: pret, ptp* ~*)* **1** *vt* **(a)** *(lit, fig)* weh tun *(+dat); (injure)* verletzen. **to** ~ **oneself** sich *(dat)* weh tun; **to** ~ **one's arm** sich *(dat)* am Arm weh tun; *(injure)* sich *(dat)* den Arm verletzen; **to get** ~ verletzt werden. **(b)** *(harm)* schaden *(+dat).* **it wouldn't** ~ **you to say sorry** du solltest dich wirklich entschuldigen; **it won't** ~ **him to wait** es schadet ihm nicht(s), wenn er etwas warten muß. **2** *vi* **(a)** *(be painful)* weh tun; *(fig also)* verletzend sein. **that** ~**s!** *(lit, fig)* das tut weh! **(b) but surely a little drink won't** ~ aber ein Gläschen kann doch wohl nicht schaden. **3** *adj limb, feelings* verletzt; *tone, look* gekränkt.

**hurtful** ['hɜːtfʊl] *adj* verletzend.

**hurtle** ['hɜːtl] *vi* rasen. **he came hurtling around the corner** er kam um die Ecke gerast.

**husband** ['hʌzbənd] *n* Ehemann *m.* **my/her** ~ mein/ ihr Mann.

**hush** [hʌʃ] **1** *n* Stille *f.* **2** *interj* pst!

▶**hush up** *vt sep scandal* vertuschen.

**hushed** [hʌʃt] *adj voices* gedämpft; *words* leise.

**hush-hush** ['hʌʃ'hʌʃ] *adj (col)* streng geheim.

**husk** [hʌsk] *n* Schale *f; (of rice also)* Hülse *f.*

**husky**[1] ['hʌskɪ] *adj (+er)* rauh.

**husky**[2] *n (dog)* Schlittenhund *m.*

**hustings** ['hʌstɪŋz] *npl (Brit)* **on the** ~ im Wahlkampf; *(at election meeting)* bei einer Wahlveranstaltung.

**hustle** ['hʌsl] **1** *n* **the** ~ **and bustle** das geschäftige Treiben; *(rush)* die Hektik *f.* **2** *vt* **to** ~ **sb out of the building** jdn schnell aus dem Gebäude bringen; **to** ~ **things (along)** die Dinge vorantreiben. **3** *vi* **(a)** *(move busily)* hasten, eilen. **(b)** *(prostitute)* auf den Strich gehen *(col).* **to** ~ **for business** *(salesman etc)* Aufträgen nachjagen.

**hut** [hʌt] *n* Hütte *f; (Mil)* Baracke *f.*

**hutch** [hʌtʃ] *n* Verschlag *m; (for rabbit)* Stall *m.*

**hyacinth** ['haɪəsɪnθ] *n* Hyazinthe *f.*

**hyaena** [haɪ'iːnə] *n* Hyäne *f.*

**hybrid** ['haɪbrɪd] *n (Bot, Zool)* Kreuzung *f; (fig)* Mischform *f.*

**hydrangea** [haɪ'dreɪndʒə] *n* Hortensie *f.*

**hydrant** ['haɪdrənt] *n* Hydrant *m.*

**hydraulic** [haɪ'drɒlɪk] *adj* hydraulisch.

**hydraulics** [haɪ'drɒlɪks] *n sing* Hydraulik *f.*

**hydro-:** ['haɪdrəʊ-] ~**carbon** *n* Kohlenwasserstoff *m;* ~**chloric acid** *n* Salzsäure *f;* ~**electric** *adj* hydroelektrisch; ~**electric power station** *n* Wasserkraftwerk *nt;* ~**foil** *n (boat)* Tragflächenboot *nt.*

**hydrogen** ['haɪdrɪdʒən] *n* Wasserstoff *m.* ~ **bomb** Wasserstoffbombe *f.*

**hydrometer** [haɪ'drɒmətəʳ] *n* Hydrometer *nt.*

**hydrophobia** [ˌhaɪdrə'fəʊbɪə] *n* Wasserscheu *f; (rabies)* Tollwut *f.*

**hydroxide** [haɪ'drɒksaɪd] *n* Hydroxyd, Hydroxid *nt.*

**hyena** [haɪ'iːnə] *n* = **hyaena.**

**hygiene** ['haɪdʒiːn] *n* Hygiene *f.* **personal** ~ Körperpflege *f.*

**hygienic** [haɪ'dʒiːnɪk] *adj* hygienisch.

**hymn** [hɪm] *n* Kirchenlied *nt.* ~ **book** Gesangbuch *nt.*

**hype** [haɪp] *(col)* **1** *n* (Werbe)rummel *m (col).* **2** *vt product, film etc* hochjubeln *(col).*

**hyper-** ['haɪpəʳ] *pref* Hyper-, hyper-, Über-, über-.

**hyper-:** ~**active** *adj* äußerst aktiv; ~**critical** *adj* übertrieben kritisch; ~**market** *n (Brit)* großer Supermarkt; ~**sensitive** *adj* überempfindlich; ~**tension** *n* Hypertonie *f,* erhöhter Blutdruck.

**hyphen** ['haɪfən] *n* Bindestrich *m; (at end of line)* Trenn(ungs)strich *m.*

**hyphenate** ['haɪfəneɪt] *vt* mit Bindestrich schreiben; *(insert hyphen)* trennen.

**hyphenation** [ˌhaɪfə'neɪʃən] *n* Silbentrennung *f.*

**hypnosis** [hɪp'nəʊsɪs] *n* Hypnose *f.*

**hypnotic** [hɪp'nɒtɪk] *adj* hypnotisch; *(hypnotizing, fig)* hypnotisierend.

**hypnotism** ['hɪpnətɪzəm] *n* Hypnotismus *m.*

**hypnotist** ['hɪpnətɪst] *n* Hypnotiseur *m,* Hypnotiseuse *f.*

**hypnotize** ['hɪpnətaɪz] *vt* hypnotisieren.

**hypochondria** [ˌhaɪpəʊ'kɒndrɪə] *n* Hypochondrie *f.*

**hypochondriac** [ˌhaɪpəʊ'kɒndrɪæk] *n* Hypochonder *m.*

**hypocrisy** [hɪ'pɒkrɪsɪ] *n* Heuchelei *f; (pretending innocence)* Scheinheiligkeit *f.*

**hypocrite** ['hɪpəkrɪt] *n* Heuchler(in *f) m.*

**hypocritical** [ˌhɪpə'krɪtɪkəl] *adj* heuchlerisch.

**hypodermic** [ˌhaɪpə'dɜːmɪk] *adj, n* ~ **(needle** or **syringe)** Spritze *f.*

**hypotenuse** [haɪ'pɒtɪnjuːz] *n* Hypotenuse *f.*

**hypothermia** [ˌhaɪpəʊ'θɜːmɪə] *n* Unterkühlung *f.*

**hypothesis** [haɪ'pɒθɪsɪs] *n, pl* **hypotheses** [haɪ'pɒθɪsiːz] Hypothese *f.*

**hypothetical** [ˌhaɪpəʊ'θetɪkəl] *adj* hypothetisch. **purely** ~ reine Hypothese.

**hysterectomy** [ˌhɪstə'rektəmɪ] *n* Hysterektomie *f,* Totaloperation *f (col).*

**hysteria** [hɪ'stɪərɪə] *n* Hysterie *f.*

**hysterical** [hɪ'sterɪkəl] *adj* hysterisch; *(col: very funny)* irrsinnig komisch *(col).*

**hysterically** [hɪ'sterɪkəlɪ] *adv* hysterisch. ~ **funny** irrsinnig komisch *(col).*

**hysterics** [hɪ'sterɪks] *npl* hysterischer Anfall. **to go into** ~ *(col: laugh)* sich (halb) totlachen.

**Hz** = **hertz** Hz.

# I

**I, i** [aɪ] *n* I, i *nt*. **I for Isaac** *(Brit)*, **I for item** *(US)* ≈ I wie Ida.

**I** *pers pron* ich. **it is ~** *(form)* ich bin es.

**I** = **Island, Isle**.

**IA** *(US Post)* = **Iowa**.

**IBA** *(Brit)* = **Independent Broadcasting Authority** *Aufsichtsgremium nt der kommerziellen Fernseh- und Rundfunkanstalten*.

**Iberian** [aɪˈbɪərɪən] *adj* iberisch. **~ Peninsula** Iberische Halbinsel.

**ib(id)** = **ibidem** ib(d).

**i/c** = **in charge** verantw.

**ICBM** = **intercontinental ballistic missile** Interkontinentalrakete *f*.

**ice** [aɪs] **1** *n* **(a)** Eis *nt*; *(on roads)* (Glatt)eis *nt*. **to be as cold as ~** eiskalt sein; **to keep** *or* **put sth on ~** *(lit)* etw kalt stellen; *(fig)* etw auf Eis legen; **to break the ~** *(fig)* das Eis brechen; **to be skating on thin ~** *(fig)* sich aufs Glatteis begeben; **to cut no ~ with sb** *(col)* auf jdn keinen Eindruck machen. **(b)** *(Brit: ice-cream)* (Speise)eis *nt*. **2** *vt* *cake* glasieren.
▶**ice over** *vi* zufrieren; *(windscreen)* vereisen.
▶**ice up** *vi (aircraft wings etc)* vereisen; *(pipes etc)* einfrieren.

**ice** *in cpds* Eis-; **~ age** *n* Eiszeit *f*; **~ axe** *(Brit) or* **~ ax** *(US) n* Eispickel *m*; **~berg** *n (lit, fig)* Eisberg *m*; **~-blue** *adj* eisblau; **~bound** *adj port* zugefroren; *ship* vom Eis eingeschlossen; *road* vereist; **~box** *n (Brit: in refrigerator)* Eisfach *nt*; *(US)* Eisschrank *m*; *(insulated box)* Kühltasche *f*; **~breaker** *n* Eisbrecher *m*; **~ bucket** *n* Eiskühler *m*; **~cap** *n* Eiskappe *f*; **~-cold** *adj* eiskalt; **~-cream** *n* Eis *nt*; **~-cream soda** *n Eisbecher m mit Sirup, Marmelade, Früchten, Milch und Ingwerlimonade*; **~ cube** *n* Eiswürfel *m*.

**iced** [aɪst] *adj* **(a)** *(cooled)* eisgekühlt; *coffee, water* Eis-. **(b)** *cake* glasiert.

**ice:** **~ floe** *n* Eisscholle *f*; **~ hockey** *n* Eishockey *nt*.

**Iceland** [ˈaɪslənd] *n* Island *nt*.

**Icelander** [ˈaɪsləndəʳ] *n* Isländer(in *f*) *m*.

**Icelandic** [aɪsˈlændɪk] **1** *adj* isländisch. **2** *n (language)* Isländisch *nt*.

**ice:** **~lolly** *(Brit) n* Eis *nt* am Stiel; **~ pack** *n (on head)* Eisbeutel *m*; **~ pick** *n* Eispickel *m*; **~ rink** *n* Schlittschuhbahn *f*; *(with seating for spectators)* Eisstadion *nt*; **~-skate** *vi* Schlittschuh laufen; **~-skating** *n* Schlittschuhlaufen *nt*.

**icicle** [ˈaɪsɪkl] *n* Eiszapfen *m*.

**icily** [ˈaɪsɪlɪ] *adv (lit, fig)* eisig. **to look ~ at sb** jdm einen eisigen Blick zuwerfen.

**icing** [ˈaɪsɪŋ] *n* **(a)** *(Cook)* Zuckerguß *m*. **~ sugar** *(Brit)* Puderzucker *m*. **(b)** *(formation of ice)* Eisbildung, Vereisung *f*.

**icon** [ˈaɪkɒn] *n* Ikone *f*; *(Comp)* Ikon *nt*.

**iconoclastic** [aɪˌkɒnəˈklæstɪk] *adj* bilderstürmerisch.

**icy** [ˈaɪsɪ] *adj (+er) (lit, fig)* eisig; *road* vereist.

**I'd** [aɪd] = **I would; I had**.

**id** [ɪd] *n (Psych)* Es *nt*.

**ID** = **(a) identification, identity**. **~ card** Ausweis *m*. **(b)** *(US Post)* **Idaho**.

**idea** [aɪˈdɪə] *n* Idee *f*. **good ~!** gute Idee!; **that's not a bad ~** das ist keine schlechte Idee; **the very ~!** (nein), so was!; **the very ~ of horsemeat revolts me** der bloße Gedanke an Pferdefleisch ekelt mich; **the ~ never entered my head!** auf den Gedanken bin ich überhaupt nicht gekommen; **to hit upon the ~ of doing sth** den plötzlichen Einfall haben, etw zu tun; **that gives me an ~, we could ...** da fällt mir ein, wir könnten ...; **the ~ for the book** die Idee zu dem Buch; **he's somehow got the ~ into his head that ...** er bildet sich *(dat)* irgendwie ein, daß ...; **don't go getting ~s about promotion** machen Sie sich *(dat)* nur keine falschen Hoffnungen auf eine Beförderung; **to put ~s into sb's head** jdm einen Floh ins Ohr setzen; **what's the big ~?** *(col)* was soll das denn?; **that's the ~** genau (das ist's)!; **if that's your ~ of fun** wenn Sie das lustig finden; **he has some very strange ~s** er hat merkwürdige Vorstellungen; **his ~ of a pleasant evening is ...** seine Vorstellung von einem angenehmen Abend ist, ...; **you've no ~ how worried I've been** du kannst dir nicht vorstellen, welche Sorgen ich mir gemacht habe; **(I've) no ~** (ich habe) keine Ahnung; **I have an ~ that ...** ich habe so das Gefühl, daß ...; **could you give me an ~ of how long ...?** könnten Sie mir ungefähr sagen, wie lange ...?

**ideal** [aɪˈdɪəl] **1** *adj* ideal. **in an ~ world** im Idealfall; *(Philos)* in einer vollkommenen Welt. **2** *n* Idealvorstellung *f*, Ideal *nt*.

**idealism** [aɪˈdɪəlɪzəm] *n* Idealismus *m*.

**idealist** [aɪˈdɪəlɪst] *n* Idealist(in *f*) *m*.

**idealistic** [aɪˌdɪəˈlɪstɪk] *adj* idealistisch.

**idealize** [aɪˈdɪəlaɪz] *vt* idealisieren.

**ideally** [aɪˈdɪəlɪ] *adv* ideal. **they are ~ suited for each other** sie passen ausgezeichnet zueinander; **~, ...** idealerweise *or* im Idealfall ...

**identical** [aɪˈdentɪkəl] *adj (exactly alike)* identisch; *(same)* derselbe/dieselbe/dasselbe. **~ twins** eineiige Zwillinge *pl*.

**identifiable** [aɪˈdentɪˌfaɪəbl] *adj* erkennbar; *(esp Sci)* identifizierbar.

**identification** [aɪˌdentɪfɪˈkeɪʃən] *n* Identifizierung *f*; *(papers)* Ausweispapiere *pl*. **he had no (means of) ~** er konnte sich nicht ausweisen.

**identify** [aɪˈdentɪfaɪ] **1** *vt* **(a)** identifizieren; *plant, species etc* bestimmen; *(mark identity of)* kennzeichnen; *(recognize, pick)* erkennen *(by an +dat)*. **(b)** *(consider as the same)* gleichsetzen *(with* mit*)*. **2** *vr* **(a) to ~ oneself** sich ausweisen. **(b) to ~ oneself with sb/sth** sich mit jdm/etw identifizieren. **3** *vi (with film hero etc)* sich identifizieren *(with* mit*)*.

**Identikit** ® [aɪˈdentɪkɪt] *n*: **~ (picture)** Phantombild *nt*.

**identity** [aɪˈdentɪtɪ] *n* Identität *f*. **to prove one's ~** sich ausweisen.

**identity**: ~ **card** n (Personal)ausweis m; ~ **parade** n Gegenüberstellung f (zur Identifizierung des Täters).
**ideological** [ˌaɪdɪə'lɒdʒɪkəl] adj ideologisch.
**ideology** [ˌaɪdɪ'ɒlədʒɪ] n Weltanschauung, Ideologie f.
**idiocy** ['ɪdɪəsɪ] n (a) no pl Idiotie f, Schwachsinn m. (b) (act) Dummheit f.
**idiom** ['ɪdɪəm] n idiomatische Wendung.
**idiomatic** [ˌɪdɪə'mætɪk] adj idiomatisch.
**idiosyncrasy** [ˌɪdɪə'sɪŋkrəsɪ] n Eigenheit, Eigenart f.
**idiosyncratic** [ˌɪdɪəsɪŋ'krætɪk] adj **he has a very ~ way of** ... er hat eine eigene Art zu ...
**idiot** ['ɪdɪət] n Idiot, Dummkopf m. **you (stupid) ~!** du Idiot!; **what an ~ I am/was!** ich Idiot!
**idiotic** [ˌɪdɪ'ɒtɪk] adj idiotisch. **don't be ~!** sei nicht so blöd!
**idle** ['aɪdl] **1** adj (a) (not working) person untätig. **the ~ rich** die reichen Müßiggänger; **in my ~ moments** in stillen Augenblicken; **~ life** faules Leben; **money lying ~** totes Kapital; **his car was lying ~ most of the time** sein Auto stand meistens unbenutzt herum. (b) (lazy) faul. (c) (in industry) person unbeschäftigt; machine außer Betrieb. **to be made ~** (worker) seine Arbeit einstellen müssen; **the whole factory stood ~** die ganze Fabrik hatte die Arbeit eingestellt; **the machine stood ~** die Maschine stand still. (d) promise, words leer; (useless) nutzlos. **~ curiosity** pure Neugier. **2** vi (engine) leerlaufen. **when the engine is idling** wenn der Motor im Leerlauf ist.
►**idle away** vt sep one's time etc vertrödeln.
**idleness** ['aɪdlnɪs] n (a) (not working) Untätigkeit f; (pleasurable) Muße f. (b) (laziness) Faulheit f.
**idler** ['aɪdlər] n (pej) Faulenzer(in f) m.
**idly** ['aɪdlɪ] adv (a) (without working) untätig; (pleasurably) müßig. **to stand ~ by** untätig danebenstehen. (b) (lazily) faul.
**idol** ['aɪdl] n (lit) Götzenbild nt; (fig) Idol nt.
**idolize** ['aɪdəlaɪz] vt vergöttern; (star) zum Idol machen.
**I'd've** ['aɪdəv] = **I would have.**
**idyll** ['ɪdɪl] n Idyll nt.
**idyllic** [ɪ'dɪlɪk] adj idyllisch.
**i.e.** abbr d.h.
**if** [ɪf] **1** conj wenn; (in case also) falls; (whether, in indirect clause) ob. **I would be pleased ~ you could do it** wenn Sie das tun könnten, wäre ich sehr froh; (even) ~ auch wenn; (even) ~ **they are poor, at least they are happy** sie sind zwar arm, aber wenigstens glücklich; ~ **only I had known!** wenn ich das nur gewußt hätte!; **I would like to see him, ~ only for a few hours** ich würde ihn gerne sehen, wenn auch nur für ein paar Stunden; **as ~** als ob; **he acts as ~ he were** or **was rich** er tut so, als ob er reich wäre; ~ **necessary** falls nötig; ~ **so** wenn ja; ~ **not** wenn nicht; ~ **I were you/him** wenn ich Sie/er wäre. **2** n **it's a big ~** das ist die große Frage; **~s and buts** Wenn und Aber nt.
**iffy** ['ɪfɪ] adj (col) zweifelhaft.
**igloo** ['ɪgluː] n Iglu m or nt.
**ignite** [ɪg'naɪt] **1** vt entzünden. **2** vi sich entzünden.
**ignition** [ɪg'nɪʃən] n Entzünden nt; (Aut) Zündung f. ~ **key** Zündschlüssel m.
**ignoble** [ɪg'nəʊbl] adj unehrenhaft.
**ignominious** [ˌɪgnə'mɪnɪəs] adj schmachvoll; behaviour schändlich.
**ignominy** ['ɪgnəmɪnɪ] n Schmach, Schande f.
**ignoramus** [ˌɪgnə'reɪməs] n Ignorant m.
**ignorance** ['ɪgnərəns] n Unwissenheit f; (of particular subject) Unkenntnis f. **to keep sb in ~ of sth** jdn

in Unkenntnis über etw (acc) lassen; ~ **is bliss** (Prov) was ich nicht weiß, macht mich nicht heiß (Prov).
**ignorant** ['ɪgnərənt] adj unwissend; (of plan etc) nicht informiert (of über +acc). **to be ~ of geography** sich in Geographie nicht auskennen; **to be ~ of the facts** die Tatsachen nicht kennen.
**ignore** [ɪg'nɔːr] vt ignorieren; (pay no attention to) nicht beachten; remark also übergehen.
**IL** (US Post) = **Illinois.**
**ilk** [ɪlk] n **people/things of that ~** solche Leute/dergleichen Dinge.
**ill** [ɪl] **1** adj (a) pred (sick) krank. **to fall** or **be taken ~** erkranken (with sth an etw dat), krank werden; **to feel ~** sich krank fühlen. (b) (bad) schlecht. ~ **feeling** böses Blut; **no ~ feeling?** Sie nehmen es mir hoffentlich nicht übel; **no ~ feeling!** ich nehme es Ihnen nicht übel; **due to ~ health** aus Gesundheitsgründen; **as ~ luck would have it** wie es der Teufel so will; ~ **will** böses Blut; **I don't bear them any ~ will** ich trage ihnen nichts nach; **it's an ~ wind (that blows nobody any good)** (Prov) so hat alles seine guten Seiten. **2** n **to think ~ of sb** schlecht von jdm denken; **to speak ~ of sb** schlecht über jdn reden. **3** adv schlecht. **he can ~ afford to refuse** er kann es sich (dat) schlecht leisten abzulehnen.
**I'll** [aɪl] = **I will; I shall.**
**ill**: ~-**advised** adj unklug; **you would be ~-advised to trust her** Sie wären schlecht beraten, wenn Sie ihr trauten; ~-**at-ease** adj unbehaglich; ~-**behaved** adj ungezogen; ~-**bred** adj schlecht erzogen; ~-**considered** adj action, words unüberlegt; ~-**defined** adj ungenau; ~-**disposed** adj to be ~-**disposed to(wards) sb** jdm übel gesinnt sein.
**illegal** [ɪ'liːgəl] adj unerlaubt; (against a specific law) gesetzwidrig; trade, possession etc illegal.
**illegality** [ˌɪliː'gælɪtɪ] n see adj Ungesetzlichkeit f; Gesetzwidrigkeit f; Illegalität f.
**illegally** [ɪ'liːgəlɪ] adv ~ **imported** illegal eingeführt; **you're ~ parked** Sie stehen im Parkverbot.
**illegible** [ɪ'ledʒəbl] adj unleserlich.
**illegitimate** [ˌɪlɪ'dʒɪtɪmɪt] adj (a) child unehelich. (b) (contrary to law) unzulässig; government unrechtmäßig.
**ill**: ~-**fated** adj (a) person vom Unglück verfolgt; (b) (doomed) unglückselig; ~-**founded** adj unbegründet; ~-**gotten gains** npl unrechtmäßiger Gewinn; ~-**humoured**, (US) ~-**humored** adj schlecht gelaunt.
**illicit** [ɪ'lɪsɪt] adj illegal; spirits schwarz gebrannt.
**ill-informed** ['ɪlɪn,fɔːmd] adj person schlecht informiert; criticism, speech wenig sachkundig.
**illiteracy** [ɪ'lɪtərəsɪ] n Analphabetentum nt.
**illiterate** [ɪ'lɪtərət] **1** adj **to be ~** Analphabet sein; (uncultured) person ungebildet. **2** n Analphabet(in f) m.
**ill**: ~-**judged** adj unklug; ~-**mannered** adj unhöflich; ~-**natured** adj bösartig.
**illness** ['ɪlnɪs] n Krankheit f.
**illogical** [ɪ'lɒdʒɪkəl] adj unlogisch.
**ill**: ~-**suited** adj (to one another) nicht zusammenpassend; (to sth) ungeeignet (to für); ~-**tempered** adj schlechtgelaunt; (habitually) übellaunig; ~-**timed** adj ungelegen; ~-**treat** vt schlecht behandeln; ~-**treatment** n schlechte Behandlung.
**illuminate** [ɪ'luːmɪneɪt] vt (a) room, street beleuchten; (spotlight etc) anstrahlen. ~**d display** Leuchtanzeige f; ~**d sign/advertisement** Leuchtzeichen nt/Leuchtreklame f. (b) (fig) question, subject erläutern.
**illuminating** [ɪ'luːmɪneɪtɪŋ] adj (instructive) auf-

schlußreich.

**illumination** [ɪˌluːmɪˈneɪʃən] *n* **(a)** *(of street etc)* Beleuchtung *f*. **(b)** ~s *pl* festliche Beleuchtung *f*. **(c)** *(fig)* Erläuterung *f*.

**illusion** [ɪˈluːʒən] *n* Illusion *f*. **to be under an** ~ einer Täuschung *(dat)* unterliegen; **to be under the** ~ **that** ... sich *(dat)* einbilden, daß ...; **to have no** ~s sich *(dat)* keine Illusionen machen.

**illusive** [ɪˈluːsɪv], **illusory** [ɪˈluːsərɪ] *adj* trügerisch.

**illustrate** [ˈɪləstreɪt] *vt* illustrieren; *(fig)* veranschaulichen. ~d **(magazine)** Illustrierte *f*.

**illustration** [ˌɪləsˈtreɪʃən] *n (picture)* Abbildung *f*, Illustration *f*. **by way of** ~ als Beispiel.

**illustrative** [ˈɪləstrətɪv] *adj* veranschaulichend.

**illustrator** [ˈɪləstreɪtəʳ] *n* Illustrator *m*.

**illustrious** [ɪˈlʌstrɪəs] *adj* glanzvoll, gefeiert; *deeds* glorreich.

**ILO** = **International Labour Organization** IAO *f*.

**I'm** [aɪm] = **I am.**

**image** [ˈɪmɪdʒ] *n* **(a)** *(carved etc)* Standbild *nt*; *(painted)* Bild *nt*; *(likeness)* Ebenbild *nt*. **he is the living** *or* **spitting** ~ **of his father** er ist seinem Vater wie aus dem Gesicht geschnitten. **(b)** *(mental picture)* Vorstellung *f*, Bild *nt*. **(c)** **(public)** ~ Image *nt*.

**imagery** [ˈɪmɪdʒərɪ] *n* Metaphorik *f*.

**imaginable** [ɪˈmædʒɪnəbl] *adj* denkbar. **the fastest way** ~ der denkbar schnellste Weg.

**imaginary** [ɪˈmædʒɪnərɪ] *adj danger* eingebildet, imaginär; *characters* frei ersonnen, erfunden.

**imagination** [ɪˌmædʒɪˈneɪʃən] *n (creative)* Phantasie, Vorstellungskraft *f*; *(self-deceptive)* Einbildung *f*. **to have (a vivid)** ~ (eine lebhafte) Phantasie haben; **use your** ~ lassen Sie Ihre Phantasie spielen; **it's only (your)** ~! das bilden Sie sich *(dat)* nur ein!

**imaginative** [ɪˈmædʒɪnətɪv] *adj* phantasievoll; *plan, idea also* einfallsreich.

**imagine** [ɪˈmædʒɪn] *vt* **(a)** *(picture)* sich *(dat)* vorstellen. **I can't** ~ **what you mean** ich kann mir nicht vorstellen, was Sie meinen; **you can't** ~ **how** ... Sie können sich nicht vorstellen, wie ...; **you can't** ~ **it!** Sie machen sich keine Vorstellung davon! **(b)** *(be under illusion)* sich *(dat)* einbilden. **don't** ~ **that** ... bilden Sie sich nur nicht ein, daß ...; **you're (just) imagining things** *(col)* Sie bilden sich das alles nur ein. **(c)** *(suppose)* annehmen. **is it time now? — I would** ~ **so** ist es soweit? — ich denke schon; **I would never have** ~d **he would have done that** ich hätte nie gedacht, daß er das tun würde.

**imbalance** [ɪmˈbæləns] *n* Unausgeglichenheit *f*.

**imbecile** [ˈɪmbəsiːl] *n* Idiot, Schwachkopf *m*; *(Med)* Schwachsinnige(r) *mf*.

**imbibe** [ɪmˈbaɪb] *vt (form, hum)* trinken, bechern *(hum)*.

**imbue** [ɪmˈbjuː] *vt (fig)* erfüllen.

**IMF** = **International Monetary Fund** IWF *m*.

**imitate** [ˈɪmɪteɪt] *vt* imitieren, nachahmen.

**imitation** [ˌɪmɪˈteɪʃən] **1** *n* Imitation, Nachahmung *f*. **to do an** ~ **of sb** jdn imitieren *or* nachahmen. **2** *adj* unecht. ~ **leather** Kunstleder *nt*.

**imitative** [ˈɪmɪtətɪv] *adj* imitativ *(geh)*.

**imitator** [ˈɪmɪteɪtəʳ] *n* Nachahmer, Imitator *m*.

**immaculate** [ɪˈmækjʊlɪt] *adj* tadellos; *(spotless)* makellos. **the I~ Conception** die Unbefleckte Empfängnis.

**immaculately** [ɪˈmækjʊlɪtlɪ] *adv* tadellos; *(spotlessly)* makellos.

**immaterial** [ˌɪməˈtɪərɪəl] *adj (unimportant)* unwesentlich. **it is quite** ~ **to me (whether)** ... es ist für mich unwichtig, (ob) ...; **that's (quite)** ~ das spielt (überhaupt) keine Rolle.

**immature** [ˌɪməˈtjʊəʳ] *adj (lit, fig)* unreif.

**immaturity** [ˌɪməˈtjʊərɪtɪ] *n* Unreife *f*.

**immeasurable** [ɪˈmeʒərəbl] *adj* unermeßlich.

**immediacy** [ɪˈmiːdɪəsɪ] *n* Unmittelbarkeit *f*; *(urgency)* Dringlichkeit *f*.

**immediate** [ɪˈmiːdɪət] *adj* **(a)** *(instant)* umgehend. **to take** ~ **action** sofort handeln. **(b)** *future etc* unmittelbar; *cause, successor also* direkt; *vicinity also* nächste. **the** ~ **family** die engste Familie.

**immediately** [ɪˈmiːdɪətlɪ] **1** *adv* sofort; *reply, return, depart also* umgehend. ~ **after/before** unmittelbar danach/davor. **2** *conj (Brit)* sobald.

**immemorial** [ˌɪmɪˈmɔːrɪəl] *adj*: **from time** ~ seit undenklichen Zeiten.

**immense** [ɪˈmens] *adj* enorm, immens.

**immensely** [ɪˈmenslɪ] *adv* unheimlich *(col)*, enorm; *grateful* äußerst.

**immensity** [ɪˈmensɪtɪ] *n* Unermeßlichkeit *f*.

**immerse** [ɪˈmɜːs] *vt* eintauchen *(in in +acc)*. **to be** ~d **in water** unter Wasser sein; **to** ~ **oneself in sth** *(fig)* sich in etw *(acc)* vertiefen.

**immersion** [ɪˈmɜːʃən] *n* **(a)** Eintauchen *nt*. ~ **heater** *(Brit)* Wasserboiler *m*; *(for jug etc)* Tauchsieder *m*. **(b)** *(fig)* Vertieftsein *nt*.

**immigrant** [ˈɪmɪgrənt] **1** *n* Einwanderer *m*, Einwanderin *f*. **2** *attr* ~ **workers** ausländische Arbeitnehmer *pl*; *(esp in western Germany also)* Gastarbeiter *pl*.

**immigrate** [ˈɪmɪgreɪt] *vi* einwandern *(to in +acc)*.

**immigration** [ˌɪmɪˈgreɪʃən] *n* Einwanderung, Immigration *f*; *(at airport etc)* Einwanderungsstelle *f*; *(~ authorities)* Einwanderungsbehörde *f*. **to go through** ~ die Einwanderungsformalitäten erledigen.

**imminent** [ˈɪmɪnənt] *adj* bevorstehend. **to be** ~ unmittelbar bevorstehen.

**immobile** [ɪˈməʊbaɪl] *adj* unbeweglich; *(not able to move) person* bewegungslos.

**immobility** [ˌɪməʊˈbɪlɪtɪ] *n see adj* Unbeweglichkeit *f*; Bewegungslosigkeit *f*.

**immobilize** [ɪˈməʊbɪlaɪz] *vt traffic* zum Erliegen bringen; *army* bewegungsunfähig machen; *(Fin) capital* festlegen.

**immoderate** [ɪˈmɒdərɪt] *adj desire* übermäßig; *demands also* überzogen; *views also* übersteigert.

**immodest** [ɪˈmɒdɪst] *adj* unbescheiden.

**immodesty** [ɪˈmɒdɪstɪ] *n* Unbescheidenheit *f*.

**immoral** [ɪˈmɒrəl] *adj action* unmoralisch; *behaviour also* unsittlich; *person also* sittenlos.

**immorality** [ˌɪməˈrælɪtɪ] *n* Unmoral *f*; *(of person also)* Sittenlosigkeit *f*; *(immoral act)* Unsittlichkeit *f*.

**immortal** [ɪˈmɔːtl] *adj* unsterblich.

**immortality** [ˌɪmɔːˈtælɪtɪ] *n* Unsterblichkeit *f*.

**immortalize** [ɪˈmɔːtəlaɪz] *vt* unsterblich machen.

**immovable** [ɪˈmuːvəbl] *adj (lit)* unbeweglich; *(fig) obstacle* unüberwindlich.

**immune** [ɪˈmjuːn] *adj (Med)* immun *(to gegen)*; *(fig)* sicher *(from vor +dat)*. ~ **system** Immunsystem *nt*; ~ **deficiency syndrome** Immunschwächekrankheit *f*.

**immunity** [ɪˈmjuːnɪtɪ] *n (Med, diplomatic)* Immunität *f*; *(fig)* Sicherheit *f*.

**immunization** [ˌɪmjʊnaɪˈzeɪʃən] *n* Immunisierung *f*.

**immunize** [ˈɪmjʊnaɪz] *vt* immunisieren.

**immunodeficiency** [ˌɪmjʊnəʊdɪˈfɪʃənsɪ] *n* Immunschwäche *f*.

**immutable** [ɪˈmjuːtəbl] *adj* unveränderlich.

**imp** [ɪmp] *n* Kobold *m*; *(col: child also)* Schlingel *m (col)*.

**impact** [ˈɪmpækt] *n* Aufprall *m (on auf +acc)*; *(of two moving objects)* Zusammenprall *m*; *(of falling object) (on house)* Einschlag *m (on in +acc)*; *(on ground)* Aufschlag *m (on auf +dat)*; *(force)* Wucht *f*;

*(fig)* (Aus)wirkung *f (on* auf *+acc).* **on ~ (with)** beim Aufprall (auf *+acc)*/Zusammenprall (mit) *etc*; **his speech had a great ~ on his audience** seine Rede machte großen Eindruck auf seine Zuhörer.
**impair** [ɪm'pɛəʳ] *vt* beeinträchtigen.
**impale** [ɪm'peɪl] *vt* aufspießen *(on* auf *+dat).*
**impart** [ɪm'pɑːt] *vt* **(a)** *information* mitteilen; *knowledge* vermitteln. **(b)** *(bestow)* verleihen *(to dat).*
**impartial** [ɪm'pɑːʃəl] *adj person, attitude* unvoreingenommen; *decision also* gerecht.
**impartiality** [ɪm,pɑːʃɪ'ælɪtɪ] *n see adj* Unvoreingenommenheit *f*; Gerechtigkeit *f.*
**impassable** [ɪm'pɑːsəbl] *adj* unpassierbar.
**impasse** [ɪm'pɑːs] *n (fig)* Sackgasse *f.* **to have reached an ~** sich festgefahren haben.
**impassioned** [ɪm'pæʃnd] *adj* leidenschaftlich.
**impassive** [ɪm'pæsɪv] *adj* gelassen.
**impatience** [ɪm'peɪʃəns] *n* Ungeduld *f*; *(intolerance)* Unduldsamkeit *f.*
**impatient** [ɪm'peɪʃənt] *adj* ungeduldig; *(intolerant)* unduldsam *(of* gegenüber*).*
**impatiently** [ɪm'peɪʃəntlɪ] *adv* ungeduldig.
**impeach** [ɪm'piːtʃ] *vt* **(a)** *(Jur: accuse) public official* (eines Amtsvergehens) anklagen. **(b)** *sb's character, motives* in Frage stellen.
**impeachment** [ɪm'piːtʃmənt] *n (Jur)* Anklage *f* (wegen eines Amtsvergehens).
**impeccable** [ɪm'pekəbl] *adj* tadellos.
**impecunious** [ɪmpɪ'kjuːnɪəs] *adj* mittellos.
**impede** [ɪm'piːd] *vt person* hindern; *action, traffic* behindern.
**impediment** [ɪm'pedɪmənt] *n* Hindernis *nt*; *(Med)* Behinderung *f.* **speech ~** Sprachfehler *m.*
**impel** [ɪm'pel] *vt* **(a)** *(force)* **to ~ sb to do sth** jdn (dazu) nötigen, etw zu tun. **(b)** *(drive on)* (voran)treiben.
**impending** [ɪm'pendɪŋ] *adj* bevorstehend; *storm also* heraufziehend; *danger* drohend.
**impenetrable** [ɪm'penɪtrəbl] *adj* undurchdringlich; *fortress* uneinnehmbar; *mind, mystery* unergründlich; *theory* undurchschaubar.
**imperative** [ɪm'perətɪv] **1** *adj* **to be ~** unbedingt nötig sein. **2** *n (Gram)* Imperativ *m.* **in the ~** im Imperativ.
**imperceptible** [,ɪmpə'septəbl] *adj* nicht wahrnehmbar; *difference also* unmerklich.
**imperceptibly** [ɪmpə'septɪblɪ] *adv* kaum wahrnehmbar; *move* kaum merklich.
**imperfect** [ɪm'pɜːfɪkt] **1** *adj* **(a)** *(faulty)* unvollkommen; *(Comm) goods* fehlerhaft. **(b)** *(incomplete)* unvollständig. **2** *n (Gram)* Imperfekt *nt.*
**imperfection** [,ɪmpə'fekʃən] *n* **(a)** *no pl see adj* Unvollkommenheit *f*; Unvollständigkeit *f.* **(b)** *(fault, defect)* Mangel *m.*
**imperfectly** [ɪm'pɜːfɪktlɪ] *adv* unvollkommen; *(esp Comm)* fehlerhaft.
**imperial** [ɪm'pɪərɪəl] *adj* **(a)** *(of empire)* Reichs-; *(of emperor)* kaiserlich, Kaiser-. **(b)** *(Brit) weights, measures* britisch.
**imperialism** [ɪm'pɪərɪəlɪzəm] *n* Imperialismus *m.*
**imperialist** [ɪm'pɪərɪəlɪst] *n* Imperialist (in *f) m.*
**imperil** [ɪm'perɪl] *vt* gefährden.
**imperious** [ɪm'pɪərɪəs] *adj* gebieterisch.
**imperishable** [ɪm'perɪʃəbl] *adj* unverderblich.
**impermeable** [ɪm'pɜːmɪəbl] *adj* undurchlässig.
**impersonal** [,ɪm'pɜːsnl] *adj* unpersönlich.
**impersonate** [ɪm'pɜːsəneɪt] *vt* sich ausgeben als; *(take off)* imitieren, nachahmen.
**impersonation** [ɪm,pɜːsə'neɪʃən] *n see vt* Verkörperung *f*; Imitation, Nachahmung *f.* **he does ~s of politicians** er imitiert Politiker.

**impersonator** [ɪm'pɜːsəneɪtəʳ] *n (Theat)* Imitator (in *f) m.*
**impertinence** [ɪm'pɜːtɪnəns] *n* Unverschämtheit *f.*
**impertinent** [ɪm'pɜːtɪnənt] *adj* unverschämt *(to* zu, gegenüber*).*
**imperturbable** [,ɪmpə'tɜːbəbl] *adj* unerschütterlich.
**impervious** [ɪm'pɜːvɪəs] *adj* undurchlässig; *(fig)* unzugänglich *(to* für*); (criticism)* unberührt *(to* von*).*
**impetuosity** [ɪm,petjʊ'ɒsɪtɪ] *n* **(a)** *see adj* Ungestüm *nt*; Impulsivität *f.* **(b)** *(impetuous behaviour)* ungestümes Handeln.
**impetuous** [ɪm'petjʊəs] *adj act, person* ungestüm; *decision* impulsiv.
**impetus** ['ɪmpɪtəs] *n (lit, fig)* Impuls *m*; *(force)* Kraft *f*; *(momentum)* Schwung *m.*
▸**impinge on** [ɪm'pɪndʒɒn] *vi +prep obj* sich auswirken auf *(+acc)*, beeinflussen; *(on sb's rights etc also)* einschränken.
**impish** ['ɪmpɪʃ] *adj* schelmisch.
**implacable** [ɪm'plækəbl] *adj* unerbittlich.
**implant** [ɪm'plɑːnt] **1** *vt* **(a)** *(fig)* einimpfen *(in sb* jdm*).* **(b)** *(Med)* einpflanzen. **2** ['ɪmplɑːnt] *n* Implantat *nt.*
**implausible** [ɪm'plɔːzəbl] *adj* nicht plausibel; *story, excuse also* unglaubwürdig.
**implement** ['ɪmplɪmənt] **1** *n* Gerät *nt*; *(tool also)* Werkzeug *nt.* **2** [ɪmplɪ'ment] *vt law* vollziehen; *promise* erfüllen; *plan etc* durchführen.
**implementation** [,ɪmplɪmen'teɪʃən] *n see vt* Vollzug *m*; Erfüllung *f*; Durchführung *f.*
**implicate** ['ɪmplɪkeɪt] *vt* **to ~ sb in sth** jdn in etw verwickeln.
**implication** [,ɪmplɪ'keɪʃən] *n* Implikation *f*; *(of law, agreement etc also)* Auswirkung *f.* **the possible ~s of his decision** die ganze Tragweite seiner Entscheidung; **by ~** implizit.
**implicit** [ɪm'plɪsɪt] *adj* **(a)** *(implied)* implizit; *threat also* indirekt; *recognition also* stillschweigend. **to be ~ in sth** durch etw impliziert werden; *(in contract etc)* in etw *(dat)* impliziert sein. **(b)** *(unquestioning) confidence* absolut.
**implicitly** [ɪm'plɪsɪtlɪ] *adv* **(a)** *(by implication)* implizit. **(b)** *(unquestioningly)* absolut.
**implore** [ɪm'plɔːʳ] *vt person* anflehen.
**imploring** *adj*, **~ly** *adv* [ɪm'plɔːrɪŋ, -lɪ] flehend; *beg also* inständig.
**imply** [ɪm'plaɪ] *vt* **(a)** andeuten, implizieren. **are you ~ing ...?** wollen Sie damit vielleicht andeuten, daß ...?; **it implies that he has changed his mind** das deutet darauf hin, daß er es sich *(dat)* anders überlegt hat. **(b)** *(involve)* bedeuten.
**impolite** [,ɪmpə'laɪt] *adj* unhöflich.
**impoliteness** [,ɪmpə'laɪtnɪs] *n* Unhöflichkeit *f.*
**imponderable** [ɪm'pɒndərəbl] *adj* unberechenbar.
**import 1** ['ɪmpɔːt] *n* **(a)** *(Comm)* Import *m*, Einfuhr *f.* **(b)** *(meaning)* Bedeutung *f.* **2** [ɪm'pɔːt] *vt (Comm)* einführen, importieren; *(Comp)* importieren.
**importance** [ɪm'pɔːtəns] *n* Wichtigkeit *f*; *(significance also)* Bedeutung *f*; *(influence also)* Einfluß *m.* **to be of no (great) ~** nicht (besonders) wichtig sein; **to attach the greatest ~ to sth** einer Sache *(dat)* größte Bedeutung beimessen.
**important** [ɪm'pɔːtənt] *adj* wichtig; *(significant also)* bedeutend; *(influential)* einflußreich. **it's not ~** *(doesn't matter)* das macht nichts; **to try to look ~** sich *(dat)* ein gewichtiges Aussehen geben.
**importantly** [ɪm'pɔːtəntlɪ] *adj (usu pej)* wichtigtuerisch *(pej).*
**import** *in cpds* Einfuhr-, Import-; **~ duty** *n* Einfuhrzoll *m.*
**importer** [ɪm'pɔːtəʳ] *n* Importeur (in *f) m (of* von*).*

**import:** ~ **licence** *(Brit)* or **license** *(US) n* Einfuhrlizenz *f*; ~ **quota** Einfuhrkontingent *nt*.

**impose** [ɪmˈpəʊz] **1** *vt task, conditions* auferlegen *(on sb* jdm*); sanctions, fine* verhängen *(on gegen); tax* erheben. **to** ~ **oneself on sb** sich jdm aufdrängen. **2** *vi* zur Last fallen *(on sb* jdm*).* **to** ~ **on sb's kindness** jds Freundlichkeit ausnützen.

**imposing** [ɪmˈpəʊzɪŋ] *adj* beeindruckend; *appearance, building also* stattlich.

**imposition** [ˌɪmpəˈzɪʃən] *n* **(a)** *no pl see vt* Auferlegung *f*; Verhängung *f*. **(b)** *(tax)* Steuer *f (on* für, auf +*dat).* **(c)** *(taking advantage)* Zumutung *f (on* für*).* **if it's not too much of an** ~ wenn es nicht zuviel Mühe macht.

**impossibility** [ɪmˌpɒsəˈbɪlɪtɪ] *n* Unmöglichkeit *f*.

**impossible** [ɪmˈpɒsəbl] **1** *adj* unmöglich. ~! ausgeschlossen! **2** *n* Unmögliche(s) *nt*. **to ask for the** ~ Unmögliches verlangen; **to do the** ~ Unmögliches tun.

**impossibly** [ɪmˈpɒsəblɪ] *adv* unmöglich.

**impostor** [ɪmˈpɒstəʳ] *n* Hochstapler(in *f*) *m*.

**impotence** [ˈɪmpətəns] *n see adj* Schwäche *f*; Impotenz *f*; Machtlosigkeit *f*.

**impotent** [ˈɪmpətənt] *adj (physically)* schwach; *(sexually)* impotent; *(fig)* machtlos; *rage* ohnmächtig.

**impound** [ɪmˈpaʊnd] *vt* **(a)** *(seize) goods* beschlagnahmen. **(b)** *cattle* einsperren; *car* abschleppen (lassen).

**impoverished** [ɪmˈpɒvərɪʃt] *adj* verarmt; *soil* ausgelaugt.

**impoverishment** [ɪmˈpɒvərɪʃmənt] *n* Verarmung *f*; *(of soil)* Auslaugung *f*.

**impracticable** [ɪmˈpræktɪkəbl] *adj* impraktikabel; *design, size* unbrauchbar; *road* schwer befahrbar.

**impractical** [ɪmˈpræktɪkəl] *adj* unpraktisch; *scheme also* unbrauchbar.

**imprecise** [ˌɪmprɪˈsaɪs] *adj* ungenau, unpräzis(e).

**imprecision** [ˌɪmprɪˈsɪʒən] *n* Ungenauigkeit *f*.

**impregnable** [ɪmˈpregnəbl] *adj fortress* uneinnehmbar; *(fig) position* unerschütterlich.

**impregnate** [ˈɪmpregneɪt] *vt* **(a)** *(saturate)* tränken. **(b)** *(Biol: fertilize)* befruchten; *humans also* schwängern.

**impresario** [ˌɪmpreˈsɑːrɪəʊ] *n* Theater-/Operndirektor *m*.

**impress** [ɪmˈpres] *vt* **(a)** beeindrucken; *(memorably also)* Eindruck machen auf *(+acc); (arouse admiration in)* imponieren *(+dat).* **he** ~**ed me favourably/unfavourably** er hat einen/keinen guten Eindruck auf mich gemacht. **(b) to** ~ **a pattern onto sth** ein Muster auf etw *(acc)* aufdrücken.

**impression** [ɪmˈpreʃən] *n* **(a)** Eindruck *m*. **to make a good** ~ **on sb** einen guten Eindruck auf jdn machen; **first** ~**s** der erste Eindruck; **to give sb the** ~ **that ...** jdm den Eindruck vermitteln, daß ...; **I was under the** ~ **that ...** ich hatte den Eindruck, daß ... **(b)** *(on wax etc)* Abdruck *m*. **(c)** *(of book etc)* Nachdruck *m*. **first** ~ Erstdruck *m*. **(d)** *(take-off)* Nachahmung, Imitation *f*. **to do an** ~ **of sb** jdn imitieren.

**impressionable** [ɪmˈpreʃnəbl] *adj* für Eindrücke empfänglich. **at an** ~ **age** in einem Alter, in dem man für Eindrücke besonders empfänglich ist.

**impressionism** [ɪmˈpreʃənɪzəm] *n* Impressionismus *m*.

**impressionist** [ɪmˈpreʃənɪst] *n* Impressionist(in *f*) *m*.

**impressive** [ɪmˈpresɪv] *adj* beeindruckend; *performance, personality also* eindrucksvoll.

**impressively** [ɪmˈpresɪvlɪ] *adv see adj*.

**imprint** [ɪmˈprɪnt] **1** *vt seal, paper etc* aufprägen *(on* auf *+acc); (on paper)* aufdrucken *(on* auf *+acc).* **to**

~ **itself on sb's mind** sich jdm einprägen. **2** [ˈɪmprɪnt] *n* **(a)** *(on wax etc)* Abdruck *m*. **(b)** *(Typ)* Impressum *nt*.

**imprison** [ɪmˈprɪzn] *(lit)* inhaftieren; *(fig)* gefangenhalten.

**imprisonment** [ɪmˈprɪznmənt] *n (action)* Inhaftierung *f*; *(state)* Gefangenschaft *f*. **to sentence sb to one month's** ~ jdn zu einem Monat Gefängnis verurteilen.

**improbability** [ɪmˌprɒbəˈbɪlɪtɪ] *n* Unwahrscheinlichkeit *f*.

**improbable** [ɪmˈprɒbəbl] *adj* unwahrscheinlich.

**impromptu** [ɪmˈprɒmptjuː] **1** *adj* improvisiert. ~ **speech** Stegreifrede *f*. **2** *adv* improvisiert; *perform* aus dem Stegreif.

**improper** [ɪmˈprɒpəʳ] *adj (unsuitable)* unpassend; *(unseemly)* unschicklich; *(indecent)* unanständig; *use* unsachgemäß; *conduct* unehrenhaft.

**improperly** [ɪmˈprɒpəlɪ] *adv see adj*.

**impropriety** [ˌɪmprəˈpraɪətɪ] *n* Unschicklichkeit *f*.

**improve** [ɪmˈpruːv] **1** *vt* verbessern; *production* steigern; *knowledge* erweitern; *low salaries* aufbessern. **to** ~ **one's mind** sich weiterbilden. **2** *vi* besser werden; *production* sich steigern; *situation, pupil* sich bessern. **the patient is improving** dem Patienten geht es besser.

▶**improve (up)on** *vi* +*prep obj* übertreffen; *offer* überbieten.

**improvement** [ɪmˈpruːvmənt] *n see vt* Verbesserung *f*; Steigerung *f*; Erweiterung *f*; Aufbesserung *f*; *(in health)* Besserung *f*; *(in studies also)* Fortschritte *pl*. **to carry out** ~**s to a house** ein Haus modernisieren; **it's an** ~ **on the old one** es ist eine Verbesserung gegenüber dem/der alten.

**improvisation** [ˌɪmprəvaɪˈzeɪʃən] *n* Improvisation *f*.

**improvise** [ˈɪmprəvaɪz] *vti* improvisieren.

**imprudent** [ɪmˈpruːdənt] *adj* unklug.

**impudence** [ˈɪmpjʊdəns] *n* Unverschämtheit, Frechheit *f*.

**impudent** [ˈɪmpjʊdənt] *adj* unverschämt.

**impugn** [ɪmˈpjuːn] *vt person* angreifen; *motives, honesty* in Zweifel ziehen.

**impulse** [ˈɪmpʌls] *n* Impuls *m*. **on** ~ aus einem Impuls heraus; ~ **buying** spontanes Kaufen.

**impulsive** *adj*, ~**ly** *adv* [ɪmˈpʌlsɪv, -lɪ] impulsiv; *act, remark also* spontan.

**impulsiveness** [ɪmˈpʌlsɪvnɪs] *n* Impulsivität *f*.

**impunity** [ɪmˈpjuːnɪtɪ] *n*: **with** ~ ungestraft.

**impure** [ɪmˈpjʊəʳ] *adj water, food* verunreinigt; *thoughts, motives* unsauber.

**impurity** [ɪmˈpjʊərɪtɪ] *n see adj* Unreinheit *f*; Unsauberkeit *f*.

**impute** [ɪmˈpjuːt] *vt* zuschreiben *(to sb/sth* jdm/einer Sache*).*

**IN** *(US Post)* = **Indiana**.

**in** = **inch**.

**in** [ɪn] **1** *prep* **(a)** *(position)* in *(+dat); (with motion)* in *(+acc).* **it was** ~ **the car** es war im Auto; **he put it** ~ **the car** er legte es ins Auto; ~ **the street** auf der/die Straße; ~ **Thompson Street** in der Thompsonstraße; ~ **bed/prison** im Bett/Gefängnis; ~ **Germany/Iran/Switzerland/the United States** in Deutschland/im Iran/in der Schweiz/in den Vereinigten Staaten.

**(b) we find it** ~ **Dickens** wir finden das bei Dickens; **rare** ~ **a child of that age** selten bei einem Kind in diesem Alter; **we've got a good recruit** ~ **her** sie ist für uns eine gute neue Mitarbeiterin.

**(c)** *(time)* in *(+dat); (within)* innerhalb von. ~ **1974** (im Jahre) 1974; ~ **the sixties** in den sechziger Jahren; ~ **June** im Juni; ~ **(the) spring** im Frühling; ~

the morning(s) morgens, am Morgen; ~ the afternoon am Nachmittag; ~ the daytime tagsüber; ~ the evening am Abend; three o'clock ~ the afternoon drei Uhr nachmittags; ~ those days damals; ~ a week('s time) in einer Woche; I haven't seen him ~ years ich habe ihn seit Jahren nicht mehr gesehen.

(d) (manner, state, condition) ~ German auf Deutsch; to pay ~ dollars in Dollar bezahlen; to walk ~ twos zu zweit gehen; ~ anger im Zorn; ~ poverty in Armut; dressed ~ white weiß gekleidet; the lady ~ green die Dame in Grün; to write ~ ink mit Tinte schreiben; to die ~ hundreds zu Hunderten sterben.

(e) (ratio) there are 12 inches ~ a foot ein Fuß hat 12 Zoll; one ~ ten jeder zehnte.

(f) (in respect of) blind ~ the left eye auf dem linken Auge or links blind; a rise ~ prices ein Preisanstieg m; ten feet ~ height zehn Fuß hoch; five ~ number fünf an der Zahl.

(g) (occupation) he is ~ the army er ist beim Militär; he is ~ banking er ist im Bankwesen (tätig).

(h) ~ saying this, I want to ... wenn ich das sage, will ich ...; ~ trying to escape beim Fluchtversuch; ~ that insofern als.

2 adv (a) da; (at home also) zu Hause. the train is ~ der Zug ist da or angekommen; the harvest is ~ die Ernte ist eingebracht; we were asked ~ wir wurden hereingebeten. (b) miniskirts are ~ Miniröcke sind in (col). (c) (phrases) he's ~ for a surprise/~ for it der kann sich auf eine Überraschung/auf was (col) gefaßt machen; we are ~ for rain uns (dat) steht Regen bevor; you don't know what you are ~ for Sie wissen nicht, was Ihnen bevorsteht; he hasn't got it ~ him er hat nicht das Zeug dazu; to have it ~ for sb (col) es auf jdn abgesehen haben (col); to be ~ on sth an einer Sache beteiligt sein; on secret etc über etw (acc) Bescheid wissen.

3 adj attr (col) in inv (col). an ~ subject ein Modefach nt; the ~ thing is to ... es ist in (col) or zur Zeit Mode, zu ...

4 n to know the ~s and outs of a matter bei einer Sache genau Bescheid wissen.

**inability** [ˌɪnəˈbɪlɪtɪ] n Unfähigkeit f.

**inaccessibility** [ˈɪnækˌsesəˈbɪlɪtɪ] n Unzugänglichkeit f.

**inaccessible** [ˌɪnækˈsesəbl] adj unzugänglich.

**inaccuracy** [ɪnˈækjʊrəsɪ] n see adj Ungenauigkeit f; Unrichtigkeit f.

**inaccurate** [ɪnˈækjʊrɪt] adj ungenau; (not correct) unrichtig.

**inaction** [ɪnˈækʃən] n Untätigkeit f.

**inactive** [ɪnˈæktɪv] adj untätig; volcano erloschen.

**inactivity** [ˌɪnækˈtɪvɪtɪ] n Untätigkeit f; (of mind) Trägheit f; (Comm) Flaute f.

**inadequacy** [ɪnˈædɪkwəsɪ] n see adj Unzulänglichkeit f; Unangemessenheit f.

**inadequate** [ɪnˈædɪkwɪt] adj unzulänglich; supplies, reasons also unzureichend; measures unangemessen. she makes him feel ~ sie gibt ihm das Gefühl der Unzulänglichkeit.

**inadmissible** [ˌɪnədˈmɪsəbl] adj unzulässig.

**inadvertent** [ˌɪnədˈvɜːtənt] adj unbeabsichtigt, ungewollt.

**inadvertently** [ˌɪnədˈvɜːtəntlɪ] adv versehentlich.

**inadvisable** [ˌɪnədˈvaɪzəbl] adj unratsam.

**inane** [ɪˈneɪn] adj dumm.

**inanimate** [ɪnˈænɪmɪt] adj leblos; nature unbelebt.

**inanity** [ɪˈnænɪtɪ] n Dummheit f.

**inapplicable** [ɪnˈæplɪkəbl] adj answer unzutreffend; rules nicht anwendbar (to auf +acc).

**inappropriate** [ˌɪnəˈprəʊprɪɪt] adj unpassend; action also unangemessen.

**inapt** [ɪnˈæpt] adj ungeschickt.

**inaptitude** [ɪnˈæptɪtjuːd] n (for work etc) Untauglichkeit f; (of remark) Ungeschicktheit f.

**inarticulate** [ˌɪnɑːˈtɪkjʊlɪt] adj sounds, writings unverständlich. she's very ~ sie kann sich nur schlecht ausdrücken.

**inartistic** [ˌɪnɑːˈtɪstɪk] adj unkünstlerisch.

**inasmuch** [ˌɪnəzˈmʌtʃ] adv: ~ as da, weil; (to the extent that) insofern als.

**inattention** [ˌɪnəˈtenʃən] n Unaufmerksamkeit f. ~ to detail Ungenauigkeit f im Detail.

**inattentive** [ˌɪnəˈtentɪv] adj unaufmerksam.

**inaudible** [ɪnˈɔːdəbl] adj unhörbar.

**inaugural** [ɪˈnɔːgjʊrəl] adj lecture Antritts-.

**inaugurate** [ɪˈnɔːgjʊreɪt] vt president, official (feierlich) in sein/ihr Amt einführen; building einweihen; exhibition eröffnen; era einleiten.

**inauguration** [ɪˈnɔːgjʊˈreɪʃən] n see vt Amtseinführung f; Einweihung f; Eröffnung f; Beginn m.

**inauspicious** [ˌɪnɔːsˈpɪʃəs] adj unheilverheißend.

**in-between** [ɪnbɪˈtwiːn] (col) adj Mittel-, Zwischen-. it is sort of ~ es ist so ein Mittelding; ~ stage Zwischenstadium nt; ~ times zwischendurch.

**inborn** [ˈɪnbɔːn] adj angeboren.

**inbred** [ˈɪnbred] adj angeboren.

**inbreeding** [ˈɪnbriːdɪŋ] n Inzucht f.

**inbuilt** [ˈɪnbɪlt] adj (Tech) integriert; (fig: inborn) angeboren.

**Inc** (US) = **Incorporated**.

**Inca** [ˈɪŋkə] n (Hist) Inka m.

**incalculable** [ɪnˈkælkjʊləbl] adj amount unermeßlich; consequences unabsehbar.

**incantation** [ˌɪnkænˈteɪʃən] n Zauber(spruch) m; (act) Beschwörung f.

**incapable** [ɪnˈkeɪpəbl] adj person unfähig; (physically) hilflos. to be ~ of doing sth unfähig sein, etw zu tun; ~ of working arbeitsunfähig; ~ of tenderness zu Zärtlichkeit nicht fähig.

**incapacitate** [ˌɪnkəˈpæsɪteɪt] vt unfähig machen. physically ~d körperlich behindert.

**incapacity** [ˌɪnkəˈpæsɪtɪ] n Unfähigkeit f (for für).

**in-car** [ˈɪnkɑːr] adj attr Auto-; entertainment während der Fahrt.

**incarcerate** [ɪnˈkɑːsəreɪt] vt einkerkern.

**incarnate** [ɪnˈkɑːnɪt] adj (Rel) menschgeworden; (personified) leibhaftig attr, in Person. the devil ~ der leibhaftige Teufel.

**incarnation** [ˌɪnkɑːˈneɪʃən] n (Rel) Menschwerdung f; (fig) Verkörperung f.

**incendiary** [ɪnˈsendɪərɪ] 1 adj (lit) bomb Brand-. ~ device Brandsatz m. 2 n (bomb) Brandbombe f.

**incense¹** [ɪnˈsens] vt wütend machen. ~d wütend, erbost (at, by über +acc).

**incense²** [ˈɪnsens] n (Eccl) Weihrauch m.

**incentive** [ɪnˈsentɪv] n Anreiz m. ~ bonus Leistungszulage f; ~ scheme (Ind) Anreizsystem nt.

**inception** [ɪnˈsepʃən] n Beginn, Anfang m. from its ~ von Anfang an.

**incessant** [ɪnˈsesnt] adj unaufhörlich; noise ununterbrochen.

**incest** [ˈɪnsest] n Inzest m.

**incestuous** [ɪnˈsestjʊəs] adj inzestuös.

**inch** [ɪntʃ] 1 n Zoll, Inch m. a few ~es ≈ ein paar Zentimeter; ~ by ~ ≈ Zentimeter um Zentimeter; he came within an ~ of victory er hätte um ein Haar gewonnen; the lorry missed me by ~es der Lastwagen hat mich um Haaresbreite verfehlt; he is every ~ a soldier er ist vom Scheitel bis zur Sohle ein Soldat; **give him an ~ and he'll take a mile** *(prov)* wenn man ihm den kleinen Finger gibt, nimmt er die ganze Hand *(prov)*. **2** *vi* **to ~ forward** sich millimeterweise vorwärtsbewegen; **because prices are ~ing up** weil die Preise allmählich ansteigen; **the Dutch swimmer is ~ing ahead** der holländische Schwimmer schiebt sich langsam an die Spitze.

**incidence** ['ɪnsɪdəns] *n (of crime)* Häufigkeit *f*. **angle of ~** *(Opt)* Einfallswinkel *m*.

**incident** ['ɪnsɪdənt] *n (event)* Ereignis *nt*, Vorfall *m*; *(diplomatic etc)* Zwischenfall *m*. **~ room** Einsatzzentrale *f*.

**incidental** [,ɪnsɪ'dentl] *adj (secondary etc)* nebensächlich; *remark* beiläufig. **~ music** Begleitmusik *f*; *(for a play)* Bühnenmusik *f*; **~ expenses** Nebenkosten *pl*.

**incidentally** [,ɪnsɪ'dentəlɪ] *adv (by the way)* übrigens.

**incinerate** [ɪn'sɪnəreɪt] *vt* verbrennen.

**incinerator** [ɪn'sɪnəreɪtər] *n* (Müll)verbrennungsanlage *f*; *(garden ~)* Verbrennungsofen *m*.

**incipient** [ɪn'sɪpɪənt] *adj* beginnend.

**incision** [ɪn'sɪʒən] *n* Schnitt *m*; *(Med)* Einschnitt *m*.

**incisive** [ɪn'saɪsɪv] *adj style* prägnant; *criticism* treffend; *mind* scharf; *person* scharfsinnig.

**incisor** [ɪn'saɪzər] *n* Schneidezahn *m*.

**incite** [ɪn'saɪt] *vt* aufhetzen *(to* zu +*dat)*.

**incitement** [ɪn'saɪtmənt] *n* Aufhetzung *f*.

**incl** = **inclusive, including** inkl.

**inclement** [ɪn'klemənt] *adj weather* unfreundlich.

**inclination** [,ɪnklɪ'neɪʃən] *n* **(a)** Neigung *f*. **he follows his (own) ~s** er tut das, wozu er Lust hat; **I have no ~ to see him again** ich habe kein Bedürfnis, ihn wiederzusehen; **he showed no ~ to leave** er machte keine Anstalten zu gehen. **(b)** *(of hill, slope etc)* Gefälle *nt*.

**incline** [ɪn'klaɪn] **1** *vt* **(a)** *head, roof* neigen. **(b)** *(dispose)* veranlassen, bewegen. **this ~s me to think that he must be lying** das läßt mich vermuten, daß er lügt. **2** *vi* **(a)** *(slope)* sich neigen; *(ground also)* abfallen. **(b)** *(tend)* **to ~ to sth** zu etw neigen. **3** ['ɪnklaɪn] *n* Neigung *f*; *(of hill)* Abhang *m*; *(gradient: Rail etc)* Gefälle *nt*.

**inclined** [ɪn'klaɪnd] *adj* **to be ~ to do sth** *(wish to)* etw tun wollen; *(tend to)* dazu neigen, etw zu tun; **they are ~ to be late** sie kommen gern zu spät; **I am ~ to think that ...** ich neige zu der Ansicht, daß ...; **if you feel ~** wenn Sie Lust haben; **if you're ~ that way** wenn Ihnen so etwas liegt; **I'm ~ to disagree** ich möchte da doch widersprechen; **it's ~ to break** das bricht leicht.

**include** [ɪn'kluːd] *vt* einschließen; *(on list, in group etc)* aufnehmen. **the tip is not ~d in the bill** Trinkgeld ist in der Rechnung nicht inbegriffen; **the invitation ~s everybody** die Einladung betrifft alle; **the children ~d** einschließlich der Kinder; **does that ~ me?** gilt das auch für mich?

**including** [ɪn'kluːdɪŋ] *prep* einschließlich *(+gen)*. **~ service** inklusive Bedienung; **not ~ service** Bedienung nicht inbegriffen; **up to and ~ March 4th** bis einschließlich 4. März.

**inclusion** [ɪn'kluːʒən] *n (in a team, list)* Aufnahme *f*; *(of an ingredient)* Beigabe *f*.

**inclusive** [ɪn'kluːsɪv] *adj* einschließlich; *price* Pauschal-. **to be ~ of** einschließlich *(+gen)* sein; **from 1st to 6th May ~** vom 1. bis einschließlich 6. Mai.

**incognito** [,ɪnkɒg'niːtəʊ] *adv* inkognito.

**incoherent** [,ɪnkəʊ'hɪərənt] *adj style, argument* zusammenhanglos; *speech also* wirr; *drunk etc*

schwer verständlich. **he was totally ~** man konnte ihn überhaupt nicht verstehen.

**incoherently** [,ɪnkəʊ'hɪərəntlɪ] *adv* zusammenhanglos.

**income** ['ɪnkʌm] *n* Einkommen *nt*; *(receipts)* Einkünfte *pl*.

**income: ~ bracket** *n* Einkommensklasse *f*; **~ group** *n* Einkommensgruppe *f*; **~s policy** *n* Lohnpolitik *f*; **~ support** *n (Brit)* ≃ Sozialhilfe *f*; **~ tax** *n* Lohnsteuer *f*; **~ tax return** *n* Steuererklärung *f*.

**incoming** ['ɪn,kʌmɪŋ] *adj* ankommend; *train also* einfahrend; *orders etc* eingehend. **~ mail** Eingänge *pl*; **~ tide** (steigende) Flut.

**incommunicado** [,ɪnkəmjʊnɪ'kɑːdəʊ] *adj pred* abgesondert. **to be ~** *(fig)* für niemanden zu sprechen sein.

**incomparable** [ɪn'kɒmpərəbl] *adj* nicht vergleichbar *(with* mit*)*; *beauty, skill* unvergleichlich.

**incomparably** [ɪn'kɒmpərəblɪ] *adv* unvergleichlich.

**incompatibility** ['ɪnkəm,pætə'bɪlɪtɪ] *n* Unvereinbarkeit *f*.

**incompatible** [,ɪnkəm'pætəbl] *adj characters, ideas* unvereinbar; *technical systems also* nicht zueinander passend; *(Comp)* nicht kompatibel; *blood groups* nicht miteinander verträglich. **they are ~** sie passen überhaupt nicht zueinander.

**incompetence** [ɪn'kɒmpɪtəns] *n* Unfähigkeit *f*; *(for job)* Untauglichkeit *f*.

**incompetent** [ɪn'kɒmpɪtənt] *adj person* unfähig; *(for sth)* untauglich; *piece of work* unzulänglich.

**incompetently** [ɪn'kɒmpɪtəntlɪ] *adv* stümperhaft.

**incomplete** [,ɪnkəm'pliːt] *adj collection, series* unvollkommen, unvollständig; *(not finished also)* *painting* unfertig.

**incompleteness** [,ɪnkəm'pliːtnɪs] *n* Unvollständigkeit *f*.

**incomprehensible** *adj*, **~bly** *adv* [ɪn,kɒmprɪ'hensəbl, -lɪ] unverständlich; *act also* unbegreiflich.

**inconceivable** [,ɪnkən'siːvəbl] *adj* unvorstellbar.

**inconclusive** [,ɪnkən'kluːsɪv] *adj result* unbestimmt; *action, investigation* ergebnislos; *(not convincing)* *argument* nicht überzeugend.

**incongruity** [,ɪnkɒŋ'gruːɪtɪ] *n (inappropriateness)* Unangebrachtsein *nt*; *(disparity)* Mißverhältnis *nt* *(of sth with sth* zwischen etw *dat* und etw *dat)*.

**incongruous** [ɪn'kɒŋgruəs] *adj couple, mixture* nicht zusammenpassend *attr*; *thing to do, behaviour, remark* unpassend; *(out of place)* fehl am Platz.

**inconsequential** [ɪn,kɒnsɪ'kwenʃəl] *adj* irrelevant; *(not logical)* unlogisch; *(unimportant)* unwichtig.

**inconsiderable** [,ɪnkən'sɪdərəbl] *adj* **a not ~ amount** ein nicht unbedeutender Betrag.

**inconsiderate** [,ɪnkən'sɪdərɪt] *adj* rücksichtslos; *(in less critical sense)* unaufmerksam.

**inconsistency** [,ɪnkən'sɪstənsɪ] *n see adj* **(a)** Widersprüchlichkeit *f*. **(b)** Unbeständigkeit *f*.

**inconsistent** [,ɪnkən'sɪstənt] *adj* **(a)** *(contradictory)* widersprüchlich. **to be ~ with sth** mit etw nicht übereinstimmen. **(b)** *(uneven, irregular)* *work* unbeständig; *person also* inkonsequent.

**inconsolable** [,ɪnkən'səʊləbl] *adj* untröstlich.

**inconspicuous** [,ɪnkən'spɪkjʊəs] *adj* unauffällig. **he tried to make himself ~** er versuchte, möglichst nicht aufzufallen.

**inconstancy** [ɪn'kɒnstənsɪ] *n* Unbeständigkeit *f*.

**inconstant** [ɪn'kɒnstənt] *adj person* unbeständig.

**incontestable** [,ɪnkən'testəbl] *adj* unbestreitbar.

**incontinence** [ɪn'kɒntɪnəns] *n (Med)* Inkontinenz *f* *(spec)*.

**incontinent** [ɪn'kɒntɪnənt] *adj (Med)* unfähig, Stuhl und/oder Harn zurückzuhalten.

**incontrovertible** [ɪn,kɒntrə'vɜːtəbl] *adj* unbestreitbar.

**inconvenience** [,ɪnkən'viːnɪəns] **1** *n* Unannehmlichkeit *f (to sb* für jdn*)*. **it was something of an ~ not having a car** es war ziemlich lästig, kein Auto zu haben; **I don't want to cause you any ~** ich möchte Ihnen keine Umstände bereiten. **2** *vt* Umstände bereiten *(+dat)*. **don't ~ yourself** machen Sie (sich *dat)* keine Umstände.

**inconvenient** [,ɪnkən'viːnɪənt] *adj time* ungelegen; *house, design* unpraktisch; *location* ungünstig; *journey* beschwerlich. **3 o'clock is very ~ for me** 3 Uhr kommt mir sehr ungelegen.

**inconveniently** [,ɪnkən'viːnɪəntlɪ] *adv timed* ungelegen; *placed* ungünstig; *laid out* unpraktisch.

**incorporate** [ɪn'kɔːpəreɪt] *vt* **(a)** *(integrate)* aufnehmen, integrieren *(into* in *+acc)*. **(b)** *(contain)* (in sich *dat)* enthalten.

**incorporated** [ɪn'kɔːpəreɪtɪd] *adj (US Comm)* als Aktiengesellschaft eingetragen.

**incorrect** [,ɪnkə'rekt] *adj* **(a)** falsch; *wording, calculation also* fehlerhaft. **that is ~** das stimmt nicht. **(b)** *dress, behaviour* inkorrekt.

**incorrectly** [,ɪnkə'rektlɪ] *adv see adj*; *assume* fälschlich(erweise).

**incorrigible** [ɪn'kɒrɪdʒəbl] *adj* unverbesserlich.

**incorruptible** [,ɪnkə'rʌptəbl] *adj* unbestechlich.

**increase** [ɪn'kriːs] **1** *vi* zunehmen; *(taxes)* erhöht werden; *(strength, friendship)* wachsen; *(price, demand)* steigen; *(business, town)* sich vergrößern. **to ~ in volume/weight** an Umfang/Gewicht zunehmen; **to ~ in size/number** sich vergrößern/vermehren.

**2** *vt* vergrößern; *possessions, riches also* vermehren; *sales also* erweitern; *numbers, taxes, price, speed* erhöhen. **he ~d his efforts** er strengte sich mehr an; **~d standard of living** höherer Lebensstandard; **~d efficiency** Leistungssteigerung *f.*

**3** *n* Zunahme, Steigerung *f; (in size)* Vergrößerung, Erweiterung *f; (in number)* Zuwachs *m,* Zunahme *f; (in speed)* Erhöhung, Steigerung *f (in gen); (of business)* Erweiterung *f; (in sales)* Aufschwung *m; (of effort etc)* Steigerung *f; (of demand)* Steigen *nt; (of violence)* Anwachsen *nt.* **to get an ~ of £15 per week** eine Lohnerhöhung von £15 pro Woche bekommen; **to be on the ~** ständig zunehmen; **rent ~** Mieterhöhung *f.*

**increasing** [ɪn'kriːsɪŋ] *adj* zunehmend, (an)wachsend. **an ever ~ number of people are changing to ...** mehr und mehr Leute steigen auf *(+acc)* ... um.

**increasingly** [ɪn'kriːsɪŋlɪ] *adv* zunehmend, immer mehr. **~, people are finding that ...** man findet in zunehmendem Maße, daß ...

**incredible** [ɪn'kredəbl] *adj* unglaublich; *(col also)* unwahrscheinlich gut/schlecht *(col)*. **this music is ~** diese Musik ist sagenhaft *(col)*; **you're ~** du bist wirklich unschlagbar.

**incredibly** [ɪn'kredəblɪ] *adv* unglaublich, unwahrscheinlich.

**incredulity** [,ɪnkrɪ'djuːlɪtɪ] *n* Ungläubigkeit, Skepsis *f.*

**incredulous** [ɪn'kredjʊləs] *adj* ungläubig, skeptisch.

**increment** ['ɪnkrɪmənt] *n (in salary)* Gehaltserhöhung *f.*

**incriminate** [ɪn'krɪmɪneɪt] *vt* belasten.

**incriminating** [ɪn'krɪmɪneɪtɪŋ] *adj* belastend.

**incubate** ['ɪnkjʊbeɪt] **1** *vt egg* ausbrüten; *bacteria* züchten. **2** *vi (lit)* ausgebrütet werden.

**incubation** [,ɪnkjʊ'beɪʃən] *n see vb* Ausbrüten *nt;* Züchten *nt.* **~ period** *(Med)* Inkubationszeit *f.*

**incubator** ['ɪnkjʊbeɪtəʳ] *n (for babies)* Brutkasten *m;*

*(for chickens)* Brutapparat *m.*

**inculcate** ['ɪnkʌlkeɪt] *vt* einimpfen *(in sb* jdm*)*.

**incumbent** [ɪn'kʌmbənt] *(form)* **1** *adj* **to be ~ upon sb** jdm obliegen *(form)*. **2** *n* Amtsinhaber *m.*

**incur** [ɪn'kɜːʳ] *vt anger, injury* sich *(dat)* zuziehen; *loss* erleiden; *debts, expenses* machen.

**incurable** [ɪn'kjʊərəbl] *adj (Med)* unheilbar; *(fig)* unverbesserlich.

**incursion** [ɪn'kɜːʃən] *n* Eindringen *nt (into* in *+acc)*.

**indebted** [ɪn'detɪd] *adj* **to be ~ to sb for sth** jdm für etw (zu Dank) verpflichtet sein.

**indecency** [ɪn'diːsnsɪ] *n* Unanständigkeit *f.*

**indecent** [ɪn'diːsnt] *adj* unanständig, anstößig; *(Jur) act* unsittlich. **~ assault** *(Brit)* Notzucht *f;* **~ exposure** Erregung *f* öffentlichen Ärgernisses; **with ~ haste** mit ungebührlicher Eile.

**indecently** [ɪn'diːsntlɪ] *adv* unanständig; *(Jur)* unsittlich. **~ fast** *(col)* ungebührlich schnell.

**indecipherable** [,ɪndɪ'saɪfərəbl] *adj* nicht zu entziffern *pred*, nicht zu entziffernd *attr*; *handwriting* unleserlich.

**indecision** [,ɪndɪ'sɪʒən] *n* Unentschlossenheit *f.*

**indecisive** [,ɪndɪ'saɪsɪv] *adj person, manner* unschlüssig, unentschlossen; *discussion* ergebnislos; *argument, battle* nicht entscheidend *attr.*

**indeed** [ɪn'diːd] *adv* **(a)** tatsächlich, wirklich. **I feel, ~ I know he is right** ich habe das Gefühl, ja ich weiß (sogar), daß er recht hat; **isn't that wrong? — ~** ist das nicht falsch? — allerdings; **are you coming? — ~ I am!** kommst du? — aber sicher *or* natürlich; **may I open the window? — you may ~** darf ich das Fenster öffnen? — ja bitte!; **very hot ~** wirklich sehr heiß; **thank you very much ~** vielen herzlichen Dank. **(b)** *(admittedly)* zwar. **there are ~ mistakes in it, but ...** es sind zwar Fehler darin, aber ... **(c)** *(expressing possibility)* **I may ~ come** es kann gut sein, daß ich komme.

**indefatigable** [,ɪndɪ'fætɪgəbl] *adj* unermüdlich.

**indefensible** [,ɪndɪ'fensəbl] *adj behaviour etc* unentschuldbar; *town etc* unhaltbar; *cause, theory* unvertretbar.

**indefinable** [,ɪndɪ'faɪnəbl] *adj* undefinierbar; *feeling* unbestimmt.

**indefinite** [ɪn'defɪnɪt] *adj* unbestimmt; *(vague)* unklar, undeutlich.

**indefinitely** [ɪn'defɪnɪtlɪ] *adv wait etc* unendlich lange, endlos; *postpone* auf unbestimmte Zeit. **we can't go on like this ~** wir können nicht endlos so weitermachen.

**indelible** [ɪn'deləbl] *adj ink* wasserfest; *(fig) impression* unauslöschlich. **~ pencil** Kopierstift *m.*

**indelicate** [ɪn'delɪkət] *adj person* taktlos; *(crude)* geschmacklos.

**indemnify** [ɪn'demnɪfaɪ] *vt* **(a)** *(compensate)* entschädigen. **to ~ sb for expenses** jdm seine Unkosten erstatten. **(b)** *(safeguard)* absichern *(from, against* gegen); *(insure)* versichern *(against, from* gegen).

**indemnity** [ɪn'demnɪtɪ] *n* **(a)** *(compensation) (for damage, loss etc)* Schadensersatz *m,* Entschädigung *f; (after war)* Wiedergutmachung *f.* **(b)** *(insurance)* Versicherung(sschutz *m) f.*

**indent** [ɪn'dent] *vt (Typ)* line einrücken.

**indentation** [,ɪnden'teɪʃən] *n (in border)* Einschnitt *m; (Typ)* Einrückung *f; (in metal)* Delle *f.*

**indented** [ɪn'dentɪd] *adj (Typ)* eingerückt; *(Geog) coastline* zerklüftet.

**independence** [,ɪndɪ'pendəns] *n see adj* Unabhängigkeit *f (of* von*)*; Selbständigkeit *f.* **I~ Day** *(US)* der Unabhängigkeitstag.

**independent** [,ɪndɪ'pendənt] *adj* unabhängig *(of* von*) (also Pol)*; parteilos *(Pol)*; *person (in attitude,* *spirit also)* selbständig; *development* eigenständig. **a man of** ~ **means** ein Mann mit Privateinkommen; ~ **suspension** *(Aut)* Einzel(rad)aufhängung *f.*

**independently** [ˌɪndɪ'pendəntlɪ] *adv (on own initiative)* von allein(e).

**in-depth** ['ɪndepθ] *adj* eingehend, tiefschürfend.

**indescribable** [ˌɪndɪ'skraɪbəbl] *adj* unbeschreiblich; *(col: terrible)* schrecklich.

**indestructible** [ˌɪndɪ'strʌktəbl] *adj* unzerstörbar.

**indeterminate** [ˌɪndɪ'tɜːmɪnɪt] *adj* unbestimmt.

**index** ['ɪndeks] *n* (**a**) *pl* **-es** *(in book)* Register *nt; (of sources)* Quellenverzeichnis *nt.* (**b**) *pl* **indices** *(on scale)* (An)zeiger *m.* **cost-of-living** ~ Lebenshaltungskosten-Index *m.*

**index card** *n* Karteikarte *f.*

**indexed** ['ɪndekst] *adj (Econ) see* **index-linked.**

**index:** ~ **finger** *n* Zeigefinger *m;* ~**-linked** *adj salaries* der Inflationsrate *(dat)* angeglichen; *pensions* dynamisch.

**India** ['ɪndɪə] *n* Indien *nt.* ~ **ink** *(esp US)* Tusche *f.*

**Indian** ['ɪndɪən] **1** *adj* (**a**) indisch. (**b**) *(American* ~*)* indianisch, Indianer-. ~ **ink** Tusche *f;* ~ **Ocean** Indischer Ozean; ~ **summer** Altweibersommer, Spätsommer *m.* **2** *n* (**a**) Inder(in *f*) *m.* (**b**) *(American* ~*)* Indianer(in *f*) *m; (Central/South American)* Indio *m.*

**India rubber** *n* Gummi, Kautschuk *m; (eraser)* Radiergummi *m.*

**indicate** ['ɪndɪkeɪt] **1** *vt* (**a**) *(point out, mark)* zeigen, bezeichnen; *(register) temperature etc* anzeigen. (**b**) *(show) feelings etc* andeuten, zeigen. (**c**) *(be a sign of, suggest)* schließen lassen auf *(+acc),* (hin)deuten auf *(+acc).* **this would definitely** ~ **that** ... das würde bestimmt darauf hindeuten, daß ...; **what does it** ~ **to you?** was schließen Sie daraus? **2** *vi (Aut)* blinken. **to** ~ **(turning) right** rechts blinken.

**indication** [ˌɪndɪ'keɪʃən] *n (sign)* (An)zeichen *nt (also Med) (of* für), Hinweis *m (of* auf *+acc).* **we had no** ~ **that** ... es gab kein Anzeichen dafür, daß ...; **if you could give me a rough** ~ **of** ... wenn Sie mir eine ungefähre Vorstellung davon geben könnten ...

**indicative** [ɪn'dɪkətɪv] **1** *adj* (**a**) **to be** ~ **of sth** auf etw *(acc)* schließen lassen; *of sb's character* für etw bezeichnend sein. (**b**) *(Gram)* indikativisch. **2** *n (Gram)* **in the** ~ im Indikativ.

**indicator** ['ɪndɪkeɪtəʳ] *n (gauge)* Anzeiger *m; (needle)* Zeiger *m; (Aut)* Blinker *m.* ~ **board** *(Rail)* Anzeigetafel *f.*

**indices** ['ɪndɪsiːz] *pl of* **index.**

**indict** [ɪn'daɪt] *vt (charge)* anklagen, unter Anklage stellen; *(US Jur)* Anklage erheben gegen *(for* wegen *+gen).*

**indictable** [ɪn'daɪtəbl] *adj offence* strafbar.

**indictment** [ɪn'daɪtmənt] *n (of person)* Anklage, Anschuldigung *f.* **to be an** ~ **of sth** *(fig)* ein Armutszeugnis für etw sein.

**indifference** [ɪn'dɪfrəns] *n see adj* (**a**) Gleichgültigkeit *f (to, towards* gegenüber*).* (**b**) Mittelmäßigkeit *f.*

**indifferent** [ɪn'dɪfrənt] *adj* (**a**) gleichgültig, indifferent *(geh) (to, towards* gegenüber*).* **he is quite** ~ **to her** sie ist ihm ziemlich gleichgültig. (**b**) *(mediocre)* mittelmäßig, durchschnittlich.

**indigenous** [ɪn'dɪdʒɪnəs] *adj* einheimisch *(to* in *+dat).*

**indigestible** [ˌɪndɪ'dʒestəbl] *adj* unverdaulich.

**indigestion** [ˌɪndɪ'dʒestʃən] *n* Magenverstimmung *f.*

**indignant** [ɪn'dɪgnənt] *adj* entrüstet, empört *(at, about, with* über *+acc).* **to be/become** ~ sich entrüsten.

**indignantly** [ɪn'dɪgnəntlɪ] *adv* entrüstet.

**indignation** [ˌɪndɪg'neɪʃən] *n* Entrüstung, Empörung *f (at, about, with* über *+acc).*

**indignity** [ɪn'dɪgnɪtɪ] *n* Demütigung *f.*

**indigo** ['ɪndɪgəʊ] **1** *n* Indigo *nt or m.* **2** *adj* indigofarben.

**indirect** [ˌɪndɪ'rekt] *adj* indirekt. **by an** ~ **route** auf einem Umweg; **to make an** ~ **reference to sth** auf etw anspielen; ~ **object** Dativobjekt *nt;* ~ **speech** *or (US)* **discourse** indirekte Rede.

**indirectly** [ˌɪndɪ'rektlɪ] *adv* indirekt; *(in a roundabout way)* auf Umwegen.

**indiscernible** [ˌɪndɪ'sɜːnəbl] *adj* nicht erkennbar.

**indiscreet** [ˌɪndɪ'skriːt] *adj* indiskret; *(tactless)* taktlos.

**indiscretion** [ˌɪndɪ'skreʃən] *n see adj* Indiskretion *f;* Taktlosigkeit *f; (affair)* Affäre *f.*

**indiscriminate** [ˌɪndɪ'skrɪmɪnɪt] *adj* wahllos; *reader, shopper* unkritisch; *tastes* unausgeprägt.

**indispensable** [ˌɪndɪ'spensəbl] *adj* unentbehrlich *(to* für*).* ~ **to life** lebensnotwendig.

**indisposed** [ˌɪndɪ'spəʊzd] *adj (unwell)* unwohl.

**indisposition** [ˌɪndɪspə'zɪʃən] *n* Unwohlsein *nt.*

**indisputable** [ˌɪndɪ'spjuːtəbl] *adj* unbestreitbar; *evidence* unanfechtbar.

**indisputably** [ˌɪndɪ'spjuːtəblɪ] *adv* unbestreitbar.

**indistinct** [ˌɪndɪ'stɪŋkt] *adj* unklar, undeutlich.

**indistinctly** [ˌɪndɪ'stɪŋktlɪ] *adv* undeutlich; *remember* schwach, dunkel.

**indistinguishable** [ˌɪndɪ'stɪŋgwɪʃəbl] *adj* nicht unterscheidbar *(from* von*).*

**individual** [ˌɪndɪ'vɪdjʊəl] **1** *adj* (**a**) *(separate)* einzeln. ~ **cases** Einzelfälle *pl;* ~ **tastes differ** die Geschmäcker sind verschieden. (**b**) *(own)* eigen; *(for one person)* portion etc einzeln, Einzel-. (**c**) *(distinctive)* eigen, individuell. **2** *n* Individuum *nt,* Einzelne(r) *mf.*

**individualism** [ˌɪndɪ'vɪdjʊəlɪzm] *n* Individualismus *m.*

**individualist** [ˌɪndɪ'vɪdjʊəlɪst] *n* Individualist(in *f*) *m.*

**individuality** ['ɪndɪˌvɪdjʊ'ælɪtɪ] *n* Individualität *f.*

**individually** [ˌɪndɪ'vɪdjʊəlɪ] *adv* individuell; *(separately)* einzeln.

**indivisible** [ˌɪndɪ'vɪzəbl] *adj* unteilbar *(also Math).*

**Indo-** ['ɪndəʊ-] *pref* Indo-. ~**china** *n* Indochina *nt.*

**indoctrinate** [ɪn'dɒktrɪneɪt] *vt* indoktrinieren.

**indoctrination** [ɪnˌdɒktrɪ'neɪʃən] *n* Indoktrination *f.*

**indolence** ['ɪndələns] *n* Trägheit *f.*

**indolent** ['ɪndələnt] *adj* träge.

**Indonesia** [ˌɪndəʊ'niːzɪə] *n* Indonesien *nt.*

**Indonesian** [ˌɪndəʊ'niːzɪən] **1** *adj* indonesisch. **2** *n* (**a**) Indonesier(in *f*) *m.* (**b**) *(language)* Indonesisch *nt.*

**indoor** ['ɪndɔːʳ] *adj plant, aerial* Zimmer-; *clothes* Haus-; *sport* Hallen-. ~ **games** Spiele *pl* für drinnen; *(Sport)* Hallenspiele *pl;* ~ **photographs/ photography** Innenaufnahmen *pl;* ~ **swimming pool** Hallenbad *nt; (private)* überdachtes Schwimmbad.

**indoors** [ɪn'dɔːz] *adv* drinnen, innen; *(at home)* zu Hause. **to stay** ~ im Haus bleiben, drin bleiben *(col);* **to go** ~ ins Haus gehen.

**indubitable** [ɪn'djuːbɪtəbl] *adj* unzweifelhaft.

**indubitably** [ɪn'djuːbɪtəblɪ] *adv* zweifellos.

**induce** [ɪn'djuːs] *vt* (**a**) *(persuade)* dazu bewegen *or* bringen. (**b**) *reaction* bewirken, hervorrufen; *sleep* herbeiführen; *birth* einleiten. **this drug** ~**s sleep** dieses Mittel hat eine einschläfernde Wirkung. (**c**) *(Elec) current* induzieren.

**inducement** [ɪn'djuːsmənt] *n (no pl: persuasion)* Überredung *f; (incentive)* Anreiz *m.* **as an added** ~ als besonderer Anreiz.

**induction** [ɪn'dʌkʃən] *n* (**a**) *(of sleep, reaction etc)*

**inferno**

Herbeiführen nt; (of birth) Einleitung f. **(b)** (Philos, Elec) Induktion f. **(c)** (of official, priest) Amtseinführung f.

**indulge** [ɪn'dʌldʒ] **1** vt desires etc nachgeben (+dat); person also nachsichtig sein mit; (over~) children verwöhnen. **to** ~ **oneself in sth** sich (dat) etw gönnen. **2** vi **to** ~ **in sth** sich (dat) etw gönnen or genehmigen (col); (in vice, drink) einer Sache (dat) frönen. **I don't** ~ (drink/smoke) ich trinke/rauche nicht.

**indulgence** [ɪn'dʌldʒəns] n **(a)** Nachsicht f; (of appetite etc) Nachgiebigkeit f (of gegenüber); (over~) Verwöhnen nt. **the** ~ **of his wishes** das Erfüllen seiner Wünsche. **(b)** (in activity, drink etc) ~ **in drink** übermäßiges Trinken. **(c)** (thing indulged in) Luxus m; (food, drink, pleasure) Genuß m.

**indulgent** [ɪn'dʌldʒənt] adj (to gegenüber) nachsichtig; mother etc also nachgiebig; (to one's own desires etc) zu nachgiebig.

**industrial** [ɪn'dʌstrɪəl] adj worker, equipment, state, town etc Industrie-; production also industriell; training, accident Betriebs-. ~ **action** Arbeitskampfmaßnahmen pl; **to take** ~ **action** in den Ausstand treten; ~ **dispute** Arbeitskonflikt m; ~ **estate** (Brit) Industriegelände nt; ~ **injury** Arbeitsverletzung f; ~ **park** (US) Industriegelände nt; ~ **relations** Beziehungen pl zwischen Arbeitgebern und Gewerkschaften; (in particular company also) Betriebsklima nt; **I~ Revolution** Industrielle Revolution; ~ **tribunal** Arbeitsgericht nt; ~ **unrest** Arbeitsunruhen pl; ~ **waste** Industriemüll m.

**industrialist** [ɪn'dʌstrɪəlɪst] n Industrielle(r) mf.

**industrialization** [ɪn,dʌstrɪəlaɪ'zeɪʃən] n Industrialisierung f.

**industrialize** [ɪn'dʌstrɪəlaɪz] vti industrialisieren. ~**d countries** Industrieländer pl.

**industrious** [ɪn'dʌstrɪəs] adj fleißig.

**industry** ['ɪndəstrɪ] n **(a)** Industrie f. **heavy/light** ~ Schwer-/Leichtindustrie f; **in certain industries** in einigen Branchen. **(b)** (industriousness) Fleiß m.

**inebriated** [ɪ'niːbrɪeɪtɪd] adj **(a)** (form) unter starkem Alkoholeinfluß (form). **(b)** (fig) berauscht.

**inedible** [ɪn'edɪbl] adj nicht eßbar; (foul-tasting) ungenießbar.

**ineffective** [,ɪnɪ'fektɪv] adj unwirksam, ineffektiv; person unfähig, untauglich.

**ineffectual** [,ɪnɪ'fektjʊəl] adj ineffektiv.

**inefficiency** [,ɪnɪ'fɪʃənsɪ] n see adj Unfähigkeit f; Inkompetenz f; Leistungsunfähigkeit f.

**inefficient** [,ɪnɪ'fɪʃənt] adj person unfähig, inkompetent; machine, company leistungsschwach; method unrationell.

**inelegant** [ɪn'elɪgənt] adj unelegant; clothes also ohne Schick.

**ineligible** [ɪn'elɪdʒəbl] adj (for benefits, grant) nicht berechtigt (for zu +dat); (for job) ungeeignet. ~ **for a pension** nicht pensionsberechtigt.

**inept** [ɪ'nept] adj ungeschickt; remark unpassend; attempt plump; comparison ungeeignet.

**ineptitude** [ɪ'neptɪtjuːd] n see adj Ungeschicktheit f; Plumpheit f; Ungeeignetheit f.

**inequality** [,ɪnɪ'kwolɪtɪ] n Ungleichheit f.

**inequitable** [ɪn'ekwɪtəbl] adj ungerecht.

**ineradicable** [,ɪnɪ'rædɪkəbl] adj disease, prejudice unausrottbar; feelings unauslöschlich.

**inert** [ɪ'nɜːt] adj unbeweglich; (Phys) matter träge; (Chem) substance inaktiv. ~ **gas** Edelgas nt.

**inertia** [ɪ'nɜːʃə] n (lit, fig) Trägheit f. ~**-reel seat belt** Automatikgurt m.

**inescapable** [,ɪnɪs'keɪpəbl] adj unvermeidlich.

**inessential** [,ɪnɪ'senʃəl] adj unwesentlich.

**inestimable** [ɪn'estɪməbl] adj unschätzbar.

**inevitability** [ɪn,evɪtə'bɪlɪtɪ] n Unvermeidlichkeit f.

**inevitable** [ɪn'evɪtəbl] adj unvermeidlich.

**inevitably** [ɪn'evɪtəblɪ] adv zwangsläufig.

**inexact** adj, ~**ly** adv [,ɪnɪg'zækt, -lɪ] ungenau.

**inexcusable** adj, ~**bly** adv [,ɪnɪks'kjuːzəbl, -ɪ] unverzeihlich.

**inexhaustible** [,ɪnɪg'zɔːstəbl] adj source nie versiegend; wealth, patience unerschöpflich.

**inexorable** adj, ~**bly** adv [ɪn'eksərəbl, -ɪ] (relentless(ly)) unerbittlich; (not to be stopped) unaufhaltsam.

**inexpensive** [,ɪnɪk'spensɪv] adj billig, preisgünstig.

**inexperience** [,ɪnɪk'spɪərɪəns] n Unerfahrenheit f.

**inexperienced** [,ɪnɪk'spɪərɪənst] adj unerfahren; skier etc ungeübt.

**inexpert** adj, ~**ly** adv [ɪn'ekspɜːt, -lɪ] unfachmännisch, laienhaft; (untrained) ungeübt.

**inexplicable** [,ɪnɪk'splɪkəbl] adj unerklärlich.

**inexplicably** [,ɪnɪk'splɪkəblɪ] adv (+adj) unerklärlich; (+vb) unerklärlicherweise.

**inexpressible** [,ɪnɪk'spresəbl] adj unbeschreiblich; pain, joy also unsagbar.

**inexpressive** [,ɪnɪk'spresɪv] adj face ausdruckslos; word nichtssagend; style ohne Ausdruckskraft.

**inextricable** [,ɪnɪk'strɪkəbl] adj tangle unentwirrbar; confusion unüberschaubar.

**inextricably** [,ɪnɪk'strɪkəblɪ] adv entangled unentwirrbar; linked untrennbar.

**infallibility** [ɪn,fælə'bɪlɪtɪ] n Unfehlbarkeit f.

**infallible** adj, ~**bly** adv [ɪn'fæləbl, -ɪ] unfehlbar.

**infamous** ['ɪnfəməs] adj berüchtigt, verrufen; deed niederträchtig.

**infamy** ['ɪnfəmɪ] n see adj Verrufenheit f; Niedertracht f.

**infancy** ['ɪnfənsɪ] n frühe Kindheit f; (fig) Anfangsstadium nt. **data processing is no longer in its** ~ die Datenverarbeitung steckt nicht mehr in den Kinderschuhen.

**infant** ['ɪnfənt] n (baby) Säugling m; (young child) Kleinkind nt. ~ **mortality** Säuglingssterblichkeit f; ~ **school** (Brit) Grundschule f für die ersten beiden Jahrgänge.

**infantile** ['ɪnfəntaɪl] adj (childish) kindisch, infantil.

**infantry** ['ɪnfəntrɪ] n (Mil) Infanterie f.

**infantryman** ['ɪnfəntrɪmən] n, pl **-men** [-mən] Infanterist m.

**infatuated** [ɪn'fætjʊeɪtɪd] adj vernarrt, verknallt (col) (with in +acc). **to become** ~ **with sb** sich in jdn vernarren; ~ **with sth** von etw besessen.

**infatuation** [ɪn,fætjʊ'eɪʃən] n Vernarrtheit f (with in +acc).

**infect** [ɪn'fekt] vt wound infizieren; water verseuchen; meat verderben; (fig: with enthusiasm etc) anstecken. **his wound became** ~**ed** seine Wunde entzündete sich.

**infection** [ɪn'fekʃən] n (illness) Infektion, Entzündung f; (of water) Verseuchung f.

**infectious** [ɪn'fekʃəs] adj (Med, fig) ansteckend.

**infer** [ɪn'fɜːʳ] vt **(a)** schließen, folgern (from aus). **(b)** (imply) andeuten.

**inference** ['ɪnfərəns] n Schluß(folgerung f) m.

**inferior** [ɪn'fɪərɪəʳ] adj (in quality) minderwertig; quality also geringer; person unterlegen; court untergeordnet.

**inferiority** [ɪn,fɪərɪ'ɒrɪtɪ] n (in quality) Minderwertigkeit f; (of person) Unterlegenheit f (to gegenüber). ~ **complex** Minderwertigkeitskomplex m.

**infernal** [ɪn'fɜːnl] adj (lit) Höllen-; (fig) scheme teuflisch; (col) noise höllisch.

**inferno** [ɪn'fɜːnəʊ] n (hell) Hölle f, Inferno nt; (blazing house etc) Flammenmeer nt. **a blazing** ~ ein flammendes Inferno.

**infertile** [ɪn'fɜːtaɪl] *adj soil, womb* unfruchtbar; *mind* ideenlos.

**infertility** [,ɪnfɜː'tɪlɪtɪ] *n see adj* Unfruchtbarkeit *f;* Ideenlosigkeit *f.*

**infest** [ɪn'fest] *vt (vermin)* herfallen über *(+acc); (plague)* befallen. **to be ~ed with disease/rats** verseucht/mit Ratten verseucht sein; **to be ~ed with lice** *etc* von Läusen *etc* befallen sein.

**infidelity** [,ɪnfɪ'delɪtɪ] *n* Untreue *f.*

**in-fighting** ['ɪnfaɪtɪŋ] *n (fig)* interner Machtkampf.

**infiltrate** ['ɪnfɪltreɪt] **1** *vt troops* infiltrieren; *(Pol)* organization *also* unterwandern; *spies* einschleusen. **2** *vi (Mil)* eindringen *(into* in *+acc); (spy also)* sich einschleusen *(into* in *+acc).*

**infiltration** [,ɪnfɪl'treɪʃən] *n (Mil)* Infiltration *f; (Pol also)* Unterwanderung *f.*

**infiltrator** ['ɪnfɪl,treɪtəʳ] *n (Mil)* Eindringling *m; (Pol)* Unterwanderer *m.*

**infinite** ['ɪnfɪnɪt] *adj (lit)* unendlich; *(fig also) trouble, pleasure* grenzenlos. **an ~ amount of time** unendlich viel Zeit.

**infinitely** ['ɪnfɪnɪtlɪ] *adv* unendlich; *(fig also)* grenzenlos; *improved* ungeheuer; *better, worse* unendlich viel.

**infinitesimal** [,ɪnfɪnɪ'tesɪməl] *adj* unendlich klein.

**infinitive** [ɪn'fɪnɪtɪv] *n* Infinitiv *m.*

**infinity** [ɪn'fɪnɪtɪ] *n (lit)* Unendlichkeit *f; (fig also)* Grenzenlosigkeit *f; (Math)* das Unendliche. **to ~** (bis) ins Unendliche; **"~"** *(Phot)* „unendlich".

**infirm** [ɪn'fɜːm] *adj* gebrechlich, schwach.

**infirmary** [ɪn'fɜːmərɪ] *n* Krankenhaus *nt; (in school etc)* Krankenzimmer *nt; (in prison, barracks)* Krankenstation *f.*

**infirmity** [ɪn'fɜːmɪtɪ] *n* Gebrechlichkeit *f.*

**inflame** [ɪn'fleɪm] *vt* **(a)** *(Med)* entzünden. **to become ~d** sich entzünden. **(b)** *person* aufbringen; *feelings* entflammen; *anger* erregen.

**inflammable** [ɪn'flæməbl] *adj (lit)* feuergefährlich, (leicht) entzündbar; *(fig) situation* brisant.

**inflammation** [,ɪnflə'meɪʃən] *n (Med)* Entzündung *f.*

**inflammatory** [ɪn'flæmətərɪ] *adj speech* aufrührerisch.

**inflatable** [ɪn'fleɪtɪbl] *adj* aufblasbar. **~ dinghy** Schlauchboot *nt.*

**inflate** [ɪn'fleɪt] *vt* **(a)** aufpumpen; *(by mouth)* aufblasen. **(b)** *(Econ) prices* steigern, hochtreiben. **(c)** *(fig)* steigern.

**inflated** [ɪn'fleɪtɪd] *adj prices* überhöht, inflationär; *pride* übersteigert; *style* geschwollen. **to have an ~ opinion of oneself** ein übertriebenes Selbstbewußtsein haben.

**inflation** [ɪn'fleɪʃən] *n (Econ)* Inflation *f.* **to fight ~** die Inflation bekämpfen; **5% ~** eine Inflationsrate von 5%.

**inflationary** [ɪn'fleɪʃənərɪ] *adj* inflationär, inflationistisch *(pej).* **the ~ spiral** die Inflationsspirale.

**inflation-proof** [ɪn'fleɪʃən,pruːf] *adj* inflationssicher.

**inflect** [ɪn'flekt] *vt (Gram)* flektieren, beugen.

**inflexibility** [ɪn,fleksɪ'bɪlɪtɪ] *n see adj* mangelnde Flexibilität *f;* Sturheit *f;* Unbiegsamkeit, Steifheit *f.*

**inflexible** [ɪn'fleksəbl] *adj attitude, opinion* wenig flexibel; *person also* stur; *substance, object* unbiegsam, steif.

**inflict** [ɪn'flɪkt] *vt punishment* verhängen *(on, upon* gegen*); suffering* zufügen *(on or upon sb* jdm*); wound* beibringen *(on or upon sb* jdm*).* **to ~ oneself on sb** sich jdm aufdrängen.

**in-flight** ['ɪnflaɪt] *adj attr* während des Fluges. **~ entertainment** Bordprogramm *nt.*

**influence** ['ɪnfluəns] **1** *n* Einfluß *m.* **to have an ~ on sb/sth** *(person)* Einfluß auf jdn/etw haben; *(fact, weather etc also)* Auswirkungen *pl* auf jdn/etw haben; **to have a great deal of ~ with sb** großen Einfluß bei jdm haben; **he's been a bad ~ on you** er war ein schlechter Einfluß für Sie; **she is a good ~ on the pupils** sie hat einen guten Einfluß auf die Schüler; **to exert an ~ on sb** Einfluß auf jdn ausüben; **under the ~ of drink** unter Alkoholeinfluß; **under the ~** *(col)* betrunken. **2** *vt* beeinflussen. **to be easily ~d** leicht beeinflußbar sein.

**influential** [,ɪnflu'enʃəl] *adj* einflußreich.

**influenza** [,ɪnflu'enzə] *n* Grippe *f.*

**influx** ['ɪnflʌks] *n (of capital)* Zufuhr *f; (of people)* Zustrom *m; (of ideas etc)* Zufluß *m.*

**info** ['ɪnfəu] *n (col)* Auskunft *f.*

**inform** [ɪn'fɔːm] **1** *vt* benachrichtigen, informieren *(about* über *+acc);* unterrichten. **to ~ sb of sth** jdn von etw unterrichten, jdn über etw informieren; **I am pleased to ~ you that** ... ich freue mich, Ihnen mitteilen zu können, daß ...; **to ~ the police** die Polizei benachrichtigen; **to keep sb/oneself ~ed** jdn/sich auf dem laufenden halten *(of* über *+acc);* **why was I not ~ed?** warum wurde mir das nicht mitgeteilt? **2** *vi* **to ~ against** *or* **on sb** jdn anzeigen *or* denunzieren *(pej).*

**informal** [ɪn'fɔːməl] *adj (not official) meeting* informell; *visit* inoffiziell; *(without ceremony) meeting, language* ungezwungen; *manner* leger; *restaurant* gemütlich. **"dress ~"** „zwanglose Kleidung".

**informality** [,ɪnfɔː'mælɪtɪ] *n see adj* informeller Charakter; inoffizieller Charakter; Ungezwungenheit *f;* legere Art; Gemütlichkeit *f.*

**informally** [ɪn'fɔːməlɪ] *adv (unofficially)* inoffiziell; *(casually, without ceremony)* zwanglos, ungezwungen.

**informant** [ɪn'fɔːmənt] *n* Informant *m.*

**informatics** [,ɪnfə'mætɪks] *n sing* Informatik *f.*

**information** [,ɪnfə'meɪʃən] *n* Auskunft *f,* Informationen *pl.* **a piece of ~** eine Auskunft, eine Information; **for your ~** zu Ihrer Information; *(indignantly)* damit Sie es wissen!; **to give sb ~ about** *or* **on sth** jdm Auskunft *or* Informationen über jdn/etw geben; **to get ~ about** *or* **on sb/sth** sich über jdn/etw informieren; **detailed ~** Einzelheiten *pl.*

**information: ~ bureau** *n* Auskunft(sbüro *nt) f; (for tourist ~)* Verkehrsbüro *nt;* **~ desk** *n* Informationsschalter *m;* **~ officer** *n* Auskunftsbeamte(r) *m;* **~ processing** *n* Informationsverarbeitung *f;* **~ retrieval** *n* Informations- *or* Datenabruf *m;* **~ science** *n* Informatik *f;* **~ superhighway** *n* Datenautobahn *f;* **~ technology** Informationstechnik *f.*

**informative** [ɪn'fɔːmətɪv] *adj* aufschlußreich; *book, lecture also* lehrreich.

**informed** [ɪn'fɔːmd] *adj observers* informiert, (gut) unterrichtet; *(educated)* gebildet.

**informer** [ɪn'fɔːməʳ] *n* Informant, Denunziant *(pej) m.* **police ~** Polizeispitzel *m (pej);* **to turn ~** seine Mittäter verraten.

**infra dig** ['ɪnfrə'dɪg] *adj (col)* **he considers it ~** er hält es für unter seiner Würde.

**infra-red** [,ɪnfrə'red] *adj* infrarot.

**infrastructure** ['ɪnfrə,strʌktʃəʳ] *n* Infrastruktur *f.*

**infrequent** [ɪn'friːkwənt] *adj* selten. **at ~ intervals** in großen Abständen.

**infrequently** [ɪn'friːkwəntlɪ] *adv* selten.

**infringe** [ɪn'frɪndʒ] **1** *vt* verstoßen gegen; *law, copyright also* verletzen. **2** *vi* **to ~ (up)on sb's privacy** in jds Privatsphäre *(acc)* eingreifen.

**infringement** [ɪn'frɪndʒmənt] *n* **(a)** **an ~ (of a rule)** ein Regelverstoß *m;* **~ of the law** Gesetzesverletzung *or* -übertretung *f*; ~ **of a patent/copyright** Patentverletzung *f*/Verletzung *f* des Urheberrechts. **(b)** *(of privacy)* Eingriff *m (of* in +*acc).*

**infuriate** [ɪn'fjʊərɪeɪt] *vt* wütend *or* rasend machen. **to be/get** ~**d** wütend *or* rasend sein/werden.

**infuriating** [ɪn'fjʊərɪeɪtɪŋ] *adj* (äußerst) ärgerlich. **an** ~ **habit** eine Unsitte; **an** ~ **person** ein Mensch, der einen zur Raserei bringen kann.

**infuse** [ɪn'fjuːz] **1** *vt* **(a)** *courage etc* einflößen *(into sb* jdm*).* **they were** ~**d with new hope** sie waren von neuer Hoffnung erfüllt. **(b)** *(Cook) tea* aufgießen. **2** *vi (tea)* ziehen.

**infusion** [ɪn'fjuːʒən] *n* **(a)** *(of hope etc)* Einflößen *nt.* **(b)** *(Cook)* Aufguß *m; (tea-like)* Tee *m.* **(c)** *(Med)* Infusion *f.*

**ingenious** [ɪn'dʒiːnɪəs] *adj* genial; *person also* erfinderisch; *device also* raffiniert.

**ingeniously** [ɪn'dʒiːnɪəslɪ] *adj* genial; *designed also* raffiniert.

**ingenuity** [ˌɪndʒɪ'njuːɪtɪ] *n* Genialität *f; (of person also)* Einfallsreichtum *m; (of device also)* Raffiniertheit *f.*

**ingenuous** [ɪn'dʒenjʊəs] *adj* **(a)** *(candid)* aufrichtig. **(b)** *(naive)* naiv.

**ingot** ['ɪŋgət] *n* Barren *m.*

**ingrained** [ˌɪn'greɪnd] *adj* **(a)** *habit* fest, eingefleischt; *belief* unerschütterlich. **(b)** *dirt* tiefsitzend *(attr).*

**ingratiate** [ɪn'greɪʃɪeɪt] *vr* **to** ~ **oneself with sb** sich bei jdm einschmeicheln.

**ingratiating** [ɪn'greɪʃɪeɪtɪŋ] *adj person, speech* schmeichlerisch; *smile* süßlich.

**ingratitude** [ɪn'grætɪtjuːd] *n* Undank *m.* **sb's** ~ jds Undankbarkeit *f.*

**ingredient** [ɪn'griːdɪənt] *n* Bestandteil *m; (for recipe)* Zutat *f.* **all the** ~**s of success** alles, was man zum Erfolg braucht.

**ingrowing** ['ɪngrəʊɪŋ] *adj toenail* eingewachsen.

**inhabit** [ɪn'hæbɪt] *vt* bewohnen; *(animals)* leben in *(+dat).*

**inhabitable** [ɪn'hæbɪtəbl] *adj* bewohnbar.

**inhabitant** [ɪn'hæbɪtənt] *n* Bewohner(in *f) m; (of island, town also)* Einwohner(in *f) m.*

**inhale** [ɪn'heɪl] **1** *vt* einatmen; *(Med)* inhalieren. **2** *vi (in smoking)* Lungenzüge machen.

**inhaler** [ɪn'heɪlər] *n* Inhalationsapparat *m.*

**inherent** [ɪn'hɪərənt] *adj* innewohnend. **the** ~ **hardness of diamonds** die den Diamanten eigene Härte; **the** ~ **risks of the test** die mit dem Test verbundenen Gefahren.

**inherently** [ɪn'hɪərəntlɪ] *adv* von Natur aus.

**inherit** [ɪn'herɪt] *vt (lit, fig)* erben.

**inheritance** [ɪn'herɪtəns] *n* Erbe *nt (also fig),* Erbschaft *f.*

**inhibit** [ɪn'hɪbɪt] *vt* hemmen. **to** ~ **sb from doing sth** jdn daran hindern, etw zu tun.

**inhibited** [ɪn'hɪbɪtɪd] *adj* gehemmt.

**inhibition** [ˌɪnhɪ'bɪʃən] *n* Hemmung *f.*

**inhospitable** [ˌɪnhɒ'spɪtəbl] *adj* ungastlich; *region* unwirtlich.

**in-house** [ɪn'haʊs] *adj, adv* hausintern.

**inhuman** [ɪn'hjuːmən] *adj cruelty etc* unmenschlich.

**inhumane** [ˌɪnhjuː'meɪn] *adj* inhuman; *(to people also)* menschenunwürdig.

**inhumanity** [ˌɪnhjuː'mænɪtɪ] *n* Unmenschlichkeit *f.* **the** ~ **of man to man** die Unmenschlichkeit der Menschen untereinander.

**inimitable** [ɪ'nɪmɪtəbl] *adj* unnachahmlich.

**iniquitous** [ɪ'nɪkwɪtəs] *adj* ungeheuerlich.

**iniquity** [ɪ'nɪkwɪtɪ] *n* Ungeheuerlichkeit *f.*

**initial** [ɪ'nɪʃəl] **1** *adj* anfänglich, Anfangs-. **my** ~ **re-**

**action** meine anfängliche Reaktion; **in the** ~ **stages** im Anfangsstadium; ~ **letter** Anfangsbuchstabe *m.* **2***n* Initiale *f.* **3** *vt letter* mit seinen Initialen unterzeichnen; *(Comm)* abzeichnen; *(Pol)* paraphieren.

**initialize** [ɪ'nɪʃəlaɪz] *vt (Comp)* initialisieren.

**initially** [ɪ'nɪʃəlɪ] *adv* anfangs, am Anfang.

**initiate** [ɪ'nɪʃɪeɪt] *vt* **(a)** *(set in motion)* den Anstoß geben zu. **to** ~ **proceedings** *(Jur)* einen Prozeß anstrengen. **(b)** *(into club)* feierlich aufnehmen; *(in tribal society)* adolescents initiieren.

**initiation** [ɪˌnɪʃɪ'eɪʃən] *n* **(a)** *(of project etc)* Initiierung *f.* **(b)** *(into society)* Aufnahme *f; (as tribal member)* Initiation *f.* ~ **ceremony** Aufnahmezeremonie *f.*

**initiative** [ɪ'nɪʃətɪv] *n* Initiative *f.* **to take the** ~ die Initiative ergreifen; **on one's own** ~ aus eigener Initiative; **use your** ~! hast du keine Initiative?

**inject** [ɪn'dʒekt] *vt* (ein)spritzen; *(fig) comment* einwerfen; *money* pumpen. **to** ~ **sb with sth** *(Med)* jdm etw einspritzen; **he** ~**ed new life into the club** er brachte neues Leben in den Verein.

**injection** [ɪn'dʒekʃən] *n (act, esp Tech)* Einspritzung *f; (esp Med)* Injektion, Spritze *f.* **an** ~ **of capital** *(Econ)* eine Finanzspritze; ~ **engine** *(Aut)* Einspritzmotor *m;* ~ **pump** Einspritzpumpe *f.*

**injector** [ɪn'dʒektər] *n (Tech) (also* ~ **nozzle)** Einspritzdüse *f.*

**injudicious** [ˌɪndʒʊ'dɪʃəs] *adj* unklug.

**injunction** [ɪn'dʒʌŋkʃən] *n* Anordnung *f; (Jur)* gerichtliche Verfügung.

**injure** ['ɪndʒər] *vt (lit, fig)* verletzen. **to** ~ **one's leg** sich *(dat)* das Bein verletzen.

**injured** ['ɪndʒəd] *adj (lit, fig)* verletzt; *(fig)* voice, *feelings* gekränkt. **he was** ~ er wurde verletzt; **the** ~ die Verletzten; **the** ~ **party** *(Jur)* der/die Geschädigte.

**injurious** [ɪn'dʒʊərɪəs] *adj* schädlich *(to* +*dat).* ~ **to health** gesundheitsschädlich.

**injury** ['ɪndʒərɪ] *n* Verletzung *f (to gen);* (fig also) Kränkung *f (to gen).* **to do sb/oneself an** ~ jdn/ sich verletzen; **to play** ~ **time** *(Brit Sport)* nachspielen.

**injustice** [ɪn'dʒʌstɪs] *n (unfairness, inequality)* Ungerechtigkeit *f; (violation of sb's rights)* Unrecht *nt no pl.* **to do sb an** ~ jdm Unrecht tun.

**ink** [ɪŋk] *n* Tinte *f; (Art)* Tusche *f.*

**ink** *in cpds* Tinten-; ~ **blot** *n* Tintenklecks *m;* ~**-jet printer** *n* Tintenstrahldrucker *m.*

**inkling** ['ɪŋklɪŋ] *n* Ahnung *f.* **he hadn't an** ~ er hatte nicht die leiseste Ahnung; **to give sb an** ~ jdm eine Andeutung geben.

**ink:** ~**pad** *n* Stempelkissen *nt;* ~ **stain** *n* Tintenfleck *m.*

**inky** ['ɪŋkɪ] *adj (+er) (lit)* tintenbeschmiert; *(fig) darkness* tintenschwarz; *black* tintig.

**inlaid** [ɪn'leɪd] *adj* eingelegt. ~ **table** Tisch *m* mit Einlegearbeit.

**inland** ['ɪnlənd] **1** *adj waterway, trade* Binnen-; *mail* Inland(s)-. **I**~ **Revenue** *(Brit)* ≈ Finanzamt *nt.* **2** *adv* landeinwärts.

**inlaws** ['ɪnlɔːz] *npl (parents-in-law)* Schwiegereltern *pl; (others)* angeheiratete Verwandte *pl.*

**inlet** ['ɪnlet] *n* **(a)** *(of sea)* Meeresarm *m; (of river)* Flußarm *m.* **(b)** *(Tech)* Zuleitung *f; (of ventilator)* Öffnung *f.* ~ **pipe** Zuleitung(srohr *nt) f;* ~ **valve** Einlaßventil *nt.*

**inmate** ['ɪnmeɪt] *n* Insasse *m,* Insassin *f.*

**inmost** ['ɪnməʊst] *adj* innerste(r, s).

**inn** [ɪn] *n* Gasthaus *nt; (old: hotel)* Herberge *f (old).*

**innards** ['ɪnədz] *npl* Innereien *pl (also fig),* Eingeweide *pl.*

**innate** [ɪ'neɪt] *adj* angeboren.

**inner** ['ɪnər] *adj* innere(r,s); *surface, door, ear also* Innen-; *meaning* verborgen; *life* Seelen-. ~ **city** Innenstadt *f;* ~ **harbour** Innenbecken *nt;* **the needs of the** ~ **man** die inneren Bedürfnisse.

**innermost** ['ɪnəməʊst] *adj* innerst; *thoughts* geheimst. **in the** ~ **depths of the forest** im tiefsten Wald.

**inner:** ~ **spring mattress** *n (US)* Federkernmatratze *f;* ~ **tube** *n* Schlauch *m.*

**innings** ['ɪnɪŋz] *n (Cricket)* Innenrunde *f.* **he has had a good** ~ *(fig col)* er war lange an der Reihe; *(life)* er hatte ein langes, ausgefülltes Leben.

**innkeeper** ['ɪn,kiːpər] *n* (Gast)wirt *m.*

**innocence** ['ɪnəsəns] *n* **(a)** Unschuld *f.* **in all** ~ in aller Unschuld. **(b)** *(ignorance)* Unkenntnis *f.*

**innocent** ['ɪnəsnt] *adj* **(a)** unschuldig *(of an +dat);* *mistake* unabsichtlich. **to put on an** ~ **air** eine Unschuldsmiene aufsetzen. **(b)** ~ **of** *(ignorant)* nicht vertraut mit; *(devoid of)* frei von.

**innocently** ['ɪnəsntlɪ] *adv* unschuldig; *(in all innocence)* in aller Unschuld.

**innocuous** [ɪ'nɒkjʊəs] *adj* harmlos.

**innovate** ['ɪnəʊveɪt] *vi* Neuerungen einführen.

**innovation** [,ɪnəʊ'veɪʃən] *n* Innovation *f;* *(introduction also)* Neueinführung *f (of gen);* *(thing introduced also)* Neuerung *f.*

**innovative** ['ɪnə,veɪtɪv] *adj* innovativ.

**innuendo** [,ɪnjʊ'endəʊ] *n, pl* **-es** versteckte Andeutung. **to make** ~**es about sb** über jdn Andeutungen fallenlassen.

**innumerable** [ɪ'njuːmərəbl] *adj* unzählig.

**inoculate** [ɪ'nɒkjʊleɪt] *vt person* impfen *(against gegen).*

**inoculation** [ɪ,nɒkjʊ'leɪʃən] *n* Impfung *f.*

**inoffensive** [,ɪnə'fensɪv] *adj* harmlos.

**inoperative** [ɪn'ɒpərətɪv] *adj law, rule* außer Kraft; *machine, radio etc* außer Betrieb, nicht funktionsfähig.

**inopportune** [ɪn'ɒpətjuːn] *adj* inopportun; *moment also* ungelegen. **to be** ~ ungelegen kommen.

**inordinate** [ɪ'nɔːdɪnɪt] *adj* unmäßig; *number, sum of money* ungeheuer.

**inorganic** [,ɪnɔː'gænɪk] *adj* anorganisch.

**in-patient** ['ɪnpeɪʃnt] *n* stationär behandelter Patient/behandelte Patientin.

**input** ['ɪnpʊt] **1** *n (Comp)* Eingabe *f,* Input *m or nt;* *(power* ~*)* Energiezufuhr *f;* *(of energy, work etc)* Aufwand *m; (Rad: Hifi: point of* ~*)* Eingang *m.* ~ **data** *(Comp)* Eingabedaten *pl.* **2** *vt (Comp)* eingeben.

**inquest** ['ɪnkwest] *n (into death)* gerichtliche Untersuchung der Todesursache.

**inquire** [ɪn'kwaɪər] *etc (esp US)* = **enquire** *etc.*

**inquisition** [,ɪnkwɪ'zɪʃən] *n (Hist, fig)* Inquisition *f.*

**inquisitive** [ɪn'kwɪzɪtɪv] *adj* neugierig; *look* forschend; *(for knowledge)* wißbegierig.

**inquisitiveness** [ɪn'kwɪzɪtɪvnɪs] *n* Neugier *f; (for knowledge)* Wißbegierde *f.*

**inroad** ['ɪnrəʊd] *n (Mil)* Einfall *m (into in +acc).* **to make** ~**s into sth** *into time* etw stark in Anspruch nehmen; *into savings* etw stark angreifen; **the Japanese are making** ~**s into the British market** die Japaner dringen in den britischen Markt ein.

**insane** [ɪn'seɪn] **1** *adj* geisteskrank; *(fig)* wahnsinnig. **2** *npl* **the** ~ die Geisteskranken *pl.*

**insanitary** [ɪn'sænɪtərɪ] *adj* unhygienisch.

**insanity** [ɪn'sænɪtɪ] *n* Geisteskrankheit *f; (fig)* Wahnsinn *m.*

**insatiable** [ɪn'seɪʃəbl] *adj* unersättlich.

**inscribe** [ɪn'skraɪb] *vt (on sth* in etw *acc) words etc (on ring etc)* eingravieren; *(on stone)* einmeißeln.

**inscription** [ɪn'skrɪpʃən] Inschrift *f; (on coin)* Aufschrift *f; (in book)* Widmung *f.*

**inscrutable** [ɪn'skruːtəbl] *adj* unergründlich. ~ **face** undurchdringlicher Gesichtsausdruck.

**inseam** ['ɪnsiːm] *n (US)* ~ **measurement** innere Beinlänge.

**insect** ['ɪnsekt] *n* Insekt *nt.* ~ **bite** Insektenstich *m;* ~ **repellent** Insektenschutzmittel *nt.*

**insecticide** [ɪn'sektɪsaɪd] *n* Insektizid *nt.*

**insecure** [,ɪnsɪ'kjʊər] *adj* unsicher.

**insecurity** [,ɪnsɪ'kjʊərɪtɪ] *n* Unsicherheit *f.*

**insensible** [ɪn'sensəbl] *adj* unempfindlich *(to gegen); (unconscious)* bewußtlos.

**insensitive** [ɪn'sensɪtɪv] *adj* **(a)** *(emotionally)* gefühllos. **(b)** *(unappreciative)* unempfänglich *(to für).* **(c)** *(physically)* unempfindlich *(to gegen).* ~ **to pain/ light** schmerz-/lichtunempfindlich.

**insensitivity** [ɪn,sensɪ'tɪvɪtɪ] *n* **(a)** *(emotional)* Gefühllosigkeit *f (towards* gegenüber*).* **(b)** *(unappreciativeness)* Unempfänglichkeit *f (to* für*).* **(c)** *(physical)* Unempfindlichkeit *f (to* gegen*).*

**inseparable** [ɪn'sepərəbl] *adj* untrennbar; *friends* unzertrennlich.

**insert** [ɪn'sɜːt] **1** *vt (stick into)* hineinstecken; *(place in)* hineinlegen; *(place between)* einfügen; *(Film, TV)* einblenden; *thermometer* einführen; *coin* einwerfen; *(Comp) disk* einlegen. **to** ~ **a paragraph** einen Absatz einfügen; **to** ~ **an advertisement in the paper** eine Anzeige in die Zeitung setzen. **2** ['ɪnsɜːt] *n (in book)* Einlage *f; (in magazine)* Beilage *f.*

**insertion** [ɪn'sɜːʃən] *n see vt* Hineinstecken *nt;* Hineinlegen *nt;* Einfügen *nt;* Einführen *nt;* Einwerfen *nt.*

**in-service** ['ɪn,sɜːvɪs] *adj attr* ~ **training** (berufsbegleitende) Fortbildung; ~ **course** Fortbildungskurs *m.*

**inset** ['ɪnset] *n (also* ~ **map)** Nebenkarte *f; (on diagram)* Nebenbild *nt.*

**inshore** ['ɪn'ʃɔːr] *adj* Küsten-. ~ **fishing** Küstenfischerei *f.*

**inside** ['ɪn'saɪd] **1** *n* **(a)** Innere(s) *nt; (of pavement)* Innenseite *f.* **on the** ~ innen; **to know a company from the** ~ interne Kenntnisse über eine Firma haben; **locked from the** ~ von innen verschlossen. **(b) the wind blew the umbrella** ~ **out** der Wind hat den Schirm umgestülpt; **your jumper's** ~ **out** du hast deinen Pullover auf links an; **to turn sth** ~ **out** etw umdrehen; *jumper etc* etw auf links drehen; *(fig) flat etc* etw auf den Kopf stellen; **to know sth** ~ **out** etw in- und auswendig kennen. **(c)** *(col) (*~**s:** *stomach)* Eingeweide, Innere(s) *nt.*

**2** *adj* Innen-, innere(r, s). ~ **information** interne Informationen *pl;* **it looks like an** ~ **job** *(crime)* es sieht nach dem Werk von Insidern aus *(col);* ~ **lane** *(Sport)* Innenbahn *f; (Aut)* Innenspur *f;* ~ **leg (measurement)** innere Beinlänge; ~ **pocket** Innentasche *f;* ~ **story** *(Press)* Inside-Story *f;* ~ **forward** Halbstürmer *m;* ~ **left** Halblinke(r) *m;* ~ **right** Halbrechte(r) *m.*

**3** *adv* innen; *(indoors)* drin(nen); *(direction)* nach innen, hinein/herein. **look** ~ sehen Sie hinein; **let's go** ~ gehen wir hinein; **there is something** ~ es ist etwas (innen) drin; **to be** ~ *(col: in prison)* sitzen *(col).*

**4** *prep* **(a)** *(place)* innen in *(+dat); (direction)* in *(+acc)* ... hinein). **he was waiting** ~ **the house** er wartete im Haus; **he went** ~ **the house** er ging ins Haus (hinein). **(b)** *(time)* innerhalb. **he was 5 seconds** ~ **the record** er ist 5 Sekunden unter dem Rekord geblieben.

**insider** [ɪn'saɪdər] *n* Eingeweihte(r) *m.* ~ **dealing** *or*

**trading** *(Fin)* Insiderhandel *m.*

**insidious** [ɪnˈsɪdɪəs] *adj* heimtückisch.

**insight** [ˈɪnsaɪt] *n* **his ~ into my problems** sein Verständnis *nt* für meine Probleme; **to gain an ~ into sth** (einen) Einblick in etw *(acc)* gewinnen.

**insignia** [ɪnˈsɪgnɪə] *npl* Insignien *pl.*

**insignificance** [ˌɪnsɪgˈnɪfɪkəns] *n see adj* Belanglosigkeit *f;* Geringfügigkeit *f;* Unscheinbarkeit *f.*

**insignificant** [ˌɪnsɪgˈnɪfɪkənt] *adj* belanglos; *sum, difference also* geringfügig; *person* unscheinbar.

**insincere** [ˌɪnsɪnˈsɪəʳ] *adj* unaufrichtig.

**insincerity** [ˌɪnsɪnˈserɪtɪ] *n* Unaufrichtigkeit *f.*

**insinuate** [ɪnˈsɪnjʊeɪt] *vt* **(a)** andeuten *(sth to sb* etw jdm gegenüber*).* **what are you insinuating?** was wollen Sie damit sagen? **(b) to ~ oneself into sb's favour** sich bei jdm einschmeicheln.

**insinuating** [ɪnˈsɪnjʊeɪtɪŋ] *adj* anzüglich.

**insinuation** [ɪnˌsɪnjʊˈeɪʃən] *n* Anspielung *f (about* auf *+acc).*

**insipid** [ɪnˈsɪpɪd] *adj* fad; *person, novel also* geistlos.

**insist** [ɪnˈsɪst] *vti* bestehen. **I ~!** ich bestehe darauf!; **if you ~** wenn Sie darauf bestehen; *(if you like)* wenn's unbedingt sein muß; **I must ~ that you stop** ich muß darauf bestehen, daß Sie aufhören; **he ~s that he is innocent** er behauptet beharrlich, unschuldig zu sein; **I ~ on the best** ich bestehe auf bester Qualität; **if you will ~ on smoking, ...** wenn Sie schon unbedingt rauchen müssen, ...

**insistence** [ɪnˈsɪstəns] *n* Bestehen *nt (on* auf *+dat).* **I did it at his ~** ich tat es, weil er darauf bestand.

**insistent** [ɪnˈsɪstənt] *adj* **(a)** *person* beharrlich; *salesman etc* aufdringlich. **he was most ~ about it** er beharrte darauf. **(b)** *(urgent) demand, tone* nachdrücklich.

**insole** [ˈɪnsəʊl] *n* Einlegesohle *f.*

**insolence** [ˈɪnsələns] *n* Unverschämtheit *f.*

**insolent** *adj,* **~ly** *adv* [ˈɪnsələnt, -lɪ] unverschämt.

**insoluble** [ɪnˈsɒljʊbl] *adj* **(a)** *substance* unlöslich. **(b)** *problem* unlösbar.

**insolvency** [ɪnˈsɒlvənsɪ] *n* Zahlungsunfähigkeit *f.*

**insolvent** [ɪnˈsɒlvənt] *adj* zahlungsunfähig.

**insomnia** [ɪnˈsɒmnɪə] *n* Schlaflosigkeit *f.*

**insomniac** [ɪnˈsɒmnɪæk] *n* **to be an ~** an Schlaflosigkeit leiden.

**inspect** [ɪnˈspekt] *vt* **(a)** *(examine)* prüfen. **to ~ sth for sth** etw auf etw *(acc)* (hin) prüfen. **(b)** *(Mil etc: review)* inspizieren.

**inspection** [ɪnˈspekʃən] *n* **(a)** Prüfung *f; (of school)* Inspektion *f.* **on ~** bei näherer Betrachtung; **for your ~** zur Prüfung. **(b)** *(Mil)* Inspektion *f.*

**inspector** [ɪnˈspektəʳ] *n (factory ~, Brit: on buses)* Kontrolleur(in *f*) *m; (of schools)* Schulrat *m,* Schulrätin *f; (of police)* Polizeiinspektor *m; (of taxes)* Steuerinspektor *m.*

**inspiration** [ˌɪnspəˈreɪʃən] *n* Inspiration *(for* zu *or* für*),* Eingebung *(for* zu*) f.* **he gets his ~ from ...** er läßt sich von ... inspirieren.

**inspire** [ɪnˈspaɪəʳ] *vt* **(a)** *respect, awe* einflößen *(in sb* jdm*).* **to ~ sb with confidence** jdm mit Vertrauen erfüllen. **(b)** *(be inspiration to) person* inspirieren.

**inspired** [ɪnˈspaɪəd] *adj* genial. **in an ~ moment** in einem Augenblick der Inspiration; *(iro)* in einem lichten Moment; **it was an ~ guess** das war genial geraten.

**inspiring** [ɪnˈspaɪərɪŋ] *adj speech* inspirierend.

**inst** *(Brit Comm dated)* = **instant** d.M.

**instability** [ˌɪnstəˈbɪlɪtɪ] *n* Instabilität *f; (of character also)* Labilität *f.*

**install** [ɪnˈstɔːl] *vt* installieren; *telephone also* anschließen; *person* (in ein Amt) einsetzen.

**installation** [ˌɪnstəˈleɪʃən] *n* **(a)** *see vt* Installation *f;*

Anschluß *m;* Amtseinsetzung *f.* **(b)** *(machine etc)* Anlage *f.* **(c)** *military ~* militärische Anlage.

**instalment,** *(US)* **installment** [ɪnˈstɔːlmənt] *n* **(a)** *(of serial)* Fortsetzung *f; (TV)* (Sende)folge *f.* **(b)** *(Fin)* Rate *f.* **monthly ~** Monatsrate *f;* **to pay in** *or* **by ~s** in Raten bezahlen.

**installment plan** *n (US)* Ratenzahlung(splan *m) f.* **to buy on the ~** auf Raten kaufen.

**instance** [ˈɪnstəns] *n (example)* Beispiel *nt; (case)* Fall *m.* **for ~** zum Beispiel; **in the first ~** zunächst (einmal).

**instant** [ˈɪnstənt] **1** *adj* **(a)** unmittelbar; *relief, result also* sofortig *attr.* **~ camera** Sofortbildkamera *f;* **~ replay** *(TV)* Wiederholung *f.* **(b)** *(Cook)* Instant-. **~ coffee** Pulverkaffee *m;* **~ food** Schnellgerichte *pl.* **2** *n* Augenblick *m.* **this (very) ~** sofort; **at that very ~** genau in dem Augenblick.

**instantaneous** [ˌɪnstənˈteɪnɪəs] *adj* unmittelbar.

**instantaneously** [ˌɪnstənˈteɪnɪəslɪ] *adv* sofort, unverzüglich.

**instantly** [ˈɪnstəntlɪ] *adv* sofort.

**instead** [ɪnˈsted] **1** *prep* **~ of** statt *(+gen or (col) +dat),* anstelle von. **~ of going to school** (an)statt zur Schule zu gehen; **his brother came ~ of him** sein Bruder kam an seiner Stelle. **2** *adv* statt dessen. **if he doesn't want to go, I'll go ~** wenn er nicht gehen will, gehe ich an seiner Stelle.

**instep** [ˈɪnstep] *n (Anat)* Spann *m; (of shoe)* Blatt *nt.*

**instigate** [ˈɪnstɪgeɪt] *vt* anstiften; *reform etc* initiieren.

**instigation** [ˌɪnstɪˈgeɪʃən] *n see vt* Anstiftung *f;* Initiierung *f.* **at sb's ~** auf jds Betreiben.

**instil** [ɪnˈstɪl] *vt* einflößen *(into sb* jdm*).*

**instinct** [ˈɪnstɪŋkt] *n* Instinkt *m.* **by** *or* **from ~** instinktiv.

**instinctive** *adj,* **~ly** *adv* [ɪnˈstɪŋktɪv, -lɪ] instinktiv.

**institute** [ˈɪnstɪtjuːt] **1** *vt* **(a)** *reforms* einführen; *search* einleiten. **(b)** *(Jur) an action* einleiten; *proceedings* anstrengen *(against* gegen*).* **2** *n* Institut *nt; (home)* Anstalt *f.*

**institution** [ˌɪnstɪˈtjuːʃən] *n (organization, custom)* Institution *f; (building, home etc)* Anstalt *f.*

**institutional** [ˌɪnstɪˈtjuːʃənl] *adj life etc* Anstalts-.

**institutionalize** [ˌɪnstɪˈtjuːʃənəlaɪz] *vt* institutionalisieren.

**in-store** [ˈɪnstɔːʳ] *adj* im Laden. **~ surveillance (system)** geschäftsinternes Überwachungssystem.

**instruct** [ɪnˈstrʌkt] *vt* **(a)** *(teach) person* unterrichten. **(b)** *(tell, direct) person* anweisen; *(command)* die Anweisung erteilen *(+dat); (appoint) lawyer* beauftragen.

**instruction** [ɪnˈstrʌkʃən] *n* **(a)** *(teaching)* Unterricht *m. (command)* Anweisung, Instruktion *f.* **~s for use** Gebrauchsanweisung *f;* **~ book** *or* **manual** Bedienungsanleitung *f.*

**instructive** [ɪnˈstrʌktɪv] *adj* aufschlußreich; *(of educational value)* lehrreich.

**instructor** [ɪnˈstrʌktəʳ] *n (also Sport)* Lehrer *m; (US)* Dozent *m; (Mil)* Ausbilder *m.*

**instrument** [ˈɪnstrʊmənt] *n (Mus, Tech)* Instrument *nt; (domestic)* Gerät *nt; (person)* Werkzeug *nt.* **to fly an aircraft on ~s** ein Flugzeug nach den (Bord)instrumenten fliegen; **~ flight** Instrumentenflug *m;* **~ panel** *(Aviat, Aut)* Armaturenbrett *nt.*

**instrumental** [ˌɪnstrʊˈmentl] *adj* **(a) he was ~ in getting her the job** er hat ihr zu dieser Stelle verholfen; **to be ~ in sth** bei etw eine entscheidende Rolle spielen. **(b)** *music* Instrumental-.

**instrumentalist** [ˌɪnstrʊˈmentəlɪst] *n* Instrumentalist(in *f*) *m.*

**insubordinate** [ˌɪnsəˈbɔːdɪnɪt] *adj* aufsässig.

**insubordination** [ˌɪnsəˌbɔːdɪˈneɪʃən] *n* Aufsässigkeit *f; (Mil)* Gehorsamsverweigerung *f.*
**insufferable** *adj* [ɪnˈsʌfərəbl] unerträglich.
**insufficient** [ˌɪnsəˈfɪʃənt] *adj* ungenügend *pred*; *work, insulation also* unzulänglich.
**insular** [ˈɪnsjələʳ] *adj (narrow)* engstirnig.
**insularity** [ˌɪnsjʊˈlærɪtɪ] *n* Engstirnigkeit *f.*
**insulate** [ˈɪnsjʊleɪt] *vt room, (Elec)* isolieren; *(fig: shelter)* abschirmen *(from gegen).*
**insulating tape** [ˈɪnsjʊleɪtɪŋˌteɪp] *n (Brit)* Isolierband *nt.*
**insulation** [ˌɪnsjʊˈleɪʃən] *n* Isolierung *f; (material also)* Isoliermaterial *nt; (fig)* Geschütztheit *f (from gegen).*
**insulator** [ˈɪnsjʊleɪtəʳ] *n (Elec)* Isolator *m; (material)* Isoliermaterial *nt.*
**insulin** [ˈɪnsjʊlɪn] *n* Insulin *nt.*
**insult** [ɪnˈsʌlt] **1** *vt* beleidigen; *(by words also)* beschimpfen. **2** [ˈɪnsʌlt] *n (to für +acc)* Beleidigung *f; (with words also)* Beschimpfung *f.* **to add ~ to injury** das Ganze noch schlimmer machen.
**insulting** [ɪnˈsʌltɪŋ] *adj* beleidigend.
**insuperable** [ɪnˈsuːpərəbl] *adj* unüberwindlich.
**insupportable** [ˌɪnsəˈpɔːtəbl] *adj* unerträglich.
**insurance** [ɪnˈʃʊərəns] *n* Versicherung *f.* **to take out ~** eine Versicherung abschließen.
**insurance: ~ agent** *n* Versicherungsvertreter(in *f*) *m;* **~ broker** *n* Versicherungskaufmann *m;* **~ company** *n* Versicherungsgesellschaft *f;* **~ policy** *n* Versicherungspolice *f; (fig)* Sicherheitsvorkehrung *f;* **~ premium** *n* Versicherungsprämie *f;* **~ salesman** Versicherungsvertreter *m.*
**insure** [ɪnˈʃʊəʳ] *vt car, house etc* versichern (lassen) *(with bei; for für).* **to ~ oneself** *or* **one's life** eine Lebensversicherung abschließen.
**insurer** [ɪnˈʃʊərəʳ] *n* Versicherer *m.*
**insurgent** [ɪnˈsɜːdʒənt] **1** *adj* aufständisch. **2** *n* Aufständische(r) *mf.*
**insurmountable** [ˌɪnsəˈmaʊntəbl] *adj* unüberwindlich.
**insurrection** [ˌɪnsəˈrekʃən] *n* Aufstand *m.*
**intact** [ɪnˈtækt] *adj* unversehrt.
**intake** [ˈɪnteɪk] *n (of water, electric current, Sch)* Aufnahme *f; (pipe)* Zuflußrohr *nt.* **food ~** Nahrungsaufnahme *f.*
**intangible** [ɪnˈtændʒəbl] *adj* **(a)** nicht greifbar. **(b)** *longings* unbestimmbar. **(c)** *(Jur, Comm)* **~ assets** immaterielle Werte *pl.*
**integer** [ˈɪntɪdʒəʳ] *n* ganze Zahl.
**integral** [ˈɪntɪgrəl] *adj (essential)* wesentlich; *(built-in)* eingebaut; *(whole)* vollständig.
**integrate** [ˈɪntɪgreɪt] *vt* integrieren *(into* in *+acc).* **to ~ sth with sth** etw auf etw *(acc)* abstimmen.
**integrated** [ˈɪntɪgreɪtɪd] *adj plan* einheitlich; *school* ohne Rassentrennung. **a fully ~ personality** eine in sich ausgewogene Persönlichkeit; **~ circuit** integrierte Schaltung.
**integration** [ˌɪntɪˈgreɪʃən] *n* Integration *f (into* in *+acc).* **(racial) ~** Rassenintegration *f.*
**integrity** [ɪnˈtegrɪtɪ] *n* **(a)** *(honesty)* Integrität *f.* **(b)** *(wholeness)* Einheit *f.*
**intellect** [ˈɪntɪlekt] *n* Intellekt *m.*
**intellectual** [ɪntɪˈlektjʊəl] **1** *adj* intellektuell; *interests also* geistig. **something a little more ~** etwas geistig Anspruchsvolleres. **2** *n* Intellektuelle(r) *mf.*
**intelligence** [ɪnˈtelɪdʒəns] *n* **(a)** Intelligenz *f.* **~ test** Intelligenztest *m.* **(b)** *(news, information)* Informationen *pl.* **(c)** *(Mil etc)* Geheimdienst *m.*
**intelligent** *adj*, **~ly** *adv* [ɪnˈtelɪdʒənt, -lɪ] intelligent.
**intelligentsia** [ɪnˌtelɪˈdʒentsɪə] *n* Intelligenz *f.*
**intelligible** [ɪnˈtelɪdʒəbl] *adj* verständlich.

**intemperate** [ɪnˈtempərɪt] *adj climate* extrem; *person* unmäßig.
**intend** [ɪnˈtend] *vt* **(a)** *(+n)* beabsichtigen, wollen. **I ~ed no harm** es war (von mir) nicht böse gemeint; *(with action)* ich hatte nichts Böses beabsichtigt; **I didn't ~ it as an insult** das sollte keine Beleidigung sein; **that remark was ~ed for you** mit dieser Bemerkung waren Sie gemeint; **this film was never ~ed for children** dieser Film war nie für Kinder gedacht. **(b)** *(+vb)* beabsichtigen, vorhaben. **he ~s to win** er hat fest vor, zu gewinnen; **I ~ to take him with me** ich habe vor, ihn mitzunehmen; *(insist)* er soll mit mir mitkommen; **what do you ~ to do about it?** was beabsichtigen Sie, dagegen zu tun?
**intense** [ɪnˈtens] *adj* intensiv; *disappointment* äußerst groß; *person* ernsthaft.
**intensely** [ɪnˈtenslɪ] *adv angry* äußerst; *study* intensiv.
**intensify** [ɪnˈtensɪfaɪ] **1** *vt* intensivieren; *meaning* verstärken. **2** *vi* zunehmen; *(pain, heat also)* stärker werden.
**intensity** [ɪnˈtensɪtɪ] *n* Intensität *f; (of feeling, storm also)* Heftigkeit *f.*
**intensive** [ɪnˈtensɪv] *adj* intensiv, Intensiv-. **in ~ care** auf der Intensivstation; **~ care unit** Intensivstation *f;* **they came under ~ fire** sie kamen unter heftigen Beschuß.
**intensively** [ɪnˈtensɪvlɪ] *adv* intensiv.
**intent** [ɪnˈtent] **1** *n* Absicht *f.* **to all ~s and purposes** im Grunde; **with ~ to** *(Jur)* mit dem Vorsatz zu. **2** *adj look* durchdringend. **to be ~ on achieving sth** fest entschlossen sein, etw zu erreichen.
**intention** [ɪnˈtenʃən] *n* Absicht *f.* **I have every ~ of doing that** ich habe die feste Absicht, das zu tun; **I have no** *or* **haven't the least ~ of staying!** ich habe nicht die geringste Absicht hierzubleiben; **with the best of ~s** in der besten Absicht; **with the ~ of …** mit dem Vorsatz zu …
**intentional** [ɪnˈtenʃənl] *adj* absichtlich, vorsätzlich *(esp Jur).* **it wasn't ~** das war keine Absicht.
**intentionally** [ɪnˈtenʃnəlɪ] *adv* absichtlich.
**intently** [ɪnˈtentlɪ] *adv* konzentriert.
**inter-** [ˈɪntəʳ] *pref* zwischen-, Zwischen-.
**interact** [ˌɪntərˈækt] *vi* aufeinander einwirken; *(Phys)* wechselwirken; *(Psychol)* interagieren.
**interaction** [ˌɪntərˈækʃən] *n see vi* gegenseitige Einwirkung, Wechselwirkung *f (also Phys);* Interaktion *f.*
**interactive** [ˌɪntərˈæktɪv] *adj* interaktiv.
**intercede** [ˌɪntəˈsiːd] *vi* sich einsetzen, sich verwenden *(with bei, on behalf of für).*
**intercept** [ˌɪntəˈsept] *vt message, plane* abfangen; *phone call also* abhören. **they ~ed the enemy** sie schnitten dem Feind den Weg ab.
**interception** [ˌɪntəˈsepʃən] *n* Abfangen *nt.*
**interceptor** [ˌɪntəˈseptəʳ] *n (Aviat)* **~ (fighter)** Abfangjäger *m.*
**interchange** [ˈɪntəˌtʃeɪndʒ] **1** *n* **(a)** *(of roads)* Kreuzung *f; (of motorways)* (Autobahn)kreuz *nt.* **(b)** *(exchange)* Austausch *m.* **2** [ˌɪntəˈtʃeɪndʒ] *vt* **(a)** *(switch round)* (aus)tauschen. **(b)** *ideas etc* austauschen *(with mit).*
**interchangeable** [ˌɪntəˈtʃeɪndʒəbl] *adj* austauschbar. **x is ~ with y** x und y sind austauschbar.
**interchangeably** [ˌɪntəˈtʃeɪndʒəblɪ] *adv* austauschbar. **they are used ~** sie können ausgetauscht werden.
**inter-city** [ˌɪntəˈsɪtɪ] *n* Intercity *m.*
**intercom** [ˈɪntəkɒm] *n* (Gegen)sprechanlage *f; (in ship, plane)* Bordverständigungsanlage *f.*

**interconnect** [ˌɪntəkə'nekt] **1** vt miteinander verbinden; (Elec also) circuits etc zusammenschalten. ~ed events zusammenhängende or miteinander in Verbindung stehende Ereignisse. **2** vi miteinander verbunden sein; (facts, events) in Zusammenhang stehen.

**intercontinental** ['ɪntə,kɒntɪ'nentl] adj interkontinental, Interkontinental-.

**intercourse** ['ɪntəkɔːs] n (sexual) ~ (Geschlechts-)verkehr m; social ~ gesellschaftlicher Verkehr.

**interdependence** [ˌɪntədɪ'pendəns] n wechselseitige Abhängigkeit.

**interdependent** [ˌɪntədɪ'pendənt] adj wechselseitig voneinander abhängig.

**interdisciplinary** [ˌɪntə'dɪsɪˌplɪnərɪ] adj fachübergreifend.

**interest** ['ɪntrɪst] **1** n (a) Interesse nt. to take an ~ in sb/sth sich für jdn/etw interessieren; just for ~ nur interessehalber; he has lost ~ er hat das Interesse verloren; his ~s are ... er interessiert sich für ...; of vital ~ to the economy von lebenswichtigem Interesse für die Wirtschaft; to act in sb's/one's own ~(s) in jds/im eigenen Interesse handeln; in the public ~ im öffentlichen Interesse. (b) (Fin) Zinsen pl. rate of ~, ~ rate Zinssatz m; to bear ~ at 4% 4% Zinsen tragen, mit 4% verzinst sein. (c) (Comm) (share, stake) Anteil m; (~ group) Kreise pl, Interessengruppe f. he has a financial ~ in the company er ist finanziell an der Firma beteiligt; British trading ~s britische Handelsinteressen pl.
**2** vt interessieren (in für, an +dat). to ~ sb in doing sth jdn dafür interessieren, etw zu tun; can I ~ you in a little drink? kann ich Sie zu etwas Alkoholischem überreden?

**interested** ['ɪntrɪstɪd] adj interessiert (in an +dat). I'm not ~ ich bin nicht (daran) interessiert; to be ~ in sb/sth sich für jdn/etw interessieren; I'm going to the cinema, are you ~ (in coming)? ich gehe ins Kino, haben Sie Lust mitzukommen?; she was ~ to see what he would do sie war gespannt, was er wohl tun würde; he is an ~ party er ist daran beteiligt.

**interest-free** ['ɪntrɪst'friː] adj loan zinsfrei.

**interesting** ['ɪntrɪstɪŋ] adj interessant.

**interestingly** ['ɪntrɪstɪŋlɪ] adv ~ enough, ... interessanterweise ...

**interface** ['ɪntəfeɪs] **1** n (Comp) Schnittstelle f, Interface nt; (fig) Grenzfläche f. the man/machine ~ die Interaktion von Mensch und Maschine. **2** [ɪntə'feɪs] vt koppeln.

**interfere** [ˌɪntə'fɪər] vi (in sb's affairs) sich einmischen (in in +acc). don't ~ with the machine laß die Finger von der Maschine; who's been interfering with my books? wer war an meinen Büchern?; to ~ with sth (disrupt, Rad) etw stören; to ~ with sb's plans jds Pläne durchkreuzen.

**interference** [ˌɪntə'fɪərəns] n (meddling) Einmischung f; (disruption, Rad) Störung f (with gen).

**interfering** [ˌɪntə'fɪərɪŋ] adj don't be so ~ misch dich nicht immer ein.

**interim** ['ɪntərɪm] **1** n in the ~ in der Zwischenzeit. **2** adj vorläufig; arrangements also, government Übergangs-; report, payment Zwischen-. ~ dividend (Fin) Abschlagsdividende f.

**interior** [ɪn'tɪərɪər] **1** adj (inside) Innen-; (inland, domestic) Binnen-. **2** n (of building, container, country) Innere(s) nt; (of car) Innenraum m; (decoration, furnishings) Innenausstattung f; (Phot) Innenaufnahme f. deep in the ~ tief im Landesinneren; Department of the I~ (US) Innenministerium nt.

**interior**: ~ decorator n Innenausstatter(in f) m; ~

**design** n Innenarchitektur f; ~ **designer** n Innenarchitekt(in f) m; ~ **light** n (Aut) Innenleuchte f; ~ **sprung mattress** n Federkernmatratze f.

**interject** [ˌɪntə'dʒekt] vt remark einwerfen.

**interjection** [ˌɪntə'dʒekʃən] n (exclamation) Ausruf m; (remark) Einwurf m.

**interlocking** [ˌɪntə'lɒkɪŋ] adj ineinandergreifend.

**interloper** ['ɪntələupər] n Eindringling m.

**interlude** ['ɪntəluːd] n Periode f; (episode) Episode f; (Theat) Wechselspiel nt; (interval) Pause f.

**intermarriage** [ˌɪntə'mærɪdʒ] n (between groups) Mischehen pl; (within the group) Heirat f untereinander.

**intermarry** [ˌɪntə'mærɪ] vi Mischehen eingehen; (within the group) untereinander heiraten.

**intermediary** [ˌɪntə'miːdɪərɪ] n (Ver)mittler(in f) m.

**intermediate** [ˌɪntə'miːdɪət] adj Zwischen-; French etc für fortgeschrittene Anfänger.

**interminable** [ɪn'tɜːmɪnəbl] adj endlos. after what seemed an ~ journey nach einer Reise, die nicht enden zu wollen schien.

**intermingle** [ˌɪntə'mɪŋgl] vi sich mischen (with unter +acc).

**intermission** [ˌɪntə'mɪʃən] n (a) Unterbrechung f. (b) (Theat, Film) Pause f.

**intermittent** [ˌɪntə'mɪtənt] adj periodisch auftretend; (Tech) intermittierend.

**intermittently** [ˌɪntə'mɪtəntlɪ] adv periodisch, (Tech) intermittierend.

**intern¹** [ɪn'tɜːn] vt person internieren.

**intern²** ['ɪntɜːn] (US) n Assistenzarzt m, Assistenzärztin f.

**internal** [ɪn'tɜːnl] adj (inner) innere(r, s); diameter Innen-; trade etc Binnen-; policy, mail intern; ~ combustion engine Verbrennungsmotor m; I~ Revenue Service (US) Finanzamt nt; ~ affairs innere Angelegenheiten pl.

**internally** [ɪn'tɜːnəlɪ] adv innen, im Inneren; (in body) innerlich; (in country) landesintern; (in organization) intern. "not to be taken ~" „nicht zur inneren Anwendung".

**international** [ˌɪntə'næʃnəl] **1** adj international. ~ call Auslandsgespräch nt; ~ law Völkerrecht nt; I~ Monetary Fund Internationaler Währungsfonds; ~ money order Auslandsanweisung f. **2** n (Sport) (match) Länderspiel nt; (player) Nationalspieler(in f) m.

**internationally** [ˌɪntə'næʃnəlɪ] adv international.

**internecine** [ˌɪntə'niːsaɪn] adj (bloody) mörderisch.

**internee** [ˌɪntɜː'niː] n Internierte(r) mf.

**internment** [ɪn'tɜːnmənt] n Internierung f. ~ camp Internierungslager nt.

**interplanetary** [ˌɪntə'plænɪtərɪ] adj interplanetar.

**interplay** ['ɪntəpleɪ] n Zusammenspiel nt.

**Interpol** ['ɪntəpɒl] n Interpol f.

**interpose** [ˌɪntə'pəuz] vt dazwischenbringen or -legen; remark einwerfen.

**interpret** [ɪn'tɜːprɪt] **1** vt (a) dolmetschen. (b) (explain) auslegen, interpretieren; (Theat, Mus) interpretieren. how would you ~ what he said? wie würden Sie seine Worte auffassen? **2** vi dolmetschen.

**interpretation** [ɪn,tɜːprɪ'teɪʃən] n see vt (b) Auslegung, Interpretation f.

**interpreter** [ɪn'tɜːprɪtər] n Dolmetscher(in f) m; (Theat, Mus) Interpret(in f) m.

**interrelated** [ˌɪntərɪ'leɪtɪd] adj to be ~ zueinander in Beziehung stehen, zusammenhängen.

**interrogate** [ɪn'terəgeɪt] vt (police) verhören.

**interrogation** [ɪn,terə'geɪʃən] n Verhör nt.

**interrogative** [ˌɪntə'rɒgətɪv] adj (Gram) Frage-, Interrogativ-.

**interrogator** [ɪn'terəgeɪtəʳ] *n* Vernehmungsbeamte(r) *mf.*

**interrupt** [ˌɪntə'rʌpt] *vti* unterbrechen *(also Elec)*; *work also* stören. **stop ~ing (me)!** fall mir nicht dauernd ins Wort!

**interruption** [ˌɪntə'rʌpʃən] *n* Unterbrechung *f; (of work also)* Störung *f.*

**intersect** [ˌɪntə'sekt] **1** *vt* durchschneiden; *(Geometry)* schneiden. **2** *vi* sich kreuzen; *(Geometry)* sich schneiden.

**intersection** [ˌɪntə'sekʃən] *n (crossroads)* Kreuzung *f; (Geometry)* Schnittpunkt *m.*

**intersperse** [ˌɪntə'spɜːs] *vt* **woods ~d with fields** Wald mit Feldern dazwischen; **a speech ~d with quotations** eine mit Zitaten gespickte Rede.

**interstate** [ˌɪntə'steɪt] *adj (US)* zwischen den (Bundes)staaten. **I~ Highway** ≈ Bundesautobahn *f.*

**intertwined** [ˌɪntə'twaɪnd] *adj* ineinander verschlungen.

**interval** ['ɪntəvəl] *n* **(a)** *(space, time)* Abstand *m.* **at ~s** in Abständen; **sunny ~s** Aufheiterungen *pl.* **(b)** *(Sch, Theat, fig)* Pause *f.* **(c)** *(Mus)* Intervall *nt.*

**intervene** [ˌɪntə'viːn] *vi (person)* einschreiten *(in bei)*, intervenieren; *(event, fate)* dazwischenkommen. **in the intervening weeks** in den dazwischenliegenden Wochen.

**intervention** [ˌɪntə'venʃən] *n* Eingreifen *nt*, Intervention *f.*

**interview** ['ɪntəvjuː] **1** *n (for job)* Vorstellungsgespräch *nt; (with authorities etc)* Gespräch *nt; (TV etc)* Interview *nt.* **2** *vt job applicant* ein/das Vorstellungsgespräch führen mit; *(TV etc)* interviewen. **he is being ~ed on Monday for the job** er hat am Montag sein Vorstellungsgespräch.

**interviewee** [ˌɪntəvjuː'iː] *n (for job)* Stellenbewerber(in *f*) *m; (TV etc)* Interviewte(r) *mf.*

**interviewer** ['ɪntəvjuːəʳ] *n (for job)* Leiter(in *f*) *m* des Vorstellungsgesprächs; *(TV etc)* Interviewer(in *f*) *m.*

**intestate** [ɪn'testɪt] *adj (Jur)* **to die ~** sterben, ohne ein Testament zu hinterlassen.

**intestinal** [ɪn'testɪnl] *adj* Darm-.

**intestine** [ɪn'testɪn] *n* Darm *m.* **~s** Eingeweide *nt*; **small/large ~** Dünn-/Dickdarm *m.*

**intimacy** ['ɪntɪməsɪ] *n* Vertrautheit *f; (euph: sexual ~)* Intimität *f.*

**intimate¹** ['ɪntɪmɪt] *adj friend* eng, vertraut; *(sexually)* intim; *knowledge* gründlich. **to be on ~ terms with sb** zu jdm ein vertrauliches Verhältnis haben; **to be/become ~ with sb** mit jdm vertraut sein/ werden.

**intimate²** ['ɪntɪmeɪt] *vt* andeuten. **he ~d to them that they should stop** er gab ihnen zu verstehen, daß sie aufhören sollten.

**intimately** ['ɪntɪmɪtlɪ] *adv acquainted* bestens; *speak* vertraulich; *connected* eng; *know* genau.

**intimation** [ˌɪntɪ'meɪʃən] *n* Andeutung *f.*

**intimidate** [ɪn'tɪmɪdeɪt] *vt* einschüchtern.

**intimidation** [ɪnˌtɪmɪ'deɪʃən] *n* Einschüchterung *f.*

**into** ['ɪntʊ] *prep* in *(+acc)*; *crash* gegen. **to translate sth ~ French** etw ins Französische übersetzen; **to divide 3 ~ 9** 9 durch 3 teilen; **far ~ the night** bis tief in die Nacht hinein; **it turned ~ a nice day** es wurde ein schöner Tag; **I'm not really ~ the job yet** *(col)* ich bin noch nicht ganz in der Arbeit drin *(col)*; **to be (heavily) ~ sth** *(col: like)* (schwer) auf etw *(acc)* stehen *(col)*, (völlig) auf etw *(acc)* abgefahren sein *(col)*; **he's ~ drugs/wine** er nimmt Drogen/ist Weinliebhaber.

**intolerable** [ɪn'tɒlərəbl] *adj* unerträglich.

**intolerance** [ɪn'tɒlərəns] *n* Intoleranz *f (of gegen-*

über*).*

**intolerant** [ɪn'tɒlərənt] *adj* intolerant *(of gegenüber).*

**intonation** [ˌɪntəʊ'neɪʃən] *n* Intonation *f.*

**intoxicate** [ɪn'tɒksɪkeɪt] *vt (lit, fig)* berauschen.

**intoxicated** [ɪn'tɒksɪkeɪtɪd] *adj* betrunken, berauscht *(also fig).*

**intoxicating** [ɪn'tɒksɪkeɪtɪŋ] *adj* berauschend. **~ liquors** *(form)* alkoholische Getränke.

**intoxication** [ɪnˌtɒksɪ'keɪʃən] *n* Rausch *m (also fig).*

**intractable** [ɪn'træktəbl] *adj problem, illness* hartnäckig; *child* widerspenstig.

**intransigence** [ɪn'trænsɪdʒəns] *n* Unnachgiebigkeit *f.*

**intransigent** [ɪn'trænsɪdʒənt] *adj* unnachgiebig.

**intransitive** [ɪn'trænsɪtɪv] *adj verb* intransitiv.

**intravenous** [ˌɪntrə'viːnəs] *adj* intravenös.

**in-tray** ['ɪntreɪ] *n* Ablage *f* für Eingänge.

**intrepid** [ɪn'trepɪd] *adj* unerschrocken.

**intricacy** ['ɪntrɪkəsɪ] *n* Kompliziertheit *f; (of a law etc)* Feinheit *f.*

**intricate** ['ɪntrɪkɪt] *adj* kompliziert; *(involved also)* verwickelt.

**intrigue** [ɪn'triːg] **1** *vi* intrigieren. **2** *vt (arouse interest of)* faszinieren; *(arouse curiosity of)* neugierig machen. **I'd be ~d to know why ...** es würde mich schon interessieren, warum ... **3** ['ɪntriːg] *n (plot)* Intrige *f; (no pl: plotting)* Intrigen(spiel *nt*) *pl.*

**intriguing** [ɪn'triːgɪŋ] *adj* faszinierend, interessant.

**intrinsic** [ɪn'trɪnsɪk] *adj value* immanent; *(essential)* wesentlich. **~ fault** grundlegender Fehler.

**introduce** [ˌɪntrə'djuːs] *vt* **(a)** *(to person)* vorstellen *(to sb* jdm*)*, bekannt machen *(to* mit*); (to subject)* einführen *(to* in *+acc).* **have you two been ~d?** hat man Sie miteinander bekannt gemacht?; **to ~ oneself** sich vorstellen. **(b)** *reform* einführen; *(Parl) bill* einbringen; *programme, (also TV)* ankündigen. **(c)** *(insert)* einführen *(into* in *+acc).*

**introduction** [ˌɪntrə'dʌkʃən] *n* **(a)** *(to person)* Vorstellung *f.* **letter of ~** Einführungsbrief *m.* **(b)** *(in book)* Einleitung *f (to* zu*).* **(c)** *(to subject, of reform etc)* Einführung *f (to* in *+acc); (of bill)* Einbringen *nt; (of speaker)* Vorstellung *f; (of programme)* Ankündigung *f.* **he needs no ~** er braucht nicht vorgestellt zu werden. **(d)** *(insertion)* Einführung *f (into* in *+acc).*

**introductory** [ˌɪntrə'dʌktərɪ] *adj chapter* einleitend; *remarks* einführend; *talk, offer* Einführungs-.

**introspection** [ˌɪntrəʊ'spekʃən] *n* Selbstbeobachtung *f.*

**introspective** [ˌɪntrəʊ'spektɪv] *adj person* in sich gekehrt; *novel* introspektiv.

**introvert** ['ɪntrəʊvɜːt] *n* Introvertierte(r) *mf.* **to be an ~** introvertiert sein.

**introverted** ['ɪntrəʊvɜːtɪd] *adj* introvertiert.

**intrude** [ɪn'truːd] *vi* eindringen. **to ~ in sb's affairs** sich in jds Angelegenheiten *(acc)* einmischen; **am I intruding?** störe ich?; **to ~ on sb's privacy** jds Privatsphäre verletzen.

**intruder** [ɪn'truːdəʳ] *n* Eindringling *m.*

**intrusion** [ɪn'truːʒən] *n (disturbance)* Störung *f.* **forgive the ~** entschuldigen Sie, wenn ich hier so eindringe.

**intrusive** [ɪn'truːsɪv] *adj person* aufdringlich.

**intuition** [ˌɪntjuː'ɪʃən] *n* Intuition *f; (of future events etc)* (Vor)ahnung *f (of* von*).*

**intuitive** *adj* [ɪn'tjuːɪtɪv] intuitiv; *guess, feeling* instinktiv.

**intuitively** [ɪn'tjuːɪtɪvlɪ] *adv* intuitiv; *feel, guess* instinktiv.

**inundate** ['ɪnʌndeɪt] *vt (lit, fig)* überschwemmen; *(with work)* überhäufen.

**inure** [ɪn'juɔr] vt gewöhnen (to an +acc); (physically) abhärten (to gegen).

**invade** [ɪn'veɪd] vt einmarschieren in (+acc); (fig) überfallen. **to ~ sb's privacy** jds Privatsphäre verletzen.

**invader** [ɪn'veɪdɔr] n Invasor m.

**invalid¹** ['ɪnvəlɪd] **1** adj krank; (disabled) körperbehindert. **~ chair** (Brit) Rollstuhl m; **~ car** Invaliden(kraft)fahrzeug nt. **2** n Kranke(r) mf; (disabled person) Invalide m, Invalidin f, Körperbehinderte(r) mf.
►**invalid out** vt sep **to be ~ed ~ of the army** wegen Dienstuntauglichkeit aus dem Heer entlassen werden.

**invalid²** [ɪn'vælɪd] adj ungültig; argument nicht stichhaltig.

**invalidate** [ɪn'vælɪdeɪt] vt ungültig machen; theory entkräften.

**invaluable** [ɪn'væljuəbl] adj unbezahlbar; service unschätzbar.

**invariable** [ɪn'veərɪəbl] adj unveränderlich.

**invariably** [ɪn'veərɪəblɪ] adv ständig. **he is ~ late** er kommt immer zu spät.

**invasion** [ɪn'veɪʒən] n (lit, fig) Invasion f; (of privacy etc) Eingriff m (of in +acc). **the German ~ of Poland** der Einmarsch der Deutschen in Polen.

**invective** [ɪn'vektɪv] n Beschimpfungen pl (against gen).

**inveigle** [ɪn'viːgl] vt **to ~ sb into doing sth** jdn dazu verlocken, etw zu tun.

**invent** [ɪn'vent] vt erfinden.

**invention** [ɪn'venʃən] n Erfindung f.

**inventive** [ɪn'ventɪv] adj (creative) mind schöpferisch; novel, design einfallsreich; (resourceful) erfinderisch.

**inventiveness** [ɪn'ventɪvnɪs] n Erfindungsgabe f.

**inventor** [ɪn'ventɔr] n Erfinder(in f) m.

**inventory** ['ɪnvəntrɪ] n Inventar nt, Bestandsaufnahme f. **to take an ~ of sth** den Bestand einer Sache (gen) aufnehmen.

**inverse** [ɪn'vɜːs] adj umgekehrt. **in ~ order** in umgekehrter Reihenfolge; **to be in ~ proportion to ...** im umgekehrten Verhältnis zu ... stehen.

**inversion** [ɪn'vɜːʃən] n Umkehrung f.

**invert** [ɪn'vɜːt] vt umkehren. **~ed commas** (Brit) Anführungszeichen pl; **~ed snob** Edelproletarier(in f) m (col).

**invertebrate** [ɪn'vɜːtɪbrɪt] n Wirbellose(r) m.

**invest** [ɪn'vest] **1** vt **(a)** (Fin, fig) investieren (in in +acc or dat); (Fin also) anlegen (in in +dat). **(b)** (form: in office) president etc einsetzen. **2** vi investieren, Geld anlegen (in in +acc or dat, with bei). **to ~ in a new car** sich (dat) ein neues Auto anschaffen.

**investigate** [ɪn'vestɪgeɪt] **1** vt untersuchen; (research also) erforschen; business affairs überprüfen; complaint nachgehen (+dat). **2** vi nachforschen; (police) Ermittlungen anstellen. **investigating officer** Ermittlungsbeamte(r) m.

**investigation** [ɪn,vestɪ'geɪʃən] n **(a)** (to determine cause) Untersuchung f (into gen); (by police) Ermittlungen pl; (of applicants, political beliefs etc) Überprüfung f. **on ~** bei näherer Untersuchung; **to be under ~** überprüft werden; **he is under ~** (by police) gegen ihn wird ermittelt. **(b)** (research) Forschung f; (of bacteria etc) Erforschung f (into gen).

**investigative** [ɪn'vestɪgətɪv] adj journalism Enthüllungs-.

**investigator** [ɪn'vestɪgeɪtɔr] n Ermittler m; (private ~) (Privat)detektiv m.

**investiture** [ɪn'vestɪtʃɔr] n Amtseinführung f.

**investment** [ɪn'vestmənt] n (Fin) Investition f. **to make an ~** investieren (of sth etw); **oil is a good ~** Öl ist eine gute (Kapital)anlage.

**investment: ~ income** n Kapitalerträge pl; **~ management** n Vermögensverwaltung f; **~ trust** n Investmenttrust m.

**investor** [ɪn'vestɔr] n Kapitalanleger, Investor m. **the small ~** der Kleinanleger.

**inveterate** [ɪn'vetərɪt] adj hatred tief verwurzelt; enemies unversöhnlich; criminal, smoker Gewohnheits-; gambler unverbesserlich.

**invidious** [ɪn'vɪdɪəs] adj remark gehässig; task unangenehm; distinctions ungerecht.

**invigilate** [ɪn'vɪdʒɪleɪt] vti (Brit) exam Aufsicht führen (bei).

**invigilator** [ɪn'vɪdʒɪleɪtɔr] n (Brit) Aufsicht, Aufsichtsperson f.

**invigorate** [ɪn'vɪgəreɪt] vt beleben; (cure etc) kräftigen.

**invigorating** [ɪn'vɪgəreɪtɪŋ] adj climate gesund; air, shower erfrischend; tonic kräftigend; (fig) attitude (herz)erfrischend.

**invincible** [ɪn'vɪnsəbl] adj army etc unbesiegbar; courage, determination unerschütterlich.

**inviolable** [ɪn'vaɪələbl] adj unantastbar.

**invisibility** [ɪn,vɪzə'bɪlɪtɪ] n Unsichtbarkeit f.

**invisible** [ɪn'vɪzəbl] adj unsichtbar (also Econ). **~ earnings** (Econ) unsichtbare Einkünfte pl; **~ ink** Geheimtinte f; **~ mending** Kunststopfen nt; **~ to the naked eye** mit dem bloßen Auge nicht erkennbar.

**invitation** [,ɪnvɪ'teɪʃən] n Einladung f. **by ~ (only)** nur auf Einladung; **at sb's ~** auf jds Aufforderung (acc) (hin).

**invite** [ɪn'vaɪt] **1** vt person einladen; suggestions bitten um. **to ~ sb to do sth** jdn bitten, etw zu tun; **to ~ sb in** jdn hereinbitten; **that's inviting trouble** das gibt bestimmt Ärger. **2** ['ɪnvaɪt] n (col) Einladung f.
►**invite out** vt sep einladen. **I ~d her ~** ich habe sie gefragt, ob sie mit mir ausgehen möchte.

**inviting** [ɪn'vaɪtɪŋ] adj einladend; prospect, meal verlockend.

**invoice** ['ɪnvɔɪs] **1** n Rechnung f. **2** vt goods in Rechnung stellen, berechnen. **to ~ sb for sth** jdm für etw eine Rechnung ausstellen.

**invoicing** ['ɪnvɔɪsɪŋ] n Fakturierung f.

**invoke** [ɪn'vəʊk] vt the law etc anrufen; treaty etc sich berufen auf (+acc).

**involuntarily** [ɪn'vɒləntərɪlɪ] adv unbeabsichtigt; (automatically) unwillkürlich.

**involuntary** [ɪn'vɒləntərɪ] adj unbeabsichtigt; reaction etc unwillkürlich.

**involve** [ɪn'vɒlv] vt **(a)** (entangle) verwickeln (sb in sth jdn in etw acc); (include) beteiligen (sb in sth jdn an etw dat); (concern) betreffen. **to get ~d in sth** in etw (acc) verwickelt werden; **I didn't want to get ~d** ich wollte damit nichts zu tun haben; **I didn't want to get too ~d** ich wollte mich nicht zu sehr engagieren; **we are all ~d in the battle against inflation** der Kampf gegen die Inflation geht uns alle an; **to be ~d with sb** mit jdm zu tun haben; (sexually) mit jdm ein Verhältnis haben; **to get ~d with sb** mit jdm Kontakt bekommen; **he got ~d with a girl** er hat eine Beziehung mit einem Mädchen angefangen.
**(b)** (entail) zur Folge haben; (mean) bedeuten. **what does your job ~?** worin besteht Ihre Arbeit?; **to ~ a lot of hard work** mit viel Arbeit verbunden sein; **it would ~ moving to Germany** das würde bedeuten, nach Deutschland zu ziehen.

**involved** [ɪn'vɒlvd] adj kompliziert, umständlich (pej); story also verwickelt; style komplex.

**involvement** [ɪn'vɒlvmənt] *n (being concerned with)* Beteiligung *f (in* an +*dat); (in quarrel, crime etc)* Verwicklung *f (in* in +*acc); (commitment)* Engagement *nt; (sexually)* Verhältnis *nt; (complexity)* Kompliziertheit *f.* **the extent of his ~ with her/with his work** das Maß, in dem er sich bei ihr/bei seiner Arbeit engagiert hat; **we don't know the extent of his ~ in the plot** wir wissen nicht, wie weit er an dem Komplott beteiligt ist/war.

**invulnerable** [ɪn'vʌlnərəbl] *adj* unverwundbar; *(lit, fig) position* unangreifbar.

**inward** ['ɪnwəd] *adj (inner)* innere(r, s); *life* innerlich; *thoughts* innerste(r, s). **~-looking** in sich gekehrt.

**inwardly** ['ɪnwədlɪ] *adv* innerlich.

**inward(s)** ['ɪnwəd(z)] *adv* nach innen.

**I/O** *(Comp)* = **input/output** E/A *f.*

**IOC** = **International Olympic Committee** IOK *nt.*

**iodine** ['aɪədiːn] *n* Jod *nt.*

**IOM** = **Isle of Man.**

**ion** ['aɪən] *n* Ion *nt.*

**Ionian** [aɪ'əʊnɪən] *adj* **~ Sea** Ionisches Meer.

**iota** [aɪ'əʊtə] *n* Jota *nt.* **not one ~** nicht ein Jota; **not an ~ of truth** kein Körnchen *nt* Wahrheit.

**IOU** [,aɪəʊ'juː] = **I owe you** Schuldschein *m.*

**IPA** = **International Phonetic Alphabet** IPA *nt.*

**IOW** = **Isle of Wight.**

**IQ** = **intelligence quotient** IQ, Intelligenzquotient *m.*

**IRA** = **Irish Republican Army** IRA *f.*

**Iran** [ɪ'rɑːn] *n* der Iran.

**Iranian** [ɪ'reɪnɪən] **1** *adj* iranisch. **2** *n* **(a)** Iraner(in *f*) *m.* **(b)** *(language)* Iranisch *nt.*

**Iraq** [ɪ'rɑːk] *n* der Irak.

**Iraqi** [ɪ'rɑːkɪ] **1** *adj* irakisch. **2** *n* Iraker(in *f*) *m.*

**irascible** [ɪ'ræsɪbl] *adj* reizbar, jähzornig.

**irate** [aɪ'reɪt] *adj* zornig; *crowd* wütend.

**Ireland** ['aɪələnd] *n* Irland *nt.*

**iris** ['aɪərɪs] *n* **(a)** *(of eye)* Iris *f.* **(b)** *(Bot)* Iris, Schwertlilie *f.*

**Irish** ['aɪərɪʃ] **1** *adj* **(a)** irisch. **~man** Ire *m;* **~ Sea** Irische See; **~woman** Irin *f.* **(b)** *(hum col: illogical)* unlogisch. **2** *n* **(a)** *pl* **the ~** die Iren *pl.* **(b)** *(language)* Irisch *nt.*

**irk** [ɜːk] *vt* verdrießen *(geh)*, ärgern.

**irksome** ['ɜːksəm] *adj* lästig.

**iron** ['aɪən] **1** *n* **(a)** Eisen *nt (also Golf).* **a will of ~** ein eiserner Wille; **to rule with a rod of ~** mit eiserner Faust herrschen; **to have more than one ~ in the fire** *(fig)* mehrere Eisen im Feuer haben; **he has too many ~s in the fire** er macht zuviel auf einmal; **to strike while the ~ is hot** *(Prov)* das Eisen schmieden, solange es heiß ist *(Prov).* **(b)** *(electric ~)* Bügeleisen *nt.* **2** *adj (lit, fig)* eisern; *(lit also)* Eisen-. **3** *vt clothes* bügeln.

▶**iron out** *vt sep (lit, fig)* ausbügeln.

**iron:** **I~ Age** *n* Eisenzeit *f;* **I~ Curtain** *n* Eiserner Vorhang; **the former I~ Curtain countries** die Länder hinter dem ehemaligen Eisernen Vorhang; **~ foundry** *n (works)* Eisenhütte *f; (workshop)* Eisengießerei *f.*

**ironic(al)** [aɪ'rɒnɪk(əl)] *adj* ironisch; *situation* paradox.

**ironically** [aɪ'rɒnɪkəlɪ] *adv* ironisch. **and then, ~ enough, he turned up** komischerweise tauchte er dann auf.

**ironing** ['aɪənɪŋ] *n (process)* Bügeln *nt; (clothes)* Bügelwäsche *f.* **to do the ~** (die Wäsche) bügeln; **~ board** Bügelbrett *nt.*

**iron:** **~ lung** *n* eiserne Lunge; **~monger** *n (Brit)* Eisen(waren)händler(in *f*) *m;* **~ ore** *n* Eisenerz *nt.*

**~works** *n sing or pl* Eisenhütte *f.*

**irony** ['aɪərənɪ] *n* Ironie *f no pl.* **the ~ of it is that ...** das Ironische daran ist, daß ...

**irrational** [ɪ'ræʃənl] *adj* irrational; *(not sensible)* unvernünftig.

**irreconcilable** [ɪ,rekən'saɪləbl] *adj enemy* unversöhnlich; *differences* unvereinbar.

**irrecoverable** [,ɪrɪ'kʌvərəbl] *adj* unwiederbringlich verloren; *loss* unersetzlich.

**irredeemable** [,ɪrɪ'diːməbl] *adj sinner* (rettungslos) verloren; *loss* endgültig.

**irrefutable** [,ɪrɪ'fjuːtəbl] *adj* unwiderlegbar.

**irregular** [ɪ'regjʊlə'] *adj* **(a)** *(uneven, Gram)* unregelmäßig; *surface* uneben. **to keep ~ hours** keine festen Zeiten haben. **(b)** *behaviour* ungehörig. **this is most ~!** das verstößt gegen die Vorschriften.

**irregularity** [ɪ,regjʊ'lærɪtɪ] *n see adj* **(a)** Unregelmäßigkeit *f;* Unebenheit *f.* **(b)** Ungehörigkeit *f.* **a slight ~ in the proceedings** ein kleiner Formfehler.

**irrelevance** [ɪ'reləvəns] *n* Irrelevanz *f no pl; (of details also)* Unwesentlichkeit *f; (of titles, individuals)* Bedeutungslosigkeit *f.*

**irrelevant** [ɪ'reləvənt] *adj* irrelevant *(to* für*); information* unwesentlich; *titles etc* bedeutungslos. **it is ~ whether he agrees or not** es ist belanglos, ob er zustimmt; **that's ~** das spielt keine Rolle.

**irreligious** [,ɪrɪ'lɪdʒəs] *adj* unreligiös; *youth etc* gottlos.

**irreparable** [ɪ'repərəbl] *adj damage* irreparabel, nicht wiedergutzumachen *attr.*

**irreplaceable** [,ɪrɪ'pleɪsəbl] *adj* unersetzlich.

**irrepressible** [,ɪrɪ'presəbl] *adj urge* unbezähmbar; *optimism* unerschütterlich; *person* nicht unterzukriegen; *delight* unbändig.

**irreproachable** [,ɪrɪ'prəʊtʃəbl] *adj* tadellos.

**irresistible** [,ɪrɪ'zɪstəbl] *adj* unwiderstehlich.

**irresolute** [ɪ'rezəluːt] *adj* unentschlossen.

**irrespective** [,ɪrɪ'spektɪv] *adj:* **~ of** ungeachtet *(+gen)*, unabhängig von; **candidates should be chosen ~ of sex** bei der Auswahl der Kandidaten sollte das Geschlecht keine Rolle spielen; **~ of whether they want to or not** gleichgültig, ob sie wollen oder nicht.

**irresponsibility** ['ɪrɪ,spɒnsə'bɪlɪtɪ] *n see adj* Unverantwortlichkeit *f;* Verantwortungslosigkeit *f.*

**irresponsible** [,ɪrɪ'spɒnsəbl] *adj behaviour* unverantwortlich; *person* verantwortungslos.

**irretrievable** [,ɪrɪ'triːvəbl] *adj* nicht mehr wiederzubekommen; *loss* unersetzlich. **~ breakdown of marriage** (unheilbare) Zerrüttung der Ehe.

**irretrievably** [,ɪrɪ'triːvəblɪ] *adv* **~ lost** für immer verloren.

**irreverence** [ɪ'revərəns] *n see adj* Respektlosigkeit *f;* Pietätlosigkeit *f.*

**irreverent** [ɪ'revərənt] *adj behaviour, remark* respektlos; *(towards religion)* pietätlos.

**irreversible** [,ɪrɪ'vɜːsəbl] *adj judgment* unwiderruflich.

**irrevocable** [ɪ'revəkəbl] *adj* unwiderruflich.

**irrigate** ['ɪrɪgeɪt] *vt land, crop* bewässern.

**irrigation** [,ɪrɪ'geɪʃən] *n (Agr)* Bewässerung *f.* **~ canal** Bewässerungskanal *m.*

**irritable** ['ɪrɪtəbl] *adj (as characteristic)* reizbar; *(on occasion)* gereizt.

**irritant** ['ɪrɪtənt] *n (Med)* Reizerreger *m.*

**irritate** ['ɪrɪteɪt] *vt (annoy)* ärgern; *(deliberately)* reizen; *(get on nerves)* irritieren.

**irritating** ['ɪrɪteɪtɪŋ] *adj* ärgerlich; *cough* lästig. **I find his jokes most ~** seine Witze regen mich wirklich auf; **you really are the most ~ person** du kannst einem wirklich auf die Nerven gehen.

**irritation** [ˌɪrɪ'teɪʃən] n (a) (state) Ärger m; (act) Ärgern nt; (deliberate) Reizen nt; (thing that irritates) Ärgernis nt. (b) (Med) Reizung f.

**IRS** (US) = **Internal Revenue Service.**

**is** [ɪz] 3rd person sing pres of **be.**

**ISBN** = **International Standard Book Number** ISBN f.

**Islam** ['ɪzlɑːm] n (religion) der Islam; (Moslems collectively) Mohammedaner pl.

**Islamic** [ɪz'læmɪk] adj islamisch.

**island** ['aɪlənd] n (lit, fig) Insel f.

**islander** ['aɪləndər] n Inselbewohner(in f) m.

**isle** [aɪl] n (poet) Eiland nt (poet). **the I~ of Man** die Insel Man.

**isn't** ['ɪznt] = **is not.**

**isobar** ['aɪsəʊbɑːr] n Isobare f.

**isolate** ['aɪsəʊleɪt] vt (a) isolieren; (cut off also) abschneiden. **to ~ oneself from the world** sich von der Welt zurückziehen. (b) (pinpoint) herausfinden; essential factor herauskristallisieren.

**isolated** ['aɪsəʊleɪtɪd] adj (a) (cut off) abgeschnitten, isoliert; (remote) abgelegen; existence zurückgezogen. (b) (single) einzeln. **~ instances** Einzelfälle pl.

**isolation** [ˌaɪsəʊ'leɪʃən] (a) (act) (separation) Absonderung, Isolierung (esp Med) f; (pinpointing) Herausfinden nt; (of essential factor) Herauskristallisierung f. (b) (state) Isolation f; (remoteness) Abgeschiedenheit f. **to keep a patient in ~** einen Patienten isolieren; **to live in ~** zurückgezogen leben; **to consider sth in ~** etw gesondert betrachten; **it doesn't make much sense in ~** ohne Zusammenhang ist es ziemlich unverständlich.

**isolation: ~ hospital** n Krankenhaus nt für ansteckende Krankheiten; **~ ward** n Isolierstation f.

**isolationism** [ˌaɪsəʊ'leɪʃənɪzəm] n Isolationismus m.

**isosceles** [aɪ'sɒsɪliːz] adj (Geom) gleichschenklig.

**isotope** ['aɪsəʊtəʊp] n Isotop nt.

**Israel** ['ɪzreɪl] n Israel nt.

**Israeli** [ɪz'reɪlɪ] **1** adj israelisch. **2** n Israeli mf.

**issue** ['ɪʃuː] **1** vt passport ausstellen; shares, banknotes, rations ausgeben; order, warning erteilen (to dat); details bekanntgeben; (publish) book herausgeben. **to ~ sth to sb/to ~ sb with sth** etw an jdn ausgeben; **to ~ sb with a visa** jdm ein Visum ausstellen; **a warrant for his arrest was ~d** gegen ihn wurde Haftbefehl erlassen.

**2** vi (liquid, gas) austreten; (smoke) (heraus)quellen; (sound) (heraus)dringen; (people etc) (heraus)strömen.

**3** n (a) (question) Frage f; (matter also) Angelegenheit f; (problematic) Problem nt. **the ~ is whether** ... die Frage ist, ob ...; **what is at ~?** worum geht es?; **that's not at ~** das steht nicht zur Debatte; **to take ~ with sb over sth** jdm in etw (dat) widersprechen; **to make an ~ of sth** etw aufbauschen; **to evade the ~** ausweichen; **to face the ~** den Tatsachen ins Auge sehen.

(b) (outcome) Ergebnis nt. **that decided the ~** das war ausschlaggebend; **to force the ~** eine Entscheidung erzwingen.

(c) (of banknotes, shares etc) Ausgabe f; (of shares also) Emission f. **place of ~** (of tickets) Ausgabestelle f; (of passports) Ausstellungsort m; **date of ~** (of tickets) Ausstellungsdatum nt; (of stamps) Ausgabetag m. **the ~ of blankets/guns to the troops** die Versorgung der Truppen mit Decken/die Ausrüstung der Truppen mit Gewehren.

(d) (of book etc) Herausgabe f; (book etc) Ausgabe f.

(e) (Jur: offspring) Nachkommenschaft f.

**Istanbul** [ˌɪstæn'buːl] n Istanbul nt.

**isthmus** ['ɪsməs] n Landenge f.

**IT** = **information technology.**

**it** [ɪt] pron (a) (when replacing noun) (subject) er/sie/es; (dir obj) ihn/sie/es; (indir obj) ihm/ihr/ihm. **of ~** davon; **behind/over** etc **~** dahinter/darüber etc; **who is ~?** – **~'s me** wer ist da? – ich (bin's); **what is ~?** was ist es or das?; (matter) was ist los?; **that's not ~** (not the trouble) das ist es (gar) nicht; **that must have been ~** das wird es wohl gewesen sein; **the worst of ~ is that** ... das Schlimmste daran ist, daß ...

(b) (indef subject) es. **~'s raining** es regnet; **if ~ hadn't been for her, we would have come** wenn sie nicht gewesen wäre, wären wir gekommen; **why is ~ always me who has to** ...? warum muß (ausgerechnet) immer ich ...?; **I've known ~ happen** ich habe es (schon) erlebt; **~'s Friday tomorrow** morgen ist Freitag; **~ was he or (col) him who asked her** er hat sie gefragt; er war es, der sie gefragt hat; **~'s his rudeness I object to** seine Unhöflichkeit ist es, woran ich Anstoß nehme; **~ was for his sake that she lied** nur um seinetwillen hat sie gelogen.

(c) (col phrases) **that's ~!** (agreement) ja, genau!; (annoyed) jetzt reicht's mir!; **that's ~ (then)!** (achievement) (so,) das wär's!; (disappointment) ja, das war's dann wohl.

**ita, ITA** (Brit) = **initial teaching alphabet** Leselernalphabet nt.

**Italian** [ɪ'tæljən] **1** adj italienisch. **2** n (a) Italiener(in f) m. (b) (language) Italienisch nt.

**italic** [ɪ'tælɪk] **1** adj kursiv. **2** n ~s pl Kursivschrift f; **in ~s** kursiv (gedruckt).

**Italy** ['ɪtəlɪ] n Italien nt.

**itch** [ɪtʃ] **1** n (a) Jucken nt, Juckreiz m. **I have an ~** mich juckt es. (b) (col: urge) Lust f. **I have an ~ to do sth** es juckt (col) mich, etw zu tun. **2** vi (a) jucken. **my back ~es** mein Rücken juckt (mich). (b) (col) **he is ~ing to ...** es juckt (col) ihn, zu ...; **he's ~ing for a fight** er ist auf Streit aus.

**itchy** ['ɪtʃɪ] adj (+er) (itching) juckend. **it's ~** es juckt; **I've got ~ feet** (col) ich will hier weg (col); (want to travel also) mich packt das Fernweh.

**it'd** ['ɪtəd] = **it would; it had.**

**item** ['aɪtəm] n (a) (on agenda etc) Punkt m; (Comm: in account book) (Rechnungs)posten m; (article) Gegenstand m; (in catalogue etc) Artikel m; (Brit: in variety show) Nummer f. (b) (of news) Bericht m; (short, Rad, TV also) Meldung f. **a short news ~** eine Zeitungsnotiz/eine Kurzmeldung.

**itemize** ['aɪtəmaɪz] vt einzeln aufführen. **~d account** spezifizierte Rechnung.

**itinerant** [ɪ'tɪnərənt] adj umherziehend, Wander-; worker Saison-. **~ theatre group** Wandertruppe f.

**itinerary** [aɪ'tɪnərərɪ] n (route) (Reise)route f.

**it'll** ['ɪtl] = **it will; it shall.**

**ITN** (Brit) = **Independent Television News** Nachrichtendienst m der Fernsehanstalt ITV.

**its** [ɪts] poss adj sein(e)/ihr(e)/sein(e).

**it's** [ɪts] = **it is; it has** (as aux).

**itself** [ɪt'self] pron (a) (reflexive) sich. (b) (emph) selbst. **and now we come to the text ~** und jetzt kommen wir zum Text selbst; **the frame ~ is worth £1,000** der Rahmen allein ist £1000 wert; **the amount in ~** der Betrag an sich. (c) **by ~** (alone) allein; (automatically) von selbst, selbsttätig.

**ITV** (Brit) = **Independent Television** kommerzielle Fernsehanstalt.

**IUD** = **intra-uterine device** Intrauterinpessar nt.

**I've** [aɪv] = **I have.**

**ivory** ['aɪvərɪ] **1** n (also colour) Elfenbein nt. **the ivo-**

ries *(col: piano keys)* die Tasten. **2** *adj* elfenbeinern; *(colour)* elfenbeinfarben.

**Ivory Coast** *n* Elfenbeinküste *f.*

**ivory tower** *n (fig)* Elfenbeinturm *m.*

**ivy** ['aɪvɪ] *n* Efeu *m.*

**Ivy League** *n (US) Eliteuniversitäten pl der USA.*

# J

**J, j** [dʒeɪ] *n* J, j *nt.* **J for Jack** *(Brit)*, **J for Jig** *(US)* ≈ J wie Julius.

**J/A** = **joint account.**

**jab** [dʒæb] **1** *vt (with stick, elbow etc)* stoßen; *(with knife also)* stechen. **he ~bed his elbow into my side** er stieß mir den Ellbogen in die Seite. **2** *vi* stoßen *(at sb with sth* mit etw nach jdm*)*. **3** *n (with stick, elbow)* Stoß *m*; *(with needle, knife)* Stich *m*; *(col: injection)* Spritze *f*; *(Boxing)* (kurze) Gerade.

**jabber** ['dʒæbə<sup>r</sup>] **1** *vt* (daher)plappern *(col)*; *poem* herunterrasseln *(col)*. **2** *vi (also ~ away)* plappern, quasseln *(col)*. **they were ~ing away in Spanish** sie quasselten *(col)* Spanisch.

**jack** [dʒæk] *n* **(a)** *(Aut)* Wagenheber *m*. **(b)** *(Cards)* Bube *m*. **(c) every man ~ of them** alle ohne Ausnahme. **(d)** *(Bowls)* Zielkugel *f*.
  ►**jack in** *vt sep (col) job etc* aufgeben; *lover* Schluß machen mit *(col)*.
  ►**jack up** *vt sep car* aufbocken; *(col: prices)* in die Höhe treiben.

**jackal** ['dʒækɔːl] *n* Schakal *m*.

**jackass** ['dʒækæs] *n (col: person)* Esel *m (col)*.

**jackdaw** ['dʒækdɔː] *n* Dohle *f*.

**jacket** ['dʒækɪt] *n* **(a)** *(garment)* Jacke *f*; *(man's also)* Jackett *nt*. **(b)** *(of book, US: of record)* Hülle *f*. **(c)** *(esp US: for papers etc)* Umschlag *m*. **(d) ~ potatoes** in der Schale gebackene Kartoffeln *pl*. **(e)** *(Tech: of boiler etc)* Mantel *m*.

**jack: ~-in-the-box** *n* Kastenteufel *m*; **~knife 1** *n* (großes) Taschenmesser; **2** *vi* **the (articulated) truck ~knifed** der Anhänger (des Lastwagens) hat sich quergestellt; **~-of-all-trades** *n* Alleskönner *m*; **to be (a) ~-of-all-trades (and master of none)** *(prov)* ein Hansdampf *m* in allen Gassen sein; **~ plug** *n* Bananenstecker *m*; *(for telephone)* Telefonstecker *m*; **~pot** *n* Pott *m (col)*; *(in lottery etc)* Hauptgewinn *m*; **to hit the ~pot** *(in lottery)* den Hauptgewinn bekommen; *(fig)* das große Los ziehen; **J~ Robinson** [,dʒæk'rɒbɪnsən] *n*: **before you could say J~ Robinson** *(col)* im Nu.

**jacuzzi** [dʒə'kuːzɪ] *n* Whirlpool *m*.

**jade** [dʒeɪd] **1** *n (stone)* Jade *m* or *f*; *(colour)* Jadegrün *nt*. **2** *adj* Jade-; *(colour)* jadegrün.

**jaded** ['dʒeɪdɪd] *adj (physically)* abgespannt; *(permanently)* verbraucht; *(mentally)* abgestumpft; *appearance* verbraucht.

**jagged** ['dʒægɪd] *adj* zackig; *wound, tear* ausgefranst; *coastline* zerklüftet.

**jaguar** ['dʒægjʊə<sup>r</sup>] *n* Jaguar *m*.

**jail** [dʒeɪl] **1** *n* Gefängnis *nt*. **in ~** im Gefängnis; **to go to ~** ins Gefängnis kommen. **2** *vt* einsperren.

**jail: ~bird** *n (col)* Knastbruder *m (col)*; **~break** *n* Ausbruch *m (aus dem Gefängnis)*.

**jailer** ['dʒeɪlə<sup>r</sup>] *n* Gefängniswärter(in *f*) *m*.

**jalop(p)y** [dʒə'lɒpɪ] *n (col)* alte Mühle *(col)*.

**jam¹** [dʒæm] *n* Marmelade *f*. **you want ~ on it too, do you?** *(Brit col)* du kriegst wohl nie genug? *(col)*.

**jam²** **1** *n* **(a)** *(crowd)* Gedränge *nt*. **(b)** *(traffic ~)*

(Verkehrs)stau *m*. **(c)** *(blockage in machine etc)* Stockung *f*. **(d)** *(col: tight spot)* **to be in a ~** in der Klemme sitzen *(col)*; **to get into a ~ with sth** mit etw Schwierigkeiten haben; **to get sb out of a ~** jdm aus der Klemme helfen *(col)*.
  **2** *vt* **(a)** *(make stick)* window etc verklemmen; brakes etc blockieren; *(wedge)* festklemmen; *(between two things)* einklemmen. **it's ~med** es klemmt; **he got his finger ~med in the door** er hat sich *(dat)* den Finger in der Tür eingeklemmt. **(b)** *(cram)* stopfen, quetschen *(into* in *+acc)*. **we were ~med together** wir waren zusammengedrängt. **(c)** *(block)* street etc verstopfen, blockieren; *radio station* stören. **a street ~med with cars** eine verstopfte Straße; **all the lines are ~med** alle Leitungen sind durch Anrufe blockiert.
  **3** *vi* **(a) the crowd ~med into the bus** die Menschenmenge zwängte sich in den Bus. **(b)** *(become stuck) (brake)* sich verklemmen; *(door, moving part etc)* klemmen.
  ►**jam in** *vt sep* **(a)** *(wedge in)* einkeilen. **he was ~med ~ by the crowd** er war in der Menge eingekeilt. **(b)** *(press in)* (herein)stopfen in *(+acc)*.
  ►**jam on** *vt sep* **to ~ ~ the brakes** auf die Bremse steigen. **2** *vi (brakes)* klemmen.

**Jamaica** [dʒə'meɪkə] *n* Jamaika *nt*.

**Jamaican** [dʒə'meɪkən] **1** *adj* jamaikanisch. **2** *n* Jamaikaner(in *f*) *m*.

**jamb** [dʒæm] *n* **(door/window) ~** (Tür-/Fenster)pfosten *m*.

**jamboree** [,dʒæmbə'riː] *n (Scouts)* Jamboree *nt*; *(spree)* Rummel *m (col)*.

**James** [dʒeɪmz] *n* ≈ Jakob *m*.

**jam: ~ jar** *n* Marmeladenglas *nt*; **~-packed** *adj* überfüllt, proppenvoll *(col)*; **~ session** *n* Jam Session *f*.

**Jan** = **January** Jan.

**jane** [dʒeɪn] *n (US col)* Weib *nt (col)*.

**jangle** ['dʒæŋgl] **1** *vi (money)* klimpern *(col)*; *(bells)* bimmeln *(col)*; *(chains)* rasseln. **2** *vt* money klimpern mit; *keys also, chains* rasseln mit. **3** *n see vi* Klimpern *nt*; Bimmeln *nt*; Rasseln *nt*.

**janitor** ['dʒænɪtə<sup>r</sup>] *n* Hausmeister *m*; *(of flats also)* Hauswart *m*.

**January** ['dʒænjʊərɪ] *n* Januar *m; see* **September.**

**Japan** [dʒə'pæn] *n* Japan *nt*.

**Japanese** [,dʒæpə'niːz] **1** *adj* japanisch. **2** *n* **(a)** Japaner(in *f*) *m*. **(b)** *(language)* Japanisch *nt*.

**jar¹** [dʒɑː<sup>r</sup>] *n (for jam etc)* Glas *nt*; *(without handle)* Topf *m*; *(with handle)* Krug *m*.

**jar²** **1** *n (jolt)* Ruck *m*; *(fig)* Schock *m*. **2** *vi (note)* schauerlich klingen; *(colours)* sich beißen *(col)*; *(ideas)* sich nicht vertragen, nicht harmonieren *(with* mit*)*. **this ~s stylistically** das fällt stilmäßig aus dem Rahmen; **this noise ~s on my nerves** dieser Lärm geht mir auf die Nerven; **her voice ~s on my ears** ihre Stimme geht mir durch und durch. **3** *vt building etc* erschüttern; *back* sich *(dat)* stauchen; *(fig)* einen Schock versetzen *(+dat)*. **don't ~ the camera** wackele nicht mit dem Fotoapparat.

**jargon** ['dʒɑːgən] *n* Jargon *m (pej)*, Fachsprache *f*.

**jarring** ['dʒɑːrɪŋ] *adj sound* gellend; *accent* störend; *colours* sich beißend *attr (col)*.

**Jas.** = **James.**

**jasmin(e)** ['dʒæzmɪn] *n* Jasmin *m*.

**jaundice** ['dʒɔːndɪs] *n* Gelbsucht *f*.

**jaundiced** ['dʒɔːndɪst] *adj* **(a)** *(lit)* gelbsüchtig. **(b)** *attitude* zynisch. **to take a ~ view of sth** in bezug auf etw *(acc)* zynisch sein.

**jaunt** [dʒɔːnt] *n* Trip *m*, Spritztour *f*. **to go for a ~** eine Spritztour machen.

**jaunty** ['dʒɔːntɪ] *adj (+er)* fröhlich; *hat* flott; *attitude* sorglos, unbekümmert. **he wore his hat at a ~ angle** er hatte den Hut keck aufgesetzt.

**Java** ['dʒɑːvə] *n* Java *nt*.

**javelin** ['dʒævlɪn] *n* Speer *m*. **(throwing) the ~** Speerwerfen *nt*; **~ thrower** Speerwerfer(in *f*) *m*.

**jaw** [dʒɔː] *n* **(a)** Kiefer *m*. **with its prey between its ~s** mit der Beute im Maul; **the ~s of death** die Klauen *pl* des Todes. **(b)** *(of vice)* Backe *f*.

**jawbone** ['dʒɔːbəʊn] *n* Kieferknochen *m*.

**jay** [dʒeɪ] *n* Eichelhäher *m*.

**jaywalker** ['dʒeɪˌwɔːkəʳ] *n* unachtsamer Fußgänger, unachtsame Fußgängerin.

**jazz** [dʒæz] **1** *n (Mus)* Jazz *m*. **... and all that ~** ... und all so'n Zeug *(col)*. **2** *attr band, music* Jazz-.
▶**jazz up** *vt sep* aufmöbeln *(col)*.

**jazzy** ['dʒæzɪ] *adj (+er) (tune)* verjazzt; *(colour)* knallig *(col)*; *(pattern)* wild; *(dress)* poppig *(col)*.

**JCB** ® [dʒeɪsiːˈbiː] *n* Erdräummaschine *f*.

**jealous** ['dʒeləs] *adj lover etc* eifersüchtig; *(envious: of sb's success etc)* neidisch. **to be ~ of sb** auf jdn eifersüchtig sein/jdn beneiden.

**jealously** ['dʒeləslɪ] *adv see adj* eifersüchtig; neidisch.

**jealousy** ['dʒeləsɪ] *n see adj (of* auf *+acc)* Eifersucht *f*; Neid *m*.

**jeans** [dʒiːnz] *npl* Jeans *pl*. **pair of ~** Jeanshose *f*.

**Jeep** ® [dʒiːp] *n* Jeep ® *m*.

**jeer** [dʒɪəʳ] **1** *n (remark)* höhnische Bemerkung; *(shout)* Buhruf *m*; *(esp pl: laughter)* Hohngelächter *nt*. **2** *vi see n* höhnische Bemerkungen machen; buhen; höhnisch lachen. **to ~ at sb** jdn (laut) verhöhnen.

**jeering** ['dʒɪərɪŋ] **1** *adj* höhnisch. **2** *n see* **jeer 1.**

**jelly** ['dʒelɪ] *n* Gelee *nt*; *(esp Brit: dessert)* Wackelpeter *m (col)*.

**jellyfish** ['dʒelɪfɪʃ] *n* Qualle *f*.

**jemmy** ['dʒemɪ] *n (Brit)* Brecheisen *nt*.

**jeopardize** ['dʒepədaɪz] *vt* gefährden.

**jeopardy** ['dʒepədɪ] *n* Gefahr *f*. **in ~** gefährdet; **to put sb/sth in ~** jdn/etw gefährden.

**jerk** [dʒɜːk] **1** *n* **(a)** Ruck *m*; *(jump)* Satz *m*; *(twitch)* Zuckung *f*. **to give sth a ~** einer Sache *(dat)* einen Ruck geben; *rope* an etw *(dat)* ruckartig ziehen; **the train stopped with a ~** der Zug hielt mit einem Ruck an. **(b)** *(col: person)* Trottel *m (col)*. **2** *vt* rucken an *(+dat)*. **the impact ~ed his head forward** beim Aufprall wurde sein Kopf nach vorn geschleudert; **he ~ed the book out of my hand** er riß mir das Buch aus der Hand. **3** *vi (rope)* rucken; *(move jerkily)* ruckeln *(col)*; *(body, muscle)* zucken; *(head)* zurückzucken. **he ~ed away from me** er zuckte vor mir zurück; **the car ~ed forward** der Wagen machte einen Satz nach vorn; **the car ~ed to a stop** das Auto hielt ruckweise an.

**jerkin** ['dʒɜːkɪn] *n* Weste *f*; *(Hist)* (Leder)wams *nt*.

**jerky** ['dʒɜːkɪ] *adj (+er)* ruckartig; *speech also, style* abgehackt. **a ~ ride** eine holprige Fahrt.

**Jerry** ['dʒerɪ] *n (col)* Deutsche(r) *m*.

**jerry:** **~ built** *adj* schlampig gebaut; **~ can** *n* großer (Blech)kanister.

**jersey** ['dʒɜːzɪ] *n* Pullover *m*; *(Ftbl etc)* Trikot *nt*.

**Jersey** ['dʒɜːzɪ] *n* Jersey *nt*.

**Jerusalem** [dʒəˈruːsələm] *n* Jerusalem *nt*. **~ artichoke** Jerusalemartischocke *f*.

**jest** [dʒest] **1** *n (joke)* Scherz, Witz *m*. **in ~** im Spaß. **2** *vi (esp liter)* scherzen. **to ~ about sth** über etw *(acc)* Witze machen.

**jester** ['dʒestəʳ] *n (Hist)* Narr *m*.

**Jesuit** ['dʒezjʊɪt] *n* Jesuit *m*.

**Jesus** ['dʒiːzəs] *n* Jesus *m*. **~ Christ** Jesus Christus; **~ Christ!** *(col)* Herrgott (noch mal)! *(col)*.

**jet¹** [dʒet] **1** *n* **(a)** Strahl *m*. **a ~ of water** ein Wasserstrahl. **(b)** *(nozzle)* Düse *f*. **(c)** *(also ~ plane)* Düsenflugzeug *nt*, Jet *m (col)*. **2** *vi (Aviat col)* jetten *(col)*.

**jet²** *n (Miner)* Gagat *m*. **~ black** pechschwarz.

**jet:** **~ engine** *n* Düsentriebwerk *nt*; **~ fighter** *n* Düsenjäger *m*; **~lag** *n* Jet-lag *nt*; **~lagged** *adj* **to be ~lagged** durch den Zeitunterschied müde sein; **~ plane** *n* Düsenflugzeug *nt*; **~-propelled** *adj* mit Düsenantrieb, Düsen-; **~ set** *n* Jet-set *m*.

**jettison** ['dʒetɪsn] *vt (lit, fig)* über Bord werfen; *unwanted articles* wegwerfen.

**jetty** ['dʒetɪ] *n (breakwater)* Hafendamm *m*; *(landing pier)* Pier *m*, Landungsbrücke *f*.

**Jew** [dʒuː] *n* Jude *m*, Jüdin *f*.

**jewel** ['dʒuːəl] *n* **(a)** *(gem)* Edelstein *m*, Juwel *nt (geh)*; *(piece of jewellery)* Schmuckstück *nt*. **(b)** *(of watch)* Stein *m*.

**jeweller,** *(US)* **jeweler** ['dʒuːələʳ] *n* Juwelier *m*; *(making jewellery)* Goldschmied *m*. **~'s (shop)** Juwelierladen *m*.

**jewellery,** *(US)* **jewelry** ['dʒuːəlrɪ] *n* Schmuck *m no pl*. **a piece of ~** ein Schmuckstück *nt*; **~ store** *(US)* Juwelierladen *m*.

**Jewess** ['dʒuːɪs] *n* Jüdin *f*.

**Jewish** ['dʒuːɪʃ] *adj* jüdisch. **he/she is ~** er ist Jude/sie ist Jüdin.

**Jewishness** ['dʒuːɪʃnɪs] *n* Judentum *nt*.

**Jewry** ['dʒuərɪ] *n* das Judentum.

**jib** [dʒɪb] **1** *n (of crane)* Ausleger *m*; *(Naut)* Klüver *m*. **2** *vi* **to ~ (at sth)** sich (gegen etw) sträuben.

**jibe** [dʒaɪb] *n, vi* = **gibe.**

**jiffy** ['dʒɪfɪ] *n (col)* Augenblick *m*, Minütchen *nt (col)*. **I won't be a ~** ich komme sofort; *(back soon)* ich bin sofort wieder da; **in a ~** sofort.

**Jiffy bag** ® *n* (gepolsterte) Versandtasche *f*.

**jig** [dʒɪg] *n* **(a)** *(dance) lebhafter Volkstanz*. **(b)** *(Tech)* Spannvorrichtung *f*.

**jiggle** ['dʒɪgl] *vt* wackeln mit.

**jigsaw** ['dʒɪgsɔː] *n (also ~ puzzle)* Puzzle(spiel) *nt*.

**jilt** [dʒɪlt] *vt lover* den Laufpaß geben *(+dat)*. **~ed** verschmäht.

**jingle** ['dʒɪŋgl] **1** *n* **(a)** *(of keys etc)* Klimpern *nt*; *(of bells)* Bimmeln *nt*. **(b)** *(catchy verse)* Spruch *m*; *(for remembering)* Merkspruch *m*. **advertising ~** Werbespruch *m*. **2** *vi (keys etc)* klimpern; *(bells)* bimmeln. **3** *vt keys* klimpern mit; *bells* bimmeln lassen.

**jingoism** ['dʒɪŋgəʊɪzm] *n* Hurrapatriotismus *m*.

**jinx** [dʒɪŋks] *n* **there's a ~ on it** das ist verhext.

**jitters** ['dʒɪtəz] *npl (col)* **the ~** das große Zittern *(col)*; **to give sb the ~** jdn ganz rappelig machen *(col)*; **to get the ~** Bammel kriegen *(col)*.

**jittery** ['dʒɪtərɪ] *adj (col)* nervös, rappelig *(col)*.

**jive** [dʒaɪv] **1** *n (dance)* Swing *m*. **2** *vi* Swing tanzen.

**job** [dʒɒb] *n* **(a)** *(piece of work)* Arbeit *f*. **I have a ~ to do** ich habe zu tun; **it's quite a ~ to paint the house** das Haus zu streichen ist ziemlich viel Arbeit; **he's on the ~** *(col: at work)* er ist bei der Arbeit; **training**

on the ~ Ausbildung *f* am Arbeitsplatz; **he made a good** ~ **of it** er hat es gut hingekriegt *(col)*; **we have a lot of** ~**s on just now** wir haben zur Zeit viele Aufträge; **he knows his** ~ er versteht sein Handwerk; **that's not my** ~ dafür bin ich nicht zuständig.

(b) *(employment)* Stelle *f*, Job *m* *(col)*. **500** ~**s lost** 500 Arbeitsplätze verlorengegangen; **to bring new** ~**s to a region** in einer Gegend neue Arbeitsplätze schaffen.

(c) *(duty)* Aufgabe *f*. **I'm only doing my** ~ ich tue nur meine Pflicht.

(d) **that's a good** ~**!** so ein Glück; **it's a good** ~ **I brought my cheque book** nur gut, daß ich mein Scheckbuch dabeihabe; **to give sb/sth up as a bad** ~ jdn/etw aufgeben; **that should do the** ~ das müßte hinhauen *(col)*; **this is just the** ~ das ist genau das richtige; **she has a** ~ **getting up the stairs** es ist gar nicht einfach für sie, die Treppe hinaufzukommen.

(e) *(col: crime)* Ding *nt* *(col)*. **remember that bank** ~**?** erinnerst du dich an das große Ding in der Bank? *(col)*.

(f) *(col: person, thing)* Ding *nt*. **his new car's a lovely little** ~ sein neues Auto ist wirklich große Klasse *(col)*.

**jobber** ['dʒɒbəʳ] *n* *(St Ex)* Effektenhändler *m*.

**jobbing** ['dʒɒbɪŋ] *adj* *gardener etc* Gelegenheits-; *printer* Akzidenz-.

**job:** ~ **centre** *n* *(Brit)* Arbeitsamt *nt*; ~ **creation scheme** *n* Arbeitsbeschaffungsprogramm *nt*; ~ **description** *n* Tätigkeitsbeschreibung *f*; ~ **hunting** *n* Arbeitssuche *f*; ~**less 1** *adj* arbeitslos; **2** *n* **the** ~**less** *pl* die Arbeitslosen *pl*; ~ **loss** *n* **there were 1,000** ~ **losses** 1 000 Arbeitsplätze gingen verloren; ~ **lot** *n* *(Comm)* (Waren)posten *m*; *(fig)* Sammelsurium *nt*; ~ **satisfaction** *n* Zufriedenheit *f* am Arbeitsplatz; ~ **security** *n* Sicherheit *f* des Arbeitsplatzes; ~**-sharing** *n* Arbeitsplatzteilung *f*.

**jockey** ['dʒɒkɪ] **1** *n* Jockey, Rennreiter(in *f*) *m*. **2** *vi* **to** ~ **for position** *(lit)* sich in eine gute Position zu drängen versuchen; *(fig)* rangeln.

**jockstrap** ['dʒɒkstræp] *n* Suspensorium *nt*.

**jocular** ['dʒɒkjʊləʳ] *adj* lustig, spaßig. **to be in a** ~ **mood** zu Scherzen aufgelegt sein.

**jodhpurs** ['dʒɒdpəz] *npl* Reithose(n *pl*) *f*.

**jog** [dʒɒg] **1** *vt* *elbow etc* stoßen an *(+acc) or* gegen; *person* anstoßen. **to** ~ **sb's memory** jds Gedächtnis *(dat)* nachhelfen. **2** *vi* trotten; *(Sport)* Dauerlauf machen, joggen. **3** *n* *(run)* trabender Lauf, Trott *m*; *(Sport)* Dauerlauf *m*. **to go for a** ~ *(Sport)* einen Dauerlauf machen, joggen (gehen).

▶**jog along** *vi* *(person, worker, industry)* vor sich *(acc)* hinwursteln *(col)*; *(work)* seinen Gang gehen.

**jogging** ['dʒɒgɪŋ] *n* Dauerlauf *m*, Joggen *nt*. **he goes** ~ er macht Jogging.

**John** [dʒɒn] *n* *(monarch etc)* Johann, Johannes. ~ **the Baptist** Johannes der Täufer.

**john** [dʒɒn] *n* *(US col: toilet)* Klo *nt* *(col)*.

**join** [dʒɔɪn] **1** *vt* **(a)** *(lit, fig: connect)* verbinden *(to* mit*)*; *(attach also)* anfügen *(to* an *+acc)*. **to** ~ **battle (with the enemy)** den Kampf (mit dem Feind) aufnehmen; **to** ~ **hands** *(lit, fig)* sich *(dat)* die Hände reichen.

(b) *(become member of)* army gehen zu; *political party, club* beitreten *(+dat)*, eintreten in *(+acc)*; *university* *(as student)* anfangen an *(+dat)*; *(as staff)* firm anfangen bei; *group of people* sich anschließen *(+dat)*.

(c) **he** ~**ed us in France** er stieß in Frankreich zu uns; **I** ~**ed him at the station** ich traf mich mit ihm am Bahnhof; **I'll** ~ **you in five minutes** ich bin in fünf Minuten bei Ihnen; *(follow you)* ich komme in fünf Minuten nach; **may I** ~ **you?** kann ich mich Ihnen anschließen?; *(sit with you)* darf ich mich zu Ihnen setzen?; **will you** ~ **us?** machen Sie mit?; *(sit with us)* wollen Sie uns nicht Gesellschaft leisten?; *(come with us)* kommen Sie mit?; **do** ~ **us for lunch** essen Sie doch mit uns (zu Mittag); **will you** ~ **me in a drink?** trinken Sie ein Glas mit mir?

(d) *(river)* another river, the sea münden *or* fließen in *(+acc)*; *(road)* another road münden in *(+acc)*.

**2** *vi* **(a)** *(also* ~ **together)** *(two parts)* *(be attached)* (miteinander) verbunden sein; *(be attachable)* sich (miteinander) verbinden lassen; *(meet, be adjacent)* zusammentreffen; *(estates)* aneinander grenzen; *(rivers)* zusammenfließen; *(roads, lines, boundaries etc)* sich treffen. **they all** ~**ed together to get her a present** sie taten sich alle zusammen, um ihr ein Geschenk zu kaufen. **(b)** *(club member)* beitreten, Mitglied werden.

**3** *n* Naht(stelle) *f*; *(in pipe, knitting)* Verbindungsstelle *f*.

▶**join in** *vi* *(in activity)* mitmachen *(prep obj* bei*)*; *(in game also)* mitspielen *(prep obj* bei*)*. ~ ~, **everybody!** *(in song etc)* alle (mitmachen)!; **everybody** ~**ed** ~ **the chorus** sie sangen alle zusammen den Refrain.

▶**join up 1** *vi* **(a)** *(Mil)* zum Militär gehen. **(b)** *(meet: roads etc)* sich treffen; *(join forces)* sich zusammenschließen, sich zusammentun *(col)*. **2** *vt sep* (miteinander) verbinden.

**joiner** ['dʒɔɪnəʳ] *n* Tischler, Schreiner *m*.

**joinery** ['dʒɔɪnərɪ] *n* *(trade)* Tischlerei *f*.

**joint** [dʒɔɪnt] **1** *n* **(a)** *(Anat)* Gelenk *nt*. **(b)** *(in woodwork)* Fuge *f*; *(in pipe etc)* Verbindung(sstelle) *f*; *(welded etc)* Naht(stelle) *f*. **(c)** *(Cook)* Braten *m*. **a** ~ **of beef** ein Rinderbraten *m*. **(d)** *(col: place)* Laden *m* *(col)*. **(e)** *(col: of marijuana)* Joint *m* *(col)*. **2** *adj attr* gemeinsam; *action, work also* Gemeinschafts-; *owner(ship)* Mit-. ~ **account** gemeinsames Konto; **the essay was a** ~ **effort** der Aufsatz ist in Gemeinschaftsarbeit entstanden; ~ **heir** Miterbe *m*, Miterbin *f*; ~ **owners** Miteigentümer *pl*; ~ **stock company** Aktiengesellschaft *f*; ~ **venture** Gemeinschaftsunternehmen, Joint-venture *nt*.

**jointly** ['dʒɔɪntlɪ] *adv* gemeinsam.

**joist** [dʒɔɪst] *n* Balken *m*; *(steel)* Träger *m*.

**joke** [dʒəʊk] **1** *n* Witz *m*; *(prank)* Streich *m*; *(laughing stock)* Gespött *nt*. **for a** ~ zum Spaß, aus Jux *(col)*; **I don't see the** ~ ich möchte wissen, was daran so lustig sein soll; **he treats it as a big** ~ für ihn ist das ein Witz; **he can't take a** ~ er versteht keinen Spaß; **it's no** ~ das ist nicht zum Lachen; **this is getting beyond a** ~ das geht (langsam) zu weit; **the** ~ **was on me** der Spaß ging auf meine Kosten; **to play a** ~ **on sb** jdm einen Streich spielen; **to make** ~**s about sth** sich über etw lustig machen. **2** *vi* Witze machen *(about* über *+acc)*; *(pull sb's leg)* Spaß machen. **I'm not joking** ich meine das ernst; **you must be joking!** das ist ja wohl nicht dein Ernst!

**joker** ['dʒəʊkəʳ] *n* **(a)** *(person)* Witzbold, Spaßvogel *m*. **(b)** *(Cards)* Joker *m*.

**joking** ['dʒəʊkɪŋ] **1** *adj tone* scherzhaft, spaßend. **2** *n* Witze *pl*. ~ **apart** Spaß beiseite.

**jokingly** ['dʒəʊkɪŋlɪ] *adv* im Spaß.

**jollity** ['dʒɒlɪtɪ] *n* Fröhlichkeit, Ausgelassenheit *f*.

**jolly** ['dʒɒlɪ] **1** *adj* *(+er)* *(merry)* fröhlich, vergnügt. **2** *adv* *(Brit col)* **you are** ~ **lucky** Sie haben vielleicht Glück *(col)*; ~ **good** prima *(col)*; **that's** ~ **kind of you** das ist furchtbar nett von Ihnen; **you** ~ **well**

**will go!** und ob du gehst! **3** *vt* **to ~ sb along** jdm aufmunternd zureden.

**jolt** [dʒəʊlt] **1** *vi (vehicle)* holpern; *(give one ~)* einen Ruck machen. **to ~ along** rüttelnd entlangfahren; **to ~ to a halt** ruckweise anhalten. **2** *vt (lit) (shake)* durchrütteln; *(once)* einen Ruck geben *(+dat)*; *(fig)* aufrütteln. **it ~ed him into action** das hat ihn aufgerüttelt. **3** *n (jerk)* Ruck *m*. **it gave me a ~** *(fig)* das hat mir einen Schock versetzt.

**Jordan** [ˈdʒɔːdn] *n* Jordanien *nt*; *(river)* Jordan *m*.

**Jordanian** [dʒɔːˈdeɪnɪən] **1** *adj* jordanisch. **2** *n* Jordanier(in *f*) *m*.

**joss stick** [ˈdʒɒsstɪk] *n* Räucherstäbchen *nt*.

**jostle** [ˈdʒɒsl] **1** *vi* drängeln. **he ~d against me** er rempelte mich an. **2** *vt* anrempeln, schubsen. **he was ~d along with the crowd** die Menge schob ihn mit sich.

**jot** [dʒɒt] *n (of truth)* Funken *m*, Körnchen *nt*.
▶**jot down** *vt sep* sich *(dat)* notieren.

**jotter** [ˈdʒɒtəʳ] *n (note pad)* Notizblock *m*; *(notebook)* Notizheft(chen) *nt*.

**jottings** [ˈdʒɒtɪŋz] *npl* Notizen *pl*.

**joule** [dʒuːl] *n* Joule *nt*.

**journal** [ˈdʒɜːnl] *n (periodical)* Zeitschrift *f*; *(diary)* Tagebuch *nt*.

**journalese** [ˌdʒɜːnəˈliːz] *n* Zeitungsjargon *m*.

**journalism** [ˈdʒɜːnəlɪzəm] *n* Journalismus *m*.

**journalist** [ˈdʒɜːnəlɪst] *n* Journalist(in *f*) *m*.

**journalistic** [ˌdʒɜːnəˈlɪstɪk] *adj* journalistisch.

**journey** [ˈdʒɜːnɪ] **1** *n* Reise *f*; *(by train, car also)* Fahrt *f*. **to go on a ~** eine Reise machen, verreisen; **it is a 50 mile ~** es liegt 50 Meilen entfernt; **a two day ~** eine Reise von zwei Tagen; **a train ~** eine Zugfahrt; **the ~ home** die Heimfahrt. **2** *vi* reisen.

**jovial** *adj*, **~ly** *adv* [ˈdʒəʊvɪəl, -ɪ] fröhlich; *welcome* herzlich.

**joviality** [ˌdʒəʊvɪˈælɪtɪ] *n see adj* Fröhlichkeit *f*; Herzlichkeit *f*.

**jowl** [dʒaʊl] *n (jaw)* (Unter)kiefer *m*; *(often pl: cheek)* Backe *f*.

**joy** [dʒɔɪ] *n* Freude *f*. **to my great ~** zu meiner großen Freude; **I wish you ~ (of it)!** *(iro)* na dann viel Spaß!; **I didn't get much ~** *(Brit col)* ich hatte nicht viel Erfolg; **did you get any ~?** hat es geklappt? *(col)*.

**joyful** *adj*, **~ly** *adv* [ˈdʒɔɪfʊl, -ɪ] freudig, froh.

**joyous** *adj*, **~ly** *adv* [ˈdʒɔɪəs, -lɪ] *(liter)* freudig, froh.

**joy: ~-ride** *n* Spritztour *f (in einem gestohlenen Auto)*; **~-rider** *n* Autodieb *m, der den Wagen nur für eine Spritztour nimmt*; **~stick** *n (Aviat)* Steuerknüppel *m*; *(Comp)* Joystick *m*.

**JP** *(Brit)* = **Justice of the Peace.**

**Jr** = **junior** jr., jun.

**jubilant** [ˈdʒuːbɪlənt] *adj mood* Jubel-; *crowd* jubelnd; *face* strahlend *attr*. **they gave him a ~ welcome** sie empfingen ihn mit Jubel; **he was ~ at the news** er war überglücklich, als er die Nachricht hörte.

**jubilation** [ˌdʒuːbɪˈleɪʃən] *n* Jubel *m*.

**jubilee** [ˈdʒuːbɪliː] *n* Jubiläum *nt*.

**judge** [dʒʌdʒ] **1** *n (Jur)* Richter(in *f*) *m*; *(of competition)* Preisrichter(in *f*) *m*; *(Sport)* Schiedsrichter(in *f*) *m*; *(fig)* Kenner *m*. **to be a good ~ of character** ein guter Menschenkenner sein; **to be a good ~ of wine** ein Weinkenner sein.
**2** *vt* **(a)** *(Jur) person* die Verhandlung führen über *(+acc)*; *case* verhandeln; *(God)* richten. **(b)** *competition* beurteilen, bewerten; *(Sport)* Schiedsrichter sein bei. **(c)** *(fig: pass judgement on)* ein Urteil fällen über *(+acc)*. **you shouldn't ~ people by appear-** ances Sie sollten Menschen nicht nach ihrem Äußeren beurteilen. **(d)** *(consider, assess)* **he ~d it to be necessary/advisable** er hielt es für nötig/ratsam; **you can ~ for yourself how upset I was** Sie können sich *(dat)* denken, wie bestürzt ich war; **I can't ~ whether he was right or wrong** ich kann nicht beurteilen, ob er recht oder unrecht hatte. **(e)** *(estimate) distance etc* einschätzen. **he ~d the moment well** er hat den richtigen Augenblick abgepaßt.

**3** *vi (Jur)* Richter sein; *(God)* richten; *(at competition)* Preisrichter sein; *(Sport)* Schiedsrichter sein; *(fig) (pass judgement)* ein Urteil fällen; *(form an opinion)* (be)urteilen. **as far as one can ~** soweit man (es) beurteilen kann; **judging by** or **from sth** nach etw zu urteilen; **judging by appearances** dem Aussehen nach; **(you can) ~ for yourself** beurteilen Sie das selbst.

**judg(e)ment** [ˈdʒʌdʒmənt] *n (Jur)* (Gerichts)urteil *nt*; *(opinion)* Ansicht *f*, Urteil *nt*; *(value ~)* Werturteil *nt*; *(estimation)* Einschätzung *f*; *(discernment)* Urteilsvermögen *nt*. **to pass ~** *(lit, fig)* ein Urteil fällen, das Urteil sprechen *(on* über *+acc)*; **an error of ~** eine Fehleinschätzung; **in my ~** meiner Meinung nach; **against my better ~** gegen meine Überzeugung; **it's a question of ~** das ist Ansichtssache.

**Judg(e)ment Day** *n* Tag *m* des Jüngsten Gerichts.

**judicial** [dʒuːˈdɪʃəl] *adj (Jur)* gerichtlich, Justiz-.

**judiciary** [dʒuːˈdɪʃɪərɪ] *n (branch of administration)* Gerichtsbehörden *pl*; *(judges)* Richterstand *m*.

**judicious** *adj*, **~ly** *adv* [dʒuːˈdɪʃəs, -lɪ] klug, umsichtig.

**judo** [ˈdʒuːdəʊ] *n* Judo *nt*.

**jug** [dʒʌg] **1** *n* **(a)** *(with lid)* Kanne *f*; *(without lid)* Krug *m*; *(small)* Kännchen *nt*. **(b)** *(col: prison)* Knast *m (col)*. **2** *vt* **~ged hare** ≈ Hasenpfeffer *m*.

**juggernaut** [ˈdʒʌgənɔːt] *n (Brit: truck)* Schwerlaster *m*.

**juggle** [ˈdʒʌgl] *vti* jonglieren. **to ~ (with) the figures** mit den Zahlen jonglieren.

**juggler** [ˈdʒʌgləʳ] *n* Jongleur *m*.

**Jugoslavia** [ˌjuːgəʊˈslɑːvɪə] *n* = **Yugoslavia.**

**jugular** [ˈdʒʌgjʊləʳ] *n (also ~ vein)* Drosselvene *f*.

**juice** [dʒuːs] *n (lit, fig col)* Saft *m*; *(fuel)* Sprit *m (col)*.

**juiciness** [ˈdʒuːsɪnɪs] *n (lit, fig of scandal)* Saftigkeit *f*; *(of story)* Pikanterie *f*.

**juicy** [ˈdʒuːsɪ] *adj (+er)* saftig; *story* pikant, schlüpfrig; *scandal also* gepfeffert *(col)*.

**jujitsu** [ˌdʒuːˈdʒɪtsuː] *n* Jiu-Jitsu *nt*.

**jukebox** [ˈdʒuːkbɒks] *n* Musikbox *f*.

**Jul** = **July** Jul.

**July** [dʒuːˈlaɪ] *n* Juli *m*; *see* **September.**

**jumble** [ˈdʒʌmbl] **1** *vt (also ~ up) (lit)* durcheinanderwerfen. **~d up** durcheinander; *(fig) facts* durcheinanderbringen. **2** *n* **(a)** Durcheinander *nt*; *(of ideas also)* Wirrwarr *m*. **(b)** *no pl (for ~ sale)* gebrauchte Sachen *pl*. **~ sale** *(Brit)* = Flohmarkt *m*; *(for charity)* Wohltätigkeitsbasar *m*.

**jumbo** [ˈdʒʌmbəʊ] **1** *n (~ jet)* Jumbo(-Jet) *m*. **2** *adj (box, sausage)* Riesen-.

**jump** [dʒʌmp] **1** *n (lit, fig)* Sprung *m*; *(with parachute)* Absprung *m*; *(on race-course)* Hindernis *nt*; *(of prices)* (sprunghafter) Anstieg. **to be one ~ ahead** *(fig)* einen Schritt voraus sein.

**2** *vi* **(a)** springen; *(parachutist)* (ab)springen; *(typewriter)* Buchstaben überspringen; *(prices, shares)* sprunghaft ansteigen. **to ~ for joy** einen Freudensprung machen; **to ~ up and down on the spot** auf der Stelle hüpfen; **she was ~ing up and down (with excitement)** *(fig)* sie war ganz aus dem Häuschen *(col)*; **to ~ to conclusions** vorschnelle

Schlüsse ziehen; **go and** ~ **in the lake!** *(col)* scher dich zum Teufel! *(col)*; ~ **to it!** mach schon!; **if you keep** ~**ing from one thing to another** wenn Sie nie bei einer Sache bleiben. **(b)** *(start)* zusammenzucken. **you made me** ~ du hast mich (aber) erschreckt.
**3** *vt* **(a)** ditch etc überspringen, hinüberspringen über *(+acc)*. **(b)** *(skip)* überspringen, auslassen. **to** ~ **the rails** *(train)* entgleisen. **(c)** *(col)* **to** ~ **bail** abhauen *(col)* *(während man auf Kaution freigelassen ist)*; **to** ~ **the lights** bei Rot über die Kreuzung fahren; **to** ~ **the queue** *(Brit)* sich vordrängeln; **to** ~ **ship** *(Naut)* *(passenger)* das Schiff vorzeitig verlassen; *(sailor)* heimlich abheuern; **to** ~ **sb** *(attack)* jdn überfallen.
▶**jump about** or **around** *vi* herumspringen.
▶**jump at** *vi* +*prep obj person (lit)* anspringen; *(fig)* anfahren; *object* zuspringen auf *(+acc)*; *offer* sofort zugreifen bei; *chance* sofort beim Schopf ergreifen.
▶**jump down** *vi* hinunter-/herunterspringen *(from* von*)*. **to** ~ ~ **sb's throat** jdn anfahren.
▶**jump in** *vi* hinein-/hereinspringen. ~ ~! *(into vehicle)* steig ein!
▶**jump off** *vi* herunterspringen *(prep obj* von*)*; *(from train, bus)* aussteigen *(prep obj* aus*)*; *(from bicycle, horse)* absteigen *(prep obj* von*)*.
▶**jump on** *vi (lit) (onto vehicle)* einsteigen *(prep obj, -to* in +*acc)*; *(onto bicycle, horse)* aufsteigen *(prep obj, -to* auf +*acc)*. **he** ~**ed** ~ **(to) his bicycle** er schwang sich auf sein Fahrrad.
▶**jump out** *vi* hinaus-/herausspringen; *(from vehicle)* aussteigen *(of* aus*)*.
▶**jump up** *vi* hochspringen; *(from sitting or lying position also)* aufspringen; *(onto sth)* hinaufspringen *(onto* auf +*acc)*.
**jumped-up** ['dʒʌmpt'ʌp] *adj (col)* eingebildet. **this new** ~ **manager** dieser kleine Emporkömmling von einem Abteilungsleiter.
**jumper** ['dʒʌmpər] *n* **(a)** *(garment) (Brit)* Pullover *m*; *(US: dress)* Trägerkleid *nt*. **(b)** *(person, animal)* Springer *m*. **(c)** ~ **cable** *(US Aut)* Starthilfekabel *nt*.
**jump:** ~ **jet** *n* Senkrechtstarter *m*; ~ **leads** *npl (Brit Aut)* Starthilfekabel *nt*; ~**-off** *n (Show-jumping)* Stechen *nt*; ~**-start** *vt (by pushing)* anschieben; *(with leads)* mit Starthilfekabel starten; ~ **suit** *n* Overall *m*.
**jumpy** ['dʒʌmpɪ] *adj (+er) (col) person* nervös; *(easily startled)* schreckhaft.
**Jun** = **(a)** **June** Jun. **(b)** **junior** jr., jun.
**junction** ['dʒʌŋkʃən] *n (Rail)* Gleisanschluß *m*; *(Brit: of roads)* Kreuzung *f*. **railway** ~ Eisenbahnknotenpunkt *m*; ~ **box** *(Elec)* Verteilerkasten *m*.
**juncture** ['dʒʌŋktʃər] *n*: **at this** ~ zu diesem Zeitpunkt.
**June** [dʒuːn] *n* Juni *m*; *see* **September**.
**jungle** ['dʒʌŋgl] *n* Dschungel *m (also fig)*, Urwald *m*.
**junior** ['dʒuːnɪər] **1** *adj* **(a)** *(younger)* jünger. **Hiram Schwarz,** ~ **Hiram Schwarz** junior; ~ **classes** *(Sch)* Unterstufe *f*; ~ **school** *(Brit)* Grundschule *f*; ~ **high (school)** *(US)* ≈ Mittelschule *f*. **(b)** *employee* untergeordnet; *officer* rangniedriger. ~ **clerk** zweiter Buchhalter; ~ **Minister** Staatssekretär(in *f*) *m*. **2** *n* **(a)** Jüngere(r) *mf*. **he is two years my** ~ er ist zwei Jahre jünger als ich. **(b)** *(Brit Sch)* Grundschüler(in *f*) *m*; *(US Univ) Student(in f) m im vorletzten Studienjahr.*
**juniper** ['dʒuːnɪpər] *n* Wacholder *m*. ~ **berry** Wacholderbeere *f*.
**junk¹** [dʒʌŋk] *n* **(a)** *(discarded objects)* Trödel *m*, Gerümpel *nt*; *(col: trash)* Schund *m*; *(pej: food)* Fraß *m (col)*. **(b)** *(col: drugs)* Stoff *m (col)*.

**junk²** *n (boat)* Dschunke *f*.
**junk:** ~ **foods** *npl (pej)* Plastikessen *nt (pej col)*; *(sweets)* Süßkram *m (col)*; ~ **heap** *n (also col: car)* Schrotthaufen *m*.
**junkie** ['dʒʌŋkɪ] *n (col)* Fixer(in *f*) *m (col)*.
**junk:** ~ **mail** *n (Post)* wurfsendungen *pl*; ~ **room** *n* Rumpelkammer *f*; ~ **shop** *n* Trödelladen *m*.
**junta** ['dʒʌntə] *n* Junta *f*.
**Jupiter** ['dʒuːpɪtər] *n* Jupiter *m*.
**jurisdiction** [,dʒʊərɪs'dɪkʃən] *n* Gerichtsbarkeit *f*; *(range of authority)* Zuständigkeit(sbereich *m*) *f*. **matters that do not fall under the** ~ **of this court** Fälle, für die dieses Gericht nicht zuständig ist; **that's not (in) my** ~ dafür bin ich nicht zuständig.
**jurisprudence** [,dʒʊərɪs'pruːdəns] *n* Jura *no art*.
**juror** ['dʒʊərər] *n* Schöffe *m*, Schöffin *f*; *(for capital crimes)* Geschworene(r) *mf*.
**jury** ['dʒʊərɪ] *n* **(a)** **the** ~ die Schöffen *pl*; *(for capital crimes)* die Geschworenen *pl*; **to sit on the** ~ Schöffe/Geschworener sein. **(b)** *(for competition)* Jury *f*.
**jury:** ~**box** *n* Schöffen-/Geschworenenbank *f*; ~**man** *n* = **juror**; ~ **service** *n* **to be called for** ~ **service** als Schöffe/Geschworener berufen werden.
**just¹** [dʒʌst] *adj* **(a)** *(with time)* gerade, (so)eben. **they have** ~ **left** sie sind gerade gegangen; **I met him** ~ **after lunch** ich habe ihn gleich nach dem Mittagessen getroffen; **hurry up, he's** ~ **going** beeilen Sie sich, er geht gerade; **I'm** ~ **coming** ich komme ja schon; **I was** ~ **going to ...** ich wollte gerade ...; ~ **as I was going** gerade, als ich gehen wollte.
**(b)** *(barely, almost not)* gerade noch. **he** ~ **escaped being run over** er wäre um ein Haar überfahren worden; **I arrived** ~ **in time** ich bin gerade noch rechtzeitig gekommen.
**(c)** *(exactly)* genau. **it is** ~ **five o'clock** es ist genau fünf Uhr; **that's** ~ **like you** das sieht dir ähnlich; ~ **as I expected** genau wie ich es erwartet hatte; **that's** ~ **it!** das ist es ja gerade!; **that's** ~ **what I was going to say** genau das wollte ich (auch) sagen; ~ **what do you mean by that?** was soll das heißen?; ~ **at that moment** genau in dem Augenblick; **everything has to be** ~ **so** es muß alles seine Ordnung haben.
**(d)** *(only, simply)* nur, bloß. ~ **you and me** nur wir beide; **he's** ~ **a boy** er ist doch noch ein Junge; ~ **like that** einfach so; **it's** ~ **not good enough** es ist einfach nicht gut genug; **I** ~ **prefer it this way** ich find's einfach besser so; ~ **round the corner** gleich um die Ecke; ~ **above the trees** direkt über den Bäumen.
**(e)** *(absolutely)* einfach, wirklich. **it was** ~ **fantastic** es war einfach prima; **it's** ~ **terrible** das ist ja schrecklich!
**(f)** ~ **as** genauso, ebenso; **the blue hat is** ~ **as nice as the red one** der blaue Hut ist genauso hübsch wie der rote; **it's** ~ **as well you didn't go out** nur gut, daß Sie nicht weggegangen sind; **it would be** ~ **as well if you came** es wäre doch besser, wenn Sie kämen; **come** ~ **as you are** kommen Sie so, wie Sie sind; ~ **as you please** wie Sie wollen; ~ **as I thought!** ich habe es mir doch gedacht!
**(g)** ~ **about** in etwa, so etwa; **I am** ~ **about ready** ich bin so gut wie fertig; **did he make it in time?** — ~ **about** hat er's (rechtzeitig) geschafft? — so gerade; **I am** ~ **about fed up with it!** *(col)* so langsam aber sicher hängt es mir zum Hals raus *(col)*.
**(h)** ~ **now** *(in past)* gerade erst; **not** ~ **now** im Moment nicht; **you can go, but not** ~ **now** Sie können gehen, aber nicht gerade jetzt; ~ **think** denk bloß; ~ **listen** hör mal; ~ **a moment** or **minute!** Mo-

ment mal!; **I can ~ see him as a soldier** ich kann ihn mir gut als Soldat vorstellen; **can I ~ finish this?** kann ich das eben noch fertigmachen?; **don't I ~!** und ob!; **~ watch it** nimm dich bloß in acht; **~ you dare!** wehe!

**just²** *adj (+er) person, decision* gerecht *(to* gegenüber*)*; *anger* berechtigt; *suspicion* begründet. **as (it) is only ~** wie es recht und billig ist.

**justice** ['dʒʌstɪs] *n* **(a)** *(quality)* Gerechtigkeit *f*; *(system)* Justiz *f*; *(of claims)* Rechtmäßigkeit *f*. **to bring a thief to ~** einen Dieb vor Gericht bringen; **to do him ~** um ihm gegenüber gerecht zu sein; **this photograph doesn't do me ~** auf diesem Foto bin ich nicht gut getroffen; **she never does herself ~** sie kommt nie richtig zur Geltung; **he complained, with ~, that ...** er hat sich zu Recht beklagt, daß ...; **there's no ~, is there?** das ist doch nicht gerecht. **(b)** *(judge)* Richter *m*. **J~ of the Peace** Friedensrichter *m*.

**justifiable** [ˌdʒʌstɪ'faɪəbl] *adj* zu rechtfertigen *pred*, berechtigt.

**justifiably** [ˌdʒʌstɪ'faɪəblɪ] *adv* zu Recht.

**justification** [ˌdʒʌstɪfɪ'keɪʃən] *n* **(a)** Rechtfertigung *f*. **(b)** *(Typ)* Blocksatz *m*; *(Comp)* Randausgleich *m*.

**justify** ['dʒʌstɪfaɪ] *vt* **(a)** rechtfertigen *(sth to sb* etw jdm gegenüber*)*. **am I justified in thinking that ...?** gehe ich recht in der Annahme, daß ...?; **he was justified in doing that** es war gerechtfertigt, daß er das tat; **you're not justified in talking to her like that** Sie haben kein Recht, so mit ihr zu reden. **(b)** *(Typ)* justieren; *(Comp)* ausrichten.

**justness** ['dʒʌstnɪs] *n* Gerechtigkeit *f*.

**jut** [dʒʌt] *vi (also ~ out)* hervorstehen, herausragen.

**jute** [dʒuːt] *n* Jute *f*.

**juvenile** ['dʒuːvənaɪl] **1** *n (Admin)* Jugendliche(r) *mf*. **2** *adj (youthful)* jugendlich; *(for young people)* Jugend-, für Jugendliche; *(pej)* kindisch, unreif.

**juvenile:** **~ court** *n* Jugendgericht *nt*; **~ crime** *or* **delinquency** *n* Jugendkriminalität *f*; **~ delinquent** *n* jugendlicher Straftäter.

**juxtapose** ['dʒʌkstə,pəʊz] *vt* nebeneinanderstellen.

**juxtaposition** [ˌdʒʌkstəpə'zɪʃən] *n (act)* Nebeneinanderstellung *f*. **in ~** (direkt) nebeneinander.

# K

**K, k** [keɪ] *n* K, k *nt.* **K for King** ≃ K wie Kaufmann.
**K** *(in salaries etc)* = **thousand** -tausend. **15 ~** 15 000.
**k** *(Comp)* = **kilobyte** KB.
**kale** [keɪl] *n* Grünkohl *m.*
**kaleidoscope** [kə'laɪdəskəup] *n* Kaleidoskop *nt.*
**Kampuchea** [ˌkæmpʊ'tʃɪə] *n* Kampuchea *nt.*
**kangaroo** [ˌkæŋgə'ruː] *n* Känguruh *nt.* **~ court** inoffizielles Gericht.
**karate** [kə'rɑːtɪ] *n* Karate *nt.*
**karting** ['kɑːtɪŋ] *n* Go-Kart-Fahren *nt.*
**Kashmir** [kæʃ'mɪər] *n* Kaschmir *nt.*
**kayak** ['kaɪæk] *n* Kajak *m or nt.*
**KC** *(Brit Jur)* = **King's Counsel** Kronanwalt *m.*
**kebab** [kə'bæb] *n* Kebab *m.*
**keel** [kiːl] *n* *(Naut)* Kiel *m.* **to be on an even ~ again** *(fig)* wieder im Lot sein; **he put the business back on an even ~** er brachte das Geschäft wieder auf die Beine *(col).*
▶**keel over** *vi (ship)* kentern; *(fig col)* umkippen.
**keen** [kiːn] *adj (+er)* **(a)** *edge, wind, competition, wit* scharf; *appetite* kräftig; *interest* stark; *desire, pain* heftig; *sight, hearing* gut; *(esp Brit) prices* günstig.
**(b)** *(enthusiastic)* begeistert; *football fan etc also* leidenschaftlich; *applicant, learner* stark interessiert; *(hardworking)* eifrig. **~ to learn** lernbegierig; **to be ~ on sb** von jdm sehr angetan sein, scharf auf jdn sein *(col);* *on actor, author* von jdm begeistert sein; **to be ~ on sth** etw sehr gern mögen; **to be ~ on doing sth** *(like to do)* etw gern tun; **to be ~ to do sth** *(want to do)* darauf erpicht sein *or* scharf darauf sein *(col),* etw zu tun; **to be ~ on mountaineering** sehr gern bergsteigen; **I'm not very ~ on him** ich bin von ihm nicht gerade begeistert; **he's not ~ on her coming** er möchte eigentlich nicht, daß sie kommt.
**keenly** ['kiːnlɪ] *adv* **(a)** *(sharply)* scharf; *feel* leidenschaftlich, stark. **(b)** *(enthusiastically)* mit Begeisterung.
**keenness** ['kiːnnɪs] *n* **(a)** *(of mind, wind)* Schärfe *f.* **(b)** *see adj (b)* Begeisterung *f;* Leidenschaftlichkeit *f;* starkes Interesse; Eifer *m.*
**keep** [kiːp] *(vb: pret, ptp* **kept)** **1** *vt* **(a)** *(retain)* behalten. **to ~ a place for sb** einen Platz für jdn freihalten; **you can ~ it!** *(col)* das kannst du dir an den Hut stecken! *(col).*
**(b)** *shop* haben, führen; *animals* halten. **to ~ house for sb** jdm den Haushalt führen.
**(c)** *(support) family etc* unterhalten. **I earn enough to ~ myself** ich verdiene genug (für mich) zum Leben; **to ~ sb in clothing** für jds Kleidung sorgen.
**(d)** *(maintain in a certain state)* halten. **to ~ one's dress clean** sein Kleid nicht schmutzig machen; **just to ~ her happy** damit sie zufrieden ist; **to ~ sb waiting** jdn warten lassen; **can't you ~ him talking?** können Sie ihn nicht in ein Gespräch verwickeln?; **to ~ sth tidy** etw sauber *or* in Ordnung halten; **the garden was well kept** der Garten war (gut) gepflegt; **to ~ a machine running** eine Maschine lau-

fen lassen; **to ~ the conversation going** das Gespräch in Gang halten.
**(e)** *(store, look after)* aufbewahren; *(put aside)* aufheben. **where does he ~ his money?** wo bewahrt er sein Geld auf?; **where do you ~ your spoons?** wo hast du die Löffel?; **I've been ~ing it for you** ich habe es für Sie aufgehoben.
**(f)** *promise* halten; *rule* befolgen; *treaty, appointment* einhalten; *obligations* nachkommen *(+dat).*
**(g)** *accounts, diary etc* führen *(of über +acc).*
**(h)** *(detain)* aufhalten. **I mustn't ~ you** ich will Sie nicht aufhalten; **what kept you?** wo waren Sie denn so lange?; **to ~ sb in prison** jdn in Haft halten.
**(i)** *(not disclose)* **can you ~ this from your mother?** können Sie das vor Ihrer Mutter geheimhalten?; **~ it to yourself** behalten Sie das für sich.
**(j) to ~ late hours** lange aufbleiben.
**2** *vi* **(a) to ~ (to the) left** sich links halten; **to ~ to the middle of the road** *(Aut)* immer in der Mitte der Straße fahren. **(b) to ~ doing sth** *(not stop)* etw weiter tun; *(repeatedly)* etw immer wieder tun; *(constantly)* etw dauernd tun; **to ~ walking** weitergehen; **he kept lying to her** er hat sie immer wieder belogen; **if you ~ complaining** wenn Sie sich weiter beschweren; **she ~s talking about you all the time** sie redet dauernd von Ihnen; **~ going** machen Sie weiter; **~ at it!** bleib am Ball! **(c)** *(remain)* bleiben. **to ~ quiet** still sein; **to ~ silent** schweigen; **to ~ calm** ruhig bleiben. **(d)** *(food etc)* sich halten. **(e)** *(state of health)* **how are you ~ing?** wie geht es Ihnen denn so?; **to ~ well** gesund bleiben; **to ~ fit** fit bleiben; **he's ~ing better now** es geht ihm wieder besser. **(f)** *(wait)* **that can ~** das kann warten.
**3** *n* **(a)** *(livelihood, food)* Unterhalt *m.* **I got £10 a week and my ~** ich bekam £ 10 pro Woche und freie Kost und Logis; **to earn one's ~** *(fig)* sein Geld verdienen; *(machine etc)* sich rentieren. **(b)** *(in castle)* Bergfried *m; (as prison)* Burgverlies *nt.* **(c) for ~s** *(col)* für immer; **it's yours for ~s** das darfst du behalten.
▶**keep away 1** *vi (lit)* wegbleiben; *(not approach)* nicht näher herankommen *(from an +acc).* **~ ~!** kommen Sie nicht näher!; **I just can't ~ ~** es zieht mich immer wieder hin; **~ ~ from him** lassen Sie die Finger von ihm. **2** *vt always separate person, children etc* fernhalten *(from von).* **to ~ sth ~ from sth** etw nicht an etw *(acc)* kommen lassen.
▶**keep back 1** *vi* zurückbleiben. **~ ~!** treten Sie zurück! **2** *vt sep* **(a)** *hair, crowds* zurückhalten; *water* stauen; *tears* unterdrücken. **(b)** *(withhold) taxes* einbehalten; *information etc* verschweigen *(from sb* jdm*); (from parent, husband etc)* verheimlichen *(from sb* jdm*); (make late)* aufhalten; *pupil* dabehalten. **(d)** *(hold up, slow down)* behindern.
▶**keep down 1** *vi* unten bleiben. **~ ~!** bleib unten! **2** *vt sep* **(a)** *(hold down)* unten halten. **~ your voices ~** reden Sie leise! **(b)** *revolt, one's anger* unterdrücken; *rabbits, weeds etc* unter Kontrolle halten.

**you can't** ~ **a good man** ~ ein tüchtiger Mann läßt sich nicht unterkriegen. **(c)** *prices* niedrig halten; *spending* einschränken. **to** ~ **one's weight** ~ nicht zunehmen. **(d)** *food etc* bei sich behalten. **(e)** *(Sch)* **he was kept** ~ er mußte das Schuljahr wiederholen.

▶**keep from 1** *vt +prep obj* **(a) I couldn't** ~ **him** ~ **going there** ich konnte ihn nicht davon abhalten, dort hinzugehen; **the bells** ~ **me** ~ **sleeping** die Glocken lassen mich nicht schlafen; **his anorak kept him** ~ **getting wet** sein Anorak schützte ihn vor dem Regen; **this will** ~ **the water** ~ **freezing** das verhindert, daß das Wasser gefriert. **(b)** *(withhold)* **to** ~ **sth** ~ **sb** jdm etw verschweigen; *piece of news also* jdm etw vorenthalten. **2** *vi +prep obj* **to** ~ ~ **doing sth** etw nicht tun; *(avoid doing also)* es vermeiden, etw zu tun; **she couldn't** ~ ~ **laughing** sie mußte einfach lachen.

▶**keep in 1** *vt sep feelings* zügeln; *pupil* nachsitzen lassen; *stomach* einziehen. **2** *vi* **he wants to** ~ ~ **with her** er will es nicht mit ihr verderben.

▶**keep off 1** *vi (person)* wegbleiben. **if the rain** ~**s** ~ wenn es nicht regnet. **2** *vt sep dog, person* fernhalten *(prep obj* von*)*. "~ ~ **the grass**" „Betreten des Rasens verboten"; ~ **your hands** ~ Hände weg! **3** *vi +prep obj* vermeiden. ~ ~ **the whisky** lassen Sie das Whiskytrinken.

▶**keep on 1** *vi* **(a)** weitermachen. **to** ~ ~ **doing sth** etw weiter tun; *(repeatedly)* etw immer wieder tun; *(incessantly)* etw dauernd tun; **if you** ~ ~ **like this** wenn du so weitermachst; **the rain kept** ~ **all night** es regnete die ganze Nacht durch. **(b)** *(keep going)* weitergehen/-fahren. ~ ~ **past the church** fahren/gehen Sie immer weiter, an der Kirche vorbei. **(c) to** ~ ~ **at sb** *(col)* dauernd an jdm herummeckern *(col)*; **to** ~ ~ **about sth** *(col)* unaufhörlich von etw reden; **don't** ~ ~ **so!** *(col)* hören Sie doch endlich auf damit! **2** *vt sep* **(a)** *employee* behalten. **(b)** *coat etc* anbehalten; *hat* aufbehalten.

▶**keep out 1** *vi (of building)* draußen bleiben; *(of property)* etw nicht betreten. "~ ~" „Zutritt verboten"; **to** ~ ~ **of danger** Gefahr meiden; **to** ~ ~ **of debt** keine Schulden machen; **that child can never** ~ ~ **of mischief** das Kind stellt dauernd etwas an; **you** ~ ~ **of this!** halten Sie sich da raus! **2** *vt sep* **(a)** *person* nicht hereinlassen *(of* in *+acc)*; *light, cold, enemy etc* abhalten. **(b) I wanted to** ~ **him** ~ **of this** ich wollte nicht, daß er da mit hineingezogen wird; ~ **him** ~ **of my way** halte ihn mir vom Leib.

▶**keep to 1** *vi +prep obj* **(a)** ~ ~ **the main road** bleiben Sie auf der Hauptstraße; **to** ~ ~ **the schedule** sich an den Zeitplan halten. **(b) to** ~ **(oneself)** ~ **oneself** nicht sehr gesellig sein; **they** ~ ~ **themselves** sie bleiben unter sich. **2** *vt +prep obj* **to** ~ **sb** ~ **his word** darauf bestehen, daß jd sein Wort hält; **to** ~ **sth** ~ **a minimum** etw auf ein Minimum beschränken.

▶**keep together 1** *vi (stay together)* zusammenbleiben. **2** *vt (fix together, unite)* zusammenhalten.

▶**keep up 1** *vi* **(a)** *(tent)* stehen bleiben. **(b)** *(rain)* (an)dauern; *(weather etc)* anhalten; *(morale, determination)* nicht nachlassen. **(c) to** ~ ~ **(with sb/sth)** *(in race, work)* (mit jdm/etw) Schritt halten; *(in comprehension)* (jdm/einer Sache) folgen können; **to** ~ ~ **with the Joneses** mit den Nachbarn mithalten; **to** ~ ~ **with the times** mit der Zeit gehen; **to** ~ ~ **with the news** sich auf dem laufenden halten.

**2** *vt sep* **(a)** *tent* aufrecht halten. **(b)** *(not stop)* nicht aufhören mit; *studies* weiterführen; *quality, prices, friendship, tradition, payments* aufrechterhal-

ten; *speed* halten. **I try to** ~ ~ **my French** ich versuche, mit meinem Französisch nicht aus der Übung zu kommen; ~ **it** ~! (machen Sie) weiter so!; **he couldn't** ~ **it** ~ er mußte aufgeben. **(c)** *(maintain)* *house* unterhalten; *road* instand halten. **(d)** *(prevent from going to bed)* am Schlafengehen hindern. **that child kept me** ~ **all night** das Kind hat mich die ganze Nacht nicht ins Bett kommen lassen.

**keeper** ['kiːpər] *n (zoo)* Wärter(in *f*) *m*; *(museum)* Aufseher(in *f*) *m*; *(goal~)* Torhüter *m*.

**keep-fit** ['kiːpˈfɪt] *n* Fitneßtraining *nt*; *(exercises)* Gymnastik *f*.

**keeping** ['kiːpɪŋ] *n* **(a)** *(care)* Obhut *f*. **to put sth in sb's** ~ jdm etw zur Aufbewahrung übergeben. **(b) in** ~ **with** in Einklang mit.

**keepsake** ['kiːpseɪk] *n* Andenken *nt*.

**keg** [keg] *n (barrel)* kleines Faß.

**kennel** ['kenl] *n* Hundehütte *f*. **to put a dog in** ~**s** einen Hund in eine Hundepension geben.

**Kenya** ['kenjə] *n* Kenia *nt*.

**Kenyan** ['kenjən] **1** *n* Kenianer(in *f*) *m*. **2** *adj* kenianisch.

**kept** [kept] *pret, ptp of* **keep.**

**kerb** [kɜːb] *n (Brit)* Randstein *m*.

**kerb:** ~**-crawler** *n* Freier *m* im Autostrich; ~**-crawling** *n* Autostrich *m*; ~**stone** *n* Bordstein, Randstein *m*.

**kernel** ['kɜːnl] *n (lit, fig)* Kern *m*.

**kerosene** ['kerəsiːn] *n* Kerosin *nt*; *(paraffin)* Paraffin *nt*.

**kestrel** ['kestrəl] *n* Turmfalke *m*.

**ketchup** ['ketʃəp] *n* Ketchup *nt or m*.

**kettle** ['ketl] *n* Kessel *m*. **I'll put the** ~ **on** ich stelle mal eben (Kaffee-/Tee)wasser auf; **the** ~**'s boiling** das Wasser kocht; **a pretty** ~ **of fish** *(col)* eine schöne Bescherung *(col)*; **that's a different** ~ **of fish** *(col)* das ist doch was ganz anderes.

**kettledrum** ['ketldrʌm] *n* (Kessel)pauke *f*.

**key** [kiː] **1** *n* **(a)** *(lit, fig)* Schlüssel *m*. **the** ~ **to the mystery** der Schlüssel zum Geheimnis. **(b)** *(for maps etc)* Zeichenerklärung *f*. **(c)** *(of piano, typewriter etc)* Taste *f*. **(d)** *(Mus)* Tonart *f*. **to sing off** ~ falsch singen; **change of** ~ Tonartwechsel *m*; **in the** ~ **of C major/minor** in C-Dur/c-Moll. **2** *adj attr (vital)* Schlüssel-. ~ **figure** *or* **person** Schlüsselfigur *f*; ~ **point** springender Punkt.

▶**key in** *vt (Comp)* eingeben.

**key:** ~**board 1** *n* Tastatur *f*; **2** *vti (Typ, Comp)* eingeben, eintippen; ~**boarder** *n (Comp)* Datentypist(in *f*) *m*; ~ **boarding** *n (Comp)* Dateneingabe *f*.

**keyed up** ['kiːd'ʌp] *adj* **she was (all)** ~ **about the interview** sie war wegen des Interviews ganz aufgedreht *(col)*.

**key:** ~**hole** *n* Schlüsselloch *nt*; ~**note** *n (Mus)* Grundton *m*; *(fig)* Leitgedanke *m*; ~**note speech** *n (Pol etc)* programmatische Rede; ~**pad** *n* Tastenfeld *nt*; ~ **ring** *n* Schlüsselring *m*; ~ **signature** *n (Mus)* Tonartvorzeichnung *f*; ~**stroke** *n* Tastenanschlag *m*.

**kg** = **kilogram(s)** kg.

**khaki** ['kɑːkɪ] **1** *n* K(h)aki *nt*. **2** *adj* k(h)aki(farben).

**kibbutz** [kɪ'bʊts] *n, pl* -**im** Kibbuz *m*.

**kick** [kɪk] **1** *n* Tritt, Stoß *m*; *(of gun)* Rückstoß *m*. **to take a** ~ **at sb/sth** nach jdm/etw treten; **to give the door a** ~ gegen die Tür treten; **it's better than a** ~ **in the pants** *(col)* das ist besser als ein Tritt in den Hintern *(col)*; **she gets a** ~ **out of it** *(col)* es macht ihr einen Riesenspaß *(col)*; **to do sth for** ~**s** *(col)* etw aus Jux *(col)* tun; **this drink has plenty of** ~ **in it** *(col)* dieses Getränk hat es in sich. **2** *vi (person)* tre-

ten; *(struggle)* um sich treten; *(animal)* ausschlagen. **3** *vt (person, horse)* sb treten; *door, ball* treten gegen; *object* einen Tritt versetzen *(+dat)*. **to ~ the bucket** *(col)* ins Gras beißen *(col)*; **I could have ~ed myself** *(col)* ich hätte mir in den Hintern treten können *(col)*; **to ~ the habit** *(col)* es aufgeben.
►**kick about** *or* **around 1** *vi (col) (person)* rumhängen *(col) (prep obj* in *+dat)*; *(thing)* rumliegen *(col) (prep obj* in *+dat)*. **2** *vt sep* **to ~ a ball** ~ einen Ball herumkicken *(col)*; **you shouldn't let them ~ you ~** Sie sollten sich nicht so herumschubsen lassen.
►**kick in** *vt sep door* eintreten. **to ~ sb's teeth ~** jdm die Zähne einschlagen.
►**kick off** *vi (Ftbl)* anstoßen; *(fig col)* anfangen.
►**kick out 1** *vi* **to ~ ~ at sb** nach jdm treten. **2** *vt sep (col)* rauswerfen *(col) (of* aus*)*. **to be ~ed ~** rausfliegen *(col)*.
►**kick up** *vt sep* **to ~ ~ a fuss** *(col)* Krach schlagen *(col)*.
**kick:** **~-off** *n (Sport)* Anpfiff, Anstoß *m; (col: beginning)* Beginn *m;* **~-starter** *n* Kickstarter *m.*
**kid** [kɪd] **1** *n* **(a)** *(young goat)* Kitz *nt; (leather)* Glacéleder *nt.* **to handle sb with ~ gloves** *(fig)* jdn mit Samthandschuhen anfassen. **(b)** *(col: child)* Kind *nt.* **it's ~'s stuff** *(for children)* das ist was für kleine Kinder *(col)*; *(easy)* das ist doch ein Kinderspiel; **his ~ brother** sein kleiner Bruder; **OK, ~!** okay, Junge/Mädchen! **2** *vt (col)* **to ~ sb (on)** *(tease)* jdn aufziehen *(col)*; *(deceive)* jdn an der Nase rumführen *(col)*; **don't ~ yourself!** machen Sie sich doch nichts vor! **3** *vi (col)* Jux machen *(col)*. **you're ~ding!** das ist doch nicht dein Ernst!; **no ~ding** ehrlich *(col)*.
**kiddy** ['kɪdɪ] *n (col)* Kind *nt,* Kleine(r) *mf.*
**kidnap** ['kɪdnæp] *vt* entführen, kidnappen.
**kidnapper** ['kɪdnæpər] *n* Entführer(in *f)*, Kidnapper(in *f) m.*
**kidnapping** ['kɪdnæpɪŋ] *n* Entführung *f.*
**kidney** ['kɪdnɪ] *n (Anat, Cook)* Niere *f.*
**kidney:** **~ bean** *n* Gartenbohne *f;* **~ machine** *n* künstliche Niere.
**kidology** [kɪ'dɒlədʒɪ] *n (col)* Bluff *m (col)*.
**kill** [kɪl] **1** *vt* **(a)** töten, umbringen; *(slaughter)* schlachten; *weeds* vernichten, vertilgen. **to be ~ed in battle** im Kampf fallen; **her brother was ~ed in a car accident** ihr Bruder ist bei einem Autounfall ums Leben gekommen; **how many were ~ed?** wieviele Todesopfer gab es?; **she ~ed herself** sie brachte sich um; **don't ~ me** lassen Sie mich leben; **he was ~ed with poison/a knife** er wurde vergiftet/(mit einem Messer) erstochen; **I'll ~ him!** *(also fig)* den bring' ich um *(col)*.
**(b)** *(fig) feelings, love etc* zerstören; *(spoil) flavour, performance* verderben, überdecken; *hopes* zunichte machen; *sound* schlucken; *(Press etc) paragraph, story* streichen; *(Tech) engine etc* abschalten. **to ~ time** die Zeit totschlagen; **we have two hours to ~** wir haben noch zwei Stunden übrig; **to ~ two birds with one stone** *(Prov)* zwei Fliegen mit einer Klappe schlagen *(Prov)*; **these stairs are ~ing me** *(col)* diese Treppe bringt mich (noch mal) um *(col)*; **she was ~ing herself (laughing)** *(col)* sie hat sich (fast) totgelacht *(col)*; **my feet are ~ing me** *(col)* mir brennen die Füße.
**2** *vi* töten. **smoking can ~** Rauchen kann tödliche Folgen haben.
**3** *n* **to be in at the ~** *(fig)* den Schlußakt miterleben.
►**kill off** *vt sep* vernichten; *cows, pigs* abschlachten; *weeds also* vertilgen.
**killer** ['kɪlər] *n (person)* Mörder(in *f) m.* **this disease**

**is a ~** diese Krankheit ist tödlich.
**killer:** **the ~ instinct** *n (lit)* der Tötungsinstinkt; **a successful businessman needs the ~ instinct** *(fig)* ein erfolgreicher Geschäftsmann muß über Leichen gehen können; **~ whale** *n* Schwertwal *m.*
**killing** ['kɪlɪŋ] **1** *n (of person)* Töten *nt.* **three more ~s in Belfast** drei weitere Todesopfer in Belfast; **to make a ~** *(fig)* einen Riesengewinn machen. **2** *adj blow etc* tödlich; *pace* mörderisch.
**killingly** ['kɪlɪŋlɪ] *adv:* **~ funny** zum Totlachen.
**killjoy** ['kɪldʒɔɪ] *n* Spielverderber *m.*
**kiln** [kɪln] *n* (Brenn)ofen *m; (for bricks)* Trockenofen *m.*
**kilo** ['kiːləʊ] *n* Kilo *nt.*
**kilobyte** ['kɪləʊbaɪt] *n* Kilobyte *nt.*
**kilogram, kilogramme** ['kɪləʊgræm] *n* Kilogramm *nt.*
**kilometre,** *(US)* **kilometer** ['kɪləʊˌmiːtər, kɪ'lɒmɪtər] *n* Kilometer *m.*
**kilowatt** ['kɪləʊwɒt] *n* Kilowatt *nt.*
**kilt** [kɪlt] *n* Kilt, Schottenrock *m.*
**kilter** ['kɪltər] *n:* **out of ~** nicht in Ordnung.
**kimono** [kɪ'məʊnəʊ] *n* Kimono *m.*
**kin** [kɪn] *n* Verwandte *pl,* Verwandtschaft *f.*
**kind¹** [kaɪnd] **1** *n* **(a)** Art *f; (of coffee etc)* Sorte *f.* **several ~s of flour** mehrere Mehlsorten; **this ~ of book** diese Art Buch; **what ~ of ...?** was für ein(e) ...?; **the only one of its ~** das einzige seiner Art; **he is not the ~ of man to refuse** er ist nicht der Typ, der nein sagt; **he's not that ~ of person** so ist er nicht; **a strange ~ of feeling** so ein seltsames Gefühl; **they're two of a ~** *(people)* sie sind vom gleichen Schlag; **I know your ~** deinen Typ kenne ich; **this ~ of thing** so etwas; **... of all ~s** alle möglichen ...; **something of the ~** so etwas Ähnliches; **nothing of the ~** nichts dergleichen; **you'll do nothing of the ~** du wirst das schön bleiben lassen!; **it's not my ~ of holiday** solche Ferien sind nicht mein Fall *(col)*; **she's my ~ of woman** sie ist mein Typ.
**(b) payment in ~** Bezahlung in Naturalien; **I shall pay you in ~** *(fig)* ich werde es Ihnen in gleicher Münze zurückzahlen.
**2** *adv (col)* **I was ~ of disappointed** *(a little)* ich war irgendwie enttäuscht; *(very)* ich war ziemlich enttäuscht.
**kind²** *adj (+er)* nett, freundlich *(to zu)*. **would you be ~ enough to open the door** wären Sie so nett *or* lieb, die Tür zu öffnen.
**kindergarten** ['kɪndəˌgɑːtn] *n* Kindergarten *m.*
**kind-hearted** [ˌkaɪnd'hɑːtɪd] *adj* gütig.
**kind-heartedness** [ˌkaɪnd'hɑːtɪdnɪs] *n* Güte *f.*
**kindle** ['kɪndl] *vt fire* anzünden; *passions* entfachen.
**kindliness** ['kaɪndlɪnɪs] *n* Liebenswürdigkeit *f.*
**kindly** ['kaɪndlɪ] **1** *adv speak, act* freundlich, nett; *treat* liebenswürdig. **they ~ put me up for a night** sie nahmen mich freundlicherweise für eine Nacht auf; **will you ~ do it now** tun Sie das sofort, wenn ich bitten darf!; **~ shut the door** machen Sie doch bitte die Tür zu!; **I don't take ~ to his smoking** sein Rauchen ist mir gar nicht angenehm; **he won't take at all ~ to that** das wird ihm gar nicht gefallen. **2** *adj (+er) person* lieb, nett; *advice* freundlich; *voice* sanft, gütig.
**kindness** ['kaɪndnɪs] *n* Freundlichkeit, Liebenswürdigkeit *f (towards* gegenüber*)*; *(goodness)* Güte *f (towards* gegenüber*)*; *(act of ~)* Gefälligkeit, Aufmerksamkeit *f.* **out of the ~ of one's heart** aus reiner Nächstenliebe; **to do sb a ~** jdm eine Gefälligkeit erweisen.
**kindred** ['kɪndrɪd] **1** *n no pl (relatives)* Verwandtschaft *f.* **2** *adj (related)* verwandt. **~ spirit** Gleichge-

sinnte(r) *mf.*

**kinetic** [kɪ'netɪk] *adj* kinetisch.

**king** [kɪŋ] *n* König *m (also Chess, Cards)*; *(Draughts)* Dame *f.* **fit for a ~** königlich.

**kingdom** ['kɪŋdəm] *n* Königreich *nt.* **you can go on doing that till ~ come** *(col)* Sie können (so) bis in alle Ewigkeit weitermachen.

**kingfisher** ['kɪŋfɪʃər] *n* Eisvogel *m.*

**king:** **~pin** *n (Aut)* Achsschenkelbolzen *m*; *(fig: person)* Stütze *f*; **~-size(d)** *adj (col)* im Großformat; *cigarettes* King-size; *bed* extra groß.

**kink** [kɪŋk] *n* **(a)** *(in rope etc)* Schlaufe *f*; *(in hair)* Welle *t.* **(b)** *(mental peculiarity)* Tick *m (col)*; *(sexual)* abartige Veranlagung.

**kinky** ['kɪŋkɪ] *adj (+er)* **(a)** *hair* wellig. **(b)** *(col) person, ideas* verdreht *(col)*; *fashion* verrückt *(col)*; *(sexually)* abartig.

**kinship** ['kɪnʃɪp] *n* Verwandtschaft *f.*

**kinsman** ['kɪnzmən] *n, pl* **-men** [-mən] Verwandte(r) *m.*

**kinswoman** ['kɪnzwumən] *n, pl* **-women** [-wɪmɪn] Verwandte *f.*

**kiosk** ['kiːɒsk] *n* Kiosk *m*; *(Brit Telec)* (Telefon)-zelle *f.*

**kip** [kɪp] *(Brit col)* **1** *n (sleep)* Schläfchen *nt.* **I've got to get some ~** ich muß mal 'ne Runde pennen *(col).* **2** *vi* pennen *(col).*

**kipper** ['kɪpər] *n* Räucherhering *m.*

**kiss** [kɪs] **1** *n* Kuß *m.* **~ of life** Mund-zu-Mund-Beatmung *f*; **~ of death** *(fig)* Todesstoß *m.* **2** *vt* küssen; *(fig: touch gently)* sanft berühren. **to ~ sb's cheek** jdn auf die Wange küssen; **they ~ed each other** sie küßten sich; **to ~ sb goodbye** jdm einen Abschiedskuß geben. **3** *vi* küssen; *(~ each other)* sich küssen.

**kissagram** ['kɪsə,græm] *n durch eine(n) Angestellte(n) einer Agentur persönlich übermittelter Kuß (zum Geburtstag etc).*

**kit** [kɪt] *n* **(a)** *(equipment)* Ausrüstung *f*; *(Brit Sport)* Sportzeug *nt*, Sportsachen *pl*; *(belongings, luggage etc)* Sachen *pl.* **(b)** *(for self-assembly)* Bausatz *m.* **model aircraft ~** Modellflugzeugbaukasten; **in ~ form** zum Selberbauen.
▶**kit out** *vt sep* ausrüsten *(esp Mil)*, ausstatten.

**kitbag** ['kɪtbæg] *n* Seesack *m.*

**kitchen** ['kɪtʃɪn] **1** *n* Küche *f.* **2** *attr* Küchen-.

**kitchenette** [,kɪtʃɪ'net] *n (separate room)* kleine Küche; *(part of one room)* Kochnische *f.*

**kitchen:** **~ foil** *n* Alufolie *f*; **~ garden** *n* Gemüsegarten *m*; **~ sink** *n* Spülbecken *nt*; **I've packed everything but the ~ sink** *(col)* ich habe den ganzen Hausrat eingepackt; **~ sink drama** *n* Alltagsdrama *nt*; **~ unit** *n* Küchenschrank *m*; **~ utensil** *n* Küchengerät *nt*; **~ware** *n* Küchengeräte *pl.*

**kite** [kaɪt] *n (Orn)* Milan *m*; *(toy)* Drachen *m.*

**kith** [kɪθ] *n*: **~ and kin** Blutsverwandte *pl.*

**kitten** ['kɪtn] *n* Kätzchen *nt.* **to have ~s** *(fig col)* Junge kriegen *(col).*

**kitty** ['kɪtɪ] *n* **(a)** *(money)* (gemeinsame) Kasse; *(Cards etc also)* Spielkasse *f.* **(b)** *(col: cat)* Mieze *f.*

**kiwi** ['kiːwiː] *n* **(a)** *(bird)* Kiwi *m.* **the K~s** *(col, esp Sport)* die Neuseeländer. **(b)** *(also ~ fruit)* Kiwi(frucht) *f.*

**KKK** *(US)* = **Ku Klux Klan.**

**kleptomaniac** [,kleptəʊ'meɪnɪæk] *n* Kleptomane *m*, Kleptomanin *f.*

**km** = **kilometre(s)** km.

**km/h** = **kilometres per hour** km/h.

**knack** [næk] *n* Trick, Kniff *m.* **there's a (special) ~ to opening it** da ist ein Trick dabei, wie man das aufbekommt; **to get the ~ of doing sth** (es) herausbe-

kommen, wie man etw macht; **you'll soon get the ~ of it** Sie werden den Dreh bald raushaben *(col)*; **I've lost the ~** ich bekomme das nicht mehr hin; **she's got a ~ of saying the wrong thing** sie hat ein Talent dafür, immer das Falsche zu sagen.

**knacker** ['nækər] *n* Abdecker *m.*

**knackered** ['nækəd] *adj (Brit col)* kaputt *(col).*

**knapsack** ['næpsæk] *n* Rucksack *m.*

**knead** [niːd] *vt dough* kneten.

**knee** [niː] **1** *n* Knie *nt.* **to be on one's ~s** *(lit, fig)* auf den Knien liegen; **on bended ~(s)** *(liter, hum)* kniefällig; **to go down on one's ~s (to sb)** *(lit, fig)* sich (vor jdm) auf die Knie werfen; **to bring sb to his ~s** *(lit, fig)* jdn in die Knie zwingen. **2** *vt* mit dem Knie stoßen.

**knee:** **~ breeches** *npl* Kniebundhose *f*; **~ cap** *n* Kniescheibe *f*; **~-deep** *adj* knietief; **~-high** *adj* in Kniehöhe; **~-jerk reaction** *n* instinktive Reaktion; **~ joint** *n* Kniegelenk *nt.*

**kneel** [niːl] *pret, ptp* **knelt** *or* **~ed** *vi (before* vor *+dat)* knien; *(also ~ down)* (sich) hinknien.

**knee-length** ['niːleŋθ] *adj skirt* knielang; *boots* kniehoch.

**knee pad** *n* Knieschützer *m.*

**knelt** [nelt] *pret, ptp of* **kneel.**

**knew** [njuː] *pret of* **know.**

**knickers** ['nɪkəz] *npl* Schlüpfer *m.* **don't get your ~ in a twist!** *(col!)* dreh nicht gleich durch! *(col).*

**knick-knack** ['nɪknæk] *n* nette Kleinigkeit. **~s** Krimskrams *m.*

**knife** [naɪf] **1** *n, pl* **knives** Messer *nt.* **~, fork and spoon** Besteck *nt*; **he's got his ~ into me** *(col)* er hat es auf mich abgesehen *(col)*; **to be balanced on a ~ edge** *(fig)* auf Messers Schneide stehen. **2** *vt* einstechen auf *(+acc)*; *(fatally)* erstechen.

**knight** [naɪt] **1** *n (title, Hist)* Ritter *m*; *(Chess)* Springer *m.* **2** *vt* adeln.

**knighthood** ['naɪthʊd] *n* **to receive a ~** in den Adelsstand erhoben werden.

**knit** [nɪt] *pret, ptp* **~ted** *or* **~ 1** *vt* **(a)** stricken. **(b) to ~ one's brow** die Stirn runzeln. **2** *vi* **(a)** stricken. **(b)** *(bones: also ~ together)* verwachsen.

**knitted** ['nɪtɪd] *adj* gestrickt; *cardigan etc* Strick-.

**knitting** ['nɪtɪŋ] *n* Stricken *nt*; *(material being knitted)* Strickzeug *nt.* **she was doing her ~** sie strickte.

**knitting:** **~ machine** *n* Strickmaschine *f*; **~ needle** *n* Stricknadel *f*; **~ pattern** *n* Strickmuster *nt.*

**knitwear** ['nɪtwɛər] *n* Strickwaren *pl.*

**knives** [naɪvz] *pl of* **knife.**

**knob** [nɒb] *n (on walking stick)* Knauf *m*; *(on door also)* Griff *m*; *(on instrument etc)* Knopf *m*; *(of butter)* Stück *nt.*

**knobbly** ['nɒblɪ] *adj (+er) wood* knorrig. **~ knees** Knubbelknie *pl (col).*

**knock** [nɒk] **1** *n (blow)* Stoß *m*; *(esp with hand, tool etc)* Schlag *m.* **I got a ~ on the head** ich habe einen Schlag auf den Kopf bekommen; **he gave himself a nasty ~** er hat sich böse angeschlagen. **(b)** *(noise)* Klopfen *nt no pl.* **there was a ~ at the door** es hat geklopft. **(c)** *(fig: setback)* (Tief)schlag *m.* **~s** *(col: criticism)* Kritik *f*; **to (have to) take a lot of ~s** viele Tiefschläge einstecken (müssen); *(be criticized)* unter starken Beschuß kommen; **to take a ~** *(pride etc)* erschüttert werden.

**2** *vt* **(a)** *(strike)* stoßen; *(with hand, tool etc)* schlagen; *(jolt)* stoßen gegen; *(collide with: car, driver)* rammen. **to ~ one's head** *etc* sich *(dat)* den Kopf *etc* anschlagen; **to ~ sb on the head** jdn an *or* auf den Kopf schlagen; **to ~ sb to the ground** jdn zu Boden werfen; **to ~ sb unconscious** jdn bewußtlos werden lassen; *(person)* jdn bewußtlos schlagen; **to ~ holes in an argument** ein Argument zerpflücken; **she ~ed the gun out of his hand** sie schlug ihm die Waffe aus der Hand; **she ~ed the glass to the ground** sie stieß gegen das Glas, und es fiel zu Boden; **to ~ some sense into sb** jdn zur Vernunft bringen. **(b)** *(col: criticize)* (he)runtermachen *(col)*.

**3** *vi* **(a)** klopfen. **to ~ at the door/window** anklopfen/gegen das Fenster klopfen. **(b)** *(collide)* stoßen *(into, against* gegen*)*. **(c)** **his knees were ~ing** ihm zitterten die Knie.

►**knock about** *or* **around 1** *vi (col) (prep obj* in +*dat) (person)* herumhängen *(col)*; *(object)* herumliegen. **2** *vt sep (ill-treat)* verprügeln; *(damage)* ramponieren *(col)*. **to ~ a ball ~** *(Tennis etc)* ein paar Bälle schlagen.

►**knock back** *vt sep (col)* **(a)** **he ~ed ~ his whisky** er kippte sich *(dat)* den Whisky hinter die Binde *(col)*. **(b)** *(cost)* **this watch ~ed me ~ £20** ich habe für die Uhr £20 hingelegt *(col)*.

►**knock down** *vt sep person, thing* umwerfen; *opponent* niederschlagen; *(car, driver)* anfahren; *(fatally)* überfahren; *building* abreißen; *door* einschlagen.

►**knock in** *vt sep nail* einschlagen.

►**knock off 1** *vi (col)* aufhören, Schluß machen *(col)*. **let's ~ ~ now** Schluß für heute *(col)*. **2** *vt sep* **(a)** *(lit) vase, person etc* hinunterstoßen. **the branch ~ed the rider ~ his horse** der Ast riß den Reiter vom Pferd. **(b)** **he ~ed £5 ~ the price** *(col)* er hat £5 vom Preis nachgelassen. **(c)** *(col: do quickly) essay* hinhauen *(col)*. **(d)** *(Brit col: steal)* klauen *(col)*. **(e)** *(col: stop)* aufhören mit. **to ~ ~ (work)** Feierabend machen; **~ it ~!** nun hör schon auf!

►**knock out** *vt sep* **(a)** *tooth* ausschlagen; *nail* herausschlagen *(of* aus*)*; *pipe* ausklopfen; *contents* herausklopfen *(of* aus*)*. **(b)** *(stun) (by hitting)* bewußtlos schlagen, k.o. schlagen *(also Boxing)*; *(col: exhaust)* fertigmachen *(col)*. **(c)** *(from contest)* besiegen *(of* in +*dat)*. **to be ~ed ~** ausscheiden *(of* aus*)*. **(d)** *(col: exhaust)* schaffen *(col)*.

►**knock over** *vt sep* umwerfen, umstoßen; *(car)* anfahren; *(fatally)* überfahren.

►**knock together** *vt sep* **(a)** *(make hurriedly)* auf die Beine stellen *(col)*. **(b)** *(lit)* aneinanderstoßen. **I'd like to ~ their heads ~** man sollte die beiden zur Räson bringen.

►**knock up** *vt sep* **(a)** *(Brit: wake)* (auf)wecken. **(b)** *meal* auf die Beine stellen *(col)*. **(c)** *(col: make pregnant)* ein Kind anhängen (+*dat) (col)*.

**knockdown** ['nɒkdaʊn] *adj* **~ price** Schleuderpreis *m*; *(at auction)* Mindestpreis *m*.

**knocker** ['nɒkəʳ] *n (door ~)* (Tür)klopfer *m*.

**knock-for-knock** ['nɒkfə'nɒk] *adj (Brit Insur)* **~ agreement** Vereinbarung, bei der jede Versicherungsgesellschaft den Schaden am von ihr versicherten Fahrzeug übernimmt.

**knocking** ['nɒkɪŋ] *n* Klopfen *nt*.

**knocking-off time** [nɒkɪŋ'ɒf,taɪm] *n (col)* Feierabend *m*.

**knock:** **~-kneed** [nɒk'niːd] *adj* **to be ~-kneed** X-Beine haben; **~-on effect** *n* Folgewirkungen *pl (on* auf +*acc)*; **~out 1** *n (Boxing)* Knockout, K.o. *m*; *(col: person, thing)* Wucht *f (col)*; **2** *attr* **~out competition** Ausscheidungskampf *m*; **~-up** *n (Brit Sport)* **to have a ~-up** ein paar Bälle schlagen.

**knot** [nɒt] **1** *n (lit, fig, Naut)* Knoten *m*; *(in muscle)* Verspannung *f*; *(in wood)* Ast *m*, Verwachsung *f*. **to tie/untie a ~** einen Knoten machen/aufmachen; **to tie oneself (up) in ~s** *(fig)* sich immer mehr verwickeln. **2** *vt* einen Knoten machen in (+*acc)*; *(~*

*together)* verknoten. **get ~ted!** *(col)* du kannst mich mal! *(col)*.

**knotty** ['nɒtɪ] *adj (+er) problem* verwickelt, verzwickt *(col)*.

**know** [nəʊ] *(vb: pret* **knew**, *ptp* **known)** **1** *vti* **(a)** *(have knowledge about)* wissen; *answer, facts etc also* kennen; *French etc* können. **to ~ how to do sth** *(in theory)* wissen, wie man etw macht; *(in practice)* etw tun können; **she ~s all the answers** sie kennt sich aus; *(pej)* sie weiß immer alles besser; **to let sb ~ sth** *(not keep back)* jdn etw wissen lassen; *(tell, inform)* jdm Bescheid geben; **as far as I ~** soviel ich weiß; **not that I ~** nicht daß ich wüßte; **who ~s?** wer weiß?; **there's no ~ing what he'll do** man weiß nie, was er noch tut; **I'd have you ~ that ...** ich möchte doch sehr betonen, daß ...; **to ~ what one is talking about** wissen, wovon man redet; **before you ~ where you are** ehe man sich's versieht; **he just didn't want to ~** er wollte einfach nicht hören; **I ~!** ich weiß!; *(having a good idea)* ich weiß was!; **I wouldn't ~** *(col)* weiß ich (doch) nicht *(col)*; **I knew it** ich wußte es doch!; **how should I ~** wie soll ich das wissen?; **well, what do you ~!** *(col)* sieh mal einer an!; **you never ~** man kann nie wissen; **you ~, we could ...** weißt du/wissen Sie, wir könnten ...; **he didn't come, you ~** er ist nämlich nicht gekommen; **I ~ better than that** ich bin ja nicht ganz dumm; **I ~ better than to say something like that** ich werde mich hüten, so etwas zu sagen; **he should have ~n better than to do that** es war dumm von ihm, das zu tun; **they don't ~ any better** sie kennen es nicht anders; **OK, you ~ best** okay, Sie müssen es wissen.

**(b)** *(be acquainted with) people, places, book* kennen. **do you ~ him to speak to?** kennen Sie ihn näher?; **if I ~ John, he'll already be there** wie ich John kenne, ist er schon da; **to get to ~ sb/a place** jdn/einen Ort kennenlernen; **to get to ~ sth** *methods etc* etw lernen; *habits, shortcuts etc* etw herausfinden.

**(c)** *(recognize)* erkennen. **to ~ sb by his voice** *etc* jdn an der Stimme *etc* erkennen; **he ~s a bargain when he sees one** er weiß, was ein guter Kauf ist; **you wouldn't ~ him from his brother** Sie könnten ihn nicht von seinem Bruder unterscheiden; **to ~ the difference between right and wrong** Gut und Böse unterscheiden können; **he wouldn't ~ the difference** das merkt er nicht.

**(d)** *(experience)* erleben. **I've never ~n it to rain so heavily** so einen starken Regen habe ich noch nie erlebt; **I've never ~n him to smile** ich habe es noch nie erlebt, daß er lächelt; **have you ever ~n such a thing to happen before?** haben Sie je schon so etwas erlebt?

**(e)** *(in passive)* **to be ~n (to sb)** (jdm) bekannt sein; **it is (well) ~n that ...** es ist (allgemein) bekannt, daß ...; **he is ~n to have been here** man weiß, daß er hier war; **he is ~n as Mr X** man kennt ihn als Herrn X; **to make sb/sth ~n** jdn/etw bekanntmachen; **to make oneself ~n** sich melden *(to sb* bei jdm*)*; **to become ~n** bekannt werden; *(famous)* berühmt werden.

**2** *n (col)* **to be in the ~** Bescheid wissen *(col)*.

►**know about** *vi* +*prep obj maths, politics* sich auskennen in (+*dat)*; *Africa* Bescheid wissen über (+*acc)*; *women, cars* sich auskennen mit; *(be aware of)* wissen von. **I didn't ~ ~ that** das wußte ich nicht; **I only knew ~ it yesterday** ich habe erst gestern davon gehört; **did you ~ ~ Maggie?** weißt du über Maggie Bescheid?; **I don't ~ ~ that** *(don't agree)* da bin ich aber nicht so sicher.

▶**know of** *vi +prep obj café, method* kennen; *(have heard of) sb* gehört haben von. **not that I** ~ ~ nicht, daß ich wüßte.

**know:** ~**-all** *n* Alleswisser *m*; ~**-how** *n* Sachkenntnis *f*, Know-how *nt*.

**knowing** [ˈnəʊɪŋ] *adj look* wissend.

**knowingly** [ˈnəʊɪŋlɪ] *adv* **(a)** *(consciously)* bewußt, absichtlich. **(b)** *look* wissend.

**know-it-all** [ˈnəʊɪtɔːl] *n (US)* = **know-all**.

**knowledge** [ˈnɒlɪdʒ] *n* **(a)** Wissen *nt*, Kenntnis *f*. **to have no** ~ **of** keine Kenntnis haben von; **to (the best of) my** ~ meines Wissens; **not to my** ~ nicht, daß ich wüßte; **without his** ~ ohne sein Wissen; **it has come to my** ~ **that ...** es ist mir zu Ohren gekommen, daß ... **(b)** *(learning)* Kenntnisse *pl*, Wissen *nt*. **my** ~ **of English** meine Englischkenntnisse *pl*.

**knowledg(e)able** [ˈnɒlɪdʒəbl] *adj person* bewandert *(about* in *+dat)*; *report* fundiert.

**known** [nəʊn] **1** *ptp of* **know. 2** *adj* bekannt; *expert also* anerkannt.

**knuckle** [ˈnʌkl] *n* (Finger)knöchel *m*; *(of meat)* Hachse, Haxe *f*.

▶**knuckle down** *vi (col)* sich dahinterklemmen *(col)*.

▶**knuckle under** *vi (col)* spuren *(col)*.

**knuckle:** ~**duster** *n* Schlagring *m*; ~ **head** *n (US col)* Blödmann *m (col)*.

**KO** *n* K.o.(-Schlag) *m*.

**koala** [kəʊˈɑːlə] *n (also* ~ **bear)** Koala(bär) *m*.

**kooky** [ˈkuːkɪ] *adj (+er) (US col)* verrückt *(col)*.

**Koran** [kɒˈrɑːn] *n* Koran *m*.

**Korea** [kəˈrɪə] *n* Korea *nt*.

**Korean** [kəˈrɪən] **1** *adj* koreanisch. **2** *n* **(a)** Koreaner(in *f*) *m*. **(b)** *(language)* Koreanisch *nt*.

**kosher** [ˈkəʊʃər] *adj* koscher.

**kph** = **kilometres per hour** km/h.

**Kraut** [kraʊt] *n (esp pej)* Deutsche(r) *mf*.

**Kremlin** [ˈkremlɪn] *n*: **the** ~ der Kreml.

**KS** *(US Post)* = **Kansas.**

**Kt** *(Brit)* = **Knight.**

**kudos** [ˈkjuːdɒs] *n* Ansehen *nt*, Ehre *f*.

**Kurd** [kɜːd] *n* Kurde *m*, Kurdin *f*.

**Kurdish** [ˈkɜːdɪʃ] *adj* kurdisch.

**Kuwait** [kʊˈweɪt] *n* Kuwait *nt*.

**Kuwaiti** [kʊˈweɪtɪ] **1** *adj* kuwaitisch. **2** *n* Kuwaiter(in *f*) *m*.

**kW** = **kilowatt(s)** kW.

**KY** *(US Post)* = **Kentucky.**

# L

**L, I** [el] *n* L, l *nt.* **L for Lucy** *(Brit),* **L for love** *(US)* ≃ L wie Ludwig.
**L** = (a) *(Brit Mot)* **Learner.** (b) **Lake.**
**l** = (a) **litre(s)** l. (b) **left** l.
**LA** = (a) **Los Angeles.** (b) *(US Post)* **Louisiana.**
**lab** [læb] = **laboratory.**
**label** ['leɪbl] **1** *n (lit, fig)* Etikett *nt; (showing contents etc)* Aufschrift *f; (on cage)* Schild *nt; (tied)* Anhänger *m; (adhesive)* Aufkleber *m; (on parcel)* Paketadresse *f.* **on the EMI ~** bei EMI erschienen. **2** *vt* (a) etikettieren, mit einem Anhänger/Aufkleber versehen; *(write on)* beschriften. **the bottle was ~led "poison"** die Flasche trug die Aufschrift „Gift". (b) *(fig) ideas* bezeichnen; *(pej)* abstempeln.
**laboratory** [lə'bɒrətərɪ, *(US)* 'læbrə,tɔːrɪ] *n* Labor *nt.* **~ assistant** Laborant (in *f*) *m.*
**Labor Day** *n (US)* der Tag der Arbeit.
**laborious** [lə'bɔːrɪəs] *adj task* mühsam; *style* schwerfällig.
**laboriously** [lə'bɔːrɪəslɪ] *adv* mühsam; *(speak)* umständlich.
**labour,** *(US)* **labor** ['leɪbər] **1** *n* (a) *(work in general)* Arbeit *f; (toil)* Mühe *f; (task)* Aufgabe *f; (cost)* Arbeitskosten *pl.* **it was a ~ of love** ich/er *etc* tat es aus Liebe zur Sache. (b) *(persons)* Arbeitskräfte *pl.* **to withdraw one's ~** die Arbeit verweigern; **organized ~** die organisierte Arbeiterschaft. (c) *(Brit Pol)* **L~** die Labour Party; **this district is L~** dies ist ein Labourbezirk. (d) *(Med)* Wehen *pl.* **to be in ~** in den Wehen liegen, Wehen haben; **to go into ~** Wehen bekommen. **2** *vt subject* auswalzen, breittreten *(col).* **I won't ~ the point** ich will nicht darauf herumreiten; **his breathing became ~ed** er begann, schwer zu atmen. **3** *vi (in fields etc)* arbeiten; *(work hard)* sich abmühen *(at,* with mit*).* **to ~ under a delusion** sich einer Täuschung *(dat)* hingeben; **to ~ up a hill** sich einen Hügel hinaufquälen.
**labour camp** *n* Arbeitslager *nt.*
**labourer,** *(US)* **laborer** ['leɪbərər] *n* (Hilfs)arbeiter *m; (farm ~)* Landarbeiter *m.*
**labour: L~ Exchange** *n (Brit dated)* Arbeitsamt *nt;* **~ force** *n* Arbeiterschaft *f;* **~-intensive** *adj* arbeitsintensiv; **~-market** *n* Arbeitsmarkt *m;* **~ movement** *n* Arbeiterbewegung *f;* **~ pains** *npl* Wehen *pl;* **~ relations** *npl* die Beziehungen *pl* zwischen Unternehmern und Arbeitern; **~-saving** *adj* arbeitssparend; **~ union** *n (US)* Gewerkschaft *f;* **~ unrest** *n* Arbeitsunruhen *pl.*
**laburnum** [lə'bɜːnəm] *n* Goldregen *m.*
**labyrinth** ['læbɪrɪnθ] *n (lit, fig)* Labyrinth *nt.*
**lace** [leɪs] **1** *n* (a) *(fabric)* Spitze *f; (as trimming)* Spitzenbesatz *m.* (b) *(of shoe)* Schnürsenkel *m.* **2** *vt* (a) schnüren. (b) **to ~ a drink** einen Schuß Alkohol in ein Getränk geben; **~d with brandy** mit einem Schuß Weinbrand.
▶**lace up 1** *vt sep* (zu)schnüren. **2** *vi* geschnürt werden.
**lacemaking** ['leɪsmeɪkɪŋ] *n* Klöppelei *f.*

**lacerate** ['læsəreɪt] *vt* verletzen; *(by glass etc)* zerschneiden; *painting* aufschlitzen. **her knee was badly ~d** sie hatte tiefe Wunden am Knie.
**laceration** [,læsə'reɪʃən] *n* Fleischwunde *f.*
**lace-up (shoe)** ['leɪsʌp(ʃuː)] *n* Schnürschuh *m.*
**lack** [læk] **1** *n* Mangel *m.* **through ~ of sth** aus Mangel an etw *(dat);* **they failed through ~ of support** sie scheiterten, weil es ihnen an Unterstützung fehlte; **~ of water** Wassermangel *m;* **there is no ~ of money in that family** in dieser Familie fehlt es nicht an Geld. **2** *vt* **they ~ the necessary talent** es fehlt ihnen an nötigem Talent; **we ~ time** uns fehlt die nötige Zeit. **3** *vi* **to be ~ing** fehlen; **to be found ~ing** zu wünschen übrig lassen; **he is ~ing in confidence** ihm fehlt es an Selbstvertrauen; **he ~ed for nothing** es fehlte ihm an nichts.
**lackadaisical** [,lækə'deɪzɪkəl] *adj* lustlos, desinteressiert; *(idle)* saumselig.
**lackey** ['lækɪ] *n (lit, fig)* Lakai *m.*
**lacklustre,** *(US)* **lackluster** ['læk,lʌstər] *adj surface* glanzlos; *style* farblos.
**laconic** [lə'kɒnɪk] *adj* lakonisch; *prose, style* knapp.
**lacquer** ['lækər] **1** *n* Lack *m; (Brit: hair ~)* Haarspray *nt.* **2** *vt* lackieren; *(Brit) hair* sprayen.
**lacrosse** [lə'krɒs] *n* Lacrosse *nt.*
**lad** [læd] *n* Junge *m; (in stable etc)* Bursche *m.* **young ~** junger Mann; **listen, ~** hör mir mal zu, mein Junge!; **all together, ~s, push!** alle Mann anschieben!; **he's a bit of a ~** *(col)* er ist ein ziemlicher Draufgänger; **he likes a night out with the ~s** *(col)* er geht abends gern mal mit seinen Kumpels weg *(col).*
**ladder** ['lædər] **1** *n* (a) *(lit, fig)* Leiter *f.* **the climb up the social ~** der gesellschaftliche Aufstieg; **it's a first step up the ~** das ist ein Anfang. (b) *(Brit: in tights etc)* Laufmasche *f.* **~proof** maschenfest. **2** *vt (Brit) tights etc* zerreißen. **3** *vi (Brit: tights etc)* Laufmaschen bekommen.
**laden** ['leɪdn] *adj (lit, fig)* beladen *(with* mit*).*
**la-di-da** ['lɑːdɪ'dɑː] *adj (col)* affektiert.
**ladle** ['leɪdl] **1** *n* (Schöpf)kelle *f,* Schöpflöffel *m.* **2** *vt* schöpfen.
**lady** ['leɪdɪ] *n* (a) Dame *f.* **"Ladies"** *(lavatory)* „Damen"; **where is the ladies or the ladies' room?** wo ist die Damentoilette?; **ladies and gentlemen!** sehr geehrte Damen und Herren!; **the old ~** *(col) (mother, wife)* meine/seine *etc* Alte *(col);* **his young ~** seine Freundin; **ladies' man** Charmeur *m;* **ladies' bicycle** Damen(fahr)rad *nt.* (b) *(noble)* Adlige *f.* **L~** *(title)* Lady *f;* **Our L~** die Jungfrau Maria.
**lady: ~bird,** *(US)* **~bug** *n* Marienkäfer *m;* **~ doctor** *n* Ärztin *f;* **~ friend** *n* Dame *f;* **~-in-waiting** *n* Ehrendame *f;* **~-killer** *n (col)* Herzensbrecher *m;* **~like** *adj* damenhaft; **~ship** *n:* **Your L~ship** Ihre Ladyschaft.
**lag¹** [læg] **1** *n (time-~)* Zeitdifferenz *f; (delay)* Verzögerung *f.* **2** *vi (time)* langsam vergehen, dahinkriechen; *(also ~ behind)* zurückbleiben; *(pej)* hinter-

herhinken. **we ~ behind in space exploration** in der Raumforschung liegen wir (weit) zurück.

**lag²** *vt pipe* isolieren.

**lager** ['lɑːgər] *n* helles Bier. **~ lout** *(Brit col)* betrunkener Rowdy *or (causing damage)* Randalierer.

**lagging** ['lægɪŋ] *n* Isolierung *f*; *(material)* Isoliermaterial *nt*.

**lagoon** [lə'guːn] *n* Lagune *f*.

**laid** [leɪd] *pret, ptp of* **lay³**.

**laid-back** ['leɪd'bæk] *adj (col)* gelassen, cool *(col)*.

**lain** [leɪn] *ptp of* **lie²**.

**lair** [lɛər] *n* Lager *nt*; *(cave)* Höhle *f*; *(den)* Bau *m*.

**laird** [lɛəd] *n (Scot)* Gutsherr *m*.

**laissez-faire** [ˌleɪseɪ'fɛər] *n* Laisser-faire *nt*.

**laity** ['leɪtɪ] *n (Eccl)* Laienstand *m*.

**lake** [leɪk] *n* See *m*. **L~ District** Lake District *m (Seengebiet nt im NW Englands)*.

**lamb** [læm] **1** *n* Lamm *nt*; *(meat)* Lamm(fleisch) *nt*. **like a ~ to the slaughter** wie das Lamm zur Schlachtbank. **2** *vi* lammen. **the ~ing season** die Lammungzeit.

**lamb: ~ chop** *n* Lammkotelett *nt*; **~skin** *n* Lammfell *nt*.

**lambswool** ['læmzwʊl] *n* Lammwolle *f*.

**lame** [leɪm] **1** *adj (+er)* **(a)** lahm; *(as result of stroke etc)* gelähmt. **the horse went ~** das Pferd fing an zu lahmen. **(b)** *(fig) excuse* faul; *argument* schwach. **~ duck** Niete *f (col)*; *(company)* unwirtschaftliche Firma. **2** *vt* lähmen; *horse* lahm machen.

**lamely** ['leɪmlɪ] *adv* lahm.

**lameness** ['leɪmnɪs] *n see adj* **(a)** Lähmung *f*; Gelähmtsein *nt*. **(b)** *(fig)* Lahmheit *f*; Schwäche *f*.

**lament** [lə'ment] **1** *n* **(a)** Klage(n *pl*), Wehklage *f*. **(b)** *(Mus)* Klagelied *nt*. **2** *vt* beklagen; *misfortune etc* bejammern. **to ~ sb** um jdn trauern. **3** *vi* (weh)klagen. **to ~ for sb** um jdn trauern; **to ~ over sth** über etw *(acc)* jammern.

**lamentable** ['læməntəbl] *adj* beklagenswert; *work* erbärmlich.

**lamentably** ['læməntəblɪ] *adv* beklagenswert; *fail* kläglich.

**lamentation** [ˌlæmən'teɪʃən] *n* (Weh)klage *f*; *(act)* Klagen, Jammern *nt*.

**laminate** ['læmɪneɪt] **1** *vt* laminieren. **2** *n* Schichtstoff *m*.

**laminated** ['læmɪneɪtɪd] *adj* geschichtet; *windscreen* Verbundglas-; *book cover* laminiert. **~ glass** Verbundglas *nt*; **~ plastic** Resopal ® *nt*; **~ wood** Sperrholz *nt*.

**lamp** [læmp] *n* Lampe *f*; *(in street)* Laterne *f*; *(on ship)* Licht *nt*; *(torch)* Taschenlampe *f*.

**lamp light** *n* Lampenlicht *nt*; *(in street)* Licht *nt* der Laterne(n). **by ~** bei Lampenlicht.

**lampoon** [læm'puːn] **1** *n* Schmähschrift *f*. **2** *vt* verspotten.

**lamp: ~post** *n* Laternenpfahl *m*; **~shade** *n* Lampenschirm *m*; **~standard** *n* = **~post**.

**lance** [lɑːns] **1** *n* Lanze *f*. **~-corporal** Obergefreite(r) *m*. **2** *vt (Med)* aufstechen.

**lancet** ['lɑːnsɪt] *n (Med)* Lanzette *f*.

**Lancs** [læŋks] *(Brit)* = **Lancashire**.

**land** [lænd] **1** *n* **(a)** *(not sea)* Land *nt*. **by ~** auf dem Landweg; **to see how the ~ lies** *(fig)* die Lage sondieren. **(b)** *(nation, region, fig)* Land *nt*. **to be in the ~ of the living** unter den Lebenden sein. **(c)** *(as property)* Grund und Boden *m*. **(d)** *(Agr)* Land *nt*; *(soil)* Boden *m*. **to work on the ~** das Land bebauen; **to live off the ~** *(grow own food)* sich von Selbstangebautem ernähren.

**2** *vt* **(a)** *passengers* absetzen; *plane, troops* landen; *goods* abladen; *boat, fish on hook* an Land zie-

hen; *fish at port* anlanden. **(b)** *(col: obtain)* kriegen *(col)*; *contract* sich *(dat)* verschaffen; *prize* sich *(dat)* holen *(col)*. **(c)** *(col)* he **~ed** him a punch on the jaw er versetzte ihm einen Kinnhaken; **it'll ~ you in jail** das wird dich noch ins Gefängnis bringen; **I've ~ed myself in a real mess** ich bin (ganz schön) in die Klemme geraten *(col)*; **I got ~ed with the job** man hat mir die Arbeit aufgehalst *(col)*; **I got ~ed with him for two hours** ich hatte ihn zwei Stunden lang auf dem Hals.

**3** *vi* landen; *(from ship)* an Land gehen. **we're coming in to ~** wir setzen zur Landung an; **to ~ on one's feet** *(lit)* auf den Füßen landen; *(fig)* auf die Füße fallen; **he ~ed awkwardly** er ist ungeschickt aufgekommen.

►**land up** *vi (col)* landen *(col)*.

**land: ~ agent** *n* Gutsverwalter(in *f*) *m*; **~ breeze** *n* Landwind *m*.

**landed** ['lændɪd] *adj* **the ~ class** die Großgrundbesitzer *pl*; **~ gentry** Landadel *m*.

**land: ~ fall** *n* Sichten *nt* von Land; **~ fill (site)** *n* Mülldeponie *f*.

**landing** ['lændɪŋ] *n* **(a)** *(of person, troops, plane)* Landung *f*. **(b)** *(on stairs) (inside house)* Flur *m*; *(outside flat door)* Treppenabsatz *m*.

**landing: ~-card** *n* Einreisekarte *f*; **~-craft** *n* Landungsboot *nt*; **~ gear** *n (Aviat)* Fahrgestell *nt*; **~ pad** *n* Landeplatz *m* (für Hubschrauber); **~-stage** *n (Brit Naut)* Landesteg *m*; **~-strip** *n* Landepiste *f*.

**land: ~-lady** *n* Vermieterin *f*; *(in pub)* Wirtin *f*; **~locked** *adj* von Land eingeschlossen; **a ~locked country** ein Binnenstaat *m*; **~lord** *n (of land)* Grundbesitzer *m*; *(of flat etc)* Vermieter *m*; *(Brit: of pub)* Wirt *m*; **~lubber** ['lænd,lʌbər] *n* Landratte *f (col)*; **~mark** *n* Wahrzeichen *nt*; *(fig)* Meilenstein *m*; **~mass** *n* Landmasse *f*; **~ mine** *n* Landmine *f*; **~-owner** *n* Grundbesitzer *m*; **~scape** ['lændskeɪp] **1** *n* Landschaft *f*; **2** *vt big area* landschaftlich gestalten; *garden* anlegen; **~scape gardening** *n* Landschafts-/Gartengestaltung *f*; **~scape painting** *n* Landschaftsmalerei *f*; **~slide** *n (lit, fig)* Erdrutsch *m*; **a ~slide victory** ein überwältigender Sieg; **~slip** *n* Erdrutsch *m*.

**lane** [leɪn] *n (in country)* (Feld)weg *m*; *(in town)* Gasse *f*; Weg *m*; *(Sport)* Bahn *f*; *(motorway)* Spur *f*. **"get in ~"** „bitte einordnen".

**language** ['læŋgwɪdʒ] *n* Sprache *f*. **bad ~** unanständige Ausdrücke *pl*; **strong ~** Kraftausdrücke *pl*; *(forceful)* harte Worte *pl*; **mind your ~!** so was sagt man nicht! *(col)*; **to talk the same ~ (as sb)** die gleiche Sprache (wie jd) sprechen.

**language: ~ course** *n* Sprachkurs(us) *m*; **~ lab(oratory)** *n* Sprachlabor *nt*; **~ teacher** *n* Sprachlehrer(in *f*) *m*.

**languid** ['læŋgwɪd] *adj* träge; *gesture* müde; *appearance, manner* gelangweilt.

**languish** ['læŋgwɪʃ] *vi* schmachten; *(pine)* sich sehnen *(for nach)*.

**languor** ['læŋgər] *n* Trägheit *f*; *(weakness)* Mattigkeit *f*.

**languorous** ['læŋgərəs] *adj* träge; *feeling* wohlig; *tone, voice* schläfrig.

**lank** [læŋk] *adj person* hager; *hair* strähnig.

**lanky** ['læŋkɪ] **1** *adj (+er)* schlaksig. **2** *n (col)* Lange(r) *mf (col)*.

**lanolin(e)** ['lænəʊlɪn] *n* Lanolin *nt*.

**lantern** ['læntən] *n* Laterne *f*.

**Laos** [laʊs] *n* Laos *nt*.

**Laotian** ['laʊʃɪən] **1** *adj* laotisch. **2** *n* Laote *m*, Laotin *f*.

**lap¹** [læp] *n* Schoß *m*. **it's in the ~ of the gods** es liegt im Schoß der Götter; **to live in the** ~ **of luxury** ein Luxusleben führen.

**lap²** *(Sport) n (round)* Runde *f*. **we're on the last** ~ **now** *(fig)* wir haben es bald geschafft.

**lap³ 1** *vt (lick)* lecken. **2** *vi (water)* klatschen *(against gegen)*.

►**lap up** *vt sep liquid* auflecken; *praise* genießen; *nonsense* schlucken. **she** ~**ped it** ~ *(fig)* das ging ihr runter wie Honig *(col)*.

**lapdog** ['læp,dɒg] *n* Schoßhund *m*.

**lapel** [lə'pɛl] *n* Revers *nt or m*.

**Lapland** ['læplænd] *n* Lappland *nt*.

**Laplander** ['læplændə¹], **Lapp** [læp] *n* Lappländer(in *f*) *m*, Lappe *m*, Lappin *f*.

**lapse** [læps] **1** *n* **(a)** *(error)* Fehler *m*; *(moral)* Fehltritt *m*; *(decline)* Absinken *nt no pl*. **he had a** ~ **of memory** es ist ihm entfallen; ~ **in standards** Niveauabfall *m*. **(b)** *(expiry)* Ablauf *m*; *(of claim)* Erlöschen *nt*; *(of time)* Zeitraum *m*. **there was a** ~ **in the conversation** es gab eine Gesprächspause. **2** *vi* **(a)** *(morally)* einen Fehltritt begehen; *(decline)* abgleiten. **to** ~ **into one's old ways** wieder in seine alten Gewohnheiten verfallen; **he** ~**d into silence** er verfiel in Schweigen; **his work is lapsing** seine Arbeit läßt nach. **(b)** *(expire)* ablaufen; *(claims)* erlöschen; *(correspondence)* einschlafen.

**lapsed** [læpst] *adj Catholic* abtrünnig; *(expired) insurance etc* abgelaufen.

**laptop** ['læp,tɒp] *n (Comp)* Laptop *m*.

**larceny** ['lɑːsənɪ] *n (Jur)* Diebstahl *m*.

**larch** [lɑːtʃ] *n* Lärche *f*.

**lard** [lɑːd] *n* Schweineschmalz *nt*.

**larder** ['lɑːdə¹] *n (room)* Speisekammer *f*; *(cupboard)* Speiseschrank *m*.

**large** [lɑːdʒ] **1** *adj (+er)* **(a)** *(big)* groß; *person* korpulent. ~ **as life** in voller Lebensgröße. **(b)** *(extensive) interests* weitreichend. **2** *adv* groß. **guilt was writ** ~ **all over his face** die Schuld stand ihm deutlich im Gesicht geschrieben. **3** *n* **at** ~ *(in general)* im großen und ganzen; **people at** ~ die Allgemeinheit; **to be at** ~ *(free)* frei herumlaufen; *(prisoner)* auf freiem Fuß sein.

**largely** ['lɑːdʒlɪ] *adv (mainly)* zum größten Teil.

**large scale** ['lɑːdʒ,skeɪl] *adj* groß angelegt. ~ **changes** Veränderungen *pl* in großem Umfang; **a** ~ **producer** ein Großhersteller *m*; ~ **rioting** Massenunruhen *pl*; **a** ~ **map** eine (Land)karte in großem Maßstab.

**largesse** [lɑː'ʒɛs] *n* Großzügigkeit *f*.

**lark¹** [lɑːk] *n (Orn)* Lerche *f*. **to get up with the** ~ mit den Hühnern aufstehen.

**lark²** *n (col) (joke)* Jux *(col)*, Spaß *m*. **to do sth for a** ~ etw (nur) aus Jux machen; **this whole agency** ~ die ganze Geschichte mit der Agentur *(col)*.

►**lark about** *or* **around** *vi (col)* herumalbern. **to** ~ ~ **with sth** mit etw herumspielen.

**larva** ['lɑːvə] *n, pl -e* ['lɑːviː] Larve *f*.

**laryngitis** [,lærɪn'dʒaɪtɪs] *n* Kehlkopfentzündung *f*.

**larynx** ['lærɪŋks] *n* Kehlkopf *m*.

**lascivious** [lə'sɪvɪəs] *adj person, behaviour* lüstern.

**laser** ['leɪzə¹] *n* Laser *m*. ~ **beam** Laserstrahl *m*; ~ **printer** Laserdrucker *m*.

**lash¹** [læʃ] *n (eye*~*)* Wimper *f*.

**lash²** **1** *n (whip)* Peitsche *f*; *(thong)* Schnur *f*; *(stroke, as punishment)* (Peitschen)schlag *m*; *(*~*ing) (of tail)* Schlagen *nt*; *(of waves, rain also)* Peitschen *nt*. **2** *vt* **(a)** *(beat)* peitschen; *(as punishment)* auspeitschen; *(rain)* peitschen gegen; *(tail)* schlagen mit. **the wind** ~**ed the sea into a fury** wütend peitschte der Wind die See. **(b)** *(tie)* festbinden *(to an +dat)*. **to** ~ **sth together** etw zusammenbinden.

►**lash down 1** *vt sep (tie down)* festbinden. **2** *vi (rain etc)* niederprasseln.

►**lash out** *vi* **(a)** *(physically)* (wild) um sich schlagen. **to** ~ ~ **at sb** auf jdn losgehen. **(b)** *(in words)* vom Leder ziehen *(col)*. **to** ~ ~ **against** *or* **at sb/sth** gegen jdn/etw wettern. **(c)** *(col: with money)* sich in Unkosten stürzen. **to** ~ ~ **on sth** sich *(dat)* etw was kosten lassen *(col)*.

**lashing** ['læʃɪŋ] *n* **(a)** *(beating)* Prügel *pl*; *(punishment)* Auspeitschung *f*. **(b)** ~**s** *pl (col)* eine Unmenge *(col)*; ~**s of money** massenhaft Geld *(col)*.

**lass** [læs] *n* (junges) Mädchen *nt*.

**lassitude** ['læsɪtjuːd] *n* Mattigkeit, Trägheit *f*.

**lasso** [læ'suː] **1** *n, pl* -**(e)s** Lasso *m or nt*. **2** *vt* mit dem Lasso einfangen.

**last¹** [lɑːst] **1** *adj* letzte(r, s). **he was (the)** ~ **to arrive** er kam als letzter an; **the** ~ **person** der letzte; **the** ~ **but one, the second** ~ **(one)** der/die/das vorletzte; ~ **Monday** letzten Montag; ~ **year** letztes Jahr; **during the** ~ **20 years** in den letzten 20 Jahren; ~ **but not least** nicht zuletzt; **that's the** ~ **thing I worry about** das ist das Letzte, worüber ich mir Sorgen machen würde; **that was the** ~ **thing I expected** damit hatte ich am wenigsten gerechnet; **he's the** ~ **person I want to see** er ist der letzte, den ich sehen möchte; **the** ~ **word** *(in fashion)* der letzte Schrei; **the** ~ **word in ...** das letzte an ... *(dat)*.

**2** *n* der/die/das letzte. **he was the** ~ **to leave** er ging als letzter; **each one is better than the** ~ eins ist besser als das andere; **this is the** ~ **of the cake** das ist der Rest des Kuchens; **that was the** ~ **we heard of him** seitdem haben wir nichts mehr von ihm gehört; **we shall never hear the** ~ **of it** das werden wir noch lange zu hören bekommen; **at** ~ endlich; **to the** ~ bis zum Schluß.

**3** *adv* **I** ~ **heard from him a month ago** vor einem Monat habe ich das letztemal von ihm gehört; **he spoke** ~ er sprach als letzter; ~ **thing (at night)** *(abends)* als letztes.

**last²** **1** *vt* **it will** ~ **me a lifetime** das hält ein Leben lang; **these cigarettes will** ~ **me a week** diese Zigaretten reichen mir eine Woche. **2** *vi (continue)* dauern; *(remain intact: flowers, food, marriage)* halten; *(rain)* anhalten. **it's too good to** ~ das ist zu schön, um von Dauer zu sein; **the previous boss** ~**ed only a week** der letzte Chef blieb nur eine Woche.

**last³** *n* Leisten *m*.

**last-ditch** ['lɑːst,dɪtʃ] *adj attr* in letzter Minute.

**lasting** ['lɑːstɪŋ] *adj relationship* dauerhaft; *shame etc* anhaltend.

**lastly** ['lɑːstlɪ] *adv* schließlich, zum Schluß.

**last:** ~**-mentioned** *adj* letztgenannt; ~**-minute** *adj* in letzter Minute; **it was a** ~**-minute decision** er/sie *etc* hat sich in letzter Minute dazu entschlossen; ~ **number redial** *n (Telec)* Letztnummernspeicher *m*; ~ **rites** *npl (Rel)* Letzte Ölung *f*; **the L**~ **Supper** *(Rel)* das (Letzte) Abendmahl.

**latch** [lætʃ] *n* Riegel *m*. **to leave the door on the** ~ die Tür nur einklinken.

►**latch on** *vi (col)* **(a)** *(get hold)* sich festhalten *(to sth an etw dat)*. **he** ~**ed** ~ **to the idea of coming with us** er hat es sich *(dat)* in den Kopf gesetzt, mitzukommen. **(b)** *(attach oneself)* sich anschließen *(to dat)*. **she** ~**ed** ~ **to me at the party** sie hängte sich auf der Party an mich *(col)*. **(c)** *(understand)* kapieren *(col)*.

**latchkey** ['lætʃ,kiː] *n* Haus-/Wohnungsschlüssel *m*. ~ **child** Schlüsselkind *nt*.

**late** [leɪt] **1** *adj (+er)* **(a)** spät. **to be** ~ **(for sth)** (zu etw) zu spät kommen; **the train was** ~ der Zug hatte Verspätung; **I was ~ (in) getting up this morning** ich bin heute morgen zu spät aufgestanden; **he is ~ with his rent** er hat seine Miete noch nicht bezahlt; **I don't want to make you ~** ich möchte Sie nicht aufhalten; **due to the ~ arrival of ...** wegen der verspäteten Ankunft ... *(+gen)*. **(b)** *hour* spät; *opening hours* lang; *bus, train* Spät-. **it's ~** es ist spät; **it's getting ~** es ist schon spät; **at this ~ hour** zu so später Stunde; **he keeps very ~ hours** er geht sehr spät ins Bett; **to have a ~ night** lange aufbleiben; **we have ~ opening on Thursdays** donnerstags haben wir länger geöffnet; **it happened in the ~ eighties** es geschah Ende der achtziger Jahre; **in the ~ morning** am späten Vormittag; **he came in ~ June** er kam Ende Juni. **(c)** *attr (deceased)* verstorben. **(d)** *(former)* **the ~ Prime Minister** der frühere *or* vorige Premierminister.

**2** *adv* spät. **to come ~** zu spät kommen; **the train arrived eight minutes ~** der Zug hatte acht Minuten Verspätung; **better ~ than never** besser spät als gar nicht; **to stay up ~** lange aufbleiben; **to work ~ at the office** länger im Büro arbeiten; **~ at night** spät abends; **~ in the afternoon** am späten Nachmittag; **~ in the year** (gegen) Ende des Jahres; **rather ~ in life** ziemlich spät; *(in old age)* im Alter; **of ~** in letzter Zeit.

**latecomer** ['leɪtkʌməʳ] *n* Nachzügler(in *f*) *m*.

**lately** ['leɪtlɪ] *adv* in letzter Zeit. **till ~** bis vor kurzem.

**lateness** ['leɪtnɪs] *n (at work etc)* Zuspätkommen *nt*; *(of train, payments)* Verspätung *f*; *(of meal)* späte Zeit; *(of harvest, seasons)* spätes Eintreten. **the ~ of the hour** die späte *or* vorgerückte Stunde.

**latent** ['leɪtənt] *adj* latent; *ability, defect, strength also* verborgen; *energy* ungenutzt.

**later** ['leɪtəʳ] **1** *adj* später. **at a ~ date** zu einem späteren Termin; **a ~ edition** eine neuere Auflage; **in his ~ years** in seinem späteren Leben. **2** *adv* später. **~ that night** später in der Nacht; **a moment ~** einen Augenblick später; **see you ~!** bis später!; **not ~ than 1995** spätestens 1995; **~ on** nachher; **~ on this month** noch in diesem Monat.

**lateral** ['lætərəl] *adj* seitlich. **~ thinking** kreatives Denken.

**laterally** ['lætərəlɪ] *adv* seitlich.

**latest** ['leɪtɪst] **1** *adj* **(a)** späteste(r, s). **what is the ~ date you can come?** wann kannst du spätestens kommen? **(b)** *(most recent) fashion, version* neu(e)ste(r, s). **the ~ news** das Neu(e)ste. **2** *adv* am spätesten. **3** *n* **(a)** **what's the ~ (about John)?** was gibt's Neues (über John)?; **wait till you hear the ~!** warte, bis du das Neueste gehört hast! **(b)** **at the (very) ~** spätestens.

**latex** ['leɪteks] *n* Latex *(spec)*, Milchsaft *m*.

**lath** [læθ] *n* Latte *f*. **~s** *pl (structure)* Lattenwerk *nt*.

**lathe** [leɪð] *n* Drehbank *f*. **~ operator** Dreher *m*.

**lather** ['lɑːðəʳ] **1** *n* *(Seifen)*schaum *m*; *(sweat)* Schweiß *m*. **the horse was in a ~** das Pferd war schweißnaß; **to get into a ~ (about sth)** *(col)* sich (über etw *acc*) aufregen. **2** *vt* einschäumen. **3** *vi* schäumen.

**Latin** ['lætɪn] **1** *adj (Roman)* civilization römisch; *poets also* lateinisch; *temperament* südländisch. **~ language** lateinische Sprache. **2** *n (language)* Latein(isch) *nt*.

**Latin America** *n* Lateinamerika *nt*.

**Latin-American** ['lætɪnə'merɪkən] **1** *adj* lateinamerikanisch. **2** *n* Lateinamerikaner(in *f*) *m*.

**latitude** ['lætɪtjuːd] *n* Breite *f*; *(fig)* Freiheit *f*.

**latrine** [lə'triːn] *n* Latrine *f*.

**latter** ['lætəʳ] **1** *adj* **(a)** *(second of two)* letztere(r, s).

**(b)** *(at the end)* **the ~ part of the book is better** gegen Ende wird das Buch besser; **the ~ part of the week** die zweite Hälfte der Woche; **in his ~ years** in den späteren Jahren seines Lebens. **2** *n* **the ~** der/die/das letztere; die letzteren.

**latterly** ['lætəlɪ] *adv* in letzter Zeit.

**lattice** ['lætɪs] *n* Gitter *nt*. **~-work** Gitterwerk *nt*.

**Latvia** ['lætvɪə] *n* Lettland *nt*.

**Latvian** ['lætvɪən] **1** *adj* lettisch. **2** *n* **(a)** Lette *m*, Lettin *f*. **(b)** *(language)* Lettisch *nt*.

**laudable** ['lɔːdəbl] *adj* lobenswert.

**laugh** [lɑːf] **1** *n* Lachen *nt*. **she gave a loud ~** sie lachte laut auf; **to have a good ~ about sth** sich köstlich über etw *(acc)* amüsieren; **it'll give us a ~** *(col)* das wird lustig; **the ~ was on me** der Witz ging auf meine Kosten; **to have the last ~** derjenige sein, der zuletzt lacht; **to have the last ~ over** *or* **on sb** es jdm zeigen *(col)*; **what a ~** (das ist ja) zum Totlachen! *(col)*; **just for a ~** nur (so) aus Spaß; **it'll be a good ~** es wird bestimmt lustig; **he's a ~** er ist zum Schreien *(col)*.

**2** *vi* lachen *(about, at, over* über *+acc)*. **to ~ at sb** sich über jdn lustig machen; **to ~ up one's sleeve** sich *(dat)* ins Fäustchen lachen; **it's all very well for you to ~** du hast gut lachen; **you'll be ~ing on the other side of your face soon** dir wird das Lachen bald vergehen; **to ~ in sb's face** jdm ins Gesicht lachen; **he who ~s last ~s longest** *(Prov)* wer zuletzt lacht, lacht am besten *(Prov)*; **don't make me ~!** *(iro col)* daß ich nicht lache! *(col)*; **you've got your own house, you're ~ing** *(col)* du hast ein eigenes Haus, du hast es gut.

**3** *vt* **to ~ oneself silly** sich tot- *or* kaputtlachen *(col)*; **he was ~ed out of court** er wurde ausgelacht. ▸**laugh off** *vt* **(a)** *always separate* **to ~ one's head ~** sich totlachen *(col)*. **(b)** *sep (dismiss)* mit einem Lachen abtun.

**laughable** ['lɑːfəbl] *adj* lächerlich.

**laughing** ['lɑːfɪŋ] **1** *adj* lachend. **it's no ~ matter** das ist nicht zum Lachen; **~ gas** Lachgas *nt*. **2** *n* Lachen *nt*.

**laughing stock** *n* Witzfigur *f*. **his ideas made him a ~** mit seinen Ideen machte er sich lächerlich.

**laughter** ['lɑːftəʳ] *n* Gelächter *nt*. **~ broke out among the audience** das Publikum brach in Gelächter aus.

**launch** [lɔːntʃ] **1** *n* **(a)** *(vessel)* Barkasse *f*. **(b)** *(~ing) (of ship)* Stapellauf *m*; *(of lifeboat)* Aussetzen *nt*; *(of rocket)* Abschuß *m*. **(c)** *(~ing) (of company)* Gründung *f*; *(of new product)* Einführung *f*. **2** *vt* **(a)** *new vessel* vom Stapel lassen; *lifeboat* aussetzen; *rocket* abschießen. **Lady X ~ed the new boat** Lady X taufte das neue Schiff. **(b)** *company* gründen; *new product* auf den Markt bringen. **to ~ an offensive against the enemy** zum Angriff gegen den Feind übergehen. ▸**launch into** *vi +prep obj* **(a)** *(attack)* anprangern. **(b)** *(start)* in Angriff nehmen. **the author ~es straight ~ his main theme** der Autor kommt gleich zum Hauptthema. ▸**launch out** *vi (diversify)* sich verlegen *(in* auf *+acc)*. **the company ~ed ~ in several new directions** die Firma stieg in einige neue Branchen ein.

**launching** ['lɔːntʃɪŋ] *n* = **launch 1 (b)**.

**launching pad** *n* Abschußrampe *f*; *(fig)* Sprungbrett *nt*.

**launder** ['lɔːndəʳ] *vti* waschen und bügeln; *(fig) money* waschen.

**laund(e)rette** [,lɔːndə'ret] *n (Brit)* Waschsalon *m*.

**laundromat** ['lɔːndrəʊmæt] *n (US)* Waschsalon *m*.

**laundry** ['lɔːndrɪ] *n (place)* Wäscherei *f*; *(clothes) (dirty)* schmutzige Wäsche; *(washed)* Wäsche *f*. **to**

do the ~ (Wäsche) waschen.
**laurel** ['lɒrəl] n Lorbeer m. **to rest on one's ~s** sich auf seinen Lorbeeren ausruhen.
**lava** ['lɑːvə] n Lava f.
**lavatory** ['lævətrɪ] n Toilette f. ~ **attendant** Toiletten-frau f/-mann m; ~ **paper** Toilettenpapier nt; ~ **seat** Toilettensitz m.
**lavender** ['lævɪndəʳ] n (flower) Lavendel m.
**lavish** ['lævɪʃ] **1** adj gifts großzügig; praise, affection überschwenglich; banquet, party üppig; (pej) verschwenderisch. **to be ~ with sth** mit etw verschwenderisch umgehen; **to be ~ with one's money/praise** das Geld mit vollen Händen ausgeben/nicht mit Lob geizen. **2** vt **to ~ sth on sb** jdn mit etw überhäufen.
**lavishly** ['lævɪʃlɪ] adv give großzügig; praise überschwenglich; put paint on reichlich; entertain sb üppig. **they entertain ~** sie geben feudale Feste; ~ **furnished** aufwendig eingerichtet.
**law** [lɔː] n Gesetz nt; (system) Recht nt; (as study) Jura no art. ~ **of nature** Naturgesetz nt; **it's the ~** das ist Gesetz; **his word is ~** sein Wort ist Gesetz; **is there a ~ against it?** ist das verboten?; **he is a ~ unto himself** er macht, was er will; **he is above the ~** er steht über dem Gesetz; **to keep within the ~** sich im Rahmen des Gesetzes bewegen; **in ~** vor dem Gesetz; **by ~** gesetzlich; **to take the ~ into one's own hands** das Recht selbst in die Hand nehmen; ~ **and order** Recht und Ordnung; **I'll have the ~ on you** (col) ich rufe die Polizei.
**law:** ~**-abiding** adj gesetzestreu; ~**breaker** n Rechtsbrecher m; ~ **court** n Gericht nt.
**lawful** adj, ~**ly** adv ['lɔːfʊl, 'lɔːfəlɪ] rechtmäßig.
**lawless** ['lɔːlɪs] adj act gesetzwidrig; person gesetzlos; country ohne Gesetzgebung.
**lawlessness** ['lɔːlɪsnɪs] n Gesetzwidrigkeit f.
**lawn** [lɔːn] n (grass) Rasen m no pl.
**lawn:** ~**mower** n Rasenmäher m; ~ **tennis** n Rasentennis nt.
**law:** ~**school** n (esp US) juristische Fakultät; (separate institution) juristische Hochschule; ~ **student** n Jurastudent(in f) m; ~**suit** n Prozeß m, Klage f; **he brought a ~suit for damages** er strengte eine Schadenersatzklage an.
**lawyer** ['lɔːjəʳ] n (Rechts)anwalt m, (Rechts)anwältin f.
**lax** [læks] adj (+er) lax; discipline lasch; morals locker. **to be ~ about sth** etw vernachlässigen; **he's ~ about washing** er nimmt's mit dem Waschen nicht so genau.
**laxative** ['læksətɪv] n Abführmittel nt.
**laxity** ['læksɪtɪ], **laxness** ['læksnɪs] n Laxheit f; (carelessness) Nachlässigkeit f.
**lay¹** [leɪ] adj Laien-.
**lay²** pret of **lie**.
**lay³** (vb: pret, ptp **laid**) **1** vt (a) (place, put) legen (sth on sth auf etw acc). **to ~ (one's) hands on** (get hold of) erwischen; (find) finden; **I never laid a hand on him** ich habe ihn überhaupt nicht angefaßt.
(b) bricks, foundations, track, mines, eggs legen; cable verlegen; carpet (ver)legen; (prepare) fire herrichten; (Brit) table decken; plans schmieden. **to ~ breakfast** den Frühstückstisch decken.
(c) (non-material things) burden auferlegen (on sb jdm). **to ~ the blame for sth on sb** jdm die Schuld an etw (dat) geben; **to ~ oneself open to criticism** sich der Kritik aussetzen; **the police laid a charge of murder against him** die Polizei erstattete Anzeige wegen Mordes gegen ihn; **he laid his case before them** er trug ihnen seinen Fall vor; **to ~ a bet on sth** auf etw (acc) wetten.

(d) ghost austreiben; fear zerstreuen.
(e) (col: sexually) aufs Kreuz legen (col).
**2** vi (hen) legen.
►**lay aside** vt sep work etc zur Seite legen; (save) beiseite legen; plans etc auf Eis legen.
►**lay down** vt sep (a) book, pen etc hinlegen (on auf +acc). (b) (give up) burden ablegen; office niederlegen. **to ~ ~ one's arms** die Waffen niederlegen; **to ~ ~ one's life** sein Leben opfern. (c) policy festsetzen; rules festlegen. **to ~ ~ the law** (col) Vorschriften machen (to sb jdm).
►**lay in** vt sep food etc einlagern; supplies also anlegen.
►**lay into** vi +prep obj (col) **to ~ ~ sb** auf jdn losgehen; (verbally) jdn fertigmachen (col).
►**lay off 1** vi (col: stop) aufhören (prep obj mit). ~ ~ **it!** hör auf damit!; ~ ~ **my little brother, will you!** laß bloß meinen kleinen Bruder in Ruhe! **2** vt sep workers entlassen; (temporarily) Feierschichten machen lassen. **to be laid ~** entlassen werden; Feierschichten einlegen müssen.
►**lay on** vt sep (a) (apply) paint auftragen. (b) hospitality bieten (for sb jdm); entertainment sorgen für; excursion veranstalten; extra buses einsetzen; water, electricity anschließen.
►**lay out** vt sep (a) clothes zurechtlegen; corpse aufbahren. (b) (design, arrange) anlegen; room aufteilen; rooms in house anordnen; page umbrechen; (in magazines) das Layout (+gen) machen. (c) money ausgeben. (d) (knock out) **to ~ sb ~** jdn erledigen (col).
►**lay over** vi (US) Station machen.
►**lay up** vt sep (a) (store) lagern; supply anlegen; (amass) anhäufen. **he's ~ing ~ trouble for himself in the future** er wird später noch (viel) Ärger bekommen. (b) (immobilize) ship auflegen; car stillegen. **to be laid ~ (in bed)** im Bett liegen.
**lay:** ~**about** n Nichtstuer, Gammler m; ~**by** n (Brit) (in town) Parkbucht f; (in country) Parkplatz m; (big) Rastplatz m.
**layer** ['leɪəʳ] **1** n Schicht (also Geol), Lage f. ~ **cake** Schichttorte f. **2** vt hair abstufen. ~**ed cut** Stufenschnitt m.
**layette** ['leɪ'et] n Babyausstattung f.
**lay:** ~**man** n Laie m; **to the ~man** für den Laien; ~**off** n further ~**offs were unavoidable** weitere Arbeiter mußten entlassen werden or (temporarily) mußten Feierschichten einlegen; ~**out** n Anordnung f; (Typ) Layout nt; **we have changed the ~out of this office** wir haben dieses Büro anders aufgeteilt; ~ **person** n Laie m.
**laze** [leɪz] vi (also: ~ **about**, ~ **around**) faulenzen.
**lazily** ['leɪzɪlɪ] adv faul; (languidly) träge.
**laziness** ['leɪzɪnɪs] n Faulheit f; (languor) Trägheit f.
**lazy** ['leɪzɪ] adj (+er) faul; (slow-moving) langsam; (lacking activity) träge. **we had a ~ holiday** wir haben im Urlaub nur gefaulenzt.
**lazybones** ['leɪzɪ,bəʊnz] n sing (col) Faulpelz m.
**lb** n (weight) = Pfd.
**lc** (Typ) = **lower case**.
**LCD** = **liquid crystal display** LCD nt.
**Ld** = **Lord**.
**L-driver** (Brit) = **learner driver**.
**LEA** (Brit) = **Local Education Authority**.
**lead¹** [led] n (metal) Blei nt; (in pencil) Graphit nt.
**lead²** [liːd] (vb: pret, ptp **led**) **1** n (a) (front position) Spitzenposition f; (Sport) Führung f; (distance, time ahead) Vorsprung m. **to have two minutes' ~ over sb** zwei Minuten Vorsprung vor jdm haben; **to be in the ~** in Führung liegen; **he took the ~ from the German runner** er ging vor dem deutschen Läufer

in Führung; **it's my** ~ *(Cards)* ich fange an. **(b)**
*(example)* Beispiel *nt.* **to follow sb's** ~ jds Beispiel
folgen. **(c)** *(clue)* Anhaltspunkt *m*; *(in guessing etc)*
Tip *m.* **the police have a** ~ die Polizei hat eine Spur.
**(d)** *(Theat) (part)* Hauptrolle *f*; *(person)* Hauptdar-
steller(in *f*) *m.* **to sing the** ~ die tragende Partie
singen. **(e)** *(leash)* Leine *f.* **on a** ~ an der Leine. **(f)**
*(Elec)* Leitung *f*, Kabel *nt.*

  **2** *vt* **(a)** *(conduct)* person, animal führen. **that road
will** ~ **you to the station** auf dieser Straße kommen
Sie zum Bahnhof; **to** ~ **the way** *(lit, fig)* vorangehen; *(fig: be superior)* führend sein.

  **(b)** *(be the leader of, direct)* (an)führen; *expedition, team* leiten; *movement, revolution* anführen;
*orchestra (conductor)* leiten; *(first violin)* führen. **to
~ a government** an der Spitze einer Regierung stehen; **to** ~ **a party** den Parteivorsitz führen.

  **(c)** *(be first in)* anführen. **they led us by 30 seconds** sie lagen 30 Sekunden vor uns *(dat)*; **Britain
led the world in textiles** Großbritannien war auf
dem Gebiet der Textilproduktion führend in der
Welt.

  **(d)** *card* ausspielen.

  **(e)** *life* führen. **to** ~ **a life of luxury** in Luxus leben, ein Luxusleben führen.

  **(f)** *(influence)* **to** ~ **sb to do sth** jdn dazu bringen,
etw zu tun; **what led him to change his mind?** wie
kam er dazu, seine Meinung zu ändern?; **he is
easily led** er läßt sich leicht beeinflussen; **this led
me to the conclusion that ...** daraus schloß ich,
daß ...

  **3** *vi* **(a)** *(go in front)* vorangehen; *(in race)* in Führung liegen. **to** ~ **by 10 metres** 10 Meter Vorsprung
haben. **(b)** *(be a leader)* führen. **(c)** *(Cards)* ausspielen *(with sth* etw*).* **(d)** *(street etc)* führen. **it** ~**s into
that room** es führt zu diesem Raum. **(e)** *(result in,
cause)* führen *(to* zu*).* **remarks like that could** ~ **to
trouble** solche Bemerkungen könnten unangenehme
Folgen haben; **what will all these strikes** ~ **to?** wo
sollen all diese Streiks hinführen?

  ►**lead away** *vt sep* wegführen; *prisoner* abführen.

  ►**lead off 1** *vt sep* abführen. **a policeman led the
drunk** ~ **the pitch** ein Polizist führte den Betrunkenen vom Platz. **2** *vi* **several streets** ~ ~ **the square**
mehrere Straßen gehen vom Platz ab.

  ►**lead on 1** *vi usu imper* ~ ~**, sergeant!** führen Sie
an, Feldwebel! **2** *vt sep (deceive)* hinters Licht führen; *(tease)* aufziehen. **he led us** ~ **to believe that
we would get the money** er hat uns vorgemacht,
wir würden das Geld bekommen *(col)*; **she's just**
~**ing him** ~ sie führt ihn nur an der Nase herum.

  ►**lead up** *vi* **the events that led** ~ **to the war** die
Ereignisse, die dem Krieg vorausgingen; **what are
you** ~**ing** ~ **to?** worauf willst du hinaus?; **what's all
this** ~**ing** ~ **to?** was soll das Ganze?

**leaded** ['ledɪd] *adj window* Bleiglas-; *petrol* verbleit.
**leaden** ['ledn] *adj* bleiern *(geh)*; *heart, limbs* blei-
schwer.
**leader** ['liːdəʳ] *n* **(a)** Führer *m*; *(of union, party also)*
Vorsitzende(r) *mf*; *(military also)* Befehlshaber *m*;
*(of gang, rebels)* Anführer *m*; *(of expedition, project)*
Leiter(in *f*) *m*; *(Sport) (in league)* Tabellenführer
*m*; *(in race)* der/die/das Erste; *(Mus) (Brit: of orchestra)* Konzertmeister *m*; *(of choir)* Leiter *m*; *(of
pop group)* Leader *m.* **to be the** ~ *(in race, competition)* in Führung liegen; **the** ~**s** *(in race, competition)* die Spitzengruppe; ~ **of the opposition** Opposi-
tionsführer(in *f*) *m*; **the product is a** ~ **in its field**
das Produkt ist auf diesem Gebiet führend. **(b)**
*(Brit Press)* Leitartikel *m.* ~ **writer** Leitartikler *m.*
**leadership** ['liːdəʃɪp] *n* **(a)** Führung *f.* **under the** ~

**of** unter (der) Führung von. **(b)** *(quality)* Führungsqualitäten *pl.*
**lead-free** ['led'friː] *adj* bleifrei.
**leading¹** ['ledɪŋ] *n (Typ)* Durchschuß *m.*
**leading²** ['liːdɪŋ] *adj* **(a)** *(first)* vorderste(r, s); *runner also* führend. **(b)** *(most important) person, company* führend; *sportsman, product* Spitzen-; *issue,
(Theat) part* Haupt-.
**leading** ['liːdɪŋ-]: ~ **lady** *n* Hauptdarstellerin *f*; ~
**light** *n (person)* Leuchte *f*; ~ **man** *n* Hauptdarstel-
ler *m*; ~ **question** *n* Suggestivfrage *f*; ~ **role** *n*
Hauptrolle *f*; *(fig)* führende Rolle.
**lead** ['led-]: ~ **pencil** *n* Bleistift *m*; ~**-poisoning** *n*
Bleivergiftung *f.*
**lead** ['liːd-]: ~ **story** *n* Hauptartikel *m*; ~ **time** *n*
*(for production)* Produktionszeit *f*; *(for delivery)* Lie-
ferzeit *f.*
**leaf** [liːf] **1** *n, pl* **leaves (a)** Blatt *nt.* **to be in** ~ grün
sein. **(b)** *(of paper)* Blatt *nt.* **to take a** ~ **out of sb's
book** sich *(dat)* von jdm eine Scheibe abschneiden;
**to turn over a new** ~ einen neuen Anfang machen.
**(c)** *(of table)* Ausziehplatte *f.* **2** *vi* **to** ~ **through a
book** ein Buch durchblättern.
**leaflet** ['liːflɪt] *n* Prospekt *m*; *(with instructions)*
Merkblatt *nt*; *(handout)* Flugblatt *nt*; *(brochure)*
Broschüre *f.*
**leafy** ['liːfɪ] *adj (+er) tree* belaubt; *lane* grün.
**league** [liːg] *n* **(a)** *(treaty)* Bündnis *nt*, Bund *m*; *(organization)* Verband *m.* **L~ of Nations** Völkerbund
*m*; **to be in** ~ **with sb** mit jdm gemeinsame Sache
machen. **(b)** *(Sport)* Liga *f.* **he's not in the same** ~
*(fig)* er hat nicht das gleiche Format.
**league**: ~ **game** *n* Meisterschaftsspiel *nt*; ~ **leaders** *npl* Tabellenführer *m*; ~ **table** *n* Tabelle *f.*
**leak** [liːk] **1** *n (lit, fig)* undichte Stelle; *(Naut)* Leck
*nt*; *(escape of liquid)* Leck *nt.* **to have a** ~ undicht
sein; **a gas** ~ eine undichte Stelle in der Gasleitung; **there's been a** ~ **to the press** der Presse sind
Informationen zugespielt worden. **2** *vt* durchlas-
sen; *(fig) information* zuspielen *(to sb* jdm*).* **3** *vi* **(a)**
*(ship, receptacle)* lecken; *(roof, shoes)* nicht dicht
sein; *(pen)* auslaufen. **(b)** *(gas)* ausströmen; *(liquid)*
auslaufen. **water is** ~**ing (in) through the roof** es
regnet durch (das Dach durch).
**leakage** ['liːkɪdʒ] *n (act)* Auslaufen *nt.* **the ground
was polluted by a** ~ **of chemicals** der Boden war
durch auslaufende Chemikalien verunreinigt.
**leakproof** ['liːkpruːf] *adj* dicht.
**leaky** ['liːkɪ] *adj (+er)* undicht; *boat also* leck.
**lean¹** [liːn] *adj (+er)* **(a)** *(thin)* dünn; *face, person*
schmal; *(through lack of food)* hager; *meat, (Aut)
mixture* mager. **(b)** *(poor) year, harvest* mager.
**lean²** [liːn] *(vb: pret, ptp* ~**ed** *or* **leant) 1** *vt (put in sloping
position)* lehnen *(against* gegen, an +*acc*); *(rest)* aufstützen *(on* auf +*dat or acc*). **to** ~ **one's head on
sb's shoulder** seinen Kopf an jds Schulter *(acc)* lehnen; **to** ~ **one's elbow on sth** sich mit dem Ellbogen auf etw *(acc)* stützen. **2** *vi* **(a)** *(be off vertical)*
sich neigen *(to* nach*)*; *(trees)* sich biegen. **he** ~**t
across the counter** er beugte sich über den Ladentisch. **(b)** *(rest)* sich lehnen *(against* gegen +*acc*).
**he** ~**t on the edge of the table** er stützte sich auf
die Tischkante. **(c)** *(tend in opinion etc)* **to** ~ **towards the left/socialism** nach links/zum Sozialismus
tendieren.

  ►**lean back** *vi* sich zurücklehnen.

  ►**lean forward** *vi* sich vorbeugen.

  ►**lean on** *vi (depend)* **to** ~ ~ **sb** sich auf jdn verlassen; *(col: put pressure on)* jdn bearbeiten *(col) or*
beknien *(col).*

  ►**lean out** *vi* sich hinauslehnen *(of aus).*

►**lean over** vi (be off vertical) sich (vor)neigen; (bend) sich vorbeugen (sth über +acc).

**lean-burn** ['li:nbɜːn] adj ~ **engine** Magermotor m.

**leaning** ['li:nɪŋ] **1** adj schräg, schief. **2** n Hang m.

**leanness** ['li:nnɪs] n Magerkeit f.

**leant** [lent] pret, ptp of **lean**.

**lean-to** ['li:ntu:] n Anbau m; (shelter) Wetterschutz m.

**leap** [li:p] (vb: pret, ptp ~ed or leapt) **1** n Sprung m. **in one ~** mit einem Satz; **a great ~ forward** (fig) ein großer Sprung nach vorn; **a ~ in the dark** (fig) ein Sprung ins Ungewisse; **by ~s and bounds** (fig) sprunghaft. **2** vt springen über (+acc). **3** vi springen. **to ~ to one's feet** aufspringen; **my heart leapt** mein Herz machte einen Sprung.

►**leap at** vi +prep obj offer, opportunity sich stürzen auf (+acc).

►**leap up** vi (person) aufspringen; (flames) hochschlagen; (prices) sprunghaft ansteigen.

**leapfrog** ['li:pfrɒg] **1** n Bockspringen nt. **2** vi **he ~ged over him** er machte einen Bocksprung über ihn.

**leapt** [lept] pret, ptp of **leap**.

**leap year** n Schaltjahr nt.

**learn** [lɜːn] pret, ptp ~ed or learnt **1** vt lernen; language also erlernen; (be informed) erfahren. **I ~t (how) to swim** ich habe schwimmen gelernt; **we ~t (how) to write business letters** wir lernten Geschäftsbriefe schreiben. **2** vi lernen; (find out) erfahren (about, of von). **I can't, but I'm hoping to ~** ich kann es nicht, aber ich hoffe, es zu lernen; **he'll never ~!** er lernt es nie!; **to ~ from experience** durch Erfahrung lernen.

**learned** ['lɜːnɪd] adj gelehrt; society also, profession akademisch. **a ~ man** ein Gelehrter m.

**learner** ['lɜːnəʳ] n Anfänger(in f) m; (Brit: also ~ driver) Fahrschüler(in f) m. **slow ~s** lernschwache Schüler.

**learning** ['lɜːnɪŋ] n (act) Lernen nt; (erudition) Gelehrsamkeit f. **a man of ~** ein Gelehrter m.

**learnt** [lɜːnt] pret, ptp of **learn**.

**lease** [li:s] **1** n (of land, business premises etc) Pacht f; (contract) Pachtvertrag m; (of house, office) Miete f; (contract) Mietvertrag m. **to take a ~ on a house** ein Haus mieten; **to let sth out on ~** etw verpachten/vermieten; **to give sb a new ~ of life** jdm (neuen) Aufschwung geben. **2** vt (take) (from von) pachten; mieten; (give: also ~ out) (to an +acc) verpachten; vermieten.

**lease:** ~**hold 1** n (property) Pachtbesitz m; **2** adj gepachtet; property Pacht-; ~**holder** n Pächter m.

**leash** [li:ʃ] n Leine f. **on a ~** an der Leine.

**least** [li:st] **1** adj geringste(r, s). **2** adv am wenigsten. **~ possible expenditure** möglichst geringe Kosten; **the ~ expensive car** das billigste Auto; **he's the ~ aggressive of men** er ist nicht im mindesten aggressiv; **not the ~ bit drunk** kein bißchen betrunken. **3** n **the ~** der/die/das Geringste; **it's the ~ one can do** es ist das wenigste, was man tun kann; **at ~ it's not raining** wenigstens regnet es nicht; **there were eight at ~** es waren mindestens acht da; **we need three at the very ~** allermindestens brauchen wir drei; **not in the ~** (upset) nicht im geringsten (verärgert); **to say the ~** gelinde gesagt; **the ~ said, the better** (Prov) je weniger man darüber spricht, desto besser.

**least-worst** adj am wenigsten schlecht.

**leather** ['leðəʳ] **1** n Leder nt. **2** adj Leder-, ledern. ~ **goods** Lederwaren pl.

**leathery** ['leðərɪ] adj ledern; meat zäh.

**leave** [li:v] (vb: pret, ptp **left**) **1** n **(a)** (permission) Er-

laubnis f. **to ask sb's ~ to do sth** jdn um Erlaubnis bitten, etw zu tun. **(b)** (permission to be absent, Mil) Urlaub m. **to be on ~** auf Urlaub sein; **to be on ~ of absence** beurlaubt sein. **(c)** **to take one's ~** sich verabschieden (of sb von jdm); **you must have taken ~ of your senses** Sie haben wohl den Verstand verloren.

**2** vt **(a)** (depart from, quit) place, person verlassen. **the train left the station** der Zug fuhr aus dem Bahnhof; **when he left Rome** als er von Rom wegging/wegfuhr etc; **to ~ home** von zu Hause weggehen; **to ~ one's job** seine Stelle aufgeben; **to ~ the road** (accidentally) von der Straße abkommen; **I'll ~ you at the station** (in car) ich setze dich am Bahnhof ab.

**(b)** (allow or cause to remain) lassen; mark, message, scar hinterlassen; meal stehenlassen. **who left the window open?** wer hat das Fenster offengelassen?; **this ~s me free for the afternoon** dadurch habe ich den Nachmittag frei; **~ me alone!** laß mich (in Ruhe)!; **to ~ well alone** die Finger davonlassen (col); **to ~ sb to himself** jdn allein lassen; **to ~ go of** loslassen; **let's ~ it at that** lassen wir es dabei (bewenden); **I was left with the bill** ich saß mit der Rechnung da.

**(c)** (forget) liegenlassen, stehenlassen.

**(d)** **to be left** (remain, be over) übrigbleiben; **all I have left** alles, was ich noch habe; **3 from 10 ~s 7** 10 minus 3 (ist) gleich 7; **nothing was left for me but to sell it** mir blieb nichts anderes übrig, als es zu verkaufen.

**(e)** (entrust) überlassen (up to sb jdm). **~ it to me** laß mich nur machen!; **I ~ it to you** das überlasse ich Ihnen; **to ~ sth to chance** etw dem Zufall überlassen.

**(f)** (after death) money, person hinterlassen.

**3** vi (weg)gehen, abfahren; (plane) abfliegen. **we ~ for Sweden tomorrow** wir fahren morgen nach Schweden.

►**leave aside** vt sep beiseite lassen.

►**leave behind** vt sep car, children dalassen; (outstrip) hinter sich (dat) lassen; (forget) liegenlassen, stehenlassen. **we've left all that ~ us** das alles liegt hinter uns.

►**leave in** vt sep scene in play etc nicht herausnehmen.

►**leave off 1** vt sep clothes nicht anziehen; lid nicht darauftun, ablassen (col); lights auslassen. **you left her name ~ the list** Sie haben ihren Namen nicht in die Liste aufgenommen. **2** vi +prep obj (col) aufhören. **we left ~ work after lunch** wir haben nach dem Mittagessen Feierabend gemacht; **~ ~ (doing that)!** hör auf (damit)!

►**leave on** vt sep clothes, lights anlassen.

►**leave out** vt sep **(a)** (not bring in) draußen lassen. **(b)** (omit) auslassen; (exclude) people ausschließen (of von). **you ~ my wife ~ of this** lassen Sie meine Frau aus dem Spiel! **(c)** (leave available) dalassen; (not put away) liegen lassen. **I'll ~ the books ~ on my desk** ich lasse die Bücher auf meinem Schreibtisch.

►**leave over** vt sep (leave surplus) übriglassen. **to be left ~** übrig(geblieben) sein.

**leaves** [li:vz] pl of **leaf**.

**leave-taking** ['li:vteɪkɪŋ] n Abschied m.

**leaving** ['li:vɪŋ] ~ **certificate** n Abgangszeugnis nt; ~ **present** n Abschiedsgeschenk nt.

**Lebanese** [ˌlebə'ni:z] **1** adj libanesisch. **2** n Libanese m, Libanesin f.

**Lebanon** ['lebənən] n **the ~** der Libanon.

**lech** [letʃ] vi (col) geilen (pej). **to ~ after sb** lüsterne

Blicke nach jdm werfen; *(desire)* geil auf jdn sein.
**lecherous** ['letʃərəs] *adj* lüstern; geil *(pej)*.
**lechery** ['letʃərɪ] *n* Lüsternheit *f*.
**lectern** ['lektɜːn] *n* Lesepult *nt*.
**lecture** ['lektʃəʳ] **1** *n* **(a)** Vortrag *m*; *(Univ)* Vorlesung *f*. **to give a ~** einen Vortrag/eine Vorlesung halten *(to* für, *on sth* über etw *acc)*. **(b)** *(scolding)* **to give sb a ~** jdm eine Strafpredigt halten *(about* wegen*)*. **2** *vt* **(a) to ~ sb on sth** jdm einen Vortrag/eine Vorlesung über etw *(acc)* halten; **he ~s us in physics** wir hören bei ihm (Vorlesungen in) Physik. **(b)** *(scold)* abkanzeln. **3** *vi* einen Vortrag halten; *(Univ)* eine Vorlesung halten; *(give ~ course)* Vorlesungen halten *(on* über +*acc)*. **he ~s in English** er ist Dozent für Anglistik.
**lecture: ~ hall** *n (Univ)* Hörsaal *m*; **~ notes** *npl (professor's)* Manuskript *nt*; *(student's)* Aufzeichnungen *pl*; **~ theatre** *n* Hörsaal *m*.
**lecturer** ['lektʃərəʳ] *n (Univ)* Dozent(in *f*) *m*; *(speaker)* Referent(in *f*) *m*.
**LED** *(Elec)* = **light-emitting diode** Leuchtdiode *f*. **~ display** Leuchtdiodenanzeige *f*.
**led** [led] *pret, ptp of* **lead²**.
**ledge** [ledʒ] *n* Leiste, Kante *f*; *(of window) (inside)* Fensterbrett *nt*; *(outside)* Sims *nt or m*; *(shelf)* Ablage *f*; *(mountain ~)* (Fels)vorsprung *m*.
**ledger** ['ledʒəʳ] *n* Hauptbuch *nt*.
**lee** [liː] **1** *adj* Lee-. **2** *n* **(a)** *(Naut)* Lee *f*. **(b)** *(shelter)* Windschatten *m*.
**leech** [liːtʃ] *n* Blutegel *m*; *(fig)* Blutsauger *m*.
**leek** [liːk] *n* Porree, Lauch *m*.
**leer** [lɪəʳ] **1** *n (knowing, sexual)* anzügliches Grinsen; *(evil)* heimtückischer Blick. **2** *vi* anzüglich grinsen; einen heimtückischen Blick haben. **he ~ed at her** er warf ihr lüsterne Blicke zu.
**lees** [liːz] *npl* Bodensatz *m*.
**leeward** ['liːwəd] **1** *adj* Lee-. **2** *n* Lee(seite) *f*. **to ~** leewärts.
**leeway** ['liːweɪ] *n* **(a)** *(Naut)* Leeweg *m*. **(b)** *(fig: flexibility)* Spielraum *m*. **to make up ~** den Zeitverlust aufholen.
**left¹** [left] *pret, ptp of* **leave**.
**left²** **1** *adj (also Pol)* linke(r, s). **2** *adv* links *(of* von*)*. **turn ~** *(Aut)* links abbiegen; **keep ~** sich links halten. **3** *n* **(a)** Linke(r, s). **on the ~** links *(of* von*)*; **on my ~** links von mir. **(b)** *(Pol)* Linke *f*. **to be on the ~** links stehen.
**left: ~-hand** *adj* Links-; **~-hand drive** Linkssteuerung *f*; **~-hand side** linke Seite; **on his ~-hand side** zu seiner Linken; **~-handed** *adj* linkshändig; *tool* für Linkshänder.
**leftie** ['leftɪ] *n (pej)* Rote(r) *mf (pej col)*.
**leftist** ['leftɪst] **1** *adj* linke(r, s), linksgerichtet. **2** *n* Linke(r) *mf*.
**left: ~-luggage (office)** *n (Brit)* Gepäckaufbewahrung *f*; **~-luggage locker** *n* Gepäckschließfach *nt*; **~-over** *adj* übriggeblieben; **~-overs** *npl* (Über)reste *pl*; **~-wing 1** *adj (Pol)* linke(r, s); **2** *n* ~ **wing** linker Flügel *(also Sport)*; **~-winger** *n (Pol)* Linke(r) *mf*.
**leg** [leg] **1** *n* Bein *nt*; *(Cook)* Keule, Hachse *f*. **to pull sb's ~** jdn auf den Arm nehmen; **to be on one's last ~s** in den letzten Zügen liegen *(col)*; *(person)* auf dem letzten Loch pfeifen *(col)*; **he hasn't a ~ to stand on** *(fig) (no excuse)* er kann sich nicht herausreden; *(no proof)* das kann er nicht belegen. **2** *vt*: **to ~ it** *(col)* laufen.
**legacy** ['legəsɪ] *n (lit, fig)* Vermächtnis *nt*; *(fig also)* Erbe *nt*; *(fig pej)* Hinterlassenschaft *f*.
**legal** ['liːgl] *adj* **(a)** *(lawful)* legal; *claim* Rechts-; *(according to the law)* tender, limit gesetzlich; *(allowed*

*by law)* speed zulässig; *will, purchase* rechtsgültig. **to become ~** rechtskräftig werden; **the ~ age for marriage** das gesetzliche Heiratsalter; **to have ~ status** rechtsfähig sein; *(document)* Rechtskraft haben. **(b)** *(relating to the law)* matters juristisch, Rechts-; *advice, mind* juristisch; *fees, decision* Gerichts-; *act, adviser* Rechts-; *inquiry* gerichtlich. **to take ~ action against sb** gegen jdn Klage erheben; **to take ~ advice** juristischen Rat einholen; **~ adviser** juristischer Berater; **~ aid** Rechtshilfe *f*; **~ holiday** *(US)* gesetzlicher Feiertag; **the ~ profession** die Juristenschaft.
**legality** [liːˈgælɪtɪ] *n* Legalität *f*; *(of claim)* Rechtmäßigkeit *f*; *(of will, marriage, purchase)* Rechtsgültigkeit *f*.
**legalize** ['liːgəlaɪz] *vt* legalisieren.
**legally** ['liːgəlɪ] *adv (lawfully)* transacted legal; *married* rechtmäßig; *guaranteed* gesetzlich; *indefensible* rechtlich. **~ binding** rechtsverbindlich; **~ valid** rechtsgültig.
**legation** [lɪˈgeɪʃən] *n (diplomats)* Gesandtschaft *f*; *(building)* Gesandtschaftsgebäude *nt*.
**legend** ['ledʒənd] *n* **(a)** Legende *f*; *(fictitious)* Sage *f*. **(b)** *(inscription, caption)* Legende *f*.
**legendary** ['ledʒəndərɪ] *adj* **(a)** legendär. **(b)** *(famous)* berühmt.
**-legged** [-'legd, -'legɪd] *adj suf* -beinig. **bare-~** ohne Strümpfe.
**leggings** ['legɪŋz] *npl (Fashion)* Leggin(g)s *pl*.
**leggy** ['legɪ] *adj (+er)* langbeinig; *(gawky)* staksig.
**legibility** [ledʒɪˈbɪlɪtɪ] *n* Lesbarkeit, Leserlichkeit *f*.
**legible** ['ledʒɪbl] *adj* lesbar; *writing also* leserlich.
**legion** ['liːdʒən] *n* Legion *f*.
**legionnaire** [ˌliːdʒəˈnɛəʳ] *n* Legionär *m*. **~'s disease** Legionärskrankheit *f*.
**legislate** ['ledʒɪsleɪt] *vi* Gesetze/ein Gesetz erlassen. **to ~ for sth** *(fig)* etw berücksichtigen.
**legislation** [ˌledʒɪsˈleɪʃən] *n (making laws)* Gesetzgebung *f*; *(laws)* Gesetze *pl*.
**legislative** ['ledʒɪslətɪv] *adj* gesetzgebend. **~ reforms** Gesetzesreformen *pl*.
**legislator** ['ledʒɪsleɪtəʳ] *n* Gesetzgeber *m*.
**legislature** ['ledʒɪsleɪtʃəʳ] *n* Legislative *f*.
**legit** [lɪˈdʒɪt] *adj (col) (legitimate)* sauber *(col)*; *(all right)* okay *(col)*.
**legitimacy** [lɪˈdʒɪtɪməsɪ] *n* Rechtmäßigkeit *f*.
**legitimate** [lɪˈdʒɪtɪmɪt] *adj (lawful)* rechtmäßig, legitim; *(born in wedlock)* ehelich; *(reasonable)* berechtigt; *excuse* begründet. **the ~ theatre** das konventionelle Sprechtheater.
**legitimize** [lɪˈdʒɪtɪmaɪz] *vt* legitimieren; *children* für ehelich erklären.
**leg: ~less** *adj* ohne Beine; *(col: drunk)* sternhagelvoll *(col)*; **~-room** *n* Platz *m* für die Beine; **~ up** *n* **to give sb a ~ up** jdm hochhelfen; **~warmer** *n* Legwarmer *m*.
**Leics** *(Brit)* = **Leicestershire.**
**leisure** ['leʒəʳ] *n* Freizeit *f*. **to lead a life of ~** ein Leben der Muße führen; **do it at your ~** *(in own time)* tun Sie es, wenn Sie Zeit dazu haben; *(at own speed)* lassen Sie sich *(dat)* Zeit damit.
**leisure: ~ activities** *npl* Freizeitbeschäftigungen *pl*; **~ hours** Freizeit *f*.
**leisurely** ['leʒəlɪ] *adj* geruhsam. **at a ~ pace** gemächlich.
**leisure: ~ time** *n* Freizeit *f*; **~ wear** *n* Freizeitkleidung *f*.
**lemon** ['lemən] *n* **(a)** Zitrone *f*; *(colour)* Zitronengelb *nt*. **(b)** *(col: fool)* Dussel *m (col)*; *(bad product)* schlechte Ware.
**lemonade** [ˌleməˈneɪd] *n* Limonade *f*.

**lemon**: ~ **curd** n zähflüssiger Brotaufstrich mit Zitronengeschmack; ~ **juice** n Zitronensaft m; ~ **tea** n Zitronentee m.

**lend** [lend] pret, ptp **lent 1** vt (loan) leihen (to sb jdm); (banks) money verleihen (to an +acc). **to ~ a hand** helfen; **it ~s it a certain credibility** das verleiht der Sache eine gewisse Glaubwürdigkeit. **2** vr **to ~ itself to sth** (be suitable) sich für etw eignen.

**lender** ['lendər] n Verleiher(in f) m.

**lending** ['lendɪŋ]: ~ **library** n Leihbücherei f; ~ **policy** n (of bank etc) Kreditpolitik f; ~ **rate** n (Darlehens)zinssatz m.

**length** [leŋθ] n (a) Länge f; (section) (of cloth, pipe) Stück nt; (of pool, wallpaper) Bahn f. **to be 4 metres in ~** 4 Meter lang sein; **what ~ is it?** wie lang ist es?; **of some ~** ziemlich lang; **along the whole ~ of the river** den ganzen Fluß entlang; **over all the ~ and breadth of England** in ganz England; (travelling) kreuz und quer durch ganz England; **at full ~** in voller Länge; **to win by half a ~** mit einer halben Länge siegen. **(b)** (of time) Dauer f; (great ~) lange Dauer. **of some ~** ziemlich lange; **at ~** (finally) schließlich; (for a long time) lange, ausführlich. **(c) to go to great ~s** sich (dat) sehr viel Mühe geben; **to go to the ~ of doing sth** so weit gehen, etw zu tun.

**lengthen** ['leŋθən] **1** vt verlängern; clothes länger machen. **2** vi länger werden.

**lengthways** ['leŋθweɪz], **lengthwise** ['leŋθwaɪz] adv der Länge nach.

**lengthy** ['leŋθɪ] adj (+er) lange; (dragging on) langwierig; speech also langatmig (pej).

**lenience** ['liːnɪəns], **leniency** ['liːnɪənsɪ] n see adj Nachsicht f; Milde f.

**lenient** ['liːnɪənt] adj nachsichtig (towards gegenüber); judge milde.

**lens** [lenz] n (Opt) Linse f; (in spectacles) Glas nt; (camera part) Objektiv nt. ~ **cap** Schutzkappe f; ~ **hood** Sonnenblende f.

**lent** [lent] pret, ptp of **lend**.

**Lent** [lent] n Fastenzeit f.

**lentil** ['lentl] n Linse f.

**Leo** ['liːəʊ] n (Astrol) Löwe m.

**leopard** ['lepəd] n Leopard m.

**leotard** ['liːətɑːd] n Trikot nt; (for gymnastics) Gymnastikanzug m.

**leper** ['lepər] n Leprakranke(r) mf. ~ **colony** Leprasiedlung f.

**leprosy** ['leprəsɪ] n Lepra f.

**lesbian** ['lezbɪən] **1** adj lesbisch. **2** n Lesbierin f.

**lesion** ['liːʒən] n Verletzung f.

**Lesotho** [lɪ'səʊtəʊ] n Lesotho nt.

**less** [les] **1** adj, adv, n weniger. **the minister, no ~** kein Geringerer als der Minister; ~ **and ~** immer weniger; **she saw him ~ and ~** (often) sie sah ihn immer seltener; **it's nothing ~ than disgraceful** es ist wirklich eine Schande; ~ **quickly** nicht so schnell; **even ~** noch weniger; **none the ~** trotzdem; **the ~ said the better** je weniger man darüber spricht, desto besser; **can't you let me have it for ~?** können Sie es mir nicht etwas billiger geben? **2** prep weniger; (Comm) abzüglich.

**lessee** [le'siː] n Pächter m; (of house, flat) Mieter m.

**lessen** ['lesn] **1** vt (make less) verringern; cost senken; effect abschwächen; (make less important etc) herabsetzen. **2** vi nachlassen; (value of money) abnehmen.

**lessening** ['lesnɪŋ] n Nachlassen nt (in sth +gen).

**lesser** ['lesər] adj geringer; (in names) klein. **to a ~ extent** in geringerem Maße.

**lesson** ['lesn] n (Sch etc) Stunde f; (unit of study)

Lektion f; (fig) Lehre f. ~**s** Unterricht m; **a French ~** eine Französischstunde; **to give a ~** eine Stunde geben; **to be a ~ to sb** jdm eine Lehre sein; **to teach sb a ~** jdm eine Lektion erteilen.

**lessor** [le'sɔːr] n (form) Verpächter m; (of flat etc) Vermieter m.

**lest** [lest] conj (form) (for fear that) aus Furcht, daß; (in order that ... not) damit ... nicht; (in case) für den Fall, daß. ~ **we forget** damit wir nicht vergessen; **I was frightened ~ he should fall** ich hatte Angst, daß er fallen könnte.

**let** [let] pret, ptp ~ vt **(a)** (permit) lassen. **to ~ sb do sth** jdn etw tun lassen; ~ **me help you** darf ich Ihnen helfen?; ~ **me know what you think** sagen Sie mir, was Sie davon halten; **to ~ sb be** jdn in Ruhe lassen; **to ~ sb/sth go, to ~ go of sb/sth** jdn/etw loslassen; **to ~ oneself go** (neglect oneself) sich gehenlassen; (relax) aus sich herausgehen; **we'll ~ it pass** or **go this once** (disregard) wir wollen es einmal durchgehen lassen; **to ~ sb/sth alone** jdn/etw in Ruhe lassen; **we'd better ~ well alone** wir lassen besser die Finger davon; ~ **alone** ... (much less) geschweige denn ...; **to ~ sb through** jdn durchlassen.

**(b)** ~**'s go!** gehen wir!; ~ **him try (it)!** das soll er nur versuchen!; ~ **me think** or **see, where did I put it?** warte mal, wo habe ich das nur hingetan?; ~ **X be 60** X sei 60.

**(c)** (esp Brit: hire out) vermieten (to an +acc). **"to ~"** „zu vermieten".

►**let down** vt sep **(a)** (lower) rope, person hinunter-/herunterlassen; seat herunterklappen; hair, window herunterlassen; (lengthen) dress länger machen. **(b) to ~ sb ~** (fail to help) jdn im Stich lassen (over mit); **to feel ~** (by sb) (von jdm) enttäuscht sein; **to ~ the school/oneself ~** die Schule/sich blamieren.

►**let in** vt sep **(a)** water durchlassen. **(b)** (admit) air, visitor hereinlassen. **just ~ yourself ~** geh einfach hinein; **I was just ~ting myself ~** ich schloß gerade die Tür auf. **(c)** (involve in) **to ~ oneself ~ for sth** sich auf etw (acc) einlassen; **to ~ oneself/sb ~ for trouble** sich/jdm Ärger einhandeln. **(d)** (allow to know) **she ~ me ~ on the secret** sie hat es mir verraten.

►**let off 1** vt sep **(a)** arrow abschießen; gun abfeuern; firework, bomb hochgehen lassen; (emit) vapour von sich geben; gases absondern. **(b)** (forgive) **to ~ sb ~** jdn laufenlassen; **to ~ sb ~ sth** jdm etw erlassen; **to ~ sb ~ with a warning** jdn mit einer Verwarnung davonkommen lassen; **to be ~ ~ lightly** glimpflich davonkommen. **(c)** (allow to go) gehen lassen. **2** vi (col: fart) einen fahren lassen (col).

►**let on 1** vi es verraten. **2** vt **(a)** don't ~ ~ you **know** (col) laß dir bloß nicht anmerken, daß du das weißt. **(b)** (pretend) **to ~ ~ that ...** vorgeben, daß ...

►**let out** vt sep **(a)** (allow to go out) hinaus-/herauslassen; (from car) absetzen; (divulge) news bekanntgeben; secret verraten, ausplaudern (col); fire ausgehen lassen. **I'll ~ myself ~** ich finde alleine hinaus; **to ~ ~ a laugh/groan** auflachen/(auf)stöhnen. **(b)** (make larger) dress auslassen. **(c)** (free from responsibility) **that ~s me ~** (of it) da komme ich (schon mal) nicht in Frage. **(d)** (Brit: rent) vermieten.

►**let up** vi (cease) aufhören; (ease up) nachlassen. **he never ~s ~ about money** er redet unaufhörlich von Geld.

**let-down** ['letdaʊn] n (col: disappointment) Enttäuschung f.

**lethal** ['liːθəl] adj tödlich.

**lethargic** [lɪ'θɑːdʒɪk] *adj person* träge, lethargisch; *(uninterested)* teilnahmslos.
**lethargy** ['leθədʒɪ] *n* Lethargie *f.*
**let's** [lets] = **let us.**
**letter** ['letəʳ] **1** *n* **(a)** *(of alphabet)* Buchstabe *m.* **the ~ of the law** der Buchstabe des Gesetzes; **to the ~** sehr genau; *(as given)* ganz nach Vorschrift. **(b)** *(written message)* Brief *m*; *(Comm etc)* Schreiben *nt (to* an *+acc).* **by ~** schriftlich; **~ of credit** Akkreditiv *nt.* **(c)** *(Liter)* **~s** Literatur *f*; **man of ~s** Belletrist *m*; *(writer)* Literat *m.*
**letter: ~ bomb** *n* Briefbombe *f*; **~ box** *n* Briefkasten *m.*
**letterhead** ['letəhed] *n* Briefkopf *m*; *(writing paper)* Geschäftspapier *nt.*
**lettering** ['letərɪŋ] *n* Beschriftung *f.*
**letter: ~-opener** *n* Brieföffner *m*; **~ press** *n* Hochdruck *m*; **~ quality** *n* Korrespondenz- *or* Briefqualität *f*; **~ quality printer** *n* Schönschreibdrucker *m.*
**lettuce** ['letɪs] *n* Kopfsalat *m.*
**let-up** ['letʌp] *n (col)* Pause *f*; *(easing up)* Nachlassen *nt.* **if there is a ~ in the rain** wenn der Regen nachläßt; **there was no ~** *(in work etc)* der Druck ließ nicht nach.
**leukaemia,** *(esp US)* **leukemia** [luːˈkiːmɪə] *n* Leukämie *f.*
**level** ['levl] **1** *adj* **(a)** *(flat)* surface eben; *spoonful* gestrichen; *(at the same height)* auf gleicher Höhe *(with* mit*)*; *(fig)* gleich gut. **the two runners are dead ~** die beiden Läufer sind genau auf gleicher Höhe; **to create a ~ playing field** *(fig)* Chancengleichheit schaffen. **(b)** *(steady)* tone of voice ruhig; *(well-balanced)* ausgeglichen; *judgement* abgewogen; *head* kühl. **(c) I'll do my ~ best** ich werde mein möglichstes tun.
**2** *adv* **~ with** in Höhe *(+gen)*; **the pipe runs ~ with the ground** *(parallel)* das Rohr verläuft parallel zum Boden; **they're running absolutely ~** sie laufen auf genau gleicher Höhe; **to draw ~ with sb** mit jdm gleichziehen.
**3** *n* **(a)** *(instrument)* Wasserwaage *f.* **(b)** *(altitude)* Höhe *f*; *(standard)* Niveau *nt.* **on a ~ (with)** auf gleicher Höhe (mit); **at eye ~** in Augenhöhe; **to be on a ~ with** auf gleichem Niveau sein wie; **a high ~ of hydrogen** ein hoher Wasserstoffanteil; **the ~ of alcohol in the blood** der Alkoholgehalt im Blut; **a high ~ of intelligence** ein hoher Intelligenzgrad; **the very high ~ of production** das hohe Produktionsniveau; **a high ~ of civilization** eine hohe Kulturstufe; **the talks were held at the highest ~** die Gespräche fanden auf höchster Ebene statt; **at ministerial ~** auf Ministerebene; **a high-~ meeting** ein Spitzentreffen; **on the moral ~** moralisch gesehen; **on a purely personal ~** auf rein persönlicher Ebene.
**(c)** *(col: straightforward, honest)* **it's on the ~** *(business)* es ist reell; **to be on the ~ (with sb)** ehrlich (mit jdm) sein.
**4** *vt* **(a)** *ground etc* einebnen; *building* abreißen; *town* dem Erdboden gleichmachen. **(b)** *blow* versetzen *(at sb* jdm*)*; *weapon* richten *(at* auf *+acc)*; *accusation* erheben *(at* gegen*)*; *remark* richten *(at* gegen*)*.
**5** *vi* **to ~ with sb** *(col)* ehrlich mit jdm sein.
▶**level out 1** *vi (also ~ off) (ground)* eben werden; *(fig)* sich ausgleichen. **2** *vt sep site* planieren, einebnen; *(fig) differences* ausgleichen.
**level: ~ crossing** *n (Brit)* (beschrankter) Bahnübergang; **~-headed** *adj person* ausgeglichen; *reply, decision* ausgewogen, überlegt.

**lever** ['liːvəʳ, *(US)* 'levəʳ] **1** *n* Hebel *m*; *(crowbar)* Brechstange *f*; *(fig)* Druckmittel *nt.* **2** *vt* (hoch)-stemmen. **he ~ed the box open** er stemmte die Kiste auf.
**leverage** ['liːvərɪdʒ] *n* Hebelkraft *f*; *(fig)* Einfluß *m.* **to use sth as ~** *(fig)* etw als Druckmittel benutzen.
**levity** ['levɪtɪ] *n* Leichtfertigkeit *f.*
**levy** ['levɪ] **1** *n (act)* (Steuer)einziehung *f*; *(tax)* Abgaben *pl.* **2** *vt tax* einziehen; *fine* auferlegen *(on sb* jdm*)*; *army* ausheben.
**lewd** [luːd] *adj (+er)* unanständig; *(lustful)* lüstern; *remark* anzüglich; *imagination* schmutzig.
**lexicographer** [ˌleksɪˈkɒgrəfəʳ] *n* Lexikograph(in *f*) *m.*
**lexicography** [ˌleksɪˈkɒgrəfɪ] *n* Lexikographie *f.*
**lhd** *(Aut)* = **left-hand drive.**
**LI** *(US Post)* = **Long Island.**
**liability** [ˌlaɪəˈbɪlɪtɪ] *n* **(a)** *(burden)* Belastung *f*; *(proneness)* Anfälligkeit *f (to* für*)*; *(responsibility)* Haftung *f.* **~ for** *or* **to tax** Steuerpflicht *f*; **we accept no ~ for ...** wir übernehmen keine Haftung für ... **(b)** *(Fin)* **liabilities** Verbindlichkeiten *pl.*
**liable** ['laɪəbl] *adj* **(a)** *(subject to)* **to be ~** unterliegen *(for sth* einer Sache *dat)*; **to be ~ for** *or* **to tax** *(things)* besteuert werden; *(person)* steuerpflichtig sein. **(b)** *(to illness)* anfällig *(to* für *+acc).* **(c)** *(responsible)* **to be ~** haften *(for* für *+acc).* **(d)** *(likely to)* **we are ~ to get wet here** wir können hier leicht naß werden; **is he ~ to come?** ist es wahrscheinlich, daß er kommt?; **he's ~ to tell the police** es wäre ihm zuzutrauen, daß er es der Polizei meldet; **the computer is still ~ to make mistakes** der Computer kann durchaus noch Fehler machen.
**liaise** [liːˈeɪz] *vi (be the contact person)* als Verbindungsperson fungieren; *(get in contact)* sich in Verbindung setzen *(with* mit*)*.
**liaison** [liːˈeɪzɒn] *n (coordination)* Zusammenarbeit *f*; *(person)* Verbindungsmann *m*; *(affair)* Liaison *f.*
**liaison officer** *n* Verbindungsperson *f.*
**liar** ['laɪəʳ] *n* Lügner(in *f*) *m.*
**Lib Dem** [ˌlɪbˈdem] *(Brit Pol)* = **Liberal Democrat.**
**libel** ['laɪbəl] **1** *n* (schriftlich geäußerte) Verleumdung *(on* gen*).* **2** *vt* verleumden.
**libellous,** *(US)* **libelous** ['laɪbələs] *adj* verleumderisch.
**liberal** ['lɪbərəl] **1** *adj* **(a)** *(generous)* offer großzügig; *helping of food* reichlich. **(b)** *(broad-minded, also Pol)* liberal. **2** *n (Pol:* **L~)** Liberale(r) *mf.* **L~ Democrat** *(Brit)* Liberaldemokrat(in *f*) *m.*
**liberalism** ['lɪbərəlɪzəm] *n* Liberalität *f*; *(Pol:* **L~)** der Liberalismus.
**liberality** [ˌlɪbəˈrælɪtɪ] *n (generosity)* Großzügigkeit *f.*
**liberalize** ['lɪbərəlaɪz] *vt* liberalisieren.
**liberally** ['lɪbərəlɪ] *adv* liberal; *(generously)* großzügig. **apply the paint ~** die Farbe reichlich auftragen.
**liberal-minded** [ˌlɪbərəlˈmaɪndɪd] *adj person* liberal (eingestellt); *views* liberal.
**liberate** ['lɪbəreɪt] *vt (free) prisoner* befreien; *gas etc* freisetzen.
**liberation** [ˌlɪbəˈreɪʃən] *n* Befreiung *f*; *(of gases)* Freisetzung *f.*
**liberator** ['lɪbəreɪtəʳ] *n* Befreier *m.*
**Liberia** [laɪˈbɪərɪə] *n* Liberia *nt.*
**Liberian** [laɪˈbɪərɪən] **1** *adj* liberianisch. **2** *n* Liberianer(in *f*) *m.*
**liberty** ['lɪbətɪ] *n* **(a)** Freiheit *f.* **basic liberties** Grundrechte *pl*; **to be at ~** *(criminal etc)* frei herumlaufen; **to be at ~ to do sth** *(be permitted)* etw tun dürfen; **I am not at ~ to comment** es ist mir nicht gestattet, darüber zu sprechen. **(b) I have taken the**

~ **of giving your name** ich habe mir erlaubt, Ihren Namen anzugeben; **to take liberties with sb** sich jdm gegenüber Freiheiten herausnehmen; **what a ~!** *(col)* so eine Frechheit!

**libido** [lɪˈbiːdəʊ] *n* Libido *f*.

**Libra** [ˈliːbrə] *n (Astrol)* Waage *f*.

**librarian** [laɪˈbrɛərɪən] *n* Bibliothekar (in *f*) *m*.

**library** [ˈlaɪbrərɪ] *n* Bibliothek, Bücherei *f*.

**library:** ~ **book** *n* Buch *nt* aus der Bücherei; ~ **ticket** *n* Leserausweis *m*.

**libretto** [lɪˈbretəʊ] *n* Libretto *nt*.

**Libya** [ˈlɪbɪə] *n* Libyen *nt*.

**Libyan** [ˈlɪbɪən] **1** *adj* libysch. **2** *n* Libyer (in *f*) *m*.

**lice** [laɪs] *pl of* **louse**.

**licence,** *(US)* **license** [ˈlaɪsəns] *n* **(a)** *(permit)* Genehmigung *f*; *(Comm)* Lizenz *f*; *(driving ~)* Führerschein *m*; *(gun ~)* Waffenschein *m*; *(marriage ~)* Eheerlaubnis *f*; *(to sell alcohol)* Schankerlaubnis *f*. **you have to have a (television) ~ ≃** man muß Fernsehgebühren bezahlen; **to manufacture sth under ~** etw in Lizenz herstellen. **(b)** *(freedom)* Freiheit *f*; *(excessive freedom)* Zügellosigkeit *f*.

**license** [ˈlaɪsəns] **1** *n (US)* = **licence**. **2** *vt* eine Lizenz/Konzession vergeben an *(+acc)*. **a car must be ~d every year** die Kfz-Steuer muß jedes Jahr bezahlt werden.

**licensed** [ˈlaɪsənst] *adj* ~ **premises** Lokal *nt* mit Schankerlaubnis.

**licensee** [ˌlaɪsənˈsiː] *n (of bar)* Inhaber (in *f*) *m* einer Schankerlaubnis. **postage paid by ~** Gebühr bezahlt Empfänger.

**license plate** *n (US)* Nummernschild *nt*.

**licensing** [ˈlaɪsənsɪŋ] *adj* ~ **hours** Ausschankzeiten *pl*.

**licentious** [laɪˈsenʃəs] *adj life* ausschweifend; *behaviour* unzüchtig; *person, look* lüstern.

**lick** [lɪk] **1** *n* **(a)** *(with tongue)* Lecken *nt*. **to give sth a ~** an etw *(dat)* lecken. **(b)** *(col: small quantity)* **it's time we gave the kitchen a ~ of paint** die Küche könnte auch mal wieder etwas Farbe vertragen *(col)*. **(c)** *(col: pace)* **at full ~** mit Volldampf *(col)*. **2** *vt* **(a)** *(with tongue)* lecken; *(flames)* züngeln an *(+dat)*. **he ~ed the stamp** er leckte an der Briefmarke; **he ~ one's lips** sich *(dat)* die Lippen lecken; *(fig)* sich *(dat)* die Finger lecken; **to ~ one's wounds** *(fig)* seine Wunden lecken; **to ~ sb's boots** *(fig)* vor jdm kriechen. **(b)** *(col: defeat)* in die Pfanne hauen *(col)*. **I think we've got it ~ed** ich glaube, wir haben die Sache jetzt im Griff.

**licorice** *n* = **liquorice**.

**lid** [lɪd] *n* **(a)** Deckel *m*. **that puts the ~ on it** *(col)* das schlägt dem Faß den Boden aus; **the press took the ~ off the whole plan** die Presse hat den ganzen Plan aufgedeckt. **(b)** *(eye~)* Lid *nt*.

**lido** [ˈliːdəʊ] *n* Freibad *nt*.

**lie¹** [laɪ] **1** *n* Lüge *f*. **to tell a ~** lügen; **to give the ~ to a report** die Unwahrheit eines Berichtes nachweisen; ~ **detector** Lügendetektor *m*. **2** *vi* lügen. **to ~ to sb** jdn anlügen. **3** *vt* **to ~ one's way out of sth** sich aus etw herauslügen.

**lie²** *pret* **lay,** *ptp* **lain** *vi* liegen; *(~ down)* sich legen. **he lay where he had fallen** er blieb liegen, wo er hingefallen war; ~ **on your back** leg dich auf den Rücken; **obstacles ~ in the way of our success** unser Weg zum Erfolg ist mit Hindernissen verstellt; **the snow didn't ~** der Schnee blieb nicht liegen; **the runner who is lying third** der Läufer, der auf dem dritten Platz liegt; **it ~s with you to solve the problem** es liegt bei dir, das Problem zu lösen; **that responsibility ~s with your department** dafür ist Ihre Abteilung verantwortlich; **to ~ asleep** schla-

fen; **to ~ helpless** hilflos daliegen; **to ~ dying** im Sterben liegen; **to ~ resting** ruhen; **the snow lay deep** es lag tiefer Schnee; **the book lay unopened** das Buch lag ungeöffnet da; **to ~ low** untertauchen; **how do things ~?** wie steht die Sache?

▶**lie about** *or* **around** *vi* herumliegen.

▶**lie back** *vi (recline)* sich zurücklehnen.

▶**lie down** *vi* sich hinlegen *(on auf +acc)*. ~ ~ *(to a dog)* leg dich!; **he won't take that lying ~!** das läßt er sich nicht gefallen!

▶**lie in** *vi (stay in bed)* im Bett bleiben.

▶**lie up** *vi (go into hiding)* untertauchen. **the robbers are lying ~** die Räuber sind untergetaucht.

**Liechtenstein** [ˈlɪktənstaɪn] **1** *n* Liechtenstein *nt*. **2** *adj* liechtensteinisch.

**lie:** ~ **detector** *n* Lügendetektor *m*; ~**-down** *n (col)* Nickerchen *nt (col)*; **to have a ~-down** sich hinlegen.

**Liège** [lɪˈeɪʒ] *n* Lüttich *nt*.

**lie-in** [ˈlaɪɪn] *n (col)* **to have a ~** (sich) ausschlafen.

**lieu** [luː] *n* **in ~ of X** anstelle von X.

**Lieut.** *(Mil)* = **Lieutenant** Lt.

**lieutenant** [lefˈtenənt, *(US)* luːˈtenənt] *n (US)* Leutnant *m*; *(Brit)* Oberleutnant *m*.

**lieutenant:** ~**-colonel** *n* Oberstleutnant *m*; ~**-general** *n* Generalleutnant *m*.

**life** [laɪf] *n*, *pl* **lives** **(a)** Leben *nt*. **bird ~** die Vogelwelt; **drawn from ~** lebensnah; **the battle resulted in great loss of ~** bei der Schlacht kamen viele ums Leben; **this is a matter of ~ and death** hier geht es um Leben und Tod; **a ~ and death struggle** ein Kampf auf Leben und Tod; **to come to ~** *(fig)* lebendig werden; **after half an hour the discussion came to ~** nach einer halben Stunde kam Leben in die Diskussion; **to put new ~ into sb** jdm wieder Auftrieb geben; **they swam for dear ~** sie schwammen um ihr Leben; **at my time of ~** in meinem Alter; **he's got a job for ~** er hat eine Stelle auf Lebenszeit; **to take one's ~ in one's hands** mit dem Leben spielen; **the murderer was imprisoned for ~** der Mörder wurde zu lebenslänglicher Freiheitsstrafe verurteilt; **he's doing ~** *(col)* er ist ein Lebenslänglicher *(col)*; **to see ~** *(fig)* die Welt sehen; **there isn't much ~ here in the evenings** hier ist abends nicht viel los; **those children are full of ~** diese Kinder sind sehr lebhaft; **he is the ~ and soul of the party** er bringt Leben in die Party.

**(b)** *(individual life)* **how many lives were lost?** wie viele (Menschen) sind ums Leben gekommen?; **to take sb's ~** jdn umbringen; **to take one's own ~** sich *(dat)* das Leben nehmen; **to save sb's ~** *(lit)* jdm das Leben retten; *(fig)* jdn retten; **early/later in ~** in frühen/späten Jahren; **his ~ won't be worth living!** er wird nichts mehr zu lachen haben!; **all his ~** sein ganzes Leben lang; **I've never been to London in my ~** ich war in meinem ganzen Leben noch nicht in London; **run for your lives!** rennt um euer Leben!; **I can't for the ~ of me ...** *(col)* ich kann beim besten Willen nicht ...; **not on your ~!** *(col)* ich bin doch nicht verrückt! *(col)*.

**(c)** *(useful or active life of sth)* Lebensdauer *f*. **during the ~ of the present Parliament** während der Legislaturperiode des gegenwärtigen Parlaments; **there's not much ~ left in the battery** die Batterie macht's nicht mehr lange *(col)*.

**life:** ~ **annuity** *n* Leibrente *f*; ~ **assurance** *n (Brit)* Lebensversicherung *f*; ~**belt** *n* Rettungsgürtel *m*; ~**blood** *n (fig)* Lebensnerv *m*; ~**boat** *n* Rettungsboot *nt*; ~**buoy** *n* Rettungsring *m*; ~ **cycle** *n* Lebenszyklus *m*; ~ **expectancy** *n* Lebenserwartung *f*; ~**guard** *n (on beach)* Rettungsschwimmer *m*; ~

**history** *n* Lebensgeschichte *f*; ~ **imprisonment** *n* lebenslängliche Freiheitsstrafe; ~ **insurance** *n* Lebensversicherung *f*; ~ **jacket** *n* Schwimmweste *f*.

**lifeless** ['laɪflɪs] *adj* leblos; *planet* ohne Leben; *(fig: dull)* lahm *(col)*, langweilig; *hair* schlaff.

**life:** ~**like** *adj* lebensecht; *imitation also* naturgetreu; ~**line** *n* Rettungsleine *f*; *(of diver)* Signalleine *f*; *(fig)* Rettungsanker *m*; ~**long** *adj* lebenslang; **they are** ~**long friends** sie sind schon seit ihrer Kindheit Freunde; ~ **membership** *n* Mitgliedschaft *f* auf Lebenszeit; ~ **preserver** *n (US)* Schwimmweste *f*; ~ **raft** *n* Rettungsfloß *nt*; ~**saver** *n (person)* Lebensretter(in *f*) *m*; **it was a real** ~**saver!** *(fig)* das hat mich gerettet; ~**saving 1** *n* Lebensrettung *f*; *(from drowning)* Rettungsschwimmen *nt*; **2** *adj* lebensrettend; *techniques, apparatus* Rettungs-; ~ **sentence** *n* lebenslängliche Freiheitsstrafe; ~**size(d)** *adj* in Lebensgröße; ~ **span** *n* Lebenserwartung *f*; *(Bot, Zool)* Lebensdauer *f*; ~ **story** *n* Lebensgeschichte *f*; ~**style** *n* Lebensstil *m*; ~ **support system** *n* Lebenserhaltungssystem *nt*; ~**time** *n* (a) Lebenszeit *f*; *(of battery, machine, animal)* Lebensdauer *f*; **once in a** ~**time** einmal im Leben; **during or in my** ~**time** während meines Lebens; **the chance of a** ~**time** eine einmalige Chance; **the work of a** ~**time** ein Lebenswerk *nt*; **(b)** *(fig)* Ewigkeit *f*.

**lift** [lɪft] **1** *n* (a) **give me a** ~ **with this trunk** hilf mir, den Koffer hochzuheben. **(b)** *(fig: emotional uplift)* **to give sb a** ~ jdn aufmuntern. **(c)** *(in car etc)* Mitfahrgelegenheit *f*. **to give sb a** ~ *(take along)* jdn mitnehmen; *(as special journey)* jdn fahren; **to get a** ~ **from sb** von jdm mitgenommen/gefahren werden; **thanks for the** ~ danke fürs Mitnehmen. **(d)** *(Brit: elevator)* Aufzug *m*. **(e)** *(Aviat)* Auftrieb *m*. **2** *vt* **(a)** *(also* ~ **up)** hochheben; *window* hochschieben; *feet, head* heben; *eyes* aufschlagen; *hat* ziehen. **it's too heavy to** ~ es ist zu schwer zum Hochheben. **(b)** *(fig: also* ~ **up)** heben; *voice* erheben. **(c)** *(remove)* *restrictions etc* aufheben. **(d)** *(col: steal)* klauen *(col)*. **3** *vi* **(a)** *(mist)* sich lichten. **(b)** = ~ **up 2**.

▶**lift down** *vt sep* herunterheben.
▶**lift off** *vti sep* abheben.
▶**lift out** *vt* herausheben.
▶**lift up 1** *vt sep* = **lift 2 (a, b)**. **to** ~ ~ **one's head** *(fig)* den Kopf hochhalten. **2** *vi* hochgeklappt werden.

**lift:** ~ **attendant** *n (Brit)* Fahrstuhlführer *m*; ~**off** *n (Space)* Start *m*; **we have** ~**off** der Start ist erfolgt; ~**shaft** *n* Aufzugsschacht *m*.

**ligament** ['lɪgəmənt] *n (Anat)* Band *nt*. **he's torn a** ~ **in his shoulder** er hat einen Bänderriß in der Schulter.

**light¹** [laɪt] *(vb: pret, ptp* **lit** *or* ~**ed)* **1** *n* (a) Licht *nt*. **at first** ~ bei Tagesanbruch; **to shed** *or* **throw** ~ **on sth** *(fig)* Licht in etw *(acc)* bringen; **to cast fresh** ~ **on sth** neues Licht auf etw *(acc)* werfen; **to stand in sb's** ~ *(lit)* jdm im Licht stehen; **in the cold** ~ **of day** *(fig)* bei Licht besehen; **this story shows him in a bad** ~ diese Geschichte wirft ein schlechtes Licht auf ihn; **it revealed him in a different** ~ es ließ ihn in einem anderen Licht erscheinen; **to see sth in a new** ~ etw mit anderen Augen betrachten; **in the** ~ **of** angesichts *(+gen)*; **to bring to** ~ ans Tageslicht bringen; **to come to** ~ ans Tageslicht kommen; **finally I saw the** ~ *(col)* endlich ging mir ein Licht auf *(col)*; *(morally)* endlich wurden mir die Augen geöffnet; **according to his** ~**s** nach bestem Wissen und Gewissen.

**(b)** *(single* ~*)* Licht *nt*; *(lamp)* Lampe *f*; *(fluorescent* ~*)* Neonröhre *f*. **(traffic)** ~**s** Ampel *f*; **the** ~**s** *(of a car)* die Beleuchtung.

**(c)** *(flame)* **have you a** ~? haben Sie Feuer?; **to set** ~ **to sth** etw anzünden.

**2** *adj (+er)* hell. **a** ~ **green dress** ein hellgrünes Kleid; **it is** ~ **now** es ist jetzt hell *or* Tag.

**3** *vt* **(a)** *(illuminate)* beleuchten; *lamp, light* anmachen. **to** ~ **the way for sb** jdm leuchten; *(fig)* jdm den Weg weisen. **(b)** *(set fire to)* anzünden; *fire also* anmachen.

**4** *vi (begin to burn)* brennen.

▶**light up 1** *vi* **(a)** *(be lit)* aufleuchten. **(b)** *(face)* sich erhellen; *(eyes)* aufleuchten. **2** *vt sep* **(a)** *(illuminate)* beleuchten; *(from inside)* erhellen *(with spotlights)* anstrahlen. **the square was all lit** ~ der Platz war hell erleuchtet. **(b)** *cigarette etc* anzünden.

**light²** **1** *adj (+er)* leicht; *taxes* niedrig; *punishment* milde. **to be a** ~ **eater** kein großer Esser sein; ~ **comedy** Lustspiel *nt*; ~ **music** Unterhaltungsmusik *f*; ~ **opera** Operette *f*; ~ **reading** Unterhaltungslektüre *f*; **as** ~ **as a feather** federleicht; **to be** ~ **on one's feet** sich leichtfüßig bewegen; **to make** ~ **of one's difficulties** seine Schwierigkeiten auf die leichte Schulter nehmen; **to make** ~ **work of** spielend fertigwerden mit. **2** *adv* **to travel** ~ mit leichtem Gepäck reisen.

**light:** ~ **bulb** *n* Glühbirne *f*; ~**-coloured** *(Brit) or* ~**-colored** *(US) adj* hell.

**lighten¹** ['laɪtn] **1** *vt* erhellen; *colour, hair* aufhellen; *gloom* aufheitern. **2** *vi* sich aufhellen.

**lighten²** **1** *vt load, (fig) heart* leichter machen. **to** ~ **sb's burden** jdn entlasten. **2** *vi (load)* leichter werden. **her heart** ~**ed** ihr wurde leichter ums Herz.

**lighter** ['laɪtə'] *n (cigarette* ~*)* Feuerzeug *nt*.

**light:** ~**-fingered** [ˌlaɪt'fɪŋgəd] *adj* langfingerig; ~ **fitting** *n (*~**bulb holder)** Fassung *f*; ~**-haired** *adj* hellhaarig; ~**-headed** *adj* benebelt *(col)*; *(dizzy also)* benommen; *(frivolous)* leichtfertig; ~**-hearted** *adj* unbeschwert; *chat* zwanglos; *reply* scherzhaft; *book* vergnüglich; ~**house** *n* Leuchtturm *m*; ~**house keeper** *n* Leuchtturmwärter *m*.

**lighting** ['laɪtɪŋ] *n* Beleuchtung *f*.

**lighting-up time** [ˌlaɪtɪŋ'ʌptaɪm] *n (Brit)* Zeitpunkt *m*, zu dem die Straßen- und Fahrzeugbeleuchtung eingeschaltet werden muß. **when is** ~? wann wird die Beleuchtung angemacht?

**lightly** ['laɪtlɪ] *adv* **(a)** *touch, rain, wounded* leicht; *tread* leise. **to sleep** ~ einen leichten Schlaf haben; **to get off** ~ glimpflich davonkommen. **(b)** *(casually)* *say* leichthin. **he spoke** ~ **of his illness** er nahm seine Krankheit auf die leichte Schulter; **to treat sth too** ~ etw nicht ernst genug nehmen; **a responsibility not to be** ~ **undertaken** eine Verantwortung, die man nicht unüberlegt auf sich nehmen sollte.

**light meter** *n* Belichtungsmesser *m*.

**lightness¹** ['laɪtnɪs] *n* Helligkeit *f*.

**lightness²** *n* **(a)** *(of weight)* geringes Gewicht; *(of task, step)* Leichtigkeit *f*; *(of punishment)* Milde *f*; *(of soil, cake)* Lockerheit *f*. **(b)** *(lack of seriousness)* Leichtfertigkeit *f*.

**lightning** ['laɪtnɪŋ] **1** *n* Blitz *m*. **as quick as** ~, **like (greased)** ~ wie der Blitz, wie ein geölter Blitz; ~ **conductor** *or (US)* **rod** Blitzableiter *m*. **2** *attr* blitzschnell, Blitz-. ~ **attack** Blitzangriff *m*; ~ **strike** *(Brit)* spontaner Streik.

**light:** ~ **pen** *n (Comp)* Lichtstift *or* -griffel *m*; ~**ship** *n* Feuerschiff *nt*; ~**weight 1** *adj* leicht; *(boxer)* Leichtgewichts-; *(fig)* schwach; **2** *n* Leichtgewicht *nt (also fig)*; *(boxer)* Leichtgewichtler *m*; ~**-year** *n* Lichtjahr *nt*.

**like¹** [laɪk] **1** adj **(a)** (similar) ähnlich. **(b)** (same) **of ~ origin** gleicher Herkunft.

**2** prep (similar to) ähnlich (+dat); (in comparisons) wie. **to be ~ sb** jdm ähnlich sein; **they are very ~ each other** sie sind sich sehr ähnlich; **who(m) is he ~?** wem sieht er ähnlich?; **what's he ~?** wie ist er?; **what's your new coat ~?** wie sieht dein neuer Mantel aus?; **she was ~ a sister to me** sie war für mich wie eine Schwester; **that's just ~ him!** das sieht ihm ähnlich!; **it's not ~ him** es ist nicht seine Art; **I never saw anything ~ it** so (et)was habe ich noch nie gesehen; **that's more ~ it!** so ist es schon besser!; **there's nothing ~ a nice cup of tea!** es geht nichts über eine gute Tasse Tee!; **the Americans are ~ that** so sind die Amerikaner; **do it ~ this** mach es so; **people ~ that** solche Leute; **it will cost something ~ £10** es wird so ungefähr £10 kosten; **that sounds ~ a good idea** das hört sich gut an; **~ mad** (col), **~ anything** (col) wie verrückt (col); **he thinks ~ us** er denkt wie wir.

**3** adv (col) **it's nothing ~ it** das ist nicht zu vergleichen; **as ~ as not** höchstwahrscheinlich.

**4** conj (strictly incorrect) **~ I said** wie gesagt.

**5** n (equal etc) **did you ever see the ~?** (col) hast du so was schon gesehen?; **and the ~, and such ~** und dergleichen; **I've met the ~s of you before** (col) solche wie dich kenne ich schon (col); **the ~s of us** unsereins sing.

**like²** **1** n usu pl **she tried to find out his ~s and dislikes** sie wollte herausbekommen, was er mochte und was nicht.

**2** vt **(a)** person mögen. **how do you ~ him?** wie gefällt er dir?; **I don't ~ him** ich mag ihn nicht; **he is well ~d here** er ist hier sehr beliebt.

**(b)** **I ~ black shoes** mir gefallen schwarze Schuhe; **I ~ it** das gefällt mir; **I ~ chocolate** ich mag Schokolade; **I ~ football** ich mag Fußball; (playing) ich spiele gerne Fußball; **I ~ this translation** ich finde diese Übersetzung gut; **how do you ~ your coffee?** wie trinken Sie Ihren Kaffee?; **how would you ~ a walk?** was hältst du von einem Spaziergang?; **well, I ~ that!** (col) das ist ein starkes Stück! (col); **to come** or **get to ~ sth** Gefallen an etw (dat) finden.

**(c)** (wish, wish for) **what would you ~?** was hätten or möchten Sie gern?; **would you ~ a drink?** möchten Sie etwas trinken?; **I should ~ more time** ich würde mir gerne noch etwas Zeit lassen; **they would have ~d to come** sie wären gern gekommen; **I should ~ to know why** ich wüßte gerne, warum; **I should ~ you to do it** ich möchte, daß du es tust; **I didn't ~ to disturb him** ich wollte ihn nicht stören.

**3** vi **as you ~** wie Sie wollen; **if you ~** wenn Sie wollen.

**lik(e)able** ['laɪkəbl] adj sympathisch.

**likelihood** ['laɪklɪhʊd] n Wahrscheinlichkeit f. **in all ~** aller Wahrscheinlichkeit nach; **there is no ~ of** **that** das ist nicht wahrscheinlich; **there is little ~ that ...** es ist kaum anzunehmen, daß ...

**likely** ['laɪklɪ] **1** adj (+er) **(a)** (probable) wahrscheinlich. **he is not ~ to come** es ist unwahrscheinlich, daß er kommt; **is it ~ that I would do that?** trauen Sie mir das zu?; **an incident ~ to cause trouble** ein Zwischenfall, der zu Schwierigkeiten führen kann; **a ~ explanation** eine wahrscheinliche Erklärung; (iro) wer's glaubt, wird selig! (col); **a ~ story!** (iro) das glaubst du doch (wohl) selber nicht! (col). **(b)** (col: suitable) **a ~ spot for a picnic** ein geeignetes Fleckchen für ein Picknick; **he is a ~ person for the job** er kommt für die Stelle in Frage. **2** adv **not ~!** (col) wohl kaum (col); **as ~ as not** höchstwahr-

scheinlich; **very ~ they've lost it** höchstwahrscheinlich haben sie es verloren.

**like-minded** ['laɪk'maɪndɪd] adj gleichgesinnt.

**liken** ['laɪkən] vt vergleichen (to mit).

**likeness** ['laɪknɪs] n (resemblance) Ähnlichkeit f; (portrait) Bild(nis) nt. **in the ~ of** in der Gestalt (+gen).

**likewise** ['laɪkwaɪz] adv ebenso. **he did ~** er machte es ebenso; **have a nice weekend — ~** schönes Wochenende! — danke gleichfalls!

**liking** ['laɪkɪŋ] n **(a)** (for particular person) Zuneigung f; (for types) Vorliebe f. **to have a ~ for sb** Zuneigung für jdn empfinden; **she took an immediate ~ to him** er war ihr gleich sympathisch. **(b)** (for thing) Vorliebe f. **to take a ~ to sth** Gefallen an etw (dat) finden; **to be to sb's ~** nach jds Geschmack m sein.

**lilac** ['laɪlək] **1** n **(a)** (plant) Flieder m. **(b)** (colour) Lila nt. **2** adj fliederfarben, lila.

**lilt** [lɪlt] n (of song) munterer Rhythmus; (of voice) singender Tonfall.

**lilting** ['lɪltɪŋ] adj tune etc beschwingt.

**lily** ['lɪlɪ] n Lilie f; (water ~) Seerose f. **~ of the valley** Maiglöckchen nt.

**limb** [lɪm] n (Anat) Glied nt. **~s** pl Gliedmaßen pl; **life and ~** Leib und Leben; **to be out on a ~** (fig) (ganz) allein (da)stehen.

▶**limber up** [ˌlɪmbər'ʌp] vi Lockerungsübungen machen; (fig) sich vorbereiten.

**limbo** ['lɪmbəʊ] n (fig) Übergangs- or Zwischenstadium nt. **our plans are in ~** unsere Pläne sind auf Eis gelegt worden; **to disappear into ~** spurlos verschwinden.

**lime¹** [laɪm] n (Geol) Kalk m.

**lime²** n (Bot: linden, also ~ tree) Linde(nbaum m) f.

**lime³** **1** n (Bot) (citrus fruit) Limone f; (tree) Limonenbaum m. **~ juice** Limonensaft m. **2** adj (also ~ green)** hellgrün.

**limelight** ['laɪmlaɪt] n Rampenlicht nt. **to be in the ~** im Rampenlicht stehen.

**limerick** ['lɪmərɪk] n Limerick m.

**limestone** ['laɪmstəʊn] n Kalkstein m.

**limey** ['laɪmɪ] n (US col) Engländer m.

**limit** ['lɪmɪt] **1** n **(a)** (limitation) Beschränkung f; (speed ~) Tempolimit nt; (Comm) Limit nt. **to put a ~ on sth, to set a ~ to** or **on sth** etw beschränken; **there's a ~!** alles hat seine Grenzen!; **there is a ~ to what one person can do** ein Mensch kann nur so viel tun und nicht mehr; **there is no ~ to his stupidity** seine Dummheit kennt keine Grenzen; **there's a ~ to the amount of money we can spend** unseren Ausgaben sind Grenzen gesetzt; **it is true within ~s** es ist bis zu einem gewissen Grade richtig; **without ~s** unbegrenzt; **to know no ~s** keine Grenzen kennen; **over the ~** zuviel; (in time) zu lange; **he was driving over the ~** er hat das Tempolimit überschritten; (after drinking) er hat sich mit zuviel Promille ans Steuer gesetzt.

**(b)** (col) **that's the ~!** das ist die Höhe! (col); **that child is the ~!** dieses Kind ist eine Zumutung! (col).

**2** vt beschränken; freedom, spending einschränken; imagination hemmen. **to ~ sth to sth** etw auf etw (acc) beschränken; **are you ~ed for time?** ist Ihre Zeit begrenzt?

**limitation** [ˌlɪmɪ'teɪʃən] n Beschränkung f; (of freedom, spending) Einschränkung f; (disadvantage) Handikap nt. **to have/know one's ~s** seine Grenzen haben/kennen.

**limited** ['lɪmɪtɪd] adj begrenzt. **in a ~ sense** in gewissem Maße; **~ company** (Brit) Gesellschaft f mit beschränkter Haftung.

**limitless** ['lɪmɪtlɪs] *adj* grenzenlos.
**limo** ['lɪməʊ] *(col)*, **limousine** ['lɪməziːn] *n* Limousine *f*.
**limp¹** [lɪmp] **1** *n* Hinken *nt*. **to walk with a ~** hinken, humpeln. **2** *vi* hinken. **the ship ~ed into port** das Schiff kam mit Müh und Not in den Hafen.
**limp²** *adj (+er)* schlapp, schlaff; *flowers* welk; *material, cloth* weich. **let your body go ~** entspannen Sie alle Muskeln.
**limpet** ['lɪmpɪt] *n* Napfschnecke *f*. **to stick to sb like a ~** *(col)* wie eine Klette an jdm hängen.
**limpid** ['lɪmpɪd] *adj* klar; *liquid also* durchsichtig.
**limply** ['lɪmplɪ] *adv* schlapp, schlaff.
**linchpin** ['lɪntʃpɪn] *n* Achs(en)nagel *m*; *(fig)* Stütze *f*. **she is the ~ of the project** mit ihr steht und fällt das Projekt.
**Lincs** *(Brit)* = **Lincolnshire**.
**linden** ['lɪndən] *n (also ~ tree)* Linde(nbaum *m*) *f*.
**line¹** [laɪn] **1** *n* **(a)** *(rope etc, fishing ~)* Leine *f*; *(on tennis court etc, on paper)* Linie *f*; *(on face)* Falte *f*. **the ~ between right and wrong** die Grenze zwischen Recht und Unrecht; **to have good ~s** formschön sein; **the ship's graceful ~s** die schnittigen Linien des Schiffes.
**(b)** *(row)* Reihe *f*; *(of people, cars also)* Schlange *f*; *(of hills)* Kette *f*; *(US: queue)* Schlange *f*. **in (a) ~** in einer Reihe; **in a straight ~** geradlinig; **John is next in ~ for promotion** John ist als nächster mit der Beförderung an der Reihe; **he was descended from a long ~ of farmers** er stammte aus einem alten Bauerngeschlecht; **who is fourth in ~ to the throne?** wer steht an vierter Stelle der Thronfolge?; **to be in/out of ~** *(buildings etc)* in einer Flucht/versetzt stehen; **to be out of ~ with sb/sth** *(fig)* mit jdm/etw nicht übereinstimmen; **to bring sth into ~ with sth** *(fig)* etw mit etw in Einklang bringen; **he refused to fall into ~ with the new proposals** er weigerte sich, mit den neuen Vorschlägen konform zu gehen; **to step out of ~** *(fig)* aus der Reihe tanzen; **to stand in ~** *(US)* Schlange stehen.
**(c)** *(air~, shipping ~)* Linie *f*.
**(d)** *(Rail)* Strecke *f*. **~s** *pl* Gleise *pl*; **to reach the end of the ~** *(fig)* am Ende sein.
**(e)** *(Telec: cable)* Leitung *f*. **the firm has 52 ~s** die Firma hat 52 Anschlüsse; **this is a very bad ~** die Verbindung ist sehr schlecht; **the ~ went dead** die Leitung war auf einmal tot; **to be on the ~ to sb** mit jdm telefonieren; **hold the ~** bleiben Sie am Apparat!; **can I have an outside ~?** geben Sie mir bitte ein Amt.
**(f)** *(Comp)* **on ~** on line, angeschlossen.
**(g)** *(written)* Zeile *f*. **~s** *(Sch)* Strafarbeit *f*; **~s** *(Theat)* Text *m*; **to drop sb a ~** jdm ein paar Zeilen schreiben; **to read between the ~s** zwischen den Zeilen lesen.
**(h)** *(direction, course)* **~ of argument** Argumentation *f*; **~ of attack** *(Mil)* Angriffslinie *f*; *(fig)* Taktik *f*; **enemy ~s** *(Mil)* feindliche Stellungen *pl*; **to be on the right ~s** *(fig)* auf dem richtigen Weg sein, richtig liegen *(col)*; **we must take a firm** *or* **strong ~ with these people** wir müssen diesen Leuten gegenüber sehr bestimmt auftreten; **to lay it on the ~** *(col)* die Karten auf den Tisch legen *(col)*; **to lay it on the ~ to sb** jdm reinen Wein einschenken *(col)*; **to put one's life/job** *etc* **on the ~** *(col)* sein Leben/seine Stelle *etc* riskieren; **the ~ of least resistance** der Weg des geringsten Widerstandes; **he took the ~ that ...** er vertrat den Standpunkt, daß ...; **to be along the ~s of ...** ungefähr so etwas wie ... sein; **I was thinking along the same ~s** ich hatte etwas Ähnliches gedacht; **it's all in the ~ of duty** das ge-

hört zu meinen/seinen *etc* Pflichten.
**(i)** *(fig: business)* Branche *f*. **what ~ is he in?**, **what's his ~?** was ist er von Beruf?; **that's not in my ~** das liegt mir nicht.
**(j)** *(Comm: stock article)* Artikel *m*; *(model)* Modell *nt*. **we have a new ~ in torches** wir führen neuartige Taschenlampen.
**2** *vt* **(a)** *(cross with ~s)* linieren. **worry had ~d his face** sein Gesicht war von Sorgen gezeichnet. **(b)** *streets* säumen. **a road ~d with trees** eine von Bäumen gesäumte Straße; **the streets were ~d with cheering crowds** eine jubelnde Menge säumte die Straßen.
▶**line up 1** *vi (stand in line)* sich aufstellen; *(queue)* sich anstellen. **2** *vt sep* **(a)** *troops, prisoners* antreten lassen; *boxes, books etc* in einer Reihe aufstellen. **(b)** *(prepare, arrange) entertainment* sorgen für; *speakers* verpflichten; *support* mobilisieren. **have you anything special ~d ~ for today?** haben Sie für heute etwas Besonderes auf dem Programm?; **have you anyone ~d ~ for the job?** haben Sie schon jemanden für die Stelle im Sinn?
**line²** *vt clothes* füttern; *box, walls, furnace etc* auskleiden. **to ~ one's own pockets** *(fig)* in die eigene Tasche arbeiten.
**lineage** ['lɪnɪɪdʒ] *n (descent)* Abstammung *f*.
**linear** ['lɪnɪəʳ] *adj motion* linear; *measure* Längen-.
**line closure** *n (Rail)* Streckenstillegung *f*.
**lined** [laɪnd] *adj face etc (of old people)* faltig; *(through worry etc)* gezeichnet; *paper* liniert.
**line: ~ drawing** *n* Zeichnung *f*; **~ feed** *n (Comp)* Zeilenvorschub *m*; **~ judge** *n (Tennis)* Linienrichter(in *f*) *m*.
**linen** ['lɪnɪn] **1** *n* Leinen *nt*; *(table ~)* Tischwäsche *f*; *(sheets, garments etc)* Wäsche *f*. **~ cupboard** Wäscheschrank *m*. **2** *adj* Leinen-.
**line printer** *n* Zeilendrucker *m*.
**liner** ['laɪnəʳ] *n (ship)* Passagierschiff *nt*.
**linesman** ['laɪnzmən], *(US also)* **lineman** ['laɪnmən] *n, pl* **-men** [-mən] *(Sport)* Linienrichter *m*; *(Rail)* Streckenwärter *m*.
**line-up** ['laɪnʌp] *n (Sport)* Aufstellung *f*; *(cast)* Besetzung *f*; *(US: queue)* Schlange *f*; *(also* **police ~)** Gegenüberstellung *f*.
**linger** ['lɪŋgəʳ] *vi (also ~ on)* (zurück)bleiben; *(delay)* sich aufhalten; *(stand around)* herumstehen; *(in dying)* zwischen Leben und Tod schweben; *(custom)* sich halten; *(doubts)* zurückbleiben; *(feeling, pain)* anhalten; *(memory)* bleiben; *(chords)* nachklingen. **to ~ on a subject** bei einem Thema verweilen; **to ~ over a meal** sich bei einer Mahlzeit lange aufhalten.
**lingerie** ['lænʒəriː] *n* (Damen)unterwäsche *f*.
**lingering** ['lɪŋgərɪŋ] *adj* lang; *death* langsam; *illness* langwierig; *doubt* verbleibend; *taste* anhaltend.
**lingo** ['lɪŋgəʊ] *n (col)* Sprache *f*.
**linguist** ['lɪŋgwɪst] *n (speaker of languages)* Sprachkundige(r) *mf*; *(specialist in linguistics)* Linguist(in *f*) *m*. **I'm no ~** ich bin nicht sprachbegabt.
**linguistic** [lɪŋ'gwɪstɪk] *adj* **(a)** sprachlich; *competence* Sprach-. **(b)** *(of linguistics)* linguistisch, sprachwissenschaftlich.
**linguistically** [lɪŋ'gwɪstɪkəlɪ] *adv see adj* **(a)** sprachlich. **~ gifted** sprachbegabt. **(b)** linguistisch.
**linguistics** [lɪŋ'gwɪstɪks] *n sing* Linguistik *f*.
**lining** ['laɪnɪŋ] *n (of clothes etc)* Futter *nt*; *(of walls, container, furnace etc)* Auskleidung *f*; *(of brake)* (Brems)belag *m*.
**link** [lɪŋk] **1** *n (of chain, fig)* Glied *nt*; *(person)* Verbindungsperson *f*. **he broke all his ~s with his family** er brach alle Beziehungen zu seiner Familie ab; **cultural ~s** kulturelle Beziehungen *pl*. **2** *vt* verbin-

den; *spaceships also* aneinanderkoppeln. **to ~ arms** sich unterhaken *(with bei)*; **do you think these two murders are ~ed?** glauben Sie, daß zwischen den beiden Morden eine Verbindung besteht? **3** *vi* **to ~ (together)** *(parts of story)* sich zusammenfügen lassen; *(railway lines)* zusammenlaufen.

►**link up** *vi* zusammenkommen; *(people)* sich zusammentun; *(facts)* übereinstimmen; *(companies)* sich zusammenschließen; *(spaceships)* ein Kopplungsmanöver durchführen.

**linkage** ['lɪŋkɪdʒ] *n (system of rods)* Gestänge *nt.*

**link man** *n, pl ~* **men** [-men] Verbindungsmann *m; (Rad, TV)* Moderator *m.*

**links** [lɪŋks] *npl (golf course)* Golfplatz *m.*

**link-up** ['lɪŋkʌp] *n (Telec, general)* Verbindung *f; (of spaceships)* Kopplung(smanöver *nt) f.*

**lino** ['laɪnəʊ] *n (Brit)* Linoleum *nt.*

**linocut** ['laɪnəʊkʌt] *n* Linolschnitt *m.*

**linoleum** [lɪ'nəʊlɪəm] *n* Linoleum *nt.*

**linseed** ['lɪnsiːd] *n* Leinsamen *m. ~* **oil** Leinöl *n.*

**lint** [lɪnt] *n* Mull *m.*

**lintel** ['lɪntl] *n (Archit)* Sturz *m.*

**lion** ['laɪən] *n* Löwe *m.* **the ~'s share** der Löwenanteil.

**lioness** ['laɪənɪs] *n* Löwin *f.*

**lip** [lɪp] *n* **(a)** *(Anat)* Lippe *f; (of jug)* Schnabel *m; (of cup)* Rand *m.* **to keep a stiff upper ~** die Haltung bewahren. **(b)** *(col: cheek)* Frechheit(en *pl) f.* **to give sb a lot of ~** jdm gegenüber eine (freche) Lippe riskieren *(col).*

**liposuction** ['lɪpəʊˌsʌkʃən] *n* Liposuktion *f,* Fettabsaugen *nt.*

**lip: ~read** *vti* von den Lippen ablesen; *~* **service** *n* **to pay ~ service to an idea** ein Lippenbekenntnis zu einer Idee ablegen; **~stick** *n* Lippenstift *m.*

**liquefy** ['lɪkwɪfaɪ] **1** *vt* verflüssigen. **2** *vi* sich verflüssigen.

**liqueur** [lɪ'kjʊəʳ] *n* Likör *m.*

**liquid** ['lɪkwɪd] **1** *adj* flüssig *(also Comm).* **2** *n* Flüssigkeit *f.*

**liquidate** ['lɪkwɪdeɪt] *vt* **(a)** *(Comm)* liquidieren; *assets also* flüssig machen; *company also* auflösen. **(b)** *enemy etc* liquidieren.

**liquidation** [ˌlɪkwɪ'deɪʃən] *n see vt* **(a)** Liquidation *f; (of company also)* Auflösung *f.* **to go into ~** in Liquidation gehen. **(b)** Liquidierung *f.*

**liquid crystal** *n* Flüssigkristall *nt.*

**liquidity** [lɪ'kwɪdɪtɪ] *n* Liquidität *f.*

**liquidize** ['lɪkwɪdaɪz] *vt* (im Mixer) pürieren.

**liquidizer** ['lɪkwɪdaɪzəʳ] *n* Mixer *m.*

**liquor** ['lɪkəʳ] *n (whisky, brandy etc)* Spirituosen *pl; (alcohol)* Alkohol *m. ~* **store** *(US)* ≈ Wein- und Spirituosengeschäft *nt.*

**liquorice, licorice** ['lɪkərɪs] *n* Lakritze *f.*

**Lisbon** ['lɪzbən] *n* Lissabon *nt.*

**lisp** [lɪsp] **1** *n* Lispeln *nt.* **to speak with a ~** lispeln. **2** *vti* lispeln.

**lissom** ['lɪsəm] *adj* geschmeidig; *person* gelenkig.

**list¹** [lɪst] **1** *n* Liste *f; (shopping ~)* Einkaufszettel *m.* **it's not on the ~** es steht nicht auf der Liste; **it's on my ~ for tomorrow** es steht für morgen auf meinem Programm. **2** *vt* notieren; *item* in die Liste aufnehmen. **it is not ~ed** es ist nicht aufgeführt; **~ed building** Gebäude *nt* unter Denkmalschutz; **~ed company** *(Fin)* börsennotierte Firma.

**list²** *(Naut)* **1** *n* Schlagseite *f.* **2** *vi* Schlagseite haben.

**listen** ['lɪsn] *vi* **(a)** hören *(to sth* etw *acc).* **to ~ to the radio** Radio hören; **to ~ for sth** auf etw *(acc)* horchen; **to ~ for sb** hören, ob jd kommt; **OK, I'm ~ing** ich höre zu. **(b)** *(heed)* zuhören. **~ to me!** hör mir

zu!; **~, I know what we'll do** hör mal, ich weiß, was wir machen; **don't ~ to him** hör nicht auf ihn; **he wouldn't ~** er wollte nicht hören.

►**listen in** *vi* (Radio) hören; *(secretly)* mithören *(on sth* etw *acc).* **to ~ ~ to sth** etw im Radio hören.

**listener** ['lɪsnəʳ] *n* Zuhörer(in *f) m; (Rad)* Hörer(in *f) m.* **to be a good ~** gut zuhören können.

**listing** ['lɪstɪŋ] *n* Auflistung *f.*

**listless** ['lɪstlɪs] *adj* lustlos; *patient* teilnahmslos.

**list price** *n* Listenpreis *m.*

**list renting** *n* Vermietung *f* von Adressenlisten.

**lists** [lɪsts] *npl (Hist)* Schranken *pl.* **to enter the ~** *(fig)* zum Kampf antreten.

**lit** [lɪt] *pret, ptp of* **light¹.**

**litany** ['lɪtənɪ] *n* Litanei *f.*

**liter** *n (US)* = **litre.**

**literacy** ['lɪtərəsɪ] *n* Fähigkeit *f,* lesen und schreiben zu können. **~ campaign** Alphabetisierungskampagne *f.*

**literal** ['lɪtərəl] *adj translation* wörtlich; *meaning also* eigentlich. **it was a ~ disaster** es war im wahrsten Sinne des Wortes eine Katastrophe.

**literally** ['lɪtərəlɪ] *adv (word for word, exactly)* (wort)wörtlich; *(really)* buchstäblich, wirklich. **to take sth ~** etw wörtlich nehmen; **he was ~ a giant** er war im wahrsten Sinne des Wortes ein Riese.

**literary** ['lɪtərərɪ] *adj* literarisch; *agent, critic, criticism, history* Literatur-. **a ~ man** ein Literaturkenner *m; (author)* ein Literat *m.*

**literate** ['lɪtərɪt] *adj* **to be ~** lesen und schreiben können; *(well-educated)* gebildet sein.

**literature** ['lɪtərɪtʃəʳ] *n* Literatur *f; (col: brochures etc)* Informationsmaterial *nt.*

**lithe** [laɪð] *adj (+er)* geschmeidig.

**lithograph** ['lɪθəʊɡrɑːf] *n* Lithographie *f,* Steindruck *m.*

**lithography** [lɪ'θɒɡrəfɪ] *n* Lithographie *f.*

**Lithuania** [ˌlɪθjʊ'eɪnɪə] *n* Litauen *nt.*

**Lithuanian** [ˌlɪθjʊ'eɪnɪən] **1** *adj* litauisch. **2** *n* **(a)** Litauer(in *f) m.* **(b)** *(language)* Litauisch *nt.*

**litigation** [ˌlɪtɪ'ɡeɪʃən] *n* Prozeß, Rechtsstreit *m.*

**litmus** ['lɪtməs] *n ~* **paper** Lackmuspapier *nt.*

**litre,** *(US)* **liter** ['liːtəʳ] *n* Liter *m* or *nt.*

**litter** ['lɪtəʳ] **1** *n* **(a)** Abfälle *pl; (papers, wrappings)* Papier *nt.* **(b)** *(Zool)* Wurf *m; (bedding for animals)* Streu *f,* Stroh *nt; (cat ~)* Katzenstreu *f.* **2** *vt* **to be ~ed with sth** *(lit, fig)* mit etw übersät sein.

**litter: ~ basket** *n* Abfallkorb *m; ~* **bin** *n* Abfalleimer *m; ~* **bug** *(col), ~* **lout** *(col) n* Schmutzfink *m (col).*

**little** ['lɪtl] **1** *adj* klein. **a ~ house** ein Häuschen *nt;* **the ~ ones** die Kleinen *pl;* **a nice ~ profit** ein hübscher Gewinn; **a ~ while ago** vor kurzem; **it's only a ~ while till I ...** es ist nicht mehr lange, bis ich ...; **in a ~ while** bald.

**2** *adv, n* **(a)** wenig. **of ~ importance** von geringer Bedeutung; **~ better than** kaum besser als; **~ more than a month ago** vor kaum einem Monat; **~ short of** fast schon, beinahe; **~ did I think that ...** ich hätte kaum gedacht, daß ...; **I walk as ~ as possible** ich laufe so wenig wie möglich; **every ~ helps** wir sind froh um jede Kleinigkeit; **I see very ~ of her nowadays** ich sehe sie in letzter Zeit sehr selten; **there was ~ we could do** wir konnten nicht viel tun; **she did what ~ she could** sie tat das Wenige, das sie tun konnte; **~ by ~** nach und nach; **to make ~ of sth** etw herunterspielen; **I could make ~ of this book** ich konnte mit diesem Buch nicht viel anfangen.

**(b) a ~** ein wenig, ein bißchen; **a ~ better** ein bißchen besser; **with a ~ effort** mit etwas Mühe; **a ~ after five** kurz nach fünf; **we walked on for a ~** wir liefen noch ein bißchen weiter; **after a ~** nach einer Weile.

**liturgical** [lɪ'tɜːdʒɪkəl] *adj* liturgisch.

**liturgy** ['lɪtədʒɪ] *n* Liturgie *f*.

**live¹** [lɪv] **1** *vt life* führen. **to ~ life to the full** sein Leben auskosten.

**2** *vi* **(a)** leben. **will he ~, doctor?** wird er (über)leben, Herr Doktor?; **don't worry, you'll ~,** it's only a broken ankle reg dich nicht auf, du stirbst schon nicht, du hast nur einen gebrochenen Knöchel; **long ~ Queen Anne!** lang lebe Königin Anne!; **we ~ and learn** man lernt nie aus; **to ~ and let ~** leben und leben lassen; **to ~ like a king** wie Gott in Frankreich leben; **to ~ to a ripe old age** ein hohes Alter erreichen; **his name will ~ for ever** sein Ruhm wird nie vergehen; **his poetry will ~ for ever** seine Dichtung ist unvergänglich; **he ~d through two wars** er hat zwei Kriege miterlebt; **to ~ beyond one's income** über seine Verhältnisse leben; **you'll ~ to regret it** das wirst du noch bereuen!; **you'll just have to ~ with it** du mußt eben damit leben; **the other athletes couldn't ~ with him** die anderen Läufer konnten mit ihm nicht mithalten.

**(b)** *(reside)* wohnen; *(in town etc)* leben. **he ~s at 19 West Avenue** er wohnt in der West Avenue Nr.19; **he ~s with his parents** er wohnt bei seinen Eltern.

▶**live down** *vt sep humiliation* hinwegkommen über *(+acc)*, verwinden; *(actively) scandal* Gras wachsen lassen über *(+acc)*. **he'll never ~ it ~** das wird ihm ewig anhängen.

▶**live in** *vi (student)* im Wohnheim/College wohnen.

▶**live off** *vi +prep obj* **to ~ ~ one's interest** von seinen Zinsen leben; **to ~ ~ one's relations** auf Kosten seiner Verwandten leben.

▶**live on 1** *vi (continue to live)* weiterleben. **2** *vi +prep obj* leben von. **to ~ ~ eggs** sich von Eiern ernähren; **he doesn't earn enough to ~ ~** er verdient nicht genug, um davon zu leben.

▶**live out 1** *vi (student)* außerhalb (des Wohnheims/Colleges) wohnen. **2** *vt sep life* verbringen; *winter* überleben. **to ~ ~ one's days** seinen Lebensabend verbringen.

▶**live together** *vi (cohabit)* zusammenleben; *(share a flat etc)* zusammenwohnen.

▶**live up** *vt always separate:* **to ~ it ~** *(col)* sich ausleben; *(extravagantly)* in Saus und Braus leben *(col)*.

▶**live up to** *vi +prep obj* **the holidays ~d ~ ~ our expectations** der Urlaub hielt, was wir uns *(dat)* davon versprochen hatten; **to ~ ~ ~ one's reputation** seinem Ruf gerecht werden; **it didn't ~ ~ ~ our hopes** es entsprach nicht dem, was wir uns *(dat)* erhofft hatten; **he's got a lot to ~ ~ ~** in ihn werden große Erwartungen gesetzt.

**live²** [laɪv] **1** *adj* **(a)** *(alive)* lebend; *issue* aktuell. **a real ~ duke** ein echter Herzog. **(b)** *(having power or energy)* *coal* glühend; *match* ungebraucht; *cartridge, shell* scharf; *(Elec)* stromführend; *fence* geladen. **"danger, ~ wires!"** *"Vorsicht Hochspannung!"*; **she's a real ~ wire** *(fig)* sie ist ein richtiges Energiebündel. **(c)** *(Rad, TV)* pred live. **a ~ programme** eine Livesendung. **2** *adv (Rad, TV)* live.

**livelihood** ['laɪvlɪhʊd] *n* Lebensunterhalt *m*. **to earn a ~** sich *(dat)* seinen Lebensunterhalt verdienen.

**liveliness** ['laɪvlɪnɪs] *n see adj* Lebhaftigkeit *f*; Lebendigkeit *f*; Dynamik *f*; Aufgewecktheit *f*.

**lively** ['laɪvlɪ] *adj (+er)* lebhaft; *scene, account* lebendig; *campaign* dynamisch; *pace* flott; *mind* aufge-

weckt. **things are getting ~** es geht hoch her *(col)*; **look ~!** mach schnell!, ein bißchen dalli! *(col)*.

▶**liven up** ['laɪvən'ʌp] **1** *vt sep* beleben, Leben bringen in *(+acc) (col)*. **2** *vi* in Schwung kommen; *(person)* aufleben.

**liver** ['lɪvəʳ] *n (Anat, Cook)* Leber *f*. **~ sausage** Leberwurst *f*.

**liverish** ['lɪvərɪʃ] *adj (bad-tempered)* mürrisch. **to be ~** etwas mit der Leber haben; **I felt a bit ~ after the party** mir ging es nach der Party ziemlich mies *(col)*.

**livery** ['lɪvərɪ] *n* Livree *f*; *(fig liter)* Kleid *nt*.

**lives** [laɪvz] *pl of* **life**.

**livestock** ['laɪvstɒk] *n* Vieh *nt*.

**livid** ['lɪvɪd] *adj* **(a)** *(col)* fuchsteufelswild *(col)*. **he was ~ with us** er hatte eine Stinkwut auf uns *(col)*. **(b)** *(of colour)* bleifarben.

**living** ['lɪvɪŋ] **1** *adj* lebend; *example, faith* lebendig. **a ~ creature** ein Lebewesen *nt*; **(with)in ~ memory** seit Menschengedenken; **he is ~ proof of ...** er ist der lebende Beweis für ... **2** *n* **(a)** **the ~** *pl* die Lebenden *pl*. **(b)** *(livelihood)* Lebensunterhalt *m*. **to earn** *or* **make a ~** sich *(dat)* seinen Lebensunterhalt verdienen; **he sells brushes for a ~** er verkauft Bürsten, um sich *(dat)* seinen Lebensunterhalt zu verdienen; **what do you do for a ~?** was machen Sie beruflich?; **to work for one's ~** sich seinen Lebensunterhalt selbst verdienen.

**living: ~ conditions** *npl* Wohnverhältnisse *pl*; **~ room** *n* Wohnzimmer *nt*; **~ wage** *n* ausreichender Lohn.

**lizard** ['lɪzəd] *n* Eidechse *f*.

**LMT** *(US)* = **Local Mean Time** Ortszeit *f*.

**lo** [ləʊ] *interj* **~ and behold!** siehe da!

**load** [ləʊd] **1** *n* **(a)** *(sth carried, burden)* Last *f*; *(cargo)* Ladung *f*; *(on axle etc, fig)* Belastung *f*; *(Elec)* Spannung *f*. **a train~ of passengers** ein Zug voll Reisender; *(work)* **~** (Arbeits)belastung *f*; **that's a ~ off my mind!** da fällt mir ein Stein vom Herzen!

**(b)** *(col usages)* **~s of, a ~ of** jede Menge *(col)*; **it's a ~ of old rubbish** das ist alles Quatsch! *(col)*; *(book)* das ist alles Mist! *(col)*; **get a ~ of this!** *(listen)* hör dir das mal an!; *(look)* guck dir das mal an! *(col)*.

**2** *vt* **(a)** *goods, software* laden; *lorry etc, (burden: also ~ down)* beladen. **the ship was ~ed with bananas** das Schiff hatte Bananen geladen. **(b)** *gun* laden; *dice* präparieren. **to ~ a camera** einen Film (in einen Fotoapparat) einlegen. **(c)** *(fig)* überhäufen. **to ~ sb with honours** jdn mit Ehrungen überschütten; **we're ~ed (down) with debts** wir stecken bis zum Hals in Schulden; **the dice were ~ed against him** *(fig)* er hatte von vornherein wenig Chancen.

**3** *vi* laden. **~ing bay** Ladeplatz *m*.

▶**load up 1** *vi* aufladen. **2** *vt sep lorry* beladen; *goods* aufladen.

**loaded** ['ləʊdɪd] *adj* beladen; *dice* präpariert; *camera* mit eingelegtem Film; *gun* geladen. **a ~ question** eine Fangfrage; **he's ~** *(col: rich)* er ist steinreich *(col)*.

**loaf** [ləʊf] *n, pl* **loaves** Brot *nt*; *(unsliced)* (Brot)laib *m*. **a ~ of bread** ein (Laib) Brot; **half a ~ is better than none** *(Prov)* (wenig ist) besser als gar nichts; **use your ~!** *(col)* streng deinen Grips an! *(col)*.

▶**loaf about** *or* **around** *vi (col)* gammeln *(col)*; *(laze)* faulenzen.

**loam** [ləʊm] *n* Lehmerde *f*.

**loan** [ləʊn] **1** *n (thing lent)* Leihgabe *f*; *(from bank etc)* Kredit *m*, Darlehen *nt*; *(public ~)* Anleihe *f*. **I asked for the ~ of the bicycle** ich bat darum, das

Fahrrad ausleihen zu dürfen; **he gave me the ~ of his bicycle** er hat mir sein Fahrrad geliehen; **it's on ~** es ist geliehen; *(in museum)* es ist eine Leihgabe; *(out on ~)* es ist verliehen. **2** *vt* leihen *(to sb* jdm*)*.

**loan:** **~ account** *n* Darlehenskonto *nt*; **~ capital** *n* Anleihekapital *nt*.

**loath** [ləʊθ] *adj* **to be ~ to do sth** etw ungern tun.

**loathe** [ləʊð] *vt thing, person* verabscheuen; *jazz etc* nicht ausstehen können. **I ~ doing it** *(in general)* ich mache das überhaupt nicht gern; *(on particular occasion)* es ist mir zuwider, das zu tun.

**loathing** ['ləʊðɪŋ] *n* Abscheu *m*.

**loathsome** ['ləʊðsəm] *adj thing, person* abscheulich, widerlich; *task* verhaßt.

**loaves** [ləʊvz] *pl of* **loaf**.

**lob** [lɒb] **1** *n (Tennis)* Lob *m*. **2** *vt ball* lobben. **to ~ sth over to sb** jdm etw zuwerfen.

**lobby** ['lɒbɪ] **1** *n (entrance hall)* Eingangshalle *f*; *(place in Parliament)* Lobby *f*; *(Pol)* Interessenverband *m*. **2** *vt* **to ~ one's MP** seinen Abgeordneten zu beeinflussen suchen. **3** *vi* **they are ~ing for this reform** die Lobbyisten versuchen, diese Reform durchzubringen.

**lobbyist** ['lɒbɪɪst] *n* Lobbyist *m*.

**lobe** [ləʊb] *n (of ear)* Ohrläppchen *nt*.

**lobster** ['lɒbstəʳ] *n* Hummer *m*. **~ pot** Hummerkorb *m*.

**local** ['ləʊkəl] **1** *adj* Orts-; *(in this area)* hiesig; *(in that area)* dortig; *radio station* Regional-; *newspaper* Lokal-; *train, bus* Nahverkehrs-; *politician, elections* Kommunal-. **he's a ~ man** er ist von hier *(col)*; **~ anaesthetic** örtliche Betäubung; **~ authorities** Kommunalbehörden *pl*; *(council)* Stadt-/Gemeinde-/Kreisverwaltung *f*; **~ branch** Zweigstelle *f*; **~ call** Ortsgespräch *nt*; **~ government** die Kommunalverwaltung; **the ~ shops** die Geschäfte am Ort. **2** *n* **(a)** *(Brit: pub)* **the ~** das Stammlokal; *(in village)* die Dorfkneipe *(col)*. **(b)** *(born in)* Einheimische(r) *mf*; *(living in)* Einwohner(in *f*) *m*. **the ~s** die Ortsansässigen *pl*.

**locality** [ləʊ'kælɪtɪ] *n* Gegend *f*. **in your ~** bei dir in der Nähe.

**localize** ['ləʊkəlaɪz] *vt* **(a)** *(detect)* lokalisieren. **(b)** **~d** *(restricted)* örtlich begrenzt.

**locally** ['ləʊkəlɪ] *adv* am Ort. **houses are dear ~** Häuser sind hier teuer; **do you live ~?** wohnen Sie hier in der Nähe?

**locate** [ləʊ'keɪt] *vt* **(a)** *(position)* legen. **to be ~d at** *or* **in** sich befinden in *(+dat)*; **the hotel is centrally ~d** das Hotel liegt zentral. **(b)** *(find)* ausfindig machen; *submarine* orten. **(c)** *(Tech: hold)* (fest)halten.

**location** [ləʊ'keɪʃən] *n* **(a)** *(position, site)* Lage *f*; *(of ship)* Position *f*. **this would be an ideal ~ for the airport/company** das wäre ein ideales Gelände für den Flughafen/ein idealer Standort für die Firma. **(b)** *(finding)* Auffinden *nt*; *(of tumour)* Lokalisierung *f*; *(of star, ship)* Ortung *f*. **(c)** *(Film)* Drehort *m*. **he's on ~ in Mexico** er ist bei Außenaufnahmen in Mexiko; **~ work** *or* **shots** Außenaufnahmen *pl*.

**loch** [lɒx] *n (Scot)* See *m*; *(sea ~)* Meeresarm *m*.

**lock¹** [lɒk] *n (of hair)* Locke *f*.

**lock²** **1** *n* **(a)** *(on door, box, gun)* Schloß *nt*. **to put sb/sth under ~ and key** jdn hinter Schloß und Riegel bringen/etw wegschließen; **he offered me the house ~, stock and barrel** er bot mir das Haus mit allem Drum und Dran an *(col)*; **they rejected the idea ~, stock and barrel** sie lehnten die Idee in Bausch und Bogen ab. **(b)** *(canal ~)* Schleuse *f*. **(c)** *(Aut)* Wendekreis *m*. **the steering wheel was on full ~** das Lenkrad war voll eingeschlagen.

**2** *vt door etc* abschließen; *steering wheel* sperren, arretieren; *wheel* blockieren. **the armies were ~ed in combat** die Armeen waren in Kämpfe verwickelt; **they were ~ed in each other's arms** sie hielten sich fest umschlungen; **this bar ~s the wheel in position** diese Stange hält das Rad fest.

**3** *vi* schließen; *(wheel)* blockieren. **a suitcase that ~s** ein verschließbarer Koffer.

►**lock away** *vt sep* wegschließen; *(in safe)* einschließen; *person* einsperren.

►**lock in** *vt sep* einschließen. **to be ~ed ~** eingesperrt sein.

►**lock out** *vt sep* aussperren.

►**lock up 1** *vt sep* **(a)** *thing, house* abschließen; *person* einsperren. **to ~ sth ~ in sth** etw in etw *(dat)* einschließen; **he ought to be ~ed ~!** den müßte man einsperren! **(b)** *(Comm) capital* fest anlegen. **2** *vi* abschließen.

**lockable** ['lɒkəbl] *adj* verschließbar.

**locker** ['lɒkəʳ] *n* Schließfach *nt*. **~ room** *(Sport)* Umkleideraum *m*.

**locket** ['lɒkɪt] *n* Medaillon *nt*.

**lock:** **~ gate** *n* Schleusentor *nt*; **~jaw** *n* Wundstarrkrampf *m*; **~out** *n* Aussperrung *f*; **~smith** *n* Schlosser *m*; **~-up** *n* **(a)** *(shop)* kleiner Laden; *(garage)* Garage *f*; **(b)** *(prison)* Gefängnis *nt*.

**locomotion** [ˌləʊkə'məʊʃən] *n* Fortbewegung *f*.

**locomotive** [ˌləʊkə'məʊtɪv] *n* Lokomotive *f*.

**locum** ['ləʊkəm] *n* Vertreter(in *f*) *m*.

**locust** ['ləʊkəst] *n* Heuschrecke *f*.

**lodge** [lɒdʒ] **1** *n (in grounds)* Pförtnerhaus *nt*; *(skiing ~ etc)* Hütte *f*; *(porter's ~)* Pförtnerloge *f*. **2** *vt person* unterbringen; *complaint* einlegen *(with bei)*; *charge* einreichen; *(insert) spear* stoßen etw; *jewellery, money* deponieren, hinterlegen. **to be ~d (fest)stecken. 3** *vi* **(a)** *(live)* (zur *or* in Untermiete) wohnen *(with sb, at sb's* bei jdm*)*; *(at boarding house)* wohnen *(in* in *+dat)*. **(b)** *(object, bullet)* steckenbleiben.

**lodger** ['lɒdʒəʳ] *n* Untermieter(in *f*) *m*. **she takes ~s** sie vermietet (Zimmer).

**lodging** ['lɒdʒɪŋ] *n* Unterkunft *f*. **~s** *pl* ein möbliertes Zimmer; möblierte Zimmer *pl*; **we took ~s with Mrs B** wir mieteten uns bei Frau B ein; **~ house** Pension *f*.

**loft** [lɒft] *n* Dachboden, Speicher *m*; *(hay~)* Heuboden *m*. **in the ~** auf dem Dachboden.

**lofty** ['lɒftɪ] *adj* (+*er*) **(a)** *(high)* hoch. **(b)** *ideals* hoch; *ambitions* hochfliegend; *sentiments* erhaben; *prose* gehoben. **(c)** *(haughty)* hochmütig.

**log¹** [lɒg] *n* Baumstamm *m*; *(short)* Holzblock *m*; *(for a fire)* Scheit *nt*. **to sleep like a ~** wie ein Stein schlafen; **~ cabin** Blockhütte *f*; **~ fire** Holzfeuer *nt*.

**log²** **1** *n (record)* Aufzeichnungen *pl*. **to make** *or* **keep a ~ of sth** über etw *(acc)* Buch führen; *see* **~book**. **2** *vt* **(a)** Buch führen über *(+acc)*; *(Naut)* (ins Logbuch) eintragen. **to ~ off/on** *(Comp)* sich ab-/anmelden, ausloggen/einloggen. **(b)** *(travel)* zurücklegen.

**log³** = **logarithm** log. **~ tables** Logarithmentafel *f*.

**logarithm** ['lɒgərɪðəm] *n* Logarithmus *m*.

**log book** *n (Naut)* Logbuch *nt*; *(Aviat)* Bordbuch *nt*; *(of trucks)* Fahrtenbuch *nt*; *(Aut: registration book)* Kraftfahrzeugbrief *m*; *(in hospitals etc)* Dienstbuch *nt*.

**loggerheads** ['lɒgəhedz] *npl:* **to be at ~ (with sb)** Streit (mit jdm) haben; **they were constantly at ~ with the authorities** sie standen mit den Behörden dauernd auf Kriegsfuß.

**logic** ['lɒdʒɪk] *n* Logik *f*.

**logical** ['lɒdʒɪkəl] *adj* logisch.

**logically** ['lɒdʒɪkəlɪ] *adv think, argue* logisch. ~, **he may be right** logisch gesehen könnte er recht haben.

**logistics** [lɒ'dʒɪstɪks] *n sing* Logistik *f.*

**log jam** *n (fig)* Engpaß *m.*

**logo** ['lɒgəʊ] *n* Firmenzeichen *nt.*

**loin** [lɔɪn] *n* Lende *f.* ~ **cloth** Lendenschurz *m.*

**loiter** ['lɔɪtər] *vi (waste time)* trödeln; *(hang around suspiciously)* herumlungern. **to** ~ **with intent** sich verdächtig machen.

**loll** [lɒl] *vi* lümmeln. **to** ~ **against sth** sich (lässig) gegen *or* an etw *(acc)* lehnen.

▶**loll about** *or* **around** *vi* herumlümmeln.

**lollipop** ['lɒlɪpɒp] *n* Lutscher *m*; *(iced* ~*)* Eis *nt* am Stiel. ~ **man/woman** *(Brit col)* ≈ Schülerlotse *m/* -lotsin *f.*

**lollop** ['lɒləp] *vi (also* ~ **along)** *(person)* zockeln; *(rabbit)* hoppeln.

**lolly** ['lɒlɪ] *n* **(a)** *(Brit col: lollipop)* Lutscher *m.* **an ice** ~ ein Eis *nt* am Stiel. **(b)** *(col: money)* Mäuse *pl (col).*

**London** ['lʌndən] **1** *n* London *nt.* **2** *adj* Londoner.

**Londoner** ['lʌndənər] *n* Londoner(in *f) m.*

**lone** [ləʊn] *adj* einzeln, einsam; *(only)* einzig. ~ **mother** alleinerziehende Mutter; ~ **wolf** *(fig)* Einzelgänger *m.*

**loneliness** ['ləʊnlɪnɪs] *n* Einsamkeit *f.*

**lonely** ['ləʊnlɪ] *adj (+er)* einsam. ~ **hearts ad** Kontaktanzeige *f.*

**lone parent family** *n* Familie *f* mit nur einem Elternteil, Einelternfamilie *f.*

**loner** ['ləʊnər] *n* Einzelgänger(in *f) m.*

**lonesome** ['ləʊnsəm] *adj (esp US)* einsam. **(all) on one's** ~ ganz allein.

**long¹** [lɒŋ] **1** *adj (+er)* **(a)** *(in size)* lang; *glass* hoch; *journey* weit. **it is 6 metres** ~ es ist 6 Meter lang; **to pull a** ~ **face** ein langes Gesicht machen; **it's a** ~ **way to Hamburg** nach Hamburg ist es weit; **to have a** ~ **memory** ein gutes Gedächtnis haben; **to be** ~ **in the tooth** *(col)* nicht mehr der/die Jüngste sein. **(b)** *(in time)* lang; *job* langwierig. **it's a** ~ **time since I saw her** ich habe sie schon seit längerer Zeit nicht mehr gesehen; **will you need it for a** ~ **time?** brauchen Sie es lange?; **he's been here (for) a** ~ **time** er ist schon lange hier; ~ **time no see** *(col)* sieht man dich auch mal wieder? *(col)*; **to take a** ~ **look at sth** etw lange betrachten; **how** ~ **is the film?** wie lange dauert der Film?; **to take the** ~ **view (of sth)** auf lange Sicht betrachten; **a** ~ **drink** *(mixed)* ein Longdrink *m.*

**2** *adv* lang(e). **to be** ~ **in doing sth** lange zu etw brauchen; **don't be** ~**!** beeil dich!; **I shan't be** ~ *(in finishing)* ich bin gleich fertig; *(in returning)* ich bin gleich wieder da; **all night** ~ die ganze Nacht; **something he had** ~ **wished to happen** etwas, was er sich *(dat)* schon lange gewünscht hatte; ~ **ago** vor langer Zeit; **not** ~ **ago** vor kurzem; ~ **before** lange vorher; **not** ~ **before that** kurz davor; **as** ~ **as** so lange wie; **we waited as** ~ **as we could** wir haben gewartet, solange wir konnten; **as** ~ **as, so** ~ **as** *(provided that)* solange; **how much** ~**er can you stay?** wie lange können Sie noch bleiben?; **no** ~**er** *(not any more)* nicht mehr; **I'll wait no** ~**er** ich warte nicht länger; **so** ~**!** *(col)* tschüs *(col).*

**3** *n* **the** ~ **and the short of it is that ...** der langen Rede kurzer Sinn (ist, daß), ...; **before** ~ bald; **are you going for** ~**?** werden Sie länger weg sein?; **it won't take** ~ das dauert nicht lange.

**long²** *vi* sich sehnen *(for* nach*)*; *(less passionately)* kaum erwarten können *(for sth* etw *acc).* **I am** ~**ing to go abroad** ich brenne darauf, ins Ausland zu ge-

hen; **I'm** ~**ing to see that film** ich will den Film unbedingt sehen.

**long:** ~**-distance 1** *adj lorry, call* Fern-; *flight, race* Langstrecken-; **2** *adv* **to call** ~ **distance** ein Ferngespräch führen; ~**-drawn-out** *adj speech* langatmig; *meeting* in die Länge gezogen.

**longevity** [lɒn'dʒevɪtɪ] *n* Langlebigkeit *f.*

**long:** ~**-haired** *adj person* langhaarig; *dog etc* Langhaar-; ~**hand** *n* in ~**hand** handschriftlich.

**longing** ['lɒŋɪŋ] **1** *adj look* sehnsüchtig; *eyes* sehnsuchtsvoll. **2** *n* Sehnsucht *f (for* nach*).* **to have a** ~ **to do sth** sich danach sehnen, etw zu tun.

**longingly** ['lɒŋɪŋlɪ] *adv* sehnsüchtig.

**longish** ['lɒŋɪʃ] *adj* ziemlich lang.

**longitude** ['lɒŋgɪtjuːd] *n* Länge *f.*

**longitudinal** [lɒŋgɪ'tjuːdɪnl] *adj* Längen-; *section, axis, stripe* Längs-.

**long:** ~ **jump** *n* Weitsprung *m*; ~**-legged** *adj* langbeinig; ~**-lost** *adj (and found)* (längst) verloren geglaubt; ~**-playing record** *n* Langspielplatte *f*; ~**-range** *adj gun* weittragend; *missile, aircraft* Langstrecken-; *forecast* langfristig; ~**-running** *adj* lang; *play* lange laufend; ~**shoreman** *n (US)* Hafenarbeiter *m*; ~ **shot** *n* **it's a** ~ **shot** das ist weit hergeholt; **not by a** ~ **shot** bei weitem nicht; ~**-sighted** *adj (lit, fig)* weitsichtig; ~**-sleeved** *adj* langärmelig; ~**-standing** *adj* alt; *friendship also* langjährig; *interest, invitation* schon lange bestehend; ~**-suffering** *adj* schwer geprüft; ~**-term 1** *adj* langfristig; *effect, memory* Langzeit-; ~**-term unemployment** Dauerarbeitslosigkeit *f*; **2** *n* **in the** ~ **term** langfristig gesehen; ~ **vacation** *n (Univ)* (Sommer)semesterferien *pl*; *(Sch)* große Ferien *pl*; ~ **wave** *n (Rad)* Langwelle *f*; ~**ways** *adv* der Länge nach; ~**-winded** *adj* umständlich; *story* langatmig.

**loo** [luː] *n (Brit col)* Klo *nt (col).* **to go to the** ~ aufs Klo gehen *(col)*; **in the** ~ auf dem Klo *(col).*

**loofah** ['luːfə] *n* ~ **(sponge)** Luffaschwamm *m.*

**look** [lʊk] **1** *n* **(a)** *(glance)* Blick *m.* **she gave me a dirty** ~ sie warf mir einen vernichtenden Blick zu; **she gave me a** ~ **of disbelief** sie sah mich ungläubig an; **to have** *or* **take a** ~ **at sth** sich *(dat)* etw ansehen; **can I have a** ~**?** darf ich mal sehen; **have a** ~ **at this!** sieh dir das mal an!; **let's have a** ~ laß mal sehen!; **to take a good** ~ **at sth** sich *(dat)* etw genau ansehen; **to have a** ~ **for sth** sich nach etw umsehen; **to have a** ~ **around** sich umsehen; **shall we have a** ~ **around the town?** sollen wir uns *(dat)* die Stadt ansehen?

**(b)** *(air, appearances)* Aussehen *nt.* **there was a** ~ **of despair in his eyes** ein verzweifelter Blick war in seinen Augen; **I don't like the** ~ **of him/this wound** er/diese Wunde gefällt mir gar nicht; **by the** ~ **of him** so, wie er aussieht.

**(c)** ~**s** *pl* Aussehen *nt*; **good** ~**s** gutes Aussehen; **she's lost her** ~**s** sie sieht nicht mehr so gut aus; **you can't go by** ~**s alone** man kann nicht nur nach dem Äußeren gehen.

**2** *vt* **he is** ~**ing his age** man sieht ihm sein Alter an; **he's not** ~**ing himself these days** er sieht in letzter Zeit ganz verändert aus; **to** ~ **one's best** besonders gut aussehen; ~ **what you've done!** sieh dir mal an, was du da angestellt hast!; ~ **where you're going!** paß auf, wo du hintrittst!

**3** *vi* **(a)** *(see, glance)* gucken *(col)*, schauen *(dial)*; *(with prep also)* sehen; *(search)* suchen, nachsehen. **to** ~ **carefully** genau hinsehen *etc*; ~ **here!** hör (mal) zu!; ~, **I know you're tired, but ...** ich weiß ja, daß du müde bist, aber ...; **just** ~**!** guck mal! *(col)*; **to** ~ **over one's shoulder** über die Schulter se-

hen; **to ~ over sb's shoulder** jdm über die Schulter sehen; **~ before you leap** *(Prov)* erst wägen, dann wagen *(Prov)*.
**(b)** *(seem)* aussehen. **it ~s all right to me** es scheint mir in Ordnung zu sein; **it ~s suspicious to me** es kommt mir verdächtig vor; **the car ~s about 10 years old** das Auto sieht so aus, als ob es etwa 10 Jahre alt wäre; **it ~s well on you** es steht dir gut; **to ~ like** aussehen wie; **the picture doesn't ~ like him** das Bild sieht ihm nicht ähnlich; **it ~s like rain** es sieht nach Regen aus; **it ~s as if we'll be late** es sieht (so) aus, als würden wir zu spät kommen.
**(c)** *(face)* gehen nach. **this window ~s north** dieses Fenster geht nach Norden.
►**look after** *vi +prep obj* **(a)** *(take care of)* sich kümmern um. **to ~ ~ oneself** *(cook etc)* für sich selbst sorgen; *(be capable, strong etc)* auf sich *(acc)* aufpassen. **(b)** *bags, children* aufpassen auf *(+acc)*.
►**look around** *vi* **(a)** sich umsehen. **(b)** *(in shop etc)* sich umsehen. **let's ~ ~ the garden** sehen wir uns den Garten an.
►**look at** *vi +prep obj (also examine)* ansehen, angucken *(col)*; *(view)* betrachten, sehen; *(consider) possibilities* sich *(dat)* überlegen; *(offer in Betracht ziehen. **he ~ed ~ his watch** er sah auf die Uhr; **he/ it isn't much to ~ ~** *(not attractive)* er/es sieht nicht besonders (gut) aus; *(nothing special)* er/es sieht nach nichts aus.
►**look away** *vi* wegsehen.
►**look back** *vi* sich umsehen; *(fig)* zurückblicken *(on sth, to sth* auf etw *acc)*. **he's never ~ed ~ since** *(col)* seitdem ist es ständig mit ihm bergauf gegangen.
►**look down** *vi* hinunter-/heruntersehen *or* -gucken *(col)*. **we ~ed ~ the hole** wir sahen ins Loch hinunter.
►**look down on** *vi +prep obj (lit, fig)* herabsehen auf *(+acc)*.
►**look for** *vi +prep obj (seek)* suchen. **he's ~ing ~ trouble** er wird sich *(dat)* Ärger einhandeln; *(actively)* er sucht Streit.
►**look forward to** *vi +prep obj* sich freuen auf *(+acc)*. **I'm so ~ing ~ ~ seeing you again** ich freue mich so darauf, dich wiederzusehen; **I ~ ~ ~ ~ hearing from you** ich hoffe, bald von Ihnen zu hören.
►**look in** *vi* **(a)** hinein-/hereinsehen *or* -gucken *(col)*. **(b)** *(visit)* vorbeikommen *(on sb* bei jdm*)*.
►**look into** *vi +prep obj* hereinsehen in *(+acc)*; *(investigate)* untersuchen; *complaint etc* prüfen.
►**look on** *vi* **(a)** *(watch)* zusehen, zugucken *(col)*. **(b) to ~ ~to** *(window)* (hinaus)gehen auf *(+acc)*; *(building)* liegen an *(+dat)*. **(c)** *+prep obj (also* **look upon)** betrachten, ansehen. **to ~ ~ sb as a friend** jdn als Freund betrachten.
►**look out 1** *vi* **(a)** hinaus-/heraussehen *or* -gucken *(col)*. **to ~ ~ (of) the window** zum Fenster hinaussehen, aus dem Fenster sehen; **to ~ ~ for sb/ troublemakers** nach jdm Ausschau halten/auf Unruhestifter achten. **(b)** *(take care)* aufpassen. **~ ~!** paß auf! **2** *vt sep* heraussuchen.
►**look over** *vt sep papers, notes etc* durchsehen; *house* sich *(dat)* ansehen.
►**look round** *vi =* **look around**.
►**look through 1** *vi* durchsehen *or* -gucken *(col) (prep obj* durch*)*. **he ~ed ~ the window** er sah zum Fenster hinein/herein; **to ~ straight ~ sb** durch jdn hindurchgucken. **2** *vt sep (examine)* durchsehen **to ~ straight ~ sb** durch jdn hindurchgucken.
►**look to** *vi +prep obj* **(a)** *(look after)* sich kümmern um. **(b)** *(rely on)* sich verlassen auf *(+acc)*. **they ~ed ~ him to solve the problem** sie verließen

sich darauf, daß er das Problem lösen würde.
►**look up 1** *vi* **(a)** aufsehen, aufblicken. **(b)** *(improve)* besser werden; *(shares, prices)* steigen. **things are ~ing ~** es geht bergauf. **2** *vt sep* **(a) to ~ sb ~ and down** jdn von oben bis unten ansehen. **(b)** *(visit)* **to ~ ~ sb ~** bei jdm vorbeischauen. **(c)** *(seek) word* nachschlagen.
**lookalike** ['lʊkə,laɪk] *n* Doppelgänger(in *f*) *m*.
**looker-on** ['lʊkə'(r)ɒn] *n* Schaulustige(r) *mf (pej)*.
**look-in** ['lʊkɪn] *n:* **he didn't get a ~** *(col)* er hatte keine Chance.
**looking glass** ['lʊkɪŋglɑːs] *n* Spiegel *m*.
**look-out** ['lʊk,aʊt] *n* **(a)** *(Mil) (tower etc)* Ausguck *m*; *(person)* Wachtposten *m*. **to keep a ~ for** Ausschau halten nach; **~ post** Beobachtungsposten *m*. **(b)** *(prospect)* Aussichten *pl*. **it's a grim ~ for us** es sieht schlecht aus für uns. **(c)** *(col: worry)* **that's his ~!** das ist sein Problem!
**loom¹** [luːm] *n* Webstuhl *m*.
**loom²** *vi (also ~ ahead* or *up) (lit, fig)* sich abzeichnen; *(storm)* heraufziehen; *(disaster)* sich zusammenbrauen; *(danger)* drohen; *(difficulties)* sich auftürmen; *(exams)* bedrohlich näherrücken. **the ship ~ed (up) out of the mist** das Schiff tauchte aus dem Nebel (auf); **to ~ large** eine große Rolle spielen.
**loony** ['luːnɪ] *(col)* **1** *adj (+er)* bekloppt *(col)*. **2** *n* Verrückte(r) *mf (col)*. **~ bin** Klapsmühle *f (col)*.
**loop** [luːp] **1** *n* **(a)** *(curved shape)* Schlaufe *f*; *(of wire)* Schlinge *f*; *(of river, also Comp, Elec)* Schleife *f*. **(b)** *(Aviat)* Looping *m*. **to ~ the ~** einen Looping machen. **2** *vt rope etc* schlingen *(around* um*)*.
**loophole** ['luːp,həʊl] *n (fig)* Hintertürchen *nt*. **a ~ in the law** eine Lücke im Gesetz.
**loose** [luːs] **1** *adj (+er)* **(a)** *board, button* lose; *dress, collar* weit; *tooth, bandage, knot, screw, soil, weave* locker; *limbs* beweglich. **~ change** Kleingeld *nt*; **a ~ connection** *(Elec)* ein Wackelkontakt *m*; **to come** or **work ~** *(screw, handle etc)* sich lockern; *(button)* abgehen; **~ chippings** *(on road)* Rollsplitt *m*.
**(b)** *(free)* **to break** or **get ~** *(person, animal)* sich losreißen *(from* von*)*; *(break out)* ausbrechen; **to run ~** frei herumlaufen; *(of children)* unbeaufsichtigt herumlaufen; **to be at a ~ end** *(fig)* nichts mit sich anzufangen wissen; **to turn** or **set ~** frei herumlaufen lassen; *prisoner* freilassen; **to tie up the ~ ends** *(fig)* ein paar offene Probleme lösen.
**(c)** *(not exact, vague) translation* frei; *account* ungenau; *connection* lose; *thinking* unlogisch.
**(d)** *(too free, immoral) conduct* lose; *morals* locker; *person* unmoralisch.
**2** *n (col)* **to be on the ~** *(prisoners, dangerous animals)* frei herumlaufen.
**3** *vt* **(a)** *(free)* befreien. **(b)** *(untie)* losmachen. **(c)** *(slacken)* lockern.
**loose:** **~ covers** *npl* Überzüge *pl*; **~-fitting** *adj* weit; **~-knit** *adj* lose zusammenhängend; **~-leaf binder** *n* Ringbuch *nt*; **~-limbed** *adj (lithe)* gelenkig.
**loosely** ['luːslɪ] *adv* lose, locker; *behave* unmoralisch. **~ speaking** grob gesagt; **I was using the word rather ~** ich habe das Wort ziemlich frei gebraucht.
**loosen** ['luːsn] **1** *vt* **(a)** *(free)* befreien; *tongue* lösen. **(b)** *(untie)* lösen. **(c)** *(slacken)* lockern; *collar* aufmachen. **2** *vi* sich lockern.
►**loosen up 1** *vt sep muscles* lockern. **2** *vi (muscles)* locker werden; *(athlete)* sich (auf)-lockern; *(relax)* auftauen.
**loot** [luːt] **1** *n* Beute *f*; *(col: money)* Zaster *m (col)*. **2** *vti* plündern.
**looter** ['luːtər] *n* Plünderer *m*.
**lop** [lɒp] *vt tree* stutzen; *(also ~ off)* abhacken.

**lope** [ləʊp] *vi* in großen Sätzen springen; *(hare)* hoppeln.

**lopsided** [ˌlɒpˈsaɪdɪd] *adj* schief; *(fig)* einseitig.

**loquacious** [ləˈkweɪʃəs] *adj* redselig.

**lord** [lɔːd] **1** *n* **(a)** *(master, ruler)* Herr *m.* ~ **and master** Herr und Meister *m.* **(b)** *(Brit)* Lord *m.* **the (House of) L~s** das Oberhaus; **my** ~ *(to noble)* *(in English contexts)* Mylord; *(to judge)* Euer Ehren; **L~ Chancellor** Lordkanzler *m*; **L~ Mayor** ≃ Oberbürgermeister *m.* **(c)** *(Rel)* **L~** Herr *m*; **the L~'s prayer** das Vaterunser; **(good) L~!** *(col)* ach, du lieber Himmel! *(col)*; **L~ knows** *(col)* wer weiß; **L~ knows I've tried often enough** ich hab's weiß Gott oft genug versucht. **2** *vt* **to ~ it** das Zepter schwingen; **to ~ it over sb** jdn herumkommandieren.

**lordship** [ˈlɔːdʃɪp] *n (Brit: title)* Lordschaft *f.* **Your L~** Eure Lordschaft; *(to judge)* Euer Ehren.

**lore** [lɔːʳ] *n* Überlieferungen *pl*; *(knowledge)* Wissen *nt.* **plant ~** Pflanzenkunde *f.*

**Lorraine** [lɒˈreɪn] *n* Lothringen *nt.*

**lorry** [ˈlɒrɪ] *n (Brit)* Last(kraft)wagen, Lkw, Laster *(col) m.* ~ **driver** Last(kraft)wagenfahrer(in *f*) *m*; **~load** Lastwagenladung *f.*

**lose** [luːz] *pret, ptp* **lost 1** *vt* **(a)** verlieren; *pursuer* abschütteln; *one's French* verlernen; *prize* nicht bekommen. **the shares have lost 15% in a month** die Aktien sind in einem Monat um 15% gefallen; **you will ~ nothing by helping them** es kann dir nicht schaden, wenn du ihnen hilfst; **that mistake lost him the game** dieser Fehler kostete ihn den Sieg; **to ~ no time in doing sth** etw sofort tun; **my watch lost three hours in a week** meine Uhr ist innerhalb einer Woche drei Stunden nachgegangen; **to ~ weight** abnehmen.

**(b)** *(not catch)* train, opportunity verpassen; *words* nicht mitbekommen. **you've lost me now with all this abstract argument** bei dieser abstrakten Argumentation komme ich nicht mehr mit.

**(c) to be lost** *(things)* verschwunden sein; *(people)* sich verlaufen haben; *(driver)* sich verfahren haben; *(fig)* verloren sein; *(words)* untergehen; **I can't follow the reasoning, I'm lost** ich kann der Argumentation nicht folgen, ich verstehe nichts mehr; **to get lost** sich verlaufen; *(driver)* sich verfahren; **get lost!** *(col)* verschwinde! *(col)*; **to give sb/sth up for lost** jdn verloren geben/etw abschreiben; **I'm lost without my watch** ohne meine Uhr bin ich verloren *or* aufgeschmissen *(col)*; **classical music is lost on him** er hat keinen Sinn für klassische Musik; **the remark was lost on her** die Bemerkung kam bei ihr nicht an.

**2** *vi* verlieren; *(watch)* nachgehen. **you can't ~** du kannst nur gewinnen.

▶**lose out** *vi (col)* den kürzeren ziehen *(on* bei*) (col)*.

**loser** [ˈluːzəʳ] *n* Verlierer(in *f*) *m.* **he's a born ~** er ist der geborene Verlierer; **to be a bad ~** ein schlechter Verlierer sein.

**losing** [ˈluːzɪŋ] *adj* team Verlierer-. **a ~ battle** ein aussichtsloser Kampf; **to fight a ~ battle** auf verlorenem Posten kämpfen.

**loss** [lɒs] *n* **(a)** Verlust *m.* **there was a heavy ~ of life** viele kamen ums Leben; **the army suffered heavy ~es** die Armee erlitt schwere Verluste; **his business is running at a ~** er arbeitet mit Verlust; **to sell sth at a ~** etw mit Verlust verkaufen; **a dead ~** *(col)* ein böser Reinfall *(col)*; *(person)* ein hoffnungsloser Fall *(col)*. **(b) to be at a ~** nicht mehr weiterwissen; **to be at a ~ to explain sth** etw nicht erklären können; **to be at a ~ for words** nicht wissen, was man sagen soll.

**loss:** ~ **leader** *n* Lockvogelangebot *nt*; ~**-making** *adj* mit Verlust arbeitend.

**lost** [lɒst] **1** *pret, ptp of* **lose. 2** *adj* verloren; *child* verschwunden; *opportunity* verpaßt. ~ **cause** aussichtslose Sache; ~**-and-found (department)** *(US)*, ~ **property office** *(Brit)* Fundbüro *nt.*

**lot¹** [lɒt] *n* **(a)** *(for deciding)* Los *nt.* **to cast** *or* **draw ~s for sth** etw verlosen. **(b)** *(destiny)* Los *nt.* **it falls to my ~ to tell him** mir fällt die Aufgabe zu, es ihm zu sagen; **to throw in one's ~ with sb** sich mit jdm zusammentun. **(c)** *(plot)* Parzelle *f.* **parking ~** *(US)* Parkplatz *m.* **(d)** *(number of articles)* Posten *m*; *(at auction)* Los *nt.* **where shall I put this ~?** *(col)* wo soll ich das hier hintun?; **divide the books up into three ~s** teile die Bücher in drei Stapel auf; **he's just given me another ~** er hat mir gerade einen neuen Stoß *or* noch eine Ladung gegeben *(col)*. **(e)** *(col: group)* Haufen *m.* **that ~ in the next office** die Typen vom Büro nebenan *(col)*. **(f) the ~** alle; *(quantity)* alles; **that's the ~** das ist alles; **the whole ~ of them** sie alle; **he's eaten the ~** er hat alles aufgegessen.

**lot²** **1** *n* **a ~, ~s** viel; **a ~ of money** viel Geld; **a ~ of books, ~s of books** *(col)* viele Bücher; **such a ~** so viel; **quite a ~ of books** ziemlich viele Bücher; **he made ~s and ~s of mistakes** *(col)* er hat eine Unmenge Fehler gemacht; **we see a ~ of John these days** wir sehen John in letzter Zeit sehr oft; **I'd give a ~ to know** ... ich würde viel darum geben, wenn ich wüßte ...; **thanks a ~!** *(also iro)* vielen Dank! **2** *adv* **a ~, ~s** *(col)* viel; **things have changed a ~** es hat sich vieles geändert; **I feel ~s** *(col) or* **a ~ better** es geht mir sehr viel besser.

**lotion** [ˈləʊʃən] *n* Lotion *f.*

**lottery** [ˈlɒtərɪ] *n* Lotterie *f.* ~ **prize** Lotteriegewinn *m*; ~ **ticket** Lotterielos *nt.*

**loud** [laʊd] **1** *adj (+er)* **(a)** laut. ~ **and clear** laut und deutlich. **(b)** *behaviour* aufdringlich; *colour* schreiend; *(in bad taste)* auffällig. **2** *adv* laut. **to say sth out ~** etw laut sagen.

**loudhailer** [ˌlaʊdˈheɪləʳ] *n* Megaphon *nt*; *(not handheld)* Lautsprecher *m.*

**loudly** [ˈlaʊdlɪ] *adv* laut. **he was ~ dressed in blue** er war in ein grelles Blau gekleidet.

**loud-mouthed** [ˈlaʊdˌmaʊðd] *adj (col)* großmäulig *(col).*

**loudness** [ˈlaʊdnɪs] *n* Lautstärke *f.*

**loudspeaker** [ˌlaʊdˈspiːkəʳ] *n* Lautsprecher *m*; *(of hi-fi, in enclosure)* Box *f.*

**lounge** [laʊndʒ] **1** *n (in house)* Wohnzimmer *nt*; *(in hotel)* Gesellschaftsraum *m*; *(also ~ bar)* Salon *m*; *(at airport)* Warteraum *m.* **2** *vi* faulenzen. **to ~ about** herumliegen/-sitzen/-stehen.

**lounger** [ˈlaʊndʒəʳ] *n (person)* Faulenzer *m*; *(chair)* Liegestuhl *m.*

**lounge suit** *n* Straßenanzug *m.*

**lour, lower** [ˈlaʊəʳ] *vi (person)* ein finsteres Gesicht machen; *(clouds)* sich türmen. **to ~ at sb** jdn finster *or* drohend ansehen.

**louse** [laʊs] *n, pl* **lice** *(Zool)* Laus *f.*

**lousy** [ˈlaʊzɪ] *adj (col: very bad)* saumäßig *(col)*, beschissen *(col!)*; *trick etc* fies *(col)*. **I'm ~ at arithmetic** in Mathe bin ich miserabel *(col)*; **a ~ $3** lausige 3 Dollar *(col).*

**lout** [laʊt] *n* Rüpel, Flegel *m.*

**louvre, (US) louver** [ˈluːvəʳ] *n* Lamelle *f*; *(for ventilation)* Luftschlitz *m.* ~ **door** Lamellentür *f.*

**lovable** [ˈlʌvəbl] *adj* liebenswert.

**love** [lʌv] **1** *n* **(a)** *(affection)* Liebe *f.* ~ **of learning** Freude *f* am Lernen; ~ **of books** Liebe *f* zu Büchern; **he studies history for the ~ of it** er studiert

Geschichte aus Liebe zur Sache; **to be in ~ (with sb)** (in jdn) verliebt sein; **to fall in ~ (with sb)** sich (in jdn) verlieben; **there is no ~ lost between them** sie können sich nicht ausstehen; **to make ~** *(sexually)* miteinander schlafen; **to make ~ to sb** *(sexually)* mit jdm schlafen. **(b)** *(greetings)* **all my ~** mit herzlichen Grüßen; **give him my ~** grüß ihn von mir; **he sends his ~** er läßt grüßen; **yes, (my) ~** ja, Liebling. **(c)** *(Tennis)* null. **fifteen ~** fünfzehn null.

2 *vt* lieben; *(like) thing* gern mögen. **I ~ tennis** ich mag Tennis sehr gern; *(to play)* ich spiele sehr gern Tennis; **I'd ~ to come** ich würde sehr gerne kommen.

**love:** **~ affair** *n* Verhältnis *nt;* **~ game** *n (Tennis)* Zu-Null-Spiel *nt;* **~-hate relationship** *n* Haßliebe *f;* **~ letter** *n* Liebesbrief *m;* **~ life** *n* Liebesleben *nt.*

**loveliness** ['lʌvlɪnɪs] *n* Schönheit *f.*

**lovely** ['lʌvlɪ] *adj (+er) (beautiful)* schön; *object also* hübsch; *baby* niedlich; *(delightful)* herrlich; *(likeable)* nett. **we had a ~ time** es war sehr schön; **it's ~ and warm in this room** es ist schön warm in diesem Zimmer; **it's been ~ to see you** es war schön, dich zu sehen.

**love-making** ['lʌv,meɪkɪŋ] *n (sexual)* Liebe *f.*

**lover** ['lʌvər] *n* **(a)** Geliebte(r) *mf.* **the ~s** das Liebespaar; **to be a good ~** gut in der Liebe sein. **(b)** **a ~ of good food** ein Freund *m* von gutem Essen; **music ~** Musikliebhaber *m;* **art ~** Kunstfreund *m.*

**love:** **~sick** *adj* liebeskrank *(geh);* **to be ~sick** Liebeskummer *m* haben; **~ song** *n* Liebeslied *nt;* **~ story** *n* Liebesgeschichte *f.*

**loving** ['lʌvɪŋ] *adj* liebend; *look, disposition* liebevoll.

**lovingly** ['lʌvɪŋlɪ] *adv* liebevoll.

**low¹** [ləʊ] 1 *adj (+er)* niedrig; *form of life* nieder; *bow, note, punch* tief; *density, intelligence* gering; *food supplies* knapp; *quality* minderwertig; *light* gedämpft; *rank, position also* untergeordnet; *tastes, manners* gewöhnlich, ordinär *(pej);* *company* schlecht; *joke, song* geschmacklos; *trick* gemein; *resistance* gering; *morale* schlecht. **~ pressure** *(Met)* Tiefdruck *m;* **to speak in a ~ voice** leise sprechen; **the lamp was ~** die Lampe brannte schwach; **to feel ~** sich nicht wohl *or* gut fühlen; *(emotionally)* niedergeschlagen sein.

2 *adv aim* nach unten; *speak, sing* leise; *fly, bow* tief. **I would never sink so ~ as to ...** so tief würde ich nie sinken, daß ich ...; **share prices went so ~ that ...** die Aktienkurse fielen so sehr, daß ...; **to run** *or* **get ~** knapp werden; **we are getting ~ on petrol** uns *(dat)* geht das Benzin aus.

3 *n* **(a)** *(Met)* Tief *nt;* *(fig also)* Tiefpunkt *m.* **to reach a new ~** einen neuen Tiefstand erreichen. **(b)** *(Aut:* **~ gear)** niedriger Gang.

**low²** 1 *n (of cow)* Muh *nt.* 2 *vi* muhen.

**low:** **~brow** *adj* (geistig) anspruchslos; **~-calorie** *adj* kalorienarm; **~-cost** *adj* preiswert; **the L~ Countries** *npl* die Niederlande *pl;* **~-cut** *adj dress* tief ausgeschnitten; **~-down** *(col)* **1** *n* Informationen *pl;* **he gave me the ~-down on it** er hat mich darüber aufgeklärt; **2** *adj (esp US)* gemein, fies *(col);* **~-emission** *adj* abgasarm.

**lower¹** ['ləʊər] **1** *adj see* **low¹** niedriger; tiefer *etc;* *jaw, arm* Unter-; *limbs, storeys* untere(r, s). **the ~ school** die Unter- und Mittelstufe; **hemlines are ~ this year** die Röcke sind dieses Jahr länger; **the ~ classes** die untere(n) Schicht(en).

2 *adv* tiefer; leiser. **~ down the mountain** weiter unten am Berg; **~ down the scale/the list** weiter unten auf der Skala/Liste.

3 *vt load* herunter-/hinunterlassen; *eyes, gun* senken; *sail, flag* einholen; *bicycle saddle* niedriger

machen; *pressure* verringern; *voice, price* senken; *morale, resistance* schwächen; *standard* herabsetzen. **~ your voice** sprich leiser!; **his behaviour ~ed him in my opinion** sein Benehmen ließ ihn in meiner Achtung sinken; **to ~ the tone of the conversation** das Gesprächsniveau senken; **to ~ oneself to do sth** sich so soweit erniedrigen, daß man etw tut.

**lower²** ['laʊər] *vi* = **lour.**

**lower case** ['ləʊəkeɪs] *n* Kleinbuchstaben *pl.*

**low:** **~-fat** *adj* fettarm; **~-flying** *adj* tiefffliegend; **~-flying aircraft** Tiefflieger *m;* **~-grade** *adj* minderwertig; **~-key** *adj approach* gelassen; *handling* besonnen; *production* einfach gehalten; *reception* reserviert; **~land** *n* Flachland *nt;* **~-level** *adj radioactivity* mit niedrigem Strahlungswert; *(Comp) language* nieder; **~-loader** *n* Tieflader *m.*

**lowly** ['ləʊlɪ] *adj (+er)* bescheiden.

**low-lying** [,ləʊ'laɪɪŋ] *adj* tiefgelegen.

**low:** **~-pitched** *adj* tief; **~-powered** *adj engine* schwach; *car etc* schwach motorisiert; **~-profile** *adj* wenig profiliert; **~-rise** *attr* niedrig (gebaut); **~ season** *n* Nebensaison *f;* **~-spirited** *adj* niedergeschlagen; **~-tech** *adj* technisch unkompliziert; **~-tension** *adj (Elec)* Niederspannungs-; **~ tide, ~ water** *n* Ebbe *f,* Niedrigwasser *nt.*

**loyal** ['lɔɪəl] *adj* treu. **he was ~ to his friends** er hielt (treu) zu seinen Freunden.

**loyalist** ['lɔɪəlɪst] **1** *n* Loyalist *m.* **2** *adj* loyal; *troops* regierungstreu.

**loyally** ['lɔɪəlɪ] *adv* treu.

**loyalty** ['lɔɪəltɪ] *n* Treue *f;* *(esp Pol also)* Loyalität *f.* **conflicting loyalties** nicht zu vereinbarende Treuepflichten; **his changing political loyalties** seine wechselnden politischen Bekenntnisse.

**lozenge** ['lɒzɪndʒ] *n* **(a)** *(Med)* Pastille *f.* **(b)** *(shape)* Raute *f.*

**LP** = **long player, long playing record** LP *f.*

**LPG** = **liquefied petroleum gas** Mischung *f* von Butan- und Propangas.

**L-plate** ['elpleɪt] *n Schild nt mit der Aufschrift „L" (für Fahrschüler).*

**LPN** *(US)* = **Licensed Practical Nurse** staatlich zugelassene Krankenschwester.

**LSD** = **lysergic acid diethylamide** LSD *nt.*

**LSE** *(Brit)* = **London School of Economics.**

**LST** *(US)* = **Local Standard Time** Ortszeit *f.*

**LT** *(Elec)* = **low tension.**

**Lt** = **Lieutenant** Lt.

**Ltd** = **Limited** GmbH.

**lubricant** ['lu:brɪkənt] *n* Schmiermittel *nt.*

**lubricate** ['lu:brɪkeɪt] *vt (lit, fig)* schmieren, ölen. **well-~d** *(hum)* gut abgefüllt *(col).*

**lubrication** [,lu:brɪ'keɪʃən] *n* Schmieren, Ölen *nt.*

**Lucerne** [lu:'sɜːn] *n* Luzern *nt.* **Lake ~** Vierwaldstätter See *m.*

**lucid** ['lu:sɪd] *adj (+er) (clear)* klar; *explanation* anschaulich. **~ intervals** lichte Augenblicke.

**lucidity** [lu:'sɪdɪtɪ] *n see adj* Klarheit *f;* Anschaulichkeit *f.*

**lucidly** ['lu:sɪdlɪ] *adv* klar; *explain* anschaulich.

**luck** [lʌk] *n* Glück *nt.* **bad ~** Unglück, Pech *nt;* **bad ~!** so ein Pech!; **good ~** Glück *nt;* **good ~!** viel Glück!; **good ~ to them!** *(iro),* **and the best of (British) ~!** *(iro)* na dann viel Glück!; **no such ~!** schön wär's! *(col);* **just my ~!** Pech (gehabt), wie immer!; **it's the ~ of the draw** man muß es eben nehmen, wie's kommt; **with any ~** mit etwas Glück; **worse ~** leider; **better ~ next time!** vielleicht klappt es beim nächsten Mal!; **to be in ~** Glück haben; **to be out of ~** kein Glück haben; **he was a bit down on his ~** er hatte eine Pechsträhne; **to bring**

**sb bad** ~ jdm Unglück bringen; **as** ~ **would have it** wie es der Zufall wollte; **for** ~ als Glücksbringer; **to try one's** ~ sein Glück versuchen.
**luckily** ['lʌkɪlɪ] *adv* glücklicherweise. ~ **for me** zu meinem Glück.
**lucky** ['lʌkɪ] *adj (+er) (having, bringing luck) person, number* Glücks-; *coincidence* glücklich. ~ **charm** Glücksbringer *m*; ~ **dip** ≈ Glückstopf *m*; **it must be my** ~ **day** ich habe wohl heute meinen Glückstag; **you** ~ **thing!, you** ~ **beggar** *(col)*! du Glückliche(r); **to be** ~ Glück haben; **I was** ~ **enough to meet him** ich hatte das Glück, ihn kennenzulernen; **you are** ~ **to be alive** du kannst von Glück sagen, daß du noch lebst; **you were** ~ **to catch him** du hast Glück gehabt, daß du ihn erwischt hast; **you'll be** ~ **to make it in time** wenn du das noch schaffst, hast du (aber) Glück; **I want another £500 — you'll be** ~! ich will nochmal £500 haben — viel Glück!; **it was** ~ **I stopped him in time** zum Glück habe ich ihn rechtzeitig aufgehalten; **that was a** ~ **escape** da habe ich/hast du *etc* nochmal Glück gehabt.
**lucrative** ['luːkrətɪv] *adj* einträglich, lukrativ.
**ludicrous** ['luːdɪkrəs] *adj* grotesk; *sight, words also* lächerlich.
**luffa** ['lʌfə] *n (US)* = **loofah.**
**lug** [lʌg] *vt* schleppen.
**luggage** ['lʌgɪdʒ] *n (esp Brit)* Gepäck *nt*.
**luggage** *(Brit)*: ~ **label** *n (stick-on)* Gepäckaufkleber *m*; ~ **locker** *n* Gepäckschließfach *nt*; ~ **rack** *n (Rail etc)* Gepäckablage *f*; *(Aut)* Gepäckträger *m*; ~ **trolley** *n* Kofferkuli *m*; ~ **van** *n (Rail)* Gepäckwagen *m*.
**lugubrious** [luˈguːbrɪəs] *adj person, song* schwermütig; *expression* kummervoll.
**Luke** [luːk] *n* ≈ Lukas *m*.
**lukewarm** ['luːkwɔːm] *adj (lit, fig)* lauwarm; *support also* mäßig; *friendship* oberflächlich.
**lull** [lʌl] **1** *n* Pause *f*; *(Comm)* Flaute *f*. **a** ~ **in the wind** eine Windstille; **a** ~ **in the conversation** eine Gesprächspause. **2** *vt baby* beruhigen; *(fig)* einlullen. **to** ~ **a baby to sleep** ein Baby in den Schlaf wiegen; **he was** ~**ed into a sense of false security** er wiegte sich in trügerischer Sicherheit.
**lullaby** ['lʌləbaɪ] *n* Wiegenlied *nt*.
**lumbago** [lʌmˈbeɪgəʊ] *n* Hexenschuß *m*.
**lumber**[1] ['lʌmbəʳ] **1** *n* **(a)** *(timber)* (Bau)holz *nt*. **(b)** *(junk)* Gerümpel *nt*. **2** *vt (Brit col)* **to** ~ **sb with sth** jdm etw aufhalsen *(col)*; **he got** ~**ed with the job** man hat ihm die Arbeit aufgehalst *(col)*; **I got** ~**ed with her for the evening** ich hatte sie den ganzen Abend auf dem Hals *(col)*.
**lumber**[2] *vi (cart)* rumpeln; *(elephant, person)* trampeln.
**lumber:** ~**jack** *n* Holzfäller *m*; ~ **room** *n* Rumpelkammer *f*; ~**yard** *n (US)* Holzlager *nt*.
**luminous** ['luːmɪnəs] *adj* leuchtend; *paint, dial* Leucht-.
**lump** [lʌmp] **1** *n* Klumpen *m*; *(of sugar)* Stück *nt*; *(swelling)* Beule *f*. **with a** ~ **in one's throat** *(fig)* mit einem Kloß im Hals. **2** *vt (col)* **if he doesn't like it he can** ~ **it** wenn's ihm nicht paßt, hat er eben Pech gehabt *(col)*.
▶**lump together** *vt sep* **(a)** *(put together)* zusammentun; *books* zusammenstellen; *expenses, money* zusammenlegen. **(b)** *(judge together) persons, topics* über einen Kamm scheren; **he** ~**ed all the soldiers** ~ **as traitors** er urteilte all die Soldaten pauschal als Verräter ab.
**lump:** ~ **sugar** *n* Würfelzucker *m*; ~ **sum** *n* Pauschalsumme *f*; **to pay sth in a** ~ **sum** etw pauschal bezahlen.

**lumpy** ['lʌmpɪ] *adj (+er)* klumpig.
**lunacy** ['luːnəsɪ] *n* Wahnsinn *m*. **it's sheer** ~! das ist reiner Wahnsinn!
**lunar** ['luːnəʳ] *adj* Mond-. ~ **eclipse** Mondfinsternis *f*; ~ **module** Mondfähre *f*.
**lunatic** ['luːnətɪk] **1** *adj* verrückt, wahnsinnig. ~ **fringe** radikale Randgruppe. **2** *n* Wahnsinnige(r), Irre(r) *mf*. ~ **asylum** Irrenanstalt *f*.
**lunch** [lʌntʃ] *n* Mittagessen *nt*. **to have** ~ (zu) Mittag essen; **he's at** ~ er ist beim Mittagessen.
**lunch break** *n* Mittagspause *f*.
**luncheon** ['lʌntʃən] *n (form)* Mittagessen *nt*. ~ **meat** Frühstücksfleisch *nt*; ~ **voucher** Essensmarke *f*.
**lunch:** ~ **hour** *n* Mittagspause *f*; ~ **table** *n* Mittagstisch *m*; ~**time** *n* Mittagspause *f*.
**lung** [lʌŋ] *n (also pl)* Lunge *f*. **to fill one's** ~**s** tief einatmen; ~ **cancer** Lungenkrebs *m*.
**lunge** [lʌndʒ] **1** *n* Satz *m* nach vorn; *(esp Fencing)* Ausfall *m*. **he made a** ~ **at his opponent** er stürzte sich auf seinen Gegner. **2** *vi* (sich) stürzen. **to** ~ **at sb** sich auf jdn stürzen.
**lupin,** *(US)* **lupine** ['luːpɪn] *n* Lupine *f*.
**lurch**[1] [lɜːtʃ] *n:* **to leave sb in the** ~ *(col)* jdn im Stich lassen, jdn hängenlassen *(col)*.
**lurch**[2] **1** *n* Ruck *m*; *(of boat)* Schlingern *nt*. **to give a** ~ einen Ruck machen; *(boat)* schlingern. **2** *vi* **(a)** *see* **to give a** ~. **(b)** *(move with* ~*es)* sich ruckartig bewegen; *(boat)* schlingern; *(person)* taumeln. **the train** ~**ed to a standstill** der Zug kam mit einem Ruck zum Stehen; **to** ~ **about** hin und her schlingern/hin und her taumeln.
**lure** [lʊəʳ] **1** *n (bait)* Köder *m*; *(person, for hawk)* Lockvogel *m*; *(general)* Lockmittel *nt*; *(fig: of city, sea etc)* Verlockungen *pl*. **2** *vt* anlocken. **to** ~ **sb/an animal into a trap** jdn/ein Tier in eine Falle locken; **to** ~ **sb/an animal out** jdn/ein Tier herauslocken.
**lurid** ['lʊərɪd] *adj (+er) colour, sky* grell; *dress* grellfarben, in grellen Farben; *posters also* schreiend; *language* reißerisch; *account* sensationslüstern; *detail* grausig; *(sordid)* widerlich.
**lurk** [lɜːk] *vi* lauern. **a doubt still** ~**ed in his mind** ein Zweifel plagte ihn noch.
**luscious** ['lʌʃəs] *adj* köstlich; *fruit also* saftig; *girl* zum Anbeißen *(col)*.
**lush** [lʌʃ] *adj grass* saftig, satt; *vegetation* üppig.
**lust** [lʌst] **1** *n (inner sensation)* Wollust *f*; *(wanting to acquire)* Begierde *f (for* nach*)*; *(greed)* Gier *f (for* nach*)*. ~ **for power** Machtgier *f*. **2** *vi* **to** ~ **after, to** ~ **for** *(sexually)* begehren *(+acc)*; *(greedily)* gieren nach.
**lustful** *adj*, ~**ly** *adv* ['lʌstfʊl, -fəlɪ] lüstern.
**lustily** ['lʌstɪlɪ] *adv* kräftig; *sing* aus voller Kehle.
**lustre,** *(US)* **luster** ['lʌstəʳ] *n* Schimmer *m*; *(in eyes)* Glanz *m*.
**lustrous** ['lʌstrəs] *adj* schimmernd, glänzend.
**lusty** ['lʌstɪ] *adj (+er) person* gesund und munter; *man also* urwüchsig; *appetite* herzhaft; *cheer, cry* kräftig; *push, kick etc* kraftvoll.
**lute** [luːt] *n* Laute *f*.
**Lutheran** ['luːθərən] **1** *adj* lutherisch. **2** *n* Lutheraner(in *f*) *m*.
**Luxembourg** ['lʌksəmbɜːg] **1** *n* Luxemburg *nt*. **2** *adj* luxemburgisch.
**luxuriant** [lʌgˈzjʊərɪənt] *adj* üppig.
**luxuriate** [lʌgˈzjʊərɪeɪt] *vi* **to** ~ **in sth** sich in etw *(dat)* aalen.
**luxurious** [lʌgˈzjʊərɪəs] *adj* luxuriös, Luxus-; *carpet, hotel also* feudal; *food* üppig.
**luxuriously** [lʌgˈzjʊərɪəslɪ] *adv* luxuriös.
**luxury** ['lʌkʃərɪ] **1** *n* Luxus *m*; *(of car, house etc)* luxuriöse Ausstattung. **to live a life of** ~ ein Luxusle-

**lyrical**

ben führen; **the little luxuries** die kleinen Genüsse. **2** *adj (cruise, tax)* Luxus-.
**LV** *(Brit)* = **luncheon voucher.**
**LW** *(Rad)* = **long wave** LW.
**Lycra** ® ['laɪkrə] *n* Lycra ® *nt.*
**lying** ['laɪɪŋ] **1** *adj* verlogen. **2** *n* Lügen *nt.* **that would be** ~ das wäre gelogen.
**lynch** [lɪntʃ] *vt* lynchen. ~ **law** Lynchjustiz *f.*

**lynx** [lɪŋks] *n* Luchs *m.*
**lyre** ['laɪə<sup>r</sup>] *n* Leier *f.*
**lyric** ['lɪrɪk] **1** *adj* lyrisch. ~ **poetry** Lyrik *f;* ~ **poet** Lyriker(in *f*) *m.* **2** *n (poem)* lyrisches Gedicht; *(often pl: words of song)* Text *m.*
**lyrical** ['lɪrɪkəl] *adj* lyrisch; *(fig)* schwärmerisch. **to get** *or* **wax** ~ **about sth** über etw *(acc)* ins Schwärmen geraten.

# M

**M, m** [em] n M, m nt. **M for Mary** (Brit), **M for Mike** (US) ≃ M wie Martha.

**m** = (a) **million(s)** Mio. (b) **metre(s)** m. (c) **mile(s)**. (d) **minute(s)** min. (e) **married** verh. (f) **masculine** m.

**M** (Brit) = **motorway**.

**MA** = (a) **Master of Arts**. (b) (US Post) = **Massachusetts**.

**ma** [mɑː] n (col) Mama (col), Mutti (col) f.

**mac** [mæk] n (Brit col) Regenmantel m.

**macabre** [mə'kɑːbrə] adj makaber.

**macaroni** [,mækə'rəʊnɪ] n Makkaroni pl. ~ **cheese** Käsenudeln pl.

**macaroon** [,mækə'ruːn] n Makrone f.

**mace¹** [meɪs] n (weapon) Streitkolben m; (mayor's) Amtsstab m.

**mace²** n (spice) Muskatblüte f.

**Macedonia** [,mæsɪ'dəʊnɪə] n Mazedonien nt.

**Macedonian** [,mæsɪ'dəʊnɪən] **1** n Mazedonier(in f) m. **2** adj mazedonisch.

**machete** [mə'ʃetɪ, mə'tʃeɪtɪ] n Machete f.

**Machiavellian** [,mækɪə'velɪən] adj machiavellistisch.

**machinations** [,mækɪ'neɪʃənz] npl Machenschaften pl.

**machine** [mə'ʃiːn] **1** n Maschine f, Apparat m; (vending ~) Automat m. **2** vt (Tech) maschinell herstellen; (treat with machine) maschinell bearbeiten; (Sew) mit der Maschine nähen.

**machine:** ~ **code** n (Comp) Maschinencode m; ~ **gun** n Maschinengewehr nt; ~ **minder** or **operative** n Maschinenarbeiter m; (skilled) Maschinist m; ~-**readable** adj maschinenlesbar, maschinell lesbar.

**machinery** [mə'ʃiːnərɪ] n (lit, fig) Maschinerie f; (mechanism) Mechanismus m. **the** ~ **of government** der Regierungsapparat.

**machine:** ~ **shop** n Maschinensaal m; ~ **tool** n Werkzeugmaschine f; ~ **translation** n maschinelle Übersetzung; ~ **washable** adj waschmaschinenfest.

**machinist** [mə'ʃiːnɪst] n (Tech) (operator) Maschinist m; (Sew) Näher(in f) m.

**macho** ['mætʃəʊ] adj macho pred, Macho-. ~ **type** Macho m.

**mackerel** ['mækrəl] n Makrele f.

**mackintosh** ['mækɪntɒʃ] n Regenmantel m.

**macro-** ['mækrəʊ-] pref makro-, Makro-.

**mad** [mæd] **1** adj (+er) (a) wahnsinnig; dog tollwütig; idea verrückt. **to go** ~ wahnsinnig werden; **to drive sb** ~ jdn wahnsinnig or verrückt machen; **he's as** ~ **as a hatter** or **a March hare** (prov) er ist total verrückt; **you must be** ~! du bist ja wahnsinnig!; **they made a** ~ **rush for the door** sie stürzten zur Tür; **you** ~ **fool!** du bist ja wahnsinnig! (b) (col: angry) sauer (col). **to be** ~ **at sb** auf jdn sauer (col) sein; **to be** ~ **about** or **at sth** über etw (acc) wütend or sauer (col) sein. (c) (col: very keen) **to be** ~

**about** or **on sth** auf etw (acc) verrückt sein. **2** adv (col) **to be** ~ **keen on sb/sth** ganz scharf auf jdn/etw sein (col); **to be** ~ **keen to do sth** ganz versessen darauf sein, etw zu tun; **like** ~ wie verrückt.

**Madagascan** [,mædə'gæskən] **1** adj madagassisch. **2** n Madagasse m, Madagassin f.

**Madagascar** [,mædə'gæskər] n Madagaskar nt.

**madam** ['mædəm] n (a) yes, ~ sehr wohl, gnädige Frau (old, form); **can I help you,** ~? kann ich Ihnen behilflich sein?; **Dear Sir or M**~ Sehr geehrte Damen und Herren; **M**~ **Chairman** Frau Vorsitzende. (b) (col: girl) kleine Madam. (c) (of brothel) Bordellwirtin f.

**madcap** ['mædkæp] adj versponnen.

**madden** ['mædn] vt (make angry) ärgern.

**maddening** ['mædnɪŋ] adj zum Verrücktwerden; delay also lästig; habit aufreizend. **isn't it** ~? ist das nicht ärgerlich?

**made** [meɪd] pret, ptp of **make**. ~ **up** erfunden.

**Madeira** [mə'dɪərə] n Madeira nt; (wine) Madeira m. ~ **cake** Sandkuchen m.

**made:** ~-**to-measure** adj maßgeschneidert; ~-**to-measure suit** Maßanzug m; ~-**to-order** adj speziell angefertigt; clothes maßgeschneidert.

**madhouse** ['mædhaʊs] n (lit, fig) Irrenhaus nt.

**madly** ['mædlɪ] adv wie verrückt; (col: extremely) wahnsinnig. **to be** ~ **in love (with sb)** total (in jdn) verschossen sein (col) ; **I'm not** ~ **keen** ich bin nicht wahnsinnig scharf darauf (col).

**madman** ['mædmən] n, pl -**men** [-mən] Verrückter m.

**madness** ['mædnɪs] n Wahnsinn m. **it's sheer** ~! das ist heller or reiner Wahnsinn!

**Madonna** [mə'dɒnə] n Madonna f.

**Madrid** [mə'drɪd] n Madrid nt.

**Mafia** ['mæfɪə] n Mafia f.

**mag** [mæg] (Brit col) = **magazine**.

**magazine** [,mægə'ziːn] n (a) Zeitschrift f, Magazin nt. (b) (in gun) Magazin nt.

**maggot** ['mægət] n Made f.

**magic** ['mædʒɪk] **1** n Magie, Zauberei f; (mysterious charm) Zauber m. **as if by** ~ wie durch Zauberei; **it worked like** ~ (col) es lief wie am Schnürchen (col). **2** adj Zauber-; powers magisch; moment zauberhaft. ~ **carpet** fliegender Teppich; **the** ~ **word** (having special effect) das Stichwort; (making sth possible) das Zauberwort.

**magical** ['mædʒɪkəl] adj magisch.

**magician** [mə'dʒɪʃən] n Zauberer m; (conjuror) Zauberkünstler m. **I'm not a** ~! ich kann doch nicht hexen!

**magistrate** ['mædʒɪstreɪt] n Friedensrichter m. ~**s' court** Schiedsgericht nt.

**magnanimity** [mægnə'nɪmɪtɪ] n Großmut f.

**magnanimous** adj, ~**ly** adv [mæg'nænɪməs, -lɪ] großmütig.

**magnate** ['mægneɪt] n Magnat m.

**magnesia** [mæg'niːʃə] n Magnesia f.

**magnesium** [mæg'niːzɪəm] n Magnesium nt.

**magnet** ['mægnɪt] n (lit, fig) Magnet m.

**magnetic** [mæg'netɪk] adj (lit) magnetisch; compass, field, mine, pole, strip Magnet-; charms unwiderstehlich. ~ **disk** (Comp) Magnetplatte f.

**magnetism** ['mægnɪtɪzəm] n Magnetismus m; (fig: of person) Anziehungskraft f.

**magnetize** ['mægnɪtaɪz] vt magnetisieren.

**magnification** [ˌmægnɪfɪ'keɪʃən] n Vergrößerung f.

**magnificence** [mæg'nɪfɪsəns] n (excellence) Größe f; (splendid appearance) Pracht f, Glanz m.

**magnificent** [mæg'nɪfɪsənt] adj (wonderful, excellent) großartig; food, meal ausgezeichnet; (of splendid appearance) prachtvoll.

**magnificently** [mæg'nɪfɪsəntlɪ] adv see adj großartig; prachtvoll.

**magnify** ['mægnɪfaɪ] vt vergrößern; (exaggerate) aufbauschen. ~**ing glass** Lupe f.

**magnitude** ['mægnɪtjuːd] n Ausmaß nt; (importance) Bedeutung f; (Astron) Größenklasse f. **operations of this** ~ Vorhaben dieser Größenordnung.

**magnolia** [mæg'nəʊlɪə] n Magnolie f.

**magpie** ['mægpaɪ] n Elster f.

**maharajah** [mɑːhə'rɑːdʒə] n Maharadscha m.

**mahogany** [mə'hogənɪ] **1** n Mahagoni nt; (tree) Mahagonibaum m. **2** adj Mahagoni-.

**maid** [meɪd] n (servant) (Dienst)mädchen nt; (in hotel) Zimmermädchen nt; (lady's ~) Zofe f; (old, poet: young girl) Maid f (poet).

**maiden** ['meɪdn] **1** n (old, poet) Mädchen nt. **2** adj flight, voyage etc Jungfern-.

**maiden:** ~ **aunt** n unverheiratete, ältere Tante; ~ **name** n Mädchenname m; ~ **speech** n Jungfernrede f.

**maid:** ~ **of honour** (Brit) or **honor** (US) n Brautjungfer f; ~**servant** n Hausangestellte f.

**mail** [meɪl] **1** n Post f. **to send sth by** ~ etw mit der Post schicken; **is there any** ~ **for me?** ist Post für mich da? **2** vt aufgeben; (put in letterbox) einwerfen; (send by ~) mit der Post schicken.

**mail:** ~**bag** n Postsack m; ~**box** n (US, also electronic) Briefkasten m.

**mailing** ['meɪlɪŋ] n (circular) Rundschreiben nt. ~ **list** Anschriftenliste f.

**mail:** ~**man** n (US) Briefträger, Postbote m; ~ **order** n: **by** ~ **order** auf dem Versandweg; ~**-order catalogue** n Versandhauskatalog m; ~**-order firm** n Versandhaus nt; ~**shot** n Mailshot m; ~ **train** n Postzug m; ~ **van** n (on roads; also (US) ~ **truck)** Postauto nt; (Brit Rail) Postwagen m.

**maim** [meɪm] vt (mutilate) verstümmeln; (cripple) zum Krüppel machen.

**main** [meɪn] **1** adj attr Haupt-. **the** ~ **thing is that ...** die Hauptsache ist, daß ...; **the** ~ **thing is to ...** das Wichtigste ist, zu ...; **the** ~ **thing is you're still alive** Hauptsache, du lebst noch. **2** n (a) (pipe) Hauptleitung f. **the** ~**s** (of town) das öffentliche Versorgungsnetz; (electricity also) das Stromnetz; **the electricity was switched off at the** ~**s** der Hauptschalter für den Strom wurde abgeschaltet. **(b) in the** ~ im großen und ganzen.

**main:** ~ **beam** n (Aut) Fernlicht nt; ~ **clause** n Hauptsatz m; ~ **course** n Hauptgericht nt; ~**frame** (computer) n (Comp) Großrechner m; ~**land** n Festland nt; **on the** ~**land of Europe** auf dem europäischen Festland; ~**line** vt (col: inject heroin etc) fixen (col); ~ **line** n (Rail) Hauptstrecke f.

**mainly** ['meɪnlɪ] adv hauptsächlich; (generally) überwiegend. **the meetings are held** ~ **on Tuesdays** die Besprechungen finden meistens dienstags statt.

**main road** n Hauptstraße f.

**mains** [meɪnz]: ~ **electricity** n Netzstrom m; ~ **gas** n Leitungsgas nt; ~**-operated** adj für Netzbetrieb; ~ **water** n Leitungswasser nt.

**main:** ~**spring** n (Mech) Triebfeder f; (fig) treibende Kraft; ~**stay** n (fig) (wichtigste) Stütze f; ~**stream** n Hauptrichtung f; **to be in the** ~**stream (of)** der Hauptrichtung (+gen) angehören; ~ **street** n Hauptstraße f.

**maintain** [meɪn'teɪn] vt **(a)** (keep up) aufrechterhalten; law and order etc wahren; quality also, speed, attitude beibehalten; life erhalten. **(b)** (support) family unterhalten. **(c)** (in good condition) machine, car warten; roads, building instand halten; (service) warten. **a well** ~**ed car** ein gut gepflegter Wagen. **(d)** (claim) behaupten.

**maintenance** ['meɪntɪnəns] n see vt **(a)** Aufrechterhaltung f; Wahrung f; Beibehaltung f; Erhaltung f. **(b)** (of family) Unterhalt m; (social security) Unterstützung f; (money paid) Unterhaltsgeld nt. **he has to pay** ~ er ist unterhaltspflichtig. **(c)** Wartung f; Instandhaltung f; Pflege f.

**maintenance:** ~ **contract** n Wartungsvertrag m; ~ **costs** npl Unterhaltskosten pl; ~**-free** adj wartungsfrei; ~ **order** n (Jur) Unterhaltsurteil nt.

**maisonette** [ˌmeɪzə'net] n (small flat) Appartement nt; (small house) Häuschen nt.

**maize** [meɪz] n (Brit) Mais m.

**Maj** = Major.

**majestic** [mə'dʒestɪk] adj majestätisch; proportions stattlich; music getragen.

**majesty** ['mædʒɪstɪ] n Majestät f. **Her M**~ Ihre Majestät; **Your M**~ Eure Majestät.

**major** ['meɪdʒəʳ] **1** adj **(a)** Haupt-; (of greater importance) bedeutend(er); (of greater extent) größer. **a** ~ **road** eine Hauptverkehrsstraße; **of** ~ **importance** von großer Bedeutung; ~ **part** Großteil m. **(b)** (Mus) key, scale Dur-. **A** ~ A-Dur nt. **2** n **(a)** (Mil) Major m. **(b)** (Jur) **to become a** ~ (come of age) mündig werden. **(c)** (US) (subject) Hauptfach nt. **3** vi (US) **to** ~ **in sth** etw als Hauptfach studieren.

**Majorca** [mə'dʒɔːkə] n Mallorca nt.

**major general** n Generalmajor m.

**majority** [mə'dʒɒrɪtɪ] n **(a)** Mehrheit f. **the** ~ **of cases** die Mehrzahl der Fälle; **to be in a** ~ in der Mehrzahl sein; **to have a** ~ **of 10** eine Mehrheit von 10 Stimmen haben; **by a small** ~ mit knapper Mehrheit. **(b)** (Jur) Mündigkeit f. **to attain one's** ~ mündig werden.

**majority:** ~ **decision** n Mehrheitsbeschluß m; ~ **holding** n (Fin) Mehrheitsbeteiligung f; ~ **rule** n Mehrheitsregierung f; ~ **verdict** n Mehrheitsentscheid m.

**make** [meɪk] (vb: pret, ptp **made) 1** vt **(a)** machen; bread backen; cars herstellen; dress nähen; coffee kochen; the world erschaffen; speech halten; choice, arrangements, decision treffen. **she made it into a suit** sie machte einen Anzug daraus; **it's made of gold** es ist aus Gold; **made in Germany** in Deutschland hergestellt; **to show what one is made of** zeigen, was in einem steckt; **they're made for each other** sie sind wie füreinander geschaffen; **this car wasn't made to carry eight people** dieses Auto ist nicht dazu gedacht, acht Leute zu transportieren.

**(b)** (cause to be) machen; (appoint) machen zu; (cause to do or happen) lassen; (compel) zwingen. **to** ~ **sb happy** etc jdn glücklich etc machen; **he was made a judge** man ernannte ihn zum Richter; **it** ~**s the room look smaller** es läßt den Raum kleiner wirken; **we decided to** ~ **a day of it** wir beschlossen, den ganzen Tag dafür zu nehmen; **let's ~ it Monday** sagen wir Montag; **it all ~s me think that ...** das alles läßt mich denken, daß ...; **to ~ sb laugh** jdn zum Lachen bringen; **what ~s you say that?** warum sagst du das?; **to ~ sb do sth** jdn dazu bringen, etw zu tun; *(force)* jdn zwingen, etw zu tun; **to ~ sth do, to ~ do with sth** mit etw auskommen; **you can't ~ things happen** man kann das nicht erzwingen; **how can I ~ you understand?** wie kann ich es Ihnen verständlich machen?; **that made the cloth shrink** dadurch lief der Stoff ein; **what ~s the car go?** wie wird der Wagen angetrieben?; **what ~s you think you can do it?** weshalb glauben Sie denn, daß Sie es schaffen können?; **the chemical ~s the plant grow faster** die Chemikalie bewirkt, daß die Pflanze schneller wächst; **what made you come to this town?** was hat Sie in diese Stadt geführt?; **to ~ oneself heard/understood** sich *(dat)* Gehör verschaffen/sich verständlich machen.

**(c)** *(earn)* money verdienen; *profit, loss, fortune* machen *(on* bei*)*; *name, reputation* sich *(dat)* verschaffen.

**(d)** *(reach, achieve, also Sport)* schaffen *(col)*, erreichen; *connection* schaffen; *summit etc* es schaffen zu *(col)*. **we made good time** wir kamen schnell voran; **he just made it** er hat es gerade noch geschafft; **sorry I couldn't ~ your party last night** tut mir leid, ich habe es gestern abend einfach nicht zu deiner Party geschafft; **his first record didn't ~ the charts** seine erste Platte schaffte es nicht bis in die Hitparade; **we've made it!** wir haben es geschafft!; **we'll never ~ the airport in time** wir schaffen es garantiert nicht mehr rechtzeitig zum Flughafen; **the story made the front page** die Geschichte kam auf die Titelseite.

**(e)** *(cause to succeed)* stars etc berühmt machen. **this film made her** dieser Film war für sie der Durchbruch; **you'll be made for life** Sie werden ausgesorgt haben; **he's got it made** *(col)* er hat ausgesorgt; **he's a made man** er ist ein gemachter Mann; **that ~s my day!** das freut mich unheimlich!; *(iro)* das hat mir gerade noch gefehlt!; **he can ~ or break you** er hat dich ganz in der Hand.

**(f)** *(equal)* sein, ergeben; *(constitute also)* machen. **2 plus 2 ~s 4** 2 und 2 ist 4; **how much does that ~ altogether?** was macht das insgesamt?; **he made a good father** er gab einen guten Vater ab; **he'll never ~ a soldier** aus ihm wird nie ein Soldat.

**(g)** *(estimate)* distance, total schätzen auf. **what time do you ~ it?** wie spät hast du es?; **I ~ it 3.15** auf meiner Uhr ist es 3¹⁵; **I ~ it 3 miles** ich schätze 3 Meilen; **how many do you ~ it?** wie viele sind es nach deiner Rechnung?

**2** *vi* **(a)** *(go)* **to ~ towards a place** auf einen Ort zuhalten; *(ship)* Kurs auf einen Ort nehmen. **(b) to ~ as if to do sth** Anstalten machen, etw zu tun; *(as deception)* so tun, als wolle man etw tun.

**3** *n* **(a)** *(brand)* Marke *f.* **what ~ of car do you run?** welche (Auto)marke fahren Sie? **(b)** *(pej col)* **on the ~** *(for profit)* profitgierig *(col)*, auf Profit aus; *(ambitious)* karrieresüchtig *(col)*; *(sexually)* sexhungrig *(col)*.

▶**make away** *vi* = **make off.**

▶**make for** *vi* +*prep obj* **(a)** *(head for)* zuhalten auf *(+acc)*; *(vehicle)* losfahren auf *(+acc)*; *(ship)* Kurs halten auf *(+acc)*. **where are you making ~?** wo willst du hin? **(b)** *(promote)* führen zu; *happy marriage etc* den Grund legen für. **the trade figures ~ ~ optimism** die Handelsziffern geben Anlaß zum Optimismus.

▶**make of** *vi* +*prep obj* halten von. **I didn't ~ much**

~ **it** ich konnte nicht viel damit anfangen.

**make off** *vi* sich davonmachen *(with sth* mit etw*)*.

**make out 1** *vt sep* **(a)** *(write out)* cheque ausstellen *(to* auf *+acc)*; *list, bill* aufstellen; *(fill out)* form ausfüllen. **to ~ ~ a case for sth** für etw argumentieren. **(b)** *(see, discern)* ausmachen; *(decipher)* entziffern; *(understand)* verstehen; *person, actions* schlau werden aus. **how do you ~ that ~?** wie kommst du darauf? **(c)** *(imply)* **to ~ ~ that ...** es so hinstellen, als ob ...; **he made ~ that he was hurt** er tat, als sei er verletzt; **to ~ sb ~ to be a genius** jdn als Genie hinstellen. **2** *vi* **(a)** *(col) (get on)* zurechtkommen; *(with people)* auskommen; *(succeed)* es schaffen.

▶**make over** *vt sep* *(assign)* überschreiben *(to sb* dat*)*; *(bequeath)* vermachen *(to sb* dat*)*.

▶**make up 1** *vt sep* **(a)** *(prepare)* food, medicine, bed zurechtmachen; *parcel also* zusammenpacken; *list, accounts, team* zusammenstellen. **to ~ material ~ into sth** Material zu etw verarbeiten. **(b)** *(constitute)* bilden. **to be made ~ of** bestehen aus. **(c)** *quarrel* beilegen. **to ~ it ~ (with sb)** sich (mit jdm) wieder vertragen. **(d)** *face* schminken. **(e) to ~ ~ one's mind (to do sth)** sich entschließen(, etw zu tun); **to ~ ~ one's mind about sb/sth** sich *(dat)* eine Meinung über jdn/etw bilden. **(f)** *(invent)* erfinden. **(g)** *(compensate for)* loss ausgleichen; *distance, time* aufholen; *sleep* nachholen. **to ~ it ~ to sb for sth** *(compensate)* jdn für etw entschädigen; *(emotionally etc)* jdm etw wiedergutmachen.

**2** *vi* **(a)** *(after quarrelling)* sich wieder vertragen. **(b)** *(apply cosmetics)* sich schminken.

▶**make up for** *vi* +*prep obj* ausgleichen. **to ~ ~ ~ lost time** verlorene Zeit aufholen; **to ~ ~ ~ the loss of sb/lack of sth** jdn/etw ersetzen.

▶**make up to** *vi* +*prep obj* *(col)* sich heranmachen an *(+acc)*.

**make-believe** ['meɪkbɪ,liːv] **1** *adj attr* Phantasie-; *world also* Schein-. **2** *n* Phantasie *f.* **a world of ~** eine Phantasiewelt; **it's only ~** das ist doch nur erfunden. **3** *vt* sich *(dat)* vorstellen.

**maker** ['meɪkə'] *n* *(manufacturer)* Hersteller *m.* **our M~** unser Schöpfer *m.*

**make:** **~shift** *adj* improvisiert; *repairs* behelfsmäßig; **~-up** *n* **(a)** Make-up *nt*; *(Theat also)* Maske *f.* **(b)** *(composition)* *(of team, party etc)* Zusammenstellung *f*; *(character)* Veranlagung *f*; **loyalty is part of his ~-up** er ist loyal veranlagt; **(c)** *(Print: page ~-up)* Umbruch *m*; **~-up bag** *n* Kosmetiktasche *f*; **~-up artist** *n* Maskenbildner(in *f*) *m.*

**making** ['meɪkɪŋ] *n* **(a)** *(production)* Herstellung *f*; *(of food)* Zubereitung *f.* **in the ~** im Entstehen; **here we have history in the ~** hier wird Geschichte gemacht; **it was the ~ of him** *(made him successful)* das hat ihn zu dem gemacht, was er (heute) ist. **(b) he has the ~s of an actor** etc er hat das Zeug zu einem Schauspieler etc; **the situation has all the ~s of a strike** die Situation bietet alle Voraussetzungen für einen Streik.

**maladjusted** [,mælə'dʒʌstɪd] *adj (Psych, Sociol)* verhaltensgestört.

**maladroit** [,mælə'drɔɪt] *adj* ungeschickt.

**malady** ['mælədɪ] *n* Leiden *nt.*

**malaise** [mæ'leɪz] *n* Unwohlsein *nt*; *(fig)* Unbehagen *nt.*

**malaria** [mə'lɛərɪə] *n* Malaria *f.*

**Malawi** [mə'lɑːwɪ] *n* Malawi *nt.*

**Malawian** [mə'lɑːwɪən] **1** *adj* malawisch. **2** *n* Malawier(in *f*) *m.*

**Malay** [mə'leɪ] **1** *adj* malaiisch. **2** *n* **(a)** Malaie *m*, Malaiin *f.* **(b)** *(language)* Malaiisch *nt.*

**Malaya** [mə'leɪə] *n* Malaya *nt.*

**Malayan** [mə'leɪən] **1** *adj* malaiisch. **2** *n* Malaie *m*, Malaiin *f*.

**Malaysia** [mə'leɪzɪə] *n* Malaysia *nt*.

**Malaysian** [mə'leɪzɪən] **1** *adj* malaysisch. **2** *n* Malaysier(in *f*) *m*.

**Maldive Islands** ['mɔːldaɪv'aɪləndz] *npl* Malediven *pl*.

**male** [meɪl] **1** *adj* männlich. ~ **friend** Männerbekanntschaft *f*; ~ **nurse** Krankenpfleger *m*; ~ **crocodile** Krokodilmännchen *nt*; ~ **chauvinist pig** *(col pej)* Chauvi *m (col)*; ~ **menopause** *(hum)* Wechseljahre *pl* (des Mannes). **2** *n (animal)* Männchen *nt*; *(col: man)* Mann *m*.

**malevolence** [mə'levələns] *n* Boshaftigkeit *f*; *(of action)* Böswilligkeit *f*.

**malevolent** [mə'levələnt] *adj* boshaft; *action* böswillig.

**malformation** [ˌmælfɔː'meɪʃən] *n* Mißbildung *f*.

**malformed** [mæl'fɔːmd] *adj* mißgebildet.

**malfunction** [ˌmæl'fʌŋkʃən] **1** *n (of liver etc)* Funktionsstörung *f*; *(of machine)* Defekt *m*. **2** *vi (liver etc)* nicht richtig arbeiten; *(machine etc)* defekt sein; *(system)* nicht richtig funktionieren.

**malice** ['mælɪs] *n* Bosheit *f*; *(of action)* Böswilligkeit *f*. **I bear him no** ~ ich bin ihm nicht böse; **with** ~ **aforethought** *(Jur)* in böswilliger Absicht.

**malicious** [mə'lɪʃəs] *adj person, words* boshaft; *slander* böswillig; *(Jur) damage* mutwillig.

**maliciously** [mə'lɪʃəslɪ] *adv see adj* boshaft; böswillig; mutwillig.

**malign** [mə'laɪn] **1** *adj (liter) intent* böse; *influence* unheilvoll. **2** *vt* verleumden; *(run down)* schlecht machen. **to** ~ **sb's character** jdm Übles nachsagen.

**malignant** [mə'lɪgnənt] *adj* bösartig. **a** ~ **growth** *(Med, fig)* ein bösartiges Geschwür.

**malinger** [mə'lɪŋgə] *vi* simulieren.

**malingerer** [mə'lɪŋgərəʳ] *n* Simulant *m*.

**mall** [mɔːl, mæl] *n (US: also shopping* ~*)* Einkaufszentrum *nt*.

**malleable** ['mælɪəbl] *adj* formbar *(also fig)*, weich.

**mallet** ['mælɪt] *n* Holzhammer *m*; *(croquet)* (Krocket)hammer *m*; *(polo)* (Polo)schläger *m*.

**malnutrition** [ˌmælnjuː'trɪʃən] *n* Unterernährung *f*.

**malpractice** [ˌmæl'præktɪs] *n* Berufsvergehen, Amtsvergehen *nt*.

**malt** [mɔːlt] *n* Malz *nt*. ~ **loaf** ≃ Malzbrot *nt*; ~ **whisky** Malt Whisky *m*.

**Malta** ['mɔːltə] *n* Malta *nt*.

**Maltese** [ˌmɔːl'tiːz] **1** *adj* maltesisch. ~ **cross** Malteserkreuz *nt*. **2** *n* **(a)** Malteser(in *f*) *m*. **(b)** *(language)* Maltesisch *nt*.

**maltreat** [ˌmæl'triːt] *vt* schlecht behandeln; *(using violence)* mißhandeln.

**maltreatment** [ˌmæl'triːtmənt] *n see vt* schlechte Behandlung; Mißhandlung *f*.

**mam(m)a** [mə'mɑː] *n (col)* Mama *(col)*.

**mammal** ['mæməl] *n* Säugetier *nt*.

**mammoth** ['mæməθ] **1** *n* Mammut *nt*. **2** *adj* Mammut-; *cost, enterprise* kolossal.

**man** [mæn] **1** *n, pl* **men** Mann *m*; *(human race: also* **M**~*)* der Mensch; die Menschen; *(Chess)* Figur *f*; *(in draughts)* Stein *m*. **to make a** ~ **out of sb** einen Mann aus jdm machen; **that's just like a** ~ das ist typisch Mann; **they are** ~ **and wife** sie sind Mann und Frau; **the** ~ **in the street** der Mann auf der Straße; ~ **of property** vermögender Mann; **he's a** ~ **about town** er kennt sich aus; **a** ~ **of the world** ein Mann von Welt; **no** ~ keiner, niemand; **any** ~ jeder; **men say that** ... die Leute sagen, daß ...; **that** ~ **Jones** dieser Jones!; **as one** ~ geschlossen, wie ein Mann; **they are socialists to a** ~ sie sind allesamt Sozialisten; **he's not the** ~ **for the job** er ist nicht der Richtige für diese Aufgabe; **he's not a** ~ **to** ... er ist nicht der Typ, der ...; **he's a family** ~ *(home-loving)* er ist sehr häuslich; **it's got to be a local** ~ es muß jemand aus dieser Gegend sein; **I'm not a drinking** ~ ich bin kein großer Trinker; **you can't do that,** ~ *(col)* Mensch *or* Mann, das kannst du doch nicht machen! *(col)*.

**2** *vt ship* bemannen; *fortress* besetzen; *pump, gun* bedienen. **the ship is** ~**ned by a crew of 30** das Schiff hat 30 Mann Besatzung; **there's someone** ~**ning the telephone all day** es ist den ganzen Tag über jemand da, der das Telefon bedient.

**Man** [mæn] *n*: **the Isle of** ~ die Insel Man.

**manacles** ['mænəklz] *n pl* Handfesseln *pl*.

**manage** ['mænɪdʒ] **1** *vt* **(a)** *company, organization* leiten; *affairs* regeln; *football team, pop group* managen. **the election was** ~**d** *(pej)* die Wahl war manipuliert.

**(b)** *(handle, control) person, animal, car* zurechtkommen mit. **I can** ~ **him** mit ihm werde ich schon fertig.

**(c)** *task, another portion* bewältigen, schaffen *(col)*. **£5 is the most I can** ~ ich kann mir höchstens £5 leisten; **I'll** ~ **it** das werde ich schon schaffen; **can you** ~ **the cases?** kannst du die Koffer (allein) tragen?; **she can't** ~ **the stairs** sie kommt die Treppe nicht hinauf/hinunter; **can you** ~ **8 o'clock?** 8 Uhr, ginge das?; **I couldn't** ~ **another thing** ich könnte keinen Bissen mehr runterbringen; **to** ~ **to do sth** es schaffen, etw zu tun; **he** ~**d not to get his feet wet** es ist ihm gelungen, keine nassen Füße zu bekommen; **how did you** ~ **to miss that?** wie konnte Ihnen das nur entgehen?; **could you possibly** ~ **to close the door?** *(iro)* wäre es vielleicht möglich, die Tür zuzumachen?

**2** *vi* zurechtkommen, es schaffen *(col)*. **can you** ~**?** geht es?; **how do you** ~**?** wie machen Sie das bloß?; **to** ~ **without sth/sb** ohne etw/jdn auskommen; **how do you** ~ **on only £20 a week?** wie kommen Sie mit nur £20 pro Woche aus?

**manageable** ['mænɪdʒəbl] *adj child, horse* fügsam; *amount, job* zu bewältigen; *hair* leicht frisierbar; *number* überschaubar; *car* leicht zu handhaben. **pieces of a more** ~ **size** Stücke, die leichter zu handhaben sind.

**management** ['mænɪdʒmənt] *n* **(a)** *(act: of company)* Leitung, Führung *f*. ~ **consultant** Unternehmensberater(in *f*) *m*; ~ **studies** Betriebswirtschaft *f*. **(b)** *(persons)* Unternehmensleitung *f*; *(of single unit or smaller factory)* Betriebsleitung *f*; *(noncommercial)* Leitung *f*; ~ **and workers** Arbeitgeber und Arbeitnehmer *pl*; **"under new** ~**"** „neuer Inhaber"; *(shop)* „neu eröffnet".

**manager** ['mænɪdʒəʳ] *n (Comm etc)* Geschäftsführer *m*; *(of smaller firm or factory)* Betriebsleiter *m*; *(of bank, chain store)* Filialleiter *m*; *(of department)* Abteilungsleiter *m*; *(of pop group etc)* Manager *m*; *(of team)* Trainer *m*. **sales/publicity** ~ Verkaufsleiter/Werbeleiter *m*.

**manageress** [ˌmænɪdʒə'res] *n* Geschäftsführerin *f*; *(of department)* Abteilungsleiterin *f*; *(of chain store)* Filialleiterin *f*.

**managerial** [ˌmænə'dʒɪərɪəl] *adj* geschäftlich; *(executive)* Management-; *post* leitend. **he has no** ~ **skills** er hat keine Führungsqualitäten.

**managing director** ['mænɪdʒɪŋdɪ'rektəʳ] *n* Geschäftsführer(in *f*) *m*.

**Mancunian** [mæn'kjuːnɪən] **1** *n* Bewohner(in *f*) *m* Manchesters. **2** *adj person* aus Manchester; *institution* Manchesters.

**mandarin** ['mændərɪn] *n* (a) *(Chinese official)* Mandarin *m.* (b) *(language)* M~ Hochchinesisch *nt.* (c) *(fruit)* Mandarine *f.*

**mandate** ['mændeɪt] *n* Auftrag *m*; *(Pol also)* Mandat *nt*; *(Hist: territory)* Mandatsgebiet *nt.* **to give sb a ~ to do sth** jdm den Auftrag geben, etw zu tun.

**mandatory** ['mændətərɪ] *adj* obligatorisch; *(Pol)* mandatorisch. **membership is ~** Mitgliedschaft ist Pflicht.

**mandolin(e)** ['mændəlɪn] *n* Mandoline *f.*

**mane** [meɪn] *n (lit, fig)* Mähne *f.*

**maneuver** *n, vti (US)* = **manoeuvre.**

**manful** *adj*, **~ly** *adv* ['mænful, -ɪ] mannhaft, mutig.

**manganese** [ˌmæŋɡə'niːz] *n* Mangan *nt.*

**mangle¹** ['mæŋɡl] *n* Mangel *f.*

**mangle²** *vt (also ~ up)* (übel) zurichten.

**mango** ['mæŋɡəʊ] *n (fruit)* Mango *f.*

**mangy** ['meɪndʒɪ] *adj dog* räudig; *(fig) thing* schäbig.

**man:** **~handle** *vt* (a) grob behandeln; **he was ~handled into the van** er wurde recht unsanft in den Wagen verfrachtet; (b) *piano etc* hieven; **~hole** *n* Kanalschacht *m.*

**manhood** ['mænhʊd] *n (state)* Mannesalter *nt.*

**man:** **~-hour** *n* Arbeitsstunde *f*; **~hunt** *n* Fahndung *f*; *(for criminal also)* Verbrecherjagd *f.*

**mania** ['meɪnɪə] *n (madness)* Manie *f*; *(col: enthusiasm)* Manie *f*, Tick *(col) m.* **he has a ~ for punctuality** er hat einen Pünktlichkeitsfimmel *(col).*

**maniac** ['meɪnɪæk] **1** *adj* wahnsinnig. **2** *n* (a) Wahnsinnige(r), Irre(r) *mf.* (b) *(fig)* **these sports ~s** diese Sportfanatiker *pl.*

**manic-depressive** ['mænɪkdɪ'presɪv] **1** *adj* manisch-depressiv. **2** *n* Manisch-Depressive(r) *mf.*

**manicure** ['mænɪˌkjʊə'] **1** *n* Maniküre *f.* **~ set** Nagelnecessaire *nt.* **2** *vt* maniküren.

**manifest** ['mænɪfest] **1** *adj* offenkundig; *(definite also)* eindeutig. **he made it ~ that ...** er machte deutlich, daß ... **2** *vr* **to ~ itself** sich zeigen.

**manifestation** [ˌmænɪfe'steɪʃən] *n (act of showing)* Ausdruck *m*, Bekundung *f*; *(sign)* Anzeichen *nt.*

**manifestly** ['mænɪfestlɪ] *adv* offensichtlich. **it's so ~ obvious** es ist so völlig offensichtlich.

**manifesto** [ˌmænɪ'festəʊ] *n, pl* **-(e)s** Manifest *nt.*

**manifold** ['mænɪfəʊld] **1** *adj* vielfältig. **~ uses** vielseitige Anwendung. **2** *n (Aut)* **inlet** *or* **intake/exhaust ~** Ansaug-/Auspuffkrümmer *m.*

**Manil(l)a** [mə'nɪlə] *n (paper)* Hartpapier *nt.* **~ envelope** brauner Umschlag.

**manipulate** [mə'nɪpjʊleɪt] *vt* (a) *machine etc* bedienen; *bones* einrenken; *(after fracture)* zurechtrücken. (b) *public opinion, prices* manipulieren; *accounts also* frisieren *(col).*

**manipulation** [məˌnɪpjʊ'leɪʃən] *n* Manipulation *f.*

**mankind** [mæn'kaɪnd] *n* die Menschheit.

**manliness** ['mænlɪnɪs] *n* Männlichkeit *f.*

**manly** ['mænlɪ] *adj (+er)* männlich.

**man-made** ['mæn'meɪd] *adj* künstlich, Kunst-. **~ fibres** Kunstfasern *pl.*

**manna** ['mænə] *n* Manna *nt.*

**manned** [mænd] *adj satellite etc* bemannt.

**mannequin** ['mænɪkɪn] *n (fashion)* Mannequin *nt*; *(Art)* Modell *nt*; *(dummy)* Schaufensterpuppe *f.*

**manner** ['mænə'] *n* (a) *(mode)* Art (und Weise) *f.* **in this ~** auf diese Art und Weise; **in such a ~ that ...** so ..., daß ...; **in a ~ of speaking** sozusagen; **as to the ~ born** als sei er/sie dafür geschaffen. (b) *(behaviour etc)* Art *f.* **he has a very kind ~** er hat ein sehr freundliches Wesen; **I don't like his ~** ich mag seine Art nicht. (c) **~s** *pl (good, bad etc)* Manieren *pl*; **that's bad ~s** das gehört sich nicht; **it's bad ~s**

**to ...** es gehört sich nicht, zu ...; **he has no ~s** er hat keine Manieren; **to teach sb some ~s** jdm Manieren beibringen. (d) *(class, type)* Art *f.* **we saw all ~ of interesting things** wir sahen allerlei Interessantes.

**mannerism** ['mænərɪzəm] *n (in behaviour)* Eigenheit *f*; *(of style)* Manieriertheit *f.* **his ~s** seine Manierismen.

**mannerly** ['mænəlɪ] *adj* wohlerzogen.

**manoeuvrable**, *(US)* **maneuverable** [mə'nuːvrəbl] *adj* wendig. **easily ~** leicht zu manövrieren.

**manoeuvre**, *(US)* **maneuver** [mə'nuːvə'] **1** *n (Mil)* Feldzug *m*; *(clever plan)* Manöver *nt*, Schachzug *m.* **~s** Manöver *nt or pl*; **the troops were out on ~s** die Truppen befanden sich im Manöver. **2** *vt* manövrieren. **to ~ a gun into position** ein Geschütz in Stellung bringen. **3** *vi* manövrieren; *(Mil)* (ein) Manöver durchführen. **to ~ for position** *(lit, fig)* sich in eine günstige Position manövrieren; **room to ~** Manövrierfähigkeit *f.*

**manor** ['mænə'] *n* Gut(shof *m*) *nt.* **lord of the ~** Gutsherr *m*; **~ house** Herrenhaus *nt.*

**manpower** ['mænˌpaʊə'] *n* Arbeitskräfte *pl*; *(Mil)* Stärke *f.* **M~ Services Commission** *(Brit)* Behörde *f für Arbeitsbeschaffung, Arbeitsvermittlung und Berufsausbildung.*

**mansion** ['mænʃən] *n* Villa *f*; *(of ancient family)* Herrenhaus *nt.*

**man-size(d)** ['mænsaɪz(d)] *adj (col: very big)* Riesen-.

**manslaughter** ['mænˌslɔːtə'] *n* Totschlag *m.*

**mantelpiece** ['mæntlpiːs] *n* Kaminsims *nt or m.*

**mantle** ['mæntl] *n* (a) Umhang *m*; *(fig)* Deckmantel *m.* **a ~ of snow** eine Schneedecke. (b) *(gas ~)* Glühstrumpf *m.*

**man-to-man** [ˌmæntə'mæn] *adj, adv* von Mann zu Mann.

**manual** ['mænjʊəl] **1** *adj* manuell; *labour* körperlich. **~ worker** (manueller) Arbeiter *m*; **~ gearbox** *or* **transmission** *(Brit)* Schaltgetriebe *nt*, Schaltung *f* von Hand. **2** *n (book)* Handbuch *nt.*

**manufacture** [ˌmænjʊ'fæktʃə'] **1** *n (act)* Herstellung *f*; *(pl: products)* Erzeugnisse *pl.* **2** *vt* herstellen. **~d goods** Fertigware *f.*

**manufacturer** [ˌmænjʊ'fæktʃərə'] *n* Hersteller *m.*

**manufacturing** [ˌmænjʊ'fæktʃərɪŋ] **1** *adj techniques* Herstellungs-; *industry* verarbeitend. **~ fault** Fabrikationsfehler *m.* **2** *n* Herstellung *f.*

**manure** [mə'njʊə'] **1** *n* Dung *m*; *(esp artificial)* Dünger *m.* **2** *vt field* düngen.

**manuscript** ['mænjʊskrɪpt] *n* Manuskript *nt*; *(ancient also)* Handschrift *f.*

**many** ['menɪ] *adj, n* viele. **~ people** viele (Menschen *or* Leute); **there were as ~ as 20** es waren sogar 20 da; **as ~ again** noch einmal so viele; **there's one too ~** einer ist zuviel; **he's had one too ~** er hat einen zuviel getrunken; **they were too ~ for us** sie waren zu viele für uns; **he made one mistake too ~** er hat einen Fehler zuviel gemacht; **~ a good soldier** so mancher gute Soldat; **~ a time** so manches Mal; **a good/great ~ houses** sehr viele Häuser.

**many:** **~-coloured** *(Brit)*, **~-colored** *(US) adj* vielfarbig; **~-sided** *adj* vielseitig.

**Manx** [mæŋks] *adj* der Insel Man.

**Manxman** ['mæŋksmən] *n* Bewohner *m* der Insel Man.

**Maori** ['maʊrɪ] **1** *adj* maorisch. **2** *n* (a) Maori *mf.* (b) *(language)* Maori *nt.*

**map** [mæp] **1** *n* (Land)karte *f*; *(of streets, town)* Stadtplan *m*; *(showing specific item)* Karte *f.* **this will put Cheam on the ~** *(fig)* das wird Cheam zu einem Namen verhelfen; **it's right off the** ~ *(fig)* das liegt (ja) am Ende der Welt; **entire cities were wiped off the** ~ ganze Städte wurden ausradiert. **2** *vt (measure)* vermessen; *(make a map of)* eine Karte anfertigen von.

►**map out** *vt sep* **(a)** *(lit)* see **map 2. (b)** *(fig: plan)* entwerfen. **our holiday schedule was all** ~**ped** ~ **in advance** der Zeitplan für unsere Ferien war schon im voraus genau festgelegt.

**maple** ['meɪpl] *n (wood, tree)* Ahorn *m.* ~ **leaf** Ahornblatt *nt;* ~ **syrup** Ahornsirup *m.*

**map:** ~**-maker** *n* Kartograph(in *f*) *m;* ~**-reading** *n* Kartenlesen *nt.*

**mar** [mɑːr] *vt* verderben; *happiness* trüben; *beauty* mindern.

**Mar** = **March** Mrz.

**marathon** ['mærəθən] **1** *n (lit)* Marathon(lauf) *m; (fig)* Marathon *nt.* **2** *adj* Marathon-.

**marauder** [mə'rɔːdər] *n* Plünderer *m.*

**marauding** [mə'rɔːdɪŋ] *adj* plündernd.

**marble** ['mɑːbl] **1** *n* Marmor *m; (glass ball)* Murmel *f,* Klicker *m (col).* **2** *adj* Marmor-. **3** *vt* marmorieren.

**March** [mɑːtʃ] *n* März *m;* see **September.**

**march** [mɑːtʃ] **1** *n* **(a)** *(Mil, Mus)* Marsch *m; (demonstration)* Demonstration *f; (fig: long walk)* Weg *m.* **we had been five days on the** ~ wir waren fünf Tage lang marschiert; **it's two days'** ~ es ist ein Zwei-Tage-Marsch. **(b)** *(of time, history, events)* Lauf *m.* **(c)** **to steal a** ~ **on sb** jdm zuvorkommen. **2** *vt soldiers* marschieren lassen; *distance* marschieren. **to** ~ **sb off** jdn abführen. **3** *vi* marschieren. **forward** ~**!** vorwärts(, marsch)!; **quick** ~**!** im Laufschritt, marsch!; **time** ~**es on** die Zeit bleibt nicht stehen; **to** ~ **past sb** an jdm vorbeimarschieren; **she** ~**ed straight up to him** sie marschierte schnurstracks auf ihn zu.

**marcher** ['mɑːtʃər] *n (demonstrator)* Demonstrant(in *f*) *m.*

**marching orders** ['mɑːtʃɪŋ'ɔːdəz] *npl (Mil)* Marschbefehl *m; (col)* Entlassung *f.* **she gave him his** ~ sie hat ihm den Laufpaß gegeben.

**marchioness** ['mɑːʃənɪs] *n* Marquise *f.*

**march past** *n* Aufmarsch *m.*

**mare** [mɛər] *n (horse)* Stute *f; (donkey)* Eselin *f.*

**margarine** [,mɑːdʒə'riːn], **marge** [mɑːdʒ] *(col)* *n* Margarine *f.*

**margin** ['mɑːdʒɪn] *n* **(a)** *(on page)* Rand *m.* **(b)** *(extra amount)* Spielraum *m.* **to allow for a** ~ **of error** etwaige Fehler mit einkalkulieren; **by a narrow** ~ knapp; **(profit)** ~ Gewinnspanne *f.*

**marginal** ['mɑːdʒɪnl] *adj* **(a)** *note* Rand-. **(b)** *improvement, difference* geringfügig; *constituency, seat* mit knapper Mehrheit.

**marginally** ['mɑːdʒɪnəlɪ] *adv* geringfügig.

**marigold** ['mærɪɡəʊld] *n* Ringelblume *f.*

**marijuana** [,mærɪ'hwɑːnə] *n* Marihuana *nt.*

**marina** [mə'riːnə] *n* Jachthafen *m.*

**marinade** [,mærɪ'neɪd] *n* Marinade *f.*

**marinate** ['mærɪneɪt] *vt* marinieren.

**marine** [mə'riːn] **1** *adj* Meeres-, See-. ~ **biologist** Meeresbiologe *m*/-biologin *f;* ~ **insurance** Seeversicherung *f;* ~ **life** Meeresfauna und -flora *f.* **2** *n* **(a)** *(fleet)* Marine *f.* **merchant** ~ Handelsmarine *f.* **(b)** **the** ~**s** die Marinetruppen *pl;* **tell that to the** ~**s!** *(col)* das kannst du deiner Großmutter erzählen! *(col).*

**mariner** ['mærɪnər] *n* Seefahrer, Seemann *m.*

**marionette** [,mærɪə'net] *n* Marionette *f.*

**marital** ['mærɪtl] *adj* ehelich; *bed, row etc* Ehe-. ~ **status** Familienstand *m.*

**maritime** ['mærɪtaɪm] *adj* See-; *region, province* Küsten-.

**marjoram** ['mɑːdʒərəm] *n* Majoran *m.*

**Mark** [mɑːk] *n* ≈ Markus *m.*

**mark¹** [mɑːk] *n (Fin)* Mark *f.*

**mark²** **1** *n* **(a)** *(stain, spot etc)* Fleck *m; (scratch)* Kratzer *m; (on person)* Mal *nt; (on plane, football pitch etc)* Markierung *f.* **to make a** ~ **on sth** einen Fleck auf etw *(acc)* machen; *(damage sth)* etw beschädigen; **dirty** ~**s** Schmutzflecken *pl;* **with not a** ~ **on it** in makellosem Zustand; **he didn't have a** ~ **on him** er wies keine Verletzungen auf; **the** ~**s of violence** die Spuren der Gewalt.

**(b)** *(in exam)* Note *f.* **high** or **good** ~**s** gute Noten *pl;* **the** ~**s are out of 100** insgesamt kann/konnte man 100 Punkte erreichen; **there are no** ~**s for guessing** *(fig)* das ist ja wohl nicht schwer zu erraten; **he gets full** ~**s for punctuality** *(fig)* in Pünktlichkeit verdient er eine Eins.

**(c)** *(sign, indication)* Zeichen *nt.* **it bears the** ~**s of genius** das trägt geniale Züge; **it's the** ~ **of a gentleman** daran erkennt man den Gentleman.

**(d)** *(level)* **expenses have reached the £100** ~ die Ausgaben haben die 100-Pfund-Grenze erreicht.

**(e) M~ IX Jaguar** Jaguar IX.

**(f)** *(phrases)* **to be quick off the** ~ *(Sport)* einen guten Start haben; *(fig)* blitzschnell reagieren; **to be up to the** ~ den Anforderungen entsprechen; **to leave one's** ~ **(on sth)** einer Sache *(dat)* seinen Stempel aufdrücken; **to make one's** ~ *(instead of signature)* drei Kreuze (als Unterschrift) machen; *(fig)* sich *(dat)* einen Namen machen; **on your** ~**s!** auf die Plätze!; **to be wide of the** ~ *(shooting)* danebenschießen; *(fig: in guessing)* danebentippen; **to hit the** ~ *(lit, fig)* ins Schwarze treffen.

**2** *vt* **(a)** *(adversely)* beschädigen; *(stain)* schmutzig machen; *(scratch)* verkratzen.

**(b)** *(for recognition, identity)* markieren; *(label)* beschriften; *(price)* auszeichnen. **the bottle was** ~**ed "poison"** die Flasche trug die Aufschrift „Gift"; **the teacher** ~**ed him absent** der Lehrer trug ihn als fehlend ein; **it's not** ~**ed on the map** es ist nicht auf der Karte eingezeichnet.

**(c)** *(characterize)* kennzeichnen. **the new bill** ~**s a change of policy** das neue Gesetz deutet auf einen politischen Kurswechsel hin.

**(d)** *exam, paper* korrigieren (und benoten). **to** ~ **sth wrong** etw anstreichen.

**(e)** *(heed)* hören auf *(+acc).* ~ **my words** eins kann ich Ihnen sagen; *(threatening, warning)* lassen Sie sich das gesagt sein!

**(f)** *(Sport) player, opponent* decken.

**(g)** **to** ~ **time** *(Mil, fig)* auf der Stelle treten.

**3** *vi (get dirty)* schmutzig werden; *(get scratched)* Kratzer bekommen. **she** ~**s easily** sie bekommt leicht blaue Flecken.

►**mark down** *vt sep (note down)* (sich *dat*) notieren; *(reduce)* prices herabsetzen.

►**mark off** *vt sep* kennzeichnen; *boundary* markieren; *danger area etc* absperren.

►**mark out** *vt sep* **(a)** *tennis court etc* abstecken. **(b)** *(note)* bestimmen *(for* für*).* **he's been** ~**ed** ~ **for promotion** er ist zur Beförderung vorgesehen.

►**mark up** *vt sep (write up)* notieren *(on* auf *+dat); (increase)* price heraufsetzen.

**marked** [mɑːkt] *adj* **(a)** *contrast, accent* deutlich; *improvement* spürbar. **(b) he's a** ~ **man** er steht auf der schwarzen Liste.

**markedly** ['mɑːkɪdlɪ] *adv* merklich. **it is** ~ **better** es ist wesentlich besser.

**marker** ['mɑːkər] *n* **(a)** Marke *f; (to turn at)* Wende-

# market

**marke** f; (on road) Schild nt; (in book) Lesezeichen nt. ~ **pen** Markierstift m. (**b**) (for exams) Korrektor(in f) m.

**market** ['mɑːkɪt] **1** n Markt m. **at the** ~ auf dem Markt; **to go to** ~ auf den Markt gehen; **to be in the** ~ **for sth** an etw (dat) interessiert sein; **to be on the** ~ auf dem Markt sein; **to come on(to) the** ~ auf den Markt kommen; **to put on the** ~ auf den Markt bringen; house zum Verkauf anbieten; **to create a** ~ Nachfrage erzeugen; **to play the** ~ (an der Börse) spekulieren. **2** vt vertreiben. **to** ~ **a (new) product** ein (neues) Produkt auf den Markt bringen.

**marketable** ['mɑːkɪtəbl] adj absetzbar, marketfähig.

**market:** ~ **analysis** n Marktanalyse f; ~ **day** n Markttag m; ~ **forces** npl Marktkräfte pl; ~ **garden** n (Brit) Gemüseanbaubetrieb m.

**marketing** ['mɑːkɪtɪŋ] n Marketing nt.

**market:** ~ **leader** n Marktführer, Spitzenreiter m; ~**place** n Marktplatz m; (world of trade) Markt m; ~ **price** n Marktpreis m; ~ **research** n Marktforschung f; ~ **share** n Marktanteil m; ~ **survey** n Marktstudie f; ~ **town** n Marktort m.

**marking** ['mɑːkɪŋ] n (**a**) Markierung f; (on animal) Zeichnung f. ~ **ink** Wäschetinte f. (**b**) (of exams) (correcting) Korrektur f; (grading) Benotung f.

**marksman** ['mɑːksmən] n, pl **-men** [-mən] Schütze m; (police etc) Scharfschütze m.

**marksmanship** ['mɑːksmənʃɪp] n Treffsicherheit f.

**mark-up** ['mɑːkʌp] n Handelsspanne f; (amount added) Preisaufschlag m. ~ **price** Verkaufspreis m.

**marmalade** ['mɑːməleɪd] n Marmelade f aus Zitrusfrüchten. (**orange**) ~ Orangenmarmelade f.

**maroon** [mə'ruːn] adj kastanienbraun.

**marooned** [mə'ruːnd] adj von der Außenwelt abgeschnitten. ~ **by floods** vom Hochwasser eingeschlossen.

**marque** [mɑːk] n (esp Aut) Marke f.

**marquee** [mɑː'kiː] n Festzelt nt.

**marquess** ['mɑːkwɪs] n Marquis m.

**marriage** ['mærɪdʒ] n (state) die Ehe; (wedding) Hochzeit, Heirat f; (~ ceremony) Trauung f. **relations by** ~ angeheiratete Verwandte.

**marriageable** ['mærɪdʒəbl] adj heiratsfähig. **of** ~ **age** im heiratsfähigen Alter.

**marriage:** ~ **bureau** n Ehevermittlung f; ~ **certificate** n Heiratsurkunde f; ~ **counseling** (US), ~ **guidance** (Brit) n Eheberatung f; ~ **licence** n Eheerlaubnis f; ~ **vow** n Ehegelübde nt.

**married** ['mærɪd] adj verheiratet; life, state Ehe-. ~ **couple** Ehepaar nt; **she is a** ~ **woman** sie ist verheiratet.

**marrow** ['mærəʊ] n (**a**) (Anat) (Knochen)mark nt. **to be frozen to the** ~ völlig durchfroren sein. (**b**) (Bot) Gartenkürbis m.

**marry** ['mærɪ] **1** vt heiraten; (priest) trauen. **2** vi (also **get married**) heiraten. **to** ~ **into a rich family** in eine reiche Familie einheiraten.

►**marry off** vt sep verheiraten.

**Mars** [mɑːz] n Mars m.

**marsh** [mɑːʃ] n Sumpf m.

**marshal** ['mɑːʃəl] **1** n (Mil etc) Marschall m; (at rally, meeting etc) Ordner m; (US) Bezirkspolizeichef m. **2** vt arguments ordnen; soldiers antreten lassen.

**marshalling yard** ['mɑːʃəlɪŋ'jɑːd] n Rangierbahnhof m.

**marsh:** ~**land** n Marschland nt; ~**mallow** n (sweet) Marshmallow nt; (Bot) Eibisch m.

**marshy** ['mɑːʃɪ] adj (+er) sumpfig.

**marsupial** [mɑː'suːpɪəl] n Beuteltier nt.

**martial** ['mɑːʃəl] adj music kriegerisch, Kampf-; bearing soldatisch. **the** ~ **arts** die Kampfkunst; ~ **law** Kriegsrecht nt.

**martin** ['mɑːtɪn] n Schwalbe f.

**martyr** ['mɑːtər] **1** n Märtyrer(in f) m. **to be a** ~ **to arthritis** entsetzlich unter Arthritis zu leiden haben. **2** vt martern.

**martyrdom** ['mɑːtədəm] n (suffering) Martyrium nt; (death) Märtyrertod m.

**marvel** ['mɑːvəl] **1** n Wunder nt. **it's a** ~ **to me how he does it** (col) es wundert mich, wie er das schafft; **you're a** ~! (col) (kind) du bist ein Engel!; (clever) du bist ein Genie! **2** vi staunen (at über +acc). **to** ~ **at a sight** einen Anblick bestaunen.

**marvellous,** (US) **marvelous** ['mɑːvələs] adj wunderbar, fabelhaft. **isn't it** ~? ist das nicht herrlich?; (iro) gut, nicht! (iro).

**marvellously,** (US) **marvelously** ['mɑːvələslɪ] adv (with adj) herrlich; (with vb) großartig, fabelhaft.

**Marxism** ['mɑːksɪzəm] n der Marxismus.

**Marxist** ['mɑːksɪst] **1** adj marxistisch. **2** n Marxist(in f) m.

**marzipan** [ˌmɑːzɪ'pæn] n Marzipan nt or m.

**mascara** [mæ'skɑːrə] n Wimperntusche f.

**mascot** ['mæskət] n Maskottchen nt.

**masculine** ['mæskjʊlɪn] **1** adj männlich; woman maskulin. **2** n (Gram) Maskulinum nt.

**masculinity** [ˌmæskjʊ'lɪnɪtɪ] n Männlichkeit f.

**mash** [mæʃ] **1** n Brei m; (for animals) Futterbrei m. **2** vt zerstampfen. ~**ed potatoes** Kartoffelbrei m or -püree nt.

**mask** [mɑːsk] **1** n (lit, fig) Maske f. **2** vt maskieren; (clouds etc) verdecken; feelings verbergen.

**masochism** ['mæsəʊkɪzəm] n Masochismus m.

**masochist** ['mæsəʊkɪst] n Masochist(in f) m.

**masochistic** [ˌmæsəʊ'kɪstɪk] adj masochistisch.

**mason** ['meɪsn] n (**a**) (builder) Steinmetz m. (**b**) (free~) Freimaurer m.

**masonic** [mə'sɒnɪk] adj Freimaurer-. ~ **lodge** Freimaurerloge f.

**masonry** ['meɪsnrɪ] n (**a**) (stonework) Mauerwerk nt. (**b**) (free~) Freimaurertum nt.

**masquerade** [ˌmæskə'reɪd] **1** n Maskerade f. **2** vi to ~ **as ...** sich ausgeben als ...

**mass**[1] [mæs] n (Eccl) Messe f. **to go to** ~ zur Messe gehen; **to say** ~ die Messe lesen.

**mass**[2] **1** n (general, Phys) Masse f; (of people) Menge f. **a** ~ **of red hair** ein Wust roter Haare; **he's a** ~ **of bruises** er ist voller blauer Flecken; **the** ~**es** die Masse(n pl); **the great** ~ **of the population** die breite Masse der Bevölkerung; ~**es (of)** massenhaft, eine Masse (col). **2** vt troops zusammenziehen. **3** vi (Mil) sich massieren; (clouds) sich (zusammen)ballen. **they're** ~**ing for an attack** sie sammeln sich zum Angriff.

**massacre** ['mæsəkər] **1** n Massaker nt. **2** vt massakrieren.

**massage** ['mæsɑːʒ] **1** n Massage f. ~ **parlour** (euph) Massagesalon m. **2** vt massieren.

**masseur** [mæ'sɜːr] n Masseur m.

**masseuse** [mæ'sɜːz] n Masseurin f; (euph) Masseuse f.

**massive** ['mæsɪv] adj riesig, enorm; wall, heart attack, support massiv; task gewaltig.

**mass:** ~ **media** npl Massenmedien pl; ~ **meeting** n Massenveranstaltung f; (demonstration) Massenkundgebung f; ~ **murderer** n Massenmörder(in f) m; ~**-produce** vt in Massenproduktion herstellen; ~**-produced** adj ~**-produced items** Massenartikel pl; ~ **production** n Massenproduktion f; ~ **unemployment** n Massenarbeitslosigkeit f.

**mast** [mɑːst] n (Naut) Mast m; (Rad etc) Sendeturm m. **10 years before the** ~ 10 Jahre auf See.

**master** ['mɑːstəʳ] **1** n **(a)** (of the house, dog, servants) Herr m. **to be** ~ **in one's own house** (also fig) Herr im Hause sein; **to be one's own** ~ sein eigener Herr sein; **to be** ~ **of sth** etw beherrschen; **to be** ~ **of the situation** Herr der Lage sein; ~ **of ceremonies** (at function) Zeremonienmeister m; (on stage) Conférencier m; (TV) Showmaster m. **(b)** (Naut) Kapitän m. **(c)** (musician, painter etc) Meister m. **(d)** (teacher) Lehrer m. **(e)** (boy's title) Master m. **(f)** (Univ) **M**~ **of Arts/Science** n Magister m der philosophischen/naturwissenschaftlichen Fakultät. **(g)** (~ copy) Original nt. **2** vt meistern; one's emotions unter Kontrolle bringen; technique beherrschen.

**master:** ~ **builder** n Baumeister m; ~ **copy** n Original nt; ~ **disk** n (Comp) Hauptplatte f; ~ **file** n (Comp) Stammdatei f.

**masterful** ['mɑːstəfʊl] adj meisterhaft; (dominating) personality gebieterisch.

**master key** n Haupt- or Generalschlüssel m.

**masterly** ['mɑːstəlɪ] adj meisterhaft.

**master:** ~ **mind 1** n (führender) Kopf; **2** vt who ~ **minded the robbery?** wer steckt hinter dem Raubüberfall?; ~ **piece** n Meisterwerk nt; ~ **plan** n Gesamtkonzept nt; ~ **stroke** n Glanzstück nt; ~ **switch** n Hauptschalter m; ~ **tape** n Originalband nt; (Comp) Stammband nt.

**mastery** ['mɑːstərɪ] n (of instrument, language etc) Beherrschung f; (skill) Können nt; (over competitors etc) Oberhand f.

**masthead** ['mɑːsthed] n (Naut) Masttopp m; (esp US: in magazine etc) Impressum nt.

**masticate** ['mæstɪkeɪt] vti kauen.

**mastiff** ['mæstɪf] n Dogge f.

**masturbate** ['mæstəbeɪt] vi masturbieren, onanieren.

**masturbation** [,mæstə'beɪʃən] n Masturbation, Onanie f.

**mat** [mæt] n Matte f; (door~) Fußabstreifer m; (on table) Untersetzer m. **place** ~ Set nt.

**match**[1] [mætʃ] n Streichholz nt.

**match**[2] **1** n **(a)** (sb/sth similar, suitable etc) **to be** or **make a good** ~ gut zusammenpassen. **(b)** (equal) **to be a/no** ~ **for sb** (be able to compete with) sich mit jdm messen/nicht messen können; (be able to handle) jdm gewachsen/nicht gewachsen sein; **to meet one's** ~ seinen Meister finden. **(c)** (marriage) Heirat f. **she made a good** ~ sie hat eine gute Partie gemacht. **(d)** (Sport) (general) Wettkampf m; (team game) Spiel nt; (Tennis) Match nt; (Boxing) Kampf m.

**2** vt **(a)** (pair off) **they're well** ~ **ed** die beiden passen gut zusammen; **the teams are well** ~ **ed** die Mannschaften sind gleichwertig; ~ **each diagram with its counterpart** ordnen Sie die Schaubilder einander (dat) zu; **to be** ~ **ed against sb** gegen jdn antreten. **(b)** (equal) gleichkommen (+dat) (in an +dat). **I can't** ~ **him in chess** im Schach kann ich es mit ihm nicht aufnehmen; **the results did not** ~ **our hopes** die Ergebnisse entsprachen nicht unseren Hoffnungen. **(c)** (clothes, colours) passen zu; (make ~; also Elec) aufeinander abstimmen.

**3** vi zusammenpassen. **with a skirt to** ~, **with a** ~ **ing skirt** mit (dazu) passendem Rock; ~ **ing outfit** Kombination f.

**matchbox** ['mætʃbɒks] n Streichholzschachtel f.

**matchless** ['mætʃlɪs] adj unvergleichlich.

**match:** ~ **maker** n Ehestifter(in f), Kuppler(in f) (pej) m; ~ **point** n (Tennis) Matchball m; ~ **stick** n

Streichholz nt; ~ **wood** n **smashed to** ~ **wood** (fig) zu Kleinholz gemacht.

**mate**[1] [meɪt] (Chess) **1** n Matt nt. **2** vt matt setzen.

**mate**[2] **1** n **(a)** (fellow worker) Kollege m; (helper) Gehilfe m. **(b)** (Naut) Maat m. **(c)** (of animal) (male) Männchen nt; (female) Weibchen nt; (person) Lebenspartner(in f) m. **his** ~ das Weibchen. **(d)** (col: friend) Kamerad(in f) m, Kumpel m (col). **listen** ~! hör mal, Freundchen! (col); **got a light** ~? hast du Feuer, Kumpel? (col). **2** vt animals paaren; female decken lassen. **3** vi (Zool) sich paaren.

**material** [mə'tɪərɪəl] **1** adj materiell. ~ **damage** Sachschaden m. **(b)** (esp Jur: important) difference wesentlich. **2** n **(a)** Material nt; (for report etc) Stoff m. ~ **s** Material nt; **he's good editorial** ~ er hat das Zeug zum Redakteur. **(b)** (cloth) Stoff m.

**materialism** [mə'tɪərɪəlɪzəm] n der Materialismus.

**materialistic** adj, ~ **ally** adv [mə,tɪərɪə'lɪstɪk, -əlɪ] materialistisch.

**materialize** [mə'tɪərɪəlaɪz] vi (idea, plan) sich verwirklichen; (promises, hopes etc) wahr werden.

**materially** [mə'tɪərɪəlɪ] adv wesentlich.

**maternal** [mə'tɜːnl] adj mütterlich. ~ **grandmother/ grandfather** Großmutter/Großvater mütterlicherseits.

**maternity** [mə'tɜːnɪtɪ] n Mutterschaft f.

**maternity:** ~ **benefit** n Mutterschaftsgeld nt; ~ **dress** n Umstandskleid nt; ~ **home**, ~ **hospital** n Entbindungsheim nt; ~ **leave** n Mutterschaftsurlaub m; ~ **ward** n Entbindungsstation f.

**matey** ['meɪtɪ] (Brit col) **1** adj kumpelhaft. **to be** ~ **with sb** mit jdm auf du und du stehen. **2** n Kumpel m (col).

**math** [mæθ] n (US col) Mathe f (col).

**mathematical** adj, ~ **ly** adv [,mæθə'mætɪkəl,- i] mathematisch.

**mathematician** [,mæθəmə'tɪʃən] n Mathematiker(in f) m.

**mathematics** [,mæθə'mætɪks] n sing Mathematik f.

**maths** [mæθs] n sing (Brit col) Mathe f (col).

**matinée** ['mætɪneɪ] n Matinee f; (in the afternoon also) Nachmittagsvorstellung f.

**mating** ['meɪtɪŋ] n Paarung f.

**mating:** ~ **call** n Lockruf m; ~ **season** n Paarungszeit f.

**matins** ['mætɪnz] n sing (Rel) Morgenandacht f.

**matriarch** ['meɪtrɪɑːk] n Matriarchin f.

**matrices** ['meɪtrɪsiːz] pl of **matrix**.

**matriculate** [mə'trɪkjʊleɪt] vi sich immatrikulieren.

**matrimonial** [,mætrɪ'məʊnɪəl] adj vows Ehe-.

**matrimony** ['mætrɪmənɪ] n (form) Ehe f.

**matrix** ['meɪtrɪks] n, pl **matrices** or **-es (a)** (mould) Matrize f. **(b)** (Geol, Math) Matrix f.

**matron** ['meɪtrən] n (in hospital) Oberschwester f; (in school) Schwester f.

**matronly** ['meɪtrənlɪ] adj matronenhaft.

**matt** [mæt] adj mattiert. ~ **paint** Mattlack m.

**matted** ['mætɪd] adj verfilzt.

**matter** ['mætəʳ] **1** n **(a)** (Phys etc: substance) die Materie; (particular kind) Stoff m. **advertising** ~ Werbung f; **printed** ~ Drucksache(n pl) f; **colouring** ~ Farbstoff(e pl) m; **reading** ~ Lektüre f.

**(b)** (Med: pus) Eiter m.

**(c)** (content) Inhalt m.

**(d)** (question, affair) Sache, Angelegenheit f; (topic) Thema nt. **in this** ~ in diesem Zusammenhang; **in the** ~ **of** ... was ... (+acc) anbelangt; **in the** ~ **of clothes** etc in puncto Kleidung etc; **there's the** ~ **of my expenses** da wären noch meine Auslagen; **that's quite another** ~ das ist etwas (ganz) anderes; **it will be no easy** ~ **(to)** ... es wird nicht einfach sein, zu ...; **it's a serious** ~ das ist eine ernste Angelegenheit; **the** ~ **in hand** die vorliegende Angelegenheit; **the** ~ **is closed** der Fall ist erledigt; **for that** ~ eigentlich; **business** ~s geschäftliche Dinge *pl*, Geschäftliche(s) *nt*; **money** ~s Geldfragen *pl*; **as** ~s **stand** wie die Dinge liegen; **to make** ~s **worse** zu allem Unglück (noch).

(e) **a** ~ **of** eine Sache von; **it's a** ~ **of time** das ist eine Frage der Zeit; **it's a** ~ **of opinion** das ist Ansichtssache; **it will be a** ~ **of a few weeks** es wird ein paar Wochen dauern; **in a** ~ **of minutes** innerhalb von Minuten; **it's a** ~ **of great concern to us** die Sache ist für uns von großer Bedeutung; **it's a** ~ **of increasing the money supply** es geht darum, die Geldzufuhr zu erhöhen; **as a** ~ **of course** selbstverständlich; **no** ~! macht nichts; **I've decided to leave, no** ~ **what** ich gehe, egal was passiert; **no** ~ **how/what/when** *etc* ... egal, wie/was/wann *etc* ...; **no** ~ **how hot it was** selbst bei der größten Hitze; **something is the** ~ **with sb/sth** etwas ist mit jdm/etw los; *(ill)* etwas fehlt jdm; **what's the** ~ **with you?** was ist denn mit dir los?; **what's the** ~ **with smoking?** was ist denn dabei, wenn man raucht?; **something's the** ~ **with the lights** mit der Beleuchtung ist irgend etwas nicht in Ordnung.

**2** *vi* **it doesn't** ~ (es *or* das) macht nichts; **what does it** ~? was macht das schon?; **I forgot it, does it** ~? ich hab's vergessen, ist das schlimm?; **does it** ~ **to you if I go?** macht es dir etwas aus, wenn ich gehe?; **it doesn't** ~ **to me what you do** es ist mir (ganz) egal, was du machst.

**matter-of-fact** ['mætərəv'fækt] *adj* sachlich.

**Matthew** ['mæθju:] *n* = Matthias *m*; *(Bibl)* Matthäus *m*.

**matting** ['mætɪŋ] *n* Matten *pl*.

**mattress** ['mætrɪs] *n* Matratze *f*.

**mature** [mə'tjʊər] **1** *adj (+er) person, cheese* reif; *child* vernünftig; *wine* ausgereift. **2** *vi (person)* reifer werden; *(wine, cheese)* reifen.

**maturity** [mə'tjʊərɪtɪ] *n* Reife *f*. **to reach** ~ *(person)* erwachsen werden; *(legally)* volljährig werden.

**maudlin** ['mɔːdlɪn] *adj story* rührselig; *person* gefühlsselig.

**maul** [mɔːl] *vt* übel zurichten.

**Mauritius** [mə'rɪʃəs] *n* Mauritius *nt*.

**mausoleum** [ˌmɔːsə'lɪəm] *n* Mausoleum *nt*.

**mauve** [məʊv] *adj* mauve.

**maverick** ['mævərɪk] *n (dissenter)* Abtrünnige(r) *m*; *(independent thinker)* Querdenker *m*.

**mawkish** ['mɔːkɪʃ] *adj* rührselig, kitschig.

**max** = **maximum** max.

**maxi** ['mæksɪ] **1** *n (skirt)* Maxirock *m*; *(dress)* Maxikleid *nt*. **2** *adj (col)* Mega-. **a** ~ **headache** Wahnsinnskopfschmerzen *pl*.

**maxim** ['mæksɪm] *n* Maxime *f*.

**maximize** ['mæksɪmaɪz] *vt* maximieren.

**maximum** ['mæksɪməm] **1** *adj attr* Höchst-; *size, costs* maximal. **the** ~ **salary is** ... das höchste Gehalt ist ...; *(top grade)* das Endgehalt ist...; ~ **security wing/prison** Hochsicherheitstrakt *m*/-gefängnis *nt*. **2** *n, pl* **-s** *or* **maxima** ['mæksɪmə] Maximum *nt*. **up to a** ~ **of £8** bis zu maximal £8; **temperatures reached a** ~ **of 34°** die Höchsttemperatur betrug 34°.

**May** [meɪ] *n* Mai *m*; *see* **September**.

**may** [meɪ] *vi pret* **might** *(see also* **might¹)** **(a)** *(possibility: also* **might)** können. **it** ~ **rain** vielleicht regnet es; **it** ~ **be that** ... könnte es sein, daß ...; **he** ~ **not be hungry** vielleicht hat er keinen Hunger; **I** ~ **have said so** es kann *or* könnte sein, daß ich das gesagt habe; **you** ~ **be right** *(doubting)* Sie haben vielleicht recht; *(tentatively*

*agreeing)* da könnten Sie recht haben; **yes, I** ~ ja, das ist möglich; **you** ~ **well ask** das ist eine gute Frage!

**(b)** *(permission)* dürfen. ~ **I go now?** darf ich jetzt gehen?; **yes, you** ~ ja, Sie dürfen.

**(c) I hope he** ~ **succeed** ich hoffe, daß es ihm gelingt; **I hoped he might succeed** ich hatte gehofft, es würde ihm gelingen; **you** ~ *or* **might as well go now** du kannst jetzt ruhig gehen; **if they don't have it we** ~ *or* **might as well go to another firm** wenn sie es nicht haben, gehen wir am besten zu einer anderen Firma.

**(d)** *(in wishes)* ~ **you be successful!** (ich wünsche Ihnen) viel Erfolg!; ~ **you be very happy together** ich wünsche euch, daß ihr sehr glücklich miteinander werdet.

**maybe** ['meɪbiː] *adv* vielleicht.

**May:** ~ **Day** *n* der 1. Mai; ~**day** *n (distress call)* Maydaysignal *nt*, SOS-Ruf *m*.

**mayhem** ['meɪhem] *n (havoc)* Chaos *nt*.

**mayonnaise** [ˌmeɪə'neɪz] *n* Mayonnaise *f*.

**mayor** [mɛər] *n* Bürgermeister(in *f*) *m*.

**mayoress** ['mɛəres] *n* Frau *f* des Bürgermeisters; *(lady mayor)* Bürgermeisterin *f*.

**maypole** ['meɪpəʊl] *n* Maibaum *m*.

**maze** [meɪz] *n* Irrgarten *m*; *(fig)* Gewirr *nt*.

**MBE** = **Member of the Order of the British Empire** *britischer Verdienstorden*.

**MC** = **(a) Master of Ceremonies**. **(b)** *(US)* **Member of Congress**.

**McCoy** [mə'kɔɪ] *see* real.

**MCP** *(Brit col)* = **male chauvinist pig**.

**MD** = **(a) Doctor of Medicine** Dr. med. **(b)** = **managing director**. **(c)** *(US Post)* = **Maryland**.

**me** [miː] *pron* **(a)** *(dir obj, with prep +acc)* mich; *(indir obj, with prep +dat)* mir. **he's older than** ~ er ist älter als ich. **(b)** *(emph)* ich. **who,** ~? wer, ich?; **it's** ~ ich bin's.

**ME** = **(a)** *(US Post)* Maine. **(b)** *(Med)* **myalgic encephalomyelitis** *krankhafter Energiemangel (oft nach Viruserkrankungen)*.

**meadow** ['medəʊ] *n* Wiese *f*.

**meagre**, *(US)* **meager** ['miːgər] *adj* spärlich; *amount* kläglich; *meal* dürftig.

**meal¹** [miːl] *n (flour etc)* Schrot(mehl *nt*) *m*.

**meal²** *n* Mahlzeit *f*; *(food)* Essen *nt*. **come around for a** ~ komm zum Essen (zu uns); **to go for a** ~ essen gehen; **to have a (good)** ~ (gut) essen; **hot** ~s warme Mahlzeiten *pl*; **to make a** ~ **of sth** *(col)* etw auf sehr umständliche Art machen.

**meal:** ~**-ticket** *n (US: lit)* Essensmarke *f*; **she's just his** ~**-ticket** er ist nur des Geldes wegen mit ihr befreundet; ~**time** *n* Essenszeit *f*.

**mealy-mouthed** [ˌmiːlɪ'maʊðd] *adj politician* schönfärberisch. **to be** ~ viele Worte machen, schwafeln.

**mean¹** [miːn] *adj (+er)* **(a)** *(miserly)* geizig. **he's** ~ **with his money** er ist geizig mit seinem Geld. **(b)** *(unkind, spiteful)* gemein. **you** ~ **thing!** du gemeines Stück!, du Miststück! *(col)*; **a** ~ **trick** eine Gemeinheit. **(c)** *(vicious)* bösartig; *look* gehässig; *criminal* niederträchtig. ~ **machine** *(col) (car)* heißer Wagen; *(motorcycle)* Feuerstuhl *m (col)*. **(d) he is no** ~ **player** er ist ein beachtlicher Spieler; **that's no** ~ **feat** diese Aufgabe ist nicht zu unterschätzen.

**mean²** **1** *n* Durchschnitt *m*. **the golden** *or* **happy** ~ der goldene Mittelweg. **2** *adj* mittlere(r, s).

**mean³** *pret, ptp* **meant** *vt* **(a)** bedeuten; *(person: have in mind)* meinen. **what do you** ~ **by that?** was willst du damit sagen?; **I** ~ **it!** ich meine das ernst!; **I** ~ **what I say** es ist mir ernst damit; **the name** ~s **nothing to me** der Name sagt mir nichts;

it ~s starting all over again das bedeutet, daß wir/sie wieder ganz von vorne anfangen müssen; **this will ~ great changes** dies wird bedeutende Veränderungen zur Folge haben; **he ~s a lot to me** er bedeutet mir viel. **(b)** *(intend)* beabsichtigen. **to ~ to do sth** etw tun wollen; *(do on purpose)* etw absichtlich tun; **to be ~t for sb/sth** für jdn/etw bestimmt sein; **to ~ sb to do sth** wollen, daß jd etw tut; **sth is ~t to be sth** etw soll etw sein; **I ~t it as a joke** das sollte ein Witz sein; **you are ~t to be on time** du solltest pünktlich sein; **he wasn't ~t to be a leader** er war nicht zum Führer bestimmt; **I ~ to be obeyed** ich verlange, daß man mir gehorcht; **this pad is ~t for drawing** dieser Block ist zum Zeichnen gedacht; **you weren't ~t to see it** du solltest das nicht zu sehen bekommen; **he ~s well/no harm** er meint es gut/nicht böse.

**meander** [mɪˈændər] *vi (river)* sich (dahin)-schlängeln; *(go off subject)* (vom Thema) abschweifen; *(walking)* schlendern.

**meaning** [ˈmiːnɪŋ] *n* Bedeutung *f*; *(sense: of words, poem etc also)* Sinn *m*. **a look full of ~** ein bedeutsamer Blick; **do you get my ~?** haben Sie mich (richtig) verstanden?; **you don't know the ~ of hunger** du weißt ja gar nicht, was Hunger bedeutet; **what's the ~ of this?** was soll denn das (heißen)?

**meaningful** [ˈmiːnɪŋfʊl] *adj* sinnvoll; *film* bedeutungsvoll; *relationship* tiefergehend.

**meaningless** [ˈmiːnɪŋlɪs] *adj sentence, statement* ohne Bedeutung; *life* sinnlos.

**meanness** [ˈmiːnnɪs] *n see adj* **(a)** Geiz *m*. **(b)** Gemeinheit *f*. **(c)** Bösartigkeit *f*; Gehässigkeit *f*; Niedertracht *f*.

**means** [miːnz] *n* **(a)** *sing (method)* Möglichkeit *f*; *(instrument)* Mittel *nt*. **a ~ of transport** ein Beförderungsmittel *nt*; **a ~ to an end** ein Mittel *nt* zum Zweck; **there is no ~ of doing it** es ist unmöglich, das zu tun; **we've no ~ of knowing that** wir können das nicht wissen; **by ~ of sth** durch etw; **by ~ of doing sth** dadurch, daß man etw tut. **(b)** *sing* **by all ~!** (aber) selbstverständlich *or* natürlich!; **by no ~** keineswegs; *(under no circumstances)* auf keinen Fall. **(c)** *pl (wherewithal)* Mittel *pl*; *(financial ~ also)* Gelder *pl*. **a man of ~** ein vermögender Mann; **private ~** private Mittel; **to live beyond/within one's ~** über seine Verhältnisse/seinen Verhältnissen entsprechend leben; **~ test** Überprüfung *f* der Einkommens- und Vermögensverhältnisse.

**meant** [ment] *pret, ptp of* **mean³**.

**meantime** [ˈmiːntaɪm] **1** *adv* inzwischen. **2** *n* **in the ~** in der Zwischenzeit, inzwischen.

**meanwhile** [ˈmiːnwaɪl] *adv* inzwischen.

**measles** [ˈmiːzlz] *n sing* Masern *pl*.

**measly** [ˈmiːzlɪ] *adj (+er) (col)* mick(e)rig *(col)*.

**measure** [ˈmeʒər] **1** *n* **(a)** *(unit of measurement)* Maß (einheit *f*) *nt*; *(amount ~d)* Menge *f*; *(fig: yardstick)* Maßstab *m (of* für*)*. **her joy was beyond ~** ihre Freude kannte keine Grenzen; **to give sb full/short ~** *(barman)* richtig/zuwenig ausschenken; **in full ~** in höchstem Maße; **for good ~** sicherheitshalber; **it gave us some ~ of the difficulty** es gab uns einen Begriff von der Schwierigkeit; **in some ~** in gewisser Hinsicht; **some ~ of** ein gewisses Maß an; **to a *or* in large ~** in hohem Maße. **(b)** *(step)* Maßnahme *f*. **to take ~s to do sth** Maßnahmen ergreifen, um etw zu tun.

**2** *vt* messen; *length* abmessen; *room* ausmessen; *(take sb's measurements)* Maß nehmen bei. **to ~ one's length** *(fig: fall)* der Länge nach hinfallen.

**3** *vi* messen. **what does it ~?** wieviel mißt es?
►**measure off** *vt sep* abmessen.
►**measure out** *vt sep* abmessen; *weights* abwiegen.
►**measure up** *vi (be good enough, compare well)* **he didn't ~ ~** er hat enttäuscht; **to ~ ~ to sth** an etw *(acc)* herankommen.

**measured** [ˈmeʒəd] *adj tread* gemessen; *tone, way of talking* bedächtig; *words* wohlüberlegt.

**measurement** [ˈmeʒəmənt] *n* **(a)** *(act)* Messung *f*. **(b)** *(measure)* Maß *nt*; *(figure)* Meßwert *m*; *(fig)* Maßstab *m*. **to take sb's ~s** bei jdm Maß nehmen.

**measuring** [ˈmeʒərɪŋ]: **~ jug** *n* Meßbecher *m*; **~ tape** *n* Bandmaß *nt*.

**meat** [miːt] *n* Fleisch *nt*. **cold ~s** Aufschnitt *m*. **one man's ~ is another man's poison** *(Prov)* des einen Freud, des andern Leid *(Prov)*.

**meat** *in cpds* Fleisch-; **~ball** *n* Fleischkloß *m*; **~ loaf** *n* ≈ Fleischkäse *m*; **~ pie** *n* Fleischpastete *f*.

**meaty** [ˈmiːtɪ] *adj (+er)* **(a)** *taste* Fleisch-. **(b)** *(fig) book* aussagestark.

**Mecca** [ˈmekə] *n (Geog, fig)* Mekka *nt*.

**mechanic** [mɪˈkænɪk] *n* Mechaniker *m*.

**mechanical** [mɪˈkænɪkəl] *adj (lit, fig)* mechanisch. **~ engineer/engineering** Maschinenbauingenieur *m*/Maschinenbau *m*; **~ pencil** *(US)* Drehbleistift *m*.

**mechanics** [mɪˈkænɪks] *n* **(a)** *sing (subject) (engineering)* Maschinenbau *m*; *(Phys)* Mechanik *f*. **(b)** *pl (technical aspects)* Mechanik *f*; *(of writing etc)* Technik *f*; *(of procedure)* Mechanismus *m*.

**mechanism** [ˈmekənɪzəm] *n* Mechanismus *m*.

**mechanization** [ˌmekənaɪˈzeɪʃən] *n* Mechanisierung *f*; *(Mil)* Motorisierung *f*.

**mechanize** [ˈmekənaɪz] *vt* mechanisieren; *(Mil)* motorisieren.

**medal** [ˈmedl] *n* Medaille *f*; *(decoration)* Orden *m*. **~ ceremony** *(Sport)* Siegerehrung *f*.

**medallion** [mɪˈdæljən] *n* Medaillon *nt*; *(medal)* Medaille *f*.

**medallist,** *(US)* **medalist** [ˈmedəlɪst] *n* Medaillengewinner(in *f*) *m*.

**meddle** [ˈmedl] *vi (interfere)* sich einmischen *(in* in *+acc)*; *(tamper)* sich zu schaffen machen *(with* an *+dat)*. **he's not a man to ~ with** mit ihm ist nicht gut Kirschen essen *(col)*.

**meddler** [ˈmedlər] *n* **he's a terrible ~** er muß sich immer in alles einmischen.

**meddlesome** [ˈmedlsəm] *adj,* **meddling** [ˈmedlɪŋ] *adj attr* **she's a ~ old busybody** sie mischt sich dauernd in alles ein.

**media** [ˈmiːdɪə] *n, pl of* **medium** Medien *pl*. **he works in the ~** er ist im Medienbereich tätig; **all the ~ were there** Presse, Funk und Fernsehen waren dort.

**media circus** *n* Medienrummel *m*.

**mediaeval** *adj* = **medieval**.

**median** [ˈmiːdɪən] *adj* mittlere(r, s). **~ strip** *(US)* Mittelstreifen *m*.

**mediate** [ˈmiːdɪeɪt] **1** *vi* vermitteln. **2** *vt settlement* aushandeln.

**mediation** [ˌmiːdɪˈeɪʃən] *n* Vermittlung *f*.

**mediator** [ˈmiːdɪeɪtər] *n* Vermittler *m*.

**Medicaid** [ˈmedɪˌkeɪd] *n (US)* staatliche *Krankenversicherung und Gesundheitsfürsorge für Einkommensschwache.*

**medical** [ˈmedɪkəl] **1** *adj* medizinisch; *examination, treatment* ärztlich; *board, inspector* Gesundheits-; **~ card** *(Brit)* Krankenversicherungsschein *m*; **~ certificate** ärztliches Attest; **~ practitioner** praktischer Arzt; **~ school** ≈ medizinische Fakultät; **~ student** Medizinstudent(in *f*) *m*. **2** *n* (ärztliche) Untersuchung.

**Medicare** ['medɪ,kɛəʳ] *n (US) staatliche Krankenversicherung und Gesundheitsfürsorge für ältere Bürger.*

**medicated** ['medɪkeɪtɪd] *adj* medizinisch.

**medication** [,medɪ'keɪʃən] *n (act)* (medizinische) Behandlung; *(drugs etc)* Medikamente *pl*; *(medicine)* Medikament *nt.*

**medicinal** [me'dɪsɪnl] *adj* Heil-, heilend.

**medicine** ['medsm, 'medɪsm] *n* **(a)** Arznei *f*; *(particular preparation)* Medikament *nt.* **to give sb a taste of his own** ~ *(fig)* es jdm mit gleicher Münze heimzahlen. **(b)** *(science)* Medizin *f.*

**medicine:** ~ **chest** *n* Hausapotheke *f*; **~-man** *n* Medizinmann *m.*

**medieval** [,medɪ'iːvəl] *adj* mittelalterlich.

**mediocre** [,miːdɪ'əʊkəʳ] *adj* mittelmäßig.

**mediocrity** [,miːdɪ'ɒkrɪtɪ] *n* Mittelmäßigkeit *f.*

**meditate** ['medɪteɪt] *vi* nachdenken *(upon, on* über *+acc)*; *(Rel, Philos)* meditieren.

**meditation** [,medɪ'teɪʃən] *n* Nachdenken *nt*; *(Rel, Philos)* Meditation *f.*

**Mediterranean** [,medɪtə'reɪnɪən] **1** *n (also* ~ **Sea)** Mittelmeer *nt.* **2** *adj* Mittelmeer-; *person* südländisch.

**medium** ['miːdɪəm] **1** *adj quality, size etc* mittlere(r, s); *steak* halbdurch; *brown, sized etc* mittel-. **of** ~ **height** mittelgroß; **at** ~ **price** in der mittleren Preislage. **2** *n, pl* **media** *or* **-s (a)** *(means)* Mittel *nt.* **through the** ~ **of the press** durch die Presse; **advertising** ~ Werbeträger *m.* **(b)** *(midpoint)* Mitte *f.* **happy** ~ goldener Mittelweg. **(c)** *(spiritualist)* Medium *nt.*

**medium** *in cpds* mittel-; **~-dry** *wine, sherry* halbtrocken; ~ **price range** *n* mittlere Preislage; **~-range** *adj aircraft etc* Mittelstrecken-; **~-sized** *adj* mittelgroß; *firm* mittelständisch; ~ **wave** *n* Mittelwelle *f.*

**medley** ['medlɪ] *n* Gemisch *nt*; *(Mus)* Medley *nt.*

**meek** [miːk] *adj (+er)* sanft(mütig); *(pej)* duckmäuserisch; *(uncomplaining)* duldsam.

**meekly** ['miːklɪ] *adv* sanft; *(pej)* duckmäuserisch.

**meet** [miːt] *(vb: pret, ptp* **met) 1** *vt* **(a)** *(encounter) person* treffen; *(by arrangement)* sich treffen mit; *difficulty* stoßen auf *(+acc).* **he met his death in 1800** im Jahre 1800 fand er den Tod; **to arrange to** ~ **sb** sich mit jdm verabreden; **his eyes met mine** unsere Blicke trafen sich; **there's more to it than** ~**s the eye** da steckt mehr dahinter, als man auf den ersten Blick meint.

**(b)** *(get to know)* kennenlernen. **come and** ~ **my brother** komm, ich mache dich mit meinem Bruder bekannt; **pleased to** ~ **you!** angenehm! *(form)*, guten Tag/Abend.

**(c)** *(await arrival, collect)* abholen *(at an +dat,* von*).* **the car will** ~ **the train** der Wagen steht am Bahnhof bereit.

**(d)** *expectations, target, deadline* erfüllen; *requirement* gerecht werden *(+dat)*; *expenses, needs* decken; *charge, criticism* begegnen *(+dat).*

**2** *vi* **(a)** *(encounter) (people)* sich begegnen; *(by arrangement)* sich treffen; *(society, committee etc)* tagen. **haven't we met before somewhere?** sind wir uns nicht schon mal begegnet?; **until we** ~ **again!** bis zum nächsten Mal! **(b)** *(join etc)* sich treffen; *(converge)* sich vereinigen; *(rivers)* ineinanderfließen; *(intersect)* sich schneiden; *(fig: come together)* sich treffen. **our eyes met** unsere Blicke trafen sich.

**3** *n (Hunt)* Jagd *f*; *(US Sport)* Sportfest *nt.*

▶**meet up** *vi* sich treffen *(with sb* mit jdm*).*

▶**meet with** *vi +prep obj* **(a)** *hostility, problems* stoßen auf *(+acc)*; *success, accident* haben; *disaster* erleiden; *approval, untimely death* finden. **(b)** *person* treffen; *(have a meeting)* (zu einer Unterredung) zusammenkommen mit.

**meeting** ['miːtɪŋ] *n* **(a)** Begegnung *f*; *(arranged)* Treffen *nt*; *(business* ~*)* Besprechung *f.* **Mr Jones is in a** ~ Herr Jones ist (gerade) bei einer Besprechung; **the minister had a** ~ **with the ambassador** der Minister traf zu Gesprächen mit dem Botschafter zusammen; ~ **of minds** Zusammentreffen *nt* von Gleichgesinnten; *(reaching agreement)* Annäherung der Standpunkte. **(b)** *(of committee)* Sitzung *f*; *(of members, citizens)* Versammlung *f.* **at the last** ~ bei der letzten Sitzung. **(c)** *(Sport)* Veranstaltung *f*; *(between teams, opponents)* Begegnung *f.*

**meeting:** ~ **place** *n* Treffpunkt *m*; ~ **point** *n* Treffpunkt *m*; *(of rivers)* Zusammenfluß *m*; *(of lines)* Schnittpunkt *m.*

**mega-** ['megə-] *pref* Mega-. **~bucks** *n (col)* ein Schweinegeld *nt (col)*; **~byte** *n (Comp)* Megabyte *nt.*

**megalomaniac** [,megələʊ'meɪnɪæk] *n* Größenwahnsinnige(r) *mf.*

**megaphone** ['megəfəʊn] *n* Megaphon *nt.*

**megastar** ['megəstɑːʳ] *n* Megastar *m.*

**melancholy** ['melənkəlɪ] **1** *adj* melancholisch; *duty, sight etc* traurig. **2** *n* Melancholie *f.*

**mêlée** ['meleɪ] *n* Gedränge, Gewühl *nt*; *(fighting)* Handgemenge *nt.*

**mellow** ['meləʊ] **1** *adj (+er) fruit, wine* ausgereift; *colour, light* warm; *sound, voice* weich; *person* gesetzt; *(fig: slightly drunk)* angeheitert. **2** *vi (wine, fruit)* reif werden, *(colours, sounds)* weicher werden, *(person)* gesetzter werden.

**melodious** *adj*, **~ly** *adv* [mɪ'ləʊdɪəs, -lɪ] melodisch.

**melodrama** ['meləʊ,drɑːmə] *n* Melodrama *nt.*

**melodramatic** [,meləʊdrə'mætɪk] *adj* melodramatisch.

**melody** ['melədɪ] *n* Melodie *f.*

**melon** ['melən] *n* Melone *f.*

**melt** [melt] **1** *vt* schmelzen; *butter* zerlassen; *(fig) heart etc* erweichen. **her tears** ~**ed my anger** beim Anblick ihrer Tränen verflog mein Zorn. **2** *vi* schmelzen; *(butter also)* zergehen; *(fig: anger)* verfliegen. **it just** ~**s in the mouth** es zergeht einem nur so auf der Zunge; **he** ~**ed into the crowd** er verschwand in der Menge.

▶**melt away** *vi (lit)* (weg)schmelzen; *(fig)* sich auflösen; *(person)* dahinschmelzen; *(anger)* verfliegen; *(suspicion, money)* zerrinnen.

▶**melt down** *vt sep* einschmelzen.

**meltdown** ['meltdaʊn] *n* Kernschmelze *f.*

**melting** ['meltɪŋ-]: ~ **point** *n* Schmelzpunkt *m*; ~ **pot** *n (lit, fig)* Schmelztiegel *m*; **to be in the** ~ **pot** in der Schwebe sein.

**member** ['membəʳ] *n* Mitglied *nt*; *(of tribe, species)* Angehörige(r) *mf*; *(Parl)* Abgeordnete(r) *mf.* **"~s only"** „nur für Mitglieder"; ~ **of the family** Familienmitglied *nt*; **a** ~ **of the audience** ein Zuschauer/Zuhörer *m*; **the** ~**s of the expedition** die Expeditionsteilnehmer *pl*; **the** ~ **countries** die Mitgliedsstaaten *pl*; ~ **of parliament** Parlamentsmitglied *nt.*

**membership** ['membəʃɪp] *n* Mitgliedschaft *f (of in +dat)*; *(number of members)* Mitgliederzahl *f.* ~ **card** Mitgliedskarte *f.*

**membrane** ['membreɪn] *n* Membran(e) *f.*

**memento** [mə'mentəʊ] *n, pl* **-(e)s** Andenken *nt (of an +acc).*

**memo** ['meməʊ] *n* **(a)** = **memorandum. (b)** ~ **pad** Notizblock *m.*

**memoir** ['memwɑːʳ] *n* **(a)** Kurzbiographie *f.* **(b)** ~**s** *pl* Memoiren *pl.*

**memorable** ['memərəbl] *adj* unvergeßlich; *(important)* denkwürdig.

**memorandum** [,memə'rændəm] *n, pl* **memoranda** [,memə'rændə] *(in business)* Mitteilung *f*; *(personal reminder)* Notiz *f*.

**memorial** [mɪ'mɔːrɪəl] **1** *adj plaque, service* Gedenk-. **2** *n* Denkmal *nt (to* für*)*.

**memorize** ['meməraɪz] *vt* sich *(dat)* einprägen.

**memory** ['memərɪ] *n* **(a)** Gedächtnis *nt*; *(faculty)* Erinnerungsvermögen *nt*. **from** ~ aus dem Kopf; **I have a bad** ~ **for faces** ich habe ein schlechtes Personengedächtnis; **if my** ~ **serves me right** wenn ich mich recht entsinne. **(b)** *(that remembered)* Erinnerung *f (of* an +*acc)*. **I have no** ~ **of it** ich kann mich nicht daran erinnern. **(c)** *(Comp)* Speicher *m*. ~ **bank** Datenspeicher *m*. **(d) in** ~ **of** zur Erinnerung *or* zum Gedenken *(form)* an *(+acc)*.

**men** [men] *pl of* **man.**

**menace** ['menɪs] **1** *n* **(a)** Bedrohung *f (to gen)*; *(imminent danger)* drohende Gefahr. **(b)** *(col: nuisance)* (Land)plage *f*. **2** *vt* bedrohen.

**menacing** *adj*, ~**ly** *adv* ['menɪsɪŋ, -lɪ] drohend.

**ménage** [me'nɑːʒ] *n* Haushalt *m*. ~ **à trois** Dreiecksverhältnis *nt*.

**mend** [mend] **1** *n* **to be on the** ~ auf dem Wege der Besserung sein. **2** *vt (repair)* reparieren; *roof, fence also* ausbessern; *hole, clothes* flicken. **my shoes need** ~**ing** ich muß meine Schuhe reparieren lassen; **to** ~ **one's ways** sich bessern. **3** *vi (bone)* (ver)heilen.

**mendacious** [men'deɪʃəs] *adj (form)* verlogen.

**mendacity** [men'dæsɪtɪ] *n (form)* Verlogenheit *f*.

**menfolk** ['menfəʊk] *npl* Männer *pl*.

**menial** ['miːnɪəl] *adj* niedrig.

**meningitis** [,menɪn'dʒaɪtɪs] *n* Hirnhautentzündung *f*.

**menopause** ['menəʊpɔːz] *n* Wechseljahre *pl*.

**men's room** *n (esp US)* Herrentoilette *f*.

**menstrual** ['menstrʊəl] *adj* Menstruations-. ~ **period** Monatsblutung *f*.

**menstruate** ['menstrʊeɪt] *vi* die Menstruation haben.

**menstruation** [,menstrʊ'eɪʃən] *n* die Menstruation *or* Periode.

**menswear** ['menzweəʳ] *n* Herrenbekleidung *f*.

**mental** ['mentl] *adj* **(a)** geistig; *cruelty* seelisch. **to make a** ~ **note of sth** sich *(dat)* etw merken; **he has a** ~ **age of ten** er ist auf dem geistigen Entwicklungsstand eines Zehnjährigen; ~ **arithmetic** Kopfrechnen *nt*; ~ **asylum** *or* **hospital** psychiatrische Klinik *f*; ~ **blackout** Bewußtseinsstörung *f*; ~ **health** Geisteszustand *m*; ~ **home** (Nerven)heilanstalt *f*; ~ **illness** Geisteskrankheit *f*; ~ **patient** Geisteskranke(r) *mf*; ~ **process** Denkprozeß *m*. **(b)** *(col: mad)* übergeschnappt *(col)*.

**mentality** [men'tælɪtɪ] *n* Mentalität *f*. **they have an aggressive** ~ sie haben eine aggressive Art.

**mentally** ['mentəlɪ] *adv* **(a)** geistig. ~ **handicapped/deficient** geistig behindert/geistesschwach; **he is** ~ **ill** er ist geisteskrank. **(b)** *(in one's head)* im Kopf.

**menthol** ['menθɒl] *n* Menthol *nt*.

**mention** ['menʃən] **1** *n* Erwähnung *f*. **to get** *or* **receive a** ~ erwähnt werden; **to give sth a** ~ etw erwähnen; **there is a/no** ~ **of it** es wird erwähnt/nicht erwähnt; **it's hardly worth a** ~ es ist kaum erwähnenswert. **2** *vt* erwähnen *(to sb* jdm gegenüber*)*. **not to** ~ ... geschweige denn ...; **too numerous to** ~ zu zahlreich, um sie einzeln erwähnen zu können; **don't** ~ **it!** (bitte,) gern geschehen!; ~**ing no names**, ohne irgendwelche Namen nennen zu wollen; ~ **me to your parents!** viele Grüße an Ihre Eltern!

**mentor** ['mentɔːʳ] *n* Mentor *m*.

**menu** ['menjuː] *n* **(a)** Speisekarte *f*. **what's on the** ~? was gibt es heute (zu essen)? **(b)** *(Comp)* Menü *nt*. ~-**driven** menügesteuert.

**MEP** = **Member of the European Parliament** Mitglied *nt* des Europäischen Parlaments.

**mercantile** ['mɜːkəntaɪl] *adj* Handels-. **the** ~ **marine** die Handelsmarine.

**mercenary** ['mɜːsɪnərɪ] **1** *adj* **(a)** *person* geldgierig. **(b)** *(Mil) troops* Söldner-. **2** *n* Söldner *m*.

**merchandise** ['mɜːtʃəndaɪs, -daɪz] *n* Ware *f*.

**merchant** ['mɜːtʃənt] *n* Kaufmann *m*. **diamond** ~ Diamantenhändler *m*.

**merchant** *in cpds* Handels-; ~ **bank** *n (Brit)* Handelsbank *f*; ~ **banker** *n (Brit)* Bankier *m* (bei einer Handelsbank); ~**man** *n* Handelsschiff *nt*; ~ **marine** *(US)*, ~ **navy** *n* Handelsmarine *f*; ~ **seaman** *n* Matrose *m* in der Handelsmarine; ~ **ship** *n* Handelsschiff *nt*.

**merciful** ['mɜːsɪfʊl] *adj* gnädig. **his death was a** ~ **release** sein Tod war für ihn eine Erlösung.

**mercifully** ['mɜːsɪfəlɪ] *adv act* barmherzig; *treat sb* gnädig; *(fortunately)* glücklicherweise.

**merciless** ['mɜːsɪlɪs] *adj* erbarmungslos; *destruction* schonungslos.

**mercilessly** ['mɜːsɪlɪslɪ] *adv* erbarmungslos.

**mercurial** [mɜː'kjʊərɪəl] *adj (volatile)* sprunghaft, wechselhaft; *(lively)* quicklebendig.

**Mercury** ['mɜːkjʊrɪ] *n* Merkur *m*.

**mercury** ['mɜːkjʊrɪ] *n* Quecksilber *nt*.

**mercy** ['mɜːsɪ] *n no pl (feeling of compassion)* Erbarmen *nt*; *(in judgment)* Gnade *f*; *(God's* ~*)* Barmherzigkeit *f*. **to have** ~ **on sb** mit jdm Erbarmen haben; **to show sb** ~/**no** ~ Erbarmen/kein Erbarmen mit jdm haben; **to be at the** ~ **of sb/sth** jdm/einer Sache *(dat)* ausgeliefert sein; **it's a** ~ **nobody was hurt** *(col)* man kann von Glück sagen, daß niemand verletzt wurde.

**mercy killing** *n* Töten *nt* aus Mitleid.

**mere** [mɪəʳ] *adj* bloß; *formality also* rein. **he's a** ~ **clerk** er ist bloß ein kleiner Angestellter; **but she's a** ~ **child** aber sie ist doch nur *or* doch noch ein Kind!

**merely** ['mɪəlɪ] *adv* lediglich, bloß.

**merge** [mɜːdʒ] **1** *vi* **(a)** zusammenkommen; *(colours)* ineinander übergehen; *(roads)* zusammenlaufen. **to** ~ **with sth** mit etw verschmelzen; *(colour)* in etw *(acc)* übergehen; **to** ~ **into sth** in etw *(acc)* übergehen. **(b)** *(Comm)* fusionieren. **2** *vt (Comm)* fusionieren; *(Comp) files* mischen.

**merger** ['mɜːdʒəʳ] *n (Comm)* Fusion *f*.

**meridian** [mə'rɪdɪən] *n (Astron, Geog)* Meridian *m*.

**meringue** [mə'ræŋ] *n* Meringe *f*, Baiser *nt*.

**merit** ['merɪt] **1** *n (achievement)* Leistung *f*, Verdienst *nt*; *(advantage)* Vorzug *m*. **to look** *or* **inquire into the** ~**s of sth** etw auf seine Vorteile untersuchen; **to treat a case on its** ~**s** einen Fall gesondert behandeln. **2** *vt* verdienen.

**meritocracy** [,merɪ'tɒkrəsɪ] *n* Leistungsgesellschaft *f*.

**mermaid** ['mɜːmeɪd] *n* Nixe, Meerjungfrau *f*.

**merrily** ['merɪlɪ] *adv* vergnügt; *boil also* munter.

**merriment** ['merɪmənt] *n* Heiterkeit *f*; *(laughter)* Gelächter *nt*.

**merry** ['merɪ] *adj (+er)* **(a)** *(cheerful)* fröhlich, vergnügt. **M**~ **Christmas!** Fröhliche *or* Frohe Weihnachten! **(b)** *(col: tipsy)* beschwipst *(col)*.

**merry:** ~-**go-round** *n* Karussell *nt*; ~**making** *n* Feiern *nt*.

**mesh** [meʃ] **1** *n (hole)* Masche *f*; *(size of hole)* Maschenweite *f*; *(wire* ~*)* Maschendraht *m*. **out of/in** ~

*(Mech)* nicht im/im Eingriff. **2** *vi* eingreifen *(with in* ~*acc)*; *(gears)* ineinandergreifen.

**mesmerize** ['mezməraɪz] *vt* hypnotisieren; *(fig)* fesseln. **the audience sat ~d** die Zuschauer saßen wie gebannt.

**mess**[1] [mes] *n* Durcheinander *nt*; *(untidy also)* Unordnung *f*; *(dirty)* Schweinerei *f*. **to be (in) a ~** unordentlich sein; *(disorganized)* ein einziges Durcheinander sein; *(fig: one's life, marriage etc)* verkorkst sein *(col)*; **to look a ~** *(person)* unmöglich aussehen; *(untidy also, room)* unordentlich aussehen; **to make a ~** *(untidy)* Unordnung machen; *(dirty)* eine Schweinerei machen; **to make a ~ of sth** *(untidy)* etw durcheinanderbringen; *(dirty)* etw verdrecken; *(bungle, botch)* etw verpfuschen; **the cat has made a ~ on the carpet** die Katze hat auf den Teppich gemacht.

▶**mess about** *or* **around** *(col)* **1** *vt sep person* an der Nase herumführen *(col)*; *(boss etc)* herumschikanieren; *(by delaying)* hinhalten. **2** *vi (play the fool)* herumalbern *or* -blödeln *(col)*; *(do nothing in particular)* herumgammeln *(col)*; *(fiddle)* herumfummeln *(col) (with an +dat)*; *(as hobby etc)* herumbasteln *(with an +dat) (col)*.

▶**mess up** *vt sep* durcheinanderbringen; *(make untidy also)* in Unordnung bringen; *(make dirty)* verdrecken; *(botch, bungle)* verpfuschen, verhunzen *(col)*; *marriage* kaputtmachen *(col)*, ruinieren; *life, person* verkorksen *(col)*.

**mess**[2] *(Mil)* *n* Kasino *nt*; *(on ships)* Messe *f*.

**message** ['mesɪdʒ] *n* Mitteilung, Nachricht, Botschaft *(form) f*. **to take a ~ to sb** jdm eine Nachricht überbringen; **can I take a ~ (for him)?** *(on telephone)* kann ich (ihm) etwas ausrichten?; **to give sb a ~** *(verbal)* jdm etwas ausrichten; *(written)* jdm eine Nachricht geben; **would you give John a ~ (for me)?** könnten Sie John etwas (von mir) ausrichten?; **to leave a ~ for sb** *(written)* jdm eine Nachricht hinterlassen; *(verbal)* jdm etwas ausrichten lassen; **to get the ~** *(fig col)* kapieren *(col)*.

**messenger** ['mesɪndʒər] *n* Bote *(form)*, Überbringer (in *f*) *m*; *(Mil)* Kurier *m*. **~ boy** Laufbursche *m*.

**Messiah** [mɪ'saɪə] *n* Messias *m*.

**Messrs** ['mesəz] *pl of* **Mr** *(on letters etc)* **to ~ ...** an die Herren ...

**mess-up** ['mesʌp] *n* Kuddelmuddel *m or nt (col)*.

**messy** ['mesɪ] *adj (+er) (dirty)* dreckig; *(untidy)* unordentlich; *(confused)* durcheinander *pred*; *(fig: unpleasant)* unschön.

**met** [met] *pret, ptp of* **meet**.

**met** *(Brit)* = **meteorological**.

**Met** *(US)* = **Metropolitan Opera** Met *f*.

**metabolism** [mə'tæbəlɪzəm] *n* Stoffwechsel *m*.

**metal** ['metl] *n* Metall *nt*; *(Brit: on road)* Asphalt *m*.

**metallic** [mɪ'tælɪk] *adj* metallisch.

**metallurgy** [me'tælədʒɪ] *n* Metallurgie *f*.

**metal** *in cpds* Metall-; **~ polish** *n* Metallpolitur *f*; **~work** *n* Metall *nt*; **we did ~work at school** wir haben in der Schule Metallarbeiten gemacht; **~ worker** *n* Metallarbeiter (in *f*) *m*.

**metamorphosis** [ˌmetə'mɔːfəsɪs] *n, pl* **metamorphoses** [ˌmetə'mɔːfəsiːz] Metamorphose *f*; *(fig)* Verwandlung *f*.

**metaphor** ['metəfər] *n* Metapher *f*.

**metaphorical** [ˌmetə'fɒrɪkəl] *adj* metaphorisch.

**metaphysical** [ˌmetə'fɪzɪkəl] *adj* metaphysisch.

**metaphysics** [ˌmetə'fɪzɪks] *n sing* Metaphysik *f*.

**mete out** ['miːt'aʊt] *vt sep* zuteil werden lassen *(to sb* jdm*)*; *praise* austeilen; *rewards* verteilen. **to ~ ~ a punishment to sb** jdn bestrafen.

**meteor** ['miːtɪər] *n* Meteor *m*.

**meteoric** [ˌmiːtɪ'ɒrɪk] *adj* meteorisch; *(fig)* kometenhaft.

**meteorite** ['miːtɪəraɪt] *n* Meteorit *m*.

**meteorological** [ˌmiːtɪərə'lɒdʒɪkəl] *adj* Wetter-, meteorologisch. **the M~ Office** *(Brit)* das Wetteramt.

**meteorologist** [ˌmiːtɪə'rɒlədʒɪst] *n* Meteorologe *m*, Meteorologin *f*.

**meteorology** [ˌmiːtɪə'rɒlədʒɪ] *n* Meteorologie *f*.

**meter**[1] ['miːtər] *n* Zähler *m*; *(parking* ~*)* Parkuhr *f*. **~ maid** *(col)* Politesse *f*.

**meter**[2] *n (US)* = **metre**.

**methane** ['miːθeɪn] *n* Methan *nt*.

**method** ['meθəd] *n* Methode *f*; *(process)* Verfahren *nt*. **~ of payment** Zahlungsweise *f*.

**methodical** [mɪ'θɒdɪkəl] *adj* methodisch.

**methodically** [mɪ'θɒdɪkəlɪ] *adv* methodisch.

**Methodist** ['meθədɪst] *n* Methodist (in *f*) *m*.

**methodology** [ˌmeθə'dɒlədʒɪ] *n* Methodik *f*.

**meths** [meθs] *n sing* Spiritus *m*.

**methylated spirits** ['meθɪleɪtɪd'spɪrɪts] *n sing* (Brenn)spiritus *m*.

**meticulous** [mɪ'tɪkjʊləs] *adj* (peinlich) genau. **to be ~ about sth** es mit etw sehr genau nehmen.

**meticulously** [mɪ'tɪkjʊləslɪ] *adv* mit äußerster Sorgfalt, (peinlich) genau. **~ clean** makellos sauber.

**metre**, *(US)* **meter** ['miːtər] *n* **(a)** *(Measure)* Meter *m or nt*. **(b)** *(Poet)* Metrum *nt*.

**metric** ['metrɪk] *adj* metrisch. **the ~ system** das metrische Maßsystem; **~ ton** Metertonne *f*.

**metrication** [ˌmetrɪ'keɪʃən] *n* Umstellung *f* auf das metrische Maßsystem.

**metronome** [metrə'nəʊm] *n* Metronom *nt*.

**metropolis** [mɪ'trɒpəlɪs] *n* Metropole, Weltstadt *f*; *(capital)* Hauptstadt *f*.

**metropolitan** [ˌmetrə'pɒlɪtən] *adj see n* weltstädtisch; der Hauptstadt. **M~ Police** *(Brit)* Londoner Polizei.

**mettle** ['metl] *n (spirit)* Stehvermögen *nt*; *(of horse)* Zähigkeit *f*; *(temperament)* Feuer *nt*. **to show one's ~ zeigen, was in einem steckt; **to be on one's ~** auf dem Posten sein.

**mew** [mjuː] **1** *n* Miau(en) *nt*. **2** *vi* miauen.

**mews** [mjuːz] *n sing or pl* Gasse *f* mit ehemaligen Kutscherhäuschen.

**Mexican** ['meksɪkən] **1** *adj* mexikanisch. **2** *n* Mexikaner(in *f*) *m*.

**Mexico** ['meksɪkəʊ] *n* Mexiko *nt*. **~ City** Mexiko City *nt*.

**mezzanine** ['mezəniːn] *n* Mezzanin *nt*.

**mezzo-soprano** [ˌmetsəʊsə'prɑːnəʊ] *n* Mezzosopran *m*.

**mfg** = **manufacturing**.

**mfr** = **manufacture(r)** Herst.

**mg** = **milligram** mg.

**MHz** = **megahertz** MHz.

**MI** *(US Post)* = **Michigan**.

**MI5** *(Brit)* = **Military Intelligence, section 5** *Spionageabwehrdienst m*; ≈ MAD *m*.

**MI6** *(Brit)* = **Military Intelligence, section 6** *Geheimdienst m*.

**miaow** [miː'aʊ] **1** *n* Miau(en) *nt*. **2** *vi* miauen.

**mica** ['maɪkə] *n* Muskovit *m*.

**mice** [maɪs] *pl of* **mouse**.

**mickey** ['mɪkɪ] *n (col)*: **to take the ~ (out of sb)** jdn auf den Arm *or* auf die Schippe nehmen *(col)*.

**micro-** ['maɪkrəʊ-] *pref* mikro-, Mikro-.

**microbe** ['maɪkrəʊb] *n* Mikrobe *f*.

**micro:** **~biology** *n* Mikrobiologie *f*; **~chip** *n* Mikrochip *m*; **~-computer** *n* Mikrocomputer *m*; **~cosm** *n* Mikrokosmos *m*; **~ dot** *n* Mikrobild *nt*; **~fiche** *n* Mikrofiche *m or nt*; **~film** *n* Mikrofilm *m*; **~light** *n*

**Milky Way**

Ultraleichtflugzeug *nt*; ~**meter** [maɪˈkrɒmɪtəʳ] *n* Meßschraube *f*; ~**organism** *n* Mikroorganismus *m*; ~**phone** *n* Mikrofon *nt*; ~**processor** *n* Mikroprozessor *m*; ~**scope** *n* Mikroskop *nt*; ~**scopic** [ˌmaɪkrəˈskɒpɪk] *adj* *details, print* mikroskopisch; *thing* mikroskopisch klein; ~**wave** *n* Mikrowelle *f*; ~**wave oven** *n* Mikrowellenherd *m*.

**mid** [mɪd] *adj* mittel-, Mittel-. **in** ~ **January** Mitte Januar; **in the** ~ **1950s** Mitte der fünfziger Jahre; **he's in his mid 30s** er ist Mitte dreißig; **temperatures in the** ~ **eighties** Temperatur um 30°C; **in** ~ **morning** am Vormittag; **in** ~ **ocean** mitten auf dem Meer; **in** ~ **air** in der Luft.

**midday** [ˈmɪdˈdeɪ] **1** *n* Mittag *m*. **at** ~ mittags, um die Mittagszeit. **2** *adj attr* mittäglich. ~ **meal** Mittagessen *nt*.

**middle** [ˈmɪdl] **1** *n* Mitte *f*; *(central section: of book, film etc)* mittlerer Teil; *(inside of fruit etc)* Innere(s) *nt*; *(waist)* Taille *f*. **in the** ~ **of the table** mitten auf dem Tisch; *(in exact centre)* in der Mitte des Tisches; **in the** ~ **of the night** mitten in der Nacht; **in the** ~ **of the day** gegen Mittag; **in the** ~ **of nowhere** am Ende der Welt; **in** *or* **about the** ~ **of May** Mitte Mai; **we were in the** ~ **of lunch** wir waren mitten beim Essen; **to be in the** ~ **of doing sth** mitten dabei sein, etw zu tun; **I'm in the** ~ **of reading it** ich bin mittendrin. **2** *adj* mittlere(r, s); *part, point, finger* Mittel-.

**middle** *in cpds* Mittel-, mittel-; ~ **age** *n* mittleres Lebensalter; ~-**aged** *adj* mittleren Alters; **M**~ **Ages** *npl* Mittelalter *nt*; ~-**brow** *adj* für den (geistigen) Normalverbraucher; ~-**class** *adj* bürgerlich, spießig *(pej)*; *(Sociol)* mittelständisch; ~ **class(es)** *n* Mittelstand *m* or -schicht *f*; ~ **distance** *n* mittlere Entfernung; ~-**distance runner** *n* Mittelstreckenläufer(in *f*) *m*; ~ **ear** *n* Mittelohr *nt*; **M**~ **East** *n* Naher Osten; **M**~ **Eastern** *adj* nahöstlich; ~**man** *n* Mittelsmann *m*; *(Comm)* Zwischenhändler *m*; ~ **name** *n* zweiter Vorname; ~-**of-the-road** *adj* gemäßigt; *policy, politician* der gemäßigten Mitte; ~ **school** *n (Brit)* Schule für 9- bis 13-jährige; ~ **weight** *n* Mittelgewicht *nt*.

**middling** [ˈmɪdlɪŋ] *adj* mittelmäßig; *(as answer)* so lala *(col)*.

**Middx** *(Brit)* = **Middlesex** *Grafschaft um London.*

**midfield** [ˌmɪdˈfiːld] **1** *n* Mittelfeld *nt*. **2** *adj* Mittelfeld-.

**midge** [mɪdʒ] *n* Mücke *f*.

**midget** [ˈmɪdʒɪt] *n* Liliputaner *m*.

**midi system** [ˈmɪdɪˌsɪstəm] *n (Hifi)* Midi-Anlage *f*.

**mid: the M**~**lands** *npl* Mittelengland *nt*; ~**night** *n* Mitternacht *f*; **at** ~**night** um Mitternacht. ~**night mass** *(at Christmas)* Christmesse *f*.

**midriff** [ˈmɪdrɪf] *n* Taille *f*.

**midst** [mɪdst] *n* **in the** ~ **of** mitten in.

**mid:** ~**stream** *n* **in** ~**stream** *(lit)* in der Mitte des Flusses; *(fig)* auf halber Strecke. ~**summer 1** *n* Hochsommer *m*; **M**~**summer's Day** Sommersonnenwende *f*; **2** *adj days, nights* Hochsommer-; ~**term** *adj* ~-**term elections** *(Pol)* Zwischenwahlen *pl*; ~**way** *adv* auf halbem Weg; ~**way through sth** mitten in etw *(dat)*; **to have reached the** ~**way point** die Hälfte geschafft haben; ~**week** *adv* mitten in der Woche; **M**~**west** *n (US)* Mittelwesten *m*.

**midwife** [ˈmɪdwaɪf] *n, pl* -**wives** Hebamme *f*.

**midwifery** [ˌmɪdˈwɪfərɪ] *n* Geburtshilfe *f*.

**midwinter** [ˌmɪdˈwɪntəʳ] *n* Mitte *f* des Winters.

**miffed** [mɪft] *adj (col)* sauer *(col)* *(at* über +*acc)*.

**might**[1] [maɪt] *pret of* **may. as you** ~ **expect** wie zu erwarten war; **you** ~ **try Smith's** Sie könnten es ja mal bei Smith versuchen; **he** ~ **at least have apolo-** gized er hätte sich wenigstens entschuldigen können.

**might**[2] *n* Macht *f*. **with all one's** ~ mit aller Kraft.

**mightily** [ˈmaɪtɪlɪ] *adv* mit aller Macht; *(col: extremely)* mächtig *(col)*; *improved* stark.

**mighty** [ˈmaɪtɪ] **1** *adj (+er)* gewaltig; *(wielding power)* mächtig; *warrior* stark. **2** *adv (col)* mächtig *(col)*. ~ **fine** *(esp US)* großartig.

**migraine** [ˈmiːgreɪn] *n* Migräne *f*.

**migrant** [ˈmaɪgrənt] **1** *adj* Wander-. ~ **bird** Zugvogel *m*; ~ **worker** Gastarbeiter *m*. **2** *n (bird)* Zugvogel *m*; *(person)* Übersiedler(in *f*) *m*.

**migrate** [maɪˈgreɪt] *vi (animals, workers)* (ab)wandern; *(birds)* nach Süden ziehen.

**migration** [maɪˈgreɪʃən] *n* Wanderung *f*; *(of birds also)* (Vogel)zug *m*; *(seasonal)* Zug *m*. ~ **of peoples** *(Hist)* Völkerwanderung *f*.

**migratory** [maɪˈgreɪtərɪ] *adj life, instinct, worker* Wander-. ~ **bird** Zugvogel *m*.

**Milan** [mɪˈlæn] *n* Mailand *nt*.

**mike** [maɪk] *n (col)* Mikrofon, Mikro *(col)* *nt*.

**mild** [maɪld] **1** *adj (+er)* mild; *breeze, criticism* leicht; *character* sanft; *(slight)* leicht. **2** *n (Brit: beer)* (leichtes) dunkles Bier.

**mildew** [ˈmɪldjuː] *n* Schimmel *m*; *(on plants)* Mehltau *m*.

**mildly** [ˈmaɪldlɪ] *adv* leicht; *say* sanft; *rebuke* milde. **to put it** ~ gelinde gesagt.

**mile** [maɪl] *n* Meile *f*. **how many** ~**s per gallon does your car do?** ≃ wieviel (Benzin) verbraucht Ihr Auto?; **a fifty-**~ **journey** eine Fahrt von fünfzig Meilen; ~**s (and** ~**s)** *(col)* meilenweit; **they live** ~**s away** sie wohnen meilenweit weg; **it sticks out a** ~ das sieht ja ein Blinder (mit Krückstock) *(col)*; **he's** ~**s better at tennis than she is** er spielt hundertmal besser Tennis als sie *(col)*.

**mileage** [ˈmaɪlɪdʒ] *n* Meilen *pl*; *(on odometer)* Meilenstand *m*. ~ **allowance** Kilometergeld *nt*; **what** ~ **does your car do?** wieviel (Benzin) verbraucht Ihr Auto?; **we got a lot of** ~ **out of it** *(fig col)* das war uns *(dat)* sehr dienlich.

**mileometer** [maɪˈlɒmɪtəʳ] *n (Brit)* ≃ Kilometerzähler *m*.

**milestone** [ˈmaɪlstəʊn] *n (lit, fig)* Meilenstein *m*.

**milieu** [ˈmiːljɜː] *n* Milieu *nt*.

**militancy** [ˈmɪlɪtənsɪ] *n* Militanz *f*.

**militant** [ˈmɪlɪtənt] **1** *adj* militant. **2** *n* militantes Mitglied/militanter Gewerkschaftler *etc*.

**militarism** [ˈmɪlɪtərɪzəm] *n* Militarismus *m*.

**militaristic** [ˌmɪlɪtəˈrɪstɪk] *adj* militaristisch.

**military** [ˈmɪlɪtərɪ] **1** *adj* militärisch; *government, band* Militär-. ~ **service** Wehrdienst *m*. **2** *n:* **the** ~ das Militär.

**militate** [ˈmɪlɪteɪt] *vi* **to** ~ **against sth** gegen etw sprechen.

**militia** [mɪˈlɪʃə] *n* Miliz, Bürgerwehr *f*.

**milk** [mɪlk] **1** *n* Milch *f*. ~ **of magnesia** Magnesiamilch *f*; **it's no use crying over spilt** ~ *(prov)* was passiert ist, ist passiert. **2** *vt (lit, fig)* melken.

**milk** *in cpds* Milch-; ~ **chocolate** *n* Vollmilchschokolade *f*; ~ **churn** *n* Milchkanne *f*; ~ **float** *n (Brit)* Milchwagen *m*.

**milking** [ˈmɪlkɪŋ] *n* Melken *nt*. ~ **machine** Melkmaschine *f*.

**milk:** ~ **jug** *n* Milchkrug *m*; ~**man** *n* Milchmann *m*; ~ **run** *n (Aviat col)* Routineflug *m*; ~ **shake** *n* Milchmixgetränk *nt*, Milchshake *m*; ~ **tooth** *n* Milchzahn *m*; ~ **truck** *n (US)* Milchwagen *m*.

**milky** [ˈmɪlkɪ] *adj (+er)* milchig. ~ **coffee** Milchkaffee *m*.

**Milky Way** [ˌmɪlkɪˈweɪ] *n* Milchstraße *f*.

**mill** [mɪl] **1** *n* Mühle *f*; *(paper, steel ~ etc)* Fabrik *f*; *(cotton~)* *(for thread)* Spinnerei *f*; *(for cloth)* Weberei *f*. **he really went through the ~** *(col)* er hat wirklich viel durchmachen müssen. **2** *vt flour, coffee etc* mahlen; *paper* walzen; *metal* fräsen; *coin* rändeln. ▶**mill about** *or* **around** *vi* umherlaufen.

**millennium** [mɪˈlenɪəm] *n, pl* -**s** *or* **millennia** [mɪˈlenɪə] *(1,000 years)* Jahrtausend *nt*; *(state of perfection)* Tausendjähriges Reich *nt*.

**miller** [ˈmɪləʳ] *n* Müller *m*.

**millet** [ˈmɪlɪt] *n* Hirse *f*.

**milli-**: **~gram(me)** *n* Milligramm *nt*; **~litre,** *(US)* **~liter** *n* Milliliter *m or nt*; **~metre,** *(US)* **~meter** *n* Millimeter *m or nt*.

**milliner** [ˈmɪlɪnəʳ] *n* Hutmacher(in *f*) *m*.

**millinery** [ˈmɪlɪnərɪ] *n (trade)* Hutmacherhandwerk *nt*.

**million** [ˈmɪljən] *n* Million *f*. **4 ~ people** 4 Millionen Menschen; **the starving ~s** die Millionen, die Hunger leiden; **she's one in a ~** *(col)* so jemanden wie sie findet man so bald nicht wieder; **to feel like a ~ dollars** *(col)* sich pudelwohl fühlen; **to look (like) a ~ dollars** *(col)* einfach fantastisch aussehen.

**millionaire** [ˌmɪljəˈnɛəʳ] *n* Millionär *m*.

**millionairess** [ˌmɪljəˈnɛərɛs] *n* Millionärin *f*.

**millipede** [ˈmɪlɪpiːd] *n* Tausendfüßler *m*.

**mill**: **~pond** *n* Mühlteich *m*; **as calm as a ~pond** spiegelglatt; **~stone** *n* Mühlstein *m*; **it's a ~stone around his neck** das ist für ihn ein Klotz am Bein; **~wheel** *n* Mühlrad *nt*.

**mime** [maɪm] **1** *n (acting)* Pantomime *f*; *(actor)* Pantomime *m*; *(ancient play, actor)* Mimus *m*. **2** *vt* pantomimisch darstellen.

**mimic** [ˈmɪmɪk] **1** *n* Imitator *m*. **2** *vt* nachahmen; *(ridicule)* nachäffen.

**mimicry** [ˈmɪmɪkrɪ] *n* Nachahmung *f*.

**min** = (a) **minute(s)** min. (b) **minimum** min.

**minaret** [ˌmɪnəˈret] *n* Minarett *nt*.

**mince** [mɪns] **1** *n (Brit) (also* **~d meat***)* Hackfleisch, Gehackte(s) *nt*. **2** *vt meat* durch den Fleischwolf drehen. **he doesn't ~ his words** er nimmt kein Blatt vor den Mund. **3** *vi (walk)* tänzeln, trippeln. **mincing steps** tänzelnde Schritte.

**mince**: **~meat** *n* süße Gebäckfüllung aus Dörrobst und Sirup; **to make ~meat of sb** *(col) (physically)* Hackfleisch aus jdm machen *(col)*; *(verbally)* jdn zur Schnecke machen *(col)*; **~ pie** *n* mit Mincemeat gefülltes Gebäck.

**mincer** [ˈmɪnsəʳ] *n* Fleischwolf *m*.

**mind** [maɪnd] **1** *n* (a) *(intellect)* Geist *(also Philos, person)*, Verstand *m*; *(type of ~ also)* Kopf *m*; *(thoughts)* Gedanken *pl*; *(memory)* Gedächtnis *nt*. **it's a question of ~ over matter** es ist eine Willensfrage; **it's all in the ~** das ist alles Einbildung; **one of the finest ~s of our times** einer der großen Geister unserer Zeit; **to be clear in one's ~ about sth** sich *(dat)* über etw im klaren sein; **he had something on his ~** ihn beschäftigte etwas; **if you put your ~ to it** wenn du dich anstrengst; **she couldn't get him out of her ~** er ging ihr nicht aus dem Kopf; **to take sb's ~ off sth** jdn auf andere Gedanken bringen; **the idea never entered my ~** daran hatte ich überhaupt nicht gedacht; **to bear** *or* **keep sth in ~** etw nicht vergessen; *facts also, application* etw im Auge behalten; **to bear** *or* **keep sb in ~** an jdn denken; **it went right out of my ~** daran habe ich überhaupt nicht mehr gedacht; **to bring** *or* **call sth to ~** etw in Erinnerung rufen.

(b) *(inclination)* Lust *f*; *(intention)* Absicht *f*. **to have sb/sth in ~** an jdn/etw denken; **to have it in ~ to do sth** beabsichtigen, etw zu tun; **I've half a ~/a**

good **~ to …** ich hätte Lust/gute Lust, zu …; **nothing was further from my ~** nichts lag mir ferner; **his ~ is set on that** er hat sich *(dat)* das in den Kopf gesetzt.

(c) *(opinion)* Meinung, Ansicht *f*. **to change one's ~** es sich *(dat)* anders überlegen; **to be in two ~s about sth** sich *(dat)* über etw *(acc)* nicht im klaren sein; **to be of one** *or* **the same ~** gleicher Meinung sein; **to my ~ he's wrong** meiner Ansicht nach irrt er sich; **to have a ~ of one's/its own** *(person: not conform)* seinen eigenen Kopf haben *(hum: machine etc)* seine Mucken haben *(col)*.

(d) *(sanity)* Verstand *m*. **to go out of** *or* **lose one's ~** den Verstand verlieren; **to be out of one's ~** nicht bei Verstand sein; *(with worry etc)* vor Sorgen ganz krank sein.

**2** *vt* (a) *(look after)* aufpassen auf (+*acc*); *sb's chair, seat* freihalten. **I'm ~ing the shop** *(fig)* ich sehe nach dem Rechten.

(b) *(be careful of)* aufpassen *(auf* +*acc*); *(pay attention to)* achten auf (+*acc*); *(act in accordance with)* beachten. **~ the step!** Vorsicht Stufe!; **~ your own business** kümmern Sie sich um Ihre eigenen Angelegenheiten.

(c) *(care, worry about)* sich kümmern um; *(object to)* etwas haben gegen. **she doesn't ~ it** es macht ihr nichts aus; *(is not bothered)* es stört sie nicht; *(is indifferent to)* es ist ihr egal; **would you ~ opening the door?** wären Sie so freundlich, die Tür aufzumachen?; **do you ~ my smoking?** macht es Ihnen etwas aus, wenn ich rauche?; **it's bad enough for the children, never ~ the parents** für die Kinder ist es schon schlimm genug, von den Eltern ganz zu schweigen; **never ~ the expense** (es ist) egal, was es kostet; **never ~ him** kümmere dich nicht um ihn!; **I wouldn't ~ a cup of tea** ich hätte nichts gegen eine Tasse Tee.

**3** *vi* (a) *(be careful)* aufpassen. **~ you get that done** sieh zu, daß du das fertigbekommst!

(b) **~ you** allerdings; **~ you, he did try** er hat es immerhin versucht.

(c) *(object)* etwas dagegen haben. **do you ~?** macht es Ihnen etwas aus?; **do you ~!** *(iro)* ich möchte doch sehr bitten!; **may I? — I don't ~** darf ich? — meinetwegen; **which one do you want? — I don't ~** welches willst du? — das ist mir egal.

(d) **never ~** macht nichts!; *(in exasperation)* ist ja auch egal!; **never ~, you'll find another** mach dir nichts draus, du findest bestimmt einen anderen; **never ~ about that now!** laß das doch jetzt!

▶**mind out** *vi* aufpassen *(for* auf +*acc*).

**mind**: **~-blowing** *adj (col)* irre *(col)*; **~-boggling** *adj (col)* irrsinnig *(col)*.

-**minded** *adj suf* **romantically/technically~** romantisch/technisch veranlagt; **evil~** übel gesinnt.

**minder** [ˈmaɪndəʳ] *n (caring for sb)* Betreuer(in *f*) *m*; *(col: aide)* Aufpasser(in *f*) *m*.

**mindful** [ˈmaɪndfʊl] *adj* **to be ~ of sth** an etw *(acc)* denken.

**mind**: **~less** *adj (stupid)* ohne Verstand; *(senseless) destruction, crime* sinnlos; *occupation* geistlos; **~ reader** *n* Gedankenleser(in *f*) *m*.

**mine¹** [maɪn] *poss pron* meine(r, s). **this car is ~** dieses Auto gehört mir; **is this ~?** gehört das mir?; **his friends and ~** seine und meine Freunde; **a friend of ~** ein Freund von mir; **a favourite expression of ~** einer meiner Lieblingsausdrücke.

**mine²** **1** *n* (a) *(Min)* Bergwerk *nt*; *(copper ~ etc also)* Mine *f*; *(coal~ also)* Zeche *f*. **to work down the ~s** unter Tage arbeiten. (b) *(Mil, Naut etc)* Mine *f*. **to lay ~s** Minen legen. (c) *(fig)* **the book is a ~ of infor-**

**mation** das Buch ist eine wahre Fundgrube; **he is a ~ of information** er ist ein wandelndes Lexikon *(col)*. **2** *vt* **(a)** *coal, metal* fördern, abbauen. **(b)** *(Mil, Naut)* verminen; *ship* eine Mine befestigen an *(+dat)*; *(blow up)* (mit einer Mine) sprengen. **3** *vi* Bergbau betreiben. **to ~ for sth** nach etw graben.

**mine:** **~-detector** *n* Minensuchgerät *nt*; **~field** *n* Minenfeld *nt*.

**miner** ['maɪnəʳ] *n* Bergarbeiter, Bergmann *m*.

**mineral** ['mɪnərəl] **1** *n* Mineral *nt*. **2** *adj deposit, resources, oil* Mineral-; *substance* mineralisch. **~ water** Mineralwasser *nt*.

**mine:** **~sweeper** *n* Minensuchboot *nt*; **~worker** *n* Bergarbeiter *m*.

**mingle** ['mɪŋgl] *vi* sich vermischen; *(people, groups)* sich untereinander vermischen. **to ~ with the crowd** sich unters Volk mischen; **you should ~ a bit** *(at party etc)* du solltest dich ein bißchen unter die Leute mischen.

**mini-** ['mɪnɪ-] *pref* Mini-.

**miniature** ['mɪnɪtʃəʳ] **1** *n* Miniaturausgabe *f*; *(Art)* Miniatur *f*. **in ~** im kleinen, in Kleinformat. **2** *adj attr* Miniatur-. **~ camera** Kleinbildkamera *f*; **~ poodle** Zwergpudel *m*.

**mini:** **~bus** *n* Kleinbus *m*; **~cab** *n* Kleintaxi *nt*; **~car** *n* Kleinwagen *m*.

**minim** ['mɪnɪm] *n (Brit Mus)* halbe Note.

**minimal** *adj*, **~ly** *adv* ['mɪnɪml, -əlɪ] minimal.

**minimize** ['mɪnɪmaɪz] *vt expenditure etc* auf ein Minimum reduzieren.

**minimum** ['mɪnɪməm] **1** *n* Minimum *nt*. **with a ~ of inconvenience** mit einem Minimum an Unannehmlichkeiten; **to reduce sth to a ~** etw auf ein Mindestmaß reduzieren. **2** *adj attr* Mindest-. **~ lending rate** Diskontsatz, Eckzins *m*; **~ temperature** Tiefsttemperatur *f*; **~ wage** Mindestlohn *m*.

**mining** ['maɪnɪŋ] *n* **(a)** *(Min)* Bergbau *m*. **(b)** *(Mil) (of area)* Verminen *nt*; *(of ship)* Sprengung *f* (mit einer Mine).

**mining:** **~ engineer** *n* Bergbauingenieur *m*; **~ industry** *n* Bergbau *m*.

**miniskirt** ['mɪnɪˌskɜːt] *n* Minirock *m*.

**minister** ['mɪnɪstəʳ] **1** *n* **(a)** *(Pol)* Minister *m*. **(b)** *(Eccl)* Pastor *m*, protestantischer Geistlicher. **2** *vi* **to ~ to sb** sich um jdn kümmern.

**ministerial** [ˌmɪnɪ'stɪərɪəl] *adj (Pol)* ministeriell, Minister-.

**ministry** ['mɪnɪstrɪ] *n* **(a)** *(Pol)* Ministerium *nt*. **~ of agriculture** Landwirtschaftsministerium. **(b)** *(Eccl)* geistliches Amt. **to join** *or* **go into the ~** Geistlicher werden.

**mink** [mɪŋk] *n* Nerz *m*. **~ coat** Nerzmantel *m*.

**minor** ['maɪnəʳ] **1** *adj* **(a)** *(of lesser extent)* kleiner; *(of lesser importance)* unbedeutend; *offence, operation* leicht; *importance* geringer; *position, road* Neben-. **a ~ role** eine Nebenrolle. **(b)** *(Mus)* Moll-. **G ~ g-Moll** *nt*. **2** *n* **(a)** *(Jur)* Minderjährige(r) *mf*. **(b)** *(US Univ)* Nebenfach *nt*.

**Minorca** [mɪ'nɔːkə] *n* Menorca *nt*.

**minority** [maɪ'nɒrɪtɪ] **1** *n* Minderheit *f*. **to be in a ~** in der Minderheit sein. **2** *adj attr* Minderheits-. **~ group** Minderheit *f*.

**minster** ['mɪnstəʳ] *n* Münster *nt*.

**minstrel** ['mɪnstrəl] *n* Spielmann *m*.

**mint¹** [mɪnt] **1** *n* Münzanstalt, Münze *f*. **a ~ of money** *(col)* ein Vermögen *nt (col)*. **2** *adj stamp* ungestempelt. **in ~ condition** neuwertig. **3** *vt coin* prägen.

**mint²** *n (Bot)* Minze *f*; *(sweet)* Pfefferminz *nt*. **~ sauce** Minzsoße *f*.

**minuet** [ˌmɪnjʊ'et] *n* Menuett *nt*.

**minus** ['maɪnəs] **1** *prep* **(a)** minus, weniger. **£100 ~**

**taxes** £100 abzüglich (der) Steuern. **(b)** *(without, deprived of)* ohne. **2** *adj quantity, value* negativ; *sign* Minus-; *temperatures* unter Null. **~ three degrees** drei Grad minus.

**minuscule** ['mɪnəˌskjuːl] *adj* winzig.

**minute¹** ['mɪnɪt] *n* **(a)** *(of time, degree)* Minute *f*. **in a ~** sofort; **this (very) ~!** auf der Stelle!; **I shan't be a ~, it won't take a ~** es dauert nicht lang; **any ~** jeden Augenblick; **tell me the ~ he comes** sag mir sofort Bescheid, wenn er kommt; **have you got a ~?** hast du mal einen Augenblick Zeit?; **at the last ~** in letzter Minute. **(b)** *(official note)* Notiz *f*. **~s** Protokoll *nt*; **to take the ~s** das Protokoll führen.

**minute²** [maɪ'njuːt] *adj (small)* winzig; *(detailed, exact)* minuziös; *detail* kleinste(r, s).

**minute hand** *n* Minutenzeiger *m*.

**minutely** [maɪ'njuːtlɪ] *adv (by a small amount)* ganz geringfügig; *(in detail)* genauestens.

**minx** [mɪŋks] *n* Biest *nt (col)*.

**miracle** ['mɪrəkl] *n* Wunder *nt*. **~ play** Mirakelspiel *nt*; **~ worker** Wundertäter(in *f*) *m*; **to work** *or* **perform ~s** *(lit)* Wunder vollbringen; **I can't work ~s** ich kann doch nicht hexen!; **it's a ~ he ...** es ist ein Wunder, daß er ....

**miraculous** [mɪ'rækjʊləs] *adj* wunderbar; *powers* Wunder-.

**miraculously** [mɪ'rækjʊləslɪ] *adv* auf wunderbare Weise; *(fig)* wie durch ein Wunder.

**mirage** ['mɪrɑːʒ] *n* Fata Morgana *f*; *(fig)* Trugbild *nt*.

**mire** ['maɪəʳ] *n (also fig)* Morast *m*.

**mirror** ['mɪrəʳ] **1** *n* Spiegel *m*. **~ image** *(lit, fig)* Spiegelbild *nt*. **2** *vt* widerspiegeln.

**mirth** [mɜːθ] *n* Frohsinn *m*; *(laughter)* Heiterkeit *f*.

**misadventure** [ˌmɪsəd'ventʃəʳ] *n* Mißgeschick *nt*. **death by ~** Tod *m* durch Unfall.

**misanthropist** [mɪ'zænθrəpɪst] *n* Misanthrop, Menschenfeind *m*.

**misapply** [ˌmɪsə'plaɪ] *vt* falsch anwenden.

**misapprehension** [ˌmɪsæprɪ'henʃən] *n* Mißverständnis *nt*. **I think you are under a ~** ich glaube, bei Ihnen liegt (da) ein Mißverständnis vor; **he was under the ~ that ...** er hatte irrtümlicherweise angenommen, daß ...

**misappropriate** [ˌmɪsə'prəʊprɪeɪt] *vt* entwenden; *money* veruntreuen.

**misappropriation** [ˌmɪsəˌprəʊprɪ'eɪʃən] *n see vt* Entwendung *f*; Veruntreuung *f*.

**misbehave** [ˌmɪsbɪ'heɪv] *vi* sich schlecht benehmen; *(child also)* ungezogen sein.

**misbehaviour,** *(US)* **misbehavior** [ˌmɪsbɪ'heɪvjəʳ] *n* schlechtes Benehmen.

**misc = miscellaneous.**

**miscalculate** [ˌmɪs'kælkjʊleɪt] **1** *vt* falsch berechnen; *(misjudge)* falsch einschätzen. **2** *vi* sich verrechnen; *(estimate wrongly)* sich verkalkulieren.

**miscalculation** [ˌmɪskælkjʊ'leɪʃən] *n* Rechenfehler *m*; *(wrong estimation)* Fehlkalkulation *f*; *(misjudgement)* Fehleinschätzung *f*.

**miscarriage** [ˌmɪs'kærɪdʒ] *n* **(a)** *(Med)* Fehlgeburt *f*. **(b)** **~ of justice** Justizirrtum *m*.

**miscarry** [mɪs'kærɪ] *vi* **(a)** *(Med)* eine Fehlgeburt haben. **(b)** *(fail: plans)* fehlschlagen.

**miscast** [ˌmɪs'kɑːst] *vt actor* die falsche Rolle geben *+dat*. **he was ~ in this part** mit ihm war die Rolle fehlbesetzt.

**miscellaneous** [ˌmɪsə'leɪnɪəs] *adj* verschieden; *poems* verschiedenerlei; *collection, crowd* bunt. **"~"** „Verschiedenes".

**miscellany** [mɪ'selənɪ] *n (collection)* (bunte) Sammlung; *(variety)* Vielfalt *f*.

**mischance** [mɪs'tʃɑːns] *n* **by some** ~ durch einen unglücklichen Zufall.

**mischief** ['mɪstʃɪf] *n (roguery)* Verschmitztheit *f*; *(naughty behaviour)* Unfug *m*. ~**-maker** Unruhestifter *m*; **he's always getting into** ~ er stellt dauernd etwas an; **to keep out of** ~ keine Dummheiten machen; **to make** ~ Unfrieden stiften; **to do sb a** ~ jdm etwas (an)tun.

**mischievous** ['mɪstʃɪvəs] *adj expression, smile* verschmitzt; *rumour* bösartig; *person* boshaft.

**mischievously** ['mɪstʃɪvəslɪ] *adv smile, say* verschmitzt; *(making trouble)* boshaft.

**misconceived** [ˌmɪskən'siːvd] *adj* schlecht konzipiert.

**misconception** [ˌmɪskən'sepʃən] *n* fälschliche Annahme; *(no pl: misunderstanding)* Verkennung *f*. **to be under a** ~ **about sth** sich *(dat)* falsche Vorstellungen von etw machen.

**misconduct** [ˌmɪs'kɒndʌkt] *n (improper behaviour)* schlechtes Benehmen; *(professional)* Berufsvergehen *nt*; *(sexual)* Fehltritt *m*.

**misconstrue** [ˌmɪskən'struː] *vt* mißverstehen.

**miscount** [ˌmɪs'kaʊnt] **1** *n* falsche Zählung. **2** *vi* sich verzählen.

**misdeed** [ˌmɪs'diːd] *n* Missetat *f (col)*.

**misdemeanour,** *(US)* **misdemeanor** [ˌmɪsdɪ'miːnəʳ] *n* schlechtes Benehmen; *(Jur)* Vergehen *nt*.

**misdirect** [ˌmɪsdɪ'rekt] *vt energies* falsch einsetzen; *person* in die falsche Richtung schicken; *operation* schlecht durchführen.

**miser** ['maɪzəʳ] *n* Geizhals, Geizkragen *m*.

**miserable** ['mɪzərəbl] *adj* **(a)** *(unhappy)* unglücklich. **I feel** ~ **today** ich fühle mich heute elend *or* miserabel. **(b)** *headache, weather* fürchterlich; *existence, spectacle* erbärmlich, elend. **(c)** *(contemptible)* miserabel, jämmerlich; *person* gemein, erbärmlich; *failure* kläglich. **a** ~ **£3** miese £3 *(col)*.

**miserably** ['mɪzərəblɪ] *adv* **(a)** *(unhappily)* unglücklich. **(b)** *(wretchedly) live, die* jämmerlich; *poor* erbärmlich. **(c)** *(contemptibly) pay* miserabel; *fail* kläglich; *treat, behave* gemein.

**miserly** ['maɪzəlɪ] *adj* geizig.

**misery** ['mɪzərɪ] *n (sadness)* Kummer *m*, Trauer *f*; *(suffering)* Qualen *pl*; *(wretchedness)* Elend *nt*. **to put an animal out of its** ~ ein Tier von seinen Qualen erlösen; **to put sb out of his** ~ *(fig)* jdn nicht länger auf die Folter spannen.

**misfire** [ˌmɪs'faɪəʳ] *vi (engine, rocket)* fehlzünden; *(plan)* fehlschlagen; *(trick)* danebengehen.

**misfit** ['mɪsfɪt] *n (person)* Außenseiter(in *f*) *m*.

**misfortune** [mɪs'fɔːtʃuːn] *n (ill fortune, affliction)* (schweres) Schicksal *or* Los *nt*; *(bad luck)* Pech *nt no pl*; *(unlucky incident)* Mißgeschick *nt*. **I had the** ~ **to ...** ich hatte das Pech, zu ....

**misgiving** [mɪs'gɪvɪŋ] *n* Bedenken *pl*. **I had (certain)** ~**s about lending him the money** mir war bei dem Gedanken, ihm das Geld zu leihen, nicht ganz wohl.

**misguided** [mɪs'gaɪdɪd] *adj* töricht; *decision also, opinions* irrig; *(misplaced) kindness, enthusiasm* unangebracht.

**mishandle** [mɪs'hændl] *vt case* falsch handhaben.

**mishap** ['mɪshæp] *n* Mißgeschick *nt*. **he's had a slight** ~ ihm ist ein kleines Mißgeschick passiert; **without** ~ ohne Zwischenfälle.

**mishear** [ˌmɪs'hɪəʳ] *pret, ptp* **misheard** [ˌmɪs'hɜːd] **1** *vt* falsch hören. **2** *vi* sich verhören.

**mishit** ['mɪshɪt] *n* Fehlschlag *m*.

**mishmash** ['mɪʃˌmæʃ] *n* Mischmasch *m*.

**misinform** [ˌmɪsɪn'fɔːm] *vt* falsch informieren.

**you've been** ~**ed** man hat Sie falsch informiert.

**misinterpret** [ˌmɪsɪn'tɜːprɪt] *vt* falsch auslegen; *novel* fehlinterpretieren. **he** ~**ed her silence as agreement** er deutete ihr Schweigen fälschlich als Zustimmung.

**misinterpretation** [ˌmɪsɪnˌtɜːprɪ'teɪʃən] *n* Fehldeutung *f*; *(Liter)* Fehlinterpretation *f*.

**misjudge** [ˌmɪs'dʒʌdʒ] *vt* falsch einschätzen, sich verschätzen in *(+dat)*; *person also* falsch beurteilen.

**misjudgement** [ˌmɪs'dʒʌdʒmənt] *n* Fehleinschätzung *f*.

**mislay** [ˌmɪs'leɪ] *pret, ptp* **mislaid** [ˌmɪs'leɪd] *vt* verlegen.

**mislead** [ˌmɪs'liːd] *pret, ptp* **misled** *vt (give wrong idea)* irreführen. **your description misled me into thinking that ...** aufgrund Ihrer Beschreibung nahm ich (irrtümlich) an, daß...

**misleading** [ˌmɪs'liːdɪŋ] *adj* irreführend. **the** ~ **simplicity of his style** die täuschende Einfachheit seines Stils.

**misled** [ˌmɪs'led] *pret, ptp of* **mislead**.

**mismanage** [ˌmɪs'mænɪdʒ] *vt company, finances* schlecht verwalten; *affair* schlecht handhaben.

**mismanagement** [ˌmɪs'mænɪdʒmənt] *n* Mißwirtschaft *f*; *(of an affair)* falsche Handhabung.

**misnomer** [ˌmɪs'nəʊməʳ] *n* unzutreffende Bezeichnung.

**misogynist** [mɪ'sɒdʒɪnɪst] *n* Frauenfeind *m*.

**misplace** [ˌmɪs'pleɪs] *vt* **(a)** *file etc* falsch einordnen; *(mislay)* verlegen. **(b) to be** ~**d** *(confidence etc)* unangebracht sein.

**misprint** ['mɪsprɪnt] *n* Druckfehler *m*.

**mispronounce** [ˌmɪsprə'naʊns] *vt* falsch aussprechen.

**misquote** [ˌmɪs'kwəʊt] *vt* falsch zitieren.

**misread** [ˌmɪs'riːd] *pret, ptp* **misread** [ˌmɪs'red] *vt* falsch lesen; *(misinterpret)* falsch verstehen.

**misrepresent** [ˌmɪsreprɪ'zent] *vt* falsch darstellen; *ideas* verfälschen.

**misrepresentation** [ˌmɪsreprɪzen'teɪʃən] *n* falsche Darstellung; *(of ideas)* Verfälschung *f*.

**miss**[1] [mɪs] **1** *n (shot)* Fehltreffer *m*. **it was a near** ~ das war sehr knapp; *(shot)* das war knapp daneben; **to give sth a** ~ *(col)* sich *(dat)* etw schenken.

**2** *vt* **(a)** *(fail to hit, catch, find etc)* verpassen; *(not hit, find)* target, ball, vocation, place* verfehlen; *(not hear etc)* nicht mitbekommen. **to** ~ **breakfast** nicht frühstücken; *(be too late for)* das Frühstück verpassen; **you haven't** ~**ed much!** da hast du nicht viel verpaßt!; **they** ~**ed each other in the crowd** sie verfehlten sich in der Menge; **to** ~ **the boat** *or* **bus** *(fig)* den Anschluß verpassen; **I wouldn't have** ~**ed it for anything** das hätte ich mir nicht entgehen lassen wollen. **(b)** *(avoid) obstacle* (noch) ausweichen können *(+dat)*; *(escape)* entgehen *(+dat)*; *(leave out)* auslassen; *(overlook)* übersehen. **my heart** ~**ed a beat** mir stockte das Herz. **(c)** *(notice or regret absence of)* vermissen. **I** ~ **my old car** mein altes Auto fehlt mir.

**3** *vi* nicht treffen; *(shooting also)* danebenschießen; *(not catch)* nicht fangen; *(ball also)* danebengehen.

▶**miss out 1** *vt sep* auslassen, weglassen. **2** *vi (col)* zu kurz kommen. **to** ~ ~ **on sth** etw verpassen; *(get less)* bei etw zu kurz kommen.

**miss**[2] *n* Fräulein *nt*. **M**~ **Smith** *(woman)* Frau Smith; *(young girl)* Fräulein Smith; **M**~ **Germany 1994** (die) Miß Germany von 1994.

**missal** ['mɪsəl] *n* Meßbuch *nt*.

**misshapen** [ˌmɪs'ʃeɪpən] *adj* mißgebildet; *plant, tree* verwachsen.

**missile** ['mɪsaɪl] n (a) (stone etc) (Wurf)geschoß nt. (b) (rocket) Rakete f. ~ **base** or **site** Raketenbasis f; ~ **launcher** Startrampe f; (vehicle) Raketenwerfer m.

**missing** ['mɪsɪŋ] adj (not able to be found) person, boat vermißt; object verschwunden; (not there) fehlend. **to be** ~/**to have gone** ~ fehlen; (mountaineer, boat etc) vermißt werden; **the coat has two buttons** ~ an dem Mantel fehlen zwei Knöpfe; ~ **person** Vermißte(r) mf; ~ **link** fehlendes Glied; (Biol) Zwischenform f.

**mission** ['mɪʃən] n (task) Auftrag m; (calling) Berufung f; (Mil) Befehl m; (operation) Einsatz m; (journey) Mission f. ~ **accomplished** (Mil, fig) Befehl ausgeführt; (fig) Auftrag ausgeführt; **he's on a secret** ~ er ist in geheimer Mission unterwegs; **the Foreign Secretary's** ~ **to the Middle East** die Nahostmission des Außenministers.

**missionary** ['mɪʃənrɪ] n Missionar(in f) m.

**missis** ['mɪsɪz] n (Brit col) **the/his** ~ meine/seine bessere Hälfte (hum col), meine/seine Alte (pej col).

**misspell** [ˌmɪs'spel] pret, ptp ~**ed** or **misspelt** vt falsch schreiben.

**misspent** [ˌmɪs'spent] adj vergeudet.

**mist** [mɪst] n Nebel m; (haze) Dunst m; (on glass etc) Beschlag m. **through a** ~ **of tears** durch einen Tränenschleier; **it is lost in the** ~**s of time** das liegt im Dunkel der Vergangenheit.

▶**mist over** vi (become cloudy) sich trüben; (glass, mirror: also **mist up**) (sich) beschlagen.

**mistake** [mɪ'steɪk] **1** n Fehler m. **to make a** ~ (in calculating etc) einen Fehler machen; (be mistaken) sich irren; **to make the** ~ **of asking too much** den Fehler machen, zuviel zu verlangen; **by** ~ aus Versehen, versehentlich; **there must be some** ~ da muß ein Irrtum vorliegen; **there's no** ~ **about it, ...** (es besteht) kein Zweifel, ...; **make no** ~**, I mean what I say** damit wir uns nicht falsch verstehen: mir ist es Ernst; **it's freezing and no** ~! (col) (ich kann dir sagen,) das ist vielleicht ein Frost! (col).

**2** vt pret **mistook**, ptp **mistaken** remarks etc falsch verstehen; house, time sich irren or vertun (col) in (+dat). **to** ~ **sb's meaning** jdn falsch verstehen; **there's no mistaking the urgency of the situation** die Dringlichkeit der Situation steht außer Frage; **to** ~ **A for B** A mit B verwechseln; **to be** ~**n** sich irren; **if I am not (very much)** ~**n** ... wenn ich mich nicht (sehr) irre ...

**mistaken** [mɪ'steɪkən] adj (wrong) idea falsch; (misplaced) loyalty, kindness unangebracht. **a case of** ~ **identity** eine Verwechslung.

**mistakenly** [mɪ'steɪkənlɪ] adv irrtümlicherweise; (by accident) versehentlich.

**mister** ['mɪstər] n (col: form of address) Meister m.

**mistletoe** ['mɪsltəʊ] n Mistel f; (sprig) Mistelzweig m.

**mistook** [mɪ'stʊk] pret of **mistake**.

**mistranslate** [ˌmɪstræns'leɪt] vt falsch übersetzen.

**mistranslation** [ˌmɪstræns'leɪʃən] n falsche Übersetzung.

**mistreat** [ˌmɪs'triːt] vt schlecht behandeln.

**mistreatment** [ˌmɪs'triːtmənt] n schlechte Behandlung.

**mistress** ['mɪstrɪs] n (a) (of house, dog) Herrin f. (b) (lover) Geliebte. (c) (Brit: teacher) Lehrerin f.

**mistrust** [ˌmɪs'trʌst] **1** n Mißtrauen nt (of gegenüber). **2** vt mißtrauen (+dat).

**mistrustful** [ˌmɪs'trʌstfʊl] adj mißtrauisch (of sb/sth jdm/einer Sache gegenüber).

**misty** ['mɪstɪ] adj (+er) day neblig; (hazy) dunstig;

glasses (misted up) beschlagen. ~-**eyed** mit verschleiertem Blick.

**misunderstand** [ˌmɪsʌndə'stænd] pret, ptp **misunderstood** vt falsch verstehen, mißverstehen.

**misunderstanding** [ˌmɪsʌndə'stændɪŋ] n Mißverständnis nt; (disagreement) Meinungsverschiedenheit f.

**misunderstood** [ˌmɪsʌndə'stʊd] **1** ptp of **misunderstand**. **2** adj unverstanden; artist verkannt.

**misuse** [ˌmɪs'juːs] **1** n Mißbrauch m. **2** [ˌmɪs'juːz] vt mißbrauchen.

**MIT** = **Massachusetts Institute of Technology**.

**mite** [maɪt] n (a) (small amount) bißchen nt. (b) (child) **poor little** ~! armes Wurm! (col).

**mitigate** ['mɪtɪgeɪt] vt punishment mildern. **mitigating circumstances** mildernde Umstände pl.

**mitigation** [ˌmɪtɪ'geɪʃən] n Milderung f.

**mitre,** (US) **miter** ['maɪtər] n (a) (Eccl) Mitra f. (b) (Tech: also ~-**joint**) Gehrung f.

**mitt** [mɪt] n (a) = **mitten**. (b) (baseball glove) Baseballhandschuh m.

**mitten** ['mɪtn] n Fausthandschuh m; (with bare fingers) Handschuh m mit halben Fingern.

**mix** [mɪks] **1** n Mischung f. **a good social** ~ ein bunt gemischtes Publikum; **cake** ~ Backmischung f. **2** vt (ver)mischen; drinks mixen; (Cook) ingredients verrühren. **you shouldn't** ~ **your drinks** man sollte nicht mehrere Sachen durcheinander trinken; **to** ~ **business with pleasure** das Angenehme mit dem Nützlichen verbinden. **3** vi (a) sich mischen lassen; (chemical substances, races) sich vermischen. (b) (go together) zusammenpassen. (c) (people) (get on) miteinander auskommen; (associate) miteinander verkehren. **to** ~ **with sb** mit jdm auskommen; mit jdm verkehren; **to** ~ **well** kontaktfreudig sein.

▶**mix in** vt sep egg, water unterrühren.

▶**mix up** vt sep (a) vermischen; ingredients verrühren; medicine mischen. (b) (get in a muddle) durcheinanderbringen; (confuse with sb/sth else) verwechseln. (c) (involve) **to** ~ **sb** ~ **in sth** jdn in etw (acc) hineinziehen; **to be** ~**ed** ~ **in sth** in etw (acc) verwickelt sein.

**mixed** [mɪkst] adj gemischt; (both good and bad) unterschiedlich. **in** ~ **company** wenn Damen dabei sind; **I have** ~ **feelings about it** ich betrachte die Sache mit gemischten Gefühlen.

**mixed:** ~ **bag** n bunte Mischung; ~ **blessing** n it's **a** ~ **blessing** das ist ein zweischneidiges Schwert; ~ **doubles** npl (Sport) gemischtes Doppel; ~ **economy** n gemischte Wirtschaftsform; ~ **grill** n Grillteller m; ~ **metaphor** n gemischte Metapher f; ~-**up** adj durcheinander pred; (muddled) person also, ideas konfus; **she's just a crazy** ~-**up kid** sie ist einfach total verdreht.

**mixer** ['mɪksər] n (a) (food ~) Mixer m; (cement ~) Mischmaschine f. (b) (drink) Tonic etc zum Auffüllen von alkoholischen Mixgetränken. (c) (Film, Rad, TV) Mixer m; (device also) Mischpult nt. (d) (sociable person) **to be a good** ~ kontaktfreudig sein.

**mixture** ['mɪkstʃər] n Mischung f; (Cook) Gemisch nt; (cake ~, dough) Teig m.

**mix-up** ['mɪksʌp] n Durcheinander nt; (confusion of two things) Verwechslung f. **there must have been a** ~ da muß irgend etwas schiefgelaufen sein (col).

**mk, Mk** = **mark, Mark**.

**MLR** (Brit Econ) = **minimum lending rate**.

**ml** = **millilitre** ml.

**mm** = **millimetre** mm.

**MN** = (a) (Brit) **Merchant Navy** HM f. (b) (US Post) = **Minnesota**.

**m.o., M.O.** = **money order**.

**MO** = (a) **medical officer. (b)** *(US Post)* **Missouri. (c)** *(US col)* **modus operandi.**

**moan** [məun] **1** *n (groan)* Stöhnen *nt; (grumble)* Gejammer *nt no pl (col).* **2** *vi (groan)* stöhnen; *(grumble)* jammern, schimpfen *(about* über +*acc).*

**moat** [məut] *n* Wassergraben *m; (of castle also)* Burggraben *m.*

**mob** [mɒb] **1** *n (crowd)* Horde *f; (riotous, violent)* Mob *m no pl.* **the** ~ *(pej: the masses)* die Masse (n *pl).* **2** *vt* herfallen über *(+acc).*

**mobile** ['məubaɪl] *adj person* beweglich; *(having means of transport)* beweglich, motorisiert; *(Sociol)* mobil; *X-ray unit etc* fahrbar. ~ **home** Wohnwagen *m;* ~ **library** Fahrbücherei *f.*

**mobility** [məu'bɪlɪtɪ] *n (of person)* Beweglichkeit *f; (of work force, Sociol)* Mobilität *f.*

**mobilization** [ˌməubɪlaɪ'zeɪʃən] *n* Mobilisierung *f; (Mil also)* Mobilmachung *f.*

**mobilize** ['məubɪlaɪz] **1** *vt* mobilisieren; *(Mil also)* mobil machen. **2** *vi* mobil machen.

**moccasin** ['mɒkəsɪn] *n* Mokassin *m.*

**mock** [mɒk] **1** *adj attr emotions* gespielt; *battle* Schein-; *examination* Probe-; *Tudor* Pseudo-. **2** *vt (ridicule)* sich lustig machen über *(+acc); (mimic)* nachäffen; *(defy)* trotzen *(+dat).* **3** *vi* **to** ~ **at** *sb/sth* sich über jdn/etw lustig machen.

**mockery** ['mɒkərɪ] *n (derision)* Spott *m; (object of ridicule)* Gespött *nt.* **they made a** ~ **of him** sie machten ihn zum Gespött; **to make a** ~ **of sth** etw zur Farce machen; **it was a** ~ **of a trial** der Prozeß war eine einzige Farce.

**mocking** ['mɒkɪŋ] *adj* spöttisch.

**mockingbird** ['mɒkɪŋbɜːd] *n* Spottdrossel *f.*

**mock:** ~ **turtle soup** *n* Mockturtlesuppe *f;* ~**-up** *n* Modell *nt* in Originalgröße.

**MOD** *(Brit)* = **Ministry of Defence** Verteidigungsministerium *nt.*

**mod cons** ['mɒd'kɒnz] = **modern conveniences** Komfort *m.*

**mode** [məud] *n* **(a)** *(way)* Art (und Weise) *f; (form)* Form *f.* **(operating)** ~ Betriebsart *f; (Comp)* Modus *m;* ~ **of transport** Transportmittel *nt.* **(b)** *(Fashion)* Mode *f.*

**model** ['mɒdl] **1** *n* Modell *nt; (perfect example)* Muster *nt (of an* +*dat); (fashion* ~*)* Mannequin *nt; (male* ~*)* Dressman *m.* **to make sth on the** ~ **of sth** etw *(acc)* einer Sache *(dat)* nachbilden; **to hold sb up as a** ~ jdn als Vorbild hinstellen. **2** *adj railway* Modell-; *home* Muster-; *(perfect)* vorbildlich, Muster-. **3** *vt* **(a)** **X is** ~**led on Y** Y dient als Vorlage *or* Muster für X; **the system was** ~**led on the American one** das System war nach amerikanischem Muster aufgebaut; **to** ~ **oneself on sb** sich *(dat)* jdn zum Vorbild nehmen. **(b)** *(make a* ~*)* modellieren, formen. **(c)** *dress etc* vorführen. **4** *vi* **(a)** *(make* ~*s)* modellieren. **(b)** *(Art, Phot)* als Modell arbeiten; *(fashion)* als Mannequin/Dressman arbeiten; ~ **for sb** jdm als Modell stehen; *(as a fashion* ~*)* jds Kreationen vorführen.

**modelling,** *(US)* **modeling** ['mɒdlɪŋ] *n* **(a)** *(Phot, Art)* Arbeit *f* als Modell; *(fashion)* Auftreten *nt* als Mannequin/Dressman. **to do** ~ als Modell/Mannequin/Dressman arbeiten. **(b)** *(model-making)* Modellbau *m.*

**modem** ['məudem] *n* Modem *nt.*

**moderate** ['mɒdərɪt] **1** *adj* gemäßigt *(also Pol); appetite, speed* mäßig; *price* vernünftig; *eater* maßvoll; *number, income, success* bescheiden; *punishment, winter* mild. **a** ~ **amount** eine kleinere Menge; *(money)* ein mäßig großer Betrag; ~**-sized** mittelgroß. **2** *n (Pol)* Gemäßigte (r) *mf.* **3** ['mɒdəreɪt] *vt*

mäßigen. **to have a moderating influence on sb** mäßigend auf jdn wirken. **4** ['mɒdəreɪt] *vi* nachlassen.

**moderately** ['mɒdərɪtlɪ] *adv* einigermaßen. **a** ~ **expensive suit** ein nicht allzu teurer Anzug; **the house was** ~ **large** das Haus war mäßig groß.

**moderation** [ˌmɒdə'reɪʃən] *n* Mäßigung *f.* **in** ~ mit Maß (en).

**modern** ['mɒdən] *adj* modern *(also Art, Liter); times, world also* heutig; *history* neuere. ~ **languages** neuere Sprachen *pl;* **M**~ **Greek** *etc* Neugriechisch *etc nt.*

**modernism** ['mɒdənɪzəm] *n* Modernismus *m.*

**modernist** ['mɒdənɪst] *n* Modernist *m.*

**modernistic** [ˌmɒdə'nɪstɪk] *adj* modernistisch.

**modernity** [mɒ'dɜːnɪtɪ] *n* Modernität *f.*

**modernization** [ˌmɒdənaɪ'zeɪʃən] *n* Modernisierung *f.*

**modernize** ['mɒdənaɪz] *vt* modernisieren.

**modest** ['mɒdɪst] *adj* bescheiden; *requirements* gering; *price* mäßig; *(chaste)* anständig. **to be** ~ **about one's successes** nicht mit seinen Erfolgen prahlen.

**modestly** ['mɒdɪstlɪ] *adv* bescheiden; *(chastely)* anständig.

**modesty** ['mɒdɪstɪ] *n* Bescheidenheit *f.* **in all** ~ bei aller Bescheidenheit.

**modicum** ['mɒdɪkəm] *n* ein wenig *or* bißchen. **a** ~ **of truth** ein Körnchen Wahrheit.

**modification** [ˌmɒdɪfɪ'keɪʃən] *n* (Ver)änderung *f; (of design)* Abänderung *f; (of contract, wording)* Modifizierung *f.* **to make** ~**s to sth** (Ver)änderungen an etw *(dat)* vornehmen; etw abändern; etw modifizieren.

**modify** ['mɒdɪfaɪ] *vt* **(a)** *(change)* (ver)ändern; *design* abändern; *contract, wording* modifizieren. **(b)** *(moderate)* mäßigen. **(c)** *(Gram)* näher bestimmen.

**modular** ['mɒdjuləʳ] *adj* aus Bauelementen (zusammengesetzt); *(Comp, Elec)* modular. **the** ~ **design of the furniture** die aus Bauelementen bestehenden Möbel.

**modulate** ['mɒdjuleɪt] *vti (Mus, Rad)* modulieren.

**modulation** [ˌmɒdju'leɪʃən] *n (Mus, Rad)* Modulation *f.*

**module** ['mɒdjuːl] *n* (Bau)element *nt; (Comp, Elec)* Modul *nt; (Sch)* Kurseinheit *f; (Space)* Raumkapsel *f.*

**mohair** ['məuhɛəʳ] *n* Mohair *m.*

**Mohammed** [məu'hæmɪd] *n* Mohammed *m.*

**Mohammedan** [məu'hæmɪdən] **1** *adj* mohammedanisch. **2** *n* Mohammedaner (in *f) m.*

**Mohican** [məu'hiːkən] *n* **(a)** Mohikaner (in *f) m;* **(b)** **m**~ *(haircut)* Irokesenschnitt *m.*

**moist** [mɔɪst] *adj (+er)* feucht *(from, with* vor +*dat).*

**moisten** ['mɔɪsn] *vt* anfeuchten. **to** ~ **sth with sth** etw mit etw befeuchten.

**moisture** ['mɔɪstʃəʳ] *n* Feuchtigkeit *f.*

**moisturizer** ['mɔɪstʃəraɪzəʳ], **moisturizing cream** ['mɔɪstʃəraɪzɪŋ'kriːm] *n* Feuchtigkeitscreme *f.*

**molar (tooth)** ['məuləʳ(ˌtuːθ)] *n* Backenzahn *m.*

**molasses** [məu'læsɪz] *n* Melasse *f.*

**mold** *etc (US)* = **mould** *etc.*

**mole¹** [məul] *n (Anat)* Leberfleck *m.*

**mole²** *n (Zool)* Maulwurf *m; (col: secret agent)* Agent *m.*

**molecular** [məu'lekjuləʳ] *adj* molekular, Molekular-.

**molecule** ['mɒlɪkjuːl] *n* Molekül *nt.*

**molehill** ['məulhɪl] *n* Maulwurfshaufen *m.*

**molest** [məu'lest] *vt* belästigen.

**moll** [mɒl] *n (col)* Gangsterbraut *f.*

**mollify** ['mɒlɪfaɪ] *vt* besänftigen.

**mollusc** ['mɒləsk] *n* Weichtier *nt.*

**mollycoddle** ['mɒlɪ,kɒdl] vt verhätscheln.
**molt** [məʊlt] (US) = **moult**.
**molten** ['məʊltən] adj geschmolzen; glass, lava flüssig.
**mom** [mɒm] n (US col) = **mum²**.
**moment** ['məʊmənt] n **(a)** Augenblick, Moment m. **at any** ~ jeden Augenblick; **at the** ~ im Augenblick, momentan; **not at the** ~ im Augenblick or zur Zeit nicht; **at the last** ~ im letzten Augenblick; **at this (particular)** ~ **in time** momentan; **for the** ~ im Augenblick; **for a** ~ (für) einen Augenblick; **not for a** or **one** ~ ... nie(mals)...; **I didn't hesitate for a** ~ ich habe keinen Augenblick gezögert; **in a** ~ gleich; **half a** ~/**one** ~! einen Moment!; **just a** ~!, **wait a** ~! Moment mal!; **I shan't be a** ~ ich bin gleich wieder da; (nearly ready) ich bin gleich soweit; **I have just this** ~ **heard of it** ich habe es eben or gerade erst erfahren; **not a** ~ **too soon** keine Minute zu früh; **the** ~ **it happened** (in dem Augenblick,) als es passierte; **tell me the** ~ **he comes** sagen Sie mir sofort Bescheid, wenn er kommt; **the man of the** ~ der Mann des Tages.
**(b)** (Phys) Moment nt.
**(c)** (importance) Bedeutung f.
**momentarily** ['məʊməntərɪlɪ] adv **(a)** (für) einen Augenblick. **(b)** (US) (very soon) jeden Augenblick; (from moment to moment) zusehends.
**momentary** ['məʊməntərɪ] adj kurz. **there was a** ~ **silence** einen Augenblick lang herrschte Stille.
**momentous** [məʊ'mentəs] adj (memorable, important) bedeutsam; (of great consequence) von großer Tragweite.
**momentum** [məʊ'mentəm] n (of moving object) Schwung m; (at moment of impact) Wucht f; (Phys) Impuls m; (fig) Schwung m. **to gather** or **gain** ~ (lit) sich beschleunigen, in Fahrt kommen (col); (fig: idea, movement, plan) in Gang kommen.
**Mon** = **Monday** Mo.
**Monaco** ['mɒnəkəʊ] n Monaco nt.
**monarch** ['mɒnək] n Monarch(in f) m.
**monarchist** ['mɒnəkɪst] **1** adj monarchistisch. **2** n Monarchist(in f) m.
**monarchy** ['mɒnəkɪ] n Monarchie f.
**monastery** ['mɒnəstərɪ] n (Mönchs)kloster nt.
**monastic** [mə'næstɪk] adj mönchisch, klösterlich; life Ordens-.
**Monday** ['mʌndɪ] n Montag m; see **Tuesday**.
**Monegasque** [mɒnə'gæsk] **1** n Monegasse m, Monegassin f. **2** adj monegassisch.
**monetarism** ['mʌnɪtərɪzəm] n Monetarismus m.
**monetarist** ['mʌnɪtərɪst] **1** adj monetaristisch. **2** n Monetarist(in f) m.
**monetary** ['mʌnɪtərɪ] adj **(a)** (Pol) währungspolitisch; crisis, unit, union, policy, system Währungs-; reserves Geld-. **(b)** (pecuniary) Geld-; considerations geldlich.
**money** ['mʌnɪ] n Geld nt. **to make** ~ (person) (viel) Geld verdienen; (business) etwas einbringen; **to lose** ~ (person) Geld verlieren; (business) Verluste machen; **there's** ~ **in it** das ist sehr lukrativ; **that's the one for my** ~! ich tippe auf ihn/sie etc; **it's** ~ **for jam** (col) or **old rope** (col) da wird einem das Geld ja nachgeworfen (col); **to be in the** ~ (col) Geld wie Heu haben; **to earn good** ~ gut verdienen; **to get one's** ~'**s worth** auf seine Kosten kommen; **do you think I'm made of** ~? (col) ich bin doch kein Krösus!; **that's throwing good** ~ **after bad** das ist rausgeschmissenes Geld (col); ~ **talks** (col) mit Geld geht alles; ~ **isn't everything** (prov) Geld allein macht nicht glücklich (prov).
**money:** ~-**back guarantee** n Geld-zurück-

Garantie f; ~ **bag** n Geldsack m; ~ **box** n Sparbüchse f; ~-**changer** n Geldwechsler m.
**moneyed** ['mʌnɪd] adj begütert.
**money:** ~**grubbing** adj geldgierig; ~**lender** n Geld(ver)leiher m; ~**maker** n (idea) einträgliche Sache; (product) Verkaufserfolg m; ~**making** adj idea, plan einträglich; ~ **market** n Geldmarkt m; ~ **order** n (from bank) Zahlungsanweisung f; (esp US Post) Postanweisung f; ~**spinner** n (col) Verkaufsschlager m (col).
**mongol** ['mɒŋgəl] n: **he's a** ~ (col: has Down's syndrome) er ist mongoloid.
**Mongol** ['mɒŋgəl] see **Mongolian**.
**Mongolia** [mɒn'gəʊlɪə] n Mongolei f.
**Mongolian** [mɒn'gəʊlɪən] **1** adj mongolisch. **2** n **(a)** Mongole m, Mongolin f. **(b)** (language) Mongolisch nt.
**mongoose** ['mɒŋguːs] n, pl **-s** Mungo m.
**mongrel** ['mʌŋgrəl] n (also ~ **dog**) Promenadenmischung f; (pej) Köter m.
**monitor** ['mɒnɪtə'] **1** n **(a)** (Sch) Schüler(in f) m mit besonderen Aufsichtspflichten. **book** ~ Bücherwart m. **(b)** (TV, Tech: screen) Monitor m; (control, observer) Überwacher m; (Rad) Mitarbeiter(in f) m am Monitor-Dienst. **2** vt foreign station abhören; product, progress überwachen.
**monk** [mʌŋk] n Mönch m.
**monkey** ['mʌŋkɪ] n Affe m; (fig: child) Schlingel m.
**monkey:** ~ **business** n (col) **no** ~ **business!** mach(t) mir keine Sachen! (col); **there's some** ~ **business going on here** da ist doch irgend etwas faul (col); ~-**nut** n Erdnuß f; ~-**tricks** npl Unfug m; ~-**wrench** n verstellbarer Schraubenschlüssel, Engländer m.
**mono** [mɒnəʊ] **1** n Mono nt. **2** adj Mono-.
**monochrome** ['mɒnəkrəʊm] adj monochrom; television Schwarzweiß-.
**monocle** ['mɒnəkəl] n Monokel nt.
**monogram** ['mɒnəgræm] n Monogramm nt.
**monolingual** [,mɒnə'lɪŋgwəl] adj einsprachig.
**monolith** ['mɒnəʊlɪθ] n Monolith m.
**monolithic** [,mɒnəʊ'lɪθɪk] adj (lit, fig) monolithisch.
**monologue** ['mɒnəlɒg] n Monolog m.
**monoplane** ['mɒnəʊpleɪn] n Eindecker m.
**monopolize** [mə'nɒpəlaɪz] vt (lit) market beherrschen; (fig) place, sb's time etc in Beschlag nehmen; conversation an sich (acc) reißen.
**monopoly** [mə'nɒpəlɪ] n (lit) Monopol nt. **to have a** ~ **of sth** (fig) etw für sich gepachtet haben (col).
**mono:** ~**rail** n Einschienenbahn f; ~**syllabic** adj (lit, fig) einsilbig; ~**syllable** n einsilbiges Wort; **to speak/answer in** ~**syllables** einsilbig sein/einsilbige Antworten geben.
**monotone** ['mɒnətəʊn] n monotoner Klang; (voice) monotone Stimme.
**monotonous** adj, ~**ly** adv [mə'nɒtənəs, -lɪ] (lit, fig) eintönig, monoton.
**monotony** [mə'nɒtənɪ] n (lit, fig) Eintönigkeit, Monotonie f.
**monoxide** [mɒ'nɒksaɪd] n Monoxyd nt.
**monsoon** [mɒn'suːn] n Monsun m.
**monster** ['mɒnstə'] **1** n (big animal, thing) Ungetüm, Monstrum nt; (animal, person also) Ungeheuer nt; (cruel person) Unmensch m. **2** attr (enormous) Riesen-.
**monstrosity** [mɒn'strɒsɪtɪ] n (quality) Ungeheuerlichkeit f; (thing) Monstrum nt.
**monstrous** ['mɒnstrəs] adj (huge) ungeheuer (groß); (shocking, horrible) abscheulich; suggestion ungeheuerlich.
**montage** [mɒn'tɑːʒ] n Montage f.

**month** [mʌnθ] *n* Monat *m*. **in the ~ of October** im Oktober; **six ~s** ein halbes Jahr, sechs Monate; **paid by the ~** monatlich bezahlt.

**monthly** ['mʌnθlɪ] **1** *adj* monatlich; *magazine, ticket* Monats-. **2** *adv* monatlich. **twice ~** zweimal im Monat. **3** *n* Monats(zeit)schrift *f*.

**monument** ['mɒnjʊmənt] *n* Denkmal *nt*; *(big also)* Monument *nt*; *(small, on grave etc)* Gedenkstein *m*; *(fig)* Zeugnis *nt (to gen)*.

**monumental** [ˌmɒnjʊ'mentl] *adj (very great)* enorm, monumental *(geh)*; *proportions, achievement* gewaltig; *ignorance* ungeheuer.

**moo** [muː] *n* Muhen *nt*. **2** *vi* muhen.

**mooch** [muːtʃ] *(col)* **1** *vi* **to ~ about** *or* **around** herumgammeln *(col)*. **2** *vt (US)* abstauben *(col)*.

**mood¹** [muːd] *n* Stimmung *f*; *(of person also)* Laune *f*; *(bad ~)* schlechte Laune. **he was in a good/bad/ foul ~** er war gut/schlecht/fürchterlich gelaunt; **to be in a festive ~** feierlich gestimmt sein; **to be in a generous ~** in Geberlaune sein; **to be in the ~ for sth/to do sth** zu etw aufgelegt sein/dazu aufgelegt sein, etw zu tun; **I'm not in the ~ for work** ich habe keine Lust zum Arbeiten; **I'm not in the ~** ich bin nicht in der richtigen Stimmung; **he's in a ~** er hat schlechte Laune.

**mood²** *n (Gram)* Modus *m*.

**moodily** ['muːdɪlɪ] *adv see adj*.

**moodiness** ['muːdɪnɪs] *n see adj* Launenhaftigkeit *f*; schlechte Laune.

**moody** ['muːdɪ] *adj (+er)* launisch; *(bad-tempered)* schlechtgelaunt *attr*, schlecht gelaunt *pred*; *look, answer* übellaunig.

**moon** [muːn] *n* Mond *m*. **you're asking for the ~!** du verlangst Unmögliches!; **to be over the ~** *(col)* überglücklich sein.

**moon** *in cpds* Mond-; **~beam** *n* Mondstrahl *m*; **~ landing** *n* Mondlandung *f*; **~less** *adj* mondlos; **~light 1** *n* Mondschein *m*; **2** *vi (col)* ≈ schwarzarbeiten; **~ lighting** *n (col)* ≈ Schwarzarbeit *f*; **~lit** *adj object* mondbeschienen; *night, lawn* mondhell; **~shine** *n (~light)* Mondschein *m*; **~shot** *n* Mondflug *m*.

**moor¹** [mʊər] *n* (Heide)moor *nt*; *(high-lying)* Hochmoor *nt*.

**moor²** **1** *vt* festmachen, vertäuen; *(at permanent moorings)* muren. **2** *vi* festmachen, anlegen.

**moorhen** ['mʊəhen] *n* Teichhuhn *nt*.

**mooring** ['mʊərɪŋ] *n (place)* Anlegeplatz *m*. **~s** *(ropes)* Verankerung *f*.

**moorland** ['mʊələnd] *n* Moor- *or* Heideland(schaft *f*) *nt*.

**moose** [muːs] *n* Elch *m*.

**moot** [muːt] **1** *adj:* **a ~ point** *or* **question** eine fragliche Sache. **2** *vt* **it has been ~ed whether ...** es wurde zur Debatte gestellt, ob ...

**mop** [mɒp] **1** *n (floor ~)* Mop *m*; *(col: hair)* Mähne *f*. **2** *vt floor* wischen. **to ~ one's face** sich *(dat)* den Schweiß vom Gesicht wischen.

▶**mop up** *vt sep* **(a)** aufwischen. **(b)** *(Mil)* säubern *(col)*.

**mope** [məʊp] *vi* Trübsal blasen *(col)*.

▶**mope about** *or* **around** *vi* mit einer Jammermiene herumlaufen.

**moped** ['məʊped] *n* Moped *nt*; *(very small)* Mofa *nt*.

**moral** ['mɒrəl] **1** *adj* moralisch; *principles, philosophy* Moral-; *(virtuous)* moralisch einwandfrei; *(sexually)* tugendhaft. **~ standards** Moral *f*; **~ courage** Charakter *m*. **2** *n* **(a)** *(lesson)* Moral *f*. **(b)** **~s** *pl (principles)* Moralvorstellungen *pl*.

**morale** [mɒ'rɑːl] *n* Moral *f*. **to boost sb's ~** jdm (moralischen) Auftrieb geben.

**morality** [mə'rælɪtɪ] *n* Moralität *f*; *(moral system)* Moral, Ethik *f*.

**moralize** ['mɒrəlaɪz] *vi* moralisieren. **to ~ about sth** sich über etw *(acc)* moralisch entrüsten.

**morally** ['mɒrəlɪ] *adv* **(a)** *(ethically)* moralisch. **(b)** *(virtuously)* moralisch einwandfrei; *(in sexual matters)* tugendhaft.

**morass** [mə'ræs] *n* Morast, Sumpf *(also fig) m*.

**moratorium** [ˌmɒrə'tɔːrɪəm] *n* Moratorium *nt*. **a ~ on nuclear armament** ein Atomwaffenstopp *m*.

**morbid** ['mɔːbɪd] *adj* **(a)** *idea etc* krankhaft; *interest* unnatürlich; *imagination, humour etc* makaber; *(gloomy) outlook, thoughts, novel, film* düster; *person* trübsinnig; *(pessimistic)* schwarzseherisch. **(b)** *(Med)* morbid; *growth* krankhaft.

**more** [mɔːr] **1** *n, pron* **(a)** *(greater amount)* mehr; *(additional amount, things)* noch mehr. **~ and ~** immer mehr; **a lot ~** viel mehr; *(in addition)* noch viel mehr; **a few ~** noch ein paar; **a little ~** etwas mehr; *(in addition)* noch etwas mehr; **no ~** nichts mehr; *(countable)* keine mehr; **some ~** noch etwas; *(countable)* noch welche; **any ~?** noch mehr?; **there isn't/aren't any ~** mehr gibt es nicht; *(here, left over)* es ist nichts mehr da/es sind keine mehr da; **is/are there any ~?** gibt es noch mehr?; *(left over)* ist noch etwas da/sind noch welche da?; **even ~** noch mehr; **what ~ can I do?** was kann ich sonst noch tun?; **what ~ do you want?** was willst du mehr?; **there's ~ to it** da steckt (noch) mehr dahinter; **and what's ~, he ...** und obendrein hat er ... (noch) ...

**(b)** **(all) the ~** um so mehr; **the ~ you give him, the ~ he wants** je mehr du ihm gibst, desto mehr verlangt er; **the ~ the merrier** je mehr desto besser.

**2** *adj* mehr; *(in addition)* noch mehr. **two ~ bottles** noch zwei Flaschen; **one ~ day** noch ein Tag; **~ and ~ money** immer mehr Geld; **a lot/a little ~ money** viel/etwas mehr Geld; *(in addition)* noch viel/noch etwas mehr Geld; **a few ~ weeks** noch ein paar Wochen; **no ~ money** kein Geld mehr; **no ~ singing!** Schluß mit der Singerei; **do you want some ~ tea** möchten Sie noch etwas Tee?; **is there any ~ wine in the bottle?** ist noch (etwas) Wein in der Flasche?; **the ~ fool you for giving him the money** du bist vielleicht dumm, ihm das Geld zu geben.

**3** *adv* **(a)** mehr. **~ and ~** immer mehr; **it will grow a bit ~** es wird noch etwas wachsen; **£5/2 hours ~ than I thought** £5 mehr/2 Stunden länger, als ich dachte; **he is ~ than satisfied** er ist mehr als zufrieden; **it will ~ than meet the demand** das wird die Nachfrage mehr als genügend befriedigen; **she's no ~ a duchess than I am** sie ist genausowenig eine Herzogin wie ich (eine bin); **once ~** noch einmal, nochmal *(col)*; **never ~** nie mehr *or* wieder; **no ~, not any ~** nicht mehr; **if he comes here any ~** ... wenn er noch weiter hierher kommt ...; **~ or less** mehr oder weniger. **(b)** *(to form comp of adj, adv)* -er *(than* als*)*. **~ beautiful/beautifully** schöner; **~ and ~ beautiful** immer schöner; **no ~ stupid than I am** (auch) nicht dümmer als ich.

**moreish** ['mɔːrɪʃ] *adj (col)* **it's rather/very ~** es schmeckt nach mehr.

**moreover** [mɔː'rəʊvər] *adv* zudem, außerdem.

**morgue** [mɔːg] *n* Leichenschauhaus *nt*.

**moribund** ['mɒrɪbʌnd] *adj customs, way of life* zum Aussterben verurteilt.

**Mormon** ['mɔːmən] *n* Mormone *m*, Mormonin *f*.

**morning** ['mɔːnɪŋ] **1** *n* Morgen *m*; *(later part also)* Vormittag *m*. **in the ~** am Morgen; am Vormittag;

*(tomorrow)* morgen früh; **early in the ~** früh(morgens); *(tomorrow)* morgen früh; **(at) 7 in the ~** (um) 7 Uhr morgens; *(tomorrow)* morgen früh um 7; **this/yesterday/tomorrow ~** heute morgen/gestern morgen/morgen früh; heute/ gestern/morgen vormittag; **on the ~ of November 28th** am Morgen des 28. November. **2** *attr* Morgen-; *train, service etc* Vormittags-; *(early ~) train, news* Früh-.

**morning: ~ after** *n (state)* Katerstimmung *f* (am nächsten Morgen); **~-after pill** *n* Pille *f* (am Morgen) danach; **~ dress** *n no pl* Cut *m*; **~ service** *n (Eccl)* Morgenandacht *f*; **~ sickness** *n* (Schwangerschafts)übelkeit *f*.

**Moroccan** [mə'rɒkən] **1** *adj* Marokkanisch. **2** *n* Marokkaner(in *f*) *m*.

**Morocco** [mə'rɒkəʊ] *n* Marokko *nt*.

**moron** ['mɔːrɒn] *n (Med)* Geistesschwache(r) *mf*; *(col)* Dummkopf *(col) m*.

**moronic** [mə'rɒnɪk] *adj (Med)* geistesschwach; *(col)* schwachsinnig *(col)*.

**morose** [mə'rəʊs] *adj* verdrießlich, mißmutig.

**morphine** ['mɔːfiːn] *n* Morphium *nt*.

**morphing** ['mɔːfɪŋ] *n (Comp)* Morphing *nt*.

**morse** [mɔːs] *n (also* M~ **code)** Morseschrift *f*.

**morsel** ['mɔːsl] *n (food)* Bissen *m*; *(fig)* bißchen *nt*.

**mortal** ['mɔːtl] **1** *adj* sterblich; *injury, combat* tödlich. **2** *n* Sterbliche(r) *mf*.

**mortality** [mɔː'tælɪtɪ] *n* **(a)** Sterblichkeit *f*. **(b)** *(number of deaths)* Todesfälle *pl*; *(rate)* Sterblichkeit(sziffer) *f*.

**mortally** ['mɔːtəlɪ] *adv (fatally)* tödlich; *(fig: extremely) shocked* zu Tode; *offended* tödlich.

**mortar**[1] ['mɔːtə<sup>r</sup>] *n* **(a)** *(bowl)* Mörser *m*. **(b)** *(cannon)* Mörser, Minenwerfer *m*.

**mortar**[2] *n (cement)* Mörtel *m*.

**mortarboard** ['mɔːtəbɔːd] *n (Univ) zu feierlichen Anlässen von Studenten und Dozenten getragene flache Kopfbedeckung.*

**mortgage** ['mɔːgɪdʒ] **1** *n* Hypothek *f (on* auf +*acc/ dat)*. **~ company** *(US)* ≃ Hypothekenbank *f*; **~ rate** Hypothekenzinssatz *m*; **~ repayment** Hypothekenzahlung *f*. **2** *vt house, land* mit einer Hypothek belasten.

**mortice** *n, vt* = **mortise.**

**mortician** [ˌmɔː'tɪʃən] *n (US)* Bestattungsunternehmer *m*.

**mortification** [ˌmɔːtɪfɪ'keɪʃən] *n* **(a)** Beschämung *f*; *(humiliation)* Demütigung *f*. **(b)** *(Rel)* Kasteiung *f*.

**mortify** ['mɔːtɪfaɪ] *vt usu pass* **(a)** beschämen. **he was mortified** er empfand das als beschämend. **(b)** *(Rel)* kasteien.

**mortise, mortice** ['mɔːtɪs] *n* Zapfenloch *nt*. **~ lock** Einsteckschloß *nt*.

**mortuary** ['mɔːtjʊərɪ] *n* Leichenhalle *f*.

**mosaic** [məʊ'zeɪɪk] **1** *n* Mosaik *nt*. **2** *attr* Mosaik-.

**Moscow** ['mɒskəʊ] *n* Moskau *nt*.

**Moslem** ['mɒzlem] *adj, n* = **Muslim.**

**mosque** [mɒsk] *n* Moschee *f*.

**mosquito** [mɒ'skiːtəʊ] *n, pl* **-es** Stechmücke *f*; *(in tropics)* Moskito *m*. **~ net** Moskitonetz *nt*.

**moss** [mɒs] *n* Moos *nt*. **~ green** *adj* moosgrün.

**mossy** ['mɒsɪ] *adj (+er) (moss-covered)* bemoost; *lawn* vermoost; *(mosslike)* moosartig.

**most** [məʊst] **1** *adj superl* **(a)** meiste(r, s); *(greatest) satisfaction, pleasure etc* größte(r, s). **who has (the) ~ money?** wer hat am meisten *or* das meiste Geld?; **for the ~ part** größtenteils; *(by and large)* im großen und ganzen. **(b)** *(the majority of)* die meisten. **~ men/people** die meisten (Menschen/Leute).
   **2** *n, pron* **~ of it/them** das meiste/die meisten; **~ of the money/his friends** das meiste Geld/die meisten seiner Freunde; **~ of the day** fast den ganzen Tag über; **~ of the time** die meiste Zeit; *(usually)* meist(ens); **do the ~ you can** machen Sie soviel (wie) Sie können; **at (the) ~** höchstens; **to make the ~ of sth** *(make good use of)* etw voll ausnützen; *(enjoy)* etw in vollen Zügen genießen.
   **3** *adv* **(a)** *superl (+vbs)* am meisten; *(+adj)* -ste(r, s); *(+adv)* am -sten. **the ~ beautiful** der/die/das schönste; **which one did it ~ easily?** wem ist es am leichtesten gefallen?; **what ~ displeased him was** ... am meisten mißfiel ihm ...; **~ of all** am allermeisten; **~ of all because** ... vor allem, weil ... **(b)** *(very)* äußerst, überaus. **~ likely** höchstwahrscheinlich.

**mostly** ['məʊstlɪ] *adv (principally)* hauptsächlich; *(most of the time)* meistens; *(by and large)* zum größten Teil.

**MOT** *(Brit)* **(a)** = **Ministry of Transport. (b)** **~ (test)** ≃ TÜV *m*. **it failed its ~** ≃ es ist nicht durch den TÜV gekommen.

**motel** [məʊ'tel] *n* Motel *nt*.

**motet** [məʊ'tet] *n* Motette *f*.

**moth** [mɒθ] *n* Nachtfalter *m*; *(wool-eating)* Motte *f*.

**moth: ~ball 1** *n* Mottenkugel *f*; **to put in ~balls** *(lit, fig)* einmotten; *ship* stillegen; **2** *vt* einmotten; *ship* stillegen; **~-eaten** *adj (fig)* ausgedient, vermottet *(col)*.

**mother** ['mʌðə<sup>r</sup>] **1** *n* Mutter *f*. **M~'s Day** Muttertag *m*; **to be (like) a ~ to sb** wie eine Mutter zu jdm sein. **2** *vt (care for) young* großziehen; *(cosset)* bemuttern.

**mother: ~board** *n (Comp)* Hauptplatine *f*; **~ country** *n (native country)* Vaterland *nt*; *(head of empire)* Mutterland *nt*; **~hood** *n* Mutterschaft *f*; **~-in-law** *n, pl* **~s-in-law** Schwiegermutter *f*; **~land** *n* Vaterland *nt*; *(of ancestors)* Land *nt* der Väter.

**motherly** ['mʌðəlɪ] *adj* mütterlich.

**mother: ~-of-pearl** *n* Perlmutt *nt*; **~ ship** *n* Mutterschiff *nt*; **~-to-be** *n, pl* **~s-to-be** werdende Mutter; **~ tongue** *n* Muttersprache *f*.

**mothproof** ['mɒθpruːf] *adj* mottenfest.

**motif** [məʊ'tiːf] *n (Art, Mus)* Motiv *nt*.

**motion** ['məʊʃən] **1** *n* **(a)** Bewegung *f*. **to be in ~** sich bewegen; *(machine etc)* laufen; *(train etc)* fahren; **to set** *or* **put sth in ~** etw in Gang bringen *or* setzen; **to go through the ~s of doing sth** etw der Form halber tun. **(b)** *(proposal)* Antrag *m*. **to propose** *or* **make** *(US)* **a ~** einen Antrag stellen. **2** *vti* **to ~ (to) sb to do sth** jdm ein Zeichen geben, daß er etw tun solle.

**motion: ~less** *adj* bewegungslos, reg(ungs)los; **~ picture** *n (esp US)* Film *m*.

**motivate** ['məʊtɪveɪt] *vt* motivieren.

**motivation** [ˌməʊtɪ'veɪʃən] *n* Motivation *f*.

**motive** ['məʊtɪv] **1** *n* Motiv *nt*. **the profit ~** Gewinnstreben *nt*. **I did it from the best of ~s** ich hatte die besten Absichten. **2** *adj force* Antriebs-.

**motley** ['mɒtlɪ] *adj* kunterbunt; *(varied also)* bunt(gemischt).

**motor** ['məʊtə<sup>r</sup>] **1** *n* **(a)** Motor *m*. **(b)** *(col: car)* Auto *nt*. **2** *vi* (mit dem Auto) fahren.

**motor: ~bike** *n* Motorrad *nt*; **~boat** *n* Motorboot *nt*; **~car** *n (form)* Personenkraftwagen *(form) m*; **~ coach** *n* Reisebus *m*; **~-cycle** *n* Motorrad *nt*; **~-cyclist** *n* Motorradfahrer(in *f*) *m*; **~ home** *n* Wohnmobil *nt*; **~ industry** *n* Automobilindustrie *f*.

**motoring** ['məʊtərɪŋ] **1** *adj attr accident, offence* Verkehrs-; *correspondent* Auto-. **~ organization** Automobilklub *m*; **the ~ public** die Autofahrer *pl*. **2** *n* Autofahren *nt*.

**motorist** ['məʊtərɪst] *n* Autofahrer(in *f*) *m*.
**motorize** ['məʊtəraɪz] *vt* motorisieren.
**motor:** ~ **mechanic** *n* Kfz-Mechaniker *m*; ~ **race** *n* Autorennen *nt*; ~ **racing** *n* Autorennsport *m*; ~ **scooter** *n* Motorroller *m*; ~ **show** *n (Brit)* Automobilausstellung *f*; ~ **vehicle** *n* Kraftfahrzeug *nt*; ~**way** *n (Brit)* Autobahn *f*; ~**way madness** Geschwindigkeitsrausch *m* (auf der Autobahn).
**mottled** ['mɒtld] *adj* gesprenkelt; *complexion* fleckig.
**motto** ['mɒtəʊ] *n, pl* **-es** Motto *nt*; *(personal also)* Devise *f*.
**mould¹,** *(US)* **mold** [məʊld] **1** *n (hollow form)* (Guß)form *f*; *(shape, Cook)* Form *f*. **to be cast in the same** ~ *(people)* vom gleichen Schlag sein. **2** *vt* formen *(into* zu*)*; *(cast)* gießen.
**mould²,** *(US)* **mold** *n (fungus)* Schimmel *m*.
**moulder,** *(US)* **molder** ['məʊldər] *vi (lit)* vermodern; *(food)* verderben; *(building)* zerfallen.
**moulding,** *(US)* **molding** ['məʊldɪŋ] *n (cast)* Abdruck *m*; *(strip of wood etc)* Zierleiste *f*; *(ceiling ~)* Deckenfries *m*.
**mouldy,** *(US)* **moldy** ['məʊldɪ] *adj (+er)* verschimmelt; *(musty)* mod(e)rig. **to go** ~ verschimmeln.
**moult,** *(US)* **molt** [məʊlt] *vi (bird)* sich mausern; *(mammals)* sich haaren.
**mound** [maʊnd] *n* **(a)** *(hill, burial ~)* Hügel *m*; *(earthwork)* Wall *m*; *(Baseball)* Wurfmal *nt*. **(b)** *(pile)* Haufen *m*; *(of books)* Stapel *m*.
**mount¹** [maʊnt] *n (poet: mountain, hill)* Berg *m*. **M~ Everest** Mount Everest *m*.
**mount²** **1** *n* **(a)** *(horse etc)* Reittier *nt*. **(b)** *(support, base)* *(of machine)* Sockel *m*; *(of colour slide)* Rahmen *m*; *(of jewel)* Fassung *f*; *(of photo, picture)* Passepartout *nt*; *(stamp* ~*)* Falz *m*. **2** *vt* **(a)** *(climb onto)* besteigen. **(b)** *(place in/on* ~*)* montieren; *picture* mit einem Passepartout versehen; *(on backing)* aufziehen; *colour slide* rahmen; *specimen* präparieren; *jewel* (ein)fassen; *stamp* aufkleben. **(c)** *(organize)* play inszenieren; *attack* organisieren. **(d) to** ~ **guard** Wache stehen *(on* vor +*dat)*. **3** *vi* **(a)** *(get on)* aufsteigen; *(on horse also)* aufsitzen. **(b)** *(increase: also* ~ **up***)* steigen.
**mountain** ['maʊntɪn] *n (lit, fig)* Berg *m*. **in the** ~**s** im Gebirge; **to make a** ~ **out of a molehill** aus einer Mücke einen Elefanten machen *(col)*; ~ **bike** Mountain-Bike *nt*; ~ **chain** Gebirgskette *f*.
**mountaineer** [ˌmaʊntɪ'nɪər] *n* Bergsteiger(in *f*) *m*.
**mountaineering** [ˌmaʊntɪ'nɪərɪŋ] *n* Bergsteigen *nt*.
**mountainous** ['maʊntɪnəs] *adj* gebirgig.
**mountain:** ~ **pasture** *n* Bergwiese *f*; *(alpine)* Alm *f*; ~ **range** *n* Gebirgszug *m*; ~ **rescue service/team** *n* Bergwacht *f*; ~**side** *n* Berghang *m*; ~ **top** *n* Berggipfel *m*.
**mounted** ['maʊntɪd] *adj (on horseback)* beritten.
**Mountie** ['maʊntɪ] *n (col)* berittener kanadischer Polizist.
**mounting** ['maʊntɪŋ] *n (support)* see **mount²** 1(b); *(Tech: of engine etc)* Aufhängung *f*.
**mourn** [mɔːn] **1** *vt person* trauern um; *sb's death* beklagen, betrauern; *(fig)* nachtrauern *(+dat)*. **2** *vi* trauern. **to** ~ **for** *or* **over sb/sth** um jdn trauern/einer Sache *(dat)* nachtrauern.
**mourner** ['mɔːnər] *n* Trauernde(r) *mf*; *(non-relative at funeral)* Trauergast *m*.
**mournful** ['mɔːnfʊl] *adj person, occasion* trauervoll; *character, voice, mood* weinerlich; *sigh, appearance* kläglich; *sound, cry* klagend.
**mourning** ['mɔːnɪŋ] *n (act)* Trauer *f*, Trauern *nt (of um)*. **to be in** ~ **for sb** um jdn trauern; **to wear/put on** ~ Trauer tragen/anlegen.

**mouse** [maʊs] *n, pl* **mice** *(also Comp)* Maus *f*.
**mouse:** ~**hole** *n* Mauseloch *nt*; ~**trap** *n* Mausefalle *f*.
**mousse** [muːs] *n* Creme(speise) *f*; *(for hair styling)* Schaumfestiger *m*.
**moustache,** *(US)* **mustache** [mə'stɑːʃ] *n* Schnurrbart *m*.
**mousy, mousey** ['maʊsɪ] *adj (+er) (timid)* schüchtern; *hair* mausgrau.
**mouth** [maʊθ] **1** *n (of person)* Mund *m*; *(of animal)* Maul *nt*; *(of bottle, cave etc)* Öffnung *f*; *(of river)* Mündung *f*; *(of harbour)* Einfahrt *f*. **to keep one's (big)** ~ **shut** *(col)* die Klappe halten *(col)*; **shut your** ~! *(col!)* halt's Maul! *(col!)*. **2** [maʊð] *vt (soundlessly)* mit Lippensprache sagen.
**mouthful** ['maʊθfʊl] *n (of drink)* Schluck *m*; *(of food)* Bissen *m*; *(fig) (difficult word)* Zungenbrecher *m*; *(long word)* Bandwurm *m*.
**mouth** *in cpds* Mund-; ~**organ** *n* Mundharmonika *f*; ~**piece** *n* Mundstück *nt*; *(of telephone)* Sprechmuschel *f*; *(fig: medium)* Sprachrohr *nt*; ~**-to-**~ **resuscitation** *n* Mund-zu-Mund-Beatmung *f*; ~**wash** *n* Mundwasser *nt*; ~**-watering** *adj* lecker; **it's really** ~**-watering** da läuft einem das Wasser im Mund zusammen.
**movable** ['muːvəbl] *adj* beweglich; *(transportable)* transportierbar.
**move** [muːv] **1** *n* **(a)** *(in game)* Zug *m*; *(fig) (step, action)* Schritt *m*; *(measure taken)* Maßnahme *f*. **it's my** *etc* ~ *(lit, fig)* ich *etc* bin am Zug; **to make a/the first** ~ *(fig)* etwas unternehmen/den ersten Schritt tun; **that was a bad/good** ~ *(fig)* das war taktisch falsch/das war ein guter Schachzug.
 **(b)** *(movement)* Bewegung *f*. **to be on the** ~ *(fig: things, developments)* im Fluß sein; *(person: in different places)* unterwegs sein; **to get a** ~ **on (with sth)** *(col: hurry up)* sich (mit etw) beeilen; **get a** ~ **on!** nun mach schon! *(col)*; **to make a** ~ **to do sth** *(fig)* Anstalten machen, etw zu tun; **it's time we made a** ~ es wird Zeit, daß wir uns auf den Weg machen.
 **(c)** *(of house etc)* Umzug *m*; *(to different job)* Stellenwechsel *m*; *(to different department)* Wechsel *m*. **2** *vt* **(a)** bewegen; *wheel etc* (an)treiben; *(shift about)* umstellen, umräumen; *(transport)* befördern; *hand* wegziehen; *chess piece etc* ziehen mit; *(out of the way)* wegräumen. **to be unable to** ~ **sth** *(lift)* etw nicht von der Stelle bringen; *screw* etw nicht losbekommen; **I can't** ~ **this handle** der Griff läßt sich nicht bewegen.
 **(b)** *(change location of)* offices, troops verlegen; *patient* bewegen; *(transport)* transportieren; *employee (to new department)* versetzen. **to** ~ **house** *(Brit)* umziehen.
 **(c)** *(fig: sway)* **to** ~ **sb to do sth** jdn veranlassen, etw zu tun; **I shall not be** ~**d** ich bleibe dabei.
 **(d)** *(cause emotion in)* bewegen; *(upset)* erschüttern, ergreifen. **to** ~ **sb to tears** jdn zu Tränen rühren.
 **(e)** *(form: propose)* beantragen. **she** ~**d an amendment to the motion** sie stellte einen Abänderungsantrag.
 **3** *vi* **(a)** sich bewegen; *(vehicle)* fahren; *(traffic)* vorankommen. **nobody** ~**d** niemand rührte sich; **the vehicle began to** ~ das Fahrzeug setzte sich in Bewegung; **don't** ~! stillhalten!; **to get moving** in Bewegung kommen; *(hurry)* sich beeilen; **to keep moving** nicht stehenbleiben; **he jumped from the moving train** er sprang aus dem fahrenden Zug; **to keep sb/sth moving** jdn/etw in Gang halten; **things are moving at last** endlich kommen die Dinge in

Gang; **to ~ with the times** mit der Zeit gehen; **they must ~ first** sie müssen den ersten Schritt tun; **he has ~d to another department** er hat die Abteilung gewechselt; **it's time we were moving** es wird Zeit, daß wir gehen; **that's really moving!** *(col: fast)* das ist aber ein ganz schönes Tempo! *(col)*.
**(b)** *(~ house)* umziehen.
**(c)** *(in games) (make a ~)* ziehen; *(have one's turn)* am Zug sein.

▶**move about 1** *vt sep furniture etc* umstellen; *parts of body* (hin und her) bewegen; *employee* versetzen. **2** *vi* sich (hin und her) bewegen; *(fidget)* herumzappeln; *(travel)* unterwegs sein.

▶**move along 1** *vt sep* weiterrücken; *bystanders etc* zum Weitergehen veranlassen. **2** *vi (along seat etc)* aufrücken; *(along bus etc)* weitergehen; *(cars)* weiterfahren.

▶**move away 1** *vt sep* wegräumen; *person* wegschicken. **to ~ sb ~ from sth** jdn von etw entfernen. **2** *vi (move aside)* aus dem Weg gehen; *(leave) (people)* weggehen; *(vehicle)* losfahren; *(move house)* wegziehen *(from aus, von)*.

▶**move back 1** *vt sep (to former place)* zurückstellen; *people* zurückbringen; *(to the rear) things* zurückschieben; *car* zurückfahren; *people* zurückdrängen; *troops* zurückziehen. **2** *vi* **(a)** *(to former place)* zurückkommen; *(into one's house)* wieder einziehen *(into* in *+acc)*. **(b)** *(to the rear)* zurückweichen; *(troops)* sich zurückziehen; *(car)* zurückfahren. **~ ~, please!** bitte zurücktreten!

▶**move down 1** *vt sep (downwards)* (weiter) nach unten stellen; *(along)* (weiter) nach hinten stellen. **2** *vi (downwards)* nach unten rücken; *(along)* weiterrücken; *(in bus etc)* nach hinten aufrücken.

▶**move forward 1** *vt sep person* vorgehen lassen; *table etc* vorrücken; *chess piece* vorziehen; *car* vorfahren; *troops* vorrücken lassen; *event, date* vorverlegen. **2** *vi (person)* vorrücken; *(crowd)* sich vorwärts bewegen; *(car)* vorwärtsfahren; *(troops)* vorrücken.

▶**move in 1** *vt sep troops* einsetzen *(-to* in *+dat)*; *(take inside)* herein-/hineinstellen *(-to* in *+acc)*. **2** *vi* **(a)** *(into house)* einziehen *(-to* in *+acc)*. **(b)** *(come closer)* näher herankommen *(on* an *+acc)*; *(police, troops)* anrücken; *(workers)* anfangen. **to ~ ~ on sb** gegen jdn vorrücken.

▶**move off 1** *vt sep people* wegschicken. **2** *vi* **(a)** *(go away)* weggehen. **(b)** *(start moving)* sich in Bewegung setzen; *(train, car also)* abfahren.

▶**move on 1** *vt sep hands of clock* vorstellen. **the policeman ~d them ~** der Polizist forderte sie auf, weiterzugehen/*(in vehicles)* weiterzufahren. **2** *vi (people)* weitergehen; *(vehicles)* weiterfahren. **it's about time I was moving ~** *(fig)* es wird Zeit, daß ich (mal) etwas anderes mache; **let's ~ ~ to the next point** gehen wir zum nächsten Punkt über.

▶**move out 1** *vt sep car* herausfahren *(of aus)*; *troops* abziehen. **~ the table ~ of the corner** rücken Sie den Tisch von der Ecke weg! **2** *vi (leave accommodation)* ausziehen; *(withdraw: troops)* abziehen.

▶**move over 1** *vt sep* herüber-/hinüberschieben. **2** *vi* zur Seite rücken. **~ ~!** rück mal ein Stück! *(col)*.

▶**move up 1** *vt sep* (weiter) nach oben stellen; *(promote)* befördern; *(Sch)* versetzen; *(Sport)* aufsteigen lassen. **2** *vi (fig)* aufsteigen; *(shares, rates etc)* steigen; *(be promoted)* befördert werden; *(Sch)* versetzt werden; *(move along)* aufrücken. **to ~ ~ the social scale** die gesellschaftliche Leiter hinaufklettern.

**movement** ['muːvmənt] *n* **(a)** Bewegung *f*; *(fig: trend)* Trend *m (towards* zu*); (of events)* Entwick-

lung *f*. **~ of the bowels** Stuhlgang *m*; **the police were investigating his ~s** die Polizei stellte Ermittlungen über ihn an. **(b)** *(political etc ~)* Bewegung *f*. **(c)** *(Mus)* Satz *m*. **(d)** *(of clock)* Uhrwerk *nt*.

**mover** ['muːvə'] *n* **(a)** *(of proposition)* Antragsteller *m*. **(b)** *(remover)* Möbelpacker *m*. **(c) she's a beautiful ~** ihre Bewegungen sind sehr schön.

**movie** ['muːvɪ] *n (esp US)* Film *m*. **(the) ~s** der Film; **to go to the ~s** ins Kino gehen.

**movie** *in cpds* Film-; **~ camera** *n* Filmkamera *f*; **~goer** *n* Kinogänger(in *f*) *m*; **~ theater** *n (US)* Kino *nt*.

**moving** ['muːvɪŋ] *adj* **(a)** beweglich. **~ staircase** Rolltreppe *f*; **~ van** *(US)* Möbelwagen *m*. **(b)** *(fig: instigating)* *force* treibend. **(c)** *(causing emotion)* ergreifend; *tribute* rührend.

**mow** [məʊ] *pret* **~ed**, *ptp* **mown** *or* **~ed** *vti* mähen.
▶**mow down** *vt (fig)* niedermähen.

**mower** ['məʊə'] *n (person)* Mäher *m*; *(for lawn)* Rasenmäher *m*.

**Mozambique** [ˌməʊzəmˈbiːk] *n* Mosambik *nt*.

**MP** = **Member of Parliament.**

**mpg** = **miles per gallon.**

**mph** = **miles per hour.**

**Mr** ['mɪstə'] = **Mister** Herr *m*.

**MRP** = **manufacturer's recommended price** empf. Preis.

**Mrs** ['mɪsɪz] *n* Frau *f*.

**MS** = **(a) manuscript** Ms. **(b)** *(Med)* **multiple sclerosis** MS *f*. **(c)** *(US Post)* **Mississippi.**

**Ms** [mɪz] Frau *f*.

**MSc** = **Master of Science.**

**MSS** = **manuscripts.**

**Mt** = **Mount.**

**MT** = **(a) machine translation. (b)** *(US Post)* **Montana.**

**much** [mʌtʃ] **1** *adj, n* **(a)** viel *inv*. **how ~** wieviel *inv*; **that ~** so viel; **~ of this is true** vieles daran ist wahr; **we don't see ~ of each other** wir sehen uns nicht oft; **he/it isn't up to ~** *(col)* er/es ist nicht gerade berühmt *(col)*; **she's not ~ of a cook** sie ist keine große Köchin; **that wasn't ~ of a party** die Party war nicht gerade besonders; **that's a bit ~!** das ist ja ein starkes Stück! *(col)*; **they are ~ of a muchness** *(things)* das ist eins wie das andere; *(people)* sie sind einer wie der andere.

**(b) too ~** zuviel *inv*; *(ridiculous)* das Letzte *(col)*; **to be too ~ for sb** *(in quantity)* zuviel für jdn sein; *(too expensive)* jdm zuviel sein; **that insult was too ~ for me** die Beleidigung ging mir zu weit.

**(c) (just) as ~** genausoviel *inv*; **not as ~** nicht soviel; **three times as ~** dreimal soviel; **as ~ as you want/can** *etc* soviel du willst/kannst *etc*; **as ~ again** noch einmal soviel; **I feared/thought ~** *(genau)* das habe ich befürchtet/mir gedacht *etc*; **it's as ~ as I can do to stand up** es fällt mir schwer genug aufzustehen.

**(d) so ~** soviel *inv*; *(emph so, with following that)* so viel; **it's not so ~ a problem of modernization as** ... es ist nicht so sehr ein Problem der Modernisierung als ...

**(e) to make ~ of sb/sth** viel Wind um jdn/etw machen; **I couldn't make ~ of that chapter** mit dem Kapitel konnte ich nicht viel anfangen *(col)*.

**2** *adv* **(a)** *(with adj, adv)* viel; *(with vb)* sehr; *(with vb of physical action)* drive, sleep, talk *etc* viel; come, visit *etc* oft, viel *(col)*. **so ~/too ~** soviel/ zuviel; **so sehr/zu sehr; I like it very/so ~** es gefällt mir sehr gut/so sehr; **I don't like him/it too ~** ich kann ihn/es nicht besonders leiden; **thank you very ~** vielen Dank; **however ~ he tries** wie sehr er sich auch bemüht; ~ **to my astonishment** zu meinem großen Erstaunen; ~ **as I should like to** so gern ich möchte; ~ **as I like him** sosehr ich ihn mag.

(b) *(by far)* weitaus, bei weitem. ~ **the biggest** weitaus der/die/das größte; **I would** ~ **rather stay** ich würde viel lieber bleiben.

(c) *(almost)* beinahe. **they are** ~ **the same** sie sind fast gleich.

**muck** [mʌk] *n* (a) *(dirt)* Dreck *m*; *(manure)* Dung *m*. (b) *(rubbish)* Mist *m*; *(food etc)* Zeug *nt (col)*.

►**muck about** *or* **around** *(col)* **1** *vt sep* to ~ **sb** ~ mit jdm machen, was man will; jdn verarschen *(col!)*; *(by not committing oneself)* jdn hinhalten. **2** *vi (lark about)* herumblödeln *(col)*; *(do nothing in particular)* herumgammeln *(col)*; *(tinker with)* herumfummeln *(with an +dat)*.

►**muck in** *vi (col)* mit anpacken *(col)*.

►**muck out** *vti sep* ausmisten.

►**muck up** *vt sep (col)* (a) *(dirty)* dreckig machen *(col)*. (b) *(spoil)* vermasseln *(col)*.

**muck-raking** ['mʌk,reɪkɪŋ] *n (fig col)* Sensationsmache *f (col)*.

**mucky** ['mʌkɪ] *adj (+er)* dreckig *(col)*, schmutzig.

**mucus** ['mjuːkəs] *n* Schleim *m*.

**mud** [mʌd] *n* Schlamm *m*. **his name is** ~ *(col)* er ist unten durch *(col)*; **to throw** ~ **at sb/sth** *(fig col)* jdn mit Schmutz bewerfen/etw in den Schmutz ziehen.

**mud bath** *n* Schlammbad *nt*; *(Med)* Moorbad *nt*.

**muddle** ['mʌdl] **1** *n* Durcheinander *nt*. **to get in(to) a** ~ *(things)* durcheinandergeraten; *(person)* konfus werden; **to be in a** ~ völlig durcheinander sein; **to make a** ~ **of sth** etw völlig durcheinanderbringen. **2** *vt (also* ~ **up)** durcheinanderbringen; *(make confused) person also* verwirren.

►**muddle along** *or* **on** *vi* vor sich *(acc)* hinwursteln *(col)*.

►**muddle through** *vi* sich durchschlagen.

**muddled** ['mʌdld] *adj* konfus; *person also* durcheinander *pred*; *ideas also* verworren.

**muddle-headed** [,mʌdl'hedɪd] *adj person* zerstreut; *ideas* verworren.

**muddy** ['mʌdɪ] *adj (+er) floor, shoes etc* schlammbeschmiert; *ground, liquid* schlammig.

**mud:** ~ **flap** *n* Schmutzfänger *m*; ~ **flats** *npl* Watt(enmeer) *nt*; ~**guard** *n (on cycles)* Schutzblech *nt*; *(on cars)* Kotflügel *m*; ~ **pack** *n* Schlammpackung *f*; ~**-slinging** *n* Schlechtmacherei *f*.

**muesli** ['mjuːzlɪ] *n* Müsli *nt*.

**muff¹** [mʌf] *n* Muff *m*.

**muff²** *(col) vt* vermasseln *(col)*; *exam also* verhauen *(col)*; *lines, text* verpatzen *(col)*.

**muffin** ['mʌfɪn] *n (Brit)* weiches, flaches Milchbrötchen, *meist warm gegessen*; *(US)* kleiner runder Rührkuchen.

**muffle** ['mʌfl] *vt* (a) *(wrap warmly: also* ~ **up)** *person* einmummen. (b) *(deaden) shot etc* dämpfen; *noise* abdämpfen; *shouts* ersticken.

**muffled** ['mʌfld] *adj sound etc* gedämpft; *shouts* erstickt.

**muffler** ['mʌflər] *n* (a) *(scarf)* (dicker) Schal. (b) *(US Aut)* Auspufftopf, Schalldämpfer *m*.

**mufti** ['mʌftɪ] *n (col)* **in** ~ in Zivil.

**mug** [mʌg] **1** *n* (a) *(cup)* Becher *m*; *(for beer)* Krug *m*. (b) *(col: fool)* Trottel *m*. **that's a** ~**'s game** das ist doch schwachsinnig *(col)*. (c) *(col: face)* Visage *f (col!)*. ~ **shot** Verbrecherfoto *nt (col)*. **2** *vt (attack and rob)* überfallen.

►**mug up** *vt sep (also* ~ ~ **on)** pauken *(col)*.

**mugger** ['mʌgər] *n* Straßenräuber *m*.

**mugging** ['mʌgɪŋ] *n* Straßenraub *m no pl*. **a lot of**

~**s** viele Überfälle auf offener Straße.

**muggins** ['mʌgɪnz] *n sing (Brit col)* Blödmann *m (col)*; *(referring to oneself)* ich Blödmann *(col)*. ~ **did all the work** ich war wieder mal der/die Dumme und habe die ganze Arbeit allein gemacht.

**muggy** ['mʌgɪ] *adj (+er)* schwül; *heat* drückend.

**mulatto** [mjuː'lætəʊ] *n, pl* **-es** Mulatte *m*, Mulattin *f*.

**mulberry** ['mʌlbərɪ] *n (fruit)* Maulbeere *f*; *(tree)* Maulbeerbaum *m*.

**mule** [mjuːl] *n* Maultier *nt*. **(as) stubborn as a** ~ (so) störrisch wie ein Maulesel.

**mull** [mʌl] *vt* ~**ed wine** Glühwein *m*.

►**mull over** *vt sep* sich *(dat)* durch den Kopf gehen lassen.

**multi-** ['mʌltɪ] *pref* mehr-, Mehr-; *(with Latin stem in German)* Multi-, multi-; ~**-access** *adj (Comp) system etc* Mehrplatz-; ~**-coloured,** *(US)* ~**-colored** *adj* mehrfarbig; *lights, decorations* bunt; *bird* buntgefiedert; ~**-faceted** *adj* vielseitig.

**multifarious** [,mʌltɪ'fɛərɪəs] *adj* vielfältig.

**multi:** ~**lateral** *adj (Pol)* multilateral; ~**level parking garage** *n (US)* Parkhaus *nt*; ~**lingual** *adj* mehrsprachig; ~**millionaire** *n* Multimillionär(in *f*) *m*; ~**national 1** *n* multinationaler Konzern, Multi *m (col)*; **2** *adj* multinational.

**multiple** ['mʌltɪpl] **1** *adj* (a) *(with sing n: of several parts)* mehrfach. ~ **choice** Multiple Choice *no art*; ~ **crash** Massenkarambolage *f*. (b) *(with pl n: many)* mehrere. **2** *n* (a) *(Math)* Vielfache(s) *nt*. (b) *(Brit: also* ~ **store)** Ladenkette *f*.

**multiple sclerosis** *n* multiple Sklerose.

**multiplex** ['mʌltɪpleks] **1** *adj (Comp)* Multiplex-. **2** *n (cinema)* Multiplex *nt*.

**multiplication** [,mʌltɪplɪ'keɪʃən] *n* (a) *(Math)* Multiplikation *f*. ~ **table** Multiplikationstabelle *f*. (b) *(fig)* Vervielfachung *f*.

**multiplicity** [,mʌltɪ'plɪsɪtɪ] *n* Vielzahl *f*. **for a** ~ **of reasons** aus vielerlei Gründen.

**multiply** ['mʌltɪplaɪ] *vt (+ Math)* multiplizieren, malnehmen. **4 multiplied by 6 is 24** 4 mal 6 ist 24. **2** *vi* (a) *(Math)* multiplizieren. (b) *(fig)* sich vervielfachen. (c) *(breed)* sich vermehren.

**multi:** ~**-purpose** *adj* Mehrzweck-; ~**racial** *adj* gemischtrassig; ~**racial policy** Politik *f* der Rassenintegration; ~**racial school** Schule *f* ohne Rassentrennung; ~**-stor(e)y** *adj* mehrstöckig; ~**-stor(e)y car-park** *(Brit)* Parkhaus *nt*.

**multitude** ['mʌltɪtjuːd] *n* Menge *f*. **a** ~ **of** ... eine Vielzahl von ..., eine ganze Menge ....

**mum¹** [mʌm] *n, adj (col)* ~**'s the word!** nichts verraten! *(col)*; **to keep** ~ den Mund halten *(about* über +*acc) (col)*.

**mum²** *n (Brit col: mother)* Mutter *f*; *(as address)* Mutti *f (col)*.

**mumble** ['mʌmbl] **1** *vt* murmeln. **2** *vi* vor sich *(acc)* hin murmeln; *(speak indistinctly)* nuscheln.

**mumbo-jumbo** ['mʌmbəʊ'dʒʌmbəʊ] *n (ritual)* Hokuspokus *m*; *(gibberish)* Kauderwelsch *nt*.

**mummify** ['mʌmɪfaɪ] *vt* mumifizieren.

**mummy¹** ['mʌmɪ] *n (corpse)* Mumie *f*.

**mummy²** *n (Brit col: mother)* Mami *f (col)*.

**mumps** [mʌmps] *n sing* Mumps *m or f (col) no art*.

**munch** [mʌntʃ] *vti* mampfen *(col)*.

**mundane** [,mʌn'deɪn] *adj (worldly)* weltlich; *(pej: humdrum)* banal.

**Munich** ['mjuːnɪk] *n* München *nt*.

**municipal** [mjuː'nɪsɪpəl] *adj* städtisch; *council, elections etc* Stadt-, Gemeinde-.

**municipality** [mjuː,nɪsɪ'pælɪtɪ] *n* Gemeinde *f*.

**munificence** [mjuː'nɪfɪsns] *n (form)* Großzügigkeit *f*.

**munitions** [mjuː'nɪʃənz] *npl* Kriegsmaterial *nt no pl*.

~ **dump** Munitionslager, -depot *nt*; ~ **factory** Munitionsfabrik *f*.

**mural** ['mjʊərəl] **1** *n* Wandgemälde *nt*. **2** *adj* Wand-.

**murder** ['mɜ:dər] **1** *n* **(a)** Mord *m*. **to commit** ~ einen Mord begehen. **(b)** *(fig col)* **it was** ~ es war mörderisch; **to cry blue** ~ ein Mordstheater machen *(col)*; **to get away with** ~ sich *(dat)* alles erlauben können. **2** *vt* ermorden, umbringen; *(slaughter)* morden; *(col) opponents* haushoch schlagen; *(col: ruin) music etc* verhunzen *(col)*.

**murderer** ['mɜ:dərər] *n* Mörder *m*.

**murderess** ['mɜ:dərɪs] *n* Mörderin *f*.

**murderous** ['mɜ:dərəs] *adj deed* Mord-; *(fig)* mörderisch.

**murk** [mɜ:k] *n* Düsternis *f (geh)*.

**murky** ['mɜ:kɪ] *adj (+er)* trübe; *fog* dicht; *photo, outline etc* unscharf; *past* dunkel.

**murmur** ['mɜ:mər] **1** *n* Murmeln *nt*; *(of discontent)* Murren *nt*; *(of water, traffic)* Rauschen *nt*. **there was a** ~ **of approval/disagreement** ein beifälliges/abfälliges Murmeln erhob sich; **not a** ~ kein Laut; **without a** ~ ohne zu murren. **2** *vt* murmeln; *(with discontent)* murren. **3** *vi* murmeln; *(with discontent)* murren *(about* über +*acc)*; *(fig)* rauschen.

**muscle** ['mʌsl] *n* Muskel *m*; *(fig: power)* Macht *f*. **to have financial/industrial** ~ finanzkräftig/wirtschaftlich einflußreich sein; **he never moved a** ~ er rührte sich überhaupt nicht.

▶**muscle in** *vi (col)* **to** ~ ~ **(on sth)** (bei etw) mitmischen.

**muscleman** ['mʌslmæn] *n* Muskelmann, Muskelprotz *m (col)*.

**Muscovite** ['mʌskəvaɪt] **1** *adj* Moskauer. **2** *n* Moskauer(in *f*) *m*.

**muscular** ['mʌskjʊlər] *adj* Muskel-; *strong* muskulös. ~ **dystrophy** Muskeldystrophie *f*.

**muse** [mju:z] **1** *vi* nachgrübeln *(about, on* über +*acc)*. **2** *vt* grüblerisch sagen.

**museum** [mju:'zɪəm] *n* Museum *nt*. ~ **piece** *(lit, hum)* Museumsstück *nt*.

**mush** [mʌʃ] *n* Brei *m*.

**mushroom** ['mʌʃrʊm] **1** *n* (eßbarer) Pilz *m*; *(button* ~*)* Champignon *m*. ~ **cloud** Atompilz *m*. **2** *vi (grow rapidly)* wie die Pilze aus dem Boden schießen. **his fame** ~**ed** er wurde schlagartig berühmt.

**mushy** ['mʌʃɪ] *adj (+er)* matschig; *liquid, consistency* breiig; *(col) film etc* schmalzig *(col)*. ~ **peas** Erbsenmus *nt*.

**music** ['mju:zɪk] *n* Musik *f*; *(written score)* Noten *pl*. **to set sth to** ~ etw vertonen; **to face the** ~ *(fig)* dafür geradestehen.

**musical** ['mju:zɪkəl] **1** *adj* musikalisch; *instrument, evening* Musik-; *(tuneful)* melodisch. ~ **box** Spieluhr *or* -dose *f*; ~ **chairs** *sing* Reise *f* nach Jerusalem. **2** *n* Musical *nt*.

**musically** ['mju:zɪkəlɪ] *adv* musikalisch.

**music** *in cpds* Musik-; ~ **cassette** *n* Musikkassette *f*; ~ **hall** *n* Varieté *nt*.

**musician** [mju:'zɪʃən] *n* Musiker(in *f*) *m*.

**music lesson** *n* Musikstunde *f*.

**musicologist** [ˌmju:zɪ'kɒlədʒɪst] *n* Musikwissenschaftler(in *f*) *m*.

**music-:** ~ **stand** *n* Notenständer *m*; ~**-stool** *n* Klavierhocker *m*; ~ **teacher** *n* Musiklehrer(in *f*) *m*.

**musk** [mʌsk] *n (secretion, smell)* Moschus *m*.

**musket** ['mʌskɪt] *n* Muskete *f*.

**musketeer** [ˌmʌskɪ'tɪər] *n* Musketier *m*.

**musk-:** ~**rat** *n* Bisamratte *f*; ~**-rose** *n* Moschusrose *f*.

**musky** ['mʌskɪ] *adj (+er) smell* Moschus-.

**Muslim** ['mʊzlɪm] **1** *adj* moslemisch. **2** *n* Moslem *m*,

Moslime *f*.

**muslin** ['mʌzlɪn] *n* Musselin *m*.

**musquash** ['mʌskwɒʃ] *n* Bisamratte *f*.

**muss** [mʌs] *vt (US col: also* ~ **up)** durcheinanderbringen *(col)*.

**mussel** ['mʌsl] *n* (Mies)muschel *f*.

**must** [mʌst] **1** *vb aux present tense only* **(a)** müssen. **if you** ~ wenn's sein muß. **(b)** *(in neg sentences)* dürfen. **I** ~**n't forget that** ich darf das nicht vergessen. **(c)** *(probability)* **he** ~ **be there by now** jetzt müßte er schon dort sein; *(more certain)* er ist inzwischen bestimmt da; **I** ~ **have lost it** ich habe es wohl verloren; **you** ~ **have heard of him** Sie haben bestimmt schon von ihm gehört; **he** ~ **be older than that** er muß älter sein; **there** ~ **be a reason for it** es muß doch eine Erklärung dafür geben! **2** *n (col)* Muß *nt*. **an umbrella is a** ~ man braucht unbedingt einen Schirm; **this programme is a** ~ **for everyone** dieses Programm muß man einfach gesehen haben.

**mustache** ['mʌstæʃ] *n (US)* = **moustache**.

**mustang** ['mʌstæŋ] *n* Mustang *m*.

**mustard** ['mʌstəd] *n* Senf *m*; *(colour)* Senfgelb *nt*. ~ **gas** Senfgas *nt*; **to cut the** ~ *(US col)* es bringen *(col)*.

**muster** ['mʌstər] **1** *n (esp Mil: assembly)* Appell *m*. **to pass** ~ *(fig)* den Anforderungen genügen. **2** *vt* **(a)** *(summon)* zusammenrufen; *(esp Mil)* antreten lassen. **(b)** *(manage to raise: also* ~ **up)** zusammenbekommen; *strength, courage* aufbringen; *all one's strength, courage* zusammennehmen. **3** *vi* sich versammeln; *(esp Mil)* (zum Appell) antreten.

**mustiness** ['mʌstɪnɪs] *n* Muffigkeit *f*.

**mustn't** ['mʌsnt] = **must not**.

**musty** ['mʌstɪ] *adj (+er) air* muffig; *books* moderig.

**mutate** [mju:'teɪt] *vi (Biol)* mutieren *(to* zu*)*.

**mutation** [mju:'teɪʃən] *n (Biol)* Mutation *f*.

**mute** [mju:t] **1** *adj* stumm *(also Ling)*; *amazement, rage* sprachlos. **2** *n (dumb person)* Stumme(r) *mf*.

**muted** ['mju:tɪd] *adj* gedämpft; *(fig) criticism etc* verhalten.

**mutilate** ['mju:tɪleɪt] *vt person, animal, story* verstümmeln; *painting etc* verschandeln *(col)*.

**mutilation** [ˌmju:tɪ'leɪʃən] *n see vt* Verstümmelung *f*; Verschandelung *f (col)*.

**mutineer** [ˌmju:tɪ'nɪər] *n* Meuterer *m*.

**mutinous** ['mju:tɪnəs] *adj (Naut)* meuterisch; *(fig)* rebellisch.

**mutiny** ['mju:tɪnɪ] *(Naut, fig)* **1** *n* Meuterei *f*. **2** *vi* meutern.

**mutter** ['mʌtər] **1** *n* Gemurmel *nt*; *(of discontent)* Murren *nt*. **2** *vt* murmeln, brummeln. **3** *vi* murmeln; *(with discontent)* murren.

**mutton** ['mʌtn] *n* Hammel(fleisch *nt*) *m*. **leg of** ~ Hammelkeule *f*; **she's** ~ **dressed as lamb** *(col)* sie macht auf jung *(col)*.

**mutual** ['mju:tjʊəl] *adj respect etc* gegenseitig; *satisfaction* beiderseitig; *friends, dislikes etc* gemeinsam. **it would be for our** ~ **benefit** es wäre für uns beide von Vorteil; **the feeling is** ~ das beruht (ganz) auf Gegenseitigkeit.

**mutually** ['mju:tjʊəlɪ] *adv* beide; *distrust* gegenseitig; *satisfactory, beneficial* für beide Seiten; *agreed* von beiden Seiten.

**muzzle** ['mʌzl] **1** *n* **(a)** *(snout, mouth)* Maul *nt*. **(b)** *(for dog etc)* Maulkorb *m*. **(c)** *(of gun)* Mündung *f*; *(barrel)* Lauf *m*. **2** *vt animal* einen Maulkorb anlegen (+*dat)*; *(fig) critics, the press* mundtot machen.

**muzzy** ['mʌzɪ] *adj (+er) (dizzy, dazed)* benommen; *(blurred) view, memory etc* veschwommen.

**MVP** *(US Sport)* = **most valuable player.**

**MW** *(Rad)* = **medium wave** MW.

**my** [maɪ] *poss adj* mein. **I've hurt** ~ **leg** ich habe mir das Bein verletzt; ~ **father and mother** mein Vater und meine Mutter; **in** ~ **country** bei uns.

**myopia** [maɪ'əʊpɪə] *n* Kurzsichtigkeit *f.*

**myopic** [maɪ'ɒpɪk] *adj* kurzsichtig.

**myriad** ['mɪrɪəd] *adj* unzählige.

**myself** [maɪ'self] *pers pron* **(a)** *(dir obj, with prep +acc)* mich; *(indir obj, with prep +dat)* mir. **I said to** ~ ich sagte mir; **I wanted to see (it) for** ~ ich wollte es selbst sehen. **(b)** *(emph)* (ich) selbst. **my wife and** ~ meine Frau und ich; **I did it** ~ ich habe es selbst gemacht; **(all) by** ~ (ganz) allein(e); **I'll go there** ~ ich gehe selbst hin. **(c)** *(one's normal self)* **I'm not (feeling)** ~ **today** ich bin heute nicht ganz auf der Höhe.

**mysterious** [mɪ'stɪərɪəs] *adj* geheimnisvoll; *(puzzling)* mysteriös.

**mysteriously** [mɪ'stɪərɪəslɪ] *adv vanish, change* auf mysteriöse Weise; *missing* unerklärlicherweise; *(secretively)* geheimnisvoll.

**mystery** ['mɪstərɪ] *n (puzzle)* Rätsel *nt*; *(secret)* Geheimnis *nt.* ~ **play** Mysterienspiel *nt*; ~ **tour** Fahrt *f* ins Blaue; **it's a** ~ **to me** das ist mir ein Rätsel.

**mystic** ['mɪstɪk] **1** *adj* mystisch. **2** *n* Mystiker(in *f*) *m.*

**mystical** ['mɪstɪkəl] *adj* mystisch.

**mysticism** ['mɪstɪsɪzəm] *n* Mystizismus *m*; *(of poetry etc)* Mystik *f.*

**mystification** [ˌmɪstɪfɪ'keɪʃən] *n (state)* Verwunderung, Verblüffung *f*; *(act)* Verwirrung *f.*

**mystify** ['mɪstɪfaɪ] *vt* vor ein Rätsel stellen. **I was mystified by the whole business** die ganze Sache war mir ein Rätsel.

**mystifying** ['mɪstɪfaɪɪŋ] *adj* rätselhaft.

**mystique** [mɪ'stiːk] *n* geheimnisvoller Nimbus.

**myth** [mɪθ] *n* Mythos *m*; *(fig)* Märchen *nt.*

**mythical** ['mɪθɪkəl] *adj* mythisch; *(fig)* erfunden. ~ **figure/character** Sagengestalt *f.*

**mythological** [ˌmɪθə'lɒdʒɪkəl] *adj* mythologisch.

**mythology** [mɪ'θɒlədʒɪ] *n* Mythologie *f.*

**myxomatosis** [ˌmɪksəʊmə'təʊsɪs] *n* Myxomatose *f.*

# N

**N, n** [en] *n* N, n *nt.* **N for Nellie** *(Brit)*, **N for Nan** *(US)* ≃ N wie Nordpol.

**N** = **north** N.

**n** = (a) **noun** Subst. (b) **neuter** *nt.*

**n/a** = **not applicable** entf.

**NAAFI, Naafi** ['næfɪ] = **Navy, Army and Air Force Institutes** *(shop/canteen)* Laden *m*/Kantine *f* der britischen Streitkräfte.

**nab** [næb] *vt (col)* (a) *(catch, speak to)* erwischen; *(police also)* schnappen *(col)*. (b) *(take for oneself)* sich *(dat)* grapschen *(col)*, klauen *(col)*.

**nadir** ['neɪdɪəʳ] *n* (a) *(Astron)* Fußpunkt *m.* (b) *(fig)* Tiefstpunkt *m.*

**naff** [næf] *adj (Brit col) (not much use)* nutzlos; *(bad style)* ordinär. **this car is pretty ~** dieses Auto bringt's nicht *(col)*.

**nag¹** [næg] **1** *vt* herumnörgeln an *(+dat)*. **she ~ged me into buying it** sie ließ mir keine Ruhe, bis ich es gekauft hatte. **2** *vi (find fault)* herumnörgeln, meckern *(col)*; *(be insistent)* keine Ruhe geben. **to ~ at sb** an jdm herumnörgeln, jdm keine Ruhe lassen. **3** *n (fault-finder)* Nörgler (in *f*) *m.*

**nag²** *n (old horse)* Klepper *m*; *(col: horse)* Gaul *m.*

**nagging** ['nægɪŋ] **1** *adj wife* meckernd *(col)*, nörglerisch; *(pestering)* ewig drängend; *pain* dumpf; *worry, doubt* quälend. **2** *n (fault-finding)* Meckern *nt (col)*, Nörgelei *f*; *(pestering)* ewiges Drängen.

**nail** [neɪl] **1** *n (Anat, Tech)* Nagel *m.* **as hard as ~s** knallhart *(col)*; *(physically)* zäh wie Leder; **to pay on the ~** *(fig col)* auf der Stelle bezahlen; **to hit the ~ on the head** *(fig)* den Nagel auf den Kopf treffen; **to be a ~ in sb's coffin** *(fig)* ein Nagel zu jds Sarg sein. **2** *vt* (a) nageln. **to ~ sth to the wall** etw an die Wand nageln. (b) *(fig col)* **to be ~ed to the spot** *or* **ground** wie auf der Stelle festgenagelt sein; **to ~ sb** sich *(dat)* jdn schnappen *(col)*; *(charge also)* jdn drankriegen *(col)*.

▶**nail down** *vt sep* (a) *(lit)* box zunageln; *carpet, lid* festnageln. (b) *person* festnageln *(to auf +acc)*.

**nail** *in cpds* Nagel-; **~-biting** *adj (col)* terror atemberaubend; *suspense also* atemlos; **~-brush** *n* Nagelbürste *f*; **~-file** *n* Nagelfeile *f*; **~ polish** *n* Nagellack *m*; **~ polish remover** *n* Nagellackentferner *m*; **~ scissors** *npl* Nagelschere *f*; **~ varnish** *n (Brit)* Nagellack *m*; **~ varnish remover** *n (Brit)* Nagellackentferner *m.*

**naïve** [naɪˈiːv] *adj (+er)* naiv.

**naïveté, naïvety** [naɪˈiːvɪtɪ] *n* Naivität *f.*

**naked** ['neɪkɪd] *adj person* nackt; *branch, countryside* kahl; *flame, light* ungeschützt; *truth, facts* nackt. **to/with the ~ eye** für das bloße/mit dem bloßen Auge.

**NALGO** ['nælgəʊ] *(Brit)* = **National and Local Government Officers' Association** Gewerkschaft *f* der staatlichen und kommunalen Verwaltungsangestellten.

**NAM** *(US)* = **National Association of Manufacturers** Herstellerverband *m.*

**name** [neɪm] **1** *n* (a) Name *m.* **what's your ~?** wie heißen Sie?, wie ist Ihr Name? *(form)*; **my ~ is ...** ich heiße ..., mein Name ist ... *(form)*; **a man by the ~ of Gunn** ein Mann namens Gunn; **I know him only by ~** ich kenne ihn nur dem Namen nach; **to refer to sb/sth by ~** jdn/etw namentlich *or* mit Namen nennen; **in ~ alone** *or* **only** nur dem Namen nach; **I won't mention any ~s** ich möchte keine Namen nennen; **he writes under the ~ of X** er schreibt unter dem Namen X; **fill in your ~(s) and address(es)** Namen und Adresse eintragen; **in the ~ of** im Namen *(+gen)*; **in the ~ of God** um Gottes willen; **all the big ~s were there** alle großen Namen waren da; **I'll put your ~ down** *(on list, in register etc)* ich trage dich ein; *(for school, excursion etc)* ich melde dich an *(for zu)*; **to call sb ~s** jdn beschimpfen; **that's the ~ of the game** *(col)* darum geht es.

(b) *(reputation)* Name, Ruf *m.* **to have a good/bad ~** einen guten/schlechten Ruf haben; **to get a bad ~ in** Verruf kommen; **to give sb a bad ~** jdn in Verruf bringen; **to make a ~ for oneself** as sich *(dat)* einen Namen machen als; **to have a ~ for sth** für etw bekannt sein.

**2** *vt* (a) *(call by a ~, give a ~ to, specify)* nennen *(as als)*; *new star etc* benennen; *ship* taufen. **a person ~d Smith** jemand namens Smith; **to ~ a child after** *or* *(US)* **for sb** ein Kind nach jdm nennen; **~ your price** nennen Sie Ihren Preis; **to ~ the day** den Hochzeitstag festsetzen; **you ~ it, he's done it** es gibt nichts, was er noch nicht gemacht hat.

(b) *(appoint, nominate)* ernennen *(as als, for für)*. **to ~ sb mayor** jdn zum Bürgermeister ernennen.

**name:** **~-drop** *vi (col)* berühmte Bekannte in die Unterhaltung einfließen lassen; **she's always ~-dropping** sie muß dauernd erwähnen, wen sie alles kennt; **~less** *adj (unknown) person* unbekannt; *(undesignated)* namenlos; *(undefined) sensation, emotion* unbeschreiblich; *(shocking) vice, crime* unaussprechlich; **a certain person who shall remain ~less** jemand, der nicht genannt werden soll.

**namely** ['neɪmlɪ] *adv* nämlich.

**name:** **~-plate** *n* Namensschild *nt*; *(on business premises)* Firmenschild *nt*; **~sake** *n* Namensvetter *m*/-schwester *f.*

**Namibia** [næˈmɪbɪə] *n* Namibia *nt.*

**nanny** ['nænɪ] *n* (a) Kindermädchen *nt.* (b) *(col: also* **nanna***)* Oma, Omi *f (col).*

**nanny goat** *n* Geiß, Ziege *f.*

**nano-** ['nænəʊ-] *in cpds* Nano-; **~second** *n* Nanosekunde *f.*

**nap¹** [næp] *n* Nickerchen *nt.* **to have** *or* **take a ~** ein Nickerchen machen.

**nap²** *n (Tex)* Flor *m.*

**napalm** ['neɪpɑːm] *n* Napalm *nt.*

**nape** [neɪp] *n*: **~ of the neck** Nacken *m*, Genick *nt.*

**napkin** ['næpkɪn] *n* (a) *(table~)* Serviette *f.* **~ ring** Serviettenring *m.* (b) *(for baby)* Windel *f*; *(US: sanitary ~)* (Damen)binde *f.*

**Naples** ['neɪplz] *n* Neapel *nt.*

**nappy** ['næpɪ] *n (Brit)* Windel *f.* ~ **liner** Windeleinlage *f.*

**narc** [nɑːk] *n (US col)* Rauschgiftfahnder (in *f*) *m.*

**narcissus** [nɑːˈsɪsəs] *n, pl* **narcissi** *(Bot)* Narzisse *f.*

**narcotic** [nɑːˈkɒtɪk] *n* Rauschgift *nt.*

**nark** [nɑːk] *n (Brit col)* Spitzel *m.*

**narked** [nɑːkt] *adj (Brit col)* **to be** *or* **feel** ~ sauer sein *(col) (about* über + *acc).*

**narrate** [nəˈreɪt] *vt* erzählen; *events etc* schildern.

**narration** [nəˈreɪʃən] *n* Erzählung *f*; *(of events etc)* Schilderung *f.*

**narrative** ['nærətɪv] **1** *n* Erzählung *f.* **three pages of** ~ drei Seiten erzählender Text. **2** *adj* erzählend; *ability etc* erzählerisch.

**narrator** [nəˈreɪtər] *n* Erzähler (in *f*) *m.*

**narrow** ['nærəʊ] **1** *adj* (+*er*) **(a)** eng; *road, valley also* schmal. **(b)** *(fig) person, attitudes* engstirnig; *sense* eng; *existence* beschränkt; *majority, victory* knapp; *scrutiny* peinlich genau. **to have a** ~ **mind** engstirnig sein; **to have a** ~ **escape** mit knapper Not davonkommen. **2** *vt road etc* enger machen. **to** ~ **the choice** *(fig)* die Auswahl reduzieren. **3** *vi* enger werden, sich verengen.
► **narrow down** *(to* auf +*acc)* **1** *vi* sich beschränken; *(be concentrated)* sich konzentrieren. **2** *vt sep (limit)* beschränken; *(concentrate)* konzentrieren. **that** ~s **it** ~ **a bit** dadurch wird die Auswahl kleiner.

**narrowly** ['nærəʊlɪ] *adv* **(a)** *beat* knapp; *escape* mit knapper Not. **he** ~ **escaped being knocked down** er wäre um ein Haar überfahren worden; **you** ~ **missed (seeing) him** du hast ihn gerade verpaßt. **(b)** *interpret* eng; *examine* peinlich genau.

**narrow:** ~ **minded** *adj* engstirnig; ~-**mindedness** *n* Engstirnigkeit *f.*

**NASA** ['næsə] = **National Aeronautics and Space Administration** NASA *f.*

**nasal** ['neɪzəl] *adj sound* nasal, Nasal-; *voice* näselnd.

**nastily** ['nɑːstɪlɪ] *adv (unpleasantly)* scheußlich; *speak, say* gehässig; *behave also* gemein.

**nastiness** ['nɑːstɪnɪs] *n no pl* Scheußlichkeit *f*; *(of person)* Gemeinheit *f*; *(behaviour)* gemeines Benehmen *(to* gegenüber*).*

**nasturtium** [nəsˈtɜːʃəm] *n* (Kapuziner)kresse *f.*

**nasty** ['nɑːstɪ] *adj* (+*er*) scheußlich, widerlich; *cough, wound* schlimm; *(offensive)* anstößig; *(dirty)* schmutzig; *(dangerous) disease, corner, fog* böse, gefährlich; *person, behaviour* gemein, fies *(col)*; *trick* übel; *(spiteful) remark* gehässig. **she had a** ~ **fall** sie ist böse hingefallen; **he had a** ~ **time of it** es ging ihm ganz übel; **to turn** ~ unangenehm werden; **he has a** ~ **temper** mit ihm ist es nicht gut Kirschen essen; **he's a** ~ **piece of work** *(col)* er ist ein übler Typ *(col).*

**nation** ['neɪʃən] *n* Volk *nt*; *(people of one country)* Nation *f.*

**national** ['næʃənəl] **1** *adj* national; *interest, debt, income* Staats-, öffentlich; *strike, scandal* landesweit; *security* Staats-; *team, character* National-; *language* Landes-; *custom, monument* Volks-. **the** ~ **papers** *or* **press** die überregionale Presse. **2** *n* **(a)** *(person)* Staatsbürger (in *f*) *m.* **foreign** ~ Ausländer (in *f*) *m.* **(b)** *(col: newspaper)* überregionale Zeitung.

**national:** ~ **anthem** *n* Nationalhymne *f*; ~ **costume,** ~ **dress** *n* Nationaltracht *f*; **N**~ **Front** *n (Brit) rechtsradikale Partei*; **N**~ **Guard** *n (US)* Nationalgarde *f*; **N**~ **Health** *adj attr (Brit)* = Kassen-; **N**~ **Health (Service)** *n (Brit)* Staatlicher Gesundheitsdienst *m*; **I got it on the N**~ **Health** = das hat

die Krankenkasse bezahlt; **N**~ **Health patient** = Kassenpatient (in *f*) *m*; ~ **insurance** *n (Brit)* Sozialversicherung *f.*

**nationalism** ['næʃnəlɪzəm] *n* Nationalismus *m.*

**nationalist** ['næʃnəlɪst] **1** *adj* nationalistisch. **2** *n* Nationalist (in *f*) *m.*

**nationality** [ˌnæʃəˈnælɪtɪ] *n* Staatsangehörigkeit, Nationalität *f.* **what** ~ **is he?** welche Staatsangehörigkeit hat er?

**nationalization** [ˌnæʃnəlaɪˈzeɪʃən] *n* Verstaatlichung *f.*

**nationalize** ['næʃnəlaɪz] *vt* verstaatlichen.

**nationally** ['næʃnəlɪ] *adv (as a nation)* als Nation; *(nationwide)* landesweit.

**national:** ~ **park** *n* Nationalpark *m*; ~ **service** *n (Brit)* Wehrdienst *m*; **N**~ **Socialism** *n* der Nationalsozialismus; **N**~ **Trust** *n (Brit) Verband m für Denkmalpflege und Naturschutz.*

**nation-wide** ['neɪʃənˌwaɪd] *adj, adv* landesweit.

**native** ['neɪtɪv] **1** *adj* **(a)** *product, costume, customs, plants* einheimisch; *(associated with natives) quarters, labour* Eingeborenen-. **a** ~ **German** ein gebürtiger Deutscher, eine gebürtige Deutsche. **(b)** *(inborn) wit, quality* angeboren. **2** *n* **(a)** *(person)* Einheimische(r) *mf*; *(in colonial contexts)* Eingeborene(r) *mf*; *(original inhabitant)* Ureinwohner (in *f*) *m.* **a** ~ **of Germany** ein gebürtiger Deutscher, eine gebürtige Deutsche. **(b) to be a** ~ **of** ... *(plant, animal)* in ... beheimatet sein.

**native:** ~ **country** *n* Heimatland *nt*; ~ **land** *n* Vaterland *nt*; ~ **language** *n* Muttersprache *f*; ~ **speaker** *n* Muttersprachler (in *f*) *m*; **I'm a** ~ **speaker of English** Englisch ist meine Muttersprache; ~ **town** *n* Heimatstadt *f.*

**nativity** [nəˈtɪvɪtɪ] *n* **the N**~ Christi Geburt *no art*; ~ **play** Krippenspiel *nt.*

**NATO** ['neɪtəʊ] = **North Atlantic Treaty Organization** NATO *f.*

**natter** ['nætər] *(Brit col)* **1** *vi* schwatzen *(col)*; *(chatter also)* quasseln *(col).* **2** *n* **to have a** ~ einen Schwatz halten *(col).*

**natural** ['nætʃərəl] **1** *adj* **(a)** natürlich; *rights* naturgegeben, Natur-; *laws, phenomena, world* Natur-. **it is** ~ **for him to think** ... es ist nur natürlich, daß er denkt ...; ~ **resources** Naturschätze *pl*; **the** ~ **world** die Natur; **in its** ~ **state** im Naturzustand; **to die a** ~ **death** *or* **of** ~ **causes** eines natürlichen Todes sterben; **death from** ~ **causes** *(Jur)* Tod durch natürliche Ursachen. **(b)** *(inborn) gift, ability* angeboren. **to have a** ~ **talent for sth** eine natürliche Begabung für etw haben. **2** *n* **(a)** *(Mus) (sign)* Auflösungszeichen *nt*; *(note)* Note *f* ohne Vorzeichen; **B** ~ **H, h** *nt*; **D**~ **D, d** *nt.* **(b)** *(col: person)* Naturtalent *nt.*

**natural:** ~ **childbirth** *n* natürliche Geburt; ~ **fibre** *n* Naturfaser *f*; ~ **gas** *n* Erdgas *nt*; ~ **history** *n* Naturkunde *f.*

**naturalism** ['nætʃrəlɪzəm] *n* Naturalismus *m.*

**naturalist** ['nætʃrəlɪst] *n* Naturforscher (in *f*) *m.*

**naturalistic** [ˌnætʃrəˈlɪstɪk] *adj (Art, Liter)* naturalistisch.

**naturalization** [ˌnætʃrəlaɪˈzeɪʃən] *n* Einbürgerung *f.*

**naturalize** ['nætʃrəlaɪz] *vt person* einbürgern; *animal, plants* heimisch machen. **to become** ~**d** eingebürgert werden.

**naturally** ['nætʃrəlɪ] *adv* **(a) he is** ~ **lazy** er ist von Natur aus faul. **(b)** *(not taught)* natürlich, instinktiv. **it comes** ~ **to him** das fällt ihm leicht. **(c)** *(unaffectedly)* natürlich, ungekünstelt. **(d)** *(of course)* natürlich.

**natural wastage** *n* natürliche Personalreduzierung.

**nature** ['neɪtʃə'] *n* (a) Natur *f*. **N~** die Natur; **laws of ~** Naturgesetze *pl*; **to paint from ~** nach der Natur malen. (b) *(of person)* Wesen(sart *f*) *nt*, Natur *f*. **to have a jealous/happy ~** eine eifersüchtige/fröhliche Natur haben; **it is not in my ~ to say things like that** es entspricht nicht meiner Art, so etwas zu sagen; **cruel by ~** von Natur aus grausam. (c) *(type, sort)* Art *f*. **things of this ~** derartiges; **something in the ~ of an apology** so etwas wie eine Entschuldigung; ... **or something of that ~** ... oder etwas in der Art.

**nature: ~ conservancy** *n* Naturschutz *m*; **~-lover** *n* Naturfreund *m*; **~ reserve** *n* Naturschutzgebiet *nt*; **~ study** *n* Naturkunde *f*; **~ trail** *n* Naturlehrpfad *m*.

**naturism** ['neɪtʃərɪzəm] *n* Freikörperkultur *f*, FKK *no art*.

**naturist** ['neɪtʃərɪst] *n* Anhänger(in *f*) *m* der Freikörperkultur.

**naughtily** ['nɔːtɪlɪ] *adv* frech; *(esp of child)* remark, behave ungezogen.

**naughtiness** ['nɔːtɪnɪs] *n see adj* (a) Frechheit *f*; Unartigkeit, Ungezogenheit *f*.

**naughty** ['nɔːtɪ] *adj (+er)* (a) frech; *child* unartig, ungezogen; *dog* ungehorsam. **you ~ boy!** du böser Junge!; **it was ~ of him to break it** das war aber gar nicht lieb von ihm, daß er das kaputtgemacht hat. (b) *joke, word, story* unanständig.

**nausea** ['nɔːsɪə] *n (Med)* Übelkeit *f*; *(fig)* Ekel *m*.

**nauseate** ['nɔːsɪeɪt] *vt* **to ~ sb** *(fig)* jdn anwidern.

**nauseating** ['nɔːsɪeɪtɪŋ] *adj sight, violence, food* ekelerregend; *film, book* gräßlich; *person* widerlich.

**nauseous** ['nɔːsɪəs] *adj* (a) *(Med)* **that made me (feel) ~** dabei wurde mir übel. (b) *(fig)* widerlich.

**nautical** ['nɔːtɪkəl] *adj* nautisch; *tradition, appearance* seemännisch. **~ mile** Seemeile *f*.

**naval** ['neɪvəl] *adj* Marine-; *base, parade* Flotten-; *battle, forces* See-. **~ superiority** Überlegenheit *f* zur See.

**naval: ~ officer** *n* Marineoffizier *m*; **~ power** *n* Seemacht *f*.

**nave** [neɪv] *n (of church)* Haupt- or Mittelschiff *nt*.

**navel** ['neɪvəl] *n (Anat)* Nabel *m*.

**navigable** ['nævɪɡəbl] *adj waterway* schiffbar.

**navigate** ['nævɪɡeɪt] **1** *vi (in plane, ship)* navigieren; *(in car)* den Fahrer dirigieren; *(in rally)* franzen. **2** *vt* (a) *aircraft, ship* navigieren. (b) *(journey through)* durchfahren; *(journey along) (river etc)* befahren.

**navigation** [ˌnævɪˈɡeɪʃən] (a) Navigation *f*. **~ light** Positionslicht *nt*. (b) *(shipping)* Schiffsverkehr *m*.

**navigator** ['nævɪɡeɪtə'] *n (Naut)* Navigationsoffizier *m*; *(Aviat)* Navigator *m*; *(Mot)* Beifahrer *m*.

**navvy** ['nævɪ] *n (Brit)* Bauarbeiter *m*.

**navy** ['neɪvɪ] **1** *n* (a) (Kriegs)marine *f*. **N~ Department** *(US)* Marineministerium *nt*. (b) *(also ~ blue)* Marineblau *nt*. **2** *adj* (a) *attr* Marine-. (b) *(also ~ blue)* marineblau.

**Nazi** ['nɑːtsɪ] **1** *n* Nazi *m*; *(fig pej)* Faschist *m*. **2** *adj* Nazi-.

**Nazism** ['nɑːtsɪzəm] *n* Nazismus *m*.

**NB** = **nota bene** NB.

**NBC** *(US)* = **National Broadcasting Company** NBC *f*.

**NC** *(US Post)* = **North Carolina.**

**NCO** = **non-commissioned officer.**

**ND** *(US Post)* = **North Dakota.**

**NE** = (a) **north-east** NO. (b) *(US Post)* **Nebraska.**

**Neapolitan** [nɪəˈpɒlɪtən] *n* **1** *adj* neapolitanisch. **2** *n* Neapolitaner(in *f*) *m*.

**near** [nɪə'] *(+er)* **1** *adv* (a) nahe. **to be ~** *(person, object)* in der Nähe sein; *(event etc)* bevorstehen; *(danger, end, help etc)* nahe sein; **to be very ~** ganz in der Nähe sein; *(in time)* unmittelbar bevorstehen; *(danger etc)* ganz nahe sein; **to be ~er/~est** näher/am nächsten sein; *(event etc)* zeitlich näher liegen/zeitlich am nächsten liegen; **to be ~ at hand** zur Hand sein; *(shops)* in der Nähe sein; *(help)* ganz nahe sein; *(event)* unmittelbar bevorstehen; **he lives quite ~** er wohnt ganz in der Nähe; **that was the ~est I ever got to seeing him** da hätte ich ihn fast gesehen.

(b) *(exactly, accurately)* genau. **as ~ as I can judge** soweit ich es beurteilen kann; **(that's) ~ enough** so geht's ungefähr.

(c) **it's nowhere ~ enough/right** das ist bei weitem nicht genug/das ist weit gefehlt; **nowhere ~ as much** bei weitem nicht soviel; **he is nowhere ~ as clever as you** er ist bei weitem nicht so klug wie du.

**2** *prep (also adv:* **~ to)** (a) *(close to) (position)* nahe an *(+dat)*, nahe *(+dat)*; *(with motion)* nahe an *(+acc)*; *(in the vicinity of)* in der Nähe von *or (+gen)*. **the hotel is very ~ (to) the station** das Hotel liegt ganz in der Nähe des Bahnhofs; **to come or get ~ (to) sth** nahe an etw herankommen; **to stand ~ (to) the table** neben dem *or* nahe am Tisch stehen; **she stood too ~ (to) the stove** sie stand zu nahe am Herd; **when we got ~ (to) the house** als wir an das Haus herankamen; **~ here/there** hier/dort in der Nähe; **take the chair ~est (to) you** nehmen Sie den Stuhl direkt neben Ihnen.

(b) *(close in time)* gegen. **come back ~er (to) 3 o'clock** kommen Sie gegen 3 Uhr wieder; **~ (to) the end of the play** gegen Ende des Stücks; **I'm ~ (to) the end of the book/my stay** ich habe das Buch fast zu Ende gelesen/mein Aufenthalt ist fast zu Ende.

(c) *(on the point of)* **to be ~ (to) doing sth** nahe daran sein, etw zu tun; **to be ~ (to) tears/despair etc** den Tränen/der Verzweiflung *etc* nahe sein; **the project is ~ (to) completion** das Projekt steht vor seinem Abschluß.

(d) *(similar to)* ähnlich *(+dat)*. **German is ~er (to) Dutch than English** ist Deutsch ist dem Holländischen ähnlicher als Englisch; **nobody comes anywhere ~ him at swimming** im Schwimmen kann es niemand mit ihm aufnehmen *(col)*.

**3** *adj* (a) *(close in space)* nahe. **it looks very ~** es sieht so aus, als ob es ganz nah wäre; **our ~est neighbours are 5 miles away** unsere nächsten Nachbarn sind 5 Meilen entfernt. (b) *relation, friend* nah. (c) *escape* knapp. **a ~ disaster** beinahe ein Unglück *nt*; **that was a ~ miss or thing** das war knapp; **a ~ contest** ein Wettkampf *m* mit knappem Ausgang; **to be in a state of ~ collapse** einem Zusammenbruch nahe sein; (d) *(close in nature)* resemblance groß. **£50 or ~(est) offer** Verhandlungsbasis £50; **this is the ~est equivalent** das kommt dem am nächsten.

**4** *vt place* sich nähern *(+dat)*. **to be ~ing sth** *(fig)* auf etw *(acc)* zugehen; **to ~ completion** kurz vor dem Abschluß stehen.

**nearby** [nɪə'baɪ] **1** *adv* in der Nähe. **2** *adj* nahe gelegen.

**near: N~East** *n* Naher Osten; **~ letter quality** *n (Comp)* Schönschrift *f*.

**nearly** ['nɪəlɪ] *adv* beinahe, fast. **I ~ laughed** ich hätte fast gelacht; **she was ~ in tears** sie war den Tränen nahe; **not ~** bei weitem nicht, nicht annähernd.

**near miss** *n (Aviat)* Beinahezusammenstoß *m*.

**nearness** ['nɪənɪs] *n* Nähe *f*.

**near:** ~**side 1** *adj* auf der Beifahrerseite, linke(r, s)/rechte(r, s); **2** *n* Beifahrerseite *f*; ~**-sighted** *adj* kurzsichtig.

**neat** [niːt] *adj* (+*er*) **(a)** *(tidy) person, house, hair-style* ordentlich; *worker, work, handwriting also* sauber; *appearance also* gepflegt. **to make a** ~ **job of sth** etwas tadellos machen. **(b)** *(pleasing)* nett; *clothes also* adrett; *person, figure also* hübsch. **(c)** *(skilful) gadget* gelungen; *style* gewandt; *solution* elegant; *trick* schlau. **that's very** ~ das ist sehr schlau. **(d)** *(undiluted) spirits* pur. **(e)** *(US col: excellent)* klasse *inv (col)*.

**neatly** [ˈniːtlɪ] *adv see adj (a-c)* **(a)** ordentlich; sauber. **(b)** nett; adrett; hübsch. **(c)** gelungen; gewandt; elegant; schlau. ~ **put** treffend ausgedrückt.

**neatness** [ˈniːtnɪs] *n see adj (a-c)* **(a)** Ordentlichkeit *f*; Sauberkeit *f*. **(b)** Nettheit *f*, nettes Aussehen; Adrettheit *f*; hübsches Aussehen. **(c)** Gelungenheit *f*; Gewandtheit *f*; Eleganz *f*; Schlauheit *f*.

**nebulous** [ˈnebjʊləs] *adj (fig)* unklar, nebulös.

**necessarily** [ˈnesɪsərɪlɪ] *adv* notwendigerweise, unbedingt. **not** ~ nicht unbedingt.

**necessary** [ˈnesɪsərɪ] **1** *adj* **(a)** notwendig, nötig *(to, for* für*)*. **it is** ~ **to ...** man muß ...; **is it** ~ **for me to come too?** muß ich auch kommen?; **it's not** ~ **for you to come** Sie brauchen nicht zu kommen; **it is** ~ **for him to be there** es ist nötig *or* notwendig, daß er da ist, er muß (unbedingt) da sein; **all the** ~ **qualifications** alle erforderlichen Qualifikationen; ~ **condition** Voraussetzung *f*; **to make it** ~ **for sb to do sth** es erforderlich machen, daß jd etw tut; **if** ~ wenn nötig, nötigenfalls; **to make the** ~ **arrangements** die erforderlichen Maßnahmen treffen; **to do what is** ~ alles Nötige tun; **to do no more than is** ~ nicht mehr tun, als unbedingt nötig ist. **(b)** *(unavoidable) conclusion, result* unausweichlich. **a** ~ **evil** ein notwendiges Übel.

**2** *n* **(a)** *(col: what is needed)* **the** ~ das Notwendige; **will you do the** ~? wirst du das Nötige erledigen? **(b)** *(col: money)* **the** ~ das nötige Kleingeld.

**necessitate** [nɪˈsesɪteɪt] *vt* notwendig machen, erfordern *(form)*.

**necessity** [nɪˈsesɪtɪ] *n* **(a)** *no pl* Notwendigkeit *f*. **from** *or* **out of** ~ aus Not; **of** ~ notgedrungen; **it is a case of absolute** ~ es ist unbedingt notwendig; **in case of** ~ im Notfall. **(b)** *(necessary thing)* Notwendigkeit *f*. **the bare necessities (of life)** das Notwendigste (zum Leben).

**neck** [nek] **1** *n* Hals *m*; *(of dress etc)* Ausschnitt *m*; *(size)* Halsweite *f*. **to break one's** ~ sich *(dat)* das Genick brechen; **to risk one's** ~ Kopf und Kragen riskieren; **to save one's** ~ seinen Hals aus der Schlinge ziehen; **a stiff** ~ ein steifer Hals *or* Nacken; **to be up to one's** ~ **in work** bis über den Hals in der Arbeit stecken; **he's in it up to his** ~ *(col)* er steckt bis über den Hals drin; **to stick one's** ~ **out** seinen Kopf riskieren; **in this** ~ **of the woods** *(col)* in diesen Breiten; **it has a high** ~ *(dress etc)* es ist hochgeschlossen. **2** *vi (col)* knutschen *(col)*.

**neck:** ~ **and neck** *(lit, fig)* **1** *adj attr* Kopf-an-Kopf-; **2** *adv* Kopf an Kopf; ~**band** *n* Besatz *m*; *(for pullover)* (Hals)bündchen *nt*.

**necklace** [ˈneklɪs] *n* (Hals)kette *f*.

**neck:** ~**line** *n* Ausschnitt *m*; ~ **size** *n* Halsweite *f*; ~**tie** *n (esp US)* Krawatte *f*, Schlips *m*.

**nectar** [ˈnektəʳ] *n (lit, fig)* Nektar *m*.

**nectarine** [ˈnektərɪn] *n (fruit)* Nektarine *f*.

**NEDC** *(Brit)* = **National Economic Development Council** *Rat m für Wirtschaftsentwicklung.*

**née** [neɪ] *adj* **Mrs Smith,** ~ **Jones** Frau Smith, geborene Jones.

**need** [niːd] **1** *n* **(a)** *no pl (necessity)* Notwendigkeit *f (for gen)*. **if** ~ **be** nötigenfalls; **in case of** ~ notfalls, im Notfall; **(there is) no** ~ **for sth** etw ist nicht nötig; **there is no** ~ **for sb to do sth** jd braucht etw nicht zu tun; **there's no** ~ **to get angry** du brauchst nicht gleich wütend zu werden; **to be (badly) in** ~ **of sth** *(person)* etw (dringend) brauchen; **to be in** ~ **of repair** reparaturbedürftig sein; **to have no** ~ **of sth** etw nicht brauchen; **to have no** ~ **to do sth** etw nicht zu tun brauchen.

**(b)** *no pl (misfortune, poverty)* Not *f*. **in time(s) of** ~ in Zeiten der Not; **those in** ~ die Notleidenden *pl*.

**(c)** *(requirement)* Bedürfnis *nt*. **the body's** ~ **for oxygen** das Sauerstoffbedürfnis des Körpers; **my** ~**s are few** ich stelle nur geringe Ansprüche.

**2** *vt* **(a)** brauchen. **to** ~ **no introduction** keine besondere Einführung brauchen; **much** ~**ed** dringend notwendig; **just what I** ~**ed** genau das richtige; **that's all I** ~**ed** *(iro)* das hat mir gerade noch gefehlt; **it** ~**s a coat of paint** es muß gestrichen werden; **a visa is** ~**ed to enter the USA** für die Einreise in die USA braucht man ein Visum; **it** ~**ed an accident to make him drive carefully** er mußte erst einen Unfall haben, bevor er vernünftig fuhr.

**(b)** **sth** ~**s doing** *or* **to be done** etw muß gemacht werden; **the book** ~**s careful reading** man muß das Buch genau lesen; **to** ~ **to do sth** *(have to)* etw tun müssen; **he doesn't** ~ **to be told** man braucht es ihm nicht zu sagen; **she** ~**s to have everything explained to her** man muß ihr alles erklären.

**3** *aux* **(a)** *(positive)* müssen. ~ **he go?** muß er gehen?; ~ **I say more?** mehr brauche ich ja wohl nicht zu sagen; **I** ~ **hardly say that ...** ich brauche wohl kaum zu erwähnen, daß ...; **you only** ~**ed (to) ask** du hättest nur (zu) fragen brauchen; **one** ~ **only look** ein Blick genügt.

**(b)** *(negative)* brauchen. **you** ~**n't wait** du brauchst nicht (zu) warten; **we** ~**n't have come** wir hätten gar nicht (zu) kommen brauchen; **I/you** ~**n't have bothered** das war nicht nötig.

**(c)** *(logical necessity)* **that** ~**n't be the case** das muß nicht unbedingt der Fall sein; **it** ~ **not follow that ...** daraus folgt nicht unbedingt, daß ...

**needle** [ˈniːdl] **1** *n* Nadel *f*. **it's like looking for a** ~ **in a haystack** es ist, als ob man eine Stecknadel im Heuhaufen suchte; **to give sb the** ~ *(col)* jdn reizen. **2** *vt (col: goad)* ärgern, piesacken *(col)*. **what's needling him?** was ist ihm über die Leber gelaufen? *(col)*.

**needle:** ~**craft** *n* Handarbeit *f*; ~ **match** *n* spannendes Spiel.

**needless** [ˈniːdlɪs] *adj* unnötig. ~ **to say** natürlich; ~ **to say, he didn't come** er kam natürlich nicht.

**needlessly** [ˈniːdlɪslɪ] *adv* unnötig(erweise).

**needlework** [ˈniːdlwɜːk] *n* Handarbeit *f*.

**needy** [ˈniːdɪ] **1** *adj* (+*er*) ärmlich, bedürftig. **2** *n* **the** ~ die Bedürftigen *pl*.

**negation** [nɪˈɡeɪʃən] *n* Verneinung *f*.

**negative** [ˈneɡətɪv] **1** *adj* negativ; *answer* verneinend; *(Gram)* form verneint. ~ **cash flow** *(Fin)* Überhang *m* der Zahlungsausgänge; ~ **sign** *(Math)* Minuszeichen *nt*. **2** *n* **(a)** *(also Gram)* Verneinung *f*. **to answer in the** ~ eine verneinende Antwort geben; *(refuse)* einen ablehnigen Bescheid geben; **his answer was a curt** ~ er antwortete mit einem knappen Nein; **put this sentence into the** ~ verneinen Sie diesen Satz. **(b)** *(Gram: word)* Negation *f*; *(Math)* negative Zahl. **(c)** *(Phot)* Negativ *nt*. **(d)** *(Elec)* negativer Pol.

**neglect** [nɪ'glekt] **1** vt vernachlässigen; *opportunity* versäumen; *advice* nicht befolgen. **to ~ to do sth** es versäumen, etw zu tun. **2** Vernachlässigung f; *(negligence)* Nachlässigkeit f. **~ of one's duties** Pflichtversäumnis nt; **to be in a state of ~** verwahrlost sein, völlig vernachlässigt sein; **the fire started through (his) ~** das Feuer ist durch seine Nachlässigkeit entstanden.

**neglected** [nɪ'glektɪd] adj vernachlässigt. **to feel ~** sich vernachlässigt fühlen.

**neglectful** [nɪ'glektfʊl] adj nachlässig; *father, government etc* pflichtvergessen. **to be ~ of sb/sth** jdn/ etw vernachlässigen.

**négligé(e)** ['neglɪʒeɪ] n Negligé nt.

**negligence** ['neglɪdʒəns] n *(carelessness)* Nachlässigkeit f; *(causing danger, Jur)* Fahrlässigkeit f.

**negligent** ['neglɪdʒənt] adj **(a)** nachlässig; *(causing danger, damage)* fahrlässig. **both drivers were ~** beide Fahrer haben sich fahrlässig verhalten. **(b)** *(off-hand)* lässig.

**negligible** ['neglɪdʒəbl] adj unwesentlich; *quantity also* geringfügig.

**negotiable** [nɪ'gəʊʃɪəbl] adj **(a)** *(Comm) (can be sold)* verkäuflich; *(can be transferred)* übertragbar. **these terms are ~** über diese Bedingungen kann verhandelt werden. **(b)** *road* befahrbar; *river, mountain pass* passierbar; *obstacle, difficulty* überwindbar.

**negotiate** [nɪ'gəʊʃɪeɪt] **1** vt **(a)** verhandeln über *(+acc)*; *(bring about)* aushandeln. **(b)** *bend, (horse) fence* nehmen; *river, mountain* passieren; *obstacle* überwinden. **2** vi verhandeln *(for* über *+acc)*.

**negotiation** [nɪ,gəʊʃɪ'eɪʃən] n **(a)** *see vt (a)* Verhandlung f; Aushandlung f. **the matter is still under ~** über diese Sache wird noch verhandelt. **(b)** *usu pl (talks)* Verhandlung f. **to enter into ~s with sb** Verhandlungen mit jdm aufnehmen. **(c)** *(of river, mountain)* Passage f, Passieren nt; *(of obstacle)* Überwindung f.

**negotiator** [nɪ'gəʊʃɪeɪtəʳ] n Unterhändler(in f) m.

**Negress** ['niːgres] n Negerin f.

**Negro** ['niːgrəʊ] **1** adj Neger-. **2** n Neger m.

**neigh** [neɪ] **1** vi wiehern. **2** n Wiehern nt.

**neighbour,** *(US)* **neighbor** ['neɪbəʳ] **1** n Nachbar(in f) m; *(at table)* Tischnachbar(in f) m; *(Bibl etc)* Nächste(r) mf. **2** vi *(US col)* **to ~ with sb** gutnachbarliche Beziehungen zu jdm haben.

**neighbourhood,** *(US)* **neighborhood** ['neɪbəhʊd] n *(district)* Gegend f; *(people)* Nachbarschaft f. **in the ~ of sth** in der Nähe von etw; **~ watch** *Vereinigung f von Bürgern, die durch erhöhte Wachsamkeit die Polizei bei der Verbrechensbekämpfung unterstützen.*

**neighbouring,** *(US)* **neighboring** ['neɪbərɪŋ] adj *house(s), village* benachbart, Nachbar-; *fields, community, country* Nachbar-.

**neighbourly,** *(US)* **neighborly** ['neɪbəlɪ] adj *action, relations* gutnachbarlich. **they are ~ people** sie sind gute Nachbarn.

**neither** ['naɪðəʳ] **1** adv **~ ... nor** weder ... noch; **he ~ knows nor cares** er weiß es nicht und will es auch nicht wissen. **2** conj auch nicht. **if you don't go, ~ shall I** wenn du nicht gehst, gehe ich auch nicht; **I'm not going — ~ am I** ich gehe nicht — ich auch nicht; **he didn't do it (and) ~ did his sister** weder er noch seine Schwester haben es getan. **3** adj keine(r, s) *(der beiden)*. **~ one of them** keiner von beiden. **4** pron keiner(r, s). **~ of them** keiner von beiden; **which one will you take? — ~** welches nehmen Sie? — keines (von beiden).

**neo-** ['niːəʊ-] pref neo-, Neo-; **~classical** adj klassizistisch; **~fascist 1** adj neofaschistisch; **2** n Neo-

faschist (in f) m.

**neolithic** [,niːəʊ'lɪθɪk] adj jungsteinzeitlich, neolithisch.

**neologism** [nɪ'ɒlədʒɪzəm] n *(Ling)* (Wort)neubildung f, Neologismus m.

**neon** ['niːɒn] n *(Chem)* Neon nt. **~ light** Neonlicht nt; **~ sign** *(name)* Neon- or Leuchtschild nt; *(advertisement)* Leuchtreklame f no pl.

**Nepal** [nɪ'pɔːl] n Nepal nt.

**Nepalese** [nepə'liːz] **1** adj nepalesisch. **2** n Nepalese m, Nepalesin f.

**nephew** ['nevjuː, 'nefjuː] n Neffe m.

**nepotism** ['nepətɪzəm] n Vetternwirtschaft f.

**Neptune** ['neptjuːn] n *(Astron, Myth)* Neptun m.

**nerd** [nɜːd] n *(col!)* Schwachkopf m *(col)*.

**nerve** [nɜːv] **1** n **(a)** *(Anat)* Nerv m. **to suffer from ~s** nervös sein; **to have an attack of ~s** in Panik geraten, durchdrehen *(col)*; **his ~s are bad** er hat schlechte Nerven; **to get on sb's ~s** *(col)* jdm auf die Nerven gehen; **to have ~s of steel** Nerven wie Drahtseile haben. **(b)** *no pl (courage)* Mut m. **to lose/keep one's ~** die Nerven verlieren/nicht verlieren; **to have the ~ to do sth** sich trauen, etw zu tun; **a test of ~** eine Nervenprobe. **(c)** *no pl (col: impudence)* Frechheit, Unverschämtheit f. **to have the ~ to do sth** die Frechheit besitzen, etw zu tun; **he's got a ~!** der hat Nerven! *(col)*. **2** vtr **to ~ oneself for sth/to do sth** sich seelisch und moralisch auf etw *(acc)* vorbereiten/darauf vorbereiten, etw zu tun.

**nerve: ~ centre** *(Brit)*, **~ center** *(US)* n Nervenzentrum nt *(Anat)*; Schaltzentrale f *(fig)*; **~-racking** ['nɜːvrækɪŋ] adj nervenaufreibend.

**nervous** ['nɜːvəs] adj **(a)** *(Anat) system etc* Nerven-; *exhaustion, reflex* nervös. **~ breakdown** Nervenzusammenbruch m; **~ energy** Vitalität f; **~ tension** Nervenanspannung f. **(b)** *(apprehensive)* nervös; *(overexcited, tense also)* aufgeregt. **to feel ~** nervös sein; **I am ~ about the exam/him** mir ist bange vor dem Examen/um ihn; **I am rather ~ about diving** ich habe eine ziemliche Angst vor dem Tauchen *(col)*.

**nervously** ['nɜːvəslɪ] adv nervös; *(excitedly also)* aufgeregt.

**nervous: ~ Nellie** n *(US col)* Flattermann m; **~ wreck** n *(col)* **to be/feel a ~ wreck** mit den Nerven völlig am Ende sein.

**nervy** ['nɜːvɪ] adj *(+er)* **(a)** *(Brit: tense)* nervös. **(b)** *(US col: cheeky)* frech.

**nest** [nest] **1** n Nest nt. **to leave the ~** *(lit, fig)* das Nest verlassen; **a ~ of tables** ein Satz m Tische. **2** vi nisten.

**nesting-box** ['nestɪŋbɒks] n Nistkasten m.

**nestle** ['nesl] vi **to ~ down in bed** sich ins Bett kuscheln; **to ~ up to sb** sich an jdn kuscheln; **the village nestling in the hills** das Dorf, das zwischen den Bergen eingebettet liegt.

**nestling** ['neslɪŋ] n Nestling m.

**net¹** [net] **1** n *(lit, fig)* Netz nt. **to be caught in the ~** *(fig)* in die Falle gehen. **2** vt *fish, butterfly* mit dem Netz fangen; *(Sport) ball* ins Netz schlagen; *(fig) criminal* fangen.

**net²** **1** adj **(a)** *price, income, weight* netto, Netto-. **~ assets** Nettovermögen nt; **~ profit** Reingewinn m; **it costs £15 ~** es kostet £15 netto. **(b)** *(fig)* **~ result** Endergebnis nt. **2** vt netto einnehmen; *(in wages, salary)* netto verdienen; *(deal etc)* einbringen.

**net: ~ball** n *(Brit)* Korbball m; **~ curtain** n Tüllgardine f, Store m.

**Netherlands** ['neðələndz] npl **the ~** die Niederlande pl.

**netting** ['netɪŋ] *n* Netz *nt; (wire ~)* Maschendraht *m.*
**nettle** ['netl] **1** *n (Bot)* Nessel *f.* **2** *vt (fig col) person* wurmen *(col)*, fuchsen *(col)*.
**nettle rash** *n* Nesselausschlag *m.*
**network** ['netwɜːk] **1** *n* **(a)** *(lit, fig)* Netz *nt.* **(b)** *(Rad, TV)* Sendenetz *nt; (Elec, Comp)* Netzwerk *nt.* **2** *vt (Comp)* vernetzen.
**networking** ['netwɜːkɪŋ] *n (Comp)* Rechnerverbund *m.*
**neuralgia** [njʊə'rældʒə] *n* Neuralgie *f,* Nervenschmerzen *pl.*
**neuro-** ['njʊərəʊ-] *in cpds* Neuro-, neuro-; **~biology** Neurobiologie *f.*
**neurosis** [njʊə'rəʊsɪs] *n, pl* **neuroses** [njʊə'rəʊsiːz] Neurose *f.*
**neurotic** [njʊə'rɒtɪk] **1** *adj* neurotisch. **to be ~ about** **sth** *(col)* in bezug auf etw *(acc)* neurotisch sein. **2** *n* Neurotiker(in *f*) *m.*
**neuter** ['njuːtəʳ] **1** *adj* **(a)** *(Gram)* sächlich. **(b)** *animal, person* geschlechtslos; *(castrated)* kastriert; *plant* ungeschlechtlich. **2** *n* **(a)** *(Gram)* Neutrum *nt.* **(b)** *(animal)* geschlechtloses Wesen; *(castrated)* kastriertes Tier. **3** *vt cat, dog* kastrieren; *female* sterilisieren.
**neutral** ['njuːtrəl] **1** *adj* neutral. **2** *n (Aut)* Leerlauf *m.* **to be in ~** im Leerlauf sein.
**neutrality** [njuː'trælɪtɪ] *n* Neutralität *f.*
**neutralize** ['njuːtrəlaɪz] *vt* neutralisieren; *(fig)* ausgleichen.
**neutron** ['njuːtrɒn] *n* Neutron *nt.*
**neutron bomb** *n* Neutronenbombe *f.*
**never** ['nevəʳ] *adv* **(a)** nie. **I have ~ seen him** ich habe ihn (noch) nie gesehen; **~ again** nie wieder; **I'll ~ try that again** das werde ich nicht noch einmal versuchen; **~ before** noch nie; **I have ~ seen him before** ich habe ihn noch nie gesehen; **~ before have men climbed this peak** nie zuvor haben Menschen diesen Gipfel erklommen; **~ even** nicht einmal; **~ ever** gar nie; **I have ~ ever been so insulted** ich bin noch nie so beleidigt worden.
  **(b)** *(emph: not)* **that will ~ do!** das geht ganz und gar nicht!; **he ~ so much as smiled** er hat nicht einmal gelächelt; **he said ~ a word** er hat kein einziges Wort gesagt; **you've ~ left it behind!** *(col)* du hast es doch wohl nicht etwa liegenlassen! *(col)*; **would you do it again? — ~!** würdest du das noch einmal machen? — bestimmt nicht; **Spurs were beaten — ~!** *(col)* Spurs sind geschlagen worden — das ist doch nicht möglich!; **well I ~ (did)!** *(col)* nein, so was!
**never: ~-ending** *adj* endlos; **~-never** *n (Brit col)*: **on the ~-never** auf Pump *(col)*.
**nevertheless** [ˌnevəðə'les] *adv* trotzdem, dennoch.
**new** [njuː] *adj (+er)* neu. **that's nothing ~** das ist nichts Neues; **that's something ~!** das ist wirklich ganz was Neues!; **what's ~?** *(col)* was gibt's Neues? *(col)*; **dressed in ~ clothes** neu eingekleidet; **to make sth (look) like ~** etw wie neu machen; **as ~** wie neu; **this system is ~ to me** dieses System ist mir neu; **he is a ~ man** *(fig)* er ist ein neuer Mensch; **that's a ~ one on me** *(col)* das ist mir ja ganz neu; **a ~ kind of engine** ein neuartiger Motor; **I'm quite ~ to this job** ich bin neu in dieser Stelle; **I am ~ to this place** ich bin erst seit kurzem hier.
**new: ~-born** *adj* neugeboren; **~comer** *n* Neuankömmling *m; (in job, subject etc)* Neuling *m (to* in *+dat)*; **N~ England** *n* Neuengland *nt;* **~-fangled** ['njuːˌfæŋgld] *adj* neumodisch; **N~foundland** ['njuːfəndlænd] *n* Neufundland *nt; (dog)* Neufundländer *m;* **N~ Guinea** *n* Neuguinea *nt;* **~-laid** ['njuːleɪd] *adj* frisch.

**newly** ['njuːlɪ] *adv* frisch. **~-made** ganz neu; *bread, cake etc* frisch gebacken.
**newlyweds** ['njuːlɪwedz] *npl (col)* Frischvermählte *pl.*
**new moon** *n* Neumond *m.* **there's a ~ tonight** heute nacht ist Neumond.
**newness** ['njuːnɪs] *n* Neuheit *f.*
**New Orleans** [ˌnjuːɔː'liːnz] *n* New Orleans *nt.*
**news** [njuːz] *n no pl* **(a)** *(report, information)* Nachricht *f; (recent development)* Neuigkeit(en *pl*) *f.* **a piece of ~** eine Neuigkeit; **I have ~/no ~ of him** ich weiß Neues/nichts Neues von ihm; **there is no ~** es gibt nichts Neues; **have you heard the ~?** haben Sie schon das Neueste gehört?; **is there any ~?** gibt es etwas Neues?; **I have ~ for you** *(iro)* ich habe eine Überraschung für dich; **bad/good ~** schlechte/gute Nachricht(en); **he's bad ~** *(col)* er bedeutet nichts als Ärger; **that is good ~** das sind ja gute Nachrichten; **who will break the ~ to him?** wer wird es ihm beibringen?; **that is ~ to me!** das ist (mir) ganz neu!
  **(b)** *(Press, Film, Rad, TV)* Nachrichten *pl.* **it was on the ~** das kam in den Nachrichten; **to be in the ~** von sich reden machen.
**news: ~ agency** *n* Nachrichtenagentur *f;* **~ agent** *n (Brit)* Zeitungshändler *m;* **~ bulletin** *n,* **~cast** *n (TV, Rad)* Nachrichtensendung *f;* **~caster** *n* Nachrichtensprecher(in *f*) *m;* **~ dealer** *n (US)* Zeitungshändler *m;* **~ desk** *n* Nachrichtenredaktion *f;* **~ editor** *n* Nachrichtenredakteur *m;* **~flash** *n* Kurzmeldung *f;* **~letter** *n* Mitteilungsblatt *nt.*
**New South Wales** *n* Neusüdwales *nt.*
**newspaper** ['njuːzˌpeɪpəʳ] *n* Zeitung *f.* **daily/weekly ~** Tageszeitung/Wochenzeitung.
**newspaper: ~ advertisement** *n* Zeitungsinserat *nt;* **~ article** *n* Zeitungsartikel *m;* **~ boy** *n* Zeitungsausträger, Zeitungsjunge *m;* **~ kiosk** *n* Zeitungskiosk *m;* **~ man** *n* Zeitungsverkäufer *m; (journalist)* Journalist *m;* **~ report** *n* Zeitungsbericht *m.*
**news: ~print** *n* Zeitungspapier *nt;* **~reader** *n* Nachrichtensprecher(in *f*) *m;* **~reel** *n* Wochenschau *f;* **~room** *n (of newspaper)* Nachrichtenredaktion *f; (TV, Rad)* Nachrichtenstudio *nt;* **~stand** *n* Zeitungsstand *m;* **~worthy** *adj* **to be ~worthy** Neuigkeitswert haben.
**newsy** ['njuːzɪ] *adj (+er) (col)* voller Neuigkeiten.
**newt** [njuːt] *n* Wassermolch *m.*
**new: N~ Testament 1** *n* **the N~ Testament** das Neue Testament; **2** *adj attr* des Neuen Testaments; **the N~ World** *n* die Neue Welt.
**New Year** *n* neues Jahr; *(~'s Day)* Neujahr *nt.* **to see in the ~** das neue Jahr begrüßen; **Happy ~!** (ein) frohes neues Jahr!; **~'s Day,** *(US also)* **~'s** Neujahr *nt;* **~'s Eve** Silvester *nt;* **~ resolution** (guter) Vorsatz für das neue Jahr.
**New: ~ York** [njuː'jɔːk] *n* New York *nt;* **~ Zealand** [njuː'ziːlənd] **1** *n* Neuseeland *nt;* **2** *adj attr* neuseeländisch; **~ Zealander** *n* Neuseeländer(in *f*) *m.*
**next** [nekst] **1** *adj* nächste(r, s). **come back ~ week/ Tuesday** kommen Sie nächste Woche/nächsten Dienstag wieder; **he came back the ~ day/week** er kam am nächsten Tag/in der nächsten Woche wieder; **(the) ~ time I see him** wenn ich ihn das nächste Mal sehe; **the ~ time I saw him** als ich ihn das nächste Mal sah; **(the) ~ moment he was gone** im nächsten Moment war er weg; **from one moment to the ~** von einem Augenblick auf den anderen; **this time ~ week** nächste Woche um diese Zeit; **the year/week after ~** übernächstes Jahr/übernächste Woche; **the ~ day but one** der übernächste Tag;

who's ~? wer ist der nächste?; you're ~ Sie sind dran *(col) or* an der Reihe; ~ please! der nächste bitte!; the ~ but one der/die/das übernächste.

2 *adv* (a) *(the ~ time)* das nächste Mal; *(afterwards)* danach. what shall we do ~? was sollen wir als nächstes machen?; whatever ~? *(in surprise)* Sachen gibt's! *(col)*; *(despairingly)* wo soll das nur hinführen? (b) ~ to sb/sth neben jdm/etw; *(with motion)* neben jdn/etw; the ~ to last row die vorletzte Reihe; he was ~ to last er war der vorletzte; the ~ to bottom shelf das zweite Brett von unten; ~ to the skin (direkt) auf der Haut; ~ to nothing so gut wie nichts; ~ to impossible nahezu unmöglich. (c) the ~ best der/die/das nächstbeste.

**next-door** ['neks'dɔːr] 1 *adv* nebenan. they live ~ to us sie wohnen (direkt) neben uns; the boy ~ der Junge von nebenan. 2 *adj* the ~ neighbour/house der Nachbar/die Nachbarin von nebenan/das Nebenhaus; we are ~ neighbours wir wohnen Tür an Tür.

**next of kin** *n* nächster Verwandte, nächste Verwandte; *pl* nächste Verwandte.

**NFL** = **National Football League** *amerikanische Fußball-Nationalliga.*

**NFU** = **National Farmers' Union** *britische Bauerngewerkschaft.*

**NH** *(US Post)* = **New Hampshire.**

**NHS** *(Brit)* = **National Health Service.**

**NI** *(Brit)* = (a) **Northern Ireland.** (b) **National Insurance.**

**Niagara Falls** [naɪˈægrəˈfɔːlz] *npl* die Niagarafälle *pl.*

**nib** [nɪb] *n* Feder *f.*

**nibble** ['nɪbl] 1 *vti* to ~ (at) sth an etw *(dat)* knabbern. 2 *vi (fig)* sich interessiert zeigen.

**NICAM** *n System nt zur Umwandlung von Audio-Signalen in digitale Form.*

**Nicaragua** [ˌnɪkəˈrægjʊə] *n* Nicaragua *nt.*

**Nicaraguan** [ˌnɪkəˈrægjʊən] 1 *adj* nicaraguanisch. 2 *n* Nicaraguaner(in *f*) *m.*

**Nice** [niːs] *n* Nizza *nt.*

**nice** [naɪs] *adj (+er)* (a) nett; *voice also* sympathisch; *(~-looking) dress, looks etc also* hübsch; *taste, smell, meal* gut; *warmth, weather, feeling, car* schön; *(skilful) workmanship, work* gut, schön. be ~ to him sei nett zu ihm; that's not ~! das ist aber nicht nett; to have a ~ time sich gut amüsieren; I had a ~ rest ich habe mich gut *or* schön ausgeruht; how ~ of you to ... wie nett von Ihnen, zu ... (b) *(intensifier)* schön. a ~ long holiday schön lange Ferien; ~ and warm/near schön warm/nahe; ~ and easy ganz leicht.

(c) *(respectable)* nett; *district* fein; *words* schön; *manners* gut.

(d) *(iro)* schön, sauber. here's a ~ state of affairs! das sind ja schöne Zustände!; you're in a ~ mess du sitzt in einem schönen Schlamassel *(col)*.

(e) *(subtle) distinction* fein, genau. that was a ~ point das war eine gute Bemerkung.

**nice-looking** ['naɪs'lʊkɪŋ] *adj* gutaussehend; *girl also* hübsch. to be ~ gut aussehen.

**nicely** ['naɪslɪ] *adv (pleasantly)* nett; *(well) go, speak, behave, placed* gut. to go ~ wie geschmiert laufen *(col)*; that will do ~ das reicht vollauf; how's it going? — ~, thank you wie geht es so? — danke, ganz gut; he's getting on ~ ihm geht's ganz gut.

**nicety** ['naɪsɪtɪ] *n* (a) *(subtlety)* Feinheit *f*; *(of judgement also)* Schärfe *f*; *(precision)* (peinliche) Genauigkeit. (b) **niceties** *pl* Feinheiten *pl.*

**niche** [niːʃ] *n (Archit)* Nische *f*; *(fig)* Plätzchen *nt.*

**nick¹** [nɪk] 1 *n* (a) Kerbe *f.* I got a little ~ on my chin ich habe mich leicht am Kinn geschnitten. (b) in

the ~ of time gerade noch (rechtzeitig). (c) *(Brit col: condition)* in good/bad ~ gut/nicht gut in Schuß *(col)*. 2 *vt* (a) *stick* einkerben. to ~ oneself *(col)* sich schneiden. (b) *(bullet) person, wall* streifen.

**nick²** *(Brit)* 1 *vt (col)* (a) *(arrest)* einsperren *(col)*; *(catch)* schnappen *(col)*. he got ~ed den haben sie sich *(dat)* geschnappt *(col)*. (b) *(steal)* klauen *(col)*. 2 *n (prison)* Knast *m (col)*; *(police station)* Wache *f.*

**nickel** ['nɪkl] *n* (a) *(metal)* Nickel *nt.* ~ silver Neusilber *nt.* (b) *(US: coin)* Fünfcentstück *nt.*

**nickname** ['nɪkneɪm] 1 *n* Spitzname *m.* 2 *vt* to ~ sb ... jdm den Spitznamen ... geben.

**nicotine** ['nɪkətiːn] *n* Nikotin *nt.*

**niece** [niːs] *n* Nichte *f.*

**nifty** ['nɪftɪ] *adj (+er) (col)* flott *(col)*; *gadget, tool* schlau *(col)*.

**Nigeria** [naɪˈdʒɪərɪə] *n* Nigeria *nt.*

**Nigerian** [naɪˈdʒɪərɪən] 1 *adj* nigerisch. 2 *n* Nigerianer(in *f*) *m.*

**niggardly** ['nɪgədlɪ] *adj person* knaus(e)rig; *amount, portion also* kümmerlich.

**nigger** ['nɪgər] *n (pej)* Nigger *m (pej col)*.

**niggle** ['nɪgl] 1 *vi (complain)* herumkritisieren *(about an +dat)*. 2 *vt (worry)* plagen, zu schaffen machen *(+dat)*.

**niggling** ['nɪglɪŋ] *adj person* überkritisch; *doubt, pain* quälend; *detail* pingelig *(col)*.

**night** [naɪt] *n* Nacht *f*; *(evening)* Abend *m.* I saw him last ~ ich habe ihn gestern abend gesehen; I'll see him tomorrow ~ ich treffe ihn morgen abend; on Friday ~ Freitag abend/nacht; on the ~ of (Saturday) the 11th am (Samstag, dem) 11. nachts/abends; 11/6 o'clock at ~ 11 Uhr nachts/6 Uhr abends; to travel/see Paris by ~ nachts reisen/Paris bei Nacht sehen; far into the ~ bis spät in die Nacht; in/during the ~ in/während der Nacht; the ~ before last they were ... vorgestern abend/vorletzte Nacht waren sie ...; to spend the ~ at a hotel in einem Hotel übernachten; I need a good ~'s sleep ich muß mal wieder ordentlich schlafen; ~ after ~ jede Nacht; all ~ (long) die ganze Nacht; to have a ~ out (abends) ausgehen; to have a late/an early ~ spät/früh ins Bett kommen, spät/früh schlafen gehen; to work ~s nachts arbeiten; ~ is falling die Nacht bricht herein; the last three ~s of Hamlet die letzten drei Abende von „Hamlet".

**night** *in cpds* Nacht-; ~-**bird** *n* Nachtvogel *m*; *(fig)* Nachtschwärmer *m (col)*; ~-**cap** *n* (a) *(garment)* Schlafmütze *f*; (b) *(drink)* Schlaftrunk *m*; ~-**club** *n* Nachtklub *m*; ~-**dress** *n (Brit)* Nachthemd *nt*; ~ **duty** *n* Nachtdienst *m*; ~-**fall** *n* Einbruch *m* der Dunkelheit; ~-**gown** *n* Nachthemd *nt.*

**nightie** ['naɪtɪ] *n (Brit: col)* Nachthemd *nt.*

**nightingale** ['naɪtɪŋgeɪl] *n* Nachtigall *f.*

**night life** *n* Nachtleben *nt.*

**nightly** ['naɪtlɪ] 1 *adj (every night)* (all)nächtlich, Nacht-; *(every evening)* (all)abendlich, Abend-. 2 *adv* jede Nacht/jeden Abend. twice ~ zweimal pro Abend.

**night:** ~**mare** *n (lit, fig)* Alptraum *m*; ~**owl** *n (col)* Nachteule *f (col)*; ~ **porter** *n* Nachtportier *m*; ~**safe** *n* Nachtsafe *m*; ~**school** *n* Abendschule *f*; ~-**shift** *n* Nachtschicht *f*; to be on ~-**shift** Nachtschicht haben *or* arbeiten; ~-**spot** *n* Nachtlokal *nt*; ~ **stand** *(US)* Nachttisch *m*; ~**stick** *n (US)* Schlagstock *m*; ~ **storage heater** *n* Nachtspeicherofen *m*; ~ **table** *n (US)* Nachttisch *m*; ~-**time** *n* Nacht *f*; at ~-**time** nachts; ~-**watchman** *n* Nachtwächter *m.*

**nihilism** ['naɪlɪzəm] *n* Nihilismus *m.*

**nil** [nɪl] *n* null *(also Sport)*; *(nothing)* nichts. the score

**was one-~** es stand eins zu null.

**Nile** [naɪl] *n* Nil *m*.

**nimble** ['nɪmbl] *adj (+er) fingers* flink; *(agile)* gelenkig, beweglich; *(skilful)* geschickt; *mind* beweglich.

**nimbly** ['nɪmblɪ] *adv work* flink; *dance* leicht(füßig).

**nimby** ['nɪmbɪ] = **not in my back yard** ≃ ohne mich!

**nincompoop** ['nɪŋkəmpuːp] *n (col)* Trottel *m*.

**nine** [naɪn] **1** *adj* neun. **~ times out of ten** so gut wie immer. **2** *n* Neun *f*. **dressed up to the ~s** in Schale *(col)*; *see* **six**.

**ninepins** ['naɪnpɪnz] *n (game)* Kegeln *nt*. **to go down like ~ *(fig)*** wie die Fliegen umfallen.

**nineteen** ['naɪn'tiːn] *adj* neunzehn. **she talks ~ to the dozen** sie redet wie ein Wasserfall *(col)*.

**nineteenth** ['naɪn'tiːnθ] *adj* neunzehnte(r, s); *see* **sixteenth**.

**nine-to-five** [,naɪntə'faɪv] *adj* **~ job** regelmäßige Arbeit, ≃ Achtstundentag *m*.

**ninety** ['naɪntɪ] **1** *adj* neunzig. **2** *n* Neunzig *f*; *see* **sixty**.

**ninth** [naɪnθ] **1** *adj* neunte(r, s). **2** *n (as fraction)* Neuntel *nt*; *(of series)* Neunte(r, s); *see* **sixth**.

**nip¹** [nɪp] **1** *n (pinch)* Kniff *m*; *(bite from animal etc)* Biß *m*. **there's a ~ in the air today** es ist heute ganz schön frisch. **2** *vt* (a) *(bite)* zwicken; *(pinch also)* kneifen; *bud, shoot* abknipsen. **to ~ sth in the bud** *(fig)* etw im Keim ersticken. (b) *(cold, frost etc) plants* angreifen. **3** *vi (Brit col)* sausen *(col)*, flitzen *(col)*. **to ~ up(stairs)/down(stairs)** hoch-/runtersausen *(col)*; **I'll just ~ down to the shops** ich gehe mal kurz einkaufen *(col)*; **I'll just ~ out for a moment** ich gehe nur mal kurz raus.

**nip²** *n (col: drink)* Schlückchen *nt*.

**nipple** ['nɪpl] *n (Anat)* Brustwarze *f*; *(on baby's bottle)* Sauger *m*.

**nippy** ['nɪpɪ] *adj (+er)* (a) *(Brit col)* flink, flott; *car* spritzig. (b) *weather* frisch.

**nit** [nɪt] *n* (a) *(Zool)* Nisse *f*. (b) *(Brit col)* Dummkopf, Blödmann *(col) m*.

**nit-picking** ['nɪtpɪkɪŋ] *adj (col)* pingelig *(col)*.

**nitrogen** ['naɪtrədʒən] *n* Stickstoff *m*.

**nitroglycerin(e)** ['naɪtrəʊ'glɪsəriːn] *n* Nitroglyzerin *nt*.

**nitty-gritty** ['nɪtɪ'grɪtɪ] *n (col)* **to get down to the ~** zur Sache kommen.

**nitwit** ['nɪtwɪt] *n (col)* Dummkopf *m*.

**NJ** *(US Post)* = **New Jersey**.

**NLQ** *(Comp)* = **near letter quality** NLQ.

**NM** *(US Post)* = **New Mexico**.

**no** = **number** Nr.

**no** [nəʊ] **1** *adv* (a) *(negative)* nein. **oh ~!** o nein!; **to answer ~ *(to question)*** mit Nein antworten; *(to request)* nein sagen; **she can't say ~** sie kann nicht nein sagen. (b) *(with comp)* nicht. **I can bear it ~ longer** ich kann es nicht länger ertragen; **I have ~ more money** ich habe kein Geld mehr; **~ fewer than 100** bestimmt 100; **~ later than Monday** spätestens Montag.

**2** *adj* kein. **~ one person could do it** keiner könnte das allein tun; **~ two men are alike** zwei Menschen sind immer verschieden; **~ other man** kein anderer; **it's of ~ interest/importance** das ist belanglos/unwichtig; **it's ~ use** *or* **good** das hat keinen Zweck; **~ parking/smoking** Parken/Rauchen verboten; **there's ~ telling what he'll do next** man kann nie wissen, was er als nächstes tut; **there's ~ denying it** es läßt sich nicht leugnen; **she's ~ beauty** sie ist nicht gerade eine Schönheit; **I'm ~ expert, but ...** ich bin zwar kein Fachmann, aber ...; **in ~ time** im Nu; **it's ~ small matter** das ist keine Kleinigkeit;

**theirs is ~ easy task** sie haben keine leichte Aufgabe; **there is ~ such thing** so etwas gibt es nicht; **it was/we did ~ such thing!** das stimmt überhaupt nicht!

**3** *n, pl* **-es** Nein *nt*; *(~ vote)* Neinstimme *f*. **I won't take ~ for an answer** ich bestehe darauf.

**no-account** ['nəʊə,kaʊnt] *adj (US col)* nichtsnutzig.

**nobble** ['nɒbl] *vt (Brit col)* (a) *horse* lahmlegen *(col)*. (b) *(catch)* sich *(dat)* schnappen *(col)*. (c) *(obtain dishonestly) votes etc* sich *(dat)* kaufen; *money* einsacken *(col)*.

**Nobel prize** ['nəʊbel'praɪz] *n* Nobelpreis *m*.

**nobility** [nəʊ'bɪlɪtɪ] *n no pl* (Hoch)adel *m*. **she is one of the ~** sie ist eine Adlige.

**noble** ['nəʊbl] **1** *adj (+er)* (a) *person, rank* adlig. **to be of ~ birth** adlig sein. (b) *(fine) person, deed etc* edel, nobel; *appearance* vornehm. (c) *(col: selfless)* edel, edelmütig. **2** *n* Adlige(r) *mf*.

**nobleman** ['nəʊblmən] *n, pl* **-men** [-mən] Adlige(r) *m*.

**noblewoman** ['nəʊblwʊmən] *n, pl* **-women** [-wɪmɪn] Adlige *f*.

**nobly** ['nəʊblɪ] *adv (aristocratically)* vornehm; *(finely)* edel; *(bravely)* wacker; *(col: selflessly)* nobel, edel(mütig).

**nobody** ['nəʊbədɪ] **1** *pron* niemand, keiner. **~ knows better than I** niemand *or* keiner weiß besser als ich; **there was ~ else** da war sonst niemand; **~ else could have done it** es kann niemand anders gewesen sein; *(capable)* das hätte sonst niemand geschafft. **2** *n* Niemand *m no pl*. **he's a ~** er ist ein Niemand.

**no-claims bonus** ['nəʊ,kleɪmz'bəʊnəs] *n (Insur)* Schadenfreiheitsrabatt *m*.

**nocturnal** [nɒk'tɜːnl] *adj* nächtlich. **~ animal/bird** Nachttier *nt*/Nachtvogel *m*.

**nocturne** ['nɒktɜːn] *n (Mus)* Nokturne *f*.

**nod** [nɒd] **1** *n* Nicken *nt*. **to give sb a ~** jdm zunicken; **to answer with a ~** *(zustimmend)* nicken. **2** *vi* nicken. **to ~ to sb** jdm zunicken; **to ~ in agreement** zustimmend nicken. **3** *vt* **to ~ one's head** mit dem Kopf nicken.

▶**nod off** *vi* einnicken *(col)*.

**node** [nəʊd] *n (all senses)* Knoten *m*.

**no-go area** ['nəʊ'gəʊ,eərɪə] *n* Sperrgebiet *nt*.

**no-good** *adj (col)* nichtsnutzig.

**noise** [nɔɪz] *n* Geräusch *nt*; *(loud, irritating sound)* Lärm, Krach *m*; *(Elec: interference)* Rauschen *nt*. **what was that ~?** was war das für ein Geräusch?; **the ~ of the traffic/bells** der Straßenlärm/der Lärm der Glocken; **it made a lot of ~** es hat viel Krach gemacht; **don't make a ~!** sei leise!; **stop that ~** hör mit dem Lärm auf; **she made ~s about leaving early** *(col)* sie gab zu verstehen, daß sie früh gehen wollte; **a big ~** *(fig col)* ein großes Tier *(col)*.

**noise abatement** *n* Lärmbekämpfung *f*.

**noiseless** ['nɔɪzlɪs] *adj* geräuschlos; *step also* lautlos.

**noise:** **~ level** *n* Geräuschpegel *m*; **~ pollution** *n* Lärmbelästigung *f*; **~ reduction** *n (in recordings)* Rauschunterdrückung *f*.

**noisily** ['nɔɪzɪlɪ] *adv see adj*.

**noisy** ['nɔɪzɪ] *adj (+er)* laut; *protest, debate* lautstark. **don't be so ~** sei nicht so laut, mach nicht so viel Lärm.

**nomad** ['nəʊmæd] *n* Nomade *m*, Nomadin *f*.

**nomadic** [nəʊ'mædɪk] *adj* nomadisch; *tribe* Nomaden-.

**no-man's-land** ['nəʊmænzlænd] *n (lit, fig)* Niemandsland *nt*.

**nom de plume** ['nɒmdə'pluːm] *n* Pseudonym *nt*.

**nomenclature** [nəʊ'menklətʃə<sup>r</sup>] n Nomenklatur f.
**nominal** ['nɒmɪnl] adj nominell.
**nominate** ['nɒmɪneɪt] vt (appoint) ernennen; (propose) nominieren, (als Kandidat) aufstellen. **he was ~d chairman** er wurde zum Vorsitzenden ernannt.
**nomination** [,nɒmɪ'neɪʃən] n (appointment) Ernennung f; (proposal) Nominierung f.
**nominative** [,nɒmmətɪv] (Gram) **1** n Nominativ m. **2** adj **(the)** ~ **case** der Nominativ.
**nominee** [,nɒmɪ'niː] n Kandidat(in f) m.
**non-** [nɒn-] in cpds Nicht-, nicht-. ~**-aggression** n Nichtangriff m; ~**-aggression pact** or **treaty** n Nichtangriffspakt m; ~ **alcoholic** adj alkoholfrei; ~**-aligned** adj blockfrei; ~**-believer** n Nichtgläubige(r) mf.
**nonce word** ['nɒnswɜːd] n Ad-hoc-Bildung f.
**nonchalance** ['nɒnʃələns] n Lässigkeit, Nonchalance f.
**nonchalant** ['nɒnʃələnt] adj lässig, nonchalant.
**non:** ~**-combatant 1** n Nichtkämpfer m; **2** adj nicht am Kampf beteiligt; ~**-commisssioned officer** n Unteroffizier m; ~**-committal** adj zurückhaltend; answer also unverbindlich; **to be** ~**-committal about whether ...** sich nicht festlegen, ob ...; ~**conformist 1** n Nonkonformist(in f) m; **2** adj nonkonformistisch; ~**-contributory pension scheme** n Rentenversicherung f ohne Eigenbeteiligung. ~**-co-operation** n unkooperative Haltung.
**nondescript** ['nɒndɪskrɪpt] adj taste, colour unbestimmbar; person, appearance unauffällig, unscheinbar (pej).
**none** [nʌn] **1** pron keine(r, s); keine; (on form) keine. ~ **of them is coming** von ihnen kommt keiner; ~ **of the boys/them** keiner der Jungen/von ihnen; ~ **of this** nichts davon; ~ **of this is any good** das ist alles nicht gut; **do you have any bread/apples? —** ~ **(at all)** haben Sie Brot/Äpfel? — nein, gar keines/keine; **there is** ~ **left** es ist nichts übrig; **their guest was** ~ **other than ...** ihr Gast war kein anderer als ...; **(we'll have)** ~ **of that!** jetzt reicht's aber!; **he would have** ~ **of it** er wollte davon nichts wissen.
**2** adv **to be** ~ **the wiser** auch nicht schlauer sein; **it's** ~ **too warm** es ist nicht zu warm; **he's** ~ **the worse for the experience** die Erfahrung hat ihm nichts geschadet; **and** ~ **too soon either** und auch keineswegs zu früh.
**nonentity** [nɒ'nentɪtɪ] n unbedeutende Figur.
**non-essential** [nɒnɪ'senʃəl] **1** adj unnötig; workers nicht unbedingt nötig; services nicht lebenswichtig. **2** n ~**s** pl nicht (lebens)notwendige Dinge pl.
**nonetheless** [,nʌnðə'les] adv nichtsdestoweniger, trotzdem.
**non:** ~**-event** n (col) Reinfall m (col), Pleite f (col); ~**-executive director** n Aufsichtsratsmitglied nt ohne Entscheidungsbefugnis; ~**-existence** n Nichtvorhandensein nt; ~**-existent** adj nicht vorhanden; **his accent is practically** ~**-existent** er hat praktisch keinen Akzent; ~**-fattening** adj nicht dickmachend attr; ~**-fiction** n Sachbücher pl; ~**-flammable** adj nichtentzündbar attr, nicht entzündbar; ~**-intervention** n (Pol etc) Nichteinmischung f (in in +acc); ~**-iron** adj bügelfrei; ~**-member** n Nichtmitglied nt; **open to** ~**-members** Gäste willkommen; ~**-nuclear** adj weapons konventionell; ~**-payment** n Nichtzahlung f.
**nonplus** ['nɒn'plʌs] vt verblüffen.
**non:** ~**-productive** adj meeting, discussion etc unergiebig; ~**-productive industries** Dienstleistungssektor m; ~**-profit** (US), ~**-profit-making** adj keinen Gewinn anstrebend attr; charity etc also gemeinnüt-

zig; ~**-proliferation** n Nichtverbreitung f; ~**-reflecting** adj spiegelfrei; ~**-resident 1** adj nicht ansässig; (in hotel) nicht im Hause wohnend; **2** n Nicht(orts)ansässige(r) mf; (in hotel) nicht im Haus wohnender Gast; **open to** ~**-residents** auch für Nichthotelgäste; ~**-returnable** adj bottle Einweg-.
**nonsense** ['nɒnsəns] n no pl (also as interjection) Unsinn, Quatsch (col) m; (verbal also) dummes Zeug; (silly behaviour) Dummheiten pl. **a piece of** ~ ein Unsinn or Quatsch (col) m; **that's a lot of** ~! das ist (ja) alles dummes Zeug!; **I've had enough of this** ~ jetzt reicht's mir aber; **to make (a)** ~ **of sth** etw unsinnig or sinnlos machen; **no more of your** ~! Schluß mit dem Unsinn!; **he will stand no** ~ **from anybody** er läßt nicht mit sich spaßen.
**nonsensical** [nɒn'sensɪkəl] adj unsinnig.
**non:** ~**-shrink** adj nicht einlaufend; ~**-skid** adj rutschsicher; ~**-slip** adj rutschfest; ~**-smoker** n **(a)** (person) Nichtraucher(in f) m; **(b)** (Rail) Nichtraucher(abteil nt) m; ~**-smoking** adj area Nichtraucher-; ~**-standard** adj part nicht serienmäßig; ~**-standard size** Sondergröße f; ~**-starter** n (in race) Nichtstartende(r) mf; (fig: person, idea) Blindgänger m; ~**-stick** adj pan, surface kunststoffbeschichtet, Teflon- ®; ~**-stop 1** adj train durchgehend; journey ohne Unterbrechung; flight, performances Nonstop-; **2** adv talk ununterbrochen; fly nonstop; travel ohne Unterbrechung; ~**-taxable** adj nichtsteuerpflichtig; ~**-U** adj (Brit) nicht vornehm; ~**-violent** adj gewaltlos; ~**-volatile** adj (Comp) memory nichtflüchtig; ~**-voting shares** npl stimmrechtslose Aktien pl; ~**-white 1** n Farbige(r) mf; **2** adj farbig; area für Farbige.
**noodle** ['nuːdl] n (Cook) Nudel f.
**nook** [nʊk] n Winkel m. **in every** ~ **and cranny** in jedem Winkel.
**noon** [nuːn] n Mittag m. **at** ~ um 12 Uhr mittags.
**no one** ['nəʊwʌn] pron = nobody 1.
**noose** [nuːs] n Schlinge f. **to put one's head in the** ~ (fig) den Kopf in die Schlinge stecken.
**nor** [nɔː<sup>r</sup>] conj **(a)** noch. **neither ...** ~ **weder ... noch.** **(b)** (and not) und ... auch nicht. **I don't like him —** ~ **do I** ich mag ihn nicht — ich auch nicht.
**norm** ['nɔːm] n Norm f.
**normal** ['nɔːməl] **1** adj person, situation normal; practice, routine also, (customary) üblich. **it's a perfectly** ~ **thing** das ist völlig normal; **he is not his** ~ **self today** er ist heute so anders. **2** n no pl (of temperature) Normalwert. **temperatures below** ~ Temperaturen unter dem Durchschnitt; **her temperature is above/below** ~ sie hat erhöhte Temperatur/sie hat Untertemperatur; **when things are back to** ~ wenn sich alles wieder normalisiert hat.
**normality** [nɔː'mælɪtɪ] n Normalität f. **to return to** ~ sich wieder normalisieren.
**normalize** ['nɔːməlaɪz] vt normalisieren; relations wiederherstellen.
**normally** ['nɔːməlɪ] adv (usually) normalerweise, gewöhnlich; (in normal way) normal.
**Norman** ['nɔːmən] **1** adj normannisch. **2** n Normanne m, Normannin f.
**Normandy** ['nɔːməndɪ] n Normandie f.
**north** [nɔːθ] **1** n Norden m. **in/from the** ~ im/aus dem Norden; **to live in the** ~ im Norden leben; **to the** ~ **of** nördlich von, im Norden von; **to veer/go to the** ~ in nördliche Richtung or nach Norden drehen/gehen; **to face (the)** ~ nach Norden liegen; **the N~ (of Scotland/England)** Nordschottland/Nordengland nt. **2** adj attr Nord-. **3** adv (towards N~) nach Norden. ~ **of** nördlich or im Norden von.

**north** *in cpds* Nord-; **N~ Africa** *n* Nordafrika *nt*; **N~ African 1** *adj* nordafrikanisch. **2** *n* Nordafrikaner(in *f*) *m*. **N~ America** *n* Nordamerika *nt*; **N~ American 1** *adj* nordamerikanisch; **2** *n* Nordamerikaner(in *f*) *m*.

**Northants** [nɔː'θænts] = **Northamptonshire.**

**north: N~ Atlantic Treaty** *n* Nordatlantikpakt *m*; **~bound** *adj carriageway* nach Norden (führend); *traffic* in Richtung Norden; **~-east 1** *adj* Nordost-, nordöstlich; **2** *adv* nach Nordosten; **~-east of** nordöstlich von; **~-easterly** *adj* nordöstlich; **~-eastern** *adj* nordöstlich.

**northerly** ['nɔːðəlɪ] *adj wind, direction, latitude* nördlich.

**northern** ['nɔːðən] *adj hemisphere, counties* nördlich; *Germany, Italy etc* Nord-. **N~ Ireland** Nordirland *nt*; **the ~ states** *(US Hist)* die Nordstaaten; **with a ~ outlook** mit Blick nach Norden.

**northerner** ['nɔːðənəʳ] *n* **(a)** Bewohner(in *f*) *m* des Nordens; *(from north of England/Germany)* Nordengländer(in *f*) *m*/-deutsche(r) *mf*. **he is a ~** er kommt aus dem Norden des Landes. **(b)** *(US)* Nordstaatler(in *f*) *m*.

**northernmost** ['nɔːðənməust] *adj* nördlichste(r, s).

**north: N~ German** *adj* norddeutsch; **N~ Korea** *n* Nordkorea *nt*; **N~ Pole** *n* Nordpol *m*; **N~ Sea 1** *n* Nordsee *f*; **2** *adj* Nordsee-; **N~ Sea gas/oil** Nordseegas *nt*/-öl *nt*; **~-south divide** *n* Nord-Süd-Gefälle *nt*; **~ward, ~wardly** *adj* nördlich; **~-west 1** *adj* Nordwest-, nordwestlich; **2** *adv* nach Nordwest(en); **~-west of** nordwestlich von; **~-westerly 1** *adj* nordwestlich; **2** *n* Nordwestwind *m*; **~western** *adj* nordwestlich.

**Norway** ['nɔːweɪ] *n* Norwegen *nt*.

**Norwegian** [nɔː'wiːdʒən] **1** *adj* norwegisch. **2** *n* **(a)** Norweger(in *f*) *m*. **(b)** *(language)* Norwegisch *nt*.

**nose** [nəuz] **1** *n* **(a)** Nase *f*; *(fig also)* Riecher *m (col)*. **to speak through one's ~** durch die Nase sprechen; **my ~ is bleeding** ich habe Nasenbluten; **follow your ~** immer der Nase nach; **to do sth under sb's very ~** etw vor jds Augen tun; **it was right under his ~ all the time** er hatte es die ganze Zeit direkt vor der Nase; **to lead sb by the ~** jdn an der Nase herumführen; **to poke** *or* **stick one's ~ into sth** *(fig)* seine Nase in etw *(acc)* stecken; **you keep your ~ out of this** *(col)* halt du dich da raus! *(col)*; **to look down one's ~ at sb/sth** auf jdn/etw herabsehen; **to pay through the ~** *(col)* sich dumm und dämlich zahlen *(col)*; **to have a ~ for sth** *(fig)* eine Nase *or* einen Riecher *(col)* für etw haben.

**(b)** *(of plane)* Nase *f*; *(of car)* Schnauze *f*; *(of boat also)* Bug *m*. **~ to tail** *(cars)* Stoßstange an Stoßstange.

**2** *vti* **the ship ~d (its way) through the fog** das Schiff tastete sich durch den Nebel.

▶**nose about** *or* **around** *vi* herumschnüffeln *(col)*; *(person also)* herumspionieren *(col)*.

▶**nose out** *vt sep* aufspüren; *secret, scandal* ausspionieren *(col)*, ausschnüffeln *(col)*.

**nose: ~bag** *n* Futtersack *m*; **~bleed** *n* Nasenbluten *nt*; **to have a ~bleed** Nasenbluten haben; **~dive 1** *n (Aviat)* Sturzflug *m*; **to go into a ~dive** zum Sturzflug ansetzen; **the company's affairs took a ~dive** mit der Firma ging es rapide bergab; **2** *vi (plane)* im Sturzflug herabgehen; **~ drops** *npl* Nasentropfen *pl*.

**nosey** *adj* = **nosy.**

**nosh** [nɒʃ] *n (Brit col) (food)* Futter *nt (col)*; *(meal)* Schmaus *m*.

**nosh-up** ['nɒʃʌp] *n (Brit col)* Schmaus *m*, Freßgelage *nt (col)*.

**nostalgia** [nɒ'stældʒɪə] *n* Nostalgie *f (for* nach*)*.

**nostalgic** [nɒ'stældʒɪk] *adj* nostalgisch, wehmütig.

**nostril** ['nɒstrəl] *n* Nasenloch *nt*; *(of horse etc)* Nüster *f*.

**nosy** ['nəuzɪ] *adj (+er) (col)* neugierig.

**not** [nɒt] *adv* **(a)** nicht. **he told me ~ to come** er sagte, ich solle nicht kommen; **do ~** *or* **don't come** kommen Sie nicht; **~ a sound/word** *etc* kein einziger Ton/einziges Wort *etc*; **~ a bit** kein bißchen; **~ a sign of ...** keine Spur von ...; **~ one of them** kein einziger, nicht einer; **~ a thing** überhaupt nichts; **~ any more** nicht mehr; **~ yet** noch nicht.

**(b)** *(in rhetorical questions)* **it's hot, isn't it?** es ist heiß, nicht wahr *or* nicht?; **isn't it hot?** ist das vielleicht heiß!; **you are coming, aren't you** *or* **are you ~?** Sie kommen doch, oder?; **you are ~ angry — or are you?** Sie sind doch nicht etwa böse?

**(c) is he coming? — I hope/I believe ~** kommt er? — ich hoffe/glaube nicht; **it would appear ~** anscheinend nicht; **he's decided not to do it — I should think/hope ~** er hat sich entschlossen, es nicht zu tun — das möchte ich auch meinen/hoffen; **are you cold? — ~ at all** ist dir kalt? — überhaupt nicht; **thank you very much — ~ at all** vielen Dank — keine Ursache; **~ in the least** überhaupt *or* gar nicht; **~ that I know of** nicht, daß ich wüßte.

**notable** ['nəutəbl] *adj person* bedeutend; *success, event also* bemerkenswert, denkwürdig; *difference, improvement* beträchtlich, beachtlich.

**notably** ['nəutəblɪ] *adv* **(a)** *(strikingly)* auffallend; *improved, different* beträchtlich. **(b)** *(in particular)* hauptsächlich, vor allem.

**notary (public)** ['nəutərɪ('pʌblɪk)] *n* Notar(in *f*) *m*.

**notation** [nəu'teɪʃən] *n (system)* Zeichensystem *nt*; *(symbols)* Zeichen *pl*; *(Mus)* Notenschrift *f*.

**notch** [nɒtʃ] **1** *n* Kerbe *f*; *(of handbrake etc)* Raste *f*; *(in belt)* Loch *nt*; *(on damaged blade etc)* Scharte *f*. **2** *vt* einkerben, einschneiden.

▶**notch up** *vt sep points* erzielen, einheimsen *(col)*; *record* verzeichnen; *success* verzeichnen können.

**notchback** ['nɒtʃbæk] *n (Aut)* Stufenheck *nt*.

**note** [nəut] **1** *n* **(a)** Notiz *f*; *(foot~)* Anmerkung, Fußnote *f*; *(informal letter)* Briefchen *nt*, paar Zeilen *pl*. **~s** *(summary)* Aufzeichnungen *pl*; *(plan, draft)* Konzept *nt*; **lecture ~s** *(professor's)* Manuskript *nt*; *(student's)* Aufzeichnungen *pl*; **to speak without ~s** ohne Vorlage sprechen; **to take ~s** Notizen machen; *(in lecture also, in interrogation)* mitschreiben; **to take** *or* **make a ~ of sth** sich *(dat)* etw notieren; **to compare ~s** *(fig)* Eindrücke *or* Erfahrungen austauschen.

**(b)** *no pl (notice)* **to take ~ of sth** von etw Notiz nehmen; *(heed)* einer Sache *(dat)* Beachtung schenken; **worthy of ~** beachtenswert, erwähnenswert.

**(c)** *no pl (importance)* **a man of ~** ein bedeutender Mann; **nothing of ~** nichts Erwähnenswertes.

**(d)** *(Mus) (sign)* Note *f*; *(sound, on piano etc)* Ton *m*. **to play the right/wrong ~** richtig/falsch spielen; **to strike the right ~** *(fig)* den richtigen Ton treffen.

**(e)** *(quality, tone)* Ton, Klang *m*. **a ~ of nostalgia** eine nostalgische Note; **there was a ~ of warning in his voice** seine Stimme hatte einen warnenden Unterton.

**(f)** *(Brit Fin)* Note *f*, Schein *m*. **a £5 ~**, **a five-pound ~** ein Fünfpfundschein *m*.

**2** *vt* bemerken; *(take note of)* zur Kenntnis nehmen; *(pay attention to)* beachten.

**note: ~book** *n* Notizbuch *or* -heft *nt*; **~case** *n (Brit)* Brieftasche *f*.

**noted** ['nəutɪd] *adj* bekannt *(for* für, wegen*)*.

**note: ~pad** *n* Notizblock *m*; **~paper** *n* Briefpapier *nt.*

**noteworthy** ['nəʊtwɜːðɪ] *adj* beachtenswert, erwähnenswert.

**nothing** ['nʌθɪŋ] **1** *n, pron, adv* nichts. **to eat ~** nichts essen; **~ could be easier** nichts wäre einfacher; **it was reduced to ~** es blieb nichts davon übrig; **she is** *or* **means ~ to him** sie bedeutet ihm nichts; **that came to ~** da ist nichts draus geworden; **I can make ~ of it** das sagt mir nichts; **he thinks ~ of doing that** er findet nichts dabei(, das zu tun); **think ~ of it** denk dir nichts dabei; *(after thanks)* keine Ursache!; **to say ~ of** ... ganz zu schweigen von ...; **~ doing!** *(col)* da ist nichts drin! *(col)*; **for ~** *(free, in vain)* umsonst; **there's ~ (else) for it but to leave** da bleibt einem nichts (anderes) übrig als zu gehen; **there's ~ in the rumour** das Gerücht ist aus der Luft gegriffen, an dem Gerücht ist nichts (Wahres); **there's ~ to it** *(col)* das ist kinderleicht *(col)*; **~ but** nur; **he does ~ but eat** er ißt nur *or* ständig; **~ else** sonst nichts; **~ more** sonst nichts; **I'd like ~ more than that** ich möchte nichts lieber als das; **~ much** nicht viel; **~ if not polite** überaus höflich; **~ new** nichts Neues; **it was ~ like as big** es war lange nicht so groß; **he has ~ on her** *(col)* er kann ihr nicht das Wasser reichen *(col)*; **in ~ flat** *(US col)* in Null Komma nichts *(col)*.

**2** *n* **(a)** *(Math)* Null *f.* **(b)** *(thing, person of no value)* Nichts *nt.* **it was a mere ~** das war doch nicht der Rede wert; **to whisper sweet ~s to sb** jdm Zärtlichkeiten ins Ohr flüstern.

**nothingness** ['nʌθɪŋnɪs] *n* Nichts *nt.*

**notice** ['nəʊtɪs] **1** *n* **(a)** *(warning, communication)* Bescheid *m*, Benachrichtigung *f*; *(written notification)* Mitteilung *f*; *(of forthcoming event, film etc)* Ankündigung *f.* **to give sb ~ of sth** jdm etw mitteilen; **without ~** ohne Ankündigung; *(of arrival also)* unangemeldet; **he didn't give us much ~, he gave us rather short ~** er hat uns nicht viel Zeit gelassen *or* gegeben; **at short ~** kurzfristig; **at a moment's ~** jederzeit, sofort; **at three days' ~** innerhalb von drei Tagen; **until further ~** bis auf weiteres.

**(b)** *(public announcement)* Bekanntmachung *f*; *(on ~-board etc)* Anschlag *m*; *(poster also)* Plakat *nt*; *(sign)* Schild *nt*; *(in newspaper)* Mitteilung *f*; *(short)* Notiz *f*; *(of wedding, vacancy etc)* Anzeige *f.* **the ~ says** ... da steht ...

**(c)** *(to end employment etc)* Kündigung *f.* **~ to quit** Kündigung *f*; **to give sb ~** jdm kündigen; **to give in one's ~** kündigen; **I am under ~ (to quit), I got my ~** mir ist gekündigt worden; **a month's ~** eine einmonatige Kündigungsfrist.

**(d)** *(review)* Kritik, Rezension *f.*

**(e)** *(attention)* **to take ~ of sth** von etw Notiz nehmen; *(heed)* etw beachten, einer Sache *(dat)* Beachtung schenken; **to take no ~ of sb/sth** von jdm/etw keine Notiz nehmen; **take no ~!** kümmern Sie sich nicht darum!; **that has escaped his ~** das hat er nicht bemerkt; **to bring sth to sb's ~** jdn auf etw *(acc)* aufmerksam machen; *(in letter)* jdn von etw in Kenntnis setzen; **it came to his ~ that** ... er hat erfahren, daß ...

**2** *vt* bemerken, *(perceive also)* wahrnehmen; *(recognize, acknowledge)* zur Kenntnis nehmen; *(difference)* feststellen; *(realize also)* merken. **without my noticing it** ohne daß ich etwas gemerkt *or* bemerkt habe; **he pretended not to ~** er tat so, als ob er es nicht bemerkt hätte; **did he wave? – I never ~d** hat er gewinkt? – ich habe es nicht gesehen.

**noticeable** ['nəʊtɪsəbl] *adj* erkennbar, wahrnehmbar; *(visible)* sichtbar; *(obvious, considerable)* deutlich; *(relief, pleasure etc)* sichtlich, merklich. **the**

**stain is very ~** der Fleck fällt ziemlich auf; **it is hardly ~** man merkt es kaum.

**notice-board** ['nəʊtɪsbɔːd] *n (Brit)* Anschlagbrett *nt*; *(in school etc also)* Schwarzes Brett.

**notification** [,nəʊtɪfɪ'keɪʃən] *n* Benachrichtigung, Mitteilung *f*; *(of loss, damage etc)* Meldung *f.* **to send written ~ of sth to sb** jdm etw schriftlich mitteilen.

**notify** ['nəʊtɪfaɪ] *vt person, candidate* benachrichtigen, unterrichten *(form)*; *change of address, loss etc* melden. **to ~ sb of sth** jdn von etw benachrichtigen; *authorities etc* jdm etw melden.

**notion** ['nəʊʃən] *n* **(a)** *(idea, thought)* Idee *f*; *(conception also)* Vorstellung *f*; *(vague knowledge also)* Ahnung *f*; *(opinion)* Meinung *f.* **I have no ~** *or* **not the slightest ~ of what he means** ich habe keine Ahnung *or* nicht die leiseste Ahnung, was er meint; **I have no ~ of time** ich habe überhaupt kein Zeitgefühl; **where did you get the ~ that I ...?** wie kommst du denn auf die Idee, daß ich ...?; **I have a ~ that ...** ich habe den Verdacht, daß .... **(b)** *(esp US col)* **~s** *pl* Kurzwaren *pl.*

**notoriety** [,nəʊtə'raɪətɪ] *n* traurige Berühmtheit.

**notorious** [nəʊ'tɔːrɪəs] *adj person, fact* berüchtigt; *place also* verrufen; *(well-known) criminal, liar* notorisch. **to be ~ for sth** für etw berüchtigt sein.

**notoriously** [nəʊ'tɔːrɪəslɪ] *adv* notorisch. **to be ~ violent** für seine Gewalttätigkeit berüchtigt sein.

**Notts** *(Brit)* = **Nottinghamshire.**

**notwithstanding** [,nɒtwɪθ'stændɪŋ] *(form)* **1** *prep* ungeachtet *(+gen) (form).* **2** *adv* nichtsdestotrotz *(form).* **3** *conj* **~ that** ... obgleich ...

**nougat** ['nuːgɑː] *n* Nougat *m.*

**nought** [nɔːt] *n* Null *f.* **~s and crosses** *(Brit)* Spiel, bei dem jeder Spieler drei Kreise bzw Kreuze in einer Reihe zu erzielen versucht.

**noun** [naʊn] *n* Substantiv (um), Hauptwort *nt.*

**nourish** ['nʌrɪʃ] *vt* nähren; *person* ernähren.

**nourishing** ['nʌrɪʃɪŋ] *adj* nahrhaft.

**nourishment** ['nʌrɪʃmənt] *n* Nahrung *f.*

**nouveau riche** [,nuːvəʊ'riːʃ] **1** *n, pl* **-x** **-s** [,nuːvəʊ'riːʃ] Neureiche(r) *mf.* **2** *adj* typisch neureich.

**Nov** = **November** Nov.

**Nova Scotia** ['nəʊvə'skəʊʃə] *n* Neuschottland *nt.*

**novel**[1] ['nɒvəl] *n* Roman *m.*

**novel**[2] *adj* neu(artig).

**novelist** ['nɒvəlɪst] *n* Romanschriftsteller(in *f*) *m.*

**novelty** ['nɒvəltɪ] *n* **(a)** *(newness)* Neuheit *f.* **(b)** *(innovation)* Neuheit *f*, Novum *nt.* **it was quite a ~** das war etwas ganz Neues. **(c)** *(Comm: trinket)* Krimskrams *m.*

**November** [nəʊ'vembər] *n* November *m*; *see* **September.**

**novice** ['nɒvɪs] *n (Eccl)* Novize *m*, Novizin *f*; *(fig)* Neuling, Anfänger(in *f*) *m (at* bei, *in* +*dat).*

**now** [naʊ] **1** *adv* **(a)** jetzt, nun; *(immediately)* sofort, gleich; *(at this very moment)* gerade, (so)eben; *(nowadays)* heute, heutzutage. **she ~ realized why** ... da erkannte sie, warum ...; **just ~** gerade; **~ is the time to do it** jetzt ist der richtige Moment dafür; **I'll do it right ~** ich mache es jetzt gleich *or* sofort; **it's ~ or never** jetzt oder nie; **by ~** inzwischen; **for ~** (jetzt) erst einmal, vorläufig; **even ~** selbst jetzt noch; **from ~ on(wards)** von nun an; **in three days from ~** (heute) in drei Tagen; **up to ~, till ~, until ~** bis jetzt; **that's all for ~** das wär's für heute. **(b)** **~ ... ~** bald ... bald; **(every) ~ and then, ~ and again** ab und zu, gelegentlich.

**2** *conj* **~ (that) you've seen him** jetzt, wo Sie ihn gesehen haben.

**3** *interj* also. ~, ~! na, na!; **well** ~ also; ~ **then** also (jetzt); **stop that** ~! Schluß jetzt!; ~, **why didn't I think of that?** warum habe ich bloß nicht daran gedacht?

**nowadays** ['nauədeiz] *adv* heute, heutzutage.

**noway** ['nou,wei], *(US also)* **noways** *adv see* **way 1(g)**.

**nowhere** ['nəuwɛəʳ] *adv* nirgends; *(with verbs of motion)* nirgendwohin. ~ **special** einfach irgendwo; *(with motion)* einfach irgendwohin; **to appear from** ~ ganz plötzlich auftauchen; **we're getting** ~ **(fast)** wir kommen nicht weiter; **rudeness will get you** ~ Grobheit bringt dir gar nichts ein.

**noxious** ['nɒkʃəs] *adj* schädlich; *habit* übel.

**nozzle** ['nɒzl] *n* Düse *f*.

**nr** = **near** bei, b.

**NSPCC** *(Brit)* = **National Society for the Prevention of Cruelty to Children** ≈ Kinderschutzbund *m*.

**NSW** = **New South Wales**.

**NT** = **New Testament** NT *nt*.

**nth** [enθ] *adj* **the** ~ **degree** die n-te Potenz; **for the** ~ **time** zum x-ten Mal *(col)*.

**nuance** ['njuːɑ̃ːns] *n* Nuance *f*.

**nubile** ['njuːbail] *adj* *(attractive) girl* gut entwickelt.

**nuclear** ['njuːkliəʳ] *adj* Kern-, Atom- *(esp Mil)*; *explosion, reaction, research* Kern-; *fuel, disarmament* nuklear, atomar; *attack, testing* Kernwaffen-, Atomwaffen-; *submarine, missile* atomgetrieben, Atom-.

**nuclear:** ~ **accident** *n* Reaktorunglück *nt*; ~ **deterrent** *n* nukleares Abschreckungsmittel; ~ **family** *n* Kleinfamilie *f*; ~ **fission** *n* Kernspaltung *f*; ~**-free zone** *n* atomwaffenfreie Zone; ~ **physics** *n* Kernphysik *f*; ~ **power** *n* Atomkraft, Kernenergie *f*; ~**-powered** *adj* atomgetrieben; ~ **power station** *n* Kern- *or* Atomkraftwerk *nt*; ~ **reactor** *n* Kern- *or* Atomreaktor *m*; ~ **war** *n* Atomkrieg *m*; ~ **waste** *n* Atommüll *m*; ~ **weapon** *n* Kern- *or* Atomwaffe *f*.

**nucleus** ['njuːkliəs] *n, pl* **nuclei** *(Phys, fig)* Kern *m*; *(Biol: of cell also)* Nukleus *m*.

**nude** [njuːd] **1** *adj* nackt; *(Art)* Akt-. ~ **figure/portrait** Akt *m*. **2** *n* *(person)* Nackte(r) *mf*; *(Art) (painting etc)* Akt *m*; *(model)* Aktmodell *nt*. **in the** ~ nackt.

**nudge** [nʌdʒ] **1** *vt* stupsen. **2** *n* **to give sb a** ~ jdm einen Stups geben.

**nudist** ['njuːdist] *n* Anhänger(in *f*) *m* der Freikörperkultur, FKK-Anhänger(in *f*) *m*. ~ **colony** FKK-Kolonie *f*.

**nudity** ['njuːditi] *n* Nacktheit *f*.

**nugget** ['nʌgit] *n* *(of gold etc)* Klumpen *m*.

**nuisance** ['njuːsns] *n* **(a)** *(person)* Plage *f*; *(esp pestering)* Nervensäge *f*; *(esp child)* Quälgeist *m*. **to make a** ~ **of oneself** lästig werden. **(b)** *(thing, event)* **to be a** ~ lästig sein; *(annoying)* ärgerlich sein; **what a** ~, **having to do it again** wie ärgerlich, das noch einmal machen zu müssen.

**NUJ** *(Brit)* = **National Union of Journalists** *Journalistengewerkschaft f*.

**nuke** [njuːk] *(col)* **1** *n* Atombombe *f*. **2** *vt* mit Atomwaffen angreifen; *(destroy)* atomar vernichten.

**null** [nʌl] *adj*: ~ **and void** *(Jur)* (null und) nichtig, ungültig.

**nullify** ['nʌlifai] *vt* annullieren, für (null und) nichtig erklären.

**NUM** *(Brit)* = **National Union of Mineworkers** *Bergarbeitergewerkschaft f*.

**numb** [nʌm] **1** *adj (+er)* taub, gefühllos; *(emotionally)* benommen, wie betäubt. **hands** ~ **with cold** Hände, die vor Kälte taub *or* gefühllos sind; ~ **with**

**grief** starr *or* wie betäubt vor Schmerz. **2** *vt (cold)* taub *or* gefühllos machen; *(injection, fig)* betäuben.

**number** ['nʌmbəʳ] **1** *n* **(a)** *(Math)* Zahl *f*; *(numeral)* Ziffer *f*; *(amount)* Anzahl *f*. **a** ~ **of applicants** eine Anzahl von Bewerbern; **large** ~**s of people/books** eine große Anzahl von Leuten/eine ganze Menge Bücher; **on a** ~ **of occasions** des öfteren; **in a small** ~ **of cases** in wenigen Fällen; **ten in** ~ zehn an der Zahl; **in small/large** ~**s** in kleinen/großen Mengen; **any** ~ **of cards** *etc (many)* sehr viele Karten *etc*.

**(b)** *(of house, phone)* Nummer *f*; *(of page)* Seitenzahl *f*; *(of car)* (Auto)nummer *f*. **N**~ **Ten (Downing Street)** Nummer Zehn (Downing Street); **to take a car's** ~ die Nummer eines Autos aufschreiben; **I dialled the wrong** ~ ich habe mich verwählt; **it was a wrong** ~ ich/er *etc* war falsch verbunden; **the** ~ **one pop star** *(col)* der Popstar Nummer Eins *(col)*; **to look after** ~ **one** *(col)* (vor allem) an sich *(acc)* selbst denken; **his** ~**'s up** *(col)* er ist dran *(col)*; **to do sth by** ~**s** *or (US)* **the** ~**s** etw nach Schema F erledigen *(esp pej)*.

**(c)** *(song, act etc)* Nummer *f*; *(issue of magazine etc also)* Ausgabe *f*, Heft *nt*; *(dress)* Kreation *f*.

**2** *vt* **(a)** *(give a number to)* numerieren; *(count)* zählen. **to be** ~**ed** *(limited)* begrenzt sein; **his days are** ~**ed** seine Tage sind gezählt. **(b)** *(include)* zählen *(among* zu**).** **we** ~ **them among our friends** wir zählen sie zu unseren Freunden. **(c)** *(amount to)* zählen. **the group** ~**ed 50** es waren 50 (Leute in der Gruppe).

**number:** ~**less** *adj* zahllos, unzählig; ~**-plate** *n (Brit)* Nummernschild *nt*.

**numbers game, numbers racket** *n illegale Lotterie, bei der Geldbeträge auf das Vorkommen bestimmter Zahlenfolgen (z.B. Aktienkurse) in einer Zeitung gesetzt werden.*

**numbness** ['nʌmnis] *n (of limbs etc)* Taubheit *f*; *(fig: of mind, senses)* Benommenheit *f*.

**numeracy** ['njuːmərəsi] *n* Rechnen *nt*. **his** ~ seine rechnerischen Fähigkeiten.

**numeral** ['njuːmərəl] *n* Ziffer *f*.

**numerate** ['njuːmərit] *adj* rechenkundig.

**numeric** [njuːˈmerik] *adj* ~ **keypad** *(Comp)* numerisches Tastenfeld.

**numerical** [njuːˈmerikəl] *adj symbols, equation* numerisch, Zahlen-; *value* Zahlen-; *superiority* zahlenmäßig. **in** ~ **order** nach Zahlen geordnet.

**numerically** [njuːˈmerikəli] *adv* zahlenmäßig.

**numerous** ['njuːmərəs] *adj* zahlreich; *family* kinderreich.

**nun** [nʌn] *n* Nonne *f*.

**NUPE** ['njuːpi] *(Brit)* **National Union of Public Employees** *Gewerkschaft f der Angestellten im öffentlichen Dienst.*

**nuptial** ['nʌpʃəl] *(liter, hum)* **1** *adj feast* Hochzeits-. ~ **bliss** das Eheglück; ~ **vow** Eheversprechen *nt*. **2** *n* ~**s** *pl* Hochzeit *f*.

**NUR** *(Brit)* = **National Union of Railwaymen** *Eisenbahnergewerkschaft f.*

**Nuremberg** ['njuərəm,bɜːg] *n* Nürnberg *nt*.

**nurse** [nɜːs] **1** *n* Schwester *f*; *(as professional title)* Krankenschwester *f*; *(nanny)* Kindermädchen *nt*. **male** ~ Krankenpfleger *m*. **2** *vt* **(a)** pflegen; *(fig) plan* hegen; *(treat carefully)* schonen. **to** ~ **sb back to health** jdn gesundpflegen; **he stood there nursing his bruised arm** er stand da und hielt behutsam seinen verletzten Arm. **(b)** *(suckle) child* stillen; *(cradle)* (in den Armen) wiegen.

**nursemaid** ['nɜːsmeid] *n (nanny, hum: servant)* Kindermädchen *nt*.

**nursery** ['nɜːsəri] *n* **(a)** *(room)* Kinderzimmer *nt*; *(in* *hospital)* Säuglingssaal *m.* **(b)** *(institution)* Kindergarten *m;* *(all-day)* Kindertagesstätte *f.* **(c)** *(Agr, Hort)* *(for plants)* Gärtnerei *f;* *(for trees)* Baumschule *f.*

**nursery:** ~ **rhyme** *n* Kinderreim *m;* ~ **school** *n* Kindergarten *m;* ~ **slope** *n (Brit)* Anfängerhügel *m.*

**nursing** ['nɜːsɪŋ] **1** *n* **(a)** *(care of invalids)* Pflege *f.* **(b)** *(profession)* Krankenpflege *f.* **she's going in for** ~ sie will in der Krankenpflege arbeiten. **2** *adj attr* **staff** Pflege-; *abilities* pflegerisch. **the** ~ **profession** die pflegerischen Berufe.

**nursing:** ~ **auxiliary** *n (Brit)* Schwesternhelferin *f;* ~ **bottle** *n (US)* Flasche *f;* ~ **home** *n* Privatklinik *f;* *(Brit: maternity hospital)* Entbindungsklinik *f;* *(convalescent home)* Pflegeheim *nt;* ~ **mother** *n* stillende Mutter; ~ **officer** *n* Oberschwester *f.*

**NUS** *(Brit)* = **National Union of Students** *Studentengewerkschaft f.*

**NUT** *(Brit)* = **National Union of Teachers** *Gewerkschaft f der Lehrer.*

**nut** [nʌt] *n* **(a)** *(Bot)* Nuß *f;* *(of coal)* kleines Stück. **a hard** ~ **to crack** *(fig)* eine harte Nuß. **(b)** *(col: head)* Nuß *(col)*, Birne *(col) f.* **use your** ~! streng deinen Grips an! *(col)*; **to do one's** ~ *(Brit col)* durchdrehen *(col)*. **(c)** *(col: person)* Spinner(in *f) m (col)*. **he's a tough** ~ *(col)* er ist ein harter Brocken *(col)*. **(d)** *(Mech)* (Schrauben)mutter *f.*

**nut:** ~**-case** *n (col)* Spinner(in *f) m (col)*; ~**cracker(s** *pl) n* Nußknacker *m;* ~**-house** *n (col) (lit, fig)* Irrenhaus *nt (col)*; ~**meg** *n* Muskat(-nuß *f) m.*

**nutrient** ['njuːtrɪənt] **1** *adj substance* nahrhaft; *properties* Nähr-. **2** *n* Nährstoff *m.*

**nutrition** [njuːˈtrɪʃən] *n (diet, science)* Ernährung *f.*

**nutritious** [njuːˈtrɪʃəs] *adj* nahrhaft.

**nuts** [nʌts] *adj pred (col)* **to be** ~ spinnen *(col)*; **to go** ~ durchdrehen *(col)*; **to be** ~ **about sb/sth** *(keen on)* ganz verrückt nach jdm/auf etw *(acc)* sein *(col)*.

**nutshell** ['nʌtˌʃel] *n* Nußschale *f.* **in a** ~ *(fig)* kurz gesagt.

**nutty** ['nʌtɪ] *adj (+er)* **(a)** *flavour* Nuß-. **(b)** *(col: crazy)* bekloppt *(col)*.

**nuzzle** ['nʌzl] *vi* ~ **(up) against sb, to** ~ **up to sb** sich an jdn schmiegen *or* drücken.

**NV** *(US Post)* = **Nevada.**

**NW** = **north-west** NW.

**NY** *(US Post)* = **New York.**

**NYC** *(US Post)* = **New York City.**

**nylon** ['naɪlɒn] **1** *n* **(a)** *(Tex)* Nylon *nt.* **(b)** ~**s** *pl* Nylonstrümpfe *pl.* **2** *adj* Nylon-.

**nymph** [nɪmf] *n (Myth)* Nymphe *f.*

**nymphomaniac** [ˌnɪmfəʊˈmeɪnɪæk] *n* Nymphomanin *f.*

**NZ** = **New Zealand.**

# O

**O, o** [əʊ] *n* (a) O, o *nt.* (b) [*(Brit)* əʊ, *(US)* 'zɪərəʊ] *(Telec)* Null *f.* **O for Oliver** *(Brit)*, **O for Oboe** *(US)* ≈ O wie Otto.

**oaf** [əʊf] *n, pl* **-s** *or* **oaves** *(fool)* Blödmann *m (col)*; *(lout)* Flegel, Lümmel *m.*

**oafish** ['əʊfɪʃ] *adj* blöd; *(loutish)* flegelhaft, lümmelhaft.

**oak** [əʊk] *n* Eiche *f; (wood also)* Eichenholz *nt.*

**oak** *in cpds* Eichen-; **~ apple** *n* Gallapfel *m.*

**OAP** *(Brit)* = **old-age pensioner.**

**oar** [ɔːʳ] *n* Ruder *nt,* Riemen *(Rowing) m.* **to put** *or* **stick one's ~ in** *(col)* sich einmischen.

**oarsman** ['ɔːzmən] *n* Ruderer *m.*

**OAS** = **Organization of American States** OAS *f.*

**oasis** [əʊ'eɪsɪs] *n, pl* **oases** [əʊ'eɪsiːz] *(lit, fig)* Oase *f.*

**oast-house** ['əʊsthaʊs] *n als Hopfendarre dienendes Gebäude.*

**oat** [əʊt] *n usu pl* Hafer *m.* **~s** *pl (Cook)* Haferflocken *pl;* **to sow one's wild ~s** *(fig)* sich *(dat)* die Hörner abstoßen.

**oath** [əʊθ] *n* (a) Schwur *m; (Jur)* Eid *m.* **to take** *or* **swear an ~** schwören; *(Jur)* einen Eid ablegen *or* leisten; **to be under ~** *(Jur)* unter Eid stehen; **to put sb on ~** *(Jur)* jdn vereidigen; **to take the ~** *(Jur)* vereidigt werden. (b) *(curse, profanity)* Fluch *m.*

**oatmeal** ['əʊtmiːl] *n no pl* Haferschrot *m.*

**OAU** = **Organization of African Unity** OAU *f.*

**obdurate** ['ɒbdjʊrɪt] *adj (stubborn)* hartnäckig; *sinner* verstockt; *(hardhearted)* unerbittlich.

**OBE** *(Brit)* = **Officer of the Order of the British Empire** *britischer Verdienstorden.*

**obedience** [ə'biːdɪəns] *n no pl* Gehorsam *m.* **in ~ to the law** dem Gesetz entsprechend.

**obedient** [ə'biːdɪənt] *adj* gehorsam; *child, dog also* folgsam. **to be ~** gehorchen *(to dat).*

**obelisk** ['ɒbɪlɪsk] *n (Archit)* Obelisk *m.*

**obese** [əʊ'biːs] *adj* fettleibig *(form, Med).*

**obesity** [əʊ'biːsɪtɪ] *n* Fettleibigkeit *f (form, Med).*

**obey** [ə'beɪ] **1** *vt* gehorchen (+*dat); law, rules, order* befolgen; *(machine)* reagieren auf (+*acc).* **2** *vi* gehorchen; *(child, dog also)* folgen.

**obituary** [ə'bɪtjʊərɪ] *n* Nachruf *m.* **~ notice** Todesanzeige *f;* **~ column** Sterberegister *nt.*

**object¹** ['ɒbdʒɪkt] *n* (a) *(thing)* Gegenstand *m; (abstract etc)* Objekt, Ding *nt.* **he was an ~ of scorn** er war die Zielscheibe der Verachtung. (b) *(aim)* Ziel *nt,* Absicht *f.* **with this ~ in mind** mit diesem Ziel vor Augen; **with the sole ~ (of doing)** mit dem einzigen Ziel(, zu ...); **what's the ~ (of staying here)?** wozu (bleiben wir hier)?; **that defeats the ~** das verfehlt seinen Sinn *or* Zweck. (c) **money/distance (is) no ~** Geld/Entfernung spielt keine Rolle. (d) *(Gram)* Objekt *nt.*

**object²** [əb'dʒekt] **1** *vi* dagegen sein; *(protest)* protestieren; *(be against: in discussion etc)* Einwände haben *(to gegen); (raise objection)* Einwände erheben; *(disapprove)* etwas dagegen haben. **to ~ to sth** *(disapprove)* etw mißbilligen; **if you don't ~** wenn Sie nichts dagegen haben; **do you ~ to my smoking?** stört es (Sie), wenn ich rauche?; **I ~ to your tone/to people smoking in my living room** ich verbitte mir diesen Ton/ich verbitte mir, daß in meinem Wohnzimmer geraucht wird. **2** *vt* einwenden.

**objection** [əb'dʒɒkʃən] *n (reason against)* Einwand *m (to gegen); (dislike)* Abneigung *f; (disapproval)* Einspruch, Widerspruch *m.* **to make** *or* **raise an ~** einen Einwand erheben; **I have no ~ to his going away** ich habe nichts dagegen (einzuwenden), daß er weggeht; **are there any ~s?** irgendwelche Einwände?; **I see no ~ to it** ich sehe nichts, was dagegen spricht; **I have no ~ to him** *(as a person)* ich habe nichts gegen ihn.

**objectionable** [əb'dʒekʃənəbl] *adj* störend; *conduct, remark, language* anstößig; *smell* übel. **he's a most ~ person** er ist unausstehlich.

**objective** [əb'dʒektɪv] **1** *adj* objektiv. **2** *n (aim)* Ziel *nt; (esp Comm)* Zielvorstellung *f; (Mil)* Angriffsziel *nt.*

**objectively** [əb'dʒektɪvlɪ] *adv* objektiv.

**objectivity** [ˌɒbdʒek'tɪvɪtɪ] *n* Objektivität *f.*

**object lesson** *n (fig)* Paradebeispiel *nt (in, on für, gen).*

**objector** [əb'dʒektəʳ] *n* Gegner(in *f) m (to gen).*

**obligation** [ˌɒblɪ'geɪʃən] *n* Verpflichtung, Pflicht *f.* **to be under an ~ to do sth** die Pflicht haben, etw zu tun; **without ~** *(Comm)* unverbindlich.

**obligatory** [ɒ'blɪgətərɪ] *adj* obligatorisch. **biology is ~** Biologie ist Pflicht; **to make it ~ for sb to do sth** vorschreiben, daß jd etw tut.

**oblige** [ə'blaɪdʒ] *vt* (a) *(compel)* zwingen; *(because of duty)* verpflichten *(sb to do sth* jdn, etw zu tun*).* **to feel ~d to do sth** sich verpflichtet fühlen, etw zu tun; **I was ~d to go** ich sah mich gezwungen zu gehen; **you are not ~d to do it** Sie sind nicht dazu verpflichtet. (b) *(do a favour to)* einen Gefallen tun (+*dat).* **could you ~ me with a light?** wären Sie so gut, mir Feuer zu geben?; **anything to ~** stets zu Diensten; **much ~d!** herzlichen Dank!; **I am much ~d to you for this** ich bin Ihnen dafür sehr verbunden *(form).*

**obliging** [ə'blaɪdʒɪŋ] *adj* entgegenkommend, gefällig; *personality* zuvorkommend.

**obligingly** [ə'blaɪdʒɪŋlɪ] *adv* entgegenkommenderweise, freundlicherweise.

**oblique** [ə'bliːk] **1** *adj line, look* schief, schräg; *angle* schief; *style, reply, hint, reference* indirekt. **2** *n* Schrägstrich *m.*

**obliquely** [ə'bliːklɪ] *adv* schräg; *(fig)* indirekt.

**obliterate** [ə'blɪtəreɪt] *vt (erase)* auslöschen; *city also* vernichten; *(hide) sun, view* verdecken.

**oblivion** [ə'blɪvɪən] *n* Vergessenheit *f.* **to sink** *or* **fall into ~** in Vergessenheit geraten.

**oblivious** [ə'blɪvɪəs] *adj* **to be ~ of sth** sich *(dat)* einer Sache *(gen)* nicht bewußt sein; **he was quite ~ of his surroundings** er nahm seine Umgebung gar nicht wahr.

**occupation**

**oblong** ['ɒblɒŋ] **1** *adj* rechteckig. **2** *n* Rechteck *nt.*
**obnoxious** [ɒb'nɒkʃəs] *adj* widerlich, widerwärtig; *person also, behaviour* unausstehlich. **an ~ person** ein Ekel *nt (col).*
**o.b.o.** *(US)* = **or best offer** oder Angebot.
**oboe** ['əʊbəʊ] *n* Oboe *f.*
**oboist** ['əʊbəʊɪst] *n* Oboist(in *f*) *m.*
**obscene** [əb'si:n] *adj* obszön; *(non-sexually, repulsive)* ekelerregend, widerlich; *prices, demands* unverschämt.
**obscenity** [əb'senɪtɪ] *n* Obszönität *f*; *(remark also)* ordinärer Ausdruck. **the ~ of these crimes** diese ekelerregenden Verbrechen.
**obscure** [əb'skjʊər] **1** *adj (+er)* **(a)** *style* unklar; *argument* verworren; *book* schwer verständlich. **(b)** *(indistinct) feeling, memory* dunkel. **for some ~ reason** aus einem unerfindlichen Grund. **(c)** *(little known) poet, village* unbekannt; *beginnings (humble)* unbedeutend; *life* wenig beachtenswert. **2** *vt* **(a)** *(hide) sun, view* verdecken. **(b)** *(confuse) issue, argument* unklar machen.
**obscurity** [əb'skjʊərɪtɪ] *n (of night, origins)* Dunkel *nt*; *(of style, argument)* Unklarheit *f.* **to live in ~** zurückgezogen leben; **to sink into ~** in Vergessenheit geraten.
**obsequious** [əb'si:kwɪəs] *adj* unterwürfig *(to, towards* gegen, gegenüber*).*
**observance** [əb'zɜ:vəns] *n* **(a)** *(of law)* Befolgung, Beachtung *f.* **(b)** *(Eccl)* Einhaltung *f.*
**observant** [əb'zɜ:vənt] *adj* aufmerksam, wachsam. **that's very ~ of you** das hast du aber gut bemerkt.
**observation** [ˌɒbzə'veɪʃən] *n* **(a)** Beobachtung *f*; *(act also)* Beobachten *nt.* **to keep sb/sth under ~** *(by police)* jdn/etw überwachen; **powers of ~** Beobachtungsgabe *f*; **he's in hospital for ~** er ist zur Beobachtung im Krankenhaus; **~ car** *(US Rail)* Panoramawagen *m*; **~ post** Beobachtungsposten *m.* **(b)** *(remark)* Bemerkung *f.*
**observatory** [əb'zɜ:vətrɪ] *n* Sternwarte *f*; *(Met)* Wetterwarte *f.*
**observe** [əb'zɜ:v] *vt* **(a)** *(watch, notice)* beobachten; *difference also* wahrnehmen; *(by police)* überwachen. **(b)** *(obey)* achten auf *(+acc)*; *rule, custom, ceasefire* einhalten.
**observer** [əb'zɜ:vər] *n (watcher)* Zuschauer(in *f*) *m*; *(Mil, Pol)* Beobachter(in *f*) *m.*
**obsess** [əb'ses] *vt* **to be ~ed by** *or* **with sb/sth** von jdn/etw besessen sein.
**obsession** [əb'seʃən] *n (fixed idea)* fixe Idee, Manie *f*; *(fear etc)* Zwangsvorstellung *f*; *(state)* Besessenheit *f (with* von*).* **it's an ~ with him** *(hobby etc)* er ist davon besessen; **this ~ with order** dieser Ordnungswahn; **because of his ~ with her** weil er ihr gänzlich verfallen ist/war.
**obsessive** [əb'sesɪv] *adj* zwanghaft. **to become ~** *(activity)* zum Zwang *or* zur Manie werden; **he is an ~ reader** er liest wie besessen.
**obsolescence** [ˌɒbsə'lesns] *n* Veralten *nt.*
**obsolescent** [ˌɒbsə'lesnt] *adj* veraltend. **to be ~** anfangen zu veralten.
**obsolete** ['ɒbsəli:t] *adj* veraltet, überholt. **to become ~** veralten.
**obstacle** ['ɒbstəkl] *n (lit, fig)* Hindernis *nt.* **~ course** Hindernisstrecke *f*; **~ race** Hindernisrennen *nt*; **to be an ~ to sb/sth** jdm/einer Sache im Weg(e) stehen; **to put an ~ in sb's way** jdm ein Hindernis in den Weg stellen; **all the ~s to peace** alles, was dem Frieden im Weg steht.
**obstetrician** [ˌɒbstə'trɪʃən] *n* Geburtshelfer(in *f*) *m.*
**obstetrics** [ɒb'stetrɪks] *n sing* Geburtshilfe *f.*
**obstinacy** ['ɒbstɪnəsɪ] *n* Hartnäckigkeit *f*, Starr-

sinn *m (pej).*
**obstinate** ['ɒbstɪnɪt] *adj* hartnäckig, starrsinnig *(pej)*; *nail etc* widerspenstig. **to remain ~** stur bleiben.
**obstreperous** [əb'strepərəs] *adj* aufmüpfig *(col)*; *child* aufsässig.
**obstruct** [əb'strʌkt] *vt* **(a)** *(block)* blockieren; *road also, view* versperren; *(Med) artery, pipe also* verstopfen. **you're ~ing my view** Sie versperren mir die Sicht. **(b)** *(hinder)* (be)hindern; *traffic, progress also* aufhalten; *(Sport)* behindern.
**obstruction** [əb'strʌkʃən] *n see vt* **(a)** Blockierung *f*; *(of view)* Versperren *nt*; Verstopfung *f.* **(b)** Behinderung *f.* **to cause an ~** *(to traffic)* den Verkehr behindern. **(c)** *(obstacle)* Hindernis, Hemmnis *(esp fig) nt.* **there is an ~ in the pipe** das Rohr ist verstopft.
**obstructive** [əb'strʌktɪv] *adj* obstruktiv *(esp Pol)*, behindernd. **to be ~** *(person)* Schwierigkeiten machen, sich querstellen *(col).*
**obtain** [əb'teɪn] *vt* erhalten; *result, votes also* erzielen; *information, goods also* beziehen. **to ~ sth by hard work** etw durch harte Arbeit erreichen; **to ~ sth for sb** jdm etw beschaffen.
**obtainable** [əb'teɪnəbl] *adj* erhältlich.
**obtrusive** [əb'tru:sɪv] *adj person* aufdringlich; *smell also* penetrant; *building, furniture* zu auffällig.
**obtuse** [əb'tju:s] *adj* **(a)** *(Geometry)* stumpf. **(b)** *person* begriffsstutzig, beschränkt.
**obviate** ['ɒbvɪeɪt] *vt* vermeiden; *need* vorbeugen *(+dat).*
**obvious** ['ɒbvɪəs] *adj* offensichtlich; *difference, fact also* eindeutig; *statement* naheliegend; *reason* (leicht) ersichtlich; *reluctance, surprise* sichtlich; *(not subtle)* plump. **an ~ truth** eine offenkundige Tatsache; **that's the ~ solution** das ist die naheliegendste Lösung; **he was the ~ choice** es lag nahe, ihn zu wählen; **it's quite ~ he doesn't understand** es ist doch klar, daß er es nicht versteht; **there's no need to make it so ~** man braucht das (doch) nicht so deutlich zu zeigen; **I would have thought that was perfectly ~** das liegt doch auf der Hand; **to state the ~** sagen/schreiben, was sich von selbst versteht.
**obviously** ['ɒbvɪəslɪ] *adv* offensichtlich, offenbar; *(noticeably)* (offen)sichtlich. **he's ~ French** er ist eindeutig ein Franzose; **he's not ~ French** man merkt ihm nicht an, daß er Franzose ist; **~!** selbstverständlich!
**occasion** [ə'keɪʒən] **1** *n* **(a)** *(point in time)* Gelegenheit *f.* **on that ~** damals, bei jener Gelegenheit; **on ~** gelegentlich; **to rise to the ~** sich der Lage gewachsen zeigen. **(b)** *(special time)* Ereignis *nt.* **on the ~ of his birthday** anläßlich seines Geburtstages; **it's an ~** es ist ein besonderer Anlaß. **(c)** *(opportunity)* Gelegenheit *f.* **(d)** *(reason)* Grund *m.* **if you have ~ to ...** sollten Sie Veranlassung haben, zu ... **2** *vt (form)* Anlaß geben zu.
**occasional** [ə'keɪʒənl] *adj* **(a)** **he likes an ~ cigar** er raucht gelegentlich eine Zigarre. **(b)** **~ table** kleiner Wohnzimmertisch.
**occasionally** [ə'keɪʒənəlɪ] *adv* gelegentlich, hin und wieder. **very ~** sehr selten.
**occult** [ɒ'kʌlt] **1** *adj* okkult. **2** *n* Okkulte(s) *nt.*
**occupant** ['ɒkjʊpənt] *n (of house)* Bewohner(in *f*) *m*; *(of post)* Inhaber(in *f*) *m*; *(of car)* Insasse *m.*
**occupation** [ˌɒkjʊ'peɪʃən] *n* **(a)** *(employment)* Beruf *m*, Tätigkeit *f.* **he is a joiner by ~** er ist Tischler von Beruf. **(b)** *(pastime)* Beschäftigung *f.* **(c)** *(Mil)* Okkupation *f*; *(act also)* Besetzung *f (of* von*)*; *(state also)* Besatzung *f (of* in *+dat).* **army of ~** Besatzungsheer

*nt.* (**d**) *(of house etc)* **ready for** ~ bezugsfertig.

**occupational** [ˌɒkjʊ'peɪʃənl] *adj* Berufs-, beruflich. ~ **guidance** *(Brit)* Berufsberatung *f*; ~ **pension scheme** *or (US)* **plan** betriebliche Altersversorgung; ~ **hazard** *or* **risk** Berufsrisiko *nt*; ~ **therapy** Beschäftigungstherapie *f*.

**occupier** ['ɒkjʊpaɪəʳ] *n (of house)* Bewohner(in *f*) *m*; *(of post)* Inhaber(in *f*) *m*.

**occupy** ['ɒkjʊpaɪ] *vt* (**a**) *house* bewohnen; *room* belegen. **is this seat occupied?** ist dieser Platz besetzt? (**b**) *(Mil etc)* besetzen. (**c**) *post, position* innehaben, bekleiden *(geh)*. (**d**) *(take up)* beanspruchen; *space also* einnehmen; *time also* in Anspruch nehmen. **to** ~ **one's time** seine Zeit verbringen. (**e**) *(busy)* beschäftigen. **to be occupied (with)** beschäftigt sein (mit); **to** ~ **oneself** sich beschäftigen; **to keep sb occupied** jdn beschäftigen; **he kept his mind occupied** er beschäftigte sich geistig; **the line is occupied** *(US)* die Nummer ist besetzt.

**occur** [ə'kɜːʳ] *vi* (**a**) *(event)* geschehen, vorkommen; *(difficulty)* sich ergeben; *(change)* stattfinden. **that doesn't** ~ **very often** das kommt nicht oft vor. (**b**) *(be found: disease)* vorkommen. (**c**) **it** ~**s to me that** ... ich habe den Eindruck, daß ...; **the idea just** ~**red to me** es ist mir gerade eingefallen; **it never** ~**red to me** darauf bin ich noch nie gekommen.

**occurrence** [ə'kʌrəns] *n (event)* Ereignis *nt*, Begebenheit *f*; *(presence, taking place)* Auftreten *nt*; *(of minerals)* Vorkommen *nt*. **an everyday** ~ ein alltägliches Ereignis.

**ocean** ['əʊʃən] *n* Ozean *m*, Meer *nt*. ~**s of** ... *(col)* jede Menge ...

**ocean:** ~ **bed** *or* **floor** *n* Meeresboden *or* -grund *m*; ~**-going** *adj* hochseetauglich.

**Oceania** [ˌəʊʃɪ'ɑːnɪə] *n* Ozeanien *nt*.

**ocean liner** *n* Ozeandampfer *m*.

**oceanography** [ˌəʊʃə'nɒgrəfɪ] *n* Meereskunde *f*.

**ochre,** *(US)* **ocher** ['əʊkəʳ] *n* Ocker *m or nt*.

**o'clock** [ə'klɒk] *adv* **at 5** ~ um 5 Uhr; **it is 5** ~ es ist 5 Uhr.

**OCR** *(Comp)* = **optical character reader; optical character recognition** OCR *f*.

**Oct** = **October** Okt.

**octagon** ['ɒktəgən] *n* Achteck, Oktagon *nt*.

**octagonal** [ɒk'tægənl] *adj* achteckig.

**octane** ['ɒkteɪn] *n* Oktan *nt*. **high-**~ **petrol** Benzin *nt* mit hoher Oktanzahl.

**octave** ['ɒktɪv] *n (Mus)* Oktave *f*.

**October** [ɒk'təʊbəʳ] *n* Oktober *m*; *see* **September.**

**octogenarian** [ˌɒktəʊdʒɪ'nɛərɪən] **1** *n* Achtzigjährige(r) *mf*. **2** *adj* achtzigjährig.

**octopus** ['ɒktəpəs] *n* Tintenfisch *m*, *(larger)* Krake *f*.

**oculist** ['ɒkjʊlɪst] *n* Augenarzt *m*, -ärztin *f*.

**odd** [ɒd] *adj* (+*er*) (**a**) *(peculiar)* merkwürdig, sonderbar; *person, thing, idea also* eigenartig. **how** ~ **that we should meet him** (wie) eigenartig *etc*, daß wir ihn trafen; **the** ~ **thing about it is that** ... das Merkwürdige *etc* daran ist, daß ...; **he's got some** ~ **ways** er hat eine verschrobene Art. (**b**) *number* ungerade. (**c**) *(one of a pair or a set)* *shoe, glove* einzeln. **he is (the)** ~ **man** *or* **one out** er ist das fünfte Rad am Wagen; **underline the word which is the** ~ **one out** unterstreichen Sie das nicht dazugehörige Wort. (**d**) **600** ~ **marks** so um die 600 Mark; **at** ~ **moments** ab und zu; ~ **job** (gelegentlich) anfallende Arbeit; ~ **job man** Mädchen *nt* für alles.

**oddball** ['ɒdbɔːl] *n (col)* Spinner *m (col)*; *(harmless)* komischer Kauz.

**oddity** ['ɒdɪtɪ] *n* (**a**) *(of person)* Eigenartigkeit *f*; *(of thing)* Ausgefallenheit *f*. (**b**) *(odd person)* komischer Kauz; *(thing)* Kuriosität *f*.

**oddly** ['ɒdlɪ] *adv speak, behave* eigenartig, sonderbar. **they are** ~ **similar** sie sind sich merkwürdig ähnlich; ~ **enough she was at home** seltsamerweise war sie zu Hause.

**oddment** ['ɒdmənt] *n usu pl* Restposten *m*; *(of cloth)* Rest *m*; *(single piece)* Einzelstück *nt*.

**oddness** ['ɒdnɪs] *n* Merkwürdigkeit, Seltsamkeit *f*.

**odd-numbered** [ˌɒd'nʌmbəd] *adj* ungerade.

**odds** [ɒdz] *npl* (**a**) *(Betting)* Gewinnquote *f*; *(of bookmaker also)* Kurse *pl*. **the** ~ **are 6 to 1** die Chancen stehen 6:1; **long/short** ~ geringe/hohe Gewinnchancen. (**b**) *(chances for or against)* Chance(n *pl*) *f*. **the** ~ **were against us** alles sprach gegen uns; **the** ~ **were in our favour** alles sprach für uns; **against all the** ~ **he won** wider Erwarten gewann er; **what are the** ~ **on/against ...?** wie stehen die Chancen, daß .../daß ... nicht?; **to struggle against impossible** ~ so gut wie keine Aussicht auf Erfolg haben; **the** ~ **are that he will come** es sieht ganz so aus, als ob er kommet. (**c**) *(col)* **to pay over the** ~ einen überhöhten Preis bezahlen. (**d**) *(difference)* **what's the** ~**?** was macht das schon (aus)?; **it makes no** ~ es spielt keine Rolle. (**e**) *(variance)* **to be at** ~ **with sb over sth** mit jdm in etw *(dat)* nicht übereinstimmen.

**odds and ends** *npl* Krimskrams *m (col)*. **there are some** ~ **still to do** es sind noch ein paar Kleinigkeiten zu erledigen.

**odds-on** ['ɒdzɒn] *adj* **the** ~ **favourite** der klare Favorit.

**ode** [əʊd] *n* Ode *f (to, on* an +*acc)*.

**odious** ['əʊdɪəs] *adj person* abstoßend, ekelhaft; *action* abscheulich.

**odometer** [əʊ'dɒmətəʳ] *n (US)* Kilometerzähler *m*.

**odour,** *(US)* **odor** ['əʊdəʳ] *n (lit, fig)* Geruch *m*; *(sweet smell)* Duft *m*; *(bad smell)* Gestank *m*. **to be in bad** ~ **with sb** schlecht bei jdm angeschrieben sein *(col)*.

**odourless,** *(US)* **odorless** ['əʊdəlɪs] *adj* geruchlos.

**Odyssey** ['ɒdɪsɪ] *n (Myth, fig)* Odyssee *f*.

**OECD** = **Organization for Economic Cooperation and Development** OECD *f*.

**Oedipus** ['iːdɪpəs] *n* Ödipus *m*. ~ **complex** Ödipuskomplex *m*.

**oesophagus,** *(US)* **esophagus** [iː'sɒfəgəs] *n* Speiseröhre *f*.

**of** [ɒv,əv] *prep* (**a**) von (+*dat)*, *use of gen.* **the wife** ~ **the doctor** die Frau des Arztes; **a friend** ~ **ours** ein Freund von uns; **a painting** ~ **him** ein Gemälde von ihm; **a painting** ~ **his** *(belonging to him)* eines seiner Gemälde; ~ **it** davon; **the first** ~ **May** der erste Mai; **it is very kind** ~ **you** es ist sehr freundlich von Ihnen; **south** ~ **Paris** südlich von Paris; **within a month** ~ **his death** (schon) einen Monat nach seinem Tod; **a quarter** ~ **four** *(US)* Viertel vor vier. (**b**) *(cause)* **he died** ~ **poison/cancer** er starb an Gift/Krebs; **it tastes** ~ **garlic** es schmeckt nach Knoblauch. (**c**) *(material)* aus. **dress made** ~ **wool** Wollkleid *nt*, Kleid *nt* aus Wolle. (**d**) *(quality, identity etc)* **a man** ~ **courage** ein mutiger Mensch; **a girl** ~ **ten** ein zehnjähriges Mädchen; **the city** ~ **Paris** die Stadt Paris. (**e**) **he is a leader** ~ **men** er hat die Fähigkeit, Menschen zu führen; **writer** ~ **legal articles** Verfasser von juristischen Artikeln; **love** ~ **money** Liebe zum Geld; **how many** ~ **them do you want?** wie viele möchten Sie (davon)?; **there were six** ~ **us** wir waren zu sechst; **he is not one** ~ **us** er gehört nicht zu uns; **today** ~ **all days** ausgerechnet heute; **you** ~ **all people ought to know** gerade Sie sollten

das wissen; **what do you think ~ him?** was halten
Sie von ihm?; **what ~ it?** ja und?

(f) *(in temporal phrases)* **he's become very quiet ~
late** er ist in letzter Zeit so ruhig; **they go out ~ an
evening** sie gehen abends (schon mal) aus.

**off** [ɒf] **1** *adv* **(a)** *(distance)* **the house is 5km ~** das
Haus ist 5 km entfernt; **it's a long way ~** das ist
weit weg; *(time)* das liegt in weiter Ferne; **the
exams aren't very far ~** es ist nicht mehr lang bis
zu den Prüfungen.

(b) *(departure)* **to be/go ~** gehen; **he's ~ to school**
er geht zur Schule; **(be) ~ with you!** fort mit dir!; **I
must be ~** ich muß gehen; **where are you ~ to?** wohin gehen Sie denn?, wohin geht's denn *(col)*?; ~
**we go!** los!, na denn man los! *(col)*; **he's ~ playing
tennis every evening** er geht jeden Abend Tennis
spielen.

(c) *(removal)* **he had his coat ~** er hatte den Mantel nicht an; ~ **with those wet clothes!** raus aus
den nassen Sachen! *(col)*; **the handle is ~** der Griff
ist ab *(col)* or ist abgegangen; **there are two buttons
~** es fehlen zwei Knöpfe.

(d) *(discount)* **3% ~** *(Comm)* 3% Nachlaß; **to give
sb £5 ~** jdm £5 Ermäßigung geben.

(e) *(not at work)* **to have time ~ to do sth** freiha-
ben, um etw zu tun; **I've got a day ~** ich habe einen
Tag frei(bekommen); **she's nearly always ~ on
Tuesdays** dienstags hat sie fast immer frei.

(f) *(in phrases)* ~ **and on, on and ~** ab und zu;
**right** or **straight ~** gleich; **3 days straight ~** 3 Tage
hintereinander.

**2** *adj* **(a)** *attr (substandard)* schlecht. **I'm having an
~ day today** ich bin heute nicht in Form.

(b) *pred (Brit: not fresh)* verdorben, schlecht.

(c) *pred (cancelled)* party, talks abgesagt; *(not
available: in restaurant)* aus. **the agreement is ~** die
Abmachung gilt nicht (mehr); **their engagement is
~** ihre Verlobung ist gelöst; **the play is ~** das Stück
wurde abgesagt; **chicken is ~** Hähnchen gibt es
nicht mehr.

(d) *TV, light, machine* aus(geschaltet); *tap*
zu(gedreht). **the gas/electricity was ~** das Gas/der
Strom war abgeschaltet; **the handbrake was ~** die
Handbremse war gelöst.

(e) **they are badly/well ~** sie sind nicht gut/(ganz)
gut gestellt; **how are we ~ for time?** wie sieht es
mit der Zeit aus?; **that's a bit ~!** das ist ein dicker
Hund! *(col)*.

**3** *prep* **(a)** *(indicating motion, removal etc)* von
*(+dat)*. **he jumped ~ the roof** er sprang vom Dach;
**they dined ~ a chicken** sie verspeisten ein Hühnchen; **he got £2 ~ the shirt** er bekam das Hemd £2
billiger; **the coat has two buttons ~ it** am Mantel
fehlen zwei Knöpfe.

(b) **a street ~ Piccadilly** eine Nebenstraße von
Piccadilly; **he lives just ~ the square** er wohnt ganz
in der Nähe des Platzes; **2 miles ~ the motorway** 2
Meilen von der Autobahn entfernt; **anchored ~ the
coast** vor der Küste liegend.

(c) ~ **the map** nicht mehr auf dieser Karte; **I'm ~
beer at the moment** Bier kann mich zur Zeit nicht
reizen; **I'm right ~ sausages** ich kann keine Wurst
mehr sehen.

(d) **to be ~ duty** (dienst)frei haben; **to be ~
school/work** schulfrei/frei haben; *(due to illness etc)*
in der Schule/bei der Arbeit fehlen.

**offal** ['ɒfəl] *n no pl* Innereien *pl*.

**off:** **~beat** *adj (unusual)* ausgefallen, ungewöhnlich;
**~-centre,** *(US)* **~-center** *adj (lit)* nicht in der Mitte;
**~-chance** *n* **I just did it on the ~-chance** ich habe es
auf gut Glück getan; **he bought it on the ~-chance**

**that it would come in useful** er kaufte es, weil es
vielleicht irgendwann mal nützlich sein könnte; **~-
colour,** *(US)* **~-color** *adj* **to be ~-colour** sich unwohl fühlen.

**offence,** *(US)* **offense** [ə'fens] *n* **(a)** *(Jur: crime)*
Straftat *f*, Delikt *nt*; *(minor also)* Vergehen *nt*. **to
commit an ~** sich strafbar machen; **it is an ~ to ...**
... ist bei Strafe verboten; **an ~ against ...** ein Verstoß *m* gegen ... **(b)** *no pl (to sb's feelings)* Kränkung *f*. **to cause** or **give ~ to sb** jdn kränken; **to
take ~ at sth** wegen etw gekränkt sein; **I meant no
~** ich habe es nicht böse gemeint

**offend** [ə'fend] **1** *vt* **(a)** *(hurt feelings of)* kränken;
*(be disagreeable to)* Anstoß erregen bei. **don't be
~ed** nehmen Sie mir *etc* das nicht übel. **(b)** *ear, eye*
beleidigen; *sense of justice* verletzen. **2** *vi* **(a)** *(give
offence)* beleidigend sein. **(b)** *(do wrong)* Unrecht
tun.

**offender** [ə'fendər] *n (law-breaker)* Täter(in *f*) *m*;
*(against traffic laws)* Verkehrssünder(in *f*) *m*. **young
~** jugendlicher Straffälliger.

**offending** [ə'fendɪŋ] *adj remark* kränkend, beleidigend. **the ~ object** der Stein des Anstoßes.

**offensive** [ə'fensɪv] **1** *adj* **(a)** *weapon (Jur)* Angriffs-;
*(Mil also)* Offensiv-. **(b)** *(unpleasant) smell, sight*
übel, abstoßend; *language, film* anstößig; *(insulting)
remark, behaviour* beleidigend. **to find sb/sth ~** jdn/
etw abstoßend finden; *behaviour, language* Anstoß
an etw *(dat)* nehmen; **he was ~ to her** er beleidigte
sie. **2** *n (Mil, Sport)* Angriff *m*, Offensive *f*. **to take
the ~** in die Offensive gehen; **on the ~** in der Offensive.

**offensively** [ə'fensɪvlɪ] *adv (unpleasantly)* übel, widerlich; *(in moral sense)* anstößig; *(abusively)* beleidigend.

**offer** ['ɒfər] **1** *n* Angebot *nt*. **to make an ~ of sth to sb**
jdm etw anbieten; **an ~ I couldn't refuse** ein Ange-
bot, zu dem ich nicht nein sagen konnte; **on ~**
*(Comm)* im Angebot. **2** *vt* **(a)** anbieten; *reward,
prize* aussetzen; *plan, suggestion* unterbreiten; *excuse* vorbringen. **to ~ to do sth** anbieten, etw zu
tun; **he ~ed to help** er bot seine Hilfe an; **to ~
one's services** anbieten. **(b)** *resistance* bieten.

**offering** ['ɒfərɪŋ] *n* Gabe *f*; *(Rel) (collection)* Opferga-
be *f*; *(sacrifice)* Opfer *nt*.

**offertory** ['ɒfətərɪ] *n (Eccl) (part of service)* Opferung
*f*; *(collection)* Kollekte *f*.

**offhand** [,ɒf'hænd] **1** *adj remark* lässig. **2** *adv* so
ohne weiteres, aus dem Stand *(col)*. **I couldn't tell
you ~** das könnte ich Ihnen auf Anhieb nicht sagen.

**offhandedly** [,ɒf'hændɪdlɪ] *adv* lässig, leichthin.

**office** ['ɒfɪs] *n* **(a)** Büro *nt*; *(of lawyer)* Kanzlei *f*;
*(part of organization)* Abteilung *f*; *(branch also)* Geschäftsstelle *f*; *(US: of doctor)* Praxis *f*. **at the ~** im
Büro. **(b)** *(public position)* Amt *nt*. **to take ~** sein
Amt antreten; *(political party)* die Regierung übernehmen; **to be in** or **hold ~** im Amt sein; *(party)* an
der Regierung sein; **to be out of ~** nicht mehr an
der Regierung sein; *(person)* nicht im Amt sein. **(c)**
*usu pl* **through his good ~s** durch seine guten Dienste; **through the ~s of ...** durch Vermittlung von ...
**(d)** *(Eccl)* Gottesdienst *m*.

**office:** **~ automation** *n* Büroautomatisierung *f*; ~
**bearer** *n* Amtsträger(in *f*) *m*; **~ block** *n* Büroge-
bäude *nt*; **~ holder** *n (US)* Amtsträger(in *f*) *m*; ~
**hours** *npl* Dienstzeit *f*; *(on sign)* Geschäftszeiten
*pl*; *(US: of doctor)* Sprechstunden *pl*; **~ job** *n* Stelle
*f* im Büro, Bürojob *m (col)*; **~ junior** Bürogehilfe
*m*, -gehilfin *f*; **~ manager** *n* Büroleiter(in *f*) *m*.

**officer** ['ɒfɪsər] *n* **(a)** *(Mil, Naut, Aviat)* Offizier *m*. **~s'
mess** Offizierskasino *nt*. **(b)** *(official)* Beamte(r) *m*,

Beamtin *f*; *(police ~)* Polizist *m.* **no,** ~ nein(, Herr Wachtmeister).

**office worker** *n* Büroangestellte(r) *mf.*

**official** [ə'fɪʃəl] **1** *adj* offiziell; *report, duties, meeting also* amtlich; *robes, visit* Amts-; *ceremony, style* formell. **is that ~?** ist das amtlich?; *(publicly announced)* ist das offiziell? ~ **strike** gewerkschaftlich genehmigter Streik. **2** *n* Beamte(r) *m,* Beamtin *f*; *(of club)* Funktionär(in *f*) *m.*

**officialdom** [ə'fɪʃəldəm] *n (pej)* Beamtentum *nt.*

**officialese** [ə,fɪʃə'liːz] *n* Amtssprache *f.*

**officially** [ə'fɪʃəlɪ] *adv* offiziell.

**officiate** [ə'fɪʃɪeɪt] *vt* amtieren, fungieren *(at* bei*).* **to ~ at a marriage** eine Trauung vornehmen.

**officious** [ə'fɪʃəs] *adj* übereifrig.

**offing** ['ɒfɪŋ] *n:* **in the ~** in Sicht.

**off:** ~**-key** *adj (Mus)* falsch; ~**-licence** *n (Brit)* Wein- und Spirituosenhandlung *f*; ~**-limits** *adj* verboten; ~**-line** *(Comp)* **1** *adj* Off-Line-; **2** *adv* off-line; **to operate** ~**-line** im Off-line-Betrieb arbeiten; ~**-load** *vt goods* ausladen, entladen; *passengers* aussteigen lassen; ~**-peak** *adj* ~**-peak rate** verbilligter Tarif; *(Elec)* ≃ Nachttarif *m*; ~**-peak electricity** Nachtstrom *m*; ~**-peak ticket** verbilligte Fahrkarte/ Flugkarte außerhalb der Stoßzeit; ~**-putting** *adj (Brit) smell, behaviour* abstoßend; *thought, story* wenig ermutigend; *(daunting)* entmutigend; ~ **ramp** *n (US)* Ausfahrt *f*; ~**-season** *n* Nebensaison *f.*

**offset** ['ɒfset] *(vb: pret, ptp* ~*)* **1** *vt* **(a)** *(financially, statistically etc)* ausgleichen; *(make up for)* aufwiegen. **(b)** *(place non-centrally)* versetzen. **2** *n (Typ)* Offsetdruck *m.*

**off:** ~**shoot** *n* **(a)** *(of plant)* Ausläufer *m*; **(b)** *(fig: of organization)* Nebenzweig *m*; ~**shore** *adj fisheries* Küsten-; *island* küstennah; *rig, installations etc* im Meer; *wind* ablandig *(Naut)*; *investment* im Ausland; ~**side 1** *adj* **(a)** *(Sport)* im Abseits; ~**side trap** Abseitsfalle *f*; **(b)** *(Aut)* auf der Fahrerseite; **2** *n (Aut)* Fahrerseite *f*; **3** *adv (Sport)* abseits, im Abseits; ~**-spring** *n* Sprößling *m*; *(of animal)* Junge(s) *nt*; ~**stage** *adv* hinter den Kulissen; ~**-the-cuff** *adj remark, speech* aus dem Stegreif; ~**-the-peg** *(Brit)*, ~**-the-rack** *(US) adj suit* von der Stange; ~**-the-shoulder** *adj* schulterfrei; ~**-white** *adj* gebrochen weiß.

**often** ['ɒfən] *adv* oft, häufig. **as ~ as twice a week** sogar zweimal in der Woche; **more ~ than not, as ~ as not** meistens; **every so ~** von Zeit zu Zeit; **how ~?** wie oft?

**ogle** ['əʊgl] *vt* kein Auge lassen von, begaffen *(pej)*; *(flirtatiously)* schöne Augen machen *(+dat).*

**ogre** ['əʊgə'] *n* Menschenfresser *m*; *(fig)* Unmensch *m.*

**OH** *(US Post)* = **Ohio.**

**oh** [əʊ] *interj* ach; *(surprised, disappointed)* oh; *(questioning)* tatsächlich.

**ohc** = **overhead camshaft.**

**ohm** [əʊm] *n (Elec)* Ohm *nt.*

**OHMS** = **On His/Her Majesty's Service** *Aufdruck auf amtlichen Sendungen.*

**ohv** = **overhead valve(s).**

**oi(c)k** [ɔɪk] *n (Brit pej col)* Prolet *m.*

**oil** [ɔɪl] **1** *n* **(a)** Öl *nt.* **to pour ~ on troubled waters** die Wogen glätten. **(b)** *(petroleum)* (Erd)öl *nt.* **to strike ~** *(lit)* auf Öl stoßen; *(fig: get rich)* das große Los ziehen. **2** *vt* ölen, schmieren.

**oil** *in cpds* Öl-; ~**can** *n* Ölkanne *f*; ~ **change** *n* Ölwechsel *m*; ~**cloth** *n* Wachstuch *nt*; ~ **company** *n* Ölkonzern *m*; ~**field** *n* Ölfeld *nt*; ~**-fired** *adj* Öl-, mit Ölfeuerung; ~ **gauge** *n (for pressure)* Öldruck-

messer *m*; *(for level)* Ölstandsanzeiger *m*; ~ **industry** *n* Ölindustrie *f*; ~ **lamp** *n* Öllampe *f*; ~ **level** *n* Ölstand *m*; ~ **painting** *n* Ölgemälde *nt*; ~ **pan** *n (US Aut)* Ölwanne *f*; ~ **pipeline** *n* Erdölleitung *f*; ~**-producing** *adj* (erd)ölproduzierend; ~**-rich** *adj* ölreich; ~ **rig** *n* (Öl)bohrinsel *f*; ~**skin** *n (cloth)* Öltuch *nt*; ~**skins** *npl (clothing)* Ölzeug *nt*; ~**slick** *n* Ölteppich *m*; ~ **tanker** *n* (Öl)tanker *m*; *(lorry)* Tankwagen *m*; ~ **well** *n* Ölquelle *f.*

**oily** ['ɔɪlɪ] *adj (+er)* ölig; *food* fettig; *clothes, fingers* voller Öl; *(fig)* aalglatt.

**ointment** ['ɔɪntmənt] *n* Salbe *f.*

**o.i.r.o.** = **offers in the region of** VB.

**OK** *(US Post)* = **Oklahoma.**

**OK, okay** ['əʊ'keɪ] *(col)* **1** *interj* okay *(col)*; *(agreed also)* in Ordnung. ~**,** ~**!** ist ja gut! *(col).* **2** *adj* in Ordnung, okay *(col).* **that's ~ with** *or* **by me** von mir aus; *(that's convenient)* das ist mir recht, mir ist's recht; **is it ~ with you if ...?** hast du was dagegen, wenn ...?; **how's your mother?** — **she's ~** wie geht's deiner Mutter? — gut *or (not too well)* so einigermaßen; **to be ~ (for time/money** *etc)* (noch) genug (Zeit/Geld *etc*) haben; **is that ~?** geht das?, ist das okay? *(col)*; **he's ~** er ist in Ordnung *(col).* **3** *adv (well)* gut; *(not too badly)* einigermaßen. **can you mend/manage it ~?** kannst du das reparieren/ kommst du damit klar? **4** *vt plan, suggestion* gutheißen, billigen. **5** *n* Zustimmung *f,* Okay *nt (col).*

**old** [əʊld] **1** *adj (+er)* **(a)** alt. ~ **people** *or* **folk(s)** alte Leute *pl*; ~ **Mr Smith** der alte (Herr) Smith; **he is 40 years ~** er ist 40 (Jahre alt); **two-year-~** Zweijährige(r) *mf*; **the ~ part of Ulm** die Ulmer Altstadt; **the ~ (part of) town** die Altstadt; **my ~ school** meine alte *or* ehemalige Schule; ~ **soldier** altgedienter Soldat; *(fig: experience person)* alter Kämpe *(hum).* **(b)** *(col: as intensifier)* **she dresses any ~ how** die ist vielleicht immer angezogen *(col)*; ~ **Mike** der Mike *(col)*; **the same ~ excuse** die gleiche alte Entschuldigung. **2** *n* **the ~** die alten Leute; **in days of ~** in früheren Zeiten; **I know him of ~** ich kenne ihn von früher.

**old:** ~ **age** *n* das Alter; **in one's ~ age** auf seine alten Tage *(also hum)*; ~**-age pension** *n* Rente *f*; ~**-age pensioner** *n (Brit)* Rentner(in *f*) *m*; ~ **boy** *n (Brit Sch)* ehemaliger Schüler; **the ~ boy network** Beziehungen *pl* (von der Schule her).

**olden** ['əʊldən] *adj (liter)* **in ~ times** *or* **days** früher, vordem *(liter).*

**old:** **O~ English 1** *n* Altenglisch *nt*; **2** *adj* altenglisch; ~**-established** *adj family, firm* alteingesessen; *custom* seit langem bestehend, alt; ~**-fashioned** *adj* altmodisch; ~ **girl** *n (Brit Sch)* ehemalige Schülerin; ~ **hat** *adj (col)* **it's ~ hat** das ist Schnee von gestern.

**oldie** ['əʊldɪ] *n (col) (song)* Oldie *m*; *(joke)* alter Witz. **the ~s** *(people)* die Alten.

**old:** ~ **maid** *n* alte Jungfer; ~ **master** *n* alter Meister; ~ **people's home** *n* Altersheim *nt*; ~ **school** *n (fig)* alte Schule; ~ **school tie** *n (fig) Einstellung f von Ehemaligen einer Public School*; **O~ Testament** *n* Altes Testament; ~**-timer** *n* Veteran *m*; ~ **wives' tale** *n* Ammenmärchen *nt*; **O~ World** *n* alte Welt.

**O Level** ['əʊlevl] *n (Brit old) ehemaliger Abschluß der Sekundarstufe 1.*

**olive** ['ɒlɪv] **1** *n* **(a)** Olive *f*; *(also ~ tree)* Olivenbaum, Ölbaum *m.* **(b)** *(colour)* Olivgrün *nt.* **2** *adj* olivgrün.

**olive:** ~ **branch** *n (lit, fig)* Ölzweig *m*; **to hold out the ~ branch to sb** *(fig)* jdm seinen Willen zum Frieden bekunden; ~ **oil** *n* Olivenöl *nt.*

**Olympic** [əʊˈlɪmpɪk] **1** *adj* olympisch. ~ **champion** Olympiasieger (in *f*) *m*. **2** *n* **the** ~**s** *pl* die Olympiade *f*, die olympischen Spiele.
**OM** *(Brit)* = **Order of Merit** *Verdienstorden m*.
**Oman** [əʊˈmɑːn] *n* Oman *nt*.
**Omani** [əʊˈmɑːnɪ] **1** *adj* omanisch. **2** *n* Omaner (-in *f*) *m*.
**ombudsman** [ˈɒmbʊdzmən] *n*, *pl* **-men** [-mən] Ombudsmann *m*.
**omelette**, *(US)* **omelet** [ˈɒmlɪt] *n* Omelett (e) *nt*.
**omen** [ˈəʊmen] *n* Omen, Zeichen *nt*.
**ominous** [ˈɒmɪnəs] *adj* bedrohlich; *sign also* verhängnisvoll. **that sounds** ~ das verspricht nichts Gutes.
**ominously** [ˈɒmɪnəslɪ] *adv* bedrohlich; *say* in einem unheilverkündenden Ton.
**omission** [əʊˈmɪʃən] *n* Auslassen *nt*; *(word etc left out)* Auslassung *f*; *(failure to do sth)* Unterlassung *f*.
**omit** [əʊˈmɪt] *vt* (a) *(leave out)* auslassen. (b) *(fail)* es unterlassen *(to do sth* etw zu tun*)*.
**omnibus** [ˈɒmnɪbəs] *n* (a) *(form: bus)* Omnibus *m*. (b) ~ **edition** *(book)* Sammelband *m*.
**omnipotent** [ɒmˈnɪpətənt] *adj* allmächtig.
**omniscient** [ɒmˈnɪsɪənt] *adj* allwissend.
**omnivorous** [ɒmˈnɪvərəs] *adj* allesfressend.
**on** [ɒn] **1** *prep* (a) *(indicating place, position)* auf *(+dat)*; *(with vb of motion)* auf *(+acc)*; *(on vertical surface, part of body)* an *(+dat/acc)*. **the book is** ~ **the table** das Buch ist auf dem Tisch; **he put the book** ~ **the table** er legte das Buch auf den Tisch; **it was** ~ **the blackboard** es stand an der Tafel; **he hung it** ~ **the wall/nail** er hängte es an die Wand/den Nagel; **he hit his head** ~ **the table/**~ **the ground** er hat sich *(dat)* den Kopf am Tisch/auf dem *or* am Boden angeschlagen; **I have no money** ~ **me** ich habe kein Geld bei mir; **we had something to eat** ~ **the train** wir haben im Zug etwas gegessen; **a house** ~ **the main road** ein Haus an der Hauptstraße.
(b) *(means)* **we went** ~ **the train** wir fuhren mit dem Zug; ~ **foot/horseback** zu Fuß/Pferd; **he lives** ~ **his income** er lebt von seinem Einkommen.
(c) *(about, concerning)* über *(+acc)*. **a book** ~ German grammar ein Buch über deutsche Grammatik; **his views** ~ **that** seine Meinung darüber.
(d) *(time)* ~ **Sunday** (am) Sonntag; ~ **Sundays** sonntags; ~ **December the first** am ersten Dezember; ~ **the minute** auf die Minute genau; ~ **my arrival** bei meiner Ankunft; ~ **examination** bei näherer Untersuchung; ~ **request** auf Wunsch; ~ **hearing this he left** als er das hörte, ging er; ~ **receiving my letter** nach Erhalt meines Briefes.
(e) **he is** ~ **the committee/the board** er gehört dem Ausschuß/Vorstand an; **I am working** ~ **a new project** ich arbeite gerade an einem neuen Projekt; **we were** ~ **page 72** wir waren auf Seite 72; **this round is** ~ **me** diese Runde geht auf meine Kosten; **prices are up** ~ **last year('s)** im Vergleich zum letzten Jahr sind sie Preise gestiegen; **he played (it)** ~ **the violin/trumpet** er spielte (es) auf der Geige/Trompete; **I'm** ~ **£15,000 a year** ich verdiene £15.000 im Jahr; **to be** ~ **a training course** an einem Lehrgang teilnehmen; **to be** ~ **drugs/pills** Drogen/Pillen nehmen.
**2** *adv see also vb* +*on* (a) **he put his hat** ~ er setzte seinen Hut auf; **he put his coat** ~ er zog seinen Mantel an; **she had nothing** ~ sie hatte nichts an; **what did he have** ~? was hatte er an?
(b) *(continuation)* **move** ~! gehen Sie weiter!; **from that day** ~ von diesem Tag an; **it was well** ~ **in the night** es war spät in der Nacht; **to keep** ~

**talking** in einem fort reden; **go** ~ **with your work** machen Sie Ihre Arbeit weiter; **life still goes** ~ das Leben geht weiter; **they talked** ~ **and** ~ sie redeten und redeten; **the film went** ~ **and** ~ der Film wollte kein Ende nehmen; **to read** ~ weiterlesen.
(c) *(in phrases)* **he's always (going)** ~ **at me to get my hair cut** er liegt mir dauernd in den Ohren, daß ich mir die Haare schneiden lassen soll; **what's he** ~ **about?** wovon redet er nun schon wieder?
**3** *adj* (a) *lights, TV, radio etc* (gestellt). *brake* angezogen; *electricity, gas* an (gestellt). **the** ~ **switch** der Einschalter; **to leave the light** ~ das Licht brennen lassen *or* anlassen.
(b) **to be** ~ *(being performed: film etc)* gezeigt werden; **what's** ~ **tonight?** was läuft heute abend?; **I have nothing** ~ **tonight** ich habe heute abend nichts vor; **what's** ~ **in London?** was läuft zur Zeit in London?
(c) *(valid)* **to be** ~ *(bet, agreement)* gelten; **you're** ~! abgemacht!; **it's just not** ~ *(not acceptable)* das geht einfach nicht.
**once** [wʌns] **1** *adv* (a) *(on one occasion)* einmal. ~ **a week** einmal in der Woche; ~ **again** *or* **more** noch einmal; ~ **again we find that** ... wir stellen erneut fest, daß ...; ~ **or twice** *(fig)* nur ein paarmal; ~ **and for all** ein für allemal; **(every)** ~ **in a while** ab und zu mal; **you can come this** ~ dieses eine Mal können Sie kommen; **for** ~ ausnahmsweise einmal.
(b) *(in past)* einmal. **he was** ~ **famous** er war früher einmal berühmt; ~ **upon a time there was** ... es war einmal ... (c) **at** ~ *(immediately)* sofort, auf der Stelle; *(at the same time)* auf einmal, gleichzeitig; **all at** ~ auf einmal; **they came all at** ~ sie kamen alle gleichzeitig. **2** *conj* wenn, *(with past tense)* als. ~ **you understand, it's easy** wenn Sie es einmal verstehen, ist es einfach.
**once-over** [ˈwʌnsəʊvəʳ] *n (col)* **to give sb/sth the** ~ *(appraisal)* jdn/etw mal kurz überprüfen; *(clean)* mal kurz über etw *(acc)* gehen *(col)*.
**oncoming** [ˈɒnkʌmɪŋ] *adj car, traffic* entgegenkommend. **the** ~ **traffic** der Gegenverkehr.
**OND** *(Brit)* = **Ordinary National Diploma** *Diplom in technischen Fächern.*
**one** [wʌn] **1** *adj* (a) *(number)* ein/eine/ein; *(counting)* eins. ~ **man in a thousand** einer von tausend; **the baby is** ~ *(year old)* das Kind ist ein Jahr (alt); **it is** ~ *(o'clock)* es ist eins, es ist ein Uhr; **there is only** ~ **way of doing it** es gibt nur eine Möglichkeit, es zu tun.
(b) *(indefinite)* ~ **morning/day he realized** ... eines Morgens/Tages bemerkte er ...; **you'll regret it** ~ **day** Sie werden das eines Tages bereuen; ~ **morning next week** nächste Woche einmal morgens.
(c) *(sole, only)* **he is the** ~ **man to tell you** er ist der einzige, der es Ihnen sagen kann; **no** ~ **man could do it** niemand konnte es allein tun; **the** ~ **and only Brigitte Bardot** die unvergleichliche Brigitte Bardot.
(d) *(same)* **they all came in the** ~ **car** sie kamen alle in dem einen Auto; **they are** ~ **and the same person** das ist ein und dieselbe Person; **it is** ~ **and the same thing** das ist ein und dasselbe; **it's all** ~ **(to me)** das ist (mir) einerlei.
**2** *pron* (a) eine(r, s). **the** ~ **who** ... der (jenige), der .../die (jenige), die .../das (jenige), das ...; **do you have** ~? haben Sie einen/eine/eins?; **the red/big** *etc* ~ der/die/das rote/große *etc*; **a bigger** ~ ein größerer/eine größere/ein größeres; **not** ~ **of them** nicht eine(r, s) von ihnen; **every** ~ jede(r, s); **this** ~ diese(r, s); **that** ~ der/die/das; **which** ~? welche(r, s)?; **I'm not** ~ **to go out often** ich bin

nicht der Typ, der oft ausgeht; **he's never ~ to say no** er sagt nie nein; **he's a great ~ for discipline** er ist ganz groß, wenn's um Disziplin geht; **she is a teacher, and he/her sister wants to be ~ too** sie ist Lehrerin, und er möchte auch gern Lehrer werden/ihre Schwester möchte auch gern eine werden; **I, for ~,** think otherwise ich zum Beispiel denke anders; **~ by ~** einzeln; **he is ~ of the family** er gehört zur Familie; **he is ~ of us** er ist einer von uns; *(member of a group)* er gehört zu uns.

(**b**) *(impers) (num)* man; *(acc)* einen; *(dat)* einem. **~ must learn to keep quiet** man muß lernen, still zu sein; **to hurt ~'s foot** sich *(dat)* den Fuß verletzen.

**3** *n (written figure)* Eins *f.* **in ~s and twos** in kleinen Gruppen; **it was bedroom and sitting-room (all) in ~** es war Schlaf- und Wohnzimmer in einem; **to be at ~ with oneself** mit sich selbst im Einklang sein; **to be ~ up on sb** *(col) (know more)* jdm eins voraussein; *(have more)* jdm etwas voraushaben.

**one another** = **each other.**

**one:** **~-armed** *adj* einarmig; **~-armed bandit** *n (col)* einarmiger Bandit; **~-day excursion** *n (US)* Tagesrückfahrkarte *f;* **~-eyed** *adj* einäugig; **~-legged** *adj* einbeinig; **~-man** *adj* Einmann-; **~-man band** Einmannkapelle *f; (fig col)* Einmannbetrieb *m;* **~-night stand** *n (Theat)* einmalige Vorstellung; *(fig)* **he's just after a ~-night stand** er sucht nur eine für eine Nacht; **~-off** *(Brit col)* **1** *adj* einmalig; **2** *n a* **~-off** etwas Einmaliges; *(product)* ein Einzelstück; **~-piece** *adj* einteilig.

**onerous** ['ɒnərəs] *adj responsibility* schwer(wiegend); *task, duty* schwer.

**oneself** [wʌn'self] *pron* (**a**) *(dir and indir, with prep)* sich; *(~ personally)* sich selbst *or* selber. (**b**) *(emph)* (sich) selbst; *see* **myself.**

**one:** **~-shot** *adj (US)* einmalig; **~-sided** *adj* einseitig; *judgement, account also* parteiisch; **~-time** *adj* ehemalig; **~-to-one** *adj correlation* eins-zu-eins; **~-to-one tuition** *n* Einzelunterricht *m;* **~-track** *adj* **he's got a ~-track mind** er denkt sehr eingleisig; **~-upmanship** [,wʌn'ʌpmənʃɪp] *n* **that's just a form of ~-upmanship** damit will er *etc* den anderen nur um eine Nasenlänge voraus sein; **~-way** *adj traffic, street* Einbahn-; **~-way ticket** *(US Rail)* einfache Fahrkarte.

**ongoing** ['ɒngəʊɪŋ] *adj (in progress)* laufend; *(long-term) development, relationship, situation* andauernd.

**onion** ['ʌnjən] *n* Zwiebel *f.*

**online** [ɒn'laɪn] **1** *adj attr* On-line-. **2** *adv* on-line. **to operate ~** im On-line-Betrieb arbeiten.

**onlooker** ['ɒnlʊkər] *n* Zuschauer(in *f*) *m.*

**only** ['əʊnlɪ] **1** *adj attr* einzige(r, s). **he's an ~ child** er ist ein Einzelkind *nt;* **he was the ~ one to leave** *or* **who left** er ist als einziger gegangen; **that's the ~ thing for it/the ~ thing to do** das ist die einzige Möglichkeit; **my ~ wish/regret** das einzige, was ich mir wünsche/was ich bedaure.

**2** *adv* nur. **it's ~ five o'clock** es ist erst fünf Uhr; **I ~ wanted to be with you** ich wollte nur mit dir zusammen sein; **~ too true** *etc* nur (all)zu wahr *etc;* **I'd be ~ too pleased to help** ich würde nur zu gerne helfen; **if ~ that hadn't happened** wenn das bloß nicht passiert wäre; **we ~ just caught the train** wir haben den Zug gerade noch gekriegt; **he has ~ just arrived** er ist gerade erst angekommen; **I've ~ just got enough** ich habe gerade genug; **not ~ ... but also ...** nicht nur ..., sondern auch ...

**3** *conj* bloß, nur. **I would do it myself, ~ I haven't time** ich würde es selbst machen, ich habe nur keine Zeit.

**o.n.o.** = **or near(est) offer** oder Angebot.

**on-off switch** ['ɒn'ɒfswɪtʃ] *n* Ein- und Ausschalter *m.*

**onomatopoeia** [,ɒnəʊmætəʊ'piːə] *n* Lautmalerei *f.*

**onrush** ['ɒnrʌʃ] *n (of people)* Ansturm *m; (of water)* Schwall *m.*

**onset** ['ɒnset] *n* Beginn *m; (of cold weather also)* Einbruch *m; (of illness)* Ausbruch *m.*

**onshore** ['ɒnʃɔr] *adj* Land-; *wind* See-, auflandig *(Naut).*

**onside** [ɒn'saɪd] *adv (Sport)* nicht im Abseits.

**on-site** [ɒn'saɪt] *in cpds* Vor-Ort-; **~ supervision** Vor-Ort-Kontrolle *f.*

**onslaught** ['ɒnslɔːt] *n (Mil)* (heftiger) Angriff *(on* auf *+acc).* **to make an ~ on sb/sth** *(fig) (verbally)* jdn/etw angreifen; *(on work)* einer Sache *(dat)* zu Leibe rücken.

**on-the-job training** ['ɒnðə,dʒɒb'treɪnɪŋ] *n* Ausbildung *f* am Arbeitsplatz.

**onto** ['ɒntʊ] *prep* (**a**) *(upon, on top of)* auf *(+acc); (on sth vertical)* an *(+acc).* (**b**) *(in verbal expressions)* **to get/come ~ a subject** auf ein Thema zu sprechen kommen; **to be/get ~** *or* **on to sb** *(find sb out)* jdm auf die Schliche gekommen sein/kommen *(col);* **I'll get ~ him about it** ich werde ihn darauf ansprechen.

**onus** ['əʊnəs] *n no pl* Pflicht *f; (burden)* Last *f.* **to shift the ~ for sth onto sb** jdm die Verantwortung für etw zuschieben; **the ~ to do it is on him** es liegt an ihm, das zu tun.

**onward** ['ɒnwəd] *adv (also* **~s)** voran, vorwärts; *march* weiter. **from today/this time ~** von heute/der Zeit an.

**onyx** ['ɒnɪks] **1** *n* Onyx *m.* **2** *adj* Onyx-.

**ooh** [uː] *interj* oh.

**oomph** [ʊmf] *n (col) (energy)* Pep *m (col); (power)* Kraft *f.*

**ooze** [uːz] **1** *n (mud)* Schlamm *m.* **2** *vi* triefen; *(wound)* nässen; *(resin, mud, glue)* (heraus)quellen. **3** *vt* (**a**) (aus)schwitzen. (**b**) *(fig) charm* triefen von *(pej),* verströmen.

**opacity** [əʊ'pæsɪtɪ] *n* Undurchsichtigkeit *f.*

**opal** ['əʊpəl] *n (stone)* Opal *m.*

**opaque** [əʊ'peɪk] *adj* (**a**) opak; *glass also, liquid* trüb; *tights* blickdicht. (**b**) *(fig) prose* undurchsichtig, unklar.

**OPEC** ['əʊpek] = **Organization of Petroleum Exporting Countries** OPEC *f.*

**open** ['əʊpən] **1** *adj* offen; *door, bottle, eye, flower also* auf *pred,* geöffnet; *lines of communication, road* frei; *(public) meeting, trial* öffentlich. **to keep/hold the door ~** die Tür offen- *or* auflassen/offen- *or* aufhalten; **I can't keep my eyes ~** ich kann die Augen nicht offenhalten; **the baker's shop is ~** der Bäckerladen hat geöffnet *or* hat auf *(col);* **to lay oneself ~ to criticism/attack** sich der Kritik/Angriffen aussetzen; **in the ~ air** im Freien; **~ to traffic/shipping** für den Verkehr/die Schiffahrt freigegeben; **to be ~ to sb** *(admission)* jdm freistehen; *(place)* für jdn geöffnet sein; **he was ~ with us** er war ganz offen mit uns; **two possibilities were ~ to him** zwei Möglichkeiten standen ihm offen; **~ day** Tag *m* der offenen Tür; **~ to the public** der Öffentlichkeit zugänglich; **to be ~ to advice/suggestions** Ratschlägen/Vorschlägen gegenüber offen sein; **I'm ~ to offers** ich lasse gern mit mir reden; **they left the matter ~** sie ließen die Angelegenheit offen; **to keep an ~ mind** alles offen lassen; **to have an ~ mind on sth** einer Sache *(dat)* aufgeschlossen gegenüberstehen; **~ verdict** *(Jur) Todesfeststellung f ohne Angabe des Grundes.*

**2** _n_ **in the** ~ _(outside)_ im Freien; _(on_ ~ _ground)_ auf freiem Feld; **to bring sth out into the** ~ mit etw nicht länger hinterm Berg halten; **to come out into the** ~ _(fig) (person)_ Farbe bekennen; _(affair)_ herauskommen.

**3** _vt_ **(a)** _door, mouth, bottle, letter etc_ öffnen, aufmachen _(col)_; _book also, newspaper_ aufschlagen; _(officially) exhibition_ eröffnen; _building_ einweihen; _road_ dem Verkehr übergeben. **to** ~ **one's heart to sb** sich jdm öffnen; ~ **your mind to new possibilities** öffnen Sie sich _(dat)_ den Blick für neue Möglichkeiten; **to** ~ **fire** _(Mil)_ das Feuer eröffnen _(on_ auf _+acc)_. **(b)** _shop, trial, school, account_ eröffnen.

**4** _vi_ **(a)** aufgehen; _(door, flower, wound also)_ sich öffnen. **(b)** _(shop, museum)_ öffnen, aufmachen. **(c)** _(door)_ führen _(into_ in _+acc)_. **(d)** _(start)_ beginnen _(with_ mit_)_; _(Cards, Chess)_ eröffnen. **the play** ~**s next week** das Stück wird ab nächster Woche gegeben.

►**open out 1** _vi (river, street)_ sich verbreitern _(into_ zu_)_; _(valley also, view)_ sich weiten, sich öffnen; _(flower)_ sich öffnen, aufgehen. **2** _vt sep (unfold) map etc_ auseinanderfalten.

►**open up 1** _vi (flower)_ sich öffnen, aufgehen; _(fig) (prospects, field, new horizons)_ sich erschließen; _(person: become expansive)_ gesprächiger werden. **2** _vt sep_ **(a)** _territory, prospects_ erschließen; _new horizons, field of research etc also_ auftun; _(unblock) disused tunnel etc_ freimachen. **(b)** _(unlock) house, shop, car etc_ aufschließen. **(c)** _(start) business_ eröffnen; _shop also_ aufmachen.

**open:** ~**-air** _adj_ im Freien; ~**-air swimming pool** _n_ Freibad _nt_; ~**-and-shut** _adj_ it's an ~**-and-shut case** es ist ein glasklarer Fall; ~**-cast** _adj coalmine_ über Tage; ~**-cast mining** Tagebau _m_; ~**-ended** _adj_ unbegrenzt; _discussion_ alles offen lassend; _contract_ unbefristet.

**opener** ['ǝupnǝ<sup>r</sup>] _n_ Öffner _m_.

**open:** ~**-handed** _adj_ freigebig; ~**-heart surgery** _n_ Eingriff _m_ am offenen Herzen; ~**-hearted** _adj_ offenherzig; _welcome_ herzlich; ~ **house** _n_ **to keep** ~ **house** ein offenes Haus führen; ~ **learning** _n_ Erwachsenenbildung _f_ durch Teilzeit- und Fernkurse.

**opening** ['ǝupnɪŋ] **1** _n_ **(a)** Öffnung _f_; _(in traffic)_ Lücke _f_; _(forest clearing)_ Lichtung _f_. **(b)** _(beginning)_ Anfang _m_; _(of debate, speech, trial also, Chess, Cards)_ Eröffnung _f_. **(c)** _(official_ ~_) (of exhibition, stores)_ Eröffnung _f_. **O**~ **of Parliament** Parlamentseröffnung _f_. **(d)** _(opportunity)_ Möglichkeit, Chance _f_; _(job vacancy)_ (freie) Stelle. **2** _attr (initial, first)_ erste(r, s); _speech also_ Eröffnungs-; _remarks_ einführend.

**opening:** ~ **ceremony** _n_ Eröffnungsfeier _f_; ~ **hours** _npl_ Öffnungszeiten _pl_; ~ **time** _n_ Öffnungszeit _f_; **what are the bank's** ~ **times?** wann hat die Bank geöffnet?

**openly** ['ǝupǝnlɪ] _adv_ offen; _(publicly)_ öffentlich.

**open:** ~**-minded** _adj_ aufgeschlossen; ~**-mindedness** _n_ Aufgeschlossenheit _f_; ~**-mouthed** [,ǝupn'mauðd] _adj (in surprise or stupidity)_ mit offenem Mund; ~**-necked** _adj shirt_ mit offenem Kragen.

**openness** ['ǝupnnɪs] _n (frankness)_ Offenheit _f_.

**open:** ~**-plan** _adj office_ Großraum-; _flat etc_ offen angelegt; ~ **prison** _n_ offenes Gefängnis; ~ **sandwich** _n_ belegtes Brot; ~ **season** _n (Hunt)_ Jagdzeit _f_; **O**~ **University** _n (Brit)_ Fernuniversität _f_.

**opera** ['ɒpǝrǝ] _n_ Oper _f_. **to go to the** ~ in die Oper gehen.

**opera** _in cpds_ Opern-; ~ **glasses** _npl_ Opernglas _nt_; ~ **house** _n_ Opernhaus _nt_; ~ **singer** _n_ Opernsänger(in _f_) _m_.

**operate** ['ɒpǝreɪt] **1** _vi_ operieren _(also Mil, Med)_; _(machine)_ funktionieren; _(be in operation)_ in Betrieb sein; _(buses, planes)_ verkehren; _(theory, plan, law)_ sich auswirken; _(organization, system)_ arbeiten. **I don't like the way he** ~**s** ich mag seine Methoden nicht; **to be** ~**d on** _(Med)_ operiert werden. **2** _vt_ **(a)** _machine_ bedienen; _(set in operation)_ in Betrieb setzen; _brakes etc also_ betätigen. **(b)** _business_ führen.

**operatic** [,ɒpǝ'rætɪk] _adj singer, music_ Opern-; _style_ opernhaft.

**operating** ['ɒpǝreɪtɪŋ] _adj attr_ **(a)** _(Tech, Comm)_ _pressure, cost_ Betriebs-. **(b)** _(Med)_ Operations-. ~ **theatre** _(Brit) or_ **room** Operationssaal, OP _m_.

**operation** [,ɒpǝ'reɪʃǝn] _n_ **(a)** _(of machine, system)_ Funktionieren _nt_; _(act of operating)_ Bedienung _f_; _(of small mechanism)_ Betätigung _f_. **to be in** ~ _(machine)_ in Betrieb sein; _(law)_ in Kraft sein; _(plan)_ durchgeführt werden; **to be out of** ~ außer Betrieb sein; **to come into** ~ _(law)_ in Kraft treten; _(plan)_ zur Anwendung gelangen; **to bring** _or_ **put a law into** ~ ein Gesetz in Kraft setzen. **(b)** _(Med)_ Operation _f (on_ an _+dat)_. **to have an** ~ **(for a hernia** _etc)_ (wegen eines Bruchs _etc)_ operiert werden. **(c)** _(enterprise)_ Unternehmen _nt_; _(task, stage in undertaking)_ Arbeitsgang _m_. **(business)** ~**s** Geschäfte _pl_; **to cease** ~**s** den Geschäftverkehr einstellen.

**operational** [,ɒpǝ'reɪʃǝnl] _adj (ready for use)_ _machine, vehicle_ betriebsbereit; _army unit, aeroplane etc_ einsatzfähig; _(in use or action) machine, vehicle etc_ in Betrieb; _army unit etc_ im Einsatz.

**operative** ['ɒpǝrǝtɪv] **1** _adj_ **(a)** _measure, laws_ wirksam. **"if" being the** ~ **word** wobei ich „wenn" betone. **(b)** _(Med) treatment_ operativ. **2** _n (of machinery)_ Maschinenarbeiter(in _f_) _m_; _(skilled)_ Maschinist(in _f_) _m_.

**operator** ['ɒpǝreɪtǝ<sup>r</sup>] _n (Telec)_ ≈ Vermittlung _f_; _(person)_ Dame _f_/Herr _m_ von der Vermittlung; _(of machinery)_ (Maschinen)arbeiter(in _f_) _m_; _(of computer etc)_ Bediener(in _f_) _m_. **smooth** ~ _(col)_ Schlawiner _m (col)_.

**operetta** [ɒpǝ'retǝ] _n_ Operette _f_.

**ophthalmic** [ɒf'θælmɪk] _adj_ Augen-.

**opinion** [ǝ'pɪnjǝn] _n_ Meinung, Ansicht _f (about, on_ zu_)_; _(political, religious)_ Anschauung _f_; _(professional advice)_ Gutachten _nt_; _(esp Med)_ Befund _m_. **in my** ~ meiner Meinung nach; **to be of the** ~ **that** ... der Ansicht sein, daß ...; **to ask sb's** ~ jdn nach seiner Meinung fragen; **it is a matter of** ~ das ist Ansichtssache; **to have a high/poor** ~ **of sb/sth** eine hohe/schlechte Meinung von jdm/etw haben; **to form an** ~ **of sb/sth** sich _(dat)_ eine Meinung über jdn/etw bilden; ~ **poll** Meinungsumfrage _f_; **to seek** _or_ **get a second** ~ _(esp Med)_ ein zweites Gutachten einholen.

**opinionated** [ǝ'pɪnjǝneɪtɪd] _adj_ rechthaberisch.

**opium** ['ǝupɪǝm] _n (lit, fig)_ Opium _nt_.

**opponent** [ǝ'pǝunǝnt] _n_ Gegner(in _f_) _m_.

**opportune** ['ɒpǝtjuːn] _adj time_ günstig; _remark_ an passender Stelle; _action, event_ rechtzeitig.

**opportunism** [,ɒpǝ'tjuːnɪzǝm] _n_ Opportunismus _m_.

**opportunist** [,ɒpǝ'tjuːnɪst] _n_ Opportunist(in _f_) _m_.

**opportunity** [,ɒpǝ'tjuːnɪtɪ] _n_ Gelegenheit _f_; _(chance to better oneself)_ Chance, Möglichkeit _f_. **at the first** _or_ **earliest** ~ bei der erstbesten Gelegenheit; **to take the** ~ **to do sth** _or_ **of doing sth** die Gelegenheit nutzen, etw zu tun; **as soon as I get the** ~ sobald sich die Gelegenheit ergibt; **opportunities for promotion** Aufstiegsmöglichkeiten _or_ -chancen _pl_.

**oppose** [ǝ'pǝuz] _vt_ ablehnen; _(fight against)_ sich entgegenstellen _(+dat)_; _leadership, orders_ sich widersetzen _(+dat)_; _government_ sich stellen gegen. **he** ~**s**

our coming er ist dagegen, daß wir kommen.
**opposed** [ə'pəʊzd] *adj pred* **to be ~ to sb/sth** gegen jdn/etw sein; **I am ~ to your going** ich bin dagegen, daß Sie gehen; **as ~ to** im Gegensatz zu.
**opposing** [ə'pəʊzɪŋ] *adj team* gegnerisch; *army* feindlich; *characters* gegensätzlich.
**opposite** ['ɒpəzɪt] **1** *adj* **(a)** *(facing)* gegenüberliegend *attr*, gegenüber *pred*. **to be ~** gegenüber liegen/stehen/sitzen *etc*; **on the ~ page** auf der Seite gegenüber, auf der gegenüberliegenden Seite. **(b)** *(other) side, end, opinion* entgegengesetzt *(to, from dat, zu)*. **the ~ sex** das andere Geschlecht; **~ number** Pendant *nt*; **they've got quite ~ characters** sie sind ganz gegensätzliche Charaktere. **2** *n* Gegenteil *nt*; *(contrasting: black/white etc)* Gegensatz *m*. **quite the ~!** ganz im Gegenteil! **3** *adv* gegenüber, auf der gegenüberliegenden Seite. **they sat ~** sie saßen uns/ihnen/sich *etc* gegenüber. **4** *prep* gegenüber *(+dat)*. **~ one another** sich gegenüber; **they live ~ us** sie wohnen uns gegenüber.
**opposition** [,ɒpə'zɪʃən] *n* **(a)** *(resistance)* Widerstand *m*; *(people resisting)* Opposition *f*. **to act in ~ to sth** einer Sache *(dat)* zuwiderhandeln. **(b)** *(esp Brit Parl)* **O~** Opposition(spartei) *f*; **to be in ~** in der Opposition sein.
**oppress** [ə'pres] *vt* **(a)** *(tyrannize)* unterdrücken. **(b)** *(weigh down)* bedrücken.
**oppression** [ə'preʃən] *n* *(tyranny)* Unterdrückung *f*.
**oppressive** [ə'presɪv] *adj regime, laws* repressiv; *taxes* (er)drückend. **(b)** *(fig) heat* drückend; *thought* bedrückend.
**oppressor** [ə'presər] *n* Unterdrücker *m*.
**opt** [ɒpt] *vi* **to ~ for sth/to do sth** sich für etw entscheiden/sich entscheiden, etw zu tun.
►**opt out** *vi* sich anders entscheiden; *(of awkward situation)* abspringen *(of bei)*; *(of responsibility, invitation)* ablehnen *(of acc)*; *(give up membership)* austreten *(of aus)*; *(of pension/insurance scheme)* kündigen *(of acc)*; *(of society)* aussteigen; *(school, hospital)* sich für die Selbstverwaltung entscheiden.
**optic** ['ɒptɪk] *adj nerve, centre* Seh-.
**optical** ['ɒptɪkəl] *adj* optisch. **~ illusion** optische Täuschung; **~ character reader** *(Comp)* optischer Klarschriftleser; **~ character recognition** *(Comp)* optische Zeichenerkennung; **~ fibre** Lichtleitfaser *f*; *(cable)* Lichtleiter *m*.
**optician** [ɒp'tɪʃən] *n* Optiker(in *f*) *m*.
**optics** ['ɒptɪks] *n sing* Optik *f*.
**optima** ['ɒptɪmə] *pl of* **optimum.**
**optimism** ['ɒptɪmɪzəm] *n* Optimismus *m*.
**optimist** ['ɒptɪmɪst] *n* Optimist(in *f*) *m*.
**optimistic** [,ɒptɪ'mɪstɪk] *adj* optimistisch *(about sth* in bezug auf *+acc)*.
**optimum** ['ɒptɪməm] *adj* optimal.
**option** ['ɒpʃən] *n* **(a)** *(choice)* Wahl *f no pl*; *(possible course of action also)* Möglichkeit *f*. **I have no ~** mir bleibt keine andere Wahl; **he had no ~ but to come** ihm blieb nichts anderes übrig, als zu kommen; **to leave one's ~s open** sich *(dat)* alle Möglichkeiten offenhalten. **(b)** *(Comm)* Option *f (on* auf *+acc)*; *(on house, goods etc also)* Vorkaufsrecht *nt (on* an *+dat)*; *(on shares)* Bezugsrecht *nt (on* für*)*. **with an ~ to buy** mit einer Kaufoption. **(c)** *(Univ, Sch)* Wahlfach *nt*.
**optional** ['ɒpʃənl] *adj (not compulsory)* freiwillig; *(Sch, Univ) subject* Wahl-; *(fitted if required)* auf Wunsch erhältlich. **~ extras** Extras *pl*.
**opulence** ['ɒpjʊləns] *n no pl see adj* Reichtum *m*; Prunk *m*; Feudalität *f*; Üppigkeit *f*.
**opulent** ['ɒpjʊlənt] *adj* reich; *clothes, decoration* prunkvoll; *chairs, carpets* feudal; *lifestyle* üppig.

**opus** ['əʊpəs] *n, pl* **opera** ['ɒpərə] *n (Mus, fig)* Opus *nt*; *(fig also)* Werk *nt*.
**OR** *(US Post)* = **Oregon.**
**or** *conj* oder; *(with neg)* noch. **he could not read ~ write** er konnte weder lesen noch schreiben; **you'd better go ~ (else) you'll be late** gehen Sie jetzt besser, sonst kommen Sie zu spät; **you'd better do it ~ else!** tu das lieber, sonst ...!; **in a day ~ two** in ein bis zwei Tagen; **the Congo, ~ rather, Zaire** der Kongo, beziehungsweise Zaire.
**oracle** ['ɒrəkl] *n* Orakel *nt*; *(person)* Seher(in *f*) *m*; *(fig)* Alleswisser *m*.
**oral** ['ɔːrəl] **1** *adj* **(a)** *(Med)* oral. **~ vaccination** Schluckimpfung *f*. **(b)** *(verbal)* mündlich. **to improve one's ~ skills in a language** eine Sprache besser sprechen lernen. **2** *n* Mündliche(s) *nt*.
**orally** ['ɔːrəlɪ] *adv* **(a)** oral. **not to be taken ~** nicht einnehmen. **(b)** *(verbally)* mündlich.
**orange** ['ɒrɪndʒ] **1** *n (fruit)* Orange, Apfelsine *f*; *(tree)* Orangenbaum *m*. **2** *adj (in colour)* orange *inv*, orange(n)farben.
**orangeade** [,ɒrɪndʒ'eɪd] *n* Orangenlimonade *f*.
**orange: ~juice** *n* Orangensaft *m*; **~ peel** *n* Orangenschale *f*.
**orang-utan(g)** [ɔː,ræŋuː'tæn, -'tæŋ] *n* Orang-Utan *m*.
**oration** [ɒ'reɪʃən] *n* Ansprache *f*. **funeral ~** Grabrede *f*.
**orator** ['ɒrətər] *n* Redner(in *f*) *m*.
**oratorio** [,ɒrə'tɔːrɪəʊ] *n (Mus)* Oratorium *nt*.
**oratory** ['ɒrətərɪ] *n (art)* Redekunst *f*.
**orbit** ['ɔːbɪt] **1** *n (Astron, Space)* Umlaufbahn *f*. **to be in ~** in der Umlaufbahn sein; **to put a satellite into ~** einen Satelliten in die Umlaufbahn schießen; **to go into ~** in die Umlaufbahn eintreten. **2** *vt* umkreisen. **3** *vi* kreisen.
**orbital road** ['ɔːbɪtl'rəʊd] *n* Ringstraße *f*, Ring *m*.
**orchard** ['ɔːtʃəd] *n* Obstgarten *m*; *(commercial)* Obstplantage *f*. **apple ~** Obstgarten *m* mit Apfelbäumen.
**orchestra** ['ɔːkɪstrə] *n* Orchester *nt*; *(US Theat: seating)* Parkett *nt*.
**orchestral** [ɔː'kestrəl] *adj* Orchester-.
**orchestra pit** *n* Orchestergraben *m*.
**orchestrate** ['ɔːkɪstreɪt] *vt (Mus, fig)* orchestrieren.
**orchestration** [,ɔːkɪs'treɪʃən] *n* Orchestrierung *f*.
**orchid** ['ɔːkɪd] *n* Orchidee *f*.
**ordain** [ɔː'deɪn] *vt* **(a)** *sb* ordinieren. **(b)** *(destine: God, fate)* wollen, bestimmen. **it was ~ed** das Schicksal hat es so gefügt *(geh)*.
**ordeal** [ɔː'diːl] *n* Tortur *f*; *(stronger, long-lasting)* Martyrium *nt*; *(torment, emotional ~)* Qual *f*.
**order** ['ɔːdər] **1** *n* **(a)** *(sequence)* (Reihen)folge *f*. **word ~** Wortstellung *f*; **in ~ of preference** *etc* in der bevorzugten Reihenfolge; **to put sth in (the right) ~** etw ordnen; **to be in the wrong ~** *or* **out of ~** durcheinander sein; *(one item)* nicht am richtigen Platz sein.
**(b)** *(system, discipline)* Ordnung *f*; *(in school also)* Disziplin *f*. **there's no ~ in his work** seiner Arbeit fehlt die Systematik; **it is in the ~ of things** es liegt in der Natur der Dinge; **his passport was in ~** sein Paß war in Ordnung; **to keep ~** die Ordnung wahren; **to keep the children in ~** die Kinder unter Kontrolle halten.
**(c)** *(working condition)* Zustand *m*. **to be in good/bad ~** in gutem/schlechtem Zustand sein; *(work well/badly)* in Ordnung/nicht in Ordnung sein; **to be out of/in ~** *(car, radio, telephone)* nicht funktionieren/funktionieren; *(machine, lift)* außer/in Betrieb sein.
**(d)** *(command)* Befehl *m*. **by ~ of the minister** auf

Anordnung des Ministers; **to be under ~s to do sth** Instruktionen haben, etw zu tun.

**(e)** *(in restaurant etc, for supplies)* Bestellung *f*; *(for goods, services)* Auftrag *m*. **two ~s of French fries** *(esp US)* zwei Portionen Pommes frites; **made to ~** auf Bestellung (gemacht); **to place an ~ with sb** eine Bestellung bei jdm aufgeben *or* machen; jdm einen Auftrag geben; **pay to the ~ of** zahlbar an *(+acc)*.

**(f) in ~ to do sth** um etw zu tun; **in ~ that** damit.

**(g)** *(correct procedure at meeting, Parl etc)* **a point of ~** eine Verfahrensfrage; **to be out of ~** *(fig)* aus dem Rahmen fallen; **to call the meeting to ~** die Versammlung zur Ordnung rufen; **a drink would seem to be in ~** ein Drink wäre angebracht; **is it in ~ for me to go to Paris?** ist es in Ordnung, wenn ich nach Paris fahre?; **to be the ~ of the day** auf dem Programm stehen *(also fig)*; *(Mil)* der Tagesbefehl sein.

**(h)** *(Biol)* Ordnung *f*; *(fig: class, degree)* Art *f*. **intelligence of a high ~** hochgradige Intelligenz; **something in the ~ of ten per cent** in der Größenordnung von zehn Prozent.

**(i)** *(Eccl)* *(of monks etc)* Orden *m*. **to take (holy) ~s** die Weihen empfangen.

**2** *vt* **(a)** *(command, decree)* sth befehlen, anordnen; *(prescribe: doctor)* verordnen *(for sb* jdm*)*. **to ~ sb to do sth** jdm befehlen, etw zu tun; *(esp Mil)* jdn dazu beordern, etw zu tun; **the referee ~ed him off the pitch** der Schiedsrichter stellte ihn vom Platz. **(b)** *(direct, arrange)* one's *affairs, life* ordnen. **(c)** *(Comm etc)* goods, *dinner, taxi* bestellen; *(to be manufactured)* in Auftrag geben *(from sb* bei jdm*)*.

**3** *vi* bestellen.

▶**order about** *or* **around** *vt sep* herumkommandieren.

**order: ~ book** *n (Comm)* Auftragsbuch *nt*; **to have a full ~ book** voll im Geschäft sein; **~ form** *n* Bestellformular *nt*, Bestellschein *m*.

**orderly** ['ɔːdəlɪ] **1** *adj* **(a)** *(tidy, methodical)* ordentlich. **(b)** *(disciplined)* ruhig, friedlich. **2** *n* **(medical)** ~ Pfleger(in *f*) *m*; *(Mil)* Sanitäter *m*.

**order number** *n (Comm)* Bestellnummer *f*.

**ordinal** ['ɔːdɪnl] *(Math)* **1** *adj* Ordnungs-, Ordinal-. **2** *n* Ordnungs- *or* Ordinalzahl *f*.

**ordinarily** ['ɔːdnrɪlɪ] *adv* gewöhnlich; *(+adj)* normal.

**ordinary** ['ɔːdnrɪ] **1** *adj* **(a)** gewöhnlich, normal. **in the ~ way I would ...** normalerweise *or* gewöhnlich würde ich ...; **my ~ doctor** der Arzt, zu dem ich normalerweise gehe; **~ seaman** *(Brit)* Leichtmatrose *m*; **~ share** *(Fin)* Stammaktie *f*. **(b)** *(average)* durchschnittlich. **2** *n* **out of the ~** außergewöhnlich, außerordentlich.

**ordination** [ˌɔːdɪ'neɪʃən] *n* Ordination *f*.

**ordnance** ['ɔːdnəns] *n (Mil)* *(artillery)* Geschütze *pl*; *(supply)* Material *nt*. **~ factory** Munitionsfabrik *f*; **O~ Survey map** *(Brit)* ≈ Meßtischblatt *nt*.

**ore** [ɔːʳ] *n* Erz *nt*.

**organ** ['ɔːgən] *n* **(a)** *(Anat)* Organ *nt*. **(b)** *(Mus)* Orgel *f*. **(c)** *(mouthpiece of opinion)* Sprachrohr *nt*; *(newspaper)* Organ *nt*.

**organ-grinder** ['ɔːgən'graɪndəʳ] *n* Drehorgelspieler *m*.

**organic** [ɔː'gænɪk] *adj (lit, fig)* organisch; *vegetables etc* aus biologischem Anbau; *farming* biologisch-dynamisch.

**organism** ['ɔːgənɪzəm] *n* Organismus *m*.

**organist** ['ɔːgənɪst] *n* Organist(in *f*) *m*.

**organization** [ˌɔːgənaɪ'zeɪʃən] *n* **(a)** *(act)* Organisation *f (also Pol)*; *(of time)* Einteilung *f*. **(b)** *(arrangement)* see *vt* (a) Ordnung *f*; Einteilung *f*; Aufbau *m*;

Planung *f*. **(c)** *(institution)* Organisation *f*; *(Comm)* Unternehmen *nt*.

**organize** ['ɔːgənaɪz] *vt* **(a)** *(systematize)* ordnen; *time, work* einteilen; *essay* aufbauen; *one's/sb's life* planen. **to get (oneself) ~d** *(get ready)* alles vorbereiten; *(sort things out)* seine Sachen in Ordnung bringen. **(b)** *(arrange)* party, meeting etc organisieren; *food for party etc* sorgen für. **to ~ things so that ...** es so einrichten, daß ...

**organized** ['ɔːgənaɪzd] *adj* organisiert; *life* geregelt. **he isn't very ~** bei ihm geht alles drunter und drüber *(col)*.

**organizer** ['ɔːgənaɪzəʳ] *n* Organisator(in *f*) *m*; *(of event also)* Veranstalter(in *f*) *m*.

**orgasm** ['ɔːgæzəm] *n* Orgasmus *m*.

**orgy** ['ɔːdʒɪ] *n (lit, fig)* Orgie *f*. **drunken ~** Sauforgie *f (col)*.

**orient** ['ɔːrɪənt] **1** *n (also* O~*)* Orient *m*; *(poet also)* Morgenland *nt*. **2** *vt see* **orientate**.

**oriental** [ˌɔːrɪ'entl] **1** *adj* orientalisch. **2** *n (person)* O~ Orientale *m*, Orientalin *f*.

**orientate** ['ɔːrɪənteɪt] *vt* ausrichten *(towards* auf *+acc)*; *thinking* orientieren *(towards* an *+dat)*. **money-~d** materiell ausgerichtet.

**orientation** [ˌɔːrɪən'teɪʃən] *n* Orientierung *f*; *(fig also)* Ausrichtung *f*.

**orienteering** [ˌɔːrɪən'tɪərɪŋ] *n* Orientierungslauf *m*.

**orifice** ['ɒrɪfɪs] *n* Öffnung *f*.

**origin** ['ɒrɪdʒɪn] *n* Ursprung *m*; *(of person, family)* Herkunft *f*. **to have its ~ in sth** auf etw *(acc)* zurückgehen; **country of ~** Herkunftsland *nt*; **of humble ~s** aus bescheidenen Verhältnissen.

**original** [ə'rɪdʒɪnl] **1** *adj* **(a)** *(first, earliest)* ursprünglich. **~ inhabitants of a country** Ureinwohner *pl* eines Landes; **~ text/version** Urtext *m*/Urfassung *f*. **(b)** *(not imitative)* painting original; *idea* originell. **~ research** eigene Forschung. **2** *n* Original *nt*; *(of model)* Vorlage *f*. **he reads Kant in the ~** er liest Kant im Original.

**originality** [əˌrɪdʒɪ'nælɪtɪ] *n* Originalität *f*.

**originally** [əˌrɪdʒənəlɪ] *adv* **(a)** ursprünglich. **(b)** *(in an original way)* originell.

**originate** [ə'rɪdʒɪneɪt] **1** *vt* hervorbringen; *policy, company* ins Leben rufen; *product* erfinden. **2** *vi* **(a)** entstehen. **to ~ from** *or* **with sb** von jdm stammen. **(b)** *(US: bus, train etc)* ausgehen *(in* von*)*.

**origination** [əˌrɪdʒɪ'neɪʃən] *n* Entstehung *f*; *(of product)* Erfindung *f*.

**originator** [ə'rɪdʒɪneɪtəʳ] *n (of plan, idea)* Urheber(in *f*) *m*; *(of product)* Erfinder(in *f*) *m*.

**Orkney Islands** ['ɔːknɪ'aɪləndz] *npl (also* **Orkneys***)* Orkneyinseln *pl*.

**ornament** ['ɔːnəmənt] **1** *n (object)* Ziergegenstand *m*. **2** *vt* verzieren; *room* ausschmücken.

**ornamental** [ˌɔːnə'mentl] *adj* dekorativ; *garden, plant etc* Zier-.

**ornamentation** [ˌɔːnəmen'teɪʃən] *n (ornamental detail)* Verzierungen *pl*; *(ornaments)* Schmuck *m*.

**ornate** [ɔː'neɪt] *adj* kunstvoll; *(of larger objects)* prunkvoll; *language* überladen *(pej)*, reich.

**ornithologist** [ˌɔːnɪ'θɒlədʒɪst] *n* Ornithologe *m*, Ornithologin *f*.

**ornithology** [ˌɔːnɪ'θɒlədʒɪ] *n* Ornithologie, Vogelkunde *f*.

**orphan** ['ɔːfən] **1** *n* Waise *f*. **2** *vt* **to be ~ed** zur Waise werden.

**orphanage** ['ɔːfənɪdʒ] *n* Waisenhaus *nt*.

**orthodontist** [ˌɔːθəʊ'dɒntɪst] *n* Kieferorthopäde *m*, -pädin *f*.

**orthodox** ['ɔːθədɒks] *adj (Rel, fig)* orthodox.

**orthodoxy** ['ɔːθədɒksɪ] *n* **(a)** Orthodoxie *f*. **(b)** *(fig)*

Konventionalität *f.*

**orthography** [ɔː'θɒɡrəfɪ] *n* Rechtschreibung, Orthographie *f.*

**orthopaedic,** *(US)* **orthopedic** [ˌɔːθəʊ'piːdɪk] *adj* orthopädisch.

**orthopaedics,** *(US)* **orthopedics** [ˌɔːθəʊ'piːdɪks] *n sing* Orthopädie *f.*

**orthopaedist,** *(US)* **orthopedist** [ˌɔːθəʊ'piːdɪst] *n* Orthopäde *m,* Orthopädin *f.*

**OS** = (a) **ordinary seaman.** (b) *(Brit)* **Ordnance Survey.** (c) **outsize.**

**Oscar** ['ɒskər] *n (Film)* Oscar *m.*

**oscillate** ['ɒsɪleɪt] *vi (lit, fig)* schwanken; *(Phys)* oszillieren, schwingen.

**oscillation** [ˌɒsɪ'leɪʃən] *n* Schwanken *nt; (individual movement etc)* Schwankung *f; (Phys)* Oszillation, Schwingung *f.*

**Oslo** ['ɒzləʊ] *n* Oslo *nt.*

**osmosis** [ɒz'məʊsɪs] *n* Osmose *f.*

**osprey** ['ɒspreɪ] *n* Fischadler *m.*

**ossify** ['ɒsɪfaɪ] *vi (lit)* verknöchern; *(fig)* erstarren; *(mind)* unbeweglich werden.

**ostensible** [ɒ'stensəbl] *adj* vorgeblich; *(alleged)* angeblich.

**ostentation** [ˌɒsten'teɪʃən] *n (display of wealth etc)* Pomp *m,* Protzerei *f (pej); (of skills etc)* Angeberei *f.*

**ostentatious** [ˌɒsten'teɪʃəs] *adj* (a) *(pretentious)* protzig *(col).* (b) *(conspicuous)* auffällig.

**osteopath** ['ɒstɪəpæθ] *n* Osteopath(in *f) m.*

**ostracism** ['ɒstrəsɪzəm] *n* Ächtung *f.*

**ostracize** ['ɒstrəsaɪz] *vt* ächten.

**ostrich** ['ɒstrɪtʃ] *n* Strauß *m.*

**OT** = **Old Testament** AT.

**other** ['ʌðər] **1** *adj* (a) andere(r, s). ~ **people** andere (Leute); **some ~ people will come later** später kommen noch ein paar; **do you have any ~ questions?** haben Sie sonst noch Fragen?; **the ~ day** neulich; **some ~ time** *(in future)* ein andermal; *(in past)* ein anderes Mal; ~ **people's property** fremdes Eigentum. (b) **every ~** *(alternate)* jede(r, s) zweite. (c) ~ **than** *(except)* außer *(+dat); (different to)* anders als. (d) **some time or ~** irgendwann (einmal); **some writer or ~** irgendein Schriftsteller *m.*

**2** *pron* andere(r, s). **he doesn't like hurting ~s** er mag niemanden verletzen; **there are 6 ~s** da sind noch 6 (andere); **are there any ~s there?** sind noch andere da?; **there were no ~s** there es waren sonst keine da; **something/someone or ~** irgend etwas/jemand; **one or ~ of them will come** einer (von ihnen) wird kommen.

**3** *adv* **somehow or ~** irgendwie; **somewhere or ~** irgendwo; **he was none ~ than the Minister** es war niemand anders als der Minister.

**otherwise** ['ʌðəwaɪz] **1** *adv* (a) *(in a different way)* anders. **I am ~ engaged** *(form)* ich bin anderweitig beschäftigt; **except where ~ stated** *(form)* sofern nicht anders angegeben; **Richard I, ~ (known as) the Lionheart** Richard I., auch als Löwenherz bekannt; **you seem to think ~** Sie scheinen anderer Meinung zu sein. (b) *(in other respects)* sonst, im übrigen. **2** *conj (or else)* sonst, andernfalls.

**other-worldly** [ˌʌðə'wɜːldlɪ] *adj attitude* weltfern; *smile, expression* entrückt.

**otter** ['ɒtər] *n* Otter *m.*

**OU** *(Brit)* = **Open University.**

**ouch** [aʊtʃ] *interj* autsch.

**ought** [ɔːt] *aux* (a) *(moral obligation)* **I ~ to do it** ich sollte *or* müßte es tun; **he ~ to have come** er hätte kommen sollen *or* müssen; **he thought you ~ to know** er meinte, Sie sollten das wissen. (b) *(desir-*

*ability)* **you ~ to see that film** den Film sollten Sie sehen; **she ~ to have been a teacher** sie hätte Lehrerin werden sollen. (c) *(probability)* **he ~ to win the race** er müßte das Rennen gewinnen; **that ~ to do** das dürfte wohl *or* müßte reichen; **... and I ~ to know!** ... und ich muß es doch wissen!

**ounce** [aʊns] *n* Unze *f.* **there's not an ~ of truth in it** daran ist kein Fünkchen Wahrheit.

**our** ['aʊər] *poss adj* unser; *see* **my.**

**ours** ['aʊəz] *poss pron* unsere(r, s); *see* **mine¹.**

**ourselves** [ˌaʊə'selvz] *pers pron (dir, indir obj +prep)* uns; *(emph)* selbst; *see* **myself.**

**oust** [aʊst] *vt object* herausbekommen; *government* absetzen; *politician, colleague etc* absägen *(col); rivals* ausschalten; *(take place of)* verdrängen.

**out** [aʊt] *see also* ~ **of 1** *adv* (a) *(not in container, car etc)* außen; *(not in building, room)* draußen; *(indicating motion) (seen from inside)* hinaus, raus *(col); (seen from ~side)* heraus, raus *(col).* **to be ~** weg sein; *(when visitors come)* nicht da sein; **they are ~ shopping** sie sind (zum) Einkaufen (gegangen); **he's ~ in his car** er ist mit dem Auto unterwegs; **it's cold ~ here/there** es ist kalt hier/da draußen; **he likes to be ~ and about** er ist gern unterwegs; **we had a day ~ in London** wir haben einen Tagesausflug nach London gemacht; **the journey ~** die Hinreise; *(seen from destination)* die Herfahrt; **the workers are ~** *(on strike)* die Arbeiter streiken; **the tide is ~** es ist Ebbe.

(b) *(indicating distance)* **to go ~ to China** nach China fahren; ~ **in the Far East** im Fernen Osten; **the boat was ten miles ~** das Schiff war zehn Meilen weit draußen; **five days ~ from Liverpool** *(Naut) (leaving)* fünf Tage nach dem Auslaufen von Liverpool; *(approaching)* fünf Tage vor Liverpool; ~ **at sea** draußen auf dem Meer.

(c) **to be ~** *(sun, stars, moon)* scheinen; *(flowers)* blühen.

(d) *(light, fire, ball, player)* aus; *(not in fashion)* aus der Mode; *(~ of the question)* ausgeschlossen, nicht drin *(col);* **to be ~** *(unconscious)* bewußtlos *or* weg *(col)* sein.

(e) **the best car ~** das beste Auto, das es zur Zeit gibt; **to be ~** *(be published)* herausgekommen sein; **their secret was ~** ihr Geheimnis war bekannt geworden; **the results are ~** die Ergebnisse sind (he)raus; ~ **with it!** heraus damit!; **before the day was ~** noch am selben Tag; **his calculations were ~** er hatte sich in seinen Berechnungen geirrt; **you're not far ~** Sie haben es fast (getroffen); **you're way ~!** weit gefehlt! *(geh),* da hast du dich völlig vertan *(col);* **we were £5/20% ~** wir hatten uns um £ 5/20% verrechnet *or* vertan *(col);* **speak ~ loud** sprechen Sie laut/lauter; **to be ~ for a good time** sich amüsieren wollen; **he's ~ for all he can get** er will haben, was er nur bekommen kann; **he's ~ to get her** er ist hinter ihr her; **he's just ~ to make money** er ist nur auf Geld aus; ~ **and away** weitaus, mit Abstand.

**2** *n* (a) *see* **in.** (b) *(esp US fig col: way ~)* Hintertür *f.*

**out-and-out** ['aʊtən'aʊt] *adj liar, fool* ausgemacht; *defeat* total.

**outback** ['aʊtbæk] *n:* **the ~** *(in Australia)* das Hinterland.

**out:** ~**bid** *pret, ptp* ~**bid** *vt* überbieten; ~**board** *adj motor* Außenbord-.

**outbreak** ['aʊtbreɪk] *n (of war, hostility, disease)* Ausbruch *m.* **a recent ~ of fire caused ...** ein Brand verursachte kürzlich ...; **at the ~ of war** bei Kriegsausbruch.

**outbuilding** ['aʊtbɪldɪŋ] n Nebengebäude nt.
**outburst** ['aʊtbɜːst] n (of joy, anger) Ausbruch m.
**outcast** ['aʊtkɑːst] n Ausgestoßene(r) mf. **social ~** Außenseiter m der Gesellschaft.
**outclass** [ˌaʊt'klɑːs] vt in den Schatten stellen.
**outcome** ['aʊtkʌm] n Ergebnis nt. **what was the ~?** was ist dabei herausgekommen?
**outcrop** ['aʊtkrɒp] n **an ~ (of rock)** eine Felsnase.
**outcry** ['aʊtkraɪ] n Aufschrei m (against über +acc); (public protest) Protestwelle f (against gegen). **there was a general ~ about the increase in taxes** eine Welle des Protests erhob sich wegen der Steuererhöhung.
**out:** **~dated** adj idea, theory überholt; machine, word, custom veraltet; **~distance** vt hinter sich (dat) lassen, abhängen (col).
**outdo** [ˌaʊt'duː] pret **outdid** [ˌaʊt'dɪd], ptp **outdone** [ˌaʊt'dʌn] vt übertreffen, überbieten (sb in sth jdn an etw dat).
**outdoor** ['aʊtdɔːr] adj life, games im Freien. **~ shoes** Straßenschuhe pl; **~ clothes** wärmere Kleidung; **~ type** sportlicher Typ; **~ swimming pool** Freibad nt.
**outdoors** ['aʊt'dɔːz] **1** adv draußen, im Freien. **to go ~** ins Freie or nach draußen gehen. **2** n **the great ~** (hum) die freie Natur.
**outer** ['aʊtər] adj attr äußere(r, s); door etc also Außen-. **~ garments** or **clothing** Oberbekleidung f; **~ space** der Weltraum.
**outfit** ['aʊtfɪt] n **(a)** (clothes) Kleidung f; (Fashion) Ensemble nt; (uniform) Uniform f; (of scout) Kluft f. **(b)** (equipment) Ausrüstung f. **(c)** (col: organization) Verein m (col). **(d)** (Mil) Einheit, Truppe f.
**outfitter** ['aʊtfɪtər] n (of ships) Ausrüster m. **gentlemen's ~'s** (esp Brit) Herrenausstatter m; **sports ~'s** (esp Brit) Sportartikelgeschäft nt.
**outgoing** ['aʊtˌgəʊɪŋ] **1** adj **(a)** tenant ausziehend; office-holder scheidend; train, boat hinausfahrend. **~ flight** Hinflug m. **(b)** personality kontaktfreudig. **2** npl **~s** (Brit) Ausgaben pl.
**outgrow** [ˌaʊt'grəʊ] pret **outgrew** [ˌaʊt'gruː], ptp **outgrown** [ˌaʊt'grəʊn] vt clothes herauswachsen aus; habit entwachsen (+dat).
**outhouse** ['aʊthaʊs] n Nebengebäude nt.
**outing** ['aʊtɪŋ] n Ausflug m. **to go on an ~** einen Ausflug machen.
**outlandish** [ˌaʊt'lændɪʃ] adj absonderlich; behaviour also malerisch; wallpaper etc ausgefallen.
**outlast** [ˌaʊt'lɑːst] vt (live longer) überleben; (endure longer) länger durchhalten als; (thing) länger halten als; (idea etc) überdauern.
**outlaw** ['aʊtlɔː] **1** n Geächtete(r) mf; (in western etc) Bandit m. **2** vt organization ächten; newspaper etc verbieten.
**outlay** ['aʊtleɪ] n (Kosten)aufwand m; (recurring, continuous) Kosten pl. **the initial ~** die anfänglichen Aufwendungen; **capital ~** Kapitalaufwand m.
**outlet** ['aʊtlet] **1** n **(a)** (for water) Abfluß m; (for steam) Abzug m; (US Elec) Steckdose f. **(b)** (Comm) Absatzmarkt m; (merchant) Abnehmer m; (shop) Verkaufsstelle f. **(c)** (fig) (for talents) Betätigungsmöglichkeit f; (for emotion) Ventil nt. **2** attr pipe Abfluß-; (for steam) Abzugs-; valve Auslaß-.
**outline** ['aʊtlaɪn] **1** n **(a)** (of objects) Umriß m; (silhouette) Silhouette f; (of face) Züge pl. **(b)** (fig: summary) Abriß m. **in (broad) ~** in groben Zügen; **just give (me) the main ~s** skizzieren Sie es mir grob. **2** vt **(a) the mountain was ~d against the sky** der Berg zeichnete sich gegen den Himmel ab. **(b)** (give summary of) umreißen, skizzieren.
**outlive** [ˌaʊt'lɪv] vt person überleben. **to have ~d its usefulness** ausgedient haben; (method, system) sich

überlebt haben.
**outlook** ['aʊtlʊk] n **(a)** (view) Aussicht f (over über +acc, on to auf +acc). **(b)** (prospects, Met) Aussichten pl. **(c)** (mental attitude) Einstellung f. **his ~ (up)on life** seine Einstellung zum Leben.
**out:** **~lying** adj (distant) entlegen, abgelegen; (outside the town boundary) umliegend; **~lying district** (of town) Außenbezirk nt; **~manoeuvre,** (US) **~maneuver** vt (Mil, fig) ausmanövrieren; (in rivalry) ausstechen; **~moded** adj unzeitgemäß; ideas, technology etc also überholt.
**outnumber** [ˌaʊt'nʌmbər] vt in der Überzahl sein gegenüber. **to be ~ed** zahlenmäßig unterlegen sein; **we were ~ed five to one** sie waren fünfmal so viele wie wir.
**out of** prep **(a)** (outside, away from) (position) nicht in (+dat), außerhalb (+gen); (motion) aus (+dat). **to go/be ~ the country** außer Landes gehen/sein; **he walked ~ the room** er ging aus dem Zimmer (hinaus); **he went ~ the door** er ging zur Tür hinaus; **to look ~ the window** aus dem Fenster sehen; **I saw him ~ the window** ich sah ihn durchs Fenster; **~ danger/sight** außer Gefahr/Sicht; **he feels ~ it** (col) er kommt sich (dat) ausgeschlossen vor; **you're well ~ it** so ist es auch besser für dich.
**(b)** (cause, motive) aus (+dat). **~ curiosity** aus Neugier.
**(c)** (indicating origins or source) aus (+dat). **to drink ~ a glass** aus einem Glas trinken; **made ~ silver** aus Silber (gemacht); **to copy sth ~ a book** etw aus einem Buch kopieren.
**(d)** (from among) von (+dat). **in seven cases ~ ten** in sieben von zehn Fällen; **one ~ every four smokers** einer von vier Rauchern.
**(e)** (without) **~ breath** außer Atem; **we are ~ money/bread** wir haben kein Geld/Brot mehr.
**out:** **~-of-date** adj, pred **~ of date** methods, ideas überholt; clothes, records altmodisch; customs veraltet; **~-of-the-way** adj, pred **~ of the way** spot abgelegen; theory ungewöhnlich; **~patient** n ambulanter Patient, ambulante Patientin; **~patients' (department)** Ambulanz f; **~play** vt besser spielen als; **~post** n (Mil, fig) Vorposten m.
**output** ['aʊtpʊt] **1** n (of machine, factory, person) Produktion f; (of engine, Elec) Leistung f; (capacity of amplifier) Ausgangsleistung f; (Comp) Ausgabe f, Output m or nt. **2** vt (Comp) ausgeben.
**outrage** ['aʊtreɪdʒ] **1** n (wicked, violent deed) Schandtat f; (cruel also) Greueltat f; (by police, demonstrators etc) Ausschreitung f; (indecency, injustice) Skandal m. **bomb ~** verbrecherischer Bombenanschlag; **an ~ against humanity** ein Verbrechen nt gegen die Menschlichkeit; **it's a public ~** es ist ein öffentlicher Skandal; **an ~ against good taste** eine unerhörte Geschmacklosigkeit. **2** [aʊt'reɪdʒ] vt sense of decency beleidigen; person empören, entrüsten.
**outrageous** [aʊt'reɪdʒəs] adj (cruel, violent) grauenhaft; (unjust) unerhört; conduct, nonsense haarsträubend; language entsetzlich; charge etc ungeheuerlich; clothes, make-up unmöglich; (indecent) geschmacklos.
**outrageously** [aʊt'reɪdʒəslɪ] adv fürchterlich; exaggerate also maßlos; dressed unmöglich.
**out:** **~ran** pret of **~run**; **~rider** n (on motorcycle) Kradbegleiter m.
**outright** [aʊt'raɪt] **1** adv (at once) kill auf der Stelle; (openly) geradeheraus. **2** ['aʊtraɪt] adj nonsense, disaster total. **that's ~ arrogance/deception** das ist die reine Arroganz/das ist glatter Betrug; **an ~ error** ganz einfach ein Fehler.

**out:** ~**run** *pret* ~**ran,** *ptp* ~**run** *vt* schneller laufen als; *(outdistance)* davonlaufen *(+dat)*; ~**set** *n* Anfang *m*; **at the** ~**set** am Anfang; **from the** ~**set** von Anfang an; ~**shine** *pret, ptp* ~**shone** *vt (fig)* in den Schatten stellen.

**outside** [‚aʊt'saɪd] **1** *n (of house, car, object)* Außenseite *f.* **to open the door from the** ~ die Tür von außen öffnen; **to overtake on the** ~ außen überholen; **he sees it from the** ~ *(fig)* er sieht es als Außenstehender; **at the (very)** ~ im äußersten Falle.

**2** *adj* **(a)** *(external)* Außen-, äußere(r, s). **an** ~ **broadcast** eine nicht im Studio produzierte Sendung; ~ **capital** Fremdkapital *nt*; **the** ~ **lane** die äußere Spur; ~ **line** *(Telec)* Amtsanschluß *m*; ~ **seat** *(in a row)* Platz *m* am Gang. **(b)** *price* äußerste(r, s). **at an** ~ **estimate** maximal. **(c)** *(very unlikely)* **an** ~ **chance** eine geringe Chance; **my horse only has an** ~ **chance** mein Pferd hat nur Außenseiterchancen.

**3** *adv (on the outer side)* außen; *(of house, vehicle)* draußen. **to be/go** ~ draußen sein/nach draußen gehen.

**4** *prep (also* ~ **of) (a)** außerhalb *(+gen)*. **to be/go** ~ **sth** außerhalb einer Sache sein/aus etw gehen; **he is waiting** ~ **the door** er wartet vor der Tür; **it is** ~ **the terms of our agreement** es geht über unsere Vereinbarung hinaus. **(b)** *(apart from)* außer *(+dat)*.

**outsider** [‚aʊt'saɪdə<sup>r</sup>] *n* Außenseiter(in *f*) *m*.

**out:** ~**size** *adj* übergroß; ~**size clothes** Kleidung *f* in Übergröße; ~**skirts** *npl (of town)* Außenbezirke *pl*, Stadtrand *m*; ~**smart** *vt (col)* überlisten, austricksen *(col)*.

**outspoken** [‚aʊt'spəʊkən] *adj* *person, criticism, book* freimütig; *remark* direkt. **he is** ~ er nimmt kein Blatt vor den Mund.

**outspread** [‚aʊt'spred] *adj* ausgebreitet.

**outstanding** [‚aʊt'stændɪŋ] *adj* **(a)** *(exceptional)* hervorragend; *talent, beauty* außerordentlich; *event* bemerkenswert; *detail* auffallend; *feature* hervorstechend. **(b)** *(Comm, Fin) business, work* unerledigt; *bill, interest* ausstehend.

**outstandingly** [‚aʊt'stændɪŋlɪ] *adv* außerordentlich; ~ **good/well** hervorragend.

**out:** ~**stay** *vt* **I don't want to** ~**stay my welcome** ich will eure Gastfreundschaft nicht zu lange in Anspruch nehmen; ~**stretched** *adj body* ausgestreckt; ~**strip** *vt* **(a)** überholen; **(b)** *(fig)* übertreffen *(in an +dat)*; ~**take** *n* nicht verwendete Filmsequenz, Nichtkopierer *m (spec)*; ~**-tray** *n* Ablage *f* für Ausgänge; ~**vote** *vt* überstimmen.

**outward** ['aʊtwəd] **1** *adj* **(a)** *appearance, form* äußere(r, s). **it was purely** ~ **show** es war alles nur Theater *or* Mache *(col)*. **(b)** *movement* nach außen gehend; *freight* ausgehend. ~ **journey/voyage** Hinfahrt/Hinreise *f.* **2** *adv* nach außen. **the door opens** ~ die Tür geht nach außen auf.

**outwardly** ['aʊtwədlɪ] *adv* nach außen hin.

**outwards** ['aʊtwədz] *adv* nach außen.

**out:** ~**weigh** *vt disadvantages* mehr Gewicht haben als; ~**wit** *vt* überlisten; *(in card games etc)* austricksen *(col)*; ~**worn** *adj idea* abgenutzt.

**oval** ['əʊvəl] **1** *adj* oval. **2** *n* Oval *nt*.

**ovary** ['əʊvərɪ] *n (Anat)* Eierstock *m*; *(Bot)* Fruchtknoten *m*.

**ovation** [əʊ'veɪʃən] *n* Ovation *f*, stürmischer Beifall. **to get an** ~ stürmischen Beifall ernten.

**oven** ['ʌvn] *n (Cook)* (Back)ofen *m*; *(cooker)* Herd *m*; *(Tech: for drying)* (Trocken)ofen *m*. **it's like an** ~ **in here** hier ist es ja wie im Backofen.

**oven:** ~**-glove** *n (Brit)* Topfhandschuh *m*; ~**proof** *adj dish* feuerfest; ~**-ready** *adj* bratfertig; ~**ware** *n* feuerfeste Formen *pl*.

**over** ['əʊvə<sup>r</sup>] **1** *prep* **(a)** *(above, across)* über *(+dat)*; *(direction)* über *(+acc)*. **he spread the blanket** ~ **the bed** er breitete die Decke über das Bett; **he spilled coffee** ~ **it** er goß Kaffee darüber; **you've got ink all** ~ **your hands** Ihre Hände sind ganz voller Tinte; **to hit sb** ~ **the head** jdm auf den Kopf schlagen; **bent** ~ **one's books** über die Bücher gebeugt; **to look** ~ **the wall** über die Mauer schauen; **the noise came from** ~ **the wall** der Lärm kam von der anderen Seite der Mauer; **it's** ~ **the page** es ist auf der nächsten Seite; **it's just** ~ **the road from us** das ist von uns (aus) nur über die Straße; **the bridge** ~ **the river** die Brücke über den Fluß; **they came from all** ~ **England/all** ~ **the place** sie kamen aus ganz England/von überall her.

**(b)** *(more than, longer than)* über *(+acc)*. ~ **and above that** darüber hinaus; **an increase of 15%** ~ **last year** ein Zuwachs von 15% im Vergleich zum letzten Jahr; **that was well** ~ **a year ago** das ist weit über ein Jahr her.

**(c)** *(during)* während *(+gen)*, in *(+dat)*. ~ **the weekend** übers Wochenende; ~ **the summer/ Christmas** den Sommer über/über Weihnachten; ~ **the years I've come to realize** ... im Laufe der Jahre ist mir klargeworden ...; **the visits were spread** ~ **several months** die Besuche verteilten sich über mehrere Monate.

**(d) they talked** ~ **a cup of coffee** sie unterhielten sich bei einer Tasse Kaffee; **they'll be a long time** ~ **it** sie werden dazu lange brauchen; **I've got an advantage** ~ **him** ich habe ihm gegenüber einen Vorteil; **he told me** ~ **the phone** er hat es mir am Telefon gesagt; **I heard it** ~ **the radio** ich habe es im Radio gehört; **it's not worth arguing** ~ es lohnt (sich) nicht, darüber zu streiten.

**2** *adv* **(a)** *(across)* **(away from speaker)* hinüber; *(towards speaker)* herüber; *(on the other side)* drüben. **they swam** ~ **to us** sie schwammen zu uns herüber; **he took the fruit** ~ **to his mother** er brachte das Obst zu seiner Mutter hinüber; **he swam** ~ **to the other side** er schwamm auf die andere Seite (hinüber); **come** ~ **tonight** kommen Sie heute abend vorbei; **he is** ~ **here/there** er ist hier/dort drüben; ~ **to you!** Sie sind daran; **and now** ~ **to our reporter in Belfast** und nun schalten wir zu unserem Reporter in Belfast um; ~ **in America** drüben in Amerika.

**(b) famous the world** ~ in der ganzen Welt berühmt; **I've been looking for it all** ~ *(esp US)* ich habe überall danach gesucht; **I am aching all** ~ mir tut alles weh; **he was shaking all** ~ er zitterte am ganzen Leib; **that's him/Fred all** ~ das ist typisch für ihn/Fred, typisch Fred.

**(c) to turn an object** ~ einen Gegenstand herumdrehen; **he knocked the vase and** ~ **it went** er stieß an die Vase, und sie fiel um.

**(d)** *(ended: film, operation etc)* zu Ende. **the rain is** ~ der Regen hat aufgehört; **the danger was** ~ die Gefahr war vorüber; **when all this is** ~ wenn das alles vorbei ist; **it's all** ~ **between us** es ist aus zwischen uns.

**(e)** *(repetition)* **to start (all)** ~ **again** noch einmal (ganz) von vorn anfangen; ~ **and** ~ **(again)** immer (und immer) wieder; **he did it five times** ~ er hat es fünfmal wiederholt.

**(f)** *(excessively)* übermäßig, allzu.

**(g)** *(remaining)* übrig. **there was no meat (left)** ~ es war kein Fleisch mehr übrig.

**(h)** *(more)* **children of 8 and** ~ Kinder über 8; **all**

**results of 5.3 and** ~ alle Ergebnisse von 5,3 und darüber. **(i)** *(Telec)* over. ~ **and out** Ende der Durchsage; *(Aviat)* over and out.

**over-** *pref* über-.

**over:** ~**abundant** *adj* überreichlich; ~**act** *vi* (die Rolle) übertrieben spielen; ~**active** *adj* zu aktiv.

**overall¹** [ˌəʊvərˈɔːl] **1** *adj* **(a)** *width, total* gesamt, Gesamt-. ~ **dimensions** Außenmaße *pl*; ~ **majority** absolute Mehrheit. **(b)** *(general)* allgemein. **the** ~ **effect of this was to** ... dies hatte das Endergebnis, daß ... **2** *adv* **(a)** insgesamt. **(b)** *(in general)* im großen und ganzen.

**overall²** [ˈəʊvərɔːl] *n (Brit)* Kittel *m*.

**overalls** [ˈəʊvərɔːlz] *npl* Overall *m*.

**over:** ~**anxious** *adj* übertrieben besorgt; *(on particular occasion)* übermäßig aufgeregt; **I'm not exactly** ~**anxious to go** ich bin nicht gerade scharf darauf zu gehen *(col)*; ~**ate** *pret of* ~**eat**; ~**awe** *vt (intimidate)* einschüchtern; *(impress)* überwältigen; ~**balance 1** *vi* aus dem Gleichgewicht kommen; **2** *vt* umwerfen; *boat* kippen.

**overbearing** [ˌəʊvəˈbɛərɪŋ] *adj* herrisch.

**overboard** [ˈəʊvəbɔːd] *adv* **(a)** *(Naut)* **to fall** ~ über Bord gehen; **man** ~! Mann über Bord! **(b)** *(fig: col)* **to go** ~ übers Ziel hinausschießen, zu weit gehen; **don't go** ~ **about it** übertreiben Sie es nicht.

**over:** ~**book** *vt* überbuchen; ~**burden** *vt (lit)* überladen; *(fig)* überlasten; ~**came** *pret of* ~**come**; ~**cast** *adj* bedeckt; *sky also* bewölkt; **it's getting rather** ~**cast** es zieht sich zu; ~**cautious** *adj* übervorsichtig.

**overcharge** [ˌəʊvəˈtʃɑːdʒ] *vt person* zuviel berechnen *(+dat)* (for für).

**overcoat** [ˈəʊvəkəʊt] *n* (Winter)mantel *m*.

**overcome** [ˌəʊvəˈkʌm] *pret* **overcame** [ˌəʊvəˈkeɪm], *ptp* ~ *vt enemy* überwältigen; *bad habit* sich *(dat)* abgewöhnen; *shyness etc* überwinden; *temptation* widerstehen *(+dat)*; *difficulty, anger* überwinden; *disappointment* hinwegkommen über *(+acc)*. **he was** ~ **by the fumes** die Dämpfe machten ihn bewußtlos; **he was quite** ~ **by grief/emotion** Schmerz/Rührung übermannte ihn; **I'm quite** ~ ich bin ganz ergriffen.

**over:** ~**confidence** *n* übersteigertes Selbstvertrauen; *(over-optimism)* zu großer Optimismus; ~**confident** *adj* übertrieben selbstsicher; *(too optimistic)* zu optimistisch; ~**cook** *vt* verbraten; *(boil)* verkochen; ~ **critical** *adj* zu kritisch; ~**crowded** *adj* überfüllt; *(overpopulated)* überbevölkert; ~**crowding** *n* Überfüllung *f*; *(of town)* Überbevölkerung *f*.

**overdo** [ˌəʊvəˈduː] *pret* **overdid** [ˌəʊvəˈdɪd], *ptp* **overdone** [ˌəʊvəˈdʌn] *vt (exaggerate)* übertreiben. **you are** ~**ing it** *or* **things** Sie übertreiben; *(tiring yourself)* Sie übernehmen sich.

**over:** ~**done** *adj* **(a)** *(exaggerated)* übertrieben; **(b)** *(Cook)* verkocht; *bacon etc* verbraten; ~**dose 1** *n* Überdosis *f*; **2** *vi* eine Überdosis nehmen; ~**draft** *n* Konto-Überziehung *f*; **to have an** ~**draft of £10** sein Konto um £10 überzogen haben; ~**draft facility** *n* Dispositionskredit *m*; ~**draw** *pret* ~**drew**, *ptp* ~**drawn** *vt one's account* überziehen; ~**dressed** *adj* übertrieben gekleidet; *(too smart)* zu elegant angezogen; ~**drive** *n (Aut)* Schnellgang (getriebe *nt*) *m*; ~**due** *adj* überfällig; **long** ~**due** schon seit langem fällig; ~**eat** *pret* ~**ate**, *ptp* ~**eaten** *vi* zuviel essen; ~**emphasize** *vt* überbetonen; ~**enthusiastic** *adj* übertrieben begeistert; ~**estimate** *vt price* zu hoch einschätzen; *importance* überbewerten; *chances, danger* überschätzen; ~**excited**

*adj person* zu aufgeregt; *children* aufgedreht; ~**exertion** *n* Überanstrengung *f*; ~**expose** *vt (Phot)* überbelichten; ~**feed** *pret, ptp* ~**fed** *vt* überfüttern; ~**fill** *vt* zu voll machen.

**overflow** [ˈəʊvəfləʊ] **1** *n (outlet)* Überlauf *m*; *(excess: of people, population)* Überschuß *m (of* an *+dat)*. **2** [ˌəʊvəˈfləʊ] *vt area* überschwemmen. **the river has** ~**ed its banks** der Fluß ist über die Ufer getreten. **3** [ˌəʊvəˈfləʊ] *vi (liquid, river etc)* überlaufen. **full to** ~**ing** *(bowl, cup)* zum Überlaufen voll; *(room)* überfüllt; **the crowd at the meeting** ~**ed into the street** die Leute bei der Versammlung standen bis auf die Straße.

**over:** ~**fly** *pret* ~**flew**, *ptp* ~**flown** *vt* **(a)** *(fly over) town* überfliegen; **(b)** *(fly beyond) runway, airport* hinausfliegen über *(+acc)*. ~**full** *adj* zu voll; ~**generous** *adj* zu großzügig; ~**grown** *adj* **(a)** überwachsen *(with* von*)*; **(b) an** ~**grown schoolboy** ein großes Kind; ~**hang** *(vb: pret, ptp* ~**hung)** **1** *vt* hängen über *(+acc)*; *(rocks, balcony)* hinausragen über *(+acc)*, vorstehen über *(+acc)*; **2** *n* Überhang *m*; ~**hanging** *adj* überhängend; ~**haul 1** *n* Überholung *f*; **2** *vt machine, vehicle engine* überholen; *plans* überprüfen.

**overhead** [ˌəʊvəˈhed] **1** *adv* oben; *(in the sky)* am Himmel. **a plane flew** ~ ein Flugzeug flog über uns *etc (acc)* (hinweg). **2** [ˈəʊvəhed] *adj* ~ **cables** Freileitungen; ~ **projector** Overheadprojektor *m*; ~ **camshaft** obenliegende Nockenwelle; ~ **valves** obengesteuerte Ventile. **3** [ˈəʊvəhed] *n (US)* = **overheads**.

**overheads** [ˈəʊvəhedz] *npl (Brit Comm)* allgemeine Unkosten *pl*.

**overhear** [ˌəʊvəˈhɪəʳ] *pret, ptp* **overheard** [ˌəʊvəˈhɜːd] *vt* zufällig mit anhören. **he was** ~**d to say that** ... jemand hat ihn sagen hören, daß ...

**over:** ~**heat 1** *vi (engine etc)* heißlaufen; *(fig: economy)* sich überhitzen; **2** *vt (lit, fig)* überhitzen; ~**hung** *pret, ptp of* ~**hang**.

**overindulge** [ˌəʊvərɪnˈdʌldʒ] *vi* zuviel genießen.

**overindulgence** [ˌəʊvərɪnˈdʌldʒəns] *n (eating)* Völlerei *f*. ~ **in wine** übermäßiger Weingenuß.

**overjoyed** [ˌəʊvəˈdʒɔɪd] *adj* überglücklich *(at, by* über *+acc)*. **he wasn't exactly** ~ er war nicht gerade erfreut.

**over:** ~**kill** *n (Mil)* Overkill *m*; *(fig)* Rundumschlag *m*; ~**land** *adv travel etc* über Land.

**overlap** [ˈəʊvəlæp] **1** *n* Überschneidung *f*; *(of concepts)* teilweise Deckung. **3 inches'** ~ 3 Zoll Überlappung; **there's quite a lot of** ~ **between their work** ihre Arbeitsbereiche überschneiden sich in vielen Punkten. **2** [ˌəʊvəˈlæp] *vi* **(a)** *(tiles, boards)* sich überlappen. **(b)** *(dates, responsibilities)* sich überschneiden; *(ideas, work)* sich teilweise decken.

**over:** ~**lay** *(pret, ptp* ~**laid)** [ˌəʊvəˈleɪ] *vt* überziehen; ~**leaf** *adv* **the illustration** ~**leaf** die umseitige Abbildung; ~**load** *vt* überladen; *(Elec, Mech)* überlasten.

**overlook** [ˌəʊvəˈlʊk] *vt* **(a)** *(have view onto)* überblicken. **a room** ~**ing the park** ein Zimmer mit Blick auf den Park; **the garden is not** ~**ed** niemand kann in den Garten hineinsehen. **(b)** *(fail to notice)* übersehen. **(c)** *(ignore) mistake* hinwegsehen über *(+acc)*, durchgehen lassen.

**overly** [ˈəʊvlɪ] *adv* übermäßig.

**over:** ~**manning** *n* Überbesetzung *f* (mit Arbeitskräften); ~**much** *adv* übermäßig viel.

**overnight** [ˌəʊvəˈnaɪt] **1** *adv* **(a)** über Nacht. **to stay** ~ **(with sb)** bei jdm übernachten. **(b)** *(fig)* von heute auf morgen. **the place had changed** ~ der Ort hatte sich über Nacht verändert. **2** [ˈəʊvəˌnaɪt] *adj* **(a)**

*journey, train etc* Nacht-. ~ **stay** Übernachtung *f*; ~ **bag** Reisetasche *f*. **(b)** *(fig: sudden)* ganz plötzlich. **the play was an ~ success** das Stück wurde über Nacht ein Erfolg.

**over:** ~**paid** *pret, ptp of* ~**pay**; ~**particular** *adj* zu genau, pingelig *(col)*; ~**pass** *n* Überführung *f*; ~**pay** *pret, ptp* ~**paid** *vt* überbezahlen; **to** ~**pay sb by £50** jdm £50 zuviel bezahlen; ~**populated** *adj* übervölkert; ~**population** *n* Übervölkerung *f*.

**overpower** [ˌəʊvə'paʊər] *vt (emotion, heat)* überwältigen.

**overpowering** [ˌəʊvə'paʊərɪŋ] *adj* überwältigend; *smell* penetrant; *heat* unerträglich. **he's a bit ~ at times** seine Art kann einem manchmal zuviel werden.

**over:** ~**price** *vt* **these goods are** ~**priced** diese Waren sind zu teuer; **at £50 it's** ~**priced** £50 ist zuviel dafür; ~**print** *vt stamp, text* überdrucken; *(Phot)* überkopieren; ~**produce** *vi* überproduzieren; ~**production** *n* Überproduktion *f*; ~**protective** *adj parent* überängstlich; ~**rate** *vt* überschätzen; *book, system etc* überbewerten; ~**reach** *vr* sich übernehmen; ~**react** *vi* übertrieben reagieren *(to* auf +*acc)*; ~**reaction** *n* übertriebene Reaktion *(to* auf +*acc)*.

**override** [ˌəʊvə'raɪd] *pret* **overrode** [ˌəʊvə'rəʊd], *ptp* **overridden** [ˌəʊvə'rɪdn] *vt decision, ruling* aufheben, außer Kraft setzen; *objection* ablehnen; *mechanism* abschalten.

**overriding** [ˌəʊvə'raɪdɪŋ] *adj principle* vorrangig, wichtigste(r, s). **of ~ importance** von allergrößter Wichtigkeit.

**overripe** [ˌəʊvə'raɪp] *adj* überreif.

**overrule** [ˌəʊvə'ruːl] *vt* ablehnen; *claim* nicht anerkennen; *verdict, decision* aufheben. **he was** ~**d by the majority** er wurde überstimmt.

**overrun** [ˌəʊvə'rʌn] *pret* **overran** [ˌəʊvə'ræn], *ptp* ~ **1** *vt* **(a)** *(weeds)* überwuchern. ~ **with tourists** von Touristen überlaufen. **(b)** *(troops etc: invade)* einfallen in (+*dat)*. **2** *vi (in time)* überziehen. **his speech overran by ten minutes** seine Rede dauerte zehn Minuten zu lang.

**overseas** ['əʊvə'siːz] **1** *adj market, state* ausländisch; *(far away)* Übersee-. **our ~ office** unsere Zweigstelle im Ausland/in Übersee; ~ **aid** Entwicklungshilfe *f*; **an ~ visitor** ein Besucher aus dem Ausland/aus Übersee. **2** [ˌəʊvə'siːz] *adv* **to be ~** im Ausland/in Übersee sein; **to go ~** ins Ausland/nach Übersee gehen.

**over:** ~**see** *pret* ~**saw**, *ptp* ~**seen** *vt* beaufsichtigen; ~**seer** *n* Aufseher(in *f*) *m*; *(foreman)* Vorarbeiter(in *f*) *m*; ~**sensitive** *adj* überempfindlich; ~**shadow** *vt (lit, fig)* überschatten.

**overshoot** [ˌəʊvə'ʃuːt] *pret, ptp* **overshot** [ˌəʊvə'ʃɒt] *vt runway* hinausschießen über (+*acc)*. **to ~ the mark** *(lit, fig)* übers Ziel hinausschießen.

**oversight** ['əʊvəsaɪt] *n* Versehen *nt*. **by** *or* **through an ~** aus Versehen.

**over:** ~**simplification** *n* (zu) grobe Vereinfachung; ~**simplify** *vt* grob vereinfachen; ~**sleep** *pret, ptp* ~**slept** *vi* verschlafen; ~**spend** *pret, ptp* ~**spent** *vi* zuviel ausgeben; ~**spending** *n* zu hohe Ausgaben *pl*; ~**spill** *n (Brit)* Bevölkerungsüberschuß *m*; ~**spill town** Trabantenstadt *f*; ~**staffed** *adj* überbesetzt; ~**state** *vt facts, case* übertreiben; ~**statement** *n* Übertreibung *f*; ~**step** *vt* **to** ~**step the mark** zu weit gehen; ~**strain** *vt person* überanstrengen; *metal, part, resources, strength* überbelasten; **to** ~**strain oneself** sich übernehmen; ~**strung** *adj person* überspannt; ~**subscribe** *vt (Fin)* überzeichnen.

**overt** [əʊ'vɜːt] *adj* offen; *hostility* unverhohlen.

**overtake** [ˌəʊvə'teɪk] *pret* **overtook** [ˌəʊvə'tʊk], *ptp* **overtaken** [ˌəʊvə'teɪkən] **1** *vt* einholen; *(pass) runner etc, (Brit) car* überholen. **events have** ~**n us** wir waren auf die Entwicklung der Dinge nicht gefaßt. **2** *vi (Brit)* überholen.

**overtaking** [ˌəʊvə'teɪkɪŋ] *n (Brit)* Überholen *nt*. **"No ~"** „Überholverbot".

**over:** ~**tax** *vt* **(a)** *(fig) person, heart* überlasten; *patience* überfordern; **to** ~**tax oneself** *or* **one's strength** sich übernehmen; **(b)** *(lit)* übermäßig besteuern; ~**throw** *(vb: pret* ~**throw**, *ptp* ~**thrown) 1** ['əʊvəˌθrəʊ] *n* Sieg *m (of* über +*acc)*; *(being* ~**thrown)** Niederlage *f*; *(of dictator etc)* Sturz *m*; *(of country)* Eroberung *f*; **2** [ˌəʊvə'θrəʊ] *vt (defeat) enemy* besiegen; *dictator* stürzen; *country* erobern.

**overtime** ['əʊvətaɪm] **1** *n* **(a)** Überstunden *pl*. **I am on ~** ich mache Überstunden; **he did four hours' ~** er hat vier (Stunden) Überstunden gemacht. **(b)** *(US Sport)* Verlängerung *f*. **2** *adv* **to work ~** Überstunden machen; **my imagination was working ~** meine Phantasie lief auf Hochtouren *(col)*.

**over:** ~**tired** *adj* übermüdet; ~**tiredness** *n* Übermüdung *f*.

**overtone** ['əʊvətəʊn] *n (fig)* Unterton *m*.

**overture** ['əʊvətjʊər] *n (Mus)* Ouvertüre *f*. **to make ~s to sb** Annäherungsversuche bei jdm machen.

**overturn** [ˌəʊvə'tɜːn] **1** *vt* **(a)** umkippen, umwerfen. **(b)** *regime* stürzen. **2** *vi (chair)* umkippen; *(boat also)* kentern.

**over:** ~**use 1** [ˌəʊvə'juːz] *vt* zu häufig gebrauchen; **2** [ˌəʊvə'juːs] *n* zu häufiger Gebrauch; ~**value** *vt goods* zu hoch schätzen; ~**view** *n* Überblick *m (of* über +*acc)*.

**overweening** [ˌəʊvə'wiːnɪŋ] *adj* überheblich, anmaßend; *ambition* maßlos.

**overweight** ['əʊvə'weɪt] *adj thing* zu schwer; *person* übergewichtig. **this box is 5 kilos ~** diese Schachtel hat 5 Kilo Übergewicht; **you're ~** Sie haben Übergewicht.

**overwhelm** [ˌəʊvə'welm] *vt* **(a)** *(overpower: strong feelings)* überwältigen. **he was** ~**ed when they gave him the present** er war zutiefst gerührt, als sie ihm das Geschenk gaben. **(b)** *enemy* überwältigen; *country* besiegen. **(c)** *(fig) (with favours, praise)* überschütten; *(with questions)* bestürmen; *(with work)* überhäufen.

**overwhelming** [ˌəʊvə'welmɪŋ] *adj* überwältigend; *desire* unwiderstehlich.

**overwhelmingly** [ˌəʊvə'welmɪŋlɪ] *adv see adj* **they voted ~ for it** sie haben mit überwältigender Mehrheit dafür gestimmt.

**overwork** [ˌəʊvə'wɜːk] **1** *n* Überarbeitung *f*. **2** *vt horse etc* schinden; *person* überanstrengen; *idea, theme* überstrapazieren. **we're** ~**ed** wir sind überarbeitet. **3** *vi* sich überarbeiten.

**overwrite** [ˌəʊvə'raɪt] *vti (Comp)* überschreiben.

**overwrought** [ˌəʊvə'rɔːt] *adj person* überreizt.

**overzealous** [ˌəʊvə'zeləs] *adj* übereifrig.

**ovulation** [ˌɒvjʊ'leɪʃən] *n* Eisprung *m*.

**ow** [aʊ] *interj* autsch.

**owe** [əʊ] *vt money* schulden, schuldig sein *(sb sth, sth to sb* jdm etw). **I ~ him a meal** ich bin ihm noch ein Essen schuldig; **how much do I ~ you?** *(in shop etc)* was bin ich (Ihnen) schuldig?; **I ~ my life to him** ich verdanke ihm mein Leben; **to what do I ~ the honour of your visit?** *(iro)* was verschafft mir die Ehre Ihres Besuches?

**owing** ['əʊɪŋ] **1** *adj* unbezahlt. **how much is still ~?** wieviel steht noch aus? **2** *prep* ~ **to** wegen *(+gen or (col) +dat)*, infolge *(+gen)*; ~ **to the circumstances** umständehalber; ~ **to his being foreign** weil er Ausländer ist/war.

**owl** [aʊl] *n* Eule *f.*

**own¹** [əʊn] *vt* (**a**) *(possess)* besitzen. **who ~s that?** wem gehört das?; **he acts as if he ~s the place** er tut, als wäre er hier zu Hause. (**b**) *(admit)* zugeben; *(recognize)* anerkennen.
►**own up** *vi* es zugeben. **to ~ ~ to sth** etw zugeben; **he ~ed ~ to stealing the money** er gab zu, das Geld gestohlen zu haben.

**own²** **1** *adj attr* eigen. **his ~ car** sein eigenes Auto; **one's ~ car** ein eigenes Auto; **he's his ~ man** er geht seinen eigenen Weg; **he does (all) his ~ cooking** er kocht für sich selbst. **2** *pron* (**a**) **that's my ~** das ist mein eigenes; **those are my ~** die gehören mir; **my ~ is bigger** meine(r, s) ist größer; **my time is my ~** ich kann frei über meine Zeit verfügen; **a house of one's ~** ein eigenes Haus; **I have money of my ~** ich habe selbst Geld; **it has a beauty all its ~** *or* **of its ~** es hat eine ganz eigene Schönheit. (**b**) *(in phrases)* **can I have it for my (very) ~?** darf ich das ganz für mich allein behalten?; **to get one's ~ back (on sb)** es jdm heimzahlen; **(all) on one's ~** (ganz) allein; **on its ~** *(alone)* allein; *(automatically)* von selbst, von allein.

**owner** ['əʊnər] *n* Besitzer(in *f*), Eigentümer(in *f*) *m*; *(of shop, factory, firm etc)* Inhaber(in *f*) *m.* **who's the ~ of this umbrella?** wem gehört dieser Schirm?; **at the ~'s risk** auf eigene Gefahr.

**owner-occupier** [,əʊnər'ɒkjʊpaɪər] *n* jd, der ein Haus/eine Wohnung besitzt und darin wohnt, Eigennutzer *m* *(form).*

**ownership** ['əʊnəʃɪp] *n* Besitz *m.* **under new ~** unter neuer Leitung.

**own goal** *n (lit, fig)* Eigentor *nt.*

**ox** [ɒks] *n, pl* **-en** Ochse *m.* **as strong as an ~** bärenstark.

**oxidation** [,ɒksɪ'deɪʃən] *n (Chem)* Oxydation *f.*

**oxide** ['ɒksaɪd] *n (Chem)* Oxyd *nt.*

**oxidize** ['ɒksɪdaɪz] *vti* oxydieren.

**Oxon** ['ɒksən] = (**a**) **Oxfordshire;** (**b**) **Oxoniensis** der Universität Oxford.

**oxtail** ['ɒksteɪl] *n:* **~ soup** Ochsenschwanzsuppe *f.*

**oxyacetylene** [,ɒksɪə'setɪliːn] *adj* Azetylensauerstoff-. **~ burner** *or* **torch** Schweißbrenner *m*; **~ welding** Autogenschweißen *nt.*

**oxygen** ['ɒksɪdʒən] *n* Sauerstoff *m.*

**oxygen:** **~ mask** *n* Sauerstoffmaske *f*; **~ tank** *n* Sauerstoffbehälter *m*; **~ tent** *n* Sauerstoffzelt *nt.*

**oyster** ['ɔɪstər] *n* Auster *f.* **the world's his ~** die Welt steht ihm offen.

**oz** = **ounce(s).**

**Oz** [ɒz] *n (col)* Australien *nt.*

**ozone** ['əʊzəʊn] *n* Ozon *nt.* **~ layer** Ozonschicht *f*; **hole in the ~ layer** Ozonloch *nt.*

# P

**P, p** [piː] *n* P, p *nt*. **P for Peter** P wie Peter; **to mind one's P's and Q's** *(col)* sich anständig benehmen.

**p** = (a) **page** S. (b) **penny, pence**. (c) *(Mus)* **piano** p.

**P** = **Prince** Pr.

**PA** = (a) **personal assistant**. (b) **public address (system)**. (c) *(US Post)* **Pennsylvania**.

**p.a.** = **per annum**.

**pa** [pɑː] *n (esp US col)* Papa *m (col)*.

**pace** [peɪs] **1** *n* (a) *(step)* Schritt *m*. **twelve ~s off** zwölf Schritt(e) entfernt; **to put sb/a new car through his/its ~s** *(fig)* jdn/ein neues Auto auf Herz und Nieren prüfen. (b) *(speed)* Tempo *nt*. **at a good** *or* **smart ~** recht schnell; **at a slow ~** langsam; **how long will he keep this ~ up?** wie lange wird er das Tempo durchhalten?; **the present ~ of development** die momentane Entwicklungsrate; **to keep ~** Schritt halten; *(in discussing)* mitkommen; **I can't keep ~ with events** ich komme mit den Ereignissen nicht mehr mit; **to make** *or* **set the ~** das Tempo angeben; **I can't stand the ~ any more** *(col)* ich kann nicht mehr mithalten. **2** *vt (measure) floor, room* mit Schritten ausmessen. **3** *vi* **to ~ up and down** auf und ab gehen.

**pace:** **~maker** *n (Med, Sport, fig)* Schrittmacher *m*; **~-setter** *n (Sport)* Schrittmacher *m*.

**Pacific** [pə'sɪfɪk] **1** *n* **the ~ (Ocean)** der Pazifische Ozean, der Pazifik. **2** *adj time, islands* Pazifisch; *coast* Pazifik-. **a ~ island** eine Insel im Pazifik.

**pacifier** ['pæsɪfaɪəʳ] *n (US: dummy)* Schnuller *m*.

**pacifism** ['pæsɪfɪzəm] *n* Pazifismus *m*.

**pacifist** ['pæsɪfɪst] **1** *adj* pazifistisch. **2** *n* Pazifist(in *f) m*.

**pacify** ['pæsɪfaɪ] *vt baby* beruhigen; *angry person* besänftigen; *area* befrieden. **just to ~ the unions** nur damit die Gewerkschaften stillhalten.

**pack** [pæk] **1** *n* (a) *(bundle)* Bündel *nt*; *(on animal)* Last *f*; *(rucksack)* Rucksack *m*; *(Mil)* Gepäck *nt no pl*. (b) *(packet) (washing powder etc)* Paket *nt*; *(US: of cigarettes)* Schachtel *f*. **in ~s of six** im Sechserpack. (c) *(Hunt)* Meute *f*. (d) *(of wolves)* Rudel *nt*. (e) *(pej: group)* Horde, Meute *f*. **he told us a ~ of lies** er tischte uns einen Sack voll Lügen auf. (f) *(of cards)* (Karten)spiel *nt*. (g) *(Rugby)* Stürmer *pl*.

**2** *vt* (a) *container etc* vollpacken; *meat in tin etc* abpacken. **~ed in dozens** im Dutzend abgepackt. (b) *case* packen; *things in case* einpacken. (c) *(wrap, put into parcel)* einpacken. **~ed in polythene** in Cellophan verpackt. (d) *(crowd)* packen; *articles also* stopfen. **the box was ~ed full of explosives** die Kiste war voll mit Sprengstoff; **the crowds that ~ed the stadium** die Menschenmassen, die sich im Stadium drängten; **to be ~ed (out)** *(full)* gerammelt voll sein *(col)*; **all this information is ~ed into one chapter** all diese Informationen sind in einem Kapitel zusammengedrängt. (e) *(make firm) soil etc* festdrücken. (f) *(US col: carry) gun* tragen, dabei haben. (g) *(col)* **to ~ a (heavy) punch** kräftig zu-

schlagen.

**3** *vi* (a) *(items)* passen; *(person)* packen. **it ~s (in) nicely** es läßt sich gut verpacken; **I'm still ~ing** ich bin noch beim Packen. (b) *(crowd)* **the crowds ~ed into the stadium** die Menge drängte sich in das Stadion; **we can't all ~ into one Mini** wir können uns nicht alle in einen Mini zwängen. (c) *(col)* **to send sb ~ing** jdn kurz abfertigen.

▶**pack in 1** *vt sep* (a) *clothes etc* einpacken. (b) *people* hineinpferchen in *(+acc)*. **we can't ~ any more ~ here** *(people)* hier geht keiner mehr rein; *(things)* hier geht nichts mehr rein. (c) *(play, actor etc)* in Scharen anziehen. (d) *(Brit col: give up) job* hinschmeißen *(col)*; *girlfriend etc* sausenlassen *(col)*; *work, activity* Feierabend machen mit *(col)*. **~ it ~!** hör auf!, laß es gut sein! **2** *vi* (a) *(crowd in)* sich hineindrängen. (b) *(Brit col: engine etc)* seinen Geist aufgeben *(hum)*.

▶**pack off** *vt sep* **she ~ed them ~ to bed/school** sie schickte sie ins Bett/in die Schule.

▶**pack up 1** *vt sep clothes etc* zusammenpacken. **2** *vi* (a) *(prepare luggage)* packen. (b) *(col: stop working) (engine)* seinen Geist aufgeben *(hum)*; *(person)* Feierabend machen *(col)*. (c) **the tent ~s ~ easily** das Zelt läßt sich gut verpacken.

**package** ['pækɪdʒ] **1** *n* (a) *(parcel, esp US: packet)* Paket *nt*; *(of cardboard)* Schachtel *f*. (b) *(esp Comm: group, set)* Paket, Bündel *nt*. **software ~** Softwarepaket *nt*. **2** *vt* (a) verpacken. (b) *(to enhance sales)* präsentieren.

**package:** **~ bomb** *n (US)* Paketbombe *f*; **~ deal** *n* Pauschalangebot *nt*; **~ holiday** *or* **tour** *n* Pauschalreise *f*.

**packaging** ['pækɪdʒɪŋ] *n see vt* (a) Verpackung *f*. (b) Präsentation *f*.

**packed lunch** ['pækt'lʌntʃ] *n* Lunchpaket *nt*.

**packer** ['pækəʳ] *n* Packer(in *f) m*.

**packet** ['pækɪt] *n* (a) Paket *nt*; *(of cigarettes)* Päckchen *nt*, Schachtel *f*; *(of potato crisps)* Tüte *f*; *(small box)* Schachtel *f*. (b) *(Brit col: lot of money)* **that must have cost a ~** das muß ein Heidengeld gekostet haben *(col)*.

**pack:** **~horse** *n* Packpferd *nt*; *(fig)* Packesel *m*; **~ice** *n* Packeis *nt*.

**packing** ['pækɪŋ] *n* (a) *(act) (in suitcases)* Packen *nt*; *(in factories etc)* Verpackung *f*. **to do one's ~** packen. (b) *(material)* Verpackung *f*.

**packing case** *n* Kiste *f*.

**pact** [pækt] *n* Pakt *m*. **to make a ~ with sb** mit jdm einen Pakt schließen.

**pad** [pæd] **1** *n* (a) *(stuffing) (for comfort etc)* Polster *nt*; *(for protection)* Schützer *m*. (b) *(of paper)* Block *m*. (c) *(for inking)* Stempelkissen *nt*. (d) *(of animal's foot)* Ballen *m*. (e) *(launching ~)* (Abschuß)rampe *f*. (f) *(col: room, home)* Bude *f (col)*. **2** *vt shoulders etc* polstern.

▶**pad about** *vi* umhertapsen.

▶**pad out** *vt sep* (a) *shoulders* polstern. (b) *essay*

*etc* auswalzen; *speech* ausdehnen.
**padded** ['pædɪd] *adj* gepolstert; *envelope* wattiert.
**padding** ['pædɪŋ] *n* (a) *(material)* Polsterung *f.* (b) *(fig: in essay etc)* Füllwerk *nt.*
**paddle** ['pædl] 1 *n* (a) *(oar)* Paddel *nt*; *(blade of wheel)* Schaufel *f*; *(wheel)* Schaufelrad *nt*; *(US: for table tennis)* Schläger *m.* (b) **to go for a** ~ durchs Wasser waten. 2 *vti* (a) paddeln. (b) *(walk in shallow water)* waten.
**paddle:** ~ **boat** *n* Raddampfer *m*; *(small, on pond)* Paddelboot *nt*; ~ **steamer** *n* Raddampfer *m.*
**paddling pool** ['pædlɪŋˌpuːl] *n* *(Brit)* Planschbecken *nt.*
**paddock** ['pædək] *n* *(field)* Koppel *f*; *(of racecourse)* Sattelplatz *m*; *(motor racing)* Fahrerlager *nt.*
**paddy** ['pædɪ] *n* *(also* ~ **field)** Reisfeld *nt.*
**padlock** ['pædlɒk] 1 *n* Vorhängeschloß *nt.* 2 *vt* (mit einem Vorhängeschloß) verschließen.
**padre** ['pɑːdrɪ] *n* *(Mil)* Feldkaplan *m.*
**paediatric,** *(US)* **pediatric** [ˌpiːdɪ'ætrɪk] *adj* Kinder-.
**paediatrician,** *(US)* **pediatrician** [ˌpiːdɪə'trɪʃən] *n* Kinderarzt *m*, -ärztin *f.*
**pagan** ['peɪgən] 1 *adj* heidnisch. 2 *n* Heide *m*, Heidin *f.*
**page¹** [peɪdʒ] 1 *n* *(also* ~-**boy)** Page *m.* 2 *vt* **to** ~ **sb** jdn ausrufen lassen.
**page²** *n* Seite *f.* **on** ~ **14** auf Seite 14; **write on both sides of the** ~ beschreiben Sie beide Seiten; **to turn over the** ~/~**s** umblättern.
**pageant** ['pædʒənt] *n* *(show)* Historienspiel *nt.*
**pageantry** ['pædʒəntrɪ] *n* Prunk *m*, Gepränge *nt.*
**page:** ~-**boy** *n* (a) Page *m*; (b) *(hairstyle)* Pagenkopf *m*; ~ **number** *n* Seitenzahl *f*; ~ **proofs** *npl* *(Print)* Umbruch *m.*
**pager** ['peɪdʒəʳ] *n* Piepser *m* *(col).*
**paginate** ['pædʒɪneɪt] *vt* paginieren.
**pagination** [ˌpædʒɪ'neɪʃən] *n* Paginierung *f.*
**pagoda** [pə'gəʊdə] *n* Pagode *f.*
**paid** [peɪd] 1 *pret, ptp of* **pay.** 2 *adj* official, work bezahlt. **to put** ~ **to sth** etw zunichte machen; **that's put** ~ **to him** das war's dann wohl für ihn *(col).*
**paid-up** [ˌpeɪd'ʌp] *adj* share eingezahlt. **a** ~ **membership of 500** 500 zahlende Mitglieder; **fully** ~ **member** Mitglied *nt* ohne Beitragsrückstände; *(fig)* überzeugtes Mitglied.
**pail** [peɪl] *n* Eimer *m.*
**pain** [peɪn] 1 *n* (a) *(physical)* Schmerz *m*; *(mental)* Qualen *pl.* **this helps the** ~ das ist gut gegen die Schmerzen; **to be in** ~ Schmerzen haben; **he screamed in** ~ er schrie vor Schmerzen; **I have a** ~ **in my leg** mein Bein tut mir weh. (b) **to be at (great)** ~**s to do sth** sich *(dat)* (große) Mühe geben, etw zu tun; **to take** ~**s over sth/to do sth** sich *(dat)* Mühe mit etw geben/sich *(dat)* Mühe geben, etw zu tun. (c) *(penalty)* **on** ~ **of death** bei Todesstrafe. (d) **to be a (real)** ~ *or* **a** ~ **in the neck** einem auf den Wecker gehen *(col).* 2 *vt (mentally)* schmerzen. **it** ~**s me to see their ignorance** ihre Unwissenheit tut schon weh.
**pain barrier** *n* Schmerzgrenze *f.*
**pained** [peɪnd] *adj expression* gequält.
**painful** ['peɪnfʊl] *adj* (a) *(physically)* schmerzhaft. **is it** ~? tut es weh? (b) *experience, memory* unangenehm. **it is my** ~ **duty to tell you that ...** ich habe die traurige Pflicht, Ihnen mitteilen zu müssen, daß ... (c) *(col: terrible)* peinlich; *(boring)* party etc zum Sterben langweilig.
**painfully** ['peɪnfəlɪ] *adv* (a) *(physically)* schmerzhaft. (b) *(col: very)* schrecklich. **it was** ~ **obvious** es war nicht zu übersehen.
**painkiller** ['peɪnˌkɪləʳ] *n* Schmerzmittel *nt.*

**painkilling** ['peɪnˌkɪlɪŋ] *adj* schmerzstillend.
**painless** ['peɪnlɪs] *adj* schmerzlos. **don't worry, it's quite** ~ *(col)* keine Angst, es ist ganz einfach.
**painstaking** ['peɪnzˌteɪkɪŋ] *adj* person, work äußerst sorgfältig; *accuracy* peinlich.
**painstakingly** ['peɪnzˌteɪkɪŋlɪ] *adv* mit äußerster Sorgfalt; *(very accurately)* peinlich genau.
**paint** [peɪnt] 1 *n* (a) Farbe *f*; *(on car, furniture also)* Lack *m*; *(make-up)* Schminke *f.* (b) ~**s** *pl* Farben *pl.* 2 *vt* (a) *wall etc* streichen; *car* lackieren. **to** ~ **the town red** *(col)* die Stadt unsicher machen *(col).* (b) *picture, person* malen. **he** ~**ed a very convincing picture** *(fig)* er zeichnete ein sehr überzeugendes Bild. 3 *vi* malen; *(decorate)* (an)streichen.
**paint:** ~**box** *n* Farbkasten *m*; ~**brush** *n* Pinsel *m.*
**painter** ['peɪntəʳ] *n* Maler(in *f*) *m.*
**pain threshold** *n* Schmerzschwelle *f.*
**painting** ['peɪntɪŋ] *n* (a) *(picture)* Bild, Gemälde *nt.* (b) *no pl (Art)* Malerei *f.* (c) *no pl (of flat etc)* Anstreichen *nt.*
**paint:** ~ **pot** *n* Farbtopf *m*; ~ **remover** *or* **stripper** *n* Abbeizmittel *nt*; ~ **roller** *n* Rolle *f*; ~**work** *n (on car etc)* Lack *m*; *(on wall, furniture)* Anstrich *m.*
**pair** [pɛəʳ] 1 *n (of shoes, people)* Paar *nt*; *(of animals, cards)* Pärchen *nt.* **a** ~ **of trousers/scissors** eine Hose/Schere; **in** ~**s** paarweise; *arrive, go out* zu zweit; *seated* in Zweiergruppen. 2 *vt* in Paaren *or* paarweise anordnen.
▶**pair off** 1 *vt sep* in Zweiergruppen einteilen. **to** ~ **sb** ~ **with sb** *(find boyfriend etc for)* jdn mit jdm zusammenbringen. 2 *vi* Paare bilden. **to** ~ ~ **with sb** mit jdm gehen.
**pajamas** [pə'dʒɑːməz] *npl (US)* = **pyjamas.**
**Paki** ['pækɪ] *n (esp pej col)* 1 *n (person)* Pakistani *mf.* 2 *adj* pakistanisch.
**Pakistan** [ˌpɑːkɪs'tɑːn] *n* Pakistan *nt.*
**Pakistani** [ˌpɑːkɪs'tɑːnɪ] 1 *adj* pakistanisch. 2 *n* Pakistani *mf*, Pakistaner(in *f*) *m.*
**pal** [pæl] *n (col)* Kumpel *m (col).*
**palace** ['pælɪs] *n (lit, fig)* Palast *m.*
**palatable** ['pælətəbl] *adj (also iro)* genießbar; *food also* schmackhaft *(to für)*; *(fig)* attraktiv.
**palate** ['pælɪt] *n (lit)* Gaumen *m.*
**palatial** [pə'leɪʃəl] *adj (spacious)* palastartig; *(luxurious)* luxuriös, feudal *(hum col).*
**palaver** [pə'lɑːvəʳ] *n* (a) *(Brit col: fuss)* Theater *nt (col).* (b) *(esp US: chatter)* Geschwätz *nt.*
**pale¹** [peɪl] 1 *adj (+er)* blaß; *face (unhealthy)* bleich. ~ **green** *etc* blaß *or* zartgrün *etc*; **to go** *or* **turn** ~ bleich werden. 2 *vi (person)* erbleichen, blaß werden. **to** ~ **into insignificance** zur Bedeutungslosigkeit herabsinken.
**pale²** *n (stake)* Pfahl *m.* **to be beyond the** ~ unmöglich sein; **those remarks were quite beyond the** ~ diese Bemerkungen haben eindeutig die Grenzen überschritten.
**paleness** ['peɪlnɪs] *n* Blässe *f.*
**Palestine** ['pælɪstaɪn] *n* Palästina *nt.*
**Palestinian** [ˌpælə'stɪnɪən] 1 *adj* palästinensisch. 2 *n* Palästinenser(in *f*) *m.*
**palette** ['pælɪt] *n* Palette *f.*
**palisade** [ˌpælɪ'seɪd] *n* (a) Palisade *f.* (b) ~**s** *pl (US)* Steilufer *nt.*
**pall¹** [pɔːl] *n (over coffin)* Sargtuch *nt.* **a** ~ **of smoke** eine Dunstglocke; *(rising)* eine Rauchwolke.
**pall²** *vi* an Reiz verlieren.
**pall-bearer** ['pɔːlˌbɛərəʳ] *n* Sargträger *m.*
**pallet** ['pælɪt] *n (for storage)* Palette *f.*
**palliative** ['pælɪətɪv] *n* Linderungsmittel *nt.*
**pallid** ['pælɪd] *adj* blaß, fahl.
**pallor** ['pæləʳ] *n* Blässe, Fahlheit *f.*

**pally** ['pælɪ] *adj (+er) (col) manner, type* kumpelhaft. **to be ~ with sb** mit jdm gut Freund sein; **to get ~ with sb** sich mit jdm anfreunden.

**palm¹** [pɑːm] *n (Bot)* Palme *f*; *(Eccl)* Palmzweig *m*.

**palm²** *n (Anat)* Handfläche *f.* **to grease sb's ~** jdn schmieren *(col)*; **to read sb's ~** jdm aus der Hand lesen.

▶**palm off** *vt sep (col) rubbish, goods* andrehen *(on/to) sb* jdm) *(col).*

**palmist** ['pɑːmɪst] *n* Handliniendeuter(in *f*) *m.*

**palmistry** ['pɑːmɪstrɪ] *n* Handliniendeutung *f.*

**palm: P~ Sunday** *n* Palmsonntag *m*; **~tree** *n* Palme *f.*

**palmy** ['pɑːmɪ] *adj (+er)* glücklich, unbeschwert.

**palpable** ['pælpəbl] *adj* greifbar; *(clear) lie, error* offensichtlich.

**palpably** ['pælpəblɪ] *adv (clearly)* eindeutig.

**palpitate** ['pælpɪteɪt] *vi (heart)* heftig klopfen; *(tremble)* zittern.

**palpitation** [,pælpɪ'teɪʃən] *n (of heart)* Herzklopfen *nt*; *(trembling)* Zittern *nt.* **to have ~s** Herzklopfen haben.

**paltry** ['pɔːltrɪ] *adj* armselig, schäbig.

**pampas** ['pæmpəs] *npl* Pampas *pl.* **~ grass** Pampasgras *nt.*

**pamper** ['pæmpər] *vt* verwöhnen; *child also, dog* verhätscheln.

**pamphlet** ['pæmflɪt] *n (informative)* Broschüre *f*; *(literary)* Druckschrift *f*; *(political)* Flugblatt *nt.*

**pan¹** [pæn] **1** *n* **(a)** *(Cook)* Pfanne *f*; *(sauce~)* Topf *m.* **(b)** *(of scales)* Waagschale *f*; *(of lavatory)* Becken *nt.* **2** *vt* **(a)** *gold* waschen. **(b)** *(US col) fish* braten. **(c)** *(US col: slate) new play etc* verreißen. **3** *vi* **to ~ for gold** Gold waschen.

▶**pan out** *vi (col)* sich entwickeln. **to ~ ~ well** klappen *(col).*

**pan²** *vi (camera)* schwenken. **a ~ning shot** ein Schwenk *m.*

**pan-** *pref* pan-, Pan-. **P~-African** panafrikanisch.

**panacea** [,pænə'sɪə] *n* Allheilmittel *nt.*

**panache** [pə'næʃ] *n* Schwung, Elan *m.* **she dresses with ~** sie kleidet sich sehr extravagant.

**Panama** [,pænə'mɑː] *n* Panama *nt.* **~ Canal** Panamakanal *m.*

**panama (hat)** *n* Panamahut *m.*

**pancake** ['pænkeɪk] *n* Pfannkuchen *m.* **P~ Day** Fastnachtsdienstag *m.*

**pancreas** ['pæŋkrɪəs] *n* Bauchspeicheldrüse *f.*

**panda** ['pændə] *n* Panda *m.*

**panda car** *n (Brit)* (Funk)streifenwagen *m.*

**pandemonium** [,pændɪ'məunɪəm] *n* Chaos *nt.*

**pander** ['pændər] *vi* nachgeben *(to dat).* **she ~ed to his every wish** sie erfüllte ihm jeden Wunsch; **to ~ to sb's ego** jdm um den Bart gehen.

**p and h, p & h** *(US)* = **postage and handling.**

**p and p, p & p** = **postage and packing.**

**pane** [peɪn] *n* Glasscheibe *f.*

**panel** ['pænl] **1** *n* **(a)** *(wood)* Platte, Tafel *f*; *(in ceiling, door)* Feld *nt*; *(Art)* Tafel *f*; *(of bodywork of a car)* Karosserieteil *nt*; *(of instruments, switches)* Schalttafel *f.* **instrument ~** Armaturenbrett *nt*; *(on machine)* Kontrolltafel *f.* **(b)** *(of interviewers etc)* Gremium *nt*; *(in discussion)* Diskussionsrunde *f*; *(in quiz game)* Rateteam *nt.* **a ~ of experts** ein Sachverständigengremium *nt.* **2** *vt wall* täfeln.

**panel: ~ beater** *n* Autoschlosser *m*; **~ discussion** *n* Podiumsdiskussion *f*; **~ game** *n* Ratespiel *nt.*

**panelling,** *(US)* **paneling** ['pænəlɪŋ] *n* Täfelung *f,* Paneel *nt*; *(to conceal radiator etc)* Verschalung *f.*

**panellist,** *(US)* **panelist** ['pænəlɪst] *n* Diskussionsteilnehmer(in *f*) *m.*

**pang** [pæŋ] *n* **~ of conscience** Gewissensbisse *pl*; **~s of hunger** quälender Hunger.

**panic** ['pænɪk] **1** *n* Panik *f.* **to flee in ~** panikartig die Flucht ergreifen; **a ~ reaction** eine panikartige Reaktion; **to hit the ~ button** *(fig col)* durchdrehen *(col).* **2** *vi* in Panik geraten. **don't ~!** nur keine Panik!

**panicky** ['pænɪkɪ] *adj person* überängstlich; *act, measure etc* panikartig.

**panic-stricken** ['pænɪk,strɪkən] *adj* von Panik ergriffen; *look* panisch.

**pannier** ['pænɪər] *n* Korb *m*; *(on motor-cycle etc)* Satteltasche *f.*

**panorama** [,pænə'rɑːmə] *n* Panorama *nt (of gen)*; *(survey)* Übersicht *f (of* über *+acc).*

**panoramic** [,pænə'ræmɪk] *adj view* Panorama-. **~ shot** *(Phot)* Panoramaaufnahme *f*; **a ~ view of the hills** ein Blick *m* auf das Bergpanorama.

**pansy** ['pænzɪ] *n* **(a)** *(Bot)* Stiefmütterchen *nt.* **(b)** *(pej) (effeminate man)* Tunte *f (col)*; *(homosexual)* Schwule(r) *m (col).*

**pant** [pænt] *vi* keuchen; *(dog)* hecheln. **to be ~ing for a drink** nach etwas zu trinken lechzen.

**pantechnicon** [pæn'teknɪkən] *n (Brit)* Möbelwagen *m.*

**panther** ['pænθər] *n* Panther *m.*

**panties** ['pæntɪz] *npl* Höschen *nt*; *(for women also)* Slip *m.* **a pair of ~** ein Höschen *nt*/ein Slip *m.*

**pantomime** ['pæntəmaɪm] *n (in GB: Theat)* Weihnachtsmärchen *nt*; *(mime)* Pantomime *f.*

**pantry** ['pæntrɪ] *n* Speisekammer *f.*

**pants** [pænts] *npl (esp US: trousers)* Hose *f*; *(Brit: under~)* Unterhose *f.* **a pair of ~** eine Hose/Unterhose; **to wear the ~** *(US fig)* die Hosen anhaben *(col).*

**pantsuit** ['pæntsuːt] *n (US)* Hosenanzug *m.*

**pantyhose** ['pæntɪhəuz] *n (US)* Strumpfhose *f.*

**papacy** ['peɪpəsɪ] *n* Papsttum *nt.*

**papal** ['peɪpəl] *adj* päpstlich.

**paparazzo** [,pæpə'rætsəu], *pl* **paparazzi** [,pæpə'rætsɪ] *n* Fotojäger, Paparazzo *m.*

**paper** ['peɪpər] **1** *n* **(a)** Papier *nt.* **a piece of ~** ein Stück *nt* Papier; **a sheet of ~** ein Blatt *nt* Papier; **to put sth down on ~** etw schriftlich festhalten; **it looks good on ~ but ...** auf dem Papier sieht es gut aus, aber ...; **it's not worth the ~ it's written on** es ist schade um das Papier, auf dem es steht. **(b)** *(newspaper)* Zeitung *f.* **to write to the ~s about sth** Leserbriefe/einen Leserbrief schreiben; **it was in the ~s** es stand in der Zeitung. **(c)** **~s** *pl (identity ~s, writings)* Papiere *pl.* **private ~s** private Unterlagen *pl.* **(d)** *(set of questions in exam)* Testbogen *m*; *(exam)* Klausur *f*; *(Sch)* Arbeit *f*; *(academic)* Referat *nt.* **to read a ~** ein Referat halten. **(e)** *(wall~)* Tapete *f.* **2** *vt wall, room* tapezieren.

**paper** *in cpds* Papier-; **~back** *n* Taschenbuch *nt*; **~ bag** *n* Tüte *f*; **~boy** *n* Zeitungsjunge *m*; **~ chase** *n* Schnitzeljagd *f*; **~-clip** *n* Büroklammer *f*; **~ cup** *n* Pappbecher *m*; **~ feed** *n (Comp)* Papiervorschub *m*; **~ girl** *n* Zeitungsausträgerin *f*; **~ handkerchief** *or* **hankie** *(col) n* Papiertaschentuch *nt*; **~ knife** *n* Brieföffner *m*; **~ mill** *n* Papierfabrik *f*; **~ money** *n* Papiergeld *nt*; **~ napkin** *n* Papierserviette *f*; **~ plate** *n* Pappteller *m*; **~ round** *n* **to do a ~ round** Zeitungen austragen; **~ shop** *n* Zeitungsladen *m*; **~-thin** *adj walls* hauchdünn; **~weight** *n* Briefbeschwerer *m*; **~work** *n* Schreibarbeit *f.*

**papier mâché** [,pæpɪer'mæʃeɪ] *n* Pappmaché *nt.*

**papist** ['peɪpɪst] *n (pej)* Papist(in *f*) *m.*

**paprika** ['pæprɪkə] *n* Paprika *m.*

**Papua** ['pæpjuə] *n* Papua *nt.*

**Papuan** ['pæpjuən] **1** *adj* papuanisch. **2** *n (person)*

**parity**

Papua *mf.*

**par** [pɑːʳ] *n* **to be on a ~ with sb/sth** sich mit jdm/ etw messen können; **below ~** *(fig)* unter Niveau; **that's ~ for the course** *(fig)* das ist normal; **I'm feeling a bit below ~ today** ich bin heute nicht ganz auf dem Posten *(col)*.

**para** ['pærə] = **(a)** **paragraph** Abs. **(b)** **paratrooper**.

**parable** ['pærəbl] *n* Parabel *f,* Gleichnis *nt.*

**parachute** ['pærəʃuːt] **1** *n* Fallschirm *m.* **by ~** mit dem Fallschirm; **~ drop** *(of supplies)* Fallschirmabwurf *m;* **~ jump** Absprung *m* (mit dem Fallschirm). **2** *vt troops* mit dem Fallschirm absetzen; *supplies* abwerfen. **3** *vi (also ~ down)* (mit dem Fallschirm) abspringen. **to ~ to safety** sich mit dem Fallschirm retten.

**parachuting** ['pærəʃuːtɪŋ] *n* Fallschirmspringen *nt.*

**parachutist** ['pærəʃuːtɪst] *n* Fallschirmspringer (in *f) m.*

**parade** [pə'reɪd] **1** *n (procession)* Umzug *m; (Mil, circus, display)* Parade *f; (political)* Demonstration *f; (fashion ~)* Modenschau *f; (of wealth etc)* Zurschaustellung *f; (Mil: review)* Truppeninspektion *f.* **to be on ~** *(Mil)* eine Parade abhalten. **2** *vt* **(a)** *troops* vorbeimarschieren lassen; *military might* demonstrieren; *placards* vor sich her tragen. **(b)** *(show off)* zur Schau stellen. **3** *vi* ziehen *(through* durch*); (Mil)* vorbeimarschieren; *(political party)* eine Demonstration veranstalten.

**parade ground** *n* Exerzierplatz *m.*

**paradigm** ['pærədaɪm] *n* Musterbeispiel *nt.*

**paradise** ['pærədaɪs] *n (lit, fig)* Paradies *nt.*

**paradox** ['pærədɒks] *n* Paradox *nt.* **life is full of ~es** das Leben steckt voller Widersprüche.

**paradoxical** [,pærə'dɒksɪkəl] *adj* paradox; *person* widersprüchlich.

**paradoxically** [,pærə'dɒksɪkəlɪ] *adv* paradoxerweise; *worded* paradox.

**paraffin** ['pærəfɪn] *n (Brit: oil)* Paraffin(öl) *nt; (US: wax)* Paraffin *nt.*

**paraffin: ~ heater** *n* = **~ stove**; **~ lamp** *n* Paraffinlampe *f;* **~ stove** *n (Brit)* Paraffinofen *m.*

**paragon** ['pærəgən] *n* Muster *nt.* **a ~ of virtue** ein Muster *nt* an Tugendhaftigkeit.

**paragraph** ['pærəgrɑːf] *n* Absatz *m.*

**Paraguay** ['pærəgwaɪ] *n* Paraguay *nt.*

**Paraguayan** [,pærə'gwaɪən] **1** *adj* paraguayisch. **2** *n* Paraguayer (in *f) m.*

**parakeet** ['pærəkiːt] *n* Sittich *m.*

**parallel** ['pærəlel] **1** *adj* **(a)** *lines, streets* parallel. **the road is ~ to the river** die Straße verläuft parallel zum Fluß; **~ bars** Barren *m.* **(b)** *(fig) case, career, development* vergleichbar. **a ~ case** ein Parallelfall *m;* **the two systems developed along ~ lines** die Entwicklung der beiden Systeme verlief parallel. **2** *adv* **to run ~** *(roads, careers)* parallel verlaufen. **3** *n* **(a)** *(Geometry)* Parallele *f;* *(Geog)* Breitenkreis *m.* **the 49th ~** der 49. Breitengrad. **(b)** *(Elec)* **connected in ~** parallel geschaltet. **(c)** *(fig)* Parallele *f.* **without ~** beispiellos; **to draw a ~ between X and Y** eine Parallele zwischen X und Y ziehen. **4** *vt (fig)* gleichen *(+dat).*

**parallelogram** [,pærə'leləʊgræm] *n* Parallelogramm *nt.*

**paralyse** ['pærəlaɪz] *vt* **(a)** lähmen. **to be ~d (with fright)** vor Schreck wie gelähmt sein. **(b)** *industry* lahmlegen.

**paralysis** [pə'ræləsɪs] *n, pl* **paralyses** [pə'rælɪsiːz] Lähmung *f; (of industry etc)* Lahmlegung *f.*

**paralytic** [,pærə'lɪtɪk] *adj* **(a)** paralytisch, Lähmungs-. **(b)** *(Brit col: drunk)* total blau *(col).*

**paralyze** *(US)* = **paralyse.**

**paramedic** [,pærə'medɪk] *n* medizinische Hilfskraft; *(for first aid etc)* Sanitäter (in *f) m.*

**parameter** [pə'ræmətəʳ] *n* **(a)** *(Math)* Parameter *m.* **(b)** **~s** *pl (framework, limits)* Rahmen *m.*

**paramilitary** [,pærə'mɪlɪtərɪ] *adj* paramilitärisch.

**paramount** ['pærəmaʊnt] *adj* Haupt-. **of ~ importance** von größter Wichtigkeit.

**paranoia** [,pærə'nɔɪə] *n* Paranoia *f; (col)* Verfolgungswahn *m.*

**paranoid** ['pærənɔɪd] *adj* paranoid. **or am I just being ~ about it?** oder bilde ich mir das nur ein?

**paranormal** [,pærə'nɔːməl] *adj* paranormal.

**parapet** ['pærəpɪt] *n* Brüstung *f.*

**paraphernalia** [,pærəfə'neɪlɪə] *npl* Utensilien *pl.* **all the ~** das ganze Drum und Dran *(col).*

**paraphrase** ['pærəfreɪz] **1** *n* Umschreibung *f.* **2** *vt* umschreiben.

**paraplegia** [,pærə'pliːdʒə] *n* doppelseitige Lähmung.

**paraplegic** [,pærə'pliːdʒɪk] **1** *adj* doppelseitig gelähmt. **2** *n* Paraplegiker (in *f) m (spec).*

**parapsychology** [,pærəsaɪ'kɒlədʒɪ] *n* Parapsychologie *f.*

**parasite** ['pærəsaɪt] *n (lit, fig)* Parasit *m.*

**parasitic(al)** [,pærə'sɪtɪk(əl)] *adj animal, plant* Schmarotzer-, parasitär *(also fig).*

**parasol** ['pærəsɒl] *n* Sonnenschirm *m.*

**paratrooper** ['pærətruːpəʳ] *n* Fallschirmjäger *m.*

**paratroops** ['pærətruːps] *npl* Fallschirmjäger *pl.*

**parcel** ['pɑːsl] *n* Paket *nt.* **to do sth up in a ~** etw als Paket verpacken.

▶**parcel up** *vt sep* als Paket verpacken.

**parcel: ~ bomb** *n (Brit)* Paketbombe *f;* **~ post** *n* Paketpost *f.*

**parched** [pɑːtʃt] *adj* ausgetrocknet. **to be ~ (with thirst)** (vor Durst) verschmachten.

**parchment** ['pɑːtʃmənt] *n* Pergament *nt.*

**pardon** ['pɑːdn] **1** *n* **(a)** *(Jur)* Begnadigung *f.* **general ~** Amnestie *f.* **(b)** **I beg your ~, but could you ...?** verzeihen Sie bitte, könnten Sie ...?; **I beg your ~!** erlauben Sie mal!; **I beg your ~?** *(Brit)* bitte?, wie bitte?; **I beg your ~** *(apology)* Verzeihung. **2** *vt* **(a)** *(Jur)* begnadigen. **(b)** *(forgive)* verzeihen *(sb* jdm, *sth* etw*).* **to ~ sb sth** jdm etw verzeihen; **~ me?** *(US)* bitte?, wie bitte?

**pardonable** ['pɑːdnəbl] *adj offence* entschuldbar; *mistake also* verzeihlich.

**pare** [peəʳ] *vt nails* schneiden; *fruit, stick* schälen.

▶**pare down** *vt sep costs etc* einschränken.

**parent** ['peərənt] **1** *n* Elternteil *m.* **~s** Eltern *pl.* **2** *attr* **~ company** Muttergesellschaft *f;* **~-teacher association** Eltern-Lehrer-Ausschuß *m.*

**parentage** ['peərəntɪdʒ] *n* Herkunft *f.*

**parental** [pə'rentl] *adj care etc* elterlich *attr.*

**parenthesis** [pə'renθɪsɪs] *n, pl* **parentheses** [pə'renθɪsiːz] Klammer *f.*

**parenthetic(al)** [,pærən'θetɪk(əl)] *adj* beiläufig.

**parenthood** ['peərənthʊd] *n* Elternschaft *f.*

**Paris** ['pærɪs] *n* Paris *nt.*

**parish** ['pærɪʃ] *n* Gemeinde *f; (district)* Pfarrbezirk *m,* Pfarrei *f.*

**parish: ~ church** *n* Pfarrkirche *f;* **~ council** *n* Gemeinderat *m.*

**parishioner** [pə'rɪʃənəʳ] *n* Gemeindemitglied *nt.*

**parish: ~ priest** *n* Pfarrer *m;* **~ register** *n* Kirchenbuch *nt.*

**Parisian** [pə'rɪzɪən] **1** *adj* Pariser *inv.* **2** *n* Pariser (in *f) m.*

**parity** ['pærɪtɪ] *n (equality)* Gleichstellung *f; (of opportunities)* Gleichheit *f; (Fin, Sci, Comp)* Parität *f.* **the ~ of the dollar** die Dollarparität.

**park** [pɑːk] **1** *n* Park *m*; *(Brit col: football pitch)* Platz *m*. **2** *vt* **(a)** *car* parken; *bike* abstellen. **a ~ed car** ein parkendes Auto. **(b)** *(col: put) luggage etc* abstellen. **he ~ed himself right in front of the fire** er pflanzte sich direkt vor den Kamin *(col)*. **3** *vi* parken. **there was nowhere to ~** es gab nirgendwo einen Parkplatz.

**parka** ['pɑːkə] *n* Parka *m*.

**park-and-ride** [ˌpɑːkən'raɪd] *n* Park-and-ride-System *nt*.

**parking** ['pɔːkɪŋ] *n* Parken *nt*.

**parking:** **~ attendant** *n* Parkplatzwächter *m*; **~ lights** *npl* Standlicht *nt*; **~ lot** *n (US)* Parkplatz *m*; **~ meter** *n* Parkuhr *f*; **~ offence** *n* Verstoß *m* gegen das Parkverbot; **~ place** *n* Parkplatz *m*; **~ space** *n* Parklücke *f*; **~ ticket** *n* Strafzettel *m*; **~ violation** *n (US)* = **~ offence**.

**Parkinson's** ['pɑːkɪnsənz] *n (also ~ disease)* Parkinsonsche Krankheit.

**park:** **~keeper** *n* Parkwächter *m*; **~land** *n* Parklandschaft *f*; **~way** *n (US)* Allee *f*.

**parky** ['pɑːkɪ] *adj (+er) (Brit col)* kühl, frisch.

**parlance** ['pɑːləns] *n* **in common ~** im allgemeinen Sprachgebrauch; **in technical ~** in der Fachsprache.

**parliament** ['pɑːləmənt] *n* Parlament *nt*. **to get into ~** ins Parlament kommen.

**parliamentarian** [ˌpɑːləmen'tɛərɪən] *n* Parlamentarier *m*.

**parliamentary** [ˌpɑːlə'mentərɪ] *adj* parlamentarisch.

**parlour,** *(US)* **parlor** ['pɑːləʳ] *n (in house, beauty ~ etc)* Salon *m*. **ice-cream ~** Eisdiele *f*.

**parlous** ['pɑːləs] *adj (old, hum)* **in a ~ state** in einem prekären Zustand.

**Parmesan** ['pɑːmɪzæn] *n (also ~cheese)* Parmesan(-käse) *m*.

**parochial** [pə'rəʊkɪəl] *adj* **(a)** *(Eccl)* Pfarr-, Gemeinde-. **(b)** *(fig) attitude, person* engstirnig; *mind, ideas* beschränkt.

**parody** ['pærədɪ] **1** *n* Parodie *f (of auf +acc)*. **2** *vt* parodieren.

**parole** [pə'rəʊl] **1** *n (Jur)* Bewährung *f*; *(temporary release)* Strafunterbrechung *f*. **let sb out on ~** jdn auf Bewährung entlassen; *(temporarily)* jdm Strafunterbrechung gewähren; **to be on ~** unter Bewährung stehen; *(temporarily)* auf Kurzurlaub sein. **2** *vt prisoner* auf Bewährung entlassen; *(temporarily)* Strafunterbrechung gewähren *(+dat)*.

**paroxysm** ['pærəksɪzəm] *n* Anfall *m*. **~s of laughter** ein Lachkrampf *m*.

**parquet** ['pɑːkeɪ] *n* Parkett *nt*.

**parrot** ['pærət] *n* Papagei *m*. **to repeat sth ~-fashion** etw wie ein Papagei nachplappern.

**parry** ['pærɪ] *vti (Fencing, fig)* parieren; *(Boxing)* abwehren.

**parsimonious** [ˌpɑːsɪ'məʊnɪəs] *adj* geizig.

**parsley** ['pɑːslɪ] *n* Petersilie *f*.

**parsnip** ['pɑːsnɪp] *n* Pastinake *f*.

**parson** ['pɑːsn] *n* Pfarrer, Pastor *m*.

**parsonage** ['pɑːsənɪdʒ] *n* Pfarrhaus *nt*.

**part** [pɑːt] **1** *n* **(a)** Teil *m*. **it is ~ and parcel of the job** das gehört zur Arbeit dazu; **in ~** teilweise, zum Teil; **it is in large ~ true** das ist zum großen Teil wahr; **for the main** *or* **most ~** in erster Linie; *(generally speaking)* im großen und ganzen; **in the latter ~ of the year** gegen Ende des Jahres; **5 ~s of sand to 1 of cement** 5 Teile Sand auf ein(en) Teil Zement.

**(b)** *(component, Mech)* Teil *nt*. **spare ~** Ersatzteil *nt*; **~ of speech** *(Gram)* Wortart *f*; **principal ~s of a**

*verb* Stammformen *pl*.

**(c)** *(of series)* Folge *f*; *(of serial)* Fortsetzung *f*; **~ one** *(TV, Rad etc)* erster Teil.

**(d)** *(share, role)* (An)teil *m*, Rolle *f*; *(Theat)* Rolle *f*; *(Mus)* Stimme *f*. **to play one's ~** *(fig)* seinen Beitrag leisten; **to take ~ in sth** an etw *(dat)* teilnehmen; **he looks the ~** *(fig)* so sieht er auch aus; **to play no ~ in sth** *(person)* nicht an etw *(dat)* beteiligt sein; *(factor etc)* bei etw keine Rolle spielen.

**(e)** **~s** *pl (region)* Gegend *f*; **he's not from these ~s** er ist nicht aus dieser Gegend.

**(f)** *(side)* Seite *f*. **to take sb's ~** sich auf jds Seite *(acc)* stellen; **for my ~** was mich betrifft; **on my ~** *etc* meinerseits *etc*; **on the ~ of** von seiten *(+gen)*, seitens *(+gen)*; **to take sth in good/bad ~** etw nicht übelnehmen/etw übelnehmen; **a man of ~s** ein vielseitiges Talent; **a man of many ~s** ein vielseitiger Mensch.

**(g)** *(US: in hair)* Scheitel *m*.

**2** *adv* teils, teilweise. **it is ~ iron and ~ copper** es ist teils aus Eisen und teils aus Kupfer; **~ eaten** halb aufgegessen; *apple, sandwich* angebissen.

**3** *vt* **(a)** *(divide)* teilen; *hair* scheiteln; *curtain* zur Seite schieben. **(b)** *(separate)* trennen. **to ~ sb from sb/sth** jdn von jdm/etw trennen; **to ~ company with sb/sth** sich von jdm/etw trennen; *(in opinion)* mit jdm nicht gleicher Meinung sein.

**4** *vi* **(a)** *(divide)* sich teilen; *(curtains)* sich öffnen. **(b)** *(separate) (person)* sich trennen; *(things)* sich lösen, abgehen. **to ~ with sth** sich von etw trennen.

**partake** [pɑː'teɪk] *pret* **partook,** *ptp* **partaken** [pɑː'teɪkn] *vi (form)* **(a)** **to ~ of** *food, drink* zu sich *(dat)* nehmen. **(b)** **to ~ in** *(an activity)* an etw *(dat)* teilnehmen.

**part exchange** *n (Brit)* **to offer/take sth in ~** etw in Zahlung geben/nehmen.

**partial** ['pɑːʃəl] *adj* **(a)** *(not complete)* Teil-, teilweise; *paralysis, eclipse* teilweise, partiell. **(b)** *(biased)* voreingenommen. **(c)** **to be ~ to sth** eine Schwäche für etw haben.

**partiality** [ˌpɑːʃɪ'ælɪtɪ] *n* **(a)** *(bias)* Voreingenommenheit *f*. **(b)** *(liking)* Vorliebe *f (for für)*.

**partially** ['pɑːʃəlɪ] *adv (partly)* zum Teil, teilweise.

**participant** [pɑː'tɪsɪpənt] *n* Teilnehmer(in *f*) *m (in gen, an +dat)*.

**participate** [pɑː'tɪsɪpeɪt] *vi (take part)* sich beteiligen, teilnehmen *(in an +dat)*.

**participation** [pɑːˌtɪsɪ'peɪʃən] *n* Beteiligung *f*; *(in competition etc)* Teilnahme *f*; *(worker ~)* Mitbestimmung *f*.

**participle** ['pɑːtɪsɪpl] *n* Partizip *nt*.

**particle** ['pɑːtɪkl] *n* **(a)** *(of sand etc, Phys)* Teilchen *nt*. **(b)** *(Gram)* Partikel *f*.

**particular** [pə'tɪkjʊləʳ] **1** *adj* **(a)** *(as against others)* **this ~ house is very nice** dies (eine) Haus ist sehr hübsch; **in this ~ instance** in diesem besonderen Fall; **is there any one ~ colour you prefer?** bevorzugen Sie eine bestimmte Farbe? **(b)** *(special)* besondere(r, s). **in ~** besonders, vor allem; **nothing in ~** nichts Besonderes *or* Bestimmtes; **is there anything in ~ you'd like?** haben Sie einen besonderen Wunsch?; **he's a ~ friend of mine** er ist ein guter Freund von mir; **for no ~ reason** aus keinem besonderen Grund. **(c)** *(fussy, fastidious)* eigen; *(choosy)* wählerisch. **he is very ~ about cleanliness** er nimmt es mit der Sauberkeit sehr genau; **you can't be too ~** man kann gar nicht wählerisch genug sein; **I'm not too ~ (about it)** es kommt mir nicht so darauf an.

**2** *n* **~s** *pl* Einzelheiten *pl*; *(about person)* Personalien *pl*; **for further ~s apply to the personnel man-**

**ager** weitere Auskünfte erteilt der Personalchef; **to give ~s** Angaben machen.

**particularly** [pə'tɪkjʊləlɪ] adv besonders, vor allem; specify, request ausdrücklich. **he was not ~ pleased** er war nicht besonders erfreut; **it's important, ~ as time is short** es ist wichtig, zumal die Zeit knapp wird.

**parting** ['pɑːtɪŋ] **1** n **(a)** Abschied m. **is this the ~ of the ways then?** das ist also das Ende (unserer Beziehung)? **(b)** (Brit: in hair) Scheitel m. **2** adj Abschieds-, abschließend. **"He knows about it already", was her ~ shot** „Er weiß es schon", schleuderte sie ihm/ihr etc nach; **his ~ words** seine Abschiesworte pl.

**partisan** [ˌpɑːtɪ'zæn] **1** adj **(a)** parteiisch (esp pej), parteilich. **~ spirit** Parteigeist m. **(b)** (Mil) Partisanen-. **2** n (Mil) Partisan(in f) m.

**partition** [pɑː'tɪʃən] **1** n **(a)** Teilung f. **(b)** (wall) Trennwand f. **(c)** (section) Abteilung f. **2** vt country spalten; room aufteilen.
▶**partition off** vt sep abteilen, abtrennen.

**partly** ['pɑːtlɪ] adv zum Teil, teilweise. **~ ..., ~ ...** teils ... teils ...

**partner** ['pɑːtnəʳ] **1** n Partner(in f) m; (in limited company also) Gesellschafter(in f) m; (in crime) Komplize m, Komplizin f. **~s in crime** Komplizen. **2** vt **to ~ sb** jds Partner sein; **to be ~ed by sb** jdn zum Partner haben.

**partnership** ['pɑːtnəʃɪp] n **(a)** Partnerschaft f; (in sport, dancing etc) Paar nt. **in ~ with sb** in Zusammenarbeit mit jdm. **(b)** (Comm) Personengesellschaft f. **to enter into a ~** in eine Gesellschaft eintreten.

**partook** [pɑː'tʊk] pret of **partake**.

**part: ~ owner** n Mitbesitzer(in f) m; **~ payment** n Teilzahlung f.

**partridge** ['pɑːtrɪdʒ] n Rebhuhn nt.

**part: ~-time 1** adj Teilzeit-; **I'm just ~-time** ich arbeite nur Teilzeit; **2** adv work stundenweise; teach als Teilzeitlehrer(in); **~-timer** n Teilzeitkraft f; **~-time work** n (Press) Lieferungswerk nt.

**party** ['pɑːtɪ] n **(a)** (Pol) Partei f. **(b)** (group) Gruppe, Gesellschaft f; (Mil) Kommando nt, Trupp m. **a ~ of tourists** eine Reisegesellschaft. **(c)** (celebration) Fest nt, Party, Fete (col) f; (more formal) Gesellschaft f. **to have** or **give a ~** eine Party geben or machen; **at the ~** auf dem Fest or der Party; **bei der Gesellschaft. (d)** (Jur, fig) Partei f. **a/the third ~** ein Dritter m/der Dritte; **the parties to a dispute** die streitenden Parteien; **to be a ~ to sth** an etw (dat) beteiligt sein.

**party: ~ line** n **(a)** (Pol) Parteilinie f; **(b)** (Telec) Gemeinschaftsanschluß m; **~ political** adj parteipolitisch; **~ politics** npl Parteipolitik f. **~ pooper** n (inf) Partymuffel m (inf).

**pass** [pɑːs] **1** n **(a)** (permit) Ausweis m; (Mil etc) Passierschein m. **(b)** (Brit Sch) **to get a ~ in German** seine Deutschprüfung bestehen; (lowest level) seine Deutschprüfung mit „ausreichend" bestehen. **(c)** (Geog, Sport) Paß m; (Ftbl: for shot at goal) Vorlage f. **(d)** things have come to a pretty **~ when ...** so weit ist es schon gekommen, daß ...; **things had come to such a ~ that ...** die Lage hatte sich so zugespitzt, daß ... **(e) to make a ~ at sb** bei jdm Annäherungsversuche machen.

**2** vt **(a)** (move past) vorbeigehen an (+dat); vorbeifahren an (+dat); (overtake) athlete, car überholen. **(b)** (cross) frontier etc überschreiten, passieren. **not a word ~ed her lips** kein Wort kam über ihre Lippen. **(c)** (reach, hand) reichen. **they ~ed the photograph around** sie reichten das Foto herum; **~**

**(me) the salt, please** reich mir doch bitte das Salz!; **to ~ the ball to sb** (Sport) jdm den Ball zuspielen. **(d) it ~es my comprehension that ...** es geht über meinen Verstand, daß ... **(e)** (Univ etc) exam bestehen; candidate bestehen lassen. **(f)** (approve) motion annehmen; plan gutheißen; (Parl) verabschieden. **(g)** (spend) time verbringen. **he did it just to ~ the time** er tat das nur, um sich (dat) die Zeit zu vertreiben; **to ~ the time of day with sb** mit jdm ein paar freundliche Worte wechseln. **(h)** remark von sich geben; opinion abgeben; (Jur) sentence verhängen; judgement fällen.

**3** vi **(a)** (move past) vorbeigehen; vorbeifahren. **we ~ed in the corridor** wir gingen im Korridor aneinander vorbei.
**(b)** (overtake) überholen.
**(c)** (move, go) **~ along** or **down the bus please!** bitte weiter durchgehen!; **words ~ed between them** es gab einige Meinungsverschiedenheiten; **to ~ out of sight** außer Sichtweite geraten; **when we ~ed over the frontier** als wir die Grenze passierten; **shall we ~ to the second subject on the agenda?** wollen wir zum zweiten Punkt der Tagesordnung übergehen?; **he ~ed under the archway** er ging/fuhr durch das Tor.
**(d)** (time) (also **~ by**) vergehen.
**(e)** (disappear, end: anger, era etc) vorübergehen; (storm) (go over) vorüberziehen; (abate) sich legen; (rain) vorbeigehen. **it'll ~** das geht vorüber!
**(f)** (be acceptable) gehen. **to let sth ~** etw durchgehen lassen; **let it ~!** vergessen wir's!; **it'll ~** das geht.
**(g)** (be considered, be accepted) angesehen werden (for or as sth als etw). **she could easily ~ for 25** sie könnte leicht für 25 durchgehen.
**(h)** (in exam) bestehen.
**(i)** (Cards, in quiz etc) passen. **(I) ~!** passe!
▶**pass away** vi **(a)** (end) zu Ende gehen. **(b)** (euph: die) entschlafen (euph).
▶**pass by 1** vi (go past) vorbeigehen; (car etc) vorbeifahren; (time, months etc) vergehen. **2** vi +prep obj **we ~ed a line of hotels** wir kamen an einer Reihe Hotels vorbei. **3** vt sep (ignore) problems übergehen. **life has ~ed her ~** das Leben ist an ihr vorübergegangen.
▶**pass down** vt sep traditions, characteristics weitergeben (to an +acc).
▶**pass off 1** vi **(a)** (take place) ablaufen. **(b)** (end) vorübergehen. **(c)** (be taken as) durchgehen (as als). **2** vt sep **to ~ oneself/sb ~ as sth** sich/jdn als or für etw ausgeben.
▶**pass on 1** vi **(a)** (euph: die) entschlafen (euph). **(b)** (proceed) übergehen (to zu). **2** vt sep news, information weitergeben; disease übertragen.
▶**pass out** vi **(a)** (become unconscious) in Ohnmacht fallen, umkippen (col). **(b)** (new officer) ernannt werden.
▶**pass over** vt sep übergehen. **he's been ~ed ~ again** er ist schon wieder übergangen worden.
▶**pass round** vt sep herumreichen.
▶**pass through** vi **I'm only ~ing** ich bin nur auf der Durchreise; **you have to ~ ~ Berlin** du mußt über Berlin fahren.
▶**pass up** vt sep chance vorübergehen lassen.

**passable** ['pɑːsəbl] adj **(a)** passierbar; road etc also befahrbar. **(b)** (tolerable) passabel.

**passably** ['pɑːsəblɪ] adv leidlich, passabel.

**passage** ['pæsɪdʒ] n **(a)** (transition) Übergang m. **with the ~ of time** mit der Zeit. **(b)** (through country) Durchreise f. **(c)** (voyage, fare) Überfahrt f. **(d)** (Parl: process) parlamentarische Behandlung;

*(final)* Verabschiedung *f.* **(e)** *(corridor)* Gang *m.* **(f)** *(in book)* Passage *f*; *(Mus also)* Stück *nt.* **a** ~ **from the Bible** eine Bibelstelle.

**passageway** ['pæsɪdʒweɪ] *n* Durchgang *m.*

**pass:** ~ **book** *n* Sparbuch *nt*; ~ **degree** *n niedrigster Grad an britischen Universitäten,* ≈ „Ausreichend".

**passenger** ['pæsɪndʒər] *n (on bus, in taxi)* Fahrgast *m*; *(on train)* Reisende(r) *mf*; *(on ship, plane)* Passagier *m*; *(in car)* Mitfahrer(in *f*) *m*; *(on motorcycle)* Beifahrer(in *f*) *m.* **he's just a** ~ *(fig pej: in team etc)* er wird von den anderen mit durchgezogen.

**passenger** *in cpds* Passagier-; ~ **liner** *n* Passagierschiff *nt*; ~ **train** *n* Personenzug *m.*

**passer-by** [ˌpɑːsə'baɪ] *n, pl* **passers-by** Passant(in *f*) *m.*

**passing** ['pɑːsɪŋ] **1** *n* **(a)** Vorübergehen *nt*; *(overtaking)* Überholen *nt.* **with the** ~ **of time** im Lauf(e) der Zeit; **I would like to mention in** ~ **that** ... ich möchte beiläufig erwähnen, daß ... **2** *adj car* vorbeifahrend; *clouds* vorüberziehend; *years* vergehend; *glance etc, thought* flüchtig; *comments, reference* beiläufig; *fancy* vorübergehend. **(b)** *(Sport)* Zuspiel *nt.*

**passing:** ~ **manoeuvre** *n* Überholmanöver *nt*; ~ **place** *n (on narrow road)* Ausweichstelle *f*; ~ **trade** *n* Laufkundschaft *f.*

**passion** ['pæʃən] *n* Leidenschaft *f*; *(Rel, Mus)* Passion *f.* **to have a** ~ **for sth** eine Passion *or* Leidenschaft für etw haben; **music is a** ~ **with him** die Musik ist bei ihm eine Leidenschaft.

**passionate** *adj*, ~**ly** *adv* ['pæʃənɪt, -lɪ] leidenschaftlich.

**passion:** ~ **flower** *n* Passionsblume *f*; ~ **fruit** *n* Passionsfrucht *f*; **P**~ **play** *n* Passionsspiel *nt.*

**passive** ['pæsɪv] **1** *adj* passiv; *acceptance* widerspruchslos. ~ **smoking** Mitrauchen, Passivrauchen *nt.* **2** *n (Gram)* Passiv *nt.* **in the** ~ im Passiv.

**passively** ['pæsɪvlɪ] *adv* passiv; *accept* widerspruchslos.

**passiveness** ['pæsɪvnɪs], **passivity** [pə'sɪvɪtɪ] Passivität *f.*

**pass:** ~ **key** *n* Hauptschlüssel *m*; ~**mark** *n* Ausreichend *nt.*

**Passover** ['pɑːsəuvər] *n* Passah *nt.*

**passport** ['pɑːspɔːt] *n (Reise)*paß *m*; *(fig)* Schlüssel *m (to* für, zu*).* ~ **control** Paßkontrolle *f*; ~ **photo** Paßbild, Paßfoto *nt.*

**password** ['pɑːswɜːd] *n* Kennwort *nt*, Parole *f*; *(Comp)* Paßwort *nt.*

**past** [pɑːst] **1** *adj* **(a)** frühe(r, s) *attr*, vergangene(r, s) *attr.* **for some time** ~ seit einiger Zeit; **in times** ~ in früheren Zeiten. **(b)** *(Gram)* ~ **tense** Vergangenheit *f*; ~ **participle** Partizip Perfekt *nt.*

**2** *n (also Gram)* Vergangenheit *f.* **in the** ~ in der Vergangenheit *(also Gram)*, früher; **to be a thing of the** ~ der Vergangenheit *(dat)* angehören.

**3** *prep* **(a)** *(motion)* an *(+dat)* ... vorbei *or* vorüber; *(position: beyond)* hinter *(+dat).* **just** ~ **the library** kurz hinter der Bücherei; **to run** ~ **sb** an jdm vorbeilaufen. **(b)** *(time)* nach *(+dat).* **ten (minutes)** ~ **three** zehn (Minuten) nach drei; **half** ~ **four** halb fünf; **a quarter** ~ **nine** Viertel nach neun. **(c)** *(beyond)* ~ **forty** über vierzig; ~ **belief** unglaublich; **we're** ~ **caring** es kümmert uns nicht mehr; **to be** ~ **sth** für etw zu alt sein; **I wouldn't put it** ~ **him** *(col)* ich würde es ihm schon zutrauen.

**4** *adv* vorbei, vorüber. **to walk/run** ~ vorbeigehen/vorbeirennen.

**pasta** ['pæstə] *n* Nudeln *pl.*

**paste** [peɪst] **1** *n* **(a)** *(for sticking)* Kleister *m.* **(b)** *(spread)* Brotaufstrich *m.* **(c)** *(jewellery)* Straß *m.* **(d)** **mix to a smooth/firm** ~ *(Cook)* zu einem glatten/festen Teig anrühren. **2** *vt (apply* ~ *to) wallpaper etc* einkleistern; *(affix)* kleben *(to* an *+acc, in* in *+acc).*

**pasteboard** ['peɪstbɔːd] *n* Karton *m*, Pappe *f.*

**pastel** ['pæstl] **1** *n (crayon)* Pastellstift *m*; *(drawing)* Pastellzeichnung *f*, Pastell *nt*; *(colour)* Pastellton *m.* **2** *adj attr* Pastell-.

**pasteurize** ['pæstəraɪz] *vt* pasteurisieren.

**pastille** ['pæstɪl] *n* Pastille *f.*

**pastime** ['pɑːstaɪm] *n* Zeitvertreib *m.*

**past master** *n* **to be a** ~ **at doing sth** ein Experte darin sein, etw zu tun.

**pastor** ['pɑːstər] *n* Pfarrer *m.*

**pastoral** ['pɑːstərəl] *adj* pastoral; *duties also* seelsorgerisch. ~ **care** Seelsorge *f.*

**pastry** ['peɪstrɪ] *n* Teig *m*; *(cake etc)* Stück, Teilchen *(dial) nt.* **pastries** *pl* Gebäck *nt.*

**pastry:** ~ **brush** *n* Backpinsel *m*; ~ **case** *n* Törtchenform *f*; ~ **cook** *n* Konditor(in *f*) *m.*

**pasture** ['pɑːstʃər] *n* **(a)** *(field)* Weide *f.* **to put out to** ~ auf die Weide treiben; **to move on to** ~**s new** *(fig)* sich *(dat)* etwas Neues suchen. **(b)** *no pl (also* ~ **land)** Weideland *nt.*

**pasty**[1] ['peɪstɪ] *adj consistency* zähflüssig; *material* klebrig; *complexion, face* bläßlich; *look also* kränklich.

**pasty**[2] ['pæstɪ] *n (esp Brit)* Pastete *f.*

**pasty-faced** ['peɪstɪ'feɪst] *adj* blaß, bleichgesichtig.

**pat**[1] [pæt] *n (of butter)* Portion *f.*

**pat**[2] **1** *adv* **to know** *or* **have sth off** ~ etw wie aus dem Effeff können *(col).* **2** *adj answer, explanation* glatt.

**pat**[3] **1** *n* Klaps *m.* **he gave him a** ~ **on the shoulder** er tippte ihm auf die Schulter; **to give the dog a** ~ den Hund tätscheln; **to give sb/oneself a** ~ **on the back** *(fig)* jdm/sich selbst auf die Schulter klopfen. **2** *vt (touch lightly)* tätscheln; *(hit gently) ball* leicht schlagen; *sand* festklopfen; *face* abtupfen.

**patch** [pætʃ] **1** *n* **(a)** *(for mending)* Flicken *m*; *(eye* ~*)* Augenklappe *f.* **(b)** **it's/he's not a** ~ **on ...** *(col)* das/er ist gar nichts gegen ... **(c)** *(small area, stain)* Fleck *m*; *(piece of land)* Stück *nt*; *(subdivision of garden)* Beet *nt*; *(part, section)* Stelle *f*; *(of time)* Phase *f.* **a** ~ **of blue sky** ein Stückchen *nt* blauer Himmel; ~**es of colour** Farbtupfer *pl*; **the cabbage** ~ das Kohlbeet; **he's going through a bad** ~ **at the moment** er hat's zur Zeit nicht leicht. **2** *vt* flicken.

▶**patch up** *vt sep* zusammenflicken; *quarrel* beilegen. **to** ~ **things** ~ **temporarily** die Dinge notdürftig zusammenflicken; *(in relationship)* die Beziehung wieder ins Lot bringen; **they managed to** ~ ~ **their relationship** sie haben sich schließlich wieder ausgesöhnt.

**patchwork** ['pætʃwɜːk] *n* ~ **quilt** Flickendecke *f*; **a** ~ **of fields** ein buntes Mosaik von Feldern.

**patchy** ['pætʃɪ] *adj (+er) work* ungleichmäßig; *knowledge, memory* lückenhaft. ~ **fog** stellenweise auftretender Nebel.

**pate** [peɪt] *n* Rübe *f (col).* **bald** ~ Glatze *f.*

**pâté** ['pæteɪ] *n* Pastete *f.*

**patent**[1] ['peɪtənt] *adj (obvious)* offensichtlich.

**patent**[2] **1** *n* Patent *nt.* ~ **applied for** *or* **pending** Patent angemeldet; **to take out a** ~ **on sth** etw patentieren lassen. **2** *vt* patentieren lassen. **3** *adj (~ed) invention* patentiert.

**patent agent** *(Brit)*, **patent attorney** *(esp US) n* Patentanwalt *m*, -anwältin *f.*

**patentee** [ˌpeɪtn'tiː] *n* Patentinhaber(in *f*) *m.*

**patent leather** n Lackleder nt.
**patently** ['peɪtəntlɪ] adv offensichtlich. **that's** ~ **obvious** das liegt doch auf der Hand.
**patent:** ~ **medicine** n patentrechtlich geschütztes Arzneimittel; ~ **office** n Patentamt nt; ~ **remedy** n Patentrezept nt; (medicine) Hausmittel nt; (fig) Patentlösung f; ~ **specification** n Patentschrift f.
**paternal** [pə'tɜːnl] adv väterlich. **my** ~ **grandmother** meine Großmutter väterlicherseits.
**paternalist(ic)** [pə'tɜːnəlɪst, pə,tɜːnə'lɪstɪk] adj patriarchalisch.
**paternity** [pə'tɜːnɪtɪ] n Vaterschaft f. ~ **leave** Vaterschaftsurlaub m. ~ **suit** Vaterschaftsprozeß m.
**path** [pɑːθ] n (lit, fig) Weg m; (smaller) Pfad m; (in field) Feldweg m; (trajectory) Bahn f. **the** ~ **of virtue** der Pfad der Tugend.
**pathetic** [pə'θetɪk] adj (a) (piteous) mitleiderregend. **it was** ~ **to see** es war ein Bild des Jammers. (b) (bad) erbärmlich. **it's** ~ es ist zum Heulen (col).
**pathetically** [pə'θetɪkəlɪ] adv (a) (piteously) mitleiderregend. ~ **thin/weak** erschreckend dünn/schwach. (b) slow, stupid, inefficient erbärmlich. **a** ~ **inadequate answer** eine äußerst dürftige Antwort.
**pathological** [,pæθə'lɒdʒɪkəl] adj (lit, fig) krankhaft; studies etc pathologisch.
**pathologist** [pə'θɒlədʒɪst] n Pathologe m, Pathologin f.
**pathology** [pə'θɒlədʒɪ] n (science) Pathologie f.
**pathos** ['peɪθɒs] n Pathos nt.
**pathway** ['pɑːθweɪ] n Weg m; (smaller) Pfad m.
**patience** ['peɪʃəns] n (a) Geduld f. **to have** ~/**no** ~ **(with sb/sth)** Geduld/keine Geduld (mit jdm/etw) haben; **to lose (one's)** ~ **(with sb/sth)** (mit jdm/etw) die Geduld verlieren. (b) (Brit Cards) Patience f. **to play** ~ eine Patience legen.
**patient** ['peɪʃənt] **1** adj geduldig. **to be** ~ **with sb** Geduld mit jdm haben. **2** n Patient(in f) m.
**patiently** ['peɪʃəntlɪ] adv geduldig.
**patina** ['pætɪnə] n Patina f.
**patio** ['pætɪəʊ] n Veranda, Terrasse f.
**patriarch** ['peɪtrɪɑːk] n Patriarch m.
**patriot** ['peɪtrɪət] n Patriot(in f) m.
**patriotic** [,pætrɪ'ɒtɪk] adj patriotisch.
**patriotism** ['pætrɪətɪzəm] n Patriotismus m.
**patrol** [pə'trəʊl] **1** n (police) Streife f; (aircraft, ship) Patrouille f. **on** ~ (Mil) auf Patrouille; (police) auf Streife; (guard dogs, squad car) im Einsatz. **2** vt (Mil) patrouillieren; (policeman) seine Runden machen in (+dat); (police car) Streife fahren in (+dat). **3** vi patrouillieren; (policemen) eine Streife/Streifen machen. **to** ~ **up and down** auf und ab gehen.
**patrol:** ~ **boat** n Patrouillenboot nt; ~ **car** n Streifenwagen m; ~**man** n Wächter m; (US: policeman) Polizist m; ~ **wagon** n (US) grüne Minna (col), Gefangenenwagen m.
**patron** ['peɪtrən] n (of shop) Kunde m, Kundin f; (of restaurant, hotel) Gast m; (of society) Schirmherr(in f) m; (of artist) Förderer, Gönner(in f) m; (~ saint) Schutzpatron(in f) m. ~ **of the arts** Kunstmäzen m.
**patronage** ['pætrənɪdʒ] n **under the** ~ **of** unter der Schirmherrschaft des/der.
**patronize** ['pætrənaɪz] vt (a) pub, cinema etc besuchen. **the shop is well** ~**d** das Geschäft hat viel Kundschaft. (b) (treat condescendingly) herablassend behandeln.
**patronizing** ['pætrənaɪzɪŋ] adj gönnerhaft, herablassend. **to be** ~ **to** or **towards sb** jdn von oben herab behandeln.
**patron saint** n Schutzheilige(r) mf.
**patter** ['pætər] **1** n (a) (of feet) Getrippel nt; (of rain)

Plätschern nt. (b) (of salesman, comedian, conjurer, disc jockey) Sprüche pl (col). **sales** ~ Vertretersprüche pl. **2** vi (person, feet) trippeln; (rain: also ~ down) plätschern.
**pattern** ['pætən] **1** n (a) Muster nt. **to make a** ~ ein Muster bilden. (b) (Sew) Schnittmuster nt; (Knitting) Strickanleitung f. (c) (fig: model) Vorbild nt. **on the Albanian** ~ nach albanischem Muster; **to set a** or **the** ~ **for sth** ein Vorbild für etw sein. (d) (fig: in events, behaviour etc) Muster nt; (recurrent) Regelmäßigkeit f. **the** ~ **of events** der Ablauf der Ereignisse; **to follow the usual** ~ nach dem üblichen Schema verlaufen; **behaviour** ~**s** Verhaltensmuster pl. **2** vt (model) machen (on nach). **to be** ~**ed on sth** einer Sache (dat) nachgebildet sein; (music, style etc) einer Sache (dat) nachempfunden sein.
**pattern book** n Musterbuch nt.
**patterned** ['pætənd] adj gemustert.
**paucity** ['pɔːsɪtɪ] n (form) Mangel m (of an +dat).
**Paul** [pɔːl] n Paul m; (Bibl) Paulus m.
**paunch** [pɔːntʃ] n Bauch, Wanst m.
**pauper** ['pɔːpər] n Arme(r) mf.
**pause** [pɔːz] **1** n Pause f. **there was a** ~ **while ...** es entstand eine Pause, während ...; **to have a** ~ (eine) Pause machen; **without (a)** ~ ununterbrochen; **a** ~ **for thought** eine Denkpause. **2** vi stehenbleiben; (speaker) innehalten. **he** ~**d for breath** er machte eine Pause, um Luft zu holen; **let's** ~ **here** machen wir hier Pause; **it made him** ~ das machte ihn nachdenklich.
**pave** [peɪv] vt pflastern. **to** ~ **the way for sb/sth** (fig) jdm/einer Sache den Weg ebnen.
**pavement** ['peɪvmənt] n (a) (Brit) Bürgersteig m, Trottoir nt. ~ **artist** Pflastermaler m. (b) (US) (paved road) Straße f; (surfacing) Straßendecke f.
**pavilion** [pə'vɪlɪən] n Pavillon m; (Sport) (changing ~) Umkleideräume pl; (clubhouse) Klubhaus nt.
**paving** ['peɪvɪŋ] n Belag m; (US: of road) Decke f; (action) Pflastern nt. ~ **stone** Platte f.
**paw** [pɔː] **1** n (of animal, col: hand) Pfote f; (of lion, bear) Pranke, Tatze f. **2** vt (a) tätscheln; (lion etc) mit der Tatze berühren. **to** ~ **the ground** (lit) scharren; (fig: be impatient) ungeduldig werden. (b) (pej col: handle) betatschen (col).
**pawn**[1] [pɔːn] n (Chess) Bauer m; (fig) Schachfigur f.
**pawn**[2] **1** n (security) Pfand nt. **to put sth in** ~ etw verpfänden. **2** vt verpfänden.
**pawn:** ~**broker** n Pfandleiher m; ~**shop** n Pfandhaus nt.
**pay** [peɪ] (vb: pret, ptp **paid**) **1** n Lohn m; (of salaried employee, civil servant) Gehalt nt; (Mil) Sold m. **to be in sb's** ~ für jdn arbeiten.
**2** vt (a) zahlen; person, bill, debt bezahlen. **to** ~ **sb £10** jdm £10 zahlen; **how much is there to** ~? was bin ich schuldig?; **to be** or **get paid** (in regular job) seinen Lohn/sein Gehalt bekommen; **savings accounts that** ~ **5%** Sparkonten, die 5% Zinsen bringen. (b) (lit, fig: be profitable to) sich lohnen für. **in future it would** ~ **you to ask** in Zukunft solltest du besser vorher fragen. (c) **to** ~ **(sb) a visit** or **call** jdn besuchen; (more formal) jdm einen Besuch abstatten.
**3** vi (a) zahlen. **they** ~ **well for this sort of work** diese Arbeit wird gut bezahlt; **no, no, I'm** ~**ing** nein, nein, ich (be)zahle; **to** ~ **for sth** etw bezahlen; **it's already paid for** es ist schon bezahlt. (b) (be profitable) sich lohnen. **it's a business that** ~**s** es ist ein rentables Geschäft; **crime doesn't** ~ (prov) Verbrechen lohnen sich nicht. (c) (fig: to suffer) **to** ~ **for sth (with sth)** für etw (mit etw) bezahlen; **you'll**

~ **for that!** dafür wirst du (mir) büßen.
▶**pay back** *vt sep money* zurückzahlen; *compliment, visit* erwidern; *insult, trick* sich revanchieren für. **to ~ sb ~** es jdm heimzahlen.
▶**pay in** *vt sep* einzahlen. **to ~ money ~to an account** Geld auf ein Konto einzahlen.
▶**pay off** *vt sep workmen* auszahlen; *debt* abbezahlen; *instalments* ab(be)zahlen; *mortgage* ablösen; *creditor* befriedigen. **to ~ sth ~ in instalments** etw in Raten ab(be)zahlen.
▶**pay out** *vt sep* (a) *money (spend)* ausgeben; *(count out)* auszahlen. (b) *rope* ablaufen lassen.
▶**pay up 1** *vt sep what one owes* zurückzahlen; *subscription* bezahlen. **his account/he is paid ~** er hat alles bezahlt. **2** *vi* zahlen. **come on, ~ ~!** los, bezahl endlich!
**payable** ['peɪəbl] *adj* zahlbar; *(due)* fällig. **to make a cheque ~ to sb** einen Scheck auf jdn ausstellen.
**pay:** **~-as-you-earn** *n (Brit)* Steuersystem *nt, bei dem die Lohnsteuer direkt einbehalten wird*; **~ award** *n* Lohn-/Gehaltserhöhung *f*; **~-claim** *n* Lohn-/Gehaltsforderung *f*; **~-day** *n* Zahltag *m*; **~ differential** *n* Lohngefälle *nt*; **~ dispute** *n* Tarifkonflikt *m*.
**PAYE** *(Brit)* = **pay-as-you-earn.**
**payee** [peɪˈiː] *n* Zahlungsempfänger *m*.
**pay:** **~ envelope** *n (US)* Lohntüte *f*; **~ freeze** *n* Lohnstopp *m*; **~ increase** *n* Lohn-/Gehaltserhöhung *f*.
**paying** ['peɪɪŋ] *adj* (a) *(profitable)* rentabel. (b) **~ guest** zahlender Gast.
**payload** ['peɪləʊd] *n* Nutzlast *f*.
**payment** ['peɪmənt] *n* Zahlung *f*; *(paying)* Bezahlung *f*; *(of debt, mortgage)* Abtragung, Rückzahlung *f*. **three monthly ~s** drei Monatsraten; **as or in ~ for his services** als Bezahlung für seine Dienste; **on ~ of** bei Bezahlung von; **to make a ~** eine Zahlung leisten.
**payoff** ['peɪɒf] *n (col: bribe)* Bestechungsgeld *nt*; *(outcome)* Quittung *f*; *(of joke)* Pointe *f*.
**pay:** **~ packet** *n (Brit)* Lohntüte *f*; **~ phone** *n* Münztelefon *nt*; **~ rise** *n* Lohn-/Gehaltserhöhung *f*; **~roll** *n* Lohnliste *f*; *(workers)* Belegschaft *f*; **to be on the (firm's) ~roll** bei der Firma fest angestellt sein; **~ round** *n* Tarifrunde *f*; **~slip** *n* Lohn-/Gehaltsstreifen *m*; **~ station** *n (US)* öffentlicher Fernsprecher; **~ talks** *npl* Lohnverhandlungen *pl*; *(for profession, area of industry)* Tarifverhandlungen *pl*.
**PC** = (a) **personal computer** PC *m*. (b) *(Brit)* **Police Constable.** (c) *(Brit)* **Privy Councillor.**
**PCB** = **printed circuit board.**
**pd** = **paid** bez.
**PDQ** *(col)* = **pretty damn quick** verdammt schnell *(col)*.
**pc** = (a) **post card.** (b) **per cent** v.H.
**PE** = **physical education.**
**pea** [piː] *n* Erbse *f*.
**peace** [piːs] *n* Frieden *m*; *(tranquillity)* Ruhe *f*. **to be at ~ with sb/sth** mit jdm/etw in Frieden leben; **he is at ~** *(euph: dead)* er ruht in Frieden; **to make (one's) ~ (with sb)** sich (mit jdm) versöhnen; **to make ~ between ...** Frieden stiften zwischen ... *(+dat)*; **to keep the ~** *(Jur) (demonstrator, citizen)* die öffentliche Ordnung wahren; *(policeman)* die öffentliche Ordnung aufrechterhalten; *(fig)* Frieden bewahren; **~ of mind** innere Ruhe; **~ and quiet** Ruhe und Frieden; **to give sb some ~** jdn in Ruhe *or* Frieden lassen; **to give sb no ~** jdm keine Ruhe lassen; **she doesn't have a moment's ~** sie hat keine ruhige Minute.

**peaceable** *adj*, **~bly** *adv* ['piːsəbl, -ɪ] friedlich.
**peace:** **~ campaigner** *n* Friedenskämpfer(in *f*) *m*; **~ conference** *n* Friedenskonferenz *f*; **P~ Corps** *n (US)* ≃ Entwicklungsdienst *m*.
**peaceful** ['piːsfʊl] *adj* friedlich; *nation, person etc* friedfertig; *holiday, sleep etc* ruhig; *death* sanft.
**peacefully** ['piːsfəlɪ] *adv* friedlich. **to die ~ (in one's sleep)** friedlich entschlafen.
**peace:** **~-keeping 1** *n* Friedenssicherung *f*; **2** *adj* Friedens-; **~-keeping force** Friedenstruppe *f*; **~-keeping role** friedenssichernde Rolle; **~-loving** *adj* friedliebend; **~maker** *n* Friedensstifter(in *f*) *m*; **~ movement** *n* Friedensbewegung *f*; **~-offering** *n (lit, fig)* Friedensangebot *nt*; **~ talks** *npl* Friedensverhandlungen *pl*; **~time** *n* Friedenszeiten *pl*, Frieden *m*.
**peach** [piːtʃ] **1** *n* (a) *(fruit)* Pfirsich *m*; *(tree)* Pfirsichbaum *m*. (b) *(col)* **she's a ~** sie ist klasse *(col)*. **2** *adj* pfirsichfarben.
**peacock** ['piːkɒk] *n* Pfau *m*.
**pea-green** ['piː,griːn] *adj* erbsengrün.
**peak** [piːk] **1** *n* (a) *(of mountain)* Gipfel *m*; *(of roof)* First *m*. (b) *(of cap)* Schirm *m*. (c) *(maximum)* Höhepunkt *m*; *(on graph)* Scheitelpunkt *m*. **he is at the ~ of fitness** er ist in Höchstform; **when demand is at its ~** wenn die Nachfrage am stärksten ist. **2** *adj attr value, power* Spitzen-; *production* Höchst-. **3** *vi* den Höchststand erreichen; *(engine)* seine Spitzenleistung erreichen.
**peaked** [piːkt] *adj* (a) **~ cap** Schirmmütze *f*. (b) *(US)* = **peaky.**
**peak:** **~ hours** *npl*, **~ period** *n (of traffic)* Hauptverkehrszeit *f*; *(Telec, Elec)* Hauptbelastungszeit *f*; **~ viewing period** *n (TV)* Hauptsendezeit *f*.
**peaky** ['piːkɪ] *adj (+er) (Brit col)* complexion blaß. **to look ~** angeschlagen aussehen *(col)*.
**peal** [piːl] **1** *n* **~ of bells** *(sound)* Glockenläuten *nt*; **~s of laughter** schallendes Gelächter; **~ of thunder** Donnerrollen *nt*. **2** *vi (bell)* läuten.
**peanut** ['piːnʌt] *n* Erdnuß *f*. **~s** *(col) (not much money)* Kleingeld *nt (to sb für jdn)*; *(not significant)* Kleinkram *m*; **the pay is ~s** die Bezahlung ist miserabel *or* lächerlich *(col)*; **~ butter** Erdnußbutter *f*.
**pear** [pɛəʳ] *n* Birne *f*; *(tree)* Birnbaum *m*.
**pearl** [pɜːl] *n (lit, fig)* Perle *f*; *(mother-of-~, colour)* Perlmutt *nt*. **string of ~s** Perlenkette *f*; **~ of wisdom** weiser Spruch.
**pearl:** **~ barley** *n* Perlgraupen *pl*; **~ fishing** *n* Perlenfischerei *f*; **~ grey** *adj* silbergrau; **~ oyster** *n* Perlenauster *f*.
**pearly** ['pɜːlɪ] *adj (+er) (in colour)* perlmuttfarben. **~ white** perlweiß; **P~ Gates** Himmelstür *f*.
**pear:** **~-shaped** *adj* birnenförmig; **~ tree** *n* Birnbaum *m*.
**peasant** ['pezənt] **1** *n (lit)* (armer) Bauer; *(pej col) (ignoramus)* Banause *m*; *(pleb)* Prolet *m*. **2** *adj attr* bäuerlich. **~ farmer** (armer) Bauer.
**peasantry** ['pezəntrɪ] *n* Bauernschaft *f*; *(class)* Bauerntum *nt*.
**pease-pudding** ['piːz'pʊdɪŋ] *n* Erbs(en)püree *nt*.
**pea:** **~-shooter** *n* Pusterohr *nt*; **~ soup** *n* Erbsensuppe *f*.
**peat** [piːt] *n* Torf *m*. **~bog** Torfmoor *nt*.
**pebble** ['pebl] *n* Kieselstein *m*. **he/she is not the only ~ on the beach** *(col)* es gibt noch andere.
**pebbly** ['peblɪ] *adj* steinig.
**peck** [pek] **1** *n* (a) *(col: kiss)* Küßchen *nt*. (b) **the hen gave him a ~** die Henne hackte nach ihm. **2** *vt (bird)* picken. **3** *vi* picken *(at nach)*. **he just ~ed at his food** er stocherte nur in seinem Essen herum.
**pecking order** ['pekɪŋ,ɔːdəʳ] *n (lit, fig)* Hackord-

**pencil**

nung f.

**peckish** ['pekɪʃ] adj (Brit col: hungry) I'm (feeling) a bit ~ ich könnte was zwischen die Zähne gebrauchen (col).

**pectin** ['pektɪn] n Pektin nt.

**peculiar** [pɪ'kju:lɪəʳ] adj (a) (strange) seltsam, eigenartig. (b) (exclusive, special) eigentümlich (to für +acc). an animal ~ to Africa ein Tier, das nur in Afrika vorkommt.

**peculiarity** [pɪ,kju:lɪ'ærɪtɪ] n (a) (strangeness) Eigenartigkeit f. (b) (unusual feature) Besonderheit f.

**pecuniary** [pɪ'kju:nɪərɪ] adj (form) penalties, affairs Geld-; gain, problem finanziell.

**pedagogic(al)** [,pedə'gɒdʒɪk(əl)] adj (form) pädagogisch.

**pedal** ['pedl] 1 n Pedal nt; (on bin etc) Trethebel m. ~ bin (Brit) Treteimer m. 2 vi (on bicycle) treten. to ~ off (mit dem Rad) wegfahren.

**pedalo** ['pedələu] n Tretboot nt.

**pedant** ['pedənt] n Pedant (in f) m.

**pedantic** [pɪ'dæntɪk] adj pedantisch.

**pedantry** ['pedəntrɪ] n Pedanterie f.

**peddle** ['pedl] vt hausieren mit (pej). to ~ drugs mit Drogen handeln.

**peddler** ['pedləʳ] n (esp US) = **pedlar**.

**pederast** ['pedəræst] n Päderast m.

**pedestal** ['pedɪstl] n Sockel m. to put sb on a ~ (fig) jdn in den Himmel heben.

**pedestrian** [pɪ'destrɪən] 1 n Fußgänger(in f) m. 2 adj (a) attr Fußgänger-. ~ crossing (Brit) Fußgängerüberweg m; ~ precinct (Brit) Fußgängerzone f. (b) (prosaic) schwunglos.

**pediatric, pediatrician** (esp US) = **paediatric, paediatrician**.

**pedicure** ['pedɪkjuəʳ] n Pediküre f.

**pedigree** ['pedɪgri:] 1 n (lit, fig) Stammbaum m; (document) Ahnentafel f. 2 attr reinrassig.

**pedlar** ['pedləʳ] n Hausierer(in f) m; (of drugs) Drogenhändler(in f) m.

**pee** [pi:] (col) 1 n (urine) Urin m, Pipi nt (baby-talk). to need/have a ~ pinkeln müssen/pinkeln (col). 2 vi pinkeln (col).

**peek** [pi:k] 1 n kurzer Blick; (furtive) verstohlener Blick. to take or have a ~ kurz/verstohlen gucken (at nach). 2 vi gucken (at nach).

**peel** [pi:l] 1 n Schale f. 2 vt schälen. 3 vi (wallpaper) sich lösen; (paint) abblättern; (skin, person) sich schälen or pellen (col).
▶**peel away** 1 vt sep wallpaper, paint abziehen (from von); wrapper abstreifen (from von). 2 vi (lit, fig) sich lösen (from von).
▶**peel back** vt sep cover, wrapping abziehen.
▶**peel off** 1 vt sep (+prep obj von) tape, wallpaper abziehen; wrapper, glove etc abstreifen. 2 vi sich lösen.

**peeler** ['pi:ləʳ] n (potato ~) Schälmesser nt.

**peelings** ['pi:lɪŋz] npl Schalen pl.

**peep¹** [pi:p] 1 n (sound) (of bird etc) Piep m; (of horn, whistle, col: of person) Ton m. we haven't had or heard a ~ out of him (col) wir haben keinen Pieps von ihm gehört (col). 2 vi (bird etc) piepen; (horn, car) tuten; (whistle) pfeifen.

**peep²** 1 n (look) kurzer Blick; (furtive) verstohlener Blick. to take or have a ~ (at sth) kurz/verstohlen (nach etw) gucken. 2 vi gucken (at nach). to ~ from behind sth hinter etw (dat) hervorschauen; to ~ over sth über etw (acc) gucken.

**peephole** ['pi:phəul] n Guckloch nt; (in door also) Spion m.

**peeping Tom** [,pi:pɪŋ'tɒm] n Spanner (col), Voyeur m.

**peer¹** [pɪəʳ] n (a) ~ (of the realm) Peer m. (b) (equal) Gleichrangige(r) mf. he was well-liked by his ~s er war bei seinesgleichen beliebt.

**peer²** vi starren; (inquiringly) schielen. to ~ (hard) at sb/sth jdn/etw anstarren.

**peerage** ['pɪərɪdʒ] n Adelsstand m, Peers pl. to give sb a ~ jdm einen Adelstitel verleihen; to raise sb to the ~ jdn in den Adelsstand erheben.

**peer group** n (age group) Altersgruppe f; (ability group) Leistungsklasse f.

**peerless** ['pɪəlɪs] adj einzigartig.

**peeved** [pi:vd] adj (col) eingeschnappt (col), verärgert.

**peevish** ['pi:vɪʃ] adj gereizt; (irritable) reizbar.

**peevishly** ['pi:vɪʃlɪ] adv gereizt.

**peevishness** ['pi:vɪʃnɪs] n Gereiztheit f; (irritability) Reizbarkeit f.

**peewit** ['pi:wɪt] n Kiebitz m.

**peg** [peg] 1 n (stake) Pflock m; (for wood joints, in games) Stift m; (Brit: clothes ~) (Wäsche)klammer f. off the ~ von der Stange; to take sb down a ~ or two (col) jdm einen Dämpfer geben; a ~ on which to hang one's prejudices etc ein guter Aufhänger für seine Vorurteile etc. 2 vt (a) (fasten) anpflocken; clothes anklammern; (tent) festpflocken. (b) prices, wages festsetzen.
▶**peg away** vi (col) nicht locker lassen (at mit).
▶**peg out** 1 vt sep washing aufhängen; (mark out) area abstecken. 2 vi (col: die) abkratzen (col).

**pejorative** [pɪ'dʒɒrɪtɪv] adj abwertend.

**pekinese** [,pi:kɪ'ni:z] n, pl - (dog) Pekinese m.

**Peking** [pi:'kɪŋ] n Peking nt.

**pelican** ['pelɪkən] n Pelikan m. ~ crossing Ampelüberweg m.

**pellet** ['pelɪt] n (for gun) Schrotkugel f.

**pell-mell** ['pel'mel] adv wie Kraut und Rüben (col).

**pelmet** ['pelmɪt] n (board) Blende f; (drapery) Schabracke f.

**pelt** [pelt] 1 vt (throw) schleudern (at nach). to ~ sb/sth (with sth) jdn/etw (mit etw) bewerfen. 2 vi (col) (a) (go fast) pesen (col). (b) it ~ed (with rain) es hat so geschüttet (col). 3 n (col) at full ~ volle Pulle (col).

**pelvic** ['pelvɪk] adj Becken-. ~ fin Bauchflosse f.

**pelvis** ['pelvɪs] n Becken nt.

**pen¹** [pen] 1 n (dip ~) Feder f; (fountain ~) Füller m; (ball-point ~) Kugelschreiber, Kuli (col) m. to put ~ to paper zur Feder greifen. 2 vt niederschreiben.

**pen²** n (a) (for cattle etc) Pferch m; (play~) Laufstall m. (b) (US col: prison) Knast (col) m.

**penal** ['pi:nl] adj law, colony etc Straf-. ~ code Strafgesetzbuch nt; ~ institution Strafanstalt f; ~ reform Strafrechtsreform f; ~ system Strafrecht nt.

**penalize** ['pi:nəlaɪz] vt bestrafen; (fig) benachteiligen.

**penalty** ['penltɪ] n (a) (punishment) Strafe f; (fig: disadvantage) Nachteil m. on ~ of death/£5/ imprisonment bei Todesstrafe/bei einer Geldstrafe von £5/bei Gefängnisstrafe; to pay the ~ dafür büßen. (b) (Sport) Strafstoß m; (Soccer also) Elfmeter m.

**penalty:** ~ area n Strafraum m; ~ clause n Strafklausel f; ~ kick n Strafstoß m; (soccer also) Elfmeter m; ~ shootout n Elfmeterschießen nt.

**penance** ['penəns] n (Rel) Buße f; (fig) Strafe f. to do ~ Buße tun; (fig) büßen.

**pence** [pens] n pl of **penny**.

**penchant** ['pɑ̃:ʃã:ŋ] n Schwäche f (for für).

**pencil** ['pensl] 1 n Bleistift m; (eyebrow ~) Augenbrauenstift *m*. **2** *vt* mit Bleistift schreiben/zeichnen. **3** *attr drawing* Bleistift-.

▶**pencil in** *vt sep (arrange provisionally)* vorläufig vormerken.

**pencil:** ~ **case** *n* Federmäppchen *nt*; ~ **sharpener** *n* (Bleistift)spitzer *m*.

**pendant** ['pendənt] *n* Anhänger *m*.

**pending** ['pendɪŋ] **1** *adj* anstehend; *lawsuit* anhängig. **to be** ~ *(decision etc)* noch anstehen; *(trial)* noch anhängig sein; ~ **tray** Ablage *f* für noch Unerledigtes. **2** *prep* ~ **his arrival/return** bis zu seiner Ankunft/Rückkehr.

**pendulum** ['pendjʊləm] *n* Pendel *nt*. **the** ~ **has swung back in the opposite direction** *(fig)* das Pendel ist in die entgegengesetzte Richtung ausgeschlagen.

**penetrate** ['penɪtreɪt] **1** *vt* eindringen in *(+acc)*; *walls etc* durchdringen; *(Mil)* enemy lines durchbrechen; *(Med)* vein durchstechen. **2** *vi* eindringen; *(go right through)* durchdringen. **the idea just didn't** ~ *(fig)* das ist mir/ihm *etc* nicht klargeworden.

**penetrating** ['penɪtreɪtɪŋ] *adj* durchdringend; *mind* scharf; *insight* scharfsinnig; *light* grell; *pain* stechend.

**penetration** [,penɪ'treɪʃən] *n see vt* Eindringen *nt (into* in *+acc)*; Durchdringen *nt (of gen)*; Durchbrechung *f*; Durchstechen *nt*.

**penfriend** ['penfrend] *n (Brit)* Brieffreund(in *f*) *m*.

**penguin** ['peŋgwɪn] *n* Pinguin *m*.

**penicillin** [,penɪ'sɪlɪn] *n* Penizillin *nt*.

**peninsula** [pɪ'nɪnsjʊlə] *n* Halbinsel *f*.

**penis** ['piːnɪs] *n* Penis *m*.

**penitence** ['penɪtəns] *n (also Eccl)* Reue *f*.

**penitent** ['penɪtənt] **1** *adj* reuig *(also Eccl)*, zerknirscht. **2** *n (Eccl)* Büßer(in *f*) *m*.

**penitentiary** [,penɪ'tenʃərɪ] *n (esp US: prison)* Strafanstalt *f*.

**pen:** ~**knife** *n* Taschenmesser *nt*; ~ **name** *n* Pseudonym *nt*.

**pennant** ['penənt] *n* Wimpel *m*.

**penniless** ['penɪlɪs] *adj* mittellos.

**Pennines** ['penaɪnz] *npl* Pennines *pl (Gebirgszug in Nordengland)*.

**penny** ['penɪ] *n*, *pl (coins)* **pennies** *or (sum)* **pence** Penny *m*; *(US)* Centstück *nt*. **in for a** ~, **in for a pound** *(prov)* wennschon, dennschon *(col)*; *(morally)* wer A sagt, muß auch B sagen *(prov)*; **I'm not a** ~ **the wiser** ich bin genauso klug wie zuvor; **take care of the pennies and the pounds will take care of themselves** *(Prov)* spare im kleinen, dann hast du im großen; **a** ~ **for your thoughts** ich möchte deine Gedanken lesen können; **he keeps turning up like a bad** ~ *(col)* der taucht immer wieder auf *(col)*; **the** ~ **dropped** *(col)* der Groschen ist gefallen *(col)*.

**penny:** ~-**farthing** *n* Hochrad *nt*; ~-**pinching** *adj* knauserig *(col)*; ~ **whistle** *n* Blechflöte *f*.

**pen pal** *n (esp US)* Brieffreund(in *f*) *m*.

**pen-pusher** ['pen,pʊʃər] *n (col)* Schreiberling *m*.

**pension** ['penʃən] *n (money)* Rente *f*.

▶**pension off** *vt sep (col)* vorzeitig pensionieren.

**pensionable** ['penʃənəbl] *adj (post)* **to be** ~ zu einer Rente berechtigen; **of** ~ **age** im Rentenalter.

**pensioner** ['penʃənər] *n* Rentner(in *f*) *m*.

**pension:** ~ **fund** *n* Rentenfonds *m*; ~ **scheme** *n* Rentenversicherung *f*.

**pensive** ['pensɪv] *adj* nachdenklich; *(sadly serious)* schwermütig.

**pentagon** ['pentəgən] *n* Fünfeck *nt*. **the P**~ das Pentagon.

**pentathlon** [pen'tæθlən] *n* Fünfkampf *m*.

**Pentecost** ['pentɪkɒst] *n (Jewish)* Erntefest *nt*;

*(Christian)* Pfingsten *nt*.

**penthouse** ['penthaʊs] *n (apartment)* Penthouse *nt*.

**pent-up** [,pent'ʌp] *adj person (with frustration, anger)* geladen *pred*; *(nervous, excited)* innerlich angespannt; *emotions, excitement* aufgestaut.

**penultimate** [pe'nʌltɪmɪt] *adj* vorletzte(r, s).

**penury** ['penjʊrɪ] *n* Armut, Not *f*.

**peony** ['piːənɪ] *n* Pfingstrose *f*.

**people** ['piːpl] **1** *npl* **(a)** Menschen *pl*; *(not in formal context)* Leute *pl*. **French** ~ die Franzosen; **Edinburgh** ~ (die) Leute aus/in Edinburg; **all** ~ **with red hair** alle Rothaarigen; **why me of all** ~**?** warum ausgerechnet ich/mich?; **what do you** ~ **think?** was haltet ihr denn davon?; **poor/blind/disabled** ~ Arme/Blinde/Behinderte; **country** ~ Menschen *pl* vom Land; **some** ~**!** Leute gibt's! **(b)** *(inhabitants)* Bevölkerung *f*. **the** ~ **of Rome** die Bevölkerung von Rom. **(c)** *(one, they)* man; *(~ in general)* die Leute. ~ **say that** ... man sagt, daß ... **(d)** *(nation, masses)* Volk *nt*. **the common** ~ das einfache Volk; **a man of the** ~ ein Mann *m* des Volkes; ~ **power** Basisdemokratie *f*; **the P**~**'s Republic of China** die Volksrepublik China. **2** *vt* bevölkern.

**pep** [pep] *n (col)* Schwung, Pep *(col)* *m*.

▶**pep up** *vt sep (col)* Schwung bringen in *(+acc)*; *food* pikanter machen; *person* munter machen.

**pepper** ['pepər] **1** *n* Pfeffer *m*; *(green, red ~)* Paprikaschote *f*. **2** *vt* pfeffern. **to** ~ **an essay with quotations** eine Arbeit mit Zitaten spicken.

**pepper:** ~**corn** *n* Pfefferkorn *nt*; ~ **mill** *n* Pfeffermühle *f*; ~**mint** *n* Pfefferminz *nt*; *(Bot)* Pfefferminze *f*; ~ **pot** *or* **shaker** *(US)* *n* Pfefferstreuer *m*.

**peppery** ['pepərɪ] *adj* gepfeffert; *(fig)* old man etc hitzköpfig.

**pep:** ~ **pill** *n* Aufputschpille *f*; ~ **talk** *n (col)* aufmunternde Worte *pl*.

**per** [pɜːr] *prep* pro. **£20** ~ **annum** £20 pro Jahr; **40 miles** ~ **hour** ≈ 60 km pro Stunde *or* in der Stunde; **$2** ~ **dozen** das Dutzend für $2; **£5** ~ **copy** £5 pro *or* je Exemplar; **as** ~ gemäß *(+dat)*.

**per capita** [pə'kæpɪtə] *adj* ~ **income** Pro-Kopf-Einkommen *nt*.

**perceive** [pə'siːv] *vt* wahrnehmen; *(understand, recognize)* erkennen.

**per cent**, *(US)* **percent** [pə'sent] *n* Prozent *nt*. **20** ~ 20 Prozent; **a 10** ~ **discount** 10 Prozent Rabatt.

**percentage** [pə'sentɪdʒ] **1** *n (in) Prozentsatz *m*; *(commission, payment)* Anteil *m*; *(proportion)* Teil *m*. **a small** ~ **of the population** ein geringer Teil der Bevölkerung; **what** ~**?** wieviel Prozent?; **to get a** ~ **on all sales** prozentual am Umsatz beteiligt sein. **2** *attr* prozentual. **on a** ~ **basis** prozentual; ~ **sign** Prozentzeichen *nt*.

**perceptible** [pə'septəbl] *adj* wahrnehmbar; *improvement, trend etc* spürbar.

**perceptibly** [pə'septəblɪ] *adv* spürbar; *(to the eye)* sichtbar.

**perception** [pə'sepʃən] *n* **(a)** *no pl* Wahrnehmung *f*. **(b)** *(mental image, conception)* Auffassung *f (of von)*. **one's** ~ **of the situation** die eigene Einschätzung der Lage. **(c)** *(no pl: perceptiveness)* Einsicht *f*; *(perceptive remark, observation)* Beobachtung *f*. **(d)** *no pl (of difficulties, meaning etc)* Erkennen *nt*.

**perceptive** [pə'septɪv] *adj (sensitive) person* einfühlsam; *(penetrating) analysis, speech* scharfsinnig; *book* aufschlußreich. **very** ~ **of you!** *(iro)* du merkst auch alles.

**perch**[1] [pɜːtʃ] *n (fish)* Barsch *m*.

**perch**[2] **1** *n (of bird)* Stange *f*; *(in tree)* Ast *m*; *(iro: for person etc)* Hochsitz *m*. **2** *vt* **to** ~ **sth on sth** etw auf etw *(acc)* setzen *or (upright)* stellen; **to be** ~**ed on**

sth auf etw *(dat)* sitzen. 3 *vi (bird, fig: person)* hocken; *(alight)* sich niederlassen.

**percolate** ['pɜːkəleɪt] 1 *vt* filtrieren; *coffee* (in einer Kaffeemaschine) zubereiten. 2 *vi (lit, fig)* durchsickern.

**percolator** ['pɜːkəleɪtər] *n* Kaffeemaschine *f*.

**percussion** [pəˈkʌʃən] *n (Mus)* Schlagzeug *nt*. ~ **instrument** Schlaginstrument *nt*.

**percussionist** [pəˈkʌʃənɪst] *n* Schlagzeuger(in *f*) *m*.

**peregrine (falcon)** ['perɪɡrɪn(ˈfɔːlkən)] *n* Wanderfalke *m*.

**peremptory** [pəˈremptərɪ] *adj command* kategorisch; *voice* gebieterisch; *person* herrisch.

**perennial** [pəˈrenɪəl] 1 *adj plant* mehrjährig; *(perpetual)* ewig; *(recurring)* immer wiederkehrend. 2 *n (Bot)* mehrjährige Pflanze.

**perestroika** [perəˈstrɔɪkə] *n* Perestroika *f*.

**perfect** ['pɜːfɪkt] 1 *adj* **(a)** perfekt; *balance, symmetry also* vollkommen; *work of art also* vollendet; *weather, day also* ideal; *(Comm: not damaged)* einwandfrei. ~ **couple** Traumpaar *nt*; **it was the** ~ **moment** es war genau der richtige Augenblick. **(b)** *(absolute, utter)* völlig. **he's a** ~ **stranger to me** er ist mir völlig fremd; **it's a** ~ **disgrace** es ist wirklich eine Schande. **(c)** *(Gram)* ~ **tense** Perfekt *nt*. 2 *n (Gram)* Perfekt *nt*. **in the** ~ im Perfekt. 3 [pəˈfekt] *vt* vervollkommnen.

**perfection** [pəˈfekʃən] *n* Vollkommenheit, Perfektion *f*. **to do sth to** ~ etw perfekt tun.

**perfectionism** [pəˈfekʃənɪzəm] *n* Perfektionismus *m*.

**perfectionist** [pəˈfekʃənɪst] *n* 1 Perfektionist *m*. 2 *adj* perfektionistisch.

**perfectly** ['pɜːfɪklɪ] *adv* **(a)** perfekt. **I understand you** ~ ich weiß genau, was Sie meinen. **(b)** *(absolutely)* absolut, vollkommen. **we're** ~ **happy about it** wir sind damit völlig zufrieden; **a** ~ **lovely day** ein wirklich herrlicher Tag; **you know** ~ **well that** ... du weißt ganz genau, daß ...

**perforate** ['pɜːfəreɪt] 1 *vt (also Med)* perforieren; *(pierce once)* durchstechen, lochen. 2 *vi (ulcer, appendix)* durchbrechen.

**perforation** [ˌpɜːfəˈreɪʃən] *n (act)* Perforieren *nt*; *(row of holes, Med)* Perforation *f*.

**perform** [pəˈfɔːm] 1 *vt play, concerto* aufführen; *solo* vortragen; *part* spielen; *trick* vorführen; *miracle* vollbringen; *task* verrichten; *duty, function* erfüllen; *operation* durchführen; *ceremony* vollziehen. 2 *vi* **(a)** *(orchestra etc)* auftreten. **to** ~ **on the violin** Geige spielen. **(b) to** ~ **well/badly** *(car, football team etc)* eine gute/schlechte Leistung zeigen; *(examination candidate etc)* gut/schlecht abschneiden; **the 2 litre version** ~s **better** die Zweiliterversion leistet mehr; **how did he** ~? *(actor, musician)* wie war er?; **how did the car** ~? wie ist der Wagen gelaufen?

**performance** [pəˈfɔːməns] *n* **(a)** *(of play, opera etc)* Aufführung *f*; *(cinema)* Vorstellung *f*; *(by actor)* Leistung *f*; *(of a part)* Darstellung *f*. **he gave an excellent** ~ er hat ausgezeichnet gespielt/gesungen *etc*; **we are going to hear a** ~ **of Beethoven's 5th** wir werden Beethovens Fünfte hören. **(b)** *(carrying out)* *see vt* Aufführung *f*; Vortrag *m*; *(of part)* Darstellung *f*; Vorführung *f*; Vollbringung *f*; Verrichtung, Erfüllung *f*; Durchführung *f*; Vollzug *m*. **in the** ~ **of his duties** in Ausübung seiner Pflicht. **(c)** *(effectiveness)* *(of machine, sportsman etc)* Leistung *f*; *(of examination candidate etc)* Abschneiden *nt*. **he put up a good** ~ er hat sich gut geschlagen *(col)*. **(d)** *(col: fuss)* **what a** ~! was für ein Umstand!

**performer** [pəˈfɔːmər] *n (Theat, Mus)* Künstler(-

in *f*) *m*.

**performing** [pəˈfɔːmɪŋ] *adj animal* dressiert. **the** ~ **arts** die darstellenden Künste; ~ **rights** Aufführungsrechte *pl*.

**perfume** ['pɜːfjuːm] 1 *n (substance)* Parfüm *nt*; *(smell)* Duft *m*. 2 [pəˈfjuːm] *vt* parfümieren.

**perfumery** [pəˈfjuːmərɪ] *n (perfume factory)* Parfümerie *f*; *(perfumes)* Parfüm *nt*.

**perfunctory** [pəˈfʌŋktərɪ] *adj* flüchtig.

**perhaps** [pəˈhæps, præps] *adv* vielleicht. ~ **so** das mag sein.

**peril** ['perɪl] *n* Gefahr *f*.

**perilous** ['perɪləs] *adj* gefährlich.

**perilously** ['perɪləslɪ] *adv* gefährlich. **she came** ~ **close to falling** sie wäre um ein Haar heruntergefallen.

**perimeter** [pəˈrɪmɪtər] *n (Math)* Umfang *m*; *(of grounds)* Grenze *f*. ~ **fence** Umzäunung *f*.

**period** ['pɪərɪəd] *n* **(a)** *(length of time)* Zeit *f*; *(age)* Zeitalter *nt*, Epoche *f*; *(Geol, Met)* Periode *f*. **for a** ~ **of eight weeks** für einen Zeitraum von acht Wochen; **at that** ~ **(of my life)** zu diesem Zeitpunkt (in meinem Leben); **a writer of the** ~ ein zeitgenössischer Schriftsteller. **(b)** *(Sch)* Stunde *f*. **(c)** *(esp US: full stop)* Punkt *m*. **you're not going,** ~ du gehst nicht, und damit hat sich's; **he just doesn't understand,** ~ er versteht einfach überhaupt nichts. **(d)** *(menstruation)* Periode *f*, Tage *pl (col)*.

**period:** ~ **costume** *n* zeitgenössische Kostüme *pl*; ~ **furniture** *n* antike Möbel *pl*; ~ **house** *n* altes Haus *(vor etwa 1800)*.

**periodic** [ˌpɪərɪˈɒdɪk] *adj* periodisch. ~ **table** *(Chem)* Periodensystem *nt*.

**periodical** [ˌpɪərɪˈɒdɪkəl] 1 *adj* = **periodic**. 2 *n* Zeitschrift *f*.

**periodically** [ˌpɪərɪˈɒdɪkəlɪ] *adv* von Zeit zu Zeit.

**period:** ~ **pains** *npl* Menstruationsschmerzen *pl*; ~ **piece** *n* antikes Stück; *(painting, music etc)* Zeitdokument *nt*.

**peripatetic** [ˌperɪpəˈtetɪk] *adj* umherreisend; *existence* rastlos; *teacher* an mehreren Schulen unterrichtend *attr*.

**peripheral** [pəˈrɪfərəl] 1 *adj* Rand-; *(Comp)* Peripherie-; *(fig also)* nebensächlich. 2 *n (Comp)* Peripheriegerät *nt*.

**periphery** [pəˈrɪfərɪ] *n* Peripherie *f*.

**periscope** ['perɪskəʊp] *n* Periskop *nt*.

**perish** ['perɪʃ] *vi* **(a)** *(die)* umkommen, sterben; *(cities, civilization)* untergehen. **(b)** *(rubber, leather etc)* verschleißen; *(food)* verderben. **(c)** *(col)* ~ **the thought!** Gott bewahre!

**perishable** ['perɪʃəbl] 1 *adj food* verderblich. 2 *npl* ~s leicht verderbliche Ware(n).

**perishing** ['perɪʃɪŋ] *adj (col: very cold)* eisig kalt. **I'm** ~ ich geh' fast ein vor Kälte *(col)*.

**peritonitis** [ˌperɪtəʊˈnaɪtɪs] *n* Bauchfellentzündung *f*.

**perjure** ['pɜːdʒər] *vr* **to** ~ **oneself** einen Meineid leisten.

**perjury** ['pɜːdʒərɪ] *n* Meineid *m*. **to commit** ~ einen Meineid leisten.

**perk** [pɜːk] *n (esp Brit: benefit)* Vergünstigung *f*.
▶**perk up** 1 *vt sep* **to** ~ **sb** ~ *(make lively)* jdn munter machen; *(make cheerful)* jdn aufheitern. 2 *vi (liven up: person, party)* munter werden; *(cheer up)* aufleben.

**perky** ['pɜːkɪ] *adj (+er) (cheerful, bright)* munter; *(cheeky, pert)* keß.

**perm** [pɜːm] 1 *n* Dauerwelle *f*. 2 *vt* **she had her hair** ~ed sie hat sich *(dat)* eine Dauerwelle machen lassen.

**permanence** ['pɜːmənəns], **permanency** ['pɜːmənənsı] *n* Dauerhaftigkeit *f.*

**permanent** ['pɜːmənənt] **1** *adj* ständig, permanent; *arrangement, position* fest; *job, relationship* dauerhaft; *agreement* unbefristet. **a ~ employee** ein Festangestellter *m*; **I'm not ~ here** ich bin hier nicht fest angestellt; **~ address** ständiger Wohnsitz; **~ memory** *(Comp)* Festspeicher *m.* **2** *n (US)* = **perm 1.**

**permanently** ['pɜːmənəntlı] *adv* permanent, ständig; *fixed* fest. **are you living ~ in Frankfurt?** ist Frankfurt Ihr ständiger Wohnsitz?

**permeability** [,pɜːmɪə'bɪlıtı] *n* Durchlässigkeit *f.*

**permeable** ['pɜːmɪəbl] *adj* durchlässig.

**permeate** ['pɜːmıeıt] **1** *vt (lit, fig)* durchdringen. **2** *vi* dringen *(into* in +*acc, through* durch*)*.

**permissible** [pə'mısıbl] *adj* erlaubt *(for sb* jdm*).*

**permission** [pə'mıʃən] *n* Erlaubnis *f.* **with your ~** mit Ihrer Erlaubnis; **to give sb ~ (to do sth)** jdm erlauben(, etw zu tun); **to ask sb's ~** jdn um Erlaubnis bitten.

**permissive** [pə'mısıv] *adj* nachgiebig, permissiv *(geh)*; *(sexually)* freizügig. **the ~ society** die permissive Gesellschaft.

**permit** [pə'mıt] **1** *vt sth* erlauben, gestatten. **to ~ sb to do sth** jdm erlauben, etw zu tun; **is it/am I ~ted to smoke?** darf man/ich rauchen? **2** *vi* **(a) if you (will) ~** wenn Sie gestatten; **weather ~ting** wenn es das Wetter zuläßt. **(b)** *(form)* **to ~ of sth** etw zulassen. **3** ['pɜːmıt] *n* Genehmigung *f.* **~ holder** Inhaber(in *f*) *m* eines Berechtigungsscheins.

**permutation** [,pɜːmjʊ'teıʃən] *n* Permutation *f.*

**pernicious** [pɜː'nıʃəs] *adj* schädlich.

**pernickety** [pə'nıkıtı] *adj (col)* pingelig *(col).*

**peroxide** [pə'rɒksaıd] *n* Peroxyd *nt.* **a ~ blonde** *(pej)* eine Wasserstoffblonde.

**perpendicular** [,pɜːpən'dıkjələ ͬ] **1** *adj* senkrecht *(to* zu*).* **2** *n* Senkrechte *f.*

**perpetrate** ['pɜːpıtreıt] *vt* begehen; *crime also* verüben.

**perpetrator** ['pɜːpıtreıtə ͬ] *n* Täter *m.* **the ~ of this crime** derjenige, der dieses Verbrechen begangen hat.

**perpetual** [pə'petjʊəl] *adj* ständig, immerwährend; *joy* stet; *ice, snow* ewig. **~ motion** Perpetuum mobile *nt.*

**perpetually** [pə'petjʊəlı] *adv* ständig.

**perpetuate** [pə'petjʊeıt] *vt* aufrechterhalten; *memory* bewahren.

**perpetuity** [,pɜːpı'tjuːıtı] *n* **in ~** auf ewig.

**perplex** [pə'pleks] *vt* verblüffen.

**perplexed** [pə'plekst] *adj* verblüfft, perplex.

**perplexing** [pə'pleksıŋ] *adj* verblüffend.

**perplexity** [pə'pleksıtı] *n* Verblüffung *f.*

**persecute** ['pɜːsıkjuːt] *vt* verfolgen.

**persecution** [,pɜːsı'kjuːʃən] *n* Verfolgung *f (of* von*).* **~ complex** Verfolgungswahn *m.*

**perseverance** [,pɜːsı'vıərəns] *n* Ausdauer *(with* mit*),* Beharrlichkeit *(with* bei*) f.*

**persevere** [,pɜːsı'vıə ͬ] *vi* durchhalten *(with* bei*),* nicht aufgeben *(with* bei*).* **to ~ in one's studies** mit seinem Studium weitermachen.

**persevering** [,pɜːsı'vıərıŋ] *adj* beharrlich.

**Persia** ['pɜːʃə] *n* Persien *nt.*

**Persian** ['pɜːʃən] **1** *adj* persisch. **~ carpet** Perser(teppich) *m*; **~ cat** Perserkatze *f*; **the P~ Gulf** der Persische Golf. **2** *n* **(a)** Perser(in *f*) *m.* **(b)** *(language)* Persisch *nt.*

**persist** [pə'sıst] *vi (persevere)* nicht lockerlassen *(with* mit*); (in belief, demand etc)* beharren *(in* auf +*dat); (fog, pain)* anhalten. **if you ~ in misbehaving** wenn du dich weiterhin so schlecht benimmst.

**persistence** [pə'sıstəns] *n* Hartnäckigkeit *f*; *(perseverance)* Ausdauer *f*; *(of pain)* Anhalten *nt.*

**persistent** [pə'sıstənt] *adj questions* beharrlich; *person* hartnäckig; *efforts* ausdauernd; *offender, drinking* gewohnheitsmäßig; *nagging, lateness, threats* ständig; *rain, illness* anhaltend. **~ offender** Gewohnheitsverbrecher *m.*

**persistently** [pə'sıstəntlı] *adv see adj.*

**persnickety** [pə'snıkıtı] *adj (US col) see* **pernickety.**

**person** ['pɜːsn] *n* **(a)** *pl* **people** *or (form)* **-s** *(human being)* Mensch *m*; *(in official contexts)* Person *f.* **I know no such ~** so jemanden kenne ich nicht; **a certain ~** ein gewisser Jemand; **~ to ~ call** *(esp US)* Gespräch *nt* mit Voranmeldung; **per ~** pro Person. **(b)** *pl* **-s** *(Gram)* Person *f.* **first ~ singular/plural** erste Person Singular/Plural. **(c)** *pl* **-s** *(body, physical presence)* Körper *m*; *(appearance)* Äußere(s) *nt.* **in ~** persönlich; **in the ~ of** in Gestalt *(+gen)*; **on** *or* **about one's ~** bei sich.

**personable** ['pɜːsnəbl] *adj (in appearance)* von angenehmer Erscheinung; *(in personality)* sympathisch.

**personage** ['pɜːsənıdʒ] *n* Persönlichkeit *f.*

**personal** ['pɜːsnl] *adj* persönlich. **it's nothing ~ but** ... nicht, daß ich etwas gegen Sie persönlich hätte, aber ...; **don't be ~** nun werden Sie mal nicht persönlich; **"~"** *(on letter)* „privat"; **~ allowance** persönlicher Freibetrag; **~ assistant** Privatsekretär(in *f*) *m*; **~ column** Familienanzeigen *pl*; **~ property** Privateigentum *nt*; **~ call** Gespräch *nt* mit Voranmeldung; *(private call)* Privatgespräch *nt*; **~ computer** Personalcomputer *m*; **~ effects** persönliches Eigentum; **~ hygiene** Körperpflege *f*; **~ identification number** Geheimnummer *f*; **~ matter** private Angelegenheit; **~ organizer** Terminplaner *m*; **~ pronoun** Personalpronomen *nt*; **~ stereo** Walkman ® *m.*

**personality** [,pɜːsə'nælıtı] *n (character, person)* Persönlichkeit *f.* **~ cult** Personenkult *m.*

**personalize** ['pɜːsənəlaız] *vt* persönlicher gestalten; *(put initials etc on)* eine persönliche Note geben *(+dat).*

**personally** ['pɜːsənəlı] *adv* persönlich. **~, I think that** ... ich persönlich bin der Meinung, daß ...

**personification** [pɜː,sɒnıfı'keıʃən] *n* Verkörperung *f.*

**personify** [pɜː'sɒnıfaı] *vt* verkörpern. **he is greed personified** er ist die Gier in Person.

**personnel** [,pɜːsə'nel] **1** *n sing or pl* **(a)** Personal *nt*; *(on plane, ship)* Besatzung *f*; *(Mil)* Leute *pl.* **(b)** *(~ department)* die Personalabteilung. **2** *attr* Personal-. **~ management** Personalführung *f*; **~ manager/officer** Personalchef(in *f*) *m*/-sachbearbeiter(in *f*) *m.*

**perspective** [pə'spektıv] *n (lit, fig)* Perspektive *f.* **try to get things in ~** versuchen Sie, das nüchtern und sachlich zu sehen.

**Perspex** ® ['pɜːspeks] *n (Brit)* ≈ Plexiglas ® *nt.*

**perspicacious** [,pɜːspı'keıʃəs] *adj person, remark etc* scharfsinnig; *decision* weitsichtig.

**perspicacity** [,pɜːspı'kæsıtı] *n* Scharfsinnn *m.*

**perspiration** [,pɜːspə'reıʃən] *n (perspiring)* Schwitzen *nt*, Transpiration *f (geh); (sweat)* Schweiß *m.*

**perspire** [pə'spaıə ͬ] *vi* schwitzen.

**persuadable** [pə'sweıdəbl] *adj* **to be ~** sich überreden lassen.

**persuade** [pə'sweıd] *vt* überreden; *(convince)* überzeugen. **to ~ sb to do sth** jdn überreden, etw zu tun; **to ~ sb into doing sth** jdn dazu überreden, etw zu tun; **to ~ sb of sth** jdn von etw überzeugen; **to ~ sb that** ... jdn davon überzeugen, daß ...; **he doesn't take much persuading** ihn braucht man nicht lange zu überreden.

**persuasion** [pə'sweɪʒən] n (a) *(persuading)* Überredung f. **she tried every possible means of** ~ sie setzte ihre ganze Überredungskunst ein. (b) *(belief)* Überzeugung f; *(sect, denomination)* Glaube(nsrichtung f) m.

**persuasive** [pə'sweɪsɪv] adj *salesman, arguments etc* überzeugend.

**persuasively** [pə'sweɪsɪvlɪ] adv überzeugend.

**persuasiveness** [pə'sweɪsɪvnɪs] n *(of person)* Überredungskunst f; *(of argument)* Überzeugungskraft f.

**pert** [pɜːt] adj *(+er)* keß; *(impudent)* keck.

**pertain** [pɜː'teɪn] vi **to** ~ **to sth** etw betreffen; *(belong to)* zu etw gehören; **all documents** ~**ing to the case** alle den Fall betreffenden Dokumente.

**pertinent** ['pɜːtɪnənt] adj relevant *(to für)*; *information* sachdienlich.

**perturb** [pə'tɜːb] vt beunruhigen.

**perturbing** [pə'tɜːbɪŋ] adj beunruhigend.

**Peru** [pə'ruː] n Peru nt.

**perusal** [pə'ruːzəl] n Lektüre f.

**peruse** [pə'ruːz] vt (durch)lesen.

**Peruvian** [pə'ruːvɪən] 1 adj peruanisch. 2 n Peruaner(in f) m.

**pervade** [pɜː'veɪd] vt erfüllen.

**pervasive** [pɜː'veɪsɪv] adj *smell etc* durchdringend; *influence, ideas* um sich greifend.

**perverse** [pə'vɜːs] adj *(contrary) idea* abwegig; *(person)* verstockt; *(perverted)* pervers.

**perversely** [pə'vɜːslɪ] adv *see adj.*

**perverseness** [pə'vɜːsnɪs] n = **perversity.**

**perversion** [pə'vɜːʃən] n *(esp sexual, Psych)* Perversion f; *(no pl: act of perverting)* Pervertierung f; *(distortion: of truth etc)* Verzerrung f.

**perversity** [pə'vɜːsɪtɪ] n *see adj* Abwegigkeit f; Verstocktheit f; Perversität f.

**pervert** [pə'vɜːt] 1 vt *(deprave) person, mind* verderben, pervertieren; *(distort) truth etc* verzerren. **to** ~ **the course of justice** *(Jur)* die Rechtsfindung behindern; *(by official)* das Recht beugen. 2 ['pɜːvɜːt] n Perverse(r) mf.

**perverted** [pə'vɜːtɪd] adj *(depraved)* verdorben; *mind* pervertiert.

**pesky** ['peskɪ] adj *(esp US col)* nervtötend *(col).*

**pessimism** ['pesɪmɪzəm] n Pessimismus m.

**pessimist** ['pesɪmɪst] n Pessimist(in f) m.

**pessimistic** adj, ~**ally** adv [,pesɪ'mɪstɪk, -əlɪ] pessimistisch.

**pest** [pest] n (a) *(Zool)* Schädling m. ~ **control** Schädlingsbekämpfung f. (b) *(fig) (person)* Nervensäge f; *(thing)* Plage f.

**pester** ['pestər] vt belästigen; *(keep on at: with requests etc)* plagen.

**pesticide** ['pestɪsaɪd] n Schädlingsbekämpfungsmittel, Pestizid *(spec)* nt.

**pestilent** ['pestɪlənt], **pestilential** [,pestɪ'lenʃəl] adj *(fig: pernicious)* schädlich; *(col: loathsome)* ekelhaft.

**pestle** ['pestl] n Stößel m.

**pet** [pet] 1 adj attr *(favourite) pupil, idea etc* Lieblings-. **he has a** ~ **monkey** er hält einen Affen als Haustier; **a** ~ **name** ein Kosename m; **this is my** ~ **aversion** or **hate** das kann ich auf den Tod nicht ausstehen. 2 n (a) *(animal)* Haustier nt. ~ **food** Tierfutter nt; ~ **shop** Zoohandlung f. (b) *(favourite)* Liebling m. **teacher's** ~ Lehrers Liebling m; **yes, (my)** ~ ja, (mein) Schatz. 3 vt *animal* streicheln; *child also* liebkosen. 4 vi *(sexually)* Petting machen.

**petal** ['petl] n Blütenblatt nt.

**Peter** ['piːtər] n Peter m; *(apostle)* Petrus m. **to rob** ~ **to pay Paul** ein Loch mit dem anderen zustopfen.

▶**peter out** [,piːtə'raʊt] vi langsam zu Ende gehen; *(mineral vein)* versiegen; *(river)* versickern; *(song, noise)* verhallen; *(interest)* sich legen.

**petit bourgeois** ['petɪ'bʊəʒwɑː] 1 n Kleinbürger(in f) m. 2 adj kleinbürgerlich.

**petite** [pə'tiːt] adj *woman, girl* zierlich.

**petition** [pə'tɪʃən] 1 n (a) *(list of signatures)* Unterschriftenliste f. **to get up a** ~ **against sth** Unterschriften gegen etw sammeln. (b) *(request)* Gesuch nt, Petition f. ~ **for divorce** Scheidungsantrag m. 2 vt *person, authorities (request, entreat)* ersuchen *(for um)*; *(hand ~ to)* eine Unterschriftenliste vorlegen *(+dat).* 3 vi **to** ~ **for divorce** die Scheidung einreichen.

**petrel** ['petrəl] n Sturmvogel m.

**petrify** ['petrɪfaɪ] vt (a) *(lit)* versteinern. (b) **to be petrified with fear** starr vor Angst sein.

**petrochemical** [,petrəʊ'kemɪkəl] adj petrochemisch.

**petrol** ['petrəl] n *(Brit)* Benzin nt.

**petrol** *(Brit)*: ~ **can** n Benzinkanister m; ~ **cap** n Tankverschluß m; ~ **engine** n Benzinmotor m.

**petroleum** [pɪ'trəʊlɪəm] n Petroleum nt. ~ **jelly** Vaseline f.

**petrol** *(Brit)*: ~ **gauge** n Benzinuhr f; ~ **pump** n *(on engine)* Benzinpumpe f; *(at garage)* Zapfsäule f; ~ **station** n Tankstelle f; ~ **tank** n Benzintank m; ~ **tanker** n (Benzin)tankwagen m.

**petticoat** ['petɪkəʊt] n Unterrock m; *(stiffened)* Petticoat m.

**pettifogging** ['petɪfɒgɪŋ] adj kleinlich; *details* belanglos.

**pettiness** ['petɪnɪs] n *(small-mindedness)* Kleinlichkeit f; *(triviality)* Belanglosigkeit f.

**petting** ['petɪŋ] n Petting nt.

**petty** ['petɪ] adj *(+er)* (a) *(trivial)* unbedeutend, belanglos; *excuse* billig; *crime* geringfügig, Bagatell-. (b) *(small-minded)* kleinlich; *(spiteful) remark* spitz. (c) *(minor) chieftain etc* untergeordnet; *(pej) official also* unbedeutend.

**petty**: ~ **cash** n ≃ Portokasse f; ~ **larceny** n leichter Diebstahl; ~ **thief** n (kleiner) Dieb(in f) m; ~ **officer** n *(Navy)* Unteroffizier m.

**petulance** ['petjʊləns] n verdrießliche Art; *(of child)* bockige Art *(col).*

**petulant** ['petjʊlənt] adj verdrießlich; *child* bockig *(col).*

**petunia** [pɪ'tjuːnɪə] n Petunie f.

**pew** [pjuː] n *(Eccl)* (Kirchen)bank f. **have** or **take a** ~! *(hum)* laß dich nieder! *(hum).*

**pewter** ['pjuːtər] n *(alloy)* Zinn nt.

**PG** *(Brit Film)* = **Parental Guidance** bedingt jugendfrei.

**PGA** = **Professional Golfers' Association** *Golfspielerverband m.*

**pH** = **potential of hydrogen** pH. ~ **value** pH-Wert m.

**phallic** ['fælɪk] adj phallisch; *symbol* Phallus-.

**phantom** ['fæntəm] 1 n Phantom nt; *(ghost: esp of particular person)* Geist m. 2 adj attr Geister-; *(mysterious)* Phantom-.

**pharmaceutical** [,fɑːmə'sjuːtɪkəl] 1 adj pharmazeutisch; *industry* Pharma-. 2 n usu pl Arzneimittel nt. ~ **company/industry** etc Pharmaunternehmen nt/-industrie f etc.

**pharmacist** ['fɑːməsɪst] n Apotheker(in f) m; *(in research)* Pharmazeut(in f) m.

**pharmacology** [,fɑːmə'kɒlədʒɪ] n Pharmakologie f.

**pharmacy** ['fɑːməsɪ] n (a) *(science)* Pharmazie f. (b) *(shop)* Apotheke f.

**phase** [feɪz] 1 n Phase f; *(of project, history also)* Abschnitt m; *(of illness)* Stadium nt. **out of/in** ~ *(Tech,*

*Elec)* phasenverschoben/phasengleich; *(fig)* unkoordiniert/koordiniert; **he's just going through a** ~ das ist nur so eine Phase bei ihm. **2** *vt (introduce gradually)* schrittweise durchführen; *(coordinate, fit to one another) starting times etc* aufeinander abstimmen; *machines etc* gleichschalten. **a** ~**d withdrawal of troops** ein schrittweiser Truppenabzug.
▶**phase in** *vt sep* allmählich einführen.
▶**phase out** *vt sep* auslaufen lassen.
**PhD** *n* ≃ Dr. phil. ~ **thesis** Doktorarbeit *f.*
**pheasant** ['feznt] *n* Fasan *m.*
**phenomenal** [fɪ'nɒmɪnl] *adj* phänomenal, sagenhaft *(col)*; *boredom, heat* unglaublich.
**phenomenally** [fɪ'nɒmɪnəlɪ] *adv* außerordentlich; *bad, boring etc* unglaublich.
**phenomenon** [fɪ'nɒmɪnən] *n, pl* **phenomena** Phänomen *nt.* **a common** ~ eine häufige Erscheinung.
**phew** [fju:] *interj* Mensch, puh.
**phial** ['faɪəl] *n* Fläschchen *nt.*
**philanderer** [fɪ'lændərəʳ] *n* Schwerenöter *m.*
**philanthropic** [ˌfɪlən'θrɒpɪk] *adj* menschenfreundlich; *person also, organization* philanthropisch *(geh).*
**philanthropist** [fɪ'lænθrəpɪst] *n* Menschenfreund, Philanthrop *(geh) m.*
**philanthropy** [fɪ'lænθrəpɪ] *n* Menschenfreundlichkeit *f.*
**philatelist** [fɪ'lætəlɪst] *n* Philatelist(in *f) m.*
**philately** [fɪ'lætəlɪ] *n* Philatelie, Briefmarkenkunde *f.*
**philharmonic** [ˌfɪlɑː'mɒnɪk] *adj* philharmonisch. **the Berlin P**~ **(Orchestra)** die Berliner Philharmoniker *pl.*
**Philippine** ['fɪlɪpiːn] *adj* philippinisch.
**Philippines** ['fɪlɪpiːnz] *npl* Philippinen *pl.*
**Phillips screw** ® *n* ['fɪlɪps'skruː] Kreuzschlitzschraube *f.*
**philistine** ['fɪlɪstaɪn] *n* (Kultur)banause *m.*
**philology** [fɪ'lɒlədʒɪ] *n* Philologie *f.*
**philosopher** [fɪ'lɒsəfəʳ] *n* Philosoph(in *f) m.*
**philosophic(al)** [ˌfɪlə'sɒfɪk(əl)] *adj* philosophisch; *(fig)* gelassen. **she's very** ~ **about it** sie nimmt es ganz gelassen.
**philosophically** [ˌfɪlə'sɒfɪkəlɪ] *adv see adj.*
**philosophize** [fɪ'lɒsəfaɪz] *vi* philosophieren *(about, on* über +*acc).*
**philosophy** [fɪ'lɒsəfɪ] *n* Philosophie *f.* ~ **of life** Lebensphilosophie *f.*
**phlegm** [flem] *n (mucus)* Schleim *m; (fig) (coolness)* Gemütsruhe *f; (stolidness)* Trägheit *f.*
**phlegmatic** [fleg'mætɪk] *adj (cool)* seelenruhig; *(stolid)* träge, phlegmatisch.
**phobia** ['fəubɪə] *n* Phobie *f.* **she has a** ~ **about it** sie hat krankhafte Angst davor.
**phoenix, *(US)* phenix** ['fiːnɪks] *n (Myth)* Phönix *m.*
**phone** [fəun] **1** *n* Telefon *nt.* **to pick up/put down the** ~ (den Hörer) abnehmen/auflegen; **he's on the** ~ er telefoniert gerade. **2** *vt person* anrufen. **3** *vi* anrufen, telefonieren.
▶**phone in 1** *vi* anrufen. **2** *vt sep* telefonisch übermitteln.
**phone:** ~ **book** *n* Telefonbuch *nt;* ~ **box,** ~ **booth** *n (Brit)* Telefonzelle *f;* ~ **call** *n* Anruf *m;* **in our** ~ **call** in unserem Telefongespräch; ~**card** *n* Telefonkarte *f;* ~**-in** ['fəunɪn] *n Rundfunk-/Fernsehprogramm nt, an dem man sich per Telefon beteiligen kann,* Phone-in *nt;* ~ **number** *n* Telefonnummer *f;* ~**tapping** *n* Anzapfen *nt* von Telefonleitungen.
**phonetic** [fəu'netɪk] *adj* phonetisch.
**phonetics** [fəu'netɪks] *n sing (subject)* Phonetik *f.*
**phon(e)y** ['fəunɪ] *(col)* **1** *adj* unecht; *excuse, deal*

faul *(col); name* falsch; *passport, money* gefälscht; *story* erfunden. **2** *n (bogus policeman etc)* Schwindler(in *f) m; (doctor)* Scharlatan *m; (pretentious person)* Angeber(in *f) m.*
**phonograph** ['fəunəgrɑːf] *n (old)* Phonograph *m; (US)* Plattenspieler *m.*
**phonology** [fəu'nɒlədʒɪ] *n* Phonologie *f.*
**phony** *adj, n* = **phon(e)y.**
**phosphate** ['fɒsfeɪt] *n (Chem)* Phosphat *nt; (Agr: fertilizer)* Phosphatdünger *m.*
**phosphorescence** [ˌfɒsfə'resns] *n* Phosphoreszenz *f.*
**phosphorescent** [ˌfɒsfə'resnt] *adj* phosphoreszierend.
**phosphorous** ['fɒsfərəs] *adj* phosphorsauer.
**phosphorus** ['fɒsfərəs] *n* Phosphor *m.*
**photo** ['fəutəu] *n* Foto *nt,* Aufnahme *f.*
**photo:** ~ **album** *n* Fotoalbum *nt;* ~ **call** *n* Fototermin *m;* ~**copier** *n* (Foto)kopiergerät *nt;* ~**copy 1** *n* Fotokopie *f;* **2** *vt* fotokopieren; ~ **corner** *n* Fotoecke *f;* ~**electric cell** *n* Photozelle *f;* ~ **finish** *n* Fotofinish *nt;* **P**~**fit (picture)** *n* Phantombild *nt.*
**photogenic** [ˌfəutəu'dʒenɪk] *adj* fotogen.
**photograph** ['fəutəgrɑːf] **1** *n* Fotografie, Aufnahme *f.* **to take a** ~ **(of sb/sth)** (jdn/etw) fotografieren, ein Bild (von jdm/etw) machen; ~ **album** Fotoalbum *nt.* **2** *vt* fotografieren.
**photographer** [fə'tɒgrəfəʳ] *n* Fotograf(in *f) m.*
**photographic** [ˌfəutə'græfɪk] *adj* fotografisch; *equipment, club* Foto-.
**photography** [fə'tɒgrəfɪ] *n* Fotografie *f; (in film, book etc)* Fotografien, Bilder *pl.*
**photo:** ~ **journalist** *n* Fotojournalist(in *f) m;* ~ **opportunity** *n* Fototermin *m; (fortuitous)* Fotogelegenheit *f;* ~**sensitive** *adj* lichtempfindlich; ~**stat** ® *n, vt* = ~**copy;** ~**synthesis** *n* Photosynthese *f.*
**phrase** [freɪz] **1** *n (Gram)* Satzteil *m; (Mus)* Phrase *f; (expression)* Ausdruck *m; (set expression)* Redewendung *f.* **2** *vt* formulieren.
**phrasebook** ['freɪzbuk] *n* Sprachführer *m.*
**phraseology** [ˌfreɪzɪ'ɒlədʒɪ] *n* Ausdrucksweise *f.*
**physical** ['fɪzɪkəl] *adj* **(a)** *(of the body)* körperlich; *(not psychological also)* physisch; *check-up* ärztlich. **(b)** *(material)* physisch; *world* faßbar. **(c)** *(of physics) laws* physikalisch. **it's a** ~ **impossibility** es ist ein Ding der Unmöglichkeit *(col).*
**physical:** ~ **education** *n (abbr* **PE***)* Sport *m,* Leibesübungen *pl (form);* ~ **jerks** *npl (col)* Gymnastik *f.*
**physically** ['fɪzɪkəlɪ] *adv* körperlich, physisch; *(Sci)* physikalisch. **it's** ~ **impossible** es ist ein Ding der Unmöglichkeit; **they removed him** ~ sie haben ihn mit Gewalt entfernt.
**physical training** *n (abbr* **PT***) see* **physical education.**
**physician** [fɪ'zɪʃən] *n* Arzt *m,* Ärztin *f.*
**physicist** ['fɪzɪsɪst] *n* Physiker(in *f) m.*
**physics** ['fɪzɪks] *n sing (subject)* Physik *f.*
**physiological** [ˌfɪzɪə'lɒdʒɪkəl] *adj* physiologisch.
**physiology** [ˌfɪzɪ'ɒlədʒɪ] *n* Physiologie *f.*
**physiotherapist** [ˌfɪzɪə'θerəpɪst] *n* Krankengymnast(in *f) m.*
**physiotherapy** [ˌfɪzɪə'θerəpɪ] *n* Krankengymnastik *f.*
**physique** [fɪ'ziːk] *n* Körperbau *m,* Statur *f.*
**pianist** ['pɪənɪst] *n* Klavierspieler(in *f) m; (concert* ~*)* Pianist(in *f) m.*
**piano** ['pjænəu] *n (upright)* Klavier *nt; (grand)* Flügel *m.*
**piano:** ~ **accordion** *n* Pianoakkordeon *nt;* ~ **lesson** *n* Klavierstunde *f;* ~ **stool** *n* Klavierhocker *m;* ~ **tuner** *n* Klavierstimmer(in *f) m.*
**pic** [pɪk] *n (col)* Bild *nt; (photo)* Foto *nt.*

**piccolo** ['pɪkələʊ] *n* Pikkoloflöte *f.*
**pick** [pɪk] **1** *n* **(a)** *(~axe)* Spitzhacke *f*, Pickel *m*; *(Mountaineering)* Eispickel *m*; *(tooth~)* Zahnstocher *m.* **(b)** *(choice)* **to have first** ~ die erste Wahl haben; **take your** ~! such dir etwas/einen *etc* aus! **(c)** *(best)* Beste(s) *nt.*
  **2** *vt* **(a)** *(choose)* (aus)wählen. **to** ~ **a team** eine Mannschaft aufstellen; **to** ~ **sides** wählen; **to** ~ **a winner** *(lit)* den Sieger erraten; *(fig)* das Große Los ziehen; **to** ~ **one's time** den richtigen Zeitpunkt wählen; **you do** ~ **'em** *(iro)* du gerätst auch immer an den Falschen. **(b)** *(pull at)* **jumper, blanket etc** zupfen an *(+dat)*; **spot, scab** kratzen an *(+dat)*; **hole** bohren. **to** ~ **one's nose** in der Nase bohren; **to** ~ **one's teeth** in den Zähnen herumstochern; **to** ~ **a lock** ein Schloß knacken; **to** ~ **holes in sth** *(fig)* etw bemäkeln; *in argument* etw in einigen Punkten widerlegen; **to** ~ **a fight** *or* **quarrel (with sb)** (mit jdm) einen Streit vom Zaun brechen; **to** ~ **sb's pocket** jdm die Geldbörse/Brieftasche stehlen; **to** ~ **sb's brains** sich bei jdm informieren. **(c)** *(pluck)* **flowers, fruit** pflücken.
  **3** *vi* **to** ~ **and choose** wählerisch sein; **to** ~ **at one's food** im Essen herumstochern.
  ▶**pick off** *vt sep* **(a)** *(remove)* **fluff etc** wegzupfen; **nail polish** abschälen. **(b)** *(shoot)* abschießen.
  ▶**pick on** *vi +prep obj* **(choose)** aussuchen; *(victimize)* herumhacken auf *(+dat)*. **why** ~ ~ **me?** *(col)* warum gerade ich?; ~ ~ **somebody your own size!** *(col)* leg dich doch mit einem Gleichstarken an! *(col)*.
  ▶**pick out** *vt sep* **(a)** *(choose)* aussuchen. **(b)** *(distinguish)* **person, face** entdecken. **(c)** *(Mus)* **to** ~ ~ **a tune** eine Melodie improvisieren.
  ▶**pick up** *vt sep* **(a)** *(take up)* aufheben; *reference, trail* aufnehmen; *(lift momentarily)* hochheben. **to** ~ ~ **a child in one's arms** ein Kind auf den Arm nehmen; **to** ~ **oneself** ~ aufstehen; **as soon as he** ~**s** ~ **a book** sobald er ein Buch in die Hand nimmt; **to** ~ ~ **the phone** den Hörer abnehmen; **to** ~ ~ **the bill** *(fig: pay)* die Rechnung bezahlen; **to** ~ ~ **the pieces** *(lit, fig)* die Scherben aufsammeln.
  **(b)** *(get)* holen; *(buy)* bekommen; *(acquire)* **habit** sich *(dat)* angewöhnen; **news, gossip** aufschnappen; **illness** sich *(dat)* holen *or* zuziehen *(col)* **girl** aufgabeln *(col)*, sich *(dat)* anlachen *(col)*. **to** ~ ~ **speed** schneller werden.
  **(c)** *(learn)* **skill etc** sich *(dat)* aneignen; **language** *also* lernen; *accent, word* aufschnappen; **information** herausbekommen. **you'll soon** ~ **it** ~ du wirst das schnell lernen.
  **(d)** *(collect)* **person, goods** abholen; *(bus etc)* **passengers** aufnehmen; *(in car)* mitnehmen; *(rescue: helicopter, lifeboat)* bergen; *(arrest, catch)* **criminal** schnappen *(col)*.
  **(e)** *(Rad)* **station** hereinbekommen; **message** empfangen; *(on radar)* ausmachen.
  **(f)** *(correct, put right)* korrigieren.
  **2** *vi* **(a)** *(improve)* besser werden; *(appetite also)* zunehmen; *(currency)* sich erholen; *(business)* florieren; *(after slump)* sich erholen. **(b)** *(continue)* **to** ~ ~ **where one left off** da weitermachen, wo man aufgehört hat.
**pickaback** ['pɪkəbæk] *n* **to give sb a** ~ jdn huckepack nehmen.
**pickaxe,** *(US)* **pickax** [pɪkæks] *n* Spitzhacke *f*, Pickel *m.*
**picket** ['pɪkɪt] **1** *n* **(a)** *(of strikers)* Streikposten *m.* **(b)** *(Mil)* Feldposten, Vorposten *m.* **2** *vt* **factory** Streikposten aufstellen vor *(+dat)*. **3** *vi* Streikposten aufstellen. **he is** ~**ing at the front entrance** er ist Streik-

posten am Vordereingang.
**picket:** ~ **duty** *n* Streikpostendienst *m*; **to be on** ~ **duty** Streikposten sein; ~ **line** *n* Streikpostenkette *f*; **to cross a** ~ **line** eine Streikpostenkette durchbrechen.
**pickings** ['pɪkɪŋz] *npl* Ausbeute *f*; *(stolen goods)* Beute *f.* **the** ~ **are good** es fällt einiges dabei ab.
**pickle** ['pɪkl] **1** *n* **(a)** *(food)* Pickles *pl.* **(b)** *(solution)* *(brine)* Salzlake *f*; *(vinegar)* Essigsoße *f.* **(c)** *(col: predicament)* Klemme *f (col)*. **he was in a** ~ er saß in der Tinte *(col)*. **2** *vt* einlegen.
**pick:** ~**-me-up** *n (col)* Muntermacher *m*; ~**pocket** *n* Taschendieb(in *f*) *m.*
**pick-up** ['pɪkʌp] *n* **(a)** *(of record deck)* Tonabnehmer *m.* ~ **arm** Tonarm *m.* **(b)** *(also* ~ **truck)** Kleintransporter *m.*
**picnic** ['pɪknɪk] **1** *n* Picknick *nt.* **to have a** ~ picknicken; **it was no** ~ *(fig col)* es war kein Honiglecken. **2** *vi* picknicken, ein Picknick machen.
**picnic basket** *or* **hamper** *n* Picknickkorb *m.*
**pictogram** ['pɪktəgræm] *n* Piktogramm *nt.*
**pictorial** [pɪk'tɔːrɪəl] *adj* **calendar** bebildert; **magazine** *also* illustriert; **description** bildhaft.
**picture** ['pɪktʃər] **1** *n* **(a)** Bild *nt*; *(mental image also)* Vorstellung *f*; *(painting also)* Gemälde *nt*; *(drawing also)* Zeichnung *f.* **these figures give the general** ~ diese Zahlen geben ein allgemeines Bild; **to be in the** ~ im Bilde sein; **to put sb in the** ~ jdn ins Bild setzen; **I get the** ~ ich hab's begriffen *or* kapiert *(col)*; **she looked a** ~ sie war bildschön; **the garden is a** ~ der Garten ist eine Pracht; **she looked** *or* **was the** ~ **of happiness** sie sah wie das Glück in Person aus. **(b)** *(Film)* Film *m.* **the** ~**s** *(Brit)* das Kino; **to go to the** ~**s** *(Brit)* ins Kino gehen. **2** *vt* *(imagine)* sich *(dat)* vorstellen.
**picture:** ~ **book** *n* Bildband *m*; *(for children)* Bilderbuch *nt*; ~ **frame** *n* Bilderrahmen *m*; ~ **gallery** *n* Gemäldegalerie *f*; ~ **hook** *n* Bilderhaken *m*; ~ **library** *n* Bildarchiv *nt*; ~ **postcard** *n* Ansichtskarte *f*; ~ **rail** *n* Bilderleiste *f.*
**picturesque** [,pɪktʃə'resk] *adj* malerisch; *(fig)* **description** anschaulich.
**piddle** ['pɪdl] *vi (col)* pinkeln *(col)*; *(esp child)* Pipi machen *(col)*.
**piddling** ['pɪdlɪŋ] *adj (col)* lächerlich; **amount** *also* lumpig *(col)*.
**pidgin** ['pɪdʒɪn] *n* Mischsprache *f.*
**pie** [paɪ] *n* Pastete *f*; *(sweet)* Obstkuchen *m*; *(individual)* Törtelett *nt.* **that's all** ~ **in the sky** *(col)* das sind doch alles nur verrückte Ideen; **as easy as** ~ *(col)* kinderleicht.
**piece** [piːs] *n* **(a)** Stück *nt*; *(part, member of a set)* Teil *nt*; *(component part)* Einzelteil *nt*; *(fragment of glass etc also)* Scherbe *f*; *(in draughts etc)* Stein *m*; *(chess)* Figur *f*; *(Press: article)* Artikel *m*; *(col!: woman)* Weib *nt.* **a 50p** ~ ein 50-Pence-Stück; **a** ~ **of cake/land/paper** ein Stück *nt* Kuchen/Land/Papier; **a** ~ **of furniture/luggage/clothing** ein Möbel-/Gepäck-/Kleidungsstück *nt*; **a ten-**~ **coffee set** ein zehnteiliges Kaffeeservice; **a** ~ **of news/information** eine Nachricht/eine Information; **a** ~ **of work** eine Arbeit; ~ **by** ~ Stück für Stück; **to take sth to** ~**s** etw in seine Einzelteile zerlegen; **to come to** ~**s** sich zerlegen lassen; *(break)* auseinanderfallen; **to fall to** ~**s** auseinanderfallen; *(glass)* zerbrechen; **to smash sth to** ~**s** etw kaputtschlagen; **he tore the letter (in)to** ~**s** er zerriß den Brief, er riß den Brief in Stücke.
  **(b)** *(phrases)* **to go to** ~**s** *(crack up)* durchdrehen *(col)*; **all in one** ~ *(intact)* heil, unversehrt; **to give sb a** ~ **of one's mind** jdm gehörig die Meinung sa-

gen; **to say one's** ~ seine Meinung sagen.

▶**piece together** *vt sep (lit)* zusammenstückeln; *(fig)* sich *(dat)* zusammenreimen; *evidence* zusammenfügen.

**piece:** ~**meal 1** *adv* stückweise; *(haphazardly)* kunterbunt durcheinander; **2** *adj* stückweise; *(haphazard)* wenig systematisch; ~ **rate** *n* Akkordlohn *m*; ~**work** *n* Akkordarbeit *f*; **to be on** ~**work** im Akkord arbeiten.

**pie:** ~ **chart** *n* Kreisdiagramm *nt*; ~ **dish** *n* Pastetenform *f*.

**pier** [pɪər] *n* Pier *m or f*; *(landing-place also)* Anlegestelle *f*.

**pierce** [pɪəs] *vt* durchstechen; *(knife, spear, bullet)* durchbohren; *(fig: sound, coldness etc)* durchdringen. **to** ~ **a hole in sth** etw durchstechen; **to have one's ears** ~**d** sich *(dat)* die Ohrläppchen durchstechen lassen.

**piercing** [ˈpɪəsɪŋ] *adj* durchdringend; *eyes also* stechend; *cold also, sarcasm* beißend; *wit* scharf.

**piety** [ˈpaɪətɪ] *n* Pietät, Frömmigkeit *f*.

**piffle** [ˈpɪfl] *n (col)* Quatsch *m (col)*.

**piffling** [ˈpɪflɪŋ] *adj (col)* lächerlich.

**pig** [pɪg] *n (lit, fig col)* Schwein *nt*; *(greedy)* Vielfraß *m (col)*. **to buy a** ~ **in a poke** *(prov)* die Katze im Sack kaufen; **to make a** ~ **of oneself** sich *(dat)* den Bauch vollschlagen *(col)*.

**pigeon** [ˈpɪdʒən] *n* **(a)** Taube *f*. **(b)** *(col)* **that's not my** ~ das ist nicht mein Bier *(col)*.

**pigeon:** ~**hole 1** *n (in desk etc)* Fach *nt*; **2** *vt (lit)* (in Fächer) einordnen; *(fig: categorize)* einordnen, aufteilen; ~ **post** *n* Taubenpost *f*.

**piggyback** [ˈpɪgɪbæk] *n* = **pickaback.**

**piggy bank** [ˈpɪgɪbæŋk] *n* Sparschwein *nt*.

**pigheaded** [ˌpɪgˈhedɪd] *adj* stur.

**piglet** [ˈpɪglɪt] *n* Ferkel *nt*.

**pigment** [ˈpɪgmənt] *n* Pigment *nt*.

**pigmentation** [ˌpɪgmənˈteɪʃən] *n* Pigmentierung *f*.

**pigmy** *n* = **pygmy.**

**pig:** ~**'s ear** *n* **to make a** ~**'s ear of sth** *(Brit col)* etw vermasseln *(col)*; ~**skin** *n* Schweinsleder *nt*; ~**sty** *n* Schweinestall *m*; *(fig also)* Saustall *m (col)*; ~**tail** *n* Zopf *m*.

**pike** [paɪk] *n (fish)* Hecht *m*.

**pilchard** [ˈpɪltʃəd] *n* Sardine *f*.

**pile¹** [paɪl] **1** *n* **(a)** *(heap)* Stapel *m*. **to put things in a** ~ etw (auf)stapeln; **her things lay** *or* **were in a** ~ ihre Sachen lagen auf einem Haufen. **(b)** *(col: large amount)* Haufen *m*, Menge *f*. ~**s of food** jede Menge Essen *(col)*; **a** ~ **of things to do** massenhaft zu tun *(col)*. **(c)** *(col: fortune)* Vermögen *nt*. **to make a** ~ einen Haufen Geld verdienen. **2** *vt* stapeln. **a table** ~**d high with books** ein Tisch mit Stapeln von Büchern.

▶**pile in** *vi (col)* *(-to* in +*acc)* hereindrängen; *(get in)* einsteigen. ~ ~! immer herein!

▶**pile up 1** *vi* **(a)** *(lit, fig)* sich anhäufen; *(traffic)* sich stauen; *(evidence)* sich verdichten; *(crash)* aufeinander auffahren. **2** *vt sep* (auf)stapeln; *money* horten; *(fig) debts* anhäufen; *evidence* sammeln.

**pile²** *n* Pfahl *m*.

**pile³** *n (of carpet, cloth)* Flor *m*.

**pile-driver** [ˈpaɪlˌdraɪvər] *n* Ramme *f*.

**piles** [paɪlz] *npl* Hämorrhoiden *pl*.

**pile-up** [ˈpaɪlʌp] *n (car crash)* (Massen)karambolage *f*.

**pilfer** [ˈpɪlfər] *vti* stehlen, klauen *(col)*. **there's a lot of** ~**ing in the office** im Büro wird viel geklaut *(col)*.

**pilgrim** [ˈpɪlgrɪm] *n* Pilger(in *f*) *m*.

**pilgrimage** [ˈpɪlgrɪmɪdʒ] *n* Wallfahrt *f*. **to go on** *or*

**make a** ~ pilgern, eine Wallfahrt machen.

**pill** [pɪl] *n* Tablette *f*. **the** ~ die Pille; **to be/go on the** ~ die Pille nehmen.

**pillage** [ˈpɪlɪdʒ] **1** *n (act)* Plünderung *f*; *(booty)* Beute *f*. **2** *vti* plündern.

**pillar** [ˈpɪlər] *n* Säule *f*. **a** ~ **of society** eine Stütze der Gesellschaft; **from** ~ **to post** von Pontius zu Pilatus.

**pillar-box** [ˈpɪləbɒks] *n (Brit)* Briefkasten *m*. ~ **red** knallrot.

**pillion** [ˈpɪljən] **1** *n (on motorbike)* Beifahrersitz *m*. ~ **passenger** Beifahrer(in *f*) *m*. **2** *adv* **to ride** ~ auf dem Beifahrersitz mitfahren.

**pillory** [ˈpɪlərɪ] *vt (fig)* anprangern.

**pillow** [ˈpɪləu] *n* (Kopf)kissen *nt*.

**pillow:** ~ **case** *or* **slip** *n* (Kopf)kissenbezug *m*; ~ **fight** *n* Kissenschlacht *f*; ~ **talk** *n* Bettgeflüster *nt*.

**pilot** [ˈpaɪlət] **1** *n (Aviat)* Pilot(in *f*) *m*; *(Naut)* Lotse *m*. **2** *vt plane* fliegen; *ship* lotsen; *(fig)* führen, leiten.

**pilot:** ~ **boat** *n* Lotsenboot *nt*; ~ **light** *n* Zündflamme *f*; ~ **scheme** *n* Pilotprojekt *nt*, Modellversuch *m*.

**pimento** [pɪˈmentəu] *n* **(a)** Paprikaschote *f*. **(b)** *(allspice)* Piment *m or nt*.

**pimp** [pɪmp] *n* Zuhälter *m*.

**pimple** [ˈpɪmpl] *n* Pickel *m*.

**pimply** [ˈpɪmplɪ] *adj (+er)* pickelig.

**PIN** = **personal identification number.**

**pin** [pɪn] **1** *n (Sew)* Stecknadel *f*; *(tie* ~, *hair* ~) Nadel *f*; *(Mech)* Bolzen, Stift *m*; *(in grenade)* Sicherungsstift *m*; *(Elec: of plug)* Pol *m*. **a two-**~ **plug** ein zweipoliger Stecker; ~**s and needles** *sing or pl* ein Kribbeln *nt*; **I've got** ~**s and needles in my foot** es kribbelt in meinem Fuß, mein Fuß ist eingeschlafen; **as neat as a new** ~ blitzsauber; **for two** ~**s I'd pack up and go** *(col)* es fehlt nicht mehr viel, dann gehe ich; **you could have heard a** ~ **drop** man hätte eine Stecknadel fallen hören können. **2** *vt* **(a)** *dress* stecken. **to** ~ **sth to sth** etw an etw *(acc)* heften. **(b)** *(fig)* **to** ~ **sb to the ground/against a wall** jdn an den Boden/an eine Wand drücken; **to** ~ **one's hopes on sb/sth** seine Hoffnungen auf jdn/etw setzen; **to** ~ **back one's ears** die Ohren spitzen *(col)*. **(c)** *(col: accuse of)* **to** ~ **sth on sb** jdm etw anhängen.

▶**pin down** *vt sep* **(a)** *(with pins)* an- *or* festheften; *(hold, weight down)* niederhalten; *(person)* zu Boden drücken. **(b)** *(fig)* **to** ~ **sb** ~ jdn festnageln *(col)* *or* festlegen; **he wouldn't be** ~**ned** ~ **to any particular date** er ließ sich nicht auf ein bestimmtes Datum festlegen; **I've seen him somewhere before but I can't** ~ **him** ~ ich habe ihn schon mal irgendwo gesehen, kann ihn aber nicht einordnen; **we can't** ~ ~ **the source of the rumours** wir können die Quelle der Gerüchte nicht lokalisieren; **there's something odd here, but I can't** ~ **it** ~ irgend etwas stimmt hier nicht, aber ich kann nicht genau sagen was.

▶**pin up** *vt sep notice* anheften; *hair* hochstecken; *dress etc* stecken.

**pinafore** [ˈpɪnəfɔːr] *n (for children)* Kinderkittel *m*; *(apron)* Schürze *f*. ~ **dress** *(Brit)* Trägerkleid *nt*.

**pin:** ~**ball** *n (also* ~**ball machine)* Flipper *m*; ~**board** *n* Pinnwand *f*.

**pincers** [ˈpɪnsəz] *npl* **(a)** Kneifzange *f*. **a pair of** ~ eine Kneifzange. **(b)** *(Zool)* Schere, Zange *f*.

**pinch** [pɪntʃ] **1** *n* **(a)** *(with fingers)* Kneifen *nt no pl*. **to give sb a** ~ jdn in den Arm *or* in den Arm kneifen. **(b)** *(Cook)* Prise *f*. **(c)** *(pressure)* **to feel the** ~ *(financially)* die schlechte Lage zu spüren bekommen; **I'm rather feeling the** ~ **at the moment** *(short of money)* ich bin im Augenblick ziemlich knapp bei Kasse *(col)*; **if it comes to the ~** wenn es zum Schlimmsten kommt; **at a ~** zur Not. **2** *vt* **(a)** *(with fingers)* kneifen; *(with tool)* wire etc zusammendrücken. **(b)** *(col: steal)* klauen *(col)*. **don't let anyone ~ my seat** paß auf, daß mir niemand den Platz wegnimmt. **3** *vi (shoe, also fig)* drücken. **to ~ and scrape** sich einschränken.

**pinched** ['pɪntʃt] *adj* **(a)** verhärmt. **~ with cold** verfroren. **(b)** *(col: short)* **to be ~ for money/time/space** knapp bei Kasse sein *(col)*/keine Zeit haben/ein wenig beengt sein.

**pincushion** ['pɪn,kʊʃn] *n* Nadelkissen *nt*.

**pine**[1] [paɪn] *n* Kiefer *f.*

**pine**[2] *vi* **to ~ for sb/sth** sich nach jdm/etw sehnen.
  ▶**pine away** *vi* sich vor Kummer verzehren.

**pineapple** ['paɪn,æpl] *n* Ananas *f.*

**pine:** **~ cone** *n* Kiefernzapfen *m*; **~ forest** *n* Tannenwald *m*; **~ kernel** *(Brit)*, **~ nut** *n* Pinienkern *m*; **~ needle** *n* Kiefernnadel *f*; **~ tree** *n* Kiefer *f.*

**ping** [pɪŋ] **1** *n (of bell)* Klingeln *nt; (of bullet)* Peng *nt.* **2** *vi (bell)* klingeln; *(bullet)* peng machen.

**ping-pong** ['pɪŋpɒŋ] *n* Pingpong *nt.* **~ table** Tischtennisplatte *f.*

**pinion** ['pɪnjən] *n (Mech)* Ritzel, Treibrad *nt.*

**pink**[1] [pɪŋk] **1** *n* **(a)** *(colour)* Rosa *nt.* **(b)** *(plant)* Gartennelke *f.* **(c)** **to be in the ~** vor Gesundheit strotzen. **2** *adj (colour)* rosa *inv*, rosafarben; *cheeks, face* rosig. **to turn ~** erröten.

**pink**[2] *vt (Sew)* mit der Zickzackschere schneiden, zacken.

**pink**[3] *vi (Aut)* klopfen.

**pinkie** ['pɪŋkɪ] *n (Scot col, US col)* kleiner Finger.

**pinking** ['pɪŋkɪŋ] *n* **(a)** *(Aut)* Klopfen *nt.* **(b)** *(Sew)* **~ shears** *or* **scissors** Zickzackschere *f.*

**pin money** *n* Taschengeld *nt.*

**pinnacle** ['pɪnəkl] *n (Archit)* Fiale *f; (of rock)* Gipfel *m*, Spitze *f; (fig)* Gipfel, Höhepunkt *m.*

**pinny** ['pɪnɪ] *n (col)* Schürze *f.*

**pin:** **~point** *vt (locate)* genau an- *or* aufzeigen; *(define, identify)* genau feststellen *or* -legen; **~prick** *n* Nadelstich *m*; **~stripe** *n (~stripe suit)* Nadelstreifenanzug *m.*

**pint** [paɪnt] *n (Measure)* Pint *nt.* **to have a ~** *(esp Brit)* ein Bier *nt* trinken.

**pinta** ['paɪntə] *n (Brit col)* ≃ halber Liter Milch.

**pin:** **~-up** *n (picture)* Pin-up-Foto *nt; (girl)* Pin-up-Girl *nt; (man)* Idol *nt;* **~wheel** *n (US: firework)* Feuerrad *nt.*

**pioneer** [,paɪə'nɪəʳ] **1** *n (also Mil)* Pionier *m; (fig also)* Wegbereiter *m.* **2** *vt way* bahnen; *(fig)* Pionierarbeit *f* leisten für.

**pious** ['paɪəs] *adj* fromm; *(pej also)* frömmlerisch. **a ~ hope** ein frommer Wunsch.

**pip**[1] [pɪp] *n* **(a)** *(Bot)* Kern *m.* **(b)** *(on dice)* Auge *nt; (Brit Mil col)* Stern *m; (radar)* Pip *m*, Echozeichen *nt.* **(c)** *(Brit Rad, Telec)* **the ~s** das Zeitzeichen; *(in public telephone)* das Tut-tut-tut. **he/she gives me the ~** *(Brit col)* ich kann ihn/sie nicht riechen *(col)*.

**pip**[2] *vt (Brit col)* knapp besiegen *or* schlagen. **to ~ sb at the post** *(in race)* jdn um Haaresbreite schlagen; *(fig)* jdm um Haaresbreite zuvorkommen.

**pipe** [paɪp] **1** *n* **(a)** *(for water, gas etc)* Rohr *nt*, Leitung *f; (fuel ~)* Leitung *f.* **(b)** *(Mus)* Flöte *f; (fife, of organ)* Pfeife *f.* **~s** *(bag~s)* Dudelsack *m.* **(c)** *(for smoking)* Pfeife *f.* **to smoke a ~** Pfeife rauchen; **put that in your ~ and smoke it!** *(col)* steck dir das hinter den Spiegel *(col)*. **2** *vt* **(a)** *water, oil etc* in Rohren leiten; *music, broadcast* ausstrahlen. **~d music** *(pej)* Musikberieselung *f (col)*. **(b)** *(Mus) tune* flöten, pfeifen; *(sing in high voice)* krähen; *(speak in high voice)* piepsen; *(Naut)* pfeifen. **to ~ sb aboard** jdn

mit Pfeifensignal an Bord empfangen. **(c)** *(Cook)* spritzen; *cake* mit Spritzguß verzieren. **3** *vi (Mus)* (die) Flöte spielen; *(young bird, anxiously)* piep(s)en.
  ▶**pipe down** *vi (col)* die Luft anhalten *(col)*.
  ▶**pipe up** *vi (col: person)* den Mund aufmachen, sich melden.

**pipe:** **~ cleaner** *n* Pfeifenreiniger *m*; **~ dream** *n* Hirngespinst *nt*; **that's just a ~ dream** das ist ja wohl nur ein frommer Wunsch; **~line** *n* (Rohr)leitung *f; (for oil, gas also)* Pipeline *f*; **to be in the ~line** *(fig)* in Vorbereitung sein.

**piper** ['paɪpəʳ] *n (bagpipes)* Dudelsackpfeifer *m.*

**piping** ['paɪpɪŋ] **1** *n* **(a)** *(pipework)* Rohrleitungssystem *nt; (pipe)* Rohrleitung *f.* **(b)** *(Sew)* Paspelierung *f.* **2** *adv:* **~ hot** kochendheiß.

**piquancy** ['piːkənsɪ] *n* Würze *f; (fig)* Pikanterie *f.*

**piquant** ['piːkənt] *adj (lit, fig)* pikant.

**pique** [piːk] **1** *n* Groll *m.* **he resigned in a fit of ~** er kündigte voller Empörung. **2** *vt (offend)* kränken, verletzen. **~d** pikiert.

**piracy** ['paɪərəsɪ] *n* Piraterie *f; (of book etc)* Raubdruck *m; (of record)* Raubpressung *f.*

**piranha** [pɪ'rɑːnjə] *n* Piranha *m.*

**pirate** ['paɪərɪt] **1** *n* Seeräuber, Pirat *m.* **~ radio** Piratensender *m.* **2** *vt book* einen Raubdruck herstellen von; *invention, idea* stehlen. **~(d) edition** Raubdruck *m.*

**pirouette** [,pɪrʊ'et] **1** *n* Pirouette *f.* **2** *vi* Pirouetten drehen.

**Pisces** ['paɪsiːz] *npl (Astrol)* Fische *pl.* **I'm (a) ~** ich bin (ein) Fisch.

**piss** [pɪs] *(col!)* **1** *n* Pisse *f (col!)*. **to take the ~ out of sb** *(col!)* jdn verarschen *(col!)*. **2** *vti* pissen *(col!)*.
  ▶**piss off** *vi (esp Brit col!)* abhauen *(col)*. **to be ~ed ~ with sb/sth** von jdm/etw die Schnauze voll haben *(col!)*.

**pissed** [pɪst] *adj (col!) (Brit: drunk)* voll *(col)*, besoffen *(col); (US: angry)* stocksauer *(col)*.

**pistachio** [pɪ'stɑːʃɪəʊ] *n* Pistazie *f.*

**pistol** ['pɪstl] *n* Pistole *f.* **~ shot** Pistolenschuß *m*; **to hold a ~ to sb's head** *(fig)* jdm die Pistole auf die Brust setzen.

**piston** ['pɪstən] *n* Kolben *m.* **~ engine** Kolbenmotor *m*; **~ rod** Kolbenstange *f.*

**pit**[1] [pɪt] **1** *n* **(a)** Grube *f; (motorracing)* Box *f; (Sport: for jump)* Sprunggrube *f; (coalmine also)* Zeche *f; (trap)* Fallgrube *f; (of stomach)* Magengrube *f.* **in the ~ of one's stomach** in der Magengegend; **he works down the ~(s)** er arbeitet unter Tage. **(b)** *(Theat) (usu pl Brit: for audience)* Parkett *nt; (orchestra ~)* Orchesterraum *m.* **(c) the ~s** *(col: very bad)* das Allerletzte.

**2** *vt* **(a)** **to be ~ted with small craters** mit kleinen Kratern übersät sein; **the car was ~ted with rustholes** der Wagen war mit Rostlöchern übersät. **(b)** **to ~ one's strength/wits against sb/sth** seine Kraft/seinen Verstand an jdm/etw messen; **in the next round A is ~ted against B** in der nächsten Runde stehen sich A und B gegenüber.

**pit**[2] *(esp US)* **1** *n (in fruit)* Stein *m.* **2** *vt* entsteinen.

**pitapat** [,pɪtə'pæt] *adv (of heart)* poch poch; *(of feet)* tapp tapp. **to go ~** *(heart)* pochen, klopfen.

**pitch**[1] [pɪtʃ] *n* Pech *nt.* **as black as ~** pechschwarz.

**pitch**[2] **1** *n* **(a)** *(esp Brit Sport)* Platz *m*, Feld *nt; (Brit: place for business)* Stand *m.* **our usual ~** *(on beach etc)* unser Stammplatz *m.* **(b)** *(angle, slope: of roof)* Neigung *f; (of propeller)* Steigung *f.* **(c)** *(of note)* Tonhöhe *f; (of instrument)* Tonlage *f; (of voice)* Stimmlage *f.* **to have perfect ~** das absolute Gehör haben. **(d)** *(fig: degree)* **we can't keep on working at**

this ~ **much longer** wir können dieses Arbeitstempo nicht mehr lange durchhalten; **matters had reached such a ~ that** ... die Sache hatte sich derart zugespitzt, daß ... **(e)** *(col: sales ~) (technique)* Verkaufstaktik *f*; *(long talk)* Sermon *m (col)*.

**2** *vt* **(a)** *(throw)* hay gabeln; *ball* werfen. **he was ~ed from** *or* **off his horse** er wurde vom Pferd geworfen. **(b)** *(Mus)* **the soprano part is ~ed too high for me** die Sopranstimme ist zu hoch für mich. **(c)** *(fig)* **to ~ one's expectations too high** seine Erwartungen zu hoch spannen; **that's ~ing it rather strong** *or* **a bit high** das ist ein bißchen übertrieben. **(d)** *(put up)* camp aufschlagen; *stand* aufstellen.

**3** *vi* **(a)** *(fall)* fallen, stürzen. **to ~ forward** vornüberfallen. **(b)** *(Naut)* stampfen; *(Aviat)* absacken. **to ~ and toss** *(ship)* von den Wellen hin und her geworfen werden; *(person)* sich wälzen.

▶**pitch in 1** *vt sep* hineinwerfen. **2** *vi (col)* einspringen. **so we all ~ed ~ together** also packten wir alle mit an.

▶**pitch into** *vi +prep obj (attack)* herfallen über *(+acc)*; *food also, work* sich hermachen über *(+acc)*.

**pitch black** *or* **dark** *adj* pechschwarz.

**pitched** ['pɪtʃt] *adj* **(a)** **~ roof** Satteldach *nt*. **(b)** *battle* offen.

**pitcher**[1] ['pɪtʃər] *n* Krug *m*.

**pitcher**[2] *n (Baseball)* Werfer *m*.

**pitchfork** ['pɪtʃfɔːk] **1** *n* Heugabel *f*; *(for manure)* Mistgabel *f*. **2** *vt (fig)* **to ~ sb into sth** jdn mitten in etw *(acc)* hineinwerfen.

**piteous** *adj*, **~ly** *adv* ['pɪtɪəs, -lɪ] mitleiderregend; *cry* kläglich.

**pitfall** ['pɪtfɔːl] *n (fig)* Falle *f*. "**P~s of English**" „Hauptschwierigkeiten der englischen Sprache".

**pith** [pɪθ] *n (Bot)* Mark *nt*; *(of orange etc)* weiße Haut; *(fig: core)* Kern *m*.

**pithead** ['pɪthed] *n* Übertageanlagen *pl*. **at the ~** über Tage; **~ ballot** Abstimmung *f* der Bergarbeiter.

**pithy** ['pɪθɪ] *adj (+er) (fig)* markig. **~ remarks** Kraftsprüche *pl*.

**pitiable** ['pɪtɪəbl] *adj* bemitleidenswert.

**pitiful** ['pɪtɪfʊl] *adj* **(a)** *sight, story* mitleiderregend; *person* bedauernswert; *cry also* jämmerlich. **(b)** *(poor, wretched)* erbärmlich, jämmerlich.

**pitifully** ['pɪtɪfəlɪ] *adv* mitleiderregend; *cry* jämmerlich; *(wretchedly)* erbärmlich.

**pitiless** ['pɪtɪlɪs] *adj* mitleidlos; *person also, heat* unbarmherzig; *cruelty also* erbarmungslos.

**pitilessly** ['pɪtɪlɪslɪ] *adv* erbarmungslos.

**pittance** ['pɪtəns] *n* Hungerlohn *m*.

**pitter-patter** ['pɪtəˈpætər] **1** *n (of rain)* Klatschen *nt*; *(of feet)* Getrappel *nt*. **2** *adv* **run** tapp tapp. **her heart went ~** ihr Herz klopfte.

**pity** ['pɪtɪ] **1** *n* **(a)** Mitleid, Erbarmen *nt*. **for ~'s sake!** Erbarmen!; *(less seriously)* um Himmels willen!; **to have** *or* **take ~ on sb, to feel ~ for sb** mit jdm Mitleid haben. **(b)** *(what a)* **~!** *(wie)* schade!; **more's the ~!** leider; **it is a ~ that** ... es ist schade, daß ... **2** *vt* bedauern.

**pitying** *adj*, **~ly** *adv* ['pɪtɪɪŋ, -lɪ] mitleidig; *(with contempt)* verächtlich.

**pivot** ['pɪvət] *(vb: pret, ptp ~ed)* **1** *n* Drehzapfen *m*; *(fig)* Dreh- und Angelpunkt *m*. **2** *vt* drehbar lagern. **3** *vi* sich drehen.

**pixel** ['pɪksl] *n (Comp)* Pixel *nt*.

**pixie, pixy** ['pɪksɪ] *n* Kobold *m*.

**pizazz** [pəˈzæz] *n* Flair *nt*, Pfiff *m (col)*.

**pizza** ['piːtsə] *n* Pizza *f*.

**Pl** = **Place** Pl.

**placard** ['plækɑːd] *n* Plakat *nt*.

**placate** [pləˈkeɪt] *vt* beschwichtigen.

**place** [pleɪs] **1** *n* **(a)** *(in general)* Platz *m*, Stelle *f*. **this is just the ~ for a picnic** das ist genau der richtige Platz für ein Picknick; **this is the ~ where he was killed** an dieser Stelle wurde er getötet; **from ~ to ~** von einem Ort zum anderen; **in another ~** woanders; **some/any ~** irgendwo; **this is no ~ for children** das ist hier für Kinder nicht geeignet; **all over the ~** überall; *(untidy)* ganz durcheinander; *(wrong)* völlig verkehrt; **his work is all over the ~** auf seine Arbeit ist kein Verlaß; **water is coming through in several ~s** an mehreren Stellen kommt Wasser durch; **do the spoons have a special ~?** haben die Löffel einen bestimmten Platz?; **make sure the screw is properly in ~** achten Sie darauf, daß die Schraube richtig sitzt; **to be out of ~** nicht an der richtigen Stelle sein; *(fig)* deplaziert sein; *(remark also)* unangebracht sein; *(person also)* fehl am Platze sein; **to feel out of ~** sich fehl am Platz fühlen; **not a hair out of ~** tadellos frisiert; **your ~ is by his side** dein Platz ist an seiner Seite; **everything was in ~** alles war an seiner Stelle; **in the right/wrong ~** an der richtigen/falschen Stelle; **to keep/lose one's ~** *(in book etc)* die richtige Stelle markieren/verlieren; **it was the last ~ I expected to find him** da hätte ich ihn am wenigsten vermutet; **this isn't the ~ to discuss politics** dies ist nicht der Ort, um über Politik zu sprechen; **to go ~s** *(travel)* herumreisen; **he's going ~s** *(fig col)* er bringt's zu was *(col)*.

**(b)** *(specific ~)* Stätte *f*, Ort *m*. **~ of birth/residence** Geburtsort *m*/Wohnort *m*; **~ of business** *or* **work** Arbeitsstelle *f*.

**(c)** *(district etc)* Gegend *f*; *(country)* Land *nt*; *(building)* Gebäude *nt*; *(town)* Ort *m*; *(home)* Haus *nt*; Wohnung *f*. **there's nothing to do in this ~** hier kann man nichts unternehmen; **at Jimmy's ~** bei Jimmy; **come round to my ~ some time** besuch mich mal, komm doch mal vorbei; **let's go back to my ~** laß uns zu mir gehen; **where's your ~?** wo wohnst du?

**(d)** *(seat, in team, school etc)* Platz *m*; *(university ~)* Studienplatz *m*; *(job)* Stelle *f*. **to take one's ~ (at table)** Platz nehmen; **~s for 500 workers** 500 Arbeitsplätze; **to lose one's ~** *(in a queue)* sich wieder hinten anstellen müssen.

**(e)** *(social position etc)* Rang *m*, Stellung *f*. **people in high ~s** Leute in hohen Positionen; **I know my ~** ich weiß, was sich für mich gehört; **it's not my ~ to comment** es steht mir nicht zu, einen Kommentar abzugeben; **to keep** *or* **put sb in his ~** jdn in seine Schranken weisen.

**(f)** *(in exam, Sport etc)* Platz *m*; *(Math)* Stelle *f*. **to three decimal ~s** *or* **~s of decimals** auf drei Dezimalstellen *or* Stellen nach dem Komma; **in the first/second ~** erstens/zweitens; **to win first ~** erste(r, s) sein.

**(g)** **in ~ of** statt *(+gen)*; **if I were in your ~** (wenn ich) an Ihrer Stelle (wäre); **to take ~** stattfinden; **to take the ~ of sb/sth** den Platz von jdm/etw einnehmen.

**2** *vt* **(a)** *(put)* setzen, stellen; *(lay down)* legen; *person at table etc* setzen; *guards* aufstellen; *(Ftbl, Tennis)* plazieren; *troops* in Stellung bringen; *announcement (in paper)* inserieren *(in in +dat)*; *advertisement* setzen *(in in +acc)*. **I shall ~ the matter in the hands of a lawyer** ich werde die Angelegenheit einem Rechtsanwalt übergeben; **to ~ too much emphasis on sth** zu großen Wert auf etw *(acc)* legen; **that should be ~d first** das sollte an erster Stelle stehen; **to ~ trust** *etc* **in sb/sth** Vertrauen in jdn/etw setzen.

**(b) to be** ~**d** *(shop, town, house etc)* liegen; **we are well** ~**d for the shops** was Einkaufsmöglichkeiten angeht, wohnen wir günstig; **how are you** ~**d for time/money?** wie sieht es mit deiner Zeit/deinem Geld aus?; **Liverpool are well** ~**d in the league** Liverpool liegt gut in der Tabelle; **we are better** ~**d now than we were last month** wir stehen jetzt besser da als vor einem Monat.

**(c)** *order* erteilen *(with sb* jdm*)*; *contract* abschließen *(with sb* mit jdm*)*; *money* deponieren; *(Comm) goods* absetzen.

**(d)** *(in race, competition etc)* **the German runner was** ~**d third** der deutsche Läufer belegte den dritten Platz.

**(e)** *(remember, identify)* einordnen. **I can't quite** ~ **him/his accent** ich kann ihn/seinen Akzent nicht einordnen.

**placebo** [plə'si:bəu] *n (Med)* Placebo *nt*.

**place:** ~ **card** *n* Tischkarte *f*; ~ **mat** *n* Set *nt*.

**placement** ['pleɪsmənt] *n* **(a)** *(act)* Plazierung *f*; *(finding job)* Vermittlung *f*. **(b)** *(training period)* Praktikum *nt*.

**place-name** ['pleɪs,neɪm] *n* Ortsname *m*.

**placenta** [plə'sentə] *n* Plazenta *f*.

**placid** ['plæsɪd] *adj* ruhig; *disposition* friedfertig.

**placidity** [plə'sɪdɪtɪ] *n* Ruhe *f*; *(of disposition)* Friedfertigkeit *f*.

**placidly** ['plæsɪdlɪ] *adv* ruhig, friedlich.

**plagiarism** ['pleɪdʒərɪzəm] *n* Plagiat *nt*.

**plagiarist** ['pleɪdʒərɪst] *n* Plagiator(in *f*) *m*.

**plagiarize** ['pleɪdʒəraɪz] *vt book, idea* plagiieren.

**plague** [pleɪg] **1** *n (Med)* Seuche *f*; *(Bibl, fig)* Plage *f*. **the** ~ die Pest; **to avoid sb/sth like the** ~ *(col)* jdn/etw wie die Pest meiden *(col)*. **2** *vt* plagen. **to** ~ **sb with questions** jdn ständig mit Fragen belästigen; **to be** ~**d by doubts** von Zweifeln geplagt werden.

**plaice** [pleɪs] *n no pl* Scholle *f*.

**plaid** [plæd] *n* Plaid *nt*. ~ **skirt** karierter Rock.

**plain** [pleɪn] **1** *adj (+er)* **(a)** klar; *(obvious also)* offensichtlich; *tracks, differences* deutlich. ~ **to see** offensichtlich; **it's as** ~ **as a pikestaff** *or* **the nose on your face** *(col)* das sieht doch ein Blinder (mit Krückstock) *(col)*; **to make sth** ~ **to sb** jdm etw klar machen; **I'd like to make it quite** ~ **that** ... ich möchte gern klarstellen, daß ...

**(b)** *(frank, straightforward) question, answer* klar; *truth* schlicht. ~ **dealing** Redlichkeit *f*; **in** ~ **language** *or* **English** unmißverständlich, ≈ auf gut Deutsch; **it was** ~ **sailing** es ging glatt (über die Bühne) *(col)*.

**(c)** *(simple, with nothing added)* einfach; *living also* schlicht, bescheiden; *cooking also* (gut)bürgerlich; *paper* unliniert; *colour* einheitlich; *(not patterned) material etc* uni *pred*, einfarbig. **under** ~ **cover** in neutralem Umschlag.

**(d)** *(sheer)* rein; *greed also* nackt; *nonsense etc also* völlig, blank *(col)*.

**(e)** *(not beautiful) person, face* wenig attraktiv; *building* unansehnlich.

**2** *adv* **(a)** *(col: simply, completely)* (ganz) einfach. **(b) I can't put it** ~**er than that** deutlicher kann ich es nicht sagen.

**3** *n* **(a)** *(Geog)* Ebene *f*. **(b)** *(Knitting)* rechte Masche.

**plain:** ~ **chocolate** *n* Zartbitterschokolade *f*; ~ **clothes** *npl* Zivil *nt*.

**plainly** ['pleɪnlɪ] *adv* **(a)** *(clearly)* eindeutig; *explain, visible* klar, deutlich. **(b)** *(frankly)* offen. **(c)** *(simply, unsophisticatedly)* einfach.

**plainness** ['pleɪnnɪs] *n* **(a)** *(frankness)* Offenheit *f*.

**(b)** *(simplicity)* Einfachheit *f*. **(c)** *(lack of beauty)* Unansehnlichkeit *f*.

**plain:** ~ **speaking** *n* Offenheit *f*; **some** ~ **speaking** ein paar offene Worte; ~**-spoken** *adj* offen, direkt; *criticism also* unverhohlen; **to be** ~**-spoken** sagen, was man denkt.

**plaintiff** ['pleɪntɪf] *n* Kläger(in *f*) *m*.

**plaintive** ['pleɪntɪv] *adj* klagend; *voice etc also* wehleidig *(pej)*.

**plait** [plæt] **1** *n* Zopf *m*. **she wears her hair in** ~**s** sie trägt Zöpfe. **2** *vt* flechten.

**plan** [plæn] **1** *n* **(a)** *(scheme)* Plan *m*; *(Pol, Econ also)* Programm *nt*. ~ **of action** *(Mil, fig)* Aktionsprogramm *nt*; ~ **of campaign** *(Mil)* Strategie *f*; **the** ~ **is to meet at six** es ist geplant, sich um sechs zu treffen; **the best** ~ **is to tell him first** am besten sagt man es ihm zuerst; **to have great** ~**s for sb** große Pläne mit jdm haben; **have you any** ~**s for tonight?** hast du (für) heute abend (schon) etwas vor?; **according to** ~ planmäßig, wie vorgesehen. **(b)** *(diagram)* Plan *m*; *(for essay, speech)* Konzept *nt*; *(town* ~*)* Stadtplan *m*.

**2** *vt* planen; *programme etc* erstellen, ausarbeiten; *(intend)* vorhaben. **we weren't** ~**ning to** wir hatten es nicht vor; **this development was not** ~**ned** diese Entwicklung war nicht eingeplant; ~**ned obsolescence** geplanter Verschleiß.

**3** *vi* planen. **to** ~ **for sth** sich auf etw *(acc)* einstellen; **to** ~ **months ahead** (auf) Monate vorausplanen; **I'm not** ~**ning on staying** ich habe nicht vor zu bleiben.

**plane¹** [pleɪn] *n (also* ~ **tree)** Platane *f*.

**plane²** **1** *adj* eben *(also Math)*. **2** *n* **(a)** *(Math, fig)* Ebene *f*; *(intellectual also)* Niveau *nt*; *(social* ~*)* Schicht *f*. **(b)** *(tool)* Hobel *m*. **(c)** *(aeroplane)* Flugzeug *nt*. **to go by** ~ fliegen. **3** *vt* hobeln. **to** ~ **sth down** etw glatt hobeln.

**planet** ['plænɪt] *n* Planet *m*.

**planetarium** [,plænɪ'tɛərɪəm] *n* Planetarium *nt*.

**plank** [plæŋk] *n* Brett *nt*. **to be as thick as two (short)** ~**s** dumm wie Bohnenstroh sein *(col)*.

**plankton** ['plæŋktən] *n* Plankton *nt*.

**planner** ['plænər] *n* Planer(in *f*) *m*; *(chart)* Jahresplaner *m*.

**planning** *in cpds* Planungs-. **to be at the** ~ **stage** *(project)* in der Planung sein; *(team)* bei der Planung sein; ~ **permission** Baugenehmigung *f*.

**plant** [plɑːnt] **1** *n* **(a)** *(Bot)* Pflanze *f*. **rare/tropical** ~**s** seltene/tropische Gewächse *pl*. **(b)** *(no pl: equipment)* Anlagen *pl*; *(equipment and buildings)* Produktionsanlage *f*; *(factory)* Werk *nt*. **2** *attr* Pflanzen-. ~ **life** Pflanzenwelt *f*. **3** *vt* **(a)** *plants, trees* (an)pflanzen; *field* bepflanzen. **to** ~ **a field with wheat** auf einem Feld Weizen anbauen. **(b)** *(place in position)* setzen; *bomb* legen; *kiss* drücken; *(in the ground) stick* stecken; *flag* pflanzen. **to** ~ **sth in sb's mind** jdm etw in den Kopf setzen; **he** ~**ed himself right in the doorway** er pflanzte sich genau in den Eingang *(col)*. **(c)** *(col)* schmuggeln; *(informer, spy etc)* (ein)schleusen. **to** ~ **sth on sb** jdm etw unterschieben.

**plantain** ['plæntɪn] *n (weed)* Wegerich *m*.

**plantation** [plæn'teɪʃən] *n* Plantage *f*; *(of trees)* Anpflanzung *f*.

**planter** ['plɑːntər] *n (person)* Pflanzer(in *f*) *m*; *(machine)* Pflanzmaschine *f*; *(outer pot)* Übertopf *m*; *(tub)* Pflanzgefäß *nt*.

**plant:** ~ **hire** *n* Baumaschinenvermietung *f*; ~ **pot** *n* Blumentopf *m*.

**plaque** [plæk] *n* **(a)** *(on building etc)* Tafel *f*. **(b)** *(Med: on teeth)* (Zahn)belag *m*.

**plasma** ['plæzmə] _n_ Plasma _nt._
**plaster** ['plɑːstəʳ] **1** _n_ **(a)** _(Build)_ (Ver)putz _m._ **(b)** _(Art, Med: also ~ of Paris)_ Gips _m; (Med: ~ cast)_ Gipsverband _m._ **to have one's leg in ~** das Bein in Gips haben; **to put a leg in ~** ein Bein eingipsen. **(c)** _(Brit: sticking ~)_ Pflaster _nt._ **2** _vt_ **(a)** _(Build)_ _wall_ verputzen. **(b)** _(col: cover)_ vollkleistern. **to ~ a wall with posters** eine Wand mit Plakaten bepflastern _(col);_ **~ed with mud** schlammbedeckt.
**plaster:** **~board** _n_ Gipskarton(platten _pl)_ _m;_ **~ cast** _n_ _(model, statue)_ Gipsform _f; (of footprint etc)_ Gipsabdruck _m; (Med)_ Gipsverband _m._
**plastered** ['plɑːstəd] _adj pred (col: drunk)_ voll _(col)._ **to get ~** sich vollaufen lassen _(col)._
**plasterer** ['plɑːstərəʳ] _n_ Gipser, Stukkateur _m._
**plastic** ['plæstɪk] **1** _n_ Plastik _nt._ **~s** Kunststoffe _pl._ **2** _adj (lit, fig)_ Plastik-; _food also_ synthetisch. **the ~ arts** die bildenden Künste.
**plastic:** **~ bag** _n_ Plastiktüte _f;_ **~ bullet** _n_ Plastikgeschoß _nt;_ **~ explosive** _n_ Plastiksprengstoff _m._
**plasticine** ® ['plæstɪsiːn] _n (Brit)_ Plastilin _nt._
**plastic:** **~ money** _n_ Kreditkarten _pl,_ Plastikgeld _nt (col);_ **~ surgeon** _n_ plastischer Chirurg; **~ surgery** _n_ plastische Chirurgie; _(cosmetic also)_ Schönheitsoperation _f;_ **he had to have ~ surgery** er mußte sich einer plastischen Operation unterziehen.
**plate** [pleɪt] **1** _n_ **(a)** _(also ~ful)_ Teller _m._ **to have sth handed to one on a ~** _(fig col)_ etw auf einem Tablett serviert bekommen _(col);_ **to have a lot on one's ~** _(fig col)_ viel am Hals haben _(col)._ **(b)** _(gold, silver)_ Tafelgold _nt;_ Tafelsilber _nt; (~d metal)_ vergoldetes/versilbertes Metall. **(c)** _(Tech, Phot, Typ)_ Platte _f; (name~, number~)_ Schild _nt._ **(d)** _(illustration)_ Tafel _f._ **(e)** _(dental ~)_ (Gaumen)platte _f._ **2** _vt (with armour-plating)_ panzern. **to ~ (with gold/silver/nickel/chrome)** vergolden/-silbern/-nickeln/-chromen.
**plateau** ['plætəʊ] _n, pl_ **-s** _or_ **-x** _(Geog)_ Plateau _nt,_ Hochebene _f._ **prices have reached a ~** die Preise haben sich eingependelt.
**plate:** **~ful** _n_ Teller _m_ (voll); **~ glass** _n_ Flachglas, Tafelglas _nt._
**platen** ['plætən] _n (of typewriter, printer)_ Walze _f._
**plate rack** _n (Brit)_ Geschirrständer _m._
**platform** ['plætfɔːm] _n_ **(a)** Plattform _f; (stage)_ Podium _nt,_ Bühne _f._ **(b)** _(Rail)_ Bahnsteig _m._ **from ~ 7** von Gleis 7. **(c)** _(Pol)_ Plattform _f._
**platform:** **~ shoe** _n_ Plateauschuh _m;_ **~ ticket** _n_ Bahnsteigkarte _f._
**plating** ['pleɪtɪŋ] _n (act) (with gold)_ Vergolden _nt; (with silver)_ Versilbern _nt; (with chrome)_ Verchromen _nt; (material)_ Auflage _f; (armour-~)_ Panzerung _f._
**platinum** ['plætɪnəm] _n_ Platin _nt._ **a ~ blonde** eine Platinblonde.
**platitude** ['plætɪtjuːd] _n_ Platitüde, Plattheit _f._
**platonic** [plə'tɒnɪk] _adj love, friendship_ platonisch.
**platoon** [plə'tuːn] _n (Mil)_ Zug _m._
**platter** ['plætəʳ] _n_ Teller _m; (wooden ~ also)_ Brett _nt; (serving dish)_ Platte _f._
**plaudits** ['plɔːdɪts] _npl (liter)_ Ovationen _pl; (also fig)_ Beifall _m._
**plausibility** [ˌplɔːzɪ'bɪlɪtɪ] _n see adj_ Plausibilität _f;_ Glaubwürdigkeit _f._
**plausible** ['plɔːzəbl] _adj_ plausibel; _argument also_ einleuchtend; _story, excuse also_ glaubwürdig.
**play** [pleɪ] **1** _n_ **(a)** _(Sport)_ Spiel _nt._ **to be at ~** beim Spielen sein; **to do/say sth in ~** etw aus Spaß tun/sagen; **~ on words** Wortspiel _nt;_ **children at ~** spielende Kinder; **to abandon ~** das Spiel abbrechen; **there was some exciting ~ towards the end** gegen Ende gab

es einige spannende (Spiel)szenen; **to be in/out of ~** _(ball)_ im Spiel/im Aus sein. **(b)** _(Tech, Mech)_ Spiel _nt._ **1 mm (of) ~** 1 mm Spiel. **(c)** _(Theat)_ (Theater)stück _nt; (Rad)_ Hörspiel _nt; (TV)_ Fernsehspiel _nt._ **(d)** _(fig phrases)_ **to come into ~** ins Spiel kommen; **to give full ~ to one's imagination** seiner Phantasie _(dat)_ freien Lauf lassen; **to bring** _or_ **call sth into ~** etw einsetzen; **to make great ~ of sth** viel Aufhebens von etw machen.
  **2** _vt game, card, role, instrument, tune_ spielen; _(direct) light, hose_ richten. **to ~ sb (at a game)** gegen jdn (ein Spiel) spielen; **to ~ ball** _(fig)_ mitmachen; **to ~ a joke on sb** jdm einen Streich spielen; **to ~ a mean trick on sb** jdn auf gemeine Art hereinlegen; **to ~ the piano** Klavier spielen.
  **3** _vi_ spielen; _(fountain)_ laufen. **to go out to ~** rausgehen und spielen; **to ~ with the idea of doing sth** mit dem Gedanken spielen, etw zu tun; **we don't have much time/money to ~ with** wir haben zeitlich/finanziell nicht viel Spielraum; **he wouldn't ~** _(fig col)_ er wollte nicht mitspielen _(col);_ **he's ~ing at being angry** seine Wut war gespielt; **he's just ~ing at it** er tut nur so; **what are you ~ing at?** _(col)_ was soll (denn) das? _(col);_ **to ~ for money** um Geld spielen; **to ~ for time** _(fig)_ Zeit gewinnen wollen; **to ~ into sb's hands** _(fig)_ jdm in die Hände spielen; **to ~ to sb** jdm vorspielen; **the firemen's hoses ~ed on the flames** die Schläuche der Feuerwehrmänner waren auf die Flammen gerichtet; **the searchlights ~ed over the roofs** die Suchscheinwerfer strichen über die Dächer; **it's playing at the Old Vic next week** _(Theat)_ es läuft nächste Woche im Old Vic.
  ▶**play about** _or_ **around** _vi_ spielen. **to ~ ~ with sth/an idea** mit etw/einer Idee spielen.
  ▶**play along 1** _vi_ mitspielen. **he ~ed ~ with the system** er arrangierte sich mit dem System. **2** _vt sep_ ein falsches Spiel spielen mit; _(in order to gain time)_ hinhalten.
  ▶**play back** _vt sep tape recording_ abspielen. **the conversation was ~ed ~ to us** man spielte uns _(dat)_ das Gespräch vor.
  ▶**play down** _vt sep_ herunterspielen.
  ▶**play off 1** _vt sep_ **to ~ X ~ against Y** X gegen Y ausspielen; **he was ~ing them ~ against each other** er spielte sie gegeneinander aus. **2** _vi (Sport)_ um die Entscheidung spielen.
  ▶**play on 1** _vi_ weiterspielen. **2** _vi +prep obj sb's fears, good nature_ geschickt ausnutzen. **the author is ~ing ~ words** der Autor spielt mit Worten.
  ▶**play out** _vt sep_ **(a)** _(Theat) scene_ darstellen. **(b)** **to be ~ed ~** _(person)_ völlig erschöpft _or_ geschafft sein _(col); (joke etc)_ abgedroschen sein. **(c)** _(Mus: accompany)_ mit Musik hinausgeleiten.
  ▶**play through** _vi +prep obj_ durchspielen.
  ▶**play up 1** _vi_ **(a)** _(Brit col: cause trouble: car, child)_ verrückt spielen _(col)._ **(b)** _(col: flatter)_ **to ~ ~ to sb** jdn umschmeicheln. **2** _vt sep (col)_ **(a)** _(cause trouble to)_ **to ~ sb ~** jdm Schwierigkeiten machen. **(b)** _(exaggerate)_ hochspielen.
  ▶**play upon** _see_ **play on.**
**play:** **~-act** _vi_ Theater spielen; **~-acting** _n (fig)_ Theater(spiel) _nt;_ **~back** _n (switch, recording)_ Wiedergabe _f;_ **~boy** _n_ Playboy _m._
**player** ['pleɪəʳ] _n (Sport, Mus)_ Spieler(in _f) m; (Theat)_ Schauspieler(in _f) m._
**playful** ['pleɪfʊl] _adj_ neckisch; _child, animal_ verspielt, munter.
**play:** **~goer** _n_ Theaterbesucher(in _f) m;_ **~ground** _n_ Spielplatz _m; (Sch)_ (Schul)hof _m;_ **~group** _n_ Spielgruppe _f;_ **~house** _n_ **(a)** _(US: doll's house)_

Puppenstube *f*; **(b)** *(Theat)* Schauspielhaus *nt.*
**playing** ['pleɪɪŋ]: ~ **card** *n* Spielkarte *f*; ~ **field** *n* Sportplatz *m.*
**play:** ~**mate** *n* Spielkamerad(in *f*) *m*; ~**off** *n* Entscheidungsspiel *nt*; ~**pen** *n* Laufstall *m*; ~**room** *n* Spielzimmer *nt*; ~ **school** *n* Kindergarten *m*; ~ **street** *n* Spielstraße *f*; ~**thing** *n (lit, fig)* Spielzeug *nt*; ~**time** *n* Zeit *f* zum Spielen; *(Sch)* große Pause.
**playwright** ['pleɪraɪt] *n* Dramatiker(in *f*) *m*; *(contemporary also)* Stückeschreiber(in *f*) *m.*
**plc, PLC** *(Brit)* = **public limited company** ≃ AG *f.*
**plea** [pliː] *n* **(a)** Bitte *f*; *(general appeal)* Appell *m.* to **make a** ~ **for sth** zu etw aufrufen; **to make a** ~ **for leniency** um Milde bitten. **(b)** *(Jur)* Plädoyer *nt.* to **enter a** ~ **of guilty/not guilty** ein Geständnis ablegen/seine Unschuld erklären; ~ **bargaining** *Verhandlungen pl zwischen Richter und Verteidigung über die Möglichkeit, bestimmte Anklagepunkte fallenzulassen, wenn der Angeklagte sich in anderen Punkten schuldig bekennt.*
**plead** [pliːd] *pret, ptp* ~**ed** *or (Scot, US)* **pled 1** *vt* **(a)** *(argue)* vertreten. **to** ~ **sb's case, to** ~ **the case for sb** *(Jur)* jdn vertreten; **to** ~ **the case for sth** *(fig)* sich für etw einsetzen; **to** ~ **sb's cause** *(fig)* für jds Sache eintreten. **(b)** *(as excuse) ignorance* sich berufen auf *(+acc).* **2** *vi* **(a)** *(beg)* bitten, nachsuchen *(for* um*).* **to** ~ **with sb to do sth** jdn bitten *or* ersuchen *(geh),* etw zu tun. **(b)** *(Jur) (counsel)* das Plädoyer halten. **to** ~ **guilty/not guilty** sich schuldig/nicht schuldig bekennen; **to** ~ **for sth** *(fig)* für etw plädieren.
**pleading** ['pliːdɪŋ] **1** *n* Bitten *nt*; *(Jur)* Plädoyer *nt.* **2** *adj look, voice* flehend.
**pleasant** ['pleznt] *adj* angenehm; *news* erfreulich; *person also, face* nett; *smile* freundlich.
**pleasantly** ['plezntlɪ] *adv* angenehm; *smile, greet etc* freundlich.
**pleasantness** ['plezntnɪs] *n* Freundlichkeit *f.*
**pleasantry** ['plezntrɪ] *n (joking remark)* Scherz *m*; *(polite remark)* Nettigkeit *f.* **to exchange pleasantries** Höflichkeiten austauschen.
**please** [pliːz] **1** *interj* bitte. **(yes,)** ~ *(acceptance)* (ja,) bitte; *(enthusiastic)* oh ja, gerne; **pass the salt,** ~ würden Sie mir bitte das Salz reichen?; **may I?** ~ ~ **do!** darf ich? – bitte sehr!; ~ **don't!** bitte nicht!
**2** *vi* **(a)** **if you** ~ *(form: in request)* wenn ich darum bitten darf; **and then, if you** ~**, he tried** ... und dann, stell dir vor, versuchte er ...; **(just) as you** ~ ganz wie Sie wollen; **to do as one** ~**s** machen *or* tun, was einem gefällt. **(b)** *(cause satisfaction)* gefallen. **anxious** *or* **eager to** ~ darum bemüht, alles richtig zu machen. **3** *vt (give pleasure to)* eine Freude machen *(+dat)*; *(satisfy)* zufriedenstellen; *(do as sb wants)* gefällig sein *(+dat).* **it** ~**s me to see him so happy** es freut mich, daß er so glücklich ist; **you can't** ~ **everybody** man kann es nicht allen recht machen; **there's no pleasing him** er ist nie zufrieden; **to be hard to** ~ schwer zufriedenzustellen sein; **I was only too** ~**d to help** es war mir wirklich eine Freude zu helfen.
**4** *vr* **to** ~ **oneself** tun, was einem gefällt; ~ **yourself, then!** wie Sie wollen!; **you can** ~ **yourself where you sit** es ist Ihnen überlassen, wo Sie sitzen.
**pleased** [pliːzd] *adj (happy)* erfreut; *(satisfied)* zufrieden. **to be** ~ **(about sth)** sich (über etw *acc*) freuen; **I'm** ~ **to hear that** ... es freut mich zu hören, daß ...; ~ **to meet you** angenehm *(form),* freut mich; **to be** ~ **with sb/sth** mit jdm/etw zufrieden sein.

**pleasing** *adj,* ~**ly** *adv* ['pliːzɪŋ, -lɪ] angenehm.
**pleasurable** *adj,* ~**bly** *adv* ['pleʒərəbl, -ɪ] angenehm.
**pleasure** ['pleʒər] *n* **(a)** Freude *f.* **it's a** ~**, (my)** ~ gern (geschehen)!; **with** ~ gern, mit Vergnügen *(form)*; **it gives me great** ~ **to be here** *(form)* es ist mir eine große Freude, hier zu sein; **it would give me great** ~ **to** ... es wäre mir ein Vergnügen, zu ...; **to have the** ~ **of doing sth** das Vergnügen haben, etw zu tun; **Mrs X requests the** ~ **of Mr Y's company** *(form)* Frau X gibt sich die Ehre, Herrn Y einzuladen *(form).* **(b)** *(source of* ~*)* Vergnügen *nt.* **he's a** ~ **to teach** es ist ein Vergnügen, ihn zu unterrichten; **the** ~**s of country life** die Freuden des Landlebens; **all the** ~**s of London** alle Vergnügungen Londons. **(c)** *(iro, form: will)* Wunsch *m.* **at one's** ~ nach Belieben; **to await sb's** ~ abwarten, was jd zu tun geruht.
**pleasure** *in cpds* Vergnügungs-; ~ **boat** *n (steamer)* Vergnügungsdampfer *m*; ~ **cruise** *n* Kreuzfahrt *f*; ~**loving** *adj* lebenslustig, leichtlebig *(pej)*; ~**seeking** *adj* vergnügungssüchtig.
**pleat** [pliːt] **1** *n* Falte *f.* **2** *vt* fälteln. ~**ed skirt** Faltenrock *m*; ~ **trousers** Bundfaltenhose *f.*
**pleb** [pleb] *n (pej col)* Plebejer(in *f*) *(pej),* Prolet(in *f*) *(pej col) m.*
**plebeian** [plɪ'biːən] **1** *adj* plebejisch. **2** *n* Plebejer(in *f*) *m.*
**plebiscite** ['plebɪsɪt] *n* Plebiszit *nt.*
**plectrum** ['plektrəm] *n* Plektron *nt.*
**pled** [pled] *(US, Scot) pret, ptp of* **plead.**
**pledge** [pledʒ] **1** *n (in pawnshop, of love)* Pfand *nt*; *(promise)* Versprechen *nt.* **as a** ~ **of** als Zeichen *(+gen)*; **under (the)** ~ **of secrecy** unter dem Siegel der Verschwiegenheit; **election** ~**s** Wahlversprechen *pl*; **to sign** *or* **take the** ~ *(hum col)* dem Alkohol abschwören *(usu hum).* **2** *vt* **(a)** *(give as security, pawn)* verpfänden. **(b)** *(promise)* versprechen, zusichern. **to** ~ **one's word** sein Wort geben; **to** ~ **support for sb/sth** jdm/einer Sache seine Unterstützung zusichern; **I am** ~**d to secrecy** ich bin zum Schweigen verpflichtet.
**plenary** ['pliːnərɪ] *adj* ~ **session** Plenarsitzung *f*; ~ **powers** unbeschränkte Vollmachten *pl.*
**plenipotentiary** [ˌplenɪpə'tenʃərɪ] *n* (General)bevollmächtigte(r) *mf.*
**plentiful** ['plentɪful] *adj* reichlich; *commodities, gold etc* reichlich vorhanden; *hair* voll. **to be in** ~ **supply** reichlich vorhanden sein.
**plenty** ['plentɪ] *n* **(a)** eine Menge. **land of** ~ Land des Überflusses; **times of** ~ Zeiten des Überflusses; **in** ~ im Überfluß; **three kilos will be** ~ drei Kilo sind reichlich; **take** ~ nimm dir reichlich; **there are still** ~ **left** es sind immer noch eine ganze Menge da. **(b)** ~ **of** viel, eine Menge; ~ **of time/milk/eggs** viel *or* eine Menge Zeit/Milch/viele *or* eine Menge Eier; **a country with** ~ **of natural resources** ein Land mit umfangreichen Bodenschätzen; **we arrived in** ~ **of time to get a good seat** wir kamen so rechtzeitig, daß wir einen guten Platz bekamen.
**plethora** ['pleθərə] *n (form)* Fülle *f (of* von*).*
**pleurisy** ['plʊərɪsɪ] *n* Brustfellentzündung *f.*
**pliability** [plaɪə'bɪlɪtɪ] *n see adj* Biegsamkeit *f*; Geschmeidigkeit *f*; Formbarkeit *f.*
**pliable** ['plaɪəbl] *adj* biegsam; *leather* geschmeidig; *mind, person* formbar.
**pliers** ['plaɪəz] *npl (also pair of* ~*)* Zange *f.*
**plight** [plaɪt] *n* Not *f,* Elend *nt*; *(of economy etc)* Verfall *m.* **to be in a sorry** ~ in einem traurigen Zustand sein.
**plimsoll** ['plɪmsəl] *n (Brit)* Turnschuh *m.*

**plinth**

**plinth** [plɪnθ] *n* Sockel *m*.
**PLO** = **Palestine Liberation Organization** PLO *f*.
**plod** [plɒd] *vi* to ~ **up a hill** einen Hügel hinaufstapfen; **to** ~ **along** *or* **on** weiterstapfen; **to** ~ **away at sth** sich mit etw herumquälen.
**plodder** ['plɒdə'] *n* zähe(r) Arbeiter(in *f*) *m*.
**plonk¹** [plɒŋk] **1** *n* Bums *m*. **it fell with a** ~ **to the floor** es fiel mit einem Bums auf den Boden. **2** *adv fall, land* bums. **3** *vt* (*col: also* ~ **down**) (*drop, put down*) hinschmeißen (*col*); (*bang down*) hinknallen (*col*). **to** ~ **oneself (down)** sich hinpflanzen (*col*).
**plonk²** *n* (*Brit col: wine*) (billiger) Wein, Gesöff *nt* (*hum, pej*).
**plonker** [plɒŋkə'] *n* (*col*) Idiot *m*.
**plop** [plɒp] **1** *n* Plumps *m*; (*in water*) Platsch *m*. **2** *vi* (*make a plopping sound*) platschen.
**plot** [plɒt] **1** *n* (a) (*Agr*) Stück *nt* Land; (*bed: in garden*) Beet *nt*; (*building* ~) Grundstück *nt*; (*allotment*) Schrebergarten *m*. **a** ~ **of land** ein Stück *nt* Land. (b) (*conspiracy*) Komplott *nt*. (c) (*Liter, Theat*) Handlung *f*. **2** *vt* (a) (*plan*) planen, aushecken (*col*). **they** ~**ted to kill him** sie planten gemeinsam, ihn zu töten. (b) *position, course* feststellen; (*draw on map*) einzeichnen; (*Math, Med*) *curve* aufzeichnen. **3** *vi* sich verschwören.
**plotter¹** ['plɒtə'] *n* Verschwörer(in *f*) *m*.
**plotter²** *n* (*Comp*) Plotter *m*.
**plotting** ['plɒtɪŋ] *n* Intrigen *pl*.
**plough**, (*US*) **plow** [plaʊ] **1** *n* Pflug *m*. **the P**~ (*Astron*) der Wagen. **2** *vt* pflügen. **3** *vi* (*vehicle*) rasen (*into* in +*acc*).
▶**plough back** *vt sep* (*Agr*) unterpflügen; (*Comm*) *profits* wieder hineinstecken (*into* in +*acc*).
▶**plough through** *vt snow, mud etc* sich kämpfen durch; *book, work* sich durchackern durch (*col*).
▶**plough up** *vt sep field* umpflügen.
**plough**, (*US*) **plow**: ~**land** *n* Ackerland *nt*; ~**man** *n* Pflüger *m*; ~**man's lunch** *n* Brot *nt* und Käse mit *Salat und Mixed Pickles*.
**ploy** [plɔɪ] *n* (*stratagem*) Trick *m*.
**pluck** [plʌk] **1** *n* (*courage*) Mut *m*. **2** *vt fruit, flower* pflücken; *chicken* rupfen; *guitar, eyebrows* zupfen. **to** ~ (**at**) **sb's sleeve** jdn am Ärmel zupfen; **to** ~ **up courage** all seinen Mut zusammennehmen.
**pluckily** ['plʌkɪlɪ] *adv* tapfer.
**plucky** ['plʌkɪ] *adj* (+*er*) *person, smile* tapfer; *action, person* mutig.
**plug** [plʌg] **1** *n* (a) (*in sink*) Stöpsel *m*; (*for stopping a leak, in barrel*) Propfen *m*. (b) (*Elec*) Stecker *m*; (*Aut: spark* ~) (Zünd)kerze *f*. (c) (*col: piece of publicity*) Schleichwerbung *f no pl*. **to give sb/sth a** ~ **für** jdn/etw Schleichwerbung machen. **2** *vt* (a) (*stop*) *gap, leak* zustopfen. (b) (*insert*) stecken. (c) (*col: publicize*) Schleichwerbung machen für (*col*). (d) (*col: push, put forward*) *idea* hausieren gehen mit.
▶**plug away** *vi* (*col*) ackern (*col*). **to** ~ ~ **at sth** sich mit etw abrackern (*col*); **he kept** ~**ging** ~ er hat nicht lockergelassen.
▶**plug in 1** *vt sep TV, heater etc* anschließen; *telephone etc* einstöpseln. **to be** ~**ged** ~ angeschlossen sein. **2** *vi* sich anschließen lassen. **where does the TV** ~ ~? wo wird der Fernseher angeschlossen?
**plughole** ['plʌɡhaʊl] *n* Abfluß(loch *nt*) *m*.
**plum** [plʌm] **1** *n* (a) (*fruit, tree*) Pflaume *f*; (*Victoria* ~, *dark blue*) Zwetsch(g)e *f*. (b) (*colour*) Pflaumenblau *nt*. (c) (*fig col*) **a real** ~ **of a job** ein Bombenjob (*col*). **2** *adj attr* (*col*) *job, position* Bomben- (*col*), Mords- (*col*).
**plumage** ['pluːmɪdʒ] *n* Gefieder *nt*.
**plumb** [plʌm] **1** *n* (~-*line*) Lot *nt*. **out of** ~ nicht im Lot. **2** *adv* (*col*) (*completely*) total (*col*); (*exactly*) ge

nau. ~ **crazy** vollkommen *or* total (*col*) verrückt; ~ **in the middle** (haar)genau in der Mitte. **3** *vt* (a) *ocean, depth* (aus)loten. (b) (*fig*) *mystery etc* ergründen. **to** ~ **the depths of despair** die tiefste Verzweiflung erleben.
▶**plumb in** *vt washing machine etc* fest anschließen.
**plumb bob** *n* Lot, Senkblei *nt*.
**plumber** ['plʌmə'] *n* Installateur, Klempner *m*.
**plumbing** ['plʌmɪŋ] *n* (a) (*work*) Installieren *nt*. (b) (*fittings*) Rohre, Leitungen *pl*.
**plumbline** ['plʌmlaɪn] *n* Lot.
**plume** [pluːm] *n* Feder *f*; (*on helmet*) Federbusch *m*. ~ **of smoke** Rauchwolke *f*.
**plummet** ['plʌmɪt] *vi* (*bird, plane etc*) hinunter-/ herunterstürzen; (*sales*) stark zurückgehen; (*currency*) fallen, absacken (*to* auf +*acc*).
**plump** [plʌmp] *adj* (+*er*) rundlich, pummelig (*col*); *legs etc* stämmig; *face* rundlich, voll.
▶**plump for** *vi* +*prep obj* sich entscheiden für.
▶**plump up** *vt sep pillow* aufschütteln; *chicken* mästen.
**plumpness** ['plʌmpnɪs] *n* Rundlichkeit *f*.
**plunder** ['plʌndə'] **1** *n* (a) (*act*) (*of place*) Plünderung *f*; (*of things*) Raub *m*. (b) (*loot*) Beute *f*. **2** *vti place* plündern (*also hum*).
**plunge** [plʌndʒ] **1** *vt* (a) (*thrust*) stecken; (*into water etc*) tauchen. **he** ~**d his knife into his victim's back** er jagte seinem Opfer das Messer in den Rücken. (b) (*fig*) **to** ~ **the country into debt** das Land in Schulden stürzen; **the room was/we were** ~**d into darkness** das Zimmer war in Dunkelheit getaucht/ tiefe Dunkelheit umfing uns.
  **2** *vi* (a) (*dive*) tauchen; (*goalkeeper*) hechten. (b) (*rush, esp downward*) stürzen. **to** ~ **to one's death** zu Tode stürzen. (c) (*share prices, currency etc*) stark fallen. (d) (*fig: into debate, studies etc*) sich stürzen (*into* in +*acc*).
  **3** *vr* (*into studies, job etc*) sich stürzen (*into* in +*acc*).
  **4** *n* (*lit, fig*) Sturz *m*; (*dive*) (Kopf)sprung *m*. **to take the** ~ (*fig col*) den Sprung wagen.
**plunger** ['plʌndʒə'] *n* (a) (*piston*) Tauchkolben *m*. (b) (*for clearing drain*) Sauger *m*.
**plunging** ['plʌndʒɪŋ] *adj neckline, back* tief ausgeschnitten.
**pluperfect** [pluː'pɜːfɪkt] *n* Plusquamperfekt *nt*.
**plural** ['plʊərəl] **1** *adj* (*Gram*) Mehrzahl-, Plural-. **2** *n* Mehrzahl *f*, Plural *m*. **in the** ~ im Plural, in der Mehrzahl.
**plus** [plʌs] **1** *prep* plus (+*dat*); (*together with*) und (außerdem). **2** *adj* ~ **sign** Pluszeichen *nt*; **a** ~ **factor** ein Pluspunkt *m*; **on the** ~ **side** auf der Habenseite; **50 hours** ~ **a week** mehr als 50 Stunden pro Woche. **3** *n* (*sign*) Pluszeichen *nt*; (*positive factor*) Pluspunkt *m*; (*extra*) Plus *nt*.
**plush** [plʌʃ] **1** *n* Plüsch *m*. **2** *adj* (+*er*) (*col: luxurious*) feudal (*col*); *hotel also* Nobel-; *furnishing also* elegant, vornehm.
**Pluto** ['pluːtəʊ] *n* (*Astron*) Pluto *m*.
**plutocrat** ['pluːtəʊkræt] *n* Plutokrat(in *f*) *m*.
**plutonium** [pluː'təʊnɪəm] *n* Plutonium *nt*.
**ply¹** [plaɪ] *n* (a) **three-**~ *wood* dreischichtig; *wool* dreifädig; *tissues* dreilagig. (b) = **plywood**.
**ply²** **1** *vt* (a) *tool, brush etc* gebrauchen; *oars* einsetzen. (b) *trade* ausüben, betreiben. (c) (*ships*) *sea, river* befahren. (d) **to** ~ **sb with questions** jdn mit Fragen überhäufen; **to** ~ **sb with drink(s)** jdm immer wieder etwas zum Trinken aufdrängen. **2** *vi* (*ship*) **to** ~ **between** verkehren zwischen; **to** ~ **for hire** seine Dienste anbieten.

**plywood** ['plaɪwʊd] n Sperrholz nt.
**PM** = Prime Minister.
**pm** = post meridiem p.m.
**PMT** n abbr (= **premenstrual tension**) prämenstruelle Spannung.
**pneumatic** [njuːˈmætɪk] adj Luft-. ~ **drill** Preßluftbohrer m.
**pneumonia** [njuːˈməʊnɪə] n Lungenentzündung f.
**PO** = (a) **post office** PA. (b) **postal order** PA.
**poach**[1] [pəʊtʃ] vt egg pochieren; fish (blau) dünsten. ~**ed eggs** verlorene Eier.
**poach**[2] vti wildern (for auf +acc); ideas etc klauen (col). **to ~ (on sb's territory)** jdm ins Gehege kommen.
**poacher** ['pəʊtʃər] n Wilderer m.
**poaching** ['pəʊtʃɪŋ] n Wildern nt, Wilderei f.
**PO Box** n Postfach nt.
**pocket** ['pɒkɪt] 1 n (a) (in garment) Tasche f. **to have sb/sth in one's ~** (fig) jdn/etw in der Tasche haben (col); **they live in each other's ~s** (fig) sie hängen ständig zusammen (col). (b) (receptacle: in suitcase, file etc) Fach nt; (Billiards) Loch nt. (c) (resources) **to ˙be a drain on one's ~** jds Geldbeutel strapazieren (col); **to be out of ~** einen Verlust machen; **to be in ~** auf sein Geld kommen (col); **I was £100 in ~ after the sale** nach dem Verkauf war ich um £100 reicher; **to put one's hand in one's ~** in die Tasche greifen. (d) (small area) Gebiet nt. ~ **of resistance** Widerstandsnest nt. 2 adj comb, edition Taschen-. 3 vt (a) (put in one's pocket) einstecken. **to ~ one's pride** seinen Stolz überwinden. (b) (gain) kassieren; (misappropriate) einstecken (col).
**pocket:** ~**book** n (a) (notebook) Notizbuch nt; (b) (US) (wallet) Brieftasche f; (handbag) Handtasche f; ~ **calculator** n Taschenrechner m; ~**ful** n a ~**ful** eine Tasche voll; ~ **handkerchief** n Taschentuch nt; ~**knife** n Taschenmesser nt; ~**money** n Taschengeld nt; ~-**size(d)** adj book im Taschenformat; camera Miniatur-.
**pock** [pɒk]: ~ **mark** n Pockennarbe f; ~**marked** adj face pockennarbig; surface narbig.
**pod** [pɒd] n (Bot) Hülse f; (of peas also) Schote f.
**podgy** ['pɒdʒɪ] adj (+er) pummelig; face schwammig.
**podiatrist** [pɒˈdiːətrɪst] n (US) Fußpfleger(in f) m.
**podium** ['pəʊdɪəm] n Podest nt.
**poem** ['pəʊɪm] n Gedicht nt.
**poet** ['pəʊɪt] n Dichter(in f) m. ~ **laureate** Hofdichter m.
**poetess** ['pəʊɪtes] n Dichterin f.
**poetic** [pəʊˈetɪk] adj poetisch; talent also dichterisch; place, scene malerisch. ~ **justice** poetische Gerechtigkeit; ~ **licence** (Brit) or **license** (US) dichterische Freiheit.
**poetically** [pəʊˈetɪkəlɪ] adv poetisch; gifted dichterisch.
**poetry** ['pəʊɪtrɪ] n Dichtung f. **to write** ~ Gedichte schreiben; ~ **reading** Dichterlesung f.
**po-faced** ['pəʊfeɪst] adj (col) grimmig.
**poignancy** ['pɔɪnjənsɪ] n see adj Ergreifende(s) nt; Wehmut f; Schmerzlichkeit f; Schärfe f. **he writes with great ~** er schreibt sehr ergreifend.
**poignant** ['pɔɪnjənt] adj ergreifend; memories, look wehmütig; distress, regret schmerzlich; wit scharf.
**poignantly** ['pɔɪnjəntlɪ] adv ergreifend; (wistfully) wehmütig.
**point** [pɔɪnt] 1 n (a) Punkt m; (place also) Stelle f; (sharp end) Spitze f; (on thermometer) Grad m. **(nought)** ~ **seven (0.7)** null Komma sieben (0,7); **from all** ~**s (of the compass)** aus allen (Himmels)richtungen; **up to a** ~ bis zu einem gewissen Grad or Punkt; **at the** ~ **of a gun** mit vorgehaltener Pistole; **not to put too fine a** ~ **on it** (fig) um ganz offen zu sein; **the train stops at Slough and all** ~**s east** der Zug hält in Slough und allen Orten östlich davon; ~ **of departure** (lit, fig) Ausgangspunkt m; ~ **of view** Gesichtspunkt m; **from my** ~ **of view** aus meiner Sicht; **from the** ~ **of view of productivity** von der Produktivität her gesehen; **at this** ~ (spatially) an dieser Stelle; (in time) (then) in diesem Augenblick; (now) jetzt; **from that** ~ **on they were friends** von da an waren sie Freunde; **at no** ~ nie; **at no** ~ **in the book** an keiner Stelle des Buches; **to be (up)on the** ~ **of doing sth** im Begriff sein, etw zu tun; **to reach the** ~ **of no return** (fig) den Punkt erreichen, von dem an es kein Zurück gibt; **they provoked him to the** ~ **where he lost his temper** sie reizten ihn so lange, bis er die Geduld verlor; **severe to the** ~ **of cruelty** streng bis an die Grenze der Grausamkeit; **when it comes to the** ~ wenn es darauf ankommt; **to win on** ~**s** nach Punkten gewinnen; **the** ~ **at issue** der strittige Punkt; **a 12-**~ **plan** ein Zwölfpunkte-Plan m; **a** ~ **of interest** ein interessanter Punkt; **to come to the** ~ zur Sache kommen; **to keep to the** ~ beim Thema bleiben; **beside the** ~ irrelevant; **his remarks are very much to the** ~ seine Bemerkungen sind sehr sachbezogen; **my** ~ **was ...** was ich sagen wollte, war ...; **to make a** ~ ein Argument nt anbringen; **he made the** ~ **that ...** er betonte, daß ...; **you have a** ~ **there** (col); **I take your** ~, ~ **taken** ich akzeptiere, was Sie sagen; (I understand) ich habe schon begriffen; **to gain** or **carry one's** ~ sich durchsetzen; **to get** or **see the** ~ verstehen, worum es geht; **to miss the** ~ nicht verstehen, worum es geht; **he missed the** ~ **of what I was saying** er begriff nicht, worauf ich hinauswollte; **that's not the** ~ darum geht es nicht; **that's the whole** ~ das ist es ja gerade; **a case in** ~ ein einschlägiger Fall; **the case in** ~ der zur Debatte stehende Punkt; **to make a** ~ **of sth** auf etw (acc) Wert legen; **he made a special** ~ **of being early** er legte besonderen Wert darauf, früh dazusein; **a** ~ **of principle** eine grundsätzliche Frage; **a** ~ **of order** eine Frage der Geschäftsordnung; **good/bad** ~**s** (characteristics) gute/schlechte Seiten pl; **he has his** ~**s** er hat auch seine guten Seiten.
(b) (purpose) Zweck, Sinn m. **there's no** ~ **in staying** es hat keinen Zweck or Sinn zu bleiben; **I don't see the** ~ **of carrying on** ich sehe keinen Sinn darin, weiterzumachen; **what's the** ~? was soll's?; **the** ~ **is that ...** die Sache ist die, daß ...; **the** ~ **of the story** die Pointe (der Geschichte).
(c) ~**s** pl (Brit Rail) Weichen pl.
(d) ~**s** pl (Aut) Unterbrecherkontakte pl.
(e) (Brit Elec: power ~) Steckdose f.
2 vt (a) (aim, direct) gun, telescope etc richten (at auf +acc). **he** ~**ed his stick in the direction of the house** er zeigte mit dem Stock auf das Haus. (b) (mark, show) zeigen. **to** ~ **the way** (lit, fig) den Weg weisen. (c) (Build) wall, brickwork verfugen.
3 vi (a) (with finger etc) zeigen, deuten (at, to auf +acc). **he** ~**ed in the direction of the house/towards the house** er zeigte in die Richtung des Hauses/zum Haus; **the compass needle** ~**s (to the) north** die Kompaßnadel zeigt nach Norden. (b) (indicate, point out) hinweisen; (facts, events also) hindeuten (to auf +acc). **everything** ~**s that way** alles weist in diese Richtung. (c) (face, be situated: building, valley etc) liegen; (be aimed: gun, vehicle etc) gerichtet sein. **in which direction is it** ~**ing?** in welche Richtung zeigt es?

▶**point out** *vt sep* zeigen auf *(+acc)*. **could you ~ him ~ to me?** kannst du mir zeigen, wer er ist?; **to ~ sth ~ (to sb)** (jdn) auf etw *(acc)* hinweisen; **she ~ed ~ that** ... sie wies darauf hin, daß ...
▶**point up** *vt sep (emphasize)* betonen.
**point-blank** [ˌpɔɪntˈblæŋk] **1** *adj* direkt; *refusal* glatt. **at ~ range** aus kürzester Entfernung. **2** *adv fire* aus kürzester Entfernung; *refuse* rundheraus.
**point duty** *n* Verkehrsdienst *m*.
**pointed** [ˈpɔɪntɪd] *adj* **(a)** *(sharp) stick, roof, nose* spitz. **~ arch** Spitzbogen *m*. **(b)** *(obvious in intention) remark, comment* scharf, spitz; *reference* unverblümt; *gesture, departure* ostentativ.
**pointedly** [ˈpɔɪntɪdlɪ] *adv refer* unverblümt; *leave* demonstrativ.
**pointer** [ˈpɔɪntər] *n* **(a)** *(indicator)* Zeiger *m*; *(stick)* Zeigestock *m*. **(b)** *(dog)* Pointer, Vorstehhund *m*. **(c)** *(fig: hint)* Hinweis *m*; *(indication also)* Anzeichen *nt*. **a ~ to a possible solution** ein Hinweis auf eine mögliche Lösung.
**pointless** *adj*, **~ly** *adv* [ˈpɔɪntlɪs, -lɪ] sinnlos.
**pointlessness** [ˈpɔɪntlɪsnɪs] *n* Sinnlosigkeit *f*.
**point of sale** *n (Comm)* Verkaufsstelle *f*.
**poise** [pɔɪz] **1** *n* **(a)** *(carriage of head, body)* Haltung *f*; *(grace)* Grazie *f*. **(b)** *(composure)* Gelassenheit *f*; *(self-possession)* Selbstsicherheit *f*. **2** *vt (balance, hold balanced)* balancieren. **we sat ~d on the edge of our chairs** wir balancierten auf den Stuhlkanten; **the enemy are ~d to attack** der Feind steht bereit zum Angriff.
**poised** [pɔɪzd] *adj* selbstsicher.
**poison** [ˈpɔɪzn] **1** *n (lit, fig)* Gift *nt*. **to hate sb like ~** jdn wie die Pest hassen *(col)*. **2** *vt (lit, fig)* vergiften; *air, rivers* verpesten; *marriage* zerrütten. **it won't ~ you** *(col)* das wird dich nicht umbringen *(col)*; **to ~ sb's mind against sb/sth** jdn gegen jdn/etw aufstacheln.
**poison gas** *n* Giftgas *nt*.
**poisoning** [ˈpɔɪznɪŋ] *n (lit, fig)* Vergiftung *f*.
**poison ivy** *n* Giftefeu *m*.
**poisonous** [ˈpɔɪznəs] *adj* **(a)** giftig; *snake, plants etc also* Gift-. **(b)** *(fig) literature, doctrine* zersetzend; *remark, tongue etc* giftig; *propaganda also* Hetz-.
**poke** [pəʊk] **1** *n (jab)* Stoß, Schubs *(col) m*. **2** *vt* **(a)** *(jab with stick)* stoßen; *(with finger)* stupsen. **to ~ the fire** das Feuer schüren; **he accidentally ~d me in the eye** er hat mir aus Versehen ins Auge gestoßen. **(b)** *(US col: punch)* hauen *(col)*. **(c)** *(thrust)* **to ~ one's head/a stick into sth** seinen Kopf/einen Stock in etw *(acc)* stecken; **he ~d his head around the door** er steckte seinen Kopf durch die Tür. **(d)** *(make by poking)* hole bohren. **3** *vi* **his elbows were poking through his sleeves** an seinen Ärmeln kamen schon die Ellenbogen durch; **to ~ at sth** *(testing)* etw prüfen; *(searching)* in etw *(dat)* stochern; **well, if you will go poking into things that don't concern you** ... na ja, wenn du deine Nase ständig in Dinge steckst, die dich nichts angehen ...
▶**poke about** or **around** *vi* **(a)** *(prod)* herumstochern. **(b)** *(col: nose about)* schnüffeln *(col)*.
▶**poke out** **1** *vi* vorstehen. **2** *vt sep* **to ~ sb's eye ~** jdm das Auge ausstechen.
**poker¹** [ˈpəʊkər] *n (for fire)* Schürhaken *m*.
**poker²** *n (Cards)* Poker *nt*.
**poker-faced** [ˈpəʊkəˌfeɪst] *adj* mit einem Pokergesicht; *(bored)* mit unbewegter Miene.
**poky** [ˈpəʊkɪ] *adj (+er) (pej) room, house* winzig. **it's so ~ in here** es ist so eng hier.
**Poland** [ˈpəʊlənd] *n* Polen *nt*.
**polar** [ˈpəʊlər] *adj* Polar-, polar. **~ bear** Polar- *or* Eisbär *m*.
**polarity** [pəʊˈlærɪtɪ] *n (Phys, fig)* Polarität *f*.
**polarization** [ˌpəʊləraɪzeɪʃən] *n (Phys)* Polarisation *f*; *(fig)* Polarisierung *f*.
**polarize** [ˈpəʊləraɪz] **1** *vt* polarisieren. **2** *vi* sich polarisieren.
**Polaroid** ® [ˈpəʊlərɔɪd] *n* Polaroidkamera ®, Sofortbildkamera *f*.
**Pole** [pəʊl] *n* Pole *m*, Polin *f*.
**pole¹** [pəʊl] *n* Stange *f*; *(flag~, telegraph ~ also)* Mast *m*; *(for vaulting)* Stab *m*.
**pole²** *n (Geog, Astron, Elec)* Pol *m*. **they are ~s apart** sie *(acc)* trennen Welten.
**pole:** **~bean** *n (US)* Strangenbohne *f*; **~cat** *n* Iltis *m*; *(US)* Skunk *m*, Stinktier *nt*.
**polemic** [pɒˈlemɪk] **1** *adj* polemisch. **2** *n* Polemik *f*.
**pole:** **~ position** *n (Motor racing)* Pole-position *f*, bester Startplatz für dem Trainingsschnellsten; **~star** *n* Polarstern *m*; **~ vault 1** *n* Stabhochsprung *m*; **2** *vi* stabhochspringen; **~ vaulter** *n* Stabhochspringer *m*.
**police** [pəˈliːs] **1** *n (+sing vb: institution, +pl vb: policemen)* Polizei *f*. **hundreds of ~** Hunderte von Polizisten; **extra ~ were called in** es wurden zusätzliche Polizeikräfte angefordert. **2** *vt road, frontier* kontrollieren.
**police:** **~ car** *n* Polizeiwagen *m*; **~ constable** *n (Brit)* Polizist *m*; **~ department** *n (US)* Polizeibehörde *f*; **~ dog** *n* Polizeihund *m*; **~ escort** *n* Polizeieskorte *f*; **~ force** *n* Polizei *f*; **~man** *n* Polizist *m*; **~ officer** *n* Polizeibeamter *m*; **~ presence** *n* Polizeiaufgebot *nt*; **~ record** *n* **to have a ~ record** vorbestraft sein; **~ state** *n* Polizeistaat *m*; **~ station** *n* (Polizei)wache *f*; **~woman** *n* Polizistin *f*.
**policy¹** [ˈpɒlɪsɪ] *n* Politik *f no pl*; *(of business also)* Geschäftspolitik *f no pl (on bei)*, Praktiken *pl (pej) (on* in bezug auf *+acc)*; *(of government, newspaper also)* Linie *f*; *(of political party also)* Programm *nt*; *(principle)* Grundsatz *m*. **our ~ on immigration/recruitment** unsere Einwanderungs-/Einstellungspolitik; **foreign ~** Außenpolitik; **my ~ is to wait and see** meine Devise heißt abwarten; **it was good/bad ~** das war (taktisch) klug/unklug.
**policy²** *n (also insurance ~)* (Versicherungs)police *f*. **~ holder** Versicherungsnehmer *m*.
**polio** [ˈpəʊlɪəʊ] *n* Polio, Kinderlähmung *f*.
**Polish** [ˈpəʊlɪʃ] **1** *adj* polnisch. **2** *n (language)* Polnisch *nt*.
**polish** [ˈpɒlɪʃ] **1** *n* **(a)** *(shoe ~)* Creme *f*; *(floor ~)* Bohnerwachs *nt*; *(furniture ~)* Politur *f*; *(metal ~)* Poliermittel *nt*; *(nail ~)* Lack *m*. **to give sth a ~** etw polieren; *shoes, silver also* etw putzen; *floor* etw bohnern. **(b)** *(shine)* Glanz *m*; *(of furniture)* Politur *f*. **high ~** Hochglanz *m*; **to put a ~ on sth** Glanz auf etw *(acc)* bringen. **(c)** *(fig: refinement)* Schliff *m*; *(of performance)* Brillanz *f*. **he lacks ~** ihm fehlt der Schliff/die Brillanz. **2** *vt* **(a)** polieren; *silver, shoes also* putzen; *floor* bohnern. **(b)** *(fig) performance* den letzten Schliff geben *(+dat)*; *manner, style also* verfeinern.
▶**polish off** *vt sep (col) food* verputzen *(col)*; *drink* wegputzen *(col)*; *work* erledigen.
▶**polish up** *vt sep* **(a)** *floor, silver etc* auf Hochglanz bringen. **(b)** *(fig: improve) style, one's French etc* aufpolieren *(col)*; *work* überarbeiten.
**polished** [ˈpɒlɪʃt] *adj* **(a)** *surface, furniture* poliert; *floor* gebohnert; *stone, glass* geschliffen. **(b)** *style etc* verfeinert; *performance, performer* brillant. **(c)** *manners* geschliffen.
**polite** [pəˈlaɪt] *adj (+er)* höflich. **it wouldn't be ~** es wäre unhöflich; **be ~ about her cooking** mach ein

paar höfliche Bemerkungen über ihre Kochkunst; **I was just being** ~ ich wollte nur höflich sein; **we sat around making** ~ **conversation** wir saßen zusammen und machten Konversation.
**politely** [pə'laɪtlɪ] adv höflich.
**politeness** [pə'laɪtnɪs] n Höflichkeit f.
**politic** ['pɒlɪtɪk] adj (taktisch) klug.
**political** [pə'lɪtɪkəl] adj politisch. ~ **asylum** politisches Asyl; ~ **prisoner** politischer Gefangener.
**politically** [pə'lɪtɪkəlɪ] adv politisch.
**politician** [,pɒlɪ'tɪʃən] n Politiker(in f) m.
**politics** ['pɒlɪtɪks] n (a) (+pl vb) Politik f. **what are his** ~? welche politischen Ansichten hat er? (b) (+ sing or pl vb) Politik f. **to go into** ~ in die Politik gehen; **to talk** ~ über Politik reden.
**polka** ['pɒlkə] n Polka f.
**polka dot 1** n Tupfen m. **2** adj gepunktet.
**poll** [pəʊl] **1** n (a) (Pol: voting) Abstimmung f; (election) Wahl f. **to take a** ~ eine Abstimmung durchführen. (b) (total of votes cast) Wahlbeteiligung f; (for candidate) Stimmenanteil m. **there was an 84%** ~ **die Wahlbeteiligung betrug** 84%; **they got 34% of the** ~ sie bekamen 34% der Stimmen. (c) ~s (voting place) Wahllokale pl; (election) Wahl f; **to go to the** ~s **zur** Wahl gehen; **a defeat at the** ~s eine Wahlniederlage. (d) (opinion ~) Umfrage f. **2** vt votes erhalten; (in opinion ~) befragen. **40% of those** ~**ed supported the Government** 40% der Befragten waren für die Regierung.
**pollen** ['pɒlən] n Blütenstaub, Pollen m. ~ **count** Pollenflug m.
**pollinate** ['pɒlɪneɪt] vt bestäuben.
**pollination** [,pɒlɪ'neɪʃən] n Bestäubung f.
**polling** ['pəʊlɪŋ] n Stimmabgabe, Wahl f. ~ **has been heavy** die Wahlbeteiligung war hoch.
**polling:** ~ **booth** n Wahlkabine f; ~ **day** n Wahltag m; ~ **station** n Wahllokal nt.
**pollster** ['pəʊlstər] n Meinungsforscher(in f) m.
**polltax** n Kopfsteuer f.
**pollutant** [pə'lu:tənt] n Schadstoff m.
**pollute** [pə'lu:t] vt verschmutzen, verunreinigen; (fig) mind verderben.
**pollution** [pə'lu:ʃən] n (a) Umweltverschmutzung f. (b) (of rivers etc) Verschmutzung, Verunreinigung f; (fig) Verpestung f.
**polo** ['pəʊləʊ] n Polo nt.
**polo:** ~ **neck** n Rollkragen m; (sweater) Rollkragenpullover m; ~ **shirt** n Polohemd nt.
**poltergeist** ['pɒltəgaɪst] n Poltergeist m.
**poly** (Brit) = **polytechnic.**
**polyester** [,pɒlɪ'estər] n Polyester m.
**polyethylene** [,pɒlɪ'eθɪli:n] n (esp US) Polyäthylen nt.
**polygamy** [pɒ'lɪgəmɪ] n Polygamie, Vielehe f.
**polyglot** ['pɒlɪglɒt] **1** adj vielsprachig. **2** n (person) Polyglotte(r) mf.
**polygon** ['pɒlɪgən] n Polygon, Vieleck nt.
**polymath** ['pɒlɪmæθ] n vielseitig Gebildete(r) mf.
**polymer** ['pɒlɪmər] n Polymer nt.
**Polynesia** [,pɒlɪ'ni:zɪə] n Polynesien nt.
**Polynesian** [,pɒlɪ'ni:zɪən] **1** adj polynesisch. **2** n Polynesier(in f) m.
**polyp** ['pɒlɪp] n Polyp m.
**polystyrene** [,pɒlɪ'staɪri:n] n Polystyrol nt; (expanded also) Styropor ® nt.
**polytechnic** [,pɒlɪ'teknɪk] n (Brit) ≃ Polytechnikum nt; (degree-awarding) Technische Hochschule, TH f.
**polythene** ['pɒlɪθi:n] n (Brit) Polyäthylen nt; (in everyday language) Plastik nt. ~ **bag** Plastiktüte f.
**polyunsaturated** [,pɒlɪʌn'sætʃəreɪtɪd] adj mehrfach ungesättigt.

**polyurethane** [,pɒlɪ'juərɪθeɪn] n Polyurethan nt.
**pomegranate** ['pɒmə,grænɪt] n Granatapfel m.
**Pomerania** [,pɒmə'reɪnɪə] n Pommern nt.
**Pomeranian** [,pɒmə'reɪnɪən] n (dog) Spitz m.
**pommy** ['pɒmɪ] n (Austral col) Engländer(in f) m.
**pomp** [pɒmp] n Pomp, Prunk m. ~ **and circumstance** Pomp und Prunk.
**pompom** ['pɒmpɒm] n (on hat etc) Troddel, Bommel (dial) f.
**pomposity** [pɒm'pɒsɪtɪ] n see adj Aufgeblasenheit, Wichtigtuerei f; Bombast m.
**pompous** ['pɒmpəs] adj person aufgeblasen, wichtigtuerisch; language, remark bombastisch.
**ponce** [pɒns] n (Brit col: effeminate type) Tunte f (col).
**poncy** ['pɒnsɪ] adj (Brit col) tuntenhaft (col).
**pond** [pɒnd] n Teich m.
**ponder** ['pɒndər] **1** vt nachdenken über (+acc). **2** vi nachdenken (on, over über +acc).
**ponderous** ['pɒndərəs] adj style etc schwerfällig.
**pong** [pɒŋ] (Brit col) **1** n Gestank, Mief (col) m. **there's a bit of a** ~ **in here** hier stinkt's. **2** vi stinken.
**pontiff** ['pɒntɪf] n Pontifex m; (pope also) Papst m.
**pontificate** [pɒn'tɪfɪkɪt] **1** n Pontifikat nt. **2** [pɒn'tɪfɪkeɪt] vi (fig) dozieren.
**pontoon¹** [pɒn'tu:n] n Ponton m. ~ **bridge** Pontonbrücke f.
**pontoon²** n (Brit Cards) Siebzehnundvier nt.
**pony** ['pəʊnɪ] n Pony nt.
**pony:** ~ **tail** n Pferdeschwanz m; ~ **trekking** n Ponyreiten nt.
**poodle** ['pu:dl] n Pudel m.
**poof** [puf] n (Brit col) Schwule(r) m (col).
**pooh** [pu:] interj (bad smell) puh; (disdain) bah.
**pooh-pooh** ['pu:'pu:] vt verächtlich abtun.
**pool¹** [pu:l] n (a) Teich m; (underground) See m; (of rain) Pfütze f; (of spilt liquid) Lache f; (in river) Loch nt. **a** ~ **of blood** eine Blutlache. (b) (swimming ~) (Schwimm)becken nt; (in private garden, hotel also) Swimming Pool m; (swimming baths) Schwimmbad nt.
**pool²** **1** n (a) (common fund) (gemeinsame) Kasse f. **each player put £10 in the** ~ jeder Spieler gab £10 in die Kasse. (b) (supply, source) typing ~ Schreibzentrale f; ~ **of labour** Arbeitskraftreserve f; **there is a great** ~ **of untapped resources** es gibt große, noch ungenutzte Reserven. (c) **the** ~**s** pl (football ~) Toto m or nt; **to do the** ~**s** Toto spielen; **to win the** ~**s** im Toto gewinnen. (d) (form of snooker) Poolbillard nt. (e) (Comm) Interessengemeinschaft f; (US: monopoly, trust) Pool m, Kartell nt. **2** vt resources, savings zusammenlegen; efforts vereinen (geh).
**pooped** [pu:pt] adj (US col) geschafft (col).
**poor** [puər] **1** adj (+er) (a) arm. **a country** ~ **in natural resources** ein an Bodenschätzen armes Land; **it's the** ~ **man's Mercedes** es ist der Mercedes des kleinen Mannes; ~ **relation** (fig) Sorgenkind nt; **to be treated as the** ~ **relation** (fig) stiefmütterlich behandelt werden; **you** ~ **(old) chap** (col) du armer Kerl (col); ~ **you!** du Ärmste(r)! (b) (not good) schlecht; performance also, leadership schwach. **a** ~ **chance of success** schlechte Erfolgsaussichten pl; **he is a** ~ **traveller** er verträgt Reisen nicht gut; **it's a** ~ **thing for Britain if ...** es steht schlecht um Großbritannien, wenn ...; **she was** ~ **at languages** sie war schlecht or schwach in Sprachen. **2** npl **the** ~ die Armen pl.
**poor box** n Almosenbüchse f.
**poorly** ['puəlɪ] **1** adv (a) arm; dressed, furnished ärmlich. ~ **off** schlecht gestellt, arm dran (col). (b)

*(badly)* schlecht. ~ **lit/**~ **paid** schlecht beleuchtet/ bezahlt; **to do** ~ **(at sth)** (in etw *dat*) schwach *or* schlecht abschneiden. **2** *adj pred (ill)* krank, elend. **to be** ~ sich schlecht fühlen.

**pop¹** [pɒp] *n (esp US col) (father)* Papa *m (col)*; *(elderly man)* Opa *m (hum col)*.

**pop²** *n (~ music)* Popmusik *f*, Pop *m*.

**pop³ 1** *n* **(a)** *(sound)* Knall *m.* **(b)** *(fizzy drink)* Brause, Limo *(col)* f. **2** *adv* **to go** ~ *(cork)* knallen; *(balloon)* platzen. **3** *vt* **(a)** *balloon, popcorn* zum Platzen bringen. **(b)** *(col: put)* stecken. **to** ~ **a letter into the postbox** einen Brief einwerfen; **he** ~**ped his head around the door** er steckte den Kopf durch die Tür; **to** ~ **the question** einen (Heirats)antrag machen. **4** *vi* **(a)** *(col: go* ~*) (cork)* knallen; *(balloon)* platzen; *(buttons, popcorn)* aufplatzen; *(ears)* knacken. **his eyes were** ~**ping out of his head** ihm fielen fast die Augen aus dem Kopf *(col)*. **(b)** *(col: go quickly or suddenly)* **to** ~ **along/down to the baker's** schnell zum Bäcker gehen; **I'll just** ~ **upstairs** ich laufe mal eben nach oben.

►**pop in** *(col)* *vi* schnell hereinkommen/ hereingehen; *(visit)* auf einen Sprung vorbeikommen *(col)*.

►**pop off** *vi (col)* **(a)** *(die)* den Löffel abgeben *(col)*. **(b)** *(go off)* verschwinden *(col) (to* nach*)*.

►**pop out** *(col)* *vi (go out)* (schnell) rausgehen *(col)*/rauskommen *(col)*; *(spring, rabbit)* herausspringen *(of aus)*. **he has just** ~**ped** ~ **to the shops** er ist eben einkaufen gegangen.

►**pop up** *(col)* *vi (appear suddenly)* auftauchen; *(toast)* hochschießen *(col)*.

**pop:** ~ **art** *n* Pop-art *f*; ~ **concert** *n* Popkonzert *nt*; ~**corn** *n* Popcorn *nt*.

**Pope** [pəʊp] *n* Papst *m*.

**pop:** ~**-eyed** *adj* glotzäugig; ~ **festival** *n* Popfestival *nt*; ~ **group** *n* Popgruppe *f*; ~ **gun** *n* Spielzeugpistole *f*.

**poplar** ['pɒplə'] *n* Pappel *f*.

**poplin** ['pɒplɪn] *n* Popeline *m or f*.

**popmobility** ['pɒpməʊˌbɪlɪtɪ] *n* Gymnastik *f* zu Popmusik.

**pop music** *n* Popmusik *f*.

**popper** ['pɒpə'] *n (Brit col: press-stud)* Druckknopf *m*.

**poppet** ['pɒpɪt] *n (col)* Schatz *m*.

**poppy** ['pɒpɪ] *n* Mohn *m*.

**poppy: P~ Day** *n (Brit)* ≃ Volkstrauertag *m (BRD)*; ~**-seed** *n* Mohn *m*.

**popsicle**® ['pɒpsɪkl] *n (US)* Eis *nt* am Stiel.

**pop:** ~ **singer** *n* Popsänger(in *f*) *m*; ~ **song** *m* Popsong *m*; *(hit)* Schlager *m*; ~ **star** *n* Popstar *m*.

**populace** ['pɒpjʊlɪs] *n* Bevölkerung *f*; *(masses)* breite Öffentlichkeit *f*.

**popular** ['pɒpjʊlə'] *adj* **(a)** beliebt *(with* bei*)*; *decision, measure* populär. **he was a very** ~ **choice** seine Wahl fand großen Anklang. **(b)** *(for the general public)* populär; *music* leicht; *prices* erschwinglich; *science* Populär-; *edition* Volks-; *lectures, journal* populärwissenschaftlich. **(c)** *(widespread)* belief, fallacy weitverbreitet; *(of or for the people)* government, approval, support des Volkes. **by** ~ **request** auf vielseitigen Wunsch.

**popularity** [ˌpɒpjʊ'lærɪtɪ] *n* Beliebtheit *f*; *(with the public also)* Popularität *f (with* bei*)*.

**popularize** ['pɒpjʊləraɪz] *vt* populär machen; *science* popularisieren.

**popularly** ['pɒpjʊlɪ] *adv* allgemein. **he is** ~ **believed to be a rich man** nach allgemeiner Ansicht ist er ein reicher Mann.

**populate** ['pɒpjʊleɪt] *vt (inhabit)* bevölkern; *(colonize)* besiedeln. **this area is** ~**d mainly by immigrants**

in diesem Gebiet leben hauptsächlich Einwanderer; **densely** ~**d cities** dicht bevölkerte Städte *pl*.

**population** [ˌpɒpjʊ'leɪʃən] *n (of region, country)* Bevölkerung *f*; *(of town)* Einwohner *pl*; *(number of inhabitants)* Bevölkerungszahl *f*. **the** ~ **explosion** die Bevölkerungsexplosion.

**populism** ['pɒpjʊlɪzəm] *n* Populismus *m*.

**populist** ['pɒpjʊlɪst] **1** *n* Populist(in *f*) *m*. **2** *adj* populistisch.

**populous** ['pɒpjʊləs] *adj* dicht besiedelt.

**pop-up** ['pɒpʌp] *adj toaster* automatisch; *book, picture* Hochklapp-.

**porage** *n* = **porridge**.

**porcelain** ['pɔːsəlɪn] **1** *n* Porzellan *nt*. **2** *adj* Porzellan-.

**porch** [pɔːtʃ] *n (of house)* Windfang *m*; *(US: veranda)* Veranda *f*; *(of church)* Portal *nt*.

**porcupine** ['pɔːkjʊpaɪn] *n* Stachelschwein *nt*.

**pore** [pɔː'] *n* Pore *f*.

►**pore over** *vi +prep obj (scrutinize)* genau studieren; *(meditate)* nachgrübeln über *(+acc)*. **to** ~ ~ **one's books** über seinen Büchern hocken.

**pork** [pɔːk] *n* Schweinefleisch *nt*.

**pork:** ~ **chop** *n* Schweinekotelett *nt*; ~ **pie** *n* Schweinefleischpastete *f*; ~ **sausage** *n* Schweinswurst *f*.

**porn** [pɔːn], *(esp US)* **porno** ['pɔːnəʊ] *n (col)* Porno *m (col)*. **hard/soft** ~ harter/weicher Porno.

**pornographic** [ˌpɔːnə'græfɪk] *adj* pornographisch.

**pornography** [pɔː'nɒɡrəfɪ] *n* Pornographie *f*.

**porous** ['pɔːrəs] *adj rock, substance* porös.

**porpoise** ['pɔːpəs] *n* Tümmler *m*.

**porridge** ['pɒrɪdʒ] *n* Haferbrei *m*. ~ **oats** Haferflocken *pl*.

**port¹** [pɔːt] *n* Hafen *m*; *(town also)* Hafenstadt *f*. **to come/put into** ~ in den Hafen einlaufen; ~ **authority** Hafenbehörde *f*; **any** ~ **in a storm** *(prov)* in der Not frißt der Teufel Fliegen *(Prov)*.

**port²** **1** *n (Naut, Aviat: left side)* Backbord *nt*. **2** *adj side* Backbord-.

**port³** *n (also* ~ **wine)** Portwein *m*.

**portability** [ˌpɔːtə'bɪlɪtɪ] *n* Tragbarkeit *f*.

**portable** ['pɔːtəbl] *adj* tragbar; *telephone* Mobil-; *typewriter* Reise-; *radio* Koffer-. **easily** ~ leicht zu tragen; **a** ~ **television** ein Portable *m or nt*, ein tragbarer Fernseher.

**portcullis** [pɔːt'kʌlɪs] *n* Fallgitter *nt*.

**portent** ['pɔːtent] *n* Zeichen, Omen *(geh)* *nt (of* für*)*.

**porter** ['pɔːtə'] *n (of office etc)* Pförtner *m*; *(hospital* ~*)* Assistent *m*; *(at hotel)* Portier *m*; *(Rail, at airport)* Gepäckträger *m*; *(US Rail: sleeper attendant)* Schlafwagenschaffner *m*.

**portfolio** [pɔːt'fəʊlɪəʊ] *n* (Akten)mappe *f*; *(Fin)* Portefeuille *nt*; *(of artist, designer)* Kollektion *f*. **minister without** ~ *(Pol)* Minister ohne Geschäftsbereich.

**porthole** ['pɔːthəʊl] *n* Bullauge *nt*.

**portion** ['pɔːʃən] *n (piece, part)* Teil *m*; *(of ticket)* Abschnitt *m*; *(of food)* Portion *f*.

**portly** ['pɔːtlɪ] *adj (+er)* beleibt, korpulent.

**portmanteau** [pɔːt'mæntəʊ] *n, pl* **-s** *or* **-x** Handkoffer *m*. ~ **word** Kombinationsform *f*.

**portrait** ['pɔːtrɪt] *n* Porträt *nt*. **to have one's** ~ **painted** sich malen lassen.

**portrait:** ~ **format** *n* Hochformat *nt*; ~ **painter** *n* Porträtmaler(in *f*) *m*.

**portray** [pɔː'treɪ] *vt* darstellen; *(paint also)* malen.

**portrayal** [pɔː'treɪəl] *n* Darstellung *f*.

**Portugal** ['pɔːtjʊɡəl] *n* Portugal *nt*.

**Portuguese** [ˌpɔːtjʊ'ɡiːz] **1** *adj* portugiesisch. ~ **man-of-war** Staatsqualle *f*. **2** *n* **(a)** Portugiese *m*,

Portugiesin f. **(b)** *(language)* Portugiesisch nt.

**pose** [pəʊz] **1** n *(position, attitude)* Haltung f; *(of model, pej also)* Pose f. **to strike a** ~ sich in Positur werfen. **2** vt *question, problem* vortragen. **3** vi *(model)* posieren; *(sitting also)* Modell sitzen; *(standing also)* Modell stehen. **to** ~ **as** *(fig)* sich ausgeben als.

**poser** ['pəʊzər] n **(a)** *(col: person)* Angeber m. **(b)** *(problem)* harte Nuß *(col)*.

**posh** [pɒʃ] *(col)* **1** adj (+er) piekfein *(col)*, vornehm; *neighbourhood, hotel also* nobel. **2** adv (+er): **to talk** ~ mit vornehmem Akzent sprechen.

**position** [pə'zɪʃən] **1** n **(a)** *(location)* *(of person)* Platz m; *(of object also)* Stelle f; *(of microphone, statue, wardrobe etc)* Standort m; *(of spotlight, table)* Anordnung f; *(of town, house etc)* Lage f; *(of plane, ship, Sport)* Position f; *(Mil)* Stellung f. **to be in/out of** ~ an der richtigen/falschen Stelle sein; **what** ~ **do you play?** auf *or* in welcher Position spielst du?; **to finish in third** ~ Dritter werden. **(b)** *(posture)* Haltung f; *(in love-making)* Stellung f. **in a reclining** ~ zurückgelehnt. **(c)** *(social standing)* Stellung, Position f; *(job)* Stelle f. **a man of** ~ eine hochgestellte Persönlichkeit; **he has a high** ~ **in the Ministry** er bekleidet eine hohe Stellung im Ministerium; **a** ~ **of trust** eine Vertrauensstellung. **(d)** *(fig: situation, circumstance)* Lage f. **to be in a** ~ **to do sth** in der Lage sein, etw zu tun; **what is the** ~ **regarding ...?** wie sieht es mit ... aus? **(e)** *(fig: point of view, attitude)* Standpunkt m, Haltung f. **to take up a** ~ **on sth** eine Haltung bei einer Sache einnehmen.

**2** vt *ladder, guards* aufstellen; *soldiers, policemen* postieren. **he** ~**ed himself where he could see her** er plazierte sich so, daß er sie sehen konnte.

**positive** ['pɒzɪtɪv] adj **(a)** *(Math, Phot, Elec)* positiv; *pole* Plus-. **(b)** *(affirmative, constructive)* positiv; *criticism, suggestion* konstruktiv. **(c)** *person, tone of voice* bestimmt; *instructions* streng; *evidence, decision* eindeutig; *rule* fest. **that is** ~ **proof** das ist der sichere Beweis; **to be** ~ **that** ... sicher sein, daß ...; **this is a** ~ **miracle/disgrace** das ist wirklich ein Wunder/eine Schande.

**positively** ['pɒzɪtɪvlɪ] adv **(a)** positiv. **(b)** *(decisively)* bestimmt; *(definitely) prove* eindeutig. **(c)** *(really, absolutely)* wirklich, echt *(col)*.

**posse** ['pɒsɪ] n *(US: sheriff's* ~*)* Aufgebot nt; *(fig)* Gruppe, Schar f.

**possess** [pə'zes] vt besitzen. **to be** ~**ed by an idea** von einer Idee besessen sein; **to fight like one** ~**ed** wie ein Besessener kämpfen; **whatever** ~**ed you to do that?** was ist bloß in dich gefahren, so etwas zu tun?

**possession** [pə'zeʃən] n **(a)** *(ownership)* Besitz m; *(Sport: of ball)* Ballbesitz m. **to have sth in one's** ~ etw in seinem Besitz haben; **to have/take** ~ **of sth** etw in Besitz haben/nehmen; **to be in** ~ **of sth** im Besitz von etw sein; **to come into** ~ **of sth** in den Besitz von etw gelangen; **to get/have** ~ **of the ball** in Ballbesitz gelangen/im Ballbesitz sein. **(b)** *(thing possessed)* Besitz m no pl; *(territory)* Besitzung f.

**possessive** [pə'zesɪv] adj **(a) to be** ~ **about sth** seine Besitzansprüche auf etw *(acc)* betonen; **to be** ~ **towards sb** an jdn Besitzansprüche stellen. **(b)** *(Gram)* ~ **pronoun/adjective** Possessivpronomen nt.

**possessor** [pə'zesər] n Besitzer(in f) m. **to be the proud** ~ **of sth** der stolze Besitzer von etw sein.

**possibility** [,pɒsə'bɪlɪtɪ] n Möglichkeit f. **there's not much** ~ **of success/of his** or **him being successful** die Aussichten auf Erfolg/darauf, daß er Erfolg hat,

sind nicht sehr groß; **within the bounds of** ~ im Bereich des Möglichen; **the** ~ **of doing sth** die Möglichkeit, etw zu tun; **it's a distinct** ~ **that** ... es besteht eindeutig die Möglichkeit, daß ...; **he is a** ~ **for the job** er kommt für die Stelle in Betracht; **there is some** or a ~ **that** ... es besteht die Möglichkeit, daß ...; **a job with real possibilities** eine Stelle mit echten Möglichkeiten.

**possible** ['pɒsəbl] **1** adj möglich. **to make sth** ~ etw möglich machen; **as soon/often as** ~ so bald/oft wie möglich; **the best/worst** ~ ... der/die/das bestmögliche/schlechtestmögliche ...; **if (at all)** ~ falls (irgend) möglich; **it's just** ~ **that I'll see you before then** eventuell sehe ich dich vorher noch; **it will be** ~ **for you to return the same day** Sie haben die Möglichkeit, am selben Tag zurückzukommen. **2** n **a long list of** ~**s** for the job eine lange Liste möglicher Kandidaten für die Stelle.

**possibly** ['pɒsəblɪ] adv **(a) that can't** ~ **be true** das kann unmöglich wahr sein; **how could he** ~ **have known that?** wie konnte er das bloß wissen?; **he did all he** ~ **could** er tat, was er nur konnte; **if I** ~ **can** wenn ich irgend kann. **(b)** *(perhaps)* vielleicht, möglicherweise.

**post¹** [pəʊst] **1** n *(pole, door* ~ *etc)* Pfosten m; *(lamp*~*)* Pfahl m; *(telegraph* ~*)* Mast m. **starting/ winning** or **finishing** ~ Start-/Zielpfosten m; **he was left at the** ~ sie ließen ihn stehen. **2** vt **(a)** *(display: also* ~ *up)* anschlagen. **(b)** *(announce) concert etc* durch Anschlag bekanntmachen. **to** ~ **(as) missing** als vermißt melden.

**post²** **1** n **(a)** *(job)* Stelle f, Posten m. **to look for/take up a** ~ eine Stelle suchen/antreten. **(b)** *(Mil)* Posten m. **at one's** ~ auf seinem Posten; **a frontier** ~ ein Grenzposten m; **last** ~ *(bugle call)* Zapfenstreich m. **2** vt **(a)** *(position)* postieren. **(b)** *(send, assign)* versetzen.

**post³** **1** n *(esp Brit: mail)* Post f. **by** ~ mit der Post; **it's in the** ~ es ist unterwegs; **to put sth in the** ~ etw aufgeben; **to catch/miss the** ~ *(letter)* noch/ nicht mehr mit der Post mitkommen; *(person)* rechtzeitig zur Leerung kommen/die Leerung verpassen; **has the** ~ **been?** war die Post schon da? **2** vt **(a)** *(put in the* ~*)* aufgeben; *(in letterbox)* einwerfen, einstecken; *(send by* ~ *also)* mit der Post schicken. **I** ~**ed it to you on Monday** ich habe es am Montag an Sie abgeschickt. **(b)** *(inform)* **to keep sb** ~**ed** jdn auf dem laufenden halten.

**post-** [pəʊst-] pref nach-.

**postage** ['pəʊstɪdʒ] n Porto nt. ~ **and packing** *(abbr* **p & p)** Porto und Verpackung; ~ **paid** or *(US)* **prepaid** portofrei.

**postage stamp** n Briefmarke f.

**postal** ['pəʊstəl] adj Post-. ~ **district** Zustellbezirk m; ~ **order** n *(Brit)* Geldgutschein, der bei der Post gekauft und eingelöst wird, ≈ Postanweisung f; ~ **vote** n to use one's ~ **vote** per Briefwahl wählen.

**post:** ~**-bag** n *(Brit)* Postsack m; ~**box** n *(Brit)* Briefkasten m; ~**card** n Postkarte f; **(picture)** ~**card** n Ansichtskarte f; ~ **code** n *(Brit)* Postleitzahl f; ~**date** vt *cheque* vordatieren.

**poster** ['pəʊstər] n *(advertising)* Plakat nt; *(for decoration also)* Poster nt.

**poste restante** ['pəʊstrе'stɑ̃t] *(Brit)* **1** n Aufbewahrungsstelle f für postlagernde Sendungen. **2** adv postlagernd.

**posterior** [pɒ'stɪərɪər] n *(hum)* Hintern m *(col)*, Allerwerteste(r) m *(hum)*.

**posterity** [pɒ'sterɪtɪ] n die Nachwelt.

**poster paint** n Plakatfarbe f.

**post:** ~**-free** adj, adv *(Brit)* portofrei; ~**graduate** n *jd, der seine Studien nach dem ersten akademischen Grad weiterführt,* Graduierte(r) *mf;* ~**haste** *adv* schnellstens.

**posthumous** *adj,* ~**ly** *adv* ['pɒstjuməs, -lɪ] postum, posthum.

**posting** ['pəʊstɪŋ] *n (transfer)* Versetzung *f; (Mil)* Abkommandierung *f.*

**post:** ~**man** *n* Briefträger *m;* ~**mark 1** *n* Poststempel *m;* **2** *vt* (ab)stempeln; **the letter is** ~**marked "Birmingham"** der Brief ist in Birmingham abgestempelt; ~**master** *n* Postmeister *m;* ~**master general** *n* ≈ Postminister *m;* ~**mistress** *n* Postmeisterin *f;* ~**modern** *adj* postmodern; ~**modernism** *n* Postmodernismus *m;* ~**-mortem** [,pəʊst'mɔːtəm] *n* Obduktion, Leichenöffnung *f; (fig)* Manöverkritik *f (fig);* **to hold** *or* **have a** ~**-mortem on sth** etw hinterher erörtern; ~**-natal** *adj* nach der Geburt, postnatal *(spec);* ~ **office** *n* Postamt *nt;* **the P**~ **Office** *(institution)* die Post; ~ **office savings bank** Postsparkasse *f;* ~ **office savings book** Postsparbuch *nt;* ~**-paid** *adj* portofrei; *envelope* frankiert.

**postpone** [pəʊst'pəʊn] *vt* aufschieben; *(for specified period)* verschieben. **it has been** ~**d till Tuesday** es ist auf Dienstag verschoben worden.

**postponement** [pəʊst'pəʊnmənt] *n (act)* Verschiebung *f; (result)* Aufschub *m.*

**postpositive** [pəʊst'pɒzɪtɪv] *adj (Gram)* nachgestellt.

**postscript** ['pəʊs,skrɪpt] *n (abbr PS: to letter)* Postskriptum *nt; (to book, article etc)* Nachwort *nt; (fig: to affair)* Nachspiel *nt.*

**postulate** ['pɒstjʊlɪt] **1** *n* Postulat *nt.* **2** ['pɒstjʊleɪt] *vt* postulieren; *theory* aufstellen.

**posture** ['pɒstʃəʳ] **1** *n (lit, fig)* Haltung *f; (pej)* Pose *f.* **2** *vi* sich in Positur werfen.

**postwar** ['pəʊst'wɔːʳ] *adj* Nachkriegs-. **the** ~ **period** *or* **years** die Nachkriegszeit; ~ **London** das London der Nachkriegszeit.

**posy** ['pəʊzɪ] *n* Sträußchen *nt.*

**pot** [pɒt] **1** *n* **(a)** Topf *m; (tea~, coffee~)* Kanne *f.* ~**s and pans** Kochgeschirr *nt;* **to go to** ~ *(col: person, business)* auf den Hund kommen *(col);* **to have** ~**s of money** *(col)* jede Menge Geld haben *(col).* **(b)** *(col: marijuana)* Gras *nt (col).* **2** *vt meat* einmachen; *jam* einfüllen; *plant* eintopfen; *(shoot) game* schießen; *(Billiards) ball* einlochen.

**potash** ['pɒtæʃ] *n* Kali *nt.*

**potassium** [pə'tæsɪəm] *n* Kalium *nt.*

**potato** [pə'teɪtəʊ] *n, pl* -**es** Kartoffel *f.* ~ **chip** *(US)* **or crisp** *(Brit)* *n* Kartoffelchip *m;* ~ **peeler** Kartoffelschäler *m.*

**potbellied** ['pɒt,belɪd] *adj person* spitzbäuchig; *(through hunger)* blähbäuchig.

**potency** ['pəʊtənsɪ] *n see adj* Stärke *f;* Durchschlagskraft *f;* Potenz *f;* Macht *f.*

**potent** ['pəʊtənt] *adj drink, motive etc* stark; *argument etc* durchschlagend; *man* potent; *ruler* mächtig.

**potentate** ['pəʊtənteɪt] *n* Potentat *m.*

**potential** [pəʊ'tenʃəl] **1** *adj* potentiell. **he is a** ~ **virtuoso** er hat das Zeug zum Virtuosen. **2** *n* Potential *nt.* **the** ~ **for growth** das Wachstumspotential *nt;* **to have** ~ ausbaufähig sein *(col);* **he shows quite a bit of** ~ es steckt einiges in ihm.

**potentially** [pəʊ'tenʃəlɪ] *adv* potentiell.

**pot:** ~**hole** *n* **(a)** *(in road)* Schlagloch *nt;* **(b)** *(Geol)* Höhle *f;* ~**holer** *n* Höhlenforscher(in *f) m;* ~**holing** *n* Höhlenforschung *f.*

**potion** ['pəʊʃən] *n* Trank *m.*

**pot:** ~**luck** *n:* **to take** ~**luck** nehmen, was es gerade gibt; **we took** ~**luck and went to the nearest pub**

wir gingen aufs Geratewohl in die nächste Kneipe; ~**pourri** [,pəʊpʊ'riː] *n* **(a)** *(lit)* Duftmischung *f;* **(b)** *(fig: mixture, medley)* bunte Mischung; *(of music)* Potpourri *nt;* ~ **roast** *n* Schmorbraten *m;* ~**shot** *n* **to take a** ~**shot at sth** aufs Geratewohl auf etw *(acc)* schießen.

**potted** ['pɒtɪd] *adj* **(a)** *meat* eingemacht; *fish* eingelegt; *plant* Topf-. **(b)** *(shortened)* **a** ~ **history of** ein kurzer Abriß der Geschichte *(+gen).*

**potter¹** ['pɒtəʳ] *n* Töpfer(in *f) m.* ~**'s wheel** Töpferscheibe *f.*

**potter²** *vi (do little jobs)* herumwerkeln; *(wander aimlessly)* herumschlendern. **she** ~**s away in the kitchen for hours** sie hantiert stundenlang in der Küche herum; **to** ~ **around the house** im Haus herumwerkeln; **to** ~ **along** *(car, driver)* dahinzuckeln.

**pottery** ['pɒtərɪ] *n (workshop, craft)* Töpferei *f; (pots)* Töpferwaren *pl; (glazed)* Keramik *f; (archaeological remains)* Tonscherbe *f.*

**potting compost** *n* Blumenerde *f.*

**potty¹** ['pɒtɪ] *n (esp Brit)* Töpfchen *nt.* ~**-trained** sauber.

**potty²** *adj (+er) (Brit col: mad)* verrückt.

**pouch** [paʊtʃ] *n* Beutel *m; (under eyes)* (Tränen)sack *m; (of hamster)* Tasche *f; (Mil)* (Patronen)tasche *f.*

**pouffe** [puːf] *n* **(a)** *(seat)* Puff *m.* **(b)** *(Brit col)* = **poof.**

**poulterer** ['pəʊltərəʳ] *n (Brit)* Geflügelhändler(in *f) m.*

**poultice** ['pəʊltɪs] *n* Umschlag, Wickel *m; (for boil)* Zugpflaster *nt.*

**poultry** ['pəʊltrɪ] *n* Geflügel *nt.* ~ **farm** Geflügelfarm *f;* ~ **farmer** Geflügelzüchter *m;* ~ **farming** Geflügelzucht *f.*

**pounce** [paʊns] **1** *n* Sprung, Satz *m; (swoop by bird)* Angriff *m.* **2** *vi (cat, lion etc)* einen Satz machen; *(bird)* niederstoßen; *(fig)* zuschlagen. **to** ~ **on sb/sth** *(lit, fig)* sich auf jdn/etw stürzen; *(bird)* auf etw *(acc)* niederstoßen; *(police)* sich *(dat)* jdn greifen/in etw *(dat)* eine Razzia machen.

**pound¹** [paʊnd] *n* **(a)** *(weight)* ≈ Pfund *nt.* **two** ~**s of apples** zwei Pfund Äpfel; **by the** ~ pfundweise. **(b)** *(money)* Pfund *nt.* **one** ~ **sterling** ein Pfund Sterling; **five** ~**s** fünf Pfund; **a five-**~ **note** ein Fünfpfundschein *m.*

**pound²** **1** *vt (hammer, strike)* hämmern; *earth* feststampfen; *meat* klopfen; *dough* kneten; *corn etc* (zer)stampfen; *piano* hämmern auf *(+dat); table* hämmern auf *(+acc); door, wall* hämmern gegen; *(waves) ship* schlagen gegen; *(guns, bombs)* ununterbrochen beschießen; *(artillery)* unter Beschuß haben. **to** ~ **sth to pieces** etw kleinstampfen; *(sea) ship* zertrümmern; **to** ~ **sth to a pulp** etw zu Brei stampfen. **2** *vi* **(a)** *(beat)* hämmern; *(heart)* (wild) pochen; *(waves, sea)* schlagen (on, against gegen); *(hooves)* stampfen. **he** ~**ed on the door/on the table** er hämmerte gegen die Tür/auf den Tisch. **(b)** *(run heavily)* stampfen; *(walk heavily, stamp)* stapfen.

**pound³** *n (for stray dogs)* städtischer Hundezwinger; *(for cars)* Abstellplatz *m (für amtlich abgeschleppte Fahrzeuge).*

**pounding** ['paʊndɪŋ] *n* Hämmern *nt; (of heart)* Pochen *nt; (of music, drums)* Dröhnen *nt; (of waves, sea)* Schlagen *nt; (of hooves, feet etc)* Stampfen *nt; (of guns, bombs)* Bombardement *nt.* **to take a** ~ *(ship in storm)* stark mitgenommen werden; *(town in war)* schwer bombardiert werden; *(Sport)* scharf angegriffen werden; *(lose heavily)* eine Schlappe einstecken müssen *(col).*

**pour** [pɔːʳ] **1** *vt liquid* gießen; *sugar, rice etc* schüt-

ten; *drink* einschenken. **can I ~ you another drink?**
kann ich Ihnen nachschenken?; **to ~ money into a**
**project** Geld in ein Projekt pumpen *(col)*. **2** *vi* **(a)**
*(lit, fig)* strömen; *(smoke also)* hervorquellen. **the**
**sweat was ~ing off him** der Schweiß floß in Strömen an ihm herunter; **cars ~ed along the road** Au-
tokolonnen rollten die Straße entlang. **(b) it's ~ing**
**(down) (with rain)** es gießt (in Strömen), es schüttet
*(col)*.
▶**pour away** *vt sep* weggießen.
▶**pour forth** *vti* = **pour out 1, 2.**
▶**pour in** *vi* hinein-/hereinströmen; *(donations, pro-*
*tests)* in Strömen eintreffen.
▶**pour off** *vt sep* abgießen.
▶**pour out 1** *vi* hinaus-/herausströmen *(of* aus*)*;
*(smoke also)* hervorquellen *(of* aus*)*; *(words)* heraus-
sprudeln *(of* aus*)*. **2** *vt sep liquid* ausgießen; *sugar*
*etc* ausschütten; *drink* einschenken; *(fig) troubles*
sich *(dat)* von der Seele reden. **to ~ ~ one's heart to**
**sb** jdm sein Herz ausschütten.
**pouring** ['pɔːrɪŋ] *adj* ~ **rain** strömender Regen; **a ~**
**wet day** ein völlig verregneter Tag.
**pout** [paʊt] **1** *n (facial expression)* Schmollmund *m*. **2**
*vi (with lips)* einen Schmollmund machen; *(sulk)*
schmollen.
**poverty** ['pɒvətɪ] *n* Armut *f (of* an +*dat)*. ~ **of** imagi-
**nation** Phantasielosigkeit *f*; ~ **line** Armutsgrenze *f*;
~ **trap** Armutsfalle *f*; ~-**stricken** notleidend; *condi-*
*tions* kümmerlich; **to be** ~-**stricken** Armut leiden.
**POW** = **prisoner of war.**
**powder** ['paʊdər] **1** *n* Pulver *nt*; *(face, talcum* ~ *etc)*
Puder *m*; *(dust)* Staub *m*. **2** *vt* **(a)** *milk* pulverisieren. ~**ed milk** Milchpulver *nt*. **(b)** *face etc* pudern.
**to ~ one's nose** *(lit)* sich *(dat)* die Nase pudern;
*(euph)* kurz verschwinden *(euph)*.
**powder:** ~ **compact** *n* Puderdose *f*; ~ **keg** *n (lit,*
*fig)* Pulverfaß *nt*; ~ **puff** *n* Puderquaste *f*; ~ **room**
*n* Damentoilette *f*.
**powdery** ['paʊdərɪ] *adj (like powder)* pulvrig;
*(crumbly)* bröckelig; *bones* morsch; *(covered with*
*powder)* gepudert.
**power** ['paʊər] **1** *n* **(a)** *no pl (physical strength)* Kraft
*f*; *(force: of blow, explosion etc)* Stärke, Wucht *f*;
*(fig: of argument etc)* Überzeugungskraft *f*. **the ~ of**
**love/tradition** die Macht der Liebe/Tradition.
**(b)** her ~**s of persuasion** ihre Überredungskünste
*pl*; **his** ~**s of hearing** sein Hörvermögen *nt*; **mental**
~**s** geistige Kräfte *pl*.
**(c)** *(capacity, authority)* Macht *f*; *(Jur, parental)* Gewalt *f*; *(usu pl: authority)* Befugnis *f*. **he did all in his**
~ **to help them** er tat (alles), was in seiner Macht
stand, um ihnen zu helfen; **to be in sb's** ~ in jds
Gewalt *(dat)* sein; **that is beyond** *or* **outside my** ~**(s)**
das überschreitet meine Befugnisse; ~ **of attorney**
*(Jur)* (Handlungs)vollmacht *f*; **the party now in** ~
die Partei, die im Augenblick an der Macht ist; **to**
**come to** ~ an die Macht kommen; **he has been**
**given full** ~**(s) to make all decisions** man hat
ihm volle Entscheidungsgewalt übertragen.
**(d)** *(person or institution having authority)* Autorität *f*. **to be the** ~ **behind the throne** die graue Eminenz sein; **the** ~**s that be** *(col)* die da oben *(col)*; **the**
~**s of darkness** die Mächte der Finsternis.
**(e)** *(nation)* Macht *f*. **a naval** ~ eine Seemacht.
**(f)** *(nuclear* ~ *etc)* Energie *f*; *(of water, steam also)*
Kraft *f*; *(of engine, transmitter)* Leistung *f*; *(of lens,*
*drug)* Stärke *f*. **they cut off the** ~ *(electricity)* sie haben den Strom abgestellt.
**(g)** *(Math)* Potenz *f*. **to the** ~ **(of)** 2 hoch 2.
**(h)** *(col: a lot of)* **that did me a** ~ **of good** das hat
mir unheimlich gutgetan *(col)*.

**2** *vt (engine)* antreiben; *(fuel)* betreiben.
**power:** ~ **base** *n* Machtbasis *f*; ~**boat** *n* Motorboot
*nt*; ~ **cut** *n (Brit)* Stromsperre *f*; *(accidental)* Stromausfall *m*; ~-**driven** *adj tool* Motor-; ~ **failure** *n*
Stromausfall *m*.
**powerful** ['paʊfʊl] *adj government etc* mächtig;
*boxer, engine, drug, emotions* stark; *punch, deter-*
*gent* kraftvoll; *build* kräftig; *(fig) actor, music, film*
mitreißend; *argument* durchschlagend.
**powerfully** ['paʊfəlɪ] *adv* kraftvoll. ~ **built** kräftig
gebaut.
**powerhouse** ['paʊhaʊs] *n (fig)* treibende Kraft *(be-*
*hind* hinter +*dat, of gen)*.
**power:** ~**less** *adj committee, person* machtlos; **to**
**be** ~**less to resist** nicht die Kraft haben, zu widerstehen; **the government is** ~**less to deal with** infla-
**tion** die Regierung steht der Inflation machtlos
gegenüber; ~ **line** *n* (Haupt)stromleitung *f*; ~
**outage** *n (US)* Stromausfall *m*; ~ **point** *n (Brit*
*Elec)* Steckdose *f*; ~ **politics** *npl* Machtpolitik *f*; ~
**saw** *n* Motorsäge *f*; *(electric)* Elektrosäge *f*; ~ **sta-**
**tion** *n* Kraftwerk *nt*; ~ **steering** *n (Aut)* Servolen-
kung *f*; ~ **tool** *n* Elektrowerkzeug *nt*.
**pp** = **(a) pages** S. **(b) on behalf of** i.A.
**PPE** *(Brit Univ)* = **Philosophy, Politics and Eco-**
**nomics.**
**PPS** = **post-postscriptum** PPS.
**PQ** = **Province of Quebec.**
**pr** = **pair.**
**PR** [piː'ɑːr] = **(a) proportional representation. (b)**
**public relations** PR *f*. ~ **work** Öffentlichkeitsarbeit
*f*. **(c)** *(US Post)* **Puerto Rico.**
**practicability** [,præktɪkə'bɪlɪtɪ] *n* Durchführbarkeit *f*.
**practicable** ['præktɪkəbl] *adj* durchführbar, praktikabel; *road* geeignet.
**practical** ['præktɪkəl] *adj* praktisch; *person* praktisch (veranlagt). **to have a** ~ **mind** praktisch denken.
**practicality** [,præktɪ'kælɪtɪ] *n (of person)* praktische
Veranlagung; *(of scheme)* Durchführbarkeit *f*;
*(practical detail)* praktische Einzelheit.
**practical:** ~ **joke** *n* Streich *m*; ~ **joker** *n* Witzbold
*m (col)*.
**practically** ['præktɪkəlɪ] *adv (all senses)* praktisch.
**practice** ['præktɪs] **1** *n* **(a)** *(habit, custom) (of individ-*
*ual)* Gewohnheit *f*; *(of group, in country)* Brauch *m*;
*(in business)* Verfahrensweise *f*. **as is my (usual)** ~
wie es meine Gewohnheit ist; **that's common** ~ das
ist allgemein üblich. **(b)** *(exercise, training)* Übung
*f*; *(rehearsal, trial run)* Probe *f*; *(Motor racing)* Training *nt*. ~ **lap** Trainingsrunde *f*; ~ **makes perfect**
*(Prov)* Übung macht den Meister *(Prov)*; **to be out**
**of/in** ~ aus der/in Übung sein; **that was just a** ~ **run**
das war nur mal zur Probe. **(c)** *(as opposed to*
*theory)* Praxis *f*. **in** ~ in der Praxis; **that won't**
**work in** ~ das läßt sich praktisch nicht durchführen; **to put one's ideas into** ~ seine Ideen in die
Praxis umsetzen. **(d)** *(of doctor etc)* Praxis *f*. **to set**
**up in** ~ eine Praxis eröffnen.
**2** *vti (US)* = **practise.**
**practise,** *(US)* **practice** ['præktɪs] **1** *vt* **(a)** *thrift, pa-*
*tience etc* üben; *self-denial* praktizieren. **to ~ what**
**one preaches** *(prov)* seine Lehren in die Tat umsetzen. **(b)** *(in order to acquire skill)* üben; *song, chorus*
proben. **to ~ the violin** Geige üben; **to ~ doing sth**
etw üben; **I'm practising my German on him** ich pro-
biere mein Deutsch an ihm aus. **(c)** *(follow, exer-*
*cise) profession, religion* ausüben, praktizieren. **to ~**
**law/medicine** als Anwalt/Arzt praktizieren. **2** *vi* **(a)**
*(in order to acquire skill)* üben; *(choir)* proben;

*(Sport)* trainieren; *(Motor racing)* Trainingsrunden drehen. **(b)** *(lawyer, doctor etc)* praktizieren.

**practised,** *(US)* **practiced** ['præktɪst] *adj* geübt. **with a ~ eye** mit geübtem Auge.

**practising,** *(US)* **practicing** ['præktɪsɪŋ] *adj doctor, Christian, homosexual* praktizierend; *socialist* aktiv.

**practitioner** [præk'tɪʃənəʳ] *n (of method)* Benutzer *m*; *(medical ~)* praktischer Arzt, praktische Ärztin; *(dental ~)* Zahnarzt *m*/-ärztin *f*; *(legal ~)* Rechtsanwalt *m*/-anwältin *f*.

**pragmatic** *adj*, **~ally** *adv* ['præg'mætɪk, -əlɪ] pragmatisch.

**pragmatism** ['prægmətɪzəm] *n* Pragmatismus *m*.

**pragmatist** ['prægmətɪst] *n* Pragmatiker(in *f*) *m*.

**Prague** [prɑːg] *n* Prag *nt*.

**prairie** ['prɛərɪ] *n* Grassteppe *f*; *(in North America)* Prärie *f*.

**praise** [preɪz] **1** *vt* loben; *(to others, worshipfully also)* rühmen *(geh)*. **to ~ sb for having done sth** jdn dafür loben, etw getan zu haben. **2** *n* Lob *nt no pl*. **a hymn of ~** eine Lobeshymne; **he spoke in ~ of their efforts** er sprach lobend von ihren Bemühungen; **I have nothing but ~ for him** ich kann ihn nur loben; **~ be to God!** gelobt sei der Herr!

**praiseworthy** ['preɪz,wɜːðɪ] *adj* lobenswert.

**pram** [præm] *n (Brit)* Kinderwagen *m*.

**prance** [prɑːns] *vi (horse)* tänzeln; *(person) (jump around)* herumhüpfen; *(walk gaily, mince)* tänzeln. **to ~ in/out** *(person)* herein-/hinausspazieren.

**prank** [præŋk] *n* Streich *m*. **to play a ~ on sb** jdm einen Streich spielen.

**prat** [præt] *n (Brit col)* Knallkopf *m (col)*.

**prattle** ['prætl] **1** *n* Geplapper *nt*. **2** *vi* plappern.

**prawn** [prɔːn] *n* Garnele *f*. **~ cocktail** Krabbencocktail *m*.

**pray** [preɪ] *vi (say prayers)* beten. **let us ~** lasset uns beten; **to ~ for sb/sth** für jdn/um etw beten.

**prayer** [prɛəʳ] *n* Gebet *nt*; *(service, ~ meeting)* Andacht *f*. **to say one's ~s** beten.

**prayer: ~ book** *n* Gebetbuch *nt*; **~ mat** *n* Gebetsteppich *m*.

**pre-** [priː-] *pref* vor-; *(esp with Latinate words in German)* prä-. **at ~-1980 prices** zu Preisen von vor 1980.

**preach** [priːtʃ] **1** *vt* predigen; *(fig) advantages etc* propagieren. **to ~ a sermon** *(lit, fig)* eine Predigt halten. **2** *vi (lit, fig)* predigen. **to ~ to/at sb** jdm eine Predigt halten; **to ~ to the converted** *(fig)* offene Türen einrennen.

**preacher** ['priːtʃəʳ] *n* Prediger *m*; *(fig: moralizer)* Moralprediger(in *f*) *m*.

**preamble** [priː'æmbl] *n* Einleitung *f*; *(of book)* Vorwort *nt*; *(Jur)* Präambel *f*.

**prearrange** ['priːə'reɪndʒ] *vt* vorher vereinbaren.

**precarious** [prɪ'kɛərɪəs] *adj* unsicher; *situation also, position, relationship* prekär; *state* gefährlich.

**precariously** [prɪ'kɛərɪəslɪ] *adv* unsicher. **to be ~ balanced** *(lit, fig)* auf der Kippe stehen; **he lived rather ~** er lebte in ziemlich ungesicherten finanziellen Verhältnissen.

**precaution** [prɪ'kɔːʃən] *n* Vorsichtsmaßnahme *f*. **to take ~s against sth** Vorsichtsmaßnahmen gegen etw treffen; **to take the ~ of doing sth** vorsichtshalber etw tun; **to take ~s** *(use contraceptives)* ein Verhütungsmittel *nt* gebrauchen.

**precautionary** [prɪ'kɔːʃənərɪ] *adj* Vorsichts-, vorbeugend.

**precede** [prɪ'siːd] *vt (in order, time)* vorangehen *(+dat)*; *(in importance)* gehen vor *(+dat)*; *(in rank)* stehen über *(+dat)*.

**precedence** ['presɪdəns] *n (of person)* vorrangige Stellung *(over gegenüber)*; *(of problem etc)* Vorrang

*m (over* vor *+dat)*. **to take ~ over sb/sth** vor jdm/ etw Vorrang haben.

**precedent** ['presɪdənt] *n* Präzedenzfall *m*. **without ~** noch nie dagewesen; **to set a ~** einen Präzedenzfall schaffen.

**preceding** [prɪ'siːdɪŋ] *adj* vorhergehend.

**precept** ['priːsept] *n* Grundsatz *m*, Prinzip *nt*.

**precinct** ['priːsɪŋkt] *n (pedestrian ~)* Fußgängerzone *f*; *(shopping ~)* Geschäftsviertel *nt*; *(US: police ~)* Revier *nt*. **~s** *pl (grounds, premises)* Gelände *nt*; *(environs)* Umgebung *f*.

**precious** ['preʃəs] **1** *adj (costly)* wertvoll, kostbar; *(treasured)* wertvoll; *(iro)* heißgeliebt. **~ stone/ metal** Edelstein *m*/Edelmetall *nt*. **2** *adv (col)* **~ little/few** herzlich wenig/wenige *(col)*.

**precipice** ['presɪpɪs] *n (lit, fig)* Abgrund *m*.

**precipitate** [prə'sɪpɪtɪt] **1** *adj (overhasty)* übereilt, überstürzt. **2** [prɪ'sɪpɪteɪt] *vt* **(a)** *(hurl)* schleudern; *(downwards)* hinunterschleudern; *(fig)* stürzen. **(b)** *(hasten)* beschleunigen. **(c)** *(Chem)* (aus)fällen; *(Met)* niederschlagen.

**precipitation** [prɪ,sɪpɪ'teɪʃən] *n* **(a)** *(haste)* Eile *f*; *(over-hastiness)* Übereile *f*. **(b)** *(Met)* Niederschlag *m*.

**precipitous** [prɪ'sɪpɪtəs] *adj* steil; *(hasty)* überstürzt.

**précis** ['preɪsiː] *n* Zusammenfassung *f*; *(Sch)* Inhaltsangabe *f*.

**precise** [prɪ'saɪs] *adj* genau; *answer, description etc, worker also* präzis. **at that ~ moment** genau in dem Augenblick; **this was the ~ amount I needed** das war genau der Betrag, den ich brauchte; **please be more ~** drücken Sie sich bitte etwas genauer aus; **or, to be more ~, ...** oder, um es genauer zu sagen, ...

**precisely** [prɪ'saɪslɪ] *adv* genau; *answer, describe, work also* präzis. **at ~ 7 o'clock, at 7 o'clock ~** Punkt 7 Uhr; **what ~ do you mean?** was meinen Sie eigentlich genau?

**precision** [prɪ'sɪʒən] *n* Genauigkeit *f*; *(of work, movement also)* Präzision *f*.

**precision: ~ instrument** *n* Präzisionsgerät *nt*; **~-made** *adj* präzisionsgefertigt.

**preclude** [prɪ'kluːd] *vt possibility* ausschließen. **to ~ sb from doing sth** jdn daran hindern, etw zu tun.

**precocious** [prɪ'kəʊʃəs] *adj teenager, behaviour* frühreif; *statement, way of speaking* altklug.

**precociousness** [prɪ'kəʊʃəsnɪs], **precocity** [prɪ'kɒsɪtɪ] *n see adj* Frühreife *f*; Altklugheit *f*.

**preconceived** [,priːkən'siːvd] *adj opinion, idea* vorgefaßt.

**preconception** [,priːkən'sepʃən] *n* vorgefaßte Meinung.

**precondition** [,priːkən'dɪʃən] *n* (Vor)bedingung *f*.

**pre-cook** [priː'kʊk] *vt* vorkochen.

**precursor** [priː'kɜːsəʳ] *n* Vorläufer *m*; *(in office)* (Amts)vorgänger(in *f*) *m*.

**predate** [,priː'deɪt] *vt (precede)* zeitlich vorangehen *(+dat)*; *cheque, letter* zurückdatieren.

**predator** ['predətəʳ] *n (animal)* Raubtier *nt*; *(person)* Plünderer *m*.

**predatory** ['predətərɪ] *adj animal instincts* Raub-; *attack, tribe* räuberisch.

**predecessor** ['priːdɪsesəʳ] *n (person)* Vorgänger(in *f*) *m*; *(thing)* Vorläufer *m*. **our ~s** *(ancestors)* unsere Vorfahren *pl*.

**predestination** [priː,destɪ'neɪʃən] *n* Vorherbestimmung *f*.

**predestine** [priː'destɪn] *vt* vorherbestimmen; *person* prädestinieren.

**predetermine** [,priːdɪ'tɜːmɪn] *vt events, sb's future etc* vorherbestimmen; *price, date etc* im voraus festlegen.

**predicament** [prɪ'dɪkəmənt] n Zwangslage f, Dilemma nt. **to be in a ~** in einer Zwangslage sein.

**predicate** ['predɪkɪt] n (Gram) Prädikat nt.

**predicative** adj, **~ly** adv [prɪ'dɪkətɪv, -lɪ] prädikativ.

**predict** [prɪ'dɪkt] vt vorhersagen.

**predictable** [prɪ'dɪktəbl] adj vorhersagbar. **you are so ~** man weiß doch genau, wie du reagierst.

**predictably** [prɪ'dɪktəblɪ] adv **~**, **he was late** wie vorauszusehen war, kam er zu spät.

**prediction** [prɪ'dɪkʃən] n Voraussage f.

**predilection** [ˌpriːdɪ'lekʃən] n Vorliebe f (for für).

**predispose** [ˌpriːdɪ'spəʊz] vt geneigt machen. **to ~ sb in favour of sb/sth** jdn für jdn/etw einnehmen; **I'm not ~d to help him** ich bin nicht geneigt, ihm zu helfen.

**predisposition** [ˌpriːdɪspə'zɪʃən] n Neigung f (to zu); (Med) Anfälligkeit f (to für).

**predominance** [prɪ'dɒmɪnəns] n (control) Vorherrschaft f; (prevalence) Überwiegen nt.

**predominant** [prɪ'dɒmɪnənt] adj (most prevalent) idea, theory vorherrschend; (dominating) person, animal beherrschend.

**predominantly** [prɪ'dɒmɪnəntlɪ] adv überwiegend.

**predominate** [prɪ'dɒmɪneɪt] vi (a) vorherrschen. **(b)** (in influence etc) überwiegen. **Good will always ~ over Evil** das Gute wird immer über das Böse siegen.

**pre-eminence** [priː'emɪnəns] n überragende Bedeutung.

**pre-eminent** [priː'emɪnənt] adj herausragend.

**pre-eminently** [priː'emɪnəntlɪ] adv hauptsächlich, vor allem; (excellently) hervorragend.

**pre-empt** [priː'empt] vt zuvorkommen (+dat).

**pre-emptive** [priː'emptɪv] adj präventiv, Präventiv-.

**preen** [priːn] 1 vt feathers putzen. 2 vr **to ~ oneself** (bird) sich putzen; (person: dress up) sich herausputzen, sich aufputzen.

**prefab** ['priːfæb] n Fertighaus nt.

**prefabricated** [ˌpriː'fæbrɪkeɪtɪd] adj vorgefertigt, Fertig-; building Fertig-.

**preface** ['prefɪs] n 1 Vorwort nt. 2 vt remarks einleiten.

**prefect** ['priːfekt] n Präfekt m; (Brit Sch) Aufsichtsschüler(in f) m. **form ~** (Sch) ≈ Klassensprecher(in f) m.

**prefer** [prɪ'fɜːʳ] vt (a) (like better) vorziehen (to dat), lieber mögen (to als); drink, food, music also lieber trinken/essen/hören (to als); applicant, solution vorziehen, bevorzugen; (be more fond of) person lieber haben (to als). **he ~s coffee to tea** er trinkt lieber Kaffee als Tee; **I'd ~ something less ornate** ich hätte lieber etwas Schlichteres; **I ~ to resign rather than ...** eher kündige ich, als daß ...; **I ~ walking/flying** ich gehe lieber zu Fuß/fliege lieber; **I ~ not to say** ich sage es lieber nicht; **I would ~ you to do it today** mir wäre es lieber, wenn Sie es heute täten. **(b)** (Jur) **to ~ a charge/charges (against sb)** Klage (gegen jdn) erheben.

**preferable** ['prefərəbl] adj **X is ~ to Y** X ist Y (dat) vorzuziehen; **it would be ~ to do it that way** es wäre besser, es so zu machen.

**preferably** ['prefərəblɪ] adv am liebsten. **tea or coffee? – coffee, ~** Tee oder Kaffee? – lieber Kaffee; **but ~ not Tuesday** aber, wenn möglich, nicht Dienstag.

**preference** ['prefərəns] n (greater liking) Vorliebe f; (greater favour) Vorzug m. **for ~** lieber; **to have a ~ for sth** eine Vorliebe für etw haben, etw bevorzugen; **I drink coffee in ~ to tea** ich trinke lieber Kaffee als Tee; **what is your ~?** was wäre Ihnen am

liebsten?; **I have no ~** mir ist das eigentlich gleich; **to show ~ to sb** jdn bevorzugen; **to give ~ to sb/sth** jdm/etw den Vorzug geben (over gegenüber); **~ shares** or **stock** (Brit Fin) Vorzugsaktien pl.

**preferential** [prefə'renʃəl] adj treatment bevorzugt; terms Sonder-. **to give sb ~ treatment** jdn bevorzugt behandeln.

**prefix** ['priːfɪks] n (Gram) Vorsilbe f, Präfix nt.

**pregnancy** ['pregnənsɪ] n Schwangerschaft f; (of animal) Trächtigkeit f. **~ test** Schwangerschaftstest m.

**pregnant** ['pregnənt] adj (a) woman schwanger; animal trächtig, tragend. **3 months ~** im dritten Monat (schwanger). **(b)** (fig) remark, silence, pause bedeutungsschwer. **~ with meaning** bedeutungsgeladen.

**preheat** [priː'hiːt] vt vorheizen.

**prehistoric** [ˌpriːhɪ'stɒrɪk] adj prähistorisch, vorgeschichtlich.

**prehistory** [ˌpriː'hɪstərɪ] n Vorgeschichte f.

**prejudge** [priː'dʒʌdʒ] vt case, issue im vorhinein beurteilen; person im voraus verurteilen.

**prejudice** ['predʒʊdɪs] 1 n (a) (biased opinion) Vorurteil nt. **his ~ against ...** seine Voreingenommenheit gegen ...; **that's pure ~** das ist reine Voreingenommenheit; **racial ~** Rassenvorurteile pl. **(b)** (esp Jur: detriment, injury) Schaden m. **to the ~ of sb/sth** (form) zu jds Schaden/unter Beeinträchtigung +gen; **without ~** (Jur) ohne Verbindlichkeit. 2 vt **(a)** (bias) beeinflussen. **(b)** (injure) case etc gefährden; chances also beeinträchtigen.

**prejudiced** ['predʒʊdɪst] adj person voreingenommen (against gegen); opinion vorgefaßt; judge befangen.

**prejudicial** [ˌpredʒʊ'dɪʃəl] adj abträglich (to sth einer Sache dat). **to be ~ to sb's chances** jds Chancen gefährden.

**prelate** ['prelɪt] n Prälat m.

**preliminary** [prɪ'lɪmɪnərɪ] 1 adj talks, enquiry etc Vor-; remarks also, chapter einleitend; measures vorbereitend. **the ~ rounds** (Sport) die Ausscheidungsrunden. 2 n Einleitung f (to zu); (Sport) Vorspiel nt. **the preliminaries** (preparatory measures) die vorbereitenden Maßnahmen.

**prelims** ['priːˌlɪmz] npl (in book) Titelei f.

**prelude** ['prelju:d] n Vorspiel nt; (fig) Auftakt m (to zu +dat).

**premarital** [priː'mærɪtl] adj vorehelich.

**premature** ['premətʃʊəʳ] adj birth, arrival vorzeitig; decision, action verfrüht. **you were a little ~** da waren Sie ein wenig voreilig; **the baby was three weeks ~** das Baby wurde drei Wochen zu früh geboren; **~ baby** Frühgeburt f.

**prematurely** ['premətʃʊəlɪ] adv vorzeitig. **to be born ~** eine Frühgeburt sein.

**premeditate** [priː'medɪteɪt] vt vorsätzlich planen.

**premeditated** [priː'medɪteɪtɪd] adj vorsätzlich.

**premeditation** [priːˌmedɪ'teɪʃən] n Vorsatz m.

**premenstrual** [priː'menstrʊəl] adj prämenstruell, vor der Menstruation auftretend.

**premier** ['premɪəʳ] n Premier(minister) m.

**première** ['premɪɛəʳ] n Uraufführung f.

**premise** ['premɪs] n (a) (esp Logic) Prämisse (spec), Voraussetzung f. (b) **~s** pl (of school, factory) Gelände nt; (building) Gebäude nt; (shop) Räumlichkeiten pl. **business ~s** Geschäftsräume pl; (building) Geschäftsgebäude nt.

**premium** ['priːmɪəm] n (a) (bonus) Bonus m, Prämie f; (surcharge) Zuschlag m; (Insur) Prämie f; (St Ex) Aufgeld, Agio nt. **~ bond** (Brit) Lotterieaktie f; **~ (gasoline)** (US) Super nt; **to sell sth at a ~** etw über seinem Wert verkaufen; **to be at a** ~ *(St Ex)* über Pari stehen; *(fig)* hoch im Kurs stehen; **to put a** ~ **on sth** *(fig)* großen Wert auf etw *(acc)* legen.

**premonition** [ˌpriːmə'nɪʃən] *n (presentiment)* (böse) Vorahnung; *(forewarning)* Vorwarnung *f.*

**prenatal** [priː'neɪtl] *adj (esp US)* = **antenatal.**

**preoccupation** [priːˌɒkjʊ'peɪʃən] *n* **her** ~ **with her appearance** ihre ständige Sorge um ihr Äußeres; **that was his main** ~ das war sein Hauptanliegen.

**preoccupied** [priː'ɒkjʊpaɪd] *adj* gedankenverloren. **to be** ~ **with sth** nur an etw *(acc)* denken.

**preoccupy** [priː'ɒkjʊpaɪ] *vt* (stark) beschäftigen.

**prep** [prep] *n (Brit Sch)* Hausaufgaben *pl.*

**prepacked** [ˌpriː'pækt] *adj* abgepackt.

**prepaid** [ˌpriː'peɪd] *adj postage, goods* vorausbezahlt; *envelope* freigemacht.

**preparation** [ˌprepə'reɪʃən] *n* **(a)** Vorbereitung *f; (of meal, medicine etc)* Zubereitung *f.* **in** ~ **for sth** als Vorbereitung für etw; **to be in** ~ in Vorbereitung sein; ~**s for war/a journey** Kriegs-/Reisevorbereitungen *pl;* **to make** ~**s** Vorbereitungen treffen. **(b)** *(Med, Sci)* Präparat *nt.*

**preparatory** [prɪ'pærətərɪ] *adj* **(a)** *step, measure* vorbereitend. ~ **to the conference** um die Konferenz vorzubereiten. **(b)** ~ **school** *(Brit)* private Vorbereitungsschule für die Public School; *(US)* private Vorbereitungsschule für die Hochschule.

**prepare** [prɪ'pɛəʳ] **1** *vt* vorbereiten *(sb for sth* jdn auf etw *acc, sth for sth* etw für etw *acc);* *meal, medicine* zubereiten; *guest-room* fertigmachen; *(Sci)* präparieren; *data* aufbereiten. ~ **yourself for a shock!** mach dich auf einen Schock gefaßt! **2** *vi* **to** ~ **for sth** Vorbereitungen für etw treffen; **to** ~ **for an exam** sich auf eine Prüfung vorbereiten; **to** ~ **for war** Kriegsvorbereitungen treffen; **to** ~ **to do sth** Anstalten machen, etw zu tun.

**prepared** [prɪ'pɛəd] *adj* **(a)** vorbereitet *(for* auf *+acc).* **you must be** ~ **for everything/the worst** du mußt dich auf alles/auf das Schlimmste gefaßt machen. **(b)** *(willing)* **to be** ~ **to do sth** bereit sein, etw zu tun.

**preponderance** [prɪ'pɒndərəns] *n* Übergewicht *nt.*

**preponderant** [prɪ'pɒndərənt] *adj* überwiegend.

**preposition** [ˌprepə'zɪʃən] *n* Präposition *f.*

**prepossessing** [ˌpriːpə'zesɪŋ] *adj* anziehend.

**preposterous** [prɪ'pɒstərəs] *adj* grotesk, absurd.

**preprogrammed** [ˌpriː'prəʊgræmd] *adj* vorprogrammiert.

**prep school** *n (Brit) see* **preparatory (b).**

**prerecord** [ˌpriːrɪ'kɔːd] *vt* (vorher) aufzeichnen. ~**ed cassette** bespielte Kassette.

**prerequisite** [ˌpriː'rekwɪzɪt] *n* Voraussetzung *f.*

**prerogative** [prɪ'rɒgətɪv] *n* Vorrecht *nt.*

**Presbyterian** [ˌprezbɪ'tɪərɪən] **1** *adj* presbyterianisch. **2** *n* Presbyterianer(in *f) m.*

**preschool** ['priːskuːl] *adj attr* vorschulisch, Vorschul-. **a child of** ~ **age** ein Kind *nt* im Vorschulalter.

**prescribe** [prɪ'skraɪb] *vt* **(a)** *(order, lay down)* vorschreiben. ~**d reading** *or* **book** Pflichtlektüre *f.* **(b)** *(Med, fig)* verschreiben *(sth for sb* jdm etw).

**prescription** [prɪ'skrɪpʃən] *n (Med)* Rezept *nt; (act of prescribing)* Verschreiben *nt.* **to make up** *or* **fill** *(US)* **a** ~ eine Medizin zubereiten; ~ **charge** Rezeptgebühr *f;* **only available on** ~ rezeptpflichtig.

**prescriptive** [prɪ'skrɪptɪv] *adj* normativ.

**presence** ['prezns] *n* Gegenwart, Anwesenheit *f.* **in sb's** ~, **in the** ~ **of sb** in jds Gegenwart *(dat);* **to make one's** ~ **felt** sich bemerkbar machen; **military** ~ Militärpräsenz *f.*

**presence of mind** *n* Geistesgegenwart *f.*

**present**[1] ['preznt] **1** *adj* **(a)** *(in attendance)* anwesend; *(existing)* vorhanden. **to be** ~ anwesend sein, da/hier sein; **to be** ~ **at sth** bei etw anwesend sein; ~ **company excepted** Anwesende ausgenommen; **all those** ~ alle Anwesenden; **carbon is** ~ **in organic matter** Kohlenstoff ist in organischen Stoffen vorhanden. **(b)** *(at the* ~ *time) moment, state of affairs etc* gegenwärtig, derzeitig; *problems, husband etc also* jetzig; *season etc* laufend. **at the** ~ **moment** zum jetzigen Zeitpunkt; **in the** ~ **circumstances** unter den gegenwärtigen Umständen; **in the** ~ **case** im vorliegenden Fall. **(c)** *(Gram)* **in the** ~ **tense** in der Gegenwart, im Präsens; ~ **participle** Partizip *nt* Präsens. **2** *n* Gegenwart *f; (Gram also)* Präsens *nt.* **at** ~ zur Zeit, im Moment; **up to the** ~ bislang, bis jetzt.

**present**[2] **1** *n (gift)* Geschenk *nt.* **to make sb a** ~ **of sth** jdm etw schenken *(also fig);* **I was given it as a** ~ das habe ich geschenkt bekommen.

**2** [prɪ'zent] *vt* **(a)** *medal, prize etc* überreichen; *(as gift)* schenken; *(put forward)* vorlegen; *cheque (for payment)* präsentieren; *proof* erbringen *(of sth* für etw); *proposal* unterbreiten. **to** ~ **sb with sth, to** ~ **sth to sb** jdm etw überreichen; *(as a gift)* jdm etw schenken; ~ **arms!** *(Mil)* präsentiert das Gewehr! **(b)** *(offer, provide) target, opportunity* bieten. **his action** ~**ed us with a problem** seine Tat stellte uns vor ein Problem. **(c)** *(Rad, TV)* präsentieren; *(Theat also)* aufführen; *(commentator)* moderieren. ~**ing Sabine Citron as ...** *(Film)* und erstmals Sabine Citron als ... **(d)** *(introduce)* vorstellen. **to** ~ **Mr X to Miss Y** Herrn X Fräulein Y *(dat)* vorstellen.

**3** [prɪ'zent] *vr (opportunity, problem etc)* sich ergeben.

**presentable** [prɪ'zentəbl] *adj* **to be** ~ sich sehen lassen können; **to make oneself** ~ sich zurechtmachen.

**presentation** [ˌprezən'teɪʃən] *n* **(a)** *(of gift etc)* Überreichung *f; (of prize, medal also, ceremony)* Verleihung *f; (gift)* Geschenk *nt.* **to make sb a** ~ jdm ein Geschenk überreichen. **(b)** *(act of presenting) (of report, voucher etc)* Vorlage *f; (of petition)* Überreichung *f; (Jur: of case, evidence)* Darlegung *f.* **on** ~ **of a certificate** gegen Vorlage einer Bescheinigung. **(c)** *(Theat)* Inszenierung *f; (TV also, Rad)* Produktion *f.* **(d)** *(style of* ~*)* Präsentation *f.*

**present-day** ['prezntdeɪ] *adj attr* heutig.

**presenter** [prɪ'zentəʳ] *n (TV, Rad)* Moderator(in *f) m.*

**presentiment** [prɪ'zentɪmənt] *n* (Vor)ahnung *f.* **to have a** ~ **that ...** das Gefühl haben, daß ...

**presently** ['prezntlɪ] *adv* **(a)** *(soon)* bald. **(b)** *(esp US: at present)* zur Zeit, gegenwärtig.

**preservation** [ˌprezə'veɪʃən] *n see vt* **(a)** Erhaltung *f;* Wahrung *f;* Aufrechterhaltung *f.* **(b)** Konservierung *f (also of leather, wood);* Präservierung *f.* **(c)** Einmachen *nt;* Einlegen *nt.* **(d)** Bewahrung *f.*

**preservative** [prɪ'zɜːvətɪv] *n (Cook)* Konservierungsmittel *nt.*

**preserve** [prɪ'zɜːv] **1** *vt* **(a)** *(keep intact, maintain) customs, building, position* erhalten; *peace also, dignity, appearances* wahren; *memory* aufrechterhalten. **(b)** *(keep from decay)* konservieren; *specimens etc* präservieren; *leather, wood* schützen. **well** ~**d** gut erhalten. **(c)** *(Cook)* einmachen; *(pickle)* einlegen. **(d)** *(keep from harm, save)* bewahren. **to** ~ **sb from sth** jdn vor etw *(dat)* bewahren. **2** *n* **(a)** *(Cook)* ~**s** *pl* Eingemachtes *nt.* **(b)** *(special domain)* Ressort *nt.* **game** ~ *(Hunt)* Jagdrevier *nt.*

**preserving** [prɪ'zɜːvɪŋ] *adj (Cook) jar, sugar* Einmach-.

**preset** [priː'set] *adj* voreingestellt.

**pre-shrunk** [pri:'ʃrʌŋk] adj vorgewaschen.

**preside** [prɪ'zaɪd] vi (at meeting etc) den Vorsitz haben (at bei). **to ~ over an organization** etc eine Organisation etc leiten.

**presidency** ['prezɪdənsɪ] n Präsidentschaft f; (esp US: of company) Aufsichtsratsvorsitz m; (US Univ) Rektorat nt.

**president** ['prezɪdənt] n Präsident(in f) m; (esp US: of company) Aufsichtsratsvorsitzende(r) mf; (US Univ) Rektor(in f) m.

**presidential** [ˌprezɪ'denʃəl] adj (Pol) Präsidenten-; election also Präsidentschafts-. **his ~ duties** seine Pflichten als Präsident.

**press** [pres] **1** n (a) (squeeze, push) Druck m. **to give sth a ~** etw drücken; dress etc etw bügeln. (b) (trouser ~, flower ~) Presse f. (c) (Typ) (Drucker-) presse f; (publishing firm) Verlag m; (newspapers) Presse f. **to go to ~** in Druck gehen; **to be in the ~** im Druck sein; **the daily ~** die Tagespresse; **the weekly ~** die Wochenzeitungen pl; **to get a good/bad ~** eine gute/schlechte Presse bekommen.
  **2** vt (a) (push, squeeze) drücken (to an +acc); button, doorbell also, brake pedal drücken auf (+acc); clutch, piano pedal treten; grapes (aus)pressen; flowers pressen. (b) (iron) clothes bügeln. (c) (urge, persuade) drängen; (harass) bedrängen; (insist on) claim, argument bestehen auf (+dat). **to ~ sb hard** jdm (hart) zusetzen; **to ~ the point** darauf beharren or herumreiten (col); **to ~ one's views on sb** jdm seine Ansichten aufdrängen; **to ~ sb for an answer** auf jds Antwort drängen; **to be ~ed (for money/time)** in Geldnot/Zeitnot sein; **to ~ sb/sth into service** jdn/etw einspannen. (d) machine part, record etc pressen. **~ed steel** Preßstahl m.
  **3** vi (a) (lit, fig: bear down, exert pressure) drücken; (urge, agitate) drängen; (be insistent also) drängeln (col). **to ~ for sth** auf etw (acc) drängen; **time ~es** die Zeit drängt. (b) (move, push) sich drängen.
  ▶**press ahead, press on** vi weitermachen; (with journey) weiterfahren. **to ~ ~ with sth** (fig) mit etw weitermachen; (with plans) etw weiterführen.

**press:** **~ agency** n Presseagentur f; **~ conference** n Pressekonferenz f; **~ coverage** n Presseberichte pl (of über +acc); **~ cutting** n (Brit) Zeitungsausschnitt m; **~ gallery** n (esp Jur, Parl) Pressetribüne f; **~-gang** vt (col) **to ~-gang sb into (doing) sth** jdn drängen, etw zu tun.

**pressing** ['presɪŋ] adj (urgent) dringend; (insistent) requests nachdrücklich.

**press:** **~ officer** n Pressesprecher(in f) m; **~ photographer** n Pressefotograf(in f) m; **~ release** n Pressemitteilung f; **~ report** n Pressebericht m; **~ stud** n (Brit) Druckknopf m; **~-up** n Liegestütz m.

**pressure** ['preʃər] **1** n (a) Druck m (also Phys, Met). **at high/full ~** (lit, fig) unter Hochdruck. (b) (compulsion, influence) Druck, Zwang m. **~ parental ~** Druck von seiten der Eltern; **social ~s** gesellschaftliche Zwänge pl; **to do sth under ~** etw unter Druck tun; **to be under ~ to do sth** unter Druck stehen, etw zu tun; **to put ~ on sb** jdn unter Druck setzen; **to put the ~ on** (col) Dampf machen (col); **~ of work prevents me** Arbeitsüberlastung hindert mich daran; **he's under a lot of ~** er ist großen Belastungen ausgesetzt. **2** vt = **pressurize** (b).

**pressure:** **~-cooker** n Druckkochtopf, Schnellkochtopf m; **~ gauge** n Druckmesser m; (for tyres) Reifendruckmesser m; **~ group** n Interessengruppe f.

**pressurize** ['preʃəraɪz] vt (a) cabin, spacesuit auf

Normaldruck halten. (b) unter Druck setzen. **to ~ sb into doing sth** jdn so unter Druck setzen, daß er etw tut.

**Prestel** ® ['prestel] n ≈ Bildschirmtext m.

**prestige** [pre'sti:ʒ] n Prestige nt.

**prestigious** [pre'stɪdʒəs] adj Prestige-. **to be (very) ~** (einen hohen) Prestigewert haben.

**prestressed** ['pri:strest] adj vorgespannt; concrete Spann-.

**presumably** [prɪ'zju:məblɪ] adv vermutlich. **~ he is very rich, is he?** ich nehme an, er ist sehr reich, oder?

**presume** [prɪ'zju:m] **1** vt (a) (suppose) annehmen, vermuten. (b) (venture) **to ~ to do sth** sich (dat) erlauben, etw zu tun. **2** vi (a) (suppose) annehmen, vermuten. (b) (take liberties) **I don't want to ~** ich wollte nicht aufdringlich sein; **to ~ on or upon sth** etw überbeanspruchen.

**presumption** [prɪ'zʌmpʃən] n (a) (assumption) Annahme, Vermutung f. (b) (boldness) Dreistigkeit f; (arrogance) Vermessenheit f.

**presumptuous** adj, **~ly** adv [prɪ'zʌmptjʊəs, -lɪ] unverschämt, vermessen.

**presuppose** [ˌpri:sə'pəʊz] vt voraussetzen.

**pre-tax** [pri:'tæks] adj unversteuert, vor Besteuerung.

**pretence,** (US) **pretense** [prɪ'tens] n (a) (story) erfundene Geschichte; (insincerity) Verstellung f; (affectation) Unnatürlichkeit f; (pretext) Vorwand m. **he didn't really shoot me, it was just ~** er hat nicht auf mich geschossen, er hat nur so getan; **to make a ~ of being sth** so tun, als sei man etw; **it's all a ~** das ist alles nur gespielt or Mache (col); **his ~ of innocence/friendship** seine gespielte Unschuld/Freundschaft; **let's stop all this ~** hören wir auf, uns (dat) etwas vorzumachen; **on or under the ~ of doing sth** unter dem Vorwand, etw zu tun. (b) **to make no ~ to sth** keinen Anspruch auf etw (acc) erheben.

**pretend** [prɪ'tend] **1** vt (a) (make believe, feign) vortäuschen, vorgeben. **to ~ to be interested** so tun, als ob man interessiert wäre; **to ~ to be sick** eine Krankheit vortäuschen; **to ~ to be asleep** sich schlafend stellen. (b) (claim) **I don't ~ to ...** ich behaupte nicht, daß ich ... **2** vi so tun, als ob; (keep up facade) sich verstellen. **he is only ~ing** er tut nur so (als ob).

**pretense** n (US) = **pretence**.

**pretension** [prɪ'tenʃən] n (a) (claim) Anspruch m; (social, cultural) Ambition f. **he makes no ~(s) to originality** er erhebt keineswegs den Anspruch, originell zu sein. (b) (ostentation) Prahlerei f; (affectation) Anmaßung f.

**pretentious** [prɪ'tenʃəs] adj anmaßend; speech, book hochtrabend; (ostentatious) angeberisch, protzig (col); restaurant, décor pompös.

**preterite** ['pretərɪt] n Imperfekt nt.

**pretext** ['pri:tekst] n Vorwand m. **on or under the ~ of doing sth** unter dem Vorwand, etw zu tun.

**prettily** ['prɪtɪlɪ] adv hübsch.

**prettiness** ['prɪtɪnɪs] n hübsches Aussehen.

**pretty** ['prɪtɪ] **1** adj (+er) (a) hübsch, nett. **to make oneself ~** sich hübsch machen; **I'm/she's not just a ~ face!** (col) ich bin gar nicht so dumm (, wie ich aussehe) (col)/sie hat auch Köpfchen; **it wasn't ~/a ~ sight** das war alles andere als schön/das war kein schöner Anblick. (b) (col) hübsch, schön (col); price, sum also stolz. **it'll cost a ~ penny** das wird eine schöne Stange Geld kosten (col). **2** adv (rather) ziemlich; good also ganz; (very also) ganz schön (col). **~ nearly** or **well finished** so gut wie fertig (col).

**pretzel** ['pretsl] *n* Brezel *f.*
**prevail** [prɪ'veɪl] *vi* **(a)** *(gain mastery)* sich durchsetzen *(over, against* gegenüber). **(b)** *(conditions, wind etc)* vorherrschen; *(be widespread: customs)* weit verbreitet sein. **(c)** *(persuade)* **to ~ (up)on sb to do sth** jdn dazu bewegen, etw zu tun.
**prevailing** [prɪ'veɪlɪŋ] *adj conditions* derzeitig; *fashion* aktuell; *opinion* herrschend; *wind* vorherrschend.
**prevalence** ['prevələns] *n (widespread occurrence)* Vorherrschen *nt; (of crime, disease)* Häufigkeit *f.*
**prevalent** ['prevələnt] *adj (widespread)* weit verbreitet; *conditions* herrschend; *fashions, style* beliebt.
**prevaricate** [prɪ'værɪkeɪt] *vi* Ausflüchte machen.
**prevarication** [pri,værɪ'keɪʃən] *n* Ausflucht *f; (prevaricating)* Ausflüchte *pl.*
**prevent** [prɪ'vent] *vt sth* verhindern, verhüten; *(through preventive measures)* vorbeugen *(+dat).* **to ~ sb (from) doing sth** jdn daran hindern, etw zu tun; **to ~ sth (from) happening** verhindern, daß etw geschieht.
**preventable** [prɪ'ventəbl] *adj* vermeidbar.
**prevention** [prɪ'venʃən] *n* Verhütung *f; (through preventive measures)* Vorbeugung *f (of gegen).*
**preventive** [prɪ'ventɪv] *adj* vorbeugend, Präventiv-. **~ medicine** Präventivmedizin *f.*
**preview** ['priːvjuː] *n* **(a)** *(of play, film)* Vorpremiere *f; (of exhibition)* Vernissage *f.* **(b)** *(Film, trailer, TV)* Vorschau *f (of auf +acc).*
**previous** ['priːvɪəs] *adj* **(a)** *(earlier)* vorherig; *page, day* vorhergehend; *year* vorangegangen; *(with indef art)* früher. **the ~ page/day** die Seite/der Tag davor; **in ~ years** in früheren Jahren; **on a ~ occasion** bei einer früheren Gelegenheit; **I have a ~ engagement** ich habe schon einen Termin; **to have a ~ conviction** vorbestraft sein; **~ owner** Vorbesitzer(in *f) m.* **(b)** **~ to** vor *(+dat);* **~ to going out** ... bevor ich/er *etc* ausging, ...
**previously** ['priːvɪəslɪ] *adv* vorher, früher.
**pre-war** [,priː'wɔːr] *adj* Vorkriegs-.
**prey** [preɪ] **1** *n (lit, fig)* Beute *f.* **bird of ~** Raubvogel *m;* **to fall ~ to sb/sth** *(fig)* ein Opfer von jdm/etw werden. **2** *vi* **to ~ (up)on** *(animals)* Jagd machen auf *(+acc); (pirates, thieves)* (aus)plündern; *(doubts)* nagen an *(+dat).* **it ~ed on his mind** der Gedanke daran quälte ihn.
**prezzie** ['prezɪ] *n (col)* Geschenk *nt.*
**price** [praɪs] **1** *n (lit, fig)* Preis *m.* **the ~ of cars** die Autopreise *pl;* **to go up/down in ~** teurer/billiger werden; **what is the ~ of that?** was kostet das?; **at a ~ of** ... zum Preis(e) von ...; **at a ~** zum entsprechenden Preis; **at a reduced ~** verbilligt, zu herabgesetztem Preis *(form);* **the ~ of fame** der Preis für den Ruhm; **at any ~** um jeden Preis; **not at any ~** um keinen Preis; **at the ~ of losing his health** um den Preis seiner Gesundheit; **it's too high a ~ to pay** das ist ein zu hoher Preis; **to put a ~ on sth** einen Preis für etw nennen; **to be beyond/without ~** nicht mit Geld zu bezahlen sein; **to put a ~ on sb's head** eine Belohnung auf jds Kopf *(acc)* aussetzen.
**2** *vt (fix ~ of)* den Preis festsetzen von; *(label)* auszeichnen *(at mit).* **it was ~d at £5** es kostete £5; **reasonably ~d** angemessen im Preis; **~d too high/low** zu teuer/billig; **to ~ oneself out of the market** sich selbst durch zu hohe Preise konkurrenzunfähig machen.
**price:** **~ bracket** *n* Preisklasse *f;* **~ control** *n* Preiskontrolle *f;* **~cut** *n* Preissenkung *f;* **~cutting** *n* Preissenkungen *pl;* **~ fixing** *n (by group of producers)* Preisabsprache *f; (by producer)* Preis-

bindung *f;* **~ freeze** *n* Preisstopp *m;* **~ increase** *n* Preiserhöhung *f.*
**priceless** ['praɪslɪs] *adj* unschätzbar, von unschätzbarem Wert; *(col: amusing) joke, film* köstlich; *person* unbezahlbar.
**price:** **~ limit** *n* Preisgrenze *f;* **~ list** *n* Preisliste *f;* **~ range** *n* Preisspanne *f;* **it's within my ~ range** es entspricht meinen Preisvorstellungen; **~ rise** *n* Preiserhöhung *f;* **~s policy** *n* Preispolitik *f;* **~ tag** *n* Preisschild *nt.*
**pricey** ['praɪsɪ] *adj (Brit col)* kostspielig.
**pricing** ['praɪsɪŋ] *n* Preisfestzetzung *f.* **~ policy** Preispolitik *f.*
**prick** [prɪk] **1** *n* **(a)** *(puncture, pricking sensation)* Stich *m.* **~s of conscience** Gewissensbisse *pl.* **(b)** *(col!: penis)* Schwanz *m (col!).* **2** *vt (puncture)* one-self, *sb* stechen; *balloon* durchstechen; **to ~ one's finger (with/on sth)** sich *(dat)* (mit etw) in den Finger stechen/sich *(dat)* (an etw *dat)* den Finger stechen. **3** *vi (thorn, injection etc)* stechen; *(eyes)* brennen.
▶**prick up** *vt sep* **to ~ ~ its/one's ears** *(lit, fig)* die Ohren spitzen.
**prickle** ['prɪkl] *n* **(a)** *(sharp point)* Stachel *m; (on plants also)* Dorn *m.* **(b)** *(sensation)* Stechen *nt; (from wool etc)* Kratzen *nt; (tingle)* Prickeln *nt.*
**prickly** ['prɪklɪ] *adj (+er)* **(a)** *plant, animal* stach(e)lig; *material* kratzig; *sensation* stechend; *(tingling)* prickelnd. **(b)** *(fig) person* bissig.
**prickly:** **~ heat** *n* Hitzepocken *pl;* **~ pear** *n (plant)* Feigenkaktus *m; (fruit)* Kaktusfeige *f.*
**pride** [praɪd] **1** *n* **(a)** Stolz *m; (arrogance)* Hochmut *m.* **to take (a) ~ in sth/in one's appearance** auf etw *(acc)* stolz sein/Wert auf sein Äußeres legen; **her ~ and joy** ihr ganzer Stolz; **the ~ of the army** der Stolz der Armee; **to have** *or* **take ~ of place** den Ehrenplatz einnehmen. **(b)** *(of lions)* Rudel *nt.* **2** *vr* **to ~ oneself on sth** sich einer Sache *(gen)* rühmen können; **I ~ myself on being something of an expert in this field** ich darf wohl behaupten, mich auf diesem Gebiet auszukennen.
**priest** [priːst] *n* Priester, Geistliche(r) *m.*
**priestess** ['priːstɪs] *n* Priesterin *f.*
**priesthood** ['priːsthʊd] *n* Priestertum *nt; (priests collectively)* Priesterschaft *f.* **to enter the ~** Priester werden.
**priestly** ['priːstlɪ] *adj* priesterlich; *robes, office also* Priester-.
**prig** [prɪg] *n (goody-goody)* Tugendlamm *nt (col); (snob)* Schnösel *m (col).*
**prim** [prɪm] *adj (+er) (also* **~ and proper**) etepetete *inv (col); (demure) person, dress* sittsam, züchtig; *(prudish)* prüde.
**prima donna** ['priːmə'dɒnə] *n (lit, fig)* Primadonna *f.*
**prima facie** ['praɪmə'feɪʃɪ] **1** *adv* allem Anschein nach. **2** *adj* **a ~ case of** ... auf den ersten Blick ein Fall von ...; **the police have a ~ case** so wie es aussieht, hat die Polizei genügend Beweise.
**primarily** ['praɪmərɪlɪ] *adv* in erster Linie.
**primary** ['praɪmərɪ] **1** *adj (chief, main)* Haupt-, wesentlich. **our ~ concern** unser Hauptanliegen; **of ~ importance** von größter Bedeutung. **2** *n (US: also* **~ election)** Vorwahl *f.*
**primary:** **~ colour** *(Brit) or* **color** *(US) n* Grundfarbe *f;* **~ education** *n* Grundschul(aus)bildung *f;* **~ product** *n* Grundstoff *m; (main product)* Hauptprodukt *m;* **~ school** *n* Grundschule *f;* **~ teacher** *n* Grundschullehrer(in *f) m;* **~ winding** *n (Elec)* Primärwicklung *f.*
**primate** ['praɪmeɪt] *n* **(a)** *(Zool)* Primat *m.* **(b)** ['praɪmɪt] *(Eccl)* Primas *m.*

**prime** [praɪm] 1 adj (a) (major, chief) Haupt-, wesentlich. ~ **time** (TV) Hauptsendezeit f; **of** ~ **importance** von größter Bedeutung. (b) (excellent) erstklassig. ~ **example** Musterbeispiel nt; **in** ~ **condition** (meat, fruit etc) von hervorragender Qualität; (athlete, car etc) in erstklassiger Verfassung. (c) (Math) Prim-. 2 n **in the** ~ **of** life in der Blüte seiner Jahre; **he is in/past his** ~ er ist in den besten Jahren/er ist über seine besten Jahre hinaus; (singer, artist) er ist an seinem Höhepunkt angelangt/er hat seine beste Zeit hinter sich. 3 vt (a) bomb scharf machen; pump vorpumpen; surface for painting grundieren. (b) (with advice, information) instruieren. **to be well** ~**d for the interview/game** für das Interview/Spiel gut gerüstet sein.

**prime:** ~ **costs** npl (Comm) Selbstkosten pl; ~ **minister** n Premierminister(in f) m; ~ **number** n Primzahl f.

**primer** ['praɪmə*r*] n (a) (paint, coat) Grundierung f. (b) (book) Fibel f. (c) (explosive) Zünder m.

**primeval** [praɪ'miːvəl] adj urzeitlich. ~ **forest** Urwald m.

**primitive** ['prɪmɪtɪv] adj primitiv; man urzeitlich.

**primly** ['prɪmlɪ] adv (demurely) sittsam; (prudishly) prüde.

**primness** ['prɪmnɪs] n (übertrieben) sittsame Art; (prudishness) Prüderie f.

**primrose** ['prɪmrəʊz] 1 n (Bot) Primel f; (colour) Blaßgelb n. 2 adj blaßgelb.

**primula** ['prɪmjʊlə] n Primel f.

**primus (stove)** ® ['praɪməs(ˌstəʊv)] n Primuskocher m.

**prince** [prɪns] n (king's son) Prinz m; (ruler) Fürst m. P~ **Charming** (fig) Märchenprinz m; ~ **consort/regent** Prinzgemahl m/-regent m.

**princely** ['prɪnslɪ] adj (lit, fig) fürstlich.

**princess** [prɪn'ses] n Prinzessin f; (wife of ruler) Fürstin f.

**principal** ['prɪnsɪpəl] 1 adj Haupt-, hauptsächlich. **the** ~ **cities of China** die wichtigsten Städte Chinas; **my** ~ **concern** mein Hauptanliegen nt; ~ **horn** erster Hornist, erste Hornistin; ~ **shareholder** Hauptaktionär m. 2 n (a) (of school, college) Rektor m; (in play) Hauptperson f. (b) (Fin, of investment) Kapital(summe f) nt.

**principality** [ˌprɪnsɪ'pælɪtɪ] n Fürstentum nt. **the** P~ (Brit) Wales nt.

**principally** ['prɪnsɪpəlɪ] adv vornehmlich, in erster Linie.

**principle** ['prɪnsɪpl] n (moral precept) Prinzip nt, Grundsatz m. **in/on** ~ im/aus Prinzip, prinzipiell; **a man of** ~(**s**) ein Mensch mit Prinzipien; **it's against my** ~**s** es geht gegen meine Prinzipien; **it's a matter of** ~, **it's the** ~ **of the thing** es geht dabei ums Prinzip.

**print** [prɪnt] 1 n (a) (typeface) Schrift f; (~ed matter) Gedruckte(s) nt. **out of/in** ~ vergriffen/gedruckt; **to see sth in cold** ~ etw schwarz auf weiß sehen; **he'll never get into** ~ er wird nie etwas veröffentlichen; **in big/small** ~ groß/klein gedruckt. (b) (picture) Druck m; (Phot) Abzug m, Kopie f; (fabric) bedruckter Stoff; (cotton ~) Kattun m. (c) (impression: of foot etc) Abdruck m. 2 vt (a) book, design drucken; fabric bedrucken. (b) (publish) story veröffentlichen. (c) (write) in Druckschrift schreiben.
▶**print out** vt sep (Comp) ausdrucken.

**printable** ['prɪntəbl] adj druckfähig.

**printed** ['prɪntɪd] adj Druck-, gedruckt; (written in capitals) in Großbuchstaben; fabric bedruckt. ~ **matter/papers** Drucksache f; ~ **circuit** gedruckte

Schaltung; ~ **circuit board** Leiterplatte f.

**printer** ['prɪntə*r*] n (a) (device) Drucker m. (b) (person) Drucker(in f) m. ~**'s error** Druckfehler m; ~**'s ink** Druckerschwärze f.

**printhead** ['prɪnt,hed] n (Comp) Druckkopf m.

**printing** ['prɪntɪŋ] n (a) (process) Drucken nt. (b) (unjoined writing) Druckschrift f; (characters, print) Schrift f. (c) (quantity printed) Auflage f.

**printing:** ~ **press** n Druckerpresse f; ~ **works** n sing or pl Druckerei f.

**printout** ['prɪntaʊt] n (Comp) Ausdruck m.

**printrun** ['prɪntrʌn] n Auflage f.

**print wheel** n (Comp) Typenrad nt.

**prior**[1] ['praɪə*r*] adj (a) knowledge, warning, agreement vorherig; (earlier) früher. ~ **claim** Vorrecht nt (to auf); **a** ~ **engagement** eine vorher getroffene Verabredung. (b) ~ **to sth** vor etw (dat); ~ **to going out** ... bevor ich/er etc ausging, ...

**prior**[2] n (Eccl) Prior m.

**prioress** ['praɪərɪs] n Priorin f.

**priority** [praɪ'ɒrɪtɪ] n Vorrang m, Priorität f; (thing having precedence) vorrangige Angelegenheit. **a top** ~ eine Sache von äußerster Dringlichkeit; **to have** ~ Vorrang or Priorität haben; **to give** ~ **to sth** etw vorrangig behandeln, einer Sache (dat) Priorität geben; ~ **treatment** Vorzugsbehandlung f; **to get** ~ **treatment** bevorzugt behandelt werden; **in order of** ~ nach Dringlichkeit; **we must get our priorities right** wir müssen unsere Prioritäten richtig setzen.

**priory** ['praɪərɪ] n Priorat nt.

**prise,** (US) **prize** [praɪz] vt **to** ~ **sth open** etw aufbrechen; **to** ~ **the lid up/off** den Deckel auf-/abbekommen.

**prism** ['prɪzəm] n Prisma nt.

**prison** ['prɪzn] 1 n (lit, fig) Gefängnis nt. **to be in** ~ im Gefängnis sein; **to go to** ~ **for 5 years** für 5 Jahre ins Gefängnis gehen; **to send sb to** ~ jdn ins Gefängnis schicken. 2 attr Gefängnis-; system, facilities Strafvollzugs-. ~ **camp** Gefangenenlager nt; ~ **life** das Leben im Gefängnis.

**prisoner** ['prɪznə*r*] n Gefangene(r) mf; (convicted also) Häftling m. ~ **(at the bar)** (Jur) Angeklagte(r) mf; **to hold** or **keep sb** ~ jdn gefangenhalten; **to take sb** ~ jdn gefangennehmen; ~ **of war** Kriegsgefangene(r) m.

**prissy** ['prɪsɪ] adj (pej) zimperlich.

**pristine** ['prɪstaɪn, -tiːn] adj beauty unberührt; condition tadellos, makellos.

**privacy** ['prɪvəsɪ, 'praɪvəsɪ] n Privatleben nt. **there is no** ~ man kann kein Privatleben führen; **in the** ~ **of one's home** in den eigenen vier Wänden (col); **in the strictest** ~ (meeting etc) unter äußerster Geheimhaltung.

**private** ['praɪvɪt] 1 adj (a) privat; letter, reasons persönlich; matter Privat-, vertraulich; place abgelegen; funeral im engsten Kreis; hearing etc nichtöffentlich attr. **they wanted to be** ~ sie wollten für sich sein; **to keep sth** ~ etw für sich behalten; **his** ~ **life** sein Privatleben nt; **with** ~ **bathroom** mit eigenem Bad. (b) ~ **car** Privatwagen m; ~ **citizen** Privatperson f; ~ **enterprise** Privatunternehmen nt; (free enterprise) freies Unternehmertum; ~ **eye** (col) Privatdetektiv m; ~ **parts** (genitals) Geschlechtsteile pl; ~ **practice** Privatpraxis f; ~ **property** Privateigentum nt; ~ **school** Privatschule f; ~ **sector** Privatwirtschaft f; ~ **view** (Art) Vernissage f. 2 n (a) (Mil) Gefreite(r) mf. (b) **in** ~ privat; **we must talk in** ~ wir müssen das unter uns besprechen.

**privately** ['praɪvɪtlɪ] adv (a) (not publicly) privat. ~ **owned** in Privatbesitz. (b) (secretly, personally) per-

sönlich; *(in confidence)* vertraulich. **but ~ he was very upset** doch innerlich war er sehr aufgebracht.
**privation** [praɪ'veɪʃən] *n* **(a)** *(state)* Armut, Not *f.* **(b)** *(hardship)* Entbehrung *f.*
**privatization** [ˌpraɪvətaɪ'zeɪʃən] *n* Privatisierung *f.*
**privatize** ['praɪvətaɪz] *vt* privatisieren.
**privet** ['prɪvɪt] *n* Liguster *m.*
**privilege** ['prɪvɪlɪdʒ] **1** *n* Privileg, Sonderrecht *nt;* *(honour)* Ehre *f;* *(Parl)* Immunität *f.* **2** *vt* privilegieren, bevorrechtigen. **I was ~d to talk to him** ich hatte die Ehre, mich mit ihm zu unterhalten.
**privileged** ['prɪvɪlɪdʒd] *adj person, classes* privilegiert. **for a ~ few** für eine kleine Gruppe von Privilegierten.
**privy** ['prɪvɪ] *adj* **(a) to be ~ to sth** *(form)* in etw *(acc)* eingeweiht sein. **(b) P~ Council, P~ Councillor** Geheimer Rat.
**prize¹** [praɪz] **1** *n* Preis *m;* *(in lottery also)* Gewinn *m.* **to win first ~** den ersten Preis gewinnen. **2** *adj* **(a)** *(awarded a ~)* entry, essay preisgekrönt. **~ idiot** *(col)* Volltrottel *m (col).* **(b)** *(awarded as a ~) trophy* Sieges-. **(c)** *(offering a ~) competition* Preis-. **~ draw** Lotterie *f.* **3** *vt* (hoch)schätzen. **his most ~d possession** sein wertvollster Besitz.
**prize²** *vt (US)* = **prise**.
**prize:** **~-fight** *n (esp Hist)* Preisboxkampf *m;* **~-fighter** *n (esp Hist)* Preisboxer *m;* **~-giving** *n (Sch)* Preisverteilung *f;* **~ money** *n* Geldpreis *m;* *(in competition)* Gewinn *m;* **~-winner** *n* (Preis)gewinner(in *f*) *m;* **~winning** *adj entry, novel* preisgekrönt; *ticket* Gewinn-.
**PRO** = **public relations officer**.
**pro¹** [prəʊ] *n (col: professional)* Profi *m.*
**pro²** **1** *prep (in favour of)* für. **2** *n* **the ~s and cons** das Für und Wider, das Pro und Kontra.
**pro-** *pref (in favour of)* pro-. **~-feminist/Arab** profeministisch/proarabisch.
**probability** [ˌprɒbə'bɪlɪtɪ] *n* Wahrscheinlichkeit *f.* **in all ~** höchstwahrscheinlich.
**probable** ['prɒbəbl] *adj* wahrscheinlich.
**probably** ['prɒbəblɪ] *adv* wahrscheinlich. **more ~ than not** höchstwahrscheinlich.
**probate** ['prəʊbɪt] *n (examination)* gerichtliche Testamentsbestätigung; *(will)* beglaubigte Testamentsabschrift.
**probation** [prə'beɪʃən] *n* **(a)** *(Jur)* Bewährung *f.* **to put sb on ~ (for a year)** jdm (ein Jahr) Bewährung geben; **to be on ~** Bewährung haben; **to be released on ~** auf Bewährung freigelassen werden; **~ officer** Bewährungshelfer(in *f*) *m.* **(b)** *(of employee)* Probe *f;* *(~ period)* Probezeit *f.*
**probationary** [prə'beɪʃnərɪ] *adj* Probe-. **~ period** Probezeit *f.*
**probationer** [prə'beɪʃnər] *n (Jur)* auf Bewährung Freigelassene(r) *mf.*
**probe** [prəʊb] **1** *n* **(a)** *(device)* Sonde *f.* **(b)** *(investigation)* Untersuchung *f (into gen).* **2** *vt* untersuchen; *space, sb's past, private life* erforschen; *mystery* ergründen. **3** *vi* suchen, forschen *(for nach);* *(Med)* untersuchen *(for auf +acc).* **to ~ into sb's private life** in jds Privatleben *(dat)* herumschnüffeln *(col).*
**probing** ['prəʊbɪŋ] **1** *n* Untersuchung *f.* **2** *adj question, study* prüfend.
**probity** ['prəʊbɪtɪ] *n* Redlichkeit *f.*
**problem** ['prɒbləm] *n* Problem *nt;* *(Math: as school exercise)* Aufgabe *f.* **what's the ~?** wo fehlt's?; **he's got a drinking ~** er trinkt (zuviel); **I had no ~ in getting the money** ich habe das Geld ohne Schwierigkeiten bekommen; **no ~!** *(col)* kein Problem!; **~ area** Problembereich *m.*
**problematic(al)** [ˌprɒblə'mætɪk(əl)] *adj* problematisch.

tisch.
**problem:** **~ child** *n* Problemkind *nt;* **~ page** *n* Problemseite *f.*
**procedural** [prə'siːdjʊrəl] *adj* verfahrenstechnisch.
**procedure** [prə'siːdʒər] *n* Verfahren *nt.* **business ~** geschäftliche Verfahrensweise; **a lengthy ~** eine langwierige Prozedur; **what is the ~ in such cases?** wie geht man in solchen Fällen vor?
**proceed** [prə'siːd] **1** *vi* **(a)** *(form: go)* gehen; *(by vehicle)* fahren. **(b)** *(form: go on) (person)* weitergehen; *(vehicle, by vehicle)* weiterfahren. **we then ~ed to London** wir fuhren dann nach London weiter. **(c)** *(set about sth)* vorgehen; *(carry on, continue)* fortfahren. **can we now ~ to the next item on the agenda?** können wir jetzt zum nächsten Punkt der Tagesordnung übergehen?; **they ~ed with their plan** sie führten ihren Plan weiter; *(start)* sie gingen nach ihrem Plan vor; **negotiations are ~ing well** die Verhandlungen kommen gut voran; **to ~ on the assumption that ...** von der Voraussetzung ausgehen, daß ... **(d)** *(originate)* **to ~ from** kommen von; *(fig)* herrühren von. **(e)** *(Jur)* **to ~ against sb** gegen jdn gerichtlich vorgehen.
  **2** *vt* **now, he ~ed** nun, fuhr er fort; **to ~ to do sth** (dann) etw tun.
**proceeding** [prə'siːdɪŋ] *n* **(a)** *(course of action)* Vorgehen *nt.* **(b)** **~s** *pl (function)* Veranstaltung *f.* **(c)** **~s** *pl (esp Jur)* Verfahren *nt;* **to take/start ~s against sb** gegen jdn gerichtlich vorgehen; **to take legal ~s** einen Prozeß anstrengen. **(d)** **~s** *pl (written minutes etc)* Protokoll *nt;* *(published report)* Tätigkeitsbericht *m.*
**proceeds** ['prəʊsiːdz] *npl (yield)* Ertrag *m;* *(from sale etc)* Erlös *m;* *(takings)* Einnahmen *pl.*
**process¹** ['prəʊses] **1** *n* **(a)** *(process)* Prozeß *m.* **in the ~ of time** im Laufe der Zeit; **in the ~ dabei; in the ~ of learning** beim Lernen; **to be in the ~ of doing sth** dabei sein, etw zu tun; **in ~ of construction** im Bau. **(b)** *(method, technique)* Verfahren *nt.* **2** *vt (treat)* *raw materials, data* verarbeiten; *food* konservieren; *milk* sterilisieren; *application, loan* bearbeiten; *film* entwickeln. **~ed cheese, (US) ~ cheese** Schmelzkäse *m.*
**process²** [prə'ses] *vi (Brit: go in procession)* ziehen, schreiten.
**processing** ['prəʊsesɪŋ] *n see vt* Verarbeitung *f;* Konservierung *f;* Sterilisierung *f;* Bearbeitung *f;* Entwicklung *f.*
**processing:** **~ language** *n (Comp)* Prozeßsprache *f;* **~ plant** *n* Aufbereitungsanlage *f.*
**procession** [prə'seʃən] *n (organized)* Umzug *m;* *(solemn)* Prozession *f;* *(line of people, cars etc)* Reihe, Schlange *f. funeral ~* Trauerzug *m.*
**processor** ['prəʊsesər] *n (Comp)* Prozessor *m.*
**proclaim** [prə'kleɪm] *vt* **(a)** erklären; *revolution* ausrufen. **to ~ sb king** jdn zum König ausrufen. **(b)** *(reveal)* verraten.
**proclamation** [ˌprɒklə'meɪʃən] *n* Erklärung *f;* *(of laws, measures)* Verkündung *f;* *(of state of emergency)* Ausrufung *f.*
**proclivity** [prə'klɪvɪtɪ] *n* Neigung *f (for zu).*
**procrastinate** [prəʊ'kræstɪneɪt] *vi* zögern, zaudern.
**procrastination** [prəʊˌkræstɪ'neɪʃən] *n* Zögern, Zaudern *nt.*
**procreation** [ˌprəʊkrɪ'eɪʃən] *n* Zeugung *f.*
**procure** [prə'kjʊər] *vt* **(a)** *(obtain)* beschaffen, sich *(dat)* verschaffen; *(bring about)* bewirken. **to ~ sth for sb/oneself** jdm/sich etw beschaffen. **(b)** *(for prostitution)* beschaffen *(for sb* jdm*).*
**procurement** [prə'kjʊəmənt] *n* Beschaffung *f.*
**prod** [prɒd] **1** *n* Stupser, Knuff *(col) m.* **to give sb a ~**

**profuse**

jdn anstupsen; *(fig)* jdm einen Stoß geben. **2** *vt* **(a)** anstupsen, knuffen *(col).* **he ~ded the donkey (on) with his stick** er trieb den Esel mit seinem Stock vorwärts. **(b)** *(fig)* anspornen *(to do sth, into sth* zu etw*).* **to ~ sb into action** jdm einen Stoß geben. **3** *vi* **to ~ at sth** an etw *(acc)* stoßen.

**prodigal** ['prɒdɪgəl] *adj* verschwenderisch. **the ~ son** *(Bibl, fig)* der verlorene Sohn.

**prodigious** [prə'dɪdʒəs] *adj (vast)* ungeheuer; *(marvellous)* erstaunlich, wunderbar.

**prodigiously** [prə'dɪdʒəslɪ] *adv* außerordentlich; *eat, drink* ungeheuer viel.

**prodigy** ['prɒdɪdʒɪ] *n* Wunder *nt.* **child ~** Wunderkind *nt.*

**produce** ['prɒdjuːs] **1** *n no pl (Agr)* Produkt (e *pl*), Erzeugnis (se *pl*) *nt.* **~ of Italy** italienisches Erzeugnis. **2** [prə'djuːs] *vt* **(a)** *(manufacture)* produzieren; *cars, steel, paper etc also* herstellen; *energy* erzeugen; *crop, return on capital* abwerfen; *coal also* fördern; *(create) book, article* schreiben; *painting* anfertigen; *ideas also, delinquents etc* hervorbringen. **(b)** *(bring forward, show) gift, wallet etc* hervorholen *(from, out of* aus*); pistol* ziehen *(from, out of* aus*); evidence* liefern; *witness* beibringen; *ticket, documents* vorzeigen. **I can't ~ it out of thin air** ich kann es doch nicht aus dem Ärmel schütteln *(col).* **(c)** *play* inszenieren; *film* produzieren. **(d)** *(cause)* bitterness, impression* hervorrufen; *interest also, spark* erzeugen.

**producer** [prə'djuːsəʳ] *n* Hersteller *m*; *(Agr)* Produzent, Erzeuger *m*; *(Theat)* Regisseur *m*; *(Film, TV)* Produzent *m.*

**product** ['prɒdʌkt] *n* Produkt, Erzeugnis *nt*; *(fig: result, Math, Chem)* Produkt *nt.* **food ~s** Nahrungsmittel *pl.*

**production** [prə'dʌkʃən] *n* **(a)** *see vt (a)* Produktion *f*; Herstellung *f*; Erzeugung *f*; Förderung *f*; Schreiben *nt*; Hervorbringung *f.* **to go into ~** *(factory)* die Produktion aufnehmen; *(model)* in Produktion gehen; **to take sth out of ~** etw aus der Produktion nehmen. **(b)** *(output)* Produktion *f.* **(c)** *see vt (b)* Hervorholen *nt*; Lieferung *f*; Vorzeigen *nt.* **on ~ of this ticket** gegen Vorlage dieser Eintrittskarte. **(d)** *(of play)* Inszenierung *f*; *(of film)* Produktion *f.*

**production: ~ line** *n* Fließband *nt*; **~ manager** *n* Produktionsleiter *m*; **~ model** *n (car)* Serienmodell *nt*; **~ platform** *n (for oil)* Förderplattform *f.*

**productive** [prə'dʌktɪv] *adj* produktiv; *land* fruchtbar; *mind* schöpferisch; *business* rentabel.

**productivity** [,prɒdʌk'tɪvɪtɪ] *n see adj* Produktivität *f*; Fruchtbarkeit *f*; schöpferische Kraft.

**productivity: ~ agreement** *n* Produktivitätsvereinbarung *f*; **~ bonus** *n* Leistungszulage *f.*

**Prof** = **Professor** Prof.

**profane** [prə'feɪn] **1** *adj* **(a)** *(secular)* weltlich, profan. **(b)** *(irreverent, sacrilegious)* (gottes)lästerlich. **2** *vt* entweihen.

**profanity** [prə'fænɪtɪ] *n* Gotteslästerlichkeit *f*; *(act, utterance)* (Gottes)lästerung *f.*

**profess** [prə'fes] *vt* **(a)** *faith, belief etc* sich bekennen zu. **(b)** *(claim to have) interest, enthusiasm* bekunden; *belief* kundtun; *ignorance* zugeben. **I do not ~ to be an expert** ich behaupte nicht, ein Fachmann zu sein.

**professed** [prə'fest] *adj* erklärt; *(pej: purported)* angeblich. **to be a ~ Christian** sich zum christlichen Glauben bekennen.

**profession** [prə'feʃən] *n* **(a)** *(occupation)* Beruf *m.* **the medical/teaching ~** der Arzt-/Lehrerberuf; *(members of the ~)* die Ärzte-/Lehrerschaft; **by ~** von Beruf; **the ~s** die gehobenen Berufe. **(b)**

*(declaration)* Bekenntnis *nt*; *(Eccl)* Gelübde *nt.* **~ of faith** Glaubensbekenntnis *nt.*

**professional** [prə'feʃənl] **1** *adj* **(a)** Berufs-, beruflich; *army, soldier, tennis player* Berufs-; *(working) lady, couple etc* berufstätig; *opinion* fachmännisch, fachlich. **~ footballer** Profifußballer *m*; **the ~ classes** die gehobenen Berufe; **to take ~ advice** fachmännischen Rat einholen; **to turn *or* go ~** Profi werden. **(b)** *(skilled, competent) piece of work etc* fachmännisch, fachgerecht; *company, approach* professionell. **it's not up to ~ standards** es ist nicht fachmännisch gemacht worden; **it wouldn't be ~ of me to ...** es wäre nicht korrekt von mir, wenn ich ... **2** *n* Fachmann *m*, Fachfrau *f*; *(esp Sport)* Profi *m*; *(working person)* Berufstätige (r) *mf.*

**professionalism** [prə'feʃnəlɪzəm] *n* Professionalismus *m*; *(of job, piece of work)* Perfektion *f.*

**professionally** [prə'feʃnəlɪ] *adv* beruflich; *(in accomplished manner)* fachmännisch; *work* professionell. **he plays ~** er ist Berufsspieler *or* Profi; **he is ~ recognized as the best ...** er ist in Fachkreisen als der beste ... bekannt.

**professor** [prə'fesəʳ] *n* Professor (in *f*) *m*; *(US also: teacher)* Dozent (in *f*) *m.*

**professorship** [prə'fesəʃɪp] *n* Professur *f*, Lehrstuhl *m.*

**proffer** ['prɒfəʳ] *vt gift, drink* anbieten; *apologies, thanks etc* aussprechen; *remark* machen.

**proficiency** [prə'fɪʃənsɪ] *n level or standard of* ~ Leistungsstand *m*; **her ~ at teaching** ihre Tüchtigkeit als Lehrerin; **~ test** Leistungstest *m.*

**proficient** [prə'fɪʃənt] *adj* tüchtig, fähig. **he is just about ~ in German** seine Deutschkenntnisse reichen gerade aus.

**profile** ['prəʊfaɪl] *n* Profil *nt*; *(picture, photograph)* Profilbild *nt*; *(biographical ~)* Porträt *nt.* **in ~** *(person, head)* im Profil; **to keep a low ~** sich zurückhalten.

**profit** ['prɒfɪt] **1** *n* Gewinn, Profit *(also pej) m.* **~ and loss account** Gewinn-und-Verlust-Rechnung *f*; **to make a ~ (out of *or* on sth)** (mit etw) einen Gewinn machen, (an etw *dat*) verdienen; **to sell sth at a ~** etw mit Gewinn verkaufen. **2** *vi (gain)* profitieren *(by, from* von*)*, Nutzen ziehen *(by, from* aus*).*

**profitability** [,prɒfɪtə'bɪlɪtɪ] *n* Rentabilität *f.*

**profitable** ['prɒfɪtəbl] *adj (Comm)* gewinnbringend, rentabel; *(fig: beneficial)* nützlich.

**profitably** ['prɒfɪtəblɪ] *adv see adj.*

**profiteer** [,prɒfɪ'tɪəʳ] **1** *n* Profitmacher *m*; *(practising extortion)* Wucherer *m.* **2** *vi* Wucher treiben.

**profiteering** [,prɒfɪ'tɪərɪŋ] *n* Wucher(ei *f*) *m.*

**profit: ~-making** *adj organization* rentabel; *(~-orientated)* gewinnorientiert; **~ margin** *n* Gewinnspanne *f*; **~-sharing** *n* Gewinnbeteiligung *f.*

**profligate** ['prɒflɪgɪt] *adj (dissolute)* lasterhaft; *(extravagant)* verschwenderisch.

**pro forma invoice** [,prəʊ'fɔːmə'ɪnvɔɪs] *n* Pro-Forma-Rechnung *f.*

**profound** [prə'faʊnd] *adj* tief; *thought, thinker* tiefgründig; *book* gehaltvoll; *knowledge* profund *(geh)*; *indifference* völlig; *interest* stark; *changes* tiefgreifend *attr.*

**profoundly** [prə'faʊndlɪ] *adv* zutiefst. **~ deaf** hochgradig schwerhörig; **~ significant** äußerst bedeutsam; **~ indifferent** vollkommen gleichgültig; **..., he said ~ ...**, sagte er tiefsinnig.

**profundity** [prə'fʌndɪtɪ] *n* **(a)** *no pl* Tiefe *f*; *(of thought, thinker, book etc)* Tiefgründigkeit *f*; *(of knowledge)* Gründlichkeit *f.* **(b)** *(profound remark)* Tiefsinnigkeit *f.*

**profuse** [prə'fjuːs] *adj vegetation* üppig; *thanks,*

*praise* überschwenglich; *apologies* überreichlich.

**profusely** [prə'fjuːslı] *adv grow* üppig; *bleed, sweat* stark; *thank, praise* überschwenglich. **he apologized** ~ er entschuldigte sich vielmals.

**profusion** [prə'fjuːʒən] *n* Überfülle *f.* **trees in** ~ Bäume in Hülle und Fülle.

**progeny** ['prɒdʒını] *n* Nachkommen *pl.*

**prognosis** [prɒg'nəʊsıs] *n, pl* **prognoses** [prɒg'nəʊsiːz] Prognose, Voraussage *f.*

**program** ['prəʊgræm] **1** *n* **(a)** *(Comp)* Programm *nt.* **(b)** *(US)* = **programme 1. 2** *vt* **(a)** *computer* programmieren. **(b)** *(US)* = **programme 2.**

**programmable** ['prəʊgræməbl] *adj* programmierbar.

**programme,** *(US)* **program** ['prəʊgræm] **1** *n* Programm *nt; (Rad, TV also)* Sendung *f.* ~ **of events** Veranstaltungsprogramm *nt;* **we've got a very heavy** ~ **of meetings** wir haben sehr viele Besprechungen auf unserem Programm; **what's the** ~ **for tomorrow?** was steht für morgen auf dem Programm? **2** *vt* programmieren.

**programmer** ['prəʊgræmər] *n* Programmierer(-in *f*) *m.*

**programming** ['prəʊgræmıŋ] *n* Programmieren *nt.* ~ **language** Programmiersprache *f.*

**progress** ['prəʊgres] **1** *n* **(a)** *no pl (movement forwards)* Vorwärtskommen *nt; (Mil)* Vorrücken *nt.* **they made good** ~ **across the open country** sie kamen im offenen Gelände gut vorwärts. **(b)** *no pl (advance)* Fortschritt *m.* **the** ~ **of events** der Gang der Ereignisse; **to make (good/slow)** ~ (gute/langsame) Fortschritte machen; ~ **report** Fortschrittsbericht *m; (of work)* Tätigkeitsbericht *m;* **in** ~ im Gange; **the work still in** ~ die noch zu erledigende Arbeit.

**2** [prə'gres] *vi* **(a)** *(move, go forward)* sich vorwärts bewegen. **(b)** *(in time)* **as the work** ~**es** mit dem Fortschreiten der Arbeit; **as the game** ~**ed** im Laufe des Spiels. **(c)** *(improve, make progress)* Fortschritte machen. **how far have you** ~**ed since our last meeting?** wie weit sind Sie seit unserer letzten Sitzung vorangekommen?; **investigations are** ~**ing well** die Untersuchungen machen gute Fortschritte.

**progression** [prə'greʃən] *n* Folge *f; (Math)* Reihe *f; (Mus)* Sequenz *f; (development)* Entwicklung *f.* **sales have shown a continuous upwards** ~ im Absatz wurde eine stete Aufwärtsentwicklung verzeichnet.

**progressive** [prə'gresıv] *adj* **(a)** *(increasing)* zunehmend; *disease etc* fortschreitend; *paralysis, taxation* progressiv. **(b)** *(favouring progress)* progressiv, fortschrittlich.

**progressively** [prə'gresıvlı] *adv* zunehmend.

**prohibit** [prə'hıbıt] *vt* **(a)** verbieten, untersagen. **to** ~ **sb from doing sth** jdm etw verbieten *or* untersagen. **"smoking** ~**ed"** „Rauchen verboten". **(b)** *(prevent)* verhindern. **to** ~ **sb from doing sth** jdn daran hindern, etw zu tun.

**prohibition** [,prəʊı'bıʃən] *n* Verbot *nt.* **(the) P**~ *(Hist)* die Prohibition; **the** ~ **of smoking** das Rauchverbot.

**prohibitive** [prə'hıbıtıv] *adj price, cost* unerschwinglich.

**prohibitively** [prə'hıbıtıvlı] *adv* ~ **expensive** unerschwinglich.

**project¹** ['prɒdʒekt] *n* Projekt *nt; (scheme)* Vorhaben *nt; (Sch, Univ)* Referat *nt.* ~ **leader** *or* **manager** Projektleiter(in *f*) *m.*

**project²** [prə'dʒekt] **1** *vt* **(a)** *film, map, figures* projizieren. **to** ~ **oneself/one's personality** sich selbst/seine eigene Person zur Geltung bringen; **to** ~

**one's voice** seine Stimme zum Tragen bringen. **(b)** *(plan)* voraussagen; *costs* überschlagen. **2** *vi (jut out)* hervorragen *(from* aus*).* **the upper storey** ~**s over the road** das obere Stockwerk ragt über die Straße.

**projectile** [prə'dʒektaıl] *n (also Mil)* Geschoß *nt.*

**projection** [prə'dʒekʃən] *n* **(a)** *(of films, map)* Projektion *f.* ~ **room** Vorführraum *m.* **(b)** *(overhang etc)* Vorsprung *m.* **(c)** *(prediction)* Prognose *f; (of cost)* Überschlagung *f.*

**projectionist** [prə'dʒekʃnıst] *n* Filmvorführer *m.*

**projector** [prə'dʒektər] *n (Film)* Projektor *m.*

**proletarian** [,prəʊlə'tɛərıən] **1** *adj* proletarisch. **2** *n* Proletarier(in *f*) *m.*

**proletariat** [,prəʊlə'tɛərıət] *n* Proletariat *nt.*

**proliferate** [prə'lıfəreıt] *vi (number)* sich stark erhöhen; *(ideas)* um sich greifen; *(animals)* sich stark vermehren; *(weeds, cells)* wuchern.

**proliferation** [prə,lıfə'reıʃən] *n (in numbers)* starke Erhöhung; *(of animals)* zahlreiche Vermehrung; *(of nuclear weapons)* Weitergabe *f; (of ideas)* Ausbreitung *f; (of weeds)* Wuchern *nt.*

**prolific** [prə'lıfık] *adj* fruchtbar; *writer* produktiv.

**prologue** ['prəʊlɒg] *n* Prolog *m; (of book)* Vorwort *nt; (fig)* Vorspiel *nt.*

**prolong** [prə'lɒŋ] *vt* verlängern; *(pej) process, pain* hinauszögern.

**prolongation** [,prəʊlɒŋ'geıʃən] *n see vt* Verlängerung *f;* Hinauszögern *nt.*

**prolonged** [prə'lɒŋd] *adj* lang anhaltend.

**prom** [prɒm] *n (col)* = **promenade 1. the P**~**s** die Promenadenkonzerte *(in der Londoner Royal Albert Hall).*

**promenade** [,prɒmı'nɑːd] **1** *n (esp Brit: esplanade)* (Strand)promenade *f; (US: ball)* Studenten-/Schülerball *m.* ~ **concert** zwangloses Konzert *(meist mit vielen Stehplätzen);* ~ **deck** Promenadendeck *nt.* **2** *vi (stroll)* promenieren.

**prominence** ['prɒmınəns] *n* **(a)** **the** ~ **of his features** seine ausgeprägten Gesichtszüge. **(b)** *(of ideas, beliefs)* Beliebtheit *f; (of writer, politician etc)* Bekanntheit *f.* **to come into** ~ in den Vordergrund rücken; *(person)* in Erscheinung treten; **to bring sb/sth into** ~ *(attract attention to)* jdn/etw herausstellen; *(make famous)* jdn/etw berühmt machen. **(c)** *(prominent part)* Vorsprung *m.*

**prominent** ['prɒmınənt] *adj* **(a)** *cheekbones, teeth* vorstehend *attr; crag* vorspringend *attr.* **to be** ~ vorstehen; vorspringen. **(b)** *(conspicuous) markings* auffällig; *feature, characteristic* hervorstechend. **the castle occupies a** ~ **position** das Schloß hat eine exponierte Lage. **(c)** *(leading) role* führend; *(significant)* wichtig. **(d)** *(well-known) personality, publisher* prominent.

**prominently** ['prɒmınəntlı] *adv display, place* deutlich sichtbar. **he figured** ~ er spielte eine bedeutende Rolle.

**promiscuity** [,prɒmı'skjuːıtı] *n* Promiskuität *f.*

**promiscuous** [prə'mıskjʊəs] *adj (sexually)* **to be** ~ häufig den Partner wechseln; ~ **behaviour** häufiger Partnerwechsel.

**promise** ['prɒmıs] **1** *n* **(a)** Versprechen *nt.* **their** ~ **of help** ihr Versprechen zu helfen; **to make sb a** ~ jdm ein Versprechen geben; **to hold** *or* **keep sb to his** ~ jdn an sein Versprechen binden. **(b)** *(hope, prospect)* Hoffnung, Aussicht *f.* **a young man of** ~ ein vielversprechender junger Mann; **to show** ~ zu den besten Hoffnungen berechtigen. **2** *vt* versprechen; *(forecast)* hindeuten auf *(+acc).* **to** ~ **(sb) to do sth** (jdm) versprechen, etw zu tun; **to** ~ **sb sth, to** ~ **sth to sb** jdm etw versprechen; **to** ~ **sb the**

**earth** jdm das Blaue vom Himmel herunter versprechen; **it ~s to be a hard day** es sieht nach einem harten Tag aus. **3** *vi* versprechen. **(do you) ~?** versprichst du es?; **I'll try, but I'm not promising** ich werde es versuchen, aber ich kann nichts versprechen.

**promising** ['prɒmɪsɪŋ] *adj* vielversprechend.

**promissory note** ['prɒmɪsərɪ'nəʊt] *n* Schuldschein *m*.

**promontory** ['prɒməntrɪ] *n* Kap *nt*.

**promote** [prə'məʊt] *vt* **(a)** *(in rank)* befördern *(to* zu +*dat)*. **our team was ~d** *(Ftbl)* unsere Mannschaft ist aufgestiegen. **(b)** *(foster)* fördern; *(organize)* conference etc veranstalten; *(advertise)* werben für; *(put on the market)* auf den Markt bringen.

**promoter** [prə'məʊtər] *n* *(Sport, of beauty contest etc)* Promoter, Veranstalter *m*; *(of company)* Mitbegründer *m*.

**promotion** [prə'məʊʃən] *n* **(a)** *(in rank)* Beförderung *f*. **to get** *or* **win ~** befördert werden; *(football team)* aufsteigen. **(b)** *(fostering)* Förderung *f*; *(organization: of conference etc)* Veranstaltung *f*; *(advertising)* Werbung, Promotion *f* *(of* für*)*; *(advertising campaign)* Werbekampagne *f*; *(marketing)* Einführung *f* auf dem Markt.

**promotional** [prə'məʊʃənəl] *adj literature etc* Werbe-.

**prompt** [prɒmpt] **1** *adj* (+*er*) prompt; *action* unverzüglich. **he is always very ~** *(on time)* er ist immer sehr pünktlich. **2** *adv* **at 6 o'clock ~** Punkt 6 Uhr. **3** *vt* **(a)** *(motivate)* veranlassen *(to* zu*)*. **to ~ sb to do sth** jdn (dazu) veranlassen, etw zu tun; **what ~ed you to do it?** was hat Sie dazu veranlaßt? **(b)** *conclusion* nahelegen. **(c)** *(help with speech)* vorsagen *(sb* jdm*)*; *(Theat)* soufflieren *(sb* jdm*)*. **he didn't need any ~ing** *(fig)* das brauchte man ihm nicht zweimal zu sagen. **4** *n* **(a) to give sb a ~** *(Theat)* jdm soufflieren; *(fig)* jdm weiterhelfen. **(b)** *(Comp)* Aufforderungsmeldung *f*, Prompt *m*.

**prompter** ['prɒmptər] *n* Souffleur *m*, Souffleuse *f*.

**promptly** ['prɒmptlɪ] *adv* prompt. **they left ~ at 6** sie gingen Punkt 6 Uhr; **of course he ~ forgot it all** er hat natürlich prompt alles vergessen.

**promptness** ['prɒmptnɪs] *n* Promptheit *f*.

**prone** [prəʊn] *adj* **(a)** *(lying)* **to be** *or* **lie ~** auf dem Bauch liegen. **(b)** *(liable)* **to be ~ to sth/to do sth** zu etw neigen/dazu neigen, etw zu tun.

**prong** [prɒŋ] *n* **(a)** *(of fork)* Zinke *f*. **(b)** *(fig)* *(of argument)* Punkt *m*; *(of attack)* (Angriffs)spitze *f*.

**-pronged** [-prɒŋd] *adj suf (of fork)* -zinkig. **a three~ attack** ein Angriff mit drei Spitzen.

**pronoun** ['prəʊnaʊn] *n* Fürwort, Pronomen *nt*.

**pronounce** [prə'naʊns] **1** *vt* **(a)** *word etc* aussprechen. **(b)** *(declare)* erklären für. **the doctors ~d him unfit for work** die Ärzte erklärten ihn für arbeitsunfähig; **to ~ sentence** das Urteil verkünden. **2** *vi* **to ~ in favour of/against sth** sich für/gegen etw aussprechen; **to ~ on sth** zu etw Stellung nehmen.

**pronounced** [prə'naʊnst] *adj (marked)* ausgesprochen; *improvement* deutlich; *views* entschieden. **he has a ~ limp** er hinkt sehr stark.

**pronouncement** [prə'naʊnsmənt] *n* Erklärung *f*; *(Jur: of sentence)* Verkündung *f*. **to make a ~** eine Erklärung abgeben.

**pronto** ['prɒntəʊ] *adv (col)* fix *(col)*. **do it ~** aber dalli! *(col)*.

**pronunciation** [prə,nʌnsɪ'eɪʃən] *n* Aussprache *f*.

**proof** [pruːf] **1** *n* **(a)** Beweis *m* *(of* für*)*. **as** *or* **in ~ of** als *or* zum Beweis für; **that is ~ that ...** das ist der Beweis dafür, daß ...; **to give** *or* **show ~ of sth** etw nachweisen; **can you give us any ~ of that?** können Sie (uns) dafür Beweise liefern? **(b)** *(test, trial)* Pro-

be *f*. **to put sth to the ~** etw auf die Probe stellen; *(Tech)* etw erproben. **(c)** *(Typ)* (Korrektur)fahne *f*; *(Phot)* Probeabzug *m*. **(d)** *(of alcohol)* Alkoholgehalt *m*. **40 ~** ≈ 40 Vol.-%. **2** *adj* **to be ~ against fire** feuersicher sein; **~ against inflation** inflationssicher.

**proof: ~-reader** *n* Korrektor(in *f*) *m*; **~-reading** *n* Korrekturlesen *nt*.

**Prop** *(Comm)* = **proprietor** Inh.

**prop** [prɒp] **1** *n* **(a)** *(lit)* Stütze *f*; *(fig also)* Halt *m*. **(b)** *(Theat)* Requisit *nt*. **2** *vt* **to ~ the door open** die Tür offenhalten; **to ~ sth against sth** etw gegen etw lehnen.

►**prop up** *vt sep* **(a)** *(rest, lean)* **to ~ oneself/sth ~ against sth** sich/etw gegen etw lehnen. **(b)** *(lit, fig: support)* stützen; *tunnel, wall* abstützen; *organization* unterstützen. **to ~ oneself ~ on sth** sich auf etw *(acc)* stützen.

**propaganda** [,prɒpə'gændə] *n* Propaganda *f*.

**propagate** ['prɒpəgeɪt] *vt* fortpflanzen; *(disseminate)* verbreiten; *views also* propagieren; *(Hort) plants* vermehren.

**propagation** [,prɒpə'geɪʃən] *n* Fortpflanzung *f*; *(dissemination)* Verbreitung *f*; *(of views)* Propagierung *f*; *(Hort: of plants)* Vermehrung *f*.

**propagator** ['prɒpəgeɪtər] *n* *(Hort)* Saatkiste *f*.

**propane** ['prəʊpeɪn] *n* *(also ~ gas)* Propan(gas) *nt*.

**propel** [prə'pel] *vt* antreiben; *(fuel)* betreiben.

**propeller** [prə'pelər] *n* Propeller *m*. **~ shaft** *(Aut)* Kardanwelle *f*; *(Naut)* Schraubenwelle *f*.

**propelling pencil** [prə,pelɪŋ'pensl] *n* *(Brit)* Drehbleistift *m*.

**propensity** [prə'pensɪtɪ] *n* Neigung *f* *(to* zu*)*. **to have a ~ to do sth** dazu neigen, etw zu tun.

**proper** ['prɒpər] **1** *adj* **(a)** *(fitting, suitable)* richtig; *(seemly)* anständig; *(prim and ~)* korrekt. **the ~ time** die richtige Zeit; **in the ~ way** richtig; **as you think ~** wie Sie es für richtig halten; **to do the ~ thing** das tun, was sich gehört; **the ~ thing to do would be to apologize** eigentlich müßte er *etc* sich entschuldigen; **we thought it only ~** wir dachten, es gehört sich einfach. **(b)** *(actual)* eigentlich. **in the ~ sense of the word** in der eigentlichen Bedeutung des Wortes; **he's not a ~ electrician** er ist kein richtiger Elektriker; **not in Berlin ~** nicht in Berlin selbst. **(c)** *(col: real) fool etc* richtig; *(thorough) beating* gehörig, tüchtig *(col)*. **we are in a ~ mess** wir sitzen ganz schön in der Patsche *(col)*. **2** *adv* **(a)** *(dial) cruel, poorly* richtig *(col)*. **(b)** *(incorrect usage) talk* richtig.

**properly** ['prɒpəlɪ] *adv* **(a)** *(correctly)* richtig. **~ speaking** genaugenommen; **not ~ dressed for walking** nicht richtig angezogen zum Wandern. **(b)** *(in seemly fashion)* anständig. **(c)** *(justifiably)* zu Recht. **(d)** *(col: really, thoroughly)* ganz schön *(col)*.

**proper noun** *n* Eigenname *m*.

**property** ['prɒpətɪ] *n* **(a)** *(thing owned)* Eigentum *nt*. **that's my ~** das gehört mir; **a man of ~** ein begüterter Mann. **(b)** *(building)* Haus *nt*; Wohnung *f*; *(office)* Gebäude *nt*; *(land)* Besitztum *nt*; *(estate)* Besitz *m*. **(c)** *(characteristic)* Eigenschaft *f*. **it has healing properties** es besitzt heilende Kräfte. **(d)** *(Theat)* Requisit *nt*.

**property: ~ developer** *n* Bauunternehmer *m*; **~ manager** *n* *(Theat)* Requisiteur *m*; **~ market** *n* Immobilienmarkt *m*; **~ owner** *n* Haus- und Grundbesitzer *m*; **~ tax** *n* Vermögenssteuer *f*.

**prophecy** ['prɒfɪsɪ] *n* Prophezeiung *f*.

**prophesy** ['prɒfɪsaɪ] *vt* prophezeien.

**prophet** ['prɒfɪt] *n* Prophet *m*. **~ of doom** Unheilsverkünder(in *f*) *m*.

**prophetic** [prə'fetɪk] *adj* prophetisch.

**propitious** [prə'pɪʃəs] *adj* günstig *(to, for* für*)*.

**proportion** [prə'pɔːʃən] **1** *n* **(a)** *(in number)* Verhältnis *nt (of x to y* zwischen x und y*)*. **~s** *(size)* Ausmaß *nt*; *(of building)* Ausmaße *pl.* **to be in/out of ~ to** *or* **with sth** im Verhältnis/in keinem Verhältnis zu etw stehen; *(in size, Art)* in den Proportionen zu etw passen/nicht zu etw passen; **to get sth in ~** *(fig)* etw objektiv betrachten; **he has let it all get out of ~** *(fig)* er hat den Blick für die Proportionen verloren; **it's out of all ~!** das geht über jedes Maß hinaus!; **he has no sense of ~** *(fig)* ihm fehlt der Sinn für das richtige Maß. **(b)** *(part, amount)* Teil *m.* **what ~ of industry is in private hands?** wie groß ist der Anteil der Industrie, der sich in privater Hand befindet?

**2** *vt* **a well ~ed woman/building** eine wohlproportionierte Frau/ein wohlausgewogenes Gebäude.

**proportional** [prə'pɔːʃənl] *adj* proportional *(to* zu*)*. **~ representation** Verhältniswahlrecht *nt*; **~ spacing** *(Typ, Comp)* Proportionalschrift *f.*

**proportionally** [prə'pɔːʃnəlɪ] *adv* proportional; *more, less* entsprechend.

**proportionate** [prə'pɔːʃnɪt] *adj* proportional. **to be/ not to be ~ to sth** im Verhältnis/in keinem Verhältnis zu etw stehen.

**proportionately** [prə'pɔːʃnɪtlɪ] *adv* proportional.

**proposal** [prə'pəʊzl] *n* Vorschlag *m (on, about* zu*)*; *(of marriage)* (Heirats)antrag *m.* **to make sb a ~** jdm einen Vorschlag machen.

**propose** [prə'pəʊz] **1** *vt* **(a)** vorschlagen; *motion* stellen, einbringen; *toast* ausbringen *(to* auf *+acc)*. **I ~ that we leave now** ich schlage vor, daß wir jetzt gehen. **(b)** *(have in mind)* beabsichtigen. **but I don't ~ to** ich habe aber nicht die Absicht; **how do you ~ to pay for it?** wie wollen Sie das bezahlen? **2** *vi (~ marriage)* einen (Heirats)antrag machen *(to sb* jdm*)*.

**proposer** [prə'pəʊzə\*] *n (in debate)* Antragsteller(in *f) m.*

**proposition** [‚prɒpə'zɪʃən] **1** *n* **(a)** *(statement)* Aussage *f.* **(b)** *(proposal)* Vorschlag *m*; *(argument)* These *f.* **(c)** *(prospect)* Aussicht *f.* **(d) he/that is a tough ~** er/das ist ein harter Brocken. **2** *vt to ~ sb (sexually)* jdm einen unanständigen Antrag machen.

**propound** [prə'paʊnd] *vt* darlegen.

**proprietary** [prə'praɪətərɪ] *adj rights* Besitz-; *medicine, article* Marken-. **~ brand of ...** Marken...; **~ goods** Markenware *f*; **~ name** Markenname *m.*

**proprietor** [prə'praɪətə\*] *n (of pub, patent)* Inhaber(in *f) m*; *(of house, newspaper)* Besitzer(in *f) m.*

**propriety** [prə'praɪətɪ] *n (correctness)* Korrektheit *f*; *(decency)* Anstand *m.* **breach of ~** Verstoß *m* gegen die guten Sitten.

**props** [prɒps] *npl (Theat)* Requisiten *pl.*

**propulsion** [prə'pʌlʃən] *n* Antrieb *m.*

**pro rata** [prəʊ'rɑːtə] *adj, adv* anteilmäßig.

**prosaic** [prəʊ'zeɪɪk] *adj* prosaisch; *(down-to-earth)* nüchtern; *life, joke* alltäglich.

**proscribe** [prəʊ'skraɪb] *vt (forbid)* verbieten; *(exile)* verbannen.

**prose** [prəʊz] *n* Prosa *f*; *(writing, style)* Stil *m*; *(Sch: translation)* Übersetzung *f* in die Fremdsprache.

**prosecute** ['prɒsɪkjuːt] *vt* **(a)** *person* strafrechtlich verfolgen *(for* wegen*)*. **(b)** *(form: carry on)* campaign etc durchführen; *claim* weiterverfolgen.

**prosecution** [‚prɒsɪ'kjuːʃən] *n (Jur) (act of prosecuting)* strafrechtliche Verfolgung; *(in court: case, side)* Anklage *f (for* wegen*)*. **(the) counsel for the ~** der Anklagevertreter.

**prosecutor** ['prɒsɪkjuːtə\*] *n* Ankläger(in *f) m.*

**prospect** ['prɒspekt] **1** *n* **(a)** *(outlook)* Aussicht *f (of* auf *+acc)*. **what a ~!** *(iro)* das sind ja schöne Aussichten!; **he has no ~s** er hat keine Zukunft; **a job with no ~s** eine Stelle ohne Zukunft; **to hold out the ~ of sth** etw in Aussicht stellen; **to have sth in ~** etw in Aussicht haben. **(b)** *(person, thing)* Arsenal **is a good ~ for the cup** Arsenal ist ein aussichtsreicher Kandidat für den Pokal. **2** [prə'spekt] *vi (Min)* nach Bodenschätzen suchen. **to ~ for gold** nach Gold suchen.

**prospecting** [prə'spektɪŋ] *n (Min)* Suche *f* nach Bodenschätzen.

**prospective** [prə'spektɪv] *adj attr (likely to happen)* voraussichtlich; *(future) son-in-law* zukünftig; *buyer* interessiert. **~ candidate** potentieller Kandidat.

**prospector** [prə'spektə\*] *n* Gold-/Erz-/Ölsucher *m.*

**prospectus** [prə'spektəs] *n* Verzeichnis *nt*; *(for holidays etc)* Prospekt *m.*

**prosper** ['prɒspə\*] *vi (country, crime)* blühen; *(financially also)* florieren.

**prosperity** [prɒs'perɪtɪ] *n* Wohlstand *m*; *(of business)* Prosperität *f.*

**prosperous** ['prɒspərəs] *adj* wohlhabend; *business* gutgehend; *economy* florierend, blühend.

**prostate (gland)** ['prɒsteɪt(‚glænd)] *n* Prostata *f.*

**prostitute** ['prɒstɪtjuːt] **1** *n* Prostituierte *f.* **male ~** Strichjunge *m (col)*. **2** *vt one's talents* verkaufen. **to ~ oneself** sich prostituieren.

**prostitution** [‚prɒstɪ'tjuːʃən] *n (lit, fig)* Prostitution *f*; *(of talents, ideals)* Verkaufen *nt.*

**prostrate** ['prɒstreɪt] **1** *adj* ausgestreckt. **2** [prɒ'streɪt] *vt usu pass (lit)* zu Boden werfen; *(fig) (with fatigue)* ermatten; *(with shock)* niederschmettern. **to be ~d by** *or* **with grief** vor Gram gebrochen sein. **3** [prɒ'streɪt] *vr* sich niederwerfen *(before* vor *+dat)*.

**protagonist** [prəʊ'tægənɪst] *n (esp Liter)* Protagonist(in *f) m*; *(champion)* Verfechter(in *f) m.*

**protect** [prə'tekt] *vt (against* gegen, *from* vor *+dat)* schützen; *(person)* beschützen.

**protection** [prə'tekʃən] *n* **(a)** Schutz *m (against* gegen, *from* vor *+dat)*; *(of rights)* Wahrung *f.* **to be under sb's ~** unter jds Schutz *(dat)* stehen. **(b)** *(also ~ money)* Schutzgeld *nt.* **~ racket** organisiertes Erpresserunwesen.

**protectionism** [prə'tekʃənɪzəm] *n* Protektionismus *m.*

**protective** [prə'tektɪv] *adj* Schutz-; *attitude* beschützend. **~ clothing** Schutzkleidung *f*; **~ custody** Schutzhaft *f*; **~ instinct** Beschützerinstinkt *m*; **she is very ~ towards her children** sie ist sehr fürsorglich ihren Kindern gegenüber.

**protector** [prə'tektə\*] *n (defender)* Beschützer *m.*

**protégé, protégée** ['prɒtəʒeɪ] *n* Schützling *m.*

**protein** ['prəʊtiːn] *n* Eiweiß, Protein *nt.* **high-/low-~** eiweißreich/eiweißarm.

**pro tem** ['prəʊ'tem] = **pro tempore** zur Zeit, z. Z(t).

**protest** ['prəʊtest] **1** *n* Protest *m*; *(demonstration)* Protestdemonstration *f*; *(rally)* Protestkundgebung *f.* **under ~** unter Protest; **in ~ against** aus Protest gegen; **to make a/one's ~** Widerspruch erheben. **2** [prə'test] *vi (against, about* gegen*)* protestieren; *(demonstrate)* demonstrieren. **3** [prəʊ'test] *vt innocence* beteuern. **it's mine, he ~ed** das gehört mir, protestierte er.

**Protestant** ['prɒtɪstənt] **1** *adj* protestantisch; *(esp Germany)* evangelisch. **2** *n* Protestant(in *f) m.*

**protestation** [‚prɒte'steɪʃən] *n* **(a)** *(of loyalty etc)* Beteuerung *f.* **(b)** *(protest)* Protest *m.*

**protester** [prə'testə\*] *n* Protestierende(r) *mf*; *(in demonstration)* Demonstrant(in *f) m.*

**protest**: ~ **march** n Protestmarsch m; ~ **song** n Protestsong m; ~ **vote** n Proteststimme f.
**protocol** ['prəʊtəkɒl] n Protokoll nt.
**proton** ['prəʊtɒn] n Proton nt.
**prototype** ['prəʊtəʊtaɪp] n Prototyp m.
**protracted** [prə'træktɪd] adj illness, discussion langwierig; dispute längere(r, s).
**protractor** [prə'træktər] n (Math) Winkelmesser m.
**protrude** [prə'truːd] 1 vi (out of, from aus) vorstehen; (eyes) vortreten; (ears) abstehen. 2 vt strecken.
**protruding** [prə'truːdɪŋ] adj vorstehend; eyes vortretend; ears abstehend.
**protuberance** [prə'tjuːbərəns] n Wölbung f; (on body, metal) Beule f.
**protuberant** [prə'tjuːbərənt] adj vorstehend; eyes vortretend.
**proud** [praʊd] 1 adj stolz (of auf +acc). **to be** ~ **that** ... stolz (darauf) sein, daß ...; **I hope you're** ~ **of yourself** (iro) ich hoffe, du bist stolz auf dich; **that's nothing to be** ~ **of** das ist nichts, worauf man stolz sein kann. 2 adv **to do sb/oneself** ~ jdn/sich verwöhnen.
**proudly** ['praʊdlɪ] adv stolz.
**prove** [pruːv] pret ~d, ptp ~d or **proven 1** vt (a) (verify) beweisen. **to** ~ **sb innocent** or **sb's innocence** jds Unschuld beweisen; **he was** ~d **right in the end** er hat schließlich doch recht behalten. **(b)** (test) rifle etc erproben; one's worth, courage beweisen. **(c)** also vi (turn out) **to** ~ **(to be) useful** etc sich als nützlich etc erweisen; **if it** ~s **otherwise** wenn sich das Gegenteil herausstellt. 2 vr (a) (show one's value, courage etc) sich bewähren. **(b) to** ~ **oneself innocent** etc sich als unschuldig etc erweisen.
**proven** ['pruːvən] adj bewährt; innocence erwiesen.
**Provence** [prɒ'vãs] n die Provence.
**proverb** ['prɒvɜːb] n Sprichwort nt.
**proverbial** adj, ~**ly** adv [prə'vɜːbɪəl, -ɪ] (lit, fig) sprichwörtlich.
**provide** [prə'vaɪd] 1 vt (a) (make available) zur Verfügung stellen; money bereitstellen; (see to, bring along) food, records etc sorgen für; (produce) ideas, specialist knowledge, electricity liefern; shade spenden; privacy, topic of conversation sorgen für. **to** ~ **sth for sb** jdm etw zur Verfügung stellen; (supply) jdm etw besorgen; **to** ~ **sb with sth** (with food etc) jdn mit etw versorgen; (equip) jdn mit etw ausstatten; (with excuse, idea) jdm etw liefern; (with opportunity, information) jdm etw verschaffen or geben; **this job** ~d **him with enough money** diese Stelle verschaffte ihm genug Geld. **(b)** (stipulate: clause, agreement) vorsehen. 2 vi **the Lord will** ~ (prov) der Herr wird's schon geben.
▶**provide for** vi +prep obj (a) family etc versorgen. **his family was well** ~d ~ seine Familie war gut versorgt. **(b) as** ~d ~ **in the contract** wie in dem Vertrag vorgesehen; **we** ~d ~ **all emergencies** wir haben für alle Notfälle vorgesorgt.
**provided (that)** [prə'vaɪdɪd('ðæt)] conj vorausgesetzt(, daß).
**providence** ['prɒvɪdəns] n (fate) die Vorsehung.
**providential** [ˌprɒvɪ'denʃəl] adj glücklich. **to be** ~ (ein) Glück sein.
**provider** [prə'vaɪdər] n (of family) Ernährer(in f) m.
**providing (that)** [prə'vaɪdɪŋ('ðæt)] conj vorausgesetzt(, daß).
**province** ['prɒvɪns] n (a) Provinz f. **(b) the** ~s pl die Provinz. **(c)** (fig: area of knowledge, activity etc) Gebiet nt, Bereich m. **it's not within my** ~ das fällt nicht in meinen Bereich; **that is outside my** ~ das ist nicht mein Gebiet. **(d)** (area of authority) Kom-

petenzbereich m. **that's not my** ~ dafür bin ich nicht zuständig.
**provincial** [prə'vɪnʃəl] **1** adj Provinz-; custom, accent ländlich; (pej) provinziell. **2** n Provinzbewohner(in f) m; (pej) Provinzler(in f) m.
**provision** [prə'vɪʒən] n (a) (act of supplying) Beschaffung f; (of food, water etc) Versorgung f (of mit, to sb jds). **(b)** (supply) Vorrat m (of an +dat). **(c)** ~s (food) Lebensmittel pl; (for journey) Proviant m. **(d)** (allowance) Berücksichtigung f; (arrangement) Vorkehrung f; (stipulation) Bestimmung f. **with the** ~ **that** ... mit der Bedingung, daß...; **there's no** ~ **for later additions** spätere Erweiterungen sind nicht vorgesehen; **to make** ~ **for the future** für die Zukunft Vorsorge treffen; **to make** ~ **for sth** etw vorsehen; for error etc einkalkulieren; **to make** ~ **against sth** gegen etw Vorkehrungen treffen.
**provisional** [prə'vɪʒənl] **1** adj provisorisch; measures also, offer, decision vorläufig. ~ **driving licence** (Brit) vorläufige Fahrerlaubnis für Fahrschüler. **2** n (Ir Pol) **the P**~s die Provisorische Irisch-Republikanische Armee.
**provisionally** [prə'vɪʒnəlɪ] adv vorläufig.
**proviso** [prə'vaɪzəʊ] n (condition) Bedingung f; (clause) Vorbehaltsklausel f.
**provocation** [ˌprɒvə'keɪʃən] n Provokation f. **at the slightest** ~ beim geringsten Anlaß.
**provocative** [prə'vɒkətɪv] adj provokatorisch; remark, behaviour also herausfordernd.
**provoke** [prə'vəʊk] vt sb provozieren, herausfordern; animal reizen; anger, criticism, smile hervorrufen; discussion, revolt auslösen. **to** ~ **sb into doing sth** or **to do sth** jdn dazu bringen, daß er etw tut; (taunt) jdn dazu treiben, daß er etw tut.
**provoking** [prə'vəʊkɪŋ] adj provozierend; (annoying) ärgerlich.
**provost** ['prɒvəst] n (Scot) Bürgermeister m; (Univ) ≃ Dekan m.
**prow** [praʊ] n Bug m.
**prowess** ['praʊɪs] n (skill) Fähigkeiten pl, Können nt; (courage) Tapferkeit f.
**prowl** [praʊl] **1** vi (also ~ **about** or **around)** herumstreichen; (boss, headmaster) herumschleichen. **2** n **to be on the** ~ herumstreichen.
**prowl car** n (US) Streifenwagen m.
**prowler** ['praʊlər] n Herumtreiber(in f) m; (peeping Tom) Spanner m (col).
**proximity** [prɒk'sɪmɪtɪ] n Nähe f. **in close** ~ **to** in unmittelbarer Nähe (+gen).
**proxy** ['prɒksɪ] n (power) (Handlungs)vollmacht f; (person) Handlungsbevollmächtigte(r) mf. **by** ~ durch einen Stellvertreter.
**prude** [pruːd] n **to be a** ~ prüde sein.
**prudence** ['pruːdəns] n see adj Umsicht f; Klugheit f; Überlegtheit f.
**prudent** ['pruːdənt] adj person umsichtig; measure, decision klug; answer wohlüberlegt.
**prudently** ['pruːdəntlɪ] adv wohlweislich; act umsichtig.
**prudish** ['pruːdɪʃ] adj prüde.
**prudishness** ['pruːdɪʃnɪs] n Prüderie f.
**prune**[1] [pruːn] n Backpflaume f.
**prune**[2] vt (also ~ **down)** stutzen; (fig) expenditure, essay kürzen; workforce reduzieren.
**pruning shears** ['pruːnɪŋʃɪəz] npl Gartenschere f.
**pry**[1] [praɪ] vi neugierig sein; (in drawers etc) (herum)schnüffeln (in in +dat). **I don't mean to** ~, **but** ... es geht mich ja nichts an, aber ...; **to** ~ **into sb's affairs** seine Nase in jds Angelegenheiten (acc) stecken.

**pry²** *vt (US)* = **prise**.
**PS** = **postscript** PS.
**psalm** [sɑːm] *n* Psalm *m*.
**PSBR** *(Brit Fin)* = **Public Sector Borrowing Requirement**.
**pseud** [sjuːd] *(col) n* Möchtegern *m (col)*.
**pseudo** ['sjuːdəu] *adj (col: pretended)* unecht; *intellectual etc* Möchtegern- *(col)*, Pseudo-.
**pseudo-** *pref* Pseudo-, pseudo.
**pseudonym** ['sjuːdənɪm] *n* Pseudonym *nt*.
**PST** *(US)* = **Pacific Standard Time**.
**PSV** *(Brit)* = **Public Service Vehicle**.
**psyche** ['saɪkɪ] *n* Psyche *f*.
▶**psyche up** [,saɪk'ʌp] *vt sep (col)* **to** ~ **oneself** ~ sich hochputschen *(col)*.
**psychedelic** [,saɪkɪ'delɪk] *adj* psychedelisch.
**psychiatric** [,saɪkɪ'ætrɪk] *adj* psychiatrisch; *illness* psychisch.
**psychiatrist** [saɪ'kaɪətrɪst] *n* Psychiater(in *f*) *m*.
**psychiatry** [saɪ'kaɪətrɪ] *n* Psychiatrie *f*.
**psychic** ['saɪkɪk] *adj* übersinnlich; *powers* übernatürlich. ~ **research** Parapsychologie *f*; **she is** ~ sie besitzt übernatürliche Kräfte; **you must be** ~! du kannst wohl hellsehen!
**psycho** ['saɪkəu] *n (US col)* Verrückte(r) *mf*.
**psychoanalyse,** *(US)* **psychoanalyze** [,saɪkəu-'ænəlaɪz] *vt* psychoanalytisch behandeln.
**psychoanalysis** [,saɪkəuə'nælɪsɪs] *n* Psychoanalyse *f*.
**psychoanalyst** [,saɪkəu'ænəlɪst] *n* Psychoanalytiker(in *f*) *m*.
**psychological** [,saɪkə'lɒdʒɪkəl] *adj (mental)* psychisch; *(concerning psychology)* psychologisch. ~ **thriller** Psychokrimi *m*; ~ **warfare** psychologische Kriegführung; **he's not really ill, it's all** ~ er ist nicht wirklich krank, das ist alles psychisch bedingt.
**psychologically** [,saɪkə'lɒdʒɪkəlɪ] *adv see adj*. ~ **unstable** psychisch labil.
**psychologist** [saɪ'kɒlədʒɪst] *n* Psychologe *m*, Psychologin *f*.
**psychology** [saɪ'kɒlədʒɪ] *n (science)* Psychologie *f*; *(make-up)* Psyche *f*.
**psychopath** ['saɪkəupæθ] *n* Psychopath(in *f*) *m*.
**psychosis** [saɪ'kəusɪs] *n, pl* **psychoses** [saɪ'kəusiːz] Psychose *f*.
**psychosomatic** [,saɪkəusəu'mætɪk] *adj* psychosomatisch. ~ **medicine** Psychosomatik *f*.
**psychotherapy** [,saɪkəu'θerəpɪ] *n* Psychotherapie *f*.
**psychotic** [saɪ'kɒtɪk] **1** *adj* psychotisch. ~ **illness** Psychose *f*. **2** *n* Psychotiker(in *f*) *m*.
**pt** = **(a) point** Pkt. **(b) part. (c) pint**.
**Pt** *(Geog)* = **Point**.
**PT** = **physical training**.
**PTA** = **parent-teacher association**.
**Pte** *(Brit Mil)* = **Private**.
**pto** = **please turn over** bitte wenden, b. w.
**pub** [pʌb] *n (Brit)* Kneipe *(col)*, Wirtschaft *f*; *(in the country also)* Gasthaus *nt*.
**pub-crawl** ['pʌbkrɔːl] *n (Brit col)* Kneipenbummel *m (col)*. **to go on a** ~ einen Zug durch die Gemeinde machen *(col)*.
**puberty** ['pjuːbətɪ] *n* die Pubertät.
**pubic** ['pjuːbɪk] *adj* Scham-.
**public** ['pʌblɪk] **1** *adj* öffentlich; *health, library also* Volks-; *spending, debts* der öffentlichen Hand, Staats-. **to be** ~ **knowledge** allgemein bekannt sein; **in the** ~ **interest** im öffentlichen Interesse; **it's rather** ~ **here** es ist nicht gerade privat hier; **he is a** ~ **figure** er ist eine Persönlichkeit des öffentlichen Lebens; **in the** ~ **eye** im Blickpunkt der Öffentlich-

keit; **to make sth** ~ etw bekanntgeben; *(officially)* etw öffentlich bekannt machen; **to create** ~ **awareness** öffentliches Interesse wecken; **to go** ~ *(Comm)* in eine Aktiengesellschaft umgewandelt werden. **2** *n sing or pl* Öffentlichkeit *f*. **in** ~ in der Öffentlichkeit; *speak also* öffentlich; **the theatregoing** ~ die theaterinteressierte Öffentlichkeit.
**public address system** *n* Lautsprecheranlage *f*.
**publican** ['pʌblɪkən] *n (Brit)* Gastwirt(in *f*) *m*.
**publication** [,pʌblɪ'keɪʃən] *n* Veröffentlichung *f*.
**public:** ~ **bar** *n* ≃ Ausschank *m*; ~ **company** *n* Aktiengesellschaft *f*; ~ **convenience** *(Brit)* öffentliche Toilette; ~ **enemy** *n* Staatsfeind *m*; ~ **health** *n* (öffentliches) Gesundheitswesen; ~ **holiday** *n* gesetzlicher Feiertag; ~ **house** *n (Brit)* Gaststätte *f*.
**publicity** [pʌb'lɪsɪtɪ] *n* Publicity *f*; *(Comm: advertising, advertisements)* Werbung *f*. ~ **agent** Publicity-manager *m*; ~ **campaign** Publicitykampagne *f*; *(Comm)* Werbekampagne *f*; ~ **material** Werbematerial *nt*.
**publicize** ['pʌblɪsaɪz] *vt* **(a)** *(make public)* bekanntmachen. **I don't** ~ **the fact** ich will das nicht an die große Glocke hängen *(col)*. **(b)** *(get publicity for)* *film, author* Publicity machen für; *new product* Werbung machen für.
**public library** *n* öffentliche Bücherei.
**publicly** ['pʌblɪklɪ] *adv* öffentlich. ~ **owned** staatseigen.
**public:** ~ **nuisance** *n* allgemeines Ärgernis; ~ **opinion** *n* die öffentliche Meinung; ~ **opinion poll** *n* Meinungsumfrage *f*; ~ **ownership** *n* **under** ~ **ownership** in öffentlichem Besitz; ~ **property** *n* Staatsbesitz *m*; ~ **prosecutor** *n* Staatsanwalt *m/*-anwältin *f*; ~ **purse** *n* Staatskasse *f*; ~ **relations** *npl* Public Relations *pl*, Öffentlichkeitsarbeit *f*; ~ **relations officer** *n* Pressesprecher(in *f*) *m*; ~ **school** *n (Brit)* Privatschule, Public School *f*; *(US)* staatliche Schule; ~ **sector** *n* öffentlicher Sektor; ~ **sector borrowing requirement** *n* Kreditaufnahme *f* durch die öffentliche Hand; ~ **service** *n* *(Civil Service)* öffentlicher Dienst; *(facility: water, transport etc)* öffentlicher Dienstleistungsbetrieb; *(work)* Dienst *m* an der Allgemeinheit; ~ **service vehicle** *n* öffentliches Verkehrsmittel *nt*; ~ **speaking** *n* **I don't like** ~ **speaking** ich halte nicht gern Reden; ~**-spirited** *adj act* von Gemeinsinn zeugend; ~ **transport** *or (US)* **transportation** *n* öffentliche Verkehrsmittel *pl*; ~ **utility** *n* öffentlicher Versorgungsbetrieb; ~ **works** *npl* öffentliche Arbeiten.
**publish** ['pʌblɪʃ] *vt* **(a)** *(issue)* veröffentlichen; *book, magazine etc also* herausbringen. ~**ed by Collins** bei Collins erschienen; "~**ed monthly**" „erscheint monatlich"; **who's that book** ~**ed by?** in welchem Verlag ist das Buch erschienen? **(b)** *(make public)* *news, banns* bekanntgeben; *decree* herausgeben; *will* eröffnen.
**publisher** ['pʌblɪʃər] *n (person)* Verleger(in *f*) *m*; *(firm: also* ~**s)** Verlag *m*.
**publishing** ['pʌblɪʃɪŋ] *n (trade)* das Verlagswesen. ~ **company** Verlagshaus *nt*.
**puce** [pjuːs] *adj* braunrot; *(with rage, shame)* rot.
**pucker** ['pʌkər] *vt (also* ~ **up)** *one's lips, mouth* verziehen; *(for kissing)* spitzen; *one's brow* runzeln; *material* Falten machen in *(+acc)*.
**pud** [pud] *(col)* = **pudding**.
**pudding** ['pudɪŋ] *n (dessert)* Nachspeise *f*. **what's for** ~**?** was gibt es als Nachtisch?
**pudding basin** *n* Puddingform *f*.
**puddle** ['pʌdl] *n* Pfütze *f*.

**puerile** ['pjʊəraɪl] adj infantil.
**Puerto Rican** ['pwɜːtəʊ'riːkən] 1 adj puertoricanisch. 2 n Puertoricaner(in f) m.
**Puerto Rico** ['pwɜːtəʊ'riːkəʊ] n Puerto Rico nt.
**puff** [pʌf] 1 n (a) (on cigarette etc) Zug m (at, of an +dat). a ~ of wind ein Windstoß m; a ~ of smoke eine Rauchwolke; **to be out of** ~ (col) außer Puste sein (col). (b) (powder ~) Quaste f. ~ **sleeve** Puffärmel m. (c) (Cook) cream ~ Windbeutel m; ~ **pastry,** (US) ~ **paste** Blätterteig m. 2 vt smoke ausstoßen; (person) blasen; cigarette paffen (col). 3 vi (person, train) schnaufen; (chimney, smoke) qualmen. **the train ~ed into the station** der Zug fuhr schnaufend in den Bahnhof ein; **to ~ at a cigar** an einer Zigarre paffen.
►**puff out** vt sep (a) (expand) chest herausstrecken; cheeks aufblasen; feathers (auf)plustern; sail blähen. (b) (emit) air, smoke ausstoßen. (c) (blow out) auspusten.
►**puff up** vt sep feathers (auf)plustern. **to be all ~ed up (with pride)** (fig) ganz aufgeblasen sein.
**puffed** [pʌft] adj (col) außer Puste (col).
**puffin** ['pʌfɪn] n Papageientaucher m.
**puffy** ['pʌfɪ] adj (+er) (swollen) geschwollen; (from crying) verquollen.
**pug** [pʌg] n (also ~ dog) Mops m.
**pugnacious** [pʌg'neɪʃəs] adj kampfeslustig; (verbally) streitsüchtig.
**pug-nosed** ['pʌgnəʊzd] adj knollennasig.
**puke** [pjuːk] vi (col!) kotzen (col).
**pull** [pʊl] 1 n (a) (tug) Ziehen nt; (short) Ruck m; (lit, fig: attraction) Anziehungskraft f; (of current) Sog m. **he gave her/the rope a** ~ er zog sie/am Seil; **I felt a ~ at my sleeve** ich spürte, wie mich jemand am Ärmel zog. (b) (at pipe, beer) Zug m. **he took a** ~ **at his pipe/glass** er zog an seiner Pfeife/nahm einen Schluck aus seinem Glas. (c) bell ~ Klingelzug m. (d) (col: influence) Beziehungen pl. **I've got no** ~ **with them** ich habe keinen Draht zu ihnen (col).
2 vt (a) (draw, drag) ziehen. **to** ~ **a door shut** eine Tür zuziehen. (b) (tug) rope, bell ziehen an (+dat); boat rudern. **he ~ed her hair** er zog sie an den Haaren; **to** ~ **sth to pieces** (lit) etw in Stücke reißen; (fig: criticize) etw verreißen; **to** ~ **sb's leg** jdn auf den Arm nehmen; ~ **the other one** (col) das glaubst du doch wohl selber nicht!; **she was the one ~ing the strings** sie war es, die alle Fäden in der Hand hielt; **to** ~ **one's punches** (fig) sich zurückhalten; see also **face**. (c) (extract, draw out) tooth, gun, knife ziehen; weeds, lettuce, cork herausziehen; beer zapfen. **to** ~ **a gun on sb** jdn mit der Pistole bedrohen. (d) (strain) muscle sich (dat) zerren; (tear) thread ziehen. (e) (attract) crowd anziehen. (f) (col) **what are you trying to ~?** was heckst du wieder aus? (col).
3 vi (a) ziehen (on, at an +dat). **to** ~ **to the left** (car) nach links ziehen; **to** ~ **on or at one's cigarette** an seiner Zigarette ziehen. (b) (move: train, car etc) fahren. **the car ~ed into the driveway** der Wagen fuhr in die Einfahrt; **he ~ed across to the left-hand lane** er wechselte auf die linke Spur über; **to** ~ **ahead (of sb)** (car, runner) (jdm) vorbeiziehen; (fig: rival etc) jdn hinter sich (dat) lassen.
►**pull apart** vt sep (a) (separate) auseinanderziehen; sheets of paper also, fighting people trennen; radio etc auseinandernehmen. (b) (fig col) (search thoroughly) auseinandernehmen (col); (criticise also) verreißen.
►**pull away** 1 vt sep wegziehen. **she ~ed it** ~ **from him** sie zog es von ihm weg; (from his hands) sie zog es ihm aus den Händen. 2 vi (move off) wegfah-

ren; (ship) ablegen.
►**pull back** 1 vt sep zurückziehen. 2 vi (lit) sich zurückziehen; (catch up) aufholen. **to** ~ ~ **(from doing sth)** (fig) einen Rückzieher machen (und etw nicht tun) (col).
►**pull down** vt sep (a) herunterziehen. (b) (demolish) buildings abreißen.
►**pull in** 1 vt sep (a) claws etc einziehen; (into swimming-pool etc) hineinziehen. (b) (rein in) horse zügeln. (c) (attract) crowds anziehen. (d) (col: take into custody) einkassieren (col). 2 vi (into station etc) einfahren, einlaufen (into in +acc); (into driveway) hineinfahren (into in +acc); (stop, park) anhalten. **he ~ed** ~ **to the side of the road** er fuhr an den Straßenrand.
►**pull off** vt sep (a) wrapping paper abziehen; cover also abnehmen; (violently) abreißen; clothes, shoes ausziehen. (b) (col: succeed in) schaffen (col); deal also zuwege bringen (col); burglary drehen (col).
►**pull on** vt sep coat etc sich (dat) überziehen; hat aufsetzen.
►**pull out** 1 vt sep (a) (extract) (of aus) herausziehen; tooth ziehen; page heraustrennen. (b) (withdraw) zurückziehen; troops abziehen. 2 vi (a) (withdraw) aussteigen (of aus) (col); (troops) abziehen. (b) (leave: train etc) herausfahren (of aus). (c) (driver) herausfahren.
►**pull over** 1 vt sep (a) hinüber-/herüberziehen (prep obj über +acc). (b) (topple) umreißen. 2 vi (car, driver) zur Seite fahren.
►**pull through** vi (fig: recover) durchkommen.
►**pull together** 1 vi (lit) gemeinsam ziehen; (fig: cooperate) am gleichen Strang ziehen. 2 vr sich zusammenreißen. ~ **yourself** ~ reiß dich zusammen.
►**pull up** 1 vt sep (a) (raise by pulling) hochziehen; (up slope also) nach oben ziehen. (b) (uproot) herausreißen. (c) (stop) anhalten. (d) (reprimand) (for behaviour) zurechtweisen; (for grammar etc) korrigieren. 2 vi (stop) anhalten.
**pulley** ['pʊlɪ] n Rolle f; (block) Flaschenzug m.
**Pullman** ® ['pʊlmən] n (~ car) Pullmanwagen ® m; (US: sleeper) Schlafwagen m.
**pull:** ~-**out** n (withdrawal) Abzug m; (supplement) heraustrennbarer Teil; ~**over** n Pullover m.
**pulmonary** ['pʌlmənərɪ] adj embolism etc Lungen-.
**pulp** [pʌlp] n (a) Brei m; (of fruit) Fruchtfleisch nt. **to beat sb to a** ~ (col) jdn zu Brei schlagen (col). 2 vt fruit zerdrücken; paper, book einstampfen; wood zu Brei verarbeiten.
**pulpit** ['pʊlpɪt] n Kanzel f.
**pulsate** [pʌl'seɪt] vi (lit, fig) pulsieren; (head, heart) klopfen; (voice, building) beben; (machine) stampfen; (music) rhythmisch klingen.
**pulse¹** [pʌls] 1 n (Anat) Puls m; (Phys) Impuls m; (fig: of music) Rhythmus m. **to feel** or **take sb's** ~ jdm den Puls fühlen. 2 vi pulsieren.
**pulse²** n (Bot, Cook) Hülsenfrucht f.
**pulverize** ['pʌlvəraɪz] vt pulverisieren.
**puma** ['pjuːmə] n Puma m.
**pumice (stone)** ['pʌmɪs(ˌstəʊn)] n Bimsstein m.
**pummel** ['pʌml] vt eintrommeln auf (+acc).
**pump** [pʌmp] 1 n Pumpe f. 2 vt pumpen; brake pedal mehrmals treten. **to** ~ **sth dry** etw leerpumpen; **to** ~ **sb dry** (fig) jdn aussaugen; **to** ~ **bullets into sb** jdn mit Blei vollpumpen (col); **to** ~ **money into sth** Geld in etw (acc) hineinpumpen; **to** ~ **information out of sb** Informationen aus jdm herausholen.
►**pump in** vt sep (lit, fig) hineinpumpen.
►**pump out** vt sep liquid, air herauspumpen; boat, cellar leerpumpen; stomach auspumpen.

►**pump up** *vt sep tyre etc* aufpumpen.
**pumpkin** ['pʌmpkɪn] *n* Kürbis *m*.
**pun** [pʌn] *n* Wortspiel *nt*.
**Punch** [pʌntʃ] *n* Kasper *m*, Kasperle *nt*. ~**-and-Judy show** Kasper(le)theater *nt*; **to be (as) pleased as** ~ *(col)* sich wie ein Schneekönig freuen *(col)*.
**punch¹** [pʌntʃ] **1** *n* (a) *(blow)* Schlag *m*. (b) *no pl (fig: vigour)* Schwung *m*. **2** *vti* boxen.
**punch²** **1** *n (for ~ing holes)* Locher *m*; *(for tickets)* Lochzange *f*; *(for stamping metal etc)* Prägestempel *m*. **2** *vt ticket etc* lochen; *metal, holes* stanzen; *(stamp) metal, pattern* prägen.
►**punch in** *vt sep (Comp) data* tasten, tippen *(col)*.
**punch³** *n (drink)* Bowle *f*; *(hot)* Punsch *m*.
**punch:** ~ **bag** *n* Sandsack *m*; ~ **ball** *n* Punchingball *m*; ~ **bowl** *n* Bowle *f*; ~ **card** *n* Lochkarte *f*; ~**-drunk** *adj* benommen; *(confused)* durcheinander *pred*; ~**-line** *n* Pointe *f*; ~ **tape** *n* Lochstreifen *m*; ~**-up** *n (Brit col)* Schlägerei *f*.
**punching bag** ['pʌntʃɪŋˌbæg] *n (esp US)* Sandsack *m*.
**punctilious** [pʌŋk'tɪlɪəs] *adj (regarding etiquette)* korrekt; *(fastidious)* peinlich genau.
**punctual** ['pʌŋktjʊəl] *adj* pünktlich. **to be** ~ pünktlich kommen.
**punctuality** [ˌpʌŋktjʊ'ælɪtɪ] *n* Pünktlichkeit *f*.
**punctually** ['pʌŋktjʊəlɪ] *adv* pünktlich.
**punctuate** ['pʌŋktjʊeɪt] *vt* (a) *(Gram)* mit Satzzeichen versehen. (b) *(intersperse)* unterbrechen. **he ~d his talk with jokes** er spickte seine Rede mit Witzen.
**punctuation** [ˌpʌŋktjʊ'eɪʃən] *n* Zeichensetzung, Interpunktion *f*. ~ **mark** Satzzeichen *nt*.
**puncture** ['pʌŋktʃəʳ] **1** *n (in tyre, balloon etc)* Loch *nt*; *(in skin)* (Ein)stich *m*; *(flat tyre)* Reifenpanne *f*. **2** *vt* stechen in (+*acc*); *membrane* durchstechen; *tyre, balloon* Löcher/ein Loch machen in (+*acc*).
**pundit** ['pʌndɪt] *n (fig)* Experte *m*, Expertin *f*.
**pungency** ['pʌndʒənsɪ] *n (lit, fig)* Schärfe *f*.
**pungent** ['pʌndʒənt] *adj (lit, fig)* scharf; *smell also* stechend.
**punish** ['pʌnɪʃ] *vt* (a) *person, offence* bestrafen. (b) *(fig col: drive hard, treat roughly)* strapazieren; *horses, oneself* schinden; *opponent* zusetzen (+*dat*).
**punishable** ['pʌnɪʃəbl] *adj* strafbar. **it is a** ~ **offence** es ist strafbar.
**punishing** ['pʌnɪʃɪŋ] **1** *adj blow* hart; *schedule, race* mörderisch. **2** *n* **to take a** ~ *(col) (car, furniture etc)* strapaziert werden; *(team, boxer etc)* vorgeführt werden *(col)*.
**punishment** ['pʌnɪʃmənt] *n* (a) *(penalty)* Strafe *f*; *(punishing)* Bestrafung *f*. (b) *(fig col)* **to take a lot of** ~ *(car, furniture etc)* stark strapaziert werden; *(Sport)* vorgeführt werden *(col)*.
**punitive** ['pjuːnɪtɪv] *adj* Straf-; *taxation* extrem hoch.
**Punjab** ['pʌndʒɑːb] *n* **the** ~ das Pandschab.
**punk** [pʌŋk] *n* (a) *(person: also* ~ **rocker)** Punker *m*; *(music: also* ~ **rock)** Punk(-Rock) *m*; *(culture)* Punk *m*. (b) *(US col: hoodlum)* Ganove *m (col)*.
**punt** [pʌnt] **1** *n (boat)* Stechkahn *m*. **2** *vti* staken. **to go** ~**ing** Stechkahn fahren.
**punter** ['pʌntəʳ] *n* (a) *(better)* Wetter *m*; *(gambler)* Spieler(in *f*) *m*. (b) *(col)* Typ *m (col)*. **the average** ~ Otto Normalverbraucher.
**puny** ['pjuːnɪ] *adj (+er) (weak) person* schwächlich; *effort* kläglich.
**pup** [pʌp] *n* Junge(s) *nt*.
**pupil¹** ['pjuːpl] *n (Sch, fig)* Schüler(in *f*) *m*.
**pupil²** *n (Anat)* Pupille *f*.
**puppet** ['pʌpɪt] *n* Puppe *f*; *(glove* ~) Handpuppe *f*; *(string* ~, *fig)* Marionette *f*.

**puppet:** ~**government** *n* Marionettenregierung *f*; ~**-show** *n* Puppenspiel *nt*; ~ **state** *n* Marionettenstaat *m*; ~ **theatre** *or (US)* **theater** *n* Marionettentheater *nt*.
**puppy** ['pʌpɪ] *n* junger Hund. ~ **fat** Babyspeck *m*; ~ **love** Schwärmerei *f*.
**purchase** ['pɜːtʃɪs] **1** *n* (a) Kauf *m*; *(of furniture, flat, car also)* Anschaffung *f*. **to make a** ~ einen Kauf tätigen; eine Anschaffung machen. (b) *(grip)* Halt *m*. **he couldn't get a** ~ **on the wet rope** er konnte an dem nassen Seil keinen Halt finden. **2** *vt (buy)* kaufen, erwerben *(form)*. **purchasing power** Kaufkraft *f*; ~ **price** Kaufpreis *m*; ~ **tax** *(Brit)* Kaufsteuer *f*.
**purchaser** ['pɜːtʃɪsəʳ] *n* Käufer(in *f*) *m*.
**pure** [pjʊəʳ] *adj (+er)* rein; *motive* ehrlich, lauter *(geh)*. **she stared at him in** ~ **disbelief** sie starrte ihn ganz ungläubig an; *malice* ~ **and simple** reine Bosheit; **a** ~ **wool dress** ein Kleid aus reiner Wolle.
**purebred** ['pjʊəbred] *adj* reinrassig.
**purée** ['pjʊəreɪ] *n* Püree *nt*, Brei *m*. **tomato** ~ Tomatenmark *nt*.
**purely** ['pjʊəlɪ] *adv* rein.
**purgative** ['pɜːgətɪv] *n* Abführmittel *nt*.
**purgatory** ['pɜːgətərɪ] *n (Rel)* das Fegefeuer; *(fig: state)* die Hölle.
**purge** [pɜːdʒ] **1** *n* (a) *(Med)* (starkes) Abführmittel. (b) *(Pol etc)* Säuberung(saktion) *f*. **2** *vt* reinigen; *body* entschlacken; *guilt, sin* büßen; *(Pol etc) party* säubern *(of von)*; *traitor* eliminieren *(from aus)*.
**purification** [ˌpjʊərɪfɪ'keɪʃən] *n* Reinigung *f*.
**purify** ['pjʊərɪfaɪ] *vt* reinigen.
**purist** ['pjʊərɪst] *n* Purist(in *f*) *m*.
**puritan** ['pjʊərɪtən] *(Rel:* P~) **1** *adj* puritanisch. **2** *n* Puritaner(in *f*) *m*.
**puritanical** [ˌpjʊərɪ'tænɪkəl] *adj* puritanisch.
**purity** ['pjʊərɪtɪ] *n* Reinheit *f*; *(of motives)* Lauterkeit *(geh)*, Ehrlichkeit *f*.
**purl** [pɜːl] *n* linke Masche. ~ **two** zwei links.
**purloin** [pɜː'lɔɪn] *vt (form, hum)* entwenden *(form, hum) (from* +*dat)*.
**purple** ['pɜːpl] **1** *adj* violett, lila; *face* hochrot; *(pej) passage* hochtrabend. **to go** ~ **(in the face)** hochrot werden. **2** *n (colour)* Violett, Lila *nt*.
**purport** ['pɜːpət] **1** *n* Tenor *m*. **2** [pɜː'pɔːt] *vt* **to** ~ **to be/do sth** *(person)* vorgeben, etw zu sein/tun; *(thing)* etw sein/tun sollen.
**purpose** ['pɜːpəs] *n* (a) *(intention)* Absicht *f*; *(goal)* Zweck *m*. **on** ~ mit Absicht, absichtlich; **he did it for** *or* **with the** ~ **of improving his image** er tat es in der Absicht, sein Image zu verbessern; **to have a** ~ **in life** ein Lebensziel haben; **to answer** *or* **serve sb's** ~**(s)** jds Zweck(en) dienen; **for our** ~**s** für unsere Zwecke; **for the** ~**s of this meeting** zum Zweck dieser Konferenz; **for all practical** ~**s** in der Praxis; **to the** ~ relevant; **to good** ~ zu einem guten Zweck; **to no** ~ umsonst. (b) *no pl* **strength of** ~ Entschlußkraft *f*; **sense of** ~ Zielbewußtsein *nt*.
**purpose-built** [ˌpɜːpəs'bɪlt] *adj* speziell angefertigt; *building* zu diesem Zweck erbaut.
**purposeful** ['pɜːpəsfʊl] *adj* entschlossen.
**purposely** ['pɜːpəslɪ] *adv* bewußt, absichtlich.
**purr** [pɜːʳ] **1** *vi (cat, fig: person)* schnurren; *(engine)* surren. **2** *n* Schnurren *nt no pl*; Surren *nt no pl*.
**purse** [pɜːs] **1** *n* (a) *(for money)* Portemonnaie *nt*, Geldbörse *f (form)*. **to hold the** ~ **strings** *(fig)* über die Finanzen bestimmen. (b) *(US: handbag)* Handtasche *f*. ~ **snatcher** Taschendieb *m*. (c) *(Sport: prize)* Preisgeld *nt*. **2** *vt* **to** ~ **one's lips** einen Schmollmund machen.
**purser** ['pɜːsəʳ] *n* Zahlmeister *m*.
**pursue** [pə'sjuː] *vt* (a) verfolgen; *pleasure, success*

nachjagen (+dat), aussein auf (+acc); happiness streben nach. **(b)** (carry on) course of action etc verfolgen; inquiry durchführen; profession, studies nachgehen (+dat); subject weiterführen.

**pursuer** [pə'sjuːəʳ] n Verfolger(in f) m.

**pursuit** [pə'sjuːt] n **(a)** (of person) Verfolgung (of gen), Jagd (of auf +acc) f; (of knowledge, happiness) Streben nt (of nach); (of pleasure) Jagd f (of nach). **in hot ~ of sb** hart auf jds Fersen (acc); **to go in ~ of sb/sth** sich auf die Jagd nach jdm/etw machen; **in (the) ~ of his goal** in Verfolgung seines Ziels. **(b)** (occupation) Beschäftigung f; (hobby, pastime) Zeitvertreib m. **his literary ~s** seine Beschäftigung mit der Literatur.

**purveyor** [pɜː'veɪəʳ] n (form) (seller) Händler m; (supplier) Lieferant m.

**pus** [pʌs] n Eiter m.

**push** [puʃ] **1** n **(a)** Schubs m (col); (short) Stoß m. **to give sb/sth a ~** jdn/etw schieben; jdm/etw einen Stoß versetzen; **to give a car a ~** einen Wagen anschieben; **to give sb the ~** (Brit col) employee jdn rausschmeißen (col); lover jdm den Laufpaß geben (col). **(b)** (effort) Anstrengung f; (sales ~) Aktion f; (Mil: offensive) Offensive f. **(c)** (drive, aggression) Durchsetzungsvermögen nt. **(d)** (col) **at a ~** notfalls, im Notfall; **if/when it comes to the ~** wenn es darauf ankommt.

**2** vt **(a)** schieben; (quickly, violently) stoßen, schubsen (col); (press) button drücken. **to ~ a door open/shut** eine Tür auf-/zudrücken; **he ~ed the book into my hand** er drückte mir das Buch in die Hand.
**(b)** (fig) claims, interests durchzusetzen versuchen; candidate die Werbetrommel rühren für; product propagieren, pushen (Comm sl); drugs schieben, pushen (Drugs sl). **to ~ home one's advantage** seinen Vorteil ausnützen; **don't ~ your luck** treib's nicht zu weit!; **he must be ~ing 70** (col) er muß auf die 70 zugehen.
**(c)** (fig: put pressure on) drängen, drängeln (col); pupil, employee antreiben. **to ~ sb to do sth** jdn dazu drängen, etw zu tun; **they ~ed him to the limit** sie trieben ihn bis an seine Grenzen; **that's ~ing it a bit** (col) das ist ein bißchen übertrieben; **to be ~ed for time/money** (col) unter Zeitdruck stehen/knapp bei Kasse sein (col); **I'm a bit ~ed just now** (col) ich habe momentan wenig Zeit.

**3** vi (shove) schieben; (quickly, violently) stoßen; (in a crowd, apply pressure) drängen, drängeln (col); (fig: be ambitious, assert oneself) kämpfen. "~" (on door) „drücken"; (on bell) „klingeln".

▶**push around** vt sep **(a)** herumstoßen. **(b)** (fig col: bully) herumschubsen.

▶**push aside** vt sep zur Seite or beiseite schieben; (fig) problems etc einfach abtun.

▶**push away** vt sep wegschieben; (quickly) wegstoßen.

▶**push back** vt sep people zurückdrängen; (with one push) zurückstoßen; curtains, hair zurückschieben.

▶**push down** vt sep nach unten drücken; (knock over) umstoßen; fence niederreißen.

▶**push down on** vi +prep obj drücken auf (+acc).

▶**push forward 1** vi (Mil) vorwärts drängen. **2** vt sep (lit) nach vorn schieben; (fig) claim geltend machen; ideas hervorheben; sb, oneself in den Vordergrund schieben.

▶**push in 1** vt sep **(a)** hineinschieben; (quickly, violently) hineinstoßen. **to ~ one's way ~** sich hineindrängen. **(b)** (break) window, sides of box eindrücken. **2** vi (lit: in queue etc) sich hineindrängen

or -drängeln (col).

▶**push off 1** vt sep hinunterschieben; (quickly, violently) hinunterstoßen; lid, cap wegdrücken. **to ~ sb/sth ~ sth** jdn/etw von etw schieben/stoßen. **2** vi **(a)** (in boat) abstoßen. **(b)** (col: leave) abhauen (col).

▶**push on 1** vi (with journey) weiterfahren; (walking) weitergehen; (with job) weitermachen. **2** vt sep top, lid festdrücken.

▶**push out** vt sep hinausschieben; (quickly, violently) hinausstoßen. **to ~ sb/sth ~ of sth** jdn/etw aus etw schieben/stoßen.

▶**push over** vt sep **(a)** (pass over) hinüber-/herüberschieben; (quickly, violently) hinüber-/herüberstoßen. **to ~ sb/sth ~ sth** jdn/etw über etw (acc) schieben/stoßen. **(b)** (knock over) umwerfen.

▶**push through 1** vt sep **(a)** (shove through) durchschieben; (quickly, violently) durchstoßen. **to ~ sb/sth ~ sth** jdn/etw durch etw schieben/stoßen; **to ~ one's way ~ the crowd** sich durch die Menge drängen. **(b)** (get done quickly) bill, decision durchpeitschen (col); business durchziehen (col). **2** vi (through crowd) sich durchschieben; (more violently) sich durchdrängen; (new shoots) austreiben.

▶**push up** vt sep **(a)** (lit) hinaufschieben; (quickly, violently) hinaufstoßen; window hochschieben/-stoßen. **(b)** (fig: raise, increase) hochtreiben.

**push:** **~-bike** n (Brit) Fahrrad nt; **~-button** n Drucktaste f, Knopf m; **~-button telephone** Tastentelefon nt; **~-button warfare** Krieg m auf Knopfdruck; **~chair** n (Brit) Sportwagen m.

**pusher** ['puʃəʳ] n (col) **(a)** (of drugs) Pusher(in f) m (col). **(b)** (ambitious person) **he's a ~** er setzt sich durch.

**push:** **~-over** n (col) (job etc) Kinderspiel nt; (person) leichtes Opfer; **~rod** n (Mech) Stößelstange f; **~-start** vt car anschieben.

**pushy** ['puʃɪ] adj (+er) (col) penetrant (pej).

**puss** [pus], **pussy** ['pusɪ] n (cat) Mieze f (col).

**pussy:** **~-cat** n (baby-talk) Miezekatze f (baby-talk); **~foot** vi (col: act cautiously) wie die Katze um den heißen Brei schleichen (col); **~ willow** n Salweide f.

**put** [put] pret, ptp **~ 1** vt **(a)** (place) tun (esp col); (~ down, position) stellen, setzen; (lay down) legen; (push in) stecken. **to ~ sth in a drawer** etw in eine Schublade tun or legen; **he ~ his hand in his pocket** er steckte die Hand in die Tasche; **he ~ some more coal on the fire** er legte Kohle nach; **to ~ sugar in one's coffee** Zucker in den Kaffee tun; **to ~ the ball in the net** (Ftbl) den Ball ins Netz setzen; **he ~ his toe in the water** er steckte seinen Zeh ins Wasser; **he ~ his hand on my shoulder** er legte seine Hand auf meine Schulter.
**(b)** (thrust) stecken. **he ~ his head around the door** er steckte den Kopf zur Tür herein; **to ~ one's fist through a window** mit der Faust ein Fenster einschlagen.
**(c)** **to stay ~** liegen-/stehen-/hängen- etc bleiben; (hair) halten; (person) (not move) hier-/dableiben; (not stand up) sitzenbleiben.
**(d)** **to ~ a child in a home** ein Kind in ein Heim stecken; **to ~ money into sth** (sein) Geld in etw (acc) stecken; **he ~ £10/money on a horse** er setzte £10/setzte auf ein Pferd; **to ~ a lot of time into sth** viel Zeit in etw (acc) stecken; **to ~ a lot of effort into one's work** viel Mühe in seine Arbeit stecken.
**(e)** (cause to be, do etc) **to ~ sb in a good/bad mood** jdn fröhlich/mißmutig stimmen; **they ~ her to work on the new project** sie wurde für das neue Projekt eingesetzt; **to be ~ to a lot of inconvenience over sth** mit etw viele Unannehmlichkeiten

haben.

  **(f)** *comma, line* machen; *(~ forward) proposal* vorbringen. **to ~ one's signature to a document** seine Unterschrift unter ein Schriftstück setzen; **to ~ a matter before a committee** eine Angelegenheit vor einen Ausschuß bringen; **to ~ the arguments for and against sth** das Für und Wider von etw *(dat)* aufzählen; **to ~ sth on the agenda** etw auf die Tagesordnung setzen; **you might ~ it to him that** ... du könntest ihm nahelegen, daß ...; **to ~ a question/ suggestion to sb** jdm eine Frage stellen/einen Vorschlag unterbreiten; **I ~ it to you that** ... ich möchte Ihnen vorhalten, daß ...

  **(g)** *(express)* ausdrücken, sagen. **that's one way of ~ting it** so kann man's auch sagen; **to ~ it bluntly** hart *or* grob ausgedrückt; **how shall I ~ it?** wie soll ich (es) sagen?; **to ~ sth into German** etw ins Deutsche übersetzen.

  **(h)** *(rate)* schätzen *(at* auf *+acc).* **he ~s money before his family's happiness** er stellt Geld über das Glück seiner Familie; **to ~ a value of £10 on sth** den Wert einer Sache *(gen)* auf £10 schätzen.

  **2** *vi (Naut)* **to ~ to sea** in See stechen.

▸**put about** *vt sep news, rumour* verbreiten, in Umlauf bringen. **he ~ it ~ that** ... er verbreitete (das Gerücht), daß ...

▸**put across** *vt sep* **(a)** *(communicate) ideas* verständlich machen *(to sb* jdm*)*, klar zum Ausdruck bringen; *knowledge* vermitteln *(to sb* jdm*)*; *(promote)* an den Mann bringen *(col).* **to ~ oneself ~** den richtigen Eindruck von sich vermitteln. **(b)** *(col)* = **put over**.

▸**put aside** *vt sep* **(a)** *book etc* beiseite legen. **(b)** *(save for later use)* zurücklegen. **(c)** *(fig: forget)* ablegen, über Bord werfen *(col); anger* begraben; *thought* aufgeben; *differences* vergessen.

▸**put away** *vt sep* **(a)** *(in usual place)* einräumen; *(tidy away)* wegräumen. **to ~ the car ~** das Auto in die Garage stellen. **(b)** *(col: consume)* schaffen *(col); food also* verputzen *(col).* **(c)** *(in prison etc)* einsperren.

▸**put back** *vt sep* **(a)** *(replace) see* **put 1 (a)** zurücktun/-stellen *or* -setzen/-legen/-stecken. **(b)** *(postpone)* verschieben; *(set back)* zurückwerfen; *(readjust) watch etc* zurückstellen.

▸**put by** *vt sep* zurücklegen, auf die hohe Kante legen.

▸**put down 1** *vt sep* **(a)** *(set down) object see* **put 1 (a)** wegtun/-setzen *or* -stellen/weglegen; *surface* verlegen. **I simply couldn't ~ that book ~** ich konnte das Buch einfach nicht aus der Hand legen.

  **(b)** *(lower) umbrella* zumachen; *aerial* einschieben; *car roof* zurückklappen; *lid* zuklappen.

  **(c)** *rebellion* niederschlagen; *rebels* niederwerfen; *crime* besiegen; *(humiliate)* demütigen.

  **(d)** *(pay)* anzahlen; *deposit* machen.

  **(e)** *pets* einschläfern; *injured horse etc* den Gnadenschuß geben *(+dat).*

  **(f)** *(write down)* aufschreiben; *(on form)* angeben. **~ me ~ for £50** für mich können Sie £50 eintragen.

  **(g)** *(attribute)* zurückführen *(to* auf *+acc),* zuschreiben *(to dat).*

  **2** *vi (Aviat)* landen.

▸**put forward** *vt sep* **(a)** *idea, suggestion* vorbringen; *(nominate)* vorschlagen. **(b)** *(advance) meeting* vorverlegen *(to* auf *+acc); (readjust) watch etc* vorstellen.

▸**put in 1** *vt sep* **(a)** *(place in) see* **put 1 (a)** hineintun/-setzen *or* -stellen/-legen/-stecken; *(pack)* einpacken.

  **(b)** *(insert in book, speech etc)* einfügen; *(add)* hin-

zufügen.

  **(c)** *(enter) application* einreichen; *claim also* stellen. **to ~ ~ a plea of not guilty** *(Jur)* auf „nicht schuldig" plädieren; **to ~ one's name ~ for sth** sich um etw bewerben; *for evening classes, exam* sich für etw anmelden; **to ~ sb ~ for an exam/an award** jdn für *or* zu einer Prüfung/für eine Ehrung vorschlagen.

  **(d)** *(install) central heating, car radio* einbauen.

  **(e)** *(Pol: elect)* an die Regierung bringen.

  **(f)** *(devote, expend) time* verbringen *(with* mit*),* verwenden *(with* auf*).* **could you ~ ~ an extra hour?** könnten Sie eine zusätzliche Stunde Arbeit einschieben?; **he ~ ~ a lot of hard work on the project** er hat eine Menge harter Arbeit in das Projekt gesteckt.

  **2** *vi* **(a) to ~ ~ for sth** *for job* sich um etw bewerben; *for leave, rise* etw beantragen. **(b)** *(Naut: enter port)* **to ~ ~ to Bremen/harbour** in Bremen/in den Hafen einlaufen.

▸**put off** *vt sep* **(a)** *(set down) passengers* aussteigen lassen *(prep obj* aus*); (forcibly)* hinauswerfen *(prep obj* aus*).* **(b)** *(postpone, delay)* verschieben; *visitors* (wieder) ausladen; *decision* aufschieben; *sth unpleasant* hinauszögern. **to ~ sth ~ till later** etw auf später verschieben. **(c)** *(prevent from coming) boyfriend, creditor* hinhalten. **to ~ sb ~ doing sth** jdn davon abbringen, etw zu tun. **(d)** *(repel)* die Lust verderben *(+dat).* **to ~ sb ~ sth** jdm etw verleiden. **(e)** *(distract)* ablenken *(prep obj* von*); (disturb)* stören.

▸**put on** *vt sep* **(a)** *coat, shoes etc* anziehen; *hat (sich dat)* aufsetzen; *make-up* auftragen; *accent, manners* annehmen; *facade, front* aufsetzen. **to ~ one's make-up** sich schminken; **to ~ ~ an air of innocence** eine unschuldige Miene aufsetzen; **his sorrow is all ~ ~** sein Kummer ist bloß Schau *(col).*

  **(b)** *(increase, add)* **to ~ ~ weight/a few pounds** zunehmen/ein paar Pfund zunehmen; **to ~ ~ speed** schneller fahren, beschleunigen; **10p was ~ ~ the price of petrol** der Benzinpreis wurde um 10 Pence erhöht.

  **(c)** *play* aufführen; *exhibition* veranstalten; *film* vorführen; *train, bus* einsetzen; *(fig) act, show* abziehen *(col).*

  **(d)** *(on telephone)* **to ~ sb ~ to sb** jdn mit jdm verbinden; **would you ~ him ~?** könnten Sie ihn mir geben?

  **(e)** *(switch on) light, TV* anmachen, einschalten. **to ~ the kettle/dinner ~** das Wasser/das Essen aufsetzen.

  **(f)** *(readjust) watch etc* vorstellen.

  **(g)** **to ~ sb ~ to sth** *(inform about)* jdm etw vermitteln; **to ~ sb ~ to a plumber/garage** *etc* jdm einen Installateur/eine Reparaturwerkstatt *etc* empfehlen; **what ~ you ~ to it?** was hat dich darauf gebracht?; **to ~ the police ~ to sb** die Polizei auf jds Spur bringen.

  **(h)** *(col: tease, trick)* auf den Arm nehmen *(col).*

▸**put out 1** *vt sep* **(a)** *rubbish etc* hinausbringen; *cat* vor die Tür setzen. **to ~ the washing ~ (to dry)** die Wäsche (zum Trocknen) raushängen; **this has ~ us ~ of business** deswegen haben wir Pleite gemacht; **she could not ~ him ~ of her thoughts** er ging ihr nicht aus dem Sinn.

  **(b)** *(stretch out) hand, foot* ausstrecken; *tongue, head* herausstrecken. **to ~ one's head ~ of the window** den Kopf zum Fenster hinausstrecken.

  **(c)** *dishes, cutlery* auflegen; *chessmen etc* aufstellen.

  **(d)** *(circulate) pamphlet* herausbringen; *propagan-*

*da* machen; *rumour* verbreiten; *regulations* erlassen; *statement* abgeben; *message, appeal* durchgeben; *description* bekanntgeben; *TV programme* bringen, senden.
 (e) *(extinguish)* löschen.
 (f) *(vex)* **to be** ~ ~ **(by sth)** (über etw *acc*) verärgert sein.
 (g) *(inconvenience)* **to** ~ **oneself** ~ **(for sb)** sich *(dat)* (wegen jdm) Umstände machen.
 (h) *(dislocate)* *knee, shoulder* ausrenken; *(more severely)* auskugeln; *back* verrenken.
 **2** *vi (Naut: set sail)* auslaufen. **to** ~ ~ **to sea** in See stechen; **to** ~ ~ **from Bremen** von Bremen auslaufen.
▶**put over** *vt sep* **to** ~ **one** ~ **on sb** *(col)* jdn anführen.
▶**put through** *vt sep* **(a)** *reform, proposal* durchbringen; *(+prep obj)* bringen durch; *claim* weiterleiten. **(b)** *person* verbinden *(to* mit*)*; *call* durchstellen *(to* zu*)*. **to** ~ **a call** ~ **to Beirut** ein Gespräch nach Beirut vermitteln *or (caller)* anmelden.
▶**put together** *vt sep* **(a)** *(in same room etc)* zusammentun; *(seat together)* zusammensetzen. **he's better than all the others** ~ ~ er ist besser als alle anderen zusammen. **(b)** *(assemble)* zusammensetzen; *furniture, machine also* zusammenbauen; *essay etc, (Jur) case* zusammenstellen; *collection, evidence* zusammentragen.
▶**put up 1** *vt sep* **(a)** *(raise)* *hand* hochheben; *car window* zumachen; *sash window* hochschieben; *umbrella* aufklappen; *hair* hochstecken; *collar* hochschlagen. **(b)** *flag, sail* aufziehen. **(c)** *picture etc* aufhängen; *notice* anschlagen. **(d)** *building, fence* errichten; *ladder, scaffolding* aufstellen; *tent* aufschlagen; *(fig)* *facade* vortäuschen. **(e)** *missile, flare* hochschießen. **(f)** *(increase)* *sales, prices* erhöhen. **(g)** = **put forward (a)**. **(h)** *(offer)* **to** ~ **sth** ~ **for sale** etw zum Verkauf anbieten; **to** ~ ~ **resistance (to sb)** (jdm) Widerstand leisten. **(i)** *(give accommodation to)* unterbringen. **(j)** *(provide)* *capital* bereitstellen; *reward* aussetzen. **(k) to** ~ **sb** ~ **to sth** jdn zu etw anstiften.
 **2** *vi* **(a)** *(stay)* wohnen; *(for the night)* übernachten. **(b) to** ~ ~ **for election** sich zur Wahl stellen.
▶**put upon** *vi +prep obj (impose on)* ausnutzen. **she felt** ~ ~ sie fühlte sich ausgenutzt.
▶**put up with** *vi +prep obj* sich abfinden mit.

**I won't** ~ ~ ~ **that** das lasse ich mir nicht gefallen.
**put:** ~**-down** *n* Abfuhr *f;* ~**-on** *adj* vorgetäuscht; *smile* falsch.
**putrefaction** [ˌpjuːtrɪˈfækʃən] *n* Verwesung *f.*
**putrefy** [ˈpjuːtrɪfaɪ] *vi* verwesen.
**putrid** [ˈpjuːtrɪd] *adj* verfault; *smell* faul.
**putt** [pʌt] **1** *n (Golf)* Schlag *m (mit dem man einlocht).* **2** *vti* putten, einlochen.
**putter** [ˈpʌtəʳ] *n (club)* Putter *m.*
**putting** [ˈpʌtɪŋ] Putten *nt.* ~ **green** kleiner Rasenplatz zum Putten.
**putty** [ˈpʌtɪ] *n* Kitt *m.* **he was** ~ **in her hands** er war Wachs in ihren Händen.
**put-up** [ˈpʊtʌp] *adj (col)* **a** ~ **job** ein abgekartetes Spiel.
**puzzle** [ˈpʌzl] **1** *n* **(a)** *(word game etc)* Rätsel *nt;* *(toy)* Geduldsspiel *nt;* *(jigsaw)* Puzzle(spiel) *nt.* **(b)** *(mystery)* Rätsel *nt.* **2** *vt* **to** ~ **over etw** *(acc)* den Kopf zerbrechen. **3** *vt* verblüffen. **I'm** ~**d about it** es ist mir ein Rätsel; **the police are** ~**d** die Polizei steht vor einem Rätsel.
▶**puzzle out** *vt sep* austüfteln.
**puzzled** [ˈpʌzld] *adj look* verdutzt, verblüfft.
**puzzlement** [ˈpʌzlmənt] *n* Verblüffung *f.*
**puzzling** [ˈpʌzlɪŋ] *adj* rätselhaft; *story, mechanism* verwirrend.
**PVC** = **polyvinyl chloride** PVC *nt.*
**Pvt** *(US Mil)* = **Private.**
**pw** = **per week** wö.
**PX** *(US Mil)* = **Post Exchange** *Laden m/Kantine f für Armeeangehörige.*
**pygmy** [ˈpɪgmɪ] *n* **(a)** P~ Pygmäe *m.* **(b)** *(small person, fig)* Zwerg *m.*
**pyjamas,** *(US)* **pajamas** [pəˈdʒɑːməz] *npl* Schlafanzug, Pyjama *m.*
**pylon** [ˈpaɪlən] *n* Mast *m.*
**pyramid** [ˈpɪrəmɪd] *n* Pyramide *f.*
**pyre** [ˈpaɪəʳ] *n* Scheiterhaufen *m (zum Verbrennen von Leichen).*
**Pyrenean** [ˌpɪrəˈniːən] *adj* pyrenäisch.
**Pyrenees** [ˌpɪrəˈniːz] *npl* Pyrenäen *pl.*
**Pyrex** ® [ˈpaɪreks] *n* ≈ Jenaer Glas ® *nt.*
**pyromaniac** [ˌpaɪərəʊˈmeɪnɪæk] *n* Pyromane *m,* Pyromanin *f.*
**pyrotechnics** [ˌpaɪrəʊˈteknɪks] *n (sing)* Pyrotechnik *f; (pl: display)* Feuerwerk *nt.*
**python** [ˈpaɪθən] *n* Python(schlange *f) m.*

# Q

**Q, q** [kjuː] n Q, q nt. **Q for Queen** ≃ Q wie Quelle.
**Q** = (a) question. (b) queen.
**Qatar** [kæ'tɑːr] n Katar nt.
**QC** (Brit) = Queen's Counsel.
**QED** (Math) = **quod erat demonstrandum** q.e.d.
**qr** = quarter.
**qt** = quart.
**qtr** = quarter.
**quack¹** [kwæk] **1** n Schnattern, Quaken nt no pl. **2** vi (duck) schnattern, quaken, quak machen (col).
**quack²** n Quacksalber, Kurpfuscher m; (hum: doctor) Doktor, Medizinmann (hum) m.
**quad** [kwɒd] n = (a) **quadrangle** Hof m. (b) **quadruplet** Vierling m. (c) **quadraphonic** quadro. (d) **quadraphony** Quadro nt.
**quadrangle** ['kwɒdræŋgl] n (a) (Math) Viereck nt. (b) (Archit) (viereckiger) (Innen)hof.
**quadraphonic** [ˌkwɒdrə'fɒnɪk] adj quadrophon. ~ **sound** Quadrosound m.
**quadraphony** [kwɒd'rɒfənɪ] n Quadrophonie f.
**quadratic** [kwɒ'drætɪk] adj (Math) quadratisch.
**quadrilateral** [ˌkwɒdrɪ'lætərəl] **1** adj (Math) vierseitig. **2** n Viereck nt.
**quadruped** ['kwɒdrʊped] n Vierfüß(l)er m.
**quadruple** ['kwɒdrʊpl] **1** adj vierfach. **2** vt vervierfachen. **3** vi sich vervierfachen.
**quadruplet** [kwɒ'druːplɪt] n (child) Vierling m.
**quaff** [kwɒf] vt (old, hum) trinken, schlürfen (hum).
**quagmire** ['kwægmaɪər] n Sumpf, Morast m; (fig) (of vice etc) Morast m; (difficult situation) Schlamassel m (col).
**quail¹** ['kweɪl] vi (vor Angst) zittern or beben (before vor +dat).
**quail²** n (Orn) Wachtel f.
**quaint** [kweɪnt] adj (+er) (picturesque) malerisch; (charmingly old-fashioned) urig; (pleasantly odd) idea kurios; (old lady, way of speaking) drollig.
**quaintly** ['kweɪntlɪ] adv see adj written schnurrig; dressed putzig; named originell.
**quaintness** ['kweɪntnɪs] n see adj malerische Art; Urigkeit f; Kuriosität f; Drolligkeit f.
**quake** [kweɪk] **1** vi beben (with vor +dat). **2** n (col: earth~) (Erd)beben nt.
**Quaker** ['kweɪkər] n Quäker(in f) m.
**qualification** [ˌkwɒlɪfɪ'keɪʃən] n (a) (on paper) Qualifikation f; (document) Zeugnis nt; (requisite quality) Voraussetzung f. **what are your ~s?** welche Qualifikationen haben Sie?; **the only ~ needed is a knowledge of French** die einzige Voraussetzung sind Französischkenntnisse. (b) (limitation) Einschränkung f; (modification) Modifikation f. **to accept a plan with/without ~(s)** einen Plan unter Vorbehalt/vorbehaltlos billigen.
**qualified** ['kwɒlɪfaɪd] adj (a) (having training) ausgebildet; engineer graduiert; (with university degree) engineer Diplom-. **highly ~** hochqualifiziert; **to be ~ to do sth** qualifiziert sein, etw zu tun; **he was not ~ for the job** ihm fehlte die Qualifikation für die Stel-

le. (b) (limited) praise, approval nicht uneingeschränkt. **a ~ success** kein voller Erfolg; ~ **acceptance** (Comm) bedingte Annahme; **in a ~ sense** mit Einschränkungen.
**qualify** ['kwɒlɪfaɪ] **1** vt (a) (make competent) qualifizieren; (make legally entitled) berechtigen. **to ~ sb to do sth** (entitle) jdn berechtigen, etw zu tun; **he is not qualified to make these decisions** er ist nicht kompetent, diese Entscheidungen zu treffen. (b) (limit) statement, criticism einschränken; (change slightly) opinion, remark modifizieren. (c) (Gram) näher bestimmen. **2** vi (also Sport) sich qualifizieren (for für); (fulfil required conditions) in Frage kommen (for für). **to ~ as a doctor/teacher** sein medizinisches Staatsexamen machen/die Lehrbefähigung erhalten; **he hardly qualifies as a poet** er kann kaum als Dichter angesehen werden.
**qualifying** ['kwɒlɪfaɪɪŋ] adj adjective erläuternd; round, heat Qualifikations-. ~ **examination** Auswahlprüfung f.
**qualitative** ['kwɒlɪtətɪv] adj qualitativ.
**quality** ['kwɒlɪtɪ] **1** n Qualität f; (of justice, education etc) (hoher) Stand; (characteristic) Eigenschaft f; (nature) Art f. **of good/poor ~** von guter/schlechter Qualität; ~ **matters more than quantity** Qualität geht vor Quantität; **they vary in ~** sie sind qualitativ unterschiedlich; ~ **of life** Lebensqualität f. **2** attr goods etc Qualitäts-; (col: good) erstklassig (col); newspaper angesehen. ~ **control** Qualitätskontrolle f; ~ **time** sinnvoll genutzte Zeit.
**qualm** [kwɑːm] n Bedenken nt; (scruple) Skrupel m. **without a ~** ohne jeden Skrupel; ~**s of conscience** Gewissensbisse pl; **I had some ~s about his future** ich hatte einige Bedenken wegen seiner Zukunft.
**quandary** ['kwɒndərɪ] n Verlegenheit f, Dilemma nt. **he was in a ~ about what to do** er wußte nicht, was er tun sollte.
**quango** ['kwæŋgəʊ] n regierungsunabhängiger Verwaltungsausschuß m.
**quantify** ['kwɒntɪfaɪ] vt quantifizieren (form).
**quantitative** ['kwɒntɪtətɪv] adj quantitativ.
**quantity** ['kwɒntɪtɪ] n Quantität f; (amount) Menge f; (proportion) Anteil m (of an +dat); (Math, Phys, fig) Größe f. **in ~**, **in large quantities** in großen Mengen; **in equal quantities** zu gleichen Teilen; **quantities of books** Unmengen von Büchern.
**quantity surveyor** n Baukostenkalkulator m.
**quantum** ['kwɒntəm] n, pl **quanta** (Phys) Quant nt. ~ **leap** (Phys) Quantensprung m; (fig) Riesenschritt m; ~ **physics** sing Quantenphysik f; ~ **theory** Quantentheorie f.
**quarantine** ['kwɒrəntiːn] n Quarantäne f. **to be in ~** in Quarantäne sein.
**quarrel** ['kwɒrəl] **1** n Streit m; (dispute) Auseinandersetzung f. **they have had a ~** sie haben Streit gehabt; **let's not have a ~ about it** wir wollen uns nicht darüber streiten; **to start** or **pick a ~** einen Streit anfangen (with mit); **I have no ~ with him** ich

habe nichts gegen ihn. **2** *vi* **(a)** *(have a dispute)* sich streiten *(with* mit, *about, over* über *+acc)*; *(more trivially also)* sich zanken. **(b)** *(find fault)* etwas auszusetzen haben *(with* an *+dat)*. **you can't ~ with that** daran kann man doch nichts aussetzen.

**quarrelling,** *(US)* **quarreling** ['kwɒrəlɪŋ] *n* Streiterei *f*.

**quarrelsome** ['kwɒrəlsəm] *adj* streitsüchtig; *woman also* zänkisch.

**quarry**[1] ['kwɒrɪ] **1** *n* **(a)** Steinbruch *m*. **sandstone ~** Sandsteinbruch *m*. **(b)** *(fig)* Fundgrube *f*. **2** *vt* brechen, hauen.

**quarry**[2] *n* **(a)** *(Hunt)* Beute *f*. **(b)** *(fig) (thing)* Ziel *nt*; *(person)* Opfer *nt*.

**quart** [kwɔːt] *n (Measure)* Quart *nt*.

**quarter** ['kwɔːtəʳ] **1** *n* **(a)** Viertel *nt*; *(fourth of a year)* Vierteljahr, Quartal *nt*; *(US: 25 cents)* Vierteldollar *m*. **to divide sth into ~s** etw in vier Teile teilen; **the bottle was a ~/three-~s full** die Flasche war zu einem Viertel/dreiviertel voll; **a ~ (of a pound) of sausages** ein Viertel(pfund) Wurst; **a mile and a ~** cineinviertel Meilen; **a ~ of a mile** eine Viertelmeile; **for a ~ of the price** zu einem Viertel des Preises; **a ~ of an hour** eine Viertelstunde; **a ~ to seven** *(Brit)*, **a ~ of seven** *(US)* Viertel vor sieben; **a ~ past six** *(Brit)*, **a ~ after six** *(esp US)* Viertel nach sechs; **an hour and a ~** eineinviertel Stunden.

**(b)** *(district, area)* Viertel *nt*. **they came from all ~s of the earth** sie kamen aus allen Teilen der Welt; **in these ~s** in dieser Gegend; **he won't get help from that ~** von dieser Seite wird er keine Hilfe bekommen; **at close ~s** in der Nähe; *(from nearby)* aus der Nähe.

**(c)** *(direction)* (Himmels)richtung *f*. **they came from all ~s** sie kamen aus allen Himmelsrichtungen.

**(d)** **~s** *pl (lodgings)* Quartier *nt (also Mil)*, Unterkunft *f*; **to be confined to ~s** *(Mil)* Stubenarrest haben.

**(e) to give sb no ~** jdn nicht schonen.

**2** *adj pound, mile etc* Viertel-.

**3** *vt* **(a)** vierteln. **(b)** *(lodge)* einquartieren *(also Mil) (on* bei).

**quarter:** **~deck** *n (Naut)* Achterdeck *nt*; **~-final** *n* Viertelfinale *nt*.

**quarterly** ['kwɔːtəlɪ] **1** *adj* vierteljährlich. **2** *n* Vierteljahresschrift *f*. **3** *adv* vierteljährlich.

**quarter:** **~master** *n (Mil)* Quartiermeister *m*; *(Navy)* Steuermannsmaat *m*; **~ note** *n (US)* Viertelnote *f*.

**quartet** [kwɔː'tet] *n (Mus)* Quartett *nt*.

**quarto** ['kwɔːtəʊ] **1** *n (Typ)* Quart(format) *nt*. **2** *attr paper, volume* in Quart.

**quartz** ['kwɔːts] *n* Quarz *m*. **~ clock** Quarzuhr *f*.

**quasar** ['kweɪzɑʳ] *n* Quasar *nt*.

**quash** [kwɒʃ] *vt* **(a)** *(Jur) verdict* aufheben, annullieren. **(b)** *rebellion* unterdrücken; *suggestion, objection* ablehnen.

**quasi-** ['kwɑːzɪ] *pref* quasi-, quasi.

**quaver** ['kweɪvəʳ] **1** *n* **(a)** *(esp Brit Mus)* Achtel(note *f) nt*. **(b)** *(in voice)* Beben *nt*. **2** *vi (voice)* beben; *(Mus)* tremolieren.

**quay** [kiː] *n* Kai *m*. **alongside the ~** am Kai.

**quayside** ['kiːsaɪd] *n* Kai *m*.

**queasiness** ['kwiːzɪnɪs] *n* Übelkeit *f*.

**queasy** ['kwiːzɪ] *adj (+er)* **I feel ~** mir ist übel.

**Quebec** [kwɪ'bek] *n* Quebec *nt*.

**queen** [kwiːn] *n* **(a)** *(also fig)* Königin *f*. **~ bee** Bienenkönigin *f*; **~ mother** Königinmutter *f*; **Q~'s Counsel** Kronanwalt *m*/-anwältin *f*; **~'s English** eng-

lische Hochsprache. **(b)** *(Cards, Chess)* Dame *f*. **~ of spades** Pik Dame. **(c)** *(col: homosexual)* Schwule(r) *m (col)*.

**queer** [kwɪəʳ] **1** *adj (+er)* **(a)** *(strange)* komisch. **(b)** *(col) (unwell)* unwohl; *(peculiar) feeling* komisch. **I feel ~** mir ist nicht gut/mir ist ganz komisch *(col)*. **(c)** *(col: homosexual)* schwul *(col)*. **2** *n (col: homosexual)* Schwule(r) *m (col)*. **3** *vt* **to ~ sb's pitch** *(col)* jdm einen Strich durch die Rechnung machen.

**quell** [kwel] *vt fear* bezwingen; *passion* zügeln; *riot* niederschlagen; *anxieties* überwinden.

**quench** [kwentʃ] *vt fire* löschen; *thirst also* stillen; *enthusiasm* dämpfen.

**querulous** ['kwerʊləs] *adj* nörglerisch. **a ~ person** ein Querulant *m*.

**query** ['kwɪərɪ] **1** *n (question)* Frage *f*; *(Comp)* Abfrage *f*. **to raise a ~** eine Frage aufwerfen. **2** *vt* **(a)** *(express doubt about)* bezweifeln; *statement, motives* in Frage stellen; *bill, item* reklamieren. **(b)** *(check)* **to ~ sth with sb** etw mit jdm abklären.

**quest** [kwest] *n (search)* Suche *f (for* nach*)*; *(for knowledge, happiness etc)* Streben *nt (for* nach*)*.

**question** ['kwestʃən] **1** *n* Frage *f (to* an *+acc)*; *(Parl also)* Anfrage *f (to* an *+acc)*; *(no pl: doubt also)* Zweifel *m*. **to ask sb a ~** jdm eine Frage stellen, jdn etwas fragen; **beyond (all)** *or* **without ~** ohne Frage, ohne (jeden) Zweifel; **without ~ he is ...** er ist zweifellos *or* ohne Zweifel ...; **his honesty is beyond ~** seine Ehrlichkeit steht außer Frage; **your sincerity is not in ~** niemand zweifelt an Ihrer Aufrichtigkeit; **to call sth into ~** etw in Frage stellen; **that's another ~ altogether** das ist etwas völlig anderes; **that's not the ~** darum geht es nicht; **it's not just a ~ of money** es ist nicht nur eine Frage des Geldes; **there's no ~ of that happening** es kann keine Rede davon sein, daß das passiert; **there's no ~ of a strike** von einem Streik kann keine Rede sein; **that's out of the ~** das kommt nicht in Frage; **the matter in ~** die in Frage stehende Angelegenheit.

**2** *vt* **(a)** *(ask ~s of)* fragen *(about* nach*)*; *(police etc)* vernehmen, befragen *(about* zu*)*; *(examiner)* prüfen *(on* über *+acc)*. **they were ~ed by the immigration authorities** ihnen wurden von der Einwanderungsbehörde viele Fragen gestellt. **(b)** *(express doubt about)* bezweifeln; *(dispute, challenge)* in Frage stellen. **I ~ whether it's worth it** ich bezweifle, daß es der Mühe wert ist.

**questionable** ['kwestʃənəbl] *adj (suspect)* fragwürdig; *(open to doubt) statement, figures* fraglich; *value, advantage also* zweifelhaft.

**questioner** ['kwestʃənəʳ] *n* Fragesteller(in *f) m*.

**questioning** ['kwestʃənɪŋ] **1** *adj look* fragend. **2** *n* Verhör *nt*; *(by police also)* Vernehmung *f*.

**question:** **~mark** *n (lit, fig)* Fragezeichen *nt*; **~master** *n* Quizmaster *m*.

**questionnaire** [ˌkwestʃə'neəʳ] *n* Fragebogen *m*.

**queue** [kjuː] **1** *n (Brit: of people, cars)* Schlange *f*. **to form a ~** eine Schlange bilden; **to stand in a ~** Schlange stehen; **to join the ~** sich (hinten) anstellen; **to jump the ~** sich vordrängeln; **a ~ of cars** eine Autoschlange. **2** *vi (Brit: also ~ up)* Schlange stehen; *(form a ~)* eine Schlange bilden; *(people)* sich anstellen. **they were queueing for bread** sie standen um Brot an.

**queue-jumping** ['kjuːˌdʒʌmpɪŋ] *n (Brit)* Vordrängeln *nt*.

**quibble** ['kwɪbl] **1** *vi (be petty-minded)* kleinlich sein *(over, about* wegen*)*; *(argue with sb)* sich herumstreiten *(over, about* wegen*)*. **to ~ over details** auf Einzelheiten herumreiten. **2** *n* **I've got a few ~s**

**about the design** ich habe ein paar Kleinigkeiten am Design auszusetzen.

**quiche** [kiːʃ] *n* Quiche *f.*

**quick** [kwɪk] **1** *adj* (+*er*) **(a)** schnell; *answer also* prompt. **be** ~**!** mach schnell!; *(on telephone etc)* faß dich kurz!; **and be** ~ **about it** aber ein bißchen dalli *(col)*; **you were** ~ das ging ja schnell; **he was too** ~ **for me** *(in speech)* das ging mir zu schnell; *(in escaping)* er war zu schnell für mich; ~ **march!** *(Mil)* im Eilschritt, marsch!; **it's** ~**er by train** mit dem Zug geht es schneller; **he is** ~ **to criticize other people** er ist mit seiner Kritik schnell bei der Hand; **what's the** ~**est way to the station?** wie komme ich am schnellsten zum Bahnhof?

**(b)** *(short)* kiss flüchtig; *speech* kurz; *rest* klein, kurz. **let me have a** ~ **look** laß mich mal schnell sehen; **could I have a** ~ **word?** könnte ich Sie mal kurz sprechen?; **I'll just write him a** ~ **note** ich schreibe ihm schnell mal; **a** ~ **one** *(drink)* einer/eins auf die Schnelle *(col)*; *(question)* eine kurze Frage.

**(c)** *(lively,* ~ *to understand)* mind wach; *person* schnell von Begriff *(col)*; *child* aufgeweckt; *temper* hitzig; *eye, ear* scharf. **he is** ~ **at figures** er kann schnell rechnen.

**2** *n (Anat)* empfindliches Fleisch *(besonders unter den Fingernägeln).* **to be cut to the** ~ *(fig)* tief getroffen sein.

**3** *adv* (+*er*) schnell.

**quicken** ['kwɪkən] **1** *vt (also* ~ **up***)* beschleunigen. **2** *vi (also* ~ **up***)* schneller werden, sich beschleunigen. **the pace** ~**ed** das Tempo nahm zu.

**quick-fire** ['kwɪk'faɪə<sup>r</sup>] *adj* ~ **questions** Fragen *pl* wie aus der Maschinenpistole.

**quickie** ['kwɪkɪ] *n (col) (drink)* einer/eins auf die Schnelle *(col)*; *(question)* kurze Frage.

**quicklime** ['kwɪklaɪm] *n* ungelöschter Kalk.

**quickly** ['kwɪklɪ] *adv* schnell.

**quickness** ['kwɪknɪs] *n* **(a)** *(speed)* Schnelligkeit *f.* **(b)** *(intelligence)* schnelle Auffassungsgabe.

**quick:** ~**sand** *n* Treibsand *m*; ~**silver** *n* Quecksilber *nt*; ~**step** *n* Quickstep *m*; ~**-tempered** *adj* hitzig, leicht erregbar; ~**-witted** *adj* geistesgegenwärtig; *answer* schlagfertig.

**quid** [kwɪd] *n, pl -* *(col)* Pfund *nt.* **20** ~ 20 Eier *(col).*

**quiet** ['kwaɪət] **1** *adj* (+*er*) **(a)** *(silent)* still; *neighbours, person also, engine* ruhig; *music, car, voice* leise. **he's very** ~ er ist sehr still; **(be)** ~**!** Ruhe!; **to keep** ~ *(not speak)* still sein; *(not make noise)* leise sein; **keep** ~**!** sei/seid still!; **can't you keep your dog** ~**!** können Sie nicht zusehen, daß Ihr Hund still ist?; **to keep** ~ **about sth** über etw *(acc)* nichts sagen.

**(b)** *(peaceful)* ruhig; *smile* leise. **things are very** ~ **at the moment** im Augenblick ist nicht viel los; **to lead a** ~ **life** ein ruhiges Leben führen; **everything was** ~ **on the Syrian border** an der syrischen Grenze herrschte Ruhe; **to have a** ~ **drink** in aller Ruhe einen trinken *(col).*

**(c)** *(gentle) character* sanft; *child* ruhig; *horse* gutwillig; *irony* leise.

**(d)** *(simple) style, elegance* schlicht; *wedding, dinner* im kleinen Rahmen.

**(e)** *(not overt) hatred, envy* still; *resentment* heimlich. **I'll have a** ~ **word with him** ich werde mal ein Wörtchen (im Vertrauen) mit ihm reden; **he kept the matter** ~ er behielt die Sache für sich.

**2** *n* Ruhe *f.* **the sudden** ~ **after the bombing** die plötzliche Stille nach dem Bombenangriff; **on the** ~ heimlich; **he left on the** ~ er ist still und heimlich weggegangen.

**3** *vt* = **quieten.**

**quieten** ['kwaɪətn] *vt sb* zum Schweigen bringen; *noisy class, dog* zur Ruhe bringen; *crying baby* beruhigen; *engine* ruhiger machen; *(calm) person, conscience* beruhigen.

▶**quieten down 1** *vi (become silent)* leiser werden; *(become calm)* sich beruhigen; *(after wild youth)* ruhiger werden. **2** *vt sep* beruhigen.

**quietly** ['kwaɪətlɪ] *adv (making little noise)* leise; *(peacefully, making little fuss)* ruhig; *(secretly)* still und heimlich; *dressed* dezent. **he's very** ~ **spoken** er hat eine sehr leise Stimme; **to be** ~ **confident** insgeheim sehr sicher sein; **I was sitting here** ~ **sipping my wine** ich saß da und trank in aller Ruhe meinen Wein; **he slipped off** ~ er machte sich in aller Stille davon.

**quietness** ['kwaɪətnɪs] *n* **(a)** Stille *f; (of engine, car)* Geräuscharmut *f; (of footsteps etc)* Lautlosigkeit *f; (of person)* stille Art. **the** ~ **of her voice** ihre leise Stimme. **(b)** *(peacefulness)* Ruhe *f.*

**quill** [kwɪl] *n (feather, pen)* Feder *f; (feather stem)* Federkiel *m; (of porcupine)* Stachel *m.*

**quilt** [kwɪlt] **1** *n (continental* ~*)* Steppdecke *f; (unstitched)* Federbett *nt.* **2** *vt* absteppen; *(with padding)* wattieren. ~**ed jacket** Steppjacke *f.*

**quilting** ['kwɪltɪŋ] *n (process)* Absteppen *nt*; Wattieren *nt.*

**quin** [kwɪn] *n (Brit)* = **quintuplet** Fünfling *m.*

**quince** [kwɪns] *n (fruit, tree)* Quitte *f.* ~ **jelly** Quittengelee *nt.*

**quinine** [kwɪ'niːn] *n* Chinin *nt.*

**quintessence** [kwɪn'tesns] *n (fig)* Quintessenz *f; (embodiment)* Inbegriff *m.*

**quintet** [kwɪn'tet] *n (Mus)* Quintett *nt.*

**quintuplet** [kwɪn'tjuːplɪt] *n* Fünfling *m.*

**quip** [kwɪp] **1** *n* witzige Bemerkung. **2** *vti* witzeln.

**quire** [kwaɪə<sup>r</sup>] *n (24 sheets)* 24 Bogen Papier.

**quirk** [kwɜːk] *n* Marotte *f; (of nature, fate)* Laune *f.* **by a strange** ~ **of fate** durch eine Laune des Schicksals.

**quirky** ['kwɜːkɪ] *adj* (+*er*) schrullig.

**quit** [kwɪt] *(vb: pret, ptp* ~**ted** *or* ~*)* **1** *vt* **(a)** *(leave)* town, army verlassen; *(give up)* job aufgeben. **(b)** *(col: stop)* aufhören mit. **to** ~ **doing sth** aufhören, etw zu tun. **2** *vi* **(a)** *(leave one's job)* kündigen. **(b)** *(go away)* weg- or fortgehen. **notice to** ~ Kündigung *f*; **they gave me notice to** ~ sie haben mir gekündigt. **(c)** *(give up)* aufgeben. **3** *adj* ~ **of** frei von, ledig (+*gen*) *(geh).* **we are** ~ **of him** wir sind ihn los.

**quite** [kwaɪt] *adv* **(a)** *(entirely)* ganz; *(emph)* völlig. ~ **unnecessary/wrong** völlig unnötig/falsch; **I am** ~ **happy where I am** ich fühle mich hier ganz wohl; **I was** ~ **happy until you came along** bevor du kamst, war ich völlig zufrieden; **it's** ~ **impossible to do that** das ist völlig unmöglich; **are you** ~ **finished!** *(iro)* bist du endlich fertig?; **he's** ~ **grown up now** er ist jetzt schon richtig erwachsen; **I** ~ **agree with you** ich stimme völlig mit Ihnen überein; **he** ~ **understands that he must go** er sieht durchaus ein, daß er gehen muß; **he has** ~ **recovered** er ist völlig wiederhergestellt; **that's** ~ **another matter** das ist doch etwas ganz anderes; **that's** ~ **enough for me** das reicht mir wirklich; **not** ~ nicht ganz; **you weren't** ~ **early/tall enough** Sie waren ein bißchen zu spät dran/zu klein; **I don't** ~ **see what he means** ich verstehe nicht ganz, was er meint; **sorry! —  that's** ~ **all right** Entschuldigung! — das macht doch nichts; **thank you — that's** ~ **all right** danke — bitte schön, gern geschehen; ~ **(so)!** genau!; ~ **the thing** *(col)* ganz große Mode.

**(b)** *(to some degree)* ziemlich. ~ **likely** sehr wahrscheinlich; **he's had** ~ **a lot to drink** er hat ganz

schön viel getrunken *(col)*; ~ **a few people** ziemlich viele Leute; **he is** ~ **a good singer** er ist ein ziemlich guter Sänger; **I** ~ **like this painting** dieses Bild gefällt mir ganz gut.
   **(c)** *(really, truly)* wirklich. **she's** ~ **a girl/cook** *etc* sie ist ein tolles Mädchen/eine tolle Köchin *etc*; **it's** ~ **delightful** es ist einfach wunderbar; **it was** ~ **a shock** es war ein ziemlicher Schock; **that's** ~ **some bill** *(col)* das ist vielleicht eine Rechnung *(col)*; **it was** ~ **an experience** das war schon ein Erlebnis; **he's** ~ **a hero now** jetzt ist er ein richtiger Held.

**quits** [kwɪts] *adj* quitt. **to be** ~ **with sb** mit jdm quitt sein; **shall we call it** ~? sagen wir, wir sind quitt?

**quiver**¹ ['kwɪvər] **1** *vi* zittern *(with* vor *+dat)*; *(eyelids etc)* zucken. **2** *n* Zittern *nt*; Zucken *nt*.

**quiver**² *n (for arrows)* Köcher *m*.

**quixotic** [kwɪk'sɒtɪk] *adj* versponnen; *ideals* schwärmerisch. **a** ~ **gesture** eine Donquichotterie.

**quiz** [kwɪz] **1** *n* **(a)** Quiz *nt*. **(b)** *(US Sch col)* Prüfung *f*. **2** *vt* **(a)** *(question closely)* ausfragen *(about* über *+acc)*. **(b)** *(US Sch col)* prüfen.

**quiz:** ~**game** *n* Ratespiel *nt*; ~**master** *n* Quizmaster *m*; ~ **show** *n* Quiz *nt*.

**quizzical** ['kwɪzɪkəl] *adj* **(a)** *air, look* fragend; *smile* zweifelnd. **(b)** *(odd)* eigenartig.

**quoit** [kwɔɪt] *n* Wurfring *m*. ~**s** *(game)* Wurfringspiel *nt*.

**quorum** ['kwɔːrəm] *n* Quorum *nt*.

**quota** ['kwəʊtə] *n* **(a)** *(of work)* Pensum *nt*. **(b)** *(of an +dat) (permitted amount)* Quantum *nt*; *(share allotted)* Anteil *m*; *(of goods)* Kontingent *nt*. **the** ~ **of immigrants allowed into the country** die zugelassene Einwanderungsquote.

**quotation** [kwəʊ'teɪʃən] *n* **(a)** *(passage cited)* Zitat *nt*; *(act)* Zitieren *nt*. **a** ~ **from Shakespeare** ein Shakespeare-Zitat. **(b)** *(St Ex)* Notierung *f*. **(c)** *(Comm)* Preisangebot *nt*; *(estimate)* Kostenvoranschlag *m*.

**quotation marks** *npl* Anführungszeichen *pl*. **open/close** ~ Anführungszeichen unten/oben.

**quote** [kwəʊt] **1** *vt* **(a)** *author, text* zitieren. **you can** ~ **me (on that)** Sie können das ruhig wörtlich wiedergeben; **he was** ~**d as saying that** ... er soll gesagt haben, daß ...; ~... **un**~ Zitat Anfang ... Zitat Ende; **don't** ~ **me on this** *(I'm not sure)* ich kann mich nicht dafür verbürgen; *(don't repeat)* das sollte unter uns bleiben; **he said, and I** ~ ... er sagte, und zwar wörtlich, ... **(b)** *(cite)* anführen. **to** ~ **sb/sth as an example** jdn/etw als Beispiel anführen. **(c)** *(Comm)* price nennen; *reference number* angeben. **how much did they** ~ **you for that?** wieviel wollten sie dafür haben? **(d)** *(St Ex)* notieren. **the shares are** ~**d at £2** die Aktien werden mit £2 notiert.
   **2** *vi* **(a)** zitieren. **to** ~ **from an author** einen Schriftsteller zitieren. **(b)** *(Comm)* ein Preisangebot machen; *(builders etc)* einen Kostenvoranschlag machen.
   **3** *n* **(a)** *(from author, politician)* Zitat *nt*. **(b)** ~**s** *pl (col)* Anführungszeichen *pl*; **in** ~**s** in Anführungszeichen. **(c)** *(Comm)* Preisangebot *nt*; *(estimate)* Kostenvoranschlag *m*.

**quotient** ['kwəʊʃənt] *n (Math)* Quotient *m*.

**qv** = **quod vide** s.d.

**qwerty keyboard** ['kwɜː,tɪ'kiːbɔːd] *n* Qwerty-Tastatur *f*.

# R

**R, r** [ɑːʳ] *n* R, r *nt.* **R for Robert** *(Brit)*, **R for Roger** *(US)* ≃ R wie Richard; **the three Rs** Lesen, Schreiben und Rechnen *(with sing or pl vb).*
**R** = **(a)** *(Brit)* **Rex**; **Regina. (b) river** Fl. **(c)** *(US Film)* **restricted** für Jugendliche nicht geeignet. **(d)** *(US Pol)* **Republican.**
**r** = **right** r.
**RA** *(Brit)* = **Royal Academy**; *(after name)* **Royal Academician.**
**RAAF** = **Royal Australian Air Force** australische Luftwaffe.
**rabbi** ['ræbaɪ] *n* Rabbiner *m*; *(as title)* Rabbi *m.*
**rabbit** ['ræbɪt] *n* Kaninchen *nt.*
**rabbit** *in cpds* Kaninchen-; ~ **burrow** *or* **hole** *n* Kaninchenbau *m*; ~ **hutch** *n* Kaninchenstall *m*; ~ **warren** *n (fig: maze)* Labyrinth *nt.*
►**rabbit on** *vi (Brit col)* schwafeln *(col).* **what's he ~ting ~ about?** was schwafelt er da? *(col).*
**rabble** ['ræbl] *n (disorderly crowd)* lärmender Haufen *(col)*; *(pej: lower classes)* Pöbel *m.*
**rabid** ['ræbɪd] *adj* **(a)** *(Vet)* tollwütig. **(b)** *(fanatical)* fanatisch; *hatred also* wild.
**rabies** ['reɪbiːz] *n* Tollwut *f.*
**RAC** = **Royal Automobile Club** britischer Automobilclub ≃ ADAC *m.*
**raccoon** *n* = **racoon.**
**race¹** [reɪs] **1** *n* Rennen *nt*; *(on foot also)* (Wett)lauf *m*; *(swimming)* Wettschwimmen *nt.* **100 metres ~** 100-Meter-Lauf *m*; **to run a ~ with** *or* **against sb** mit jdm um die Wette laufen; **to go to the ~s** zum Pferderennen gehen; **a ~ against time** *(fig)* ein Wettlauf *m* gegen die Zeit.
**2** *vt (compete with)* um die Wette laufen/fahren/schwimmen *etc* mit; *(Sport)* laufen/fahren/schwimmen *etc* gegen. **I'll ~ you to school** ich mache mit dir ein Wettrennen bis zur Schule.
**3** *vi* **(a)** *(compete)* laufen/fahren/schwimmen *etc.* **to ~ with** *or* **against sb** mit jdm um die Wette laufen *etc.* **(b)** *(rush)* rasen, jagen; *(on foot also)* rennen; *(with work)* hetzen. **to ~ after sb/sth** hinter jdm/etw herjagen; **to ~ ahead with sth** etw vorantreiben; **the project is racing ahead** die Arbeit am Projekt geht mit Riesenschritten voran. **(c)** *(engine)* durchdrehen; *(pulse)* jagen, fliegen.
**race²** *n (ethnic group, species)* Rasse *f.* **of mixed ~** gemischtrassig.
**race:** ~ **car** *n (US)* Rennwagen *m*; ~ **car driver** *n* Rennfahrer *m*; ~**course** *n* Rennbahn *f*; ~ **hatred** *n* Rassenhaß *m*; ~**horse** *n* Rennpferd *nt*; ~ **meeting** *n* Rennveranstaltung *f*; ~ **relations** *n* **(a)** *pl* Beziehungen *pl* zwischen den Rassen; **(b)** *sing (subject)* Rassenintegration *f*; ~**track** *n* Rennbahn *f.*
**racial** ['reɪʃəl] *adj* rassisch; *conflict, disturbances etc* Rassen-. ~ **discrimination** Rassendiskriminierung *f*; ~ **equality** Rassengleichheit *f*; ~ **integration** Rassenintegration *f.*
**racialism** ['reɪʃəlɪzəm] *n* Rassismus *m.*
**racialist** ['reɪʃəlɪst] **1** *n* Rassist(in *f*) *m.* **2** *adj* rassi-

stisch.
**racially** ['reɪʃəlɪ] *adv* in bezug auf die Rasse; *superior* rassenmäßig. ~ **mixed** gemischtrassig.
**racial:** ~ **minority** *n* rassische Minderheit; ~ **prejudice** *n* Rassenvorurteil *nt*; ~ **segregation** *n* Rassentrennung *f.*
**racing** ['reɪsɪŋ] *n* Rennsport *m*; *(races)* Rennen *pl*; *(horse-~)* Pferderennsport *m*; *(motor ~)* Motorrennen *nt.*
**racing** *in cpds* Renn-. ~ **car** *n (Brit)* Rennwagen *m*; ~ **driver** *n (Brit)* Rennfahrer *m.*
**racism** ['reɪsɪzəm] *n* = **racialism.**
**racist** ['reɪsɪst] *n, adj* = **racialist.**
**rack¹** [ræk] **1** *n* **(a)** *(for hats, toast, pipes etc)* Ständer *m*; *(for bottles, plates also)* Gestell *nt*; *(shelves)* Regal *nt*; *(luggage ~)* Gepäcknetz *nt*; *(on car, bicycle)* Gepäckträger *m*; *(Tech)* Zahnstange *f.* **(b)** *(Hist)* Folter(bank) *f.* **2** *vt* **(a)** *(pain)* quälen. ~**ed with pain/remorse** von Schmerzen/Gewissensbissen geplagt. **(b) to ~ one's brains** sich *(dat)* den Kopf zerbrechen.
**rack²** *n*: **to go to ~ and ruin** *(country, economy)* herunterkommen, vor die Hunde gehen *(col)*; *(building)* verfallen.
**rack-and-pinion steering** ['rækən'pɪnjən,stiːrɪŋ] *n (Aut)* Zahnstangenlenkung *f.*
**racket¹** ['rækɪt] *n (Sport)* Schläger *m.*
**racket²** *n* **(a)** *(uproar)* Krach, Lärm *m.* **to make a ~** Krach machen. **(b)** *(col) (dishonest business)* Schwindelgeschäft *nt (col)*; *(making excessive profit)* Wucher *m.* **the drugs ~** das Drogengeschäft.
**racketeer** [,rækɪ'tɪəʳ] *n* Gauner *m (col)*; *(making excessive profit)* Halsabschneider *m (col).*
**raconteur** [,rækɒn'tɜːʳ] *n* Erzähler(in *f*) *m* von Anekdoten.
**racoon, raccoon** [rə'kuːn] *n* Waschbär *m.*
**racquet** ['rækɪt] *n* = **racket¹.**
**racy** ['reɪsɪ] *adj (+er) speech, style* schwungvoll, feurig; *(risqué)* gewagt.
**RADA** ['rɑːdə] *(Brit)* = **Royal Academy of Dramatic Art** bekannteste britische Schauspielschule.
**radar** ['reɪdɑːʳ] *n* Radar *nt or m.*
**radar** *in cpds* Radar-; ~ **operator** *n* Bediener(in *f*) *m* eines/des Radargerätes; ~ **scanner** *n* Rundsuchradargerät *nt*; ~ **screen** *n* Radarschirm *m*; ~ **trap** *n* Radarfalle *f.*
**radial** ['reɪdɪəl] *adj (Tech)* radial. ~**(-ply) tyre** *(Brit) or* **tire** *(US)* Gürtelreifen *m.*
**radiance** ['reɪdɪəns] *n* Leuchten *nt.*
**radiant** ['reɪdɪənt] *adj (lit, fig)* strahlend *(with vor +dat).* **to be ~ with health/joy** vor Gesundheit strotzen/vor Freude strahlen.
**radiate** ['reɪdɪeɪt] **1** *vi* **(a)** Strahlen aussenden; *(emit heat)* Wärme ausstrahlen; *(heat)* ausgestrahlt werden. **(b)** *(lines, roads)* strahlenförmig ausgehen *(from von).* **2** *vt (lit, fig)* ausstrahlen.
**radiation** [,reɪdɪ'eɪʃən] *n (of heat etc)* (Aus)strahlung *f*; *(rays)* radioaktive Strahlung; *(absorbed by body)*

Strahlenbelastung f. ~ **sickness** Strahlenkrankheit f.

**radiator** ['reɪdɪeɪtəʳ] n (heating) Heizkörper, Radiator m; (Aut) Kühler m. ~ **grille** Kühlergrill m; ~ **mascot** Kühlerfigur f.

**radical** ['rædɪkəl] **1** adj (basic) fundamental; (extreme) reform radikal, grundlegend; rethinking total; (Pol) radikal. **2** n (Pol) Radikale(r) mf.

**radically** ['rædɪkəlɪ] adv see adj. **there's something** ~ **wrong with this** hier stimmt etwas ganz und gar nicht.

**radio** ['reɪdɪəʊ] **1** n (a) Rundfunk m; (also ~ set) Radio(gerät) nt. **to listen to the** ~ Radio hören; **to hear sth on the** ~ etw im Radio hören. (b) no pl (telegraphy) Funk m. **over the** or **by** ~ über or per Funk. **2** vt person über Funk verständigen; message funken, durchgeben. **3** vi **to** ~ **for help** per Funk einen Hilferuf durchgeben.

**radio:** ~**active** adj radioaktiv; ~**activity** n Radioaktivität f; ~ **announcer** n Rundfunksprecher(in f) m; ~ **beacon** n (Aviat, Naut) Funkfeuer nt; ~ **broadcast** n Rundfunkübertragung f; ~-**cassette recorder** n Radiorecorder m; ~ **contact** n Funkverbindung f; ~-**controlled** adj ferngesteuert; ~ **engineer** n Rundfunktechniker(in f) m.

**radiographer** [reɪdɪ'ɒɡrəfəʳ] n Röntgenassistent(in f) m.

**radiography** [,reɪdɪ'ɒɡrəfɪ] n Röntgenographie f.

**radiology** [,reɪdɪ'ɒlədʒɪ] n Radiologie f; (X-ray also) Röntgenologie f.

**radio:** ~ **pager** n Funkrufempfänger m; ~ **play** n Hörspiel nt; ~ **programme** or **program** (US) n Rundfunksendung f; ~ **station** n Radio- or Rundfunksender m; ~ **taxi** n Funktaxi nt; ~ **telephone** n Funksprechgerät nt; ~ **telescope** n Radioteleskop nt; ~**therapy** n Strahlentherapie f.

**radish** ['rædɪʃ] n Rettich m; (small red) Radieschen nt.

**radium** ['reɪdɪəm] n Radium nt.

**radius** ['reɪdɪəs] n, pl **radii** ['reɪdɪaɪ] (Math) Radius m. **within a 5 mile** ~ **(of Hamburg)** im Umkreis von 8 km (um Hamburg).

**radon** ['reɪdɒn] n (Chem) Radon nt.

**RAF** = **Royal Air Force** königliche (britische) Luftwaffe.

**raffia** ['ræfɪə] n (for handicraft) Bast m.

**raffle** ['ræfl] **1** n Tombola, Verlosung f. ~ **ticket** Los nt. **2** vt (also ~ **off**) verlosen.

**raft** [rɑːft] n Floß nt.

**rafter** ['rɑːftəʳ] n (Dach)sparren m.

**rag¹** [ræg] n (a) Lumpen, Fetzen m; (for cleaning) Lappen m. ~**s** Lumpen pl; (col: clothes) Klamotten pl (col); **in** ~**s** zerlumpt; **to go from** ~**s to riches** vom Tellerwäscher zum Millionär werden. (b) (pej col: newspaper) Käseblatt nt.

**rag²** **1** n (Brit col: joke) Jux m (col). ~ **week** (Univ) Woche, in der Studenten durch Aufführungen Geld für Wohltätigkeitszwecke sammeln. **2** vt (tease) aufziehen, foppen.

**ragamuffin** ['ræɡə,mʌfɪn] n Vogelscheuche f (col); (child) Gassenkind n.

**rag:** ~-**and-bone man** n Lumpensammler m; ~**bag** n (fig) Sammelsurium nt (col); ~ **doll** n Flickenpuppe f.

**rage** [reɪdʒ] **1** n Wut f, Zorn m. **to be in a** ~ wütend sein; **to fly into a** ~ einen Wutanfall bekommen; **to be (all) the** ~ (col) der letzte Schrei sein (col). **2** vi toben.

**ragged** ['ræɡɪd] adj person, clothes zerlumpt; beard zottig; coastline, rocks zerklüftet; edge, cuff ausgefranst. **to run sb** ~ (col: exhaust) jdn fertigmachen (col).

**raging** ['reɪdʒɪŋ] adj person wütend; fever heftig; thirst brennend; sea, wind tobend. **he was** ~ er tobte.

**rag trade** n (col) Modebranche f.

**raid** [reɪd] **1** n Überfall m; (Mil also) Angriff m; (air ~) Luftangriff m; (police ~) Razzia f; (by thieves also) Einbruch m. **2** vt (a) überfallen; (police) eine Razzia durchführen in (+dat); (thieves) einbrechen in (+acc). (b) (fig hum) plündern.

**raider** ['reɪdəʳ] n (bandit) Gangster m; (thief) Einbrecher m; (in bank) Bankräuber m; (looter) Plünderer m.

**rail¹** [reɪl] n (a) (on bridge, stairs etc) Geländer nt; (Naut) Reling f; (curtain ~) Schiene f; (towel-~) Handtuchhalter m. ~**s** (fence) Umzäunung f. (b) (for train, tram) Schiene f, Gleis m. **to go off the** ~**s** (lit) entgleisen; (fig: morally) auf die schiefe Bahn geraten. (c) (~ travel, ~way) die (Eisen)bahn. **to travel by** ~ mit der Bahn fahren.

**rail²** vi **to** ~ **at/against sb** jdn beschimpfen/über jdn schimpfen.

**railcar** ['reɪlkɑːʳ] n Triebwagen m.

**railing** ['reɪlɪŋ] n (rail) Geländer nt; (Naut) Reling f; (fence: ~s) Zaun m.

**railroad** ['reɪlrəʊd] **1** n (US) (Eisen)bahn f. ~ **station** Bahnhof m; ~ **tracks** Gleise pl. **2** vt **to** ~ **a bill** eine Gesetzesvorlage durchpeitschen; **to** ~ **sb into doing sth** jdn so unter Druck setzen, daß er etw tut.

**railroader** ['reɪlrəʊdəʳ] n (US) Eisenbahner m.

**rail:** ~ **strike** n Bahnstreik m; ~ **traffic** n Bahnverkehr m.

**railway** ['reɪlweɪ] n (Brit) (Eisen)bahn f; (track) Gleise pl.

**railway** (Brit): ~ **carriage** n Eisenbahnwagen m; ~ **compartment** n Zugabteil nt; ~ **crossing** n Bahnübergang m; ~ **engine** n Lokomotive f; ~ **line** n (Eisen)bahnlinie f; (track) Gleis nt; ~**man** n Eisenbahner m; ~ **station** n Bahnhof m.

**railworker** ['reɪlwɜːkəʳ] n Bahnarbeiter(in f) m.

**rain** [reɪn] **1** n Regen m. **in the** ~ im Regen; **come** ~ **or shine** (fig) was auch geschieht; **the** ~**s** die Regenzeit. **2** vti impers (lit, fig) regnen. **it is** ~**ing** es regnet; **it never** ~**s but it pours** (prov) ein Unglück kommt selten allein (prov); **it's** ~**ing cats and dogs** (col) es gießt wie aus Kübeln.

▶**rain down** vi (blows etc) niederprasseln (upon auf +acc).

▶**rain off**, (US) **rain out** vt sep **to be** ~**ed** ~ wegen Regen nicht stattfinden.

**rainbow** ['reɪnbəʊ] n Regenbogen m. **in all the colours of the** ~ in allen Regenbogenfarben.

**rain:** ~-**check** n (US) **to take a** ~-**check on sth** (col) etw auf ein andermal verschieben; ~**coat** n Regenmantel m; ~**drop** n Regentropfen m; ~**fall** n Niederschlag m; ~**forest** n Regenwald m; ~**proof** adj regendicht; ~**storm** n schwere Regenfälle pl; ~**water** n Regenwasser nt.

**rainy** ['reɪnɪ] adj (+er) regnerisch, Regen-; area regenreich. ~ **season** Regenzeit f; **to keep sth for a** ~ **day** (fig) etw für schlechte Zeiten aufheben.

**raise** [reɪz] **1** vt (a) (lift) object, arm heben; blinds, eyebrow, (Theat) curtain hochziehen; (Naut) anchor lichten; sunken ship heben. **to** ~ **one's hat to sb** den Hut vor jdm ziehen; **to** ~ **sb from the dead** jdn von den Toten erwecken; **to** ~ **one's voice** lauter sprechen; (get angry) laut werden; **to** ~ **the roof** (fig) (with anger) fürchterlich toben; (audience) vor Begeisterung toben.

(b) (increase) (to auf +acc) salary, temperature erhöhen; price also, standard anheben. **to** ~ **the tone** das Niveau heben; **to** ~ **to the power of 2** (Math) in die 2. Potenz erheben.

   (**c**) _(promote)_ (er) heben _(to in +acc)._

   (**d**) _(build, erect)_ errichten.

   (**e**) _(create, evoke)_ problem, question aufwerfen; _objection_ erheben; _suspicion, hope_ (er)wecken; _spirits_ (herauf)beschwören. **to ~ sb's/one's hopes** jdm/sich Hoffnung machen; **to ~ a laugh/smile** _(in others)_ Gelächter/ein Lächeln hervorrufen; _(oneself)_ lachen/lächeln; **to ~ a protest** protestieren; **to ~ hell** _(col)_ einen Höllenspektakel machen _(col)._

   (**f**) _(grow, breed)_ children, animals aufziehen; _crops_ anbauen. **to ~ a family** Kinder großziehen.

   (**g**) _army_ aufstellen; _taxes_ erheben; _funds, money_ aufbringen; _loan_ aufnehmen.

   (**h**) _(end)_ siege, embargo aufheben.

   **2** _n (in salary)_ Gehaltserhöhung _f; (in wages)_ Lohnerhöhung _f._

**raisin** ['reɪzən] _n_ Rosine _f._

**rajah** ['rɑːdʒə] _n_ Radscha _m._

**rake¹** [reɪk] **1** _n_ Harke _f (esp N Ger)_, Rechen _m (S Ger)._ **2** _vt_ (**a**) _garden, leaves_ harken _(esp N Ger)_, rechen _(S Ger)._ (**b**) _(machine gun, searchlight)_ bestreichen.

   ▶**rake in** _vt sep (col)_ money kassieren _(col)._ **he's raking it ~** er scheffelt das Geld nur so.

   ▶**rake up** _vt sep_ memories, grievance aufwärmen. **to ~ ~ the past** in der Vergangenheit wühlen.

**rake²** _n (person)_ Lebemann _m._

**rake-off** ['reɪkɒf] _n (col)_ (Gewinn)anteil _m._

**rakish** ['reɪkɪʃ] _adj person_ flott, verwegen. **his hat was at a ~ angle** er hatte den Hut flott aufgesetzt.

**rally** ['rælɪ] **1** _n_ (**a**) Versammlung _f; (with speaker)_ Kundgebung _f; (Aut)_ Rallye _f._ (**b**) _(Tennis)_ Ballwechsel _m._ **2** _vt_ troops, supporters (ver)sammeln. **to ~ one's strength** all seine Kräfte sammeln. **3** (**a**) _vi (St Ex)_ sich erholen. (**b**) _(troops, people)_ sich versammeln. **~ing point** Sammelplatz _m;_ **to ~ to the support of sb** _(fig)_ sich geschlossen hinter jdn stellen.

   ▶**rally around** _vi +prep obj_ leader sich scharen um; _person in distress_ sich annehmen _(+gen)._

**ram** [ræm] **1** _n_ (**a**) _(animal)_ Widder, Schafbock _m._ (**b**) _(Tech)_ Ramme _f,_ Rammbock _m; (hydraulic)_ Stößheber _m._ **2** _vt_ (**a**) _(push)_ stick, post, umhertun stoßen; _(with great force)_ rammen; _(pack)_ zwängen; _(Tech)_ pile rammen. **to ~ sth down sb's throat** _(col)_ jdm etw unter die Nase reiben _(col)._ (**b**) _(crash into)_ ship, car rammen. **the car ~med a lamppost** das Auto prallte gegen einen Laternenpfahl.

**RAM** _(Comp)_ = **random access memory** RAM _m or nt._

**ramble** ['ræmbl] **1** _n_ Streifzug _m; (hike)_ Wanderung _f._ **to go for or on a ~** einen Streifzug/eine Wanderung machen. **2** _vi_ (**a**) _(wander about)_ Streifzüge/einen Streifzug machen; _(go on hike)_ wandern. (**b**) _(in speech)_ faseln _(col); (pej: also_ ~ **on**) schwafeln _(col)._

**rambler** ['ræmblər] _n_ Wanderer _m,_ Wanderin _f; (rose)_ Kletterrose _f._

**rambling** ['ræmblɪŋ] _adj_ speech weitschweifig; _person_ schwafelnd _(col); building_ weitläufig. **~ rose** Kletterrose _f._

**rambunctious** [ræm'bʌŋkʃəs] _adj (US)_ = **rumbustious.**

**ramification** [ˌræmɪfɪ'keɪʃən] _n_ Verzweigung _f; (smaller, of arteries)_ Verästelung _f._ **the race question and its ~s** die Rassenfrage und die damit verbundenen Probleme.

**ramify** ['ræmɪfaɪ] _vi (lit, fig)_ sich verzweigen.

**ramp** [ræmp] _n_ Rampe _f; (hydraulic ~)_ Hebebühne _f; (Aviat: also_ **boarding ~**) Gangway _f._

**rampage** ['ræmpeɪdʒ] **1** _n_ **to be/go on the ~** randalieren. **2** [ræm'peɪdʒ] _vi (also ~_ **about)** herumtoben.

**rampant** ['ræmpənt] _adj_ plants, growth üppig; _evil etc_ wild wuchernd _attr._ **to be ~** (wild) wuchern.

**rampart** ['ræmpɑːt] _n_ Wall _m._

**ram raid** ['ræmreɪd] _n_ Raubüberfall _m, bei dem eine Geschäftsfront mit einem Fahrzeug gerammt wird._

**ramrod** ['ræmrɒd] _n:_ **he's as stiff as a ~** er ist steif wie ein Besenstiel.

**ramshackle** ['ræmˌʃækl] _adj_ building baufällig; _car etc_ klapprig.

**ran** [ræn] _pret of_ **run.**

**ranch** [rɑːntʃ] _n_ Ranch, Viehfarm _f._ **~ house** _(US)_ Bungalow _m._

**rancher** [rɑːntʃər] _n_ Rancher, Viehzüchter _m._

**rancid** ['rænsɪd] _adj_ ranzig.

**rancour,** _(US)_ **rancor** ['ræŋkər] _(of tone)_ Verbitterung _f; (of attack)_ Boshaftigkeit _f._

**R & B** = **rhythm and blues** R & B _m._

**R & D** = **research and development.**

**random** ['rændəm] **1** _n_ **at ~** speak, walk, drive aufs Geratewohl; _shoot, drop bombs_ ziellos; _take_ wahllos; **a few examples taken at ~** ein paar willkürlich gewählte Beispiele; **I (just) chose one at ~** ich wählte einfach irgendeine (beliebige). **2** _adj_ selection willkürlich, Zufalls-. **a ~ bullet** eine verirrte Kugel; **a ~ shot** ein Schuß _m_ ins Blaue; **he was killed by a ~ shot** er wurde von einer verirrten Kugel getötet; **to make a ~ guess** auf gut Glück raten; **~ sample** Stichprobe _f;_ **~ access** _(Comp)_ Direktzugriff _m;_ **~ access memory** _(Comp)_ Direktzugriffsspeicher _m._

**randy** ['rændɪ] _adj (+er) (Brit)_ scharf _(col)_, geil.

**rang** [ræŋ] _pret of_ **ring².**

**range** [reɪndʒ] **1** _n_ (**a**) _(scope, distance covered)_ Aktionsradius _m; (of missile, gun, telescope also)_ Reichweite _f; (of vehicle also)_ Fahrbereich _m; (of plane also)_ Flugbereich _m._ **at a ~ of** auf eine Entfernung von; **at short/long ~** auf kurze/große Entfernung; **to be out of ~** außer Reichweite sein; **within (firing) ~** in Schußweite; **~ of vision** Gesichtsfeld _nt._ (**b**) _(spread, selection)_ Reihe _f; (of goods also)_ Sortiment _nt; (of colours also)_ Skala _f; (of sizes, models)_ Auswahl _f (of an +dat)._ **a wide ~** eine große Auswahl; **in this price ~** in dieser Preisklasse; **out of/within my price ~** außerhalb/innerhalb meiner (finanziellen) Möglichkeiten. (**c**) _(also_ **shooting ~**) _(Mil)_ Schießplatz _m; (rifle ~)_ Schießstand _m._ (**d**) _(row)_ Reihe _f; (mountain ~)_ Kette _f._ (**e**) _(US: grazing land)_ Weideland _nt._

   **2** _vt (place in a row)_ aufstellen; _objects also_ anordnen. **~d right/left** _(Typ)_ rechtsbündig/linksbündig.

   **3** _vi_ (**a**) _(extend) (from ... to)_ gehen (von ... bis); _(temperature, value)_ liegen (zwischen ... und). **his interests ~ from skiing to chess** seine Interessen reichen vom Skifahren bis zum Schachspielen; **the conversation ~d over a number of subjects** die Unterhaltung kreiste um mehrere Themen. (**b**) _(roam)_ streifen. **to ~ over the area** im Gebiet umherstreifen.

**range-finder** ['reɪndʒˌfaɪndər] _n_ Entfernungsmesser _m._

**ranger** ['reɪndʒər] _n_ (**a**) _(of forest etc)_ Förster _m._ (**b**) _(US: mounted patrolman)_ Ranger _m; (commando)_ Überfallkommando _nt._

**Rangoon** [ræŋ'guːn] _n_ Rangun _nt._

**rangy** ['reɪndʒɪ] _adj (+er)_ langglied(e)rig.

**rank¹** [ræŋk] **1** _n_ (**a**) _(Mil: grade)_ Rang _m._ (**b**) _(class, status)_ Stand _m,_ Schicht _f._ **people of all ~s** Leute _pl_ aus allen (Gesellschafts)schichten. (**c**) _(row)_ Reihe _f; (Brit: taxi ~)_ Taxistand _m._ (**d**) _(Mil: formation)_

Glied *nt.* **to break ~(s)** aus dem Glied treten; **the ~s** *(Brit)* die Mannschaften und die Unteroffiziere; **the ~ and file of the party/union** die Basis der Partei/ Gewerkschaft; **the ~ and file workers** die einfachen Arbeiter; **to rise from the ~s** aus dem Mannschaftsstand zum Offizier aufsteigen; *(fig)* sich hocharbeiten. **2** *vt (class, consider)* **to ~ sb among the best/great** *etc* jdn zu den Besten/Großen *etc* zählen. **3** *vi* **to ~ among** zählen zu; **to ~ above sb** bedeutender als jd sein; *(officer)* rangmäßig über jdm liegen; **to ~ 6th** den 6. Rang belegen; **he ~s as a great composer** er gilt als großer Komponist.

**rank²** *adj (+er)* **(a)** *plants* üppig; *grass* verwildert. **to grow ~** wuchern. **(b)** *smell* übel; *fat* ranzig. **(c)** *attr injustice* schreiend; *nonsense* rein; *traitor, liar* übel; *stupidity* ausgesprochen.

**rankings** ['ræŋkɪŋz] *npl (Sport)* Rangliste *f.*

**rankle** ['ræŋkl] *vi* **to ~ (with sb)** (jdn) wurmen *(col).*

**ransack** ['rænsæk] *vt (search)* durchwühlen; *(pillage) house* plündern; *region* herfallen über *(+acc).*

**ransom** ['rænsəm] **1** *n* Lösegeld *nt.* **to hold sb to ~** *(lit)* jdn als Geisel halten; *(fig)* jdn erpressen; **~ note** Erpresserbrief *m.* **2** *vt (buy free)* Lösegeld bezahlen für; *(set free)* gegen Lösegeld freilassen.

**rant** [rænt] *vi (angrily)* eine Schimpfkanonade loslassen; *(talk nonsense)* irres Zeug reden *(col).* **to ~ (and rave)** *(be angry)* herumschimpfen; **~ at sb** mit jdm schimpfen.

**ranting** ['ræntɪŋ] *n see vi* Geschimpfe *nt*; irres Zeug *(col).*

**rap** [ræp] **1** *n (noise, blow)* Klopfen *nt no pl.* **there was a ~ at the door** es hat geklopft; **to take the ~** *(col)* den Kopf hinhalten müssen *(col).* **2** *vt table* klopfen auf *(+acc)*; *window* klopfen an *(+acc).* **to ~ sb's knuckles** *(lit, fig)* jdm auf die Finger klopfen. **3** *vi* klopfen. **to ~ at the door** kurz (an die Tür) klopfen.

**rapacious** [rə'peɪʃəs] *adj* habgierig.

**rape¹** [reɪp] **1** *n* Vergewaltigung *f.* **2** *vt* vergewaltigen.

**rape²** *n (plant)* Raps *m.* **~ (seed) oil** Rapsöl *nt.*

**rapid** ['ræpɪd] **1** *adj* schnell; *change also* rapide; *descent, decline, rise* steil. **2** *n* **~s** *pl* Stromschnellen *pl.*

**rapidity** [rə'pɪdɪtɪ] *n see adj* Schnelligkeit *f*; Rapidheit *f*; Steilheit *f.*

**rapidly** ['ræpɪdlɪ] *adv see adj.*

**rapier** ['reɪpɪər] *n* Rapier *nt.*

**rapist** ['reɪpɪst] *n* Vergewaltiger *m.*

**rapport** [ræ'pɔːr] *n (good)* ~ gutes Verhältnis; **the ~ I have with my father** das enge Verhältnis zwischen mir und meinem Vater; **in ~ with** in Harmonie mit.

**rapprochement** [ræ'prɒʃmɑ̃ːŋ] *n* Annäherung *f.*

**rapt** [ræpt] *adj* **(a)** *interest* gespannt; *attention* atemlos. **~ in contemplation** in Betrachtungen versunken. **(b)** *look, smile* verzückt.

**rapture** ['ræptʃər] *n (delight)* Entzücken *nt*; *(ecstasy)* Verzückung *f.* **to be in ~s** entzückt sein *(over über +acc, about von)*; **to go into ~s** ins Schwärmen geraten.

**rapturous** ['ræptʃərəs] *adj applause, reception* stürmisch; *exclamation* entzückt; *look* verzückt.

**rare** [rɛər] *adj (+er)* **(a)** selten. **it's ~ for her to come** sie kommt nur selten. **(b)** *atmosphere* dünn. **(c)** *meat* roh; *steak* blutig, englisch.

**rarebit** ['rɛəbɪt] *n* = **Welsh ~.**

**rarefied** ['rɛərɪfaɪd] *adj atmosphere, air* dünn; *(fig)* exklusiv.

**rarely** ['rɛəlɪ] *adv* selten.

**raring** ['rɛərɪŋ] *adj:* **to be ~ to go** *(col)* in den Startlöchern sein *(col).*

**rarity** ['rɛərɪtɪ] *n* Seltenheit *f*; *(rare occurrence also)* Rarität *f.*

**rascal** ['rɑːskəl] *n* Gauner *m*; *(child)* Schlingel *m.*

**rash¹** [ræʃ] *n (Med)* Ausschlag *m.* **to break out in a ~** einen Ausschlag bekommen.

**rash²** *adj (+er) person* unbesonnen; *act also* überstürzt; *words, decision* voreilig.

**rasher** ['ræʃər] *n* **~ of bacon** Speckstreifen *m.*

**rashly** ['ræʃlɪ] *adv see adj.*

**rashness** ['ræʃnɪs] *n see adj* Unbesonnenheit *f*; Überstürztheit *f*; Voreiligkeit *f.*

**rasp** [rɑːsp] **1** *n (tool)* Raspel *f*; *(noise)* Kratzen *nt no pl.* **2** *vt* **(a)** *(Tech)* raspeln. **(b)** ... **he rasped** ..., krächzte er.

**raspberry** ['rɑːzbərɪ] **1** *n* Himbeere *f.* **to blow a ~** *(col)* verächtlich schnauben. **2** *adj jam* Himbeer-.

**rasping** ['rɑːspɪŋ] **1** *adj sound* kratzend; *voice* krächzend; *cough, breath* keuchend. **2** *n (sound)* Kratzen *nt*; *(of voice)* Krächzen *nt.*

**rat** [ræt] *n* Ratte *f*; *(pej col: person)* elender Verräter *(col).* **to smell a ~** den Braten riechen *(col).*

**ratchet** ['rætʃɪt] *n* Ratsche *f.* **~ wheel** Sperrad *nt.*

**rate** [reɪt] **1** *n* **(a)** *(ratio, proportion, frequency)* Rate *f*; *(speed)* Tempo *nt.* **at a ~ of 5 per hour** (in einem Tempo von) 5 pro Stunde; **~ of flow** *(of water etc)* Fluß *m*; **pulse ~** Puls *m*; **at a great** *(col)* **~, at a ~ of knots** *(col)* in irrsinnigem Tempo *(col)*; **at this ~** *(fig)* wenn das so weitergeht; **if you continue at this ~** *(lit, fig)* wenn du in diesem Tempo weitermachst; **at any ~** auf jeden Fall. **(b)** *(Comm, Fin)* Satz *m*; *(St Ex)* Kurs *m.* **~ of exchange** Wechselkurs *m*; **what's the ~ of pay?** wie hoch ist die Bezahlung?; **~ of interest** Zinssatz *m*; **postage ~s** Postgebühren *pl*; **there is a reduced ~ for children** Kinderermäßigung wird gewährt. **(c)** **~s** *pl (Brit old: municipal tax)* Kommunalabgaben *pl.*

**2** *vt* **(a)** *(estimate value or worth of)* (ein)schätzen. **to ~ sb/sth among** ... jdn/etw zu ... zählen; **how do you ~ these results?** was halten Sie von diesen Ergebnissen?; **to ~ sb/sth as sth** jdn/etw für etw halten; **he is generally ~d as** ... er gilt allgemein als ...; **to ~ sb/sth highly** jdn/etw hoch einschätzen. **(b)** *(Brit old)* **a house ~d at £500 per annum** ein Haus, dessen steuerbarer Wert £500 pro Jahr ist.

**3** *vi* **to ~ as/among** ... gelten als .../zählen zu ...

**ratepayer** ['reɪtˌpeɪər] *n (Brit old)* Steuerzahler *m (von Kommunalabgaben).*

**rather** ['rɑːðər] *adv* **(a)** *(for preference)* lieber. **~ than wait, he went away** er ging lieber, als daß er wartete; **I would ~ have the blue dress** ich hätte lieber das blaue Kleid; **I would ~ be happy than rich** ich wäre lieber glücklich als reich; **I would ~ you came yourself** mir wäre es lieber, Sie kämen selbst; **I'd ~ not** lieber nicht; **he expects me to phone ~ than (to) write** er erwartet eher, daß ich anrufe, als daß ich schreibe.

**(b)** *(more accurately)* vielmehr. **he is, or ~ was, a soldier** er ist, beziehungsweise or vielmehr war, Soldat; **a car, or ~ an old banger** ein Auto, genauer gesagt eine alte Kiste.

**(c)** *(to a considerable degree)* ziemlich; *(somewhat)* etwas. **he felt ~ better** er fühlte sich bedeutend wohler; **it's ~ more difficult than you think** es ist um einiges schwieriger, als du denkst; **she's ~ an idiot/a killjoy** sie ist reichlich doof *(col)*/ein richtiger Spielverderber; **I ~ think he's wrong** ich glaube fast, er hat unrecht; **~!** *(col)* und ob! *(col)*, klar! *(col).*

**ratification** [rætɪfɪ'keɪʃən] *n* Ratifizierung *f.*

**ratify** ['rætɪfaɪ] *vt* ratifizieren.

**rating** ['reɪtɪŋ] *n* **(a)** *(assessment)* (Ein)schätzung *f.*

**(b)** *(class) (Sport: of yacht, car)* Klasse *f*; *(Fin: also credit ~)* Kreditfähigkeit *f*. **(c)** *(Naut) (rank)* Rang *m*; *(sailor)* Matrose *m*. **(d)** *(TV)* ~s Einschaltquote *f*.

**ratio** ['reɪʃɪəʊ] *n* Verhältnis *nt*. **the ~ of men to women** das Verhältnis von Männern zu Frauen; **in the** *or* **a ~ of 100 to 1** *(written* 100:1*)* im Verhältnis 100 zu 1.

**ration** ['ræʃən] **1** *n* Ration *f*; *(fig)* Quantum *nt*. **~s** *(food)* Rationen *pl*; **to put sb on short ~s** jdn auf halbe Ration setzen; **~ book** Bezugsscheinheft *nt*; *(for food)* ≃ Lebensmittelkarte *f*. **2** *vt goods, food* rationieren. **he was ~ed to 1 kg** ihm wurde nur 1 kg erlaubt.

**rational** ['ræʃənl] *adj (having reason)* vernunftbegabt, rational; *(reasonable)* vernünftig; *person, action also* rational; *(Med: lucid, sane) person* bei klarem Verstand.

**rationale** [ræʃə'nɑːl] *n* Gründe *pl*.

**rationalization** [ˌræʃnəlaɪ'zeɪʃən] *n* Rationalisierung *f*.

**rationalize** ['ræʃnəlaɪz] *vt* rationalisieren; *problem* vernünftig betrachten.

**rationing** ['ræʃənɪŋ] *n* Rationierung *f*.

**rat:** **~pack** *n (Brit col: journalists)* Journalistenmeute *f (pej col)*; **~ poison** *n* Rattengift *nt*; **~-race** *n* ständiger Konkurrenzkampf.

**rattle** ['rætl] **1** *vi* klappern; *(chains)* rasseln; *(bottles)* klirren; *(gunfire)* knattern. **there's something rattling** da klappert etwas. **2** *vt* **(a)** *dice, keys* schütteln; *chains* rasseln mit; *windows* rütteln an *(+dat)*. **(b)** *(col: alarm) person* durcheinanderbringen. **don't get ~d!** reg dich nicht auf! **3** *n* **(a)** *(sound) see vi* Klappern *nt no pl*; Rasseln *nt no pl*; Klirren *nt no pl*; Knattern *nt no pl*. **(b)** *(child's)* Rassel *f*; *(sports fan's)* Schnarre *f*.

▶**rattle off** *vt sep speech, list* herunterrasseln.

▶**rattle on** *vi (col)* (unentwegt) quasseln *(col) (about* über *+acc)*.

**rattle:** **~snake** *n* Klapperschlange *f*; **~trap** *n (hum col)* Klapperkiste *f (hum col)*.

**ratty** ['rætɪ] *adj (+er)* **(a)** *(Brit col: irritable)* gereizt. **don't get ~** sei nicht so gereizt. **(b)** *(US col: shabby)* schäbig.

**raucous** *adj*, **~ly** *adv* ['rɔːkəs, -lɪ] rauh, heiser.

**raunchy** ['rɔːntʃɪ] *adj (+er) (col) (lecherous)* geil; *(vulgar)* vulgär; *novel* rasant.

**ravage** ['rævɪdʒ] **1** *n* **~s** *(of war)* Verheerung *f (of* durch*)*; **the ~s of time** die Spuren *pl* der Zeit. **2** *vt (ruin)* verwüsten; *(plunder)* plündern.

**rave** [reɪv] **1** *vi* phantasieren; *(speak furiously)* toben; *(col: speak, write enthusiastically)* schwärmen *(about, over* von*)*. **2** *n (dance)* wilde Fete *or* Party *(bei der Drogen genommen werden)*. **3** *attr* **~ review** *(col)* begeisterte Kritik.

**raven** ['reɪvən] *n* Rabe *m*.

**ravenous** ['rævənəs] *adj animal* ausgehungert; *person also* heißhungrig; *appetite* gewaltig. **I'm ~** ich habe einen Bärenhunger *(col)*.

**ravine** [rə'viːn] *n* Schlucht *f*.

**raving** ['reɪvɪŋ] **1** *adj (frenzied)* wahnsinnig, verrückt; *(delirious)* im Delirium. **a ~ lunatic** *(col)* ein kompletter Idiot *(col)*. **2** *adv* **~ mad** *(col)* total verrückt *(col)*. **3** *n* **~(s)** Phantasien *pl*.

**ravioli** [rævɪ'əʊlɪ] *n* Ravioli *pl*.

**ravishing** *adj*, **~ly** *adv* ['rævɪʃɪŋ, -lɪ] atemberaubend.

**raw** [rɔː] **1** *adj (+er)* **(a)** *(uncooked)* roh; *(unprocessed) ore, sugar also* Roh-; *spirit* rein; *cloth* ungewalkt; *leather* ungegerbt; *(fig) statistics* nackt. **to give sb a ~ deal** *(col)* jdn unfair behandeln; **to get a ~ deal** *(col)* schlecht wegkommen *(col)*; **~ material**

Rohstoff *m*. **(b)** *(inexperienced) troops* neu, unerfahren. **~ recruit** *(fig)* blutiger Anfänger *(col)*. **(c)** *(sore) wound* offen; *skin* wund. **(d)** *wind, air* rauh. **(e)** *(esp US: coarse)* derb. **2** *n* **(a) to touch sb on the ~** *(Brit)* bei jdm einen wunden Punkt berühren. **(b) nature in the ~** die rauhe Seite der Natur.

**ray¹** [reɪ] *n* Strahl *m*. **a ~ of hope** ein Hoffnungsschimmer *m*.

**ray²** *n (fish)* Rochen *m*.

**rayon** ['reɪɒn] **1** *n* Reyon *nt*. **2** *adj* Reyon-.

**raze** [reɪz] *vt* **to ~ to the ground** dem Erdboden gleichmachen.

**razor** ['reɪzəʳ] *n* Rasierapparat *m*; *(cutthroat)* Rasiermesser *nt*. **electric ~** (elektrischer) Rasierapparat; **to be on a ~'s edge** auf Messers Schneide stehen.

**razor:** **~ blade** *n* Rasierklinge *f*; **~-sharp** *adj knife* scharf (wie ein Rasiermesser); *(fig) person* sehr scharfsinnig; *mind, wit* messerscharf; **~ wire** *n* Bandstacheldraht, Nato-Draht *(col) m*.

**razzmatazz** ['ræzmə'tæz] *n (col)* Rummel *m*, Tamtam *nt (col)*.

**RC** = **Roman Catholic** rk, r.-k.

**Rd** = **Road** Str.

**RD** *(US)* = **rural delivery** Landpostzustellung *f*.

**RDC** *(Brit)* = **rural district council**.

**RE** = **Religious Education**.

**re** [riː] *prep (Comm)* betreffs *(+gen)*. **~ your letter of the 16th** Betr(eff): Ihr Brief vom 16.

**re-** [riː-] *pref* wieder-.

**reach** [riːtʃ] **1** *n* **(a)** *within/out of sb's* ~ in/außer jds Reichweite *(dat)*; **keep out of ~ of children** von Kindern fernhalten; **within easy ~ of the sea** in unmittelbarer Nähe des Meeres; **I keep it within easy ~** ich habe es in greifbarer Nähe. **(b)** *(of river)* Strecke *f*. **the upper ~es** der Oberlauf.

**2** *vt* **(a)** *(arrive at)* erreichen; *town* ankommen in *(+dat)*; *agreement* erzielen; *conclusion* kommen zu. **when the news ~ed my ears** als mir die Nachricht zu Ohren kam; **to ~ page 50** bis Seite 50 kommen; **you can ~ me at my hotel** Sie erreichen mich in meinem Hotel. **(b)** *(stretch to get or touch)* **to be able to ~ sth** an etw *(acc)* (heran)reichen können; **can you ~ it?** kommen Sie dran? **(c)** *(come up to, go down to)* reichen bis zu. **he ~es her shoulder** er geht ihr bis zur Schulter.

**3** *vi* **(a)** *(to, as far as bis)* reichen; *(territory etc also)* sich erstrecken. **(b)** *(stretch out hand or arm)* greifen. **to ~ for sth** nach etw greifen *or* langen *(col)*.

▶**reach out 1** *vt sep* **he ~ed ~ his hand to take the book** er streckte die Hand aus, um das Buch zu nehmen. **2** *vi* die Hand/Hände ausstrecken. **to ~ ~ for sth** nach etw greifen *or* langen *(col)*.

**reachable** ['riːtʃəbl] *adj* erreichbar.

**react** [ri'ækt] *vi* reagieren *(to auf +acc)*. **to ~ against** negativ reagieren auf *(+acc)*.

**reaction** [ri'ækʃən] *n* Reaktion *f (to auf +acc, against gegen)*; *(Mil)* Gegenschlag *m*. **what was his ~ to your suggestion?** wie hat er auf Ihren Vorschlag reagiert?

**reactionary** [ri'ækʃənrɪ] *adj* reaktionär.

**reactor** [ri'æktəʳ] *n (Phys)* Reaktor *m*.

**read¹** [riːd] *(vb: pret, ptp* read [red]*)* **1** *vt* **(a)** lesen; *(to sb)* vorlesen *(to dat)*. **do you ~ music?** können Sie Noten lesen?; **to take sth as read** *(fig) (as self-evident)* etw als selbstverständlich voraussetzen; *(as agreed)* etw für abgemacht halten. **(b)** *(interpret) thoughts, feelings* lesen; *dream* deuten; *words* verstehen. **to ~ sb's thoughts/mind** jds Gedanken lesen; **to ~ sb's hand** jdm aus der Hand lesen;

**these words can be read in several ways** diese Wörter können unterschiedlich verstanden werden; **to ~ something into a text** etwas in einen Text (hinein)lesen. **(c)** *(Univ: study)* studieren. **(d)** *thermometer etc* ablesen. **to ~ a meter** einen Zähler(-stand) ablesen; **to ~ the gas meter** das Gas ablesen.

**2** *vi* lesen; *(to sb)* vorlesen *(to dat)*; *(have wording)* lauten. **to ~ aloud** laut lesen; **to ~ to oneself** für sich lesen; **he likes being read to** er läßt sich *(dat)* gern vorlesen; **this book ~s well** das Buch liest sich gut; **the letter ~s as follows** der Brief besagt folgendes *or* hat folgenden Wortlaut *(form)*.

**3** *n* **she enjoys a good ~** sie liest gern; **this book is quite a good ~** das Buch liest sich gut.

▶**read in** *vt sep (Comp)* einlesen.

▶**read off** *vt sep* ablesen; *(without pause)* herunterlesen.

▶**read on** *vi* weiterlesen.

▶**read out** *vt sep* vorlesen.

▶**read over** *or* **through** *vt sep* durchlesen.

▶**read up 1** *vt sep* nachlesen über (+*acc*). **2** *vi* nachlesen *(on* über +*acc)*.

**read²** [red] **1** *pret, ptp of* **read¹**. **2** *adj* **he is well ~** er ist sehr belesen.

**readable** ['riːdəbl] *adj (legible)* lesbar; *(worth reading)* lesenswert.

**readdress** [ˌriːə'dres] *vt* umadressieren.

**reader** ['riːdər] *n* **(a)** Leser(in *f*) *m.* **(b)** *(Brit Univ)* ≈ Dozent(in *f*) *m.* **(c)** *(schoolbook)* Lesebuch *nt*; *(to teach reading)* Fibel *f*; *(foreign language text)* Text *m*; *(anthology)* Sammelband *m.*

**readership** ['riːdəʃɪp] *n* Leserschaft *f.* **a wide ~** eine große Leserschaft.

**readies** ['redɪz] *npl (col: cash)* Bare(s) *nt (col).* **100 in ~** 100 bar auf die Hand *(col).*

**readily** ['redɪlɪ] *adv* bereitwillig; *(easily)* leicht.

**readiness** ['redɪnɪs] *n* Bereitschaft *f.* **to be (kept) in ~ (for sth)** (für etw) bereitgehalten werden; **his ~ to help** seine Hilfsbereitschaft.

**reading** ['riːdɪŋ] *n* **(a)** *(action)* Lesen *nt*; *(by author)* Lesung *f.* **(b)** *(~ matter)* Lektüre *f.* **this book makes very interesting ~** dieses Buch ist sehr interessant zu lesen. **(c)** *(interpretation)* Interpretation *f.* **my ~ of this sentence** mein Verständnis des Satzes. **(d)** *(from thermometer/meter)* Thermometer-/Zählerstand *m*; *(from instruments)* Anzeige *f.* **to take a ~** den Thermometerstand/Zählerstand/die Anzeige ablesen.

**reading:** **~ glasses** *npl* Lesebrille *f*; **~ knowledge** *n* **to have a ~ knowledge of a language** eine Sprache lesen können; **~ lamp** *n* Leselampe *f*; **~ list** *n* Lektüreliste *f*; **~ matter** *n* Lesestoff *m*; **~ room** *n* Lesesaal *m.*

**readjust** [ˌriːə'dʒʌst] **1** *vt instrument, mechanism* neu einstellen; *(correct)* nachstellen. **2** *vi* sich wieder anpassen *(to* an +*acc).*

**read:** **~-only memory** *n (Comp)* Lesespeicher, Festwertspeicher *m*; **~-out** *n (Comp)* Anzeige *f.*

**ready** ['redɪ] **1** *adj* **(a)** fertig; *(prepared also)* bereit. **~ for use** gebrauchsfertig; **~ to serve** tischfertig; **~ for battle** kampfbereit; **~ for anything** zu allem bereit; **are you ~ to go?** sind Sie soweit?; **I'm ~ for him!** er soll nur kommen!; **everything is ~ for his visit** alles ist für seinen Besuch bereit; **to be ~ with an excuse** eine Entschuldigung bereit haben; **to get (oneself) ~** sich fertigmachen; **to get ~ to do sth** sich bereitmachen, etw zu tun; **to get ~ to go out** sich zum Ausgehen fertigmachen. **(b)** **~ to do sth** *(willing)* bereit, etw zu tun; *(quick)* schnell dabei, etw zu tun; **I'm ~ to believe it** ich möchte das fast glauben; **he was ~ to cry** er war den Tränen nahe.

**(c)** *(available)* **~ money** jederzeit verfügbares Geld; **~ cash** Bargeld *nt.*

**2** *n* **at the ~** *(Mil)* mit dem Gewehr im Anschlag; *(fig)* marsch-/fahrbereit *etc*; **with his pen at the ~** mit gezücktem Federhalter.

**ready** *in cpds* fertig-; **~-made** *adj curtains* fertig; *clothes* Konfektions-; *solution* Patent-; **~ reckoner** *n* Rechentabelle *f*; **~-to-wear** *adj* Konfektions-, von der Stange *(col).*

**reaffirm** [ˌriːə'fɜːm] *vt* erneut versichern.

**real** ['rɪəl] **1** *adj* **(a)** wirklich; *(genuine) gold, flowers, joy* echt; *(as opposed to substitute)* *(true, actual) owner, reason, purpose also* eigentlich; *(not imaginary) creature, world also, (Econ)* real. **~ ale** *(Brit)* nach altem Rezept gebrautes Bier; **~ coffee** Bohnenkaffee *m*; **in ~ life** im wirklichen Leben; **in ~ terms** effektiv; **it's the ~ thing** *or* **McCoy, this whisky!** dieser Whisky ist das einzig Wahre; **~ time** *(Comp)* Echtzeit *f.* **(b)** **~ estate** Immobilien *pl.* **2** *adv (esp US col)* echt *(col)*, wirklich. **3** *n* **for ~** *(col)* wirklich, echt *(col)*; **is that invitation for ~?** ist die Einladung ernst gemeint?; **this time it's for ~** diesmal ist es ernst.

**realism** ['rɪəlɪzəm] *n* Realismus *m.*

**realist** ['rɪəlɪst] *n* Realist *m.*

**realistic** [rɪə'lɪstɪk] *adj* realistisch.

**reality** [riː'ælɪtɪ] *n* **(a)** Wirklichkeit, Realität *f.* **to become ~** sich verwirklichen; **(the) ~ is somewhat different** die Wirklichkeit sieht etwas anders aus; **in ~** *(in fact)* in Wirklichkeit; *(actually)* eigentlich. **(b)** *(trueness to life)* Naturtreue *f.*

**realization** [ˌrɪəlaɪ'zeɪʃən] *n* **(a)** *(of assets)* Realisation *f*; *(of hope, plan)* Realisierung, Verwirklichung *f.* **(b)** *(awareness)* Erkenntnis *f.*

**realize** ['rɪəlaɪz] *vt* **(a)** *(become aware of)* erkennen, sich *(dat)* bewußt werden (+*gen*); *(be aware of)* sich *(dat)* klar sein über (+*acc*); *(appreciate)* begreifen; *(notice)* bemerken; *(discover)* feststellen. **does he ~ the problems?** sind ihm die Probleme bewußt?; **I ~d what he meant** ich begriff, was er meinte; **I ~d how he had done it** ich erkannte, wie er es gemacht hatte; **I'd ~d it was raining** ich hatte gemerkt, daß es regnete; **I ~d I didn't have any money on me** ich stellte fest, daß ich kein Geld dabei hatte; **you couldn't be expected to ~ that** das konnten Sie nicht wissen; **he came to ~ that ...** er kam zu der Erkenntnis, daß .... **(b)** *hope, plan* verwirklichen. **(c)** *(Fin) assets* realisieren; *price* erzielen; *interest* abwerfen; *(goods)* einbringen.

**really** ['rɪəlɪ] **1** *adv* **(a)** *(in reality)* wirklich, tatsächlich. **I don't ~ think so** das glaube ich eigentlich nicht. **(b)** *(intensifier)* wirklich, echt *(col).* **you ~ must visit Paris** Sie müssen wirklich Paris besuchen. **2** *interj* wirklich, ehrlich.

**realm** [relm] *n (liter: kingdom)* Königreich *nt*; *(fig)* Reich *nt.* **within the ~s of possibility** im Bereich des Möglichen.

**realtor** ['rɪəltɔːr] *n (US)* Grundstücksmakler *m.*

**ream** [riːm] *n (of paper)* Ries *nt.* **he always writes ~s** *(col)* er schreibt immer ganze Bände *(col).*

**reap** [riːp] *vt* **(a)** *corn (cut)* schneiden, mähen; *(harvest)* ernten. **(b)** *(fig) profit* ernten; *reward* bekommen.

**reaper** ['riːpər] *n* Mähmaschine *f.*

**reappear** [ˌriːə'pɪər] *vi* wiederauftauchen.

**reappearance** [ˌriːə'pɪərəns] *n* Wiederauftauchen *nt.*

**reapply** [ˌriːə'plaɪ] *vi (for job)* sich erneut bewerben *(for* um).

**reappraisal** [ˌriːə'preɪzəl] *n* Neubeurteilung *f.*

**rear¹** [rɪər] **1** *n (back part)* hinterer Teil; *(col: buttocks)* Hintern *m (col).* **to be situated at the ~ of the**

**plane** *(inside)* hinten im Flugzeug sein; *(outside)* am hinteren Ende des Flugzeugs sein; **at the ~ of the building** *(outside)* hinter dem Haus; *(inside)* hinten im Haus; **from the ~** von hinten; **to bring up the ~** *(Mil)* die Nachhut bilden; *(fig)* das Schlußlicht bilden. **2** *adj* Hinter-, hintere(r, s); *(Aut) engine, window* Heck-. **~ door** *(of car)* hintere Tür; **~ wheel/ lights** *(Aut)* Hinterrad *nt*/Rücklichter *pl*.

**rear²** **1** *vt* (a) *animals, family* großziehen, aufziehen. **(b) to ~ its head** *(animal)* den Kopf zurückwerfen; *racialism* **~ed its ugly head** der Rassismus kam zum Durchbruch. **2** *vi (also ~ up) (horse)* sich aufbäumen.

**rear:** **~-engined** *adj (Aut)* mit Heckmotor; **~ guard** *n (Mil)* Nachhut *f*.

**rearm** [ˌriːˈɑːm] **1** *vt country* wiederbewaffnen; *forces* neu ausrüsten. **2** *vi* wieder aufrüsten; sich neu ausrüsten.

**rearmament** [ˌriːˈɑːməmənt] *n see vb* Wiederaufrüstung *f*; Neuausrüstung *f*.

**rearrange** [ˌriːəˈreɪndʒ] *vt furniture, system* umstellen; *plans also, order, ideas* ändern; *meeting* verlegen.

**rearrangement** [ˌriːəˈreɪndʒmənt] *n see vt* Umstellung *f*; Änderung *f*; Verlegung *f*.

**rear-view mirror** [ˈrɪəˌvjuːˈmɪrəʳ] *n* Rückspiegel *m*.

**reason** [ˈriːzn] **1** *n* (a) *(cause, justification)* Grund *m (for* für*)*. **to give sb ~ for complaint** jdm Anlaß *or* Grund zur Klage geben; **you have no ~ to interfere** Sie haben keinen Grund, sich einzumischen; **I want to know the ~ why** ich möchte wissen, weshalb; **and that's the ~ why ...** und deshalb ...; **I have (good) ~ to believe that ...** ich habe (guten) Grund zu der Annahme, daß ...; **there is every ~ to believe (that) ...** es spricht alles dafür, daß ...; **for that very ~ eben deswegen; for the very ~ that she was there** gerade weil sie da war; **with (good) ~** mit gutem Grund; **for no particular ~** ohne bestimmten Grund; **all the more ~ for doing** um so mehr Grund, das zu tun; **by ~ of** wegen (+*gen*).

(b) *no pl (faculty)* Verstand *m*; *(common sense)* Vernunft *f*. **to lose one's ~** den Verstand verlieren; **he won't listen to ~** er läßt sich *(dat)* nichts sagen; **that stands to ~** das ist logisch; **you can have anything within ~** Sie können alles haben, solange es sich in Grenzen hält.

**2** *vi* (a) *(think logically)* vernünftig *or* logisch denken. (b) *(argue)* diskutieren. **to ~ with sb** vernünftig mit jdm reden.

**3** *vt* (a) **to ~ why/what ...** sich *(dat)* klarmachen, warum/was ... (b) *(also ~ out) (deduce)* folgern; *(verbally)* argumentieren.

**reasonable** [ˈriːznəbl] *adj* (a) vernünftig; *chance* reell; *claim, doubt* berechtigt; *amount* angemessen; *(acceptable) excuse, offer* akzeptabel. **beyond (all) ~ doubt** ohne (jeden) Zweifel. (b) *(quite good)* ordentlich, ganz gut.

**reasonably** [ˈriːznəbli] *adv* (a) *behave, act, think* vernünftig. **one could ~ think that ...** man könnte durchaus annehmen, daß ...; **~ priced** preiswert. (b) *(quite)* ziemlich, ganz.

**reasoned** [ˈriːznd] *adj* durchdacht.

**reasoning** [ˈriːznɪŋ] *n* Argumentation *f*. **~ is not his strong point** logisches Denken ist nicht gerade seine starke Seite.

**reassemble** [ˌriːəˈsembl] *vi* sich wieder versammeln.

**reassert** [ˌriːəˈsɜːt] *vt* **to ~ oneself** *or* **one's authority** seine Autorität wieder geltend machen.

**reassurance** [ˌriːəˈʃʊərəns] *n* (a) *(feeling of security)* Beruhigung *f*. **to give sb ~** jdn beruhigen. (b) *(re-*

*newed confirmation)* Bestätigung *f*. **despite his ~(s)** trotz seiner Versicherungen.

**reassure** [ˌriːəˈʃʊəʳ] *vt* (a) *(relieve sb's mind)* beruhigen; *(give feelings of security to)* das Gefühl der Sicherheit geben (+*dat*). (b) *(verbally)* versichern (+*dat*). **to ~ sb of sth** jdm etw versichern.

**reassuring** [ˌriːəˈʃʊərɪŋ] *adj* beruhigend.

**reawakening** [ˌriːəˈweɪknɪŋ] *n* Wiedererwachen *nt*.

**rebate** [ˈriːbeɪt] *n (money back)* Rückvergütung *f*.

**rebel** [ˈrebl] **1** *n* Rebell(in *f*) *m*. **2** *adj attr* rebellisch. **3** [rɪˈbel] *vi* rebellieren.

**rebellion** [rɪˈbeljən] *n* Rebellion *f*, Aufstand *m*.

**rebellious** [rɪˈbeljəs] *adj* rebellisch.

**rebirth** [ˌriːˈbɜːθ] *n* Wiedergeburt *f*.

**reborn** [ˌriːˈbɔːn] *adj* **to be ~** wiedergeboren werden; **to be ~ in** *(fig)* weiterleben in (+*dat*).

**rebound** [rɪˈbaʊnd] **1** *vi* zurückprallen *(against, off* von*)*. **your violent methods will ~ on you** Ihre rauhen Methoden werden auf Sie zurückfallen. **2** [ˈriːbaʊnd] *n (of ball, bullet)* Rückprall *m*. **she married him on the ~** sie heiratete ihn, um sich über einen anderen hinwegzutrösten.

**rebuff** [rɪˈbʌf] **1** *n* Abfuhr *f*. **to meet with a ~** abgewiesen werden, eine Abfuhr bekommen; *(from opposite sex)* einen Korb bekommen *(col)*. **2** *vt* abweisen; einen Korb geben (+*dat*) *(col)*.

**rebuild** [ˌriːˈbɪld] *vt house* wieder aufbauen; *(fig) country, relationship* wiederaufbauen.

**rebuilding** [ˌriːˈbɪldɪŋ] *n* Wiederaufbau *m*.

**rebuke** [rɪˈbjuːk] **1** *n* Zurechtweisung *f*. **2** *vt* zurechtweisen *(for* wegen*)*, tadeln *(for* für*)*.

**rebut** [rɪˈbʌt] *vt contention* widerlegen.

**rebuttal** [rɪˈbʌtl] *n* Widerlegung *f*.

**recalcitrant** [rɪˈkælsɪtrənt] *adj* aufsässig.

**recall** [rɪˈkɔːl] **1** *vt* (a) *(summon back, evoke)* zurückrufen; *ambassador* abberufen; *library book, (Fin) capital* zurückfordern. (b) *(remember)* sich erinnern an (+*acc*). **I cannot ~ meeting him** ich kann mich nicht daran erinnern, daß ich ihn kennengelernt habe. **2** *n see vt* (a) Rückruf *m*; Abberufung *f*; Rückforderung *f*. **beyond ~** für immer vorbei.

**recant** [rɪˈkænt] **1** *vt religious belief* widerrufen; *statement also* zurücknehmen. **2** *vi* widerrufen.

**recap** [ˈriːkæp] *(col)* **1** *n* kurze Zusammenfassung. **2** *vti* rekapitulieren, kurz zusammenfassen.

**recapitulate** [ˌriːkəˈpɪtjʊleɪt] *vti* rekapitulieren, kurz zusammenfassen.

**recapitulation** [ˌriːkəˌpɪtjʊˈleɪʃən] *n* kurze Zusammenfassung; *(Mus)* Reprise *f*.

**recapture** [ˌriːˈkæptʃəʳ] *vt animal* wieder einfangen; *prisoner* wiederergreifen; *territory* wiedererobern; *(fig) atmosphere* wieder wachwerden lassen.

**recd** = **received** erh.

**recede** [rɪˈsiːd] *vi (tide, price)* zurückgehen; *(fig)* sich entfernen; *(hope)* schwinden. **to ~ into the distance** in der Ferne verschwinden.

**receding** [rɪˈsiːdɪŋ] *adj chin, forehead* fliehend; *hairline* zurückweichend.

**receipt** [rɪˈsiːt] *n* (a) *no pl* Empfang *m*; *(Comm also)* Erhalt, Eingang *m*. **to acknowledge ~ of sth** den Empfang *etc* einer Sache *(gen)* bestätigen; **I am in ~ of your letter** *(Comm)* ich habe Ihren Brief erhalten. (b) *(paper)* Quittung *f*; *(from till)* Kassenbeleg *m*. (c) *(Comm, Fin: money taken)* **~s** Einnahmen *pl*.

**receive** [rɪˈsiːv] *vt* (a) *(get)* bekommen, erhalten; *punch* (ab)bekommen; *refusal, setback* erfahren; *impression* gewinnen; *recognition* finden; *(Jur) stolen goods* Hehlerei (be)treiben mit. **"~d with thanks"** *(Comm)* „dankend erhalten". (b) *(welcome) person* empfangen; *(into group)* aufnehmen *(in* in +*acc*)*; *offer, news* aufnehmen. **to ~ a warm wel-**

**come** herzlich empfangen werden; **the play has been well ~d** das Stück wurde gut aufgenommen. **(c)** *(Rad, TV)* empfangen.

**receiver** [rɪ'siːvəʳ] *n* **(a)** *(of letter, goods)* Empfänger(in *f*) *m*; *(Jur: of stolen goods)* Hehler(in *f*) *m*. **(b)** *(Fin, Jur)* **(official)** ~ Konkursverwalter *m*; **to call in the** ~ Konkurs anmelden. **(c)** *(Telec)* Hörer *m*. **(d)** *(Rad)* Empfänger *m*.

**receivership** [rɪ'siːvəʃɪp] *n*: **to go into** ~ in Konkurs gehen.

**recent** ['riːsənt] *adj* kürzlich *(usu adv)*; *event, development, news* neueste(r, s); *edition, addition* neu; *publication* Neu-. **the** ~ **improvement** die vor kurzem eingetretene Verbesserung; **most** ~ neueste(r, s); **his** ~ **arrival** seine Ankunft vor kurzem; **in** ~ **years** in den letzten Jahren; ~ **developments** jüngste Entwicklungen.

**recently** ['riːsəntlɪ] *adv (a short while ago)* vor kurzem, kürzlich; *(during the last few days or weeks)* in letzter Zeit. ~ **he has been doing it differently** seit kurzem macht er das anders; **as** ~ **as** erst; **quite** ~ erst kürzlich; **until (quite)** ~ (noch) bis vor kurzem.

**receptacle** [rɪ'septəkl] *n* Behälter *m*.

**reception** [rɪ'sepʃən] *n (welcome, ceremony, in hotel, Rad, TV)* Empfang *m*; *(into group, of play etc)* Aufnahme *f*. **to give sb a warm** ~ jdm einen herzlichen Empfang bereiten; jdn herzlich empfangen; ~ **camp,** ~ **centre** *(Brit)* or **center** *(US)* Aufnahmelager *nt*; ~ **desk** Empfang *m*; *(in hotel)* Rezeption *f*.

**receptionist** [rɪ'sepʃənɪst] *n (in hotel)* Empfangschef *m*, Empfangsdame *f*; *(with firm)* Herr *m*/Dame *f* am Empfang; *(at airport)* Bodenhostess *f*; *(at doctor's etc)* Sprechstundenhilfe *f*.

**receptive** [rɪ'septɪv] *adj person, mind* aufnahmefähig; *audience* empfänglich. ~ **to** empfänglich für.

**recess** [rɪ'ses] *n* **(a)** *(of Parliament)* (Sitzungs)pause *f*; *(of lawcourts)* Ferien *pl*; *(US Law, Sch)* Pause *f*. **(b)** *(alcove)* Nische *f*.

**recession** [rɪ'seʃən] *n* **(a)** *no pl* Rückgang *m*. **(b)** *(Econ)* Rezession *f*.

**recharge** [ˌriː'tʃɑːdʒ] *vt battery* (wieder)aufladen; *gun* nachladen.

**rechargeable** [ˌriː'tʃɑːdʒəbl] *adj battery* (wieder) aufladbar.

**recherché** [rə'ʃɛəʃeɪ] *adj* gewählt; *book, subject* ausgefallen.

**recipe** ['resɪpɪ] *n* Rezept *nt*. ~ **for success** Erfolgsrezept *nt*; **that's a** ~ **for disaster** das führt mit Sicherheit in die Katastrophe.

**recipient** [rɪ'sɪpɪənt] *n* Empfänger(in *f*) *m*.

**reciprocal** [rɪ'sɪprəkəl] *adj (mutual)* gegenseitig; *(Gram, Math)* reziprok.

**reciprocate** [rɪ'sɪprəkeɪt] **1** *vt smiles, wishes, help* erwidern. **2** *vi* sich revanchieren. **but she didn't** ~ *(emotionally)* aber sie erwiderte seine/ihre Gefühle nicht.

**recital** [rɪ'saɪtl] *n (of poetry)* Vortrag *m*; *(piano ~ etc)* Konzert *nt*; *(account)* Schilderung *f*.

**recitation** [ˌresɪ'teɪʃən] *n* Vortrag *m*.

**recite** [rɪ'saɪt] **1** *vt* **(a)** *poetry* vortragen, rezitieren. **(b)** *facts* hersagen; *details* aufzählen. **2** *vi* vortragen, rezitieren.

**reckless** ['reklɪs] *adj* leichtsinnig; *driver, driving* rücksichtslos; *speed* gefährlich.

**recklessly** ['reklɪslɪ] *adv see adj.*

**recklessness** ['reklɪsnɪs] *n see adj* Leichtsinn *m*; Rücksichtslosigkeit *f*; Gefährlichkeit *f*.

**reckon** ['rekən] *vt* **(a)** *(calculate)* berechnen. **he ~ed the cost to be £40.51** er berechnete die Kosten auf £40,51. **(b)** *(judge)* rechnen, zählen *(among zu)*. **she is ~ed a beautiful woman** sie gilt als schöne Frau.

**(c)** *(think, suppose)* glauben; *(estimate)* schätzen. **what do you ~?** was meinen Sie?; **I ~ we can start** ich glaube, wir können anfangen; **I ~ he must be about forty** ich schätze, er müßte so um die Vierzig sein.

►**reckon on** *vi +prep obj* zählen auf *(+acc)*. **you can ~ ~ 30** Sie können mit 30 rechnen; **I wasn't ~ing ~ having to do that** ich habe nicht damit gerechnet, daß ich das tun muß.

►**reckon up** *vt sep* zusammenrechnen.

►**reckon with** *vi +prep obj* rechnen mit. **he's a person to be ~ed ~** er ist jemand, den man nicht unterschätzen sollte.

►**reckon without** *vt* nicht rechnen mit.

**reckoning** ['rekənɪŋ] *n (calculation)* (Be)rechnung *f*. **to be out in one's** ~ sich ziemlich verrechnet haben; **the day of** ~ der Tag der Abrechnung.

**reclaim** [rɪ'kleɪm] **1** *vt* **(a)** *land* gewinnen; *(by irrigation etc)* kultivieren. **(b)** *baggage etc* abholen. **2** *n* **past** ~ für immer verloren.

**reclamation** [ˌreklə'meɪʃən] *n see vt* **(a)** Gewinnung *f*; Kultivierung *f*.

**recline** [rɪ'klaɪn] **1** *vt arm* legen *(on auf +acc)*; *head* also zurücklehnen *(on an +acc)*; *seat* zurückstellen. **2** *vi (person)* liegen; *(seat)* sich verstellen lassen. **reclining chair** Ruhesessel *m*; **reclining seat** *(in car, on boat)* Liegesitz *m*.

**recluse** [rɪ'kluːs] *n* Einsiedler(in *f*) *m*.

**recognition** [ˌrekəg'nɪʃən] *n* **(a)** *(acknowledgement, Pol)* Anerkennung *f*. **in** ~ **of** in Anerkennung *(+gen)*; **by your own** ~ wie Sie selbst zugeben; **to gain** ~ Anerkennung finden. **(b)** *(identification)* Erkennen *nt*. **he/it has changed beyond all** or **out of all** ~ er/es ist nicht wiederzuerkennen.

**recognizable** ['rekəgnaɪzəbl] *adj* erkennbar. **you're scarcely ~ with that beard** Sie sind mit dem Bart kaum wiederzuerkennen.

**recognize** ['rekəgnaɪz] *vt* **(a)** *(know again)* wiedererkennen; *(identify)* erkennen *(by an +dat)*. **(b)** *(acknowledge, Pol)* anerkennen *(as, to be als)*. **(c)** *(be aware)* erkennen; *(be prepared to admit)* zugeben, eingestehen.

**recognized** ['rekəgnaɪzd] *adj* anerkannt.

**recoil** [rɪ'kɔɪl] *vi* **(a)** *(person) (from vor +dat)* zurückweichen; *(in fear)* zurückschrecken; *(in disgust)* zurückschaudern. **he ~ed from doing it** ihm graute davor, das zu tun. **(b)** *(gun)* zurückstoßen; *(spring)* zurückschnellen.

**recollect** [ˌrekə'lekt] *vt* sich erinnern an *(+acc)*. **as far as I can** ~ soweit ich mich erinnern kann.

**recollection** [ˌrekə'lekʃən] *n (memory)* Erinnerung *f (of an +acc)*. **I have no** ~ **of it** ich kann mich daran nicht erinnern.

**recommend** [ˌrekə'mend] *vt* empfehlen *(as als)*. **what do you ~ for a cough?** was empfehlen Sie gegen Husten?; **to ~ sth to sb** jdm etw empfehlen; **it is not to be ~ed** es ist nicht zu empfehlen; **~ed (retail) price** unverbindlicher Richtpreis; **she has much to ~ her** es spricht sehr viel für sie.

**recommendation** [ˌrekəmen'deɪʃən] *n* Empfehlung *f*. **on the ~ of** auf Empfehlung von; **can you make a ~?** können Sie jemanden/etwas empfehlen?

**recompense** ['rekəmpens] **1** *n* **(a)** *(reward)* Belohnung *f*. **in ~ for** als Belohnung für. **(b)** *(Jur, fig)* Entschädigung *f*. **2** *vt* **(a)** *(reward)* belohnen. **(b)** *(Jur, fig: repay)* person entschädigen.

**reconcilable** ['rekənˌsaɪləbl] *adj people* versöhnbar; *ideas* miteinander vereinbar.

**reconcile** ['rekənsaɪl] *vt* **(a)** *people* aussöhnen; *differences* beilegen; *dispute* schlichten. **they became ~d** sie versöhnten sich; **to ~ oneself to sth, to become**

~d to sth sich mit etw abfinden. **(b)** *(make compatible) facts, ideas* miteinander in Einklang bringen, miteinander vereinbaren. **to ~ sth with sth** etw mit etw in Einklang bringen.

**reconciliation** [‚rekənsılı'eıʃən] *n (of persons)* Aussöhnung *f; (of opinons, principles)* Versöhnung *f; (of differences)* Beilegung *f.*

**recondite** [rı'kɒndaıt] *adj* abstrus.

**recondition** [‚riːkən'dıʃən] *vt* generalüberholen. **a ~ed engine** ein Austauschmotor *m.*

**reconnaissance** [rı'kɒnısəns] *n (Aviat, Mil)* Aufklärung *f.* **~ plane** Aufklärungsflugzeug *nt;* **to be on ~** bei einem Aufklärungseinsatz sein.

**reconnoitre,** *(US)* **reconnoiter** [‚rekə'nɔıtə^r] **1** *vt (Aviat, Mil) region* auskundschaften, aufklären. **2** *vi* das Gelände erkunden.

**reconsider** [‚riːkən'sıdə^r] **1** *vt* noch einmal überdenken; *(change)* revidieren; *(Jur) case* wiederaufnehmen. **2** *vi* **there's still time to ~** es ist noch nicht zu spät, es sich *(dat)* anders zu überlegen.

**reconstruct** [‚riːkən'strʌkt] *vt* rekonstruieren; *building* wiederaufbauen.

**reconstruction** [‚riːkən'strʌkʃən] *n see vt* Rekonstruktion *f;* Wiederaufbau *m.*

**record** [rı'kɔːd] **1** *vt* **(a)** *(diarist etc)* aufzeichnen; *(documents, diary etc)* dokumentieren; *(in register)* eintragen; *(keep minutes of)* protokollieren; *one's thoughts, feelings etc* niederschreiben; *protest* zum Ausdruck bringen.

**(b)** *(on tape etc)* aufnehmen. **a ~ed programme** eine Aufzeichnung; **~ed music** Musikaufnahmen *pl.*

**2** ['rekɔːd] *n* **(a)** *(account)* Aufzeichnung *f; (of attendance)* Liste *f; (of meeting)* Protokoll *nt; (official document)* Unterlage *f; (Comp)* Datensatz *m; (lit, fig: of the past)* Dokument *nt.* **to keep a ~ of sth** über etw *(acc)* Buch führen; *(official, registrar)* etw registrieren; **it is on ~ that** ... es gibt Belege dafür, daß ...; *(in files)* es ist aktenkundig, daß ...; **there is no similar example on ~** es ist kein ähnliches Beispiel bekannt; **he's on ~ as saying** ... es ist belegt, daß er gesagt hat, ...; **to put sth on ~** etw schriftlich festhalten; **there is no ~ of his having said it** es ist nirgends belegt, daß er es gesagt hat; **to set the ~ straight** für klare Verhältnisse sorgen; **for the ~** der Ordnung halber; **(strictly) off the ~, he did come** ganz im Vertrauen: er ist doch gekommen.

**(b)** *(history)* Vorgeschichte *f; (achievements)* Leistungen *pl; (police ~)* Vorstrafen *pl.* **to have an excellent ~** ausgezeichnete Leistungen vorweisen können; **he's got a ~** er ist vorbestraft; **she has a good ~ of service** sie ist eine verdiente Mitarbeiterin; **he has a bad attendance ~** er fehlt oft; **her past ~** ihre bisherigen Leistungen; **to have a good ~ at school** ein guter Schüler sein; **to have a good safety ~** in bezug auf Sicherheit einen guten Ruf haben.

**(c)** *(Mus)* (Schall)platte *f; (compact disc)* CD *f; (~ing)* Aufnahme *f.*

**(d)** *(Sport, fig)* Rekord *m.* **to beat** *or* **break the ~** den Rekord brechen; **to hold the ~** den Rekord halten; **long-jump ~** Rekord im Weitsprung; **a ~ time** eine Rekordzeit.

**record-breaking** ['rekɔːd‚breıkıŋ] *adj (Sport, fig)* Rekord-.

**recorded delivery** [rı'kɔːdıd dı'lıvrı] *n (Brit)* eingeschriebene Sendung (ohne Versicherung). **by ~** per Einschreiben.

**recorder** [rı'kɔːdə^r] *n* **(a)** *(apparatus)* Registriergerät *nt.* **cassette/tape ~** Kassettenrecorder *m*/Tonbandgerät *nt.* **(b)** *(Mus)* Blockflöte *f.*

**record holder** *n (Sport)* Rekordinhaber(in *f) m.*

**recording** [rı'kɔːdıŋ] *n (of sound)* Aufnahme *f; (pro-*

*gramme)* Aufzeichnung *f.* **~ engineer** Aufnahmetechniker *m;* **~ studio** Aufnahmestudio *nt.*

**record** ['rekɔːd]: **~ library** *n* Plattenverleih *m; (collection)* Plattensammlung *f;* **~-player** *n* Plattenspieler *m;* **~ sleeve** *n* Schallplattenhülle *f;* **~ token** *n* Plattengutschein *m.*

**recount** [rı'kaunt] *vt (relate)* erzählen, wiedergeben.

**re-count** [‚riː'kaunt] **1** *vt* nachzählen. **2** ['riː‚kaunt] *n (of votes)* Nachzählung *f.*

**recoup** [rı'kuːp] *vt money, amount* wieder hereinbekommen; *losses* wiedergutmachen, wettmachen.

**recourse** [rı'kɔːs] *n* Zuflucht *f.* **to have ~ to sb/sth** sich an jdn wenden/Zuflucht zu etw nehmen; **without ~** *(Fin)* ohne Regreß.

**recover** [rı'kʌvə^r] **1** *vt* wiederfinden; *goods, property* zurückbekommen; *health* wiedererlangen; *wreck* bergen; *(Ind etc) materials* gewinnen; *debt* eintreiben; *(Jur) damages* Ersatz erhalten für; *losses* wiedergutmachen; *expenses* decken. **to ~ one's breath/strength** wieder zu Atem/Kräften kommen; **to ~ consciousness** das Bewußtsein wiedererlangen; **to ~ one's sight** wieder sehen können; **to be quite ~ed** sich ganz erholt haben. **2** *vi (after accident etc, from illness, Fin)* sich erholen; *(regain consciousness)* wieder zu sich kommen.

**re-cover** [‚riː'kʌvə^r] *vt chairs etc* neu beziehen; *book* neu einbinden.

**recovery** [rı'kʌvərı] *n* **(a)** *see vt* Wiederfinden *nt;* Zurückbekommen *nt;* Wiedererlangung *f;* Bergung *f;* Gewinnung *f;* Eintreibung *f;* Ersatz *m (of für);* Wiedergutmachung *f;* Deckung *f.* **~ vehicle/service** Abschleppwagen *m*/-dienst *m.* **(b)** *see vi* Erholung *f.* **(economic) ~** Aufschwung *m;* **he is making a good ~** er erholt sich gut; **past ~** nicht mehr zu retten.

**recreation** [‚rekrı'eıʃən] *n* **(a)** *(leisure)* Erholung *f; (pastime)* Hobby *nt.* **for ~ I go fishing** zur Erholung gehe ich angeln; **~ period** Freistunde *f;* **~ ground** Freizeitgelände *nt.* **(b)** *(Sch)* Pause *f.*

**recreational** [‚rekrı'eıʃənəl] *adj* Freizeit-. **~ drug** Freizeitdroge *f.*

**recriminations** [rı‚krımı'neıʃənz] *npl* gegenseitige Beschuldigungen *pl.*

**recruit** [rı'kruːt] **1** *n (Mil)* Rekrut *m (to gen); (to party, club)* neues Mitglied *(to* in +*dat); (to staff)* Neue(r) *mf (to* in +*dat).* **2** *vt soldier* rekrutieren; *member* werben; *staff* einstellen. **he ~ed me to help** er hat mich dazu herangezogen.

**recruiting** [rı'kruːtıŋ] *adj* **~ office** Rekrutierungsbüro *nt.*

**recruitment** [rı'kruːtmənt] *n (of soldiers)* Rekrutierung *f; (of members)* Werbung *f; (of staff)* Einstellung *f.*

**rectangle** ['rek‚tæŋgl] *n* Rechteck *nt.*

**rectangular** [rek'tæŋgjulə^r] *adj* rechteckig.

**rectifier** ['rektı‚faıə^r] *n (Elec)* Gleichrichter *m.*

**rectify** ['rektıfaı] *vt* korrigieren.

**rector** ['rektə^r] *n* **(a)** *(Rel)* Pfarrer *m (der Anglikanischen Kirche).* **(b)** *(Scot) (Sch)* Direktor(in *f) m; (Univ)* Rektor(in *f) m.*

**rectory** ['rektərı] *n (house)* Pfarrhaus *nt.*

**rectum** ['rektəm] *n, pl* **-s** *or* **recta** Mastdarm *m.*

**recuperate** [rı'kuːpəreıt] **1** *vi* sich erholen. **2** *vt losses* wettmachen.

**recuperation** [rı‚kuːpə'reıʃən] *n see vb* Erholung *f;* Wiedergutmachung *f.*

**recur** [rı'kɜː^r] *vi* wiederkehren; *(error also, event)* sich wiederholen; *(opportunity)* sich noch einmal bieten; *(idea, theme also)* wieder auftauchen.

**recurrence** [rı'kʌrəns] *n see vi* Wiederkehr *f;* Wiederholung *f;* Wiederauftauchen *nt.*

**recurrent** [rı'kʌrənt] *adj idea, illness* (ständig) wiederkehrend *attr*; *error, problem also* häufig (vorkommend).

**recurring** [rɪ'kɜːrɪŋ] *adj attr* (**a**) = **recurrent**. (**b**) *(Math)* **four point nine three** ~ vier Komma neun Periode drei.

**recyclable** [ˌriː'saɪkləbl] *adj* wiederverwertbar.

**recycle** [ˌriː'saɪkl] *vt waste* wiederaufbereiten, recyceln.

**recycling** [ˌriː'saɪklɪŋ] *n* Wiederaufbereitung *f*, Recycling *nt*. ~ **plant** Wiederaufbereitungsanlage *f*.

**red** [red] **1** *adj* (+*er*) *(also Pol)* rot. ~ **meat** Rind-/Lammfleisch *nt*; ~ **as a beetroot** rot wie eine Tomate; **she turned** ~ **with embarrassment** sie wurde vor Verlegenheit rot; **it's like a** ~ **rag to a bull** das ist ein rotes Tuch für ihn/sie *etc*. **2** *n* Rot *nt*; *(Pol: person)* Rote(r) *mf*. **to underline sth in** ~ etw rot unterstreichen; **to be (£100) in the** ~ (mit £100) in den roten Zahlen sein; **to see** ~ rot sehen.

**red** *in cpds* Rot-, rot; ~ **beet** *n (US)* rote Rübe; ~-**blooded** *adj* heißblütig; ~**breast** *n* Rotkehlchen *nt*; ~-**brick university** *n (Brit) verhältnismäßig moderne britische Universität*; ~ **carpet** *n (lit, fig)* roter Teppich; **a** ~-**carpet reception** ein Empfang *m* mit rotem Teppich; *(fig also)* ein großer Bahnhof; **R**~ **Cross** *n* Rotes Kreuz; ~**currant** *n* rote Johannisbeere; ~ **deer** *n* Rothirsch *m*; *pl* Rotwild *nt*.

**redden** ['redn] **1** *vt* röten; *sky, foliage* rot färben. **2** *vi (face)* sich röten; *(person)* rot werden; *(sky, foliage)* sich rot färben.

**reddish** ['redɪʃ] *adj* rötlich.

**redecorate** [ˌriː'dekəreɪt] *vt* neu streichen; *(repaint and wallpaper)* neu streichen und tapezieren.

**redecoration** [ˌriːdekə'reɪʃən] *n see vb* Neuanstrich *m* (und -tapezieren *nt*).

**redeem** [rɪ'diːm] *vt trading stamps, coupons etc* einlösen *(for gegen)*; *(Fin) debt, mortgage* abzahlen; *shares* verkaufen; *(US) banknote* wechseln *(for in* +*acc)*; *one's honour* retten; *(Rel) sinner* erlösen; *(compensate for) failing* wettmachen. **to** ~ **oneself** sich reinwaschen.

**redeemable** [rɪ'diːməbl] *adj* einlösbar. ~ **for cash** gegen Bargeld einzulösen.

**Redeemer** [rɪ'diːmər] *n (Rel)* Erlöser *m*.

**redeeming** [rɪ'diːmɪŋ] *adj quality* ausgleichend. ~ **feature** aussöhnendes Moment; **the only** ~ **feature of this novel is** ... das einzige, was einen mit diesem Roman aussöhnt, ist ...

**redemption** [rɪ'dempʃən] *n see vt* Einlösung *f*; Abzahlung *f*; Verkauf *m*; Wechsel *m*; Rettung *f*; *(Rel)* Erlösung *f*. **beyond** *or* **past** ~ *(fig)* nicht mehr zu retten.

**redeploy** [ˌriːdɪ'plɔɪ] *vt troops, weapons* umstationieren; *staff* anderweitig einsetzen.

**redevelop** [ˌriːdɪ'veləp] *vt building, area* sanieren.

**redevelopment** [ˌriːdɪ'veləpmənt] *n* Sanierung *f*.

**red:** ~-**eye** *n (Phot)* Rotfärbung *f der Augen auf Blitzlichtfotos*; ~-**faced** *adj* mit rotem Kopf; ~-**haired** *adj* rothaarig; ~-**handed** *adv*: **to catch sb** ~-**handed** jdn auf frischer Tat ertappen; ~-**head** *n* Rothaarige(r) *mf*; ~ **herring** *n (fig)* Ablenkungsmanöver *nt*; *(in thrillers, research)* falsche Spur; ~-**hot** *adj (lit)* rotglühend; *(very hot)* glühend heiß; *(fig col) (enthusiastic)* Feuer und Flamme *pred (col)*; *news* brandaktuell; **R**~ **Indian** *n* Indianer(in *f*) *m*.

**redirect** [ˌriːdaɪ'rekt] *vt letter* umadressieren; *(forward)* nachsenden; *traffic* umleiten.

**rediscover** [ˌriːdɪ'skʌvər] *vt* wiederentdecken.

**rediscovery** [ˌriːdɪ'skʌvərɪ] *n* Wiederentdeckung *f*.

**redistribute** [ˌriːdɪ'strɪbjuːt] *vt* umverteilen.

**red:** ~-**letter day** *n* besonderer Tag; ~ **light** *n (lit) (warning light)* rotes Licht; *(traffic light)* Rotlicht *nt*;

**to go through the** ~ **light** *(Mot)* bei Rot über die Ampel fahren; **the** ~-**light district** das Amüsierviertel, der Strich *(col)*.

**redness** ['rednɪs] *n* Röte *f*.

**redo** [ˌriː'duː] *vt* noch einmal machen; *(redecorate)* neu machen.

**redolent** ['redəulənt] *adj (liter)* **to be** ~ **of sth** an etw *(acc)* erinnern.

**redouble** [ˌriː'dʌbl] *vt efforts, zeal etc* verdoppeln.

**redoubtable** [rɪ'dautəbl] *adj (formidable) task* gewaltig; *person* respektgebietend *attr*.

**red pepper** *n* rote Paprikaschote.

**redraft** [ˌriː'drɑːft] *vt* neu entwerfen.

**redress** [rɪ'dres] **1** *vt errors etc* wiedergutmachen; *situation* bereinigen; *grievance* beseitigen; *balance* wiederherstellen. **2** *n* **to seek** ~ **for** Wiedergutmachung verlangen für; **there is no** ~ das steht unumstößlich fest; **to have no** ~ **in law** keinen Rechtsanspruch haben.

**red:** ~-**rimmed** *adj* rotgerändert; **R**~ **Sea** *n* Rotes Meer; ~**skin** *n* Rothaut *f*; ~ **tape** *n (fig)* Papierkrieg *m (col)*; *(with authorities also)* Behördenkram *m (col)*.

**reduce** [rɪ'djuːs] *vt pressure, swelling* verringern, reduzieren; *standards, goods, prices* herabsetzen; *taxes, temperature* senken; *(shorten)* verkürzen; *expenses, wages* kürzen; *width, staff, photo* verkleinern; *scale of operations* einschränken; *output* drosseln. **to** ~ **one's weight** abnehmen; **to** ~ **speed** *(Mot)* langsamer fahren; **to** ~ **sth to a powder/to its parts** etw pulverisieren/in seine Einzelteile zerlegen; **it has been** ~**d to nothing** es ist zu nichts zusammengeschmolzen; **to** ~ **sb to silence/despair/tears** jdn zum Schweigen/zur Verzweiflung/zum Weinen bringen; **to** ~ **sb to begging** jdn zum Betteln zwingen; **are we** ~**d to this!** so weit ist es also gekommen!

**reduced** [rɪ'djuːst] *adj price, fare* ermäßigt; *goods* herabgesetzt; *scale, version* kleiner.

**reduction** [rɪ'dʌkʃən] *n* (**a**) *no pl (in sth gen)* Reduzierung, Verringerung *f*; *(in authority)* Schwächung *f*; *(in prices also, of goods, items)* Herabsetzung *f*; *(in expenses, wages)* Kürzung *f*; *(in size)* Verkleinerung *f*; *(shortening)* Verkürzung *f*; *(in output also)* Drosselung *f*. **to make a** ~ **on an article** einen Artikel heruntersetzen; ~ **of taxes** Steuersenkung *f*. (**b**) *(amount reduced) (in sth gen)* Abnahme *f*, Rückgang *m*; *(in size)* Verkleinerung *f*; *(in length)* Verkürzung *f*; *(in taxes)* Nachlaß *m*; *(in prices)* Ermäßigung *f*; *(Jur: of sentence)* Kürzung *f*; *(of swelling)* Rückgang *m*.

**redundancy** [rɪ'dʌndənsɪ] *n* Überflüssigkeit *f*; *(Brit Ind)* Arbeitslosigkeit *f*. **redundancies** Entlassungen *pl*; ~ **payment** Abfindung *f*.

**redundant** [rɪ'dʌndənt] *adj* überflüssig; *(Brit Ind: out of work)* arbeitslos. **to be made** ~ *(Brit Ind)* den Arbeitsplatz verlieren.

**red:** ~ **wine** *n* Rotwein *m*; ~**wood** *n* Redwood *nt*.

**reed** [riːd] *n (Bot)* Schilf(rohr), Ried *nt*; *(of wind instrument)* Rohrblatt *nt*.

**reef**¹ [riːf] *n (in sea)* Riff *nt*.

**reef**² *n (Naut)* Reff *nt*. ~ **knot** Kreuzknoten *m*.

**reek** [riːk] **1** *n* Gestank *m*. **2** *vi* stinken *(of nach)*.

**reel** [riːl] **1** *n* (**a**) Spule *f*; *(of thread etc also)* Rolle *f*; *(Fishing)* (Angel)rolle *f*. (**b**) *(dance)* Reel *m*. **2** *vi (person)* taumeln; *(drunk also)* torkeln. **the blow sent him** ~**ing** er taumelte unter dem Schlag; **my head is** ~**ing** mir dreht sich der Kopf.

▶**reel in** *vt sep (Fishing)* einrollen; *fish* einholen.

▶**reel off** *vt sep list* herunterrasseln *(col)*.

**re-elect** [ˌriːɪ'lekt] *vt* wiederwählen.

**re-election** [ˌriːɪ'lekʃən] *n* Wiederwahl *f.*
**reel-to-reel** ['riːltə'riːl] *adj:* ~ **tape recorder** Tonbandgerät *nt.*
**re-enact** [ˌriːɪ'nækt] *vt* **(a)** *(Jur)* wieder in Kraft setzen. **(b)** *(repeat)* scene, crime nachstellen.
**re-enter** [ˌriː'entər] *vti* wieder eintreten (in +*acc*).
**re-entry** [ˌriː'entrɪ] *n (also Space)* Wiedereintritt *m.*
**re-examine** [ˌriːɪg'zæmɪn] *vt* erneut prüfen.
**ref¹** [ref] *n (Sport col)* = **referee** Schiedsrichter *m,* Schiri *m (Sport col).*
**ref²** = **reference (number).**
**refectory** [rɪ'fektərɪ] *n (in college)* Mensa *f.*
**refer** [rɪ'fɜːʳ] **1** *vt (pass) matter, problem* weiterleiten *(to an +acc); decision* übergeben *(to sb* jdm*); patient* überweisen *(to an +acc).* **I ~red him to the manager** ich verwies ihn an den Geschäftsführer; **to ~ sb to the article on ...** jdn auf den Artikel über *(+acc)* ... verweisen. **2** *vi* **(a) to ~ to** *(allude to)* sprechen von; *(mention also)* erwähnen; *(words)* sich beziehen auf *(+acc);* **I am not ~ring to you** ich meine nicht Sie; **~ring to your letter** *(Comm)* mit Bezug auf Ihren Brief. **(b)** *(apply)* **to ~ to** *(orders, rules)* gelten für; *(criticism, remark)* sich beziehen auf *(+acc).* **(c)** *(consult)* **to ~ to** *to notes, book* nachschauen in *(+dat); to person* sich wenden an *(+acc).*
**referee** [ˌrefə'riː] **1** *n* **(a)** *(Ftbl, fig)* Schiedsrichter *m;* *(Boxing)* Ringrichter *m;* *(Judo, Wrestling)* Kampfrichter *m.* **(b)** *(Brit: person giving a reference)* Referenz *f.* **2** *vt (Sport, fig)* Schiedsrichter sein bei; *(Ftbl also)* pfeifen *(col).*
**reference** ['refrəns] *n* **(a)** *(act of mentioning)* Erwähnung *f (to sb/sth* jds/einer Sache*); (allusion) (direct)* Bemerkung *f (to* über *+acc); (indirect)* Anspielung *f (to* auf *+acc); (in book etc)* Verweis *m.* **to make (a) ~ to sth** etw erwähnen; **in** *or* **with ~ to** was ... anbetrifft; *(Comm)* bezüglich *(+gen).* **(b)** *(connection)* **to have (no) ~ to** in (keiner) Beziehung stehen zu. **(c)** *(testimonial: also* ~**s)** Referenz(en *pl*) *f.* **to give sb a good ~** jdm ein gutes Zeugnis ausstellen.
**reference:** ~ **book** *n* Nachschlagewerk *nt;* ~ **library** *n* Präsenzbibliothek *f;* ~ **number** *n* Nummer *f; (file number)* Aktenzeichen *nt; (of machine)* Seriennummer *f.*
**referendum** [ˌrefə'rendəm] *n, pl* **referenda** [ˌrefə'rendə] Volksentscheid *m,* Referendum *nt.* **to hold a ~** einen Volksentscheid durchführen.
**referral** [rɪ'fɜːrəl] *n (esp Med)* Überweisung *f (to an +acc).*
**refill** [ˌriː'fɪl] **1** *vt* nachfüllen. **2** ['riːfɪl] *n (for fountain pen, lighter)* Nachfüllpatrone *f; (for ballpoint)* Ersatzmine *f.* **would you like a ~?** *(col: drink)* darf ich nachschenken?
**refine** [rɪ'faɪn] *vt oil, sugar* raffinieren; *techniques* verfeinern.
 ▶**refine upon** *vi +prep obj detail* näher ausführen; *method* verfeinern.
**refined** [rɪ'faɪnd] *adj* **(a)** *metal, oil* raffiniert, rein. ~ **sugar** (Zucker)raffinade *f.* **(b)** *taste* fein; *person, style* vornehm.
**refinement** [rɪ'faɪnmənt] *n no pl (of oil, sugar)* Raffination, Reinigung *f; (no pl: of person, language, style)* Vornehmheit, Feinheit *f; (improvement: in technique, machine etc)* Verfeinerung, Verbesserung *f (in sth gen).*
**refinery** [rɪ'faɪnərɪ] *n (oil, sugar* ~*)* Raffinerie *f.*
**refit** [ˌriː'fɪt] **1** *vt ship* neu ausrüsten; *factory* neu ausstatten. **2** ['riːfɪt] *n (Naut)* Neuausrüstung *f.*
**reflate** [ˌriː'fleɪt] *vt (Econ)* ankurbeln.
**reflation** [riː'fleɪʃən] *n (Econ)* Ankurbelung *f* der Konjunktur.

**reflationary** [riː'fleɪʃnərɪ] *adj (Econ)* reflationär.
**reflect** [rɪ'flekt] **1** *vt* **(a)** *light etc* reflektieren; *(surface, mirror also)* spiegeln; *(fig) views, reality etc* widerspiegeln. **the moon was ~ed in the lake** der Mond spiegelte sich im See; **I saw him ~ed in the mirror** ich sah ihn im Spiegel; **the difficulties ~ed in his report** die Schwierigkeiten, die in seinem Bericht zum Ausdruck kommen. **(b)** *(think)* **do you ever ~ that ...?** denken Sie je darüber nach, daß ...? **2** *vi (meditate)* nachdenken, reflektieren *(geh) (on, about* über *+acc).*
**reflection** [rɪ'flekʃən] *n* **(a)** *no pl (reflecting)* Reflexion *f; (by mirror)* Spiegelung *f; (fig)* Widerspiegelung *f.* **(b)** *(image)* Spiegelbild *nt; (fig)* Widerspiegelung *f.* **to see one's ~ in a mirror** sich im Spiegel sehen; **a pale ~ of ...** ein matter Abglanz *(+gen).* **(c)** *no pl (consideration)* Überlegung *f; (contemplation)* Reflexion, Betrachtung *f.* **on ~** wenn ich *etc* mir das recht überlege; **this is no ~ on your motives** damit soll gar nichts über Ihre Motive gesagt sein.
**reflective** [rɪ'flektɪv] *adj person* nachdenklich.
**reflectively** [rɪ'flektɪvlɪ] *adv say, speak* überlegt.
**reflector** [rɪ'flektər] *n (on car)* Rückstrahler *m; (telescope)* Reflektor *m.*
**reflex** ['riːfleks] **1** *adj* Reflex-. ~ **action** Reflex *m;* ~ **camera** *(Phot)* Spiegelreflexkamera *f.* **2** *n (Physiol, Psych, fig)* Reflex *m.*
**reflexive** [rɪ'fleksɪv] *(Gram) adj* reflexiv.
**refloat** [ˌriː'fləʊt] *vt ship, business* wieder flottmachen.
**reform** [rɪ'fɔːm] **1** *n* Reform *f (in sth gen); (of person)* Besserung *f.* **2** *vt institutions, society* reformieren; *person* bessern. **3** *vi (person)* sich bessern.
**reformat** [ˌriː'fɔːmæt] *vt (Comp)* umformatieren.
**reformation** [ˌrefə'meɪʃən] *n (of person)* Besserung *f.* **the R~** die Reformation.
**reformatory** [rɪ'fɔːmətərɪ] *n (dated)* Besserungsanstalt *f (dated).*
**reformed** [rɪ'fɔːmd] *adj church, spelling* reformiert; *person* gewandelt. **he's a ~ character** er hat sich gebessert.
**reformer** [rɪ'fɔːmər] *n (Pol)* Reformer *m; (Rel)* Reformator *m.*
**refraction** [rɪ'frækʃən] *n* Brechung *f.* **angle of ~** Brechungswinkel *m.*
**refractory** [rɪ'fræktərɪ] *adj* **(a)** *person* störrisch. **(b)** *(Chem, Miner)* hitzebeständig.
**refrain¹** [rɪ'freɪn] *vi* **please ~!** bitte unterlassen Sie das!; **he ~ed from comment** er enthielt sich eines Kommentars; **I couldn't ~ from laughing** ich konnte mir das Lachen nicht verkneifen; **please ~ from smoking** bitte nicht rauchen!
**refrain²** *n (Mus, Poet, fig)* Refrain *m.*
**refresh** [rɪ'freʃ] *vt (drink, rest)* erfrischen; *(meal)* stärken. **to ~ oneself** *(with drink)* eine Erfrischung zu sich nehmen; *(with a bath)* sich erfrischen; *(with rest)* sich ausruhen; **to ~ one's memory** sein Gedächtnis auffrischen.
**refresher** [rɪ'freʃər] *n (col: drink)* Erfrischung *f.* ~ **course** *(Univ etc)* Auffrischungskurs *m.*
**refreshing** [rɪ'freʃɪŋ] *adj (lit, fig)* erfrischend.
**refreshment** [rɪ'freʃmənt] *n* **(a)** *(of mind, body)* Erfrischung *f.* **(b)** *(food, drink) (light)* ~**s** (kleine) Erfrischungen *pl;* ~ **bar** *or* **stall** Büfett *nt;* ~ **room** Erfrischungsraum *m.*
**refrigerate** [rɪ'frɪdʒəreɪt] *vt (chill)* kühlen; *(freeze)* tiefkühlen.
**refrigeration** [rɪˌfrɪdʒə'reɪʃən] *n see vt* Kühlung *f;* Tiefkühlung *f.* ~ **plant** Kühlanlage *f.*
**refrigerator** [rɪ'frɪdʒəreɪtər] *n* Kühlschrank *m.*

**refuel** [‚riːˈfjʊəl] *vti* auftanken.
**refuelling** [‚riːˈfjʊəlɪŋ] *n* Auftanken *nt*.
**refuge** [ˈrefjuːdʒ] *n* **(a)** *(lit, fig)* Zuflucht *f (from* vor
*+dat)*. **place of** ~ Zufluchtsort *m*; **to seek** ~ Zuflucht
suchen; **to take** ~ sich flüchten *(in* in *+acc)*. **(b)** *(for
climbers etc)* Unterstand *m*.
**refugee** [‚refjʊdʒiː] *n* Flüchtling *m*. ~ **camp** Flücht-
lingslager *nt*.
**refund** [rɪˈfʌnd] **1** *vt money, postage* zurückerstat-
ten; *expenses* erstatten. **2** [ˈriːfʌnd] *n see vt* Rückerstattung *f*; Erstattung *f*. **they wouldn't give me a**
~ man wollte mir das Geld nicht zurückgeben.
**refurbish** [‚riːˈfɜːbɪʃ] *vt* aufpolieren; *dress, furniture
also* verschönern; *house* renovieren.
**refurnish** [‚riːˈfɜːnɪʃ] *vt* neu möblieren.
**refusal** [rɪˈfjuːzəl] *n* Ablehnung *f*; *(of offer also)* Zurückweisung *f*; *(of permission, visa, also Show-
jumping)* Verweigerung *f*; *(to do sth)* Weigerung *f*.
**to meet with** *or* **get a** ~ eine Absage erhalten; **to
have (the) first** ~ **of sth** etw als erster angeboten bekommen.
**refuse¹** [rɪˈfjuːz] **1** *vt invitation, candidate, proposal*
ablehnen; *(stronger)* zurückweisen; *offer also* ausschlagen; *permit, permission* verweigern. **to** ~ **to
do sth** sich weigern, etw zu tun; **he was** ~**d a visa**
ihm wurde das Visum verweigert; **to be** ~**d sth** etw
nicht bekommen; **his request was** ~**d** seine Bitte
wurde abgelehnt; **the car** ~**s to start** das Auto will
einfach nicht anspringen. **2** *vi* ablehnen; *(to do sth)*
sich weigern; *(horse)* verweigern.
**refuse²** [ˈrefjuːs] *n* Müll *m*; *(food waste)* Abfall *m*.
**refuse** [ˈrefjuːs] *in cpds* Müll-; ~ **bin** *n* Mülleimer
*m*; ~ **collection** *n* Müllabfuhr *f*; ~ **collector** *n*
Müllwerker *m*; ~ **disposal** *n* Müllbeseitigung *f*; ~
**disposal unit** *n* Müllschlucker *m*; ~ **dump** *n*
Müllabladeplatz *m*.
**refusenik** [rɪˈfjuːznɪk] *n* Verweigerer *m*.
**refute** [rɪˈfjuːt] *vt* widerlegen.
**regain** [rɪˈgeɪn] *vt* wiedererlangen; *lost time* aufholen; *territory* zurückbekommen. **to** ~ **possession of**
**sth** wieder in den Besitz einer Sache *(gen)* gelangen.
**regal** [ˈriːgəl] *adj* königlich; *(fig)* hoheitsvoll.
**regale** [rɪˈgeɪl] *vt (with food, drink)* verwöhnen; *(with
stories)* ergötzen *(geh)*.
**regalia** [rɪˈgeɪlɪə] *npl* Insignien *pl*. **she was in full** ~
*(hum)* sie war in großer Aufmachung *(hum)*.
**regard** [rɪˈgɑːd] **1** *vt* **(a)** *(consider)* betrachten. **to** ~
**sb/sth as sth** jdn/etw für etw halten; **to** ~ **sb/sth
with favour** jdn/etw wohlwollend betrachten; **to** ~
**sth with horror** mit Schrecken an etw *(acc)* denken;
**to be** ~**ed as ...** als ... gelten, als ... angesehen werden; **to** ~ **sb/sth highly** jdn/etw sehr schätzen; **he is
highly** ~**ed** er ist hoch angesehen. **(b)** *(concern)* **as**
~**s your application** was Ihren Antrag betrifft. **(c)**
*(heed)* berücksichtigen. **without** ~**ing his wishes**
ohne Rücksicht auf seine Wünsche.
**2** *n* **(a)** *(attention, concern)* Rücksicht *f (for* auf
*+acc)*. **to show no** ~ **for sb/sth** keine Rücksichtnahme für jdn/etw zeigen; **with no** ~ **for his safety**
ohne Rücksicht auf seine Sicherheit. **(b) in this** ~
diesbezüglich *(form)*, in diesem Zusammenhang;
**with** *or* **in** ~ **to** in bezug auf *(+acc)*. **(c)** *(respect)*
Achtung *f*. **to hold sb in high** ~ jdn sehr schätzen.
**(d)** ~**s** *pl (in message)* Gruß *m*; **to send sb one's** ~**s**
jdn grüßen lassen; **give him my** ~**s** grüßen Sie ihn
von mir; **(kindest)** ~**s, with kind** ~**s** mit freundlichen Grüßen.
**regarding** [rɪˈgɑːdɪŋ] *prep* in bezug auf *(+acc)*, bezüglich *(+gen)*.
**regardless** [rɪˈgɑːdlɪs] **1** *adj* ~ **of** ohne Rücksicht auf

*(+acc)*, ungeachtet *(+gen)*; **to do sth** ~ **of the consequences** etw ohne Rücksicht auf die Folgen tun; ~
**of what it costs** egal, was es kostet; ~ **of the fact
that ...** ungeachtet der Tatsache, daß ... **2** *adv*
trotzdem. **he did it** ~ er hat es trotzdem getan.
**regatta** [rɪˈgætə] *n* Regatta *f*.
**regenerate** [rɪˈdʒenəreɪt] *vt (renew, re-create)* erneuern; *tissue also* neu bilden.
**regeneration** [rɪ‚dʒenəˈreɪʃən] *n see vt* Erneuerung
*f*; Neubildung *f*.
**reggae** [ˈregeɪ] *n* Reggae *m*.
**regime** [reɪˈʒiːm] *n (Pol)* Regime *nt*; *(fig: management, social system etc)* System *nt*.
**regiment** [ˈredʒɪmənt] **1** *n (Mil)* Regiment *nt*. **2** *vt
(fig)* reglementieren.
**regimental** [‚redʒɪˈmentl] *adj (Mil)* Regiments-.
**regimentation** [‚redʒɪmenˈteɪʃən] *n (fig)* Reglementierung *f*.
**region** [ˈriːdʒən] *n (of country)* Region *f*; *(of body
also)* Gegend *f*; *(of atmosphere, fig)* Bereich *m*. **in
the** ~ **of 5 pounds** um die 5 Pfund; **offers in the** ~ **of
£150,000** Verhandlungsbasis £150 000.
**regional** [ˈriːdʒənl] *adj* regional. ~ **development** Ge-
bietserschließung *f*.
**register** [ˈredʒɪstər] **1** *n (book)* Register *nt*; *(at
school)* Namensliste *f*; *(in hotel)* Gästebuch *nt*; *(of
members etc)* Mitgliedsbuch *nt*. **electoral** ~ Wählerverzeichnis *nt*; ~ **of births, deaths and marriages**
Personenstandsbuch *nt*.
**2** *vt* **(a)** *(authorities: record formally)* registrieren;
*(in book, files)* eintragen; *fact, figure also* erfassen.
**he is** ~**ed as disabled** er ist anerkannter Schwerbe-
schädigter. **(b)** *(individual: have recorded)* birth,
*(Comm)* company, trademark, vehicle etc anmelden.
**to** ~ **a protest** Protest anmelden. **(c)** *(indicate)*
*speed* anzeigen; *(expression) happiness* zum Ausdruck bringen. **he** ~**ed surprise** er zeigte sich überrascht. **(d)** *letter* einschreiben lassen.
**3** *vi* **(a)** *(on electoral list etc)* sich eintragen; *(in
hotel)* sich anmelden; *(student)* sich einschreiben.
**to** ~ **with a doctor** sich bei einem Arzt auf die Pa-
tientenliste setzen lassen. **(b)** *(col: be understood)* **it
hasn't** ~**ed (with him)** er hat es noch nicht regi-
striert.
**registered** [ˈredʒɪstəd] *adj* **(a)** *student* eingeschrieben; *voter, company* eingetragen; *design* gesetzlich
geschützt; *vehicle* amtlich zugelassen. ~ **nurse** *(US)*
staatlich geprüfte Krankenschwester; *(male)* staatlich geprüfter Pfleger; ~ **trademark** eingetragenes
Warenzeichen. **(b)** *letter, parcel* eingeschrieben. **by**
~ **post** per Einschreiben.
**registrar** [‚redʒɪˈstrɑːr] *n (Admin)* Standesbeamte(r)
*m*; *(Univ)* Kanzler *m*; *(Med)* Krankenhausarzt *m/*
-ärztin *f*.
**registration** [‚redʒɪˈstreɪʃən] *n see vt* **(a)** Registrierung *f*; Eintragung *f*; Erfassung *f*. **(b)** Anmeldung
*f*. ~ **document** (Kraft)fahrzeugbrief *m*; ~ **number**
*(Brit Aut)* polizeiliches Kennzeichen.
**registry** [ˈredʒɪstrɪ] *n* Sekretariat *nt*; *(in church)* Sakristei *f*; *(Brit: also* ~ **office)** Standesamt *nt*. **to get
married in a** ~ **office** standesamtlich heiraten.
**regret** [rɪˈgret] **1** *vt* bedauern; *lost opportunity* nachtrauern *(+dat)*. **I** ~ **that we will not be coming** ich
bedaure, daß wir nicht kommen können; **I** ~ **to say
that ...** ich muß Ihnen leider mitteilen, daß ... **2** *n*
Bedauern *nt no pl*. **much to my** ~ sehr zu meinem
Bedauern; **I have no** ~**s** ich bereue nichts.
**regretful** [rɪˈgretfʊl] *adj* bedauernd.
**regretfully** [rɪˈgretfəlɪ] *adv (sadly)* mit Bedauern;
*(reluctantly)* widerstrebend.
**regrettable** [rɪˈgretəbl] *adj* bedauerlich.

**regrettably** [rɪ'gretəblɪ] *adv* bedauerlicherweise.
**regroup** [,riː'gruːp] **1** *vt* um- *or* neugruppieren. **2** *vi* sich umgruppieren, sich neu gruppieren.
**regt** = **regiment** Reg.
**regular** ['regjʊləʳ] **1** *adj* (a) regelmäßig; *features also* ebenmäßig; *surface* gleichmäßig; *employment* fest; *way of life* geregelt. **to keep ~ hours** feste Zeiten haben; **she is as ~ as clockwork** bei ihr geht alles auf die Minute genau. (b) *(habitual) size, price, time* normal; *staff, customer, pub, seat* Stamm-; *listener* regelmäßig. **our ~ cleaning woman** unsere normale Reinemachefrau; **my ~ doctor** mein Hausarzt *m*. (c) *(permissible, accepted) action, procedure* richtig. **it is quite ~ to apply in person** es ist ganz in Ordnung, sich persönlich zu bewerben. (d) *(Mil) soldier, army* Berufs-. (e) *(col) disaster, clown etc* regelrecht. **2** *n (Mil)* Berufssoldat *m*; *(customer etc)* Stammkunde *m*, Stammkundin *f*; *(in pub, hotel)* Stammgast *m*.
**regularity** [,regjʊ'lærɪtɪ] *n* (a) *see adj (a)* Regelmäßigkeit *f*; Ebenmäßigkeit *f*; Gleichmäßigkeit *f*; *(of procedure etc)* Festheit *f*; Geregeltheit *f*. (b) *(of action, procedure)* Richtigkeit *f*.
**regularize** ['regjʊləraɪz] *vt breathing, service* regulieren; *situation, relationship* normalisieren.
**regularly** ['regjʊlɒlɪ] *adv* regelmäßig; *breathe, beat also* gleichmäßig.
**regulate** ['regjʊleɪt] *vt* regulieren; *life-style* regeln; *clock* richtig stellen.
**regulation** [,regjʊ'leɪʃən] **1** *n* (a) *(of machine)* Regulierung *f*. (b) *(rule)* Vorschrift *f*. **2** *attr boots, dress* vorgeschrieben.
**regulator** ['regjʊleɪtəʳ] *n (instrument)* Regler *m*.
**rehabilitate** [,riːhə'bɪlɪteɪt] *vt refugee, ex-soldier* (in die Gesellschaft) eingliedern; *the disabled also* rehabilitieren; *ex-prisoner* resozialisieren.
**rehabilitation** ['riːhə,bɪlɪ'teɪʃən] *n see vt* Eingliederung *f* in die Gesellschaft; Rehabilitation *f*; Resozialisierung *f*. **~ centre** *(Admin, Med)* Rehabilitationszentrum *nt*.
**rehash** [,riː'hæʃ] **1** *vt literary material etc* aufbereiten. **2** ['riːhæʃ] *n* Aufguß *m (pej)*.
**rehearsal** [rɪ'hɜːsəl] *n (Theat, Mus)* Probe *f*.
**rehearse** [rɪ'hɜːs] *vti (Theat, Mus)* proben. **to ~ what one is going to say** einüben, was man sagen will.
**reheat** [,riː'hiːt] *vt* aufwärmen.
**rehouse** [,riː'haʊz] *vt* unterbringen.
**reign** [reɪn] **1** *n (lit, fig)* Herrschaft *f*. **in the ~ of** während der Herrschaft *(+gen)*. **2** *vi (lit, fig)* herrschen *(over* über *+acc)*. **silence ~s** es herrscht Ruhe; **~ing champion** amtierender Meister.
**reimburse** [,riːɪm'bɜːs] *vt person* entschädigen; *loss, costs* ersetzen; *expenses* erstatten.
**reimbursement** [,riːɪm'bɜːsmənt] *n see vt* Entschädigung *f*; Ersatz *m*; Erstattung *f*.
**rein** [reɪn] *n (lit, fig)* Zügel *m*. **~s** *(for child)* Laufgurt *m*; **to hold the ~s** *(lit, fig)* die Zügel in der Hand haben; **to keep a tight ~ on sb/sth** *(lit, fig)* bei jdm/etw die Zügel kurz halten; **to allow sb/sth free ~** *(fig)* jdm/einer Sache freien Lauf lassen.
▶**rein in** *vt sep (lit, fig)* zügeln.
**reincarnation** [,riːɪnkɑː'neɪʃən] *n* die Wiedergeburt.
**reindeer** ['reɪndɪəʳ] *n, pl* - Ren(tier) *nt*.
**reinforce** [,riːɪn'fɔːs] *vt (lit, fig, Psych)* verstärken; *sb's demands* stärken, stützen; *evidence, opinion* bestätigen. **~d concrete** Stahlbeton *m*.
**reinforcement** [,riːɪn'fɔːsmənt] *n* (a) *no pl (act) see vt* Verstärkung *f*; Stärkung, Stützung *f*; Bestätigung *f*. (b) *(thing)* Verstärkung *f*. **~s** *(Mil, fig)* Verstärkung *f*.
**reinstate** [,riːɪn'steɪt] *vt person* wieder einstellen *(in*

in *+acc)*; *law and order* wiederherstellen *(in* in *+dat)*.
**reinvest** [,riːɪn'vest] *vt* reinvestieren.
**reissue** [,riː'ɪʃjuː] **1** *vt book* neu auflegen; *stamps, recording, coins* neu herausgeben. **2** *n see vt* Neuauflage *f*; Neuausgabe *f*.
**reiterate** [riː'ɪtəreɪt] *vt* wiederholen.
**reject** [rɪ'dʒekt] **1** *vt* (a) *damaged goods etc (customer)* zurückweisen; *(maker)* aussortieren. (b) *(turn down) application, request etc* ablehnen; *suitor, advances* zurückweisen; *offer also* ausschlagen; *possibility* verwerfen. (c) *(Med) transplant* abstoßen; *(stomach) food* verweigern. **2** ['riːdʒekt] *n (Comm)* Ausschuß *m no pl*. **~ goods** Ausschußware *f*.
**rejection** [rɪ'dʒekʃən] *n see vt* (a) Zurückweisung *f*; Aussortierung *f*. (b) Ablehnung *f*; Zurückweisung *f*; Verwerfen *nt*. (c) *(Med)* Abstoßung *f*; Verweigerung *f*.
**rejoice** [rɪ'dʒɔɪs] *vi* sich freuen; *(jubilate)* jubeln; *(Rel)* jauchzen.
**rejoicing** [rɪ'dʒɔɪsɪŋ] *n* Jubel *m*. **~s** Jubel *m*.
**rejoin¹** [,riː'dʒɔɪn] *vt person, regiment* sich wieder anschließen *(+dat)*. **to ~ one's ship** *(Naut)* wieder aufs Schiff kommen; **then we ~ed the motorway** danach fuhren wir wieder auf die Autobahn.
**rejoin²** [rɪ'dʒɔɪn] *vt (reply)* erwidern.
**rejoinder** [rɪ'dʒɔɪndəʳ] *n* Erwiderung *f*.
**rejuvenate** [rɪ'dʒuːvɪneɪt] *vt* verjüngen; *(fig)* erfrischen.
**rekindle** [,riː'kɪndl] *vt (lit, fig) fire, passions* wieder anzünden; *hope* wiedererwecken.
**relapse** [rɪ'læps] **1** *n (Med, into vice, crime)* Rückfall *m*; *(in economy)* Rückschlag *m*. **2** *vi (Med)* einen Rückfall haben. **to ~ (into crime)** rückfällig werden.
**relate** [rɪ'leɪt] **1** *vt* (a) *(recount) story* erzählen; *details* aufzählen. (b) *(associate)* in Verbindung bringen *(to, with* mit*)*. **2** *vi* (a) zusammenhängen *(to* mit*)*. (b) *(form relationship)* eine Beziehung finden *(to* zu*)*.
**related** [rɪ'leɪtɪd] *adj* (a) *(in family)* verwandt *(to* mit*)*. (b) *(connected)* zusammenhängend; *theories, languages etc* verwandt. **to be ~d to sth** mit etw zusammenhängen/verwandt sein.
**relating** [rɪ'leɪtɪŋ] *adj* **~ to** in Zusammenhang mit.
**relation** [rɪ'leɪʃən] *n* (a) *(relative)* Verwandte(r) *mf*. **he's a/no ~ (of mine)** er ist/ist nicht mit mir verwandt; **what ~ is she to you?** wie ist sie mit Ihnen verwandt? (b) *(relationship)* Beziehung *f*. **to bear a ~ to** in Beziehung stehen zu; **in ~ to** *(as regards)* in bezug auf *(+acc)*; *(compared with)* im Verhältnis zu. (c) **~s** *pl (dealings, ties, sexual ~s)* Beziehungen *pl*.
**relationship** [rɪ'leɪʃənʃɪp] *n (in family)* Verwandtschaft *f (to* mit*)*; *(connection: between events etc)* Beziehung *f*; *(relations)* Verhältnis *nt*, Beziehungen *pl*; *(in business)* Verbindung *f*. **to have a (sexual) ~ with** ein Verhältnis haben mit; **to have a good ~ with sb** ein gutes Verhältnis zu jdm haben.
**relative** ['relətɪv] **1** *adj* (a) relativ; *(respective)* jeweilig. **to live in ~ luxury** verhältnismäßig *or* relativ luxuriös leben; **the ~ merits of A and B** die jeweiligen Verdienste von A und B. (b) *(relevant)* **~ to** sich beziehend auf *(+acc)*. (c) *(Gram) clause, pronoun* Relativ-. **2** *n (person)* = **relation** (a).
**relatively** ['relətɪvlɪ] *adv* relativ, verhältnismäßig. **~ speaking** relativ gesehen.
**relativity** [,relə'tɪvɪtɪ] *n (Phys, Philos)* Relativität *f*. **the theory of ~** die Relativitätstheorie.
**relax** [rɪ'læks] **1** *vt* lockern; *muscles also, person* entspannen; *attention, effort* nachlassen in *(+dat)*. **2** *vi*

(sich) entspannen; *(rest)* (sich) ausruhen; *(calm down)* sich beruhigen.

**relaxation** [,ri:læk'seɪʃən] *n* **(a)** *see vt* Lockerung *f*; Entspannung *f*; Nachlassen *nt*. **(b)** *(rest)* Entspannung *f*; *(recreation also)* Erholung *f*.

**relaxed** [rɪ'lækst] *adj* locker; *person, smile, voice* ruhig; *atmosphere* gelockert. **to feel ~** *(physically)* entspannt sein; *(mentally)* sich wohl fühlen.

**relaxing** [rɪ'læksɪŋ] *adj* entspannend; *climate* erholsam.

**relay** ['ri:leɪ] **1** *n* **(a)** *(of workers)* Ablösung *f*; *(of horses)* frisches Gespann. **to work in ~s** sich ablösen. **(b)** *(Sport: also ~ race)* Staffel(lauf *m*) *f*. **(c)** *(Rad, TV)* Relais *nt*. **2** *vt* **(a)** *(Rad, TV)* (weiter)übertragen. **(b)** *message* ausrichten *(to sb jdm)*.

**release** [rɪ'li:s] **1** *vt* **(a)** *animal, person* freilassen; *(from prison also)* entlassen; *(rescue)* befreien; *(from obligation)* entbinden, befreien. **(b)** *(let go of)* loslassen; *handbrake* lösmachen; *(Phot) shutter* auslösen; *grip, clasp* lösen; *confiscated articles* freigeben. **to ~ the clutch** die Kupplung kommen lassen. **(c)** *news, statement* veröffentlichen. **(d)** *(emit) gas, energy* freisetzen; *smell* ausströmen; *pressure, steam* ablassen. **2** *n* **(a)** *see vt (a)* Freilassung *f*; Entlassung *f*; Befreiung *f*; Entbindung *f*. **(b)** *(mechanism)* Auslöser *m*. **(c)** *(of statement etc)* Veröffentlichung *f*; *(statement)* Verlautbarung *f*. **(d)** *(of gas, energy)* Freisetzung *f*. **(e)** *(film)* Film *m*; *(record)* Platte *f*. **this film is now on general ~** dieser Film ist nun überall zu sehen; **a new ~** *(record)* eine Neuerscheinung; *(film)* ein neu herausgekommener Film.

**relegate** ['relɪgeɪt] *vt (lit, fig: downgrade)* degradieren; *(Sport) team* absteigen lassen *(to in +acc)*. **to be ~d** *(Sport)* absteigen.

**relegation** [,relɪ'geɪʃən] *n see vt* Degradierung *f*; *(Sport)* Abstieg *m*.

**relent** [rɪ'lent] *vi (person)* nachgeben; *(pace, pain)* nachlassen; *(weather)* sich bessern.

**relentless** [rɪ'lentlɪs] *adj* erbarmungslos; *person also* unerbittlich; *pain, cold* nicht nachlassend.

**relentlessly** [rɪ'lentlɪslɪ] *adv* unerbittlich, erbarmungslos; *oppose* unnachgiebig; *rain* unaufhörlich.

**relevance** ['reləvəns] *n* Relevanz *f*.

**relevant** ['reləvənt] *adj* relevant *(to für)*; *knowledge, question* sachbezogen; *authority, person* zuständig.

**reliability** [rɪ,laɪə'bɪlɪtɪ] *n see adj* Zuverlässigkeit *f*; Seriosität *f*.

**reliable** [rɪ'laɪəbl] *adj* zuverlässig; *firm* seriös.

**reliably** [rɪ'laɪəblɪ] *adv* zuverlässig. **I am ~ informed that** ... ich weiß aus zuverlässiger Quelle, daß ...

**reliance** [rɪ'laɪəns] *n* Vertrauen *nt (on auf +acc)*.

**reliant** [rɪ'laɪənt] *adj* angewiesen *(on, upon auf +acc)*.

**relic** ['relɪk] *n* Überbleibsel, Relikt *nt*; *(Rel)* Reliquie *f*.

**relief** [rɪ'li:f] **1** *n* **(a)** *(from anxiety, pain)* Erleichterung *f*. **to bring sb ~** *(drug)* jdm Erleichterung verschaffen; **that's a ~!** mir fällt ein Stein vom Herzen; **it was a ~ to find it** ich/er etc war erleichtert, als ich/er *etc* es fand; **a little light ~** eine kleine Abwechslung. **(b)** *(assistance)* Hilfe *f*. **to provide ~ for the poor** für die Armen sorgen. **(c)** *(esp Mil: act of relieving, replacement forces)* Entsatz *m*; *(substitute)* Ablösung *f*. **(d)** *(Art, Geog)* Relief *nt*; *(Typ also)* Hochdruck *m*. **to throw sth into ~** *(fig)* etw hervorheben. **2** *attr* **(a)** *fund, organization* Hilfs-. **~ supplies** Hilfsgüter *pl*. **(b)** *driver* Ablöse-; *troops* Entsatz-; *(Brit) bus, road* Entlastungs-. **(c)** *map* Relief-; *printing also* Hoch-.

**relieve** [rɪ'li:v] *vt* **(a)** *person* erleichtern. **he was ~d to learn that** er war erleichtert, als er das hörte; **to**

**~ sb's mind** jdn beruhigen; **to ~ sb of sth** *of burden, pain* jdn von etw befreien; *of duty, command* jdn einer Sache *(gen)* entheben *(geh)*; *of suitcase etc* jdm etw abnehmen; *(hum) of wallet* jdn um etw erleichtern. **(b)** *(mitigate) anxiety* mildern, schwächen; *pain* lindern; *(completely)* stillen; *tension* abbauen; *poverty* erleichtern; *(Med) congestion* abhelfen *(+dat)*; *(completely)* beheben. **to ~ oneself** *(euph)* sich erleichtern; **it ~s the monotony** das ist eine Abwechslung. **(c)** *(take over from, also Mil)* ablösen. **(d)** *(Mil) town* entsetzen.

**religion** [rɪ'lɪdʒən] *n* Religion *f*; *(creed)* Glaube(n) *m*. **the Christian ~** der christliche Glaube.

**religious** [rɪ'lɪdʒəs] *adj* **(a)** religiös; *person also* gläubig; *order* geistlich; *freedom also, wars* Glaubens-. **~ instruction** *(Sch)* Religionsunterricht *m*; **~ leader** Religionsführer *m*. **(b)** *(fig: conscientious)* gewissenhaft.

**religiously** [rɪ'lɪdʒəslɪ] *adv* live fromm; *(fig: conscientously)* gewissenhaft, treu und brav.

**relinquish** [rɪ'lɪŋkwɪʃ] *vt hope, plan* aufgeben; *right, possessions also* verzichten auf *(+acc)*. **to ~ one's hold on sb/sth** *(lit, fig)* jdn/etw loslassen.

**relish** ['relɪʃ] **1** *n* **(a)** *(enjoyment)* Gefallen *m (for an +dat)*. **to do sth with (great) ~** etw mit (großem) Genuß tun. **(b)** *(Cook)* Soße *f*. **2** *vt* genießen; *food, wine also* sich *(dat)* schmecken lassen. **I don't ~ doing that** *(enjoy)* das ist gar nicht nach meinem Geschmack; *(look forward to)* darauf freue ich mich überhaupt nicht.

**relive** [,ri:'lɪv] *vt youth etc* noch einmal erleben.

**reload** [,ri:'ləud] *vt gun* nachladen.

**relocate** [,ri:ləu'keɪt] **1** *vt* verlegen. **2** *vi* den Standort wechseln.

**reluctance** [rɪ'lʌktəns] *n* Widerwillen *m*. **to do sth with ~** etw widerwillig *or* ungern tun.

**reluctant** [rɪ'lʌktənt] *adj* widerwillig. **he is ~ to do it** es widerstrebt ihm, es zu tun; **he seems ~ to admit it** er scheint es nicht zugeben zu wollen.

**reluctantly** [rɪ'lʌktəntlɪ] *adv* widerwillig.

**rely** [rɪ'laɪ] *vi* **to ~ (up)on sb/sth** sich auf jdn/etw verlassen; *(be dependent on)* auf jdn/etw angewiesen sein; **she relied on the trains being on time** sie verließ sich darauf, daß die Züge pünktlich waren; **she is not to be relied upon** man kann sich nicht auf sie verlassen.

**remain** [rɪ'meɪn] *vi* bleiben; *(be left over)* übrigbleiben. **much ~s to be done** es bleibt noch viel zu tun; **all that ~s is for me to wish you every success** ich möchte Ihnen nur noch viel Erfolg wünschen; **that ~s to be seen** das bleibt abzuwarten; **the fact ~s that** ... das ändert nichts an der Tatsache, daß ...; **to ~ silent** weiterhin schweigen; **to ~ behind** zurückbleiben; **I ~ yours faithfully John Smith** „ich verbleibe hochachtungsvoll Ihr John Smith".

**remainder** [rɪ'meɪndəʳ] *n* Rest *m (also Math)*. **~s** *pl (Comm)* Restbestände *pl*.

**remaining** [rɪ'meɪnɪŋ] *adj* übrig, restlich. **I have only two ~** ich habe nur noch zwei (übrig).

**remains** [rɪ'meɪnz] *npl (of meal)* Reste *pl*; *(of building)* Überreste *pl*; *(archaeological ~)* Ruinen *pl*. **human ~** menschliche Überreste *pl*.

**remake** ['ri:meɪk] *n (Film)* Neuverfilmung *f*, Remake *nt (spec)*.

**remand** [rɪ'mɑ:nd] **1** *vt (Jur)* **to ~ sb (in custody/on bail)** jdn weiterhin in Untersuchungshaft behalten/ unter Kaution halten. **2** *n* **to be on ~** in Untersuchungshaft sein; *(on bail)* auf Kaution freigelassen sein; **~ home** *(Brit Hist)* Untersuchungsgefängnis *nt* für Jugendliche.

**remark** [rɪ'mɑ:k] **1** *n* Bemerkung *f*. **worthy of ~** be-

merkenswert. **2** *vt (say)* bemerken. **3** *vi* **to ~ (up)on sth** über etw *(acc)* eine Bemerkung machen.
**remarkable** [rɪ'mɑːkəbl] *adj (notable)* bemerkenswert; *intelligence, talent also* beachtlich; *(extraordinary)* außergewöhnlich. **to be ~ for sth** sich durch etw auszeichnen.
**remarkably** [rɪ'mɑːkəblɪ] *adv* außergewöhnlich.
**remarry** [,riː'mærɪ] *vi* wieder heiraten.
**remedial** [rɪ'miːdɪəl] *adj attr action, measures* Hilfs-; *(Med)* Heil-. **~ teaching** Förderunterricht *m*; **~ class** Förderklasse *f* (für Lernschwache).
**remedy** ['remədɪ] **1** *n (Med, fig)* Mittel *nt (for* gegen*)*; *(medication)* Heilmittel *nt (for* gegen*)*. **the situation is beyond ~** die Lage ist hoffnungslos. **2** *vt (Med)* heilen; *(fig) fault* beheben; *situation* bessern.
**remember** [rɪ'membər] **1** *vt* **(a)** *(recall)* sich erinnern an *(+acc)*; *(bear in mind)* denken an *(+acc)*; *(learn) facts* sich *(dat)* merken. **I ~ that he was very tall** ich erinnere mich, daß er sehr groß war; **I ~ her as a beautiful girl** ich habe sie als schönes Mädchen in Erinnerung; **we must ~ that he's only a child** wir sollten bedenken, daß er noch ein Kind ist; **to ~ to do sth** daran denken, etw zu tun; **I can't ~ the word at the moment** das Wort fällt mir im Moment nicht ein; **here's something to ~ me by** da hast du etwas, das dich (immer) an mich erinnern wird; **I can never ~ phone numbers** ich kann mir Telefonnummern einfach nicht merken; **to ~ sb in one's will** jdn in seinem Testament bedenken. **(b)** *(commemorate)* gedenken *(+gen)*. **(c)** *(give good wishes to)* **~ me to your mother** grüßen Sie Ihre Mutter von mir; **he asks to be ~ed to you** er läßt Sie grüßen. **2** *vi* sich erinnern. **if I ~ right(ly)** *or* **aright** wenn ich mich recht erinnere *or* entsinne.
**remembrance** [rɪ'membrəns] *n* Erinnerung *f (of* an *+acc)*. **R~ Day** *(Brit)* ≃ Volkstrauertag *m*; **in ~ of** zur Erinnerung an *(+acc)*.
**remind** [rɪ'maɪnd] *vt* erinnern *(of* an *+acc)*. **to ~ sb to do sth** jdn daran erinnern, etw zu tun; **that ~s me!** da(bei) fällt mir etwas ein.
**reminder** [rɪ'maɪndər] *n (note etc)* Gedächtnisstütze *f*. **(letter of) ~** *(Comm)* Mahnung *f*; **to give sb a ~ to do sth** jdn daran erinnern, etw zu tun.
**reminisce** [,remɪ'nɪs] *vi* sich in Erinnerungen ergehen *(about* über *+acc)*.
**reminiscence** [,remɪ'nɪsəns] *n* Erinnerung *f (of* an *+acc)*.
**reminiscent** [,remɪ'nɪsənt] *adj* **to be ~ of sth** an etw *(acc)* erinnern.
**remiss** [rɪ'mɪs] *adj* nachlässig.
**remission** [rɪ'mɪʃən] *n (Jur)* (Straf)erlaß *m*; *(Rel)* Nachlaß *m*. **he got 3 years' ~** ihm wurden 3 Jahre erlassen.
**remit** [rɪ'mɪt] *vt* **(a)** *(cancel, pardon) debt, sentence, sins* erlassen. **(b)** *(send) money* überweisen. **(c)** *(Jur: transfer) case* verweisen *(to* an *+acc)*.
**remittance** [rɪ'mɪtəns] *n* Überweisung *f (to* an *+acc)*.
**remnant** ['remnənt] *n* Rest *m*; *(fig: of splendour, custom)* Überrest *m*.
**remold** ['riːməuld] *n (US)* = **remould**.
**remonstrance** [rɪ'mɒnstrəns] *n* Protest *m (with* bei, *against* gegen*)*.
**remonstrate** ['remənstreɪt] *vi* protestieren *(against* gegen*)*. **to ~ with sb (about sth)** jdm Vorhaltungen (wegen etw) machen.
**remorse** [rɪ'mɔːs] *n* Reue *f (at, over* über *+acc)*. **without ~** *(merciless)* erbarmungslos.
**remorseful** [rɪ'mɔːsful] *adj* reumütig, reuig.
**remorseless** [rɪ'mɔːslɪs] *adj* reuelos; *(fig: merciless)* unbarmherzig.
**remorselessly** [rɪ'mɔːslɪslɪ] *adv* unbarmherzig.

**remote** [rɪ'məut] *adj (+er)* **(a)** entfernt; *(isolated)* abgelegen; *(in time)* fern; *(person)* unnahbar. **(b)** *(slight) possibility, resemblance* entfernt; *chance* gering.
**remote: ~ control** *n* Fernlenkung *f*; *(Rad, TV)* Fernbedienung *f*; **~-controlled** *adj* ferngesteuert; *(Rad, TV)* mit Fernbedienung.
**remotely** [rɪ'məutlɪ] *adv situated, related* entfernt. **it's just ~ possible** es ist gerade eben noch möglich; **they're not even ~ similar** sie sind sich nicht im entferntesten ähnlich.
**remould** ['riːməuld] *n (Brit)* runderneuerter Reifen.
**remount** [,riː'maunt] **1** *vt horse, bicycle* wieder steigen auf *(+acc)*. **2** *vi* wieder aufsitzen.
**removable** [rɪ'muːvəbl] *adj cover, attachment* abnehmbar; *lining* abknöpfbar.
**removal** [rɪ'muːvəl] *n see vt* **(a)** Entfernung *f*; Abnahme *f*; Herausnehmen *nt*; Ausbau *m*. **(b)** Beseitigung *f*; Zerstreuung *f*. **(c)** Entfernung *f*. **(d)** *(move from house)* Umzug *m*.
**removal: ~ expenses** *npl* Umzugskosten *pl*; **~ firm** *n* Spedition *f*; **~ man** *n* Möbelpacker *m*; **~ van** *n (Brit)* Möbelwagen *m*.
**remove** [rɪ'muːv] **1** *vt* **(a)** *(take off/away, Med)* entfernen *(from* aus*)*; *cover, attachments also, bandage, tie* abnehmen; *(take out)* herausnehmen *(from* aus*)*; *(Tech)* ausbauen *(from* aus*)*. **to ~ sth from sb** jdm etw wegnehmen; **to ~ a child from school** ein Kind von der Schule nehmen. **(b)** *(eradicate) threat, obstacle, problem* beseitigen; *doubt, suspicion* zerstreuen. **(c)** *(form: dismiss) official* entfernen. **(d) to be far ~d from** ... weit entfernt sein von ...; **a cousin twice ~d** ein Vetter zweiten Grades. **2** *vi (form: move house)* **to ~ to London** nach London (um-) ziehen.
**remover** [rɪ'muːvər] *n* **(a)** *(for nail varnish, stains etc)* Entferner *m*. **(b)** *(removal man)* Möbelpacker *m*. **~s** *(removal firm)* Spedition *f*.
**remunerate** [rɪ'mjuːnəreɪt] *vt* bezahlen, vergüten.
**remuneration** [rɪ,mjuːnə'reɪʃən] *n* Bezahlung, Vergütung *f*.
**renaissance** [rɪ'neɪsãːns] *n* **the R~** *(Hist)* die Renaissance.
**rename** [,riː'neɪm] *vt* umbenennen. **Leningrad was ~d St Petersburg** Leningrad wurde in St Petersburg umbenannt.
**render** ['rendər] *vt* **(a)** *(form: give) service* leisten; *judgement* abgeben; *homage* erweisen. **(b)** *(interpret, translate)* wiedergeben; *(in writing)* übertragen; *music, poem also* vortragen. **(c)** *(form: make)* machen. **to ~ a bomb harmless** eine Bombe entschärfen. **(d)** *(also ~ down) fat* auslassen. **(e)** *(Build)* verputzen.
**rendering** ['rendərɪŋ] *n* Wiedergabe *f*; *(in writing)* Übertragung *f*; *(of piece of music, poem)* Vortrag *m*.
**rendez-vous** ['rɒndɪvuː] **1** *n (place)* Treffpunkt *m*; *(agreement to meet)* Rendezvous *nt*. **2** *vi* sich treffen *(with* mit*)*; *(spaceships)* ein Rendezvousmanöver durchführen.
**rendition** [ren'dɪʃən] *n (form)* = **rendering**.
**renegade** ['renɪgeɪd] **1** *n* Abtrünnige(r) *mf*. **2** *adj* abtrünnig.
**renew** [rɪ'njuː] *vt* erneuern; *contract, passport etc (authority)* verlängern; *(holder)* verlängern lassen; *discussions, attempts* wiederaufnehmen; *one's strength* wiederherstellen; *supplies* auffrischen. **to ~ a library book** ein Buch verlängern lassen; **to ~ one's acquaintance with sb** seine Bekanntschaft mit jdm auffrischen.
**renewable** [rɪ'njuːəbl] **1** *adj* erneuerbar; *contract,*

*passport, library book* verlängerbar. **2** *npl* ~**s** erneuerbare Energien *pl.*

**renewal** [rɪ'njuːəl] *n see vt* Erneuerung *f*; Verlängerung *f*; Wiederaufnahme *f*; Wiederherstellung *f*; Auffrischung *f.*

**renounce** [rɪ'naʊns] *vt right, one's liberty* aufgeben; *religion, devil, opinions, cause* abschwören *(+dat)*; *(Rel)* world entsagen *(+dat)*.

**renovate** ['renəʊveɪt] *vt building* renovieren; *painting, furniture* restaurieren.

**renovation** [,renəʊ'veɪʃən] *n see vt* Renovierung *f*; Restaurierung *f.*

**renown** [rɪ'naʊn] *n* guter Ruf, Ansehen *nt.*

**renowned** [rɪ'naʊnd] *adj* berühmt *(for* für*)*.

**rent** [rent] **1** *n (for house, room)* Miete *f*; *(for farm, factory)* Pacht *f.* **for** ~ zu vermieten/verpachten/verleihen. **2** *vt* **(a)** *(also vi) house, room* mieten; *farm, factory* pachten; *TV, car etc* leihen. **(b)** *(also* ~ *out)* vermieten; verpachten; verleihen.

**rental** ['rentl] *n (amount paid) (for house)* Miete *f*; *(for TV, car, boat etc also)* Leihgebühr *f*; *(for land)* Pacht *f*; *(income from rents)* Miet-/Pacht-/Leihgebühreinnahmen *pl.* ~ **car** *(US)* Mietauto *nt*; ~ **library** *(US)* Leihbücherei *f.*

**rent:** ~ **boy** *n* Strichjunge *m (col)*; ~ **collector** *n* Mietkassierer(in *f*) *m*; ~**-controlled** *adj* mit gebundener Miete; ~**-free** *adj* mietfrei; ~ **tribunal** *n* Mieterschiedsgericht *nt.*

**renunciation** [rɪ,nʌnsɪ'eɪʃən] *n see* **renounce** Aufgabe *f*; Abschwören *nt*; Entsagung *f.*

**reopen** [,riː'əʊpən] **1** *vt* wieder öffnen; *shop, theatre, hostilities* wiedereröffnen; *debate, negotiations, (Jur) case* wiederaufnehmen. **2** *vi* wieder aufgehen; *(shop, theatre etc)* wieder aufmachen; *(negotiations)* wiederbeginnen.

**reorder** [,riː'ɔːdəʳ] *vti* nachbestellen; *(if first order is lost)* neu bestellen.

**reorganization** [riː,ɔːɡənaɪ'zeɪʃən] *n see vt* Umorganisation *f*; Umordnung *f*; Neueinteilung *f*; Neuaufbau *m.*

**reorganize** [,riː'ɔːɡənaɪz] *vt* umorganisieren; *furniture, books* umordnen; *work* neu einteilen; *essay* neu aufbauen.

**rep** [rep] = **(a)** *(Theat)* **repertory. (b)** *(Comm)* **representative.**

**Rep** *(US Pol)* = **(a) Republican. (b) Representative.**

**repaid** [,riː'peɪd] *pret, ptp of* **repay.**

**repaint** [,riː'peɪnt] *vt* neu streichen.

**repair** [rɪ'pɛəʳ] **1** *vt (lit, fig)* reparieren; *tyre also, clothes* flicken; *roof, wall also, road* ausbessern; *(fig) wrong, damage* wiedergutmachen. **2** *n see vt* Reparatur *f*; Flicken *nt*; Ausbesserung *f.* **to be under** ~ *(car, machine)* in Reparatur sein; **to put sth in for** ~ etw zur Reparatur bringen; **beyond** ~ nicht mehr zu reparieren; **closed for** ~**s** wegen Reparaturarbeiten geschlossen; **to be in good** ~ in gutem Zustand sein; **state of** ~ Zustand *m.*

**repairable** [rɪ'pɛərəbl] *adj* reparabel.

**repair:** ~ **kit** *or* **outfit** *n* Flickzeug *nt*; ~ **shop** *n* Reparaturwerkstatt *f.*

**reparation** [,repə'reɪʃən] *n (for damage)* Entschädigung *f*; *(usu pl: after war)* Reparationen *pl*; *(for wrong)* Wiedergutmachung *f.* **to make** ~ **for sth** etw wiedergutmachen.

**repartee** [,repɑː'tiː] *n* Schlagabtausch *m*; *(retort)* schlagfertige Antwort.

**repast** [rɪ'pɑːst] *n (liter, hum)* Mahl *nt (geh).*

**repatriate** [,riː'pætrɪeɪt] *vt* in das Heimatland zurücksenden, repatriieren.

**repatriation** ['riː,pætrɪ'eɪʃən] *n* Repatriierung *f.*

**repay** [,riː'peɪ] *pret, ptp* **repaid** *vt money* zurückzahlen; *expenses* erstatten; *debt* abzahlen; *kindness* vergelten; *visit* erwidern. **how can I ever** ~ **you?** wie kann ich das jemals wiedergutmachen?

**repayable** [,riː'peɪəbl] *adj* rückzahlbar.

**repayment** [,riː'peɪmənt] *n (of money)* Rückzahlung *f*; *(of effort, kindness)* Lohn *m.*

**repeal** [rɪ'piːl] **1** *vt law* aufheben. **2** *n* Aufhebung *f.*

**repeat** [rɪ'piːt] **1** *vt* wiederholen; *(tell to sb else)* weitersagen *(to sb* jdm*).* **to** ~ **oneself** sich wiederholen; **don't** ~ **it to anyone** sag es nicht weiter; **to** ~ **an order** *(Comm)* nachbestellen; **this offer will never be** ~**ed!** dies ist ein einmaliges Angebot! **2** *n (Rad, TV)* Wiederholung *f.*

**repeated** *adj*, ~**ly** *adv* [rɪ'piːtɪd, -lɪ] wiederholt.

**repeat:** ~ **offender** *n* Mehrfachtäter *m*; ~ **order** *n (Comm)* Nachbestellung *f*; ~ **performance** *n (Theat)* Wiederholungsvorstellung *f.*

**repel** [rɪ'pel] *vt enemy* zurückschlagen; *sb's advance* abwehren; *water* abstoßen; *(disgust)* abstoßen.

**repellent** [rɪ'pelənt] **1** *adj* **(a)** ~ **to water** wasserabstoßend. **(b)** *(disgusting)* abstoßend. **2** *n* **insect** ~ Insektenschutzmittel *nt.*

**repent** [rɪ'pent] *vi* Reue empfinden *(of* über *+acc).*

**repentance** [rɪ'pentəns] *n* Reue *f.*

**repentant** [rɪ'pentənt] *adj look* reuevoll. **he was very** ~ es reute ihn sehr.

**repercussion** [,riːpə'kʌʃən] *n (consequence)* Auswirkung *f (on* auf *+acc).* ~**s** *pl (of misbehaviour etc)* Nachspiel *nt*; **that is bound to have** ~**s** das geht nicht ohne Nachspiel ab.

**repertoire** ['repətwɑːʳ] *n* Repertoire *nt.*

**repertory** ['repətərɪ] *n (also* ~ **theatre***)* Repertoire-Theater *nt.* ~ **company** Repertoire-Ensemble *nt.*

**repetition** [,repɪ'tɪʃən] *n* Wiederholung *f.*

**repetitious** [,repɪ'tɪʃəs] *adj* sich wiederholend.

**repetitive** [rɪ'petɪtɪv] *adj* sich dauernd wiederholend; *work also* monoton. **to be** ~ sich dauernd wiederholen.

**rephrase** [riː'freɪz] *vt* anders formulieren.

**replace** [rɪ'pleɪs] *vt* **(a)** zurückstellen; *(put flat)* zurücklegen. **to** ~ **the receiver** *(Telec)* (den Hörer) auflegen. **(b)** *(substitute, renew)* ersetzen; *(employee: temporarily)* vertreten.

**replacement** [rɪ'pleɪsmənt] *n* **(a)** *see vt* **(a)** Zurückstellen *nt*; Zurücklegen *nt.* **(b)** *(substituting)* Ersatz *m*; *(by deputy)* Vertretung *f.* ~ **cost** Wiederbeschaffungskosten *pl*; ~ **part** Ersatzteil *nt.*

**replay** ['riːpleɪ] *(Sport)* **1** *n (recording)* Wiederholung *f*; *(match)* Wiederholungsspiel *nt.* **2** [,riː'pleɪ] *vt match, game* wiederholen.

**replenish** [rɪ'plenɪʃ] *vt* ergänzen; *glass* auffüllen.

**replete** [rɪ'pliːt] *adj (form: supplied)* reichlich versehen *(with* mit*).*

**replica** ['replɪkə] *n* Kopie *f*; *(of ship, building etc)* Nachbildung *f.*

**reply** [rɪ'plaɪ] **1** *n (letter)* Antwort *f*; *(spoken also)* Erwiderung *f.* **in** ~ (als Antwort) darauf; **in** ~ **to your letter** in Beantwortung Ihres Briefes *(form).* **2** *vti* antworten; *(spoken also)* erwidern.

**reply:** ~ **coupon** *n* Antwortschein *m*; ~**-paid** *adj envelope* freigemacht, frei-; ~**-paid postcard** Rückantwortkarte *f.*

**report** [rɪ'pɔːt] **1** *n* **(a)** *(account, statement)* Bericht *m (on* über *+acc)*; *(Press, Rad, TV also)* Reportage *f (on* über *+acc).* **to give a** ~ **on sth** Bericht über etw *(acc)* erstatten/eine Reportage über etw *(acc)* machen; **(school)** ~ Zeugnis *nt*; **there is a** ~ **that ...** *(rumour)* es wird gesagt, daß ... **(b)** *(of gun)* Knall *m.*

**2** *vt* **(a)** *results, findings* berichten über *(+acc)*; *(announce also)* melden *(to sb* jdm*).* **he** ~**ed to me**

that … er meldete mir, daß …; **the papers ~ed the crime as solved** laut Presseberichten ist das Verbrechen aufgeklärt; **he is ~ed as having said …** er soll gesagt haben …; **~ed speech** *(Gram)* indirekte Rede. **(b)** *(to sb jdm)* *(notify authorities of)* *accident, crime* melden; *(to police also)* anzeigen; *one's position* angeben. **to ~ sb for sth** jdn wegen etw melden *or (to the police)* anzeigen.
    **3** *vi* **(a)** *(announce oneself)* sich melden. **to ~ for duty** sich zum Dienst melden; **to ~ sick** sich krank melden. **(b)** *(give a ~)* berichten, Bericht erstatten *(on über +acc)*. **(c)** *(be subordinate to)* **to ~ to sb** jdm unterstellt sein.
    ►**report back** *vi* **(a)** *(announce one's return)* sich zurückmelden. **(b)** *(give report)* Bericht erstatten *(to sb* jdm*)*.

**reportedly** [rɪˈpɔːtɪdlɪ] *adv* wie verlautet.
**reporter** [rɪˈpɔːtə*] *n (Press, Rad, TV)* Reporter(in *f)*; *(on the spot)* Korrespondent(in *f)* *m.*
**repose** [rɪˈpəʊz] **1** *n (liter)* *(rest, peace)* Ruhe *f*; *(composure)* Gelassenheit *f.* **2** *vi (form, liter: rest, be buried)* ruhen.
**repossess** [ˌriːpəˈzes] *vt* wieder in Besitz nehmen.
**reprehensible** [ˌreprɪˈhensɪbl] *adj* tadelnswert.
**represent** [ˌreprɪˈzent] *vt* darstellen; *(symbolize also)* symbolisieren; *(act or speak for, Parl, Jur)* vertreten.
**representation** [ˌreprɪzenˈteɪʃən] *n* **(a)** *no pl see vt* Darstellung *f*; Symbolisierung *f*; Vertretung *f.* **(b)** *(drawing, description, Theat)* Darstellung *f.* **(c)** ~**s** *pl (esp Pol: remonstrations)* Vorhaltungen *pl*; **the ambassador made ~s to the government** der Botschafter wurde bei der Regierung vorstellig.
**representative** [ˌreprɪˈzentətɪv] **1** *adj (of* für*)* repräsentativ; *attitude also* typisch; *(symbolize also)* symbolisch. **2** *n (Comm)* Vertreter(in *f)* *m*; *(Jur)* Bevollmächtigte(r) *mf*; *(US Pol)* Abgeordnete(r) *mf* des Repräsentantenhauses.
**repress** [rɪˈpres] *vt revolt, population, laugh* unterdrücken; *emotions, desires also* zurückdrängen; *(Psych)* verdrängen.
**repressed** [rɪˈprest] *adj* unterdrückt; *(Psych)* verdrängt.
**repression** [rɪˈpreʃən] *n* Unterdrückung *f*; *(Psych)* Verdrängung *f.*
**repressive** [rɪˈpresɪv] *adj* repressiv.
**reprieve** [rɪˈpriːv] **1** *n (Jur)* Begnadigung *f*; *(postponement)* Strafaufschub *m*; *(fig)* Gnadenfrist *f.* **2** *vt* **he was ~d** *(Jur)* er wurde begnadigt; *(sentence postponed)* seine Strafe wurde aufgeschoben; **the building/firm has been ~d for a while** das Gebäude/die Firma ist vorerst noch einmal verschont geblieben.
**reprimand** [ˈreprɪmɑːnd] **1** *n* Tadel *m*; *(official also)* Verweis *m.* **2** *vt* tadeln.
**reprint** [ˌriːˈprɪnt] **1** *vt* neu auflegen, nachdrucken. **2** [ˈriːprɪnt] *n* Neuauflage *f*, Nachdruck *m.*
**reprisal** [rɪˈpraɪzəl] *n (for* gegen*)* Vergeltungsmaßnahme *f*, Repressalie *f.* **to take ~s** zu Repressalien greifen; **as a ~ for** als Vergeltung für.
**reproach** [rɪˈprəʊtʃ] **1** *n (rebuke)* Vorwurf *m.* **above *or* beyond ~** über jeden Vorwurf erhaben. **2** *vt* Vorwürfe machen *(+dat)*. **to ~ sb for a mistake** jdm einen Fehler vorwerfen; **to ~ sb for having done sth** jdm Vorwürfe dafür machen, daß er etw getan hat.
**reproachful** [rɪˈprəʊtʃfʊl] *adj* vorwurfsvoll.
**reprobate** [ˈreprəʊbeɪt] *n* verkommenes Subjekt.
**reprocessing plant** [rɪˈprəʊsesɪŋˌplɑːnt] *n* Wiederaufbereitungsanlage *f.*
**reproduce** [ˌriːprəˈdjuːs] **1** *vt* wiedergeben; *(Art, mechanically also)* reproduzieren. **2** *vi (Biol)* sich

vermehren.
**reproduction** [ˌriːprəˈdʌkʃən] *n* **(a)** *(procreation)* Fortpflanzung *f.* **(b)** *(copy)* Reproduktion *f*; *(photo)* Kopie *f*; *(sound~)* Wiedergabe *f.* ~ **furniture** Stilmöbel *pl.*
**reproof¹** [ˌriːˈpruːf] *vt garment* frisch imprägnieren.
**reproof²** [rɪˈpruːf] *n* Tadel *m*, Rüge *f.*
**reprove** [rɪˈpruːv] *vt person, action* tadeln.
**reptile** [ˈreptaɪl] *n* Reptil *nt.*
**republic** [rɪˈpʌblɪk] *n* Republik *f.*
**republican, Republican** [rɪˈpʌblɪkən] **1** *adj* republikanisch. **2** *n* Republikaner(in *f)* *m.*
**repudiate** [rɪˈpjuːdɪeɪt] *vt person* verstoßen; *authorship, debt, obligation* nicht anerkennen; *accusation* zurückweisen.
**repudiation** [rɪˌpjuːdɪˈeɪʃən] *n see vt* Verstoßung *f*; Nichtanerkennung *f*; Zurückweisung *f.*
**repugnance** [rɪˈpʌɡnəns] *n* Widerwille *m (towards, for* gegen*)*.
**repugnant** [rɪˈpʌɡnənt] *adj* widerlich, abstoßend.
**repulse** [rɪˈpʌls] *vt (Mil)* enemy abwehren.
**repulsion** [rɪˈpʌlʃən] *n (distaste)* Widerwille *m (for* gegen*)*.
**repulsive** [rɪˈpʌlsɪv] *adj (loathsome)* abstoßend.
**repurchase** [riːˈpɜːtʃəs] *n* Rückkauf *m.*
**reputable** [ˈrepjʊtəbl] *adj* ehrenhaft; *occupation* ordentlich, anständig; *dealer, firm* seriös.
**reputation** [ˌrepjʊˈteɪʃən] *n* Ruf *m*; *(bad ~)* schlechter Ruf. **what sort of ~ does she have?** wie ist ihr Ruf?; **to have a ~ for honesty** als ehrlich gelten.
**repute** [rɪˈpjuːt] **1** *n* Ruf *m*, Ansehen *nt.* **to be of good ~** einen guten Ruf genießen; **to be held in high ~** in hohem Ansehen stehen. **2** *vt (pass only)* **he is ~d to be …** man sagt, daß er … ist.
**reputedly** [rɪˈpjuːtɪdlɪ] *adj* wie man annimmt. **he is ~ the best player** er gilt als der beste Spieler.
**request** [rɪˈkwest] **1** *n* Bitte *f*, Ersuchen *nt (geh)*. **at sb's ~** auf jds Bitte; **by ~** auf Wunsch; **to make a ~ for sth** um etw bitten. **2** *vt* bitten um; *(Rad)* record sich *(dat)* wünschen. **to ~ sth of sb** *(form)* jdn um etw bitten *or* ersuchen *(geh)*; **to ~ sb to do sth** jdn darum bitten, etw zu tun; **"you are ~ed not to smoke"** „bitte nicht rauchen".
**request stop** *n (Brit)* Bedarfshaltestelle *f.*
**requiem** [ˈrekwɪem] *n* Requiem *nt.*
**require** [rɪˈkwaɪə*] *vt* **(a)** *(need)* brauchen, benötigen; *action, care* erfordern; *(desire)* wünschen. **I have all I ~** ich habe alles, was ich brauche; **what qualifications are ~d?** welche Qualifikationen werden verlangt?; **it ~s attention** *or* **repairing** es müßte repariert werden; **to be ~d to do sth** etw machen müssen; **if ~d** falls erforderlich; **as and when ~d** nach Bedarf. **(b)** *(order)* **to ~ sb to do sth** von jdm verlangen, daß er/sie etw tut; **to ~ sth of sb** etw von jdm verlangen.
**required** [rɪˈkwaɪəd] *adj* erforderlich; *date* vorgeschrieben; *(desired)* gewünscht. **the ~ amount** die benötigte Menge.
**requirement** [rɪˈkwaɪəmənt] *n (need)* Bedarf *m no pl*; *(desire)* Wunsch *m*; *(condition, thing required)* Erfordernis *nt.* **to meet sb's ~s** jds Ansprüchen gerecht werden; **to fit the ~s** den Erfordernissen entsprechen.
**requisite** [ˈrekwɪzɪt] **1** *n* Erfordernis *nt.* **toilet ~s** Toilettenartikel *pl.* **2** *adj* erforderlich.
**requisition** [ˌrekwɪˈzɪʃən] *n* Anforderung *f*; *(Mil)* Requisition *f.* **to make a ~ for sth** etw anfordern. **2** *vt* anfordern; *(Mil)* supplies requirieren.
**reroute** [ˌriːˈruːt] *vt train, bus* umleiten.
**rerun** [ˌriːˈrʌn] **1** *vt race* wiederholen. **2** [ˈriːrʌn] *n* Wiederholung *f.*

**resale** ['riːˌseɪl] *n* Weiterverkauf *m*. ~ **price maintenance** Preisbindung *f*.

**reschedule** [riːˈʃedjuːl] *vt* auf eine neue Zeit festlegen. **to be ~d for tomorrow morning** auf morgen früh verlegt werden.

**rescind** [rɪˈsɪnd] *vt* rückgängig machen; *law* aufheben.

**rescue** ['reskjuː] **1** *n (saving)* Rettung *f*; *(freeing)* Befreiung *f*. ~ **party** Rettungsmannschaft *f*; **to go/come to sb's** ~ jdm zu Hilfe kommen. **2** *vt (save)* retten; *(free)* befreien. **you ~d me from a difficult situation** du hast mich aus einer schwierigen Lage gerettet.

**rescuer** ['reskjʊəʳ] *n see vt* Retter(in *f*) *m*; Befreier(in *f*) *m*.

**research** [rɪˈsɜːtʃ] **1** *n* Forschung *f (into, on* über +*acc)*. **a piece of** ~ eine Forschungsarbeit; **to do** ~ forschen, Forschung betreiben; ~ **and development** Forschung und Entwicklung. **2** *vi* forschen. **3** *vt* erforschen, untersuchen. **a well-~ed book** ein Buch das auf solider Forschungsarbeit beruht.

**research assistant** *n* wissenschaftliche Hilfskraft.

**researcher** [rɪˈsɜːtʃəʳ] *n* Forscher(in *f*) *m*.

**research:** ~ **student** *n (Univ)* Student, der *Forschungen für einen höheren akademischen Grad betreibt*; ~ **worker** *n* Forscher *m*.

**resemblance** [rɪˈzembləns] *n* Ähnlichkeit *f*. **to bear a strong/no** ~ **to sb/sth** starke/keine Ähnlichkeit mit jdm/etw haben.

**resemble** [rɪˈzembl] *vt* gleichen *(+dat)*, ähnlich sein *(+dat)*.

**resent** [rɪˈzent] *vt remarks, behaviour* sich ärgern über *(+acc)*; *person* eine Abneigung haben gegen. **he ~ed the fact that ...** er ärgerte sich darüber, daß ...; **to** ~ **sb's success** jdm seinen Erfolg mißgönnen; **I** ~ **that** das gefällt mir nicht.

**resentful** [rɪˈzentfʊl] *adj* verärgert *(of* über +*acc)*; *(jealous)* neidisch *(of* auf +*acc)*. **he felt** ~ **about her promotion** er nahm es ihr übel, daß sie befördert worden war.

**resentment** [rɪˈzentmənt] *(of* über +*acc)* Verärgerung *f*; *(jealousy)* Neid *m*.

**reservation** [ˌrezəˈveɪʃən] *n* **(a)** *(qualification of opinion)* Vorbehalt *m*. **without** ~ ohne Vorbehalt. **with ~s** unter Vorbehalt(en); **to have ~s about sb/sth** Bedenken in bezug auf jdn/etw haben. **(b)** *(booking)* Reservierung *f*. **to make a** ~ **at the hotel** ein Zimmer im Hotel reservieren lassen; **to have a** ~ **(for a room)** ein Zimmer reserviert haben; ~ **desk** Reservierungsschalter *m*; *(US: in hotel)* Rezeption *f*. **(c)** *(area of land)* Reservat *nt*. **(central)** ~ *(Brit: on motorway)* Mittelstreifen *m*.

**reserve** [rɪˈzɜːv] **1** *vt* **(a)** *(keep)* aufsparen, aufheben. **to** ~ **one's strength** seine Kräfte sparen; **to** ~ **judgement** mit einem Urteil zurückhalten; **to** ~ **the right to do sth** sich *(dat)* (das Recht) vorbehalten, etw zu tun. **(b)** *(book in advance)* reservieren lassen. **2** *n* **(a)** *(store) (of* an +*dat)* Reserve *f*, Vorrat *m*; *(Fin)* Reserve *f*. **cash** ~ Barreserve *f*; **world ~s of copper** die Weltreserven *pl* an Kupfer; **to have/keep in** ~ in Reserve haben/halten. **(b) without** ~ ohne Vorbehalt. **(c)** *(piece of land)* Reservat *nt*. **(d)** *(coolness, reticence)* Reserve *f*. **he treated me with some** ~ er behandelte mich etwas reserviert. **(e)** *(Mil: force)* Reserve *f*. **the ~s** die Reserveeinheiten. **(f)** *(Sport)* Reservespieler(in *f*) *m*. **the ~s** die Reserve(mannschaft).

**reserved** [rɪˈzɜːvd] *adj* **(a)** *(reticent)* zurückhaltend *(about* in bezug auf +*acc)*. **(b)** *room, seat* reserviert. **(c) all rights** ~ alle Rechte vorbehalten.

**reserve:** ~ **price** *n* Mindest- *or* Ausrufpreis *m*; ~

**team** *n* Reserve(mannschaft) *f*.

**reservist** [rɪˈzɜːvɪst] *n (Mil)* Reservist *m*.

**reservoir** ['rezəvwɑːʳ] *n (lit) (for water)* Reservoir *nt*; *(fig: of talent etc)* Fundgrube *f (of* an +*dat)*.

**reset** [ˌriːˈset] *pret, ptp* ~ *vt (readjust)* neu einstellen; *watch etc* neu stellen *(to* auf +*acc)*; *(put back) dial, mileometer* zurückstellen *(to* auf +*acc)*; *(Comp)* rücksetzen.

**resettle** [ˌriːˈsetl] *vt refugees* umsiedeln.

**reshape** [ˌriːˈʃeɪp] *vt* umformen.

**reshuffle** [ˌriːˈʃʌfl] *n* **Cabinet** ~ *(Pol)* Kabinettsumbildung *f*.

**reside** [rɪˈzaɪd] *vi* **(a)** *(form: live)* seinen Wohnsitz haben; *(monarch etc)* residieren. **(b)** *(fig)* **the power ~s in the President** die Macht ruht beim Präsidenten.

**residence** ['rezɪdəns] *n* **(a)** *(house)* Wohnhaus *nt*; *(hostel: for students, nurses)* Wohnheim *nt*; *(of monarch, ambassador etc)* Residenz *f*. **(b)** *no pl* **country/place of** ~ Aufenthaltsland *nt*/Wohnort *m*; **after 5 years'** ~ **in Britain** nach 5 Jahren Aufenthalt in Großbritannien; **to take up** ~ **in the capital** sich in der Hauptstadt niederlassen; **to be in** ~ *(monarch, governor etc)* anwesend sein; ~ **permit** Aufenthaltsgenehmigung *f*.

**resident** ['rezɪdənt] **1** *n* Bewohner(in *f*) *m*; *(in town also)* Einwohner(in *f*) *m*; *(of institution also)* Insasse *m*, Insassin *f*; *(in hotel)* Gast *m*. **2** *adj (in country, town)* wohnhaft; *tutor* Haus-; *physician* Anstalts-. **they are ~ in Germany** sie haben ihren Wohnsitz in Deutschland.

**residential** [ˌrezɪˈdenʃəl] *adj area* Wohn-; *job* im Haus; *college* mit einem Wohnheim verbunden; *course* mit Wohnung im Heim.

**residual** [rɪˈzɪdjʊəl] *adj* restlich, Rest-.

**residue** ['rezɪdjuː] *n* Rest *m*; *(Chem)* Rückstand *m*.

**resign** [rɪˈzaɪn] **1** *vt* **(a)** *(give up)* office, post zurücktreten von; *claim, rights* verzichten auf *(+acc)*. **to** ~ **power** abtreten. **(b) to** ~ **oneself to sth/to doing sth** sich mit etw abfinden/sich damit abfinden, etw zu tun. **2** *vi (from public appointment)* zurücktreten; *(employee)* kündigen. **to** ~ **from office** sein Amt niederlegen.

**resignation** [ˌrezɪgˈneɪʃən] *n* **(a)** *see vi* Rücktritt *m*; Kündigung *f*. **to hand in** *or* **tender** *(form)* **one's** ~ seinen Rücktritt/seine Kündigung einreichen/sein Amt niederlegen. **(b)** *(mental state)* Resignation *f (to* gegenüber +*dat)*.

**resigned** [rɪˈzaɪnd] *adj smile* resigniert. **to become** ~ **to sth** sich mit etw abfinden; **to be** ~ **to one's fate** sich in sein Schicksal ergeben haben.

**resilience** [rɪˈzɪlɪəns] *n see adj* Federn *nt*; Unverwüstlichkeit *f*.

**resilient** [rɪˈzɪlɪənt] *adj* **(a)** *material* federnd attr. **to be** ~ federn. **(b)** *(fig)* person, nature unverwüstlich.

**resin** ['rezɪn] *n* Harz *nt*.

**resist** [rɪˈzɪst] **1** *vt* **(a)** sich widersetzen *(+dat)*; *arrest, advances, attack, proposal, change also* sich wehren gegen. **(b)** *temptation, sb* widerstehen *(+dat)*. **I couldn't** ~ **(eating) another piece of cake** ich konnte der Versuchung nicht widerstehen, noch ein Stück Kuchen zu essen. **(c)** *(wall, door)* standhalten *(+dat)*. **2** *vi see vt* **(a)** sich widersetzen; sich wehren. **(b)** widerstehen.

**resistance** [rɪˈzɪstəns] *n (to* gegen) Widerstand *m (also Elec, Phys, Mil)*; *(Med)* Widerstandsfähigkeit *f (to* gegen). **(powers of)** ~ Widerstandskraft *f*; ~ **to water/heat** Wasser-/Hitzebeständigkeit *f*; **to meet with** ~ auf Widerstand stoßen; **to offer no** ~ **(to sb/sth)** *(to attacker, advances etc)* (jdm/gegen etw) keinen Widerstand leisten.

**resistant** [rɪ'zɪstənt] *adj material* strapazierfähig; *(Med)* immun *(to* gegen). **water-~** wasserbeständig.
**resit** [,ri:'sɪt] *(pret, ptp resat) vt exam* wiederholen.
**resolute** ['rezəlu:t] *adj* energisch; *answer* entschieden, bestimmt.
**resolution** [,rezə'lu:ʃən] *n* **(a)** *(decision)* Beschluß *m*; *(Pol, Admin etc also)* Resolution *f*; *(governing one's behaviour)* Vorsatz *m.* **good ~s** gute Vorsätze *pl.* **(b)** *no pl (resoluteness)* Entschlossenheit *f.* **(c)** *no pl (of problem)* Lösung *f.* **(d)** *(Phys, Mus)* Auflösung *f (into* in *+acc); (TV, Comp)* (Bild)auflösung *f.*
**resolve** [rɪ'zɒlv] **1** *vt* **(a)** *problem* lösen; *doubt* zerstreuen. **(b)** *(decide)* **to ~ that** ... beschließen, daß ...; **to ~ to do sth** beschließen, etw zu tun. **2** *n* **(a)** *(decision)* Beschluß *m.* **to make a ~ to do sth** den Beschluß fassen, etw zu tun. **(b)** *(resoluteness)* Entschlossenheit *f.*
**resolved** [rɪ'zɒlvd] *adj* (fest) entschlossen.
**resonance** ['rezənəns] *n* Resonanz *f; (of voice)* voller Klang.
**resonant** ['rezənənt] *adj sound* voll; *voice* klangvoll; *room* mit Resonanz.
**resort** [rɪ'zɔːt] **1** *n* **(a)** *(recourse)* Ausweg *m; (thing, action resorted to also)* Rettung *f.* **without ~ to violence** ohne Gewaltanwendung; **as a last ~** wenn es nicht anders geht; **in the last ~** im schlimmsten Fall. **(b)** *(place)* Urlaubsort *m.* **seaside ~** Seebad *nt*; **ski ~** Wintersportort *m.* **2** *vi* **to ~ to sth/sb** zu etw greifen/sich an jdn wenden; **to ~ to violence/theft** gewalttätig/zum Dieb werden; **to ~ to lying/swearing** sich aufs Lügen/Fluchen verlegen.
**resound** [rɪ'zaʊnd] *vi* (wider)hallen *(with* von).
**resounding** [rɪ'zaʊndɪŋ] *adj noise, shout* widerhallend; *(fig) victory* gewaltig; *success* durchschlagend; *defeat* haushoch. **the response was a ~ "no"** die Antwort war ein überwältigendes „Nein".
**resource** [rɪ'sɔːs] *n* **(a)** **~s** *pl (wealth, supplies, money etc)* Mittel, Ressourcen *pl*; **financial/mineral/natural ~s** Geldmittel *pl*/Bodenschätze *pl*/Naturschätze *pl*; **left to one's own ~s** sich *(dat)* selbst überlassen. **(b)** *(expedient)* Mittel *nt.* **as a last ~** wenn es nicht anders geht; **a valuable (teaching) ~** ein nützliches Lehrmittel.
**resourceful** [rɪ'sɔːsfʊl] *adv person* einfallsreich, findig; *scheme* genial.
**resourcefulness** [rɪ'sɔːsfʊlnɪs] *n* Einfallsreichtum *m*, Findigkeit *f.*
**respect** [rɪ'spekt] **1** *n* **(a)** *(esteem)* Respekt *m*, Achtung *f (for* vor *+dat).* **to have/show ~ for** Respekt haben/zeigen vor *(+dat);* **I have the highest ~ for his ability** ich halte ihn für außerordentlich fähig; **to hold sb in great ~** jdn sehr achten. **(b)** *(consideration)* Rücksicht *f (for* auf *+acc).* **to treat with ~** *person* rücksichtsvoll behandeln; *dangerous person etc* sich in acht nehmen vor *(+dat);* **out of ~ for** aus Rücksicht auf *(+acc);* **with (due) ~, I still think that** ... bei allem Respekt meine ich dennoch, daß ... **(c)** *(reference)* **with ~ to** ... was ... anbetrifft, in bezug auf ... *(+acc).* **(d)** *(aspect)* Hinsicht, Beziehung *f.* **in many ~s** in vielerlei Hinsicht. **(e)** **~s** *pl (regards)* Empfehlungen *(geh)*, Grüße *pl*; **to pay one's last ~s to sb** jdm die letzte Ehre erweisen.
**2** *vt* respektieren; *person, customs, privacy also* achten; *ability* anerkennen. **a ~ed company** eine angesehene Firma.
**respectability** [rɪ,spektə'bɪlɪtɪ] *n see adj* **(a)** Ehrbarkeit *f*; Ehrenhaftigkeit *f*; Anständigkeit *f*; Korrektheit *f.*
**respectable** [rɪ'spektəbl] *adj* **(a)** *person* ehrbar; *motives also* ehrenhaft; *district* anständig; *clothes, behaviour* korrekt. **in ~ society** in guter Gesellschaft.

**(b)** *(large) income* ansehnlich. **(c)** *(fairly good) advantage* beträchtlich; *score* beachtlich.
**respectably** [rɪ'spektəblɪ] *adv dress, behave* anständig.
**respectful** *adj*, **~ly** *adv* [rɪ'spektfʊl, -əlɪ] respektvoll *(towards* gegenüber).
**respecting** [rɪ'spektɪŋ] *prep* bezüglich *(+gen).*
**respective** [rɪ'spektɪv] *adj* jeweilig.
**respectively** [rɪ'spektɪvlɪ] *adv* **they cost £50 and £60 ~** sie kosten £50 beziehungsweise £60.
**respiration** [,respɪ'reɪʃən] *n (Bot, Med)* Atmung *f.*
**respirator** ['respɪreɪtər] *n (Med)* Beatmungsgerät *nt*; *(Mil)* Atemschutzgerät *nt.*
**respiratory** [rɪ'spaɪərətərɪ] *adj* Atem-; *organs, problem* Atmungs-.
**respite** ['respaɪt] *n (easing off)* Nachlassen *nt.* **without ~** ohne Unterbrechung; **to give sb no ~** jdm keine Ruhe lassen.
**resplendent** [rɪ'splendənt] *adj* glänzend, strahlend; *clothes* prächtig.
**respond** [rɪ'spɒnd] *vi* **(a)** *(reply)* antworten. **to ~ to a question** eine Frage beantworten. **(b)** *(show reaction)* reagieren *(to* auf *+acc).* **to ~ to an appeal** einen Appell beantworten; **to ~ to a call** einem Ruf folgen; **the patient did not ~ to the treatment** der Patient sprach auf die Behandlung nicht an.
**response** [rɪ'spɒns] *n (reply)* Antwort, Erwiderung *f*; *(reaction)* Reaktion *f*; *(Eccl)* Antwort *f.* **in ~ (to)** in Erwiderung *(+gen)* (geh).
**responsibility** [rɪ,spɒnsə'bɪlɪtɪ] *n* **(a)** *no pl* Verantwortung *f.* **to take (full) ~ (for sth)** die (volle) Verantwortung (für etw) übernehmen; **that's his ~** dafür ist er verantwortlich. **(b)** *(duty, burden)* Verpflichtung *f (to* für).
**responsible** [rɪ'spɒnsəbl] *adj* **(a)** verantwortlich; *(to blame also)* schuld *(for* an *+dat).* **what's ~ for the hold-up?** woran liegt die Verzögerung?; **she is not ~ for her actions** *(esp Jur)* sie ist nicht zurechnungsfähig. **to hold sb ~ for sth** jdn für etw verantwortlich machen; **to be directly ~ to sb** jdm unmittelbar unterstellt sein. **(b)** *(trustworthy)* verantwortungsbewußt; *(involving responsibility) job* verantwortungsvoll.
**responsibly** [rɪ'spɒnsəblɪ] *adv act* verantwortungsbewußt.
**responsive** [rɪ'spɒnsɪv] *adj person, audience* interessiert; *steering* leicht ansprechend. **to be ~ to sth** auf etw *(acc)* reagieren *or* ansprechen; **he wasn't very ~ (to my complaint)** er ging kaum darauf ein.
**rest¹** [rest] **1** *n* **(a)** *(relaxation)* Ruhe *f; (pause)* Pause *f; (on holiday etc)* Erholung *f.* **a day of ~** ein Ruhetag *m*; **to need ~** Ruhe brauchen; **I need a ~** ich muß mich ausruhen; *(vacation)* ich brauche Urlaub; **to have a ~** *(relax)* (sich) ausruhen; *(pause)* (eine) Pause machen.
**(b)** **to be at ~** *(peaceful)* ruhig sein; *(immobile)* sich in Ruhelage/-stellung befinden; *(euph: dead)* ruhen; **to put** *or* **set sb's mind at ~** jdn beruhigen; **to come to ~** *(ball, car etc)* zum Stillstand kommen; *(bird, insect)* sich niederlassen; *(gaze, eyes)* hängenbleiben *(upon* an *+dat).*
**(c)** *(Mus)* Pause *f.*
**2** *vi* **(a)** sich ausruhen; *(pause)* Pause machen; *(euph: be buried)* ruhen. **he will not ~ until he discovers the truth** er wird nicht (eher) ruhen, bis er die Wahrheit herausgefunden hat; **to let a matter ~** eine Sache auf sich beruhen lassen; **may he ~ in peace** er ruhe in Frieden.
**(b)** *(decision, responsibility etc)* liegen *(with* bei). **the matter must not ~ there** man kann die Sache so nicht belassen; **~ assured that** ... Sie können ver-

sichert sein, daß ...

  (c) *(lean: person, head, ladder)* lehnen *(on* an *+dat, against* gegen*)*; *(roof etc, eyes, gaze)* ruhen *(on* auf *+dat)*; *(fig: be based) (argument, case)* sich stützen *(on* auf *+acc)*; *(reputation)* beruhen *(on* auf *+dat)*.

  **3** *vt* one's eyes ausruhen; *voice* schonen; *horses* ausruhen lassen; *ladder* lehnen *(against* gegen, *on* an *+acc)*; *elbow, (fig)* theory, suspicions stützen *(on* auf *+acc)*. **God ~ his soul** Gott hab ihn selig!

**rest²** *n (remainder)* **the ~** der Rest, das übrige/die übrigen; **the ~ of the money/meal** das übrige Geld/Essen; **the ~ of us/them** die übrigen, die anderen; **all the ~ of the money** das ganze übrige Geld; **all the ~ of the books** alle übrigen Bücher; **and all the ~ of it** *(col)* und so weiter und so fort; **for the ~** im übrigen.

**restart** [ˌriːˈstɑːt] **1** *vt* activity wieder aufnehmen; *engine* wieder anlassen; *machine* wieder anschalten. **2** *vi* wieder anfangen; *(engine)* wieder anspringen.

**restaurant** [ˈrɛstərɔ̃ːŋ] *n* Restaurant *nt*. **~ car** *(Brit Rail)* Speisewagen *m*.

**restaurateur** [ˌrɛstərəˈtɜːʳ] *n* Gastwirt, Gastronom*m*.

**rest:** **~ cure** *n* Erholung *f*; *(in bed)* Liegekur *f*; **~ day** *n* Ruhetag *m*.

**restful** [ˈrɛstful] *adj* occupation, pastime etc erholsam; *colour* ruhig; *place* friedlich.

**rest-home** [ˈrɛstˌhəʊm] *n* Pflegeheim *nt*.

**resting place** [ˈrɛstɪŋˌpleɪs] *n* Rastplatz *m*. **last ~** letzte Ruhestätte *f*.

**restive** [ˈrɛstɪv] *adj* unruhig; *(restless)* person, manner rastlos.

**restless** [ˈrɛstlɪs] *adj* person, sea unruhig; *(not wanting to stay in one place)* rastlos.

**restock** [ˌriːˈstɒk] *vt* **to ~ (a shop)** die Bestände (eines Geschäfts) wieder auffüllen.

**restoration** [ˌrɛstəˈreɪʃən] *n* **(a)** *(return)* Rückgabe *f (to* an *+acc)*; *(of property also)* Rückerstattung *f (to* an *+acc)*; *(of confidence, order)* Wiederherstellung *f*; *(to office)* Wiedereinsetzung *f (to* in *+acc)*. **(b) the R~** *(Hist)* die Restauration. **(c)** *(of monument, work of art etc)* Restaurierung, Restauration *f*.

**restorative** [rɪˈstɔːrətɪv] *adj* stärkend.

**restore** [rɪˈstɔːʳ] *vt* **(a)** *(give back)* zurückgeben; *confidence, order* wiederherstellen. **to ~ sb to health** jds Gesundheit wiederherstellen; **~d to health** wiederhergestellt; **to ~ sth to its former condition** etw wiederherstellen. **(b)** *(to former post)* wiedereinsetzen *(to* in *+acc)*. **to ~ to power** wieder an die Macht bringen. **(c)** *(renovate)* restaurieren.

**restorer** [rɪˈstɔːrəʳ] *n (Art)* Restaurator(in *f) m*.

**restrain** [rɪˈstreɪn] *vt* person zurückhalten; *prisoner* mit Gewalt festhalten; *animal, children* bändigen. **to ~ sb from doing sth** jdn davon abhalten, etw zu tun; **to ~ oneself** sich beherrschen.

**restrained** [rɪˈstreɪnd] *adj* emotions unterdrückt; *manner, words* beherrscht; *tone* verhalten; *criticism* maßvoll.

**restraint** [rɪˈstreɪnt] *n* **(a)** *(restriction)* Einschränkung, Beschränkung *f*. **without ~** unbeschränkt; **develop ungehemmt; wage ~** Zurückhaltung *f* bei Lohnforderungen. **(b)** *(moderation)* Beherrschung *f*. **to show a lack of ~** wenig Beherrschung zeigen. **(c)** *(head ~)* Kopfstütze *f*.

**restrict** [rɪˈstrɪkt] *vt* beschränken *(to* auf *+acc)*; *time, number also* begrenzen *(to* auf *+acc)*.

**restricted** [rɪˈstrɪktɪd] *adj* view beschränkt, begrenzt; *(Admin, Mil)* information geheim; *locality* nur bestimmten Gruppen zugänglich. **~ area** *(Brit Mot)* Strecke *f* mit Geschwindigkeitsbeschränkung;

*(Mil etc)* Sperrgebiet *nt*.

**restriction** [rɪˈstrɪkʃən] *n see vt (on gen)* Beschränkung *f*; Begrenzung *f*. **without ~s** uneingeschränkt; **price ~** Preisbeschränkung *f*.

**restrictive** [rɪˈstrɪktɪv] *adj* restriktiv, einschränkend *attr*.

**rest room** [ˈrɛstˌruːm] *n (US)* Toilette *f*.

**restructure** [ˌriːˈstrʌktʃəʳ] *vt* umstrukturieren.

**rest stop** *n (US Mot)* Rastplatz *m*.

**restyle** [ˌriːˈstaɪl] *vt* neu stylen.

**result** [rɪˈzʌlt] **1** *n* **(a)** Folge *f*. **as a ~ he failed** folglich fiel er durch; **as a ~ of which he ...** was zur Folge hatte, daß er ...; **to be the ~ of** resultieren aus. **(b)** *(outcome)* Ergebnis, Resultat *nt*. **~s** *(of test, experiment)* Werte *pl*; **to get ~s** *(person)* Resultate erzielen; **as a ~ of my inquiry** auf meine Anfrage (hin); **what was the ~?** *(Sport)* wie ist es ausgegangen?; **without ~** ergebnislos. **2** *vi* sich ergeben, resultieren *(from* aus*)*.

  ▶**result in** *vi +prep obj* führen zu. **this ~ed ~ his being late** das führte dazu, daß er zu spät kam.

**resultant** [rɪˈzʌltənt] *adj* resultierend.

**resume** [rɪˈzjuːm] **1** *vt* **(a)** *(restart)* activity wiederaufnehmen; *journey* fortsetzen. **to ~ work** die Arbeit wiederaufnehmen. **(b)** *command, possession* wieder übernehmen. **to ~ one's seat** seinen Platz wieder einnehmen. **2** *vi (classes, work etc)* wieder beginnen.

**résumé** [ˈreɪzjuːmeɪ] *n* Zusammenfassung *f*; *(US: curriculum vitae)* Lebenslauf *m*.

**resumption** [rɪˈzʌmpʃən] *n (of activity)* Wiederaufnahme *f*; *(of command, possession)* erneute Übernahme *f*; *(of journey)* Fortsetzung *f*; *(of classes)* Wiederbeginn *m*.

**resurface** [ˌriːˈsɜːfɪs] *vt* **to ~ a road** den Belag einer Straße erneuern.

**resurgence** [rɪˈsɜːdʒəns] *n* Wiederaufleben *nt*.

**resurrection** [ˌrɛzəˈrɛkʃən] *n (revival)* Wiederbelebung *f*; *(Rel)* Auferstehung *f*.

**resuscitate** [rɪˈsʌsɪteɪt] *vt (Med)* wiederbeleben; *(fig)* beleben.

**resuscitation** [rɪˌsʌsɪˈteɪʃən] *n (Med)* Wiederbelebung *f*; *(fig)* Belebung *f*.

**retail** [ˈriːteɪl] **1** *n* Einzelhandel *m*. **2** *vt* im Einzelhandel verkaufen. **3** *vi (goods)* **to ~ at ...** im Einzelhandel ... kosten. **4** *adv* im Einzelhandel.

**retailer** [ˈriːteɪləʳ] *n* Einzelhändler *m*.

**retail:** **~ outlet** *n* Einzelhandelsverkaufsstelle *f*; **~ price** *n* Einzelhandelspreis *m*; **~ price index** *n* Einzelhandelspreisindex *m*.

**retain** [rɪˈteɪn] *vt* **(a)** *(keep)* behalten; *money, possession, person* zurück(be)halten; *custom* bewahren; *(dam)* water stauen. **to ~ control (of sth)** etw weiterhin in der Gewalt haben. **(b)** *(remember)* sich *(dat)* merken; *(computer)* information speichern.

**retainer** [rɪˈteɪnəʳ] *n (fee)* Honorar *nt*; *(advance)* Vorschuß *m*.

**retake** [riːˈteɪk] *pret* **retook,** *ptp* **retaken** *vt (Mil)* town zurückerobern; *(Film)* nochmals aufnehmen; *(Sch, Sport)* exam, penalty wiederholen.

**retaliate** [rɪˈtælɪeɪt] *vi* Vergeltung üben; *(for bad treatment, insults etc)* sich revanchieren *(against sb* an jdm*)*; *(in battle)* zurückschlagen; *(Sport, in fight, in argument)* kontern.

**retaliation** [rɪˌtælɪˈeɪʃən] *n* Vergeltung *f*; *(in fight also)* Vergeltungsschlag *m*; *(in argument, diplomacy etc)* Konterschlag *m*. **in ~** zur Vergeltung; **that's my ~ for what you did** das ist meine Revanche für das, was du getan hast.

**retarded** [rɪˈtɑːdɪd] *adj (Med)* zurückgeblieben.

**retch** [rɛtʃ] *vi* würgen.

**retd** = **retired** a.D.

**retell** [rɪ'tel] *vt pret, ptp* **retold** wiederholen; *old legend* nacherzählen.

**retention** [rɪ'tenʃən] *n* Beibehaltung *f*; *(of possession)* Zurückhaltung *f*; *(of water, Comp: information)* Speicherung *f*.

**retentive** [rɪ'tentɪv] *adj memory* aufnahmefähig.

**rethink** [,ri:'θɪŋk] *vt pret, ptp* **rethought** [ri:'θɔːt] überdenken.

**reticence** ['retɪsəns] *n* Zurückhaltung *f*.

**reticent** ['retɪsənt] *adj* zurückhaltend.

**retina** ['retɪnə] *n, pl* **-e** ['retɪniː] *or* **-s** Netzhaut *f*.

**retinue** ['retɪnjuː] *n* Gefolge *nt*.

**retire** [rɪ'taɪəʳ] **1** *vi* **(a)** *(give up work)* aufhören zu arbeiten; *(civil servant)* sich pensionieren lassen; *(self-employed)* sich zur Ruhe setzen; *(soldier)* aus der Armee ausscheiden; *(singer, player etc)* (zu singen/spielen *etc)* aufhören. **(b)** *(withdraw, Mil)* sich zurückziehen; *(Sport)* aufgeben; *(Ftbl etc)* vom Feld gehen. **to ~ into oneself** sich in sich *(acc)* (selbst) zurückziehen. **2** *vt* aus Altersgründen entlassen; *civil servant, military officer* pensionieren, in den Ruhestand versetzen.

**retired** [rɪ'taɪəd] *adj* **(a)** pensioniert, im Ruhestand; *soldier* aus der Armee ausgeschieden. **(b)** *(secluded)* life zurückgezogen.

**retiree** [,rɪtaɪ'riː] *n (US)* Rentner(in *f*) *m*.

**retirement** [rɪ'taɪəmənt] *n (stopping work)* Ausscheiden *nt* aus dem Arbeitsleben *(form)*; *(of civil servant, military officer)* Pensionierung *f*; *(state)* Ruhestand *m*. **~ at 65** Altersgrenze bei 65; **to announce one's ~** sein Ausscheiden (aus seinem Beruf/seiner Stellung *etc)* ankündigen; **how will you spend your ~?** was tun Sie, wenn Sie pensioniert *or* im Ruhestand sind?

**retirement: ~ age** *n* Rentenalter *nt*; *(of civil servant)* Pensionsalter *nt*; **~ pension** *n* Altersrente *f*; *(for civil servant)* Pension *f*.

**retiring** [rɪ'taɪərɪŋ] *adj* **(a)** *(shy)* zurückhaltend. **(b)** **~ age** = **retirement age.**

**retort** [rɪ'tɔːt] **1** *n* **(a)** *(answer)* scharfe Erwiderung *or* Antwort. **(b)** *(Chem)* Retorte *f*. **2** *vti* scharf erwidern.

**retouch** [,ri:'tʌtʃ] *vt (Art, Phot)* retuschieren.

**retrace** [rɪ'treɪs] *vt past, development* zurückverfolgen. **to ~ one's steps** denselben Weg zurückgehen.

**retract** [rɪ'trækt] **1** *vt (withdraw)* offer zurückziehen; *statement* zurücknehmen; *claws, undercarriage* einziehen. **2** *vi (claws)* eingezogen werden.

**retractable** [rɪ'træktəbl] *adj* einziehbar; *headlamp* versenkbar.

**retrain** [ri:'treɪn] *vt* umschulen.

**retraining** [ri:'treɪnɪŋ] *n* Umschulung *f*.

**retread** ['ri:,tred] *n (tyre)* laufflächenerneuerter Reifen.

**retreat** [rɪ'triːt] **1** *n* **(a)** *(Mil)* Rückzug *m*. **to beat a ~** *(Mil)* den Rückzug antreten; *(fig)* das Feld räumen. **(b)** *(place)* Zuflucht(sort *m) f*. **he has gone to his country ~** er hat sich aufs Land zurückgezogen. **2** *vi (Mil)* den Rückzug antreten; *(in fear)* zurückweichen; *(flood, glacier)* zurückgehen.

**retrench** [rɪ'trentʃ] **1** *vt expenditure* einschränken; *personnel* einsparen. **2** *vi* sich einschränken.

**retrial** [ri:'traɪəl] *n (Jur)* Wiederaufnahmeverfahren *nt*.

**retribution** [,retrɪ'bjuːʃən] *n* Vergeltung *f*. **in ~** als Vergeltung.

**retrieval** [rɪ'triːvəl] *n see vt* **(a)** Zurück-/Hervor-/Heraus-/Herunterholen *nt*; Rettung *f*; Bergung *f*; Rückgewinnung *f*; Abfragen *nt*; Wiedererlangen

*nt*; Wiedergutmachung *f*.

**retrieve** [rɪ'triːv] *vt* **(a)** *(recover)* zurück-/hervor-/heraus-/herunterholen; *(rescue)* retten; *(from wreckage etc)* bergen; *material from waste* zurückgewinnen; *(Comp)* information abfragen; *honour, position* wiedererlangen; *loss* wiedergutmachen. **(b)** *(dog)* apportieren.

**retriever** [rɪ'triːvəʳ] *n (dog)* Retriever *m*.

**retroactive** [,retrəu'æktɪv] *adj* rückwirkend.

**retrograde** ['retrəugreɪd] *adj* rückläufig; *policy* rückschrittlich. **~ step** Rückschritt *m*.

**retrorocket** ['retrəu'rɒkɪt] *n* Bremsrakete *f*.

**retrospect** ['retrəuspekt] *n* **in ~** im Rückblick; **everything looks different in ~** im nachhinein sieht alles anders aus.

**retrospective** [,retrəu'spektɪv] **1** *adj thought* rückblickend; *(Admin, Jur)* pay rise rückwirkend. **2** *n (also ~ exhibition)* Retrospektive *f*.

**retrospectively** [,retrəu'spektɪvlɪ] *adv* rückwirkend.

**return** [rɪ'tɜːn] **1** *vi (come back: person, vehicle)* zurück- *or* wiederkommen; *(go back)* *(person)* zurückgehen; *(vehicle)* zurückfahren; *(symptoms, doubts, fears)* wieder auftreten. **to ~ to a subject** auf ein Thema zurückkommen; **to ~ home** nach Hause kommen/gehen, heimkehren *(geh)*.

**2** *vt* **(a)** *(give back)* zurückgeben *(to sb* jdm*)*; *(bring or take back)* zurückbringen *(to sb* jdm*)*; *(put back)* zurücksetzen/-stellen/-legen; *(send back)* *(to an +acc)* letter etc zurückschicken; *(refuse)* cheque zurückweisen; *ball* zurückschlagen/-werfen; *salute, visit, compliment* erwidern. **to ~ goods to the shop** Waren in das Geschäft zurückbringen; **to ~ fire** *(Mil)* das Feuer erwidern.

**(b)** *(reply)* erwidern.

**(c)** *(declare)* details of income angeben. **to ~ a verdict of guilty/not guilty (on sb)** *(Jur)* (jdn) schuldig sprechen/freisprechen.

**(d)** *(Fin)* income einbringen; *profit, interest* abwerfen.

**(e)** *(Brit Parl)* candidate wählen.

**3** *n* **(a)** *(of person, vehicle, seasons)* Rückkehr *f*; *(of illness)* Wiederauftreten *nt*. **on my ~** bei meiner Rückkehr; **by ~ (of post)** postwendend; **many happy ~s (of the day)!** herzlichen Glückwunsch zum Geburtstag!

**(b)** *(giving/bringing/taking/sending back) see vt* **(a)** Rückgabe *f*; Zurückbringen *nt*; Zurücksetzen/-stellen/-legen *nt*; Zurückweisen *nt*; Zurückschlagen *nt*/-werfen *nt*; Erwiderung *f*.

**(c)** *(profit)* Einkommen *nt (on aus)*; *(from land, mine etc)* Ertrag *m*. **~s** *(profits)* Gewinn *m*; *(receipts)* Einkünfte *pl*; **~ on capital** *(Fin)* Kapitalertrag *m*.

**(d)** *(fig: recompense)* **in ~** dafür; **in ~ for** für; **to do sb a kindness in ~** sich bei jdm für einen Gefallen revanchieren.

**(e)** *(act of declaring: of verdict, election results)* Verkündung *f*. **the (election) ~s** das Wahlergebnis; **tax ~** Steuererklärung *f*.

**(f)** = **~ ticket**.

**(g)** *(Comm: ~ed item)* zurückgebrachte Ware; *(Theat)* zurückgebrachte Karte.

**returnable** [rɪ'tɜːnəbl] *adj bottle* Mehrweg-; *(with deposit)* Pfand-.

**return: ~ fare** *n* Preis *m* für eine Rückfahrkarte *or (Aviat)* einen Rückflugschein; **~ flight** *n* Rückflug *m*; *(both ways)* Hin- und Rückflug *m*.

**returning officer** [rɪ'tɜːnɪŋ'ɒfɪsəʳ] *n (Brit Parl)* Wahlleiter *m*.

**return: ~ journey** *n* Rückreise *f*; *(both ways)* Hin- und Rückreise *f*; **~ key** *n (Comp)* Return-Taste *f*;

~ **match** n Rückspiel nt; ~ **ticket** n (Brit) Rückfahrkarte f; (Aviat) Rückflugschein m.
**retype** [ˌriːˈtaɪp] vt neu tippen.
**reunification** [riːˌjuːnɪfɪˈkeɪʃən] n Wiedervereinigung f.
**reunion** [rɪˈjuːnjən] n (a) (coming together) Wiedervereinigung f. (b) (gathering) Zusammenkunft f. a family ~ ein Familientreffen nt.
**reunite** [ˌriːjuːˈnaɪt] 1 vt wiedervereinigen. they were ~d at last sie waren endlich wieder vereint. 2 vi (countries, parties) sich wiedervereinigen; (people) wieder zusammenkommen.
**re-usable** [ˌriːˈjuːzəbl] adj wiederverwendbar; packaging etc Mehrweg-.
**Rev** [rev] = **Reverend**.
**rev** [rev] 1 n = **revolution** (Aut) Umdrehung f. ~ **counter** Drehzahlmesser m. 2 vti to ~ (up) (driver) den Motor auf Touren bringen; (noisily) den Motor aufheulen lassen; (engine) auf Touren kommen.
**revalue** [ˌriːˈvæljuː] vt (Fin) aufwerten
**revaluation** [riːˌvæljuˈeɪʃən] n (Fin) Aufwertung f.
**revamp** [ˌriːˈvæmp] vt (col) book, play neu bearbeiten (col); house, room umgestalten.
**reveal** [rɪˈviːl] vt (make visible) zum Vorschein bringen; (show) zeigen; (make known) truth, facts enthüllen; one's identity zu erkennen geben; ignorance, knowledge erkennen lassen. I cannot ~ to you what he said ich kann Ihnen nicht verraten, was er gesagt hat.
**revealing** [rɪˈviːlɪŋ] adj aufschlußreich; dress, neckline offenherzig (hum).
**reveille** [rɪˈvælɪ] n (Mil) Wecksignal nt.
**revel** [ˈrevl] vi (make merry) feiern. to ~ in doing sth seine wahre Freude daran haben, etw zu tun.
**revelation** [ˌrevəˈleɪʃən] n Enthüllung f; (Rel) Offenbarung f. it was a ~ to me das hat mir die Augen geöffnet.
**reveller**, (US) **reveler** [ˈrevlər] n Feiernde(r) mf.
**revelry** [ˈrevlrɪ] n Festlichkeiten pl. drunken ~ feuchtfröhliche Feiern.
**revenge** [rɪˈvendʒ] 1 n Rache f; (Sport) Revanche f. to take ~ on sb (for sth) sich an jdm (für etw) rächen; to get one's ~ sich rächen. 2 vt insult, murder, sb rächen. to ~ oneself on sb (for sth) sich (für etw) an jdm rächen.
**revengeful** [rɪˈvendʒful] adj rachsüchtig.
**revenue** [ˈrevənjuː] n (of state) Staatseinkünfte pl; (tax ~) Steueraufkommen nt; (of individual) Einkünfte pl; (department) Finanzbehörde f.
**reverberate** [rɪˈvɜːbəreɪt] vi (sound) widerhallen.
**reverberation** [rɪˌvɜːbəˈreɪʃən] n (of sound) Widerhall m.
**revere** [rɪˈvɪər] vt verehren.
**reverence** [ˈrevərəns] n Ehrfurcht f.
**Reverend** [ˈrevərənd] adj the ~ Robert Martin ≈ Pfarrer Robert Martin.
**reverent** [ˈrevərənt] adj ehrfürchtig.
**reverie** [ˈrevərɪ] n (liter) Träumereien pl. he fell into a ~ er kam ins Träumen.
**reversal** [rɪˈvɜːsəl] n Umkehrung f; (of verdict also) Umstoßung f.
**reverse** [rɪˈvɜːs] 1 adj (opposite) umgekehrt; direction entgegengesetzt; (Opt) image seitenverkehrt. in ~ **order** in umgekehrter Reihenfolge; ~ **gear** (Aut) Rückwärtsgang m.
2 n (a) (opposite) Gegenteil nt. quite the ~! ganz im Gegenteil! (b) (back) Rückseite f; (of cloth also) linke Seite f; (setback, loss) Rückschlag m; (defeat) Niederlage f. (d) (Aut) Rückwärtsgang m. in ~ im Rückwärtsgang.
3 vt (a) (turn about) order, situation umkehren;

objects, sentences also umstellen; garment wenden; result also umdrehen. to ~ **the charges** (Brit Telec) ein R-Gespräch führen; ~d **charge call** R-Gespräch nt. (b) to ~ one's car into the garage/into a tree rückwärts in die Garage/gegen einen Baum fahren. (c) trend, policy umkehren; verdict also umstoßen. 4 vi (car, driver) zurücksetzen. **reversing lights** Rückfahrscheinwerfer pl.
**reversible** [rɪˈvɜːsəbl] adj decision umstoßbar; (Phys, Chem) umkehrbar; garment Wende-. ~ **cloth** Doubleface m or nt.
**reversion** [rɪˈvɜːʃən] n Umkehr f (to zu); (to bad state) Rückfall m (to in +acc). ~ **to type** (Biol) (Arten)rückschlag m; **his** ~ **to type** das Durchbrechen seiner alten Natur.
**revert** [rɪˈvɜːt] vi (to former state) zurückkehren (to zu); (to bad state) zurückfallen (to in +acc); (to topic) zurückkommen (to auf +acc); (Jur: property) zurückfallen (to an +acc).
**review** [rɪˈvjuː] 1 n (a) (looking back) Rückblick m (of auf +acc); (report) Überblick m (of über +acc). I shall keep your case under ~ ich werde Ihren Fall im Auge behalten. (b) (re-examination) nochmalige Prüfung. the agreement comes up for ~ next year das Abkommen wird nächstes Jahr nochmals geprüft; ~ **body** Untersuchungsausschuß m. (c) (Mil: inspection) Inspektion f. (d) (of book, play etc) Kritik, Rezension f. ~ **copy** Besprechungsexemplar nt. (e) (magazine) Zeitschrift f. (f) (US Sch) Wiederholung f (des Stoffs). 2 vt (a) (look back at) one's life etc zurückblicken auf (+acc). (b) (re-examine) case erneut (über)prüfen. (c) (Mil) troops inspizieren. (d) book, play, film besprechen, rezensieren. (e) (US Sch: learn up) wiederholen.
**reviewer** [rɪˈvjuːər] n Rezensent(in f) m.
**revile** [rɪˈvaɪl] vt schmähen, verunglimpfen.
**revise** [rɪˈvaɪz] 1 vt (a) opinion, estimate überholen, revidieren; text revidieren, überarbeiten. ~d **edition** überarbeitete Ausgabe. (b) (Brit Sch: learn up) wiederholen. 2 vi (Brit) (den Stoff) wiederholen.
**revision** [rɪˈvɪʒən] n (a) (of opinion, estimate) Revidieren nt. (b) (of proofs) Revision, Überarbeitung f. (c) (Brit: for exam) Wiederholung f (des Stoffs). (d) (revised version) überarbeitete Ausgabe.
**revisit** [ˌriːˈvɪzɪt] vt wieder besuchen.
**revitalize** [ˌriːˈvaɪtəlaɪz] vt neu beleben.
**revival** [rɪˈvaɪvəl] n (from faint) Wiederbelebung f. there has been a ~ of interest in ... das Interesse an ... ist wieder wach geworden; an **economic** ~ ein wirtschaftlicher Wiederaufschwung.
**revive** [rɪˈvaɪv] 1 vt person (from fainting, fatigue) (wieder or neu) beleben; (from near death) wiederbeleben; custom, hatred wiederaufleben lassen; friendship, word, old play wiederaufnehmen. 2 vi (person) (from fainting) wieder zu sich kommen; (from fatigue) wieder aufleben, wieder munter werden; (hope, feelings) wiederaufleben; (business, trade) wiederaufblühen.
**revoke** [rɪˈvəuk] vt law aufheben; order, promise zurückziehen; decision rückgängig machen; licence entziehen.
**revolt** [rɪˈvəult] 1 n Revolte f, Aufstand m. to be in ~ (against) rebellieren (gegen). 2 vi (rebel) rebellieren (against gegen). 3 vt abstoßen, anekeln (col). I was ~ed by it es hat mich angeekelt.
**revolting** [rɪˈvəultɪŋ] adj (repulsive) abstoßend; meal, story ekelhaft; (col: unpleasant) weather, colour scheußlich; person widerlich.
**revolution** [ˌrevəˈluːʃən] n (a) (Pol, fig) Revolution f. (b) (turn) Umdrehung f. 4,000 ~s per minute (eine Drehzahl von) 4.000 Umdrehungen pro Minute.

**revolutionary** [ˌrevəˈluːʃnərɪ] **1** *adj (lit, fig)* revolutionär. **2** *n* Revolutionar *m*.

**revolutionize** [ˌrevəˈluːʃənaiz] *vt* revolutionieren.

**revolve** [rɪˈvɒlv] **1** *vt* drehen. **2** *vi* sich drehen. **to ~ on an axis/around the sun** sich um eine Achse/um die Sonne drehen; **he thinks everything ~s around him** *(fig)* er glaubt, alles drehe sich nur um ihn.

**revolver** [rɪˈvɒlvər] *n* Revolver *m*.

**revolving** [rɪˈvɒlvɪŋ] *in cpds* Dreh-.

**revue** [rɪˈvjuː] *n (Theat)* Revue *f*; *(satirical)* Kabarett *nt*.

**revulsion** [rɪˈvʌlʃən] *n (disgust)* Abscheu, Ekel *m (at* vor *+dat)*.

**reward** [rɪˈwɔːd] **1** *n* Belohnung *f*. **one of the ~s of this job** einer der Vorzüge dieser Arbeit; **~ offered for the return of ...** Finderlohn für ... **2** *vt* belohnen.

**rewarding** [rɪˈwɔːdɪŋ] *adj (financially)* lohnend, einträglich; *(morally)* lohnend; *work* dankbar.

**rewind** [ˌriːˈwaind] *pret, ptp* **rewound** *vt thread* wieder aufwickeln; *film, tape* zurückspulen. **~ button** Rückspultaste *f*.

**rewire** [ˌriːˈwaiər] *vt* neu verkabeln.

**reword** [ˌriːˈwɜːd] *vt* umformulieren.

**rewrite** [ˌriːˈrait] *vt pret* **rewrote** [ˌriːˈrəut], *ptp* **rewritten** [ˌriːˈritn] *(write again)* neu schreiben; *(recast)* umschreiben.

**rhapsody** [ˈræpsədɪ] *n (Mus)* Rhapsodie *f*; *(fig)* Schwärmerei *f*.

**rhd** = **right-hand drive.**

**rhesus** [ˈriːsəs] *n* **~ monkey** Rhesusaffe *m*; **~ factor** Rhesusfaktor *m*.

**rhetoric** [ˈretərɪk] *n* Rhetorik *f*; *(pej)* Phrasendrescherei *f (pej)*.

**rhetorical** [rɪˈtɒrɪkəl] *adj* rhetorisch; *(pej)* phrashaft. **~ question** rhetorische Frage.

**rheumatic** [ruːˈmætɪk] *adj pains* rheumatisch; *joint* rheumakrank.

**rheumatism** [ˈruːmətɪzəm] *n* Rheuma(tismus *m)* nt.

**rheumatoid** [ˈruːmətɔɪd] *adj* **~ arthritis** Gelenkrheumatismus *m*.

**Rhine** [rain] *n* Rhein *m*.

**rhino** [ˈrainəu] *n* = **rhinoceros.**

**rhinoceros** [raiˈnɒsərəs] *n* Nashorn, Rhinozeros *nt*.

**Rhodes** [rəudz] *n* Rhodos *nt*.

**Rhodesia** [rəuˈdiːʒə] *n (Hist)* Rhodesien *nt*.

**Rhodesian** [rəuˈdiːʒən] *(Hist)* **1** *adj* rhodesisch. **2** *n* Rhodesier(in *f) m*.

**rhododendron** [ˌrəudəˈdendrən] *n* Rhododendron *m or nt*.

**rhubarb** [ˈruːbɑːb] *n* Rhabarber *m*.

**rhyme** [raim] **1** *n* Reim *m*; *(poem)* Gedicht *nt*. **without ~ or reason** ohne Sinn und Verstand; **in ~** in Versen. **2** *vi* sich reimen.

**rhythm** [ˈrɪðm] *n* Rhythmus *m*.

**rhythmic(al)** *adj*, **~ally** *adv* [ˈrɪðmɪk(əl), -əlɪ] rhythmisch.

**RI** = **(a)** *(Brit)* **religious instruction. (b)** *(US Post)* **Rhode Island.**

**rib** [rɪb] **1** *n* **(a)** *(Anat, Cook, of leaf)* Rippe *f*. **~ cage** Brustkorb *m*. **(b)** *(Knitting)* Rippen *pl.* **2** *vt (tease)* necken, foppen.

**ribald** [ˈrɪbəld, ˈraibəld] *adj joke, humour* deftig; *behaviour* derb; *company* rüde.

**ribbon** [ˈrɪbən] *n (for hair, dress)* Band *nt*; *(for typewriter)* Farbband *nt*; *(on medal)* Ordensband *nt*; *(fig: narrow strip)* Streifen *m*.

**rice** [rais] *n* Reis *m*.

**rice** *in cpds* Reis-; **~ field** *or* **paddy** *n* Reisfeld *nt*; **~ paper** *n* Reispapier *nt*; **~ pudding** *n* Milchreis *m*.

**rich** [rɪtʃ] **1** *adj (+er)* reich; *decoration, clothes* prächtig; *food* schwer; *soil* fett; *land* fruchtbar;

*colour* satt; *sound, voice* voll; *wine* schwer. **~ in vitamins** vitaminreich; **~ in minerals** reich an Bodenschätzen; **~ in examples** mit vielen Beispielen; **that's ~!** *(iro)* das ist ja großartig! **2** *n* **(a) the ~** *pl* die Reichen *pl.* **(b)** **~es** *pl* Reichtümer *pl.*

**richly** [ˈrɪtʃlɪ] *adv dress, decorate* prächtig. **he was ~ rewarded** *(lit)* er wurde reich belohnt; *(fig)* er wurde reichlich belohnt; **~ deserved** wohlverdient.

**richness** [ˈrɪtʃnɪs] *n see adj* Reichtum *m*; Pracht *f*; Schwere *f*; Fruchtbarkeit *f*; Sattheit *f*; Fülle *f*; Schwere *f*.

**rickets** [ˈrɪkɪts] *n sing* Rachitis *f*.

**rickety** [ˈrɪkɪtɪ] *adj furniture etc* wackelig.

**rickshaw** [ˈrɪkʃɔː] *n* Rikscha *f*.

**ricochet** [ˈrɪkəʃeɪ] **1** *n* Abprall *m*. **2** *vi* abprallen *(off* von*)*.

**rid** [rɪd] *pret, ptp* **~** *or* **~ded** *vt* **to ~ oneself of sb/sth** jdn/etw loswerden; *of pests also* sich von etw befreien; *of ideas, prejudice etc* sich von etw lösen; **to get ~ of sb/sth** jdn/etw loswerden; **get ~ of it** sieh zu, daß du das loswirst; *(throw it away)* schmeiß es weg *(col)*.

**riddance** [ˈrɪdəns] *n* **good ~!** *(col)* ein Glück, daß wir das/den *etc* los sind.

**ridden** [ˈrɪdn] **1** *ptp of* **ride. 2** *adj* **fear-~** angsterfüllt; **disease-~** von Krankheiten befallen; **doubt-~** von Zweifeln zernagt.

**riddle¹** [ˈrɪdl] *vt* **to ~ sb/sth with bullets** jdn/etw mit Kugeln durchlöchern; **~d with holes** völlig durchlöchert.

**riddle²** *n* Rätsel *nt*. **to speak in ~s** in Rätseln sprechen.

**ride** [raid] *(vb: pret* **rode**, *ptp* **ridden) 1** *n (in vehicle, on bicycle)* Fahrt *f*; *(on horse)* Ritt *m*; *(for pleasure)* Ausritt *m*. **to go for a ~** eine Fahrt machen; *(on horse)* reiten gehen; **to go for a ~ in the car** eine Fahrt (mit dem Auto) machen; **to take sb for a ~** *(in car etc)* mit jdm eine Fahrt machen; *(col)* jdn anschmieren *(col)*; **he gave me a ~ into town in his car** er nahm mich im Auto in die Stadt mit; **thanks for the ~** danke fürs Mitnehmen.

**2** *vi* **(a)** *(on a horse etc)* reiten *(on* auf *+dat)*; *(go in vehicle, by cycle etc)* fahren. **to go riding** reiten gehen; **to ~ on a bus/in a car/in a train** in einem Bus/Wagen/Zug fahren. **(b) he's riding high** *(fig)* er schwimmt ganz oben; **to ~ at anchor** *(ship)* vor Anker liegen; **to let things ~** den Dingen ihren Lauf lassen.

**3** *vt horse* reiten. **to ~ a bike** Fahrrad fahren; **they had ridden 10 km** sie waren 10 km geritten/gefahren; **we rode the bus into town** *(esp US)* wir fuhren mit dem Bus in die Stadt.

▶**ride out** *vt sep* überstehen. **to ~ ~ the storm** *(lit, fig)* den Sturm überstehen.

▶**ride up** *vi* **(a)** *(horseman)* heranreiten; *(motorcyclist etc)* heranfahren. **(b)** *(skirt etc)* hochrutschen.

**rider** [ˈraidər] *n* **(a)** *(on horse)* Reiter(in *f) m*; *(on bicycle, motorcycle)* Fahrer(in *f) m*. **(b)** *(addition)* Zusatz *m*; *(to document)* Zusatzklausel *f*.

**ridge** [rɪdʒ] *n (of hills, mountains)* Rücken, Kamm *m*; *(pointed, steep)* Grat *m*; *(of roof)* First *m*; *(of nose)* Rücken *m*; *(raised edge)* Rand *m*. **a ~ of hills** eine Hügelkette; **a ~ of high pressure** *(Met)* ein Hochdruckkeil *m*.

**ridge pole** *n (of tent)* Firststange *f*.

**ridicule** [ˈrɪdɪkjuːl] *n* Spott *m*. **to hold sb/sth up to ~** sich über jdn/etw lustig machen.

**ridiculous** [rɪˈdɪkjuləs] *adj* lächerlich. **don't be ~** red keinen Unsinn.

**ridiculously** [rɪˈdɪkjuləslɪ] *adv* lächerlich; *expensive* wahnsinnig *(col)*.

**riding** ['raɪdɪŋ] n Reiten nt. **I enjoy** ~ ich reite gern.
**riding** in cpds Reit-; ~ **breeches** npl Reithose f; ~ **school** n Reitschule f.
**rife** [raɪf] adj disease, corruption weitverbreitet. **to be** ~ grassieren; (rumour) umgehen.
**riffraff** ['rɪfræf] n Pöbel m, Gesindel nt.
**rifle**¹ ['raɪfl] vt (also ~ **through**) sb's pockets, drawer, house durchwühlen.
**rifle**² n (gun) Gewehr nt; (for hunting) Büchse f.
**rifle range** n Schießstand m.
**rift** [rɪft] n (a) Spalt m. (b) (fig: in friendship) Riß m; (Pol also) Spalt m.
**rig** [rɪg] **1** n (oil ~) (Öl)förderturm m; (offshore) Ölbohrinsel f; (US col: truck and trailer) Sattelschlepper m. **2** vt (fig) election, market etc manipulieren.
▶**rig out** vt sep (col: clothe) ausstaffieren (col).
▶**rig up** vt sep ship auftakeln; equipment aufbauen; (fig) (make) improvisieren; (arrange) arrangieren.
**rigging** ['rɪgɪŋ] n (Naut) Tauwerk nt.
**right** [raɪt] **1** adj (a) (just, fair) richtig. **he thought it** ~ **to warn me** er hielt es für richtig, mich zu warnen; **it's only** ~ **(and proper)** es ist nur recht und billig.
(b) (true, correct) answer, time richtig. **to be** ~ (person) recht haben; (answer, solution) richtig sein; (clock) richtig gehen; **you're quite** ~ Sie haben ganz recht; **let's get it** ~ **this time** diesmal muß es klappen; **you were** ~ **to refuse** Sie hatten recht, als Sie ablehnten; **on the** ~ **track** (fig) auf dem rechten Weg; **to put** ~ error korrigieren; clock richtig stellen; situation wieder in Ordnung bringen; **to put sb** ~ jdn berichtigen.
(c) (proper) clothes, document richtig. **what's the** ~ **thing to do in this case?** was tut man da am besten?; **to come at the** ~ **time** zur rechten Zeit kommen; **to do sth the** ~ **way** etw richtig machen; **the** ~ **word** das rechte or richtige Wort; **the** ~ **man for the job** der richtige Mann für die Aufgabe; **to know the** ~ **people** die richtigen Leute kennen.
(d) (well) **the medicine soon put him** ~ die Medizin hat ihn schnell wieder auf die Beine gebracht; **I don't feel quite** ~ **today** ich fühle mich heute nicht ganz wohl; **to be** ~ **as rain** (Brit) kerngesund sein; **to be in one's** ~ **mind** klar bei Verstand sein.
(e) (phrases) ~! ~**-oh!** (Brit col), ~ **you are!** (Brit col) gut, okay (col); **that's** ~! (correct, true) das stimmt!; ~ **enough!** (das) stimmt!; **it's a** ~ **mess in here** (col) das ist vielleicht ein Durcheinander hier (col); **he's a** ~ **fool!** (col) er ist wirklich doof (col); **you're a** ~ **one** (col) du bist mir der Richtige (col).
(f) (opposite of left) rechte(r, s). ~ **hand** rechte Hand; **I'd give my** ~ **hand to know the answer** ich würde es darum geben, wenn ich die Antwort wüßte (col).
**2** adv (a) (straight, directly) direkt; (exactly also) genau. ~ **in front of you** direkt vor Ihnen; ~ **away** (immediately) sofort; ~ **off** (at the first attempt) auf Anhieb (col); ~ **now** (at this very moment) in diesem Augenblick; (immediately) sofort; ~ **here** genau hier; ~ **in the middle** genau in der/die Mitte; ~ **at the beginning** gleich am Anfang.
(b) (completely, all the way) ganz. **rotten** ~ **through** durch und durch verfault or (fig) verdorben; ~ **the way around the city** um die ganze Stadt.
(c) (correctly) richtig. **to answer** ~ richtig antworten; **if I remember** ~ wenn ich mich recht erinnere; **if everything goes** ~ wenn alles klappt (col).
(d) (Pol) **the R~ Honourable John Jones MP** der Abgeordnete John Jones.

(e) (opposite of left) rechts. **turn** ~ biegen Sie rechts ab; ~ **of centre** (Pol) rechts von der Mitte; ~**, left and centre** (everywhere) überall.
**3** n (a) no pl (moral, legal) Recht nt. **he doesn't know** ~ **from wrong** er kann Recht und Unrecht nicht auseinanderhalten; **to be in the** ~ im Recht sein.
(b) (entitlement) Recht nt; (to sth also) Anrecht nt. **(to have) a** or **the** ~ **to do sth** ein or das Recht haben, etw zu tun; **what** ~ **have you to say that?** mit welchem Recht sagen Sie das?; **he is within his** ~s das ist sein gutes Recht; **by** ~s von Rechts wegen; **in one's own** ~ selber, selbst.
(c) **to put** or **set sth to** ~s etw (wieder) in Ordnung bringen.
(d) (not left) rechte Seite; (punch) Rechte f. **to drive on the** ~ rechts fahren; **to keep to the** ~ sich rechts halten; **on my** ~ rechts (von mir); **the R~** (Pol) die Rechte.
**4** vt (a) (return to upright position) aufrichten.
(b) (make amends for) wrong wiedergutmachen. **the problem should** ~ **itself** (fig) das Problem müßte sich von selbst lösen.
**right:** ~ **angle** n rechter Winkel; **at** ~ **angles (to)** rechtwinklig (zu); ~**-angled** ['raɪt,æŋgld] adj rechtwinklig.
**righteous** ['raɪtʃəs] adj rechtschaffen; (pej: self-~) selbstgerecht (pej); indignation gerecht.
**righteousness** ['raɪtʃəsnɪs] n Rechtschaffenheit f.
**rightful** ['raɪtfʊl] adj heir, owner rechtmäßig; punishment gerecht.
**rightfully** ['raɪtfʊlɪ] adv see adj rechtmäßig; gerechterweise.
**right:** ~**-hand** adj rechte(r, s); bend Rechts-; thread rechtsgängig; ~**-hand drive** adj rechtsgesteuert; ~**-handed** adj person rechtshändig; ~**-hand man** n rechte Hand (fig); ~**-hand side** n rechte Seite.
**rightly** ['raɪtlɪ] adv (a) (correctly) he said, ~, that ... er sagte sehr richtig, daß ...; **I don't** ~ **know** ich weiß nicht genau. (b) (justifiably) mit or zu Recht. ~ **or wrongly** ob das nun richtig ist/war oder nicht; **and** ~ **so** und zwar mit Recht.
**right:** ~**-minded** adj vernünftig; ~ **of way** n (across property) Durchgangsrecht nt; (Mot: priority) Vorfahrt f; **he has the** ~ **of way** (Mot) er hat Vorfahrt; ~ **wing** n (Sport, Pol) rechter Flügel; ~**-wing** adj (Pol) Rechts-; ~**-winger** n (Sport) Rechtsaußen m; (Pol) Rechte(r) mf.
**rigid** ['rɪdʒɪd] adj (lit) material, frame starr, steif; (fig) person streng, stur (pej); discipline, principles streng, strikt; (inflexible) unbeugsam; specifications genau festgelegt, strikt; system starr, unbeugsam.
**rigidity** [rɪ'dʒɪdɪtɪ] n see adj Starrheit, Steifheit f; Strenge, Striktheit f; Unbeugsamkeit f.
**rigidly** [rɪ'dʒɪdlɪ] adv see adj.
**rigmarole** ['rɪgmərəʊl] n Gelaber nt; (process) Theater (col), Gedöns (col) nt. **to go through the whole** ~ **again** nochmal mit demselben Gelaber/Gedöns anfangen.
**rigor mortis** ['rɪgə'mɔːtɪs] n die Leichenstarre.
**rigorous** ['rɪgərəs] adj character, discipline streng, strikt; measures rigoros; (accurate) peinlich genau; analysis, tests gründlich; climate streng.
**rigorously** ['rɪgərəslɪ] adv streng, strikt; (accurately) peinlich genau.
**rigour,** (US) **rigor** ['rɪgər] n (a) no pl (strictness) Strenge, Striktheit f. (b) ~s pl (of climate, famine etc) Unbilden pl.
**rig-out** ['rɪgaʊt] n (col) Aufmachung f.
**rile** [raɪl] vt ärgern.

**rim** [rɪm] *n (of cup, bowl)* Rand *m*; *(of hat also)* Krempe *f*; *(of spectacles also)* Fassung *f*; *(of wheel)* Felge *f*.

**rimless** ['rɪmlɪs] *adj spectacles* randlos.

**rind** [raɪnd] *n (of cheese)* Rinde *f*; *(of bacon)* Schwarte *f*; *(of fruit)* Schale *f*.

**ring¹** [rɪŋ] **1** *n* **(a)** Ring *m*; *(in tree trunk)* Jahresring *m*. **to stand in a ~** im Kreis stehen; **to run ~s around sb** *(col)* jdn in die Tasche stecken *(col)*. **(b)** *(group) (Pol)* Gruppe *f*; *(of dealers, spies)* Ring *m*. **(c)** *(enclosure) (at circus)* Manege *f*; *(Sport, at exhibition)* Ring *m*. **2** *vt (surround)* umringen; *(put ~ on or round)* item on list etc einkreisen; *bird* beringen.

**ring²** *(vb: pret* **rang**, *ptp* **rung)** **1** *n* **(a)** *(sound)* Klang *m*; *(~ing: of bell, alarm)* Läuten *nt*; *(of electric bell, alarm clock, phone)* Klingeln *nt*; *(metallic sound: of swords etc)* Klirren *nt*. **there was a ~ at the door** es hat geklingelt. **(b)** *(esp Brit Telec col)* Anruf *m*. **to give sb a ~** jdn anrufen. **(c)** *(fig)* Klang *m*. **his voice had an angry ~ (in** *or* **to it)** seine Stimme klang etwas böse; **that has the ~ of truth (about it)** das klingt sehr wahrscheinlich.

**2** *vi* **(a)** *see n (a)* klingen; läuten; klingen; klirren; *(hammers)* schallen. **the (door)bell rang** es hat geklingelt; **to ~ for sb** (nach) jdm klingeln; **please ~ for attention** bitte klingeln. **(b)** *(esp Brit Telec)* anrufen. **(c)** *(sound, resound) (words, voice)* tönen; *(music, singing also)* erklingen *(geh)*. **to ~ false/true** falsch/wahr klingen; **my ears are ~ing** mir klingen die Ohren.

**3** *vt* **(a)** *bell* läuten. **~ the doorbell** (an der Tür) klingeln; **his name ~s a bell** *(fig col)* sein Name kommt mir bekannt vor; **to ~ the changes (on sth)** *(fig)* bei etw für Abwechslung sorgen. **(b)** *(esp Brit Telec: also* **~ up)** anrufen.

►**ring back** *vti sep (esp Brit)* zurückrufen.

►**ring off** *vi (esp Brit Telec)* auflegen.

►**ring out** *vi* ertönen; *(bell also)* laut erklingen; *(shot also)* krachen; *(sound above others)* herausklingen.

►**ring up** *vt sep (esp Brit Telec)* anrufen.

**ring binder** *n* Ringbuch *nt*.

**ringfinger** ['rɪŋˌfɪŋgər] *n* Ringfinger *m*.

**ringing** ['rɪŋɪŋ] **1** *adj voice, tone* schallend. **~ tone** *(Brit Telec)* Rufzeichen *nt*. **2** *n (of bell)* Läuten *nt*; *(of electric bell also, of phone)* Klingeln *nt*; *(in ears)* Klingen *nt*.

**ringleader** ['rɪŋˌliːdər] *n* Anführer(in *f*) *m*.

**ringlet** ['rɪŋlɪt] *n* Ringellocke *f*.

**ring: ~master** *n* Zirkusdirektor *m*; **~-pull can** *n* Aufreißdose *f*; **~ road** *n (Brit)* Umgehung(sstraße) *f*.

**rink** [rɪŋk] *n* Eisbahn *f*; *(roller-skating ~)* Rollschuhbahn *f*.

**rinse** [rɪns] **1** *n* Spülung *f*; *(colorant)* Tönung *f*. **2** *vt* **(a)** *clothes, hair* spülen; *plates* abspülen; *cup, mouth, basin* ausspülen. **to ~ one's hands** sich *(dat)* die Hände abspülen. **(b)** *(colour with a ~)* hair tönen.

►**rinse out** *vt sep* ausspülen, auswaschen. **to ~ ~ one's mouth** sich *(dat)* den Mund ausspülen.

**Rio (de Janeiro)** ['riːəʊ(dədʒeɪ'nɪərəʊ)] *n* Rio (de Janeiro) *nt*.

**riot** ['raɪət] **1** *n (Pol)* Aufstand, Aufruhr *m no pl*; *(by mob etc)* Krawall *m*; *(fig: wild occasion)* Orgie *f*. **to run ~** *(people)* randalieren; *(vegetation)* wuchern; **his imagination runs ~** seine Phantasie geht mit ihm durch; **to read sb the ~ act** *(fig)* jdm die Leviten lesen; **the ~ police** die Bereitschaftspolizei; **~ shield** Schutzschild *nt*. **2** *vi* randalieren; *(revolt)* einen Aufruhr machen.

**rioter** ['raɪətər] *n* Randalierer *m*; *(Pol)* Aufrührer *m*.

**riotous** ['raɪətəs] *adj* **(a)** *person, crowd* randalierend; *living, behaviour, child* wild. **(b)** *(col)* wild *(col)*; *(hilarious)* urkomisch *(col)*.

**riotously** ['raɪətəslɪ] *adv behave* wild. **it was ~ funny** *(col)* es war zum Schreien *(col)*.

**RIP** = **rest in peace** R.I.P.

**rip** [rɪp] **1** *n* Riß *m*; *(made by knife etc)* Schlitz *m*. **2** *vt material* einen Riß machen in *(+acc)*; *(stronger)* zerreißen; *(vandalize) pictures etc* zerschlitzen. **you've ~ped your jacket** du hast dir die Jacke zerrissen; **to ~ open** aufreißen; *(with knife)* aufschlitzen. **3** *vi* **(a)** *(cloth)* reißen. **(b)** *(col)* **he let ~ at me** er ist auf mich losgegangen *(col)*.

►**rip off** *vt sep* **(a)** *(lit)* abreißen *(prep obj* von*)*; *clothing* herunterreißen. **(b)** *(col) person* ausnehmen *(col)*.

►**rip up** *vt sep* zerreißen; *road* aufreißen.

**ripcord** ['rɪpˌkɔːd] *n* Reißleine *f*.

**ripe** [raɪp] *adj (+er) fruit, cheese* reif. **to live to a ~ old age** ein hohes Alter erreichen; **to be ~ for sth** *(fig)* für etw reif sein.

**ripen** ['raɪpən] **1** *vt (lit, fig)* reifen lassen. **2** *vi* reifen.

**ripeness** ['raɪpnɪs] *n* Reife *f*.

**rip-off** ['rɪpɒf] *n (col)* Wucher *m*; *(cheat)* Schwindel *m*. **it's a ~** das ist Wucher/Schwindel.

**riposte** [rɪ'pɒst] *n (retort)* schlagfertige Antwort.

**ripple** ['rɪpl] **1** *n* kleine Welle; *(noise)* Plätschern *nt*; *(of waves)* Klatschen *nt*. **2** *vi (undulate: water)* sich kräuseln; *(murmur: water)* plätschern; *(waves)* klatschen. **3** *vt water* kräuseln.

**rip-roaring** ['rɪp'rɔːrɪŋ] *adj (col)* sagenhaft *(col)*.

**rise** [raɪz] *(vb: pret* **rose**, *ptp* **risen)** **1** *n* **(a)** *(increase) (in gen)* Anstieg *m*, Steigen *nt no pl*; *(in number)* Zunahme *f*; *(in prices, wages, bank rate also)* Steigerung *f*; *(St Ex)* Aufschwung *m*. **a (pay) ~** *(Brit)* eine Gehaltserhöhung; **a ~ in the population** ein Bevölkerungszuwachs *m*; **to take a ~ out of sb** *(col)* jdn auf den Arm nehmen *(col)*.

**(b)** *(of theatre curtain)* Heben *nt*; *(of sun)* Aufgang *m*; *(to fame, power etc)* Aufstieg *m (to zu)*.

**(c)** *(small hill)* Erhebung *f*; *(slope)* Steigung *f*.

**(d)** *(origin) (of river)* Ursprung *m*. **to give ~ to sth** etw verursachen; **to questions** etw aufwerfen; **to complaints** Anlaß zu etw geben.

**2** *vi* **(a)** *(get up) (from sitting, lying)* aufstehen, sich erheben *(geh)*; *(from the dead)* auferstehen. **to ~ from the table** vom Tisch aufstehen.

**(b)** *(go up)* steigen; *(smoke also)* aufsteigen; *(prices, temperature etc also)* ansteigen *(to auf +acc)*; *(theatre curtain)* sich heben; *(sun, bread)* aufgehen; *(voice) (in volume)* sich erheben; *(in pitch)* höher werden; *(fig) (hopes)* steigen; *(anger)* wachsen. **to ~ to the surface** an die Oberfläche kommen; **he won't ~ to any of your taunts** er läßt sich von dir nicht reizen; **to ~ in price** im Preis steigen; **her spirits rose** ihre Stimmung hob sich.

**(c)** *(ground)* ansteigen; *(mountains)* sich erheben. **the mountain ~s to 3,000 metres** der Berg ragt 3.000 Meter hoch auf.

**(d)** *(fig: in society, rank)* **to ~ from nothing** sich aus dem Nichts hocharbeiten; **he rose to be President** er stieg zum Präsidenten auf.

**(e)** *(adjourn) (assembly)* auseinandergehen; *(meeting)* beendet sein. **the House rose at 2 a.m.** *(Parl)* das Haus beendete die Sitzung um 2 Uhr morgens.

**(f)** *(originate: river)* entspringen.

**(g)** *(also ~ up) (revolt: people)* sich empören, sich erheben. **to ~ (up) in protest/anger (at sth)** *(people)* sich protestierend (gegen etw) erheben/sich (gegen etw) empören. **to ~ (up) in revolt (against sb/sth)** (gegen jdn/etw) rebellieren.

**risen** ['rɪzn] *ptp of* **rise. Christ is** ~ *(Bibl)* Christ ist erstanden.

**riser** ['raɪzə'] *n (person)* **to be an early/late** ~ Frühaufsteher (in *f*)/Langschläfer (in *f*) *m* sein.

**rising** ['raɪzɪŋ] **1** *n* **(a)** *(rebellion)* Aufstand *m*. **(b)** *(of sun)* Aufgang *m*; *(of barometer, prices)* (An)steigen *nt*; *(from dead)* Auferstehung *f*. **2** *adj* **(a)** *sun* aufgehend; *tide, barometer, prices, hopes* steigend; *anger, fury* wachsend. ~ **damp** Bodenfeuchtigkeit *f*. **(b)** *(fig)* **a** ~ **politician** ein kommender Politiker; **the** ~ **generation** die kommende Generation; ~ **fives** Kinder, die bald fünf werden.

**risk** [rɪsk] **1** *n* Risiko *nt*. **to take** *or* **run** ~**s/a** ~ Risiken/ein Risiko eingehen; **to take** *or* **run the** ~ **of doing sth** das Risiko eingehen, etw zu tun; **there is no** ~ **of his coming** *or* **that he will come** es ist nicht zu befürchten, daß er kommt; **at one's own** ~ auf eigene Gefahr; **at the** ~ **of seeming stupid** auf die Gefahr hin, dumm zu erscheinen; **to put sb/sth at** ~ jdn gefährden/etw riskieren; **fire** ~ Feuerrisiko *nt*; **to be a good/bad** ~ *(Fin)* gute/schlechte Bonität haben. **2** *vt* riskieren, aufs Spiel setzen; *life also* wagen; *defeat, accident* riskieren. **she won't** ~ **coming today** sie wird es heute nicht riskieren zu kommen; **I'll** ~ **it** das riskiere ich, ich lasse es darauf ankommen.

**risky** ['rɪskɪ] *adj (+er) enterprise, deed* riskant. **it's a** ~ **business** das ist riskant.

**risqué** ['riːskeɪ] *adj joke, story* pikant, gewagt.

**rissole** ['rɪsəʊl] *n* ≃ Frikadelle *f*.

**rite** [raɪt] *n* Ritus *m*. **burial** ~**s** Bestattungsriten *pl*; **last** ~**s** *(Rel)* Letzte Ölung *f*.

**ritual** ['rɪtjʊəl] **1** *adj* rituell; *laws, objects, killing* Ritual-. **2** *n* Ritual *nt*.

**rival** ['raɪvəl] **1** *n* Rivale *m*, Rivalin *f* (*for* um, *to* für*)*; *(Comm)* Konkurrent (in *f*) *m*. **2** *adj (for)* claims, attraction* konkurrierend; *firm* Konkurrenz-. **3** *vt (in love, for affections)* rivalisieren mit; *(Comm)* konkurrieren mit. **I can't** ~ **that** da kann ich nicht mithalten.

**rivalry** ['raɪvəlrɪ] *n* Rivalität *f*; *(Comm)* Konkurrenzkampf *m*.

**river** ['rɪvə'] *n* Fluß *m*; *(major)* Strom *m*. **down/up** ~ flußabwärts/-aufwärts; **the** ~ **Rhine** *(Brit)*, **the Rhine** ~ *(US)* der Rhein.

**river** *in cpds* Fluß-; ~ **bank** *n* Flußufer *nt*; ~**bed** *n* Flußbett *nt*; ~**side 1** *n* Flußufer *nt*; **by the** ~**side** am Fluß; **2** *adj* am Ufer gelegen, Ufer-.

**rivet** ['rɪvɪt] **1** *n* Niete *f*. **2** *vt (lit)* nieten; *two things* vernieten; *(fig)* audience, attention* fesseln. **his eyes were** ~**ed to the screen** sein Blick war auf den Bildschirm geheftet; ~**ed (to the spot) with fear** vor Angst wie festgenagelt.

**rivet(t)ing** ['rɪvɪtɪŋ] *adj (fig)* fesselnd.

**Riviera** [ˌrɪvɪ'ɛərə] *n* **the (French)/Italian** ~ die französische/italienische Riviera.

**rm** = **room** Zi.

**RN** = **(a) Royal Navy. (b)** *(US)* **registered nurse.**

**RNA** = **ribonucleic acid** RNS *f*.

**RNLI** *(Brit)* = **Royal National Lifeboat Institution.**

**road** [rəʊd] *n* **(a)** Straße *f*. **"** ~ **up"** „Straßenarbeiten"; **by** ~ *(send sth)* per Spedition; *(travel)* mit dem Bus/Auto *etc*; **she lives across the** ~ *(from us)* sie wohnt (bei uns) gegenüber; **my car is off the** ~ **just now** mein Auto ist momentan in der Werkstatt; **this vehicle shouldn't be on the** ~ das Fahrzeug ist nicht verkehrstüchtig; **to be on the** ~ *(travelling)* unterwegs sein; *(theatre company)* auf Tournee sein; *(car)* fahren; **is this the** ~ **to London?** geht es hier nach London?; **the London** ~ die Straße nach London; **to have one for the** ~ *(col)* zum Ab-

schluß noch einen trinken. **(b)** *(fig)* Weg *m*. **you're on the right** ~ Sie sind auf dem richtigen Weg; **on the** ~ **to success** auf dem Weg zum Erfolg; **(get) out of the** ~! *(dial col)* weg da!; **any**~ *(dial col)* = **anyhow.**

**road** *in cpds* Straßen-; ~ **accident** *n* Verkehrsunfall *m*; ~ **atlas** *n* Autoatlas *m*; ~**block** *n* Straßensperre *f*; ~ **haulage** *n* Spedition *f*; ~**hog** *n (col)* Verkehrsrowdy *m (col)*; ~**holding** *n* Straßenlage *f*; ~ **map** *n* Straßenkarte *f*; ~ **marking** *n* Fahrbahnmarkierung *f*; ~**roller** *n* Straßenwalze *f*; ~ **safety** *n* Verkehrssicherheit *f*; ~ **salt** *n* Streusalz *nt*; ~ **sense** *n* Verkehrssinn *m*; ~**side 1** *n* Straßenrand *m*; **by the** ~**side** am Straßenrand; **2** *adj stall* an der Straße; ~**side inn** Rasthaus *nt*; ~**sign** *n* Verkehrsschild *nt*; ~**sweeper** *n* Straßenkehrer (in *f*) *m*; ~ **test** *n* Fahrtest *m*; ~ **transport** *n* Straßengüterverkehr *m*; ~**user** *n* Verkehrsteilnehmer *m*; ~**way** *n* Fahrbahn *f*; ~**works** *npl* Straßenbauarbeiten *pl*; *(on sign)* Baustelle *f*; ~**worthy** *adj* verkehrstüchtig.

**roam** [rəʊm] **1** *vt streets, countryside* wandern *or* ziehen durch. **2** *vi* (herum) wandern.

**roar** [rɔː'] **1** *vi (person, crowd, lion)* brüllen *(with* vor *+dat)*; *(fire)* prasseln; *(wind, engine)* heulen; *(sea)* tosen; *(thunder)* toben. **to** ~ **at sb** jdn anbrüllen; **the trucks** ~**ed past** die Lastwagen donnerten vorbei; **they** ~**ed with laughter** sie brüllten vor Lachen. **2** *n no pl see vi* Gebrüll *nt*; Prasseln *nt*; Heulen *nt*; Tosen *nt*; Toben *nt*. ~**s of laughter** brüllendes Gelächter.

**roaring** ['rɔːrɪŋ] *adj see vi* brüllend; prasselnd; heulend; tosend; tobend. **the** ~ **Twenties** die wilden zwanziger Jahre; **a** ~ **success** ein Bombenerfolg *m (col)*; **to do a** ~ **trade (in sth)** ein Bombengeschäft *nt* (mit etw) machen.

**roast** [rəʊst] **1** *n* Braten *m*. **pork** ~ Schweinebraten *m*. **2** *adj pork, veal* gebraten; *chicken* Brat-, gebraten; *potatoes* in Fett im Backofen gebraten. ~ **beef** Roastbeef *nt*. **3** *vt meat (im Backofen)* braten; *coffee beans* rösten. **to be** ~**ed (alive)** *(fig)* sich totschwitzen *(col)*. **4** *vi (meat)* braten; *(col: person)* irrsinnig schwitzen *(col)*; *(in sun)* in der Sonne braten.

**rob** [rɒb] *vt person* bestehlen; *(more seriously)* berauben; *shop, bank* ausrauben. **to** ~ **sb of sth** *(lit, fig)* jdm etw rauben; *(lit also)* jdm etw stehlen; **I've been** ~**bed!** ich bin bestohlen worden!; *(had to pay too much)* das war Nepp! *(col)*.

**robber** ['rɒbə'] *n* Räuber *m*.

**robbery** ['rɒbərɪ] *n* Raub *m no pl*; *(burglary)* Einbruch *m (of* in *+acc)*. ~ **with violence** *(Jur)* Raubüberfall *m*.

**robe** [rəʊb] *n (of office)* Robe *f*; *(esp US: for house wear)* Morgenrock, Bademantel *m*.

**robin** ['rɒbɪn] *n* Rotkehlchen *nt*.

**robot** ['rəʊbɒt] *n* Roboter *m*; *(fig also)* Automat *m*.

**robotics** [rəʊ'bɒtɪks] *n sing or pl* Robotertechnik *f*.

**robust** [rəʊ'bʌst] *adj* robust; *build also* kräftig; *structure* stabil.

**rock¹** [rɒk] **1** *vt* **(a)** *(swing)* schaukeln; *(gently: lull)* wiegen. **(b)** *(shake)* town erschüttern; *ship* hin und her werfen; *(fig col)* person* erschüttern. **to** ~ **the boat** *(fig)* für Unruhe sorgen. **2** *vi* schaukeln; *(building, tree)* schwanken; *(ship)* hin und her geworfen werden; *(gently)* sich wiegen; *(ground)* beben. **3** *n (Mus)* Rock *m*; *(dance)* Rock 'n' Roll *m*. ~ **and roll** Rock and Roll *m*.

**rock²** *n* **(a)** *(substance)* Stein *m*; *(~ face)* Fels (en) *m*; *(Geol)* Gestein *nt*. **(b)** *(large mass)* Fels (en) *m*; *(boulder also)* Felsbrocken *m*; *(smaller)* (großer) Stein. **as solid as a** ~ *(structure)* massiv wie ein

Fels; *(business)* sehr stabil; *(person)* absolut zuverlässig; **on the ~s** *(ship)* aufgelaufen; *(col) (with ice)* mit Eis; *(ruined: marriage etc)* kaputt *(col)*. **(c)** *(col: diamond)* Diamant *m.* **~s** *(jewels)* Klunker *pl (col)*. **(d)** *(Brit: sweet)* Zuckerstange *f.*

**rock:** **~-bottom** *n* der Tiefpunkt; **to touch/reach ~-bottom** den Tiefpunkt erreichen; **~ cake** *n (Brit)* ≈ Rosinenhäufchen *nt*; **~-climber** *n* (Felsen)kletterer(in *f*) *m*; **~ climbing** *n* Klettern *nt* (im Fels).

**rocker** ['rɒkəʳ] *n* to be/go off one's **~** *(col)* übergeschnappt sein *(col)*/überschnappen *(col)*.

**rockery** ['rɒkərɪ] *n* Steingarten *m.*

**rocket** ['rɒkɪt] **1** *n* **(a)** Rakete *f.* **(b)** *(Brit col: reprimand)* **to give sb a ~** jdm eine Zigarre verpassen *(col)*. **2** *vi (prices)* hochschießen. **to ~ to fame** über Nacht berühmt werden.

**rocket** *in cpds* Raketen-; **~ engine** *n* Raketentriebwerk *nt*; **~ launcher** *n* Raketenabschußgerät *nt*; *(on plane)* Raketenwerfer *m*; *(multiple)* Stalinorgel *f*; **~-propelled** *adj* raketengetrieben.

**rock:** **~ face** *n* Felswand *f*; **~ fall** *n* Steinschlag *m*; **~-hard** *adj* steinhart.

**Rockies** ['rɒkɪz] *npl* = **Rocky Mountains**.

**rocking** ['rɒkɪŋ]: **~ chair** *n* Schaukelstuhl *m*; **~ horse** *n* Schaukelpferd *nt.*

**rock:** **~ plant** *n* Steinpflanze *f*; **~ salt** *n* Steinsalz *nt.*

**rocky**[1] ['rɒkɪ] *adj (unsteady)* wackelig.

**rocky**[2] *adj (+er)* hill felsig; *road* steinig. **the R~ Mountains** die Rocky Mountains *pl.*

**rococo** [rəʊ'kəʊkəʊ] **1** *n* Rokoko *nt.* **2** *adj* Rokoko-.

**rod** [rɒd] *n* Stab *m*; *(longer)* Stange *f*; *(in machinery)* Stange *f*; *(for punishment, fishing)* Rute *f.*

**rode** [rəʊd] *pret of* **ride**.

**rodent** ['rəʊdənt] *n* Nagetier *nt.*

**rodeo** ['rəʊdɪəʊ] *n* Rodeo *nt.*

**roe**[1] [rəʊ] *n, pl* **-(s)** *(species: also ~ deer)* Reh *nt.* **~ buck** Rehbock *m.*

**roe**[2] *n, pl* - *(of fish)* Rogen *m.* **hard ~** Rogen *m*; **soft ~** Milch *f.*

**roger** ['rɒdʒəʳ] *interj* "~" „verstanden".

**rogue** [rəʊg] *n* Schurke *m*; *(scamp)* Schlingel *m.* **~s' gallery** *(Police col)* Verbrecheralbum *nt*; **~ elephant** Einzelgängerelefant *m.*

**roguish** ['rəʊgɪʃ] *adj* spitzbübisch.

**role** [rəʊl] *n (Theat, fig)* Rolle *f.* **~ model** Identifikationsfigur *f*; **~-play(ing)** Rollenspiel *nt*; **~ reversal** Rollentausch *m.*

**roll** [rəʊl] **1** *n* **(a)** *(of paper, wire etc)* Rolle *f*; *(of fabric)* Ballen *m*; *(of banknotes)* Bündel *nt*; *(of butter, flesh, fat)* Röllchen *nt.* **a ~ of paper** eine Rolle Papier. **(b)** *(Cook) (also* **bread ~)** Brötchen *nt.* **ham/cheese ~** Schinken-/Käsebrötchen *nt.* **(c)** *(movement, of sea)* Rollen *nt*; *(of ship also)* Schlingern *nt*; *(of person's gait)* Wiegen *nt.* **(d)** *(sound) (of thunder)* Rollen *nt*; *(of drums)* Wirbel *m.* **(e)** *(list, register)* Liste *f*, Register *nt.* **we have 60 pupils on our ~(s)** bei uns sind 60 Schüler angemeldet; **to call the ~** die Namensliste verlesen, die Namen aufrufen; **~ of honour** *(Brit) or* **honor** *(US)* Ehrenliste *f*; *(plaque)* Ehrentafel *f.*

    **2** *vi* **(a)** rollen; *(ship)* schlingern; *(presses)* laufen; *(Aviat)* eine Rolle machen. **the stones ~ed down the hill** die Steine rollten den Berg hinunter; **tears were ~ing down her cheeks** Tränen rollten ihr über die Wangen; **heads will ~!** *(fig)* da werden Köpfe rollen!; **he's ~ing in money or in it** *(col)* er schwimmt im Geld *(col)*. **(b)** *(thunder)* grollen; *(drum)* wirbeln.

    **3** *vt* rollen; *cigarette* drehen; *pastry* ausrollen; *metal, lawn* walzen. **to ~ one's eyes** die Augen rol-

len; **to ~ one's r's** das R rollen; **the hedgehog ~ed itself into a ball** der Igel rollte sich zu einer Kugel zusammen.

▶**roll about** *vi (balls)* herumrollen *or* -kugeln *(col)*; *(ship)* schlingern; *(person, dog)* sich wälzen; *(col: with laughter)* sich kugeln (vor Lachen) *(col)*.

▶**roll away 1** *vi (ball, vehicle)* wegrollen; *(clouds)* abziehen. **2** *vt sep trolley* wegrollen.

▶**roll back** *vt sep* zurückrollen.

▶**roll by** *vi (vehicle, procession)* vorbeirollen; *(clouds)* vorbeiziehen; *(time, years)* dahinziehen.

▶**roll in** *vi* herein-/hineinrollen; *(letters, money)* hereinströmen; *(col: person)* eintrudeln *(col)*.

▶**roll on** *vi* weiterrollen; *(time)* verfliegen. **~ ~ the holidays!** wenn doch nur schon Ferien wären!

▶**roll out** *vt sep barrel* hinaus-/herausrollen; *pastry, dough* ausrollen; *metal* auswalzen.

▶**roll over 1** *vi (vehicle)* sich überschlagen; *(person)* sich umdrehen. **the dog ~ed ~ onto his back** der Hund rollte auf den Rücken. **2** *vt sep person, animal, object* umdrehen.

▶**roll up 1** *vi* **(a)** *(animal)* sich zusammenrollen *(into* zu*).* **(b)** *(col: arrive)* auftauchen. **2** *vt sep* auf- *or* zusammenrollen; *sleeves* hochkrempeln.

**roll:** **~bar** *n (Aut)* Überrollbügel *m*; **~call** *n (Sch)* Namensaufruf *m*; *(Mil)* (Anwesenheits)appell *m.*

**roller** ['rəʊləʳ] *n* **(a)** Rolle *f*; *(pastry ~)* Teigrolle *f*; *(for lawn, road)* Walze *f*; *(paint ~)* Rolle *f.* **(b)** *(hair ~)* (Locken)wickler *m.* **with her ~s in** mit Lockenwicklern (im Haar). **(c)** *(wave)* Brecher *m.*

**roller:** **~ blind** *n* Rollo *nt*; **~ coaster** *n* Achterbahn *f*; **~ skate** *n* Rollschuh *m*; **~-skating** *m* Rollschuhlaufen *nt*; **~ towel** *n* Rollhandtuch *nt.*

**roll film** *n* Rollfilm *m.*

**rollicking** ['rɒlɪkɪŋ] **1** *adj* ausgelassen. **2** *n (Brit col)* **to give sb/get a ~** jdn herunterputzen/heruntergeputzt werden *(col)*.

**rolling** ['rəʊlɪŋ] *adj sea* wogend; *waves* rollend; *countryside* wellig. **a ~ stone gathers no moss** *(Prov)* nur mit Ausdauer bringt man es zu etwas.

**rolling:** **~ mill** *n (factory)* Walzwerk *nt*; *(machine)* Walze *f*; **~ pin** *n* Teigrolle *f*; **~ stock** *n (Rail)* rollendes Material.

**ROM** [rɒm] *(Comp)* = **read only memory** ROM *m or nt.*

**romaine** [ˌrəʊ'meɪn] *n (US)* Romagna-Salat *m*, römischer Salat.

**Roman** ['rəʊmən] **1** *n (Hist)* Römer(in *f*) *m.* **2** *adj* römisch; *(~ Catholic)* römisch-katholisch. **~ numeral** römische Ziffer; **r~ type** Magerdruck *m.*

**Roman Catholic 1** *adj* (römisch-)katholisch. **2** *n* Katholik(in *f*) *m*, (Römisch-)Katholische(r) *mf.*

**romance** [rəʊ'mæns] **1** *n* **(a)** *(book)* Roman *m*; *(love-story)* Liebesroman *m.* **(b)** *(Mus, love affair)* Romanze *f.* **(c)** *no pl (romanticism)* Romantik *f.* **2** *adj* **R~** *language etc* romanisch.

**Romanesque** [ˌrəʊmə'nesk] *adj* romanisch.

**Romania** [rəʊ'meɪnɪə] *n* Rumänien *nt.*

**Romanian** [rəʊ'meɪnɪən] **1** *adj* rumänisch. **2** *n* **(a)** Rumäne *m*, Rumänin *f.* **(b)** *(language)* Rumänisch *nt.*

**romantic** [rəʊ'mæntɪk] **1** *adj (Art etc: also* R~) romantisch; *person also* romantisch veranlagt. **~ novel** Liebesroman *m.* **2** *n (Art etc: also* R~) Romantiker(in *f*) *m.*

**romanticism** [rəʊ'mæntɪsɪzəm] *n (Art, Liter, Mus: also* R~) Romantik *f.*

**romanticize** [rəʊ'mæntɪsaɪz] *vt* romantisieren.

**Romany** ['rəʊmənɪ] **1** *n* **(a)** Zigeuner(in *f*) *m*, Roma *mf.* **(b)** *(language)* die Zigeunersprache, Romani *nt.* **2** *adj* Zigeuner-.

**Rome** [rəum] *n* Rom *nt.* **when in ~ do as the Romans do** *(prov)* ≈ andere Länder, andere Sitten *(Prov)*; **~ wasn't built in a day** *(Prov)* Rom ist auch nicht an einem Tag erbaut worden *(Prov)*.

**romp** [rɒmp] **1** *n* Tollerei *f.* **to have a ~** herumtollen *or* -toben. **2** *vi (children, puppies)* herumtollen *or* -toben. **to ~ home** *(fig: win)* spielend gewinnen; **to ~ through an exam** eine Prüfung spielend schaffen.

**rompers** ['rɒmpəz] *npl* Strampelhöschen *nt.*

**roof** [ru:f] **1** *n* Dach *nt; (of car also)* Verdeck *nt; (of cave)* Gewölbe *nt.* **the ~ of the mouth** der Gaumen; **without a ~ over one's head** ohne ein Dach über dem Kopf; **a room in the ~** ein Zimmer unter dem Dach; **to go through the ~** *(col) (person)* an die Decke gehen *(col); (prices etc)* in die Höhe schießen. **2** *vt house* mit einem Dach decken. **red-~ed** mit rotem Dach.

**roofing** ['ru:fɪŋ] *n (work)* Dachdeckerarbeiten *pl; (material)* Material *nt* zum Dachdecken. **~ felt** Dachpappe *f.*

**roof:** **~-rack** *n* Dachgepäckträger *m;* **~ tile** *n* Dachziegel *m;* **~top** *n* Dach *nt;* **to shout sth from the ~tops** *(fig)* etw überall herumposaunen *(col);* **~ truss** *n* Dachstuhl *m.*

**rook** [ruk] **1** *n (bird)* Saatkrähe *f; (Chess)* Turm *m.* **2** *vt (swindle)* übers Ohr hauen *(col),* betrügen.

**room** [ru:m] **1** *n* **(a)** Zimmer *nt,* Raum *m; (public hall, ball~ etc)* Saal *m; (office)* Büro *nt.* **the whole ~ laughed** der ganze Saal lachte; **to live in ~s** zur Untermiete wohnen. **(b)** *no pl (space)* Platz *m; (fig)* Spielraum *m.* **is there (enough) ~?** ist da genügend Platz?; **there is no ~ (for you)** es ist nicht genug Platz (für dich); **to make ~ for sb/sth** für jdn/etw Platz machen; **there is no ~ for doubt** es kann keinen Zweifel geben; **there is ~ for improvement in your work** Ihre Arbeit könnte um einiges besser sein. **2** *vi* zur Untermiete wohnen.

**roominess** ['ru:mɪnɪs] *n* Geräumigkeit *f.*

**rooming house** ['ru:mɪŋ'haus] *n (esp US)* Mietshaus *nt (mit möblierten Zimmern).*

**room:** **~mate** *n* Zimmergenosse *m,* Zimmergenossin *f;* **~ service** *n* Zimmerservice *m;* **~ temperature** *n* Zimmertemperatur *f;* **wine at ~ temperature** Wein mit Zimmertemperatur.

**roomy** ['ru:mɪ] *adj (+er)* geräumig; *garment* weit.

**roost** [ru:st] **1** *n (pole)* Stange *f; (henhouse)* Hühnerstall *m.* **to come home to ~** *(fig)* auf den Urheber zurückfallen. **2** *vi (bird)* sich niederlassen.

**rooster** ['ru:stər] *n* Hahn *m.*

**root** [ru:t] **1** *n* Wurzel *f.* **~s** *(fig: of person)* Wurzeln; **by the ~s** mit der Wurzel; **to take ~** *(lit, fig)* Wurzeln schlagen; **the ~ of the matter** der Kern der Sache; **to get to the ~(s) of the problem** dem Problem auf den Grund gehen. **2** *vt* **deeply ~ed** *(fig)* tief verwurzelt; **to be** *or* **stand ~ed to the spot** *(fig)* wie angewurzelt dastehen. **3** *vi (plants etc)* Wurzeln schlagen.

▶**root for** *vi +prep obj* anfeuern.

▶**root out** *vt sep* **(a)** *(lit) plant* herausreißen; *(dig up)* ausgraben. **(b)** *(fig) evil* mit der Wurzel ausreißen; *(find)* aufspüren, ausgraben *(col).*

**root:** **~ cause** *n* eigentlicher Grund; **~ crop** *or* **vegetable** *n* Wurzelgemüse *nt.*

**rope** [rəup] **1** *n* Seil *nt; (Naut)* Tau *nt; (of bell)* Glockenstrang *m.* **to give sb more ~** *(fig)* jdm mehr Freiheit lassen; **to know the ~s** *(col)* sich auskennen; **to show sb the ~s** *(col)* jdn in alles einweihen. **2** *vt box, case* verschnüren.

▶**rope in** *vt sep (fig)* rankriegen *(col).* **how did you get ~d ~ to that?** wie bist du denn da reingeraten? *(col).*

▶**rope off** *vt sep area* mit einem Seil abgrenzen.

▶**rope up** *vi (climber)* sich anseilen.

**rope** *in cpds* Seil-; **~ ladder** *n* Strickleiter *f.*

**ropy** ['rəupɪ] *adj (+er) (col) (bad)* miserabel *(col); (worn)* mitgenommen.

**rosary** ['rəuzərɪ] *n (Rel)* Rosenkranz *m.*

**rose¹** [rəuz] *pret of* **rise.**

**rose²** **1** *n* **(a)** Rose *f.* **my life isn't a bed of ~s** *or* **all ~s** *(col)* ich bin auch nicht auf Rosen gebettet. **(b)** *(nozzle)* Brause *f.* **(c)** *(colour)* Rosarot *nt.* **2** *adj* rosarot.

**rosé** ['rəuzeɪ] *n* Rosé *m.*

**rose** *in cpds* Rosen-; **~bed** *n* Rosenbeet *nt;* **~bud** *n* Rosenknospe *f;* **~bush** *n* Rosenstrauch *m;* **~-coloured,** *(US)* **~-colored** *adj* rosarot; **to see life through ~-coloured spectacles** das Leben durch eine rosarote Brille sehen; **~hip** *n* Hagebutte *f.*

**rosemary** ['rəuzmərɪ] *n* Rosmarin *m.*

**rose:** **~-pink** *adj* rosarot; **~-red** *adj* rosenrot; **~-tinted** *adj* = **~-coloured.**

**rosette** [rəu'zet] *n* Rosette *f.*

**roster** ['rɒstər] *n* Dienstplan *m.*

**rostrum** ['rɒstrəm] *n, pl* **rostra** ['rɒstrə] Rednerpult *nt; (for conductor)* Dirigentenpult *nt.*

**rosy** ['rəuzɪ] *adj (+er) (pink)* rosarot; *cheeks, future* rosig. **to paint a ~ picture of sth** etw in den rosigsten Farben ausmalen.

**rot** [rɒt] **1** *n* **(a)** Fäulnis *f no pl; (in wood also)* Moder *m no pl.* **we must stop the ~** *(fig)* wir müssen energisch durchgreifen; **then the ~ set in** *(fig)* dann setzte der Verfall ein. **(b)** *(col: rubbish)* Blödsinn *m (col).* **2** *vi (wood, material, rope)* verrotten, faulen; *(teeth, plant)* verfaulen; *(fig)* verrotten.

**rota** ['rəutə] *n* Dienstplan *m.*

**Rotarian** [rəu'tɛərɪən] *n* Rotarier *m.*

**rotary** ['rəutərɪ] **1** *adj* **(a)** *motion* rotierend, Dreh-. **(b)** **R~ Club** Rotary Club *m.* **2** *n (US)* Kreisverkehr *m.*

**rotate** [rəu'teɪt] **1** *vt* **(a)** *(around axis)* drehen, rotieren lassen. **(b)** *crops* im Wechsel anbauen; *work* turnusmäßig erledigen. **2** *vi* **(a)** sich drehen; *(Math)* rotieren. **(b)** *(crops)* im Wechsel angebaut werden; *(gently)* sich wiegen; *(people: take turns)* sich abwechseln.

**rotation** [rəu'teɪʃən] *n* **(a)** *no pl* Drehung, Rotation *f; (of crops)* Wechsel *m; (taking turns)* turnusmäßiger Wechsel. **in ~** abwechselnd im Turnus. **(b)** *(turn)* (Um)drehung *f.*

**rote** [rəut] *n:* **by ~** *learn* auswendig; *recite* mechanisch.

**rotor** ['rəutər] *n (Aviat, Elec, Aut)* Rotor *m.*

**rotten** ['rɒtn] *adj* **(a)** faul; *wood also* morsch; *fruit also* verdorben; *(fig: corrupt)* korrupt, verdorben. **(b)** *(col) (bad)* scheußlich *(col); weather, book, film, piece of work also* mies *(col); (mean)* gemein; *(unwell)* elend, mies *(col).* **what ~ luck!** so ein Pech!; **it's a ~ business** das ist eine üble Sache.

**rotund** [rəu'tʌnd] *adj person* rund(lich).

**rouble,** *(US)* **ruble** ['ru:bl] *n* Rubel *m.*

**rouge** [ru:ʒ] *n* Rouge *nt.*

**rough** [rʌf] **1** *adj (+er)* **(a)** *(uneven) ground* uneben; *surface, skin, hands* rauh. **(b)** *(coarse, unrefined) person* ungehobelt; *manners also, speech* grob, roh; *taste* sauer. **(c)** *(harsh, unpleasant) person* grob, roh; *treatment, words* grob, hart; *life* wüst; *sport, work, sound* hart; *neighbourhood, manners, voice, weather* rauh; *sea crossing* stürmisch. **to be ~ with sb** grob mit jdm umgehen; **to feel ~** sich mies fühlen; **he had a ~ time (of it)** *(fig col)* es ging ihm ziemlich dreckig *(col);* **to make things ~ for sb** *(col)* jdm

Schwierigkeiten machen; **it's ~ on him** *(Brit col)* das ist hart für ihn.

**(d)** *(approximate) plan, calculation, estimate* grob, ungefähr. **~ copy** *or* **draft** Konzept *nt*; **~ sketch** Faustskizze *f*; **~ paper** Konzeptpapier *nt*; **this was ~ justice** das war ein willkürliches Urteil.

**2** *adv live* wüst; *play* wild. **to sleep ~** im Freien übernachten.

**3** *n* **(a)** unwegsames Gelände; *(Golf)* Rauh *nt*.

**(b)** *(unpleasant aspect)* **to take the ~ with the smooth** das Leben nehmen, wie es kommt.

**4** *vt* **to ~ it** *(col)* primitiv leben.

▸**rough out** *vt sep plan, drawing* grob entwerfen.

**roughage** ['rʌfɪdʒ] *n* Ballaststoffe *pl*.

**rough: ~-and-ready** *adj method, equipment* provisorisch; *work* zusammengehauen *(col)*; *person* rauh(beinig); **~-and-tumble** *n (play)* Balgerei *f*; *(fighting)* Keilerei *f*; **~cast** *n* Rauhputz *m*; **~ diamond** *n* **he's a ~ diamond** er ist rauh aber herzlich.

**roughen** ['rʌfn] *vt skin, cloth* rauh machen; *surface* aufrauhen.

**roughhouse** ['rʌfhaʊs] *n (col)* Keilerei *f (col)*.

**roughly** ['rʌflɪ] *adv* **(a)** grob; *play* rauh; *answer, order also* hart. **(b)** *(approximately)* ungefähr. **~ (speaking)** grob gesagt.

**roughness** ['rʌfnɪs] *n see adj* **(a)** Unebenheit *f*; Rauheit *f*. **(b)** Ungehobeltheit *f*; Grobheit, Roheit *f*; saurer Geschmack. **(c)** Grobheit, Roheit *f*; Härte *f*; Rauheit *f*.

**rough: ~ note book** *n (Sch)* Schmierheft *nt*; **~shod** *adv:* **to ride ~shod over sb** rücksichtslos über jdn hinweggehen; **~ stuff** *n (col)* Handgreiflichkeiten *pl*.

**roulette** [ruː'let] *n* Roulett(e) *nt*.

**round** [raʊnd] **1** *adj (+er)* rund. **~ number** runde Zahl; **in ~ figures, that will cost 20 million** es kostet rund *or* runde 20 Millionen.

**2** *adv (esp Brit)* **to go** *or* **take the long way ~** einen Umweg machen, den längeren Weg nehmen; **to be going ~ and ~ (in circles)** sich nur im Kreis bewegen *(fig)*; **I asked him ~ for a drink** ich lud ihn auf ein Glas Wein/Bier *etc* bei mir ein; **I'll be ~ at 8 o'clock** ich werde um 8 Uhr da sein; **for the second time ~** zum zweitenmal; **all (the) year ~** das ganze Jahr über; **all ~** *(lit)* ringsherum; *(fig: for everyone)* für alle; **drinks all ~!** eine Runde!

**3** *prep (esp Brit)* **(a)** *(of place etc)* um (... herum). **~ the table** um den Tisch (herum); **all ~ the house** *(inside)* im ganzen Haus; *(outside)* um das ganze Haus herum; **to go ~ a corner** um eine Ecke gehen/fahren *etc*; **to look ~ a house** sich *(dat)* ein Haus ansehen; **to show sb ~ a town** jdn in einer Stadt herumführen. **(b)** *(approximately)* **~ (about) 7 o'clock** ungefähr um 7 Uhr; **~ (about) £800** um die £800.

**4** *n* **(a)** *(slice: of bread, meat)* Scheibe *f*. **a ~ of toast** eine Scheibe Toast. **(b)** *(delivery ~, Sport, of election, talks)* Runde *f*. **~(s)** *(of policeman, doctor)* Runde *f*; **to do one's ~(s)** seine Runde machen; *(doctor also)* Hausbesuche machen; **he does a paper ~** er trägt Zeitungen aus; **the daily ~** *(fig)* die tägliche Arbeit, der tägliche Trott *(pej)*; **to go the ~s** *(story etc)* reihum gehen; **a ~ (of drinks)** eine Runde; **a new ~ of negotiations** eine neue Verhandlungsrunde; **~ of ammunition** Ladung *f*; **a ~ of applause** Applaus *m*.

**5** *vt* **(a)** *(make ~)* runden. **(b)** *(go ~)* bend gehen/fahren um; *obstacle* herumgehen/-fahren *etc* um.

▸**round off** *vt sep* **(a)** *edges etc* abrunden. **(b)** *list, series* voll machen; *speech, meal* abrunden; *debate,*

*meeting* abschließen.

▸**round on** *vi +prep obj (verbally)* anfahren; *(in actions)* losgehen auf *(+acc)*.

▸**round up** *vt sep* **(a)** *people* zusammentrommeln *(col)*; *cattle* zusammentreiben; *criminals* hochnehmen *(col)*. **(b)** *price, number* aufrunden.

**roundabout** ['raʊndəbaʊt] **1** *adj* **~ route** Umweg *m*; **we came a ~ way** wir haben einen Umweg gemacht; **I found out in a ~ way** ich habe es auf Umwegen herausgefunden. **2** *n (Brit) (merry-go-round)* Karussell *nt*; *(Mot)* Kreisverkehr *m*.

**rounders** ['raʊndəz] *n sing (Brit)* ≃ Schlagball *m*.

**round: ~-eyed** *adj* großäugig; **~-faced** *adj* rundgesichtig.

**roundly** ['raʊndlɪ] *adv (bluntly)* ohne Umschweife.

**roundnecked** [ˌraʊnd'nekt] *adj* mit rundem Ausschnitt.

**roundness** ['raʊndnɪs] *n* Rundheit *f*.

**round: ~-shouldered** ['raʊnd'ʃəʊldəd] *adj* mit runden Schultern; **~-the-clock** *adj* rund um die Uhr *not attr*; **~ trip** *n (tour)* Rundreise *f*; *(return trip)* Hin- und Rückfahrt *f*; **~-trip ticket** *n (US)* Rückfahrkarte *f*; *(Aviat)* Hin- und Rückflug-Ticket *nt*; **~-up** *n (of cattle)* Zusammentreiben *nt*; *(of criminals)* Hochnehmen *nt (col)*; **a ~-up of today's news** eine Zusammenfassung der Nachrichten vom Tage.

**rouse** [raʊz] *vt* **(a)** *(from sleep)* wecken. **(b)** *(stimulate) person* bewegen; *feeling* wachrufen; *hatred, suspicions* erregen. **to ~ sb (to anger)** jdn reizen; **~ sb to action** jdn zum Handeln bewegen; **to ~ the masses** die Massen aufrütteln.

**rousing** ['raʊzɪŋ] *adj speech* zündend, mitreißend; *applause* stürmisch; *music* rauschend.

**rout**[1] [raʊt] **1** *n (defeating)* Sieg *m (of* über *+acc)*; *(being defeated)* vernichtende Niederlage. **2** *vt (defeat)* in die Flucht schlagen.

**rout**[2] *vi (pig etc: also* **~ about***)* herumwühlen.

▸**rout out** *vt sep (find)* aufstöbern; *(force out)* (heraus)jagen *(of aus)*.

**route** [ruːt], *(US)* [raʊt] **1** *n* Strecke, Route *f*; *(bus service)* Linie *f*. **shipping/air ~s** Schiffahrtsstraßen *or* -wege/Fluglinien; **we live on a bus ~** wir wohnen an einer Buslinie; **the ~ to the coast** der Weg zur Küste. **2** *vt train, coach, bus* legen. **my baggage was ~d through Amsterdam** mein Gepäck wurde über Amsterdam geschickt.

**route: ~ map** *n* Streckenkarte *f*; **~ march** *n* Übungsmarsch *m*.

**routine** [ruː'tiːn] **1** *n* **(a)** Routine *f*. **(b)** *(Dancing)* Figur *f*; *(Gymnastics)* Übung *f*. **2** *adj* Routine-, routinemäßig. **~ duties** tägliche Pflichten *pl*; **to be ~ procedure** Routine(sache) sein.

**rover** ['rəʊvə<sup>r</sup>] *n (wanderer)* Vagabund *m*.

**roving** ['rəʊvɪŋ] *adj* **he has a ~ eye** er riskiert gern ein Auge; **~ ambassador** Botschafter *m* für mehrere Vertretungen; **~ reporter** *Reporter, der ständig unterwegs ist.*

**row**[1] [rəʊ] *n* Reihe *f*. **4 failures in a ~** 4 Mißerfolge hinter- *or* nacheinander; **arrange them in ~s** stell sie in Reihen auf; **~ house** *(US)* Reihenhaus *nt*.

**row**[2] [rəʊ] **1** *vti (in boat)* rudern. **to ~ sb across** jdn hinüber-/herüberrudern. **2** *n* **to go for a ~** rudern gehen.

**row**[3] [raʊ] **1** *n* **(a)** *(noise)* Lärm, Krach *(col) m*. **to make a** *or* **kick up** *(col)* **a ~** Krach schlagen *(col)*. **(b)** *(quarrel)* Streit, Krach *(col) m*. **to have a ~ with sb** mit jdm Streit *or* Krach *(col)* haben. **2** *vi (quarrel)* (sich) streiten.

**rowan** ['raʊən] *n (tree)* Eberesche, Vogelbeere *f*.

**rowboat** ['rəʊ,bəʊt] *n (US)* Ruderboot *nt*.

**rowdy** ['raʊdɪ] **1** *adj (+er) (noisy)* laut; *football fans* randalierend. **2** *n* Krawallmacher *m*. **football rowdies** Fußballrowdys *pl*.

**rowdyism** ['raʊdɪɪzəm] *n* Rowdytum *nt*.

**rower** ['rəʊəʳ] *n* Ruderer *m*, Ruderin *f*.

**rowing¹** ['rəʊɪŋ] *n* Rudern *nt*. ~ **boat** Ruderboot *nt*.

**rowing²** ['raʊɪŋ] *n (quarrelling)* Streiterei *f*.

**rowlock** ['rɒlək] *n (esp Brit)* Dolle *f*.

**royal** ['rɔɪəl] **1** *adj* königlich; *family, palace also* Königs-; *(fig also)* fürstlich. **2** *n (col)* Angehörige(r) *mf* der königlichen Familie.

**royal: R~ Air Force** *n (Brit)* Königliche Luftwaffe; ~ **blue 1** *adj* königsblau; **2** *n* Königsblau *nt*.

**royalist** ['rɔɪəlɪst] **1** *adj* royalistisch. **2** *n* Royalist(in *f*) *m*.

**Royal Navy** *(Brit)* **1** *n* Königliche Marine. **2** *attr* der Königlichen Marine.

**royalty** ['rɔɪəltɪ] *n* **(a)** *(rank)* das Königtum; *(collectively)* das Königshaus. **(b) royalties** *pl (from book, records)* Tantiemen *pl (on* auf *+acc)*.

**RP** = **received pronunciation** Standardaussprache *f* (des Englischen).

**rpm** = **revolutions per minute** U/min, UpM.

**RR** *(US)* = **railroad**.

**RRP** *(Brit Comm)* = **recommended retail price**.

**RSI** = **repetitive strain injury** RSI *f*, Verletzung *f* durch wiederholte Anstrengung.

**RSPB** *(Brit)* = **Royal Society for the Protection of Birds** Vogelschutzverein *m*.

**RSPCA** = **Royal Society for the Prevention of Cruelty to Animals** = Tierschutzverein *m*.

**RSVP** = **répondez s'il vous plaît** u.A.w.g.

**Rt Hon** = **Right Honourable**.

**Rt Rev** = **Right Reverend**.

**rub** [rʌb] **1** *n* **(a)** to give sth a ~ etw reiben; *furniture, shoes, silver* etw polieren. **(b)** *(fig)* there's the ~! *(old, hum)* da liegt der Hase im Pfeffer. **2** *vt* reiben; *(with towel also)* frottieren; *(polish)* polieren. to ~ one's hands **(together)** sich *(dat)* die Hände reiben; to ~ sth dry etw trockenreiben; to ~ shoulders with all sorts of people *(fig)* mit allen möglichen Leuten in Berührung kommen. **3** *vi (thing) (against* an *+dat)* reiben; *(shoes, collar)* scheuern. you must have ~bed against some wet paint da mußt du an feuchte Farbe gekommen sein.

▶**rub down** *vt sep horse (dry)* abreiben; *(clean)* striegeln; *person* abrubbeln *(col)*; *wall, paint (clean)* abwaschen; *(sandpaper)* abschmirgeln.

▶**rub in** *vt sep* **(a)** *lotion* einreiben *(to* in *+acc)*. **(b)** *(fig)* herumreiten auf *(+dat)*. don't ~ it ~ mußt du auch noch Salz in die Wunde streuen?

▶**rub off 1** *vt sep dirt etc* abreiben; *tape* löschen; *(from blackboard)* aus- or wegwischen. **2** *vi (lit, fig)* abgehen. to ~ ~ on sb *(fig)* auf jdn abfärben.

▶**rub out 1** *vt sep stain etc* herausreiben; *(with eraser)* ausradieren. **2** *vi* herausgehen; *(with eraser)* sich ausradieren lassen.

▶**rub up** *vt sep* **(a)** *table* blank reiben, *(auf)*polieren. **(b)** to ~ sb ~ the wrong way jdn aufreizen.

**rubber¹** ['rʌbəʳ] **1** *n (material)* Gummi *m*; *(Brit: eraser)* (Radier)gummi *m*. **2** *adj* Gummi-.

**rubber²** *n (Cards)* Rubber, Robber *m*.

**rubber:** ~ **band** *n* Gummiband *nt*; ~ **bullet** *n* Gummi(wucht)geschoß *nt*; ~ **plant** *n* Gummibaum *m*; ~ **stamp** *n* Stempel *m*; ~**-stamp** *vt (lit)* stempeln; *(fig)* absegnen *(fig col)*.

**rubbery** ['rʌbərɪ] *adj material* gummiartig; *meat* zäh, wie Gummi *pred*.

**rubbish** ['rʌbɪʃ] *n* Abfall *m*, Abfälle *pl*; *(household ~, in factory also)* Müll *m*; *(on building site)* Schutt

*m*; *(trashy goods, record etc)* Mist *m (col)*; *(nonsense)* Quatsch *(col)*, Blödsinn *m*. don't talk ~! red keinen Quatsch! *(col)*; ~! (so ein) Quatsch!

**rubbish** *in cpds (esp Brit)* Müll-; ~ **bin** *n* Mülleimer *m*; ~ **cart** *n* Müllwagen *m*; ~ **chute** *n* Müllschlucker *m*; ~ **collection** *n* Müllabfuhr *f*; ~ **dump** *n* Müllkippe *f*; ~ **heap** *n* Abfallhaufen *m*; ~ **tip** *n* Müllkippe *f*.

**rubbishy** ['rʌbɪʃɪ] *adj (col) goods* wertlos. ~ **novel** Schundroman *m*.

**rubble** ['rʌbl] *n* Trümmer *pl*; *(smaller pieces)* Schutt *m*.

**ruble** ['ru:bl] *n (US)* Rubel *m*.

**ruby** ['ru:bɪ] **1** *n (stone)* Rubin *m*; *(colour: also* ~ *red)* Rubinrot *nt*. **2** *adj (~-coloured)* rubinrot; *(made of rubies)* Rubin-. ~ **wedding** vierzigster Hochzeitstag.

**RUC** = **Royal Ulster Constabulary** nordirische Polizei.

**rucksack** ['rʌksæk] *n (esp Brit)* Rucksack *m*.

**ruction** ['rʌkʃən] *n (col: usu pl)* Krach *m no pl*. that'll cause ~s das gibt Zoff *(col)*.

**rudder** ['rʌdəʳ] *n (Naut, Aviat)* Ruder *nt*.

**ruddy** ['rʌdɪ] *adj (+er)* **(a)** *complexion* gesund, rot; *glow* rötlich. **(b)** *(Brit col!)* verdammt *(col)*.

**rude** [ru:d] *adj (+er)* **(a)** *(bad-mannered)* unhöflich; *(stronger)* unverschämt; *(uncouth)* grob. it's ~ to stare es gehört sich nicht, Leute anzustarren; don't be so ~! so was sagt man/tut man nicht! **(b)** *(obscene)* unanständig. **(c)** *(harsh) shock* hart; *reminder* unsanft.

**rudely** ['ru:dlɪ] *adv* **(a)** unhöflich. **(b)** to be ~ awoken unsanft aus dem Schlaf geholt werden.

**rudeness** ['ru:dnɪs] *n see adj* **(a)** Unhöflichkeit *f*; Unverschämtheit *f*; Grobheit *f*. **(b)** Unanständigkeit *f*. **(c)** Härte *f*.

**rudiment** ['ru:dɪmənt] *n* ~s *pl* Anfangsgründe *pl*.

**rudimentary** [,ru:dɪ'mentərɪ] *adj knowledge* elementar; *system* rudimentär. a ~ sort of building ein primitives Gebäude.

**rueful** *adj*, ~**ly** *adv* ['ru:fʊl, -fəlɪ] reuevoll.

**ruff** [rʌf] *n (on dress etc, of bird)* Halskrause *f*.

**ruffian** ['rʌfɪən] *n* Rüpel *m*; *(violent)* Schläger *m*.

**ruffle** ['rʌfl] *vt* **(a)** *hair, feathers* zerzausen; *surface, water* kräuseln. **(b)** *(fig) (upset, disturb)* aus der Ruhe bringen; *(annoy also)* verärgern. to get ~d aus der Ruhe kommen.

**rug** [rʌg] *n* **(a)** Teppich *m*; *(long also)* Läufer *m*; *(valuable also)* Brücke *f*; *(bedside)* (Bett)vorleger *m*. **fireside** ~ Kaminvorleger *m*. **(b)** *(blanket)* (Woll)decke *f*.

**rugby** ['rʌgbɪ] *n* Rugby *nt*. ~ **footballer** or **player** Rugbyspieler *m*; ~ **tackle** Angriff *m, bei dem der Gegner umklammert und zu Boden geworfen wird*.

**rugged** ['rʌgɪd] *adj* rauh; *mountains* zerklüftet; *ground* felsig; *features* markig; *determination* wild; *individualism* unverwüstlich.

**rugger** ['rʌgəʳ] *n (Brit col)* = **rugby**.

**ruin** ['ru:ɪn] **1** *n* **(a)** *no pl* Untergang *m*; *(of event)* Ende *nt*; *(financial, social)* Ruin *m*. **the palace was going to** ~ der Palast verfiel (zur Ruine); you'll be the ~ of me du bist noch mein Ruin. **(b)** *(ruined building)* Ruine *f*. ~**s** *(of building)* Ruinen *pl*; *(of reputation, beauty)* Reste *pl*; *(of hopes, career)* Trümmer *pl*; to be or lie in ~s *(lit)* eine Ruine sein; *(fig)* zerstört sein; *(life: financially, socially)* ruiniert sein. **2** *vt (destroy) building, hopes* zerstören; *reputation, health also* ruinieren; *(financially, socially)* ruinieren, zugrunde richten; *(spoil) clothes, event, child* verderben.

**ruination** [,ru:ɪ'neɪʃən] *n see vt* Zerstörung *f*; Ruinierung *f*; Verderben *nt*.

**ruinous** ['ruːɪnəs] *adj (financially)* ruinös; *price* extrem.

**rule** [ruːl] **1** *n* **(a)** Regel *f*; *(Admin also)* Bestimmung *f*. **the ~s of the game** *(lit, fig)* die Spielregeln; **to play by the ~s** *(lit, fig)* die Spielregeln einhalten; **running is against the ~s** Rennen ist nicht erlaubt; **by ~ of thumb** über den Daumen gepeilt; **~ book** Regelheft *nt*; **work to ~** Dienst *m* nach Vorschrift; **I make it a ~ to get up early** ich habe es mir zur Regel gemacht, früh aufzustehen; **as a ~** in der Regel. **(b)** *(authority, reign)* Herrschaft *f*; *(period also)* Regierungszeit *f*. **the ~ of law** die Rechtsstaatlichkeit. **(c)** *(for measuring)* Metermaß *nt*, Maßstab *m*.

**2** *vt* **(a)** beherrschen; *(individual also)* herrschen über; *(fig)* emotion also zügeln; **to ~ the roost** *(col)* Herr im Haus sein *(col)*. **(b)** *(Jur, Sport, Admin: give decision)* entscheiden. **his question was ~d out of order** seine Frage wurde als unzulässig abgewiesen. **(c)** *(draw lines on)* paper linieren; *(draw)* line ziehen.

**3** *vi* **(a)** *(lit, fig: reign)* herrschen *(over* über *+acc)*, regieren *(over acc)*. **(b)** *(Jur)* entscheiden *(against* gegen, *in favour of* für, *on* über *+acc)*.

▶**rule out** *vt sep (fig: exclude)* ausschließen.

**ruled** [ruːld] *adj paper* liniert.

**ruler** ['ruːlər] *n* **(a)** *(for measuring)* Lineal *nt*. **(b)** *(sovereign)* Herrscher *m*.

**ruling** ['ruːlɪŋ] **1** *adj principle* leitend, Leit-. **the ~ class** die herrschende Klasse. **2** *n (Admin, Jur)* Entscheid *m*. **to give a ~** einen Entscheid fällen.

**rum** [rʌm] *n* Rum *m*.

**Rumania** [ruːˈmeɪnɪə] *etc see* **Romania** *etc.*

**rumble** ['rʌmbl] **1** *n see vi* Grollen *nt*; Donnern *nt*; Knacken *nt*; Knurren *nt*; Rumpeln *nt (all no pl)*. **2** *vi (thunder)* grollen; *(cannon)* donnern; *(pipes)* knacken; *(stomach)* knurren; *(train, truck)* rumpeln. **to ~ past** vorbeirumpeln. **3** *vt (col: see through)* trick, person durchschauen.

**rumbustious** [rʌmˈbʌstʃəs] *adj* derb.

**ruminate** ['ruːmɪneɪt] *vi (lit)* wiederkäuen; *(fig)* grübeln *(over, about, on* über *+acc)*.

**rummage** ['rʌmɪdʒ] *vi (also ~ about, ~ around)* herumstöbern; *(in bag, pocket)* herumkramen *(among, in* in *+dat, for* nach*)*.

**rummage sale** *n (US)* ≃ Flohmarkt *m*; *(for charity)* Wohltätigkeitsbasar *m*.

**rumour, (US) rumor** ['ruːmər] **1** *n* Gerücht *nt*. **~ has it that ...** es geht das Gerücht, daß ... **2** *vt* **it is ~ed that ...** es geht das Gerücht, daß ...; *(through gossip)* man munkelt, daß ...; **he is ~ed to be rich** er soll angeblich reich sein.

**rump** [rʌmp] *n (of animal)* Hinterbacken *pl*; *(col: of person)* Hinterteil *nt*. **~ (steak)** Rumpsteak *nt*.

**rumple** ['rʌmpl] *(also ~ up)* clothes, paper zerknittern; *hair* zerzausen.

**rumpus** ['rʌmpəs] *n (col)* Krach *m*. **to kick up a ~** *(make noise)* einen Heidenlärm machen *(col)*; *(complain)* Krach schlagen *(col)*; **~ room** *(US)* Spielzimmer *nt*.

**run** [rʌn] *(vb: pret* ran, *ptp ~)* **1** *n* **(a)** *(act of running, Cricket, Baseball)* Lauf *m*. **to go for a 2-km ~** einen 2 km-Lauf machen; **he came in at a ~** er kam hereingelaufen; **he took the fence at a ~** er nahm die Hürde im Lauf; **to break into a ~** zu rennen anfangen; **to make a ~ for it** weglaufen; **on the ~** *(from the police etc)* auf der Flucht; **he has had a good ~ for his money** *(col)* er ist auf seine Kosten gekommen; *(on death)* er hatte ein ausgefülltes Leben.

**(b)** *(in vehicle)* Fahrt *f*; *(outing also)* Ausflug *m*. **to go for a ~ in the car** eine Fahrt/einen Ausflug im

Auto machen; **on the outward/inward ~** auf der Hinfahrt/Rückfahrt; *(in plane)* auf dem Hinflug/Rückflug; **the ferries on the Dover-Calais ~** die Fähren der Linie Dover-Calais.

**(c)** **to have the ~ of a place** einen Ort zur freien Verfügung haben; **to give sb the ~ of one's house** jdm sein Haus überlassen.

**(d)** **in the short/long ~** fürs nächste/auf die Dauer; *plan etc* auf kurz/lange Sicht.

**(e)** *(series)* Folge, Reihe *f*; *(Cards)* Sequenz *f*; *(Theat)* Spielzeit *f*; *(of film)* Laufzeit *f*. **the play had a long ~** das Stück lief sehr lange; **a ~ of bad luck** eine Pechsträhne; **a ~ of misfortunes** eine Serie von Mißgeschicken.

**(f)** *(great demand)* ~ **on** Ansturm *m* auf *(+acc)*; *(Comm, Fin also)* Run *m* auf *(+acc)*.

**(g)** *(track for skiing etc)* Bahn *f*. **ski ~** Abfahrt(sstrecke) *f*.

**(h)** *(animal enclosure)* Gehege *nt*; *(chicken ~)* Hühnerhof *m*.

**(i)** *(in tights)* Laufmasche *f*.

**2** *vi* **(a)** laufen, rennen; *(in race)* laufen. **to ~ past/off** vorbei-/davonlaufen *or* -rennen; **she came ~ning out** sie kam herausgelaufen *or* -gerannt; **to ~ down a slope** einen Abhang hinunterlaufen *or* -rennen; **to ~ for the bus** zum Bus laufen *or* rennen; **she ran to meet him** sie lief ihm entgegen; **she ran to help him** sie kam ihm schnell zu Hilfe; **to ~ for one's life** um sein Leben rennen; **to ~ for President** *or* **for the Presidency** für die Präsidentschaft kandidieren; **a rumour ran through the school** ein Gerücht ging in der Schule um; **a shiver ran down her spine** ein Schauer lief ihr über den Rücken; **don't come ~ning to me if ...** du brauchst nicht bei mir anzukommen, wenn ...

**(b)** *(become)* **to ~ dry** *(river)* austrocknen; *(pen)* leer werden; *(resources)* ausgehen; **he ran short of ideas** ihm gingen die Ideen aus; **supplies are ~ning low** die Vorräte werden knapp.

**(c)** *(flow) (river, electric current)* fließen; *(eyes)* tränen; *(nose, tap)* laufen; *(paint)* zerfließen, ineinanderfließen; *(dye: in washing)* färben; *(ink)* fließen. **where the river ~s into the sea** wo der Fluß ins Meer mündet; **the street ~s into the square** die Straße mündet auf den Platz; **inflation is ~ning at 20%** die Inflationsrate beträgt 20%; **your bath is ~ning** Ihr Badewasser läuft ein; **the floor was ~ning with water** der Fußboden schwamm vor Wasser; **his blood ran cold** das Blut gefror ihm in den Adern.

**(d)** *(play, contract, Jur: sentence)* laufen; *(Fin: interest rate)* gelten. **the contract has 10 months to ~** der Vertrag läuft noch 10 Monate; **the expenditure ~s into thousands of pounds** die Ausgaben gehen in die Tausende (von Pfund); **I can't ~ to a new car** ich kann mir kein neues Auto leisten.

**(e)** *(bus, train etc)* fahren. **this train ~s between London and Manchester** dieser Zug verkehrt zwischen London und Manchester; **the buses ~ once an hour** die Busse fahren stündlich.

**(f)** *(function; also Comp)* laufen; *(factory)* arbeiten. **when the central heating is ~ning** wenn die Zentralheizung angeschaltet ist; **the car is ~ning smoothly** der Wagen läuft ohne Schwierigkeiten; **if everything ~s smoothly** wenn alles glatt geht; **you mustn't leave the engine ~ning** Sie dürfen den Motor nicht laufen lassen; **this model ~s on diesel** dieses Auto fährt mit Diesel; **the radio ~s off the mains/off batteries** das Radio läuft auf Netz/Batterie; **all trains are ~ning late** alle Züge haben Verspätung; **the project is ~ning late** das Projekt hat sich verzögert; **this story will ~ and ~** diese Story ist ein Dauerbrenner *(col)*.

**(g)** *(road)* gehen, führen; *(mountains)* sich erstrecken; *(river)* fließen; *line* sich ziehen. **the main road ~s north and south** die Hauptstraße führt von Norden nach Süden; **the river ~s for 300 km** der Fluß ist 300 km lang; **this theme ~s through his work** dieses Thema zieht sich durch sein ganzes Werk.

**(h) to ~ in the family** in der Familie liegen.

**(i)** *(stocking)* eine Laufmasche bekommen.

**(j)** *(roll, slide)* *(drawer, curtains)* laufen, gleiten; *(vehicle)* rollen.

**3** *vt* **(a)** *distance* laufen, rennen; *race* laufen. **he ~s 3 km every day** er läuft jeden Tag 3 km; **to ~ errands** Botengänge machen; **to ~ a stoplight** *(US)* bei Rot über die Kreuzung fahren; **to ~ its course** *(event, disease)* seinen Lauf nehmen; **to ~ a temperature** Fieber haben; **to ~ sb off his feet** *(col)* jdn ständig in Trab halten *(col)*; **to ~ sb into debt** jdn in Schulden stürzen.

**(b) I'll ~ you a bath** ich lasse Ihnen ein Bad einlaufen; **he ~s his words together** bei ihm fließen alle Wörter ineinander über.

**(c)** *(transport)* *person, thing* fahren, bringen; *(drive)* *vehicle* fahren. **he ran her home** er brachte sie nach Hause; **this company ~s a bus service** diese Firma unterhält einen Busdienst; **they ~ trains to London every hour** es besteht stündlicher Zugverkehr nach London.

**(d)** *(operate)* *machine* betreiben *(on mit)*; *(person)* bedienen. **to ~ a radio off the mains** ein Radio auf Netz laufen lassen; **I can't afford to ~ a car** ich kann es mir nicht leisten, ein Auto zu unterhalten; **he ~s a Rolls** er fährt einen Rolls Royce; **this car is cheap to ~** dieses Auto ist billig im Unterhalt; **to ~ a program** *(Comp)* ein Programm laufen lassen.

**(e)** *(manage, be in charge of)* leiten; *shop* führen; *(organize)* *course of study, competition* durchführen. **a well-~ hotel** ein gutgeführtes Hotel; **I want to ~ my own life** ich möchte mein eigenes Leben leben; **she's the one who really ~s everything** sie ist diejenige, die den Laden schmeißt *(col)*.

**(f)** *(move, put)* **to ~ one's finger down a list** mit dem Finger eine Liste durchgehen; **to ~ a comb through one's hair** sich *(dat)* mit einem Kamm durch die Haare fahren; **to ~ one's eye over a page** eine Seite überfliegen.

**(g)** *(take, lead etc)* *rope, road* führen; *line, ditch* ziehen; *pipe, wires* (ver)legen; *(above ground)* führen.

**(h)** *(Press: publish)* *article, series* bringen.

▶**run about** *or* **around** *vi (lit, fig)* herumlaufen *or* -rennen.

▶**run across 1** *vi* **(a)** *(lit)* hinüber-/herüberlaufen. **(b)** *(go to see)* kurz rüberlaufen *(to zu)*. **2** *vi +prep obj (meet)* *person* zufällig treffen; *(find)* *object, reference* stoßen auf *(+acc)*.

▶**run along** *vi* laufen, rennen; *(go away)* gehen. **~ ~!** *(to children)* nun geht mal schön!

▶**run away** *vi* **(a)** *(person, animal)* weglaufen; *(horse)* durchgehen. **to ~ ~ from home** von zu Hause weglaufen. **(b)** *(water)* auslaufen.

▶**run away with** *vi +prep obj (steal)* *money, object* durchbrennen mit *(col)*; *(Sport etc: win easily)* *race, prize* spielend gewinnen. **don't ~ ~ ~ the idea that ...** *(fig)* kommen Sie nur nicht auf den Gedanken, daß ...; **he lets his imagination ~ ~ ~ him** seine Phantasie geht leicht mit ihm durch.

▶**run down 1** *vi* **(a)** *(lit: person)* hinunter-/herunterlaufen. **(b)** *(watch, clock)* ablaufen; *(bat-*

*tery)* leer werden. **to let stocks ~ ~** das Lager leer werden lassen; *(deliberately)* die Vorräte abbauen. **2** *vt sep* **(a)** *(knock down)* umfahren; *(run over)* überfahren. **(b)** *factory, shop* (allmählich) auflösen; *department, stocks, staff* abbauen; *battery* zu stark belasten. **(c)** *(disparage)* schlechtmachen *(col)*.

▶**run in** *vt sep* **(a)** *(Brit)* *car* einfahren. **(b)** *(col: arrest)* schnappen *(col)*.

▶**run into** *vi +prep obj (meet)* zufällig treffen; *(collide with)* rennen/fahren gegen. **to ~ ~ trouble/problems** Ärger bekommen/auf Probleme stoßen; **to ~ ~ danger/debt** in Gefahr/Schulden geraten.

▶**run off 1** *vi* = **run away (a)**. **2** *vt sep* **(a)** *water* ablassen. **(b)** *(reproduce)* *copy* abziehen.

▶**run on** *vi* **(a)** *(lit)* weiterlaufen. **you ~ ~, I'll catch up** geh schon mal voraus, ich komme nach. **(b) it ran ~ for four hours** das zog sich über vier Stunden hin.

▶**run out** *vi* **(a)** *(person)* hinaus-/herauslaufen; *(rope, chain)* ablaufen; *(liquid)* herauslaufen; *(through leak)* auslaufen. **(b)** *(come to an end)* *contract, period of time* ablaufen; *(money, supplies)* zu Ende gehen. **my patience is ~ning ~** mir geht langsam die Geduld aus.

▶**run out of** *vi +prep obj* **he ran ~ ~ money/patience/time** ihm ging das Geld/die Geduld aus/er hatte keine Zeit mehr.

▶**run over 1** *vi* **(a)** *(to neighbour etc)* kurz hinübergehen *or* rübergehen *(col)*. **(b)** *(overflow: liquid, container)* überlaufen. **(c)** *(Rad, TV etc)* überziehen. **2** *vi +prep obj* *story, part in play, details* durchgehen; *text, notes* durchsehen. **3** *vt sep (in vehicle)* überfahren.

▶**run through** *vi +prep obj* **(a)** *(use up)* *money* durchbringen. **(b)** *(rehearse)* *play* durchspielen; *ceremony also, part* durchgehen. **(c)** = **run over 2**.

▶**run up 1** *vi (lit)* *(upstairs etc)* hinauf-/herauflaufen; *(towards sb/sth)* hin-/herlaufen *(to zu)*. **to ~ ~ against difficulties** auf Schwierigkeiten stoßen. **2** *vt sep* machen. **to ~ ~ a debt** Schulden machen.

**run:** **~about** *n (car)* Kleinwagen *m*, Autochen *nt (col)*; **~around** *n (col)* **to give sb the ~around** jdn an der Nase herumführen *(col)*; **~away** **1** *n* Ausreißer(in *f*) *m*; **2** *adj* *slave* entlaufen; *person, horse* ausgerissen; *car etc* der/die/das sich selbständig gemacht hat; *inflation* unkontrollierbar; **he had a ~away victory** er hatte einen sehr leichten Sieg; **~-down** **1** *n (col: summary)* Zusammenfassung *f*; **to give sb a ~-down on sth** jdm einen Überblick über etw *(acc)* geben; **2** *adj* *(dilapidated)* heruntergekommen; *(tired)* abgespannt; *battery* leer; **to be (feeling) ~-down** abgespannt sein.

**rune** [ruːn] *n* Rune *f*.

**rung¹** [rʌŋ] *ptp of* **ring²**.

**rung²** *n (of ladder)* Sprosse *f*; *(of chair)* Querstab *m*.

**runner** ['rʌnə<sup>r</sup>] *n* **(a)** *(athlete)* Läufer(in *f*) *m*. **(b)** *(on sledge)* Kufe *f*; *(for curtain)* Röllchen *nt*; *(for drawer, machine part)* Laufschiene *f*. **(c)** *(Bot)* **~ bean** *(Brit)* Stangenbohne *f*.

**runner-up** ['rʌnər'ʌp] *n* Zweite(r) *mf*. **the runners-up** die weiteren Plätze; *(in competition)* die weiteren Gewinner.

**running** ['rʌnɪŋ] **1** *n* **(a)** Laufen, Rennen *nt*. **to make the ~** *(lit, fig)* das Rennen machen; **to be in the ~ (for sth)** im Rennen (für etw) liegen. **(b)** *(functioning: of machine)* Laufen *nt*. **in ~ order** betriebsbereit. **(c)** *(management)* see **run 3 (e)** Leitung *f*; Führung *f*; Durchführung *f*. **2** *adj* **(a)** **~ jump** Sprung *m* mit Anlauf; **go and take a ~ jump** *(col)* du kannst mich (mal) gern haben *(col)*; **~ commen-**

**tary** *(Rad, TV)* fortlaufender Kommentar. **(b) 4 days** ~ 4 Tage hintereinander. **(c)** *(flowing) water etc* fließend; *tap, nose* laufend; *eyes* tränend. ~ **sore** *(Med)* eiternde Wunde; *(fig)* Eiterbeule *f.*

**running:** ~ **battle** *n (Mil)* Gefecht *nt*; *(fig)* Kleinkrieg *m*; ~ **costs** *npl* Betriebskosten *pl*; *(of car)* Unterhaltskosten *pl*; ~ **head** *n (Typ)* Kolumnentitel *m*; ~ **mate** *n (US Pol) Kandidat m für die Vizepräsidentschaft*; ~ **shoe** *n* Rennschuh *m*; ~ **shorts** *npl* (kurze) Sporthose *f.*

**runny** [ˈrʌnɪ] *adj (+er)* flüssig; *honey* dünnflüssig; *nose* laufend; *eyes* wässerig.

**run:** ~**-off** *n (Sport)* Entscheidungslauf *m*, Stechen *nt*; ~**-of-the-mill** *adj* durchschnittlich; *theme, novel* Feld-Wald-und-Wiesen *(col)*; ~**-up** *n (Sport)* Anlauf *m*; **in the final** ~**-up to** ... in der letzten Phase vor *(+dat)* ...

**runway** [ˈrʌnweɪ] *n (Aviat)* Start- und Landebahn *f*, Runway *f or m.*

**rupee** [ruːˈpiː] *n* Rupie *f.*

**rupture** [ˈrʌptʃər] **1** *n (lit, fig)* Bruch *m*; *(Pol: of relations)* Abbruch *m.* **2** *vt* brechen. **to** ~ **oneself** *(col)* sich *(dat)* einen Bruch heben *(col).*

**rural** [ˈrʊərəl] *adj* ländlich; *life also* Land-.

**ruse** [ruːz] *n* List *f.*

**rush¹** [rʌʃ] **1** *n* **(a)** *(of crowd)* Gedränge *nt*; *(of air)* Stoß *m*; *(Mil: attack)* Sturm *m.* **they made a** ~ **for the door** sie drängten zur Tür; **to make a** ~ **at** losstürzen auf *(+acc)*; **there's been a** ~ **on these goods** diese Waren sind rasend schnell weggegangen; **we have a** ~ **on in the office just now** bei uns im Büro herrscht zur Zeit Hochbetrieb; **the Christmas** ~ der Weihnachtsbetrieb; **we've had a** ~ **of orders** wir hatten eine Flut von Aufträgen; **water streamed out in a** ~ das Wasser schoß in einem Schwall heraus.

**(b)** *(hurry)* Eile *f*; *(stronger)* Hetze *f.* **to be in a** ~ in Eile sein; **I did it in a** ~ ich habe es sehr hastig gemacht; **what's the** ~? wozu die Eile/Hetzerei?; **is there any** ~ **for this?** eilt das?; **it all happened in such a** ~ das ging alles so plötzlich.

**2** *vi (hurry)* eilen; *(stronger)* hetzen; *(run)* stürzen; *(wind)* brausen; *(water)* schießen. **they** ~**ed to help her** sie eilten ihr zu Hilfe; **I'm** ~**ing to finish it** ich beeile mich, es fertigzumachen; **don't** ~, **take your time** überstürzen Sie nichts, lassen Sie sich Zeit; **to** ~ **through** *book* hastig lesen; *meal* hastig essen; *museum, town* hetzen durch; *work* hastig erledigen; **to** ~ **past** *(person)* vorbeistürzen; *(vehicle)* vorbeischießen; **to** ~ **in/out** *etc* hinein-/hinausstürzen; **the ambulance** ~**ed to the scene** der Krankenwagen raste zur Unfallstelle.

**3** *vt* **(a)** **to** ~ **sb to hospital** jdn schnellstens ins Krankenhaus bringen; **they** ~**ed more troops to the front** sie schickten eilends mehr Truppen an die Front; **they** ~**ed the bill through Parliament** sie peitschten die Gesetzesvorlage durch das Parlament.

**(b)** *(force to hurry)* hetzen, drängen. **don't** ~ **me!** hetz mich nicht; **he won't be** ~**ed** er läßt sich nicht drängen; **to be** ~**ed off one's feet** dauernd auf Trab sein; **to** ~ **sb off his feet** jdn dauernd auf Trab hal-

ten; **to** ~ **sb into doing sth** jdn dazu drängen, etw zu tun.

**(c)** *(charge at)* stürmen; *fence* zustürmen auf *(+acc).* **the mob** ~**ed the line of policemen** der Mob stürmte auf die Polizeikette zu.

**(d)** *(do hurriedly) job, task* hastig machen; *(do badly)* schludern bei *(col).* **you can't** ~ **this sort of work** für solche Arbeit muß man sich *(dat)* Zeit lassen.

▶**rush about** *or* **around** *vi* herumhetzen.

▶**rush out 1** *vi* hinaus-/herauseilen; *(very fast)* hinaus-/herausstürzen. **he** ~**ed** ~ **and bought one** er kaufte sofort eines. **2** *vt sep troops, supplies* eilends hintransportieren.

▶**rush through** *vt sep order* durchjagen; *goods, supplies* eilends durchschleusen.

▶**rush up** *vi (lit)* hinauf-/heraufeilen; *(very fast)* hinauf-/heraufstürzen.

**rush²** *n (Bot)* Binse *f.*

**rush:** ~**-hour(s** *pl)* *n* Hauptverkehrszeit(en *pl*), Rush-hour *f*; ~**-hour traffic** Stoßverkehr *m*; ~ **job** *n* eiliger Auftrag; *(pej: bad work)* Schluderarbeit *f (col)*; ~ **matting** *n* Binsenmatte *f.*

**rusk** [rʌsk] *n* Zwieback *m.*

**russet** [ˈrʌsɪt] *adj* rostfarben.

**Russia** [ˈrʌʃə] *n* Rußland *nt.*

**Russian** [ˈrʌʃən] **1** *adj* russisch. **2** *n* **(a)** Russe *m*, Russin *f.* **(b)** *(language)* Russisch *nt.*

**rust** [rʌst] **1** *n* Rost *m.* ~**-proof** rostfrei. **2** *adj (also* ~**-coloured)* rostfarben. **3** *vi* rosten.

▶**rust through** *vi* durchrosten.

**rustic** [ˈrʌstɪk] **1** *n* Bauer *m.* **2** *adj* bäuerlich; *furniture, style* rustikal; *manners* bäurisch *(pej).*

**rustle** [ˈrʌsl] **1** *n* Rascheln *nt*; *(of foliage)* Rauschen *nt.* **2** *vi (leaves, silk, papers)* rascheln; *(foliage, skirts)* rauschen. **3** *vt* **(a)** *paper, leaves on ground etc* rascheln mit; *(wind) leaves on tree* rauschen in *(+dat).* **(b)** *(US: steal) cattle* klauen *(col).*

▶**rustle up** *vt sep (col) meal* improvisieren *(col).*

**rustler** [ˈrʌslər] *n (US: cattle-thief)* Viehdieb *m.*

**rust:** ~**proof** *adj* rostfrei; ~**proofing** *n* Rostschutz *m*; *(substance)* Rostschutzmittel *nt.*

**rusty** [ˈrʌstɪ] *adj (+er) (lit)* rostig; *(fig) French, maths* eingerostet; *talent* verkümmert. **I'm a bit** ~ ich bin etwas aus der Übung.

**rut¹** [rʌt] *n (in track, path)* Spur, Furche *f*; *(fig: routine)* Trott *m (col).* **to be in a** ~ *(fig)* im Trott sein *(col)*; **to get into a** ~ *(person)* in einen Trott geraten *(col).*

**rut²** *n (Zool)* Brunst *f.*

**rutabaga** [ˌruːtəˈbeɪgə] *n (US)* Steckrübe *f.*

**ruthless** [ˈruːθlɪs] *adj person* rücksichtslos; *treatment, irony* schonungslos. **you'll have to be** ~ da müssen Sie ganz hart sein.

**ruthlessly** [ˈruːθlɪslɪ] *adv see adj.*

**ruthlessness** [ˈruːθlɪsnɪs] *n see adj* Rücksichtslosigkeit *f*; Schonungslosigkeit *f.*

**rutted** [ˈrʌtɪd] *adj* zerfurcht.

**RV** *(US)* = **recreational vehicle** Wohnmobil *nt*; *(trailer)* Wohnwagen *m.*

**rye** [raɪ] *n (grain)* Roggen *m*; *(US col)* Rye(whisky) *m.* ~**(bread)** Roggenbrot *nt.*

# S

**S, s** [es] n S, s nt. **S for Sugar** ≃ S wie Samuel.
**S** = **(a) south** S. **(b) Saint** St. **(c)** *(on clothes)* **small. (d)** *(US Sch)* **satisfactory** ≃ 3.
**s** = **seconds** Sek.
**SA** = **(a) South Africa. (b) South America.**
**Sabbath** ['sæbθ] n Sabbat m.
**sabbatical** [sə'bætɪkəl] n Bildungsurlaub m; *(for research)* Forschungsurlaub m. **to be on** ~ Bildungsurlaub/Forschungsurlaub haben; **to take a** ~ sich beurlauben lassen.
**sable** ['seɪbl] n Zobel m; *(fur)* Zobelpelz m.
**sabotage** ['sæbətɑː3] **1** n Sabotage f. **2** vt *(lit, fig)* sabotieren.
**saboteur** [,sæbə'tɜːʳ] n Saboteur m.
**sabre,** *(US)* **saber** ['seɪbəʳ] n Säbel m. **~-rattling** Säbelrasseln nt.
**saccharin** ['sækərɪn] n Saccharin nt.
**sachet** ['sæʃeɪ] n Beutel m; *(of powder)* Päckchen nt; *(of shampoo, cream)* Beutelchen nt.
**sack** [sæk] **1** n **(a)** Sack m. **two ~s of coal** zwei Sack Kohlen. **(b)** *(col: dismissal)* Entlassung f, Rausschmiß m *(col).* **to get the** ~ rausfliegen *(col)*; **to give sb the** ~ jdn rausschmeißen *(col).* **(c)** *(col: bed)* **to hit the** ~ sich in die Falle hauen *(col).* **2** vt *(col: dismiss)* rausschmeißen *(col)*, entlassen.
**sackful** ['sækfʊl] n Sack m. **two ~s of potatoes** zwei Sack Kartoffeln.
**sacking** ['sækɪŋ] n **(a)** *(material)* Sackleinen nt. **(b)** *(col: dismissal)* Entlassung f.
**sacrament** ['sækrəmənt] n Sakrament nt.
**sacred** ['seɪkrɪd] adj heilig; *music* geistlich; *building* sakral. **is nothing ~?** *(col)* ist denn nichts mehr heilig?; ~ **cow** *(lit, fig)* heilige Kuh.
**sacrifice** ['sækrɪfaɪs] **1** n *(lit, fig)* Opfer nt. **to make ~s** Opfer bringen. **2** vt opfern *(sth to sb* jdm etw*).*
**sacrificial** [,sækrɪ'fɪʃəl] adj Opfer-.
**sacrilege** ['sækrɪlɪdʒ] n Sakrileg nt; *(fig also)* Frevel m. **that's** ~ das ist ein Sakrileg.
**sacrilegious** [,sækrɪ'lɪdʒəs] adj *(lit)* gotteslästerlich; *(fig)* frevelhaft.
**sacristy** ['sækrɪstɪ] n Sakristei f.
**sacrosanct** ['sækrəʊ,sæŋkt] adj *(lit, fig)* sakrosankt.
**SAD** abbr (= **seasonal affective disorder**) jahreszeitlich bedingte Depression.
**sad** [sæd] adj (+er) traurig; *loss* schmerzlich; *colour* trist; *result also, mistake, lack* bedauerlich. **to feel** ~ traurig sein; **a** ~ **state of affairs** eine traurige Sache.
**sadden** ['sædn] vt betrüben.
**saddle** ['sædl] **1** n *(also of hill)* Sattel m; *(of meat)* Rücken m. **to be in the** ~ *(lit)* im Sattel sein; *(fig)* im Sattel sitzen. **2** vt **(a)** *horse* satteln. **(b)** *(col)* **to ~ sb with sb/sth** jdm jdn/etw aufhalsen *(col).*
**saddlebag** ['sædlbæg] n Satteltasche f.
**sadism** ['seɪdɪzəm] n Sadismus m.
**sadist** ['seɪdɪst] n Sadist(in f) m.
**sadistic** [sə'dɪstɪk] adj sadistisch.
**sadly** ['sædlɪ] adv **(a)** traurig; *(unfortunately)* traurigerweise. **(b)** *(regrettably)* bedauerlich. **he is** ~ **lacking in any sense of humour** ihm fehlt leider jeglicher Humor; **she will be** ~ **missed** sie wird uns allen sehr fehlen.
**sadness** ['sædnɪs] n Traurigkeit f. **our** ~ **at his death** unsere Trauer über seinen Tod.
**sae** = **stamped addressed envelope.**
**safari** [sə'fɑːrɪ] n Safari f. **to be/go on** ~ auf Safari sein/gehen; ~ **park** Safaripark m.
**safe¹** [seɪf] n *(for valuables)* Safe m or nt, Tresor m.
**safe²** **1** adj (+er) sicher; *method also, player* zuverlässig; *(cautious) policy* vorsichtig; *estimate* realistisch; *(not dangerous)* ungefährlich; *(out of danger)* in Sicherheit; *(not injured)* unverletzt. ~ **sex** geschützter Sex; **to be** ~ **from sb/sth** vor jdm/etw sicher sein; **to keep sth** ~ etw sicher aufbewahren; **all the passengers are** ~ alle Passagiere sind in Sicherheit or *(not injured)* unverletzt; ~ **journey!** gute Fahrt/Reise!; ~ **journey home!** komm gut nach Hause!; **thank God you're** ~ Gott sei Dank ist dir nichts passiert; ~ **and sound** gesund und wohlbehalten; **the patient is** ~ **now** der Patient ist jetzt außer Gefahr; **the secret is** ~ **with me** bei mir ist das Geheimnis gut aufgehoben; **this car is not** ~ **to drive** das Auto ist nicht verkehrssicher; **she is not** ~ **on the roads** sie ist eine Gefahr im Straßenverkehr; **it's a** ~ **bet** or **assumption that ...** man kann mit ziemlicher Sicherheit annehmen, daß ...; **it's a** ~ **guess** es ist so gut wie sicher; **I think it's** ~ **to say** ... ich glaube, man kann wohl sagen ...; **better** ~ **than sorry** Vorsicht ist besser als Nachsicht *(Prov)*; **just to be on the** ~ **side** um ganz sicher zu sein.
**2** adv **to play (it)** ~ *(col)* auf Nummer Sicher gehen *(col).*
**safe:** **~-breaker** n Safeknacker m *(col)*; **~-conduct** n freies Geleit; **~-cracker** n *(US)* = **~-breaker**; **~-deposit** n Tresorraum m; **~-deposit box** n Banksafe m or nt, Schließfach nt; **~guard 1** n Schutz m; **as a ~guard against** zum Schutz gegen; **2** vt schützen *(against* vor +*dat)*; *interests* wahrnehmen; **3** vi **to ~guard against sth** sich gegen etw absichern; ~ **house** n Zufluchtsort m; *(used by terrorists)* ≃ konspirative Wohnung; **~-keeping** n sichere Verwahrung; **to give sb sth for ~-keeping** jdm etw zur (sicheren) Aufbewahrung geben.
**safely** ['seɪflɪ] adv *(unharmed) arrive* wohlbehalten; *(without problems also)* sicher, gut; *(without risk)* gefahrlos; *drive* vorsichtig; *(solidly, firmly)* sicher, fest; *(not dangerously)* ungefährlich. **I think I can** ~ **say** ... ich glaube, ich kann wohl sagen ...; **I got** ~ **through the first interview** ich bin gut or heil durch das erste Gespräch gekommen; **to put sth away** ~ etw an einem sicheren Ort verwahren.
**safeness** ['seɪfnɪs] n Sicherheit f.
**safety** ['seɪftɪ] n Sicherheit f. **in a place of** ~ an einem sicheren Ort; **for ~'s sake** aus Sicherheitsgründen; **with complete** ~ vollkommen sicher; ~ **first!** Sicherheit geht vor!; **to play for** ~ *(fig)* sicher-

gehen; **(there's)** ~ **in numbers** zu mehreren ist man sicherer; **when we reached the** ~ **of the opposite bank** als wir sicher das andere Ufer erreicht hatten; **to leap to** ~ sich in Sicherheit bringen.

**safety:** ~ **belt** *n* Sicherheitsgurt *m*; ~ **catch** *n (on gun)* (Abzugs)sicherung *f*; ~ **curtain** *n (Theat)* eiserner Vorhang; ~ **factor** *n* Sicherheitsfaktor *m*; ~ **glass** *n* Sicherheitsglas *nt*; ~ **helmet** *n* Schutzhelm *m*; ~ **margin** *n* Sicherheitsspielraum *m*; ~ **match** *n* Sicherheitszündholz *nt*; ~ **measure** *n* Sicherheitsmaßnahme *f*; ~ **net** *n* Sprungnetz *nt*; ~ **pin** *n* Sicherheitsnadel *f*; ~ **valve** *n* Sicherheitsventil *nt*; *(fig)* Ventil *nt*.

**saffron** ['sæfrən] **1** *n* Safran *m*. **2** *adj* Safran-; *(in colour)* safrangelb.

**sag** [sæg] *vi* absacken; *(in the middle)* durchhängen; *(shoulders)* herabhängen; *(production, rate)* zurückgehen; *(price, spirit)* sinken; *(conversation)* stocken.

**saga** ['sɑːgə] *n* Saga *f*; *(novel also)* Generationsroman *m*; *(fig)* Geschichte *f*.

**sagacious** [sə'geɪʃəs] *adj* weise, klug.

**sage¹** [seɪdʒ] *n* Weise(r) *m*.

**sage²** *n (Bot)* Salbei *m*.

**Sagittarius** [,sædʒɪ'tɛərɪəs] *n* Schütze *m*.

**sago** ['seɪgəu] *n* Sago *m*.

**Sahara** [sə'hɑːrə] *n* Sahara *f*.

**said** [sed] **1** *pret, ptp of* **say**. **2** *adj (form)* besagt.

**sail** [seɪl] **1** *n* Segel *nt*; *(of windmill)* Flügel *m*; *(trip)* Fahrt *f*. **under** ~ mit aufgezogenen Segeln; **in** *or* **under full** ~ mit vollen Segeln; **to set** ~ **(for ...)** los- *or* abfahren (nach ...); *(with yacht)* absegeln (nach ...); **it's (a) 3 days'** ~ **from here** von hier aus fährt *or (in yacht)* segelt man 3 Tage dorthin; **to go for a** ~ segeln gehen.

**2** *vt* boat segeln mit; *liner etc* steuern. **they** ~**ed the ship to Cadiz** sie segelten nach Cadiz; **to** ~ **the seas** die Meere befahren.

**3** *vi* **(a)** *(Naut)* fahren; *(with yacht)* segeln. **are you flying** *or* ~**ing?** fliegen Sie, oder fahren Sie mit dem Schiff?; **I went** ~**ing for a week** ich ging eine Woche segeln; **to** ~ **around the world** um die Welt segeln. **(b)** *(leave)* *(for* nach*)* abfahren; *(yacht, person in yacht)* absegeln. **passengers** ~**ing for New York** Passagiere nach New York. **(c)** *(fig: glider, swan etc)* gleiten; *(moon, clouds)* ziehen; *(ball, object)* fliegen. **she** ~**ed past/out of the room** sie rauschte vorbei *(col)*/aus dem Zimmer *(col)*; **she** ~**ed through all her exams** sie schaffte alle Prüfungen spielend; **the holidays just** ~**ed by** *(col)* die Ferien vergingen wie im Flug.

**sail:** ~**board 1** *n* Windsurfbrett *nt*; **2** *vi* windsurfen; ~**boarding** *n* Windsurfen *nt*; ~**boat** *n (US)* Segelboot *nt*.

**sailing** ['seɪlɪŋ] *n* **(a)** Segeln *nt*; *(as sport also)* Segelsport *m*. **(b) when is the next** ~ **for Arran?** wann fährt das nächste Schiff nach Arran?

**sailing:** ~ **boat** *n (Brit)* Segelboot *nt*; ~ **ship** *n* Segelschiff *nt*.

**sailor** ['seɪlər] *n* **(a)** Seemann *m*; *(in navy)* Matrose *m*; *(sportsman)* Segler(in *f*) *m*. **(b) to be a bad** ~ *(get seasick)* nicht seefest sein.

**saint** [seɪnt] *n (also fig)* Heilige(r) *mf*; *(before name abbr to* **St** [snt]*)* Sankt. **St John** der heilige Johannes, St. Johannes; **St. Mark's (Church)** die Markuskirche.

**saintliness** ['seɪntlɪnɪs] *n* Heiligmäßigkeit *f*.

**saintly** ['seɪntlɪ] *adj (+er)* heiligmäßig; *(fig pej)* smile lammfromm.

**sake** [seɪk] *n* **for the** ~ **of ...** um *(+gen)* ... willen; **for your own** ~ dir selbst zuliebe; **for your family's** ~ um Ihrer Familie willen; **for heaven's** ~! *(col)* um

Gottes willen!; **for heaven's** *or* **Christ's** ~ **shut up** *(col)* nun halt doch endlich die Klappe *(col)*; **for old times'** ~ in Erinnerung an alte Zeiten; **for the** ~ **of those who ...** für diejenigen, die ...; **and all for the** ~ **of a few pounds** und alles wegen ein paar Pfund.

**salacious** [sə'leɪʃəs] *adj* schlüpfrig.

**salad** ['sæləd] *n* Salat *m*.

**salad:** ~ **bowl** *n* Salatschüssel *f*; ~ **cream** *n (Brit)* ≃ Mayonnaise *f*; ~ **dressing** *n* Salatsoße *f*; ~ **oil** *n* Salatöl *nt*; ~ **servers** *npl* Salatbesteck *nt*; ~ **spinner** *n* Salatschleuder *f*.

**salami** [sə'lɑːmɪ] *n* Salami *f*.

**salaried** ['sælərɪd] *adj* ~ **post** Angestelltenposten *m*; ~ **staff** Gehaltsempfänger *pl*.

**salary** ['sælərɪ] *n* Gehalt *nt*. ~ **earner** Gehaltsempfänger(in *f*) *m*; ~ **increase** Gehaltserhöhung *f*; ~ **scale** Gehaltsskala *f*.

**sale** [seɪl] *n* **(a)** *(selling)* Verkauf *m*; *(instance)* Geschäft *nt*; *(of insurance, bulk order)* Abschluß *m*. ~**s** *pl (turnover)* der Absatz; **for** ~ zu verkaufen; **to put sth up for** ~ etw zum Verkauf anbieten; **not for** ~ nicht verkäuflich; **to be on** ~ verkauft werden; **on** ~ **at all bookshops** in allen Buchhandlungen erhältlich; **on a** ~ **or return basis** auf Verkaufsbasis mit Rückgaberecht. **(b)** *(at reduced prices)* Ausverkauf *m*; *(at end of season)* Schlußverkauf *m*; *(clearance* ~*)* Räumungsverkauf *m*. **to go to the** ~**s** zum Ausverkauf *etc* gehen; **they've got a** ~ **on** da ist Ausverkauf *etc*; **to buy in the** ~**s** im Ausverkauf *etc* kaufen.

**saleable,** *(US)* **salable** ['seɪləbl] *adj (marketable)* absatzfähig; *(in* ~ *condition)* verkäuflich.

**sale:** ~ **price** *n* Ausverkaufspreis *m*; ~**room** *n (Brit)* Auktionsraum *m*.

**sales:** ~ **assistant** *(Brit)*, ~ **clerk** *n (US)* Verkäufer(in *f*) *m*; ~ **conference** *n* Vertreterversammlung *f*; ~ **department** *n* Verkaufsabteilung *f*; ~ **drive** *n* Verkaufskampagne *f*; ~ **figures** *npl* Verkaufs- *or* Absatzziffern *pl*; ~ **force** *n* Vertreterstab *m*; ~**man** *n* Verkäufer *m*; *(representative)* Vertreter *m*; ~ **manager** *n* Verkaufsleiter *m*.

**salesmanship** ['seɪlzmənʃɪp] *n* Verkaufstechnik *f*.

**sales:** ~ **patter** *n* = ~ **talk**; ~**person** *n* Verkäufer(in *f*) *m*; ~**room** *n (US)* Verkaufsraum *m*; ~ **talk** *n* Verkaufsgespräch *nt*; ~ **tax** *n (US)* Verkaufssteuer *f*; ~**woman** *n* Verkäuferin *f*.

**salient** ['seɪlɪənt] *adj (lit)* hervorstehend; *(fig)* hervorstechend. **the** ~ **points of his argument** die Hauptpunkte *pl* seiner Argumentation.

**saline** ['seɪlaɪn] *adj* salzig. ~ **solution** Salzlösung *f*.

**saliva** [sə'laɪvə] *n* Speichel *m*.

**salivate** ['sælɪveɪt] *vi* Speichel produzieren; *(animal)* geifern; *(old people, baby)* sabbern.

**sallow** ['sæləu] *adj* bleich; *colour* fahl.

**sally** ['sælɪ] *vi:* **sally forth** *(old, hum: set out)* sich aufmachen.

**salmon** ['sæmən] **1** *n, pl* - Lachs *m*. **2** *adj (in colour)* lachs(farben).

**salmonella** [,sælmə'nelə] *n (also* ~ **poisoning***)* Salmonellenvergiftung *f*.

**salon** ['sælɒn] *n (all senses)* Salon *m*.

**saloon** [sə'luːn] *n* Saal *m*; *(Naut)* Salon *m*; *(US: bar)* Wirtschaft *f*; *(in Westerns)* Saloon *m*.

**saloon:** ~ **bar** *n (Brit) vornehmerer Teil eines Lokals*; ~ **car** *n (Brit)* Limousine *f*.

**Salop** ['sæləp] *(Brit)* = **Shropshire.**

**salt** [sɔːlt] **1** *n (Cook, Chem)* Salz *nt*. ~ **of the earth** *(fig)* Salz der Erde; **to take sth with a pinch of** ~ *(fig)* etw nicht ganz so wörtlich nehmen; **to rub** ~ **into the wound** *(fig)* Salz in die Wunde streuen. **2** *adj* meat, water *etc* Salz-; *butter* gesalzen; *taste* sal-

zig. **3** *vt (cure)* einsalzen; *(flavour)* salzen.
►**salt away** *vt sep money* auf die hohe Kante legen *(col)*.
**SALT** = Strategic Arms Limitation Talks/Treaty SALT(-Verhandlungen *pl*/-Vertrag *m*).
**salt:** ~ **cellar** *n* Salzfäßchen *nt*; *(shaker)* Salzstreuer *m*; ~ **lake** *n* Salzsee *m*; ~ **mine** *n* Salzbergwerk *nt*; ~ **shaker** *n* Salzstreuer *m*; ~ **water** *n* Salzwasser *nt*; ~**-water** *adj fish* Meeres-; *lake* Salz-.
**salty** ['sɔːltɪ] *adj (+er)* salzig.
**salubrious** [sə'luːbrɪəs] *adj* **(a)** *(form)* air, climate gesund. **(b)** *(col)* district, person angenehm. **not very** ~ etwas zweifelhaft.
**salutary** ['sæljʊtərɪ] *adj* **(a)** *(healthy)* gesund. **(b)** *(beneficial) advice* nützlich; *experience* lehrreich; *effect* günstig.
**salute** [sə'luːt] **1** *n* Gruß *m*; *(of guns)* Salut *m*. **to take the** ~ die Parade abnehmen. **2** *vt (Mil)* grüßen; *person also* salutieren vor *(+dat)*; *courage* bewundern.
**salvage** ['sælvɪdʒ] **1** *n (act)* Bergung *f*; *(objects)* Bergungsgut *nt*. **2** *vt (from wreck, building)* bergen *(from aus)*; *(fig)* retten *(from von)*. **to** ~ **sth from the fire** etw aus den Flammen retten; ~ **what you can** *(lit, fig)* rettet, was ihr retten könnt.
**salvage:** ~ **operation** *n* Bergungsaktion *f*; *(fig)* Rettungsaktion *f*; ~ **vessel** *n* Bergungsschiff *nt*.
**salvation** [sæl'veɪʃən] *n* Rettung *f*.
**Salvation Army 1** *n* Heilsarmee *f*. **2** *attr hostel, band, meeting* der Heilsarmee.
**salvo** ['sælvəʊ] *n (of guns, fig)* Salve *f*.
**Samaritan** [sə'mærɪtən] *n* Samariter *m*. **good** ~ *(lit, fig)* barmherziger Samariter; **the** ~**s** ≈ die Telefonseelsorge.
**same** [seɪm] **1** *adj* **the** ~ der/die/das gleiche; *(one and the* ~, *identical)* derselbe/dieselbe/dasselbe; **they were both wearing the** ~ **dress** sie hatten beide das gleiche Kleid an; **they both live in the** ~ **house** sie wohnen beide in demselben Haus; **they are all the** ~ sie sind alle gleich; **she just wasn't the** ~ **person** sie war ein anderer Mensch; **it's the** ~ **thing** das ist das gleiche; **see you tomorrow,** ~ **time** ~ **place** bis morgen, gleicher Ort, gleiche Zeit; **we sat at the** ~ **table as usual** wir saßen an unserem üblichen Tisch; **he is the** ~ **age as his wife** er ist (genau) so alt wie seine Frau; **it happened the** ~ **day** es ist am gleichen *or* selben Tag passiert; **in the** ~ **way** (genau) gleich; *(by the* ~ *token)* ebenso.
**2** *pron* **(a) the** ~ der/die/das gleiche; derselbe/dieselbe/dasselbe; **the** ~ **again, please** *(Brit)* das gleiche noch mal bitte; **and I would do the** ~ **again** und ich würde es wieder tun; **he left and I did the** ~ er ist gegangen, und ich auch; **they are one and the** ~ das ist doch dasselbe; *(people)* das ist doch ein und derselbe/dieselbe; **she's much the** ~ sie hat sich kaum geändert; *(in health)* es geht ihr kaum besser; **it's always the** ~ es ist immer das gleiche.
**(b) the** ~ gleich; **to pay/treat everybody the** ~ alle gleich bezahlen/behandeln; **things go on just the** ~ **(as always)** es ändert sich nichts; **it's not the** ~ **as before** es ist nicht wie früher; **if it's all the** ~ **to you** wenn es Ihnen egal ist; **it's all the** ~ **to me (what you do)** es ist mir egal(, was du tust); **it amounts to the** ~ das kommt *or* läuft aufs gleiche hinaus; **all** *or* **just the** ~ *(nevertheless)* trotzdem; ~ **here** ich/wir auch; ~ **to you** (danke) gleichfalls.
**sameness** ['seɪmnɪs] *n* Gleichheit *f*; *(monotony)* Eintönigkeit *f*.
**sample** ['saːmpl] **1** *n (example)* Beispiel *nt (of für)*; *(for tasting, fig: of talent, behaviour)* Kostprobe *f*; *(Comm) (of cloth etc)* Muster *nt*; *(of commodities,*

*blood etc)* Probe *f*; *(Statistics)* Stichprobe *f*, Sample *nt*. **a representative** ~ **of the population** eine repräsentative Auswahl aus der Bevölkerung. **2** *vt wine, food* probieren, kosten; *pleasures* kosten.
**sanatorium** [ˌsænə'tɔːrɪəm] *n*, *pl* **sanatoria** [ˌsænə'tɔːrɪə] *(Brit)* Sanatorium *nt*; *(in cpds)* -heilanstalt *f*.
**sanctify** ['sæŋktɪfaɪ] *vt (to make holy)* heiligen; *(fig)* sanktionieren; *(consecrate)* weihen.
**sanctimonious** [ˌsæŋktɪ'məʊnɪəs] *adj* frömmlerisch. **don't be so** ~ tu doch nicht so fromm.
**sanctimoniously** [ˌsæŋktɪ'məʊnɪəslɪ] *adv* frömmlerisch.
**sanctimoniousness** [ˌsæŋktɪ'məʊnɪəsnɪs] *n* Frömmelei *f*.
**sanction** ['sæŋkʃən] **1** *n* **(a)** *(permission, approval)* Zustimmung *f*. **(b)** *(enforcing measure)* Sanktion *f*. **to impose (economic)** ~**s on a country** (wirtschaftliche) Sanktionen gegen ein Land verhängen. **2** *vt* sanktionieren.
**sanctity** ['sæŋktɪtɪ] *n* Heiligkeit *f*; *(of rights)* Unantastbarkeit *f*.
**sanctuary** ['sæŋktjʊərɪ] *n* **(a)** *(holy place)* Heiligtum *nt*; *(altar* ~*)* Altarraum *m*. **(b)** *(refuge)* Zuflucht *f*. **to seek** ~ **with** Zuflucht suchen bei. **(c)** *(for animals)* Schutzgebiet *nt*.
**sand** [sænd] **1** *n* Sand *m no pl*. ~**s** *(of desert)* Sand *m*; *(beach)* Sandstrand *m*. **2** *vt (smooth)* schmirgeln; *(sprinkle with* ~*)* streuen.
**sandal** ['sændl] *n* Sandale *f*.
**sand:** ~**bag** *n* Sandsack *m*; ~**bank** *n* Sandbank *f*; ~**blast** *vt* sandstrahlen; ~**box** *n (US)* = ~**pit**; ~**boy** *n*: **as happy as a** ~**boy** quietschvergnügt; ~**castle** *n* Sandburg *f*; ~ **dune** *n* Sanddüne *f*.
**sander** ['sændər] *n (tool)* Schwingschleifer *m*.
**sand:** ~**paper 1** *n* Sand- *or* Schmirgelpapier *nt*; **2** *vt* schmirgeln; ~**pit** *n (Brit)* Sandkasten *m*; ~**shoe** *n* Stoffschuh *m*; *(for beach)* Strandschuh *m*; ~**stone 1** *n* Sandstein *m*; **2** *adj* Sandstein-, aus Sandstein; ~**storm** *n* Sandsturm *m*.
**sandwich** ['sænwɪdʒ] **1** *n* belegtes Brot, Sandwich *nt*. **open** ~ belegtes Brot. **2** *vt (also* ~ **in)** hineinzwängen. **to be** ~**ed between two things/people** zwischen zwei Dingen/Menschen eingekeilt sein.
**sandwich:** ~**board** *n* Reklametafel *f*; ~ **course** *n* Ausbildungsgang *m, bei dem sich Theorie und Praxis abwechseln.*
**sandy** ['sændɪ] *adj (+er)* sandig; *beach, soil* Sand-, sandig *pred*; *(in colour)* rötlich; *hair* rotblond.
**sane** [seɪn] *adj (+er) person* normal; *(Med, Psych etc)* geistig gesund; *(Jur)* zurechnungsfähig; *society etc* gesund; *(sensible) advice, person* vernünftig.
**sang** [sæŋ] *pret of* **sing**.
**sangfroid** ['sãːŋ'frwɑː] *n* Seelenruhe *f*.
**sanguine** ['sæŋgwɪn] *adj (optimistic)* optimistisch.
**sanitarium** [ˌsænɪ'tɛərɪəm] *n (US)* = **sanatorium**.
**sanitary** ['sænɪtərɪ] *adj* hygienisch; *arrangements, installations* sanitär *attr*; *regulations, expert* Gesundheits-; *questions, principles* der Hygiene.
**sanitary napkin** *(US) or* **towel** *n* Damenbinde *f*.
**sanitation** [ˌsænɪ'teɪʃən] *n* Hygiene *f*; *(toilets etc)* sanitäre Anlagen *pl*; *(sewage disposal)* Kanalisation *f*. **the** ~ **department** *(esp US)* die Stadtreinigung.
**sanity** ['sænɪtɪ] *n* **(a)** *(mental balance)* geistige Gesundheit; *(of individual also)* gesunder Verstand; *(Jur)* Zurechnungsfähigkeit *f*. **to lose one's** ~ den Verstand verlieren; **to doubt sb's** ~ an jds Verstand *(dat)* zweifeln. **(b)** *(sensibleness)* Vernünftigkeit *f*. **to return to** ~ Vernunft annehmen.
**sank** [sæŋk] *pret of* **sink**[1].
**Santa (Claus)** ['sæntə('klɔːz)] *n* der Weihnachts-

mann.

**sap**[1] [sæp] n (Bot) Saft m; (fig) Lebenskraft f.

**sap**[2] vt (weaken, Mil) untergraben; confidence also schwächen. **to ~ sb's strength** jdn entkräften, jds Kräfte angreifen.

**sapling** ['sæplɪŋ] n junger Baum.

**sapper** ['sæpər] n (Mil) Pionier m.

**sapphire** ['sæfaɪər] **1** n Saphir m; (colour) Saphirblau nt. **2** adj ring Saphir-.

**sarcasm** ['sɑːkæzəm] n Sarkasmus m.

**sarcastic** [sɑːˈkæstɪk] adj sarkastisch. **are you being ~?** das soll wohl ein Witz sein (col).

**sarcophagus** [sɑːˈkɒfəgəs] n, pl **sarcophagi** [sɑːˈkɒfəgaɪ] Sarkophag m.

**sardine** [sɑːˈdiːn] n Sardine f. **packed in like ~s** wie die Ölsardinen.

**Sardinia** [sɑːˈdɪnɪə] n Sardinien nt.

**Sardinian** [sɑːˈdɪnɪən] **1** adj sardinisch. **2** n Sardinier(in f) m.

**sardonic** [sɑːˈdɒnɪk] adj höhnisch; smile sardonisch.

**sari** ['sɑːrɪ] n Sari m.

**SAS** (Brit Mil) = **Special Air Service**.

**SASE** (US Post) = **self-addressed stamped envelope**.

**sash**[1] [sæʃ] n Schärpe f.

**sash**[2] n (in window) Gewichtsschnur f.

**sash: ~-cord** n Gewichtsschnur f; **~-window** n Schiebefenster nt.

**sassy** ['sæsɪ] adj (US col) frech.

**sat** [sæt] pret, ptp of **sit**.

**Sat** = **Saturday** Sa.

**Satan** ['seɪtən] n Satan m.

**satanic** [səˈtænɪk] adj satanisch.

**satchel** ['sætʃəl] n Schultasche f.

**sated** ['seɪtɪd] adj gesättigt; (to excess) übersättigt (with von).

**satellite** ['sætəlaɪt] n Satellit m.

**satellite: ~ broadcasting** n Satellitenfunk m; **~ dish** n Parabolantenne f, Satellitenschüssel f (col); **~ state** n Satellitenstaat m; **~ town** n Trabantenstadt f.

**satiate** ['seɪʃɪeɪt] vt appetite, desires etc stillen (geh); person, animal sättigen; (to excess) übersättigen.

**satin** ['sætɪn] **1** n Satin m. **2** adj Satin-; skin samtig. **~ finish** Seidenglanz m.

**satire** ['sætaɪər] n Satire f (on auf +acc).

**satirical** [səˈtɪrɪkəl] adj literature, film etc satirisch; (mocking, joking) ironisch.

**satirically** [səˈtɪrɪkəlɪ] adv see adj.

**satirist** ['sætərɪst] n Satiriker(in f) m.

**satirize** ['sætəraɪz] vt satirisch darstellen.

**satisfaction** [ˌsætɪsˈfækʃən] n (a) (act: of person, needs, curiosity etc) Befriedigung f; (of ambition) Verwirklichung f; (of conditions, contract) Erfüllung f. (b) (state) Zufriedenheit f (at mit). **the ~ of having solved a difficult problem** das befriedigende Gefühl, ein schwieriges Problem gelöst zu haben; **to feel a sense of ~ at sth** Genugtuung über etw (acc) empfinden; **has it been done to your ~?** ist es zu Ihrer Zufriedenheit erledigt worden? (form); **to get ~ out of sth** Befriedigung in etw (dat) finden; (find pleasure) Freude an etw (dat) haben; **he proved to my ~ that ...** er hat (mir) überzeugend bewiesen, daß ...

**satisfactorily** [ˌsætɪsˈfæktərɪlɪ] adv zufriedenstellend.

**satisfactory** [ˌsætɪsˈfæktərɪ] adj (good enough) befriedigend; (only just good enough) ausreichend; account, completion of contract zufriedenstellend; reason triftig; excuse angemessen.

**satisfy** ['sætɪsfaɪ] **1** vt (a) (make contented) befriedi-

gen; employer, customers etc zufriedenstellen; (meal) person sättigen. **not satisfied with that he asked** ... damit noch immer nicht zufrieden, fragte er ...; **he's never satisfied** (always wants more) er ist mit nichts zufrieden. (b) needs, demand, sb (sexually) befriedigen; hunger stillen; conditions erfüllen; requirements genügen (+dat); ambitions verwirklichen. (c) (convince) überzeugen. **they were not satisfied with the answers** sie waren mit den Antworten nicht zufrieden.

**2** vr **to ~ oneself about sth** sich von etw überzeugen; **to ~ oneself that ...** sich davon überzeugen, daß ...

**satisfying** ['sætɪsfaɪɪŋ] adj befriedigend; food, meal sättigend. **a cool ~ lager** ein kühles, durststillendes Bier.

**saturate** ['sætʃəreɪt] vt (durch)tränken; (rain) durchnässen; (Chem, fig) solution, market sättigen.

**saturation** [ˌsætʃəˈreɪʃən] n Sättigung f. **to have reached ~ point** (fig) seinen Sättigungsgrad erreicht haben.

**Saturday** ['sætədɪ] n Samstag, Sonnabend (esp N Ger) m; see **Tuesday**.

**Saturn** ['sætən] n (Astron) Saturn m.

**sauce** [sɔːs] n (a) Soße, Sauce f. **white ~** Mehlsoße f; **what's ~ for the goose is ~ for the gander** (Prov) was dem einen recht ist, ist dem anderen billig (prov). (b) no pl (col: cheek) Frechheit f. **none of your ~!** werd bloß nicht frech! (col).

**saucepan** ['sɔːspən] n Kochtopf m.

**saucer** ['sɔːsər] n Untertasse f.

**saucily** ['sɔːsɪlɪ] adv frech.

**sauciness** ['sɔːsɪnɪs] n, no pl Frechheit f.

**saucy** ['sɔːsɪ] adj (+er) frech.

**Saudi Arabia** ['saʊdɪəˈreɪbɪə] n Saudi-Arabien nt.

**Saudi (Arabian)** ['saʊdɪ(əˈreɪbɪən)] **1** n Saudi-(araber) m, Saudiaraberin f. **2** adj saudiarabisch.

**sauna** ['sɔːnə] n Sauna f. **to have a ~** in die Sauna gehen.

**saunter** ['sɔːntər] vi schlendern. **he ~ed up to me** er schlenderte auf mich zu.

**sausage** ['sɒsɪdʒ] n Wurst f.

**sausage: ~ dog** n (Brit hum) Dackel m; **~meat** n Wurstmasse f, Wurstbrät nt; **~ roll** n ≈ Bratwurst f im Schlafrock.

**sauté** ['səʊteɪ] **1** adj **~ potatoes** Brat- or Röstkartoffeln pl. **2** vt potatoes rösten; (sear) (kurz) anbraten.

**savage** ['sævɪdʒ] **1** adj wild; fighter, punch, revenge brutal; custom grausam; animal gefährlich; competition scharf; (drastic) cuts, measures, changes drastisch; criticism schonungslos, brutal (col). **to make a ~ attack on sb** brutal über jdn herfallen; (fig) jdn scharf angreifen. **2** n Wilde(r) mf. **3** vt (animal) anfallen; (fatally) zerfleischen.

**savagely** ['sævɪdʒlɪ] adv brutal; (drastically) drastisch; criticize schonungslos.

**savagery** ['sævɪdʒərɪ] n see adj Wildheit f; Brutalität f; Grausamkeit f.

**savanna(h)** [səˈvænə] n Savanne f.

**save** [seɪv] **1** n (Ftbl etc) Ballabwehr f.

**2** vt (a) (rescue, Rel) retten. **to ~ sb from sth** jdn vor etw (dat) retten; **to ~ sb from disaster/ruin** jdn vor einer Katastrophe/dem Ruin bewahren; **he ~d me from falling/making that mistake** er hat mich davor bewahrt, hinzufallen/den Fehler zu machen; **to ~ sth from sth** etw aus etw retten; **to ~ the day (for sb)** jds Rettung sein; **God ~ the Queen** Gott schütze die Königin.

(b) (put by) aufheben, aufsparen; money sparen; (collect) stamps etc sammeln. **~ some of the cake for me** laß mir etwas Kuchen übrig; **~ me a seat** halte mir einen Platz frei; ~ **it!** *(col)* spar dir das! *(col)*.

**(c)** *(avoid using up)* *time, money* sparen; *(spare)* *eyes, battery* schonen; *(~ up) strength, fuel etc* aufsparen. **that will ~ you £2 a week** dadurch sparen Sie £2 pro Woche.

**(d)** *(prevent)* *bother, trouble* ersparen. **it'll ~ a lot of work if we** ... es erspart uns *(dat)* sehr viel Arbeit, wenn wir ...

**(e)** *goal* verhindern; *penalty* halten.

**(f)** *(Comp)* *data* (ab)speichern.

**3** *vi* **(a)** *(with money)* sparen. **to ~ for sth** für *or* auf etw *(acc)* sparen. **(b) to ~ on sth** etw sparen.

▶**save up 1** *vi* sparen *(for* für, auf *+acc)*. **2** *vt sep* *(not spend)* sparen; *(not use)* aufheben, aufbewahren. **he's saving himself ~ for the big match** er schont sich für das große Spiel.

**saveloy** ['sævələɪ] *n* Zervelatwurst *f.*

**saver** ['seɪvər] *n* *(of money)* Sparer(in *f) m.*

**saving** ['seɪvɪŋ] **1** *adj* *(redeeming)* **its/his ~ grace** was einen damit/mit ihm versöhnt. **2** *n* **(a)** *no pl (act: rescue, Rel)* Rettung *f; (of money)* Sparen *nt.* **(b)** *(of cost etc) (act)* Einsparung *f; (amount saved)* Ersparnis *f.* **(c) ~s** *pl* Ersparnisse *pl; (in account)* Spareinlagen *pl;* **post-office ~s** Postspargutguthaben *nt.*

**savings** *in cpds* Spar-; **~ and loan association** *n (US)* Bausparkasse *f;* **~ bank** *n* Sparkasse *f;* **~ book** *n* Sparkassenbuch *nt;* **~ certificate** *n* Sparbrief *m;* **~ deposit** *n* Spareinlage *f.*

**saviour,** *(US also)* **savior** ['seɪvjər] *n* Retter(in *f) m;* *(Rel also)* Erlöser *m.*

**savour,** *(US)* **savor** ['seɪvər] **1** *n* Geschmack *m;* *(slight trace)* Spur *f; (enjoyable quality)* Reiz *m.* **2** *vt* **(a)** *(form)* kosten *(geh); aroma (of food)* riechen. **(b)** *(fig liter)* genießen, auskosten.

**savoury,** *(US)* **savory** ['seɪvərɪ] **1** *adj* **(a)** *(appetizing)* lecker; *meal also* schmackhaft. **(b)** *(not sweet)* pikant. **~ omelette** pikant gefülltes Omelett; **~ biscuits** Salzgebäck *nt.* **(c)** *(fig)* angenehm; *sight also* einladend. **2** *n* Häppchen *nt.*

**saw¹** [sɔː] *pret of* **see¹.**

**saw²** *(vb: pret* ~**ed,** *ptp* ~**ed** *or* **sawn) 1** *n* Säge *f.* **2** *vt* sägen. **to ~ sth through** etw durchsägen; **to ~ sth in two** etw entzweisägen.

▶**saw off** *vt sep* absägen. **a ~n-~** *or (US)* ~**ed-~ shotgun** ein Gewehr *nt* mit abgesägtem Lauf.

**saw:** ~**dust** *n* Sägemehl *nt;* ~**mill** *n* Sägewerk *nt.*

**sawn** [sɔːn] *(esp Brit) ptp of* **saw².**

**Saxon** ['sæksn] **1** *n* Sachse *m,* Sächsin *f; (Hist)* (Angel)sachse *m/*-sächsin *f.* **2** *adj* sächsisch; *(Hist)* (angel)sächsisch.

**Saxony** ['sæksənɪ] *n* Sachsen *nt.*

**saxophone** ['sæksəfəʊn] *n* Saxophon *nt.*

**saxophonist** [sæk'sɒfənɪst] *n* Saxophonist(in *f) m.*

**say** [seɪ] *(vb: pret, ptp* **said) 1** *n* Mitspracherecht *nt* *(in* bei*).* **let him have his ~** laß ihn mal reden *or* seine Meinung äußern; **you've had your ~** Sie haben Ihre Meinung äußern können; **to have no/a ~ in sth** bei etw nichts/etwas zu sagen haben, bei etw kein/ein Mitspracherecht haben.

**2** *vti* **(a)** sagen; *poem* aufsagen; *prayer, text* sprechen; *(pronounce)* aussprechen; *(dial, gauge)* anzeigen. **~ after me** ... sprechen Sie mir nach ...; **what have you got to ~ for yourself?** was hast du zu deiner Verteidigung zu sagen?; **that's not for him to ~** es steht ihm nicht zu, sich darüber zu äußern; *(to decide)* das kann er nicht entscheiden; **he said to wait here** er hat gesagt, ich soll/wir sollen *etc* hier warten; **do it this way — if you ~ so** machen Sie es so — wenn Sie meinen; **why didn't you ~ so?** warum hast du das nicht (gleich) gesagt?; **you'd bet-**

ter **do it — who ~s?** tun Sie das lieber — wer sagt das?; **what does it mean? — I wouldn't like to ~** was bedeutet das? — das kann ich auch nicht sagen; **so ~ing, he sat down** und mit diesen Worten setzte er sich; **it ~s in the papers that** ... in den Zeitungen steht, daß ...; **what does the paper/this book ~?** was steht in der Zeitung/diesem Buch?; **the rules ~ that** ... in den Regeln heißt es, daß ...; **what does the weather forecast ~?** wie ist der Wetterbericht?; **what does your watch ~?** wie spät ist es auf deiner Uhr?; **that ~s a lot about his character** das läßt tief auf seinen Charakter schließen; **and that's ~ing a lot** und das will schon etwas heißen; **that doesn't ~ much for him** das spricht nicht für ihn.

**(b) what would you ~ to a whisky?** wie wär's mit einem Whisky?; **I wouldn't ~ no to a cup of tea** ich hätte nichts gegen eine Tasse Tee; **he never ~s no to a drink** einen Drink lehnt er nie ab; **what did he ~ to your plan?** was hat er zu Ihrem Plan gesagt?; **I'll offer £500, what do you ~ to that?** ich biete £500, was meinen Sie dazu?; **what do you ~?** was meinen Sie?; **I ~!** *(to attract attention)* hallo!; **I should ~ (so)!** das möchte ich doch meinen!; **you don't ~!** *(also iro)* nein wirklich?, was du nicht sagst!; **well said!** (ganz) richtig!; **you('ve) said it!** Sie sagen es!; **you can ~ that again!** das kann man wohl sagen!; **~ no more!** ich weiß Bescheid!; **(it's) easier said than done** das ist leichter gesagt als getan; **when all is said and done** letzten Endes; **he is said to be very rich** er soll sehr reich sein; **it goes without ~ing that** ... es versteht sich von selbst, daß ...; **that is to ~** das heißt; *(correcting also)* beziehungsweise; **to ~ nothing of the costs** *etc* von den Kosten *etc* ganz zu schweigen; **that's not to ~ that** ... das soll nicht heißen, daß ...; **they ~ ..., it is said** ... es heißt ...

**saying** ['seɪɪŋ] *n* Redensart *f; (proverb)* Sprichwort *nt.* **as the ~ goes** wie es so schön heißt.

**say-so** ['seɪsəʊ] *n (col) (assertion)* Wort *nt; (authority)* Genehmigung *f.* **on whose ~?** wer sagt das?; *(permission)* wer hat das genehmigt?; *(order)* auf wessen Anweisung?

**s/c** = **self-contained.**

**SC** *(US Post)* = **South Carolina.**

**scab** [skæb] *n* **(a)** *(on cut)* Schorf, Grind *m.* **(b)** *(col: strikebreaker)* Streikbrecher(in *f) m.*

**scaffold** ['skæfəʊld] *n (on building)* Gerüst *nt; (for execution)* Schafott *nt.*

**scaffolding** ['skæfəldɪŋ] *n* Gerüst *nt.* **to put up ~** ein Gerüst aufbauen.

**scald** [skɔːld] **1** *n* Verbrühung *f.* **2** *vt* **(a)** *oneself, skin etc* verbrühen. **(b)** *instruments, vegetables* abbrühen; *milk* abkochen.

**scalding** ['skɔːldɪŋ] *adj* siedend.

**scale¹** [skeɪl] *n (of fish)* Schuppe *f; (of rust)* Flocke *f; (kettle ~)* Kesselstein *m no pl.*

**scale²** *n* **(a)** Skala *f; (on ruler)* *(Maß)*einteilung *f; (fig)* Leiter *f; (social ~)* Stufenleiter *f.* **~ of charges** Gebührenordnung *f,* Tarife *pl.* **(b)** *(instrument)* Meßgerät *nt.* **(c)** *(Mus)* Tonleiter *f.* **the ~ of G** die G(-Dur)-Tonleiter. **(d)** *(of map etc)* Maßstab *m.* **on a ~ of 5 km to the cm** in einem Maßstab von 5 km zu 1 cm; **to draw sth to ~** etw im Maßstab *or* maßstabgerecht zeichnen. **(e)** *(fig: size, extent)* Umfang *m,* Ausmaß *nt.* **to entertain on a large/small ~** Feste im größeren/kleineren Rahmen geben; **inflation on an unprecedented ~** Inflation von bisher nie gekanntem Ausmaß; **it's similar but on a smaller ~** es ist ähnlich, nur kleiner; **on a national ~** auf nationaler Ebene.

▶**scale down** *vt sep* *(lit)* verkleinern; *(fig)* verringern.

**scale³** *vt mountain, wall* erklettern.

**scale:** ~ **drawing** *n* maßstabgetreue Zeichnung; ~ **model** *n* maßstabgetreues Modell.

**scales** [skeɪlz] *npl* **(pair of)** ~**s** Waage *f*; **to tip the** ~ **in favour of sb/sth** für jdn/etw den Ausschlag geben.

**scallop** ['skɒləp] *n (Zool)* Kammuschel *f.*

**scalp** [skælp] **1** *n* Kopfhaut *f*; *(as Indian trophy)* Skalp *m*. **2** *vt* skalpieren; *(hum: by barber)* kahlscheren *(hum).*

**scalpel** ['skælpəl] *n* Skalpell *nt.*

**scaly** ['skeɪlɪ] *adj (+er)* schuppig.

**scam** [skæm] *n (col)* Betrug, Beschiß *m (col).*

**scamp** [skæmp] *n* Frechdachs *m (col).*

**scamper** ['skæmpəʳ] *vi (person, child, puppy)* trappeln; *(squirrel, rabbit)* hoppeln; *(mice)* huschen.

**scan** [skæn] **1** *vt* **(a)** *(search with sweeping movement)* schwenken über *(+acc)*; *(person)* seine Augen wandern lassen über *(+acc)*; *newspaper, book* überfliegen; *(examine closely) horizon* absuchen; *(by radar)* absuchen, abtasten. **(b)** *(TV)* abtasten. **(c)** *verse* in Versfüße zerlegen. **2** *vi (verse)* das richtige Versmaß haben. **3** *n (Med)* Scan *m*; *(in pregnancy)* Ultraschalluntersuchung *f.*

**scandal** ['skændl] *n* **(a)** Skandal *m*. **to create a** ~ einen Skandal verursachen; *(amongst neighbours etc)* allgemeines Aufsehen erregen; **it is a** ~ **that** ... es ist skandalös, daß ... **(b)** *no pl (gossip)* Skandalgeschichten *pl*; *(piece of gossip)* Skandalgeschichte *f*. **the latest** ~ der neueste Klatsch *(col).*

**scandalize** ['skændəlaɪz] *vt* schockieren. **she was** ~**d** sie war empört *(by* über *+acc).*

**scandalous** ['skændələs] *adj* skandalös. **a** ~ **report/tale** eine Skandalgeschichte.

**Scandinavia** [ˌskændɪˈneɪvɪə] *n* Skandinavien *nt.*

**Scandinavian** [ˌskændɪˈneɪvɪən] **1** *adj* skandinavisch. **2** *n* Skandinavier(in *f*) *m.*

**scanner** ['skænəʳ] *n (Rad)* Richtantenne *f*; *(Med, Comp)* Scanner *m.*

**scant** [skænt] *adj (+er)* wenig *inv*; *attention, respect also, chance* gering; *success* mager.

**scantily** ['skæntɪlɪ] *adv* spärlich.

**scantiness** ['skæntɪnɪs] *n see adj* Spärlichkeit *f*; Kärglichkeit *f*; Knappheit *f.*

**scanty** ['skæntɪ] *adj (+er) amount, clothing* spärlich; *vegetation, meal also* kärglich; *bikini etc* knapp.

**scapegoat** ['skeɪpgəʊt] *n* Sündenbock *m*. **to make a** ~ **of sb** jdn zum Sündenbock machen.

**scar** [skɑːʳ] **1** *n (on skin, tree)* Narbe *f*; *(scratch)* Kratzer *m*; *(burn)* Brandfleck *m*; *(fig) (emotional)* Wunde *f*; *(on good name)* Makel *m*. **2** *vt skin, tree* Narben/eine Narbe hinterlassen auf *(+dat)*; *furniture* zerkratzen; Brandflecken hinterlassen auf *(+dat)*; *(fig) person* zeichnen. **he was** ~**red for life** *(lit)* er behielt bleibende Narben zurück; *(fig)* er war fürs Leben gezeichnet; **her** ~**red face** ihr narbiges Gesicht. **3** *vi* Narben/eine Narbe hinterlassen.

**scarce** [skɛəs] *adj (+er) (in short supply)* knapp; *(rare)* selten. **to make oneself** ~ *(col)* verschwinden *(col).*

**scarcely** ['skɛəslɪ] *adv* kaum. ~ **anybody** kaum jemand; ~ **anything** fast nichts; ~ **ever** fast nie; **you can** ~ **expect him to believe that** Sie erwarten doch wohl kaum, daß er das glaubt.

**scarceness** ['skɛəsnɪs], **scarcity** ['skɛəsɪtɪ] *n (shortage)* Knappheit *f*; *(rarity)* Seltenheit *f*. ~ **value** Seltenheitswert *m*; **a** ~ **of qualified people** ein Mangel *m* an qualifizierten Kräften; **in times of** ~ in schlechten Zeiten.

**scare** [skɛəʳ] **1** *n (fright, shock)* Schreck(en) *m*; *(gen-*

*eral alarm)* Hysterie *f (about* wegen). **to give sb a** ~ jdm einen Schrecken einjagen; **to cause a** ~ eine Panik auslösen. **bomb** ~ Bombenalarm *m*. **2** *vt* einen Schrecken einjagen *(+dat)*; *(worry also)* Angst machen *(+dat)*; *(frighten physically) person, animal* erschrecken; *birds* aufschrecken.

▶**scare away** *vt sep* verscheuchen; *people* verjagen.

**scarecrow** ['skɛəkrəʊ] *n (lit, fig)* Vogelscheuche *f.*

**scared** ['skɛəd] *adj person* erschrocken; *face, voice* verängstigt. **to be** ~ Angst haben *(of* vor *+dat)*; **to be easily** ~ sehr schreckhaft sein; *(easily worried)* sich *(dat)* leicht Angst machen lassen; *(timid: deer etc)* sehr scheu sein; **to be** ~ **stiff** *or* **to death** *or* **out of one's wits** *(all col)* Todesängste ausstehen; **he's** ~ **of telling her the truth** er traut sich nicht, ihr die Wahrheit zu sagen.

**scare:** ~**monger** *n* Bangemacher *m (col)*; ~ **story** *n* Schauergeschichte *f.*

**scarf** [skɑːf] *n, pl* **scarves** Schal *m*; *(neck ~)* Halstuch *nt*; *(head~)* Kopftuch *nt*; *(round the shoulders)* Schultertuch *nt.*

**scarlet** ['skɑːlɪt] **1** *n* Scharlach(rot) *nt*. ~ **fever** Scharlach *m*. **2** *adj* (scharlach)rot. **to turn** ~ hochrot werden, rot anlaufen *(col).*

**scarper** ['skɑːpəʳ] *vi (Brit col)* abhauen *(col).*

**scarves** [skɑːvz] *pl of* **scarf.**

**scary** ['skɛərɪ] *adj (+er) (col)* unheimlich; *film also* grus(e)lig *(col)*. **it was pretty** ~ da konnte man schon Angst kriegen *(col).*

**scathing** ['skeɪðɪŋ] *adj* bissig; *attack* scharf; *look, criticism* vernichtend. **to be** ~ bissige Bemerkungen *pl* machen *(about* über *+acc).*

**scatter** ['skætəʳ] **1** *vt* **(a)** verstreuen; *seeds, gravel, (Phys) light* streuen *(on, onto* auf *+acc)*. **the books were** ~**ed (about) all over the room** die Bücher lagen im ganzen Zimmer verstreut; **his friends were** ~**ed all over the country** seine Freunde waren über das ganze Land verstreut. **(b)** *(disperse)* auseinandertreiben; *army etc also* zersprengen. **2** *vi* sich zerstreuen *(to* in *+acc)*; *(in a hurry, in fear)* auseinanderlaufen.

**scatter:** ~**brain** *n (col)* Schussel *m (col)*, Chaot(in *f*) *m (col)*; ~**brained** ['skætəˌbreɪnd] *adj (col)* schusselig *(col).*

**scattered** ['skætəd] *adj population* weit verstreut; *villages* verstreut; *clouds, showers* vereinzelt.

**scatty** ['skætɪ] *adj (+er) (col)* **(a)** *(scatterbrained)* schusselig *(col)*. **(b)** *(mad)* verrückt.

**scavenge** ['skævɪndʒ] **1** *vt (lit, fig)* ergattern. **2** *vi (lit)* Nahrung suchen. **jackals live by scavenging** Schakale leben von Aas.

**scavenger** ['skævɪndʒəʳ] *n (animal)* Aasfresser *m*; *(fig: person)* Dreckwühler *m.*

**scenario** [sɪˈnɑːrɪəʊ] *n* Szenar(ium) *nt*; *(fig)* Szenario *nt.*

**scene** [siːn] *n* **(a)** *(place, setting)* Schauplatz *m*; *(of play, novel)* Ort *m* der Handlung. **the** ~ **of the crime** der Tatort, der Schauplatz des Verbrechens; **the** ~ **of the battle was a small hill** die Schlacht fand auf einem kleinen Hügel statt; **the** ~ **was set for ...** die Voraussetzungen für ... waren gegeben; **the** ~ **is set in Padua** das Stück/der Roman *etc* spielt in Padua; **to appear on the** ~ auftauchen, auf der Bildfläche erscheinen; **the police were first on the** ~ die Polizei war als erste zur Stelle. **(b)** *(Theat)* Szene *f*. **Act II,** ~ **i** Akt II, 1. Szene. **behind the** ~**s** *(lit, fig)* hinter den Kulissen. **(c)** *(sight)* Anblick *m*; *(landscape)* Landschaft *f*. **(d)** *(fuss, argument)* Szene *f*. **to make a** ~ eine Szene machen. **(e)** *(col)* **the drug** *etc* ~ die Drogenszene *etc (col)*; **that's not my** ~ da steh' ich nicht drauf *(col)*.

**scenery** ['siːnərɪ] *n (landscape)* Landschaft *f; (Theat)* Kulissen *pl; (set)* Bühnenbild *nt*.

**scenic** ['siːnɪk] *adj route etc* landschaftlich schön; *(picturesque)* malerisch. ~ **railway** *(roller coaster)* Achterbahn *f*.

**scent** [sent] **1** *n (smell)* Duft, Geruch *m; (perfume)* Parfüm *nt; (of animal)* Fährte *f*. **to be on the** ~ *(lit, fig)* auf der Spur sein *(of sb/sth* jdm/einer Sache*)*; **to lose the** ~ *(lit, fig)* die Spur verlieren; **to put** *or* **throw sb off the** ~ *(lit, fig)* jdn von der Spur abbringen. **2** *vt* **(a)** *(smell, suspect)* wittern. **(b)** *(perfume)* parfümieren. **roses** ~**ed the air** der Duft von Rosen erfüllte die Luft.

**sceptic,** *(US)* **skeptic** ['skeptɪk] *n* Skeptiker(in *f*) *m*.

**sceptical,** *(US)* **skeptical** ['skeptɪkəl] *adj* skeptisch. **he was** ~ **about ...** er war skeptisch, was ... angeht.

**scepticism,** *(US)* **skepticism** ['skeptɪsɪzəm] *n* Skepsis *f (about* gegenüber*)*.

**sceptre,** *(US)* **scepter** ['septər] *n* Szepter *nt*.

**schedule** ['ʃedjuːl *(esp Brit)*, 'skedʒʊəl] **1** *n (of events)* Programm *nt; (of work)* Zeitplan *m; (US: timetable)* Fahr-/Flugplan *m; (list)* Verzeichnis *nt*. **what's on the** ~ **for today?** was steht für heute auf dem Programm?; **according to** ~ *(work also)* nach Plan; **the train is behind** ~ der Zug hat Verspätung; **the bus was on** ~ der Bus war pünktlich; **ahead of** ~ dem Zeitplan voraus; **behind** ~ im Rückstand; **we are working to a very tight** ~ wir arbeiten nach einem sehr knappen Zeitplan. **2** *vt* planen; *(put on programme, timetable)* ansetzen; *(US: list)* aufführen. **the work is** ~**d for completion in 3 months** die Arbeit soll (laut Zeitplan) in 3 Monaten fertig sein; **this stop was not** ~**d** dieser Aufenthalt war nicht eingeplant.

**scheduled** ['ʃedjuːld *(esp Brit)*, 'skedʒʊəld] *adj* vorgesehen, geplant; *departure etc* planmäßig. ~ **flight** *(not charter)* Linienflug *m; (on timetable)* planmäßiger Flug.

**schematic** [skɪ'mætɪk] *adj* schematisch.

**scheme** [skiːm] **1** *n* **(a)** *(plan)* Plan *m*, Programm *nt; (project)* Projekt *nt; (idea)* Idee *f*. **savings** ~ Sparprogramm *nt*; **pension** ~ Rentenschema *nt;* **the** ~ **for the new ring road** das neue Umgehungsstraßenprojekt; **a** ~ **of work** ein Arbeitsprogramm *nt*. **(b)** *(plot)* (raffinierter) Plan; *(political also)* Komplott *nt; (at court, in firm etc)* Intrige *f*. **(c)** *(arrangement) (of town etc)* Anlage *f; (of room)* Einrichtung *f; (colour* ~*)* Farbzusammenstellung *f*. **2** *vi* Pläne schmieden; *(at court, in firm etc)* intrigieren.

**scheming** ['skiːmɪŋ] **1** *n* Tricks *pl (col); (of politicians etc)* Machenschaften *pl; (in firm etc)* Intrigen *pl*. **2** *adj methods, businessman* raffiniert; *politician* gewieft *(col)*.

**schism** ['sɪzəm] *n (Eccl)* Schisma *nt; (general)* Spaltung *f*.

**schizophrenia** [ˌskɪtsəʊ'friːnɪə] *n* Schizophrenie *f*.

**schizophrenic** ['skɪtsəʊ'frenɪk] **1** *adj person, reaction* schizophren. **2** *n* Schizophrene(r) *mf*.

**schnap(p)s** [ʃnæps] *n* Schnaps *m*.

**scholar** ['skɒlər] *n (learned person)* Gelehrte(r) *mf; (student)* Student(in *f*) *m;* Schüler(in *f*) *m*. **the foremost** ~**s of our time** die führenden Wissenschaftler unserer Zeit; **a famous Shakespeare** ~ ein berühmter Shakespeareexperte.

**scholarly** ['skɒləlɪ] *adj thesis etc* wissenschaftlich; *(learned)* gelehrt; *interests* hochgeistig.

**scholarship** ['skɒləʃɪp] *n (learning)* Gelehrsamkeit *f; (money award)* Stipendium *nt*.

**scholastic** [skə'læstɪk] *adj (relative to school)* schu-

lisch, Schul-; *(Univ)* Studien-.

**school¹** [skuːl] **1** *n* **(a)** Schule *f; (US: college, university)* College *nt;* Universität *f*. **at** ~ in der Schule/im College/an der Universität; **to go to** ~ in die Schule/ins College/zur Universität gehen; **there's no** ~ **tomorrow** morgen ist schulfrei *or* keine Schule. **(b)** *(Univ: department)* Fachbereich *m; (of medicine, law)* Fakultät *f*. **(c)** *(group of artists etc)* Schule *f*. **he's a diplomat of the old** ~ er ist ein Diplomat der alten Schule. **2** *vt* lehren; *animal* dressieren. **to** ~ **sb in a technique** jdn in einer Technik unterrichten.

**school²** *n (of fish)* Schwarm *m*.

**school** *in cpds* Schul-; ~ **age** *n* schulpflichtiges Alter, Schulalter *nt;* ~ **book** *n* Schulbuch *nt;* ~ **boy** *n* Schüler *m;* ~**child** *n* Schulkind *nt;* ~**days** *npl* Schulzeit *f;* ~ **dinner** *n* Schulessen *nt;* ~ **fees** *npl* Schulgeld *nt;* ~**friend** *n* Schulfreund(in *f*) *m;* ~**girl** *n* Schülerin *f*.

**schooling** ['skuːlɪŋ] *n (education)* Ausbildung *f*. **compulsory** ~ die Schulpflicht.

**school:** ~ **inspector** *n* Schulrat *m;* ~**-leaver** *n* Schulabgänger(in *f*) *m;* ~**-leaving age** *n* Schulabgangsalter *nt;* ~ **magazine** *n* Schülerzeitung *f;* ~**master** *n* Lehrer *m;* ~ **meals** *npl* Schulessen *nt;* ~**mistress** *n (Brit)* Lehrerin *f;* ~**room** *n* Klassenzimmer *nt;* ~**teacher** *n* Lehrer(in *f*) *m;* ~**work** *n* Schularbeiten *pl;* ~ **year** *n* Schuljahr *nt*.

**schooner** ['skuːnər] *n* **(a)** *(boat)* Schoner *m*. **(b)** *(sherry glass)* großes Sherryglas; *(US, Austral: beer* ~*)* hohes Bierglas.

**sciatica** [saɪ'ætɪkə] *n* Ischias *m or nt*.

**science** ['saɪəns] *n* **(a)** Wissenschaft *f; (natural* ~*)* Naturwissenschaft *f*. **to study** ~ Naturwissenschaften studieren; **a man of** ~ ein Wissenschaftler *m*. **(b)** *(systematic knowledge or skill)* Technik *f*.

**science fiction** *n* Science-fiction *f*. ~ **novel** Science-fiction-Roman *m*.

**science park** *n* Technologiepark *m*.

**scientific** [ˌsaɪən'tɪfɪk] *adj* wissenschaftlich; *(of natural sciences)* naturwissenschaftlich.

**scientist** ['saɪəntɪst] *n* Wissenschaftler(in *f*) *m; (natural* ~*)* Naturwissenschaftler(in *f*) *m*.

**sci-fi** ['saɪ'faɪ] = **science fiction** Sci-Fi *f*.

**Scillies** ['sɪlɪz], **Scilly Isles** ['sɪlɪ,aɪlz] *npl* Scilly-Inseln *pl*.

**scintillating** ['sɪntɪleɪtɪŋ] *adj* funkelnd *attr; (fig) (witty, lively)* wit, *humour* sprühend *attr*.

**scissors** ['sɪzəz] *npl* Schere *f*. **a pair of** ~ eine Schere. ~ **kick** *(Swimming, Ftbl)* Scherenschlag *m*.

**sclerosis** [sklɪ'rəʊsɪs] *n* Sklerose *f*.

**scoff¹** [skɒf] *vi* spotten. **to** ~ **at sb/sth** jdn/etw verachten; *(verbally)* sich verächtlich über jdn/etw äußern.

**scoff²** *vt (col)* futtern *(col)*. **she** ~**ed the lot** sie hat alles verputzt *(col)*.

**scold** [skəʊld] *vt* ausschimpfen *(for wegen)*. **she** ~**ed him for coming home late** sie schimpfte ihn aus, weil er so spät heimkam.

**scolding** ['skəʊldɪŋ] *n* Schelte *f no pl; (act)* Schimpferei *f*. **to give sb a** ~ jdn ausschimpfen.

**scollop** *n* = **scallop**.

**scone** [skɒn] *n* ≈ Milchbrötchen *nt; (with sultanas)* ≈ Rosinenbrötchen *nt*.

**scoop** [skuːp] **1** *n* **(a)** *(instrument)* Schaufel *f; (for ice cream, potatoes etc)* Portionierer *m*. **(b)** *(col: lucky gain)* Fang *m (col)*. **(c)** *(Press)* Knüller *m (col)*. **2** *vt* **(a)** schaufeln; *liquid* schöpfen. **(b) The Times** ~**ed the other papers** die Times ist den anderen Zeitungen zuvorgekommen.

▶**scoop out** *vt sep* **(a)** *(take out)* herausschaufeln;

*liquid* herausschöpfen. **(b)** *(hollow out) marrow etc* aushöhlen; *hole* graben.

►**scoop up** *vt sep* aufschaufeln; *liquid* aufschöpfen. **she** ~ed ~ **the cards/money** sie raffte die Karten/das Geld an sich *(acc)*.

**scoot** [skuːt] *vi (col) (scram)* abzischen *(col)*; *(walk quickly)* rennen.

**scooter** ['skuːtəʳ] *n* (Tret)roller *m*; *(motor* ~*)* Motorroller *m*.

**scope** [skəʊp] *n* **(a)** *(of topic, investigation, knowledge)* Umfang *m*; *(of law, measures)* Reichweite *f*; *(of sb's duties, tribunal)* Kompetenzbereich *m*. **sth is within the** ~ **of sth** etw hält sich im Rahmen einer Sache *(gen)*; **sth is beyond the** ~ **of sth** etw geht über etw *(acc)* hinaus; **that is beyond my** ~ das übersteigt mein Fassungsvermögen. **(b)** *(opportunity)* Möglichkeit(en *pl*) *f*; *(to develop one's talents)* Entfaltungsmöglichkeit *f*; *(to use one's talents)* Spielraum *m*. **there is** ~ **for improvement** es könnte noch verbessert werden; **to give sb** ~ **to do sth** jdm den nötigen Spielraum geben, etw zu tun.

**scorch** [skɔːtʃ] **1** *n (also* ~ **mark***)* Brandfleck *m*. **2** *vt* versengen. **the sun** ~ed **our faces** die Sonne brannte auf unsere Gesichter.

**scorcher** ['skɔːtʃəʳ] *n (col)* **yesterday/last summer was a real** ~ gestern/im letzten Sommer war es wirklich heiß.

**scorching** ['skɔːtʃɪŋ] *adj (very hot) sun, iron* glühend heiß; *day, weather* brütend heiß; *(col: very fast) speed* rasend.

**score** [skɔːʳ] **1** *n* **(a)** *(number of points)* (Punkte)stand *m*; *(of game, Sport)* Spielstand *m*; *(final* ~*)* Spielergebnis *nt*. **the** ~ **was Motherwell 2, Rangers 1** es stand 2:1 *or* zwei zu eins für Motherwell (gegen Rangers); *(final* ~*)* Motherwell schlug Rangers (mit) 2:1; **to keep (the)** ~ (mit)zählen; *(officially)* Punkte zählen; *(on scoreboard)* Punkte anschreiben; **what's the** ~? wie steht es?; *(fig also)* wie sieht es aus? *(on* mit*) (col)*; **to make a** ~ **with sb** *(fig: impress)* jdn stark beeindrucken.

**(b)** *(reckoning, grudge)* **to pay off old** ~s alteu Schulden begleichen; **to have a** ~ **to settle with sb** mit jdm eine alte Rechnung zu begleichen haben.

**(c)** *(Mus) (printed music)* Noten *pl*; *(of classical music also)* Partitur *f*; *(of film, musical)* Musik *f*.

**(d)** *(line, cut)* Kerbe *f*; *(on body)* Kratzer *m*; *(weal)* Striemen *m*.

**(e)** *(20)* **a** ~ zwanzig; ~**s of** ... *(many)* Hunderte von ..., jede Menge ... *(col)*; **by the** ~ massenweise *(col)*.

**(f)** *(reason, ground)* Grund *m*. **on that** ~ *(connection)* in diesem Zusammenhang.

**2** *vt* **(a)** erzielen; *points also* bekommen; *goals also* schießen; *runs also* schaffen. **he** ~d **an advantage over his opponent** er war gegenüber seinem Gegner im Vorteil; **each correct answer** ~s **five points** jede richtige Antwort zählt fünf Punkte; **to** ~ **a point off sb** *(fig)* jdn ausstechen; **to** ~ **a hit with sb** jdn stark beeindrucken. **(b)** *(groove)* einkerben, Kerben/eine Kerbe machen in *(+acc)*; *(mark)* Kratzer/einen Kratzer machen in *(+acc)*.

**3** *vi* **(a)** einen Punkt erzielen; *(Ftbl etc)* ein Tor schießen. **to** ~ **well/badly** gut/schlecht abschneiden; **that's where he** ~s *(fig)* das ist sein großes Plus. **(b)** *(keep* ~*)* (mit)zählen. **(c) to** ~ **with sb** *(col: have sex)* mit jdm bumsen *(col)*.

►**score off 1** *vt sep (delete)* ausstreichen. **2** *vi +prep obj* **to** ~ ~ **sb** jdn als dumm hinstellen.

**score:** ~**board** *n* Anzeigetafel *f*; ~ **card** *n* Spielprotokoll *nt*; *(Golf)* Zählkarte *f*; ~**keeper** *n (official) (Sport)* Anschreiber *m*; *(in quiz etc)* Punktezäh-

ler *m*.

**scorer** ['skɔːrəʳ] *n* **(a)** *(Ftbl etc: player)* Torschütze *m*. **Chelsea were the highest** ~s Chelsea schoß die meisten Tore; **the leading** ~ **in the quiz** der, der die meisten Punkte im Quiz erzielt hat. **(b)** = **scorekeeper**.

**scorn** [skɔːn] **1** *n (disdain)* Verachtung *f*; *(verbal also)* Hohn *m*. **to pour** ~ **on sth** etw verächtlich abtun. **2** *vt (treat scornfully)* verachten; *(condescendingly)* verächtlich behandeln; *(turn down) gift, advice* verschmähen; *idea* mit Verachtung von sich weisen.

**scornful** ['skɔːnfʊl] *adj* verächtlich; *laughter also, person* spöttisch, höhnisch. **to be** ~ **of sb/sth** jdn/etw verachten; *(verbally)* jdn/etw verhöhnen.

**Scorpio** ['skɔːpɪəʊ] *n (Astrol)* Skorpion *m*.

**scorpion** ['skɔːpɪən] *n* Skorpion *m*.

**Scot** [skɒt] *n* Schotte *m*, Schottin *f*.

**Scotch** [skɒtʃ] **1** *adj* schottisch. ~ **egg** *hartgekochtes Ei in Wurstbrät, paniert und ausgebacken*; ~ **tape** ® Tesafilm ® *m*. **2** *n* **(a)** *(~ whisky)* Scotch *m*. **(b) the** ~ *pl* die Schotten *pl*.

**scotch** [skɒtʃ] *vt rumour* aus der Welt schaffen; *idea, plan* unterbinden.

**scot-free** ['skɒt'friː] *adv:* **to get off** ~ ungeschoren davonkommen.

**Scotland** ['skɒtlənd] *n* Schottland *nt*.

**Scots** [skɒts] **1** *adj* schottisch. **2** *n (dialect)* Schottisch *nt*.

**Scots:** ~**man** *n* Schotte *m*; ~**woman** *n* Schottin *f*.

**Scottish** ['skɒtɪʃ] **1** *adj* schottisch. **2** *n* **(a)** *(dialect)* Schottisch *nt*. **(b) the** ~ *pl* die Schotten *pl*; ~ **National Party** Schottische Nationalpartei.

**scoundrel** ['skaʊndrəl] *n (dated)* Schurke *m*; *(col)* Bengel *m*.

**scour¹** ['skaʊəʳ] *vt pans* scheuern.

**scour²** *vt area* absuchen *(for nach)*.

**scourer** ['skaʊərəʳ] *n* Topfkratzer *m*.

**scourge** [skɜːdʒ] **1** *n (lit, fig)* Geißel *f*. **2** *vt* **(a)** geißeln. **(b)** *(fig: punish)* strafen.

**Scouse** [skaʊs] *(Brit col)* **1** *adj* Liverpooler. **2** *n (person)* Liverpooler(in *f*) *m*; *(dialect)* Liverpooler Dialekt *m*.

**scout** [skaʊt] **1** *n* **(a)** *(Mil)* Späher *m*. **(b)** Pfadfinder *m*; *(US: girl* ~*)* Pfadfinderin *f*. **2** *vi* erkunden. **to** ~ **(around) for sth** nach etw Ausschau halten.

**Scouter** ['skaʊtəʳ] *n* Gruppenführer *m*.

**scout:** ~ **master** *n (old)* Gruppenführer *m*; ~ **troop** *n* Pfadfindergruppe *f*.

**scowl** [skaʊl] **1** *n* finsterer Blick, böses Gesicht. **to give sb a** ~ jdn böse ansehen. **2** *vi* ein finsteres Gesicht machen. **to** ~ **at sb** jdn böse ansehen.

**scrabble** ['skræbl] *vi (also* ~ **about***)* (herum)tasten; *(among movable objects)* (herum)wühlen.

**scraggy** ['skrægɪ] *adj (+er)* dürr; *meat* sehnig.

**scram** [skræm] *vi (col)* abhauen *(col)*. ~! hau ab!, verschwinde/verschwindet!

**scramble** ['skræmbl] **1** *vt* **(a)** *pieces, letters* (ver)mischen. **(b)** *eggs* verrühren. ~d **eggs** Rührei(er *pl*) *nt*. **(c)** *(Telec) message* verschlüsseln.

**2** *vi* **(a)** *(climb)* klettern. **he** ~d **to his feet** er rappelte sich auf *(col)*; **to** ~ **through the hedge** durch die Hecke krabbeln *(col)*; **to** ~ **up sth** auf etw *(acc)* hinaufklettern. **(b)** *(struggle)* **to** ~ **for sth/to get sth** sich um etw raufen/sich raufen, um etw zu bekommen; **for ball etc** um etw kämpfen/darum kämpfen, etw zu bekommen; **for bargains, job, good site** sich um etw drängeln/sich drängeln, um etw zu bekommen.

**3** *n* **(a)** *(rush)* Gedrängel *nt (for nach)*. **(b)** *(motorcycle* ~*)* Querfeldeinrennen *nt*.

**scrambler** ['skræmblə<sup>r</sup>] n (Telec) Chiffriergerät nt.
**scrap¹** [skɪæp] **1** n **(a)** (small piece) Stückchen nt; (fig) bißchen nt no pl; (of papers also, of conversation, news) Fetzen m; (of truth) Fünkchen nt, Spur f. there isn't a ~ of food in the house es ist überhaupt nichts zu essen im Haus; not a ~! nicht die Spur!; not a ~ of evidence nicht der geringste Beweis. **(b)** (usu pl: leftover) Rest m. **(c)** (waste material) Altmaterial nt; (metal) Schrott m; (paper) Altpapier nt. are these notes ~? können die Notizen weggeworfen werden?; to sell a ship for ~ ein Schiff zum Verschrotten verkaufen. **2** vt car, ship etc verschrotten; furniture, clothes ausrangieren; idea, plan etc fallenlassen; piece of work wegwerfen.
**scrap²** (col) **1** n Balgerei f; (verbal) Streiterei f. **2** vi sich balgen; (verbally) sich streiten.
**scrap:** ~book n Sammelalbum nt; ~ dealer n (in metal) Schrotthändler m.
**scrape** [skreɪp] **1** n **(a)** (act) to give sth a ~ see vt (a). **(b)** (mark, graze) Schramme f. **(c)** (sound) Kratzen nt. **(d)** (difficulty) Schwulitäten pl (col). to get sb out of a ~ jdm aus der Klemme helfen (col). **2** vt **(a)** (make clean or ˈsmooth) potatoes etc schaben; plate, wall abkratzen; saucepan auskratzen. that's really scraping the barrel (fig) das ist wirklich das Letzte vom Letzten. **(b)** gatepost etc streifen; paintwork ankratzen; knee aufschürfen. **(c)** (grate against) kratzen an (+dat). **(d)** (make by scraping) hole scharren. to ~ a living gerade so sein Auskommen haben. **3** vi he ~d at the paint for hours er kratzte stundenlang an der Farbe herum.
▶**scrape along** or **by** vi sich schlecht und recht durchschlagen (col) (on mit).
▶**scrape off** vt sep abkratzen (prep obj von).
▶**scrape through 1** vi (lit) (object) gerade so durchgehen; (person) sich durchzwängen; (in exam) gerade noch durchkommen (col). **2** vi +prep obj narrow gap sich durchzwängen durch; exam gerade noch durchkommen durch (col).
▶**scrape together** vt sep leaves zusammenharken; money zusammenkratzen; people zusammenbringen; support (mit einigen Schwierigkeiten) organisieren.
**scraper** ['skreɪpə<sup>r</sup>] n (tool) Spachtel m; (at door) Kratzeisen nt.
**scrapheap** ['skræp‚hiːp] n Schrotthaufen m. to be thrown on the ~ (thing) zum Schrott geworfen werden; (person) zum alten Eisen geworfen werden; (idea) über Bord geworfen werden.
**scrap:** ~ merchant n (in metal) Schrotthändler m; ~ metal n Schrott m, Altmetall nt; ~ paper n Schmierpapier nt.
**scrappy** ['skræpɪ] adj (+er) zusammengestoppelt (col); knowledge lückenhaft.
**scrap yard** n Schrottplatz m.
**scratch** [skrætʃ] **1** n **(a)** (mark) Kratzer m. **(b)** (act) the dog enjoys a ~ der Hund kratzt sich gern. **(c)** to start from ~ (ganz) von vorn(e) anfangen; to start sth from ~ etw ganz von vorne anfangen; business etw aus dem Nichts aufbauen; to learn a language/a new trade from ~ eine Sprache von Grund auf erlernen/einen neuen Beruf von der Pike auf erlernen; to come up to ~ (col) den Anforderungen entsprechen. **2** adj attr meal improvisiert; crew, team zusammengewürfelt. **3** vt kratzen; hole scharren; (leave ~es on) zerkratzen. to ~ one's head (lit, fig) sich (dat) den Kopf kratzen; if you ~ my back, I'll ~ yours (fig) eine Hand wäscht die andere; to ~ the surface of sth (fig) etw (nur) oberflächlich berühren.

**4** vi **(a)** (make ~ing movement/noise) kratzen; (in soil etc) scharren; (~ oneself) sich kratzen. **(b)** (become ~ed) the new paint ~s easily der neue Lack bekommt leicht Kratzer.
▶**scratch out** vt sep auskratzen; (cross out) ausstreichen.
**scratch:** ~ card n (for lottery etc) Rubbelkarte f; ~ pad n (US Comp) Notizblock m.
**scratchy** ['skrætʃɪ] adj (+er) sound, pen kratzend attr; record zerkratzt; feel, sweater kratzig.
**scrawl** [skrɔːl] **1** n Gekrakel nt (col); (handwriting) Klaue f (col); (col: message) gekritzelte Nachricht. **2** vt hinkritzeln.
**scrawny** ['skrɔːnɪ] adj (+er) dürr.
**scream** [skriːm] **1** n **(a)** Schrei m; (screech) Kreischen nt; (of engine, siren) Heulen nt. there were ~s of laughter from the audience das Publikum kreischte vor Lachen; to give a ~ einen Schrei ausstoßen. **(b)** (fig col) to be a ~ zum Schreien sein (col). **2** vt schreien; command brüllen; (fig: headlines) ausschreien. to ~ sth at sb jdm etw zuschreien; you idiot, she ~ed at me du Idiot, schrie sie mich an. **3** vi schreien; kreischen; (wind, engine, siren) heulen. to ~ at sb jdn anschreien; to ~ with laughter vor Lachen kreischen.
**scree** [skriː] n Geröll nt.
**screech** [skriːtʃ] **1** n Kreischen nt no pl; (of tyres also, of brakes) Quietschen nt no pl; (of owl) Schrei m. the car stopped with a ~ of brakes das Auto hielt mit quietschenden Bremsen. **2** vi kreischen; (brakes, tyres also) quietschen.
**screen** [skriːn] **1** n **(a)** (protective) Schirm m; (for privacy etc) Wandschirm m; (as partition) Trennwand f; (against insects) Fliegenfenster nt; (fig) (for protection) Schutz m; (of trees) Wand f; (of mist, secrecy) Schleier m. **(b)** (Film) Leinwand f; (TV, radar ~, Comp) (Bild)schirm m. the big/small ~ die Leinwand/der Fernsehschirm; to edit on ~ (Comp) am Bildschirm editieren. **2** vt **(a)** (hide) verdecken; (protect) abschirmen (from gegen). he ~ed his eyes from the sun er schützte die Augen vor der Sonne. **(b)** TV programme senden; film vorführen. **(c)** (sift) sieben. **(d)** (investigate) applicants, security risks überprüfen.
**screening** ['skriːnɪŋ] n **(a)** (of applicants, security risks) Überprüfung f; (Med) Untersuchung f. **(b)** (of film) Vorführung f; (TV) Sendung f.
**screen:** ~ memory n (Comp) Bildschirmspeicher m; ~play n Drehbuch nt; ~ printing n Siebdruck(verfahren nt) m; ~ test n Probeaufnahmen pl.
**screw** [skruː] **1** n **(a)** (Mech, Naut, Aviat) Schraube f. he's got a ~ loose (col) bei dem ist eine Schraube locker (col); to put the ~s on sb (col) jdm die Daumenschrauben anlegen. **(b)** (Brit col: prison officer) Schließer m (col). **2** vt **(a)** schrauben (to an +acc, onto auf +acc). **(b)** (col: put pressure on) to ~ sb for sth etw aus jdm herausquetschen (col). **(c)** (col!: have sex with) bumsen (col), vögeln (col!).
▶**screw together** vt sep zusammenschrauben.
▶**screw up** vt sep **(a)** paper, material zerknüllen; eyes zusammenkneifen; face verziehen. to ~ one's courage seinen ganzen Mut zusammennehmen. **(b)** (col) (spoil) vermasseln (col); (make uptight) sb neurotisch machen. to get ~ed ~ about sth sich wegen etw ganz verrückt machen.
**screw:** ~ball (esp US col) n Spinner(in f) m (col); ~cap n Schraubverschluß m; ~driver n Schraubenzieher m; ~ top n Schraubverschluß m.
**screwy** ['skruːɪ] adj (+er) (col) verrückt, bekloppt (col); (weird) person, humour komisch.

**scribble** ['skrɪbl] **1** *n* Gekritzel *nt no pl*; *(note)* schnell hingekritzelte Nachricht. **2** *vt (also ~ down)* hinkritzeln. **to ~ sth on sth** etw auf etw *(acc)* kritzeln. **3** *vi* kritzeln.

**scribbler** ['skrɪblər] *n (pej col)* Schreiberling *m (pej)*.

**scribe** [skraɪb] *n* Schreiber *m*; *(Bibl)* Schriftgelehrte(r) *m*.

**scrimmage** ['skrɪmɪdʒ] *n (US Ftbl)* Gedränge *nt*; *(Rugby)* offenes Gedränge; *(col: struggle also)* Rangelei *f (col)*.

**scrimp** [skrɪmp] *vi* sparen, knausern. **to ~ and save** geizen und sparen.

**script** [skrɪpt] *n* **(a)** *(style of writing)* Schrift *f*; *(handwriting)* Handschrift *f*. **(b)** *(of play, documentary)* Text *m*; *(for film)* Drehbuch *nt*.

**scripted** ['skrɪptɪd] *adj discussion* vorbereitet.

**scripture** ['skrɪptʃər] *n* **(a)** S~, **the** S~s die (Heilige) Schrift. **(b)** *(Sch)* Religion *f*.

**scriptwriter** ['skrɪpt,raɪtər] *n (Film)* Drehbuchautor(in *f*) *m*.

**scroll** [skrəʊl] **1** *n* Schriftrolle *f*; *(decorative)* Schnörkel *m*. **2** *vi (Comp)* blättern.

**scrotum** ['skrəʊtəm] *n (Anat)* Hodensack *m*.

**scrounge** [skraʊndʒ] *(col)* **1** *vi (sponge)* schnorren *(col) (off, from* bei*)*. **he ~d off his parents for years** er lag seinen Eltern jahrelang auf der Tasche *(col)*. **2** *vt* schnorren *(col)*, abstauben *(col) (from, off* bei*)*. **3** *n (col)* **to be on the ~** am Schnorren sein *(col)*.

**scrounger** ['skraʊndʒər] *n (col)* Schnorrer(in *f*) *m (col)*.

**scrub¹** [skrʌb] *nt (Bot)* Gebüsch, Gestrüpp *nt*.

**scrub²** **1** *n* Schrubben *nt no pl*. **to give sth a ~/a good ~** etw schrubben/gründlich abschrubben. **2** *vt* schrubben; *vegetables* putzen; *(col: cancel)* abblasen *(col)*; *idea* abschreiben *(col)*. **to ~ oneself down** sich abschrubben.

**scrub brush** *(US)*, **scrubbing brush** *(Brit)* ['skrʌbɪŋ,brʌʃ] *n* Scheuerbürste *f*.

**scruff¹** [skrʌf] *n* **by the ~ of the neck** am Genick.

**scruff²** *n (col: scruffy person) (man)* abgerissener Typ; *(woman)* Schlampe *f (pej col)*.

**scruffily** ['skrʌfɪlɪ] *adv (col)* gammelig *(col)*.

**scruffiness** ['skrʌfɪnɪs] *n (col)* vergammelter Zustand.

**scruffy** ['skrʌfɪ] *adj (+er) (col)* vergammelt *(col)*; *house also* verlottert *(col)*, verwahrlost.

**scrum** [skrʌm] *n (Rugby)* Gedränge *nt*.

**scrumptious** ['skrʌmpʃəs] *adj (col) meal etc* lecker.

**scruple** ['skru:pl] *n* Skrupel *m usu pl*. **~s** *(doubts)* (moralische) Bedenken *pl*; **to have no ~s** keine Skrupel haben.

**scrupulous** ['skru:pjʊləs] *adj (person)* gewissenhaft; *honesty, fairness* unbedingt; *cleanliness* peinlich; *account* (peinlich) genau.

**scrupulously** ['skru:pjʊləslɪ] *adv (honestly, conscientiously)* gewissenhaft; *(meticulously)* exact, clean peinlich; *fair, careful* äußerst.

**scrutinize** ['skru:tɪnaɪz] *vt (examine)* (genau) untersuchen; *(check)* genau prüfen; *votes* prüfen; *(stare at)* mustern. **to ~ sth for sth** etw auf etw *(acc)* prüfen.

**scrutiny** ['skru:tɪnɪ] *n* **(a)** *(examination)* Untersuchung *f*; *(checking)* (Über)prüfung *f*; *(of person)* Musterung *f*; *(stare)* musternder Blick. **it does not stand up to ~** es hält keiner genauen Prüfung stand. **(b)** *(Pol)* Wahlprüfung *f*.

**scuba** ['sku:bə] *n* (Schwimm)tauchgerät *nt*. **~ diver** *(Sport)* taucher(in *f*) *m*; **~ diving** Sporttauchen *nt*.

**scuff** [skʌf] **1** *vt* abwetzen. **2** *n (~ mark)* abgewetzte Stelle.

**scuffle** ['skʌfl] **1** *n (skirmish)* Rauferei *f (col)*. **2** *vi*

*(have skirmish)* sich raufen. **to ~ with the police** ein Handgemenge *nt* mit der Polizei haben.

**scullery** ['skʌlərɪ] *n* Spülküche *f*.

**sculpt** [skʌlpt] **1** *vt* = **sculpture 2**. **2** *vi* bildhauern *(col)*.

**sculptor** ['skʌlptər] *n* Bildhauer(in *f*) *m*.

**sculptress** ['skʌlptrɪs] *n* Bildhauerin *f*.

**sculpture** ['skʌlptʃər] **1** *n (art)* Bildhauerkunst *f*; *(work)* Bildhauerei *f*; *(object)* Skulptur, Plastik *f*. **2** *vt* formen; *(in stone)* hauen, meißeln; *(in clay etc)* modellieren. **he ~d the tombstone out of marble** er haute den Grabstein in Marmor.

**scum** [skʌm] *n* **(a)** *(on liquid)* Schaum *m*; *(residue)* Rand *m*. **(b)** *(pej col) (collective)* Abschaum *m*; *(one individual)* Dreckskerl *m (col)*. **the ~ of the earth** der Abschaum der Menschheit.

**scupper** ['skʌpər] *vt (Naut)* versenken; *(Brit col: ruin)* zerschlagen. **if he finds out, we'll be ~ed** wenn er das erfährt, sind wir erledigt *(col)*.

**scurrilous** ['skʌrɪləs] *adj (abusive)* verleumderisch; *(indecent)* unflätig.

**scurry** ['skʌrɪ] *vi (person)* hasten; *(with small steps)* trippeln; *(animals)* huschen. **to ~ along** entlanghasten/entlangtrippeln/entlanghuschen.

**scurvy** ['skɜːvɪ] *n* Skorbut *m*.

**scuttle¹** ['skʌtl] *n* Kohleneimer *m*.

**scuttle²** *vi (person)* trippeln; *(animals)* hoppeln; *(spiders, crabs etc)* krabbeln. **she ~d off in a hurry** sie flitzte davon.

**scuttle³** *(Naut) vt* versenken.

**scythe** [saɪð] **1** *n* Sense *f*. **2** *vt* (mit der Sense) mähen.

**SD** *(US Post)* = **South Dakota**.

**SDI** = **strategic defence initiative** SDI *f*.

**SDLP** *(Brit Pol)* = **Social Democratic and Labour Party** *sozialistische Partei Nordirlands*.

**SDP** *(Brit Pol Hist)* = **Social Democratic Party**.

**sea** [si:] *n* **(a)** Meer *nt*, See *f*. **by ~** auf dem Seeweg; **to travel by ~** mit dem Schiff fahren; **a town by the ~** eine Stadt am Meer; **(out) at ~** auf See; **as I looked out to ~** als ich aufs Meer hinausblickte; **to be all at ~** *(fig)* nicht durchblicken *(col) (with* bei*)*; **to go to ~** zur See gehen; **to put to ~** in See stechen; **heavy/strong ~s** schwere/rauhe See; **a ~ of faces** ein Meer von Gesichtern; **a ~ of flame** ein Flammenmeer.

**sea:** **~ air** *n* Seeluft *f*; **~ anemone** *n* Seeanemone *f*; **~bed** *n* Meeresboden *m*; **~ bird** *n* Seevogel *m*; **~board** *n (US)* Küste *f*; **~ breeze** *n* Seewind *m*; **~ change** *n* totale Veränderung; **~farer** *n* Seefahrer *m*; **~faring** *adj nation, people* seefahrend; **~food** *n* Meeresfrüchte *pl*; **~ front** *n* Strandpromenade *f*; **~going** *adj boat etc* hochseetüchtig; *nation, family* Seefahrer-; **~-green** *adj* meergrün; **~gull** *n* Möwe *f*; **~horse** *n* Seepferdchen *nt*.

**seal¹** [si:l] *n (Zool)* Seehund *m*; *(~skin)* Seal *m*.

**seal²** **1** *n* **(a)** *(impression in wax etc)* Siegel *nt*; *(against unauthorized opening)* Versiegelung *f*; *(die)* Stempel *m*; *(decorative label)* Aufkleber *m*. **under the ~ of secrecy** unter dem Siegel der Verschwiegenheit; **~ of quality** Gütesiegel *nt*; **to put one's ~ of approval on sth** einer Sache *(dat)* seine offizielle Zustimmung geben. **(b)** *(airtight closure)* Verschluß *m*; *(washer)* Dichtung *f*. **2** *vt* versiegeln; *envelope, parcel also* zukleben; *(make air- or watertight) joint etc* abdichten; *(fig: finalize)* besiegeln. **~ed envelope** verschlossener Briefumschlag; **my lips are ~ed** meine Lippen sind versiegelt; **this ~ed his fate** dadurch war sein Schicksal besiegelt.

▶**seal off** *vt sep* absperren, abriegeln.

▶**seal up** *vt sep* versiegeln; *parcel, letter* zukleben;

**secondary**

*crack, windows* abdichten.
**sealant** ['si:lənt] *n* Dichtungsmasse *f.*
**sea:** ~ **legs** *npl:* **to find one's** ~ **legs** (auf dem/ einem Schiff) standfest werden; ~ **level** *n* Meeresspiegel *m;* **above/below** ~ **level** über/unter dem Meeresspiegel.
**sealing wax** ['si:lɪŋ,wæks] *n* Siegelwachs *nt.*
**sea lion** *n* Seelöwe *m.*
**sealskin** ['si:lskɪn] *n* Seehundfell *nt,* Seal *m.*
**seam** [si:m] *n* **(a)** Naht *f.* **to come apart at the** ~s *(lit, fig)* aus den Nähten gehen; **to be bursting at the** ~s *(lit, fig)* aus allen Nähten platzen *(col).* **(b)** *(Geol)* Flöz *nt.*
**seaman** ['si:mən] *n, pl* **-men** [-mən] Seemann *m.*
**seamanship** ['si:mənʃɪp] *n* Seemannschaft *f.*
**sea:** ~ **mile** *n* Seemeile *f;* ~ **mist** *n* Küstennebel *m.*
**seamless** ['si:mlɪs] *adj* nahtlos.
**seamstress** ['semstrɪs] *n* Näherin *f.*
**seamy** ['si:mɪ] *adj* (+er) *(down-at-heel)* heruntergekommen; *(dubious)* zwielichtig. **the** ~ **side of life** die Schattenseite des Lebens.
**séance** ['seɪɑ̃:ns] *n* spiritistische Sitzung, Séance *f.*
**sea:** ~ **plane** *n* Wasserflugzeug *nt;* ~ **port** *n* Seehafen *m;* ~ **power** *n* Seemacht *f.*
**search** [sɜ:tʃ] **1** *n (hunt: for lost object, person etc)* Suche *f (for* nach); *(examination: of luggage etc)* Durchsuchung *f (of gen);* *(Comp, Rad)* Suchlauf *m.* **to go in** ~ **of sb/sth** auf die Suche nach jdm/etw gehen. **2** *vt (for* nach) durchsuchen; *archives etc* suchen in (+*dat),* durchforschen; *conscience* erforschen; *memory etc* durchforschen. **to** ~ **a place for sb/sth** einen Ort nach jdm/etw absuchen; ~ **me!** *(col)* was weiß ich? *(col).* **3** *vi* suchen *(for* nach).
▶**search through** *vi* +*prep obj* durchsuchen; *papers, books* durchsehen.
**searcher** ['sɜ:tʃəʳ] *n* Suchende(r) *mf.* **the** ~s *(search party)* die Suchmannschaft.
**searching** ['sɜ:tʃɪŋ] *adj look* forschend; *question* durchdringend.
**search:** ~**light** *n* Suchscheinwerfer *m;* ~ **party** *n* Suchmannschaft *f;* ~ **warrant** *n* Durchsuchungsbefehl *m.*
**searing** ['sɪərɪŋ] *adj heat* glühend; *pain also* scharf.
**sea:** ~ **salt** *n* Meersalz *nt;* ~**scape** *n* Seestück *nt;* ~ **shell** *n* Muschel *f;* ~**shore** *n* Strand *m;* **on the** ~**shore** am Strand; ~**sick** *adj* seekrank; ~**sickness** *n* Seekrankheit *f;* ~**side 1** *n* **at the** ~**side** am Meer; **to go to the** ~**side** ans Meer fahren; **2** *attr town* Küsten-; *holiday* am Meer; ~**side resort** Badeort *m.*
**season** ['si:zn] **1** *n* **(a)** *(of the year)* Jahreszeit *f.* **rainy/monsoon** ~ Regen-/Monsunzeit *f.* **(b)** *(sporting* ~ *etc)* Saison *f.* **holiday** ~ Urlaubszeit *f;* *(Hunt)* Schonzeit *f;* **nesting/hunting** ~ Brut-/Jagdzeit *f;* **the football** ~ die Fußballsaison; **strawberries are in** ~**/out of** ~ **now** für Erdbeeren ist jetzt die richtige/nicht die richtige Zeit; **"S**~**'s greetings"** „fröhliche Weihnachten und ein glückliches neues Jahr". **2** *vt* **(a)** *food* würzen; *(fig: temper)* durchsetzen. **(b)** *wood* ablagern; *(fig: inure)* troops stählen.
**seasonable** ['si:zənbl] *adj dress, weather etc* der Jahreszeit entsprechend *attr.* **to be** ~ der Jahreszeit entsprechen.
**seasonal** ['si:zənl] *adj employment etc* Saison-.
**seasonally** ['si:zənəlɪ] *adv:* ~ **adjusted** saisonbereinigt.
**seasoned** ['si:znd] *adj* **(a)** *food* gewürzt. **(b)** *timber* abgelagert. **(c)** *(fig: experienced)* erfahren.
**seasoning** ['si:znɪŋ] *n (Cook)* Gewürz *nt.*
**season ticket** *n (Rail)* Zeitkarte *f;* *(Theat)* Abonnement *nt.*

**seat** [si:t] **1** *n* **(a)** *(place to sit)* (Sitz)platz *m;* *(piece of furniture)* Sitz *m;* *(usu pl:* ~*ing)* Sitzgelegenheit *f.* **driving** ~ Fahrersitz *m;* **we haven't enough** ~s wir haben nicht genügend Sitzgelegenheiten; **to lose one's** ~ seinen Platz verlieren; **will you keep my** ~ **for me?** würden Sie mir meinen Platz freihalten?; **I've booked two** ~s ich habe zwei Plätze reservieren lassen. **(b)** *(of chair etc)* Sitz *m,* Sitzfläche *f;* *(of trousers)* Hosenboden *m;* *(buttocks)* Gesäß *nt.* **(c)** *(on committee, of government, in parliament)* Sitz *m;* *(of fire, trouble)* Herd *m.* **to win a** ~ ein Mandat gewinnen; **his** ~ **is in Devon** sein Wahlkreis *m* ist in Devon; ~ **of emotions** Sitz der Gefühle; ~ **of learning** Lehrstätte *f.*
**2** *vt* **(a)** *person etc* setzen. **to** ~ **oneself** sich setzen; **to be** ~**ed** sitzen; **please be** ~**ed** bitte, setzen Sie sich; **to remain** ~**ed** sitzen bleiben. **(b)** *(have sitting room for)* **the car/table** ~s **4** im Auto/am Tisch ist Platz für 4 Personen; **the theatre** ~s **900** das Theater hat 900 Sitzplätze.
**seat belt** *n* Sicherheitsgurt *m.* **to fasten one's** ~ sich anschnallen.
**-seater** [-si:təʳ] *suf* **1** *n* -sitzer *m.* **2** *attr car, plane* -sitzig.
**seating** ['si:tɪŋ] *n* Sitzplätze *pl.* ~ **arrangements** Sitzordnung *f;* ~ **capacity** (Zahl *f* der) Sitzplätze.
**sea:** ~ **urchin** *n* Seeigel *m;* ~ **wall** *n* Deich *m;* ~ **water** *n* Meerwasser *nt;* ~**weed** *n* (See)tang *m,* Seegras *nt;* ~**worthy** *adj* seetüchtig.
**sec** [sek] = **second(s)** Sek.
**Sec** = **Secretary** Sekr.
**secateurs** [,sekə'tɜ:z] *npl (Brit)* Gartenschere *f.*
**secede** [sɪ'si:d] *vi* sich abspalten.
**secession** [sɪ'seʃən] *n* Abspaltung *f;* *(US Hist)* Sezession *f.*
**secluded** [sɪ'klu:dɪd] *adj spot, house* abgelegen; *life* zurückgezogen.
**seclusion** [sɪ'klu:ʒən] *n (of house, spot)* Abgelegenheit *f.*
**second**[1] ['sekənd] **1** *adj* zweite(r, s). **the** ~ **floor** *(Brit)* der zweite Stock; *(US)* der erste Stock; **a** ~ **Goethe** ein zweiter Goethe; **every** ~ **house** jedes zweite Haus; **to be** ~ Zweite(r, s) sein; **to be** ~ **to none** unübertroffen sein; **in** ~ **place** *(Sport etc)* an zweiter Stelle; **in the** ~ **place** *(secondly)* zweitens; **to be** ~ **in command** *(Mil)* stellvertretender Kommandeur sein; *(fig)* der zweite Mann sein; **will you have a** ~ **cup?** möchten Sie noch eine Tasse? **2** *adv* (+*adj)* zweit-; (+*vb)* an zweiter Stelle. **to come/lie** ~ *(in race, competition)* Zweite(r) werden. **3** *vt motion, proposal* unterstützen. **I'll** ~ **that!** *(at meeting)* ich unterstütze das; *(in general)* meine Meinung. **4** *n* **(a)** *(of time, Math, Sci)* Sekunde *f;* *(col: short time)* Augenblick *m.* **just a** ~! (einen) Augenblick!; **it won't take a** ~ es dauert nicht lange; **I'll only be a** ~ **(or two)** ich komme gleich; *(back soon)* ich bin gleich wieder da; **at that very** ~ genau in dem Augenblick. **(b)** **the** ~ *(in order)* der/die/das zweite; *(in race, class etc)* der/die/das Zweite; **to come a poor/ good** ~ einen schlechten/guten zweiten Platz belegen; **Elizabeth the S**~ Elisabeth die Zweite. **(c)** *(Brit Univ: degree)* **she got a** ~ ≃ sie bestand (ihr Examen) mit „gut". **(d)** ~s *pl (col:* ~ *helping)* Nachschlag *m (col);* **can I have** ~s? kann ich noch etwas nachbekommen? **(e)** *(Comm)* ~s *pl* Waren zweiter Wahl. **(f)** *(Boxing, duelling)* Sekundant *m.*
**second**[2] [sɪ'kɒnd] *vt (Brit)* abordnen.
**secondary** ['sekəndərɪ] *adj* **(a)** sekundär, Sekundär-*(also Sci);* *road, effect* Neben-; *industry* verarbeitend; *reason* weniger bedeutend. **of** ~ **importance**

von untergeordneter Bedeutung. **(b)** *(higher) education, school* höher. ~ **modern (school)** *(Brit)* ≈ Realschule *f.*

**second:** ~-**best 1** *n* Zweitbeste(r, s); **(the)** ~-**best isn't good enough for him** das Beste ist gerade gut genug für ihn; **2** *adj* zweitbeste(r, s); **3** *adv* **to come off** ~-**best** *(come off badly)* den kürzeren ziehen; ~ **class** *n (Rail etc, mail)* zweite Klasse; ~-**class** *adj* **(a)** *also adv travel, mail, citizen* zweiter Klasse *(after noun)*; **(b)** = ~-**rate**; ~ **cousin** *n* Cousin *m*/Cousine *f* zweiten Grades.

**seconder** ['sekəndər] *n* Befürworter(in *f*) *m.*

**second:** ~-**guess** *vt* **to** ~-**guess sb** vorhersagen, was jd machen/sagen wird; ~ **hand** *n (of watch)* Sekundenzeiger *m*; ~-**hand 1** *adj* gebraucht; *car also* Gebraucht-; *dealer* Gebrauchtwaren-; *(for cars)* Gebrauchtwagen-; *bookshop* Antiquariats-; *clothes* getragen, Secondhand- *(esp Comm)*; *(fig) information, knowledge* aus zweiter Hand; **2** *adv* gebraucht, aus zweiter Hand; **I only heard it** ~-**hand** ich habe es nur aus zweiter Hand; ~ **home** *n* Zweitwohnung *f.*

**secondly** ['sekəndlı] *adv* zweitens; *(secondarily)* an zweiter Stelle, in zweiter Linie.

**secondment** [sɪ'kɒndmənt] *n (Brit)* Abordnung *f.* **to be on** ~ abgeordnet sein.

**second:** ~ **nature** *n* zweite Natur; **to become** ~ **nature (to sb)** (jdm) in Fleisch und Blut übergehen; ~-**rate** *adj (pej)* zweitklassig; ~ **sight** *n* das Zweite Gesicht; **you must have** ~ **sight** du mußt hellsehen können; ~ **thoughts** *npl* **to have** ~ **thoughts about sth** sich *(dat)* etw anders überlegen; **on** ~ **thoughts I decided not to** dann habe ich mich doch dagegen entschieden.

**secrecy** ['si:krəsı] *n (of person)* Verschwiegenheit *f*; *(secretiveness)* Heimlichtuerei *f*; *(of event, talks)* Heimlichkeit *f.* **in** ~ im geheimen.

**secret** ['si:krɪt] **1** *adj* geheim; *weapon, negotiations, code* Geheim-; *drinker, admirer* heimlich. **the** ~ **ingredient** die geheimnisvolle Zutat; *(fig: of success etc)* die Zauberformel; **to keep sth** ~ **(from sb)** etw (vor jdm) geheimhalten; **it's all highly** ~ es ist alles streng geheim. **2** *n* Geheimnis *nt.* **in** ~ im geheimen; **I told you that in** ~ **or as a** ~ ich habe Ihnen das im Vertrauen erzählt; **they always met in** ~ sie trafen sich immer heimlich; *(society etc)* sie hatten immer geheime Versammlungen; **there's no** ~ **about it** das ist kein Geheimnis; **to keep a** ~ ein Geheimnis bewahren; **can you keep a** ~**?** kannst du schweigen?; **to make no** ~ **of sth** kein Geheimnis aus etw machen.

**secret agent** *n* Geheimagent(in *f*) *m.*

**secretarial** [,sekrə'tɛərıəl] *adj* Sekretärinnen-; *job, qualifications* als Sekretärin.

**secretariat** [,sekrə'tɛərıət] *n* Sekretariat *nt.*

**secretary** ['sekrətrı] *n* Sekretär(in *f*) *m*; *(of society)* Geschäftsführer(in *f*) *m*; *(keeping minutes etc)* Schriftführer(in *f*) *m*; *(esp US Pol: minister)* Minister(in *f*) *m.*

**secretary:** ~ **bird** *n* Sekretär *m*; **S**~ **General** *n, pl* **Secretaries General** *or* **S**~ **Generals** Generalsekretär *m*; **S**~ **of State** *(Brit)* Minister(in *f*) *m*; *(US)* Außenminister(in *f*) *m*; ~ **pool** *n (US)* = **typing pool.**

**secrete** [sɪ'kri:t] *vt* **(a)** *(hide)* verbergen. **(b)** *(Med)* absondern.

**secretion** [sɪ'kri:ʃən] *n* **(a)** *(hiding)* Verbergen *nt.* **(b)** *(Med) (act)* Absonderung *f*; *(substance)* Sekret *nt.*

**secretive** ['si:krətıv] *adj person (by nature)* verschlossen; *(in action)* geheimnistuerisch; *smile, behaviour* geheimnisvoll. **to be** ~ **about sth** mit etw

geheimnisvoll tun.

**secretly** ['si:krətlı] *adv (in secrecy)* im geheimen; *meet* heimlich; *(privately)* insgeheim. **he was** ~ **concerned** insgeheim war er beunruhigt.

**secret:** ~ **police** *n* Geheimpolizei *f*; ~ **service** *n* Geheimdienst *m.*

**sect** [sekt] *n* Sekte *f.*

**sectarian** [sek'tɛərıən] *adj policy, views* religiös beeinflußt; *school also* konfessionell; *war, differences* Konfessions-; *groups* sektiererisch. ~ **violence** (gewalttätige) Konfessionsstreitigkeiten; **it was a** ~ **bombing** der Bombenanschlag hing mit den Konfessionsstreitigkeiten zusammen.

**section** ['sekʃən] *n* **(a)** *(part)* Teil *m*; *(of book, motorway)* Abschnitt *m*; *(of document, law)* Absatz *m*; *(of railway)* Streckenabschnitt *m.* **the string** ~ **of the orchestra** die Streicher *pl* des Orchesters; **the sports** ~ *(Press)* der Sportteil; **the black** ~ **of the community** die Gruppe der Schwarzen in der Gesellschaft. **(b)** *(department, Mil)* Abteilung *f.* **(c)** *(diagram)* Schnitt *m.* **vertical/longitudinal** ~ Quer-/Längsschnitt *m.*

**sectional** ['sekʃənl] *adj* **(a)** *(in sections) furniture, pipe* zerlegbar, zusammensetzbar. ~ **drawing** Darstellung *f* im Schnitt. **(b)** *rivalries* zwischen den Gruppen; *interests* partikularistisch.

**sector** ['sektər] *n* Sektor *m.*

**secular** ['sekjulər] *adj* weltlich; *music, art* profan.

**secure** [sɪ'kjuər] **1** *adj (+er)* sicher; *(emotionally)* geborgen; *existence, income* gesichert; *(firm) grip, knot* fest. ~ **in the knowledge that ...** ruhig in dem Bewußtsein, daß ...; **to be** ~ **against sth** vor etw *(dat)* sicher sein; **to feel** ~ sich sicher fühlen; *(emotionally)* sich geborgen fühlen; **is the window/lid** ~**?** ist das Fenster fest zu/ist der Deckel fest drauf? **2** *vt* **(a)** *festmachen; (tie up also)* befestigen; *window, door* fest zumachen; *(with bolt etc)* sichern; *tile* befestigen; *(make safe)* sichern *(from, against* gegen*)*, schützen *(from, against* vor +*dat)*. **(b)** *(obtain)* sich *(dat)* sichern; *votes, order* erhalten; *profits* erzielen; *share, interest in business* erwerben; *(buy)* erstehen; *employee* verpflichten. **(c)** *(guarantee)* sichern; *loan* (ab)sichern.

**securely** [sɪ'kjuəlı] *adv (firmly)* fest; *(safely)* sicher.

**security** [sɪ'kjuərıtı] *n* **(a)** Sicherheit *f*; *(emotional)* Geborgenheit *f*; *(~ measures)* Sicherheitsvorkehrungen *pl.* **for** ~ zur Sicherheit. **(b)** *(~ department)* Sicherheitsdienst *m.* **(c)** *(Fin) (guarantee)* Sicherheit *f*; *(guarantor)* Bürge *m.* **to lend money on** ~ Geld gegen Sicherheit leihen. **(d)** *(Fin)* **securities** *pl* (Wert)papiere *pl.*

**security** *in cpds* Sicherheits-; *(Fin)* Wertpapier-; ~ **check** *n* Sicherheitskontrolle *f*; **S**~ **Council** *n* Sicherheitsrat *m*; ~ **firm** *n* Wach- und Sicherheitsdienst *m*; ~ **forces** *npl* Sicherheitskräfte *pl*; ~ **guard** *n* Sicherheitsbeamte(r) *m*; ~ **risk** *n* Sicherheitsrisiko *nt.*

**sedan** [sɪ'dæn] *n (US)* Limousine *f.*

**sedate** [sɪ'deıt] **1** *adj (+er)* gesetzt; *colour* ruhig; *life* geruhsam; *speed* gemächlich. **2** *vt* Beruhigungsmittel geben *(+dat).* **he was heavily** ~**d** er stand stark unter dem Einfluß von Beruhigungsmitteln.

**sedation** [sɪ'deıʃən] *n* Beruhigungsmittel *pl.* **to put sb under** ~ jdm Beruhigungsmittel geben.

**sedative** ['sedətıv] **1** *n* Beruhigungsmittel *nt.* **2** *adj* beruhigend.

**sedentary** ['sedntərı] *adj job* sitzend *attr*; *worker* Sitz-. **to lead a** ~ **life** sehr viel sitzen.

**sediment** ['sedımənt] *n* (Boden)satz *m*; *(in river)* Ablagerung *f*; *(in solution)* Sediment *nt.*

**sedimentary** [,sedı'mentərı] *adj* sedimentär. ~

rocks Sedimentgestein *nt.*
**sedition** [sə'dɪʃən] *n* Aufwiegelung *f.*
**seditious** [sə'dɪʃəs] *adj* aufrührerisch.
**seduce** [sɪ'djuːs] *vt* verführen. **to ~ sb into doing sth** jdn zu etw verleiten.
**seducer** [sɪ'djuːsər] *n* Verführer *m.*
**seduction** [sɪ'dʌkʃən] *n* Verführung *f.*
**seductive** [sɪ'dʌktɪv] *adj* verführerisch; *offer* verlockend.

**see**[1] [siː] *pret* **saw,** *ptp* **seen** *vt* (a) sehen; *(in book etc also)* lesen; *(check also)* nachsehen, gucken *(col)*; *film* sich *(dat)* ansehen. **worth ~ing** sehenswert; **to ~ sb do sth** sehen, wie jd etw macht; **I've never ~n him swim** ich habe ihn nie schwimmen sehen; **he was ~n to enter the building** man hat ihn gesehen, wie er das Gebäude betrat; **I saw it happen** ich habe gesehen, wie es passiert ist; **I don't like to ~ people mistreated** ich kann es nicht sehen, wenn Menschen schlecht behandelt werden; **I'll go and ~ who it is** ich sehe mal nach(, wer das ist); **~ page 8** siehe Seite 8; **there was nothing to be ~n** es war nichts zu sehen; **I don't know what she ~s in him** ich weiß nicht, was sie an ihm findet; **we don't ~ much of them nowadays** wir sehen sie zur Zeit nur selten; **I shall be ~ing them for dinner** ich treffe sie beim Abendessen; **~ you (soon)!** bis bald!; **be ~ing you!, ~ you later!** bis später!; **~ you on Sunday!** bis Sonntag!; **you must be ~ing things** du siehst wohl Gespenster!; **that remains to be ~n** das wird sich zeigen; **now let me ~ how we can solve this** lassen Sie mich mal überlegen, wie wir das lösen können; **let me ~ if I can't find a better way** mal sehen, ob ich nicht etwas Besseres finden kann; **as I ~ it** so, wie ich das sehe; **try to ~ it my way** versuchen Sie doch einmal, es aus meiner Sicht zu sehen; **I don't ~ it that way** ich sehe das anders.

(b) *(visit)* besuchen; *(on business)* aufsuchen. **to go and ~ sb** jdn besuchen (gehen); **to ~ the doctor** zum Arzt gehen; **he is the man to ~ about this** Sie sollten sich damit an ihn wenden.

(c) *(meet with)* sehen; *(talk to)* sprechen; *(receive visit of)* empfangen. **the boss will ~ you now** der Chef läßt jetzt bitten; **I'll have to ~ my wife about that** das muß ich mit meiner Frau besprechen; **have you ~n Personnel yet?** waren Sie schon bei der Personalabteilung?

(d) *(accompany)* begleiten, bringen. **to ~ sb to the door** jdn zur Tür bringen; **to ~ sb home** jdn heimbegleiten.

(e) *(visualize)* sich *(dat)* vorstellen. **I can't ~ that working** ich kann mir kaum vorstellen, daß das klappt; **I can't ~ myself in that job** ich glaube nicht, daß das eine Stelle für mich wäre.

(f) *(understand)* verstehen; *(understand the reason for)* einsehen; *(realize)* erkennen. **I don't ~ the need for the change** ich sehe nicht ein, warum das geändert werden muß; **I can ~ that it might be a good thing** ich sehe ja ein, daß das eine gute Idee wäre; **I can ~ I'm going to be busy** ich sehe schon, ich werde viel zu tun haben; **I fail to or don't ~ how anyone could ...** ich begreife einfach nicht, wie jemand nur ... kann; **I don't ~ how it works** es ist mir nicht klar, wie das funktioniert; **I ~ from this report that ...** ich ersehe aus diesem Bericht, daß ...; **(do you) ~ what I mean?** verstehst du(, was ich meine)?; *(didn't I tell you!)* siehst du's jetzt!; **I ~ what you mean** ich verstehe, was du meinst; *(you're quite right)* ja, du hast recht; **to make sb ~ sth** jdm etw klarmachen.

(g) *(ensure)* **~ that it is done by tomorrow** sieh zu,

daß es bis morgen fertig ist.

**2** *vi* (a) sehen. **let me ~, let's ~** laß mich mal sehen; **who was it? – I couldn't/didn't ~** wer war das? – ich konnte es nicht sehen; **can you ~ to read?** ist es Ihnen hell genug zum Lesen?; **as far as the eye can ~** so weit das Auge reicht; **~ for yourself!** sieh doch selbst!

(b) *(check, find out)* nachsehen, gucken *(col)*. **is he there? – I'll ~** ist er da? – ich sehe mal nach; **let me ~** lassen Sie mich mal nachsehen.

(c) *(understand)* verstehen. **as far as I can ~ ...** soweit ich sehen kann ...; **it's all over, ~?** es ist vorbei, verstehst du?; **as I ~ from your report** wie ich aus Ihrem Bericht ersehe; **(you) ~, it's like this** es ist nämlich so; **I ~!** aha!; *(after explanation)* ach so!

(d) *(consider)* **we'll ~** (wir werden *or* wollen) mal sehen; **I don't know, I'll have to ~** ich weiß nicht, ich muß mal sehen; **let me ~, let's ~** lassen Sie mich mal überlegen.

▶**see about** *vi +prep obj* (a) *(attend to)* sich kümmern um. **he came to ~ ~ the TV** er kam, um sich *(dat)* den Fernseher anzusehen; **he came to ~ ~ the rent** er ist wegen der Miete gekommen. (b) *(consider)* **I'll ~ ~ it** ich will mal sehen; **we'll ~ ~ that!** *(iro)* das wollen wir mal sehen.

▶**see in 1** *vi* herein-/hineinsehen. **2** *vt sep New Year* begrüßen.

▶**see off** *vt sep* (a) *(bid farewell to)* verabschieden. **are you coming to ~ me ~** *(at the airport)?* kommt ihr mit mir (zum Flughafen)? (b) *(chase off)* Beine machen *(+dat) (col)*.

▶**see out 1** *vi* *(look out)* heraus-/hinaussehen. **I can't ~ ~ of the window** ich kann nicht zum Fenster hinaussehen. **2** *vt sep* (a) *(show out)* hinausbegleiten *(of aus)*. **I'll ~ myself ~** ich finde (schon) alleine hinaus. (b) *(last to the end of)* *(coat, car)* winter *etc* überdauern; *(invalid)* year *etc* überleben.

▶**see over** *vi +prep obj* house *etc* sich *(dat)* ansehen.

▶**see through 1** *vi* (a) *(lit)* (hin)durchsehen *(prep obj* durch*)*. (b) *+prep obj* *(fig: not be deceived by)* durchschauen. **I can ~ right ~ you** ich habe dich durchschaut. **2** *vt always separate* (a) *(help through difficult time)* beistehen *(+dat)*. **I hope £10 will ~ you ~** die £10 reichen dir hoffentlich. (b) *job* zu Ende bringen; *(Parl)* bill durchbringen.

▶**see to** *vi +prep obj* sich kümmern um. **these shoes need/that cough needs ~ing ~** die Schuhe müssen repariert werden/um den Husten muß man sich kümmern; **please ~ ~ it that ...** bitte sorgen Sie dafür, daß ...

**see**[2] *n* Bistum *nt.* **Holy S~** Heiliger Stuhl.

**seed** [siːd] **1** *n* *(Bot)* *(one single)* Same(n) *m*; *(of grain, poppy etc)* Korn *nt*; *(within fruit)* (Samen)kern *m*; *(collective)* Samen *m*; *(for birds)* Körner *pl*; *(grain)* Saat *f*; *(fig: of unrest, idea etc)* Keim *m* *(of* zu*)*. **to go to ~** *(vegetables)* schießen; *(flowers)* einen Samenstand bilden; *(fig: person)* herunterkommen. **2** *vt* (a) *(sow with ~)* besäen. (b) *(extract ~s from)* entkernen. (c) *(Sport)* setzen, plazieren. **~ed number one** als Nummer eins gesetzt. **3** *vi* *(vegetables)* schießen; *(flowers)* Samen entwickeln.

**seed:** **~bed** *n* Saatbeet *nt*; **~ box** *n* Setzkasten *m*; **~ corn** *n* Saatkorn *nt.*
**seediness** ['siːdɪnɪs] *n see adj* (a) Zwielichtigkeit *f*; Schäbigkeit *f.*
**seed:** **~less** *adj* kernlos; **~ling** *n* Sämling *m*; **~ potato** *n* Saatkartoffel *f.*
**seedy** ['siːdɪ] *adj* (+er) (a) *(disreputable)* person, area,

*place* zwielichtig; *clothes* schäbig, abgerissen. **(b)** *(dated col: unwell)* **I feel** ~ mir ist flau.
**seeing** ['si:ɪŋ] *conj* ~ **(that)** da.
**seek** [si:k] *pret, ptp* **sought** *vt* suchen; *fame, wealth* streben nach. **to** ~ **sb's advice** jdn um Rat fragen.
▶**seek for** *vi* +*prep obj* suchen nach; *reforms, changes* anstreben.
▶**seek out** *vt sep* ausfindig machen; *opinion* herausfinden.
**seem** [si:m] *vi* scheinen. **he** ~**s (to be) honest** er scheint ehrlich zu sein; **he** ~**s younger than he is** er wirkt jünger, als er ist; **that makes it** ~ **longer** dadurch wirkt es länger; **things aren't always what they** ~ vieles ist anders, als es aussieht; **what** ~**s to be the trouble?** worum geht es denn?; *(doctor)* was fehlt Ihnen denn?; **he has left, it** ~**s** er ist anscheinend weggegangen; **so it** ~**s** es sieht (ganz) so aus; **it would** ~ **that he is coming after all** es sieht so aus, als ob er doch noch kommt; **how does it** ~ **to you?** was meinen *Sie?*; **it just doesn't** ~ **right somehow** das ist doch irgendwie nicht richtig; **it only** ~**s like it** das kommt einem nur so vor; **it all** ~**s so unreal to me** es kommt mir alles so unwirklich vor; **I** ~ **to have heard his name before** sein Name kommt mir bekannt vor.
**seeming** ['si:mɪŋ] *adj attr* scheinbar.
**seemingly** ['si:mɪŋlɪ] *adv* anscheinend.
**seemly** ['si:mlɪ] *adj (+er)* schicklich. **it isn't** ~ **(for sb to do sth)** es schickt sich nicht (für jdn, etw zu tun).
**seen** [si:n] *ptp of* **see**[1].
**seep** [si:p] *vi* sickern. **to** ~ **away** *or* **out** versickern; **to** ~ **through/into sth** durch etw durchsickern/in etw *(acc)* hineinsickern.
**seer** [sɪə[r]] *n* Seher(in *f*) *m.*
**seersucker** ['sɪə,sʌkə[r]] *n* Krepp, Seersucker *m.*
**seesaw** ['si:sɔ:] **1** *n* Wippe *f.* **2** *vi* wippen; *(fig) (emotional states)* auf und ab gehen; *(prices, public opinion)* schwanken.
**seethe** [si:ð] *vi (boil)* sieden; *(fig) (be crowded)* wimmeln *(with von)*; *(be angry)* kochen *(col)*. **to** ~ **with anger** vor Wut kochen.
**see-through** ['si:θru:] *adj* durchsichtig. ~ **pack** Klarsichtpackung *f.*
**segment** ['segmənt] *n* Teil *m*; *(of worm)* Glied, Segment *nt*; *(of orange)* Stück *nt*; *(of circle)* Abschnitt *m*, Segment *nt.*
**segregate** ['segrɪgeɪt] *vt individuals* absondern; *(according to race/religion) groups of population* nach Rassen/Konfessionen trennen. **to be** ~**d from sb/sth** von jdm/etw abgesondert sein; ~**d** *(racially) school, church* nur für Weiße/Schwarze; *schools* mit Rassentrennung; *society* nach Rassen getrennt.
**segregation** [,segrɪ'geɪʃən] *n* Trennung *f*; *(racial)* Rassentrennung *f.*
**seismograph** ['saɪzməgrɑ:f] *n* Seismograph *m.*
**seize** [si:z] **1** *vt* **(a)** *(grasp)* packen, ergreifen; *(as hostage)* nehmen; *(confiscate)* beschlagnahmen; *passport* einziehen; *ship (authorities)* beschlagnahmen; *(capture) town* einnehmen; *train, building* besetzen; *criminal* fassen. **to** ~ **sb's arm** jdn am Arm packen. **(b)** *(fig) (panic, fear)* packen; *power* an sich *(acc)* reißen; *(leap upon) idea* aufgreifen; *opportunity* ergreifen. **2** *vi (also* ~ **up)** *engine, part* sich festfressen.
▶**seize on** *or* **upon** *vi* +*prep obj* **(a)** *(clutch at) idea, offer* sich stürzen auf *(+acc)*. **(b)** *(pick out for criticism)* herausgreifen.
**seizure** ['si:ʒə[r]] *n* **(a)** Beschlagnahmung *f*; *(of passport)* Einzug *m*; *(capture)* Einnahme *f*; *(of train, building)* Besetzung *f.* **(b)** *(Med)* Anfall *m*; *(apo-*

*plexy)* Schlaganfall *m.*
**seldom** ['seldəm] *adv* selten. ~ **have I** ... ich habe selten ...
**select** [sɪ'lekt] **1** *vti* auswählen; *(in buying also)* aussuchen. **2** *adj* exklusiv; *(carefully chosen)* auserlesen. ~ **committee** Sonderausschuß *m.*
**selection** [sɪ'lekʃən] *n* **(a)** *(choosing)* (Aus)wahl *f*; *(Biol)* Auslese *f.* **(b)** *(person, thing selected)* Wahl *f*; *(likely winner)* Tip *m.* **to make one's** ~ seine Wahl treffen; ~ **committee** Auswahlkomitee *nt.* **(c)** *(range, assortment)* Auswahl *f (of* an +*dat).*
**selective** [sɪ'lektɪv] *adj* wählerisch; *reader* kritisch, anspruchsvoll; *school* Elite-. ~ **service** *(US)* Wehrdienst *m.*
**selectively** [sɪ'lektɪvlɪ] *adv* wählerisch; *read, operate* selektiv. **to buy** ~ beim Einkaufen kritisch sein.
**selector** [sɪ'lektə[r]] *n* **(a)** *(Tech)* Wählschalter *m*; *(knob)* Schaltknopf *m.* **(b)** *(Sport)* jd, der die Mannschaftsaufstellung vornimmt.
**self** [self] *n, pl* **selves** Ich, Selbst *(esp Psych)* no pl *nt*; *(side of character)* Seite *f.* **one's other/better** ~ sein anderes/besseres Ich; **he's quite his old** ~ **again** er ist wieder ganz der alte *(col).*
**self:** ~**-addressed envelope** *n* adressierter Rückumschlag; ~**-adhesive** *adj* selbstklebend; ~**-adjusting** *adj* selbstregulierend *attr*; *brakes* selbstnachstellend *attr*; ~**-appointed** *adj* selbsternannt; ~**-assertion** *n* Durchsetzungsvermögen *nt*; ~**-assertive** *adj* selbstbewußt; *(pej)* von sich selbst eingenommen; ~**-assurance** *n* Selbstsicherheit *f*; ~**-assured** *adj* selbstsicher; ~**-awareness** *n* Selbsterfahrung *f*; ~**-catering** *adj (Brit)* für Selbstversorger; ~**-centred**, *(US)* ~**-centered** *adj* egozentrisch, ichbezogen; ~**-cleaning** *adj* selbstreinigend; ~**-coloured**, *(US)* ~**-colored** *adj* einfarbig, uni; ~**-confessed** *adj* erklärt *attr*; ~**-confidence** *n* Selbstvertrauen *nt*; ~**-confident** *adj* selbstbewußt; ~**-conscious** *adj* befangen, gehemmt; *piece of writing, style etc* bewußt; ~**-consciousness** *n see adj* Befangenheit, Gehemmtheit *f*; Bewußtheit *f*; ~**-contained** *adj (esp Brit) flat* separat; ~**-control** *n* Selbstbeherrschung *f*; ~**-critical** *adj* selbstkritisch; ~**-criticism** *n* Selbstkritik *f*; ~**-defeating** *adj* unsinnig; *argument* sich selbst widerlegend *attr*; ~**-defence,** *(US)* ~**-defense** *n* Selbstverteidigung *f*; *(Jur)* Notwehr *f*; **to act in** ~**-defence** in Notwehr handeln; ~**-discipline** *n* Selbstdisziplin *f*; ~**-effacing** *adj* zurückhaltend; ~**-employed** *adj* selbständig; *artist* freischaffend; *journalist* freiberuflich; ~**-esteem** *n (*~**-respect)** Selbstachtung *f*; ~**-evident** *adj* offensichtlich; *(not needing proof)* selbstverständlich; ~**-explanatory** *adj* unmittelbar verständlich; **this word is** ~**-explanatory** das Wort erklärt sich selbst; ~**-expression** *n* Selbstdarstellung *f*; ~**-financing** *adj* selbstfinanzierend; ~**-governing** *adj* selbstverwaltet; **to become** ~**-governing** eine eigene Regierung bekommen; ~**-government** *n* Selbstverwaltung *f*; ~**-help** *n* Selbsthilfe *f*; ~**-importance** *n* Aufgeblasenheit *f*; ~**-important** *adj* aufgeblasen; ~**-imposed** *adj* selbstauferlegt *attr*; ~**-indulgent** *adj* genießerisch; *(in eating, drinking also)* maßlos; ~**-inflicted** *adj wounds* sich *(dat)* selbst zugefügt *attr*; *task, punishment* sich *(dat)* freiwillig auferlegt; ~**-interest** *n (selfishness)* Eigennutz *m*; *(personal advantage)* eigenes Interesse.
**selfish** ['selfɪʃ] *adj* selbstsüchtig; *(self-centred)* egoistisch.
**selfishness** ['selfɪʃnɪs] *n see adj* Selbstsucht *f*; Egoismus *m.*

**self-justification** n Rechtfertigung f. ..., **he said in** ~ ..., sagte er zu seiner eigenen Rechtfertigung.
**selfless** adj, ~**ly** adv ['selflɪs, -lɪ] selbstlos.
**self:** ~-**made** adj dress etc selbstgemacht; ~-**made man** Selfmademan m; ~-**opinionated** adj rechthaberisch; nonsense, drivel selbstherrlich; ~-**pity** n Selbstmitleid nt; ~-**portrait** n Selbstporträt nt; ~-**possessed** adj selbstbeherrscht; ~-**preservation** n Selbsterhaltung f; ~-**propelled** adj selbstangetrieben; ~-**raising**, (US) ~-**rising** adj flour selbsttreibend, mit bereits beigemischtem Backpulver; ~-**reliance** n Selbständigkeit f; ~-**reliant** adj selbständig; ~-**respect** n Selbstachtung f; **have you no** ~-**respect?** schämen Sie sich gar nicht?; ~-**respecting** adj anständig; **no** ~-**respecting person would** ... niemand, der etwas auf sich hält, würde ...; ~-**restraint** n Selbstbeherrschung f; ~-**righteous** adj selbstgerecht; ~-**righteousness** n Selbstgerechtigkeit f; ~-**sacrifice** n Selbstaufopferung f; ~**same** adj **the** ~**same** genau der-/die-/dasselbe; **on the** ~**same day** noch am selben Tag; ~-**satisfied** adj (smug) selbstgefällig; ~-**service 1** n Selbstbedienung f; **2** adj Selbstbedienungs-; ~-**styled** adj selbsternannt; ~-**sufficiency** n (of person) Selbständigkeit f; (emotional) Selbstgenügsamkeit f; (of country) Autarkie f; ~-**sufficient** adj person selbständig; (emotionally) selbstgenügsam; country autark; **they are** ~-**sufficient in oil** sie können ihren Ölbedarf selbst decken; ~-**supporting** adj person finanziell unabhängig; structure freitragend; chimney freistehend; **the newspaper is** ~-**supporting** die Zeitung trägt sich selbst; ~-**tapping screw** n selbstschneidende Schraube; ~-**taught** adj skills selbsterlernt; **he is** ~-**taught** er hat sich (dat) das selbst beigebracht; (intellectually) er hat sich durch Selbstunterricht gebildet; ~-**test** n Selbsttest m; ~-**willed** adj eigenwillig.
**sell** [sel] (vb: pret, ptp **sold**) **1** vt (a) verkaufen (sb sth, sth to sb jdm etw, etw an jdn); insurance policy abschließen (to mit); (business) goods also absetzen. **I was sold this in Valencia** man hat mir das in Valencia verkauft; **the book sold 3,000 copies** von dem Buch wurden 3.000 Exemplare verkauft; **to be sold on sb/sth** (col) von jdm/etw begeistert sein. (b) (stock) führen, haben (col); (deal in) vertreiben. **to** ~ **oneself** (put oneself across) sich profilieren (to bei), sich verkaufen (to an +acc). (c) (fig: betray) verraten. **to** ~ **sb down the river** (col) jdn verschaukeln (col).
**2** vi (person) verkaufen (to sb an jdn); (article) sich verkaufen (lassen). **his book is** ~**ing well/won't** ~ sein Buch verkauft sich gut/läßt sich nicht verkaufen; **the house sold for £130,000** das Haus wurde für £130.000 verkauft.
►**sell off** vt sep verkaufen; (get rid of quickly, cheaply) abstoßen.
►**sell out 1** vt sep ausverkaufen. **sorry, sold** ~ wir sind leider ausverkauft; **we're sold** ~ **of ice-cream** das Eis ist ausverkauft. **2** vi (a) (sell entire stock) alles verkaufen. (b) (in business) sein Geschäft/seine Firma/seinen Anteil etc verkaufen. (c) (col: betray) **he sold** ~ **to the enemy** er hat sich an den Feind verkauft.
►**sell up 1** vt sep zu Geld machen (col); (Brit Fin) zwangsverkaufen. **2** vi seinen Besitz/seine Firma etc verkaufen.
**sell-by date** ['selbaɪˌdeɪt] n ≃ Haltbarkeitsdatum nt.
**seller** ['selə'] n (a) Verkäufer(in f) m. **it's a** ~'**s market in housing just now** zur Zeit bestimmen die Verkäufer die Hauspreise. (b) (thing sold) **big** ~ Verkaufsschlager m; **bad** ~ schlecht gehender Ar-

tikel; (in shop also) Ladenhüter m; **this book is a good/slow** ~ das Buch verkauft sich gut/schlecht.
**selling** ['selɪŋ] adj Verkaufs-. ~ **point** Verkaufsanreiz m; ~ **price** Verkaufspreis m.
**sellotape** ® ['seləʊteɪp] (Brit) **1** n Klebeband nt; ≃ Tesafilm ® m. **2** vt mit Klebeband festkleben.
**sellout** ['selaʊt] n (a) (col: betrayal) fauler Handel (to mit); (of one's ideals etc) Ausverkauf m (to an +acc). (b) (Theat, Sport) ausverkauftes Haus. **to be a** ~ ausverkauft sein.
**selvage, selvedge** ['selvɪdʒ] n Webkante f.
**selves** [selvz] pl of **self**.
**semantic** [sɪ'mæntɪk] adj semantisch.
**semantics** [sɪ'mæntɪks] n sing Semantik f.
**semaphore** ['seməfɔ:'] n Signalsprache f.
**semblance** ['sembləns] n Anflug m (of von); (of order) Anschein m.
**semen** ['si:mən] n Sperma nt.
**semester** [sɪ'mestə'] n Semester nt.
**semi** ['semɪ] n = (a) (Brit col) **semidetached (house)**. (b) (US) **semi-trailer**.
**semi:** ~-**bold** adj (Typ) halbfett; ~**breve** n (esp Brit) ganze Note; ~**circle** n Halbkreis m; ~**circular** adj halbkreisförmig; ~**colon** n Semikolon nt; ~**conductor** n Halbleiter m; ~**conscious** adj halb bewußtlos; ~**detached (house)** n Doppelhaus(hälfte f) nt; ~-**detached houses** Doppelhäuser pl; ~**final** n Halbfinale nt; ~**finalist** n Teilnehmer(in f) m am Halbfinale; ~**finals** npl Halbfinale nt.
**seminal** ['semɪnl] adj **to be present in a** ~ **state** im Keim vorhanden sein.
**seminar** ['semɪnɑ:'] n Seminar nt.
**seminary** ['semɪnərɪ] n Priesterseminar nt.
**semi:** ~**precious** adj ~**precious stone** Halbedelstein m; ~**quaver** n (esp Brit) Sechzehntel(note f) nt; ~**skilled** adj worker angelernt; job Anlern-; ~**skilled labour** (workforce) Angelernte pl; (work) Arbeit f für Angelernte; ~**tone** n (Mus) Halbton m; ~**trailer** n Sattelanhänger m.
**semolina** [ˌsemə'li:nə] n Grieß m.
**Sen, sen** = **senior**.
**Sen** (US) = **senator**.
**SEN** (Brit old) = **State Enrolled Nurse**.
**senate** ['senɪt] n Senat m.
**senator** ['senɪtə'] n Senator m; (as address) Herr Senator.
**send** [send] pret, ptp **sent** vt (a) schicken; letter, messenger also senden; (~ off) letter abschicken; (Rad) radio wave ausstrahlen; signal senden; (through wires) übermitteln. **to** ~ **sb to prison/to his death** jdn ins Gefängnis/in den Tod schicken; **to** ~ **sb to university** jdn studieren lassen; **to** ~ **sb for sth** jdn nach etw schicken; **she** ~**s her love/congratulations/apologies** etc sie läßt grüßen/Ihnen ihre Glückwünsche ausrichten/sich entschuldigen etc; ~ **him my love/best wishes** grüßen Sie ihn von mir.
(b) (propel, make go) ball schießen; (hurl) schleudern; (conveyor belt) befördern. **the blow sent him sprawling** der Schlag schleuderte ihn zu Boden; **the fire sent everyone running out of the building** das Feuer ließ alle das Gebäude fluchtartig verlassen; **his speech sent a wave of excitement through the audience** seine Rede ließ eine Woge der Aufregung durch die Zuschauer gehen; **this sent him into fits of laughter** das ließ ihn in einen Lachkrampf ausbrechen.
►**send away 1** vt sep wegschicken; letter etc also abschicken. **I had to** ~ **him** ~ **without an explanation** ich mußte ihn ohne Erklärung weggehen las-

sen. **2** *vi* **to** ~ **for sth** etw (per Post) anfordern.
►**send back** *vt sep* zurückschicken; *food in res-*
*taurant* zurückgehen lassen.

►**send down** *vt sep* **(a)** *temperature, prices* fallen
lassen; *(gradually)* senken. **(b)** *(Brit Univ: expel)* re-
legieren. **(c)** *prisoner* verurteilen *(for* zu*)*.

►**send for** *vi +prep obj* **(a)** kommen lassen; *doctor,*
*police, priest also* rufen; *help* herbeirufen; *(person*
*in authority)* pupil, minister zu sich bestellen. **(b)**
*copy, catalogue* anfordern.

►**send in** *vt sep* einsenden; *person* herein-/
hineinschicken; *troops* einsetzen.

►**send off 1** *vt sep* **(a)** *letter* abschicken. **(b)** *chil-*
*dren to school* wegschicken. **(c)** = **send away 1**.
**(d)** *(Sport)* vom Platz weisen *(for* wegen*)*. **2** *vi* =
**send away 1**.

►**send on** *vt sep* **(a)** *(Brit: forward)* letter nachschicken; *(pass on)* memo weiterleiten. **(b)** *(in ad-*
*vance)* troops, luggage vorausschicken. **(c)** *(Sport)*
substitute einsetzen; *(Theat)* actor auf die Bühne
schicken.

►**send out** *vt sep* **(a)** *(of house, room)* hinaus-/
herausschicken *(of* aus*)*. **he sent me** ~ **to buy a pa-**
**per** er hat mich losgeschickt, um eine Zeitung zu
kaufen. **(b)** *(emit)* rays, radio signals aussenden;
*light, heat, smoke* abgeben. **(c)** *leaflets, invitations,*
*application forms* verschicken.

►**send up** *vt sep* **(a)** *rocket* hochschießen; *balloon*
steigen lassen. **(b)** *prices* hochtreiben. **(c)** **to** ~ **sth**
~ **in flames** etw in Flammen aufgehen lassen. **(d)**
*(Brit col: satirize)* verulken *(col)*.

**sender** ['sendə<sup>r</sup>] *n* Absender(in *f*) *m*. **return to** ~ zurück an Absender.

**send:** ~**-off** *n* Verabschiedung *f*; **to give sb a good**
~**-off** jdn ganz groß verabschieden *(col)*; ~**-up** *n*
*(Brit col)* Verulkung *f (col)*; **to do a** ~**-up of sb/sth**
jdn/etw verulken *(col)*.

**Senegal** [,senɪ'gɔːl] *n* Senegal *nt*.

**Senegalese** [,senɪgə'liːz] **1** *adj* senegalesisch. **2** *n*
Senegalese *m*, Senegalesin *f*.

**senile** ['siːnaɪl] *adj person* senil; *(physically)* altersschwach.

**senility** [sɪ'nɪlɪtɪ] *n* Senilität *f*; *(physical)* Alters-
schwäche *f*.

**senior** ['siːnɪə<sup>r</sup>] **1** *adj (in age)* älter; *(in rank)* vorge-
setzt, übergeordnet; *(with longer service)* dienstäl-
ter; *rank, civil servant* höher; *officer* ranghöher; *po-*
*sition, editor, executive etc* leitend; *doctor, nurse etc*
Ober-. **he is** ~ **to me** *(in age)* er ist älter als ich; *(in*
*rank)* er ist mir übergeordnet; *(in length of service)*
er arbeitet schon länger hier als ich; **(the)** ~ **man-**
**agement** die Geschäftsleitung; ~ **partner** Hauptge-
sellschafter *m*; ~ **consultant** Chefarzt *m*/-ärztin *f*;
~ **citizen** älterer Mitbürger, ältere Mitbürgerin; ~
**citizens** Senioren *pl*; ~ **school**, ~ **high school** *(US)*
Oberstufe *f*; ~ **executive** leitender Angestellter;
**can I speak to somebody more** ~? könnte ich bitte
Ihren Vorgesetzten sprechen?; **J. B. Schwartz, S~**
J. B. Schwartz senior.

   **2** *n (Sch)* Oberstufenschüler(in *f*) *m*; *(US Univ)*
Student(in *f*) *m* im 4./letzten Studienjahr. **he is my**
~ *(in age)* er ist älter als ich; *(in rank)* er ist mir
übergeordnet; *(in length of service)* er arbeitet
schon länger hier als ich; **he is two years my** ~ er
ist zwei Jahre älter als ich.

**seniority** [,siːnɪ'ɒrɪtɪ] *n (in age)* (höheres) Alter; *(in*
*rank)* (höhere) Position; *(Mil)* (höherer) Rang; *(in*
*civil service etc)* (höherer) Dienstgrad; *(in service)*
(längere) Betriebszugehörigkeit; *(in civil service*
*etc)* (höheres) Dienstalter.

**sensation** [sen'seɪʃən] *n* **(a)** *(feeling)* Gefühl *nt*; *(of*

*heat etc)* Empfindung *f*. **a/the** ~ **of falling** das Gefühl
zu fallen; **a** ~ **of fear** ein Angstgefühl *nt*. **(b)** *(great*
*success)* Sensation *f*. **to cause a** ~ (großes) Aufsehen erregen.

**sensational** [sen'seɪʃənl] *adj* **(a)** sensationell; *news*
*item* Sensations-; *style, film* reißerisch. **(b)** *(col:*
*very good etc)* sagenhaft *(col)*.

**sensationally** [sen'seɪʃnəlɪ] *adv* **(a)** *write* in einem
reißerischen Stil. **(b)** *(col: amazingly)* sagenhaft
*(col)*.

**sense** [sens] **1** *n* **(a)** *(bodily)* Sinn *m*. ~ **of hearing** Ge-
hör(sinn *m*) *nt*; ~ **of sight** Sehvermögen *nt*; ~ **of**
**smell** Geruchssinn *m*; ~ **of taste** Geschmackssinn
*m*; ~ **of touch** Tastsinn *m*; ~**s** *pl (right mind)* Verstand *m*; **to be out of one's** ~**s** nicht ganz bei Trost
sein *(col)*, von Sinnen sein *(geh)*; **to bring sb to his**
~**s** jdn zur Besinnung bringen; **to come to one's** ~**s**
zur Besinnung kommen, Vernunft annehmen.

   **(b)** *(feeling)* Gefühl *nt*. ~ **of duty** Pflichtgefühl *nt*;
**a** ~ **of pleasure** *etc* ein Gefühl der Freude *etc*; ~ **of**
**justice** Gerechtigkeitssinn *m*; ~ **of humour** Sinn *m*
für Humor; **these buildings create a** ~ **of space** diese Gebäude vermitteln den Eindruck von Weite.

   **(c)** *(good* ~*) (common)* gesunder Menschenverstand; **he had the (good)** ~ **to ...** er war so vernünftig und ...; **she didn't even have the** ~ **to take a key**
sie war auch noch zu dumm dazu, einen Schlüssel
mitzunehmen; **you should have had more** ~ **than to**
**...** du hättest vernünftiger sein sollen und nicht ...;
**there is no** ~ **in that** das hat keinen Sinn; **what's**
**the** ~ **of doing this?** welchen Sinn hat es denn, das
zu tun?; **to talk** ~ vernünftig sein; **to make sb see**
~ jdn zur Vernunft bringen.

   **(d) to make** ~ *(sentence etc)* (einen) Sinn ergeben; *(be sensible, rational etc)* sinnvoll *or* vernünftig
sein; **it doesn't make** ~ **to spend all that money** es
ist doch Unsinn, soviel Geld auszugeben; **it makes**
**good** ~ das scheint sehr vernünftig; **it makes good**
**financial** ~ **to ...** aus finanzieller Sicht gesehen ist es
sehr vernünftig, zu ...; **it all makes** ~ **now** jetzt
wird einem alles klar; **to make** ~ **of sth** etw verstehen, aus etw schlau werden *(col)*.

   **(e)** *(meaning)* Sinn *m no pl*. **in the full** ~ **of the**
**word** im wahrsten Sinne des Wortes; **it has three**
**distinct** ~**s** es hat drei verschiedene Bedeutungen;
**in every** ~ **of the word** in der vollen Bedeutung des
Wortes; **in a** ~ in gewisser Hinsicht; **in every** ~ in
jeder Hinsicht; **in what** ~? inwiefern?

   **2** *vt* fühlen, spüren. **I could** ~ **someone there in**
**the dark** ich fühlte *or* spürte, daß da jemand in der
Dunkelheit war.

**senseless** ['senslɪs] *adj* **(a)** *(unconscious)* besinnungs-
los, bewußtlos. **to knock sb** ~ jdn bewußtlos schlagen. **(b)** *(stupid)* unvernünftig, unsinnig; *(futile)*
*waste, discussion* sinnlos.

**senselessly** ['senslɪslɪ] *adv see adj (b)*.

**senselessness** ['senslɪsnɪs] *n see adj (b)* Unvernunft,
Unsinnigkeit *f*; Sinnlosigkeit *f*.

**sensibility** [,sensɪ'bɪlɪtɪ] *n (to beauty etc)* Empfindsamkeit *f*; *(artistic* ~ *also)* Sensibilität *f*; *(emotional*
~*, susceptibility to insult)* Empfindlichkeit *f*. **sen-**
**sibilities** Zartgefühl *nt*.

**sensible** ['sensəbl] *adj* **(a)** vernünftig. **be** ~ **about it**
seien Sie vernünftig. **(b)** *(appreciable)* spürbar.

**sensibly** ['sensəblɪ] *adv* vernünftig; *(as sentence*
*modifier)* vernünftigerweise.

**sensitive** ['sensɪtɪv] *adj* **(a)** *(emotionally)* person sensibel, empfindsam; *(easily hurt)* empfindlich;
*(understanding)* einfühlsam. **to be** ~ **about sth** in
bezug auf etw *(acc)* empfindlich sein. **(b)** *instru-*
*ments, plants, film* empfindlich; *(fig)* topic, issue hei-

kel. ~ **to light** lichtempfindlich.
**sensitively** ['sensɪtɪvlɪ] adv react empfindlich; treat, portray einfühlsam.
**sensitivity** [sensɪ'tɪvɪtɪ] n see adj Sensibilität, Empfindsamkeit f; Empfindlichkeit f; Einfühlsamkeit f; (fig) heikle Natur.
**sensitize** ['sensɪtaɪz] vt sensibilisieren.
**sensual** adj, **~ly** adv ['sensjʊəl, -ɪ] sinnlich.
**sensuality** [sensjʊ'ælɪtɪ] n Sinnlichkeit f.
**sensuous** adj, **~ly** adv ['sensjʊəs, -lɪ] sinnlich.
**sent** [sent] pret, ptp of **send**.
**sentence** ['sentəns] **1** n (a) (Gram) Satz m. ~ **structure** Satzbau m. (b) (Jur) Strafe f. **to be under ~ of death** zum Tode verurteilt sein; **the judge gave him a 6-month ~** der Richter verurteilte ihn zu 6 Monaten Haft; **to pass ~ (on sb)** (über jdn) das Urteil verkünden; (fig) jdn verurteilen. **2** vt (Jur) verurteilen (to zu).
**sentiment** ['sentɪmənt] n (a) (feeling, emotion) Gefühl nt. (b) (sentimentality) Sentimentalität f. (c) (opinion) Ansicht f. **my ~s exactly!** genau meine Meinung!
**sentimental** [sentɪ'mentl] adj sentimental; person, mood also gefühlvoll; value Gefühls-. **for ~ reasons** aus Sentimentalität.
**sentimentality** [sentɪmen'tælɪtɪ] n Sentimentalität f.
**sentimentally** [sentɪ'mentəlɪ] adv (esp pej) sentimental; important, attached etc gefühlsmäßig.
**sentinel** ['sentɪnl] n Wache f.
**sentry** ['sentrɪ] n Wachtposten m. **to be on ~ duty** auf Wache sein; **~ box** Wachhäuschen nt.
**Seoul** [səʊl] n Seoul nt.
**separable** ['sepərəbl] adj trennbar.
**separate** ['seprət] **1** adj (a) gesondert (from von); section, piece also extra attr inv; organization, unit also, existence eigen attr; provisions, regulations also besondere(r, s) attr; beds, accounts getrennt; entrance, flat separat. **that is a ~ issue** das ist eine Frage für sich; **on two ~ occasions** bei zwei verschiedenen Gelegenheiten; **on a ~ occasion** bei einer anderen Gelegenheit; **they live ~ lives** sie gehen getrennte Wege; **to keep two things ~** zwei Dinge auseinanderhalten. (b) (individual) einzeln. **all the ~ questions** alle einzelnen Fragen; **everybody has a ~ task** jeder hat seine eigene Aufgabe. **2** n **~s** pl (Fashion) kombinierbare Einzelteile.
**3** ['sepəreɪt] vt trennen; (divide up) aufteilen (into in +acc). **he is ~d from his wife** er lebt von seiner Frau getrennt.
**4** ['sepəreɪt] vi sich trennen.
**separately** ['seprətlɪ] adv getrennt, separat; live getrennt; (singly) einzeln.
**separation** [sepə'reɪʃən] n Trennung f; (of rocket etc) Abtrennung f (from von).
**separatist** ['sepərətɪst] **1** adj separatistisch. **2** n Separatist(in f) m.
**sepia** ['siːpjə] n Sepia f.
**sepsis** ['sepsɪs] n Vereiterung, Sepsis (spec) f.
**Sept** = **September** Sept.
**September** [sep'tembər] **1** n September m. **the first of ~** der erste September; **on ~ 19th** (written), **on 19th ~** (written), **on the 19th of ~** (spoken) am 19. September, am neunzehnten September; **~ 3rd, 1993, 3rd ~ 1993** (on letter) 3. September 1993; **in ~** im September; **at the beginning/end of ~** Anfang/Ende September; **there are 30 days in ~** der September hat 30 Tage. **2** adj attr September-; mists etc also septemberlich.
**septic** ['septɪk] adj vereitert, septisch. **the wound turned ~** die Wunde eiterte; **~ tank** Klärbehäl-

ter m.
**septicaemia**, (US) **septicemia** [septɪ'siːmɪə] n Blutvergiftung f.
**sepulchre**, (US) **sepulcher** ['sepəlkər] n Grabstätte f.
**sequel** ['siːkwəl] n Folge f (to von); (of book, film) Fortsetzung f (to von). **it had a tragic ~** es hatte ein tragisches Nachspiel.
**sequence** ['siːkwəns] n (a) (order) Folge, Reihenfolge f. **in ~** der Reihe nach; **to do sth in ~** etw in der richtigen Reihenfolge tun. (b) (things following) Reihe, Folge f; (Mus, Cards) Sequenz f; (Math) Reihe f.
**sequential** [sɪ'kwenʃəl] adj (form) der Reihe nach; (Comp) sequentiell.
**sequin** ['siːkwɪn] n Paillette f.
**Serb** [sɜːb] n Serbe m, Serbin f.
**Serbia** ['sɜːbɪə] n Serbien nt.
**Serbian** ['sɜːbɪən] adj serbisch.
**Serbo-Croat** ['sɜːbəʊ'krəʊæt] n (language) Serbokroatisch nt.
**serenade** [serə'neɪd] **1** n Serenade f. **2** vt ein Ständchen nt bringen (+dat).
**serene** [sə'riːn] adj gelassen; sea ruhig; sky heiter.
**serenely** [sə'riːnlɪ] adv gelassen.
**serenity** [sɪ'renɪtɪ] n Gelassenheit f.
**serf** [sɜːf] n Leibeigene(r) mf.
**serge** [sɜːdʒ] n Serge f.
**sergeant** ['sɑːdʒənt] n (Mil) Feldwebel m; (police) Polizeimeister m. **~ major** Oberfeldwebel m.
**serial** ['sɪərɪəl] **1** n (novel) Fortsetzungsroman m; (Rad) Sendereihe f; (TV) Serie f. **2** adj Serien-; story, programme in Fortsetzungen; (Comp, Mus) seriell. **~ killer** Serienmörder(in f) m; **~ number** fortlaufende Nummer; (on manufactured goods) Fabrikationsnummer f.
**serialize** ['sɪərɪəlaɪz] vt in Fortsetzungen bringen; (put into serial form) in Fortsetzungen umarbeiten.
**series** ['sɪəriːz] n, pl - Serie f; (Rad) Sendereihe f; (of books, lectures, films) Reihe f. **a ~ of articles** eine Artikelserie; **in ~** der Reihe nach; **~ production** Serienherstellung f.
**serious** ['sɪərɪəs] adj (a) ernst; person, manner (not frivolous) ernsthaft; newspaper, interest seriös; offer, suggestion ernstgemeint attr, ernst gemeint pred, seriös; doubts also ernsthaft. **to be ~ about doing sth** etw im Ernst tun wollen; **I'm ~ (about it)** das ist mein Ernst; **he is ~ about her** er meint es ernst mit ihr; **you can't be ~!** das kann nicht dein Ernst sein! (b) (critical) ernst; accident, mistake, injury damage, loss schwer; situation also bedenklich. **it's ~** das ist schlimm; **it's getting ~** es wird ernst; **inflation is getting ~** die Inflation nimmt ernste Ausmaße an.
**seriously** ['sɪərɪəslɪ] adv (a) ernst; talk, interested ernsthaft; (not jokingly) im Ernst. **to take sb/sth ~** jdn/etw ernst nehmen; **do you ~ want to do that?** wollen Sie das wirklich or im Ernst tun?; **~ though** ... aber mal ganz im Ernst ...; **do you mean that ~?** meinen Sie das ernst?, ist das Ihr Ernst? (b) wounded schwer; ill also ernstlich; deteriorate bedenklich.
**seriousness** ['sɪərɪəsnɪs] n see adj (a) Ernst m; Ernsthaftigkeit f; Seriosität f. **in all ~** ganz im Ernst. (b) Ernst m; Schwere f; Bedenklichkeit f.
**sermon** ['sɜːmən] n (Eccl) Predigt f; (moralizing) Moralpredigt f; (scolding) Strafpredigt f.
**serpent** ['sɜːpənt] n Schlange f (also fig).
**Serps** [sɜːps] (Brit) = **state earnings-related pension scheme** staatliche Rentenversicherung.
**serrated** [se'reɪtɪd] adj gezackt. **~ knife** Sägemes-

ser *nt.*

**serum** ['sɪərəm] *n* Serum *nt.*

**servant** ['sɜːvənt] *n (lit, fig)* Diener(in *f*) *m*; *(also ~ girl)* Dienstmädchen *nt*; *(domestic)* Dienstbote *m.*

**serve** [sɜːv] **1** *vt* **(a)** dienen *(+dat)*; *(be of use)* nützen *(+dat)*. **he ~d his country well** er hat sich um sein Land verdient gemacht; **if my memory ~s me right** wenn ich mich recht erinnere; **to ~ its/sb's purpose** seinen Zweck erfüllen/jds Zwecken *(dat)* dienen; **it ~s no useful purpose** es hat keinen praktischen Wert; **to ~ sb as sth** jdm als etw dienen; **it has ~d us well** es hat uns gute Dienste geleistet.

**(b)** *years in army etc* ableisten; *term of office* durchlaufen; *apprenticeship* durchmachen; *sentence* verbüßen, absitzen *(col).*

**(c)** *(in shop)* bedienen; *(bus, gas etc)* versorgen. **I'm being ~d, thank you** danke, ich werde schon bedient.

**(d)** *(esp in restaurant) food, drink* servieren; *guests* bedienen; *(waiter)* bedienen; *(pour drink for)* einschenken *(+dat)*; *wine etc* einschenken. **dinner is ~d** *(butler)* das Essen ist aufgetragen; *(hostess)* darf ich zu Tisch bitten?; *"~s three" (on packet etc)* „(ergibt) drei Portionen".

**(e)** *(Tennis etc) ball* aufschlagen.

**(f)** *(Jur)* zustellen *(on sb* jdm*).* **to ~ a summons on sb, to ~ sb with a summons** jdn vor Gericht laden; **the landlord ~d notice on his tenants** der Vermieter kündigte den Mietern.

**(g) (it) ~s you right!** *(col)* das geschieht dir (ganz) recht!; **it ~s him right for being so greedy** *(col)* das geschieht ihm ganz recht, was muß er auch so gierig sein!

**2** *vi* **(a)** dienen. **to ~ on the jury** Geschworene(r) *mf* sein; **to ~ on a committee** einem Ausschuß angehören; **to ~ as chairman** das Amt des Vorsitzenden innehaben. **(b)** *(Mil)* dienen. **(c)** *(waiter, butler etc)* servieren *(at table* bei Tisch*)*. **(d) to ~ as, to ~ for** dienen als; **it ~s to show/explain ...** das zeigt/ erklärt ... **(e)** *(Tennis etc)* aufschlagen.

**3** *n (Tennis etc)* Aufschlag *m.* **whose ~ is it?** wer hat Aufschlag?

▸**serve up** *vt sep food* servieren; *rations* verteilen.

**server** ['sɜːvəʳ] *n* **(a)** *(fork etc)* Servierlöffel *m/* Vorlegegabel *f*; *(pie ~)* Tortenheber *m.* **salad ~s** Salatbesteck *nt.* **(b)** *(Tennis)* Aufschläger(in *f*) *m.*

**service** ['sɜːvɪs] *n* **(a)** Dienst *m.* **his faithful ~** seine treuen Dienste; **his ~s to industry/the country** seine Verdienste in der Industrie/um das Land; **he has ten years' ~ behind him** er hat zehn Jahre Dienstzeit hinter sich *(dat)*; **to do sb a ~** jdm einen Dienst erweisen; **to do good ~** gute Dienste leisten; **to be of ~ to sb** jdm nützen; **to be at sb's ~** jdm zur Verfügung stehen; **can I be of ~ to you?** kann ich Ihnen behilflich sein?; **out of ~** außer Betrieb; **to need the ~s of a lawyer** einen Anwalt brauchen.

**(b)** *(Mil)* Militärdienst *m.* **the (armed) ~s** die Streitkräfte; **when I was in the ~s** als ich beim Militär war.

**(c)** *(to customers)* Service *m*; *(in shop, restaurant etc)* Bedienung *f.*

**(d)** *(bus, train, plane etc)* Bus-/Zug-/Flugverbindung *f.* **there's no ~ to X on Sundays** sonntags fährt kein Bus/Zug *etc* nach X.

**(e)** *(Eccl)* Gottesdienst *m.*

**(f)** *(of machines)* Wartung *f*; *(Aut: major ~)* Inspektion *f.* **my car is in for a ~** mein Auto wird gewartet; mein Auto ist bei der Inspektion.

**(g)** *(tea, coffee etc set)* Service *nt.*

**(h)** *(Tennis)* Aufschlag *m.*

**(i) ~s** *pl (commercial)* Dienstleistungen *pl*; *(gas*

*etc)* Versorgungsnetz *nt.*

**2** *vt car, machine* warten. **to have a car ~d** ein Auto warten lassen; *(major ~)* ein Auto zur Inspektion geben.

**serviceable** ['sɜːvɪsəbl] *adj (practical)* zweckmäßig; *(usable)* brauchbar.

**service:** **~ area** *n* Raststätte *f*; **~ charge** *n (Brit)* Bedienung(sgeld *nt*) *f*; *(of bank)* Bearbeitungsgebühr *f*; **~ industry** *n* Dienstleistungsbranche *f*; **the ~ industries** das Dienstleistungsgewerbe *nt*; **~man** *n* Militärangehörige(r) *m*; **~ station** *n* Tankstelle *f* (mit Reparaturwerkstatt).

**servicing** ['sɜːvɪsɪŋ] *n* Wartung *f.*

**serviette** [ˌsɜːvɪ'et] *n* Serviette *f.*

**servile** ['sɜːvaɪl] *adj* unterwürfig; *obedience* sklavisch.

**servility** [sɜː'vɪlɪtɪ] *n* Unterwürfigkeit *f.*

**serving** ['sɜːvɪŋ] *n (of food)* Portion *f.*

**serving:** **~ cart** *n (US)* Servierwagen *m*; **~ dish** *n* (Servier)platte *f*; **~ hatch** *n* Durchreiche *f*; **~ spoon** *n* Vorlegelöffel *m.*

**servo** ['sɜːvəʊ] *n* Servomechanismus *m*; *(brake ~)* Bremskraftverstärker *m.*

**session** ['seʃən] *n* **(a)** *(meeting)* Sitzung *f*; *(Jur, Parl: period)* Sitzungsperiode *f*; *(Parl: term of office)* Legislaturperiode *f.* **to be in ~** eine Sitzung abhalten; *(Jur, Pol)* tagen; **a ~ of talks/negotiations** Gespräche *pl*/Verhandlungen *pl*; **recording ~** Aufnahme *f*; **we're in for a long ~** das wird lange dauern; **I had a long ~ with him** *(talk)* ich habe lange mit ihm gesprochen. **(b)** *(academic year) (Univ)* Studienjahr *nt*; *(Sch)* Schuljahr *nt*; *(term)* Semester/Trimester *nt*; *(division of course)* Stunde, Sitzung *(esp Univ) f.*

**set** [set] *(vb: pret, ptp ~)* **1** *n* **(a)** Satz *m*; *(of two)* Paar *nt*; *(of cutlery, furniture etc)* Garnitur *f*; *(tea-~ etc)* Service *nt*; *(of tablemats etc)* Set *nt*; *(chess or draughts ~ etc)* Spiel *nt*; *(painting ~)* Malkasten *m*; *(Meccano ®, chemistry ~)* Baukasten *m*; *(gift or presentation ~)* Kassette *f.* **~ of rooms** Zimmerflucht *f*; **a ~ of tools** Werkzeug *nt*; **a ~ of teeth** ein Gebiß *nt.*

**(b)** *(group of people)* Kreis *m*; *(pej)* Bande *f*; *(Brit Sch: stream)* Kurs *m.* **the literary ~** die Literaten *pl*; **the golfing ~** die Golffreunde *pl.*

**(c)** *(Tennis)* Satz *m*; *(Table-tennis)* Spiel *nt.* **~ point** Satzpunkt *m.*

**(d)** *(Telec, Rad, TV)* Gerät *nt*, Apparat *m.*

**(e)** *(hair~)* Frisur, Form *f.* **to have a (shampoo and) ~** sich *(dat)* die Haare (waschen und) legen lassen.

**(f)** *(Theat)* Bühnenbild *nt*; *(Film)* Szenenaufbau *m.* **to be on the ~** bei den Dreharbeiten sein.

**(g)** *(Math)* Menge *f.*

**2** *adj* **(a)** *pred (ready)* fertig, bereit. **all ~?** alles klar?; **to be all ~ to do sth** sich darauf eingerichtet haben, etw zu tun. **(b)** *(rigid)* starr; *expression* feststehend; *forms also, habit, custom* fest; *(prescribed)* festgesetzt; *essay topic* vorgegeben; *(prearranged) time, place* bestimmt, ausgemacht *(col).* **~ book(s)** Pflichtlektüre *f*; **~ lunch/meal** Tagesgericht *nt*; **~ menu** Tageskarte *f*; **~ phrase** feste Redewendung; **~ piece** Standardstück *nt*; *(Ftbl)* Standardsituation *f*; **to be ~ in one's ways** in seinen Gewohnheiten festgefahren sein. **(c)** *(resolved)* entschlossen. **to be (dead) ~ on sth/doing sth** etw unbedingt haben/tun wollen; **to be (dead) ~ against sth/doing sth** (total) gegen etw sein/etw (absolut) nicht tun wollen.

**3** *vt* **(a)** *(put, place)* stellen; *(on its side, flat)* legen; *(deliberately, carefully)* setzen.

**(b)** *(regulate, adjust)* einstellen *(at* auf *+acc)*; *clock* stellen *(by* nach, *to* auf *+acc)*; *(fix) trap, snare* aufstellen; *(fig)* stellen *(for sb* jdm*)*. **to ~ the alarm for a certain time** den Wecker auf eine bestimmte Zeit stellen.

(c) *(prescribe, impose) target, limit etc* festlegen; *task, question* stellen *(sb* jdm*)*; *homework* aufgeben; *exam* zusammenstellen; *(arrange) time, date* festsetzen, ausmachen *(col)*; *(establish) record* aufstellen; *fashion* bestimmen. **to ~ the date (of the wedding)** das Hochzeitsdatum festsetzen; **to ~ a value on sth** einen Wert für etw festsetzen; **to ~ a high value on sth** einer Sache *(dat)* großen Wert beimessen; **to ~ sb a problem** *(lit)* jdm ein Problem aufgeben; *(fig)* jdn vor ein Problem stellen.

(d) *(mount) gem* fassen *(in* in +*dat)*; *piece of jewellery* besetzen *(with* mit*)*; *windowpane* einsetzen *(in* in +*acc)*; *(embed firmly)* einlegen *(in* in +*dat)*; *(in ground)* einlassen *(in* in +*acc)*.

(e) *(Liter)* **the book** *etc* **is ~ in Rome** das Buch *etc* spielt in Rom; **he ~ the book in Rome** er wählte Rom als Schauplatz für sein Buch.

(f) *(Med) bone* einrichten; *dislocated joint* einrenken.

(g) *(lay with cutlery) table* decken. **to ~ places for 14** für 14 decken.

(h) *hair* legen, eindrehen.

(i) **to ~ the police/dogs on sb** die Polizei/Hunde auf jdn hetzen.

(j) *(Mus)* **to ~ sth to music** etw vertonen.

(k) *(Typ)* setzen.

(l) **to ~ sth going/in motion** etw in Gang/Bewegung bringen; **to ~ sb doing sth** jdn dazu veranlassen, etw zu tun; **to ~ sb laughing** jdn zum Lachen bringen; **that ~ me thinking** das gab mir zu denken; **that ~ me thinking that ...** das ließ mich denken, daß ...; **to ~ people talking** Anlaß zu Gerede geben; **to ~ sb/oneself to do sth** jdn etw tun lassen/sich daranmachen, etw zu tun.

**4** *vi* (a) *(sun etc)* untergehen. (b) *(jelly, cement)* fest werden; *(jam also)* gelieren; *(bone)* zusammenwachsen.

►**set about** *vi* +*prep obj* (a) *(begin)* anfangen; *(tackle)* anfassen, anpacken *(col)*. **to ~ ~ doing sth** *(begin)* sich daranmachen, etw zu tun; **how do I ~ ~ getting a loan?** wie fasse *or* packe *(col)* ich es an, ein Darlehen zu bekommen? (b) *(attack)* herfallen über (+*acc)*.

►**set against** *vt sep* +*prep obj* (a) *(influence against)* einnehmen gegen; *(cause trouble between)* Zwietracht säen zwischen (+*dat)*. (b) *(balance against) evidence etc* gegenüberstellen (+*dat)*.

►**set aside** *vt sep* (a) *work, money* beiseite legen; *time* einplanen; *plans* aufschieben; *differences* beiseite schieben; *dislike* vergessen; *mistrust, bitterness* sich freimachen von; *formality* verzichten auf (+*acc)*; *rules, protest* übergehen. (b) *(Jur)* aufheben; *will* für ungültig erklären.

►**set back** *vt sep* (a) *(place at a distance)* zurücksetzen. **the house is ~ ~ from the road** das Haus liegt etwas von der Straße ab. (b) *(retard)* verzögern, behindern. **the programme has been ~ ~ (by) 2 years** das Programm ist um 2 Jahre zurückgeworfen worden. (c) *(col: cost)* kosten. **the dinner ~ me ~ £35** das Essen hat mich 35 Pfund gekostet *or* ärmer gemacht *(col)*.

►**set down** *vt sep* (a) *(put down) suitcase* absetzen; *passenger also* aussteigen lassen. (b) *(in writing)* (schriftlich) niederlegen.

►**set in** *vi (start) (frost etc)* einsetzen; *(panic)* ausbrechen; *(night)* anbrechen; *(Med: gangrene, complications)* sich einstellen. **the rain has ~ ~** es hat sich eingeregnet.

►**set off 1** *vt sep* (a) *bomb* losgehen lassen; *alarm, mechanism* auslösen. (b) *(offset)* **to ~ sth ~ against sth** etw einer Sache *(dat)* gegenüberstellen. (c) *(enhance)* hervorheben. **to ~ sth ~ from sth** etw von etw abheben. **2** *vi (depart)* aufbrechen; *(car, in car etc)* losfahren. **to ~ ~ on a journey** eine Reise antreten; **to ~ ~ for Spain** nach Spanien abfahren *or* losfahren.

►**set out 1** *vt sep (display)* ausbreiten; *(arrange) chess pieces* aufstellen; *essay* anlegen. **2** *vi* (a) *(depart)* = **set off 2.** (b) *(intend)* beabsichtigen. **I didn't ~ ~ to do that** ich hatte nicht vor, das zu tun.

►**set to 1** *vi (start working etc)* loslegen *(col)*. **they ~ ~ and repaired it** sie machten sich an die Arbeit und reparierten es. **2** *vi* +*prep obj* **to ~ ~ work** sich an die Arbeit machen.

►**set up 1** *vi (establish oneself)* **to ~ ~ as a doctor** sich als Arzt niederlassen; **to ~ ~ in business** sein eigenes Geschäft aufmachen; **to ~ ~ on one's own** sich selbständig machen. **2** *vt sep* (a) *(place in position) statue, post* aufstellen; *(assemble) tent, stall, apparatus* aufbauen; *(fig: arrange) meeting* vereinbaren; *robbery* planen. **to ~ sth ~ for sb** etw für jdn vorbereiten. (b) *(establish)* gründen; *school, office* einrichten; *inquiry* anordnen. **to ~ sb ~ in business** jdm zu einem Geschäft verhelfen; **to ~ sb ~ as sth** (es) jdm ermöglichen, etw zu werden; **to be ~ ~ for life** für sein ganzes Leben ausgesorgt haben. (c) *(col: frame)* **to ~ sb ~** jdm etwas anhängen; **I've been ~ ~** das will mir einer anhängen *(col)*.

►**set upon** *vi* +*prep obj* überfallen; *(animal)* anfallen.

**set:** **~back** *n* Rückschlag *m*; **~ square** *n (esp Brit)* Zeichendreieck *nt*; **~ theory** *n* Mengenlehre *f*.

**settee** [se'tiː] *n* Couch *f*, Sofa *nt*.

**setter** ['setə<sup>r</sup>] *n (dog)* Setter *m*.

**setting** ['setɪŋ] *n* (a) *(of sun, moon)* Untergang *m*. (b) *(background, atmosphere)* Rahmen *m*; *(surroundings)* Umgebung *f*; *(of novel etc)* Schauplatz *m*. **a film with a medieval ~** ein Film, der im Mittelalter spielt. (c) *(of jewel)* Fassung *f*. (d) *(at table)* Gedeck *nt*. (e) *(position on dial etc)* Einstellung *f*. (f) *(musical arrangement)* Vertonung *f*. (g) *(hair)* Legen *nt*. **~ lotion** (Haar)festiger *m*.

**settle** ['setl] **1** *vt* (a) *(decide)* entscheiden; *(sort out)* regeln; *problem* klären; *dispute, differences* beilegen; *doubts* ausräumen; *date, place* festlegen, ausmachen *(col)*; *venue* festlegen; *deal* abschließen; *price, terms* aushandeln. **when my future is ~d** wenn sich meine Zukunft entschieden hat; **to ~ one's affairs** seine Angelegenheiten in Ordnung bringen; **to ~ an estate** *(Jur)* die Verteilung des Nachlasses regeln; **to ~ a case out of court** einen Fall außergerichtlich klären; **that's ~d then** das ist also klar; **that ~s it** damit wäre der Fall (ja wohl) erledigt; *(angry)* jetzt reicht's.

(b) *(pay) bill* begleichen; *account* ausgleichen.

(c) *(place carefully)* legen; *(in upright position)* stellen; *(make comfortable) baby* schlafen legen; *invalid* bequem hinlegen; *(calm) nerves, stomach* beruhigen. **to ~ oneself comfortably in an armchair** es sich *(dat)* in einem Sessel bequem machen.

(d) *(colonize) land* besiedeln.

(e) *(form)* **to ~ money/property on sb** jdm Geld/Besitz überschreiben; *(in will)* jdm Geld/Besitz vermachen.

**2** *vi* (a) *(in country, town, profession)* sich niederlassen; *(as settler)* sich ansiedeln; *(in house)* sich einrichten; *(feel at home in house, town)* sich einleben *(into* an +*dat)*; *(in job, surroundings)* sich eingewöhnen *(into* in +*dat)*; *(permanently in area)* seßhaft werden. **to ~ into a habit** sich *(dat)* etw angewöhnen.

 **(b)** *(become less variable: weather)* beständig werden. **if the weather would only ~** wenn das Wetter nicht mehr so unbeständig wäre.

 **(c)** *(become calm) (child, matters, stomach)* sich beruhigen; *(panic, excitement)* sich legen; *(become less excitable)* ruhiger werden. **he couldn't ~ to anything** er konnte sich auf nichts konzentrieren.

 **(d)** *(come to rest, sit down) (person, bird)* sich niederlassen *or* setzen; *(dust)* sich setzen *or* legen; *(sink slowly) (building)* sich senken; *(ground, sediment)* sich setzen.

 **(e)** *(Jur)* **to ~ (out of court)** sich vergleichen.

 **(f)** *(pay)* bezahlen. **can I ~ with you later?** kann ich später mit Ihnen abrechnen?

►**settle down** *vi* **(a)** = **settle 2 (a)**. **it's time he ~d ~** es wird Zeit, daß er zur Ruhe kommt; *(got married)* es wird Zeit, daß er heiratet; **to ~ ~ at school/a job** sich an einer Schule/in einer Stellung eingewöhnen. **(b)** = **settle 2 (c)**. **(c) to ~ ~ to work** sich an die Arbeit machen *or* setzen; **to ~ ~ for the night** sich schlafen legen.

►**settle for** *vi* +*prep obj* sich zufriedengeben mit. **she won't ~ ~ anything less** mit weniger gibt sie sich nicht zufrieden.

►**settle in** *vi (in house, town)* sich einleben; *(in job, school)* sich eingewöhnen.

►**settle on** *vi* +*prep obj* sich entscheiden für; *(agree on)* sich einigen auf (+*acc)*.

►**settle up 1** *vi* (be)zahlen. **to ~ ~ with sb** *(lit, fig)* mit jdm abrechnen. **2** *vt sep bill* bezahlen.

**settled** ['setld] *adj way of life* geregelt; *(Brit) weather* beständig. **to be ~** in geregelten Verhältnissen leben; *(established)* etabliert sein; *(in place)* seßhaft sein; *(have permanent job etc)* festen Fuß gefaßt haben; *(in a house)* sich häuslich niedergelassen haben; *(be less restless)* ruhiger sein.

**settlement** ['setlmənt] *n* **(a)** *(act) (deciding)* Entscheidung *f*; *(sorting out)* Regelung *f*; *(of problem etc)* Klärung *f*; *(of dispute etc)* Beilegung *f*; *(of estate)* Regelung *f*; *(of bill, claim)* Bezahlung *f*; *(of account)* Ausgleich *m*. **a ~ out of court** *(Jur)* ein außergerichtlicher Vergleich; **to reach a ~** sich einigen, einen Vergleich treffen; **in ~ of our account** zum Ausgleich unseres Kontos. **(b)** *(colony, village)* Siedlung, Niederlassung *f*; *(colonization)* Besiedlung *f*. **(c)** *(contract, agreement etc)* Übereinkunft *f*.

**settler** ['setlər] *n* Siedler(in *f*) *m*.

**set:** **~-to** *n* *(col)* Krach *m* *(col)*; **to have a ~-to with sb** sich mit jdm in die Wolle kriegen *(col)*; **~-up** *n* **(a)** *(col: situation)* Zustände *pl*; **I don't like the whole ~-up** mir gefällt das ganze Drum und Dran nicht *(col)*; **(b)** *(col: rigged contest)* abgekartete Sache.

**seven** ['sevn] *adj* sieben; *see* **six.**

**seventeen** ['sevn'ti:n] *adj* siebzehn.

**seventeenth** ['sevn'ti:nθ] *adj* siebzehnte(r, s); *see* **sixteenth.**

**seventh** ['sevnθ] **1** *adj* siebte(r, s). **2** *n* *(fraction)* Siebtel *nt*; *(in series)* Siebte(r, s); *(Mus)* Septime *f*; *(chord)* Septimenakkord *m*; *see* **sixth.**

**seventieth** ['sevntɪɪθ] *adj* siebzigste(r, s); *see* **sixtieth.**

**seventy** ['sevntɪ] *adj* siebzig; *see* **sixty.**

**sever** ['sevər] *vt (cut through)* durchtrennen; *(violently)* durchschlagen; *(cut off)* abtrennen; *(violently)* abschlagen; *(fig: break off) ties* lösen; *relations* abbrechen; *communications* unterbrechen.

**several** ['sevrəl] **1** *adj (some)* einige, mehrere; *(various)* verschiedene. **I've seen him ~ times/~ times**

**already** ich habe ihn einige Male gesehen/schon mehrere Male gesehen; **I'll need ~ more** ich brauche noch einige. **2** *pron* einige. **~ of the houses** einige (der) Häuser; **~ of us** einige von uns.

**severance pay** ['sevərəns,peɪ] *n* eine Abfindung.

**severe** [sɪ'vɪər] *adj* (+*er)* *person, appearance* streng; *punishment, competition, test* hart; *criticism, reprimand* scharf; *crime, warning* ernst; *illness, injury, blow, frost, loss* schwer, schlimm; *pain, storm* stark, heftig; *weather* rauh. **to be ~ with sb** streng mit jdm sein.

**severely** [sɪ'vɪəlɪ] *adv see adj.* **to be ~ critical of sth** sich äußerst kritisch über etw *(acc)* äußern; **~ handicapped** schwerbehindert.

**severity** [sɪ'verɪtɪ] *n see adj* Strenge *f*; Härte *f*; Schärfe *f*; Ernst *m*; Schwere *f*; Stärke, Heftigkeit *f*; Rauheit *f*. **the ~ of the cold/drought/frost/loss** die schwere Kälte/Dürre/der starke Frost/der schwere Verlust.

**sew** [səʊ] *pret* **~ed**, *ptp* **~n** *vti* nähen. **to ~ sth on/together** etw annähen/zusammennähen.

►**sew up** *vt sep* **(a)** nähen *(also Med)*; *opening* zunähen. **(b)** *(fig)* unter Dach und Fach bringen. **it's all ~n ~** es ist unter Dach und Fach.

**sewage** ['sju:ɪdʒ] *n* Abwasser *nt*. **~ farm/works** Kläranlage *f*.

**sewerage** ['sjʊərɪdʒ] *n (system)* Kanalisation *f*; *(service)* Abwasserbeseitigung *f*.

**sewer** ['sjʊər] *n (pipe)* Abwasserleitung *f*; *(main ~)* Abwasserkanal *m*; *(fig: smelly place)* Kloake *f*.

**sewing** ['səʊɪŋ] *n (activity)* Nähen *nt*; *(piece of work)* Näharbeit *f*. **~ basket** Nähkorb *m*; **~ cotton** Nähgarn *nt*; **~ machine** Nähmaschine *f*.

**sewn** [səʊn] *ptp of* **sew.**

**sex** [seks] **1** *n* **(a)** *(Biol)* Geschlecht *nt*. **what ~ is the baby?** welches Geschlecht hat das Baby? **(b)** *(sexuality)* Sexualität *f*, Sex *m*; *(sexual intercourse)* Sex *(col)*, Geschlechtsverkehr *(form)* *m*. **to have ~** (Geschlechts)verkehr haben. **2** *adj attr* Geschlechts-; *hygiene, crime* Sexual-; *film, scandal* Sex-.

**sex:** **~ act** *n* Geschlechtsakt *m*; **~ appeal** *n* Sex-Appeal *m*; **~ change** *n* Geschlechtsumwandlung *f*; **~ discrimination** *n* Diskriminierung *f* auf Grund des Geschlechts; **~ education** *n* Sexualerziehung *f*.

**sexily** ['seksɪlɪ] *adv* aufreizend, sexy *(col)*.

**sexism** ['seksɪzm] *n* Sexismus *m*.

**sexist** ['seksɪst] **1** *n* Sexist(in *f*) *m*. **2** *adj* sexistisch.

**sex:** **~less** *adj* geschlechtslos; **~ life** *n* Geschlechtsleben *nt*; **~ maniac** *n (criminal)* Triebtäter *m*; *(hum col) (man)* Lustmolch *m (hum)*; *(woman)* Nymphomanin *f*; **~ object** *n* Sexualobjekt *nt*; **~ offence** *n* Sexualverbrechen *nt*; **~ offender** *n* Sexualtäter *m*; **~ shop** *n* Sexshop *m*.

**sextant** ['sekstənt] *n* Sextant *m*.

**sextet** [seks'tet] *n* Sextett *m*.

**sexton** ['sekstən] *n* Küster *m*.

**sexual** ['seksjʊəl] *adj* sexuell; *maturity* Geschlechts-; *partner* Sexual-; *crime* Sexual-, Trieb-. **~ harassment** sexuelle Belästigung; **~ intercourse** Geschlechtsverkehr *m*.

**sexuality** [,seksjʊ'ælɪtɪ] *n* Sexualität *f*.

**sexy** ['seksɪ] *adj* (+*er) (col)* sexy *pred*; *smile, pose also* aufreizend; *joke, film* erotisch; *(product etc)* geil *(col)*.

**Seychelles** [seɪ'ʃelz] *npl* Seychellen *pl*.

**SF** = **science fiction.**

**sgd** = **signed** gez.

**Sgt** = **sergeant.**

**shabbily** ['ʃæbɪlɪ] *adv (lit, fig)* schäbig.

**shabbiness** ['ʃæbɪnɪs] *n (lit, fig)* Schäbigkeit *f.*
**shabby** ['ʃæbɪ] *adj (+er) (lit, fig)* schäbig.
**shack** [ʃæk] **1** *n* Hütte *f.* **2** *vi (col)* **to ~ up with sb** mit jdm zusammenziehen.
**shackle** ['ʃækl] **1** *n usu pl* Kette, Fessel *(also fig) f.* **2** *vt* in Ketten legen.
**shade** [ʃeɪd] **1** *n* **(a)** Schatten *m.* **30° in the ~** 30 Grad im Schatten; **to give ~** Schatten spenden; **to put sb/sth in the ~** *(fig)* jdn/etw in den Schatten stellen. **(b)** *(lamp~)* (Lampen)schirm *m; (esp US: blind)* Jalousie *f; (roller blind)* Rollo *nt; (outside house)* Markise *f.* **~s** *(col: sunglasses)* Sonnenbrille *f.* **(c)** *(of colour)* (Farb)ton *m; (fig) (of opinion)* Schattierung *f; (of meaning)* Nuance *f.* **a bright ~ of red** ein leuchtender Rotton. **(d)** *(small quantity)* **it's a ~ long/too long** es ist eine Spur zu lang. **2** *vt* **(a)** *(protect from light)* abschirmen; *lamp, window* abdunkeln. **that part is ~d by a tree** der Teil liegt im Schatten eines Baumes. **(b)** *(Art)* schattieren; *(hatch)* schraffieren.
**shading** ['ʃeɪdɪŋ] *n (Art)* Schattierung *f; (hatching)* Schraffierung *f.*
**shadow** ['ʃædəʊ] **1** *n (lit, fig)* Schatten *m; (fig: threat)* (Be)drohung *f.* **in the ~** im Schatten; **in the ~s** im Dunkel; **sb lives under the ~ of sth** etw lastet wie ein Schatten auf jdm; **to be just a ~ of one's former self** nur noch ein Schatten seiner selbst sein; **without a ~ of a doubt** ohne den geringsten Zweifel. **2** *attr (Brit Pol)* Schatten-. **the ~ Foreign Secretary** der Außenminister im Schattenkabinett. **3** *vt (follow)* beschatten *(col).*
**shadow:** **~-boxing** *n (lit, fig)* Schattenboxen *nt;* **~ cabinet** *n (Brit)* Schattenkabinett *nt;* **~ play** *n* Schattenspiel *nt.*
**shadowy** ['ʃædəʊɪ] *adj* schattig; *(blurred)* verschwommen. **to lead a ~ existence** ein undurchsichtiges Dasein führen.
**shady** ['ʃeɪdɪ] *adj (+er)* **(a)** *place* schattig; *tree* schattenspendend. **(b)** *(col: dubious)* zwielichtig.
**shaft** [ʃɑːft] *n* Schaft *m; (of tool, golf club etc)* Stiel *m; (of light)* Strahl *m; (Mech)* Welle *f.*
**shaggy** ['ʃægɪ] *adj (+er) (long-haired)* zottig; *(unkempt)* zottelig.
**Shah** [ʃɑː] *n* Schah *m.*
**shake** [ʃeɪk] *(vb: pret* **shook,** *ptp* **shaken) 1** *n (act of shaking)* Schütteln *nt.* **to give a rug a ~** einen Läufer ausschütteln; **to give the paint a ~** die Farbe (gut) durchschütteln; **to give sb/oneself a good ~** sich kräftig schütteln; **with a ~ of the head** mit einem Kopfschütteln; **to be no great ~s** *(col)* nicht umwerfend sein *(at* in *+dat).*
**2** *vt* **(a)** schütteln; *building* erschüttern; *cocktail* durchschütteln. **"~ well before using"** „vor Gebrauch gut schütteln"; **to be ~n to pieces** total durchgeschüttelt werden; **to ~ one's fist at sb** jdm mit der Faust drohen; **to ~ one's head** den Kopf schütteln; **to ~ oneself/itself free** sich losmachen; **to ~ hands with sb** jdm die Hand schütteln. **(b)** *(weaken) faith etc* erschüttern; *evidence, reputation, resolve* ins Wanken bringen. **(c)** *(shock, amaze)* erschüttern. **that shook him!** da war er platt *(col);* **it was a nasty accident, he's still rather badly ~n** es war ein schlimmer Unfall, der Schreck sitzt ihm noch in den Knochen.
**3** *vi* wackeln; *(hand)* zittern; *(earth, voice)* beben. **the whole boat shook as the waves hit it** das ganze Boot wurde vom Aufprall der Wellen erschüttert; **to ~ like a leaf** zittern wie Espenlaub; **to ~ with fear** vor Angst zittern; **he was shaking all over** er zitterte am ganzen Körper.
▶**shake off** *vt sep dust, pursuer* abschütteln; *head-*

*ache* loswerden.
▶**shake out** *vt sep* **(a)** herausschütteln; *rug* ausschütteln. **(b)** *(fig: out of complacency etc)* aufrütteln *(of aus).*
▶**shake up** *vt sep* **(a)** *bottle, liquid* schütteln; *pillow* aufschütteln. **(b)** *(upset)* erschüttern. **she's still a bit ~n ~** sie ist immer noch ziemlich mitgenommen. **(c)** *management, recruits* auf Zack bringen *(col); ideas* revidieren.
**shaken** ['ʃeɪkən] *ptp of* **shake.**
**shake-up** ['ʃeɪkʌp] *n (col) (reorganization)* Umbesetzung *f.* **to give a department a good ~** eine Abteilung umkrempeln *(col).*
**shakily** ['ʃeɪkɪlɪ] *adv* wacklig; *talk* mit zittriger Stimme; *walk* mit wackligen Schritten.
**shakiness** ['ʃeɪkɪnɪs] *n see adj* Wackeligkeit *f;* Fragwürdigkeit *f;* Zittrigkeit *f;* Unsicherheit *f.*
**shaky** ['ʃeɪkɪ] *adj (+er) chair, position* wacklig; *evidence* fragwürdig; *voice, hands, writing* zittrig; *knowledge* unsicher. **his Spanish is rather ~** sein Spanisch ist ziemlich holprig; **to feel ~** sich ganz schwach fühlen.
**shale** [ʃeɪl] *n* Schiefer *m.*
**shall** [ʃæl] *pret* **should** *modal aux* **(a)** *(future)* **we ~** *or* **we'll go to France this year** wir werden dieses Jahr nach Frankreich fahren, wir fahren dieses Jahr nach Frankreich; **no, I ~ not** *or* **I shan't** nein, das werde ich nicht tun *or* das tue ich nicht; **yes, I ~** ja, das werde ich tun *or* das tue ich! **(b)** *(determination, obligation)* **you ~ pay for this!** dafür wirst du büßen!; **but I say you shall do it!** aber ich; sage dir, du wirst das machen!; **the directors ~ not be disturbed** *(form)* die Direktoren dürfen nicht gestört werden; **I want to go too — and so you ~** ich will auch mitkommen — aber gewiß doch. **(c)** *(in questions, suggestions)* **what ~ we do?** was sollen wir machen?; **let's go in, ~ we?** komm, gehen wir hinein!; **I'll buy 3, ~ I?** soll ich 3 kaufen?, ich kaufe 3, oder?
**shallot** [ʃə'lɒt] *n* Schalotte *f.*
**shallow** ['ʃæləʊ] **1** *adj* flach; *water also* seicht; *(fig) talk, person* oberflächlich. **in the ~ end of the pool** am flachen Ende des Beckens. **2** *n* **~s** *pl* Untiefe *f.*
**shalt** [ʃælt] *(obs) 2nd pers sing of* **shall.**
**sham** [ʃæm] **1** *n* **(a)** *(pretence)* Heuchelei *f.* **their marriage had become a ~** ihre Ehe war zur Farce geworden. **(b)** *(person)* Scharlatan *m.* **2** *adj diamonds etc* unecht, imitiert; *sympathy etc* vorgetäuscht, gespielt. **~ battle** Scheingefecht *nt.* **3** *vt* vortäuschen; *sympathy* heucheln. **4** *vi* so tun; *(esp with illness)* simulieren; *(with feelings)* heucheln. **he's just ~ming** er tut nur so.
**shamble** ['ʃæmbl] *vi* schlurfen.
**shambles** ['ʃæmblz] *n sing* heilloses Durcheinander. **the room was a ~** im Zimmer herrschte ein heilloses Durcheinander; **the economy is in a ~** die Wirtschaft befindet sich im Chaos.
**shambolic** [ʃæm'bɒlɪk] *adj (col)* chaotisch *(col).*
**shame** [ʃeɪm] **1** *n* **(a)** *(feeling of ~)* Scham *f; (cause of ~)* Schande *f.* **to feel ~ at sth** sich für etw schämen; **he hung his head in ~** er senkte beschämt den Kopf; *(fig)* er schämte sich; **to bring ~ upon sb/oneself** jdm/sich Schande machen; **to put sb/sth to ~** *(fig)* jdn/etw in den Schatten stellen; **~ on you!** du solltest dich/ihr solltet euch schämen! **(b)** *(pity)* **it's a ~ you couldn't come** schade, daß du nicht kommen konntest; **what a ~!** (das ist aber) schade!; **what a ~ he ...** schade, daß er ... **2** *vt* Schande machen *(+dat); (fig: by excelling)* in den Schatten stellen. **he ~d us by working so hard** er hat uns alle durch sein hartes Arbeiten beschämt.

**shamefaced** ['ʃeɪm,feɪst] *adj* betreten.
**shameful** ['ʃeɪmfʊl] *adj* schändlich. **how ~!** was für eine Schande!; **what ~ behaviour!** dieses Benehmen ist eine Schande.
**shamefully** ['ʃeɪmfəlɪ] *adv* schändlich. **I am ~ ignorant** es ist eine Schande, wie wenig ich weiß.
**shameless** ['ʃeɪmlɪs] *adj* schamlos. **he was quite ~ about it** er schämte sich überhaupt nicht.
**shamelessly** ['ʃeɪmlɪslɪ] *adv* schamlos.
**shammy (leather)** ['ʃæmɪ('leðəʳ)] *n* Fenster-/Autoleder *nt*.
**shampoo** [ʃæm'puː] **1** *n (liquid)* Shampoo, Schampon *nt*; *(act of washing)* Reinigung *f*; *(of hair)* Waschen *nt*. **to have a ~** sich *(dat)* die Haare waschen lassen. **2** *vt person* die Haare waschen *(+dat)*; *hair* waschen; *carpet* reinigen.
**shamrock** ['ʃæmrɒk] *n* Klee *m*; *(leaf)* Kleeblatt *nt*.
**shandy** ['ʃændɪ] *n* Bier *nt* mit Limonade, Radler *m (SGer)*, Alsterwasser *nt (NGer)*.
**shandygaff** ['ʃændɪ,gæf] *n (US)* = **shandy**.
**shank** [ʃæŋk] *n* **(to go) on S~s' pony** auf Schusters Rappen (reiten).
**shan't** [ʃɑːnt] = **shall not**.
**shanty**[1] ['ʃæntɪ] *n (hut)* Baracke, Hütte *f*. **~ town** Slum(vor)stadt *f*.
**shanty**[2] *n (Mus)* Seemannslied, Shanty *nt*.
**shape** [ʃeɪp] **1** *n* **(a)** Form *f*. **what ~ is it?** welche Form hat es?; **it's rectangular** *etc* **in ~** es ist rechteckig *etc*; **she's the right ~ for a model** sie hat die richtige Figur für ein Mannequin; **to hammer metal into ~** Metall zurechthämmern; **to knock sth out of ~** etw zerbeulen; **to take ~** *(lit, fig)* Gestalt annehmen; **of all ~s and sizes** jeder Art, in allen Variationen; **I don't accept gifts in any ~ or form** ich nehme überhaupt keine Geschenke an; **we do not know the ~ of things to come** wir wissen nicht, wie sich die Zukunft gestalten wird.
**(b)** *(unidentified figure)* Gestalt *f*; *(object)* Form *f*.
**(c)** *(fig: order, condition)* **in good/bad ~** *(sportsman)* in Form/nicht in Form; *(mentally, healthwise)* in guter/schlechter Verfassung; *(things, business)* in gutem/schlechtem Zustand; **to get into ~** *(sportsman etc)* in Form kommen; **to get a house into ~** ein Haus in Ordnung bringen; **to get one's affairs into ~** seine Angelegenheiten ordnen; **to knock sb/sth into ~** jdn/etw auf Vordermann bringen.
**2** *vt (lit) stone etc* bearbeiten; *clay etc* formen *(into* zu); *(fig) character, ideas* formen, prägen; *one's life* gestalten; *course of history* bestimmen.
**3** *vi (also ~ up)* sich entwickeln. **to ~ up well** sich gut entwickeln.
**SHAPE** = **Supreme Headquarters Allied Powers, Europe** Hauptquartier *nt* der NATO in Europa.
**shaped** [ʃeɪpt] *adj* geformt. **an oddly ~ hat** ein Hut mit einer komischen Form.
**-shaped** [-ʃeɪpt] *adj suf* -förmig.
**shapeless** ['ʃeɪplɪs] *adj* formlos; *(ugly)* unförmig.
**shapelessness** ['ʃeɪplɪsnɪs] *n* Formlosigkeit *f*; *(ugly)* Unförmigkeit *f*.
**shapeliness** ['ʃeɪplɪnɪs] *n see adj* Wohlproportioniertheit *f*; Wohlgeformtheit *f*.
**shapely** ['ʃeɪplɪ] *adj (+er) figure, woman* wohlproportioniert; *legs, bust* wohlgeformt.
**share** [ʃɛəʳ] **1** *n* **(a)** *(portion)* Anteil *m (in or of* an *+dat)*. **I want my fair ~** ich will meinen (An)teil; **he didn't get his fair ~** er ist zu kurz gekommen; **I've had more than my fair ~ of bad luck** ich habe aber auch wirklich Pech gehabt; **I'll give you a ~ in the profit** ich beteilige Sie am Gewinn; **in equal ~s** zu gleichen Teilen; **to take one's ~ of the**

**proceeds/blame** sich *(dat)* seinen Anteil am Gewinn nehmen/sich mitschuldig erklären; **to pay one's ~** seinen (An)teil bezahlen; **to do one's ~** sein(en) Teil beitragen; **to have a ~ in sth** an etw *(dat)* beteiligt sein; **I had no ~ in that** damit hatte ich nichts zu tun. **(b)** *(Fin)* (Geschäfts)anteil *m*; *(in a public limited company)* Aktie *f*.
**2** *vt (divide)* teilen; *(have in common also)* gemeinsam haben; *responsibility* gemeinsam tragen. **we ~ the same name/birthday** wir haben den gleichen Namen/am gleichen Tag Geburtstag; **they ~ a room** sie haben ein gemeinsames Zimmer; **I do not ~ that view** diese Ansicht teile ich nicht.
**3** *vi* **(a)** teilen. **children have to learn to ~** Kinder müssen lernen, mit anderen zu teilen; **to ~ and ~ alike** (brüderlich) mit (den) anderen teilen. **(b) to ~ in sth** sich an etw *(dat)* beteiligen; *(in profit)* an etw *(dat)* beteiligt sein; *(in enthusiasm)* etw teilen; *(in success, sorrow)* an etw *(dat)* Anteil nehmen.
**share:** ~ **certificate** *n* Aktie(nurkunde) *f*; ~**holder** *n* Aktionär(in *f*) *m*; ~ **index** *n* Aktienindex *m*; ~**out** *n* Verteilung *f*; *(St Ex)* (Dividenden)-ausschüttung *f*; ~ **price** *n* Aktienkurs *m*.
**shark** [ʃɑːk] *n* **(a)** Hai(fisch) *m*. **(b)** *(col: swindler)* Schlitzohr *nt (col)*. **loan ~** Kredithai *m (col)*.
**sharp** [ʃɑːp] **1** *adj (+er)* **(a)** scharf; *needle, angle* spitz; *air, wind* schneidend; *apple* sauer; *wine* herb; *nose* empfindlich; *(intelligent) person* schlau, auf Draht *(col)*; *child* aufgeweckt; *remark* scharfsinnig. **that was pretty ~ of you** das war ganz schön schlau *or* clever *(col)* von dir; **to keep a ~ watch for mistakes** scharf auf Fehler aufpassen. **(b)** *(sudden, intense) whistle, cry* durchdringend, schrill; *drop in prices* steil; *frost* scharf; *shower, desire, pain* heftig. **after a short, ~ struggle** nach kurzem, heftigem Kampf. **(c)** *(pej: cunning) person* gerissen, raffiniert; *trick etc* raffiniert. ~ **practice(s)** unsaubere Geschäfte *pl*. **(d)** *(harsh, fierce) tongue, retort, tone of voice* scharf; *person* schroff. **he has a ~ temper** er ist jähzornig. **(e)** *(Mus) note (too high)* zu hoch; *(raised a semitone)* (um einen Halbton) erhöht.
**2** *adv (+er)* **(a)** *(Mus)* zu hoch. **(b) at 5 o'clock ~** Punkt 5 Uhr; **to turn ~ right** scharf nach rechts abbiegen; **look ~!** dalli! *(col)*, zack, zack! *(col)*.
**3** *n (Mus)* Kreuz *nt*. **you played F natural instead of a ~** du hast f statt fis gespielt.
**sharpen** ['ʃɑːpən] *vt* **(a)** *knife* schleifen; *razor* wetzen; *pencil* spitzen; *(fig) appetite* anregen; *wits* schärfen. **(b)** *(Mus) (by a semitone)* (um einen Halbton) erhöhen; *(raise pitch)* höher singen/spielen/stimmen.
**sharp end** *n* **at the ~** *(fig)* in vorderster Front.
**sharpener** ['ʃɑːpnəʳ] *n* Schleifgerät *nt*; *(in rod shape)* Wetzstahl *m*; *(pencil ~)* (Bleistift)spitzer *m*.
**sharp:** ~**-eyed** *adj* scharfsichtig; **to be ~-eyed** scharfe Augen haben; ~**-featured** *adj* mit scharfen (Gesichts)zügen.
**sharpish** ['ʃɑːpɪʃ] *adv (col: promptly)* schnellstens.
**sharply** ['ʃɑːplɪ] *adv* scharf; *drop, rise* steil; *(harshly) speak, reply* schroff. ~ **angled** spitzwinklig; **the road bends ~ to the left** die Straße macht eine scharfe Linkskurve.
**sharpness** ['ʃɑːpnɪs] *n see adj* **(a)** Schärfe *f*; Spitzheit *f*; schneidende Kälte; Säure *f*; Herbheit *f*; *(intelligence)* Schläue *f*; Aufgewecktheit *f*; Scharfsinnigkeit *f*. **(b)** Schrillheit *f*; Schärfe *f*; Heftigkeit *f*. **(c)** *(pej)* Gerissenheit, Raffiniertheit *f*. **(d)** Schärfe *f*; Schroffheit *f*.
**sharp:** ~**shooter** *n* Scharfschütze *m*; ~**-sighted** *adj* = ~**-eyed**; ~**-tempered** *adj* jähzornig; ~**-tongued** *adj* scharfzüngig; ~**-witted** *adj* scharf-

sinnig.

**shatter** ['ʃætər] **1** vt **(a)** (lit) zertrümmern; hopes, dreams zunichte machen; nerves zerrütten. **the blast ~ed all the windows** durch die Explosion zersplitterten alle Fensterscheiben; **his hopes were ~ed** seine Hoffnungen hatten sich zerschlagen. **(b)** (fig col: exhaust) fertigmachen (col); (mentally) mitnehmen. **2** vi zerbrechen, zerspringen; (windscreen) (zer)splittern.

**shattered** ['ʃætəd] adj (col) (exhausted) fertig (col); (amazed) platt (col); (emotionally exhausted) mitgenommen.

**shattering** ['ʃætərɪŋ] adj **(a)** blow, explosion gewaltig; defeat vernichtend. **(b)** (fig col: exhausting) anstrengend; (psychologically) niederschmetternd.

**shatterproof** ['ʃætəpruːf] adj splitterfrei.

**shave** [ʃeɪv] (vb: pret ~d, ptp ~d or **shaven**) **1** n Rasur f. **to have a ~** sich rasieren; (at a barber's) sich rasieren lassen; **to have a close ~** (fig) mit knapper Not davonkommen; **that was a close ~** das war knapp. **2** vt face, legs rasieren; wood hobeln. **3** vi (person) sich rasieren; (razor) rasieren.

▶**shave off** vt sep beard sich (dat) abrasieren; sb's beard abrasieren; wood abhobeln.

**shaven** ['ʃeɪvn] adj head (kahl)geschoren.

**shaver** ['ʃeɪvər] n (razor) Rasierapparat m. **~ point** Steckdose f für Rasierapparate.

**shaving** ['ʃeɪvɪŋ] n ~s pl Späne pl.

**shaving** in cpds Rasier-; **~ brush** n Rasierpinsel m; **~ foam** n Rasierschaum m; **~ point** n (Brit) Steckdose f für Rasierapparate.

**shawl** [ʃɔːl] n (Umhänge)tuch nt; (covering head) (Kopf)tuch nt.

**she** [ʃiː] **1** pron sie; (of boats, cars) es. **~ who ...** (liter) diejenige, die ... **2** n Sie f.

**she-** pref weiblich. **~-bear** Bärin f.

**sheaf** [ʃiːf] n, pl **sheaves** (of wheat, corn) Garbe f; (of arrows etc, papers, notes) Bündel nt.

**shear** [ʃɪər] pret ~ed, ptp **shorn** vt sheep scheren; wool (ab)scheren.

**shears** [ʃɪəz] npl (große) Schere; (for hedges etc) Heckenschere f; (for metal) Metallschere f.

**sheath** [ʃiːθ] n (for sword etc) Scheide f; (Bot) (Blatt)scheide f; (on cable) Mantel m; (Brit: contraceptive) Kondom m or nt.

**sheathe** [ʃiːð] vt sword in die Scheide stecken; cable armieren. **~d in metal** mit Metall verkleidet.

**sheath knife** n Fahrtenmesser nt.

**sheaves** [ʃiːvz] pl of **sheaf**.

**shed**[1] [ʃed] pret, ptp ~ vt **(a)** leaves, hair etc verlieren; horns abwerfen; clothes ausziehen. **to ~ its skin** sich häuten; **you should ~ a few pounds** Sie sollten ein paar Pfund abnehmen or loswerden. **(b)** tears, blood vergießen. **I won't ~ any tears over him** ich weine ihm keine Träne nach. **(c)** burden, leader loswerden; cares ablegen; friend fallenlassen. **(d)** light, perfume verbreiten. **to ~ light on sth** (fig) etw erhellen.

**shed**[2] n Schuppen m; (industrial) Halle f; (cattle ~) Stall m.

**she'd** [ʃiːd] = **she would**; **she had**.

**sheen** [ʃiːn] n Glanz m.

**sheep** [ʃiːp] n, pl - (lit, fig) Schaf nt. **to separate the ~ from the goats** (fig) die Schafe von den Böcken trennen.

**sheep: ~dip** n Desinfektionsbad nt für Schafe; **~dog** nt Hütehund m; **~ farmer** n Schafzüchter m; **~fold** n Schafstall m.

**sheepish** ['ʃiːpɪʃ] adj look verlegen. **I felt a bit ~ about it** das war mir ein bißchen peinlich.

**sheep: ~-shearing** n Schafschur f; **~skin** n **(a)**

Schaffell nt; **(b)** (US col: diploma) Pergament nt.

**sheer** [ʃɪər] adj (+er) **(a)** (absolute) rein; nonsense also bar, glatt. **by ~ chance** rein zufällig; **by ~ hard work** durch nichts als harte Arbeit. **(b)** (steep) cliff, drop steil, jäh (geh). **there is a ~ drop of 200 metres** es fällt 200 Meter steil ab. **(c)** (of cloth etc) (hauch)dünn. **~ tights** Feinstrumpfhose f.

**sheet** [ʃiːt] n **(a)** (for bed) (Bett)laken, Bettuch nt; (for covering furniture) Tuch nt. **the furniture was covered with (dust)~s** die Möbel waren verhängt. **(b)** (of paper, col: a newspaper) Blatt nt; (big, as of wrapping paper, stamps etc, Typ) Bogen m. **~ of music** Notenblatt nt. **(c)** (of plywood) Platte f; (of glass also) Scheibe f; (of metal also) Blech nt; (baking ~) (Back)blech nt; (of water, ice etc) Fläche f. **a ~ of ice covered the lake** eine Eisschicht bedeckte den See; **a ~ of flame** eine riesige Flamme.

**sheet: ~ feed** n (for printer) Papierzuführung f; **~ lightning** n Wetterleuchten nt; **~ metal** n Walzblech nt; **~ music** n Notenblätter pl.

**sheik(h)** [ʃeɪk] n Scheich m.

**shelf** [ʃelf] n, pl **shelves** **(a)** Brett, Bord nt; (for books) Bücherbrett nt. **shelves** (unit of furniture) Regal nt; **she was left on the ~** (col: single woman) sie ist sitzengeblieben. **(b)** (ledge of rock etc) Gesims nt, (Fels)vorsprung m.

**shelf: ~ life** n Lagerfähigkeit f; **~ mark** n Standortzeichen nt.

**shell** [ʃel] n **(a)** (of egg, nut, mollusc) Schale f; (on beach) Muschel f; (of snail) (Schnecken)haus nt; (of tortoise, insect) Panzer m; (pastry ~) Form f. **to come out of one's ~** (fig) aus sich (dat) herausgehen; **to withdraw into one's ~** (fig) sich in sein Schneckenhaus verkriechen. **(b)** (frame) (of building) Mauerwerk nt; (unfinished) Rohbau m; (ruin) Gemäuer nt; (of car) (unfinished) Karosserie f; (gutted) Wrack nt; (of ship) Gerippe nt; (gutted) Wrack nt. **(c)** (Mil) Granate f; (esp US: cartridge) Patrone f. **2** vt **(a)** peas etc enthülsen; eggs, nuts schälen. **(b)** (Mil) (mit Granaten) beschießen.

▶**shell out** (col) **1** vt sep blechen (col). **2** vi **to ~ ~ for sth** für etw blechen (col).

**she'll** [ʃiːl] = **she will**; **she shall**.

**shellfish** ['ʃelfɪʃ] n Schaltier(e pl) nt; (Cook) Meeresfrüchte pl.

**shelling** ['ʃelɪŋ] n Granatfeuer nt (of auf +acc).

**shell: ~proof** adj bombensicher; **~ shock** n Kriegsneurose f; **~ suit** n Trilobal-Anzug m.

**shelter** ['ʃeltər] **1** n (protection) Schutz m; (place) Unterstand m; (air-raid ~) (Luftschutz)keller m; (bus ~) Wartehäuschen nt; (for the night) Unterkunft f. **a night ~ for homeless people** ein Obdachlosenasyl nt; **in the ~ of one's home** in der Geborgenheit seines Heims; **under the ~ of the rock** im Schutze des Felsens; **to take ~** sich in Sicherheit bringen; (from rain, hail etc) sich unterstellen; **to give sb ~** jdn beherbergen; (from vor +dat); criminal verstecken. **to ~ sb from blame** jdn gegen Vorwürfe in Schutz nehmen. **to ~ sb from harm** jdn vor Schaden bewahren. **3** vi **there was nowhere to ~** man konnte nirgends Schutz finden; (from rain etc) man konnte sich nirgends unterstellen; **a good place to ~** eine Stelle, wo man gut geschützt ist.

**sheltered** ['ʃeltəd] adj place geschützt; life behütet. **~ from the wind** windgeschützt; **~ housing** (for old people) Altenwohnungen pl; (for handicapped people) Behindertenwohnungen pl.

**shelve** [ʃelv] **1** vi (slope) abfallen. **2** vt problem aufschieben; plan ad acta legen.

**shelves** [ʃelvz] pl of **shelf**.

**shelving** ['ʃelvɪŋ] *n* Regale *pl.*
**shepherd** ['ʃepəd] **1** *n* Schäfer *m.* ~'s **pie** *Auflauf m aus Hackfleisch und Kartoffelbrei.* **2** *vt* führen.
**sherbet** ['ʃɜːbət] *n (powder)* Brausepulver *nt; (drink)* Brause *f; (US: water ice)* Fruchteis *nt.*
**sheriff** ['ʃerɪf] *n* Sheriff *m; (Scot)* Friedensrichter *m.*
**sherry** ['ʃerɪ] *n* Sherry *m.*
**she's** [ʃiːz] = **she is**; **she has.**
**Shetland Islands** ['ʃetlənd'aɪləndz], **Shetlands** ['ʃetləndz] *npl* Shetlandinseln *pl.*
**Shetland pony** ['ʃetlənd'pəʊnɪ] *n* Shetlandpony *nt.*
**shield** [ʃiːld] **1** *n (Mil, Her)* Schild *m; (sporting trophy also)* Trophäe *f; (on machine)* Schutzschirm *m; (eye~, radiation ~)* Schirm *m; (fig)* Schutz *m.* **riot ~** Schutzschild *m.* **2** *vt* schützen *(sb from sth jdn vor etw dat).*
**shift** [ʃɪft] **1** *n* **(a)** *(change)* Änderung *f; (in policy, opinion also)* Wandel *m; (from one place to another)* Verlegung *f.* **a ~ in direction** eine Richtungsände-rung; **a ~ in public opinion** ein Meinungsum-schwung *m* in der Bevölkerung; **a ~ of emphasis** eine Gewichtsverlagerung. **(b)** *(US Aut: gear~)* Schaltung *f; (on typewriter: also ~ key)* Umschalttas-te *f.* **(c)** *(period at work, group of workers)* Schicht *f.* **to work in ~s** in Schichten arbeiten; **to do ~ work** Schicht arbeiten. **(d)** *(stratagem)* List *f; (expedient)* Ausweg *m.* **to make ~ with sth** sich mit etw behel-fen.
**2** *vt* **(a)** *(move)* bewegen; *furniture also* ver-rücken; *head, arm* wegnehmen; *(from one place to another)* verschieben; *offices etc* verlegen; *rubble* wegräumen; *(with difficulty)* von der Stelle bewe-gen; *nail, cork* rauskriegen; *lid* abkriegen *(col).* **to ~ scenery** Kulissen schieben; **to ~ one's ground** sei-nen Standpunkt ändern; **to ~ sb from an opinion** jdn von einer Meinung abbringen; **to ~ the blame onto somebody else** die Verantwortung auf jemand anders schieben. **(b)** *(col: get rid of)* loswerden. **(c)** *(US Aut)* **to ~ gears** schalten.
**3** *vi* **(a)** *(move)* sich bewegen; *(cargo, scene)* sich verlagern; *(scene)* wechseln; *(wind)* umspringen; *(from one's position)* abgehen. **he ~ed out of the way** er ging aus dem Weg; **he ~ed onto his back** er drehte sich auf den Rücken; **~ing sands** *(Geol)* Flugsand *m.* **(b)** *(Aut)* schalten. **(c)** *(col: person: hurry)* sich beeilen; *(car, driver: go very fast)* einen Affenzahn draufhaben *(col).* **his Porsche can really ~** sein Porsche geht ab wie eine Rakete *(col).*
**shift:** **~ key** *n* Umschalttaste *f;* **~less** *adj* träge, energielos; **~ work** *n* Schichtarbeit *f;* **~ worker** *n* Schichtarbeiter(in *f*) *m.*
**shifty** ['ʃɪftɪ] *adj (+er) (not honest)* unehrlich; *(not re-liable)* unzuverlässig; *glance* verstohlen; *reply* aus-weichend.
**Shiite** ['ʃiːaɪt] **1** *n* Schiit(in *f*) *m.* **2** *adj* schiitisch.
**shilling** ['ʃɪlɪŋ] *n (Brit old)* Shilling *m.*
**shilly-shally** ['ʃɪlɪ,ʃælɪ] *vi (col)* hin und her überlegen.
**shimmer** ['ʃɪmər] **1** *n* Schimmer *m.* **2** *vi* schimmern.
**shin** [ʃɪn] **1** *n* Schienbein *nt; (of meat)* Hachse *f.* **2** *vi* **to ~ up/down** (geschickt) hinauf-/hinunterklettern.
**shinbone** ['ʃɪnbəʊn] *n* Schienbein *nt.*
**shindig** ['ʃɪndɪɡ] *n (col)* Remmidemmi *nt (col).*
**shindy** ['ʃɪndɪ] *n (col)* Radau *m (col); (noise also, dis-pute)* Krach *m (col).*
**shine** [ʃaɪn] *(vb: pret, ptp* **shone**) **1** *n* Glanz *m.* **to give one's shoes a ~** seine Schuhe polieren; **to take the ~ off sth** *(lit, fig)* einer Sache *(dat)* den Glanz nehmen; **she's taken a real ~ to my brother** *(col)* mein Bruder hat es ihr wirklich angetan. **2** *vt* **(a)** *pret, ptp usu* **~d** *(polish: also ~ up)* blank putzen; *shoes also* polieren. **(b)** **to ~ a light on sth** etw be-

leuchten; **~ the torch this way!** leuchte einmal hier-her!; **don't ~ it in my eyes!** blende mich nicht! **3** *vi* **(a)** leuchten; *(stars, eyes also, paint)* glänzen; *(sun, lamp)* scheinen; *(glass)* blitzblank sein. **her face shone with happiness** ihr Gesicht strahlte vor Glück. **(b)** *(fig: excel)* glänzen. **to ~ at/in sth** bei/in etw *(dat)* glänzen.
**shingle**[1] ['ʃɪŋɡl] *n (tile)* Schindel *f; (US col: sign-board)* Schild *nt.*
**shingle**[2] *n no pl (pebbles)* Kieselsteine *pl.*
**shingles** ['ʃɪŋɡlz] *n sing (Med)* Gürtelrose *f.*
**shin-guard** ['ʃɪnɡɑːd] *n* = **shin-pad.**
**shininess** ['ʃaɪnɪnɪs] *n* Glanz *m.*
**shining** ['ʃaɪnɪŋ] *adj (lit, fig)* leuchtend; *light* strah-lend; *eyes also, paint* glänzend; *car* blitzblank.
**shin-pad** ['ʃɪnpæd] *n* Schienbeinschützer *m.*
**shiny** ['ʃaɪnɪ] *adj (+er)* glänzend.
**ship** [ʃɪp] **1** *n* **(a)** Schiff *nt.* **on board ~** an Bord; **~'s company** (Schiffs)besatzung *f;* **~'s papers** Schiffs-papiere *pl.* **(b)** *(US col: plane)* Maschine *f; (space~)* Raumschiff *nt.* **2** *vt* **(a)** *(take on board)* goods an Bord bringen, laden; *crew, passengers* an Bord nehmen. **to ~ oars** die Riemen einlegen; **to ~ water** leck sein. **(b)** *(transport)* versenden; *grain etc* ver-frachten; *(by sea also)* verschiffen.
▶**ship out** *vt sep* versenden; *coal, grain etc* ver-frachten. **to ~ supplies ~ to sb** jdn (per Schiff) mit Vorräten versorgen.
**ship:** **~builder** *n* Schiffbauer *m;* **~building** *n* Schiffbau *m;* **~ canal** *n* Seekanal *m;* **~load** *n* Schiffsladung *f;* **~mate** *n* Schiffskamerad *m.*
**shipment** ['ʃɪpmənt] *n* Sendung *f; (act)* Transport *m; (transporting by sea)* Verschiffung *f.*
**shipowner** ['ʃɪpəʊnər] *n* Schiffseigner *m; (of many ships)* Reeder *m.*
**shipper** ['ʃɪpər] *n (company)* Speditionsfirma *f; (sender)* Absender *m.*
**shipping** ['ʃɪpɪŋ] **1** *n no pl* **(a)** Schiffahrt *f; (ships)* Schiffe *pl.* **(b)** *(transportation)* Verschiffung *f; (by rail etc)* Versand *m.* **2** *adj attr* **~ agent** Spediteur *m;* **~ company**, **~ line** Schiffahrtslinie, Reederei *f;* **~ forecast** Seewetterbericht *m;* **~ lane** Schiffahrts-straße *f.*
**ship:** **~shape** *adj, adv* tipptopp *(col);* **~wreck 1** *n (lit, fig)* Schiffbruch *m; (fig also)* Scheitern *nt;* **2** *vt* **to be ~wrecked** schiffbrüchig sein; *(fig)* Schiffbruch erleiden, scheitern; **~yard** *n* (Schiffs)werft *f.*
**shire** ['ʃaɪər] *n (Brit old)* Grafschaft *f.* **~ horse** Zug-pferd *nt.*
**shirk** [ʃɜːk] **1** *vt* sich drücken vor *(+dat),* ausweichen *(+dat).* **2** *vi* sich drücken.
**shirker** ['ʃɜːkər] *n* Drückeberger(in *f*) *m.*
**shirt** [ʃɜːt] *n (men's)* (Ober)hemd *nt; (Ftbl)* Hemd, Trikot *nt; (woman's: also US ~waist)* Hemdbluse *f.* **keep your ~ on** *(col)* reg dich nicht auf!
**shirt-sleeves** ['ʃɜːtsliːvz] *npl* Hemdsärmel *pl.* **in his/their ~** in Hemdsärmeln.
**shirty** ['ʃɜːtɪ] *adj (+er) (esp Brit col)* sauer *(col),* ver-ärgert. **don't get ~ with me** werd mir nicht frech.
**shit** [ʃɪt] *(vb: pret, ptp* **~** *or (hum)* **shat**) *(col!)* **1** *n* **(a)** Scheiße *f (col!); (nonsense also)* Scheiß *m (col!).* **(b)** *(person)* Arschloch *nt (col!).* **(c)** **~s** *pl (state of fear)* **to have/get the ~s** Schiß haben/kriegen *(col).* **2** *vi* scheißen *(col!).* **3** *interj* Scheiße *(col!).*
**shiver** ['ʃɪvər] **1** *n (of cold)* Schauer *m; (of horror also)* Schauder *m.* **the sight sent ~s down my spine** bei dem Anblick lief es mir kalt den Rücken hinun-ter; **it gives me the ~s** ich kriege davon eine Gän-sehaut. **2** *vi* zittern *(with vor +dat); (with fear also)* schaudern.
**shivery** ['ʃɪvərɪ] *adj* **to feel ~** frösteln.

**shoal** [ʃəʊl] *n (of fish)* Schwarm *m*.
**shock** [ʃɒk] **1** *n* **(a)** *(of explosion, impact)* Wucht *f*;
*(of earthquake)* (Erd)stoß *m*. **(b)** *(Elec)* Schlag *m*;
*(Med)* (Elektro)schock *m*. **to get a ~** einen Schlag
bekommen. **(c)** *(emotional disturbance)* Schock,
Schlag *m*; *(state)* Schock (zustand) *m*. **to be suffering from ~** einen Schock (erlitten) haben; **to be in
(a state of) ~** unter Schock stehen; **the ~ killed him**
den Schock hat er nicht überlebt; **to give sb a ~**
jdn erschrecken; **it gave me a nasty ~** es hat mir
einen bösen Schreck(en) eingejagt; **to get the ~ of
one's life** den Schock seines Lebens kriegen; **he is
in for a ~!** *(col)* der wird sich wundern! *(col)*.
　**2** *vt (affect emotionally)* erschüttern; *(make indignant)* schockieren, schocken *(col)*. **to be ~ed by
sth** über etw *(acc)* bestürzt sein; *(morally)* über etw
*(acc)* schockiert sein; **she is easily ~ed** sie ist leicht
schockiert; **I was ~ed at the news** ich war bestürzt
über die Nachricht.
　**3** *vi (film, writer etc)* schockieren, schocken *(col)*.
**shock absorber** ['ʃɒkəbˌzɔːbəʳ] *n* Stoßdämpfer *m*.
**shocking** ['ʃɒkɪŋ] *adj* **(a)** *news* erschütternd,
schockierend. **(b)** *(very bad)* entsetzlich, furchtbar.
**isn't it ~!** es ist doch furchtbar!
**shock:** **~proof** *adj* stoßfest; **~ therapy** *or* **treatment** *n* Schocktherapie *f*; **~ wave** *n (lit)* Druckwelle *f*; *(fig)* Erschütterung *f*.
**shod** [ʃɒd] *pret, ptp of* **shoe.**
**shoddiness** ['ʃɒdɪnɪs] *n see adj* Schäbigkeit *f*;
Schludrigkeit *f*; Minderwertigkeit *f*.
**shoddy** ['ʃɒdɪ] *adj* (+er) schäbig; *work* schludrig;
*goods also* minderwertig.
**shoe** [ʃuː] *(vb: pret, ptp* **shod) 1** *n* **(a)** Schuh *m*. **I
wouldn't like to be in his ~s** ich möchte nicht in seiner Haut stecken; **to put oneself in sb's ~s** sich in
jds Lage *(acc)* versetzen. **(b)** *(horse~)* (Huf)eisen
*nt*. **(c)** *(brake ~)* Bremsbacke *f*. **2** *vt horse* beschlagen.
**shoe:** **~brush** *n* Schuhbürste *f*; **~horn** *n* Schuhan-
zieher, Schuhlöffel *m*; **~lace** *n* Schnürsenkel *m*;
**~maker** *n* Schuhmacher, Schuster *m*; **~ polish** *n*
Schuhcreme *f*; **~ repairer** *n* Schuster *m*; **~shine** *n*
*(US)* **to have a ~shine** sich *(dat)* die Schuhe putzen
lassen; **~shop** *n* Schuhgeschäft *nt*; **~ size** *n*
Schuhgröße *f*; **~string** *n* **(a)** *(US: ~lace)* Schnürsenkel *m*; **(b)** *(fig)* **to live on a ~string** von der
Hand in den Mund leben; **~string budget** *n* Mini-
budget *nt (col)*; **~tree** *n* (Schuh)spanner *m*.
**shone** [ʃɒn] *pret, ptp of* **shine.**
**shoo** [ʃuː] **1** *interj* sch; *(to dog etc)* pfui; *(to child)*
husch. **2** *vt* **to ~ sb away** jdn verscheuchen.
**shook** [ʃʊk] *pret of* **shake.**
**shoot** [ʃuːt] *(vb: pret, ptp* **shot) 1** *n* **(a)** *(Bot)* Trieb
*m*; *(from seed etc also)* Keim *m*; *(of bushes, trees)*
Schößling *m*; *(young branch)* Reis *nt*. **(b)** *(hunting
expedition)* Jagd *f*; *(~ing party)* Jagdgesellschaft *f*;
*(competition)* (Wett)schießen *nt*.
　**2** *vt* **(a)** *(Mil etc)* schießen; *bullet, gun* abfeuern.
**(b)** *person, animal (hit)* anschießen; *(wound seriously)* niederschießen; *(kill)* erschießen. **to ~ sb
dead** jdn erschießen; **he shot himself** er hat sich erschossen; **he shot himself in the foot** er schoß sich
*(dat)* in den Fuß; *(fig col)* er hat ein Eigentor geschossen *(col)*; **he was shot in the leg** er wurde ins
Bein getroffen; **you'll get shot for doing that!** *(fig
col)* das kann dich Kopf und Kragen kosten! *(col)*.
**(c)** *(throw, propel)* schleudern; *(Sport)* schießen. **to
~ a question at sb** eine Frage auf jdn abfeuern; **to
~ a glance at sb** jdm einen (schnellen) Blick zuwerfen. **(d)** *(Phot) film, scene* drehen; *snapshot* schießen; *subject* aufnehmen.

　**3** *vi* **(a)** schießen; *(as hunter)* jagen. **to ~ to kill**
gezielt schießen; *(police)* einen gezielten
Todesschuß/gezielte Todesschüsse abgeben; **don't
~!** nicht schießen!; **stop or I'll ~!** stehenbleiben
oder ich schieße!; **to ~ at sb/sth** auf jdn/etw schießen; **to ~ at goal** aufs Tor schießen. **(b)** **to ~ into
the lead** an die Spitze vorpreschen; **he shot down
the stairs** er schoß *or* jagte die Treppe hinunter; **to
~ by** *or* **past** vorbeischießen *or* -jagen; **the pain
shot up his leg** der Schmerz durchzuckte sein Bein.
▸**shoot down** *vt sep plane* abschießen; *person* erschießen; *(fig col) person* fertigmachen *(col)*; *suggestion* abschmettern *(col)*; *argument* in der Luft
zerreißen.
▸**shoot off** *vi* davonschießen *(col)*.
▸**shoot out 1** *vi (emerge swiftly)* herausschießen
*(of aus)*. **2** *vt sep* **(a)** *(put out swiftly) hand etc* blitzschnell ausstrecken; *tongue etc* hervorschnellen
(lassen). **(b)** **to ~ it ~** sich *(dat)* ein (Feuer)gefecht
liefern.
▸**shoot up** *vi (hand, prices)* in die Höhe schnellen;
*(grow rapidly) (children, plant)* in die Höhe schießen;
*(new towns, buildings etc)* aus dem Boden schießen.
**shooting** ['ʃuːtɪŋ] *n* **(a)** *(shots)* Schießen *nt*; *(by artillery)* Feuer *nt*. **there was some ~** es wurde geschossen; **there was a ~ last night** gestern nacht ist
jemand erschossen worden. **(b)** *(Sport: Ftbl etc,
with guns)* Schießen *nt*; *(Hunt)* Jagen *nt*, Jagd *f*. **(c)**
*(Film)* Drehen *nt*.
**shooting:** **~ brake** *n (Aut old)* Kombiwagen *m*; **~
gallery** *n* Schießstand *m*; **~ match** *n:* **the whole ~
match** *(col)* der ganze Laden *(col)*; **~ party** *n* Jagdgesellschaft *f*; **~ range** *n* Schießstand *m*; **~ star** *n*
Sternschnuppe *f*; **~ stick** *n* Jagdstuhl *m*.
**shootout** ['ʃuːtaʊt] *n* Schießerei *f*.
**shop** [ʃɒp] **1** *n* **(a)** Geschäft *nt*, Laden *m*; *(esp Brit:
large store)* Kaufhaus *nt*. **I have to go to the ~s** ich
muß einkaufen gehen; **to set up ~** ein Geschäft
eröffnen; **all over the ~** *(col)* überall; *(wrong)* völlig
verkehrt; **to talk ~** über die Arbeit reden; *(professional people also)* fachsimpeln. **(b)** *(work~)* Werkstatt *f*; *(workers)* Arbeiterschaft *f*. **2** *vi* einkaufen,
Einkäufe machen. **to go ~ping** einkaufen gehen. **3**
*vt (Brit col: betray)* **to ~ sb (to sb)** jdn (bei jdm) verpfeifen *(col)*.
▸**shop around** *vi (lit, fig)* sich umsehen *(for nach)*.
**shop:** **~ assistant** *n (Brit)* Verkäufer(in *f*) *m*; **~
floor** *n* **(a)** *(place)* Produktionsstätte *f*; *(for heavier
work)* Werkstatt *f*; **he started off working on the ~
floor** er hat (ganz unten) in der Fabrik *or* Produktion angefangen; **on the ~ floor** in der Werkstatt/
Fabrik; unter den Arbeitern; **(b)** *(Brit: workers)* Arbeiter *pl*, Leute *pl* in der Produktion; **~keeper** *n*
Ladenbesitzer(in *f*), Geschäftsinhaber(in *f*) *m*;
**~lifter** *n* Ladendieb(in *f*) *m*; **~lifting** *n* Ladendieb-
stahl *m*.
**shopper** ['ʃɒpəʳ] *n* Käufer(in *f*) *m*.
**shopping** ['ʃɒpɪŋ] *n (act)* Einkaufen *nt*; *(goods
bought)* Einkäufe *pl*. **to do one's ~** einkaufen, Einkäufe machen.
**shopping:** **~ bag** *n* Einkaufstasche *f*; **~ basket** *n*
Einkaufskorb *m*; **~ centre,** *(US)* **~ center** *n* Einkaufszentrum *nt*; **~ list** *n* Einkaufszettel *m*; **~
mall** *n (esp US)* Einkaufszentrum *nt*; **~ spree** *n*
Einkaufsbummel *m*; **~ street** *n* Geschäftsstraße *f*;
**~ trolley** *n* Einkaufswagen *m*.
**shop:** **~-soiled** *adj (Brit) clothes, furniture* angeschmutzt; *goods, material* leicht beschädigt; **~
steward** *n* (gewerkschaftlicher) Vertrauensmann
*(im Betrieb)*; **~ window** *n (lit, fig)* Schaufenster *nt*;
**~worn** *adj (US)* = **~-soiled.**

**shore¹** [ʃɔːʳ] *n (sea ~, lake ~)* Ufer *nt*; *(beach)* Strand *m*; *(coast)* Küste *f.* **these ~s** *(fig)* dieses Land; **on the ~s of the lake** am Seeufer; **on ~** an Land.

**shore²** *vt (also ~ up)* (ab)stützen; *(fig)* stützen.

**shore:** **~ leave** *n (Naut)* Landurlaub *m*; **~line** *n* Uferlinie *f.*

**shorn** [ʃɔːn] *ptp of* **shear**.

**short** [ʃɔːt] **1** *adj (+er)* **(a)** kurz; *steps also, person* klein. **a ~ way off** nicht weit entfernt; **to be ~ in the leg** *(person)* kurze Beine haben; *(trousers)* zu kurz sein; **a ~ time ago** vor kurzer Zeit, vor kurzem; **in a ~ while** in Kürze; **time is getting/is ~** die Zeit wird/ist knapp; **to take the ~ view of sth** etw auf kurze Sicht betrachten; **in ~ order** *(esp US col)* sofort; **~ and sweet** schön kurz; **the ~ answer is that he refused** kurz gesagt, er lehnte ab; **in ~** kurz gesagt; **Pat is ~ for Patricia** Pat ist die Kurzform von Patricia.

**(b)** *(curt) reply* knapp; *(rude)* barsch, schroff; *manner, person* schroff, kurz angebunden *(col).* **to have a ~ temper** unbeherrscht sein; **to be ~ with sb** jdn schroff behandeln, jdm gegenüber kurz angebunden sein *(col).*

**(c)** *(insufficient)* zuwenig *inv*; *rations* knapp. **to be in ~ supply** knapp sein; *(Comm)* beschränkt lieferbar sein; **to be ~ (in ~ supply)** knapp sein; *(shot, throw)* nicht weit genug sein; **we are (five/£3) ~** wir haben (fünf/£3) zuwenig, uns *(dat)* fehlen fünf/£3; **we are ~ of books** wir haben zuwenig Bücher; **to be ~ of time** wenig Zeit haben; **I'm a bit ~ (of cash)** *(col)* ich bin etwas knapp bei Kasse *(col)*; **we are £2,000 ~ of our target** wir liegen £2.000 unter unserem Ziel; **not far ~ of £100** nicht viel weniger als £100, knapp unter £100; **to be ~ on experience** wenig Erfahrung haben.

**2** *adv* **(a) to fall ~** *(arrow, missile etc)* vor dem Ziel landen. **that's where the book falls ~** daran fehlt es dem Buch; **to fall ~ of sth** etw nicht erreichen; *of expectations* etw nicht erfüllen; **it falls far ~ of what we require** das bleibt weit hinter unseren Bedürfnissen zurück; **to go ~ (of money/food etc)** zuwenig (Geld/zu essen *etc)* haben; **we are running ~ (of petrol/time)** wir haben nicht mehr viel (Benzin/Zeit); **I'm running ~ of ideas** mir gehen die Ideen aus; **my patience is running ~** meine Geduld ist bald zu Ende; **to sell sb ~** *(in shop)* jdm zuwenig geben; *(betray, cheat)* jdn betrügen.

**(b)** *(abruptly, suddenly)* plötzlich, abrupt. **to stop ~** *(while driving)* plötzlich stehenbleiben; *(while talking)* plötzlich *or* unvermittelt innehalten; **I'd stop ~ of** *or* **at murder** vor Mord würde ich haltmachen.

**(c) ~ of** *(except)* außer *(+dat)*; **it is nothing ~ of robbery** das ist glatter Diebstahl; **nothing ~ of a revolution can** ... nur eine Revolution kann ...; **it's little ~ of madness** das grenzt an Wahnsinn; **I don't see what you can do ~ of asking him yourself** ich sehe keine andere Möglichkeit, als daß Sie ihn selbst fragen; **~ of telling him a lie** ... außer ihn zu belügen ...

**3** *(~ circuit)* Kurzschluß, Kurze(r) *(col) m*; *(col: ~ drink)* Kurze(r) *m (col).*

**4** *vt (Elec)* kurzschließen.

**5** *vi (Elec)* einen Kurzschluß haben.

**shortage** [ʃɔːtɪdʒ] *n (of goods, objects)* Knappheit *f* no *pl (of an +dat)*; *(of people)* Mangel *m* no *pl (of an +dat)*. **the housing ~** die Wohnungsknappheit; **a ~ of staff** Personalmangel *m.*

**short:** **~bread** *n* Mürb(e)teiggebäck *nt*; **~cake** *n (Brit:* **~bread)** Mürb(e)teiggebäck *nt*; *(US: sponge)* Biskuittörtchen *nt*; **~-change** *vt to* **~-change sb**

jdm zuwenig herausgeben; *(fig col)* jdn übers Ohr hauen *(col)*; **~-circuit 1** *n* Kurzschluß *m*; **2** *vt* kurzschließen; **3** *vi* einen Kurzschluß haben; **~coming** *n (esp pl)* Mangel *m*; *(of person)* Fehler *m*; **~crust** *n (also* **~crust pastry)** *(esp Brit)* Mürbeteig *m*; **~ cut** *n* Abkürzung *f*; *(easy solution)* Patentlösung *f*; **~ drink** *n* hochprozentiges Getränk.

**shorten** [ʃɔːtn] **1** *vt* verkürzen; *dress, rope* kürzer machen; *book, syllabus etc* kürzen. **2** *vi (days)* kürzer werden.

**short:** **~fall** *n* Defizit *nt*; **~hand** *n* Kurzschrift, Stenographie *f*; **in ~hand** in Kurzschrift; **to write ~hand** stenographieren; **to take sth down in ~hand** etw stenographieren; **~-handed** *adj* **to be ~-handed** zu wenig Personal haben; **~hand notebook** *n* Stenoblock *m*; **~hand typist** *n (Brit)* Stenotypist(in *f) m*; **~-haul** *adj aircraft, flight* Kurzstrecken-; *transport* Nah-; **~-haul routes** kurze Strecken; **~ list** *n (esp Brit)* Auswahlliste *f*; **to be on the ~ list** in der engeren Wahl sein; **~-list** *vt (esp Brit)* **to ~-list sb** jdn in die engere Wahl ziehen; **~-lived** *adj (lit, fig)* kurzlebig; *protests, attempts* nicht lange andauernd; **to be ~-lived** *(success, happiness)* von kurzer Dauer sein.

**shortly** [ʃɔːtlɪ] *adv* **(a)** *(soon)* bald, in Kürze; *after, before* kurz. **(b)** *(curtly)* barsch.

**shortness** [ʃɔːtnɪs] *n* Kürze *f*; *(of person)* Kleinheit *f*; *(shortage)* Knappheit *f*; *(curtness)* Schroffheit *f.*

**short:** **~ pastry** *n* Mürbeteig *m*; **~-range** *adj aircraft, missile etc* Kurzstrecken-; *gun* Nahkampf-; *planning, forecast* kurzfristig.

**shorts** [ʃɔːts] *npl* **(a)** Shorts *pl*, kurze Hose(n *pl*). **(b)** *(esp US: underpants)* Unterhose *f.*

**short:** **~-sighted** *adj*, **~-sightedly** *adv (lit, fig)* kurzsichtig; **~-sightedness** *n (lit, fig)* Kurzsichtigkeit *f*; **~-sleeved** *adj* kurzärmelig; **~-staffed** *adj* **to be ~-staffed** zuwenig Personal haben; **~-stay parking** *n* Kurzparken *nt*; **~ story** *n* Kurzgeschichte, Short story *f*; **~-tempered** *adj (in general)* unbeherrscht; *(in a bad temper)* gereizt; **to be ~-tempered with sb** mit jdm ungeduldig sein; **~ term** *n* **in the ~ term** auf kurze Sicht; **~-term** *adj* kurzfristig; **~ time (working)** *n* Kurzarbeit *f*; **to be on ~ time (working)** kurzarbeiten, Kurzarbeit haben; **~wave 1** *n (also* **~wave radio)** Kurzwelle *f*; **2** *adj transmission* auf Kurzwelle.

**shot¹** [ʃɒt] **1** *pret, ptp of* **shoot**.

**2** *n* **(a)** *(from gun, bow etc)* Schuß *m.* **to fire** *or* **take a ~ at sb/sth** einen Schuß auf jdn/etw abfeuern *or* abgeben; **he's a good/bad ~** er ist ein guter/ schlechter Schütze. **(b)** *(attempt)* Versuch *m.* **at the first ~** *(col)* auf Anhieb *(col)*; **to take a ~ (at it)** *(try)* es *(mal)* versuchen; *(guess)* (auf gut Glück) raten. **(c)** *(col: quickly)* **like a ~** *run away* wie der Blitz *(col)*; *do sth* sofort; *agree* sofort, ohne zu überlegen. **(d)** *(injection)* Spritze *f*; *(immunization)* Impfung *f.* **to give a company a ~ in the arm** *(fig)* einer Firma eine Finanzspritze geben. **(e)** *(Sport) (Ftbl, Hockey etc)* Schuß *m*; *(throw)* Wurf *m*; *(Tennis, Golf)* Schlag *m.* **to take a ~ at goal** aufs Tor schießen. **(f)** *(~-putting)* **the ~** *(discipline)* Kugelstoßen *nt*; *(weight)* die Kugel; **to put the ~** kugelstoßen. **(g)** *(Phot)* Aufnahme *f.*

**shot²** *adj* **(a)** *(variegated)* durchzogen *(with* mit*)*; *silk* changierend. **(b)** *(col: rid)* **to be/get ~ of sb/sth** jdn/etw los sein/loswerden.

**shot:** **~gun** *n* Schrotflinte *f*; **~gun wedding** *n* Mußheirat *f*; **~-put** *n (event)* Kugelstoßen *nt*; **~-putter** *n* Kugelstoßer(in *f) m.*

**should** [ʃʊd] *pret of* **shall** *modal aux vb* **(a)** *(expressing duty, advisability, command)* **you ~ do that** du solltest das tun; **you ~n't do that** Sie sollten das nicht tun; **I ~ have done it** ich hätte es tun sollen or müssen; **I ~n't have done it** ich hätte es nicht tun sollen or dürfen; **he ~ know that it's wrong to lie** er sollte or müßte wissen, daß man nicht lügen darf; **you really ~ see that film** den Film sollten or müssen Sie wirklich sehen; **~ I go too?** – **yes you ~** sollte ich auch gehen? – ja, das sollten Sie schon; **was it a good film?** – **I ~ think it was** war der Film gut? – und ob; **he's coming to apologize** – **I ~ think so** er will sich entschuldigen – das möchte ich auch hoffen; ... **and I ~ know** ... und ich müßte es ja wissen; **how ~ I know?** woher soll ich das wissen?

(b) (expressing probability) **he ~ be there by now** er müßte eigentlich schon da sein; **why ~ he suspect me?** warum sollte er mich verdächtigen?; **this book ~ help you** dieses Buch wird Ihnen bestimmt helfen.

(c) (in tentative statements) **I ~n't like to say** ich möchte mich nicht festlegen; **I ~ hardly have called him an idiot** ich hätte ihn wohl kaum einen Idioten genannt; **I ~ think there were about 40** ich schätze, daß etwa 40 dort waren; **I ~ like to disagree** da möchte ich widersprechen; **I ~ like to know** ich wüßte gern; **I ~ like to apply for the job** ich würde mich gern um die Stelle bewerben; **thanks, I ~ like to** danke, gern.

(d) (subjunc, conditional) **I ~ go if ...** ich würde gehen, wenn ...; **we ~ have come if ...** wir wären gekommen, wenn ...; **I don't know why he ~ behave so strangely** ich weiß nicht, warum er sich so eigenartig benimmt; **if he ~ come, ~ he come** falls er kommen sollte, sollte er kommen; **I ~n't be surprised if he comes** or **were to come** ich wäre keineswegs überrascht, wenn er kommen würde; **I ~n't (do it) if I were you** ich würde das an Ihrer Stelle nicht tun; **I ~n't worry about it** ich würde mir darüber keine Gedanken machen; **it is necessary that he ~ be told** es ist nötig, daß man es ihm sagt.

**shoulder** ['ʃəʊldəʳ] **1** n (also of meat) Schulter f. **to shrug one's ~s** mit den Schultern or Achseln zucken; **to have broad ~s** (lit) breite Schultern haben; (fig) einen breiten Rücken haben; **to cry on sb's ~** sich an jds Brust (dat) ausweinen; **~ to ~** Schulter an Schulter; **he's head and ~s above the rest** er ist einen ganzen Kopf größer als die anderen; **to put one's ~ to the wheel** (fig) sich ins Zeug legen. **2** vt **(a)** schultern, auf die Schulter nehmen; (fig) responsibilities auf sich (acc) nehmen; expense tragen. **(b)** (push) (mit der Schulter) stoßen. **to ~ sb aside** (lit) jdn zur Seite stoßen.

**shoulder: ~ bag** n Umhängetasche f; **~ blade** n Schulterblatt nt; **~-length** adj hair schulterlang; **~ strap** n (Mil) Schulterklappe f; (of dress) Träger m; (of bag etc) (Schulter)riemen m.

**shouldn't** ['ʃʊdnt] = **should not**.

**shout** [ʃaʊt] **1** n Ruf, Schrei m. **a ~ of protest/pain** ein Protestruf m/Schmerzensschrei m; **a ~ of excitement** ein aufgeregter Schrei; **~s of applause/laughter** Beifallsrufe pl/brüllendes Gelächter; **to give a ~** einen Schrei ausstoßen; **to give sb a ~** jdn rufen; **give me a ~ when you're ready** (col) sag mir Bescheid, wenn du fertig bist. **2** vt schreien; (call) rufen; order brüllen. **to ~ abuse at sb** jdn (laut) beschimpfen. **to ~ a warning to sb** jdm eine Warnung zurufen. **3** vi (call out) rufen; (very loudly) schreien; (angrily, commanding) brüllen. **to ~ for sb/sth** nach jdm/etw rufen or schreien; **to ~ at sb** jdn anschreien or anbrüllen; **to ~ for help** um Hilfe rufen. **4** vr **to ~ oneself hoarse** sich heiser schreien.

▶**shout down** vt sep person niederbrüllen.
▶**shout out 1** vi einen Schrei ausstoßen; (in pain, rage, protest) aufschreien. **2** vt sep ausrufen; order brüllen.

**shouting** ['ʃaʊtɪŋ] n (act) Schreien nt; (sound) Geschrei nt. **it's all over bar the ~** (col) es ist so gut wie gelaufen (col).

**shove** [ʃʌv] **1** n Schubs (col), Stoß m. **to give sb a ~** jdn schubsen (col) or stoßen; **to give sth a ~** etw rücken; door gegen etw stoßen; car etw anschieben. **2** vt **(a)** (push) schieben; (with one short push) stoßen, schubsen (col); (jostle) drängen. **to ~ one's way forward** sich nach vorn durchdrängen. **(b)** (col: put) **to ~ sth on(to) sth** etw auf etw (acc) werfen (col); **to ~ sth in(to) sth/between sth** etw in etw (acc)/zwischen etw (acc) stecken; **he ~d a book into my hand** er drückte mir ein Buch in die Hand. **3** vi stoßen; (to move sth) schieben; (jostle) drängeln. **to ~ past sb** sich an jdm vorbeidrängen.

▶**shove off** vi (col) abschieben (col).
▶**shove over** (col) **1** vt sep rüberwerfen (col). **2** vi (also shove up) rutschen.

**shovel** ['ʃʌvl] **1** n Schaufel f; (with long handle also) Schippe f. **2** vt schaufeln; coal, snow also schippen. **to ~ food into one's mouth** (col) Essen in sich (acc) hineinschaufeln (col).

**shovelful** ['ʃʌvlfʊl] n Schaufel f. **a ~ of coal** eine Schaufel Kohle.

**show** [ʃəʊ] (vb: pret ~ed, ptp ~n) **1** n **(a)** (display) a fine **~ of roses** eine Rosenpracht; **~ of force** Machtdemonstration f; **to have a ~ of hands** eine Abstimmung per Handzeichen vornehmen.

**(b)** (outward appearance) Schau f. **to do sth for ~** etw tun, um Eindruck zu machen; **to make a great ~ of being impressed/overworked** sich (dat) ganz den Anschein geben, beeindruckt/überarbeitet zu sein; **without any ~ of emotion** ohne irgendwelche Gefühle zu zeigen; **it was all ~** es war alles nur Schau (col).

**(c)** (exhibition) Ausstellung f. **flower/dog ~** Blumen-/Hundeschau f; **to be on ~** ausgestellt sein.

**(d)** (Theat) Aufführung f; (TV, variety ~) Show f; (Rad) Sendung f; (Film) Vorstellung f. **to go to a ~** ins Theater gehen; **the ~ must go on** (fig) es muß trotz allem weitergehen.

**(e)** (col: organization) Laden m (col). **he runs the ~** er schmeißt hier den Laden (col); **to give the (whole) ~ away** alles verraten.

**(f)** good **~!** (dated col) bravo!; **it's a poor ~ when ...** (col) es ist ein schwaches Bild, wenn ...; **to put up a good ~** eine gute Leistung zeigen.

**2** vt **(a)** zeigen; (at exhibition also) ausstellen; passport vorzeigen; profit verzeichnen; kindness, favour erweisen; courage also, loyalty, taste beweisen; proof erbringen. **to ~ sth to sb** jdm etw zeigen; **~ me how to do it** zeigen Sie mir, wie man das macht; **to ~ one's face** sich zeigen; **he had nothing to ~ for it** er hatte am Ende nichts vorzuweisen; **I'll ~ him!** (col) dem werd' ich's zeigen!; **it ~s that ...** es zeigt, daß ...; **as ~n in the illustration** wie in der Illustration dargestellt; **the roads are ~n in red** die Straßen sind rot (eingezeichnet); **it just goes to ~ that ...** das zeigt doch nur, daß ...; **it was ~ing signs of rain** es sah nach Regen aus; **to ~ signs of wear** Abnutzungserscheinungen aufweisen; **she's beginning to ~ her age** man sieht ihr allmählich das Alter an; **the carpet ~s the dirt** auf dem Teppich sieht man den Schmutz; **to ~ sb the way** jdm den Weg zeigen; **to ~ sb in/out** jdn hereinbringen/hinausbegleiten; **to ~ sb to his seat** jdn an seinen Platz bringen; **to ~ sb to the door**

jdn zur Tür bringen; *(eject)* jdm die Tür weisen; **they were ~n over** *or* **around the factory** sie wurden in der Fabrik herumgeführt.

(b) *(prove)* beweisen. **this ~s him to be a thief** das beweist, daß er ein Dieb ist.

**3** *vi* (a) *(be visible)* zu sehen sein, sichtbar sein; *(petticoat etc)* vorsehen, rausgucken *(col)*; *(film)* gezeigt werden, laufen; *(exhibit: artist)* ausstellen. **it doesn't ~** man sieht es nicht; **the dirt doesn't ~** man sieht den Schmutz nicht; **his anger ~ed in his eyes** man konnte ihm seinen Ärger von den Augen ablesen; **to ~ through** durchscheinen. (b) *(prove)* **it just goes to ~!** da sieht man's mal wieder!

►**show in** *vt sep* hereinbringen.

►**show off 1** *vi* angeben *(to, in front of* vor +*dat)*. **2** *vt sep* *knowledge, medal* angeben mit; *new car, baby etc* vorführen *(to sb* jdm*)*.

►**show out** *vt sep* hinausbegleiten.

►**show up 1** *vi* (a) *(be seen)* zu sehen *or* zu erkennen sein; *(stand out)* hervorstechen. **the tower ~ed ~ clearly against the sky** der Turm zeichnete sich deutlich gegen den Himmel ab; **to ~ ~ well/badly** *(fig)* ein gute/schlechte Figur machen. (b) *(col: turn up)* auftauchen, sich blicken lassen *(col)*. **2** *vt sep* (a) *(highlight)* (deutlich) erkennen lassen. (b) *(reveal)* zum Vorschein bringen; *sb's character, intentions* deutlich zeigen; *impostor* entlarven; *fraud* aufdecken; *(humiliate)* bloßstellen; *(shame)* blamieren.

**show: ~biz** ['ʃəʊbɪz] *(col)*, **~ business** *n* Showbusiness, Showgeschäft *nt*; **~case** *n* Schaukasten *m*, Vitrine *f*; *(fig)* Schaufenster *nt*; **~down** *n (col)* Kraftprobe, Machtprobe *f*; **to have a ~down with sb** sich mit jdm auseinandersetzen.

**shower** ['ʃaʊəʳ] **1** *n* (a) *(of rain etc)* Schauer *m*; *(of arrows, blows etc)* Hagel *m*; *(of questions)* Schwall *m*. (b) *(~ bath)* Dusche *f*. **to take** *or* **have a ~** duschen. (c) *(US col: party)* Party, *auf der jeder ein Geschenk für den Ehrengast mitbringt*; *(for bride-to-be)* ≈ Polterabend *m*. **2** *vt* **to ~ sb with sth** *with curses, blows* etw auf jdn niederprasseln lassen; *with honours, presents, abuse* jdn mit etw überschütten. **3** *vi (wash)* duschen.

**shower: ~ cap** *n* Duschhaube *f*; **~ curtain** *n* Duschvorhang *m*; **~ gel** *n* Duschgel *nt*; **~proof** *adj* regenfest.

**showery** ['ʃaʊərɪ] *adj* regnerisch.

**show: ~girl** *n* Revuegirl *nt*; **~ground** *n* Ausstellungsgelände *nt*; *(for circus)* Zirkusgelände *nt*; **~ house** *n* Musterhaus *nt*.

**showily** ['ʃaʊɪlɪ] *adv* protzig; *behave* theatralisch. **~ dressed** aufgeputzt.

**showing** ['ʃaʊɪŋ] *n* (a) *(exhibition)* Ausstellung *f*. (b) *(performance)* Aufführung *f*; *(of film)* Vorstellung *f*; *(of programme)* Ausstrahlung *f*. (c) *(standard of performance)* **to make a good/poor ~** eine gute/ schwache Leistung zeigen.

**show: ~-jumper** *n (rider)* Springreiter(in *f*) *m*; *(horse)* Springpferd *nt*; **~-jumping** *n* Springreiten *nt*.

**showman** ['ʃəʊmən] *n, pl* **-men** [-mən] Showman *m*; *(fig)* Schauspieler *m*.

**showmanship** ['ʃəʊmənʃɪp] *n* (Talent *nt* für) effektvolle Darbietung.

**shown** [ʃəʊn] *ptp of* **show**.

**show: ~-off** *n (col)* Angeber(in *f*) *m*; **~piece** *n* Schaustück *nt*; *(fine example)* Paradestück *nt*; **~place** *n (tourist attraction)* Sehenswürdigkeit *f*; **~room** *n* Ausstellungsraum *m*; **~ trial** *n* Schauprozeß *m*.

**showy** ['ʃaʊɪ] *adj (+er)* protzig; *person, colour* auf-

fallend; *manner* theatralisch; *production, decor* bombastisch.

**shrank** [ʃræŋk] *pret of* **shrink**.

**shrapnel** ['ʃræpnl] *n* Schrapnell *nt*.

**shred** [ʃred] **1** *n (scrap)* Fetzen *m*; *(of vegetable, meat)* Stückchen *nt*; *(fig)* Spur *f*; *(of truth)* Fünkchen *nt*. **not a ~ of evidence** keinerlei Beweis; **to be in ~s** zerfetzt sein; **to tear sth to ~s** etw in Stücke reißen; *(fig)* etw verreißen; *argument* etw total zerpflücken; **to tear sb to ~s** keinen guten Faden an jdm lassen. **2** *vt* (a) *food, paper* schnitzeln; *carrot* raspeln; *cabbage* hobeln; *(in shredder)* paper in den Papierwolf geben. (b) *(tear)* in kleine Stücke reißen; *(with claws)* zerfetzen.

**shredder** ['ʃredəʳ] *n (grater)* Reibe *f*; *(in food processor)* Schnitzelwerk *nt*; *(for waste paper)* Reißwolf *m*; *(for garden waste)* Häcksler *m*.

**shrew** [ʃruː] *n* Spitzmaus *f*; *(fig)* Xanthippe *f*.

**shrewd** [ʃruːd] *adj (+er) person* gewitzt, clever *(col)*; *businessman also, plan* clever *(col)*, raffiniert; *investment, argument* taktisch geschickt; *assessment, mind* scharf. **that was a ~ guess** das war gut geraten; **I have a ~ idea that ...** ich habe so das Gefühl, daß ...

**shrewdly** ['ʃruːdlɪ] *adv* geschickt, clever *(col)*.

**shrewdness** ['ʃruːdnɪs] *n see adj* Gewitztheit *f*; Cleverness *(col)*, Raffiniertheit *f*; Geschicktheit *f*; Schärfe *f*; *(of guess)* Treffsicherheit *f*.

**shriek** [ʃriːk] **1** *n* (schriller) Schrei; *(of whistle)* schriller Ton; *(of brakes)* Quietschen *nt*. **a ~ of pain/horror** ein Schmerzens-/Schreckensschrei *m*; **~s of laughter** kreischendes Lachen; **to give a ~** einen schrillen Schrei ausstoßen. **2** *vi* aufschreien. **to ~ at sb** jdn ankreischen; **to ~ with laughter** vor Lachen quietschen.

**shrift** [ʃrɪft] *n* **to give sb/sth short ~** jdn/etw kurz abfertigen.

**shrill** [ʃrɪl] *adj (+er)* schrill.

**shrimp** [ʃrɪmp] *n* Garnele, Krevette *f*.

**shrine** [ʃraɪn] *n* Schrein *m*; *(tomb)* Grabstätte *f*; *(chapel)* Grabkapelle *f*; *(altar)* Grabaltar *m*.

**shrink** [ʃrɪŋk] *(vb: pret* **shrank**, *ptp* **shrunk***)* **1** *vt* einlaufen lassen. **2** *vi* (a) schrumpfen; *(clothes etc)* einlaufen; *(wood)* schwinden; *(fig) (popularity)* abnehmen, schwinden; *(trade)* zurückgehen. **~-proof** nicht einlaufend. (b) *(fig: recoil)* **to ~ from doing/ saying sth** davor zurückschrecken, etw zu tun/sich davor scheuen, etw zu sagen; **to ~ from the truth** vor der Wahrheit die Augen verschließen; **to ~ back** zurückweichen; **to ~ away from sb** vor jdm zurückweichen.

**shrinkage** ['ʃrɪŋkɪdʒ] *n (of material, clothes)* Einlaufen *nt*; *(fig: of economic growth etc)* Rückgang *m*; *(Comm)* Einbußen *pl*.

**shrink: ~proof, ~-resistant** *adj* schrumpfbeständig; **~-wrap** *vt* einschweißen; **~-wrapping** *n (process)* Einschweißen *nt*; *(material)* Einschweißfolie *f*.

**shrivel** ['ʃrɪvl] *(also ~ up)* **1** *vt plants (frost, dryness)* welk werden lassen; *(heat)* austrocknen; *skin, fruit* runzlig werden lassen; *nylon* zusammenschrumpfen lassen. **2** *vi* schrumpfen; *(balloon, nylon)* zusammenschrumpfen; *(plants)* welk werden; *(through heat)* austrocknen; *(fruit, skin)* runzlig werden.

**shroud** [ʃraʊd] **1** *n* (a) Leichentuch *nt*. (b) *(fig)* Schleier *m*. **a ~ of mist** ein Nebelschleier *m*. **2** *vt (fig)* hüllen. **the whole thing is ~ed in mystery** die ganze Angelegenheit ist von einem Geheimnis umgeben.

**Shrove Tuesday** [ˌʃrəʊvˈtjuːzdeɪ] *n* Faschingsdienstag *(S Ger)*, Fastnachtsdienstag *m*.

**shrub** [ʃrʌb] n Busch, Strauch m.
**shrubbery** ['ʃrʌbərɪ] n (shrub bed) Strauchrabatte f; (shrubs) Büsche, Sträucher pl.
**shrug** [ʃrʌg] 1 n Achselzucken nt no pl. **to give a ~** die or mit den Achseln zucken. 2 vt shoulders zucken (mit).
► **shrug off** vt sep mit einem Achselzucken abtun; illness abschütteln.
**shrunk** [ʃrʌŋk] ptp of **shrink**.
**shrunken** ['ʃrʌŋkən] adj (ein)geschrumpft. old person geschrumpft. **~ head** Schrumpfkopf m.
**shudder** ['ʃʌdər] 1 n Schauer, Schauder m. **to give a ~** (person) sich schütteln, erschaudern (geh); (ground) beben. 2 vi (person) schaudern, schauern; (house, ground) beben, zittern; (car, train) rütteln. **the train ~ed to a halt** der Zug kam rüttelnd zum Stehen; **I ~ to think** mir graut, wenn ich nur daran denke.
**shuffle** ['ʃʌfl] 1 n (a) **to walk with a ~** schlurfen. (b) (Cards) **to give the cards a ~** die Karten mischen. 2 vt (a) **he ~d his feet as he walked** er schlurfte beim Gehen. (b) cards mischen. **he ~d the papers on his desk together** er raffte die Papiere auf seinem Schreibtisch zusammen. 3 vi (walk) schlurfen.
**shun** [ʃʌn] vt meiden; publicity, light scheuen.
**shunt** [ʃʌnt] vt (a) (Rail) rangieren. **they ~ed the train off the main line** sie schoben den Zug auf ein Nebengleis. (b) (col) person schieben.
**shunter** ['ʃʌntər] n Rangierlokomotive f.
**shunting** ['ʃʌntɪŋ] n Rangieren nt. **~ engine** Rangierlokomotive f; **~ yard** Rangierbahnhof m.
**shush** [ʃuʃ] 1 interj pst, sch. 2 vt zum Schweigen auffordern.
**shut** [ʃʌt] (vb: pret, ptp ~) 1 vt (a) zumachen; door, book, shop also schließen. **they ~ the office at 6.00** das Büro wird um 18⁰⁰ geschlossen; **~ your eyes** mach die Augen zu; **~ your mouth** (col!) or face (col!) halt's Maul! (col!). (b) **to ~ sb/sth in(to) sth** jdn/etw in etw (dat) einschließen; **she was ~ in the cellar** sie wurde im Keller eingesperrt; **to ~ one's fingers in the door** sich (dat) die Finger in der Tür einklemmen.
2 vi (door, window, box) schließen, zugehen; (shop, factory) schließen, geschlossen werden. **it ~s very easily** es läßt sich ganz leicht schließen or zumachen (col); **when do the shops ~?** wann schließen die Geschäfte?, wann machen die Geschäfte zu? (col).
3 adj geschlossen, zu pred (col). **sorry sir, we're ~** wir haben leider geschlossen; **the door swung ~** die Tür schlug zu; **to find the door ~** vor verschlossener Tür stehen.
► **shut away** vt sep (put away) wegschließen; (in sth) einschließen (in in +dat); (keep locked away) books, papers etc aufbewahren; (safely) verwahren; persons verborgen halten.
► **shut down** 1 vt sep shop, factory zumachen (col), schließen. **the airport is completely ~ ~** der Flughafen hat den gesamten Flugverkehr eingestellt. 2 vi (shop, factory etc) zumachen (col), schließen. **the television service ~s ~ at midnight** um Mitternacht ist Sendeschluß im Fernsehen.
► **shut in** vt sep einschließen (also fig), einsperren (col) (prep obj, to in +dat).
► **shut off** vt sep (a) water, electricity abstellen; light, engine ab- or ausschalten; street (ab)sperren. **the kettle ~s itself ~** der Wasserkessel schaltet von selbst ab. (b) (isolate) (ab)trennen. **I feel ~ ~ from civilization** ich komme mir von der Zivilisation abgeschnitten vor.
► **shut out** vt sep (a) person, oneself aussperren (of

aus); view versperren; light nicht hereinlassen (of in +acc). **don't ~ the sun** ~ laß doch die Sonne herein! (b) (fig) foreign competition ausschalten; memory, foreign broadcasts unterdrücken. **I can't ~ her ~ of my life** sie spielt immer noch eine Rolle in meinem Leben.
► **shut up** 1 vt sep (a) house verschließen. **to ~ ~ shop** (lit) das Geschäft schließen; (fig) Feierabend machen (col). (b) (imprison) einsperren. (c) (col: silence) zum Schweigen bringen. **that'll soon ~ him ~** das wird ihm schon den Mund stopfen (col). 2 vi (col) den Mund halten (col). **~ ~!** halt die Klappe! (col!), halt's Maul! (col!).
**shut: ~down** n Stillegung f; (TV, Rad) Sendeschluß m; **~-eye** n (col) Schlaf m; **~-in** adj (a) (US) ans Haus/ans Bett gefesselt; (b) **a ~-in feeling** ein Gefühl des Eingeschlossenseins.
**shutter** ['ʃʌtər] 1 n (Fenster)laden m; (Phot) Verschluß m. **to put up the ~s** (fig) den Laden dichtmachen (col); **~ release** (Phot) Auslöser m; **~ speed** Verschlußzeit f. 2 vt **~ed windows** geschlossene (Fenster)läden.
**shuttle** ['ʃʌtl] 1 n (a) (of loom etc) Schiffchen nt. (b) (plane, train etc) Pendelflugzeug nt/-zug m etc; (space ~) Raumtransporter m. 2 vt passengers, goods hin- und hertransportieren.
**shuttle: ~cock** n Federball m; **~ diplomacy** n Pendeldiplomatie f; **~ service** n Pendelverkehr m.
**shy** [ʃaɪ] 1 adj (+er) (a) schüchtern; animal scheu. **don't be ~** nur keine Hemmungen! (col!); **to be ~ of/with sb** Hemmungen vor/gegenüber jdm haben; **to be ~ of doing sth** Hemmungen haben, etw zu tun; **to feel ~** schüchtern sein. (b) (esp US col: short) **we're $3 ~** wir haben 3 Dollar zuwenig. 2 vi (horse) scheuen (at vor +dat).
► **shy away** vi (horse) zurückscheuen; (person) zurückweichen. **to ~ ~ from sb/sth** vor jdm zurückweichen/vor etw (dat) zurückschrecken.
**shyly** ['ʃaɪlɪ] adv see adj schüchtern; scheu.
**shyness** ['ʃaɪnɪs] n Schüchternheit f; (esp of animals) Scheu f.
**shyster** ['ʃaɪstər] n (US col) Gauner m; (lawyer) Rechtsverdreher m (col).
**Siamese** [,saɪə'miːz] 1 adj siamesisch. **~ cat** Siamkatze f, siamesische Katze; **~ twins** siamesische Zwillinge pl. 2 n (dated) Siamese m, Siamesin f.
**Siberia** [saɪ'bɪərɪə] n Sibirien nt.
**Siberian** [saɪ'bɪərɪən] 1 adj sibirisch. 2 n Sibirier(in f) m.
**sibling** ['sɪblɪŋ] n Bruder m/Schwester f. **~s** Geschwister pl.
**Sicilian** [sɪ'sɪlɪən] 1 adj sizilianisch. 2 n Sizilianer(in f) m.
**Sicily** ['sɪsɪlɪ] n Sizilien nt.
**sick** [sɪk] adj (+er) (a) (ill) krank (also fig). **the ~** die Kranken pl; **to be (off) ~** (wegen Krankheit) fehlen; **to fall** or **take ~** krank werden; **to go ~** krank werden; **to make sb ~** (fig col) jdn (ganz) krank machen (col); **it makes you ~ the way he's always right** (col) es ist zum Auswachsen, daß er immer recht hat (col); **to be ~ at** or **about sth** (fig) (disgusted) von etw angewidert sein; (upset) wegen etw geknickt sein. (b) (Brit: vomiting) **to be ~** brechen, sich übergeben; (esp cat, baby) spucken; **I felt ~** mir war schlecht or übel; **that food makes me ~** von dem Essen wird mir übel or schlecht. (c) (col: fed up) **to be ~ of doing sth** es satt haben, etw zu tun; **I'm ~ and tired of it** ich habe davon die Nase voll (col), ich habe es gründlich satt. (d) (col) joke etc geschmacklos; person abartig, pervers.
► **sick up** vt sep (Brit) erbrechen.

**sick:** ~**bay** *n* Krankenrevier *nt*; ~**bed** *n* Kranken-
bett *nt*.
**sicken** ['sɪkn] **1** *vt (turn sb's stomach)* anekeln, anwidern; *(upset greatly)* erschüttern, krank machen
*(col)*; *(disgust)* anwidern. **2** *vi* **he's definitely** ~**ing
for something** er wird bestimmt krank; **to** ~ **of sth**
*(tire)* einer Sache *(gen)* müde sein *(geh)*, etw satt
haben.
**sickening** ['sɪknɪŋ] *adj (lit)* ekelerregend; *smell, sight
also* widerlich, ekelhaft; *(upsetting)* entsetzlich, erschütternd; *(disgusting, annoying)* ekelhaft; *treatment* abscheulich; *delays* unerträglich.
**sickle** ['sɪkl] *n* Sichel *f*.
**sick:** ~ **leave** *n* **to be on** ~ **leave** krank geschrieben
sein; ~ **list** *n* **to be on/off the** ~ **list** auf der/nicht
mehr auf der Krankenliste stehen; *(with injury)* auf
der/nicht mehr auf der Verletztenliste stehen.
**sickly** ['sɪklɪ] *adj (+er) person* kränklich; *complexion,
light* blaß; *smell, taste, colour* widerlich, ekelhaft;
*smile* matt; *grin* schwach; *climate* ungesund.
**sickness** ['sɪknɪs] *n (Med)* Krankheit *f (also fig)*;
*(nausea)* Übelkeit *f*; *(Brit: vomiting)* Erbrechen *nt*;
*(of joke etc)* Geschmacklosigkeit *f*. ~ **benefit** *(Brit)*
Krankengeld *nt*.
**sick:** ~**pay** *n* Lohnfortzahlung *f* im Krankheitsfall;
~**room** *n* Krankenzimmer *nt*.
**side** [saɪd] **1** *n* **(a)** Seite *f*; *(of cave, trench, mining
shaft, boat, caravan)* Wand *f*; *(of cliff, mountain)*
Hang *m*. **this** ~ **up!** *(on parcel etc)* oben!; **right/
wrong** ~ *(of cloth)* rechte/linke Seite.
  **(b)** *(edge)* Rand *m*. **at the** ~ **of the road** am Straßenrand; **at the** ~ **of the plate** auf dem Tellerrand.
  **(c)** *(not back or front)* Seite *f*. **by/at the** ~ **of sth**
seitlich von etw; **to drive on the left** ~ **of the road**
auf der linken Straßenseite fahren; **the path goes
down the** ~ **of the house** der Weg führt seitlich am
Haus entlang; **it's this/the other** ~ **of London** *(out of
town)* es ist auf dieser/auf der anderen Seite Londons; *(in town)* es ist in diesem Teil/am anderen
Ende von London; **from all** ~**s** von allen Seiten;
**from** ~ **to** ~ von einer Seite zur anderen; **he moved
to one** ~ er trat zur Seite; **to put sth on one** ~ etw
beiseite legen; *(shopkeeper)* etw zurücklegen; **to
take sb on one** ~ jdn beiseite nehmen; **just this** ~
**of the boundary** (noch) diesseits der Grenze; **on the
other** ~ **of the boundary** jenseits der Grenze; **with
one's head on one** ~ mit zur Seite geneigtem Kopf;
**by sb's** ~ neben jdm; ~ **by** ~ nebeneinander, Seite
an Seite; **to stand/sit** ~ **by** ~ **with sb** direkt neben
jdm stehen/sitzen; **I'll be by your** ~ *(fig)* ich werde
Ihnen zur Seite stehen; **to be on the safe** ~ sichergehen; **we'll take an extra £50 just to be on the safe**
~ wir nehmen vorsichtshalber 50 Pfund mehr mit;
**to get on the wrong** ~**/stay on the right** ~ **of sb** es
(sich *dat*) mit jdm verderben/nicht verderben; **on
the right** ~ **of the law** auf dem Boden des Gesetzes;
**on the right/wrong** ~ **of 40** diesseits/jenseits der 40,
unter/über 40; **on his mother's** ~ mütterlicherseits;
**to make a bit (of money) on the** ~ *(col)* sich *(dat)* etwas nebenbei verdienen; **to have a bit on the** ~ einen Seitensprung machen; **a problem with many** ~**s**
**to it** ein vielschichtiges Problem; **there are always
two** ~**s to every story** alles hat seine zwei Seiten;
**let's hear your** ~ **of the story** erzählen Sie mal Ihre
Version (der Geschichte); **to look on the bright** ~
*(be optimistic)* zuversichtlich sein; *(look on the positive* ~*)* etw von der positiven Seite betrachten.
  **(d) (a bit) on the large/formal** *etc* ~ etwas groß/
förmlich *etc*; *(for somebody)* etwas zu groß/
förmlich *etc*.
  **(e)** *(opposing team)* *(Sport, in quiz)* Mannschaft *f*;

*(fig)* Seite *f*. **there are two** ~**s in the dispute** in dem
Streit stehen sich zwei Parteien gegenüber; **to
change** ~**s** sich auf die andere Seite schlagen;
*(Sport)* die Seiten wechseln; **to take** ~**s** parteiisch
sein; **to take** ~**s with sb** für jdn Partei ergreifen;
**he's on our** ~ er steht auf unserer Seite; **whose** ~
**are you on?** *(supporting team)* für wen sind Sie?; *(in
argument)* zu wem halten Sie eigentlich?
  **2** *adj attr (on one* ~*) entrance, door, road, street*
Seiten-; *(not main) entrance, room, road, street, job*
Neben-.
  **3** *vi* **to** ~ **with/against sb** jds Partei *(acc)*/Partei
gegen jdn ergreifen.
**side:** ~**board** *n* Anrichte *f*, Sideboard *nt*; ~**boards,**
~**burns** *npl* Koteletten *pl*; *(longer)* Backenbart *m*;
~**car** *n* Beiwagen *m*; *(esp Sport)* Seitenwagen *m*;
~**dish** *n* Beilage *f*; ~**door** *n* Seitentür *f*; ~**drum** *n*
kleine Trommel; ~ **effect** *n* Nebenwirkung *f*; ~
**kick** *n (esp US col)* Kumpel *m (col)*; *(assistant)*
Handlanger *m (pej)*; ~**light** *n (Aut)* Begrenzungsleuchte *f*; *(incorporated in headlight)* Standlicht *nt*;
~**line** *n (job etc)* Nebenerwerb *m*; **to do sth as a**
~**line** etw nebenbei tun; ~**lines** *npl* Seitenlinien *pl*;
**to be or stand on the** ~**lines** *(fig)* unbeteiligter Zuschauer sein; ~**long** *adj, adv glance* Seiten-; *(surreptitious)* verstohlen; **to give sb a** ~**long glance, to
glance** ~**long at sb** jdn kurz aus den Augenwinkeln
anblicken; ~ **plate** *n* kleiner Teller; ~**saddle** *adv*
**to ride** ~**saddle** im Damensitz reiten; ~ **salad** *n*
Salat *m* (als Beilage); ~ **show** *n* Nebenvorstel-
lung *f*; *(fig: lesser event)* Nebenattraktion *f*; ~
**splitting** *adj* urkomisch, zum Totlachen *(col)*; ~
**step 1** *vt tackle, punch* (seitwärts) ausweichen
(+*dat*); *person, question* ausweichen (+*dat*); **2** *vi (lit,
fig)* ausweichen; ~ **street** *n* Seitenstraße *f*; *(not
main)* Nebenstraße *f*; ~**track 1** *n (esp US)* = **siding; 2** *vt* ablenken; **I got** ~**tracked onto something
else** ich wurde durch irgend etwas abgelenkt; *(from
topic)* ich wurde irgendwie vom Thema abge-
bracht; ~**walk** *n (US)* Bürgersteig, Gehsteig *m*;
~**ways 1** *adj movement* zur Seite; *glance* von der
Seite; **to give sb/sth a** ~**ways glance** jdn/etw von
der Seite ansehen; **2** *adv move* zur Seite, seitwärts; *look at sb* von der Seite.
**siding** ['saɪdɪŋ] *n (Rail)* Rangiergleis *nt*.
**sidle** ['saɪdl] *vi* (sich) schleichen. **to** ~ **away** (sich)
wegschleichen; **to** ~ **up to sb** sich an jdn heranschleichen.
**SIDS** (= **sudden infant death syndrome**) Krippentod *m*, plötzlicher Kindstod.
**siege** [si:dʒ] *n (of town)* Belagerung *f*; *(by police)*
Umstellung *f*. **to lay** ~ **to a town/a house** eine
Stadt/ein Haus belagern/umstellen; ~ **economy** Be-
lagerungswirtschaft *f*.
**siesta** [sɪ'estə] *n* Siesta *f*. **to have a** ~ Siesta halten.
**sieve** [sɪv] **1** *n* Sieb *nt*. **to have a memory like a** ~
*(col)* ein Gedächtnis wie ein Sieb haben *(col)*. **2** *vt*
= **sift 1 (a)**.
**sift** [sɪft] **1** *vt* **(a)** sieben; *coal* schütteln. **(b)** *(fig)
(search)* sichten, durchgehen; *(separate)* trennen. **2**
*vi (fig)* **to** ~ **through the evidence** das Beweismaterial durchgehen.
**sigh** [saɪ] **1** *n (of person)* Seufzer *m*; *(of wind)* Säuseln *nt no pl*. **to heave a** ~ **of relief** einen Seufzer
der Erleichterung ausstoßen. **2** *vti* seufzen; *(wind)*
säuseln. **to** ~ **with relief** erleichtert aufatmen.
**sighing** ['saɪɪŋ] *n see vti* Seufzen *nt*; Säuseln *nt*.
**sight** [saɪt] **1** *n* **(a)** *(faculty)* Sehvermögen *nt*. **to have
long/short** ~ weit-/kurzsichtig sein; **to lose/regain
one's** ~ sein Augenlicht verlieren/wiedergewinnen;
**he has very good** ~ er sieht sehr gut.

**(b) to hate sb at first** ~ jdn vom ersten Augenblick an nicht leiden können; **love at first** ~ Liebe auf den ersten Blick; **at first** ~ **it seemed easy** auf den ersten Blick erschien es einfach; **to shoot on** ~ sofort schießen; **he played the music at** ~ er hat vom Blatt gespielt; **at the** ~ **of the police they ran away** als sie die Polizei sahen, rannten sie weg; **to know sb by** ~ jdn vom Sehen kennen; **to catch** ~ **of sb/sth** jdn/etw sehen; **to have** ~ **of sth** *(form)* etw zu Gesicht bekommen; **to lose** ~ **of sb/sth** *(lit, fig)* jdn/ etw aus den Augen verlieren; **don't lose** ~ **of the fact that** ... Sie dürfen nicht außer acht lassen, daß ...; **payable at** ~ *(Comm)* zahlbar bei Sicht; **30 days'** ~ *(Comm)* 30 Tage nach Sicht.

**(c)** *(sth seen)* Anblick *m*. **the** ~ **of blood makes me sick** wenn ich Blut sehe, wird mir übel; **the most beautiful** ~ **I've ever seen** das Schönste, was ich je gesehen habe; **I can't bear the** ~ **of him** ich kann ihn (einfach) nicht ausstehen; **what a horrible** ~! das sieht ja furchtbar aus!; **to be** *or* **look a** ~ *(funny)* zum Schreien aussehen *(col)*; *(horrible)* fürchterlich aussehen.

**(d)** *(range of vision)* Sicht *f*. **to be in** *or* **within** ~ in Sicht *or* in Sichtweite sein; **our goal is in** ~ unser Ziel ist in greifbarer Nähe; **we came in** ~ **of the coast** die Küste kam in Sicht; **to keep sb in** ~ jdn im Auge behalten; **to keep out of** ~ sich verborgen halten; **to keep sb/sth out of** ~ jdn/etw versteckt halten; **keep out of my** ~! laß dich bloß bei mir nicht mehr blicken!; **to be out of** ~ nicht mehr zu sehen sein; **don't let the children out of your** ~ laß die Kinder nicht aus den Augen!; **out of** ~, **out of mind** *(Prov)* aus den Augen, aus dem Sinn *(Prov)*.

**(e)** *usu pl (of city etc)* Sehenswürdigkeit *f*. **to see the** ~**s of a town** eine Stadt besichtigen.

**(f)** *(on gun etc)* Visier *nt*. **to set one's** ~**s too high** *(fig)* seine Ziele zu hoch stecken; **to set one's** ~**s on sth** *(fig)* ein Auge auf etw *(acc)* werfen.

**(g)** *(col)* **not by a long** ~ bei weitem nicht; **we're not finished yet, not by a long** ~ wir sind noch lange nicht fertig; **he's a damn** ~ **cleverer than you think** er ist verdammt *(col)* *or* um einiges klüger als du denkst.

**2** *vt (see)* sichten *(also Mil)*; *person* ausmachen.

**sighted** ['saɪtɪd] *adj* sehend. **partially** ~ sehbehindert.

**sighting** ['saɪtɪŋ] *n* Sichten *nt*. **another** ~ **of the monster was reported** das Ungeheuer soll erneut gesichtet worden sein.

**sight:** ~**-read** *vti* vom Blatt spielen/lesen/singen; ~**seeing** *n* Besichtigungen *pl*; **to go** ~**seeing** auf Besichtigungstour gehen; ~**seer** *n* Tourist(in *f*) *m* (auf Besichtigungstour).

**sign** [saɪn] **1** *n* **(a)** *(with hand etc)* Zeichen *nt*. **he nodded as a** ~ **of agreement/recognition** er nickte zum Zeichen der Zustimmung, daß er mich/ihn *etc* erkannt hatte; **to give sb a** ~, **to make a** ~ **to sb** jdm ein Zeichen geben.

**(b)** *(indication, Med)* Anzeichen *nt (of* für *or* gen)*; *(evidence)* Zeichen *nt (of* von *or* gen)*; *(trace)* Spur *f*. **a sure/good** ~ ein sicheres/gutes Zeichen; **it's a** ~ **of the true expert** daran erkennt man den wahren Experten; **at the first** ~ **of disagreement** beim ersten Anzeichen von Uneinigkeit; **there is no** ~ **of their agreeing** nichts deutet darauf hin, daß sie zustimmen werden; **to show** ~**s of sth** Anzeichen von etw erkennen lassen; **our guest showed no** ~**s of leaving** unser Gast machte keine Anstalten zu gehen; **the rain showed no** ~**s of stopping** nichts deutete darauf hin, daß der Regen aufhören würde; **there was no** ~ **of life in the village** das Dorf war

wie ausgestorben; **there was no** ~ **of him anywhere** er war nirgends zu sehen.

**(c)** *(road*~, *shop*~*)* Schild *nt*.

**(d)** *(written symbol, Astrol)* Zeichen *nt*.

**2** *vt* **(a) to** ~ **one's name** unterschreiben; **to** ~ **one's name in a book** sich in ein Buch eintragen; **he** ~**s himself J.G. Jones** er unterschreibt mit J.G. Jones. **(b)** *letter etc* unterschreiben, unterzeichnen *(form)*; *picture, book* signieren. **to** ~ **the register** sich eintragen.

**3** *vi* **(a)** *(signal)* **to** ~ **to sb to do sth** jdm Zeichen/ ein Zeichen geben, etw zu tun. **(b)** *(with signature)* unterschreiben.

►**sign away** *vt sep* verzichten auf *(+acc)*. **she felt she was** ~**ing** ~ **her life** sie hatte das Gefühl, ihr ganzes Leben zu überschreiben.

►**sign for** *vi* +*prep obj* den Empfang *(+gen)* bestätigen.

►**sign in 1** *vt sep person* eintragen. **to** ~ **sb** ~ **at a club** jdn als Gast in einen Klub mitnehmen. **2** *vi* sich eintragen.

►**sign off** *vi (in letter)* Schluß machen; *(Rad, TV)* sich verabschieden.

►**sign on 1** *vt sep* = **sign up 1. 2** *vi* **(a)** = **sign up 2. (b)** *(for unemployment benefit)* sich arbeitslos melden. **to be** ~**ing** ~ Arbeitslosenunterstützung beziehen.

►**sign out** *vi* sich austragen. **to** ~ ~ **of a hotel** sich aus dem Hotelgästebuch austragen.

►**sign over** *vt sep* überschreiben *(to sb* jdm)*.

►**sign up 1** *vt sep (employ, enlist) actors* verpflichten; *workers, employees* anstellen; *sailors* anheuern. **2** *vi* sich verpflichten; *(employees, players also)* unterschreiben; *(sailors)* anheuern; *(for evening class etc)* sich einschreiben.

**signal** ['sɪgnl] **1** *n* **(a)** *(sign)* Zeichen *nt*; *(as part of code)* Signal *nt*; *(message)* Nachricht *f*. **engaged** *(Brit)* *or* **busy** ~ *(Telec)* Besetztzeichen *nt*; **to give the** ~ **for sth** das Zeichen/Signal zu etw geben; **the** ~ **is very weak** *(TV, Rad)* der Empfang ist sehr schlecht. **(b)** *(apparatus, Rail)* Signal *nt*. **the** ~ **is at red** das Signal steht auf Rot. **2** *vt* **(a)** *(indicate)* anzeigen; *arrival, (fig) future event etc* ankündigen. **to** ~ **sb to do sth** jdm ein/das Zeichen geben, etw zu tun. **(b)** *message* signalisieren. **3** *vi* Zeichen/ein Zeichen geben. **he** ~**led for his bill** er winkte zum Zeichen, daß er zahlen wollte; **the driver didn't** ~ der Fahrer hat kein Zeichen gegeben.

**signal:** ~**box** *n* Stellwerk *nt*; ~**man** *n (Rail)* Stellwerkswärter *m*; *(Mil)* Fernmelder, Funker *m*.

**signatory** ['sɪgnətərɪ] *n* Unterzeichnete(r) *mf (form)*.

**signature** ['sɪgnətʃər] *n* **(a)** Unterschrift *f*; *(of artist)* Signatur *f*. **(b)** *(Mus)* Vorzeichnung *f*. **(c)** *(Rad, TV)* ~ **tune** *(Brit)* Erkennungsmelodie *f*.

**signboard** ['saɪnbɔːd] *n* Schild *nt*.

**signet ring** ['sɪgnɪt,rɪŋ] *n* Siegelring *m*.

**significance** [sɪg'nɪfɪkəns] *n* Bedeutung *f*; *(of action also)* Tragweite *f*. **of no** ~ belanglos, bedeutungslos.

**significant** [sɪg'nɪfɪkənt] *adj (considerable, having consequence)* bedeutend; *(important)* wichtig; *(meaningful)* bedeutungsvoll; *look* vielsagend, bedeutsam. **it is** ~ **that** ... es ist bezeichnend, daß ...; **to be** ~ **to** *or* **for sth** eine bedeutende *or* wichtige Rolle in etw *(dat)* spielen; ~ **other** Partner(in *f*) *m*.

**significantly** [sɪg'nɪfɪkəntlɪ] *adv (considerably)* bedeutend; *(meaningfully)* bedeutungsvoll; *look* vielsagend, bedeutsam. **it is not** ~ **different** da besteht kein wesentlicher Unterschied; ~ **enough,** ... bezeichnenderweise ...

**signify** ['sɪgnɪfaɪ] *vt* **(a)** *(mean)* bedeuten. **(b)** *(indicate)* andeuten, erkennen lassen; *(person also)* zu erkennen geben.

**sign:** ~ **language** Zeichensprache *f*; ~**post 1** *n* Wegweiser *m*; **2** *vt way* beschildern; *diversion* ausschildern; ~**writer** *n* Schildermaler(in *f*) *m*.

**silage** ['saɪlɪdʒ] *n* Silage *f*, Silofutter *nt*.

**silence** ['saɪləns] **1** *n* Stille *f*; *(quietness also)* Ruhe *f*; *(absence of talk also, of letters etc)* Schweigen *nt*; *(on a particular subject)* (Still)schweigen *nt*. ~! Ruhe!; **in** ~ still; *(not talking also)* schweigend; **there was** ~ alles war still; **radio** ~ *(Mil)* Funkstille *f*. **2** *vt (lit, fig)* zum Schweigen bringen.

**silencer** ['saɪlənsəʳ] *n (on gun, Brit: on car)* Schalldämpfer *m*; *(part of exhaust)* Auspufftopf *m*.

**silent** ['saɪlənt] *adj* still; *(not talking also)* schweigsam; *engine etc* ruhig; *agreement etc* (still)schweigend *attr*. ~ **movie** Stummfilm *m*; ~ **letter** stummer Buchstabe; ~ **partner** *(US)* stiller Teilhaber; **the** ~ **majority** die schweigende Mehrheit; **to be** ~ **(about sth)** (über etw *acc*) schweigen; **to keep** *or* **remain** ~ still sein *or* bleiben; *(about sth)* sich nicht äußern.

**silently** ['saɪləntlɪ] *adv* lautlos; *(without talking)* schweigend; *(with little noise)* leise.

**Silesia** [saɪ'liːzɪə] *n* Schlesien *nt*.

**Silesian** [saɪ'liːzɪən] **1** *adj* schlesisch. **2** *n* Schlesier(in *f*) *m*.

**silhouette** [ˌsɪluː'et] **1** *n* Silhouette *f*; *(picture)* Scherenschnitt *m*. **2** *vt* **to be** ~**d against sth** sich (als Silhouette) gegen etw abzeichnen.

**silicon** ['sɪlɪkən] *n* Silizium *nt*. ~ **chip** Siliziumscheibe *f*.

**silicone** ['sɪlɪkəun] *n* Silikon *nt*.

**silicosis** [ˌsɪlɪ'kəusɪs] *n* Staublunge, Silikose *f*.

**silk** [sɪlk] **1** *n* **(a)** Seide *f*; *(~ dress)* Seidenkleid *nt*. **(b)** *(Brit Jur: barrister)* Kronanwalt *m*. **2** *adj* Seiden-, seiden. **the dress is** ~ das Kleid ist aus Seide.

**silkiness** ['sɪlkɪnɪs] *n (gleam)* seidiger Glanz; *(softness)* seidige Weichheit; *(of voice)* Sanftheit *f*.

**silk:** ~ **screen** *n* Seidensieb *nt*; *(also* ~-**screen printing)** Seidensiebdruck *m*; ~**worm** *n* Seidenraupe *f*.

**silky** ['sɪlkɪ] *adj (+er)* seidig; *voice* samtig.

**sill** [sɪl] *n* Sims *m or nt*; *(window~)* (Fenster)sims *m or nt*; *(esp of wood)* Fensterbrett *nt*; *(on car)* Türleiste *f*.

**silly** ['sɪlɪ] *adj (+er)* dumm, doof *(col)*.

**silliness** ['sɪlɪnɪs] *n* Albernheit *f*; *(act also)* Dummheit *f*. ~ **season** *(Press)* Sauregurkenzeit *f*; *(col)* Sommerloch *nt (col)*; **don't be** ~ *(do* ~ *things)* mach keinen Quatsch *(col)*; *(say* ~ *things)* red keinen Unsinn; *(ask* ~ *questions)* frag nicht so dumm; **that was a** ~ **thing to do** das war dumm (von dir); **to make sb look** ~ jdn lächerlich machen.

**silo** ['saɪləu] *n* Silo *nt*; *(for missile)* unterirdische Startrampe, Raketensilo *nt*.

**silt** [sɪlt] **1** *n* Schwemmsand *m*; *(river mud)* Schlick *m*. **2** *vi (also* ~ **up)** verschlammen.

**silver** ['sɪlvəʳ] **1** *n* **(a)** *(metal, tableware)* Silber *nt*. **(b)** *(coins)* Silbergeld *nt*. **2** *adj* Silber-, silbern.

**silver:** ~ **birch** *n* Weißbirke *f*; ~ **foil** *n (kitchen foil)* Alufolie *f*; *(~ paper)* Silberpapier *nt*; ~ **jubilee** *n* 25-jähriges Jubiläum; ~ **medal** *n* Silbermedaille *f*; ~ **paper** *n (Brit)* Silberpapier *nt*; ~ **plate** *n (plating)* Silberauflage *f*; *(articles)* versilberte Sachen *pl*; ~-**plated** *adj* versilbert; ~ **screen** *n* Leinwand *f*; ~**smith** *n* Silberschmied *m*; ~**ware** *n* Silber *nt*; ~ **wedding** *n* silberne Hochzeit, Silberhochzeit *f*.

**silvery** ['sɪlvərɪ] *adj* silbern; *voice* silberhell.

**similar** ['sɪmɪləʳ] *adj* ähnlich. ~ **amount, size** ungefähr gleich. **she and her sister are very** ~ ihre Schwester und sie sind sich sehr ähnlich; ~ **in size** ungefähr gleich groß.

**similarity** [ˌsɪmɪ'lærɪtɪ] *n* Ähnlichkeit *f (to mit)*.

**similarly** ['sɪmɪləlɪ] *adv* ähnlich; *(equally)* genauso. ~, **you could maintain** ... genausogut könnten Sie behaupten ...

**simile** ['sɪmɪlɪ] *n* Gleichnis *nt*.

**simmer** ['sɪməʳ] **1** *vt* auf kleiner Flamme kochen lassen. **2** *vi* auf kleiner Flamme kochen; *(fig) (with rage)* kochen *(col)*; *(with excitement)* fiebern.

▶**simmer down** *vi* sich beruhigen, sich abregen *(col)*.

**simper** ['sɪmpəʳ] **1** *n* ..., **she said with a** ~ ..., sagte sie affektiert. **2** *vi (smile)* geziert lächeln; *(talk)* säuseln. ~**ing** geziert.

**simple** ['sɪmpl] *adj (+er)* **(a)** einfach; *decor, dress also* schlicht. **the** ~ **fact is** ... es ist einfach so, daß ...; **it's as** ~ **as ABC** das ist kinderleicht. **(b)** *(foolish, mentally deficient)* einfältig.

**simple-minded** [ˌsɪmpl'maɪndɪd] *adj* einfältig.

**simpleton** ['sɪmpltən] *n* Einfaltspinsel *m*.

**simplicity** [sɪm'plɪsɪtɪ] *n* Einfachheit *f*; *(lack of sophistication, of decor etc also)* Schlichtheit *f*. **it's** ~ **itself** das ist die einfachste Sache der Welt.

**simplification** [ˌsɪmplɪfɪ'keɪʃən] *n* Vereinfachung *f*.

**simplify** ['sɪmplɪfaɪ] *vt* vereinfachen.

**simplistic** [sɪm'plɪstɪk] *adj* simpel.

**simply** ['sɪmplɪ] *adv* einfach; *(merely)* nur, bloß.

**simulate** ['sɪmjuleɪt] *vt emotions* vortäuschen; *enthusiasm also* spielen; *illness also, conditions, environment* simulieren. ~**d leather/sheepskin** Lederimitation *f*/falsches Schaffell.

**simulation** [ˌsɪmju'leɪʃən] *n* Vortäuschung *f*; *(reproduction)* Simulation *f*.

**simulator** ['sɪmjuleɪtəʳ] *n* Simulator *m*.

**simultaneous** [ˌsɪməl'teɪnɪəs] *adj* gleichzeitig. ~ **equations** *(Math)* Simultangleichungen *pl*; ~ **interpreting** Simultandolmetschen *nt*.

**simultaneously** [ˌsɪməl'teɪnɪəslɪ] *adv* gleichzeitig, simultan *(geh)*.

**sin** [sɪn] **1** *n (Rel, fig)* Sünde *f*. **to live in** ~ *(col)* in wilder Ehe leben; *(Rel)* in Sünde leben; **to cover a multitude of** ~**s** *(hum)* viele Schandtaten verdecken. **2** *vi* sündigen *(against* gegen, an +*dat)*, sich versündigen *(against* an +*dat)*; *(against principles etc)* verstoßen *(against* gegen*)*.

**since** [sɪns] **1** *adv (in the meantime)* inzwischen; *(up to now)* seitdem. **ever** ~ seither; **long** ~ schon lange; **he died long** ~ er ist schon lange tot; **not long** ~ erst vor kurzem. **2** *prep* seit. **ever** ~ **1900** (schon) seit 1900; **he had been living there** ~ **1900** er lebte da schon seit 1900; **I've been coming here** ~ **1972** ich komme schon seit 1972 hierher; **it's a long time** ~ **then** das ist schon lange her. **3** *conj* **(a)** *(time)* seit(dem). **ever** ~ **I've known him** seit(dem) ich ihn kenne. **(b)** *(because)* da.

**sincere** [sɪn'sɪəʳ] *adj* aufrichtig; *person also* offen; *intention also* ernst, ehrlich.

**sincerely** [sɪn'sɪəlɪ] *adv see adj* aufrichtig; offen; ernsthaft. **yours** ~ *(esp Brit)* mit freundlichen Grüßen.

**sincerity** [sɪn'serɪtɪ] *n see adj* Aufrichtigkeit *f*; Offenheit *f*; Ernsthaftigkeit *f*. **in all** ~ in aller Offenheit.

**sine** [saɪn] *n (Math)* Sinus *m*.

**sinecure** ['sɪnɪkjuəʳ] *n* Sinekure *f (geh)*.

**sinew** ['sɪnjuː] *n* Sehne *f*.

**sinewy** ['sɪnjuɪ] *adj* sehnig; *(fig) plant, tree* knorrig.

**sinful** ['sɪnful] *adj* sündig; *person, act, thought also* sündhaft *(geh)*.

**sing** [sɪŋ] *pret* **sang**, *ptp* **sung 1** *vt* singen. **to** ~ **the praises of sb/sth** ein Loblied auf jdn/etw singen. **2** *vi* singen; *(ears)* dröhnen; *(kettle)* summen.

▶**sing out** *vi* **(a)** *(sing loudly)* laut *or* aus voller

Kehle singen. **(b)** *(col: shout)* schreien *(col)*.
**Singapore** [ˌsɪŋgə'pɔːr] *n* Singapur *nt*.
**singe** [sɪndʒ] *vt* sengen; *clothes* versengen; *(slightly)* ansengen.
**singer** ['sɪŋər] *n* Sänger(in *f*) *m*.
**Singhalese** [ˌsɪŋgə'liːz] **1** *adj* singhalesisch. **2** *n* **(a)** Singhalese *m*, Singhalesin *f*. **(b)** *(language)* Singhalesisch *nt*.
**singing** ['sɪŋɪŋ] *n* Singen *nt*; *(of person, bird also)* Gesang *m*; *(in the ears)* Dröhnen *nt*; *(of kettle)* Summen *nt*. **he teaches** ~ er gibt Gesangstunden; **do you like my ~?** gefällt dir mein Gesang?
**single** ['sɪŋgl] **1** *adj* **(a)** *(one only)* einzige(r, s). **not a ~ one spoke up** nicht ein einziger äußerte sich dazu; **every ~ day was precious** jeder (einzelne) Tag war kostbar; **not a ~ thing** überhaupt nichts. **(b)** *(not double etc)* einzeln; *bed, room* Einzel-; *carburettor, spacing, (Brit) ticket* einfach. **(c)** *(not married)* unverheiratet, ledig; *parent* alleinstehend, alleinerziehend. ~ **people** Unverheiratete *pl*; **I'm** ~ ich bin nicht verheiratet. **2** *n* **(a)** *(Brit: ticket)* Einzelfahrkarte *f*; *(room)* Einzelzimmer *nt*; *(CD, record)* Single *f*. **a ~/two ~s to Bonn** einmal/zweimal einfach nach Bonn. **(b)** *(unmarried person)* Single *m*. ~**s bar** Singles-Bar *f*.
▶**single out** *vt sep* *(choose)* auswählen; *victim, prey* sich *(dat)* herausgreifen; *(distinguish, set apart)* herausheben *(from* über +*acc)*. **to** ~ **sb** ~ **for special attention** jdm besondere Aufmerksamkeit zuteil werden lassen.
**single:** ~**-breasted** *adj jacket* einreihig; ~**-cell(ed)** *adj (Biol)* einzellig; ~ **cream** *n* Sahne *f (mit geringem Fettgehalt)*; ~**-decker** *n* einstöckiger Omnibus; ~**-density** *adj (Comp) disk* mit einfacher Dichte; ~**-entry book-keeping** *n* einfache Buchführung; ~ **European market** *n* europäischer Binnenmarkt; ~ **file** *n* **in** ~ **file** im Gänsemarsch; ~**-handed** *adj* (ganz) allein *(after noun)*; *achievement* ohne (fremde) Hilfe vollbracht; *struggle* einsam; **2** *adv (also* ~**-handedly)* ohne Hilfe, im Alleingang; ~**-lens-reflex (camera)** *n* Spiegelreflexkamera *f*; ~**-line** *adj* eingleisig; *railway also, traffic* einspurig; ~**-minded** *adj* zielstrebig; *devotion* unbeirrbar.
**singleness** ['sɪŋglnɪs] *n* ~ **of purpose** Zielstrebigkeit *f*.
**single-parent** [ˌsɪŋgl'pɛərənt] *adj* ~ **family** Familie *f* mit nur einem Elternteil, Einelternfamilie *f*.
**singles** ['sɪŋglz] *n sing or pl (Sport)* Einzel *nt*. **the** ~ **finals** das Finale im Einzel; **men's** ~ Herreneinzel *nt*.
**single:** ~**-seater** *n* Einsitzer *m*; ~**-sex** *adj education* nach Geschlechtern getrennt; ~**-sided** *adj (Comp etc)* einseitig; ~**-storey** *adj* eingeschossig.
**singlet** ['sɪŋglɪt] *n (Brit) (Sport)* ärmelloses Trikot; *(underclothing)* (ärmelloses) Unterhemd, Trikothemd *nt*.
**single-track** ['sɪŋglˌtræk] *adj* einspurig; *(Rail also)* eingleisig.
**singly** ['sɪŋglɪ] *adv* einzeln; *(solely)* allein.
**singsong** ['sɪŋsɒŋ] *n* **we often have a** ~ **at the pub** in der Kneipe singen wir oft zusammen.
**singular** ['sɪŋgjʊlər] **1** *adj* **(a)** *(Gram)* im Singular. **(b)** *(odd)* sonderbar, eigenartig. **(c)** *(outstanding)* einzigartig, einmalig. **2** *n* Singular *m*. **in the** ~ im Singular.
**singularity** [ˌsɪŋgjʊ'lærɪtɪ] *n (oddity)* Sonderbarkeit, Eigenartigkeit *f*.
**singularly** ['sɪŋgjʊlərlɪ] *adv* außerordentlich.
**Sinhalese** [ˌsɪnhə'liːz] *see* **Singhalese**.
**sinister** ['sɪnɪstər] *adj* unheimlich; *person, scheme*

*also* finster; *music, look also* düster; *fate* böse.
**sink¹** [sɪŋk] *pret* sank, *ptp* sunk **1** *vt* **(a)** *ship* versenken. **(b)** *(fig: ruin)* theory zerstören; *hopes also* zunichte machen. **now we're sunk!** *(col)* jetzt sind wir geliefert *(col)*. **(c)** *shaft* senken; *hole* ausheben; *foundations* absenken. **to** ~ **a post in the ground** einen Pfosten in den Boden einlassen. **(d)** *teeth, claws* schlagen. **(e)** *differences* begraben. **(f) to** ~ **money in sth** Geld in etw *(acc)* stecken. **(g) to be sunk in thought** in Gedanken versunken sein.
**2** *vi* sinken; *(ship also)* untergehen; *(sun also)* versinken; *(voice, building, land etc)* sich senken; *(shares, prices)* fallen. **to** ~ **to the bottom** auf den Grund sinken; **he was left to** ~ **or swim** *(fig)* er war ganz auf sich allein angewiesen; **to** ~ **into a chair** in einen Sessel (nieder)sinken; **the sun sank beneath the horizon** die Sonne versank am Horizont; **to** ~ **to one's knees** auf die Knie sinken; **to** ~ **into a deep sleep** in tiefen Schlaf versinken; **my heart sank at the sight of the work** beim Anblick der Arbeit verließ mich der Mut; **with** ~**ing heart** mutlos; **she has sunk in my estimation** sie ist in meiner Achtung gesunken.
▶**sink in** *vi* **(a)** *(into mud etc)* einsinken *(prep obj, -to* in +*acc)*. **(b)** *(col: be understood)* kapiert werden *(col)*. **it's only just sunk** ~ **that it really did happen** ich kapiere erst jetzt, daß das tatsächlich passiert ist *(col)*.
**sink²** *n* Ausguß *m*; *(in kitchen also)* Spülbecken *nt*. ~ **unit** Spüle *f*.
**sinking** ['sɪŋkɪŋ] **1** *n (of ship)* Untergang *m*; *(deliberate)* Versenkung *f*; *(of shaft)* Senken *nt*; *(of well)* Bohren *nt*. **2** *adj* ~ **feeling** flaues Gefühl (im Magen) *(col)*; ~ **fund** Tilgungsfonds *m*.
**sinner** ['sɪnər] *n* Sünder(in *f*) *m*.
**sinuous** ['sɪnjʊəs] *adj (lit, fig)* gewunden; *motion of snake* schlängelnd *attr*; *dancing etc* geschmeidig.
**sinus** ['saɪnəs] *n (in head)* (Nasen)nebenhöhle *f*; *(frontal)* Stirnhöhle *f*.
**sip** [sɪp] **1** *n* Schluck *m*; *(very small)* Schlückchen *nt*. **2** *vt* in kleinen Schlucken trinken; *(suspiciously, daintily)* nippen an *(+dat)*; *(savour)* schlürfen.
**siphon** ['saɪfən] **1** *n* Heber *m*; *(soda* ~*)* Siphon *m*. **2** *vt* absaugen; *(into tank)* umfüllen.
▶**siphon off** *vt sep* **(a)** *(lit)* absaugen; *petrol* abzapfen; *(into container)* umfüllen, abfüllen. **(b)** *(fig) staff* abziehen; *profits* abschöpfen.
**sir** [sɜːr] *n* **(a)** *(in direct address)* mein Herr *(form)*, Herr X. **Dear S~ (or Madam),** ... sehr geehrte (Damen und) Herren! **(b)** *(knight etc)* S~ Sir *m*. **(c)** *(Sch: teacher)* **please** ~**!** Herr X!; **I'll tell** ~ ich sag's dem Lehrer.
**sire** ['saɪər] **1** *n (Zool)* Vatertier *nt*. **2** *vt* zeugen.
**siren** ['saɪərən] *n (also Myth)* Sirene *f*.
**sirloin** ['sɜːlɔɪn] *n* Filet *nt*.
**sis** [sɪs] *n (col)* Schwesterherz *nt (col)*.
**sissy** ['sɪsɪ] *n* Waschlappen *m (col)*, Memme *f*.
**sister** ['sɪstər] *n* **(a)** Schwester *f*; *(in trade union)* Kollegin *f*. **(b)** *(nun)* (Ordens)schwester *f*; *(before name)* Schwester *f*. **(c)** *(Brit: senior nurse)* Oberschwester *f*.
**sister** *in cpds company, party, ship etc* Schwester-; ~**-in-law** *n, pl* ~**s-in-law** Schwägerin *f*.
**sisterly** ['sɪstəlɪ] *adj* schwesterlich.
**sit** [sɪt] *(vb: pret, ptp* sat*)* **1** *vi* **(a)** *(be* ~*ting)* sitzen *(in/on* in/auf +*dat)*; *(*~ *down)* sich setzen *(in/on* in/auf +*acc)*. **a place to** ~ ein Sitzplatz *m*; ~ **by/with me** setz dich zu mir/neben mich; **to** ~ **for a painter** einem Maler Modell sitzen; **to** ~ **for an exam** eine Prüfung ablegen *(form)* or machen; **to be** ~**ting pretty** *(fig col)* gut dastehen *(col)*. **(b)** *(assembly)* ta-

gen; *(have a seat)* einen Sitz haben. **to ~ on a committee** in einem Ausschuß sitzen. **(c)** *(bird: hatch)* sitzen, brüten. **(d)** *(fig: clothes)* sitzen *(on sb* bei jdm*)*.

**2** *vt* **(a)** setzen *(in* in *+acc, on* auf *+acc)*; *(place)* *object also* stellen. **to ~ a child on one's knees** sich *(dat)* ein Kind auf den Schoß setzen; **the table ~s 5 people** an dem Tisch haben 5 Leute Platz. **(b)** *(esp Brit) examination* ablegen *(form)*, machen.

►**sit about** *or* **around** *vi* herumsitzen.

►**sit back** *vi* *(lit, fig)* sich zurücklehnen; *(fig: do nothing)* die Hände in den Schoß legen.

►**sit down** *vi* sich (hin)setzen. **to ~ ~ in a chair** sich auf einen Stuhl setzen.

►**sit in** *vi* **(a)** *(demonstrators)* ein Sit-in veranstalten. **(b)** *(attend as visitor)* dabeisein, dabeisitzen *(on sth* bei etw*)*.

►**sit on** *vi +prep obj* *(not deal with)* sitzen auf *(+dat)*; *(col: suppress) idea, product* unterdrücken; *person* einen Dämpfer aufsetzen *(+dat) (col)*.

►**sit out 1** *vi* draußen sitzen. **2** *vt sep* **(a)** *(stay to end) play* bis zum Ende (sitzen)bleiben bei, bis zum Ende durchhalten *(pej)*; *storm* auf das Ende *(+gen)* warten. **(b)** *dance* auslassen. **I'll ~ this one ~** ich setze diesmal aus.

►**sit through** *vi +prep obj* durchhalten, aushalten *(pej)*.

►**sit up 1** *vi* **(a)** aufrecht sitzen; *(action)* sich aufrichten. **~ ~!** setz dich gerade hin!; **to make sb ~ ~ (and take notice)** *(fig col)* jdn aufhorchen lassen. **(b)** *(not go to bed)* aufbleiben. **she sat ~ with the sick child** sie wachte bei dem kranken Kind. **2** *vt sep* aufrichten; *doll also, baby* hinsetzen.

**sitcom** ['sɪtkɒm] *n (col)* Situationskomödie *f*.

**sit-down** ['sɪtdaυn] *adj attr* **to have a ~ strike** einen Sitzstreik machen; **a ~ meal** eine richtige Mahlzeit.

**site** [saɪt] **1** *n* **(a)** Stelle *f*, Platz *m*. **(b)** *(Archeol)* Stätte *f*. **(c)** *(building ~)* Baustelle *f*. **~ hut** Baubude *f*; **~ manager** Bauleiter(in *f*) *m*; **missile ~** Raketenbasis *f*. **(d)** *(camping ~)* Campingplatz *m*. **2** *vt* legen, anlegen. **to be ~d** liegen, (gelegen) sein.

**sit-in** ['sɪtɪn] *n* Sit-in *nt*, Sitzblockade *f*. **to hold** *or* **stage a ~** ein Sit-in veranstalten.

**sitter** ['sɪtə<sup>r</sup>] *n (Art)* Modell *nt*; *(baby-~)* Babysitter *m*.

**sitting** ['sɪtɪŋ] *n (of committee, for portrait)* Sitzung *f*. **they have two ~s for lunch** sie servieren das Mittagessen in zwei Schüben.

**sitting:** **~ duck** *n (fig)* leichte Beute; **~ member** *n (Parl)* derzeitiger Abgeordneter, derzeitige Abgeordnete; **~ room** *n (lounge)* Wohnzimmer *nt*; *(in guest house etc)* Aufenthaltsraum *m*; **~ target** *n (lit, fig)* leichte Beute; **~ tenant** *n* (derzeitiger) Mieter.

**situate** ['sɪtjʊeɪt] *vt* legen.

**situated** ['sɪtjʊeɪtɪd] *adj* gelegen; *person (financially)* gestellt, situiert *(geh)*. **it is ~ in the High Street** es liegt an der Hauptstraße; **a pleasantly ~ house** ein schön gelegenes Haus; **how are you ~ (for money)?** wie ist Ihre finanzielle Lage?

**situation** [ˌsɪtjʊ'eɪʃən] *n* **(a)** *(state of affairs)* Lage, Situation *f*; *(financial, marital etc)* Lage *f*, Verhältnisse *pl*; *(in play, novel)* Situation *f*. **to save the ~** die Situation retten; **~ comedy** Situationskomödie *f*. **(b)** *(of house etc)* Lage *f*. **(c)** *(job)* Stelle *f*. **"~s vacant/wanted"** „Stellenangebote/Stellengesuche".

**six** [sɪks] **1** *adj* sechs. **she is ~ (years old)** sie ist sechs (Jahre alt); **at (the age of) ~** im Alter von sechs Jahren; **it's ~ (o'clock)** es ist sechs (Uhr); **there are ~ of us** wir sind sechs; **~ and a half/quarter** sechseinhalb/sechseinviertel; **to be ~ feet under**

*(hum)* sich *(dat)* die Radieschen von unten besehen *(hum)*; **it's ~ of one and half a dozen of the other** *(col)* das ist Jacke wie Hose *(col)*. **2** *n* Sechs *f*. **to divide sth into ~** etw in sechs Teile teilen; **they are sold in ~es** sie werden in Sechserpackungen verkauft; **to be at ~es and sevens** *(things)* wie Kraut und Rüben durcheinanderliegen *(col)*; *(person)* völlig durcheinander sein; **to knock sb for ~** *(col)* jdn umhauen.

**six:** **~fold 1** *adj* sechsfach; **2** *adv* um das Sechsfache; **~ footer** *n* **to be a ~ footer** über 1,80 *(gesprochen:* einsachtzig*)* sein; **~ hundred 1** *adj* sechshundert; **2** *n* Sechshundert *f*; **~ million** *adj, n* sechs Millionen; **~-pack** *n* Sechserpackung *f*; **~-shooter** *n (col)* sechsschüssiger Revolver.

**sixteen** ['sɪks'tiːn] **1** *adj* sechzehn. **2** *n* Sechzehn *f*.

**sixteenth** ['sɪks'tiːnθ] **1** *adj* sechzehnte(r, s). **a ~ part** ein Sechzehntel *nt*; **~ note** *(US Mus)* Sechzehntelnote *f*. **2** *n* **(a)** *(fraction)* Sechzehntel *nt*; *(in series)* Sechzehnte(r, s). **(b)** *(date)* der Sechzehnte.

**sixth** [sɪksθ] **1** *adj* sechste(r, s). **a ~ part** ein Sechstel *nt*; **he was** *or* **came ~** er wurde Sechster; **she was ~ from the left** sie war die Sechste von links. **2** *n* **(a)** *(fraction)* Sechstel *nt*; *(in series)* Sechste(r, s). **(b)** *(date)* **the ~** der Sechste; **on the ~** am Sechsten; **the ~ of September** der sechste September.

**sixth:** **~ form** *n (Brit)* Abschlußklasse, ≈ 13. Klasse *f*; **~-former** *n (Brit)* Schüler(in *f*) *m* der Abschlußklasse.

**six thousand 1** *adj* sechstausend. **2** *n* Sechstausend *f*.

**sixth sense** *n* sechster Sinn.

**sixtieth** ['sɪkstɪθ] **1** *adj* sechzigste(r, s). **2** *n* *(fraction)* Sechzigstel *nt*; *(in series)* Sechzigste(r, s).

**sixty** ['sɪkstɪ] **1** *adj* sechzig. **2** *n* Sechzig *f*. **the sixties** die sechziger Jahre; **to be in one's sixties** in den Sechzigern sein; **to be in one's late/early sixties** Ende/Anfang sechzig sein; **~-four thousand dollar question** *n (hum)* große Frage, Zehntausendmarkfrage *f (hum)*.

**sixty-one** ['sɪkstɪ'wʌn] *adj* einundsechzig.

**six-year-old** ['sɪksjɪəˌəυld] **1** *adj* sechsjährig *attr*, sechs Jahre alt *pred*. **2** *n* Sechsjährige(r) *mf*.

**size** [saɪz] **1** *n* Größe *f*; *(of problem, operation also)* Ausmaß *nt*. **collar/hip/waist ~** Kragen-/Hüft-/Taillenweite *f*; **it's the ~ of a brick** es ist so groß wie ein Ziegelstein; **he's about your ~** er ist ungefähr so groß wie du; **what ~ is it?** wie groß ist es?; *(clothes, shoes, gloves etc)* welche Größe ist es?; **it's quite a ~** es ist ziemlich groß; **it's two ~s too big** es ist zwei Nummern zu groß; **to cut sth to ~** etw auf die richtige Größe zurechtschneiden; **that's about the ~ of it** *(col)* ja, so ungefähr kann man es sagen. **2** *vt* größenmäßig ordnen.

►**size up** *vt sep* abschätzen.

**sizeable** ['saɪzəbl] *adj* ziemlich groß, größer; *car, estate, jewel also* ansehnlich.

**sizzle** ['sɪzl] *vi* brutzeln.

**skate¹** [skeɪt] *n (fish)* Rochen *m*.

**skate²** **1** *n (shoe)* Schlittschuh *m*; *(blade)* Kufe *f*. **put** *or* **get your ~s on** *(fig col)* mach/macht mal ein bißchen dalli! *(col)*. **2** *vi* eislaufen, Schlittschuh laufen; *(figure-~)* eislaufen; *(roller-~)* Rollschuh laufen. **it went skating across the room** *(fig)* es rutschte durch das Zimmer.

►**skate around** *or* **over** *vi +prep obj difficulty, problem* einfach übergehen.

**skate:** **~board** *n* Skateboard, Rollbrett *nt*; **~boarder** *n* Skateboardfahrer(in *f*) *m*; **~boarding** *n* Skateboardfahren *nt*.

**skater** ['skeɪtə<sup>r</sup>] *n (ice-~)* Schlittschuhläufer(in *f*) *m*;

*(figure-~)* Eiskunstläufer(in *f*) *m*; *(roller-~)* Rollschuhläufer(in *f*) *m*.

**skating** ['skeɪtɪŋ] *n (ice-~)* Eislauf *m*; *(figure-~)* Eiskunstlauf *m*; *(roller-~)* Rollschuhlauf *m*. ~ **rink** Eisbahn/Rollschuhbahn *f*.

**skein** [skeɪn] *n (of wool etc)* Strang *m*.

**skeleton** ['skelɪtn] **1** *n (lit, fig)* Skelett *nt*; *(esp of ship)* Gerippe *nt*. **a ~ in one's cupboard** *(of public figure)* eine Leiche im Keller. **2** *adj staff, service* Minimal-; *(emergency)* Not-. ~ **crew** Minimalbesatzung *f*; ~ **key** Dietrich, Nachschlüssel *m*.

**skeptic** *etc (US)* = **sceptic** *etc*.

**sketch** [sketʃ] **1** *n (Art, Liter)* Skizze *f*; *(Theat)* Sketch *m*; *(design also)* Entwurf *m*. **2** *vt (lit, fig)* skizzieren.
►**sketch in** *vt sep details (verbally)* umreißen.

**sketch:** ~-**book** *n* Skizzenbuch *nt*; ~ **map** *n* Kartenskizze *f*; ~ **pad** *n* Skizzenblock *m*.

**sketchy** ['sketʃɪ] *adj (+er) (inadequate)* flüchtig, oberflächlich; *(incomplete)* bruchstückhaft.

**skewer** ['skjʊəʳ] **1** *n* Spieß *m*. **2** *vt* aufspießen.

**skew-whiff** [,skjuː'wɪf] *adj (Brit col)* (wind)schief.

**ski** [skiː] **1** *n* Ski, Schi *m*. **2** *vi* Ski laufen *or* fahren. **they ~ed down the slope/over the hill** sie fuhren (auf ihren Skiern) den Hang hinunter/sie liefen (mit ihren Skiern) über den Hügel.

**ski boot** *n* Skistiefel *m*.

**skid** [skɪd] **1** *n (Aut etc)* Schleudern *nt*. **to go into a ~** ins Schleudern kommen; **to correct a ~** das Fahrzeug wieder in seine Gewalt bekommen. **2** *vi (car, objects)* schleudern; *(person)* ausrutschen. **to ~ across the floor** über den Boden rutschen; **the car ~ded into a tree** der Wagen schleuderte gegen einen Baum.

**skid:** ~**mark** *n* Reifenspur *f*; *(from braking)* Bremsspur *f*; ~ **row** *n (esp US col)* Pennergegend *f (col)*; **to be on ~ row** heruntergekommen sein.

**skier** ['skiːəʳ] *n* Skifahrer(in *f*) *m*.

**skiff** [skɪf] *n* Skiff *nt*; *(Sport)* Einer *m*.

**skiing** ['skiːɪŋ] *n* Skilaufen, Skifahren *nt*. **to go ~** Skilaufen gehen; ~ **goggles** Skibrille *f*; ~ **holiday** Skiurlaub *m*; ~ **instructor** Skilehrer(in *f*) *m*.

**ski** *in cpds* Ski-; ~-**jump** *n (action)* Skisprung *m*; *(place)* Sprungschanze *f*; ~-**jumping** *n* Skispringen *nt*.

**skilful,** *(US)* **skillful** ['skɪlfʊl] *adj* geschickt; *player etc also* gewandt; *painting etc* kunstvoll.

**skilfully,** *(US)* **skillfully** ['skɪlfəlɪ] *adv see adj*.

**skilfulness,** *(US)* **skillfulness** ['skɪlfəlnɪs] *n see* **skill (a)**.

**ski-lift** ['skiːlɪft] *n* Skilift *m*.

**skill** [skɪl] *n* **(a)** *no pl (skilfulness)* Geschick *nt*, Geschicklichkeit *f*; *(of sculptor etc)* Kunst(fertigkeit) *f*. **his ~ at billiards/in persuading people** sein Geschick beim Billiard/seine Fähigkeit, andere zu überreden. **(b)** *(acquired technique)* Fertigkeit *f*; *(ability)* Fähigkeit *f*.

**skilled** [skɪld] *adj (skilful)* geschickt, gewandt *(at in +dat)*; *(trained)* ausgebildet, Fach-; *(requiring skill)* fachmännisch.

**skillet** ['skɪlɪt] *n* Bratpfanne *f*.

**skillful** *(US)* = **skilful**.

**skim** [skɪm] **1** *vt* **(a)** *(remove floating matter)* abschöpfen; *milk* entrahmen. ~**med** *or (US)* ~ **milk** Magermilch *f*. **(b)** *(pass low over)* streifen über *(+acc)*; *(fig: touch on)* berühren. **the book merely** ~**s the surface of the problem** das Buch berührt das Problem nur an der Oberfläche. **(c)** *(read quickly) (also ~ through)* überfliegen. **2** *vi (across, over)* über *+acc) (move quickly)* fliegen; *(aircraft also)* gleiten; *(stones)* springen.

**skimp** [skɪmp] **1** *vt food, material* sparen an *(+dat)*;

*work* nachlässig erledigen; *details* zu kurz kommen lassen. **2** *vi* sparen *(on an +dat)*.

**skimpy** ['skɪmpɪ] *adj (+er)* dürftig; *meal, existence also* kärglich; *clothing* spärlich; *bikini etc* knapp. **to be ~ with sth** mit etw sparsam sein.

**skin** [skɪn] **1** *n* **(a)** Haut *f*. **to be soaked to the ~** bis auf die Haut naß sein; **he's nothing but ~ and bone(s) nowadays** er ist nur noch Haut und Knochen; **that's no ~ off my nose** *(col)* das juckt mich nicht *(col)*; **to save one's own ~** die eigene Haut retten; **to jump out of one's ~** *(col)* erschreckt hochfahren; **to get under sb's ~** *(col) (irritate)* jdm auf die Nerven gehen *(col)*; *(fascinate) (music)* jdm unter die Haut gehen; *(person)* jdn faszinieren; **I've got you under my ~** *(col)* du hast mir's angetan; **to have a thick ~** *(fig)* ein dickes Fell haben *(col)*; **by the ~ of one's teeth** *(col)* mit knapper Not. **(b)** *(hide)* Haut *f*; *(fur)* Fell *nt*. **(c)** *(of fruit etc)* Schale *f*; *(on sausage, milk)* Haut *f*.

**2** *vt animal* häuten; *fruit* schälen; *grapes, tomatoes* enthäuten. **to ~ sb alive** *(col)* jdm den Kopf abreißen *(hum col)*; **to keep one's eyes ~ned (for sth)** die Augen (nach etw) offenhalten.

**skin:** ~ **cream** *n* Hautcreme *f*; ~-**deep** *adj see* **beauty;** ~-**diver** *n* Sporttaucher(in *f*) *m*; ~-**diving** *n* Sporttauchen *nt*; ~**flint** *n (col)* Geizkragen *m (col)*.

**skinful** ['skɪnfʊl] *n (col)* **to have had a ~** einen über den Durst getrunken haben *(col)*.

**skin:** ~ **graft** *n* Hauttransplantation *f*; ~**head** *n (Brit col)* Skinhead *m*.

**skinny** ['skɪnɪ] *adj (+er) (col) person, legs* dünn.

**skint** [skɪnt] *adj (Brit col)* **to be ~** pleite *or* blank sein *(col)*.

**skin-tight** ['skɪn,taɪt] *adj* hauteng.

**skip¹** [skɪp] **1** *n* (kleiner) Sprung *m*; *(in dancing)* Hüpfschritt *m*. **2** *vi* **(a)** hüpfen; *(jump, gambol)* springen; *(with rope)* seilspringen. **(b)** *(move from subject to subject)* springen. **3** *vt* **(a)** *(omit, miss) school etc* schwänzen *(col)*; *chapter etc* auslassen, überspringen. **to ~ lunch** das Mittagessen ausfallen lassen; **let's ~ it** lassen wir das. **(b)** *(US)* **to ~ rope** seilspringen.
►**skip about** *vi* herumhüpfen.
►**skip through** *vi +prep obj book* durchblättern.

**skip²** *n (esp Brit) (Build)* Container *m*; *(Min)* Förderkorb *m*.

**ski:** ~ **pants** *npl* Skihose(n *pl*) *f*; ~ **pole** *n* Skistock *m*.

**skipper** ['skɪpəʳ] **1** *n* Kapitän *m*. **2** *vt* führen.

**skipping** ['skɪpɪŋ] *n* Seilspringen *nt*. ~ **rope** *(Brit)* Sprungseil *nt*.

**ski resort** *n* Skiurlaubsort *m*.

**skirmish** ['skɜːmɪʃ] *n (Mil)* Geplänkel *nt*; *(scrap, fig)* Zusammenstoß *m*.

**skirt** [skɜːt] **1** *n* Rock *m*; *(of jacket, coat)* Schoß *m*. **2** *vt (also ~ round)* umgehen.

**skirting (board)** ['skɜːtɪŋ(,bɔːd)] *n (Brit)* Fußleiste *f*.

**ski:** ~-**run** *n* Skipiste *f*; ~ **stick** *n* Skistock *m*; ~ **suit** *n* Skianzug *m*.

**skit** [skɪt] *n* (satirischer) Sketch *(on über +acc)*.

**skittish** ['skɪtɪʃ] *adj (playful)* übermütig; *(flirtatious) woman* neckisch, kokett.

**skittle** ['skɪtl] *n (Brit)* Kegel *m*. **to play ~s** kegeln.

**skive** [skaɪv] *(Brit col) vi* blaumachen *(col)*; *(from school etc)* schwänzen *(col)*.
►**skive off** *vi (Brit col)* sich drücken *(col) (prep obj* vor *+dat)*.

**skulk** [skʌlk] *vi (move)* schleichen; *(lurk)* sich herumdrücken.

**skull** [skʌl] *n* Schädel *m*. ~ **and crossbones** Totenkopf *m*; ~**cap** Scheitelkäppchen *nt.*

**skunk** [skʌŋk] *n* Skunk *m*, Stinktier *nt.*

**sky** [skaɪ] *n* Himmel *m*. **under the open** ~ unter freiem Himmel; **in the** ~ am Himmel; **the** ~**'s the limit!** nach oben sind keine Grenzen gesetzt; **to praise sb to the skies** jdn über den grünen Klee loben *(col)*.

**sky:** ~ **blue** *n* Himmelblau *nt*; ~**-blue** *adj* himmelblau; ~**-diver** *n* Fallschirmspringer(in *f*) *m*; ~**-diving** *n* Fallschirmspringen *nt*; ~**-high 1** *adj prices* schwindelnd hoch; **2** *adv* zum Himmel; **to blow a bridge** ~**-high** *(col)* eine Brücke in die Luft sprengen; **to blow a theory** ~**-high** *(col)* eine Theorie zum Einsturz bringen; ~**lark 1** *n* Feldlerche *f*; **2** *vi (col) (frolic)* tollen; *(fool around)* blödeln *(col)*; ~**light** *n* Oberlicht *nt*; *(in roof also)* Dachfenster *nt*; ~**line** *n (horizon)* Horizont *m*; *(of hills etc)* Silhouette *f*; ~**scraper** *n* Wolkenkratzer *m.*

**slab** [slæb] *n (of wood etc)* Tafel *f*; *(of stone etc)* Platte *f*; *(in mortuary)* Tisch *m*; *(of cake)* großes Stück; *(of chocolate)* Tafel *f.*

**slack** [slæk] **1** *adj (+er)* **(a)** *(not tight)* locker. **(b)** *(lazy)* bequem, träge; *(negligent)* nachlässig, schlampig *(col)*. **to be** ~ **about one's work** in bezug auf seine Arbeit nachlässig sein. **(c)** *(Comm) market* flau; *season also* ruhig. **business is** ~ das Geschäft geht schlecht. **2** *n* **(a)** *(of rope etc)* **to take up the** ~ **(on a rope/sail)** ein Seil/Segel straffen *or* spannen; **there is too much** ~ das Seil/Segel hängt zu sehr durch; **to take up the** ~ **in the economy** die brachliegenden Kräfte der Wirtschaft nutzen. **(b)** *(coal)* Grus *m.* **3** *vi* bummeln.

**slacken** ['slækn] **1** *vt* **(a)** *(loosen)* lockern. **(b)** *(reduce)* vermindern, verringern. **2** *vi* **(a)** *(become loose)* sich lockern. **(b)** *(also* ~ **off)** *(speed)* sich verringern; *(rate of development)* sich verlangsamen; *(wind, demand, market)* abflauen.

**slackness** ['slæknɪs] *n (of rope)* Schlaffheit *f*; *(of business, market etc)* Flaute *f*; *(laziness)* Bummelei *f*; *(negligence)* Nachlässigkeit *f.*

**slacks** [slæks] *npl* Hose *f.*

**slag** [slæg] **1** *n* Schlacke *f.* ~ **heap** Schlackenhalde *f.* **2** *vt (col: run down)* *(also* ~ **off)** (he)runtermachen *(col)*.

**slain** [sleɪn] *ptp of* **slay.**

**slake** [sleɪk] *vt thirst* stillen.

**slalom** ['slɑːləm] *n* Slalom *m.*

**slam** [slæm] **1** *n* **(a)** *(of door etc)* Zuschlagen *nt no pl.* **with a** ~ mit voller Wucht. **(b)** *(Cards)* Schlemm *m.* **2** *vt* **(a)** *(close violently)* zuknallen. **to** ~ **sth shut** etw zuknallen; **to** ~ **the door in sb's face** jdm die Tür vor der Nase zumachen; **he** ~**med his fist on the table** er knallte mit der Faust auf den Tisch *(col)*; **to** ~ **the brakes on** *(col)* auf die Bremse latschen *(col)*. **(b)** *(col: criticize harshly)* verreißen; *person* herunterputzen *(col)*. **3** *vi (door)* zuschlagen.

**slander** ['slɑːndər] **1** *n* Verleumdung *f.* **2** *vt* verleumden.

**slanderous** ['slɑːndərəs] *adj* verleumderisch.

**slang** [slæŋ] **1** *n* Slang *m*; *(army* ~, *schoolboy etc)* Jargon *m.* **2** *adj* Slang-. **3** *vt (esp Brit col)* **to** ~ **sb/ sth** jdn beschimpfen/über etw *(acc)* schimpfen; **they were having a** ~**ing match** sie beschimpften sich um die Wette.

**slangy** ['slæŋɪ] *adj (+er)* salopp.

**slant** [slɑːnt] **1** *n* **(a)** Schräge *f.* **to be on the** ~ sich neigen, schräg sein. **(b)** *(fig) (bias, leaning)* Tendenz, Neigung *f*; *(point of view)* Anstrich *m.* **a right-wing** ~ ein Rechtsdrall *m.* **2** *vt (lit)* verschieben; *report* färben. **the book is** ~**ed towards women** das Buch ist auf Frauen ausgerichtet. **3** *vi* sich neigen.

**slanting** ['slɑːntɪŋ] *adj* schräg.

**slap** [slæp] **1** *n* Schlag, Klaps *m.* **to give sb a** ~ jdm einen Klaps geben; **a** ~ **in the face** *(lit, fig)* ein Schlag ins Gesicht *(lit also)* eine Ohrfeige; **to give sb a** ~ **on the back** jdm (anerkennend) auf den Rücken klopfen; *(fig)* jdn loben; **to give sb a** ~ **on the wrist** *(fig col)* jdm einen Anpfiff geben *(col)*. **2** *adv (col)* direkt. **3** *vt* **(a)** schlagen. **to** ~ **sb's face** jdn ohrfeigen, jdm eine runterhauen *(col)*. **(b)** *(put noisily)* knallen *(on/to)* auf *(+acc)*. **he just** ~**ped the paint on** er klatschte die Farbe einfach drauf *(col)*. ►**slap down** *vt sep (col)* hinknallen; *(fig)* **to** ~ **sb** ~ jdm eins aufs Dach geben *(col)*.

**slap:** ~**-bang** *adv (col) crash* mit Karacho *(col)*; **it was** ~**-bang in the middle** es war genau in der Mitte; ~**-dash** *adj* flüchtig, schludrig *(pej)*; ~**-happy** *adj* unbekümmert; ~**stick** *n* Klamauk *m (col)*; ~**stick comedy** Slapstick *m*; ~**-up** *adj (col) meal* mit allem Drum und Dran *(col)*.

**slash** [slæʃ] **1** *n* **(a)** *(action)* Streich *m*; *(wound)* Schnitt *m.* **(b)** *(Typ: oblique stroke)* Schrägstrich *m.* **2** *vt* **(a)** *(cut)* zerfetzen; *face also* aufschlitzen; *undergrowth* abhauen; *(with sword)* hauen auf *(+acc)*. **(b)** *(col) price* radikal herabsetzen.

**slat** [slæt] *n* Leiste *f*; *(in grid etc)* Stab *m.*

**slate** [sleɪt] **1** *n* **(a)** *(rock)* Schiefer *m*; *(roof* ~) Schieferplatte *f.* **put it on the** ~ *(col)* schreiben Sie es an; **to wipe the** ~ **clean** *(fig)* reinen Tisch machen. **(b)** *(US Pol)* (Kandidaten)liste *f.* **2** *adj* Schiefer-. **3** *vt* **(a)** *roof* (mit Schiefer) decken. **(b)** *(esp Brit col: criticize harshly)* verreißen; *person* zusammenstauchen *(col)*.

**slate:** ~**-blue** *adj* blaugrau; ~**-coloured,** *(US)* ~**-colored** *adj* schieferfarben; ~**-grey,** *(US)* ~**-gray** *adj* schiefergrau.

**slaughter** ['slɔːtər] **1** *(of animals)* Schlachten *nt no pl*; *(of persons)* Gemetzel *nt.* **the** ~ **on the roads** das Massensterben auf den Straßen. **2** *vt* schlachten; *persons (lit)* abschlachten; *(fig)* fertigmachen *(col)*.

**slaughterhouse** ['slɔːtəhaus] *n* Schlachthof *m.*

**Slav** [slɑːv] **1** *adj* slawisch. **2** *n* Slawe *m*, Slawin *f.*

**slave** [sleɪv] **1** *n* Sklave *m*, Sklavin *f.* **to be a** ~ **to sb/sth** jds Sklave sein/Sklave von etw sein. **2** *vi* sich abplagen, schuften *(col)*. **to** ~ **(away) at sth** sich mit etw herumschlagen.

**slave:** ~ **driver** *n (lit, fig)* Sklaventreiber *m*; ~ **labour** *(Brit) or* **labor** *(US) n (work)* Sklavenarbeit *f*; **he uses** ~ **labour** sein Leute müssen wie die Sklaven arbeiten.

**slavery** ['sleɪvərɪ] *n* Sklaverei *f*; *(condition)* Sklavenleben *nt*; *(fig: addiction)* sklavische Abhängigkeit *(to von)*.

**slave trade** *n* Sklavenhandel *m.*

**slavish** *adj*, ~**ly** *adv* ['sleɪvɪʃ, -lɪ] sklavisch.

**Slavonic** [slə'vɒnɪk] *adj* slawisch.

**slay** [sleɪ] *pret* **slew,** *ptp* **slain** *vt* erschlagen; *(with gun etc)* ermorden.

**sleazy** ['sliːzɪ] *adj (+er) (col)* schäbig; *(disreputable)* anrüchig.

**sled** [sled] *(Brit),* **sledge** [sledʒ] *n* Schlitten *m.*

**sledge(hammer)** ['sledʒ(ˌhæmər)] *n* Vorschlaghammer *m.*

**sleek** [sliːk] **1** *adj (+er) hair, fur, animal* geschmeidig; *(of general appearance)* gepflegt; *car also* schnittig, elegant. **2** *vt* **to** ~ **one's hair down** sich *(dat)* die Haare glätten.

**sleep** [sliːp] *(vb: pret, ptp* **slept) 1** *n* Schlaf *m.* **to go to** ~ *(person, limb)* einschlafen; **to have a** ~ (etwas) schlafen; **to have a good night's** ~ sich richtig ausschlafen; **to put sb to** ~ jdn zum Schlafen bringen; *(drug)* jdn einschläfern; **to put an animal to** ~

*(euph)* ein Tier einschläfern; **that film sent me to ~** bei dem Film bin ich eingeschlafen. **2** *vt* **the house ~s 10** in dem Haus können 10 Leute schlafen *or* übernachten. **3** *vi* schlafen. **to ~ late** lange schlafen.

▶**sleep around** *vi (col)* mit jeder/jedem schlafen *(col)*.

▶**sleep in** *vi* ausschlafen; *(col: oversleep)* verschlafen.

▶**sleep off** *vt sep* hangover etc ausschlafen. **to ~ it ~** seinen Rausch ausschlafen.

▶**sleep on** *vi +prep obj* problem, decision überschlafen. **why don't you ~ ~ it** schlafen Sie doch erst einmal darüber.

▶**sleep with** *vi +prep obj (have sex)* schlafen mit.

**sleeper** ['sli:pǝr] *n* **(a) to be a heavy/light ~** einen festen/leichten Schlaf haben. **(b)** *(Brit Rail: on track)* Schwelle *f.* **(c)** *(Brit Rail) (train)* Schlafwagenzug *m; (coach)* Schlafwagen *m; (berth)* Platz *m* im Schlafwagen.

**sleepily** ['sli:pɪlɪ] *adv see adj (a)* verschlafen.

**sleepiness** ['sli:pɪnɪs] *n see adj (a)* Schläfrigkeit *f;* Verschlafenheit *f.*

**sleeping** ['sli:pɪŋ] *adj* schlafend. **S~ Beauty** Dornröschen *nt;* **let ~ dogs lie** *(Prov)* schlafende Hunde soll man nicht wecken *(Prov).*

**sleeping: ~ bag** *n* Schlafsack *m;* **~ car** *n* Schlafwagen *m;* **~ partner** *n (Brit)* stiller Teilhaber; **~ pill** *n* Schlaftablette *f;* **~ policeman** *n (traffic hump)* Bodenschwelle *f;* **~ quarters** *npl* Schlafräume *pl.*

**sleepless** ['sli:plɪs] *adj* schlaflos.

**sleeplessness** ['sli:plɪsnɪs] *n* Schlaflosigkeit *f.*

**sleep: ~walk** *vi* schlafwandeln; **~walker** *n* Schlafwandler (in *f) m.*

**sleepy** ['sli:pɪ] *adj (+er)* **(a)** *(drowsy)* person, voice etc schläfrig; *(not yet awake)* verschlafen. **to be/look ~** *(tired)* müde sein/aussehen. **(b)** *(inactive)* person lahm *(col);* place, atmosphere verschlafen; *climate* schläfrig machend; *afternoons* schläfrig.

**sleet** [sli:t] **1** *n* Schneeregen *m.* **2** *vi* **it was ~ing** es gab Schneeregen.

**sleeve** [sli:v] *n* **(a)** *(on garment)* Ärmel *m.* **to roll up one's ~s** *(lit, fig)* die Ärmel aufkrempeln *(col);* **to have sth up one's ~** *(fig col)* etw in petto haben *or* auf Lager haben. **(b)** *(for record)* Hülle *f.*

**sleeveless** ['sli:vlɪs] *adj* ärmellos.

**sleigh** [sleɪ] *n* (Pferde)schlitten *m.* **~ ride** Schlittenfahrt *f.*

**sleight** [slaɪt] *n:* **by ~ of hand** durch Taschenspielertricks.

**slender** ['slendǝr] *adj* schlank; *hand, waist also* schmal; *resources, majority* knapp; *hope* schwach, gering.

**slenderness** ['slendǝnɪs] *n see adj* Schlankheit *f;* Schmalheit *f;* Knappheit *f.*

**slept** [slept] *pret, ptp of* **sleep.**

**sleuth** [slu:θ] *n (col)* Spürhund *m (col).*

**slew¹,** *(US)* **slue** [slu:] *vti* (herum)schwenken.

**slew²** *pret of* **slay.**

**slice** [slaɪs] **1** *n* **(a)** Scheibe *f;* *(of bread also)* Schnitte *f; (fig: of population, profit)* Teil *m.* **a ~ of life** ein Ausschnitt aus dem Leben. **2** *(esp Brit: food server)* Wender *m.* **cake ~** Tortenheber *m.* **2** *vt* **(a)** *bread, meat etc* (in Scheiben) schneiden. **to ~ sth in two** etw durchschneiden. **(b)** *ball* anschneiden. **3** *vi* **to ~ through sth** etw durchschneiden.

▶**slice off** *vt sep* abschneiden.

▶**slice up** *vt sep* (ganz) in Scheiben schneiden; *(divide)* aufteilen.

**sliced** [slaɪst] *adj* (in Scheiben) geschnitten; *bread*

(auf)geschnitten.

**slicer** ['slaɪsǝr] *n (cheese-~ etc)* Hobel *m; (machine) (bread-~)* Brotschneider *m; (bacon-~)* ≈ Wurstschneidemaschine *f.*

**slick** [slɪk] **1** *adj (+er) (col)* **(a)** *(usu pej: clever, smart)* clever *(col);* answer, solution, performance, style glatt. **(b)** *hair* geschniegelt. **(c)** *(US: slippery)* glatt, schlüpfrig. **2** *n* **(a)** *(oil-~)* Ölteppich *m.* **(b)** *(US col: glossy magazine)* Hochglanzmagazin *nt.*

**slide** [slaɪd] *(vb: pret, ptp* **slid** [slɪd]*)* **1** *n* **(a)** *(chute, in playground etc)* Rutschbahn *f.* **(b)** *(fig: fall, drop)* Abfall *m.* **the ~ in share prices** der Preisrutsch bei den Aktien; **his gradual ~ into alcoholism** sein allmählicher Abstieg zum Alkoholiker. **(c)** *(esp Brit: for hair)* Spange *f.* **(d)** *(Phot)* Dia *nt; (microscope ~)* Objektträger *m.* **a lecture with ~s** ein Diavortrag *m.* **2** *vt (push)* schieben; *(slip)* gleiten lassen. **3** *vi* **(a)** rutschen; *(deliberately also)* schlittern. **to ~ down the banisters** das Treppengeländer hinunterrutschen. **(b)** *(move smoothly: machine part etc)* sich schieben lassen. **it slid into place** es rutschte an die richtige Stelle. **(c)** *(person: move quietly etc)* schleichen. **(d)** *(fig)* **the days slid by** *or* **past** die Tage vergingen schnell; **to let things ~** die Dinge laufen lassen.

**slide: ~ film** *n* Diafilm *m;* **~ projector** *n* Diaprojektor *m;* **~ rule** *n* Rechenschieber *m;* **~ show** *n* Diavortrag *m.*

**sliding** ['slaɪdɪŋ] *adj part, scale* gleitend; *door, roof etc* Schiebe-. **~ seat** Schiebesitz *m; (in boat)* Rollsitz *m.*

**slight** [slaɪt] **1** *adj (+er)* **(a)** *person, build* zierlich. **(b)** *(small, trivial)* leicht; *improvement also, change, possibility* geringfügig; *importance, intelligence* gering; *error also* klein; *acquaintance* flüchtig. **he showed some ~ optimism** er zeigte gewisse Ansätze von Optimismus; **he takes offence at the ~est thing** er ist wegen jeder (kleinsten) Kleinigkeit gleich beleidigt; **I haven't the ~est (idea)** ich habe nicht die geringste Ahnung; **not in the ~est** nicht im geringsten. **2** *n (affront)* Affront *m (on gegen).* **a ~ on one's/sb's character** eine persönliche Kränkung. **3** *vt (offend)* kränken; *(ignore)* ignorieren.

**slighting** ['slaɪtɪŋ] *adj (offensive)* kränkend; *remark* abfällig.

**slightly** ['slaɪtlɪ] *adv* **(a)** **~ built** *person* zierlich. **(b)** *(to a slight extent)* etwas, ein kleines bißchen; *know* flüchtig; *smell* leicht, etwas.

**slim** [slɪm] **1** *adj (+er)* **(a)** schlank; *waist etc* schmal. **(b)** *resources, profits* mager; *hope also* schwach; *chances* gering; *evidence* dürftig. **2** *vi* eine Schlankheitskur machen.

**slime** [slaɪm] *n* Schleim *m.*

**slimline** ['slɪm,laɪn] *adj dress* schlank geschnitten; *TV, PC etc* flach; *(low-calorie)* kalorienarm.

**slimming** ['slɪmɪŋ] *adj* schlankmachend *attr.* **crispbread is ~** Knäckebrot macht schlank; **~ foods** kalorienarme Nahrungsmittel *pl.*

**slimness** ['slɪmnɪs] *n see adj* **(a)** Schlankheit *f;* Schmalheit *f.* **(b)** Magerkeit *f;* Dürftigkeit *f.*

**slimy** ['slaɪmɪ] *adj (+er) (lit, fig)* schleimig; *wall* glitschig; *hands* schmierig.

**sling** [slɪŋ] *(vb: pret, ptp* **slung)** **1** *n* Schlinge *f; (for rifle)* (Trag)riemen *m.* **to have one's arm in a ~** den Arm in der Schlinge tragen. **2** *vt (throw)* schleudern, schmeißen *(col).* **he slung his coat over his arm** er warf sich *(dat)* den Mantel über den Arm.

▶**sling out** *vt sep (col)* rausschmeißen *(col).*

**sling: ~back shoes, ~backs** *npl* Slingpumps *pl;* **~shot** *n (US)* Schleuder *f.*

**slink** [slɪŋk] *pret, ptp* **slunk** *vi* schleichen. **to ~ away** *or* **off** sich davonschleichen.

**slinky** ['slɪŋkɪ] *adj (+er) (col)* aufreizend; *(clothes)* hauteng.

**slip** [slɪp] **1** *n* **(a)** *(slide)* he had a nasty ~ er ist ausgerutscht und bös gefallen. **(b)** *(mistake)* Ausrutscher, Patzer *m.* **to make a (bad)** ~ sich (übel) vertun *(col)*; **a** ~ **of the pen/tongue** ein Flüchtigkeitsfehler *m*/Versprecher *m*; **it was just a** ~ **of the pen** da habe ich mich nur verschrieben. **(c) to give sb the** ~ jdm entwischen. **(d)** *(pillow ~)* Kissenbezug *m.* **(e)** *(undergarment)* Unterrock *m.* **(f)** *(of paper)* Zettel *m.* **~s of paper** Zettel *pl.* **(g) a (mere)** ~ **of a girl** *(slightly built)* ein zierliches Persönchen.

**2** *vt* **(a)** schieben; *(slide)* gleiten lassen; *(Aut) clutch* schleifen lassen. **to** ~ **sth across to sb** jdm etw zuschieben; *(unobtrusively)* jdm etw zustecken; **to** ~ **sth into sb's pocket** jdm etw in die Tasche gleiten lassen; **she** ~**ped the dress over her head** sie streifte sich *(dat)* das Kleid über den Kopf; **to** ~ **a disc** *(Med)* sich *(dat)* einen Bandscheibenschaden zuziehen; **to** ~ **sb a fiver** jdm einen Fünfpfundschein zustecken. **(b)** *(escape from)* sich losreißen. **the dog** ~**ped its chain** der Hund hat sich (von der Kette) losgerissen; **the boat had** ~**ped its moorings** das Boot hatte sich losgerissen; **it** ~**ped my mind** ich habe es vergessen; **it** ~**ped my notice** es ist mir entgangen.

**3** *vi* **(a)** *(person)* (aus)rutschen; *(feet, tyres)* (weg)rutschen; *(become loose: knot, nut)* sich lösen; *(Aut: clutch)* schleifen. **the knife** ~**ped** das Messer rutschte ab; **it** ~**ped from her hand** es rutschte ihr aus der Hand; **to** ~ **into a dress** in ein Kleid schlüpfen; **suddenly everything** ~**ped into place** plötzlich paßte alles zusammen. **(b)** *(move quickly)* schlüpfen; *(move smoothly)* rutschen. **I'll** ~ **around to the shop** ich springe schnell zum Laden. **(c) to let (it)** ~ **that** ... fallenlassen, daß...; **the police let the thief** ~ **through their fingers** die Polizei ließ sich *(dat)* den Dieb durch die Finger schlüpfen. **(d)** *(decline: standards, morals etc)* fallen. **you're** ~**ping!** *(col)* du läßt nach *(col)*.

▶**slip away** *vi* sich wegschleichen; *(time)* verstreichen; *(chances)* (allmählich) schwinden; *(opportunity)* dahinschwinden.

▶**slip by** *vi (person)* sich vorbeischleichen *(prep obj* an *+dat)*; *(years)* verfliegen, nur so dahinschwinden.

▶**slip in 1** *vi (person)* (sich) hineinschleichen. **2** *vt sep remark* einfließen lassen.

▶**slip off 1** *vi (person)* sich wegschleichen. **2** *vt sep clothes* ausziehen, abstreifen.

▶**slip on** *vt sep* schlüpfen in *(+acc)*; *dress also* überstreifen; *ring* aufziehen; *lid* drauftun *(prep obj* auf *+acc)*.

▶**slip out** *vi* **(a)** *(leave unobtrusively)* kurz weggehen. **(b)** *(be revealed)* herauskommen. **the secret** ~**ped** ~ **before he realized** ehe er sich's versah, war ihm das Geheimnis herausgerutscht.

▶**slip up** *vi (col: err)* sich vertun *(col) (over, in* bei).

**slip:** ~ **case** *n* Schuber *m*; ~**cover** *n (esp US)* Schonbezug *m*; ~**knot** *n* Schlaufenknoten *m*; ~**ons** *npl (also* ~**-on shoes)** Slipper *pl*; ~**over** *n* Pullunder *m.*

**slipped disc** [slɪpt'dɪsk] *n* Bandscheibenschaden *m.*

**slipper** ['slɪpər] *n* Pantoffel, Hausschuh *m.*

**slippery** ['slɪpərɪ] *adj* **(a)** schlüpfrig; *rope, road* glatt, rutschig; *fish* glitschig. **he's on the** ~ **slope** *(col)* er ist auf der schiefen Bahn. **(b)** *(pej col) person* glatt, windig *(col)*. **a** ~ **customer** ein aalglatter Typ *(col)*.

**slip-road** ['slɪprəud] *n (Brit)* Zufahrtsstraße *f*; *(for entering motorway)* (Autobahn)auffahrt *f*; *(for leaving motorway)* (Autobahn)ausfahrt *f.*

**slipshod** ['slɪpʃɒd] *adj* schludrig.

**slip:** ~**stream** *n (Aviat)* Sog *m*; *(Aut)* Windschatten *m*; ~**up** *n* Schnitzer *m*; *(less serious)* Patzer *m*; ~**way** *n (Naut)* Gleitbahn *f*; **to come off the** ~**way** vom Stapel laufen.

**slit** [slɪt] *(vb: pret, ptp* ~*)* **1** *n* Schlitz *m.* **2** *vt* (auf)schlitzen. **to** ~ **a sack open** einen Sack aufschlitzen; **to** ~ **sb's throat** jdm die Kehle aufschlitzen.

**slither** ['slɪðər] *vi* rutschen. **to** ~ **about on the ice** auf dem Eis herumschlittern.

**sliver** ['slɪvər] *n (of wood etc)* Splitter *m*; *(thin slice)* Scheibchen *nt.*

**slob** [slɒb] *n (col)* Drecksau *f (col!)*.

**slobber** ['slɒbər] *vi* sabbern, sabbeln *(also fig)*; *(dog)* geifern.

**sloe** [sləu] *n* Schlehe *f.*

**slog** [slɒg] *(col)* **1** *n (effort)* Schinderei *f (col)*. **it's a hard** ~ **to the top** man muß ganz schön schuften, um nach oben zu kommen. **2** *vt ball* dreschen *(col)*; *opponent* hart treffen. **to** ~ **away at sth** *(col)*. **3** *vi* **to** ~ **away at sth** *(work)* an etw *(dat)* schuften *(col)*; **we** ~**ged on for another 5 miles** wir kämpften uns noch 5 Meilen weiter.

**slogan** ['sləugən] *n* Slogan *m*; *(motto)* Motto *nt*; *(political also)* Parole *f.*

**slogger** ['slɒgər] *n (col: worker)* Arbeitstier *nt.*

**slop** [slɒp] **1** *vi (spill)* (über)schwappen. **to** ~ **over (into sth)** überschwappen (in etw *acc*). **2** *vt (spill)* verschütten; *(pour out)* schütten.

**slope** [sləup] **1** *n* **(a)** *(angle)* Neigung *f*; *(downwards also)* Gefälle *nt*; *(of roof also)* Schräge *f.* **(b)** *(sloping ground)* (Ab)hang *m.* **on a** ~ am Hang; **halfway up the** ~ auf halber Höhe; **the (ski)** ~**s** die Pisten. **2** *vi* geneigt sein; *(road, floor)* sich neigen. **the ground** ~**s down to the stream** das Land senkt sich zum Fluß hin ab.

▶**slope off** *vi (col: person)* abziehen *(col)*.

**sloping** ['sləupɪŋ] *adj road (upwards)* ansteigend; *(downwards)* abfallend; *roof, floor* schräg; *garden etc* am Hang; *(not aligned)* schief.

**sloppily** ['slɒpɪlɪ] *adv see adj (a)*.

**sloppiness** ['slɒpɪnɪs] *n see adj* **(a)** Schlampigkeit *f (col)*. **(b)** Rührseligkeit *f.*

**sloppy** ['slɒpɪ] *adj (+er)* **(a)** *(col: careless)* schlampig *(col)*; *work also* schlud(e)rig *(col)*. **(b)** *(col: sentimental)* rührselig; *novel also* schmalzig.

**slops** [slɒps] *npl (dirty water)* Schmutzwasser *nt*; *(food waste)* Abfallbrühe *f*; *(in teapot)* Satz *m.*

**slosh** [slɒʃ] *(col)* **1** *vt* **(a) to** ~ **some water over sth** Wasser über etw *(acc)* schütten. **(b)** *(Brit: hit)* hauen. **2** *vi* **to** ~ **about in the water** im Wasser herumplanschen.

**sloshed** [slɒʃt] *adj pred (esp Brit col)* blau *(col)*. **to get** ~ sich besaufen *(col)*.

**slot** [slɒt] *n (opening)* Schlitz *m*; *(groove)* Rille *f*; *(col: place)* Plätzchen *nt (col)*; *(TV col)* (gewohnte) Sendezeit. ~ **machine** Münzautomat *m*; *(for gambling)* Spielautomat *m*; ~ **meter** Münzzähler *m.*

▶**slot in 1** *vt sep* hineinstecken. **to** ~ **sth** ~**to sth** etw in etw *(acc)* stecken. **2** *vi* sich einfügen lassen. **suddenly everything** ~**ted** ~**to place** plötzlich paßte alles zusammen.

**sloth** [sləuθ] *n* **(a)** *(laziness)* Faulheit *f.* **(b)** *(Zool)* Faultier *nt.*

**slothful** ['sləuθful] *adj* faul; *person, life also* träge.

**slouch** [slautʃ] **1** *n* krumme Haltung; *(of shoulders)* Hängen *m.* **to be no** ~ **at sth** *(col)* etw ganz schön gut können *(col)*. **2** *vi (stand, sit)* herumhängen *(col)*; *(move)* latschen. **to** ~ **off** davonzockeln *(col)*; **he was** ~**ed over his desk** er hing über seinem Schreibtisch; **he sat ~ed on a chair** er hing auf einem Stuhl.

**Slovak** ['sləʊvæk] **1** adj slowakisch. **2** n **(a)** Slowake m, Slowakin f. **(b)** (language) Slowakisch nt.

**Slovakia** [sləʊ'vækɪə] n die Slowakei.

**Slovene** ['sləʊviːn] **1** adj slowenisch. **2** n Slowene m, Slowenin f.

**Slovenia** [sləʊ'viːnɪə] n Slowenien nt.

**slovenly** ['slʌvnlɪ] adj schlampig (col).

**slow** [sləʊ] **1** adj (+er) langsam. **it's ~ work** das braucht seine Zeit; **he is a ~ worker/learner/reader** er arbeitet/lernt/liest langsam; **to get off to a ~ start** (race) schlecht vom Start kommen; (project) nur langsam in Gang kommen; **to be ~/not to be ~ to do sth** sich (dat) mit etw Zeit lassen/etw prompt erledigen; **he is ~ to make up his mind/~ to anger** er braucht lange, um sich zu entscheiden/er wird nicht so leicht wütend; **they were ~ to act** sie ließen sich (dat) Zeit; **they were ~ to react** sie reagierten nur langsam; **to be (20 minutes) ~** (clock) (20 Minuten) nachgehen; **bake in a ~ oven** bei schwacher Hitze backen. **2** adv (+er) langsam. **to go ~** (driver) langsam fahren; (workers) einen Bummelstreik machen. **3** vi **to ~** (to a stop/standstill) langsam zum Stehen/zum Stillstand kommen.

►**slow down** or **up 1** vi sich verlangsamen; (drive/walk) langsamer fahren/gehen; (worker) langsamer arbeiten. **2** vt sep verlangsamen; engine drosseln; machine herunterschalten; programme, project verzögern.

**slow:** **~coach** n (Brit col) Langweiler m; (mentally) Transuse f (col); **~down** n (US: go-slow) Bummelstreik m; **~ lane** n (driving on right) rechte Spur; (driving on left) linke Spur; (on hill) Kriechspur f.

**slowly** ['sləʊlɪ] adv langsam.

**slow:** **~ motion** n Zeitlupe f; **in ~ motion** in Zeitlupe; **~-moving** adj sich (nur) langsam fortbewegend; traffic zähflüssig.

**slowness** ['sləʊnɪs] n Langsamkeit f. **their ~ to act** ihr Zaudern; **~ of mind** Begriffsstutzigkeit f.

**slow:** **~poke** n (US) see **~coach**; **~-witted** adj begriffsstutzig; **~worm** n Blindschleiche f.

**SLR** (Phot) = single-lens reflex.

**sludge** [slʌdʒ] n Schlamm m.

**slue** [sluː] (US) = **slew**[1].

**slug**[1] [slʌg] n Nacktschnecke f. **~s and snails** Schnecken pl (mit und ohne Gehäuse).

**slug**[2] **1** n (bullet) Kugel f; (blow) Schlag m. **a ~ of whisky** ein Schluck m Whisky. **2** vt (col: hit) eine knallen (+dat) (col).

**sluggish** ['slʌgɪʃ] adj (indolent, Med) träge; engine, car lahm, langsam; business flau; market lustlos.

**sluggishly** ['slʌgɪʃlɪ] adv move, flow träge; (Comm) flau, lustlos.

**sluggishness** ['slʌgɪʃnɪs] n see adj Trägheit f; Lahmheit f. **the ~ of the market** die Flaute am Markt.

**sluice** [sluːs] **1** n Schleuse f. **2** vt **to ~ sth (down)** etw abspritzen.

**sluice gate** n Schleusentor nt.

**slum** [slʌm] **1** n (usu pl: area) Slum m, Elendsviertel nt; (house) Elendsquartier nt. **~ clearance** ≈ (Stadt)sanierung f.

**slumber** ['slʌmbəʳ] (liter) **1** n Schlummer (geh), Schlaf m. **~s** Träume pl. **2** vi schlummern (geh).

**slump** [slʌmp] **1** n (in gen) (in numbers, popularity etc) (plötzliche) Abnahme f; (in production) Rückgang m; (state) Tiefstand m; (Fin) Sturz m, Baisse f (spec). **~ in prices** Preissturz m (of bei); **~ in sales** Absatzflaute f; **the 1929 S~** die Weltwirtschaftskri-

se von 1929. **2** vi **(a)** (Fin, Comm) (prices) stürzen, fallen; (sales, production) plötzlich zurückgehen; (fig: morale etc) sinken. **(b)** (sink) fallen, sinken. **to ~ into a chair** sich in einen Sessel fallen lassen; **he was ~ed over the wheel** er war über dem Steuer zusammengesackt.

**slung** [slʌŋ] pret, ptp of **sling**.

**slunk** [slʌŋk] pret, ptp of **slink**.

**slur** [slɜːʳ] **1** n **(a)** Makel m; (insult) Beleidigung f. **to cast a ~ on sb/sth** jdn/etw in einem schlechten Licht erscheinen lassen; (person) jdn/etw verunglimpfen. **(b)** (Mus) Bindung f. **(c)** **to speak with a ~** undeutlich sprechen. **2** vt (pronounce indistinctly) undeutlich aussprechen, lallen.

**slurp** [slɜːp] vti schlürfen.

**slurred** [slɜːd] adj undeutlich; (Mus) gebunden.

**slush** [slʌʃ] n (watery snow) (Schnee)matsch m; (mud) Morast m; (col: sentimental nonsense) Kitsch m. **~ fund** Schmiergeldfonds m.

**slushy** ['slʌʃɪ] adj (+er) snow, mud, path matschig; (col: sentimental) kitschig.

**slut** [slʌt] n (liederliche) Schlampe.

**sly** [slaɪ] **1** adj (+er) schlau, gerissen; look, wink verschmitzt. **2** n **on the ~** heimlich, still und leise (hum), ganz heimlich.

**slyly** ['slaɪlɪ] adv see adj.

**slyness** ['slaɪnɪs] n see adj Schlauheit, Gerissenheit f; Verschmitztheit f.

**smack**[1] [smæk] vi **to ~ of** (taste) leicht schmecken nach; (fig) riechen nach.

**smack**[2] **1** n (klatschender) Schlag m; (slap also) fester Klaps; (sound) Klatschen nt. **to give a child/the ball a ~** einem Kind eine knallen (col)/auf den Ball dreschen (col); **you'll get a ~** du kriegst gleich eine (col); **a ~ in the eye** (fig) ein Schlag ins Gesicht. **2** vt (slap) knallen (col). **to ~ a child's bottom** einem Kind den Hintern versohlen (col); **he ~ed his lips** er leckte sich (dat) die Lippen. **3** adv (col) direkt. **he ran ~ into the door** sie rannte voll gegen die Tür (col).

**smacker** ['smækəʳ] n (col) **(a)** (kiss) Schmatz m (col). **(b)** (money) (pound) Pfund nt; (dollar) Dollar m.

**small** [smɔːl] **1** adj (+er) **(a)** klein; supply also, importance gering; waist schmal; letter also Klein-; sum also bescheiden. **the ~est possible number of books** so wenig Bücher wie möglich; **to have a ~ appetite/be a ~ eater** wenig Appetit haben/kein großer Esser sein; **no ~ success** ein beachtlicher Erfolg; **to feel/look ~** (fig) sich (ganz) klein (und häßlich) vorkommen/schlecht dastehen; **a few ~ matters** ein paar Kleinigkeiten; **to help in a ~ way** bescheidene Hilfe leisten; **to start in a ~ way** klein anfangen. **(b)** (fig: mean, petty) person kleinlich. **2** n **(a)** **the ~ of the back** das Kreuz. **(b)** **~s** pl (Brit col) Unterwäsche f. **3** adv **to chop sth up ~** etw kleinhacken.

**small:** **~ ad** n (Brit) Kleinanzeige f; **~ arms** npl Handfeuerwaffen pl; **~ change** n Kleingeld nt; **~holder** n (Brit) Kleinbauer m; **~holding** n (Brit) kleiner Landbesitz; **~ hours** npl früher Morgen; **in the ~ hours** in den frühen Morgenstunden.

**smallish** ['smɔːlɪʃ] adj eher klein, eher kleiner. **he is ~** er ist eher klein.

**small-minded** [ˌsmɔːl'maɪndɪd] adj engstirnig.

**smallness** ['smɔːlnɪs] n Kleinheit f; (of waist) Schmalheit f; (of sum, present) Bescheidenheit f; (pettiness) Kleinlichkeit f.

**small:** **~pox** n Pocken pl; **~ print** n das Kleingedruckte; **~-scale** adj map, model in verkleinertem Maßstab; project kleinangelegt; **~ screen** n (TV) **on the ~ screen** auf dem Bildschirm; **~ talk** n oberflächliche Konversation; **~-time** *adj (col)* armselig; *crook* klein; *politician* Schmalspur-; *actor* drittrangig; **~-town** *adj* Kleinstadt-, kleinstädtisch; *mentality also* kleinbürgerlich.

**smarmy** ['smɑːmɪ] *adj (+er) (Brit col)* schmierig; *(servile)* kriecherisch *(pej)*; *voice* einschmeichelnd.

**smart** [smɑːt] **1** *adj (+er)* **(a)** schick; *person, clothes, car also* flott; *society* fein. **a ~-looking girl/garden** ein flott aussehendes Mädchen/ein gepflegter Garten; **the ~ set** die Schickeria *(col)*. **(b)** *(bright, clever)* clever *(col)*, schlau; *thief, trick also* raffiniert; *(pej) person, answer* neunmalklug *(pej col)*; *(Comp) card etc* intelligent. **to get ~** *(col)* sich am Riemen reißen *(col)*; *(get cheeky)* frech kommen *(with dat)*. **(c)** *(quick)* (blitz)schnell; *pace* flott *(col)*. **and look ~ (about it)**! und zwar ein bißchen fix *or* plötzlich! *(col)*. **2** *vi* brennen. **it will make your cut ~** es wird (dir) in der Wunde brennen; **to ~ from sth** *(from blow etc)* von etw brennen; *(fig)* unter etw *(dat)* leiden.

**smart:** **~-aleck** ['smɑːt,ælɪk] *(col)* **1** *n* Schlauberger *m (col)*; **2** *adj remarks* besserwisserisch; **~-arse**, *(US)* **~-ass** *n (col!)* Klugscheißer *m (col!)*.

**smarten** ['smɑːtn] *(also ~ up)* **1** *vt house, room* herausputzen; *appearance* aufmöbeln *(col)*. **to ~ oneself up** *(dress up)* sich in Schale werfen *(col)*; *(generally improve appearance)* mehr Wert auf sein Äußeres legen; **you'd better ~ up your ideas** *(col)* du solltest dich am Riemen reißen *(col)*. **2** *vi* = **~ oneself up**.

**smartly** ['smɑːtlɪ] *adv* **(a)** schick; *dress also* flott. **(b)** clever *(col)*, schlau. **(c)** (blitz)schnell; *walk* rasch.

**smartness** ['smɑːtnɪs] *n* **(a)** Schick *m*. **(b)** *(cleverness)* Cleverness *(col)*, Schlauheit *f*; *(of thief, trick)* Raffiniertheit *f*.

**smash** [smæʃ] **1** *vt* **(a)** zerschlagen; *window also* einschlagen. **I ~ed my glasses** die Brille ist mir kaputtgegangen. **(b)** *(defeat or destroy)* zerschlagen; *rebellion also* niederschlagen; *opponent* zerschmettern; *record* haushoch schlagen. **(c)** *(strike, also Tennis)* schmettern.

**2** *vi* **(a)** *(break)* zerbrechen. **it ~ed into a thousand pieces** es (zer)sprang in tausend Stücke. **(b)** *(crash)* prallen. **the car ~ed into the wall** das Auto krachte gegen die Mauer; **the plane ~ed into the houses** das Flugzeug raste in die Häusergruppe.

**3** *n* **(a)** *(noise)* Krachen *nt*; *(of waves)* Klatschen *nt*. **there was a ~** es hat gekracht. **(b)** *(collision)* Unfall *m*. **(c)** *(blow)* Schlag *m*; *(Tennis)* Schmetterball *m*.

**4** *adv (col)* mit Karacho *(col)*.

►**smash down** *vt sep door* einschlagen.

►**smash in** *vt sep* einschlagen. **the firemen had to ~ their way** ~ die Feuerwehrleute mußten gewaltsam eindringen; **to ~ sb's face** ~ *(col)* jdm die Schnauze einschlagen *(col!)*.

►**smash up** *vt sep* zertrümmern; *car* kaputtfahren.

**smash-and-grab (raid)** [ˌsmæʃən'græb(reɪd)] *n* Schaufenstereinbruch *m*.

**smashed** [smæʃt] *adj (col)* stockbesoffen *(col)*.

**smasher** ['smæʃəʳ] *n (esp Brit col)* toller Typ *(col)*; *(woman)* Klassefrau *f (col)*.

**smash hit** *n (col)* Superhit *m (col)*.

**smashing** ['smæʃɪŋ] *adj (esp Brit col)* klasse *inv*, Klasse *pred*, dufte *(all col)*.

**smattering** ['smætərɪŋ] *n* **a ~ of French** ein paar Brocken Französisch.

**smear** [smɪəʳ] **1** *n* verschmierter Fleck; *(fig)* Beschmutzung *f*; *(defamation)* Verleumdung *f*; *(Med)* Abstrich *m*. **this left a ~ on his name** das schadete sei-

nem Namen; **~ campaign** Verleumdungskampagne *f*; **~ test** *(Med)* Abstrich *m*. **2** *vt* **(a)** *cream, ointment* schmieren; *(spread)* verschmieren; *(mark, make dirty)* beschmieren; *face* einschmieren. **(b)** *(fig) person* verunglimpfen; *sb's reputation* beschmutzen. **3** *vi (glass)* verschmieren; *(print)* verschmiert *or* verwischt werden; *(biro)* schmieren; *(paint, ink)* verlaufen.

**smell** [smel] *(vb: pret, ptp ~ed or esp Brit* **smelt***)* **1** *n (sense of ~, odour)* Geruch *m*; *(unpleasant also)* Gestank *m*; *(fragrant also)* Duft *m*. **it ~s ~** es riecht gut *or* angenehm; **there's a ~ of gas** hier riecht es nach Gas. **2** *vt* **(a)** riechen. **can you ~ burning?** riechst du, daß etwas brennt *or (Cook)* anbrennt? **(b)** *(fig) danger, treason* wittern. **to ~ trouble** Ärger kommen sehen. **3** *vi* riechen; *(unpleasantly also)* stinken; *(fragrantly also)* duften. **to ~ of sth** *(lit, fig)* nach etw riechen; **his breath ~s** er hat Mundgeruch.

►**smell out** *vt sep* **(a)** *rabbit, traitor etc* aufspüren; *plot* aufdecken. **(b)** **these onions are ~ing the house ~!** die Zwiebeln verpesten das ganze Haus!

**smelling salts** ['smelɪŋˌsɒlts] *npl* Riechsalz *nt*.

**smelly** ['smelɪ] *adj (+er)* übelriechend, stinkend. **it's ~ in here** hier riecht es drin stinkt es.

**smelt¹** [smelt] *pret, ptp of* **smell**.

**smelt²** *vt ore* schmelzen; *(refine)* verhütten.

**smidgen, smidgin** ['smɪdʒən] *n (col)* **a ~** ein klitzekleines bißchen *(col)*.

**smile** [smaɪl] **1** *n* Lächeln *nt*. **to be all ~s** übers ganze Gesicht strahlen; **to give sb a ~** jdm zulächeln; **take that ~ off your face!** hör auf, so zu grinsen!; **that soon wiped the ~ off his face** dabei verging ihm bald das Lachen. **2** *vi* lächeln. **come on, ~ ~** lach mal!; **to ~ at sb** jdn anlächeln; *(cheerfully)* jdn anlachen; **to ~ at sth** über etw *(acc)* lächeln; **to ~ with joy/happiness** *etc* vor Freude/Glück *etc* strahlen; **fortune ~d on him** *(liter)* ihm lachte das Glück.

**smiling** ['smaɪlɪŋ] *adj* lächelnd.

**smirk** [smɜːk] **1** *n* Grinsen *nt*. **2** *vi* grinsen.

**smite** [smaɪt] *pret* **smote**, *ptp* **smitten** *vt (old, liter)* schlagen.

**smith** [smɪθ] *n* Schmied *m*.

**smithereens** [ˌsmɪðə'riːnz] *npl* **to smash sth to ~** etw in tausend Stücke schlagen.

**smithy** ['smɪðɪ] *n* Schmiede *f*.

**smitten** ['smɪtn] **1** *ptp of* **smite**. **2** *adj* **to be ~ with the plague/remorse** von der Pest heimgesucht/von Reue geplagt werden; **he's really ~ with her** *(col)* er ist wirklich vernarrt in sie *(col)*.

**smock** [smɒk] *n* Kittel *m*.

**smog** [smɒg] *n* Smog *m*.

**smoke** [sməuk] **1** *n* **(a)** Rauch *m*. **there's no ~ without fire** *(prov)* kein Rauch ohne Flamme *(prov)*; **to go up in ~** in Rauch (und Flammen) aufgehen. **(b)** *(cigarette etc)* **have you got a ~?** hast du was zu rauchen? *(col)*; *(act)* **to have a ~** eine rauchen. **2** *vt* **(a)** *cigarette* rauchen. **(b)** *fish etc* räuchern. **3** *vi* rauchen; *(oil-lamp etc)* qualmen. **to ~ like a chimney** wie ein Schlot rauchen.

**smoke-bomb** ['sməukbɒm] *n* Rauchbombe *f*.

**smoked** [sməukt] *adj bacon, fish* geräuchert, Räucher-. **~ glass** Rauchglas *nt*.

**smoke detector** *n* Rauchmelder *m*.

**smokeless** ['sməuklɪs] *adj zone* rauchfrei; *fuel* rauchlos.

**smoker** ['sməukəʳ] *n* **(a)** *(person)* Raucher(in *f*) *m*. **to be a heavy ~** stark rauchen, ein starker Raucher sein. **(b)** *(Rail)* Raucher(abteil *nt*) *m*.

**smoke:** **~-ring** *n* (Rauch)ring *m*; **~screen** *n* Rauchvorhang *m*; *(fig)* Deckmantel, Vorwand *m*; **~**

**shop** n (US) Tabakladen m; ~ **signal** n Rauchzeichen nt.
**smoking** ['sməʊkɪŋ] **1** adj rauchend. **2** n Rauchen nt. "no ~" „Rauchen verboten".
**smoking:** ~ **compartment,** (US) ~ **car** n Raucherabteil nt; ~ **jacket** n Hausjacke f.
**smoky** ['sməʊkɪ] adj (+er) chimney, fire rauchend; room, atmosphere verraucht; flavour rauchig.
**smolder** vi (US) = **smoulder.**
**smooch** [smu:tʃ] (col) vi knutschen (col).
**smooth** [smu:ð] **1** adj (+er) **(a)** (in texture, surface etc) glatt; sea also ruhig; outline sanft; skin also, hair weich. **as** ~ **as glass** spiegelglatt; **worn** ~ **steps** glattgetreten; knife abgeschliffen; tyre abgefahren. **(b)** (in consistency) paste sämig; sauce glatt. **(c)** motion, flight, crossing ruhig; gear-change weich; landing glatt; breathing gleichmäßig; (trouble-free) transition, functioning reibungslos, glatt. **the bill had a** ~ **passage through Parliament** der Gesetzentwurf kam glatt durchs Parlament. **(d)** (polite, often pej) manners, salesman glatt; person also schmierig (pej); (unruffled) kühl, cool (col). **to be a** ~ **talker** ein Schönredner sein; **a** ~ **operator** ein Schlawiner m (col).
**2** vt surface, dress, hair glätten; wood glatthobeln; (fig) feelings beruhigen. **to** ~ **the way for sb** jdm den Weg ebnen.
►**smooth down** vt sep glatt machen; hair, dress glattstreichen; (fig) person, feelings beruhigen.
►**smooth out** vt sep (make smooth) crease, surface glätten; (fig) difficulty aus dem Weg räumen.
►**smooth over** vt sep quarrel in Ordnung bringen. **to** ~ **things** ~ die Sache geradebiegen (col).
**smoothly** ['smu:ðlɪ] adv land weich; change gear leicht; drive ruhig; fit genau; make transition unmerklich; talk schön; handle situation kühl; behave aalglatt (pej). **to go** ~ (without problems) glatt über die Bühne gehen; **to run** ~ (engine) rund laufen.
**smoothness** ['smu:ðnɪs] n see adj **(a)** Glätte f; Ruhe f; Sanftheit f; Weichheit f. **(b)** Sämigkeit f; Glätte f. **(c)** Ruhe f; Weichheit f; Glätte f; Gleichmäßigkeit f; Reibungslosigkeit f; (of fit) Genauigkeit f.
**smote** [sməʊt] pret of smite.
**smother** ['smʌðəʳ] vt **(a)** (stifle) person, fire ersticken; (fig) criticism also, yawn, sob etc unterdrücken. **to** ~ **sb with affection** jdn mit seiner Liebe erdrücken. **(b)** (cover) (ganz) bedecken (in mit).
**smoulder,** (US) **smolder** ['sməʊldəʳ] vi (lit, fig) glimmen, schwelen. ~**ing hatred** schwelender Haß.
**smudge** [smʌdʒ] **1** n Fleck m; (of ink) Klecks m. **2** vt verwischen. **3** vi verschmieren.
**smug** [smʌg] adj (+er) selbstgefällig; remark, expression also süffisant.
**smuggle** ['smʌgl] vti (lit, fig) schmuggeln. **to** ~ **sb/sth in** jdn/etw einschmuggeln; **to** ~ **sb/sth out** jdn/etw herausschmuggeln.
**smuggler** ['smʌgləʳ] n Schmuggler(in f) m.
**smuggling** ['smʌglɪŋ] n Schmuggel m.
**smugly** ['smʌglɪ] adv selbstgefällig; grin, say also süffisant.
**smugness** ['smʌgnɪs] n Selbstgefälligkeit f.
**smut** [smʌt] n **(a)** (piece of dirt) Rußflocke f. **(b)** (fig) Schmutz m.
**smutty** ['smʌtɪ] adj (+er) (lit, fig) schmutzig.
**snack** [snæk] n Imbiß m. **to have a** ~ eine Kleinigkeit essen; ~ **bar** Imbißstube f.
**snafu** [snæ'fu:] n (US col) Schlamassel m (col).
**snag** [snæg] n Haken m, Schwierigkeit f. **there's a** ~ die Sache hat einen Haken; **what's the** ~? was ist das Problem?; **to run into** or **hit a** ~ in Schwierig-

keiten (acc) kommen.
**snail** [sneɪl] n Schnecke f. **at a** ~'**s pace** im Schneckentempo.
**snake** [sneɪk] n Schlange f. **a** ~ **in the grass** (fig) (woman) eine listige Schlange; (man) ein heimtückischer Kerl.
**snake:** ~**bite** n Schlangenbiß m; ~ **charmer** n Schlangenbeschwörer m; ~**skin** n Schlangenhaut f; (leather) Schlangenleder nt; **2** adj Schlangenleder-, aus Schlangenleder.
**snap** [snæp] **1** n **(a)** (sound) Schnappen nt; (with fingers) Schnippen nt; (of sth breaking) Knacken nt. **(b)** (Phot) Schnappschuß m. **(c)** (Cards) ≃ Schnippschnapp nt. **2** adj attr plötzlich, spontan. ~ **decision** plötzlicher Entschluß. **3** vt **(a)** fingers schnipsen mit. **to** ~ **a book shut** ein Buch zuklappen; **to** ~ **sth into place** etw einschnappen lassen. **(b)** (break) zerbrechen. **(c)** (also ~ out) **to** ~ **an order** bellend etwas befehlen; **she** ~**ped a few words at the children** sie pfiff die Kinder an. **(d)** (Phot) knipsen. **4** vi **(a)** (click) (zu)schnappen; (crack, break) zerbrechen. **to** ~ **shut** zuschnappen; **my patience finally** ~**ped** dann ist mir aber der Geduldsfaden gerissen. **(b)** (speak sharply) bellen (col). **to** ~ **at sb** jdn anschnauzen (col). **(c)** (of dog etc, fig) schnappen (at nach).
►**snap off** vt sep (break off) abbrechen; (bite off) abbeißen. **to** ~ **sb's head** ~ (fig col) jdm ins Gesicht springen (col).
►**snap out 1** vt sep order brüllen. **2** vi ~ ~ **of it!** reiß dich zusammen!; (cheer up) Kopf hoch!
►**snap up** vt sep (lit, fig) wegschnappen.
**snapdragon** ['snæp,drægən] n (Bot) Löwenmaul nt.
**snappish** ['snæpɪʃ] adj (lit, fig) bissig.
**snappy** ['snæpɪ] adj (+er) **(a)** (col) flott (col). **and make it** ~! und zwar ein bißchen flott! (col). **(b)** (lit, fig) dog, person bissig. **(c)** (col) translation kurz und treffend; phrase zündend.
**snapshot** ['snæpʃɒt] n Schnappschuß m.
**snare** [sneəʳ] **1** n (lit, fig: trap) Falle f; (fig also) Fallstrick m. **2** vt (lit, fig) (ein)fangen.
**snarl** [snɑ:l] **1** n Knurren nt no pl. **2** vi knurren. **to** ~ **at sb** jdn anknurren.
►**snarl up** vt sep (col) **I got** ~**ed** ~ **in a traffic jam** ich bin im Verkehr steckengeblieben.
**snarl-up** ['snɑ:lʌp] n (col) (in traffic) Verkehrschaos nt. **there's a** ~ **in the system** das System ist zum Erliegen gekommen.
**snatch** [snætʃ] **1** n **(a)** (act) Griff m. **to make a** ~ **at sth** nach etw greifen; (animal) zuschnappen. **(b)** (Brit col) (robbery) Raub m; (kidnapping) Entführung f. **(c)** (snippet) Stück nt; (of conversation) Fetzen m. **2** vt **(a)** (grab) greifen. **to** ~ **sth from sb** jdm etw entreißen; **to** ~ **hold of sth** etw greifen, etw schnappen; **to** ~ **sth out of sb's hand** jdm etw aus der Hand reißen. **(b)** some sleep etc ergattern. **to** ~ **a quick meal** schnell etwas essen. **(c)** (Brit col) (steal) money klauen (col); handbag aus der Hand reißen; (kidnap) entführen. **3** vi greifen (at nach). **don't** ~! nicht grapschen! (col).
►**snatch away** vt sep wegreißen (sth from sb jdm etw).
►**snatch up** vt sep schnappen. **he** ~**ed** ~ **his camera** er schnappte sich (dat) seine Kamera; **the mother** ~**ed** ~ **her child** die Mutter riß ihr Kind an sich (acc).
**sneak** [sni:k] **1** n Schleicher m; (Sch col) Petze(r) mf (Sch col). ~ **preview** (Film) Vorschau f; (of new car etc) Vorbesichtigung f; ~ **thief** Langfinger m (col). **2** vt **he** ~**ed a cake off the counter** er klaute (col) einen Kuchen vom Ladentisch; **to** ~ **sth into a room** etw in ein Zimmer schmuggeln; **to** ~ **a look**

**at sb/sth** auf jdn/etw schielen *(col)*. **3** *vi* **(a) to ~ away** *or* **off** sich wegschleichen; **to ~ in** sich einschleichen; **to ~ past sb** (sich) an jdm vorbeischleichen; **to ~ out of doing sth** *(US)* sich vor etw *(dat)* drücken. **(b)** *(Sch col: tell tales)* petzen *(col)*. **to ~ on sb** jdn verpetzen *(col)*.

**sneakers** ['sniːkəz] *npl (US)* Turnschuhe *pl*.

**sneaking** ['sniːkɪŋ] *adj attr* geheim *attr*. **I have a ~ feeling that ...** ich habe das unbestimmte Gefühl, daß ...

**sneaky** ['sniːkɪ] *adj (+er) (col)* raffiniert, schlau.

**sneer** [snɪər] **1** *n (expression)* spöttisches Lächeln; *(remark)* spöttische Bemerkung. **2** *vi* spotten; *(look sneering)* spöttisch grinsen. **to ~ at sb** jdn verhöhnen; *(laugh at)* jdn auslachen.

**sneeze** [sniːz] **1** *n* Nieser *m (col)*. **2** *vi* niesen. **not to be ~d at** nicht zu verachten.

**snide** [snaɪd] *adj (col)* abfällig.

**sniff** [snɪf] **1** *n* Schniefen *nt no pl (col)*; *(disdainful)* Naserümpfen *nt no pl*; *(of dog)* Schnüffeln *nt no pl*. **we never got a ~ of the vodka** *(col)* wir durften noch nicht einmal an dem Wodka riechen; **have a ~ at this** riech mal hieran! **2** *vt (test by smelling)* riechen, schnuppern an *(+dat) (col)*; *smelling salts* einziehen; *glue* einatmen, schnüffeln *(col)*; *(fig: detect)* wittern, riechen. **3** *vi (person)* schniefen *(col)*; *(dog)* schnuppern. **to ~ at sth** *(lit)* an etw *(dat)* schnuppern; *(fig)* die Nase über etw *(acc)* rümpfen. **not to be ~ed at** nicht zu verachten.

▶**sniff out** *vt sep (lit, fig)* aufspüren; *crime, plot* aufdecken.

**sniffer dog** ['snɪfə͵dɒg] *n* Spürhund *m*.

**sniffle** ['snɪfl] *n, vi* = **snuffle**.

**snigger** ['snɪgər] **1** *n* Kichern, Gekicher *nt*. **2** *vi* kichern *(at, about* wegen*)*.

**snip** [snɪp] **1** *n* **(a)** *(cut, cutting action)* Schnitt *m*. **(b)** *(of cloth)* Stück *nt*; *(of paper)* Schnipsel *m (col)*; *(from newspaper)* Ausschnitt *m*. **(c)** *(esp Brit col: bargain)* Geschäft, Schnäppchen *nt (col)*. **it's a ~ at only £2** für nur £2 ist es unheimlich günstig. **(d)** *(US col: insignificant person)* Würstchen *nt (pej col)*. **2** *vt* schnippeln *(col)*. **to ~ sth off** etw abschnippeln *(col)*.

**snipe** [snaɪp] **1** *n, pl - (Orn)* Schnepfe *f*. **2** *vi* **to ~ at sb** *(lit, fig)* aus dem Hinterhalt auf jdn schießen.

**sniper** ['snaɪpər] *n* Heckenschütze *m*. **~-fire** Heckenschützenfeuer *nt*.

**snippet** ['snɪpɪt] *n* Stückchen *nt*; *(of paper also)* Schnipsel *m or nt*; *(of information)* (Bruch)stück *nt*. **~s of a conversation** Gesprächsfetzen *pl*.

**snivel** ['snɪvl] *vi* heulen, flennen *(col)*.

**snivelling**, *(US)* **sniveling** ['snɪvlɪŋ] *adj* heulend.

**snob** [snɒb] *n* Snob *m*. **~ value** Snobappeal *m*.

**snobbery** ['snɒbərɪ] *n* Snobismus *m*.

**snobbish** *adj*, **~ly** *adv* ['snɒbɪʃ, -lɪ] snobistisch, versnobt *(col)*.

**snobbishness** ['snɒbɪʃnɪs] *n* Snobismus *m*, Versnobtheit *f (col)*.

**snog** [snɒg] *vi (Brit col)* rumknutschen *(col)*.

**snooker** ['snuːkər] **1** *n* Snooker *nt*. **2** *vt* **to be ~ed** *(fig col)* festsitzen *(col)*.

**snoop** [snuːp] **1** *n* **(a)** = **snooper**. **(b)** *(act)* I'll have **a ~ around** ich gucke mich mal (ein bißchen) um. **2** *vi* schnüffeln. **to ~ around** herumschnüffeln.

**snooper** ['snuːpər] *n* Schnüffler(in *f*) *m*.

**snootily** ['snuːtɪlɪ] *adv (col)* hochnäsig, von oben herab.

**snooty** ['snuːtɪ] *adj (+er) (col)* hochnäsig.

**snooze** [snuːz] **1** *n* Schläfchen, Nickerchen *nt*. **to have a ~** ein Schläfchen machen; **~ button** *(on radio alarm)* Schlummertaste *f*. **2** *vi* ein Nickerchen

machen.

**snore** [snɔːr] **1** *n* Schnarchen *nt no pl*. **2** *vi* schnarchen.

**snoring** ['snɔːrɪŋ] *n* Schnarchen *nt*.

**snorkel** ['snɔːkl] **1** *n* Schnorchel *m*. **2** *vi* **to go ~ling** *(Brit) or* **~ing** *(US)* schnorcheln gehen.

**snort** [snɔːt] **1** *n* Schnauben *nt no pl*; *(of boar)* Grunzen *nt no pl*. **he gave a ~ of contempt** er schnaubte verächtlich. **2** *vti* schnauben; *(boar)* grunzen.

**snot** [snɒt] *n (col)* Rotz *m (col)*.

**snotty** ['snɒtɪ] *adj (+er) (col)* **(a)** Rotz- *(col)*; *child* rotznäsig *(col)*. **(b)** *(fig: snooty)* hochnäsig; *(insolent)* rotzig *(col)*.

**snout** [snaʊt] *n (of animal)* Schnauze *f*; *(col: of person)* Rüssel *(col)*.

**snow** [snəʊ] **1** *n* **(a)** *(also col: cocaine or heroin)* Schnee *m*; *(~fall)* Schneefall *m*. **the heavy ~s last winter** die heftigen Schneefälle im letzten Winter; **as white as ~** schneeweiß. **(b)** *(TV)* Geflimmer *nt*, Schnee *m*. **2** *vi* schneien.

▶**snow in** *vt sep (usu pass)* **to be** *or* **get ~ed ~** eingeschneit sein.

▶**snow under** *vt sep (col: usu pass)* **to be ~ed ~** *(with work)* reichlich eingedeckt sein; *(with requests)* überhäuft werden.

**snow: ~ball 1** *n* Schneeball *m*; *(drink)* Snowball *m*; **2** *vi* eskalieren; **~ blind** *adj* schneeblind; **~ blindness** *n* Schneeblindheit *f*; **~bound** *adj* eingeschneit; **~-capped** *adj* schneebedeckt; **~-covered** *adj* verschneit; **~drift** *n* Schneewehe *f*; **~drop** *n (Bot)* Schneeglöckchen *nt*; **~fall** *n* Schneefall *m*; **~flake** *n* Schneeflocke *f*; **~line** *n* Schneegrenze *f*; **~man** *n* Schneemann *m*; **~mobile** *n* Schneemobil *nt*; **~plough**, *(US)* **~plow** *n (also Ski)* Schneepflug *m*; **~shoe** *n* Schneeschuh *m*; **~storm** *n* Schneesturm *m*; **~-white** *adj* schneeweiß.

**snowy** ['snəʊɪ] *adj (+er)* **(a)** *weather, region* schneereich; *hills* verschneit. **it was very ~ yesterday** gestern hat es viel geschneit. **(b)** *(white as snow)* schneeweiß.

**SNP** *n abbr of* **Scottish National Party**.

**snub** [snʌb] **1** *n* Brüskierung *f*. **to give sb a ~** jdn brüskieren, jdn vor den Kopf stoßen; *subordinate, pupil etc (verbally)* jdm über den Mund fahren. **2** *vt* **(a)** *person* brüskieren, vor den Kopf stoßen; *subordinate, pupil etc (verbally)* über den Mund fahren *(+dat)*; *proposal* kurz abtun. **(b)** *(ignore, not greet)* schneiden.

**snub: ~nose** *n* Stupsnase *f*; **~-nosed** *adj* stupsnasig.

**snuff** [snʌf] **1** *n* Schnupftabak *m*. **to take ~** schnupfen. **2** *vt candle (extinguish: also ~ out)* auslöschen. **to ~ it** *(Brit col!: die)* abkratzen *(col!)*.

**snuff box** *n* Schnupftabakdose *f*.

**snuffle** ['snʌfl] **1** *n* Schniefen *nt no pl*. **to have the ~s** *(col)* einen leichten Schnupfen haben. **2** *vi* schnüffeln; *(with cold, from crying)* schniefen.

**snug** [snʌg] *adj (+er) (cosy)* behaglich, gemütlich; *bed, garment, room etc* mollig warm; *(sheltered) spot* geschützt; *(close-fitting)* gutsitzend *attr*; *(tight)* eng. **to be ~ in bed** es im Bett mollig warm haben; **it is a good ~ fit** es paßt gut.

**snuggle** ['snʌgl] *vi* sich kuscheln. **to ~ down in bed** sich ins Bett kuscheln; **to ~ up (to sb)** sich (an jdn) ankuscheln.

**snugly** ['snʌglɪ] *adv* gemütlich, behaglich; *fit* wie angegossen.

**SO** *(Fin)* = **standing order** DA.

**so** [səʊ] **1** *adv* **(a)** so. **~ much tea/~ many flies** so viel Tee/so viele Fliegen; **he was ~ stupid (that)** er war so dumm(, daß); **I am not ~ stupid as to believe**

**that** so dumm bin ich nicht, daß ich das glaube(n würde); **would you be** ~ **kind as to open the door?** wären Sie bitte so freundlich, die Tür zu öffnen?; ~ **great a writer as Shakespeare** ein so großer Dichter wie Shakespeare; **he's not been** ~ **well recently** in letzter Zeit geht es ihm nicht besonders gut; **how are things? – not** ~ **bad!** wie geht's? – nicht schlecht!

**(b)** *(emphatic)* glad, sorry etc so; *pleased, relieved, hope, wish* sehr; *love* so sehr; *hate* so sehr, derart. **I'm** ~ **very tired** ich bin ja so müde; **it would be** ~ **much better/easier** es wäre so viel besser/einfacher; ~ **much the better/worse (for sb)** um so besser/schlechter (für jdn); **that's** ~ **kind of you** das ist wirklich sehr nett von Ihnen.

**(c)** *(replacing longer sentence)* das, es. **I hope** ~ hoffentlich; *(emphatic)* das hoffe ich doch sehr; **I think** ~ ich glaube schon; **I never said** ~ das habe ich nie gesagt; **I told you** ~ ich habe es dir doch gesagt; **why should I do it? – because I say** ~ warum muß ich das tun? – weil ich es sage, darum; **I didn't say** ~ das habe ich nicht gesagt; ~ **I believe** ja, ich glaube schon; ~ **I see** ja, das sehe ich; **please, do** ~ bitte(, tun Sie es ruhig); **it may be** ~ es kann schon sein; ~ **be it** nun gut; **if** ~ wenn ja; **or** ~ **they say** oder so heißt es jedenfalls; **that is** ~ das stimmt; **if that's** ~ wenn das stimmt; **he's coming by plane – is that** ~**?** er kommt mit dem Flugzeug – tatsächlich?; **I didn't say that – you did** ~ *(esp US col)* das habe ich nicht gesagt – doch(, hast du wohl).

**(d)** *(thus, in this way)* so. **perhaps it was better** ~ vielleicht war es auch besser so; ~ **it was that** ... so kam es, daß ...; **and** ~ **it was** und so war es auch; **by** ~ **doing he has** ... dadurch hat er ..., indem er das tat, hat er ...; ... **and** ~ **saying he walked out** ... und damit ging er hinaus; **the article is** ~ **written as to** ... der Artikel ist so geschrieben, daß ...

**(e)** *(unspecified amount)* **how high is it? – oh, about** ~ **high** wie hoch ist das? – oh, ungefähr so; ~ **much per head** soviel pro Kopf; **they behaved like** ~ **many children** sie benahmen sich wie die Kinder; **a week or** ~ so (etwa) eine Woche; **50 or** ~ etwa 50.

**(f)** *(likewise)* auch. ~ **am/would/do/could** *etc* **I** ich auch; **he's wrong and** ~ **are you** ihr irrt euch beide.

**(g)** **he walked past and didn't** ~ **much as look at me** er ging vorbei, ohne mich auch nur anzusehen; ~ **much for that!** *(col)* das wär's ja wohl gewesen! *(col)*; ~ **much for him** *(col)* das war ja wohl nichts mit ihm! *(col)*; ~ **much for his help** *(col)* er war eine schöne Hilfe! *(col)*.

**2** *conj* **(a)** *(expressing purpose)* damit. ~ **(that) you don't have to do it again** damit Sie es nicht noch einmal machen müssen; **we hurried** ~ **as not to be late** wir haben uns beeilt, um nicht zu spät zu kommen.

**(b)** *(expressing result, therefore)* also. **it rained (and)** ~ **we couldn't go out** es regnete und deshalb konnten wir nicht weggehen; **he was standing in the doorway** ~ **(that) no one could get past** er stand in der Tür, so daß niemand vorbeikonnte; **I told him to leave and** ~ **he did** ich habe ihm gesagt, er solle gehen, und das hat er auch getan; **the roads are busy** ~ **be careful** es ist viel Verkehr, also sei vorsichtig; ~ **you see** ... wie du siehst, ...

**(c)** *(in questions, exclamations)* also. ~ **that's his wife/the reason!** das ist also seine Frau/der Grund!; ~ **you did do it!** du hast es also doch gemacht!; ~ **(what)?** *(col)* (na) und?; **I'm not going,** ~ **there!** *(col)* ich geh' nicht, fertig, aus!

**soak** [səʊk] **1** *vt (wet)* durchnässen. **to be/get** ~**ed** völlig durchnäßt sein/werden; **to be** ~**ed to the skin, to be** ~**ed through** bis auf die Haut durchnäßt sein. **2** *vi* **(a)** *(steep)* **leave it to** ~ weichen Sie es ein; *(in dye)* lassen Sie die Farbe einziehen; **to** ~ **in a bath** sich in der Badewanne aalen *(col)*. **(b)** *(penetrate)* **rain has** ~**ed through the ceiling** der Regen ist durch die Decke gesickert; **the coffee was** ~**ing into the carpet** der Kaffee zog in den Teppich ein.

►**soak in** *vi (stain, dye etc)* einziehen.

►**soak up** *vt sep liquid* aufsaugen; *sunshine* genießen; *sound* schlucken; *(fig) information* aufsaugen, in sich *(acc)* aufnehmen.

**soaking** ['səʊkɪŋ] **1** *adj* klitschnaß *(col)*, patschnaß *(col)*. **2** *adv* ~ **wet** triefend naß, klitschnaß *(col)*; **a** ~ **wet day** ein völlig verregneter Tag. **3** *n* **to get a** ~ patschnaß werden *(col)*.

**so-and-so** ['səʊənsəʊ] *n (col)* **(a)** *(unspecified)* ~ **up at the shop** Herr/Frau Soundso im Laden. **(b)** *(pej)* **he's an old** ~ das ist ein gemeiner Kerl.

**soap** [səʊp] **1** *n* Seife *f*. **2** *vt* einseifen, abseifen.

**soap:** ~**box** *n (lit: packing case)* Seifenkiste *f*; *(fig: platform)* Apfelsinenkiste *f*; ~ **bubble** *n* Seifenblase *f*; ~ **dish** *n* Seifenschale *f*; ~ **dispenser** *n* Seifenspender *m*; ~**flakes** *npl* Seifenflocken *pl*; ~ **opera** *n (TV, Rad)* Fernseh-/Hörspielserie, Seifenoper *(col) f*; ~ **powder** *n* Seifenpulver *nt*; ~**suds** *npl (foam)* Seifenschaum *m*.

**soapy** ['səʊpɪ] *adj (+er)* seifig. ~ **water** Seifenwasser *nt*.

**soar** [sɔːʳ] *vi* **(a)** *(rise: also* ~ **up)** aufsteigen; *(bird also)* sich in die Lüfte schwingen. **to** ~ **(up) into the sky** zum Himmel steigen. **(b)** *(fig) (building)* hochragen; *(price)* hochschnellen; *(popularity, hopes)* einen Aufschwung nehmen.

**soaring** ['sɔːrɪŋ] *adj bird, plane* in die Luft steigend; *tower* hoch aufragend; *imagination* hochfliegend; *popularity* schnell zunehmend; *prices* in die Höhe schnellend; *inflation* unaufhaltsam; *hopes* wachsend.

**s.o.b.** *(US col!)* = **son of a bitch.**

**sob** [sɒb] **1** *n* Schluchzer *m*, Schluchzen *nt no pl*. **to give a** ~ (auf)schluchzen; ..., **he said with a** ~ ..., sagte er schluchzend. **2** *vi* schluchzen *(with* vor +*dat)*. **3** *vt* **to** ~ **one's heart out** sich *(dat)* die Seele aus dem Leib weinen.

**sober** ['səʊbəʳ] *adj* **(a)** *(not drunk)* nüchtern. **to be as** ~ **as a judge** stocknüchtern sein *(col)*. **(b)** *(sedate, serious) life, mood, occasion* ernst; *(sensible, moderate) opinion, judgement* vernünftig; *assessment, facts* nüchtern. **(c)** *(not bright or showy)* schlicht; *colour* gedeckt.

►**sober up 1** *vt sep (lit)* nüchtern machen; *(fig)* zur Vernunft bringen. **2** *vi (lit)* nüchtern werden; *(fig) (after laughing etc)* sich beruhigen.

**sobering** *adj* ernüchternd.

**soberly** ['səʊbəlɪ] *adv* nüchtern; *behave* vernünftig; *dress, furnish* schlicht.

**sobriety** [sə'braɪɪtɪ] *n* **(a)** *(not being drunk)* Nüchternheit *f*. **(b)** *(seriousness, sedateness)* Solidität *f*; *(of dress)* Schlichtheit *f*; *(of colour)* Gedecktheit *f*.

**soc** [sɒk] = **society** Ges.

**so-called** [,səʊ'kɔːld] *adj* sogenannt; *(supposed)* angeblich.

**soccer** ['sɒkəʳ] *n* Fußball *m*. ~ **player** Fußballer, Fußballspieler(in *f*) *m*.

**sociability** [,səʊʃə'bɪlɪtɪ] *n* Geselligkeit *f*.

**sociable** ['səʊʃəbl] *adj (gregarious)* gesellig; *(friendly)* freundlich. ... **just to be** ~ ..., man möchte sich ja nicht ausschließen; **I'm not feeling very** ~

**today** mir ist heute nicht nach Geselligkeit (zumute).

**social** ['səʊʃəl **1** *adj* **(a)** *(relating to community, Admin, Pol)* sozial; *history, reform, legislation, policy* Sozial-; *system, realism, class* Gesellschafts-; *structure, conditions, evils also* gesellschaftlich. **the ~ services** die Sozialeinrichtungen *pl*.

**(b)** *engagements, life, superior* gesellschaftlich; *behaviour* in Gesellschaft; *advancement, status also* sozial. **~ climber** Emporkömmling *m (pej)*, sozialer Aufsteiger; **there isn't much ~ life around here** hier kommen die Leute nicht viel zusammen; **a job which leaves no time for one's ~ life** ein Beruf, bei dem man keine Zeit für andere Leute hat.

**(c)** *(gregarious) evening, person* gesellig; *(living in groups) animals* gesellig lebend.

**2** *n* geselliger Abend.

**social: ~ club** *n* Klub *m* für geselliges Beisammensein; **~ democrat** *n* Sozialdemokrat(in *f*) *m*; **~ democratic** *adj* sozialdemokratisch; **~ insurance** *n (US)* Sozialversicherung *f*.

**socialism** ['səʊʃəlɪzəm] *n* Sozialismus *m*.

**socialist** ['səʊʃəlɪst] **1** *adj* sozialistisch. **2** *n* Sozialist(in *f*) *m*.

**socialite** ['səʊʃəlaɪt] *n (col)* Angehörige(r) *mf* der Schickeria *(col)*; *(man also)* Salonlöwe *m (col)*.

**socialize** ['səʊʃəlaɪz] **1** *vt* sozialisieren; *means of production* vergesellschaften. **2** *vi* **to ~ with sb** *(meet socially)* mit jdm gesellschaftlich verkehren; *(chat to)* sich mit jdm unterhalten; **she ~s a lot** sie hat ein reges gesellschaftliches Leben.

**socially** ['səʊʃəlɪ] *adv* gesellschaftlich; *deprived etc* sozial; *meet* privat.

**social: ~ science** *n* Sozialwissenschaft *f*; **~ security** *n* Sozialhilfe *f*; *(scheme)* Sozialversicherung *f*; **to be on ~ security** Sozialhilfeempfänger sein; **~ studies** *npl* Sozialkunde *f*; **~ work** *n* Sozialarbeit *f*; **~ worker** *n* Sozialarbeiter(in *f*) *m*.

**society** [sə'saɪətɪ] *n* **(a)** Gesellschaft *f; (also high ~)* High-Society *f.* **modern industrial ~** die moderne Industriegesellschaft. **(b)** *(club, organization)* Verein *m*; *(learned, Comm)* Gesellschaft *f.*

**society** *in cpds* Gesellschafts-; **~ column** *n* Gesellschaftsspalte *f.*

**socio-** [ˌsəʊsɪəʊ-] *pref* sozio-. **~economic** sozioökonomisch.

**sociological** [ˌsəʊsɪə'lɒdʒɪkəl] *adj* soziologisch.

**sociologist** [ˌsəʊsɪ'ɒlədʒɪst] *n* Soziologe *m*, Soziologin *f.*

**sociology** [ˌsəʊsɪ'ɒlədʒɪ] *n* Soziologie *f.*

**sock¹** [sɒk] *n* Socke *f*, Socken *m (col)*; *(knee-length)* Kniestrumpf *m.* **to pull one's ~s up** *(col)* sich am Riemen reißen *(col)*.

**sock²** **1** *n (col)* Schlag *m* (mit der Faust). **to give sb a ~ in the eye** jdm eine aufs Auge verpassen *(col)*. **2** *vt (col: hit)* hauen *(col)*. **~ him one!** knall ihm eine! *(col)*.

**socket** ['sɒkɪt] *n* **(a)** *(of eye)* Augenhöhle *f; (of joint)* Gelenkpfanne *f; (of tooth)* Zahnhöhle *f.* **(b)** *(Brit Elec)* Steckdose *f; (for lightbulb, Mech)* Fassung *f*; **~ spanner** *(Brit)*, **~ wrench** *(US)* Steckschlüssel *m.*

**sod¹** [sɒd] *n (turf)* Grassode *f.*

**sod²** *n (Brit col!)* Sau *f (col!)*. **the poor ~s** die armen Schweine *(col)*.

**soda** ['səʊdə] *n* **(a)** *(Chem)* Soda *nt; (sodium oxide)* Natriumoxyd *nt.* **(b)** *(drink)* Soda(wasser) *nt.*

**soda: ~-fountain** *n (US: café)* Erfrischungshalle *f*; **~ siphon** *n* Siphon *m*; **~-water** *n* Sodawasser *nt.*

**sodden** ['sɒdn] *adj* durchnäßt.

**sodium** ['səʊdɪəm] *n* Natrium *nt.* **~ chloride** Natriumchlorid, Kochsalz *nt.*

**sodomy** ['sɒdəmɪ] *n* Analverkehr *m.*

**sofa** ['səʊfə] *n* Sofa *nt*, Couch *f.* **~ bed** Bettsofa, Sofabett *nt.*

**Sofia** ['səʊfɪə] *n* Sofia *nt.*

**soft** [sɒft] *adj (+er)* **(a)** weich; *meat* zart; *(pej: flabby) muscle* schlaff. **~ currency** weiche Währung; **~ fruit** Beerenobst *nt*; **~ furnishings** Raumtextilien *pl*; **~ ice-cream** Softeis *nt*; **~ water** weiches Wasser. **(b)** *(smooth) skin* zart; *surface* glatt; *material* weich. **(c)** *(gentle, not harsh)* sanft; *(subdued) music* gedämpft; *(not loud)* leise; *rain, breeze, tap, steps* leicht. **(d)** *character, government* schwach; *treatment, teacher* nachsichtig; *punishment* mild(e). **to be ~ on sb** jdm gegenüber nachgiebig sein. **(e)** *(not tough)* verweichlicht; *(easy) job, life* bequem. **that's a ~ option** das ist der Weg des geringsten Widerstandes. **(f)** *drink* alkoholfrei; *drug* weich. **(g)** *(col: foolish)* doof *(col)*. **you must be ~!** du spinnst wohl! *(col)*. **(h)** *(col: feeling affection)* **to be ~ on sb** für jdn schwärmen; **to have a ~ spot for sb** eine Schwäche für jdn haben. **(i)** *(Typ, Comp)* hyphen etc weich.

**soft: ~-boiled** *adj* egg weich(gekocht); **~-centred** *adj* Praline mit Cremefüllung.

**soften** ['sɒfn] **1** *vt* weich machen; *light, sound, colour* dämpfen; *effect, sb's anger, reaction, impression* mildern; *outline* weicher machen; *resistance* schwächen; *person* verweichlichen. **to ~ the blow** *(fig)* den Schock mildern. **2** *vi (material, person, heart)* weich werden; *(voice, look)* sanft werden; *(anger, resistance)* nachlassen.

▶**soften up** *vt sep* weich machen; *(fig) person* mild stimmen; *(flatter)* schmeicheln (+*dat*); *(by bullying, in fight)* weichmachen; *enemy, resistance* zermürben.

**softener** ['sɒfnər] *n (for water)* Enthärtungsmittel *nt*; *(fabric ~)* Weichspüler *m.*

**soft-hearted** [ˌsɒft'hɑːtɪd] *adj* weichherzig.

**softie** ['sɒftɪ] *n (col)* Softy *m (col)*; *(weakling)* Weichling *m.*

**softly** ['sɒftlɪ] *adv (gently, tenderly)* sanft; *(not loud)* leise; *rain, blow* leicht.

**softness** ['sɒftnɪs] *n see adj* **(a)** Weichheit *f*; Zartheit *f*; Schlaffheit *f.* **(b)** Zartheit *f*; Glätte *f*; Weichheit *f.* **(c)** Sanftheit *f*; Gedämpftheit *f*; leiser Klang; Leichtheit *f.* **(d)** Schwäche *f*; Nachsichtigkeit *f*; Milde *f.*

**soft: ~-pedal** *vi* zurückstecken; **~ porn** *n* Softpornographie *f*; **~ sell** *n* weiche Verkaufstaktik, Soft selling *nt*; **~-soap** *(fig col)* **1** *n* Schmeichelei *f*, Schmus *m (col)*; **2** *vt* einseifen *(col)*; **~-spoken** *adj* person leise sprechend *attr*; **to be ~-spoken** eine leise Stimme haben; **~ target** *n* leicht verwundbares Ziel; **~ touch** *n* **to be a ~ touch** nachgiebig sein; **~ toy** *n* Stofftier *nt*; **~ verge** *n* "~ verges" „Seitenstreifen nicht befahrbar"; **~ware** *n* Software *f*; **~wood** *n* Weichholz *nt.*

**softy** *n (col)* = **softie**.

**soggy** ['sɒgɪ] *adj (+er)* durchnäßt, triefnaß; *soil* durchweicht; *food* matschig *(col)*.

**soil¹** [sɔɪl] *n (earth, ground)* Erde *f*, Erdreich *nt*, Boden *m.* **cover it with ~** bedecken Sie es mit Erde; **native/foreign ~** heimatlicher/fremder Boden; **the ~** *(fig: farmland)* die Scholle.

**soil²** **1** *vt (lit, fig)* beschmutzen; *honour* beflecken; *oneself* besudeln; *minds* verderben. **2** *vi* schmutzig werden.

**soiled** [sɔɪld] *adj* schmutzig, verschmutzt.

**sojourn** ['sɒdʒɜːn] *n (liter)* Aufenthalt *m.*

**solace** ['sɒlɪs] *n* Trost *m.*

**solar** ['səʊlər] *adj* Sonnen-. **~ cell** Solarzelle *f*; **~ eclipse** Sonnenfinsternis *f*; **~ energy** Sonnenenergie f; ~ **heating** Solarheizung f; ~ **panel** Sonnenkollektor m; ~ **plexus** Magengrube f; ~ **system** Sonnensystem nt.

**solarium** [səʊ'lɛərɪəm] n, pl **solaria** [səʊ'lɛərɪə] Solarium nt.

**sold** [səʊld] pret, ptp of **sell**.

**solder** ['səʊldər] **1** n Lötmittel nt. **2** vt löten; (~ together) verlöten.

**soldering-iron** ['səʊldərɪŋ,aɪən] n Lötkolben m.

**soldier** ['səʊldʒər] **1** n Soldat m. **old** ~ altgedienter Soldat; (fig: experienced person) alter Hase (col). **2** vi Soldat sein.
▶**soldier on** vi unermüdlich weitermachen.

**sole**¹ [səʊl] **1** n Sohle f. **2** vt besohlen.

**sole**² n (fish) Seezunge f.

**sole**³ adj einzig; heir also, rights Allein-. ~ **agency** Alleinvertretung f; ~ **agent** Alleinvertreter (in f) m.

**solely** ['səʊllɪ] adv (einzig und) allein, nur. **she is** ~ **responsible** sie allein trägt die Verantwortung.

**solemn** ['sɒləm] adj feierlich; person, plea, warning, expression ernst; architecture erhaben; promise, oath heilig; (drab) colour trist.

**solemnity** [sə'lemnɪtɪ] n see adj Feierlichkeit f; Ernst m; Erhabenheit f; heiliger Ernst; Tristheit f.

**solemnize** ['sɒləmnaɪz] vt to ~ **a marriage** eine Trauung feierlich vollziehen.

**solemnly** ['sɒləmlɪ] adv feierlich; walk gemessenen Schrittes; warn, plead ernst; promise hoch und heilig. **I** ~ **swear that** ... ich schwöre bei allem, was mir heilig ist, daß ...

**solenoid** ['səʊlənɔɪd] n Magnetspule f.

**solicit** [sə'lɪsɪt] **1** vt support etc bitten um; person inständig bitten; votes werben; (prostitute) ansprechen. **2** vi (prostitute) Kunden anwerben.

**solicitor** [sə'lɪsɪtər] n (Jur) (Brit) Rechtsanwalt m/ -anwältin f (der/die nicht vor Gericht plädiert); (US) Justizbeamte (r) m/-beamtin f.

**solicitous** [sə'lɪsɪtəs] adj (form) (concerned) besorgt (about um); (eager) dienstbeflissen.

**solid** ['sɒlɪd] **1** adj **(a)** (firm, not liquid) fuel, food, substance fest. ~ **body** Festkörper m; **to be frozen** ~ hartgefroren sein.
**(b)** (pure, not hollow, not broken) block, gold, silver, rock massiv; matter fest; crowd etc dicht; row ununterbrochen; line of people etc geschlossen; week ganz. **the square was packed** ~ **with cars** die Autos standen dicht an dicht auf dem Platz; **for two** ~ **days** or **for two days** ~ zwei Tage ununterbrochen.
**(c)** (stable, secure) bridge, house, car, relationship stabil; piece of work, character, education solide; foundations also, (lit, fig) ground fest; business solide, reell. **a good** ~ **meal** eine kräftige Mahlzeit.
**(d)** reason, argument handfest, stichhaltig; grounds fundiert.
**(e)** (unanimous) vote einstimmig; support geschlossen. **Newtown is** ~ **for Labour** in Newtown wählt fast jeder Labour.
**2** n **(a)** fester Stoff. ~**s and liquids** feste und flüssige Stoffe pl; (Sci) Festkörper und Flüssigkeiten pl. **(b)** (usu pl: food) feste Nahrung no pl.

**solidarity** [,sɒlɪ'dærɪtɪ] n Solidarität f.

**solidify** [sə'lɪdɪfaɪ] **1** vi fest werden; (lava etc) erstarren; (fig: support) sich festigen. **2** vt see vi fest werden lassen; erstarren lassen; festigen.

**solidity** [sə'lɪdɪtɪ] n Festigkeit f; (of structure) Stabilität f; (fig) (of vote) Einstimmigkeit f; (of support) Geschlossenheit f.

**solidly** ['sɒlɪdlɪ] adv **(a)** (firmly) secured fest. ~ **built** house solide gebaut; person kräftig gebaut. **(b)** (uninterruptedly) work ununterbrochen. **(c)** vote ein-

stimmig; support geschlossen. **to be** ~ **behind sb** geschlossen hinter jdm stehen.

**solid-state** [,sɒlɪd'steɪt] adj (Phys) Festkörper-; (Elec) Halbleiter-.

**soliloquy** [sə'lɪləkwɪ] n Monolog m (also Theat).

**solitaire** [,sɒlɪ'tɛər] n (game, gem) Solitär m.

**solitary** ['sɒlɪtərɪ] adj (a) (alone, secluded) life, person einsam; place also abgeschieden. **a few** ~ **houses** ein paar vereinzelte Häuser; **in** ~ **confinement** in Einzelhaft. **(b)** (sole) case, example einzig. **not a** ~ **one** kein einziger.

**solitude** ['sɒlɪtjuːd] n Einsamkeit f; (of place also) Abgeschiedenheit f.

**solo** ['səʊləʊ] **1** n Solo nt. **2** adj flight Allein-; violinist, violin, part, dance etc Solo-. **3** adv allein; (Mus) solo. **to fly** ~ einen Alleinflug machen.

**soloist** ['səʊləʊɪst] n Solist (in f) m.

**Solomon** ['sɒləmən] n (Bibl) Salomo (n) m. **a judgement of** ~ ein salomonisches Urteil.

**solstice** ['sɒlstɪs] n Sonnenwende f.

**soluble** ['sɒljʊbl] adj (a) löslich. ~ **in water** wasserlöslich. **(b)** problem lösbar.

**solution** [sə'luːʃən] n **(a)** Lösung f (to gen); (of crime) Aufklärung f. **(b)** (Chem) Lösung f.

**solve** [sɒlv] vt problem, equation lösen; mystery enträtseln; crime aufklären.

**solvency** ['sɒlvənsɪ] n (Fin) Zahlungsfähigkeit, Solvenz f.

**solvent** ['sɒlvənt] **1** adj **(a)** (Chem) lösend; agent Lösungs-. **(b)** (Fin) zahlungsfähig, solvent. **2** n (Chem) Lösungsmittel nt. ~ **abuse** Lösungsmittelmißbrauch m, Schnüffeln nt (col).

**Som** (Brit) = **Somerset**.

**Somali** [səʊ'mɑːlɪ] **1** adj somalisch. **2** n Somali mf, Somalier (in f) m.

**Somalia** [səʊ'mɑːlɪə] n Somalia nt.

**sombre,** (US) **somber** ['sɒmbər] adj (dark) dunkel; (gloomy) düster.

**some** [sʌm] **1** adj **(a)** (with plural nouns) einige; (a few, emphatic) ein paar; (any: in "if" clauses, questions) usu not translated. **if you have** ~ **questions** wenn Sie Fragen haben; **did you bring** ~ **records?** hast du Schallplatten mitgebracht?; ~ **records of mine** einige meiner Platten; **would you like** ~ **more biscuits?** möchten Sie noch (ein paar) Kekse?; ~ **few people** einige wenige Leute.
**(b)** (with singular nouns) etwas, usu not translated; (a little, emph) etwas, ein bißchen. **there's** ~ **ink on your shirt** Sie haben Tinte auf dem Hemd; **would you like** ~ **cheese?** möchten Sie (etwas) Käse?; ~ **more tea?** möchten Sie noch Tee?; **leave** ~ **cake for me** laß mir ein Stück Kuchen übrig.
**(c)** (certain, in contrast) manche (r, s). ~ **people say** ... manche Leute sagen ...; **in** ~ **ways** in gewisser Weise; **to** ~ **extent** in gewissem Maße.
**(d)** (vague, indeterminate) irgendein. ~ **book/man or other** irgendein Buch/Mann; ~ **woman rang up** da hat eine Frau angerufen; **in** ~ **way or another** irgendwie; **or** ~ **such** oder so etwas ähnliches; **or** ~ **such name** oder so ein ähnlicher Name; ~ **time before midnight** irgendwann vor Mitternacht; ~ **time or other** irgendwann einmal; ~ **other time** ein andermal; ~ **day** eines Tages; ~ **day next week** irgendwann nächste Woche.
**(e)** (intensifier) ziemlich; (in exclamations) vielleicht ein (col). **(that was)** ~ **party!** das war vielleicht eine Party! (col); **this might take** ~ **time** das könnte einige Zeit dauern; **quite** ~ **time** ziemlich lange; **to speak at** ~ **length** ziemlich lange sprechen; **it's** ~ **distance from the house** es ist ziemlich weit vom Haus entfernt.

**(f)** *(iro)* vielleicht ein *(col)*. ~ **experts!** das sind vielleicht Experten! *(col)*; ~ **help you are/this is** du bist/das ist mir vielleicht eine Hilfe *(col)*; ~ **people!** Leute gibt's!

**2** *pron* **(a)** *(~ people)* einige; *(certain people)* manche; *(in "if" clauses, questions)* welche. ~ ..., others ... manche ..., andere ...; ~ **of my friends** einige meiner Freunde; **there are still** ~ **who will never understand** es gibt immer noch Leute, die das nie begreifen werden; **do you have** ~? haben Sie welche?

**(b)** *(referring to plural nouns) (a few)* einige; *(certain ones)* manche; *(in "if" clauses, questions)* welche. ~ **of these books** einige dieser Bücher; **they're lovely, try** ~ die schmecken gut, probieren Sie mal; **if I've still got** ~ wenn ich noch welche habe.

**(c)** *(referring to singular nouns) (a little)* etwas; *(a certain amount, in contrast)* manches; *(in "if" clauses, questions)* welche(r, s). **I drank** ~ **of the milk** ich habe (etwas) von der Milch getrunken; **have** ~! nehmen Sie sich *(dat)*, bedienen Sie sich; **it's good cake, would you like** ~? das ist ein guter Kuchen, möchten Sie welchen?; **would you like** ~ **tea?** — **no, I've got** ~ möchten Sie Tee? — nein, ich habe noch; ~ **of it had been eaten** einiges (davon) war gegessen worden; **this is** ~ **of the finest scenery in Scotland** dies ist eine der schönsten Landschaften Schottlands.

**3** *adv* **(a)** ungefähr, etwa, zirka. ~ **20 people** ungefähr 20 Leute. **(b)** *(esp US col) (a little)* etwas, ein bißchen; *(a lot)* viel. **he's traveling** ~ *(US)* er fährt aber ganz schön schnell *(col)*; **that's going** ~ das ist ganz schön schnell *(col)*.

**somebody** ['sʌmbədɪ] **1** *pron* jemand; *(dir obj)* jemand(en); *(indir obj)* jemandem. ~ **else** jemand anders; ~ **or other** irgend jemand; ~ **knocked at the door** es klopfte jemand an die Tür; **we need** ~ **German** wir brauchen einen Deutschen; **everybody needs** ~ **to talk to** jeder braucht einen, mit dem er sprechen kann. **2** *n* **she's (really)** ~ sie ist jemand, sie ist schon wer *(col)*; **he thinks he's really** ~ er denkt, er ist sonst wer.

**somehow** ['sʌmhaʊ] *adv* irgendwie. **it must be done** ~ **or other** es muß irgendwie gemacht werden.

**someone** ['sʌmwʌn] *pron* = **somebody 1.**

**someplace** ['sʌmpleɪs] *adv (US col)* **be** irgendwo; **go** irgendwohin. = **somebody 1.**

**somersault** ['sʌməsɔːlt] **1** *n* Purzelbaum *m*; *(Sport, fig)* Salto *m*. **to do a** ~ einen Purzelbaum schlagen/ einen Salto machen; *(car)* sich überschlagen. **2** *vi (person)* einen Purzelbaum schlagen; *(Sport)* einen Salto machen; *(car)* sich überschlagen.

**something** ['sʌmθɪŋ] **1** *pron* etwas. ~ **serious** *etc* etwas Ernstes; ~ **or other** irgend etwas, irgendwas; ~ **of the sort** *or* **kind** so (et)was Ähnliches; **she has a certain** ~ sie hat ein gewisses Etwas; **a little** ~ *(gift)* eine Kleinigkeit; **there's** ~ **in what you say** an dem, was du sagst, ist (schon) was dran; **well, that's** ~ das ist immerhin etwas; **she's called Rachel** ~ sie heißt Rachel Soundso; **it was** ~ **else** *or* **quite** ~ das war schon toll *(col)*; **or** ~ *(col)* oder so (was); **are you drunk or** ~? *(col)* bist du betrunken oder was? *(col)*.

**2** *adv* **(a)** ~ **over 200** etwas über 200; ~ **like 200** ungefähr 200; **you look** ~ **like him** du siehst ihm irgendwie ähnlich; **this is** ~ **like the one I wanted** so (et)was Ähnliches wollte ich haben; **this is** ~ **like!** *(col)* das ist wirklich toll! *(col)*. **(b)** **it's** ~ **of a problem** das ist schon ein Problem; **I feel** ~ **of a stranger here** ich fühle mich hier irgendwie fremd; **he's** ~ **of a musician** er ist ein recht guter Musiker;

~ **of a surprise/drunkard** eine ziemliche Überraschung/ein ziemlicher Säufer. **(c)** *(col)* **the weather was** ~ **shocking** das Wetter war einfach schrecklich.

**sometime** ['sʌmtaɪm] **1** *adv* irgendwann. **write to me** ~ **soon** schreib mir (doch) bald (ein)mal; ~ **next year** irgendwann nächstes Jahr. **2** *adj attr (form)* früher, einstig.

**sometimes** ['sʌmtaɪmz] *adv* manchmal.

**somewhat** ['sʌmwɒt] *adv* ein wenig. ~ **of a surprise** eine ziemliche Überraschung.

**somewhere** ['sʌmweər] *adv* **(a) be** irgendwo; **go** irgendwohin. **I left it** ~ **or other** ich habe es irgendwo liegen-/stehenlassen; **I know** ~ **where** ... ich weiß, wo ... **(b)** *(fig)* ~ **about £50,** ~ **in the region of £50** um (die) £50 herum; **she is** ~ **in her fifties** sie muß in den Fünfzigern sein; ~ **between midnight and one o'clock** irgendwann zwischen Mitternacht und ein Uhr.

**somnambulist** [sɒm'næmbjʊlɪst] *n* Schlafwandler(in *f*) *m*.

**somnolent** ['sɒmnələnt] *adj* **(a)** *(sleepy)* schläfrig. **(b)** *(causing sleep)* einschläfernd.

**son** [sʌn] *n (lit, fig)* Sohn *m*; *(as address)* mein Junge.

**sonar** ['səʊnɑːr] *n* Sonar(gerät), Echolot *nt*.

**sonata** [sə'nɑːtə] *n* Sonate *f*.

**song** [sɒŋ] *n* Lied *nt*; *(folk~ also, blues-~)* Song *m*; *(singing)* Gesang *m*. **to burst into** ~ ein Lied anstimmen; **to make a** ~ **and dance about sth** *(col)* eine Haupt- und Staatsaktion aus etw machen *(col)*; **buy sth for a** ~ *(col)* etw für ein Butterbrot kaufen.

**song:** **~bird** *n* Singvogel *m*; **~book** *n* Liederbuch *nt*; ~ **cycle** *n* Liederzyklus *m*; ~ **recital** *n (evening)* Liederabend *m*.

**songwriter** ['sɒŋˌraɪtər] *n* Texter(in *f*) und Komponist(in *f*) *m*; *(of modern ballads)* Liedermacher(in *f*) *m*.

**sonic** ['sɒnɪk] *adj* Schall-. ~ **boom** Überschallknall *m*.

**son-in-law** ['sʌnɪnlɔː] *n, pl* **sons-in-law** Schwiegersohn *m*.

**sonnet** ['sɒnɪt] *n* Sonett *nt*.

**sonny** ['sʌnɪ] *n (col)* (mein) Junge *m*.

**sonority** [sə'nɒrɪtɪ] *n* Klangfülle *f*.

**sonorous** ['sɒnərəs] *adj* volltönend, sonor *(geh)*; *language, poem* klangvoll.

**soon** [suːn] *adv* **(a)** *(in a short time from now)* bald; *(early)* früh; *(quickly)* schnell. **it will** ~ **be Christmas** bald ist Weihnachten; ~ **after his death** kurz nach seinem Tode; ~ **afterwards** kurz *or* bald danach; **how** ~ **can you be ready?** wann kannst du fertig sein?; ~ **is the next performance?** wann fängt die nächste Vorstellung an?; **we got there too** ~ wir waren zu früh dort; **he** ~ **changed his mind** er blieb nicht lange bei seiner Meinung; **all too** ~ viel zu schnell; **we were none too** ~ wir kamen gerade rechtzeitig; **as** ~ **as** sobald; **as** ~ **as possible** so schnell wie möglich. **(b)** **I would as** ~ **not go** *(prefer not to)* ich würde lieber nicht gehen; **I would as** ~ **you didn't tell him** es wäre mir lieber, wenn du es ihm nicht erzählen würdest.

**sooner** ['suːnər] *adv* **(a)** *(time)* früher. ~ **or later** früher oder später; **the** ~ **the better** je eher *or* früher, desto besser; **no** ~ **had we arrived than** ... wir waren kaum angekommen, da ...; **no** ~ **said than done** gesagt, getan. **(b)** *(preference)* lieber. **I would** ~ **not do it** ich würde es lieber nicht tun.

**soot** [sʊt] *n* Ruß *m*. **black as** ~ rußschwarz.

**soothe** [suːð] *vt* beruhigen; *pain* lindern, mildern.

**soothing** ['suːðɪŋ] *adj* beruhigend; *(pain-relieving)* schmerzlindernd; *massage* wohltuend.

**sooty** ['sʊtɪ] *adj (+er)* rußig; *deposit* Ruß-.
**sop** [sɒp] *n* **(a)** *(food)* eingetunktes Brotstück. **(b)** *(to pacify)* **as a ~** zur Beschwichtigung.
**sophisticated** [sə'fɪstɪkeɪtɪd] *adj* **(a)** *(worldly, cultivated)* kultiviert; *person, restaurant also* gepflegt, elegant; *dress* raffiniert, schick. **(b)** *(complex, advanced)* hochentwickelt; *method also* durchdacht; *device also* ausgeklügelt. **(c)** *(subtle, refined)* subtil; *prose, style also, discussion* anspruchsvoll; *plan* ausgeklügelt, raffiniert; *system* differenziert.
**sophistication** [sə,fɪstɪ'keɪʃən] *n see adj* **(a)** Kultiviertheit *f*; Gepflegtheit, Eleganz *f*; Raffiniertheit *f*, Schick *m*. **(b)** hoher Entwicklungsstand; Durchdachtheit *f*; Ausgeklügeltheit *f*. **(c)** Subtilität *f*; hohe Ansprüche *pl*; Ausgeklügeltheit, Raffiniertheit *f*; Differenziertheit *f*.
**sophomore** ['sɒfəmɔːr] *n (US)* Student(in *f*) *m* im 2. *Jahr*.
**soporific** [,sɒpə'rɪfɪk] *adj* einschläfernd.
**sopping** ['sɒpɪŋ] *adj (also ~ wet)* durchnäßt; *person* klitschnaß *(col)*.
**soppy** ['sɒpɪ] *adj (col) (sentimental)* *book, song* schmalzig *(col)*; *person* sentimental; *look* schmachtend; *(effeminate)* weibisch; *(silly)* doof *(col)*.
**soprano** [sə'prɑːnəʊ] **1** *n (also part)* Sopran *m*; *(person also)* Sopranist(in *f*) *m*. **2** *adj* Sopran-. **3** *adv* im Sopran.
**sorbet** ['sɔːbeɪ] *n* Sorbet *nt or m*, Fruchteis *nt*.
**sorcerer** ['sɔːsərər] *n* Hexenmeister, Hexer *m*.
**sorcery** ['sɔːsərɪ] *n* Hexerei *f*.
**sordid** ['sɔːdɪd] *adj* eklig; *place also* verkommen; *motive* niedrig; *conditions, life, story* erbärmlich; *details* unerfreulich; *crime* gemein.
**sore** [sɔːr] **1** *adj (+er)* **(a)** *(inflamed)* wund, entzündet. **to have a ~ throat** Halsschmerzen haben; **my eyes are ~** mir tun die Augen weh. **(b)** *(fig)* **a ~ point** ein wunder Punkt. **(c)** *(col: angry, upset)* verärgert, sauer *(col) (about sth* über etw *(acc), at sb* über jdn). **now don't get ~ at me** werd doch nicht gleich sauer! *(col)*. **2** *n* wunde Stelle.
**sorely** ['sɔːlɪ] *adv tempted* sehr, arg *(S Ger, Aus, Sw)*; *needed* dringend; *missed* schmerzlich; *(liter) afflicted, offended* zutiefst; *wounded* schwer.
**soreness** ['sɔːnɪs] *n (pain)* Schmerz *m*; *(rawness)* Wundsein *nt*.
**sorrel** ['sɒrəl] *n* **(a)** *(Bot)* Sauerampfer *m*; *(wood-~)* Sauerklee *m*. **(b)** *(horse)* Fuchs *m*.
**sorrow** ['sɒrəʊ] *n (no pl: sadness)* Traurigkeit *f*; *(no pl: grief)* Kummer *m*; *(care)* Sorge, Kümmernis *f*; *(affliction)* Leiden *nt*. **this was a great ~ to me** das hat mir großen Kummer bereitet; **her ~ at his death** ihre Trauer über seinen Tod; **to drown one's ~s** seine Sorgen ertränken.
**sorrowful** *adj*, **~ly** *adv* ['sɒrəʊfʊl, -fəlɪ] traurig.
**sorry** ['sɒrɪ] *adj (+er)* **(a)** *pred (sad)* traurig. **this work is no good, I'm ~ to say** diese Arbeit taugt nichts, das muß ich leider sagen; **to feel ~ for sb/oneself** jdn/sich selbst bemitleiden; **I feel ~ for the child** das Kind tut mir leid; **you'll be ~ for this!** das wird dir noch leid tun! **(b)** *(in apologizing)* **~!** Entschuldigung!, Verzeihung!; **I'm ~** es tut mir leid; **can you lend me £5? — ~** kannst du mir £5 leihen? — bedaure, leider nicht; **~?** *(pardon)* wie bitte?; **to say ~ (to sb for sth)** sich (bei jdm für etw) entschuldigen; **I'm ~ about that vase/your dog** es tut mir leid wegen der Vase/um Ihren Hund. **(c)** *(pitiful) condition, plight* traurig; *excuse* faul.
**sort** [sɔːt] **1** *n* **(a)** *(kind)* Art *f*; *(species, type, model also)* Sorte *f*. **a ~ of ...** eine Art ..., so ein(e) ...; **this ~ of house** diese Art Haus; **what ~ of** was für ein; **he's not the ~ of man to do that** er ist nicht der

Mensch, der das täte; **this ~ of thing** so etwas; **all ~s of things** alles mögliche; **people of all ~s** alle möglichen Leute; **he's a painter of a ~** *or* **of ~s** er ist so eine Art Maler; **something of the ~** so (et)was Ähnliches; **nothing of the ~!** von wegen!; **you'll do nothing of the ~!** das wirst du schön bleiben lassen! **(b)** *(person)* **he's a good ~** er ist ein prima Kerl; **he's not my ~** er ist nicht mein Typ; **I don't trust his ~** solchen Leuten traue ich nicht; **I know your ~** euch Brüder kenn' ich! *(col)*; **it takes all ~s** (to make a world) es gibt solche und solche. **(c) to be out of ~s** nicht ganz auf der Höhe sein. **(d)** *(esp Comp: sorting)* Sortieren *nt*. **to do a ~** *(Comp)* sortieren.
**2** *adv* **~ of** *(col)* irgendwie; **it's ~ of heavy** es ist irgendwie schwer *(col)*; **is this how he did it? — well, ~ of** hat er das so gemacht? — ja, so ungefähr.
**3** *vt (also Comp)* sortieren.
▶**sort out** *vt sep* **(a)** *(arrange)* sortieren; *(select)* aussortieren. **to ~ sth ~ from sth** etw von etw trennen. **(b)** *(straighten out)* muddle in Ordnung bringen; *problem* lösen; *situation* klären. **the problem will ~ itself ~** das Problem wird sich von selbst lösen; **to ~ oneself ~** mit sich ins reine kommen. **(c)** *(col)* **to ~ sb ~** sich *(dat)* jdn vorknöpfen *(col)*.
**sort code** *n (Fin)* Bankleitzahl *f*.
**sortie** ['sɔːtɪ] *n (Mil)* Ausfall *m*; *(Aviat)* (Einzel)einsatz *m*.
**sorting:** **~ machine** *n* Sortiermaschine *f*; **~ office** *n* Postverteilstelle *f*.
**so-so** ['səʊsəʊ] *adj pred, adv (col)* so la la.
**soufflé** ['suːfleɪ] *n* Soufflé *nt*.
**sought** [sɔːt] *pret, ptp of* **seek**.
**sought-after** ['sɔːtɑːftər] *adj* begehrt. **much ~** vielbegehrt; *rare object* gesucht.
**soul** [səʊl] *n* **(a)** Seele *f*. **All S~s' Day** Allerheiligen *nt*; **God rest his ~!** Gott hab ihn selig! **(b)** *(inner being)* Innerste(s), Wesen *nt*; *(finer feelings)* Herz, Gefühl *nt*. **he loved her with all his ~** er liebte sie von ganzem Herzen. **(c)** *(person)* Seele *f*. **you poor ~!** *(col)* du Ärmste(r)!; **not a ~** keine Menschenseele; **the ship was lost with all ~s** das Schiff ging mit allen Passagieren unter; **he's the ~ of discretion** er ist die Diskretion in Person. **(d)** *(music)* Soul *m*.
**soul-destroying** ['səʊldɪ,strɔɪŋ] *adj* geisttötend; *factory work etc* nervtötend.
**soulful** ['səʊlfʊl] *adj look* seelenvoll; *person* gefühlvoll.
**soul:** **~mate** *n* **they are ~mates** sie sind verwandte Seelen; **~-searching** *n* Gewissensprüfung *f*.
**sound¹** [saʊnd] **1** *adj (+er)* **(a)** *(in good condition)* *person, animal* gesund; *health* gut; *condition, building, appliance* einwandfrei. **to be as ~ as a bell** kerngesund sein; **to be of ~ mind** *(esp Jur)* bei klarem Verstand sein, im Vollbesitz seiner geistigen Kräfte sein *(Jur)*. **(b)** *(valid, dependable)* solide; *argument, analysis also* fundiert; *economy also* stabil; *person* verläßlich; *idea, move, advice* vernünftig. **to be ~ on sth** *(have good knowledge)* gründliche Kenntnisse in etw *(dat)* haben. **(c)** *(thorough)* gründlich; *beating* gehörig; *defeat* vernichtend. **(d)** *(Jur) decision* rechtmäßig. **(e)** *(deep) sleep* tief, fest. **2** *adv (+er)* **to be ~ asleep** fest schlafen.
**sound²** **1** *n (noise)* Geräusch *nt*; *(Ling)* Laut *m*; *(Phys)* Schall *m*; *(Mus, of instruments)* Klang *m*; *(TV, Rad)* Ton *m*. **don't make a ~** still!; **the speed of ~** (die) Schallgeschwindigkeit; **within ~ of** in Hörweite *(+gen)*; **to the ~(s) of the national anthem** zu den Klängen der Nationalhymne; **not a ~ was to be heard** man hörte keinen Ton; **~s/the ~ of laugh-**

ter Gelächter *nt*; **we heard the ~ of voices on the terrace** wir hörten Stimmen auf der Terrasse; **I don't like the ~ of it** das klingt gar nicht gut.

**2** *vt* **(a)** **~ your horn** hupen!; **to ~ the alarm** Alarm schlagen; *(mechanism)* die Alarmanlage auslösen; **to ~ the retreat** zum Rückzug blasen; **to ~ the "r" in "cover"** das „r" in „cover" aussprechen; **his speech ~ed a note of warning** in seiner Rede klang eine Warnung an. **(b)** *(test by tapping, Med)* abklopfen.

**3** *vi* **(a)** *(emit ~)* erklingen, ertönen. **feet ~ed in the corridor** im Flur waren Schritte zu hören. **(b)** *(give impression)* klingen, sich anhören. **it ~s hollow** es klingt hohl; **the children ~ happy** es hört sich so an, als ob die Kinder ganz vergnügt sind; **he ~s French (to me)** er hört sich (für mich) wie ein Franzose an; **that ~s very odd** das hört sich sehr seltsam an; **he ~s like a nice man** nach dem, was man hört, ist er ein netter Mensch; **it ~s like a sensible idea** das klingt ganz vernünftig.
▶**sound off** *vi (col)* sich auslassen *(about* über *+acc)*.

**sound³** *vt (Naut)* loten, ausloten.
▶**sound out** *vt sep person* aushorchen; *opinions* herausfinden. **to ~ sb ~ on sth** bei jdm in bezug auf etw *(acc)* vorfühlen.

**sound⁴** *n (Geog)* Meerenge *f,* Sund *m.*

**sound:** ~ **archives** *npl* Tonarchiv *nt*; ~ **barrier** *n* Schallmauer *f*; ~**bite** *n (Rad, TV)* prägnantes Zitat; ~ **broadcasting** *n* Hörfunk *m*; ~ **effects** *npl* Toneffekte *pl*; ~ **engineer** *n* Toningenieur(in *f*) *m.*

**sounding** ['saʊndɪŋ] *n (Naut)* Loten *nt,* Peilung *f.* **to take ~s** *(lit)* Lotungen vornehmen; *(fig)* sondieren.

**sounding board** *n (on instrument, fig)* Resonanzboden *m.*

**soundless** *adj,* ~**ly** *adv* ['saʊndlɪs, -lɪ] lautlos.

**soundly** ['saʊndlɪ] *adv built, made* solide; *argue, invest also* vernünftig; *thrash* tüchtig, gehörig. **our team was ~ beaten** unsere Mannschaft wurde eindeutig geschlagen; **to sleep ~** tief und fest schlafen.

**soundness** ['saʊndnɪs] *n* **(a)** *(good condition)* guter Zustand; *(healthiness)* gesunder Zustand. **(b)** *(dependability)* Solidität *f*; *(of economy)* Stabilität *f*; *(of person)* Verläßlichkeit *f*; *(validity) (of argument)* Fundiertheit *f*; *(of idea, advice)* Vernünftigkeit *f*; *(Jur: of decision)* Rechtmäßigkeit *f.* **(c)** *(of sleep)* Tiefe *f.*

**sound:** ~**proof 1** *adj* schalldicht; **2** *vt* schalldicht machen; ~ **recording** *n* Tonaufnahme *f*; ~**track** *n* Ton(spur *f*) *m*; *(music)* Filmmusik *f,* Soundtrack *m*; ~ **wave** *n* Schallwelle *f.*

**soup** [suːp] *n* Suppe *f.* **to be in the ~** *(col)* in der Tinte sitzen *(col).*
▶**soup up** *vt sep (col) car* frisieren *(col).*

**soupçon** ['suːpsɔːŋ] *n (of spice etc)* Spur *f*; *(of irony etc)* Anflug *m.*

**soup:** ~-**kitchen** *n* Volksküche *f*; *(for disaster area etc)* Feldküche *f*; ~-**plate** *n* Suppenteller *m*; ~**spoon** *n* Suppenlöffel *m.*

**sour** ['saʊər] **1** *adj (+er)* **(a)** *fruit* sauer; *wine* säuerlich. **(b)** *(bad) milk* sauer; *smell* säuerlich. **to go ~** *(lit)* sauer werden; *(fig) (relationship, marriage)* sich radikal verschlechtern; *(project)* sich als Fehlschlag erweisen. **(c)** *(fig) person* verdrießlich, griesgrämig; *remark* bissig. **he's feeling ~ about being demoted** er ist über seine Absetzung verbittert; **it's just ~ grapes** die Trauben hängen zu hoch. **2** *vt milk* sauer werden lassen; *person* griesgrämig machen; *relations* trüben.

**source** [sɔːs] *n (of river, light, information)* Quelle *f*;

*(of troubles, problems etc)* Ursache *f.* ~ **language** Ausgangssprache *f*; **a ~ of vitamin C** ein Vitamin-C-Spender *m*; **I have it from a good ~ that** ... ich habe es aus sicherer Quelle, daß ...; **at ~** *(tax)* unmittelbar, direkt; **from reliable ~s** aus zuverlässiger Quelle.

**sour(ed) cream** ['saʊə(d)'kriːm] *n* saure Sahne.

**sourness** ['saʊənɪs] *n* saurer Geschmack; *(of wine, smell)* Säuerlichkeit *f*; *(fig) (of person)* Verdrießlichkeit, Griesgrämigkeit *f*; *(of remark)* Bissigkeit *f.*

**souse** [saʊs] *vt* übergießen. **he ~d himself with water** er übergoß sich mit Wasser.

**south** [saʊθ] **1** *n* Süden *m.* **in the ~ of** im Süden *+gen*; **to the ~ of** im Süden *or* südlich von; **from the ~** aus dem Süden; *(wind)* von Süden; **to veer to the ~** nach Süden drehen; **the S~ of France** Südfrankreich *nt.* **2** *adj* südlich, Süd-; *(in names)* Süd-. **3** *adv* im Süden; *(towards the ~)* nach Süden. **to be further ~** weiter südlich sein; **~ of** südlich von, im Süden von.

**south** *in cpds* Süd-; **S~ Africa** *n* Südafrika *nt*; **S~ African 1** *adj* südafrikanisch; **2** *n* Südafrikaner(in *f*) *m*; **S~ America** *n* Südamerika *nt*; **S~ American 1** *adj* südamerikanisch; **2** *n* Südamerikaner(in *f*) *m*; ~**bound** *adj* (in) Richtung Süden; ~-**east 1** *n* Südosten *m*; **2** *adj* südöstlich; *(in names)* Südost-; **3** *adv* nach Südosten; ~-**east of** südöstlich von; ~-**easterly** *adj direction* südöstlich; ~-**easterly wind** Südostwind *m*; ~-**eastern** *adj* südöstlich, im Südosten.

**southerly** ['sʌðəlɪ] *adj* südlich; *wind* aus südlicher Richtung.

**southern** ['sʌðən] *adj* südlich; *(in names)* Süd-; *(Mediterranean)* südländisch. **S~ Africa** das südliche Afrika; **S~ Europe** Südeuropa *nt*; **S~ Ireland** (Süd)irland *nt*; **S~ States** Südstaaten *pl.*

**southerner** ['sʌðənər] *n* Bewohner(in *f*) *m* des Südens; Südengländer(in *f*) *m/*-deutsche(r) *mf etc*; *(from the Mediterranean)* Südländer(in *f*) *m*; *(US)* Südstaatler(in *f*) *m.*

**southernmost** ['sʌðənməʊst] *adj* südlichste(r, s).

**south:** **S~ German** *adj* süddeutsch; **S~ Korea** *n* Südkorea *nt*; **S~ Pole** *n* Südpol *m*; **S~ Seas** *npl* Südsee *f*; ~**ward(s)** **1** *adj* südlich; **2** *adv* nach Süden, südwärts; ~-**west 1** *n* Südwesten *m*; **2** *adj* Südwest-, südwestlich; *wind* aus südwestlicher Richtung; **3** *adv* nach Südwest(en); ~-**west of** südwestlich von; **S~-West Africa** *n* Südwestafrika *nt*; ~-**westerly** *adj* südwestlich; *wind* Südwest-; ~-**western** *adj* südwestlich.

**souvenir** [ˌsuːvəˈnɪər] *n* Andenken, Souvenir *nt (of* an *+acc).*

**sou'wester** [saʊˈwestər] *n (hat)* Südwester *m.*

**sovereign** ['sɒvrɪn] **1** *n (monarch)* Souverän *m,* Herrscher(in *f*) *m*; *(Brit old: coin)* 20-Shilling-Münze *f.* **2** *adj (supreme)* höchste(r, s), oberste(r,s); *state, power* souverän; *contempt* tiefste(r, s), äußerste(r, s).

**sovereignty** ['sɒvrəntɪ] *n* Oberhoheit *f*; *(right of self-determination)* Souveränität *f.*

**soviet** ['səʊvɪət] *(Hist)* **1** *n* Sowjet *m.* **the S~s** *(people)* die Sowjetbürger. **2** *adj attr* sowjetisch, Sowjet-. **the S~ Union** *n* die Sowjetunion.

**sow¹** [səʊ] *pret* ~**ed,** *ptp* ~**n** *or* ~**ed** *vt* **(a)** *corn, plants* säen; *seed* aussäen. **(b)** *(fig)* **to ~ (the seeds of) hatred/discord/rebellion** Haß/Zwietracht säen/ Aufruhr stiften.

**sow²** [saʊ] *n* Sau *f.*

**sown** [səʊn] *ptp of* **sow¹.**

**soya** ['sɔɪə], *(US)* **soy** [sɔɪ] *n* Soja *f.* ~ **bean** Sojabohne *f*; ~ **sauce** Sojasoße *f.*

**sozzled** ['sɒzld] *adj (Brit col)* **to be** ~ einen sitzen haben *(col)*; **to get** ~ beschwipst werden *(col)*; *(deliberately)* sich besaufen *(col)*.

**spa** [spɑː] *n (town)* Kurort *m*; *(spring)* (Mineral)quelle *f*.

**space** [speɪs] **1** *n* (a) Raum *m (also Phys)*; *(outer* ~ *also)* der Weltraum, das Weltall. **to stare into** ~ ins Leere starren. (b) *no pl (room)* Platz, Raum *m*. **to take up a lot of** ~ viel Platz einnehmen; **to clear/ leave some** ~ **for sb/sth** für jdn/etw Platz schaffen/ lassen; **to buy** ~ *(Press)* Platz für Anzeigen kaufen; **parking** ~ Platz *m* zum Parken. (c) *(gap, empty area)* Platz *m no art*; *(between objects, words, lines)* Zwischenraum *m*; *(parking* ~*)* Lücke *f*. **please answer in the** ~ **provided** bitte an der dafür vorgesehenen Stelle beantworten. (d) *(of time)* Zeitraum *m*. **in a short** ~ **of time** in kurzer Zeit; **in the** ~ **of one hour** innerhalb einer Stunde.
 **2** *vt (also* ~ **out)** in Abständen verteilen; *visits* verteilen; *words* Abstand lassen zwischen *(+dat)*. **~d out** *(col) (on drugs)* high *(col)*; *(confused etc)* geistig weggetreten *(col)*.

**space** *in cpds* (Welt)raum-; ~ **age** *n* Weltraumzeitalter *nt*; **~-age** *adj attr* des Weltraumzeitalters; **~-bar** *n (Typ)* Leertaste *f*; **~craft** *n* Raumfahrzeug *nt*; *(unmanned)* Raumkörper *m*; ~ **heater** *n (esp US)* Heizgerät *nt*; **~man** *n* (Welt)raumfahrer *m*; ~ **rocket** *n* Weltraumrakete *f*; **~-saving** *adj equipment, gadget* platzsparend; **~ship** *n* Raumschiff *nt*; ~ **shuttle** *n* Raumtransporter *m*; ~ **station** *n* (Welt)raumstation *f*; ~ **suit** *n* Raumanzug *m*; ~ **travel** *n* die Raumfahrt; ~ **walk** *n* Weltraumspaziergang *m*.

**spacing** ['speɪsɪŋ] *n* Abstände *pl*; *(between two objects)* Abstand *m*; *(also* ~ **out)** Verteilung *f*; *(of payments)* Verteilung *f* über längere Zeit.

**spacious** ['speɪʃəs] *adj* geräumig; *park* weitläufig.

**spade** [speɪd] *n* (a) *(tool)* Spaten *m*; *(children's* ~*)* Schaufel *f*. **to call a** ~ **a** ~ *(prov)* das Kind beim Namen nennen *(prov)*. (b) *(Cards)* Pik *nt*. **the Queen/ two of** ~**s** die Pik-Dame/Pik-Zwei.

**spadework** ['speɪdwɜːk] *n (fig)* Vorarbeit *f*.

**spaghetti** [spəˈgetɪ] *n* Spaghetti *pl*; *(fig col: cables)* Kabelsalat *m (col)*. ~ **junction** *n (col)* Autobahnknoten(punkt) *m*.

**Spain** [speɪn] *n* Spanien *nt*.

**span¹** [spæn] **1** *n* (a) *(of hand)* Spanne *f*; *(wing~, of bridge etc)* Spannweite *f*. **a single-~ bridge** eine eingespannte Bogenbrücke. (b) *(time* ~*)* Zeitspanne *f*; *(of memory)* Gedächtnisspanne *f*; *(of attention)* Konzentrationsspanne *f*; *(range)* Umfang *m*. **2** *vt (rope, rainbow)* sich spannen über *(+acc)*; *(plank)* führen über *(+acc)*; *(Mus)* octave etc greifen; *(encircle)* umfassen; *(in time)* sich erstrecken über *(+acc)*.

**span²** *(old)* pret of **spin**.

**Spaniard** ['spænjəd] *n* Spanier(in *f*) *m*.

**spaniel** ['spænjəl] *n* Spaniel *m*.

**Spanish** ['spænɪʃ] **1** *adj* spanisch. **the** ~ die Spanier *pl*. **2** *n (language)* Spanisch *nt*.

**Spanish onion** *n* Gemüsezwiebel *f*.

**spank** [spæŋk] **1** *n* Klaps *m*. **to give sb a** ~ jdm einen Klaps geben; *(spanking)* jdm den Hintern versohlen. **2** *vt* versohlen.

**spanking** ['spæŋkɪŋ] **1** *n* Tracht *f* Prügel. **2** *adj pace* scharf. **3** *adv (col)* ~ **new** funkelnagelneu *(col)*.

**spanner** ['spænə'] *n (Brit)* Schraubenschlüssel *m*. **to throw a** ~ **in the works** *(fig)* Sand ins Getriebe streuen *(col)*; **that's a real** ~ **in the works** das ist wirklich ein Hemmschuh.

**spar¹** [spɑː'] *n (Naut)* Rundholz *nt*.

**spar²** *vi (Boxing)* ein Sparring *nt* machen; *(fig)* sich

kabbeln *(col) (about* um).

**spare** [speə'] **1** *adj* (a) den/die/das man nicht braucht, übrig *pred*; *(surplus)* überzählig, übrig *pred*; *bed, room* Gäste-; *(replacement)* part etc Ersatz-. **have you any** ~ **string?** hast du (mal) eine Schnur?; **I can give you a racket, I have a** ~ **one** ich kann dir einen Schläger geben, ich habe noch einen; **take some** ~ **clothes** nehmen Sie Sachen zum Wechseln mit; **it's all the** ~ **cash I have** mehr Bargeld habe ich nicht übrig; **should you have any** ~ **time** sollten Sie noch Zeit haben; **we have two** ~ **seats** wir haben zwei Plätze übrig. (b) **to go** ~ *(col)* durchdrehen *(col)*.
 **2** *n (*~ *part)* Ersatzteil *nt*; *(*~ *wheel)* Reserverad *nt*; *(*~ *tyre)* Reservereifen *m*. **I always carry a** ~ ich habe immer eins als Reserve dabei.
 **3** *vt* (a) *usu neg (grudge)* **we must** ~ **no effort in trying to finish this job** wir dürfen keine Mühe scheuen, um diese Arbeit zu erledigen; **no expense was ~d** es wurden keine Kosten gescheut.
 (b) **to** ~ **sb sth** *(give)* jdm etw überlassen *or* geben; *money* jdm etw geben; **can you** ~ **the time to do it?** haben Sie Zeit, das zu machen?; **I can** ~ **you five minutes** ich habe fünf Minuten Zeit für Sie (übrig); **to have sth to** ~ etw übrig haben; **there are three to** ~ es sind drei übrig; **to have a few minutes to** ~ ein paar Minuten Zeit haben; **I got to the station with two minutes to** ~ ich war zwei Minuten vor der Abfahrt am Bahnhof.
 (c) *(do without)* person, object entbehren, verzichten auf *(+acc)*. **I can't** ~ **it** ich kann es nicht entbehren, ich kann darauf nicht verzichten; **can you** ~ **this for a moment?** kannst du mir das kurz geben?; **to** ~ **a thought for sb/sth** an jdn/etw denken.
 (d) *(show mercy to)* verschonen; *(refrain from upsetting sb, sb's feelings)* schonen.
 (e) *(save)* **to** ~ **sb/oneself sth** jdm/sich etw ersparen; ~ **me the details** verschone mich mit den Einzelheiten; **to** ~ **him embarrassment** um ihn nicht in Verlegenheit zu bringen.

**spare:** ~ **part** *n* Ersatzteil *nt*; ~ **rib** *n* Rippchen *nt*; ~ **room** *n* Gästezimmer *nt*; ~ **time 1** *n (leisure time)* Freizeit *f*; **2** *adj attr* Freizeit-; ~ **tyre** *(Brit)* or **tire** *(US)* *n* Reservereifen *m*; *(fig col)* Rettungsring *m (col)*; ~ **wheel** *n* Reserverad *nt*.

**sparing** ['speərɪŋ] *adj* sparsam. **to be** ~ **of (one's) praise** mit Lob geizen.

**sparingly** ['speərɪŋlɪ] *adv* sparsam; *spend, drink, eat* in Maßen. **to use sth** ~ mit etw sparsam umgehen.

**spark** [spɑːk] **1** *n (from fire, Elec)* Funke *m*; *(fig: glimmer)* Fünkchen *nt*, Funke(n) *m*. **not a** ~ **of life** kein Fünkchen Leben; **when the ~s start to fly** *(fig)* wenn die Funken anfangen zu fliegen; **a bright** ~ *(iro)* ein Intelligenzbolzen *m (iro)*. **2** *vt (also* ~ **off)** entzünden; *explosion* verursachen; *(fig)* auslösen; *interest, enthusiasm* wecken. **3** *vi* Funken sprühen; *(Elec)* zünden.

**spark(ing) plug** ['spɑːk(ɪŋ)'plʌg] *n* Zündkerze *f*.

**sparkle** ['spɑːkl] **1** *n* Funkeln *nt*. **he lacks** ~ ihm fehlt der (rechte) Schwung. **2** *vi* funkeln *(with* vor *+dat)*; *(fig: person)* vor Leben(sfreude) sprühen; *(with intelligence, wit etc)* brillieren.

**sparkler** ['spɑːklə'] *n* (a) *(firework)* Wunderkerze *f*. (b) *(col: diamond)* Klunker *m (col)*.

**sparkling** ['spɑːklɪŋ] *adj lights* glänzend, funkelnd; *eyes* funkelnd; *wit* sprühend; *(lively) person* vor Leben sprühend; *(witty) person, speech* vor Geist sprühend; *(bubbling) mineral water etc* mit Kohlensäure; ~ **wine** *(as type)* Schaumwein *m*; *(slightly* ~*)* Perlwein *m*; ~ **white** blütenweiß; **to be** ~ **clean** vor Sauberkeit blitzen.

**sparring partner** ['spɑːrɪŋ'pɑːtnər] *n* Sparringpartner *m*; *(fig also)* Kontrahent(in *f*) *m*.
**sparrow** ['spærəʊ] *n* Sperling, Spatz *m*.
**sparrowhawk** ['spærəʊhɔːk] *n (European)* Sperber *m*.
**sparse** [spɑːs] *adj (+er)* spärlich; *covering, population* dünn; *(infrequent) references also* rar.
**sparsely** ['spɑːslɪ] *adv* spärlich; *wooded also, populated* dünn.
**spartan** ['spɑːtən] *adj (fig)* spartanisch.
**spasm** ['spæzəm] *n (Med)* Krampf *m*; *(of asthma, coughing, fig)* Anfall *m*. **to work in** ~s sporadisch arbeiten.
**spasmodic** [spæz'mɒdɪk] *adj (Med)* krampfartig; *(fig: occasional)* sporadisch; *growth* schubweise.
**spastic** ['spæstɪk] **1** *adj* spastisch. **2** *n* Spastiker(in *f*) *m*.
**spat** *pret, ptp of* **spit**[1].
**spate** [speɪt] *n (of river)* Hochwasser *nt*; *(fig) (of letters, orders etc)* Flut *f*; *(of burglaries, accidents)* Serie *f*; *(of words, abuse)* Schwall *m*. **the river is in (full)** ~ der Fluß führt Hochwasser.
**spatial** ['speɪʃəl] *adj* räumlich.
**spatter** ['spætər] *vt* bespritzen. **to** ~ **water over sb, to** ~ **sb with water** jdn naß spritzen.
**spatula** ['spætjʊlə] *n* Spachtel *m*; *(Med)* Spatel *m*.
**spawn** [spɔːn] **1** *n (of fish, frogs)* Laich *m*. **2** *vi* laichen. **3** *vt (fig)* erzeugen.
**spay** [speɪ] *vt cat* sterilisieren.
**SPCA** *(US)* = **Society for the Prevention of Cruelty to Animals** Tierschutzverein *m*.
**SPCC** *(US)* = **Society for the Prevention of Cruelty to Children** Kinderschutzbund *m*.
**speak** [spiːk] *pret* **spoke**, *ptp* **spoken 1** *vt* **(a)** *(utter)* sagen; *one's thoughts* äußern; *one's lines* aufsagen. **to** ~ **one's mind** seine Meinung sagen; **nobody spoke a word** niemand sagte ein Wort. **(b)** *language* sprechen. **English spoken here** hier spricht man Englisch.
    **2** *vi* **(a)** *(talk, be on* ~*ing terms)* sprechen, reden *(about* über *+acc*, von; *on* zu*)*; *(converse)* reden, sich unterhalten *(with* mit*)*; *(give opinion)* sich äußern *(on, to* zu*)*. **to** ~ **to** *or* **with sb** mit jdm sprechen; **did you** ~? haben Sie etwas gesagt?; **to** ~ **in a whisper** flüstern; **I'm not** ~**ing to you** mit dir rede ich nicht mehr; **I wasn't** ~**ing to you** das war nicht für dich gemeint; **I'll** ~ **to him about it** *(euph: tell off)* ich werde ein Wörtchen mit ihm reden; **I don't know him to** ~ **to** ich kenne ihn nicht näher; ~**ing of dictionaries** ... da wir gerade von Wörterbüchern sprechen ...; **not to** ~ **of** ... ganz zu schweigen von ...; **it's nothing to** ~ **of** es ist nicht weiter erwähnenswert; **no money** *etc* **to** ~ **of** so gut wie kein Geld *etc*; **to** ~ **well of sb/sth** Gutes über jdn/etw sagen; **so to** ~ sozusagen; **strictly** ~**ing** genau genommen; **legally** ~**ing** rechtlich gesehen; **generally** ~**ing** im allgemeinen; ~**ing personally** ... was mich betrifft ...
    **(b) to** ~ **in public** in der Öffentlichkeit reden; **to** ~ **in the debate** in der Debatte das Wort ergreifen; **to ask sb to** ~ jdm das Wort erteilen.
    **(c)** *(Telec)* ~**ing!** am Apparat!; **Jones** ~**ing!** (hier) Jones!; **who is** ~**ing?** wer ist da, bitte?; *(on extension phone, in office)* wer ist am Apparat?
    ▶**speak against** *vi +prep obj (in debate)* sich aussprechen gegen; *(criticize)* kritisieren.
    ▶**speak for** *vi +prep obj* **(a)** *(in debate)* unterstützen. **(b) to** ~ ~ **sb** *(on behalf of)* in jds Namen *(dat)* sprechen; *(in favour of)* ein gutes Wort für jdn einlegen; ~**ing** ~ **myself** ... was mich angeht ...; **let her** ~ ~ **herself** laß sie selbst reden; ~ ~ **yourself!** *(I*

*don't agree)* das meinst auch nur du!; *(don't include me)* du vielleicht!; **to** ~ **well** ~ **sth** ein Beweis *m* für etw sein; **to** ~ ~ **itself** *(be obvious)* für sich sprechen; **that's already spoken** ~ das ist schon vergeben.
    ▶**speak out** *vi (audibly)* deutlich sprechen; *(give opinion)* seine Meinung deutlich vertreten. **to** ~ ~ **against sth** sich gegen etw aussprechen.
    ▶**speak up** *vi* **(a)** *(raise one's voice)* lauter sprechen; *(talk loudly)* laut (und verständlich) sprechen. **(b)** *(fig)* seine Meinung sagen *or* äußern. **don't be afraid to** ~ ~ sagen Sie ruhig Ihre Meinung; **to** ~ ~ **for sb/sth** für jdn/etw eintreten.
**speaker** ['spiːkər] *n* **(a)** *(of language)* Sprecher *m*. **all** ~**s of German** alle Deutschsprechenden. **(b)** Sprecher(in *f*) *m*; *(in discussion also, in lecture)* Redner(in *f*) *m*. **the last** *or* **previous** ~ der Vorredner; **our** ~ **today is** ... der heutige Referent ist ... **(c)** *(loud*~*, in record-player)* Lautsprecher *m*; *(separate enclosure)* Box *f*. **(d)** *(Parl)* **S**~ Sprecher(in *f*) *m*.
**speaking** ['spiːkɪŋ] *n (act of* ~*)* Sprechen *nt*; *(speeches)* Reden *pl*.
**-speaking** *adj suf* -sprechend; *(with native language also)* -sprachig.
**speaking:** ~ **clock** *n (Brit)* Zeitansage *f*; ~ **terms** *npl* **to be on** ~ **terms with sb** mit jdm reden.
**spear** [spɪər] *n* Speer *m*.
**spear:** ~**head 1** *n (of spear)* Speerspitze *f*; *(Mil)* Angriffsspitze *f*; *(fig: person, thing)* Bahnbrecher *m (of* für*)*; **2** *vt (lit, fig)* anführen; ~**mint** *n* Grüne Minze.
**spec** [spek] *n (col)* **on** ~ auf gut Glück.
**special** ['speʃəl] **1** *adj* **(a)** besondere(r, s); *(specific, exceptional) purpose, use, friend, favour, occasion also* speziell. **I have no** ~ **person in mind** ich habe eigentlich an niemanden Bestimmtes gedacht; **take** ~ **care of it** passen Sie besonders gut darauf auf; **nothing** ~ nichts Besonderes; **he expects** ~ **treatment** er will besonders behandelt werden; **what's so** ~ **about her?** was ist denn an ihr so besonders?; **what's so** ~ **about that?** na und? *(col)*, das ist doch nichts Besonderes! **(b)** *(out of the ordinary) permission, edition, powers* Sonder-; *subject, dictionary* Spezial-. ~ **feature** *(Press)* Sonderartikel *m*. **2** *n (constable)* Hilfspolizist(in *f*) *m*; *(train)* Sonderzug *m*; *(Cook)* Tagesgericht *nt*; *(edition)* Sonderausgabe *f*; *(product)* Sonderausführung *f*; *(unique)* Einzelanfertigung *f*.
**special:** ~ **agent** *n (spy)* Agent(in *f*) *m*; **S**~ **Branch** *n (Brit)* Sicherheitspolizei *f*; ~ **case** *n (also Jur)* Sonderfall *m*; ~ **correspondent** *n (Press)* Sonderberichterstatter(in *f*) *m*; ~ **delivery** *n* Eilzustellung *f*; **by** ~ **delivery** durch Eilboten; ~ **effects** *npl* Spezialeffekte, Tricks *pl*.
**specialist** ['speʃəlɪst] **1** *n* Spezialist(in *f*) *m*, Fachmann *m*/-frau *f (in* für*)*; *(Med)* Facharzt *m*/-ärztin *f (in* für*)*. **2** *adj attr knowledge, dictionary, training* Fach-.
**speciality** [ˌspeʃɪ'ælɪtɪ], *(US)* **specialty** ['speʃəltɪ] *n* Spezialität *f*; *(subject also)* Spezialgebiet *nt*. **to make a** ~ **of sth** sich auf etw *(acc)* spezialisieren.
**specialize** ['speʃəlaɪz] *vi* sich spezialisieren *(in* auf *+acc)*. **we** ~ **in** ... wir haben uns auf ... spezialisiert.
**specialized** ['speʃəlaɪzd] *adj* spezialisiert. **a** ~ **knowledge of biology** Fachkenntnisse *pl* in Biologie.
**specially** ['speʃəlɪ] *adv* besonders; *(specifically)* speziell, extra. **a** ~ **difficult task** eine besonders schwierige Aufgabe; **I had it** ~ **made** ich habe es extra machen lassen.
**special:** ~ **offer** *n* Sonderangebot *nt*; **to be on** ~ **offer** im Sonderangebot sein; ~ **school** *n* Sonderschule *f*; *(for physically handicapped)* Behinderten-

schule *f*; ~ **subject** *n (Sch)* Leistungsfach *nt.*

**specialty** ['speʃəltɪ] *(US)* **1** *n* = **speciality. 2** *adj store, tool* Spezial-.

**species** ['spiːʃiːz] *n, pl* - Art *f; (Biol also)* Spezies *f.*

**specific** [spə'sɪfɪk] **1** *adj* **(a)** *(definite)* speziell; *(precise) statement, instructions* genau; *example* ganz bestimmt. **9.3, to be** ~ 9,3, um genau zu sein; **can you be a bit more** ~? können Sie sich etwas genauer äußern? **(b)** *(Sci)* spezifisch. ~ **gravity** spezifisches Gewicht. **2** *n* ~**s** *pl* nähere Einzelheiten *pl.*

**specifically** [spə'sɪfɪkəlɪ] *adv warn, order, state* ausdrücklich; *(specially) designed, request* speziell; *(precisely)* genau.

**specification** [ˌspesɪfɪ'keɪʃən] *n (detail)* Angabe *f; (stipulation)* Bedingung *f; (of requirements)* genaue Angabe; *(technical description)* (genaue) Beschreibung; *(design) (for car, machine)* (detaillierter) Entwurf; *(for building)* Bauplan *m; (also* ~**s** *pl)* genaue Angaben *pl; (of car, machine)* technische Daten *pl; (of new building)* Baubeschreibung *f.*

**specify** ['spesɪfaɪ] **1** *vt* angeben; *(in detail)* detaillieren; *(list)* (einzeln) aufführen; *(stipulate)* vorschreiben; *(blueprint, contract etc)* vorsehen. **2** *vi* genaue Angaben machen. **unless otherwise specified** wenn nicht anders angegeben.

**specimen** ['spesɪmɪn] **1** *n* Exemplar *nt; (of urine, blood etc)* Probe *f; (sample)* Muster *nt.* **a beautiful or fine** ~ ein Prachtexemplar *nt; he's a pretty poor* ~ *(col)* er hat nicht viel zu bieten *(col).* **2** *adj attr page* Probe-. **a** ~ **copy** ein Probeexemplar *nt; a* ~ **signature** eine Unterschriftenprobe.

**specious** ['spiːʃəs] *adj argument* vordergründig bestechend, Schein-; *claim* fadenscheinig.

**speck** [spek] *n* Fleck *m; (of blood, paint also)* Spritzer *m; (of soot)* Flocke *f; (of gold, colour etc)* Sprenkel *m.* ~ **of dust** Stäubchen *nt,* Staubkorn *nt; a* ~ **on the horizon** ein Punkt *m* am Horizont.

**speckle** ['spekl] *vt* sprenkeln. **to be** ~**d with sth** mit etw gesprenkelt sein.

**specs** [speks] *npl (col)* Brille *f.*

**spectacle** ['spektəkl] *n* **(a)** *(show)* Schauspiel *nt.* **a sad** ~ ein trauriger Anblick; **to make a** ~ **of oneself** unangenehm auffallen. **(b)** ~**s** *pl (also* **pair of** ~**s)** Brille *f.*

**spectacle case** *n* Brillenetui *nt.*

**spectacular** [spek'tækjʊləʳ] **1** *adj* sensationell; *improvement, success also* spektakulär. **2** *n (Theat)* Show *f.*

**spectator** [spek'teɪtəʳ] *n* Zuschauer(in *f*) *m.* ~ **sport** Publikumssport *m.*

**spectre,** *(US)* **specter** ['spektəʳ] *n* Gespenst *nt; (fig)* (Schreck)gespenst *nt.*

**spectrum** ['spektrəm] *n, pl* **spectra** Spektrum *nt; (fig: range also)* Skala *f.*

**speculate** ['spekjʊleɪt] *vi* **(a)** Überlegungen anstellen, spekulieren *(about, on* über *+acc).* **(b)** *(Fin)* spekulieren *(in* mit, *on* an *+dat).*

**speculation** [ˌspekjʊ'leɪʃən] *n* Spekulation *f (on* über *+acc); (guesswork also)* Vermutung *f.* **it is the subject of much** ~ darüber sind viele Vermutungen angestellt worden.

**speculative** ['spekjʊlətɪv] *adj* **(a)** spekulativ; *ideas* rein theoretisch. **(b)** *(Fin)* Spekulations-.

**speculator** ['spekjʊleɪtəʳ] *n* Spekulant(in *f*) *m.*

**sped** [sped] *pret, ptp of* **speed.**

**speech** [spiːtʃ] *n no pl* Sprache *f; (act of speaking)* Sprechen *nt; (manner of speaking)* Sprechweise *f; (oration, Theat)* Rede *f (on, about* über *+acc); (address)* Ansprache *f.* **to lose/recover the power of** ~ die Sprache verlieren/zurückgewinnen; **freedom of** ~ Redefreiheit *f;* **to give** *or* **make a** ~ eine Rede *etc*

halten; **direct/indirect** *or* **reported** ~ *(Brit Gram)* direkte/indirekte Rede.

**speech:** ~ **balloon** *n* Sprechblase *f;* ~ **day** *n (Brit)* Schulfeier *f;* ~ **defect,** ~ **impediment** *n* Sprachfehler *m.*

**speechless** ['spiːtʃlɪs] *adj (at a loss for words)* sprachlos *(with* vor *+dat); anger* stumm. **his remark left me** ~ seine Bemerkung verschlug mir die Sprache.

**speech:** ~ **synthesizer** *n* Sprachsynthesizer *m;* ~ **therapist** *n* Logopäde *m,* Logopädin *f;* ~ **therapy** *n* Sprachtherapie *f; (treatment)* logopädische Behandlung.

**speed** [spiːd] *(vb: pret, ptp* **sped** *or* ~**ed)* **1** *n* **(a)** Geschwindigkeit *f; (fast* ~ *also)* Schnelligkeit *f; (of moving object or person also)* Tempo *nt.* **at** ~ bei hoher Geschwindigkeit; **at a high/low** ~ mit hoher/ niedriger Geschwindigkeit; **at full** *or* **top** ~ mit Höchstgeschwindigkeit; **at a** ~ **of 50 mph** mit einem Tempo von 50 Meilen pro Stunde; **at the** ~ **of light** mit Lichtgeschwindigkeit; **to pick up** *or* **gather** ~ schneller werden; *(fig: development)* sich beschleunigen; **to lose** ~ (an) Geschwindigkeit verlieren; **what** ~ **were you doing?** wie schnell sind Sie gefahren?; **what is her shorthand/typing** ~? wieviele Silben/Anschläge pro Minute schreibt sie? **(b)** *(Aut, Tech: gear)* Gang *m.* **a three-** ~ **gear/gearbox** ein Dreiganggetriebe *nt.* **(c)** *(Phot) (film* ~*)* Lichtempfindlichkeit *f; (shutter* ~*)* Belichtungszeit *f.*

**2** *vt* **to** ~ **sb on his way** *(person)* jdn verabschieden; *(iro)* jdn hinauskomplimentieren; *(good wishes etc)* jdn auf seinem Weg begleiten.

**3** *vi* **(a)** *pret, ptp* **sped** *(move quickly)* jagen; *(arrow)* sausen. **the years sped by** die Jahre vergingen wie im Fluge. **(b)** *pret, ptp* ~**ed** *(Aut: exceed* ~ *limit)* zu schnell fahren.

▶**speed up** *pret, ptp* ~**ed** ~ **1** *vi (car, driver etc)* beschleunigen; *(person)* Tempo zulegen; *(work, production etc)* schneller werden. **2** *vt sep* beschleunigen; *person* antreiben; *research also* vorantreiben.

**speed:** ~**boat** *n* Rennboot *nt;* ~ **bump** *or* **hump** *n* Bodenschwelle *f.*

**speedily** ['spiːdɪlɪ] *adv* schnell; *reply, return* prompt.

**speeding** ['spiːdɪŋ] *n* Tempoüberschreitung *f.*

**speed limit** *n* Geschwindigkeitsbegrenzung *f,* Tempolimit *nt.* **a 30 mph** ~ eine Geschwindigkeitsbegrenzung von 50 km/h.

**speedometer** [spɪ'dɒmɪtəʳ] *n* Tachometer *m.*

**speed:** ~ **skater** *n* Eisschnellläufer(in *f*) *m;* ~ **skating** *n* Eisschnelllauf *m;* ~ **trap** *n* Radarfalle *f (col);* ~**way** *n* **(a)** *(Sport)* Speedwayrennen *nt; (track)* Speedwayrennbahn *f;* **(b)** *(US) (race-track)* Rennstrecke *f; (expressway)* Schnellstraße *f.*

**speedy** ['spiːdɪ] *adj (+er)* schnell; *answer, service also* prompt; *remedy* schnell wirkend.

**spell**¹ [spel] *n (lit, fig)* Zauber *m; (incantation)* Zauberspruch *m.* **to be under a** ~ *(lit)* verzaubert *or* verhext sein; *(fig)* wie verzaubert sein; **to cast a** ~ **over sb** *(lit, fig)* jdn verzaubern; **to be under sb's** ~ *(fig)* in jds Bann *(dat)* stehen; **to break the** ~ *(lit, fig)* den Bann brechen.

**spell**² *n (period)* Weile *f.* **for a** ~ eine Weile, eine Zeitlang; **cold/hot** ~ Kälte-/Hitzewelle *f;* **a short** ~ **of sunny weather** eine kurze Schönwetterperiode.

**spell**³ *pret, ptp* ~**ed** *or* **spelt 1** *vi (in writing)* richtig schreiben; *(aloud)* buchstabieren. **she can't** ~ sie kann keine Rechtschreibung. **2** *vt* **(a)** schreiben; *(aloud)* buchstabieren. **how do you** ~ **"onyx"?** wie schreibt man „onyx"?; **how do you** ~ **your name?** wie schreibt sich Ihr Name?, wie schreiben Sie sich? **(b)** *(denote)* bedeuten. **this** ~**s disaster (for**

us) das bedeutet nichts Gutes (für uns).
▶**spell out** *vt sep (spell aloud)* buchstabieren; *(read slowly)* entziffern; *(explain)* verdeutlichen. **do I have to ~ it ~ for you?** *(col)* muß ich noch deutlicher werden?

**spell:** ~**binding** *adj* fesselnd; ~**bound** *adj, adv (fig)* wie verzaubert, gebannt; **to hold sb ~bound** jdn fesseln; *(person also)* jdn in seinen Bann schlagen.
**spell-check(er)** ['speltʃek(ər)] *n (Comp)* Rechtschreibprüfung f.
**spelling** ['spelɪŋ] *n* Rechtschreibung f; *(of a word)* Schreibweise f. ~ **check** Rechtschreibprüfung f; ~ **mistake** (Recht)schreibfehler *m*.
**spelt** [spelt] *pret, ptp of* **spell³**.
**spend** [spend] *pret, ptp* **spent** *vt* (a) *money* ausgeben *(on für)*; *energy, strength* verbrauchen; *time* brauchen. **time well spent** sinnvoll genutzte Zeit. **(b)** *(pass) time, evening etc* verbringen. **he ~s his time reading** er verbringt seine Zeit mit Lesen; **to ~ money/time on sth** *(devote to)* Geld/Zeit für etw aufbringen.
**spending** ['spendɪŋ] *n no pl* Ausgaben *pl*. **government ~ cuts** Kürzungen im Etat; ~ **money** Taschengeld *nt*; ~ **power** Kaufkraft f; ~ **spree** *n* Kauforgie f.
**spendthrift** ['spendθrɪft] **1** *adv* verschwenderisch. **2** *n* Verschwender(in f) *m*.
**spent** [spent] **1** *pret, ptp of* **spend**. **2** *adj ammunition, cartridge, match* verbraucht; *person* erschöpft. **to be a ~ force** nichts mehr zu sagen haben; *(movement)* sich totgelaufen haben.
**sperm** [spɜːm] *n* Samenfaden *m*, Spermium *nt*; *(fluid)* Sperma *nt.* ~ **bank** Samenbank f; ~ **donor** Samenspender *m*; ~ **duct** Samenleiter *m*; ~ **whale** *n* Pottwal *m*.
**spew** [spjuː] **1** *vi (col: vomit)* brechen, spucken. **2** *vt* **(a)** *(also ~ up) (col: vomit)* erbrechen, ausspucken. **(b)** *(fig: also ~ out) flames* speien; *smoke, lava also* ausstoßen.
**sphere** [sfɪər] *n* **(a)** Kugel f; *(heavenly ~)* Gestirn *nt (geh).* **(b)** *(fig)* Sphäre f; *(of person, experience)* Bereich *m*; *(of knowledge etc)* Gebiet, Feld *nt; (social etc circle)* Kreis *m.* **in the ~ of politics** in der Welt der Politik; **his ~ of influence** sein Einflußbereich; ~ **of activity** *(job, specialism)* Wirkungskreis *m*; **that's outside my ~** *(not my responsibility)* das ist nicht mein Gebiet.
**spherical** ['sferɪkəl] *adj (in shape)* kugelförmig.
**sphinx** [sfɪŋks] *n* Sphinx f.
**spice** [spaɪs] **1** *n* **(a)** Gewürz *nt.* ~ **rack** Gewürzbord *nt*; **mixed ~(s)** Gewürzmischung f. **(b)** *(fig)* Würze f. **variety is the ~ of life** *(prov)* über mal was Neues *(col).* **2** *vt (lit, fig)* würzen. **a highly ~d account** *(fig)* ein reichlich ausgeschmückter Bericht.
**spiciness** ['spaɪsɪnɪs] *n* Würze f; *(fig)* Pikanterie f.
**spick-and-span** ['spɪkən'spæn] *adj house etc* blitzsauber, tipptopp in Ordnung *pred; person* wie aus dem Ei gepellt *(col).*
**spicy** ['spaɪsɪ] *adj (+er)* würzig; *sauce, food also* stark gewürzt; *(fig) story etc* pikant.
**spider** ['spaɪdər] *n* Spinne f. ~'**s web** Spinnwebe f, Spinnennetz *nt*.
**spidery** ['spaɪdərɪ] *adj writing* krakelig; *limbs etc* spinnenhaft.
**spiel** [ʃpiːl] *n (col)* Blabla *nt (col); (tall story, excuse)* Geschichte f *(col).*
**spike** [spaɪk] **1** *n (on railing, helmet etc)* Spitze f; *(nail)* Nagel *m; (on plant)* Stachel *m; (on shoe etc)* Spike *m; (for papers)* Dorn *m.* **2** *vt* **(a)** aufspießen. **(b)** *(fig: frustrate) rumours* den Boden entziehen *(+dat).* **to ~ sb's guns** jdm einen Strich durch die

Rechnung machen *(col).* **(c)** *(US: lace)* drink einen Schuß zusetzen *(+dat).* ~**d with rum** mit einem Schuß Rum.
**spikes** [spaɪks] *npl (Sport)* Spikes *pl*.
**spiky** ['spaɪkɪ] *adj (+er) railings* mit Metallspitzen; *bush, grass, animal* stach(e)lig; *branch* dornig; *flower* mit spitzen Blütenblättern; *leaf* spitz; *writing* steil.
**spill** [spɪl] *pret, ptp* ~**ed** *or* **spilt 1** *vt* verschütten; *blood* vergießen. **to ~ the beans (to sb)** *(col)* (jdm gegenüber) nicht dichthalten *(col);* **the lorry ~ed its load onto the road** die Ladung des Lastwagens fiel auf die Straße. **2** *vi* verschüttet werden; *(large quantity)* sich ergießen; *(fig: people)* strömen. **the blood ~ed onto the floor** das Blut floß auf den Boden.
▶**spill out 1** *vi (of aus) (liquid)* herausschwappen; *(grain)* herausrieseln; *(money, jewels)* herausfallen; *(fig: people)* (heraus)strömen. **2** *vt sep* ausschütten; *(by accident)* verschütten.
▶**spill over** *vi (liquid)* überlaufen; *(grain etc, assembly)* überquellen; *(fig: population)* sich ausbreiten *(into auf +acc).*
**spillage** ['spɪlɪdʒ] *n (act)* Verschütten *nt; (of oil)* Auslaufen *nt; (quantity)* verschüttete Menge.
**spilt** [spɪlt] *pret, ptp of* **spill**.
**spin** [spɪn] *(vb: pret, ptp* **spun) 1** *n* **(a)** *(revolution)* Drehung f; *(washing machine programme)* Schleudern *nt no pl.* **to give sth a ~** etw (schnell) drehen; *(in washing machine)* etw schleudern; **to be in a (flat) ~** *(fig col)* rotieren *(col) (about wegen).* **(b)** *(on ball)* Drall *m; (Billiards)* Effet *m.* **(c)** *(Aviat)* Trudeln *nt no pl.* **to go into a ~** zu trudeln anfangen. **(d)** *(trip)* Spritztour f. **to go for a ~** (ein bißchen) spazierenfahren.
**2** *vt* **(a)** spinnen. **(b)** *(turn) wheel* drehen; *(fast)* herumwirbeln; *(in washing machine)* schleudern; *(toss) coin* werfen; *(Sport) ball* einen Drall/Effet geben *(+dat); (with racket)* (an)schneiden.
**3** *vi* **(a)** spinnen. **(b)** *(revolve)* sich drehen; *(fast)* (herum)wirbeln; *(plane etc)* trudeln; *(in washing machine)* schleudern. **the car spun out of control** der Wagen geriet stark ins Schleudern; **my head is ~ning** mir dreht sich alles.
▶**spin out** *vt sep (col) money, food* strecken *(col); holiday, meeting* in die Länge ziehen; *story* ausspinnen.
**spinach** ['spɪnɪtʃ] *n* Spinat *m*.
**spinal** ['spaɪnl] *adj vertebrae* Rücken-; *injury, muscle* Rückgrat-. ~ **column** Wirbelsäule f; ~ **cord** Rückenmark *nt*.
**spindle** ['spɪndl] *n (for spinning, Mech)* Spindel f.
**spindly** ['spɪndlɪ] *adj (+er) legs, arms, plant* spindeldürr; *chairs* zierlich.
**spin:** ~**-drier,** ~**-dryer** *n (Brit)* (Wäsche)schleuder f; ~**-dry** *vti* schleudern.
**spine** [spaɪn] *n* **(a)** *(Anat)* Rückgrat *nt; (of book)* (Buch)rücken *m.* **(b)** *(spike)* Stachel *m; (of plant also)* Dorn *m.*
**spine:** ~**-chiller** *n (col)* Gruselgeschichte f; Gruselfilm *m;* ~**-chilling** *adj (col)* gruselig; *noise* unheimlich.
**spineless** ['spaɪnlɪs] *adj (fig) person* ohne Rückgrat; *compromise, refusal* feige.
**spinner** ['spɪnər] *n* **(a)** *(of cloth)* Spinner(in f) *m.* **(b)** *(col)* = **spin-drier**.
**spinney** ['spɪnɪ] *n (esp Brit)* Dickicht *nt*.
**spinning** *in cpds* Spinn-; ~ **top** *n* Kreisel *m;* ~ **wheel** *n* Spinnrad *nt*.
**spin-off** ['spɪnɒf] *n (side-product)* Nebenprodukt *nt*.
**spinster** ['spɪnstər] *n* Unverheiratete f; *(pej)* alte

Jungfer *(pej)*. **to be a** ~ unverheiratet *or* eine alte Jungfer *(pej)* sein.

**spiral** ['spaɪərəl] **1** *adj* spiralförmig; *shell also* gewunden; *spring* Spiral-; *movement* in Spiralen. ~ **staircase** Wendeltreppe *f*. **2** *n (lit, fig)* Spirale *f*. **inflationary** ~ Inflationsspirale *f*. **3** *vi (also* ~ **up)** sich hochwinden; *(smoke also)* spiralförmig aufsteigen; *(prices)* (nach oben) klettern.

**spire** [spaɪə*r*] *n (of church)* Turmspitze *f*.

**spirit** ['spɪrɪt] *n (soul, ghost)* Geist *m*. **I'll be with you in** ~ im Geiste werde ich bei euch sein.

(b) *no pl (courage)* Mut *m*; *(vitality)* Elan *m*. **a man of** ~ *(courageous)* ein mutiger Mensch; **to break sb's** ~ jds Mut brechen; **to sing with** ~ mit Inbrunst singen.

(c) *(attitude: of country, group of people etc)* Geist *m*; *(mood)* Stimmung *f*. **team/community** ~ Mannschaftsgeist *m*/Gemeinschaftssinn *m*; **Christmas** ~ *(mood)* weihnachtliche Stimmung; **party** ~ Partystimmung *f*; **fighting** ~ Kampfgeist *m*; **a** ~ **of optimism** eine optimistische Stimmung; **the** ~ **of the age** der Zeitgeist; **he has the right** ~ er hat die richtige Einstellung; **to enter into the** ~ **of sth** bei etw mitmachen; **that's the** ~! *(col)* so ist's recht! *(col)*; **the** ~ **of the law** der Geist des Gesetzes; **to take sth in the right** ~ etw richtig auffassen.

(d) ~**s** *pl (state of mind)* Stimmung *f*. **to be in good/bad** ~**s** guter/schlechter Laune sein; **to keep up one's** ~**s** den Mut nicht verlieren; **to raise sb's** ~**s** jdn aufmuntern.

(e) ~**s** *pl (alcohol)* Spirituosen *pl*.

**spirited** ['spɪrɪtɪd] *adj* temperamentvoll; *performance* lebendig; *(courageous) person, attempt* mutig; *defence, resistance* beherzt.

**spirit:** ~ **lamp** *n* Petroleumlampe *f*; ~ **level** *n* Wasserwaage *f*.

**spiritual** ['spɪrɪtjʊəl] **1** *adj* geistig; *(Eccl)* geistlich. **2** *n (Mus)* Spiritual *nt*.

**spiritualism** ['spɪrɪtjʊəlɪzəm] *n* Spiritismus *m*.

**spiritualist** ['spɪrɪtjʊəlɪst] *n* Spiritist(in *f*) *m*.

**spit**[1] [spɪt] *(vb: pret, ptp* **spat)** **1** *n (saliva)* Spucke *f*. **2** *vt* spucken. **3** *vi* spucken; *(fat)* spritzen; *(fire)* zischen; *(person: verbally, cat)* fauchen. **it is** ~**ting (with rain)** es tröpfelt.

► **spit out** *vt sep* ausspucken; *words* ausstoßen. ~ **it** ~! *(fig col)* heraus mit der Sprache!

**spit**[2] *n* (a) *(Cook)* (Brat)spieß *m*. **on the** ~ am Spieß. (b) *(of land)* Landzunge *f*.

**spite** [spaɪt] *n* (a) *(ill will)* Gehässigkeit *f*. **to do sth out of** *or* **from** ~ etw aus reiner Boshaftigkeit tun. (b) **in** ~ **of** *(despite)* trotz *(+gen)*; **we went in** ~ **of everything** wir gingen dennoch; **he did it in** ~ **of himself** er konnte nicht anders; **in** ~ **of the fact that he ...** obwohl er ... **2** *vt* ärgern. **she just does it to** ~ **me** sie tut es nur, um mich zu ärgern.

**spiteful** *adj*, ~**ly** *adv* ['spaɪtfʊl, -fəlɪ] boshaft, gemein.

**spitting image** ['spɪtɪŋ'ɪmɪdʒ] *n (col)* Ebenbild *nt*. **to be the** ~ **of sb** jdm wie aus dem Gesicht geschnitten sein.

**spittle** ['spɪtl] *n* Speichel *m*, Spucke *f*.

**splash** [splæʃ] **1** *n* (a) *(spray)* Spritzen *nt no pl*; *(noise)* Platschen *nt no pl*. **to make a** ~ *(fig)* Furore machen; *(news)* wie eine Bombe einschlagen; *(book)* einschlagen. (b) *(small amount)* Spritzer *m*; *(in drink etc also)* Schuß *m*; *(of colour, light)* Tupfen *m*. ~**es of paint** Farbspritzer *pl*. **2** *vt water etc* spritzen; *(pour)* gießen; *person, object* bespritzen. **to** ~ **water over sb** jdn mit Wasser bespritzen; **the story was** ~**ed all over the papers** die Geschichte wurde in allen Zeitungen groß rausgebracht *(col)*. **3** *vi*

*(liquid)* spritzen; *(rain, waves)* klatschen; *(tears)* tropfen; *(when diving, walking etc)* platschen; *(when playing)* planschen.

► **splash down** *vi (Space)* wassern.

► **splash out** *vi (col)* tüchtig in die Tasche greifen *(col)*; *(giving presents etc)* sich nicht lumpen lassen *(col)*. **to** ~ ~ **on sth** sich *(dat)* etw spendieren *(col)*.

**splashdown** ['splæʃdaʊn] *n (Space)* Wasserung *f*.

**splatter** ['splætə*r*] *vt* bespritzen; *(with ink, paint etc)* beklecksen.

**splay** [spleɪ] *(also* ~ **out)** *vt (spread out) legs, fingers, toes* spreizen; *feet* nach außen stellen.

**splayfoot** ['spleɪˌfʊt] *n* Spreizfuß *m*.

**spleen** [spliːn] *n (Anat)* Milz *f*; *(fig)* Zorn *m*. **to vent one's** ~ seinem Ärger Luft machen.

**splendid** ['splendɪd] *adj* (a) *(magnificent)* herrlich; *occasion, scale* großartig. (b) *(excellent)* hervorragend; *rider etc, idea* glänzend.

**spendidly** ['splendɪdlɪ] *adv* (a) *(magnificently)* herrlich. (b) *(excellently)* hevorragend, glänzend.

**splendour,** *(US)* **splendor** ['splendə*r*] *n* Pracht *f no pl*; *(of music, achievement)* Großartigkeit *f*.

**splice** [splaɪs] *vt ropes* spleißen *(spec)*; *tapes, film* (zusammen)kleben; *pieces of wood etc* verfugen.

**splicer** ['splaɪsə*r*] *n (for films)* Klebepresse *f*.

**splint** [splɪnt] *n* Schiene *f*. **to put a** ~ **on sth** etw schienen; **to be in** ~**s** geschient sein.

**splinter** ['splɪntə*r*] **1** *n* Splitter *m*. **2** *vt* (zer)splittern; *(with axe) wood* zerhacken. **3** *vi* (zer)splittern.

**splinter group** *n* Splittergruppe *f*.

**split** [splɪt] *(vb: pret, ptp* ~**)** **1** *n* (a) *(Riß *m (in* in *+dat)*; *(in rock, wood also)* Spalt *m (in* in *+dat)*. (b) *(fig: division)* Bruch *m (in* in *+dat)*; *(Pol, Eccl)* Spaltung *f (in gen)*. **there is a** ~ **in the party over ...** die Partei ist in der Frage *(+gen)* ... gespalten. (c) *(distinction: in meaning)* Aufteilung *f*. (d) *pl* **the** ~**s** Spagat *m*; **to do the** ~**s** einen Spagat machen. (e) *(col: sweet) (also* **banana** ~**)** Bananen-Split *m*. **jam/cream** ~ mit Marmelade/Sahne gefülltes Gebäckstück.

**2** *adj* gespalten *(on, over* in *+dat)*.

**3** *vt* (a) *(cleave)* (zer)teilen; *wood also, atom* spalten; *fabric* zerreißen; *seam* aufplatzen lassen. **to** ~ **hairs** *(col)* Haarspalterei treiben *(col)*; **to** ~ **one's sides (laughing)** *(col)* vor Lachen fast platzen *(col)*; **to** ~ **sth open** etw aufbrechen; **his head was** ~ **open when he fell** er hatte sich *(dat)* beim Fallen den Kopf aufgeschlagen. (b) *(divide)* spalten; *(share) work, costs etc* (sich *dat*) teilen. **to** ~ **sth into three parts** etw in drei Teile aufteilen; **to** ~ **the vote** die Stimmen spalten; **a party** ~ **three ways** eine in drei Lager gespaltene Partei; **they** ~ **the profit three ways** sie haben den Gewinn in drei Teile geteilt; **to** ~ **the difference** *(fig: in argument etc)* sich auf halbem Wege einigen; *(lit: with money etc)* sich *(dat)* die Differenz teilen.

**4** *vi* (a) *(wood)* sich spalten; *(trousers, seam etc)* platzen; *(fabric)* zerreißen. **to** ~ **open** aufplatzen; **my head is** ~**ting** *(fig)* mir platzt der Kopf. (b) *(col: tell tales)* **to** ~ **on sb** jdn verpfeifen *(col)*.

► **split off 1** *vt sep* abtrennen *(prep obj* von*)*; *(break)* abbrechen *(prep obj* von*)*. **2** *vi* abbrechen; *(fig)* sich trennen *(from* von*)*.

► **split up 1** *vt sep money, work* (auf)teilen; *party, organization* spalten; *meeting* ein Ende machen *(+dat)*; *two people* trennen; *crowd* zerstreuen. **2** *vi* zerbrechen; *(divide)* sich teilen; *(meeting, crowd)* sich spalten; *(partners)* sich trennen.

**split:** ~ **infinitive** *n (Gram)* getrennter Infinitiv; ~**level** *adj (Archit)* mit versetzten Geschossen; ~ **peas** *npl* getrocknete (halbe) Erbsen *pl*; ~

**personality** *n* gespaltene Persönlichkeit; ~ **second 1** *n* **in a** ~ **second** in Sekundenschnelle; **2** *adj* ~-**second timing** Abstimmung *f* auf die Sekunde; *(of actor)* Gefühl *nt* für den richtigen Moment; ~ **time** *n (Ski)* Zwischenzeit *f.*

**splitting** ['splɪtɪŋ] **1** *n* Zerteilung *f; (of wood)* Spalten *nt.* **the** ~ **of the atom** die Kernspaltung. **2** *adj headache* rasend.

**splodge** [splɒdʒ], **splotch** [splɒtʃ] *n* Klecks *m; (of cream etc)* Klacks *m.*

**splutter** ['splʌtər] *vi (person) (spit)* prusten; *(stutter)* stottern; *(engine)* stottern; *(fire, fat)* zischen.

**spoil** [spɔɪl] *[vb: pret, ptp* ~**ed** *or* **spoilt***)* **1** *n usu pl* Beute *f no pl; (fig: profits also)* Gewinn *m.* **the** ~**s of war** die Kriegsbeute. **2** *vt* **(a)** *(ruin, detract from)* verderben; *view also, town, looks etc* verschandeln; *peace of mind* zerstören; *life* ruinieren; *ballot papers* ungültig machen. **to** ~ **one's appetite** sich *(dat)* den Appetit verderben; **it** ~**ed our evening** das hat uns *(dat)* den Abend verdorben. **(b)** *person* verwöhnen; *children also* verziehen. **to be** ~**t for choice** die Qual der Wahl haben. **3** *vi (food)* verderben. **to be** ~**ing for a fight** Streit suchen.

**spoiler** ['spɔɪlər] *n (Aut)* Spoiler *m.*

**spoilsport** ['spɔɪlspɔːt] *n (col)* Spielverderber *m (col).*

**spoilt** [spɔɪlt] **1** *pret, ptp of* **spoil. 2** *adj child* verwöhnt, verzogen.

**spoke¹** [spəʊk] *n* Speiche *f.* **to put a** ~ **in sb's wheel** *(col)* jdm Knüppel zwischen die Beine werfen *(col).*

**spoke²** *pret of* **speak.**

**spoken** ['spəʊkən] **1** *ptp of* **speak. 2** *adj language* gesprochen.

**spokesman** ['spəʊksmən] *n, pl* -**men** [-mən] Sprecher *m.*

**spokesperson** ['spəʊkspɜːsn] *n* Sprecher(in *f*) *m.*

**spokeswoman** ['spəʊkswʊmən] *n, pl* -**women** [-wɪmɪn] Sprecherin *f.*

**sponge** [spʌndʒ] **1** *n* **(a)** Schwamm *m.* **(b)** *(Cook) (also* ~ **cake)** Rührkuchen *m; (fatless)* Biskuitkuchen *m.* **2** *vt* **(a)** *(clean)* abwischen; *(wound)* abtupfen. **(b)** *(col: scrounge)* schnorren *(col) (from* bei*).*

► **sponge down** *vt sep person* (mit dem Schwamm) waschen; *walls also* abwaschen.

**sponge:** ~ **bag** *n (Brit)* Kulturbeutel *m;* ~ **cake** *n* Rührkuchen *m; (fatless)* Biskuitkuchen *m.*

**sponger** ['spʌndʒər] *n (col)* Schnorrer *m (col).*

**spongy** ['spʌndʒɪ] *adj (+er)* weich; *(light) pudding* locker; *skin etc* schwammig.

**sponsor** ['spɒnsər] **1** *n* Förderer *m,* Förderin *f; (for membership)* Bürge *m,* Bürgin *f; (for event)* Schirmherr(in *f*) *m; (Rad, TV, Sport etc)* Sponsor(in *f*) *m; (for fund raising)* Spender(in *f*) *m.* **2** *vt* unterstützen; *(financially also)* fördern, sponsern; *future member* bürgen für; *membership, bill* befürworten; *(Rad, TV, Sport etc)* sponsern. **he** ~**ed him at 5p a mile** er verpflichtete sich, ihm 5 Pence pro Meile zu geben.

**sponsored** ['spɒnsəd] *adj (for charity etc) walk etc: zur Geldbeschaffung abgehalten, wobei die Leistung vom Sponsor honoriert wird.*

**sponsorship** ['spɒnsəʃɪp] *n see vt* Unterstützung *f;* Förderung *f;* Schirmherrschaft *f;* Bürgschaft *f;* Befürwortung *f; (Rad, TV, Sport etc)* Finanzierung *f.*

**spontaneity** [ˌspɒntəˈneɪətɪ] *n see adj* Spontaneität *f;* Ungezwungenheit *f.*

**spontaneous** [spɒnˈteɪnɪəs] *adj* spontan; *style* ungezwungen. ~ **combustion** Selbstentzündung *f.*

**spoof** [spuːf] *(col) n* **(a)** *(parody)* Parodie *f (of* auf +*acc).* **(b)** *(hoax)* Scherz *m (col).*

**spook** [spuːk] *n (col)* Gespenst *nt.*

**spooky** ['spuːkɪ] *adj (+er) (col) castle etc* gruselig *(col).*

**spool** [spuːl] **1** *n (Phot, on sewing machine)* Spule *f; (on fishing line, for thread)* Rolle *f.* **2** *vt (film, Comp etc)* spulen.

**spoon** [spuːn] **1** *n* Löffel *m.* **to be born with a silver** ~ **in one's mouth** *(fig)* mit einem silbernen Löffel im Mund geboren sein *(col).* **2** *vt* löffeln.

**spoonerism** ['spuːnərɪzəm] *n* lustiger Versprecher.

**spoon-feed** ['spuːnfiːd] *pret, ptp* **spoon-fed** ['spuːnfed] *vt baby, invalid* füttern; *(fig) (do thinking for)* gängeln; *(supply with)* füttern *(col).*

**spoonful** ['spuːnfʊl] *n* Löffel *m.* **a** ~ **of soup** ein Löffel Suppe.

**sporadic** [spəˈrædɪk] *adj* sporadisch.

**spore** [spɔːr] *n* Spore *f.*

**sport** [spɔːt] **1** *n* **(a)** Sport *m no pl; (type of* ~*)* Sportart *f.* **to be good at** ~**(s)** sportlich sein; **outdoor/ indoor** ~**s** Sport *m* im Freien/Hallensport *m.* **(b)** *(amusement)* Spaß *m.* **to do sth for/in** ~ etw zum Spaß tun. **(c)** *(col: person)* feiner Kerl *(col); (Austral)* Junge *m.* **to be a (good)** ~ alles mitmachen; **be a** ~! sei kein Spielverderber! **2** *vt tie, dress* anhaben; *(show off) ring etc* protzen mit. **3** *adj attr (US)* = **sports.**

**sporting** ['spɔːtɪŋ] *adj* **(a)** *person, interests* sportlich; *gun* Jagd-. ~ **events** Wettkämpfe *pl.* **(b)** *(sportsmanlike)* sportlich; *spirit also* Sports-; *(fig) offer, solution* fair; *(decent)* anständig. **to give sb a** ~ **chance** jdm eine faire Chance geben.

**sportingly** ['spɔːtɪŋlɪ] *adv* fair; *(decently)* anständig; *(as sporting gesture)* fairerweise, anständigerweise.

**sports,** *(US also)* **sport** *in cpds* Sport-; ~ **car** *n* Sportwagen *m;* ~ **complex** *n* Sportanlage *f;* ~ **day** *n (Brit Sch)* Sportfest *nt;* ~ **field,** ~ **ground** *n* Sportplatz *m;* ~ **jacket** *n (Brit)* Sakko *m;* ~**man** [-mən] *n (player)* Sportler *m;* ~**manship** [-mənʃɪp] *n (skill)* Sportlichkeit *f; (fairness also)* Sportgeist *m;* ~**woman** *n* Sportlerin *f.*

**sporty** ['spɔːtɪ] *adj (+er) (col)* **(a)** *person, car, clothes* sportlich. **(b)** *(jaunty)* flott.

**spot** [spɒt] **1** *n* **(a)** *(dot)* Tupfen, Punkt *m; (on dice)* Punkt *m; (stain, on fruit)* Fleck *m; (fig: on reputation)* Makel *m (on* an +*dat).* **a dress with** ~**s** ein getupftes *or* gepunktetes Kleid; ~**s of blood/grease** Blutflecken *pl*/Fettflecken *pl;* ~**s of ink** Tintenkleckse *pl;* **to knock** ~**s off sb/sth** *(fig col)* jdn/etw in den Schatten stellen; **to have** ~**s before one's eyes** Sternchen sehen.

**(b)** *(Med etc)* Fleck *m; (pimple)* Pickel *m.* **to break** *or* **come out in** ~**s** Flecken/Pickel bekommen.

**(c)** *(place)* Stelle *f; (point)* Punkt *m.* **this is the** ~ **where Karl was murdered** an dieser Stelle ist Karl ermordet worden; **a pleasant** ~ ein schönes Fleckchen *(col);* **on the** ~ *(at the scene)* an Ort und Stelle; *(at once)* auf der Stelle; **on-the-**~ **investigation** Untersuchung *f* an Ort und Stelle; *(immediate)* sofortige Untersuchung; **an on-the-**~ **report** ein Bericht *m* vom Ort des Geschehens; **weak** ~ schwache Stelle.

**(d)** *(Brit col: small quantity)* **a** ~ **of** ein bißchen; **we had a** ~ **of rain/a few** ~**s of rain** wir hatten ein paar Tropfen Regen; **there was a** ~ **of trouble/ bother** es gab etwas Ärger; **would you like to do a** ~ **of driving?** möchten Sie ein bißchen fahren?

**(e)** *(difficulty)* Klemme *f.* **to be in a (tight)** ~, **to be on the** ~ in der Klemme sitzen *(col);* **to put sb on the** ~ jdn in Verlegenheit bringen.

**(f)** *(in show)* Nummer *f; (Rad, TV: for advertisement)* Werbespot *m.* **a three-minute TV** ~ drei Minu-

ten Sendezeit im Fernsehen.
(g) *(col: ~light)* Scheinwerfer *m*; *(in room)* Strahler *m*.
2 *vt* (a) *(notice, see)* entdecken, sehen; *(pick out)* erkennen; *(find) mistake, bargain* finden. (b) *(stain)* bespritzen. **blue material ~ted with white** blauer Stoff mit weißen Tupfen.
3 *vi* **it's ~ting (with rain)** es tröpfelt.
**spot:** ~ **cash** *n:* **for** ~ **cash** gegen sofortige Bezahlung; ~ **check** *n* Stichprobe *f*.
**spotless** ['spɒtlɪs] *adj* tadellos sauber, picobello *inv (col)*; *(fig) reputation* makellos.
**spotlessly** ['spɒtlɪslɪ] *adv:* ~ **clean** blitzsauber.
**spot:** ~**light** *n (lamp)* Scheinwerfer *m*; *(in room)* Strahler *m*; **to be in the ~light** *(fig)* im Rampenlicht der Öffentlichkeit stehen; **to turn the ~light on sb/sth** *(fig)* die Aufmerksamkeit auf jdn/etw lenken; ~**-on** *adj (Brit col) answer, analysis* exakt, genau, richtig; ~ **remover** *n* Fleckenentferner *m*.
**spotted** ['spɒtɪd] *adj* gefleckt; *(with dots)* getüpfelt; *material* getupft; *(marked, stained)* fleckig.
**spotty** ['spɒtɪ] *adj (+er)* fleckig; *(pimply)* pick(e)lig, voller Pickel.
**spouse** [spaʊs] *n (form)* Gatte *m (form)*, Gattin *f (form)*.
**spout** [spaʊt] 1 *n* (a) Ausguß *m*; *(on watering can)* Rohr *nt*; *(of teapot etc)* Tülle *f*. **up the** ~ *(col: plans etc)* im Eimer *(col)*. (b) *(jet of water etc)* Fontäne *f*.
2 *vt* (a) *water etc* (heraus)spritzen; *(whale also)* ausstoßen; *(volcano)* speien. (b) *(col: declaim) poetry, speeches* loslassen *(col) (at sb* auf jdn*)*; *words* hervorsprudeln; *figures* herunterrasseln *(col)*; *nonsense* von sich geben.
**sprain** [spreɪn] 1 *n* Verstauchung *f*. 2 *vt* verstauchen. **to** ~ **one's ankle** sich *(dat)* den Fuß verstauchen.
**sprang** [spræŋ] *pret of* **spring**.
**sprat** [spræt] *n* Sprotte *f*. **to set a** ~ **to catch a mackerel** *(prov)* mit der Wurst nach dem Schinken werfen *(prov)*.
**sprawl** [sprɔːl] 1 *n (of town etc)* Ausbreitung *f*. **urban** ~ wild wuchernde Ausbreitung des Stadtgebietes.
2 *vi (person) (fall)* der Länge nach hinfallen; *(lounge)* sich hinflegeln; *(plant, town)* (wild) wuchern. **to send sb ~ing** jdn zu Boden werfen.
**sprawling** ['sprɔːlɪŋ] *adj city, suburbs* wild wuchernd; *figure* hingeflegelt.
**spray**[1] [spreɪ] *n (bouquet)* Strauß *m*; *(buttonhole)* Ansteckblume *f*.
**spray**[2] 1 *n* (a) Sprühregen *m*; *(of sea)* Gischt *m*. **the ~ from the lorries makes it difficult to see** die Lastwagen spritzen so, daß man kaum etwas sehen kann. (b) *(implement) (also* ~ **can)** Sprühdose *f*; *(insecticide* ~, *for irrigation)* Spritze *f*; *(scent~)* Zerstäuber *m*. (c) *(hair-~ etc)* Spray *m or nt*. (d) **to give sth a** ~ etw besprühen; *(with paint, insecticide)* etw spritzen; *(with hair-~ etc)* etw sprayen. 2 *vt plants, insects etc* besprühen; *(with paint, insecticide)* spritzen; *hair* sprayen; *room* aussprühen; *water, paint, foam* sprühen; *perfume* (ver)sprühen. **to** ~ **sth with water/bullets** etw mit Wasser besprühen/mit Kugeln übersäen. 3 *vi* sprühen; *(water, mud)* spritzen.
**sprayer** ['spreɪə<sup>r</sup>] *n* = **spray**[2] **1** (b).
**spraygun** ['spreɪgʌn] *n* Spritzpistole *f*.
**spread** [spred] *(vb: pret, ptp* ~*)* 1 *n* (a) *(of wings)* Spannweite *f*; *(range) (of marks)* Verteilung *f*; *(of prices)* Spanne *f*; *(of ideas, interests)* Spektrum *nt*. **middle-age** ~ Altersspeck *m (col)*.
(b) *(growth)* Ausbreitung *f*; *(spatial)* Ausdehnung *f*. **the** ~ **of nuclear weapons** die zunehmende Verbreitung von Atomwaffen.

(c) *(col: of food etc)* Festessen *nt*; *(for bread)* (Brot)aufstrich *m*. **cheese** ~ Streichkäse *m*.
(d) *(Press, Typ: also* **double-page** ~*)* Doppelseite *f*; *(report)* zweiseitiger Bericht; *(advertisement)* zweiseitige Anzeige.
2 *vt* (a) *(open or lay out: also* ~ **out)** ausbreiten; *fan* öffnen; *hands, legs* spreizen. **the peacock** ~ **its tail** der Pfau schlug ein Rad; **the view which was** ~ **out before us** die Sicht, die sich uns bot.
(b) *bread, surface* bestreichen; *butter, paint etc* streichen. ~ **the paint evenly** verteilen Sie die Farbe gleichmäßig; **to** ~ **a blanket on sth** eine Decke über etw *(acc)* breiten; **the table was** ~ **with food** der Tisch war reichlich gedeckt.
(c) *(distribute: also* ~ **out)** *forces, objects, payments* verteilen; *sand, fertilizer also, muck* streuen. **our resources are** ~ **very thinly** unsere Mittel sind maximal beansprucht.
(d) *news, panic, rumour* verbreiten.
3 *vi* (a) *(extend) (spatially)* sich erstrecken *(over, across* über *+acc)*; *(with movement) (weeds, fire, smile, industry)* sich ausbreiten *(over, across* über *+acc)*; *(towns)* sich ausdehnen; *(knowledge, fear etc, smell, disease, trouble, fire)* sich verbreiten. **to** ~ **to sth** etw erreichen; *(disease etc)* auf etw *(acc)* übergreifen. (b) *(butter etc)* sich streichen lassen.
▶**spread out** 1 *vt sep* = **spread** 2 (a, c). 2 *vi* (a) *(countryside etc)* sich ausdehnen. (b) *(troops, runners)* sich verteilen.
**spread-eagle** ['spred,iːgl] *vt* **to lie ~d** mit ausgestreckten Armen und Beinen daliegen.
**spreader** ['spredə<sup>r</sup>] *n* Spachtel *m*.
**spreadsheet** ['spredʃiːt] *n* Arbeitsblatt *nt*; *(Comp)* Tabellenkalkulation *f*.
**spree** [spriː] *n* **spending** *or* **shopping** ~ Großeinkauf *m*; **to be/go on a** ~ *(drinking)* eine Zechtour machen; *(spending)* groß einkaufen gehen.
**sprig** [sprɪg] *n* Zweig *m*. ~ **of flowers** Blütenzweig.
**sprightly** ['spraɪtlɪ] *adj (+er) person, tune* munter; *old person* rüstig; *walk* schwungvoll.
**spring** [sprɪŋ] *(vb: pret* **sprang** *or (US)* **sprung**, *ptp* **sprung)** 1 *n* (a) *(lit, fig liter: source)* Quelle *f*.
(b) *(season)* Frühling *m*. ~ **is in the air** der Frühling liegt in der Luft.
(c) *(leap)* Sprung *m*. **in one** ~ mit einem Satz.
(d) *(Mech)* Feder *f*. ~**s** *(Aut)* Federung *f*.
(e) *no pl (bounciness) (of chair)* Federung *f*; *(of wood etc)* Elastizität *f*. **to walk with a** ~ **in one's step** mit federnden Schritten gehen.
2 *vt (cause to operate)* auslösen; *mine also* explodieren lassen; *lock, mousetrap etc* zuschnappen lassen. **to** ~ **a leak** *(pipe)* (plötzlich) undicht werden; *(ship)* (plötzlich) ein Leck bekommen; **to** ~ **sth on sb** *(fig) idea, decision* jdn mit etw konfrontieren; **to** ~ **a surprise on sb** jdn völlig überraschen.
3 *vi* (a) *(leap)* springen; *(be activated)* ausgelöst werden; *(mousetrap)* zuschnappen. **to** ~ **at sb** jdn anspringen; **to** ~ **out at sb** auf jdn losspringen; **to** ~ **open** aufspringen; **to** ~ **to one's feet** aufspringen; **to** ~ **into action** aktiv werden; *(police, fire brigade etc)* in Aktion treten; **to** ~ **into view** plötzlich in Sicht kommen; **to** ~ **to mind** einem einfallen; **to** ~ **to sb's aid/defence** jdm zu Hilfe eilen; **he sprang to fame** er wurde plötzlich berühmt; **to** ~ **(in)to life** (plötzlich) lebendig werden; *(engine)* anspringen.
(b) *(issue: also* ~ **forth)** *(liter) (water, blood)* (hervor)quellen *(from* aus*)*; *(fire, sparks)* sprühen *(from* aus*)*.
(c) *(fig) (idea)* entstehen *(from* aus*)*; *(interest, irritability etc)* herrühren *(from* von*)*. **where did you** ~ **from?** *(col)* wo kommst du denn her?; **to** ~ **into ex-**

**istence** (plötzlich *or* rasch) entstehen.
►**spring back** *vi (person)* zurückspringen; *(object)* zurückschnellen.
►**spring up** *vi (plant)* hervorsprießen; *(weeds, buildings)* aus dem Boden schießen; *(person)* aufspringen; *(fig) (friendship, firm)* (plötzlich) entstehen; *(problem, rumour)* auftauchen.
**spring:** ~**binder** *n* Klemmhefter *m*; ~**board** *n (lit, fig)* Sprungbrett *nt*; ~ **chicken** *n* he's no ~ chicken er ist nicht mehr der Jüngste *(col)*; ~-**clean** *vt* Frühjahrsputz machen in *(+dat)*; ~-**cleaning** *n* Frühjahrsputz *m*.
**springiness** ['sprɪŋɪnɪs] *n* Elastizität *f*.
**springing** ['sprɪŋɪŋ] *n (of car, bed etc)* Federung *f*.
**spring:** ~-**loaded** *adj* mit einer Sprungfeder; ~ **onion** *n* Frühlingszwiebel *f*; ~ **tide** *n* Springflut *f*; ~**time** *n* Frühling *m*.
**springy** ['sprɪŋɪ] *adj (+er) step* federnd; *plank, turf, grass also* nachgiebig, elastisch; *rubber, wood, plastic etc, hair* elastisch; *bed* weich gefedert.
**sprinkle** ['sprɪŋkl] *vt water* sprenkeln; *lawn* sprengen; *plant* besprengen; *salt, dust, sugar etc* streuen; *cake* bestreuen.
**sprinkler** ['sprɪŋklə<sup>r</sup>] *n (Hort, Agr)* Berieselungsapparat *m*; *(in garden also)* (Rasen)sprenger *m*; *(for fire-fighting)* Sprinkler *m*; *(on watering can etc)* Sprenger *m*; *(sugar ~)* Streuer *m*.
**sprinkling** ['sprɪŋklɪŋ] *n (of rain, dew etc)* ein paar Tropfen; *(of sugar etc)* Prise *f*; *(fig: of humour etc)* Anflug *m*. there was a ~ of young people es waren ein paar vereinzelte junge Leute da.
**sprint** [sprɪnt] **1** *n* Lauf *m*; *(race)* Sprint *m*; *(burst of speed)* Spurt *m*. the 100-meter(s) ~ der 100-Meter-Lauf. **2** *vi (in race)* sprinten; *(dash)* rennen; *(for train etc also)* spurten *(for* zu*)*.
**sprinter** ['sprɪntə<sup>r</sup>] *n* Sprinter(in *f*) *m*.
**spritzer** ['sprɪtsə<sup>r</sup>] *n* (Wein)schorle *f*.
**sprocket** ['sprɒkɪt] *n (on bicycle etc)* Kettenrad *nt*; *(on projector)* Greifer *m*; *(on printer)* Stachelrad *nt*.
**sprout** [spraut] **1** *n* **(a)** *(of plant)* Trieb *m*; *(of tree also)* Schößling, Sproß *m*; *(from seed)* Keim *m*. **(b)** *(Brussels ~)* (Rosenkohl)röschen *nt*. ~s *pl* Rosenkohl *m*. **2** *vt leaves, buds etc* treiben; *horns etc* entwickeln; *seeds etc* keimen lassen; *(col) beard sich (dat)* wachsen lassen. **3** *vi* **(a)** *(grow)* sprießen; *(seed, wheat etc)* keimen; *(potatoes, trees etc)* Triebe bekommen. **(b)** *(lit, fig: also* ~ up*) (plants, weeds)* sprießen; *(new sects, new buildings)* wie Pilze aus dem Boden schießen.
**spruce**¹ [spruːs] *n (also* ~ fir*)* Fichte *f*.
**spruce**² *adj (+er)* gepflegt; *(neat)* adrett.
►**spruce up** *vt sep child* herausputzen; *house, garden* auf Vordermann bringen *(col)*. to ~ oneself *(get dressed up)* sich in Schale werfen; *(woman)* sich zurechtmachen.
**sprung** [sprʌŋ] **1** *ptp of* **spring**. **2** *adj* gefedert.
**spry** [spraɪ] *adj* rüstig.
**spud** [spʌd] *n (col: potato)* Kartoffel *f*.
**spun** [spʌn] *pret, ptp of* **spin**.
**spunk** [spʌŋk] *n (col)* Courage *f*.
**spur** [spɜː<sup>r</sup>] **1** *n* Sporn *m*; *(fig)* Ansporn *m (to* für*)*; *(Geog)* Vorsprung *m*. to win *or* gain one's ~s *(fig)* sich *(dat)* die Sporen verdienen; on the ~ of the moment ganz spontan. **2** *vt (also* ~ on*) horse* die Sporen geben *(+dat)*; *(fig)* anspornen. ~red (on) by greed von Habgier getrieben.
**spurious** ['spjʊərɪəs] *adj claim* unberechtigt; *document, account* falsch; *emotion* nicht echt.
**spurn** [spɜːn] *vt* verschmähen.
**spurt** [spɜːt] **1** *n* **(a)** *(flow)* Strahl *m*. ~s of flame Stichflammen. **(b)** *(of speed)* Spurt *m*. to put a ~ on

*(lit, fig)* einen Spurt vorlegen; **there was a ~ of activity** es brach plötzlich Aktivität aus. **2** *vi (gush: also* ~ out*)* (heraus)spritzen *(from* aus*)*.
**sputum** ['spjuːtəm] *n (Med)* Auswurf *m*.
**spy** [spaɪ] **1** *n* Spion(in *f*) *m*; *(police* ~*)* Spitzel *m*. **2** *vt* sehen. **3** *vi* spionieren. to ~ on sb jdn bespitzeln; on neighbours jdm nachspionieren.
►**spy out** *vt sep* to ~ ~ the land *(Mil)* die Gegend auskundschaften; *(fig)* die Lage peilen.
**spying** ['spaɪɪŋ] *n* Spionage *f*.
**spy:** ~ **network** *n* Agentennetz *nt*; ~ **ring** *n* Spionagering *m*; ~ **satellite** *n* Spionagesatellit; ~ **story** *n* Spionagegeschichte *f*.
**Sq** = **Square.**
**sq** = **square.** ~ **m** qm, m².
**squabble** ['skwɒbl] **1** *n* Zank, Streit *m*. **2** *vi* (sich) zanken, (sich) streiten *(about, over* um*)*.
**squabbling** ['skwɒblɪŋ] *n* Zankerei, Streiterei *f*.
**squad** [skwɒd] *n (Mil, police unit etc)* Kommando *nt*; *(drug/fraud* ~*)* Dezernat *nt*; *(of workmen)* Trupp *m*; *(Sport)* Spielerstamm *m*.
**squad car** *n* Streifenwagen *m*.
**squadron** ['skwɒdrən] *n (of cavalry)* Schwadron *f*; *(Aviat)* Staffel *f*; *(Naut)* Geschwader *nt*.
**squalid** ['skwɒlɪd] *adj room, house* schmutzig und verwahrlost; *existence, conditions* elend; *deed, idea etc* niederträchtig; *dispute, gossip* entwürdigend; *affair* schmutzig.
**squall** [skwɔːl] **1** *n (storm)* Bö(e) *f*; *(fig)* Gewitter *nt*. **2** *vi* schreien.
**squalor** ['skwɒlə<sup>r</sup>] *n* Schmutz *m*; *(moral* ~*)* Verkommenheit *f*.
**squander** ['skwɒndə<sup>r</sup>] *vt* verschwenden *(on* an *+acc)*; *opportunity* vertun.
**square** [skwɛə<sup>r</sup>] **1** *n* **(a)** Quadrat *nt*; *(piece of material, paper etc also)* Viereck *nt*; *(on chessboard etc)* Feld *nt*; *(on paper, in crossword)* Kästchen *nt*; *(on material etc)* Karo *nt*. cut it in ~s schneiden Sie es quadratisch zu; **we're back to** ~s jetzt sind wir wieder da, wo wir angefangen haben. **(b)** *(in town, Mil)* Platz *m*; *(US: of houses)* Block *m*. **(c)** *(Math)* Quadrat(zahl *f*) *nt*. **the** ~ **of 3 is 9** 3 hoch 2 ist 9. **(d)** *(col: old-fashioned person)* Spießer *m (col)*. to be a ~ von *(vor)*gestern sein.
   **2** *adj (+er)* **(a)** *(in shape)* quadratisch; *picture, lawn etc also, nib* viereckig; *file* Vierkant-; *block of wood etc* vierkantig. to be a ~ **peg in a round hole** am falschen Platz sein. **(b)** *(forming right angle) corner* rechtwinklig; *shoulder* eckig; *build* vierschrötig. ~ **angle** rechter Winkel. ~ **brackets** eckige Klammern. **(c)** *(Math)* Quadrat-. **3** ~ **kilometers** 3 Quadratkilometer; **3 metres** ~ 3 Meter im Quadrat; ~ **root** Quadratwurzel *f*. **(d)** *attr (complete) meal* ordentlich. **(e)** *(fair) deal* gerecht, fair; *game, person* ehrlich. to give sb a ~ **deal** jdn fair behandeln; **I'll be** ~ **with you** ich will ehrlich mit dir sein. **(f)** *(fig: even)* to be ~ *(accounts etc)* in Ordnung sein; to get ~ **with sb** mit jdm abrechnen. **(g)** *(col: old-fashioned)* überholt; *person, ideas* spießig *(col)*. he's ~ er ist von *(vor)*gestern.
   **3** *adv (+er)* **(a)** *(at right angles)* rechtwinklig. ~ **with sth** senkrecht zu etw. **(b)** *(directly)* direkt, genau.
   **4** *vt* **(a)** *(make* ~*)* quadratisch machen; to ~ one's **shoulders** die Schultern straffen. **(b)** *(Math) number* quadrieren. **3** ~**d is 9** 3 hoch 2 ist 9. **(c)** *(adjust) debts* begleichen; *creditors* abrechnen mit; *(reconcile)* in Einklang bringen. to ~ one's **accounts** abrechnen *(with* mit*)*; to ~ **sth with one's conscience** etw mit seinem Gewissen vereinbaren; **I'll** ~ **it with the boss** *(col)* ich mache das mit dem

Chef ab *(col)*.
 **5** *vi* übereinstimmen *(with* mit*)*.
►**square off** *vt sep (make square) corner* rechtwinklig machen.
►**square up** *vi* (a) Kampfstellung annehmen. **to** ~ ~ **to sb** sich vor jdm aufpflanzen *(col)*; *(boxer)* vor jdm in Kampfstellung gehen; *(fig)* jdm die Stirn bieten. **(b)** *(lit, fig: settle)* abrechnen.
**squarely** ['skwɛəlɪ] *adj* (a) *(directly)* direkt, genau; *(fig: firmly)* fest. **we must face this** ~ wir müssen dieser Sache *(dat)* (fest) ins Auge sehen. **(b)** *(honestly)* ehrlich; *(fairly)* gerecht, fair.
**squash¹** [skwɒʃ] **1** *n* (a) *(Brit) (fruit concentrate)* Fruchtsaftkonzentrat *nt*; *(drink)* Fruchtsaftgetränk *nt*. **(b)** *(crowd)* Gedränge *nt*. **it's a bit of a** ~ es ist ziemlich eng. **2** *vt* (a) *(also* ~ **up)** zerdrücken; *box etc* zusammendrücken. **(b)** *(fig col) (silence)* person über den Mund fahren *(+dat)*; *(quash)* protest, argument vom Tisch fegen *(col)*. **(c)** *(squeeze)* quetschen. **to** ~ **sb/sth in** jdn/etw hineinquetschen; **to be** ~**ed together** eng zusammengequetscht sein. **3** *vi* (a) *(get* ~*ed)* zerdrückt werden. **(b)** *(squeeze)* sich quetschen. **to** ~ **in** sich hinein-/ hereinquetschen; **could you** ~ **up?** könnt ihr etwas zusammenrücken.
**squash²** *n (Sport)* Squash *nt*. ~ **court** Squashfeld *nt*.
**squat** [skwɒt] **1** *adj (+er) chair* niedrig; *figure, person* gedrungen. **2** *vi* (a) *(person) (animal)* hocken; *(also* ~ **down***)* sich (hin)hocken. **(b)** *(on land)* sich (illegal) ansiedeln. **to** ~ **(in a house)** ein Haus besetzt haben.
**squatter** ['skwɒtəʳ] *n (on land)* illegaler Siedler; *(in house)* Hausbesetzer(in *f*) *m*.
**squaw** [skwɔː] *n* Squaw *f*.
**squawk** [skwɔːk] **1** *n* heiserer Schrei; *(of hens)* Gackern *nt*. **2** *vi (bird, person)* kreischen.
**squeak** [skwiːk] **1** *n (of hinge etc, shoe, pen)* Quietschen *nt no pl*; *(of person, small animal)* Quieken *nt no pl*; *(of bird)* Piepsen *nt no pl*; *(fig col: sound)* Pieps *m (col)*. **the door opened with a** ~ die Tür ging quietschend auf. **2** *vi (door, hinge, shoes etc)* quietschen; *(person, small animal)* quieken; *(mouse, bird)* piepsen.
**squeaky** ['skwiːkɪ] *adj (+er)* quietschend; *voice* piepsig.
**squeaky-clean** [ˌskwiːkɪ'kliːn] *adj (col)* blitzsauber *(col)*.
**squeal** [skwiːl] **1** *n (of person, tyre, brakes)* Quietschen *nt no pl*; *(of protest)* (Auf)schrei *m*; *(of pig)* Quieken *nt no pl*. **a** ~ **of pain** ein Schmerzensschrei *m*; ~**s/a** ~ **of laughter** schrilles Gelächter. **2** *vi* (a) *(person, brakes, tyres)* quietschen; *(pig, puppy)* quieksen; *(fig col)* jammern. **to** ~ **with pain/ pleasure** vor Schmerz kreischen/vor Vergnügen quietschen. **(b)** *(col: confess, inform) (criminal)* singen *(col)* (to bei); *(schoolboy etc)* petzen *(col)* (to bei).
**squeamish** ['skwiːmɪʃ] *adj person (easily nauseated or shocked)* empfindlich. **I felt a bit** ~ *(sick)* mir war leicht übel.
**squeamishness** ['skwiːmɪʃnɪs] *n (nausea)* Übelkeit *f*; *(disgust)* Ekel *m*; *(prudishness)* Zimperlichkeit *f*.
**squeegee** ['skwiːdʒiː] *n* (Gummi)wischer *m*; *(Phot)* Rollenquetscher *m*.
**squeeze** [skwiːz] **1** *n* (a) *(act of squeezing)* Drücken *nt no pl*; *(hug)* Umarmung *f*; *(of hand)* Händedruck *m*; *(in bus etc)* Gedränge *nt*. **to give sth a** ~ etw drücken, etw pressen; *lemon, sponge* etw ausdrücken; **to give sb/sb's hand a** ~ jdn an sich *(acc)* drücken/jdm die Hand drücken; **it was a tight** ~ es war fürchterlich eng; **put a** ~ **of toothpaste on the**

**brush** drücken Sie etwas Zahnpasta auf die Bürste; **to put the** ~ **on sb** *(col)* jdm die Daumenschrauben anlegen *(col)*. **(b)** *(credit* ~*)* Kreditbeschränkung *f*.
 **2** *vt* drücken; *sponge, tube* ausdrücken; *orange* auspressen; *(squash) person, hand* einquetschen. **to** ~ **clothes into a case** Kleider in einen Koffer zwängen; **to** ~ **out water/juice** Wasser/Saft herauspressen *(from aus)*; **he** ~**d the trigger** er drückte ab; **to** ~ **money/information** *etc* **out of sb** Geld/ Informationen *etc* aus jdm herausquetschen.
 **3** *vi* **to** ~ **in/out** sich hinein-/hinausdrängen; **to** ~ **past sb** sich an jdm vorbeidrücken; **to** ~ **through a crowd** sich durch eine Menge zwängen; **you'll have to** ~ **up a bit** Sie müssen ein bißchen zusammenrücken.
**squelch** [skweltʃ] *vi* platschen; *(shoes, mud)* quatschen.
**squib** [skwɪb] *n* Knallfrosch *m*.
**squid** [skwɪd] *n* Tintenfisch *m*.
**squiggle** ['skwɪgl] *n (also signature)* Schnörkel *m*. **(messy)** ~**s** Gekritzel *nt*.
**squint** [skwɪnt] **1** *n (Med)* Schielen *nt no pl*. **to have a** ~ leicht schielen; **to take a** ~ **at sb/sth** einen Blick auf jdn/etw werfen *(col)*. **2** *vi* schielen; *(in strong light etc)* blinzeln. **to** ~ **at sb/sth** nach jdm/ etw schielen; *(quickly)* einen kurzen Blick auf jdn/ etw werfen.
**squire** ['skwaɪəʳ] *n (esp Brit: landowner)* Gutsherr *m*.
**squirm** [skwɜːm] *vi* sich winden; *(in distaste)* schaudern; *(with embarrassment)* sich (drehen und) winden. **spiders make me** ~ vor Spinnen graust es mir.
**squirrel** ['skwɪrəl] *n* Eichhörnchen *nt*.
**squirt** [skwɜːt] **1** *n* (a) Spritzer *m*. **(b)** *(pej col: person)* Pimpf *m (col)*. **2** *vt liquid* spritzen; *object, person* bespritzen. **to** ~ **water at sb** jdn mit Wasser bespritzen. **3** *vi* spritzen.
**Sr** = **senior** sen.
**Sri Lanka** [ˌsriː'læŋkə] *n* Sri Lanka *nt*.
**Sri Lankan** [ˌsriː'læŋkən] **1** *adj* srilankisch. **2** *n* Srilanker(in *f*) *m*.
**SRN** *(Brit)* = **State Registered Nurse**.
**SS** = **steamship**.
**ST** *(US)* = **Standard Time**.
**st** *(Brit)* = **stone**.
**St.** = (a) **Street** Str. (b) **Saint** hl., St.
**stab** [stæb] **1** *n* (a) *(with knife etc, wound, of pain)* Stich *m*. ~ **wound** Stichwunde *f*; **to feel a** ~ **of pain** einen stechenden Schmerz empfinden; **a** ~ **in the back** *(fig)* ein Dolchstoß *m*. **(b)** *(col: try)* Versuch *m*. **to have a** ~ **at sth** etw probieren. **2** *vt person* einen Stich versetzen *(+dat)*; *(several times)* einstechen auf *(+acc)*; *(wound seriously)* niederstechen. **to** ~ **sb (to death)** jdn erstechen; **to** ~ **sb with a knife** jdn mit einem Messerstich/mit Messerstichen verletzen; **he was** ~**bed through the arm/heart** er hatte eine Stichwunde am Arm/der Stich traf ihn ins Herz; **to** ~ **sb in the back** *(lit)* jdm in den Rücken stechen; *(fig)* jdm in den Rücken fallen. **3** *vi* **to** ~ **at sb/sth** *(with knife etc)* nach jdm/etw stechen; *(with finger)* auf jdn/etw zeigen.
**stabbing** ['stæbɪŋ] **1** *n* Messerstecherei *f*. **2** *adj pain* stechend.
**stability** [stə'bɪlɪtɪ] *n* Stabilität *f*; *(of relationship also, of job)* Beständigkeit *f*. **(mental)** ~ (seelische) Ausgeglichenheit.
**stabilize** ['steɪbəlaɪz] **1** *vt (Fin, Naut, Aviat)* stabilisieren. **2** *vi* sich stabilisieren.
**stabilizer** ['steɪbəlaɪzəʳ] *n (Naut)* Stabilisator *m*; *(Aviat)* Stabilisierungsfläche *f*.
**stable¹** ['steɪbl] *adj (+er)* stabil; *relationship also, job* beständig; *character* gefestigt. **mentally** ~ ausgegli-

chen.

**stable²** *n (building)* Stall *m; (group of racehorses)* (Renn)stall *m. riding* ~s Reitstall *m.*

**staccato** [stə'kɑ:təʊ] *adj, adv (Mus)* staccato; *(fig)* abgehackt.

**stack** [stæk] **1** *n* **(a)** *(pile)* Haufen *m; (neatly piled)* Stoß, Stapel *m.* **to join the** ~ *(Aviat)* kreisen. **(b)** *(col: lots)* Haufen *m (col).* ~s jede Menge *(col);* **we have ~s of time** wir haben jede Menge Zeit. **2** *vt* **(a)** stapeln. **to ~ up** aufstapeln. **(b)** *(US Cards)* präparieren. **the odds are ~ed against us** *(fig)* wir haben keine großen Chancen. **3** *vi* sich stapeln lassen.

**stadium** ['steɪdɪəm] *n* Stadion *nt.*

**staff** [stɑ:f] **1** *n* **(a)** Personal *nt; (Sch, Univ)* Kollegium *nt,* Lehrkörper *m (form); (of department, on project)* Mitarbeiterstab *m.* **a large** ~ viel Personal/ ein großes Kollegium/ein großer Mitarbeiterstab; **a member of** ~ ein Mitarbeiter *m; (Sch)* ein Kollege *m;* **we have 30 typists on the** ~ bei uns sind 30 Schreibkräfte angestellt; **to be on the** ~ zum Personal/Kollegium/Mitarbeiterstab gehören. **(b)** *(stick, symbol of authority)* Stab *m.* **(c)** *pl* **staves** *(Mus)* Notenlinien *pl.* **2** *vt department* Mitarbeiter finden für; *hospital, shop* mit Personal besetzen; *school* mit Lehrpersonal besetzen. **to be well ~ed** gut besetzt sein; **the kitchens are ~ed by foreigners** das Küchenpersonal besteht aus Ausländern.

**staff:** ~ **canteen** *n* Betriebskantine *f;* ~ **meeting** *n* Lehrerkonferenz *f;* ~ **nurse** *n* ausgebildete Krankenschwester; ~ **officer** *n* Stabsoffizier *m;* ~**room** *n* Lehrerzimmer *nt.*

**Staffs** *(Brit)* = **Staffordshire.**

**stag** [stæg] *n (deer)* Hirsch *m.*

**stage** [steɪdʒ] **1** *n* **(a)** *(Theat, fig)* Bühne *f; (platform in hall)* Podium *nt.* **the** ~ *(profession)* das Theater; **to be on/go on the** ~ *(as career)* beim Theater sein/ zum Theater gehen; **to go on** ~ *(actor)* die Bühne betreten; **the** ~ **was set** *(fig)* alles war vorbereitet. **(b)** *(period)* Stadium *nt; (of disease, process also, of development)* Phase *f.* **at this** ~ **in the negotiations** an diesem Punkt der Verhandlungen; **at this** ~ **in the game** *(fig)* zu diesem Zeitpunkt; **in the early/ final ~(s)** im Anfangs-/Endstadium; **to go through a difficult** ~ eine schwierige Phase durchmachen. **(c)** *(part of journey, race etc)* Abschnitt *m,* Etappe *f; (fare~)* Fahrzone *f.* **in** *or* **by (easy)** ~**s** *(lit, fig)* etappenweise. **(d)** *(section of rocket)* Stufe *f.*

    **2** *vt play* aufführen; *(fig) accident, scene etc* inszenieren; *welcome* arrangieren; *demonstration, strike etc* veranstalten. **to ~ a recovery/comeback** sich erholen/ein Comeback machen.

**stage:** ~**coach** *n* Postkutsche *f;* ~ **door** *n* Bühneneingang *m;* ~ **fright** *n* Lampenfieber *nt;* ~**hand** *n* Bühnenarbeiter(in *f) m;* ~**manage** *vt (lit)* Inspizient sein bei; *(fig) demonstration, argument* inszenieren; ~ **manager** *n* Inspizient *m;* ~ **name** *n* Künstlername *m;* ~-**struck** *adj* theaterbesessen; ~ **whisper** *n* to say sth in a ~ **whisper** etw hörbar flüstern.

**stagger** ['stægə'] **1** *vi* taumeln; *(because of illness, weakness)* wanken; *(drunkenly)* torkeln. **2** *vt* **(a)** *(fig: amaze)* den Atem verschlagen *(+dat),* umhauen *(col).* **(b)** *hours, holidays* staffeln; *seats etc* versetzt anordnen.

**staggered** ['stægəd] *adj* **(a)** *(amazed)* verblüfft. **(b)** *working hours etc* gestaffelt.

**staggering** ['stægərɪŋ] *adj (amazing)* umwerfend *(col).*

**staging** ['steɪdʒɪŋ] *n* Inszenierung *f.*

**stagnant** ['stægnənt] *adj (still) air, water* stehend *attr; (foul, stale) water* abgestanden; *air* verbraucht;

*trade* stagnierend; *mind* träge.

**stagnate** [stæg'neɪt] *vi (not circulate, business)* stagnieren; *(become foul) (water)* stagnieren; *(air)* verbraucht werden; *(person)* verdummen, versauern *(col); (mind)* einrosten.

**stagnation** [stæg'neɪʃən] *n (of water)* Stagnieren *nt; (of air)* Stau *m; (of trade also)* Stagnation *f; (of person)* Verdummung *f; (of mind)* Verlangsamung *f.*

**stag:** ~ **night** *n* Zechabend *m des Bräutigams mit seinen Freunden;* ~ **party** *n* **(a)** Herrenabend *m;* **(b)** = ~ **night.**

**staid** [steɪd] *adj (+er)* gesetzt; *colour* gedeckt.

**stain** [steɪn] **1** *n* **(a)** *(lit)* Fleck *m; (fig also)* Makel *m.* **a blood** ~ ein Blutfleck *m;* ~ **remover** Fleckenentferner *m.* **(b)** *(colorant)* (Ein)färbemittel *nt; (wood~)* Beize *f.* **2** *vt beflecken; (colour)* einfärben; *(with wood~)* beizen. **3** *vi* **(a)** *leave a* ~ Flecken hinterlassen. **(b)** *(get ~ed)* Flecken bekommen.

**stained** [steɪnd] *adj dress, floor* fleckig; *glass* bemalt; *reputation* befleckt. ~-**glass window** Buntglasfenster *nt;* ~ **with blood** blutbefleckt.

**stainless** ['steɪnlɪs] *adj (rust-resistant)* rostfrei. ~ **steel** Edelstahl *m;* "~ **steel**" „rostfrei"; ~ **steel cutlery** rostfreies Besteck.

**stair** [stɛə'] *n* **(a)** *(step)* Stufe *f.* **(b)** *usu pl (~way)* Treppe *f.* **at the top of the ~s** oben an der Treppe.

**stair:** ~ **carpet** *n* Treppenläufer *m;* ~**case** *n* Treppe *f;* ~**way** *n* Treppe *f;* ~**well** *n* Treppenhaus *nt.*

**stake** [steɪk] **1** *n* **(a)** *(post)* Pfahl *m; (for plant)* Stange *f; (for animal)* Pflock *m.* **(b)** *(place of execution)* Scheiterhaufen *m.* **to be burnt at the** ~ auf dem Scheiterhaufen verbrannt werden. **(c)** *(bet)* Einsatz *m; (financial interest)* Anteil *m.* **to be at** ~ auf dem Spiel stehen; **he has a lot at** ~ er hat viel zu verlieren; **to have a** ~ **in sth** *in business* einen Anteil an etw *(dat)* haben; **that's precisely the issue at** ~ genau darum geht es. **2** *vt* **(a)** *animal* anpflocken. **(b)** *(also* ~ **up)** *plant* hochbinden; *fence* abstützen. **(c)** *(bet, risk)* setzen *(on* auf *+acc); (US: back financially)* finanziell unterstützen. **to ~ one's life/reputation on sth** seine Hand für etw ins Feuer legen/sich mit seinem guten Namen für etw verbürgen; **to ~ a/one's claim to sth** sich *(dat)* ein Anrecht auf etw *(acc)* sichern.

►**stake off** *or* **out** *vt sep land* abstecken.

**stalactite** ['stæləktaɪt] *n* Stalaktit *m.*

**stalagmite** ['stæləgmaɪt] *n* Stalagmit *m.*

**stale** [steɪl] *adj (+er)* **(a)** *(old, musty)* alt; *cake also* trocken; *(in taste, smell also)* muffig; *water, beer* schal; *air* verbraucht. **(b)** *(fig) news* überholt; *joke* abgedroschen; *athlete, pianist* verbraucht.

**stalemate** ['steɪlmeɪt] *n (Chess, fig)* Patt *nt.* **to reach** ~ *(lit)* ein Patt erreichen; *(fig)* in eine Sackgasse geraten.

**stalk¹** [stɔ:k] **1** *vt game* sich anpirschen an *(+acc); person* sich anschleichen an *(+acc); (animal)* sich heranschleichen an *(+acc).* **2** *vi (walk haughtily)* stolzieren.

**stalk²** *n (of plant, leaf)* Stiel *m; (cabbage ~)* Strunk *m.* **his eyes popped out on ~s** *(col)* er bekam Stielaugen *(col).*

**stall** [stɔ:l] **1** *n* **(a)** *(in stable)* Box *f.* **(b)** *(at market etc)* Stand *m.* **(c)** ~**s** *pl (Brit Theat, Film)* Parkett *nt;* **in the ~s** im Parkett. **2** *vt (Aut)* abwürgen; *(Aviat)* überziehen. **3** *vi* **(a)** *(engine)* absterben; *(Aviat)* überziehen. **(b)** *(delay)* Zeit schinden *(col).* **to ~ on a decision** eine Entscheidung hinauszögern; **to ~ for time** versuchen, Zeit zu gewinnen; **stop** ~**ing** versuchen Sie auf auszuweichen; ~**ing tactics** Hinhaltetaktik *f.*

**stallholder** ['stɔ:lhəʊldə'] *n* Standinhaber(in *f) m.*

**stallion** ['stæljən] *n* Hengst *m.*

**stalwart** ['stɔːlwət] **1** *adj* **(a)** *(in spirit)* treu; *belief* unerschütterlich. **(b)** *(in build)* robust. **2** *n (supporter)* (getreuer) Anhänger.

**stamen** ['steɪmen] *n* Staubgefäß *nt.*

**stamina** ['stæmɪnə] *n* Ausdauer *f.*

**stammer** ['stæmə<sup>r</sup>] **1** *n* Stottern *nt.* **to speak with a** ~ stottern. **2** *vt* stammeln. **3** *vi* stottern.

**stamp** [stæmp] **1** *n* **(a)** *(postage ~)* (Brief)marke *f;* *(insurance* ~ *etc)* Marke *f;* *(trading ~)* (Rabatt)marke *f; (airmail* ~*, sticker)* Aufkleber *m.* **(b)** *(rubber* ~ *etc)* Stempel *m.* **(c)** *(fig)* **to bear the** ~ **of authenticity** authentischen Charakter haben. **2** *vt* **(a) to** ~ **one's foot** (mit dem Fuß) aufstampfen; **to** ~ **the ground** (mit dem Fuß/den Füßen) auf den Boden stampfen. **(b)** *(put postage* ~ *on)* freimachen. **a** ~**ed addressed envelope** ein frankierter Rückumschlag. **(c)** *document etc (with rubber* ~*)* stempeln; *(with embossing machine)* prägen; *name, pattern* aufstempeln; aufprägen *(on* auf +*acc); (fig)* ausweisen *(as* als*).* **the new leader has** ~**ed his personality on the party** der neue Vorsitzende hat der Partei seine Persönlichkeit aufgeprägt. **3** *vi (walk)* sta(m)pfen; *(disapprovingly, in dancing)* (auf)-stampfen; *(horse)* aufstampfen. **you** ~**ed on my foot!** Sie haben mir auf den Fuß getreten!

▶**stamp out 1** *vt sep* **(a)** *fire* austreten; *(fig: eradicate) epidemic, crime* ausrotten; *opposition* unterdrücken; *trouble* niederschlagen; *rebels* unschädlich machen. **(b)** *(cut out) pattern* ausstanzen. **2** *vi* herausstampfen.

**stamp:** ~ **album** *n* Briefmarkenalbum *nt;* ~ **collection** *n* Briefmarkensammlung *f;* ~ **collector** *n* Briefmarkensammler(in *f) m;* ~ **duty** *n* (Stempel)gebühr *f.*

**stampede** [stæm'piːd] **1** *n (of cattle)* wilde Flucht; *(of people)* Massenansturm *m (on* auf +*acc); (to escape)* wilde Flucht. **2** *vt horses, crowd* in (wilde *or* helle) Panik versetzen. **to** ~ **sb into doing sth** *(fig)* jdn dazu drängen, etw zu tun. **3** *vi* durchgehen; *(crowd)* losstürmen *(for* auf +*acc).*

**stamp machine** *n* Briefmarkenautomat *m.*

**stance** [stæns] *n (posture, Sport)* Haltung *f; (mental attitude also)* Einstellung *f.*

**stand** [stænd] *(vb: pret, ptp* **stood)** **1** *n* **(a) to take a** ~ **(on a matter)** (zu einer Angelegenheit) eine Einstellung vertreten; **to take a firm** ~ einen festen Standpunkt vertreten *(on* zu*).* **(b)** *(Mil) (resistance)* Widerstand *m; (battle)* Gefecht *nt.* **to make a** ~ *(lit, fig)* Widerstand leisten. **(c)** *(taxi ~)* Stand *m.* **(d)** *(furniture, music ~)* Ständer *m.* **(e)** *(market stall etc)* Stand *m.* **(f)** *(band~)* Podium *nt.* **(g)** *(Sport)* Tribüne *f; (US Jur)* Zeugenstand *m.* **(we sat) in the** ~ (wir saßen) auf der Tribüne.

**2** *vt* **(a)** *(place)* stellen. **(b)** *(withstand) pressure, close examination etc (object)* standhalten *(+dat); (person)* gewachsen sein *(+dat); test* bestehen; *climate* vertragen; *heat, noise* aushalten; *loss, cost* verkraften. **(c)** *(col: put up with) person, noise etc* aushalten. **I can't** ~ **him/it** *(don't like)* ich kann ihn/es nicht ausstehen; **I can't** ~ **being kept waiting** ich kann es nicht leiden, wenn man mich warten läßt; **I can't** ~ **it any longer** ich halte das nicht mehr (länger) aus. **(d) to** ~ **sb a drink** *(col)* jdm einen Drink spendieren.

**3** *vi* **(a)** *(be situated, be upright)* stehen; *(get up)* aufstehen. **don't just** ~ **there!** stehen Sie nicht nur (dumm) rum! *(col);* **to** ~ **still** stillstehen; **we stood talking** wir standen da und unterhielten uns; **to be left** ~**ing** *(house etc)* stehenbleiben; *(fig)* weit zurückfallen *(by* hinter +*dat).*

   **(b) he** ~**s over 6 feet** er ist über 1,80 m groß; **the**

**tree** ~**s 70 feet high** der Baum ist 20 m hoch. **(c) to** ~ **as a candidate** kandidieren.

   **(d)** *(continue to be valid) (offer, argument, contract)* gelten; *(decision, record, account)* stehen. **the theory** ~**s or falls by this** damit steht und fällt die Theorie.

   **(e)** *(fig: be in a position)* **we** ~ **to lose/gain a lot** wir laufen Gefahr, eine Menge zu verlieren/wir können sehr viel gewinnen.

   **(f)** *(fig: be placed)* **how do we** ~**?** wie stehen wir?; **I'd like to know where I** ~ **(with him)** ich möchte wissen, woran ich (bei ihm) bin; **to** ~ **accused of sth** einer Sache *(gen)* angeklagt sein; **as things** ~ nach Lage der Dinge.

   **(g)** *(fig: be, continue to be)* **to** ~ **firm** *or* **fast** festbleiben; **to** ~ **ready** sich bereithalten; **to** ~ **together** zusammenhalten; **to** ~ **(as) security for sb** für jdn bürgen; **nothing now** ~**s between us** es steht nichts mehr zwischen uns.

▶**stand about** *or* **around** *vi* herumstehen.

▶**stand aside** *vi (lit)* zur Seite treten; *(fig: withdraw)* zurücktreten.

▶**stand back** *vi (move back)* zurücktreten; *(be situated at a distance)* abliegen; *(fig: distance oneself)* Abstand nehmen. **to** ~ ~ **and do nothing** tatenlos zusehen.

▶**stand by 1** *vi* **(a)** *(remain uninvolved)* (unbeteiligt) danebenstehen. **(b)** *(be on alert)* sich bereithalten. **2** *vi* +*prep obj* **to** ~ ~ **a promise/sb** ein Versprechen/zu jdm halten.

▶**stand down** *vi (retire, withdraw)* zurücktreten; *(before appointment)* verzichten; *(Jur)* den Zeugenstand verlassen.

▶**stand for** *vi* +*prep obj* **(a)** *(be candidate for)* kandidieren für. **to** ~ ~ **election** sich zur Wahl stellen. **(b)** *(represent)* stehen für. **(c)** *(put up with)* hinnehmen.

▶**stand in** *vi* einspringen *(for* für*).*

▶**stand out** *vi* **(a)** *(project)* hervorstehen; *(land, balcony)* herausragen. **(b)** *(contrast, be noticeable)* auffallen. **to** ~ ~ **against sth** sich von etw abheben; *(oppose)* gegen etw Widerstand leisten; **to** ~ ~ **for sth** auf etw *(acc)* bestehen.

▶**stand up 1** *vi* **(a)** *(get up)* aufstehen; *(be standing)* stehen. **(b)** *(argument)* überzeugen; *(Jur)* bestehen. **(c) to** ~ ~ **for sb/sth** für jdn/etw eintreten; **to** ~ ~ **to sth** *to test, pressure (object)* einer Sache *(dat)* standhalten; *(person)* einer Sache *(dat)* gewachsen sein; *to hard wear etw (acc)* aushalten; **to** ~ ~ **to sb** sich jdm gegenüber behaupten. **2** *vt sep* **(a)** *(put upright)* hinstellen. **(b)** *(col) boyfriend etc* versetzen.

**stand-alone** [ˌstændə'ləʊn] *adj (Comp)* eigenständig.

**standard** ['stændəd] **1** *n* **(a)** *(average, established norm)* Norm *f; (criterion)* Maßstab *m.* **to set a good** ~ Maßstäbe setzen; **to be above/below** ~ über/unter der Norm sein; **to be up to** ~ den Anforderungen genügen. **(b)** *usu pl (moral* ~*s)* (sittliche) Maßstäbe *pl.* **he sets himself very high** ~**s** er stellt hohe Anforderungen an sich *(acc)* selbst. **(c)** *(degree, level)* Niveau *nt.* ~ **of living** Lebensstandard *m;* **first-year university** ~ Wissensstand *m* des ersten Studienjahrs; **of high/low** ~ von hohem/ niedrigem Niveau. **(d)** *(measurement)* (Maß)einheit *f; (monetary* ~*)* (Währungs)standard *m.* **(e)** *(flag)* Flagge *f; (on car)* Stander *m.* ~~**bearer** Fahnenträger *m.*

**2** *adj (usual, customary)* üblich; *model, price, practice, reply, reference work* Standard-; *equipment* serienmäßig; *size* Normal-; *(established) weight, size* Norm-. ~ **letter** *(Comm)* Schemabrief *m;* ~ **English** korrektes Englisch; ~ **German** Hochdeutsch *nt;* **S**~ **Time** *(US)* Normalzeit *f;* **it's** ~ **practice/procedure** es ist allgemein üblich/das übliche Verfahren; **it's fitted as** ~ es wird serienmäßig eingebaut.

**standardize** ['stændədaız] *vt education, style* vereinheitlichen; *format, sizes etc* normen.

**standard:** ~ **lamp** *n (Brit)* Stehlampe *f*; ~ **rose** *n* Rosenstock *m*.

**stand-by** ['stændbaı] **1** *n* **(a)** *(person)* Ersatz, Ersatzmann *m*; *(Sport also)* Auswechselspieler(in *f*) *m*; *(thing)* Reserve *f*; *(Aviat) (plane)* Entlastungsflugzeug *nt*; *(ticket)* Standby-Ticket *nt*. **(b)** *(state of readiness)* **on** ~ in Bereitschaft; *(ready for action)* in Einsatzbereitschaft; **to be on 24-hour** ~ 24 Stunden Bereitschaftsdienst haben. **2** *adj attr troops, player* Reserve-; *(Aviat) plane* Entlastungs-; *ticket, flight* Standby-. ~ **generator** Notstromaggregat *nt*.

**stand-in** ['stændın] *n (Film, Theat)* Ersatz *m*.

**standing** ['stændıŋ] **1** *n* **(a)** *(social)* Rang *m*, (gesellschaftliche) Stellung; *(professional)* Position *f*; *(financial)* (finanzielle) Verhältnisse *pl*; *(repute)* Ruf *m*. **of high** ~ von hohem Rang; *(repute)* von hohem Ansehen; **a man of some** ~ ein angesehener Mann; **what is his** ~ **locally?** was hält man in der Gegend von ihm? **(b)** *(duration)* Dauer *f*. **a treaty of only six months'** ~ ein Vertrag, der erst seit sechs Monaten besteht; **of long** ~ alt, langjährig.

**2** *adj attr* **(a)** *(established, permanent)* ständig; *rule, custom* bestehend; *army also* stehend. **it's a** ~ **joke** das ist schon zu einem Witz geworden; **to pay sth by** ~ **order** etw per Dauerauftrag bezahlen. **(b)** *(from a standstill) start, jump* aus dem Stand; *(not sitting) ticket* Stehplatz-; *(erect) corn* auf dem Halm (stehend); *stone* (aufrecht) stehend. ~ **room only** nur Stehplätze; **to give sb a** ~ **ovation** jdm eine stehende Ovation darbringen.

**stand:** ~-**offish** [ˌstænd'ɒfıʃ] *adj (col)* distanziert; ~**pat** *adj (US)* erzkonservativ; ~**pipe** *n* Steigrohr *nt*; ~**point** *n* Standpunkt *m*; **from the** ~**point of the teacher** von Standpunkt des Lehrers gesehen; ~**still** *n* Stillstand *m*; **to be at a** ~**still** *(plane, train)* stehen; *(machines, traffic, factory)* stillstehen; *(trade)* ruhen; **to bring production to a** ~**still** die Produktion zum Erliegen bringen; **to come to a** ~**still** *(person, vehicle)* anhalten; *(traffic, machines)* zum Stillstand kommen; *(industry etc)* zum Erliegen kommen; ~-**up** *adj attr buffet, collar* Steh-; *meal* im Stehen; ~-**up fight** Schlägerei *f*; ~-**up comic** *or* **comedian** Bühnenkomiker(in *f*) *m*.

**stank** [stæŋk] *pret of* **stink**.

**stanza** ['stænzə] *n* Strophe *f*.

**staple¹** ['steɪpl] **1** *n* Heftklammer *f*; *(for wires, cables etc)* Krampe *f*. **2** *vt* heften; *wire* mit Krampen befestigen. **to** ~ **sth together** etw zusammenheften.

**staple²** *adj diet, food* Grund-, Haupt-.

**stapler** ['steɪpləʳ] *n* Heftmaschine *f*.

**star** [stɑːʳ] **1** *n* **(a)** Stern *m*; *(asterisk also, Sch)* Sternchen *nt*. **the S**~**s and Stripes** das Sternenbanner; **you can thank your lucky** ~**s that** ... Sie können von Glück sagen, daß ...; **it's all in the** ~**s** es steht (alles) in den Sternen; **to see** ~**s** Sterne sehen; **a four-**~ **hotel** ein Vier-Sterne-Hotel *nt*. **(b)** *(person)* Star *m*. **2** *adj attr attraction* Haupt-; *performer, pupil* Star-. **3** *vt (Film also)* **to** ~ **sb** in der Hauptrolle zeigen; ~**ring** ... in der Hauptrollen/den Hauptrollen ... **4** *vi (Film etc)* die Hauptrolle spielen.

**starboard** ['stɑːbəd] **1** *n* Steuerbord *nt*. **2** *adj* Steuerbord-.

**starch** [stɑːtʃ] **1** *n* Stärke *f*. ~-**reduced** stärkearm. **2** *vt* stärken.

**starchy** ['stɑːtʃı] *adj (+er)* stärkehaltig; *(fig)* steif.

**stardom** ['stɑːdəm] *n* Ruhm *m*. **where he hoped to find** ~ wo er hoffte, ein Star zu werden.

**stare** [stɛəʳ] **1** *n* (starrer) Blick. **to give sb a** ~ jdn anstarren. **2** *vt* **the answer was staring us in the face** die Antwort lag klar auf der Hand. **3** *vi (vacantly etc)* (vor sich hin) starren; *(cow, madman)* stieren; *(in surprise)* große Augen machen; *(eyes)* weit aufgerissen sein. **he** ~**d in disbelief** er starrte ungläubig; **to** ~ **at sb/sth** jdn/etw anstarren.

**star:** ~**fish** *n* Seestern *m*; ~**gazer** *n (hum col)* Sterngucker *m (hum col)*.

**stark** [stɑːk] **1** *adj (+er) realism, contrast* kraß; *reality, poverty also, truth, terror* nackt; *landscape, cliffs, branches* kahl; *colour* kräftig; *(glaring)* grell. **2** *adv* ~ **raving** *or* **staring mad** *(col)* total verrückt *(col)*; ~ **naked** *(also* **starkers** *col)* splitternackt.

**starkly** ['stɑːklı] *adv lit* grell; *contrasted* scharf; *described* kraß.

**starless** ['stɑːlıs] *adj* stern(en)los.

**starlet** ['stɑːlıt] *n* (Film)sternchen *nt*.

**starlight** ['stɑːlaıt] *n* Sternenlicht *nt*.

**starling** ['stɑːlıŋ] *n* Star *m*.

**starlit** ['stɑːlıt] *adj sky, night* stern(en)klar.

**starry** ['stɑːrı] *adj (+er) night* stern(en)klar.

**starry-eyed** [ˌstɑːrı'aıd] *adj idealist* blauäugig. **to go all** ~ glänzende Augen kriegen.

**star:** **S**~-**spangled Banner** *n* Sternenbanner *nt*; ~-**studded** *adj* **(a)** *(liter) night* stern(en)klar; **(b)** *(fig)* ~-**studded cast** Starbesetzung *f*.

**start¹** [stɑːt] **1** *n (fright etc)* **to give a** ~ zusammenfahren; *(start up)* aufschrecken; *(horse)* scheuen; **to give sb a** ~ jdn erschrecken; **to wake with a** ~ aus dem Schlaf hochschrecken. **2** *vi* zusammenfahren; *(start up)* aufschrecken. **to** ~ **from one's chair/out of one's sleep** aus dem Stuhl hochfahren/aus dem Schlaf hochschrecken.

**start²** **1** *n* **(a)** *(beginning)* Beginn, Anfang *m*; *(departure)* Aufbruch *m*; *(of race)* Start *m*; *(of rumour, trouble, journey)* Ausgangspunkt *m*. **at the** ~ am Anfang, zu Beginn; *(Sport)* am Start; **for a** ~ *(to begin with)* fürs erste; *(firstly)* zunächst einmal; **from the** ~ von Anfang an; **from** ~ **to finish** von Anfang bis Ende; **to make a** ~ **(on sth)** (mit etw) anfangen; **to make an early** ~ frühzeitig aufbrechen; **to make a fresh** ~ **(in life)** (noch einmal) von vorn anfangen. **(b)** *(advantage, Sport)* Vorsprung *m (over* vor *+dat)*.

**2** *vt* **(a)** *(begin)* anfangen mit; *argument, career, new life, negotiations* beginnen, anfangen; *new job, journey* antreten. **to** ~ **work** anfangen zu arbeiten; **he** ~**ed life as a miner** er hat als Bergmann angefangen; **you** ~**ed it!** du hast angefangen!; **don't** ~ **that again!** fang nicht schon wieder (damit) an! **(b)** *(cause to begin) runners, race* starten; *train* abfahren lassen; *rumour* in Umlauf setzen; *conversation* anfangen, anknüpfen; *fight* anfangen; *blaze, collapse, chain reaction* auslösen; *fire* anzünden; *(arsonist)* legen; *(found) enterprise* gründen. **to** ~ **sb thinking/on a subject** jdn nachdenklich machen/jdn auf ein Thema bringen; **to** ~ **sb on a career** jdm zu einer Karriere verhelfen. **(c)** *car, machine* starten; *engine also* anlassen; *clock* in Gang setzen.

**3** *vi* **(a)** *(begin)* anfangen, beginnen; *(car, engine)* anspringen; *(plane)* starten; *(move off)* anfahren; *(bus, train)* abfahren; *(rumour)* in Umlauf kommen; *(violins etc)* einsetzen. ~**ing from Tuesday** ab Dienstag; **to** ~ **for home** sich auf den Heimweg machen; **to** ~ **(off) with** *(firstly)* erstens; *(at the beginning)* zunächst; **to** ~ **after sb** jdn verfolgen; **to get** ~**ed** anfangen; *(on trip)* aufbrechen; **to** ~ **on a task/the food** sich an eine Aufgabe/ ans Essen machen; **to** ~ **talking** zu sprechen anfangen; **he** ~**ed by saying** ... er sagte zunächst ...; **don't you** ~! fang du nicht auch noch an! **(b)** *(give a* ~*)* zusammenfahren.

▶**start off 1** *vi (begin)* anfangen; *(begin moving: person)* losgehen; *(on journey)* aufbrechen; *(run)* loslaufen; *(drive)* losfahren; *(esp Sport)* starten; *(begin talking etc)* anfangen *(on mit)*. **2** *vt sep sth* anfangen. **to ~ sb ~ (talking)** jdm das Stichwort geben; **a few stamps to ~ you** ~ ein paar Briefmarken für den Anfang.

▶**start out** *vi (begin)* (zunächst) beginnen *or* anfangen; *(begin a journey)* aufbrechen *(for* nach*)*. **we ~ed ~ on a long journey** wir machten uns auf eine lange Reise.

▶**start over** *vi (US)* noch (ein)mal von vorn anfangen.

▶**start up 1** *vi* (a) *(begin: music etc)* anfangen; *(machine)* angehen *(col)*, in Gang kommen; *(motor)* anspringen; *(siren)* losheulen. (b) *(move suddenly)* hochschrecken. **2** *vt sep* (a) *(cause to function)* in Gang bringen; *engine also* anlassen. (b) *(begin)* eröffnen; *business also, conversation* anfangen.

**starter** ['stɑːtə*] *n* (a) *(Sport)* Starter(in *f*) *m*. (b) *(Aut etc: self-~)* Anlasser *m*. (c) *(child)* **to be a late** *or* **slow ~** Spätentwickler *m* sein. (d) *(Brit col: first course)* Vorspeise *f*. (e) **for ~s** *(col)* für den Anfang *(col)*.

**starter: ~ drug** *n* Einstiegsdroge *f*; **~ home** *n* erstes (eigenes) Haus; *(apartment)* erste (eigene) Wohnung.

**starting** ['stɑːtɪŋ] *in cpds (Sport) block, signal, line, post* Start-; **~ grid** *n* Start(platz) *m*; **~ gun** *n* Startpistole *f*; **~ handle** *n* Anlasserkurbel *f*; **~ point** *n (lit, fig)* Ausgangspunkt *m*; **~ post** *n* Startpflock *m*.

**startle** ['stɑːtl] *vt* erschrecken. **I was ~d to see how old he looked** ich stellte entsetzt fest, wie alt er aussah.

**startling** ['stɑːtlɪŋ] *adj news* überraschend; *(bad)* alarmierend, bestürzend; *resemblance* erstaunlich; *originality, discovery* aufregend.

**start-up** ['stɑːtʌp] *n (Tech, Comp)* Start *m*. **~ costs** Startkosten *pl*.

**star turn** *n* Sensation, Hauptattraktion *f*.

**starvation** [stɑːˈveɪʃən] *n (act)* Hungern *nt*; *(of besieged people)* Aushungern *nt*; *(condition)* Hunger *m*. **to die of ~** verhungern; **to go on a ~ diet** *(hum)* eine Hungerkur machen.

**starve** [stɑːv] **1** *vt* (a) *(deprive of food)* hungern lassen; *(also ~ out)* aushungern; *(kill: also ~ to death)* verhungern lassen; **to ~ oneself** hungern. (b) *(fig)* **to ~ sb of sth** jdm etw vorenthalten *or* verweigern; **to be ~d of capital** an akutem Kapitalmangel leiden; **to be ~d of affection** keine Zuwendung erfahren. **2** *vi* hungern; *(die: also ~ to death)* verhungern. **I'm simply starving!** *(col)* ich sterbe vor Hunger! *(col)*; **to ~ for sth** *(fig)* nach etw hungern.

**starving** ['stɑːvɪŋ] *adj (lit)* hungernd *attr*; *(fig)* hungrig.

**stash** [stæʃ] *vt (also ~ away) (col) loot* verschwinden lassen *(col)*; *money* beiseite schaffen.

**state** [steɪt] **1** *n* (a) *(condition)* Zustand *m*. **~ of health/mind** Gesundheits-/Geisteszustand *m*; **the ~ of the nation** die Lage der Nation; **the present ~ of the economy** die gegenwärtige Wirtschaftslage; **where animals live in their natural ~** wo Tiere im Naturzustand leben; **in a good/bad ~** in gutem/schlechtem Zustand; **he's in no (fit) ~ to do that** er ist nicht in dem (richtigen) Zustand dafür; **look at the ~ of your hands!** guck dir bloß mal deine Hände an!; **the room was in a terrible ~** im Zimmer herrschte ein fürchterliches Durcheinander.
  (b) *(col: anxiety)* **to get into a ~ (about sth)** *(col)* wegen etw durchdrehen *(col)*.

(c) *(pomp)* Aufwand, Pomp *m*. **to be received in great ~** mit großem Staat empfangen werden; **to travel in ~** pompös reisen; **to lie in ~** (feierlich) aufgebahrt sein.
  (d) *(Pol)* Staat *m*; *(federal ~)* (Bundes)staat *m*; *(in BRD, Austria)* (Bundes)land *nt*. **the S~s** die (Vereinigten) Staaten; **the S~ of Florida** der Staat Florida; **affairs of ~** Staatsangelegenheiten *pl*.
  **2** *vt* darlegen, vortragen; *name, price* nennen; *purpose* angeben. **to ~ that ...** feststellen, daß ...; **to ~ one's case** seine Sache vortragen; **to ~ the case for the prosecution** *(Jur)* die Anklage vortragen; **unless otherwise ~d** wenn nicht anders angegeben; **as ~d in my letter, I ...** wie in meinem Brief erwähnt, ... ich ...

**state** *in cpds* Staats-; *control, industry* staatlich; *(US etc)* bundesstaatlich.

**stated** ['steɪtɪd] *adj* (a) *(declared) sum, date* genannt; *limits* bestimmt. (b) *(fixed, regular) times, amount* fest(gesetzt).

**state: S~ Department** *n (US)* Außenministerium *nt*; **~ education** *n* staatliche Erziehung; *(system)* staatliches Erziehungswesen; **~house** *n (US)* Parlamentsgebäude, Kapitol *nt*; **~less** *adj* staatenlos; **~less person** Staatenlose(r) *mf*.

**stateliness** ['steɪtlɪnɪs] *n see adj* Würde *f*; Gemessenheit *f*.

**stately** ['steɪtlɪ] *adj (+er) person, bearing* würdevoll; *pace* gemessen. **~ home** herrschaftliches Anwesen, Schloß *nt*.

**statement** ['steɪtmənt] *n* (a) *(of thesis etc)* Darstellung *f*; *(of problem also)* Darlegung *f*. (b) *(that said)* Feststellung *f*; *(claim)* Behauptung *f*; *(official ~)* Erklärung *f*; *(in court, to police)* Aussage *f*; *(written)* Protokoll *nt*. **to make a ~** eine Presseerklärung abgeben. (c) *(Fin) (tradesman's)* Rechnung *f*; *(bank ~)* Kontoauszug *m*.

**state: ~-of-the-art** *adj* neueste(r, s); *technology* Spitzen-; **to be ~-of-the-art** dem neuesten Stand der Technik entsprechen; **~-owned** *adj* staatseigen; **~room** *n (in palace)* Empfangssaal *m*; *(on ship)* Kabine *f*; **~ school** *n* öffentliche Schule; **~ secret** *n* Staatsgeheimnis *nt*; **S~'s evidence** *n (US)* Aussage *f* eines Kronzeugen; **to turn S~'s evidence** als Kronzeuge auftreten; **s~side** *(US col)* **1** *adj* in den Staaten *(col)*; **2** *adv (to the USA)* nach Hause (in die Staaten); *(in the USA)* zu Hause (in den Staaten).

**statesman** ['steɪtsmən] *n, pl* **-men** [-mən] Staatsmann *m*.

**statesmanship** ['steɪtsmənʃɪp] *n* Staatskunst *f*.

**static** ['stætɪk] **1** *adj* (a) *(Phys)* statisch. (b) *(not moving or changing)* konstant; *(stationary)* feststehend *attr*; *condition, society* statisch. **2** *n (Phys)* Reibungselektrizität *f*; *(Rad)* atmosphärische Störungen *pl*.

**station** ['steɪʃən] **1** *n* (a) *(railway ~, bus ~)* Bahnhof *m*; *(stop)* Station *f*. (b) *(police ~, fire ~)* Wache *f*; *(space ~)* (Raum)station *f*; *(US: gas ~)* Tankstelle *f*. (c) *(Mil: post)* Stellung *f*, Posten *m*. (d) *(Rad, TV)* Sender *m*. (e) *(rank)* Stand *m*. **~ in life** Stellung *f* (im Leben), Rang *m*; **he has got ideas above his ~** er hat Ideen, die jemandem aus seinem Stand gar nicht zukommen. **2** *vt (Mil) troops* stationieren; *sentry* aufstellen.

**stationary** ['steɪʃənərɪ] *adj (not moving) car* haltend *attr*; *(not movable)* fest(stehend *attr*). **to be ~** *(vehicles)* stehen; *(traffic, fig)* stillstehen; **to remain ~** sich nicht bewegen; *(traffic)* stillstehen.

**stationer** ['steɪʃənə*] *n* Schreibwarenhändler *m*. **~'s (shop)** *(Brit)* Schreibwarenhandlung *f*.

**stationery** ['steɪʃənərɪ] *n (notepaper)* Briefpapier *nt*;

*(writing materials)* Schreibwaren *pl.*
**station:** ~ **house** *n (US: police)* (Polizei)wache *f;*
~**master** *n* Bahnhofsvorsteher *m;* ~ **wagon** *n*
*(US)* Kombi(wagen) *m.*
**statistic** [stə'tɪstɪk] *n* Statistik *f.*
**statistical** [stə'tɪstɪkəl] *adj* statistisch.
**statistician** [ˌstætɪ'stɪʃən] *n* Statistiker(in *f*) *m.*
**statistics** [stə'tɪstɪks] *n* **(a)** *sing* Statistik *f.* **(b)** *pl*
*(data)* Statistiken *pl.*
**statuesque** [ˌstætjʊ'esk] *adj* standbildhaft; *person,*
*figure* stattlich; *beauty* klassisch.
**statuette** [ˌstætjʊ'et] *n* Statuette *f.*
**stature** ['stætʃər] *n* **(a)** Wuchs *m; (esp of man)* Statur
*f.* **(b)** *(fig)* Format *nt.*
**status** ['steɪtəs] *n* Stellung *f; (legal ~, social ~ also)*
Status *m.* **equal** ~ Gleichstellung *f;* **marital** ~ Familienstand *m.*
**status line** *n (Comp)* Statuszeile *f.*
**status quo** ['steɪtəs'kwəʊ] *n* Status quo *m.*
**status:** ~ **report** *n* Zwischenbericht *m;* ~ **symbol**
*n* Statussymbol *nt.*
**statute** ['stætjuːt] *n* Gesetz *n; (of organization)* Satzung *f,* Statut *nt.* ~ **book** Gesetzbuch *nt;* **to put sth**
**in the** ~ **book** etw zum Gesetz machen.
**statutory** ['stætjʊtərɪ] *adj* gesetzlich; *(in organiza-*
*tion)* satzungsgemäß; *right also* verbrieft; *punish-*
*ment* (vom Gesetz) vorgesehen. ~ **declaration** *(Jur)*
eidesstattliche Erklärung.
**staunch**¹ [stɔːntʃ] *adj (+er) Catholic, loyalist* überzeugt; *member, supporter* getreu; *support* standhaft.
**staunch**² *vt flow* stauen; *bleeding* stillen.
**stave** [steɪv] *n (Mus: staff)* Notenlinien *pl.*
▸**stave in** *pret, ptp* **stove in** *vt sep* eindrücken.
▸**stave off** *pret, ptp* ~**d off** *vt sep attack* zurückschlagen; *crisis, cold* abwehren; *hunger* lindern.
**staves** [steɪvz] *pl of* **staff 1 (c).**
**stay** [steɪ] **1** *n* **(a)** Aufenthalt *m.* **a short** ~ **in hospital**
ein kurzer Krankenhausaufenthalt. **(b)** *(Jur)* Aus-
setzung *f.* ~ **of execution** Vollstreckungsaufschub
*m.*
**2** *vt* **(a)** *(Jur) order, sentence* aussetzen. **(b) to** ~
**the course** *(lit, fig)* durchhalten.
**3** *vi* **(a)** *(remain)* bleiben. **to** ~ **for** *or* **to supper**
zum Abendessen bleiben; **unemployment has come**
**to** ~ die Arbeitslosigkeit ist zum Dauerzustand geworden; **if it** ~**s fine** wenn es schön bleibt; ~ **with**
**it!** nun gut aufgeben! **(b)** *(reside)* wohnen; *(at youth*
*hostel etc)* übernachten. **to** ~ **at a hotel** im Hotel
wohnen; **I** ~**ed in Italy for a few weeks** ich habe
mich ein paar Wochen in Italien aufgehalten; **he is**
~**ing at Chequers for the weekend** er verbringt das
Wochenende in Chequers; **to** ~ **with friends** bei
Freunden wohnen; **my brother came to** ~ mein
Bruder ist zu Besuch gekommen.
▸**stay away** *vi (from* von*)* wegbleiben; *(from per-*
*son)* sich fernhalten.
▸**stay behind** *vi* zurückbleiben; *(Sch: as punish-*
*ment)* nachsitzen.
▸**stay in** *vi (at home)* zu Hause bleiben; *(in position*
*etc)* drinbleiben; *(Sch)* nachsitzen.
▸**stay on** *vi (lid etc)* draufbleiben; *(light)* anblei-
ben; *(people)* (noch) bleiben. **to** ~ ~ **at school/as**
**manager** (in der Schule) weitermachen/(weiterhin)
Geschäftsführer bleiben.
▸**stay out** *vi (person)* draußen bleiben; *(on strike)* weiter-
streiken; *(not come home)* wegbleiben. **to** ~ ~ **of**
**sth** sich aus etw heraushalten; **he never managed**
**to** ~ ~ **of trouble** er war dauernd in Schwierigkeiten.
▸**stay up** *vi* **(a)** *(person)* aufbleiben. **don't** ~ ~ **for**

**me!** bleib nicht meinetwegen auf! **(b)** *(tent, fence,*
*pole)* stehen bleiben; *(picture, decorations)* hängen
bleiben.
**stay-at-home** ['steɪət,həʊm] *n* Stubenhocker *m.*
**stayer** ['steɪər] *n (horse)* Steher *m.* **to be a** ~ *(person)*
Stehvermögen *nt* haben.
**staying power** ['steɪɪŋ,paʊər] *n* Durchhaltevermögen *nt,* Ausdauer *f.*
**St Bernard** [sənt'bɜːnəd] *n (dog)* Bernhardiner *m.*
**STD** *(Brit Telec)* = **subscriber trunk dialling.** ~
**code** Vorwahl(nummer) *f.*
**stead** [sted] *n* **in his** ~ **an** seiner Stelle; **to stand sb**
**in good** ~ jdm zugute kommen.
**steadfast** ['stedfɑːst] *adj* fest; *person, refusal also*
standhaft; *belief* unerschütterlich.
**steadfastness** ['stedfɑːstnɪs] *n see adj* Festigkeit *f;*
Standhaftigkeit *f;* Unerschütterlichkeit *f.*
**steadily** ['stedɪlɪ] *adv* **(a)** *(firmly)* ruhig; *balanced*
fest; *gaze* unverwandt. **(b)** *(constantly)* ständig; *rain*
ununterbrochen. **(c)** *(reliably)* zuverlässig.
**steadiness** ['stedɪnɪs] *n* Festigkeit *f; (of hand, eye)*
Ruhe *f; (regularity)* Stetigkeit *f; (of gaze)* Unver-
wandtheit *f; (of character)* Zuverlässigkeit *f.*
**steady** ['stedɪ] **1** *adj (+er)* **(a)** *(firm, not wobbling)*
*hand, nerves, eye* ruhig; *gaze* unverwandt. **with a** ~
**hand** mit ruhiger Hand; **to hold sth** ~ etw ruhig
halten; *ladder* etw festhalten; **the chair is not very**
~ der Stuhl ist wacklig. **(b)** *(constant) wind, pro-*
*gress, demand etc* ständig, stet *(geh); drizzle* ununterbrochen; *temperature* beständig. **to drive at a**
**pace/70 (mph)** in gleichmäßigem Tempo/ständig
mit 110 (km/h) fahren. **(c)** *(reliable, regular) worker*
zuverlässig. **(d)** *job, boyfriend* fest. **2** *adv* ~! *(care-*
*fully, gently)* vorsichtig!; *(Naut)* Kurs halten!; ~
**(on)!** sachte! *(col);* **to go** ~ **(with sb)** *(col)* mit jdm
(fest) zusammen sein. **3** *vt plane, boat* wieder ins
Gleichgewicht bringen; *(stabilize) nerves, person* beruhigen; *(in character)* ausgleichen. **to** ~ **oneself**
festen Halt finden; **she had a** ~**ing influence on him**
durch sie wurde er ausgeglichener.
**steak** [steɪk] *n* Steak *nt; (of fish)* Filet *nt.* ~ **and kid-**
**ney pie** Fleischpastete *f* mit Nieren.
**steal** [stiːl] *(vb: pret* **stole,** *ptp* **stolen) 1** *vt object,*
*idea, heart* stehlen. **to** ~ **sth from sb** jdm etw stehlen; **to** ~ **the show/sb's thunder** die Schau stehlen/
jdm den Wind aus den Segeln nehmen; **the baby**
**stole all the attention** das Baby zog die ganze Aufmerksamkeit auf sich. **2** *vi* **(a)** *(thieve)* stehlen. **(b)**
*(move quietly)* sich stehlen, (sich) schleichen. **to** ~
**away** sich davonstehlen; **to** ~ **up on sb** sich an jdn
heranschleichen. **3** *n (US col: bargain)* Geschenk *nt*
*(col).* **it's a** ~! das ist (ja) geschenkt! *(col).*
**stealth** [stelθ] *n* List *f.* **by** ~ durch List.
**stealthy** ['stelθɪ] *adj (+er)* verstohlen; *footsteps* verhalten.
**steam** [stiːm] **1** *n* Dampf *m.* **the windows were cov-**
**ered with** ~ die Fensterscheiben waren beschlagen; **full** ~ **ahead!** *(Naut)* volle Kraft voraus!; **to**
**get up** ~ *(fig)* in Schwung kommen; **to let off** ~ *(lit,*
*fig)* Dampf ablassen; **to run out of** ~ *(fig)* den
Schwung verlieren; **under one's own** ~ *(fig)* allein,
ohne Hilfe. **2** *vt* dämpfen; *food* dünsten. **to** ~ **open**
**an envelope** einen Briefumschlag über Dampf öffnen; ~**ed pudding** gedämpfter Pudding *m.* **3** *vi* **(a)**
*(give off* ~*)* dampfen. **(b)** *(move)* dampfen. **the ship**
~**ed into the harbour** das Schiff lief in den Hafen
ein.
▸**steam up 1** *vt sep window* beschlagen lassen. **to**
**be/get** ~**ed** ~ *(fig col)* hochgehen *(col) (about* wegen*).* **2** *vi (window)* beschlagen.
**steam:** ~**boat** *n* Dampfschiff *nt,* Dampfer *m;* ~

**engine** *n* Dampfmaschine *f*; *(Rail: locomotive)* Dampflok *f*.

**steamer** ['sti:mər] *n* *(ship)* Dampfer *m*; *(Cook)* Dampfkochtopf *m*.

**steam**: ~ **iron** *n* Dampfbügeleisen *nt*; ~**roller** *n* Dampfwalze *f*; ~**ship** *n* Dampfschiff *nt*; ~ **train** *n* Dampfzug *m*.

**steamy** ['sti:mɪ] *adj (+er)* dunstig; *room, atmosphere* voll Dampf; *window* beschlagen.

**steed** [sti:d] *n (liter)* Roß *nt*.

**steel** [sti:l] **1** *n* Stahl *m*. **2** *adj attr* Stahl-. **3** *vt* to ~ **oneself** sich wappnen *(for gegen)*; *(physically)* sich stählen *(for für)*; **to** ~ **oneself to do sth** allen Mut zusammennehmen, um etw zu tun.

**steel** *in cpds* Stahl-, stahl-; ~ **band** *n* Steelband *f*; ~ **mill** *n* Stahlwalzwerk *nt*; ~**works** *n sing or pl* Stahlwerk *nt*.

**steely** ['sti:lɪ] *adj (+er)* grip stahlhart; *gaze* hart; *determination* eisern; *blue* Stahl-.

**steep¹** [sti:p] *adj (+er)* **(a)** steil. **it's a** ~ **climb** es geht steil hinauf; **there's been a** ~ **drop in the value of the pound** das Pfund ist stark gefallen. **(b)** *(fig col)* demand unverschämt; *price also, bill* gesalzen *(col)*. **it seems a bit** ~ **that** ... es ist ein starkes Stück, daß ...

**steep²** *vt* **(a)** *(in liquid)* eintauchen; *(in marinade, dye)* ziehen lassen; *dried food* einweichen. **(b)** *(fig)* **to be** ~**ed in sth** von etw durchdrungen sein; ~**ed in history** geschichtsträchtig.

**steeple** ['sti:pl] *n* Kirchturm *m*.

**steeple**: ~**chase** *n (for horses)* Hindernisrennen *nt*; *(for runners)* Hindernislauf *m*; ~**jack** *n* Turmarbeiter *m*.

**steeply** ['sti:plɪ] *adv* steil.

**steepness** ['sti:pnɪs] *n* Steilheit *f*.

**steer¹** [stɪər] **1** *vt (lit, fig)* lenken; *ship* steuern; *person also* lotsen. **2** *vi (in car)* lenken; *(in ship)* steuern. **to** ~ **due north** Kurs nach Norden halten; **to** ~ **for or towards sth** auf etw *(acc)* zuhalten; *(Naut)* etw ansteuern; *(fig)* auf etw *(acc)* zusteuern.

**steer²** *n* junger Ochse.

**steering** ['stɪərɪŋ] *n (in car etc)* Lenkung *f*; *(Naut)* Steuerung *f*.

**steering**: ~ **column** *n* Lenksäule *f*; ~ **committee** *n* vorbereitender Ausschuß; ~ **lock** *n* Lenkradschloß *nt*; ~ **wheel** *n* Steuer(rad) *nt*; *(of car also)* Lenkrad *nt*.

**stem** [stem] **1** *n (of plant, glass)* Stiel *m*; *(of shrub, word)* Stamm *m*; *(of grain)* Halm *m*; *(of pipe)* Hals *m*. **2** *vt (check, stop)* aufhalten; *flood, tide* eindämmen; *bleeding* zum Stillstand bringen. **3** *vi* **to** ~ **from sth** *(result from)* von etw herrühren; *(have as origin)* auf etw *(acc)* zurückgehen.

**stench** [stentʃ] *n* Gestank *m*.

**stencil** ['stensl] *n* Schablone *f*; *(Printing: for duplicating)* Matrize *f*.

**stenographer** [ste'nɒgrəfər] *n* Stenograph(in *f*) *m*.

**stenography** [ste'nɒgrəfɪ] *n* Stenographie *f*.

**step** [step] **1** *n* **(a)** *(pace, in dancing)* Schritt *m*. **to take a** ~ einen Schritt machen; ~ **by** ~ *(lit, fig)* Schritt für Schritt; **to be in/out of** ~ *(fig)* im/nicht im Gleichklang sein *(with mit)*.

**(b)** *(move)* Schritt *m*; *(measure also)* Maßnahme *f*. **it's a great** ~ **forward** es ist ein großer Schritt nach vorn; **that would be a** ~ **back/in the right direction for him** das wäre für ihn ein Rückschritt/ein Schritt in die richtige Richtung; **to take** ~**s to do sth** Maßnahmen ergreifen, (um) etw zu tun.

**(c)** *(in process, experiment, scale, hierarchy)* Stufe *f*. ~**s** *(outdoors)* Treppe *f*; **mind the** ~ Vorsicht Stufe.

**(d)** ~**s** *pl (~-ladder: also pair of* ~**s)** Stufenleiter *f*.

**2** *vt* ~ **two paces to the left** treten Sie zwei Schritte nach links.

**3** *vi* gehen. **to** ~ **into/out of sth** *house, room, puddle* in etw *(acc)*/aus etw treten; *train, dress* in etw *(acc)*/aus etw steigen; **to** ~ **on(to) sth** *plane, train* in etw *(acc)* steigen; *platform, ladder* auf etw *(acc)* steigen; **to** ~ **on sth** *object, toy* auf etw *(acc)* treten; **to** ~ **over sb/sth** über jdn/etw steigen; ~ **this way, please** hier entlang, bitte!; **to** ~ **inside** herein-/hineintreten; **to** ~ **outside** heraus-/hinaustreten; ~ **on it!** mach mal ein bißchen schneller! *(col)*; *(in car)* gib Gas!

▶**step aside** *vi (lit)* zur Seite treten; *(fig)* Platz machen.

▶**step back** *vi (lit)* zurücktreten. **to** ~ ~ **from sth** *(fig)* von etw Abstand gewinnen.

▶**step down** *vi (fig)* **to** ~ ~ **in favour of sb** jdm Platz machen.

▶**step forward** *vi* vortreten; *(fig)* sich melden.

▶**step in** *vi (lit)* eintreten *(-to, +prep obj* in *+acc)*; *(fig)* einschreiten.

▶**step off** *vi +prep obj (off bus, plane, boat)* aussteigen *(prep obj* aus*)*. **to** ~ ~ **the pavement** vom Bürgersteig treten.

▶**step up** *vt sep* steigern; *efforts also, campaign* verstärken; *volume* erhöhen.

**step-** *pref brother, mother, daughter etc* Stief-. ~**child** Stiefkind *nt*.

**step-ladder** ['step,lædər] *n* Stufenleiter *f*.

**steppe** [step] *n* Steppe *f*.

**stepping stone** ['stepɪŋ,stəʊn] *n* (Tritt)stein *m*; *(fig)* Sprungbrett *nt (to* für*)*.

**stereo** ['sterɪəʊ] **1** *n* Stereo *nt*; *(hi-fi system)* Stereoanlage *f*. **in** ~ in Stereo. **2** *adj* Stereo-.

**stereophonic** [,sterɪəʊ'fɒnɪk] *adj* stereophon.

**stereoscopic** [,sterɪəʊ'skɒpɪk] *adj* stereoskopisch.

**stereotype** ['sterɪə,taɪp] *n (fig)* Klischee(vorstellung *f*) *nt*; *(~ character)* stereotype Figur.

**stereotyped** ['sterɪə,taɪpt] *adj* stereotyp; *thinking* schablonenhaft.

**sterile** ['steraɪl] *adj* **(a)** *(lit, fig)* unfruchtbar. **(b)** *(germ-free)* steril, keimfrei; *(fig) décor etc* steril.

**sterility** [ste'rɪlɪtɪ] *n see adj* **(a)** Unfruchtbarkeit *f*; **(b)** Sterilität *f*.

**sterilization** [,sterɪlaɪ'zeɪʃən] *n* Sterilisation *f*.

**sterilize** ['sterɪlaɪz] *vt person, instruments* sterilisieren.

**sterling** ['stɜːlɪŋ] **1** *adj* **(a)** *(Fin)* Sterling-. **in pounds** ~ in Pfund Sterling. **(b)** *(fig)* gediegen; *character* lauter. **(c)** ~ **silver** Sterlingsilber *nt*. **2** *n no art (money)* das Pfund Sterling. **in** ~ in Pfund Sterling. **3** *adj attr* aus (Sterling)silber.

**stern¹** [stɜːn] *n (Naut)* Heck *nt*.

**stern²** *adj (+er) (strict)* streng; *words also, character, warning* ernst. **made of** ~**er stuff** aus härterem Holz geschnitzt.

**sternly** ['stɜːnlɪ] *adv see adj*.

**sternness** ['stɜːnnɪs] *n see adj* Strenge *f*; Ernst *m*.

**steroid** ['stɪərɔɪd] *n* Steroid *nt*.

**stet** [stet] *interj (Typ)* stehenlassen.

**stethoscope** ['steθəskəʊp] *n* Stethoskop *nt*.

**stevedore** ['sti:vɪdɔːr] *n* Stauer *m*.

**stew** [stju:] **1** *n* **(a)** Eintopf(gericht *nt*) *m*. **(b)** *(col)* **to be in a** ~ **(about sth)** (über etw *(acc)* or wegen etw) ganz aufgeregt sein. **2** *vt meat* schmoren; *fruit* dünsten. ~**ed apples** Apfelkompott *nt*. **3** *vi (meat)* schmoren; *(fruit)* dünsten; *(col: tea)* bitter werden. **to let sb** ~ **(in his/her own juice)** jdn (im eigenen Saft) schmoren lassen.

**steward** ['stjuːəd] *n* Steward *m*; *(on estate etc)* Verwalter *m*; *(at dance, meeting)* Ordner *m*.

**stewardess** ['stjuːədes] *n* Stewardess *f*.

**stewing steak** ['stjuːɪŋ'steɪk], **stewmeat** *(US)* ['stjuːmiːt] *n* (Rinder)schmorfleisch *nt*.

**stick¹** [stɪk] *n* (a) Stock *m*; *(twig)* Zweig *m*; *(hockey ~)* Schläger *m*; *(drum~)* Schlegel *m*. **to give sb/sth (a lot of)** ~ *(col: criticize)* jdn/etw heruntermachen *(col)*; **just a few ~s of furniture** nur ein paar Möbelstücke; **to get hold of the wrong end of the** ~ *(fig col)* es/das falsch verstehen; **to live (out) in the ~s** *(fig)* weit vom Schuß wohnen. (b) *(of sealing wax, celery, rhubarb, dynamite)* Stange *f*; *(of chalk, shaving soap)* Stück *nt*.

**stick²** *pret, ptp* **stuck 1** *vt* (a) *(with glue etc)* kleben. **to ~ an envelope down** einen Briefumschlag zukleben. (b) *(pin)* stecken. **he stuck a badge on his lapel** er steckte sich *(dat)* ein Abzeichen ans Revers. (c) *(jab) knife, sword etc* stoßen. (d) *(col: place, put)* tun *(col)*; *(in sth also)* stecken *(col)*. ~ **it on the shelf** tu's aufs Regal; **he stuck his head around the corner** er steckte seinen Kopf um die Ecke; **you know where you can ~ that** *(col!)* du kannst mich mal! *(col!)*. (e) *(esp Brit col: tolerate)* aushalten; *pace, pressure of work* durchhalten. **I can't ~ him/that** ich kann ihn/das nicht ausstehen *(col)*.

**2** *vi* (a) *(glue, object)* kleben *(to* an *+dat)*. **the name seems to have stuck** der Name scheint an ihm/ihr *etc* hängengeblieben zu sein. (b) *(become caught, wedged etc)* steckenbleiben; *(drawer, window)* klemmen. (c) *(sth pointed)* stecken *(in* in *+dat)*. **it stuck in my foot** das ist mir im Fuß steckengeblieben. (d) *(project)* **his toes are ~ing through his socks** seine Zehen kommen durch die Socken. (e) *(stay)* bleiben; *(slander)* haftenbleiben. **to ~ in sb's mind** jdm im Gedächtnis bleiben; **to make sth ~ (in one's mind)** sich *(dat)* etw einprägen.

▶**stick around** *vi (col)* hier/da bleiben.

▶**stick at** *vi +prep obj* (a) *(persist)* bleiben an *(+dat) (col)*. **to ~ it** dranbleiben *(col)*. (b) **he will ~ ~ nothing** er macht vor nichts halt.

▶**stick by** *vi +prep obj sb* halten zu; *promise* stehen zu.

▶**stick on 1** *vt sep label, cover* aufkleben *(prep obj* auf *+acc)*. **2** *vi (label etc)* kleben, haften *(prep obj* an *+dat)*.

▶**stick out 1** *vi* (her)vorstehen *(of* aus*)*; *(ears, hair)* abstehen; *(fig: be noticeable)* auffallen. **2** *vt sep* (a) *tongue etc* hinaus-/herausstrecken. (b) **to ~ it ~** durchhalten.

▶**stick out for** *vi +prep obj* sich stark machen für.

▶**stick to** *vi +prep obj* bleiben bei; *(remain faithful to) principles etc* treu bleiben *(+dat)*.

▶**stick together** *vi* zusammenkleben; *(fig: partners etc)* zusammenhalten.

▶**stick up 1** *vt sep* (a) *(with tape etc)* zukleben. (b) *(col: raise)* ~ **'em** ~! Hände hoch! (c) *(col) notice etc* aufhängen, anbringen. **2** *vi (nail etc)* vorstehen; *(hair)* abstehen; *(collar)* hochstehen.

▶**stick up for** *vi +prep obj sb, one's principles* eintreten für. **to ~ ~ ~ oneself** sich behaupten.

**sticker** ['stɪkəʳ] *n* (a) *(label)* Aufkleber *m*. (b) *(col: determined person)* **he's a ~** er ist zäh.

**stickiness** ['stɪkɪnɪs] *n (lit)* Klebrigkeit *f*; *(of atmosphere, weather)* Schwüle *f*.

**sticking plaster** ['stɪkɪŋ,plɑːstəʳ] *n (Brit)* Heftpflaster *nt*.

**stick-in-the-mud** ['stɪkɪnðə,mʌd] *(col) n* Muffel *m (col)*.

**stickleback** ['stɪklbæk] *n* Stichling *m*.

**stickler** ['stɪkləʳ] *n* **to be a ~ for sth** es mit etw peinlich genau nehmen.

**stick:** ~-**on** *adj label* (Auf)klebe-; ~-**up** *n (col)* bewaffneter Überfall.

**sticky** ['stɪkɪ] *adj (+er)* (a) klebrig; *label* Klebe-; *paint* feucht; *atmosphere* schwül; *air* stickig; *(sweaty) hands* feucht. ~ **tape** Klebeband *nt*. (b) *(fig col) problem, person* schwierig; *moment* heikel. **to come to a ~ end** ein böses Ende nehmen; **to be on a ~ wicket** in einer schwierigen Lage sein.

**stiff** [stɪf] **1** *adj (+er)* (a) steif; *brush* hart; *dough, paste* fest. (b) *resistance, drink* stark; *competition* hart; *breeze* steif; *climb, test* schwierig; *examination, punishment* schwer; *price, demand* hoch. **that's a bit ~** das ist ganz schön happig *(col)*. **2** *n (col)* Leiche *f*.

**stiffen** ['stɪfn] *(also ~ up)* **1** *vt* steif machen; *shirt etc* stärken; *(disease) limb* steif werden lassen; *resistance etc* verstärken. **2** *vi* steif werden; *(fig: resistance)* sich verhärten; *(breeze)* auffrischen.

**stiffly** ['stɪflɪ] *adv* steif.

**stiffness** ['stɪfnɪs] *n see adj* (a) Steifheit *f*; Härte *f*; Festigkeit *f*. (b) Stärke *f*; Härte *f*; Schwierigkeit *f*; Schwere *f*; Höhe *f*.

**stifle** ['staɪfl] **1** *vt (suffocate)* ersticken; *(fig) yawn, cough also, opposition* unterdrücken. **2** *vi* ersticken.

**stifling** ['staɪflɪŋ] *adj fumes* erstickend; *heat* drückend. **it's ~ in here** es ist ja zum Ersticken hier drin *(col)*.

**stigma** ['stɪgmə] *n* Brandmal, Stigma *nt*.

**stigmatize** ['stɪgmətaɪz] *vt* brandmarken.

**stile** [staɪl] *n* (Zaun)übertritt *m*.

**stiletto** [stɪ'letəʊ] *n* (a) *(knife)* Stilett *nt*. (b) *(esp Brit: also ~ heel)* Pfennigabsatz *m*.

**still¹** [stɪl] **1** *adj, adv (+er)* (a) *(motionless)* bewegungslos; *person also* reglos; *sea, waters* ruhig. **to keep ~** stillhalten; **to hold sth ~** etw ruhig halten; **to be ~** *(vehicle, needle etc)* stillstehen; **to lie ~** reglos daliegen; **to stand ~** still stehen; **my heart stood ~** mir stockte das Herz; ~ **waters run deep** *(Prov)* stille Wasser sind tief *(Prov)*. (b) *(quiet, calm)* still. **be ~!** sei still! **2** *adj wine* nicht moussierend; *drink* ohne Kohlensäure. **a ~ photograph** ein Standfoto *nt*. **3** *n* (a) **in the ~ of the night** in der Stille der Nacht. (b) *(Film)* Standfoto *nt*.

**still²** [stɪl] *adv* (a) *(temporal)* noch; *(for emphasis, in exasperation, used on its own)* immer noch; *(in negative sentences)* noch immer, immer noch; *(now as in the past)* nach wie vor. **there will ~ be objections** es wird nach wie vor Einwände geben. (b) *(nevertheless, all the same)* trotzdem. ~, **it was worth it** es hat sich trotzdem gelohnt; ~, **he is my brother** er ist trotz allem mein Bruder; **rich but ~ not happy** reich und doch nicht glücklich; ~, **at least we didn't lose anything** na ja, wir haben wenigstens nichts dabei verloren; ~, **what can you expect?** was kann man auch anderes erwarten? (c) *(with comp)* noch. ~ **better** noch besser; **better** ~, **do it this way** oder noch besser, mach es so. **2** *conj* (und) doch.

**still³** *n (for alcohol)* Destillierapparat *m*.

**still:** ~**birth** *n* Totgeburt *f*; ~**born** *adj (lit, fig)* totgeboren *attr*; **the child was ~born** das Kind kam tot zur Welt; ~ **life** *n, pl* ~ **lifes** Stilleben *nt*.

**stillness** ['stɪlnɪs] *n* (a) *(motionlessness)* Unbewegtheit *f*; *(of person)* Reglosigkeit *f*. (b) *(quietness)* Stille, Ruhe *f*.

**stilt** [stɪlt] *n* Stelze *f*; *(Archit)* Pfahl *m*.

**stilted** ['stɪltɪd] *adj* gestelzt, gespreizt.

**stimulant** ['stɪmjʊlənt] *n* Anregungsmittel *nt*; *(fig)* Ansporn *m*.

**stimulate** ['stɪmjʊleɪt] *vt* (a) *(excite) circulation, mind* anregen; *(cold shower, coffee)* beleben; *(Med also)* stimulieren; *nerve* reizen; *(sexually)* erregen; *(fig)* *person* anspornen; *(intellectually)* stimulieren; *sb's interest* erregen. **to ~ sb to do sth** jdn anspornen, etw zu tun. **(b)** *(increase) economy, sales etc* ankurbeln; *(incite) response* hervorrufen; *criticism* anregen zu.

**stimulating** ['stɪmjʊleɪtɪŋ] *adj* anregend; *walk* belebend; *prospect* ermunternd; *experience (physically)* erfrischend; *(mentally)* stimulierend.

**stimulation** [ˌstɪmjʊ'leɪʃən] *n* **(a)** *(act) (physical, mental)* Anregung *f*; *(from shower, walk etc)* belebende Wirkung; *(state)* Angeregtheit *f*; *(sexual)* Erregung *f*; *(fig: incentive)* Anreiz *m*; *(intellectual)* Stimulation *f*. **(b)** *(of economy, sales etc)* Ankurbelung *f (to gen)*.

**stimulus** ['stɪmjʊləs] *n, pl* **stimuli** ['stɪmjʊlaɪ] Anreiz *m*; *(inspiration)* Anregung *f*; *(Physiol)* Reiz *m*. **it gave trade new ~** das hat dem Handel neuen Aufschwung gegeben.

**sting** [stɪŋ] *(vb: pret, ptp* **stung***)* **1** *n* **(a)** *(organ: of insect)* Stachel *m*. **(b)** *(wound) (of insect)* Stich *m*; *(of nettle, jellyfish)* Quaddel *f*. **(c)** *(pain) (from needle etc)* Stechen *nt*; *(of antiseptic, ointment, from nettle etc)* Brennen *nt*; *(of whip)* brennender Schmerz. **(d)** *(fig) (of remark, irony)* Stachel *m*; *(of attack, criticism etc)* Schärfe *f*. **to take the ~ out of sth** etw entschärfen; *(out of remark, criticism also)* einer Sache *(dat)* den Stachel nehmen.

**2** *vt* **(a)** *(insect)* stechen; *(jellyfish)* verbrennen. **(b)** *(comments etc)* treffen; *(remorse, conscience)* quälen. **(c)** *(col)* **they really stung you for that** sie haben dich dabei ganz schön ausgenommen; **can I ~ you for a fiver?** kann ich dich um fünf Pfund erleichtern?

**3** *vi (insect)* stechen; *(nettle, jellyfish etc)* brennen; *(burn: eyes, cut, ointment etc)* brennen; *(comments etc)* schmerzen. **smoke makes your eyes ~** Rauch brennt in den Augen.

**stinginess** ['stɪndʒɪnɪs] *n (col)* Geiz *m*, Knickerigkeit *f (col)*.

**stinging nettle** ['stɪŋɪŋˌnetl] *n* Brennessel *f*.

**stingy** ['stɪndʒɪ] *adj (+er) (col) person* geizig, knickerig *(col)*; *sum, portion, donation* schäbig. **to be ~ with sth** mit etw knausern.

**stink** [stɪŋk] *(vb: pret* **stank***, ptp* **stunk***)* **1** *n* Gestank *m*. **to kick up a ~** *(col)* Stunk machen *(col)*. **2** *vi* **(a)** stinken *(of nach)*. **it ~s in here** hier (drin) stinkt's. **(b)** *(fig col) (be disgusting)* zum Kotzen sein *(col)*; *(be suspicious)* stinken *(col)*.

▶**stink out** *vt sep (col) room* verstänkern *(col)*.

**stink bomb** *n* Stinkbombe *f*.

**stinker** ['stɪŋkər] *n (col) (problem)* harte Nuß *(col)*; *(person)* Ekel *nt*.

**stinking** ['stɪŋkɪŋ] **1** *adj (col)* beschissen *(col!)*. **keep your ~ money!** du kannst dein Scheißgeld behalten! *(col!)* **2** *adv (col)* **~ rich** stinkreich *(col)*.

**stint** [stɪnt] **1** *n (period)* Zeit *f*. **to do one's ~** *(work)* seine Arbeit tun; *(share)* sein(en) Teil beitragen; **would you like to do a ~ at the wheel?** möchtest du auch mal das Steuer übernehmen? **2** *vt* knausern mit. **to ~ sb of sth** *of praise, reward* jdm etw vorenthalten; **to ~ oneself (of sth)** sich (mit etw) einschränken.

**stipulate** ['stɪpjʊleɪt] *vt* **(a)** *(make a condition)* zur Auflage machen. **(b)** *delivery date, amount, price* festsetzen; *size* vorschreiben; *conditions* stellen.

**stipulation** [ˌstɪpjʊ'leɪʃən] *n* **(a)** *(condition)* Auflage *f*. **(b)** *see vt (b)* Festsetzung *f*; Vorschreiben *nt*; Stellen *nt*.

**stir** [stɜːr] **1** *n* **(a)** **to give sth a ~** etw rühren; *tea etc* etw umrühren. **(b)** *(fig: excitement)* Aufruhr *m*. **to cause** *or* **create a ~** Aufsehen erregen.

**2** *vt* **(a)** umrühren; *cake mixture* rühren. **~ sugar into the mixture** den Zucker darunterrühren. **(b)** *(move)* bewegen; *limbs* rühren; *water, waves* kräuseln. **come on, ~ yourself** *(col)* komm, beweg dich! *(col)*. **(c)** *(fig) emotions* aufwühlen; *passion* wachrufen; *imagination* anregen; *curiosity* erregen; *(incite) person* anstacheln; *(move) person, heart* rühren. **to ~ sb to do sth** jdn bewegen, etw zu tun; *(incite)* jdn dazu anstacheln, etw zu tun; **to ~ sb into action** jdn zum Handeln bewegen.

**3** *vi* **(a)** sich regen; *(person also)* sich rühren; *(leaves, animal etc)* sich bewegen. **(b)** *(col: through gossip etc)* stänkern *(col)*.

▶**stir up** *vt sep (fig) anger* erregen; *memories* wachrufen; *opposition, discord* erzeugen; *hatred* schüren; *revolution* anzetteln; *mob* aufstacheln. **to ~ ~ trouble** Unruhe stiften; **that'll ~ things ~** das kann heiter werden!

**stir-fry** ['stɜːfraɪ] *vt* (unter Rühren) kurz anbraten.

**stirring** ['stɜːrɪŋ] *adj speech, music* bewegend; *(stronger)* aufwühlend.

**stirrup** ['stɪrəp] *n* Steigbügel *m*.

**stitch** [stɪtʃ] **1** *n* **(a)** Stich *m*; *(in knitting etc)* Masche *f*; *(kind of ~)* *(in knitting etc)* Muster *nt*; *(in embroidery)* Stichart *f*. **to put a few ~es in sth** etw mit ein paar Stichen nähen; **he needed ~es in his arm** sein Arm mußte genäht werden; **to have one's ~es out** die Fäden gezogen bekommen; **a ~ in time saves nine** *(Prov)* was du heute kannst besorgen, das verschiebe nicht auf morgen *(Prov)*. **(b)** *(col: piece of clothing)* **she hadn't a ~ on** sie war splitter(faser)nackt *(col)*. **(c)** *(pain)* Seitenstiche *pl*. **(d)** **to be in ~es** *(col: from laughing)* sich schieflachen *(col)*. **2** *vt (Sew, Med) (also ~ up)* nähen; *tear* zunähen. **I've been ~ed up** *(col: framed)* man hat mich reingelegt *(col)*.

**stoat** [stəʊt] *n* Wiesel *nt*.

**stock** [stɒk] **1** *n* **(a)** *(supply)* Vorrat *m (of an +dat)*; *(Comm)* Bestand *m (of an +dat)*. **to have sth in ~** etw vorrätig haben; **to be in ~/out of ~** *(goods)* vorrätig/nicht vorrätig sein; **to take ~** *(Comm)* Inventur machen; **to take ~ of sb** jdn abschätzen; **to take ~ of the situation** sich *(dat)* über die Situation klarwerden. **(b)** *(live~)* Viehbestand *m*. **(c)** *(Cook)* Brühe *f*. **(d)** *(Fin) (capital)* Aktienkapital *nt*; *(shares held by investor)* Anteil *m*; *(government ~)* Staatsanleihe *f*. **~s and shares** (Aktien und) Wertpapiere *pl*, Effekten *pl*. **(e)** **to be on the ~s** *(ship)* im Bau sein; *(book etc)* in Arbeit sein. **(f)** **~s** *pl (Hist: for punishment)* Stock *m*. **(g)** *(Rail)* **rolling ~** rollendes Material.

**2** *adj attr phrase etc* Standard-.

**3** *vt* **(a)** *(shop etc) goods* führen. **(b)** *cupboard* füllen; *shop also, library* ausstatten; *pond, river* (mit Fischen) besetzen; *farm* mit einem Viehbestand versehen.

▶**stock up** *vi* sich eindecken *(on mit)*.

**stockade** [stɒ'keɪd] *n* Palisade(nzaun *m*) *f*.

**stock:** **~broker** *n* Börsenmakler *m*; **~broking** *n* Effektenhandel *m*; **~ car** *n* **(a)** *(for racing)* Stock Car *m (frisierter, verstärkter älterer Serienwagen)*; **(b)** *(US Rail: cattle truck)* Viehwaggon *m*; **~ company** *n (US)* **(a)** *(Fin)* Aktiengesellschaft *f*; **(b)** *(Theat)* Repertoiretheater *nt*; **~ control** *n* Bestandsüberwachung *f*; **~ cube** *n* Brüh- *or* Suppenwürfel *m*; **~ exchange** *n* Börse *f*; **~holder** *n* Aktionär(in *f*) *m*.

**Stockholm** ['stɒkhəʊm] *n* Stockholm *nt*.

**stocking** ['stɒkɪŋ] **1** *n* Strumpf *m*. **2** *vt* **in one's ~ed feet** in Strümpfen.

**stocking filler** *n* kleines Geschenk *(für den Weihnachtsstrumpf)*.

**stock-in-trade** [ˌstɒkɪn'treɪd] *n (tools, materials, fig)* Handwerkszeug *nt.*

**stockist** ['stɒkɪst] *n (Brit)* Händler *m.*

**stock:** ~ **market** *n* Börse(nmarkt *m*) *f*; ~**pile 1** *n* Vorrat *m (of an +dat)*; *(of weapons)* Lager *nt*; **2** *vt* Vorräte an *(+dat)* ... anlegen; *(pej)* horten; ~**room** *n* Lager(raum *m*) *nt*; ~**taking** *n (Brit)* Inventur *f*; *(fig)* Bestandsaufnahme *f.*

**stocky** ['stɒkɪ] *adj (+er)* stämmig.

**stockyard** ['stɒkjɑːd] *n* Viehhof *m*; *(abattoir)* Schlachthof *m.*

**stodge** [stɒdʒ] *n (col)* Pampe *f (col).*

**stodgy** ['stɒdʒɪ] *adj (+er) food* pampig *(col)*, schwer; *subject* trocken; *book* schwer verdaulich.

**stoic** ['stəʊɪk] **1** *n* Stoiker *m.* **2** *adj* stoisch.

**stoical** ['stəʊɪkəl] *adj* stoisch.

**stoicism** ['stəʊɪsɪzəm] *n* stoische Ruhe.

**stoke** [stəʊk] *vt furnace* (be)heizen; *fire* schüren.

**stoker** ['stəʊkər] *n* Heizer *m.*

**stole** *pret of* **steal.**

**stolen** ['stəʊlən] **1** *ptp of* **steal. 2** *adj* gestohlen. ~ **goods** Diebesgut *nt.*

**stolid** ['stɒlɪd] *adj person* phlegmatisch, stur *(pej).*

**stomach** ['stʌmək] **1** *n (abdomen)* Magen *m*; *(belly, paunch)* Bauch *m*; *(fig: appetite)* Lust *f (for auf +acc).* **to hit sb in the** ~ jdn in die Bauchgegend schlagen; **on an empty** ~ *drink etc* auf leeren *or* nüchternen Magen; **on an empty/a full** ~ *swim, drive etc* mit leerem/vollem Magen; **I have no** ~ **for that** das ist mir zuwider; **he doesn't have the** ~ **for it** *(guts)* dazu hat er nicht den Mumm *(col).* **2** *vt (col) behaviour, cruelty* vertragen; *person, film etc* ausstehen.

**stomach** *in cpds* Magen-; ~**-ache** *n* Magenschmerzen *pl*; ~ **trouble** *n* Magenbeschwerden *pl*; ~ **ulcer** *n* Magengeschwür *nt*; ~ **upset** *n* Magenverstimmung *f.*

**stomp** [stɒmp] *vi* stapfen.

**stone** [stəʊn] **1** *n* (a) Stein *m.* **a** ~**'s throw from the station** nur einen Steinwurf *or* Katzensprung vom Bahnhof entfernt; **to leave no** ~ **unturned** nichts unversucht lassen. **(b)** *(Brit: weight)* 6,35 kg. **2** *adj* Stein-, aus Stein. **3** *vt* (a) *(throw ~s at)* mit Steinen bewerfen; *(kill)* steinigen. **(b)** *fruit* entsteinen. **(c)** *(col)* **to be** ~**d (out of one's mind)** total weg sein *(col).*

**stone: S**~ **Age** *n* Steinzeit *f*; ~**-cold 1** *adj* eiskalt; **2** *adv* ~**-cold sober** stocknüchtern *(col)*; ~**-dead** *adj* mausetot *(col)*; ~**-deaf** *adj* stocktaub *(col)*; ~**mason** *n* Steinmetz *m*; ~**wall** *vi (fig: esp Parl)* obstruieren; *(in answering questions)* ausweichen; *(Sport)* mauern *(Sport sl)*; ~**ware** *n* Steingut *nt*; ~**work** *n* Mauerwerk *nt.*

**stony** ['stəʊnɪ] *adj (+er) ground* steinig; *(fig) glance, silence* steinern.

**stony-broke** ['stəʊnɪ'brəʊk] *adj (Brit col)* völlig abgebrannt.

**stood** [stʊd] *pret, ptp of* **stand.**

**stooge** [stuːdʒ] *n (col)* Handlanger *m*; *(comedian's)* Stichwortgeber *m.*

**stool** [stuːl] *n (seat)* Hocker *m*; *(foot* ~, *kitchen* ~, *milking* ~ *also)* Schemel *m*; *(folding)* Klappstuhl *m.* **to fall between two** ~**s** sich zwischen zwei Stühle setzen; *(be neither one thing nor the other)* weder dem einen noch dem anderen gerecht werden.

**stool pigeon** *n (col) (decoy)* Lockvogel *m*; *(informer)* Spitzel *m.*

**stoop** [stuːp] **1** *n* Gebeugtheit *f*; *(deformity)* krummer Rücken, Buckel *m.* **to walk with a** ~ gebeugt gehen. **2** *vi* sich beugen *(over über +acc)*; *(also* ~ **down)** sich bücken; *(have a* ~*)* gebeugt gehen. **to** ~

**to sth/to doing sth** *(fig)* sich zu etw hergeben/sich dazu hergeben, etw zu tun.

**stop** [stɒp] **1** *n* (a) *(act of* ~*ping)* Halt *m.* **to bring sth to a** ~ *(lit)* etw anhalten *or* stoppen; *traffic* etw zum Erliegen bringen; *(fig) meeting, development* einer Sache *(dat)* ein Ende machen; *conversation* etw verstummen lassen; **to come to a** ~ *(car, machine)* anhalten; *(traffic)* stocken; *(meeting, rain)* aufhören; *(conversation)* verstummen; **to put a** ~ **to sth** einer Sache *(dat)* einen Riegel vorschieben.

**(b)** *(stay)* Aufenthalt *m*; *(break)* Pause *f*; *(Aviat)* Zwischenlandung *f.* **to make a** ~ *(bus, train, tram)* (an)halten; *(plane, ship)* (Zwischen)station machen; **to have a** ~ **for coffee** eine Kaffeepause machen; **to have a** ~ haltmachen; **to work without a** ~ ohne Unterbrechung arbeiten.

**(c)** *(~ping place)* Station *f*; *(for bus)* Haltestelle *f.*

**(d)** *(esp Brit: punctuation mark)* Punkt *m.*

**(e)** *(stopper) (for door etc)* Sperre *f*; *(on typewriter)* Feststelltaste *f.*

**(f)** *(on organ)* Registerzug *m.* **to pull out all the** ~**s** *(fig)* alle Register ziehen.

**2** *vt* (a) *(when moving) person* anhalten; *engine, machine etc* abstellen; *blow* auffangen; *traffic (hold up)* aufhalten; *(bring to standstill)* zum Erliegen bringen; *(policeman)* anhalten; *(keep out) noise, light* abfangen, auffangen. ~ **thief!** haltet den Dieb!

**(b)** *(from continuing) rumour, crime* ein Ende machen *(+dat)*; *nonsense, noise* unterbinden; *match, conversation, work* beenden; *development, attack* aufhalten; *(temporarily)* unterbrechen; *flow of blood* stillen; *speaker, speech* unterbrechen; *production* zum Stillstand bringen; *(temporarily)* unterbrechen.

**(c)** *(cease)* aufhören mit. **to** ~ **doing sth** aufhören, etw zu tun; **she never** ~**s talking** sie redet ununterbrochen; **to** ~ **smoking** mit dem Rauchen aufhören; *(put out cigarette etc)* das Rauchen einstellen; ~ **it!** hör auf!

**(d)** *(suspend)* stoppen; *payments, production etc* einstellen; *cheque, electricity* sperren; *subsidy, grant etc* streichen; *proceedings* abbrechen; *(cancel) subscription* kündigen.

**(e)** *(prevent from happening) sth* verhindern; *(prevent from doing) sb* abhalten. **to** ~ **oneself** sich zurückhalten, sich bremsen *(col)*; **there's no** ~**ping him** *(col)* er ist nicht zu bremsen *(col)*; **to** ~ **sb (from) doing sth** jdn davon abhalten *or (physically)* daran hindern, etw zu tun; *(put a* ~ *to)* dafür sorgen, daß jd etw nicht mehr tut; **to** ~ **sth (from) happening** *(prevent)* (es) verhindern, daß etw geschieht; **how can we** ~ **the baby (from) crying?** *(prevent)* was können wir tun, damit das Baby nicht schreit?; **to** ~ **the thief (from) escaping** den Dieb an der Flucht hindern.

**(f)** *(block)* verstopfen; *(fill) tooth* plombieren; *(fig) gap* füllen; *leak of information* stopfen.

**3** *vi* (a) *(halt)* anhalten; *(train, car also)* halten; *(traveller)* haltmachen; *(pedestrian, clock)* stehenbleiben; *(engine, machine)* stillstehen. ~**!** halt!, stopp!; **we** ~**ped for a drink at the pub** wir machten in der Kneipe Station, um etwas zu trinken; **to** ~ **at nothing (to do sth)** *(fig)* vor nichts haltmachen(, um etw zu tun). **(b)** *(finish, cease)* aufhören; *(pain also)* weggehen; *(also fig: heart)* stillstehen; *(production, payments)* eingestellt werden; *(show, match, film)* zu Ende sein; *(music, speaker also)* verstummen. **to** ~ **doing sth** aufhören, etw zu tun, mit etw aufhören; **he never knows when to** ~ er weiß nie, wann er aufhören muß. **(c)** *(col: stay)* bleiben *(at in +dat, with bei, at home zu Hause).*

▶**stop away** *vi (col)* wegbleiben.
▶**stop by** *vi* kurz vorbeischauen. **to ~ ~ (at) sb's house** bei jdm hereinschauen *(col)*.
▶**stop down** *vi (Phot)* die Blende schließen.
▶**stop in** *vi (col)* zu Hause bleiben.
▶**stop off** *vi (kurz)* haltmachen *(at sb's* bei jdm*)*.
▶**stop over** *vi* kurz haltmachen; *(on travels)* Zwischenstation machen *(in* in +*dat)*; *(Aviat)* zwischenlanden.
▶**stop up 1** *vt sep* verstopfen; *crack, hole also* zustopfen. **2** *vi (col: stay up)* aufbleiben.
**stop:** ~**cock** *n* Absperrhahn *m*; ~**gap** *n (thing)* Notbehelf *m*; *(scheme)* Notlösung *f*; *(person)* Lückenbüßer *m*; ~**light** *n (brake light)* Bremslicht *nt*; *(US: traffic light)* rotes Licht; ~**over** *n* Zwischenstation *f*; *(Aviat)* Zwischenlandung *f*.
**stoppage** ['stɒpɪdʒ] *n* **(a)** *(in work)* Unterbrechung *f*; *(in traffic)* Stockung *f*; *(because of strike etc)* Stopp *m*; *(strike)* Streik *m*. **(b)** *(of pay, cheque)* Sperrung *f*; *(deduction)* Abzug *m*. **(c)** *(blockage)* Verstopfung *f*, Stau *m*.
**stopper** ['stɒpəʳ] *n (plug)* Stöpsel *m*.
**stopping train** ['stɒpɪŋˌtreɪn] *n* Nahverkehrszug, Bummelzug *(col) m*.
**stop:** ~**press** *n (esp Brit) (news)* letzte Meldungen *pl*; ~ **sign** *n* Stoppschild *nt*; ~**watch** *n* Stoppuhr *f*.
**storage** ['stɔːrɪdʒ] *n* **(a)** *(of goods, food)* Lagerung *f*; *(of books, documents)* Aufbewahrung *f*; *(of electricity, data)* Speicherung *f*, Speichern *nt*. **to put sth into ~** etw unterstellen, etw (ein)lagern. **(b)** = ~ **space**.
**storage:** ~ **battery** *n* Akkumulator *m*; ~ **capacity** *n (of warehouse etc)* Lagerfläche *f*; *(of computer)* Speicherkapazität *f*; ~ **heater** *n* (Nacht)speicherofen *m*; ~ **space** *n* Lagerraum *m*; *(in house)* Stauraum *m*; ~ **tank** *n* Sammelbehälter *m*.
**store** [stɔːʳ] **1** *n* **(a)** *(stock)* Vorrat *m (of an* +*dat)*; *(fig)* Fülle *f*, Reichtum *m (of an* +*dat)*. ~**s** *pl (supplies)* Vorräte *pl*; **to lay** *or* **get in a ~ of food** einen Lebensmittelvorrat anlegen; **to be in ~ for sb** jdm bevorstehen; **to have a surprise in ~ for sb** für jdn eine Überraschung auf Lager haben; **what has the future in ~ for us?** was wird uns *(dat)* die Zukunft bringen?; **to set great/little ~ by sth** viel/wenig von etw halten. **(b)** *(esp US: shop)* Laden *m*, Geschäft *nt*; *(department ~)* Kaufhaus *nt*. **2** *vt* lagern; *documents* aufbewahren; *furniture* unterstellen; *(in depository)* einlagern; *information, heat* speichern; *(keep in reserve, collect: also ~ up)* Vorräte an (+*dat*) ... anschaffen. **to ~ sth away** etw verwahren. **to ~ up trouble for oneself** sich *(dat)* nur Schwierigkeiten einhandeln.
**store:** ~**house** *n* Lager (haus) *nt*; *(fig)* Fundgrube *f*; ~ **keeper** *n (in ~house)* Lagerverwalter *m*; *(esp US: shopkeeper)* Ladenbesitzer (in *f*) *m*; ~**room** *n* Lagerraum *m*; *(for food)* Vorratskammer *f*.
**storey, (US) story** ['stɔːrɪ] *n, pl* -**s** *or (US)* **stories** Stock (werk *nt*) *m*, Etage *f*. **a nine-~ building** ein neunstöckiges Gebäude; **on the second ~** im zweiten Stock; *(US)* im ersten Stock.
**stork** [stɔːk] *n* Storch *m*.
**storm** [stɔːm] **1** *n* **(a)** *(lit)* Unwetter *nt*; *(thunder~)* Gewitter *nt*; *(strong wind)* Sturm *m*. **there is a ~ blowing** es stürmt; **a ~ in a teacup** *(fig)* ein Sturm im Wasserglas. **(b)** *(fig) (of abuse)* Flut *f (of von)*; *(of applause, criticism)* Sturm *m (of gen)*; *(of blows, missiles)* Hagel *m (of von)*; *(outcry)* Aufruhr *m*. ~ **of protest** Proteststurm *m*. **(c)** **to take sth/sb by ~** *(Mil, fig)* etw/jdn im Sturm erobern. **2** *vt* stürmen. **3** *vi* **(a)** *(talk angrily)* wüten *(at gegen)*. **(b)** *(move violently)* stürmen.

**storm:** ~ **cloud** *n (lit, fig)* Gewitterwolke *f*; ~ **cone** *n* Sturmkegel *m*; ~ **door** *n* äußere Windfangtür; ~ **force** *n* Windstärke *f* 10; ~ **force wind** *n* schwerer Sturm; ~ **troops** *npl* Sturmtruppe *f*.
**stormy** ['stɔːmɪ] *adj (+er) (lit, fig)* stürmisch; *discussion also, temper* hitzig; *protests* heftig.
**story¹** ['stɔːrɪ] *n* **(a)** *(tale, account)* Geschichte *f*; *(Liter also)* Erzählung *f*; *(joke)* Witz *m*. **it's a long ~** das ist eine lange Geschichte; **the ~ of her life** ihre Lebensgeschichte; **that's the ~ of my life** *(fig)* das war schon immer mein Problem; **that's another ~** das ist eine andere Geschichte; **his ~ is that ...** er behauptet, daß ...; **that's not the whole ~** das ist nicht die ganze Wahrheit; **the marks tell their own ~** die Spuren sprechen für sich; **to cut a long ~ short** um es kurz zu machen, der langen Rede kurzer Sinn; **it's the (same) old ~** es ist (immer) das alte Lied; **but it's another ~ now** aber jetzt sieht die Sache anders aus. **(b)** *(Press) (event)* Geschichte *f*; *(newspaper ~)* Artikel *m*. **(c)** *(plot)* Handlung *f*. **(d)** *(col: lie)* Märchen *nt*. **to tell stories** Märchen erzählen.
**story²** *n (US)* = **storey**.
**story:** ~**board** *n (TV, Film)* Storyboard *nt*; ~**book 1** *n* Geschichtenbuch *nt*; **2** *adj attr castles, romance etc* märchenhaft; ~**line** *n* Handlung *f*; ~**teller** *n (narrator)* Geschichtenerzähler (in *f*) *m*.
**stout** [staʊt] **1** *adj (+er)* **(a)** *(corpulent)* korpulent. **(b)** *(strong) stick, horse etc* kräftig; *door, rope, gate* stark. **(c)** *(brave) denial* entschieden. **2** *n* Starkbier *nt*; *(sweet ~)* ≈ Malzbier *nt*.
**stout-hearted** [ˌstaʊtˈhɑːtɪd] *adj* tapfer.
**stoutly** ['staʊtlɪ] *adv (strongly) made* solide; *(resolutely) resist, defend* tapfer, beherzt; *refuse, deny* entschieden.
**stoutness** ['staʊtnɪs] *n see adj* **(a)** Korpulenz *f*. **(b)** Kräftigkeit *f*; Stärke *f*. **(c)** Tapferkeit *f*; Entschiedenheit *f*.
**stove** [staʊv] *n* Ofen *m*; *(for cooking)* Herd *m*. **electric/gas ~** Elektro-/Gasherd *m*.
**stove in** *pret, ptp of* **stave in**.
**stow** [staʊ] *vt* **(a)** *(Naut) cargo* verladen, (ver)stauen. **(b)** *(put away: also ~ away)* verstauen *(in in +dat)*.
▶**stow away** *vi* als blinder Passagier fahren.
**stowaway** ['staʊəweɪ] *n* blinder Passagier.
**straddle** ['strædl] *vt (standing)* breitbeinig stehen über (+*dat)*; *(sitting)* rittlings sitzen auf (+*dat)*; *(jumping)* grätschen über (+*acc)*; *(fig) differences* überbrücken; *two continents* überspannen. **to ~ the border/river** sich über beide Seiten der Grenze/beide Ufer des Flusses erstrecken.
**strafe** [streɪf] *vt* unter Beschuß nehmen.
**straggle** ['strægl] *vi (spread untidily) (houses, trees)* verstreut liegen; *(hair)* (unordentlich) hängen; *(plant)* in alle Richtungen wuchern. **to ~ behind** zurückbleiben, hinterherzockeln *(col)*.
**straggler** ['stræglə'] *n* Nachzügler *m*.
**straggling** ['stræglɪŋ] *adj* **(a)** *children, cattle etc* weit verteilt; *(~ behind)* zurückgeblieben; *village* sich lang hinziehend; *houses* zerstreut liegend; *group, row* auseinandergezogen. **(b)** *(col: also* **straggly)** *hair* zottig; *plant* wuchernd.
**straight** [streɪt] **1** *adj (+er)* **(a)** gerade; *posture also* aufrecht; *hair* glatt; *skirt, trousers* gerade geschnitten. **your tie isn't ~** deine Krawatte sitzt schief; **the picture isn't ~** das Bild hängt schief; **as ~ as a die** kerzengerade; *road* schnurgerade; **to keep a ~ face** keine Miene verziehen; **to be (all) ~** *(in order)* in Ordnung sein; *(fig: clarified also)* (völlig) geklärt sein; **to put things ~** *(tidy)* alles in Ordnung brin-

gen; *(clarify)* alles klären; **to put sb ~ about sth** jdm etw klarmachen; **he soon put me ~!** er hat mich eines Besseren belehrt.

   **(b)** *(frank) answer, talking* offen; *denial, refusal* direkt; *(honest) person, dealings, advice* ehrlich. **to be ~ with sb** offen zu jdm sein.

   **(c)** *(plain) drink* pur; *(Pol) fight* direkt; *choice* einfach; *(col) (heterosexual)* normal, hetero *(col)*; *(conventional)* etabliert, spießig *(pej)*. **to have a ~ choice between A and B** nur die Wahl zwischen A und B haben.

   **(d)** *(continuous)* ununterbrochen. **~ run** *(Cards)* Sequenz *f*; **our team had ten ~ wins** unsere Mannschaft gewann zehnmal hintereinander.

   **(e)** *(Theat) production* konventionell; *actor* ernsthaft. **a ~ play** ein reines Drama.

   **2** *adv* **(a)** *hold, walk, shoot* gerade; *stand up also* aufrecht; *leap at, aim for, above, across* direkt. **~ through sth** glatt durch etw; **he came ~ at me** er kam direkt auf mich zu; **it went ~ up in the air** es flog senkrecht in die Luft; **to look ~ ahead** geradeaus sehen; **the town lay ~ ahead of us** die Stadt lag direkt vor uns; **to drive ~ on** geradeaus weiterfahren; **to be going ~** *(criminal)* keine krummen Sachen (mehr) machen *(col)*.

   **(b)** *(directly)* direkt; *(immediately)* sofort. **I went ~ home** ich ging direkt nach Hause; **to look sb ~ in the eye** jdm direkt in die Augen sehen; **~ after this** sofort danach; **~ away** *or* **off** sofort, auf der Stelle; **to come ~ to the point** gleich zur Sache kommen; **ten wins ~ off** zehn Siege hintereinander.

   **(c)** *(clearly) think, see* klar; *(frankly)* offen, ohne Umschweife. **~ out** *(col)* rundheraus.

   **(d)** *drink* pur.

   **3** *n* **(~ part, on race track)** Gerade *f*; *(road, rail)* gerade Strecke. **the final ~** die Zielgerade; **to keep on the ~ and narrow** dafür sorgen, daß man nicht auf die schiefe Bahn gerät; **to cut sth on the ~** etw gerade (ab)schneiden.

**straighten** ['streɪtn] **1** *vt* **(a)** *hat* gerade aufsetzen; *tie* geradeziehen; *shoulders* straffen. **(b)** *(also ~ out: make straight)* gerademachen; *picture* gerade hinhängen; *road, river* begradigen; *tablecloth* geradeziehen; *wire* geradebiegen; *hair* glätten. **(c)** *(also ~ up: tidy)* in Ordnung bringen. **(d)** *(also ~ out: put right) problem, situation* klären. **2** *vi (also ~ out: road, plant etc)* gerade werden; *(hair)* glatt werden. **to ~ up** *(person)* sich aufrichten. **3** *vr* **to ~ oneself (up)** sich aufrichten; **the problem will soon ~ itself out** das Problem wird sich bald von selbst erledigen.

**straight: ~faced** [streɪt'feɪst] **1** *adv* ohne eine Miene zu verziehen; **2** *adj* **to be ~faced** keine Miene verziehen; **~forward** *adj (honest) person* aufrichtig; *explanation, look also* offen, freimütig; *(simple) question, problem* einfach.

**strain¹** [streɪn] **1** *n* **(a)** *(Mech)* Belastung *f*; *(on beams, floor also)* Druck *m*. **the ~ on a rope** die Seilspannung; **can you take some of the ~?** können Sie mal mit festhalten/mit ziehen?; **to put a (great) ~ on sth** etw (stark) belasten; **to show signs of ~** Zeichen von Überlastung zeigen.

   **(b)** *(fig: mental, economic etc)* Belastung *f (on* für*)*; *(effort)* Anstrengung *f*; *(pressure) (of job etc also)* Beanspruchung *f (of* durch*)*; *(of responsibility)* Last *f*; *(muscle-~)* (Muskel)Überanstrengung *f (on* gen*)*. **to be under a lot of ~** stark beansprucht sein; **I find her/that a bit of a ~** ich finde sie/das ziemlich anstrengend; **to put a (great) ~ on sb/sth** jdn/etw stark belasten; **to show signs of ~** Zeichen von Überlastung zeigen;

**to be under ~** großen Belastungen ausgesetzt sein; **the ~s of modern life** die Belastungen *or* der Streß des heutigen Lebens.

   **(c)** **~s** *pl (of instrument, tune)* Klänge *pl*; **to the ~s of** zu den Klängen *(+gen)*.

   **2** *vt* **(a)** *(stretch)* spannen. **(b)** *(put ~ on) rope, relationship, budget* belasten; *nerves, patience also* strapazieren; *(put too much ~ on)* überlasten; *meaning* dehnen. **to ~ one's ears/eyes to ...** angestrengt lauschen/gucken, um zu ...; **to ~ every nerve** jeden Nerv anspannen; **to ~ oneself** sich anstrengen; *(excessively)* sich überanstrengen. **(c)** *(Med) muscle* zerren; *back, eyes, voice* strapazieren; *(excessively)* überanstrengen; *heart* belasten; *(excessively)* überlasten. **(d)** *(filter)* (durch)sieben; *(pour water off) vegetables* abgießen. **to ~ off water** Wasser abgießen.

   **3** *vi (exert effort)* sich anstrengen; *(pull)* zerren, ziehen; *(fig: strive)* sich bemühen. **to ~ to do sth** sich anstrengen, etw zu tun; **to ~ at sth** sich mit etw abmühen; *(pull)* an etw *(dat)* ziehen.

**strain²** *n* **(a)** *(streak)* Hang, Zug *m*; *(hereditary)* Veranlagung *f*. **a ~ of madness** eine Veranlagung zum Wahnsinn. **(b)** *(breed) (animals)* Rasse *f*; *(of plants)* Sorte *f*; *(of virus etc)* Art *f*.

**strained** [streɪnd] *adj* **(a)** *muscle* gezerrt; *back, eyes* überanstrengt. **(b)** *expression, style* unnatürlich; *smile, conversation* gezwungen; *meeting* steif; *voice, relations, atmosphere, nerves* (an)gespannt. **he looked rather ~** er sah ziemlich abgespannt aus.

**strainer** ['streɪnəʳ] *n (Cook)* Sieb *nt*.

**strait** [streɪt] *n (Geog)* Meerenge *f*. **the ~s of Dover** die Straße von Dover; **to be in dire ~s** in großen Nöten sein.

**straitened** ['streɪtnd] *adj* **in ~ circumstances** in eingeschränkten Verhältnissen.

**strait: ~jacket** *n (lit, fig)* Zwangsjacke *f*; **~-laced** [streɪt'leɪst] *adj* prüde, spießig *(col)*.

**strand** [strænd] *n* Strang *m*; *(of hair)* Strähne *f*; *(of thread)* Faden *m*; *(of wire)* Litze *f*; *(of beads)* Schnur *f*.

**stranded** ['strændɪd] *adj* **to be ~** *(ship, fish, shipwrecked person)* gestrandet sein; **to be (left) ~** *(person)* festsitzen; *(without money also)* auf dem trockenen sitzen *(col)*.

**strange** [streɪndʒ] *adj (+er)* **(a)** seltsam, merkwürdig. **(b)** *(unfamiliar) surroundings* fremd; *(unaccustomed) work* ungewohnt. **I felt rather ~ at first** zuerst fühlte ich mich ziemlich fremd; **I feel ~ in a skirt** ich komme mir in einem Rock komisch vor *(col)*.

**strangely** ['streɪndʒlɪ] *adv (oddly)* seltsam, merkwürdig; *act, behave also* komisch *(col)*. **~ enough** seltsamerweise, merkwürdigerweise.

**strangeness** ['streɪndʒnɪs] *n see adj* **(a)** Seltsamkeit, Merkwürdigkeit *f*. **(b)** Fremdheit *f*; Ungewohntheit *f*.

**stranger** ['streɪndʒəʳ] *n* Fremde(r) *mf*. **he's a perfect ~ to me** ich kenne ihn überhaupt nicht; **I'm a ~ here myself** ich bin selbst fremd hier; **he is no ~ to London** er kennt sich in London aus; **he is no ~ to suffering** Leid ist ihm nicht fremd; **hullo, ~!** *(col)* hallo, lange nicht gesehen.

**strangle** ['stræŋgl] *vt (murder)* erwürgen; *(fig) cry* ersticken.

**stranglehold** ['stræŋgl,həʊld] *n (fig)* absolute Machtposition *(on* gegenüber*)*. **they have a ~ on us** *(fig)* sie haben uns in der Zange.

**strangler** ['stræŋgləʳ] *n* Würger(in *f*) *m*.

**strangulation** [ˌstræŋgjʊ'leɪʃən] *n* Erwürgen *nt*. **death was due to ~** der Tod trat durch Ersticken ein.

**strap** [stræp] **1** *n* Riemen *m*; *(for safety also)* Gurt *m*; *(watch ~)* Band *nt*; *(shoulder ~)* Träger *m*. **to give sb the ~** jdn verprügeln. **2** *vt* **to ~ sth onto sth** etw auf etw *(acc)* schnallen; **to ~ sb/sth down** jdn/ etw festschnallen; **to ~ sb/oneself in** *(in car, plane)* jdn/sich anschnallen.

**strap-hanging** ['stræp,hæŋɪŋ] *n* Pendeln *nt* *(als stehender Fahrgast)*.

**strapless** ['stræplɪs] *adj* trägerlos; *dress also* schulterfrei.

**strapping** ['stræpɪŋ] *adj (col)* stramm.

**Strasbourg** ['stræzbɜːg] *n* Straßburg *nt*.

**strata** ['strɑːtə] *pl of* **stratum**.

**stratagem** ['strætɪdʒəm] *n (Mil)* Kriegslist *f*; *(artifice)* List *f*.

**strategic** [strə'tiːdʒɪk] *adj* strategisch; *(strategically important)* strategisch wichtig; *(fig also)* taktisch.

**strategically** [strə'tiːdʒɪkəlɪ] *adv* strategisch; *(fig also)* taktisch. **to be ~ placed** eine strategisch günstige Stellung haben.

**strategist** ['strætɪdʒɪst] *n* Stratege *m*; *(fig also)* Taktiker(in *f*) *m*.

**strategy** ['strætɪdʒɪ] *n* **(a)** *(Mil)* Strategie *f*; *(Sport, fig also)* Taktik *f*. **(b)** *(art of ~)* *(Mil)* Kriegskunst *f*; *(fig)* Taktieren *nt*.

**stratosphere** ['strætəʊsfɪər] *n* Stratosphäre *f*.

**stratum** ['strɑːtəm] *n, pl* **strata** *(Geol, fig)* Schicht *f*.

**straw** [strɔː] **1** *n* **(a)** *(stalk)* Strohhalm *m*; *(collectively)* Stroh *nt no pl*. **it's the last ~!** *(col)* das ist der Gipfel! *(col)*; **to clutch at ~s** sich an einen Strohhalm klammern. **(b)** *(drinking ~)* Strohhalm *m*. **2** *adj attr* Stroh-; *basket* aus Stroh.

**strawberry** ['strɔːbərɪ] *n* Erdbeere *f*.

**straw:** **~-coloured, ~-colored** *(US) adj* strohfarben; *hair* strohblond; **~ hat** *n* Strohhut *m*.

**stray** [streɪ] **1** *vi (also ~ away)* sich verirren; *(also ~ about)* (umher)streunen; *(fig: thoughts, speaker)* abschweifen. **to ~ (away) from sth** *(lit, fig)* von etw abkommen. **2** *adj child, bullet, cattle* verirrt; *cat, dog etc* streunend *attr*; *(ownerless)* herrenlos; *(isolated) remarks, houses* vereinzelt; *(single) remark* einzeln; *(occasional)* gelegentlich; *thoughts* flüchtig. **3** *n (dog, cat)* streunendes Tier; *(ownerless)* herrenloses Tier.

**streak** [striːk] **1** *n* Streifen *m*; *(of light)* Strahl *m*; *(in hair)* Strähne *f*; *(of fat also)* Schicht *f*; *(fig) (trace)* Spur *f*; *(of jealousy, meanness etc)* Zug *m*; *(of madness, humour)* Anflug *m*. **like a ~ of lightning** wie der Blitz; **a winning/losing ~** eine Glücks-/ Pechsträhne. **2** *vt* streifen. **the sky was ~ed with red** der Himmel hatte rote Streifen; **~ed with dirt/ paint** schmutzverschmiert/mit Farbe beschmiert; **to have one's hair ~ed** sich *(dat)* Strähnen ins Haar färben lassen. **3** *vi* **(a)** *(lightning)* zucken; *(col: move quickly)* flitzen *(col)*. **to ~ along/past** entlang-/ vorbeiflitzen *(col)*. **(b)** *(run naked)* blitzen.

**streaker** ['striːkər] *n* Blitzer(in *f*) *m*.

**streaky** ['striːkɪ] *adj (+er) bacon* durchwachsen.

**stream** [striːm] **1** *n* **(a)** *(small river)* Bach *m*; *(current)* Strömung *f*. **to go with/against the ~** *(lit, fig)* mit dem/gegen den Strom schwimmen. **(b)** *(of liquid, people)* Strom *m*; *(of light, tears)* Flut *f*; *(of words, abuse)* Schwall *m*. **(c)** *(Brit Sch)* Leistungsgruppe *f*. **2** *vt* **(a)** **the walls ~ed water** von den Wänden rann das Wasser; **his face ~ed blood** Blut strömte ihm übers Gesicht. **(b)** *(Brit Sch)* in (Leistungs)gruppen einteilen. **3** *vi (lit, fig)* strömen; *(eyes)* tränen. **the walls were ~ing with water** die Wände trieften vor Nässe; **the rain was ~ing down** es regnete in Strömen; **tears ~ed down her face**

Tränen rannen über ihr Gesicht.

▶**stream in** *vi* herein-/hineinströmen.

▶**stream out** *vi* heraus-/hinausströmen *(of* aus*)*.

▶**stream past** *vi* vorbeiströmen *(prep obj* an +*dat)*.

**streamer** ['striːmər] *n (flag)* Banner *nt*; *(made of paper)* Luftschlange *f*.

**stream feed** *n (on photocopier)* automatischer Papiereinzug.

**streamline** ['striːmlaɪn] *vt (lit)* Stromlinienform geben (+*dat)*; *(fig)* rationalisieren.

**streamlined** ['striːmlaɪnd] *adj wing* windschlüpfig; *car, plane* stromlinienförmig; *(fig)* rationalisiert.

**street** [striːt] **1** *n* Straße *f*. **in** *or* **on the ~** auf der Straße; **it's right up my ~** *(fig col)* das ist genau mein Fall *(col)*; **to be ~s ahead of** *or* **better than sb** *(fig col)* jdm haushoch überlegen sein *(col)*; **to take to the ~s** *(demonstrators)* auf die Straße gehen; **to be on the ~s** *(prostitute)* auf den Strich gehen *(col)*; *(homeless)* auf der Straße stehen. **2** *adj attr* Straßen-.

**street:** **~car** *n (US)* Straßenbahn *f*; **~ cleaner** *n (esp US)* Straßenkehrer(in *f*) *m*; **~ cred** *n (col)* Image *nt*; **~ fighting** *n* Straßenkämpfe *pl*; **~ lamp** *n* Straßenlaterne *f*; **~ level** *n* **at ~ level** zu ebener Erde; **~ light** *n* Straßenlaterne *f*; **~ lighting** *n* Straßenbeleuchtung *f*; **~ map** *n* Stadtplan *m*; **~ market** *n* Straßenmarkt *m*; **~ plan** *n* **= ~ map**; **~ sweeper** *n* Straßenkehrer(in *f*) *m*; **~ trader** *n* Straßenhändler(in *f*) *m*; **~ value** *n* Verkaufswert *m*; **~walker** *n* Prostituierte *f*; **~wise** *adj* **to be ~wise** wissen, wo's lang geht *(col)*.

**strength** [streŋθ] *n* **(a)** *(lit, fig)* Stärke *f*; *(of person, feelings)* Kraft *f*; *(of table, wall)* Stabilität *f*; *(of conviction, views)* Festigkeit *f*; *(of argument, evidence)* Überzeugungskraft *f*; *(of mixture)* Konzentration *f*. **~ of character/will** Charakter-/Willensstärke *f*; **on the ~ of sth** auf Grund einer Sache *(gen)*; **his ~ failed him** ihn verließen die Kräfte; **to save one's ~** mit seinen Kräften haushalten; **when she has her ~ back** wenn sie wieder bei Kräften ist; **to go from ~ to ~** einen Erfolg nach dem anderen haben. **(b)** *(numbers)* (An)zahl *f*; *(Mil)* Stärke *f*. **to be up to/ below ~** (die) volle Stärke/nicht die volle Stärke haben; **the police were there in ~** ein starkes Polizeiaufgebot war anwesend; **they came in ~** sie kamen in großer Zahl.

**strengthen** ['streŋθən] **1** *vt* stärken; *building, protest* verstärken; *person (lit)* Kraft geben (+*dat)*; *(fig: in opinion)* bestärken (in in +*dat)*; *currency, market* festigen; *affection also, effect* vergrößern. **2** *vi* stärker werden.

**strenuous** ['strenjʊəs] *adj* **(a)** *(exhausting)* anstrengend; *march, game also* ermüdend. **(b)** *(energetic) supporter, support* unermüdlich; *effort, denial* hartnäckig; *conflict, protest* heftig.

**strenuously** ['strenjʊəslɪ] *adv see adj* (b).

**stress** [stres] **1** *n* **(a)** *(strain)* Belastung *f*, Streß *m*; *(Med)* Überlastung *f*, Streß *m*. **the ~es and strains of modern life** die Belastungen des heutigen Lebens; **times of ~** Zeiten *pl* großer Belastung; **to be under ~** großen Belastungen ausgesetzt sein; *(as regards work)* unter Streß stehen, im Streß sein. **(b)** *(accent)* Betonung *f*; *(fig: emphasis)* Akzent *m*. **to put** *or* **lay (great) ~ on sth** großen Wert auf etw *(acc)* legen; *on fact, detail* etw (besonders) betonen. **(c)** *(Mech)* Belastung *f*. **2** *vt (lit, fig: emphasize)* betonen; *good manners, subject* großen Wert legen auf (+*acc)*.

**stressed** [strest] *adj person* gestreßt *(col)*, überlastet.

**stressful** ['stresfʊl] *adj* anstrengend, stressig *(col)*; *situation* angespannt.

**stress mark** n Akzent m, Betonungszeichen nt.

**stretch** [stretʃ] **1** n **(a)** *(elasticity)* **to be at full ~** *(lit: material)* bis zum äußersten gedehnt sein; *(fig) (person)* mit aller Kraft arbeiten; *(factory etc)* auf Hochtouren arbeiten *(col)*; *(engine, production, work)* auf Hochtouren laufen; **by no ~ of the imagination** beim besten Willen nicht. **(b)** *(of road etc)* Strecke f; *(of river, countryside etc)* Stück nt; *(of journey)* Abschnitt m. **a straight ~ of road** eine gerade Strecke; **in that ~ of the river** in dem Teil des Flusses; **for a long ~** über eine weite Strecke. **(c)** *(~ of time)* Zeit(raum m) f. **for a long ~ of time** für (eine) lange Zeit; **for hours at a ~** stundenlang; **three days at a ~** drei Tage an einem Stück; **to do a ~** *(col: in prison)* im Knast sein *(col)*.

**2** adj attr dehnbar, Stretch-.

**3** vt **(a)** *(extend)* strecken; *(widen)* jumper also, elastic, shoes dehnen; *(spread)* wings etc ausbreiten; *(tighten)* rope spannen. **to ~ one's legs** *(go for a walk)* sich *(dat)* die Beine vertreten *(col)*. **(b)** *(make go further)* money strecken; *(use fully)* resources voll (aus)nutzen; credit voll beanspruchen; athlete, student etc fordern; one's abilities bis zum äußersten fordern. **(c)** *(strain)* meaning äußerst weit fassen; truth, rules großzügig auslegen. **to ~ a point** großzügig sein; **that's ~ing it a bit (far)** das geht fast zu weit.

**4** vi *(after sleep etc)* sich strecken; *(be elastic)* sich dehnen, dehnbar sein; *(extend) (time, area, influence)* sich erstrecken *(to* bis, *over* über *+acc)*; *(be enough: food, money)* reichen *(to* für); *(become looser)* weiter werden; *(become longer)* länger werden. **to ~ to reach sth** sich recken, um etw zu erreichen; **the fields ~ed away into the distance** die Felder dehnten sich bis in die Ferne aus; **I can't ~ to that** so viel kann ich mir nicht erlauben.

▶**stretch out 1** vt sep arms, wings ausbreiten; leg, hand ausstrecken; foot vorstrecken; rope spannen; meeting, essay ausdehnen. **to ~ oneself** sich ausgestreckt hinlegen. **2** vi sich strecken; *(col: lie down)* sich hinlegen; *(countryside)* sich ausbreiten; *(in time)* sich erstrecken *(over* über *+acc)*. **he lay ~ed ~ on the bed** er lag ausgestreckt auf dem Bett.

**stretcher** ['stretʃər] n (Med) Trage f.

**stretcher: ~-bearer** n Krankenträger m; **~ case** n Kranke(r) mf/Verletzte(r) mf, der/die nicht gehen kann; *(Mil)* Schwerverwundete(r) mf.

**stretch marks** npl Schwangerschaftsstreifen pl.

**strew** [struː] ptp **strewn** [struːn] vt *(scatter)* verstreuen; flowers, sand streuen. **the floor was ~n with ... ...** lag/lagen überall auf dem Boden verstreut.

**stricken** ['strɪkən] **1** *(old)* ptp of **strike**. **2** adj *(liter: wounded)* verwundet; *(afflicted)* leidgeprüft; *(ill)* leidend *(geh)*; ship, plane in Not. **~ with grief/fear** etc schmerzerfüllt/von Angst etc erfüllt.

**strict** [strɪkt] adj *(+er)* **(a)** law, parent etc streng; order, discipline also, obedience strikt; Catholic strenggläubig. **(b)** *(precise)* streng; meaning genau. **in the ~ sense of the word** genau genommen; **in ~ confidence** streng vertraulich.

**strictly** ['strɪktlɪ] adv **(a)** streng. **smoking is ~ forbidden** Rauchen ist strengstens verboten. **(b)** *(precisely)* genau; *(absolutely)* absolut. **~ confidential** streng vertraulich; **~ speaking** genau genommen; **not ~ true** nicht ganz richtig; **~ between you and me** ganz unter uns.

**strictness** ['strɪktnɪs] n **(a)** Strenge f. **(b)** *(preciseness)* Genauigkeit f.

**stricture** ['strɪktʃər] n usu pl *(criticism)* (scharfe) Kri-

tik no pl.

**stride** [straɪd] *(vb: pret* **strode**, *ptp* **stridden** ['strɪdn])* **1** n *(step)* Schritt m; *(gait also)* Gang m. **to get into one's ~** *(fig)* in Schwung or in Fahrt kommen; **to take sth in one's ~** mit etw spielend fertigwerden; exam, interview etw spielend schaffen; **to make (great) ~s** (große) Fortschritte machen; **this is a giant ~ (forward)** das ist ein riesiger Fortschritt. **2** vi schreiten *(geh)*, mit großen Schritten gehen. **to ~ off** davonschreiten *(geh)*; **to ~ up to sb** auf jdn zuschreiten *(geh)*.

**strident** ['straɪdənt] adj sound schrill, durchdringend; colour grell; criticism, tone scharf; demand, protest lautstark.

**strife** [straɪf] n Unfriede m; *(in family, between friends)* Zwietracht f *(geh)*. **armed ~** bewaffneter Konflikt; **internal ~** innere Kämpfe pl.

**strike** [straɪk] *(vb: pret* **struck**, *ptp* **struck** or *(old)* **stricken)* **1** n **(a)** Streik m. **to be on ~** streiken; **to come out or go on ~** in den Streik treten. **(b)** *(discovery of oil, gold etc)* Fund m. **to make a ~** fündig werden; **a lucky ~** ein Treffer, ein Glücksfall m. **(c)** *(Mil: attack)* Angriff m. **(d)** *(act of striking)* Schlag m.

**2** vt **(a)** *(hit)* schlagen; door schlagen an *(+acc)*; nail, table schlagen auf *(+acc)*; metal, hot iron etc hämmern; *(bullet, lightning, misfortune)* treffen; *(disease)* befallen. **to ~ sb/sth a blow** jdm/einer Sache einen Schlag versetzen; **who struck the first blow?** wer hat zuerst (zu)geschlagen?; **to ~ a blow for sth** *(fig)* eine Lanze für etw brechen.

**(b)** *(collide with, meet)* *(spade)* stoßen auf *(+acc)*; *(car)* fahren gegen; ground aufschlagen auf *(+acc)*; *(ship)* auflaufen auf *(+acc)*; *(sound, light)* ears, eyes treffen. **to ~ one's head against sth** sich *(dat)* den Kopf an etw *(acc)* stoßen; **to ~ difficulties/obstacles** *(fig)* in Schwierigkeiten geraten/auf Hindernisse stoßen; **a terrible sight struck my eyes** plötzlich sah ich etwas Schreckliches.

**(c)** *(sound)* string, chord, note anschlagen; *(clock)* schlagen.

**(d)** *(occur to)* in den Sinn kommen *(+dat)*. **to ~ sb as unlikely** etc jdm unwahrscheinlich etc vorkommen; **that ~s me as a good idea** das kommt mir sehr vernünftig vor; **has it ever struck you that ...?** *(occurred to you)* haben Sie je daran gedacht, daß ...?; *(have you noticed)* ist Ihnen je aufgefallen, daß ...?; **to be struck by sth** von etw beeindruckt sein; **how does it ~ you?** was halten Sie davon?; **how does she ~ you?** welchen Eindruck haben Sie von ihr?

**(e)** *(produce, make)* coin prägen; *(fig)* agreement aushandeln. **to ~ a light/match** Feuer machen/ein Streichholz anzünden; **to be struck dumb** stumm werden; **to ~ fear into sb** jdn mit Angst erfüllen.

**(f)** *(find)* oil stoßen auf *(+acc)*. **to ~ it rich** das große Geld machen.

**(g)** *(remove)* streichen. **to be struck** or *(US)* **stricken from a list/the record** von einer Liste/aus dem Protokoll gestrichen werden.

**3** vi **(a)** *(hit)* treffen; *(lightning)* einschlagen; *(snake)* zubeißen; *(attack, Mil etc)* angreifen; *(criminal, disease)* zuschlagen; *(panic)* ausbrechen. **to ~ against sth** gegen etw stoßen; **to ~ at sb/sth** *(lit)* nach jdm/etw schlagen; **to ~ at the roots of democracy** an den Wurzeln der Demokratie rütteln. **(b)** *(clock)* schlagen. **(c)** *(workers)* streiken *(for* für). **(d) to ~ lucky** Glück haben; **to ~ on a new idea** auf eine neue Idee kommen.

▶**strike back** vi zurückschlagen; *(fig also)* sich wehren. **to ~ ~ at sb** jds Angriff *(acc)* erwidern; *(fig)* sich gegen jdn wehren.

▶**strike down** vt sep niederschlagen; (God) enemies vernichten; (fig) zu Fall bringen. **to be struck** ~ niedergeschlagen werden; (by illness) niedergeworfen werden.

▶**strike off** vt sep **(a)** (cut off) abschlagen. **(b)** (from list) (aus)streichen; solicitor die Lizenz entziehen (+dat); doctor die Zulassung entziehen (+dat).

▶**strike out 1** vi **(a)** (hit out) schlagen. **to** ~ ~ **at sb** (lit, fig) jdn angreifen. **(b)** (change direction) zuhalten (for, towards auf +acc); (set out) sich aufmachen (for zu). **to** ~ ~ **on one's own** (lit) allein losziehen; (fig) eigene Wege gehen; **to** ~ ~ **in a new direction** (fig) neue Wege gehen. **2** vt sep name, entry (aus)streichen.

▶**strike up 1** vi (band etc) anfangen (zu spielen). **2** vt insep **(a)** (band) tune anstimmen. **(b)** friendship schließen; conversation anfangen.

**strike:** ~ **action** n Streikmaßnahmen pl; ~ **ballot** n Urabstimmung f; ~**-bound** adj bestreikt, vom Streik betroffen; ~**breaker** n Streikbrecher m; ~ **force** n (Mil) Kampftruppe f; ~ **pay** n Streikgeld nt.

**striker** ['straɪkə'] n **(a)** (worker) Streikende(r) mf. **(b)** (Ftbl) Stürmer m.

**striking** ['straɪkɪŋ] adj **(a)** colour etc auffallend; resemblance frappierend; difference erstaunlich; beauty eindrucksvoll. **a** ~ **example of sth** ein hervorragendes Beispiel für etw. **(b)** within ~ distance in greifbarer Nähe.

**strikingly** ['straɪkɪŋlɪ] adv see adj (a).

**string** [strɪŋ] (vb: pret, ptp strung) **1** n **(a)** (cord) Schnur f, Bindfaden m; (on apron etc) Band nt; (on anorak) Kordel f; (of puppet) Faden m. **to pull** ~**s** (fig col) Fäden ziehen, Beziehungen spielen lassen; **with no** ~**s attached** ohne Bedingungen. **(b)** (row) (of beads) Schnur f; (of onions) Zopf m; (of racehorses etc) Reihe f; (of people, vehicles) Schlange f; (fig: series) Reihe f; (of lies, curses) Serie f. **(c)** (of musical instrument, tennis racket etc) Saite f. (of bow) Sehne f. **the** ~**s** pl (instruments) die Streichinstrumente pl; (players) die Streicher pl; **to have more than one** ~ **to one's bow** mehrere Eisen im Feuer haben.

**2** vt **(a)** (put on ~) aufreihen. **to** ~ **objects/sentences** etc **together** Gegenstände zusammenbinden/Sätze etc aneinanderreihen; **she can't even** ~ **two sentences together** sie bringt keinen vernünftigen Satz zusammen. **(b)** violin etc, tennis racket (mit Saiten) bespannen. **(c)** (space out) aufreihen.

▶**string along** (col) **1** vt sep to ~ **sb** ~ jdn hinhalten. **2** vi (go along with) sich anschließen (with dat).

**string bag** n Einkaufsnetz m.

**stringed** [strɪŋd] adj instrument Saiten-; (played with bow also) Streich-.

**stringency** ['strɪndʒənsɪ] n see adj Strenge f; Härte f; (of measures) Schärfe f.

**stringent** ['strɪndʒənt] adj standards, laws streng; testing, training etc also hart; measures also energisch. ~ **economies** schärfste Sparmaßnahmen pl.

**string:** ~ **instrument** n Saiteninstrument nt; (played with bow also) Streichinstrument nt; ~**-pulling** n Spielenlassen nt von Beziehungen; ~ **quartet** n Streichquartett nt; ~ **vest** n Netzhemd nt.

**stringy** ['strɪŋɪ] adj (+er) meat sehnig, faserig; vegetable faserig.

**strip** [strɪp] **1** n **(a)** (narrow piece) Streifen m; (of land also) (schmales) Stück nt; (of metal) Band nt. **(b)** (Brit Sport) Trikot nt. **2** vt **(a)** (remove clothes etc from) person ausziehen; bed abziehen; wall (remove

paint from) abkratzen; (with chemical) abbeizen; (remove paper from) die Tapeten abziehen von; wallpaper abziehen; (remove contents from) ausräumen. **to** ~ **a house of its contents** ein Haus ausräumen; **to** ~ **sth from** or **off sth** etw von etw entfernen; ~**ped of sth** ganz ohne etw. **(b)** (fig: deprive of) berauben (of gen). **(c)** (Tech: dismantle) engine, car, gun auseinandernehmen. **3** vi (remove clothes) sich ausziehen; (at doctor's) sich freimachen; (perform ~tease) strippen (col). **to** ~ **naked** sich ganz ausziehen; **to** ~ **to the waist** den Oberkörper freimachen.

▶**strip off** vi = **strip 3**.

**strip cartoon** n Comic m.

**stripe** [straɪp] n **(a)** Streifen m. **(b)** (US: kind) (of politics) Richtung f; (of character, opinion) Art f.

**striped** [straɪpt] adj gestreift.

**strip:** ~ **light** n (esp Brit) Neonröhre f; ~ **lighting** n (esp Brit) Neonbeleuchtung f.

**stripper** ['strɪpə'] n **(a)** (performer) Stripteasetänzer(in f) m. **(b)** (paint-~) Abbeizmittel nt; (wallpaper ~) Tapetenlöser m.

**strip:** ~**-search 1** n Leibesvisitation f, zu der sich der/die Durchsuchte ausziehen muß; **2** vt ausziehen lassen und durchsuchen; **he was** ~**-searched** er mußte sich ausziehen und einer Leibesvisitation unterziehen; ~**tease** n Striptease m or nt.

**stripy** ['straɪpɪ] adj (col) gestreift.

**strive** [straɪv] pret **strove**, ptp **striven** ['strɪvn] vi (exert oneself) sich bemühen; (fight) kämpfen. **to** ~ **to do sth** bestrebt sein, etw zu tun; **to** ~ **for sth** nach etw streben; **to** ~ **against sth** gegen etw (an)kämpfen.

**strobe** [strəʊb] n **(a)** = **stroboscope**. **(b)** (also ~ lighting) stroboskopische Beleuchtung.

**stroboscope** ['strəʊbəskəʊp] n Stroboskop nt.

**strode** [strəʊd] pret of **stride**.

**stroke** [strəʊk] **1** n **(a)** (blow) Schlag, Hieb m. **(b)** (Cricket, Golf, Rowing, Tennis) Schlag m; (Swimming) (movement) Zug m; (type of ~) Stil m. **to put sb off his** ~ (fig) jdn aus dem Konzept bringen. **(c)** (of pen etc) Strich m. **he doesn't do a** ~ **(of work)** er tut keinen Schlag (col); **a** ~ **of genius** ein genialer Einfall; **a** ~ **of luck** ein Glücksfall m; **we had a** ~ **of luck** wir hatten Glück; **at a** or **one** ~ mit einem Schlag. **(d)** (of clock) Schlag m. **on the** ~ **of twelve** Punkt zwölf (Uhr). **(e)** (of piston) Hub m. **two-**~ **engine** Zweitaktmotor m. **(f)** (Med) Schlag m. **to have a** ~ einen Schlaganfall bekommen. **(g)** (caress) Streicheln nt no pl. **to give sb/sth a** ~ jdn/etw streicheln. **2** vt streicheln. **he** ~**d his chin** er strich sich (dat) übers Kinn.

**stroll** [strəʊl] **1** n Spaziergang m. **to go for a** ~, **to take a** ~ einen Bummel machen. **2** vi spazieren. **to** ~ **along** bummeln; **to** ~ **along the road** die Straße entlangspazieren; **to** ~ **up to sb** auf jdn zuschlendern.

**stroller** ['strəʊlə'] n (person) Bummler(in f) m; (US: for babies) Sportwagen m.

**strong** [strɒŋ] **1** adj (+er) **(a)** stark; material, grip also, kick, voice kräftig; table, wall stabil; shoes fest; (Fin) economy gesund; (strongly marked) features ausgeprägt. **you need a** ~ **stomach to be a nurse** als Krankenschwester darf man nicht empfindlich sein.

**(b)** (healthy) kräftig; constitution also robust; teeth also, eyes, eyesight, heart, nerves gut.

**(c)** (powerful, effective) stark; character, views fest; country mächtig; candidate, case aussichtsreich; argument, evidence überzeugend; protest energisch; measure drastisch; letter geharnischt.

**to have** ~ **feelings/views about sth** in bezug auf etw

*(acc)* stark engagiert sein; **to have ~ feelings for sth** eine starke Bindung an etw *(acc)* haben; **~ language** starke Worte; **to protest in ~ terms** energisch protestieren; **a group 20 ~** eine 20 Mann starke Gruppe; **he is ~ in/on sth** etw ist seine Stärke.

**(d)** *curry* scharf; *spice, smell, taste* kräftig; *(pungent) smell, taste* streng; *colour, light* kräftig; *acid* stark; *solution* konzentriert. **a ~ drink/whisky** ein harter Drink/ein starker Whisky.

**2** *adv (+er) (col)* **to be going ~** *(old person, thing)* gut in Schuß sein *(col)*; *(runner)* eine gute Kondition zeigen; *(party, rehearsals)* in Schwung sein *(col)*.

**strong:** **~-arm** *adj (col) tactics etc* brutal, Gewalt-; **~-box** *n* (Geld)kassette *f*; **~hold** *n (castle, fortress)* Festung *f; (town etc)* Stützpunkt *m; (fig)* Hochburg *f.*

**strongly** ['strɒŋlɪ] *adv* **(a)** *(physically)* stark; *kick, grip* kräftig; *fight* energisch; *built* stabil; *built (person)* kräftig. **(b)** *influence, suspect, tempt* stark; *interest also* brennend; *believe* fest. **to feel very ~ about sth** in bezug auf etw *(acc)* stark engagiert sein; **I didn't know that you felt so ~ about it** ich habe nicht gewußt, daß Ihnen das so viel bedeutet; *(against it)* ich habe nicht gewußt, daß Sie so dagegen sind. **(c)** *(powerfully)* stark; *protest* heftig, energisch; *plead* inständig; *support* kräftig; *answer, worded* in starken Worten. **I ~ advise you ...** ich möchte Ihnen dringend(st) raten ...

**strong:** **~-man** *n, pl* **~-men** *[-men] (lit, fig)* starker Mann; **~-minded** *adj* willensstark; **~ point** *n* Stärke *f*; **~room** *n* Stahlkammer *f*; **~-willed** ['strɒŋ'wɪld] *adj* willensstark; *(pej)* eigensinnig.

**strontium** ['strɒntɪəm] *n* Strontium *nt.*

**stroppy** ['strɒpɪ] *adj (+er) (Brit col)* fuchtig *(col)*; *answer, child* pampig *(col)*.

**strove** [strəʊv] *pret of* **strive.**

**struck** [strʌk] **1** *pret, ptp of* **strike. 2** *adj* **(a)** *pred* **to be ~ with sb/sth** *(impressed)* von jdm/etw begeistert *or* angetan sein; **I wasn't very ~ with him** er hat keinen großen Eindruck auf mich gemacht; **to be ~ on sb/sth** *(keen)* auf jdn/etw stehen *(col)*, auf jdn/etw versessen sein. **(b)** *(US attr) (striking) workers* streikend; *factory, employers* vom Streik betroffen.

**structural** ['strʌktʃərəl] *adj* **(a)** strukturell; *(of building) alterations, damage* baulich; *defect* Konstruktions-. **(b)** *(weight-bearing) wall, beam* tragend.

**structurally** ['strʌktʃərəlɪ] *adv* strukturell. **~ sound** statisch einwandfrei.

**structure** ['strʌktʃəʳ] **1** *n* **(a)** Struktur *f; (Liter)* Aufbau *m; (Tech: of bridge, car etc)* Konstruktion *f.* **(b)** *(thing constructed)* Konstruktion *f.* **2** *vt* strukturieren; *essay, argument* gliedern; *layout, life* gestalten.

**struggle** ['strʌgl] **1** *n (lit, fig)* Kampf *m (for* um*); (fig: effort)* Anstrengung *f.* **without a ~** *surrender* kampflos; **to put up a ~** sich wehren; **the ~ for survival** der Überlebenskampf; **it was a ~** es war mühsam; **I had a ~ to persuade him** es war gar nicht einfach, ihn zu überreden.

**2** *vi* **(a)** *(contend)* kämpfen; *(in self-defence)* sich wehren; *(financially)* in Schwierigkeiten sein; *(fig: strive)* sich sehr anstrengen. **to ~ to do sth** sich sehr anstrengen, etw zu tun; **to ~ for sth** um etw kämpfen; **to ~ with sth** *with problem* sich mit etw herumschlagen; *with language, homework* sich mit etw abmühen; *with doubts, conscience* mit etw ringen. **(b)** *(move with difficulty)* sich quälen. **to ~ to one's feet** mühsam aufstehen; **to ~ on** *(lit)* sich weiterkämpfen; *(fig)* weiterkämpfen.

**strum** [strʌm] *vt tune* klimpern; *guitar* klimpern auf

*(+dat).*

**strung** [strʌŋ] *pret, ptp of* **string.**

**strut¹** [strʌt] *vi* stolzieren. **to ~ about (the yard)** (auf dem Hof) herumstolzieren; **to ~ past** vorbeistolzieren.

**strut²** *n (horizontal)* Strebe *f; (vertical)* Pfeiler *m.*

**strychnine** ['strɪkniːn] *n* Strychnin *nt.*

**stub** [stʌb] **1** *n (of candle, pencil, tail, cigarette)* Stummel *m; (of cheque, ticket)* Abschnitt *m; (of tree)* Stumpf *m.* **2** *vt* **to ~ one's toe** *(on or against sth)* sich *(dat)* den Zeh *(an etw dat)* stoßen; **to ~ out a cigarette** eine Zigarette ausdrücken.

**stubble** ['stʌbl] *n no pl* Stoppeln *pl.*

**stubbly** ['stʌblɪ] *adj (+er) field, beard* Stoppel-; *chin* stoppelig.

**stubborn** ['stʌbən] *adj person, insistence* starrsinnig, stur; *animal also, child* störrisch; *refusal, weeds, cough* hartnäckig; *lock* widerspenstig. **to be ~ about sth** stur auf etw *(dat)* beharren.

**stubbornly** ['stʌbənlɪ] *adv stur; refuse* hartnäckig.

**stubbornness** ['stʌbənnɪs] *n see adj* Starrsinn *m*, Sturheit *f*; störrische Art; Hartnäckigkeit *f*; Widerspenstigkeit *f.*

**stubby** ['stʌbɪ] *adj (+er) revolver etc* kurz; *tail* stummelig; *pencil* kurz und dick; *person* gedrungen, untersetzt; *legs* kurz und stämmig.

**stucco** ['stʌkəʊ] *n, pl* **-(e)s** Stuck *m.*

**stuck** [stʌk] **1** *pret, ptp of* **stick². 2** *adj* **(a)** *(baffled)* **to be ~** nicht klarkommen. **(b)** *(col)* **he/she is ~ for sth** es fehlt ihm/ihr an etw *(dat)*; **I'm a bit ~ for cash** ich bin ein bißchen knapp bei Kasse. **(c)** *(col)* **to get ~ into sth** sich in etw *(acc)* richtig reinknien *(col)*; **to be ~ with sb/sth** jdn/etw am Hals haben *(col)*.

**stuck-up** [stʌk'ʌp] *adj (col) person* hochnäsig.

**stud¹** [stʌd] **1** *n (nail)* Beschlagnagel *m; (decorative)* Ziernagel *m.* **2** *vt* **~ded with ...** mit ... übersät; *with jewels* mit ... besetzt.

**stud²** *n (group of horses) (for breeding)* Gestüt *nt*, Zucht *f; (for racing etc)* Stall *m; (stallion)* (Zucht)hengst *m.*

**student** ['stjuːdənt] **1** *n (Univ)* Student(in *f*) *m; (esp US: at school, night school)* Schüler(in *f*) *m.* **he is a ~ of French** *or* **a French ~** er studiert Französisch; **medical/law ~s** Medizin-/Jurastudenten *pl.* **2** *adj attr* Studenten-; *activities also, movement* studentisch. **~ driver** *(US)* Fahrschüler(in *f*) *m.*

**student:** **~ nurse** *n* Schwesternschülerin *f/* Pflegeschüler *m*; **~ teacher** *n* Referendar(in *f*) *m*; **~ or ~s' union** *n* **(a)** *(organization)* Studentenvereinigung *f*; **(b)** *(building)* Gebäude *nt* der Studentenvereinigung.

**stud:** **~ farm** *n* Gestüt *nt*; **~ horse** *n* Zuchthengst *m.*

**studied** ['stʌdɪd] **1** *pret, ptp of* **study. 2** *adj reply* wohlüberlegt; *prose* kunstvoll.

**studio** ['stjuːdɪəʊ] *n* Studio *nt; (of painter also)* Atelier *nt; (broadcasting ~ also)* Senderaum *m.*

**studio:** **~ audience** *n* Publikum *nt* im Studio; **~ flat** *or* **apartment** *(US) n* Appartementwohnung *f.*

**studious** ['stjuːdɪəs] *adj person* fleißig, eifrig; *attention, piece of work* gewissenhaft, sorgfältig.

**studiously** ['stjuːdɪəslɪ] *adv* fleißig, eifrig; *(painstakingly)* sorgfältig; *polite, cool* bewußt; *avoid* gezielt, sorgsam.

**study** ['stʌdɪ] **1** *n* **(a)** *(studying) (esp Univ)* Studium *nt; (at school)* Lernen *nt; (of situation, evidence, case)* Untersuchung *f; (of nature)* Beobachtung *f.* **the ~ of cancer** die Krebsforschung; **African studies** *(Univ)* afrikanische Sprache und Kultur, Afrikanistik *f*; **to make a ~ of sth** etw untersuchen; *(academic)* etw studieren; **during my studies** während meines Studiums. **(b)** *(piece of work)* Studie *f (of über +acc)*; *(Art, Phot)* Studie *f (of gen)*; *(Mus)* Etüde *f.* **(c)** *(room)* Arbeitszimmer *nt.* **2** *vt* studieren; *(Sch)* lernen; *nature also, stars* beobachten; *author, text etc* sich befassen mit; *(research into)* erforschen; *(examine also)* untersuchen; *evidence* prüfen. **3** *vi* studieren; *(esp Sch)* lernen. **to ~ to be a teacher/doctor** ein Lehrer-/Medizinstudium machen; **to ~ under sb** bei jdm studieren.

**study:** **~ group** *n* Arbeitsgemeinschaft *f*; **~ leave** *n* Bildungsurlaub *m.*

**stuff** [stʌf] **1** *n* **(a)** Zeug *nt.* **the ~ that heroes are made of** der Stoff, aus dem Helden gemacht sind; **it's poor/good ~** das ist schlecht/gut; **books and ~** *(col)* Bücher und so *(col)*; **and ~ like that** und so was *(col)*; **all that ~ about how he wants to help us** *(col)* all das Gerede, daß er uns helfen will; **~ and nonsense** Quatsch *(col).* **(b)** *(col)* **that's the ~** so ist's richtig!, weiter so!; **to do one's ~** seine Nummer abziehen *(col)*; **he did his ~ well** er hat seine Sache gut gemacht; **to know one's ~** sich auskennen.

**2** *vt* **(a)** *(fill)* vollstopfen; *hole* zustopfen; *object* (hinein)stopfen *(into* in *+acc)*; *(into envelope)* stecken *(into* in *+acc).* **to ~ sth away** etw wegstecken; **he ~ed it away in his pocket** er stopfte es in seine Tasche; **to be ~ed up (with a cold)** verschnupft sein, eine verstopfte Nase haben. **(b)** *(Cook)* füllen. **(c)** *cushion etc* füllen; *toy also* (aus)stopfen; *(in taxidermy)* ausstopfen. **a ~ed toy** ein Stofftier *nt.* **(d)** *(col!)* **~ it** *(be quiet)* halt's Maul! *(col!)*; **get ~ed!** du kannst mich mal *(col!).*

**3** *vr* **to ~ oneself (with cakes)** sich (mit Kuchen) vollstopfen *(col).*

**stuffing** ['stʌfɪŋ] *n (of pillow, Cook)* Füllung *f*; *(of furniture)* Polstermaterial *nt*; *(in taxidermy, toys)* Füllmaterial *nt.*

**stuffy** ['stʌfɪ] *adj (+er)* **(a)** *room, atmosphere* stickig, dumpf. **(b)** *(narrow-minded)* spießig; *(prudish)* prüde; *(stiff)* steif; *(dull)* langweilig, öde.

**stultify** ['stʌltɪfaɪ] *vt mind, person* verkümmern lassen. **to become stultified** verkümmern.

**stumble** ['stʌmbl] *vi (lit, fig)* stolpern; *(in speech)* stocken. **to ~ against sth** gegen etw stoßen; **to ~ on** *or* **across sth** *(fig)* auf etw *(acc)* stoßen.

**stumbling-block** ['stʌmblɪŋblɒk] *n (fig)* Hindernis *nt.* **to be a ~ to sth** einer Sache *(dat)* im Weg stehen.

**stump** [stʌmp] **1** *n* **(a)** *(of tree, limb, tooth, candle)* Stumpf *m*; *(of pencil, tail)* Stummel *m*; *(Cricket)* Stab *m.* **(b)** *(US Pol: platform)* Rednertribüne *f.* **~ speaker** Wahlredner(in *f*) *m.* **2** *vt (fig col)* **you've got me ~ed** da bin ich überfragt; **I'm ~ed** ich bin mit meinem Latein am Ende *(col)*; **to be ~ed for an answer** um eine Antwort verlegen sein. **3** *vi (col)* stapfen. **to ~ along/about** entlang-/herumstapfen.

**stumpy** ['stʌmpɪ] *adj (+er)* kurz; *person* stämmig, untersetzt; *tree* klein und gedrungen. **~ tail** Stummelschwanz *m.*

**stun** [stʌn] *vt (make unconscious)* betäuben; *(daze)* benommen machen; *(fig) (shock)* fassungslos machen; *(amaze)* verblüffen. **he was ~ned by the news** *(bad news)* er war von der Nachricht wie betäubt; *(good news)* die Nachricht hat ihn überwältigt.

**stung** [stʌŋ] *pret, ptp of* **sting.**

**stunk** [stʌŋk] *ptp of* **stink.**

**stunning** ['stʌnɪŋ] *adj dress, girl etc* toll *(col)*, atemberaubend.

**stunt¹** [stʌnt] *n (in film)* Action-Szene *f*; *(publicity ~, trick)* Gag *m*; *(Aviat)* Kunststück *nt.*

**stunt²** *vt (lit, fig) growth, development* hemmen; *trees, mind etc* verkümmern lassen.

**stunted** ['stʌntɪd] *adj plant, mind* verkümmert; *child* unterentwickelt.

**stuntman** ['stʌntmæn] *n, pl* **-men** [-ˌmen] *n* Stuntman *m.*

**stupefaction** [ˌstjuːpɪˈfækʃən] *n* Verblüffung *f.*

**stupefy** ['stjuːpɪfaɪ] *vt* benommen machen; *(fig: amaze, surprise)* verblüffen.

**stupefying** ['stjuːpɪfaɪɪŋ] *adj (amazing)* verblüffend.

**stupendous** [stjuːˈpendəs] *adj* phantastisch; *effort* enorm.

**stupid** ['stjuːpɪd] *adj* dumm. **don't be ~** sei nicht so blöd *(col)*; **I've done a ~ thing** ich habe etwas ganz Dummes gemacht; **you ~ idiot!** du blöder Idiot!; **that was a ~ thing to do** das war dumm (von dir); **to drink oneself ~** sich sinnlos betrinken.

**stupidity** [stjuːˈpɪdɪtɪ] *n* Dummheit *f.*

**stupidly** ['stjuːpɪdlɪ] *adv* dumm. **~ I forgot** dummerweise habe ich es vergessen.

**stupor** ['stjuːpər] *n* Benommenheit *f.* **to be in a drunken ~** im Vollrausch sein.

**sturdily** ['stɜːdɪlɪ] *adv* stabil. **he is ~ built** er ist kräftig gebaut.

**sturdiness** ['stɜːdɪnɪs] *n see adj* **(a)** Kräftigkeit *f*; Robustheit *f*; Stabilität *f.*

**sturdy** ['stɜːdɪ] *adj (+er)* **(a)** *person, plant* kräftig; *material* robust; *building, car* stabil. **(b)** *(fig) opposition* standhaft.

**sturgeon** ['stɜːdʒən] *n* Stör *m.*

**stutter** ['stʌtər] **1** *n (of person, engine)* Stottern *nt no pl.* **he has a bad ~** er stottert sehr. **2** *vti* stottern.

**stutterer** ['stʌtərər] *n* Stotterer *m*, Stotterin *f.*

**sty** [staɪ] *n (lit, fig)* Schweinestall *m.*

**sty(e)** [staɪ] *n (Med)* Gerstenkorn *nt.*

**style** [staɪl] *n* **(a)** Stil *m.* **~ of painting** Malstil *m*; **the ~ of his writing** sein Stil *m*; **~ of life** Lebensstil *m*; **a poem in the Romantic ~** ein Gedicht im Stil der Romantik; **he won in fine ~** er gewann überlegen; **that house is not my ~** so ein Haus ist nicht mein Stil; **hillwalking/flattering people is not his ~** Bergwanderungen liegen ihm nicht/es ist nicht seine Art zu schmeicheln; **the man has ~** der Mann hat Format; **in ~** stilvoll; **to do things in ~** alles im großen Stil tun; **to celebrate in ~** groß feiern. **(b)** *(Fashion)* Stil *m no pl*, Mode *f*; *(cut)* Schnitt *m*; *(hair~)* Frisur *f.* **all the latest ~s** die neueste Mode.

**styli** ['staɪlaɪ] *pl of* **stylus.**

**styling** ['staɪlɪŋ] *n (of car etc)* Design *nt*; *(of dress, hair)* Schnitt *m.*

**stylish** ['staɪlɪʃ] *adj person, dress etc* elegant; *car, hotel, district also* edel; *furnishings* stilvoll; *(fashionable)* modisch; *way of life* großartig.

**stylishly** ['staɪlɪʃlɪ] *adv* elegant; *furnished* stilvoll; *(fashionably)* modisch; *live* im großen Stil.

**stylishness** ['staɪlɪʃnɪs] *n see adj* Eleganz *f*; Vornehmheit *f*; stilvolle Art; modische Finesse; großangelegter Stil.

**stylist** ['staɪlɪst] *n (Fashion)* Designer(in *f*) *m*; *(hair~)* Friseur *m*, Friseuse *f.*

**stylistic** [staɪˈlɪstɪk] *adj* stilistisch. **~ device** Stilmittel *nt.*

**stylized** ['staɪlaɪzd] *adj* stilisiert.

**stylus** ['staɪləs] *n, pl* **styli** *(on record-player)* Nadel *f.*

**styptic** ['stɪptɪk] *adj* **~ pencil** Blutstillstift *m.*

**suave** [swɑːv] *adj* weltmännisch, aalglatt *(pej).*

**sub** [sʌb] = **(a)** submarine. **(b)** subscription. **(c)** substitute.

**sub-** *pref* Unter-, unter-; *(esp with foreign words)* Sub-, sub-.

**subaltern** ['sʌbltən] *n (Brit Mil)* Subalternoffizier *m.*

**sub:** **~committee** *n* Unterausschuß *m*; **~conscious 1** *adj* unterbewußt; **2** *n* **the ~conscious** das

Unterbewußtsein; ~**consciously** *adv* im Unterbewußtsein; ~**continent** *n* Subkontinent *m*; ~**contract 1** ['sʌbkəntrækt] *vt* (vertraglich) weitervergeben *(to an +acc)*; **2** [sʌb'kɒntrækt] *n* Nebenvertrag *m*; ~**contractor** *n* Subunternehmer *m*; ~**culture** *n* Subkultur *f*, Szene *f (col)*; ~**divide** *vt* unterteilen; ~**division** *n (act)* Unterteilung *f (into in +acc)*; *(~group)* Unterabteilung *f*.

**subdue** [səb'djuː] *vt rebels, country* unterwerfen; *rioters* überwältigen; *(fig) anger, desire* unterdrücken; *noise, light, high spirits* dämpfen; *animals, children* bändigen.

**subdued** [səb'djuːd] *adj colour, lighting, voice* gedämpft; *manner, person* ruhig; *mood, atmosphere* gedrückt; *(submissive) voice, manner, person* fügsam, gehorsam; *(repressed) feelings, excitement* unterdrückt.

**sub:** ~**-editor** *n (esp Brit)* Redakteur(in *f*) *m*; ~**frame** *n (Aut)* Hilfsrahmen *m*; ~**group** *n* Unterabteilung *f*; ~**heading** *n* Untertitel *m*; ~**human** *adj* unmenschlich.

**subject** ['sʌbdʒɪkt] **1** *n* **(a)** *(Pol)* Staatsbürger(in *f*) *m*; *(of king etc)* Untertan *m*, Untertanin *f*. **(b)** *(Gram)* Subjekt *nt*, Satzgegenstand *m*. **(c)** *(topic, Mus)* Thema *nt*; *(Art)* Motiv *nt*. **to change the ~** das Thema wechseln; **on the ~ of ...** zum Thema *(+gen)* ...; **while we're on the ~** da wir gerade beim Thema sind. **(d)** *(discipline) (Sch, Univ)* Fach *nt*; *(specialist ~)* (Spezial)gebiet *nt*. **(e)** *(object)* Gegenstand *m (of gen)*; *(in experiment) (person)* Versuchsperson *f*; *(animal)* Versuchstier *nt*. **he is the ~ of much criticism** er wird stark kritisiert.
**2** *adj* **(a)** *(conquered)* unterworfen. **(b) to be ~ to** *sth to law, change, sb's will* einer Sache *(dat)* unterworfen sein; *to illness* für etw anfällig sein; *to consent, approval* von etw abhängig sein; **northbound trains are ~ to delays** bei Zügen in Richtung Norden muß mit Verspätung gerechnet werden; **prices are ~ to alteration without notice** Preisänderungen sind vorbehalten; **~ to confirmation in writing** vorausgesetzt, es wird schriftlich bestätigt.
**3** [səb'dʒekt] *vt* **(a)** *(subjugate)* unterwerfen; *terrorists, guerillas* zerschlagen. **(b) to ~ sb to sth** *to questioning, analysis* jdn einer Sache *(dat)* unterziehen; *to torture, criticism* jdn einer Sache *(dat)* aussetzen; **to ~ sb/a book to criticism** jdn/ein Buch kritisieren.

**subjection** [səb'dʒekʃən] *n* **(a)** *(state)* Abhängigkeit *f*. **to hold a people in ~** ein Volk unterdrücken. **(b)** *(act)* Unterwerfung *f*; *(of terrorists etc)* Zerschlagung *f*.

**subjective** *adj*, ~**ly** *adv* [səb'dʒektɪv, -lɪ] subjektiv.
**subjectivity** [ˌsʌbdʒek'tɪvɪtɪ] *n* Subjektivität *f*.
**subject-matter** ['sʌbdʒɪkt'mætər] *n (theme)* Stoff *m*; *(content)* Inhalt *m*.
**sub judice** [ˌsʌb'dʒuːdɪsɪ] *adj* **to be ~** verhandelt werden.
**subjugate** ['sʌbdʒʊgeɪt] *vt* unterwerfen.
**subjugation** [ˌsʌbdʒʊ'geɪʃən] *n* Unterwerfung *f*.
**subjunctive** [səb'dʒʌŋktɪv] **1** *adj* konjunktivisch. **the ~ mood** der Konjunktiv. **2** *n (mood, verb)* Konjunktiv *m*.
**sub:** ~**let** *pret, ptp* ~**let** *vti* untervermieten *(to an +acc)*; ~**lieutenant** *n (Brit Naut)* Leutnant *m* zur See.
**sublimate** ['sʌblɪmeɪt] *vt* sublimieren.
**sublime** [sə'blaɪm] *adj beauty, scenery, thoughts* erhaben; *achievement, genius also* überragend; *indifference, contempt* vollkommen.
**sublimely** [sə'blaɪmlɪ] *adv* erhaben; *unaware, indifferent etc* vollkommen.

**subliminal** [ˌsʌb'lɪmɪnl] *adj (Psych)* unterschwellig.
**submachine gun** [ˌsʌbmə'ʃiːn'gʌn] *n* Maschinenpistole *f*.
**submarine** ['sʌbməˌriːn] *n* Unterseeboot, U-Boot *nt*.
**submerge** [səb'mɜːdʒ] **1** *vt* untertauchen; *(flood)* überschwemmen. **the house was completely ~d** das Haus stand völlig unter Wasser. **2** *vi (diver, submarine)* tauchen.
**submersion** [səb'mɜːʃən] *n* Untertauchen *nt*; *(of submarine)* Tauchen *nt*; *(by flood)* Überschwemmung *f*.
**submission** [səb'mɪʃən] *n* **(a)** *(yielding)* Unterwerfung *f (to unter +acc)*; *(submissiveness)* Gehorsam *m*; *(Sport)* Aufgabe *f*. **(b)** *(presentation)* Eingabe *f*; *(documents)* Vorlage *f*.
**submissive** *adj*, ~**ly** *adv* [səb'mɪsɪv, -lɪ] demütig, unterwürfig *(pej) (to gegenüber)*.
**submissiveness** [səb'mɪsɪvnɪs] *n* Demut *f*, Unterwürfigkeit *f (pej)*.
**submit** [səb'mɪt] **1** *vt* **(a)** *(put forward)* vorlegen *(to dat)*; *application etc* einreichen *(to bei)*. **to ~ that ...** *(esp Jur)* behaupten, daß ... **(b) to ~ sth to scrutiny etc** etw einer Prüfung *etc* unterziehen; **to be ~ted to sth** *to sth unpleasant* einer Sache *(dat)* ausgesetzt sein. **2** *vi (yield)* nachgeben; *(Mil)* sich ergeben *(to dat)*; *(Sport)* aufgeben. **to ~ to sth** *to sb's orders, judgement* sich einer Sache *(dat)* beugen; *to indignity* etw erdulden; *to demands, threats* einer Sache *(dat)* nachgeben; **to ~ to blackmail** sich erpressen lassen.
**subnormal** [ˌsʌb'nɔːməl] *adj intelligence, temperature* unterdurchschnittlich; *person* minderbegabt. **mentally ~** geistig minderbemittelt.
**subordinate** [sə'bɔːdɪnɪt] **1** *adj officer* rangniedriger; *position, importance* untergeordnet. ~ **clause** *(Gram)* Nebensatz *m*; **to be ~ to sb/sth** jdm/einer Sache untergeordnet sein. **2** *n* Untergebene(r) *mf*. **3** [sə'bɔːdɪneɪt] *vt* unterordnen *(to dat)*.
**subpoena** [səb'piːnə] *(Jur)* **1** *n* Vorladung *f*. **to serve a ~ on sb** jdn vorladen. **2** *vt* vorladen.
**sub:** ~**-post office** *n (Brit)* Poststelle *f*; ~**routine** *n (Comp)* Unterprogramm *nt*.
**subscribe** [səb'skraɪb] **1** *vt money* spenden *(to für)*. ~**d capital** *(Fin)* gezeichnetes Kapital. **2** *vi* **to ~ to an appeal** sich an einer Spendenaktion beteiligen; **to ~ to a magazine** *etc* eine Zeitschrift *etc* abonnieren; **to ~ to sth** *to proposal* etw gutheißen, etw billigen; *to opinion, theory* etw vertreten.
**subscriber** [səb'skraɪbər] *n (to paper)* Abonnent(in *f*) *m*; *(to fund)* Spender(in *f*) *m*; *(Telec)* Teilnehmer(in *f*) *m*; *(of shares)* Zeichner *m*. ~ **trunk dialling** *(Brit)* der Selbstwählferndienst.
**subscript** ['sʌbskrɪpt] *adj (Typ)* tiefgestellt.
**subscription** [səb'skrɪpʃən] *n (money subscribed)* Beitrag *m*; *(to newspaper, concert etc)* Abonnement *nt (to gen)*. **to take out a ~ to sth** etw abonnieren; **to pay one's ~ (to a club)** seinen (Vereins)beitrag bezahlen.
**subsection** ['sʌbˌsekʃən] *n* Unterabteilung *f*; *(Jur)* Paragraph *m*.
**subsequent** ['sʌbsɪkwənt] *adj* (nach)folgend. ~ **to** *(form)* im Anschluß an *(+acc)*.
**subsequently** ['sʌbsɪkwəntlɪ] *adv (afterwards)* später; *(from that time also)* von da an.
**subservient** [səb'sɜːvɪənt] *adj (pej)* unterwürfig *(to gegenüber)*.
**subside** [səb'saɪd] *vi (flood)* sinken; *(land, building)* sich senken, absacken *(col)*; *(storm, wind, anger etc)* nachlassen, sich legen.
**subsidence** [səb'saɪdəns] *n* Senkung *f*.
**subsidiarity** [ˌsəbsɪdɪ'ærɪtɪ] *n* Subsidiarität *f*.

**subsidiary** [səb'sɪdɪərɪ] **1** *adj role, subject etc* Neben-; *company* Tochter-. **2** *n* Tochtergesellschaft *f*.

**subsidize** ['sʌbsɪdaɪz] *vt company etc* subventionieren; *(col) person* unterstützen.

**subsidy** ['sʌbsɪdɪ] *n* Subvention *f*. **there is a ~ on butter** Butter wird subventioniert; **housing subsidies** Wohnungsbauförderung *f (durch öffentliche Mittel)*.

**subsist** [səb'sɪst] *vi* sich ernähren, leben *(on von)*.

**subsistence** [səb'sɪstəns] *n (living)* Leben *nt (on von)*; *(means of ~)* (Lebens)unterhalt *m*.

**subsistence:** **~ allowance** *n* Unterhaltszuschuß *m*; **~ farming** *n* Ackerbau *m* für den Eigenbedarf; **~ level** *n* Existenzminimum *nt*; **at ~ level** auf dem Existenzminimum; **~ wage** *n* Minimallohn *m*.

**sub:** **~soil** *n* Untergrund *m*; **~sonic** *adj* Unterschall-; **~species** *n* Unterart *f*.

**substance** ['sʌbstəns] *n* Substanz *f*. **in ~** im wesentlichen; **the argument lacks ~** das Argument hat keine Substanz; **there is some ~ in his claim** seine Behauptung ist nicht unfundiert; **a man of ~** ein vermögender Mann.

**substandard** [ˌsʌb'stændəd] *adj work, goods, quality* minderwertig; *housing* unzulänglich.

**substantial** [səb'stænʃəl] *adj* **(a)** *meal, person, cloth* kräftig; *furniture, building, firm* solide; *book* umfangreich. **(b)** *(considerable) loss, part, improvement, amount* beträchtlich; *sum also* namhaft; *(rich) landowner* vermögend. **(c)** *(weighty)* bedeutend; *proof, argument* überzeugend; *difference* wesentlich.

**substantially** [səb'stænʃəlɪ] *adv* **(a)** *(solidly)* solide; *(considerably)* erheblich, beträchtlich. **~ built** *house* solide gebaut; *person* kräftig gebaut. **(b)** *(essentially, basically)* im wesentlichen.

**substantiate** [səb'stænʃɪeɪt] *vt* erhärten.

**substantive** ['sʌbstəntɪv] *adj evidence, argument, reason* überzeugend, stichhaltig.

**substation** ['sʌbˌsteɪʃən] *n (Elec)* Umspannwerk *nt*.

**substitute** ['sʌbstɪtjuːt] **1** *n* Ersatz *m no pl*; *(representative also)* Vertretung *f*; *(Sport)* Ersatzspieler(in *f*) *m*. **2** *adj attr* Ersatz-. **~ teacher** *(US)* Vertretung *f*. **3** *vt* **to ~ A for B** B durch A ersetzen; *(Sport also)* B gegen A auswechseln. **4** *vi* **to ~ for sb/sth** für jdn einspringen/etw ersetzen.

**substitution** [ˌsʌbstɪ'tjuːʃən] *n* Ersetzen *nt (of X for Y* von Y durch X); *(Sport)* Austausch *m (of X for Y* von Y gegen X). **to make a ~** *(Sport)* auswechseln.

**subtenant** [ˌsʌb'tenənt] *n (of flat etc)* Untermieter(in *f*) *m*; *(of land)* Unterpächter(in *f*) *m*.

**subterfuge** ['sʌbtəfjuːdʒ] *n (trickery)* Täuschung *f*; *(trick)* Trick *m*.

**subterranean** [ˌsʌbtə'reɪnɪən] *adj* unterirdisch.

**subtitle** ['sʌbˌtaɪtl] **1** *n* Untertitel *m*. **2** *vt film* mit Untertiteln versehen; *book etc* einen Untertitel geben *(+dat)*.

**subtle** ['sʌtl] *adj fein; hint* zart; *charm* unaufdringlich; *(not obvious) remark, point* scharfsinnig; *design, proof* raffiniert.

**subtlety** ['sʌtltɪ] *n see adj* Feinheit *f*; Zartheit *f*; Unaufdringlichkeit *f*; Scharfsinn(igkeit *f*) *m*; Raffiniertheit *f*.

**subtly** ['sʌtlɪ] *adv fein; flavoured also* delikat; *argue, analyse* scharfsinnig; *achieve one's ends* auf raffinierte Weise. **~ different** auf subtile Weise verschieden.

**subtotal** ['sʌbˌtəʊtl] *n* Zwischen- *or* Teilsumme *f*.

**subtract** [səb'trækt] *vti* abziehen, subtrahieren *(from von)*.

**subtraction** [səb'trækʃən] *n* Subtraktion *f*.

**subtropical** [ˌsʌb'trɒpɪkəl] *adj* subtropisch.

**suburb** ['sʌbɜːb] *n* Vorort *m*.

**suburban** [sə'bɜːbən] *adj* Vorort-; *(pej)* kleinbürgerlich. **~ line** *(Rail)* Vorortbahn *f*.

**suburbia** [sə'bɜːbɪə] *n (usu pej)* die Vororte *pl*. **to live in ~** in einem (typischen) Vorort wohnen.

**subversion** [səb'vɜːʃən] *n no pl* Subversion *f*; *(of rights, freedom etc)* Untergrabung *f*.

**subversive** [səb'vɜːsɪv] **1** *adj* subversiv. **~ elements** subversive Kräfte *pl*. **2** *n* Umstürzler(in *f*) *m*.

**subway** ['sʌbweɪ] *n* Unterführung *f*; *(US Rail)* U-Bahn *f*.

**subzero** [sʌb'zɪərəʊ] *adj temperatures* unter Null.

**succeed** [sək'siːd] **1** *vi* **(a)** *(person)* erfolgreich sein, Erfolg haben; *(plan etc also)* gelingen. **to ~ in business/in a plan** geschäftlich/mit einem Plan erfolgreich sein; **I ~ed in doing it** es gelang mir, zu tun; **you'll only ~ in making things worse** damit erreichst du nur, daß alles noch schlimmer wird. **(b)** *(come next)* **to ~ to an office** in einem Amt nachfolgen; **he ~ed to his father's position** er trat die Nachfolge seines Vaters an *(geh)*. **2** *vt (come after, take the place of)* folgen *(+dat)*; *(person also)* Nachfolger(in *f*) *m* werden *(+gen)*. **to ~ sb in a post/in office** jds Stelle *(acc)* übernehmen/jdm im Amt nachfolgen.

**succeeding** [sək'siːdɪŋ] *adj* folgend. **~ generations** nachfolgende Generationen *pl*.

**success** [sək'ses] *n* Erfolg *m*. **without ~** ohne Erfolg, erfolglos; **to make a ~ of sth** mit *or* bei etw erfolgreich sein; **to meet with ~** Erfolg haben, erfolgreich sein; **~ story** Erfolgsstory *f*; *(person, thing)* Erfolg *m*.

**successful** [sək'sesfʊl] *adj* erfolgreich. **to be ~** erfolgreich sein, Erfolg haben *(in* mit, bei*)*; **I was ~ in doing it** es gelang mir, es zu tun.

**successfully** [sək'sesfəlɪ] *adv* erfolgreich, mit Erfolg.

**succession** [sək'seʃən] *n* **(a)** Folge, Serie *f*; *(with no intervening period)* (Aufeinander)folge *f*. **in ~** hintereinander; **in quick ~** schnell hintereinander. **(b)** *(to post)* Nachfolge *f*. **fourth in ~ to the throne** an vierter Stelle in der Thronfolge.

**successive** [sək'sesɪv] *adj* **four ~ days** vier Tage hintereinander, vier aufeinanderfolgende Tage; **~ generations have ...** eine Generation nach der anderen hat ...

**successively** [sək'sesɪvlɪ] *adv* nacheinander.

**successor** [sək'sesər] *n* Nachfolger(in *f*) *m (to gen)*; *(to throne)* Thronfolger(in *f*) *m*. **~ organization** Nachfolgeorganisation *f*.

**succinct** [sək'sɪŋkt] *adj* knapp.

**succinctly** [sək'sɪŋktlɪ] *adv* kurz und bündig; *write* in knappen Worten. **as he very ~ put it** wie er so treffend bemerkte.

**succinctness** [sək'sɪŋktnɪs] *n* Knappheit, Kürze *f*.

**succulent** ['sʌkjʊlənt] **1** *adj peach, steak* saftig. **2** *n (Bot)* Sukkulente *f (spec)*.

**succumb** [sə'kʌm] *vi* erliegen *(to dat)*; *(to threats)* sich beugen *(to dat)*.

**such** [sʌtʃ] **1** *adj* **(a)** *(of that kind)* solche(r, s). **~ a person** so ein Mensch, ein solcher Mensch; **~ people/books** solche Leute/Bücher; **many/all ~ people** viele/all solche Leute; **do you have ~ a book?** haben Sie so ein Buch?; **~ a thing (as)** so etwas (wie); **I said no ~ thing** das habe ich nie gesagt; **no ~ thing** nichts dergleichen; **you'll do no ~ thing** du wirst dich hüten; **there's no ~ thing as a unicorn** so etwas wie ein Einhorn gibt es nicht; **... or some ~ thing ...** oder so etwas, ... oder so ähnlich; **... or some ~ name/place** ... oder so (ähnlich); **in ~ a case** in einem solchen Fall; **books ~ as**

**these, ~ books as these** Bücher wie diese, solche Bücher.

**(b)** *(so much, so great etc)* solche(r, s). **he's ~ a liar** er ist ein derartiger *or* so ein Lügner; **he's not ~ a fool as you think** er ist nicht so dumm, wie Sie denken; **he did it in ~ a way that** ... er machte es so, daß ...; **~ wealth/beauty!** was für ein Reichtum/welche Schönheit!; **he's always in ~ a hurry** er hat es immer so eilig.

**(c)** *pred* **his surprise was ~ that** ... er war so überrascht, daß ...; **his manner was ~ that** ... er benahm sich so, daß ...

**2** *adv* so, solch *(geh)*. **~ a big house** so ein großes Haus; **nobody else makes ~ a good cup of tea as you** niemand kocht so guten Tee wie du; **it's ~ a long time ago** es ist so lange her.

**3** *pron* **rabbits and hares and ~** Kaninchen, Hasen und dergleichen; **~ being the case** ... in diesem Fall ...; **~ was not my intention** dies war nicht meine Absicht; **~ is not the case** dies ist nicht der Fall; **~ is life!** so ist das Leben!; **as ~** an sich; **~ as?** zum Beispiel?; **~ as it is** so, wie es nun mal ist.

**such-and-such** ['sʌtʃən'sʌtʃ] *(col)* **1** *adj* **~ a time/town** die und die Zeit/Stadt. **2** *n* **Mr ~** Herr Soundso.

**suchlike** ['sʌtʃˌlaɪk] *(col)* **1** *adj* solche. **2** *pron* dergleichen.

**suck** [sʌk] **1** *vt* saugen; *sweet, pastille* lutschen; *lollipop, thumb* lutschen an (+*dat*). **to ~ sb dry** *(fig)* jdn bis aufs Blut aussaugen. **2** *vi (at* an +*dat)* saugen; *(at lollipop, thumb)* lutschen; *(at pipe, through straw)* ziehen.

▶**suck down** *vt sep (current etc)* hinunterziehen.

▶**suck in** *vt sep liquid, dust* aufsaugen; *air (ventilator)* ansaugen; *(person)* in tiefen Zügen einatmen; *cheeks* einziehen.

▶**suck up 1** *vt sep liquid, dust* aufsaugen. **2** *vi (col)* **to ~ to sb** vor jdm kriechen *(col)*.

**sucker** ['sʌkər] *n* **(a)** *(col: fool)* Trottel *m (col)*. **to be a ~ for sth** (immer) auf etw *(acc)* hereinfallen; *(be partial to)* eine Schwäche für etw haben. **(b)** *(US col: lollipop)* Lutscher *m*.

**suckle** ['sʌkl] *vt child* stillen; *animal* säugen.

**sucrose** ['suːkrəʊz] *n* Saccharose *f*, pflanzlicher Zucker.

**suction** ['sʌkʃən] *n* Saugwirkung *f*. **~-pump** Saugpumpe *f*.

**Sudan** [sʊ'dɑːn] *n (the)* **~** der Sudan.

**Sudanese** [ˌsuːdə'niːz] **1** *adj* sudanesisch. **2** *n* Sudanese *m*, Sudanesin *f*.

**sudden** ['sʌdn] **1** *adj* plötzlich; *movement also* jäh, abrupt; *(unexpected) bend, change of direction* unerwartet. **~ death play-off** Entscheidungskampf *m*. **2** *n* **all of a ~** (ganz) plötzlich.

**suddenly** ['sʌdnlɪ] *adv* plötzlich; *move also* abrupt.

**suddenness** ['sʌdnnɪs] *n* Plötzlichkeit *f*.

**suds** [sʌdz] *npl* Seifenlauge *f*; *(lather)* (Seifen)schaum *m*.

**sue** [suː] **1** *vt (Jur)* **to ~ sb for sth** jdn wegen etw verklagen; **to ~ sb for divorce** gegen jdn die Scheidung einreichen; **to ~ sb for damages** jdn auf Schadenersatz verklagen. **2** *vi (Jur)* klagen, Klage erheben. **to ~ for divorce** die Scheidung einreichen.

**suede** [sweɪd] **1** *n* Wildleder *nt*. **2** *adj* Wildleder-.

**suet** ['sʊɪt] *n* Nierenfett *nt*.

**Suez** ['suːɪz] *n* Suez *m*. **~ Canal** Suezkanal *m*.

**suffer** ['sʌfər] **1** *vt* **(a)** *pain, setback* erleiden; *hardship also, hunger* leiden; *headache, effects etc* leiden unter (+*dat*); *shock* haben. **the pound ~ed further losses** das Pfund mußte weitere Einbußen hinnehmen. **(b)** *(tolerate)* dulden, ertragen. **he doesn't ~**

**fools gladly** Dummheit ist ihm ein Greuel. **2** *vi (physically, mentally, fig)* leiden *(from* unter +*dat, from illness* an +*dat)*; *(as punishment, in hell etc)* büßen. **he was ~ing from shock** er hatte einen Schock (erlitten); **your health will ~** deine Gesundheit wird darunter leiden; **you'll ~ for this!** das wirst du büßen!

**sufferance** ['sʌfərəns] *n* **he's only here on ~** er wird hier nur geduldet.

**sufferer** ['sʌfərər] *n (Med)* Leidende(r) *mf (from* an +*dat)*. **diabetes ~s, ~s from diabetes** Zuckerkranke *pl*.

**suffering** ['sʌfərɪŋ] *n* Leiden *nt*; *(hardship, deprivation)* Leid *nt no pl*.

**suffice** [sə'faɪs] *(form)* **1** *vi* (aus)reichen. **2** *vt* **~ it to say** ... es reicht wohl, wenn ich sage, ...

**sufficiency** [sə'fɪʃənsɪ] *n (adequacy)* Hinlänglichkeit *f*. **to have a ~** genügend haben.

**sufficient** [sə'fɪʃənt] *adj* genügend; *reason, condition* hinreichend. **to be ~** genügen, ausreichen; **thank you, that's ~** danke, das genügt.

**sufficiently** [sə'fɪʃəntlɪ] *adv* genug. **~ good/warm** *etc* gut/warm *etc* genug *pred*; **a ~ large number** eine ausreichend große Anzahl.

**suffix** ['sʌfɪks] *n (Ling)* Suffix *nt*, Nachsilbe *f*; *(in code etc)* Zusatz *m*.

**suffocate** ['sʌfəkeɪt] *vti (lit, fig)* ersticken. **he was ~d by the smoke** er erstickte am Rauch.

**suffocating** ['sʌfəkeɪtɪŋ] *adj (lit)* erstickend *attr*; *(fig also)* erdrückend *attr*; *heat* drückend *attr*.

**suffocation** [ˌsʌfə'keɪʃən] *n (lit, fig)* Ersticken *nt*.

**suffrage** ['sʌfrɪdʒ] *n* Wahlrecht *nt*.

**suffragette** [ˌsʌfrə'dʒet] *n* Suffragette *f*.

**suffuse** [sə'fjuːz] *vt* erfüllen; *(light)* durchfluten. **~d with light** in Licht getaucht.

**sugar** ['ʃʊɡər] **1** *n* **(a)** Zucker *m*. **(b)** *(col: term of affection)* Schätzchen *nt (col)*. **2** *vt* zuckern, süßen. **to ~ the pill** die bittere Pille versüßen.

**sugar** *in cpds* Zucker-; **~ basin** *n* Zuckerdose *f*; **~ beet** *n* Zuckerrübe *f*; **~ bowl** *n* Zuckerdose *f*; **~ candy** *n (US: sweet)* Bonbon *nt or m*; **~ cane** *n* Zuckerrohr *nt*; **~-coated** *adj* mit Zucker überzogen.

**sugared** ['ʃʊɡəd] *adj* gezuckert; *almonds* Zucker-; *words* (honig)süß.

**sugar: ~ lump** *n* Stück *nt* Zucker; **~ refinery** *n* Zuckerraffinerie *f*; **~ sprinkler** *n* Zuckerstreuer *m*.

**sugary** ['ʃʊɡərɪ] *adj taste* süß; *(full of sugar)* zuckrig; *(fig) style etc* süßlich.

**suggest** [sə'dʒest] **1** *vt* **(a)** *(propose)* vorschlagen; *plan, idea also* anregen; *explanation, theory* vorbringen. **I ~ that we go, I ~ going** ich schlage vor, (daß) wir gehen; **what do you ~ we do?** was schlagen Sie vor?; **are you ~ing I should tell a deliberate lie?** soll das heißen, daß ich bewußt lügen soll?; **I am ~ing nothing of the kind** ich habe nichts dergleichen gesagt. **(b)** *(indicate, hint at)* andeuten; *(unpleasantly)* unterstellen; *(evoke) (music, poem)* denken lassen an *(+acc)*. **what are you trying to ~?** was wollen Sie damit sagen?; **the symptoms would ~ an operation** die Symptome lassen eine Operation angeraten erscheinen. **2** *vr* **to ~ itself** *(idea, thought)* sich anbieten, naheliegen.

**suggestion** [sə'dʒestʃən] *n* **(a)** *(proposal)* Vorschlag *m*. **my ~ is that** ... mein Vorschlag lautet ..., ich schlage vor, daß ...; **following your ~** auf Ihren Vorschlag *or* Ihre Anregung hin; **I'm open to ~s** Vorschläge sind willkommen. **(b)** *(insinuation)* Andeutung *f*; *(unpleasant)* Unterstellung *f*. **I resent that ~** ich weise diese Unterstellung zurück; **there is no ~ that he was involved** es gibt keinen Anhaltspunkt

**sundial**

dafür, daß er beteiligt war. **(c)** *(hint: of irony etc)* Anflug *m*. **(d)** *(also indecent* ~*)* unsittlicher Antrag.
**suggestive** [sə'dʒestɪv] *adj* **(a)** to be ~ of sth auf etw *(acc)* hindeuten; *(create impression of)* den Eindruck von etw vermitteln. **(b)** *(indecent) joke, remark etc* zweideutig.
**suicidal** [ˌsʊɪ'saɪdl] *adj* selbstmörderisch; *person* selbstmordgefährdet. to have ~ tendencies zum Selbstmord neigen; that would be ~ *(also fig)* das wäre glatter Selbstmord.
**suicide** ['sʊɪsaɪd] *n* Selbstmord *m*; *(person)* Selbstmörder(in *f*) *m*. to commit ~ Selbstmord begehen; ~ attempt Selbstmordversuch *m*.
**suit** [suːt] **1** *n* **(a)** Anzug *m*; *(woman's)* Kostüm *nt*. ~ of clothes Garnitur *f*. **(b)** *(Jur)* Verfahren *nt*. to bring a ~ **(against sb for sth)** (wegen etw gegen jdn) einen Prozeß anstrengen. **(c)** *(Cards)* Farbe *f*. to follow ~ *(lit)* Farbe bedienen; *(fig)* jds Beispiel *(dat)* folgen.
**2** *vt* **(a)** *(be convenient to) (arrangement, date, price)* passen *(+dat)*; *(climate, food)* bekommen *(+dat)*; *(occupation)* gefallen *(+dat)*. that ~s me fine! *(col)* das ist mir recht; that would ~ me nicely *(time, arrangement)* das würde mir gut passen; *(house, job etc)* das wäre genau das richtige für mich; when would it ~ you to come? wann wäre es Ihnen recht? **(b)** *(be suitable, right for)* geeignet sein für. he is very well ~ed to the job er eignet sich sehr gut für die Stelle; they are well ~ed (to each other) sie passen gut zusammen. **(c)** *(clothes, hairstyle)* (gut) stehen *(+dat)*. **(d)** *(adapt)* anpassen *(to dat)*. **(e)** *(please)* gefallen *(+dat)*. you can't ~ everybody man kann es nicht jedem recht machen; ~ yourself! wie du willst!
**suitability** [ˌsuːtə'bɪlɪtɪ] *n* Angemessenheit *f*; *(of person for job)* Eignung *f*.
**suitable** ['suːtəbl] *adj (convenient, practical)* geeignet, passend; *(socially, culturally appropriate)* angemessen. to be ~ for sb *(date, place)* jdm passen; *(film, job)* für jdn geeignet sein; the most ~ man for the job der für die Stelle am besten geeignete Mann; would 8 o'clock be a ~ time (for you)? wäre Ihnen 8 Uhr recht?; Tuesday is the most ~ day Dienstag ist der günstigste Tag; she's not ~ for him sie paßt nicht zu ihm.
**suitably** ['suːtəblɪ] *adv* angemessen; *behave also, apologize* wie es sich gehört. he was ~ impressed er war gehörig beeindruckt.
**suitcase** ['suːtˌkeɪs] *n* Koffer *m*. to live out of a ~ aus dem Koffer leben.
**suite** [swiːt] *n* *(of furniture)* Garnitur *f*; *(of rooms)* Suite, Zimmerflucht *f*; *(Mus)* Suite *f*. bedroom ~ Schlafzimmergarnitur *f*; 3-piece ~ dreiteilige Sitzgarnitur.
**suitor** ['suːtər] *n* **(a)** *(old: of woman)* Freier *m* *(old)*. **(b)** *(Jur)* Kläger(in *f*) *m*.
**sulfate** *etc (US) see* sulphate *etc*.
**sulk** [sʌlk] **1** *vi* schmollen, beleidigt sein. **2** *n* Schmollen *nt*. to have the ~s schmollen.
**sulkily** ['sʌlkɪlɪ] *adv* schmollend.
**sulkiness** ['sʌlkɪnɪs] *n* Schmollen *nt*.
**sulky** ['sʌlkɪ] *adj (+er)* schmollend.
**sullen** ['sʌlən] *adj* **(a)** *(morose)* mürrisch. **(b)** *sky etc* düster, finster.
**sully** ['sʌlɪ] *vt reputation* besudeln.
**sulphate**, *(US)* **sulfate** ['sʌlfeɪt] *n* Sulfat *nt*.
**sulphide**, *(US)* **sulfide** ['sʌlfaɪd] *n* Sulfid *nt*.
**sulphur**, *(US)* **sulfur** ['sʌlfər] *n* Schwefel *m*.
**sulphuric**, *(US)* **sulfuric** [sʌl'fjʊərɪk] *adj* Schwefel-. ~ acid Schwefelsäure *f*.
**sultan** ['sʌltən] *n* Sultan *m*.

**sultana** [sʌl'tɑːnə] *n (fruit)* Sultanine *f*.
**sultry** ['sʌltrɪ] *adj weather* schwül; *woman* temperamentvoll; *beauty, look* glutvoll.
**sum** [sʌm] *n* **(a)** *(total)* Summe *f*; *(of money also)* Betrag *m*. that was the ~ **(total)** of his achievements das war alles, was er geschafft hatte. **(b)** *(esp Brit: calculation)* Rechenaufgabe *f*. to do ~s (in one's head) (im Kopf) rechnen.
▶**sum up 1** *vt sep* **(a)** *(summarize)* zusammenfassen. **(b)** *(evaluate rapidly)* ab- or einschätzen. **2** *vi (also Jur)* zusammenfassen. to ~ ~, we can say that ... zusammenfassend können wir feststellen, daß ...
**Sumatra** [suː'mɑːtrə] *n* Sumatra *nt*.
**summarize** ['sʌməraɪz] *vt* zusammenfassen.
**summary** ['sʌmərɪ] **1** *n* Zusammenfassung *f*. he gave us a short ~ of the film er gab uns eine kurze Inhaltsangabe des Films. **2** *adj* **(a)** *(brief) account* knapp, kurzgefaßt. **(b)** *(fast) treatment* kurz, knapp; *perusal* flüchtig; *(Jur) trial, punishment* summarisch; *dismissal* fristlos.
**summer** ['sʌmər] **1** *n* Sommer *m*. in (the) ~ im Sommer; two ~s ago im Sommer vor zwei Jahren; a ~'s day ein Sommertag *m*. **2** *adj attr* Sommer-.
**summer:** ~ camp *n (US)* Ferienlager *nt*; ~ house *n* Gartenhaus *nt*; ~time *n* Sommer *m*; *(daylight-saving time)* Sommerzeit *f*.
**summery** ['sʌmərɪ] *adj* sommerlich.
**summing-up** ['sʌmɪŋ'ʌp] *n (Jur)* Resümee *nt*.
**summit** ['sʌmɪt] **1** *n* Gipfel *m*; *(fig also)* Höhepunkt *m*; *(~ conference)* Gipfel(konferenz *f*) *m*. **2** *adj attr* Gipfel-.
**summon** ['sʌmən] *vt* **(a)** *servant, police etc* (herbei)rufen; *help* holen; *meeting, Parliament* einberufen. **(b)** *(Jur)* vorladen.
▶**summon up** *vt sep courage* zusammennehmen; *strength* aufbieten; *enthusiasm, energy* aufbringen.
**summons** ['sʌmənz] **1** *n (Jur)* Vorladung *f*. to take out a ~ against sb jdn vorladen lassen. **2** *vt (Jur)* vorladen.
**sump** [sʌmp] *n (Brit Aut)* Ölwanne *f*.
**sumptuous** ['sʌmptjʊəs] *adj (splendid)* luxuriös; *(extravagant)* aufwendig; *food etc* üppig, verschwenderisch.
**sumptuously** ['sʌmptjʊəslɪ] *adv see adj*.
**sumptuousness** ['sʌmptjʊəsnɪs] *n see adj* Luxus *m*; Aufwendigkeit *f*; Üppigkeit *f*.
**Sun** = Sunday So.
**sun** [sʌn] **1** *n* Sonne *f*. I've got the ~ in my eyes die Sonne blendet mich; he was up with the ~ er stand in aller Frühe auf; there is no reason under the ~ why ... es gibt absolut keinen Grund, warum ...; he's tried everything under the ~ er hat alles Menschenmögliche versucht; there's nothing new under the ~ *(prov)* es ist alles schon mal dagewesen; a place in the ~ *(fig)* ein Platz an der Sonne. **2** *vr* to ~ oneself sich sonnen.
**sun:** ~bathe *vi* sonnenbaden; ~bather *n* Sonnenanbeter(in *f*) *m (col)*; ~bathing *n* Sonnenbaden *nt*; ~beam *n* Sonnenstrahl *m*; ~bed *n* Sonnenbank *f*; ~ blind *n (awning)* Markise *f*; *(venetian blind)* Jalousie *f*; ~block *n* Sonnencreme *f mit hohem Lichtschutzfaktor*; ~burn *n* Bräune *f*; *(painful)* Sonnenbrand *m*; ~burnt *adj* sonnengebräunt; *(painfully)* von der Sonne verbrannt; to get ~burnt braun werden; (einen) Sonnenbrand bekommen.
**sundae** ['sʌndeɪ] *n* Eisbecher *m*.
**Sunday** ['sʌndɪ] **1** *n* Sonntag *m*. a month of ~s *(col)* eine Ewigkeit; never in a month of ~s *(col)* nie im Leben; *see* Tuesday. **2** *adj attr* Sonntags-. ~ best Sonntagsstaat *m*; ~ school Sonntagsschule *f*.
**sun:** ~ deck *n* Sonnendeck *nt*; ~dial *n* Sonnenuhr *f*;

~**down** *n (esp US)* Sonnenuntergang *m*.
**sundry** ['sʌndrɪ] **1** *adj* verschiedene. **2** *pron* all and ~ jedermann. **3** *n* **sundries** *pl* Verschiedenes (+sing vb).
**sunflower** ['sʌn,flaʊəʳ] *n* Sonnenblume *f*.
**sung** [sʌŋ] *ptp of* sing.
**sun:** ~**glasses** *npl* Sonnenbrille *f*; ~**-god** *n* Sonnengott *m*; ~ **hat** *n* Sonnenhut *m*.
**sunk** [sʌŋk] *ptp of* sink¹.
**sunken** ['sʌŋkən] *adj ship, treasure* versunken; *garden* tiefliegend *attr*; *bath* eingelassen; *cheeks* hohl; *eyes* eingesunken.
**sun:** ~ **lamp** *n* Höhensonne *f*; ~**less** *adj garden* ohne Sonne; *room also* dunkel; *day also* trübe; ~**light** *n* Sonnenlicht *nt*; **in the** ~**light** in der Sonne; ~**lit** *adj* sonnig; ~ **lounge** *n* Glasveranda *f*.
**sunny** ['sʌnɪ] *adj (+er) place, day etc* sonnig; *(fig) smile, disposition also* heiter. ~ **intervals** *(Met)* Aufheiterungen *pl*; **to look on the** ~ **side (of things)** die Dinge von der angenehmen Seite sehen.
**sun:** ~ **ray** *n* Sonnenstrahl *m*; ~**rise 1** *n* Sonnenaufgang *m*; **at** ~**rise** bei Sonnenaufgang; **2** *adj attr industries* der Spitzentechnologie; ~**roof** *n (of car)* Schiebedach *nt*; *(of hotel etc)* Sonnenterrasse *f*; ~**set** *n* Sonnenuntergang *m*; **at** ~**set** bei Sonnenuntergang; ~**shade** *n* Sonnenschirm *m*; *(awning)* Markise *f*; ~**shine** *n* Sonnenschein *m*; **hours of** ~**shine** Sonnenstunden *pl*; ~**spot** *n* **(a)** Sonnenfleck *m*; **(b)** *(col: for holiday)* Sonnenparadies *nt*; ~**stroke** *n* Sonnenstich *m*; **to get** ~**stroke** einen Sonnenstich bekommen; ~**tan** *n* Sonnenbräune *f*; **to get a** ~**tan** braun werden; ~**tan lotion** *n* Sonnenmilch *f*; ~**tan oil** *n* Sonnenöl *nt*; ~**tanned** *adj* braungebrannt; ~**trap** *n* sonniges Eckchen; ~**-up** *n (esp US)* Sonnenaufgang *m*; **at** ~**-up** bei Sonnenaufgang; ~ **visor** *n (Aut)* Sonnenblende *f*.
**super** ['suːpəʳ] *adj (col)* phantastisch, klasse *inv (col)*. ~! Klasse! *(col)*; **we had a** ~ **time** es war große Klasse *(col)* or phantastisch.
**superabundance** [,suːpərə'bʌndəns] *n (of an +dat)* großer Reichtum; *(excessive amount)* Überfluß *m*.
**superannuation** [,suːpə,rænjʊ'eɪʃən] *n* Rente *f*.
**superb** [suː'pɜːb] *adj* großartig; *design, painting also* meisterhaft.
**superbly** [suː'pɜːblɪ] *adv see adj* ~ **fit** ungemein fit.
**supercharger** ['suːpə,tʃɑːdʒəʳ] *n* Lader *m*.
**supercilious** [,suːpə'sɪlɪəs] *adj* hochnäsig.
**superficial** [,suːpə'fɪʃəl] *adj person, injury* oberflächlich; *characteristics, resemblance* äußerlich.
**superficiality** ['suːpə,fɪʃɪ'ælɪtɪ] *n see adj* Oberflächlichkeit *f*; Äußerlichkeit *f*.
**superficially** [,suːpə'fɪʃəlɪ] *adv see adj* oberflächlich; äußerlich. ~ **this may be true** oberflächlich gesehen mag das stimmen.
**superfluous** [suː'pɜːflʊəs] *adj* überflüssig.
**super:** ~**glue** *n* Sekundenkleber *m*; ~**grass** *n* Topinformant *m*; ~**highway** *n (US)* ≈ Autobahn *f*; ~**human** *adj* übermenschlich.
**superimpose** [,suːpərɪm'pəʊz] *vt* **to** ~ **sth on sth** etw auf etw *(acc)* legen; *(Phot)* etw über etw *(acc)* fotografieren; *(Film)* etw über etw *(acc)* filmen.
**superintend** [,suːpərɪn'tend] *vt* überwachen.
**superintendent** [,suːpərɪn'tendənt] *n* Aufsicht *f*; *(in swimming-pool)* Bademeister *m*; *(of police) (Brit)* ≈ Kommissar(in *f*) *m*; *(US)* ≈ Polizeipräsident *m*.
**superior** [suː'pɪərɪəʳ] **1** *adj* **(a)** *(better) quality, equipment* besser *(to* als*)*; *intellect, skill* überlegen *(to sb/ sth* jdm/einer Sache*)*. **(b)** *(excellent) work(manship), technique* großartig, hervorragend. ~ **quality goods** Waren *pl* bester Qualität. **(c)** *(higher in rank etc)* höher. ~ **officer** Vorgesetzte(r) *mf*; **to be** ~ **to sb/sth**

jdm/einer Sache übergeordnet sein. **(d)** *(greater)* überlegen *(to sb/sth* jdm/einer Sache*)*; *forces also* stärker *(to* als*)*; *strength also* größer *(to* als*)*. **they were** ~ **to us in number(s)** sie waren uns zahlenmäßig überlegen. **(e)** *(snobbish) person* überheblich; *smile also* überlegen; *(smart) restaurant, clientele* fein, vornehm. **2** *n* **(a)** *(in rank)* Vorgesetzte(r) *mf*. **to be sb's** ~ *(in ability)* jdm überlegen sein. **(b)** *(Eccl)* **Mother S**~ Mutter Oberin *f*.
**superiority** [su,pɪərɪ'ɒrɪtɪ] *n* **(a)** *(of cloth etc)* bessere Qualität; *(of technique, ability, in numbers)* Überlegenheit *f*. **(b)** *(in rank)* höhere Stellung. **(c)** *(conceitedness)* Überheblichkeit *f*.
**superlative** [suː'pɜːlətɪv] **1** *adj (excellent)* überragend; *(Gram)* superlativisch. **2** *n* Superlativ *m*.
**superman** ['suːpəmæn] *n, pl* **-men** [-men] Übermensch *m*. **S**~ *(in comics)* Supermann *m*.
**supermarket** ['suːpə,mɑːkɪt] *n* Supermarkt *m*.
**supernatural** [,suːpə'nætʃərəl] *adj* übernatürlich. **the** ~ das Übernatürliche.
**superpower** ['suːpə,paʊəʳ] *n (Pol)* Supermacht *f*.
**superscript** ['suːpə,skrɪpt] *adj (Typ)* hochgestellt.
**supersede** [,suːpə'siːd] *vt* ablösen; *person, belief also* an die Stelle treten von. ~**d ideas** überholte Ideen.
**supersonic** [,suːpə'sɒnɪk] *adj* Überschall-.
**superstar** ['suːpə,stɑːʳ] *n* Superstar *m*.
**superstition** [,suːpə'stɪʃən] *n* Aberglaube *m no pl*.
**superstitious** [,suːpə'stɪʃəs] *adj* abergläubisch.
**superstore** ['suːpə,stɔː] *n* Großmarkt *m*.
**superstructure** ['suːpə,strʌktʃəʳ] *n* Überbau *m*; *(of ship)* Aufbauten *pl*.
**supertanker** ['suːpə,tæŋkəʳ] *n* Supertanker *m*.
**supertax** ['suːpə,tæks] *n* Höchststeuer *f*.
**supervise** ['suːpəvaɪz] **1** *vt* beaufsichtigen. **2** *vi* Aufsicht führen, die Aufsicht haben.
**supervision** [,suːpə'vɪʒən] *n* Aufsicht *f*; *(action)* Beaufsichtigung *f*. **under the** ~ **of** unter der Aufsicht von.
**supervisor** ['suːpəvaɪzəʳ] *n (of work)* Aufseher(in *f*) *m*, Aufsicht *f*; *(of research)* Leiter(in *f*) *m*; *(Brit Univ)* ≈ Tutor(in *f*) *m*; *(for PhD)* Doktorvater *m*.
**supervisory** ['suːpəvaɪzərɪ] *adj role* beaufsichtigend. **in a** ~ **post** in einer Aufsichtsposition.
**supine** ['suːpaɪn] *adj* **to be** ~ auf dem Rücken liegen.
**supper** ['sʌpəʳ] *n (evening meal)* Abendessen *nt*; *(late evening snack)* (später) Imbiß. **at** ~ beim Abendessen; **to have** ~ zu Abend essen.
**suppertime** ['sʌpətaɪm] *n* Abendessenszeit *f*.
**supplant** [sə'plɑːnt] *vt* ablösen, ersetzen; *(forcibly)* verdrängen; *(by ruse) rival* ausstechen.
**supple** ['sʌpl] *adj (+er)* geschmeidig, elastisch; *shoes* weich; *mind* beweglich.
**supplement** ['sʌplɪmənt] **1** *n* **(a)** Ergänzung *f (to gen)*; *(of book)* Ergänzungsband *m (to zu)*; *(at end of book)* Anhang *m*; *(additional charge)* Zuschlag *m*. **a** ~ **to his income** eine Aufbesserung seines Einkommens. **(b)** *(colour* ~ *etc)* Beilage *f*. **2** *vt* ergänzen; *income* aufbessern.
**supplementary** [,sʌplɪ'mentərɪ] *adj* zusätzlich, ergänzend; *volume, report also* Zusatz-, Ergänzungs-. ~ **benefit** *(Brit Hist)* ≈ Sozialhilfe *f*; ~ **fare** Zuschlag *m*.
**supplication** [,sʌplɪ'keɪʃən] *n* Flehen *nt no pl*.
**supplier** [sə'plaɪəʳ] *n (Comm)* Lieferant(in *f*) *m*.
**supply** [sə'plaɪ] **1** *n* **(a)** *(supplying)* Versorgung *f*; *(Comm: delivery)* Lieferung *f (to an +acc)*; *(Econ)* Angebot *nt*. **electricity** ~ Stromversorgung *f*; **the** ~ **of blood to the brain** die Versorgung des Gehirns mit Blut; ~ **and demand** Angebot und Nachfrage *(+pl vb)*. **(b)** *(that supplied)* Lieferung *f*. **to cut off**

**the** ~ *(of gas, water etc)* das Gas/Wasser *etc* abstellen. **(c)** *(stock)* Vorrat *m.* **supplies** *pl (food)* Vorräte *pl*; *(for expedition also, for journey)* Proviant *m*; **to get** *or* **lay in supplies** *or* **a** ~ **of** sich *(dat)* einen Vorrat an *(+dat)* anlegen; **a month's** ~ ein Monatsbedarf *m*; **to be in short** ~ knapp sein; **fresh supplies** *(Mil)* Nachschub *m*; **office supplies** Bürobedarf *m*; **medical supplies** medizinischer Bedarf.

**2** *vt* **(a)** *material, food etc* sorgen für; *(deliver) goods* liefern; *evidence, gas* liefern; *(put at sb's disposal)* stellen. **(b)** *(with mit)* versorgen; *(Comm)* beliefern. **this supplied me with the chance** ... das gab mir die Chance ...; **we have not been supplied with a radio** wir haben kein Radio bekommen. **(c)** *(satisfy, make good) need* befriedigen; *want* abhelfen *(+dat)*; *(Comm)* demand decken.

**supply:** ~ **industry** *n* Zulieferungsindustrie *f*; ~ **lines,** ~ **routes** *npl (Mil, fig)* Versorgungslinien *pl*; ~ **ship** *n* Versorgungsschiff *nt*; ~ **teacher** *n (Brit)* Vertretung *f.*

**support** [sə'pɔːt] **1** *n* **(a)** *(lit)* Stütze *f.* **to give** ~ **to sb/sth** jdn/etw stützen; **to lean on sb for** ~ sich auf jdn stützen. **(b)** *(fig) (no pl: moral, financial backing)* Unterstützung *f*; *(person)* Stütze *f.* **in** ~ **of** zur Unterstützung *(+gen)*; **in** ~ **of an allegation** zur Untermauerung einer Behauptung; **to speak in** ~ **of a candidate** einen Kandidaten unterstützen; **there was a lot of** ~ **for his views** viele stimmten seiner Meinung bei.

**2** *attr (Mil)* troops, vessel etc Hilfs-.

**3** *vt* **(a)** *(lit)* stützen; *(Tech also)* abstützen; *(bear the weight of)* tragen. **(b)** *(fig)* unterstützen; *plan, motion, sb's application also* befürworten; *party, cause also* eintreten für; *(give moral* ~ *to also)* beistehen *(+dat)*, Rückhalt geben *(+dat)*; *(corroborate)* erhärten, untermauern; *(financially) family* unterhalten; *party, orchestra* finanziell unterstützen. **he** ~**s Arsenal** er ist Arsenal-Anhänger *m*; **which team do you** ~**?** für welche Mannschaft bist du?

**4** *vr* **to** ~ **oneself** *(physically)* sich stützen *(on* auf *+acc)*; *(financially)* seinen Unterhalt (selbst) bestreiten.

**supporter** [sə'pɔːtəʳ] *n* Anhänger(in *f*) *m*; *(of theory, cause also)* Befürworter(in *f*) *m*; *(Sport also)* Fan *m.* ~**s' club** Fanclub *m.*

**supporting** [sə'pɔːtɪŋ] *adj* film Vor-; *role, programme etc* Neben-. ~ **actor/actress** Nebendarsteller *m*/Nebendarstellerin *f*; **the** ~ **cast** die Nebendarsteller *pl.*

**supportive** [sə'pɔːtɪv] *adj* stützend *attr.* **my parents were very** ~ meine Eltern waren mir eine große Stütze.

**suppose** [sə'pəuz] *vt* **(a)** *(imagine)* sich *(dat)* vorstellen; *(assume, postulate also)* annehmen. **let us** ~ **that X equals 3** angenommen, X sei gleich 3; **even supposing it were** *or* **was true** (sogar) angenommen, daß es wahr ist; **always supposing he comes** immer vorausgesetzt, (daß) er kommt.

**(b)** *(believe, think)* annehmen, denken. **I** ~ **he'll come** ich nehme an, (daß) er kommt; **I don't** ~ **he'll come** ich glaube kaum, daß er kommt; **I** ~ **he won't come** ich denke, er wird nicht kommen, er wird wohl nicht kommen; **I** ~ **that's the best thing** das ist vermutlich das Beste; **I don't** ~ **you could lend me a pound?** Sie könnten mir nicht zufällig ein Pfund leihen?; **will he be coming?** — **I** ~ **so** ich komme er? — ich denke schon; **you ought to be leaving** — **I** ~ **so** du solltest jetzt gehen — stimmt wohl; **I don't** ~ **so** ich glaube kaum; **he is generally** ~**d to be rich** er gilt als reich; **he's** ~**d to be coming** er soll (angeblich) kommen.

**(c)** *(in passive: ought)* **to be** ~**d to do sth** etw tun sollen; **he's the one who's** ~**d to do it** *er* müßte es eigentlich tun; **you're** ~**d to be in bed** du solltest eigentlich im Bett sein; **he isn't** ~**d to find out** er darf es nicht erfahren; **you're not** ~**d to (do that)** das darfst du nicht tun.

**(d)** *(in imper: I suggest)* ~ **we have a go?** warum versuchen wir es nicht einmal?; ~ **we buy it?** wie wäre es, wenn wir es kauften?

**(e)** *(presuppose)* voraussetzen. **that** ~**s unlimited resources** das setzt unbegrenzte Vorräte voraus.

**supposed** [sə'pəuzd] *adj* vermutet; *date, site, author also* mutmaßlich.

**supposedly** [sə'pəuzɪdlɪ] *adv* angeblich. **the atom was** ~ **indivisible** das Atom galt als unteilbar.

**supposing** [sə'pəuzɪŋ] *conj* angenommen. **but** ~ ... aber wenn ...

**supposition** [ˌsʌpə'zɪʃən] *n (no pl: hypothesizing)* Mutmaßung, Spekulation *f*; *(thing supposed)* Annahme *f.* **acting on the** ~ **that you are right** vorausgesetzt, daß Sie recht haben.

**suppository** [sə'pozɪtərɪ] *n* Zäpfchen *nt.*

**suppress** [sə'pres] *vt* unterdrücken.

**suppression** [sə'preʃən] *n* Unterdrückung *f.*

**suppressor** ['sə'presəʳ] *n (Elec)* Entstörungselement *nt.*

**supra-** ['suːprə-] *pref* über-; *(esp with foreign words)* supra-. ~**national** überstaatlich.

**supremacy** [su'preməsɪ] *n* Vormachtstellung *f*; *(Pol, Eccl, fig)* Supremat *nt* or *m.* **air/naval** ~ Luft-/Seeherrschaft *f.*

**supreme** [su'priːm] **1** *adj (highest, ultimate)* höchste(r, s); *(very great) courage etc* äußerste(r, s), größte(r, s). **with** ~ **indifference** völlig unbeteiligt; **S**~ **Court** Oberster Gerichtshof. **2** *adv* **to rule** *or* **reign** ~ *(monarch)* absolut herrschen; *(champion, justice)* unangefochten herrschen.

**supremely** [su'priːmlɪ] *adv beautiful* unvergleichlich; *gifted* außerordentlich; *confident* zutiefst.

**Supt** = **superintendent.**

**surcharge** ['sɜːtʃɑːdʒ] *n* Zuschlag *m*; *(postal)* Nachporto, Strafporto *(col)* nt.

**sure** [ʃuəʳ] **1** *adj (+er)* sicher; *proof, facts also* eindeutig; *method also, remedy* zuverlässig, verläßlich. **I'm perfectly** ~ ich bin (mir da) ganz sicher; **to be** ~ **about sth** sich *(dat)* einer Sache *(gen)* sicher sein; **I'm not so** ~ **about that** da bin ich nicht so sicher; **to be** ~ **of oneself** sich *(dat)* seiner Sache sicher sein; *(generally self-confident)* selbstsicher sein; **it is** ~ **that he will come** er kommt ganz bestimmt; **it's** ~ **to rain** es regnet ganz bestimmt; **be** ~ **to turn the gas off** vergiß nicht, das Gas abzudrehen; **you're** ~ **of success** der Erfolg ist Ihnen sicher; **I want to be** ~ **of seeing him** ich möchte ihn auf jeden Fall sehen; **to make** ~ *(check)* nachsehen; **make** ~ **you get the leads the right way round** achten Sie darauf, daß die Kabel richtig herum sind; **make** ~ **you take your keys** denk daran, deine Schlüssel mitzunehmen; **it's best to make** ~ sicher ist sicher; **to make** ~ **of one's facts** sicherstellen, daß die Angaben stimmen; **to make** ~ **of a seat** sich *(dat)* einen Platz sichern; ~ **thing!** *(esp US col)* klare Sache! *(col)*; **he'll quit for** ~ er kündigt ganz bestimmt; **I'll find out for** ~ ich werde das genau herausfinden; **do you know for** ~**?** wissen Sie das ganz sicher?; **with a** ~ **hand** mit sicherer Hand.

**2** *adv (esp US)* **will you do it?** — ~**!** machst du das? — klar! *(col)*; **that meat** ~ **was tough** das Fleisch war vielleicht zäh!; **and** ~ **enough he did come** und er ist tatsächlich gekommen; **he'll come** ~ **enough** er kommt ganz bestimmt.

**sure:** ~-**fire** *adj (col)* todsicher *(col)*; ~-**footed** *adj* (tritt)sicher.

**surely** ['ʃʊəlɪ] *adv* **(a)** bestimmt, sicher. ~ **you don't mean it?** das meinen Sie doch bestimmt nicht (so)?; ~ **not!** das kann doch nicht stimmen!; ~ **someone must know the answer** irgend jemand muß doch die Antwort wissen. **(b)** *(esp US: gladly)* gern, mit Vergnügen.

**sureness** ['ʃʊənɪs] *n* **(a)** *(positiveness)* Überzeugung, Sicherheit *f*. **(b)** *(reliability, steadiness)* Sicherheit *f*; *(of method)* Verläßlichkeit *f*; *(of sb's judgement also)* Untrüglichkeit *f*.

**surety** ['ʃʊərətɪ] *n (sum)* Bürgschaft, Sicherheit *f*; *(person)* Bürge *m*. **to go** *or* **stand** ~ **for sb** für jdn bürgen.

**surf** [sɜːf] **1** *n* Brandung *f*. **2** *vi* surfen.

**surface** ['sɜːfɪs] **1** *n* **(a)** *(lit, fig)* Oberfläche *f*; *(of road)* Decke *f*, Belag *m*. **on the** ~ **it seems that ...** oberflächlich sieht es so aus, als ob ...; **on the** ~ **he is friendly enough** nach außen hin ist er ganz freundlich. **(b)** *(Math: of cube etc)* Fläche *f*. **(c)** *(Min)* **at/on/up to the** ~ über Tage. **2** *adj attr* **(a)** oberflächlich; *measurements* Oberflächen-. **(b)** *travel* auf dem Land-/Seeweg. **(c)** *(Min) worker, job* über Tage. **3** *vt road* mit einem Belag versehen; *wall* verblenden. **4** *vi (lit, fig)* auftauchen.

**surface:** ~ **area** *n* Fläche *f*; *(Math)* Flächeninhalt *m*; ~ **mail** *n* **by** ~ **mail** auf dem Land-/Seeweg, nicht per Luftpost; ~-**to-air** *adj attr missile* Boden-Luft-.

**surfboard** ['sɜːfbɔːd] *n* Surfbrett *nt*.

**surfeit** ['sɜːfɪt] *n* Übermaß, Zuviel *nt (of an +dat)*.

**surfer** ['sɜːfəʳ] *n* Wellenreiter(in *f*), Surfer(in *f*) *m*.

**surfing** ['sɜːfɪŋ] *n* Wellenreiten, Surfen *nt*.

**surge** [sɜːdʒ] **1** *n (of sea)* Wogen *nt*; *(of floodwater)* Schwall *m*; *(Elec)* Spannungsstoß *m*. **a** ~ **of people** eine wogende Menschenmenge; **he felt a sudden** ~ **of rage** er fühlte, wie die Wut in ihm aufstieg. **2** *vi (sea)* branden; *(floods, river)* anschwellen. **blood** ~**d into her face** ihr schoß das Blut ins Gesicht; **they** ~**d towards/round him** sie drängten auf ihn zu/sie umdrängten ihn; **people** ~**d in/out** eine Menschenmenge flutete herein/heraus.

**surgeon** ['sɜːdʒən] *n* Chirurg(in *f*) *m*.

**surgery** ['sɜːdʒərɪ] *n* **(a)** Chirurgie *f*. **to have** ~ operiert werden; **to need (heart)** ~ (am Herzen) operiert werden müssen. **(b)** *(Brit) (room)* Sprechzimmer *nt*; *(consultation)* Sprechstunde *f*. ~ **hours** Sprechstunden *pl*.

**surgical** ['sɜːdʒɪkəl] *adj treatment* operativ; *technique, instrument* chirurgisch; *training, skill* Chirurgen-, eines Chirurgen. ~ **spirit** Wundbenzin *nt*; ~ **ward** chirurgische Station, Chirurgie *f (col)*.

**surliness** ['sɜːlɪnɪs] *n* Verdrießlichkeit, Mißmutigkeit *f*.

**surly** ['sɜːlɪ] *adj (+er)* verdrießlich, mißmutig.

**surmise** [sɜːˈmaɪz] *vt* vermuten, mutmaßen.

**surmount** [sɜːˈmaʊnt] *vt obstacle* überwinden.

**surname** ['sɜːneɪm] *n* Nachname *m*. **what is his** ~? wie heißt er mit Nachnamen?

**surpass** [sɜːˈpɑːs] **1** *vt* **(a)** *(be better than)* übertreffen. **(b)** *(exceed) comprehension* hinausgehen über *(+acc)*. **2** *vr* **to** ~ **oneself** sich selbst übertreffen.

**surplice** ['sɜːplɪs] *n* Chorrock *m*.

**surplus** ['sɜːpləs] **1** *n* Überschuß *m (of an +dat)*. **2** *adj* überschüssig; *(of countable objects)* überzählig. **sale of** ~ **stock** Verkauf *m* von Lagerbeständen; **it is** ~ **to my requirements** das benötige ich nicht.

**surprise** [səˈpraɪz] **1** *n* Überraschung *f*. **in** ~ überrascht; **much to my** ~, **to my great** ~ zu meiner großen Überraschung; **with a look of** ~ mit überraschtem Gesicht; **what a** ~! was für eine Überraschung!; **to give sb a** ~ jdn überraschen; **to take sb by** ~ jdn überraschen. **2** *attr attack, visit* Überraschungs-; *parcel etc* überraschend. **3** *vt* überraschen; *(catch unawares also)* überrumpeln. **I wouldn't be** ~**d if ...** es würde mich nicht wundern, wenn ...; **don't be** ~**d if he refuses** wundern Sie sich nicht, wenn er ablehnt; **I'm** ~**ed at you!** du überraschst mich sehr!

**surprising** [səˈpraɪzɪŋ] *adj* überraschend, erstaunlich. **it's hardly** ~ **he said no** es ist kaum verwunderlich, daß er nein gesagt hat.

**surprisingly** [səˈpraɪzɪŋlɪ] *adv* ~ **(enough), he was right** er hatte erstaunlicherweise recht; **and then** ~ **he left** und dann ist er zu unserer/ihrer *etc* Überraschung gegangen.

**surreal** [səˈrɪəl] *adj* unwirklich.

**surrealism** [səˈrɪəlɪzəm] *n* Surrealismus *m*.

**surrealist** [səˈrɪəlɪst] *n* Surrealist(in *f*) *m*.

**surrealistic** [sə,rɪəˈlɪstɪk] *adj* surrealistisch.

**surrender** [səˈrendəʳ] **1** *vi* sich ergeben *(to dat)*; *(to police)* sich stellen *(to dat)*. **I** ~! ich ergebe mich! **2** *vt (Mil)* übergeben; *goods, firearms also* ausliefern; *insurance policy* einlösen; *lease* kündigen; *claim, right* aufgeben. **3** *vr* **to** ~ **oneself to sth** sich einer Sache *(dat)* hingeben; **to fate** sich in etw *(acc)* ergeben. **4** *n* **(a)** Kapitulation *f (to vor +dat)*. **(b)** *see vt* Übergabe *f (to an +acc)*; Auslieferung *f (to an +acc)*; Einlösen *nt*; Kündigung *f*; Aufgabe *f*. ~ **value** *(Insur)* Rückkaufswert *m*.

**surreptitious** *adj*, ~**ly** *adv* [,sʌrəpˈtɪʃəs, -lɪ] heimlich.

**surrogate** ['sʌrəgɪt] **1** *n (substitute)* Ersatz *m*. **2** *attr* Ersatz-. ~ **mother** Leihmutter *f*.

**surround** [səˈraʊnd] **1** *n* Umrandung *f*. **2** *vt* umgeben; *(Mil)* umstellen.

**surrounding** [səˈraʊndɪŋ] *adj* umliegend. **in the** ~ **countryside** in der Umgebung.

**surroundings** [səˈraʊndɪŋz] *npl* Umgebung *f*.

**surtax** ['sɜːtæks] *n* Steuerzuschlag *m*.

**surveillance** [sɜːˈveɪləns] *n* Überwachung *f*. **to be under** ~ überwacht werden; **to keep sb under** ~ jdn überwachen.

**survey** ['sɜːveɪ] **1** *n* **(a)** *(of land)* Vermessung *f*; *(report)* (Vermessungs)gutachten *nt*; *(of house)* Begutachtung *f*; *(report)* Gutachten *nt*. **to have a** ~ **done on a house** ein Gutachten über ein Haus erstellen lassen. **(b)** *(review: of subject, development)* Überblick *m (of über +acc)*. **(c)** *(inquiry)* Untersuchung *f (of, on über +acc)*; *(by opinion poll etc)* Umfrage *f (of, on über +acc)*.

**2** [sɜːˈveɪ] *vt* **(a)** *(look at) scene, person, prospects* sich *(dat)* ansehen; *(appraisingly also)* begutachten; *person, goods* mustern. **(b)** *(study) prospects, plans* untersuchen; *events, trends* einen Überblick geben über *(+acc)*. **(c)** *(Surv) site* vermessen; *building* inspizieren.

**surveying** [sɜːˈveɪɪŋ] *n (of land)* Vermessung *f*; *(Brit: of buildings)* Inspektion *f*.

**surveyor** [səˈveɪəʳ] *n (land* ~) Landvermesser(in *f*) *m*; *(Brit: building* ~) Bauinspektor(in *f*) *m*.

**survival** [səˈvaɪvəl] *n (of person etc)* Überleben *nt*; *(of species also)* Fortbestand *m*; *(of customs)* Weiterleben *nt*. **the** ~ **of the fittest** das Überleben der Stärkeren; ~ **course** Überlebenstraining *nt no pl*; ~ **kit** Überlebensausrüstung *f*.

**survive** [səˈvaɪv] **1** *vi (person, animal etc)* überleben; *(in job)* sich halten (können); *(treasures, play)* erhalten bleiben; *(custom)* fortbestehen. **you'll** ~ *(iro)* das wirst du schon überleben! **2** *vt* überleben; *(house, objects)* fire etc überstehen; *(col)* heat, boredom etc aushalten.

**survivor** [sə'vaɪvər] n Überlebende(r) mf. **to be a ~** *(fig: in politics etc)* nicht unterzukriegen sein.

**susceptibility** [sə,septə'bɪlɪtɪ] n no pl see adj Beeindruckbarkeit f. **~ to sth** Empfänglichkeit f für etw; Ausgesetztsein nt gegenüber etw; Anfälligkeit f für etw.

**susceptible** [sə'septəbl] adj *(impressionable)* beeindruckbar. **~ to sth** *to charms etc* für etw empfänglich; *to attack* einer Sache *(dat)* ausgesetzt; *to colds, influence* für etw anfällig.

**suspect** ['sʌspekt] **1** adj verdächtig. **2** n Verdächtige(r) mf. **3** [sə'spekt] vt **(a)** *person* verdächtigen *(of sth* einer Sache *gen)*, in Verdacht haben. **I ~ her of having stolen it** ich habe sie im Verdacht, es gestohlen zu haben; **the ~ed bank robber** der mutmaßliche Bankräuber; **he ~s nothing** er ahnt nichts. **(b)** *(doubt) truth* anzweifeln; *motive* argwöhnisch sein gegenüber. **(c)** *(think likely)* vermuten. **I ~ed as much** das habe ich doch vermutet; **a ~ed case of measles** ein Fall, bei dem der Verdacht auf Masern besteht.

**suspend** [sə'spend] vt **(a)** *(hang)* (auf)hängen *(from an +dat)*. **to hang ~ed from sth/in sth** von/in etw *(dat)* hängen. **(b)** *(stop, defer) publication, payment* (zeitweilig) einstellen; *judgement* aufschieben; *sentence* zur Bewährung aussetzen. **he was given a ~ed sentence** seine Strafe wurde zur Bewährung ausgesetzt. **(c)** *person* suspendieren; *member, pupil* zeitweilig ausschließen; *(Sport)* sperren; *licence* zeitweilig einziehen; *law, privileges* aussetzen. **to ~ from duty** suspendieren.

**suspender** [sə'spendər] n usu pl **(a)** *(Brit) (for stockings)* Strumpfhalter, Straps m; *(for socks)* Sockenhalter m. **~ belt** Strumpf(halter)gürtel m. **(b)** *(US)* **~s** pl Hosenträger pl.

**suspense** [sə'spens] n *(in book, film etc)* Spannung f. **full of ~** spannungsgeladen; **the ~ is killing me** ich bin gespannt wie ein Regenschirm *(hum col)*; **to keep sb in ~** jdn auf die Folter spannen *(col)*.

**suspension** [sə'spenʃən] n **(a)** see **suspend (b)** zeitweilige Einstellung; Aufschub m; Aussetzung f (zur Bewährung). **(b)** see **suspend (c)** Suspendierung f; zeitweiliger Ausschluß; Sperrung f; zeitweiliger Einzug; Aussetzen nt. **(c)** *(Aut)* Federung f. **independent ~** Einzelradaufhängung f.

**suspension bridge** n Hängebrücke f.

**suspicion** [sə'spɪʃən] n Verdacht, Argwohn *(geh)* m no pl; *(trace)* Hauch m, Spur f. **to arouse sb's ~s** jds Verdacht erregen; **I have a ~ that ...** ich habe den Verdacht, daß ...; **to have one's ~s about sth** seine Zweifel bezüglich einer Sache *(gen)* haben; **to be above (all)/under ~** über jeden Verdacht erhaben sein/unter Verdacht stehen; **to arrest sb on ~/on ~ of murder** jdn wegen Tatverdachts/Mordverdachts festnehmen.

**suspicious** [sə'spɪʃəs] adj **(a)** *(feeling suspicion)* argwöhnisch, mißtrauisch *(of gegenüber)*. **to be ~ about sth** etw mit Mißtrauen betrachten. **(b)** *(causing suspicion)* verdächtig.

**suspiciously** [sə'spɪʃəslɪ] adv see adj **(a)** argwöhnisch, mißtrauisch. **(b)** verdächtig. **it looks ~ like measles to me** das sieht mir verdächtig nach Masern aus.

**suspiciousness** [sə'spɪʃəsnɪs] n see adj **(a)** Argwohn m *(geh)*, Mißtrauen nt. **(b)** Verdächtigkeit f.

**suss** [sʌs] **suss out**: vt sep *(Brit col)* **to ~ sb** jdm auf den Zahn fühlen *(col)*; **to ~ sth** etw herausbekommen; **to ~ things ~** die Lage peilen *(col)*.

**sustain** [sə'steɪn] vt **(a)** *(support) load, weight* aushalten, tragen; *life* erhalten; *family* unterhalten; *(nourish) body* bei Kräften halten. **(b)** *(maintain) pretence, argument* aufrechterhalten; *effort also* nicht nachlassen in *(+dat)*; *(Jur) objection* stattgeben *(+dat)*. **(c)** *(receive) injury* erleiden.

**sustained** [sə'steɪnd] adj *effort etc* ausdauernd; *applause* anhaltend.

**sustaining** [sə'steɪnɪŋ] adj *food* nahrhaft. **~ pedal** *(Mus)* Fortepedal nt.

**sustenance** ['sʌstɪnəns] n *(food and drink)* Nahrung f; *(nutritive quality)* Nährwert m.

**suture** ['suːtʃər] *(Med)* **1** n Naht f. **2** vt nähen.

**SW** = **(a)** South-West SW. **(b)** short wave KW.

**swab** [swɒb] **1** n *(Med)* Tupfer m; *(specimen)* Abstrich m. **to take a ~** einen Abstrich machen. **2** vt **(a)** *(Med) wound etc* (ab)tupfen. **(b)** *(Naut: also ~ down)* wischen.

**Swabia** ['sweɪbɪə] n Schwaben nt.

**swag** [swæg] n *(col)* Beute f.

**swagger** ['swægər] vi **(a)** stolzieren. **(b)** *(boast, act boastfully)* angeben.

**Swahili** [swɑ'hiːlɪ] n *(language)* Swahili nt.

**swallow**[1] ['swɒləʊ] **1** n Schluck m. **2** vt *food, drink* (hinunter)schlucken; *(fig) story, evidence, insult* schlucken. **to ~ sth whole** *(lit)* etw ganz schlucken; *(fig)* etw ohne weiteres schlucken; **to ~ one's words** *(retract)* seine Worte zurücknehmen. **3** vi schlucken. **to ~ hard** *(fig)* kräftig schlucken. **▶swallow up** vt sep *(fig)* verschlingen. **the mist seemed to ~ them ~** der Nebel schien sie zu verschlucken; **I wished the ground would open and ~ me ~** ich wäre am liebsten in den Boden versunken.

**swallow**[2] n *(bird)* Schwalbe f.

**swam** [swæm] pret of **swim**.

**swamp** [swɒmp] **1** n Sumpf m. **2** vt unter Wasser setzen; *(fig)* überschwemmen.

**swampy** ['swɒmpɪ] adj *(+er)* sumpfig.

**swan** [swɒn] **1** n Schwan m. **2** vi *(col)* **to ~ off** abziehen *(col)*; **to ~ around New York** in New York herumziehen *(col)*.

**swank** [swæŋk] vi *(col)* angeben *(about mit)*.

**swanky** ['swæŋkɪ] adj *(+er) (col) manner, words* großspurig; *car etc* protzig *(col)*, Angeber-.

**swansong** ['swɒnsɒŋ] n *(fig)* Schwanengesang m.

**swap** [swɒp] **1** n Tausch m. **to do a ~ (with sb)** (mit jdm) tauschen. **2** vt *stamps, cars, houses etc* tauschen; *stories* austauschen. **to ~ sth for sth** etw gegen etw eintauschen; **to ~ places with sb** mit jdm tauschen. **3** vi tauschen.

**SWAPO** ['swɑːpəʊ] = **South-West Africa People's Organization** SWAPO f.

**swarm** [swɔːm] **1** n *(of insects, birds)* Schwarm m; *(of people also)* Schar f. **2** vi *(bees, flies, people)* schwärmen. **the place was ~ing with insects/people** es wimmelte von Insekten/Leuten.

**swarthy** ['swɔːðɪ] adj *(+er) skin* dunkel.

**swashbuckling** ['swɒʃbʌklɪŋ] adj verwegen.

**swastika** ['swɒstɪkə] n Hakenkreuz nt.

**SWAT** n abbr (= **Special Weapons and Tactics**) *(US)* Spezialeinheit f der amerikanischen Polizei.

**swat** [swɒt] vt *fly* totschlagen.

**swathe** [sweɪð] vt wickeln *(in in +acc)*.

**sway** [sweɪ] **1** n *(influence, rule)* Macht f *(over über +acc)*. **to hold ~ over sb** jdn beherrschen, jdn in seiner Macht haben. **2** vi *(trees)* sich wiegen; *(hanging object)* schwingen; *(building, bridge etc, person)* schwanken; *(train, boat)* schaukeln; *(hips)* wackeln. **3** vt **(a)** schwenken; *(wind)* hin und her bewegen. **(b)** *(influence)* beeinflussen; *(change sb's mind)* umstimmen.

**Swaziland** ['swɑːzɪlænd] n Swasiland nt.

**swear** [swɛəʳ] *(vb: pret* **swore,** *ptp* **sworn)** **1** *vt allegiance* schwören; *oath also* leisten, ablegen. **I ~ it!** ich kann das beschwören!; **to ~ sb to secrecy** jdn schwören lassen, daß er nichts verrät; **I could have sworn that was Louise** *(am almost sure)* ich könnte schwören, daß das Louise war; *(but it wasn't)* ich hätte schwören können, daß das Louise war. **2** *vi* **(a)** *(use solemn oath)* schwören. **to ~ on the Bible** auf die Bibel schwören; **to ~ to sth** etw beschwören. **(b)** *(use swearwords)* fluchen *(about* über *+acc).* **to ~ at sb/sth** jdn/etw beschimpfen.
▶**swear by** *vi +prep obj (col)* schwören auf *(+acc).*
▶**swear in** *vt sep witness etc* vereidigen.
**swearword** ['swɛə,wɜːd] *n* Fluch, Kraftausdruck *m.*
**sweat** [swet] **1** *n* Schweiß *m no pl.* **by the ~ of one's brow** *(fig)* im Schweiße seines Angesichts *(liter);* **to get into a ~ about sth** *(fig)* wegen etw ins Schwitzen geraten *or* kommen; **no ~** *(col)* kein Problem; **it was a real ~** *(col)* wir haben wirklich geschuftet *(col).* **2** *vi* schwitzen *(with* vor *+dat); (fig col) (work hard)* sich abrackern *(col) (over* mit*); (worry)* zittern *(with* vor *+dat).* **to ~ like a pig** *(col)* wie ein Affe schwitzen *(col).* **3** *vt* **to ~ blood** *(with worry)* Blut und Wasser schwitzen; *(with effort)* sich abrackern *(col);* **to ~ it out** *(fig col)* durchhalten; *(sit and wait)* abwarten.
**sweatband** ['swet,bænd] *n* Schweißband *nt.*
**sweated labour** ['swetɪd'leɪbəʳ] *n* ausgebeutete Arbeitskräfte *pl.* **that was ~!** *(col)* das war Ausbeutung!
**sweater** ['swetəʳ] *n* Pullover *m.*
**sweat:** **~shirt** *n* Sweatshirt *nt; (Sport)* Trainingspullover *m;* **~shop** *n (pej, hum col)* Ausbeuterbetrieb *m (pej).*
**sweaty** ['swetɪ] *adj (+er) hands* schweißig; *feet, smell also* Schweiß-; *person, socks* verschwitzt; *weather, work* zum Schwitzen.
**swede** [swiːd] *n (Brit)* Kohlrübe, Steckrübe *f.*
**Swede** [swiːd] *n* Schwede *m,* Schwedin *f.*
**Sweden** ['swiːdn] *n* Schweden *nt.*
**Swedish** ['swiːdɪʃ] **1** *adj* schwedisch. **2** *n* Schwedisch *nt.*
**sweep** [swiːp] *(vb: pret, ptp* **swept)** **1** *n* **(a) to give the floor a ~** den Boden kehren *or* fegen. **(b)** *(chimney ~)* Schornsteinfeger *m.* **(c)** *(of arm, pendulum)* Schwung *m; (of sword also)* Streich *m; (of dress)* Rauschen *nt no pl; (of light, radar)* Strahl *m.* **this magnificent ~ of countryside** diese herrliche Landschaft; **a long ~ of motorway** eine weitgestreckte Autobahn; **at one ~** *(fig)* auf einen Schlag; **to make a clean ~** *(fig)* gründlich aufräumen *(of sth* bei etw*).*
**2** *vt* **(a)** kehren, fegen; *dust, snow* wegfegen. **to ~ sth under the carpet** *(fig)* etw unter den Teppich kehren. **(b)** *(scan)* absuchen *(for* nach*); (lights also, bullets)* streichen über *(+acc); minefield* durchkämmen; *mines* räumen. **(c)** *(move quickly over) (wind, skirt)* fegen über *(+acc); (waves)* deck etc überschwemmen; *(glance)* gleiten über *(+acc); (fig) (violence, fashion)* überrollen; *(disease)* um sich greifen in *(+dat).* **(d)** *(remove with ~ing movement) (wave)* spülen, schwemmen; *(current)* reißen; *(wind)* fegen; *person* reißen. **to ~ sth off the table/into a bag** etw vom Tisch fegen/etw in eine Tasche raffen; **the crowd swept him into the square** er wurde von der Menge zum Platz hin mitgerissen; **he swept her off her feet** *(fig)* er eroberte sie im Sturm; **to ~ the board** *(fig)* alle Preise/Medaillen gewinnen, abräumen *(col).*
**3** *vi* **(a)** *(with broom)* kehren, fegen. **(b)** *(move) (person)* rauschen; *(vehicle, plane) (quickly)* schießen; *(majestically)* gleiten; *(skier)* fegen; *(road, river)*

in weitem Bogen führen. **to ~ in/out/by** *or* past hinein-/hinaus-/vorbeirauschen; *(majestically)* hinein-/hinaus-/vorbeigleiten; **panic swept through Europe** eine Welle der Panik ging durch Europa.
▶**sweep aside** *vt sep (lit, fig)* beiseite fegen.
▶**sweep away 1** *vi* davonrauschen; *(car, plane)* davonschießen; *(majestically)* davongleiten; *(skier)* davonfegen. **2** *vt sep dust, leaves etc* wegfegen; *(avalanche)* wegreißen; *(flood etc)* wegspülen; *(fig) old laws* aufräumen mit.
▶**sweep up 1** *vi (with broom)* zusammenkehren *or* -fegen. **2** *vt sep* zusammenkehren *or* -fegen; *(collect up) objects* zusammenraffen; *person* hochreißen; *hair* hochbinden.
**sweeper** ['swiːpəʳ] *n (road ~)* Straßenkehrer(in *f) m; (machine)* Kehrmaschine *f; (carpet ~)* Teppichkehrer *m.*
**sweeping** ['swiːpɪŋ] *adj* **(a)** *gesture* weitausholend. **(b)** *(fig) change* radikal, drastisch; *statement* pauschal; *victory* überragend.
**sweepstake** ['swiːpsteɪk] *n Rennen nt etc, bei dem die Preise aus den Einsätzen gebildet werden,* Sweepstake *nt.*
**sweet** [swiːt] **1** *adj (+er)* **(a)** süß. **to have a ~ tooth** gern Süßes essen. **(b)** *(fresh) food, water* frisch; *(fragrant) smell* süß. **(c)** *(fig: pleasant etc)* süß; *(kind also)* lieb. **~ dreams!** träume süß!, träum was Schönes! *(col);* **that's very ~ of you** das ist sehr lieb von dir; **once he caught the ~ smell of success** als erst der Erfolg lockte; **the words were ~ to his ear** die Worte klangen lieblich in seinen Ohren; **in his own ~ way** *(iro)* auf seine unübertroffene Art. **2** *n* **(a)** *(Brit: candy)* Bonbon *nt.* **(b)** *(Brit: dessert)* Nachtisch *m,* Dessert *nt.* **for ~** zum Nachtisch. **(c) yes, (my) ~** ja, (mein) Schätzchen *or* Liebling.
**sweet:** **~ and sour** *adj* süß-sauer; **~bread** *n* Bries *nt;* **~ chestnut** *n* Eßkastanie *f;* **~ corn** *n* Mais *m.*
**sweeten** ['swiːtn] *vt coffee, sauce* süßen; *(fig) temper* bessern; *task* versüßen. **to ~ sb** *(col)* jdn gnädig stimmen.
**sweetener** ['swiːtnəʳ] *n (Cook)* Süßungsmittel *nt; (artificial)* Süßstoff *m; (col: bribe)* Schmiergeld *nt.*
**sweetheart** ['swiːt,hɑːt] *n* Schatz *m,* Liebste(r) *mf.*
**sweetie** ['swiːtɪ] *n* **(a)** *(col: person)* Schatz *m.* **(b)** *(baby talk, Scot: candy)* Bonbon *m.*
**sweetly** ['swiːtlɪ] *adv* süß. *(engine)* **to run ~** prächtig laufen.
**sweetness** ['swiːtnɪs] *n* Süße *f; (of smile, nature)* Liebenswürdigkeit *f; (of person)* liebe Art. **now all is ~ and light** *(usu iro)* nun herrscht eitel Freude und Sonnenschein.
**sweet:** **~ pea** *n* Gartenwicke *f;* **~ potato** *n* Süßkartoffel *f;* **~-shop** *n (Brit)* Süßwarenladen *m or* -geschäft *nt;* **~-smelling** *adj* süß duftend *attr;* **~talk** *vt (US)* beschwatzen *(into doing sth* etw zu tun*);* **~-tempered** *adj* verträglich; **~ william** *n* Bartnelke *f.*
**swell** [swel] *(vb: pret* **~ed,** *ptp* **swollen** *or* **~ed)** **1** *n (of sea)* Wogen *nt no pl.* **there was a heavy ~** es herrschte hoher Seegang. **2** *adj (US col: excellent)* klasse *(col),* prima *(col).* **3** *vt river, sound etc* anschwellen lassen; *stomach* (auf)blähen; *wood* (auf)quellen; *sail* blähen; *numbers* anwachsen lassen; *sales* steigern. **to be swollen with pride** stolzgeschwellt sein. **4** *vi* **(a)** *(ankle, arm, eye etc: also ~ up)* (an)schwellen; *(balloon etc)* sich füllen. **(b)** *(river, lake, sound etc)* anschwellen; *(sails: also ~ out)* sich blähen; *(wood)* quellen; *(in size, number)* anwachsen.
**swelling** ['swelɪŋ] *n (Med)* Schwellung *f.*
**swelter** ['sweltəʳ] *vi* **to ~ (in the heat)** vor Hitze ver-

gehen.

**sweltering** ['sweltərɪŋ] *adj day, weather* glühend heiß; *heat* glühend. **it's ~ in here** *(col)* hier verschmachtet man ja! *(col)*.

**swept** [swept] *pret, ptp of* **sweep**.

**swerve** [swɜːv] **1** *n* Bogen *m*; *(of car etc also)* Schlenker *m (col)*. **2** *vi* einen Bogen machen *(around sth* um etw*)*; *(car, driver)* ausschwenken; *(fig) (from truth)* abweichen; *(from chosen path)* abschwenken. **the car was swerving all over the road** der Wagen schwenkte von einer Straßenseite zur anderen.

**swift** [swɪft] **1** *adj (+er)* schnell; *reaction also, revenge* prompt. **2** *n (bird)* Mauersegler *m*.

**swiftly** ['swɪftlɪ] *adv* schnell.

**swiftness** ['swɪftnɪs] *n see adj* Schnelligkeit *f*; Promptheit *f*.

**swig** [swɪg] *(col)* **1** *n* Schluck *m*. **to have** *or* **take a ~ of beer** einen Schluck Bier trinken. **2** *vt (also ~ down)* beer herunterkippen *(col)*.

**swill** [swɪl] **1** *n (animal food)* (Schweine)futter *nt*; *(garbage, slops) (solid)* Abfälle *pl*; *(liquid)* Schmutzwasser *nt*. **2** *vt* **(a)** *(also ~ out)* auswaschen; *cup, dish* ausschwenken. **(b)** *(col) beer etc* kippen *(col)*.

**swim** [swɪm] *(vb: pret* **swam***, ptp* **swum***)* **1** *n* **(a)** **it's a long ~** es ist weit (zu schwimmen); **to go for a ~** schwimmen gehen; **to have a ~** schwimmen. **(b)** *(col)* **to be in the ~** up to date sein; *(socially active)* mitmischen *(col)*. **2** *vt* schwimmen; *river, Channel* durchschwimmen. **3** *vi* schwimmen. **she can't ~ a stroke** sie kann sich keinen Meter über Wasser halten; **my head is ~ming** mir dreht sich alles; **it was absolutely ~ming in oil** es schwamm in Öl.

**swimmer** ['swɪmər] *n* Schwimmer(in *f*) *m*.

**swimming** ['swɪmɪŋ] **1** *n* Schwimmen *nt*; *(as sport)* Schwimmsport *m*. **do you like ~?** schwimmen Sie gern? **2** *adj (for ~)* Schwimm-; *(dizzy) feeling* Schwindel-.

**swimming: ~ bath** *n usu pl (Brit)* = **~ pool**; **~ cap** *n* Badekappe *f*; **~ costume** *n* Badeanzug *m*; **~ lesson** *n* Schwimmstunde *f*; **~ lessons** Schwimmunterricht *m*.

**swimmingly** ['swɪmɪŋlɪ] *adv (col)* glänzend.

**swimming: ~ pool** *n* Schwimmbad *nt*; *(outdoor also)* Freibad *nt*; *(indoor also)* Hallenbad *nt*; **~ trunks** *npl* Badehose *f*.

**swimsuit** ['swɪmsuːt] *n* Badeanzug *m*.

**swindle** ['swɪndl] **1** *n* Schwindel, Betrug *m*. **it's a ~!** das ist (der reinste) Schwindel! **2** *vt person* beschwindeln. **to ~ sb out of sth** *(take from)* jdm etw abgaunern *(col)*; *(withhold from)* jdn um etw betrügen.

**swindler** ['swɪndlər] *n* Schwindler(in *f*) *m*.

**swine** [swaɪn] *n* **(a)** *pl* - *(old, form)* Schwein *nt*. **(b)** *pl* -**s** *(pej col)* Schwein *nt*; *(woman also)* Sau *f*.

**swing** [swɪŋ] *(vb: pret, ptp* **swung***)* **1** *n* **(a)** *(movement)* Schwung *m*; *(to and fro)* Schwingen *nt*; *(of needle)* Ausschlag *m*; *(Boxing etc: blow)* Schwinger *m*; *(fig, Pol)* (Meinungs)umschwung *m (to* zugunsten *+gen, away from* zuungunsten *+gen)*. **to take a ~ at sb** nach jdm schlagen; **a ~ in opinion** ein Meinungsumschwung. **(b)** *(rhythm)* Schwung *m*; *(kind of music, dance)* Swing *m*. **to go with a ~** *(fig)* ein voller Erfolg sein *(col)*; **to be in full ~** voll im Gang sein; **to get into the ~ of things** *(col)* reinkommen *(col)*. **(c)** *(seat for ~ing)* Schaukel *f*. **to have a ~** schaukeln; **it's ~s and roundabouts** *(col)* es ist gehüpft wie gesprungen.

**2** *vt* **(a)** schwingen; *(to and fro)* hin und her schwingen; *(on swing)* schaukeln; *arms and legs (vigorously)* schwingen (mit); *(dangle)* baumeln

mit; *propeller* einen Schwung geben *(+dat)*. **he swung his racket at the ball** er holte mit dem Schläger aus; **he swung the case (up) onto his shoulder** er schwang sich *(dat)* die Kiste auf die Schulter. **(b)** *(influence) election* beeinflussen; *opinion* umschlagen lassen; *person* umstimmen, herumkriegen *(col)*. **his speech swung the decision in our favour** seine Rede ließ die Entscheidung zu unseren Gunsten ausfallen; **he managed to ~ the deal** *(col)* er hat das Geschäft gemacht *(col)*; **if you can ~ it so that ...** *(col)* wenn du es so hinkriegen kannst, daß ... **(c)** *(turn: also ~ around)* plane, car herumschwenken.

**3** *vi* **(a)** schwingen; *(to and fro)* (hin und her) schwingen; *(hanging object also)* pendeln; *(pivot)* sich drehen; *(on swing)* schaukeln; *(arms, legs: dangle)* baumeln. **(b)** *(move: into saddle, along rope)* sich schwingen. **to ~ open/shut** aufschwingen/zuschlagen; **to ~ into action** in Aktion treten; **the car swung into the square** der Wagen schwenkte auf den Platz ein; **he swung around on his chair** er drehte sich auf seinem Stuhl herum; **the party has swung to the right** in der Partei hat es einen Rechtsruck gegeben; **he'll ~ for it** *(col: hang)* dafür wird er hängen *or* baumeln *(col)*.

**swing: ~ bridge** *n* Drehbrücke *f*; **~-door** *n (Brit)* Pendeltür *f*.

**swingeing** ['swɪndʒɪŋ] *adj (Brit) blow* hart; *attack* scharf; *defeat* vernichtend; *taxation, price increases* extrem hoch; *cuts* extrem.

**swinging** ['swɪŋɪŋ] *adj step, music* schwungvoll; *movement* schaukelnd. **the ~ sixties** die „Swinging Sixties".

**swipe** [swaɪp] **1** *n (blow)* Schlag *m*. **to take a ~ at sb/sth** nach jdm/etw schlagen. **2** *vt* **(a)** *person, ball etc* schlagen. **(b)** *(col: steal)* mopsen *(col)*, klauen *(col)*. **3** *vi* **to ~ at sb/sth** nach jdm/etw schlagen.

**swirl** [swɜːl] **1** *n* Wirbel *m*. **2** *vti* wirbeln. **to ~ around** herumwirbeln.

**swish** [swɪʃ] **1** *n see vi* Zischen *nt*; Rascheln *nt*; Rauschen *nt*. **2** *adj (Brit col: plush)* edel *(col)*. **3** *vt cane* zischen lassen; *tail* schlagen mit; *skirt* rauschen mit; *water* schwenken. **4** *vi (whip, cane, tyres)* zischen; *(grass, skirts)* rascheln; *(water)* rauschen.

**Swiss** [swɪs] **1** *adj* Schweizer, schweizerisch. **~ cheese** Schweizer Käse *m*; **~ roll** Biskuitrolle *f*. **2** *n* Schweizer(in *f*) *m*. **the ~** *pl* die Schweizer *pl*; **~ French/German** *(person)* Französisch-/Deutschschweizer(in *f*) *m*; *(language)* Schweizer Französisch *nt*/Schweizerdeutsch, Schwyzerdütsch *nt (Swiss)*.

**switch** [swɪtʃ] **1** *n* **(a)** *(Elec etc)* Schalter *m*. **(b)** *(US Rail)* Weiche *f*. **(c)** *(change)* Wechsel *m*; *(in plans, policies)* Änderung *f (in gen)*; *(exchange)* Tausch *m*. **a rapid ~ of plan** eine schnelle Änderung der Pläne; **to make a ~** tauschen. **(d)** *(stick, cane)* Rute, Gerte *f*.

**2** *vt* **(a)** *(change)* wechseln; *direction, plans* ändern; *allegiance* übertragen *(to* auf *+acc)*; *attention, conversation* lenken *(to* auf *+acc)*. **(b)** *(move) production* verlegen; *object* umstellen. **(c)** *(exchange)* tauschen; *(transpose: also ~ over, ~ around) objects, figures in column* vertauschen. **I ~ed hats with him** ich tauschte meinen Hut mit ihm; **to ~ A for B** A für *or* gegen B (ein)tauschen. **(d)** *(Elec)* (um)schalten. **~ the radio to another programme** schalten Sie auf ein anderes Radioprogramm um. **(e)** *(esp US Rail)* rangieren.

**3** *vi (change: also ~ over)* (über)wechseln *(to* zu*)*; *(Elec, TV, Rad)* umschalten *(to* auf *+acc)*; *(exchange: also ~ around, ~ over)* tauschen. **he ~ed to**

another line of attack er wechselte seine Angriffstaktik.

▶**switch off 1** *vt sep light* ausschalten; *radio, TV, machine also, engine* abschalten. **the oven ~es itself ~** der Backofen schaltet sich selbsttätig ab. **2** *vi* **(a)** *see vt* ausschalten; abschalten. **(b)** *(col: person)* abschalten.

▶**switch on 1** *vt sep gas etc* anstellen; *machine, TV also, light* einschalten; *engine also* anlassen. **please leave the TV ~ed ~** laß den Fernseher bitte an. **2** *vi see vt* anstellen; einschalten; anlassen; *(automatically)* sich einschalten, angehen *(col)*.

**switch:** ~**back** *n* Berg- und Talbahn *f*; *(Brit: roller-coaster also)* Achterbahn *f*; ~**blade** *n* *(esp US)* Schnappmesser *nt*; ~**board** *n* *(Telec) (exchange)* Vermittlung *f*; *(in office etc)* Zentrale *f*; *(actual panel, Elec)* Schalttafel *f*; ~**board operator** *n* *(in office)* Telefonist(in *f*) *m*; ~**yard** *n* *(US Rail)* Rangierbahnhof *m*.

**Switzerland** ['swɪtsələnd] *n* die Schweiz. **to ~ in** die Schweiz; **in ~ in** der Schweiz.

**swivel** ['swɪvl] **1** *n* Drehgelenk *nt*. **~ chair** Drehstuhl *m*. **2** *(also ~ around)* *vt* (herum)drehen. **3** *vi* sich drehen; *(person)* sich herumdrehen.

**swivelling** ['swɪvəlɪŋ] *adj* schwenkbar.

**swollen** ['swəʊlən] **1** *ptp of* **swell. 2** *adj ankle, face, glands etc* geschwollen; *stomach* aufgedunsen; *wood* gequollen; *river* angeschwollen. **her eyes were ~** with tears ihre Augen waren verweint; **he has a ~ head** *or* **is ~-headed** *(fig)* er ist so aufgeblasen.

**swoon** [swuːn] **1** *n (old)* Ohnmacht *f*. **2** *vi (old: faint)* in Ohnmacht fallen; *(fig: over pop star etc)* beinahe ohnmächtig werden *(over sb* wegen jdm*)*.

**swoop** [swuːp] **1** *vi (lit: also ~ down) (bird)* herabstoßen, niederstoßen *(on* auf *+acc)*; *(plane)* einen Sturzflug machen; *(fig) (police)* einen Überraschungsangriff machen *(on* auf *+acc) or* landen *(col) (on* bei*)*; *(person)* sich stürzen *(on* auf *+acc)*. **the plane ~ed (down) low over the village** das Flugzeug flog im Tiefflug über das Dorf hinweg. **2** *n (of bird, plane)* Sturzflug *m*. **at one (fell) ~** auf einen Schlag.

**swop** [swɒp] = **swap.**

**sword** [sɔːd] *n* Schwert *nt*. **to cross ~s with sb** *(lit, fig)* mit jdm die Klinge(n) kreuzen.

**swordfish** ['sɔːdfɪʃ] *n* Schwertfisch *m*.

**swordsman** ['sɔːdzmən] *n, pl* **-men** [-mən] Schwertkämpfer *m*; *(fencer)* Fechter *m*.

**swore** [swɔːʳ] *pret of* **swear.**

**sworn** [swɔːn] **1** *ptp of* **swear. 2** *adj enemy* eingeschworen; *(Jur) statement* eidlich, unter Eid.

**swot** [swɒt] *(Brit col)* **1** *vti* büffeln *(col)*, pauken *(col)*. **to ~ up on** *one's* **maths** Mathe pauken *(col)*. **2** *n (pej: person)* Streber(in *f*) *m*.

**swum** [swʌm] *ptp of* **swim.**

**swung** [swʌŋ] *pret, ptp of* **swing.**

**sycamore** ['sɪkəmɔːʳ] *n* Bergahorn *m*; *(US: plane tree)* nordamerikanische Platane *f*.

**sycophant** ['sɪkəfənt] *n* Kriecher *m*.

**sycophantic** [ˌsɪkə'fæntɪk] *adj* kriecherisch.

**Sydney** ['sɪdnɪ] *n* Sydney *nt*.

**syllable** ['sɪləbl] *n* Silbe *f*. **a two-~(d) word** ein zweisilbiges Wort; **in words of one ~** *(hum)* in einfachen Worten.

**syllabus** ['sɪləbəs] *n, pl* **-es** *or* **syllabi** ['sɪləbaɪ] *(Sch, Univ)* Lehrplan *m*; *(lecture timetable)* Vorlesungsverzeichnis *nt*.

**symbiosis** [ˌsɪmbɪ'əʊsɪs] *n* Symbiose *f*.

**symbiotic** [ˌsɪmbɪ'ɒtɪk] *adj* symbiotisch.

**symbol** ['sɪmbəl] *n* Symbol, Zeichen *nt* *(of* für*)*.

**symbolic(al)** [sɪm'bɒlɪk(l)] *adj* symbolisch *(of* für*)*.

**to be ~ of sth** etw symbolisieren.

**symbolism** ['sɪmbəlɪzəm] *n* Symbolik *f*; *(Art, Liter: movement)* Symbolismus *m*.

**symbolize** ['sɪmbəlaɪz] *vt* symbolisieren.

**symmetrical** *adj*, ~**ly** *adv* [sɪ'metrɪkəl, -ɪ] symmetrisch.

**symmetry** ['sɪmɪtrɪ] *n* Symmetrie *f*.

**sympathetic** [ˌsɪmpə'θetɪk] *adj (showing pity)* mitfühlend; *(understanding)* verständnisvoll; *(well-disposed)* wohlwollend; *look, smile* freundlich. **to be** *or* **feel ~ to(wards) sb** mit jdm mitfühlen; für jdn Verständnis haben; *(Pol etc)* mit jdm sympathisieren; **a ~ ear** ein offenes Ohr.

**sympathize** ['sɪmpəθaɪz] *vi (feel compassion)* mitfühlen *(with* mit*)*; *(understand)* Verständnis haben *(with* für*)*; *(agree)* sympathisieren *(with* mit*) (esp Pol)*; *(express sympathy)* sein Mitgefühl aussprechen; *(on bereavement)* sein Beileid aussprechen. **to ~ with sb's views** jds Ansichten teilen; **I really do ~** *(have pity)* das tut mir wirklich leid; *(understand your feelings)* ich habe wirklich vollstes Verständnis.

**sympathizer** ['sɪmpəθaɪzəʳ] *n* Mitfühlende(r) *mf*; *(with cause)* Sympathisant(in *f*) *m*.

**sympathy** ['sɪmpəθɪ] *n* **(a)** *(pity, compassion)* Mitgefühl, Mitleid *nt (for* mit*)*; *(at death)* Beileid *nt*. **to feel** *or* **have ~ for sb** Mitleid mit jdm haben; **a letter of ~** ein mitfühlender Brief; *(of condolence)* ein Beileidsbrief *m*; **you have my ~!** *(hum)* herzliches Beileid *(hum)*; **you won't get any ~ from me** erwarte kein Mitleid von mir. **(b)** *(understanding)* Verständnis *nt*; *(fellow-feeling, agreement)* Sympathie *f*. **to be in/out of ~ with sb/sth** mit jdm/etw einhergehen/nicht einhergehen; **to come out in ~** *(Ind)* in Sympathiestreik treten; **~ strike** Sympathiestreik *m*.

**symphonic** [sɪm'fɒnɪk] *adj* symphonisch, sinfonisch.

**symphony** ['sɪmfənɪ] *n* Symphonie, Sinfonie *f*. **~ orchestra** Symphonie- *or* Sinfonieorchester *nt*.

**symposium** [sɪm'pəʊzɪəm] *n, pl* **-s** *or* **symposia** [sɪm'pəʊzɪə] Symposium, Symposion *nt*.

**symptom** ['sɪmptəm] *n (lit, fig)* Symptom *nt*.

**symptomatic** [ˌsɪmptə'mætɪk] *adj* symptomatisch *(of* für*)*.

**synagogue** ['sɪnəgɒg] *n* Synagoge *f*.

**sync** [sɪŋk] *n (Film, TV, Comp)* **in/out of ~** synchron/nicht synchron.

**synchromesh** ['sɪŋkrəʊˌmeʃ] *n* Synchrongetriebe *nt*.

**synchronize** ['sɪŋkrənaɪz] *vt* abstimmen *(with* auf *+acc)*; *two actions, movements* aufeinander abstimmen; *clocks* gleichstellen *(with* mit*)*. ~**d swimming** Synchronschwimmen *nt*; **to ~ a film** Bild und Ton eines Films aufeinander abstimmen.

**syncopated** ['sɪŋkəpeɪtɪd] *adj (Mus)* synkopiert.

**syndicate** ['sɪndɪkɪt] *n* Interessengemeinschaft *f*; *(for gambling)* Wettgemeinschaft *f*; *(Comm)* Syndikat *nt*, Verband *m*; *(Press)* (Presse)zentrale *f*; *(crime ~)* Ring *m*.

**syndrome** ['sɪndrəʊm] *n (Med)* Syndrom *nt*; *(fig, Sociol)* Phänomen *nt*.

**synod** ['sɪnəd] *n* Synode *f*.

**synonym** ['sɪnənɪm] *n* Synonym *nt*.

**synonymous** [sɪ'nɒnɪməs] *adj* synonym. **to be ~ with sth** *(fig)* gleichbedeutend mit etw sein.

**synopsis** [sɪ'nɒpsɪs] *n, pl* **synopses** [sɪ'nɒpsiːz] Abriß *m* der Handlung; *(of article, book)* Zusammenfassung *f*.

**syntax** ['sɪntæks] *n* Syntax *f*.

**synthesis** ['sɪnθəsɪs] *n, pl* **syntheses** ['sɪnθəsiːz] Synthese *f*.

**synthesize** ['sɪnθəsaɪz] *vt* synthetisieren; *speech*

synthetisch bilden; *theories etc* zusammenfassen.

**synthesizer** ['sɪnθəˌsaɪzə'] *n (Mus)* Synthesizer *m*.

**synthetic** [sɪn'θetɪk] **1** *adj* synthetisch; *fibre, silk* Kunst-. **2** *n* Kunststoff *m*, Synthetik *f*.

**syphilis** ['sɪfɪlɪs] *n* Syphilis *f*.

**syphon** *n* = **siphon**.

**Syria** ['sɪrɪə] *n* Syrien *nt*.

**Syrian** ['sɪrɪən] **1** *adj* syrisch. **2** *n* Syrer(in *f*) *m*.

**syringe** [sɪ'rɪndʒ] **1** *n (Med)* Spritze *f*. **2** *vt (Med)* (aus)spülen.

**syrup,** *(US also)* **sirup** ['sɪrəp] *n* Sirup *m*. **cough ~** *(Med)* Hustensaft *m*.

**system** ['sɪstəm] *n* System *nt*. **new teaching ~s** neue Lehrmethoden *pl*; **it was a shock to his ~** er hatte schwer damit zu schaffen; **to get sth out of one's ~** *(fig col)* sich *(dat)* etw von der Seele schaffen *(col)*; **you can't beat the ~** gegen das System kommst du einfach nicht an.

**systematic** [ˌsɪstə'mætɪk] *adj* systematisch; *liar, cruelty* ständig. **he works in a ~ way** er arbeitet mit System.

**systematically** [ˌsɪstə'mætɪkəlɪ] *adv* systematisch.

**systematize** ['sɪstəmətaɪz] *vt* systematisieren.

**systems: ~ analyst** *n (Comp)* Systemanalytiker(in *f*) *m*; **~ disk** *n (Comp)* Systemdiskette *f*.

# T

**T, t** [tiː] *n* T, t *nt*. **T for Tommy** ≈ T wie Theodor; **that's him/it to a T** das ist er, wie er leibt und lebt/ genau so ist es.

**ta** [tɑː] *interj (Brit col)* danke.

**TA** *(Brit)* = **Territorial Army.**

**tab¹** [tæb] *n* **(a)** *(loop on coat etc)* Aufhänger *m*; *(fastener on coat etc)* Riegel *m*; *(name ~)* *(of owner)* Namensschild *nt*; *(of maker)* Etikett *nt*; *(Mil)* Spiegel *m*; *(on filing cards)* Reiter *m*. **to keep ~s on sb/ sth** *(col)* jdn/etw genau im Auge behalten. **(b)** *(US col: bill)* Rechnung *f*.

**tab²** *(Comp, on typewriter)* **1** *n* Tabulator *m*. **~ key** Tabulatortaste *f*. **2** *vt columns* tabulieren.

**tabby** ['tæbɪ] *n (also ~ cat)* getigerte Katze; *(female)* weibliche Katze.

**table** ['teɪbl] **1** *n* **(a)** Tisch *m*; *(banquet ~)* Tafel *f*. **at the ~** am Tisch; **at ~** bei Tisch; **to sit down to** *or* **at ~** sich zu Tisch setzen; **to be under the ~** *(drunk)* unter dem Tisch liegen; **to turn the ~s (on sb)** (gegenüber jdm) den Spieß umdrehen; **the whole ~ laughed** die ganze Runde lachte. **(b)** *(of figures, prices etc, Sport)* Tabelle *f*. **(multiplication)** ~s Einmaleins *nt*; **~ of contents** Inhaltsverzeichnis *nt*. **(c)** *(Geog)* **water ~** Grundwasserspiegel *m*. **2** *vt* **(a)** *motion* einbringen. **(b)** *(US: postpone) bill* zurückstellen.

**tableau** ['tæbləʊ] *n, pl* **-s** *or* **-x** ['tæbləʊ(z)] *(Art, Theat)* Tableau *nt*; *(fig)* Bild *nt*, Szene *f*.

**table: ~ cloth** *n* Tischdecke *f or* -tuch *nt*; **~ lamp** *n* Tischlampe *f*; **~land** *n* Tafelland *nt*, Hochebene *f*; **~ manners** *npl* Tischmanieren *pl*; **~ mat** *n* Untersetzer *m*; *(of cloth)* Set *nt*; **~ salt** *n* Tafelsalz *nt*; **~spoon** *n* Eßlöffel *m*; **~spoonful** *n* Eßlöffel *m* (voll).

**tablet** ['tæblɪt] *n* **(a)** *(Pharm)* Tablette *f*. **(b)** *(of wax, clay)* Täfelchen *nt*; *(of soap)* Stückchen *nt*. **(c)** *(on wall etc)* Tafel *f*.

**table: ~ talk** *n* Tischgespräch *nt*; **~ tennis** *n* Tischtennis *nt*; **~ware** *n no pl* Tafelgeschirr *nt* und -besteck *nt*; **~ wine** *n* Tafelwein *m*.

**tabloid** ['tæblɔɪd] *n (also ~ newspaper)* kleinformatige Zeitung; *(pej)* Boulevardzeitung *f*. **the ~ press, the ~s** die Boulevardpresse.

**taboo** [tə'buː] **1** *n* Tabu *nt*. **2** *adj* tabu *pred*.

**tabulate** ['tæbjʊleɪt] *vt* tabellarisch darstellen.

**tabulation** ['tæbjʊleɪʃən] *n* Tabulation *f*.

**tabulator** ['tæbjʊleɪtəʳ] *n (on typewriter)* Tabulator *m*.

**tachograph** ['tækəʊɡrɑːf] *n* Fahrtenschreiber *m*.

**tachometer** [tæ'kɒmɪtəʳ] *n* Drehzahlmesser *m*.

**tacit** *adj*, **~ly** *adv* ['tæsɪt, -lɪ] stillschweigend.

**taciturn** ['tæsɪtɜːn] *adj* schweigsam.

**tack** [tæk] **1** *n* **(a)** *(nail)* kleiner Nagel; *(with small head also)* Stift *m*; *(esp US: drawing pin)* Heftzwecke *f*. **(b)** *(Brit Sew)* Heftstich *m*. **(c)** *(Naut: course)* Schlag *m*; *(fig)* Richtung *f*, Weg *m*. **to be on the port/starboard ~** auf Backbord-/Steuerbordbug segeln; **to be on the right/wrong ~** *(fig)* auf der

richtigen/falschen Spur sein; **to try another ~** *(fig)* es anders versuchen. **2** *vt* **(a)** *(with nail)* annageln *(to* an *+dat or acc)*; *(with clip, pin)* feststecken *(to* an *+dat)*. **(b)** *(Brit Sew)* heften. **3** *vi (Naut)* aufkreuzen.

▶**tack on** *vt sep (fig)* anhängen *(-to* dat).

**tackle** ['tækl] **1** *n* **(a)** *(lifting gear)* Flaschenzug *m*; *(Naut)* Talje *f*, Takel *nt*. **(b)** *(equipment)* Ausrüstung *f*. **fishing ~** Angelausrüstung *f*. **(c)** *(Sport)* Angriff *m*, Tackling *nt*. **2** *vt* **(a)** *(physically, Sport)* angreifen; *(Rugby)* fassen; *thief also* sich stürzen auf *(+acc)*; *(verbally)* zur Rede stellen *(about* wegen*)*. **(b)** *(undertake) job* in Angriff nehmen; *new challenge* sich versuchen an *(+dat)*; *problem* angehen; *(manage to cope with)* fertig werden mit. **3** *vi* angreifen.

**tacky¹** ['tækɪ] *adj (+er)* klebrig. **the paint is still ~** die Farbe klebt noch.

**tacky²** *adj (+er) (col) (cheap)* billig; *(down-at-heel)* heruntergekommen; *(tasteless)* geschmacklos.

**tact** [tækt] *n no pl* Takt *m*.

**tactful** *adj*, **~ly** *adv* ['tæktfʊl, -fəlɪ] taktvoll.

**tactfulness** ['tæktfʊlnɪs] *n* Takt *m*; *(sensitivity)* Feingefühl *nt*.

**tactic** ['tæktɪk] *n* Taktik *f*.

**tactical** ['tæktɪkəl] *adj (Mil, fig)* taktisch. **~ vote** Leihstimme *f*.

**tactics** ['tæktɪks] *n sing (Mil, fig)* Taktik *f*.

**tactile** ['tæktaɪl] *adj* Tast-; *(tangible)* fühlbar.

**tactless** *adj*, **~ly** *adv* ['tæktlɪs, -lɪ] taktlos.

**tactlessness** ['tæktlɪsnɪs] *n* Taktlosigkeit *f*.

**tadpole** ['tædpəʊl] *n* Kaulquappe *f*.

**taffeta** ['tæfɪtə] *n* Taft *m*.

**taffy** ['tæfɪ] *n (US)* Toffee *nt*.

**tag** [tæg] **1** *n* **(a)** *(label)* Schild(chen) *nt*; *(on clothes) (maker's name)* Etikett *nt*; *(owner's name)* Namensschild *nt*; *(loop)* Aufhänger *m*. **(b)** *(game)* Fangen *nt*. **2** *vi* **to ~ behind** *or* **after sb** hinter jdm herzockeln *(col)*.

▶**tag along** *vi* mitzockeln *(col)*. **why don't you ~ ~?** *(col)* warum kommst du nicht mit?

**tag question** *n* Bestätigungsfrage *f*.

**tail** [teɪl] **1** *n* **(a)** *(of animal)* Schwanz *m*. **with his ~ between his legs** *(fig)* mit eingezogenem Schwanz *(col)*; **to turn ~** die Flucht ergreifen; **he was right on my ~** er saß mir direkt im Nacken; **to put a ~ on sb** jdn beschatten lassen. **(b)** *(of aeroplane, procession)* Schwanz *m*; *(of comet)* Schweif *m*; *(of shirt)* Zipfel *m*; *(of jacket, coat)* Schoß *m*. **~s** *pl (jacket)* Frack *m*. **(c)** **~s** *(on coin)* Rückseite *f*; **~s I win!** bei Zahl gewinne ich. **2** *vt suspect* beschatten *(col)*; *car etc* folgen *(+dat)*.

▶**tail away** *vi* = **tail off (a)**.

▶**tail back** *vi (Brit: traffic)* sich gestaut haben.

▶**tail off** *vi* **(a)** *(diminish)* abnehmen; *(interest also)* schwinden; *(sounds)* schwächer werden; *(sentence)* abbrechen. **(b)** *(deteriorate)* sich verschlechtern.

**tail: ~back** *n (Brit)* Rückstau *m*; **a 5-mile ~back** ein Stau von 8 km; **~board** *n* Ladeklappe *f*; **~ coat** *n*

Frack *m*; ~ **end** *n* Ende *nt*; ~**fin** *n* *(Aut)* Heckflosse *f*; ~**gate** *n* *(of car)* Hecktür *f*; *(of lorry)* Ladeklappe *f*; ~-**light** *n* *(Aut)* Rücklicht *nt*.
**tailor** ['teɪlər] **1** *n* Schneider *m*. ~'**s dummy** *(lit)* Schneiderpuppe *f*. **2** *vt* **(a)** *dress etc* schneidern. **(b)** *(fig) plans* zuschneiden *(to* auf *+acc)*; *products etc* abstimmen *(to* auf *+acc)*. ~**ed to meet his needs** auf seine Bedürfnisse abgestimmt.
**tailoring** ['teɪlərɪŋ] *n* Schnitt *m*; *(profession)* Schneiderei *f*.
**tailor-made** [,teɪlə'meɪd] *adj (lit, fig)* maßgeschneidert; *role also* zugeschnitten *(for* auf *+acc)*. ~ **suit/ costume** Maßanzug *m*/Schneiderkostüm *nt*; **the job was** ~ **for him** die Stelle war ihm wie auf den Leib geschnitten.
**tail:** ~**piece** *n* Anhang *m*, Anhängsel *nt (col)*; ~**pipe** *n* *(Aut)* Endrohr *nt*; ~**plane** *n* *(Aviat)* Höhenleitwerk *nt*; ~**wind** *n* Rückenwind *m*.
**taint** [teɪnt] **1** *n (lit: of food etc)* Stich *m*; *(fig) (blemish)* Makel *m*; *(trace)* Spur *f*. **2** *vt food* verderben; *air, atmosphere* verpesten; *(fig) reputation* beschmutzen.
**Taiwan** [taɪ'wɑːn] *n* Taiwan *nt*.
**Taiwanese** [,taɪwɑː'niːz] **1** *adj* taiwanisch. **2** *n* Taiwaner(in *f) m*.
**take** [teɪk] *(vb: pret* **took***, ptp* **taken***)* **1** *vt* **(a)** nehmen; *(for oneself)* sich *(dat)* nehmen; *(~ away with one)* mitnehmen; *(remove from its place)* wegnehmen. **to** ~ **sth from sb** jdm etw wegnehmen; *(steal)* jdm etw stehlen; ~ **three eggs** *(Cook)* man nehme drei Eier; ~ **a seat/chair!** nehmen Sie Platz!; ~ **your seats!** nehmen Sie Ihre Plätze ein!; **this seat is** ~**n** dieser Platz ist besetzt; **I'll** ~ **a pound of apples** ich nehme ein Pfund Äpfel.
**(b)** *(transport, accompany)* bringen; *(~ along with one) person, things* mitnehmen. **I'll** ~ **you to the station** ich bringe Sie zum Bahnhof; **I'll** ~ **you (with me) to the party** ich nehme dich zur Party mit; **let me** ~ **your case** komm, ich nehme *or* trage deinen Koffer; **to** ~ **sb/the dog for a walk** mit jdm spazierengehen/den Hund ausführen; **to** ~ **sb to the cinema** *(treat)* jdn ins Kino einladen; *(~ along with one)* mit jdm ins Kino gehen; **this bus will** ~ **you to the town hall** der Bus fährt zum Rathaus; **this road will** ~ **you to Bath** diese Straße führt nach Bath.
**(c)** *(capture) person* fassen; *animal* fangen; *town, country etc* einnehmen; *(Chess etc)* schlagen; *(Cards) trick* machen.
**(d)** *(accept, receive)* nehmen; *job, dye, perm* annehmen; *command, role* übernehmen; *prize* gewinnen. **I won't** ~ **less than £200** ich verkaufe es nicht unter £200; **we** ~ **the Guardian** wir bekommen den „Guardian"; **to** ~ **things as they come** die Dinge nehmen, wie sie kommen; ~ **it from me!** das können Sie mir glauben; **(you can)** ~ **it or leave it** die Entscheidung liegt bei Ihnen; **he took the blow on his left arm** der Schlag traf ihn am linken Arm; *(in defence)* er wehrte den Schlag mit dem linken Arm ab; **do you** ~ **my meaning?** verstehen Sie, was ich meine?
**(e)** *exam, driving test, course, French* machen; *(as optional subject)* wählen; *lessons, tuition* nehmen; *(teach) lesson, subject* geben; *class* unterrichten. **he took his degree in 1965** er hat 1965 Examen gemacht *or* sein Examen abgelegt; **who** ~**s you for Latin?** wer unterrichtet bei euch Latein?
**(f)** *(consume) drink, food* zu sich *(dat)* nehmen; *drugs, medicine* nehmen; *(on directions for use)* einnehmen. **to** ~ **sugar in one's tea** den Tee mit Zucker trinken; **do you** ~ **sugar?** nehmen Sie Zucker?; **will you** ~ **coffee or tea?** möchten Sie Kaf-

fee oder Tee?; **not to be** ~**n (internally)** *(Med)* nur zur äußerlichen Anwendung.
**(g)** *photo* machen. **he took the whole group** er nahm die ganze Gruppe auf.
**(h)** *(put up with)* sich *(dat)* gefallen lassen; *(endure) alcohol, climate* vertragen; *long journey* aushalten; *emotional experience, shock* verkraften; *(thing)* aushalten. **I just can't** ~ **any more** das halte ich nicht mehr aus.
**(i)** *(respond to, regard) news, blow* aufnehmen; *person* nehmen; *(understand, interpret)* auffassen, verstehen. **she knows how to** ~ **him** sie versteht es, ihn von der richtigen Seite zu nehmen; **she took his death very badly** sie hat seinen Tod schlecht verkraftet; **I would** ~ **that to mean that ...** ich würde das so auffassen *or* verstehen, daß...; **to** ~ **sb/sth for** *or* **to be ...** jdn/etw für ... halten; **what do you** ~ **me for?** wofür hältst du mich eigentlich?; **may I** ~ **it that ...?** darf ich annehmen, daß ...?
**(j)** *(require)* brauchen; *clothes size* haben. **it** ~**s five hours/men ...** man braucht fünf Stunden/Leute ...; **it** ~**s me five hours ...** ich brauche fünf Stunden ...; **it took ten men to complete the job** zehn Leute waren nötig, um diese Arbeit zu erledigen; **the journey** ~**s 3 hours** die Fahrt dauert 3 Stunden; **the wound took five weeks to heal** es dauerte fünf Wochen, bis die Wunde verheilt war; **it took a lot of courage/intelligence** dazu gehörte viel Mut/ Intelligenz; **it** ~**s time** es braucht (seine) Zeit, es dauert (eine Weile); **it took a long time** es hat lange gedauert; **it won't** ~ **long** das dauert nicht lange; **that'll** ~ **some explaining** das wird schwer zu erklären sein; **she's got what it** ~**s** *(col)* sie ist nicht ohne *(col)*; *(is capable also)* sie kann was *(col)*; *(for job)* sie hat das Zeug dazu.
**(k)** *(support) weight* aushalten; *(have capacity or room for) 50 people, 200 books* Platz haben für.
**(l)** *walk* machen; *trip also* unternehmen; *taxi, train, motorway* nehmen. **to** ~ **the plane/next plane** fliegen/das nächste Flugzeug nehmen.
**(m) to be** ~**n sick** *or* **ill** krank werden; **to be** ~**n with sb/sth** *(attracted by)* von jdm/etw angetan sein.
**2** *vi (fire)* angehen; *(dye, graft)* angenommen werden; *(vaccination)* anschlagen; *(plant)* anwachsen; *(seeds)* kommen; *(fish: bite)* anbeißen.
**3** *n* **(a)** *(Film)* Aufnahme *f*. **(b)** *(US col: takings)* Einnahmen *pl*.
▶**take after** *vi +prep obj* nachschlagen *(+dat)*; *(in looks)* ähneln *(+dat)*. **he** ~**s** ~ **his mother** er ist nach seiner Mutter geraten.
▶**take along** *vt sep* mitnehmen.
▶**take apart** *vt sep (also fig col)* auseinandernehmen.
▶**take aside** *vt sep* beiseite nehmen.
▶**take away 1** *vi* **to** ~ ~ **from sth** etw schmälern; *from worth* etw mindern. **2** *vt sep* **(a)** *(subtract)* abziehen. **6** ~ ~ **2** 6 weniger 2. **(b)** *(remove) child, thing, privilege* wegnehmen *(from sb* jdm)*; *(lead, transport, carry away)* wegbringen *(from* von)*; *prisoner* abführen *(to* in *+acc)*. **they took the child** ~ **from the school** sie haben das Kind aus der Schule genommen; **to** ~ ~ **sb's pleasure/freedom** *etc* jdm die Freude/Freiheit *etc* nehmen. **(c)** *(Brit) food* mitnehmen. **pizza to** ~ ~ Pizza zum Mitnehmen.
▶**take back** *vt sep* **(a)** *(reclaim, get back)* sich *(dat)* zurückgeben lassen; *toy etc* wieder wegnehmen; *(fig: retract) threat, statement* zurücknehmen. **(b)** *(return)* zurückbringen. **he took us** ~ **(home)** er brachte uns (nach Hause) zurück. **(c)** *(agree to receive again) thing* zurücknehmen; *employee* wieder einstellen. **(d)** *(remind)* **to** ~ **sb** ~ **to his childhood**

jdn an seine Kindheit erinnern.

▶**take down** *vt sep* (**a**) *(lit) (off shelf etc)* herunternehmen; *curtains, decorations* abnehmen; *picture* abhängen; *flag* einholen. (**b**) *(dismantle) scaffolding etc* abbauen; *tent also* abbrechen; *railing, gate* entfernen. (**c**) *(write down)* (sich *dat*) notieren; *notes* (sich *dat*) machen; *letter* aufnehmen; *lecture* mitschreiben.

▶**take home** *vt insep* mit nach Hause nehmen; *(earn) £100 per week* netto verdienen.

▶**take in** *vt sep* (**a**) *(bring in) thing, person* hinein-/hereinbringen; *harvest* einbringen. **when are you taking the car ~ (to the garage)?** wann bringen Sie das Auto in die Werkstatt? (**b**) *(receive in one's home) refugee* (bei sich) aufnehmen; *child* zu sich nehmen; *(for payment) student* vermieten an *(+acc)*. **she ~s ~ lodgers** sie vermietet (Zimmer). (**c**) *(make narrower) dress* enger machen. (**d**) *(usu insep: include, cover)* einschließen. (**e**) *(note)* wahrnehmen; *area, room* überblicken; *(grasp) meaning, lecture, sb's death* begreifen; *impressions, sights etc* aufnehmen; *situation* erfassen. (**f**) *(deceive)* hereinlegen. **to be ~n ~** hereingelegt werden; **to be ~n ~ by sb/sth** auf jdn/etw hereinfallen; **to be ~n ~ by appearances** sich vom äußeren Schein täuschen lassen.

▶**take off 1** *vi (plane, passengers)* starten, abfliegen; *(plane: leave the ground)* abheben; *(Sport)* abspringen; *(fig) (project, sales)* anlaufen; *(film, product)* ankommen.

**2** *vt sep* (**a**) *(remove, cut off: person)* abmachen *(prep obj* von*)*; *hat, lid* abnehmen *(prep obj* von*)*; *tablecloth* herunternehmen *(prep obj* von*)*; *coat, gloves etc* ausziehen; *leg* abnehmen; *play* absetzen; *food from menu, bus* streichen *(prep obj* von*)*; *service, tax* abschaffen; *(remove from duty, job) detective etc* abziehen *(prep obj* von*)*; *driver* ablösen. **to ~ sth ~ sb** jdm etw abnehmen; **to ~ the receiver ~ (the hook)** den Hörer abnehmen; **he/she took her dress ~** er zog ihr das Kleid aus/sie zog ihr Kleid aus; **he took his/her clothes off** er zog sich/sie aus; **would you like to ~ your coat ~?** möchten Sie ablegen?

(**b**) *(deduct)* abziehen *(prep obj* von*)*; *(from price)* 5%, 50p nachlassen.

(**c**) *(lead away, go away with)* mitnehmen; *(under arrest etc)* abführen. **he was ~n ~ to hospital** er wurde ins Krankenhaus gebracht; **to ~ oneself ~** *(col)* sich auf den Weg machen.

(**d**) *(have free) week, Monday* frei nehmen. **to ~ time ~ work** sich *(dat)* frei nehmen.

(**e**) *(imitate)* nachmachen.

(**f**) **to ~ sb's mind ~ sth** jdn von etw ablenken; **to ~ sb/sth ~ sb's hands** jdm jdn/etw abnehmen.

▶**take on 1** *vi* (**a**) *(col: become upset)* sich aufregen. (**b**) *(become popular: song, fashion etc)* sich durchsetzen. **2** *vt sep* (**a**) *(undertake) job, work* übernehmen; *responsibility* auf sich *(acc)* nehmen; *bet* annehmen. (**b**) *(Sport etc: accept as opponent)* antreten gegen; *opponent, authorities* sich anlegen mit. (**c**) *(employ)* einstellen; *apprentice* annehmen. (**d**) *(take aboard) (coach, train etc) passengers* aufnehmen; *(plane, ship also)* an Bord nehmen; *cargo, stores* laden; *fuel* tanken. (**e**) *(assume) colour, expression* bekommen, annehmen. **he took ~ an air of importance** er gab sich *(dat)* eine gewichtige Miene.

▶**take out** *vt sep* (**a**) *(bring or carry out)* (hinaus)bringen *(of* aus*)*; *(out of garage) car* hinaus-/herausfahren *(of* aus*)*; *(for drive etc) car, boat* wegfahren mit.

(**b**) *(to theatre etc)* ausgehen mit. **to ~ the dog ~** *(for a walk)* den Hund ausführen; **to ~ sb ~ to** *or* **for dinner/to the cinema** jdn zum Essen/ins Kino einladen.

(**c**) *(pull out, extract)* herausnehmen; *tooth also* ziehen; *nail* herausziehen *(of* aus *+dat)*. **to ~ sth ~ of** *or* **from sth** etw aus etw *(dat)* (heraus)nehmen.

(**d**) *(withdraw from bank etc)* abheben.

(**e**) *(procure) insurance* abschließen. **to ~ ~ a subscription for sth** etw abonnieren.

(**f**) **to ~ sb ~ of himself** jdn auf andere Gedanken bringen; **to ~ sth ~ on sb** *(col)* etw an jdm auslassen *(col)*; **to ~ it ~ on sb** sich an jdm abreagieren; **to ~ it/a lot ~ of sb** *(tire)* jdn ziemlich/sehr schlauchen *(col)*.

▶**take over 1** *vi (assume government)* an die Macht kommen; *(military junta etc)* die Macht ergreifen; *(party)* an die Regierung kommen; *(new boss etc)* die Leitung übernehmen; *(in a place: tourists, guests etc)* sich breitmachen *(col)*. **to ~ ~ (from sb)** jdn ablösen; **the next shift ~s ~ at 6 o'clock** die nächste Schicht übernimmt um 6 Uhr. **2** *vt sep* (**a**) *(take control or possession of)* übernehmen. **tourists ~ ~ Edinburgh in the summer** im Sommer machen sich die Touristen in Edinburgh breit *(col)*. (**b**) *(escort or carry across) person* hinüberbringen; *(+prep obj)* bringen über *(+acc)*. (**c**) **to ~ sb ~ sth** *(show round)* jdm etw zeigen.

▶**take to** *vi +prep obj* (**a**) *(form liking for) person* mögen. **the children soon took ~ their new surroundings** den Kindern gefiel es bald in der neuen Umgebung; **I don't know how she'll ~ ~ him/it** ich weiß nicht, wie sie auf ihn/darauf reagieren wird; **I don't ~ kindly ~ that** ich kann das nicht leiden. (**b**) *(form habit of)* **to ~ ~ doing sth** anfangen, etw zu tun; **to ~ ~ drink** zu trinken anfangen (**c**) *(escape to) hills* sich zurückziehen in *(+acc)*, Zuflucht suchen in *(+dat)*.

▶**take up** *vt sep* (**a**) *(raise, lift)* aufnehmen; *carpet, floorboards* hochnehmen; *road* aufreißen; *dress* kürzer machen; *pen* greifen zu.

(**b**) *(lead or carry upstairs etc) invalid, child* hinauf-/heraufbringen; *visitor* (mit) hinauf-/heraufnehmen.

(**c**) *time, attention* in Anspruch nehmen; *space* einnehmen.

(**d**) *(absorb)* (in sich *acc*) aufnehmen.

(**e**) *matter, point (raise)* zur Sprache bringen *(with sb* bei jdm*)*; *(go into)* eingehen auf *(+acc)*.

(**f**) *photography, archaeology* zu seinem Hobby machen; *a hobby* sich *(dat)* zulegen; *a language* anfangen zu lernen. **to ~ ~ painting/the guitar** anfangen zu malen/Gitarre zu spielen.

(**g**) *(adopt) cause* sich einsetzen für; *idea* aufgreifen; *case* sich annehmen *(+gen)*. **to ~ ~ a position** *(lit)* eine Stellung einnehmen; *(fig: attitude)* eine Haltung einnehmen.

(**h**) *(accept) challenge, invitation, suggestion* annehmen.

(**i**) *(start) job, employment* annehmen; *new job, post* antreten; *one's duties* übernehmen; *career* einschlagen.

(**j**) *(continue) story* aufnehmen; *conversation* weiterführen; *(join in) chorus, chant* einstimmen in *(+acc)*.

(**k**) **I'll ~ you ~ on that** *(on invitation, offer)* ich werde davon Gebrauch machen; *(on promise etc)* ich nehme Sie beim Wort.

▶**take upon** *vt +prep obj* **he has ~n it ~ himself to ...** er hat die Verantwortung auf sich genommen, zu ...; **he took it ~ himself to answer for me** er meinte, er müsse für mich antworten.

▶**take up with** vi +prep obj person sich anfreunden mit.

**take:** ~**-away** (esp Brit) **1** n (a) (meal) Essen nt zum Mitnehmen; (b) (restaurant) Restaurant nt mit Außer-Haus-Verkauf; **2** adj attr meal zum Mitnehmen; ~**-home pay** n Nettoverdienst m.

**taken** ['teɪkən] ptp of **take**.

**take:** ~**-off** n (Aviat) Start, Abflug m. ~**-over** n (Fin, Comm) Übernahme f; ~**-over bid** n Übernahmeangebot nt.

**taker** ['teɪkə<sup>r</sup>] n (at auction, fig) Interessent(in f) m. **there were no** ~s (esp fig) niemand war interessiert.

**taking** ['teɪkɪŋ] **1** n (a) it's yours for the ~ das können Sie (umsonst) haben. (b) ~s pl (Comm) Einnahmen pl. **2** adj person anziehend.

**talc** [tælk], **talcum powder** ['tælkəm,paʊdə<sup>r</sup>] n Talkumpuder m; (perfumed) (Körper)puder m.

**tale** [teɪl] n (a) Geschichte f; (Liter) Erzählung f. (b) **to tell** ~s petzen (col) (to bei); **to tell** ~**s about sb** jdn verpetzen (col) (to bei).

**talent** ['tælənt] n (a) Talent nt. **to have a** ~ **for drawing/mathematics** Begabung zum Zeichnen/für Mathematik haben. (b) (talented people) Talente pl. ~ **scout** Talentsucher m.

**talented** ['tæləntɪd] adj begabt, talentiert.

**talk** [tɔːk] **1** n (a) Gespräch nt (also Pol); (conversation also) Unterhaltung f. **to have a** ~ ein Gespräch führen/sich unterhalten (with sb about sth mit jdm über etw acc); **could I have a** ~ **with you?** könnte ich Sie mal sprechen?; **to hold** or **have** ~s Gespräche führen. (b) no pl (~ing) Rederei f; (rumour) Gerede nt. **there is some** ~ **of his returning** es heißt, er kommt zurück; **she's the** ~ **of the town** sie ist zum Stadtgespräch geworden; **he's all** ~ er ist ein Schwätzer. (c) (lecture) Vortrag m. **to give a** ~ einen Vortrag halten (on über +acc).

**2** vi sprechen, reden (of von, about über +acc); (have conversation also) sich unterhalten (of, about über +acc). **to** ~ **to** or **with sb** mit jdm reden (about über +acc); (converse also) sich mit jdm unterhalten (about über +acc); **could I** ~ **to Mr Smith please?** kann ich bitte Herrn Smith sprechen?; **it's easy for you to** ~ (col) du hast gut reden (col); **don't (you)** ~ **to me like that!** wie redest du denn mit mir?; **he knows/doesn't know what he's** ~**ing about** er weiß (schon)/weiß nicht, wovon er spricht; **you can** ~! (col) du kannst gerade reden!; **to keep sb** ~**ing** jdn (mit einem Gespräch) hinhalten; **to** ~ **to oneself** Selbstgespräche führen; **now you're** ~**ing!** das läßt sich schon eher hören!; **he's been** ~**ing of going abroad** er hat davon geredet, daß er ins Ausland fahren will; ~**ing of films** ... da wir gerade von Filmen sprechen ...; **stop** ~**ing!** sei/seid ruhig!; **everyone was** ~**ing about them** sie waren in aller Munde; (because of scandal) alle haben über sie geredet; **you're** ~**ing about at least £100** Sie müssen mit wenigstens 100 Pfund rechnen.

**3** vt (a) a language, slang sprechen; nonsense reden; (discuss) politics sich unterhalten über (+acc). (b) (persuade) **to** ~ **sb into doing sth** jdn überreden or dazu bringen, etw zu tun; (against better judgement) jdm einreden, etw zu tun; **to** ~ **sb out of sth/doing sth** jdm etw ausreden/jdm ausreden, etw zu tun; **he** ~**ed himself out of trouble** er redete sich (geschickt) heraus.

▶**talk down 1** vi to ~ ~ **to sb** mit jdm herablassend sprechen. **2** vt sep pilot zur Landung einweisen.

▶**talk over** vt sep problem besprechen.

▶**talk round** vt always separate umstimmen. **I** ~**ed**

**her** ~ **to my way of thinking** ich habe sie zu meiner Anschauung bekehrt.

**talkative** ['tɔːkətɪv] adj person gesprächig.

**talked-of** ['tɔːktɒv] adj: **much** ~ berühmt.

**talker** ['tɔːkə<sup>r</sup>] n Redner(in f) m; (pej) Schwätzer(in f) m.

**talking** ['tɔːkɪŋ] n Reden, Sprechen nt. **I'll let you do the** ~ ich überlasse das Reden Ihnen; **he did all the** ~ er übernahm das Reden.

**talking:** ~ **point** n Gesprächsthema nt; ~ **shop** n (pej) Quasselbude f; ~**-to** n **to give sb a good** ~**-to** jdm eine Standpauke halten (col).

**talk show** n Talkshow f.

**tall** [tɔːl] adj (+er) (a) person groß; building, tree hoch. **how** ~ **are you?** wie groß sind Sie?; **he is 6 foot** ~ er ist 1,80 m groß. (b) (col) **that's a** ~ **order** das ist ganz schön viel verlangt; **a** ~ **story** ein Märchen nt (col).

**tallboy** ['tɔːlbɔɪ] n (Brit) hohe Schlafzimmerkommode.

**tallness** ['tɔːlnɪs] n see adj Größe f; Höhe f.

**tallow** ['tæləʊ] n Talg m.

**tally** ['tælɪ] **1** n (a) **to keep a** ~ **of** Buch führen über (+acc). (b) (result of counting) (An)zahl f. **2** vi **they don't** ~ sie stimmen nicht überein.

**talon** ['tælən] n (also fig: of person) Kralle f.

**tambourine** [,tæmbə'riːn] n Tamburin nt.

**tame** [teɪm] **1** adj (+er) (a) animal, person zahm. (b) (dull) person, life, story, film etc lahm (col). **2** vt animal, person zähmen, bändigen; passion zügeln.

**tameness** ['teɪmnɪs] n Zahmheit f; (fig) Lahmheit f.

**tamer** ['teɪmə<sup>r</sup>] n (of animals) Dompteur m/ Dompteuse f.

**tamper** ['tæmpə<sup>r</sup>] vi +prep obj **tamper with** sich (dat) zu schaffen machen an (+dat). **the lock had been** ~**ed with** jemand hatte sich an dem Schloß zu schaffen gemacht.

**tampon** ['tæmpən] n Tampon m.

**tan** [tæn] **1** n (a) (suntan) Bräune f. **to get a** ~ braun werden. (b) (colour) Hellbraun nt. **2** adj hellbraun. **3** vt (a) skins gerben. **to** ~ **sb's hide** (fig col) jdm das Fell gerben. (b) (sun) face, body etc bräunen. **4** vi braun werden. **she** ~s **easily** sie wird schnell braun.

**tandem** ['tændəm] **1** n (cycle) Tandem nt. **2** adv **in** ~ aligned hintereinander; work zusammen.

**tang** [tæŋ] n (smell) scharfer Geruch; (taste) starker Geschmack.

**tangent** ['tændʒənt] n (Math) Tangente f. **to go** or **fly off at a** ~ (fig) (plötzlich) vom Thema abschweifen.

**tangerine** [,tændʒə'riːn] n Mandarine f.

**tangible** ['tændʒəbl] adj (lit, fig) greifbar; proof also handfest; assets real.

**Tangier(s)** [tæn'dʒɪə(z)] n Tanger nt.

**tangle** ['tæŋgl] **1** n (lit) Gewirr nt; (fig: muddle) Durcheinander nt. **to get into a** ~ (lit, fig) sich verheddern; **he got into a** ~ **with the police** er hat Schwierigkeiten mit der Polizei gehabt. **2** vt (also ~ up) (lit, fig) durcheinanderbringen; wool, string also verheddern. **to get** ~**d** (lit, fig) sich verheddern; (ropes) sich verknoten; **a** ~**d web** ein Gespinst nt.

▶**tangle with** vi +prep obj (col) aneinandergeraten mit. **I'm not tangling** ~ **him** mit ihm laß ich mich (doch) nicht ein.

**tango** ['tæŋgəʊ] **1** n Tango m. **2** vi Tango tanzen. **it takes two to** ~ (fig col) es gehören immer zwei dazu.

**tangy** ['tæŋɪ] adj (+er) taste scharf; (sour) sauer; smell durchdringend.

**tank** [tæŋk] n (a) (container) Tank m; (for water also)

Wasserspeicher *m*; *(of boiler also)* Kessel *m*; *(for diver: oxygen ~)* Flasche *f*. **(b)** *(Mil)* Panzer *m*.
▶**tank up 1** *vi (ship, plane)* auftanken. **2** *vt sep (Brit col)* **to get ~ed ~** sich vollaufen lassen *(col) (on mit/)*; **to be ~ed ~** voll sein.

**tankard** ['tæŋkəd] *n* Krug *m*.

**tanker** ['tæŋkər] *n* **(a)** *(boat)* Tanker *m*. **(b)** *(vehicle)* Tankwagen *m*.

**tankful** ['tæŋkfʊl] *n* Tank(voll) *m*.

**tanned** [tænd] *adj person* braun(gebrannt).

**tanner** ['tænər] *n* Gerber *m*.

**tannery** ['tænərɪ] *n* Gerberei *f*.

**tannin** ['tænɪn] *n* Tannin *nt*.

**Tannoy** ® ['tænɔɪ] *n* Lautsprecheranlage *f*. **over** *or* **on the ~** über den Lautsprecher.

**tantalize** ['tæntəlaɪz] *vt* reizen; *(torment)* quälen.

**tantalizing** *adj*, **~ly** *adv* ['tæntəlaɪzɪŋ, -lɪ] verlockend, verführerisch.

**tantamount** ['tæntəmaʊnt] *adj:* **to be ~ to sth** einer Sache *(dat)* gleichkommen.

**tantrum** ['tæntrəm] *n* Wutanfall, Koller *(col) m*. **to have** *or* **throw a ~** einen Wutanfall bekommen.

**Tanzania** [tænzə'nɪə] *n* Tansania *nt*.

**Tanzanian** [tænzə'nɪən] **1** *adj* tansanisch. **2** *n* Tansanier(in *f*) *m*.

**tap¹** [tæp] **1** *n (esp Brit)* Hahn *m*. **on ~** *(lit: beer etc)* vom Faß; *(fig)* zur Hand. **2** *vt cask, barrel* anzapfen; *telephone lines* abhören, anzapfen *(col)*; *resources* erschließen. **the wires are ~ped here** die Leitung hier wird abgehört.

**tap²** **1** *n (light knock)* Klopfen *nt*; *(light touch)* Klaps *m*. **2** *vti* klopfen. **he ~ped me on the shoulder** er klopfte mir auf die Schulter; **he ~ped his foot impatiently** er klopfte ungeduldig mit dem Fuß auf den Boden; **to ~ at the door** leise anklopfen.

**tap:** **~-dance** *vi* steppen; **~-dancing** *n* Steppen *nt*.

**tape** [teɪp] **1** *n* **(a)** Band *nt*; *(sticky paper)* Klebeband *nt*; *(Sellotape* ® *etc)* Kleb(e)streifen *m*; *(punch~)* Lochstreifen *m*; *(Sport)* Zielband *nt*. **to break** *or* **breast the ~** *(Sport)* durchs Ziel gehen. **(b)** *(magnetic)* (Ton)band *nt*. **on ~** auf Band; **to put** *or* **get sth on ~** etw auf Band aufnehmen. **2** *vt* **(a)** *parcel* (mit Kleb(e)streifen/-band) zukleben. **(b)** *(~-record) song, message* (auf Band) aufnehmen. **(c)** *(col)* **I've got the situation ~d** ich habe die Sache im Griff *(col)*; **I've got him ~d** ich kenne mich mit ihm aus.

**tape:** **~ deck** *n* Tapedeck *nt*; **~ measure** *n* Bandmaß *nt*.

**taper** ['teɪpər] **1** *n (candle)* (dünne) Kerze. **2** *vt end of plank, stick etc* zuspitzen; *edge* abschrägen; *pair of trousers* (nach unten) verengen. **3** *vi (also ~ off)* sich zuspitzen; *(trousers)* nach unten enger werden.

**tape:** **~-record** *vt* auf Band aufnehmen; **~ recorder** *n* Tonbandgerät *nt*; **~ recording** *n* Bandaufnahme *f*.

**tapering** ['teɪpərɪŋ] *adj* spitz zulaufend.

**tapestry** ['tæpɪstrɪ] *n* Wandteppich, Gobelin *m*.

**tapeworm** ['teɪpwɜːm] *n* Bandwurm *m*.

**tapioca** [ˌtæpɪ'əʊkə] *n* Tapioka *f*.

**tappet** ['tæpɪt] *n (Aut)* Stößel *m*.

**tap water** *n* Leitungswasser *nt*.

**tar** [tɑːr] **1** *n* Teer *m*. **2** *vt fence* teeren. **they are all ~red with the same brush** *(fig)* sie sind alle vom gleichen Schlag.

**tarantula** [tə'ræntjʊlə] *n* Tarantel *f*.

**tardy** ['tɑːdɪ] *adj (+er)* zu spät.

**target** ['tɑːgɪt] **1** *n* **(a)** *(person, object, Mil)* Ziel *nt*; *(Sport: board, fig: of joke, criticism etc)* Zielscheibe *f*. **his shot was off/on ~** *(Mil)* sein Schuß ist daneben gegangen/hat getroffen; **she is on ~ for a world record** der Weltrekord liegt für sie in greifbarer

Nähe. **(b)** *(objective, goal)* Ziel *nt*; *(in production)* (Plan)soll *nt*. **production is above/on/below ~** das Produktionssoll ist überschritten/erfüllt/nicht erfüllt; **we set ourselves the ~ of £10,000** wir haben uns £10.000 zum Ziel gesetzt. **2** *vt group etc* abzielen auf *(+acc)*.

**target:** **~ date** *n* angestrebter Termin; **~ figure** *n (amount)* angestrebte Summe; *(number)* angestrebte Zahl; **~ group** *n* Zielgruppe *f*; **~ language** *n* Zielsprache *f*; **~ practice** *n* Zielschießen *nt*.

**targetted** ['tɑːgɪtɪd] *adj publicity* gezielt.

**targetting** ['tɑːgɪtɪŋ] *n* Zielsetzung *f*. **the ~ of teenagers as customers** das Abzielen auf Teenager als Kunden.

**tariff** ['tærɪf] *n* **(a)** Tarif *m*; *(in hotels)* Preisliste *f*. **(b)** *(Econ: tax)* Zoll *m*; *(table)* Zolltarif *m*.

**tarmac** ['tɑːmæk] *n* Asphalt *m*; *(esp Brit Aviat)* Rollfeld *nt*.

**tarn** [tɑːn] *n* kleiner Bergsee.

**tarnish** ['tɑːnɪʃ] **1** *vt* **(a)** *metal* stumpf werden lassen. **(b)** *(fig) reputation* beflecken; *ideals* trüben. **2** *vi (metal)* anlaufen. **3** *n* Beschlag *m*.

**tarot card** ['tærəʊkɑːd] *n* Tarockkarte *f*.

**tarpaulin** [tɑː'pɔːlɪn] *n (waterproof sheet)* Plane *f*; *(Naut)* Persenning *f*.

**tarragon** ['tærəgən] *n* Estragon *m*.

**tart¹** [tɑːt] *adj (+er)* **(a)** *flavour, wine* herb, sauer *(pej); fruit* sauer. **(b)** *(fig) remark, manner* scharf.

**tart²** *n (Cook)* Obsttorte *f*; *(individual)* Obsttörtchen *nt*. **apple/jam ~** Apfelkuchen *m*/Marmeladentörtchen *nt*.

**tart³** *n (col) (prostitute)* Nutte *f (col!); (loose woman)* Flittchen *nt (pej)*.
▶**tart up** *vt sep (esp Brit col)* aufmachen *(col)*; oneself auftakeln *(col)*. **there she was, all ~ed ~** da stand sie, aufgetakelt wie eine Fregatte *(col)*.

**tartan** ['tɑːtən] **1** *n (pattern)* Schottenkaro *nt*; *(material)* Schottenstoff *m*. **2** *adj skirt* mit Schottenkaro *or* -muster.

**tartar** ['tɑːtər] *n (of wine)* Weinstein *m*; *(in kettle)* Kesselstein *m*; *(on teeth)* Zahnstein *m*.

**Tartar** ['tɑːtər] *n* Tatar *m*. **t~** *(fig)* Tyrann *m*.

**tartar sauce** *n* ≈ Remouladensoße *f*.

**tartly** ['tɑːtlɪ] *adv remark* scharf.

**tartness** ['tɑːtnɪs] *n see adj* **(a)** Herbheit *f*; Säure *f*. **(b)** Schärfe *f*.

**task** [tɑːsk] *n* Aufgabe *f*. **it is the ~ of the politician to ...** es ist Aufgabe des Politikers, zu ...; **to take sb to ~** sich *(dat)* jdn vornehmen *(col) (for, about* wegen*)*.

**task:** **~ force** *n* Spezialeinheit *f*; **~master** *n* (strenger) Arbeitgeber; **he's a hard ~master** er ist ein strenger Meister.

**Tasmania** [tæz'meɪnɪə] *n* Tasmanien *nt*.

**tassel** ['tæsəl] *n* Quaste, Troddel *f*.

**taste** [teɪst] **1** *n (lit, fig)* Geschmack *m*; *(small amount, fig: as an example)* Kostprobe *f*; *(of sth in the future)* Vorgeschmack *m*. **I don't like the ~ of it** das schmeckt mir nicht; **a ~ of onions** ein Zwiebelgeschmack *m*; **to have a ~ (of sth)** *(lit)* (etw) probieren; *(fig)* eine Kostprobe (von etw) bekommen; *(of sth to come)* einen Vorgeschmack (von etw) haben; **in good/bad ~** geschmackvoll/geschmacklos; **to have a ~ for sth** eine Vorliebe für etw haben; **it's an acquired ~** das ist etwas für Kenner; **she has expensive ~s** sie hat einen teuren Geschmack; **my ~ in music has changed** mein musikalischer Geschmack hat sich geändert; **to be to sb's ~** nach jds Geschmack sein; **it is a matter of ~** das ist Geschmack(s)sache; **sweeten to ~** *(Cook)* nach Geschmack süßen.

**2** *vt* **(a)** *(perceive flavour of)* schmecken; *(fig)*

*blood* lecken. **(b)** *(test) wine, food products* probieren; *(official)* prüfen. **(c)** *(fig) power, freedom* erleben.
**3** *vi* schmecken. **to ~ good** (gut) schmecken; **to ~ of sth** nach etw schmecken.
**taste bud** *n* Geschmacksknospe *f.*
**tasteful** *adj,* **~ly** *adv* ['teɪstful, -fəlɪ] geschmackvoll.
**tasteless** ['teɪstlɪs] *adj* geschmacklos; *food also* fade.
**tastelessly** ['teɪstlɪslɪ] *adv* geschmacklos.
**tastelessness** ['teɪstlɪsnɪs] *n see adj* Geschmacklosigkeit *f;* Fadheit *f.*
**tastily** ['teɪstɪlɪ] *adv* schmackhaft.
**tastiness** ['teɪstɪnɪs] *n* Schmackhaftigkeit *f.*
**tasty** ['teɪstɪ] *adj (+er) dish* schmackhaft.
**ta-ta** ['tæ'tɑː] *interj (Brit col)* tschüs *(col).*
**tattered** ['tætəd] *adj clothes* zerlumpt; *book, sheet* zerfleddert; *(fig) reputation* angeschlagen.
**tatters** ['tætəz] *npl* Lumpen, Fetzen *pl.* **to be in ~** in Fetzen sein; **his jacket hung in ~** sein Jackett war zerrissen.
**tattoo¹** [tə'tuː] **1** *vt* tätowieren. **2** *n* Tätowierung *f.*
**tattoo²** *n* **(a)** *(military pageant)* Musikparade *f.* **(b)** *(Mil: on drum or bugle)* Zapfenstreich *m.*
**tatty** ['tætɪ] *adj (+er) (col)* schmuddelig; *clothes* schäbig.
**taught** [tɔːt] *pret, ptp of* **teach.**
**taunt** [tɔːnt] **1** *n* Spöttelei *f,* höhnische Bemerkung. **2** *vt person* verspotten *(about* wegen*).* **to ~ sb with cowardice** jdm höhnisch Feigheit vorwerfen.
**Taurus** ['tɔːrəs] *n (Astron, Astrol)* Stier *m.*
**taut** [tɔːt] *adj (+er) rope* straff (gespannt); *muscles* gestrafft; *(fig) (tense) nerves, situation* (an)gespannt; *(economical) prose* knapp.
**tautological** [ˌtɔːtə'lɒdʒɪkəl] *adj* tautologisch, doppelt gemoppelt *(col).*
**tautology** [tɔː'tɒlədʒɪ] *n* Tautologie *f.*
**tavern** ['tævən] *n (old)* Schenke *f (old).*
**tawdry** ['tɔːdrɪ] *adj (+er) clothes* billig und geschmacklos; *jewellery, decorations* ordinär; *person* aufgedonnert.
**tawny** ['tɔːnɪ] *adj (+er)* goldbraun.
**tax** [tæks] **1** *n* **(a)** *(Fin, Econ)* Steuer *f;* *(on a company's profit)* Abgabe *f.* **before/after ~** vor/nach Abzug der Steuern; **to put a ~ on sb/sth** jdn/etw besteuern. **(b)** *(fig)* Belastung *f (on sth gen, on sb* für jdn*).* **2** *vt* **(a)** *(Fin, Econ)* besteuern; *country* mit Steuern belegen. **(b)** *(fig) brain, imagination* strapazieren; *one's patience also* auf eine harte Probe stellen; *strength* stark beanspruchen; *resources* angreifen. **(c)** *(accuse)* **to ~ sb with sth** jdn einer Sache *(gen)* beschuldigen.
**taxable** ['tæksəbl] *adj person* steuerpflichtig; *income also* steuerbar *(form); goods* abgabenpflichtig.
**tax** *in cpds* Steuer-; **~ allowance** *n* Steuerfreibetrag *m;* **~ assessment** *n* Steuerbescheid *m.*
**taxation** [tæk'seɪʃən] *n* Besteuerung *f; (taxes also)* Steuern *pl.* **exempt from ~** steuerfrei; **subject to ~** steuerpflichtig.
**tax:** **~ avoidance** *n* Steuerumgehung *f;* **~ bill** *n (assessment)* Steuerbescheid *m; (amount)* Steuerschuld *f;* **~ bracket** *n* Steuerklasse *f;* **~ collector** *n* Steuerbeamte(r) *m; (Bibl, Hist)* Zöllner *m;* **~ cut** *n* Steuersenkung *f;* **~-deductible** *adj* (von der Steuer) absetzbar; **~ disc** *n (Brit Aut)* Steuermarke *f;* **~ evasion** *n* Steuerhinterziehung *f; (by going abroad)* Steuerflucht *f;* **~ exemption** *n* Steuerfreiheit *f;* **~ exile** *n* Steuerexil *nt; (person)* Steuerflüchtling *m;* **~-free** *adj, adv* steuerfrei; **~ haven** *n* Steuerparadies *nt.*
**taxi** ['tæksɪ] **1** *n* Taxi *nt.* **to go by ~** mit dem Taxi

fahren. **2** *vi (Aviat)* rollen. **the plane ~ed to a halt** das Flugzeug rollte aus.
**taxidermist** ['tæksɪ'dɜːmɪst] *n* Präparator *m.*
**taxi:** **~-driver** *n* Taxifahrer(in *f) m;* **~ meter** *n* Fahrpreisanzeiger *m.*
**tax increase** *n* Steuererhöhung *f.*
**taxing** ['tæksɪŋ] *adj* anstrengend.
**tax inspector** *n* Steuerprüfer(in *f) m.*
**taxi:** **~plane** *n (US)* Lufttaxi *nt;* **~ rank** *(Brit),* **~ stand** *n* Taxistand *m.*
**tax:** **~man** *n* Steuer- *or* Finanzbeamte(r) *m;* **the ~man gets 35%** das Finanzamt bekommt 35%; **~ office** *n* Finanzamt *nt;* **~payer** *n* Steuerzahler *m;* **~ rebate** *n* Steuervergütung *f;* **~ relief** *n* Steuervergünstigung *f;* **~ return** *n* Steuererklärung *f.*
**TB** = **tuberculosis** Tb, Tbc *f.*
**tbsp** = **tablespoon(ful)(s)** Eßl.
**T.D.** *(US)* = **Treasury Department.**
**T-bone steak** ['tiːbəʊn'steɪk] *n* T-bone-Steak *nt.*
**tea** [tiː] *n* **(a)** Tee *m.* **to make (the) ~** (den) Tee machen; **a cup of ~** eine Tasse Tee; **not for all the ~ in China** nicht um alles Gold der Welt. **(b)** *(afternoon ~)* Nachmittagstee *m; (meal)* Abendbrot *nt.* **we have ~ at six** wir essen um 6 Uhr zu Abend.
**tea:** **~ bag** *n* Teebeutel *m;* **~ break** *n (Brit)* Pause *f;* **~ caddy** *n* Teedose *f;* **~cake** *n* Rosinenbrötchen *nt (zum Toasten);* **~ cart** *n (US)* Tee- *or* Servierwagen *m.*
**teach** [tiːtʃ] *(vb: pret, ptp* **taught)** **1** *vt subject, person* unterrichten; *animal* abrichten. **to ~ sth to sb** jdm etw beibringen; *(teacher)* jdn in etw *(dat)* unterrichten; **to ~ sb to do sth** jdm beibringen, etw zu tun; **to ~ sb how to do sth** jdm etw beibringen; **he ~es French** er unterrichtet *or* gibt *(col)* Französisch; **to ~ oneself sth** sich *(dat)* etw beibringen; **let that ~ you not to ...** laß dir das eine Lehre sein, nicht zu ...; **that'll ~ you to break the speed limit** das hast du (nun) davon, daß du das Tempolimit überschritten hast. **2** *vi* unterrichten, Unterricht geben. **he wants to ~** er möchte Lehrer werden.
**teacher** ['tiːtʃər] *n* Lehrer(in *f) m.* **she is a German ~** sie ist Deutschlehrerin.
**teacher-training** ['tiːtʃə'treɪnɪŋ] *n* Lehrerausbildung *f.* **~ college** *(primary)* pädagogische Hochschule; *(secondary)* Studienseminar *nt.*
**tea-chest** ['tiːtʃest] *n* Kiste *f.*
**teaching** ['tiːtʃɪŋ] *n* **(a)** das Unterrichten; *(as profession)* der Lehrberuf. **to take up ~** Lehrer werden; **she enjoys ~** sie unterrichtet gern. **(b)** *(doctrine: also* **~s)** Lehre *f.*
**teaching:** **~ aid** *n* Lehrmittel *nt;* **~ hospital** *n* Ausbildungskrankenhaus *nt;* **~ qualification** *n* Lehrbefähigung *f;* **~ staff** *n* Lehrerkollegium *nt,* Lehrkörper *m (form).*
**tea:** **~ cloth** *n (Brit)* Geschirrtuch *nt;* **~ cosy** *n* Teewärmer *m;* **~cup** *n* **(a)** Teetasse *f;* **(b)** *(also* **~cupful)** Tasse *f* (voll).
**teak** [tiːk] *n* Teak(holz) *nt; (tree)* Teakbaum *m.*
**tea:** **~ lady** *n* Frau, die in Büros etc für die Angestellten Tee zubereitet; **~-leaf** *n* Teeblatt *nt.*
**team** [tiːm] *n* **(a)** Team *nt; (Sport also)* Mannschaft *f.* **football ~** Fußballmannschaft *f.* **(b)** *(of horses, oxen etc)* Gespann *nt.*
▶**team up** *vi* sich zusammentun *(with* mit*); (join group)* sich anschließen *(with sb* jdm, an jdn*).*
**tea-maker** *n* Teemaschine *f.*
**team:** **~ effort** *n* Teamarbeit *f;* **~ game** *n* Mannschaftsspiel *nt;* **~-mate** *n* Mannschaftskamerad *m;* **~ member** *n* Teammitglied *nt; (Sport also)* Mannschaftsmitglied *nt;* **~ spirit** *n* Gemeinschaftsgeist *m; (Sport)* Mannschaftsgeist *m;* **~work** *n* Ge-

meinschaftsarbeit, Teamarbeit *f.*

**tea:** ~ **party** *n* Teegesellschaft *f;* ~**pot** *n* Teekanne *f.*

**tear¹** [tɛəʳ] *(vb: pret* **tore,** *ptp* **torn/ 1** *vt* **(a)** *paper, dress* zerreißen; *flesh* aufreißen; *hole* reißen. **I've torn a muscle** ich habe mir einen Muskel gezerrt; **to** ~ **sth to pieces** etw in Stücke reißen; **the critics tore him/the play to pieces** die Kritiker haben ihn in der Luft zerrissen *(col)/*das Stück total verrissen; **to** ~ **sth open** etw aufreißen; **that's torn it!** *(fig col)* das hat alles verdorben! **(b)** *(pull away)* reißen. **her child was torn from her/her arms** das Kind wurde ihr entrissen/ihr aus den Armen gerissen; **he tore it out of my hand** er riß es mir aus der Hand. **(c)** *(fig: usu pass)* **a country torn by war** ein vom Krieg zerrissenes Land; **to be torn between two things/ people** zwischen zwei Dingen/Menschen hin- und hergerissen sein.

 **2** *vi* **(a)** *(material etc)* (zer)reißen. **her coat tore on a nail** sie zerriß sich *(dat)* den Mantel an einem Nagel; ~ **along the dotted line** an der gestrichelten Linie abtrennen. **(b)** *(move quickly)* rasen. **to** ~ **past** vorbeirasen.

 **3** *n (in material etc)* Riß *m.*

▶**tear along** *vi* entlangrasen. **he tore** ~ **the street** er raste die Straße entlang.

▶**tear apart** *vt sep house (thieves etc)* völlig durcheinanderbringen; *(bomb etc)* völlig zerstören; *meat, country* zerreißen.

▶**tear away 1** *vi* davonrasen. **2** *vt sep wrapping* abreißen *(from* von*).* **if you can** ~ **yourself** ~ **from the paper** wenn du dich von der Zeitung losreißen kannst.

▶**tear down** *vt sep poster* herunterreißen; *house* abreißen.

▶**tear off 1** *vi* **(a)** wegrasen. **he tore** ~ **down the street** er raste die Straße hinunter. **(b) the carbon** ~**s** ~ die Durchschrift läßt sich abtrennen. **2** *vt sep label, wrapping, cover* abreißen; *clothes* herunterreißen. **he tore me** ~ **a strip** *(col)* er hat mich zur Schnecke gemacht *(col).*

▶**tear out 1** *vi* heraus-/hinausrasen. **he tore** ~ **through the front door** er raste zur Haustür hinaus. **2** *vt sep* (her)ausreißen *(of* aus*).*

▶**tear up 1** *vi* angerast kommen. **he tore** ~ **the hill/road** er raste den Berg hinauf/die Straße entlang. **2** *vt sep* **(a)** *paper, (fig) contract* zerreißen. **(b)** *stake, plant* (her)ausreißen.

**tear²** [tɪəʳ] *n* Träne *f.* **in** ~**s** in Tränen aufgelöst; **the news brought** ~**s to her eyes** als sie das hörte, stiegen ihr die Tränen in die Augen; **moved to** ~**s** zu Tränen gerührt; **you are bringing** ~**s to my eyes** *(iro)* mir kommen die Tränen *(iro);* ~ **drop** Träne *f.*

**tearaway** ['tɛərəweɪ] *n (col)* Rabauke *m (col).*

**tearful** ['tɪəfʊl] *adj look* tränenfeucht; *face* tränenüberströmt. **...,** **she said in a** ~ **voice ...,** sagte sie unter Tränen.

**tearfully** ['tɪəfəlɪ] *adv say etc* unter Tränen.

**teargas** ['tɪəɡæs] *n* Tränengas *nt.*

**tearing** ['tɛərɪŋ] *adj (col):* **to be in a** ~ **hurry** es schrecklich eilig haben.

**tear-jerker** ['tɪə,dʒɜːkəʳ] *n (col)* Schmachtfetzen *m (col).*

**tear-off** ['tɛərɒf] *adj* zum Abtrennen. ~ **calendar** Abreißkalender *m.*

**tearoom** ['tiːrʊm] *n* Teestube *f,* Café *nt.*

**tease** [tiːz] **1** *vt person* necken; *animal* reizen; *(torment)* quälen; *(make fun of)* aufziehen, hänseln *(about* wegen*);* *(have on)* auf den Arm nehmen *(col).* **2** *n (col: person)* Scherzbold *m (col).*

▶**tease out** *vt sep (fig) information* ablocken *(out of sb* jdm*).*

**teaser** ['tiːzəʳ] *n (difficult question)* harte Nuß *(col);* *(riddle)* Denksportaufgabe *f.*

**tea:** ~ **service,** ~ **set** *n* Teeservice *nt;* ~ **shop** *n (Brit)* Teestube *f;* ~**spoon** *n* **(a)** Teelöffel *m;* **(b)** *(also* ~**spoonful)* Teelöffel *m* (voll); ~ **strainer** *n* Teesieb *nt.*

**teat** [tiːt] *n (of animal)* Zitze *f; (of woman)* Brustwarze *f; (Brit: on baby's bottle)* (Gummi)sauger *m.*

**tea:** ~**time** *n (for afternoon* ~*)* Teestunde *f; (North Brit: evening mealtime)* Abendessenszeit *f;* ~ **towel** *n (Brit)* Geschirrtuch *nt;* ~ **tray** *n* Tablett *nt;* ~ **trolley** *(Brit),* ~ **wagon** *(US) n* Teewagen *m.*

**tech** [tek] *(Brit)* = **technical college.**

**technical** ['teknɪkəl] *adj* **(a)** *(concerning technology)* technisch. ~ **hitch** technisches Problem. **(b)** *(of particular branch)* fachlich, Fach-; *adviser, dictionary* Fach-; *problems, vocabulary* fachspezifisch; *details* formal. ~ **term** Fachausdruck *m;* ~ **terminology** Fachsprache *f;* ~ **question** *(Jur)* Verfahrensfrage *f;* **for** ~ **reasons** aus technischen *or (Jur)* aus verfahrenstechnischen Gründen.

**technical:** ~ **college** *n (Brit)* Technische Fachschule; ~ **drawing** *n* technisches Zeichnen.

**technicality** [,teknɪ'kælɪtɪ] *n (technical detail, difficulty)* technische Einzelheit; *(fig, Jur)* Formsache *f.* **that's just a** ~ das ist bloß ein Detail.

**technically** ['teknɪkəlɪ] *adv* **(a)** technisch. **(b)** *(strictly speaking)* ~ **you're right** genaugenommen haben Sie recht.

**technician** [tek'nɪʃən] *n* Techniker(in *f) m; (skilled worker)* Facharbeiter(in *f) m.*

**technique** [tek'niːk] *n* Technik *f; (method)* Methode *f.*

**technocrat** ['teknəʊkræt] *n* Technokrat(in *f) m.*

**technological** [,teknə'lɒdʒɪkəl] *adj* technologisch; *details* technisch.

**technologist** [tek'nɒlədʒɪst] *n* Technologe *m,* Technologin *f.*

**technology** [tek'nɒlədʒɪ] *n* Technologie *f.* **the** ~ **of printing** die Drucktechnik; **the age of** ~ das technische Zeitalter.

**teddy (bear)** ['tedɪ(,bɛəʳ)] *n* Teddy(bär) *m.*

**tedious** ['tiːdɪəs] *adj* langweilig, öde.

**tediousness** ['tiːdɪəsnɪs] *n* Langeweile *f.*

**tedium** ['tiːdɪəm] *n* Langeweile *f.*

**tee** [tiː] *(Golf)* **1** *n* Tee *nt.* **2** *vt ball* auf das Tee legen. ▶**tee off** *vi* einen Ball vom (ersten) Abschlag spielen.

**teem** [tiːm] *vi* **(a)** *(with people, insects etc)* wimmeln *(with* von*).* **(b) it's** ~**ing (with rain)** es regnet *or* gießt *(col)* in Strömen.

**teenage** ['tiːn,eɪdʒ] *adj* Jugend-, Teenager-; *child, son* halbwüchsig.

**teenager** ['tiːn,eɪdʒəʳ] *n* Teenager *m.*

**teens** [tiːnz] *npl* Teenageralter *nt.* **to be in one's** ~ im Teenageralter sein.

**teenybopper** ['tiːnɪ,bɒpəʳ] *n (col)* Teeny *m (col).*

**teeny(weeny)** ['tiːnɪ('wiːnɪ)] *adj (col)* winzig (klein), klitzeklein *(col).*

**tee-shirt** *n* = **T-shirt.**

**teeter** ['tiːtəʳ] *vi* **(a)** taumeln, schwanken. **to** ~ **on the brink** *or* **edge of sth** *(lit)* am Rand von etw taumeln; *(fig)* am Rand von etw sein. **(b)** *(US: seesaw)* schaukeln.

**teeth** [tiːθ] *pl* of **tooth.**

**teethe** [tiːð] *vi* zahnen.

**teething** ['tiːðɪŋ] *n* Zahnen *nt.* ~ **ring** Beißring *m;* ~ **troubles** *pl (fig)* Kinderkrankheiten *pl.*

**teetotal** [tiː'təʊtl] *adj person* abstinent; *party etc* ohne Alkohol. **to be** ~ keinen Alkohol trinken, Antialkoholiker(in *f) m* sein.

**teetotaller,** *(US)* **teetotaler** [tiː'təʊtləʳ] *n* Absti-

nenzler(in *f*), Antialkoholiker(in *f*) *m*.
**TEFL** = **Teaching (of) English as a Foreign Language.**
**Teh(e)ran** [tɛəˈrɑːn] *n* Teheran *nt*.
**tel** = **telephone (number)** Tel.
**telecast** [ˈtelɪkɑːst] *n* Fernsehsendung *f*.
**telecommunications** [ˌtelɪkəˌmjuːnɪˈkeɪʃənz] *n* (a) *pl* Fernmeldewesen *nt*. (b) *sing (science)* Fernmeldetechnik *f*.
**telecommute** [ˈtelɪkəˌmjuːt] *vi* Teleheimarbeit machen.
**telecommuting** [ˈtelɪkəˌmjuːtɪŋ] *n* Teleheimarbeit *f*.
**telegram** [ˈtelɪɡræm] *n* Telegramm *nt*.
**telegraph**: ~ **pole** *n* Telegrafenmast *m*; ~ **wire** *n* Telegrafenleitung *f*.
**telepathic** [ˌtelɪˈpæθɪk] *adj* telepathisch. **you must be** ~! du mußt Hellseher sein!
**telepathy** [tɪˈlepəθɪ] *n* Telepathie *f*.
**telephone** [ˈtelɪfəʊn] **1** *n* Telefon *nt*. **you're wanted on the** ~ Sie werden am Telefon verlangt; **are you on the** ~? haben Sie Telefon?; **(can you be reached by** ~) sind Sie telefonisch zu erreichen?; **he's on the** ~ *(is using the* ~) er telefoniert gerade; *(wants to speak to you)* er ist am Telefon; **by** ~ telefonisch; **I've just been/I'll get on the** ~ **to him** ich habe eben mit ihm telefoniert/ich werde ihn anrufen. **2** *vt* anrufen; *message, reply* telefonisch übermitteln. **would you** ~ **the office to say ...** würden Sie im Büro anrufen und sagen ... **3** *vi* anrufen, telefonieren; *(make* ~ *call)* telefonieren. **to** ~ **for a taxi** ein Taxi rufen.
**telephone** *in cpds* Telefon-, Fernsprech- *(form)*; ~ **booth** *or* **box** *(Brit)* *n* Telefonzelle *f*; ~ **call** *n* Telefongespräch *nt*; ~ **directory** *n* Telefonbuch *nt*; ~ **exchange** *n* Vermittlungsstelle *f (form)*; ~ **kiosk** *n* *(Brit)* Telefonzelle *f*; ~ **line** *n* Telefonleitung *f*; ~ **message** *n* telefonische Nachricht; ~ **number** *n* Telefonnummer, Rufnummer *f*; ~ **operator** *n* Telefonist(in *f*) *m*; ~ **subscriber** *n* Fernsprechteilnehmer(in *f*) *m*.
**telephonist** [tɪˈlefənɪst] *n* *(Brit)* Telefonist(in *f*) *m*.
**telephoto (lens)** [ˈtelɪˌfəʊtəʊ(ˈlenz)] *n* Teleobjektiv *nt*.
**teleprinter** [ˈtelɪˌprɪntər] *n* Fernschreiber *m*.
**telescope** [ˈtelɪskəʊp] **1** *n* Teleskop *nt*. **2** *vi* sich ineinanderschieben lassen.
**telescopic** [ˌtelɪˈskɒpɪk] *adj aerial etc* ausziehbar.
**teletext** [ˈtelɪtekst] *n* Videotext *m*.
**televise** [ˈtelɪvaɪz] *vt* (im Fernsehen) übertragen. ~**d debate** Fernsehdebatte *f*.
**television** [ˈtelɪˌvɪʒən] *n* Fernsehen *nt*; *(set)* Fernsehapparat, Fernseher *(col)* *m*. **to watch** ~ fernsehen; **to be on** ~ im Fernsehen kommen; *(person)* im Fernsehen sein.
**television** *in cpds* Fernseh-; ~ **camera** *n* Fernsehkamera *f*; ~ **company** *n* Fernsehanstalt *f*; ~ **licence** *n (Brit)* Fernsehgenehmigung *f*; ~ **personality** *n* bekannte Fernsehpersönlichkeit; ~ **programme** *n* Fernsehsendung *f*; ~ **screen** *n* Bildschirm *m*, Mattscheibe *f (col)*; ~ **set** *n* Fernsehapparat, Fernseher *(col)* *m*; ~ **studio** *n* Fernsehstudio *nt*.
**telex** [ˈteleks] **1** *n* Fernschreiben, Telex *nt*; *(machine)* Fernschreiber *m*. **2** *vt message* per Telex mitteilen; *person* ein Telex schicken *(+dat)*.
**tell** [tel] *pret, ptp* **told 1** *vt* (a) *(relate) story, experiences, adventures* erzählen *(sb sth, sth to sb* jdm etw*)*; *(inform, say, announce)* sagen *(sb sth* jdm etw*)*. **to** ~ **lies/fortunes** lügen/wahrsagen; **to** ~ **sb about** *or* **of sth** jdm von etw erzählen; **I can't** ~ **you how pleased I am** ich kann Ihnen gar nicht sagen,

wie sehr ich mich freue; **who told you that?** wer hat Ihnen denn das erzählt?; **to** ~ **sb the way** jdm den Weg sagen; **could you** ~ **me the way to the station, please?** könn(t)en Sie mir bitte sagen, wie ich zum Bahnhof komme?; **(I'll)** ~ **you what, let's go to the cinema** weißt du was, gehen wir doch ins Kino!; **don't** ~ **me you can't come!** sagen Sie bloß nicht, daß Sie nicht kommen können!; **I won't do it, I** ~ **you!** und ich sage dir, das mache ich nicht!; **let me** ~ **you ...** lassen Sie sich von mir sagen, daß ...; **it was cold, I can** ~ **you** ich kann dir sagen, das war vielleicht kalt!; **I told you so** ich habe es (dir) ja gesagt; ~ **me another!** wer's glaubt! *(col)*; **don't** ~ **me, let me guess** sag's mir nicht, laß mich raten; **you're** ~**ing me!** wem sagen Sie das!
   (b) *(distinguish, discern)* **to** ~ **the time** *(child)* die Uhr kennen; **I had no way of** ~**ing the time** ich konnte nicht wissen, wie spät es war; **to** ~ **the difference** den Unterschied erkennen; **you can** ~ **that he's a foreigner** man sieht *or* merkt, daß er Ausländer ist; **to** ~ **sb/sth by sth** jdn/etw an etw *(dat)* erkennen; **to** ~ **right from wrong** Recht von Unrecht unterscheiden; **how can/could I** ~ **that?** wie soll ich das wissen?/wie hätte ich das wissen können?
   (c) *(order)* sagen *(sb* jdm*)*. **we were told to bring sandwiches with us** man hat uns gesagt, wir sollten belegte Brote mitbringen; ~ **him to stop singing** sagen Sie ihm, er soll aufhören zu singen; **do as** *or* **what you are told!** tu, was man dir sagt!; **I won't** ~ **you again** ich sage es dir nicht noch einmal.
   **2** *vi* (a) *(discern, be sure)* wissen. **who can** ~? wer weiß?; **how can I** ~? *(how should I know)* woher soll ich das wissen?; **you never can** ~ man kann nie wissen. (b) *(talk,* ~ *tales of)* sprechen. **that would be** ~**ing!** das kann ich nicht verraten; **promise you won't** ~ du mußt versprechen, daß du nichts sagst; **it hurt me more than words can** ~ es hat mich mehr verletzt, als ich mit Worten ausdrücken kann. (c) *(have effect)* sich bemerkbar machen. **his age told against him** *(in applying for job)* sein Alter sprach gegen ihn; *(in competition)* sein Alter machte sich bemerkbar.
   ▶**tell off** *vt sep (col: scold)* ausschimpfen *(for we-gen)*. **he told me** ~ **for being late** er schimpfte (mich aus), weil ich zu spät kam.
**teller** [ˈtelər] *n* (a) *(in bank)* Kassierer(in *f*) *m*. (b) *(vote counter)* Stimmenauszähler(in *f*) *m*. (c) *(of story)* Erzähler(in *f*) *m*.
**telling** [ˈtelɪŋ] **1** *adj (effective)* wirkungsvoll; *argument also* schlagend; *blow (lit, fig)* empfindlich; *(revealing)* aufschlußreich. **2** *n* (a) *(narration)* Erzählen *nt*. (b) **there is no** ~ **what he may do** man kann nicht wissen, was er tut.
**telling-off** [ˈtelɪŋˈɒf] *n (col)* Standpauke *f (col)*. **to give sb a good** ~ jdn kräftig ausschimpfen.
**telltale** [ˈtelteɪl] **1** *n* Petzer *m*, Petze *f*. **2** *adj attr* verräterisch.
**telly** [ˈtelɪ] *n (Brit col)* Fernseher *m (col)*. **on (the)** ~ im Fernsehen, **to watch** ~ fernsehen.
**temerity** [tɪˈmerɪtɪ] *n* Kühnheit *f*.
**temp¹** = (a) **temporary.** (b) **temperature.**
**temp²** [temp] *(Brit)* **1** *n* Aushilfskraft *f*. **2** *vi* als Aushilfskraft arbeiten.
**temper** [ˈtempər] **1** *n (disposition)* Wesen, Naturell *nt*; *(angry mood)* Wut *f*. **to be in a** ~/**good/bad** ~ wütend sein/guter/schlechter Laune sein; **she's got a quick/vicious** ~ sie kann sehr jähzornig sein/tückisch werden; **to lose one's** ~ die Beherrschung verlieren *(with sb* bei jdm*)*; **to keep one's** ~ sich beherrschen *(with sb* bei jdm*)*; **to fly into a** ~ einen Wutanfall bekommen; **a fit of** ~ ein Wutanfall *m*. **2**

*vt* (**a**) *metal* tempern. (**b**) *(fig) action, passion* mäßigen; *criticism* mildern.

**temperament** ['tempərəmənt] *n* Temperament *nt*; *(disposition)* Veranlagung *f.* **he has an artistic** ~ **er** ist eine Künstlernatur.

**temperamental** [,tempərə'mentl] *adj* temperamentvoll, launenhaft *(pej); car* launisch *(hum)*.

**temperance** ['tempərəns] *n* (**a**) *(moderation)* Mäßigung *f; (in speech etc also)* Zurückhaltung *f; (in eating, drinking also)* Maßhalten *nt.* (**b**) *(teetotalism)* Enthaltsamkeit *f.*

**temperate** ['tempərɪt] *adj person, climate* gemäßigt; *(in eating, demands)* maßvoll.

**temperature** ['temprɪtʃər] *n* Temperatur *f; (Med: above normal* ~ *also)* Fieber *nt.* **to take sb's** ~ bei jdm Fieber messen; **he has a** ~**/a slight/high** ~ **er** hat Fieber/erhöhte Temperatur/hohes Fieber; **he has a** ~ **of 39°C** er hat 39° Fieber.

**tempered** ['tempəd] *adj steel* gehärtet.

**-tempered** *adj suf* -gelaunt.

**tempest** ['tempɪst] *n (liter)* Sturm *m (also fig).*

**tempestuous** [,tem'pestjuəs] *adj (lit liter, fig)* stürmisch; *speech* leidenschaftlich.

**tempi** ['tempiː] *pl of* **tempo.**

**template** ['templɪt] *n* Schablone *f.*

**temple**[1] ['templ] *n (Rel)* Tempel *m.*

**temple**[2] *n (Anat)* Schläfe *f.*

**tempo** ['tempəu] *n, pl* **-s** *or* **tempi** ['tempiː] *(Mus, fig)* Tempo *nt.*

**temporal** ['tempərəl] *adj* (**a**) zeitlich; *(Gram)* Zeit-, temporal. (**b**) *(Rel)* weltlich.

**temporarily** [,tempə'rɛərɪlɪ] *adv* vorübergehend.

**temporary** ['tempərərɪ] *adj* vorübergehend; *job also* befristet; *arrangement also, road surface* provisorisch; *powers also* befristet. ~ **staff** Aushilfskräfte *pl;* ~ **solution** Übergangslösung *f;* **he's looking for** ~ **work** er sucht eine Stelle auf Zeit *(col).*

**tempt** [tempt] *vt* in Versuchung führen; *(successfully)* verführen; *(Rel also)* versuchen. **to** ~ **sb to do** *or* **into doing sth** jdn dazu verleiten, etw zu tun; **don't** ~ **me** bring mich nicht in Versuchung!; **to** ~ **fate** *(fig)* sein Schicksal herausfordern; *(in words)* den Teufel an die Wand malen; **I'm** ~**ed** es reizt mich.

**temptation** [temp'teɪʃən] *n* Versuchung *f (also Rel).* **to yield to** ~ der Versuchung erliegen.

**tempting** ['temptɪŋ] *adj* verlockend.

**ten** [ten] **1** *adj* zehn. ~ **to one he won't come** (ich wette) zehn zu eins, daß er nicht kommt; **nine out of** ~ **people would agree with you** neun von zehn Leuten würden Ihnen zustimmen. **2** *n* Zehn *f.* ~**s** *(Math)* Zehner *pl; see* **six.**

**tenable** ['tenəbl] *adj (Mil) position* haltbar; *(fig) opinion, theory also* vertretbar.

**tenacious** [tɪ'neɪʃəs] *adj* zäh; *character, person also* beharrlich.

**tenacity** [tɪ'næsɪtɪ] *n see adj* Zähigkeit *f;* Beharrlichkeit *f.* **the** ~ **of his grip** sein eiserner Griff.

**tenancy** ['tenənsɪ] *n see* **tenant** Miet-/Pachtverhältnis *nt.* **during his** ~ während er dort Mieter/Pächter ist/war.

**tenant** ['tenənt] *n* Mieter(in *f*) *m; (of farm)* Pächter(in *f*) *m.* ~ **farmer** Pächter(in *f*) *m.*

**tend**[1] [tend] *vt* sich kümmern um; *sheep* hüten; *sick person* pflegen; *machine* bedienen.

**tend**[2] *vi* **to** ~ **to be/do sth** *(have habit)* gern etw sein/tun; *(person also)* dazu neigen *or* tendieren, etw zu sein/tun; *(thing)* ~**s to stick** der Hebel bleibt oft hängen; **I** ~ **to believe him** ich neige dazu, ihm zu glauben; **to** ~ **towards** *(incline) (person, views etc)* neigen *or* tendieren zu.

**tendency** ['tendənsɪ] *n* Tendenz *f (geh); (physical predisposition)* Neigung *f.* **to have a** ~ **to be/do sth** gern etw sein/tun; *(person, style of writing also)* dazu neigen *or* tendieren, etw zu sein/zu tun; **he had an annoying** ~ **to forget things** er hatte die ärgerliche Angewohnheit, alles zu vergessen.

**tendentious** [ten'denʃəs] *adj* tendenziös.

**tender**[1] ['tendər] *n (Naut, Rail)* Tender *m.*

**tender**[2] **1** *vt money, services* (an)bieten; *thanks* aussprechen; *resignation* einreichen. **"please** ~ **exact fare"** „bitte Fahrgeld abgezählt bereithalten". **2** *vi (Comm)* sich bewerben *(for* um*).* **3** *n* (**a**) *(Comm)* Angebot *nt.* **to invite** ~**s for a job** Angebote *pl* für eine Arbeit einholen; **to put in a** ~ **for sth** ein Angebot für etw einreichen. (**b**) *legal* ~ gesetzliches Zahlungsmittel.

**tender**[3] *adj* (**a**) *spot, bruise* empfindlich; *skin, plant also* zart; *(fig) subject* heikel. (**b**) *meat* zart. (**c**) *(affectionate) person, look* zärtlich, liebevoll; *memories* lieb. **to bid sb a** ~ **farewell** liebevoll(en) Abschied von jdm nehmen; **to be in need of** ~ **loving care** *(hum)* liebevolle Zuwendung brauchen.

**tender-hearted** [,tendə'hɑːtɪd] *adj* gutherzig.

**tenderize** ['tendəraɪz] *vt meat* zart *or* weich machen; *(by beating)* klopfen.

**tenderly** ['tendəlɪ] *adv* zärtlich, liebevoll.

**tenderness** ['tendənɪs] *n see adj* (**a**) Empfindlichkeit *f;* Zartheit *f.* (**b**) Zartheit *f.* (**c**) Zärtlichkeit *f.*

**tendon** ['tendən] *n* Sehne *f.*

**tendril** ['tendrɪl] *n* Ranke *f.*

**tenement** ['tenɪmənt] *n* Mietshaus *nt.*

**Tenerife** [,tenə'riːf] *n* Teneriffa *nt.*

**tenet** ['tenət] *n* Lehrsatz *m; (Rel)* Glaubenssatz *m.*

**tenner** ['tenər] *n (col)* Zehner *m (col).*

**tennis** ['tenɪs] *n* Tennis *nt.*

**tennis** *in cpds* Tennis-; ~ **club** *n* Tennisclub *m;* ~ **court** *n* Tennisplatz *m;* ~ **elbow** *n (Med)* Tennisarm *m;* ~ **player** *n* Tennisspieler(in *f*) *m;* ~ **racket** *n* Tennisschläger *m.*

**tenor** ['tenər] **1** *n* (**a**) *(voice)* Tenor(stimme *f*) *m; (person)* Tenor *m.* (**b**) *(purport)* Tenor *m; (of theory)* Tendenz *f; (general nature: of life)* Stil *m.* **2** *adj (Mus)* Tenor-.

**tenpin bowling** [,tenpɪn'bəulɪŋ], *(US)* **tenpins** ['tenpɪnz] *n* Bowling *nt.*

**tense**[1] [tens] *n (Gram)* Zeit *f,* Tempus *nt.*

**tense**[2] **1** *adj (+er) rope, atmosphere, moment* gespannt; *muscles also, person, expression (through stress etc)* angespannt; *(through fear etc)* verkrampft; *voice* nervös; *(thrilling) scene* spannungsgeladen. **2** *vt muscles* anspannen.

**tensely** ['tenslɪ] *adv listen* angespannt; *speak, wait (nervously)* nervös; *(excitedly)* gespannt.

**tenseness** ['tensnɪs] *n see adj* Gespanntheit *f;* Angespanntheit *f;* Verkrampftheit *f;* Nervosität *f;* Spannung *f.*

**tension** ['tenʃən] *n* (**a**) *(lit)* Spannung *f; (of muscle)* Anspannung *f; (Knitting)* Festigkeit *f.* (**b**) *(nervous strain)* Anspannung *f.* (**c**) *(strain: in relationship)* Spannungen *pl.*

**tent** [tent] *n* Zelt *nt.* ~ **peg** *(Brit)* or **stake** *(US)* Zeltpflock, Hering *m;* ~ **pole** Zeltstange *f.*

**tentacle** ['tentəkl] *n* Fangarm *m; (fig)* Klaue *f.*

**tentative** ['tentətɪv] *adj (provisional)* vorläufig; *offer* unverbindlich; *(hesitant)* vorsichtig; *steps, questions* tastend.

**tentatively** ['tentətɪvlɪ] *adv see adj.*

**tenterhooks** ['tentəhuks] *npl:* **to be on** ~ wie auf glühenden Kohlen sitzen *(col);* **to keep sb on** ~ jdn zappeln lassen.

**tenth** [tenθ] **1** *adj (in series)* zehnte(r, s). **2** *n (frac-*

*tion)* Zehntel *nt;* *(in series)* Zehnte(r, s); *see* **sixth.**
**tenuous** ['tenjʊəs] *adj (a) (lit) thread etc* dünn, fein.
**(b)** *(fig) connection, argument* schwach.
**tenuousness** ['tenjʊəsnɪs] *n see adj* **(a)** Dünne,
Feinheit *f.* **(b)** Schwäche *f.*
**tenure** ['tenjʊər] *n (period of office)* Amtszeit *f.* **to
have security of** ~ *(esp US)* fest angestellt sein.
**tepid** ['tepɪd] *adj (lit, fig)* lau(warm).
**term** [tɜːm] **1** *n* **(a)** *(period of time)* Zeitraum *m; (of
contract)* Laufzeit *f; (limit)* Frist *f.* ~ **of
government/office** Regierungszeit *f*/Amtszeit *f;* **in
the long/short** ~ auf lange/kurze Sicht.
**(b)** *(Sch, Univ) (three in one year)* Trimester *nt;
(two in one year)* Semester *nt.* **in** ~**(-time)** während
der Schulzeit/des Semesters; **out of** ~**(-time)** in den
Ferien.
**(c)** *(expression)* Ausdruck *m.* **in plain** ~**s** in einfachen Worten; **technical** ~**s** Fachausdrücke *pl;* **a
contradiction in** ~**s** ein Widerspruch in sich.
**(d)** *(Math, Logic)* Term *m.* **to express one thing in**
~**s of another** eine Sache mit einer anderen erklären; **in** ~**s of production we are doing well** was die
Produktion betrifft, stehen wir gut da; **in** ~**s of
money/time** finanziell/zeitlich.
**(e)** ~**s** *pl (conditions)* Bedingungen *pl;* ~**s of reference** *(of committee etc)* Aufgabenbereich *m; (of thesis etc)* Themenbereich *m;* **to buy sth on credit/easy**
~**s** etw auf Kredit/auf Raten kaufen; **the hotel offered reduced** ~**s in winter** das Hotel bot ermäßigte
Winterpreise an; **on what** ~**s?** zu welchen Bedingungen?; **to come to** ~**s (with sb)** sich (mit jdm)
einigen; **to come to** ~**s with sth** sich mit etw abfinden.
**(f)** ~**s** *pl (relations)* **to be on good/bad** ~**s with sb**
gut/nicht (gut) mit jdm auskommen; **they are not
on speaking** ~**s** sie reden nicht miteinander.
**2** *vt* nennen, bezeichnen.
**terminal** ['tɜːmɪnl] **1** *adj syllable, station* End-; *cancer, patient* unheilbar. **to have a** ~ **illness** unheilbar
krank sein. **2** *n* **(a)** *(Rail)* Endbahnhof *m; (of buses)*
Endstation *f; (airport* ~, *container* ~*)* Terminal *m or
nt.* **(b)** *(Elec)* Pol *m.* **(c)** *(Comp)* Terminal *nt.*
**terminally** ['tɜːmɪnəlɪ] *adv* ~ **ill** unheilbar krank.
**terminate** ['tɜːmɪneɪt] **1** *vt* beenden; *contract, lease
etc* lösen; *pregnancy* abbrechen. **2** *vi* enden; *(contract, lease)* ablaufen.
**termination** [ˌtɜːmɪ'neɪʃən] *n* Ende *nt; (bringing to
an end)* Beendigung *f; (of a pregnancy)* (Schwangerschafts)abbruch *m; (expiry)* Ablauf *m; (of contract)*
Lösung *f.*
**terminology** [ˌtɜːmɪ'nɒlədʒɪ] *n* Terminologie *f.* **technical** ~ Fachausdrücke *pl.*
**terminus** ['tɜːmɪnəs] *n, pl* **terminuses** *or* **termini**
['tɜːmɪnaɪ] *(Rail, Bus)* Endstation *f.*
**termite** ['tɜːmaɪt] *n* Termite *f.*
**tern** [tɜːn] *n (Orn)* Seeschwalbe *f.*
**Terr** = **Terrace.**
**terrace** ['terəs] *n* Terrasse *f.* **(a)** ~**s** *pl (Sport)* Ränge
*pl.* **(b)** *(Brit: row of houses)* Häuserreihe *f.* ~ **house**
*(Brit)* Reihenhaus *nt.*
**terraced** ['terəst] *adj* **(a)** *hillside etc* terrassenförmig
angelegt. **(b)** ~ **house** *(Brit)* Reihenhaus *nt.*
**terracotta** [ˌterə'kɒtə] *n* Terrakotta *f.*
**terra firma** [ˌterə'fɜːmə] *n* **to be on** ~ **again** wieder
festen Boden unter den Füßen haben.
**terrain** [te'reɪn] *n* Terrain *(esp Mil)*, Gelände *nt; (fig)*
Boden *m.*
**terrapin** ['terəpɪn] *n* Sumpfschildkröte *f.*
**terrestrial** [tɪ'restrɪəl] *adj* **(a)** *(of land) plants, animals*
Land-, auf dem Land lebend. **(b)** *(of the planet
Earth)* irdisch.

**terrible** ['terəbl] *adj* schrecklich, furchtbar. **he is** ~
**at golf** er spielt furchtbar schlecht Golf.
**terribly** ['terəblɪ] *adv (badly, col: very)* schrecklich,
furchtbar.
**terrier** ['terɪər] *n* Terrier *m.*
**terrific** [tə'rɪfɪk] *adj shame, shock* unheimlich *(col);
person, success, idea also* klasse *inv (col); speed,
strength* unwahrscheinlich *(col).*
**terrifically** [tə'rɪfɪkəlɪ] *adv (col) (very)* unheimlich
*(col); (very well)* unheimlich gut *(col).*
**terrify** ['terɪfaɪ] *vt (person)* in Angst versetzen. **to be
terrified of sth** vor etw *(dat)* schreckliche Angst haben.
**terrifying** ['terɪfaɪɪŋ] *adj film* grauenerregend;
*thought, sight* entsetzlich; *speed* angsterregend.
**territorial** [ˌterɪ'tɔːrɪəl] **1** *adj* territorial, Gebiets-. ~
**waters** Territorialgewässer *pl;* **T**~ **Army** *(Brit)* Ter-
ritorialheer *nt.* **2** *n* **the T**~**s** *(Brit)* das Territorial-
heer; *(soldiers)* die Soldaten des Territorialheeres.
**territory** ['terɪtərɪ] *n* Territorium *nt; (of animals
also)* Revier *nt; (Comm: of agent etc)* Bezirk *m;
(fig)* Revier, Gebiet *nt.*
**terror** ['terər] *n* **(a)** *no pl (great fear)* panische Angst
*(of* vor +*dat).* **in** ~ in panischer Angst. **(b)** *(col) (person)* Teufel *m; (child)* Ungeheuer *nt.* **she's a** ~ **on
the roads** *(hum)* sie ist der Schrecken der Landstraße *(hum).*
**terrorism** ['terərɪzəm] *n* Terrorismus *m; (acts of* ~*)*
Terror *m.* **an act of** ~ ein Terrorakt *m.*
**terrorist** ['terərɪst] **1** *n* Terrorist(in *f*) *m.* **2** *attr* terroristisch.
**terrorize** ['terəraɪz] *vt* terrorisieren.
**terror-stricken** ['terəˌstrɪkən] *adj* starr vor
Schreck(en).
**terse** [tɜːs] *adj (+er)* knapp.
**tertiary** ['tɜːʃərɪ] *adj* tertiär; *colour* Misch-. ~ **education** Hochschulausbildung *f.*
**Terylene®** ['terɪliːn] *n* ≈ Trevira®, Diolen® *nt.*
**test** [test] **1** *n* **(a)** *(Sch)* Klassenarbeit *f; (Univ)* Klausur *f; (short)* Test *m; (intelligence* ~ *etc)* Test *m;
(driving* ~*)* (Fahr)prüfung *f.* **he gave them a vocabulary** ~ er ließ sie eine Vokabelarbeit schreiben;
*(orally)* er hat sie Vokabeln abgefragt; **to put sb/sth
to the** ~ jdn/etw auf die Probe stellen; **to stand the**
~ die Probe bestehen; **to stand the** ~ **of time** die
Zeit überdauern. **(b)** *(of vehicle, product etc, chemical* ~*)* Test *m; (check)* Kontrolle *f; (Aut: road* ~*)*
Testfahrt *f.*
**2** *vt* **(a)** *(examine, check)* testen, prüfen; *(Sch)* pu-
*pil* prüfen; *(orally)* abfragen; *intelligence etc* testen;
*(fig)* auf die Probe stellen. **the teacher** ~**ed them on
that chapter** der Lehrer fragte sie das Kapitel ab;
**to** ~ **sth for accuracy** etw auf Genauigkeit prüfen.
**(b)** *(chemically)* gold, water, chemical etc untersuchen. **to** ~ **sth for sugar** etw auf seinen
Zuckergehalt untersuchen.
**3** *vi* Tests/einen Test machen; *(chemically also)*
untersuchen *(for* auf +*acc).*
**testament** ['testəmənt] *n* **(a)** *(old)* Testament *nt.* **(b)**
*(Bibl)* **Old/New T**~ Altes/Neues Testament.
**test:** ~ **ban** *n* Teststopp *m;* ~ **ban treaty** *n* Test-
stoppabkommen *nt;* ~ **bed** *n* Prüfstand *m;* ~ **card**
*n (TV)* Testbild *nt;* ~ **case** *n* Musterfall *m;* ~ **drive**
*n* Probefahrt *f;* ~**-drive** *vt* probefahren; ~ **flight** *n*
Testflug *m.*
**testicle** ['testɪkl] *n* Hoden *m.*
**testify** ['testɪfaɪ] **1** *vt* **to** ~ **that ...** *(Jur)* bezeugen, daß
... **2** *vi (Jur)* eine Zeugenaussage machen, aussa-
gen. **to** ~ **against/in favour of sb** gegen/für jdn aussagen; **to** ~ **to sth** *(speak for)* etw bezeugen *(also
Jur); (be sign of) sincerity etc* von etw zeugen.

**testimonial** [ˌtestɪ'məunɪəl] *n (character recommendation)* Referenz *f.*

**testimony** ['testɪmənɪ] *n* Aussage *f.*

**testiness** ['testɪnɪs] *n* Gereiztheit *f.*

**testing** ['testɪŋ] **1** *n see vt* **(a)** Testen *nt*; Prüfung *f.* **(b)** Untersuchung *f.* **2** *adj* hart. **I had a ~ time** es war hart (für mich).

**testing ground** *n* Testgebiet *nt*; *(fig)* Versuchsfeld *nt.*

**test:** **~ match** *n (Brit)* Testmatch *nt*; **~ paper** *n (Sch)* Klassenarbeit *f*; *(Chem)* Reagenzpapier *nt*; **~ pattern** *n (US)* = **~ card**; **~ pilot** *n* Testpilot *m*; **~ tube** *n* Reagenzglas *nt*; **~-tube baby** *n* Retortenbaby *nt.*

**testy** ['testɪ] *adj (+er)* gereizt.

**tetanus** ['tetənəs] *n* Wundstarrkrampf, Tetanus *m.*

**tetchy** ['tetʃɪ] *adj (+er) (generally)* reizbar; *(on one occasion)* gereizt.

**tête-à-tête** ['teɪtɑː'teɪt] *n* Tête-à-tête *nt.*

**tether** ['teðər] **1** *n (lit)* Strick *m*; *(chain)* Kette *f.* **to be at the end of one's ~** *(fig col)* mit seiner Geduld am Ende sein *(col).* **2** *vt (also ~ up)* animal an- or festbinden.

**Teutonic** [tjʊ'tɒnɪk] *adj (Hist, hum)* teutonisch.

**text** [tekst] *n* Text *m*; *(of document also)* Wortlaut *m.*

**textbook** ['tekstbʊk] **1** *n* Lehrbuch *nt.* **2** *attr landing etc* Bilderbuch-. **~ case** Paradefall *m.*

**textile** ['tekstaɪl] **1** *adj* Textil-, textil. **2** *n* Stoff *m*. **~s** Textilien *pl.*

**text:** *(Comp)* **~ input** *n* Texteingabe *f*; **~ processing** *n* Textverarbeitung *f.*

**textual** ['tekstjʊəl] *adj* Text-.

**texture** ['tekstʃər] *n* Beschaffenheit *f*; *(of food)* Substanz, Textur *f*; *(of material, paper)* Textur *f*; *(of minerals also, fig: of music, poetry etc)* Gestalt *f.*

**textured** ['tekstʃəd] *adj* strukturiert, Struktur-.

**TGWU** *(Brit)* = **Transport and General Workers' Union** *Transportarbeitergewerkschaft f.*

**Thai** [taɪ] **1** *adj* thailändisch. **2** *n* **(a)** Thailänder(in *f*) *m*, Thai *mf.* **(b)** *(language)* Thai *nt.*

**Thailand** ['taɪlænd] *n* Thailand *nt.*

**thalidomide** [θə'lɪdəʊmaɪd] *n* Contergan *nt* ®. **~ baby** Contergankind *nt.*

**Thames** [temz] *n* Themse *f.* **he'll never set the ~ on fire** *(prov)* er hat das Pulver auch nicht erfunden *(prov).*

**than** [ðæn, *weak form* ðən] *conj* als. **I'd rather do anything ~ that** das wäre das letzte, was ich tun wollte; **no sooner had I sat down ~ he began to talk** kaum hatte ich mich hingesetzt, als er auch schon anfing zu reden; **who better to help us ~ he?** wer könnte uns besser helfen als er?

**thank** [θæŋk] *vt* danken *(+dat)*, sich bedanken bei. **I don't know how to ~ you** ich weiß nicht, wie ich Ihnen danken soll; **I'll ~ you to mind your own business** ich wäre Ihnen dankbar, wenn Sie sich nicht einmischen würden; **he has his brother/he only has himself to ~ for this** das hat er seinem Bruder zu verdanken/sich selbst zuzuschreiben; **~ you** danke (schön); **~ you very much** vielen Dank; **no ~ you/yes, ~ you** nein, danke/ja, bitte *or* danke; **~ you for the present** vielen Dank für Ihr Geschenk; **~ you for nothing** *(iro)* danke bestens!; **~ goodness** *or* **God** *(col)* Gott sei Dank! *(col).*

**thankful** ['θæŋkfʊl] *adj* dankbar *(to sb* jdm*).* **I'm only ~ that it didn't happen** ich bin bloß froh, daß es nicht passiert ist.

**thankfully** ['θæŋkfəlɪ] *adv* dankbar, voller Dankbarkeit. **~, no real harm has been done** zum Glück ist kein wirklicher Schaden entstanden.

**thankfulness** ['θæŋkfʊlnɪs] *n* Dankbarkeit *f.*

**thankless** ['θæŋklɪs] *adj* undankbar. **a ~ task** eine undankbare Aufgabe.

**thanks** [θæŋks] **1** *npl* **(a)** Dank *m.* **to accept sth with ~ etw** dankend annehmen; **and that's all the ~ I get** und das ist jetzt der Dank dafür. **(b)** **~ to** wegen *(+gen)*; *(with positive cause also)* dank *(+gen)*; **it's all ~ to you that we're so late** bloß deinetwegen kommen wir so spät; **it was no ~ to him that ...** es war nicht ihm zu verdanken, daß ... **2** *interj (col)* danke *(for* für*).* **many ~** vielen Dank; **~ a lot** *or* **a million** vielen *or* tausend Dank; *(iro)* (na,) vielen Dank *(col)*; **~, but no ~** *(hum)* danke, lieber nicht.

**thanksgiving** ['θæŋks,gɪvɪŋ] *n* **(a)** Danksagung *f.* **(b)** *(US)* **T~ (Day)** Thanksgiving Day *m.*

**thank-you** ['θæŋkju:] *n* Dankeschön *nt.* **~ letter** Dankbrief *m.*

**that¹** [ðæt, *weak form* ðət] **1** *dem pron, pl* **those** **(a)** das. **what is ~?** was ist das?; **who is ~?** wer ist das?; **who is ~ speaking?** wer spricht da?; *(on phone)* wer ist am Apparat?; **~'s what they've been told** das hat man ihnen gesagt; **she's not as stupid as all ~** so dumm ist sie nun auch (wieder) nicht; **I didn't think she'd get/be as angry as ~** ich hätte nicht gedacht, daß sie so böse wird; **... and all ~ ...** und so *(col)*; **like ~** so; **with weather like ~ ...** bei so einem Wetter ...; **~ is (to say)** das heißt; **oh well, ~'s** nun ja, damit ist der Fall erledigt; **you can't go and ~'s ~** du darfst nicht gehen, und damit hat sich's; **~'s it!** das ist es!; *(the right way)* richtig!; *(finished)* so, das wär's!; *(the last straw)* jetzt reicht's; **after/below ~** danach/darunter; **you can get it in any supermarket and quite cheaply at ~** man kann es in jedem Supermarkt bekommen, und sogar ganz billig; **with ~ she got up and left** damit stand sie auf und ging.

**(b)** *(opposed to "this" and "these")* das (da), jenes *(geh).* **I prefer this to ~** dies ist mir lieber als das (da); **~'s the one I like, not this one** das (dort) mag ich, nicht dies (hier).

**2** *dem adj, pl* **those** **(a)** der/die/das, jene(r, s) *(old, liter).* **what was ~ noise?** was war das für ein Geräusch?; **~ poor girl!** das arme Mädchen!; **I like ~ one** ich mag das da; **I'd like ~ one, not this one** ich möchte das da, nicht dies hier; **she was rushing this way and ~** sie rannte hierhin und dorthin; **what about ~ plan of yours now?** was ist denn nun mit Ihrem Plan?

**3** *dem adv (col)* so. **he was at least ~ much taller than me** er war mindestens soviel größer als ich; **it's not ~ cold** so kalt ist es auch wieder nicht; **he was ~ angry** er hat sich dermaßen geärgert.

**that²** *rel pron* **(a)** der/die/das; die. **all/nothing/everything etc ~ ...** alles/nichts/alles etc, was ...; **the best etc ~ ...** das Beste etc, das *or* was ...; **fool ~ I am** ich Idiot; **the girl ~ I told you about** das Mädchen, von dem ich Ihnen erzählt habe. **(b)** *(with expressions of time)* **the minute ~ he came the phone rang** genau in dem Augenblick, als er kam, klingelte das Telefon; **the day ~ ...** an dem Tag, als ...

**that³** *conj* daß. **~ he should behave like this is quite incredible** daß er sich so benehmen kann, ist kaum zu glauben; **he said ~ it was wrong** er sagte, es sei *or* wäre *(col)* falsch; **er sagte, daß es falsch sei** *or* **wäre** *(col)*; **not ~ I want to do it** nicht (etwa), daß ich das tun wollte.

**thatch** [θætʃ] **1** *n (roof)* Strohdach *nt.* **2** *vt roof* mit Stroh decken.

**thatched** [θætʃt] *adj roof* Stroh-; *cottage* mit Strohdach.

**thaw** [θɔː] **1** *vt* auftauen (lassen); *ice, snow also* tauen lassen; *(make warm) person, hands* aufwärmen; *(fig) relations* entspannen. **2** *vi (lit, fig)* auftauen; *(ice, snow)* tauen. **it is** ~**ing** es taut. **3** *n (lit, fig)* Tauwetter *nt.* **before the** ~ bevor das Tauwetter einsetzt.

▶**thaw out 1** *vi (lit, fig)* auftauen. **2** *vt sep (lit) frozen food etc* auftauen (lassen); *person, hands* aufwärmen; *(fig) person* aus der Reserve locken.

**the** [ðə, *before vowels, stressed* ðiː] **1** *def art* **(a)** der/die/das. **in** ~ **room** im *or* in dem Zimmer; **he went up on** ~ **stage** er ging aufs *or* auf das Podium; **to play** ~ **piano** Klavier spielen; **all** ~ **windows** alle Fenster; **have you invited** ~ **Browns?** haben Sie die Browns *or* die Familie Brown eingeladen?; **in** ~ **20s** in den zwanziger Jahren; **Henry** ~ **Eighth** Heinrich der Achte.

**(b)** *(with adj used as n)* das; *(pl)* die; *(with comp or superl)* der/die/das. ~ **Good** das Gute; ~ **poor** die Armen *pl*; **translated from** ~ **German** aus dem Deutschen übersetzt.

**(c)** *(distributive use)* **twenty pence** ~ **pound** zwanzig Pence das *or* pro Pfund; **paid by** ~ **hour** stundenweise *or* pro Stunde bezahlt.

**2** *adv* ~ **bigger** ~ **better** je größer, desto besser.

**theatre,** *(US)* **theater** [ˈθɪətəʳ] *n* **(a)** Theater *nt*; *(esp in names,* ~ *company also)* Bühne *f*. **to go to the** ~ ins Theater gehen; **what's on at the** ~**?** was wird im Theater gespielt? **(b)** *(Brit: operating* ~*)* Operationssaal *m*. **(c)** *(scene of events)* Schauplatz *m*. ~ **of war** Kriegsschauplatz *m*.

**theatre:** ~ **company** *n* Theaterensemble *nt*; *(touring)* Schauspieltruppe *f*; ~**goer** *n* Theaterbesucher(in *f*) *m*.

**theatrical** [θɪˈætrɪkəl] *adj* Theater-; *company also* Schauspiel-; *experience also* schauspielerisch; *(pej) behaviour etc* theatralisch.

**thee** [ðiː] *pron (old)* dich; dir.

**theft** [θeft] *n* Diebstahl *m*.

**their** [ðɛəʳ] *poss adj* **(a)** ihr. **(b)** *(his or her)* seine(r, s). **everyone knows** ~ **rights nowadays** jeder kennt heutzutage seine Rechte.

**theirs** [ðɛəz] *poss pron* ihre(r, s).

**them** [ðem, *weak form* ðəm] *pers pron pl (dir obj, with prep +acc)* sie; *(indir obj, with prep +dat)* ihnen. **both/neither of** ~ **saw me** beide haben/keiner von beiden hat mich gesehen; **give me a few of** ~ geben Sie mir ein paar davon; **none of** ~ keine(r, s) (von ihnen); **it's** ~ sie sind's; **it's** ~ **who did it** *sie* haben es getan.

**theme** [θiːm] *n* **(a)** *(subject)* Thema *nt*. **(b)** *(US Sch: essay)* Aufsatz *m*. **(c)** *(Mus)* Thema *nt*; *(Film, TV also)* Musik *f (from aus)*.

**theme:** ~ **music** *n (Film)* Titelmusik *f*; *(TV)* Erkennungsmelodie *f*; ~ **park** *n* (thematisch gestalteter) Freizeitpark; ~ **song** *n (Film)* Titelsong *m*; *(TV)* Erkennungssong *m*; ~ **tune** *n see* ~ **music.**

**themselves** [ðəmˈselvz] *pers pron pl* **(a)** *(reflexive)* sich. **(b)** *(emph)* selbst. **the figures** ~ die Zahlen selbst *or* an sich; *see* **myself.**

**then** [ðen] **1** *adv* **(a)** *(next)* dann; *(at this particular time)* da; *(in those days also)* damals. **and** ~ **what happened?** und was geschah dann?; **it was** ~ **8 o'clock** da war es 8 Uhr; **I was/will be on holiday** ~ ich war da (gerade) in Urlaub/werde da in Urlaub sein; **he did it there and** ~ er hat es auf der Stelle getan.

**(b)** *(after prep) from* ~ **on(wards)** von da an; **before** ~ vorher, zuvor; **but they had gone by** ~ da waren sie schon weg; **we'll be ready by** ~ bis dahin sind wir fertig; **since** ~ seitdem; **between now and** ~ bis dahin; **(up) until** ~ **I had never tried it** bis dahin hatte ich es nie versucht.

**(c)** *(in that case)* dann. **what are you going to do,** ~**?** was wollen Sie dann tun?; **all right,** ~ also *or* dann meinetwegen; **so it's true** ~ dann ist es (also) wahr.

**(d)** *(furthermore, and also)* dann, außerdem. **(and)** ~ **there's my aunt** und dann ist da noch meine Tante; **but** ~ ... **aber** ... auch; **but** ~ **again he is my friend** aber andererseits ist er mein Freund.

**2** *adj attr* **the** ~ **Prime Minister** der damalige Premierminister.

**theologian** [θɪəˈləʊdʒɪən] *n* Theologe *m*, Theologin *f*.

**theological** [θɪəˈlɒdʒɪkəl] *adj* theologisch. ~ **college** Priesterseminar *nt*.

**theology** [θɪˈɒlədʒɪ] *n* Theologie *f*.

**theorem** [ˈθɪərəm] *n (also Math)* Satz *m*.

**theoretical** *adj*, ~**ly** *adv* [θɪəˈretɪkəl, -ɪ] theoretisch.

**theorist** [ˈθɪərɪst] *n* Theoretiker(in *f*) *m*.

**theorize** [ˈθɪəraɪz] *vi* theoretisieren.

**theory** [ˈθɪərɪ] *n* Theorie *f*. **in** ~ theoretisch.

**therapeutic(al)** [ˌθerəˈpjuːtɪk(əl)] *adj* therapeutisch. **to be** ~ therapeutisch wirken.

**therapist** [ˈθerəpɪst] *n* Therapeut(in *f*) *m*.

**therapy** [ˈθerəpɪ] *n* Therapie *f*.

**there** [ðɛəʳ] **1** *adv* **(a)** dort, da; *(with movement)* dorthin, dahin. **it's over/in** ~ es liegt da drüben/drin; **put it under/in** ~ stellen Sie es da drunter/hinein; ~ **and back** hin und zurück; **so** ~ **we were** da waren wir nun also.

**(b)** *(fig: on this point)* da. ~ **you are wrong** da irren Sie sich.

**(c)** *(in phrases)* ~ **is/are** es *or* da ist/sind; *(*~ *exists/exist also)* es gibt; ~ **is a mouse in the room** es ist eine Maus im Zimmer; ~ **was once a castle here** hier war *or* stand einmal eine Burg; **is** ~ **any wine left?** — **well,** ~ **was** ist noch Wein da? — gerade war noch welcher da; **how many mistakes were** ~**?** wie viele Fehler waren es?; ~ **comes a time when** ... es kommt eine Zeit, wo ...; ~ **being no alternative solution** da es keine andere Lösung gibt/gab; ~ **we go again** *(col)* jetzt geht's schon wieder los; ~ **you are** *(giving sb sth)* hier(, bitte)!; *(on finding sb)* da sind Sie ja!; **you press the switch and** ~ **you are!** Sie brauchen nur den Schalter zu drücken, das ist alles.

**2** *interj* ~**!** ~**!** na, na!; **stop crying now,** ~**'s a good boy** hör auf zu weinen, na komm.

**thereabouts** [ˌðɛərəˈbaʊts] *adv* **(a)** *(place)* dort in der Nähe, dort irgendwo. **(b)** **five pounds/fifteen or** ~ so um die fünf Pfund/fünfzehn (herum).

**thereafter** [ˌðɛərˈɑːftəʳ] *adv (form)* danach, darauf *(geh)*.

**thereby** [ˌðɛəˈbaɪ] *adv* dadurch, damit.

**therefore** [ˈðɛəfɔːʳ] *adv* deshalb, daher; *(as logical consequence)* also.

**there's** [ðɛəz] = **there is**; **there has.**

**thereupon** [ˌðɛərəˈpɒn] *adv* **(a)** *(at that point)* darauf(hin). **(b)** *(form: on that subject)* darüber.

**thermal** [ˈθɜːməl] *adj* **(a)** *(Phys)* **capacity, unit** Wärme-; *reactor* thermisch. ~ **power station** Wärmekraftwerk *nt*. **(b)** ~ **spring** Thermalquelle *f*; ~ **underwear** Thermo-Unterwäsche *f*.

**thermo** [ˌθɜːməʊ-]: ~**dynamic** *adj* thermodynamisch; ~**dynamics** *npl* Thermodynamik *f*.

**thermometer** [θəˈmɒmɪtəʳ] *n* Thermometer *nt*.

**thermos** ® [ˈθɜːməs] *n (also* ~ **flask** *or* **bottle** US) Thermosflasche *f*.

**thermostat** [ˈθɜːməstæt] *n* Thermostat *m*.

**thesaurus** [θɪˈsɔːrəs] *n* Thesaurus *m*.

**these** [ðiːz] *adj, pron* diese; *see* **this.**

**thesis** [ˈθiːsɪs] *n, pl* **theses** [ˈθiːsiːz] **(a)** *(argument)* These *f*. **(b)** *(Univ) (for PhD)* Dissertation, Doktorarbeit *(col)* f; *(for diploma)* Diplomarbeit f.

**they** [ðeɪ] *pers pron pl* **(a)** sie. ~ **are very good people** es sind sehr gute Leute; **it is** ~ *(form)* sie sind es; ~ **who** diejenigen, die. **(b)** *(people in general)* ~ **say that** ... man sagt, daß ...; ~ **want to build a new road** man will *or* sie wollen eine neue Straße bauen. *(c) (he or she)* **if anyone reads this,** ~ **will notice** ... wenn jemand das liest, wird er bemerken ...

**they'd** [ðeɪd] = **they had**; **they would.**

**they'll** [ðeɪl] = **they will.**

**they're** [ðɛər] = **they are.**

**they've** [ðeɪv] = **they have.**

**thick** [θɪk] **1** *adj* **(a)** *(+er)* dick; *wall, legs also* stark; *hair, fog, smoke also, forest, hedge, beard* dicht; *liquid, sauce etc* dick(flüssig); *darkness* tief; *crowd* dicht(gedrängt); *air* schlecht. **a wall three feet** ~ eine drei Fuß dicke *or* starke Wand; **the shelves were** ~ **with dust** auf den Regalen lag dick der Staub; **the hedgerows were** ~ **with flowers** die Hecken strotzten von wilden Blumen; **the air was** ~ **with fumes/smoke** die Luft war voller Abgase/Rauch. **(b)** *(col: stupid) person* dumm, doof *(col).* **(c)** *(col: intimate)* **they are very** ~ sie sind dicke Freunde *(col).* **(d)** *(col: much)* **that's a bit** ~! das ist ein starkes Stück *(col).*

**2** *n* **in the** ~ **of the crowd/it** mitten in der Menge/mittendrin; **to stick together through** ~ **and thin** zusammen durch dick und dünn gehen.

**3** *adv (+er) spread, lie, cut* dick; *grow* dicht. **the snow lay** ~ es lag eine dichte Schneedecke; **offers of help poured in** ~ **and fast** es kam eine Flut von Hilfsangeboten; **to lay it on** ~ *(col)* (zu) dick auftragen *(col).*

**thicken** [ˈθɪkən] **1** *vt sauce etc* eindicken. **2** *vi* **(a)** dicker werden; *(fog, hair, crowd, forest)* dichter werden; *(darkness)* sich verdichten; *(sauce)* dick werden. **(b)** *(fig: plot, mystery)* immer undurchsichtiger werden. **aha, the plot** ~**s!** aha, jetzt wird's interessant!

**thicket** [ˈθɪkɪt] *n* Dickicht *nt.*

**thick:** ~**head** *n (col)* Dummkopf *m;* ~**-headed** *adj (col)* dumm, doof *(col).*

**thickie** [ˈθɪkɪ] *n (col)* Dummkopf, Doofi *(col) m.*

**thickly** [ˈθɪklɪ] *adv spread, cut* dick; *wooded* dicht. **snow was falling** ~ dichter Schnee fiel.

**thickness** [ˈθɪknɪs] *n* **(a)** *see adj (a)* Dicke *f;* Stärke *f;* Dichte *f;* Dickflüssigkeit *f.* **(b)** *(layer)* Lage, Schicht *f.*

**thick:** ~**-set** *adj* gedrungen; ~**-skinned** *adj (fig)* dickfellig.

**thief** [θiːf] *n, pl* **thieves** [θiːvz] Dieb(in f) m. **to be as thick as thieves** dicke Freunde sein *(col).*

**thieve** [θiːv] *vti* stehlen.

**thieving** [ˈθiːvɪŋ] **1** *adj* diebisch. **keep your** ~ **hands off my cigarettes** laß die Finger weg von meinen Zigaretten *(col).* **2** *n* Diebstähle *pl.*

**thigh** [θaɪ] *n* (Ober)schenkel *m.* ~ **bone** Oberschenkelknochen *m.*

**thimble** [ˈθɪmbl] *n* Fingerhut *m.*

**thin** [θɪn] **1** *adj (+er)* **(a)** dünn; *material, clothes also* leicht; *vegetation* gering, spärlich; *population, crowd* klein; *fog* leicht; *column* schmal. **his hair is getting** ~ sein Haar lichtet sich; **to be** ~ **on the ground** *(fig)* dünn gesät sein; **to vanish into** ~ **air** *(fig)* sich in Luft auflösen. **(b)** *(fig: weak, poor) voice, smile, disguise, plot* schwach; *excuse also* fadenscheinig. **2** *adv (+er) spread, cut, lie* dünn. **3** *vt paint, sauce* verdünnen; *trees* lichten; *blood* dünner werden lassen. **4** *vi (fog, crowd)* sich lichten; *(hair also)* schütter werden.

►**thin out 1** *vi (audience, crowd)* sich lichten. **the houses started** ~**ning** ~ die Häuser wurden immer spärlicher. **2** *vt sep hair, seedlings* ausdünnen; *forest* lichten; *population* verkleinern.

**thine** [ðaɪn] *(old)* **1** *poss pron* der/die/das deine. **2** *poss adj* dein/deine/dein.

**thing** [θɪŋ] *n* **(a)** Ding *nt.* **a** ~ **of beauty/great value** etwas Schönes/etwas sehr Wertvolles; **I don't have a** ~ **to wear** ich habe nichts zum Anziehen; **poor little** ~ das arme (kleine) Ding!; **you poor** ~! du Arme(r)!

**(b)** *(clothes, equipment, belongings)* ~**s** *pl* Sachen *pl;* **have you got your swimming** ~**s?** hast du dein Badezeug dabei?; **they washed up the breakfast** ~**s** sie spülten das Frühstücksgeschirr.

**(c)** *(non-material: affair, subject)* Sache *f.* **the odd/best** ~ **about it is** ... das Seltsame/Beste daran ist, ...; **it's a good** ~ **I came** nur gut, daß ich gekommen bin; **he's on to a good** ~ *(col)* er hat da was Gutes aufgetan *(col);* **what a (silly)** ~ **to do** wie kann man nur so etwas (Dummes) tun!; **there is one/another** ~ **I want to ask you** eines/und noch etwas möchte ich Sie fragen; **the** ~**s you do/say!** was du so machst/sagst!; **I must be hearing/seeing** ~**s!** ich glaube, ich höre/sehe nicht richtig; **all the** ~**s I meant to do** alles, was ich tun wollte; **to expect great** ~**s of sb/sth** Großes *or* große Dinge von jdm/etw erwarten; **I must think** ~**s over** ich muß mir die Sache überlegen; ~**s are going from bad to worse** es wird immer schlimmer; **as** ~**s stand at the moment** so wie die Dinge im Moment liegen; **how are** ~**s with you?** wie geht's (bei) Ihnen?; **to talk of one** ~ **and another** von diesem und jenem reden; **for one** ~ **it doesn't make sense** erst einmal ergibt das überhaupt keinen Sinn; **to tell sb a** ~ **or two** jdm einiges erzählen; **he knows a** ~ **or two** er hat etwas auf dem Kasten *(col);* **it's just one of those** ~**s** so was kommt eben vor *(col).*

**(d)** *(what is suitable, best)* **that's just the** ~ **for me** das ist genau das richtige für mich; **that's not the** ~ **to do** so was tut man nicht; **the latest** ~ **in ties** der letzte Schrei in der Krawattenmode; **that would be the honourable** ~ **to do** es wäre nur anständig, das zu tun; **I'll do that first** ~ **in the morning** ich werde das gleich morgen früh tun; **I'll do it first** ~ ich werde das als erstes tun; **last** ~ **at night** vor dem Schlafengehen; **the** ~ **is we haven't got enough money** die Sache ist die, wir haben nicht genug Geld; **to do one's own** ~ *(col)* tun, was man will; **she's got this** ~ **about Sartre** *(col) (can't stand)* sie kann Sartre einfach nicht ausstehen; *(is fascinated by)* sie hat einen richtigen Sartrefimmel *(col);* **she's got a** ~ **about spiders** *(col)* bei Spinnen dreht sie durch *(col).*

**thingummybob** [ˈθɪŋəmɪˌbɒb], **thingamajig** [ˈθɪŋəmɪˌdʒɪg], **thingummy** [ˈθɪŋəmɪ] *n (col)* Dings, Dingsbums, Dingsda *nt or (for people) mf (all col).*

**think** [θɪŋk] *(vb: pret, ptp* **thought)** **1** *vi* denken. **to** ~ **to oneself** sich *(dat)* denken; ~ **before you speak/act** denk nach, bevor du sprichst/handelst; **to act without** ~**ing** unüberlegt handeln; ~ **again!** denk noch mal nach; **well, you'd better** ~ **again!** das hast du dir (wohl) gedacht!; **it makes you** ~ es macht einen nachdenklich; **I need time to** ~ ich brauche Zeit zum Nachdenken; **now let me** ~ laß mich mal überlegen; **it's a good idea, don't you** ~? es ist eine gute Idee, findest du nicht auch?; **just** ~ stellen Sie sich *(dat)* bloß mal vor; **listen, I've been** ~**ing,** ... hör mal, ich habe mir überlegt, ...

**2** *vt* **(a)** denken; *(be of opinion also)* glauben, meinen. **I** ~ **it's too late** ich glaube, es ist zu spät; **I** ~ **I**

can do it ich denke, daß ich es schaffen kann; **well, I *think* it was there!** nun, ich glaube zumindest, daß es da war!; **and what do you ~? asked the interviewer** und was meinen Sie?, fragte der Interviewer; **I ~ you'd better go/accept** ich denke, Sie gehen jetzt besser/Sie stimmen lieber zu; **I ~ so** ich denke *or* glaube (schon); **I don't ~ so** ich denke *or* glaube nicht; **I should ~ so/not!** das will ich (aber) auch gemeint haben/das will ich auch nicht hoffen; **I hardly ~ that/~ it likely that ...** ich glaube kaum, daß .../ich halte es für unwahrscheinlich, daß ...; **I wouldn't have thought you would do such a thing** ich hätte nie geglaubt, daß Sie so etwas tun würden; **I ~ I'll go for a walk** ich glaube, ich mache einen Spaziergang; **you must ~ me very rude** Sie müssen mich für sehr unhöflich halten; **he ~s he's intelligent, he ~s himself intelligent** er hält sich für intelligent; **they are thought to be rich** man hält sie für reich.

(b) *(imagine)* sich *(dat)* denken, sich *(dat)* vorstellen. **I don't know what to ~** ich weiß nicht, was ich davon halten soll; **that's what you ~!** denkste! *(col)*; **that's what he ~s** hat der eine Ahnung! *(col)*; **who do you ~ you are!** wofür hältst du dich eigentlich?; **anyone would ~ he was dying** man könnte beinahe glauben, er läge im Sterben; **who would have thought it?** wer hätte das gedacht?; **to ~ that she's only ten!** wenn man sich *(dat)* vorstellt, daß sie erst zehn ist; **to ~ how to do sth** sich *(dat)* überlegen, wie man etw macht; **I never thought to ask you** ich habe gar nicht daran gedacht, Sie zu fragen; **I thought as much/I thought so** das habe ich mir schon gedacht.

**3** *n* **to have a ~** es sich überlegen; **have a ~ about it** überlegen Sie es sich.

▶**think about** *vi +prep obj* **(a)** *(reflect on)* idea, suggestion nachdenken über *(+acc)*. **OK, I'll ~ ~ it** okay, ich überlege es mir; **what are you ~ing ~?** woran denken Sie gerade?; **it's worth ~ing ~** das ist überlegenswert, das wäre zu überlegen; **to ~ twice ~ sth** sich *(dat)* etw zweimal überlegen; **that'll give him something to ~ ~** das wird ihm zu denken geben. **(b)** we're **~ing ~ a holiday in Spain** wir denken daran, in Spanien Urlaub zu machen. **(c) =** think of (a, f).

▶**think ahead** *vi* vorausdenken; *(anticipate: driver etc)* Voraussicht walten lassen.

▶**think of** *vi +prep obj* **(a)** *(consider)* denken an *(+acc)*. **he has his family to ~** er muß an seine Familie denken; **to ~ ~ sb's feelings** auf jds Gefühle *(acc)* Rücksicht nehmen; **he ~s ~ nobody but himself** er denkt bloß an sich; **what can you be ~ing ~?** wo denkst du hin? *(col)*.

**(b)** *(remember)* denken an *(+acc)*. **will you ~ ~ me sometimes?** wirst du manchmal an mich denken?; **I can't ~ ~ her name** ich kann mich nicht an ihren Namen erinnern.

**(c)** *(imagine)* sich *(dat)* vorstellen, bedenken. **~ ~ the cost of all that!** denk dir bloß, was das alles kostet.

**(d)** *(entertain possibility of)* **she'd never ~ ~ getting married** sie denkt gar nicht daran zu heiraten; **he'd never ~ ~ such a thing** so etwas würde ihm nicht im Traum einfallen.

**(e)** *(devise, suggest)* solution, idea, scheme sich *(dat)* ausdenken. **who thought ~ that idea/plan?** wer ist auf diese Idee gekommen/wer hat sich diesen Plan ausgedacht?

**(f)** *(have opinion of)* halten von. **what do you ~ ~ it/him?** was halten Sie davon/von ihm?; **to ~ highly ~ sb/sth** viel von jdm/etw halten; **I told him what I**

**thought ~ him** ich habe ihm gründlich die *or* meine Meinung gesagt.

▶**think out** *vt sep* plan durchdenken; *(come up with)* solution sich *(dat)* ausdenken.

▶**think over** *vt sep* offer sich *(dat)* überlegen.

▶**think through** *vt sep* (gründlich) durchdenken.

▶**think up** *vt sep* sich *(dat)* ausdenken. **who thought ~ that idea?** wer ist auf die Idee gekommen?

**thinkable** ['θɪŋkəbl] *adj* denkbar.

**thinker** ['θɪŋkəʳ] *n* Denker(in *f*) *m*.

**thinking** ['θɪŋkɪŋ] **1** *adj* denkend. **all ~ men will agree with me** alle vernünftigen Menschen werden mit mir übereinstimmen; **to put one's ~ cap on** scharf nachdenken. **2** *n* **to my way of ~** meiner Meinung nach; **this calls for some quick ~** hier muß eine schnelle Lösung gefunden werden.

**think tank** ['θɪŋktæŋk] *n* Expertenkommission *f*.

**thinly** ['θɪnlɪ] *adv* **(a)** dünn; *wooded* spärlich. **(b)** *(fig) disguised* kaum, dürftig; *smile* schwach.

**thinner** ['θɪnəʳ] *n (also ~s)* Verdünner *m*.

**thinness** ['θɪnnɪs] *n* Dünne *f*; *(of dress, material)* Leichtigkeit *f*; *(of liquid)* Dünnflüssigkeit *f*; *(of line, thread)* Feinheit *f*; *(of person)* Magerkeit *f*; *(of vegetation)* Spärlichkeit *f*.

**thin-skinned** [ˌθɪn'skɪnd] *adj (fig)* dünnhäutig.

**third** [θɜːd] **1** *adj* dritte(r, s). **she was** *or* **came ~ in her class/in the race** sie war die Drittbeste in der Klasse/sie belegte den dritten Platz bei dem Rennen; **~ time lucky** aller guten Dinge sind drei. **2** *n* **(a)** *(of series)* Dritte(r, s); *(fraction)* Drittel *nt*. **(b)** *(Mus)* Terz *f*. **(c)** *(Aut: ~ gear)* dritter Gang; *see* **sixth.**

**third: ~-class 1** *adv* dritter Klasse; **2** *adj (lit)* dritter Klasse; *(fig)* drittklassig; **~-degree** *n* **to give sb the ~-degree** jdn in die Zange nehmen; **~-degree burns** *npl (Med)* Verbrennungen *pl* dritten Grades.

**thirdly** ['θɜːdlɪ] *adv* drittens.

**third: ~ party** *n* Dritte(r) *m*, dritte Person; **~-party 1** *adj attr* Haftpflicht-; **2** *adv* **to be insured ~-party** haftpflichtversichert sein; **~-party fire and theft** *n (Brit Insur)* ≃ Teilkaskoversicherung *f*; **~ person** *adj* in der dritten Person; **~-rate** *adj* drittklassig; **T~ World 1** *n* Dritte Welt; **2** *attr* der Dritten Welt.

**thirst** [θɜːst] **1** *n* Durst *m*. **~ for knowledge/revenge/adventure/love** Wissensdurst *m*/Rachsucht *f*/Abenteuerlust *f*/Liebeshunger *m*; **to die of ~** verdursten. **2** *vi (fig)* **to ~ for revenge** *etc* nach Rache *etc* dürsten.

**thirsty** ['θɜːstɪ] *adj (+er)* durstig. **to be ~** Durst haben; **~ for praise/love** begierig auf Lob/nach Liebe; **it's ~ work** diese Arbeit macht durstig.

**thirteen** [ˌθɜː'tiːn] **1** *adj* dreizehn. **2** *n* Dreizehn *f*.

**thirteenth** [ˌθɜː'tiːnθ] *adj* dreizehnte(r, s); *see* **sixteenth.**

**thirtieth** ['θɜːtɪɪθ] *adj* dreißigste(r, s); *see* **sixtieth.**

**thirty** ['θɜːtɪ] **1** *adj* dreißig. **2** *n* Dreißig *f*; *see* **sixty.**

**this** [ðɪs] **1** *dem pron, pl* **these** dies, das. **what is ~?** was ist das (hier)?; **who is ~?** wer ist das?; **these are my children** das sind meine Kinder; **~ is where I live** hier wohne ich; **do you like ~?** gefällt dir das?; **I prefer ~** ich mag dies(es) lieber; **~ is to certify that ...** hiermit wird bestätigt, daß ...; **under/in front of** *etc* **~** darunter/davor *etc*; **what's all ~?** was soll das?; **we were talking of ~ and that** wir haben über dies und das geredet; **this, that and the other** alles mögliche; **will you take ~ or that?** nehmen Sie dieses hier oder das da?; **it was like ~** es war so; **~ is Mary (speaking)** hier (ist) Mary.

**2** *dem adj, pl* **these** diese(r, s). **he's coming ~ week/month/year** er kommt diese Woche/diesen Monat/dieses Jahr; **~ evening** heute abend; **~ time last week** letzte Woche um diese Zeit; **~ time** diesmal, dieses Mal; **these days** heutzutage.

**3** *dem adv* so. **it was ~ long** es war so lang; **~ far** *(time)* bis jetzt; *(place)* so weit; **~ much is certain** soviel ist sicher.

**thistle** [ˈθɪsl] *n* Distel *f.*

**thong** [θɒŋ] *n (of whip)* Peitschenschnur *f; (fastening)* Lederriemen *m.*

**thorax** [ˈθɔːræks] *n* Brustkorb *m.*

**thorn** [θɔːn] *n* Dorn *m; (shrub)* Dornenstrauch *m.* **to be a ~ in sb's flesh** *or* **side** *(fig)* jdm ein Dorn im Auge sein.

**thorny** [ˈθɔːnɪ] *adj (+er) (lit)* dornig; *(fig)* haarig.

**thorough** [ˈθʌrə] *adj* gründlich; *knowledge also* solide; *rascal* ausgemacht.

**thorough:** **~bred 1** *n* reinrassiges Tier; *(horse)* Vollblüter *m;* **2** *adj* reinrassig; *horse* Vollblut-; *dog* Rasse-; **~fare** *n* Durchgangsstraße *f;* **"no ~fare"** „Durchfahrt verboten"; **~going** *adj changes* gründlich; *revision* grundlegend; *reform* durchgreifend.

**thoroughly** [ˈθʌrəlɪ] *adv* **(a)** gründlich. **(b)** *(extremely)* durch und durch, von Grund auf. **~ boring** ausgesprochen langweilig; **I'm ~ ashamed** ich schäme mich zutiefst.

**thoroughness** [ˈθʌrənɪs] *n* Gründlichkeit *f.*

**those** [ðəʊz] *pl of* **that 1** *dem pron* **whose are ~?** wem gehören diese da?; **~ are the girls** das (da) *or* dies(es) sind die Mädchen; **above ~** darüber; **~ who want to go, may** wer möchte, kann gehen; **one of ~ who** ... einer/eine von denjenigen, die ...; **two of ~ please** zwei davon bitte; **there are ~ who say** ... einige sagen ... **2** *dem adj* diese *or* die (da), jene *(old, liter)*. **what are ~ men doing?** was machen diese Männer da?; **it was just one of ~ days/things** das war wieder so ein Tag/so eine Sache.

**thou** [ðaʊ] *pers pron (old)* du.

**though** [ðəʊ] **1** *conj* **(a)** obwohl. **even ~** obwohl; **~ poor she is generous** obwohl sie arm ist, ist sie großzügig; **strange ~ it may seem** ... so seltsam es auch scheinen mag ... **(b)** **as ~** als ob. **2** *adv* **(a)** *(nevertheless)* doch. **he didn't do it ~** er hat es aber (doch) nicht gemacht; **nice day ~ – rather windy ~** schönes Wetter – aber ziemlich windig. **(b)** *(really)* **but will he ~?** aber wird er das auch machen?

**thought** [θɔːt] **1** *pret, ptp of* **think.**

**2** *n* **(a)** *no pl* Denken *nt.* **to spend hours in ~** stundenlang in Gedanken (vertieft) sein; **to be lost in ~** in Gedanken sein; **modern ~** das moderne Denken.

**(b)** *(idea, opinion)* Gedanke *m; (sudden)* Einfall *m.* **he didn't express any ~s on the matter** er hat keine Ansichten zu diesem Thema geäußert; **that's** *or* **there's a ~!** *(amazing)* man stelle sich das mal vor!; *(problem to be considered)* das ist wahr!; *(good idea)* das ist ein guter Gedanke; **what a ~!** was für eine Vorstellung!; **I've just had a ~** *(col)* mir ist gerade etwas eingefallen; **on second ~s** wenn man sich das noch mal überlegt; **his one ~ was ...** sein einziger Gedanke war ...; **it's the ~ that counts, not how much you spend** es kommt nur auf die Idee an, nicht auf den Preis; **to collect one's ~s** sich sammeln; **the very ~ of it** der bloße Gedanke (daran).

**(c)** *no pl (care, consideration)* Nachdenken *nt.* **to give some ~ to sth** sich *(dat)* Gedanken über etw *(acc)* machen; **after much ~** nach langer Überlegung; **without ~ for sb/oneself** ohne an jdn/sich selbst zu denken; **I never gave it a ~** ich habe mir nie Gedanken darüber gemacht.

**thoughtful** [ˈθɔːtfʊl] *adj* **(a)** *(full of thought)* expression, person nachdenklich; *remark, analysis, book* gut durchdacht; *present* gut ausgedacht. **(b)** *(considerate)* rücksichtsvoll; *(attentive, helpful)* aufmerksam. **it was very ~ of you to ...** es war sehr aufmerksam von Ihnen, zu ...

**thoughtfully** [ˈθɔːtfəlɪ] *adv* **(a)** *say, look* nachdenklich. **(b)** *(with much thought)* mit viel Überlegung. **a ~ written book** ein wohldurchdachtes Buch. **(c)** *(considerately)* rücksichtsvoll; *(attentively, helpfully)* aufmerksam.

**thoughtless** [ˈθɔːtlɪs] *adj* **(a)** gedankenlos; *(inconsiderate also)* rücksichtslos. **(b)** **~ of the danger, he** leapt ungeachtet der Gefahr sprang er.

**thoughtlessly** [ˈθɔːtlɪslɪ] *adv* gedankenlos; *(inconsiderately also)* rücksichtslos.

**thought:** **~-provoking** *adj* nachdenklich stimmend; **~-reader** Gedankenleser(in *f*) *m.*

**thousand** [ˈθaʊzənd] **1** *adj* tausend. **a ~/two ~** (ein)tausend/zweitausend; **a ~ times** tausendmal; **a ~ and one/two** tausend(und)eins/tausend(und)zwei. **2** *n* Tausend *nt.* **the ~s** *(Math)* die Tausender *pl;* **there were ~s of people** es waren Tausende (von Menschen) da; **people arrived in their ~s** die Menschen kamen zu Tausenden.

**thousandth** [ˈθaʊzənθ] **1** *adj* tausendste(r, s). **2** *n (in series)* Tausendste(r, s); *(fraction)* Tausendstel *nt; see* **sixth.**

**thrash** [θræʃ] **1** *vt* **(a)** *(beat)* verprügeln; *donkey etc* einschlagen auf *(+acc).* **(b)** *(Sport col)* opponent vernichtend schlagen. **(c)** *(move wildly)* arms schlagen mit; *legs* strampeln mit. **2** *vi* **to ~ about** *or* **around** um sich schlagen; *(in bed)* sich herumwerfen; *(fish)* zappeln.

▶**thrash out** *vt sep problem* ausdiskutieren.

**thrashing** [ˈθræʃɪŋ] *n* **(a)** *(beating)* Prügel, Schläge *pl.* **to give sb a good ~** jdm eine ordentliche Tracht Prügel verpassen. **(b)** *(Sport col)* Schlappe *f.* **to give sb a ~** jdn vernichtend schlagen.

**thread** [θred] **1** *n* **(a)** *(Sew)* Garn *nt;* **(~ of cotton, wool etc)** Faden *m; (strong ~)* Zwirn *m.* **to hang by a ~** *(fig)* an einem (seidenen) Faden hängen. **(b)** *(fig: of story)* (roter) Faden. **to follow the ~ of an argument/a story** dem Gedankengang einer Argumentation/dem roten Faden (in) einer Geschichte folgen; **he lost the ~ of what he was saying** er verlor den Faden; **to pick up the ~s of a conversation** den Gesprächsfaden wiederaufnehmen. **(c)** *(Tech: of screw)* Gewinde *nt.* **2** *vt* **(a)** *needle* einfädeln; *beads* aufreihen *(on* auf *+acc); necklace* aufziehen. **(b)** **to ~ one's way through the crowd/ trees** sich durch die Menge/zwischen den Bäumen hindurchschlängeln.

**threadbare** [ˈθredbɛəʳ] *adj* abgewetzt; *clothes also* abgetragen; *carpet also* abgelaufen.

**threat** [θret] *n* Drohung *f; (danger)* Bedrohung *(to* gen*)*, Gefahr *(to* für*) f.* **is that a ~?** soll das eine Drohung sein?; **to make a ~** drohen *(against sb* jdm*);* **under ~ of sth** unter Androhung von etw.

**threaten** [ˈθretn] *vt* **(a)** *person* bedrohen, drohen *(+dat); revenge* androhen. **to ~ to do sth** (an)drohen, etw zu tun; **to ~ sb with sth** jdm mit etw drohen. **(b)** *(put in danger)* bedrohen, gefährden. **the rain ~ed to spoil the harvest** der Regen drohte die Ernte zu verderben.

**threatening** [ˈθretnɪŋ] *adj* drohend; *weather, clouds also* bedrohlich. **a ~ letter** ein Drohbrief *m;* **~ behaviour** aggressives Verhalten.

**three** [θriː] **1** *adj* drei. **2** *n* Drei *f; see* **six.**

**three:** **~-D 1** *n* **to be in ~-D** dreidimensional sein; **2** *adj (also* **~-dimensional)** dreidimensional; *film also*

3-D- *attr*; ~**fold** *adj, adv* dreifach; ~**-piece suit** *n* *(man's)* Anzug *m* mit Weste; *(lady's)* dreiteiliges Ensemble; ~**-piece suite** *n* dreiteilige Sitzgarnitur; ~**-pin plug** *n* Stecker *m* mit drei Kontakten; ~**-ply** *attr wool* dreifach, Dreifach-; *wood* dreischichtig; ~**-point turn** *n (Aut)* Wenden *nt* in drei Zügen; ~**-quarter** *attr* dreiviertel-; ~**-quarter length** dreiviertellang; ~ **quarters 1** *n* Dreiviertel *nt*; ~ **quarters of an hour** eine Dreiviertelstunde; **2** *adv* dreiviertel; ~**some** *n* Trio *nt*, Dreiergruppe *f*; **in a** ~**some** zu dritt; ~**-storey** *adj* dreistöckig; ~**-way adaptor** *n (Elec)* Dreifachstecker *m*; ~**-wheeler** *n (Aut)* dreirädriges Auto; *(tricycle)* Dreirad *nt*.

**thresh** [θreʃ] *vti* dreschen.

**threshing** ['θreʃɪŋ] *n* Dreschen *nt*. ~ **machine** Dreschmaschine *f*.

**threshold** ['θreʃhəʊld] *n (lit, fig, Psych)* Schwelle *f*. **we are on the** ~ **of a great discovery** wir stehen unmittelbar an der Schwelle zu einer großen Entdeckung.

**threw** [θruː] *pret of* **throw**.

**thrift** [θrɪft] *n* Sparsamkeit *f*. ~ **account** *(US)* Sparkonto *nt*.

**thrifty** ['θrɪftɪ] *adj (+er)* **(a)** *(careful, economical)* sparsam, wirtschaftlich. **(b)** *(US: thriving)* blühend.

**thrill** [θrɪl] **1** *n* Erregung *f*. **the** ~ **of her touch** der erregende Reiz ihrer Berührung; **it was quite a** ~ **for me** es war ein richtiges Erlebnis. **2** *vt person (story, crimes)* mitreißen, fesseln; *(experience)* eine Sensation sein für; *(sb's touch, voice etc)* freudig erzittern lassen; *(sexually)* erregen. **I was** ~**ed to get your letter** ich habe mich riesig über deinen Brief gefreut.

**thriller** ['θrɪlər] *n* Reißer *m (col)*; *(whodunnit)* Krimi, Thriller *m*.

**thrilling** ['θrɪlɪŋ] *adj* aufregend; *book, film* spannend; *sensation* überwältigend; *music* mitreißend; *(sexually)* erregend.

**thrive** [θraɪv] *vi (be in good health: animal, plant)* (gut) gedeihen; *(child also)* sich gut entwickeln; *(do well) (business)* blühen, florieren; *(businessman)* erfolgreich sein.
▶**thrive on** *vi +prep obj* **the baby** ~**s** ~ **milk** mit Milch gedeiht das Baby prächtig; **this plant** ~**s** ~ **sun and light** bei Sonne und Licht gedeiht diese Pflanze prächtig; **he** ~**s** ~ **hard work** harte Arbeit ist sein Lebenselixier.

**thriving** ['θraɪvɪŋ] *adj plant* prächtig gedeihend; *person, business* blühend; *child* gut gedeihend; *businessman* erfolgreich.

**throat** [θrəʊt] *n* Kehle *f*. **cancer of the** ~, ~ **cancer** Kehlkopfkrebs *m*; **to grab sb by the** ~ jdn bei der Gurgel packen; **to cut sb's/one's** ~ jdm/sich die Kehle durchschneiden; **to cut one's own** ~ *(fig)* sich *(dat)* selbst das Wasser abgraben; **to clear one's** ~ sich räuspern; **to ram** *or* **force one's ideas down sb's** ~ *(col)* jdm seine eigenen Ideen aufzwingen.

**throaty** ['θrəʊtɪ] *adj (+er)* rauh; *laugh* kehlig.

**throb** [θrɒb] **1** *vi (engine, heart, pulse)* klopfen; *(very strongly)* hämmern; *(drums, gunfire)* dröhnen; *(painfully: wound also)* pochen; *(fig: with life, activity)* pulsieren *(with* vor *+dat,* mit*)*. **my head is** ~**bing** ich habe rasende Kopfschmerzen. **2** *n see vi* Klopfen *nt*; Hämmern *nt*; Pochen *nt*.

**throes** [θrəʊz] *npl* **in the** ~ **of death** in Todesqualen *pl*; **to be in its final** ~ *(fig)* in den letzten Zügen liegen; **we are in the** ~ **of moving** wir stecken mitten im Umzug.

**thrombosis** [θrɒm'bəʊsɪs] *n* Thrombose *f*.

**throne** [θrəʊn] *n* Thron *m*; *(Eccl)* Stuhl *m*. **to come to**

**the** ~ den Thron besteigen.

**throng** [θrɒŋ] **1** *n* **a** ~ **of people** Scharen *pl* von Menschen. **2** *vi* sich drängen. **to** ~ **around sb/sth** um jdn/etw scharen. **3** *vt* **people** ~**ed the streets** die Menschen drängten sich in den Straßen; **to be** ~**ed with** wimmeln von.

**throttle** ['θrɒtl] **1** *vt* **(a)** erdrosseln, erwürgen. **(b)** *(fig)* opposition unterbinden. **2** *n (on engine)* Drossel *f*; *(Aut etc) (pedal)* Gaspedal *nt*; *(twist grip)* Gasgriff *m*; *(lever)* Geshebel *m*. **at full** ~ mit Vollgas; **to open the** ~ Gas geben.

**through** [θruː] **1** *prep* **(a)** *(place)* durch. **he went right** ~ **the red lights** er ist einfach bei Rot durchgefahren; **we're** ~ **that stage now** wir sind jetzt durch dieses Stadium hindurch; **to be halfway** ~ **a book** ein Buch zur Hälfte durchhaben *(col)*; **that happens halfway** ~ **the book** das passiert in der Mitte des Buches.
**(b)** *(time)* **all** ~ **his life** sein ganzes Leben lang; **he worked** ~ **the night** er hat die Nacht durchgearbeitet; **he slept** ~ **the film** er hat den ganzen Film hindurch geschlafen; **all** ~ **the autumn** den ganzen Herbst über.
**(c)** *(US)* **Monday** ~ **Friday** von Montag bis (einschließlich) Freitag.
**(d)** *(means, agency)* durch. ~ **the post** mit der Post; **absent** ~ **illness** abwesend wegen Krankheit; ~ **neglect** durch Nachlässigkeit; **to act** ~ **fear** aus Angst handeln.
**2** *adv (time, place)* durch. **he's a liar** ~ **and** ~ er ist durch und durch verlogen; **to sleep all night** ~ die ganze Nacht durchschlafen; **did you stay right** ~**?** sind Sie bis zum Schluß geblieben?; **to let sb** ~ jdn durchlassen; **to be wet** ~ durch und durch naß sein; **to read sth** ~ etw durchlesen; ~ **in the other office** (drüben) im anderen Büro; **the train goes** ~ **to Berlin** der Zug fährt bis nach Berlin durch.
**3** *adj pred* **(a)** *(finished)* **to be** ~ **with sb/sth** mit jdm/etw fertig sein *(col)*; **we're** ~ *(have finished relationship)* es ist aus zwischen uns; *(have finished job)* wir sind fertig; **I'm** ~ **with that kind of work** ich habe genug von dieser Arbeit; **are you** ~**?** sind Sie fertig? **(b)** *(Brit Telec)* **to be** ~ *(to sb/London)* mit jdm/London verbunden sein; **to get** ~ *(to sb/London)* zu jdm/nach London durchkommen; **you're** ~ **Ihre Verbindung!**

**through:** ~ **coach** *n (Rail)* Kurswagen *m (for* nach*)*; *(bus)* direkte Busverbindung; ~ **flight** *n* Direktflug *m.*

**throughout** [θruː'aʊt] **1** *prep* **(a)** *(place)* überall in *(+dat).* ~ **the country/world** im ganzen Land/in der ganzen Welt. **(b)** *(time)* ~ **the war** den ganzen Krieg hindurch *or* über; ~ **his life** sein ganzes Leben lang. **2** *adv* **(a)** *(in every part)* **the house is carpeted** ~ das Haus ist ganz mit Teppichboden ausgelegt; **a house with double glazing** ~ ein Haus, das in jedem Raum Doppelverglasung hat. **(b)** *(time)* die ganze Zeit hindurch *or* über.

**through:** ~**put** *n (Ind)* Durchsatz *m*; ~ **ticket** *n* **can I get a** ~ **ticket to London?** kann ich bis London (durch)lösen?; ~ **traffic** *n* Durchgangsverkehr *m*; ~ **train** *n* durchgehender Zug; ~**way** *n (US)* Schnellstraße *f.*

**throw** [θrəʊ] *(vb: pret* **threw**, *ptp* **thrown)* **1** *n (of ball, dice)* Wurf *m*. **it's your** ~ du bist dran; **have another** ~ werfen Sie noch einmal; **a 30-metre** ~ ein Wurf *m* von 30 Metern; **at 10 dollars a** ~ zu 10 Dollar das Stück. **2** *vt* **(a)** *ball, stone* werfen; *rider* abwerfen; *opponent* zu Boden werfen. **to** ~ **the dice/a six** würfeln/eine Sechs würfeln; **to** ~ **sth to sb** jdm etw zuwerfen; **to** ~ **sth at sb** etw nach jdm werfen;

*mud, paint etc* jdn mit etw bewerfen; **he threw himself to the floor/out of the window** er warf sich zu Boden/er stürzte sich aus dem Fenster; **to be ~n from the saddle** aus dem Sattel geworfen werden; **to ~ a glance at sb/sth** einen Blick auf jdn/etw werfen; **to ~ sb off the scent** jdn abhängen. **(b)** *switch, lever* betätigen. **(c)** *(fig col: disconcert)* aus dem Konzept bringen. **she was ~n by the question** die Frage brachte sie aus dem Konzept. **(d)** *party* geben; *fit* bekommen, kriegen *(col)*. **(e)** *pot etc* formen.

▶**throw about** *or* **around** *vt always separate* **(a)** *(scatter)* verstreuen; *(fig) money* um sich werfen mit. **(b)** *(toss)* herumwerfen; *one's arms* fuchteln mit; *one's legs* strampeln mit.

▶**throw away** *vt sep* **(a)** *(discard) rubbish* wegwerfen. **(b)** *(waste)* verschenken; *money* verschwenden *(on sth* auf etw, *on sb* an jdn*)*. **(c)** *(say casually) remark* beiläufig *or* nebenbei machen.

▶**throw back** *vt sep ball, head, enemy* zurückwerfen; *curtains* aufreißen. **to be ~n ~ upon sth** auf etw *(acc)* zurückgreifen müssen.

▶**throw in** *vt sep* **(a)** *extra* (gratis) dazugeben. **with a tour of London ~n ~** mit einer Gratistour durch London. **(b)** *(Sport) ball* einwerfen. **(c)** *(fig)* **to ~ ~ one's hand** aufgeben; **to ~ ~ the sponge** *or* **towel** das Handtuch werfen *(col)*. **(d)** *(say casually) remark* einwerfen *(to* in *+acc)*.

▶**throw off** *vt sep* **(a)** *(get rid of) clothes* abwerfen; *disguise, habits* ablegen; *pursuer* abschütteln; *cold* loswerden.

▶**throw on** *vt sep clothes* sich *(dat)* überwerfen.

▶**throw out** *vt sep* **(a)** *(discard) rubbish etc* wegwerfen. **(b)** *(reject) suggestion, (Parl) bill* ablehnen. **(c)** *person* hinauswerfen, rauswerfen *(col) (of* aus*)*. **(d)** *(make wrong) calculations etc* über den Haufen werfen *(col)*, durcheinanderbringen. **to ~ sb ~ in his calculations** jdn bei seinen Berechnungen durcheinanderbringen. **(e)** *chest* herausdrücken.

▶**throw together** *vt sep* **(a)** *(put hastily together) ingredients* zusammenwerfen; *clothes* zusammenpacken; *(make quickly)* hinhauen *(col)*; *essay* runterschreiben *(col)*. **(b)** *(fate) people* zusammenbringen.

▶**throw up 1** *vi* sich übergeben. **2** *vt sep* **(a)** *ball, hands* hochwerfen. **(b)** *(abandon) job* aufgeben; *opportunity etc* verschenken. **(c)** *(produce)* hervorbringen. **the meeting threw ~ several good ideas** bei der Versammlung kamen ein paar gute Ideen zutage.

**throw:** **~away** *adj* **(a)** *(casual) remark* nebenbei gemacht; **(b)** *packet* Wegwerf-; *bottle* Einweg-; **~away society** Wegwerfgesellschaft *f*; **(c)** *(cheap)* **~away prices** Schleuderpreise *pl*; **~back** *n* **(a)** his **selfishness is a ~back to an earlier generation** in ihm schlägt die Selbstsucht seiner Vorfahren wieder durch; **(b)** *(fig)* Rückkehr *f (to* zu*)*.

**thrower** ['θrəʊəʳ] *n* Werfer(in *f*) *m*.

**throw-in** ['θrəʊɪn] *n (Sport)* Einwurf *m*.

**thrown** [θrəʊn] *ptp of* **throw**.

**thru** *pref, adv, adj (US)* = **through**.

**thrush¹** [θrʌʃ] *n (Orn)* Drossel *f*.

**thrush²** *n (Med)* Soor *m (spec)*, Pilzkrankheit *f*.

**thrust** [θrʌst] *(vb: pret, ptp ~)* **1** *n* **(a)** Stoß *m*; *(of knife also)* Stich *m*. **the main ~ of the argument was that ...** das Argument ging hauptsächlich dahin, daß ... **(b)** *(Tech)* Druckkraft *f*; *(in rocket, turbine)* Schub(kraft *f*) *m*. **(c)** *(Mil: also ~* **forward)** Vorstoß *m*. **(d)** *(fig: of speech etc)* Tenor *m*. **2** *vt* **(a)** *(push, drive)* stoßen. **to ~ one's hands into one's pockets** die Hände in die Tasche stecken. **(b)** *(fig)*

**to ~ oneself (up)on sb** sich jdm aufdrängen; **I had the job ~ upon me** die Arbeit wurde mir aufgezwungen; **to ~ one's way to the front** sich nach vorne kämpfen. **3** *vi* stoßen *(at* nach*)*; *(with knife)* stechen *(at* nach*)*.

▶**thrust out** *vt sep leg, hand* ausstrecken; *head* vorstrecken; *chest* wölben. **she ~ her head ~ (of the window)** sie streckte den Kopf (zum Fenster) hinaus.

**thrusting** ['θrʌstɪŋ] *adj* energisch, zielstrebig.

**thruway** ['θruːweɪ] *n (US)* Schnellstraße *f*.

**thud** [θʌd] **1** *n* dumpfes Geräusch. **the ~ of his footsteps** seine dumpfen Schritte; **he fell to the ground with a ~** er fiel mit einem Plumps *(col) or* dumpfen Aufschlag zu Boden. **2** *vi* dumpf aufschlagen; *(move heavily)* stampfen. **the heavy door ~ded into place** mit einem dumpfen Knall fiel die Tür zu.

**thug** [θʌg] *n* Schläger(typ) *m*.

**thuggery** ['θʌgərɪ] *n* Schlägertum *nt*.

**thuggish** ['θʌgɪʃ] *adj* gewalttätig. **~ type** Schlägertyp *m*.

**thumb** [θʌm] **1** *n* Daumen *m*. **to be under sb's ~** unter jds Fuchtel *(dat)* stehen; **he gave me the ~s up/down** er gab mir zu verstehen, daß alles in Ordnung war/daß es nicht in Ordnung war; **it sticks out like a sore ~** das springt einem direkt ins Auge. **2** *vt* **(a)** *(col)* **to ~ a lift** per Anhalter fahren. **(b)** a **well ~ed book** ein zerlesenes Buch.

**thumb:** **~ index** *n* Daumenregister *nt*; **~nail** *n* Daumennagel *m*; **~nail sketch** *(drawing)* kleine Skizze; *(description)* kurze Skizze; **~ print** *n* Daumenabdruck *m*; **~tack** *n (US)* Reiß- *or* Heftzwecke *f*.

**thump** [θʌmp] **1** *n (blow)* Schlag *m*; *(noise)* (dumpfes) Krachen. **2** *vt table* schlagen auf *(+acc)*; *door* klopfen *or* schlagen an *(+acc)*; *(repeatedly)* trommeln auf/an *(+acc)*; *(accidentally) one's head* sich *(dat)* anschlagen. **he ~ed the box down on my desk** er knallte die Schachtel auf meinen Tisch; **I ~ed him (one) on the nose** *(col)* ich habe ihm eins auf die Nase verpaßt *(col)*. **3** *vi (person)* schlagen *(on the door/table* an die Tür/auf den Tisch*)*; *(heart)* heftig schlagen; *(move heavily)* stapfen; *(object: fall loudly)* plumpsen *(col)*.

▶**thump out** *vt sep tune* hämmern.

**thumping** ['θʌmpɪŋ] *adj (also ~* **great)** *(col)* kolossal.

**thunder** ['θʌndəʳ] **1** *n* **(a)** Donner *m*. **there is ~ in the air** es liegt ein Gewitter *nt* in der Luft. **(b)** *(fig) (of applause)* Sturm *m*; *(of cannons)* Donnern *nt*; *(of waves)* Tosen *nt*. **2** *vi (lit, fig)* donnern; *(waves, sea)* tosen. **3** *vt (shout)* brüllen, donnern.

**thunder:** **~bolt** *n (lit)* Blitz *m*; **the news came as something of a ~bolt** *(fig)* die Nachricht schlug wie ein Blitz ein; **~clap** *n* Donnerschlag *m*; **~cloud** *n* Gewitterwolke *f*.

**thunderous** ['θʌndərəs] *adj* stürmisch; *voice* donnernd.

**thunder:** **~storm** *n* Gewitter *nt*; **~struck** *adj (fig)* wie vom Donner gerührt.

**thundery** ['θʌndərɪ] *adj weather* gewittrig.

**Thuringia** [θjʊˈrɪndʒɪə] *n* Thüringen *nt*.

**Thurs** = **Thursday** Do.

**Thursday** ['θɜːzdɪ] *n* Donnerstag *m*; *see* **Tuesday**.

**thus** [ðʌs] *adv* **(a)** *(in this way)* so, auf diese Art. **~ it was that ...** so kam es, daß ... **(b)** *(consequently)* folglich. **(c)** *(+ptp or adj) reassured, encouraged etc* derart *(geh)*. **~ far** so weit.

**thwart** [θwɔːt] *vt* vereiteln; *robbery, attack also* verhindern; *person* einen Strich durch die Rechnung machen *(+dat)*. **to ~ sb in sth** jdm etw vereiteln.

**thy** [ðaɪ] *poss adj (old) (before vowel* **thine)** dein/ deine/dein; *(to God)* Dein/Deine/Dein.

**tie up**

**thyme** [taɪm] *n* Thymian *m*.
**thyroid** ['θaɪrɔɪd] **1** *n (also ~ gland)* Schilddrüse *f*. **2** *adj* Schilddrüsen-.
**tiara** [tɪ'ɑːrə] *n* Diadem *nt*.
**Tibet** [tɪ'bet] *n* Tibet *nt*.
**Tibetan** [tɪ'betən] **1** *adj* tibetanisch, tibetisch. **2** *n* **(a)** Tibetaner(in *f*) *m*. **(b)** *(language)* Tibetanisch *nt*.
**tibia** ['tɪbɪə] *n, pl* **-s** Schienbein *nt*.
**tic** [tɪk] *n (Med)* Tick *m*, nervöses Zucken.
**tick¹** [tɪk] **1** *n* **(a)** *(of clock etc)* Ticken *nt*. **(b)** *(col: moment)* Augenblick *m*, Minütchen *nt (col)*. **half a ~** eine Sekunde; **I'll be ready in a ~** or **two ~s** bin sofort fertig *(col)*. **(c)** *(mark)* Haken *m*. **to put a ~ against a name/an answer** einen Namen/eine Antwort abhaken. **2** *vi* **(a)** *(clock)* ticken. **the minutes ~ed away** or **by** or **past** die Minuten verstrichen. **(b)** *(col)* **what makes him ~?** was geht in ihm vor? **3** *vt name, answer* abhaken.
▶**tick off** *vt sep* **(a)** *name etc* abhaken. **(b)** *(col: scold)* ausschimpfen *(col)*.
▶**tick over** *vi* **(a)** *(idle: engine)* im Leerlauf sein. **the engine is ~ing ~ nicely** der Motor läuft gut. **(b)** *(fig: business etc)* ganz ordentlich laufen; *(pej)* auf Sparflamme sein *(col)*. **to keep things ~ing ~ alles** in Gang halten.
**tick²** *n (Zool)* Zecke *f*.
**tick³** *n (Brit col)*: **on ~** auf Pump *(col)*.
**ticker** ['tɪkər] *n (col: heart)* Pumpe *f (col)*.
**ticker tape** *n* Lochstreifen *m*.
**ticket** ['tɪkɪt] *n* **(a)** *(rail, bus)* Fahrkarte *f*, Fahrschein *m*; *(plane ~)* Ticket *m*, Flugschein *m*; *(Theat, for football match etc)* (Eintritts)karte *f*; *(cloakroom)* Garderobenmarke *f*; *(library)* ≈ Buchzettel *m*; *(for dry cleaners etc)* Zettel *m*; *(luggage office)* (Gepäck)schein *m*; *(raffle ~)* Los *nt*; *(price ~)* Preisschild *nt*; *(for car park)* Parkschein *m*. **(b)** *(US Pol)* Wahlliste *f*. **he's running on the Democratic ~** er kandidiert für die Demokratische Partei. **(c)** *(Jur: parking ~)* Strafzettel *m*. **to give sb a ~** jdm einen Strafzettel geben or verpassen *(col)*.
**ticket: ~ agency** *n (Theat)* Vorverkaufsstelle *f*; **~ barrier** *n (Brit Rail)* Fahrkartenschranke *f*; **~ collector** *n (Brit Rail)* Fahrkartenkontrolleur *m*; *(on train also)* Schaffner(in *f*) *m*; **~holder** *n* **~holders only through this door** *(Theat etc)* Eingang nur für Besucher mit Eintrittskarten; **~ inspector** *n (Brit)* (Fahrkarten)kontrolleur *m*; **~ office** *n (Rail)* Fahrkartenschalter *m*; *(Theat)* Kasse *f*; **~ window** *n (Rail)* (Fahrkarten)schalter *m*; *(Theat)* Kasse *f*.
**ticking-off** ['tɪkɪŋ'ɒf] *n (col)* Anpfiff *(col)* *m*. **to give sb a ~** jdm den Marsch blasen *(col)*.
**tickle** ['tɪkl] **1** *vti* **(a)** kitzeln; *(wool)* kratzen. **this wool ~s my skin** diese Wolle kratzt (auf der Haut). **(b)** *(fig col) person* amüsieren. **to be ~ed** sich gebauchpinselt fühlen *(col)*; **to be ~d pink** sich wie ein Schneekönig freuen *(col)*. **2** *vi* kitzeln. **3** *n* Kitzeln *nt*. **to give sb a ~** jdn kitzeln; **to have a ~ in one's throat** einen Hustenreiz haben.
**ticklish** ['tɪklɪʃ] *adj (lit) person* kitz(e)lig; *(fig) situation* heikel.
**tidal** ['taɪdl] *adj river, harbour* Tide- *(Naut)*; *energy, power station* Gezeiten-. **~ wave** *(lit)* Flutwelle *f*.
**tidbit** *n (US)* Leckerbissen *m*.
**tiddler** ['tɪdlər] *n (Brit)* **(a)** *(fish)* winziger Fisch. **(b)** *(col: child)* Knirps *m*.
**tiddly** ['tɪdlɪ] *adj (+er)* **(a)** *(tiny)* winzig, klitzeklein *(col)*. **(b)** *(tipsy)* angesäuselt *(col)*, beschwipst.
**tiddlywinks** ['tɪdlɪwɪŋks] *n* Floh(hüpf)spiel *nt*. **to play ~** Flohhüpfen spielen.
**tide** [taɪd] *n* **(a)** *(lit)* Gezeiten *pl*, Tide *(N Ger) f*. **(at) high/low ~** (bei) Hochwasser *nt* or Flut *f*/Niedrig-

wasser *nt* or Ebbe *f*; **the ~ is in/out** es ist Flut/Ebbe; **the ~ has turned** *(at high/low ~)* die Ebbe/die Flut hat eingesetzt; *(fig)* das Blatt hat sich gewendet. **(b)** *(fig: trend)* **the ~ of history** der Lauf der Geschichte; **the ~ of public opinion** der Trend der öffentlichen Meinung; **to go** or **swim against/with the ~** *(lit, fig)* gegen den/mit dem Strom schwimmen.
▶**tide over** *vt always separate* **that will ~ me ~ until tomorrow** damit werde ich bis morgen auskommen.
**tidemark** ['taɪdmɑːk] *n* Flutmarke *f*; *(man-made)* Pegelstand *m*.
**tidily** ['taɪdɪlɪ] *adv* ordentlich.
**tidiness** ['taɪdɪnɪs] *n see adj* Ordentlichkeit *f*; Sauberkeit *f*; Gepflegtheit *f*.
**tidings** ['taɪdɪŋz] *npl (old, liter)* Botschaft *(liter)*.
**tidy** ['taɪdɪ] **1** *adj (+er)* **(a)** *(orderly)* ordentlich; *(of ~ habits also)* sauber; *appearance* gepflegt. **to keep sth ~** etw in Ordnung halten; **to get a room ~** ein Zimmer aufräumen; **to make oneself ~** sich zurechtmachen. **(b)** *(col)* **a ~ sum** eine ordentliche Stange Geld *(col)*. **2** *vt hair* in Ordnung bringen; *room also* aufräumen.
▶**tidy away** *vt sep* wegräumen, aufräumen.
▶**tidy out** *vt sep* aufräumen, ausmisten *(col)*.
▶**tidy up 1** *vi* **(a)** *(clear away)* aufräumen. **(b)** *(clean oneself)* sich zurechtmachen. **2** *vt sep books, room* aufräumen; *piece of work* in Ordnung bringen.
**tie** [taɪ] **1** *n* **(a)** *(also esp US: neck ~)* Krawatte *f*, Schlips *m (col)*. **(b)** *(US Rail)* Schwelle *f*. **(c)** *(fig: bond)* Beziehung, Bindung *f*; *(hindrance)* Belastung *f*. **~s of friendship** freundschaftliche Beziehungen *pl*; **business ~s** Geschäftsverbindungen *pl*; **family ~s** familiäre Bindungen *pl*; **I don't want any ~s** ich will keine Bindung; **pets can be a ~** Haustiere können eine Belastung sein. **(d)** *(Sport etc: result of match)* Unentschieden *nt*; *(match, competition ending in a draw)* unentschiedenes Spiel. **the match ended in a ~** das Spiel endete unentschieden; **there was a ~ for second place** es gab zwei zweite Plätze. **(e)** *(esp Ftbl: match)* Spiel *nt*.
**2** *vt* **(a)** binden *(to an +acc)*; *(fasten also)* befestigen *(to an +dat)*. **my hands are ~d** *(fig)* mir sind die Hände gebunden; **to ~ a knot in sth** einen Knoten in etw *(acc)* machen; **we're very ~d in the evenings** wir sind abends sehr gebunden. **(b)** *(fig: unite, link)* verbinden.
**3** *vi* **(a)** *(ribbon etc)* **it won't ~ properly** es läßt sich nicht richtig binden; **it ~s at the back** es wird hinten (zu)gebunden. **(b)** *(Sport)* unentschieden spielen; *(in competition, vote)* gleich stehen. **they ~d for the first place** *(Sport, competition)* sie belegten gemeinsam den ersten Platz.
▶**tie back** *vt sep hair, door* zurückbinden.
▶**tie down** *vt sep* **(a)** *(lit)* festbinden *(to an +dat)*; *tents* verankern *(to in +dat)*. **(b)** *(fig: restrict)* binden *(to an +acc)*; *meaning* genau bestimmen.
▶**tie in 1** *vi* dazu passen. **to ~ ~ with sth** zu etw passen; **it all ~s ~** das paßt alles zusammen; **the new evidence didn't ~ ~** das neue Beweismaterial paßte nicht ins Bild. **2** *vt sep plans* in Einklang bringen.
▶**tie on** *vt sep* anbinden. **to ~ sth ~(to) sth** etw an etw *(dat)* anbinden.
▶**tie up 1** *vi* **(a)** **now it all ~s ~** jetzt paßt alles zusammen. **(b)** *(Naut)* festmachen. **2** *vt sep parcel* verschnüren; *shoelaces* binden; *boat* festmachen; *animal* anbinden *(to an +dat)*; *prisoner, hands etc* fesseln. **(b)** *(settle) deal etc* unter Dach und Fach

bringen. **to ~ ~ a few loose ends (of sth)** (bei einer
Sache) ein paar offene Probleme lösen. **(c)** *(Fin)*
*capital* (fest) anlegen. **(d)** *(link)* **to be ~d ~ with sth**
mit etw zusammenhängen. **(e)** *(keep busy)* beschäftigen; *machines* auslasten. **he's ~d ~ all tomorrow**
er ist morgen den ganzen Tag beschäftigt.

**tie:** **~ break(er)** *n (Tennis)* Tiebreak *m or nt*; **~ clip**
*n* Krawattennadel *f*; **~-on** *adj attr* Anhänge-, zum
Anbinden; **~pin** *n* Krawattennadel *f*.

**tier** [tɪər] *n (of cake)* Etage, Stufe *f; (Theat, of sta-*
*dium)* Rang *m; (fig: in hierarchy etc)* Stufe *f,* Rang
*m.* **a three-~ hierarchy** eine dreigestufte Hierarchie; **to arrange sth in ~s** etw stufenförmig aufbauen.

**tie:** **~ tack** *n (US)* Krawattennadel *f*; **~-up** *n* **(a)**
*(connection)* Verbindung *f;* **(b)** *(US: stoppage)* Stillstand *m.*

**tiff** [tɪf] *n (col)* Krach *m (col).* **to have a ~ with sb** mit
jdm Krach haben *(col).*

**tiger** ['taɪɡər] *n* Tiger *m.*

**tight** [taɪt] **1** *adj (+er)* **(a)** *clothes* eng; *join* dicht.
**(b)** *(stiff, difficult to move) screw, bolt* festsitzend.
**the tap/cork is (too) ~** der Hahn ist zu fest zu/der
Korken sitzt fest; **the drawer is a bit ~** die Schublade klemmt ein bißchen.
**(c)** *(firm) screw, knot* fest angezogen; *tap, window*
dicht; *lid, embrace* fest; *control, discipline* streng;
*organization* straff. **to run a ~ ship** *(lit, fig)* ein strenges Regiment führen.
**(d)** *(taut) rope, skin* straff.
**(e)** *(leaving little space)* eng; *weave also* dicht.
**(f)** *timing, race, match, money* knapp; *schedule*
knapp bemessen.
**(g)** *(difficult) situation* schwierig. **in a ~ spot** *(fig)*
in der Klemme *(col).*
**(h)** *(col: miserly)* knick(e)rig *(col),* geizig.
**(i)** *(col: drunk)* voll *(col).* **to get ~** blau sein *(col);*
*(intentionally)* sich vollaufen lassen.
**2** *adv (+er) hold, shut, screw* fest; *stretch* straff.
**to hold sb/sth ~** jdn/etw festhalten; **to do sth up ~**
etw gut befestigen; **sleep ~!** schlaf(t) gut!; **hold ~!**
festhalten!; **to sit ~** sich nicht rühren.
**3** *adj suf* **water~/air~** wasser-/luftdicht.

**tighten** ['taɪtn] **1** *adj (also ~ up)* **1** *vt* **(a)** *knot* fester machen; *screw* anziehen; *(re-tighten)* nachziehen; *rope*
straffen; *(stretch tighter)* straffer spannen. **(b)** *re-*
*strictions* verschärfen. **2** *vi (rope)* sich spannen;
*(knot)* sich zusammenziehen.
►**tighten up** **1** *vi* **(a)** = **tighten 2.** **(b)** *(in disci-*
*pline)* strenger werden, härter durchgreifen.
**they've ~ed ~ on security** sie haben die Sicherheitsvorkehrungen verschärft. **2** *vt sep* **(a)** = **tighten 1**
**(a).** **(b)** *organization, procedure* straffen; *discipline,*
*controls* verschärfen.

**tight:** **~-fisted** [,taɪt'fɪstɪd] *adj* knauserig *(col);* **~-**
**fitting** *adj* eng anliegend; **~-knit** *adj community*
eng miteinander verwachsen; **~-lipped** *adj (lit)* mit
schmalen Lippen; *(silent)* verschlossen.

**tightly** ['taɪtlɪ] *adv fest; stretched* straff. **to fit ~**
*(clothes)* eng anliegen; *(part in hole etc)* fest sitzen;
**~ packed** vollgestopft.

**tightness** ['taɪtnɪs] *n see adj* **(a)** enges Anliegen;
Dichtheit *f.* **(b)** Festsitzen *nt.* **(c)** fester Sitz; Dicht-
heit *f;* Strenge *f;* Straffheit *f.* **(d)** Straffheit *f.* **(e)**
Enge *f;* Dichte *f.* **(f)** Knappheit *f.* **(g)** *(with money)*
Knick(e)rigkeit *f (col),* Geiz *m.*

**tightrope** ['taɪtrəʊp] *n* Seil *nt.* **to walk a ~** *(fig)* einen
Balanceakt vollführen; **~ walker** Seiltänzer(in *f*) *m.*

**tights** [taɪts] *npl (esp Brit)* Strumpfhose *f.* **a pair of ~**
eine Strumpfhose.

**tigress** ['taɪɡrɪs] *n* Tigerin *f.*

**tilde** ['tɪldə] *n* Tilde *f.*

**tile** [taɪl] **1** *n (on roof)* (Dach)ziegel *m; (ceramic ~)*
Fliese *f; (on wall)* Kachel *f; (lino ~, polystyrene ~*
*etc)* Platte *f; (carpet ~)* (Teppich)fliese *f.* **to have a**
**night on the ~s** *(col)* einen draufmachen *(col).* **2** *vt*
*roof* (mit Ziegeln) decken; *floor* mit Fliesen/
Platten auslegen; *wall, bathroom* kacheln. **~d roof**
Ziegeldach *nt.*

**tiler** ['taɪlər] *n* Fliesenleger *m.*

**till¹** [tɪl] *prep, conj* = **until.**

**till²** *n (cash-register)* Kasse *f.*

**till³** *vt (Agr)* bestellen.

**tiller** ['tɪlər] *n (Naut)* Ruderpinne *f.*

**tilt** [tɪlt] **1** *n (slope)* Neigung *f.* **2** *vt* kippen, schräg
stellen; *head* (seitwärts) neigen. **3** *vi (slant)* sich
neigen. **this part ~s to the left** dieser Teil läßt sich
nach links kippen; **he ~ed back/forward in his chair**
er kippte mit seinem Stuhl nach hinten/vorne.

**timber** ['tɪmbər] *n* **(a)** Holz *nt; (for buildings also)*
Bauholz *nt; (land planted with trees)* (Nutz)wald *m.*
**(b)** *(beam)* Balken *m.*

**timbered** ['tɪmbəd] *adj house* Fachwerk-; *land*
Wald-.

**timbre** ['tɪmbər] *n* Timbre *nt.*

**time** [taɪm] **1** *n* **(a)** Zeit *f.* **how ~ flies!** wie die Zeit
vergeht!; **only ~ will tell whether ...** es muß sich
erst herausstellen, ob ...; **it takes ~ to do that** das
braucht (seine) Zeit; **to take (one's) ~ (over sth)**
sich *(dat)* (bei etw) Zeit lassen; **it took me all my ~**
**to finish** ich bin gerade noch fertig geworden; **in**
**(the course of) ~** mit der Zeit; **in (next to) no ~** im
Nu, im Handumdrehen; **to have a lot of/no ~ for**
**sb/sth** viel/keine Zeit für jdn/etw haben; *(fig: be*
*for/against)* viel/nichts für jdn/etw übrig haben; **to**
**find/make ~ (for sb/sth)** Zeit finden/sich *(dat)* Zeit
nehmen (für jdn/etw); **to have ~ on one's hands**
viel freie Zeit haben; **he lost no ~ in telling her** er
sagte es ihr unverzüglich; **to be in good ~** rechtzeitig dran sein; **don't rush, do it in your own ~** nur
keine Hast, tun Sie es, wie Sie es können; **let me**
**know in good ~** sagen Sie mir rechtzeitig Bescheid; **(for) a long/short ~** lange/kurz; **I'm going**
**away for a long ~** ich fahre für längere Zeit weg;
**it's a long ~ (since ...)** es ist schon lange her(, seit
...); **what a (long) ~ you have been!** du hast (aber)
lange gebraucht!; **a short ~ later/ago** kurz darauf/
vor kurzem; **in a short ~ they were all gone** nach
kurzer Zeit waren sie alle gegangen; **for some ~ (past)**
seit einiger Zeit; **all the ~** die ganze Zeit; **in two**
**weeks' ~** in zwei Wochen; **for a ~** eine Zeitlang; **for**
**the ~ being** *(provisionally)* vorläufig; *(temporarily)*
vorübergehend; **to buy sth on ~** *(US)* etw auf Raten
kaufen; **to do ~** *(col: in prison)* sitzen *(col).*
**(b)** *(of clock, moment, season)* **what ~ is it?,**
**what's the ~?** wie spät ist es?, wieviel Uhr ist es?;
**my watch keeps good ~** meine Uhr geht genau; **it's**
**~ (for me/us etc) to go, it's ~ I was/we were** *etc*
**going** es wird Zeit, daß ich gehe/wir gehen *etc;* **on**
**~/ahead of ~/behind ~** pünktlich/zu früh/zu spät;
**the project is ahead of ~/behind ~** das Projekt ist
dem Zeitplan voraus/zeitlich im Rückstand; **to**
**make good ~** gut vorankommen; **the trains are on**
**~** die Züge fahren pünktlich; **to be in ~ for sth**
rechtzeitig zu etw kommen; **it's about ~ he was**
**here** *(he has arrived)* es wird (aber) auch Zeit, daß
er kommt; *(he has not arrived)* es wird langsam
Zeit, daß er kommt; **(and) about ~ too!** das wird
aber auch Zeit!; **at all ~s** jederzeit; **at any ~ during**
**the day** zu jeder Tageszeit; **not at this ~ of night!**
nicht zu dieser nachtschlafenden Zeit!; **there are**
**~s when ...** es gibt Augenblicke, wo ...; **at the** *or*

that ~ damals, zu der Zeit; **at the present** ~ zur Zeit; **at one** ~ früher, einmal; **at any/no** ~ jederzeit/niemals; **at the same** ~ *(lit)* gleichzeitig; **they arrived at the same** ~ **as us** sie kamen zur gleichen Zeit an wie wir; **but at the same** ~, **you must admit that** ... aber andererseits müssen Sie zugeben, daß ...; **at** ~**s** manchmal; **by the** ~ **it had finished** als es zu Ende war; **by the** ~ **we arrive, there's not going to be anything left** bis wir ankommen, ist nichts mehr übrig; **by this** ~ inzwischen; **by this** ~ **next year/tomorrow** nächstes Jahr/morgen um diese Zeit; **from** ~ **to** ~ von Zeit zu Zeit; **from that** ~ **on** von der Zeit an; **since that** ~ seit der Zeit; **until such** ~ **as** ... so lange, bis ...; **this** ~ **of the day/year** diese Tages-/Jahreszeit; **this** ~ **last year/week** letztes Jahr/letzte Woche um diese Zeit; **to die before one's** ~ zu früh sterben; **when the** ~ **comes** wenn es soweit ist; **the** ~ **has come (to do sth)** es ist an der Zeit (, etw zu tun); **the** ~ **has come for us to leave** es ist Zeit für uns zu gehen; **my** ~ **is (almost) up** meine *or* die Zeit ist (gleich) um; *(fig: life)* meine Zeit ist gekommen.

(c) *(occasion)* **this** ~ diesmal, dieses Mal; **(the) next** ~ nächstes Mal; **(the) next** ~ **I see you** wenn ich dich das nächste Mal sehe; **(the) last** ~ letztes Mal; **(the) last** ~ **he was here** das letzte Mal, als er hier war; **every** *or* **each** ~ ... jedesmal, wenn ...; **many a** ~, **many** ~**s** viele Male; **for the last** ~ zum letzten Mal; **he's not very bright at the best of** ~**s** er ist sowieso nicht sehr intelligent; ~ **and (**~**) again,** ~ **after** ~ immer wieder; **they came in one/three at a** ~ sie kamen einzeln/jeweils zu dritt herein; **four at a** ~ vier auf einmal; **for weeks at a** ~ wochenlang.

(d) *(multiplication)* **2** ~**s 3 is 6** 2 mal 3 ist 6; **it was ten** ~**s as big** es war zehnmal so groß.

(e) *(rate)* **you're paid** ~ **and a half for overtime** Sie bekommen 50% Zuschlag für Überstunden.

(f) *(era)* **in Victorian** ~**s** im Viktorianischen Zeitalter; **in olden** ~**s** in alten Zeiten; **in my** ~ zu meiner Zeit; **he is ahead of his** ~ er ist seiner Zeit (weit) voraus; **to be behind the** ~**s** rückständig sein; **to keep up with the** ~**s** mit der Zeit gehen; *(keep in touch)* auf dem laufenden bleiben; ~**s are hard** die Zeiten sind schlecht; ~**s are changing** es kommen andere Zeiten.

(g) *(experience)* **we had a good** ~ es hat uns *(dat)* gut gefallen; **have a good** ~! viel Spaß!; **to have the** ~ **of one's life** eine herrliche Zeit verbringen; **to have an easy/a hard** ~ es leicht/schwer haben; **we had an easy/a hard** ~ **getting to the finals** es war leicht für uns/wir hatten Schwierigkeiten, in die Endrunde zu kommen; **to have a bad/rough** ~ **(of it)** viel mitmachen; **to give sb a hard** *or* **rough** ~ jdm das Leben schwermachen.

(h) *(rhythm)* Takt *m*. **(to be) in** ~ **(with)** im Takt (sein) (mit); **(to be/get) out of** ~ aus dem Takt (sein/kommen); **3/4** ~ Dreivierteltakt *m*; **to keep** ~ *(beat* ~*)* den Takt angeben; *(keep in* ~*)* (den) Takt halten.

**2** *vt* **(a)** *(choose* ~ *of)* **to** ~ **sth perfectly** genau den richtigen Zeitpunkt für etw wählen; **he** ~**d his arrival to coincide with** ... er legte seine Ankunft so, daß sie mit ... zusammenfiel; **the bomb is** ~**d to explode at 5 o'clock** die Bombe ist so eingestellt, daß sie um 5 Uhr explodiert; **you** ~**d that well** *(also iro)* du hast dir den richtigen Zeitpunkt ausgesucht. **(b)** *(with stop-watch etc)* stoppen; *speed also* messen.

**time:** ~ **and motion expert** *n* Fachmann *m* für Zeitstudien, ≈ REFA-Fachmann *m*; ~ **and mo-tion study** *n* Zeitstudie, Bewegungsstudie *f*; ~

**bomb** *n (lit, fig)* Zeitbombe *f*; ~**card** *n (for workers)* Stechkarte *f*; *(US:* ~*table)* Fahrplan *m*; ~ **clock** *n* Stechuhr *f*; ~**-consuming** *adj* zeitraubend; ~ **exposure** *n (photo)* Zeitaufnahme *f*; ~ **fault** *n (Showjumping)* Zeitfehler *m*; ~**-honoured** *or (US)* **-honored** *adj* althergebracht; ~**keeper** *n (Sport)* Zeitnehmer *m*; **this watch is a good/bad** ~**keeper** diese Uhr geht richtig/nicht richtig; ~**keeping** *n (Sport)* Zeitnahme *f*; *(Ind: of worker)* Einhaltung *f* der Arbeitszeiten; ~**-lag** *n* Zeitdifferenz *f*; *(delay)* Verzögerung *f*.

**timeless** ['taɪmlɪs] *adj* zeitlos; *(everlasting)* immerwährend.

**time limit** *n* zeitliche Begrenzung; *(for the completion of a job)* Frist *f*. **to put a** ~ **on sth** etw befristen.

**timely** ['taɪmlɪ] *adj* rechtzeitig. **a** ~ **piece of advice** ein Rat zur rechten Zeit; **that was very** ~ das war genau zur rechten Zeit.

**time:** ~ **off** *n* freie Zeit; ~**-out** *n (US)* **(a)** *(Sport)* Auszeit *f*; **(b)** *(break)* **to take** ~**-out** Pause machen; ~**piece** *n* Uhr *f*.

**timer** ['taɪmər] *n* Zeitmesser *m*; *(switch)* Schaltuhr *f*; *(person)* Zeitnehmer *m*.

**time:** ~**saving** *adj* zeitsparend; ~**scale** *n* zeitlicher Rahmen; *(perception of time)* Zeitbegriff *m*; ~**sharing** *n* Timesharing *nt*; ~ **signal** *n* Zeitzeichen *nt*; ~ **signature** *(Mus)* *n* Taktvorzeichnung *f*; ~ **switch** *n* Schaltuhr *f*, Zeitschalter *m*; ~**table** *n (transport)* Fahrplan *m*; *(Brit Sch)* Stundenplan *m*; **to have a busy** ~**table** ein volles Programm haben; **what's on the** ~**table?** was steht auf dem Programm? ~ **trial** *n (Cycling)* Zeitfahren *nt*; ~ **warp** *n* **we were in a** ~ **warp** wir hatten einen Zeitsprung gemacht; ~ **zone** *n* Zeitzone *f*.

**timid** ['tɪmɪd] *adj* ängstlich; *animal* scheu; *person, behaviour, words also* schüchtern.

**timidity** [tɪ'mɪdɪtɪ] *n see adj* Ängstlichkeit *f*; Scheu *f*; Schüchternheit *f*.

**timidly** ['tɪmɪdlɪ] *adv* ängstlich; *(shyly)* schüchtern.

**timing** ['taɪmɪŋ] *n* **(a)** *(choice of time)* Wahl *f* des richtigen Zeitpunkts *(of für)*; *(also Theat)* Timing *nt*. **perfect** ~, **I'd just opened a bottle** ihr kommt gerade richtig, ich habe eben eine Flasche aufgemacht; **the** ~ **was unfortunate** der Zeitpunkt war schlecht gewählt. **(b)** *(Aut) (mechanism)* Steuerung *f*; *(adjustment)* Einstellung *f*. **(c)** *(measuring of time)* Zeitmessung *f (of bei)*; *(of race etc)* Stoppen *nt*.

**timorous** ['tɪmərəs] *adj* furchtsam, scheu.

**timpani** ['tɪmpənɪ] *npl (Mus)* Kesselpauken *pl*.

**tin** [tɪn] **1** *n* **(a)** Blech *nt*; *(Chem: metal)* Zinn *nt*. **(b)** *(esp Brit: can)* Dose, Büchse *f*. **a** ~ **of beans/biscuits** ein Dose Bohnen/Kekse. **2** *vt (esp Brit) fruit etc* in Dosen konservieren.

**tinfoil** ['tɪnfɔɪl] *n (wrapping)* Stanniolpapier *nt*; *(aluminium foil)* Alufolie *f*.

**tinge** [tɪndʒ] **1** *n* **(a)** *(of colour)* Hauch *m*, Spur *f*. **(b)** *(fig: hint, trace)* Spur *f*; *(of sadness also)* Anflug *m*. **2** *vt* **(a)** *(colour)* (leicht) tönen. **(b)** *(fig)* ~**d with** ... mit einer Spur von ...; **our happiness was** ~**d with sorrow** unser Glück war getrübt.

**tingle** ['tɪŋgl] **1** *vi* kribbeln *(col) (with* vor +*dat)*; *(with blows)* leicht brennen *(with* von*)*. **to** ~ **with excitement** vor Aufregung beben. **2** *n see vi* Kribbeln *(col) nt*; leichtes Brennen. **she felt a** ~ **of excitement** sie war ganz kribbelig *(col)*.

**tinker** ['tɪŋkər] **1** *n* Kesselflicker *m*. **2** *vi (also* ~ **about)** herumbasteln; *(making repair)* herumdoktern *(with, on* an +*dat)*.

**tinkle** ['tɪŋkl] **1** *vi (bells etc)* klingen, bimmeln *(col)*; *(on piano)* klimpern; *(breaking glass)* klirren. **2** *n*

Klingen, Bimmeln *(col)* nt no pl; *(of breaking glass)* Klirren nt no pl. **to give sb a ~** *(Brit col: on telephone)* jdn anbimmeln *(col)*.

**tinkling** ['tɪŋklɪŋ] **1** n *(of bells etc)* Klingen, Bimmeln *(col)* nt; *(of piano)* Klimpern nt; *(of broken glass)* Klirren nt. **2** adj see n klingend, bimmelnd *(col)*; klimpernd; klirrend.

**tin mine** n Zinnbergwerk nt.

**tinned** [tɪnd] adj *(esp Brit)* Dosen-, Büchsen-.

**tinny** ['tɪnɪ] adj *(+er) sound* blechern; *instrument* blechern klingend; *taste* nach Blech; *(pej) typewriter etc* schäbig.

**tin:** **~-opener** n *(esp Brit)* Dosenöffner m; **~ plate** n Zinnblech nt; **~-pot** adj *(Brit col)* mickrig *(col)*; **~pot dictator** Westentaschen-Diktator m *(col)*.

**tinsel** ['tɪnsəl] n *(foil)* Girlanden pl aus Lametta *etc*.

**tin:** **~smith** n Blechschmied m; **~ soldier** n Zinnsoldat m.

**tint** [tɪnt] **1** n Ton m; *(product for hair)* Tönung(smittel nt) f. **2** vt tönen.

**tiny** ['taɪnɪ] adj *(+er)* winzig, sehr klein; *baby, child* ganz klein. **~ little** winzig klein; **a ~ mind** *(pej)* ein Zwergenverstand m.

**tip¹** [tɪp] n Spitze f; *(of cigarette)* Filter m; *(col: cigarette)* Filter(zigarette) f. **from ~ to toe** von Kopf bis Fuß; **it's on the ~ of my tongue** es liegt mir auf der Zunge; **it's just the ~ of the iceberg** *(fig)* das ist nur die Spitze des Eisbergs.

**tip²** **1** n (a) *(gratuity)* Trinkgeld nt. (b) *(warning, advice, Racing)* Tipp m. **2** vt (a) *(give gratuity to)* Trinkgeld geben *(+dat)*. **to ~ sb £1** jdm £1 Trinkgeld geben. (b) *(Racing)* tippen or setzen auf *(+acc)*. **they are ~ped to win the election** *(fig)* sie sind die Favoriten für die Wahl.

►**tip off** vt sep einen Tip geben *(+dat) (about* über *+acc)*. **he ~ped ~ the police as to her whereabouts** er verriet der Polizei, wo sie war.

**tip³** **1** vt *(tilt, incline)* kippen; *(overturn)* umkippen; *(pour, empty) liquid, load, sand, rubbish* schütten. **to ~ sth backwards/forwards** etw nach hinten/vorne kippen *or* neigen; **he ~s the scales at 11 stone** er bringt 70 Kilo auf die Waage; **it ~ped the scales in his favour** *(fig)* das hat für ihn den Ausschlag gegeben; **~ the case upside down** stell die Kiste auf den Kopf; **to ~ sb off his chair** jdn vom Stuhl kippen. **2** vi *(incline)* kippen; *(dump rubbish)* Schutt abladen. **3** n *(Brit) (for rubbish)* Müllkippe f; *(for coal)* Halde f; *(col: untidy place)* Saustall m *(col)*.

►**tip back** vti sep nach hinten kippen.

►**tip over** vti sep *(overturn)* umkippen.

►**tip up** vti sep *(tilt)* kippen; *(overturn)* umkippen; *(folding seat)* hochklappen.

**tip-off** ['tɪpɒf] n *(col)* Tip, Wink m.

**tipped** [tɪpt] adj *(Brit)* **~ cigarette** Filterzigarette f.

**tipper** ['tɪpər] n *(also* **~ truck)** Kipplaster, Kipper m.

**tipple** ['tɪpl] *(col)* **1** n **he enjoys a ~** er trinkt ganz gerne mal einen. **2** vi picheln *(col)*.

**tippler** ['tɪplər] n *(col)* Schluckspecht m *(col)*.

**tippy-toe** ['tɪpɪ'təʊ] n *(US col)* = **tiptoe**.

**tipsy** ['tɪpsɪ] adj *(+er)* beschwipst *(col)*.

**tip:** **~toe 1** n **on ~toe** auf Zehenspitzen. **2** vi auf Zehenspitzen gehen; **~toe** adv; **~top** adj *(col: first-rate)* tipptopp pred *(col)*, erstklassig.

**tirade** [taɪ'reɪd] n Tirade, Schimpfkanonade f.

**tire¹** [taɪər] **1** vt müde machen. **2** vi (a) müde werden. (b) *(become bored)* **to ~ of sb/sth** jdn/etw satt haben; jds/einer Sache *(gen)* überdrüssig werden *(geh)*; **she never ~s of talking about her son** sie redet ständig über ihren Sohn.

**tire²** n *(US)* = **tyre**.

**tired** ['taɪəd] adj (a) *(fatigued)* müde; *cliché* abgegrif-

fen. **~ out** völlig erschöpft. (b) **to be ~ of sb/sth** jdn/etw leid sein; **to get ~ of sb/sth** jdn/etw satt bekommen; **I'm ~ of telling you** ich habe es satt, dir das zu sagen.

**tiredness** ['taɪədnɪs] n Müdigkeit f. **the accident was a result of (his) ~** (seine) Übermüdung war die Unfallursache.

**tireless** adj, **~ly** adv ['taɪəlɪs, -lɪ] unermüdlich.

**tiresome** ['taɪəsəm] adj *(irritating)* lästig, leidig; *(boring)* langweilig.

**tiring** ['taɪərɪŋ] adj anstrengend, ermüdend.

**tissue** ['tɪʃuː] n (a) *(Anat, Bot, fig)* Gewebe nt. **a ~ of lies** ein Lügengespinst nt. (b) *(handkerchief)* Papier(taschen)tuch nt. (c) *(also* **~ paper)** Seidenpapier nt.

**tit¹** [tɪt] n *(bird)* Meise f.

**tit²** n: **~ for tat** wie du mir, so ich dir; **he was repaid ~ for tat** er bekam es mit gleicher Münze heimgezahlt.

**tit³** n *(col!: breast)* Titte f *(col!)*.

**titbit** ['tɪtbɪt] n *(esp Brit)* Leckerbissen m.

**titchy** ['tɪtʃɪ] adj *(Brit col) person* winzig; *things* klitzeklein *(col)*.

**titillate** ['tɪtɪleɪt] vt *person, senses* anregen; *interest* erregen. **it ~s the palate** es kitzelt den Gaumen.

**titillation** [tɪtɪ'leɪʃən] n *see vt* Anregung f; Erregen nt; *(thrill)* Kitzel m.

**titivate** ['tɪtɪveɪt] vt herausputzen, verschönern.

**title** ['taɪtl] n (a) Titel m *(also Sport)*; *(of chapter)* Überschrift f; *(form of address)* Anrede f. (b) *(Jur) (right)* (Rechts)anspruch *(to* auf *+acc)*, Titel *(spec)* m; *(document)* Eigentumsurkunde f.

**titled** ['taɪtld] adj *person, classes* mit (Adels)titel. **is he ~?** hat er einen Titel?

**title:** **~ deed** n Eigentumsurkunde f; **~ holder** n *(Sport)* Titelträger(in f) m; **~ page** n *(Typ)* Titelseite f; **~ role** n *(Theat, Film)* Titelrolle f.

**titter** ['tɪtər] **1** vti kichern. **2** n Gekicher nt.

**tittle-tattle** ['tɪtl,tætl] n Geschwätz nt; *(gossip also)* Klatsch m.

**titular** ['tɪtjʊlər] adj *(without real authority)* nominell, Titular-.

**tizz** [tɪz], **tizzy** ['tɪzɪ], **tizwoz** ['tɪzwɒz] n *(col)* **to be in/get into a ~** höchst aufgeregt sein/sich schrecklich aufregen.

**T-junction** ['tiː,dʒʌŋkʃən] n Einmündung f in eine Vorfahrtsstraße.

**TM** = **trade mark** Wz.

**TN** *(US Post)* = **Tennessee**.

**TNT** = **trinitrotoluene** TNT nt.

**to** [tuː] **1** prep (a) *(in direction of, towards)* zu. **to go ~ the station** zum Bahnhof gehen/fahren; **to go ~ the theatre/cinema** *etc* ins Theater/Kino gehen; **to go ~ France/London** nach Frankreich/London gehen/fahren; **to go ~ Switzerland** in die Schweiz gehen/fahren; **to go ~ school** zur Schule *or* in die Schule gehen; **to go ~ bed** ins *or* zu Bett gehen; **~ the left** nach links; **~ the west** nach Westen; **I have never been ~ Spain** ich war noch nie in Spanien; **hold it ~ the light** halte es gegen das Licht.

(b) *(as far as, until)* bis. **to count (up) ~ 20** bis 20 zählen; **there were (from) 40 ~ 60 people** es waren 40 bis 60 Leute da; **it's 90 kms ~ Paris** nach Paris sind es 90 km.

(c) *(+indir obj)* **to give sth ~ sb** jdm etw geben; **a present from me ~ you** ein Geschenk für dich von mir; **who did you give it ~?**, **~ who(m) did you give it?** wem haben Sie es gegeben?; **what is it ~ you?** was geht dich das an?; **he is kind ~ everyone** er ist zu allen freundlich; **he has been a good friend ~ us** er war uns *(dat)* ein guter Freund; **to address sth ~**

**toilet seat**

sb etw an jdn adressieren; "To ..." *(on envelope etc)* „An ..." *(+acc)*; **to pray ~ God** zu Gott beten; ~ **Lorna** *(toast)* auf Lorna *(acc)*.

  **(d)** *(next ~, with position)* **bumper ~ bumper** Stoßstange an Stoßstange; **at right angles/parallel ~ the wall** im rechten Winkel/parallel zur Wand; ~ **the west (of)/the left (of)** westlich/links (von).

  **(e)** *(with expressions of time)* vor. **20 (minutes) ~ 2** 20 (Minuten) vor 2; **at (a) quarter ~ 2** um Viertel vor 2; **25 ~ 3** 5 nach halb 3; **it was five ~** es war fünf vor.

  **(f)** *(in relation ~)* **3 ~ the 4th** *(Math)* 3 hoch 4; **by a majority of 10 ~ 7** mit einer Mehrheit von 10 zu 7; **they won by 4 goals ~ 2** sie haben mit 4:2 *(spoken:* vier zu zwei*)* gewonnen.

  **(g)** *(per)* pro; *(in recipes, when mixing)* auf *(+acc)*. **one person ~ a room** eine Person pro Zimmer.

  **(h)** *(in comparison ~)* **that's nothing ~ what is to come** das ist gar nichts verglichen mit dem, was noch kommt.

  **(i)** *(concerning)* **there's nothing ~ it** *(it's very easy)* es ist nichts dabei; **that's all there is ~ it** das ist alles.

  **(j)** *(accompanied by)* **to sing ~ the guitar** zur Gitarre singen; **to sing sth ~ the tune of ...** etw nach der Melodie von ... singen.

  **2** *(in infin)* **(a)** ~ **begin ~ do sth** anfangen, etw zu tun; **he decided ~ come** er beschloß zu kommen; **I want ~ do it** ich will es tun; **I want him ~ do it** ich will, daß er es tut.

  **(b)** *(in order ~)* **I did it ~ help you** ich tat es, um dir zu helfen.

  **(c)** *(until)* **he lived ~ be 100** er wurde 100 Jahre alt; **the firm grew ~ be the biggest in the world** die Firma wurde zur größten der Welt.

  **(d)** *(other uses)* ~ **see him now, one would never think ...** wenn man ihn jetzt sieht, würde man nicht glauben, ...; ~ **be honest, ...** ehrlich gesagt, ...; **well, not ~ exaggerate ...** ohne zu übertreiben, ...; **he is not the sort ~ do that** er ist nicht der Typ dazu; **I have done nothing ~ deserve this** ich habe nichts getan, womit ich das verdient hätte; **who is he ~ order you around?** wer ist er denn, daß er dich so herumkommandiert?; **there's no-one ~ help us** es ist niemand da, der uns helfen könnte; **what is there ~ do here?** was gibt es hier zu tun?; **the book is still ~ be written** das Buch muß noch geschrieben werden; **he's a big boy ~ be still in short trousers** er ist so ein großer Junge und trägt noch kurze Hosen; **I arrived ~ find she had gone** als ich ankam, war sie weg; **are you ready ~ go at last?** bist du endlich fertig?; **you are foolish ~ try it** du bist dumm, daß du das versuchst; **is it good ~ eat?** schmeckt es gut?; **it's too heavy ~ lift** es ist zu schwer zum Heben; **I'll try ~** ich werde es versuchen; **you have ~** du mußt; **I should love ~** sehr gerne.

  **3** *adj (slightly ajar)* **door** angelehnt; *(shut)* zu.

  **4** *adv* ~ **and fro** hin und her; *walk* auf und ab.

**toad** [təʊd] *n* Kröte *f*; *(fig: repulsive person)* Ekel *nt*.

**toad-in-the-hole** [,təʊdɪnðə'həʊl] *n* in *Pfannkuchenteig eingebackene Würste*.

**toadstool** ['təʊdstuːl] *n* Giftpilz *m*.

**toady** ['təʊdɪ] **1** *n (pej)* Kriecher *m*. **2** *vi* radfahren *(pej col)*. **to ~ to sb** vor jdm kriechen.

**toast**[1] [təʊst] **1** *n* Toast *m*. **a piece of ~** eine Scheibe Toast; **on ~** auf Toast; **as warm as ~** *(fig)* mollig warm; ~ **rack** Toastständer *m*. **2** *vt bread* toasten; *(on open fire)* rösten.

**toast**[2] **1** *n* Toast, Trinkspruch *m*. **to drink a ~ to sb** auf jdn trinken; **to propose a ~** einen Toast aus-

bringen *(to* auf *+acc)*. **2** *vt* **to ~ sb/sth** auf jds Wohl *or* auf jdn/etw trinken.

**toaster** ['təʊstəʳ] *n* Toaster *m*.

**toast:** ~**master** *n jd, der bei Diners Toasts ankündigt oder ausbringt und Tischreden ansagt*; ~ **rack** *n* Toastständer *m*.

**tobacco** [tə'bækəʊ] *n* Tabak *m*.

**tobacconist** [tə'bækənɪst] *n (Brit)* Tabak(waren)-händler *m*; *(shop)* Tabakladen *m*.

**to-be** [tə'biː] *adj pred* zukünftig. **the mother-/bride-/husband-~** die werdende Mutter/zukünftige Braut/der zukünftige Mann.

**toboggan** [tə'bɒgən] **1** *n* Rodel(schlitten) *m*. **2** *vi* Schlitten fahren, rodeln. **to go ~ing** Schlitten fahren, rodeln.

**today** [tə'deɪ] *adv, n* **(a)** heute. **a week/fortnight ~** heute in einer Woche/zwei Wochen; **a year ago ~** heute vor einem Jahr; ~ **is Monday** heute ist Montag; **from ~** von heute an, ab heute; ~**'s paper/news** die Zeitung/Nachrichten von heute. **(b)** *(these days)* heutzutage. **the cinema/world ~** das Kino/die Welt von heute.

**toddle** ['tɒdl] *vi* **(a) the little boy ~d into the room** der kleine Junge kam ins Zimmer gewackelt. **(b)** *(col) (walk)* gehen; *(leave: also ~ off)* abzwitschern *(col)*.

**toddler** ['tɒdləʳ] *n* Kleinkind *nt*.

**toddy** ['tɒdɪ] *n* Grog *m*.

**to-do** [tə'duː] *n (col)* Theater *(col)*, Gedöns *(col) nt*. **to make a ~** ein Theater machen *(about* um*)*.

**toe** [təʊ] **1** *n* **(a)** Zehe *f*, Zeh *m*. **to tread** *or* **step on sb's ~s** *(lit)* jdm auf die Zehen treten; *(fig)* jdm ins Handwerk pfuschen *(col)*; **to keep sb on his ~s** *(fig)* jdn auf Zack halten *(col)*. **(b)** *(of sock, shoe)* Spitze *f*. **2** *vt (fig)* **to ~ the line** spuren *(col)*; **to ~ the party line** *(Pol)* sich nach der Parteilinie richten.

**toe:** ~**cap** *n* (Schuh)kappe *f*; ~**hold** *n* Halt *m* für die Fußspitzen; *(fig)* Einstieg *m*; ~**nail** *n* Zehennagel *m*.

**toffee** ['tɒfɪ] *n (substance)* Karamel *m*; *(sweet)* Toffee *nt*. **he can't sing for ~** *(col)* er kann überhaupt nicht *or* nicht die Bohne *(col)* singen.

**toffee:** ~ **apple** *n (Brit)* kandierter Apfel; ~**-nosed** *adj (Brit col)* hochnäsig.

**toga** ['təʊgə] *n* Toga *f*.

**together** [tə'geðəʳ] *adv* zusammen. **to do sth ~** etw zusammen tun; *(jointly)* **try, achieve sth etc** also etw gemeinsam tun; **to sit/stand etc ~** zusammen *or* beieinander sitzen/stehen *etc*; **to tie/fit etc two things ~** zwei Dinge zusammenbinden/-setzen *etc*; **all ~ now!** jetzt alle zusammen!

**togetherness** [tə'geðənɪs] *n (physical)* Beisammensein *nt*; *(mental, emotional)* Zusammengehörigkeit *f*.

**toggle** ['tɒgl] **1** *n* Knebel *m*; *(on clothes)* Knebelknopf *m*. ~ **switch** Kippschalter *m*. **2** *vi (Comp)* hin-und herschalten.

**togs** [tɒgz] *npl (col)* Klamotten *pl (col)*.

▶**tog up** *vt sep (col)* **to ~ oneself ~**, **to get ~ged ~** sich in Schale werfen *(col)*.

**toil** [tɔɪl] **1** *vi (liter: work)* sich plagen *(at, over* mit*)*. **2** *n (liter: work)* Mühe, Plage *(geh) f*.

**toilet** ['tɔɪlɪt] *n (lavatory)* Toilette *f*. **to go to the ~** auf die Toilette gehen; **she's in the ~/~s** sie ist auf der Toilette.

**toilet** *in cpds* Toiletten-; ~ **attendant** *n* Toilettenfrau *f*/-mann *m*; ~ **bag** *or* **case** *n* Kulturbeutel *m*; ~ **paper** *n* Toilettenpapier *nt*; ~ **requisites** *npl* Toilettenartikel *pl*.

**toiletries** ['tɔɪlɪtrɪz] *npl* Toilettenartikel *pl*.

**toilet:** ~ **roll** *n* Rolle *f* Toilettenpapier; ~ **seat** *n*

Klosettbrille *f (col)*; ~ **soap** *n* Toilettenseife *f*; ~ **tissue** *n* Toilettenpapier *nt*; ~ **water** *n* Duftwasser, Eau de Toilette *nt*.

**toing and froing** ['tu:ɪŋən'frəʊɪŋ] *n* Hin und Her *nt*.

**token** ['təʊkən] **1** *n* **(a)** *(sign)* Zeichen *nt*. **as a ~ of/in ~ of** zum Zeichen *(+gen)*; **by the same ~** ebenso; **then by the same ~ you can't object to ...** dann können Sie aber auch nichts gegen ... einwenden. **(b)** *(counter)* Spielmarke *f*. **(c)** *(voucher, gift ~)* Gutschein *m*. **2** *attr* Schein-, pro forma. **it was just a ~ offer** das hat er/sie *etc* nur pro forma *or* so zum Schein angeboten; ~ **gesture** leere Geste; ~ **payment** symbolische Bezahlung; ~ **resistance** Scheinwiderstand *m*; ~ **strike** Warnstreik *m*; ~ **rent/fine** nominelle *or* symbolische Miete/symbolische Strafe; ~ **woman** Alibifrau *f*; *(in quota system)* Quotenfrau *f*.

**Tokyo** ['təʊkɪəʊ] *n* Tokio *nt*.

**told** [təʊld] *pret, ptp of* **tell**. **there were 50 people there all** ~ es waren alles in allem 50 Leute da.

**tolerable** ['tɒlərəbl] *adj (lit)* erträglich; *(fig: not too bad also)* annehmbar, passabel *(col)*.

**tolerably** ['tɒlərəblɪ] *adv* ziemlich. ~ **well** ganz annehmbar, ziemlich gut.

**tolerance** ['tɒlərəns] *n (also Tech)* Toleranz *f (of, for, towards* gegenüber*)*; *(towards children)* Nachsicht *f (of* mit*)*.

**tolerant** ['tɒlərənt] *adj (of, towards, with* gegenüber*)* tolerant; *(towards children)* nachsichtig.

**tolerantly** ['tɒlərəntlɪ] *adv see adj* tolerant; nachsichtig.

**tolerate** ['tɒləreɪt] *vt pain, noise, weather etc* ertragen; *person* dulden; *ideas* tolerieren; *behaviour, injustice etc also* hinnehmen.

**toleration** [,tɒlə'reɪʃən] *n* Duldung *f*.

**toll¹** [təʊl] **1** *vti (bell)* läuten. **2** *n* Läuten *nt*; *(single stroke)* Glockenschlag *m*.

**toll²** *n* **(a)** *(bridge ~, road ~)* Maut *f (esp Aus)*, Benutzungsgebühr *f*; *(US Telec)* (Fernsprech)gebühr *f*. **(b)** *(deaths, loss etc)* **the death** ~ **on the roads** die Zahl der Verkehrsopfer; **the earthquake took a heavy ~ of human life** das Erdbeben forderte viele Menschenleben.

**toll:** ~ **bridge** *n* gebührenpflichtige Brücke; ~ **call** *n (US)* Ferngespräch *nt*; ~**-free call** *n (US)* gebührenfreier Anruf; ~**gate** *n* Schlagbaum *m*; ~ **road** *n* gebührenpflichtige Straße.

**Tom** [tɒm] *n* **any** ~, **Dick or Harry** *(col)* jeder x-beliebige.

**tom** [tɒm] *n (cat)* Kater *m*.

**tomato** [tə'mɑ:təʊ, *(US)* tə'meɪtəʊ] *n, pl* **-es** Tomate *f*.

**tomato** *in cpds* Tomaten-; ~ **juice** *n* Tomatensaft *m*; ~ **ketchup** *n* (Tomaten)ketchup *m or nt*; ~ **puree** *n* Tomatenmark *nt*; ~ **sauce** *n* Tomatensoße *f*; *(ketchup)* (Tomaten)ketchup *m or nt*.

**tomb** [tu:m] *n* Grab *nt*; *(building)* Grabmal *nt*.

**tombola** [tɒm'bəʊlə] *n* Tombola *f*.

**tomboy** ['tɒmbɔɪ] *n* Wildfang *m*.

**tombstone** ['tu:mstəʊn] *n* Grabstein *m*.

**tomcat** ['tɒmkæt] *n* Kater *m*.

**tome** [təʊm] *n* dickes Buch, Wälzer *m (col)*.

**tomfoolery** [tɒm'fu:lərɪ] *n* Unsinn *m*.

**tomorrow** [tə'mɒrəʊ] *adv, n* morgen. **the day after ~** übermorgen; ~ **morning** morgen früh; **(as) from ~** ab morgen, von morgen an; **see you ~!** bis morgen!; ~**'s paper** die Zeitung von morgen.

**tomtom** ['tɒmtɒm] *n* Tomtom *nt*.

**ton** [tʌn] *n* **(a)** Tonne *f*. **(b)** ~**s** *pl (col: lots)* jede Menge *(col)*; **to have** ~**s of time/friends** jede Menge Zeit/Freunde haben *(col)*; **it weighs a ~** *(fig col)* es

ist ganz schön schwer *(col)*.

**tonal** ['təʊnl] *adj* klanglich, Klang-; *(Mus: regarding harmony)* tonal; *(Art: regarding colour)* farblich, Farb-.

**tone** [təʊn] **1** *n* **(a)** *(lit, fig)* Ton *m*; *(of colour also)* Farbton *m*; *(of neighbourhood)* Ansehen *nt*. **don't speak to me in that ~ (of voice)** in diesem Ton kannst du mit mir nicht reden; **Trevor lowered the ~ (of the conversation)** Trevor mußte natürlich wieder ausfallend werden. **(b)** *(Mus)* Ton *m*; *(US: note)* Note *f*. **2** *vt (Phot: tint)* einfärben, tonen *(spec)*.

▶**tone down** *vt sep (lit, fig)* abmildern; *colour also* abschwächen; *criticism also, language* mäßigen.

▶**tone in** *vi* (im Farbton) harmonieren.

▶**tone up** *vt sep muscles* kräftigen; *person* in Form bringen. **cycling keeps you ~d** ~ Radfahren hält einen in Form.

**tone:** ~ **control** *n* Klangregler *m*; ~**-deaf** *adj*: **he's** ~**-deaf** er hat kein musikalisches Gehör; ~ **poem** *n* Tondichtung *f*.

**toner** ['təʊnə*ʳ*] *n (for copier etc)* Toner *m*.

**tongs** [tɒŋz] *npl* Zange *f*; **a pair of** ~ eine Zange.

**tongue** [tʌŋ] *n* **(a)** Zunge *f*. **to put** *or* **stick one's ~ out at sb** jdm die Zunge herausstrecken; **to lose one's ~** *(fig)* die Sprache verlieren; **to hold one's ~** den Mund halten; **her remark was ~ in cheek** ihre Bemerkung war ironisch gemeint; **to have a sharp ~** eine scharfe Zunge haben. **(b)** *(liter: language)* Sprache *f*; *(old, Bibl)* Zunge *f*. **(c)** *(of shoe)* Zunge, Lasche *f*; *(of land)* Landzunge *f*.

**tongue:** ~**-in-cheek** *adj attr remark* witzelnd; ~**-tied** *adj* **to be** ~**-tied** keinen Ton herausbringen; ~**-twister** *n* Zungenbrecher *m*.

**tonic** ['tɒnɪk] *n* **(a)** *(Med)* Tonikum *nt*; *(hair ~)* Haarwasser *nt*; *(skin ~)* Lotion *f*. **it was a real ~ to see him again** *(fig)* es hat richtig gutgetan, ihn wiederzusehen. **(b)** ~ **(water)** Tonic(water) *nt*; **gin and ~** Gin Tonic *m*.

**tonight** [tə'naɪt] *adv (this evening)* heute abend; *(during the coming night)* heute nacht. **see you ~!** bis heute abend!

**tonnage** ['tʌnɪdʒ] *n* Tonnage *f*.

**tonne** [tʌn] *n (metric ton)* Tonne *f*.

**tonsil** ['tɒnsl] *n* Mandel *f*. **to have one's ~s out** sich *(dat)* die Mandeln herausnehmen lassen.

**tonsillectomy** [,tɒnsɪ'lektəmɪ] *n* Mandeloperation *f*.

**tonsillitis** [,tɒnsɪ'laɪtɪs] *n* Mandelentzündung *f*.

**too** [tu:] *adv* **(a)** zu. **that's ~ difficult a question to answer** diese Frage ist zu schwer zu beantworten; ~ **much/many** zuviel *inv*/zu viele; **it's ~ much for her** es ist zuviel für sie; **don't worry ~ much** mach dir nicht zuviel Sorgen; ~ **right!** *(col)* das kannst du laut sagen *(col)*; **all ~ ...** allzu ...; **only ~ ...** nur zu ...; **none ~ ...** gar nicht ..., keineswegs ...; **not ~/ not any ~ ...** nicht zu/nicht allzu ...; **he wasn't ~ interested** er war nicht allzu interessiert; **I'm not/ none ~ sure** ich bin nicht ganz/gar nicht sicher; **you're ~ kind** *(iro)* (das ist) wirklich zu nett von Ihnen; **none ~ soon** keineswegs zu früh.

**(b)** *(also)* auch. **he can swim ~, he ~ can swim** er kann *auch* schwimmen; **he can *swim* ~** schwimmen kann er auch.

**(c)** *(moreover, into the bargain)* auch noch. **it was really cheap, and it works ~!** es war wirklich billig, und es funktioniert sogar!

**took** [tʊk] *pret of* **take**.

**tool** [tu:l] *n (lit, fig)* Werkzeug *nt*; *(gardening ~)* (Garten)gerät *nt*. ~**s** Werkzeuge *pl*; *(set)* Werkzeug *nt*; **that's one of the ~s of the trade** das gehört zum Handwerkszeug; **to have the ~s for the job** das nötige Werkzeug haben.

**tool:** ~bag *n* Werkzeugtasche *f*; ~box *n* Werkzeugkasten *m*; ~ kit *n* Werkzeug(ausrüstung *f*) *nt*; ~shed *n* Geräteschuppen *m*.
**toot** [tuːt] *vt* to ~ one's horn *(driver)* hupen.
**tooth** [tuːθ] *n, pl* **teeth** *(Anat, Tech)* Zahn *m*. **to have a ~ out/filled** sich *(dat)* einen Zahn ziehen/plombieren lassen; **to get one's teeth into sth** *(lit)* etw zwischen die Zähne bekommen; *(fig)* sich in etw *(dat)* festbeißen; **to show one's teeth** die Zähne zeigen *(also fig)*; **to fight ~ and nail** bis aufs Blut kämpfen; **to kick sb in the teeth** *(fig)* jdn vor den Kopf stoßen; **armed to the teeth** bis an die Zähne bewaffnet; **in the teeth of great opposition** trotz großen Widerstandes.
**tooth** *in cpds* Zahn-; ~ache *n* Zahnschmerzen *pl*; ~brush *n* Zahnbürste *f*; ~ decay *n* Zahnfäule *f*.
**toothed** [tuːθt] *adj* gezahnt, mit Zähnen.
**tooth:** ~less *adj* zahnlos; ~ mug *n* Zahnputzbecher *m*; ~paste *n* Zahnpasta *or* -creme *f*; ~pick *n* Zahnstocher *m*; ~ powder *n* Zahnpulver *nt*.
**toothy** ['tuːθɪ] *adj (+er)* **to be ~** ein Pferdegebiß haben *(col)*.
**top¹** [tɒp] **1** *n* **(a)** *(highest part)* oberer Teil; *(of spire, tree etc, fig: of league etc)* Spitze *f*; *(of mountain)* Gipfel *m*; *(of carrots)* Ende *nt*; *(of table, bed)* Kopfende *nt*; *(of road, beach)* oberes Ende. **which is the ~?** wo ist oben?; **the ~ of the milk** die Rahmschicht (auf der Milch); **at the ~** oben; **at the ~ of the page/league/pile/stairs** *etc* oben auf der Seite/in der Tabelle/auf dem Stapel/an der Treppe *etc*; **to be (at the) ~ of the class** der/die Beste in der Klasse sein; **near the ~** (ziemlich) weit oben; **he's near the ~ in English** in Englisch gehört er zu den Besten; **he aims to reach the ~** er will an die Spitze; **five lines from the ~** in der fünften Zeile von oben; **from ~ to bottom** von oben bis unten; **to scream at the ~ of one's voice** aus Leibeskräften brüllen; **they were talking at the ~(s) of their voices** sie haben sich in voller Lautstärke unterhalten; **off the ~ of my head** *(fig)* grob gesagt; *(with figures also)* über den Daumen gepeilt *(col)*; **to go over the ~** *(exaggerate)* zu viel des Guten tun; **to be over the ~** *(exaggerated)* übertrieben sein; *(past it: person)* auf dem absteigenden Ast sein.
  **(b)** *(upper surface)* Oberfläche *f*. **to be on ~** oben liegen; *(fig)* obenauf sein; **it was on ~ of the cupboard** es war oben auf dem Schrank; **put it on ~ of the cupboard leg** es oben auf den Schrank; **on ~ of** *(in addition to)* zusätzlich zu; **things are getting on ~ of me** die Dinge wachsen mir über den Kopf; **and, on ~ of that ...** und zusätzlich ...; **it's just one thing on ~ of another** es kommt eines zum anderen; **he didn't see it until he was right on ~ of it** er sah es erst, als er ganz nah dran war; **to come out on ~** sich durchsetzen; *(over rival)* die Oberhand gewinnen; **to talk off the ~ of one's head** *(col)* nur so daherreden; **to blow one's ~** aus der Haut fahren *(col)*.
  **(c)** *(working surface)* Arbeitsfläche *f*.
  **(d)** *(bikini ~, blouse)* Oberteil *nt*.
  **(e)** *(of jar, suitcase)* Deckel *m*; *(of bottle)* Verschluß *m*; *(of pen)* Hülle *f*; *(of car)* Dach *nt*; *(of open car)* Verdeck *nt*. **hard/soft ~** Hardtop/Softtop *nt*.
  **(f)** *(Brit Aut: ~ gear)* höchster Gang. **in ~** im höchsten Gang.
  **2** *adj (upper)* obere(r, s); *(highest)* oberste(r, s); *branches, note, honours, price* höchste(r, s); *(best) driver, athlete, job* Spitzen-; *pupil, marks* beste(r, s); *entertainer, management* Top-. **~ prices** Höchstpreise *pl*; **on the ~ floor** im obersten Stockwerk; **a ~-**

**floor flat** eine Dachgeschoßwohnung; **the ~ right-hand corner** die obere rechte Ecke; **at ~ speed** mit Höchstgeschwindigkeit; **in ~ form** in Höchstform; **to be ~** *(Sch)* Beste(r) sein; **the ~ people** *(in a company)* die Leute an der Spitze; *(in society)* die oberen Zehntausend.
  **3** *adv* **to come ~** *(Sch)* Beste(r) werden.
  **4** *vt* **(a)** *(cover, cap)* bedecken. **~ped by a dome** gekrönt von einer Kuppel.
  **(b)** *(be higher than, fig: surpass)* übersteigen. **that ~s the lot** *(col)* das übertrifft alles; **and to ~ it all ...** *(col)* und um das Maß vollzumachen ...
  **(c)** **to ~ a tree** die Spitze eines Baumes abschneiden; **to ~ and tail gooseberries** Stachelbeeren putzen.
►**top up** *vt sep glass, battery, tank* auffüllen. **to ~ the oil** Öl nachfüllen; **can I ~ you ~?** *(col: at party etc)* darf ich Ihnen (noch) nachschenken?
**top²** *n* Kreisel *m*. **to sleep like a ~** wie ein Murmeltier schlafen.
**topaz** ['təʊpæz] *n* Topas *m*.
**top:** ~ **brass** *n* hohe Tiere *pl (col)*; ~coat *n* **(a)** *(overcoat)* Mantel *m*; **(b)** *(coat of paint)* Deckanstrich *m*; ~ **copy** *n* Original *nt*; ~ **dog** *n (fig)* Boß *m (col)*; ~-**flight** *adj* Spitzen-, erstklassig; ~ **gear** *n* höchster Gang; ~ **hat** *n* Zylinder *m*; ~-**heavy** *adj (lit, fig)* kopflastig.
**topic** ['tɒpɪk] *n* Thema *nt*. ~ **of conversation** Gesprächsthema *nt*.
**topical** ['tɒpɪkəl] *adj problem, speech, event* aktuell.
**topicality** [ˌtɒpɪ'kælɪtɪ] *n* Aktualität *f*.
**top:** ~less *adj* (mit) oben ohne, Oben-ohne-; ~-**level** *adj* Spitzen-; ~-**level talks** Gespräche auf höchster Ebene; ~**most** *adj* oberste(r, s); ~-**notch** *adj (col)* erstklassig; *attr* Top- *(col)*.
**topographic(al)** [ˌtɒpə'græfɪk(əl)] *adj* topographisch.
**topography** [tə'pɒgrəfɪ] *n* Topographie *f*.
**topping** ['tɒpɪŋ] *n (Cook)* with a ~ **of cream/nuts** *etc* mit Sahne/Nüssen *etc* obendrauf *or* darauf.
**topple** ['tɒpl] **1** *vi (fall)* (um)fallen. **2** *vt* umwerfen; *(from a height)* hinunterkippen; *(fig) government* stürzen.
►**topple over** *vi* fallen *(prep obj* über +*acc)*.
**top:** ~-**quality** *adj* erster Qualität; ~-**ranking** *adj* von hohem Rang; *civil servant, officer also* hohe(r); *author, singer* Spitzen-; ~-**secret** *adj* streng geheim; ~-**security prison** *n (Brit)* Hochsicherheitsgefängnis *nt*; ~**soil** *n* Mutterboden *m*; *(Agr)* Ackerkrume *f*.
**topsy-turvy** ['tɒpsɪ'tɜːvɪ] *(col)* **1** *adj (in disorder)* kunterbunt durcheinander *pred*; *(fig)* auf den Kopf gestellt. **it's a ~ world** es ist eine verkehrte Welt. **2** *adv* **to turn sth ~** *(lit, fig)* etw auf den Kopf stellen.
**top-up** ['tɒpʌp] *n (col)* **would you like a ~?** darf ich Ihnen (noch) nachschenken?; ~ **loan** Zusatzdarlehen *nt*.
**torch** [tɔːtʃ] *n (lit, fig)* Fackel *f*; *(Brit: flashlight)* Taschenlampe *f*; *(blowlamp)* Schweißbrenner *m*.
**tore** [tɔːʳ] *pret of* **tear¹**.
**torment** ['tɔːment] **1** *n* Qual *f*. **to be in ~** Qualen leiden. **2** [tɔː'ment] *vt* quälen; *(annoy, tease)* plagen.
**tormentor** [tɔː'mentəʳ] *n* Peiniger(in *f*) *m*.
**torn** [tɔːn] *ptp of* **tear¹**.
**tornado** [tɔː'neɪdəʊ] *n, pl* -**es** Tornado *m*.
**torpedo** [tɔː'piːdəʊ] **1** *n, pl* -**es** Torpedo *m*. ~ **boat** Torpedoboot *nt*. **2** *vt* torpedieren.
**torpid** ['tɔːpɪd] *adj (lethargic)* träge.
**torpor** ['tɔːpəʳ] *n* Trägheit *f*.
**torque** [tɔːk] *n (Mech)* Drehmoment *nt*. ~ **wrench** Drehmomentschlüssel *m*.

**torrent** ['tɒrənt] *n (river)* reißender Strom; *(mountain* ~*)* Gießbach *m.* **the rain came down in** ~**s** der Regen kam in wahren Sturzbächen herunter; **a** ~ **of abuse** eine Flut von Beschimpfungen.

**torrential** [tɒ'renʃəl] *adj rain* sintflutartig.

**torrid** ['tɒrɪd] *adj (lit, fig)* heiß; *heat, air, sun* sengend.

**torso** ['tɔːsəʊ] *n* Rumpf *m*; *(Art)* Torso *m.* **bare** ~ nackter Oberkörper.

**tortoise** ['tɔːtəs] *n* Schildkröte *f.*

**tortoiseshell** ['tɔːtəʃel] *n* Schildpatt *nt.*

**tortuous** ['tɔːtjʊəs] *adj (lit) path* gewunden; *(fig)* verwickelt; *methods also, person* umständlich.

**torture** ['tɔːtʃər] **1** *n* Folter *f*; *(fig)* Qual *f.* ~ **chamber** Folterkammer *f.* **2** *vt (lit)* foltern; *(fig: torment)* quälen, peinigen *(geh)*; *(fig: distort)* verzerren.

**torturer** ['tɔːtʃərər] *n (lit)* Folterknecht *m*; *(fig: tormentor)* Peiniger(in *f*) *m.*

**Tory** ['tɔːrɪ] *(Brit Pol)* **1** *n* Konservative(r) *mf*, Tory *m.* **2** *adj* konservativ, Tory-. **the** ~ **party** die Konservativen *pl.*

**toss** [tɒs] **1** *n* Wurf *m.* **with a proud** ~ **of her head** mit einer stolzen Kopfbewegung; **to win/lose the** ~ *(Ftbl, Hockey etc)* die Seitenwahl gewinnen/verlieren; **there is no point in arguing the** ~ **(with me)** es hat keinen Sinn, (mit mir) darüber zu streiten; **I don't give a** ~ **about him/it** *(col)* er/es ist mir völlig schnuppe *(col).* **2** *vt* **(a)** *(throw) ball* werfen; *salad* anmachen; *(Brit) pancake* wenden *(durch Hochwerfen)*; *rider* abwerfen. **to** ~ **sth to sb** jdm etw zuwerfen. **(b)** *(move: wind)* schütteln, zerren an *(+dat).* **the boat,** ~**ed (about) by the waves** ... das Boot, von den Wellen hin und her geworfen, ...; **to** ~ **(back) one's head** den Kopf zurückwerfen. **(c) to** ~ **a coin** eine Münze (zum Losen) hochwerfen; **I'll** ~ **you for it** laß uns darum knobeln. **3** *vi* **(a)** *(ship)* rollen. **to** ~ **and turn (in bed)** sich (im Bett) hin und her werfen. **(b) to** ~ **for sth** um etw knobeln.

▶**toss up 1** *vi* knobeln *(for* um*).* **2** *vt sep* werfen. **to** ~ **sth** ~ **(into the air)** etw hochwerfen.

**toss-up** ['tɒsʌp] *n* **it was a** ~ **whether** ... *(col)* es war völlig offen, ob ...

**tot** [tɒt] *n* **(a)** *(child: also* **tiny** ~*)* Knirps *m (col).* **(b)** *(esp Brit: of alcohol)* Schlückchen *nt.*

▶**tot up** *vt sep (esp Brit col)* zusammenzählen.

**total** ['təʊtl] **1** *adj* völlig, absolut; *sum, loss, number* Gesamt-; *war, eclipse, disaster* total. **what is the** ~ **number of rooms you have?** wie viele Zimmer haben Sie (insgesamt)?; **to be in** ~ **ignorance (of sth)** (von etw) überhaupt nichts wissen; **to have** ~ **recall** ein absolutes Erinnerungsvermögen haben. **2** *n* Gesamtmenge *f*; *(money, figures)* Endsumme *f.* **a** ~ **of 50 people** insgesamt 50 Leute. **3** *vt* **(a)** *(amount to)* sich belaufen auf *(+acc).* **(b)** *(add: also* ~ **up)** zusammenzählen *or* -rechnen.

**totalitarian** [ˌtəʊtælɪ'tɛərɪən] *adj* totalitär.

**totality** [təʊ'tælɪtɪ] *n* Gesamtheit *f.*

**totally** ['təʊtəlɪ] *adv* völlig, total.

**tote**[1] [təʊt] *n (col)* **the** ~ der Totalisator.

**tote**[2] *vt (col: carry) sth heavy* schleppen; *gun* bei sich haben.

**tote bag** *n* größere Stofftasche *f.*

**totem pole** ['təʊtəmˌpəʊl] *n* Totempfahl *m.*

**totter** ['tɒtər] *vi (wobble before falling)* wanken; *(stagger)* taumeln; *(old man, toddler)* tapsen; *(invalid, fig)* schwanken; *(economy)* kränkeln.

**tottery** ['tɒtərɪ] *adj* wack(e)lig; *person* tatterig. **a** ~ **old man** ein Tattergreis *m (col).*

**toucan** ['tuːkən] *n* Tukan *m.*

**touch** [tʌtʃ] **1** *n* **(a)** *(sense of* ~*)* (Tast)gefühl *nt.* **to be cold/soft to the** ~ sich kalt/weich anfühlen.

  **(b)** *(act of* ~*ing)* Berühren *nt*, Berührung *f*; *(of*

*pianist, typist, piano, typewriter)* Anschlag *m.* **I felt a** ~ **on my arm** ich spürte, daß jd/etw meinen Arm berührte; **it opens at a** ~ es öffnet sich auf leichten Druck; **at the** ~ **of a button** auf Knopfdruck.

  **(c)** *(skill)* Hand *f*; *(style also)* Stil *m.* **the** ~ **of a master** die Hand eines Meisters; **it has the** ~ **of genius/the professional** ~ es hat etwas Geniales/Professionelles; **he's losing his** ~ er wird langsam alt; **a personal** ~ eine persönliche Note.

  **(d)** *(stroke) (Art)* Strich *m*; *(fig)* Einfall *m.* **a book with humorous** ~**es** ein stellenweise humorvolles Buch; **a nice** ~ eine hübsche Note; *(gesture)* eine nette Geste; **to put the finishing** ~**es to sth** einer Sache *(dat)* den letzten Schliff geben.

  **(e)** *(small quantity)* Spur *f*; *(of irony, sadness etc also)* Anflug *m.* **a** ~ **of flu** eine leichte Grippe.

  **(f)** *(contact)* **to be in** ~ **with sb** mit jdm in Verbindung stehen; **they were** *or* **got in** ~ **with us yesterday** sie haben sich gestern mit uns in Verbindung gesetzt; **to be/keep in** ~ **with (political) developments** (politisch) auf dem laufenden sein/bleiben; **I'll be in** ~**!** ich lasse von mir hören!; **keep in** ~**!** laß/laßt wieder einmal von dir/euch hören!; **to be out of** ~ **with sb** keine Verbindung mehr zu jdm haben; **to be completely out of** ~ **(with sth)** (in bezug auf etw *acc*) überhaupt nicht auf dem laufenden sein; **to lose** ~ **with sb** den Kontakt zu jdm verlieren.

  **(g)** *(Ftbl)* **to be in** ~ im Aus sein.

  **2** *vt* **(a)** berühren; *(get hold of also)* anfassen; *(press lightly also)* piano keys anschlagen; *brakes* antippen; *(brush against)* streifen. **to** ~ **glasses** anstoßen; **don't** ~ **that!** faß das nicht an!; **I was** ~**ing 100 most of the way** ich fuhr fast ständig 160. **(b)** *(lay hands on)* anrühren. **the police/tax authorities can't** ~ **me** die Polizei/das Finanzamt kann mir nichts anhaben; **the paintings weren't** ~**ed by the fire** die Gemälde blieben vom Feuer verschont; **I never** ~ **whisky** ich rühre keinen Whisky an; **I don't want to** ~ **my savings** ich will meine Ersparnisse nicht anbrechen; **I wouldn't** ~ **those shares** ich würde meine Finger von diesen Aktien lassen. **(c)** *(concern)* berühren. **(d)** *(move emotionally)* rühren, bewegen; *(affect)* berühren; *(wound) pride* treffen. **deeply** ~**ed** tief gerührt *or* bewegt. **(e)** *(equal)* **nobody can** ~ **him (for** ...**)** bei ... kommt keiner an ihn heran.

  **3** *vi (come into contact)* sich berühren; *(estates etc: be adjacent also)* aneinandergrenzen. *"***please do not** ~*"* „bitte nicht berühren".

▶**touch down 1** *vi* **(a)** *(Aviat, Space)* aufsetzen. **(b)** *(Rugby, US Ftbl)* einen Versuch erzielen. **2** *vt sep ball* niederlegen.

▶**touch (up)on** *vi +prep obj subject* kurz berühren, antippen.

**touch and go** ['tʌtʃən'gəʊ] *adj* **to be** ~ riskant sein; **it's** ~ **whether** ... es steht auf des Messers Schneide, ob ...

**touchdown** ['tʌtʃdaʊn] *n* **(a)** *(Aviat, Space)* Aufsetzen *nt.* **(b)** *(Rugby, US Ftbl)* Versuch *m (Niederlegen des Balles im Malfeld des Gegners).*

**touched** [tʌtʃt] *adj pred (moved)* gerührt, bewegt.

**touchiness** ['tʌtʃɪnɪs] *n* Empfindlichkeit *f (on* in bezug auf +*acc)*; *(irritability also)* Reizbarkeit *f*; *(on one occasion)* Gereiztheit *f.*

**touching** ['tʌtʃɪŋ] **1** *adj* rührend. **2** *prep (form)* bezüglich (+*gen) (form).*

**touch:** ~**line** *n (Sport)* Seitenlinie *f*; ~**paper** *n* Zündpapier *nt*; ~**-sensitive** *adj* berührungsempfindlich; ~**-sensitive button** Sensortaste *f*; ~**-sensitive screen** Kontaktbildschirm *m*; ~**stone** *n* *(fig)* Prüfstein *m*; ~-**type** *vti* blindschreiben.

**touchy** ['tʌtʃɪ] *adj* empfindlich *(about* in bezug auf +*acc)*; *(irritable also)* leicht reizbar; *subject* heikel.

**tough** [tʌf] *adj (+er)* **(a)** zäh; *resistant* widerstandsfähig; *cloth* strapazierfähig; *(towards others)* hart; *bargaining, opponent, struggle, district, policy, controls* hart. **to get ~ (with sb)** hart durchgreifen (gegen jdn); **~ guy** *(col)* (knall)harter Bursche *(col)*. **(b)** *(difficult) task, problem* hart; *journey* strapaziös, anstrengend. **it was ~ going** *(lit, fig)* es war eine Strapaze; **to have a ~ time of it** nichts zu lachen haben; **it was ~ on the others** das war hart für die anderen; **~ (luck)!** Pech!

**toughen** ['tʌfn] *vt* **(a)** *glass, metal* härten. **(b)** *(fig) person* zäh machen; *(physically)* abhärten.

**toughness** ['tʌfnɪs] *n see adj* **(a)** Zähigkeit *f*; Widerstandsfähigkeit *f*; Strapazierfähigkeit *f*; Härte *f*. **(b)** *(difficulty)* Schwierigkeit *f*; *(of journey)* Strapazen *pl*.

**toupee** ['tuːpeɪ] *n* Toupet *nt*.

**tour** [tʊər] **1** *n (journey, walking ~ etc)* Tour *f*; *(of town, building etc)* Rundgang *m (of durch)*; *(also guided ~)* Führung *f (of durch)*; *(by bus)* Rundfahrt *f (of durch)*; *(Theat, Sport)* Tournee *f*. **to go on a ~ of Scotland/the castle** eine Schottlandreise machen/an einer Schloßführung teilnehmen; **to go/be on ~** *(Theat)* auf Tournee gehen/sein. **2** *vt* **(a)** *country etc* fahren durch *(col)*; *(on foot)* ziehen durch *(col)*; *(visit) town, building* einen Rundgang machen durch; *(by bus etc)* eine Rundfahrt machen durch. **(b)** *(Theat)* eine Tournee machen durch. **3** *vi* **(a)** *(on holiday)* eine Reise *or* Tour machen. **we're ~ing (around)** wir reisen herum; **to go ~ing** Touren/eine Tour machen. **(b)** *(Theat, Sport)* eine Tournee machen.

**tour guide** *n* Reiseleiter(in *f*) *m*.

**touring** ['tʊərɪŋ]: **~ car** *n (Motor racing)* Tourenwagen *m*; **~ company** *n (Theat)* Gastspieltruppe *f*.

**tourism** ['tʊərɪzəm] *n* Fremdenverkehr, Tourismus *m*.

**tourist** ['tʊərɪst] **1** *n (person)* Tourist(in *f*) *m*; *(Sport)* Gast *m*. **2** *attr attraction, class, hotel, shop* Touristen-; *guide* Fremden-. **~ bureau** *or* **office** Fremdenverkehrsbüro *nt*; **~ season** Reisezeit *f*; **~ industry** *or* **trade** Fremdenverkehrsgewerbe *nt*, Touristik *f*.

**tournament** ['tʊənəmənt] *n (Sport, Hist)* Turnier *nt*.

**tourniquet** ['tʊənɪkeɪ] *n* Aderpresse *f*.

**tour operator** *n* Reiseveranstalter *m*.

**tousled** ['taʊzld] *adj hair* zerzaust. **~ head** Wuschelkopf *m (col)*.

**tout** [taʊt] *(col)* **1** *n (esp Brit) (tipster)* Wettberater *m*; *(ticket ~)* Schwarzmarkthändler *m*; *(for business)* Kundenfänger *m*. **2** *vi* **to ~ for business/customers** (aufdringlich) Reklame machen/auf Kundenfang sein *(col)*.

**tow** [təʊ] **1** *n* **to give sb/a car a ~** jdn/ein Auto abschleppen; **to give sb/a yacht a ~** jdn/eine Jacht ins Schlepptau nehmen; **to have sb in ~** *(fig)* jdn im Schlepptau haben; **"on ~"** „Fahrzeug wird abgeschleppt". **2** *vt boat, glider* schleppen; *car also* abschleppen; *trailer* ziehen.

▶**tow away** *vt sep* abschleppen.

**toward(s)** [tə'wɔːd(z)] *prep* **(a)** *(in direction of) (with verbs of motion)* auf *(+acc)* ... zu. **they walked ~ the town** sie gingen auf die Stadt zu; **it's further north, ~ Dortmund** es liegt weiter nördlich, Richtung Dortmund; **~ the south** nach Süden; **he turned ~ her** er wandte sich ihr zu; **they are working ~ a solution** sie arbeiten an einer Lösung hin. **(b)** *(in relation to)*

... *(dat)* gegenüber. **what are your feelings ~ him?** was empfinden Sie ihm gegenüber? **(c)** **~ ten o'clock** gegen zehn Uhr; **~ the end of the year** gegen Ende des Jahres. **(d)** **the money will go ~ ...** das Geld wird für ... verwendet; **most of my salary goes ~ the rent** der größte Teil meines Gehalts geht für die Miete drauf *(col)*.

**tow:** **~bar** *n* Anhängerkupplung *f*; **~-car** *n (US)* Abschleppwagen *m*.

**towel** ['taʊəl] *n* Handtuch *nt*. **~ rail** *or* **rack** *(US)* Handtuchhalter *m*.

**towelette** ['taʊəlet] *n* Erfrischungstuch *nt*.

**towelling** ['taʊəlɪŋ] *n* Frottee(stoff) *m*.

**tower** ['taʊər] *n* **(a)** Turm *m*. **(b)** *(fig: person)* **a ~ of strength** ein starker (Rück)halt. **(c)** *(Comp)* Tower, Turm *m*.

▶**tower above** *or* **over** *vi* +*prep obj* **(a)** *(buildings etc)* emporragen über *(+acc)*. **(b)** *(lit, fig: people)* überragen.

**tower block** *n (Brit)* Hochhaus *nt*.

**towering** ['taʊərɪŋ] *adj building* hochragend; *mountain* (steil) aufragend; *tree* hochgewachsen. **one of the ~ giants of literature** eine der einsamen Größen der Literatur.

**town** [taʊn] *n* Stadt *f*. **the ~ of Brighton** (die Stadt) Brighton; **to go into ~** in die Stadt gehen; **to live in ~** in der Stadt wohnen; **he's out of ~** er ist nicht in der Stadt; **to have a night on the ~** *(col)* die Nacht durchmachen *(col)*; **to go to ~ on sth** *(fig col)* sich bei etw ins Zeug legen.

**town:** **~ centre** *(Brit)* or **center** *(US)* *n* Stadtmitte *f*, (Stadt)zentrum *nt*; **~ clerk** *n* Stadtdirektor *m*; *(of bigger town)* Oberstadtdirektor *m*; **~ council** *n* Stadtrat *m*; **~-dweller** *n* Stadtbewohner(in *f*) *m*; **~ hall** *n* Rathaus *nt*; **~ house** *n (in town)* Stadthaus *nt*; *(terrace house)* Reihenhaus *nt*; **~ plan** *n* Stadtplan *m*; **~ planning** *n* Stadtplanung *f*; **~scape** *n* Stadtlandschaft *f*; *(Art)* Stadtansicht *f*.

**townspeople** ['taʊnz,piːpl] *npl* Städter, Stadtmenschen *pl*; *(citizens)* Bürger *pl*.

**tow:** **~path** *n* Treidelpfad *m*; **~rope** *n* Abschleppseil *nt*; **~-truck** *n (US)* Abschleppwagen *m*.

**toxic** ['tɒksɪk] *adj* giftig, Gift-, toxisch. **~ waste** Giftmüll *m*.

**toxin** ['tɒksɪn] *n* Gift(stoff *m*), Toxin *nt*.

**toy** [tɔɪ] **1** *n* Spielzeug *nt*. **~s** Spielsachen *pl*, Spielzeug *nt*. **2** *vi* **to ~ with an object/idea** *etc* mit einer Sache/Idee *etc* spielen; **to ~ with one's food** mit dem Essen (herum)spielen.

**toy** *in cpds car, soldier* Spielzeug-; **~ boy** *n (col)* wesentlich jüngerer Liebhaber; **~ shop** *(Brit)* or **store** *(US)* *n* Spielwarenladen *m*; **~ train** *n* Spielzeugeisenbahn *f*.

**trace** [treɪs] **1** *n (sign, small amount)* Spur *f*. **to vanish without ~** spurlos verschwinden; **to lose ~ of sb/sth** jdn/etw aus den Augen verlieren. **2** *vt* **(a)** *(draw)* zeichnen; *(copy)* nachziehen; *(with tracing paper)* durchpausen. **(b)** *(follow trail of)* verfolgen; *steps* folgen *(+dat)*. **she was ~d to a house in Soho** ihre Spur führte zu einem Haus in Soho. **(c)** *(find)* ausfindig machen, auffinden.

▶**trace back** *vt sep descent* zurückverfolgen; *rumour* auf seinen Ursprung zurückverfolgen; *neurosis etc* zurückführen *(to* auf +*acc)*.

**traceable** ['treɪsəbl] *adj* auffindbar. **to be ~ to sth** sich auf etw *(acc)* zurückführen lassen.

**trace element** *n* Spurenelement *nt*.

**tracer** ['treɪsər] *n (Mil: also ~ bullet)* Leuchtspurgeschoß *nt*.

**trachea** [trə'kɪə] *n* Luftröhre *f*.

**tracing** ['treɪsɪŋ] *n (drawing)* Durchpausen *nt*; *(result)*

Pause f. ~ **paper** Pauspapier nt.

**track** [træk] **1** n **(a)** (trail) Fährte, Spur f; (of tyres) (Fahr)spur f. **to be on sb's** ~ jdm auf der Spur sein; **to keep** ~ **of sb/sth** jdn/etw im Auge behalten; **I can't keep** ~ **of your girlfriends** du hast so viele Freundinnen, da komme ich nicht mit (col); **no-one can keep** ~ **of the situation** niemand hat mehr einen Überblick über die Lage; **to lose** ~ **of sb/sth** (lose sight of) jdn/etw aus den Augen verlieren; (lose count of, be confused about) über Leute/etw den Überblick verlieren; **we must be making** ~**s** (col) wir müssen uns auf die Socken machen (col); **he stopped dead in his** ~**s** er blieb abrupt stehen; **to cover (up) one's** ~**s** seine Spuren verwischen.

**(b)** (path) Weg, Pfad m. **off the** ~ (fig) abwegig; **to be on the right/wrong** ~ (fig) auf der richtigen/ falschen Spur sein.

**(c)** (Rail) Gleise pl; (US: platform) Bahnsteig m. **to leave the** ~**(s)** entgleisen.

**(d)** (Sport) Rennbahn f; (Athletics) Bahn f; (Motorsport) Piste f; (circuit) Rennstrecke f.

**(e)** (on tape) Spur f; (song etc) Stück nt.

**(f)** (also **caterpillar** ~) Raupenkette f.

**2** vt (follow) person, animal verfolgen; (Space) rocket die Flugbahn (+gen) verfolgen.

▶**track down** vt sep aufspüren (to in +dat); thing aufstöbern, auftreiben (col); reference, source ausfindig machen.

**tracker dog** ['trækə<sup>r</sup>,dɒg] n Spürhund m.

**track event** n Laufwettbewerb m.

**tracking** ['trækɪŋ] n Verfolgen nt. ~ **station** Bodenstation f.

**track:** ~ **record** n (fig) **she has a good** ~ **record** sie hat gute Leistungen vorzuweisen; **what's his** ~ **record?** was hat er vorzuweisen?; ~ **shoe** n Rennschuh m; ~**suit** n Trainingsanzug m.

**tract**[1] [trækt] n **(a)** (of land) Gebiet nt. **narrow** ~ Streifen m. **(b)** (respiratory) Wege pl; (digestive) Trakt m.

**tract**[2] n (pamphlet) Traktat nt, Schrift f.

**traction** ['trækʃən] n Zugkraft, Zugleistung f; (of wheels) Bodenhaftung f; (Med) Streckverband m. ~ **engine** Zugmaschine f.

**tractor** ['træktə<sup>r</sup>] n Traktor m.

**tractor:** ~ **feed** n (Comp) Traktor m; ~ **unit** n Sattelschlepper m.

**trade** [treɪd] **1** n **(a)** (commerce) Handel m, Gewerbe nt; (turnover: of shop etc) die Geschäfte pl. **to do a good** ~ gute Geschäfte machen; **to do a brisk** ~ **in sth** einen reißenden Absatz an etw (dat) haben. **(b)** (line of business) Branche f, Geschäftszweig m; (job) Handwerk nt. **he's in the wool** ~ er ist in der Wollbranche; **he's in the** ~ er ist vom Fach; **as we call it in the** ~ wie es in unserer Branche heißt; **he's a bricklayer by** ~ er ist Maurer von Beruf; **he's a lawyer by** ~ (hum) er ist Rechtsanwalt. **(c)** (exchange) Tausch(handel) m. **2** vt tauschen. **to** ~ **sth for sth else** etw gegen etw anderes (ein)tauschen. **3** vi **(a)** (Comm) Handel treiben, handeln. **to** ~ **in sth** mit etw handeln; **to** ~ **with sb** mit jdm Geschäfte machen. **(b)** (US col) einkaufen (at bei).

▶**trade in** vt sep in Zahlung geben (for für).

▶**trade on** vi +prep obj ausnutzen.

**trade:** ~ **association** n Fachverband m; ~ **barrier** n Handelsschranke f; ~ **cycle** n Konjunkturzyklus m; ~ **deficit** n Handelsdefizit nt; **T**~ **Descriptions Act** n (Brit) Gesetz nt über die korrekte Beschreibung von Waren; ~ **directory** n Branchenverzeichnis nt; ~ **discount** n Händlerrabatt m; ~ **fair** n Handelsmesse f; ~ **figures** npl Handelsziffern pl; ~ **gap** n Außenhandelsdefizit nt; ~**in** n to take/offer sth as a

~**-in** etw in Zahlung nehmen/geben; ~ **journal** n Fachzeitschrift f; ~**mark** n (lit) Warenzeichen nt; **honesty was his** ~**mark** er war für seine Ehrlichkeit bekannt; ~ **mission** n Handelsmission f; ~ **name** n Handelsname m; ~ **price** n Händlerpreis, Einkaufspreis m.

**trader** ['treɪdə<sup>r</sup>] n (person) Händler(in f) m.

**trade:** ~ **route** n Handelsweg m, Handelsstraße f; ~ **secret** n (lit, fig) Betriebsgeheimnis nt.

**trades:** ~**man** n (delivery man) Lieferant m; (shopkeeper) Händler m; (plumber, electrician etc) Handwerker m; ~**man's entrance** Lieferanteneingang m; ~ **union** n = **trade union**; **T**~ **Union Congress** (britischer) Gewerkschaftsbund.

**trade:** ~ **union** n Gewerkschaft f; ~ **unionism** n Gewerkschaftsbewegung f; ~ **unionist** n Gewerkschaft(l)er(in f) m; ~ **wind** n Passat m.

**trading** ['treɪdɪŋ] **1** adj handeltreibend. **2** n Handel m, Handeln nt (in mit).

**trading** in cpds Handels-; ~ **account** n Geschäftskonto nt; ~ **estate** n Gewerbegebiet nt; ~ **loss** n Betriebsverlust m; ~ **results** npl Betriebsergebnis nt; ~ **stamp** n Rabattmarke f.

**tradition** [trə'dɪʃən] n Tradition f. ~ **has it that he ...** es ist überliefert, daß er ...

**traditional** [trə'dɪʃənl] adj traditionell; virtues also überkommen; jazz Old-time-.

**traditionally** [trə'dɪʃnəlɪ] adv traditionell; (customarily) üblicherweise.

**traffic** ['træfɪk] **1** n **(a)** Verkehr m; (Aviat) Flugverkehr m. **closed to heavy** ~ gesperrt für den Schwerlastverkehr. **(b)** (business: of port, airport) Umschlag m. ~ **in steel** Stahlumschlag m. **(c)** (usu pej: trading) Handel m (in mit); (in pornography) Vertrieb m (in von). **2** vi (usu pej) handeln (in mit).

**traffic** in cpds Verkehrs-; ~ **calming** n Verkehrsberuhigung f; ~ **circle** n (US) Kreisverkehr m; ~ **cone** n Leitkegel m; ~ **cop** n (col) Verkehrspolizist m; ~ **island** n Verkehrsinsel f; ~ **jam** n Verkehrsstau m.

**trafficker** ['træfɪkə<sup>r</sup>] n (usu pej) Händler m; (in drugs also) Dealer m.

**traffic:** ~ **lights** (Brit) npl, ~ **light** n (US) Verkehrsampel f; ~ **offence** (Brit) or **offense** (US) n Verkehrsdelikt nt; ~ **police** npl Verkehrspolizei f; ~ **policeman** n Verkehrspolizist m; ~ **sign** n Verkehrszeichen nt; ~ **violation** n (US) Verkehrsdelikt nt; ~ **warden** n (Brit) ≈ Verkehrspolizist m ohne amtliche Befugnisse; (woman issuing parking tickets) Politesse f.

**tragedy** ['trædʒɪdɪ] n Tragödie f. **six killed in holiday crash** ~ tragischer Urlaubsunfall forderte sechs Todesopfer; **the** ~ **of it is that ...** das Tragische daran ist, daß ...

**tragic** ['trædʒɪk] adj tragisch.

**tragically** ['trædʒɪkəlɪ] adv ~, **he was killed before ...** tragischerweise kam er ums Leben, bevor ...

**tragicomic** [,trædʒɪ'kɒmɪk] adj tragikomisch.

**trail** [treɪl] **1** n **(a)** Spur f. ~ **of blood** Blutspur f; ~ **of smoke/dust** Rauchfahne f/Staubwolke f. **(b)** (track) Fährte, Spur f. **hot on the** ~ dicht auf den Fersen; **to be on the** ~ **of an animal** die Spur eines Tieres verfolgen; **the police are on his** ~ die Polizei ist ihm auf der Spur. **(c)** (path) Weg, Pfad m; (nature ~ etc) (Wander)weg m. **2** vt **(a)** (follow) person folgen (+dat); animal verfolgen. **(b)** (drag) schleppen, schleifen. **the bird** ~**ed its broken wing** der Vogel zog seinen gebrochenen Flügel nach. **(c)** (US: tow) ziehen, schleppen. **3** vi **(a)** (on floor) schleifen. **(b)** (plant) sich ranken. **(c)** (walk) trotten. **(d)** (be behind: in competition etc) weit zurückliegen; (Sport)

weit zurückgefallen sein.
►**trail away** or **off** vi (voice) sich verlieren (into in +dat).
**trailer** ['treɪləʳ] n (a) (Aut) Anhänger m; (semi-~) Sattelauflieger m. (b) (US) Wohnwagen, Caravan m. ~ **park** Campingplatz m für Wohnwagen. (c) (Film, TV) Vorschau f.
**train**¹ [treɪn] n (a) (Rail) Zug m. **to go/travel by** ~ mit dem Zug or der Bahn fahren/reisen; **a** ~ **journey** eine Bahn- or Zugfahrt; **to take** or **get the 11 o'clock** ~ den Elfuhrzug nehmen; **to change** ~**s** umsteigen; **on the** ~ im Zug. (b) (line) Kolonne f; (of people) Schlange f; (retinue) Gefolge nt. **the war brought famine in its** ~ der Krieg brachte eine Hungersnot mit sich. (c) (of events) Folge, Kette f. **he interrupted my** ~ **of thought** er unterbrach meinen Gedankengang. (d) (of dress) Schleppe f.
**train**² **1** vt (a) ausbilden; child erziehen; animal abrichten, dressieren; mind schulen; (Sport) trainieren. **to** ~ **sb as sth** jdn als or zu etw ausbilden; **to** ~ **an animal to do sth** ein Tier dazu abrichten, etw zu tun; **this dog has been** ~**ed to kill** dieser Hund ist aufs Töten abgerichtet. (b) (aim) gun richten (on auf +acc). (c) plant wachsen lassen (over über +acc). **2** vi (a) (esp Sport) trainieren (for für). (b) (study) ausgebildet werden. **he** ~**ed as a teacher** er hat eine Lehrerausbildung gemacht.
**train:** ~ **attendant** n (US Rail) Schlafwagenschaffner m; ~ **driver** n Zug- or Lokführer(in f) m.
**trained** [treɪnd] adj worker gelernt, Fach-; nurse, teacher, voice ausgebildet; animal dressiert; mind, ear, eye geschult.
**trainee** [treɪ'niː] n Anlernling m; (gaining qualification) Auszubildende(r) mf; (academic, technical) Praktikant(in f) m; (nurse) Krankenpflegeschüler(in f) m, Schwesternschülerin f; (management) Trainee mf.
**trainee:** ~ **manager** n Management-Trainee mf; ~ **teacher** n (in primary school) ≈ Praktikant(in f) m; (in secondary school) ≈ Referendar(in f) m.
**trainer** ['treɪnəʳ] n (a) (Sport, of racehorse) Trainer m; (of animals) Dresseur m. (b) (shoe) Turnschuh m. (c) (aircraft) Schulflugzeug nt.
**train:** ~ **fare** n Fahrpreis m; ~ **ferry** n Eisenbahnfähre f.
**training** ['treɪnɪŋ] n Ausbildung f (also Mil); (of staff) Schulung f; (of animal) Dressur f; (Sport) Training nt. **to be in** ~ im Training sein, trainieren; (be fit) gut in Form or durchtrainiert sein; **to be out of** ~ nicht in Form sein, aus dem Training sein.
**training:** ~ **college** n (for teachers) ≈ Pädagogische Hochschule; ~ **course** n Ausbildungskurs m; ~ **scheme** n Ausbildungsprogramm nt; ~ **shoes** npl Trainingsschuhe pl.
**train:** ~ **journey** n Bahnfahrt f; (long) Bahnreise f; ~**load** n (of goods) Zugladung f; ~**loads of holidaymakers** ganze Züge voller Urlauber; ~ **service** n Zugverkehr m; (between two places) (Eisen)bahnverbindung f; ~ **set** n (Spielzeug)eisenbahn f; ~**sick** adj **he gets** ~ **sick** ihm wird beim Zugfahren schlecht or übel; ~**spotter** n ≈ Eisenbahnfan m; ~**spotting** n Hobby nt, bei dem Züge beobachtet und deren Nummern notiert werden; ~ **station** n (US) Bahnhof m.
**traipse** [treɪps] (col) vi latschen (col). **to** ~ **around the shops** in den Geschäften rumlatschen (col).
**trait** [treɪt, treɪ] n Eigenschaft f.
**traitor** ['treɪtəʳ] n Verräter m. **to be a** ~ **to one's country** sein Vaterland verraten; **to turn** ~ zum Verräter werden.
**trajectory** [trə'dʒektərɪ] n Flugbahn f.

**tram** [træm] n (Brit) Straßenbahn f.
**tram** (Brit): ~ **car** n (single car) Straßenbahnwagen m; ~ **driver** n Straßenbahnfahrer(in f) m; ~**line** n (track) Straßenbahnschiene f; (route) Straßenbahnlinie f; ~**lines** npl (Tennis) Linien pl des Doppelspielfelds.
**tramp** [træmp] **1** vi (a) (walk heavily, trudge) stapfen, stampfen. (b) (hike) wandern; (as vagabond) umherziehen. **he** ~**ed all over Europe** er zog durch ganz Europa. **2** vt (a) (spread by walking) herumtreten. **don't** ~ **that mud into the carpet** tritt den Dreck nicht in den Teppich. (b) (walk) streets latschen durch (col). **3** n (vagabond) Landstreicher(in f), Tramp m; (in town) Stadtstreicher(in f) m.
**trample** ['træmpl] **1** vt niedertrampeln, zertrampeln. **to** ~ **sth underfoot** auf etw (dat) herumtrampeln; ~**d to death** zu Tode getrampelt; **to** ~ **sth into the ground** etw in den Boden trampeln. **2** vi **he lets his wife** ~ **all over him** (fig) er läßt sich (dat) von seiner Frau auf dem Kopf herumtanzen.
►**trample on** vi +prep obj herumtreten auf (+dat). **to** ~ ~ **sb** (fig) jdn herumschikanieren; **to** ~ ~ **sb's feelings** (fig) jds Gefühle mit Füßen treten.
**trampoline** ['træmpəlɪn] n Trampolin nt.
**trance** [trɑːns] n Trance f. **to go into a** ~ in einen Trancezustand verfallen.
**tranquil** ['træŋkwɪl] adj ruhig.
**tranquillity**, (US) **tranquility** [træŋ'kwɪlɪtɪ] n Ruhe f.
**tranquillize**, (US) **tranquilize** ['træŋkwɪlaɪz] vt beruhigen.
**tranquillizer**, (US) **tranquilizer** ['træŋkwɪlaɪzəʳ] n Beruhigungsmittel nt.
**trans-** [trænz-] pref trans-, Trans-.
**transact** [træn'zækt] vt abwickeln; deal abschließen.
**transaction** [træn'zækʃən] n (a) (act) see vt Abwicklung f; Abschluß m. ~ **of business** Geschäftsbetrieb m. (b) (piece of business) Geschäft nt; (Fin, St Ex) Transaktion f. (c) ~**s** pl (of society) Sitzungsbericht m.
**transatlantic** ['trænzət'læntɪk] adj transatlantisch, Transatlantik-; customs auf der anderen Seite (des Atlantiks); cousins, accent amerikanisch; (for Americans) britisch.
**transcend** [træn'send] vt übersteigen, überschreiten.
**transcendental** [ˌtrænsen'dentl] adj überirdisch; (Philos) transzendental.
**transcontinental** [ˌtrænzkɒntɪ'nentl] adj transkontinental.
**transcribe** [træn'skraɪb] vt manuscripts abschreiben; (from shorthand) (in Langschrift) übertragen; proceedings etc niederschreiben; (Mus) transkribieren.
**transcript** ['trænskrɪpt] n (of court proceedings) Protokoll nt; (of tapes) Niederschrift f; (copy) Kopie, Abschrift f.
**transcription** [træn'skrɪpʃən] n (Mus, Phon) Transkription f; (copy, of shorthand notes) Abschrift f; (act) Abschreiben nt; (of speech, proceedings) Niederschrift f, Protokoll nt; (Rad, TV: recording) Aufnahme f.
**transept** ['trænsept] n Querschiff nt.
**transfer** [træns'fɜːʳ] **1** vt übertragen (to auf +acc); prisoner überführen (to in +acc); premises, troops, account verlegen (to in +acc, to town nach); soldier, employee versetzen (to in +acc, to town, country nach); (Sport) player abgeben (to an +acc); (Fin) funds, money überweisen (to auf +acc); (Jur) property überschreiben (to auf +acc). **he** ~**red the money from the box to his pocket** er nahm das Geld aus der Schachtel und steckte es in die Tasche.
**2** vi (a) überwechseln (to zu); (to new system,

*working conditions)* umstellen *(to* auf *+acc).* **(b)** *(in travelling)* umsteigen *(to* in *+acc); (Univ)* das Studienfach wechseln, umsatteln *(col) (from ... to* von ... auf *+acc).*

**3** ['trænsfɜːʳ] *n* **(a)** *see vt* Übertragung *f;* Überführung *f;* Verlegung *f;* Versetzung *f; (of footballer)* Transfer *m;* Überweisung *f;* Überschreibung *f.* **he asked for a** ~ *(soldier, employee)* er bat um Versetzung; *(footballer)* er bat, auf die Transferliste gesetzt zu werden. **(b)** *(picture)* Abziehbild *nt.* **(c)** *(~ ticket)* Umsteige(fahr)karte *f.*

**transferable** [træns'fɜːrəbl] *adj* übertragbar; *money, stocks* transferierbar.

**transfer:** ~ **desk** *n (Aviat)* Transitschalter *m;* ~ **fee** *n (Ftbl)* Transfersumme *f;* ~ **list** *n (Ftbl)* Transferliste *f;* ~ **lounge** *n (Aviat)* Transitraum *m.*

**transfigure** [træns'fɪgəʳ] *vt* verklären; *(transform)* verwandeln.

**transfix** [træns'fɪks] *vt* **(a)** *(fix)* annageln, feststecken *(to* an *+acc).* **(b)** *(fig)* lähmen *or* **stand** ~**ed with horror** starr vor Entsetzen sein; **he stood as though** ~**ed** er stand da wie angewurzelt.

**transform** [træns'fɔːm] *vt* umwandeln, umformen *(into* zu); *ideas, views* (von Grund auf) verändern; *person* verwandeln; *(Phys)* umwandeln *(into* in *+acc); (Elec)* (um)wandeln *(into* in *+acc),* transformieren *(into* in *+acc).* **the old house was** ~**ed into three flats** aus dem alten Haus wurden drei Wohnungen gemacht; **the caterpillar was** ~**ed into a butterfly** die Raupe verwandelte sich in einen Schmetterling.

**transformation** [ˌtrænsfə'meɪʃən] *n* Umwandlung, Umformung *f; (of ideas, views etc)* (grundlegende) Veränderung; *(of person, caterpillar etc)* Verwandlung *f; (Phys)* Umwandlung *f; (Elec)* Umwandlung, Transformation *f.*

**transformer** [træns'fɔːməʳ] *n (Elec)* Transformator *m.*

**transfusion** [træns'fjuːʒən] *n (also* **blood** ~*)* Blutübertragung, Transfusion *f.* **to give sb a** ~ jdm eine Blutübertragung geben.

**transgress** [træns'gres] **1** *vt standards* verstoßen gegen, verletzen. **2** *vi* sündigen.

**transgression** [træns'greʃən] *n* **(a)** *(of law)* Verstoß *m,* Verletzung *f.* **(b)** *(sin)* Sünde *f,* Verstoß *m.*

**transience** ['trænzɪəns] *n (of life)* Vergänglichkeit *f; (of grief, joy)* Kurzlebigkeit *f; (of interest)* Flüchtigkeit *f.*

**transient** ['trænzɪənt] **1** *adj* **(a)** *life* vergänglich; *grief, joy* kurzlebig, vorübergehend; *interest* flüchtig. **(b)** *(US)* ~ **population** nichtansässiger Teil der Bevölkerung. **2** *n (US)* Durchreisende(r) *mf.*

**transistor** [træn'zɪstəʳ] *n* **(a)** *(Elec)* Transistor *m.* **(b)** *(also* ~ **radio)** Transistorradio *nt,* Transistor *m (col).*

**transistorized** [træn'zɪstəraɪzd] *adj circuit* transistorisiert.

**transit** ['trænzɪt] *n* Durchfahrt *f,* Transit *m; (of goods)* Transport *m.* **the books were damaged in** ~ die Bücher wurden beim Transport beschädigt; ~ **camp** Durchgangslager *nt.*

**transition** [træn'zɪʃən] *n* Übergang *m (from ... to* von ... zu).

**transitional** [træn'zɪʃənl] *adj* Übergangs-.

**transitive** *adj,* ~**ly** *adv* ['trænzɪtɪv, -lɪ] transitiv.

**transitory** ['trænzɪtərɪ] *adj life* vergänglich; *grief, joy* kurzlebig, vorübergehend; *interest* flüchtig.

**transit visa** *n* Durchreisevisum *nt.*

**translate** [trænz'leɪt] *vti* **(a)** übersetzen; *work of literature also* übertragen. **to** ~ **a text from German (in)to English** einen Text aus dem Deutschen ins Englische übersetzen; **it is** ~**d as ...** es wird mit ...

übersetzt; **his novels** ~ **well (into English)** seine Romane lassen sich gut (ins Englische) übersetzen *or* übertragen. **(b) to** ~ **words into action** Worte in die Tat umsetzen.

**translation** [trænz'leɪʃən] *n* Übersetzung *f (from* aus*); (of work of literature also)* Übertragung *f.* **it loses in** ~ es verliert bei der Übersetzung.

**translator** [trænz'leɪtəʳ] *n* Übersetzer(in *f) m.*

**translucent** [trænz'luːsnt] *adj glass etc* lichtdurchlässig; *skin* durchsichtig.

**transmission** [trænz'mɪʃən] *n* **(a)** *(transmitting)* Übertragung *f; (through heredity)* Vererbung *f; (of news)* Übermittlung *f; (of heat)* Leitung *f; (programme also)* Sendung *f.* **(b)** *(Aut)* Getriebe *nt.* ~ **shaft** Kardanwelle *f.*

**transmit** [trænz'mɪt] *vt (convey) message, information* übermitteln; *sound waves, programme, illness* übertragen; *(by heredity)* vererben; *heat etc* leiten.

**transmitter** [trænz'mɪtəʳ] *n (Tech)* Sender *m; (in telephone)* Mikrofon *nt.*

**transmute** [trænz'mjuːt] *vt* umwandeln *(into* in *+acc); metal* verwandeln *(into* in *+acc).*

**transom** ['trænsəm] *n (crosspiece)* Querbalken *m; (US: fanlight)* Oberlicht *nt.*

**transparency** [træns'pærənsɪ] *n* **(a)** Transparenz, Durchsichtigkeit *f.* **(b)** *(of lies, excuses etc)* Durchschaubarkeit *f.* **(c)** *(Brit Phot)* Dia(positiv) *nt.* **colour** ~ Farbdia *nt.*

**transparent** [træns'pærənt] *adj* **(a)** durchsichtig, transparent. **(b)** *(fig) lie, intentions, personality* durchschaubar; *meaning* klar, eindeutig.

**transpire** [træn'spaɪəʳ] *vi* **(a)** *(become known)* **it now** ~**s that ...** jetzt hat sich herausgestellt, daß ... **(b)** *(happen)* passieren *(col).*

**transplant** [træns'plɑːnt] **1** *vt* **(a)** *(Hort)* umpflanzen. **(b)** *(Med)* verpflanzen. **2** ['trænsplɑːnt] *n (operation)* Verpflanzung, Transplantation *f; (organ)* Transplantat *nt,* verpflanztes Organ. **to have a** ~ sich einer Organverpflanzung unterziehen.

**transport** ['trænspɔːt] **1** *n* **(a)** *(of goods, of troops)* Transport *m.* **Ministry of T**~ Verkehrsministerium *nt;* **have you got your own** ~? bist du motorisiert?; **public** ~ öffentliche Verkehrsmittel *pl.* **(b)** *(US: shipment)* (Schiffs)fracht, Ladung *f.* **(c)** *(liter)* **it sent her into** ~**s of delight** es erfüllte sie mit freudigem Entzücken *(liter).* **2** [træns'pɔːt] *vt* **(a)** *goods* transportieren; *people* befördern; *(Hist) convict* deportieren. **(b)** *(liter)* **to be** ~**ed with joy** freudig entzückt sein *(liter).*

**transportation** [ˌtrænspɔː'teɪʃən] *n* **(a)** Transport *m; (means)* Beförderungsmittel *nt; (public)* Verkehrsmittel *nt; (cost)* Transportkosten *pl.* **Department of T**~ *(US)* Verkehrsministerium *nt.* **(b)** *(Hist: of criminal)* Deportation *f.*

**transport café** *n (Brit)* Fernfahrerlokal *nt.*

**transpose** [træns'pəʊz] *vt* umstellen; *(Mus)* transponieren.

**transship** [træns'ʃɪp] *vt* umschiffen.

**transverse** ['trænzvɜːs] *adj beam, bar, section* Quer-; *position* horizontal; *engine* querstehend.

**transvestite** [trænz'vestaɪt] *n* Transvestit *m.*

**trap** [træp] **1** *n* **(a)** *(for animal, fig)* Falle *f.* **to set** *or* **lay a** ~ **for an animal** eine Falle für ein Tier (auf)stellen; **to set a** ~ **for sb** *(fig)* jdm eine Falle stellen; **he is caught in a** ~ er sitzt in der Falle; **to fall into a** ~ in die Falle gehen. **(b)** *(vehicle)* zweirädriger Pferdewagen. **(c)** *(col: mouth)* Klappe *(col).* **shut your** ~! halt die Klappe! *(col).*

**2** *vt* **(a)** *animal* (mit einer Falle) fangen. **(b)** *(fig) person* in die Falle locken. **he realized he was** ~**ped** er merkte, daß er in der Falle saß; **to** ~ **sb into**

**saying sth** jdn dazu bringen, etw zu sagen. **(c)** *(block off, leave no escape)* in die Enge treiben. **the miners are ~ped** die Bergleute sind eingeschlossen; **my arm was ~ped** mein Arm war eingeklemmt. **(d)** *(catch)* *(Sport)* **ball** stoppen. **to ~ one's finger in the door** sich *(dat)* den Finger in der Tür einklemmen. **(e)** *gas, liquid* stauen.

**trapdoor** [ˌtræpˈdɔːr] *n* Falltür *f*; *(Theat)* Versenkung *f*.

**trapeze** [trəˈpiːz] *n* *(in circus)* Trapez *nt*. **~ artist** Trapezkünstler(in *f*) *m*.

**trapper** [ˈtræpər] *n* Fallensteller, Trapper *m*.

**trappings** [ˈtræpɪŋz] *npl* (äußeres) Drum and Dran *(col)*; *(of power)* Insignien *pl*. **~ of office** Amtsinsignien *pl*.

**trash** [træʃ] *n* **(a)** *(US: refuse)* Abfall *m*. **(b)** *(goods)* Ramsch *m*; *(book, play etc)* Schund *m*; *(pop group etc)* Mist, Schrott *m* *(col)*. **don't talk ~** red nicht so einen Quatsch *(col)*.

**trashcan** [ˈtræʃkæn] *n* *(US)* Mülltonne *f*. **~ liner** Müllsack *m*.

**trashy** [ˈtræʃɪ] *adj* *(+er)* **goods** minderwertig; **play** *also* Schund-.

**trauma** [ˈtrɔːmə] *n* *(Psych)* Trauma *nt*.

**traumatic** [trɔːˈmætɪk] *adj* traumatisch.

**travel** [ˈtrævl] *(vb: pret, ptp* **travelled**, *(US)* **traveled)* **1** *vi* **(a)** *(make a journey)* reisen. **he ~s to work by car** er fährt mit dem Auto zur Arbeit; **she is ~ling to London tomorrow** sie fährt morgen nach London; **they ~led for 500 miles** sie fuhren 800 km; **to ~ around a country** ein Land bereisen. **(b)** *(go, move)* sich bewegen; *(sound, light)* sich fortpflanzen. **light ~s at …** die Lichtgeschwindigkeit beträgt …; **we were ~ling at 50 mph** wir fuhren 80 km/h; **the electricity ~s along the wire** der Strom fließt durch den Draht; **that's ~ling!** *(col)* das ist aber schnell! **(c)** *(Comm)* Vertreter sein. **he ~s in ladies' underwear** er reist in Damenunterwäsche. **(d)** *(Tech)* **as the piston ~s from A to B** während sich der Kolben von A nach B bewegt.

**2** *vt* **area** bereisen; **distance** zurücklegen; **route** fahren.

**3** *n* **(a)** Reisen *nt*. **to be fond of ~** gerne reisen; **if you meet him on your ~s** wenn Sie mit einer Ihrer Reisen begegnen; **he's off on his ~s again** er verreist wieder. **(b)** *(Tech: distance moved)* Weg *m*; *(of piston)* Hub *m*.

**travel: ~ agency** *n* Reisebüro *nt*; **~ agent** *n* Reisebürokaufmann *m*; *(of package tours)* Reiseveranstalter *m*; **~ brochure** *n* Reiseprospekt *m*; **~ insurance** *n* Reiseversicherung *f*.

**travelled**, *(US)* **traveled** [ˈtrævld] *adj* **well-~** *person* weitgereist *attr*, weit gereist *pred*; *route* vielbefahren *attr*, viel befahren *pred*.

**traveller**, *(US)* **traveler** [ˈtrævlər] *n* **(a)** Reisende(r) *mf*. **I am a very poor** *or* **bad ~** ich vertrage das Reisen nicht. **(b)** *(also* **commercial ~)** Vertreter *m*.

**traveller's cheque**, *(US)* **traveler's check** *n* Reisescheck, Travellerscheck *m*.

**travelling**, *(US)* **traveling** [ˈtrævlɪŋ] *n* Reisen *nt*. **I hate ~** ich hasse das Reisen.

**travelling: ~ bag** *n* Reisetasche *f*; **~ circus** *n* Wanderzirkus *m*; **~ clock** *n* Reisewecker *m*; **~ exhibition** *n* Wanderausstellung *f*; **~ expenses** *npl* Reisekosten *pl*; *(on business)* Reisespesen *pl*; **~ salesman** *n* Vertreter, Handelsreisende(r) *m*.

**travelogue,** *(US)* **travelog** [ˈtrævəlɒg] *n* Reisebericht *m*.

**travel: ~-sick** *adj* reisekrank; **~-sickness** *n* Reisekrankheit *f*.

**traverse** [ˈtrævɜːs] *vt* *(cross)* **land** durchqueren; *(bridge, person)* **water** überqueren; *(Mountaineering)* **ice, slope** queren.

**travesty** [ˈtrævɪstɪ] *n* *(Liter)* Travestie *f*. **a ~ of justice** ein Hohn *m* auf die Gerechtigkeit; **the elections were a ~** die Wahlen waren ein Hohn *m* *or* eine Farce.

**trawl** [trɔːl] **1** *n* *(net)* Schleppnetz, Trawl *nt*; *(US: ~ line)* Grundleine *f*. **2** *vi* mit dem Schleppnetz fischen; *(US)* mit einer Grundleine fischen.

**trawler** [ˈtrɔːlər] *n* Fischdampfer, Trawler *m*.

**trawlerman** [ˈtrɔːləmən] *n*, *pl* **-men** [-mən] Trawlerfischer *m*.

**tray** [treɪ] *n* Tablett *nt*; *(of cakes)* *(small)* Platte *f*; *(big)* Brett *nt*; *(for display)* Auslagekästchen *nt*; *(baking ~)* (Back)blech *nt*; *(for papers, mail)* Ablage(korb *m*) *f*.

**treacherous** [ˈtretʃərəs] *adj* **(a)** *person, action* verräterisch. **(b)** *(unreliable)* trügerisch. **(c)** *(dangerous)* tückisch; *ice, smile* trügerisch.

**treacherously** [ˈtretʃərəslɪ] *adv see adj*.

**treachery** [ˈtretʃərɪ] *n* Verrat *m*.

**treacle** [ˈtriːkl] *n* *(Brit)* Sirup *m*.

**tread** [tred] *(vb: pret* **trod**, *ptp* **trodden)* **1** *n* **(a)** Schritt *m*. **to walk with a heavy ~** mit schweren Schritten gehen; **I could hear his ~ on the stairs** ich konnte seine Schritte auf der Treppe hören. **(b)** *(of stair)* Stufe *f*; *(of shoe, tyre)* Profil *nt*. **2** *vi* **(a)** *(walk)* gehen. **(b)** *(bring foot down)* treten *(on auf +acc)*. **he trod on my foot** er trat mir auf den Fuß; **to ~ softly** leise auftreten; **to ~ carefully** *(lit)* vorsichtig gehen; *(fig)* vorsichtig vorgehen. **3** *vt* **paint** treten; *(follow)* gehen. **it got trodden underfoot** es wurde zertreten; **to ~ grapes** Trauben stampfen; **to ~ water** Wasser treten; **don't ~ that earth into the carpet** treten Sie die Erde nicht in den Teppich.

**treadle** [ˈtredl] *n* *(of sewing machine)* Tretkurbel *f*.

**treadmill** [ˈtredmɪl] *n* *(lit)* Tretwerk *nt*; *(fig)* Tretmühle *f*.

**treason** [ˈtriːzn] *n* Verrat *m* *(to an +dat)*. **an act of ~** Verrat *m*.

**treasure** [ˈtreʒər] **1** *n* *(lit, fig)* Schatz *m*. **2** *vt* (hoch)schätzen. **I shall always ~ this memory** ich werde das immer in lieber Erinnerung behalten.

**treasure: ~ house** *n* **a ~ house of knowledge** eine Fundgrube des Wissens; **~ hunt** *n* Schatzsuche *f*.

**treasurer** [ˈtreʒərər] *n* *(of club)* Kassenwart *m*; *(city ~)* Stadtkämmerer *m*; *(of business)* Leiter *m* der Finanzabteilung.

**treasure trove** *n* Schatzfund *m*; *(place where treasures are found)* Fundgrube *f*.

**treasury** [ˈtreʒərɪ] *n* **(a)** *(Pol)* T~, *(US also)* T~ Department Finanzministerium *nt*; **~ bill** *(Brit)* kurzfristiger Schatzwechsel. **(b)** *(anthology)* Schatzkästlein *nt*.

**treat** [triːt] **1** *vi* **(a)** *(behave towards, handle, process, Med)* behandeln; **sewage** klären; **wastepaper** verarbeiten. **he is being ~ed for thrombosis** er ist wegen einer Thrombose in Behandlung. **(b)** *(consider)* betrachten *(as als)*. **you should ~ your work more seriously** Sie sollten Ihre Arbeit ernster nehmen. **(c)** *(pay for, give)* einladen. **to ~ sb to sth** jdn zu etw einladen, jdm etw spendieren; **I'm ~ing you** ich lade Sie ein; **to ~ oneself to sth** sich *(dat)* etw gönnen.

**2** *n* **(a)** besondere Freude. **children's ~** Kinderfest *nt*; **it's my ~** das geht auf meine Kosten; **it's a ~ in store** das ist etwas, worauf wir uns noch freuen können; **it's a (real) ~ to see you again** was für eine Freude, Sie mal wiederzusehen! **(b)** *(col)* **it's coming on a ~** es macht sich prima *(col)*.

**treatise** [ˈtriːtɪz] *n* Abhandlung *f* *(on über +acc)*.

**treatment** ['triːtmənt] *n* **(a)** *(of person, object)* Behandlung *f.* **their** ~ **of foreigners** ihre Art, Ausländer zu behandeln; **to give sb the** ~ *(col: violently, sexually)* es jdm ordentlich besorgen *(col)*; **when the delegates visited the factory, they were given the full** ~ *(col)* als die Delegierten die Fabrik besichtigten, wurde eine große Schau abgezogen *(col)*. **(b)** *(Med)* Behandlung *f.* **there are many** ~**s for rheumatism** es gibt viele Behandlungsarten für Rheumatismus; **to be having** ~ **for sth** wegen etw in Behandlung sein. **(c)** *(processing)* Behandlung *f*; *(of leather also)* Bearbeitung *f*; *(of sewage)* Klärung *f*; *(of wastepaper)* Verarbeitung *f.* **(d)** *(of subject)* Bearbeitung *f.*

**treaty** ['triːtɪ] *n* Vertrag *m.*

**treble**[1] ['trebl] **1** *adj* dreifach. **the country's inflation rate is in** ~ **figures** das Land hat eine dreistellige Inflationsrate. **2** *adv* **clothes are** ~ **the price here** Kleidung kostet hier dreimal soviel. **3** *vt* verdreifachen. **4** *vi* sich verdreifachen.

**treble**[2] **1** *n* *(Mus)* *(boy's voice)* Knabensopran *m or* -stimme *f*; *(part)* Oberstimme *f*; *(range: of voice, piano)* Diskant *m.* **the** ~ *(in recording etc)* die Höhen *pl.* **2** *adj voice* Knabensopran-. ~ **clef** Violinschlüssel *m*; ~ **part** Oberstimme *f.*

**tree** [triː] *n* **(a)** Baum *m.* **an oak/a cherry** ~ eine Eiche/ein Kirschbaum *m*; **money doesn't grow on** ~**s** das Geld fällt nicht vom Himmel. **(b)** *(family* ~*)* Stammbaum *m.*

**tree** *in cpds* Baum-; ~ **house** *n* Baumhaus *nt*; ~**less** *adj* baumlos; ~ **line** *n* Baumgrenze *f*; ~**lined** *adj* baumbestanden; ~**top** *n* Baumkrone *f*, Wipfel *m*; ~ **trunk** *n* Baumstamm *m.*

**trek** [trek] **1** *vi* trecken; *(col: traipse)* latschen *(col)*. **they** ~**ked across the desert** sie zogen durch die Wüste. **2** *n* Treck, Zug *m*; *(col)* anstrengender Marsch.

**trellis** ['trelɪs] *n* Gitter *nt*; *(for plants)* Spalier *nt.*

**tremble** ['trembl] **1** *vi* *(person, hand etc)* zittern *(with* vor*)*; *(voice also)* beben *(with* vor*)*; *(ground, building)* beben, zittern. **2** *n* Zittern, Beben *nt.* **to be all of a** ~ *(col)* am ganzen Körper zittern.

**trembling** ['tremblɪŋ] *see vi* **1** *adj* zitternd; bebend. **2** *n* Zittern, Beben *nt.*

**tremendous** [trə'mendəs] *adj* **(a)** gewaltig, enorm; *size, crowd also* riesig; *success* Riesen-. **(b)** *(very good)* klasse *(col)*, toll *(col)*. **we had a** ~ **time** wir haben uns ganz toll amüsiert.

**tremendously** [trə'mendəslɪ] *adv* sehr; *fat, tall etc also* enorm; *relieved, grateful, dangerous also* ungeheuer; *intelligent, difficult also* äußerst. **they enjoyed themselves** ~ sie haben sich prächtig amüsiert *(col)*.

**tremor** ['tremər] *n* Zittern, Beben *nt*; *(Med)* Tremor *m*; *(of emotion)* Zucken *nt*; *(earth* ~*)* Beben *nt.*

**tremulous** ['tremjʊləs] *adj voice* bebend; *(timid)* *smile, person* zaghaft.

**trench** [trentʃ] *n* Graben *m*; *(Mil)* Schützengraben *m.* **in the** ~**es** *(Mil)* im Schützengraben.

**trenchant** ['trentʃənt] *adj language* treffsicher; *style* prägnant; *satire* beißend; *speech* pointiert; *wit, criticism* scharf.

**trench:** ~ **coat** *n* Trenchcoat *m*; ~ **warfare** *n* Grabenkrieg *m.*

**trend** [trend] **1** *n* **(a)** *(tendency)* Tendenz *f*, Trend *m.* **the** ~ **towards violence** die Tendenz zur Gewalttätigkeit; **upward** ~ steigende Tendenz, Aufwärtstrend *m*; **the downward** ~ **in the birth rate** die Rückläufigkeit der Geburtenrate; **to set a** ~ richtungweisend sein. **(b)** *(fashion)* Mode *f*, Trend *m.* **2** *vi* verlaufen *(towards* nach*)*.

**trend:** ~**setter** *n* Trendsetter *m*; ~**setting** *adj* richtungweisend, tonangebend.

**trendy** ['trendɪ] **1** *adj (+er)* in *pred (col)*; *(fashionable)* modisch. **to be** ~ als schick gelten; *(clothes etc also)* gerade modern sein. **2** *n* *(person)* Schicki(micki) *m (col)*.

**trepidation** [ˌtrepɪ'deɪʃən] *n* Beklommenheit, Ängstlichkeit *f.* **full of** ~ **he knocked on the door** voll ängstlicher Erwartung klopfte er an die Tür.

**trespass** ['trespəs] **1** *vi* *(on property)* unbefugt betreten *(on sth* etw *acc)*. **to** ~ **(up)on sb's privacy** jds Privatsphäre verletzen; **to** ~ **(up)on sb's time** jds Zeit beanspruchen; **"no** ~**ing"** „Betreten verboten". **2** *n (Jur)* unbefugtes Betreten.

**trespasser** ['trespəsər] *n* Unbefugte(r) *mf.* **"**~**s will be prosecuted"** „Betreten durch Unbefugte wird strafrechtlich verfolgt".

**trestle** ['tresl] *n* Bock *m.* ~ **table** auf Böcken stehender Tisch; *(decorator's)* Tapeziertisch *m.*

**trial** ['traɪəl] *n* **(a)** *(Jur)* (Gerichts)verfahren *nt*, Prozeß *m*; *(actual hearing)* Verhandlung *f.* **to be on** ~ angeklagt sein; **to be on** ~ **for theft** des Diebstahls angeklagt sein; **at the** ~ bei der Verhandlung; **to bring sb to** ~ jdm den Prozeß machen; ~ **by jury** Schwurgerichtsverfahren *nt.* **(b)** *(test)* Versuch *m*, Probe *f.* ~**s** *(of machine, aeroplane)* Test(s *pl*) *m*; *(Sport)* Qualifikationsspiel *nt*; **horse** ~**s** Querfeldeinrennen *nt*; **to give sth a** ~ etw ausprobieren; **to give sb a** ~ *(for job)* jdn auf Probe anstellen; **to take sth on** ~ etw zur Probe *or* etw probeweise nehmen; ~ **of strength** Kraftprobe *f*; **by** ~ **and error** durch Ausprobieren. **(c)** *(hardship)* Unannehmlichkeit *f*; *(nuisance)* Plage *f*, Problem *nt* *(to* für*)*. **he's a** ~ **to his mother** er macht seiner Mutter sehr viel Kummer; ~**s and tribulations** Schwierigkeiten *pl.*

**trial:** ~ **basis** *n* **on a** ~ **basis** auf Probe; ~ **offer** *n* Einführungsangebot *nt*; ~ **pack** *n* Probepackung *f*; ~ **period** *n* Probezeit *f*; ~ **run** *n* Generalprobe *f*; *(with car etc)* Probefahrt *f*; *(of machine)* Probelauf *m*; **give the new method a** ~ **run** probieren Sie die neue Methode einmal aus.

**triangle** ['traɪæŋgl] *n* Dreieck *nt*; *(set square)* (Zeichen)dreieck *nt*; *(Mus)* Triangel *m*; *(fig: relationship)* Dreiecksbeziehung *f.*

**triangular** [traɪ'æŋgjʊlər] *adj (Math)* dreieckig. ~ **relationship** Dreiecksverhältnis *nt.*

**tribal** ['traɪbəl] *adj customs, dance* Stammes-.

**tribalism** ['traɪbəlɪzəm] *n* Tribalismus *m.*

**tribe** [traɪb] *n* Stamm *m.*

**tribesman** ['traɪbzmən] *n, pl* **-men** [-mən] Stammesangehörige(r) *m.*

**tribulation** [ˌtrɪbjʊ'leɪʃən] *n* Kummer *m no pl.* ~**s** Sorgen *pl*; *(less serious)* Kümmernisse *pl.*

**tribunal** [traɪ'bjuːnl] *n* Gericht(shof *m*) *nt*; *(inquiry)* Untersuchungsausschuß *m.*

**tributary** ['trɪbjʊtərɪ] *n (river)* Nebenfluß *m.*

**tribute** ['trɪbjuːt] *n* Tribut *m.* **to pay** ~ **to sb/sth** jdm/einer Sache (den schuldigen) Tribut zollen; **in** ~ **to sb** jdm zu Ehren; ~**s have been coming in from all over the world** aus der ganzen Welt kamen Zeichen der Anerkennung.

**trice** [traɪs] *n:* **in a** ~ im Handumdrehen, im Nu.

**trick** [trɪk] **1** *n* **(a)** *(ruse)* Trick *m.* **be careful, it's a** ~ paß auf, das ist eine Falle!; **he knows a** ~ **or two** *(col)* der kennt sich aus; **he knows all the** ~**s of the trade** er ist ein alter Hase; *(is crafty)* er ist mit allen Wassern gewaschen. **(b)** *(mischief)* Streich *m.* **to play a** ~ **on sb** jdm einen Streich spielen; **the car's started playing** ~**s again** der Wagen fängt wieder an zu mucken *(col)*; **a dirty** ~ ein ganz gemeiner Trick; **how's** ~**s?** *(col)* wie geht's? **(c)** *(skilful act)* Kunststück *nt.* **to teach a dog to do** ~**s** einem Hund

Kunststücke beibringen; **there's a special ~ to it** da ist ein Trick dabei; **that should do the ~** *(col)* das müßte eigentlich hinhauen *(col)*; **he doesn't miss a ~** *(col)* er läßt sich nichts entgehen. **(d)** *(habit)* Eigenart *f.* **to have a ~ of doing sth** die Eigenart haben, etw zu tun. **(e)** *(Cards)* Stich *m.* **to take a ~** einen Stich machen.
  **2** *attr cigar, spider* als Scherzartikel.
  **3** *vt* hereinlegen *(col)*. **I've been ~ed!** ich bin hereingelegt *or* übers Ohr gehauen *(col)* worden!; **to ~ sb into doing sth** jdn (mit einem Trick) dazu bringen, etw zu tun.

**trickery** ['trɪkərɪ] *n* Tricks *pl (col)*. **a piece of ~** ein Trick *m*; **that's just verbal ~** das ist bloß ein raffinierter Trick mit Worten.

**trickle** ['trɪkl] **1** *vi* **(a)** *(liquid)* tröpfeln, tropfen; *(sand)* rieseln; *(ball)* trudeln *(col)*. **tears ~d down her cheeks** Tränen kullerten ihr über die Wangen; **the rain ~d down his neck** der Regen tropfte ihm in den Kragen. **(b)** *(fig)* **people began to ~ back in** die Leute begannen, vereinzelt wieder hereinzukommen; **reports are beginning to ~ in** langsam treffen die ersten Berichte ein. **3** *n* **(a)** *(of liquid)* Tröpfeln *nt*; *(stream)* Rinnsal *nt.* **(b)** *(fig)* **a constant ~ of people gradually filled the lecture hall** der Hörsaal füllte sich langsam aber stetig mit Leuten; **profits have been reduced to a ~** die Gewinne sind spärlich geworden.

**trick: ~ photography** *n* Trickfotografie *f*; **~ question** *n* Fangfrage *f.*

**trickster** ['trɪkstə<sup>r</sup>] *n* Schwindler(in *f*) *m.*

**tricky** ['trɪkɪ] *adj (+er)* **(a)** *(difficult)* schwierig; *(fiddly also)* knifflig. **(b)** *situation, problem* heikel, kitzlig. **(c)** *(sly, crafty) person, plan* durchtrieben, gerissen.

**tricolour,** *(US)* **tricolor** ['trɪkələ<sup>r</sup>] *n* Trikolore *f.*

**tricycle** ['traɪsɪkl] *n* Dreirad *nt.*

**tried** [traɪd] *adj* erprobt, bewährt.

**trier** ['traɪə<sup>r</sup>] *n:* **to be a (hard) ~** sich *(dat)* (ernsthaft) Mühe geben.

**trifle** ['traɪfl] *n* **(a)** Kleinigkeit *f*; *(trivial matter also)* Lappalie *(col)*, Nichtigkeit *f.* **more cake? — just a ~, thank you** noch etwas Kuchen? — bloß ein ganz kleines Stückchen, bitte; **a ~ hot/small** ein bißchen heiß/klein; **a ~ too ...** ein wenig *or* eine Spur zu ... **(b)** *(Cook)* Trifle *nt, kuchenartige Süßspeise.*
  ►**trifle with** *vi* +*prep obj affections* spielen mit. **he is not to be ~d** ~ mit ihm ist nicht zu spaßen.

**trifling** ['traɪflɪŋ] *adj* unbedeutend, geringfügig.

**trigger** ['trɪgə<sup>r</sup>] **1** *n (of gun)* Abzug *m*; *(of cine-camera, machine)* Auslöser *m*; *(Elec)* Trigger *m.* **to pull the ~** abdrücken. **2** *vt (also ~ off)* auslösen.

**trigger-happy** ['trɪgə,hæpɪ] *adj (col)* schießfreudig *(col)*, schießwütig *(pej)*.

**trigonometry** [,trɪgə'nɒmɪtrɪ] *n* Trigonometrie *f.*

**trike** [traɪk] *n (col)* Dreirad *nt.*

**trilby** ['trɪlbɪ] *n (also ~ hat)* weicher Filzhut.

**trill** [trɪl] **1** *n* **(a)** *(of bird)* Trillern *nt*; *(of voice)* Tremolo *nt.* **(b)** *(Mus)* Triller *m.* **2** *vti (birds, Mus)* trillern; *(person)* trällern.

**trillion** ['trɪljən] *n (Brit)* Trillion *f*; *(US)* Billion *f.*

**trilogy** ['trɪlədʒɪ] *n* Trilogie *f.*

**trim** [trɪm] **1** *adj (+er)* sauber; *appearance also* adrett; *haircut* gepflegt. **he keeps his garden very ~** sein Garten ist immer sehr gepflegt. **2** *n* **(a) in good ~** *(house, car etc)* in gutem Zustand; *(person)* gut in Form; **to get into ~** sich in Form bringen. **(b)** *(col)* **to give sth a ~** etw schneiden; *(tree, hedge, beard also)* etw stutzen; **your hair needs a ~** du mußt dir die Haare etwas nachschneiden lassen. **(c)** *(in car)* Innenausstattung *f.* **3** *vt* **(a)** *(cut) hair* nachschneiden; *beard, hedge* stutzen; *dog* trim-

men; *wick, roses* beschneiden; *piece of wood* zurechtschneiden. **(b)** *(fig: cut down) budget, essay* kürzen. **(c)** *(decorate) dress* besetzen; *Christmas tree* schmücken. **(d)** *boat, plane* trimmen; *sails* richtig stellen. **(e)** *(US col) (defeat)* schlagen; *(cheat)* übers Ohr hauen *(col)*.

**trimming** ['trɪmɪŋ] *n* **(a)** *(on clothes)* Besatz *m.* **~s** Verzierung(en *pl*) *f.* **(b)** **~s** *pl (cuttings)* Abfälle *pl*; *(of paper also)* Papierschnitzel *pl.* **(c)** **~s** *pl (accessories)* Zubehör *nt*; **roast beef with all the ~s** Roastbeef mit allem Drum und Dran *(col)*.

**Trinidad** ['trɪnɪdæd] *n* Trinidad *nt.*

**Trinidadian** [trɪnɪ'dædɪən] **1** *adj* trinidadisch. **2** Trinidader(in *f*) *m.*

**Trinity** ['trɪnɪtɪ] *n* Dreifaltigkeit *f.* **~ Sunday** Trinitatis, Dreifaltigkeitsfest *nt.*

**trinket** ['trɪŋkɪt] *n* Schmuckstück *nt.* **~ box** Schmuckkästchen *nt.*

**trio** ['trɪəʊ] *n* Trio *nt*; *(for/of singers)* Terzett *nt.*

**trip** [trɪp] **1** *n* **(a)** *(journey)* Reise *f*; *(excursion)* Ausflug *m*, Tour *f*; *(shorter also)* Trip *m (col)*. **when was your last ~ to the dentist's?** wann waren Sie zuletzt beim Zahnarzt?; **he is away on a ~/a ~ to Canada** er ist auf Reisen/macht zur Zeit eine Reise nach Kanada; **to take a ~** eine Reise machen, verreisen. **(b)** *(col: on drugs)* Trip *m (col)*. **2** *vi* **(a)** *(stumble)* stolpern *(on, over* über *+acc)*. **(b)** *(skip)* trippeln. **to ~ in/out** hinein-/hinaustrippeln. **3** *vt* **(a)** *(make fall)* stolpern lassen; *(deliberately also)* ein Bein stellen *(+dat)*. **(b)** *(Mech) lever* betätigen; *mechanism* auslösen.
  ►**trip over** *vi* stolpern *(+prej obj* über *+acc)*.
  ►**trip up 1** *vi* **(a)** stolpern. **(b)** *(fig)* sich vertun. **2** *vt sep* **(a)** *(make fall)* zum Stolpern bringen. **(b)** *(fig: cause to make mistake)* eine Falle stellen *(+dat)*.

**tripartite** [,traɪ'pɑːtaɪt] *adj agreement, talks* dreiseitig; *division* Drei-.

**tripe** [traɪp] *n* **(a)** *(Cook)* Kaldaunen, Kutteln *(SGer, Aus, Sw) pl.* **(b)** *(fig col)* Quatsch *m.*

**triple** ['trɪpl] **1** *adj* dreifach. **~ jump** Dreisprung *m.* **2** *adv* dreimal soviel. **it's ~ the distance** es ist dreimal so weit. **3** *n* Dreifache(s) *nt.* **4** *vt* verdreifachen. **5** *vi* sich verdreifachen.

**triplet** ['trɪplɪt] *n* **(a)** *(baby)* Drilling *m.* **(b)** *(Mus)* Triole *f.*

**triplicate** ['trɪplɪkɪt] *n:* **in ~** in dreifacher Ausfertigung.

**tripod** ['traɪpɒd] *n (Phot)* Stativ *nt.*

**Tripoli** ['trɪpəlɪ] *n* Tripolis *nt.*

**tripper** ['trɪpə<sup>r</sup>] *n* Ausflügler(in *f*) *m.*

**trip: ~ recorder** *n (Aut)* Tageszähler *m*; **~ wire** *n* Stolperdraht *m.*

**trite** [traɪt] *adj (+er) (trivial, banal)* banal; *(hackneyed)* abgedroschen.

**triumph** ['traɪʌmf] **1** *n* Triumph *m (over* über *+acc)*. **in ~** triumphierend, im Triumph; **shouts of ~** Triumphgeschrei *nt.* **2** *vi* den Sieg davontragen *(over* über *+acc)*. **to ~ over sb/sth** über jdn/etw triumphieren.

**triumphal** [traɪ'ʌmfəl] *adj* triumphal. **~ arch** Triumphbogen *m.*

**triumphant** [traɪ'ʌmfənt] *adj (victorious)* siegreich; *(rejoicing)* triumphierend; *moment, success* triumphal. **to be ~ (over sth)** (über etw *acc*) triumphieren.

**triumphantly** [traɪ'ʌmfəntlɪ] *adv* triumphierend.

**trivia** ['trɪvɪə] *npl* Belanglosigkeiten *pl.*

**trivial** ['trɪvɪəl] *adj* **(a)** trivial; *objection, loss, details also* belanglos. **(b)** *person* oberflächlich.

**triviality** [,trɪvɪ'ælɪtɪ] *n see adj* **(a)** Trivialität *f*; Belanglosigkeit *f.*

**trivialize** ['trɪvɪəlaɪz] *vt* trivialisieren.
**trod** [trɒd] *pret of* **tread.**
**trodden** ['trɒdn] *ptp of* **tread.**
**trolley** ['trɒlɪ] *n* (a) *(Brit: cart) (four wheels)* Handwagen *m*; *(in supermarket)* Einkaufswagen *m*; *(in station)* Gepäckwagen *m*; *(for passengers)* Kofferkuli *m*; *(two wheels) (for golf clubs)* Caddy *m*; *(in station, factory etc)* Sackkarre *f*; *(tea-~)* Teewagen *m*. (b) *(Rail)* Lore *f*, Förderkarren *m*. (c) **to be off one's ~** *(col)* nicht mehr alle Tassen im Schrank haben *(col)*.
**trolley: ~bus** *n* Obus, Oberleitungsomnibus *(form) m*; **~-car** *n (US)* Straßenbahn *f*.
**trombone** [trɒm'bəʊn] *n (Mus)* Posaune *f*.
**trombonist** [trɒm'bəʊnɪst] *n* Posaunist (in *f*) *m*.
**troop** [truːp] **1** *n* (a) *(Mil: of cavalry)* Trupp *m*; *(unit)* Schwadron *f*. (b) *(Mil)* **~s** *pl* Truppen *pl*; **200 ~s** 200 Soldaten. (c) *(of scouts)* Stamm *m*. (d) *(of people)* Horde *(pej)*, Schar *f*. **2** *vi* **to ~ out/in** hinaus-/hineinströmen; **to ~ past sth** an etw *(dat)* vorbeiziehen. **3** *vi (Mil)* **to ~ the colours** die Fahnenparade abhalten.
**troop-carrier** ['truːpˌkærɪər] *n (vehicle)* Truppentransporter *m*.
**trooper** ['truːpər] *n (Mil)* Kavallerist *m*; *(US: state ~)* Polizist *m*. **to swear like a ~** wie ein Kutscher fluchen.
**troop-ship** ['truːpˌʃɪp] *n* (Truppen)transportschiff *nt*.
**trophy** ['trəʊfɪ] *n (Mil, Sport)* Trophäe *f*.
**tropic** ['trɒpɪk] *n* (a) Wendekreis *m*. **T~ of Cancer/Capricorn** Wendekreis des Krebses/Steinbocks. (b) **~s** *pl* Tropen *pl*.
**tropical** ['trɒpɪkəl] *adj* tropisch, Tropen-.
**trot** [trɒt] **1** *n* (a) *(pace)* Trab *m*. **to go at a ~** traben; **to go for a ~** einen Ausritt machen; **I've been on the ~ all day** *(fig col)* ich bin schon den ganzen Tag auf Trab. (b) *(Brit col)* **for five days on the ~** fünf Tage lang in einer Tour. **2** *vi (horse, person)* traben; *(pony)* zockeln; *(small child)* trippeln.
▶**trot out** *vt sep excuses, list* aufwarten mit.
**trotter** ['trɒtər] *n (of animal)* Fuß *m*. **pigs' ~s** *(Cook)* Schweinsfüße *pl*.
**trouble** ['trʌbl] **1** *n* (a) Ärger *m*; *(difficulties)* Schwierigkeiten *pl*. **did you have any ~ (in) getting it?** hatten Sie Schwierigkeiten, es zu bekommen?; **to be in ~** in Schwierigkeiten sein; **to be in ~ with sb** mit jdm Schwierigkeiten *or* Ärger haben; **to get into ~** in Schwierigkeiten geraten; *(with authority)* Ärger bekommen *(with mit)*; **to get sb into ~** jdn in Schwierigkeiten bringen *(with mit)*; **to get a girl into ~** *(euph)* ein Mädchen ins Unglück bringen; **to make ~** *(cause a row etc)* Krach schlagen *(col)*, Ärger machen; **that's/you're asking for ~** das kann ja nicht gutgehen; **what's the ~?** was ist los?; *(to sick person)* wo fehlt's?; **the ~ is that ...** das Problem ist, daß ...; **that's the ~** das ist das Problem; **family/money ~s** Familien-/Geldsorgen *pl*; **heart/back ~** ein Herz-/Rückenleiden *nt*; **engine ~** (ein) Motorschaden *m*.
(b) *(bother, effort)* Mühe *f*. **it's no ~ (at all)!** das mache ich doch gern; **thank you — (it was) no ~** vielen Dank — (das ist) gern geschehen; **it's not worth the ~** das ist nicht der Mühe wert; **nothing is too much ~ for her** nichts ist ihr zuviel; **to go to the ~ (of doing sth), to take the ~ (to do sth)** sich *(dat)* die Mühe machen (, etw zu tun); **to take a lot of ~ (over *or* with sth)** sich *(dat)* (mit etw) viel Mühe geben; **to put sb to a lot of ~** jdm viel Mühe machen.
(c) *(unrest, upheaval)* Unruhe *f*. **labour ~s** Arbeiterunruhen *pl*; **he made ~ between them** er hat Unruhe zwischen ihnen gestiftet.
**2** *vt* (a) *(worry)* beunruhigen; *(disturb, grieve)* bekümmern. **to be ~d by sth** wegen etw besorgt sein; **his eyes ~ him** seine Augen machen ihm zu schaffen. (b) *(bother)* bemühen, belästigen. **I'm sorry to ~ you, but could you tell me if ...** entschuldigen Sie die Störung, aber könnten Sie mir sagen, ob ...; **may I ~ you for a light?** darf ich Sie um Feuer bitten?; **I shan't ~ you with the details** ich werde Ihnen die Einzelheiten ersparen; **to ~ to do sth** sich bemühen, etw zu tun; **please don't ~ yourself** bitte bemühen Sie sich nicht.
**troubled** ['trʌbld] *adj person, look* unruhig, beunruhigt; *(grieved)* bekümmert; *times* unruhig. **the ~ waters of race relations** die gestörten Beziehungen zwischen den Rassen.
**trouble: ~-free** *adj period, process, car* problemlos; *relationship also* reibungslos; *area* ruhig; *machine* störungsfrei; **~maker** *n* Unruhestifter(in *f*) *m*; **~shooter** *n (Pol, Ind: mediator)* Vermittler(in *f*) *m*; **~some** *adj (bothersome)* lästig; *person, problem* schwierig; **~ spot** *n* Unruheherd *m*; *(in system)* Störung *f*.
**trough** [trɒf] *n* (a) *(container)* Trog *m*. **drinking ~** Wassertrog *m*. (b) *(depression)* Rille *f*; *(between waves, on graph)* Tal *nt*; *(Met)* Tiefdruckkeil *m*.
**troupe** [truːp] *n (Theat)* Truppe *f*.
**trouser** ['traʊzə]: **~ leg** *n* Hosenbein *nt*; **~ pocket** *n* Hosentasche *f*; **~ press** *n* Hosenpresse *f*.
**trousers** ['traʊzɪz] *npl (esp Brit: also pair of ~)* Hose *f*. **she was wearing ~** sie trug eine Hose; **to wear the ~** *(fig col)* die Hosen anhaben *(col)*.
**trouser suit** ['traʊzə,suːt] *n (Brit)* Hosenanzug *m*.
**trousseau** ['truːsəʊ] *n* Aussteuer *f*.
**trout** [traʊt] *n* Forelle *f*. **fishing** Forellenfang *m*.
**trowel** ['traʊəl] *n* Kelle *f*. **to lay sth on with a ~** *(fig col)* bei etw dick auftragen.
**truancy** ['truːənsɪ] *n* (Schule)schwänzen *nt (col)*.
**truant** ['truːənt] *n* (Schul)schwänzer(in *f*) *m (col)*. **to play ~** unentschuldigt fehlen, schwänzen *(col)*.
**truce** [truːs] *n (Mil, fig)* Waffenstillstand *m*; *(Mil: interrupting fighting)* Waffenruhe *f*. **~!** Friede!
**truck¹** [trʌk] **1** *n* (a) *(Rail)* Güterwagen *m*. (b) *(barrow)* Karren *m*. (c) *(lorry)* Last(kraft)wagen *m*; *(van, pick-up)* Lieferwagen *m*. **2** *vt (US)* transportieren. **3** *vi (US)* Lastwagen fahren.
**truck²** *n* (a) *(fig: dealings)* **to have no ~ with sb/sth** mit jdm/etw nichts zu tun haben. (b) *(US: garden produce) (für den Verkauf angebautes)* Gemüse.
**truck driver** *n* Lastwagenfahrer(in *f*) *m*.
**trucker** ['trʌkər] *n (US)* (a) *(truck driver)* Lastwagenfahrer(in *f*) *m*; *(haulage contractor)* Spediteur *m*. (b) *(vegetable farmer)* Gemüsegärtner(in *f*) *m*.
**truck** *(US)*: **~ farm** *n* Gemüsefarm *f*; **~ farmer** *n* Gemüsegärtner(in *f*) *m*.
**trucking** ['trʌkɪŋ] *n (US)* Spedition *f*, Transport *m*. **~ company** Speditionsfirma *f*, Transportunternehmen *nt*.
**truck: ~load** *n* Wagenladung *f*; **~stop** *n (US)* Fernfahrerlokal *nt*.
**truculent** ['trʌkjʊlənt] *adj* trotzig, aufsässig.
**trudge** [trʌdʒ] *vi* **to ~ in/out/along** *etc* hinein-/hinaus-/entlangtrotten *etc*.
**true** [truː] **1** *adj* (a) wahr. **to come ~** *(dream, wishes)* wahr werden; *(prophecy)* sich verwirklichen; *(fears)* sich bewahrheiten; **that's ~** das stimmt, das ist wahr; **the same is *or* holds ~ for ...** dasselbe gilt auch für ...; **~!** richtig!; **too ~!** (das ist nur) zu wahr!
(b) *(accurate)* description wahrheitsgetreu; *likeness* (lebens)getreu; *copy* getreu.

**(c)** *(real, genuine)* feeling, friend, opinion wahr, echt; *reason* wirklich; *antique* echt. ~ **love** die wahre Liebe; *(person)* Herzallerliebste(r) *mf (old)*.

**(d)** *(faithful)* friend, follower treu. **to be ~ to sb** jdm treu sein/bleiben; **to be ~ to one's word** (treu) zu seinem Wort stehen, seinem Wort treu bleiben; ~ **to life** lebensnah; *(Art)* lebensecht; **the horse ran ~ to form** das Pferd lief erwartungsgemäß.

**(e)** *wall, surface* gerade; *join* genau; *circle* rund; *(Mus)* note rein.

**2** *n* **out of ~** *beam, wheels* schief.

**true-blue** *adj* waschecht.

**truffle** ['trʌfl] *n* Trüffel *f or m*.

**truism** ['truːɪzəm] *n (obvious truth)* Binsenwahrheit *f*; *(platitude)* Platitüde *f*, Gemeinplatz *m*.

**truly** ['truːlɪ] *adv* **(a)** *(genuinely)* wirklich, wahrhaftig. **a ~ great writer** ein wahrhaft großer Schriftsteller. **(b)** *(faithfully)* serve treu; *reflect* wahrheitsgetreu.

**trump** [trʌmp] **1** *n (Cards, fig)* Trumpf *m*. **spades are ~s** Pik ist Trumpf; **to hold all the ~s** *(fig)* alle Trümpfe in der Hand halten; ~ **card** *(Cards)* Trumpf(karte *f*) *m*; *(fig)* Trumpf *m*; **to play one's ~ card** *(lit, fig)* seinen Trumpf ausspielen; **to turn up ~s** *(col)* die Lage retten. **2** *vt (Cards)* stechen; *(fig)* übertrumpfen.

▶**trump up** *vt sep* erfinden.

**trumpet** ['trʌmpɪt] **1** *n (Mus)* Trompete *f*. **to blow one's own ~** sich selbst loben. **2** *vi (elephant)* trompeten.

**trumpeter** ['trʌmpɪtə<sup>r</sup>] *n* Trompeter(in *f*) *m*.

**truncate** [trʌŋ'keɪt] *vt* beschneiden.

**truncheon** ['trʌntʃən] *n (esp Brit)* Knüppel *m*; *(esp of riot police)* Schlagstock *m*.

**trundle** ['trʌndl] **1** *vt (push)* rollen; *(pull)* ziehen. **2** *vi* **to ~ along/down** entlang-/hinunterzockeln; *(clatter)* entlang-/hinunterrumpeln.

**trunk** [trʌŋk] *n* **(a)** *(of tree)* Stamm *m*; *(of body)* Rumpf *m*. **(b)** *(of elephant)* Rüssel *m*. **(c)** *(case)* Schrankkoffer *m*; *(US Aut)* Kofferraum *m*. **(d)** ~**s** *pl (for swimming)* Badehose *f*; *(for sport)* Shorts *pl*; **a pair of ~s** eine Badehose/(ein Paar *nt*) Shorts.

**trunk:** ~ **call** *n (Brit Telec)* Ferngespräch *nt*; ~ **line** *n (Rail)* Hauptstrecke *f*; *(Telec)* Fernleitung *f*; ~ **road** *n (Brit)* Fernstraße *f*.

**truss** [trʌs] **1** *n* **(a)** *(Build)* Binder *m*. **(roof)** ~ Dachstuhl *m*. **(b)** *(Med)* Bruchband *nt*. **2** *vt* **(a)** *(tie)* hay bündeln. **(b)** *(Cook)* chicken etc dressieren.

▶**truss up** *vt sep* person fesseln.

**trust** [trʌst] **1** *n* **(a)** *(have confidence in)* Vertrauen *nt (in* zu*)*. **I have every ~ in him** ich habe volles Vertrauen zu ihm; **to put or place one's ~ in sb** Vertrauen in jdn setzen; **to take sth on ~** etw einfach glauben; **position of ~** Vertrauensstellung *f*. **(b)** *(charge)* Verantwortung *f*. **to commit sth to or place sth in sb's ~** jdm etw anvertrauen. **(c)** *(Jur, Fin)* Treuhand(schaft) *f*; *(property)* Treuhandeigentum *nt*; *(charitable fund)* Fonds *m*, Stiftung *f*. **to hold sth in ~ for sb** etw für jdn treuhänderisch verwalten. **(d)** *(Comm: also ~ company)* Trust *m*.

**2** *vt* **(a)** *(have confidence in)* trauen *(+dat)*; *person also* vertrauen *(+dat)*; *words* glauben. **to ~ sb to do sth** jdm zutrauen, daß er etw tut; **to ~ sb with sth, to ~ sth to sb** jdm etw anvertrauen; **can he be ~ed not to lose it?** kann man sich darauf verlassen, daß er es nicht verliert?; **can we ~ him to go shopping alone?** können wir ihn allein einkaufen gehen lassen?; **I wouldn't ~ him an inch** *(col)* ich traue ihm nicht über den Weg *(col)*. **(b)** *(iro col)* ~ **you/ him!** typisch!; ~ **him to break it!** er muß es natürlich kaputtmachen. **(c)** *(hope)* hoffen. **I ~ not** ich

hoffe nicht.

**3** *vi* **to ~ in sb** auf jdn vertrauen; **to ~ to luck *or* chance** sich auf sein Glück verlassen.

**trusted** ['trʌstɪd] *adj method* bewährt; *friend, servant* (ge)treu.

**trustee** [trʌs'tiː] *n* **(a)** *(of estate)* Treuhänder(in *f*) *m*. **(b)** *(of institution)* Verwalter *m*. ~**s** Vorstand *m*.

**trustful** ['trʌstfʊl], **trusting** ['trʌstɪŋ] *adj look* vertrauensvoll; *person also* gutgläubig, arglos.

**trust:** ~ **fund** *n* Treuhandvermögen *nt*; *(of charity)* Stiftungsgelder *pl*; ~ **territory** *n* Treuhandgebiet *nt*.

**trustworthy** ['trʌst,wɜːðɪ] *adj person* vertrauenswürdig; *statement, account* glaubwürdig.

**trusty** ['trʌstɪ] *adj (+er) (liter, hum)* getreu *(liter)*.

**truth** [truːθ] *n, pl* **-s** [truːðz] *no pl* Wahrheit *f*. **you must always tell the ~** du mußt immer die Wahrheit sagen; **to tell the ~ ...** um ehrlich zu sein ...; **the ~ of the matter is that ...** die Wahrheit ist, daß ...; **there's no ~ in what he says** es ist kein Wort wahr von dem, was er sagt; **there's some ~ in that** da ist etwas Wahres dran *(col)*; **the ~, the whole and nothing but the ~** *(Jur)* die Wahrheit, die reine Wahrheit und nichts als die Wahrheit; **in ~** in Wahrheit, in Wirklichkeit.

**truthful** ['truːθʊl] *adj person* ehrlich; *statement* wahrheitsgetreu. **to be ~ about it** ehrlich sein.

**truthfully** ['truːθʊlɪ] *adv* ehrlich; *say also, explain* wahrheitsgemäß.

**truthfulness** ['truːθʊlnɪs] *n see adj* Ehrlichkeit *f*; Wahrheit *f*.

**try** [traɪ] **1** *n* **(a)** Versuch *m*. **to have a ~** es versuchen; **let me have a ~** laß mich mal versuchen!; **to have a ~ at doing sth** versuchen *or* probieren, etw zu tun; **have another ~ (at it)** versuch's noch mal; **I'll give it a ~** *(will attempt it)* ich werde es mal versuchen; *(will test it out)* ich werde es ausprobieren; **it was a good ~** das war schon ganz gut; **it's worth a ~** es ist einen Versuch wert. **(b)** *(Rugby)* Versuch *m*. **to score a ~** einen Versuch erzielen.

**2** *vt* **(a)** *(attempt)* versuchen. **to ~ one's hardest *or* one's best** sein Bestes tun *or* versuchen; **it's ~ing to rain** *(col)* es fängt an zu regnen; **to ~ one's hand at sth** etw probieren; **just you ~ it!** *(dare)* versuch's bloß!

**(b)** *(~ out)* new product etc ausprobieren; *job applicant* eine Chance geben *(+dat)*, es versuchen mit *(col)*; *(~ using)* glue, aspirin es versuchen mit; *(~ to buy or get at)* newsagent, next door es versuchen bei; *(~ to open)* door, window ausprobieren. ~ **this for size** *(fig col)* wie wär's denn damit? *(col)*.

**(c)** *(sample, taste)* probieren.

**(d)** *(test)* courage, patience auf die Probe stellen; *(strain)* nerves anstrengen. **(just)** ~ **me!** *(col)* wetten?; **tried and tested** *(Comm)* erprobt, bewährt; **a sorely tried father** ein schwer geprüfter Vater.

**(e)** *(Jur)* person unter Anklage stellen; *case* verhandeln. **he is being tried for theft** er steht wegen Diebstahls vor Gericht.

**3** *vi* versuchen. ~ **and arrive on time** versuche, pünktlich zu sein; **he wasn't even ~ing** er hat sich *(dat)* überhaupt keine Mühe gegeben; *(didn't attempt it)* er hat es überhaupt nicht versucht.

▶**try for** *vi +prep obj* sich bemühen um.

▶**try on** *vt sep* **(a)** *clothes* anprobieren; *hat* aufprobieren. **(b)** *(fig col)* **to ~ it ~ with sb** probieren, wie weit man bei jdm gehen kann.

▶**try out** *vt sep* ausprobieren *(on bei, an +dat)*; *person* eine Chance geben *(+dat)*.

**trying** ['traɪɪŋ] *adj* anstrengend; *(nerve-wracking)* aufreibend. **they've had a ~ time of it recently** sie haben es in letzter Zeit sehr schwer gehabt.

**tryout** ['traɪaʊt] *n* Versuch *m*; *(of vehicle)* Probefahrt *f*; *(of player)* Probespiel *nt*. **to give sth/sb a ~** etw ausprobieren/es mit jdm versuchen.

**tsar** [zɑːʳ] *n* Zar *m*.

**tsarina** [zɑːˈriːnə] *n* Zarin *f*.

**tsetse (fly)** ['tsetsɪ('flaɪ)] *n* Tsetsefliege *f*.

**T-shirt** ['tiːʃɜːt] *n* T-Shirt *nt*.

**T-square** ['tiːskwɛəʳ] *n* Reißschiene *f*.

**TT** = (a) **teetotal**. (b) *(Mot)* **Tourist Trophy** *jährlich auf der Insel Man abgehaltenes Motorradrennen*. (c) *(Agr)* **tuberculin-tested**.

**tub** [tʌb] *n* Kübel *m*; *(for rainwater)* Tonne, Traufe *f*; *(for washing)* Zuber, Bottich *m*; *(of ice-cream, margarine)* Becher *m*.

**tuba** ['tjuːbə] *n* Tuba *f*.

**tubby** ['tʌbɪ] *adj (+er) (col)* dick, rundlich.

**tube** [tjuːb] *n* (a) *(pipe)* Rohr *nt*; *(of rubber, plastic)* Schlauch *m*. (b) *(of toothpaste etc)* Tube *f*; *(of sweets)* Rolle *f*. (c) *(London underground)* U-Bahn *f*. **by ~** mit der U-Bahn; **~ station** U-Bahnstation *f*. (d) *(Elec, TV, US Rad)* Röhre *f*. **the ~** *(US col)* die Röhre *(col)*.

**tubeless** ['tjuːblɪs] *adj* tyre schlauchlos.

**tuber** ['tjuːbəʳ] *n (Bot)* Knolle *f*.

**tuberculosis** [tjʊ,bɜːkjuˈləʊsɪs] *n* Tuberkulose *f*.

**tubing** ['tjuːbɪŋ] *n* Schlauch *m*.

**tubular** ['tjuːbjʊləʳ] *adj* röhrenförmig. **~ frame** Rohrrahmen *m*; **~ bells** *(Mus)* Röhrenglocken *pl*.

**TUC** *(Brit)* = **Trades Union Congress**.

**tuck** [tʌk] **1** *n (Sew)* Saum *m*; *(ornamental)* Biese *f*. **to put a ~ in sth** einen Saum in etw *(acc)* nähen. **2** *vt (put)* stecken. **he ~ed his umbrella under his arm** er steckte *or* klemmte *(col)* sich den Regenschirm unter den Arm. **3** *vi* **your bag will ~ under the seat** Sie können Ihre Tasche unter dem Sitz verstauen.

▶**tuck away** *vt sep (hide)* wegstecken. **he ~ed it ~ in his pocket** er steckte es in die Tasche; **she has a few thousand ~ed ~** sie hat ein paar tausend auf der hohen Kante; **the hut is ~ed ~ among the trees** die Hütte liegt versteckt zwischen den Bäumen.

▶**tuck in 1** *vi (col)* zulangen, reinhauen *(col)*. **~ ~!** langt zu!, haut rein! *(col)*; **to ~ ~to sth** sich *(dat)* etw schmecken lassen. **2** *vt sep flap etc* hineinstecken, reinstecken *(col)*. **to ~ one's shirt ~** das Hemd in die Hose stecken; **to ~ sb ~(to bed)** jdn zudecken.

▶**tuck up** *vt sep skirt, hair* hochnehmen; *sleeve* hochkrempeln; *legs* unterschlagen. **to ~ sb ~ (in bed)** jdn zudecken.

**Tue(s)** = **Tuesday** Di.

**Tuesday** ['tjuːzdɪ] *n* Dienstag *m*. **on ~** *(am)* Dienstag; **~ December 5th** *(in letter)* Dienstag, den 5. Dezember; **on ~s** dienstags; **I met her on a ~** ich habe sie an einem Dienstag kennengelernt; **on ~ morning/evening** *(am)* Dienstag morgen/abend; **on ~ mornings/evenings** dienstags *or* Dienstag morgens/abends; **last/next/this ~** letzten/nächsten/ diesen Dienstag; **a year last/next ~** letzten/ nächsten Dienstag vor einem Jahr; **our ~ meeting** *(this week)* unser Treffen am Dienstag; *(every week)* unser Dienstagstreffen.

**tuft** [tʌft] *n* Büschel *nt*. **a ~ of hair/feathers** ein Haarbüschel *nt*/Federbusch *m*.

**tufted** ['tʌftɪd] *adj*: **~ carpet** Tuftingteppich *m*.

**tug** [tʌg] **1** *vt* zerren, ziehen. **she ~ged his sleeve** sie zog an seinem Ärmel. **2** *vi* ziehen, zerren *(at an* +*dat)*. **3** *n* (a) *(pull)* **to give sth a ~** an etw *(dat)* ziehen; **~ of war** *(Sport, fig)* Tauziehen *nt*. (b) *(also* **~boat)** Schlepper *m*.

**tuition** [tjuˈɪʃən] *n* (a) Unterricht *m*. **extra ~** Nachhilfeunterricht. (b) *(US: school fees)* Schulgeld *nt*.

**tulip** ['tjuːlɪp] *n* Tulpe *f*.

**tumble** ['tʌmbl] **1** *n (fall)* Sturz *m*. **to take a ~** stürzen, straucheln; *(fig)* fallen. **2** *vi (fall)* straucheln, (hin)fallen; *(move quickly)* stürzen; *(fig: prices)* fallen. **he ~d off his bicycle** er stürzte vom Fahrrad; **to ~ out of/into bed** aus dem Bett/ins Bett fallen.

**tumble: ~down** *adj* verfallen, baufällig; **~-drier** *n* Trockenautomat *m*.

**tumbler** ['tʌmbləʳ] *n* (a) *(glass)* (Becher)glas *nt*. (b) *(tumble drier)* Trockenautomat *m*.

**tummy** ['tʌmɪ] *n (col)* Bauch *m*. (a) **~ ache** Bauchschmerzen *pl*, Bauchweh *nt*.

**tumour**, *(US)* **tumor** ['tjuːməʳ] *n* Geschwulst *f*, Tumor *m*.

**tumult** ['tjuːmʌlt] *n (uproar)* Tumult *m*. **the ~ of battle** das Schlachtgetümmel.

**tumultuous** [tjuˈmʌltjʊəs] *adj* tumultartig; *applause* stürmisch. **they gave him a ~ welcome** sie begrüßten ihn stürmisch.

**tuna (fish)** ['tjuːnə('fɪʃ)] *n* Thunfisch *m*.

**tundra** ['tʌndrə] *n* Tundra *f*.

**tune** [tjuːn] **1** *n* (a) *(melody)* Melodie *f*. **sung to the ~ of ...** gesungen nach der Melodie (von) ...; **to change one's ~** *(fig)* seine Meinung ändern; **to the ~ of £100** in Höhe von £100. (b) **to sing in ~/out of ~** richtig/falsch singen; **the piano is out of ~** das Klavier ist verstimmt; **to be in/out of ~ with sb/ sth** *(fig)* mit jdm/etw harmonieren/nicht harmonieren; **the engine's out of ~** der Motor müßte neu eingestellt werden; **he's in ~ with young people** er ist auf einer Wellenlänge mit der Jugend *(col)*; **he felt out of ~ with his new environment** er fühlte sich in seiner neuen Umgebung fehl am Platze. **2** *vt* (a) *(Mus) instrument* stimmen. (b) *(Rad, Aut)* einstellen; *(Aut: for high performance)* frisieren.

▶**tune in 1** *vi (Rad)* einschalten. **to ~ ~ to Radio London** Radio London einschalten *or* hören. **2** *vt sep radio* einschalten *(to acc)*. **you are ~d ~ to Radio 2** Sie hören Radio 2.

▶**tune up 1** *vi (Mus)* (sein Instrument/die Instrumente) stimmen. **2** *vt sep engine* einstellen; *(for high performance)* frisieren.

**tuneful** ['tjuːnfʊl] *adj* melodisch.

**tuneless** ['tjuːnlɪs] *adj* unmelodisch.

**tuner** ['tjuːnəʳ] *n* (a) *(Mus)* Stimmer *m*. (b) *(Rad etc)* Tuner *m*.

**tungsten** ['tʌŋstən] *n* Wolfram *nt*.

**tunic** ['tjuːnɪk] *n* Kasack *m*, Hemdbluse *f*; *(of uniform)* Uniformrock *m*.

**tuning** ['tjuːnɪŋ] *n* (a) *(Mus)* Stimmen *nt*. **~-fork** Stimmgabel *f*. (b) *(Rad)* Einstellen *nt*. **~ knob** Stationswahlknopf *m*. (c) *(Aut)* Einstellen *nt*; *(for high performance)* Frisieren, Tuning *nt*.

**Tunisia** [tjuˈnɪzɪə] *n* Tunesien *nt*.

**Tunisian** [tjuˈnɪzɪən] **1** *n* Tunesier(in *f*) *m*. **2** *adj* tunesisch.

**tunnel** ['tʌnl] *(vb: pret, ptp (Brit)* **tunnelled,** *(US)* **tunneled)** **1** *n* Tunnel *m*; *(Min)* Stollen *m*. **~ vision** (röhrenförmige) Gesichtsfeldeinengung; *(fig)* Engstirnigkeit *f*, beschränkter Horizont. **2** *vi (into* +*acc, through* durch*)* einen Tunnel bauen; *(rabbit)* einen Bau graben; *(mole)* Gänge graben. **3** *vt* **they ~led a passage under the prison wall** sie gruben sich unter der Gefängnismauer durch; **to ~ one's way through sth** sich durch etw hindurchgraben.

**tunny (fish)** ['tʌnɪ('fɪʃ)] *n* Thunfisch *m*.

**tuppence** ['tʌpəns] *n* zwei Pence. **I don't care ~** das interessiert mich nicht für fünf Pfennig *(col)*.

**turban** ['tɜːbən] *n* Turban *m*.

**turbid** ['tɜːbɪd] *adj liquid* trübe.
**turbine** ['tɜːbaɪn] *n* Turbine *f*.
**turbo** ['tɜːbəʊ] *n (Aut)* Turbo *m*.
**turbo**: ~ **charger** *n* Turbolader *m*; ~**jet** *n (engine)* Turbotriebwerk *nt*; *(aircraft)* Turbojet *m*; ~**prop** *n (engine)* Turboprop(-Triebwerk) *nt*; *(aircraft)* Turboprop-Flugzeug *nt*.
**turbot** ['tɜːbət] *n* Steinbutt *m*.
**turbulence** ['tɜːbjʊləns] *n (of emotions)* Aufgewühltheit *f*; *(of career, period)* Turbulenz *f*. **air** ~ Turbulenz *f*.
**turbulent** ['tɜːbjʊlənt] *adj* stürmisch; *emotions also* aufgewühlt; *career, period also* turbulent.
**tureen** [tə'riːn] *n* (Suppen)terrine *f*.
**turf** [tɜːf] **1** *n, pl* -s *or* **turves (a)** *(no pl: lawn)* Rasen *m*; *(no pl: squares of grass)* Soden *pl*; *(square of grass)* Sode *f*. **(b)** *(Sport)* **the T~** die (Pferde)rennbahn; ~ **accountant** Buchmacher *m*. **2** *vt* **(a)** **he** ~**ed the garden** er verlegte (Gras)soden im Garten. **(b)** *(col)* **to** ~ **sb down the stairs** jdn die Treppe hinunterscheuchen *(col)*; **to** ~ **sth into the corner** etw in die Ecke schmeißen *(col)*.
▶**turf out** *vt sep (col) person* rauswerfen; *plan* umschmeißen *(col)*, verwerfen; *(throw away)* wegschmeißen *(col)*.
**turgid** ['tɜːdʒɪd] *adj (swollen)* (an)geschwollen; *(fig) style* schwülstig, überladen.
**Turk** [tɜːk] *n* Türke *m*, Türkin *f*.
**Turkey** ['tɜːkɪ] *n* die Türkei.
**turkey** ['tɜːkɪ] *n* Truthahn *m*/-henne *f*, Pute(r) *mf (esp Cook)*.
**Turkish** ['tɜːkɪʃ] **1** *adj* türkisch. ~ **bath** türkisches Bad; ~ **delight** Lokum *nt*. **2** *n (language)* Türkisch *nt*.
**turmeric** ['tɜːmərɪk] *n* Kurkuma *nt*.
**turmoil** ['tɜːmɔɪl] *n* Aufruhr *m*; *(confusion)* Durcheinander *nt*. **everything is in a** ~ alles ist in Aufruhr; **her mind was in a** ~ sie war völlig verwirrt.
**turn** [tɜːn] **1** *n* **(a)** *(movement)* Drehung *f*. **to give sth a** ~ etw (einmal) drehen.
**(b)** *(change of direction) (in road)* Kurve *f*; *(Sport)* Wende *f*. **to make a** ~ **to the left** nach links einbiegen; *(driver, car also, road)* nach links abbiegen; *(road)* eine Linkskurve machen; **take the left-hand** ~ biegen Sie links ab; **"no left** ~**"** „Linksabbiegen verboten"; **the** ~ **of the tide** *(lit)* der Gezeitenwechsel; **the tide is on the** ~ *(lit)* die Ebbe/Flut setzt ein; *(fig)* es tritt eine Wende ein; **at the** ~ **of the century** um die Jahrhundertwende; **at every** ~ *(fig)* auf Schritt und Tritt; **things took a** ~ **for the worse/the better** die Dinge wendeten sich zum Schlechten/zum Guten; **the patient took a** ~ **for the worse/the better** das Befinden des Patienten wendete sich zum Schlechteren/zum Besseren; **things took a new** ~ die Dinge nahmen eine neue Wendung; ~ **of phrase** Ausdrucksweise *f*.
**(c)** *(in game, queue, series)* **in** ~ der Reihe nach; **out of** ~ außer der Reihe; **it's your** ~ du bist an der Reihe, du bist dran; **it's your** ~ **to do the dishes** du bist mit (dem) Abwaschen dran; **it's my** ~ **next** ich komme als nächste(r) an die Reihe; **wait your** ~ warten Sie, bis Sie an der Reihe sind; **your** ~ **will come** du kommst auch noch mal dran; **sorry, have I spoken out of** ~? Entschuldigung, habe ich etwas Falsches gesagt?; **in** ~, **by** ~**s** abwechselnd; **to take** ~**s at doing sth** etw abwechselnd tun; **to take** ~**s at the wheel** sich beim Fahren abwechseln; **to take a** ~ **at the wheel** (für eine Weile) das Steuer übernehmen.
**(d)** *(service)* **to do sb a good/bad** ~ jdm einen guten/schlechten Dienst erweisen; **one good** ~ **de-**

**serves another** *(Prov)* eine Hand wäscht die andere *(prov)*.
**(e)** *(tendency, talent)* **to have a mathematical** ~ **of mind** mathematisch begabt sein; **an optimistic/a strange** ~ **of mind** eine optimistische/seltsame Einstellung; **a melancholy** ~ **of mind** ein Hang zur Melancholie.
**(f)** *(Med col)* **he had one of his** ~**s last night** er hatte letzte Nacht wieder einen Anfall; **you/it gave me quite a** ~ du hast/es hat mir einen schönen Schrecken eingejagt.
**(g)** *(Theat)* Nummer *f*. **they got him to do a** ~ **at the party** sie brachten ihn dazu, auf der Party etwas zum besten zu geben.
**2** *vt* **(a)** *(revolve) key, screw, steering wheel* drehen. **to** ~ **the key in the lock** den Schlüssel im Schloß herumdrehen; **what** ~**s the wheel?** wie wird das Rad angetrieben?; **he** ~**ed the wheel sharply** er riß das Steuer herum.
**(b)** *(~ over, ~ round) mattress, car, soil* wenden; *page* umblättern; *record, chair, picture etc* umdrehen.
**(c)** *(transform, make become)* verwandeln *(in(to)* in +*acc)*. **the play was** ~**ed into a film** das Stück wurde verfilmt; **this hot weather has** ~**ed the milk (sour)** bei dieser Hitze ist die Milch sauer geworden.
**(d)** **she** ~**ed her head towards me** sie wandte mir den Kopf zu; **he** ~**ed his back to the wall** er kehrte den Rücken zur Wand; **success has** ~**ed her head** der Erfolg ist ihr zu Kopf gestiegen; **she seems to have** ~**ed his head** sie scheint ihm den Kopf verdreht zu haben; **she can still** ~ **a few heads** die Männer schauen sich immer noch nach ihr um; **as soon as his back is** ~**ed** sobald er den Rücken kehrt; **the sight of all that food quite** ~**ed my stomach** beim Anblick des vielen Essens drehte sich mir regelrecht der Magen um; **without** ~**ing a hair** ohne mit der Wimper zu zucken; **she can** ~ **her hand to anything** sie kann alles; **he** ~**ed his hand to cooking** er versuchte sich im Kochen; **to** ~ **one's thoughts/attention to sth** seine Gedanken/Aufmerksamkeit einer Sache *(dat)* zuwenden; **to** ~ **a gun on sb** ein Gewehr auf jdn richten; **she has** ~**ed forty** sie ist vierzig geworden; **it is** *or* **has** ~**ed 2 o'clock** es ist 2 Uhr vorbei; **the car** ~**ed the corner** das Auto bog um die Ecke; **to have** ~**ed the corner** *(fig)* über den Berg sein; **nothing will** ~ **him from his purpose** nichts wird ihn von seinem Vorhaben abbringen; **to** ~ **a dog on sb** einen Hund auf jdn hetzen.
**3** *vi* **(a)** *(revolve, move round: key, wheel)* sich drehen. **she** ~**ed to me and smiled** sie wandte sich mir zu und lächelte; **to** ~ **upside down** umkippen; **my head is** ~**ing** in meinem Kopf dreht sich alles.
**(b)** *(change direction) (to one side) (person, car)* abbiegen; *(plane, boat)* abdrehen; *(~ around)* wenden; *(person: on the spot)* sich umdrehen; *(wind)* drehen. **to** ~ **and go back** umkehren; **to** ~ **(to the) left** links abbiegen; **our luck** ~**ed** unser Glück wendete sich.
**(c)** *(go)* **to** ~ **to sb/sth** sich an jdn wenden/sich einer Sache *(dat)* zuwenden; **after her death, he** ~**ed to his books for comfort** nach ihrem Tod suchte er Trost bei seinen Büchern; **this job would make anyone** ~ **to drink!** bei dieser Arbeit muß man ja zum Trinker werden!; **the conversation** ~**ed to the accident** das Gespräch kam auf den Unfall; **I don't know which way to** ~ ich weiß nicht, was ich machen soll.
**(d)** *(leaves)* sich (ver)färben; *(milk)* sauer werden; *(meat)* schlecht werden; *(weather)* umschla-

gen. **to ~ into sth** sich in etw *(acc)* verwandeln; *(develop into)* sich zu etw entwickeln; **their short holiday ~ed into a three-month visit** aus ihrem Kurzurlaub wurde ein Aufenthalt von drei Monaten; **to ~ to stone** zu Stein werden; **to ~ traitor** zum Verräter werden; **to ~ red** *(leaves etc)* sich rot färben; *(person: blush)* rot werden; *(traffic lights)* auf Rot umspringen; **his hair is ~ing grey** sein Haar wird grau.
▶**turn against 1** *vi* +*prep obj* sich wenden gegen. **2** *vt sep* +*prep obj* **they ~ed him ~ his parents** sie brachten ihn gegen seine Eltern auf; **she ~ed his argument ~ him** sie verwendete sein Argument gegen ihn.
▶**turn around 1** *vi (face other way)* sich umdrehen; *(go back)* umkehren. **we ~ed ~ the corner** wir bogen um die Ecke. **2** *vt sep* **head** drehen; **box** umdrehen. **~ the picture ~ the other way** dreh das Bild andersherum.
▶**turn aside 1** *vi* sich abwenden *(from* von*)*. **2** *vt sep* abwenden.
▶**turn away 1** *vi* sich abwenden. **2** *vt sep* **(a)** *(move)* **head, eyes** abwenden. **(b)** *(send away)* **person** abweisen; **business** ablehnen.
▶**turn back 1** *vi* **(a)** *(traveller, aeroplane)* umkehren; *(look back)* sich umdrehen. **there can be no ~ing ~ now** *(fig)* jetzt gibt es kein Zurück mehr. **(b)** *(in book)* **to ~ ~ to page 100** auf Seite 100 zurückblättern. **2** *vt sep* **(a)** *(fold)* **bedclothes** zurückschlagen; **corner** umknicken; **hem** umschlagen. **(b)** *(send back)* **person** zurückschicken. **they were ~ed ~ at the frontier** sie wurden an der Grenze zurückgewiesen. **(c)** **clock** zurückstellen. **to ~ the clock ~ fifty years** die Uhr um fünfzig Jahre zurückdrehen.
▶**turn down 1** *vt sep* **(a)** *(fold down)* **bedclothes** zurückschlagen; **collar, brim** herunterklappen; **corner of a page** umknicken. **(b)** **gas, heat, lights** herunterdrehen; **volume** leiser stellen. **(c)** **candidate, novel etc** ablehnen; **offer also** zurückweisen; **suitor** abweisen. **2** *vi* +*prep obj* **I ~ed ~ a side street** ich bog in eine Seitenstraße ab.
▶**turn in 1** *vi* **(a)** *(drive in)* **the car ~ed ~ at the top of the drive** das Auto bog in die Einfahrt ein. **(b)** *(col: go to bed)* sich hinhauen *(col)*. **2** *vt sep (col: to police)* **to ~ sb ~** jdn anzeigen *or* verpfeifen *(col)*.
▶**turn off 1** *vi* abbiegen *(for* nach, *prep obj* von*)*. **2** *vt sep* **(a)** **light, gas, radio** ausmachen; **tap** zudrehen; **TV** abschalten; **water, electricity, engine, machine** abstellen. **(b)** *(col)* **to ~ sb ~** *(disgust)* jdn anwidern; *(put off)* jdm die Lust verderben.
▶**turn on 1** *vt sep* **(a)** **gas, heat, engine** anstellen, anmachen; **light, radio, television, the news also** einschalten; **tap, central heating** aufdrehen. **(b)** *(col: appeal to:* **music, novel etc)** **sth ~s sb ~** jd steht auf etw *(acc) (col)*; **she/it doesn't ~ me ~** sie/das läßt mich kalt *(also sexually)*; **that ~s me ~** *(sexually)* das macht mich ganz scharf *(col)*. **2** *vi* +*prep obj* **(a)** *(attack)* angreifen. **(b)** *(depend on)* abhängen von.
▶**turn out 1** *vi* **(a)** *(firemen)* ausrücken; *(doctor)* einen Krankenbesuch machen. **(b)** *(point)* **my toes ~ ~** ich laufe nach außen. **(c)** **the car ~ed ~ of the drive** das Auto bog aus der Einfahrt. **(d)** *(transpire)* sich herausstellen. **he ~ed ~ to be the murderer himself** es stellte sich heraus, daß er selbst der Mörder war; **as it ~ed ~** wie sich herausstellte. **(e)** *(develop, progress)* sich entwickeln. **everything will ~ ~ all right** es wird sich schon alles ergeben; **it's ~ed ~ nice again** es ist wieder schön geworden.
 **2** *vt sep* **(a)** **light** ausmachen; **gas also** abstellen. **(b)** *(produce)* produzieren; **novel etc** schreiben; **good students** hervorbringen. **(c)** *(expel)* vertreiben

*(of* aus*)*, hinauswerfen *(col) (of* aus*)*; **tenant** kündigen (+*dat*). **(d)** *(tip out)* **cake** stürzen; **pockets** (aus)leeren. **she ~ed the photos ~ of the box** sie kippte die Fotos aus der Schachtel. **(e)** *(clean)* **room** gründlich saubermachen. **(f)** **guard** antreten lassen. **(g)** **well ~ed-~** gut gekleidet.
▶**turn over 1** *vi* **(a)** *(person, stomach)* sich umdrehen; *(car, place etc)* sich überschlagen; *(boat)* kentern. **I ~ed ~ on(to) my back** ich drehte mich auf den Rücken. **(b)** *(with pages)* **please ~ ~** bitte wenden. **2** *vt sep* **(a)** umdrehen; *(turn upside down)* umkippen; **page** umblättern; **soil** umgraben; **mattress, steak** wenden. **the police ~ed the whole house ~** *(search)* die Polizei durchsuchte das ganze Haus; **to ~ an idea ~ in one's mind** sich *(dat)* eine Idee durch den Kopf gehen lassen. **(b)** *(hand over)* übergeben *(to* dat*)*.
▶**turn round** *vti* = **turn around**.
▶**turn up 1** *vi* **(a)** *(arrive)* erscheinen, auftauchen *(col)*. **I was afraid you wouldn't ~ ~** ich hatte Angst, du würdest nicht kommen. **(b)** *(be found)* (wieder) auftauchen *(col)*. **something is sure to ~ ~** irgend etwas findet sich schon. **(c)** *(point up)* **a ~ed-~ nose** eine Stupsnase; **to ~ ~ at the ends** sich an den Enden hochbiegen. **2** *vt sep* **(a)** *(fold)* **collar** hochklappen; **hem** annähen. **to ~ ~ one's nose at sth** *(fig)* die Nase über etw *(acc)* rümpfen. **(b)** **heat, gas** höher drehen; **radio** lauter drehen; **volume** aufdrehen; **light** heller machen.

**turn:** **~about, ~around** *n* **(a)** *(in position, fig: in opinion etc)* Kehrtwendung *f*; **(b)** *(also* **~around time)** Bearbeitungszeit *f*; *(production time)* Produktionszeit *f*; **(c)** *(of situation, company)* Umschwung *m*, Wende *f*; **(d)** *(of ship, aircraft)* Abfertigung *f*; **~coat** *m* Überläufer *m*.
**turning** [ˈtɜːnɪŋ] *n (in road)* Abzweigung *f*. **take the second ~ on the left** nimm die zweite Straße links.
**turning:** **~ circle** *n (Aut)* Wendekreis *m*; **~ lane** *n (Mot)* Abbiegerspur *f*; **~ point** *n* Wendepunkt *m*.
**turnip** [ˈtɜːnɪp] *n* Rübe *f*.
**turn:** **~-off** *n* **(a)** Abzweigung *f*; *(on motorway)* Abfahrt, Ausfahrt *f*; **the Birmingham ~-off** die Abfahrt *or* Ausfahrt Birmingham; **(b)** *(col: source of distaste)* **to be a ~-off** einem die Lust verderben; **~-on** *n (col)* **to be a ~-on** einen anmachen *(col)*.
**turnout** [ˈtɜːnaʊt] *n* **(a)** *(attendance)* Teilnahme, Beteiligung *f*; *(for an election)* Wahlbeteiligung *f*. **in spite of the rain there was a big ~ for the match** trotz des Regens war das Spiel gut besucht. **(b)** *(clean)* **to give sth a good ~** etw gründlich säubern. **(c)** *(dress)* Aufmachung *f*.
**turnover** [ˈtɜːnˌəʊvəʳ] *n (total business)* Umsatz *m*; *(Comm, Fin: of capital)* Umlauf *m*; *(Comm: of stock)* (Lager)umschlag *m*; *(of staff)* Fluktuation *f*.
**turn:** **~pike** *n (Brit Hist)* Mautschranke *f*; *(US)* gebührenpflichtige Autobahn; **~ signal** *n (US Aut)* Blinker *m*; **~stile** *n* Drehkreuz *nt*; **~table** *n* Drehscheibe *f*; *(on record player)* Plattenteller *m*; **~-up** *n* **(a)** *(Brit: on trousers)* Aufschlag *m*; **(b)** *(col: event)* **that was a ~-up for the book** das war eine (echte) Überraschung.
**turpentine** [ˈtɜːpəntaɪn], **turps** [tɜːps] *(col)* *n* Terpentin *nt*.
**turquoise** [ˈtɜːkwɔɪz] **1** *n* **(a)** *(gem)* Türkis *m*. **(b)** *(colour)* Türkis *nt*. **2** *adj* türkis(farben).
**turret** [ˈtʌrɪt] *n (Archit)* Mauerturm *m*; *(on tank)* Turm *m*; *(on ship)* Gefechtsturm *m*.
**turtle** [ˈtɜːtl] *n* (Wasser)schildkröte *f*; *(US also)* (Land)schildkröte *f*. **to turn ~** kentern.
**turtle:** **~-dove** *n (lit, fig col)* Turteltaube *f*; **~-neck (pullover)** *n* Stehkragenpullover *m*.

**Tuscany** ['tʌskənɪ] *n* die Toskana.

**tusk** [tʌsk] *n (of elephant)* Stoßzahn *m*; *(of walrus)* Eckzahn *m*; *(of boar)* Hauer *m*.

**tussle** ['tʌsl] **1** *n (lit, fig)* Gerangel *nt.* **2** *vi* sich rangeln *(with sb for sth* mit jdm um etw*).

**tussock** ['tʌsək] *n* (Gras)büschel *nt.*

**tutor** ['tjuːtər] **1** *n* (a) Privatlehrer *m.* (b) *(Brit Univ)* Tutor *m.* **2** *vt (as private teacher)* privat unterrichten; *(give extra lessons to)* Nachhilfe(unterricht) geben *(+dat).* **to** ~ **sb in Latin** jdm Privatunterricht/Nachhilfe in Latein geben.

**tutorial** [tjuː'tɔːrɪəl] *n (Brit Univ)* ≈ Kolloquium *nt.*

**tut-tut** ['tʌt'tʌt] *interj (in disapproval)* na, na.

**tuxedo** [tʌk'siːdəʊ] *n (US)* Smoking *m.*

**TV** *n (col)* = **television.** ~ **guide** Fernsehzeitung *f.*

**twaddle** ['twɒdl] *n (col)* Gewäsch *nt (col).*

**twang** [twæŋ] **1** *n (of wire, guitar string)* Doing *nt; (of rubber band, bowstring)* scharfer Ton; *(of voice)* Näseln *nt,* näselnder Tonfall. **2** *vt* zupfen; *guitar, banjo also* klimpern auf *(+dat).* **3** *vi* einen scharfen Ton von sich geben; *(rubber band)* pitschen *(col).*

**tweak** [twiːk] **1** *vt* kneifen. **to** ~ **sb's ear** jdn am Ohr ziehen. **2** *n* **to give sb's ear/nose a** ~ jdn am Ohr/an der Nase ziehen.

**twee** [twiː] *adj (+er) (col)* niedlich; *manner* geziert; *expression* gekünstelt.

**tweed** [twiːd] **1** *n* (a) *(cloth)* Tweed *m.* (b) ~s *pl (clothes)* Tweedkleidung *f.* **2** *adj* Tweed-.

**tweet** [twiːt] **1** *n* Piepsen *nt no pl.* **2** *vi* piepsen.

**tweeter** ['twiːtər] *n* Hochtöner *m.*

**tweezers** ['twiːzəz] *npl (also pair of* ~*)* Pinzette *f.*

**twelfth** [twelfθ] **1** *adj* zwölfte(r, s). **2** *n (in series)* Zwölfte(r, s); *(fraction)* Zwölftel *nt; see* **sixth.**

**twelve** [twelv] *adj* zwölf. ~ **noon** zwölf Uhr (mittags); *see* **six.**

**twentieth** ['twentɪɪθ] **1** *adj* zwanzigste(r, s). **2** *n (in series)* Zwanzigste(r, s); *(fraction)* Zwanzigstel *nt; see* **sixtieth.**

**twenty** ['twentɪ] *adj* zwanzig; *see* **sixty.**

**twenty-four** ['twentɪ'fɔːr] *adj:* ~ **hour service** Tag-und Nachtdienst *m;* **open** ~ **hours a day** rund um die Uhr geöffnet.

**twerp** [twɜːp] *n (col)* Knallkopf *m (col).*

**twice** [twaɪs] *adv* zweimal. ~ **as much/many** doppelt *or* zweimal soviel/so viele; ~ **as much bread** doppelt soviel Brot; ~ **as long as ...** zweimal so lange wie ...; **at** ~ **the speed of sound** mit doppelter Schallgeschwindigkeit; **she is** ~ **your age** sie ist doppelt so alt wie du; ~ **2 is 4** zweimal 2 ist 4; ~ **a week** zweimal wöchentlich, zweimal pro Woche; **I'd think** ~ **before trusting him with it** ihm würde ich das nicht so ohne weiteres anvertrauen.

**twiddle** ['twɪdl] **1** *vt* herumdrehen an *(+dat).* **she** ~**d the pencil in her fingers** ihre Finger spielten mit dem Bleistift; **to** ~ **one's thumbs** *(lit, fig)* Däumchen drehen. **2** *vi* **to** ~ **with a knob** an einem Knopf herumdrehen.

**twig¹** [twɪg] *n (thin branch)* Zweig *m.*

**twig²** *(Brit col)* **1** *vt (realize)* mitkriegen *(col),* mitbekommen. **he's** ~**ged it** er hat's kapiert *(col).* **2** *vi* schalten *(col),* es mitkriegen *(col).*

**twilight** ['twaɪlaɪt] *n* Dämmerung *f.* **at** ~ in der Dämmerung; **in the** ~ im Zwielicht.

**twill** [twɪl] *n (Tex)* Köper *m.*

**twin** [twɪn] **1** *n* Zwilling *m; (of vase, object)* Gegenstück, Pendant *nt.* **her** ~ **(sister/brother)** ihre Zwillingsschwester/ihr Zwillingsbruder *m.* **2** *vt (Brit)* **Oxford is** ~**ned with Bonn** Oxford ist die Partnerstadt von Bonn.

**twin:** ~**-bedded room** *n* Zweibettzimmer *nt;* ~ **beds** *npl* zwei (gleiche) Einzelbetten; ~ **brother** *n*

Zwillingsbruder *m;* ~ **carburettors** *(Brit) or* **carburetors** *(US) npl* Doppelvergaser *m.*

**twine** [twaɪn] **1** *n* Schnur *f,* Bindfaden *m.* **2** *vt* winden. **to** ~ **one's arms around sb** seine Arme um jdn schlingen. **3** *vi* **to** ~ **around sth** sich um etw winden.

**twin-engined** [,twɪn'endʒɪnd] *adj* zweimotorig.

**twinge** [twɪndʒ] *n (of pain)* Zucken *nt,* leichtes Stechen. **a** ~ **of pain** ein zuckender Schmerz; **a** ~ **of conscience/remorse** Gewissensbisse *pl.*

**twinkle** ['twɪŋkl] **1** *vi* funkeln; *(stars also)* glitzern. **2** *n* Funkeln, Glitzern *nt.* **there was a** ~ **in her eye** man sah den Schalk in ihren Augen.

**twinkling** ['twɪŋklɪŋ] *n* **in the** ~ **of an eye** im Nu, im Handumdrehen.

**twinning** ['twɪnɪŋ] *n (of towns)* Städtepartnerschaft *f.*

**twin:** ~**set** *n (Brit)* Twinset *nt;* ~ **sister** *n* Zwillingsschwester *f;* ~ **town** *n (Brit)* Partnerstadt *f;* ~**-tub (washing-machine)** *n* Waschmaschine *f* mit getrennter Schleuder.

**twirl** [twɜːl] **1** *vt* (herum)wirbeln; *skirt* herumwirbeln; *moustache* zwirbeln. **2** *vi* wirbeln. **3** *n* Wirbel *m; (in dance)* Drehung *f; (of moustache)* hochgezwirbelte Spitze.

**twist** [twɪst] **1** *n* (a) *(action)* **to give sth a** ~ etw (herum)drehen; **with a quick** ~ **of the hand** mit einer schnellen Handbewegung. (b) *(bend)* Kurve, Biegung *f; (fig: in story etc)* Wendung *f.* (c) *(Brit col)* **to be/go round the** ~ verrückt sein/werden; **it's driving me round the** ~**!** das macht mich wahnsinnig! (d) *(dance)* Twist *m.*

  **2** *vt* (a) *(wind, turn)* drehen; *(coil)* wickeln *(into* zu *+dat).* **to** ~ **threads** *etc* **together** Fäden *etc* zusammendrehen; **to** ~ **the top off a jar** den Deckel von einem Glas abdrehen. (b) *(bend, distort) key* verbiegen; *part of body, (fig) meaning, words* verdrehen. **to** ~ **sth out of shape** etw verbiegen; **to** ~ **sb's arm** *(lit)* jdn den Arm verdrehen; *(fig)* jdn überreden; **I suppose you could** ~ **my arm** ja, ehe ich mich schlagen lasse *(hum col);* **to** ~ **one's ankle** sich *(dat)* den Fuß vertreten; **his face was** ~**ed with pain** sein Gesicht war schmerzverzerrt.

  **3** *vi* (a) *(smoke)* sich ringeln; *(plant)* sich ranken; *(road, river, person: wriggle)* sich schlängeln. (b) *(dance)* Twist tanzen.

  ▶**twist off** *vt sep* abdrehen; *lid* abschrauben; *flowerheads* abknipsen.

**twisted** ['twɪstɪd] *adj* (a) *wires, rope* (zusammen)gedreht; *(bent)* verbogen. (b) *ankle* verrenkt. (c) *(fig) mind, logic* verdreht.

**twit** [twɪt] *(Brit col: person)* Trottel *m (col).*

**twitch** [twɪtʃ] **1** *n* (a) *(tic)* Zucken *nt; (individual spasm)* Zuckung *f.* **to give a** ~ zucken. (b) *(pull)* Ruck *m (of an +dat).* **to give sth a** ~ an etw *(dat)* rucken. **2** *vi (face, muscles)* zucken. **the cat's nose** ~**ed** die Katze schnupperte.

**twitter** ['twɪtər] **1** *vti (lit, fig)* zwitschern. **2** *n* (a) *(of birds)* Gezwitscher *nt.* (b) *(col)* **to be all of a** ~ ganz aufgeregt sein.

**two** [tuː] **1** *adj* zwei. **to cut sth in** ~ etw in zwei Teile schneiden; ~ **by** ~, **in** ~**s** zu zweit, zu zweien; **the** ~ **of them** die beiden; **to put** ~ **and** ~ **together** *(fig)* seine Schlüsse ziehen; ~ **can play (at) that game** *(col)* den Spieß kann man auch umdrehen; *see* **six.** **2** *n* Zwei *f;* **just the** ~ **of us/them** nur wir beide/die beiden.

**two:** ~**-bit** *adj (US col)* mies *(col);* ~**-cylinder (engine)** *n* Zweizylinder(motor) *m;* ~**-dimensional** *adj* zweidimensional; ~**-door** *adj* zweitürig; ~**-edged** *adj (lit, fig)* zweischneidig; ~**-faced** *adj (lit)* doppelgesichtig; *(fig)* falsch; ~**fold 1** *adj* zweifach, doppelt; **a** ~**fold increase** ein Anstieg um das Doppelte; **2** *adv* **to increase** ~**fold** sich um das Doppelte steigern; ~**-legged** *adj* zweibeinig; **a** ~**-legged animal** ein Zweibeiner *m*; ~**-party system** *n* Zweiparteiensystem *nt*; ~**-piece 1** *adj* zweiteilig; **2** *n (suit)* Zweiteiler *m*; *(swimming costume)* zweiteiliger Badeanzug; ~**-pin plug** *n* Stecker *m* mit zwei Kontakten; ~**-ply** *adj wool* zweifädig; *wood* aus zwei Lagen bestehend; *tissue* zweilagig; ~**-seater** *n (car, plane)* Zweisitzer *m*; ~**some** *n* (a) *(people)* Paar, Pärchen *nt*; (b) *(game)* **to have a** ~**some at golf** zu zweit Golf spielen; ~ **star petrol** *n (Brit old)* Normalbenzin *nt*; ~**-storey** *adj* zweistöckig; ~**-stroke 1** *adj* Zweitakt-; **2** *n* Zweitakter *m*. ~**-time** *vt (col) boy-/girlfriend, accomplice* betrügen; ~**-tone** *adj (in colour)* zweifarbig; ~**-track decision** *n (Pol)* Doppelbeschluß *m*; ~**-up** ~**-down** *n (Brit col)* kleines Reihenhäuschen; ~**-way** *adj* ~**-way (radio)** Funksprechgerät *nt*; ~**-way mirror** Einwegspiegel *m*; ~**-way traffic** Verkehr *m* in beiden Richtungen; ~**-wheeler** *n* Zweirad, Fahrrad *nt*.

**tycoon** [taɪ'kuːn] *n* Magnat *m*.

**TX** *(US Post)* = **Texas.**

**type¹** [taɪp] *n* (a) *(kind)* Art *f*; *(of produce, plant also)* Sorte *f*; *(esp of people)* Typ, Typus *m*. **different** ~**s of cow/rose** verschiedene Arten von Rindern/ verschiedene Rosensorten; **what** ~ **of car is it?** was für ein Auto(typ) ist das?; **they're totally different** ~**s of person** sie sind völlig verschiedene Typen; **I object to that** ~ **of behaviour** ich protestiere gegen ein solches Benehmen; **it's not my** ~ **of film** diese Art Film gefällt mir nicht; **he's not my** ~ er ist nicht mein Typ; **she's my** ~ **of girl** sie ist mein Typ; **he's not the** ~ **to hit a lady** er ist nicht der Mensch, der eine Frau schlägt. **(b)** *(col: man)* Typ *m*.

**type²** **1** *n (Typ)* Type *f*. **small/large** ~ kleine/große Schrift. **2** *vt* tippen *(col)*, (mit der Maschine) schreiben. **a badly** ~**d letter** ein schlecht getippter Brief. **3** *vi* maschineschreiben, tippen *(col)*.

▶**type out** *vt sep letter* (mit der Maschine) schreiben, tippen *(col)*.

**type:** ~**-cast** *vt (Theat)* (auf eine bestimmte Rolle) festlegen; ~**face** *n* Schrift *f*; ~**script** *n* (mit Maschine geschriebenes) Manuskript, Typoskript *nt*; ~**set** *vt* setzen; ~**setter** *n (person)* Setzer(in *f*) *m*; *(firm)* Setzerei *f*; ~**setting** *n* Setzen *nt*, (Schrift)satz *m*; ~**setting machine** Setzmaschine *f*; ~**setting firm** Setzerei *f*.

**typewriter** ['taɪp‚raɪtəʳ] *n* Schreibmaschine *f*. ~ **ribbon** Farbband *nt*.

**typewritten** ['taɪp‚rɪtn] *adj* maschinengeschrieben, getippt *(col)*.

**typhoid** ['taɪfɔɪd] *n (also* ~ *fever)* Typhus *m*.

**typhoon** [taɪ'fuːn] *n* Taifun *m*.

**typhus** ['taɪfəs] *n* Fleckfieber *nt*, Flecktyphus *m*.

**typical** ['tɪpɪkəl] *adj* typisch *(of für)*. **a** ~ **English town** eine typisch englische Stadt; **that's** ~ **of you** das ist typisch für dich.

**typically** ['tɪpɪkəlɪ] *adv see adj.* ~, **he did nothing but complain** es war typisch für ihn, daß er sich ständig beschwerte.

**typify** ['tɪpɪfaɪ] *vt* bezeichnend sein für. **he typifies the reserved Englishman** er verkörpert den Typ des zurückhaltenden Engländers.

**typing** ['taɪpɪŋ] **1** *n* Maschineschreiben, Tippen *(col) nt.* **her** ~ **isn't very good** sie kann nicht besonders gut maschineschreiben. **2** *attr* Schreibmaschinen-. ~ **error** Tippfehler *m*; ~ **pool** Schreibzentrale *f*.

**typist** ['taɪpɪst] *n (professional)* Schreibkraft *f*, Stenotypist(in *f*) *m*.

**typo** ['taɪpəʊ] *n (Typ col)* Druckfehler *m*.

**typographic(al)** [‚taɪpə'græfɪk(əl)] *adj* typographisch. ~ **error** Druckfehler *m*.

**tyrannical** [tɪ'rænɪkəl] *adj* tyrannisch.

**tyrannize** ['tɪrənaɪz] *vt (lit, fig)* tyrannisieren.

**tyranny** ['tɪrənɪ] *n (lit, fig)* Tyrannei *f*.

**tyrant** ['taɪərənt] *n (lit, fig)* Tyrann(in *f*) *m*.

**tyre,** *(US)* **tire** [taɪəʳ] *n* Reifen *m*. ~ **gauge** Reifendruckmesser *m*; ~ **pressure** Reifendruck *m*.

**tyro** ['taɪərəʊ] *n* Anfänger(in *f*) *m*.

**Tyrol** [tɪ'rəʊl] *n* **the** ~ Tirol *nt*.

**Tyrolean** ['tɪrəlɪən], **Tyrolese** [tɪrə'liːz] *adj* Tiroler.

**tzar** *n* = **tsar.**

# U

**U, u** [juː] *n* U, u *nt.* **U for Uncle** ≃ U wie Ulrich.
**U** *(Brit Cin)* = **universal** jugendfrei.
**UAE** = **United Arab Emirates** VAE.
**UB40** [ˌjuːbiːˈfɔːtɪ] *n* Ausweis *m* für Arbeitslose.
**U-bend** [ˈjuːbend] *n* *(in pipe)* U-Bogen *m.*
**ubiquitous** [juːˈbɪkwɪtəs] *adj* allgegenwärtig.
**U-boat** [ˈjuːbəut] *n* U-Boot *nt.*
**UCCA** [ˈʌkə] *(Brit)* = **Universities Central Council on Admissions** ≃ ZVS *f.*
**UDC** *(Brit)* = **Urban District Council.**
**udder** [ˈʌdər] *n* Euter *nt.*
**UDR** *(Brit)* = **Ulster Defence Regiment** *Verband m von Teilzeitsoldaten in Nordirland.*
**UEFA** [juːˈeɪfə] *n* = **Union of European Football Associations** die UEFA.
**UFO** [ˈjuːfəu] = **unidentified flying object** Ufo, UFO *nt.*
**Uganda** [juːˈgændə] *n* Uganda *nt.*
**Ugandan** [juˈgændən] **1** *adj* ugandisch. **2** *n* Ugander(in *f*) *m.*
**UGC** *(Brit)* = **University Grants Committee** *Ausschuß m für die Verteilung von Geldern an die Universitäten.*
**ugh** [ɜːh] *interj* i, igitt.
**ugliness** [ˈʌglɪnɪs] *n* Häßlichkeit *f.*
**ugly** [ˈʌglɪ] *adj (+er)* **(a)** *(not pretty)* häßlich. **as ~ as sin** häßlich wie die Nacht. **(b)** *(unpleasant, nasty)* übel; *news, wound also* schlimm; *scenes, vice, clouds* häßlich; *crime also* gemein; *sky* bedrohlich. **an ~ customer** ein übler Kunde.
**UHF** = **ultra-high frequency** UHF.
**UHT** = **ultra-heat treated** ultrahocherhitzt. **~ milk** H-Milch *f.*
**UK** = **United Kingdom** Vereinigtes Königreich.
**Ukraine** [juːˈkreɪn] *n* **the ~** die Ukraine.
**Ukrainian** [juːˈkreɪnɪən] **1** *adj* ukrainisch. **2** *n* **(a)** Ukrainer(in *f*) *m.* **(b)** *(language)* Ukrainisch *nt.*
**ulcer** [ˈʌlsər] *n (Med)* Geschwür *nt*; *(stomach ~)* Magengeschwür *nt*; *(fig)* Übel *nt.*
**Ulster** [ˈʌlstər] *n* Ulster, Nordirland *nt.* **U~man/woman** Einwohner(in *f*) *m* von Ulster.
**ulterior** [ʌlˈtɪərɪər] *adj* **~ motive** Hintergedanke *m.*
**ultimate** [ˈʌltɪmɪt] **1** *adj* **(a)** *(final)* letzte(r, s); *destiny, solution, decision* endgültig; *result, outcome, aim* End-; *control* oberste(r, s); *authority* höchste(r, s). **what is your ~ ambition in life?** was streben Sie letzten Endes im Leben an?; **although they had no ~ hope of escape** obwohl im Endeffekt keine Hoffnung auf Flucht bestand.
**(b)** *(that cannot be improved on)* vollendet, perfekt. **the ~ insult** der Gipfel der Beleidigung; **the ~ deterrent** *(Mil, fig)* das äußerste Abschreckungsmittel; **the ~ weapon** *(Mil)* die Superwaffe; *(fig)* das letzte und äußerste Mittel; **death is the ~ sacrifice** der Tod ist das allergrößte Opfer.
**(c)** *(basic)* Grund-; *cause* eigentlich; *explanation* grundsätzlich; *truth* letzte(r, s).
**(d)** *(furthest)* entfernteste(r, s); *ancestors* frü-

heste(r, s). **the ~ origins of man** die frühesten Ursprünge des Menschen.
**2** *n* Nonplusultra *nt.* **the ~ in comfort** das Höchste an Komfort.
**ultimately** [ˈʌltɪmɪtlɪ] *adv (in the end)* letztlich, letzten Endes; *(eventually)* schließlich; *(fundamentally)* im Grunde genommen. **it's ~ your decision** letztlich müssen Sie das entscheiden.
**ultimatum** [ˌʌltɪˈmeɪtəm] *n, pl* **-s** *or* **ultimata** *(Mil, fig)* Ultimatum *nt.* **to deliver an ~ to sb** jdm ein Ultimatum stellen.
**ultra-** [ˈʌltrə] *pref* ultra; **~ modern** *adj* ultra- *or* hypermodern; **~sound** *n* Ultraschall *m*; **~violet** *adj* ultraviolett.
**umbilical** [ʌmˈbɪlɪkəl] *adj* **~ cord** Nabelschnur *f.*
**umbrage** [ˈʌmbrɪdʒ] *n:* **to take ~ at sth** an etw *(dat)* Anstoß nehmen.
**umbrella** [ʌmˈbrelə] *n* (Regen)schirm *m*; *(sun ~)* (Sonnen)schirm *m.* **collapsible** *or* **telescopic ~** Taschenschirm *m*; **under the ~ of** *(fig)* unter der Schirmherrschaft von.
**umbrella: ~ organization** *n* Dachorganisation *f*; **~ stand** *n* Schirmständer *m.*
**umpire** [ˈʌmpaɪər] **1** *n (lit, fig)* Schiedsrichter(in *f*) *m.* **2** *vt (Sport)* Schiedsrichter sein bei; *(fig)* schlichten. **3** *vi* Schiedsrichter sein *(in* bei).
**umpteen** [ˌʌmpˈtiːn] *adj (col)* zig *(col)*, x *(col).* **I've told you ~ times** ich habe es dir x-mal gesagt *(col).*
**umpteenth** [ˌʌmpˈtiːnθ] *adj (col)* x-te(r, s). **for the ~ time** zum x-ten Mal.
**UN** = **United Nations** UNO *f.* **~ troops** UNO-Truppen *pl.*
**unabashed** [ˌʌnəˈbæʃt] *adj (not ashamed)* dreist; *(not overawed)* unbeeindruckt.
**unabated** [ˌʌnəˈbeɪtɪd] *adj* unvermindert. **the rain continued ~** der Regen ließ nicht nach.
**unable** [ʌnˈeɪbl] *adj pred* **to be ~ to do sth** etw nicht tun können; *(not be in a position to)* außerstande sein, etw zu tun.
**unabridged** [ˌʌnəˈbrɪdʒd] *adj* ungekürzt.
**unacceptable** [ˌʌnəkˈseptəbl] *adj* plans, terms unannehmbar; *excuse, offer, behaviour* nicht akzeptabel; *standard, conditions* untragbar. **it's quite ~ that we should be expected to ...** es kann doch nicht von uns verlangt werden, daß ...; **it's quite ~ for young children to ...** es kann nicht zugelassen werden, daß kleine Kinder ...; **the ~ face of capitalism** die Kehrseite des Kapitalismus.
**unaccompanied** [ˌʌnəˈkʌmpənɪd] *adj* person, child, singing ohne Begleitung; *instrument* Solo-. **~ luggage** aufgegebenes Reisegepäck.
**unaccountable** [ˌʌnəˈkauntəbl] *adj* unerklärlich.
**unaccountably** [ˌʌnəˈkauntəblɪ] *adv* unerklärlicherweise; *disappear* auf unerklärliche Weise.
**unaccounted for** [ˌʌnəˈkauntɪdˈfɔːr] *adj* ungeklärt. **the £30 is still ~** es ist noch ungeklärt, wo die £30 geblieben sind; **three of the passengers are still ~** drei Passagiere werden noch vermißt.

**unaccustomed** [ˌʌnə'kʌstəmd] *adj* **(a)** *(unusual)* ungewohnt. **(b)** *(of person: unused)* **to be ~ to sth** etw nicht gewohnt sein, an etw *(acc)* nicht gewöhnt sein; **to be ~ to doing sth** nicht daran gewöhnt sein, etw zu tun.

**unacquainted** [ˌʌnə'kweɪntɪd] *adj pred* **to be ~ with poverty** die Armut nicht kennen; **to be ~ with the facts** mit den Tatschen nicht vertraut sein.

**unadulterated** [ˌʌnə'dʌltəreɪtɪd] *adj* **(a)** unverfälscht, rein; *wine* rein, ungepanscht; *(hum) whisky* unverdünnt. **(b)** *(fig) nonsense* absolut; *bliss* ungetrübt.

**unadventurous** [ˌʌnəd'ventʃərəs] *adj time, life* ereignislos; *tastes* bieder; *style, performance* einfallslos; *person* wenig unternehmungslustig.

**unaffected** [ˌʌnə'fektɪd] *adj* **(a)** *(sincere)* ungekünstelt, natürlich; *pleasure, gratitude* echt. **(b)** *(not damaged)* nicht angegriffen *(also Med)*, nicht beeinträchtigt; *(not influenced)* unbeeinflußt; *(not involved)* nicht betroffen; *(unmoved)* ungerührt. **she remained quite ~ by his tears** sie blieb beim Anblick seiner Tränen völlig ungerührt.

**unafraid** [ˌʌnə'freɪd] *adj* furchtlos. **to be ~ of sb/sth** vor jdm/etw keine Angst haben.

**unaided** [ʌn'eɪdɪd] **1** *adv* ohne fremde Hilfe. **2** *adj* **his own ~ work** seine eigene Arbeit.

**unalike** [ˌʌnə'laɪk] *adj pred* unähnlich.

**unalterable** [ʌn'ɒltərəbl] *adj intention, decision* unabänderlich; *laws* unveränderlich.

**unaltered** [ʌn'ɒltəd] *adj* unverändert.

**unambiguous** [ˌʌnæm'bɪgjʊəs] *adj* eindeutig, unzweideutig.

**unambitious** [ˌʌnæm'bɪʃəs] *adj person, plan* 'nicht ehrgeizig (genug); *performance* anspruchslos.

**un-American** [ˌʌnə'merɪkən] *adj* unamerikanisch.

**unanimity** [juːnə'nɪmɪtɪ] *n see adj* Einmütigkeit *f*; Einstimmigkeit *f*.

**unanimous** [juː'nænɪməs] *adj* einmütig; *decision also, (Jur)* einstimmig. **we were ~ in thinking ...** wir waren einmütig der Ansicht ...; **by a ~ vote** einstimmig.

**unanimously** [juː'nænɪməslɪ] *adv* einstimmig.

**unanswerable** [ʌn'ɑːnsərəbl] *adj question* nicht zu beantworten(d *attr*) *pred*; *argument, case* unwiderlegbar.

**unanswered** [ʌn'ɑːnsəd] *adj* unbeantwortet.

**unappealing** [ˌʌnə'piːlɪŋ] nicht reizvoll; *person* unansehnlich; *prospect, sight* nicht verlockend.

**unappetizing** [ʌn'æpɪtaɪzɪŋ] *adj* unappetitlich; *prospect, thought* wenig verlockend.

**unappreciative** [ˌʌnə'priːʃɪətɪv] *adj* undankbar; *audience* verständnislos. **to be ~ of sth** etw nicht zu würdigen wissen.

**unapproachable** [ˌʌnə'prəʊtʃəbl] *adj place* unzugänglich; *person also* unnahbar.

**unarmed** [ʌn'ɑːmd] *adj* unbewaffnet. **~ combat** Nahkampf *m* ohne Waffe.

**unashamed** [ˌʌnə'ʃeɪmd] *adj* schamlos. **his ~ curiosity** seine unverhohlene Neugier; **he was quite ~ about it** er schämte sich dessen überhaupt nicht.

**unashamedly** [ˌʌnə'ʃeɪmɪdlɪ] *adv* ungeniert; *say, admit* ohne Scham; *in favour of, partisan* unverhohlen.

**unasked** [ʌn'ɑːskt] *adj (unrequested)* unaufgefordert, ungefragt; *(uninvited)* ungebeten.

**unassailable** [ˌʌnə'seɪləbl] *adj* unangreifbar; *fortress* uneinnehmbar; *position, reputation* unanfechtbar; *conviction* unerschütterlich; *argument* unwiderlegbar, zwingend.

**unassisted** [ˌʌnə'sɪstɪd] *adj, adv* = **unaided**.

**unassuming** [ˌʌnə'sjuːmɪŋ] *adj* bescheiden.

**unattached** [ˌʌnə'tætʃt] *adj* **(a)** *(not fastened)* unbefestigt; *(Mil)* keinem Regiment/keiner Einheit *etc* zugeteilt. **(b)** *(with no partner)* ungebunden.

**unattended** [ˌʌnə'tendɪd] *adj children* unbeaufsichtigt; *car, luggage* unbewacht; *wound, patient* unbehandelt; *shop* ohne Bedienung; *customer* nicht bedient; *business* unerledigt.

**unattractive** [ˌʌnə'træktɪv] *adj sight, place* unschön, wenig reizvoll; *offer, woman* unattraktiv; *trait, scar* unschön; *character* unsympathisch.

**unauthorized** [ʌn'ɔːθəraɪzd] *adj* unbefugt. **no entry for ~ persons** Zutritt für Unbefugte verboten!

**unavailable** [ˌʌnə'veɪləbl] *adj* nicht erhältlich; *person* nicht zu erreichen *pred*; *library book* nicht verfügbar.

**unavailing** [ˌʌnə'veɪlɪŋ] *adj* vergeblich.

**unavenged** [ˌʌnə'vendʒd] *adj* ungerächt.

**unavoidable** [ˌʌnə'vɔɪdəbl] *adj* unvermeidlich; *conclusion* zwangsläufig.

**unavoidably** [ˌʌnə'vɔɪdəblɪ] *adv* notgedrungen. **to be ~ detained** verhindert sein.

**unaware** [ˌʌnə'wɛəʳ] *adj pred* **to be ~ of sth** sich *(dat)* einer Sache *(gen)* nicht bewußt sein; **I was ~ of his presence** ich hatte nicht bemerkt, daß er da war; **I was ~ that he was interested** es war mir nicht bewußt, daß er (daran) interessiert war.

**unawares** [ˌʌnə'wɛəz] *adv (by surprise)* unerwartet; *(accidentally)* unbeabsichtigt, versehentlich; *(without knowing)* unwissentlich. **to catch** *or* **take sb ~** jdn überraschen.

**unbalanced** [ʌn'bælənst] *adj* **(a)** unausgewogen; *diet, report also, view* einseitig; *ship etc* nicht im Gleichgewicht. **(b)** *(also mentally ~) (erratic)* unausgeglichen; *(slightly crazy)* nicht ganz normal. **(c)** *account* nicht ausgeglichen.

**unbearable** [ʌn'bɛərəbl] *adj* unerträglich.

**unbearably** [ʌn'bɛərəblɪ] *adv* unerträglich.

**unbeatable** [ʌn'biːtəbl] *adj* unschlagbar; *record also* nicht zu überbieten(d *attr*) *pred*.

**unbeaten** [ʌn'biːtn] *adj* ungeschlagen; *record* ungebrochen.

**unbecoming** [ˌʌnbɪ'kʌmɪŋ] *adj behaviour, language etc* unschicklich; *clothes* unvorteilhaft; *beard* unschön.

**unbeknown(st)** [ˌʌnbɪ'nəʊn(st)] *adv (dated, hum)* **~ to me/his father** ohne mein Wissen/ohne Wissen seines Vaters.

**unbelievable** [ˌʌnbɪ'liːvəbl] *adj* unglaublich.

**unbelievably** [ˌʌnbɪ'liːvəblɪ] *adv* unglaublich.

**unbeliever** [ˌʌnbɪ'liːvəʳ] *n* Ungläubige(r) *mf*.

**unbelieving** [ˌʌnbɪ'liːvɪŋ] *adj* ungläubig.

**unbend** [ʌn'bend] *pret, ptp* **unbent** **1** *vt (straighten) metal etc* geradebiegen; *arms* strecken. **2** *vi (person, relax)* aus sich herausgehen; *(straighten body)* sich aufrichten.

**unbending** [ʌn'bendɪŋ] *adj person, attitude* unnachgiebig; *determination* unbeugsam.

**unbent** [ʌn'bent] *pret, ptp of* **unbend**.

**unbias(s)ed** [ʌn'baɪəst] *adj* unvoreingenommen; *opinion, report also* unparteiisch.

**unblemished** [ʌn'blemɪʃt] *adj (lit, fig)* makellos.

**unblock** [ʌn'blɒk] *vt* frei machen; *sink, pipe* die Verstopfung in *(+dat)* ... beseitigen.

**unbolt** [ʌn'bəʊlt] *vt* aufriegeln. **he left the door ~ed** er verriegelte die Tür nicht.

**unborn** [ʌn'bɔːn] *adj* ungeboren. **generations yet ~** kommende Generationen.

**unbound** [ʌn'baʊnd] *adj book* ungebunden.

**unbounded** [ʌn'baʊndɪd] *adj* grenzenlos.

**unbreakable** [ʌn'breɪkəbl] *adj glass, toy* unzerbrechlich; *record* nicht zu brechen(d *attr*) *pred*; *rule* unumstößlich; *promise* unverbrüchlich.

**unbridled** [ʌn'braɪdld] *adj passion* ungezügelt; *anger* hemmungslos; *tongue* lose; *capitalism* ungehemmt.

**un-British** [ʌn'brɪtɪʃ] *adj* unbritisch.

**unbroken** [ʌn'brəʊkən] *adj* (a) *(intact)* unbeschädigt; *heart, promise* nicht gebrochen. (b) *(continuous)* ununterbrochen; *(Mil)* ranks geschlossen; *line of descent* direkt. **an ~ night's sleep** eine ungestörte Nacht. (c) *(unbeaten) record* ungebrochen. (d) *horse* nicht zugeritten; *pride* ungebeugt. **his spirit remained ~** er war ungebrochen.

**unbuckle** [ʌn'bʌkl] *vt* aufschnallen.

**unburden** [ʌn'bɜːdn] *vt* **to ~ oneself/one's heart to sb** jdm sein Herz ausschütten.

**unbusinesslike** [ʌn'bɪznɪslaɪk] *adj* wenig geschäftsmäßig. **in spite of his ~ appearance** ... obwohl er gar nicht wie ein Geschäftsmann aussieht ...

**unbutton** [ʌn'bʌtn] *vt* aufknöpfen.

**uncalled-for** [ʌn'kɔːldfɔːʳ] *adj (unjustified) criticism* ungerechtfertigt; *(unnecessary)* unnötig; *(rude) remark* deplaziert. **that was quite ~** das war nun wirklich nicht nötig.

**uncanny** [ʌn'kænɪ] *adj* unheimlich.

**uncared-for** [ʌn'kɛədfɔːʳ] *adj garden, hands* ungepflegt; *child* vernachlässigt.

**uncaring** [ʌn'kɛərɪŋ] *adj* gleichgültig; *parents* lieblos.

**uncarpeted** [ʌn'kɑːpɪtɪd] *adj* ohne Teppich, nicht ausgelegt.

**unceasing** [ʌn'siːsɪŋ] *adj* unaufhörlich.

**uncensored** [ʌn'sensəd] *adj film* unzensiert.

**unceremonious** [ˌʌnserɪ'məʊnɪəs] *adj* (a) *(abrupt, rude) dismissal* brüsk, barsch; *exit, departure* überstürzt; *haste* unfein. (b) *(informal, simple) greeting* zwanglos.

**unceremoniously** [ˌʌnserɪ'məʊnɪəslɪ] *adv* kurzerhand.

**uncertain** [ʌn'sɜːtn] *adj* (a) *(unsure)* unsicher; *light* undeutlich, schwach. **to be ~ whether ...** sich *(dat)* nicht sicher sein, ob ...; **to be ~ of or about sth** sich *(dat)* einer Sache *(gen)* nicht sicher sein; **I was ~ as to what to do** ich war mir *(dat)* nicht sicher, was ich tun sollte. (b) *(unknown) date, result* ungewiß; *origins* unbestimmt. **the cause of death remains ~** die Todesursache ist weiterhin ungeklärt. (c) *(unreliable) weather, prices* unbeständig; *temper* unberechenbar; *judgement* unzuverlässig. (d) *(unclear)* vage. **in no ~ terms** klipp and klar.

**uncertainly** [ʌn'sɜːtnlɪ] *adv say* unbestimmt; *look, move* unsicher.

**uncertainty** [ʌn'sɜːtntɪ] *n (state)* Ungewißheit *f*; *(indefiniteness)* Unbestimmtheit *f*; *(doubt)* Unsicherheit *f*. **there is still some ~ (as to) whether ...** es besteht noch Ungewißheit, ob ...

**unchallenged** [ʌn'tʃælɪndʒd] *adj* unbestritten; *(Jur) evidence* unangefochten. **to go ~** *(Mil)* ohne Anruf passieren; **the record was** *or* **went ~ for several years** jahrelang versuchte niemand, den Rekord zu überbieten; **I cannot let that remark go ~** diese Bemerkung kann ich nicht unwidersprochen hinnehmen.

**unchanged** [ʌn'tʃeɪndʒd] *adj* unverändert.

**unchanging** [ʌn'tʃeɪndʒɪŋ] *adj* unveränderlich.

**uncharacteristic** [ˌʌnkærəktə'rɪstɪk] *adj* uncharakteristisch, untypisch (*of* für).

**uncharitable** [ʌn'tʃærɪtəbl] *adj* hartherzig; *remark* unfreundlich, lieblos; *view* herzlos; *criticism* unbarmherzig.

**uncharitably** [ʌn'tʃærɪtəblɪ] *adv* lieblos; *(as sentence-modifier)* liebloserweise.

**uncharted** [ʌn'tʃɑːtɪd] *adj (not explored)* uner-

forscht; *(not on map)* nicht eingezeichnet.

**unchecked** [ʌn'tʃekt] *adj* (a) *(unrestrained)* unkontrolliert; *advance* ungehindert; *anger* ungezügelt. **to go ~** *(abuse)* geduldet werden; *(advance)* nicht gehindert werden; *(inflation)* nicht eingedämmt werden; **if the epidemic goes ~** wenn der Epidemie nicht Einhalt geboten wird. (b) *(not verified)* ungeprüft.

**unchristian** [ʌn'krɪstjən] *adj* unchristlich.

**uncivil** [ʌn'sɪvɪl] *adj* unhöflich.

**uncivilized** [ʌn'sɪvɪlaɪzd] *adj country, tribe, behaviour* unzivilisiert; *(col) habit* barbarisch.

**unclaimed** [ʌn'kleɪmd] *adj prize* nicht abgeholt; *property also* herrenlos; *right* nicht geltend gemacht; *social security etc* nicht beansprucht.

**unclassified** [ʌn'klæsɪfaɪd] *adj* (a) *(not arranged)* nicht klassifiziert. **~ road** *(Brit)* (nicht numerierte) Nebenstraße. (b) *(not secret)* nicht geheim.

**uncle** ['ʌŋkl] *n* Onkel *m*. **U~ Sam** Onkel Sam; **to say** *or* **cry ~** *(US)* aufgeben.

**unclean** [ʌn'kliːn] *adj* unsauber *(also Bibl)*; *(Rel) animal* unrein; *thoughts* unkeusch; *(fig: contaminated)* schmutzig.

**unclear** [ʌn'klɪəʳ] *adj* unklar; *essay etc* undurchsichtig. **to be ~ about sth** sich *(dat)* über etw *(acc)* im unklaren sein.

**unclothed** [ʌn'kləʊðd] *adj* unbekleidet.

**unclouded** [ʌn'klaʊdɪd] *adj sky* unbewölkt; *(fig) happiness, vision* ungetrübt; *mind* klar.

**uncluttered** [ʌn'klʌtəd] *adj (tidy)* ordentlich.

**uncoil** [ʌn'kɔɪl] **1** *vt* abwickeln. **2** *vir (snake)* sich strecken; *(person)* sich ausstrecken; *(wire etc)* sich abspulen.

**uncollected** [ˌʌnkə'lektɪd] *adj tax* nicht eingezogen; *fare* nicht kassiert.

**uncombed** [ʌn'kəʊmd] *adj* ungekämmt.

**uncomfortable** [ʌn'kʌmfətəbl] *adj* (a) unbequem; *chair, position also* ungemütlich. **I feel ~ sitting like this** es ist unbequem, so zu sitzen; **I feel ~ in this jacket** in dieser Jacke fühle ich mich nicht wohl; **it feels ~** es ist unbequem. (b) *(uneasy) feeling* unangenehm, ungut; *silence (awkward)* peinlich. **to feel ~** sich unbehaglich fühlen; **I felt ~ about it** mir war nicht wohl dabei. (c) *(unpleasant) time, position* unerfreulich. **to make life ~ for sb** jdm das Leben schwer machen.

**uncomfortably** [ʌn'kʌmfətəblɪ] *adv* (a) unbequem. (b) *(uneasily)* unbehaglich. (c) *(unpleasantly)* unangenehm. **it's getting ~ close** es rückt bedrohlich näher.

**uncommitted** [ˌʌnkə'mɪtɪd] *adj* nicht engagiert; *party, country* neutral. **we want to remain ~** *(not decide)* wir wollen uns nicht festlegen.

**uncommon** [ʌn'kɒmən] *adj* (a) *(unusual)* ungewöhnlich. **it is not ~ for her to be late** es ist nichts Ungewöhnliches, daß sie zu spät kommt; **a not ~ occurrence** eine häufige Erscheinung. (b) *(outstanding)* außergewöhnlich.

**uncommunicative** [ˌʌnkə'mjuːnɪkətɪv] *adj (by nature)* verschlossen; *(temporarily)* schweigsam.

**uncompetitive** [ˌʌnkɒm'petɪtɪv] *adj athlete, racing car etc* nicht konkurrenzfähig.

**uncomplaining** [ˌʌnkəm'pleɪnɪŋ] *adj* duldsam.

**uncomplainingly** [ˌʌnkəm'pleɪnɪŋlɪ] *adv* geduldig, klaglos.

**uncompleted** [ˌʌnkəm'pliːtɪd] *adj* unvollendet.

**uncomplicated** [ʌn'kɒmplɪkeɪtɪd] *adj* unkompliziert.

**uncomplimentary** [ˌʌnkɒmplɪ'mentərɪ] *adj* unschmeichelhaft. **to be ~ about sb/sth** sich nicht sehr schmeichelhaft über jdn/etw äußern.

**uncomprehending** [ˌʌnkɒmprɪˈhendɪŋ] *adj* verständnislos.

**uncompromising** [ʌnˈkɒmprəmaɪzɪŋ] *adj* kompromißlos; *dedication, honesty* rückhaltlos; *commitment* hundertprozentig.

**unconcealed** [ˌʌnkənˈsiːld] *adj joy* offen, unverhüllt; *hatred, distaste etc also* unverhohlen.

**unconcerned** [ˌʌnkənˈsɜːnd] *adj (unworried)* unbekümmert; *(indifferent)* gleichgültig. **to be ~ about sth** sich nicht um etw kümmern.

**unconditional** [ˌʌnkənˈdɪʃənl] *adj* vorbehaltlos. **~ surrender** bedingungslose Kapitulation.

**unconditionally** [ˌʌnkənˈdɪʃnəlɪ] *adv* vorbehaltlos; *surrender* bedingungslos.

**unconfirmed** [ˌʌnkənˈfɜːmd] *adj* unbestätigt.

**uncongenial** [ˌʌnkənˈdʒiːnɪəl] *adj person* unliebenswürdig; *work, surroundings* unerfreulich.

**unconnected** [ˌʌnkəˈnektɪd] *adj* **(a)** *(unrelated)* nicht miteinander in Beziehung stehend *attr.* **the two events are ~** es besteht keine Beziehung zwischen den beiden Ereignissen. **(b)** *(incoherent)* unzusammenhängend.

**unconscious** [ʌnˈkɒnʃəs] **1** *adj* **(a)** *(Med)* bewußtlos. **the blow knocked him ~** durch den Schlag wurde er bewußtlos. **(b)** *pred (unaware)* **to be ~ of sth** sich *(dat)* einer Sache *(gen)* nicht bewußt sein; **I was ~ of the fact that ...** es war mir nicht bewußt, daß ... **(c)** *(unintentional) insult, allusion etc* unbeabsichtigt; *blunder also* ungewollt; *humour* unfreiwillig. **(d)** *(Psych)* unbewußt. **2** *n (Psych)* **the ~** das Unbewußte.

**unconsciously** [ʌnˈkɒnʃəslɪ] *adv* unbewußt. **an ~ funny remark** eine ungewollt lustige Bemerkung.

**unconstitutional** [ˌʌnkɒnstɪˈtjuːʃənl] *adj* verfassungswidrig.

**uncontaminated** [ˌʌnkənˈtæmɪneɪtɪd] *adj* nicht verseucht; *(fig)* unverdorben.

**uncontested** [ˌʌnkənˈtestɪd] *adj* unbestritten; *election, seat* ohne Gegenkandidat. **the chairmanship was ~** in der Wahl für den Vorsitz gab es keinen Gegenkandidaten.

**uncontrollable** [ˌʌnkənˈtrəʊləbl] *adj* unkontrollierbar; *child* nicht zu bändigen(d *attr*) *pred*; *horse, dog* nicht unter Kontrolle zu bringen(d *attr*) *pred*; *desire, urge* unwiderstehlich; *(physical)* unkontrollierbar; *twitch* unkontrolliert; *laughter, mirth* unbezähmbar. **to become ~** außer Kontrolle geraten.

**uncontrolled** [ˌʌnkənˈtrəʊld] *adj* ungehindert; *dogs, children* unbeaufsichtigt; *laughter* unkontrolliert; *weeping* haltlos. **if inflation is allowed to go ~** wenn die Inflation nicht unter Kontrolle gebracht wird.

**uncontroversial** [ˌʌnkɒntrəˈvɜːʃəl] *adj* unverfänglich.

**unconventional** *adj,* **~ly** *adv* [ˌʌnkənˈvenʃənl, -əlɪ] unkonventionell.

**unconvinced** [ˌʌnkənˈvɪnst] *adj* **I remain ~** ich bin noch immer nicht überzeugt.

**unconvincing** *adj,* **~ly** *adv* [ˌʌnkənˈvɪnsɪŋ, -lɪ] nicht überzeugend. **rather ~** wenig überzeugend.

**uncooked** [ʌnˈkʊkt] *adj* ungekocht, roh.

**uncooperative** [ˌʌnkəʊˈɒpərətɪv] *adj attitude* stur, wenig entgegenkommend; *witness, colleague* wenig hilfreich, nicht hilfsbereit. **the government remained ~** die Regierung war auch weiterhin nicht zur Kooperation bereit.

**uncork** [ʌnˈkɔːk] *vt bottle* entkorken.

**uncorroborated** [ˌʌnkəˈrɒbəreɪtɪd] *adj* unbestätigt; *evidence* nicht bekräftigt.

**uncountable** [ʌnˈkaʊntəbl] *adj (Gram)* unzählbar.

**uncouple** [ʌnˈkʌpl] *vt train etc* abkoppeln.

**uncouth** [ʌnˈkuːθ] *adj* ungehobelt; *expression, word* unflätig, unfein.

**uncover** [ʌnˈkʌvəʳ] *vt* **(a)** *(remove cover from)* aufdecken; *head* entblößen *(liter).* **(b)** *scandal, plot* aufdecken; *ancient ruins* zum Vorschein bringen.

**uncritical** [ʌnˈkrɪtɪkəl] *adj* unkritisch *(of, about* in bezug auf *+acc).*

**uncrossed** [ʌnˈkrɒst] *adj (Brit) cheque* Bar-.

**uncrowded** [ʌnˈkraʊdɪd] *adj* nicht überlaufen.

**unction** [ˈʌŋkʃən] *n* **extreme ~** *(Rel)* Letzte Ölung.

**uncultivated** [ʌnˈkʌltɪveɪtɪd] *adj land* unbebaut; *person, behaviour* unkultiviert; *mind* nicht ausgebildet.

**uncultured** [ʌnˈkʌltʃəd] *adj person, mind* ungebildet; *behaviour* unkultiviert.

**uncurl** [ʌnˈkɜːl] **1** *vt* auseinanderrollen. **to ~ oneself** sich strecken. **2** *vi (cat, snake)* sich langsam strecken; *(person)* sich ausstrecken.

**uncut** [ʌnˈkʌt] *adj* ungeschnitten; *diamond* ungeschliffen; *film, play etc* ungekürzt.

**undamaged** [ʌnˈdæmɪdʒd] *adj* unbeschädigt; *(fig) reputation* makellos.

**undated** [ʌnˈdeɪtɪd] *adj* undatiert.

**undaunted** [ʌnˈdɔːntɪd] *adj (not discouraged)* nicht entmutigt, unverzagt; *(fearless)* unerschrocken. **he carried on ~** er machte unverzagt weiter.

**undecided** [ˌʌndɪˈsaɪdɪd] *adj* **(a)** *person* unentschlossen. **he is ~ (as to) whether he should go or not** er ist (sich *dat*) noch unschlüssig, ob er gehen soll oder nicht. **(b)** *question* unentschieden.

**undefeated** [ˌʌndɪˈfiːtɪd] *adj army, team* unbesiegt; *spirit* ungebrochen.

**undefined** [ˌʌndɪˈfaɪnd] *adj* nicht definiert; *(vague)* undefinierbar.

**undelivered** [ˌʌndɪˈlɪvəd] *adj mail* nicht zugestellt. **if ~ return to sender** falls unzustellbar, bitte an Absender zurück.

**undemanding** [ˌʌndɪˈmaːndɪŋ] *adj* anspruchslos; *task* wenig fordernd, keine großen Anforderungen stellend *attr.*

**undemocratic** [ˌʌndeməˈkrætɪk] *adj* undemokratisch.

**undemonstrative** [ˌʌndɪˈmɒnstrətɪv] *adj* zurückhaltend.

**undeniable** [ˌʌndɪˈnaɪəbl] *adj* unbestreitbar. **it is ~ that ...** es läßt sich nicht bestreiten, daß ...

**undeniably** [ˌʌndɪˈnaɪəblɪ] *adv* zweifellos; *successful, proud* unbestreitbar.

**under** [ˈʌndəʳ] **1** *prep* **(a)** *(beneath) (place)* unter *(+dat); (direction)* unter *(+acc).* **~ it** darunter; **to come out from ~ the bed** unter dem Bett hervorkommen; **it's ~ there** es ist da drunter *(col);* **field ~ barley** mit Gerste bebautes Feld. **(b)** *(less than)* unter *(+dat).* **it took ~ an hour** es dauerte weniger als eine Stunde. **(c)** *(subordinate to, influence of etc)* unter *(+dat).* **he had 50 men ~ him** er hatte 50 Männer unter sich; **he studied ~ Popper** er hat bei Popper studiert; **he was born ~ Virgo** *(Astrol)* er ist im Zeichen der Jungfrau geboren; **the matter ~ discussion** der Diskussionsgegenstand; **to be ~ the doctor** in (ärztlicher) Behandlung sein; **it's classified ~ history** es ist unter „Geschichte" eingeordnet. **(d)** *(according to)* nach, gemäß *(+dat).* **~ the terms of the contract** gemäß den Vertragsbedingungen.

**2** *adv* **(a)** *(beneath)* unten; *(unconscious)* bewußtlos. **he came to the fence and crawled ~** er kam zum Zaun und kroch darunter durch; **to go ~** untergehen. **(b)** *(less)* darunter.

**under-** *pref (in rank)* Unter-. **for the ~-twelves/-eighteens/-forties** für Kinder unter zwölf/Jugendliche unter achtzehn/Leute unter vierzig.

**under: ~age** *adj attr* minderjährig; **~age drinking**

Alkoholgenuß *m* Minderjähriger; ~**arm** *adj throw* von unten; *hair* Achsel-; ~**capitalized** *adj (Fin)* unterkapitalisiert; ~**carriage** *n (Aviat)* Fahrwerk *nt*; ~**charge** *vt* zuwenig berechnen *(sb* jdm*)*; **he** ~**charged me by 10p** er berechnete mir 10 Pence zuwenig; ~**clothes** *npl* Unterwäsche *f*; ~**coat** *n (paint)* Grundierfarbe *f*; *(coat of paint)* Grundierung *f*; ~**cooked** *adj* (noch) nicht gar; ~**cover** *adj agent* Geheim-; ~**cover operation** verdeckter Polizeieinsatz; ~**current** *n (lit, fig)* Unterströmung *f*; *(fig: in sb's words)* Unterton *m*; ~**cut** *pret, ptp* ~**cut** *vt competitor* unterbieten; ~**developed** *adj* unterentwickelt; *resources* ungenutzt; ~**development** *n* Unterentwicklung *f*; ~**dog** *n* Benachteiligte(r) *m*; *(in game also)* Unterlegene(r) *m*; ~**done** *adj* nicht gar; *(deliberately)* nicht durchgebraten; ~**emphasize** *vt* nicht ausreichend betonen; *(intentionally)* herunterspielen; ~**employed** *adj* unterbeschäftigt; ~**employment** *n* Unterbeschäftigung *f*; ~**estimate 1** *vt cost, person* unterschätzen; **2** *n* Unterschätzung *f*; ~**exposed** *adj (Phot)* unterbelichtet; ~**exposure** *n (Phot)* Unterbelichtung *f*; ~**fed** *adj* unterernährt; ~**floor heating** *n* Fußbodenheizung *f*; ~**foot** *adv* am Boden; **it is wet** ~**foot** der Boden ist naß; **to trample sb/sth** ~**foot** *(lit, fig)* auf jdm/etw herumtrampeln; ~**funded** *adj* unterfinanziert; ~**go** *pret* ~**went**, *ptp* ~**gone** *vt suffering* durchmachen; *change also* erleben; *test, treatment, (Med)* operation sich unterziehen *(+dat)*; *(machine)* test unterzogen werden *(+dat)*; **to be** ~**going repairs** in Reparatur sein; ~**grad** *(col)*, ~**graduate 1** *n* Student(in *f*) *m*; **2** *attr* Studenten-.
**underground** ['ʌndəgraʊnd] **1** *adj* **(a)** unterirdisch; *(Min)* Untertage-. **(b)** *(fig)* press, movement Untergrund-. **2** *adv* **(a)** unterirdisch; *(Min)* unter Tage. **10 feet** ~ 3 Meter unter der Erde. **(b)** *(fig)* **to go** ~ untertauchen. **3** *n* **(a)** *(Brit Rail)* U-Bahn, Untergrundbahn *f*. **(b)** *(movement)* Untergrundbewegung *f*; *(subculture)* Underground *m*.
**under:** ~**growth** *n* Gestrüpp *nt*; *(under trees)* Unterholz *nt*; ~**hand** *adj (sly)* hinterhältig; ~**insured** *adj* unterversichert; ~**lay** *n* Unterlage *f*; ~**lie** *pret* ~**lay**, *ptp* ~**lain** *vt (lit)* liegen unter *(+dat)*; *(fig: be basis for or cause of)* zugrunde liegen *(+dat)*; ~**line** *vt (lit, fig)* unterstreichen.
**underling** ['ʌndəlɪŋ] *n (pej)* Untergebene(r) *mf*, Befehlsempfänger(in *f*) *m (pej)*.
**under:** ~**lying** *adj* **(a)** *soil, rocks* tieferliegend; **(b)** *cause* eigentlich; *(deeper also)* tiefer; *problem* zugrundeliegend; ~**manned** *adj* unterbesetzt; ~**manning** *n* Personalmangel *m*; *(deliberate)* Unterbesetzung *f*; ~**mentioned** *adj* untengenannt; ~**mine** *vt* **(a)** *(tunnel under)* unterhöhlen; *(Mil)* unterminieren; **(b)** *(fig: weaken)* authority, confidence untergraben; *health* angreifen; ~**most** *adj* unterste(r, s).
**underneath** [ʌndə'niːθ] **1** *prep (place)* unter *(+dat)*; *(direction)* unter *(+acc)*. ~ **it** darunter. **2** *adv* darunter. **the ones** ~ die darunter. **3** *n* Unterseite *f*.
**under:** ~**nourished** *adj* unterernährt; ~**paid** *adj* unterbezahlt; ~**pants** *npl* Unterhose (*n pl*) *f*; **a pair of** ~**pants** eine Unterhose, ein Paar Unterhosen; ~**pass** *n* Unterführung *f*; ~**pay** *pret, ptp* ~**paid** *vt* unterbezahlen; ~**payment** *n* Unterbezahlung *f*; **there was an** ~**payment of £10 in your salary** Sie bekamen £10 zuwenig Gehalt ausbezahlt; ~**pin** *vt wall, argument* untermauern; *economy etc* stützen; ~**play** *vt (Cards)* hand nicht voll ausspielen; **to** ~**play one's hand** *(fig)* nicht alle Trümpfe ausspielen; ~**populated** *adj* unterbevölkert; ~**price** *vt* zu billig anbieten, unter Preis anbieten; **to be** ~**priced**

zu billig gehandelt werden; ~**privileged** *adj* unterprivilegiert; **the** ~**privileged** die Unterprivilegierten *pl*; ~**rate** *vt (~estimate)* danger, chance, person unterschätzen; *(~value)* qualities unterbewerten; ~**score** *vt* unterstreichen; ~**seal** *n (Aut)* Unterbodenschutz *m*; ~**secretary** *n (also* **Parliamentary U~secretary)** (parlamentarischer) Staatssekretär; ~**sell** *pret, ptp* ~**sold** *vt (sell at lower price)* competitor unterbieten; *goods* unter Preis verkaufen; **he tends to** ~**sell himself/his ideas** er kann sich/ seine Ideen nicht verkaufen; ~**shirt** *n (US)* Unterhemd *nt*; ~**shorts** *npl (US)* Unterhose(n *pl*) *f*; ~**side** *n* Unterseite *f*; ~**signed** *adj (form)* unterzeichnet; **we the** ~**signed** wir, die Unterzeichneten; ~**sized** *adj* klein; *(less than proper size)* zu klein; *(pej)* person also zu kurz geraten *(hum)*; ~**skirt** *n* Unterrock *m*; ~**sold** *pret, ptp of* ~**sell**; ~**staffed** *adj office* unterbesetzt; **we are** ~**staffed at the moment** wir haben momentan zu wenig Personal.
**understand** [ˌʌndə'stænd] *pret, ptp* **understood 1** *vt* **(a)** verstehen; *action, event, person, difficulty also* begreifen. **I don't** ~ **Russian** ich verstehe kein Russisch; **I can't** ~ **his agreeing to do it** es ist mir unbegreiflich, warum er sich dazu bereit erklärt hat; **what do you** ~ **by "pragmatism"?** was verstehen Sie unter „Pragmatismus"?; **to** ~ **one another** sich verstehen. **(b)** *(believe)* **we understood we were to be paid for it** wir hatten angenommen, daß wir dafür bezahlt werden; **I** ~ **that you are going to Australia** ich höre, Sie gehen nach Australien; **I** ~ **you've already met** wenn ich mich nicht irre, kennen Sie sich schon; **am I/are we to** ~ ...? soll das etwa heißen, daß ...?; **to give sb to** ~ **that** ... jdm zu verstehen geben, daß ...; **I understood from his speech that** ... ich entnahm seiner Rede, daß ...
**2** *vi* **(a)** verstehen. ~? verstanden?; **you don't** ~! du verstehst das nicht!; **I quite** ~ ich verstehe schon. **(b)** **so I** ~ es scheint so; **he was, I** ~, **a widower** wie ich hörte, war er Witwer.
**understandable** [ˌʌndə'stændəbl] *adj* verständlich.
**understandably** [ˌʌndə'stændəblɪ] *adv* verständlicherweise.
**understanding** [ˌʌndə'stændɪŋ] **1** *adj* verständnisvoll. **he asked me to be** ~ er bat mich um Verständnis. **2** *n* **(a)** *(knowledge)* Kenntnisse *pl*; *(comprehension, sympathy)* Verständnis *nt*. **her** ~ **of children** ihr Verständnis für Kinder; **my** ~ **of the situation is that** ... ich verstehe die Situation so, daß ...; **he has a good** ~ **of the problem** er kennt sich mit dem Problem gut aus; **in order to promote international** ~ um die internationale Verständigung zu fördern. **(b)** *(agreement)* Abmachung, Vereinbarung *f*. **to come to or reach an** ~ **with sb** eine Vereinbarung mit jdm treffen. **(c)** *(assumption)* Voraussetzung *f*. **on the** ~ **that** ... unter der Voraussetzung, daß ...
**understate** [ˌʌndə'steɪt] *vt* untertreiben, herunterspielen. **to** ~ **one's case** untertreiben.
**understated** [ˌʌndə'steɪtɪd] *adj picture, music, colours* gedämpft; *film etc* subtil.
**understatement** [ˌʌndə'steɪtmənt] *n* Untertreibung *f*, Understatement *nt*.
**understood** [ˌʌndə'stʊd] **1** *pret, ptp of* **understand**. **2** *adj* **(a)** *(clear)* klar. **to make oneself** ~ sich verständlich machen; **do I make myself** ~? ist das klar?; **I wish it to be** ~ **that** ... ich möchte klarstellen, daß ...; ~? klar?; ~! gut! **(b)** *(believed)* **he is** ~ **to have left** es heißt, daß er gegangen ist; **it is** ~ **that** ... es heißt *or* man hört, daß ...; **he let it be** ~ **that** ... er gab zu verstehen, daß ...
**understudy** ['ʌndəˌstʌdɪ] *n (Theat)* zweite Beset-

zung.

**undertake** [ˌʌndə'teɪk] *pret* **undertook** [ˌʌndə'tʊk], *ptp* **undertaken** [ˌʌndə'teɪkn] *vt* (a) *job, duty, responsibility* übernehmen; *risk* eingehen, auf sich *(acc)* nehmen. **he undertook to be our guide** er übernahm es, unser Führer zu sein. (b) *(agree, promise)* sich verpflichten; *(guarantee)* garantieren.

**undertaker** ['ʌndəˌteɪkəʳ] *n (esp Brit)* Beerdigungsunternehmer *m*.

**undertaking** [ˌʌndə'teɪkɪŋ] *n* (a) *(enterprise)* Unternehmen *nt*; *(Comm: project also)* Projekt *nt*. (b) *(promise)* Zusicherung *f*. **I give you my solemn ~ that I will never do it again** ich verpflichte mich feierlich, es nie wieder zu tun; **I have an ~ from him** er hat mir sein Wort gegeben; **I can give no such ~** das kann ich nicht versprechen.

**under:** **~tone** *n* (a) *(of voice)* **in an ~tone** mit gedämpfter Stimme; (b) *(fig: of criticism, discontent)* Unterton *m*; **an ~tone of racialism** ein rassistischer Unterton; **~took** *pret of* **~take**; **~tow** *n* Unterströmung *f*; **~used** *adj* nicht voll genutzt; **~value** *vt artist* unterbewerten; *(price too low)* zu niedrig schätzen; *person* zu wenig schätzen; **~water 1** *adj diving, exploration* Unterwasser-; **2** *adv* unter Wasser; **~wear** *n* Unterwäsche *f*; **~weight** *adj* untergewichtig; **to be ~weight** Untergewicht haben; **~went** *pret of* **~go**; **~world** *n (criminals, Myth)* Unterwelt *f*; **~write** *pret* **~wrote**, *ptp* **~written** *vt (finance)* company, loss tragen, garantieren; *insurance policy* bürgen für; *(insure)* shipping versichern; *(St Ex)* shares zeichnen; **~writer** *n (Insur)* Versicherer *m*.

**undeserved** [ˌʌndɪ'zɜːvd] *adj* unverdient.

**undeserving** [ˌʌndɪ'zɜːvɪŋ] *adj* person, cause unwürdig. **to be ~ of sth** *(form)* einer Sache *(gen)* unwürdig sein *(form)*.

**undesirability** [ˌʌndɪzaɪərə'bɪlɪtɪ] *n* Unerwünschtheit *f*.

**undesirable** [ˌʌndɪ'zaɪərəbl] **1** *adj* policy, effect unerwünscht; *influence, characters, area* übel. **it is ~ that ... es wäre unerwünscht, wenn ...** **2** *n (person)* unerwünschtes Element.

**undetectable** [ˌʌndɪ'tektəbl] *adj* nicht nachweisbar.

**undetected** [ˌʌndɪ'tektɪd] *adj* **to go ~** nicht entdeckt werden.

**undeterred** [ˌʌndɪ'tɜːd] *adj* keineswegs entmutigt. **to carry on ~** unverzagt weitermachen.

**undeveloped** [ˌʌndɪ'veləpt] *adj* unentwickelt; *land, resources* ungenutzt.

**undid** [ʌn'dɪd] *pret of* **undo**.

**undies** ['ʌndɪz] *npl (col)* (Unter)wäsche *f*.

**undignified** [ʌn'dɪgnɪfaɪd] *adj* person, behaviour würdelos; *(inelegant)* way of sitting etc unelegant.

**undiluted** [ˌʌndaɪ'luːtɪd] *adj* unverdünnt; *(fig)* truth, version unverfälscht; *pleasure* rein, voll.

**undiminished** [ˌʌndɪ'mɪnɪʃt] *adj* unvermindert.

**undiplomatic** [ˌʌndɪplə'mætɪk] *adj* undiplomatisch.

**undipped** [ʌn'dɪpt] *adj (Brit Aut)* **~ headlights** Fernlicht *nt*.

**undiscerning** [ˌʌndɪ'sɜːnɪŋ] *adj* reader, palate anspruchslos, unkritisch; *critic* unbedarft.

**undischarged** [ˌʌndɪs'tʃɑːdʒd] *adj* debt unbezahlt. **~ bankrupt** nicht entlasteter Konkursschuldner.

**undisciplined** [ʌn'dɪsɪplɪnd] *adj* undiszipliniert.

**undisclosed** [ˌʌndɪs'kləʊzd] *adj* secret (bisher) unaufgedeckt; *details* geheimgehalten; *sum* ungenannt.

**undiscovered** [ˌʌndɪs'kʌvəd] *adj* unentdeckt.

**undiscriminating** [ˌʌndɪ'skrɪmɪneɪtɪŋ] *adj* anspruchslos, unkritisch.

**undisguised** [ˌʌndɪs'gaɪzd] *adj* ungetarnt; *(fig)* truth

unverhüllt; *dislike, affection* unverhohlen.

**undisputed** [ˌʌndɪs'pjuːtɪd] *adj* unbestritten.

**undistinguished** [ˌʌndɪ'stɪŋgwɪʃt] *adj* performance (mittel)mäßig; *appearance* durchschnittlich.

**undisturbed** [ˌʌndɪ'stɜːbd] *adj* (a) *(untouched)* papers, dust unberührt; *(uninterrupted)* person, sleep etc ungestört. (b) *(unworried)* unberührt.

**undivided** [ˌʌndɪ'vaɪdɪd] *adj* country, *(fig)* opinion, attention ungeteilt; *support* voll; *loyalty* absolut.

**undo** [ʌn'duː] *pret* **undid**, *ptp* **undone** **1** *vt* (a) *(unfasten)* aufmachen; *button, dress, parcel also* öffnen; *knitting also* aufziehen; *sewing also* auftrennen. (b) *wrong* ungeschehen machen; *work* ruinieren. **2** *vi (dress etc)* aufgehen.

**undoing** [ʌn'duːɪŋ] *n* Ruin *m*, Verderben *nt*.

**undone** [ʌn'dʌn] **1** *ptp of* **undo**. **2** *adj* (a) *(unfastened)* offen. **to come ~** aufgehen. (b) *(neglected)* task, work unerledigt.

**undoubted** [ʌn'daʊtɪd] *adj* unbestritten; *success also* zweifelhaft.

**undoubtedly** [ʌn'daʊtɪdlɪ] *adv* zweifellos.

**undreamed-of** [ʌn'driːmdɒv], **undreamt-of** [ʌn'dremtəv] *adj* ungeahnt. **in their time this was ~** zu ihrer Zeit hätte man sich *(dat)* das nie träumen lassen.

**undress** [ʌn'dres] **1** *vt* ausziehen. **to get ~ed** sich ausziehen. **2** *vi* sich ausziehen.

**undressed** [ʌn'drest] *adj* (a) *person* unbekleidet; *(still)* (noch) nicht angezogen; *(already)* schon ausgezogen. (b) *wound* unverbunden.

**undrinkable** [ʌn'drɪŋkəbl] *adj* ungenießbar.

**undue** [ʌn'djuː] *adj (excessive)* übermäßig; *(improper)* ungebührlich.

**undulating** ['ʌndjʊleɪtɪŋ] *adj* movement, line Wellen-; *waves, sea* wogend; *countryside* hügelig; *hills* sanft.

**undulation** [ˌʌndjʊ'leɪʃən] *n (of waves, countryside)* Auf und Ab *nt*; *(curve)* Rundung *f*.

**unduly** [ʌn'djuːlɪ] *adv* übermäßig; *punished* übermäßig streng. **you're worrying ~** Sie machen sich *(dat)* unnötige Sorgen.

**undying** [ʌn'daɪɪŋ] *adj* unsterblich.

**unearned** [ʌn'ɜːnd] *adj (Fin, fig)* unverdient. **~ income** Kapitaleinkommen *nt*.

**unearth** [ʌn'ɜːθ] *vt* ausgraben; *(fig)* book etc aufstöbern; *evidence* ausfindig machen.

**unearthly** [ʌn'ɜːθlɪ] *adj (eerie)* calm, scream unheimlich; *beauty* überirdisch. **at some ~ hour** *(col)* zu nachtschlafender Stunde; **an ~ din** *(col)* ein Riesenlärm *m*.

**unease** [ʌn'iːz] *n* Unbehagen *nt*, Beklommenheit *f*.

**uneasily** [ʌn'iːzɪlɪ] *adv* sit unbehaglich; *smile, speak etc also* unsicher; *sleep* unruhig. **to be ~ balanced** sehr prekär sein.

**uneasiness** [ʌn'iːzɪnɪs] *n see adj* Unruhe *f*; Unbehaglichkeit *f*; Unsicherheit *f*; *(of person)* Beklommenheit *f*; Unruhe *f*.

**uneasy** [ʌn'iːzɪ] *adj* sleep, night unruhig; *conscience* schlecht; *(worried)* laugh, look, *(awkward)* silence, atmosphere unbehaglich; *peace, balance* unsicher; *(worrying)* suspicion, feeling beunruhigend. **he was ~** *(ill at ease)* ihm war unbehaglich zumute; *(worried)* er war beunruhigt; **I am ~ about it** mir ist nicht wohl dabei; **to make sb ~** jdn beunruhigen; **I have an ~ feeling that ...** ich habe das ungute Gefühl, daß ...; **to become ~** unruhig werden.

**uneaten** [ʌn'iːtn] *adj* nicht gegessen. **he left the frogs' legs ~** er ließ die Froschschenkel auf dem Teller; **the ~ food** das übriggebliebene Essen.

**uneconomic** [ʌnˌiːkə'nɒmɪk] *adj* unwirtschaftlich.

**uneconomical** [ʌnˌiːkə'nɒmɪkəl] *adj* unwirtschaftlich; *person* verschwenderisch.

**uneducated** [ˌʌn'edjʊkeɪtɪd] *adj person* ungebildet; *speech also* unkultiviert.

**unemotional** [ˌʌnɪ'məʊʃənl] *adj person, reaction, description* nüchtern; *(without passion)* leidenschaftslos, kühl *(pej).*

**unemployable** [ˌʌnɪm'plɔɪəbl] *adj* als Arbeitskraft nicht brauchbar.

**unemployed** [ˌʌnɪm'plɔɪd] *adj person* arbeitslos; *(unused) machinery* ungenutzt; *(Fin) capital* tot. **the ~ pl** die Arbeitslosen *pl.*

**unemployment** [ˌʌnɪm'plɔɪmənt] **1** *n* Arbeitslosigkeit *f.* **~ has risen this month** die Arbeitslosenziffer ist diesen Monat gestiegen. **2** *attr* **~ benefit** *(Brit)* or **compensation** *(US)* Arbeitslosenunterstützung *f;* **~ figures** Arbeitslosenziffer *f;* **~ rate** Arbeitslosenquote *f.*

**unending** [ʌn'endɪŋ] *adj (everlasting)* ewig; *stream* endlos; *(incessant)* unaufhörlich. **it seems ~** es scheint nicht enden zu wollen.

**unendurable** [ˌʌnɪn'djʊərəbl] *adj* unerträglich.

**unenterprising** [ˌʌn'entəpraɪzɪŋ] *adj person, policy* ohne Unternehmungsgeist.

**unenthusiastic** [ˌʌnɪnθjuːzɪ'æstɪk] *adj* kühl, wenig begeistert.

**unenviable** [ʌn'envɪəbl] *adj position, task* wenig beneidenswert.

**unequal** [ʌn'iːkwəl] *adj* ungleich; *standard, quality* unterschiedlich. **to be ~ to a task** einer Aufgabe *(dat)* nicht gewachsen sein.

**unequalled,** *(US)* **unequaled** [ʌn'iːkwəld] *adj* unübertroffen; *skill, record also* unerreicht; *ignorance* beispiellos. **he is ~ by any other player** kein anderer Spieler kommt ihm gleich.

**unequivocal** [ˌʌnɪ'kwɪvəkəl] *adj* unmißverständlich, eindeutig. **he was quite ~ about it** er sagte es ganz unmißverständlich *or* klar.

**unerring** [ʌn'ɜːrɪŋ] *adj judgement, accuracy* unfehlbar; *instinct* untrüglich; *aim* treffsicher.

**UNESCO** [juː'neskəʊ] = **United Nations Educational, Scientific and Cultural Organization** UNESCO *f.*

**unethical** [ʌn'eθɪkəl] *adj* unmoralisch; *(in more serious matters)* unethisch.

**uneven** [ʌn'iːvən] *adj (not level) surface* uneben; *(irregular) line* ungerade; *thickness* ungleich; *pulse* unregelmäßig; *voice* unsicher; *colour, distribution* ungleichmäßig; *quality* unterschiedlich; *temper* unausgeglichen.

**unevenly** [ʌn'iːvənlɪ] *adv see adj* **the teams were ~ matched** die Mannschaften waren sehr ungleich.

**uneventful** [ˌʌnɪ'ventfʊl] *adj day, meeting* ereignislos; *career* wenig bewegt; *life also* ruhig, eintönig *(pej).*

**unexceptionable** [ˌʌnɪk'sepʃnəbl] *adj* einwandfrei; *person* solide.

**unexceptional** [ˌʌnɪk'sepʃənl] *adj* durchschnittlich.

**unexciting** [ˌʌnɪk'saɪtɪŋ] *adj time* nicht besonders aufregend.

**unexpected** [ˌʌnɪk'spektɪd] *adj* unerwartet. **this is an ~ pleasure** *(also iro)* welch eine Überraschung!

**unexpectedly** [ˌʌnɪk'spektɪdlɪ] *adv* unerwartet; *arrive, happen also* plötzlich.

**unexplainable** [ˌʌnɪk'spleɪnəbl] *adj* unerklärlich.

**unexplained** [ˌʌnɪk'spleɪnd] *adj phenomenon* ungeklärt; *mystery* unaufgeklärt; *lateness, absence* unentschuldigt.

**unexploded** [ˌʌnɪk'spləʊdɪd] *adj* nicht explodiert.

**unexposed** [ˌʌnɪk'spəʊzd] *adj* **(a)** *villain* nicht entlarvt; *crime* unaufgedeckt. **(b)** *(Phot)* unbelichtet.

**unexpressed** [ˌʌnɪk'sprest] *adj sorrow, wish* unausgesprochen.

**unexpressive** [ˌʌnɪk'spresɪv] *adj* ausdruckslos.

**unfailing** [ʌn'feɪlɪŋ] *adj source, interest* unerschöpflich; *remedy* unfehlbar; *friend* treu.

**unfailingly** [ʌn'feɪlɪŋlɪ] *adv* immer, stets.

**unfair** [ʌn'feər] *adj* unfair; *decision, method, remark also* ungerecht; *dismissal* ungerechtfertigt; *(Comm) competition also* unlauter. **to be ~ to sb** jdm gegenüber unfair sein.

**unfairly** [ʌn'feəlɪ] *adv* unfair; *treat, criticize etc also* ungerecht; *accuse, dismiss* zu Unrecht.

**unfairness** [ʌn'feənɪs] *n* Ungerechtigkeit *f.*

**unfaithful** [ʌn'feɪθfʊl] *adj wife, lover* untreu; *friend* treulos. **to be ~ to sb** jdm untreu sein.

**unfamiliar** [ˌʌnfə'mɪljər] *adj* **(a)** *experience, sight* ungewohnt; *surroundings also, subject, person* unbekannt. **it is ~ to me** es ist ungewohnt für mich; es ist mir unbekannt. **(b)** *(unacquainted)* **to be ~ with sth** mit etw nicht vertraut sein.

**unfamiliarity** [ˌʌnfəmɪlɪ'ærɪtɪ] *n see adj* **(a)** Ungewohntheit *f;* Unbekanntheit *f.* **(b)** mangelnde Vertrautheit. **his ~ with economics** sein Mangel *m* an ökonomischem Wissen.

**unfashionable** [ʌn'fæʃnəbl] *adj* unmodern; *district* unbeliebt; *hotel, habit* nicht in Mode.

**unfasten** [ʌn'fɑːsn] **1** *vt* aufmachen; *(detach) tag, dog* losbinden; *bonds* lösen. **2** *vi* aufgehen. **how does this dress ~?** wie macht man das Kleid auf?

**unfathomable** [ʌn'fæðəməbl] *adj* unergründlich.

**unfavourable,** *(US)* **unfavorable** [ʌn'feɪvərəbl] *adj* ungünstig; *conditions also, wind* widrig; *opinion, reaction, reply* negativ; *trade balance* passiv.

**unfavourably,** *(US)* **unfavorably** [ʌn'feɪvərəblɪ] *adv* ungünstig; *(react)* negativ. **to look ~ on sth** einer Sache *(dat)* ablehnend gegenüberstehen.

**unfeeling** [ʌn'fiːlɪŋ] *adj* gefühllos.

**unfinished** [ʌn'fɪnɪʃt] *adj* **(a)** *(incomplete)* unfertig; *work of art* unvollendet; *business* unerledigt. **(b)** *(Tech)* unbearbeitet; *cloth* Natur-.

**unfit** [ʌn'fɪt] *adj* **(a)** *(unsuitable) person, thing* ungeeignet, untauglich; *(incompetent)* unfähig. **~ to drive** fahruntüchtig; **~ to eat** ungenießbar. **(b)** *(esp Sport: injured)* nicht fit; *(in health also)* schlecht in Form, unfit. **~ (for military service)** untauglich; **to be ~ for work** arbeitsunfähig sein.

**unfitness** [ʌn'fɪtnɪs] *n see adj* **(a)** mangelnde Eignung, Untauglichkeit *f;* Unfähigkeit *f.* **(b)** mangelnde Fitneß; *(Mil)* Untauglichkeit *f.*

**unflagging** [ʌn'flægɪŋ] *adj person, zeal* unermüdlich; *enthusiasm* unerschöpflich; *devotion, interest* unverändert stark.

**unflappable** [ʌn'flæpəbl] *adj (col)* unerschütterlich. **to be ~** die Ruhe selbst sein.

**unflattering** [ʌn'flætərɪŋ] *adj portrait, comments* wenig schmeichelhaft; *dress, light also* unvorteilhaft.

**unflinching** [ʌn'flɪntʃɪŋ] *adj* unerschrocken; *determination* unbeirrbar.

**unfold** [ʌn'fəʊld] **1** *vt* **(a)** *paper, cloth* auseinanderfalten; *(spread out) map also, wings* ausbreiten; *arms* lösen; *chair* auseinanderklappen. **(b)** *(fig) story* entwickeln *(to* vor *+dat); plans, ideas also* darlegen *(to dat); secret* enthüllen. **2** *vi (story, plot)* sich abwickeln; *(truth)* an den Tag kommen; *(view, personality)* sich entfalten; *(countryside)* sich ausbreiten.

**unforeseeable** [ˌʌnfɔː'siːəbl] *adj* unvorhersehbar.

**unforeseen** [ˌʌnfɔː'siːn] *adj* unvorhergesehen.

**unforgettable** [ˌʌnfə'getəbl] *adj* unvergeßlich.

**unforgivable** [ˌʌnfə'gɪvəbl] *adj* unverzeihlich.

**unforgiving** [ˌʌnfə'gɪvɪŋ] *adj* unversöhnlich.

**unformatted** [ʌn'fɔːmætɪd] *adj (Comp) disk* nicht

formatiert, unformatiert.

**unformed** [ʌnˈfɔːmd] *adj clay, foetus* ungeformt; *character, idea* unfertig.

**unfortunate** [ʌnˈfɔːtʃənɪt] *adj* unglücklich; *person* glücklos; *day, event, error* unglückselig; *turn of phrase* ungeschickt; *time* ungünstig. **to be ~** *(person)* Pech haben; **it is most ~ that** ... es ist höchst bedauerlich, daß ...; **the ~ Mr Brown** der bedauernswerte Herr Brown.

**unfortunately** [ʌnˈfɔːtʃənɪtlɪ] *adv* leider; *worded* ungeschickt. **an ~ chosen expression** ein unglücklicher Ausdruck.

**unfounded** [ʌnˈfaʊndɪd] *adj* unbegründet; *allegations* aus der Luft gegriffen.

**unfreeze** [ʌnˈfriːz] *vt* **(a)** *(thaw)* auftauen. **(b)** *(Fin)* *wages, prices* freigeben.

**unfriendliness** [ʌnˈfrendlɪnɪs] *n see adj* Unfreundlichkeit *f*; Feindseligkeit *f*.

**unfriendly** [ʌnˈfrendlɪ] *adj* unfreundlich *(to sb* zu jdm*)*; *(hostile also)* natives, country, act feindselig.

**unfulfilled** [ˌʌnfʊlˈfɪld] *adj* unerfüllt; *person* unausgefüllt.

**unfurl** [ʌnˈfɜːl] *vt flag* aufrollen; *sail* losmachen; *(peacock) tail* entfalten.

**unfurnished** [ʌnˈfɜːnɪʃt] *adj* unmöbliert.

**ungainly** [ʌnˈɡeɪnlɪ] *adj* unbeholfen; *appearance* unelegant, unschön.

**ungentlemanly** [ʌnˈdʒentlmənlɪ] *adj* unfein; *(impolite)* unhöflich. **it is ~ (to do so)** das gehört sich nicht für einen Gentleman.

**un-get-at-able** [ˌʌnɡetˈætəbl] *adj (col)* unerreichbar; *place, part* unzugänglich.

**ungodly** [ʌnˈɡɒdlɪ] *adj* gottlos; *(col) hour* unchristlich *(col)*; *noise* Heiden-.

**ungracious** [ʌnˈɡreɪʃəs] *adj* unhöflich; *refusal* schroff; *answer* rüde.

**ungraded** [ʌnˈɡreɪdɪd] *adj (Sch)* nicht zensiert.

**ungrammatical** [ˌʌnɡrəˈmætɪkəl] *adj* ungrammatisch.

**ungrateful** [ʌnˈɡreɪtfʊl] *adj* undankbar *(to* gegenüber*)*.

**ungrudging** [ʌnˈɡrʌdʒɪŋ] *adj help* bereitwillig; *admiration* neidlos; *contribution* großzügig; *praise* von ganzem Herzen kommend *attr*.

**unguarded** [ʌnˈɡɑːdɪd] *adj* **(a)** *(undefended)* unbewacht. **(b)** *(fig: careless)* unvorsichtig, unachtsam. **in an ~ moment he** ... als er einen Augenblick nicht aufpaßte, ... er ...

**unhappily** [ʌnˈhæpɪlɪ] *adv (unfortunately)* unglücklicherweise; *(miserably)* unglücklich.

**unhappiness** [ʌnˈhæpɪnɪs] *n* Traurigkeit *f*; *(discontent)* Unzufriedenheit *f (with* mit*)*.

**unhappy** [ʌnˈhæpɪ] *adj (+er)* **(a)** *(sad)* unglücklich; *look, voice also, state of affairs* traurig. **(b)** *(not pleased)* unzufrieden *(about* mit*)*; *(uneasy)* unwohl. **if you feel ~ about it** wenn Sie darüber nicht glücklich sind; *(worried)* wenn Ihnen dabei nicht wohl ist. **(c)** *(unfortunate) coincidence, phrasing* unglücklich; *person* glücklos.

**unharmed** [ʌnˈhɑːmd] *adj person* unverletzt; *thing, reputation* unbeschädigt. **to be ~ by sth** durch etw nicht gelitten haben.

**UNHCR** = **United Nations High Commission for Refugees** UNHCR *f, hohe Flüchtlingskommission der Vereinten Nationen.*

**unhealthy** [ʌnˈhelθɪ] *adj* **(a)** *person* nicht gesund; *climate, place, life, complexion* ungesund. **the car sounds ~** *(hum)* das Auto macht ein komisches Geräusch. **(b)** *curiosity, interest* krankhaft; *influence* schädlich. **it's an ~ relationship** das ist eine ungesunde Beziehung. **(c)** *(col: dangerous)* ungesund

*(col)*.

**unheard-of** [ʌnˈhɜːdɒv] *adj (unknown)* gänzlich unbekannt; *(unprecedented)* noch nie dagewesen; *(outrageous)* unerhört.

**unheated** [ʌnˈhiːtɪd] *adj* ungeheizt.

**unheeded** [ʌnˈhiːdɪd] *adj* unbeachtet. **to go ~** keine Beachtung finden.

**unhelpful** [ʌnˈhelpfʊl] *adj person* nicht hilfreich; *advice, book* wenig hilfreich. **that is very ~ of you, you are being very ~** du bist aber wirklich keine Hilfe.

**unhesitating** [ʌnˈhezɪteɪtɪŋ] *adj (immediate) answer, offer* prompt; *help also, generosity* bereitwillig; *(steady) steps* stet; *(undoubting) answer* fest.

**unhesitatingly** [ʌnˈhezɪteɪtɪŋlɪ] *adv* ohne zu zögern; *(undoubtingly also)* ohne zu zweifeln.

**unhinge** [ʌnˈhɪndʒ] *vt* **to ~ sb/sb's mind** jdn aus der Bahn werfen; **his mind was ~d** er hatte den Verstand verloren.

**unholy** [ʌnˈhəʊlɪ] *adj (+er) (col) mess* heillos; *din* Riesen-.

**unhook** [ʌnˈhʊk] *vt latch, gate* loshaken; *dress* aufhaken; *(take from hook) picture* abhaken.

**unhoped-for** [ʌnˈhəʊptfɔːr] *adj* unverhofft.

**unhurried** [ʌnˈhʌrɪd] *adj pace, person* gelassen; *steps, movement* gemächlich; *meal, journey, life* geruhsam.

**unhurt** [ʌnˈhɜːt] *adj* unverletzt.

**unhygienic** [ˌʌnhaɪˈdʒiːnɪk] *adj* unhygienisch.

**UNICEF** [ˈjuːnɪsef] = **United Nations International Children's Emergency Fund** UNICEF *f*.

**unicorn** [ˈjuːnɪˌkɔːn] *n* Einhorn *nt*.

**unidentified** [ˌʌnaɪˈdentɪfaɪd] *adj* unbekannt; *body* nicht identifiziert; *belongings* herrenlos. **~ flying object** unbekanntes Flugobjekt.

**unification** [ˌjuːnɪfɪˈkeɪʃən] *n (of country)* Einigung *f*; *(of system)* Vereinheitlichung *f*. **~ treaty** Einigungsvertrag *m*.

**uniform** [ˈjuːnɪfɔːm] **1** *adj (unvarying) length, colour* einheitlich; *treatment also* gleich; *temperature also, pace* gleichbleibend *attr*; *(lacking variation) life, thinking* gleichförmig. **2** *n* Uniform *f*. **in/out of ~** in Uniform/in Zivil.

**uniformed** [ˈjuːnɪfɔːmd] *adj* uniformiert.

**uniformity** [ˌjuːnɪˈfɔːmɪtɪ] *n see adj* Einheitlichkeit *f*; Gleichheit *f*; Gleichmäßigkeit *f*; Gleichförmigkeit *f*.

**uniformly** [ˈjuːnɪfɔːmlɪ] *adv* einheitlich; *treat* gleich; *heat* gleichmäßig.

**unify** [ˈjuːnɪfaɪ] *vt* einigen, einen *(geh)*; *systems* vereinheitlichen.

**unilateral** [ˌjuːnɪˈlætərəl] *adj (Jur, Pol)* einseitig; *(Pol also)* unilateral.

**unimaginable** [ˌʌnɪˈmædʒməbl] *adj* unvorstellbar.

**unimaginative** *adj*, **~ly** *adv* [ˌʌnɪˈmædʒmətɪv, -lɪ] phantasielos.

**unimpaired** [ˌʌnɪmˈpɛəd] *adj quality, prestige* unbeeinträchtigt. **to be ~ self-confidence, health etc** nicht gelitten haben.

**unimpeachable** [ˌʌnɪmˈpiːtʃəbl] *adj reputation, conduct* untadelig; *proof, honesty* unanfechtbar; *source* absolut zuverlässig.

**unimportant** [ˌʌnɪmˈpɔːtənt] *adj* unwichtig.

**unimpressed** [ˌʌnɪmˈprest] *adj* unbeeindruckt, nicht beeindruckt. **I remain ~** das beeindruckt mich überhaupt nicht.

**unimpressive** [ˌʌnɪmˈpresɪv] *adj* wenig beeindruckend; *person, building also* unscheinbar.

**uninformed** [ˌʌnɪnˈfɔːmd] *adj* nicht informiert *or* unterrichtet *(about* über *+acc)*.

**uninhabitable** [ˌʌnɪnˈhæbɪtəbl] *adj* unbewohnbar.

**uninhabited** [ˌʌnɪnˈhæbɪtɪd] *adj* unbewohnt.

**uninhibited** [ˌʌnɪn'hɪbɪtɪd] *adj person* ohne Hemmungen; *greed, laughter* hemmungslos. **to be** ~ keine Hemmungen haben.
**uninitiated** [ˌʌnɪ'nɪʃɪeɪtɪd] **1** *adj* nicht eingeweiht. ~ **members of a tribe** nicht initiierte Mitglieder eines Stammes. **2** *n* **the** ~ *pl* Nichteingeweihte *pl*.
**uninjured** [ʌn'ɪndʒəd] *adj person* unverletzt; *reputation* nicht beeinträchtigt.
**uninspired** [ˌʌnɪn'spaɪəd] *adj* einfallslos. **I was** ~ **by the subject** das Thema hat mich nicht inspiriert.
**uninspiring** [ˌʌnɪn'spaɪərɪŋ] *adj* trocken; *idea* nicht gerade aufregend; *leader* langweilig.
**unintelligent** [ˌʌnɪn'telɪdʒənt] *adj person, remark* unintelligent; *approach* ungeschickt.
**unintelligible** [ˌʌnɪn'telɪdʒɪbl] *adj person* nicht zu verstehen; *speech, writing* unverständlich.
**unintended** [ˌʌnɪn'tendɪd], **unintentional** [ˌʌnɪn'tenʃənl] *adj* unbeabsichtigt; *joke also* unfreiwillig.
**unintentionally** [ˌʌnɪn'tenʃnəlɪ] *adv* unabsichtlich; *funny* unfreiwillig.
**uninterested** [ʌn'ɪntrɪstɪd] *adj* interessnlos. **to be** ~ **in sth** an etw *(dat)* nicht interessiert sein.
**uninteresting** [ʌn'ɪntrɪstɪŋ] *adj* uninteressant.
**uninterrupted** [ˌʌnɪntə'rʌptɪd] *adj (continuous) line* ununterbrochen, kontinuierlich; *noise, rain also* anhaltend; *(undisturbed) rest* ungestört.
**uninvited** [ˌʌnɪn'vaɪtɪd] *adj guest* ungeladen, ungebeten; *criticism* ungebeten.
**uninviting** [ˌʌnɪn'vaɪtɪŋ] *adj appearance, atmosphere* nicht (gerade) einladend; *prospect* nicht (gerade) verlockend; *food, sight* unappetitlich.
**union** ['juːnjən] **1** *n* **(a)** Vereinigung *f*; *(uniting also)* Zusammenschluß *m*; *(Pol also)* Union *f*. **the U~** *(US)* die Vereinigten Staaten; *(in Civil War)* die Unionsstaaten *pl*; **U~ of Soviet Socialist Republics** *(Hist)* Union *f* der Sozialistischen Sowjetrepubliken. **(b)** *(trade ~)* Gewerkschaft *f*. **(c)** *(association)* Vereinigung *f*; *(customs ~)* Union *f*; *(students' ~ also)* Studentenvereinigung *f*; ≃ AStA *m*. **(d)** *(harmony)* Eintracht, Harmonie *f*. **2** *adj attr (trade ~)* Gewerkschafts-. ~ **card** Gewerkschaftsausweis *m*.
**unionist** ['juːnjənɪst] *n* **(a)** *(trade ~)* Gewerkschaftler(in *f*) *m*. **(b)** *(Pol)* Unionsanhänger(in *f*) *m*.
**unionize** ['juːnjənaɪz] *vt* gewerkschaftlich organisieren.
**union: U~ Jack** *n* Union Jack *m*; ~ **shop** *n* gewerkschaftspflichtiger Betrieb.
**unique** [juː'niːk] *adj* einzig *attr*; *(outstanding)* einzigartig, einmalig. **such cases are not** ~ **to Britain** solche Fälle sind nicht nur auf Großbritannien beschränkt.
**uniquely** [juː'niːklɪ] *adv (solely)* einzig und allein, nur; *(outstandingly)* einmalig.
**unisex** ['juːnɪseks] *adj* Unisex-, unisex.
**unison** ['juːnɪzn] *n (Mus)* Gleichklang, Einklang *m (also fig)*. ~ einstimmig.
**unit** ['juːnɪt] *n* **(a)** *(section, Mil)* Einheit *f*; *(set of equipment also)* Anlage *f*; *(of furniture, machine)* Element *nt*; *(of organization also)* Abteilung *f*. **X-ray** ~ Röntgenabteilung *f*. **(b)** *(measure)* Einheit *f*. ~ **of length** Längeneinheit *f*; **monetary** ~ Währungseinheit *f*. **(c)** *(Math)* Einer *m*.
**unit cost** *n (Fin)* Stückkosten *pl*.
**unite** [juː'naɪt] **1** *vt (join)* verbinden; *party, country* (ver)einigen; *(emotions, ties)* (ver)einen. **2** *vi* sich zusammenschließen. **to** ~ **in doing sth** gemeinsam etw tun; **to** ~ **in opposition to sth** sich gemeinsam gegen etw stellen.
**united** [juː'naɪtɪd] *adj* verbunden; *group, nation* geschlossen; *(unified) people, nation* einig; *efforts* vereint. **to present a** ~ **front** eine geschlossene Front bieten.
**United:** ~ **Arab Emirates** *npl* Vereinigte Arabische Emirate *pl*; ~ **Kingdom** *n* Vereinigtes Königreich; ~ **Nations (Organization)** *n* Vereinte Nationen *pl*; ~ **States (of America)** *npl* Vereinigte Staaten *pl* (von Amerika).
**unit:** ~ **furniture** *n* Anbaumöbel *pl*; ~ **price** *n* Stückpreis *m*; ~ **trust** *n (Brit)* Investmentfonds *m*.
**unity** ['juːnɪtɪ] *n* Einheit *f*; *(harmony)* Einigkeit *f*; *(of a novel, painting etc)* Einheitlichkeit *f*. **this** ~ **of purpose** diese gemeinsamen Ziele; **to live in** ~ **with** in Eintracht leben mit.
**Univ** = **University** Univ.
**universal** [ˌjuːnɪ'vɜːsəl] *adj phenomenon, applicability, remedy* universal, universell; *language* Universal-; *custom also* allgemein verbreitet; *truth, rule also* allgemein gültig; *approval, peace* allgemein. ~ **joint** *(Tech)* Kardangelenk *nt*; ~ **remedy** Allheilmittel *nt*; **to be a** ~ **favourite** überall beliebt sein; **to become** ~ sich allgemein verbreiten.
**universally** [ˌjuːnɪ'vɜːsəlɪ] *adv* allgemein. ~ **applicable** allgemeingültig.
**universe** ['juːnɪvɜːs] *n (cosmos)* (Welt)all, Universum *nt*; *(world)* Welt *f*.
**university** [ˌjuːnɪ'vɜːsɪtɪ] **1** *n* Universität *f*. **to be at** ~/**to go to** ~ studieren; **to go to London U~** an der Universität (in) London studieren. **2** *adj attr town, library* Universitäts-; *qualifications, education also* akademisch. ~ **entrance (examination)** Aufnahmeprüfung *f* zum Studium; ~ **teacher** Hochschullehrer *m*.
**unjust** [ʌn'dʒʌst] *adj* ungerecht *(to gegen)*.
**unjustifiable** [ʌn'dʒʌstɪfaɪəbl] *adj* nicht zu rechtfertigen(d *attr) pred*, unvertretbar.
**unjustifiably** [ʌn'dʒʌstɪfaɪəblɪ] *adv expensive, severe, critical* ungerechtfertigt; *rude* unnötig; *criticize* zu Unrecht.
**unjustified** [ʌn'dʒʌstɪfaɪd] *adj* **(a)** ungerechtfertigt. **to be** ~ **in thinking that** ... zu Unrecht denken, daß ... **(b)** *(Print)* nicht bündig. **to set sth** ~ etw im Flattersatz setzen.
**unjustly** [ʌn'dʒʌstlɪ] *adv* zu Unrecht; *judge, treat* ungerecht.
**unjustness** [ʌn'dʒʌstnɪs] *n* Ungerechtigkeit *f*.
**unkempt** [ʌn'kempt] *adj hair* ungekämmt; *appearance, garden etc* ungepflegt.
**unkind** [ʌn'kaɪnd] *adj (+er) person, remark, action (not nice)* unfreundlich; *(cruel)* lieblos, gemein; *remark also* spitz. ~ **to the skin** nicht hautfreundlich.
**unkindly** [ʌn'kaɪndlɪ] *adv* unfreundlich; *(cruelly)* lieblos, gemein. **don't take it** ~ **if** ... nimm es nicht übel, wenn ...
**unkindness** [ʌn'kaɪndnɪs] *n* Unfreundlichkeit *f*; *(cruelty)* Lieblosigkeit, Gemeinheit *f*.
**unknowing** [ʌn'nəʊɪŋ] *adj agent* unbewußt.
**unknowingly** [ʌn'nəʊɪŋlɪ] *adv* unbewußt, ohne es zu wissen.
**unknown** [ʌn'nəʊn] **1** *adj* unbekannt. ~ **quantity** *(Math, fig)* unbekannte Größe; ~ **territory** *(lit, fig)* Neuland *nt*; **to be** ~ **to sb** *(feeling, territory)* jdm fremd sein; **it's** ~ **for him to get up so early** man ist es von ihm gar nicht gewohnt, daß er so früh aufsteht. **2** *n (person)* Unbekannte(r) *mf*; *(factor, Math)* Unbekannte *f*. **a voyage into the** ~ *(lit, fig)* eine Reise ins Ungewisse. **3** *adv* ~ **to me** *etc* ohne daß ich *etc* es wußte.
**unlace** [ʌn'leɪs] *vt* aufschnüren.
**unladen** [ʌn'leɪdn] *adj* ~ **weight, weight** ~ Leergewicht *nt*.
**unladylike** [ʌn'leɪdɪlaɪk] *adj* nicht damenhaft.

**unlawful** [ʌn'lɔːfʊl] *adj* gesetzwidrig; *means, assembly* illegal; *wedding* ungültig.

**unleaded** [ʌn'ledɪd] **1** *adj* bleifrei. **2** *n* bleifreies Benzin. **I use** ~ ich fahre bleifrei.

**unleash** [ʌn'liːʃ] *vt dog* von der Leine lassen; *(fig) outburst, tirade* entfesseln. **to** ~ **one's fury on sb** seine Wut an jdm auslassen.

**unleavened** [ʌn'levnd] *adj bread* ungesäuert.

**unless** [ən'les] *conj* es sei denn; *(at beginning of sentence)* wenn ... nicht. **don't do it** ~ **I tell you to** mach das nur, wenn ich es dir sage; ~ **I tell you to, don't do it** wenn ich es dir nicht sage, mach das nicht; ~ **I am mistaken** ... wenn ich mich nicht irre ...; ~ **otherwise stated** sofern nicht anders angegeben.

**unlicensed** [ʌn'laɪsənst] *adj car, dog, TV* nicht angemeldet; *premises* ohne (Schank)konzession; *(unauthorized)* unbefugt.

**unlike** [ʌn'laɪk] **1** *adj* unähnlich. **2** *prep* **(a)** im Gegensatz zu, anders als. **(b)** *(uncharacteristic of, photo etc)* **to be quite** ~ **sb** jdm (gar) nicht ähnlich sehen; *(behaviour also)* überhaupt nicht zu jdm passen.

**unlikelihood** [ʌn'laɪklɪhʊd], **unlikeliness** [ʌn'laɪklɪnɪs] *n* Unwahrscheinlichkeit *f*.

**unlikely** [ʌn'laɪklɪ] *adj (+er) happening, outcome* unwahrscheinlich; *explanation also* unglaubwürdig; *clothes* komisch. **it is (most)** ~/**not** ~ **that** ... es ist (höchst) unwahrscheinlich/es kann durchaus sein, daß ...; **she is** ~ **to come** sie kommt höchstwahrscheinlich nicht; **it looks an** ~ **place for mushrooms** es sieht mir nicht nach der geeigneten Stelle für Pilze aus; **in the** ~ **event that it does happen** in dem unwahrscheinlichen Fall, daß das geschieht.

**unlimited** [ʌn'lɪmɪtɪd] *adj wealth, time* unbegrenzt; *power also* schrankenlos; *patience* unendlich.

**unlined** [ʌn'laɪnd] *adj paper* unliniert; *face* faltenlos; *(without lining) dress* ungefüttert.

**unlisted** [ʌn'lɪstɪd] *adj* nicht verzeichnet.

**unlit** [ʌn'lɪt] *adj road* unbeleuchtet; *lamp* nicht angezündet.

**unload** [ʌn'ləʊd] *vt* **(a)** *ship, gun* entladen; *car also, luggage* ausladen; *truck, luggage* abladen; *cargo* löschen. **to be** ~**ed** *gun* nicht geladen sein; *truck etc* nicht beladen sein. **(b)** *(col: get rid of) children, problems* abladen *(on/to* bei*)*.

**unlock** [ʌn'lɒk] *vt door etc* aufschließen. **the door is** ~**ed** die Tür ist nicht abgeschlossen; **to leave a door** ~**ed** eine Tür nicht abschließen.

**unloose** [ʌn'luːs] *vt* **(a)** *(also* ~**n)** *knot, grasp* lösen; *rope also* losmachen. **(b)** *prisoner, dog* losbinden.

**unlovable** [ʌn'lʌvəbl] *adj* wenig liebenswert, unsympathisch.

**unloved** [ʌn'lʌvd] *adj* ungeliebt.

**unluckily** [ʌn'lʌkɪlɪ] *adv* unglücklicherweise. ~ **for him** zu seinem Pech.

**unlucky** [ʌn'lʌkɪ] *adj (+er)* unglückselig; *choice* unglücklich. **to be** ~ *(person)* Pech haben; *(not succeed)* keinen Erfolg haben; **he was** ~ **enough to meet her** er hatte das Pech, sie zu treffen; **broken mirrors are** ~ zerbrochene Spiegel bringen Unglück.

**unmade** [ʌn'meɪd] *adj bed* ungemacht; *road* unbefestigt.

**unmanageable** [ʌn'mænɪdʒəbl] *adj (unwieldy) vehicle* schwer zu handhaben; *parcel, size* unhandlich; *(uncontrollable) animal, person, hair* widerspenstig; *situation* unkontrollierbar.

**unmanly** [ʌn'mænlɪ] *adj behaviour* unmännlich; *(cowardly)* feige; *(effeminate)* weibisch.

**unmanned** [ʌn'mænd] *adj (not requiring crew) level*

crossing, space flight unbemannt; *(lacking crew) telephone exchange, lighthouse* unbesetzt.

**unmarked** [ʌn'mɑːkt] *adj* **(a)** *(unstained)* ohne Flecken, fleckenlos; *(without marking) face* ungezeichnet *(also fig)*; *suitcase etc* ohne Namen *or* Adresse; *police car* nicht gekennzeichnet. **(b)** *(Sport) player* ungedeckt. **(c)** *(Sch) work* unkorrigiert.

**unmarried** [ʌn'mærɪd] *adj* unverheiratet. ~ **mother** ledige Mutter.

**unmask** [ʌn'mɑːsk] **1** *vt (lit)* demaskieren; *(fig)* entlarven. **2** *vi* die Maske abnehmen.

**unmatched** [ʌn'mætʃt] *adj* einmalig, unübertroffen *(for* in bezug auf *+acc)*.

**unmentionable** [ʌn'menʃənəbl] *adj* tabu *pred*; *word also* unaussprechlich. **to be** ~ tabu sein.

**unmerciful** [ʌn'mɜːsɪfʊl] *adj* erbarmungslos.

**unmerited** [ʌn'merɪtɪd] *adj* unverdient.

**unmetalled** [ʌn'metld] *adj (Brit) road* unbefestigt.

**unmethodical** [ˌʌnmɪ'θɒdɪkəl] *adj* unmethodisch.

**unmindful** [ʌn'maɪndfʊl] *adj* **to be** ~ **of sth** nicht auf etw *(acc)* achten, etw nicht beachten.

**unmistak(e)able** [ˌʌnmɪ'steɪkəbl] *adj* unverkennbar; *(visually)* nicht zu verwechseln.

**unmitigated** [ʌn'mɪtɪgeɪtɪd] *adj wrath, severity* ungemildert; *(col: complete) disaster* total; *liar, rogue* Erz- *(col)*.

**unmotivated** [ʌn'məʊtɪveɪtɪd] *adj* unmotiviert.

**unmoved** [ʌn'muːvd] *adj person* ungerührt. **they were** ~ **by his playing** sein Spiel(en) ergriff sie nicht; **it leaves me** ~ das (be)rührt mich nicht.

**unmusical** [ʌn'mjuːzɪkəl] *adj* unmusikalisch.

**unnamed** [ʌn'neɪmd] *adj (nameless)* namenlos; *(anonymous)* ungenannt.

**unnatural** [ʌn'nætʃərəl] *adj* unnatürlich; *(abnormal also) relationship, crime* nicht normal *pred*, widernatürlich.

**unnaturally** [ʌn'nætʃrəlɪ] *adv* unnatürlich. **not** ~, **we were worried** es war nur natürlich, daß wir uns Sorgen machten.

**unnecessarily** [ʌn'nesɪserɪlɪ] *adv* unnötigerweise; *strict, serious* unnötig, übertrieben.

**unnecessary** [ʌn'nesɪsərɪ] *adj* unnötig; *(not requisite) visa* nicht notwendig; *(superfluous also)* überflüssig. **really, that was quite** ~ **of you!** das hättest du dir aber sparen können.

**unnerve** [ʌn'nɜːv] *vt* entnerven; *(gradually)* zermürben; *(discourage)* entmutigen.

**unnerving** [ʌn'nɜːvɪŋ] *adj (worrying)* beängstigend; *(discouraging)* entmutigend.

**unnoticed** [ʌn'nəʊtɪst] *adj* unbemerkt. **to go** *or* **pass** ~ unbemerkt bleiben.

**UNO** = **United Nations Organization** UNO *f.*

**unobjectionable** [ˌʌnəb'dʒekʃənəbl] *adj* einwandfrei.

**unobservant** [ˌʌnəb'zɜːvənt] *adj* unaufmerksam. **to be** ~ ein schlechter Beobachter sein.

**unobserved** [ˌʌnəb'zɜːvd] *adj (not seen)* unbemerkt; *(not celebrated)* nicht (mehr) eingehalten.

**unobstructed** [ˌʌnəb'strʌktɪd] *adj view, passage* ungehindert; *pipe, road* frei.

**unobtainable** [ˌʌnəb'teɪnəbl] *adj* nicht erhältlich. **number** ~ *(Telec)* kein Anschluß unter dieser Nummer.

**unobtrusive** [ˌʌnəb'truːsɪv] *adj* unauffällig.

**unoccupied** [ʌn'ɒkjʊpaɪd] *adj person* unbeschäftigt; *house* unbewohnt; *seat* frei; *(Mil) zone* unbesetzt.

**unofficial** [ˌʌnə'fɪʃəl] *adj* inoffiziell. **to take** ~ **action** *(Ind)* inoffiziell streiken.

**unofficially** [ˌʌnə'fɪʃəlɪ] *adv* inoffiziell.

**unopened** [ʌn'əʊpənd] *adj* ungeöffnet.

**unopposed** [ˌʌnəˈpəʊzd] *adj* **elected** ~ ohne Gegenstimme gewählt; **they marched on** ~ sie marschierten weiter, ohne auf Widerstand zu treffen; ~ **by the committee** ohne Widerspruch seitens des Ausschusses.

**unorganized** [ʌnˈɔːgənaɪzd] *adj* unsystematisch; *life* ungeregelt. **he is so** ~ er hat überhaupt kein System.

**unoriginal** [ˌʌnəˈrɪdʒɪnəl] *adj* wenig originell.

**unorthodox** [ʌnˈɔːθədɒks] *adj* unkonventionell, unorthodox.

**unpack** [ʌnˈpæk] *vti* auspacken.

**unpaid** [ʌnˈpeɪd] *adj* unbezahlt.

**unpalatable** [ʌnˈpælɪtəbl] *adj* *food, drink* ungenießbar; *(fig) fact, truth, mixture* unverdaulich, schwer zu verdauen.

**unparalleled** [ʌnˈpærəleld] *adj* einmalig, beispiellos. **an** ~ **success** ein Erfolg ohnegleichen.

**unpardonable** [ʌnˈpɑːdnəbl] *adj* unverzeihlich.

**unpatriotic** [ˌʌnpætrɪˈɒtɪk] *adj* unpatriotisch.

**unpaved** [ʌnˈpeɪvd] *adj* *road* nicht gepflastert.

**unperceptive** [ˌʌnpəˈseptɪv] *adj* unaufmerksam.

**unperturbed** [ˌʌnpəˈtɜːbd] *adj* nicht beunruhigt *(by* von, durch*)*, gelassen.

**unpick** [ʌnˈpɪk] *vt* auftrennen.

**unpin** [ʌnˈpɪn] *vt* *dress, hair* die Nadeln entfernen aus; *notice* abnehmen.

**unplaced** [ʌnˈpleɪst] *adj* *(Sport)* nicht plaziert. **to be** ~ sich nicht plaziert haben.

**unplanned** [ʌnˈplænd] *adj* ungeplant.

**unpleasant** [ʌnˈpleznt] *adj* unangenehm; *person, remark* unfreundlich *(to sb* jdm gegenüber*)*.

**unpleasantly** [ʌnˈplezntlɪ] *adv* *reply* unfreundlich; *warm, smell* unangenehm.

**unpleasantness** [ʌnˈplezntnɪs] *n* **(a)** *(quality)* see *adj* Unangenehmheit *f*; Unfreundlichkeit *f*. **(b)** *(bad feeling, quarrel)* Verstimmung *f*.

**unplug** [ʌnˈplʌg] *vt* *radio, lamp* den Stecker herausziehen von.

**unpolished** [ʌnˈpɒlɪʃt] *adj* unpoliert; *stone, (fig) person, manners* ungeschliffen; *performance, style* unausgefeilt.

**unpolluted** [ˌʌnpəˈluːtɪd] *adj* sauber, unverschmutzt.

**unpopular** [ʌnˈpɒpjʊlər] *adj* *person* unbeliebt *(with sb* bei jdm*)*; *decision, move* unpopulär.

**unpopularity** [ˌʌnpɒpjuˈlærɪtɪ] *n* see *adj* Unbeliebtheit *f*; Unpopularität *f*.

**unprecedented** [ʌnˈpresɪdəntɪd] *adj* noch nie dagewesen; *profit, step* unerhört. **this event is** ~ dieses Ereignis ist bisher einmalig; **an** ~ **success** ein beispielloser Erfolg.

**unpredictable** [ˌʌnprɪˈdɪktəbl] *adj* unvorhersehbar; *result* nicht vorherzusagen(d *attr*) *pred*; *behaviour, person, weather* unberechenbar.

**unprejudiced** [ʌnˈpredʒʊdɪst] *adj* *(impartial)* objektiv, unparteiisch; *(not having prejudices)* vorurteilslos.

**unpremeditated** [ˌʌnprɪˈmedɪteɪtɪd] *adj* unüberlegt; *crime* nicht vorsätzlich.

**unprepared** [ˌʌnprɪˈpɛəd] *adj* nicht vorbereitet; *person also* unvorbereitet. **to be** ~ **for sth** für etw nicht vorbereitet sein; *(be surprised)* auf etw *(acc)* nicht vorbereitet *or* gefaßt sein.

**unprepossessing** [ˌʌnpriːpəˈzesɪŋ] *adj* wenig einnehmend.

**unpretentious** [ˌʌnprɪˈtenʃəs] *adj* schlicht, bescheiden; *style, book* einfach.

**unprincipled** [ʌnˈprɪnsɪpld] *adj* prinzipienlos.

**unprintable** [ʌnˈprɪntəbl] *adj* nicht druckfähig; *(fig) answer* nicht druckreif.

**unproductive** [ˌʌnprəˈdʌktɪv] *adj* *capital* nicht gewinnbringend; *soil* ertragsarm; *meeting* unergiebig.

**unprofessional** [ˌʌnprəˈfeʃənl] *adj* *conduct* berufswidrig; *work* unfachmännisch.

**unprofitable** [ʌnˈprɒfɪtəbl] *adj* *(financially)* keinen Profit bringend; *mine etc* unrentabel; *(fig)* nutzlos.

**unpromising** [ʌnˈprɒmɪsɪŋ] *adj* nicht sehr vielversprechend.

**unpronounceable** [ˌʌnprəˈnaʊnsɪbl] *adj* unaussprechbar.

**unprotected** [ˌʌnprəˈtektɪd] *adj* ohne Schutz, schutzlos; *machine, sex* ungeschützt; *(by insurance)* ohne Versicherungsschutz.

**unproved** [ʌnˈpruːvd] *adj* unbewiesen; *(untested)* noch nicht bewährt. **he's still** ~ er hat sich noch nicht bewährt.

**unprovided for** [ˌʌnprəˈvaɪdɪdˌfɔːʳ] *adj* *children etc* unversorgt.

**unprovoked** [ˌʌnprəˈvəʊkt] *adj* grundlos.

**unpublished** [ʌnˈpʌblɪʃt] *adj* unveröffentlicht.

**unpunished** [ʌnˈpʌnɪʃt] *adj* unbestraft. **to go** ~ ohne Strafe bleiben.

**unputdownable** [ˌʌnpʊtˈdaʊnəbl] *adj* *(col)* **to be** ~ *(book)* einen nicht loslassen.

**unqualified** [ʌnˈkwɒlɪfaɪd] *adj* **(a)** *(person)* unqualifiziert. **to be** ~ nicht qualifiziert sein. **(b)** *(absolute) praise, acceptance* uneingeschränkt; *success* voll(ständig); *(col) idiot, liar* ausgesprochen.

**unquestionable** [ʌnˈkwestʃənəbl] *adj* *authority* unbestritten, unangefochten; *evidence, fact* unbezweifelbar; *sincerity, honesty* fraglos. **his honesty is** ~ seine Ehrlichkeit steht außer Frage.

**unquestionably** [ʌnˈkwestʃənəblɪ] *adv* fraglos, zweifellos.

**unquestioned** [ʌnˈkwestʃənd] *adj* unbestritten, außer Frage *pred*. **to let sth pass** ~ etw fraglos hinnehmen.

**unquestioning** *adj*, ~**ly** *adv* [ʌnˈkwestʃənɪŋ, -lɪ] bedingungslos.

**unravel** [ʌnˈrævəl] *vt* *knitting* aufziehen; *(lit, fig: untangle)* entwirren; *mystery* lösen.

**unread** [ʌnˈred] *adj* ungelesen.

**unreadable** [ʌnˈriːdəbl] *adj* *writing* unleserlich; *book, text* unverständlich.

**unready** [ʌnˈredɪ] *adj* (noch) nicht fertig. ~ **to do sth** nicht bereit, etw zu tun; ~ **for sth** auf etw *(acc)* nicht eingestellt *or* vorbereitet; *(not mature enough)* noch nicht reif genug für etw.

**unreal** [ʌnˈrɪəl] *adj* unwirklich. **this is just** ~! *(col: unbelievable)* das darf doch nicht wahr sein!

**unrealistic** [ˌʌnrɪəˈlɪstɪk] *adj* unrealistisch.

**unreality** [ˌʌnrɪˈælɪtɪ] *n* Unwirklichkeit *f*.

**unreasonable** [ʌnˈriːznəbl] *adj* *demand, price etc* übertrieben; *person* uneinsichtig; *(showing lack of sense)* unvernünftig. **to be** ~ **about sth** *(not be understanding)* kein Verständnis für etw zeigen; *(be overdemanding)* in bezug auf etw *(acc)* zuviel verlangen; **it is** ~ **to ...** es ist zuviel verlangt, zu ...; **am I being** ~? verlange ich zuviel?

**unrecognizable** [ʌnˈrekəgnaɪzəbl] *adj* nicht wiederzuerkennen(d *attr*) *pred*. **he was totally** ~ **in his disguise** man konnte ihn in seiner Verkleidung überhaupt nicht erkennen.

**unrecognized** [ʌnˈrekəgnaɪzd] *adj* *(not noticed)* person, danger, value unbemerkt; *(not acknowledged)* government, record nicht anerkannt; *genius, talent* ungewürdigt, unerkannt.

**unrecorded** [ˌʌnrɪˈkɔːdɪd] *adj* nicht aufgenommen; *(Rad, TV)* nicht aufgezeichnet; *(in documents)* nicht schriftlich erfaßt.

**unrefined** [ˌʌnrɪ'faɪnd] *adj* (a) *petroleum etc* nicht raffiniert. (b) *person* unkultiviert.

**unrehearsed** [ˌʌnrɪ'hɜːst] *adj (Theat etc)* nicht geprobt; *(spontaneous) incident* spontan.

**unrelated** [ˌʌnrɪ'leɪtɪd] *adj (unconnected)* ohne Beziehung *(to zu)*; *(by family)* nicht verwandt.

**unrelenting** [ˌʌnrɪ'lentɪŋ] *adj pressure* unablässig; *opposition, struggle* unerbittlich; *determination* hartnäckig; *pace* unvermindert; *rain* anhaltend *attr*, nicht nachlassend *attr*; *(not merciful) person, heat* unbarmherzig.

**unreliable** [ˌʌnrɪ'laɪəbl] *adj* unzuverlässig.

**unrelieved** [ˌʌnrɪ'liːvd] *adj pain, gloom* ungemindert; *grey* eintönig; *monotony, boredom* tödlich. **a life of ~ drudgery** ein Leben, das eine einzige Schinderei ist; **to be ~ by** nicht aufgelockert sein durch or von.

**unremitting** [ˌʌnrɪ'mɪtɪŋ] *adj efforts, toil* unablässig; *zeal* unermüdlich; *hatred* unversöhnlich.

**unrepeatable** [ˌʌnrɪ'piːtəbl] *adj words, views* nicht wiederholbar; *offer* einmalig.

**unrepentant** [ˌʌnrɪ'pentənt] *adj* nicht reumütig, reu(e)los. **he is ~ about it** er bereut es nicht.

**unrepresentative** [ˌʌnreprɪ'zentətɪv] *adj (Pol) government* nicht frei gewählt; *(untypical)* nicht repräsentativ *(of für)*.

**unrequited** [ˌʌnrɪ'kwaɪtɪd] *adj love* unerwidert.

**unreserved** [ˌʌnrɪ'zɜːvd] *adj* (a) *(frank) person* nicht reserviert, offen. (b) *(complete) approval* uneingeschränkt. (c) *(not booked)* nicht reserviert.

**unresolved** [ˌʌnrɪ'zɒlvd] *adj* (a) *problem etc* ungelöst. (b) *(uncertain) person* unschlüssig.

**unresponsive** [ˌʌnrɪ'spɒnsɪv] *adj (physically)* nicht reagierend *attr*; *(emotionally, intellectually)* gleichgültig, unempfänglich. **to be ~** nicht reagieren *(to* auf *+acc); (engine)* nicht ansprechen; **an ~ audience** ein Publikum, das nicht mitgeht; **I suggested it but he was fairly ~** ich habe es vorgeschlagen, aber er zeigte sich nicht sehr interessiert.

**unrest** [ʌn'rest] *n* Unruhen *pl*; *(discontent)* Unzufriedenheit *f*.

**unrestrained** [ˌʌnrɪ'streɪnd] *adj* uneingeschränkt; *feelings* offen, ungehemmt; *enthusiasm, atmosphere* ungezügelt; *behaviour* unbeherrscht.

**unrestricted** [ˌʌnrɪ'strɪktɪd] *adj power, use, growth* unbeschränkt; *access* ungehindert.

**unrewarded** [ˌʌnrɪ'wɔːdɪd] *adj* unbelohnt. **to go ~** unbelohnt bleiben; *(not gain recognition)* keine Anerkennung finden.

**unrewarding** [ˌʌnrɪ'wɔːdɪŋ] *adj work* undankbar; *(financially)* wenig einträglich.

**unripe** [ʌn'raɪp] *adj* unreif.

**unrivalled**, *(US)* **unrivaled** [ʌn'raɪvəld] *adj* unübertroffen. **~ in** or **for quality** von unübertroffener Qualität.

**unroadworthy** [ʌn'rəʊd,wɜːðɪ] *adj* nicht verkehrssicher.

**unroll** [ʌn'rəʊl] **1** *vt carpet, map* aufrollen. **2** *vi* sich aufrollen; *(fig) (plot)* sich abwickeln; *(landscape)* sich ausbreiten.

**unromantic** [ˌʌnrə'mæntɪk] *adj* unromantisch.

**unruffled** [ʌn'rʌfld] *adj person* gelassen; *sea* ruhig, unbewegt; *hair* ordentlich; *calm* unerschütterlich. **she was quite ~** sie blieb ruhig und gelassen.

**unruled** [ʌn'ruːld] *adj paper* unliniert.

**unruly** [ʌn'ruːlɪ] *adj (+er)* wild, ungebärdig.

**unsafe** [ʌn'seɪf] *adj ladder, machine, car, person* nicht sicher; *(dangerous) journey, toy, wiring* gefährlich. **to feel ~** sich nicht sicher fühlen.

**unsaid** [ʌn'sed] *adj* ungesagt, unausgesprochen. **to leave sth ~** etw unausgesprochen lassen; **it's best**

**left ~** das bleibt besser ungesagt.

**unsaleable** [ʌn'seɪləbl] *adj* unverkäuflich. **to be ~** sich nicht verkaufen lassen.

**unsatisfactory** [ˌʌnsætɪs'fæktərɪ] *adj* unbefriedigend; *profits etc* nicht ausreichend; *service, hotel* unzulänglich; *(Sch)* mangelhaft. **this is most ~** das läßt sehr zu wünschen übrig.

**unsatisfied** [ʌn'sætɪsfaɪd] *adj person* unzufrieden; *(not convinced)* nicht überzeugt; *appetite, desire, curiosity* unbefriedigt.

**unsatisfying** [ʌn'sætɪsfaɪŋ] *adj* unbefriedigend; *meal* unzureichend.

**unsavoury**, *(US)* **unsavory** [ʌn'seɪvərɪ] *adj smell, sight* widerlich; *appearance (repulsive)* abstoßend; *(dishonest, shady etc)* fragwürdig; *subject, details* unerfreulich; *joke* unfein; *district, characters* zwielichtig, übel; *reputation* zweifelhaft.

**unscathed** [ʌn'skeɪðd] *adj (lit)* unverletzt, unversehrt; *(fig)* unbeschadet; *relationship* heil. **to escape ~** *(fig)* ungeschoren davonkommen.

**unscented** [ʌn'sentɪd] *adj* nicht parfümiert.

**unscheduled** [ʌn'ʃedjuːld] *adj stop etc* außerfahrplanmäßig; *meeting* außerplanmäßig.

**unscientific** [ˌʌnsaɪən'tɪfɪk] *adj* unwissenschaftlich.

**unscramble** [ʌn'skræmbl] *vt* entwirren; *(decode) message* entschlüsseln.

**unscrew** [ʌn'skruː] **1** *vt (loosen)* losschrauben. **to come ~ed** sich lösen. **2** *vi* sich los- or abschrauben lassen; *(become loose)* sich lösen.

**unscrupulous** [ʌn'skruːpjʊləs] *adj person, behaviour* skrupellos, gewissenlos.

**unseal** [ʌn'siːl] *vt* öffnen; *(remove wax seal)* entsiegeln.

**unseasoned** [ʌn'siːznd] *adj timber* nicht abgelagert; *food* ungewürzt; *(fig: inexperienced) troops* unerfahren.

**unseaworthy** [ʌn'siː,wɜːðɪ] *adj* seeuntüchtig.

**unsecured** [ˌʌnsɪ'kjʊəd] *adj (Fin) loan* ohne Sicherheiten.

**unseeded** [ʌn'siːdɪd] *adj (Tennis)* nicht gesetzt.

**unseemly** [ʌn'siːmlɪ] *adj* unschicklich.

**unseen** [ʌn'siːn] **1** *adj* ungesehen; *(invisible)* unsichtbar; *(unobserved) escape* unbemerkt. **2** *n (esp Brit Sch)* unvorbereitete Übersetzung in die Muttersprache.

**unselfconscious** *adj*, **~ly** *adv* [ˌʌnself'kɒnʃəs, -lɪ] unbefangen.

**unselfish** [ʌn'selfɪʃ] *adj* uneigennützig, selbstlos.

**unserviceable** [ʌn'sɜːvɪsəbl] *adj* unbrauchbar.

**unsettle** [ʌn'setl] *vt* durcheinanderbringen; *(upset)* aufregen; *(disturb emotionally)* verstören; *(news)* beunruhigen; *(defeat, criticism)* verunsichern; *animal* beunruhigen.

**unsettled** [ʌn'setld] *adj* (a) *(unpaid)* unbeglichen; *(undecided) question* ungeklärt; *future* unbestimmt, ungewiß. (b) *(changeable) weather, (Fin) market* unbeständig; *(Pol) conditions also* unsicher; *life, character* unstet. **to be ~** durcheinander sein; *(thrown off balance)* aus dem Gleis geworfen sein; *(emotionally disturbed)* verstört sein. (c) *(unpopulated) territory* unbesiedelt.

**unsettling** [ʌn'setlɪŋ] *adj change, influence* destabilisierend; *defeat, knowledge* verunsichernd; *news* beunruhigend.

**unshak(e)able** [ʌn'ʃeɪkəbl] *adj* unerschütterlich.

**unshaken** [ʌn'ʃeɪkən] *adj* unerschüttert. **his nerve was ~** er behielt seine Kaltblütigkeit.

**unshaven** [ʌn'ʃeɪvn] *adj* unrasiert; *(bearded)* bärtig.

**unsigned** [ʌn'saɪnd] *adj painting* unsigniert; *letter* nicht unterschrieben.

**unsightly** [ʌn'saɪtlɪ] *adj* unansehnlich; *(stronger)*

häßlich.

**unskilled** [ʌn'skɪld] *adj* (a) *work, worker* ungelernt. (b) *(inexperienced)* ungeübt, unerfahren.

**unslept-in** [ʌn'sleptɪn] *adj* unberührt.

**unsociable** [ʌn'səʊʃəbl] *adj* ungesellig.

**unsocial** [ʌn'səʊʃəl] *adj* to work ~ hours außerhalb der normalen Arbeitszeiten arbeiten; visitors at this ~ hour Besuch um diese Zeit!

**unsold** [ʌn'səʊld] *adj* unverkauft.

**unsolicited** [ˌʌnsə'lɪsɪtɪd] *adj* unerbeten; *manuscript* unverlangt eingesandt.

**unsolved** [ʌn'sɒlvd] *adj* ungelöst.

**unsophisticated** [ˌʌnsə'fɪstɪkeɪtɪd] *adj (simple)* einfach; *(naïve)* naiv, simpel; *(undiscriminating)* unkritisch.

**unsound** [ʌn'saʊnd] *adj heart, teeth* krank; *health* angegriffen; *timber* morsch; *construction, design* unsolide; *foundations, finances* unsicher; *argument* nicht stichhaltig, anfechtbar; *advice* unvernünftig; *judgement* unzuverlässig; *doctrine* unvertretbar; *policy, move* unklug. of ~ mind *(Jur)* unzurechnungsfähig; the book is ~ on some points das Buch ist in einigen Punkten nicht korrekt.

**unsparing** [ʌn'spɛərɪŋ] *adj* (a) *(lavish)* großzügig, verschwenderisch. to be ~ with sth mit etw nicht geizen. (b) *criticism* schonungslos.

**unspeakable** [ʌn'spiːkəbl] *adj* entsetzlich.

**unspeakably** [ʌn'spiːkəblɪ] *adv* unsagbar.

**unspecified** [ʌn'spesɪfaɪd] *adj time, amount* nicht (genau) genannt.

**unspectacular** [ˌʌnspek'tækjʊləʳ] *adj* wenig eindrucksvoll; *career* wenig aufsehenerregend.

**unspoiled** [ˌʌn'spɔɪld], **unspoilt** [ˌʌn'spɔɪlt] *adj countryside* unberührt; *child* nicht verwöhnt.

**unspoken** [ʌn'spəʊkən] *adj words, thought* unausgesprochen; *agreement, consent* stillschweigend.

**unsporting** [ʌn'spɔːtɪŋ] *adj* unsportlich, unfair.

**unstable** [ʌn'steɪbl] *adj structure* nicht stabil; *area, economy* unsicher; *(Chem, Phys)* instabil; *(mentally)* labil.

**unstamped** [ʌn'stæmpt] *adj letter* unfrankiert; *document, passport* ungestempelt.

**unsteadily** [ʌn'stedɪlɪ] *adv see adj.*

**unsteadiness** [ʌn'stedɪnɪs] *n see adj* Unsicherheit *f*; Wackeligkeit *f*; Schwanken *nt*; Unregelmäßigkeit *f*.

**unsteady** [ʌn'stedɪ] *adj hand* unsicher; *ladder* wack(e)lig; *voice, economy* schwankend; *growth* unregelmäßig. to be ~ on one's feet unsicher auf den Beinen sein; the £ is still ~ das Pfund schwankt noch.

**unstinting** [ʌn'stɪntɪŋ] *adj person* großzügig; *kindness, generosity, support* uneingeschränkt. to be ~ in one's efforts keine Kosten und Mühen scheuen; he was ~ in his praise er geizte nicht mit Lob; to be ~ of one's time unendlich viel Zeit opfern.

**unstressed** [ʌn'strest] *adj (Phon)* unbetont.

**unstuck** [ʌn'stʌk] **1** *pret, ptp of* **unstick**. **2** *adj* to come ~ *(stamp, notice)* sich lösen; *(col) (plan)* schiefgehen *(col)*; *(person)* baden gehen *(col)*; *(speaker, actor)* steckenbleiben; *(in exam)* ins Schwimmen geraten.

**unsubstantiated** [ˌʌnsəb'stænʃɪeɪtɪd] *adj accusation, testimony, rumour* unbegründet.

**unsubtle** [ʌn'sʌtl] *adj* plump.

**unsuccessful** [ˌʌnsək'sesfʊl] *adj venture, meeting, person etc* erfolglos; *candidate* abgewiesen; *attempt* vergeblich; *marriage, outcome* unglücklich. to be ~ in doing sth keinen Erfolg damit haben, etw zu tun; he is ~ in everything he does nichts gelingt ihm; he was ~ in his exam er hat seine Prüfung nicht bestanden.

**unsuccessfully** [ˌʌnsək'sesfəlɪ] *adv* erfolglos; *try* vergeblich; *apply* vergebens.

**unsuitability** [ˌʌnsuːtə'bɪlɪtɪ] *n* Ungeeignetsein *nt*. his ~ for the job seine mangelnde Eignung für die Stelle; the ~ of her clothes ihre unpassende Kleidung.

**unsuitable** [ʌn'suːtəbl] *adj* unpassend. it would be ~ at this moment to ... es wäre im Augenblick unangebracht, ...; this film is ~ for children dieser Film ist für Kinder nicht geeignet; we're ~ for each other wir passen nicht zusammen; he's ~ for the job er ist für die Arbeit ungeeignet.

**unsuitably** [ʌn'suːtəblɪ] *adv* unpassend.

**unsuited** [ʌn'suːtɪd] *adj* to be ~ for *or* to sth für etw ungeeignet sein.

**unsung** [ʌn'sʌŋ] *adj hero, deed* unbesungen.

**unsure** [ʌn'ʃʊəʳ] *adj person* unsicher. to be ~ of oneself unsicher sein; to be ~ (of sth) sich *(dat)* (einer Sache *gen*) nicht sicher sein; I'm ~ of him ich bin mir bei ihm nicht sicher.

**unsurpassed** [ˌʌnsə'pɑːst] *adj* unübertroffen. to be ~ by anybody von niemandem übertroffen werden.

**unsuspected** [ˌʌnsə'spektɪd] *adj presence etc* unvermutet; *consequences, wealth* ungeahnt.

**unsuspecting** *adj*, **~ly** *adv* [ˌʌnsə'spektɪŋ, -lɪ] ahnungslos, nichtsahnend.

**unsweetened** [ˌʌn'swiːtnd] *adj* ungesüßt.

**unswerving** [ʌn'swɜːvɪŋ] *adj loyalty* unwandelbar.

**unsympathetic** [ˌʌnsɪmpə'θetɪk] *adj* (a) *(unfeeling)* wenig mitfühlend; *attitude, response* ablehnend, abweisend. (b) *(unlikeable)* unsympathisch.

**unsystematic** [ˌʌnsɪstɪ'mætɪk] *adj* unsystematisch.

**untalented** [ʌn'tælɪntɪd] *adj* unbegabt.

**untamed** [ʌn'teɪmd] *adj (lit, fig)* ungezähmt.

**untangle** [ʌn'tæŋgl] *vt (lit, fig)* entwirren.

**untapped** [ʌn'tæpt] *adj barrel* unangezapft; *resources, talent* ungenutzt.

**untaxed** [ʌn'tækst] *adj goods, income* steuerfrei; *car* unversteuert.

**untenable** [ʌn'tenəbl] *adj (lit, fig)* unhaltbar.

**untended** [ʌn'tendɪd] *adj patient* unbewacht; *garden* ungepflegt.

**untested** [ʌn'testɪd] *adj* unerprobt.

**unthinkable** [ʌn'θɪŋkəbl] *adj* undenkbar; *(too horrible)* unvorstellbar.

**unthinking** [ʌn'θɪŋkɪŋ] *adj* unbedacht, gedankenlos.

**untidily** [ʌn'taɪdɪlɪ] *adv* unordentlich.

**untidiness** [ʌn'taɪdɪnɪs] *n (of room)* Unordnung *f*; *(of person, dress)* Unordentlichkeit *f*.

**untidy** [ʌn'taɪdɪ] *adj (+er)* unordentlich.

**untie** [ʌn'taɪ] *vt knot* lösen; *parcel* aufknoten; *person, animal, hands* losbinden.

**until** [ən'tɪl] **1** *prep* (a) bis. from morning ~ night von morgens bis abends; ~ now bis jetzt; ~ then bis dahin. (b) not ~ *(in future)* nicht vor *(+dat)*; *(in past)* erst; I didn't leave him ~ the following day ich habe ihn erst am folgenden Tag verlassen. **2** *conj* (a) bis. wait ~ I come warten Sie, bis ich komme. (b) not ~ *(in future)* nicht bevor, erst wenn; *(in past)* nicht bis, erst als; he won't come ~ you invite him er kommt erst, wenn Sie ihn einladen; they did nothing ~ we came bis wir kamen, taten sie nichts; they didn't start ~ we came sie fingen erst an, als wir da waren.

**untimely** [ʌn'taɪmlɪ] *adj death* vorzeitig; *(inopportune) moment* unpassend; *remark* zur falschen Zeit.

**untiring** [ʌn'taɪərɪŋ] *adj work, effort* unermüdlich. to be ~ in one's efforts unermüdliche Anstrengungen machen.

**untold** [ʌn'təʊld] *adj story* nicht erzählt; *secret* ungelüftet; *wealth* unermeßlich; *agony, delights* unsäglich; *stars etc* unzählig. ~ **thousands** unzählig viele.

**untouchable** [ʌn'tʌtʃəbl] **1** *adj* unberührbar. **2** *n* Unberührbare(r) *mf.*

**untouched** [ʌn'tʌtʃt] *adj* **(a)** unberührt, unangetastet; *bottle etc also* nicht angebrochen; *(unmentioned)* nicht erwähnt. ~ **by human hand** nicht von Menschenhand berührt. **(b)** *(unharmed)* heil, unversehrt; *(unaffected)* unberührt; *(unmoved)* ungerührt. **(c)** *(unequalled)* ~ **for quality** in der Qualität unerreicht.

**untoward** [ˌʌntə'wɔːd] *adj (unfortunate) event* unglücklich, bedauerlich; *(unseemly)* unpassend. **nothing** ~ **had happened** es war nichts Schlimmes passiert.

**untraceable** [ʌn'treɪsɪbl] *adj* unauffindbar.

**untrained** [ʌn'treɪnd] *adj person, teacher* unausgebildet; *voice* ungeschult; *animal* undressiert. **to the** ~ **eye** dem ungeschulten Auge.

**untrammelled,** *(US also)* **untrammeled** [ʌn'træməld] *adj* unbeschränkt.

**untranslatable** [ˌʌntrænz'leɪtəbl] *adj* unübersetzbar.

**untried** [ʌn'traɪd] *adj* **(a)** *(not tested)* unerprobt; *(not attempted)* unversucht. **(b)** *(Jur) case* nicht verhandelt; *person* nicht vor Gericht gestellt.

**untroubled** [ʌn'trʌbld] *adj period* friedlich, ruhig. **the children seemed** ~ **by the heat** die Hitze schien den Kindern nichts auszumachen.

**untrue** [ʌn'truː] *adj* **(a)** *(false)* unwahr. **(b)** *(unfaithful) person* untreu. **to be** ~ **to sb** jdm untreu sein.

**untrustworthy** [ʌn'trʌst,wɜːðɪ] *adj (not reliable) book, person* unzuverlässig; *(not worthy of confidence) person* nicht vertrauenswürdig.

**untruth** [ʌn'truːθ] *n* Unwahrheit *f.*

**untruthful** [ʌn'truːθʊl] *adj statement* unwahr; *person* unaufrichtig. **you're being** ~ was du da sagst, ist nicht ganz wahr.

**unusable** [ʌn'juːzəbl] *adj* unbrauchbar.

**unused¹** [ʌn'juːzd] *adj (new)* unbenutzt, ungebraucht; *(not made use of)* ungenutzt; *(no longer used)* nicht mehr benutzt.

**unused²** [ʌn'juːst] *adj* **to be** ~ **to sth** etw *(acc)* nicht gewohnt sein; **to be** ~ **to doing sth** nicht daran gewöhnt sein, etw zu tun.

**unusual** [ʌn'juːʒʊəl] *adj (uncommon)* ungewöhnlich; *(exceptional)* außergewöhnlich. **it's** ~ **for him to be late** er kommt normalerweise nicht zu spät; **how** ~! das kommt selten vor; **that's** ~ **for him** das ist sonst nicht seine Art.

**unusually** [ʌn'juːʒʊəlɪ] *adv see adj* **most** ~, **he was late** ganz gegen seine Gewohnheit kam er zu spät.

**unutterable** *adj,* ~**bly** *adv* [ʌn'ʌtərəbl, -ɪ] unsäglich.

**unvaried** [ʌn'vɛərɪd] *adj* unverändert; *(pej)* eintönig.

**unvarnished** [ʌn'vɑːnɪʃt] *adj wood* unlackiert; *(fig) truth* ungeschminkt.

**unvarying** [ʌn'vɛərɪɪŋ] *adj* gleichbleibend, unveränderlich.

**unveil** [ʌn'veɪl] *vt statue, plan* enthüllen; *(Comm) new product* vorstellen; *face* entschleiern.

**unversed** [ʌn'vɜːst] *adj* ~ **in** nicht vertraut mit, unbewandert in *(+dat).*

**unvoiced** [ʌn'vɔɪst] *adj* unausgesprochen.

**unwanted** [ʌn'wɒntɪd] *adj furniture, clothing* unerwünscht. **he feels** ~ er kommt sich unerwünscht vor.

**unwarranted** [ʌn'wɒrəntɪd] *adj* ungerechtfertigt.

**unwary** [ʌn'wɛərɪ] *adj* unvorsichtig, unachtsam.

**unwashed** [ʌn'wɒʃt] *adj* ungewaschen; *dishes* ungespült.

**unwavering** [ʌn'weɪvərɪŋ] *adj faith, resolve* unerschütterlich; *course* beharrlich.

**unwelcome** [ʌn'welkəm] *adj visitor* unwillkommen; *news, memories* unerfreulich.

**unwell** [ʌn'wel] *adj pred* unwohl, nicht wohl. **to be** *or* **feel (a little)** ~ sich nicht (ganz) wohl fühlen.

**unwholesome** [ʌn'həʊlsəm] *adj* ungesund; *influence* ungut; *appearance, character* schmierig.

**unwieldy** [ʌn'wiːldɪ] *adj tool* unhandlich; *object also* sperrig; *(clumsy) body* schwerfällig.

**unwilling** [ʌn'wɪlɪŋ] *adj helper, pupil* widerwillig; *accomplice* unfreiwillig. **to be** ~ **to do sth** nicht bereit *or* gewillt sein, etw zu tun.

**unwillingly** [ʌn'wɪlɪŋlɪ] *adv* widerwillig.

**unwillingness** [ʌn'wɪlɪŋnɪs] *n* Widerwille *m.* **their** ~ **to compromise** ihre mangelnde Kompromißbereitschaft.

**unwind** [ʌn'waɪnd] *pret, ptp* **unwound 1** *vt thread, tape* abwickeln; *(untangle)* entwirren. **2** *vi* **(a)** sich abwickeln; *(fig: plot)* sich entwickeln. **(b)** *(col: relax)* abschalten *(col).*

**unwise** [ʌn'waɪz] *adj* unklug. **they were** ~ **enough to believe him** sie waren so töricht, ihm zu glauben.

**unwitting** [ʌn'wɪtɪŋ] *adj accomplice* unwissentlich; *action also* unabsichtlich; *victim* ahnungslos.

**unwittingly** [ʌn'wɪtɪŋlɪ] *adv (innocently)* ahnungslos; *(unknowingly)* unbewußt.

**unwonted** [ʌn'wəʊntɪd] *adj* ungewohnt. **he worked with** ~ **speed/enthusiasm** er arbeitete ungewöhnlich schnell/mit einer Begeisterung, die man sonst nicht an ihm kannte.

**unworkable** [ʌn'wɜːkəbl] *adj scheme* undurchführbar; *mine* nicht abbaubar.

**unworldly** [ʌn'wɜːldlɪ] *adj life* weltabgewandt; *(naïve)* weltfremd.

**unworn** [ʌn'wɔːn] *adj clothes* ungetragen; *carpet* nicht abgetreten; *tyres* nicht abgefahren.

**unworried** [ʌn'wʌrɪd] *adj* unbekümmert.

**unworthy** [ʌn'wɜːðɪ] *adj person* nicht wert *(of gen);* *conduct also* unwürdig *(of gen).* **this is** ~ **of you** das ist deiner unwürdig.

**unwound** [ʌn'waʊnd] *pret, ptp of* **unwind.**

**unwrap** [ʌn'ræp] *vt* auspacken, auswickeln.

**unwritten** [ʌn'rɪtn] *adj book, law* ungeschrieben; *agreement* stillschweigend.

**unyielding** [ʌn'jiːldɪŋ] *adj* unnachgiebig.

**unzip** [ʌn'zɪp] *vt zip* aufmachen; *dress, case* den Reißverschluß aufmachen an *(+dat).*

**up** [ʌp] **1** *adv* **(a)** *(in high or higher position)* oben; *(to higher position)* nach oben. ~ **there** dort oben; ~ **here on the roof** hier oben auf dem Dach; **on your way** ~ **(to see us/them)** auf dem Weg (zu uns/ihnen) herauf/hinauf; **he climbed all the way** ~ **(to us/them)** er ist den ganzen Weg (zu uns/ihnen) hochgeklettert; **to throw sth** ~ etw hochwerfen; **it's five floors** ~ es ist im fünften Stock; *(higher)* es ist fünf Stockwerke höher; **the road goes** ~ **and** ~ die Straße steigt immer weiter an; **we were 10,000 feet** ~ **when** ... wir waren 3.000 Meter hoch, als ...; **a little further** ~ ein bißchen weiter oben; **the sun/moon is** ~ die Sonne/der Mond ist aufgegangen; **with his collar** ~ mit hochgeschlagenem Kragen; **the road is** ~ die Straße ist aufgerissen; **to be** ~ **with the leaders** vorn bei den Führenden sein; **then** ~ **jumps Richard and says** ... und dann springt Richard auf und sagt ...; ~ **with the Liberals!** hoch die Liberalen; **from £10** ~ ab £10.

**(b)** *(installed, built)* **to be** ~ *(building)* stehen; *(scaffolding)* aufgestellt sein; *(shutters)* zu sein; *(wallpaper, curtains, pictures)* hängen; **they're putting** ~ **a new cinema** sie bauen ein neues Kino; **stick the notice** ~ **here** häng den Anschlag hier hin.

**(c)** *(not in bed)* auf. **to get** ~ aufstehen; **to be** ~

**and about** auf sein; *(after illness also)* auf den Beinen sein; **to be ~ late** lange aufbleiben.

**(d)** *(geographically)* oben. **~ in Inverness** oben in Inverness; **we are going ~ to Hamburg** wir fahren nach Hamburg (hinauf); **to be/go ~ north** im Norden sein/in den Norden fahren; **we're ~ for the day** wir sind (nur) für heute hier; **he was ~ at Susie's place** er war bei Susie (zu Hause).

**(e)** *(in price, value)* gestiegen *(on* gegenüber). **potatoes are ~ again** die Kartoffelpreise sind wieder gestiegen.

**(f)** *(in score)* **to be 3 goals ~** mit 3 Toren führen *or* vorn liegen *(on* gegenüber*)*; **to be one ~ on sb** jdm um einen Schritt voraus sein.

**(g)** *(col: wrong)* **what's ~?** was ist los?; **there's something ~** *(wrong)* da stimmt irgend etwas nicht; *(happening)* da ist irgend etwas im Gange.

**(h)** *(knowledgeable)* **to be well ~ in sth** gut über etw *(acc)* informiert sein; **he's well ~ in** *or* **on foreign affairs** in Auslandsfragen kennt er sich aus.

**(i)** *(finished)* **time's ~** die Zeit ist um *or* abgelaufen; **the lease is ~ next month** das Mietverhältnis endet nächsten Monat; **to eat/use sth ~** etw aufessen/aufbrauchen; **it's all ~ with him** *(col)* es ist aus mit ihm *(col)*.

**(j)** **~ to** *(as far as)* bis; **~ to now** bis jetzt; **~ to then** bis dann *or* dahin.

**(k)** **~ to:** *(col: doing)* **what's he ~ to?** *(actually doing)* was macht er da?; *(planning etc)* was hat er vor?; *(suspiciously)* was führt er im Schilde?; **he's ~ to no good** er führt nichts Gutes im Schilde.

**(l)** **~ to: I don't feel ~ to it** ich fühle mich dem nicht gewachsen; *(not well enough)* ich fühle mich nicht wohl genug dazu; **he's not/it isn't ~ to much** mit ihm/damit ist nicht viel los *(col)*; **it isn't ~ to his usual standard** es entspricht nicht seinem sonstigen Niveau; **it's ~ to us to help him** wir sollten ihm helfen; **if it was ~ to me** wenn es nach mir ginge; **it's ~ to you whether you go or not** es liegt an *or* bei dir, ob du gehst oder nicht; **shall I take it? — that's entirely ~ to you** soll ich es nehmen? — das müssen Sie selbst wissen; **it's ~ to the government to put things right** es ist Sache der Regierung, das richtigzustellen.

**(m)** **~ and down** auf und ab; **he's been ~ and down for months** seit Monaten geht es ihm mal besser, mal schlechter.

**(n)** **it was ~ against the wall** es war an die Wand gelehnt; **to be ~ against a difficulty/an opponent** einem Problem/Gegner gegenüberstehen; **I fully realize what I'm ~ against** mir ist völlig klar, womit ich es hier zu tun habe; **they were really ~ against it** sie hatten wirklich schwer zu schaffen.

**2** *prep* **further ~ the page** weiter oben auf der Seite; **to live/go ~ the hill** am Berg wohnen/den Berg hinaufgehen; **they live further ~ the hill/street** sie wohnen weiter oben am Berg/weiter die Straße entlang; **~ the road from me** bei mir in der Nähe; **he went off ~ the road** er ging die Straße hinauf; **he hid it ~ the chimney** er versteckte es (oben) im Kamin; **the water goes ~ this pipe** das Wasser geht durch dieses Rohr; **~ a tube** *(position)* in einer Röhre; *(motion)* in eine Röhre; **to go/march ~ to sb** auf jdn zugehen/zumarschieren.

**3** *n* **~s and downs** gute und schlechte Zeiten *pl*; *(of life)* Höhen und Tiefen *pl*; **to be on the ~ and ~** *(col: improving)* auf dem aufsteigenden Ast sein *(col)*; **his career is on the ~ and ~** *(col)* mit seiner Karriere geht es aufwärts.

**4** *adj* *(going up)* escalator nach oben; *(Rail)* train, line zur (nächsten größeren) Stadt.

**5** *vt* *(col)* price, offer hinaufsetzen; *production* ankurbeln; *bet* erhöhen *(to* auf *+acc)*.

**6** *vi* *(col)* **she ~ped and hit him** sie knallte ihm ganz plötzlich eine *(col)*; **he ~ped and ran** er rannte ganz plötzlich davon.

**up-and-coming** [ˈʌpənˈkʌmɪŋ] *adj* Nachwuchs-; *business* aufstrebend.

**upbeat** [ˈʌpbiːt] **1** *n (Mus)* Auftakt *m*. **2** *adj (col)* *(cheerful)* fröhlich; *(optimistic)* optimistisch.

**upbraid** [ʌpˈbreɪd] *vt* rügen.

**upbringing** [ˈʌpbrɪŋɪŋ] *n* Erziehung *f*. **to have a good ~** eine gute Kinderstube haben.

**upcoming** [ʌpˈkʌmɪŋ] *adj (esp US: coming soon)* kommend, bevorstehend.

**up-country** [ˌʌpˈkʌntrɪ] *adv* landeinwärts.

**update** [ʌpˈdeɪt] **1** *vt* aktualisieren; *person, file, book* auf den neuesten Stand bringen. **2** [ˈʌpdeɪt] *n* Aktualisierung *f*; *(new version)* Neufassung *f*. **to give sb an ~** jdn auf den neuesten Stand bringen.

**up-end** [ʌpˈend] *vt box, sofa* hochkant stellen.

**up-front** [ˌʌpˈfrʌnt] *adv pay money* im voraus.

**upgrade** [ʌpˈgreɪd] *vt employee* befördern; *job* höher einstufen; *product* verbessern; *(Hi-fi, Phot, Comp)* equipment ausbauen, nachrüsten.

**upheaval** [ʌpˈhiːvəl] *n* Aufruhr *m*. **emotional ~** Aufruhr der Gefühle; **social/political ~s** soziale/politische Umwälzungen *pl*.

**upheld** [ʌpˈheld] *pret, ptp of* **uphold**.

**uphill** [ˈʌpˈhɪl] **1** *adv* bergauf. **to go ~** bergauf gehen; *(car)* den Berg hinauffahren. **2** *adj road* bergauf (führend); *(fig)* work, struggle mühsam, mühselig. **it's ~ all the way** *(lit)* es geht die ganze Strecke bergauf; *(fig)* es ist ein harter Kampf.

**uphold** [ʌpˈhəʊld] *pret, ptp* **upheld** *vt (sustain)* tradition, honour wahren; *the law* hüten; *(support)* person, decision, objection (unter)stützen; *(Jur)* verdict bestätigen.

**upholster** [ʌpˈhəʊlstəʳ] *vt* polstern.

**upholstery** [ʌpˈhəʊlstərɪ] *n (interior)* Polsterung *f*; *(cover)* Bezug *m*; *(trade)* Polsterei *f*; *(skill)* das Polstern.

**upkeep** [ˈʌpkiːp] *n (running)* Unterhalt *m*; *(cost)* Unterhaltskosten *pl*; *(maintenance)* Instandhaltung *f*; *(of garden etc)* Pflege *f*.

**uplift** [ˈʌplɪft] *n (exaltation)* Erhebung *f*; *(moral inspiration)* Erbauung *f*.

**uplifting** [ʌpˈlɪftɪŋ] *adj* erhebend.

**up-market** [ˌʌpˈmaːkɪt] *adj* exklusiv.

**upon** [əˈpɒn] *prep see on* 1.

**upper** [ˈʌpəʳ] **1** *adj* obere(r, s); *lip, arm, jaw, deck* Ober-. **temperatures in the ~ thirties** Temperaturen über 35 Grad; **U~ Egypt/the ~ Loire** Oberägypten *nt*/die obere Loire; **~ storey** *(of house)* oberes Stockwerk; **~ circle** *(Brit Theat)* zweiter Rang; **the ~ ranks of the Civil Service** das gehobene Beamtentum; **~ school** Oberschule *f*; **U~ House** *(Parl)* Oberhaus *nt*. **2** *n* **~s** *pl (of shoe)* Obermaterial *nt*; **to be on one's ~s** *(col)* auf den Hund gekommen sein *(col)*.

**upper:** **~ case** *n (Typ)* *(also* **~-case letter)** Großbuchstabe *m*; **~ class** *n* **the ~ classes** die Oberschicht; **~-class** *adj accent, district, person* vornehm; *sport, expression, attitude* der Oberschicht; **to be ~-class** *(person)* zur Oberschicht gehören; **~classman** *n (US)* Mitglied *nt* einer High School oder eines College; **~ crust** *n (col)* **the ~ crust** die oberen Zehntausend *pl (col)*; **~-crust** *adj (col)* (schrecklich) vornehm *(col)*; **~most 1** *adj* oberste(r, s); *(fig)* ambition größte(r, s), höchste(r, s); **safety should be ~most in your minds** Sicherheit sollte für Sie an erster Stelle stehen; **2** *adv* **the blue side**

~**most** mit der blauen Seite nach oben.
**uppish** ['ʌpɪʃ], **uppity** ['ʌpɪtɪ] *adj (col: arrogant)* hochnäsig *(col).* **to get** ~ **with sb** jdm gegenüber anmaßend werden.
**upright** ['ʌpraɪt] **1** *adj* **(a)** *(erect)* aufrecht; *(vertical) post* senkrecht. ~ **piano** Klavier *nt;* ~ **chair** Stuhl *m.* **(b)** *(fig: honest) person* aufrecht. **2** *adv (erect)* aufrecht, gerade; *(vertical)* senkrecht. **to hold oneself** ~ sich gerade halten. **3** *n* **(a)** *(post)* Pfosten *m.* **(b)** *(piano)* Klavier *nt.*
**uprising** ['ʌpraɪzɪŋ] *n* Aufstand *m,* Erhebung *f.*
**upriver** [ʌp'rɪvəʳ] *adv* flußaufwärts *(from* von*).*
**uproar** ['ʌprɔːʳ] *n* Aufruhr *m.* **in** ~ in Aufruhr.
**uproarious** [ʌp'rɔːrɪəs] *adj meeting* tumultartig; *laughter* brüllend; *success, welcome* überwältigend; *joke* zum Schreien *pred.*
**uproot** [ʌp'ruːt] *vt plant* entwurzeln; *(fig: eradicate) evil* ausmerzen. ~**ed by the war** durch den Krieg entwurzelt; **to** ~ **sb from his familiar surroundings** jdn aus seiner gewohnten Umgebung herausreißen.
**upset** [ʌp'set] *(vb: pret, ptp* ~**) 1** *vt* **(a)** *(knock over, spill)* umstoßen; *boat* umkippen. **she** ~ **the milk all over the best carpet** sie stieß die Milch um, und alles lief auf den guten Teppich. **(b)** *(make sad: news, death)* bestürzen, erschüttern; *(question, insolence etc)* aus der Fassung bringen; *(experience, accident etc)* mitnehmen *(col); (distress, excite) patient, parent etc* aufregen; *(offend etc)* verletzen; *(annoy)* ärgern. **(c)** *(disorganize) calculations, balance etc* durcheinanderbringen. **(d)** *(make ill)* **the rich food** ~ **his stomach** das schwere Essen ist ihm auf den Magen geschlagen.
   **2** *adj* **(a)** *(about divorce, accident etc)* mitgenommen *(col) (about* von*); (about death, bad news etc)* bestürzt *(about* über *+acc); (sad)* betrübt, geknickt *(col) (about* über *+acc); (distressed)* aufgeregt *(about* wegen*); child* durcheinander *pred; (annoyed)* aufgebracht *(about* über *+acc); (hurt)* gekränkt, verletzt *(about* über *+acc); (hurt)* verletzt werden. **to get** ~ sich aufregen *(about* über *+acc); (hurt)* verletzt werden. **(b)** ['ʌpset] *stomach* verdorben *attr.* **to have an** ~ **stomach** sich *(dat)* den Magen verdorben haben.
   **3** ['ʌpset] *n* **(a)** *(disturbance)* Störung *f; (emotional)* Aufregung *f; (col: quarrel)* Verstimmung *f,* Ärger *m; (unexpected defeat etc)* böse Überraschung. **(b)** *(of stomach)* Magenverstimmung *f,* verdorbener Magen.
**upset price** *n (Comm)* Mindestpreis *m.*
**upsetting** [ʌp'setɪŋ] *adj (saddening)* traurig; *(stronger)* bestürzend; *(disturbing) changes* störend; *situation* unangenehm; *(offending)* beleidigend; *(annoying)* ärgerlich.
**upshot** ['ʌpʃɒt] *n (result)* Ergebnis *nt.* **the** ~ **of it all was that ...** es lief darauf hinaus, daß ...
**upside down** ['ʌpsaɪd'daʊn] **1** *adv* verkehrt herum. **to turn sth** ~ *(lit)* etw umdrehen; *(fig)* etw auf den Kopf stellen *(col).* **2** *adj* **in an** ~ **position** verkehrt herum; **to be** ~ *(picture)* verkehrt herum hängen; *(world)* kopfstehen.
**upstage** [ʌp'steɪdʒ] **1** *adv (Theat)* im Hintergrund der Bühne; *(with movement)* in den Hintergrund der Bühne. **2** *vt* **to** ~ **sb** *(Theat)* jdn zwingen, dem Publikum den Rücken zuzukehren; *(fig)* jdm die Schau stehlen.
**upstairs** [ʌp'stɛəz] **1** *adv* oben; *(with movement)* nach oben. **2** *adj window* im oberen Stock(werk); *room also* obere(r, s). **3** *n* Obergeschoß *nt.*
**upstanding** [ʌp'stændɪŋ] *adj (strong)* kräftig; *(honourable)* rechtschaffen.
**upstart** ['ʌpstɑːt] *n* Emporkömmling *m.*
**upstate** [ʌp'steɪt] *(US)* **1** *adj* im Norden (des Bun-

desstaates). **2** *adv* im Norden (des Bundesstaates); *(with movement)* in den Norden (des Bundesstaates).
**upstream** ['ʌp'striːm] *adv* flußaufwärts. **3 miles** ~ **from Henley** 3 Meilen flußaufwärts von Henley.
**upsurge** ['ʌpsɜːdʒ] *n* Zunahme, Eskalation *(pej) f.* **she felt an** ~ **of revulsion** sie fühlte Ekel in sich *(dat)* aufwallen.
**uptake** ['ʌpteɪk] *n (col):* **to be quick/slow on the** ~ schnell verstehen/schwer von Begriff sein *(col).*
**uptight** [ʌp'taɪt] *adj (col) (nervous)* nervös; *(inhibited)* verklemmt *(col); (angry)* sauer *(col).*
**up-to-date** ['ʌptə'deɪt] *adj* auf dem neuesten Stand; *fashion also, book, news* aktuell; *person, method, technique also* up to date *pred (col).* **to keep** ~ **with sth** mit *or* bei etw auf dem laufenden bleiben.
**up-to-the-minute** ['ʌptəðə'mɪnɪt] *adj news* allerneuste(r, s), allerletzte(r, s); *report* hochaktuell. **her clothes are** ~ ihre Kleider sind immer der allerletzte Schrei.
**uptown** ['ʌp'taʊn] *(US) adj, adv* im Villenviertel.
**upturn** ['ʌptɜːn] *n (fig: improvement)* Aufschwung *m.*
**upturned** ['ʌptɜːnd] *adj box etc* umgedreht; *face* nach oben gewandt. ~ **nose** Stupsnase *f (col).*
**upward** ['ʌpwəd] **1** *adj* aufwärts-, nach oben; *glance* nach oben. ~ **movement** Aufwärtsbewegung *f;* ~ **slope** Steigung *f.* **2** *adv (also* ~**s)** **(a)** *move* aufwärts, nach oben. **to look** ~ hochsehen, nach oben sehen; **face** ~ mit dem Gesicht nach oben. **(b)** *(with numbers) prices from 50p* ~ Preise von 50 Pence an, Preise ab 50 Pence; **and** ~ und darüber; ~ **of 3000** über 3000.
**upwardly** ['ʌpwədlɪ] *adv* aufwärts, nach oben. **to be** ~ **mobile** ein Aufsteiger/eine Aufsteigerin sein.
**Ural** ['jʊərəl] *n* **the** ~ **Mountains, the** ~**s** das Uralgebirge, der Ural.
**uranium** [jʊə'reɪnɪəm] *n* Uran *nt.*
**Uranus** [jʊə'reɪnəs] *n (Astron)* Uranus *m.*
**urban** ['ɜːbən] *adj* städtisch; *traffic, planning, district etc* Stadt-. ~ **renewal** Stadtsanierung *f.*
**urbane** [ɜː'beɪn] *adj person, style* weltmännisch; *(civil)* höflich; *manner, words* verbindlich.
**urbanization** [ˌɜːbənaɪ'zeɪʃən] *n* Urbanisierung, Verstädterung *(pej) f.*
**urchin** ['ɜːtʃɪn] *n* Straßen- *or* Gassenkind *nt; (mischievous)* Range *f.*
**Urdu** ['ʊəduː] *n* Urdu *nt.*
**urge** [ɜːdʒ] **1** *n (need)* Verlangen, Bedürfnis *nt; (drive)* Drang *m no pl; (physical, sexual)* Trieb *m.* **to feel an** ~ **to do sth** das Bedürfnis verspüren, etw zu tun; **I resisted the** ~ **(to contradict him)** ich habe mich beherrscht (und ihm nicht widersprochen); **come and stay with us if you get the** ~ *(col)* komm uns besuchen, wenn du Lust hast. **2** *vt* **(a)** **to** ~ **sb to do sth** *(plead with)* jdn eindringlich bitten, etw zu tun; *(earnestly recommend)* darauf dringen, daß jd etw tut; **to** ~ **sb to accept** jdn drängen, anzunehmen; **he needed no urging** er ließ sich nicht lange bitten. **(b)** *(advocate) caution, acceptance* drängen auf *(+acc).* **to** ~ **that sth should be done** darauf drängen, daß etw getan wird.
▶**urge on** *vt sep* antreiben.
**urgency** ['ɜːdʒənsɪ] *n* Dringlichkeit *f; (of tone, pleas also)* Eindringlichkeit *f.* **it's a matter of** ~ es ist dringend; **there's no** ~ es eilt nicht; **there was a note of** ~ **in his voice** es klang sehr dringend.
**urgent** ['ɜːdʒənt] *adj* dringend; *letter, parcel* Eil-. **to be in** ~ **need of medical attention** dringend ärztliche Hilfe benötigen.
**urgently** ['ɜːdʒəntlɪ] *adv required* dringend; *requested also* dringlich; *talk* eindringlich. **he is** ~ **in**

**need of help** er braucht dringend Hilfe.

**urinal** [juˈraɪnl] n (room) Pissoir nt; (vessel) Becken nt.

**urinate** [ˈjuərɪneɪt] vi Wasser lassen, urinieren.

**urine** [ˈjuərɪn] n Urin, Harn m.

**urn** [ɜːn] n (a) Urne f. (b) (also tea ~, coffee ~) Tee-/Kaffeekessel m.

**Uruguay** [ˈjuərəgwaɪ] n Uruguay nt.

**Uruguayan** [ˌjuərəˈgwaɪən] 1 n (person) Uruguayer(in f) m. 2 adj uruguayisch.

**US** = United States USA pl.

**us** [ʌs] pers pron (a) (dir and indir obj) uns. **give it (to) ~** gib es uns; **younger than ~** jünger als wir; **it's ~** wir sind's; **he is one of ~** er ist einer von uns; **this table shows ~ the tides** an dieser Tafel sieht man die Gezeiten; **~ and them** wir und die. (b) (col: me) (dir obj) mich; (indir obj) mir; (pl subj) wir. **give ~ a look** laß (mich) mal sehen; **~ English** wir Engländer.

**USA** = (a) United States of America USA pl. (b) United States Army.

**usable** [ˈjuːzəbl] adj verwendbar; ideas brauchbar. **no longer ~** nicht mehr zu gebrauchen.

**USAF** = United States Air Force.

**usage** [ˈjuːsɪdʒ] n (a) (treatment, handling) Behandlung f. **it's had some rough ~** es ist ziemlich unsanft behandelt worden. (b) (custom, practice) Brauch m, Sitte f. **it's common ~** es ist allgemein üblich. (c) (Ling: use, way of using) Sprachgebrauch m no pl, Anwendung f. **words in common ~** allgemein gebräuchliche Wörter pl.

**use¹** [juːz] 1 vt (a) benutzen, gebrauchen; means, materials also, personnel, idea verwenden; system, force, one's abilities, strength anwenden; tact, care walten lassen; drugs einnehmen. **~ only in emergencies** nur im Notfall gebrauchen; **what's this ~d for?** wofür wird das benutzt?; **to ~ sth for sth** etw zu etw verwenden.
(b) (make use of, exploit) information, talents, resources, chances (aus)nutzen; advantage nutzen; waste products verwerten. **you can ~ the leftovers to make a soup** Sie können die Reste zu einer Suppe verwerten.
(c) (~ up, consume) petrol, electricity etc verbrauchen.
(d) (pej: exploit) ausnutzen. **I feel (I've just been) ~d** ich fühle mich ausgenutzt.
2 [juːs] n (a) Verwendung f; (operation: of machines etc) Benutzung f; (of calculator etc, of word, arms, intelligence) Gebrauch m; (of method, force) Anwendung f; (of personnel, truncheons etc) Einsatz m; (of drugs) Einnahme f. Gebrauchsanweisung f; **for the ~ of** für; **for ~ in case of emergency** für Notfälle; **for external ~** zur äußerlichen Anwendung; **ready for ~** gebrauchsfertig; (machine) einsatzbereit; **to make ~ of sth** von etw Gebrauch machen, etw benutzen; **in ~/out of ~** in/außer Gebrauch; (machines) in/außer Betrieb; **to be in daily ~/no longer in ~** täglich/nicht mehr benutzt werden.
(b) (exploitation, making ~ of) Nutzung f; (way of using) Verwendung f; (of waste products, left-overs etc) Verwertung f. **to make ~ of sth** etw nutzen; **to make good/bad ~ of sth** etw gut/schlecht nutzen; **to have no ~ for** (lit, fig) keine Verwendung haben für; **to have no further ~ for sth** etw nicht mehr brauchen.
(c) (usefulness) Nutzen m. **to be of ~ to sb/for doing sth** für jdn von Nutzen sein/nützlich sein, um etw zu tun; **this is no ~ any more** das ist zu nichts mehr zu gebrauchen; **is this (of) any ~ to you?** kön-

nen Sie das brauchen?, können Sie damit etwas anfangen?; **can I be of any ~?** kann ich irgendwie behilflich sein?; **this is no ~, we must do something** so hat das keinen Sinn, wir müssen etwas tun; **it's no ~ you** or **your protesting** es hat keinen Sinn or es nützt nichts, daß du protestierst; **what's the ~ of telling him?** was nützt es, wenn man es ihm sagt?; **it's no ~** es hat keinen Zweck; **ah, what's the ~!** ach, was soll's!
(d) (right) Nutznießung f (Jur). **to have ~ of a car** einen Wagen benutzen können; **to give sb the ~ of sth** jdn etw benutzen lassen; (of car also, of money) jdm etw zur Verfügung stellen; **to have lost the ~ of one's left arm** seinen linken Arm nicht mehr gebrauchen können.
▶**use up** vt sep food, objects, one's strength verbrauchen; (finish also) aufbrauchen; scraps, leftovers etc verwerten. **the butter is all ~d ~** die Butter ist alle (col) or aufgebraucht.

**use²** [juːs] aux as in **I didn't ~ to like it** see **used²**.

**used¹** [juːzd] adj clothes etc gebraucht; (soiled) towel etc benutzt. **~ car** Gebrauchtwagen m.

**used²** [juːst] aux only in past **I ~ to swim every day** ich bin früher täglich geschwommen; **I ~ not to smoke, I didn't ~ to smoke** ich habe früher nicht geraucht; **I don't now but I ~ to** früher schon, jetzt nicht mehr; **as my mother ~ to say** wie meine Mutter zu sagen pflegte; **he ~ to be a good singer** er war einmal ein guter Sänger; **there ~ to be a field here** hier war (früher) einmal ein Feld; **things aren't what they ~ to be** es ist alles nicht mehr (so) wie früher.

**used³** [juːst] adj **to be ~ to sth** an etw (acc) gewöhnt sein, etw gewohnt sein; **to be ~ to doing sth** es gewohnt sein, etw zu tun; **I'm not ~ to it** ich bin das nicht gewohnt; **to get ~ to sth/doing sth** sich an etw (acc) gewöhnen/sich daran gewöhnen, etw zu tun.

**useful** [ˈjuːsful] adj (a) nützlich; person, contribution also wertvoll; (handy) tool also praktisch; size zweckmäßig; discussion fruchtbar; life, employment nutzbringend. **it is ~ for him to be able to ...** es ist günstig or praktisch, daß er ... kann; **to make oneself ~** sich nützlich machen; **to come in ~** sich als nützlich erweisen; **he's a ~ man to know** es ist sehr nützlich, ihn zu kennen; **it has a ~ life of 10 years** es hat eine Nutzdauer von 10 Jahren. (b) (col: capable) player brauchbar, fähig. **he's quite ~ with a gun** er kann ziemlich gut mit der Pistole umgehen.

**usefully** [ˈjuːsfəlɪ] adv employed nutzbringend. **is there anything I can ~ do?** kann ich mich irgendwie nützlich machen?

**usefulness** [ˈjuːsfəlnɪs] n see adj Nützlichkeit f; Wert m; Zweckmäßigkeit f; Nutzen m.

**useless** [ˈjuːslɪs] adj (a) nutzlos; (unusable) unbrauchbar; person also zu nichts nütze; remedy also wirkungslos. **it's ~ without a handle** ohne Griff nützt es nichts; **I'm ~ at languages** Sprachen kann ich überhaupt nicht. (b) (pointless) zwecklos, sinnlos.

**uselessly** [ˈjuːslɪslɪ] adv nutzlos.

**uselessness** [ˈjuːslɪsnɪs] n see adj (a) Nutzlosigkeit f; Unbrauchbarkeit f; Unwirksamkeit f. (b) Zwecklosigkeit, Sinnlosigkeit f.

**user** [ˈjuːzər] n Benutzer(in f) m.

**user:** **~-friendliness** n Benutzerfreundlichkeit f; **~-friendly** adj benutzerfreundlich; **~ interface** n (esp Comp) Benutzeroberfläche f; **~ software** n Anwendersoftware f.

**usher** [ˈʌʃər] 1 n (Theat etc) Platzanweiser m; (Jur)

Gerichtsdiener *m*. **2** *vt* **to ~ sb into a room/to his seat** jdn in ein Zimmer/zu seinem Platz bringen; **to ~ sb out** jdn hinauskomplimentieren; **to ~ in a new era** ein neues Zeitalter einleiten.

**usherette** [ˌʌʃəˈret] *n* Platzanweiserin *f*.

**USM** = **(a) United States Mail** amerikanische Bundespost. **(b) United States Mint** Münzanstalt *f* der USA.

**USN** = **United States Navy**.

**USS** = **(a) United States Ship**. **(b) United States Senate**.

**USSR** *(Hist)* = **Union of Soviet Socialist Republics** UdSSR *f*.

**usual** [ˈjuːʒʊəl] **1** *adj (customary)* üblich; *(normal also)* gewöhnlich, normal. **when shall I come?** – **oh, the ~ time** wann soll ich kommen? – oh, wie immer; **it's the ~ thing nowadays** das ist heute so üblich; **it's ~ to ask first** normalerweise fragt man erst; **as ~**, **as per ~** *(col)* wie üblich, wie gewöhnlich; **business as ~** normaler Betrieb; *(in shop)* Verkauf geht weiter; **later/less/more than ~** später/weniger/mehr als sonst; **it's not ~ for him to be late** er kommt normalerweise nicht zu spät. **2** *n (col)* **the ~** der/die/das Übliche. **the ~ please!** *(drink)* dasselbe wie immer, bitte!

**usually** [ˈjuːʒʊəlɪ] *adv* gewöhnlich, normalerweise. **do you fly to Spain?** – **~ fliegen** Sie nach Spanien? – meist(ens); **is he ~ so rude?** ist er immer so unhöflich?

**usurer** [ˈjuːʒərəʳ] *n* Wucherer *m*.

**usurp** [juːˈzɜːp] *vt* sich *(dat)* widerrechtlich aneignen; *power, title, inheritance also* an sich *(acc)* reißen; *throne* sich bemächtigen *(+gen)* *(geh)*; *role* sich *(dat)* anmaßen; *person* verdrängen.

**usurper** [juːˈzɜːpəʳ] *n* Usurpator *m (liter)*.

**usury** [ˈjuːʒʊrɪ] *n* Wucher *m*.

**UT** *(US Post)* = **Utah**.

**utensil** [juːˈtensl] *n* Gerät, Utensil *nt*.

**uterus** [ˈjuːtərəs] *n* Gebärmutter *f*.

**utilitarian** [ˌjuːtɪlɪˈtɛərɪən] *adj* auf Nützlichkeit ausgerichtet; *qualities* nützlich; *(Philos)* utilitaristisch.

**utility** [juːˈtɪlɪtɪ] **1** *n* **(a)** *(usefulness)* Nützlichkeit *f*, Nutzen *m*. **(b) public ~** *(company)* Versorgungsbetrieb *m*; *(service)* Leistung *f* der Versorgungsbetriebe. **2** *adj goods, vehicle* Gebrauchs-. **~ (program)** *(Comp)* Dienstprogramm *nt*; **~ room** (Haus)wirtschaftsraum *m*.

**utilization** [ˌjuːtɪlaɪˈzeɪʃən] *n see vt* Verwendung *f*; Nutzung *f*; Verwertung *f*.

**utilize** [ˈjuːtɪlaɪz] *vt* verwenden; *situation, time, opportunity, talent* nutzen; *waste paper etc* verwerten.

**utmost** [ˈʌtməʊst] **1** *adj* **(a)** *(greatest)* *ease, danger* größte(r, s); *caution, candour also* äußerste(r, s). **they used their ~ skill** Sie taten ihr Äußerstes; **with the ~ speed/care** so schnell/sorgfältig wie nur möglich; **matters of the ~ importance** Angelegenheiten von äußerster Wichtigkeit. **(b)** *(furthest)* äußerste(r, s). **2** *n* **to do/try one's ~** sein möglichstes *or* Bestes tun; **to the ~ of one's ability** so gut man nur kann; **one should enjoy life to the ~** man sollte das Leben in vollen Zügen genießen.

**Utopia** [juːˈtəʊpɪə] *n* Utopia *nt*.

**Utopian** [juːˈtəʊpɪən] *adj* utopisch, utopistisch *(pej)*.

**utter**[1] [ˈʌtəʳ] *adj* total *(col)*, vollkommen; *rogue* Erz-. **what ~ nonsense!** so ein totaler Blödsinn!

**utter**[2] *vt* von sich *(dat)* geben; *word* sagen; *cry, threat* ausstoßen.

**utterance** [ˈʌtərəns] *n* Äußerung *f*. **his last ~** seine letzten Worte.

**utterly** [ˈʌtəlɪ] *adv* total *(col)*, völlig; *depraved also, despise* zutiefst. **~ beautiful** ausgesprochen schön.

**uttermost** [ˈʌtəməʊst] *n, adj* = **utmost**.

**U-turn** [ˈjuːtɜːn] *n (lit, fig)* Wende *f*. **no ~s** Wenden verboten; **the government has done a ~ over pensions** die Rentenpolitik der Regierung hat sich um 180 Grad gedreht.

**UV** = **ultraviolet** UV.

# V

**V, v** [viː] *n* V, v *nt.* **V for Victor** ≃ V wie Viktor.

**V, v** = **volt(s)** V.

**v** = **(a) verse(s). (b)** vide s. **(c) versus. (d) very** s.

**VA** *(US Post)* = **Virginia.**

**vac** [væk] *n (Brit Univ col)* Semesterferien *pl.*

**vacancy** ['veɪkənsɪ] *n* **(a)** *(emptiness)* Leere *f; (of look also)* Ausdruckslosigkeit *f.* **(b)** *(in boarding house)* (freies) Zimmer. **have you any vacancies for August?** haben Sie im August noch Zimmer frei?; **"vacancies"** „Zimmer frei"; **"no vacancies"** „belegt". **(c)** *(job)* offene *or* freie Stelle. **to fill a** ~ eine Stelle besetzen; **vacancies** Stellenangebote, offene Stellen.

**vacant** ['veɪkənt] *adj* **(a)** *post* frei, offen; *WC, seat, hotel room* frei; *chair* unbesetzt; *house* unbewohnt; *site, lot* unbebaut. **to become** *or* **fall** ~ frei werden. **(b)** *mind, stare* leer.

**vacate** [və'keɪt] *vt seat* frei machen; *post* aufgeben; *house* räumen.

**vacation** [və'keɪʃən] **1** *n* **(a)** *(Univ)* Semesterferien *pl.* **(b)** *(US)* Ferien *pl,* Urlaub *m.* **on** ~ im *or* auf Urlaub; **to take a** ~ Urlaub machen; **to go on** ~ auf Urlaub *or* in die Ferien gehen; ~ **course** Ferienkurs *m.* **2** *vi (US)* Urlaub machen.

**vacationist** [və'keɪʃənɪst] *n (US)* Urlauber(in *f*) *m.*

**vacation:** ~ **pay** *n (US)* Urlaubsgeld *nt;* ~ **resort** *n (US)* Ferienort *m;* ~ **season** *n* Urlaubszeit *f;* ~ **trip** *n* Urlaubsreise *f.*

**vaccinate** ['væksɪneɪt] *vt* impfen.

**vaccination** [ˌvæksɪ'neɪʃən] *n* (Schutz)impfung *f.*

**vaccine** ['væksiːn] *n* Impfstoff *m.*

**vacillate** ['væsɪleɪt] *vi (lit, fig)* schwanken.

**vacuous** ['vækjuəs] *adj face, stare* ausdruckslos, leer; *remarks* nichtssagend.

**vacuum** ['vækjuəm] *n* **1** *n (Phys, fig)* (luft)leerer Raum, Vakuum *nt.* **to live in a** ~ im luftleeren Raum leben; **cultural** ~ kulturelles Vakuum. **2** *vt carpet* saugen.

**vacuum:** ~ **bottle** *n (US)* = ~ **flask;** ~ **cleaner** *n* Staubsauger *m;* ~ **flask** *n (Brit)* Thermosflasche *f;* ~**-packed** *adj* vakuumverpackt.

**vagabond** ['vægəbɒnd] *n* Vagabund *m.*

**vagary** ['veɪgərɪ] *n usu pl* Laune *f; (strange idea)* verrückter Einfall.

**vagina** [və'dʒaɪnə] *n* Scheide, Vagina *f.*

**vagrancy** ['veɪgrənsɪ] *n* Landstreicherei *f; (in cities)* Stadtstreicherei *f.*

**vagrant** ['veɪgrənt] *n* Landstreicher(in *f*) *m; (in cities)* Stadtstreicher(in *f*) *m.*

**vague** [veɪg] *adj (+er)* **(a)** *(not clear)* vage, unbestimmt; *outline, shape, photograph* verschwommen; *report, question* ungenau; *murmur* undeutlich. **I haven't the** ~**st idea** ich habe nicht die leiseste Ahnung; **there's a** ~ **resemblance** es besteht eine entfernte Ähnlichkeit; **I had a** ~ **idea she would come** ich hatte so eine (dunkle) Ahnung, daß sie kommen würde; **he was** ~ **about the time of his arrival** er äußerte sich nur unbestimmt über seine Ankunftszeit. **(b)** *(absent-minded)* geistesabwesend.

**vaguely** ['veɪglɪ] *adv* vage; *remember also* dunkel; *speak also* unbestimmt; *understand* ungefähr, in etwa. **to look** ~ **at sb** jdn verständnislos ansehen; **they're** ~ **similar** sie haben eine entfernte Ähnlichkeit.

**vagueness** ['veɪgnɪs] *n see adj* **(a)** Unbestimmtheit, Vagheit *f;* Verschwommenheit *f;* Ungenauigkeit *f.* **(b)** Geistesabwesenheit *f.*

**vain** [veɪn] *adj* **(a)** *(+er) (about looks)* eitel; *(about qualities)* eingebildet. **he's very** ~ **about his musical abilities** er bildet sich *(dat)* auf sein musikalisches Können viel ein. **(b)** *(useless, empty)* eitel *(liter);* *attempt also* vergeblich; *hope also* töricht. **in** ~ umsonst; **to take God's name in** ~ Gott lästern.

**vainly** ['veɪnlɪ] *adv* **(a)** *(to no effect)* vergeblich, vergebens. **(b)** *(conceitedly) (about looks)* eitel; *(about qualities also)* eingebildet.

**valance** ['væləns] *n (for bed frame)* Volant *m; (on window)* Querbehang *m; (wooden)* Blende *f.*

**valedictory** [ˌvælɪ'dɪktərɪ] *adj (form)* Abschieds-.

**valentine** ['væləntaɪn] *n (person)* jd, *dem man eine Valentinskarte schickt.* **St V~'s Day** Valentinstag *m;* ~ **(card)** Valentinskarte *f.*

**valet** ['væleɪ] *n* Kammerdiener *m.* ~ **parking** *(esp US)* Einparkservice *m;* ~ **service** Reinigungsdienst *m.*

**valiant** ['væljənt] *adj* **(a)** *(liter) soldier, deed* tapfer, kühn *(geh).* **(b) he made a** ~ **effort to save them** er unternahm einen kühnen Versuch, sie zu retten; **she made a** ~ **effort to smile** sie versuchte tapfer zu lächeln.

**valiantly** ['væljəntlɪ] *adv* tapfer.

**valid** ['vælɪd] *adj* **(a)** *ticket, passport* gültig; *(Jur) document, marriage* rechtsgültig; *contract* bindend; *claim* begründet. **(b)** *argument* stichhaltig; *excuse, reason* einleuchtend; *objection* begründet. **that's a very** ~ **point** das ist ein sehr wertvoller Hinweis.

**validate** ['vælɪdeɪt] *vt document (check validity)* für gültig erklären; *(with stamp, sign)* (rechts)gültig machen; *claim* bestätigen; *(Jur)* Rechtskraft verleihen *(+dat).*

**validity** [və'lɪdɪtɪ] *n* **(a)** *(Jur etc: of document)* Rechtsgültigkeit *f; (of ticket etc)* Gültigkeit *f; (of claim)* Berechtigung *f.* **(b)** *(of argument)* Stichhaltigkeit *f; (of excuse etc)* Triftigkeit *f.*

**valise** [və'liːz] *n* Reisetasche *f.*

**valley** ['vælɪ] *n* Tal *nt.* **up/down the** ~ talaufwärts/talabwärts.

**valour,** *(US)* **valor** ['vælər] *n (liter)* Tapferkeit *f.*

**valuable** ['væljuəbl] **1** *adj* **(a)** *jewel* wertvoll; *time, resource* kostbar. **(b)** *(useful)* wertvoll; *help, advice also* nützlich. **2** *n* ~**s** *pl* Wertsachen *pl.*

**valuation** [ˌvælju'eɪʃən] *n* Schätzung *f; (fig: of person's character)* Einschätzung *f.*

**valuator** ['væljuˌeɪtər] *n* Gutachter(in *f*), Schätzer(in *f*) *m.*

**value** ['væljuː] **1** *n* **(a)** Wert *m; (usefulness)* Nutzen *m.* **to be of** ~ wertvoll/nützlich sein; **of little** ~ nicht

sehr wertvoll/nützlich; **of no** ~ wertlos/nutzlos; **of great** ~ sehr wertvoll; **to put a** ~ **on sth** etw schätzen; *(on leisure etc)* einer Sache *(dat)* (hohen) Wert beimessen; **he attaches no/great** ~ **to it** er legt keinen/großen Wert darauf; **what's the** ~ **of your house?** wieviel ist Ihr Haus wert?; **it's good** ~ es ist preisgünstig; **in our shop you get** ~ **for money in** unserem Geschäft bekommen Sie etwas für Ihr Geld *(col)*; **goods to the** ~ **of £100** Waren im Wert von £100; **they put a** ~ **of £50 on it** sie haben es auf £50 geschätzt. **(b)** ~**s** *pl (moral standards)* (sittliche) Werte *pl.*
  **2** *vt* **(a)** *house, jewels* schätzen *(at* auf *+acc).* **(b)** *friendship, person, opinion, advice* schätzen. **I** ~ **it (highly)** ich weiß es zu schätzen; **if you** ~ **my opinion** ... wenn Sie Wert auf meine Meinung legen ...; **if you** ~ **your life** wenn Ihnen Ihr Leben lieb ist.
**value-added tax** ['væljuːædɪd'tæks] *n (Brit)* Mehrwertsteuer *f.*
**valued** ['væljuːd] *adj friend* geschätzt, lieb.
**value judgement** *n* Werturteil *nt.*
**valueless** ['væljuːlɪs] *adj* wertlos.
**valuer** ['væljuːər] *n* Schätzer(in *f*) *m.*
**valve** [vælv] *n (Anat)* Klappe *f; (Tech, on musical instrument)* Ventil *nt; (Brit: Rad, TV)* Röhre *f.*
**vamoose** [vəˈmuːs] *vi (US col)* abhauen *(col).*
**vamp¹** [væmp] *n (woman)* Vamp *m.*
**vamp²** *vti (Mus)* improvisieren.
**vampire** ['væmpaɪər] *n (lit, fig)* Vampir *m.*
**van¹** [væn] *n* **(a)** *(Brit Aut)* Transporter *m; (delivery* ~*)* Lieferwagen *m.* **(b)** *(Rail)* Waggon, Wagen *m.*
**van²** *n* = **vanguard.**
**V and A** ['viːənˈeɪ] *(Brit)* = **Victoria and Albert Museum.**
**vandal** ['vændəl] *n* **(a)** *(fig)* Rowdy *m.* **it was damaged by** ~**s** es ist mutwillig beschädigt worden. **(b)** *(Hist)* **V**~ Wandale *m.*
**vandalism** ['vændəlɪzəm] *n* Vandalismus *m; (Jur)* mutwillige Beschädigung.
**vandalize** ['vændəlaɪz] *vt* mutwillig beschädigen; *building* verwüsten; *(wreck)* demolieren.
**vane** [veɪn] *n* **(a)** *(also* **weather** ~*)* Wetterfahne *f.* **(b)** *(of windmill, propeller)* Flügel *m.*
**vanguard** ['vænɡɑːd] *n (Mil, Naut)* Vorhut *f.* **in the** ~ **of progress** an der Spitze des Fortschritts.
**vanilla** [vəˈnɪlə] **1** *n* Vanille *f.* **2** *adj* Vanille-.
**vanish** ['vænɪʃ] *vi* verschwinden; *(traces also)* sich verlieren; *(fears)* sich legen; *(hopes)* schwinden; *(become extinct)* untergehen.
**vanishing** ['vænɪʃɪŋ]: ~ **act** *n see* ~ **trick;** ~ **cream** *n* (Haut)pflegecreme *f;* ~ **point** *n (fig)* Nullpunkt *m;* ~ **trick** *n* **to do a** ~ **trick** *(col) (person)* sich verdrücken *(col); (thing)* Beine bekommen *(col).*
**vanity** ['vænɪtɪ] *n (concerning looks)* Eitelkeit *f; (concerning own value)* Eingebildetheit *f.*
**vanity:** ~ **case** *n* Kosmetikkoffer *m;* ~ **unit** *n* Waschbecken *nt* mit Unterschrank.
**vanquish** ['væŋkwɪʃ] *vt (liter)* bezwingen *(geh).*
**vantage** ['vɑːntɪdʒ] *n (Tennis)* Vorteil *m.*
**vantage point** *n (Mil)* (günstiger) Aussichtspunkt. **our window is a good** ~ **for watching the procession** von unserem Fenster aus hat man einen guten Blick auf die Prozession; **from our modern** ~ aus heutiger Sicht.
**vapid** ['væpɪd] *adj (liter) remark* nichtssagend, geistlos; *style* kraftlos; *taste* schal.
**vaporize** ['veɪpəraɪz] **1** *vt (by boiling etc)* verdampfen; *(naturally)* verdunsten lassen. **2** *vi see vt* verdampfen; verdunsten.
**vapour,** *(US)* **vapor** ['veɪpər] *n* Dunst *m; (steamy)*

Dampf *m.* ~ **trail** Kondensstreifen *m.*
**variability** [ˌvɛərɪəˈbɪlɪtɪ] *n see adj* **(a)** Veränderlichkeit *f;* Variabilität *f;* Wechselhaftigkeit *f.* **(b)** Regulierbarkeit *f.*
**variable** ['vɛərɪəbl] **1** *adj* **(a)** veränderlich; *(also Math, Biol)* variabel; *mood* wechselhaft. ~ **winds** wechselnde Winde *pl;* **his work is very** ~ er arbeitet sehr unterschiedlich. **(b)** *speed* regulierbar; *salary level* flexibel. **2** *n (Math, Phys, fig)* Variable *f.*
**variance** ['vɛərɪəns] *n* **(a) to be at** ~ **with sb** anderer Meinung sein als jd *(about* hinsichtlich *+gen);* **this is at** ~ **with what he said earlier** dies stimmt nicht mit dem überein, was er vorher gesagt hat. **(b)** *(difference)* Unterschied *m.*
**variant** ['vɛərɪənt] **1** *n* Variante *f.* **2** *adj (alternative)* andere(r, s). **there are two** ~ **spellings** es gibt zwei verschiedene Schreibweisen.
**variation** [ˌvɛərɪˈeɪʃən] *n* **(a)** *(varying)* Veränderung *f; (Sci)* Variation *f; (Met, of temperature, of prices)* Schwankung *f.* ~ **in opinions** unterschiedliche Auffassungen. **(b)** *(Mus)* Variation *f.* ~**s on a theme** Variationen über ein Thema. **(c)** *(different model, Biol)* Variante *f (on* von*).* **(d)** *(deviation)* Abweichung *f.*
**varicose** ['værɪkəʊs] *adj:* ~ **veins** Krampfadern *pl.*
**varied** ['vɛərɪd] *adj* unterschiedlich; *career, life* bewegt; *selection* reichhaltig. **a** ~ **group of people** eine gemischte Gruppe.
**variegated** ['vɛərɪɡeɪtɪd] *adj (coloured)* buntscheckig; *leaves* panaschiert.
**variety** [vəˈraɪətɪ] *n* **(a)** *(diversity)* Abwechslung *f.* **to give** *or* **add** ~ **to sth** Abwechslung in etw *(acc)* bringen; **a job with a lot of** ~ eine sehr abwechslungsreiche Arbeit. **(b)** *(assortment)* Vielfalt *f; (Comm)* Auswahl *f (of* an *+dat).* **in a great** ~ **of ways** auf die verschiedensten Arten; **in a** ~ **of colours** in den verschiedensten Farben; **for a** ~ **of reasons** aus verschiedenen Gründen. **(c)** *(type)* Art *f; (of cigarette, plant)* Sorte *f.* **a new** ~ **of tulip** eine neue Tulpensorte. **(d)** *(esp Brit Theat)* Varieté *nt.*
**variety:** ~ **act** *n* Variaténummer *f;* ~ **artist** *n (esp Brit)* Varietékünstler(in *f*) *m;* ~ **show** *n (esp Brit)* Varietévorführung *f; (Rad, TV)* Unterhaltungssendung *f;* ~ **theatre** *n* Varieté(theater) *nt.*
**various** ['vɛərɪəs] *adj* verschieden.
**variously** ['vɛərɪəslɪ] *adv* unterschiedlich.
**varnish** ['vɑːnɪʃ] **1** *n* Lack *m; (on furniture also, on painting)* Firnis *m.* **2** *vt* lackieren; *painting* firnissen.
**vary** ['vɛərɪ] **1** *vi* **(a)** *(diverge, differ)* sich unterscheiden, abweichen *(from* von*).* **they** ~ **in price from the others** sie unterscheiden sich im Preis von den anderen; **opinions** ~ **on this point** in diesem Punkt gehen die Meinungen auseinander. **(b)** *(be different)* unterschiedlich sein. **the price varies from shop to shop** der Preis ist von Geschäft zu Geschäft verschieden. **(c)** *(change, fluctuate)* sich (ver)ändern; *(pressure, prices)* schwanken. **to** ~ **with the weather** sich nach dem Wetter richten. **2** *vt (alter)* verändern, abwandeln; *(give variety)* variieren.
**varying** ['vɛərɪɪŋ] *adj (changing)* veränderlich; *(different)* unterschiedlich. **with** ~ **degrees of success** mit unterschiedlichem Erfolg *m.*
**vase** [vɑːz, *(US)* veɪz] *n* Vase *f.*
**vasectomy** [væˈsektəmɪ] *n* Sterilisation *f (des Mannes).*
**vaseline** ® ['væsɪliːn] *n* Vaseline *f.*
**vassal** ['væsəl] *n (lit, fig)* Vasall *m.*
**vast** [vɑːst] *adj (+er)* gewaltig, riesig; *knowledge* enorm; *majority* überwältigend. **a** ~ **expanse** eine weite Fläche.
**vastly** ['vɑːstlɪ] *adv* erheblich, bedeutend. **it is** ~ **dif-**

ferent da besteht ein erheblicher Unterschied.

**vastness** ['vɑːstnɪs] n (of size) riesige Größe; (of distance) ungeheures Ausmaß; (of ocean, plain) unermeßliche Weite; (of wealth) gewaltiger Umfang.

**vat** [væt] n Faß nt; (without lid) Bottich m.

**VAT** ['viːeɪ'tiː, væt] (Brit) = **value-added tax** MwSt.

**Vatican** ['vætɪkən] n Vatikan m.

**vaudeville** ['vəʊdəvɪl] n (esp US) Varieté nt.

**vault**[1] [vɔːlt] n (a) (cellar) (Keller)gewölbe nt; (tomb) Gruft f; (in bank) Tresor(raum) m. **in the ~s** im Gewölbe etc. (b) (Archit) Gewölbe nt.

**vault**[2] 1 n Sprung m. 2 vi springen. 3 vt überspringen.

**vaulted** ['vɔːltɪd] adj (Archit) gewölbt.

**vaunt** [vɔːnt] vt rühmen, preisen (geh). **much-~ed** vielgepriesen.

**V-belt** ['viːbelt] n Keilriemen m.

**VC** = **Victoria Cross** Viktoriakreuz nt (höchste britische Tapferkeitsauszeichnung).

**VCR** = **video cassette recorder**.

**VD** = **venereal disease**.

**VDU** = **visual display unit**. **~ operator** Bildschirmarbeiter(in f) m.

**veal** [viːl] n Kalbfleisch nt.

**vector** ['vektər] n (Math, Aviat) Vektor m.

**veer** [vɪər] vi (wind) (sich) drehen (to nach); (ship) abdrehen; (car) ausscheren; (road) scharf abbiegen. **to ~ off course** vom Kurs abkommen; **public opinion has ~ed to the right** die öffentliche Meinung ist nach rechts geschwenkt.

**veg** [vedʒ] n, no pl = **vegetable**. **meat and two ~** Fleisch nt mit Kartoffeln und Gemüse.

**vegan** ['viːgən] n Veganer(in f) m.

**vegeburger** ['vedʒɪˌbɜːgər] n vegetarische Frikadelle f.

**vegetable** ['vedʒtəbl] n (a) Gemüse nt. **cabbage is a ~** Kohl ist eine Gemüsepflanze. (b) (generic term: plant) Pflanze f. (c) **he's just a ~** er vegetiert nur vor sich hin; **she's become a ~** sie ist zum körperlichen und geistigen Krüppel geworden.

**vegetable: ~ dish** n (bowl) Gemüseschüssel f; (to eat) Gemüsegericht nt; **~ garden** n Gemüsegarten m; **~ oil** n Pflanzenöl m.

**vegetarian** [ˌvedʒɪ'tɛərɪən] 1 n Vegetarier(in f) m. 2 adj vegetarisch.

**vegetarianism** [ˌvedʒɪ'tɛərɪənɪzəm] n Vegetarismus m.

**vegetate** ['vedʒɪteɪt] vi (fig) dahinvegetieren.

**vegetation** [ˌvedʒɪ'teɪʃən] n Vegetation f.

**veggieburger** n = **vegeburger**.

**vehemence** ['viːɪməns] n Vehemenz f (geh); (of actions, feelings, protests also) Heftigkeit f; (of love, hatred) Leidenschaftlichkeit f.

**vehement** ['viːɪmənt] adj vehement (geh); feelings, speech leidenschaftlich; attack, desire, dislike, opposition heftig.

**vehicle** ['viːɪkl] n Fahrzeug nt; (fig) Mittel nt.

**vehicular** [vɪ'hɪkjʊlər] adj traffic etc Fahrzeug-.

**veil** [veɪl] 1 n Schleier m. **to take the ~** ins Kloster gehen; **under a ~ of secrecy** unter dem Mantel der Verschwiegenheit. 2 vt (lit, fig) verschleiern; feelings verbergen. **the town was ~ed by mist** die Stadt lag in Nebel gehüllt.

**veiled** [veɪld] adj reference versteckt; face verschleiert.

**vein** [veɪn] n (Anat, Bot, Min) Ader f; (fig: mood) Stimmung, Laune f. **in a humorous ~** in lustiger Stimmung; **in the same ~** in derselben Art.

**Velcro** ® ['velkrəʊ] n Velcro ® nt; (fastener) Klettverschluß m.

**vellum** ['veləm] n Pergament nt.

**velocity** [və'lɒsɪtɪ] n Geschwindigkeit f.

**velvet** ['velvɪt] 1 n Samt m. 2 adj jacket Samt-; skin, feel samtweich, samten (geh).

**velveteen** ['velvɪtiːn] n Veloursamt m.

**velvety** ['velvɪtɪ] adj samtig.

**venal** ['viːnl] adj (liter) person käuflich; practices korrupt.

**vendetta** [ven'detə] n Fehde f; (in family) Blutrache f; (of gangsters) Vendetta f. **to carry on a ~ against sb** mit jdm in Fehde liegen/an jdm Blutrache üben.

**vending machine** ['vendɪŋmə'ʃiːn] n Automat m.

**vendor** ['vendɔːr] n (esp Jur) Verkäufer m.

**veneer** [və'nɪər] n (lit) Furnier nt; (fig) Politur f; (of civilization) (An)schein m. **it's just a ~** es ist nur äußerer Schein.

**venerable** ['venərəbl] adj ehrwürdig.

**venerate** ['venəreɪt] vt verehren, hochachten; sb's memory ehren.

**venereal disease** [vɪ'nɪərɪəldɪ'ziːz] n Geschlechtskrankheit f.

**Venetian blind** [vɪ'niːʃən'blaɪnd] n Jalousie f.

**Venezuela** [ˌvene'zweɪlə] n Venezuela nt.

**Venezuelan** [ˌvene'zweɪlən] 1 adj venezolanisch. 2 n Venezolaner(in f) m.

**vengeance** ['vendʒəns] n (a) Vergeltung, Rache f. **to take ~ (up)on sb** Vergeltung an jdm üben (geh), sich an jdm rächen. (b) (col) **with a ~** gewaltig (col); **to work with a ~** hart or mächtig (col) arbeiten.

**vengeful** ['vendʒfʊl] adj rachsüchtig.

**venial** ['viːnɪəl] adj verzeihlich, entschuldbar.

**Venice** ['venɪs] n Venedig nt.

**venison** ['venɪsən] n Reh(fleisch) nt.

**venom** ['venəm] n (lit) Gift nt; (fig) Bosheit, Gehässigkeit f. **he spoke with real ~ in his voice** er sprach mit haßerfüllter Stimme.

**venomous** ['venəməs] adj (lit, fig) giftig; snake Gift-; tone also gehässig; sarcasm beißend.

**vent** [vent] 1 n (for gas, liquid) Öffnung f; (in chimney) Abzug m; (in coat) Schlitz m; (for feelings) Ventil nt. **to give ~ to sth** (fig) einer Sache (dat) Ausdruck verleihen; **to give ~ to one's feelings** seinen Gefühlen freien Lauf lassen. 2 vt feelings, anger abreagieren (on an +dat).

**ventilate** ['ventɪleɪt] vt (control air flow) belüften; (let fresh air in) lüften.

**ventilation** [ˌventɪ'leɪʃən] n see vt Belüftung f; Lüften nt. **~ shaft** Luftschacht m.

**ventilator** ['ventɪleɪtər] n Ventilator m.

**ventriloquism** [ven'trɪləkwɪzəm] n Bauchreden nt.

**ventriloquist** [ven'trɪləkwɪst] n Bauchredner(in f) m.

**venture** ['ventʃər] 1 n Unternehmen nt. **a new ~ in publishing** ein neuer verlegerischer Vorstoß; **this was a disastrous ~ for the company** dieses Projekt war für die Firma ein Fiasko.

2 vt (a) life, reputation aufs Spiel setzen; money also riskieren (on bei). **nothing ~d nothing gained** (Prov) wer nicht wagt, der nicht gewinnt (Prov). (b) guess, explanation wagen; opinion zu äußern wagen. **if I may ~ an opinion** wenn ich mir erlauben darf, meine Meinung zu sagen.

3 vi sich wagen. **to ~ out of doors** sich vor die Tür wagen; **the company ~d into a new field** die Firma wagte sich in ein neues Gebiet vor.

**venture capital** n Risikokapital nt.

**venue** ['venjuː] n (for event) Schauplatz m; (Sport) Austragungsort m; (Jur) Verhandlungsort m.

**Venus** ['viːnəs] n Venus f.

**veracity** [və'ræsɪtɪ] n (of report etc) Richtigkeit f.

**veranda(h)** [və'rændə] n Veranda f.

**verb** [vɜːb] n Verb, Zeitwort nt.

**verbal** ['vɜːbəl] *adj* mündlich; *error, skills* sprachlich. ~ **noun** Verbalsubstantiv *nt.*

**verbally** ['vɜːbəlɪ] *adv (spoken)* mündlich.

**verbatim** [vɜː'beɪtɪm] *adj, adv* (wort)wörtlich.

**verbiage** ['vɜːbɪɪdʒ] *n* Wortfülle *f,* Blabla *nt (col).*

**verbose** [vɜː'bəʊs] *adj* wortreich, weitschweifig.

**verdict** ['vɜːdɪkt] *n* Urteil *nt; (of electors)* Entscheidung *f.* ~ **of guilty/not guilty** Schuldspruch *m/* Freispruch *m;* **what's the ~?** wie lautet das Urteil?; **to give one's ~ about** *or* **on sth** sein Urteil über etw *(acc)* abgeben.

**verge** [vɜːdʒ] *n (lit, fig)* Rand *m; (Brit: of road)* Bankett *nt.* **to be on the ~ of ruin/war** am Rande des Ruins/eines Krieges stehen; **to be on the ~ of a discovery** kurz vor einer Entdeckung stehen; **to be on the ~ of tears** den Tränen nahe sein; **to be on the ~ of doing sth** im Begriff sein, etw zu tun.

►**verge on** *vi +prep obj (ideas, actions)* grenzen an *(acc).* **he's verging ~ bankruptcy** er steht kurz vor dem Bankrott; **she is verging ~ fifty** sie geht auf die Fünfzig zu.

**verger** ['vɜːdʒəʳ] *n (Eccl)* Küster *m.*

**verifiable** ['verɪfaɪəbl] *adj* nachprüfbar.

**verification** [ˌverɪfɪ'keɪʃən] *n (check)* Überprüfung *f; (confirmation)* Bestätigung *f; (proof)* Nachweis *m.*

**verify** ['verɪfaɪ] *vt (check)* (über)prüfen; *(confirm)* bestätigen; *theory* beweisen.

**veritable** ['verɪtəbl] *adj genius* wahr. **a ~ disaster** die reinste Katastrophe.

**vermilion** [və'mɪljən] *adj* zinnoberrot.

**vermin** ['vɜːmɪn] *n no pl (animal)* Schädling *m; (insects)* Ungeziefer *nt; (pej: people)* Pack *nt.*

**vermouth** ['vɜːməθ] *n* Wermut *m.*

**vernacular** [və'nækjʊləʳ] *n (dialect)* Mundart *f; (language of the country)* Landessprache *f.*

**versatile** ['vɜːsətaɪl] *adj* vielseitig. **he has a very ~ mind** er ist geistig sehr flexibel.

**versatility** [ˌvɜːsə'tɪlɪtɪ] *n see adj* Vielseitigkeit *f;* Flexibilität *f.*

**verse** [vɜːs] *n (a) (stanza)* Strophe *f.* **(b)** *no pl (poetry)* Dichtung *f.* **in ~** in Versform. **(c)** *(of Bible, Koran)* Vers *m.*

**versed** [vɜːst] *adj (also* **well ~)** bewandert, beschlagen *(in* in *+dat).*

**version** ['vɜːʃən] *n (a) (account: of event, of facts)* Darstellung *f.* **(b)** *(variant)* Version *f; (of text also)* Fassung *f; (of car)* Modell *nt.*

**versus** ['vɜːsəs] *prep* gegen *(+acc).*

**vertebra** ['vɜːtɪbrə] *n, pl* **-e** [-briː] Rückenwirbel *m.*

**vertebrate** ['vɜːtɪbrət] **1** *n* Wirbeltier *nt.* **2** *adj* Wirbel-.

**vertex** ['vɜːteks] *n, pl* **vertices** Scheitel(punkt) *m.*

**vertical** ['vɜːtɪkəl] **1** *adj line* senkrecht, vertikal. ~ **cliffs** senkrecht abfallende Klippen; ~ **take-off aircraft** Senkrechtstarter *m.* **2** *n (line)* Vertikale, Senkrechte *f.*

**vertigo** ['vɜːtɪgəʊ] *n* Schwindel *m; (Med)* Gleichgewichtsstörung *f.*

**verve** [vɜːv] *n* Schwung *m.*

**very** ['verɪ] **1** *adv* **(a)** *(extremely)* sehr. **that's not ~ funny** das ist überhaupt nicht lustig; **it's ~ possible** es ist gut möglich; ~ **probably** höchstwahrscheinlich; **he is so ~ lazy** er ist *so* faul; **how ~ odd** wie eigenartig; **I liked it ~ much** es hat mir sehr gut gefallen; **he doesn't work ~ much** er arbeitet nicht sehr viel; ~ **much so** sehr (sogar).

**(b)** *(absolutely)* aller-. ~ **best quality** allerbeste Qualität; ~ **last/first** allerletzte(r, s)/ allererste(r, s); **at the ~ latest** allerspätestens; **to do one's ~ best** sein Äußerstes tun; **at the ~ most/least** allerhöchstens/allerwenigstens.

**(c)** *(for emphasis)* **he fell ill and died the ~ same day** er wurde krank und starb noch am selben Tag; **he died the ~ same day as Kennedy** er starb genau am selben Tag wie Kennedy; **the ~ same hat** genau der gleiche Hut; **we met again the ~ next day** wir trafen uns am nächsten Tag schon wieder; **the ~ next day he walked under a bus** schon einen Tag später kam er unter einen Bus; **it's my ~ own car** das Auto gehört mir höchstpersönlich.

**2** *adj* **(a)** *(precise)* genau. **that ~ day** genau an diesem Tag; **in the ~ centre of the picture** genau in der Mitte des Bildes; **at the ~ heart of the organization** direkt im Zentrum der Organisation; **those were his ~ words** genau das waren seine Worte; **you are the ~ person I wanted to speak to** (genau) mit *Ihnen* wollte ich sprechen; **the ~ thing!** genau das richtige!

**(b)** *(extreme)* äußerste(r, s). **in the ~ beginning/at the ~ end** ganz am Anfang/Ende; **at the ~ back/front** ganz hinten/vorn(e).

**(c)** *(mere)* **the ~ thought of it** allein schon der Gedanke daran; **the ~ idea!** nein, so etwas!

**vespers** ['vespəz] *npl* Vesper *f.*

**vessel** ['vesl] *n* **(a)** *(Naut)* Schiff *nt.* **(b)** *(form: receptacle)* Gefäß *nt.*

**vest¹** [vest] *n* **(a)** *(Brit)* Unterhemd *nt.* **(b)** *(US: waistcoat)* Weste *f.* ~**-pocket** *(US)* Taschen-.

**vest²** *vt (form)* **the powers ~ed in me** die mir verliehene Macht; **he has ~ed interests in the oil business** er ist (finanziell) am Ölgeschäft beteiligt; **she has a ~ed interest in the play** *(fig)* sie hat ein persönliches Interesse an dem Stück.

**vestibule** ['vestɪbjuːl] *n* Vorhalle *f.*

**vestige** ['vestɪdʒ] *n* Spur *f.* **there is not a ~ of truth in what he says** es ist kein Körnchen Wahrheit an dem, was er sagt.

**vestment** ['vestmənt] *n* Ornat *m.*

**vestry** ['vestrɪ] *n* Sakristei *f.*

**Vesuvius** [vɪ'suːvɪəs] *n* der Vesuv.

**vet** [vet] **1** *n* = **veterinary surgeon** Tierarzt *m/* -ärztin *f.* **2** *vt* überprüfen.

**veteran** ['vetərən] *n (Mil, fig)* Veteran(in *f) m.* ~ **car** vor 1905 gebauter Oldtimer.

**veterinarian** [vetərɪ'nɛərɪən] *n (US)* Tierarzt *m/* -ärztin *f.*

**veterinary** ['vetərɪnərɪ] *adj medicine, science* Veterinär-; *training* tierärztlich. ~ **surgeon** Tierarzt *m/*-ärztin *f.*

**veto** ['viːtəʊ] **1** *n, pl* **-es** Veto *nt.* **power of ~** Vetorecht *nt;* **to have a ~** das Vetorecht haben; **to use one's ~** von seinem Vetorecht Gebrauch machen. **2** *vt* sein Veto einlegen gegen.

**vex** [veks] *vt (annoy)* ärgern, irritieren; *animals* quälen. **to be ~ed with sb** ärgerlich auf jdn sein; **to be ~ed about sth** sich über etw *(acc)* ärgern.

**vexation** [vek'seɪʃən] *n* Ärger *m; (act)* Ärgern *nt; (of animal)* Quälerei *f.*

**vexatious** [vek'seɪʃəs] *adj* ärgerlich; *regulations, headache* lästig.

**vexed** [vekst] *adj* **(a)** *(annoyed)* verärgert. **(b)** *question* umstritten.

**vexing** ['veksɪŋ] *adj* irritierend; *problem* verzwickt.

**vg** = **very good.**

**VGA** *(Comp)* = **video graphics array** VGA.

**VHF** *(Rad)* = **very high frequency** UKW.

**VI** *(US Post)* = **Virgin Islands.**

**via** ['vaɪə] *prep* über *(+acc).* **they got in ~ the window** sie kamen durchs Fenster herein.

**viability** [ˌvaɪə'bɪlɪtɪ] *n* **(a)** *(of life forms)* Lebensfähigkeit *f.* **(b)** *(of plan)* Durchführbarkeit *f; (of firm)* Rentabilität *f.* **the ~ of the EC** die Existenzfähigkeit der EG.

**viable** ['vaɪəbl] *adj* **(a)** *plant, foetus* lebensfähig. **(b)** *company* rentabel; *economy* lebensfähig; *suggestion* brauchbar; *plan* durchführbar. **not economically** ~ unrentabel.

**viaduct** ['vaɪədʌkt] *n* Viadukt *m*.

**vibes** [vaɪbz] *npl see* **vibration (b)**.

**vibrant** ['vaɪbrənt] *adj personality etc* dynamisch; *voice* volltönend, sonor. **the ~ life of the city** das pulsierende Leben der Großstadt.

**vibrate** [vaɪ'breɪt] **1** *vi (lit, fig)* zittern, beben *(with* vor *+dat)*; *(machine, string, air)* vibrieren; *(notes)* schwingen. **2** *vt* zum Vibrieren bringen; *string* zum Schwingen bringen.

**vibration** [vaɪ'breɪʃən] *n* **(a)** *(of string, sound waves)* Schwingung *f*; *(of machine)* Vibrieren *nt*; *(of voice, ground)* Beben *nt*. **(b)** *(col, usu pl)* **I get good/bad ~s from him** *(col)* er ist mir sympathisch/unsympathisch.

**vibrato** [vɪ'brɑːtəʊ] *n* Vibrato *nt*.

**vicar** ['vɪkər] *n* Pfarrer *m*.

**vicarage** ['vɪkərɪdʒ] *n* Pfarrhaus *nt*.

**vicarious** [vɪ'kɛərɪəs] *adj pleasure* indirekt, nachempfunden; *experience* ersatzweise.

**vice¹** [vaɪs] *n* Laster *nt*. **his main ~ is laziness** sein größter Fehler ist die Faulheit; **~ squad** Sittenpolizei *f*.

**vice²**, *(US)* **vise** *n* Schraubstock *m*. **to hold sth in a ~-like grip** etw fest umklammern.

**vice-** *pref* **~-chairman** *n* stellvertretender Vorsitzender; **~-chancellor** *n (Univ)* ≈ Rektor *m*; **~-president** *n* Vizepräsident *m*.

**vice versa** ['vaɪsɪ'vɜːsə] *adv* umgekehrt.

**vicinity** [vɪ'sɪnɪtɪ] *n* Umgebung *f*. **in the ~** in der Nähe *(of* von, *gen)*; **in the ~ of £500** um die £500.

**vicious** ['vɪʃəs] *adj* boshaft; *remark* gehässig; *habit* lasterhaft; *animal* bösartig; *dog* bissig; *blow, criminal, murder* brutal; *(col) headache* gemein *(col)*. **~ circle** Teufelskreis *m*.

**viciously** ['vɪʃəslɪ] *adv see adj* boshaft; gehässig; bösartig; brutal.

**viciousness** ['vɪʃəsnɪs] *n see adj* Boshaftigkeit *f*; Gehässigkeit *f*; Bösartigkeit *f*; Brutalität *f*.

**vicissitude** [vɪ'sɪsɪtjuːd] *n usu pl* Wandel *m*. **the ~s of life** die Wechselfälle des Lebens.

**victim** ['vɪktɪm] *n* Opfer *nt*. **he was the ~ of a practical joke** ihm wurde ein Streich gespielt; **to fall ~ to sth** Opfer einer Sache *(gen)* werden.

**victimization** [ˌvɪktɪmaɪ'zeɪʃən] *n see vt* ungerechte Behandlung; Schikanierung *f*.

**victimize** ['vɪktɪmaɪz] *vt* ungerecht behandeln; *(pick on)* schikanieren. **she feels ~d** sie fühlt sich ungerecht behandelt.

**victor** ['vɪktər] *n* Sieger(in *f*) *m*.

**Victorian** [vɪk'tɔːrɪən] **1** *n* Viktorianer(in *f*) *m*. **2** *adj* viktorianisch; *(fig)* (sitten)streng.

**victorious** [vɪk'tɔːrɪəs] *adj army* siegreich; *smile* siegesbewußt. **to be ~ over sb/sth** jdn/etw besiegen; **~ power** *(Pol)* Siegermacht *f*.

**victory** ['vɪktərɪ] *n* Sieg *m*. **to win a ~ over sb** einen Sieg über jdn erringen, jdn besiegen.

**victuals** ['vɪtlz] *npl* Lebensmittel *pl*.

**video** ['vɪdɪəʊ] **1** *n* **(a)** *(film)* Video *nt*. **on ~ watch, release** als Video; *record* auf Video. **(b)** *(recorder)* Videorekorder *m*. **(c)** *(US TV)* Fernsehen *nt*. **on ~ im** Fernsehen. **2** *vt* auf Video aufnehmen.

**video-** *in cpds camera, conference, tape etc* Video-; **~ cassette** Videokassette *f*; **~ disc** *n* Bildplatte *f*; **~ game** *n* Telespiel *nt*; **~ nasty** *n* Horrorvideo *nt*; **~-recorder** Videorekorder *m*; **~-recording** *n* Videoaufnahme *f*; **~tape** *n* Videoband *nt*.

**vie** [vaɪ] *vi* wetteifern; *(Comm)* konkurrieren. **to ~ with sb for sth** mit jdm um etw wetteifern.

**Vienna** [vɪ'enə] *n* Wien *nt*.

**Viennese** [ˌvɪə'niːz] **1** *adj* Wiener, wienerisch. **2** *n* Wiener(in *f*) *m*.

**Vietnam** [ˌvjet'næm] *n* Vietnam *nt*.

**Vietnamese** [ˌvjetnə'miːz] **1** *adj* vietnamesisch. **2** *n* **(a)** Vietnamese *m*, Vietnamesin *f*. **(b)** *(language)* Vietnamesisch *nt*.

**view** [vjuː] **1** *n (range of vision)* Sicht *f*; *(prospect, sight)* Aussicht *f*. **in full ~ of thousands of people** vor den Augen von Tausenden von Menschen; **the ship came into ~** das Schiff kam in Sicht; **to keep sth in ~** etw im Auge behalten; **the house is within ~ of the sea** vom Haus aus ist das Meer zu sehen; **hidden from ~** verborgen, versteckt; **on ~** *(for purchasing)* zur Ansicht; *(of exhibits)* ausgestellt; **there is a splendid ~ from here** von hier hat man einen herrlichen Blick; **a good ~ of the sea** ein schöner Blick auf das Meer; **a room with a ~** ein Zimmer mit Aussicht; **an idealistic ~ of the world** eine idealistische Weltsicht; **a general ~ of a problem** ein allgemeiner Überblick über ein Problem; **in ~ of** angesichts *(+gen)*.

**(b)** *(photograph etc)* Ansicht *f*.

**(c)** *(opinion)* Ansicht, Meinung *f*. **in my ~** meiner Ansicht nach; **what are his ~s on this problem?** was meint er zu diesem Problem?; **I have no ~s on that** ich habe keine Meinung dazu; **to take the ~ that ...** die Ansicht vertreten, daß ...; **to take a poor ~ of sth** etw mißbilligen.

**(d)** *(intention, plan)* **to have sth in ~** etw beabsichtigen; **with a ~ to doing sth** mit der Absicht, etw zu tun.

**2** *vt (see)* betrachten; *house* besichtigen; *(consider) problem etc* sehen. **he ~s the prospect with dismay** er sieht dieser Sache mit Schrecken entgegen.

**viewdata** ® ['vjuːˌdeɪtə] *n* Bildschirmtext *m*.

**viewer** ['vjuːər] *n* **(a)** *(TV)* Zuschauer(in *f*) *m*. **(b)** *(for slides)* Diabetrachter *m*.

**viewfinder** ['vjuːˌfaɪndər] *n* Sucher *m*.

**viewing** ['vjuːɪŋ] *n* **(a)** *(of house, at auction)* Besichtigung *f*. **(b)** *(TV)* Fernsehen *nt*. **I don't do much ~** ich sehe nicht viel fern; **~ peak ~ time** Haupteinschaltzeit *f*; **~ figures** Einschaltquoten *pl*.

**viewpoint** ['vjuːpɔɪnt] *n* Standpunkt *m*. **from the ~ of economic growth** unter dem Gesichtspunkt des Wirtschaftswachstums; **to see sth from sb's ~** etw aus jds Sicht sehen.

**vigil** ['vɪdʒɪl] *n* (Nacht)wache *f*. **to keep ~ over sb** bei jdm wachen.

**vigilance** ['vɪdʒɪləns] *n* Wachsamkeit *f*. **~ committee** *(US)* Bürgerwehr *f*.

**vigilant** ['vɪdʒɪlənt] *adj* wachsam.

**vigilante** [ˌvɪdʒɪ'læntɪ] *n* Mitglied *nt* einer Bürgerwehr. **~s** Bürgerwehr *f*.

**vigilantly** ['vɪdʒɪləntlɪ] *adv* wachsam.

**vignette** [vɪ'njet] *n* Vignette *f*; *(character sketch)* Skizze *f*.

**vigorous** ['vɪgərəs] *adj* kräftig; *prose, tune* kraftvoll; *protest, measures, exercises* energisch; *walk* forsch, flott.

**vigorously** ['vɪgərəslɪ] *adv see adj*.

**vigour**, *(US)* **vigor** ['vɪgər] *n* Kraft, Energie *f*; *(of protest)* Heftigkeit *f*; *(of prose)* Ausdruckskraft *f*. **youthful ~** jugendliche Spannkraft; **to speak with ~** mit Nachdruck sprechen.

**Viking** ['vaɪkɪŋ] *n* Wikinger *m*.

**vile** [vaɪl] *adj* abscheulich; *language also* unflätig; *weather, food also* scheußlich. **that was a ~ thing to say** es war gemein, so etwas zu sagen.

**vilify** ['vɪlɪfaɪ] *vt* diffamieren, verleumden.
**villa** ['vɪlə] *n* Villa *f*; *(holiday ~)* Ferienhaus *nt*.
**village** ['vɪlɪdʒ] *n* Dorf *nt*.
**village** *in cpds* Dorf-; ~ **green** *n* Dorfwiese *f*; ~ **idiot** *n* Dorftrottel *m (col)*.
**villager** ['vɪlɪdʒəʳ] *n* Dorfbewohner(in *f*) *m*.
**villain** ['vɪlən] *n (scoundrel)* Schurke *m*; *(col: criminal)* Verbrecher, Ganove *(col) m*; *(in drama, novel)* Bösewicht *m*.
**villainous** ['vɪlənəs] *adj* böse; *deed* gemein.
**villainy** ['vɪlənɪ] *n* Gemeinheit *f*.
**Vilnius** ['vɪlnɪʊs] *n* Wilna *nt*.
**VIN** *(US)* = **vehicle identification number** Fahrgestellnummer *f*.
**vindicate** ['vɪndɪkeɪt] *vt* (a) *opinion, action* rechtfertigen. (b) *(from suspicion)* rehabilitieren.
**vindication** [,vɪndɪ'keɪʃən] *n see vt* (a) Rechtfertigung *f*. **in ~ of** zur Rechtfertigung *(+gen)*. (b) Rehabilitation *f*.
**vindictive** [vɪn'dɪktɪv] *adj speech, person* rachsüchtig; *mood* unversöhnlich. **to feel ~ towards sb** Rachegefühle gegen jdn haben.
**vindictively** [vɪn'dɪktɪvlɪ] *adv* rachsüchtig.
**vindictiveness** [vɪn'dɪktɪvnɪs] *n* Rachsucht *f*; *(of mood)* Unversöhnlichkeit *f*.
**vine** [vaɪn] *n (grapevine)* Rebe *f*.
**vinegar** ['vɪnɪgəʳ] *n* Essig *m*.
**vine:** ~ **grower** *n* Weinbauer *m*; ~ **harvest** *n* Weinlese *f*; **~yard** ['vɪnjəd] *n* Weinberg *m*.
**vintage** ['vɪntɪdʒ] **1** *n* (a) *(of wine, fig)* Jahrgang *m*. **the 1972 ~** der Jahrgang 1972. (b) *(harvesting, season)* Weinlese *f*. **2** *adj attr (old)* uralt; *(high quality)* glänzend.
**vintage:** ~ **car** *n* (zwischen 1918 und 1930 gebauter) Oldtimer *m*; ~ **wine** *n* edler Wein; ~ **year** *n*: **a ~ year for ...** ein besonders gutes Jahr für ...
**vinyl** ['vaɪnɪl] *n* Vinyl *nt*.
**viola** [vɪ'əʊlə] *n (Mus)* Bratsche *f*.
**violate** ['vaɪəleɪt] *vt* (a) *treaty, promise* brechen; *(partially)* verletzen; *law, rule* verstoßen gegen; *rights* verletzen. (b) *holy place* schänden; *peacefulness* stören. **to ~ sb's privacy** in jds Privatsphäre eindringen.
**violation** [,vaɪə'leɪʃən] *n* (a) *(of law, rule)* Verstoß *m (of gegen)*; *(of rights)* Verletzung *f*. **a ~ of a treaty** ein Vertragsbruch *m*; **he did this in ~ of the conditions agreed** er verstieß damit gegen die Vereinbarungen. (b) *(of holy place)* Schändung *f*; *(of peacefulness)* Störung *f*.
**violence** ['vaɪələns] *n* (a) *(forcefulness, strength)* Heftigkeit *f*; *(of protest also)* Schärfe *f*. (b) *(brutality)* Gewalt *f*; *(of people)* Gewalttätigkeit *f*; *(of actions)* Brutalität *f*. **act of ~** Gewalttat *f*; **robbery with ~** Raubüberfall *m*; **to use ~ against sb** Gewalt gegen jdn anwenden; **was there any ~?** kam es zu Gewalttätigkeiten?; **outbreak of ~** Ausbruch von Gewalttätigkeiten; **to do ~ to sth** *(fig)* etw verletzen.
**violent** ['vaɪələnt] *adj person, action* brutal, gewalttätig; *feeling, speech* leidenschaftlich; *storm, dislike, attack, pain* heftig; *death* gewaltsam; *contrast* kraß. **to have a ~ temper** jähzornig sein; **to get ~** gewalttätig werden.
**violently** ['vaɪələntlɪ] *adv beat, attack etc* brutal; *react, speak, protest etc* heftig; *(passionately)* leidenschaftlich.
**violet** ['vaɪəlɪt] **1** *n (Bot)* Veilchen *nt*; *(colour)* Violett *nt*. **2** *adj* violett.
**violin** [,vaɪə'lɪn] *n* Geige, Violine *f*; *(player)* Geiger(in *f*) *m*. ~ **case** Geigenkasten *m*.
**violinist** [,vaɪə'lɪnɪst] *n* Geiger(in *f*) *m*.
**VIP** [vi:aɪ'pi:] *n* Prominente(r) *mf*, VIP *m*. **to get ~**

**treatment** als Ehrengast behandelt werden.
**viper** ['vaɪpəʳ] *n (Zool)* Viper *f*; *(fig)* Schlange *f*.
**viral** ['vaɪərəl] *adj* Virus-.
**virgin** ['vɜːdʒɪn] **1** *n* Jungfrau *f*. **the (Blessed) V~** *(Rel)* die (heilige) Jungfrau Maria; **he's still a ~** er ist noch unschuldig. **2** *adj (fig) forest, snow* unberührt. ~ **birth** unbefleckte Empfängnis; **the V~ Islands** die Jungferninseln.
**virginity** [vɜː'dʒɪnɪtɪ] *n* Unschuld *f*; *(of girls also)* Jungfräulichkeit *f*.
**Virgo** ['vɜːgəʊ] *n (Astrol)* Jungfrau *f*.
**virile** ['vɪraɪl] *adj (lit)* männlich; *(fig)* kraftvoll.
**virility** [vɪ'rɪlɪtɪ] *n (lit)* Männlichkeit *f*; *(sexual power)* Potenz *f*; *(fig)* Ausdruckskraft *f*.
**virtual** ['vɜːtjʊəl] *adj attr* **he is the ~ leader** er ist praktisch der Führer; **it was a ~ disaster** es war praktisch eine Katastrophe; ~ **reality** virtuelle Realität.
**virtually** ['vɜːtjʊəlɪ] *adv* praktisch. **to be ~ certain** sich *(dat)* so gut wie sicher sein.
**virtue** ['vɜːtjuː] *n* (a) *(moral quality)* Tugend *f*. **a life of ~** ein tugendhaftes Leben; **a woman of easy ~** *(euph)* ein leichtes Mädchen. (b) *(advantage, point)* Vorteil *m*. **there is no ~ in doing that** es scheint nicht sehr zweckmäßig, das zu tun; **by ~ of** aufgrund *(+gen)*.
**virtuoso** [,vɜːtjʊ'əʊzəʊ] *n (esp Mus)* **1** *n* Virtuose *m*. **2** *adj performance, playing* virtuos.
**virtuous** ['vɜːtjʊəs] *adj* tugendhaft.
**virulence** ['vɪrʊləns] *n* (a) *(Med)* Virulenz *f*; *(of poison)* Stärke *f*. (b) *(fig)* Schärfe *f*.
**virulent** ['vɪrʊlənt] *adj* (a) *(Med)* virulent; *poison* stark, tödlich. (b) *(fig)* geharnischt, scharf.
**virus** ['vaɪərəs] *n (Med, Comp)* Virus *m*.
**visa** ['viːzə] *n* Visum *nt*.
**vis-à-vis** ['viːzəviː] **1** *prep* in bezug auf *(+acc)*. **2** *adv* gegenüber.
**viscose** ['vɪskəʊs] *n* Viskose *f*.
**viscount** ['vaɪkaʊnt] *n* Viscount *m*.
**viscous** ['vɪskəs] *adj* zähflüssig; *(Phys)* viskos.
**vise** [vaɪs] *n (US)* = **vice²**.
**visibility** [,vɪzɪ'bɪlɪtɪ] *n* (a) *(Met)* Sichtbarkeit *f*. (b) *(Met)* Sichtweite *f*. **poor/good ~** schlechte/gute Sichtverhältnisse *pl*; **low ~** geringe Sichtweite.
**visible** ['vɪzəbl] *adj* sichtbar; *(obvious)* sichtlich. ~ **to the naked eye** mit dem bloßen Auge zu erkennen.
**visibly** ['vɪzəblɪ] *adv* sichtlich; *deteriorate* zusehends.
**vision** ['vɪʒən] *n* (a) *(power of sight)* Sehvermögen *nt*. **within the range of ~** in Sichtweite. (b) *(foresight)* Weitblick *m*. **a man of ~** ein Mann mit Weitblick. (c) *(in dream, trance)* Vision *f*; *(image)* Vorstellung *f*. **I had ~s of having to walk all the way home** *(col)* ich sah mich im Geiste schon den ganzen Weg nach Hause laufen.
**visionary** ['vɪʒənərɪ] **1** *adj (of visions)* vorhersehend; *(unreal)* eingebildet. **2** *n* Seher(in *f*) *m (geh)*.
**visit** ['vɪzɪt] **1** *n* Besuch *m*; *(of doctor)* Hausbesuch *m*; *(of inspector)* Kontrolle *f*; *(stay also)* Aufenthalt *m*. **to pay sb/sth a ~** jdn/etw besuchen; **to have a ~ from sb** von jdm besucht werden; **to be on a ~ to London** zu einem Besuch in London sein. **2** *vt* (a) *person, museum* besuchen. **3** *vi* (a) einen Besuch machen. (b) *(US col: chat)* ein Schwätzchen halten. ►**visit with** *vi + prep obj (US) (call on)* vorbeikommen bei; *(col: chat with)* schwatzen mit.
**visiting:** ~ **card** *n (Brit)* Visitenkarte *f*; ~ **hours** *npl* Besuchszeiten *pl*; ~ **professor** *n* Gastprofessor *m*; ~ **team** *n* Gastmannschaft *f*, Gäste *pl*.
**visitor** ['vɪzɪtəʳ] *n* Besucher(in *f*) *m*; *(in hotel)* Gast *m*. **to have ~s** *or* **a ~** Besuch haben; **~s' book**

Gästebuch *nt*.

**visor** ['vaɪzəʳ] *n (on helmet)* Visier *nt*; *(on cap)* Schirm *m*; *(Aut)* Blende *f*.

**vista** ['vɪstə] *n* Aussicht *f*, Blick *m*.

**visual** ['vɪzjʊəl] *adj field, nerve* Seh-; *memory, impression* visuell. ~ **aids** Anschauungsmaterial *nt*; ~ **display unit** Bildschirmgerät *nt*.

**visualize** ['vɪzjʊəlaɪz] *vt (see in mind)* sich *(dat)* vorstellen; *(foresee)* erwarten.

**visually** ['vɪzjʊəlɪ] *adv* visuell. ~ **handicapped** sehbehindert.

**vital** ['vaɪtl] *adj* (a) *(of life)* vital, Lebens-; *(necessary for life)* lebenswichtig. ~ **force** Lebenskraft *f*; ~ **organs** lebenswichtige Organe *pl*; ~ **statistics** *(col: of woman)* Maße *pl*. (b) *(essential)* unerläßlich. **of** ~ **importance** von größter Wichtigkeit; **this is** ~ das ist unbedingt notwendig; **your support is** ~ **to us** wir brauchen unbedingt Ihre Unterstützung. (c) *(critical) error* schwerwiegend; *problem* Kern-. **at the** ~ **moment** im entscheidenden Moment. (d) *(lively) person* vital; *artistic style also* lebendig.

**vitality** [vaɪ'tælɪtɪ] *n (energy)* Energie, Vitalität *f*; *(of prose)* Lebendigkeit *f*; *(of company)* Dynamik *f*.

**vitally** ['vaɪtəlɪ] *adv important* äußerst, ungeheuer.

**vitamin** ['vɪtəmɪn] *n* Vitamin *nt*.

**vitamin:** ~ **deficiency** *n* Vitaminmangel *m*; ~ **pill** *n* Vitamintablette *f*.

**vitiate** ['vɪʃɪeɪt] *vt (spoil)* beeinträchtigen; *(invalidate)* ungültig machen.

**vitreous** ['vɪtrɪəs] *adj* Glas-. ~ **china** Porzellanemail *nt*.

**vitriolic** [‚vɪtrɪ'ɒlɪk] *adj (fig) remark, criticism* beißend; *attack, speech* haßerfüllt.

**vituperate** [vɪ'tjuːpəreɪt] *vi* wettern *(against* gegen*)*.

**viva** ['vaɪvə] *n (Univ)* mündliche Prüfung.

**vivacious** [vɪ'veɪʃəs] *adj* lebhaft.

**vivacity** [vɪ'væsɪtɪ] *n* Lebhaftigkeit *f*.

**vivid** ['vɪvɪd] *adj light* hell; *colour* kräftig, lebhaft; *(lively) imagination* lebhaft; *description* anschaulich; *emotions* stark. **the memory of that day is still** ~ der Tag ist mir/uns *etc* noch in lebhafter Erinnerung.

**vividly** ['vɪvɪdlɪ] *adv* lebhaft; *shine* hell, leuchtend; *describe* anschaulich.

**vividness** ['vɪvɪdnɪs] *n (of colour, imagination etc)* Lebhaftigkeit *f*; *(of light)* Helligkeit *f*; *(of description)* Lebendigkeit *f*.

**vivisection** [‚vɪvɪ'sekʃən] *n* Vivisektion *f*.

**vixen** ['vɪksn] *n (Zool)* Füchsin *f*.

**viz** [vɪz] *adv* nämlich.

**V-neck** ['viːnek] *n* V-Ausschnitt *m*. ~**(ed)** pullover Pullover *m* mit V-Ausschnitt.

**vocabulary** [vəʊ'kæbjʊlərɪ] *n* Wortschatz *m*, Vokabular *nt (geh)*; *(in textbook)* Wörterverzeichnis *nt*. **legal** ~ juristisches Vokabular.

**vocal** ['vəʊkəl] **1** *adj* (a) Stimm-; *music, part* Vokal-. ~ **cords** Stimmbänder *pl*. (b) *(voicing one's opinions)* lautstark. **2** *n (of pop song)* Vokalpartie *f*. ~**: Van Morrison** Gesang: Van Morrison.

**vocalist** ['vəʊkəlɪst] *n* Sänger(in *f*) *m*.

**vocation** [vəʊ'keɪʃən] *n (Rel etc)* Berufung *f*; *(form: profession)* Beruf *m*. **to have a** ~ **for teaching** zum Lehrer berufen sein.

**vocational** [vəʊ'keɪʃənl] *adj* Berufs-. ~ **guidance** Berufsberatung *f*; ~ **school** *(US)* ≃ Berufsschule *f*; ~ **training** Berufsausbildung *f*.

**vociferous** *adj*, ~**ly** *adv* [vəʊ'sɪfərəs, -lɪ] laut; *protest* lautstark.

**vodka** ['vɒdkə] *n* Wodka *m*.

**vogue** [vəʊg] *n* Mode *f*. **to be in** ~ Mode sein; ~ **word** Modewort *nt*.

**voice** [vɔɪs] **1** *n* (a) Stimme *f*. **to lose one's** ~ die Stimme verlieren; **I've lost my** ~ ich habe keine Stimme mehr; **to be in (good)/poor** ~ gut/nicht gut bei Stimme sein; **in a deep** ~ mit tiefer Stimme; **with one** ~ einstimmig; **to give** ~ **to sth** einer Sache *(dat)* Ausdruck verleihen; **we have no** ~ **in the matter** wir haben in dieser Angelegenheit kein Mitspracherecht *nt*. (b) *(Gram)* **the active/passive** ~ das Aktiv/Passiv. **2** *vt opinion* zum Ausdruck bringen.

**voice:** ~**-over** *n* Begleitkommentar *m*; ~ **production** *n* Stimmbildung *f*.

**void** [vɔɪd] **1** *n (lit, fig)* Leere *f*. **2** *adj (empty)* leer; *(Jur)* ungültig, nichtig. ~ **of hope** hoffnungslos.

**vol** = **volume** Bd.

**volatile** ['vɒlətaɪl] *adj* (a) *(Chem)* flüchtig. (b) *(Comp)* ~ **memory** flüchtiger Speicher. (c) *person* impulsiv; *political situation* brisant.

**vol-au-vent** ['vɒləʊvã:] *n* Königinpastete *f*.

**volcanic** [vɒl'kænɪk] *adj dust* vulkanisch; *region, eruption* Vulkan-.

**volcano** [vɒl'keɪnəʊ] *n* Vulkan *m*.

**vole** [vəʊl] *n* Wühlmaus *f*; *(common* ~*)* Feldmaus *f*.

**Volga** ['vɒlgə] *n* Wolga *f*.

**volition** [və'lɪʃən] *n* Wille *m*. **of one's own** ~ aus freiem Willen, aus freien Stücken.

**volley** ['vɒlɪ] *n* (a) *(of shots)* Salve *f*; *(of arrows, stones)* Hagel *m*; *(fig: of insults)* Flut *f*. (b) *(Tennis)* Volley, Flugball *m*.

**volleyball** ['vɒlɪ‚bɔːl] *n* Volleyball *m*.

**volt** [vəʊlt] *n* Volt *nt*. ~ **meter** Voltmeter *nt*.

**voltage** ['vəʊltɪdʒ] *n* Spannung *f*.

**volte-face** ['vɒlt'fɑːs] *n (fig)* Kehrtwendung *f*.

**voluble** ['vɒljʊbl] *adj speaker* redselig *(esp pej)*; *account, protest* wortreich.

**volume** ['vɒljuːm] *n* (a) Band *m*. **a six-**~ **dictionary** ein sechsbändiges Wörterbuch; **to write** ~**s** ganze Bände *pl* schreiben; **that speaks** ~**s** *(fig)* das spricht Bände *(for* über +*acc)*. (b) *(space occupied by sth)* Volumen *nt*. (c) *(size, amount)* Ausmaß *nt (of* an +*dat)*. **the** ~ **of traffic** das Verkehrsaufkommen; **trade has increased in** ~ das Handelsvolumen hat sich vergrößert; ~ **discount** Mengenrabatt *m*. (d) *(sound)* Lautstärke *f*. **turn the** ~ **up/down** *(Rad, TV)* stell (das Radio/den Fernseher) lauter/leiser; ~ **control** *(Rad, TV)* Lautstärkeregler *m*.

**voluminous** [və'luːmɪnəs] *adj figure* üppig; *writings* umfangreich; *dress* wallend.

**voluntarily** ['vɒləntərɪlɪ] *adv* freiwillig.

**voluntary** ['vɒləntərɪ] *adj* freiwillig. ~ **worker** freiwilliger Helfer, freiwillige Helferin; *(overseas)* Entwicklungshelfer(in *f*) *m*; **a** ~ **organization** ein freiwilliger Wohlfahrtsverband; ~ **redundancy** freiwilliger Verzicht auf den Arbeitsplatz.

**volunteer** [‚vɒlən'tɪəʳ] **1** *n (also Mil)* Freiwillige(r) *mf*. **any** ~**s?** wer meldet sich freiwillig? **2** *vt help* anbieten; *suggestion* machen; *information* geben. **3** *vi* (a) sich (freiwillig) melden. **to** ~ **for sth** sich freiwillig für etw zur Verfügung stellen; **to** ~ **to do sth** sich anbieten, etw zu tun. (b) *(Mil)* sich freiwillig melden *(for* zu, *for places* nach*)*.

**voluptuous** [və'lʌptjʊəs] *adj woman, movement* sinnlich; *curves* üppig.

**vomit** ['vɒmɪt] **1** *n* Erbrochene(s) *nt*. **2** *vt* erbrechen; *(fig)* spucken. **3** *vi* sich übergeben.

**voracious** [və'reɪʃəs] *adj person* gefräßig. **she is a** ~ **reader** sie verschlingt die Bücher geradezu; **to have a** ~ **appetite** einen Riesenappetit haben.

**vortex** ['vɔːteks] *n, pl* **-es** *or* **vortices** ['vɔːtɪsiːz] *(lit)* Wirbel, Strudel *(also fig) m*.

**Vosges** [vəʊʒ] *npl* Vogesen *pl*.

**vote** [vəut] **1** *n* Stimme *f; (act of voting)* Abstimmung *f; (result)* Abstimmungsergebnis *nt.* **to put sth to the ~** über etw *(acc)* abstimmen lassen; **the Labour ~** die Labourstimmen *pl;* **to have the ~** das Wahlrecht haben. **2** *vti (elect)* wählen; *(approve)* bewilligen. **he was ~d chairman** er wurde zum Vorsitzenden gewählt; **to ~ Labour** Labour wählen; **to ~ for/against sth** für/gegen etw stimmen; **I ~ we leave now** ich schlage vor, daß wir jetzt gehen; **to ~ with one's feet** abwandern.
▶**vote in** *vt sep law* beschließen; *person* wählen.
▶**vote on** *vi +prep obj* abstimmen über *(+acc).*
**voter** ['vəutər] *n* Wähler(in *f*) *m.*
**voting** ['vəutɪŋ] *n* Wahl *f.* **~ booth** Wahlkabine *f;* **~ paper** Stimmzettel *m;* **~ system** Wahlsystem *nt.*
**vouch** [vautʃ] *vi* **to ~ for sb/sth** sich für jdn/etw verbürgen; *(legally)* für jdn/etw bürgen.
**voucher** ['vautʃər] *n* **(a)** *(for cash, petrol, meals)* Gutschein *m; (cigarette ~)* Coupon *m.* **(b)** *(receipt)* Beleg *m; (for debt)* Schuldschein *m.*
**vow** [vau] **1** *n* Versprechen *nt; (Rel)* Gelübde *nt.* **to make a ~ to do sth** geloben, etw zu tun; **to take one's ~s** sein Gelübde ablegen. **2** *vt obedience* geloben.
**vowel** ['vauəl] *n* Vokal, Selbstlaut *m.* **~ sound** Vokallaut *m.*
**voyage** ['vɔɪdʒ] *n* Reise, Fahrt *f; (by sea also)* Seereise *f; (Space also)* Flug *m.* **to go on a ~** auf eine

Reise *etc* gehen; **the ~ out** die Hinreise/der Hinflug; **the ~ back** die Rückreise/der Rückflug; **~ of discovery** *(fig)* Entdeckungsreise *f.*
**voyager** ['vɔɪədʒər] *n* Passagier *m; (Space)* Raumfahrer *m.*
**vs** = **versus.**
**V-:** **~-shaped** *adj* pfeilförmig, V-förmig; **~-sign** *n* **to give sb the ~-sign** ≈ jdm den Vogel zeigen *(col).*
**VSO** *(Brit)* = **Voluntary Service Overseas** ≈ Entwicklungsdienst *m.*
**VT** *(US Post)* = **Vermont.**
**VTOL** ['viːtɒl] *(Aviat)* = **vertical take-off and landing** Senkrechtstart und -landung.
**vulcanize** ['vʌlkənaɪz] *vt* vulkanisieren.
**vulgar** ['vʌlɡər] *adj (pej)* ordinär; *(tasteless)* geschmacklos. **~ fraction** *(Math)* gemeiner Bruch.
**vulgarity** [vʌl'ɡærɪti] *n* Vulgarität *f; (of gesture, joke also)* Anstößigkeit *f; (of colour etc)* Geschmacklosigkeit *f.*
**vulnerability** [ˌvʌlnərə'bɪlɪti] *n see adj* Verwundbarkeit *f;* Verletzlichkeit *f;* Verletzbarkeit *f;* Ungeschütztheit *f.*
**vulnerable** ['vʌlnərəbl] *adj* verwundbar; *(exposed)* verletzlich; *(fig)* verletzbar; *troops, fortress* ungeschützt. **to be ~ to temptation** für Versuchungen anfällig sein.
**vulture** ['vʌltʃər] *n (lit, fig)* Geier *m.*

# W

**W, w** ['dʌblju:] *n* W, w *nt.* **W for William** ≈ W wie Wilhelm.

**W** = **(a)** west W. **(b)** watt(s) W.

**WA** *(US Post)* = **Washington.**

**WAAF** [wæf] *(Brit)* = **Women's Auxiliary Air Force** *weibliche Einheiten der Luftwaffe.*

**WAC** [wæk] *(US)* = **Women's Army Corps** *weibliches Armeekorps.*

**wacky** ['wækɪ] *adj* (+er) *(col)* verrückt *(col).*

**wad** [wɒd] *n (compact mass)* Knäuel *m or nt; (of cotton wool etc)* Bausch *m; (of papers, banknotes)* Bündel *nt.*

**wadding** ['wɒdɪŋ] *n (for packing)* Material *nt* zum Ausstopfen; *(Sew)* Wattierung *f.*

**waddle** ['wɒdl] *vi* watscheln.

**wade** [weɪd] **1** *vt* durchwaten. **2** *vi* waten. **to ~ into** *sb/sth (col: attack)* auf jdn losgehen/etw in Angriff nehmen; **they all ~d in and helped** sie haben sich alle in die Arbeit hineingekniet; **to ~ through a book** sich durch ein Buch kämpfen.

**wader** ['weɪdər] *n* **(a)** *(Orn)* Watvogel *m.* **(b)** **~s** *pl (boots)* Watstiefel *pl.*

**wading pool** ['weɪdɪŋ'pu:l] *n (US)* Planschbecken *nt.*

**wafer** ['weɪfər] *n* **(a)** *(biscuit)* Waffel *f.* **a vanilla ~** eine Vanillewaffel. **(b)** *(Eccl)* Hostie *f.* **(c)** *(silicone ~)* Wafer *f.*

**wafer-thin** ['weɪfə'θɪn] *adj* hauchdünn.

**waffle¹** ['wɒfl] *n (Cook)* Waffel *f.* **~ iron** Waffeleisen *nt.*

**waffle²** *(Brit col)* **1** *n* Geschwafel *nt (col).* **2** *vi (also ~ on)* schwafeln *(col).*

**waft** [wɑːft] *vti* wehen. **a delicious smell ~ed up from the kitchen** ein köstlicher Geruch zog aus der Küche herauf.

**wag¹** [wæg] **1** *n* **with a ~ of its tail** mit einem Schwanzwedeln. **2** *vt tail* wedeln mit; *(bird)* wippen mit. **to ~ one's finger at sb** jdm mit dem Finger drohen. **3** *vi (tail)* wedeln; *(of bird)* wippen. **that'll set the tongues ~ging** dann geht das Gerede los.

**wag²** *n (joker)* Witzbold *m (col).* **a bit of a ~** ein alter Witzbold.

**wage¹** [weɪdʒ] *n usu pl* Lohn *m.*

**wage²** *vt war, campaign* führen.

**wage** *in cpds* Lohn-; **~ claim** *or* **demand** *n* Lohnforderung *f*; **~ differential** *n* Lohngefälle *nt*; **~ earner** *n* Lohnempfänger *m*; **~ freeze** *n* Lohnstopp *m*; **~ increase** *n* Lohnerhöhung *f*; **~ packet** *n (Brit)* Lohntüte *f.*

**wager** ['weɪdʒər] **1** *n* Wette *f (on* auf +acc). **to lay a ~** eine Wette abschließen. **2** *vti* wetten *(on* auf +acc).

**wages** ['weɪdʒɪz] *npl* Lohn *m.* **~ bill** Lohnkosten *pl*; **~ clerk** Lohnbuchhalter(in *f*) *m.*

**wage settlement** *n* Tarifabschluß *m.*

**waggle** ['wægl] **1** *vt* wackeln mit; *tail* wedeln mit; *(bird)* wippen mit. **he ~d his finger at me disapprovingly** er drohte mir mißbilligend mit dem Finger. **2** *vi* wackeln; *(tail)* wedeln. **3** *n* **with a ~ of its tail** mit einem Schwanzwedeln.

**waggon** *(Brit)*, **wagon** ['wægən] *n* **(a)** *(horse-drawn)* Wagen *m; (covered ~)* Planwagen *m; (US: delivery truck)* Lieferwagen *m; (US col: police car)* Streifenwagen *m; (US col: for transporting prisoners)* ≈ grüne Minna *(col).* **(b)** *(Brit Rail)* Waggon *m.* **(c)** *(col)* **I'm on the ~** ich trinke nichts.

**wagtail** ['wægteɪl] *n (Orn)* Bachstelze *f.*

**waif** [weɪf] *n* heimatloses Kind. **~s and strays** heimatlose Kinder *pl.*

**wail** [weɪl] **1** *n (of baby)* Geschrei *nt; (of mourner, music)* Klagen *nt; (of sirens, wind)* Heulen *nt; (col: complaint)* Gejammer *nt (col).* **2** *vi (baby, cat)* schreien; *(mourner, music)* klagen; *(sirens, wind)* heulen; *(col: complain)* jammern *(over* über +acc).

**waist** [weɪst] *n* Taille *f.* **stripped to the ~** mit nacktem Oberkörper.

**waist: ~band** *n (of trousers)* Hosenbund *m; (of dress)* Rockbund *m*; **~coat** *n (Brit)* Weste *f*; **~deep** *adj* hüfthoch, bis zur Taille reichend; **we stood ~-deep in ...** wir standen bis zur Hüfte im ...; **~line** *n* Taille *f*; **~ measurement** *n* Taillenweite *f.*

**wait** [weɪt] **1** *vi* **(a)** warten *(for* auf +acc). **to ~ for sb to do sth** darauf warten, daß jd etw tut; **it was definitely worth ~ing for** es hat sich wirklich gelohnt, darauf zu warten; **well, what are you ~ing for?** worauf wartest du denn (noch)?; **let him ~!** laß ihn warten, soll er warten!; **this work will have to ~ till later** diese Arbeit muß bis später warten; **~ a minute** *or* **moment** (einen) Moment (mal); **(just) you ~!** warte nur ab!; *(threatening)* warte nur!; **I can't ~** ich kann's kaum erwarten; *(out of curiosity)* ich bin gespannt; **I can't ~ to see his face** da bin ich (aber) auf sein Gesicht gespannt. **(b)** **to ~ at table** servieren.

**2** *vt* **to ~ one's turn** (ab)warten, bis man an der Reihe ist; **to ~ one's chance** eine günstige Gelegenheit abwarten; **to ~ dinner for sb** mit dem Essen auf jdn warten.

**3** *n* **(a)** Wartezeit *f.* **did you have a long ~?** mußten Sie lange warten? **(b)** **to lie in ~ for sb/sth** jdm/einer Sache auflauern.

▶**wait behind** *vi* zurückbleiben. **to ~ ~ for sb** zurückbleiben und auf jdn warten.

▶**wait in** *vi* zu Hause bleiben *(for* wegen).

▶**wait on** *vi +prep obj* **(a)** *(also ~ upon) (serve)* bedienen. **(b)** *(US)* **to ~ ~ table** servieren, bei Tisch bedienen.

▶**wait up** *vi* aufbleiben *(for* wegen, für).

**waiter** ['weɪtər] *n* Kellner, Ober *m.* **~!** (Herr) Ober!

**waiting** ['weɪtɪŋ] *n* Warten *nt.* **"no ~"** „Halteverbot".

**waiting: ~ game** *n*: **to play a ~ game** sich gedulden; **~ list** *n* Warteliste *f*; **~ room** *n* Warteraum *m; (at doctor's)* Wartezimmer *nt; (in station)* Wartesaal *m.*

**waitress** ['weɪtrɪs] *n* Kellnerin *f.* **~!** Fräulein!

**waive** [weɪv] *vt* **(a)** *rights, claim* verzichten auf (+acc); *rule, age limit etc* außer acht lassen. **(b)** *(put*

*aside, dismiss) question, objection* abtun.
**waiver** ['weɪvəʳ] *n (Jur)* Verzicht *m (of* auf *+acc);*
*(document)* Verzichterklärung *f; (of law, contract)*
Außerkraftsetzung *f.*
**wake¹** [weɪk] *n (Naut)* Kielwasser *nt.* **in the ~ of** *(fig)*
nach; **to follow in sb's ~** in jds Kielwasser segeln;
**X leaves Y in its ~** X hinterläßt Y; **to bring sth in its**
**~** etw mit sich bringen.
**wake²** *n (esp Ir: over corpse)* Totenwache *f.*
**wake³** *pret* **woke**, *ptp* **woken 1** *vt* wecken. **2** *vi* aufwachen. **he woke to find himself in prison** als er auf-
wachte, fand er sich im Gefängnis wieder.
▶**wake up 1** *vi (lit, fig)* aufwachen. **to ~ ~ to sth**
*(fig)* sich *(dat)* einer Sache *(gen)* bewußt werden. **2**
*vt sep (lit)* aufwecken; *(fig: rouse from sloth)* aufrütteln. **to ~ sb ~ to sth** *(fig)* jdm etw bewußt machen; **to ~ one's ideas ~** sich zusammenreißen.
**wakeful** ['weɪkfʊl] *adj (sleepless)* schlaflos; *(alert)*
wachsam.
**waken** ['weɪkən] *vt* (auf)wecken.
**waking** ['weɪkɪŋ] *adj* **to spend (all) one's ~ hours**
**doing sth** den (ganzen) Tag damit verbringen, etw
zu tun.
**Wales** [weɪlz] *n* Wales *nt.*
**walk** [wɔːk] **1** *n* **(a)** *(stroll)* Spaziergang *m; (hike)*
Wanderung *f; (charity ~)* Marsch *m (für Wohltätig-*
*keitszwecke);* *(signposted route)* Wanderweg *m;*
*(path in park etc)* Spazierweg *m.* **it's only 2 minutes'**
**~** es sind nur 2 Minuten zu Fuß; **it's a long/short ~**
**to the shops** zu den Geschäften ist es weit/nicht
weit zu Fuß; **to go for a ~** einen Spaziergang machen; **to take sb/the dog for a ~** mit jdm/dem Hund
spazierengehen; **there are some good ~s in the hills**
in den Bergen gibt es einige gute Wandermöglich-
keiten. **(b)** *(gait)* Gang *m; (of horse also)* Gangart *f.*
**the horse went at a ~** das Pferd ging im Schritt. **(c)**
**~ of life** Milieu *nt;* **people from all ~s of life** Leute
aus allen Schichten und Berufen. **(d)** *(US: Baseball)*
Walk *m,* Freibase *nt.*
 **2** *vt* **(a)** *(lead)* person, horse (spazieren)führen;
*dog* ausführen; *(ride at a ~)* im Schritt gehen lassen. **to ~ sb home/to the bus** jdn (zu Fuß) nach
Hause/zum Bus bringen. **(b)** *distance* laufen, gehen.
**I've ~ed this road many times** ich bin diese Straße
oft gegangen. **(c) to ~ the streets** *(prostitute)* auf
den Strich gehen *(col); (in search of sth)* durch die
Straßen irren; *(aimlessly)* durch die Straßen gehen;
**let's ~ it** gehen wir doch zu Fuß.
 **3** *vi* **(a)** gehen, laufen. **~ a little with me** gehen
Sie ein Stück mit mir; **to ~ in one's sleep** schlafwandeln. **(b)** *(not ride)* zu Fuß gehen, laufen *(col);*
*(stroll)* spazierengehen; *(hike)* wandern. **you can ~**
**there in 5 minutes** da ist man in 5 Minuten zu Fuß;
**to ~ home** zu Fuß nach Hause gehen.
▶**walk about** *or* **around** *vi* herumlaufen *(col).* **to**
**~ ~ sth** um etw herumgehen; *(about room etc)* in
etw *(dat)* herumgehen.
▶**walk away** *vi* weggehen, davongehen. **he ~ed ~**
**from the crash unhurt** er ist bei dem Unfall ohne
Verletzungen davongekommen; **to ~ ~ with a prize**
*etc* einen Preis *etc* kassieren *(col).*
▶**walk in** *vi* herein-/hineinkommen; *(casually)*
herein-/hineinspazieren *(col).*
▶**walk into** *vi +prep obj room* herein-/hinein-
kommen in *(+acc); person* anrempeln; *wall* laufen
gegen. **to ~ ~ sb** *(meet unexpectedly)* jdn zufällig
treffen; **to ~ ~ a trap** in eine Falle gehen; **to ~ ~ a**
**job** eine Stelle ohne Schwierigkeiten bekommen; **to**
**~ right ~ sth** *(lit)* mit voller Wucht gegen etw rennen; **you ~ed right ~ that one, didn't you?** da bist
du aber ganz schön reingefallen *(col).*

▶**walk off 1** *vt sep* **to ~ ~ one's hangover** einen
Spaziergang machen, um seinen Kater loszuwer-
den. **2** *vi* weggehen. **he ~ed ~ in the opposite direc-**
**tion** er ging in die andere Richtung davon.
▶**walk off with** *vi +prep obj (col) (take) (uninten-*
*tionally)* abziehen mit *(col); (intentionally)* abhauen
mit *(col); (win easily) prize* kassieren *(col).*
▶**walk on** *vi* **(a)** *+prep obj grass etc* betreten. **(b)**
*(continue walking)* weitergehen.
▶**walk out** *vi* **(a)** *(quit)* gehen. **to ~ ~ of a**
**meeting/room** eine Versammlung/einen Saal verlassen; **to ~ ~ on sb** jdn verlassen; *(let down)* jdn
im Stich lassen; *on girlfriend etc* jdn sitzenlassen
*(col);* **to ~ ~ on sth** aus etw aussteigen *(col).* **(b)**
*(strike)* streiken, in Streik treten.
▶**walk over** *vi +prep obj* **(a)** *(defeat)* in die Tasche
stecken *(col).* **(b) to ~ ~ all ~ sb** *(col) (dominate)* jdn
unterbuttern *(col); (in competition, match etc)* jdn
fertigmachen *(col).*
▶**walk up** *vi (go up, ascend)* (zu Fuß) hinaufgehen; *(approach)* zugehen *(to* auf *+acc).* **a man ~ed ~**
**to me/her** ein Mann kam auf mich zu/ging auf sie
zu; **~ ~!, ~ ~!** treten Sie näher!
**walk:** **~about** *n* Rundgang *m;* **the Queen went (on**
**a) ~about** die Königin nahm ein Bad in der Menge;
**to go ~about** *(col: get lost) (thing)* Beine bekommen
*(col); (person)* sich auf- und davonmachen; **~away**
*n (US) =* **~over.**
**walker** ['wɔːkəʳ] *n (stroller)* Spaziergänger(in *f) m;*
*(hiker)* Wanderer *m,* Wanderin *f; (Sport)* Geher(in *f)*
*m.* **to be a fast ~** schnell gehen.
**walkie-talkie** ['wɔːkɪ'tɔːkɪ] *n* (Hand-)Funksprechge-
rät *nt.*
**walking** ['wɔːkɪŋ] **1** *n* Gehen *nt; (as recreation)* Spazierengehen *nt; (hiking)* Wandern *nt.* **we did a lot of**
**~ on holiday** in den Ferien sind wir viel gewandert.
**2** *adj attr (esp hum) encyclopaedia, miracle etc* wan-
delnd; *doll* Lauf-. **at a ~ pace** im Schrittempo; **it's**
**within ~ distance** dahin kann man zu Fuß gehen.
**walking:** **~ holiday** *n* Wanderferien *pl;* **~ shoes**
*npl* Wanderschuhe *pl;* **~ stick** *n* Spazierstock *m;* **~**
**tour** *n* Wanderung *f.*
**walk:** **W~man** ® *n* Walkman ® *m;* **~-on** *adj part,*
*role* Statisten-; **~out** *n (strike)* Streik *m;* **to stage a**
**~out** *(from conference)* demonstrativ den Saal verlassen; **~over** *n (easy victory)* Spaziergang *m (col);*
*(fig)* Kinderspiel *nt;* **~way** *n* Fußweg *m;* **a pedes-**
**trian ~way** ein Fuß(gänger)weg *m.*
**wall** [wɔːl] *n (outside)* Mauer *f; (inside, of mountain)*
Wand *f.* **a ~ of fire** eine Feuerwand; **a ~ of**
**policemen/troops** eine Mauer von Polizisten/
Soldaten; **to go up the ~** *(col)* die Wände hochgehen
*(col);* **he drives me up the ~** *(col)* er bringt mich auf
die Palme *(col);* **to go to the ~** *(firm etc)* kaputtgehen *(col).*
▶**wall in** *vt sep* mit einer Mauer umgeben.
▶**wall off** *vt sep (cut off)* durch eine Mauer
(ab)trennen.
▶**wall up** *vt sep* zumauern.
**wallaby** ['wɒləbɪ] *n* Wallaby *nt.*
**wall:** **~bars** *npl* Sprossenwand *f;* **~ chart** *n* Schau-
tafel *f;* **~ covering** *n* Tapete *f; (tapestry)* Wandbehang *m;* **~ cupboard** *n* Wandschrank *m; (hanging)*
Hängeschrank *m.*
**walled** [wɔːld] *adj* von Mauern umgeben.
**wallet** ['wɒlɪt] *n* Brieftasche *f.*
**wall:** **~flower** *n (Bot)* Goldlack *m; (fig col)* Mauerblümchen *nt (col);* **~ hanging** *n* Wandbehang *m;* **~**
**light** *n* Wandleuchte *f;* **~ map** *n* Wandkarte *f.*
**wallop** ['wɒləp] *(col)* **1** *n (blow)* Schlag *m.* **to give**
**sb/sth a ~** jdm/einer Sache einen Schlag versetzen.

**2** vt (hit) schlagen; (punish) versohlen (col).

**walloping** ['wɒləpɪŋ] (col) n Prügel pl (col); (defeat) Schlappe f. **to give sb a ~** jdm eine Tracht Prügel geben (col).

**wallow** ['wɒləʊ] vi **(a)** (lit) (animal) sich wälzen; (boat) rollen. **(b) to ~ in luxury/self-pity** etc im Luxus/Selbstmitleid etc schwelgen.

**wall: ~ painting** n Wandgemälde nt; **~paper 1** n Tapete f; **2** vt tapezieren; **~ socket** n Wandsteckdose f; **~-to-~** adj **~-to-~ carpeting** Teppichboden m; **~ unit** n (covering whole wall) Schrankwand f; (hanging) Hängeschrank m.

**wally** ['wɒlɪ] n (Brit col) Vollidiot m (col).

**walnut** ['wɔːlnʌt] n (nut) Walnuß f; (tree, wood) Nußbaum m.

**walrus** ['wɔːlrəs] n Walroß nt.

**waltz** [wɔːls] **1** n Walzer m. **2** vi **(a)** Walzer tanzen. **(b)** (col: move, come etc) tanzen (col). **he came ~ing up** er kam angetanzt (col).

**wan** [wɒn] adj bleich; light, smile, look matt.

**wand** [wɒnd] n (magic ~) Zauberstab m; (Comp: for bar codes) Lesestift m.

**wander** ['wɒndə'] **1** n Spaziergang m; (through town, park also) Bummel m. **I'm going for a ~ around the shops** ich mache einen Ladenbummel.
**2** vt hills, world durchstreifen (geh). **to ~ the streets** durch die Straßen wandern.
**3** vi **(a)** herumlaufen; (more aimlessly) umherwandern (through, about in +dat); (leisurely) schlendern; (to see the shops) bummeln. **he ~ed over to speak to me** er kam zu mir herüber, um mit mir zu reden. **(b)** (go off, stray) **to ~ from the path** vom Wege abkommen; **he ~ed too near the edge of the cliff** er geriet zu nahe an den Rand des Abhangs. **(c)** (fig: thoughts, eye) schweifen, wandern. **to let one's mind ~** seine Gedanken schweifen lassen; **the old man's mind is beginning to ~ a bit** der alte Mann wird ein wenig wirr im Kopf; **to ~ from** or **off the point/subject** vom Punkt/Thema abschweifen or abkommen.
▶**wander off** vi weggehen; (col: leave) allmählich gehen.

**wanderer** ['wɒndərə'] n Wandervogel m.

**wandering** ['wɒndərɪŋ] **1** adj tribesman umherziehend; minstrel fahrend; thoughts (ab)schweifend; path gewunden. **2** n **~s** pl Herumziehen nt; (mental) wirre Gedanken pl.

**wanderlust** ['wɒndəlʌst] n Fernweh nt.

**wane** [weɪn] **1** n **to be on the ~** (fig) im Schwinden sein. **2** vi (moon) abnehmen; (fig) (influence, strength) schwinden; (reputation) verblassen; (daylight) nachlassen.

**wangle** ['wæŋgl] (col) **1** n Schiebung f (col). **2** vt job, ticket etc organisieren (col), besorgen. **to ~ oneself/sb in** sich hineinmogeln (col)/jdn einschleusen (col); **he'll ~ it for you** er wird das schon für dich drehen (col).

**wangler** ['wæŋglə'] n (col) Schlawiner m (col).

**wank** [wæŋk] vi (col!) wichsen (col!).

**wanly** ['wɒnlɪ] adv matt.

**want** [wɒnt] **1** n **(a)** (lack) Mangel m (of an +dat). **for ~ of** aus Mangel an (+dat); **for ~ of anything better to do, I went for a walk** weil es nichts Besseres zu tun gab, ging ich spazieren; **it wasn't for ~ of trying** es lag nicht daran, daß ich mich nicht bemüht hätte. **(b)** (poverty) Not f. **to be/live in ~** Not leiden. **(c)** (need) Bedürfnis nt; (wish) Wunsch m. **the farm supplied all their ~s** der Bauernhof versorgte sie mit allem Notwendigen; **to be in ~ of sth** etw benötigen.
**2** vt **(a)** (wish, desire) wollen. **to ~ to do sth** etw

tun wollen; **I ~ you to come here** ich will or (more polite) möchte, daß du herkommst; **I ~ it done now** ich will/möchte das sofort erledigt haben; **I don't ~ you interfering** ich will nicht, daß Sie sich einmischen. **(b)** (need, require) brauchen. **you ~ to see a doctor** Sie sollten zum Arzt gehen; **you ~ to be careful!** (col) du mußt aufpassen; **it ~s cutting** es müßte geschnitten werden; **that's all we ~ed!** (iro col) das hat uns gerade noch gefehlt!; **it only ~ed the police to turn up ...** es hätte gerade noch gefehlt, daß auch noch die Polizei anrückt ...; **"~ed"** „gesucht"; **he's a ~ed man** er wird (polizeilich) gesucht; **you're ~ed on the phone** Sie werden am Telefon verlangt.
**3** vi **(a)** (wish, desire) wollen. **you can go if you ~ (to)** wenn du willst, kannst du gehen; **I don't ~ to** ich will or (more polite) möchte nicht. **(b)** (dated) **he does not ~ for friends** es fehlt or mangelt (geh) ihm nicht an Freunden; **they ~ for nothing** es fehlt ihnen an nichts.

**want ad** n (esp US) Kaufgesuch nt.

**wanting** ['wɒntɪŋ] adj fehlend. **humour is ~ in the novel** diesem Roman fehlt es an Humor; **he is ~ in confidence** es fehlt or mangelt (geh) ihm an Selbstvertrauen; **his courage/the new engine was found ~** sein Mut war nicht groß genug/der neue Motor hat sich als unzulänglich erwiesen; **he was tried and found ~** er konnte sich nicht bewähren.

**wanton** ['wɒntən] adj **(a)** (licentious) life liederlich; behaviour, woman, pleasures schamlos; looks, thoughts lüstern. **(b)** (wilful) cruelty mutwillig; disregard, waste sträflich.

**war** [wɔː'] **1** n Krieg m. **this is ~!** (fig) das bedeutet Krieg!; **the ~ against poverty** der Kampf gegen die Armut; **~ of nerves** Nervenkrieg m; **~ of words** Wortgefecht nt; **to be at ~** sich im Krieg(szustand) befinden; **to declare ~** den Krieg erklären (on dat); (fig also) den Kampf ansagen (on dat); **to make** or **wage ~** Krieg führen (on, against gegen); **he/this car has been in the ~s a bit** er/dieses Auto sieht ziemlich mitgenommen aus. **2** vi sich bekriegen.

**warble** ['wɔːbl] vti trällern.

**warbler** ['wɔːblə'] n (Orn) Grasmücke f; (wood~) Waldsänger m.

**war: ~ correspondent** n Kriegsberichterstatter (in f) m; **~ crime** n Kriegsverbrechen nt; **~ criminal** n Kriegsverbrecher m; **~ cry** n Kriegsruf m; (fig) Schlachtruf m.

**ward** [wɔːd] n **(a)** (part of hospital) Station f; (room) (small) Krankenzimmer nt; (large) Krankensaal m. **(b)** (Jur: person) Mündel nt. **~ of court** Mündel unter Amtsvormundschaft. **(c)** (Admin) Stadtbezirk m; (election) Wahlbezirk m.
▶**ward off** vt sep attack, blow, person abwehren; danger also abwenden; depression nicht aufkommen lassen.

**war dance** n Kriegstanz m.

**warden** ['wɔːdn] n (of youth hostel) Herbergsvater m, Herbergsmutter f; (game ~) Jagdaufseher m; (traffic ~) Verkehrspolizist m, ≈ Politesse f; (of museum etc) Aufseher m; (Univ) Heimleiter (in f) m; (of Oxbridge college) Rektor m; (US: of prison) Gefängnisdirektor m.

**warder** ['wɔːdə'] n (Brit) Wärter, Aufseher m.

**wardress** ['wɔːdrɪs] n (Brit) Wärterin, Aufseherin f.

**wardrobe** ['wɔːdrəʊb] n **(a)** (cupboard) Kleiderschrank m. **(b)** (clothes) Garderobe f. **(c)** (Theat) (clothes) Kostüme pl; (room) Kleiderkammer f. **~ mistress** Gewandmeisterin f.

**wardroom** ['wɔːdruːm] n (Naut) Offiziersmesse f.

**-ward(s)** [-wəd(z)] adv suf -wärts. **town~** in Rich-

tung Stadt.
**warehouse** ['wɛəhaʊs] *n* Lager(haus) *nt.*
**wares** [wɛəz] *npl* Waren *pl.*
**warfare** ['wɔːfɛəʳ] *n* Krieg *m*; *(techniques)* Kriegs-kunst *f.*
**war:** ~ **game** *n* Kriegsspiel *nt*; ~**head** *n* Sprengkopf *m*; ~**horse** *n (lit, fig)* Schlachtroß *nt.*
**warily** ['wɛərɪlɪ] *adv* vorsichtig; *(suspiciously)* mißtrauisch, argwöhnisch. **to tread** ~ *(lit, fig)* sich vorsehen.
**wariness** ['wɛərɪnɪs] *n* Vorsicht *f*; *(mistrust)* Mißtrauen *nt (of gegenüber).*
**warlike** ['wɔːlaɪk] *adj* kriegerisch; *tone* militant.
**warm** [wɔːm] **1** *adj (+er)* **(a)** warm. **I am** *or* **feel** ~ mir ist warm. **(b)** *(in games)* **am I** ~**?** ist es (hier) warm?; **you're getting** ~ es wird schon wärmer. **(c)** *(hearty) person, welcome* herzlich, warm. **(d)** *(heated) dispute, words* hitzig. **2** *n* **we were glad to get into the** ~ wir waren froh, daß wir ins Warme kamen; **to give sth a** ~ etw wärmen. **3** *vt* wärmen. **it** ~**s my heart to ...** mir wird (es) ganz warm ums Herz, wenn ... **4** *vi* **the milk was** ~**ing on the stove** die Milch wurde auf dem Herd erwärmt; **I** ~**ed to him** er wurde mir sympathischer; **to** ~ **to one's work** sich mit seiner Arbeit anfreunden.
▶**warm up 1** *vi (lit, fig)* warm werden; *(engine)* warmlaufen; *(party, game, speaker)* in Schwung kommen; *(Sport)* sich aufwärmen. **things are** ~**ing** ~ es kommt Schwung in die Sache; *(becoming dangerous)* es wird allmählich brenzlig *(col)*. **2** *vt sep engine* warmlaufen lassen; *food etc* aufwärmen; *(fig) party* in Schwung bringen; *audience* in Stimmung bringen.
**warm-blooded** [,wɔːm'blʌdɪd] *adj* warmblütig; *(fig)* heißblütig. ~ **animal** Warmblüter *m.*
**war memorial** *n* Kriegerdenkmal *nt.*
**warm front** *n (Met)* Warm(luft)front *f.*
**warm-hearted** [,wɔːm'hɑːtɪd] *adj person* warmherzig; *gesture* großzügig.
**warmly** ['wɔːmlɪ] *adv* warm; *welcome* herzlich; *recommend* wärmstens. **we** ~ **welcome it** wir begrüßen es sehr.
**warmonger** ['wɔː,mʌŋgəʳ] *n* Kriegshetzer *m.*
**warmongering** ['wɔː,mʌŋgərɪŋ] **1** *adj* kriegshetzerisch; **2** *n* Kriegshetze *f.*
**warmth** [wɔːmθ] *n (lit, fig)* Wärme *f*; *(of welcome)* Herzlichkeit *f.*
**warm-up** ['wɔːmʌp] *n (Sport)* Aufwärmen *nt*; *(before motor race)* Aufwärmtraining *nt.*
**warn** [wɔːn] *vt* warnen *(of, about, against* vor *+dat)*; *(police, judge etc)* verwarnen. **to** ~ **sb not to do sth** jdn davor warnen, etw zu tun; **be** ~**ed** sei gewarnt!; **he had** ~**ed me off** er hatte mich davor gewarnt; **she** ~**ed us not to be late** sie ermahnte uns, nicht zu spät zu kommen; **to** ~ **sb that ...** *(inform)* jdn darauf hinweisen, daß ...
**warning** ['wɔːnɪŋ] **1** *n* Warnung *f*; *(from police, judge etc)* Verwarnung *f.* **without** ~ ohne Vorwarnung; *(unexpectedly)* unerwartet; **to give sb a** ~ jdn warnen; *(police, judge etc)* jdn verwarnen; **let this be a** ~ **to you** lassen Sie sich *(dat)* das eine Warnung sein!; **to give sb due** ~ *(inform)* jdm rechtzeitig Bescheid sagen. **2** *adj light, triangle etc* Warn-; *look, tone* warnend. **a** ~ **sign** ein erstes Anzeichen; *(signboard etc)* ein Warnzeichen *nt*/-schild *nt.*
**warp** [wɔːp] **1** *n (in weaving)* Kette *f*; *(in wood etc)* Welle *f.* **2** *vt wood* wellen; *character* entstellen; *judgement* verzerren. **3** *vi (wood)* sich wellen, sich verziehen.
**war:** ~**paint** *n (lit, fig col)* Kriegsbemalung *f*; ~**path** *n* Kriegspfad *m*; **on the** ~**path** auf dem Kriegspfad.

**warped** [wɔːpt] *adj* **(a)** *(lit)* wellig. **(b)** *(fig) sense of humour* abartig; *character also* verbogen; *judgement* verzerrt.
**warplane** ['wɔːpleɪn] *n* Kampfflugzeug *nt.*
**warrant** ['wɒrənt] **1** *n (Comm)* Garantie *f*; *(Mil)* Patent *nt*; *(search* ~*)* Durchsuchungsbefehl *m*; *(death* ~*)* Hinrichtungsbefehl *m.* **there is a** ~ **out for his arrest** gegen ihn ist Haftbefehl erlassen worden. **2** *vt* **(a)** *(justify) action etc* rechtfertigen. **to** ~ **sb doing sth** jdn dazu berechtigen, etw zu tun. **(b)** *(merit)* verdienen. **(c)** *(guarantee)* gewährleisten. **it'll work, I** ~ **you that** es funktioniert, das garantiere ich Ihnen.
**warranty** ['wɒrəntɪ] *n (Comm)* Garantie *f.* **it's still under** ~ darauf ist noch Garantie.
**warren** ['wɒrən] *n (rabbit* ~*)* Kaninchenbau *m*; *(fig)* Labyrinth *nt.*
**warring** ['wɔːrɪŋ] *adj nations* kriegführend; *interests* gegensätzlich; *factions* sich bekriegend.
**warrior** ['wɒrɪəʳ] *n* Krieger *m.*
**Warsaw** ['wɔːsɔː] *n* Warschau *nt.* ~ **Pact** *(Hist)* Warschauer Pakt *m.*
**warship** ['wɔːʃɪp] *n* Kriegsschiff *nt.*
**wart** [wɔːt] *n* Warze *f.* ~**s and all** *(hum col)* mit allen Fehlern.
**wart-hog** ['wɔːthɒg] *n* Warzenschwein *nt.*
**wartime** ['wɔːtaɪm] **1** *n* Kriegszeit *f.* **in** ~ in Kriegszeiten. **2** *adj* Kriegs-. **in** ~ **England** in England während des Krieges.
**wary** ['wɛərɪ] *adj (+er)* vorsichtig; *(looking and planning ahead)* umsichtig, klug; *look* mißtrauisch. **to be** ~ **of sb/sth** vor jdm/einer Sache auf der Hut sein; **to be** ~ **about doing sth** seine Zweifel haben, ob man etw tun soll.
**was** [wɒz] *1st, 3rd pers sing pret of* **be.**
**wash** [wɒʃ] **1** *n* **(a)** *(act of* ~*ing)* **it needs a** ~ es müßte gewaschen werden; **I need a** ~ ich muß mich waschen; **to give sb/sth a (good)** ~ jdn/etw (gründlich) waschen; **to have a** ~ sich waschen. **(b)** *(laundry)* Wäsche *f.* **to be in the** ~ in der Wäsche sein; **it will all come out in the** ~ *(fig col) (become known)* es wird schon alles rauskommen; *(work out)* es wird sich schon noch alles regeln. **(c)** *(of ship)* Kielwasser *nt.*
**2** *vt* **(a)** waschen; *dishes* spülen; *floor* aufwischen; *hands etc* sich *(dat)* waschen. **to** ~ **one's hands of sb/sth** mit jdm/etw nichts mehr zu tun haben wollen; **I** ~ **my hands of it** ich wasche meine Hände in Unschuld; **to** ~ **sth clean** etw reinwaschen. **(b)** *(sea etc)* umspülen; *cliffs etc* schlagen gegen; *(carry)* spülen. **it was** ~**ed ashore** es wurde an Land gespült.
**3** *vi* **(a)** *(have a* ~*)* sich waschen. **(b)** **a material that** ~**es well/won't** ~ ein Stoff, der sich gut wäscht/den man nicht waschen kann; **that excuse won't** ~ *(Brit fig col)* diese Entschuldigung kauft dir keiner ab! *(col).*
▶**wash away** *vt sep* (hin)wegspülen. **to** ~ ~ **sb's sins** jdn von seinen Sünden reinwaschen.
▶**wash down** *vt sep (clean)* abwaschen; *meal* hinunterspülen.
▶**wash off 1** *vi (stain, dirt)* sich herauswaschen lassen. **most of the pattern has** ~**ed** ~ das Muster ist fast ganz verwaschen. **2** *vt sep* abwaschen.
▶**wash out 1** *vi* sich auswaschen lassen. **2** *vt sep (clean)* auswaschen; *mouth* ausspülen.
▶**wash over** *vi +prep obj (sea, waves)* überspülen. **to** ~ ~ **sb** *(fig: criticism etc)* an jdm abprallen.
▶**wash up 1** *vi* **(a)** *(Brit: clean dishes)* abwaschen, spülen. **(b)** *(US: have a wash)* sich waschen. **2** *vt sep* **(a)** *(Brit) dishes* spülen. **(b)** *(sea etc)* anspülen.

**washable** ['wɒʃəbl] adj waschbar; *wallpaper* abwaschbar.
**wash:** ~**bag** n (US) Kulturbeutel m; ~**basin** n Waschbecken nt; ~**bowl** n Waschschüssel f; *(in unit)* Waschbecken nt; ~ **cloth** n (US) Waschlappen m; ~**day** n Waschtag m.
**washed out** ['wɒʃt'aʊt] adj *(col)* erledigt *(col)*. **to look** ~ mitgenommen aussehen.
**washer** ['wɒʃər] n (a) *(Tech)* Dichtung(sring m) f. (b) *(clothes* ~*)* Waschmaschine f; *(dish*~*)* (Geschirr)spülmaschine f.
**washhand basin** ['wɒʃˌhænd,beɪsn] n Handwaschbecken nt.
**washing** ['wɒʃɪŋ] n Waschen nt; *(clothes)* Wäsche f. **to do the** ~ Wäsche waschen.
**washing:** ~ **line** n (Brit) Wäscheleine f; ~ **machine** n Waschmaschine f; ~ **powder** n (Brit) Waschpulver nt; ~**-up** n (Brit) Abwasch m; **to do the** ~**-up** spülen, den Abwasch machen; ~**-up bowl** n (Brit) Spülschüssel f; ~**-up liquid** n (Brit) Spülmittel nt.
**wash:** ~ **leather** n Waschleder nt; ~**out** n *(col)* Reinfall m *(col)*; *(person)* Flasche *(col)*, Niete *(col)* f; ~ **room** n Waschraum m.
**wasn't** ['wɒznt] = **was not**.
**WASP, Wasp** [wɒsp] *(US)* = **white Anglo-Saxon Protestant**.
**wasp** [wɒsp] n Wespe f.
**waspish** ['wɒspɪʃ] adj giftig.
**wastage** ['weɪstɪdʒ] n Schwund m; *(action)* Verschwendung f; *(amount also)* Materialverlust m; *(from container also)* Verlust m; *(unusable products etc also)* Abfall m.
**waste** [weɪst] **1** adj *(superfluous)* überschüssig, überflüssig; *(left over)* ungenutzt; *land* brachliegend. **to lay** ~ verwüsten; **to lie** ~ brachliegen.
**2** n (a) Verschwendung f; *(unusable materials)* Abfall m. **it's a** ~ **of time/money** es ist Zeit-/Geldverschwendung; **it's a** ~ **of effort** das ist nicht der Mühe wert; **to go to** ~ *(food)* ungenutzt umkommen; *(money, land, talent)* ungenutzt sein/bleiben, brachliegen. (b) *(~ material)* Abfallstoffe pl; *(rubbish)* Abfall m. **radioactive** ~ Atommüll m. (c) *(land, expanse)* Wildnis no pl, Einöde f.
**3** vt verschwenden *(on an +acc, für)*; *life, time* vergeuden; *opportunity* vertun. **you're wasting your time** das ist reine Zeitverschwendung; **don't** ~ **my time** stiehl mir nicht meine Zeit; **you didn't** ~ **much time, did you?** *(col)* das ging aber schnell!; **Beethoven/she is** ~**d on him** Beethoven ist an ihn verschwendet/sie ist zu schade für ihn.
**4** vi *(food)* umkommen; *(skills)* verkümmern; *(body)* verfallen; *(strength, assets)* schwinden. ~ **not, want not** *(Prov)* spare in der Zeit, so hast du in der Not *(Prov)*.
▶**waste away** vi *(physically)* dahinschwinden *(geh)*, immer weniger werden *(col)*.
**waste:** ~**bin** n (Brit) Abfalleimer m; ~ **disposal** n Müllbeseitigung f; ~ **disposal unit** n Müllschlucker m.
**wasteful** ['weɪstfʊl] adj verschwenderisch; *method, process* unwirtschaftlich. **to be** ~ **with sth** verschwenderisch mit etw umgehen.
**wastefully** ['weɪstfəlɪ] adv verschwenderisch; *organized* unwirtschaftlich.
**wastefulness** ['weɪstfʊlnɪs] n see adj verschwenderische Art; Unwirtschaftlichkeit f. **this is sheer** ~ das ist reine Verschwendung.
**waste:** ~**ground** n verwahrlostes unbebautes Grundstück; ~ **heat** n *(Tech)* Abwärme f; ~**land** n Ödland nt; *(fig)* Einöde f; ~ **management** n Abfallentsorgung f; ~**paper** n Papierabfall m; *(for

recycling)* Altpapier nt; ~**paper basket** n (Brit) Papierkorb m; ~ **pipe** n Abflußrohr nt; ~ **product** n Abfallprodukt nt.
**waster** ['weɪstər] n (a) **it's a real time-/money-**~ das ist wirklich Zeit-/Geldverschwendung. (b) *(good-for-nothing)* Taugenichts m.
**watch¹** [wɒtʃ] n (Armband)uhr f.
**watch²** **1** n (a) **to be on the** ~ **for sb/sth** nach jdm/etw Ausschau halten; **to keep** ~ Wache halten; **to keep a close** ~ **on sb/sth** jdn/etw scharf bewachen; **to keep** ~ **over sb/sth** bei jdm/etw Wache halten; **to set a** ~ **on sb/sth** jdn/etw überwachen lassen. (b) *(period of duty, Naut, people)* Wache f; *(people also)* Wachmannschaft f. **to be on** ~ Wache haben; **officer of the** ~ wachhabender Offizier.
**2** vt (a) *(guard)* aufpassen auf *(+acc)*; *(police etc)* überwachen.
(b) *(observe)* beobachten; *match* zusehen or zuschauen bei; *film, play, TV programme* sich *(dat)* ansehen. **to** ~ **TV** fernsehen; **to** ~ **sb doing sth** jdm bei etw zuschauen; **I** ~**ed her coming down the street** ich habe sie beobachtet, wie sie die Straße entlang kam; **we are being** ~**ed** wir werden beobachtet; ~ **this!** paß auf!; **a new actor to be** ~**ed** ein Nachwuchsschauspieler, den man im Auge behalten sollte.
(c) *(be careful of)* achten auf *(+acc)*, aufpassen auf *(+acc)*. **(you'd better)** ~ **it!** *(col)* paß (bloß) auf! *(col)*; ~ **your manners/language!** bitte benimm dich!/drück dich bitte etwas gepflegter aus!; ~ **how you drive, the roads are icy** paß beim Fahren auf, die Straßen sind vereist!
**3** vi *(observe)* zusehen, zuschauen. **to** ~ **for sb/sth** nach jdm/etw Ausschau halten.
▶**watch out** vi (a) *(look carefully)* Ausschau halten *(for sb/sth* nach jdm/etw*)*. (b) *(be careful)* aufpassen, achtgeben *(for auf +acc)*. ~ ~! Achtung!; ~ ~ **for him, he's crafty** nimm dich vor ihm in acht, er ist gerissen.
▶**watch over** vi +prep obj wachen über *(+acc)*.
**watchable** ['wɒtʃəbl] adj sehenswert.
**watch:** ~**band** n (US) Uhrarmband nt; ~ **chain** n Uhrkette f; ~**dog** n *(lit)* Wachhund m; *(fig)* Aufpasser m *(col)*.
**watcher** ['wɒtʃər] n Schaulustige(r) mf; *(observer)* Beobachter(in f) m.
**watchful** ['wɒtʃfʊl] adj wachsam. **to be** ~ **for** wachsam Ausschau halten nach.
**watchfully** ['wɒtʃfəlɪ] adv wachsam.
**watchfulness** ['wɒtʃfʊlnɪs] n Wachsamkeit f.
**watching brief** ['wɒtʃɪŋ'briːf] n **to hold a** ~ eine Kontrollfunktion ausüben.
**watch:** ~**maker** n Uhrmacher m; ~**man** n *(night-* ~*man etc)* (Nacht)wächter m; ~**strap** n Uhrarmband nt; ~**tower** n Wachtturm m; ~**word** n Parole f.
**water** ['wɔːtər] **1** n Wasser nt. **the field is under** ~ das Feld steht unter Wasser; **to make** ~ *(ship)* lecken; **in American** ~**s** in amerikanischen Hoheitsgewässern; **by** ~ auf dem Wasserweg; **to make or pass** ~ Wasser lassen; **to drink or take the** ~**s** eine Kur machen; **a lot of** ~ **has flowed under the bridge since then** *(fig)* seitdem ist viel Wasser den Bach hinuntergeflossen; **to stay above** ~ *(fig)* sich über Wasser halten; **to pour cold** ~ **on sb's idea** jds Vorschlag miesmachen *(col)*; **to get into deep** ~(**s**) *(fig)* ins Schwimmen kommen; **to hold** ~ *(lit)* wasserdicht sein; **that argument won't hold** ~ *(col)* dieses Argument ist nicht hieb- und stichfest *(col)*; **to be in/get into hot** ~ *(fig col)* in Teufels Küche sein/

geraten *(col)* *(over* wegen *+gen)*; **to spend money like ~** *(col)* mit dem Geld nur so um sich werfen *(col)*.

**2** *vt* **(a)** *garden* sprengen; *field* bewässern; *plant* (be)gießen. **(b)** *horses, cattle* tränken.

**3** *vi (mouth)* wässern; *(eye)* tränen. **the smoke made his eyes ~** ihm tränten die Augen vom Rauch; **my mouth ~ed** mir lief das Wasser im Mund zusammen; **to make sb's mouth ~** jdm den Mund wässerig machen.

►**water down** *vt sep (lit, fig pej)* verwässern; *(fig also)* abschwächen; *liquids* verdünnen.

**water:** ~**bed** *n* Wasserbett *nt*; ~**-bottle** *n* Wasserflasche *f*; *(for troops etc)* Feldflasche *f*; ~ **butt** *n* Regentonne *f*; ~ **cannon** *n* Wasserwerfer *m*; ~**colour** *(Brit)*, ~**color** *(US)* **1** *n* Wasserfarbe, Aquarellfarbe *f*; *(picture)* Aquarell *nt*; **2** *attr* Aquarell-; ~**-cooled** *adj* wassergekühlt; ~**course** *n (stream)* Wasserlauf *m*; *(bed)* Flußbett *nt*; *(artificial)* Kanal *m*; ~**cress** *n* (Brunnen)kresse *f*; ~**fall** *n* Wasserfall *m*; ~**front 1** *n* Hafenviertel *nt*; **we drove along the ~front/down to the ~front** wir fuhren am Wasser entlang/hinunter zum Wasser; **2** *attr* am Wasser; ~ **heater** *n* Heißwasserbereiter *m*; ~ **hole** *n* Wasserloch *nt*.

**watering** ['wɔːtərɪŋ]: ~ **can** *n* Gießkanne *f*; ~ **hole** *n (for animals)* Wasserstelle *f*; *(Brit hum: pub)* Pinte *(col)*, Kneipe *(col)* *f*.

**water:** ~ **level** *n* Wasserstand *m*; *(of river etc also)* Pegelstand *m*; ~**lily** *n* Seerose *f*; ~**line** *n* Wasserlinie *f*; ~**logged** *adj* **the fields are ~logged** die Felder stehen unter Wasser; **the ship was completely ~logged** das Schiff war voll Wasser gelaufen; ~ **main** *n* Haupt(wasser)leitung *f*; ~**mark** *n* **(a)** *(on wall)* Wasserstandsmarke *f*; **(b)** *(on paper)* Wasserzeichen *nt*; ~**melon** *n* Wassermelone *f*; ~ **meter** *n* Wasseruhr *f*; ~ **pipe** *n* Wasserrohr *nt*; ~**-pistol** *n* Wasserpistole *f*; ~**-polo** *n* Wasserball *m*; ~**-power** *n* Wasserkraft *f*; ~**proof 1** *adj* wasserdicht; *paint* wasserfest; **2** *n (esp Brit)* Regenhaut ® *f*; **3** *vt* wasserundurchlässig machen; ~ **rat** *n* Wasserratte *f*; ~**-repellent** *adj* wasserabstoßend; ~**shed** *n (Geol)* Wasserscheide *f*; *(fig)* Wendepunkt *m*; ~**side 1** *n* Ufer *nt*; *(at sea)* Strand *m*; **2** *attr* am Wasser wachsend/lebend *etc*; ~**-ski** *vi* Wasserski laufen; ~**-skiing** *n* Wasserskilaufen *nt*; ~ **softener** *n* Wasserenthärter *m*; ~ **supply** *n* Wasserversorgung *f*; ~**table** *n* Grundwasserspiegel *m*; ~ **tank** *n* Wassertank *m*; ~ **tap** *n* Wasserhahn *m*; ~**tight** *adj (lit)* wasserdicht; *(fig) argument etc also* hieb- und stichfest; ~**-tower** *n* Wasserturm *m*; ~ **vapour** *(Brit)* or **vapor** *(US)* *n* Wasserdampf *m*; ~**way** *n* Wasserstraße *f*; *(channel)* Fahrrinne *f*; ~**wheel** *n (Mech)* Wasserrad *nt*; *(Agr)* Wasserschöpfrad *nt*; ~**-wings** *npl* Schwimmflügel *pl*; ~**works** *npl* or *sing* Wasserwerk *nt*; **to turn on the ~works** *(fig col)* zu heulen anfangen; **to have trouble with one's ~works** *(fig col)* was an der Blase haben *(col)*.

**watery** ['wɔːtərɪ] *adj soup, colour* wäßrig; *eye* tränend; *(pale) sky* blaß.

**watt** [wɒt] *n* Watt *nt*.

**wattage** ['wɒtɪdʒ] *n* Wattzahl *f*.

**wattle** ['wɒtl] *n* Flechtwerk *nt*.

**wave** [weɪv] **1** *n* **(a)** *(of water, Phys, Rad, in hair, fig)* Welle *f*. **a ~ of strikes/enthusiasm** eine Streikwelle/ Welle der Begeisterung; **the new ~** *(Mus, Film)* die Neue Welle; **to make ~s** *(fig col)* Staub aufwirbeln *(fig)*; *(cause trouble)* Unruhe stiften. **(b)** *(movement of hand)* **to give sb a ~** jdm (zu)winken; **with a ~ of his hand** mit einer Handbewegung.

**2** *vt* **(a)** *(as a sign or greeting)* winken mit *(at, to*

sb jdm*)*; *(~ about)* schwenken. **to ~ one's hand to sb** jdm winken; **to ~ goodbye to sb** jdm zum Abschied winken; **she ~d her umbrella threateningly at him** sie drohte ihm mit ihrem Schirm; **he ~d me over** er winkte mich zu sich herüber. **(b)** *hair* wellen.

**3** *vi* **(a)** winken. **to ~ at** *or* **to sb** jdm winken; *(greeting)* jdm zuwinken. **(b)** *(flag)* wehen; *(branches)* sich hin und her bewegen; *(corn)* wogen. **(c)** *(hair)* sich wellen.

►**wave around** *vt sep* herumfuchteln mit.

►**wave aside** *vt sep (lit) person* zur Seite winken; *(fig) person, objection etc* zurückweisen; *help also* ausschlagen.

►**wave away** *vt sep* wegwinken.

►**wave on** *vt sep* **the policeman ~d us ~** der Polizist winkte uns weiter.

**wave:** ~**band** *n (Rad)* Wellenbereich *m*; ~**length** *n (Rad, fig)* Wellenlänge *f*; **we're not on the same ~length** *(fig)* wir haben nicht die gleiche Wellenlänge.

**waver** ['weɪvəʳ] *vi* **(a)** *(light, flame, eyes)* flackern; *(voice)* zittern. **(b)** *(courage, self-assurance)* ins Wanken geraten; *(support)* nachlassen. **(c)** *(hesitate)* schwanken *(between* zwischen *+dat)*.

**wavy** ['weɪvɪ] *adj (+er) hair, surface* wellig, gewellt. **~ line** Schlangenlinie, Wellenlinie *f*.

**wax¹** [wæks] **1** *n* Wachs *nt*; *(ear~)* Ohrenschmalz *nt*; *(sealing ~)* Siegellack *m*. **2** *adj* Wachs-. **3** *vt* wachsen; *floor also* bohnern.

**wax²** *vi* **(a)** *(moon)* zunehmen. **to ~ and wane** *(lit)* ab- und zunehmen; *(fig)* schwanken. **(b)** *(liter: become)* werden. **to ~ enthusiastic** in Begeisterung geraten.

**wax(ed) paper** *n* Wachspapier *nt*.

**waxen** ['wæksən] *adj (fig: pale)* wachsbleich, wächsern.

**wax:** ~ **work** *n* Wachsfigur *f*; ~ **works** *n sing or pl* Wachsfigurenkabinett *nt*.

**waxy** ['wæksɪ] *adj (+er)* wächsern.

**way** [weɪ] **1** *n* **(a)** *(road)* Weg *m*. **across** *or* **over the ~** gegenüber, vis-à-vis; *(motion)* rüber *(col)*; **to fall by the ~** *(fig)* auf der Strecke bleiben.

**(b)** *(route)* Weg *m*. **the ~ to the station** der Weg zum Bahnhof; **by ~ of** *(via)* über *(+acc)*; **which is the ~ to the town hall, please?** wo geht es hier zum Rathaus, bitte?; ~ **in/out** *(also on signs)* Ein-/ Ausgang *m*; **can you find your own ~ out?** finden Sie selbst hinaus?; **on the ~ out/in** beim Hinaus-/ Hereingehen; **to be on the ~ in** *(fig col)* im Kommen sein; **to be on the ~ out** *(fig col)* am Verschwinden sein; **there's no ~ out** *(fig)* es gibt keinen Ausweg; ~ **up/down** Weg nach oben/unten; *(climbing)* Aufstieg/Abstieg *m*; ~ **there/back** Hinweg/Rückweg *m*; **prices are on the ~ up/down** die Preise steigen/fallen; **the shop is on the ~** der Laden liegt auf dem Weg; **to stop on the ~** unterwegs anhalten; **on the ~ to London** auf dem Weg nach London; **he's on the ~ to becoming an alcoholic** er ist auf dem besten Weg, Alkoholiker zu werden; **we had to go out of our ~** wir mußten einen Umweg machen; **to go out of one's ~ to do sth** *(fig)* sich *(dat)* besondere Mühe geben, etw zu tun; **to feel one's ~** sich weiter-/vorwärts-/entlangtasten; **I know my ~ about town** ich finde mich in der Stadt zurecht; **she knows her ~ about** *(fig col)* sie kennt sich aus, sie weiß Bescheid *(col)*; **to lose one's ~** sich verlaufen; *(driving)* sich verfahren; **to make one's ~ to somewhere** sich an einen Ort begeben; **can you make your own ~ to the theatre?** kannst du allein zum Theater kommen?; **to make one's ~ home** nach Hause gehen; *(start)* sich auf den Heimweg begeben; **to push one's ~ through the crowd** sich durch die Menge drängen; **to make one's ~ in the world** seinen Weg machen; **to go one's own ~** *(fig)* eigene Wege gehen; **they went their separate ~s** *(lit, fig)* ihre Wege trennten sich; **to pay one's ~** für sich selbst bezahlen; *(company, machine)* sich rentieren; **the ~ forward** der Weg vorwärts; **to go down the wrong ~** *(food, drink)* in die falsche Kehle kommen; **to prepare the ~** *(fig)* den Weg bereiten *(for sb/sth* jdm/einer Sache*)*; **could you see your ~ to lending me a pound?** wäre es Ihnen wohl möglich, mir ein Pfund zu leihen?; **to get under ~** in Gang kommen; *(Naut)* Fahrt aufnehmen *or* machen; **to be (well) under ~** im Gang/in vollem Gang sein; *(Naut)* in (voller) Fahrt sein; *(with indication of place)* unterwegs sein.

   **(c)** *(room for movement, path)* Weg *m.* **to block the ~** den Weg versperren; **to leave the ~ open** *(fig)* einen Weg frei lassen *(for sth* für etw*)*; **to make ~ for sb/sth** *(lit, fig)* für jdn/etw Platz machen; **to be in sb's ~** jdm im Weg sein; **to get in sb's ~** sich jdm in den Weg stellen; **it's in the ~ there** es ist dort im Weg; **I don't want to get in your ~ when you're working** ich will dich nicht beim Arbeiten stören; **to get sth out of the ~** *(move)* etw aus dem Weg räumen; *problem also, work* etw hinter sich *(acc)* bringen; **get out of the/my ~!** weg da!; **to keep out of sb's/the ~** *(not get in the ~)* (jdm) aus dem Weg bleiben; *(avoid)* (jdm) aus dem Weg gehen; **to put difficulties in sb's ~** jdm Hindernisse in den Weg stellen; **to stand in sb's ~** *(lit, fig)* jdm im Weg sein.

   **(d)** *(direction)* Richtung *f.* **this ~, please** hier entlang, bitte; **he went that ~** er ging in diese Richtung; **this ~ and that** hierhin und dorthin; **which ~ are you going?** in welche Richtung gehen Sie?; **she didn't know which ~ to look** *(fig)* sie wußte nicht, wo sie hinsehen sollte; **to look the other ~** *(fig)* wegsehen; **this one is better, there are no two ~s about it** *(col)* dieses hier ist besser, da gibt es gar keinen Zweifel; **it does not matter (to me) one ~ or the other** es ist mir gleich; **either ~, we're bound to lose** (so oder so,) wir verlieren auf jeden Fall; **it's the wrong ~ up** es steht verkehrt herum; **"this ~ up"** „hier oben"; **it's the other ~ around** es ist (genau) umgekehrt.

   **(e)** *(distance)* Weg *m,* Strecke *f.* **it rained all the ~** es hat auf der ganzen Strecke geregnet; **I'm behind you all the ~** *(fig)* ich stehe voll (und ganz) hinter Ihnen; **a little/long ~ off** nicht/sehr weit entfernt; **that's a long ~ back** *(in time)* das war schon vor einer ganzen Weile; **he'll go a long ~** *(fig)* er wird es weit bringen; **to have (still) a long ~ to go** (noch) weit vom Ziel entfernt sein; *(with practice)* (noch) viel vor sich haben; **it should go some/a long ~ towards solving the problem** das sollte bei dem Problem schon etwas/ein gutes Stück weiterhelfen; **a little kindness goes a long ~** ein bißchen Freundlichkeit hilft viel; **not by a long ~** bei weitem nicht.

   **(f)** *(method, manners)* Art, Weise *f.* **do it this ~** machen Sie es so; **it's not the right ~ to do it** so kann man das nicht machen; **what's the best ~ to do it?** wie macht man das am besten?; **you could tell by the ~ he was dressed** das merkte man schon an seiner Kleidung; **the ~ she walks/talks** (so) wie sie geht/spricht; **do you remember the ~ it was?** erinnerst du dich noch (daran), wie es war?; **to show sb the ~ to do sth** jdm zeigen, wie *or* auf welche Art und Weise etw gemacht wird; **to do sth the hard ~** etw auf die schwierige Art (und Weise) machen; **to learn the hard ~** aus den eigenen schlech-

ten Erfahrungen lernen; **we'll find a ~** wir werden (schon) einen Weg finden; **I'd rather do it my ~** ich möchte es lieber auf meine (eigene) Art machen; **that's his ~ of saying thank you** das ist seine Art, sich zu bedanken; **~s and means** Mittel und Wege; **~ of life** Lebensstil *m; (of nation)* Lebensart *f;* **~ of thinking** Denk(ungs)art *f;* **to my ~ of thinking** meiner Meinung *or* Auffassung nach; **a funny ~ of talking** eine komische Art, sich auszudrücken; **there are many ~s of solving the problem** es gibt viele Wege, das Problem zu lösen; **that's one ~ of doing it!** *(iro)* das ist auch eine Methode!; **that's the ~ it goes!** so ist das eben, so ist das nun mal; **the ~ things are** so, wie die Dinge liegen; **in one ~ or another** so oder so, irgendwie; **to get** *or* **have one's (own) ~** seinen Willen durchsetzen; **have it your own ~!** wie du willst!; **you can't have it both ~s** beides zugleich geht nicht; **what a ~ to speak!** so spricht man doch nicht!; **the ~s of the Spaniards** die spanische Lebensweise; **the ~ of the world** der Lauf der Dinge; **he has a ~ with children** er versteht es, mit Kindern umzugehen; **to get out of/into the ~ of sth** sich *(dat)* etw ab-/angewöhnen.

   **(g)** *(respect)* Hinsicht *f.* **in a ~** in gewisser Hinsicht *or* Weise; **in no ~** in keiner Weise; **no ~!** ausgeschlossen!; **there's no ~ she's going to agree** sie wird auf keinen Fall zustimmen; **what have you got in the ~ of drink?** was haben Sie an Getränken?; **in every possible ~** auf jede mögliche *or* denkbare Art; **in many/some ~s** in vieler/gewisser Hinsicht; **in a big ~** *(not petty)* im großen Stil; *(on a large scale)* im großen; **in the ordinary ~** normalerweise.

   **(h)** *(state)* Zustand *m.* **he's in a bad ~** es geht ihm schlecht; **things are in a bad ~** die Dinge stehen schlecht.

   **(i)** *(with by)* **by the ~** übrigens; **all this is by the ~** *(irrelevant)* das ist alles nebensächlich; *(extra)* das nur nebenbei; **by ~ of an answer/excuse** als Antwort/Entschuldigung; **by ~ of illustration** zur Illustration.

   **2** *adv (col)* **~ back/up** weit zurück/oben; **~ back when ...** vor langer Zeit, als ...; **since ~ back** seit Urzeiten; **that was ~ back** das ist schon lange her; **his guess was ~ out** seine Annahme war weit gefehlt.

**way:** **~bill** *n* Frachtbrief *m;* **~farer** ['weɪˌfɛərər] *n (liter)* Wanderer *m;* **~lay** *pret, ptp* **~laid** *vt (ambush)* überfallen; *(col)* abfangen; **~-out** *adj (col)* irre *(col);* **~side 1** *n (of path, track)* Wegrand *m; (of road)* Straßenrand *m;* **by the ~side** am Weges-/Straßenrand; **to fall by the ~side** auf der Strecke bleiben; **2** *adj café (col),* **inn** am Weg/an der Straße gelegen; **~ station** *n (US)* Zwischenstation *f;* **~ward** ['weɪwəd] *adj (self-willed)* eigenwillig; *(capricious)* abwegig.

**WBA** = **World Boxing Association.**
**WBC** = **World Boxing Council.**
**WC** [ˌdʌblju:'si:] *n* WC *nt.*
**we** [wi:] *pron* wir.
**weak** [wi:k] *adj (+er)* schwach; *character* labil; *tea, solution etc* dünn; *stomach* empfindlich. **the ~er sex** das schwache Geschlecht; **he must be a bit ~ in the head** *(col)* er ist wohl nicht ganz bei Trost *(col).*
**weaken** ['wi:kən] **1** *vt (lit, fig)* schwächen; *control etc* verringern; *foundations* angreifen; *hold* lockern. **2** *vi (lit, fig)* schwächer werden, nachlassen; *(person)* schwach werden; *(foundations)* nachgeben; *(defence, strength also)* erlahmen. **his grip on my arm ~ed** er hielt meinen Arm nicht mehr ganz so fest.

**weak-kneed** [ˌwiːkˈniːd] *adj (fig col)* schwach, feige.
**weakling** [ˈwiːklɪŋ] *n* Schwächling *m*.
**weakly** [ˈwiːklɪ] **1** *adj (dated)* schwächlich. **2** *adv* schwach.
**weak-minded** [ˌwiːkˈmaɪndɪd] *adj* **(a)** *(feebleminded)* schwachsinnig. **(b)** *(weak-willed)* willensschwach.
**weakness** [ˈwiːknɪs] *n* Schwäche *f*; *(weak point)* schwacher Punkt. **to have a ~ for sth** eine Schwäche für etw haben.
**weak-willed** [ˌwiːkˈwɪld] *adj* willensschwach.
**weal** [wiːl] *n* Striemen *m*.
**wealth** [welθ] *n* **(a)** Reichtum *m*. **~ tax** Vermögenssteuer *f*. **(b)** *(fig: abundance)* Fülle *f* *(of von)*.
**wealthy** [ˈwelθɪ] *adj (+er)* wohlhabend, reich. **the ~** *pl* die Reichen *pl*.
**wean** [wiːn] *vt baby* entwöhnen. **to ~ sb from** *or* **off sth** jdm etw abgewöhnen.
**weapon** [ˈwepən] *n (lit, fig)* Waffe *f*.
**weaponry** [ˈwepənrɪ] *n* Waffen *pl*.
**wear** [wɛəʳ] *(vb: pret* **wore**, *ptp* **worn)** **1** *n* **(a)** *(use)* **I've had a lot of ~ out of this jacket** ich habe diese Jacke viel getragen; **there isn't much ~ left in this carpet** dieser Teppich hält nicht mehr lange; **for casual/evening/everyday ~** für die Freizeit/den Abend/jeden Tag. **(b)** *(clothing)* Kleidung *f*. **(c)** **~ and tear** Abnutzung *f*, Verschleiß *m*; **fair ~ and tear** normale Abnutzungserscheinungen; **to show signs of ~** *(lit)* anfangen, abgenutzt *or (clothes, curtains)* verschlissen auszusehen; *(fig)* angegriffen aussehen; **to look the worse for ~** *(lit) (clothes, curtains etc)* verschlissen aussehen; *(clothes)* abgetragen aussehen; *(furniture etc)* abgenutzt aussehen; *(fig)* verbraucht aussehen; **I felt a bit the worse for ~** ich fühlte mich etwas angegriffen.
**2** *vt* **(a)** *clothing, jewellery etc* tragen. **what shall I ~?** was soll ich anziehen?; **I haven't a thing to ~!** ich habe nichts anzuziehen. **(b)** *(~ down, ~ out)* abnutzen; *clothes* abtragen; *sleeve etc* durchwetzen; *steps* austreten; *tyres* abfahren; *engine* kaputtmachen. **to ~ holes in sth** etw durchwetzen; *(in shoes)* etw durchlaufen; **to ~ smooth** *(by handling)* abgreifen; *(by walking)* austreten; *rocks* glätten. **(c)** *(col: accept, tolerate)* hinnehmen.
**3** *vi* **(a)** *(last)* halten; *(dress, shoes etc also)* sich tragen. **she has worn well** *(col)* sie hat sich gut gehalten *(col)*; **the theory has worn well** die Theorie hat sich bewährt. **(b)** *(become worn)* kaputtgehen; *(engine, material also)* sich abnutzen, verbraucht sein; *(tyres also)* abgefahren sein. **to have worn smooth** *(by water)* glattgewaschen sein; *(by weather)* verwittert sein; *(pattern)* abgegriffen sein; **to ~ thin** *(lit)* dünn werden; **my patience is ~ing thin** meine Geduld geht langsam zu Ende.
▶**wear away 1** *vt sep (erode) steps* austreten; *rock* abschleifen, abtragen; *(hollow out)* aushöhlen; *inscription* tilgen *(geh)*, verwischen; *(fig) determination* untergraben. **2** *vi (rocks, rough edges etc)* sich abschleifen; *(inscription)* verwittern; *(pattern)* verwischen; *(fig: patience etc)* schwinden.
▶**wear down 1** *vt sep* **(a)** *(reduce by friction)* abnutzen; *heel* ablaufen, abtreten; *tyre tread* abfahren. **(b)** *(fig) person, opposition etc* zermürben. **2** *vi* sich abnutzen; *(heels)* sich abtreten; *(tyre tread)* sich abfahren.
▶**wear off** *vi* **(a)** *(diminish)* nachlassen. **the novelty has worn ~** der Reiz des Neuen ist vorbei; **don't worry, it'll ~ ~!** keine Sorge, das gibt sich. **(b)** *(paint)* abgehen; *(plating, gilt)* sich abwetzen.
▶**wear on** *vi* sich hinziehen; *(year)* voranschreiten. **as the evening/year etc wore ~** im Laufe des Abends/Jahres *etc*.
▶**wear out 1** *vt sep* **(a)** kaputtmachen; *carpet also* abtreten; *clothes* auftragen; *shoes* ablaufen; *record, machinery* abnutzen. **(b)** *(exhaust) (physically)* erschöpfen, erledigen *(col)*; *(mentally)* fertigmachen *(col)*. **to be worn ~** erschöpft *or* erledigt sein; *(mentally)* am Ende sein *(col)*; **to ~ oneself ~** sich überanstrengen, sich kaputtmachen *(col)*. **2** *vi* kaputtgehen; *(clothes, carpets also)* verschleißen. **my patience is rapidly ~ing ~** ich bin mit meiner Geduld bald am Einde.
▶**wear through 1** *vt sep* durchwetzen; *soles of shoes* durchlaufen. **2** *vi* sich durchwetzen; *(soles of shoes)* sich durchlaufen.
**wearable** [ˈwɛərəbl] *adj* tragbar.
**wearer** [ˈwɛərəʳ] *n* Träger(in *f*) *m*.
**wearily** [ˈwɪərɪlɪ] *adv see adj (a)*.
**weariness** [ˈwɪərɪnɪs] *n see adj (a)* Müdigkeit *f*; Lustlosigkeit *f*; Mattheit *f*.
**wearing** [ˈwɛərɪŋ] *adj* anstrengend.
**wearisome** [ˈwɪərɪsəm] *adj* ermüdend; *(bothersome) questions* lästig; *(tedious) discussion* langweilig.
**weary** [ˈwɪərɪ] **1** *adj (+er)* **(a)** *(tired)* müde; *(fed up)* lustlos; *smile, groan* matt. **to feel ~** müde sein; **to be/grow ~ of sth** etw leid sein/werden. **(b)** *(tiring)* ermüdend. **for three ~ hours** drei endlose Stunden (lang). **2** *vt* ermüden. **3** *vi* **to ~ of sth** einer Sache *(gen)* müde werden *(geh)*.
**weasel** [ˈwiːzl] *n* Wiesel *nt*.
**weather** [ˈweðəʳ] **1** *n* Wetter *nt*. **in cold/this ~** bei kaltem/diesem Wetter; **what's the ~ like?** wie ist das Wetter?; **in all ~s** bei jedem Wetter; **to be** *or* **feel under the ~** *(col)* angeschlagen sein *(col)*; **to make heavy ~ of sth** *(col)* sich mit etw fürchterlich anstellen *(col)*. **2** *vt* **(a)** *(storms, winds etc)* angreifen. **(b)** *(survive: also ~ out) crisis etc* überstehen. **to ~ the storm** *(fig)* den Sturm überstehen. **3** *vi (rock etc)* verwittern; *(paint etc)* verblassen. **to ~ well** *(paint etc)* wetterfest sein.
**weather** *in cpds* Wetter-; **~-beaten** *adj face* vom Wetter gegerbt; *house* verwittert; *skin* wettergegerbt; **~ chart** *n* Wetterkarte *f*; **~cock** *n* Wetterhahn *m*.
**weathered** [ˈweðəd] *adj* verwittert; *skin* wettergegerbt.
**weather:** **~ forecast** *n* Wettervorhersage *f*; **~man** *n* Mann *m* vom Wetteramt; **~proof** *adj* wetterfest; **~ report** *n* Wetterbericht *m*; **~ satellite** *n* Wettersatellit *m*; **~vane** *n* Wetterfahne *f*.
**weave** [wiːv] *(vb: pret* **wove**, *ptp* **woven)** **1** *n (pattern of threads)* Webart *f*; *(fabric)* Gewebe *nt*. **2** *vt* **(a)** *cloth etc* weben *(into* zu*)*; *cane, flowers* flechten *(into* zu*)*. **(b)** *(fig) plot* ersinnen, erfinden; *details* einflechten *(into* in +*acc)*. **(c)** *(pret also ~d)* **to ~ one's way through the traffic** sich durch den Verkehr schlängeln. **3** *vi* **(a)** *(lit)* weben. **(b)** *(pret also ~d) (twist and turn)* sich schlängeln. **to ~ in and out through the traffic** sich durch den Verkehr schlängeln. **(c)** *(col)* **to get weaving** sich ranhalten *(col)*.
**weaver** [ˈwiːvəʳ] *n* Weber(in *f*) *m*.
**weaving** [ˈwiːvɪŋ] *n* Weberei *f*; *(as craft)* Webkunst *f*.
**web** [web] *n (lit, fig)* Netz *nt*; *(of lies also)* Gespinst, Gewebe *nt*.
**webbed** [webd] *adj foot* Schwimm-.
**webbing** [ˈwebɪŋ] *n* Gurte *pl*; *(material)* Gurtband *nt*.
**web:** **~ foot** *n* Schwimmfuß *m*; **~ offset** *n (Print)* Rollenrotations-Offsetdruck *m*.
**Wed** = **Wednesday** Mi.
**wed** [wed] *(old, form) pret, ptp ~* or *~ded* **1** *vi* sich vermählen *(form)*, heiraten. **2** *vt (bride, bridegroom)*

sich vermählen mit *(form)*; *(priest)* vermählen *(form)*, trauen. **to be ~ded to one's job/an idea** mit seinem Beruf verheiratet sein/einer Idee verfallen sein.

**we'd** [wiːd] = **we would**; **we had**.

**wedded** ['wedɪd] *adj bliss, life* Ehe-.

**wedding** ['wedɪŋ] *n (ceremony)* Trauung *f; (ceremony and festivities)* Hochzeit *f.* **to have a church ~** sich kirchlich trauen lassen.

**wedding** *in cpds* Hochzeits-; **~ anniversary** *n* Hochzeitstag *m;* **~ breakfast** *n* Hochzeitsessen *nt;* **~ cake** *n* Hochzeitskuchen *m;* **~ day** *n* Hochzeitstag *m;* **~ dress** *m* Brautkleid *nt;* **~ night** *n* Hochzeitsnacht *f;* **~ present** *n* Hochzeitsgeschenk *nt;* **~ reception** *n* Hochzeit(sfeier) *f;* **~ ring** *n* Trauring, Ehering *m.*

**wedge** [wedʒ] **1** *n (of wood etc, fig)* Keil *m; (of cake etc)* Stück *nt; (of cheese)* Ecke *f.* **it's the thin end of the ~** das ist nur der Anfang. **2** *vt* **(a)** verkeilen, (mit einem Keil) festklemmen. **to ~ a door/window open/shut** eine Tür/ein Fenster festklemmen, damit sie/es auf-/zubleibt. **(b)** *(pack tightly)* **to ~ oneself/sth** sich/etw zwängen *(in in +acc);* **to be ~d between two things/people** zwischen zwei Dingen/Personen eingekeilt sein.

**wedge-shaped** ['wedʒʃeɪpt] *adj* keilförmig.

**wedlock** ['wedlɒk] *n (form)* Ehe *f.* **to be born in/out of ~** ehelich/unehelich geboren sein.

**Wednesday** ['wenzdɪ] *n* Mittwoch *m; see* **Tuesday**.

**wee**[1] [wiː] *adj (+er) (col)* winzig; *(Scot)* klein. **a ~ bit** ein kleines bißchen.

**wee**[2] *(col)* **1** *n* **to have** *or* **do a ~** pinkeln *(col).* **2** *vi* pinkeln *(col).*

**weed** [wiːd] **1** *n* **(a)** Unkraut *nt no pl.* **(b)** *(col: person)* Schwächling *m.* **2** *vti (lit)* jäten.
►**weed out** *vt sep (fig)* aussondern.

**weeding** ['wiːdɪŋ] *n* **to do the ~** Unkraut jäten.

**weedkiller** ['wiːdkɪlə'] *n* Unkrautbekämpfungsmittel *nt.*

**weedy** ['wiːdɪ] *adj (+er) (col) person (in appearance)* schmächtig.

**week** [wiːk] *n* Woche *f.* **it'll be ready in a ~** in einer Woche ist es fertig; **~ in, ~ out** Woche für Woche; **twice/£15 a ~** zweimal/£15 in der Woche *or* pro Woche; **a ~ today** heute in einer Woche *or* in acht Tagen; **tomorrow ~, a ~ tomorrow** morgen in einer Woche; **for ~s** wochenlang; **a ~'s/a two ~ holiday** ein einwöchiger/zweiwöchiger Urlaub; **in the ~ ending May 15** in der Woche vom 11. Mai; **to knock sb into the middle of next ~** *(col)* jdn windelweich schlagen *(col).*

**week:** **~day 1** *n* Wochentag *m;* **2** *attr* Wochentags-, Werktags-; **~end** *n* Wochenende *nt;* **to go/be away for the ~end** übers Wochenende verreisen/nicht da sein; **at** *or (esp US)* **on the ~end** am Wochenende; **~end case** *n* (Kurz)reisekoffer *m.*

**weekly** ['wiːklɪ] **1** *adj* Wochen-; *visit* allwöchentlich. **2** *adv* wöchentlich. **3** *n (also ~ newspaper)* Wochenzeitschrift *f.*

**weeny** ['wiːnɪ] *adj (+er) (col)* klitzeklein *(col).*

**weep** [wiːp] *(vb: pret, ptp* **wept) 1** *vi* **(a)** weinen *(over über +acc).* **to ~ for joy/rage** vor Freude/Wut weinen; **I could have wept!** ich hätte heulen mögen. **(b)** *(wound, cut etc)* nässen. **2** *vt tears* weinen. **3** *n* **to have a good ~** sich ausweinen.

**weepie** ['wiːpɪ] *n see* **weepy 2**.

**weeping** ['wiːpɪŋ] *n* Weinen *nt.*

**weeping willow** *n* Trauerweide *f.*

**weepy** ['wiːpɪ] *(col)* **1** *adj (+er) person* weinerlich; *film etc* rührselig. **2** *n (film etc)* Schmachtfetzen *m (col).*

**wee-wee** ['wiːwiː] *n (baby-talk)* **to go for a ~** Pipi machen *(col).*

**weft** [weft] *n* Einschlagfaden, Schußfaden *m.*

**weigh** [weɪ] **1** *vt* **(a)** wiegen. **could you ~ these bananas for me?** könnten Sie mir diese Bananen auswiegen? **(b)** *(fig) problem, merits etc* abwägen. **to ~ sth in one's mind** etw erwägen; **to ~ A against B** A und B gegeneinander abwägen. **2** *vi* **(a)** wiegen. **(b)** *(fig: be a burden)* lasten *(on* auf *+dat).* **it's been ~ing on my mind** es liegt mir auf der Seele. **(c)** *(fig: be important)* gelten. **to ~ with sb** Gewicht bei jdm haben; **his age ~ed against him** sein Alter sprach gegen ihn.
►**weigh down** *vt sep (lit, fig)* niederbeugen. **she was ~ed ~ with parcels** sie war mit Paketen überladen; **to be ~ed ~ with sorrows** mit Sorgen beladen sein.
►**weigh in 1** *vi (Sport)* **he ~ed ~ at 70 kilos** er brachte 70 Kilo auf die Waage. **2** *vt sep luggage* wiegen lassen.
►**weigh out** *vt sep* abwiegen.
►**weigh up** *vt sep alternatives, situation* abwägen; *person* einschätzen.

**weigh:** **~bridge** *n* Brückenwaage *f;* **~-in** *n (Sport)* Wiegen *nt.*

**weighing machine** ['weɪɪŋməˌʃiːn] *n* Waage *f.*

**weight** [weɪt] **1** *n* **(a)** Gewicht *nt; (Sport, esp Boxing)* Gewichtsklasse *f; (of blow)* Wucht, Heftigkeit *f.* **to be 3 kilos in ~** ein Gewicht von 3 Kilo haben; **to put on/lose ~** zunehmen/abnehmen; **I hope the chair takes my ~** ich hoffe, der Stuhl hält mein Gewicht aus; **she's quite a ~** sie ist ganz schön schwer. **(b)** *(fig) (burden)* Last *f; (importance)* Bedeutung *f,* Gewicht *nt.* **the ~ of evidence** die Beweislast; **he/his opinion carries no ~** seine Stimme/Meinung fällt nicht ins Gewicht; **to add ~ to sth** einer Sache *(dat)* zusätzliches Gewicht geben; **to pull one's ~** seinen Beitrag leisten; **to throw one's ~ about** *(col)* sich wichtig machen.

**2** *vt* beschweren; *(fig) statistics* gewichten. **to be ~ed in favour of/against sb** jdn bevorzugen/benachteiligen.
►**weight down** *vt sep person (with parcels etc)* überladen; *corpse* beschweren.

**weighting** ['weɪtɪŋ] *n (Brit: supplement)* Zulage *f.*

**weight:** **~less** *adj* schwerelos; **~lessness** *n* Schwerelosigkeit *f;* **~lifter** *n* Gewichtheber *m;* **~lifting** *n* Gewichtheben *nt;* **~ limit** *n* Höchstgewicht *nt;* **~ training** *n* Krafttraining *nt;* **~-watcher** *n* Figurbewußte(r) *mf.*

**weighty** ['weɪtɪ] *adj (+er)* **(a)** *(lit)* schwer. **(b)** *(fig)* gewichtig; *responsibility* schwer.

**weir** [wɪə'] *n (barrier)* Wehr *nt.*

**weird** [wɪəd] *adj (+er) (uncanny)* unheimlich; *(col: odd)* seltsam.

**weirdo** ['wɪədəu] *n (col)* verrückter Typ *(col).*

**welcome** ['welkəm] **1** *n* Willkommen *nt.* **to give sb a warm ~** jdm einen herzlichen Empfang bereiten; **to meet with a cold/warm ~** einen kühlen/herzlichen Empfang bekommen; **to bid sb ~** *(form)* jdn willkommen heißen; **what sort of a ~ will this product get from the public?** wie wird das Produkt von der Öffentlichkeit aufgenommen werden?

**2** *adj* willkommen; *visitor also* gerngesehen *attr; news also* angenehm. **the money is very ~ just now** das Geld kommt gerade jetzt sehr gelegen; **to make sb ~** jdn sehr freundlich empfangen; **you're ~!** nichts zu danken!, aber gerne!; *(iro)* wenn's Ihnen Spaß macht!; **you're ~ to use my room** Sie können gerne mein Zimmer benutzen.

**3** *vt (lit, fig)* begrüßen, willkommen heißen.
**4** *interj* ~ **home/to Scotland!** willkommen daheim/in Schottland!
**welcoming** ['welkəmɪŋ] *adj* zur Begrüßung; *smile, gesture* einladend.
**weld** [weld] **1** *vt* **(a)** *(Tech)* schweißen. **to** ~ **parts together** Teile zusammenschweißen *or* verschweißen; **to** ~ **sth on** etw anschweißen *(to* an *+acc).* **(b)** *(fig: also* ~ **together)** zusammenschmieden *(into* zu*).* **2** *n (seam)* Schweißnaht *f.*
**welder** ['weldər] *n (person)* Schweißer(in *f) m*; *(machine)* Schweißgerät *nt.*
**welding** ['weldɪŋ] *n* Schweißen *nt.* ~ **torch** Schweißbrenner *m.*
**welfare** ['welfɛər] *n* **(a)** *(well-being)* Wohl, Wohlergehen *nt.* **(b)** *(~ work)* Fürsorge *f.* **child** ~ Kinderfürsorge *f.* **(c)** *(US: social security)* Sozialhilfe *f.*
**welfare:** ~ **state** *n* Wohlfahrtsstaat *m*; ~ **work** *n* Fürsorgearbeit *f*; ~ **worker** *n* Fürsorger(in *f) m.*
**well¹** [wel] *n (water ~)* Brunnen *m*; *(oil ~)* Ölquelle *f*; *(fig: source)* Quelle *f*; *(for lift)* Schacht *m*; *(of stairs)* Treppenhaus *nt.*
▶**well up** *vi (water)* emporsteigen, emporquellen; *(fig)* aufsteigen. **tears** ~**ed** ~ **in her eyes** Tränen stiegen ihr in die Augen.
**well²** *comp* **better,** *superl* **best 1** *adv* **(a)** gut. **he did it as** ~ **as he could** er machte es so gut er konnte; **he's doing** ~ **at school** er ist gut in der Schule; **he did** ~ **in the exam** er hat in der Prüfung gut abgeschnitten; **his business is doing** ~ sein Geschäft geht gut; **the patient is doing** ~ dem Patienten geht es gut; **if you do** ~ **you'll be promoted** wenn Sie sich bewähren, werden Sie befördert; **he has done** ~ **for himself** er hat es zu etwas gebracht; **you did** ~ **to help** es war gut, daß du geholfen hast; **he really did** ~ **there** das war wirklich eine Leistung von ihm; ~ **done!** gut gemacht!, bravo!; ~ **played!** gut gespielt!; **to do oneself** ~ *(col)* es sich *(dat)* gut gehen lassen; **everything went** ~ es ging alles gut; **to speak/think** ~ **of sb** über jdn Gutes sagen/viel von jdm halten; **to be** ~ **in with sb** *(col)* auf gutem Fuß mit jdm stehen; **to do** ~ **out of sth** von etw ganz schön *or* ordentlich profitieren; **we were** ~ **beaten** wir sind gründlich geschlagen worden; **all** *or* **only too** ~ nur (all)zu gut; ~ **and truly** (ganz) gründlich; *married, settled in* richtig; **he was** ~ **away** *(col)* er war in Fahrt *(col)*; *(drunk)* er hatte einen sitzen *(col)*; **it was** ~ **worth the trouble** das hat sich sehr gelohnt; ~ **out of sight** weit außer Sichtweite; ~ **within ...** durchaus in ... *(+dat)*; ~ **past midnight** weit nach Mitternacht; **he's** ~ **over fifty** er ist einiges *or* weit über fünfzig; ~ **over a thousand** weit über tausend.
**(b)** *(probably, reasonably)* ohne weiteres, gut, wohl. **I may** ~ **not come** es kann durchaus sein, daß ich nicht komme; **it may** ~ **be that ...** es ist gut *or* durchaus möglich, daß ...; **you may** ~ **be right** Sie mögen wohl recht haben; **she cried, as** ~ **she might** sie weinte, wozu sie auch allen Grund hatte; **you may** ~ **ask!** *(iro)* das kann man wohl fragen; **you might as** ~ **have stayed at home** du hättest genausogut zu Hause bleiben können; **I couldn't very** ~ **stay** ich konnte schlecht bleiben; **you might as** ~ **go** du könntest eigentlich ebensogut gehen; **are you coming? — I might as** ~ kommst du? — ach, warum nicht.
**(c)** *(in addition)* **as** ~ auch; **x as** ~ **as y** x sowohl als auch y.
**2** *adj* **(a)** *(in good health)* gesund. **get** ~ **soon!** gute Besserung; **I'm very** ~, **thanks** danke, es geht mir sehr gut; **she's not been** ~ **lately** ihr ging es in

letzter Zeit (gesundheitlich) gar nicht gut; **I don't feel at all** ~ ich fühle mich gar nicht gut *or* wohl.
**(b)** *(satisfactory)* gut. **all is not** ~ **with him** mit ihm steht es nicht zum besten; **that's all very** ~, **but ...** das ist ja alles schön und gut, aber ...; **it's all very** ~ **for you to say that** Sie haben gut reden; **it would be as** ~ **to ask first** es wäre wohl besser, sich erst mal zu erkundigen; **it's just as** ~ **he came** es ist (nur) gut, daß er gekommen ist; **you're** ~ **out of it** seien Sie froh, daß Sie nichts (mehr) damit zu tun haben; **all's** ~ **that ends** ~ Ende gut, alles gut.
**3** *interj* also; *(expectantly also)* na; *(doubtfully)* na ja. ~ ~!, ~ **I never** also so was!, na so was!; ~ **now** also; ~ **then** also (gut); *(in question)* na?, also?; **very** ~ **then!** na gut, also gut; *(indignantly)* also bitte.
**4** *n* Gute(s) *nt.* **to wish sb** ~ *(in general)* jdm alles Gute wünschen; *(in an attempt, iro)* jdm Glück wünschen *(in* bei*).*
**we'll** [wiːl] = **we shall**; **we will.**
**well** *in cpds* gut; ~**-advised** *adj* **you'd be** ~**-advised to ...** du tätest gut daran, zu ...; ~**-aimed** *adj* gutgezielt *attr*; ~**-balanced** *adj person* ausgeglichen; *scheme, diet* (gut) ausgewogen; ~**-behaved** *adj child* artig, wohlerzogen; *animal* guterzogen *attr*; ~**-being** *n* Wohl, Wohlergehen *nt*; ~**-bred** *adj person* wohlerzogen; *accent* distinguiert; ~**-built** *adj house* gut *or* solide gebaut; *person* stämmig, kräftig; ~**-chosen** *adj words* gut gewählt; ~**-connected** *adj* **to be** ~**-connected** Beziehungen zu höheren Kreisen haben; ~**-deserved** *adj* wohlverdient; ~**-developed** *adj muscle* gutentwickelt *attr*; *sense* (gut) ausgeprägt; ~**-disposed** *adj* **to be** ~**-disposed towards sb/sth** jdm/einer Sache freundlich gesonnen sein; ~**-done** *adj steak* durchgebraten; ~**-dressed** *adj* gut angezogen *or* gekleidet; ~**-earned** *adj* wohlverdient; ~**-educated** *adj person* gebildet; ~**-established** *adj* bewährt; ~**-fed** *adj* wohlgenährt; ~**-founded** *adj* wohlbegründet *attr*; ~**-groomed** *adj* gepflegt; ~**-heeled** *adj (col)* betucht.
**wellies** ['welɪz] *npl (Brit col)* Gummistiefel *pl.*
**well-informed** *adj* gutinformiert *attr*; *sources also* gutunterrichtet *attr*. **to be** ~ **about sth** über etw gut informiert sein.
**wellington (boot)** ['welɪŋtən('buːt)] *n (Brit)* Gummistiefel *m.*
**well:** ~**-intentioned** *adj see* ~**-meaning;** ~**-judged** *adj shot, remark* gut gezielt; *response* angemessen; ~**-kept** *adj garden, hair etc* gepflegt; *secret* streng gehütet; ~**-known** *adj* bekannt; **it's** ~**-known that ...** es ist allgemein bekannt, daß ...; ~**-made** *adj* solide gearbeitet; ~**-mannered** *adj* wohlerzogen; ~**-meaning** *adj* wohlmeinend *attr*; ~**-meant** *adj action* gutgemeint *attr*; ~**-nigh** *adv* nahezu, beinahe; ~**-off** *adj (affluent)* reich, gut daran *(col)*; **you don't know when you're** ~**-off** *(col)* du weißt (ja) nicht, wann es dir gut geht; ~**-preserved** *adj* guterhalten *attr*; ~**-read** *adj* belesen; ~**-spent** *adj time* gut genützt *or* verbracht; *money* sinnvoll ausgegeben; ~**-spoken** *adj* mit gutem Deutsch/Englisch *etc*; **to be** ~**-spoken** gutes Deutsch/Englisch *etc* sprechen; ~**-stocked** *adj* gutbestückt *attr*; *(Comm also)* mit gutem Sortiment; *larder, shelves also* reichlich gefüllt; ~**-thumbed** *adj book* zerlesen; ~**-timed** *adj* gut abgepaßt; ~**-to-do** *adj* wohlhabend, reich; ~**-tried** *adj* erprobt; *method* bewährt; ~**-wisher** *n* **our cause has many** ~**-wishers** unsere Sache hat viele Sympathisanten; **"from a** ~**-wisher"** „jemand, der es gut mit Ihnen meint"; ~**-woman clinic** *n* Frauen-

sprechstunde f (für Vorsorgeuntersuchungen); ~-
**worn** adj garment abgetragen; carpet etc abgetreten; path ausgetreten; saying etc abgedroschen.
**welsh** [welʃ] vi **to ~ on sb** (col) jdn (auf)sitzen
lassen.
**Welsh** [welʃ] **1** adj walisisch. **2** n **(a)** (language) Walisisch nt. **(b) the ~** pl die Waliser pl.
**Welsh:** **~man** n Waliser m; **~ rarebit** n über-
backene Käseschnitte; **~woman** n Waliserin f.
**welter** ['weltər] n Unzahl f; (of emotions) Sturm, Tumult m; (of words) Flut f.
**welterweight** ['weltəweit] n Weltergewicht nt.
**wend** [wend] vt **to ~ one's way home** sich auf den
Heimweg begeben.
**Wendy house** ['wendɪˌhaʊs] n Spielhaus nt.
**went** [went] pret of **go.**
**wept** [wept] pret, ptp of **weep.**
**were** [wɜː] 2nd pers sing, 1st, 2nd, 3rd person pl pret of
**be.**
**we're** [wɪər] = **we are.**
**weren't** [wɜːnt] = **were not.**
**werewolf** ['wɪəwʊlf] n Werwolf m.
**west** [west] **1** n **(a)** Westen m. **in/to the ~** im/nach
Westen; **from the ~** von Westen; **to the ~ of** westlich von, im Westen von. **(b)** (~ern world) **the W~**
der Westen. **2** adv nach Westen, westwärts. **it faces
~** es geht nach Westen; **~ of** westlich von; **to go ~**
(fig col) flöten gehen (col). **3** adj West-, westlich.
**West** in cpds West-. **~ Africa** n Westafrika nt; **~
Bank** n (in Middle East) Westjordanland nt.
**westbound** ['westbaʊnd] adj traffic in Richtung
Westen.
**westerly** ['westəlɪ] adj westlich.
**western** ['westən] **1** adj westlich. **W~ Europe**
Westeuropa nt. **2** n (film) Western m.
**westerners** ['westənəz] npl Europäer und Nord-
amerikaner.
**westernized** ['westənaɪzd] adj culture vom Westen
beeinflußt; (pej) verwestlicht.
**West:** **~ German 1** adj westdeutsch; **2** n Westdeut-
sche(r) mf; **~ Germany** n Westdeutschland nt; **~
Indian 1** adj westindisch; **2** n Westindier(in f) m;
**~ Indies** npl Westindische Inseln pl.
**Westphalia** [west'feɪlɪə] n Westfalen nt.
**Westphalian** [west'feɪlɪən] **1** adj westfälisch. **2** n
Westfale m, Westfälin f.
**west:** **~ward(s)** ['westwəd(z)], **~wardly** [-wədlɪ] **1**
adj westlich; **in a ~wardly direction** (in) Richtung
Westen; **2** adv westwärts, nach Westen.
**wet** [wet] (vb: pret, ptp **~** or **~ted**) **1** adj (+er) **(a)**
naß. **to be ~ through** durch und durch naß sein,
völlig durchnäßt sein; "**~ paint**" „frisch gestrichen"; **to get one's feet ~** sich (dat) nasse Füße holen (col). **(b)** (rainy) naß, feucht; climate, country
feucht. **the ~ season** die Regenzeit; **in ~ weather**
bei nassem Wetter. **(c)** (Brit col: weak, spiritless)
weichlich, lasch. **2** n **(a)** (moisture) Feuchtigkeit f.
**(b)** (rain) Nässe f. **it's out in the ~** es ist draußen im
Nassen. **(c)** (Brit col: person) Waschlappen m (col).
**3** vt naß machen; lips, washing befeuchten. **to ~
the bed/one's pants/oneself** ins Bett/in die Hose(n)
machen/sich naß machen.
**wet:** **~back** n (US col) illegal eingewanderter Mexi-
kaner; **~ blanket** n (col) Miesmacher(in f) m (col);
**~ look** n Hochglanz m.
**wetness** ['wetnɪs] n Nässe f; (of weather, climate)
Feuchtigkeit f.
**wet:** **~ nurse** n Amme f; **~suit** n Taucheranzug m.
**we've** [wiːv] = **we have.**
**whack** [wæk] **1** n **(a)** (blow) (knallender) Schlag. **(b)**
(col: attempt) Versuch m. **to have a ~ at sth** etw

probieren or versuchen. **(c)** (col: share) (An)teil m.
**the top ~** (amount) der Spitzenbetrag; (salary) das
Spitzengehalt. **2** vt **(a)** (hit) schlagen, hauen (col).
**(b)** (col: defeat) (haushoch) schlagen.
**whacked** [wækt] adj (col: exhausted) kaputt (col).
**whacking** ['wækɪŋ] adv (Brit col): **a ~ great ...** ein(e)
Mords- ... (col).
**whale** [weɪl] n **(a)** Wal m. **(b)** (col) **to have a ~ of a
time** sich prima amüsieren.
**whaler** ['weɪlər] n (person, ship) Walfänger m.
**wham** [wæm] **1** interj wumm. **2** n (blow) heftiger
Schlag; (bang) Knall m. **3** vt hauen. **to ~ the door
(shut)** die Tür zuknallen.
**wharf** [wɔːf] n, pl **-s** or **wharves** [wɔːvz] Kai m.
**what** [wɒt] **1** pron **(a)** (interrog) was. **~'s the weather
like?** wie ist das Wetter?; **~'s that to you?** was geht
dich das an?; **~ for?** wozu?, wofür?; **~'s that tool
for?** wofür ist das Werkzeug?; **~ did you do that
for?** warum hast du das gemacht?; **~'s the German
for ...?** wie heißt ... auf deutsch?; **~ did he agree to?**
wozu hat er zugestimmt?; **~ about ...?** wie wär's
mit ...?; **you know that pub? — ~ about it?** kennst
du die Kneipe? — was ist damit?; **~ if ...?** was ist,
wenn ...?; **so ~?** (col) na und?; **~ does it matter?**
was macht das schon?; **~'s-his/-her/-its name** (col)
der/die/das Dings(da) (col).
  **(b)** (rel) was. **that is not ~ I asked for** danach
habe ich nicht gefragt; **he agrees with ~ I say** er
stimmt mit dem überein, was ich sage; **that's exactly ~ I said** genau das habe ich gesagt; **do you
know ~ you are looking for?** weißt du, wonach du
suchst?; **come ~ may** komme was wolle; **and ~'s
more** und außerdem, und noch dazu; **~ with one
thing and another I didn't have time** wie es sich so
ergab, hatte ich keine Zeit; **he knows ~'s ~** (col) er
kennt sich aus, der weiß Bescheid (col); **and ~
have you** (col), **and ~ not** (col) und was sonst noch
alles; **(I'll) tell you ~** (col) weißt du was?; **to give sb
~ for** (col) es jdm ordentlich geben (col).
  **2** adj **(a)** (interrog) welche(r, s), was für ein/eine
(col). **~ age is he?** wie alt ist er?; **~ good would
that be?** (col) wozu sollte das gut sein? **(b)** (rel)
der/die/das. **~ little I had** das wenige, das ich hatte;
**eat ~ food you like** iß, was du möchtest. **(c)** (in set
constructions) **~ sort of** was für ein/eine; **~ else** was
sonst; see also **more. (d)** (in interj) **~ a man!** was
für ein Mann!; **~ luck!** was für ein Glück, so ein
Glück; **~ a fool I've been/I am!** ich Idiot!; **~ terrible
weather** was für ein scheußliches Wetter.
  **3** interj was!
**whatever** [wɒt'evər] **1** pron **(a) ~ you like** was (immer) du (auch) möchtest; **~ you say** wie du willst;
**... or ~ they're called ...** oder wie sie sonst heißen;
**or ~** oder sonst (so) etwas; **do you want jam or
honey? — ~** (col) möchtest du Marmelade oder Honig? — ist egal (col). **(b)** (interrog) **~ does he want?**
was will er wohl?; (impatiently) was, zum Kuckuck,
will er denn?; **~ do you mean?** was meinst du denn
bloß?; **~ shall I do?** was soll ich bloß machen? **2**
adj **(a)** welche(r, s) (auch). **~ book you choose** welches Buch Sie auch wählen; **for ~ reasons** aus welchen Gründen auch immer. **(b)** (with neg) überhaupt, absolut. **nothing/no man ~** überhaupt gar
nichts/niemand überhaupt; **it's of no use ~** es hat
absolut keinen Sinn. **(c)** (interrog) **~ reason can he
have?** was für einen Grund kann er bloß or wohl
haben?; **~ else will he do?** was wird er wohl noch
alles machen?
**whatnot** ['wɒtnɒt] n (col) Dingsbums nt (col). **... and
~ ...** und so.
**what's** [wɒts] = **what is; what has.**

**whatsit** ['wɒtsɪt] *n (col)* Dingsbums *nt (col)*.

**whatsoever** [ˌwɒtsəʊ'evər] *pron, adj see* **whatever 1 (a), 2 (a, b).**

**wheat** [wiːt] **1** *n* Weizen *m*. **2** *attr* ~**germ** Weizenkeim *m*; ~ **meal** *(Brit)* Weizenmehl *nt*.

**wheedle** ['wiːdl] *vt* **to** ~ **one's way into sth** *into organization, sb's confidence* sich in etw *(acc)* einschleichen; *into position* sich in etw *(acc)* hineinmanövrieren; **to** ~ **sth out of sb** jdm etw abschmeicheln.

**wheel** [wiːl] **1** *n* **(a)** Rad *nt*; *(steering* ~*)* Lenkrad *nt*; *(Naut)* Steuer(rad) *nt*; *(roulette* ~*)* Drehscheibe *f*; *(potter's* ~*)* (Töpfer)scheibe *f*. **at the** ~ *(lit)* am Steuer; *(fig also)* am Ruder; **to take the** ~ das Steuer übernehmen; ~ **of fortune** Glücksrad *nt*. **(b)** *(Mil)* Schwenkung *f*. **2** *vt* **(a)** *(push)* bicycle, pram schieben; *(pull)* ziehen; *(invalid)* wheelchair fahren. **(b)** *(cause to turn)* drehen. **3** *vi (turn)* drehen; *(birds, planes)* kreisen; *(Mil)* schwenken. **left** ~! links schwenkt!

▶**wheel around** *vi* sich (rasch) umdrehen; *(troops)* (ab)schwenken.

**wheel:** ~**barrow** *n* Schubkarre *f*, Schubkarren *m*; ~**base** *n* Rad(ab)stand *m*; ~ **brace** *n* Kreuzschlüssel *m*; ~**chair** *n* Rollstuhl *m*; ~ **clamp** *n (Brit)* (Park)kralle *f*.

**wheeler-dealer** ['wiːlə'diːlər] *n (col)* Schlitzohr *nt (col)*; *(in finance also)* Geschäftemacher *m*.

**wheelie** ['wiːlɪ] *n* Fahren *nt* auf dem Hinterrad.

**wheeling and dealing** ['wiːlɪŋən'diːlɪŋ] *n* Machenschaften *pl*; *(Comm)* Geschäftemacherei *f*.

**wheeze** [wiːz] *vi* pfeifend atmen; *(machines, asthmatic)* keuchen.

**whelk** [welk] *n* Wellhornschnecke *f*.

**when** [wen] **1** *adv* **(a)** wann. **since** ~ **have you been here?** seit wann sind Sie hier?; **since** ~ **do you give the orders?** seit wann hast du hier zu sagen?; **say** ~! *(col)* sag' halt! **(b)** *(rel)* **on the day** ~ an dem Tag, an dem *or* als; **at the time** ~ zu der Zeit, als *or* wo *(col)*; **during the time** ~ **he was in Germany** während der Zeit, als *or* wo *(col)* er in Deutschland war; **that's** ~ **it's important** genau dann ist es wichtig.

**2** *conj* **(a)** wenn; *(with past reference)* als. **you can go** ~ **I have finished** du kannst gehen, sobald *or* wenn ich fertig bin; ~ **I was in London** als ich in London war; **each time** ~ **I was in London** jedesmal, wenn ich in London war. **(b) be careful** ~ **crossing the road** seien Sie vorsichtig, wenn Sie über die Straße gehen; **the Prime Minister is coming here in May,** ~ **he'll** ... der Premier kommt im Mai hierher und wird dann ... **(c)** *(although, whereas)* wo ... doch. **why do you do it that way** ~ **it would be much easier like this?** warum machst du es denn auf die Art, wo es doch so viel einfacher wäre?

**whence** [wens] *adv (old)* woher.

**whenever** [wen'evər] *adv* **(a)** *(each time)* jedesmal wenn. **(b)** *(at whatever time)* wann (auch) immer; *(as soon as)* sobald. ~ **you like!** wann du willst! **(c)** *(emph)* ~ **can he have done it?** wann kann er das nur *or* wohl getan haben?

**where** [wɛər] **1** *adv* wo. ~ **(to)** wohin, wo ... hin; ~ **(from)** woher, wo ... her; ~ **are you going (to)?** wohin gehst du, wo gehst du hin?; ~ **to, sir?** wohin (wollen Sie) bitte?; ~ **are you from?** wo kommen Sie her?; **from** ~ **I'm sitting I can see the church** von meinem Platz aus kann ich die Kirche sehen; **from** ~ **I'm standing it looks like cheating** von meiner Warte aus ist das Mogelei; ~ **should we be if ...?** was wäre nur, wenn ...?

**2** *conj* wo; *(in the place where)* da, wo ..., an der Stelle, wo ... **go** ~ **you like** geh, wohin du willst;

**the bag is** ~ **you left it** die Tasche ist da, wo du sie liegengelassen hast; **this is** ~ **we got out** hier sind wir ausgestiegen; **that's** ~ **Nelson fell/I used to live** hier *or* an dieser Stelle fiel Nelson/hier *or* da habe ich (früher) gewohnt; **I've read up to** ~ **the king** ... ich habe bis dahin gelesen, wo der König ...; **we succeeded** ~ **we expected to fail** wir hatten da Erfolg, wo wir ihn nicht erwartet hatten; ~ **money is concerned** wo es ums Geld geht.

**whereabouts** [ˌwɛərə'baʊts] **1** *adv* wo, in welcher Gegend. **2** ['wɛərəbaʊts] *n sing or pl* Verbleib *m*; *(of people also)* Aufenthaltsort *m*.

**whereas** [wɛər'æz] *conj (whilst)* während; *(while on the other hand)* wohingegen.

**whereby** [wɛə'baɪ] *adv (form)* **the sign** ~ **you will recognize him** das Zeichen, an dem *or* woran Sie ihn erkennen; **the rule** ~ **it is not allowed** die Vorschrift, wonach es verboten ist.

**whereupon** [wɛərə'pɒn] *adv* worauf.

**wherever** [wɛər'evər] **1** *conj* ~ **it came from** egal, woher es kommt; woher es auch kommt; **we'll go** ~ **you like** wir gehen, wohin Sie wollen; ~ **you see this sign** überall, wo Sie dieses Zeichen sehen. **2** *adv* ~ **have I seen that before?** wo habe ich das nur *or* bloß schon gesehen?; **in London or Liverpool or** ~ in London oder Liverpool oder sonstwo.

**wherewithal** ['wɛəwɪðɔːl] *n (implements)* Utensilien *pl*. **the** ~ *(money)* das nötige Kleingeld.

**whet** [wet] *vt knife* wetzen; *axe* schleifen, schärfen; *appetite, curiosity* anregen.

**whether** ['weðər] *conj* ob. **I am not certain** ~ **or not they're coming** ich bin nicht sicher, ob sie kommen oder nicht; ~ **they come or not, we'll** ... ob sie kommen oder nicht, wir ...; **he's not sure** ~ **to go or stay** er weiß nicht, ob er gehen oder bleiben soll.

**whew** [hwuː] *interj* puh, uff.

**whey** [weɪ] *n* Molke *f*.

**which** [wɪtʃ] **1** *adj* **(a)** *(interrog)* welche(r, s). ~ **one?** welche(r, s)?; *(of people also)* wer? **(b)** *(rel)* welche(r, s). ... **by** ~ **time I was asleep** ... und zu dieser Zeit schlief ich bereits; **look at it** ~ **way you will** ... man kann es sehen, wie man will ...

**2** *pron* **(a)** *(interrog)* welche(r, s); *(of people also)* wer. ~ **of the children/books?** wer von den Kindern/welches Buch? ~ **is** ~? *(of people)* wer ist wer? *(of things)* welche(r, s) ist welche(r, s)? **(b)** *(rel)* der/die/das, welche(r, s) *(geh)*. **the bear** ~ **I saw** der Bär, den ich sah; **at** ~ **he remarked** ... worauf er bemerkte, ...; **it rained hard,** ~ **upset her** es regnete stark, was sie aufregte; **from** ~ **we deduce that** ... woraus wir ableiten, daß ...; **after** ~ **we went to bed** worauf *or* wonach wir zu Bett gingen; **the shelf on** ~ **I put it** das Brett, auf das *or* worauf ich es gelegt habe.

**whichever** [wɪtʃ'evər] **1** *adj* welche(r, s) auch immer; *(no matter which)* ganz gleich *or* egal welche(r, s). **2** *pron* welche(r, s) auch immer. ~ **(of you) has the most money** wer immer (von euch) das meiste Geld hat.

**whiff** [wɪf] *n (puff)* Zug *m*; *(wisp)* kleine Fahne, Wolke *f*; *(smell)* Hauch *m*; *(fig: trace)* Spur *f*. **to catch a** ~ **of sth** den Geruch von etw wahrnehmen.

**while** [waɪl] **1** *n* Weile *f*, Weilchen *nt (col)*. **for a** ~ (für) eine Weile, eine Zeitlang; *(a short moment)* (für) einen Moment; **a good** *or* **long** ~ eine ganze Weile *or* Zeitlang; **for/after quite a** ~ ziemlich lange/nach einer ziemlich langen Zeit; **a little** *or* **short** ~ ein Weilchen *(col)*, kurze Zeit; **it'll be ready in a short** ~ es wird bald fertig sein; **a little/long** ~ **ago** vor kurzem/vor längerer *or* langer Zeit; **some** ~ **ago** vor einiger Zeit; **all the** ~ die ganze Zeit

(über); **to be worth (one's)** ~ **to** ... sich (für jdn) lohnen, zu ...; **we'll make it worth your** ~ es soll Ihr Schaden nicht sein.
   **2** *conj* (**a**) während; *(as long as)* solange. **she fell asleep** ~ **reading** sie schlief beim Lesen ein. (**b**) *(although)* obwohl. ~ **there are difficulties, it is still worth the effort** trotz aller Schwierigkeiten lohnt es sich doch. (**c**) *(whereas)* während. **I always drink tea** ~ **she drinks coffee** ich bin Teetrinker, während sie Kaffeetrinkerin ist.
   ▶**while away** *vt sep time* sich *(dat)* vertreiben.
**whilst** [waɪlst] *conj* = **while 2**.
**whim** [wɪm] *n* Laune *f*. **her every** ~ jede ihrer Launen.
**whimper** ['wɪmpəʳ] **1** *n (of dog)* Winseln *nt no pl*; *(of person)* Wimmern *nt no pl*. **without a** ~ ohne einen (Klage)laut. **2** *vti (dog)* winseln; *(person)* wimmern.
**whimsical** ['wɪmzɪkəl] *adj* wunderlich; *look, remark* neckisch; *idea, tale* schnurrig.
**whine** [waɪn] **1** *n (of dog)* Jaulen, Heulen *nt no pl*; *(complaining cry)* Jammern, Gejammer *nt no pl*; *(of child)* Quengelei *f no pl*; *(of siren, jet engine)* Heulen *nt no pl*; *(of bullet)* Pfeifen *nt no pl*. **2** *vi (dog)* jaulen; *(person: speak, complain)* jammern, klagen; *(child)* quengeln; *(siren, jet engine)* heulen; *(bullet)* pfeifen. **don't come whining to me if** ... du brauchst mir nichts vorzujammern, wenn ...
**whinge** [wɪndʒ] *vi (col)* meckern *(col)*; *(baby)* plärren. **whinging child** knatschiges Kind.
**whinny** ['wɪnɪ] **1** *n* Wiehern *nt no pl*. **2** *vi* wiehern.
**whip** [wɪp] **1** *n* (**a**) *(Peitsche f; (riding ~)* Reitgerte *f*. (**b**) *(Parl) (person)* Fraktionsführer *m*; *(call)* Anordnung *f* des Fraktionsführers. **three-line** ~ Fraktionszwang *m*. (**c**) *(Cook)* Creme, Speise *f*. **2** *vt* (**a**) *(with whip) people* auspeitschen; *horse* peitschen; *(with stick etc)* schlagen. (**b**) *(Cook)* schlagen. (**c**) *(fig: move quickly)* **he** ~**ped the book off the desk** er schnappte sich *(dat)* das Buch vom Schreibtisch; **he** ~**ped his hand out of the way** er zog blitzschnell seine Hand weg; **he** ~**ped a gun out of his pocket** er zog rasch eine Pistole aus der Tasche. (**d**) *(col: steal)* mitgehen lassen *(col)*. **3** *vi* **he** ~**ped around when he heard** ... er fuhr herum, als er hörte ...; **he's just** ~**ped out for a minute** *(col)* er ist nur schnell mal rausgegangen *(col)*.
   ▶**whip up** *vt sep* (**a**) *(pick up)* schnappen. (**b**) *(set in motion) horses* antreiben; *(Cook) cream* schlagen; *mixture* verrühren; *(col: prepare quickly) meal* hinzaubern; *(fig: stir up) feeling* anheizen, entfachen; *support* finden; *audience, crowd* mitreißen.
**whip:** ~**cord** *n (rope)* Peitschenschnur *f*; *(fabric)* Whipcord *m*; ~ **hand** **to have the** ~ **hand (over sb)** (über jdn) die Oberhand haben; ~**lash** *n* (Peitschen)riemen *m*; *(Med)* Schleudertrauma *nt*.
**whipped cream** [ˌwɪpt'kriːm] *n* Schlagsahne *f*.
**whippet** ['wɪpɪt] *n* Whippet *m (eine Hundeart)*.
**whipping** ['wɪpɪŋ] *n (beating)* Tracht *f* Prügel; *(col: defeat)* Schlappe *f (col)*; *(fig: in debate etc)* Pleite *f (col)*.
**whipping:** ~ **boy** *n* Prügelknabe *m*; ~ **cream** *n* Schlagsahne *f*.
**whip-round** ['wɪpraʊnd] *n (esp Brit col)* **to have a** ~ den Hut herumgehen lassen.
**whirl** [wɜːl] **1** *n (spin)* Wirbeln *nt no pl*; *(of dust, water etc, also fig)* Wirbel *m*; *(of cream etc)* Tupfer *m*. **to give sb/sth a** ~ *(fig col: try out)* jdn/etw ausprobieren; **the social** ~ das gesellschaftliche Leben; **my head is in a** ~ mir schwirrt der Kopf. **2** *vt (make turn)* wirbeln. **to** ~ **sb/sth around** jdn/etw herumwirbeln. **3** *vi (spin)* wirbeln; *(water)* strudeln. **to** ~

**around** herumwirbeln; *(water)* strudeln; *(person: turn quickly)* herumfahren; **my head is** ~**ing** mir schwirrt der Kopf; **to** ~ **past** *(time)* verfliegen; *(countryside)* vorbeifliegen.
**whirlpool** ['wɜːlpuːl] *n* Strudel *m*.
**whirlwind** ['wɜːlwɪnd] *n* Wirbelwind *m*. **like a** ~ wie der Wirbelwind; **a** ~ **romance** eine stürmische Romanze.
**whirr** [wɜːʳ] **1** *n (of wings)* Schwirren *nt*; *(of wheels, machine) (quiet)* Surren *nt*; *(louder)* Dröhnen *nt*. **2** *vi see n* schwirren; surren; dröhnen.
**whisk** [wɪsk] **1** *n (Cook)* Schneebesen *m*; *(electric)* Rührgerät *nt*. **give the eggs a good** ~ schlagen Sie die Eier gut durch; **with a** ~ **of its tail** mit einem Schwanzschlag. **2** *vt (Brit Cook)* schlagen; *eggs* verquirlen. **to** ~ **the eggs into the mixture** die Eier in die Masse einrühren.
   ▶**whisk away** *vt sep* **the magician** ~**ed** ~ **the table-cloth** der Zauberer zog das Tischtuch schnell weg; **the kidnappers** ~**ed him** ~ die Entführer sausten mit ihm davon.
**whisker** ['wɪskəʳ] *n* Schnurrhaar *nt*; *(of person)* Barthaar *nt*. ~**s** *(moustache, Zool)* Schnurrbart *m*; *(side ~s)* Backenbart *m*. **to win/miss sth by a** ~ etw fast gewinnen/etw um Haaresbreite verpassen.
**whisky,** *(US, Ir)* **whiskey** ['wɪskɪ] *n* Whisky *m*. **two whiskies, please** zwei Whisky, bitte.
**whisper** ['wɪspəʳ] **1** *n* (**a**) Geflüster, Flüstern *nt no pl*; *(of wind)* Wispern *nt no pl*; *(mysterious)* Raunen *nt no pl*. **to speak in a** ~ im Flüsterton sprechen. (**b**) *(rumour)* Gerücht *nt*. **there are** ~**s (going around) that** ... es geht das Gerücht, daß ... **2** *vt* (**a**) flüstern, wispern. **to** ~ **sth to sb** jdm etw zuflüstern. (**b**) *(rumour)* **it's (being)** ~**ed that** ... es geht das Gerücht, daß ..., man munkelt, daß ... **3** *vi* flüstern, wispern *(also fig)*; *(wind)* säuseln; *(schoolchildren)* tuscheln. **to** ~ **to sb** jdm zuflüstern; mit jdm tuscheln.
**whispering** ['wɪspərɪŋ]: ~ **campaign** *n* Verleumdungskampagne *f*; ~ **gallery** *n* Flüstergalerie *f*.
**whist** [wɪst] *n* Whist *nt*.
**whistle** ['wɪsl] **1** *n* (**a**) *(sound)* Pfiff *m*; *(of wind)* Pfeifen *nt*; *(of kettle)* Pfeifton *m*. **to give a** ~ pfeifen. (**b**) *(instrument)* Pfeife *f*. **to blow a** ~ pfeifen; **to blow the** ~ **on sb/sth** *(fig col)* jdn verpfeifen *(col)*/über etw *(acc)* auspacken *(col)*; **they searched him but he was as clean as a** ~ *(col)* sie durchsuchten ihn, aber er war blitzsauber *(col)*; **it broke off as clean as a** ~ *(col)* es ist ganz glatt abgebrochen. **2** *vti* pfeifen. **the boys** ~**d at her** die Jungen pfiffen ihr nach; **the crowd** ~**d at the referee** die Menge pfiff den Schiedsrichter aus; **the referee** ~**d for a foul** der Schiedsrichter pfiff ein Foul; **he can** ~ **for it** *(col)* da kann er lange warten.
**whistle-stop** ['wɪslˌstɒp] *adj* ~ **tour** *(US Pol)* Wahlkampfreise *f*; *(fig)* Reise *f* mit Kurzaufenthalten an allen Orten.
**whistling kettle** ['wɪslɪŋ'ketl] *n* Pfeifkessel *m*.
**whit** [wɪt] *n* **not a** ~ keine Spur; *(of truth, common sense)* kein Gramm *or* Körnchen.
**Whit** [wɪt] *n (Brit) see* **Whitsun**.
**white** [waɪt] **1** *adj* weiß; *(with fear, anger etc)* blaß, kreidebleich. **to go** *or* **turn** ~ *(thing)* weiß werden; *(person)* bleich *or* blaß werden. **2** *n (colour)* Weiß *nt*; *(person)* Weiße(r) *mf*; *(of egg)* Eiweiß *nt*; *(of eye)* Weiße(s) *nt*. ~**s** *(household)* Weißwäsche *f*; *(Sport)* weiße Kleidung.
**white:** ~**bait** *n, pl* ~**bait** Breitling *m*; ~ **bread** *n* Weißbrot *nt*; ~ **coffee** *n (Brit)* Kaffee *m* mit Milch; ~**-collar** *adj* ~**-collar crime** Wirtschaftskriminalität *f*; ~**-collar job** Angestelltenstelle *f*, Büroposten *m*;

~-**collar worker** Angestellte(r) *mf*; ~ **elephant** *n* nutzloser Gegenstand; *(waste of money)* Fehlinvestition *f*; ~ **elephant stall** *n* Stand *m* mit allerlei Krimskrams; ~-**faced** *adj* kreidebleich; ~ **goods** *npl (Comm: linen)* Weißwaren *pl*; ~-**haired** *adj* weißhaarig; **W~hall** *n (Brit)* die Ministerien *pl*; ~ **horse** *n* Schimmel *m*; *(wave)* Welle *f* mit einer Schaumkrone; ~-**hot** *adj* weißglühend; *(fig)* glühend; **the W~ House** *n* das Weiße Haus; ~ **lie** *n* kleine Unwahrheit, Notlüge *f*; ~ **man** *n* Weiße(r) *m*; ~ **meat** *n* helles Fleisch.

**whiten** ['waɪtn] **1** *vt* weiß machen. **2** *vi* weiß werden.

**whiteness** ['waɪtnɪs] *n* Weiße *f*; *(of skin)* Helligkeit *f*; *(due to illness etc)* Blässe *f*.

**whitening** ['waɪtnɪŋ] *n* weiße Farbe, Schlämmkreide *f*.

**white:** ~ **noise** *n (Hifi, Rad)* weißes Rauschen; ~ **paper** *n (Pol)* Weißbuch *nt*; ~ **sauce** *n* Mehlsoße *f*, helle Soße; ~ **slave trade** *n* Mädchenhandel *m*; ~ **spirit** *n* Terpentinersatz *m*; ~ **stick** *n* Blindenstock *m*; ~**wash 1** *n* Tünche *f*; *(fig)* Schönfärberei *f*; **2** *vt walls* tünchen; *(fig)* beschönigen; ~ **water** *n* Wildwasser *nt*; ~ **wedding** *n* Hochzeit *f* in Weiß; ~ **wine** *n* Weißwein *m*; ~ **woman** *n* Weiße *f*.

**whither** ['wɪðəʳ] *adv* **(a)** *(old)* wohin. **(b)** *(journalese)* ~ **socialism?** Sozialismus, was nun?

**whiting** ['waɪtɪŋ] *n, pl* - Weißling, Weißfisch *m*.

**whitish** ['waɪtɪʃ] *adj colour* weißlich.

**Whit Monday** [,wɪt'mʌndɪ] *n* Pfingstmontag *m*.

**Whitsun** ['wɪtsən] **1** *n* Pfingsten *nt*. **2** *attr* Pfingst-.

**Whit Sunday** *n* Pfingstsonntag *m*.

**whittle** ['wɪtl] *vt* schnitzen.

▶**whittle away** *vt sep* **(a)** *bark etc* wegschneiden. **(b)** *(gradually reduce)* allmählich abbauen; *rights, power etc also* allmählich beschneiden.

▶**whittle down** *vt sep* **(a)** *piece of wood* herunterschneiden. **to** ~ ~ **to size** zurechtschneiden. **(b)** *(reduce)* kürzen, stutzen; *gap, difference* verringern. **to** ~ **sth** ~ **to sth** etw auf etw *(acc)* reduzieren; **to** ~ **sb** ~ **to size** *(fig)* jdn zurechtstutzen.

**whiz(z)** [wɪz] **1** *n* **(a)** *(of arrow)* Schwirren *nt*. **(b)** *(col)* Kanone *f (col)*. **2** *vi (of arrow)* schwirren. **the cars whizzed past** die Autos sausten vorbei.

**whiz(z)-kid** ['wɪz,kɪd] *n (col: in career)* Senkrechtstarter *m*. **financial** ~ Finanzgenie *nt*.

**WHO** = **World Health Organization** Weltgesundheitsorganisation *f*.

**who** [huː] *pron* **(a)** *(interrog)* wer; *(acc)* wen; *(dat)* wem. ~ **do you think you are?** was glaubst du, wer du bist?, für wen hältst du dich eigentlich?; ~ **are you looking for?** wen suchen Sie?; ~ **did you stay with?** bei wem haben Sie gewohnt?; **you'll soon find out** ~'**s** ~ Sie werden bald alle kennenlernen. **(b)** *(rel)* der/die/das, welche(r, s). **any man** ~ ... jeder (Mensch), der ...; **he** ~ **wishes/those** ~ **wish to go** ... wer gehen will ...

**who'd** [huːd] = **who had; who would.**

**whodun(n)it** [huː'dʌnɪt] *n (col)* Krimi *m*.

**whoever** [huː'evəʳ] *pron* wer (auch immer); *(acc)* wen (auch immer); *(dat)* wem (auch immer); *(no matter who)* ganz gleich wer/wen/wem. ~ **told you that?** wer hat dir das denn (bloß) gesagt?

**whole** [həʊl] **1** *adj* ganz; *truth* voll. **but the** ~ **purpose was to** ... aber der ganze Sinn der Sache war, daß ...; **three** ~ **weeks** drei volle *or* ganze Wochen; **the** ~ **lot** das Ganze; *(of people)* alle, der ganze Verein *(col)*; **a** ~ **lot of people** eine ganze Menge Leute; **a** ~ **lot better** *(col)* ein ganzes Stück besser; **not a cup was left** ~ nicht eine Tasse blieb heil; **she swallowed it** ~ sie schluckte es ganz (hinunter). **2**

*n* Ganze(s) *nt.* **the** ~ **of the month/London** der ganze Monat/ganz London; **nearly the** ~ **of our production** fast unsere gesamte Produktion; **as a** ~ als Ganzes; **on the** ~ im großen und ganzen, alles in allem.

**whole:** ~**foods** *npl* Vollwertkost *f*; ~**food shop** *n* Bioladen *m*; ~**hearted** *adj* völlig, uneingeschränkt; ~**hearted thanks to X** X *(dat)* danken wir von ganzem Herzen; ~**heartedly** *adv* voll und ganz; ~ **hog** *n*: **to go the** ~ **hog** *(col)* aufs Ganze gehen; ~**meal** *(Brit)* **1** *adj* Vollkorn-; **2** *n* feiner Vollkornschrot; ~ **milk** *n* Vollmilch *f*; ~ **note** *n (esp US Mus)* ganze Note; ~ **number** *n* ganze Zahl.

**wholesale** ['həʊlseɪl] **1** *n* Großhandel *m*. **2** *adj attr* **(a)** *(Comm)* Großhandels-. **(b)** *(fig: widespread)* umfassend, massiv; *slaughter, redundancies* Massen-; *(indiscriminate)* wild, generell. **3** *adv* **(a)** im Großhandel. **(b)** *(fig)* in Bausch und Bogen; *(in great numbers)* massenhaft; *(without modification)* (so) ohne weiteres.

**wholesaler** ['həʊlseɪləʳ] *n* Großhändler *m*.

**wholesome** ['həʊlsəm] *adj* gesund.

**wholewheat** ['həʊlwiːt] *n, adj (US)* = **wholemeal.**

**who'll** [huːl] = **who will; who shall.**

**wholly** ['həʊlɪ] *adv* völlig, gänzlich.

**whom** [huːm] *pron* **(a)** *(interrog) (acc)* wen; *(dat)* wem. **(b)** *(rel) (acc)* den/die/das; *(dat)* dem/der/dem. ..., **all of** ~ **were drunk** ..., die alle betrunken waren; **none/all of** ~ ... von denen keine(r, s)/alle ...

**whoop** [wuːp] **1** *n* Ruf, Schrei *m*. **2** *vi* rufen, schreien; *(with whooping cough)* pfeifen; *(with joy)* jauchzen.

**whoopee** [wʊ'piː] *interj* hurra, juchhe.

**whooping cough** ['huːpɪŋ,kɒf] *n* Keuchhusten *m*.

**whoops** [wuːps] *interj* hoppla.

**whoosh** [wuːʃ] **1** *n (of water)* Rauschen *nt*; *(of air)* Zischen *nt*. **2** *vi* rauschen; zischen.

**whopper** ['wɒpəʳ] *n (col) (sth big)* Brocken *m (col)*; *(lie)* faustdicke Lüge.

**whopping** ['wɒpɪŋ] *adj (col)* Mords- *(col)*, Riesen-; *lie* faustdick.

**whore** [hɔːʳ] *n* Hure *f*.

**whorl** [wɜːl] *n* Kringel *m*; *(of shell)* (Spiral)windung *f*.

**who's** [huːz] = **who has; who is.**

**whose** [huːz] *poss pron* **(a)** *(interrog)* wessen. ~ **is this?** wem gehört das?; ~ **car did you go in?** in wessen Auto sind Sie gefahren? **(b)** *(rel)* dessen; *(after f and pl)* deren. **the man** ~ **wife** ... der Mann, dessen Frau ...

**why** [waɪ] **1** *adv* warum, weshalb; *(asking for the purpose)* wozu; *(how come that ...)* wieso. ~ **not ask him?** warum fragst du/fragen wir *etc* ihn nicht?; ~ **ever** *or* **on earth not?** warum denn bloß nicht?; ~ **wait?** wozu (noch) warten?; ~ **do it this way?** warum denn so?; **that's** ~ darum, deswegen; **that's exactly** ~ ... genau deshalb *or* deswegen ... **2** *interj* **are you sure?** — ~ **yes** sind Sie sicher? — (aber) ja; ~ **that's easy!** na, das ist doch einfach!; **who did it?** ~ **it's obvious** wer das war? also, das ist doch klar. **3** *n*: **the** ~**s and (the) wherefores** das Warum und Weshalb.

**WI** = **(a) West Indies. (b)** *(US Post)* **Wisconsin. (c)** *(Brit)* **Women's Institute.**

**wick** [wɪk] *n* Docht *m*. **to get on sb's** ~ *(col)* jdm auf den Wecker gehen *(col)*.

**wicked** ['wɪkɪd] *adj person etc* böse; *(immoral)* schlecht, gottlos; *(indulging in vices)* lasterhaft; *(col: scandalous) price etc* unverschämt; *smile, look, grin* frech, boshaft; *satire* boshaft; *blow, frost also* gemein *(col)*. **that was a** ~ **thing to do** das war aber gemein (von dir/ihm *etc*); **he/the dog has a ~ temper** er ist unbeherrscht *or* aufbrausend/der Hund ist bösartig; **he has a ~ sense of humour** er hat einen boshaften Humor.

**wickedly** ['wɪkɪdlɪ] *adv see adj* böse; schlecht, gottlos; lasterhaft; unverschämt; boshaft.

**wickedness** ['wɪkɪdnɪs] *n (of person)* Schlechtigkeit *f*; *(immorality)* Verderbtheit *f*; *(indulgence in vices)* Lasterhaftigkeit *f*; *(of look etc)* Boshaftigkeit *f*; *(mischievousness)* Bosheit *f*.

**wicker** ['wɪkər] **1** *n* Korbgeflecht *nt*. **2** *adj attr* Korb-.

**wicker: ~ basket** *n* (Weiden)korb *m*; **~work** *n (material)* Korbgeflecht *nt*; *(articles)* Korbwaren *pl*; **~work furniture** *n* Korbmöbel *pl*.

**wicket** ['wɪkɪt] *n (Cricket) (stumps: also ~s)* Mal, Pfostentor *nt*; *(pitch)* Spielbahn *f*.

**wicket-keeper** ['wɪkɪt,ki:pər] *n (Cricket)* Torwächter *m*.

**wide** [waɪd] **1** *adj* **(a)** *road, smile* breit; *skirt, plain* weit; *eyes* groß. **it is three metres ~** es ist drei Meter breit; **the ~ screen** die Breitwand; **the big ~ world** die (große) weite Welt. **(b)** *variety* groß; *experience, choice* reich; *public, knowledge, range* breit; *interests* vielfältig; *coverage of report* umfassend; *network* weitverzweigt *attr*; *circulation* weit, groß; *question* weitreichend. **~ reading is the best education** die beste Bildung bekommt man, indem man viel liest; **his ~ reading** seine große Belesenheit. **(c)** *(missing the target)* daneben *pred*. **you're a bit ~ of the mark there** da liegst du etwas daneben; **~ of the truth** nicht ganz wahrheitsgetreu.

**2** *adv* **(a)** *(extending far)* weit. **they are set ~ apart** sie liegen weit auseinander. **(b)** *(fully)* weit. **open ~!** bitte weit öffnen; **~ open** *(door)* weit offen; **the law is ~ open to criticism** das Gesetz bietet viele Ansatzpunkte für Kritik; **the game is still ~ open** der Spielausgang ist noch völlig offen; **to be ~ awake** hellwach sein; *(alert)* wach sein. **(c)** *(far from the target)* daneben. **to go ~ of sth** an etw *(dat)* vorbeigehen.

**wide: ~-angle (lens)** *n (Phot)* Weitwinkel(objektiv *nt*) *m*; **~-awake** *adj (fully awake)* hellwach; *(alert)* wach; **~-eyed** *adj* mit großen Augen; **in ~-eyed amazement** mit großen, erstaunten Augen.

**widely** ['waɪdlɪ] *adv* weit; *(by or to many people)* weit und breit, allgemein; *differing* völlig. **the opinion is ~ held** ... es herrscht in weiten Kreisen die Ansicht ...; **it is ~ believed that** ... es wird allgemein angenommen, daß ...; **he became ~ known as** ... er wurde überall *or* in weiten Kreisen bekannt als ...; **a ~ read student** ein sehr belesener Student.

**widen** ['waɪdn] **1** *vt road* verbreitern; *passage, knowledge* erweitern. **2** *vi* breiter werden; *(interests etc)* sich ausweiten.

▶**widen out** *vi (valley etc)* sich erweitern *(into zu)*.

**wide: ~-open** *adj* weit offen; *beak* weit aufgerissen; **the ~-open spaces** die Weite *f*; **~-ranging** *adj* weitreichend; **~-spread** *adj* weitverbreitet *attr*; **to become ~spread** weite Verbreitung erlangen.

**widow** ['wɪdəʊ] **1** *n* Witwe *f*. **golf ~** *(hum)* Golfwitwe *f*. **2** *vt* zur Witwe/zum Witwer machen. **she was twice ~ed** sie ist zweimal verwitwet.

**widower** ['wɪdəʊər] *n* Witwer *m*.

**width** [wɪdθ] *n* Breite *f*; *(of trouser legs etc)* Weite *f*; *(of interests also)* Vielfalt *f*. **six centimetres in ~** sechs Zentimeter breit.

**widthways** ['wɪdθweɪz] *adv* der Breite nach.

**wield** [wi:ld] *vt pen, sword* führen; *axe* schwingen; *power* ausüben.

**wiener** ['wi:nər] *n (US)* Wiener Würstchen *nt*.

**wife** [waɪf] *n, pl* **wives** Frau, Gattin *(form) f*.

**wifely** ['waɪflɪ] *adj* **~ duties** Pflichten *pl* als Ehefrau; **~ devotion** Hingabe *f* einer Ehefrau.

**wife-swapping** ['waɪf,swɒpɪŋ] *n* Partnertausch *m*.

**wig** [wɪg] *n* Perücke *f*.

**wiggle** ['wɪgl] **1** *n* Wackeln *nt no pl*; *(in line)* Welle *f*. **give it a ~ and it might come free** wackeln Sie mal daran, dann löst es sich vielleicht. **2** *vt* wackeln mit. **3** *vi* wackeln.

**wiggly** ['wɪglɪ] *adj (+er)* wackelnd; *line* Schlangen-.

**wigwam** ['wɪgwæm] *n* Wigwam *m*.

**wild** [waɪld] **1** *adj* **(a)** *(not domesticated)* wild; *people* unzivilisiert; *garden, wood* verwildert; *flowers* wildwachsend *attr*. **the W~ West** der Wilde Westen; **~ animals** Tiere *pl* in freier Wildbahn; **the plant in its ~ state** die Pflanze im Naturzustand. **(b)** *(stormy) weather, wind, sea* rauh, stürmisch. **(c)** *(excited, riotous)* wild *(with* vor *+dat)*; *(disordered) hair also* wirr, unordentlich; *children also, desire* unbändig. **I'm not ~ about the idea** *(col)* auf die Idee bin ich nicht gerade versessen *(col)*; **to be ~ about sb** *(col)* verrückt nach jdm sein *(col)*; **the audience went ~** das Publikum raste. **(d)** *(col: angry)* wütend *(with, at* mit, auf *+acc)*, rasend. **it drives me ~** das macht mich ganz wild *or* rasend; **to get ~** wild werden *(col)*. **(e)** *(rash, extravagant)* verrückt; *exaggeration, allegation* maßlos, wild; *fluctuations* stark; *expectations* kühn; *shot* Fehl-. **never in my ~est dreams** auch in meinen kühnsten Träumen nicht.

**2** *adv grow* wild; *run* frei. **to let one's imagination run ~** seiner Phantasie *(dat)* freien Lauf lassen; **the roses/the children have run ~** die Rosen/die Kinder sind verwildert.

**3** *n* Wildnis *f*. **in the ~** in der Wildnis, in freier Wildbahn; **out in the ~s of Berkshire** *(hum)* im hintersten Berkshire.

**wild: ~ boar** *n* Wildschwein *nt*; **~ cat** *n (Zool)* Wildkatze *f*; **~cat strike** *n* wilder Streik.

**wilderness** ['wɪldənɪs] *n* Wildnis *f*; *(fig)* Wüste *f*.

**wild: ~fire** *n* **to spread like ~fire** sich wie ein Lauffeuer ausbreiten; **~fowl** *n no pl* Wildgeflügel *nt*; **~-goose chase** *n* fruchtloses Unterfangen; **to send sb out on a ~-goose chase** jdn für nichts und wieder nichts losschicken; **~ life** *n* die Tierwelt; **~life sanctuary** Wildreservat *nt*.

**wildly** ['waɪldlɪ] *adv* **(a)** wild. **(b)** *(in disorder)* wirr. **(c)** *(extravagantly) guess* drauflos, ins Blaue hinein; *talk* wirr; *exaggerated* stark, maßlos. **not ~ enthusiastic** nicht allzu begeistert.

**wildness** ['waɪldnɪs] *n* Wildheit *f*; *(of storm etc also)* Heftigkeit *f*; *(of allegation)* Maßlosigkeit *f*.

**wiles** [waɪlz] *npl* Schliche *pl*.

**wilful,** *(US)* **willful** ['wɪlfʊl] *adj* **(a)** *(self-willed)* eigenwillig. **(b)** *(deliberate) neglect, damage* mutwillig; *murder* vorsätzlich; *disobedience* wissentlich.

**will¹** [wɪl] *pret* **would 1** *modal aux* **(a)** *(forming future)* werden. **I'm sure that he ~ come** ich bin sicher, daß er kommt; **you ~ come to see us, won't you** Sie kommen uns doch besuchen, ja?; **I'll be right there** komme sofort!, bin gleich da!; **he'll be there — he won't** er wird dort sein — nein; **I ~ have finished by Tuesday** bis Dienstag bin ich fertig; **you won't lose it, ~ you?** du wirst es doch nicht verlieren, oder?

**(b)** *(emphatic)* **I ~ not have it!** das kommt nicht in Frage *(col)*; **~ you be quiet!** bist du *or* sei jetzt endlich ruhig!; **well, if you won't take advice** wenn du (eben) keinen Rat annimmst, na bitte; **he ~ interrupt all the time** er muß ständig dazwischenreden.

**(c)** *(expressing willingness, capability etc)* wollen. **he won't sign** er will nicht unterschreiben; **wait a moment, ~ you?** warten Sie bitte einen Moment;

*(impatiently)* jetzt warte doch mal einen Moment!; **the car won't start** das Auto springt nicht an; **the cut won't heal** die Schnittwunde will nicht (ver)heilen; **the car ~ do up to 120 mph** das Auto fährt bis zu 190 km/h.

**(d)** *(in questions)* **~ you have some more tea?** möchten Sie noch Tee?; **~ you accept these conditions?** akzeptieren Sie diese Bedingungen?

**(e)** *(assumption)* **he'll be there by now** jetzt ist er schon da *or* dürfte er schon da sein; **this ~ be our bus** das wird *or* dürfte unser Bus sein.

**(f)** *(tendency)* **sometimes he ~ sit in his room for hours** manchmal sitzt er stundenlang in seinem Zimmer; **accidents ~ happen** Unfälle passieren nun (ein)mal.

**2** *vi* wollen. **say what you ~** du kannst sagen, was du willst; **as you ~!** wie du willst!

**will²** **1** *n* **(a)** Wille *m.* **to have a ~ of one's own** (s)einen eigenen Willen haben; *(hum)* so seine Mucken haben *(col)*; **the ~ to win** der Wille, zu gewinnen; **(to go) against sb's ~** gegen jds Willen (handeln); **at ~** nach Belieben; **of one's own free ~** aus freien Stücken *or* freiem Willen; **with the best ~ in the world** beim (aller)besten Willen; **where there's a ~ there's a way** *(Prov)* wo ein Wille ist, ist auch ein Weg *(Prov)*. **(b)** *(testament)* Letzter Wille, Testament *nt.* **the last ~ and testament of ...** der Letzte Wille *or* das Testament des/der ...; **to make one's ~** sein Testament machen.

**2** *vt (urge by willpower)* (durch Willenskraft) erzwingen. **to ~ sb to do sth** jdn durch die eigene Willensanstrengung dazu bringen, daß er etw tut; **he ~ed himself to stay awake** er hat sich (dazu) gezwungen, wach zu bleiben; **he ~ed the ball into the net** er hat den Ball ins Netz hypnotisiert *(col)*; **the crowd were ~ing him on** das Publikum feuerte ihn an.

**willful** *(US) see* **wilful**.

**William** [ˈwɪljəm] *n* ≃ Wilhelm.

**willie** [ˈwɪlɪ] *n (hum: penis)* Pimmel *m (col)*.

**willies** [ˈwɪlɪz] *npl (col)* **it/he gives me the ~** da/bei ihm wird mir ganz anders *(col)*.

**willing** [ˈwɪlɪŋ] *adj* **(a)** *(prepared)* **to be ~ to do sth** bereit *or* gewillt *(geh)* sein, etw zu tun; **God ~** so Gott will; **he was ~ for me to take it** es war ihm recht, daß ich es nahm; **she was not ~ for us to go** sie war nicht gewillt, uns gehen zu lassen *(geh)*. **(b)** *workers, assistance* bereitwillig. **there were plenty of ~ hands** es gab viele, die helfen wollten; **to show ~** Bereitschaft zeigen.

**willingly** [ˈwɪlɪŋlɪ] *adv* bereitwillig, gerne. **will you help? — yes, ~** wollen Sie helfen? — (ja,) gerne.

**willingness** [ˈwɪlɪŋnɪs] *n see adj* **(a)** Bereitschaft *f.* **(b)** Bereitwilligkeit *f.*

**will-o'-the-wisp** [ˌwɪləðəˈwɪsp] *n* Irrlicht *nt*; *(fig)* Trugbild *nt.*

**willow** [ˈwɪləʊ] *n (also ~ tree)* Weide *f*; *(wood)* Weidenholz *nt.*

**willow pattern** *n* Weidenmotiv *nt (auf Porzellan)*.

**willowy** [ˈwɪləʊɪ] *adj* gertenschlank.

**willpower** [ˈwɪlˌpaʊəʳ] *n* Willenskraft *f.*

**willy-nilly** [ˈwɪlɪˈnɪlɪ] *adv* wohl oder übel; *(at random)* aufs Geratewohl.

**wilt** [wɪlt] *vi* **(a)** *(flowers)* welken, verwelken. **(b)** *(person: after exercise)* schlapp werden; *(enthusiasm, energy)* abflauen.

**Wilts** [wɪlts] *(Brit)* = **Wiltshire**.

**wily** [ˈwaɪlɪ] *adj (+er)* schlau, hinterlistig *(pej)*.

**wimp** [wɪmp] *n (col)* Schlappschwanz *m (col)*.

▶**wimp out** *vi (inf)* kneifen *(inf)*. **to ~ ~ of sth** bei etw kneifen.

**wimpish** [ˈwɪmpɪʃ] *adj (col)* weichlich, schlapp *(col)*.

**win** [wɪn] *(vb: pret, ptp* **won)** **1** *n* Sieg *m.* **to have a ~** *(money)* einen Gewinn machen; *(victory)* einen Sieg erzielen. **2** *vt* gewinnen; *reputation* erwerben; *scholarship, contract* bekommen; *victory* erringen. **land won from the sea** dem Meer abgewonnenes Land. **3** *vi* gewinnen, siegen. **OK, you ~, I was wrong** okay, du hast recht, ich habe mich geirrt.

▶**win back** *vt sep* zurück- *or* wiedergewinnen.

▶**win over** *or* **round** *vt sep* für sich gewinnen. **to ~ sb ~ to one's way of thinking** jdn überzeugen.

▶**win through** *vi (patient)* durchkommen. **we'll ~ ~ in the end** wir werden es schon schaffen *(col)*.

**wince** [wɪns] **1** *n* **to give a ~ (of pain)** (vor Schmerz) zusammenzucken. **2** *vi* zusammenzucken *(at bei)*.

**winch** [wɪntʃ] **1** *n* Winde *f.* **2** *vt* winden. **to ~ sth up** etw hochwinden.

**wind¹** [wɪnd] **1** *n* **(a)** Wind *m.* **the ~ is from the east** der Wind kommt von Osten; **(to run) like the ~** (rennen) wie der Wind; **a ~ of change** *(fig)* ein frischer Wind; **there's something in the ~** (irgend) etwas liegt in der Luft; **to see which way the ~ blows** *(fig)* sehen, woher der Wind weht; **to take the ~ out of sb's sails** *(fig)* jdm den Wind aus den Segeln nehmen; **to get ~ of sth** von etw Wind bekommen; **to throw caution to the ~s** Bedenken in den Wind schlagen; **to sail close to the ~** *(fig)* sich hart an der Grenze des Erlaubten bewegen.

**(b)** *(Med)* Blähungen *pl.* **to break ~** einen Wind entweichen lassen; **to get/have the ~ up** *(col) (nervous)* Angst *or* Schiß *(col)* kriegen/haben; **to put the ~ up sb** *(col)* jdm Angst machen.

**(c)** *(breath)* Atem *m*, Luft *f (col)*. **to be short of ~** außer Atem sein; **to get one's ~ back** wieder zu Atem kommen.

**(d)** *(Mus: ~ instruments)* Bläser *pl.*

**2** *vt (knock breathless)* den Atem nehmen *(+dat)*.

**wind²** [waɪnd] *(vb: pret, ptp* **wound) 1** *vt* **(a)** *wool, bandage* wickeln; *(once round)* winden; *(on to a reel)* spulen. **(b)** *handle* drehen; *clock etc* aufziehen. **(c) to ~ one's way** sich schlängeln. **2** *vi (river etc)* sich winden *or* schlängeln.

▶**wind down** *vt sep* **(a)** *car windows etc* herunterkurbeln. **(b)** *operations* reduzieren; *production* zurückschrauben.

▶**wind in** *vt sep fish* einholen; *rope* aufspulen.

▶**wind on** *vt sep film, tape* weiterspulen.

▶**wind up 1** *vt sep* **(a)** *bucket* heraufholen; *car window* hinaufkurbeln. **(b)** *clock* aufziehen. **to be wound ~ about sth** *(fig)* sich über etw *(acc)* aufregen. **(c)** *meeting, speech* beschließen, zu Ende bringen. **(d)** *company* auflösen; *service, series* auslaufen lassen. **2** *vi* **(a)** *(col: end up)* enden. **to ~ ~ in hospital** im Krankenhaus landen. **(b) to ~ ~ for the government** die abschließende Rede für die Regierung halten. **(c)** *(road)* sich hinaufschlängeln.

**wind** [ˈwɪnd-]: **~bag** *n (col)* Schaumschläger *m (col)*; **~blown** *adj* windzerzaust; **~break** *n* Windschutz *m*; **~breaker** ® *(US)*, **~cheater** *(Brit) n* Windjacke *f*; **~-chill factor** *n* Wind-Kälte-Faktor *m.*

**winder** [ˈwaɪndəʳ] *n (of watch)* Rädchen *nt*; *(of alarm clock, toy etc)* Aufziehschraube *f.*

**wind:** [ˈwɪnd-] **~fall** *n* Stück *nt* Fallobst; *(fig)* unverhoffter Glücksfall; **~falls** Fallobst *nt*; **~ farm** *n* Windpark *m.*

**winding** [ˈwaɪndɪŋ] **1** *adj river* gewunden; *road also* kurvenreich. **2** *n (Elec)* Wicklung *f.*

**winding:** **~ shaft** *n* Förderschacht *m*; **~ tower** *n* Förderturm *m.*

**wind instrument** [ˈwɪnd-] *n* Blasinstrument *nt.*

**windlass** ['wɪndləs] *n (winch)* Winde *f*; *(Naut)* Ankerwinde *f.*

**wind** ['wɪnd-]: **~less** *adj* windstill; **~mill** *n* Windmühle *f.*

**window** ['wɪndəʊ] *n (also Comp)* Fenster *nt*; *(shop ~)* (Schau)fenster *nt*; *(of bank etc)* Schalter *m.* **a ~ on the world** *(fig)* ein Fenster zur Welt.

**window:** **~ box** *n* Blumenkasten *m*; **~-cleaner** *n* Fensterputzer *m*; **~-dressing** *n* Schaufensterdekoration *f*; *(fig)* Schau *(col)*, Augenwischerei *(pej) f*; **~ envelope** *n* Fensterumschlag *m*; **~ frame** *n* Fensterrahmen *m*; **~ ledge** *n* = **~sill**; **~ pane** *n* Fensterscheibe *f*; **~ seat** *n (in house)* Fensterbank *f or* -sitz *m*; *(Rail etc)* Fensterplatz *m*; **~-shopping** *n* Schaufensterbummel *m*; **to go ~-shopping** einen Schaufensterbummel machen; **~sill** *n* Fensterbank *f.*

**wind** ['wɪnd-]: **~pipe** *n* Luftröhre *f*; **~screen**, *(US)* **~shield** *n* Windschutzscheibe *f*; **~screen** *or (US)* **~shield washer** *n* Scheibenwaschanlage *f*; **~· screen** *or (US)* **~shield wiper** *n* Scheibenwischer *m*; **~sock** *n* Luft- *or* Windsack *m*; **~surfer** *n* Windsurfer(in *f*) *m*; **~surfing** *n* Windsurfen *nt*; **~swept** *adj plains etc* über den/die/das der Wind fegt; *person, hair* (vom Wind) zerzaust; **~-tunnel** *n* Windkanal *m.*

**windward** ['wɪndwəd] **1** *adj side* Wind-; *direction* zum Wind. **2** *n* Windseite *f.* **to ~ of the island** auf der Windseite der Insel.

**windy** ['wɪndɪ] *adj (+er)* windig.

**wine** [waɪn] **1** *n* Wein *m.* **2** *vt* **to ~ and dine sb** jdn in großem Stil zum Essen ausführen; *(at home)* jdn in großem Stil bewirten.

**wine:** **~ bar** *n* Weinstube *f*; **~ bottle** *n* Weinflasche *f*; **~ box** *n* Zapfpack *m*; **~ cellar** *n* Weinkeller *m*; **~glass** *n* Weinglas *nt*; **~-grower** *n* Winzer, Weinbauer *m*; **~-growing** *n* Weinanbau *m*; **~-growing area** *n* Weingegend *f*; **~ list** *n* Weinkarte *f*; **~ merchant** *n* Weinhändler *m*; **~-taster** *n* Weinprüfer *m*; **~-tasting** *n* Weinprobe *f*; **~ waiter** *n* Weinkellner *m.*

**wing** [wɪŋ] *n* **(a)** *(of bird, plane, building, Mil, Pol, Sport)* Flügel *m*; *(Brit Aut)* Kotflügel *m.* **on the ~** im Flug(e); **to take sb under one's ~** *(fig)* jdn unter seine Fittiche nehmen; **to spread one's ~s** *(fig: young people)* flügge werden. **(b)** **~s** *pl (Theat)* Kulisse *f*; **to wait in the ~s** *(lit, fig)* in den Kulissen warten.

**wing:** **~ chair** *n* Ohrensessel *m*; **~-commander** *n (Brit)* Oberstleutnant *m* (der Luftwaffe).

**winger** ['wɪŋə'] *n (Sport)* Flügelspieler(in *f*) *m.*

**wing:** **~mirror** *n* Außenspiegel *m*; **~ nut** *n* Flügelmutter *f*; **~-span, ~spread** *n* Flügelspannweite *f.*

**wink** [wɪŋk] **1** *n (with eye)* Zwinkern, Blinzeln *nt.* **to give sb a ~** jdm zuzwinkern; **to tip sb the ~** *(col)* jdm einen Wink geben; **I didn't sleep a ~** ich habe kein Auge zugetan. **2** *vi (meaningfully)* zwinkern, blinzeln; *(light, star etc)* blinken, funkeln. **to ~ at sb** jdm zuzwinkern.

**winker** ['wɪŋkə'] *n (Brit Aut col)* Blinker *m.*

**winkle** ['wɪŋkl] **1** *n* Strandschnecke *f.* **2** *vt* **to ~ a secret out of sb** jdm ein Geheimnis entlocken.

**winner** ['wɪnə'] *n (in race, competition)* Sieger(in *f*) *m*; *(of bet, pools etc)* Gewinner(in *f*) *m*; *(col: sth successful)* Renner *(col)*, Erfolg *m.* **to be onto a ~** *(col)* das große Los gezogen haben *(col)*.

**winning** ['wɪnɪŋ] **1** *adj (a) person, entry* der/die gewinnt; *horse, team* siegreich; *goal* Sieges-; *point, stroke* entscheidend. **~ number** Gewinnzahl *f*; **~ ticket** Gewinnlos *nt*; **the ~ time** die beste Zeit; **~ post** Zielpfosten *m.* **(b)** *(charming)* smile, ways ge-

winnend, einnehmend. **2** *n* **~s** *pl* Gewinn *m.*

**winsome** ['wɪnsəm] *adj girl* reizend; *ways, smile* gewinnend, einnehmend.

**winter** ['wɪntə'] **1** *n (lit, fig)* Winter *m.* **2** *adj attr* Winter-. **~ coat** Wintermantel *m*; *(of animal)* Winterfell *nt*; **~ sports** Wintersport *m*; **~time** Winter *m*; *(for clocks)* Winterzeit *f.*

**winterize** ['wɪntəraɪz] *vt (esp US)* winterfest machen.

**wint(e)ry** ['wɪnt(ə)rɪ] *adj* winterlich; *(fig) look* eisig. **~ showers** Schneeregen *m.*

**wipe** [waɪp] **1** *n* Wischen *nt.* **to give sth a ~** etw abwischen. **2** *vt* wischen; *floor* aufwischen; *hands, feet* abwischen, abputzen; *(erase) tape, recording* löschen. **to ~ sb/sth clean** jdn/etw abwischen; **to ~ sth with/on a cloth** etw mit/an einem Tuch abwischen; **to ~ one's brow/nose** sich *(dat)* die Stirn abwischen/die Nase putzen; **to ~ one's feet** sich *(dat)* die Füße abwischen; **to ~ the tears from one's eyes** sich *(dat)* die Tränen aus den Augen wischen; **to ~ the floor with sb** *(fig col)* jdn fertigmachen *(col)*.

▶**wipe away** *vt sep (lit, fig)* wegwischen.

▶**wipe off** *vt sep mark* weg- *or* abwischen. **to be ~d ~ the face of the earth** von der Erdoberfläche verschwinden.

▶**wipe out** *vt sep* **(a)** *(clean)* auswischen. **(b)** *(erase)* (aus)löschen; *guilt* verschwinden lassen. **(c)** *(cancel) debt* bereinigen; *gain* zunichte machen. **(d)** *(destroy) disease, village* ausrotten; *enemy* aufreiben.

▶**wipe up 1** *vt sep liquid, mess* aufwischen; *dishes* abtrocknen. **2** *vi* abtrocknen.

**wiper** ['waɪpə'] *n* (Scheiben)wischer *m.* **~ blade** Wischerblatt *nt.*

**wiping-up** ['waɪpɪŋ'ʌp] *n* **to do the ~** abtrocknen.

**wire** [waɪə'] **1** *n* **(a)** Draht *m*; *(cable, on appliance)* Leitung *f*; *(in circus: high ~)* (Hoch)seil *nt.* **you've got your ~s crossed there** *(col)* Sie verwechseln da etwas; **to get in under the ~** *(US col)* etwas gerade (eben) noch rechtzeitig schaffen. **(b)** *(Telec)* Telegramm *nt.* **2** *vt* **(a)** *(put in wiring) house* die (elektrischen) Leitungen verlegen in *(+dat)*; *(connect to electricity)* (an das Stromnetz) anschließen. **(b)** *(Telec)* telegrafieren. **(c)** *(fix with ~)* mit Draht zusammenbinden.

▶**wire up** *vt sep lights, battery, speakers* anschließen; *house* elektrische Leitungen verlegen in *(+dat)*.

**wire:** **~ brush** *n* Drahtbürste *f*; **~-cutters** *npl* Drahtschere *f*; **~-haired** *adj terrier* Drahthaar-.

**wireless** ['waɪəlɪs] *(esp Brit dated) n* **(a)** *(also ~ set)* Radio, Rundfunkgerät *nt.* **(b)** *(radio)* Rundfunk *m*; *(also ~ telegraphy)* drahtlose Telegrafie.

**wire:** **~ mesh, ~ netting** *n* Maschendraht *m*; **~-pulling** *n (col)* Drahtziehen *nt*; **~ rope** *n* Drahtseil *nt*; **~ stripper** *n* Abisolierzange *f*; **~-tapping** *n* Abhören *nt*, Anzapfen *nt* von Leitungen; **~ wheel** *n (Aut)* Drahtspeichenrad *nt.*

**wiring** ['waɪərɪŋ] *n* elektrische Leitungen *pl.*

**wiring diagram** *n* Schaltplan *m.*

**wiry** ['waɪərɪ] *adj (+er)* drahtig; *hair also* borstig.

**wisdom** ['wɪzdəm] *n* Weisheit *f*; *(prudence)* Einsicht *f.*

**wisdom tooth** *n* Weisheitszahn *m.*

**wise** [waɪz] *adj (+er)* weise; *move etc* klug, vernünftig; *(col: smart)* klug, schlau. **a ~ choice** eine kluge *or* gute Wahl; **the Three W~ Men** die drei Weisen; **he's always ~ after the event** hinterher spielt er immer den Schlauen; **I'm none the ~r** *(col)* ich bin nicht klüger als zuvor; **nobody will be any the ~r**

*(col)* niemand wird etwas (davon) merken; **to get** ~ **to sb/sth** *(col)* dahinterkommen, wie jd/etw ist; **to put sb** ~ **to sb/sth** *(col)* jdn über jdn/etw aufklären.

**wise:** ~**crack** *(esp US)* n Witzelei f; *(pej)* Stichelei f; ~**guy** n *(esp US col)* Klugschwätzer *(col)*, Klugscheißer *(col!)* m.

**wisely** ['waɪzlɪ] *adv* weise; *(sensibly)* klugerweise.

**wish** [wɪʃ] **1** n (a) Wunsch m *(for* nach). **your** ~ **is my command** dein Wunsch ist mir Befehl; **I have no great** ~ **to see him** ich habe keine große Lust, ihn zu sehen; **to make a** ~ sich *(dat)* etwas wünschen; **you shall have your** ~ dein Wunsch soll in Erfüllung gehen. (b) ~**es** *pl (in greetings)* **with best** ~**es** mit den besten Grüßen; **please give him my good** ~**es** bitte grüßen Sie ihn (vielmals) von mir.

**2** vt wünschen. **he** ~**es to be alone** er möchte allein sein; **I** ~ **you to be present** ich wünsche, daß Sie anwesend sind; **do you** ~ **more coffee, sir?** *(Scot, form)* hätten Sie gern noch Kaffee?; ~ **you were here** ich wünschte, du wärest hier; ~ **he'd be quiet** ich wollte *or* wünschte, er wäre still; **to** ~ **sb well/ ill** jdm Glück *or* alles Gute/Schlechte wünschen; **to** ~ **sb a pleasant journey/a happy Christmas** jdm eine gute Reise/frohe Weihnachten wünschen; **he** ~**ed himself anywhere but there** er wünschte sich nur möglichst weit weg.

**3** vi *(make a wish)* sich *(dat)* etwas wünschen.

▶**wish for** vi +prep obj **to** ~ ~ **sth** sich *(dat)* etw wünschen; **she had everything she could** ~ ~ sie hatte alles, was man sich nur wünschen kann.

**wishbone** ['wɪʃbəʊn] n Gabelbein nt.

**wishful** ['wɪʃfʊl] *adj* **that's just** ~ **thinking** das ist reines Wunschdenken.

**wishing well** ['wɪʃɪŋˌwel] n Wunschbrunnen m.

**wishy-washy** ['wɪʃɪˌwɒʃɪ] *adj* soup labberig *(col)*, wäßrig; *person* farblos, lasch; *colour* verwaschen; *argument* schwach *(col)*; *story* ungenau, wischiwaschi *pred (col)*.

**wisp** [wɪsp] n *(of straw, hair etc)* kleines Büschel; *(of cloud)* Fetzen m; *(of smoke)* Wölkchen nt.

**wisteria** [wɪsˈtɪərɪə] n Glyzinie f.

**wistful** ['wɪstfʊl] *adj* wehmütig; *song also* schwermütig.

**wit** [wɪt] n (a) *(understanding)* Verstand m. **a battle of** ~**s** ein geistiges Kräftemessen; **to be at one's** ~**s' end** am Ende seiner Weisheit sein, mit seinem Latein am Ende sein *(hum col)*; **to scare sb out of his** ~**s** jdn zu Tode erschrecken; **to keep one's** ~**s about one** seine (fünf) Sinne beisammenhalten, einen klaren Kopf behalten; **to live by one's** ~**s** sich schlau durchs Leben schlagen. (b) *(humour)* Geist, Witz m. **full of** ~ geistreich; **there's a lot of** ~ **in the book** das Buch ist sehr geistreich. (c) *(person)* geistreicher Kopf.

**witch** [wɪtʃ] n *(lit, fig)* Hexe f.

**witch:** ~**craft** n Hexerei, Zauberei f; ~ **doctor** n Medizinmann m.

**witch-hunt** ['wɪtʃˌhʌnt] n *(lit, fig)* Hexenjagd f.

**with** [wɪð, wɪθ] *prep* (a) mit. **are you pleased** ~ **it?** bist du damit zufrieden?; **bring a book** ~ **you** bring ein Buch mit; ~ **no ... ohne ...; put it** ~ **the rest** leg es zu den anderen; **how are things** ~ **you?** wie geht's?

(b) *(at house of, in company of etc)* bei. **I'll be** ~ **you in a moment** einen Augenblick bitte, ich bin gleich da; **10 years** ~ **the company** 10 Jahre bei *or* in der Firma.

(c) *(on person, in bag etc)* bei. **I haven't got my cheque book** ~ **me** ich habe mein Scheckbuch nicht dabei *or* bei mir.

(d) *(cause)* vor *(+dat)*. **to shiver** ~ **cold** vor Kälte zittern; **the hills are white** ~ **snow** die Berge sind weiß vom Schnee; **to be ill** ~ **measles** die Masern haben.

(e) *(in the case of)* bei, mit. **it's always the same** ~ **you** es ist (doch) immer dasselbe mit dir; **the trouble** ~ **him is that he ...** die Schwierigkeit bei *or* mit ihm ist (die), daß er ...; **I cannot concentrate** ~ **all this noise going on** bei diesem Lärm kann ich mich nicht konzentrieren; ~ **the window open** bei offenem Fenster; ~ **her being ill** (jetzt,) wo sie krank ist/war; **it varies** ~ **the temperature** es verändert sich je nach Temperatur; **wine improves** ~ **age** Wein wird mit zunehmendem Alter immer besser; ~ **all his faults** bei allen seinen Fehlern, trotz aller seiner Fehler.

(f) *(expressing agreement, comprehension)* **I'm** ~ **you there** *(col)* da stimme ich dir zu; **are you** ~ **me?** verstehen Sie?, kapierst du? *(col)*.

**withdraw** [wɪðˈdrɔː] pret **withdrew**, ptp **withdrawn 1** vt *object, motion, charge* zurückziehen; *troops, team also* abziehen; *ambassador* zurückbeordern; *coins* einziehen, aus dem Verkehr ziehen; *(from bank)* money abheben; *words, comment* zurücknehmen, widerrufen; *privileges* entziehen. **the workers withdrew their labour** die Arbeiter legten ihre Arbeit nieder. **2** vi sich zurückziehen; *(Sport also)* zurücktreten *(from* von), nicht antreten *(from* von/bei*)*; *(move away)* zurücktreten *or* -gehen. **to** ~ **in favour of sb else** zu Gunsten eines anderen zurücktreten; **to** ~ **into oneself** sich in sich *(acc)* zurückziehen.

**withdrawal** [wɪðˈdrɔːəl] n *(of objects, charge)* Zurückziehen nt; *(of ambassador)* Abziehen nt; *(of coins)* Einziehen nt; *(of money)* Abheben nt; *(of words)* Zurücknahme f; *(of troops)* Rückzug m; *(from drugs)* Entzug m. **to make a** ~ **from the bank** Geld von der Bank abheben.

**withdrawal:** ~ **slip** n Auszahlungsschein m; ~ **symptoms** npl Entzugserscheinungen pl.

**withdrawn** [wɪðˈdrɔːn] **1** ptp of **withdraw. 2** adj *person* verschlossen; *manner also* zurückhaltend.

**withdrew** [wɪðˈdruː] pret of **withdraw.**

**wither** ['wɪðər] vi (a) verdorren, ausdorren; *(limb)* verkümmern. (b) *(fig)* welken; *(religion)* dahinschwinden.

**withered** ['wɪðəd] *adj* plant verdorrt, vertrocknet; *skin, person* verschrumpelt; *limb* verkümmert.

**withering** ['wɪðərɪŋ] *adj* look vernichtend.

**withhold** [wɪðˈhəʊld] pret, ptp **withheld** [wɪðˈheld] vt vorenthalten; *truth also* verschweigen; *(refuse)* consent, help verweigern, versagen *(geh)*. **to** ~ **sth from sb** jdm etw vorenthalten/verschweigen/verweigern; ~**ing tax** *(US)* (vom Arbeitgeber) einbehaltene Steuer.

**within** [wɪðˈɪn] *prep* innerhalb *(+gen)*; *(temporal also)* binnen *(+dat)*. **a voice** ~ **him** seine innere Stimme; **we were/came** ~ **100 metres of the summit** wir waren auf den letzten 100 Metern vor dem Gipfel/wir kamen bis auf 100 Meter an den Gipfel heran; **accurate to** ~ **10 mm** auf 10 mm genau; ~ **his power** in seiner Macht; **to keep** ~ **the law** sich im Rahmen des Gesetzes bewegen; **to live** ~ **one's income** im Rahmen seiner finanziellen Möglichkeiten leben.

**with it** ['wɪðɪt] *adj (col)* (a) *(attr* with-it*)* *(trendy)* person up to date; *clothes etc* in *(col)*. (b) pred *(awake, alert)* **to be** ~ da sein *(col)*.

**without** [wɪðˈaʊt] *prep* ohne. ~ **a tie** ohne Krawatte; ~ **speaking** ohne zu sprechen, wortlos; ~ **my noticing it** ohne daß ich es bemerke/bemerkte; **he left**

~ **telling us** er ging, ohne es uns zu sagen.
**with-profits** ['wɪð,prɒfɪts] *adj policy etc* mit Gewinnbeteiligung.
**withstand** [wɪð'stænd] *pret, ptp* **withstood**
[wɪð'stʊd] *vt cold* standhalten *(+dat); climate, attack
also* trotzen *(+dat); persuasion etc* widerstehen
*(+dat).*
**witless** ['wɪtlɪs] *adj* schwachsinnig; *(stupid)* dumm.
**to be scared** ~ zu Tode erschrocken sein.
**witness** ['wɪtnɪs] **1** *n* **(a)** *(person: Jur, fig)* Zeuge *m,*
Zeugin *f.* ~ **for the defence/prosecution** Zeuge/
Zeugin der Verteidigung/Anklage; **to call sb as a** ~
jdn als Zeugen vorladen. **(b)** *(evidence)* Zeugnis *nt.*
**to give** ~ **for/against sb** für/gegen jdn aussagen; **to
bear** ~ **to sth** *(lit, fig)* Zeugnis über etw *(acc)* ablegen. **2** *vt* **(a)** *(see) accident* Zeuge sein bei *or
(+gen); scenes also* (mit)erleben; *changes* erleben.
**(b)** *(testify)* bezeugen; *(attest by signature)* bestätigen. **3** *vi (testify)* **to** ~ **to sth** etw bezeugen.
**witness box** *or (US)* **stand** *n* Zeugenstand *m.*
**witter** ['wɪtər] *vi (col: also* ~ **on)** labern *(col).*
**witticism** ['wɪtɪsɪzəm] *n* geistreiche Bemerkung.
**wittily** ['wɪtɪlɪ] *adv* witzig, geistreich.
**wittiness** ['wɪtɪnɪs] *n* Witzigkeit *f.*
**wittingly** ['wɪtɪŋlɪ] *adv* bewußt, wissentlich.
**witty** ['wɪtɪ] *adj (+er)* witzig, geistreich.
**wives** [waɪvz] *pl of* **wife.**
**wizard** ['wɪzəd] *n* Zauberer, Hexenmeister *m; (col)*
Genie *nt.* **a financial** ~ ein Finanzgenie *nt.*
**wizardry** ['wɪzədrɪ] *n* Hexerei, Zauberei *f; (great
skill)* Zauberkünste *pl.*
**wizened** ['wɪznd] *adj* verhutzelt, verschrumpelt.
**wk** = **week** Wo.
**Wm** = **William.**
**WO** = **Warrant Officer.**
**w/o** = **without.**
**wobble** ['wɒbl] **1** *n* Wackeln *nt.* **the chair has a** ~
der Stuhl wackelt. **2** *vi* wackeln; *(cyclist)* schwanken; *(voice, hand, compass needle)* zittern; *(wheel)*
eiern *(col); (chin, jelly etc)* wabbeln.
**wobbly** ['wɒblɪ] **1** *adj (+er)* wackelig; *voice also,
hand* zitterig, zitternd; *jelly* wabbelig; *wheel* eiernd
*(col).* **to be** ~ *(col: after illness)* wackelig auf den
Beinen sein *(col).* **2** *n (col: agitation or anger)* **to
throw a** ~ ausrasten *(col).*
**woe** [wəʊ] *n* **(a)** *(liter, hum: sorrow)* Jammer *m.* ~
**betide him who ...!** wehe dem, der ...! **(b)** *(esp pl:
trouble)* Kummer *m.* **to tell sb one's** ~**s** jdm sein
Leid klagen.
**woebegone** ['wəʊbɪ,gɒn] *adj* kläglich, jämmerlich.
**woeful** ['wəʊfʊl] *adj (sad)* traurig; *neglect also, ignorance* beklagenswert.
**wog** [wɒg] *n (Brit pej col!)* Kaffer *m (pej col).*
**woke** [wəʊk] *pret of* **wake.**
**woken** ['wəʊkn] *ptp of* **wake.**
**wolf** [wʊlf] **1** *n, pl* **wolves** Wolf *m; (col: womanizer)*
Don Juan *m.* **a** ~ **in sheep's clothing** ein Wolf im
Schafspelz; **to cry** ~ blinden Alarm schlagen; **to
keep the** ~ **from the door** sich über Wasser halten.
**2** *vt (also* ~ **down)** *food* hinunterschlingen.
**wolf-whistle** ['wʊlf,wɪsl] *n* **they gave her a** ~ sie
pfiffen ihr nach.
**wolves** [wʊlvz] *pl of* **wolf.**
**woman** ['wʊmən] **1** *n, pl* **women** Frau *f; (domestic
help)* (Haushalts)hilfe *f; (mistress)* Geliebte *f.* **2** *adj
attr* ~ **doctor** Ärztin *f;* ~ **driver** Frau *f* am Steuer; ~
**friend** Freundin *f.*
**womanhood** ['wʊmənhʊd] *n (state, quality)* Weiblichkeit *f.* **to reach** ~ (zur) Frau werden.
**womanize** ['wʊmənaɪz] *vi* hinter den Frauen her
sein.

**womanizer** ['wʊmənaɪzər] *n* Schürzenjäger *m.*
**womanly** ['wʊmənlɪ] *adj figure, person* fraulich;
*qualities* weiblich.
**womb** [wuːm] *n* Mutterleib *m,* Gebärmutter *f (Med);
(fig)* Schoß *m.*
**women** ['wɪmɪn] *pl of* **woman.**
**womenfolk** ['wɪmɪnfəʊk] *npl* Frauen *pl.*
**women's** ['wɪmɪnz] *in cpds* Frauen-; ~ **hurdles** *npl*
Hürdenlauf *m* der Damen. **W~ Institute** *n britischer Frauenverband;* ~ **lib** *n (col)* Frauenrechts-
bewegung *f;* ~ **libber** *n (col)* Frauenrechtlerin,
Emanze *(esp pej col) f;* ~ **magazine** *n* Frauen-
zeitschrift *f;* ~ **page** *n* Frauenseite *f;* ~ **rights** *npl*
die Rechte *pl* der Frau; ~ **toilet** *n* Damentoilette *f.*
**won** [wʌn] *pret, ptp of* **win.**
**wonder** ['wʌndər] **1** *n* **(a)** *(feeling)* Staunen *nt,* Verwunderung *f.* **in** ~ voller Staunen. **(b)** *(object or
cause of* ~*)* Wunder *nt.* **the** ~ **of electricity** das Wunder der Elektrizität; **the seven** ~**s of the world** die
sieben Weltwunder; **it is a** ~ **that ...** es ist ein Wunder, daß ...; **it is no** *or* **little** ~ (es ist) kein Wunder;
**no** ~ **(he refused)!** kein Wunder(, daß er abgelehnt
hat)!; **to work** ~**s** Wunder wirken.
**2** *vt* **I** ~ **what he'll do now** ich bin gespannt, was
er jetzt tun wird *(col);* **I** ~ **who first said that** ich
wüßte (zu) gern, wer das zuerst aufgebracht hat; **I
was** ~**ing if you'd like to come too** möchten Sie
nicht vielleicht auch kommen?; **I was** ~**ing if I
could come tomorrow** könnte ich vielleicht morgen
kommen?
**3** *vi* **(a)** *(ask oneself, speculate)* **why do you ask?
— oh, I was just** ~**ing** warum fragst du? — ach, nur
so; **what will happen next, I** ~? ich bin gespannt,
was als nächstes kommt; **I was** ~**ing about that** ich
habe mich das auch schon gefragt; **I've been** ~**ing
about him** ich habe mir auch schon über ihn Gedanken gemacht; **I was** ~**ing about going to the
cinema** ich habe mir überlegt, ob ich ins Kino gehen soll; **could you possibly help me, I** ~ könnten
Sie mir vielleicht helfen? **(b)** *(be surprised)* sich
wundern. **I** ~ **(that)** **he didn't tell me** es wundert
mich, daß er es mir nicht gesagt hat; **to** ~ **at sth**
sich über etw *(acc)* wundern, über etw *(acc)* erstaunt sein; **she'll be married by now, I shouldn't** ~
es würde mich nicht wundern, wenn sie inzwischen
verheiratet wäre.
**wonder** *in cpds* Wunder-; ~ **boy** *n* Wunderknabe
*m;* ~ **drug** *n* Wunderheilmittel *nt.*
**wonderful** *adj,* ~**ly** *adv* ['wʌndəfʊl, -fəlɪ] wunderbar.
**wondering** ['wʌndərɪŋ] *adj (astonished) tone, look*
verwundert, erstaunt; *(doubtful)* fragend.
**wonderland** ['wʌndə,lænd] *n (fairyland)* Wunderland
*nt; (wonderful place)* Paradies *nt.*
**wonderment** ['wʌndəmənt] *n* Verwunderung *f.*
**wonky** ['wɒŋkɪ] *adj (+er) (Brit col) table, marriage,
grammar* wackelig. **your hat's a bit** ~ dein Hut sitzt
schief.
**wont** [wəʊnt] **1** *adj* **to be** ~ **to do sth** etw zu tun pflegen. **2** *n* **as is/was his** ~ wie er zu tun pflegt/pflegte.
**won't** [wəʊnt] = **will not.**
**woo** [wuː] *vt* **(a)** *(dated: court) woman* den Hof machen *(+dat),* umwerben; *(fig) person* umwerben. **(b)**
*(fig) stardom etc* suchen.
**wood** [wʊd] **1** *n* **(a)** *(material)* Holz *nt.* **touch** ~! dreimal auf Holz geklopft!; **beer from the** ~ Bier vom
Faß. **(b)** *(small forest)* Wald *m.* ~**s** Wald *m;* **we're
not out of the** ~ **yet** *(fig)* wir sind noch nicht über
den Berg *or* aus dem Schneider *(col);* **he can't see
the** ~ **for the trees** *(prov)* er sieht den Wald vor lauter Bäumen nicht *(prov).* **(c)** *(Bowls)* Kugel *f; (Golf)*

Holz *nt*. **2** *adj attr* (**a**) *(made of ~)* Holz-. (**b**) *(living etc in a ~)* Wald-.

**wood:** ~ **carving** *n* (Holz)schnitzerei *f*; ~**cock** *n no pl* Waldschnepfe *f*; ~**cut** *n* Holzschnitt *m*; ~**cutter** *n* (**a**) Holzfäller *m*; *(of logs)* Holzhacker *m*; (**b**) *(Art)* Holzschnitzer *m*.

**wooded** ['wʊdɪd] *adj* bewaldet; *countryside* Wald-.

**wooden** ['wʊdn] *adj* (**a**) Holz-. ~ **leg** Holzbein *nt*; ~ **spoon** *(lit)* Holzlöffel *m*; *(fig: consolation prize)* Trostpreis *m* für den Letztplazierten. (**b**) *(fig) expression, manner* hölzern; *personality* steif.

**wood:** ~**land** *n* Waldland *nt*; ~ **louse** *n* Kellerassel *f*; ~**pecker** *n* Specht *m*; ~ **pigeon** *n* Ringeltaube *f*; ~ **pulp** *n* Holzschliff *m*; ~ **screw** *n* Holzschraube *f*; ~**shed** *n* Holzschuppen *m*.

**woodsman** ['wʊdzmən] *n, pl* **-men** [-mən] Waldarbeiter *m*.

**wood:** ~**wind** *n (also* ~**wind instrument)* Holzblasinstrument *nt*; **the** ~**wind(s), the** ~**wind section** die Holzbläser *pl*; ~**work** *n* (**a**) Holzarbeit *f*; *(craft)* Tischlerei *f*; (**b**) *(wooden parts)* Holzteile *pl*; ~**worm** *n* Holzwurm *m*; **it's got** ~**worm** da ist der Holzwurm driñ.

**woof** [wʊf] *interj* ~, ~! wau, wau!

**woofer** ['wʊfə*r*] *n* Tieftöner *m*.

**wool** [wʊl] **1** *n* Wolle *f*; *(cloth also)* Wollstoff *m*. **pure new** ~ reine Schurwolle; **to pull the** ~ **over sb's eyes** *(col)* jdm Sand in die Augen streuen *(col)*. **2** *adj* Woll-.

**woollen,** *(US)* **woolen** ['wʊlən] **1** *adj* Woll-, wollen. **2** *n* ~**s** *pl (garments)* Wollsachen *pl*; *(fabrics, blankets)* Wollwaren *pl*.

**woolly,** *(US)* **wooly** ['wʊlɪ] **1** *adj (+er)* wollig; *(soft also)* flauschig; *(fig) outline* verschwommen; *sound* undeutlich; *(pej) mind, thinking* verworren, wirr. **2** *n (col: sweater etc)* Pulli *m (col)*. **winter woollies** *(esp Brit: sweaters etc)* dicke Wollsachen *(col)*; *(esp US: underwear)* wollene Unterwäsche.

**woozy** ['wuːzɪ] *adj (+er)* *(col)* benommen.

**wop** [wɒp] *n (pej col)* Kanake *m (pej col)*.

**word** [wɜːd] **1** *n* (**a**) Wort *nt*. ~**s** Wörter *pl*; *(meaningful sequence)* Worte *pl*; **foreign** ~**s** Fremdwörter *pl*; **the W**~ **of God** das Wort Gottes; ~ **for** ~ Wort für Wort; **cold isn't the** ~ **for it** kalt ist gar kein Ausdruck (dafür); **too funny for** ~**s** unbeschreiblich komisch; **to put one's thoughts into** ~**s** seine Gedanken in Worte fassen; ~**s fail me** mir fehlen die Worte; **in a** ~ mit einem Wort, kurz gesagt; **in so many** ~**s** direkt, ausdrücklich; **in other** ~**s** mit anderen Worten; **the last** ~ *(fig)* der letzte Schrei *(in* an +*dat)*; **he had the last** ~ er hatte das letzte Wort; **in the** ~**s of Goethe** um mit Goethe zu sprechen; **a** ~ **of advice** ein Rat(schlag) *m*; **a** ~ **of warning** eine Warnung; **fine** ~**s** schöne Worte *pl*; **a man of few** ~**s** ein Mann, der nicht viele Worte macht; **by** ~ **of mouth** durch mündliche Überlieferung; **to take sb at his** ~ jdn beim Wort nehmen; **to have a** ~ **with sb (about sth)** mit jdm (über etw) sprechen; *(reprimand, discipline)* jdn ins Gebet nehmen; **you took the** ~**s out of my mouth** du hast mir das Wort aus dem Mund genommen; **I wish you wouldn't put** ~**s into my mouth** ich wünschte, Sie würden mir nicht das Wort im Munde herumdrehen; **to put in a (good)** ~ **for sb** ein gutes für jdn Wort einlegen; **without a** ~ ohne ein Wort; **don't say** *or* **breathe a** ~ **about it** sag aber bitte keinen Ton davon; **to have** ~**s with sb** mit jdm eine Auseinandersetzung haben; ~ **of honour** Ehrenwort *nt*; **to keep one's** ~ sein Wort halten; **I give you my** ~ ich gebe dir mein (Ehren)wort; **to go back on one's** ~ sein Wort nicht halten; **to break one's** ~ sein

Wort brechen; **take my** ~ **for it** das kannst du mir glauben; **my** ~! meine Güte!; **to give the** ~ *(to do sth)* das Kommando geben(, etw zu tun); **just say the** ~ sag nur ein Wort.

(**b**) ~**s** *pl (text, lyrics)* Text *m*.

(**c**) *no pl (message, news)* Nachricht *f*. ~ **went around that** ... es ging die Nachricht um, daß ...; *(rumour)* es ging das Gerücht um, daß ...; **to leave** ~ **(with sb/for sb) that** ... (bei jdm/für jdn) (die Nachricht) hinterlassen, daß ...; **is there any** ~ **from John yet?** hat John schon von sich *(dat)* hören lassen?; **to send** ~ Nachricht geben; **to send** ~ **to sb** jdn benachrichtigen; **to send sb** ~ **of sth** jdn von etw benachrichtigen.

**2** *vt* formulieren, in Worte fassen; *letter* formulieren; *speech* abfassen.

**word:** ~**-blind** *adj* wortblind; ~ **game** *n* Buchstabenspiel *nt*.

**wording** ['wɜːdɪŋ] *n* Formulierung *f*; *(text)* Text *m*; *(on label)* Aufschrift *f*.

**word:** ~ **order** *n* Wortstellung *f*; ~**-perfect** *adj* sicher im Text; ~ **processing** *n* Textverarbeitung *f*; ~ **processor** *n (machine)* Textverarbeitungsanlage *f*; ~ **wrap** *n (Comp)* (automatischer) Zeilenumbruch.

**wordy** ['wɜːdɪ] *adj (+er)* wortreich, langatmig *(pej)*.

**wore** [wɔː*r*] *pret of* **wear**.

**work** [wɜːk] **1** *n* (**a**) *(labour, task)* Arbeit *f*. **he doesn't like** ~ er arbeitet nicht gern; **that's a good piece of** ~ das ist gute Arbeit; **is this all your own** ~? haben Sie das alles selbst gemacht?; **to be at** ~ **(on sth)** (an etw *dat*) arbeiten; **you need to do some more** ~ **on your pronunciation** Sie müssen noch an Ihrer Aussprache arbeiten; **to put a lot of** ~ **into sth** eine Menge Arbeit in etw *(acc)* stecken; **to get on with one's** ~ sich (wieder) an die Arbeit machen; **to make short** ~ **of sth** mit etw kurzen Prozeß machen; **the medicine had done its** ~ die Arznei hatte ihre Wirkung getan; **the forces at** ~ **here** die Kräfte, die hier am Werk sind; **it was hard** ~ **for the old car to get up the hill** das alte Auto hatte beim Anstieg schwer zu schaffen.

(**b**) *(employment, job)* Arbeit *f*. **to be (out) at** ~ bei der Arbeit sein, arbeiten sein *(col)*; **to go out to** ~ arbeiten gehen; **to be out of/in** ~ arbeitslos sein/ eine Stelle haben; **he travels to** ~ **by car** er fährt mit dem Auto zur Arbeit; **at** ~ am Arbeitsplatz; **what is your** ~? was tun Sie beruflich?; **to put sb out of** ~ jdn arbeitslos machen; **to be off** ~ (am Arbeitsplatz) fehlen.

(**c**) *(product)* Arbeit *f*; *(Art, Liter)* Werk *nt*. ~ **of art/reference** Kunstwerk *nt*/Nachschlagewerk *nt*; **a** ~ **of literature** ein literarisches Werk; **good** ~**s** gute Werke *pl*.

(**d**) ~**s** *pl (Build)* Bauarbeiten *pl*; *(Mil)* Befestigungen *pl*; *(Mech)* Getriebe, Innere(s) *nt*; *(of watch, clock)* Uhrwerk *nt*.

(**e**) ~**s** *sing or pl (factory)* Betrieb *m*, Fabrik *f*; **gas** ~**s/steel** ~**s** Gas-/Stahlwerk *nt*.

(**f**) *(col)* **the** ~**s** *pl* alles Drum und Dran; **to give sb the** ~**s** *(treat harshly)* jdn gehörig in die Mangel nehmen *(col)*; *(treat generously)* jdn gründlich verwöhnen *(col)*.

**2** *vi* (**a**) arbeiten *(at an* +*dat)*. **to** ~ **towards/for sth** auf etw *(acc)* hin/für etw arbeiten; **to** ~ **for better conditions** *etc* sich für bessere Bedingungen *etc* einsetzen. (**b**) *(function, operate)* funktionieren; *(marriage, plan also, be successful)* klappen *(col)*; *(medicine, spell)* wirken. **it won't** ~ das klappt nicht; **to get sth** ~**ing** etw in Gang bringen; **it** ~**s by electricity** es wird elektrisch angetrieben; **it** ~**s**

**both ways** es trifft auch andersherum zu. **(c)** *(mouth, face)* zucken; *(jaws)* mahlen. **(d)** *(move gradually)* **to ~ loose/along** sich lockern/sich entlangarbeiten.

**3** *vt* **(a)** *(make ~)* employees arbeiten lassen, schinden *(pej)*. **to ~ oneself to death** sich zu Tode arbeiten.

**(b)** *(operate) machine* bedienen; *lever, brake* betätigen. **to ~ sth by hand** etw mit Hand betreiben.

**(c)** *change, cure* bewirken. **to ~ mischief** Unheil anrichten; **to ~ it (so that ...)** *(col)* es so deichseln(, daß ...) *(col)*; **to ~ one's passage** seine Überfahrt abarbeiten; **to ~ one's hands free** seine Hände freibekommen; **to ~ sth into the conversation** etw in das Gespräch einfließen lassen; **to ~ oneself into a rage** fürchterlich wütend werden; **to ~ one's way through a book** sich durch ein Buch arbeiten; **to ~ one's way to the top** sich nach oben arbeiten *or* kämpfen; **he ~ed his way across the rock face** er überquerte die Felswand; **he had to ~ his way through college** er mußte sich sein Studium durch eigene Arbeit finanzieren.

**(d)** *(shape) wood, metal* bearbeiten; *dough, clay also* kneten, durcharbeiten. **he ~ed the clay into a human shape** er formte den Ton zu einer menschlichen Gestalt.

**(e)** *(exploit) mine* ausbeuten, abbauen; *land* bearbeiten; *smallholding* bewirtschaften; *(salesman) area* bereisen.

►**work around to** *vi +prep obj* **what are you ~ing ~ ~?** worauf wollen Sie hinaus?

►**work in** *vt sep* **(a)** *(rub in)* einarbeiten; *lotion* einmassieren. **(b)** *(in book, speech) reference* einbauen, einarbeiten. **(c)** *(in schedule etc)* einschieben.

►**work off** *vt sep debts, fat* abarbeiten; *energy* loswerden; *feelings* abreagieren *(on* an *+dat)*.

►**work on 1** *vi* weiterarbeiten. **2** *vi +prep obj* **(a)** *car, accent* arbeiten an *(+dat)*. **who's ~ing ~ this case?** wer bearbeitet diesen Fall?; **we haven't solved it yet but we're still ~ing ~ it** wir haben es noch nicht gelöst, aber wir sind dabei; **I'll work on him** *(try to persuade)* ich werde ihn bearbeiten. **(b)** *assumption, evidence* ausgehen von; *principle (person)* ausgehen von; *(machine)* arbeiten nach.

►**work out 1** *vi* **(a)** *(amount to)* **that ~s ~ at £105** das gibt *or* macht £105; **how much does that ~ ~ at?** was macht das? **(b)** *(succeed: plan, marriage)* funktionieren, klappen *(col)*. **how's your new job ~ing ~?** was macht die neue Arbeit?; **I hope it all ~s ~ for you** ich hoffe, daß dir alles gelingt; **things didn't ~ ~ that way** es kam ganz anders. **(c)** *(in gym etc)* trainieren.

**2** *vt sep* **(a)** *(solve, calculate)* herausbringen; *code* entschlüsseln; *mathematical problem* lösen; *problem* fertig werden mit *(+dat)*; *sum* ausrechnen. **you can ~ that ~ for yourself** das kannst du dir (doch) selbst denken; **things will always ~ themselves ~** Probleme lösen sich stets von selbst. **(b)** *(devise) scheme* (sich *dat)* ausdenken; *(in detail)* ausarbeiten. **(c)** *(understand) person* schlau werden aus *(+dat)*. **I can't ~ ~ why it went wrong** ich kann nicht verstehen, wieso es nicht geklappt hat. **(d)** *(exhaust) mine* ausbeuten; *minerals* abbauen.

►**work up** *vt sep* **(a)** *(develop) business* zu etwas bringen, entwickeln; *enthusiasm (in oneself)* aufbringen; *appetite* sich *(dat)* holen. **to ~ one's way ~** *(in career)* sich hocharbeiten. **(b)** *(stimulate) audience* aufstacheln. **to ~ ~ feelings against sb** gegen jdn Stimmung machen; **to get ~ed ~** sich aufregen.

►**work up to** *vi +prep obj question etc* zusteuern

auf *(+acc)*. **I know what you're ~ing ~ ~** ich weiß, worauf Sie hinauswollen.

**workable** ['wɜːkəbl] *adj mine* abbaufähig; *land* bebaubar; *clay* formbar; *plan* durchführbar; *majority* tragfähig.

**workaday** ['wɜːkədeɪ] *adj* Alltags-.

**workaholic** [ˌwɜːkə'hɒlɪk] *n (col)* Arbeitswütige(r) *mf*.

**work:** **~ basket** *n* Nähkorb *m*; **~bench** *n* Werkbank *f*; **~day** *n (esp US)* Arbeitstag *m*; *(day of week)* Werktag *m*.

**worker** ['wɜːkər] *n* **(a)** Arbeiter(in *f*) *m*. **(b)** *(also ~ ant/bee)* Arbeiterin *f*.

**work:** **~ flow** *n* Arbeitsablauf *m*; **~ force** *n* Arbeiterschaft *f*; **~house** *n (Brit Hist)* Armenhaus *nt*; **~in** *n (Brit)* Work-in *nt*.

**working** ['wɜːkɪŋ] **1** *adj* **(a)** *population* arbeitend, berufstätig; *mother* berufstätig. **~ man/woman** *(worker)* Arbeiter(in *f*) *m*; **I'm a ~ man!** ich gehöre zur arbeitenden Bevölkerung. **(b)** *day, conditions, clothes* Arbeits-. **~ capital** Betriebskapital *nt*; **~ hours** Arbeitszeit *f*; **~ life** Erwerbsleben *nt*; **~ lunch** Arbeitsessen *nt*; **~ party** (Arbeits)ausschuß *m*; **~ week** *(~ hours)* Wochenarbeitszeit *f*. **(c)** *(functioning) hypothesis, model* Arbeits-; *(sufficient) majority* tragfähig. **in ~ order** in betriebsfähigem Zustand; **~ knowledge** Grundkenntnisse *pl*. **2** *n* **(a)** *(work)* Arbeiten *nt*, Arbeit *f*. **(b)** **~s** *pl (way sth works)* Arbeitsweise *f*; **the ~s of his mind** seine Gedankengänge *pl*; **~s of fate** Wege *pl* des Schicksals. **(c)** **~s** *pl (Min)* Schächte *pl*; *(of quarry)* Grube *f*.

**working class** *n (also ~es)* Arbeiterklasse *f*.

**working-class** ['wɜːkɪŋ'klɑːs] *adj* der Arbeiterklasse, Arbeiter-; *(pej)* ordinär, proletenhaft. **to be ~** zur Arbeiterklasse gehören.

**work:** **~ in progress** *n* laufende Arbeiten *pl*; **~ load** *n* Arbeit(slast) *f*; **~man** *n* Handwerker(in *f*) *m*; **~manlike** ['wɜːkmən,laɪk] *adj attitude, job* fachmännisch; *product* fachmännisch gearbeitet; **~manship** ['wɜːkmənʃɪp] *n* Arbeit(squalität) *f*; **~mate** *n* (Arbeits)kollege *m*, (Arbeits)kollegin *f*; **~out** *n (Sport)* **to have a ~out** trainieren; **~ permit** *n* Arbeitserlaubnis *f*; **~place** *n* Arbeitsplatz *m*.

**works** [wɜːks]: **~ committee** *or* **council** *n* Betriebsrat *m*.

**work:** **~ sheet** *n (Sch)* Übungsblatt *nt*; **~shop** *n* Werkstatt *f*; **a music ~shop** ein Musik-Workshop *m*; **~shy** *adj* arbeitsscheu.

**works manager** *n* Werksleiter *m*.

**work:** **~ station** *n* Arbeitsplatz *m*; **~ study** *n* Arbeitsstudie *f*; **~ surface, ~ top** *n* Arbeitsfläche *f*; **~-to-rule** *n (Brit)* Dienst *m* nach Vorschrift; **~week** *n (esp US)* Arbeitswoche *f*.

**world** [wɜːld] *n* Welt *f*. **in the ~** auf der Welt; **all over the ~** auf der ganzen Welt; **he sails all over the ~** er segelt in der Weltgeschichte herum *(hum col)*; **it's the same all the ~ over** es ist (doch) überall das Gleiche; **to go around the ~** eine Weltreise machen; **to feel on top of the ~** sich glänzend fühlen; **it's a small ~** die Welt ist klein; **it's not the end of the ~!** *(col)* davon geht die Welt nicht unter! *(col)*; **to live in a ~ of one's own** in seiner eigenen (kleinen) Welt leben; **the New/Third W~** die Neue/Dritte Welt; **the business/literary ~** die Geschäftswelt/die literarische Welt; **man/woman of the ~** Mann *m*/Frau *f* von Welt; **to come down in the ~** herunterkommen; **to go up in the ~** es (in der Welt) zu etwas bringen; **to lead the ~ in sth** in etw *(dat)* in der Welt führend sein; **to have the best of both ~s** das eine tun und das andere nicht lassen; **out of this ~** *(col)* phantastisch; **not for (all) the**

~ nicht um alles in der Welt; **what/who in the** ~ was/wer in aller Welt; **it did him a** ~ **of good** es hat ihm (unwahrscheinlich) gut getan; **a** ~ **of difference** ein himmelweiter Unterschied; **they're** ~**s apart** sie sind total verschieden; **for all the** ~ **like ...** beinahe wie ...; **to think the** ~ **of sb/sth** große Stücke auf jdn halten/etw über alles stellen; **she/it means the** ~ **to him** sie/es bedeutet ihm alles.

**world** *in cpds* Welt-; ~**-beater** *n* **to be a** ~**-beater** führend in der Welt sein; ~ **champion** *n* Weltmeister(in *f*) *m*; **W**~ **Cup** *n* Fußballweltmeisterschaft *f*; *(cup)* Weltmeisterschaftspokal *m*; ~**-famous** *adj* weltberühmt.

**worldly** ['wɜːldlɪ] *adj (+er)* weltlich; *person* weltlich gesinnt. ~**-wise** weltklug.

**world:** ~ **rankings** *npl* Weltrangliste *f*; ~ **record** *n* Weltrekord *m*; ~ **record holder** *n* Weltrekordinhaber(in *f*) *m*; ~ **war** *n* Weltkrieg *m*; **W**~ **War One/ Two** der Erste/Zweite Weltkrieg; ~**-wide** *adj, adv* weltweit.

**worm** [wɜːm] **1** *n (lit, fig col)* Wurm *m*; *(wood*~*)* Holzwurm *m*. ~**s** *(Med)* Würmer *pl*; **to get a** ~**'s eye view of sth** etw aus der Froschperspektive sehen. **2** *vt* zwängen. **to** ~ **one's way into sth** sich in etw *(acc)* hineinzwängen; **to** ~ **one's way into sb's confidence** sich in jds Vertrauen einschleichen; **to** ~ **sth out of sb** jdm etw entlocken.

**worn** [wɔːn] **1** *ptp of* **wear**. **2** *adj (*~*-out) coat* abgetragen; *book* zerlesen; *carpet* abgetreten; *tyre* abgefahren; *person* angegriffen. **to look** ~ **(with care)** abgehärmt aussehen.

**worn-out** *adj attr*, **worn out** ['wɔːn,aʊt] *adj pred coat* abgetragen; *carpet* abgetreten; *phrase* abgedroschen; *(exhausted) person* erschöpft.

**worried** ['wʌrɪd] *adj* besorgt *(about, by* wegen*)*; *(anxious also)* beunruhigt. **to be** ~ **sick** krank vor Sorge(n) sein.

**worrier** ['wʌrɪəʳ] *n* **to be a** ~ sich *(dat)* ständig Sorgen machen.

**worrisome** ['wʌrɪsəm] *adj* beunruhigend; *(annoying)* lästig.

**worry** ['wʌrɪ] **1** *n* Sorge *f*. **what's your** ~? was drückt dich?; **that's the least of my worries** das macht mir noch am wenigsten Sorgen. **2** *vt* **(a)** *(cause concern)* beunruhigen, Sorgen machen *(+dat)*. **to** ~ **oneself sick (about sth)** vor Sorge (um *or* wegen etw) krank werden. **(b)** *(bother)* **to** ~ **sb with sth** jdn mit etw stören. **(c)** *(dog etc) sheep* nachstellen *(+dat)*; *(bite)* reißen. **3** *vi* sich sorgen, sich *(dat)* Sorgen machen *(about, over* um, wegen*)*. **don't** ~!, **not to** ~! keine Angst *or* Sorge!; **don't** ~, **I'll do it** laß mal, das mach ich schon.

**worry beads** *npl* Betperlen *pl*.

**worrying** ['wʌrɪɪŋ] *adj problem* beunruhigend. **it's very** ~ es macht mir große Sorge.

**worse** [wɜːs] **1** *adj, comp of* **bad** schlechter; *(morally, with bad consequences)* schlimmer, ärger. **it gets** ~ **and** ~ es wird immer schlimmer; **and to make matters** ~ und zu allem Übel; **it could have been** ~ es hätte schlimmer kommen können; ~ **luck!** (so ein) Pech!; **the patient is getting** ~ der Zustand des Patienten verschlechtert sich; **to be the** ~ **for drink** betrunken sein; **he's none the** ~ **for it** es ist ihm nichts dabei passiert; **you'll be none the** ~ **for it** das wird dir nicht schaden; **I don't think any the** ~ **of you for it** ich halte deswegen aber nicht weniger von dir.

**2** *adv, comp of* **badly** schlechter; schlimmer. **to be** ~ **off than ...** schlechter dran sein *(col) or* in einer schlechteren Lage sein als ...; **I could do a lot** ~ **than accept their offer** es wäre bestimmt kein

Fehler, wenn ich das Angebot annähme.

**3** *n* Schlechteres *nt*; Schlimmeres *nt*. **there is** ~ **to come** es kommt noch schlimmer; **it's changed for the** ~ es hat sich zum Schlechteren gewendet.

**worsen** ['wɜːsn] **1** *vt* verschlechtern. **2** *vi* sich verschlechtern, schlechter werden.

**worship** ['wɜːʃɪp] **1** *n* **(a)** Verehrung *f*; *(services)* Gottesdienste *pl*. **place of** ~ Andachtsstätte *f*; *(non-Christian)* Kultstätte *f*. **(b)** *(Brit: in titles)* **Your W**~ *(to judge)* Euer Ehren; *(to mayor)* (sehr geehrter) Herr Bürgermeister. **2** *vt (lit, fig)* anbeten. **3** *vi (Rel)* den Gottesdienst abhalten; *(RC)* die Messe feiern.

**worshipper** ['wɜːʃɪpəʳ] *n (churchgoer)* Gottesdienstbesucher(in *f*) *m*; *(of deity)* Anbeter(in *f*) *m*.

**worst** [wɜːst] **1** *adj, superl of* **bad** schlechteste(r, s); *(morally, in consequence)* schlimmste(r, s). **the** ~ **possible time** die ungünstigste Zeit. **2** *adv, superl of* **badly** am schlechtesten; am schlimmsten. **3** *n* **the** ~ **is over** das Schlimmste *or* Ärgste ist vorbei; **at** ~ schlimmstenfalls; **the** ~ **of it is ...** das Schlimmste daran ist, ...; **if the** ~ **comes to the** ~ wenn alle Stricke reißen *(col)*; **to get the** ~ **of it** den kürzeren ziehen.

**worsted** ['wɜːstɪd] *n* Kammgarn *nt*.

**worth** [wɜːθ] **1** *adj* **(a)** wert. **it's** ~ **£5** es ist £5 wert; **it's not** ~ **£5** es ist keine £5 wert; **what's this** ~? was *or* wieviel ist das wert?; **it's** ~ **a great deal to me** es ist mir viel wert; *(sentimentally)* es bedeutet mir sehr viel; **what's it** ~ **to me to do that?** was springt für mich dabei heraus? *(col)*; **he was** ~ **a million** er besaß eine Million; **for all one is** ~ so sehr man nur kann; **that's my opinion for what it's** ~ das ist meine bescheidene Meinung; **it's more than my job is** ~ **to tell you** ich sage es dir nicht, dazu liegt mir zu viel an meiner Stelle.

**(b) to be (well)** ~ **it** sich (sehr) lohnen; **to be** ~ **sth** etw wert sein; **it's not** ~ **it** es lohnt sich nicht; **it's not** ~ **the trouble** es ist nicht der Mühe wert; **the book is** ~ **reading** das Buch ist lesenswert; **is there anything** ~ **seeing in this town?** gibt es in dieser Stadt etwas Sehenswertes?; **it's a film** ~ **seeing** es ist ein sehenswerter Film; **hardly** ~ **mentioning** kaum der Rede wert.

**2** *n* Wert *m*. **£10's** ~ **of books** Bücher im Werte von £10; **to show one's true** ~ seinen wahren Wert zeigen; **to increase in** ~ im Wert steigen.

**worthless** ['wɜːθlɪs] *adj* wertlos.

**worthwhile** ['wɜːθ'waɪl] *adj* **(a)** lohnend *attr*. **to be** ~ sich lohnen; *(worth the trouble also)* der Mühe *(gen)* wert sein. **(b)** *(useful) contribution* wertvoll. **to do sth** ~ **with one's life** etwas Nützliches mit seinem Leben anfangen.

**worthy** ['wɜːðɪ] *adj (+er)* **(a)** ehrenwert, achtbar; *opponent* würdig; *motive, cause* lobenswert. **(b)** *pred* wert, würdig. ~ **of mention** erwähnenswert; **to be** ~ **of sb/sth** jds/einer Sache würdig sein *(geh)*.

**would** [wʊd] *pret of* **will**[1] *modal aux vb* **(a)** *(conditional)* **if you asked him he** ~ **do it** wenn du ihn fragtest, würde er es tun; **if you had asked him he** ~ **have done it** wenn du ihn gefragt hättest, hätte er es getan; **I thought you** ~ **want to know** ich dachte, du würdest es gerne wissen; **you** ~ **think ...** man sollte meinen ...

**(b)** *(in indirect speech)* **she said she** ~ **come** sie sagte, sie würde kommen *or* sie käme.

**(c)** *(emph)* **you** ~ **be the one to get hit** typisch, daß ausgerechnet du getroffen worden bist; **I** ~**n't know** keine Ahnung; **you** ~! das sieht dir ähnlich!; **he** ~ **have to come right now** ausgerechnet jetzt muß er kommen.

**(d)** *(insistence)* **I warned him, but he ~ do it** ich habe ihn gewarnt, aber er mußte es ja unbedingt tun; **he ~n't listen** er wollte absolut nicht zuhören.
**(e) it ~ seem so** es sieht wohl so aus; **it ~ have been about 8 o'clock** es war (wohl) so ungefähr 8 Uhr; **you ~n't have a cigarette, ~ you?** Sie hätten nicht zufällig eine Zigarette?; **what ~ you have me do?** was soll ich Ihrer Meinung nach tun?; **~ you mind closing the window?** würden *or* könnten Sie bitte das Fenster schließen?; **~ you care for some tea?** möchten Sie gerne etwas Tee?
**(f)** *(habit)* **he ~ paint it each year** er pflegte es jedes Jahr zu streichen.

**would-be** ['wʊdbiː] *adj attr* **(a)** *(pej) salesman, contract etc* angeblich. **a ~ poet** ein Möchtegern-Dichter. **(b)** *(training as, wanting to be)* angehend.

**wouldn't** ['wʊdnt] = **would not.**

**wound¹** [wuːnd] **1** *n* *(lit)* Wunde *f*; *(fig also)* Kränkung *f*. **2** *vt* *(lit, fig)* verletzen. **the ~ed** *pl* die Verwundeten *pl*; **~ed pride/vanity** verletzter Stolz/gekränkte Eitelkeit.

**wound²** [waʊnd] *pret, ptp of* **wind².**

**wove** [wəʊv] *pret of* **weave.**

**woven** ['wəʊvən] *ptp of* **weave.**

**wow** [waʊ] **1** *interj* hui *(col)*, Mann *(col)*. **2** *vt* *(col)* umhauen *(col)*.

**WP** = **(a) word processor. (b)** *(Brit col)* **weather permitting** bei gutem Wetter.

**WPC** *(Brit)* = **woman police constable** Polizistin *f*.

**wpm** = **words per minute** WpM.

**WRAC** *(Brit)* = **Women's Royal Army Corps** *Frauenkorps nt der Armee.*

**WRAF** *(Brit)* = **Women's Royal Air Force** *Frauenkorps nt der Luftwaffe.*

**wrangle** ['ræŋgl] *vi* streiten, rangeln *(about* um*)*; *(in bargaining)* feilschen.

**wrap** [ræp] **1** *n* **(a)** *(garment)* Umhangtuch *nt*; *(for child)* Wickeltuch *nt*; *(cape)* Cape *nt*; *(coat)* Mantel *m*. **(b) to keep sth under ~s** etw geheimhalten. **2** *vt* einwickeln. **shall I ~ it for you?** soll ich es Ihnen einpacken *or* einwickeln?; **to ~ sth around sth** etw um etw wickeln; **he ~ped his car around a lamppost** *(col)* er hat sein Auto an einen Laternenpfahl gesetzt *(col)*; **~ped in mystery** geheimnisumwittert.
▶**wrap up 1** *vt sep* **(a)** *(lit, fig)* einwickeln, verpacken. **(b)** *(col: finalize) deal* unter Dach und Fach bringen. **that just about ~s it ~ for today** das wäre alles für heute. **(c)** *(be involved)* **to be ~ped ~ in sb/sth** in jdm/etw aufgehen. **2** *vi* **(a)** *(dress warmly)* sich warm einpacken *(col)*. **(b)** *(col!: be quiet)* den Mund halten *(col)*.

**wrapper** ['ræpər] *n* Verpackung *f*; *(of sweets)* Papier(chen) *nt*; *(of cigar)* Deckblatt *nt*; *(of book)* (Schutz)umschlag *m*; *(postal)* Streifband *nt*.

**wrapping** ['ræpɪŋ] *n* Verpackung *f*. **~ paper** Packpapier *nt*; *(decorative)* Geschenkpapier *nt*.

**wrath** [rɒθ] *n* Zorn *m*; *(liter: of storm)* Wut *f*.

**wreak** [riːk] *vt* *(liter) destruction* anrichten; *chaos also* stiften; *vengeance* üben *(on* an +*dat)*.

**wreath** [riːθ] *n, pl* **-s** [riːðz] Kranz *m*; *(of smoke etc)* Kringel *m*.

**wreathe** [riːð] *vt* *(encircle)* (um)winden; *(clouds, mist)* umhüllen. **his face was ~d in smiles** er strahlte über das ganze Gesicht.

**wreck** [rek] **1** *n* *(ship~)* Schiffbruch *m*; *(ship itself)* Wrack *nt*; *(US: car crash etc)* Zusammenstoß *m*; *(fig) (old bicycle etc)* Trümmerhaufen *m*; *(person)* Wrack *nt*; *(of hopes, life etc)* Trümmer, Ruinen *pl*. **2** *vt* **(a)** *ship, train* zum Wrack machen; *car* kaputtfahren *(col)*, zu Schrott fahren *(col)*; *machine, furniture* zerstören; *(person)* kurz und klein schlagen

*(col)*. **to be ~ed** *(Naut)* Schiffbruch erleiden; **~ed ship/car** wrackes Schiff/zu Schrott gefahrenes Auto. **(b)** *(fig) hopes, plans* zunichte machen; *marriage* zerrütten; *career, health* zerstören, ruinieren; *person* kaputtmachen *(col)*; *holiday* verderben.

**wreckage** ['rekɪdʒ] *n* *(lit, fig: remains)* Trümmer *pl*; *(washed ashore)* Strandgut *nt*; *(of house, town also)* Ruinen *pl*.

**wrecker** ['rekər] *n* **(a)** *(Naut: salvager)* Bergungsarbeiter *m*; *(vessel)* Bergungsschiff *nt*. **(b)** *(US: breaker, salvager)* Schrotthändler *m*; *(for buildings)* Abbrucharbeiter *m*; *(breakdown truck)* Abschleppwagen *m*.

**wren** [ren] *n* Zaunkönig *m*.

**Wren** [ren] *n* *(Brit) weibliches Mitglied der britischen Marine.*

**wrench** [rentʃ] **1** *n* **(a)** *(tug)* Ruck *m*; *(Med)* Verrenkung *f*. **(b)** *(tool)* Schraubenschlüssel *m*. **(c)** *(fig)* **to be a ~** weh tun. **2** *vt* **(a)** reißen. **to ~ sth (away) from sb** jdm etw entwinden *or* entreißen; **to ~ a door open** eine Tür aufzwingen. **(b)** *(Med)* **to ~ one's ankle** sich *(dat)* den Fuß verrenken.

**wrest** [rest] *vt* **to ~ sth from sb** jdm etw entreißen.

**wrestle** ['resl] **1** *n* Ringkampf *m*. **to have a ~ with sb** mit jdm ringen. **2** *vt* ringen mit. **3** *vi* ringen.

**wrestler** ['reslər] *n* Ringkämpfer *m*; *(modern)* Ringer(in *f*) *m*.

**wrestling** ['reslɪŋ] *n* Ringen *nt*. **~ match** Ringkampf *m*.

**wretch** [retʃ] *n* **(a)** *(miserable)* armer Teufel. **(b)** *(contemptible)* Schuft *m*; *(child)* Schlingel *m*.

**wretched** ['retʃɪd] *adj* elend; *conditions, clothing etc also* erbärmlich; *(unhappy)* (tod)unglücklich; *housing, weather* erbärmlich, miserabel *(col)*; *(col: damned)* verflixt *(col)*, Mist- *(col)*. **I feel ~** *(ill)* mir geht es miserabel *(col)*.

**wretchedly** ['retʃɪdlɪ] *adv* erbärmlich; *(col: extremely)* verflixt *(col)*.

**wretchedness** ['retʃɪdnɪs] *n* Erbärmlichkeit *f*; *(misery)* Elend *nt*.

**wrick** [rɪk] *vt* **to ~ one's neck/shoulder** sich *(dat)* den Hals/die Schulter ausrenken.

**wriggle** ['rɪgl] **1** *vi* *toes, ears* wackeln mit. **to ~ one's way through sth** sich durch etw (hin)durchwinden. **2** *vi* *(also ~ about or around) (snake)* sich schlängeln; *(fish)* sich winden, zappeln; *(person) (restlessly)* zappeln; *(in embarrassment)* sich winden. **to ~ along/down** sich vorwärts schlängeln/sich nach unten schlängeln; **she managed to ~ free** es gelang ihr, sich loszuwinden.
▶**wriggle out** *vi* *(lit)* sich herauswinden *(of* aus*)*; *(fig also)* sich herausmanövrieren *(of* aus*)*. **he's ~d (his way) ~ of it** er hat sich davor gedrückt.

**wring** [rɪŋ] *(vb: pret, ptp* **wrung)** *vt* **(a)** *(also ~ out) clothes etc* auswringen, auswinden. **do not ~** *(on washing instructions)* nicht wringen. **(b)** *hands (in distress)* ringen. **I could have wrung his neck** ich hätte ihm den Hals umdrehen können. **(c)** *(extract)* **to ~ sth out of sb** etw aus jdm herausquetschen *(col)*, jdm etw abringen.

**wringer** ['rɪŋər] *n* (Wäsche)mangel *f*.

**wringing** ['rɪŋɪŋ] *adj (also ~* **wet)** tropfnaß.

**wrinkle** ['rɪŋkl] **1** *n* **(a)** *(in clothes, paper)* Knitter(falte *f*) *m*. **(b)** *(on face, skin, in stocking)* Falte *f*. **2** *vt* *fabric, paper* zerknittern; *skin* faltig machen. **to ~ one's nose/brow** die Nase rümpfen/die Stirn runzeln. **3** *vi* *(material)* knittern; *(stockings)* Falten schlagen; *(skin etc)* Falten bekommen.

**wrinkled** ['rɪŋkld] *adj sheet, paper* zerknittert; *stockings* Ziehharmonika- *(col)*; *skin* faltig; *brow* gerunzelt; *apple, old lady* verschrumpelt.

**wrinkly** ['rɪŋklɪ] *adj (+er)* schrumpelig; *(fabric)* zerknittert.
**wrist** [rɪst] *n* Handgelenk *nt.*
**wristband** ['rɪst‚bænd] *n* Armband *nt*; *(Sport)* Schweißband *nt.*
**wristwatch** ['rɪst‚wɒtʃ] *n* Armbanduhr *f.*
**writ** [rɪt] *n (Jur)* Verfügung *f.* **to issue a ~ against sb** jdn vorladen *(for wegen).*
**write** [raɪt] *pret* **wrote,** *ptp* **written 1** *vt* schreiben; *cheque also* ausstellen; *notes* sich *(dat)* machen. **he wrote me a letter** er schrieb mir einen Brief; **he wrote five sheets of paper** er schrieb fünf Seiten voll; **how is that written?** wie schreibt man das?; **to be writ(ten) large** *(fig)* klar zu erkennen sein; **it was written all over his face** es stand ihm im Gesicht geschrieben. **2** *vi* schreiben. **to ~ to sb** jdm schreiben; **we ~ to each other** wir schreiben uns; **that's nothing to ~ home about** *(col)* das ist nichts Weltbewegendes; **I'll ~ for it at once** *(order)* ich bestelle es sofort.
▶**write away** *vi* **to ~ ~ for sth** etw (schriftlich) anfordern.
▶**write back** *vi* zurückschreiben, antworten.
▶**write down** *vt sep (make a note of)* aufschreiben; *(put in writing)* niederschreiben.
▶**write in 1** *vt sep word etc* hineinschreiben, einfügen *(prep obj* in +*acc).* **2** *vi* schreiben *(to an* +*acc).* **to ~ ~ for sth** etw (schriftlich) anfordern.
▶**write off 1** *vi* = **write away. 2** *vt sep debt, losses, (fig: regard as failure)* abschreiben; *car etc (driver)* zu Schrott fahren; *(insurance company)* als Totalschaden abschreiben.
▶**write out** *vt sep notes* ausarbeiten; *name etc* ausschreiben; *cheque* ausstellen.
▶**write up** *vt sep notes* ausarbeiten; *report, diary* schreiben; *event* schreiben über (+*acc*); *(review) play, film* eine Kritik schreiben über (+*acc).*
**write-off** ['raɪtɒf] *n (car etc)* Totalschaden *m*; *(Comm)* Abschreibung *f.*
**writer** ['raɪtər] *n* Schriftsteller(in *f*) *m*; *(of report etc)* Autor(in *f*) *m*; *(of music)* Komponist(in *f*) *m.* **he's a very poor ~** er schreibt sehr schlecht; *(correspondent)* er ist kein großer Briefschreiber; **~'s cramp** Schreibkrampf *m.*
**write-up** ['raɪtʌp] *n* Pressebericht *m*; *(of play etc)* Kritik *f.*
**writhe** [raɪð] *vi* sich krümmen, sich winden *(with, in* vor +*dat).*
**writing** ['raɪtɪŋ] *n* **(a)** Schrift *f*; *(act, profession)* Schreiben *nt*; *(inscription)* Inschrift *f.* **in ~** schriftlich; **permission in ~** schriftliche Genehmigung; **in sb's own ~** *(not typewritten)* handgeschrieben; *(not written by sb else)* in jds eigener (Hand)schrift *(dat);* **the ~ is on the wall for them** ihre Stunde hat geschlagen; **he had seen the ~ on the wall** er hatte die Zeichen erkannt. **(b)** *pl (written works)* **his ~s** seine Werke *or* Schriften.
**writing** *in cpds* Schreib-; **~ case** *n* Schreibmappe *f*; **~ desk** *n* Schreibtisch *m*; **~ pad** *n* Notizblock *m*; **~ paper** *n* Schreibpapier *nt.*
**written** ['rɪtn] **1** *ptp of* **write. 2** *adj examination, statement* schriftlich; *language* Schrift-; *word* geschrieben. **~ notice** schriftliche Kündigung; *(letter)* Kündigungsschreiben *nt.*
**WRNS** *(Brit)* = **Women's Royal Naval Service** *Frauenkorps nt der Marine.*
**wrong** [rɒŋ] **1** *adj* **(a)** falsch; *(when choice is given also)* verkehrt. **to be ~** nicht stimmen; *(person)* unrecht haben; *(answer also)* falsch *or* verkehrt sein; *(watch)* falsch gehen; **it's all ~ that I should have to** ... das ist doch nicht richtig, daß ich ... muß; **I was**

**~ about him** ich habe mich in ihm geirrt; **you were ~ in thinking he did it** du hast unrecht gehabt, als du dachtest, er sei es gewesen; **I took a ~ turning** ich bin falsch abgebogen; **to say/do the ~ thing** das Falsche sagen/tun; **the ~ side of the fabric** die linke Seite des Stoffes; **to do sth the ~ way** etw falsch *or* verkehrt machen.
**(b)** *(morally)* schlecht, unrecht; *(unfair)* ungerecht, unfair. **it's ~ to steal** Stehlen ist Unrecht; **you were ~ to do that** es war nicht richtig von dir, das zu tun; **what's ~ with a drink now and again?** was ist schon (Schlimmes) dabei, wenn man ab und zu einen trinkt?
**(c)** *pred (amiss)* **something is ~** (irgend) etwas stimmt nicht *or* ist nicht in Ordnung; *(suspiciously)* irgend etwas stimmt da nicht *or* ist da faul *(col);* **is anything ~?** ist was? *(col);* **there's nothing ~** (es ist) alles in Ordnung; **what's ~?** was ist los?; **what's ~ with you?** was fehlt Ihnen?; **something's ~ with my watch** mit meiner Uhr stimmt etwas nicht.
**2** *adv* falsch. **you did ~ to do it** es war unrecht *or* nicht richtig von dir, das zu tun; **to get sth ~** sich mit etw vertun; **to get one's sums ~** sich verrechnen; **don't get me ~** verstehen Sie mich nicht falsch; **to go ~** *(on route)* falsch gehen/fahren; *(plan)* schiefgehen; *(affair etc)* schieflaufen; **my washing-machine has gone ~** meine Waschmaschine ist nicht in Ordnung; **you can't go ~** du kannst gar nichts verkehrt machen; *(in telling sb the way)* du kannst dich nicht verlaufen/verfahren.
**3** *n* Unrecht *nt no pl.* **(social) ~s** (soziale) Ungerechtigkeiten *pl*; **to be in the ~** im Unrecht sein; **to put sb in the ~** jdn ins Unrecht setzen; **two ~s don't make a right** ein zweites Unrecht hebt das erste nicht auf; **she, of course, can do no ~** sie macht natürlich nie einen Fehler.
**4** *vt* **to ~ sb** jdm unrecht tun; **to be ~ed** ungerecht behandelt werden.
**wrongdoer** ['rɒŋ‚duːər] *n* Übeltäter(in *f*) *m.*
**wrongdoing** ['rɒŋ‚duːɪŋ] *n* Missetaten *pl*; *(single act)* Missetat *f.*
**wrong-foot** [‚rɒŋ'fʊt] *vt (Sport)* auf dem falschen Fuß erwischen; *(fig)* unvorbereitet treffen.
**wrongful** ['rɒŋfʊl] *adj* ungerechtfertigt.
**wrongfully** ['rɒŋfəlɪ] *adv* zu Unrecht.
**wrong-headed** [‚rɒŋ'hedɪd] *adj* verbohrt.
**wrongly** ['rɒŋlɪ] *adv* **(a)** *(unjustly, improperly)* unrecht; *punished* zu Unrecht. **(b)** *(incorrectly)* falsch, verkehrt; *maintain* zu Unrecht; *believe* fälschlicherweise.
**wrote** [rəʊt] *pret of* **write.**
**wrought** [rɔːt] **1** *vt* **(a)** *(obs, liter) pret, ptp of* **work.** **(b) great changes have been ~** große Veränderungen wurden herbeigeführt; **the storm ~ great destruction** der Sturm richtete große Verheerungen an. **2** *adj iron* Schmiede-; *silver* gehämmert.
**wrought: ~-iron** *adj* schmiedeeisern *attr,* aus Schmiedeeisen; **~-up** *adj* **to be ~-up** aufgeregt sein.
**wrung** [rʌŋ] *pret, ptp of* **wring.**
**WRVS** *(Brit)* = **Women's Royal Voluntary Service** *freiwilliger Frauendienst.*
**wry** [raɪ] *adj (+er) (ironical)* ironisch; *joke, humour etc* trocken.
**wryly** ['raɪlɪ] *adv* ironisch.
**wt** = **weight** Gew.
**WV** *(US Post)* = **West Virginia.**
**WW1** = **World War 1.**
**WW2** = **World War 2.**
**WY** *(US Post)* = **Wyoming.**

# XYZ

**X, x** [eks] *n* X, x *nt.* ~ **for Xmas** ≃ X wie Xanthippe; ~ **pounds** x Pfund; ~ **marks the spot** die Stelle ist mit einem Kreuz gekennzeichnet; ~**-certificate film** für Jugendliche nicht geeigneter Film.

**Xerox** ® [ˈzɪərɒks] **1** *n (copy)* Xerokopie *f.* **2** *vt* xerokopieren.

**XL** = **extra large** XL.

**Xmas** [ˈeksməs, ˈkrɪsməs] *n* = **Christmas** Weihnachten *nt.*

**X-rated** [ˈeksˈreɪtɪd] *adj (US Film)* für Jugendliche nicht geeignet.

**X-ray** [ˈeksˌreɪ] **1** *n* Röntgenstrahl *m; (also* ~ **photograph/** Röntgenaufnahme *f.* **to have an** ~ geröntgt werden. **2** *vt person, organ* röntgen; *luggage, envelope* durchleuchten.

**xylophone** [ˈzaɪləfəʊn] *n* Xylophon *nt.*

**Y, y** [waɪ] *n* Y, y *nt.* ~ **for Yellow,** ~ **for Yoke** *(US)* ≃ Y wie Ypsilon.

**yacht** [jɒt] *nt* Jacht, Yacht *f.* ~ **club** Jacht- *or* Segelklub *m;* ~ **harbour** Jachthafen *m;* ~ **race** (Segel)-regatta *f.*

**yachting** [ˈjɒtɪŋ] *n* Segeln *nt.* **to go** ~ segeln gehen.

**yachtsman** [ˈjɒtsmən] *n, pl* **-men** [-mən] Segler *m.*

**yachtswoman** [ˈjɒtswʊmən] *n, pl* **-women** [-wɪmɪn] Seglerin *f.*

**yak** [jæk] *n (Zool)* Jak, Grunzochse *m.*

**yam** [jæm] *n* **(a)** *(plant)* Yamswurzel *f.* **(b)** *(US: sweet potato)* Süßkartoffel *f.*

**yank** [jæŋk] **1** *n* Ruck *m.* **give it a good** ~ zieh mal kräftig dran. **2** *vt* **to** ~ **sth** mit einem Ruck an etw *(dat)* ziehen.

▶**yank out** *vt sep* ausreißen; *tooth* ziehen.

**Yank** [jæŋk] **1** *n* Ami *m (col).* **2** *adj attr* Ami- *(col).*

**Yankee** [ˈjæŋkɪ] *(col)* **1** *n* Yankee *m (col).* **2** *adj attr* Yankee- *(col).*

**yap** [jæp] *vi (dog)* kläffen; *(talk noisily)* schnattern *(col).*

**yard¹** [jɑːd] *n (Measure)* Yard *nt.* **to buy cloth by the** ~ ≃ Stoff meterweise kaufen.

**yard²** *n* **(a)** Hof *m.* **back** ~ Hinterhof *m;* **in the** ~ auf dem Hof. **(b)** *(worksite)* Werksgelände *nt; (for storage)* Lagerplatz *m.* **builder's** ~ Bauhof *m;* **shipbuilding** ~ Werft *f;* **naval (dock)**~, **navy** ~ Marinewerft *f.* **(c)** *(US: garden)* Garten *m.*

**yard:** ~**-arm** *n (Naut)* Nock *f;* ~**stick** *n (measuring rod)* Elle *f; (fig)* Maßstab *m.*

**yarn** [jɑːn] *n* **(a)** *(Tex)* Garn *nt.* **(b)** *(tale)* Seemannsgarn *nt.* **to spin a** ~ Seemannsgarn spinnen; **to spin sb a** ~ **about sth** jdm eine Lügengeschichte über etw *(acc)* erzählen.

**yawn** [jɔːn] **1** *vt (lit, fig)* gähnen. **to** ~ **one's head off** fürchterlich gähnen *(col).* **2** *n* Gähnen *nt.* **to give a** ~ gähnen; **to be a** ~ *(col)* langweilig sein.

**yawning** [ˈjɔːnɪŋ] *adj chasm etc* gähnend.

**yd** = **yard(s).**

**yea** [jeɪ] **1** *adv (obs: yes)* ja. **2** *n* **the** ~**s and the nays** die Jastimmen und die Neinstimmen.

**yeah** [jeə] *adv (col)* ja.

**year** [jɪəʳ] *n* **(a)** Jahr *nt.* **last** ~ letztes Jahr; **this** ~ dieses Jahr; **every other** ~ jedes zweite Jahr; **in the** ~ **1969** im Jahr(e) 1969; ~ **after** ~ Jahr für Jahr; ~ **by** ~, **from** ~ **to** ~ von Jahr zu Jahr; ~ **in,** ~ **out** jahrein, jahraus; **all (the)** ~ **round** das ganze Jahr über; ~**s (and** ~**s) ago** vor (langen) Jahren; **I haven't seen her in** ~**s** ich habe sie jahrelang *or* seit Jahren nicht mehr gesehen; **a** ~ **last January** (im) Januar vor einem Jahr; **a** ~ **from now** nächstes Jahr um diese Zeit; **a hundred-**~**-old tree** ein hundertjähriger Baum; **he is six** ~**s old** er ist sechs Jahre (alt); **it costs £100 a** ~ es kostet £100 pro *or* im Jahr; **it has put** ~**s on me** es hat mich (um) Jahre älter gemacht; **it takes** ~**s off you** es macht dich um Jahre jünger; **he looks old for his** ~**s** er sieht älter aus als er ist; **well on in** ~**s** im vorgerückten Alter; **to get on in** ~**s** in die Jahre kommen.

**(b)** *(Univ, Sch, of wine)* Jahrgang *m.* **first-**~ **student** Student(in *f*) *m* im ersten Jahr; *(in first term)* ≃ Erstsemester *nt.*

**yearbook** [ˈjɪəbʊk] *n* Jahrbuch *nt.*

**yearling** [ˈjɪəlɪŋ] *n (animal)* Jährling *m; (racehorse also)* Einjährige(r) *mf.*

**year-long** [ˈjɪəˈlɒŋ] *adj* einjährig, ein Jahr dauernd.

**yearly** [ˈjɪəlɪ] **1** *adj* jährlich. **2** *adv* jährlich, einmal im Jahr. **twice** ~ zweimal im Jahr.

**yearn** [jɜːn] *vi* sich sehnen *(after, for nach).* **to** ~ **to do sth** sich danach sehnen, etw zu tun.

**yearning** [ˈjɜːnɪŋ] **1** *n* Sehnsucht *f,* Verlangen *nt (to do sth* etw zu tun, *for* nach). **2** *adj desire, look* sehnsüchtig.

**year-round** [ˌjɪəˈraʊnd] *adj* ganzjährig.

**yeast** [jiːst] *n no pl* Hefe *f.*

**yell** [jel] **1** *n* Schrei *m.* **to let out a** ~ einen Schrei ausstoßen, schreien. **2** *vt (also* ~ **out)** schreien, brüllen *(with* vor *+dat).* **he** ~**ed at her** er schrie *or* brüllte sie an; **he** ~**ed abuse at the teacher** er beschimpfte den Lehrer wüst.

**yellow** [ˈjeləʊ] **1** *adj (+er)* **(a)** gelb. **to turn** ~ gelb werden; *(paper)* vergilben; ~ **fever** Gelbfieber *nt;* ~ **light** *(US Aut)* Gelb *nt;* **(double)** ~ **line** *(Brit)* (absolutes) Halteverbot; ~ **pages** Branchenverzeichnis *nt,* Gelbe Seiten *pl.* **(b)** *(col: cowardly)* feige. **2** *n (colour)* Gelb *nt; (of egg)* Eigelb *nt.* **3** *vi* gelb werden; *(pages)* vergilben.

**yellowish** [ˈjeləʊɪʃ] *adj* gelblich.

**yelp** [jelp] **1** *n (of animal)* Jaulen *nt no pl; (of person)* Aufschrei *m.* **2** *vi (animal)* (auf)jaulen; *(person)* aufschreien.

**Yemen** [ˈjemən] *n* **(the)** ~ (der) Jemen.

**Yemeni** [ˈje+mənɪ] **1** *adj* jemenitisch. **2** *n* Jemenit(in *f*) *m.*

**yen¹** [jen] *n (Fin)* Yen *m.*

**yen²** *n (col)* Lust *f (for* auf *+acc).* **to have a ~ to do sth** Lust haben, etw zu tun.

**yeoman** ['jəumən] *n, pl* **-men** [-mən] **(a)** *(Hist: small landowner)* Freibauer *m.* **(b)** **Y~ of the Guard** *(Brit)* königlicher Leibgardist.

**yes** [jes] **1** *adv* ja; *(answering neg question)* doch. **to say ~ to a demand** einer Forderung *(dat)* zustimmen; **if management says ~ to an increase** wenn die Betriebsleitung eine Lohnerhöhung bewilligt; **~ sir!** jawohl, mein Herr; *(Mil)* jawohl, Herr General/Leutnant *etc;* **I didn't say that — oh ~, you did** das habe ich nicht gesagt — o doch, das hast du. **2** *n* Ja *nt.*

**yes man** ['jesmæn] *n, pl* **~ men** [-men] Jasager *m.*

**yesterday** ['jestədeɪ] **1** *n* Gestern *nt.* **the fashions of ~** die Mode von gestern. **2** *adv (lit, fig)* gestern. **~ morning/evening** gestern morgen/abend; **he was at home all (day) ~** er war gestern den ganzen Tag zu Hause; **the day before ~** vorgestern; **a week ago ~** gestern vor einer Woche; **~'s paper** die Zeitung von gestern.

**yet** [jet] **1** *adv* **(a)** *(still)* noch; *(thus far)* bis jetzt, bisher. **they haven't returned ~** sie sind noch nicht zurückgekommen; **this is his best book ~** das ist sein bisher bestes Buch; **as ~** *(with present tenses)* bis jetzt, bisher; *(with past)* bis dahin; **no, not ~** nein, noch nicht; **not just ~** jetzt noch nicht; **they have a few days ~** sie haben noch ein paar Tage; **I've ~ to learn how to do it** ich muß erst noch lernen, wie man es macht; **he may ~ come** er kann noch kommen; **I may ~ go to Italy** ich fahre vielleicht noch nach Italien; **I'll do it ~** ich schaffe es schon noch. **(b)** *(with interrog)* schon. **has he arrived ~?** ist er schon angekommen?; **do you have to go just ~?** müssen Sie jetzt schon gehen? **(c)** *(with comp)* noch. **this is ~ more difficult** dies ist (sogar) noch schwieriger; **he wants ~ more money** er will noch mehr Geld. **(d)** *(in addition)* **(and) ~ again** und wieder, und noch einmal; **another arrived and ~ another** es kam noch einer und noch einer. **2** *conj* doch, dennoch, trotzdem. **and ~** und doch *or* dennoch; **it's strange ~ true** es ist seltsam, aber wahr.

**yeti** ['jetɪ] *n* Yeti, Schneemensch *m.*

**yew** [ju:] *n (also ~ tree)* Eibe *f; (wood)* Eibe(nholz *nt) f.*

**YHA** *(Brit)* **= Youth Hostels Association** Jugendherbergsverband *m.*

**Yiddish** ['jɪdɪʃ] **1** *adj* jiddisch. **2** *n (language)* Jiddisch *nt.*

**yield** [ji:ld] **1** *vt* **(a)** *crop, result* hervorbringen; *(tree) fruit* tragen; *(mine)* bringen; *(shares) interest* (ein)bringen. **the information ~ed by the poll** die Informationen, die die Meinungsumfrage ergeben hat. **(b)** *(surrender)* aufgeben. **to ~ sth to sb** etw an jdn abtreten; **to ~ ground to the enemy** vor dem Feind zurückweichen. **2** *vi* **(a)** *(surrender, give way)* **they ~ed to us** sie haben nachgegeben; *(Mil)* sie haben sich uns *(dat)* ergeben; **to ~ to force** der Gewalt nachgeben; **to ~ to reason** sich der Vernunft beugen; **to ~ to sb's entreaties/threats** jds Bitten *(dat)* nachgeben/sich jds Drohungen *(dat)* beugen. **(b)** *(give way: branch, ground)* nachgeben. **(c)** *(Mot)* **to ~ to oncoming traffic** den Gegenverkehr vorbeilassen; *"~" (US, Ir)* „Vorfahrt beachten!" **3** *n (of land, tree)* Ertrag *m; (of work also)* Ergebnis *nt; (of mine, well)* Ausbeute *f; (of industry: goods)* Produktion *f; (profit)* Gewinne, Erträge *pl;*

*(Fin: of shares, business)* Ertrag, Gewinn *m.*

**yippee** [jɪ'pi:] *interj* juchhe, hurra.

**YMCA = Young Men's Christian Association** CVJM *m.*

**yob(bo)** ['jɒb(əu)] *n (Brit col)* Halbstarke(r), Rowdy *m.*

**yodel** ['jəudl] *vti* jodeln.

**yoga** ['jəugə] *n* Joga, Yoga *m or nt.*

**yog(h)urt** ['jɒgət] *n* Joghurt *m or nt.*

**yoke** [jəuk] **1** *n (for oxen etc, fig)* Joch *nt.* **to throw off the ~** *(fig)* das Joch abschütteln. **2** *vt (also ~ up)* **oxen** (ins Joch) einspannen.

**yokel** ['jəukəl] *n (pej)* Bauerntölpel *m.*

**yolk** [jəuk] *n (of egg)* Eigelb *nt.*

**yonder** ['jɒndər] *adv (poet, dial)* **(over) ~** dort drüben.

**yonks** [jɒŋks] *npl (col: ages)* eine (halbe) Ewigkeit *(col).*

**Yorks** [jɔ:ks] *(Brit)* **= Yorkshire.**

**you** [ju:] *pron* **(a)** *(German familiar form, in letter-writing usu with a capital) (sing) (nom)* du; *(acc)* dich; *(dat)* dir; *(pl) (nom)* ihr; *(acc, dat)* euch; *(German polite form: sing, pl) (nom, acc)* Sie; *(dat)* Ihnen. **all of ~** *(pl)* ihr alle/Sie alle; **if I were ~** wenn ich du/Sie wäre; **~ Germans** ihr Deutschen; **is that ~?** bist du's/seid ihr's/sind Sie's?; **it's ~** du bist es/ihr seid's/Sie sind's; **that hat just isn't ~** *(col)* der Hut paßt einfach nicht zu dir/zu Ihnen; **now there's a car for ~!** das ist mal ein tolles Auto. **b)** *(indef) (nom)* man; *(acc)* einen; *(dat)* einem. **~ never know** man kann nie wissen, man weiß nie; **it's not good for ~** es ist nicht gut.

**you'd** [ju:d] **= you would; you had.**

**you'd've** ['ju:dəv] **= you would have.**

**you'll** [ju:l] **= you will; you shall.**

**young** [jʌŋ] **1** *adj (+er)* jung; *wine, grass also* neu. **~ people** junge Leute *pl;* **~ people's fashions** Jugendmoden *pl;* **~ lady/man** junge Dame/junger Mann; *(girl-/boyfriend)* Freundin *f*/Freund *m;* **they have a ~ family** sie haben kleine Kinder; **he is ~ at heart** er ist innerlich jung geblieben; **~ Mr Brown** der junge Herr Brown; **Pitt the Y~er** Pitt der Jüngere; **he's a very ~ forty** er ist ein jugendlicher Vierziger; **in her ~ days** in ihrer Jugend; **I'm not getting any ~er** ich werde auch nicht jünger. **2** *npl* **(a)** *(people)* **the ~** die Jugend, die jungen Leute; **books for the ~** Jugendbücher *pl.* **(b)** *(animals)* Junge *pl.* **with ~** trächtig.

**youngish** ['jʌŋɪʃ] *adj* ziemlich jung.

**youngster** ['jʌŋstər] *n (boy)* Junge *m; (child)* Kind *nt.*

**your** [jɔ:r] *poss adj* **(a)** *(German familiar form, in letter-writing usu with a capital) (sing)* dein/deine/dein; *(pl)* euer/eure/euer; *(German polite form: sing, pl)* Ihr/Ihre/Ihr. **(b)** **the climate here is bad for ~ health** das Klima hier ist nicht gut für die Gesundheit; **~ typical American** der typische Amerikaner.

**you're** [juər] **= you are.**

**yours** [jɔ:z] *poss pron (German familiar form, in letter-writing usu with a capital) (sing)* deiner/deine/deins; *(pl)* eurer/eure/eures; *(German polite form: sing, pl)* Ihrer/Ihre/Ihr(e)s. **this is my book and that is ~** dies ist mein Buch und das (ist) deins/Ihres; **the idea was ~** es war deine/Ihre Idee, die Idee stammt von dir/Ihnen; **she is a cousin of ~** sie ist deine Kusine, sie ist eine Kusine von dir; **that is no business of ~** das geht dich/Sie nichts an; **that dog of ~!** dein/Ihr blöder Hund!; **~** *(in letter-writing)* Ihr/Ihre; **~ sincerely, ~ truly** *(esp US) (on letter)* mit freundlichen Grüßen; **~ truly** *(col: I, me)* meine Wenigkeit; **what's ~?** *(to drink)* was trinkst du/was trinken Sie?

**yourself** [jə'self] pron, pl **yourselves** (a) (reflexive) (German familiar form) (sing) (acc) dich; (dat) dir; (pl) euch; (German polite form: sing, pl) sich. **have you hurt** ~? hast du dir/haben Sie sich weh getan?; **you never speak about** ~ du redest nie über dich (selbst)/Sie reden nie über sich (selbst). (b) (emph) selbst. **you told me** ~ du hast/Sie haben es mir selbst gesagt; **you will see for** ~ du wirst/Sie werden es selbst sehen; **did you do it by** ~? hast du/ haben Sie das allein gemacht?

**youth** [juːθ] n (a) no pl Jugend f. **in my** ~ in meiner Jugend(zeit); **she has kept her** ~ sie ist jung geblieben. (b) pl **-s** [juːðz] (young man) junger Mann, Jugendliche(r) m. (c) ~ pl (young men and women) die Jugend. ~ **club** Jugendklub m; ~ **hostel** Jugendherberge f; ~ **movement** Jugendbewegung f.

**youthful** ['juːθfʊl] adj jugendlich. ~ **memories** Jugenderinnerungen pl.

**youthfulness** ['juːθfʊlnɪs] n Jugendlichkeit f.

**you've** [juːv] = **you have**.

**yowl** [jaʊl] **1** n (of person) Heulen nt no pl; (of dog) Jaulen nt no pl; (of cat) klägliches Miauen no pl. **2** vi (person) heulen; (dog) jaulen; (cat) kläglich miauen.

**yo-yo** ['jəʊjəʊ] n Jojo nt.

**yr(s)** = (a) **year(s)**. (b) **your(s)**.

**YTS** (Brit) = **Youth Training Scheme**.

**yucca** ['jʌkə] n Yucca, Palmlilie f.

**Yugoslav** ['juːgəʊˌslɑːv] (Hist) **1** adj jugoslawisch. **2** n Jugoslawe m, Jugoslawin f.

**Yugoslavia** [ˌjuːgəʊ'slɑːvɪə] n (Hist) Jugoslawien nt.

**Yugoslavian** [ˌjuːgəʊ'slɑːvɪən] adj (Hist) jugoslawisch.

**yuk** [jʌk] interj i, igitt.

**yukky** ['jʌkɪ] adj (+er) eklig, fies (col).

**Yule** [juːl] n (old) Weihnachten nt. ~**tide** Weihnachtszeit f.

**yummy** ['jʌmɪ] **1** adj (+er) (col) food lecker; man toll. **2** interj ~!, ~ ~! lecker! (col).

**yuppie** ['jʌpɪ] n (col) Yuppie m.

**YWCA** = **Young Women's Christian Association** CVJF m.

**Z, z** [(Brit) zed, (US) ziː] n Z, z nt. ~ **for Zebra** ≈ Z wie Zacharias.

**Zaire** [zɑː'iːəʳ] n Zaire nt.

**Zambia** ['zæmbɪə] n Sambia nt.

**Zambian** ['zæmbɪən] **1** adj sambisch. **2** n Sambier(in f) m.

**zany** ['zeɪnɪ] adj (+er) humour verrückt; person also irrsinnig komisch.

**zap** [zæp] vt (col) (hit) schlagen; (kill) ausradieren (col); (erase) data löschen.
▶**zap up** vt sep (col) aufmotzen (col).

**zappy** ['zæpɪ] adj (+er) (col) pace, car fetzig (col); style spritzig.

**zeal** [ziːl] n no pl Eifer m. **to work with great** ~ mit Feuereifer arbeiten.

**zealot** ['zelət] n Fanatiker(in f) m; (religious also) (Glaubens)eiferer(in f) m.

**zealous** ['zeləs] adj worker eifrig, emsig. ~ **for sth** eifrig um etw bemüht; **to be** ~ **to begin** erpicht darauf sein, anzufangen.

**zebra** ['zebrə] n Zebra nt. ~ **crossing** (Brit) Zebrastreifen m.

**zenith** ['zenɪθ] n (Astron, fig) Zenit m.

**zeppelin** ['zepəlɪn] n Zeppelin m.

**zero** ['zɪərəʊ] **1** n, pl **-(e)s** Null f; (point on scale) Nullpunkt m. **15 degrees below** ~ 15 Grad unter Null.
**2** adj ~ **degrees** null Grad; ~ **gravity** Schwerelosigkeit f; **at** ~ **gravity** unter Schwerelosigkeit; ~ **hour** (Mil, fig) die Stunde X; ~ **option** Nullösung f; ~**-rated** (Brit: for VAT) mehrwertsteuerfrei.
▶**zero in on** vi +prep obj main point etc herausgreifen.

**zest** [zest] n (enthusiasm) Begeisterung f; (in style, of food etc) Pfiff (col), Schwung m. ~ **for life** Lebensfreude f; **a story full of** ~ eine Geschichte mit Schwung.

**zigzag** ['zɪgzæg] **1** n Zickzack m or nt. **the river cuts a** ~ **through the rocks** der Fluß bahnt sich im Zickzack einen Weg durch die Felsen. **2** adj course, line Zickzack-; road, path zickzackförmig. **3** adv zickzackförmig, im Zickzack. **4** vi im Zickzack laufen/fahren etc.

**zilch** [zɪltʃ] n (col) Null Komma nichts (col).

**zillion** ['zɪljən] n (US col) ~**s of dollars** zig Milliarden Dollar (col).

**Zimbabwe** [zɪm'bɑːbwɪ] n Simbabwe nt.

**Zimbabwean** [zɪm'bɑːbwɪən] **1** adj simbabwisch. **2** n Simbabwer(in f) m.

**Zimmer frame** ® ['zɪməʳˌfreɪm] n Laufgestell nt.

**zinc** [zɪŋk] n Zink nt. ~ **ointment** Zinksalbe f; ~ **oxide** Zinkoxyd nt.

**Zionism** ['zaɪənɪzəm] n Zionismus m.

**Zionist** ['zaɪənɪst] **1** adj zionistisch. **2** n Zionist(in f) m.

**zip** [zɪp] **1** n (a) (Brit: fastener) Reißverschluß m. (b) (col: energy) Schwung m. **2** vi (col: car, person) flitzen (col). **to** ~ **past/along** etc vorbei-/daherflitzen etc (col).
▶**zip up 1** vt sep **to** ~ ~ **a dress** den Reißverschluß eines Kleides zumachen. **2** vi **the dress** ~**s** ~ das Kleid hat einen Reißverschluß.

**zip:** ~ **code** n (US) Postleitzahl f; ~ **fastener** n Reißverschluß m.

**zipper** ['zɪpəʳ] n Reißverschluß m.

**zippy** ['zɪpɪ] adj (+er) (col) flott.

**zit** [zɪt] n (esp US col) Pickel m.

**zither** ['zɪðəʳ] n Zither f.

**zodiac** ['zəʊdɪæk] n Tierkreis m. **signs of the** ~ Tierkreiszeichen pl.

**zombie** ['zɒmbɪ] n (a) (lit: revived corpse) Zombie m. (b) (fig) Idiot (col), Schwachkopf (col) m. **like a** ~/ **like** ~**s** wie im Tran.

**zone** ['zəʊn] **1** n (a) Zone f; (fig also) Gebiet nt. **no-parking** ~ Parkverbot nt; **time** ~ Zeitzone f. (b) (US: postal ~) Postbezirk m. **2** vt (a) town in Zonen aufteilen. (b) **to** ~ **a district for industry** einen Bezirk zur Industriezone erklären.

**zonked** [zɒŋkt] adj (col) (drunk, high) total ausgeflippt (col); (tired) total geschafft (col).

**zonk out** vi (col) umkippen (col).

**zoo** [zuː] n Zoo, Tierpark m. ~ **keeper** Tierpfleger(in f), Wärter(in f) m.

**zoological** [ˌzʊə'lɒdʒɪkəl] adj zoologisch. ~ **gardens** zoologischer Garten.

**zoologist** [zʊ'ɒlədʒɪst] n Zoologe m, Zoologin f.

**zoology** [zʊ'ɒlədʒɪ] n Zoologie f.

**zoom** [zuːm] **1** n (Phot: also ~ **lens**) Zoom(objektiv) nt, Gummilinse f (col). **2** vi (col) sausen (col). **the car** ~**ed past us** der Wagen sauste an uns vorbei (col); **to** ~ **off** davonrasen.
▶**zoom in** vi **to** ~ ~ **on sth** (Phot) etw heranholen.

**zucchini** [zuː'kiːnɪ] n (US) Zucchini f.

**Zulu** ['zuːluː] **1** adj Zulu-. **2** n Zulu mf; (language) Zulu nt.

**Zurich** ['zjʊərɪk] **1** n Zürich nt. **2** adj attr Züricher.

# IRREGULAR GERMAN VERBS

| Infinitive | Present Indicative<br>*2nd pers sing ♦ 3rd pers sing* | Imperfect<br>Indicative | Past<br>Participle |
|---|---|---|---|
| backen | bäckst, backst ♦ bäckt, backt | backte | gebacken |
| befehlen | befiehlst ♦ befiehlt | befahl | befohlen |
| beginnen | beginnst ♦ beginnt | begann | begonnen |
| beißen | beißt ♦ beißt | biß | gebissen |
| bergen | birgst ♦ birgt | barg | geborgen |
| bersten | birst ♦ birst | barst | geborsten |
| bewegen² | bewegst ♦ bewegt | bewog | bewogen |
| biegen | biegst ♦ biegt | bog | gebogen |
| bieten | bietest ♦ bietet | bot | geboten |
| binden | bindest ♦ bindet | band | gebunden |
| bitten | bittest ♦ bittet | bat | gebeten |
| blasen | bläst ♦ bläst | blies | geblasen |
| bleiben | bleibst ♦ bleibt | blieb | geblieben |
| braten | brätst ♦ brät | briet | gebraten |
| brechen | brichst ♦ bricht | brach | gebrochen |
| brennen | brennst ♦ brennt | brannte | gebrannt |
| bringen | bringst ♦ bringt | brachte | gebracht |
| denken | denkst ♦ denkt | dachte | gedacht |
| dreschen | drischst ♦ drischt | drosch | gedroschen |
| dringen | dringst ♦ dringt | drang | gedrungen |
| dürfen | *1st* darf ♦ *2nd* darfst<br>♦ *3rd* darf | durfte | gedurft ♦ *(after<br>infin)* dürfen |
| empfangen | empfängst ♦ empfängt | empfing | empfangen |
| empfehlen | empfiehlst ♦ empfiehlt | empfahl | empfohlen |
| empfinden | empfindest ♦ empfindet | empfand | empfunden |
| erschrecken | erschrickst ♦ erschrickt | erschrak | erschrocken |
| essen | ißt ♦ ißt | aß | gegessen |
| fahren | fährst ♦ fährt | fuhr | gefahren |
| fallen | fällst ♦ fällt | fiel | gefallen |
| fangen | fängst ♦ fängt | fing | gefangen |
| fechten | fichtst ♦ ficht | focht | gefochten |
| finden | findest ♦ findet | fand | gefunden |
| flechten | flichtst ♦ flicht | flocht | geflochten |
| fliegen | fliegst ♦ fliegt | flog | geflogen |
| fliehen | fliehst ♦ flieht | floh | geflohen |
| fließen | fließt ♦ fließt | floß | geflossen |
| fressen | frißt ♦ frißt | fraß | gefressen |
| frieren | frierst ♦ friert | fror | gefroren |
| gebären | gebierst ♦ gebiert | gebar | geboren |
| geben | gibst ♦ gibt | gab | gegeben |
| gedeihen | gedeihst ♦ gedeiht | gedieh | gediehen |
| gehen | gehst ♦ geht | ging | gegangen |
| gelingen | gelingt | gelang | gelungen |
| gelten | giltst ♦ gilt | galt | gegolten |
| genesen | genest ♦ genest | genas | genesen |
| genießen | genießt ♦ genießt | genoß | genossen |
| geschehen | geschieht | geschah | geschehen |
| gewinnen | gewinnst ♦ gewinnt | gewann | gewonnen |
| gießen | gießt ♦ gießt | goß | gegossen |
| gleichen | gleichst ♦ gleicht | glich | geglichen |
| gleiten | gleitest ♦ gleitet | glitt | geglitten |
| glimmen | glimmst ♦ glimmt | glomm | geglommen |
| graben | gräbst ♦ gräbt | grub | gegraben |
| greifen | greifst ♦ greift | griff | gegriffen |
| haben | hast ♦ hat | hatte | gehabt |
| halten | hältst ♦ hält | hielt | gehalten |
| hängen | hängst ♦ hängt | hing | gehangen |
| hauen | haust ♦ haut | haute | gehauen |

1

| Infinitive | Present Indicative<br>2nd pers sing ♦ 3rd pers sing | Imperfect<br>Indicative | Past<br>Participle |
|---|---|---|---|
| heben | hebst ♦ hebt | hob | gehoben |
| heißen | heißt ♦ heißt | hieß | geheißen |
| helfen | hilfst ♦ hilft | half | geholfen |
| kennen | kennst ♦ kennt | kannte | gekannt |
| klingen | klingst ♦ klingt | klang | geklungen |
| kneifen | kneifst ♦ kneift | kniff | gekniffen |
| kommen | kommst ♦ kommt | kam | gekommen |
| können | 1st kann ♦ 2nd kannst<br>♦ 3rd kann | konnte | gekonnt ♦ (after<br>infin) können |
| kriechen | kriechst ♦ kriecht | kroch | gekrochen |
| laden | lädst ♦ lädt | lud | geladen |
| lassen | läßt ♦ läßt | ließ | gelassen ♦ (after<br>infin) lassen |
| laufen | läufst ♦ läuft | lief | gelaufen |
| leiden | leidest ♦ leidet | litt | gelitten |
| leihen | leihst ♦ leiht | lieh | geliehen |
| lesen | liest ♦ liest | las | gelesen |
| liegen | liegst ♦ liegt | lag | gelegen |
| lügen | lügst ♦ lügt | log | gelogen |
| mahlen | mahlst ♦ mahlt | mahlte | gemahlen |
| meiden | meidest ♦ meidet | mied | gemieden |
| melken | melkst ♦ melkt | melkte | gemolken |
| messen | mißt ♦ mißt | maß | gemessen |
| mißlingen | mißlingt | mißlang | mißlungen |
| mögen | 1st mag ♦ 2nd magst<br>♦ 3rd mag | mochte | gemocht ♦ (after<br>infin) mögen |
| müssen | 1st muß ♦ 2nd mußt<br>♦ 3rd muß | mußte | müssen |
| nehmen | nimmst ♦ nimmt | nahm | genommen |
| nennen | nennst ♦ nennt | nannte | genannt |
| pfeifen | pfeifst ♦ pfeift | pfiff | gepfiffen |
| preisen | preist ♦ preist | pries | gepriesen |
| quellen | quillst ♦ quillt | quoll | gequollen |
| raten | rätst ♦ rät | riet | geraten |
| reiben | reibst ♦ reibt | rieb | gerieben |
| reißen | reißt ♦ reißt | riß | gerissen |
| reiten | reitest ♦ reitet | ritt | geritten |
| rennen | rennst ♦ rennt | rannte | gerannt |
| riechen | riechst ♦ riecht | roch | gerochen |
| ringen | ringst ♦ ringt | rang | gerungen |
| rinnen | rinnst ♦ rinnt | rann | geronnen |
| rufen | rufst ♦ ruft | rief | gerufen |
| salzen | salzt ♦ salzt | salzte | gesalzen |
| saufen | säufst ♦ säuft | soff | gesoffen |
| saugen | saugst ♦ saugt | sog | gesogen ♦ gesaugt |
| schaffen[1] | schaffst ♦ schafft | schuf | geschaffen |
| scheiden | scheidest ♦ scheidet | schied | geschieden |
| scheinen | scheinst ♦ scheint | schien | geschienen |
| scheißen | scheißt ♦ scheißt | schiß | geschissen |
| schelten | schiltst ♦ schilt | schalt | gescholten |
| scheren | scherst ♦ schert | schor | geschoren |
| schieben | schiebst ♦ schiebt | schob | geschoben |
| schießen | schießt ♦ schießt | schoß | geschossen |
| schinden | schindest ♦ schindet | schindete | geschunden |
| schlafen | schläfst ♦ schläft | schlief | geschlafen |
| schlagen | schlägst ♦ schlägt | schlug | geschlagen |
| schleichen | schleichst ♦ schleicht | schlich | geschlichen |
| schleifen | schleifst ♦ schleift | schliff | geschliffen |
| schließen | schließt ♦ schließt | schloß | geschlossen |
| schlingen | schlingst ♦ schlingt | schlang | geschlungen |

| Infinitive | Present Indicative<br>*2nd pers sing* ♦ *3rd pers sing* | Imperfect<br>Indicative | Past<br>Participle |
|---|---|---|---|
| schmeißen | schmeißt ♦ schmeißt | schmiß | geschmissen |
| schmelzen | schmilzt ♦ schmilzt | schmolz | geschmolzen |
| schneiden | schneid(e)st ♦ schneidet | schnitt | geschnitten |
| schreiben | schreibst ♦ schreibt | schrieb | geschrieben |
| schreien | schreist ♦ schreit | schrie | geschrie(e)n |
| schreiten | schreitest ♦ schreitet | schritt | geschritten |
| schweigen | schweigst ♦ schweigt | schwieg | geschwiegen |
| schwellen | schwillst ♦ schwillt | schwoll | geschwollen |
| schwimmen | schwimmst ♦ schwimmt | schwamm | geschwommen |
| schwinden | schwindest ♦ schwindet | schwand | geschwunden |
| schwingen | schwingst ♦ schwingt | schwang | geschwungen |
| schwören | schwörst ♦ schwört | schwor | geschworen |
| sehen | siehst ♦ sieht | sah | gesehen ♦ *(after<br>infin)* sehen |
| sein | *1st* bin ♦ *2nd* bist ♦ *3rd* ist<br>*1st pl* sind ♦ *2nd pl* seid<br>♦ *3rd pl* sind | war | gewesen |
| senden *(send)* | sendest ♦ sendet | sandte | gesandt |
| singen | singst ♦ singt | sang | gesungen |
| sinken | sinkst ♦ sinkt | sank | gesunken |
| sinnen | sinnst ♦ sinnt | sann | gesonnen |
| sitzen | sitzt ♦ sitzt | saß | gesessen |
| sollen | *1st* soll ♦ *2nd* sollst ♦ *3rd* soll | sollte | gesollt ♦ *(after<br>infin)* sollen |
| spalten | spaltest ♦ spaltet | spaltete | gespalten<br>♦ gespaltet |
| speien | speist ♦ speit | spie | gespie(e)n |
| spinnen | spinnst ♦ spinnt | spann | gesponnen |
| sprechen | sprichst ♦ spricht | sprach | gesprochen |
| sprießen | sprießt ♦ sprießt | sprießte | gesprossen |
| springen | springst ♦ springt | sprang | gesprungen |
| stechen | stichst ♦ sticht | stach | gestochen |
| stecken *(vi)* | steckst ♦ steckt | steckte ♦ stak | gesteckt |
| stehen | stehst ♦ steht | stand | gestanden |
| stehlen | stiehlst ♦ stiehlt | stahl | gestohlen |
| steigen | steigst ♦ steigt | stieg | gestiegen |
| sterben | stirbst ♦ stirbt | starb | gestorben |
| stieben | stiebst ♦ stiebt | stob ♦ stiebte | gestoben ♦ gestiebt |
| stinken | stinkst ♦ stinkt | stank | gestunken |
| stoßen | stößt ♦ stößt | stieß | gestoßen |
| streichen | streichst ♦ streicht | strich | gestrichen |
| streiten | streitest ♦ streitet | stritt | gestritten |
| tragen | trägst ♦ trägt | trug | getragen |
| treffen | triffst ♦ trifft | traf | getroffen |
| treiben | treibst ♦ treibt | trieb | getrieben |
| treten | trittst ♦ tritt | trat | getreten |
| trinken | trinkst ♦ trinkt | trank | getrunken |
| trügen | trügst ♦ trügt | trog | getrogen |
| tun | *1st* tue ♦ *2nd* tust ♦ *3rd* tut | tat | getan |
| verderben | verdirbst ♦ verdirbt | verdarb | verdorben |
| verdrießen | verdrießt ♦ verdrießt | verdroß | verdrossen |
| vergessen | vergißt ♦ vergißt | vergaß | vergessen |
| verlieren | verlierst ♦ verliert | verlor | verloren |
| verschleißen | verschleißt ♦ verschleißt | verschliß | verschlissen |
| verzeihen | verzeihst ♦ verzeiht | verzieh | verziehen |
| wachsen | wächst ♦ wächst | wuchs | gewachsen |
| wägen | wägst ♦ wägt | wog | gewogen |
| waschen | wäschst ♦ wäscht | wusch | gewaschen |
| weben | webst ♦ webt | webte, wob *(liter,<br>fig)* | gewebt, gewoben<br>*(liter, fig)* |
| weichen | weichst ♦ weicht | wich | gewichen |
| weisen | weist ♦ weist | wies | gewiesen |

| Infinitive | Present Indicative 2nd pers sing ♦ 3rd pers sing | Imperfect Indicative | Past Participle |
|---|---|---|---|
| **wenden** | wendest ♦ wendet | wendete | gewendet ♦ gewandt |
| **werben** | wirbst ♦ wirbt | warb | geworben |
| **werden** | wirst ♦ wird | wurde | geworden ♦ *(after ptp)* worden |
| **werfen** | wirfst ♦ wirft | warf | geworfen |
| **wiegen** | wiegst ♦ wiegt | wog | gewogen |
| **winden** | windest ♦ windet | wand | gewunden |
| **winken** | winkst ♦ winkt | winkte | gewinkt ♦ gewunken |
| **wissen** | *1st* weiß ♦ *2nd* weißt ♦ *3rd* weiß | wußte | gewußt |
| **wollen** | *1st* will ♦ *2nd* willst ♦ *3rd* will | wollte | gewollt ♦ *(after infin)* wollen |
| **wringen** | wringst ♦ wringt | wrang | gewrungen |
| **ziehen** | ziehst ♦ zieht | zog | gezogen |
| **zwingen** | zwingst ♦ zwingt | zwang | gezwungen |

# UNREGELMÄSSIGE ENGLISCHE VERBEN

| Präsens | Imperfekt | Partizip Perfekt | Präsens | Imperfekt | Partizip Perfekt |
|---|---|---|---|---|---|
| arise | arose | arisen | flee | fled | fled |
| awake | awoke | awoken | fling | flung | flung |
| be (am, is, are; being) | was, were | been | fly | flew | flown |
| | | | forbid | forbad(e) | forbidden |
| bear | bore | born(e) | forecast | forecast | forecast |
| beat | beat | beaten | forget | forgot | forgotten |
| become | became | become | forgive | forgave | forgiven |
| befall | befell | befallen | forsake | forsook | forsaken |
| begin | began | begun | freeze | froze | frozen |
| behold | beheld | beheld | get | got | got, (US) gotten |
| bend | bent | bent | | | |
| beset | beset | beset | give | gave | given |
| bet | bet, betted | bet, betted | go (goes) | went | gone |
| bid (at auction, cards) | bid | bid | grind | ground | ground |
| | | | grow | grew | grown |
| | | | hang | hung | hung |
| bid (say) | bade | bidden | hang (execute) | hanged | hanged |
| bind | bound | bound | | | |
| bite | bit | bitten | have | had | had |
| bleed | bled | bled | hear | heard | heard |
| blow | blew | blown | hide | hid | hidden |
| break | broke | broken | hit | hit | hit |
| breed | bred | bred | hold | held | held |
| bring | brought | brought | hurt | hurt | hurt |
| build | built | built | keep | kept | kept |
| burn | burnt, burned | burnt, burned | kneel | knelt, kneeled | knelt, kneeled |
| burst | burst | burst | know | knew | known |
| buy | bought | bought | lay | laid | laid |
| can | could | (been able) | lead | led | led |
| cast | cast | cast | lean | leant, leaned | leant, leaned |
| catch | caught | caught | leap | leapt, leaped | leapt, leaped |
| choose | chose | chosen | learn | learnt, learned | learnt, learned |
| cling | clung | clung | | | |
| come | came | come | leave | left | left |
| cost | cost | cost | lend | lent | lent |
| cost (work out price of) | costed | costed | let | let | let |
| | | | lie (lying) | lay | lain |
| | | | light | lit, lighted | lit, lighted |
| creep | crept | crept | lose | lost | lost |
| cut | cut | cut | make | made | made |
| deal | dealt | dealt | may | might | — |
| dig | dug | dug | mean | meant | meant |
| do (3rd person: he/she/it does) | did | done | meet | met | met |
| | | | mistake | mistook | mistaken |
| | | | mow | mowed | mown, mowed |
| draw | drew | drawn | | | |
| dream | dreamed, dreamt | dreamed, dreamt | must | (had to) | (had to) |
| | | | pay | paid | paid |
| drink | drank | drunk | put | put | put |
| drive | drove | driven | quit | quit, quitted | quit, quitted |
| dwell | dwelt | dwelt | read | read | read |
| eat | ate | eaten | rid | rid | rid |
| fall | fell | fallen | ride | rode | ridden |
| feed | fed | fed | ring | rang | rung |
| feel | felt | felt | rise | rose | risen |
| fight | fought | fought | run | ran | run |
| find | found | found | saw | sawed | sawed, sawn |

| Präsens | Imperfekt | Partizip Perfekt | Präsens | Imperfekt | Partizip Perfekt |
|---------|-----------|------------------|---------|-----------|------------------|
| say | said | said | spread | spread | spread |
| see | saw | seen | spring | sprang | sprung |
| seek | sought | sought | stand | stood | stood |
| sell | sold | sold | steal | stole | stolen |
| send | sent | sent | stick | stuck | stuck |
| set | set | set | sting | stung | stung |
| sew | sewed | sewn | stink | stank | stunk |
| shake | shook | shaken | stride | strode | stridden |
| shear | sheared | shorn, sheared | strike | struck | struck |
| | | | strive | strove | striven |
| shed | shed | shed | swear | swore | sworn |
| shine | shone | shone | sweep | swept | swept |
| shoot | shot | shot | swell | swelled | swollen, swelled |
| show | showed | shown | | | |
| shrink | shrank | shrunk | swim | swam | swum |
| shut | shut | shut | swing | swung | swung |
| sing | sang | sung | take | took | taken |
| sink | sank | sunk | teach | taught | taught |
| sit | sat | sat | tear | tore | torn |
| slay | slew | slain | tell | told | told |
| sleep | slept | slept | think | thought | thought |
| slide | slid | slid | throw | threw | thrown |
| sling | slung | slung | thrust | thrust | thrust |
| slit | slit | slit | tread | trod | trodden |
| smell | smelt, smelled | smelt, smelled | wake | woke, waked | woken, waked |
| sow | sowed | sown, sowed | wear | wore | worn |
| speak | spoke | spoken | weave | wove | woven |
| speed | sped, speeded | sped, speeded | weave (wind) | weaved | weaved |
| | | | wed | wedded, wed | wedded, wed |
| spell | spelt, spelled | spelt, spelled | weep | wept | wept |
| spend | spent | spent | win | won | won |
| spill | spilt, spilled | spilt, spilled | wind | wound | wound |
| spin | spun | spun | wring | wrung | wrung |
| spit | spat | spat | write | wrote | written |
| spoil | spoiled, spoilt | spoiled, spoilt | | | |

# WEIGHTS AND MEASURES
# MASSE UND GEWICHTE

## METRIC SYSTEM — METRISCHES SYSTEM

### Linear measures — Längenmaße

| | | |
|---|---|---|
| 1 millimetre (Millimeter) | = | 0.03937 inch |
| 1 centimetre (Zentimeter) | = | 0.3937 inch |
| 1 metre (Meter) | = | 39.37 inches |
| | = | 1.094 yards |
| 1 kilometre (Kilometer) | = | 0.6214 mile ($\frac{5}{8}$ mile) |

### Square measures — Flächenmaße

| | | |
|---|---|---|
| 1 square centimetre (Quadratzentimeter) | = | 0.155 square inch |
| 1 square metre (Quadratmeter) | = | 10.764 square feet |
| | = | 1.196 square yards |
| 1 square kilometre (Quadratkilometer) | = | 0.3861 square mile |
| | = | 247.1 acres |
| 1 are (Ar) = 100 square metres | = | 119.6 square yards |
| 1 hectare (Hektar) = 100 ares | = | 2.471 acres |

### Measures of capacity — Hohlmaße

| | | |
|---|---|---|
| 1 litre (Liter) | = | 1.76 pints |
| | = | 0.22 gallon |

### Weights — Gewichte

| | | |
|---|---|---|
| 1 gramme (Gramm) | = | 15.4 grains |
| 1 kilogramme (Kilogramm) | = | 2.2046 pounds |
| 1 metric ton (Tonne) = 1000 kilogrammes | = | 0.9842 ton |

## NON-METRIC SYSTEM — NICHT-METRISCHES SYSTEM

### Linear measures — Längenmaße

| | | |
|---|---|---|
| 1 inch (Zoll) | = | 2,54 Zentimeter |
| 1 foot (Fuß) = 12 inches | = | 30,48 Zentimeter |
| 1 yard (Yard) = 3 feet | = | 91,44 Zentimeter |
| 1 furlong = 220 yards | = | 201,17 Meter |
| 1 mile (Meile) = 1760 yards | = | 1,609 Kilometer |

### Square measures — Flächenmaße

| | | |
|---|---|---|
| 1 square inch (Quadratzoll) | = | 6,45 cm² |
| 1 square foot (Quadratfuß) = 144 square inches | = | 929,03 cm² |
| 1 square yard (Quadratyard) = 9 square feet | = | 0,836 m² |
| 1 square rod = 30.25 square yards | = | 25,29 m² |
| 1 acre = 4840 square yards | = | 40,47 Ar |
| 1 square mile (Quadratmeile) = 640 acres | = | 2,59 km² |

**Liquid measures — Flüssigkeitsmaße**

| | | |
|---|---|---|
| 1 gill | = | 0,142 Liter |
| 1 pint = 4 gills | = | 0,57 Liter |
| 1 quart = 2 pints | = | 1,136 Liter |
| 1 gallon (Gallone) = 4 quarts | = | 4,546 Liter |

**Weights — Avoirdupois system — Handelsgewichte**

| | | |
|---|---|---|
| 1 ounce (Unze) | = | 28,35 Gramm |
| 1 pound (britisches Pfund) = 16 ounces | = | 453,6 Gramm |
| | = | 0,453 Kilogramm |
| 1 stone = 14 pounds | = | 6,348 Kilogramm |
| 1 quarter = 28 pounds | = | 12,7 Kilogramm |
| 1 hundredweight = 112 pounds | = | 50,8 Kilogramm |
| 1 ton (Tonne) = 2240 pounds = 20 hundred-weight | = | 1016 Kilogramm |

## US MEASURES — AMERIKANISCHE MASSE

**Liquid measures — Flüssigkeitsmaße**

| | | |
|---|---|---|
| 1 US liquid gill | = | 0,118 Liter |
| 1 US liquid pint = 4 gills | = | 0,473 Liter |
| 1 US liquid quart = 2 pints | = | 0,946 Liter |
| 1 US gallon = 4 quarts | = | 3,785 Liter |

**Weights — Gewichte**

| | | |
|---|---|---|
| 1 hundredweight (*or* short hundredweight) = 100 pounds | = | 45,36 Kilogramm |
| 1 ton (*or* short ton) = 2000 pounds = 20 short hundredweights | = | 907,18 Kilogramm |

## TEMPERATURE CONVERSION — TEMPERATURUMRECHNUNG

**Fahrenheit — Centigrade (Celsius)**

Subtract 32 and multiply by 5/9
32 abziehen und mit 5/9 multiplizieren

| °F | | °C |
|---|---|---|
| 0 | | 17.8 |
| 32 | | 0 |
| 50 | | 10 |
| 70 | | 21.1 |
| 90 | | 32.2 |
| 98.4 | ≈ | 37 |
| 212 | | 100 |

**Centigrade (Celsius) — Fahrenheit**

Multiply by 9/5 and add 32
Mit 9/5 multiplizieren und 32 addieren

| °C | | °F |
|---|---|---|
| −10 | | 14 |
| 0 | | 32 |
| 10 | | 50 |
| 20 | | 68 |
| 30 | | 86 |
| 37 | ≈ | 98.4 |
| 100 | | 212 |